WHITAKER'S ALMANACK 1998

AN

Almanack

For the Year of Our Lord

1998

ESTABLISHED 1868

BY

JOSEPH WHITAKER, FSA

CONTAINING AN ACCOUNT OF THE

ASTRONOMICAL AND OTHER PHENOMENA

AND

A vast Amount of INFORMATION respecting the
GOVERNMENT, FINANCES, POPULATION,
COMMERCE, and GENERAL STATISTICS of
the various Nations of the WORLD
with an INDEX containing

over 7,000

References

LONDON

OFFICE: 12 DYOTT STREET
LONDON WC1A 1DF

The traditional design of the title page for Whitaker's Almanack which has appeared in each edition since 1868

Whitaker's Almanack

1998

LONDON:

THE STATIONERY OFFICE

THE STATIONERY OFFICE LTD

51 Nine Elms Lane, London sw8 5DR

Whitaker's Almanack published annually since 1868

© 130th edition The Stationery Office Ltd 1997

Standard edition (1,280 pages)
Cloth covers
011 702179 2

Leather binding
011 702181 4

Designed by Douglas Martin
Jacket designed by Bob Eames
Typeset by Page Bros (Norwich) Ltd
Printed and bound in Great Britain by
Clays Ltd, part of St Ives PLC, Bungay, Suffolk

EDITORIAL CONSULTANTS
Sally Whitaker
Gyles Brandreth
Rupert Pennant-Rea

EDITORIAL STAFF
Hilary Marsden (*Editor*)
Bridie Macmahon (*Assistant Editor, UK*)
Joanna Carpenter (*Assistant Editor, International*)
Marian Sheil (*Editorial Assistant*)

Published by The Stationery Office and available from:

The Publications Centre
(mail, telephone and fax orders only)
PO Box 276, London sw8 5DT
General enquiries 0171 873 0011
Telephone orders 0171 873 9090
Fax orders 0171 873 8200

The Stationery Office Bookshops
59–60 Holborn Viaduct, London ECIA 2FD
temporary until mid 1998
(counter service and fax orders only)
Fax 0171 831 1326
68–69 Bull Street, Birmingham B4 6AD
0121 236 9696   Fax 0121 236 9699
33 Wine Street, Bristol BSI 2BQ
0117 9264306   Fax 0117 9294515
9–21 Princess Street, Manchester M60 8AS
0161 834 7201   Fax 0161 833 0634
16 Arthur Street, Belfast BTI 4GD
01232 238451   Fax 01232 235401
The Stationery Office Oriel Bookshop
The Friary, Cardiff CFI 4AA
01222 395548   Fax 01222 384347
71 Lothian Road, Edinburgh EH3 9AZ
(counter service only)

Customers in Scotland may
mail, telephone or fax their orders to:
Scottish Publications Sales
South Gyle Crescent, Edinburgh EHI2 9EB
0131 622 7050   Fax 0131 622 7017

The Stationery Office's Accredited Agents
(see Yellow Pages)

and through good booksellers

Contents

CONTENTS CONTINUED

Preface

TO THE 130TH ANNUAL VOLUME 1998

Recent months have seen two momentous events in national life: the Labour Party landslide in the general election in May, and the shocking death of Diana, Princess of Wales in a car crash in August.

Nearly half of the Princess's short life was lived in the public eye, and the main events of her life are recalled in the Obituaries and illustrations. Another international figure, Mother Teresa, died within a week of the Princess, and her achievements are similarly recorded.

The general election, the results of which are recorded in full, is just one of a number of far-reaching changes in British political life. The new administration has already made changes to the machinery of government and these are reflected in the Government Departments and Public Offices section. The results of the referendums in Scotland and Wales, which will profoundly affect the nature of the United Kingdom, are recorded in the Stop-press. Progress towards European Monetary Union is recorded in the European Union section, and continuing changes in local government in England are illustrated with a map of new local authority areas.

The Countries of the World information has been radically revised and standardized in content and presentation, with increased statistical data on each country. A new section on Prisons draws together and expands previous coverage of this subject, and the Energy section has been revised and now includes data about renewable forms of energy generation. The information about national insurance and related benefits has been rewritten completely, and a description has been added of the Internet, outlining its origins and operation.

The 1998 edition is the last to be prepared under the auspices of J. Whitaker and Sons Ltd, the company founded in the 1850s by Joseph Whitaker, as shortly before this edition went to press Whitaker's Almanack was bought by The Stationery Office. Inevitably there are regrets at parting from the firm which has provided a secure home for 130 years. However, The Stationery Office recognizes the strengths and traditions of Whitaker's Almanack and wishes to build on these; we look forward to developments which will keep Whitaker's Almanack at the forefront of the rapidly changing information market. I should like to place on record here my thanks to Sally Whitaker and David Whitaker for their support and encouragement over the years.

My thanks also go, as ever, to my staff and our specialist contributors. In addition, I wish to thank the many individuals and organizations who provide us with information each year.

12 DYOTT STREET
LONDON WCIA IDF
TEL 0171-420 6000
(*until December 1997*)

51 NINE ELMS LANE
LONDON SW8 5DR
(*from January 1998*)

HILARY MARSDEN
Editor
OCTOBER 1997

The Year 1998

CHRONOLOGICAL CYCLES AND ERAS

Dominical Letter	D
Epact	2
Golden Number (Lunar Cycle)	IV
Julian Period	6711
Roman Indiction	6
Solar Cycle	19

	Beginning
Japanese year Heisei 10	1 January
Chinese year of the Tiger	28 January
Regnal year 47	6 February
Indian (Saka) year 1920	22 March
Hindu new year	28 March
Sikh new year	13 April
Muslim year AH 1419	28 April
Jewish year AM 5759	21 September
Roman year 2751 AUC	

RELIGIOUS CALENDARS

Epiphany	6 January
Makara Sankranti	14 January
Id al-Fitr	*c.*30 January
Vasant Panchami (Sarasvati-puja)	1 February
Ash Wednesday	25 February
Mahashivaratri	25 February
Holi	12 March
Ramanavami	5 April
Good Friday	10 April
Passover, first day	11 April
Easter Day (western churches)	12 April
Baisakhi Mela (Sikh new year)	13 April
Easter Day (Greek Orthodox)	19 April
Rogation Sunday	17 May
Ascension Day	21 May
Trinity Sunday	25 May
Corpus Christi	29 May
Martyrdom of Guru Arjan Dev Ji	29 May
Pentecost (Whit Sunday)	31 May
Feast of Weeks, first day	31 May
Raksha-bandhan	7 August
Janmashtami	14 August
Ganesh Chaturthi, first day	26 August
Ganesh festival, last day	5 September
Durga-puja	21 September
Navaratri festival, first day	21 September
Sarasvati-puja	29 September
Yom Kippur (Day of Atonement)	30 September
Dasara	1 October
Feast of Tabernacles, first day	5 October
Diwali (Hindu), first day	17 October
Diwali (Hindu), last day	22 October
Birthday of Guru Nanak Dev Ji	4 November
Martyrdom of Guru Tegh Bahadur Ji	24 November
First Sunday in Advent	29 November
Chanucah, first day	14 December
Ramadan, first day	*c.*20 December
Christmas Day	25 December
Birthday of Guru Gobind Singh Ji	25 December

CIVIL CALENDAR

Accession of Queen Elizabeth II	6 February
Duke of York's birthday	19 February
St David's Day	1 March
Commonwealth Day	9 March
Prince Edward's birthday	10 March
St Patrick's Day	17 March
Birthday of Queen Elizabeth II	21 April
St George's Day	23 April
Coronation of Queen Elizabeth II	2 June
Duke of Edinburgh's birthday	10 June
The Queen's Official Birthday	13 June
Queen Elizabeth the Queen Mother's birthday	4 August
Princess Royal's birthday	15 August
Princess Margaret's birthday	21 August
Remembrance Sunday	8 November
Prince of Wales's birthday	14 November
Lord Mayor's Day	14 November
Wedding Day of Queen Elizabeth II	20 November
St Andrew's Day	30 November

LEGAL CALENDAR

LAW TERMS

Hilary Term	12 January to 8 April
Easter Term	21 April to 22 May
Trinity Term	2 June to 31 July
Michaelmas Term	1 October to 21 December

QUARTER DAYS

England, Wales and Northern Ireland

Lady	25 March
Midsummer	24 June
Michaelmas	29 September
Christmas	25 December

TERM DAYS

Scotland

Candlemas	28 February
Whitsunday	28 May
Lammas	28 August
Martinmas	28 November
Removal Terms	28 May, 28 November

1998

JANUARY

Sunday		4	11	18	25
Monday		5	12	19	26
Tuesday		6	13	20	27
Wednesday		7	14	21	28
Thursday	1	8	15	22	29
Friday	2	9	16	23	30
Saturday	3	10	17	24	31

FEBRUARY

Sunday	1	8	15	22
Monday	2	9	16	23
Tuesday	3	10	17	24
Wednesday	4	11	18	25
Thursday	5	12	19	26
Friday	6	13	20	27
Saturday	7	14	21	28

MARCH

Sunday	1	8	15	22	29
Monday	2	9	16	23	30
Tuesday	3	10	17	24	31
Wednesday	4	11	18	25	
Thursday	5	12	19	26	
Friday	6	13	20	27	
Saturday	7	14	21	28	

APRIL

Sunday		5	12	19	26
Monday		6	13	20	27
Tuesday		7	14	21	28
Wednesday	1	8	15	22	29
Thursday	2	9	16	23	30
Friday	3	10	17	24	
Saturday	4	11	18	25	

MAY

Sunday		3	10	17	24	31
Monday		4	11	18	25	
Tuesday		5	12	19	26	
Wednesday		6	13	20	27	
Thursday		7	14	21	28	
Friday	1	8	15	22	29	
Saturday	2	9	16	23	30	

JUNE

Sunday		7	14	21	28
Monday	1	8	15	22	29
Tuesday	2	9	16	23	30
Wednesday	3	10	17	24	
Thursday	4	11	18	25	
Friday	5	12	19	26	
Saturday	6	13	20	27	

JULY

Sunday		5	12	19	26
Monday		6	13	20	27
Tuesday		7	14	21	28
Wednesday	1	8	15	22	29
Thursday	2	9	16	23	30
Friday	3	10	17	24	31
Saturday	4	11	18	25	

AUGUST

Sunday		2	9	16	23	30
Monday		3	10	17	24	31
Tuesday		4	11	18	25	
Wednesday		5	12	19	26	
Thursday		6	13	20	27	
Friday		7	14	21	28	
Saturday	1	8	15	22	29	

SEPTEMBER

Sunday		6	13	20	27
Monday		7	14	21	28
Tuesday	1	8	15	22	29
Wednesday	2	9	16	23	30
Thursday	3	10	17	24	
Friday	4	11	18	25	
Saturday	5	12	19	26	

OCTOBER

Sunday		4	11	18	25
Monday		5	12	19	26
Tuesday		6	13	20	27
Wednesday		7	14	21	28
Thursday	1	8	15	22	29
Friday	2	9	16	23	30
Saturday	3	10	17	24	31

NOVEMBER

Sunday	1	8	15	22	29
Monday	2	9	16	23	30
Tuesday	3	10	17	24	
Wednesday	4	11	18	25	
Thursday	5	12	19	26	
Friday	6	13	20	27	
Saturday	7	14	21	28	

DECEMBER

Sunday		6	13	20	27
Monday		7	14	21	28
Tuesday	1	8	15	22	29
Wednesday	2	9	16	23	30
Thursday	3	10	17	24	31
Friday	4	11	18	25	
Saturday	5	12	19	26	

PUBLIC HOLIDAYS

	England and Wales	Scotland	Northern Ireland
New Year	1 January	1, 2 January	1 January
St Patrick's Day	—	—	17 March
*Good Friday	10 April	10 April	10 April
Easter Monday	13 April	—	13 April
May Day	4 May	25 May	4 May
Spring	25 May	4 May	25 May
Battle of the Boyne	—	—	13 July†
Summer	31 August	3 August	31 August
*Christmas	25, 28 December	25, 28 December	25, 28 December

*In England, Wales and Northern Ireland, Christmas Day and Good Friday are common law holidays
In the Channel Islands, Liberation Day (9 May) is a bank and public holiday
†provisional date

1999

JANUARY					
Sunday		3	10	17	24	31
Monday		4	11	18	25
Tuesday		5	12	19	26
Wednesday		6	13	20	27
Thursday		7	14	21	28
Friday	1	8	15	22	29
Saturday	2	9	16	23	30

FEBRUARY					
Sunday			7	14	21	28
Monday	1	8	15	22
Tuesday	2	9	16	23
Wednesday	3	10	17	24
Thursday	4	11	18	25
Friday	5	12	19	26
Saturday	6	13	20	27

MARCH					
Sunday			7	14	21	28
Monday	1	8	15	22	29
Tuesday	2	9	16	23	30
Wednesday	3	10	17	24	31
Thursday	4	11	18	25
Friday	5	12	19	26
Saturday	6	13	20	27

APRIL				
Sunday		4	11	18	25
Monday		5	12	19	26
Tuesday		6	13	20	27
Wednesday		7	14	21	28
Thursday	1	8	15	22	29
Friday	2	9	16	23	30
Saturday	3	10	17	24

MAY					
Sunday	2	9	16	23	30
Monday	3	10	17	24	31
Tuesday	4	11	18	25
Wednesday	5	12	19	26
Thursday	6	13	20	27
Friday	7	14	21	28
Saturday	1	8	15	22	29

JUNE				
Sunday		6	13	20	27
Monday		7	14	21	28
Tuesday	1	8	15	22	29
Wednesday	2	9	16	23	30
Thursday	3	10	17	24
Friday	4	11	18	25
Saturday	5	12	19	26

JULY				
Sunday		4	11	18	25
Monday		5	12	19	26
Tuesday		6	13	20	27
Wednesday		7	14	21	28
Thursday	1	8	15	22	29
Friday	2	9	16	23	30
Saturday	3	10	17	24	31

AUGUST					
Sunday	1	8	15	22	29
Monday	2	9	16	23	30
Tuesday	3	10	17	24	31
Wednesday	4	11	18	25
Thursday	5	12	19	26
Friday	6	13	20	27
Saturday	7	14	21	28

SEPTEMBER				
Sunday		5	12	19	26
Monday		6	13	20	27
Tuesday		7	14	21	28
Wednesday	1	8	15	22	29
Thursday	2	9	16	23	30
Friday	3	10	17	24
Saturday	4	11	18	25

OCTOBER					
Sunday		3	10	17	24	31
Monday		4	11	18	25
Tuesday		5	12	19	26
Wednesday		6	13	20	27
Thursday		7	14	21	28
Friday	1	8	15	22	29
Saturday	2	9	16	23	30

NOVEMBER					
Sunday			7	14	21	28
Monday	1	8	15	22	29
Tuesday	2	9	16	23	30
Wednesday	3	10	17	24
Thursday	4	11	18	25
Friday	5	12	19	26
Saturday	6	13	20	27

DECEMBER					
Sunday		5	12	19	26
Monday		6	13	20	27
Tuesday		7	14	21	28
Wednesday	1	8	15	22	29
Thursday	2	9	16	23	30
Friday	3	10	17	24	31
Saturday	4	11	18	25

PUBLIC HOLIDAYS

	England and Wales	Scotland	Northern Ireland
New Year	1 January	1, 4 January	1 January
St Patrick's Day	—	—	17 March
*Good Friday	2 April	2 April	2 April
Easter Monday	5 April	—	5 April
May Day	3 May	31 May	3 May
Spring	31 May	3 May	31 May
Battle of the Boyne	—	—	12 July
Summer	30 August	2 August	30 August
*Christmas	27, 28 December	27, 28 December	27, 28 December

FORTHCOMING EVENTS 1998

This is the UN International Year for the Oceans and the Arts Council Year for Photography and the Electronic Image
The European City of Culture is Stockholm
* Provisional dates

9–18 January	London International Boat Show Earl's Court, London
5–8 March	Cruft's Dog Show National Exhibition Centre, Birmingham
13–15 March	Liberal Democrat Party Spring Conference Floral Hall, Southport
18 March– 13 April	Ideal Home Exhibition Earls Court, London
21–22 March	London International Book Fair Olympia, London
April–October	Chichester Festival Theatre season
1–23 May	Mayfest 1998 Glasgow
1 May– 10 October	Pitlochry Festival Theatre season Tayside
15–31 May	Bath International Music Festival
21–22 May	Chelsea Flower Show Royal Hospital, Chelsea
*21 May– 28 August	Glyndebourne Festival Opera season Lewes, E. Sussex
22–31 May	Hay Festival of Literature Hay-on-Wye, Hereford
7 June–16 August	Royal Academy Summer Exhibition Piccadilly, London
12–28 June	Aldeburgh Festival of Music and Arts Suffolk
13 June	Trooping the Colour Horse Guards Parade, London
3–12 July	York Early Music Festival
4–19 July	Cheltenham International Festival of Music
6–9 July	The Royal Show Stoneleigh Park, Kenilworth, Warks
*9–12 July	Hampton Court Palace Flower Show East Molesey, Surrey
10–26 July	Buxton Festival Derbyshire
17 July– 12 September	Promenade Concerts season Royal Albert Hall, London
*17–25 July	Welsh Proms 1997 St David's Hall, Cardiff
19 July–9 August	The Lambeth Conference University of Kent, Canterbury
21 July–2 August	Royal Tournament Earls Court, London
*28–30 July	Wisley Flower Show RHS Garden, Wisley, Surrey
1–8 August	Royal National Eisteddfod of Wales Bro Ogwr, Bridgend
7–29 August	Edinburgh Military Tattoo Edinburgh Castle
13–14 August	Battle of the Flowers Jersey
15–22 August	Three Choirs Festival Gloucester
16 August– 5 September	Edinburgh International Festival
30–31 August	Notting Hill Carnival Notting Hill, London
4 September– 8 November	Blackpool Illuminations
5 September	Braemar Royal Highland Gathering Aberdeenshire
*12–20 September	Southampton International Boat Show, Western Esplanade, Southampton
14–17 September	TUC Annual Congress Blackpool
20–24 September	Liberal Democrat Party Autumn Conference Brighton
*28 September– 2 October	Labour Party Conference Blackpool
6–9 October	Conservative Party Conference Bournemouth
1 November	London to Brighton Veteran Car Run
*1–3 November	CBI Annual Conference Birmingham
6–23 November	London International Film Festival
11 November	Two Minute Silence at 11a.m.
14 November	Lord Mayor's Procession and Show City of London
18–29 November	Huddersfield Contemporary Music Festival
29 November– 2 December	Smithfield Show Earls Court, London

SPORTS EVENTS

7 February	Rugby Union: Ireland v. Scotland Lansdowne Road, Dublin France v. England Parc des Princes, Paris
7–22 February	Winter Olympic Games Nagano, Japan
21 February	Rugby Union: Scotland v. France Murrayfield, Edinburgh England v. Wales Twickenham, London
7 March	Rugby Union: France v. Ireland Parc des Princes, Paris
8 March	Rugby Union: Wales v. Scotland Wembley Stadium, London
21 March	Rugby Union: Ireland v. Wales Lansdowne Road, Dublin
22 March	Rugby Union: Scotland v. England Murrayfield, Edinburgh
28 March	Oxford and Cambridge Boat Race Putney to Mortlake, London
4 April	Rugby Union: England v. Ireland Twickenham, London
5 April	Rugby Union: Wales v. France Wembley Stadium, London
18 April	Rugby Union: County Championship finals Twickenham, London
*18 April–4 May	Snooker: World Professional Championship Crucible Theatre, Sheffield
*26 April	Athletics: London Marathon
May	Football: Welsh FA Cup final Wembley Stadium, London

2 May	Rugby League: Challenge Cup final Wembley Stadium, London
7–10 May	Badminton Horse Trials Badminton
9 May	Rugby Union: Pilkington Cup final Twickenham, London
13–17 May	Royal Windsor Horse Show Home Park, Windsor
16 May	Football: FA Cup final Wembley Stadium, London
16 May	Football: Scottish FA Cup final
21 May	Cricket: One-day International England v. South Africa The Oval, London
23 May	Cricket: One-day International England v. South Africa Old Trafford, Manchester
24 May	Cricket: One-day International England v. South Africa Headingley, Leeds
1–6 June	Golf: British Amateur Championship Muirfield and Gullane, East Lothian
4–8 June	Cricket: 1st Test Match England v. South Africa Edgbaston, Birmingham
7 June	TT Motorcycle Races: 'Mad Sunday' Isle of Man
18–22 June	Cricket: 2nd Test Match England v. South Africa Lord's, London
22 June–5 July	Lawn Tennis Championships Wimbledon, London
July	Cricket: Benson and Hedges Cup final Lord's, London
1–5 July	Henley Royal Regatta Henley-on-Thames
2–6 July	Cricket: 3rd Test Match England v South Africa Old Trafford, Manchester
11–25 July	Shooting: NRA Imperial Meeting Bisley Camp, Woking, Surrey
*12 July	British Formula 1 Grand Prix Silverstone, Northants
12 July	Football: World Cup final France
16–19 July	Golf: The Open Royal Birkdale, Merseyside
23–27 July	Cricket: 4th Test Match England v. South Africa Trent Bridge, Nottingham
1–8 August	Yachting: Cowes Week Isle of Wight
6–10 August	Cricket: 5th Test Match England v. South Africa Headingley, Leeds
27–31 August	Cricket: Test Match England v. Sri Lanka The Oval, London
September	Cricket: Natwest Trophy final Lord's, London
*3–6 September	Eventing: Burghley Horse Trials Burghley, Lincs
11–21 September	Commonwealth Games Kuala Lumpur, Malaysia
18–20 September	Golf: Solheim Cup Muirfield Village, Dublin, Ohio
*23–27 September	Horse of the Year Show Wembley Arena, London
October	Rugby League: World Cup Australia/New Zealand

HORSE-RACING

19 March	Cheltenham Gold Cup
28 March	Lincoln Handicap Doncaster
4 April	Grand National Aintree
2 May	Two Thousand Guineas Newmarket
3 May	One Thousand Guineas Newmarket
5 June	The Oaks Epsom
5 June	Coronation Cup Epsom
6 June	The Derby Epsom
16–19 June	Royal Ascot
25 July	King George VI and Queen Elizabeth Diamond Stakes Ascot
12 September	St Leger Doncaster
3 October	Cambridgeshire Handicap Newmarket
17 October	Cesarewitch Newmarket

The horse-racing fixtures are the copyright of the British Horse-racing Board

CENTENARIES OF 1998

1498

23 May   Girolamo Savonarola, Italian religious
              and political reformer, martyred

1598

13 April   Edict of Nantes, ending civil war in
              France
19 July   Gilbert Sheldon, Archbishop of
              Canterbury 1663–78, born

1798

19 January   Auguste Comte, French philosopher,
              born
26 April   Eugène Delacroix, French romantic
              painter, born
10 May   George Vancouver, British explorer,
              died
4 June   Giovanni Casanova, Italian adventurer
              and spy, died
1 August   Battle of The Nile
4 December   Luigi Galvani, Italian scientist and
              anatomist, died

1898

9 January   Dame Gracie Fields, singer and
              comedienne, born
14 January   Lewis Carroll, novelist, died
15 January   Uffa Fox, yachtsman, born
15 March   Sir Henry Bessemer, inventor and
              engineer, died

16 March   Aubrey Beardsley, illustrator, died
9 April   Paul Robeson, American singer and
              black activist, born
3 May   Golda Meir, Prime Minister of Israel
              1969–74, born
19 May   William Gladstone, statesman and
              Prime Minister 1868–74, 1880–5, 1886
              and 1892–4, died
3 June   Samuel Plimsoll, social reformer and
              inventor of the 'Plimsoll line' for the
              safe loading of ships, died
6 June   Dame Ninette de Valois, Irish dancer
              and choreographer, founder of the
              Royal Ballet, born
9 June   Hong Kong leased by Britain from
              China for 99 years
17 June   Sir Edward Burne-Jones, painter, died
30 July   Otto von Bismarck, Prusso-German
              statesman, died
              Henry Moore, sculptor, born
8 August   Waterloo and City Line on London
              Underground opened
2 September   Battle of Omdurman
26 September George Gershwin, American composer,
              born
20 November   Sir John Fowler, civil engineer and co-
              designer of the Forth Bridge, died
26 December   Radium discovered by Pierre and
              Marie Curie

CENTENARIES OF 1999

1499

23 November   Perkin Warbeck, pretender to the
              throne of Henry VII, died

1599

25 April   Oliver Cromwell, Lord Protector
              1653–8, born

1799

18 May   Pierre de Beaumarchais, French author,
              died
14 December   George Washington, first president of
              the United States of America, died

1899

7 January   Francis Poulenc, French composer,
              born
17 January   Nevil Shute Norway, English-born
              Australian novelist, born

29 January   Alfred Sisley, Impressionist painter,
              died
23 April   Dame Ngaio Marsh, author, born
29 April   Duke Ellington, American jazz pianist
              and composer, born
8 May   Friedrich von Hayek, Austrian-born
              British winner of Nobel Prize for
              Economics in 1974, born
10 May   Fred Astaire, American dancer, born
24 May   Suzanne Lenglen, French tennis player
              who won Wimbledon six times, born
3 June   Johann Strauss (the younger), composer
              of Viennese waltzes and operettas, died
24 August   Jorge Luis Borges, Argentine poet,
              born
27 August   C. S. Forester, novelist and journalist,
              born
11 October   Boer War began
16 December   Sir Noel Coward, playwright and actor,
              born
25 December   Humphrey Bogart, American actor,
              born

Astronomy

The following pages give astronomical data for each month of the year 1998. There are four pages of data for each month. All data are given for 0h Greenwich Mean Time (GMT), i.e. at the midnight at the beginning of the day named. This applies also to data for the months when British Summer Time is in operation (for dates, *see* below).

The astronomical data are given in a form suitable for observation with the naked eye or with a small telescope. These data do not attempt to replace the *Astronomical Almanac* for professional astronomers.

A fuller explanation of how to use the astronomical data is given on pages 71–3.

CALENDAR FOR EACH MONTH

The calendar for each month shows dates of religious, civil and legal significance for the year 1998.

The days in bold type are the principal holy days and the festivals and greater holy days of the Church of England as set out in the calendar of the Alternative Service Book 1980, and the calendar of Sundays set out in the Book of Common Prayer. Observance of certain festivals and greater holy days is transferred if the day falls on a principal holy day. The calendar shows the date on which holy days and festivals are to be observed in 1998.

The days in small capitals are dates of significance in the calendars of non-Anglican denominations and non-Christian religions.

The days in italic type are dates of civil and legal significance. The royal anniversaries shown in italic type are the days on which the Union flag is to be flown.

The rest of the calendar comprises days of general interest and the dates of birth or death of well-known people.

Fuller explanations of the various calendars can be found under Time Measurement and Calendars (pages 81–9).

The zodiacal signs through which the Sun is passing during each month are illustrated. The date of transition from one sign to the next, to the nearest hour, is given under Astronomical Phenomena.

JULIAN DATE

The Julian date on 1998 January 0.0 is 2450813.5. To find the Julian date for any other date in 1998 (at 0h GMT), add the day-of-the-year number on the extreme right of the calendar for each month to the Julian date for January 0.0.

SEASONS

The seasons are defined astronomically as follows:

Spring from the vernal equinox to the summer solstice
Summer from the summer solstice to the autumnal equinox
Autumn from the autumnal equinox to the winter solstice
Winter from the winter solstice to the vernal equinox

The seasons in 1998 are:

Northern hemisphere

Vernal equinox	March 20d 20h GMT
Summer solstice	June 21d 14h GMT
Autumnal equinox	September 23d 06h GMT
Winter solstice	December 22d 02h GMT

Southern hemisphere

Autumnal equinox	March 20d 20h GMT
Winter solstice	June 21d 14h GMT
Vernal equinox	September 23d 06h GMT
Summer solstice	December 22d 02h GMT

The longest day of the year, measured from sunrise to sunset, is at the summer solstice. For the remainder of this century the longest day in the United Kingdom will fall each year on 21 June. *See also* page 81.

The shortest day of the year is at the winter solstice. For the remainder of this century the shortest day in the United Kingdom will fall on 21 December in 2000, and on 22 December in 1998 and 1999. *See also* page 81.

The equinox is the point at which day and night are of equal length all over the world. *See also* page 81.

In popular parlance, the seasons in the northern hemisphere comprise the following months:

Spring	March, April, May
Summer	June, July, August
Autumn	September, October, November
Winter	December, January, February

BRITISH SUMMER TIME

British Summer Time is the legal time for general purposes during the period in which it is in operation (*see also* page 75). During this period, clocks are kept one hour ahead of Greenwich Mean Time. The hour of changeover is 01h Greenwich Mean Time. The duration of Summer Time in 1998 is set provisionally to start March 29 01h GMT and end October 25 01h GMT, but these dates were subject to confirmation at the time of going to press.

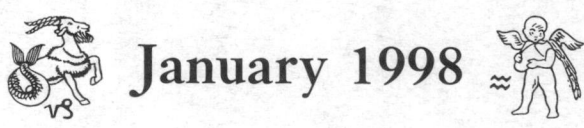

January 1998

FIRST MONTH, 31 DAYS. *Janus*, god of the portal, facing two ways, past and future

1	*Thursday*	**The Naming of Jesus.** *Bank Holiday in the UK*	*week 52 day* 1
2	*Friday*	*Bank Holiday in Scotland.* David Bailey b. 1938	2
3	*Saturday*	Josiah Wedgwood d. 1795. J. R. R. Tolkien b. 1892	3
4	*Sunday*	**2nd S. after Christmas.** T. S. Eliot d. 1965	*week* 1 *day* 4
5	*Monday*	Twelfth Night. Amy Johnson d. 1941	5
6	*Tuesday*	**The Epiphany.** Joan of Arc b. 1412	6
7	*Wednesday*	First manned balloon crossing of the English Channel 1785	7
8	*Thursday*	Elvis Presley b. 1935. Richard Tauber d. 1948	8
9	*Friday*	Dame Gracie Fields b. 1898. Richard Nixon b. 1913	9
10	*Saturday*	Carl Linnaeus d. 1778. Penny Post introduced 1840	10
11	*Sunday*	**1st S. after Epiphany.** Thomas Hardy d. 1928	*week* 2 *day* 11
12	*Monday*	*Hilary Law Sittings begin.* Jack London b. 1876	12
13	*Tuesday*	Stephen Foster d. 1864. James Joyce d. 1941	13
14	*Wednesday*	Lewis Carroll d. 1898. Sir Cecil Beaton b. 1904	14
15	*Thursday*	Molière bapt. 1622. British Museum opened 1759	15
16	*Friday*	Amilcare Ponchielli d. 1886. Start of Prohibition in USA 1920	16
17	*Saturday*	Leonhard Fuchs b. 1501. Benjamin Franklin b. 1706	17
18	*Sunday*	**2nd S. after Epiphany.** Capt. Scott reaches the South Pole 1912	*week* 3 *day* 18
19	*Monday*	Edgar Allen Poe b. 1809. Patricia Highsmith b. 1921	19
20	*Tuesday*	George Burns b. 1896. Federico Fellini b. 1920	20
21	*Wednesday*	Lenin d. 1924. George Orwell d. 1950	21
22	*Thursday*	⚔ Rorke's Drift 1879. Lyndon B. Johnson d. 1973	22
23	*Friday*	Gustave Doré d. 1883. Dame Clara Butt d. 1936	23
24	*Saturday*	⚔ Spion Kop 1900. Sir Winston Churchill d. 1965	24
25	*Sunday*	**Conversion of St Paul. 3rd S. after Epiphany**	*week* 4 *day* 25
26	*Monday*	Julia Margaret Cameron d. 1879. Republic of India proclaimed 1950	26
27	*Tuesday*	Wolfgang Amadeus Mozart b. 1756. Lewis Carroll b. 1832	27
28	*Wednesday*	*Chinese Year of the Tiger.* Sir Francis Drake d. 1596	28
29	*Thursday*	Alfred Sisley d. 1899. Germaine Greer b. 1939	29
30	*Friday*	Mahatma Ghandi assass. 1948. Orville Wright d. 1948	30
31	*Saturday*	Jean Simmons b. 1929. Samuel Goldwyn d. 1974	31

ASTRONOMICAL PHENOMENA

d	h	
1	01	Mars in conjunction with Moon. Mars 4° S.
1	21	Jupiter in conjunction with Moon. Jupiter 3° S.
4	21	Earth at perihelion (147 million km)
5	12	Saturn in conjunction with Moon. Saturn 0°.2 N.
6	15	Mercury at greatest elongation W.23°
16	11	Venus in inferior conjunction
19	23	Neptune in conjunction
20	07	Sun's longitude 300° ♒
21	04	Jupiter in conjunction with Mars. Jupiter 0°.2 N.
26	23	Mercury in conjunction with Moon. Mercury 5° S.
27	00	Venus in conjunction with Moon. Venus 3° N.
27	08	Venus in conjunction with Mercury. Venus 8° N.
28	20	Uranus in conjunction
29	16	Jupiter in conjunction with Moon. Jupiter 2° S.
30	00	Mars in conjunction with Moon. Mars 2° S.

MINIMA OF ALGOL

d	h	d	h	d	h
3	12.5	14	23.8	26	11.1
6	09.4	17	20.6	29	07.9
9	06.2	20	17.5		
12	03.0	23	14.3		

CONSTELLATIONS

The following constellations are near the meridian at

d	h		d	h
December	1	24	January	16	21
December	16	23	February	1	20
January	1	22	February	15	19

Draco (below the Pole), Ursa Minor (below the Pole), Camelopardus, Perseus, Auriga, Taurus, Orion, Eridanus and Lepus

THE MOON

Phases, Apsides and Node	d	h	m
☽ First Quarter	5	14	18
○ Full Moon	12	17	24
☾ Last Quarter	20	19	40
● New Moon	28	06	01
Perigee (369,272 km)	3	08	22
Apogee (404,597 km)	18	20	35
Perigee (363,820 km)	30	14	02

Mean longitude of ascending node on January 1, 164°

THE SUN   s.d. 16′.3

Day	Right Ascension	Dec.	Equation of time	Rise 52°	Rise 56°	Transit	Set 52°	Set 56°	Sidereal time	Transit of First Point of Aries
	h m s	° ′	m s	h m	h m	h m	h m	h m	h m s	h m s
1	18 45 04	23 02	− 3 17	8 08	8 31	12 04	15 59	15 36	6 41 47	17 15 23
2	18 49 28	22 57	− 3 45	8 08	8 31	12 04	16 00	15 37	6 45 43	17 11 27
3	18 53 53	22 52	− 4 13	8 08	8 31	12 04	16 01	15 39	6 49 40	17 07 32
4	18 58 17	22 46	− 4 41	8 08	8 30	12 05	16 02	15 40	6 53 36	17 03 36
5	19 02 41	22 39	− 5 08	8 07	8 30	12 05	16 04	15 41	6 57 33	16 59 40
6	19 07 04	22 33	− 5 35	8 07	8 29	12 06	16 05	15 43	7 01 29	16 55 44
7	19 11 27	22 25	− 6 01	8 07	8 29	12 06	16 06	15 44	7 05 26	16 51 48
8	19 15 50	22 18	− 6 27	8 06	8 28	12 07	16 08	15 46	7 09 22	16 47 52
9	19 20 11	22 09	− 6 52	8 06	8 27	12 07	16 09	15 47	7 13 19	16 43 56
10	19 24 33	22 01	− 7 17	8 05	8 26	12 07	16 10	15 49	7 17 16	16 40 00
11	19 28 53	21 52	− 7 41	8 04	8 26	12 08	16 12	15 51	7 21 12	16 36 04
12	19 33 14	21 43	− 8 05	8 04	8 25	12 08	16 13	15 52	7 25 09	16 32 08
13	19 37 33	21 33	− 8 28	8 03	8 24	12 09	16 15	15 54	7 29 05	16 28 12
14	19 41 52	21 22	− 8 50	8 02	8 23	12 09	16 16	15 56	7 33 02	16 24 17
15	19 46 10	21 12	− 9 12	8 01	8 21	12 09	16 18	15 58	7 36 58	16 20 21
16	19 50 28	21 01	− 9 33	8 00	8 20	12 10	16 19	16 00	7 40 55	16 16 25
17	19 54 45	20 49	− 9 53	8 00	8 19	12 10	16 21	16 02	7 44 51	16 12 29
18	19 59 01	20 37	−10 13	7 59	8 18	12 10	16 23	16 03	7 48 48	16 08 33
19	20 03 17	20 25	−10 32	7 57	8 17	12 11	16 24	16 05	7 52 45	16 04 37
20	20 07 31	20 13	−10 50	7 56	8 15	12 11	16 26	16 07	7 56 41	16 00 41
21	20 11 46	20 00	−11 08	7 55	8 14	12 11	16 28	16 09	8 00 38	15 56 45
22	20 15 59	19 46	−11 25	7 54	8 12	12 12	16 29	16 11	8 04 34	15 52 49
23	20 20 12	19 32	−11 41	7 53	8 11	12 12	16 31	16 13	8 08 31	15 48 53
24	20 24 24	19 18	−11 56	7 52	8 09	12 12	16 33	16 16	8 12 27	15 44 57
25	20 28 35	19 04	12 11	7 50	8 08	12 12	16 35	16 18	8 16 24	15 41 02
26	20 32 45	18 49	−12 25	7 49	8 06	12 13	16 37	16 20	8 20 20	15 37 06
27	20 36 55	18 34	−12 38	7 48	8 04	12 13	16 38	16 22	8 24 17	15 33 10
28	20 41 03	18 18	−12 50	7 46	8 03	12 13	16 40	16 24	8 28 14	15 29 14
29	20 45 11	18 02	−13 01	7 45	8 01	12 13	16 42	16 26	8 32 10	15 25 18
30	20 49 18	17 46	−13 12	7 43	7 59	12 13	16 44	16 28	8 36 07	15 21 22
31	20 53 25	17 30	−13 21	7 42	7 57	12 13	16 46	16 30	8 40 03	15 17 26

DURATION OF TWILIGHT (in minutes)

Latitude	52°	56°	52°	56°	52°	56°	52°	56°
	1 January		11 January		21 January		31 January	
Civil	41	47	40	45	38	43	37	41
Nautical	84	96	82	93	80	90	78	87
Astronomical	125	141	123	138	120	134	117	130

THE NIGHT SKY

Mercury is at its greatest western elongation on the 6th and is therefore visible as a morning object, magnitude − 0.1 to − 0.3, during the first ten days of the month. It is visible low in the south-eastern sky at the beginning of morning civil twilight.

Venus, magnitude − 4.3, is a brilliant object in the south-western sky in the early evenings for the first two weeks of the month, though drawing noticeably closer and closer to the Sun. It passes rapidly through inferior conjunction on the 16th, becoming visible in the mornings before dawn low above the east-south-eastern horizon, for the last two weeks of the month. Its magnitude is − 4.3. Both in the evening and morning apparitions, Venus exhibits a slender crescent appearance in the telescope. The thin crescent Moon may be seen near Venus on the morning of the 27th,

though this will be a difficult observation since it occurs only about 23 hours before New Moon.

Mars is unsuitably placed for observation.

Jupiter, magnitude − 2.0, is an evening object, visible low in the south-western sky for a short time in the early evening. By the end of the month it is becoming a difficult object to locate. The thin crescent Moon, only three days old, will be seen approaching Jupiter on the evening of the 1st, whilst on the evening of the 29th the Moon passes only about 1° north of the planet.

Saturn is an evening object in the southern and western skies, magnitude +0.7, moving slowly eastwards in the southern part of Pisces. The Moon, near First Quarter, is in the vicinity of the planet on the evenings of the 4th and 5th.

THE MOON

Day	RA h m	Dec. °	Hor. par. '	Semi-diam. '	Sun's co-long. °	PA of Bright Limb °	Phase %	Age d	Rise 52° h m	Rise 56° h m	Transit h m	Set 52° h m	Set 56° h m
1	20 47	−15.1	59.0	16.1	303	250	7	2.3	9 42	9 54	14 37	19 41	19 29
2	21 44	−12.0	59.3	16.1	315	249	13	3.3	10 16	10 25	15 32	20 57	20 49
3	22 39	− 8.1	59.4	16.2	327	248	22	4.3	10 46	10 51	16 24	22 14	22 11
4	23 34	− 3.8	59.4	16.2	339	247	32	5.3	11 13	11 15	17 16	23 31	23 32
5	0 28	+ 0.7	59.2	16.1	351	247	43	6.3	11 41	11 38	18 08	—	—
6	1 21	+ 5.1	59.1	16.1	4	248	55	7.3	12 08	12 02	18 59	0 48	0 52
7	2 15	+ 9.3	58.8	16.0	16	249	66	8.3	12 39	12 29	19 52	2 03	2 12
8	3 10	+12.9	58.5	15.9	28	252	76	9.3	13 12	12 59	20 45	3 17	3 29
9	4 06	+15.7	58.2	15.8	40	254	85	10.3	13 52	13 36	21 40	4 28	4 43
10	5 02	+17.6	57.7	15.7	52	257	92	11.3	14 37	14 20	22 34	5 34	5 51
11	5 58	+18.6	57.3	15.6	64	257	97	12.3	15 30	15 11	23 28	6 33	6 51
12	6 54	+18.5	56.8	15.5	76	249	99	13.3	16 28	16 10	—	7 24	7 41
13	7 48	+17.4	56.3	15.3	88	149	100	14.3	17 30	17 14	0 20	8 06	8 22
14	8 41	+15.4	55.7	15.2	101	115	98	15.3	18 34	18 21	1 10	8 42	8 55
15	9 31	+12.8	55.2	15.0	113	112	95	16.3	19 38	19 29	1 58	9 12	9 22
16	10 20	+ 9.6	54.8	14.9	125	112	90	17.3	20 42	20 37	2 44	9 38	9 45
17	11 06	+ 6.1	54.5	14.8	137	112	83	18.3	21 46	21 43	3 28	10 02	10 06
18	11 52	+ 2.4	54.3	14.8	149	113	75	19.3	22 48	22 50	4 10	10 24	10 25
19	12 37	− 1.3	54.2	14.8	161	112	67	20.3	23 51	23 56	4 52	10 46	10 44
20	13 22	− 5.0	54.3	14.8	173	111	58	21.3	—	—	5 35	11 09	11 03
21	14 08	− 8.6	54.6	14.9	186	110	48	22.3	0 55	1 02	6 18	11 34	11 25
22	14 55	−11.8	55.0	15.0	198	108	39	23.3	1 58	2 09	7 03	12 02	11 50
23	15 44	−14.6	55.7	15.2	210	105	30	24.3	3 02	3 16	7 51	12 34	12 20
24	16 36	−16.8	56.4	15.4	222	102	21	25.3	4 06	4 22	8 42	13 14	12 57
25	17 30	−18.2	57.2	15.6	234	99	13	26.3	5 07	5 25	9 35	14 02	13 43
26	18 27	−18.6	58.0	15.8	246	96	7	27.3	6 03	6 21	10 30	14 59	14 41
27	19 25	−17.9	58.8	16.0	259	95	2	28.3	6 53	7 10	11 27	16 06	15 49
28	20 24	−16.1	59.5	16.2	271	119	0	29.3	7 37	7 51	12 24	17 19	17 06
29	21 23	−13.3	60.0	16.3	283	241	1	0.7	8 14	8 25	13 21	18 37	18 27
30	22 21	− 9.6	60.2	16.4	295	247	4	1.7	8 47	8 54	14 16	19 57	19 51
31	23 18	− 5.3	60.2	16.4	307	248	10	2.7	9 17	9 20	15 11	21 16	21 15

MERCURY

Day	RA h m	Dec. °	Diam. "	Phase %	Transit h m	5° high 52° h m	5° high 56° h m
1	17 11	−20.4	7	48	10 28	7 04	7 33
3	17 17	−20.8	7	55	10 27	7 05	7 35
5	17 24	−21.2	7	60	10 26	7 08	7 38
7	17 32	−21.6	7	65	10 27	7 12	7 43
9	17 41	−22.0	6	69	10 28	7 17	7 49
11	17 51	−22.3	6	72	10 30	7 22	7 55
13	18 02	−22.6	6	76	10 33	7 27	8 01
15	18 13	−22.9	6	78	10 37	7 33	8 08
17	18 24	−23.1	6	81	10 40	7 38	8 14
19	18 36	−23.2	6	83	10 45	7 43	8 19
21	18 49	−23.3	5	85	10 49	7 48	8 24
23	19 01	−23.2	5	86	10 54	7 52	8 28
25	19 14	−23.1	5	88	10 58	7 56	8 31
27	19 27	−23.0	5	89	11 03	7 59	8 34
29	19 40	−22.7	5	91	11 09	8 02	8 36
31	19 53	−22.3	5	92	11 14	8 04	8 37

VENUS

Day	RA h m	Dec. °	Diam. "	Phase %	Transit h m	5° high 52° h m	5° high 56° h m
1	20 21	−17.4	56	8	13 36	17 23	17 01
6	20 13	−16.5	59	4	13 09	17 01	16 41
11	20 02	−15.8	62	1	12 38	16 35	16 15
16	19 49	−15.2	63	1	12 05	16 05	15 47
21	19 36	−14.9	62	1	11 33	15 35	15 17
26	19 26	−14.8	59	4	11 03	15 06	14 48
31	19 19	−14.9	56	8	10 37	14 39	14 21

MARS

Day	RA h m	Dec. °	Diam. "	Phase %	Transit h m	5° high 52° h m	5° high 56° h m
1	20 54	−18.7	4	97	14 12	17 51	17 27
6	21 10	−17.5	4	97	14 08	17 55	17 33
11	21 26	−16.3	4	97	14 04	17 59	17 39
16	21 41	−15.0	4	97	14 00	18 04	17 45
21	21 57	−13.7	4	98	13 55	18 08	17 51
26	22 12	−12.3	4	98	13 51	18 12	17 57
31	22 27	−10.8	4	98	13 46	18 16	18 03

SUNRISE AND SUNSET

	London		Bristol		Birmingham		Manchester		Newcastle		Glasgow		Belfast	
	0°05′	51°30′	2°35′	51°28′	1°55′	52°28′	2°15′	53°28′	1°37′	54°59′	4°14′	55°52′	5°56′	54°35′
	h m	h m	h m	h m	h m	h m	h m	h m	h m	h m	h m	h m	h m	h m
1	8 06	16 02	8 16	16 12	8 18	16 04	8 25	16 00	8 31	15 49	8 47	15 54	8 46	16 09
2	8 06	16 03	8 16	16 13	8 18	16 05	8 25	16 01	8 31	15 50	8 47	15 55	8 46	16 10
3	8 06	16 04	8 16	16 14	8 18	16 07	8 25	16 03	8 31	15 51	8 47	15 56	8 46	16 11
4	8 05	16 05	8 15	16 15	8 18	16 08	8 24	16 04	8 30	15 53	8 46	15 58	8 45	16 12
5	8 05	16 06	8 15	16 17	8 17	16 09	8 24	16 05	8 30	15 54	8 46	15 59	8 45	16 14
6	8 05	16 08	8 15	16 18	8 17	16 10	8 23	16 06	8 29	15 55	8 45	16 00	8 44	16 15
7	8 04	16 09	8 14	16 19	8 17	16 12	8 23	16 08	8 29	15 57	8 45	16 02	8 44	16 16
8	8 04	16 10	8 14	16 20	8 16	16 13	8 22	16 09	8 28	15 58	8 44	16 04	8 43	16 18
9	8 04	16 12	8 13	16 22	8 15	16 14	8 22	16 11	8 28	16 00	8 43	16 05	8 43	16 19
10	8 03	16 13	8 13	16 23	8 15	16 16	8 21	16 12	8 27	16 01	8 42	16 07	8 42	16 21
11	8 02	16 14	8 12	16 25	8 14	16 17	8 21	16 14	8 26	16 03	8 42	16 08	8 41	16 23
12	8 02	16 16	8 12	16 26	8 14	16 19	8 20	16 15	8 25	16 05	8 41	16 10	8 40	16 24
13	8 01	16 17	8 11	16 28	8 13	16 20	8 19	16 17	8 24	16 06	8 40	16 12	8 39	16 26
14	8 00	16 19	8 10	16 29	8 12	16 22	8 18	16 18	8 23	16 08	8 39	16 14	8 38	16 27
15	7 59	16 20	8 09	16 31	8 11	16 23	8 17	16 20	8 22	16 10	8 38	16 15	8 37	16 29
16	7 59	16 22	8 08	16 32	8 10	16 25	8 16	16 22	8 21	16 12	8 36	16 17	8 36	16 31
17	7 58	16 24	8 08	16 34	8 09	16 27	8 15	16 23	8 20	16 13	8 35	16 19	8 35	16 33
18	7 57	16 25	8 07	16 35	8 08	16 28	8 14	16 25	8 19	16 15	8 34	16 21	8 34	16 35
19	7 56	16 27	8 06	16 37	8 07	16 30	8 13	16 27	8 18	16 17	8 33	16 23	8 33	16 36
20	7 55	16 28	8 05	16 39	8 06	16 32	8 12	16 29	8 16	16 19	8 31	16 25	8 32	16 38
21	7 54	16 30	8 03	16 40	8 05	16 33	8 11	16 31	8 15	16 21	8 30	16 27	8 30	16 40
22	7 52	16 32	8 02	16 42	8 04	16 35	8 09	16 32	8 14	16 23	8 29	16 29	8 29	16 42
23	7 51	16 34	8 01	16 44	8 02	16 37	8 08	16 34	8 12	16 25	8 27	16 31	8 28	16 44
24	7 50	16 35	8 00	16 45	8 01	16 39	8 07	16 36	8 11	16 27	8 25	16 33	8 26	16 46
25	7 49	16 37	7 59	16 47	8 00	16 41	8 05	16 38	8 09	16 29	8 24	16 35	8 25	16 48
26	7 48	16 39	7 57	16 49	7 59	16 42	8 04	16 40	8 08	16 31	8 22	16 37	8 23	16 50
27	7 46	16 40	7 56	16 51	7 57	16 44	8 02	16 42	8 06	16 33	8 21	16 39	8 22	16 52
28	7 45	16 42	7 55	16 52	7 56	16 46	8 01	16 44	8 05	16 35	8 19	16 42	8 20	16 54
29	7 43	16 44	7 53	16 54	7 54	16 48	7 59	16 46	8 03	16 37	8 17	16 44	8 18	16 56
30	7 42	16 46	7 52	16 56	7 53	16 50	7 58	16 47	8 01	16 39	8 15	16 46	8 17	16 58
31	7 41	16 48	7 50	16 58	7 51	16 52	7 56	16 49	7 59	16 41	8 14	16 48	8 15	17 00

JUPITER

Day	RA	Dec.	Transit	5° high	
				52°	56°
	h m	° ′	h m	h m	h m
1	21 39.6	−14 55	14 56	18 59	18 41
11	21 47.9	−14 13	14 25	18 33	18 15
21	21 56.6	−13 27	13 54	18 07	17 50
31	22 05.6	−12 39	13 24	17 41	17 26

Diameters – equatorial 34″ polar 32″

SATURN

Day	RA	Dec.	Transit	5° high	
				52°	56°
	h m	° ′	h m	h m	h m
1	0 54.5	+ 3 07	18 10	23 52	23 52
11	0 55.8	+ 3 18	17 32	23 15	23 15
21	0 57.8	+ 3 33	16 55	22 39	22 39
31	1 00.3	+ 3 51	16 18	22 04	22 04

Diameters – equatorial 17″ polar 16″
Rings – major axis 40″ minor axis 6″

URANUS

Day	RA	Dec.	Transit	10° high	
				52°	56°
	h m	° ′	h m	h m	h m
1	20 38.7	−19 04	13 55	16 43	16 06
11	20 41.0	−18 56	13 18	16 07	15 30
21	20 43.3	−18 47	12 41	15 32	14 55
31	20 45.7	−18 38	12 04	14 56	14 20

Diameter 4″

NEPTUNE

Day	RA	Dec.	Transit	10° high	
				52°	56°
	h m	° ′	h m	h m	h m
1	20 04.0	−20 01	13 20	16 00	15 18
11	20 05.5	−19 56	12 42	15 23	14 41
21	20 07.1	−19 52	12 05	14 46	14 04
31	20 08.7	−19 47	11 27	14 09	13 28

Diameter 2″

 # February 1998

SECOND MONTH, 28 or 29 DAYS. *Februa*, Roman festival of Purification

1	*Sunday*	**4th S. after Epiphany.** John Ford b. 1895	*week 5 day* 32
2	*Monday*	**Presentation of Christ.** Bertrand Russell d. 1970	33
3	*Tuesday*	Felix Mendelssohn b. 1809. Woodrow Wilson d. 1924	34
4	*Wednesday*	Charles Lindbergh b. 1902. End of sweet rationing 1953	35
5	*Thursday*	John Boyd Dunlop b. 1840. Sir John Pritchard b. 1921	36
6	*Friday*	*Queen's Accession 1952.* Ronald Reagan b. 1911	37
7	*Saturday*	Sinclair Lewis b. 1885. Adolphe Sax d. 1894	38
8	*Sunday*	**9th S. before Easter/Septuagesima**	*week 6 day* 39
9	*Monday*	Edward Carson b. 1854. Brendan Behan b. 1923	40
10	*Tuesday*	Joseph Lister d.1912. Larry Adler b. 1914	41
11	*Wednesday*	René Descartes d. 1650. Mary Quant b. 1934	42
12	*Thursday*	Lady Jane Grey exec. 1554. Charles Darwin b. 1809	43
13	*Friday*	Catherine Howard exec. 1542. Christabel Pankhurst d. 1958	44
14	*Saturday*	St Valentine's Day. Capt. James Cook killed 1779	45
15	*Sunday*	**8th S. before Easter/Sexagesima**	*week 7 day* 46
16	*Monday*	John McEnroe b. 1959	47
17	*Tuesday*	Johann Pestalozzi d. 1827. Ruth Rendell b. 1930	48
18	*Wednesday*	Martin Luther d. 1546. Michelangelo d. 1564	49
19	*Thursday*	*Duke of York b. 1960.* Nicolas Copernicus b. 1473	50
20	*Friday*	Enzo Ferrari b. 1898. Sidney Poitier b. 1927	51
21	*Saturday*	W. H. Auden b. 1907. Malcolm X assass. 1965	52
22	*Sunday*	**7th S. before Easter/Quinquagesima**	*week 8 day* 53
23	*Monday*	Stan Laurel d. 1965. L. S. Lowry d. 1976	54
24	*Tuesday*	Shrove Tuesday. Thomas Bowdler d. 1825	55
25	*Wednesday*	**Ash Wednesday.** Sir David Puttnam b. 1941	56
26	*Thursday*	Victor Hugo b. 1802. Sir Harry Lauder d. 1950	57
27	*Friday*	Labour Party founded 1900. John Steinbeck b. 1902	58
28	*Saturday*	Charles Blondin b. 1824. Henry James d. 1916	59

ASTRONOMICAL PHENOMENA

d	h	
1	21	Saturn in conjunction with Moon. Saturn 0°.6 N.
5	21	Venus at stationary point
18	21	Sun's longitude 330°)-(
20	01	Venus at greatest brilliancy
22	08	Mercury in superior conjunction
22	20	Jupiter in conjunction with Mercury. Jupiter 1° N.
23	09	Jupiter in conjunction
23	17	Venus in conjunction with Moon. Venus 2° N.
26	13	Jupiter in conjunction with Moon. Jupiter 1° S.
26	17	Total eclipse of Sun (*see* page 66)
27	00	Mercury in conjunction with Moon. Mercury 1° S.
27	23	Mars in conjunction with Moon. Mars 0°.7 N.

MINIMA OF ALGOL

d	h	d	h	d	h
1	04.7	12	16.0	24	03.3
4	01.6	15	12.9	27	00.1
6	22.4	18	09.7		
9	19.2	21	06.5		

CONSTELLATIONS

The following constellations are near the meridian at

	d	h		d	h
January	1	24	February	15	21
January	16	23	March	1	20
February	1	22	March	16	19

Draco (below the Pole), Camelopardus, Auriga, Taurus, Gemini, Orion, Canis Minor, Monoceros, Lepus, Canis Major and Puppis

THE MOON

Phases, Apsides and Node	d	h	m
☽ First Quarter	3	22	53
○ Full Moon	11	10	23
☾ Last Quarter	19	15	27
● New Moon	26	17	26
Apogee (405,467 km)	15	14	37
Perigee (359,097 km)	27	19	47

Mean longitude of ascending node on February 1, 162°

THE SUN

s.d. 16'.2

Day	Right Ascension	Dec. —	Equation of time	Rise 52°	Rise 56°	Transit	Set 52°	Set 56°	Sidereal time	Transit of First Point of Aries
	h m s	° '	m s	h m	h m	h m	h m	h m	h m s	h m s
1	20 57 30	17 13	−13 30	7 40	7 55	12 14	16 47	16 33	8 44 00	15 13 30
2	21 01 35	16 56	−13 38	7 39	7 53	12 14	16 49	16 35	8 47 56	15 09 34
3	21 05 39	16 38	−13 46	7 37	7 51	12 14	16 51	16 37	8 51 53	15 05 38
4	21 09 42	16 21	−13 52	7 35	7 49	12 14	16 53	16 39	8 55 49	15 01 42
5	21 13 44	16 03	−13 58	7 34	7 47	12 14	16 55	16 41	8 59 46	14 57 47
6	21 17 45	15 45	14 02	7 32	7 45	12 14	16 57	16 44	9 03 43	14 53 51
7	21 21 45	15 26	−14 06	7 30	7 43	12 14	16 59	16 46	9 07 39	14 49 55
8	21 25 45	15 07	−14 09	7 29	7 41	12 14	17 00	16 48	9 11 36	14 45 59
9	21 29 44	14 48	−14 12	7 27	7 39	12 14	17 02	16 50	9 15 32	14 42 03
10	21 33 42	14 29	−14 13	7 25	7 37	12 14	17 04	16 52	9 19 29	14 38 07
11	21 37 39	14 10	−14 14	7 23	7 35	12 14	17 06	16 55	9 23 25	14 34 11
12	21 41 36	13 50	−14 14	7 21	7 33	12 14	17 08	16 57	9 27 22	14 30 15
13	21 45 32	13 30	−14 13	7 19	7 30	12 14	17 10	16 59	9 31 18	14 26 19
14	21 49 27	13 10	−14 12	7 17	7 28	12 14	17 12	17 01	9 35 15	14 22 23
15	21 53 21	12 49	−14 09	7 16	7 26	12 14	17 14	17 03	9 39 12	14 18 27
16	21 57 14	12 29	−14 06	7 14	7 24	12 14	17 15	17 05	9 43 08	14 14 32
17	22 01 07	12 08	−14 03	7 12	7 21	12 14	17 17	17 08	9 47 05	14 10 36
18	22 04 59	11 47	−13 58	7 10	7 19	12 14	17 19	17 10	9 51 01	14 06 40
19	22 08 51	11 26	−13 53	7 08	7 17	12 14	17 21	17 12	9 54 58	14 02 44
20	22 12 42	11 04	−13 47	7 06	7 14	12 14	17 23	17 14	9 58 54	13 58 48
21	22 16 32	10 43	−13 41	7 03	7 12	12 14	17 25	17 16	10 02 51	13 54 52
22	22 20 22	10 21	−13 34	7 01	7 09	12 14	17 26	17 19	10 06 47	13 50 56
23	22 24 10	9 59	−13 26	6 59	7 07	12 13	17 28	17 21	10 10 44	13 47 00
24	22 27 59	9 37	−13 18	6 57	7 05	12 13	17 30	17 23	10 14 41	13 43 04
25	22 31 47	9 15	−13 09	6 55	7 02	12 13	17 32	17 25	10 18 37	13 39 08
26	22 35 34	8 52	−13 00	6 53	7 00	12 13	17 34	17 27	10 22 34	13 35 12
27	22 39 20	8 30	−12 50	6 51	6 57	12 13	17 36	17 29	10 26 30	13 31 17
28	22 43 06	8 07	−12 40	6 49	6 55	12 13	17 37	17 31	10 30 27	13 27 21

DURATION OF TWILIGHT (in minutes)

Latitude	52°	56°	52°	56°	52°	56°	52°	56°
	1 February		11 February		21 February		28 February	
Civil	37	41	35	39	34	38	34	38
Nautical	77	86	75	83	74	81	73	81
Astronomical	117	130	114	126	113	125	112	124

THE NIGHT SKY

Mercury is unsuitably placed for observation, superior conjunction occurring on the 22nd.

Venus, magnitude −4.6, is a brilliant object in the morning skies, visible in the east-south-east before dawn. Telescopically it appears as a thin crescent, waxing noticeably during the month as the area illuminated increases from 9 per cent to 34 per cent. The old crescent Moon is near Venus on the mornings of the 23rd and 24th.

Mars is too close to the Sun for observation.

Jupiter, magnitude −2.0, may only be glimpsed with difficulty for the first few days of the month, low above the south-western horizon at the end of evening civil twilight. Thereafter it is too close to the Sun for observation as it passes through conjunction on the 23rd.

Saturn, magnitude +0.7, continues to be visible as an evening object in the south-western skies, in the constellation of Pisces. The crescent Moon passes about 1° south of Saturn on the evening of the 1st.

Zodiacal Light. The evening cone may be observed stretching up from the western horizon, along the ecliptic after the end of twilight from the 13th to the 27th. This faint phenomenon is only visible under good conditions and in the absence of both moonlight and artificial lighting.

THE MOON

Day	RA	Dec.	Hor. par.	Semi-diam.	Sun's co-long.	PA of Bright Limb	Phase	Age	Rise 52°	Rise 56°	Transit	Set 52°	Set 56°
	h m	°	'	'	°	°	%	d	h m	h m	h m	h m	h m
1	0 13	− 0.7	60.1	16.4	320	248	19	3.7	9 45	9 44	16 04	22 35	22 38
2	1 08	+ 3.9	59.7	16.3	332	249	28	4.7	10 13	10 09	16 56	23 52	23 59
3	2 03	+ 8.2	59.2	16.1	344	251	39	5.7	10 43	10 35	17 49	—	—
4	2 58	+11.9	58.7	16.0	356	253	51	6.7	11 16	11 04	18 42	1 07	1 18
5	3 53	+15.0	58.1	15.8	8	257	62	7.7	11 53	11 38	19 35	2 19	2 33
6	4 49	+17.1	57.5	15.7	20	260	72	8.7	12 35	12 18	20 29	3 26	3 42
7	5 44	+18.3	57.0	15.5	33	264	81	9.7	13 24	13 06	21 22	4 26	4 44
8	6 39	+18.5	56.5	15.4	45	268	88	10.7	14 19	14 01	22 14	5 19	5 36
9	7 33	+17.7	56.0	15.3	57	272	94	11.7	15 18	15 02	23 04	6 03	6 20
10	8 25	+16.1	55.6	15.1	69	273	98	12.7	16 21	16 08	23 52	6 41	6 55
11	9 16	+13.7	55.1	15.0	81	264	100	13.7	17 25	17 15	—	7 13	7 25
12	10 05	+10.7	54.8	14.9	93	119	100	14.7	18 29	18 22	0 38	7 41	7 49
13	10 52	+ 7.3	54.5	14.8	105	112	98	15.7	19 33	19 29	1 23	8 06	8 11
14	11 38	+ 3.7	54.2	14.8	118	111	94	16.7	20 36	20 36	2 06	8 29	8 31
15	12 23	− 0.1	54.1	14.7	130	111	89	17.7	21 39	21 42	2 48	8 51	8 50
16	13 08	− 3.8	54.1	14.7	142	110	82	18.7	22 42	22 48	3 31	9 13	9 09
17	13 53	− 7.4	54.2	14.8	154	108	74	19.7	23 44	23 54	4 13	9 37	9 29
18	14 39	−10.7	54.5	14.8	166	106	66	20.7	—	—	4 57	10 03	9 52
19	15 27	−13.6	54.9	15.0	178	104	56	21.7	0 47	1 00	5 43	10 33	10 19
20	16 17	−16.0	55.5	15.1	190	100	47	22.7	1 49	2 05	6 31	11 08	10 52
21	17 09	−17.6	56.3	15.3	203	97	37	23.7	2 50	3 07	7 21	11 51	11 33
22	18 03	−18.5	57.2	15.6	215	92	27	24.7	3 47	4 06	8 15	12 42	12 23
23	19 00	−18.3	58.1	15.8	227	88	18	25.7	4 40	4 58	9 10	13 42	13 25
24	19 58	−17.0	59.0	16.1	239	83	10	26.7	5 26	5 42	10 06	14 52	14 37
25	20 57	−14.7	59.9	16.3	251	80	4	27.7	6 07	6 20	11 03	16 08	15 56
26	21 55	−11.3	60.6	16.5	264	77	1	28.7	6 43	6 52	12 00	17 28	17 20
27	22 54	− 7.2	61.0	16.6	276	250	0	0.3	7 15	7 20	12 56	18 50	18 47
28	23 52	− 2.6	61.1	16.6	288	251	2	1.3	7 45	7 46	13 52	20 12	20 13

MERCURY

Day	RA	Dec.	Diam.	Phase	Transit	5° high 52°	5° high 56°
	h m	°	"	%	h m	h m	h m
1	19 59	−22.1	5	92	11 17	8 05	8 37
3	20 13	−21.6	5	93	11 22	8 06	8 37
5	20 26	−21.0	5	94	11 28	8 06	8 36
7	20 39	−20.3	5	95	11 33	8 07	8 34
9	20 53	−19.6	5	96	11 39	8 06	8 32
11	21 07	−18.7	5	97	11 45	8 06	8 30
13	21 20	−17.7	5	98	11 50	8 04	8 27
15	21 34	−16.7	5	99	11 56	8 03	8 24
17	21 48	−15.5	5	99	12 02	16 04	15 46
19	22 01	−14.3	5	100	12 08	16 19	16 01
21	22 15	−13.0	5	100	12 14	16 33	16 18
23	22 29	−11.5	5	100	12 20	16 48	16 34
25	22 43	−10.0	5	100	12 26	17 03	16 51
27	22 57	− 8.4	5	99	12 32	17 18	17 08
29	23 11	− 6.7	5	98	12 38	17 33	17 25
31	23 24	− 5.0	5	96	12 44	17 49	17 42

VENUS

Day	RA	Dec.	Diam.	Phase	Transit	5° high 52°	5° high 56°
	h m	°	"	%	h m	h m	h m
1	19 18	−14.9	55	9	10 32	6 29	6 48
6	19 16	−15.1	51	13	10 11	6 09	6 28
11	19 18	−15.4	47	18	9 54	5 54	6 13
16	19 24	−15.6	43	22	9 40	5 42	6 01
21	19 34	−15.8	40	26	9 30	5 33	5 53
26	19 46	−15.9	37	30	9 23	5 26	5 46
31	20 00	−15.9	34	34	9 17	5 20	5 40

MARS

Day	RA	Dec.	Diam.	Phase	Transit	52°	56°
1	22 30	−10.5	4	98	13 45	18 16	18 04
6	22 44	− 9.0	4	98	13 40	18 20	18 09
11	22 59	− 7.5	4	98	13 35	18 24	18 14
16	23 13	− 5.9	4	99	13 30	18 27	18 19
21	23 28	− 4.3	4	99	13 24	18 30	18 23
26	23 42	− 2.8	4	99	13 19	18 33	18 28
31	23 56	− 1.2	4	99	13 13	18 36	18 32

SUNRISE AND SUNSET

	London		Bristol		Birmingham		Manchester		Newcastle		Glasgow		Belfast	
	0°05′	51°30′	2°35′	51°28′	1°55′	52°28′	2°15′	53°28′	1°37′	54°59′	4°14′	55°52′	5°56′	54°35′
	h m	h m	h m	h m	h m	h m	h m	h m	h m	h m	h m	h m	h m	h m
1	7 39	16 49	7 49	17 00	7 50	16 54	7 54	16 51	7 58	16 43	8 12	16 50	8 13	17 02
2	7 37	16 51	7 47	17 01	7 48	16 55	7 53	16 53	7 56	16 45	8 10	16 52	8 12	17 04
3	7 36	16 53	7 46	17 03	7 46	16 57	7 51	16 55	7 54	16 47	8 08	16 54	8 10	17 06
4	7 34	16 55	7 44	17 05	7 45	16 59	7 49	16 57	7 52	16 49	8 06	16 57	8 08	17 08
5	7 33	16 57	7 43	17 07	7 43	17 01	7 47	16 59	7 50	16 52	8 04	16 59	8 06	17 10
6	7 31	16 59	7 41	17 09	7 41	17 03	7 46	17 01	7 48	16 54	8 02	17 01	8 04	17 12
7	7 29	17 00	7 39	17 10	7 39	17 05	7 44	17 03	7 46	16 56	8 00	17 03	8 02	17 14
8	7 28	17 02	7 37	17 12	7 38	17 07	7 42	17 05	7 44	16 58	7 58	17 05	8 00	17 16
9	7 26	17 04	7 36	17 14	7 36	17 09	7 40	17 07	7 42	17 00	7 56	17 08	7 58	17 19
10	7 24	17 06	7 34	17 16	7 34	17 11	7 38	17 09	7 40	17 02	7 53	17 10	7 56	17 21
11	7 22	17 08	7 32	17 18	7 32	17 13	7 36	17 11	7 38	17 04	7 51	17 12	7 54	17 23
12	7 20	17 10	7 30	17 20	7 30	17 14	7 34	17 13	7 36	17 06	7 49	17 14	7 52	17 25
13	7 18	17 11	7 28	17 21	7 28	17 16	7 32	17 15	7 34	17 08	7 47	17 16	7 50	17 27
14	7 17	17 13	7 27	17 23	7 26	17 18	7 30	17 17	7 32	17 10	7 45	17 18	7 48	17 29
15	7 15	17 15	7 25	17 25	7 24	17 20	7 28	17 19	7 29	17 13	7 42	17 21	7 46	17 31
16	7 13	17 17	7 23	17 27	7 22	17 22	7 26	17 21	7 27	17 15	7 40	17 23	7 43	17 33
17	7 11	17 19	7 21	17 29	7 20	17 24	7 24	17 23	7 25	17 17	7 38	17 25	7 41	17 35
18	7 09	17 20	7 19	17 31	7 18	17 26	7 22	17 25	7 23	17 19	7 35	17 27	7 39	17 37
19	7 07	17 22	7 17	17 32	7 16	17 28	7 20	17 27	7 21	17 21	7 33	17 29	7 37	17 39
20	7 05	17 24	7 15	17 34	7 14	17 30	7 17	17 29	7 18	17 23	7 31	17 32	7 35	17 41
21	7 03	17 26	7 13	17 36	7 12	17 31	7 15	17 31	7 16	17 25	7 28	17 34	7 32	17 43
22	7 01	17 28	7 11	17 38	7 10	17 33	7 13	17 33	7 14	17 27	7 26	17 36	7 30	17 45
23	6 59	17 30	7 09	17 40	7 08	17 35	7 11	17 35	7 11	17 29	7 24	17 38	7 28	17 47
24	6 57	17 31	7 07	17 41	7 06	17 37	7 09	17 37	7 09	17 31	7 21	17 40	7 25	17 49
25	6 55	17 33	7 05	17 43	7 03	17 39	7 06	17 39	7 07	17 33	7 19	17 42	7 23	17 51
26	6 52	17 35	7 02	17 45	7 01	17 41	7 04	17 41	7 04	17 35	7 16	17 44	7 21	17 53
27	6 50	17 37	7 00	17 47	6 59	17 43	7 02	17 42	7 02	17 38	7 14	17 47	7 18	17 55
28	6 48	17 38	6 58	17 48	6 57	17 44	7 00	17 44	6 59	17 40	7 11	17 49	7 16	17 57

JUPITER

Day	RA	Dec.	Transit	5° high	
				52°	56°
	h m	° ′	h m	h m	h m
1	22 06.5	−12 34	13 21	17 39	17 23
11	22 15.6	−11 44	12 51	17 13	16 59
21	22 24.7	−10 53	12 20	16 48	16 35
31	22 33.8	−10 00	11 50	16 23	16 11

Diameters – equatorial 33″ polar 31″

SATURN

Day	RA	Dec.	Transit	5° high	
				52°	56°
	h m	° ′	h m	h m	h m
1	1 00.6	+ 3 53	16 14	22 01	22 01
11	1 03.6	+ 4 14	15 38	21 26	21 27
21	1 07.2	+ 4 38	15 02	20 53	20 53
31	1 11.1	+ 5 03	14 27	20 19	20 20

Diameters – equatorial 17″ polar 15″
Rings – major axis 38″ minor axis 7″

URANUS

Day	RA	Dec.	Transit	10° high	
				52°	56°
	h m	° ′	h m	h m	h m
1	20 45.9	−18 37	12 00	9 08	9 44
11	20 48.3	−18 28	11 23	8 29	9 05
21	20 50.6	−18 19	10 46	7 51	8 26
31	20 52.8	−18 10	10 09	7 13	7 47

Diameter 4″

NEPTUNE

Day	RA	Dec.	Transit	10° high	
				52°	56°
	h m	° ′	h m	h m	h m
1	20 08.9	−19 47	11 23	8 41	9 22
11	20 10.4	−19 42	10 45	8 03	8 43
21	20 11.8	−19 38	10 07	7 24	8 04
31	20 13.1	−19 33	9 29	6 46	7 25

Diameter 2″

March 1998

THIRD MONTH, 31 DAYS. *Mars*, Roman god of battle

1	*Sunday*	**1st S. in Lent.** St David's Day	*week* 9 *day* 60
2	*Monday*	Cardinal Archbishop Hume b. 1923. D. H. Lawrence d. 1930	61
3	*Tuesday*	Thomas Otway b. 1652. Robert Adam d. 1792	62
4	*Wednesday*	Prince Henry the Navigator b. 1394. Patrick Moore b. 1923	63
5	*Thursday*	Sir Rex Harrison b. 1908. Stalin d. 1953	64
6	*Friday*	Cyrano de Bergerac b. 1619. Davy Crockett killed 1836	65
7	*Saturday*	First patent of Bell telephone 1876. Lord Snowdon b. 1930	66
8	*Sunday*	**2nd S. in Lent.** Sir Thomas Beecham d. 1961	*week* 10 *day* 67
9	*Monday*	Commonwealth Day. Ernest Bevin b. 1881	68
10	*Tuesday*	*Prince Edward b. 1964.* Jan Masaryk d. 1948	69
11	*Wednesday*	Sir Malcolm Campbell b. 1885. Sir Alexander Fleming d. 1955	70
12	*Thursday*	Cesare Borgia d. 1507. Thomas Arne b. 1710	71
13	*Friday*	Uranus discovered 1781. Sir Hugh Walpole b. 1884	72
14	*Saturday*	Mrs Isabella Beeton b. 1836. Karl Marx d. 1883	73
15	*Sunday*	**3rd S. in Lent.** Sir Henry Bessemer d. 1898	*week* 11 *day* 74
16	*Monday*	Aubrey Beardsley d. 1898. Sir Austen Chamberlain d. 1937	75
17	*Tuesday*	St Patrick's Day. *Bank Holiday in Northern Ireland*	76
18	*Wednesday*	Ivan the Terrible d. 1584. Rudolf Diesel b. 1858	77
19	*Thursday*	**St Joseph of Nazareth.** Sir Richard Burton b. 1821	78
20	*Friday*	Henry IV d. 1413. Henrik Ibsen b. 1828	79
21	*Saturday*	Robert Southey d. 1843. Sharpeville massacre, South Africa 1960	80
22	*Sunday*	**4th S. in Lent.** Mothering Sunday	*week* 12 *day* 81
23	*Monday*	Sir Roger Bannister b. 1929. Princess Eugenie of York b. 1990	82
24	*Tuesday*	Union of English and Scottish Crowns 1603. Jules Verne d. 1905	83
25	*Wednesday*	**The Annunciation.** Sir David Lean b. 1908	84
26	*Thursday*	Cecil Rhodes d. 1902. Sir Noël Coward d. 1973	85
27	*Friday*	John Bright d. 1889. Yuri Gregarin d. 1968	86
28	*Saturday*	HINDU NEW YEAR. Dirk Bogarde b. 1921	87
29	*Sunday*	**5th S. in Lent.** John Major b. 1943	*week* 13 *day* 88
30	*Monday*	Vincent Van Gogh b. 1853. Sean O'Casey b. 1880	89
31	*Tuesday*	Eiffel Tower completed 1889. Robert Bunsen b. 1811	90

ASTRONOMICAL PHENOMENA

d	h	
1	10	Saturn in conjunction with Moon. Saturn 0°.9 N.
11	03	Mars in conjunction with Mercury. Mars 1° S.
11	05	Pluto at stationary point
20	04	Mercury at greatest elongation E.19°
20	20	Sun's longitude 0° ♈
24	16	Saturn in conjunction with Mercury. Saturn 5° S.
24	19	Venus in conjunction with Moon. Venus 0°.07 S.
26	11	Jupiter in conjunction with Moon. Jupiter 0°.8 S.
27	19	Venus at greatest elongation W.47°
27	20	Mercury at stationary point
28	21	Mars in conjunction with Moon. Mars 3° N.
29	01	Saturn in conjunction with Mercury. Saturn 6° S.
29	02	Mercury in conjunction with Moon. Mercury 7° N.
29	02	Saturn in conjunction with Moon. Saturn 1° N.
31	15	Mars in conjunction with Mercury. Mars 4° S.

MINIMA OF ALGOL

d	h	d	h	d	h
1	21.0	13	08.2	24	19.5
4	17.8	16	05.1	27	16.4
7	14.6	19	01.9	30	13.2
10	11.4	21	22.7		

CONSTELLATIONS

The following constellations are near the meridian at

	d	h		d	h
February	1	24	March	16	21
February	15	23	April	1	20
March	1	22	April	15	19

Cepheus (below the Pole), Camelopardus, Lynx, Gemini, Cancer, Leo, Canis Minor, Hydra, Monoceros, Canis Major and Puppis

THE MOON

Phases, Apsides and Node	d	h	m
☽ First Quarter	5	08	41
○ Full Moon	13	04	34
☾ Last Quarter	21	07	38
● New Moon	28	03	14
Apogee (406,174 km)	15	00	24
Perigee (357,027 km)	28	06	57

Mean longitude of ascending node on March 1, 161°

THE SUN

s.d. 16'.1

Day	Right Ascension	Dec.	Equation of time	Rise 52°	Rise 56°	Transit	Set 52°	Set 56°	Sidereal time	Transit of First Point of Aries
	h m s	° '	m s	h m	h m	h m	h m	h m	h m s	h m s
1	22 46 52	− 7 45	−12 29	6 46	6 52	12 12	17 39	17 34	10 34 23	13 23 25
2	22 50 37	− 7 22	−12 17	6 44	6 50	12 12	17 41	17 36	10 38 20	13 19 29
3	22 54 21	− 6 59	−12 05	6 42	6 47	12 12	17 43	17 38	10 42 16	13 15 33
4	22 58 05	− 6 36	11 52	6 40	6 45	12 12	17 45	17 40	10 46 13	13 11 37
5	23 01 49	− 6 13	−11 39	6 38	6 42	12 12	17 46	17 42	10 50 10	13 07 41
6	23 05 32	− 5 50	−11 26	6 35	6 39	12 11	17 48	17 44	10 54 06	13 03 45
7	23 09 14	− 5 26	−11 12	6 33	6 37	12 11	17 50	17 46	10 58 03	12 59 49
8	23 12 57	− 5 03	−10 58	6 31	6 34	12 11	17 52	17 48	11 01 59	12 55 53
9	23 16 38	− 4 40	−10 43	6 29	6 32	12 11	17 54	17 50	11 05 56	12 51 57
10	23 20 20	− 4 16	−10 28	6 26	6 29	12 10	17 55	17 53	11 09 52	12 48 02
11	23 24 01	− 3 53	−10 12	6 24	6 27	12 10	17 57	17 55	11 13 49	12 44 06
12	23 27 42	− 3 29	− 9 56	6 22	6 24	12 10	17 59	17 57	11 17 45	12 40 10
13	23 31 22	− 3 06	− 9 40	6 19	6 21	12 10	18 01	17 59	11 21 42	12 36 14
14	23 35 02	− 2 42	− 9 24	6 17	6 19	12 09	18 02	18 01	11 25 38	12 32 18
15	23 38 42	− 2 18	− 9 07	6 15	6 16	12 09	18 04	18 03	11 29 35	12 28 22
16	23 42 22	− 1 55	− 8 50	6 13	6 14	12 09	18 06	18 05	11 33 32	12 24 26
17	23 46 01	− 1 31	− 8 33	6 10	6 11	12 08	18 08	18 07	11 37 28	12 20 30
18	23 49 40	− 1 07	− 8 16	6 08	6 08	12 08	18 09	18 09	11 41 25	12 16 34
19	23 53 19	− 0 43	− 7 58	6 06	6 06	12 08	18 11	18 11	11 45 21	12 12 38
20	23 56 58	− 0 20	− 7 41	6 03	6 03	12 08	18 13	18 13	11 49 18	12 08 43
21	0 00 37	+ 0 04	− 7 23	6 01	6 00	12 07	18 14	18 15	11 53 14	12 04 47
22	0 04 16	+ 0 28	− 7 05	5 59	5 58	12 07	18 16	18 17	11 57 11	12 00 51
23	0 07 54	+ 0 51	− 6 47	5 56	5 55	12 07	18 18	18 19	12 01 07	11 56 55
24	0 11 33	1 1 15	− 6 29	5 54	5 52	12 06	18 20	18 21	12 05 04	11 52 59
25	0 15 12	+ 1 39	− 6 11	5 52	5 50	12 06	18 21	18 23	12 09 01	11 49 03
26	0 18 50	+ 2 02	− 5 53	5 49	5 47	12 06	18 23	18 26	12 12 57	11 45 07
27	0 22 28	+ 2 26	− 5 35	5 47	5 45	12 05	18 25	18 28	12 16 54	11 41 11
28	0 26 07	+ 2 49	− 5 17	5 45	5 42	12 05	18 26	18 30	12 20 50	11 37 15
29	0 29 45	+ 3 13	− 4 59	5 43	5 39	12 05	18 28	18 32	12 24 47	11 33 19
30	0 33 24	+ 3 36	− 4 41	5 40	5 37	12 05	18 30	18 34	12 28 43	11 29 23
31	0 37 03	+ 3 59	− 4 23	5 38	5 34	12 04	18 32	18 36	12 32 40	11 25 28

DURATION OF TWILIGHT (in minutes)

Latitude	52°	56°	52°	56°	52°	56°	52°	56°
	1 March		11 March		21 March		31 March	
Civil	34	38	34	37	34	37	34	38
Nautical	73	81	73	80	74	82	76	84
Astronomical	112	124	113	125	116	129	120	136

THE NIGHT SKY

Mercury is an evening object, magnitude − 1.2 to +1.5, after the first ten days of the month. It is visible low in the western sky at the end of evening civil twilight. Mercury is at greatest eastern elongation on the 20th and this is the only evening apparition of the year for observers in northern temperate latitudes. During the last week of the month Mercury's magnitude is fading rapidly and the planet is then unlikely to be seen against the twilit sky.

Venus continues to be visible as a magnificent object in the morning skies, magnitude − 4.5, though only visible for about an hour before sunrise, low above the east-south-east horizon. The old crescent Moon will be seen in the vicinity of the planet on the mornings of the 24th and 25th.

Mars is unsuitably placed for observation.

Jupiter is too close to the Sun for observation. However, telescopic observers should refer to page 67 for details of a lunar occultation of Jupiter during daylight on the 26th.

Saturn is an evening object, magnitude +0.7, visible in the south-western sky in the early part of the evening. As it moves closer to the Sun it becomes increasingly difficult to observe and is unlikely to be seen after the middle of the month. The crescent Moon is in the vicinity of the planet on the evening of the 1st.

Zodiacal Light. The evening cone may be observed stretching up from the western horizon, along the ecliptic, after the end of twilight from the 14th to the 28th.

THE MOON

Day	RA	Dec.	Hor. par.	Semi- diam.	Sun's co- long.	PA of Bright Limb	Phase	Age	Rise 52°	Rise 56°	Transit	Set 52°	Set 56°
	h m	°	′	′	°	°	%	d	h m	h m	h m	h m	h m
1	0 49	+ 2.2	60.9	16.6	300	252	8	2.3	8 14	8 11	14 47	21 33	21 39
2	1 45	+ 6.8	60.4	16.5	312	253	15	3.3	8 44	8 37	15 42	22 52	23 02
3	2 42	+10.9	59.7	16.3	325	255	25	4.3	9 17	9 06	16 36	—	—
4	3 39	+14.2	59.0	16.1	337	258	35	5.3	9 53	9 39	17 31	0 08	0 21
5	4 35	+16.7	58.2	15.9	349	262	46	6.3	10 34	10 18	18 25	1 18	1 34
6	5 31	+18.1	57.4	15.6	1	266	57	7.3	11 22	11 04	19 18	2 21	2 38
7	6 26	+18.5	56.7	15.4	13	271	67	8.3	12 14	11 57	20 10	3 16	3 34
8	7 20	+18.0	56.0	15.3	26	275	76	9.3	13 12	12 56	21 01	4 03	4 20
9	8 13	+16.5	55.5	15.1	38	279	84	10.3	14 13	13 59	21 49	4 42	4 57
10	9 03	+14.3	55.0	15.0	50	283	91	11.3	15 16	15 05	22 35	5 16	5 28
11	9 52	+11.5	54.7	14.9	62	287	96	12.3	16 19	16 11	23 20	5 44	5 54
12	10 39	+ 8.3	54.4	14.8	74	291	99	13.3	17 23	17 18	—	6 10	6 16
13	11 25	+ 4.7	54.2	14.8	86	316	100	14.3	18 26	18 25	0 04	6 33	6 36
14	12 10	+ 1.0	54.0	14.7	98	101	99	15.3	19 29	19 31	0 46	6 55	6 55
15	12 55	− 2.8	54.0	14.7	111	105	97	16.3	20 32	20 37	1 28	7 18	7 14
16	13 40	− 6.4	54.0	14.7	123	105	93	17.3	21 35	21 43	2 11	7 41	7 34
17	14 26	− 9.8	54.2	14.8	135	104	88	18.3	22 37	22 49	2 54	8 06	7 56
18	15 13	−12.9	54.5	14.8	147	102	81	19.3	23 39	23 53	3 39	8 34	8 21
19	16 02	−15.4	54.9	15.0	159	99	72	20.3	—	—	4 25	9 06	8 51
20	16 53	−17.2	55.4	15.1	171	95	63	21.3	0 39	0 56	5 14	9 45	9 28
21	17 45	−18.3	56.1	15.3	184	91	53	22.3	1 37	1 55	6 04	10 31	10 13
22	18 39	−18.5	57.0	15.5	196	87	43	23.3	2 30	2 48	6 57	11 26	11 08
23	19 35	−17.7	57.9	15.8	208	82	33	24.3	3 17	3 34	7 51	12 29	12 13
24	20 32	−15.8	58.9	16.0	220	78	23	25.3	3 59	4 14	8 46	13 40	13 26
25	21 29	−13.0	59.8	16.3	232	74	14	26.3	4 36	4 47	9 42	14 57	14 47
26	22 27	− 9.2	60.6	16.5	245	69	7	27.3	5 10	5 17	10 38	16 17	16 12
27	23 25	− 4.8	61.1	16.7	257	64	2	28.3	5 40	5 44	11 34	17 40	17 39
28	0 23	0.0	61.4	16.7	269	18	0	29.3	6 10	6 09	12 30	19 03	19 07
29	1 21	+ 4.9	61.3	16.7	281	263	1	0.9	6 40	6 35	13 26	20 26	20 34
30	2 19	+ 9.3	60.9	16.6	293	259	5	1.9	7 13	7 04	14 23	21 46	21 58
31	3 18	+13.1	60.3	16.4	306	261	12	2.9	7 48	7 36	15 20	23 02	23 17

MERCURY

Day	RA	Dec.	Diam.	Phase	Transit	5° high 52°	5° high 56°
	h m	°	″	%	h m	h m	h m
1	23 11	− 6.7	5	98	12 38	17 33	17 25
3	23 24	− 5.0	5	96	12 44	17 49	17 42
5	23 38	− 3.2	5	94	12 49	18 04	17 59
7	23 51	− 1.4	5	90	12 55	18 19	18 15
9	0 04	+ 0.4	6	85	13 00	18 34	18 31
11	0 17	+ 2.2	6	80	13 04	18 47	18 46
13	0 29	+ 3.9	6	73	13 08	18 59	19 00
15	0 40	+ 5.6	6	65	13 11	19 10	19 12
17	0 49	+ 7.1	7	57	13 12	19 19	19 22
19	0 58	+ 8.4	7	49	13 12	19 25	19 29
21	1 05	+ 9.5	8	40	13 11	19 29	19 33
23	1 10	+10.4	8	32	13 07	19 29	19 35
25	1 13	+11.0	9	25	13 02	19 26	19 32
27	1 14	+11.4	9	18	12 55	19 21	19 27
29	1 14	+11.5	10	12	12 47	19 12	19 18
31	1 12	+11.3	10	7	12 37	19 00	19 05

VENUS

Day	RA	Dec.	Diam.	Phase	Transit	5° high 52°	5° high 56°
	h m	°	″	%	h m	h m	h m
1	19 54	−15.9	35	33	9 19	5 23	5 43
6	20 09	−15.8	33	36	9 15	5 17	5 37
11	20 26	−15.5	30	40	9 12	5 12	5 32
16	20 44	−15.0	28	43	9 10	5 07	5 26
21	21 03	−14.4	27	46	9 09	5 02	5 20
26	21 22	−13.5	25	49	9 09	4 57	5 13
31	21 42	−12.4	24	51	9 09	4 50	5 05

MARS

Day	RA	Dec.	Diam.	Phase	Transit	5° high 52°	5° high 56°
1	23 51	− 1.8	4	99	13 16	18 35	18 30
6	0 05	− 0.2	4	99	13 10	18 37	18 34
11	0 19	+ 1.4	4	99	13 05	18 40	18 38
16	0 33	+ 2.9	4	99	12 59	18 42	18 42
21	0 47	+ 4.5	4	99	12 53	18 45	18 45
26	1 01	+ 6.0	4	100	12 48	18 47	18 49
31	1 15	+ 7.5	4	100	12 42	18 49	18 52

SUNRISE AND SUNSET

	London		Bristol		Birmingham		Manchester		Newcastle		Glasgow		Belfast	
	0°05'	51°30'	2°35'	51°28'	1°55'	52°28'	2°15'	53°28'	1°37'	54°59'	4°14'	55°52'	5°56'	54°35'
	h m	h m	h m	h m	h m	h m	h m	h m	h m	h m	h m	h m	h m	h m
1	6 46	17 40	6 56	17 50	6 55	17 46	6 57	17 46	6 57	17 42	7 09	17 51	7 14	18 00
2	6 44	17 42	6 54	17 52	6 52	17 48	6 55	17 48	6 55	17 44	7 06	17 53	7 11	18 02
3	6 42	17 44	6 52	17 54	6 50	17 50	6 53	17 50	6 52	17 46	7 04	17 55	7 09	18 04
4	6 40	17 45	6 50	17 56	6 48	17 52	6 50	17 52	6 50	17 48	7 01	17 57	7 06	18 06
5	6 37	17 47	6 47	17 57	6 46	17 54	6 48	17 54	6 47	17 50	6 59	17 59	7 04	18 08
6	6 35	17 49	6 45	17 59	6 43	17 55	6 46	17 56	6 45	17 52	6 56	18 01	7 02	18 09
7	6 33	17 51	6 43	18 01	6 41	17 57	6 43	17 58	6 42	17 54	6 54	18 03	6 59	18 11
8	6 31	17 52	6 41	18 02	6 39	17 59	6 41	18 00	6 40	17 56	6 51	18 05	6 57	18 13
9	6 29	17 54	6 39	18 04	6 37	18 01	6 39	18 01	6 37	17 58	6 49	18 08	6 54	18 15
10	6 26	17 56	6 36	18 06	6 34	18 03	6 36	18 03	6 35	18 00	6 46	18 10	6 52	18 17
11	6 24	17 58	6 34	18 08	6 32	18 04	6 34	18 05	6 32	18 02	6 43	18 12	6 49	18 19
12	6 22	17 59	6 32	18 09	6 30	18 06	6 32	18 07	6 30	18 04	6 41	18 14	6 47	18 21
13	6 20	18 01	6 30	18 11	6 27	18 08	6 29	18 09	6 27	18 06	6 38	18 16	6 44	18 23
14	6 17	18 03	6 27	18 13	6 25	18 10	6 27	18 11	6 25	18 08	6 36	18 18	6 42	18 25
15	6 15	18 04	6 25	18 15	6 23	18 12	6 24	18 13	6 22	18 10	6 33	18 20	6 39	18 27
16	6 13	18 06	6 23	18 16	6 20	18 13	6 22	18 15	6 20	18 12	6 30	18 22	6 37	18 29
17	6 11	18 08	6 21	18 18	6 18	18 15	6 19	18 16	6 17	18 14	6 28	18 24	6 34	18 31
18	6 08	18 10	6 18	18 20	6 16	18 17	6 17	18 18	6 15	18 16	6 25	18 26	6 32	18 33
19	6 06	18 11	6 16	18 21	6 13	18 19	6 15	18 20	6 12	18 18	6 23	18 28	6 29	18 35
20	6 04	18 13	6 14	18 23	6 11	18 20	6 12	18 22	6 10	18 20	6 20	18 30	6 27	18 37
21	6 01	18 15	6 11	18 25	6 09	18 22	6 10	18 24	6 07	18 22	6 17	18 32	6 24	18 39
22	5 59	18 16	6 09	18 26	6 06	18 24	6 07	18 26	6 04	18 23	6 15	18 34	6 22	18 41
23	5 57	18 18	6 07	18 28	6 04	18 26	6 05	18 27	6 02	18 25	6 12	18 36	6 19	18 43
24	5 55	18 20	6 05	18 30	6 02	18 27	6 03	18 29	5 59	18 27	6 09	18 38	6 17	18 45
25	5 52	18 21	6 02	18 31	5 59	18 29	6 00	18 31	5 57	18 29	6 07	18 40	6 14	18 46
26	5 50	18 23	6 00	18 33	5 57	18 31	5 58	18 33	5 54	18 31	6 04	18 42	6 12	18 48
27	5 48	18 25	5 58	18 35	5 55	18 33	5 55	18 35	5 52	18 33	6 02	18 44	6 09	18 50
28	5 45	18 26	5 55	18 36	5 52	18 35	5 53	18 37	5 49	18 35	5 59	18 46	6 07	18 52
29	5 43	18 28	5 53	18 38	5 50	18 36	5 50	18 38	5 47	18 37	5 56	18 48	6 04	18 54
30	5 41	18 30	5 51	18 40	5 47	18 38	5 48	18 40	5 44	18 39	5 54	18 50	6 02	18 56
31	5 39	18 32	5 49	18 42	5 45	18 40	5 46	18 42	5 42	18 41	5 51	18 53	5 59	18 58

JUPITER

Day	RA	Dec.	Transit	5° high	
				52°	56°
	h m	° '	h m	h m	h m
1	22 32.0	−10 11	11 56	7 24	7 37
11	22 41.1	− 9 18	11 26	6 49	7 01
21	22 50.0	− 8 25	10 55	6 14	6 24
31	22 58.6	− 7 33	10 25	5 38	5 48

Diameters – equatorial 33″ polar 31″

SATURN

Day	RA	Dec.	Transit	5° high	
				52°	56°
	h m	° '	h m	h m	h m
1	1 10.3	+ 4 58	14 34	20 26	20 27
11	1 14.4	+ 5 25	13 59	19 53	19 54
21	1 10.0	+ 5 53	13 24	19 21	19 22
31	1 23.4	+ 6 21	12 49	18 48	18 50

Diameters – equatorial 16″ polar 15″
Rings – major axis 37″ minor axis 7″

URANUS

Day	RA	Dec.	Transit	10° high	
				52°	56°
	h m	° '	h m	h m	h m
1	20 52.4	−18 12	10 16	7 20	7 55
11	20 54.4	−18 04	9 39	6 42	7 16
21	20 56.3	−17 56	9 02	6 03	6 37
31	20 57.9	−17 50	8 24	5 25	5 58

Diameter 4″

NEPTUNE

Day	RA	Dec.	Transit	10° high	
				52°	56°
	h m	° '	h m	h m	h m
1	20 12.9	−19 34	9 37	6 53	7 33
11	20 14.1	−19 30	8 59	6 15	6 54
21	20 15.2	−19 27	8 21	5 36	6 15
31	20 16.0	−19 24	7 42	4 57	5 36

Diameter 2″

April 1998

FOURTH MONTH, 30 DAYS. *Aperire*, to open; Earth opens to receive seed

1	Wednesday	Royal Air Force formed 1918. VAT introduced 1973	*week* 13 *day* 91
2	Thursday	C. S. Forester d. 1966. Argentine invasion of the Falklands 1982	92
3	Friday	First run of the Pony Express 1860. Leslie Howard b. 1893	93
4	Saturday	North Atlantic Treaty signed 1949. Martin Luther King assass. 1968	94
5	Sunday	**Palm Sunday.** Spencer Tracy b. 1900	*week* 14 *day* 95
6	Monday	Cdr. Peary reaches North Pole 1909	96
7	Tuesday	Dick Turpin exec. 1739. Phineas T. Barnum d. 1891	97
8	Wednesday	*Hilary Law Sittings end.* Pablo Picasso d. 1973	98
9	Thursday	**Maundy Thursday.** Paul Robeson b. 1898	99
10	Friday	**Good Friday.** *Public Holiday in the UK*	100
11	Saturday	**Easter Eve.** Passover begins	101
12	Sunday	**Easter Day** (Western churches)	*week* 15 *day* 102
13	Monday	Sikh New Year. *Bank Holiday in England, Wales and Northern Ireland*	103
14	Tuesday	Sir John Gielgud b. 1904. *Titanic* sank 1912	104
15	Wednesday	Abraham Lincoln assass. 1865. Jean-Paul Sartre d. 1980	105
16	Thursday	Mme Marie Tussaud d. 1850. Kingsley Amis b. 1922	106
17	Friday	Benjamin Franklin d. 1790. Clare Francis b. 1946	107
18	Saturday	Irish Free State became Republic of Ireland 1949. Einstein d. 1955	108
19	Sunday	**1st. S. after Easter.** Easter Day (Greek Orthodox)	*week* 16 *day* 109
20	Monday	Harold Lloyd b. 1893. Bram Stoker d. 1912	110
21	Tuesday	*Queen Elizabeth II b. 1926. Easter Law Sittings begin*	111
22	Wednesday	Henry Fielding b. 1707. Yehudi Menuhin b. 1916	112
23	Thursday	St George's Day. Shakespeare b. 1564 and d. 1616	113
24	Friday	Daniel Defoe d. 1731. Marie Taglioni d. 1884	114
25	Saturday	**St Mark.** Patrick Lichfield b. 1939	115
26	Sunday	**2nd S. after Easter.** Eugène Delacroix b. 1798	*week* 17 *day* 116
27	Monday	Ferdinand Magellan killed 1521. Samuel Morse b. 1791	117
28	Tuesday	Muslim New Year (1419). Mutiny on *The Bounty* 1789	118
29	Wednesday	Jules Henri Poincaré b. 1854. Duke Ellington b. 1899	119
30	Thursday	Edouard Manet d. 1883. A. E. Housman d. 1936	120

Astronomical Phenomena

d h
2 07 Saturn in conjunction with Mars. Saturn 2° S.
6 17 Mercury in inferior conjunction
13 12 Saturn in conjunction
20 07 Sun's longitude 30° ♉
20 08 Mercury at stationary point
22 23 Jupiter in conjunction with Venus. Jupiter 0°.3 S.
23 07 Jupiter in conjunction with Moon. Jupiter 0°.2 S.
23 08 Venus in conjunction with Moon. Venus 0°.00 N.
24 19 Mercury in conjunction with Moon. Mercury 0°.8 N.
25 18 Saturn in conjunction with Moon. Saturn 1° N.
26 18 Mars in conjunction with Moon. Mars 4° N.

Minima of Algol

d	h	d	h	d	h
2	10.0	13	21.3	25	08.5
5	06.8	16	18.1	28	05.4
8	03.6	19	14.9		
11	00.5	22	11.7		

Constellations

The following constellations are near the meridian at

	d	h		d	h
March	1	24	April	15	21
March	16	23	May	1	20
April	1	22	May	16	19

Cepheus (below the Pole), Cassiopeia (below the Pole), Ursa Major, Leo Minor, Leo, Sextans, Hydra and Crater

The Moon

Phases, Apsides and Node	d	h	m
☽ First Quarter	3	20	18
○ Full Moon	11	22	23
☾ Last Quarter	19	19	53
● New Moon	26	11	41

| Apogee (406,353 km) | 11 | 01 | 31 |
| Perigee (358,036 km) | 25 | 17 | 46 |

Mean longitude of ascending node on April 1, 159°

THE SUN

s.d. 16'.0

Day	Right Ascension	Dec. +	Equation of time	Rise 52°	Rise 56°	Transit	Set 52°	Set 56°	Sidereal time	Transit of First Point of Aries
	h m s	° '	m s	h m	h m	h m	h m	h m	h m s	h m s
1	0 40 41	4 23	− 4 05	5 36	5 31	12 04	18 33	18 38	12 36 36	11 21 32
2	0 44 20	4 46	− 3 47	5 33	5 29	12 04	18 35	18 40	12 40 33	11 17 36
3	0 47 59	5 09	− 3 29	5 31	5 26	12 03	18 37	18 42	12 44 30	11 13 40
4	0 51 38	5 32	− 3 12	5 29	5 24	12 03	18 38	18 44	12 48 26	11 09 44
5	0 55 17	5 55	− 2 54	5 26	5 21	12 03	18 40	18 46	12 52 23	11 05 48
6	0 58 56	6 18	− 2 37	5 24	5 18	12 02	18 42	18 48	12 56 19	11 01 52
7	1 02 36	6 40	− 2 20	5 22	5 16	12 02	18 44	18 50	13 00 16	10 57 56
8	1 06 15	7 03	− 2 03	5 20	5 13	12 02	18 45	18 52	13 04 12	10 54 00
9	1 09 55	7 25	− 1 46	5 17	5 11	12 02	18 47	18 54	13 08 09	10 50 04
10	1 13 35	7 47	− 1 30	5 15	5 08	12 01	18 49	18 56	13 12 05	10 46 08
11	1 17 16	8 10	− 1 14	5 13	5 05	12 01	18 50	18 58	13 16 02	10 42 13
12	1 20 56	8 32	− 0 58	5 11	5 03	12 01	18 52	19 00	13 19 58	10 38 17
13	1 24 37	8 54	− 0 42	5 08	5 00	12 01	18 54	19 02	13 23 55	10 34 21
14	1 28 18	9 15	− 0 27	5 06	4 58	12 00	18 56	19 04	13 27 52	10 30 25
15	1 32 00	9 37	− 0 12	5 04	4 55	12 00	18 57	19 06	13 31 48	10 26 29
16	1 35 42	9 58	+ 0 03	5 02	4 53	12 00	18 59	19 08	13 35 45	10 22 33
17	1 39 24	10 20	+ 0 17	5 00	4 50	12 00	19 01	19 10	13 39 41	10 18 37
18	1 43 07	10 41	+ 0 31	4 57	4 48	11 59	19 02	19 12	13 43 38	10 14 41
19	1 46 50	11 02	+ 0 44	4 55	4 45	11 59	19 04	19 14	13 47 34	10 10 45
20	1 50 34	11 22	+ 0 57	4 53	4 43	11 59	19 06	19 16	13 51 31	10 06 49
21	1 54 18	11 43	+ 1 10	4 51	4 40	11 59	19 08	19 19	13 55 27	10 02 54
22	1 58 02	12 03	+ 1 22	4 49	4 38	11 59	19 09	19 21	13 59 24	9 58 58
23	2 01 47	12 23	+ 1 34	4 47	4 35	11 58	19 11	19 23	14 03 21	9 55 02
24	2 05 32	12 43	+ 1 45	4 45	4 33	11 58	19 13	19 25	14 07 17	9 51 06
25	2 09 18	13 03	+ 1 56	4 43	4 31	11 58	19 14	19 27	14 11 14	9 47 10
26	2 13 04	13 23	+ 2 06	4 41	4 28	11 58	19 16	19 29	14 15 10	9 43 14
27	2 16 51	13 42	+ 2 15	4 39	4 26	11 58	19 18	19 31	14 19 07	9 39 18
28	2 20 39	14 01	+ 2 25	4 37	4 24	11 58	19 19	19 33	14 23 03	9 35 22
29	2 24 26	14 20	+ 2 33	4 35	4 21	11 57	19 21	19 35	14 27 00	9 31 26
30	2 28 15	14 39	+ 2 42	4 33	4 19	11 57	19 23	19 37	14 30 56	9 27 30

DURATION OF TWILIGHT (in minutes)

Latitude	52°	56°	52°	56°	52°	56°	52°	56°
	1 April		11 April		21 April		30 April	
Civil	34	38	35	40	37	42	39	44
Nautical	76	85	79	90	84	96	89	105
Astronomical	121	137	128	148	138	167	152	200

THE NIGHT SKY

Mercury is unsuitably placed for observation throughout the month, inferior conjunction occurring on the 6th.

Venus, magnitude − 4.2, is still visible as a brilliant object in the morning skies but only visible for a short time before sunrise, low above the east-south-eastern horizon. On the morning of the 23rd the old crescent Moon will be seen about 1½° to the right of the planet.

Mars remains too close to the Sun for observation.

Jupiter is unsuitably placed for observation at first but gradually becomes visible as a morning object, magnitude − 2.1, during the last few days of the month, low above the east-south-eastern horizon for a short time before twilight inhibits observation.

Saturn passes through conjunction on the 13th and therefore is too close to the Sun for observation.

THE MOON

Day	RA	Dec.	Hor. par.	Semi- diam.	Sun's co- long.	PA of Bright Limb	Phase	Age	Rise 52°	Rise 56°	Transit	Set 52°	Set 56°
	h m	°	'	'	°	°	%	d	h m	h m	h m	h m	h m
1	4 16	+16.0	59.4	16.2	318	264	21	3.9	8 29	8 13	16 16	—	—
2	5 14	+17.8	58.5	15.9	330	268	31	4.9	9 16	8 58	17 12	0 11	0 28
3	6 11	+18.6	57.6	15.7	342	272	41	5.9	10 08	9 50	18 06	1 11	1 29
4	7 07	+18.3	56.7	15.5	354	276	52	6.9	11 05	10 48	18 58	2 01	2 19
5	8 00	+17.0	55.9	15.2	7	281	62	7.9	12 06	11 51	19 47	2 44	2 59
6	8 51	+15.0	55.3	15.1	19	285	71	8.9	13 08	12 56	20 34	3 19	3 32
7	9 40	+12.3	54.8	14.9	31	288	80	9.9	14 12	14 02	21 19	3 49	3 59
8	10 28	+ 9.2	54.4	14.8	43	291	87	10.9	15 15	15 09	22 02	4 15	4 22
9	11 14	+ 5.7	54.2	14.8	55	294	93	11.9	16 18	16 15	22 45	4 38	4 42
10	11 59	+ 1.9	54.0	14.7	68	298	97	12.9	17 21	17 22	23 27	5 01	5 02
11	12 44	− 1.8	54.0	14.7	80	308	99	13.9	18 24	18 28	—	5 23	5 20
12	13 29	− 5.5	54.0	14.7	92	33	100	14.9	19 27	19 34	0 09	5 45	5 40
13	14 15	− 9.1	54.1	14.7	104	90	99	15.9	20 30	20 41	0 52	6 09	6 01
14	15 02	−12.2	54.3	14.8	116	95	96	16.9	21 32	21 46	1 37	6 36	6 25
15	15 50	−14.9	54.6	14.9	128	95	91	17.9	22 33	22 50	2 22	7 07	6 53
16	16 40	−17.0	55.0	15.0	141	93	85	18.9	23 31	23 49	3 10	7 43	7 26
17	17 31	−18.3	55.5	15.1	153	90	78	19.9	—	—	4 00	8 26	8 08
18	18 24	−18.7	56.2	15.3	165	86	69	20.9	0 25	0 44	4 51	9 17	8 58
19	19 18	−18.2	56.9	15.5	177	82	59	21.9	1 14	1 31	5 43	10 15	9 58
20	20 13	−16.7	57.7	15.7	189	77	48	22.9	1 56	2 12	6 36	11 21	11 06
21	21 09	−14.2	58.5	15.9	202	74	37	23.9	2 34	2 47	7 30	12 33	12 21
22	22 05	−10.9	59.4	16.2	214	70	27	24.9	3 07	3 16	8 23	13 49	13 42
23	23 01	− 6.8	60.2	16.4	226	67	17	25.9	3 38	3 43	9 17	15 09	15 06
24	23 57	− 2.2	60.8	16.6	238	64	9	26.9	4 07	4 08	10 12	16 31	16 32
25	0 54	+ 2.7	61.2	16.7	250	60	3	27.9	4 36	4 33	11 08	17 54	17 59
26	1 52	+ 7.4	61.2	16.7	263	40	0	28.9	5 07	5 00	12 04	19 16	19 26
27	2 51	+11.6	61.0	16.6	275	285	1	0.5	5 40	5 30	13 02	20 37	20 50
28	3 51	+15.0	60.4	16.5	287	270	4	1.5	6 19	6 05	14 01	21 51	22 08
29	4 51	+17.4	59.7	16.3	299	270	9	2.5	7 04	6 47	14 59	22 58	23 16
30	5 50	+18.6	58.8	16.0	312	273	17	3.5	7 55	7 37	15 55	23 55	—

MERCURY

Day	RA	Dec.	Diam.	Phase	Transit	5° high 52°	5° high 56°
	h m	°	"	%	h m	h m	h m
1	1 11	+11.1	10	6	12 31	18 53	18 58
3	1 07	+10.5	11	3	12 19	18 37	18 42
5	1 02	+ 9.7	11	1	12 06	18 20	18 24
7	0 57	+ 8.8	11	0	11 53	5 43	5 39
9	0 51	+ 7.7	12	1	11 40	5 35	5 32
11	0 47	+ 6.7	12	3	11 28	5 28	5 26
13	0 43	+ 5.7	11	5	11 16	5 22	5 20
15	0 40	+ 4.8	11	8	11 06	5 15	5 15
17	0 38	+ 4.0	11	11	10 56	5 10	5 10
19	0 37	+ 3.4	11	15	10 48	5 04	5 05
21	0 38	+ 2.9	10	19	10 41	4 59	5 00
23	0 39	+ 2.6	10	22	10 35	4 55	4 56
25	0 42	+ 2.5	10	26	10 30	4 50	4 52
27	0 46	+ 2.6	9	30	10 26	4 46	4 47
29	0 51	+ 2.8	9	33	10 23	4 42	4 43
31	0 56	+ 3.1	9	37	10 21	4 38	4 38

VENUS

Day	RA	Dec.	Diam.	Phase	Transit	5° high 52°	5° high 56°
	h m	°	"	%	h m	h m	h m
1	21 46	−12.2	23	52	9 10	4 49	5 04
6	22 06	−10.9	22	54	9 10	4 42	4 55
11	22 27	− 9.5	21	57	9 11	4 34	4 46
16	22 48	− 7.9	20	59	9 12	4 26	4 37
21	23 09	− 6.1	19	61	9 13	4 18	4 26
26	23 29	− 4.3	18	63	9 14	4 09	4 16
31	23 50	− 2.4	18	65	9 16	4 00	4 05

MARS

Day	RA	Dec.	Diam.	Phase	Transit	5° high 52°	5° high 56°
	h m	°	"	%	h m	h m	h m
1	1 18	+ 7.8	4	100	12 41	18 49	18 52
6	1 32	+ 9.2	4	100	12 35	18 51	18 55
11	1 46	+10.7	4	100	12 30	18 53	18 58
16	2 00	+12.0	4	100	12 24	18 54	19 01
21	2 15	+13.3	4	100	12 19	18 56	19 04
26	2 29	+14.6	4	100	12 13	18 57	19 06
31	2 43	+15.7	4	100	12 08	18 58	19 08

SUNRISE AND SUNSET

	London		Bristol		Birmingham		Manchester		Newcastle		Glasgow		Belfast	
	0°05′	51°30′	2°35′	51°28′	1°55′	52°28′	2°15′	53°28′	1°37′	54°59′	4°14′	55°52′	5°56′	54°35′
	h m	h m	h m	h m	h m	h m	h m	h m	h m	h m	h m	h m	h m	h m
1	5 36	18 33	5 46	18 43	5 43	18 42	5 43	18 44	5 39	18 43	5 48	18 55	5 57	19 00
2	5 34	18 35	5 44	18 45	5 40	18 43	5 41	18 46	5 36	18 45	5 46	18 57	5 54	19 02
3	5 32	18 37	5 42	18 47	5 38	18 45	5 38	18 47	5 34	18 47	5 43	18 59	5 52	19 04
4	5 30	18 38	5 40	18 48	5 36	18 47	5 36	18 49	5 31	18 49	5 41	19 01	5 49	19 06
5	5 27	18 40	5 37	18 50	5 33	18 48	5 34	18 51	5 29	18 51	5 38	19 03	5 47	19 08
6	5 25	18 42	5 35	18 52	5 31	18 50	5 31	18 53	5 26	18 53	5 35	19 05	5 44	19 09
7	5 23	18 43	5 33	18 53	5 29	18 52	5 29	18 55	5 24	18 55	5 33	19 07	5 42	19 11
8	5 21	18 45	5 31	18 55	5 27	18 54	5 26	18 57	5 21	18 57	5 30	19 09	5 39	19 13
9	5 18	18 47	5 28	18 57	5 24	18 55	5 24	18 58	5 19	18 59	5 28	19 11	5 37	19 15
10	5 16	18 48	5 26	18 58	5 22	18 57	5 22	19 00	5 16	19 01	5 25	19 13	5 34	19 17
11	5 14	18 50	5 24	19 00	5 20	18 59	5 19	19 02	5 14	19 02	5 23	19 15	5 32	19 19
12	5 12	18 52	5 22	19 02	5 17	19 01	5 17	19 04	5 11	19 04	5 20	19 17	5 29	19 21
13	5 10	18 53	5 20	19 03	5 15	19 02	5 15	19 06	5 09	19 06	5 17	19 19	5 27	19 23
14	5 07	18 55	5 18	19 05	5 13	19 04	5 12	19 08	5 07	19 08	5 15	19 21	5 25	19 25
15	5 05	18 57	5 15	19 07	5 11	19 06	5 10	19 09	5 04	19 10	5 12	19 23	5 22	19 27
16	5 03	18 58	5 13	19 08	5 09	19 08	5 08	19 11	5 02	19 12	5 10	19 25	5 20	19 29
17	5 01	19 00	5 11	19 10	5 06	19 09	5 05	19 13	4 59	19 14	5 07	19 27	5 17	19 30
18	4 59	19 02	5 09	19 12	5 04	19 11	5 03	19 15	4 57	19 16	5 05	19 29	5 15	19 32
19	4 57	19 03	5 07	19 13	5 02	19 13	5 01	19 17	4 54	19 18	5 03	19 31	5 13	19 34
20	4 55	19 05	5 05	19 15	5 00	19 15	4 59	19 18	4 52	19 20	5 00	19 33	5 10	19 36
21	4 53	19 07	5 03	19 17	4 58	19 16	4 56	19 20	4 50	19 22	4 58	19 35	5 08	19 38
22	4 51	19 08	5 01	19 18	4 55	19 18	4 54	19 22	4 47	19 24	4 55	19 37	5 06	19 40
23	4 49	19 10	4 59	19 20	4 53	19 20	4 52	19 24	4 45	19 26	4 53	19 39	5 03	19 42
24	4 46	19 12	4 57	19 22	4 51	19 22	4 50	19 26	4 43	19 28	4 50	19 41	5 01	19 44
25	4 44	19 13	4 55	19 23	4 49	19 23	4 48	19 28	4 40	19 30	4 48	19 43	4 59	19 46
26	4 42	19 15	4 53	19 25	4 47	19 25	4 45	19 29	4 38	19 32	4 46	19 45	4 57	19 48
27	4 40	19 17	4 51	19 27	4 45	19 27	4 43	19 31	4 36	19 34	4 43	19 47	4 54	19 50
28	4 39	19 18	4 49	19 28	4 43	19 28	4 41	19 33	4 34	19 36	4 41	19 49	4 52	19 51
29	4 37	19 20	4 47	19 30	4 41	19 30	4 39	19 35	4 31	19 38	4 39	19 51	4 50	19 53
30	4 35	19 22	4 45	19 31	4 39	19 32	4 37	19 37	4 29	19 39	4 36	19 53	4 48	19 55

JUPITER

Day	RA	Dec.	Transit	5° high	
				52°	56°
	h m	° ′	h m	h m	h m
1	22 59.5	− 7 28	10 22	5 34	5 44
11	23 07.8	− 6 38	9 50	4 59	5 08
21	23 15.7	− 5 50	9 19	4 23	4 31
31	23 23.1	− 5 05	8 47	3 47	3 55

Diameters – equatorial 34″ polar 32″

SATURN

Day	RA	Dec.	Transit	5° high	
				52°	56°
	h m	° ′	h m	h m	h m
1	1 23.9	+ 6 24	12 45	6 46	6 44
11	1 28.6	+ 6 52	12 11	6 09	6 07
21	1 33.3	+ 7 20	11 36	5 32	5 29
31	1 38.0	+ 7 47	11 02	4 55	4 52

Diameters – equatorial 16″ polar 14″
Rings – major axis 36″ minor axis 8″

URANUS

Day	RA	Dec.	Transit	10° high	
				52°	56°
	h m	° ′	h m	h m	h m
1	20 58.0	−17 49	8 20	5 21	5 54
11	20 59.4	−17 44	7 42	4 42	5 15
21	21 00.4	−17 40	7 04	4 03	4 36
31	21 01.1	−17 38	6 25	3 24	3 57

Diameter 4″

NEPTUNE

Day	RA	Dec.	Transit	10° high	
				52°	56°
	h m	° ′	h m	h m	h m
1	20 16.1	−19 24	7 38	4 53	5 32
11	20 16.7	−19 23	7 00	4 14	4 53
21	20 17.2	−19 21	6 21	3 35	4 14
31	20 17.4	−19 20	5 42	2 56	3 34

Diameter 2″

May 1998

FIFTH MONTH, 31 DAYS. *Maia*, goddess of growth and increase

1	*Friday*	**SS Philip and James.** Great Exhibition opened 1851	*week* 17 *day* 121
2	*Saturday*	Leonardo da Vinci d. 1519. Bing Crosby b. 1904	122
3	*Sunday*	**3rd S. after Easter.** Golda Meir b. 1898	*week* 18 *day* 123
4	*Monday*	*Bank Holiday in the UK.* ⚔ Coral Sea began 1942	124
5	*Tuesday*	Napoleon d. 1821. Moya Hidalgo b. 1920	125
6	*Wednesday*	Orson Welles b. 1915. Tony Blair b. 1953	126
7	*Thursday*	Gary Cooper b. 1901. *Lusitania* torpedoed 1915	127
8	*Friday*	Antoine-Laurent Lavoisier exec. 1794. John Stuart Mill d. 1873	128
9	*Saturday*	Glenda Jackson b. 1936. Channel Islands liberated 1945	129
10	*Sunday*	**4th S. after Easter.** George Vancouver d. 1798	*week* 19 *day* 130
11	*Monday*	Spencer Perceval assass. 1812. Salvador Dali b. 1904	131
12	*Tuesday*	Gabriel Fauré b. 1845. John Masefield d. 1967	132
13	*Wednesday*	Fridtjof Nansen d. 1930. Dame Daphne du Maurier b. 1907	133
14	*Thursday*	**St Matthias.** State of Israel proclaimed 1948	134
15	*Friday*	Edwin Muir b. 1887. Joseph Cotten b. 1905	135
16	*Saturday*	Sir John Hare b. 1844. Film Academy Awards first presented 1929	136
17	*Sunday*	**5th S. after Easter.** Summer Time Act came into force 1916	*week* 20 *day* 137
18	*Monday*	Frank Capra b. 1897. Pope John Paul II b. 1920	138
19	*Tuesday*	Anne Boleyn exec. 1536. William Gladstone d. 1898	139
20	*Wednesday*	First Chelsea Flower Show 1913. Sir Max Beerbohm d. 1956	140
21	*Thursday*	**Ascension Day.** Manchester Ship Canal opened 1894	141
22	*Friday*	*Easter Law Sittings end.* Blackwall Tunnel opened 1897	142
23	*Saturday*	Thomas Hood b. 1799. Douglas Fairbanks b. 1883	143
24	*Sunday*	**S. after Ascension Day.** Suzanne Lenglen b. 1899	*week* 21 *day* 144
25	*Monday*	*Bank Holiday in the UK.* Lord Beaverbrook b. 1879	145
26	*Tuesday*	Last public hanging in England 1868	146
27	*Wednesday*	Evacuation from Dunkirk began 1940. *Bismarck* sank 1941	147
28	*Thursday*	Ian Fleming b. 1908. Patrick White b. 1912	148
29	*Friday*	Bartolomeu Diaz d. 1500. Mt. Everest conquered 1953	149
30	*Saturday*	Joan of Arc exec. 1431. Alexander Pope d. 1744	150
31	*Sunday*	**Pentecost/Whit Sunday.** FEAST OF WEEKS begins	*week* 22 *day* 151

ASTRONOMICAL PHENOMENA

d h
4 11 Neptune at stationary point
4 17 Mercury at greatest elongation W.27°
12 20 Mars in conjunction
12 22 Saturn in conjunction with Mercury. Saturn 0°.8 N.
17 15 Uranus at stationary point
21 00 Jupiter in conjunction with Moon. Jupiter 0°.3 N.
21 06 Sun's longitude 60° II
22 23 Venus in conjunction with Moon. Venus 2° N.
23 09 Saturn in conjunction with Moon. Saturn 2° N.
24 12 Mercury in conjunction with Moon. Mercury 3° N.
25 14 Mars in conjunction with Moon. Mars 5° N.
28 05 Pluto at opposition
28 23 Saturn in conjunction with Venus. Saturn 0°.3 S.

MINIMA OF ALGOL

Algol is inconveniently situated for observation during May.

CONSTELLATIONS

The following constellations are near the meridian at

	d	h		d	h
April	1	24	May	16	21
April	15	23	June	1	20
May	1	22	June	15	19

Cepheus (below the Pole), Cassiopeia (below the Pole), Ursa Minor, Ursa Major, Canes Venatici, Coma Berenices, Bootes, Leo, Virgo, Crater, Corvus and Hydra

THE MOON

Phases, Apsides and Node	d	h	m
☽ First Quarter	3	10	04
○ Full Moon	11	14	29
☾ Last Quarter	19	04	35
● New Moon	25	19	32
Apogee (405,884 km)	8	08	45
Perigee (361,645 km)	23	23	53

Mean longitude of ascending node on May 1, 157°

THE SUN
s.d. 15'.8

Day	Right Ascension h m s	Dec. + ° '	Equation of time m s	Rise 52° h m	Rise 56° h m	Transit h m	Set 52° h m	Set 56° h m	Sidereal time h m s	Transit of First Point of Aries h m s
1	2 32 04	14 57	+ 2 49	4 31	4 17	11 57	19 24	19 39	14 34 53	9 23 34
2	2 35 53	15 15	+ 2 57	4 29	4 14	11 57	19 26	19 41	14 38 50	9 19 39
3	2 39 43	15 33	+ 3 03	4 27	4 12	11 57	19 28	19 43	14 42 46	9 15 43
4	2 43 33	15 51	+ 3 09	4 25	4 10	11 57	19 29	19 45	14 46 43	9 11 47
5	2 47 24	16 08	+ 3 15	4 23	4 08	11 57	19 31	19 47	14 50 39	9 07 51
6	2 51 16	16 25	+ 3 20	4 22	4 06	11 57	19 33	19 49	14 54 36	9 03 55
7	2 55 08	16 42	+ 3 25	4 20	4 04	11 57	19 34	19 51	14 58 32	8 59 59
8	2 59 00	16 58	+ 3 29	4 18	4 02	11 56	19 36	19 53	15 02 29	8 56 03
9	3 02 53	17 15	+ 3 32	4 16	3 59	11 56	19 38	19 55	15 06 25	8 52 07
10	3 06 47	17 31	+ 3 35	4 15	3 57	11 56	19 39	19 57	15 10 22	8 48 11
11	3 10 41	17 46	+ 3 37	4 13	3 55	11 56	19 41	19 59	15 14 19	8 44 15
12	3 14 36	18 02	+ 3 39	4 11	3 53	11 56	19 42	20 01	15 18 15	8 40 19
13	3 18 31	18 17	+ 3 40	4 10	3 51	11 56	19 44	20 02	15 22 12	8 36 24
14	3 22 27	18 31	+ 3 41	4 08	3 50	11 56	19 46	20 04	15 26 08	8 32 28
15	3 26 24	18 46	+ 3 41	4 07	3 48	11 56	19 47	20 06	15 30 05	8 28 32
16	3 30 21	19 00	+ 3 40	4 05	3 46	11 56	19 49	20 08	15 34 01	8 24 36
17	3 34 19	19 14	+ 3 39	4 04	3 44	11 56	19 50	20 10	15 37 58	8 20 40
18	3 38 17	19 27	+ 3 37	4 02	3 42	11 56	19 52	20 12	15 41 54	8 16 44
19	3 42 16	19 40	+ 3 35	4 01	3 41	11 56	19 53	20 14	15 45 51	8 12 48
20	3 46 15	19 53	+ 3 32	3 59	3 39	11 56	19 55	20 15	15 49 48	8 08 52
21	3 50 15	20 06	+ 3 29	3 58	3 37	11 57	19 56	20 17	15 53 44	8 04 56
22	3 54 16	20 18	+ 3 25	3 57	3 36	11 57	19 57	20 19	15 57 41	8 01 00
23	3 58 17	20 30	+ 3 20	3 55	3 34	11 57	19 59	20 20	16 01 37	7 57 04
24	4 02 19	20 41	+ 3 15	3 54	3 33	11 57	20 00	20 22	16 05 34	7 53 09
25	4 06 21	20 52	+ 3 09	3 53	3 31	11 57	20 01	20 24	16 09 30	7 49 13
26	4 10 24	21 03	+ 3 03	3 52	3 30	11 57	20 03	20 25	16 13 27	7 45 17
27	4 14 27	21 13	+ 2 57	3 51	3 28	11 57	20 04	20 27	16 17 23	7 41 21
28	4 18 30	21 23	+ 2 50	3 50	3 27	11 57	20 05	20 28	16 21 20	7 37 25
29	4 22 34	21 33	+ 2 42	3 49	3 26	11 57	20 07	20 30	16 25 17	7 33 29
30	4 26 39	21 42	+ 2 34	3 48	3 25	11 57	20 08	20 31	16 29 13	7 29 33
31	4 30 44	21 51	+ 2 26	3 47	3 23	11 58	20 09	20 33	16 33 10	7 25 37

DURATION OF TWILIGHT (in minutes)

Latitude	52°	56°	52°	56°	52°	56°	52°	56°
	1 May		11 May		21 May		31 May	
Civil	39	45	41	49	44	53	46	57
Nautical	90	106	97	121	106	143	116	TAN
Astronomical	154	209	179	TAN	TAN	TAN	TAN	TAN

THE NIGHT SKY

Mercury is too close to the Sun for observation.

Venus continues to be visible as a splendid object in the morning skies, magnitude −4.1, though only visible for about half an hour before dawn, low above the eastern horizon. On the morning of the 23rd the old crescent Moon will be seen about 3° below and to the left of the planet. On the morning of the 29th Saturn is only 0°.3 to the right of Venus.

Mars passes through conjunction on the 12th and is therefore too close to the Sun for observation.

Jupiter, magnitude −2.2, is a morning object, though only visible low in the south-eastern sky for a short time before dawn. The old crescent Moon will be seen within a degree of Jupiter on the morning of the 21st. Jupiter passes from Aquarius into Pisces during the month. The four Galilean satellites are readily observable with a small telescope, or even a good pair of binoculars provided that they are held rigidly.

Saturn remains too close to the Sun for observation.

THE MOON

Day	RA		Dec.	Hor. par.	Semi- diam.	Sun's co- long.	PA of Bright Limb	Phase	Age	Rise 52°	Rise 56°	Transit	Set 52°	Set 56°
	h	m	°	′	′	°	°	%	d	h m	h m	h m	h m	h m
1	6	48	+18.7	57.8	15.8	324	277	26	4.5	8 53	8 35	16 50	—	0 13
2	7	44	+17.7	56.9	15.5	336	281	36	5.5	9 54	9 38	17 41	0 42	0 59
3	8	37	+15.9	56.1	15.3	348	285	46	6.5	10 58	10 44	18 30	1 21	1 35
4	9	27	+13.3	55.3	15.1	0	288	56	7.5	12 02	11 51	19 16	1 53	2 04
5	10	16	+10.2	54.8	14.9	13	291	65	8.5	13 06	12 58	20 01	2 20	2 28
6	11	02	+ 6.7	54.4	14.8	25	293	74	9.5	14 09	14 05	20 43	2 44	2 49
7	11	47	+ 3.0	54.1	14.8	37	295	82	10.5	15 12	15 12	21 25	3 07	3 09
8	12	32	− 0.8	54.0	14.7	49	296	89	11.5	16 15	16 18	22 08	3 28	3 27
9	13	17	− 4.5	54.0	14.7	61	298	94	12.5	17 18	17 25	22 50	3 50	3 46
10	14	03	− 8.2	54.2	14.8	74	302	98	13.5	18 22	18 31	23 34	4 14	4 06
11	14	49	−11.5	54.4	14.8	86	321	99	14.5	19 25	19 38	—	4 39	4 29
12	15	38	−14.4	54.7	14.9	98	56	100	15.5	20 27	20 43	0 20	5 09	4 55
13	16	27	−16.7	55.0	15.0	110	82	98	16.5	21 27	21 45	1 07	5 43	5 27
14	17	19	−18.2	55.4	15.1	122	85	94	17.5	22 23	22 42	1 57	6 24	6 06
15	18	12	−18.9	55.9	15.2	135	83	89	18.5	23 13	23 32	2 48	7 12	6 53
16	19	06	−18.6	56.5	15.4	147	80	82	19.5	23 58	—	3 40	8 08	7 50
17	20	00	−17.4	57.1	15.5	159	77	73	20.5	—	0 14	4 32	9 11	8 55
18	20	55	−15.2	57.7	15.7	171	73	63	21.5	0 36	0 50	5 24	10 19	10 06
19	21	49	−12.1	58.4	15.9	183	70	52	22.5	1 10	1 20	6 17	11 32	11 23
20	22	44	− 8.3	59.0	16.1	196	68	41	23.5	1 40	1 47	7 09	12 48	12 43
21	23	38	− 4.0	59.6	16.3	208	66	30	24.5	2 08	2 11	8 01	14 07	14 05
22	0	33	+ 0.7	60.2	16.4	220	65	20	25.5	2 35	2 35	8 54	15 26	15 30
23	1	29	+ 5.4	60.5	16.5	232	64	11	26.5	3 04	2 59	9 49	16 47	16 55
24	2	26	+ 9.8	60.6	16.5	244	62	5	27.5	3 35	3 26	10 45	18 08	18 20
25	3	25	+13.6	60.5	16.5	257	53	1	28.5	4 10	3 58	11 42	19 26	19 41
26	4	25	+16.6	60.1	16.4	269	324	0	0.2	4 52	4 36	12 41	20 38	20 56
27	5	25	+18.4	59.5	16.2	281	283	2	1.2	5 40	5 22	13 40	21 41	22 00
28	6	25	+19.0	58.7	16.0	293	280	7	2.2	6 35	6 17	14 37	22 35	22 53
29	7	23	+18.4	57.8	15.8	306	282	13	3.2	7 37	7 19	15 31	23 18	23 34
30	8	18	+16.9	57.0	15.5	318	285	21	4.2	8 41	8 26	16 23	23 54	—
31	9	11	+14.5	56.1	15.3	330	288	30	5.2	9 47	9 35	17 11	—	0 07

MERCURY

Day	RA		Dec.	Diam.	Phase	Transit	5° high 52°	5° high 56°
	h	m	°	″	%	h m	h m	h m
1	0	56	+ 3.1	9	37	10 21	4 38	4 38
3	1	03	+ 3.6	8	40	10 20	4 34	4 34
5	1	10	+ 4.2	8	43	10 19	4 30	4 30
7	1	18	+ 4.9	8	46	10 19	4 26	4 26
9	1	26	+ 5.7	7	50	10 20	4 23	4 21
11	1	35	+ 6.6	7	53	10 21	4 19	4 17
13	1	45	+ 7.6	7	56	10 23	4 16	4 13
15	1	55	+ 8.7	7	59	10 26	4 13	4 09
17	2	06	+ 9.8	7	63	10 29	4 10	4 05
19	2	18	+11.0	6	66	10 33	4 08	4 02
21	2	30	+12.2	6	70	10 37	4 05	3 59
23	2	43	+13.5	6	74	10 42	4 04	3 56
25	2	56	+14.8	6	77	10 48	4 02	3 53
27	3	10	+16.1	6	81	10 54	4 02	3 51
29	3	25	+17.4	5	85	11 02	4 02	3 50
31	3	41	+18.6	5	89	11 10	4 02	3 49

VENUS

Day	RA		Dec.	Diam.	Phase	Transit	5° high 52°	5° high 56°
	h	m	°	″	%	h m	h m	h m
1	23	50	− 2.4	18	65	9 16	4 00	4 05
6	0	11	− 0.4	17	67	9 17	3 51	3 54
11	0	33	+ 1.7	16	69	9 18	3 42	3 44
16	0	54	+ 3.8	16	70	9 20	3 33	3 33
21	1	15	+ 5.9	15	72	9 22	3 24	3 22
26	1	37	+ 7.9	15	74	9 24	3 15	3 12
31	1	59	+10.0	14	75	9 26	3 07	3 02

MARS

Day	RA		Dec.	Diam.	Phase	Transit	5° high 52°	5° high 56°
1	2	43	+15.7	4	100	12 08	5 19	5 09
6	2	58	+16.9	4	100	12 03	5 07	4 56
11	3	12	+17.9	4	100	11 58	4 56	4 44
16	3	27	+18.9	4	100	11 53	4 46	4 33
21	3	42	+19.8	4	100	11 48	4 35	4 21
26	3	57	+20.6	4	100	11 43	4 26	4 11
31	4	11	+21.3	4	100	11 38	4 17	4 01

SUNRISE AND SUNSET

	London		Bristol		Birmingham		Manchester		Newcastle		Glasgow		Belfast	
	0°05'	51°30'	2°35'	51°28'	1°55'	52°28'	2°15'	53°28'	1°37'	54°59'	4°14'	55°52'	5°56'	54°35'
	h m	h m	h m	h m	h m	h m	h m	h m	h m	h m	h m	h m	h m	h m
1	4 33	19 23	4 43	19 33	4 37	19 34	4 35	19 38	4 27	19 41	4 34	19 55	4 46	19 57
2	4 31	19 25	4 41	19 35	4 35	19 35	4 33	19 40	4 25	19 43	4 32	19 57	4 44	19 59
3	4 29	19 26	4 39	19 36	4 33	19 37	4 31	19 42	4 23	19 45	4 30	19 59	4 42	20 01
4	4 27	19 28	4 37	19 38	4 31	19 39	4 29	19 44	4 21	19 47	4 28	20 01	4 40	20 03
5	4 25	19 30	4 36	19 40	4 29	19 40	4 27	19 45	4 19	19 49	4 25	20 03	4 37	20 05
6	4 24	19 31	4 34	19 41	4 28	19 42	4 25	19 47	4 17	19 51	4 23	20 05	4 35	20 06
7	4 22	19 33	4 32	19 43	4 26	19 44	4 23	19 49	4 15	19 53	4 21	20 07	4 33	20 08
8	4 20	19 34	4 30	19 44	4 24	19 45	4 21	19 51	4 13	19 55	4 19	20 09	4 32	20 10
9	4 19	19 36	4 29	19 46	4 22	19 47	4 20	19 52	4 11	19 56	4 17	20 11	4 30	20 12
10	4 17	19 38	4 27	19 48	4 20	19 49	4 18	19 54	4 09	19 58	4 15	20 13	4 28	20 14
11	4 15	19 39	4 25	19 49	4 19	19 50	4 16	19 56	4 07	20 00	4 13	20 15	4 26	20 16
12	4 14	19 41	4 24	19 51	4 17	19 52	4 14	19 58	4 05	20 02	4 11	20 17	4 24	20 17
13	4 12	19 42	4 22	19 52	4 15	19 54	4 13	19 59	4 03	20 04	4 09	20 19	4 22	20 19
14	4 10	19 44	4 21	19 54	4 14	19 55	4 11	20 01	4 01	20 06	4 07	20 21	4 20	20 21
15	4 09	19 45	4 19	19 55	4 12	19 57	4 09	20 03	3 59	20 07	4 05	20 22	4 19	20 23
16	4 07	19 47	4 18	19 57	4 11	19 58	4 08	20 04	3 58	20 09	4 03	20 24	4 17	20 24
17	4 06	19 48	4 16	19 58	4 09	20 00	4 06	20 06	3 56	20 11	4 02	20 26	4 15	20 26
18	4 05	19 50	4 15	20 00	4 08	20 01	4 04	20 07	3 54	20 13	4 00	20 28	4 14	20 28
19	4 03	19 51	4 13	20 01	4 06	20 03	4 03	20 09	3 53	20 14	3 58	20 30	4 12	20 29
20	4 02	19 53	4 12	20 02	4 05	20 04	4 01	20 11	3 51	20 16	3 57	20 31	4 10	20 31
21	4 01	19 54	4 11	20 04	4 04	20 06	4 00	20 12	3 49	20 18	3 55	20 33	4 09	20 33
22	3 59	19 55	4 10	20 05	4 02	20 07	3 59	20 14	3 48	20 19	3 53	20 35	4 07	20 34
23	3 58	19 57	4 08	20 07	4 01	20 09	3 57	20 15	3 47	20 21	3 52	20 37	4 06	20 36
24	3 57	19 58	4 07	20 08	4 00	20 10	3 56	20 17	3 45	20 22	3 50	20 38	4 05	20 37
25	3 56	19 59	4 06	20 09	3 59	20 11	3 55	20 18	3 44	20 24	3 49	20 40	4 03	20 39
26	3 55	20 01	4 05	20 11	3 57	20 13	3 53	20 19	3 42	20 25	3 47	20 41	4 02	20 40
27	3 54	20 02	4 04	20 12	3 56	20 14	3 52	20 21	3 41	20 27	3 46	20 43	4 01	20 42
28	3 53	20 03	4 03	20 13	3 55	20 15	3 51	20 22	3 40	20 28	3 45	20 45	4 00	20 43
29	3 52	20 04	4 02	20 14	3 54	20 17	3 50	20 23	3 39	20 30	3 44	20 46	3 58	20 45
30	3 51	20 06	4 01	20 15	3 53	20 18	3 49	20 25	3 38	20 31	3 42	20 47	3 57	20 46
31	3 50	20 07	4 00	20 17	3 52	20 19	3 48	20 26	3 36	20 33	3 41	20 49	3 56	20 47

JUPITER

Day	RA	Dec.	Transit	5° high	
				52°	56°
	h m	° '	h m	h m	h m
1	23 23.1	− 5 05	8 47	3 47	3 55
11	23 30.0	− 4 23	8 15	3 11	3 18
21	23 36.3	− 3 45	7 41	2 34	2 41
31	23 41.8	3 12	7 08	1 58	2 04

Diameters – equatorial 37″ polar 34″

SATURN

Day	RA	Dec.	Transit	5° high	
				52°	56°
	h m	° '	h m	h m	h m
1	1 38.0	+ 7 47	11 02	4 55	4 52
11	1 42.7	+ 8 13	10 27	4 18	4 15
21	1 47.1	+ 8 37	9 52	3 41	3 37
31	1 51.3	+ 8 59	9 17	3 04	3 00

Diameters – equatorial 16″ polar 15″
Rings – major axis 37″ minor axis 9″

URANUS

Day	RA	Dec.	Transit	10° high	
				52°	56°
	h m	° '	h m	h m	h m
1	21 01.1	−17 38	6 25	3 24	3 57
11	21 01.5	−17 36	5 46	2 45	3 18
21	21 01.6	−17 37	5 07	2 06	2 39
31	21 01.3	−17 38	4 27	1 27	1 59

Diameter 4″

NEPTUNE

Day	RA	Dec.	Transit	10° high	
				52°	56°
	h m	° '	h m	h m	h m
1	20 17.4	−19 20	5 42	2 56	3 34
11	20 17.3	−19 20	5 02	2 16	2 55
21	20 17.1	−19 21	4 23	1 37	2 16
31	20 16.6	−19 22	3 43	0 57	1 36

Diameter 2″

 # June 1998

SIXTH MONTH, 30 DAYS. *Junius*, Roman *gens* (family)

1	*Monday*	Sir David Wilkie d. 1841. Marilyn Monroe b. 1926	*week 22 day* 152
2	*Tuesday*	*Coronation Day 1953.Trinity Law Sittings begin*	153
3	*Wednesday*	Samuel Plimsoll d. 1898. ⚔ Midway began 1942	154
4	*Thursday*	Casanova d. 1798. ⚔ Magenta 1859	155
5	*Friday*	World Environment Day. Margaret Drabble b. 1939	156
6	*Saturday*	Arthur Askey b. 1900. Dame Ninette de Valois b. 1898	157
7	*Sunday*	**Trinity Sunday.** Paul Gauguin b. 1848	*week 23 day* 158
8	*Monday*	John Smeaton b. 1724. Gerard Manley Hopkins d. 1889	159
9	*Tuesday*	Charles Dickens d. 1870. Frank Chacksfield b. 1914	160
10	*Wednesday*	*Duke of Edinburgh b. 1921.* Judy Garland b. 1922	161
11	*Thursday*	**Corpus Christi. St Barnabas.** Jacques Cousteau b. 1910	162
12	*Friday*	George Bush b. 1924. Anne Frank b. 1929	163
13	*Saturday*	*Queen's Official Birthday.* W. B. Yeats b. 1865	164
14	*Sunday*	**2nd S. after Pentecost/1st S. after Trinity**	*week 24 day* 165
15	*Monday*	Magna Carta sealed 1215. Wat Tyler exec. 1381	166
16	*Tuesday*	Valentina Tereshkova becomes first woman in space 1963	167
17	*Wednesday*	Sir Edward Burne-Jones d. 1898. Ken Loach b. 1936	168
18	*Thursday*	⚔ Waterloo 1815. Capt. Matthew Webb b. 1848	169
19	*Friday*	Sir Joseph Banks d. 1820. Metropolitan Police founded 1829	170
20	*Saturday*	Willem Barents d. 1597. Jacques Offenbach b. 1819	171
21	*Sunday*	**3rd S. after Pentecost/2nd S. after Trinity.** Prince William b. 1982	*week 25 day* 172
22	*Monday*	Sir Peter Pears b. 1910. Meryl Streep b. 1949	173
23	*Tuesday*	Sir Leonard Hutton b. 1916. Cecil Sharp d. 1924	174
24	*Wednesday*	**St John the Baptist.** Issue of the Book of Common Prayer 1559	175
25	*Thursday*	Col. George Custer d. 1876. George Orwell b. 1903	176
26	*Friday*	Francisco Pizarro d. 1541. United Nations Charter signed 1945	177
27	*Saturday*	Charles Stewart Parnell b. 1846. Harriet Martineau d. 1876	178
28	*Sunday*	**4th S. after Pentecost/3rd S. after Trinity**	*week 26 day* 179
29	*Monday*	**St Peter.** Trades unions legalized 1871	180
30	*Tuesday*	Tower Bridge opened 1894. Nancy Mitford d. 1973	181

ASTRONOMICAL PHENOMENA

d h
5 12 Mars in conjunction with Mercury. Mars 0°.3 N.
10 07 Mercury in superior conjunction
17 12 Jupiter in conjunction with Moon. Jupiter 0°.8 N.
19 21 Saturn in conjunction with Moon. Saturn 2° N.
21 14 Sun's longitude 90° ♋.
21 16 Venus in conjunction with Moon. Venus 3° N.
23 09 Mars in conjunction with Moon. Mars 5° N.
25 11 Mercury in conjunction with Moon. Mercury
        5° N.

MINIMA OF ALGOL

Algol is inconveniently situated for observation during June.

CONSTELLATIONS

The following constellations are near the meridian at

	d	h		d	h
May	1	24	June	15	21
May	16	23	July	1	20
June	1	22	July	16	19

Cassiopeia (below the Pole), Ursa Minor, Draco, Ursa Major, Canes Venatici, Bootes, Corona, Serpens, Virgo and Libra

THE MOON

Phases, Apsides and Node	d	h	m
☽ First Quarter	2	01	45
○ Full Moon	10	04	18
☾ Last Quarter	17	10	38
● New Moon	24	03	50
Apogee (404,959 km)	4	23	38
Perigee (366,567 km)	20	17	13

Mean longitude of ascending node on June 1, 156°

THE SUN   s.d. 15'.8

Day	Right Ascension h m s	Dec. + ° '	Equation of time m s	Rise 52° h m	Rise 56° h m	Transit h m	Set 52° h m	Set 56° h m	Sidereal time h m s	Transit of First Point of Aries h m s
1	4 34 49	22 00	+ 2 17	3 46	3 22	11 58	20 10	20 34	16 37 06	7 21 41
2	4 38 55	22 08	+ 2 08	3 45	3 21	11 58	20 11	20 35	16 41 03	7 17 45
3	4 43 01	22 15	+ 1 58	3 45	3 20	11 58	20 12	20 37	16 44 59	7 13 49
4	4 47 07	22 23	+ 1 49	3 44	3 19	11 58	20 13	20 38	16 48 56	7 09 54
5	4 51 14	22 30	+ 1 38	3 43	3 18	11 58	20 14	20 39	16 52 52	7 05 58
6	4 55 21	22 36	+ 1 28	3 43	3 18	11 59	20 15	20 40	16 56 49	7 02 02
7	4 59 29	22 43	+ 1 17	3 42	3 17	11 59	20 16	20 41	17 00 46	6 58 06
8	5 03 36	22 48	+ 1 06	3 42	3 16	11 59	20 17	20 42	17 04 42	6 54 10
9	5 07 44	22 54	+ 0 54	3 41	3 16	11 59	20 18	20 43	17 08 39	6 50 14
10	5 11 52	22 59	+ 0 43	3 41	3 15	11 59	20 18	20 44	17 12 35	6 46 18
11	5 16 01	23 03	+ 0 31	3 40	3 14	12 00	20 19	20 45	17 16 32	6 42 22
12	5 20 09	23 07	+ 0 19	3 40	3 14	12 00	20 20	20 46	17 20 28	6 38 26
13	5 24 18	23 11	+ 0 07	3 40	3 14	12 00	20 20	20 47	17 24 25	6 34 30
14	5 28 27	23 14	− 0 06	3 40	3 13	12 00	20 21	20 47	17 28 21	6 30 34
15	5 32 36	23 17	− 0 18	3 39	3 13	12 00	20 22	20 48	17 32 18	6 26 38
16	5 36 46	23 20	− 0 31	3 39	3 13	12 01	20 22	20 49	17 36 15	6 22 43
17	5 40 55	23 22	− 0 44	3 39	3 13	12 01	20 23	20 49	17 40 11	6 18 47
18	5 45 05	23 24	− 0 57	3 39	3 13	12 01	20 23	20 49	17 44 08	6 14 51
19	5 49 14	23 25	− 1 10	3 39	3 13	12 01	20 23	20 50	17 48 04	6 10 55
20	5 53 24	23 26	− 1 23	3 40	3 13	12 01	20 24	20 50	17 52 01	6 06 59
21	5 57 34	23 26	− 1 36	3 40	3 13	12 02	20 24	20 50	17 55 57	6 03 03
22	6 01 43	23 26	− 1 50	3 40	3 13	12 02	20 24	20 51	17 59 54	5 59 07
23	6 05 53	23 26	− 2 03	3 40	3 14	12 02	20 24	20 51	18 03 50	5 55 11
24	6 10 03	23 25	− 2 16	3 41	3 14	12 02	20 24	20 51	18 07 47	5 51 15
25	6 14 12	23 24	− 2 29	3 41	3 14	12 03	20 24	20 51	18 11 44	5 47 19
26	6 18 22	23 22	− 2 41	3 41	3 15	12 03	20 24	20 51	18 15 40	5 43 23
27	6 22 31	23 20	− 2 54	3 42	3 15	12 03	20 24	20 50	18 19 37	5 39 28
28	6 26 40	23 18	− 3 07	3 42	3 16	12 03	20 24	20 50	18 23 33	5 35 32
29	6 30 49	23 15	− 3 19	3 43	3 17	12 03	20 24	20 50	18 27 30	5 31 36
30	6 34 57	23 12	− 3 31	3 43	3 17	12 04	20 23	20 49	18 31 26	5 27 40

DURATION OF TWILIGHT (in minutes)

Latitude	52°	56°	52°	56°	52°	56°	52°	56°
	1 June		11 June		21 June		30 June	
Civil	47	58	48	61	49	63	49	62
Nautical	117	TAN	125	TAN	128	TAN	125	TAN
Astronomical	TAN	TAN	TAN	TAN	TAN	TAN	TAN	TAN

THE NIGHT SKY

Mercury is unsuitably placed for observation, superior conjunction occurring on the 10th.

Venus, magnitude − 3.9, is a splendid object in the early morning skies, low above the eastern horizon before sunrise. For observers in the British Isles, its movement towards the Sun is more than offset by its northward motion in declination so that it gradually becomes visible for longer each morning throughout the month. The old crescent Moon, three days before New, will be seen about 8° to the right of the planet on the morning of the 21st.

Mars continues to be unsuitably placed for observation.

Jupiter continues to be visible as a morning object, magnitude − 2.4, in the south-eastern sky. The Moon, near Last Quarter, is in the vicinity of the planet on the mornings of the 17th and 18th.

Saturn is not visible during the first part of the month but gradually becomes a morning object low in the eastern sky towards the end of June, magnitude + 0.5.

Twilight. Reference to the section above shows that astronomical twilight lasts all night for a period around the summer solstice (i.e. in June and July), even in southern England. Under these conditions the sky never gets completely dark since the Sun is always less than 18° below the horizon.

THE MOON

Day	RA	Dec.	Hor. par.	Semi-diam.	Sun's co-long.	PA of Bright Limb	Phase	Age	Rise 52°	Rise 56°	Transit	Set 52°	Set 56°
	h m	°	'	'	°	°	%	d	h m	h m	h m	h m	h m
1	10 01	+11.5	55.4	15.1	342	290	40	6.2	10 53	10 44	17 57	0 24	0 34
2	10 49	+ 8.1	54.9	14.9	355	292	49	7.2	11 57	11 52	18 40	0 49	0 56
3	11 35	+ 4.4	54.5	14.8	7	294	59	8.2	13 01	12 59	19 23	1 12	1 16
4	12 20	+ 0.5	54.2	14.8	19	294	68	9.2	14 04	14 06	20 05	1 34	1 34
5	13 04	− 3.3	54.1	14.8	31	295	77	10.2	15 07	15 12	20 47	1 56	1 53
6	13 50	− 7.0	54.2	14.8	43	294	84	11.2	16 11	16 19	21 31	2 18	2 12
7	14 36	−10.5	54.4	14.8	56	294	90	12.2	17 14	17 26	22 16	2 43	2 33
8	15 24	−13.5	54.7	14.9	68	295	95	13.2	18 18	18 32	23 03	3 10	2 58
9	16 13	−16.1	55.1	15.0	80	300	98	14.2	19 20	19 37	23 52	3 43	3 27
10	17 05	−17.9	55.6	15.1	92	342	100	15.2	20 18	20 37	—	4 21	4 03
11	17 58	−18.9	56.1	15.3	104	65	99	16.2	21 11	21 30	0 43	5 07	4 48
12	18 53	−18.9	56.6	15.4	117	75	96	17.2	21 59	22 16	1 35	6 01	5 42
13	19 48	−17.9	57.1	15.6	129	75	92	18.2	22 39	22 54	2 29	7 02	6 45
14	20 43	−16.0	57.6	15.7	141	73	85	19.2	23 14	23 26	3 22	8 10	7 56
15	21 37	−13.1	58.1	15.8	153	71	76	20.2	23 45	23 53	4 14	9 22	9 11
16	22 31	− 9.5	58.5	15.9	165	68	66	21.2	—	—	5 06	10 36	10 29
17	23 25	− 5.3	58.9	16.1	178	67	55	22.2	0 13	0 18	5 57	11 52	11 49
18	0 18	− 0.8	59.3	16.2	190	66	44	23.2	0 40	0 41	6 48	13 09	13 11
19	1 12	+ 3.8	59.6	16.2	202	66	33	24.2	1 07	1 04	7 40	14 28	14 33
20	2 07	+ 8.3	59.8	16.3	214	67	22	25.2	1 35	1 28	8 34	15 46	15 56
21	3 04	+12.3	59.8	16.3	227	69	13	26.2	2 07	1 56	9 29	17 03	17 17
22	4 02	+15.5	59.7	16.3	239	70	6	27.2	2 44	2 30	10 26	18 17	18 34
23	5 01	+17.8	59.4	16.2	251	67	2	28.2	3 28	3 11	11 24	19 25	19 43
24	6 01	+18.9	58.9	16.0	263	25	0	29.2	4 20	4 01	12 22	20 23	20 42
25	7 00	+18.9	58.2	15.9	276	295	1	0.8	5 18	5 00	13 18	21 12	21 29
26	7 57	+17.7	57.5	15.7	288	288	4	1.8	6 22	6 05	14 11	21 52	22 06
27	8 51	+15.6	56.8	15.5	300	288	9	2.8	7 29	7 15	15 02	22 25	22 36
28	9 43	+12.8	56.0	15.3	312	290	16	3.8	8 36	8 25	15 50	22 53	23 01
29	10 32	+ 9.5	55.4	15.1	325	291	24	4.8	9 42	9 35	16 35	23 17	23 22
30	11 20	+ 5.8	54.9	15.0	337	293	33	5.8	10 47	10 43	17 18	23 39	23 41

MERCURY

Day	RA	Dec.	Diam.	Phase	Transit	5° high 52°	5° high 56°
	h m	°	"	%	h m	h m	h m
1	3 49	+19.2	5	91	11 14	4 03	3 49
3	4 06	+20.4	5	94	11 23	4 05	3 50
5	4 24	+21.5	5	97	11 33	4 08	3 52
7	4 42	+22.5	5	99	11 44	4 13	3 55
9	5 01	+23.4	5	100	11 55	4 18	4 00
11	5 20	+24.1	5	100	12 06	19 48	20 07
13	5 39	+24.6	5	99	12 17	20 02	20 22
15	5 58	+24.9	5	97	12 28	20 15	20 35
17	6 17	+25.0	5	95	12 39	20 26	20 47
19	6 35	+25.0	5	91	12 50	20 35	20 56
21	6 53	+24.8	5	88	12 59	20 43	21 03
23	7 10	+24.4	5	84	13 08	20 49	21 09
25	7 26	+23.9	6	81	13 17	20 54	21 12
27	7 42	+23.3	6	77	13 24	20 57	21 15
29	7 56	+22.6	6	73	13 31	20 59	21 15
31	8 10	+21.8	6	70	13 36	20 59	21 15

VENUS

Day	RA	Dec.	Diam.	Phase	Transit	5° high 52°	5° high 56°
	h m	°	"	%	h m	h m	h m
1	2 04	+10.4	14	76	9 27	3 06	3 00
6	2 26	+12.3	14	77	9 29	2 58	2 51
11	2 49	+14.2	13	79	9 33	2 51	2 43
16	3 12	+15.9	13	80	9 36	2 46	2 35
21	3 36	+17.5	13	82	9 40	2 41	2 29
26	4 00	+18.9	13	83	9 45	2 37	2 24
31	4 25	+20.1	12	84	9 50	2 35	2 21

MARS

Day	RA	Dec.	Diam.	Phase	Transit	5° high 52°	5° high 56°
1	4 14	+21.5	4	100	11 37	4 15	3 59
6	4 29	+22.1	4	100	11 32	4 06	3 49
11	4 44	+22.6	4	100	11 27	3 58	3 41
16	4 59	+23.1	4	100	11 23	3 50	3 32
21	5 14	+23.5	4	100	11 18	3 43	3 25
26	5 29	+23.7	4	100	11 13	3 37	3 18
31	5 44	+23.9	4	100	11 08	3 31	3 12

SUNRISE AND SUNSET

	London 0°05' 51°30'		Bristol 2°35' 51°28'		Birmingham 1°55' 52°28'		Manchester 2°15' 53°28'		Newcastle 1°37' 54°59'		Glasgow 4°14' 55°52'		Belfast 5°56' 54°35'	
	h m	h m	h m	h m	h m	h m	h m	h m	h m	h m	h m	h m	h m	h m
1	3 49	20 08	3 59	20 18	3 51	20 20	3 47	20 27	3 35	20 34	3 40	20 50	3 55	20 49
2	3 48	20 09	3 58	20 19	3 51	20 21	3 46	20 28	3 34	20 35	3 39	20 52	3 54	20 50
3	3 48	20 10	3 58	20 20	3 50	20 22	3 45	20 29	3 34	20 36	3 38	20 53	3 53	20 51
4	3 47	20 11	3 57	20 21	3 49	20 23	3 45	20 31	3 33	20 38	3 37	20 54	3 53	20 52
5	3 46	20 12	3 56	20 22	3 48	20 24	3 44	20 32	3 32	20 39	3 36	20 55	3 52	20 53
6	3 46	20 13	3 56	20 23	3 48	20 25	3 43	20 33	3 31	20 40	3 35	20 56	3 51	20 54
7	3 45	20 14	3 55	20 23	3 47	20 26	3 43	20 34	3 30	20 41	3 35	20 57	3 50	20 55
8	3 45	20 14	3 55	20 24	3 47	20 27	3 42	20 34	3 30	20 42	3 34	20 58	3 50	20 56
9	3 44	20 15	3 54	20 25	3 46	20 28	3 42	20 35	3 29	20 43	3 33	20 59	3 49	20 57
10	3 44	20 16	3 54	20 26	3 46	20 29	3 41	20 36	3 29	20 44	3 33	21 00	3 49	20 58
11	3 43	20 17	3 54	20 27	3 45	20 30	3 41	20 37	3 28	20 44	3 32	21 01	3 48	20 59
12	3 43	20 17	3 53	20 27	3 45	20 30	3 40	20 38	3 28	20 45	3 32	21 02	3 48	21 00
13	3 43	20 18	3 53	20 28	3 45	20 31	3 40	20 38	3 28	20 46	3 32	21 03	3 48	21 00
14	3 43	20 19	3 53	20 28	3 45	20 31	3 40	20 39	3 27	20 46	3 31	21 03	3 47	21 01
15	3 43	20 19	3 53	20 29	3 44	20 32	3 40	20 39	3 27	20 47	3 31	21 04	3 47	21 02
16	3 43	20 20	3 53	20 29	3 44	20 32	3 40	20 40	3 27	20 48	3 31	21 04	3 47	21 02
17	3 42	20 20	3 53	20 30	3 44	20 33	3 39	20 40	3 27	20 48	3 31	21 05	3 47	21 02
18	3 42	20 20	3 53	20 30	3 44	20 33	3 39	20 41	3 27	20 48	3 31	21 05	3 47	21 03
19	3 43	20 21	3 53	20 31	3 44	20 34	3 39	20 41	3 27	20 49	3 31	21 06	3 47	21 03
20	3 43	20 21	3 53	20 31	3 44	20 34	3 40	20 41	3 27	20 49	3 31	21 06	3 47	21 04
21	3 43	20 21	3 53	20 31	3 45	20 34	3 40	20 42	3 27	20 49	3 31	21 06	3 47	21 04
22	3 43	20 21	3 53	20 31	3 45	20 34	3 40	20 42	3 27	20 49	3 31	21 06	3 47	21 04
23	3 43	20 22	3 54	20 31	3 45	20 34	3 40	20 42	3 28	20 50	3 32	21 07	3 48	21 04
24	3 44	20 22	3 54	20 31	3 45	20 35	3 41	20 42	3 28	20 50	3 32	21 07	3 48	21 04
25	3 44	20 22	3 54	20 31	3 46	20 35	3 41	20 42	3 28	20 50	3 32	21 07	3 48	21 04
26	3 44	20 22	3 55	20 31	3 46	20 35	3 41	20 42	3 29	20 50	3 33	21 06	3 49	21 04
27	3 45	20 22	3 55	20 31	3 47	20 34	3 42	20 42	3 29	20 49	3 33	21 06	3 49	21 04
28	3 45	20 21	3 56	20 31	3 47	20 34	3 42	20 42	3 30	20 49	3 34	21 06	3 50	21 04
29	3 46	20 21	3 56	20 31	3 48	20 34	3 43	20 41	3 31	20 49	3 35	21 06	3 51	21 03
30	3 47	20 21	3 57	20 31	3 48	20 31	3 44	20 41	3 31	20 49	3 35	21 05	3 51	21 03

JUPITER

Day	RA	Dec.	Transit	5° high 52°	56°
	h m	° '	h m	h m	h m
1	23 42.3	− 3 09	7 04	1 54	2 00
11	23 46.9	− 2 42	6 29	1 17	1 22
21	23 50.5	− 2 21	5 54	0 39	0 45
31	23 53.2	− 2 07	5 17	0 01	0 06

Diameters equatorial 40" polar 38"

SATURN

Day	RA	Dec.	Transit	5° high 52°	56°
	h m	° '	h m	h m	h m
1	1 51.7	+ 9 01	9 13	3 00	2 56
11	1 55.6	+ 9 21	8 38	2 23	2 19
21	1 59.1	+ 9 38	8 02	1 46	1 41
31	2 02.2	+ 9 53	7 26	1 08	1 01

Diameters – equatorial 17" polar 15"
Rings – major axis 38" minor axis 10"

URANUS

Day	RA	Dec.	Transit	10° high 52°	56°
	h m	° '	h m	h m	h m
1	21 01.3	-17 38	4 23	1 23	1 55
11	21 00.7	-17 41	3 44	0 43	1 16
21	20 59.8	-17 45	3 03	0 03	0 37
31	20 58.6	-17 50	2 23	23 20	23 53

Diameter 4"

NEPTUNE

Day	RA	Dec.	Transit	10° high 52°	56°
	h m	° '	h m	h m	h m
1	20 16.5	−19 22	3 39	0 53	1 32
11	20 15.9	−19 25	2 59	0 14	0 53
21	20 15.0	−19 27	2 19	23 30	0 13
31	20 14.1	−19 30	1 38	22 50	23 30

Diameter 2"

July 1998

SEVENTH MONTH, 31 DAYS. *Julius* Caesar, formerly *Quintilis*, fifth month of Roman pre-Julian calendar

1	*Wednesday*	Diana, Princess of Wales b. 1961. Amy Johnson b. 1903	*week* 26 *day* 182
2	*Thursday*	Sir Robert Peel d. 1850. Ernest Hemingway d. 1961	183
3	*Friday*	**St Thomas.** Betty Grable d. 1973	184
4	*Saturday*	William Byrd d. 1623. Louis Armstrong b. 1900	185
5	*Sunday*	**5th S. after Pentecost/4th S. after Trinity**	*week* 27 *day* 186
6	*Monday*	Guy de Maupassant d. 1893. Aneurin Bevan d. 1960	187
7	*Tuesday*	Sir Arthur Conan Doyle d. 1930. Ernest Newman d. 1959	188
8	*Wednesday*	Count von Zeppelin b. 1838. Vivien Leigh d. 1967	189
9	*Thursday*	Edmund Burke d. 1797. David Hockney b. 1937	190
10	*Friday*	Camille Pissarro b. 1830. Louis-Jacques Daguerre d. 1851	191
11	*Saturday*	Robert the Bruce b. 1274. Paul Nash d. 1946	192
12	*Sunday*	**6th S. after Pentecost/5th S. after Trinity**	*week* 28 *day* 193
13	*Monday*	*Bank Holiday in Northern Ireland.* Marat assass. 1793	194
14	*Tuesday*	Storming of the Bastille 1789. Leon Garfield b. 1921	195
15	*Wednesday*	St Swithin's Day. Gen. John J. Pershing d. 1948	196
16	*Thursday*	Capt. Roald Amundsen b. 1872. Miles Copeland b. 1913	197
17	*Friday*	Paul Delaroche b. 1797. First issue of *Punch* 1841	198
18	*Saturday*	Jane Austen d. 1817. Dr W. G. Grace b. 1848	199
19	*Sunday*	**7th S. after Pentecost/6th S. after Trinity**	*week* 29 *day* 200
20	*Monday*	Paul Valéry d. 1945. Calouste Gulbenkian d. 1955	201
21	*Tuesday*	Bread rationing began 1946. Henry Longhurst d. 1978	202
22	*Wednesday*	**St Mary Magdalen.** Tate Gallery opened 1897	203
23	*Thursday*	Raymond Chandler b. 1888. Marshal Philippe Pétain d. 1951	204
24	*Friday*	Ernest Bloch b. 1880. Amelia Earhart b. 1897	205
25	*Saturday*	**St James.** First cross-Channel flight by Bleriot 1909	206
26	*Sunday*	**8th S. after Pentecost/7th S. after Trinity**	*week* 30 *day* 207
27	*Monday*	Charter establishing the Bank of England sealed 1694	208
28	*Tuesday*	Robespierre exec. 1794. Sir Garfield Sobers b. 1936	209
29	*Wednesday*	Spanish Armada defeated 1588 (os). William Wilberforce d. 1833	210
30	*Thursday*	Henry Moore b. 1898. Count von Bismarck d. 1898	211
31	*Friday*	*Trinity Law Sittings end.* Franz Liszt d. 1886	212

ASTRONOMICAL PHENOMENA

d	h	
4	00	Earth at aphelion (152 million km)
14	19	Jupiter in conjunction with Moon. Jupiter 0°.9 N.
17	03	Mercury at greatest elongation E.27°
17	06	Saturn in conjunction with Moon. Saturn 2° N.
18	02	Jupiter at stationary point
21	12	Venus in conjunction with Moon. Venus 4° N.
22	02	Mars in conjunction with Moon. Mars 5° N.
23	01	Sun's longitude 120° ♌
23	20	Neptune at opposition
25	15	Mercury in conjunction with Moon. Mercury 2° S.
31	02	Mercury at stationary point

MINIMA OF ALGOL

d	h	d	h	d	h
3	04.1	14	15.3	26	02.6
6	00.9	17	12.1	28	23.4
8	21.7	20	09.0	31	20.2
11	18.5	23	05.8		

CONSTELLATIONS

The following constellations are near the meridian at

	d	h		d	h
June	1	24	July	16	21
June	15	23	August	1	20
July	1	22	August	16	19

Ursa Minor, Draco, Corona, Hercules, Lyra, Serpens, Ophiuchus, Libra, Scorpius and Sagittarius

THE MOON

Phases, Apsides and Node	d	h	m
☽ First Quarter	1	18	43
○ Full Moon	9	16	01
☾ Last Quarter	16	15	13
● New Moon	23	13	44
☽ First Quarter	31	12	05
Apogee (404,259 km)	2	17	27
Perigee (369,664 km)	16	13	52
Apogee (404,339 km)	30	12	10

Mean longitude of ascending node on July 1, 154°

THE SUN

s.d. 15'.8

Day	Right Ascension	Dec. +	Equation of time	Rise 52°	Rise 56°	Transit	Set 52°	Set 56°	Sidereal time	Transit of First Point of Aries
	h m s	° '	m s	h m	h m	h m	h m	h m	h m s	h m s
1	6 39 06	23 08	− 3 43	3 44	3 18	12 04	20 23	20 49	18 35 23	5 23 44
2	6 43 14	23 04	− 3 55	3 45	3 19	12 04	20 23	20 49	18 39 19	5 19 48
3	6 47 22	22 59	− 4 06	3 46	3 20	12 04	20 22	20 48	18 43 16	5 15 52
4	6 51 29	22 55	− 4 17	3 46	3 21	12 04	20 22	20 47	18 47 13	5 11 56
5	6 55 37	22 49	− 4 27	3 47	3 22	12 05	20 21	20 47	18 51 09	5 08 00
6	6 59 44	22 44	− 4 38	3 48	3 23	12 05	20 21	20 46	18 55 06	5 04 04
7	7 03 50	22 38	− 4 48	3 49	3 24	12 05	20 20	20 45	18 59 02	5 00 08
8	7 07 56	22 31	− 4 57	3 50	3 25	12 05	20 20	20 44	19 02 59	4 56 13
9	7 12 02	22 24	− 5 07	3 51	3 26	12 05	20 19	20 43	19 06 55	4 52 17
10	7 16 07	22 17	− 5 15	3 52	3 28	12 05	20 18	20 42	19 10 52	4 48 21
11	7 20 12	22 09	− 5 24	3 53	3 29	12 05	20 17	20 41	19 14 48	4 44 25
12	7 24 17	22 01	− 5 32	3 54	3 30	12 06	20 16	20 40	19 18 45	4 40 29
13	7 28 21	21 53	− 5 39	3 55	3 32	12 06	20 16	20 39	19 22 42	4 36 33
14	7 32 24	21 44	− 5 46	3 56	3 33	12 06	20 15	20 38	19 26 38	4 32 37
15	7 36 27	21 35	− 5 53	3 58	3 34	12 06	20 14	20 36	19 30 35	4 28 41
16	7 40 30	21 26	− 5 59	3 59	3 36	12 06	20 12	20 35	19 34 31	4 24 45
17	7 44 32	21 16	− 6 04	4 00	3 37	12 06	20 11	20 34	19 38 28	4 20 49
18	7 48 34	21 06	− 6 09	4 01	3 39	12 06	20 10	20 32	19 42 24	4 16 53
19	7 52 35	20 55	− 6 14	4 03	3 41	12 06	20 09	20 31	19 46 21	4 12 58
20	7 56 35	20 44	− 6 18	4 04	3 42	12 06	20 08	20 29	19 50 17	4 09 02
21	8 00 36	20 33	− 6 22	4 05	3 44	12 06	20 07	20 28	19 54 14	4 05 06
22	8 04 35	20 21	− 6 24	4 07	3 46	12 06	20 05	20 26	19 58 11	4 01 10
23	8 08 34	20 09	− 6 27	4 08	3 47	12 06	20 04	20 25	20 02 07	3 57 14
24	8 12 32	19 57	− 6 29	4 09	3 49	12 06	20 03	20 23	20 06 04	3 53 18
25	8 16 30	19 44	− 6 30	4 11	3 51	12 07	20 01	20 21	20 10 00	3 49 22
26	8 20 27	19 32	− 6 31	4 12	3 52	12 07	20 00	20 19	20 13 57	3 45 26
27	8 24 24	19 18	− 6 31	4 14	3 54	12 07	19 58	20 18	20 17 53	3 41 30
28	8 28 20	19 05	− 6 30	4 15	3 56	12 06	19 57	20 16	20 21 50	3 37 34
29	8 32 15	18 51	− 6 29	4 17	3 58	12 06	19 55	20 14	20 25 46	3 33 38
30	8 36 10	18 37	− 6 27	4 18	4 00	12 06	19 54	20 12	20 29 43	3 29 43
31	8 40 04	18 22	− 6 25	4 20	4 02	12 06	19 52	20 10	20 33 40	3 25 47

DURATION OF TWILIGHT (in minutes)

Latitude	52°	56°	52°	56°	52°	56°	52°	56°
	1 July		11 July		21 July		31 July	
Civil	48	61	46	58	44	53	41	49
Nautical	124	TAN	116	TAN	107	144	98	122
Astronomical	TAN	TAN	TAN	TAN	TAN	TAN	180	TAN

THE NIGHT SKY

Mercury is too close to the Sun for observation.

Venus is still a splendid object in the morning skies, magnitude − 3.9. By the end of the month it is visible above the east-north-eastern horizon for almost an hour and a half before sunrise. On the morning of the 21st the old crescent Moon will be seen about 6° to the right of the planet. Venus passes 4° north of Aldebaran on the 3rd.

Mars is still unsuitably placed for observation.

Jupiter, magnitude − 2.6, is a morning object in the south-eastern sky and is now becoming visible low above the eastern horizon before midnight. The gibbous Moon is near the planet on the mornings of the 14th and 15th. Jupiter reaches its first stationary point on the 18th.

Saturn, magnitude + 0.5, is a morning object, moving slowly on the borders of three constellations (Pisces, Cetus and Aries). By the end of the month it is visible low above the eastern horizon shortly after 23h. The Moon, at Last Quarter, is close to Saturn on the morning of the 17th.

Neptune is at opposition on the 23rd, in the eastern part of Sagittarius. It is not visible to the naked eye as its magnitude is + 7.8.

THE MOON

Day	RA h m	Dec. °	Hor. par. '	Semi- diam. '	Sun's co- long. °	PA of Bright Limb °	Phase %	Age d	Rise 52° h m	Rise 56° h m	Transit h m	Set 52° h m	Set 56° h m
1	12 05	+ 2.0	54.5	14.8	349	293	43	6.8	11 50	11 50	18 01	—	23 59
2	12 50	− 1.9	54.3	14.8	1	293	52	7.8	12 54	12 57	18 43	0 01	—
3	13 35	− 5.6	54.2	14.8	14	292	62	8.8	13 57	14 04	19 26	0 23	0 18
4	14 21	− 9.2	54.4	14.8	26	291	71	9.8	15 01	15 11	20 10	0 46	0 38
5	15 08	−12.5	54.7	14.9	38	289	79	10.8	16 04	16 17	20 56	1 12	1 01
6	15 57	−15.2	55.1	15.0	50	287	86	11.8	17 07	17 23	21 44	1 42	1 28
7	16 48	−17.3	55.6	15.1	62	285	92	12.8	18 07	18 26	22 35	2 18	2 01
8	17 41	−18.6	56.2	15.3	75	285	97	13.8	19 04	19 23	23 28	3 00	2 42
9	18 36	−19.0	56.8	15.5	87	293	99	14.8	19 55	20 13	—	3 51	3 32
10	19 31	−18.4	57.4	15.6	99	42	100	15.8	20 39	20 55	0 21	4 51	4 33
11	20 28	−16.7	57.9	15.8	111	68	98	16.8	21 17	21 30	1 16	5 58	5 42
12	21 23	−14.1	58.4	15.9	123	70	94	17.8	21 49	21 59	2 09	7 10	6 58
13	22 19	−10.6	58.8	16.0	135	69	87	18.8	22 19	22 25	3 02	8 25	8 17
14	23 13	− 6.5	59.0	16.1	148	68	79	19.8	22 46	22 48	3 54	9 41	9 37
15	0 07	− 2.0	59.2	16.1	160	68	68	20.8	23 12	23 11	4 46	10 58	10 58
16	1 00	+ 2.6	59.3	16.2	172	68	57	21.8	23 40	23 34	5 37	12 16	12 20
17	1 54	+ 7.1	59.3	16.2	184	69	46	22.8	—	—	6 30	13 33	13 41
18	2 49	+11.1	59.2	16.1	197	71	35	23.8	0 10	0 00	7 23	14 49	15 01
19	3 46	+14.6	59.1	16.1	209	74	24	24.8	0 44	0 31	8 18	16 02	16 18
20	4 43	+17.1	58.8	16.0	221	77	15	25.8	1 24	1 07	9 14	17 11	17 29
21	5 41	+18.6	58.5	15.9	233	81	8	26.8	2 10	1 52	10 10	18 12	18 31
22	6 39	+19.0	58.0	15.8	246	83	3	27.8	3 05	2 46	11 06	19 04	19 22
23	7 36	+18.3	57.5	15.7	258	75	0	28.8	4 06	3 48	12 00	19 48	20 03
24	8 32	+16.6	56.9	15.5	270	307	0	0.4	5 11	4 56	12 52	20 24	20 37
25	9 25	+14.0	56.3	15.3	282	292	2	1.4	6 18	6 06	13 42	20 54	21 04
26	10 15	+10.9	55.7	15.2	295	291	6	2.4	7 25	7 16	14 28	21 20	21 26
27	11 04	+ 7.3	55.2	15.0	307	291	12	3.4	8 31	8 26	15 13	21 43	21 46
28	11 50	+ 3.5	54.7	14.9	319	292	19	4.4	9 36	9 34	15 56	22 05	22 05
29	12 36	− 0.4	54.4	14.8	331	292	27	5.4	10 40	10 42	16 38	22 27	22 24
30	13 21	− 4.3	54.2	14.8	344	291	36	6.4	11 43	11 48	17 21	22 50	22 43
31	14 06	− 7.9	54.2	14.8	356	289	45	7.4	12 46	12 55	18 04	23 14	23 04

MERCURY

Day	RA h m	Dec. °	Diam. "	Phase %	Transit h m	5° high 52° h m	5° high 56° h m
1	8 10	+21.8	6	70	13 36	20 59	21 15
3	8 23	+20.9	6	66	13 41	20 59	21 13
5	8 36	+20.0	6	63	13 46	20 57	21 11
7	8 47	+19.0	7	60	13 49	20 55	21 07
9	8 58	+18.0	7	57	13 52	20 51	21 03
11	9 08	+17.0	7	53	13 53	20 47	20 58
13	9 17	+15.9	7	50	13 54	20 42	20 52
15	9 25	+14.9	8	47	13 54	20 37	20 46
17	9 32	+13.9	8	44	13 54	20 31	20 39
19	9 39	+13.0	8	41	13 52	20 24	20 31
21	9 44	+12.0	8	37	13 49	20 16	20 23
23	9 49	+11.2	9	34	13 46	20 08	20 14
25	9 53	+10.4	9	30	13 41	20 00	20 05
27	9 55	+ 9.7	9	27	13 36	19 51	19 55
29	9 57	+ 9.1	10	23	13 29	19 41	19 45
31	9 57	+ 8.7	10	19	13 21	19 31	19 34

VENUS

Day	RA h m	Dec. °	Diam. "	Phase %	Transit h m	5° high 52° h m	5° high 56° h m
1	4 25	+20.1	12	84	9 50	2 35	2 21
6	4 50	+21.1	12	86	9 55	2 34	2 19
11	5 15	+21.9	12	87	10 01	2 35	2 19
16	5 41	+22.5	12	88	10 07	2 38	2 21
21	6 07	+22.8	11	89	10 13	2 43	2 25
26	6 33	+22.8	11	90	10 20	2 49	2 32
31	7 00	+22.5	11	91	10 26	2 57	2 40

MARS

Day	RA h m	Dec. °	Diam. "	Phase %	Transit h m	5° high 52° h m	5° high 56° h m
1	5 44	+23.9	4	100	11 08	3 31	3 12
6	5 59	+24.0	4	99	11 03	3 25	3 06
11	6 14	+24.0	4	99	10 58	3 20	3 01
16	6 28	+24.0	4	99	10 53	3 16	2 57
21	6 43	+23.8	4	99	10 48	3 12	2 53
26	6 57	+23.6	4	99	10 43	3 08	2 50
31	7 12	+23.2	4	99	10 38	3 05	2 47

SUNRISE AND SUNSET

	London 0°05' 51°30'		Bristol 2°35' 51°28'		Birmingham 1°55' 52°28'		Manchester 2°15' 53°28'		Newcastle 1°37' 54°59'		Glasgow 4°14' 55°52'		Belfast 5°56' 54°35'	
	h m	h m	h m	h m	h m	h m	h m	h m	h m	h m	h m	h m	h m	h m
1	3 47	20 21	3 57	20 31	3 49	20 33	3 44	20 41	3 32	20 48	3 36	21 05	3 52	21 03
2	3 48	20 20	3 58	20 30	3 50	20 33	3 45	20 40	3 33	20 48	3 37	21 04	3 53	21 02
3	3 49	20 20	3 59	20 30	3 51	20 33	3 46	20 40	3 34	20 47	3 38	21 04	3 54	21 02
4	3 49	20 20	4 00	20 29	3 51	20 32	3 47	20 39	3 34	20 47	3 39	21 03	3 54	21 01
5	3 50	20 19	4 00	20 29	3 52	20 32	3 48	20 39	3 35	20 46	3 40	21 03	3 55	21 01
6	3 51	20 18	4 01	20 28	3 53	20 31	3 49	20 38	3 36	20 45	3 41	21 02	3 56	21 00
7	3 52	20 18	4 02	20 28	3 54	20 30	3 50	20 38	3 37	20 45	3 42	21 01	3 57	20 59
8	3 53	20 17	4 03	20 27	3 55	20 30	3 51	20 37	3 39	20 44	3 43	21 00	3 58	20 58
9	3 54	20 17	4 04	20 26	3 56	20 29	3 52	20 36	3 40	20 43	3 44	20 59	4 00	20 58
10	3 55	20 16	4 05	20 26	3 57	20 28	3 53	20 35	3 41	20 42	3 45	20 58	4 01	20 57
11	3 56	20 15	4 06	20 25	3 58	20 27	3 54	20 34	3 42	20 41	3 47	20 57	4 02	20 56
12	3 57	20 14	4 07	20 24	3 59	20 27	3 55	20 33	3 43	20 40	3 48	20 56	4 03	20 55
13	3 58	20 13	4 08	20 23	4 00	20 26	3 56	20 32	3 45	20 39	3 49	20 55	4 04	20 54
14	3 59	20 12	4 09	20 22	4 02	20 25	3 57	20 31	3 46	20 38	3 51	20 54	4 06	20 53
15	4 00	20 11	4 11	20 21	4 03	20 24	3 59	20 30	3 47	20 37	3 52	20 53	4 07	20 51
16	4 02	20 10	4 12	20 20	4 04	20 23	4 00	20 29	3 49	20 35	3 54	20 51	4 08	20 50
17	4 03	20 09	4 13	20 19	4 05	20 21	4 01	20 28	3 50	20 34	3 55	20 50	4 10	20 49
18	4 04	20 08	4 14	20 18	4 07	20 20	4 03	20 27	3 52	20 33	3 57	20 48	4 11	20 48
19	4 05	20 07	4 15	20 17	4 08	20 19	4 04	20 25	3 53	20 31	3 58	20 47	4 13	20 46
20	4 07	20 06	4 17	20 16	4 09	20 18	4 06	20 24	3 55	20 30	4 00	20 45	4 14	20 45
21	4 08	20 05	4 18	20 15	4 11	20 17	4 07	20 23	3 56	20 28	4 02	20 44	4 16	20 43
22	4 09	20 03	4 19	20 13	4 12	20 15	4 09	20 21	3 58	20 27	4 03	20 42	4 17	20 42
23	4 11	20 02	4 21	20 12	4 14	20 14	4 10	20 20	3 59	20 25	4 05	20 41	4 19	20 40
24	4 12	20 01	4 22	20 11	4 15	20 12	4 11	20 18	4 01	20 24	4 07	20 39	4 21	20 39
25	4 13	19 59	4 24	20 09	4 16	20 11	4 13	20 17	4 03	20 22	4 08	20 37	4 22	20 37
26	4 15	19 58	4 25	20 08	4 18	20 09	4 15	20 15	4 04	20 20	4 10	20 36	4 24	20 36
27	4 16	19 56	4 26	20 06	4 19	20 08	4 16	20 14	4 06	20 19	4 12	20 34	4 25	20 34
28	4 18	19 55	4 28	20 05	4 21	20 06	4 18	20 12	4 08	20 17	4 14	20 32	4 27	20 32
29	4 19	19 53	4 29	20 03	4 22	20 05	4 19	20 11	4 10	20 15	4 15	20 30	4 29	20 30
30	4 21	19 52	4 31	20 02	4 24	20 03	4 21	20 09	4 11	20 13	4 17	20 28	4 31	20 29
31	4 22	19 50	4 32	20 00	4 26	20 02	4 23	20 07	4 13	20 11	4 19	20 26	4 32	20 27

JUPITER

Day	RA	Dec.	Transit	5° high 52°	56°
	h m	° '	h m	h m	h m
1	23 53.2	− 2 07	5 17	0 01	0 06
11	23 54.7	− 2 01	4 39	23 19	23 24
21	23 55.0	− 2 02	4 00	22 40	22 45
31	23 54.1	− 2 11	3 20	22 01	22 06

Diameters – equatorial 44" polar 41"

SATURN

Day	RA	Dec.	Transit	5° high 52°	56°
	h m	° '	h m	h m	h m
1	2 02.2	+ 9 53	7 26	1 08	1 04
11	2 01.8	+10 04	6 49	0 31	0 26
21	2 06.8	+10 12	6 12	23 49	23 44
31	2 08.2	+10 17	5 34	23 11	23 05

Diameters – equatorial 18" polar 16"
Rings – major axis 40" minor axis 11"

URANUS

Day	RA	Dec.	Transit	10° high 52°	56°
	h m	° '	h m	h m	h m
1	20 58.6	−17 50	2 23	23 20	23 53
11	20 57.3	−17 56	1 42	22 40	23 14
21	20 55.8	−18 02	1 01	22 00	22 34
31	20 54.2	−18 09	0 20	21 20	21 54

Diameter 4"

NEPTUNE

Day	RA	Dec.	Transit	10° high 52°	56°
	h m	° '	h m	h m	h m
1	20 14.1	−19 30	1 38	22 50	23 30
11	20 13.0	−19 34	0 58	22 10	22 50
21	20 11.9	−19 37	0 18	21 31	22 11
31	20 10.8	19 41	23 33	20 51	21 31

Diameter 2"

August 1998

EIGHTH MONTH, 31 DAYS. Julius, Caesar *Augustus*, formerly *Sextilis*, sixth month of Roman pre-Julian calendar

1	*Saturday*	Yves St. Laurent b. 1936. ⚔ The Nile (Aboukir Bay) 1798	*week* 30 *day* 213
2	*Sunday*	**9th S. after Pentecost/8th S. after Trinity**	*week* 31 *day* 214
3	*Monday*	*Bank Holiday in Scotland.* Rupert Brooke b. 1887	215
4	*Tuesday*	*Queen Elizabeth the Queen Mother b. 1900.* William Cecil d. 1598	216
5	*Wednesday*	Jacquetta Hawkes b. 1910. Neil Armstrong b. 1930	217
6	*Thursday*	**The Transfiguration.** Diego Velazquez d. 1660	218
7	*Friday*	Joseph Jacquard d. 1834. Oliver Hardy d. 1957	219
8	*Saturday*	Great Train Robbery 1963. Princess Beatrice of York b. 1988	220
9	*Sunday*	**10th S. after Pentecost/9th S. after Trinity**	*week* 32 *day* 221
10	*Monday*	James Whistler b. 1834. Herbert Hoover b. 1874	222
11	*Tuesday*	Sir Angus Wilson b. 1913. Edith Wharton d. 1937	223
12	*Wednesday*	William Blake d. 1827. Thomas Mann d. 1955	224
13	*Thursday*	Sir Alfred Hitchcock b. 1899. H. G. Wells d. 1946	225
14	*Friday*	John Galsworthy b. 1867. William Randolph Hearst d. 1951	226
15	*Saturday*	*Princess Royal b. 1950.* First ship passed through Panama Canal 1914	227
16	*Sunday*	**11th S. after Pentecost/10th S. after Trinity**	*week* 33 *day* 228
17	*Monday*	Davy Crockett b. 1786. Honoré de Balzac d. 1850	229
18	*Tuesday*	Godfrey Evans b. 1920. George Frederick Stout d. 1944	230
19	*Wednesday*	Blaise Pascal b. 1662. President Bill Clinton b. 1946	231
20	*Thursday*	Raymond Poincaré b. 1860. Gen. William Booth d. 1912	232
21	*Friday*	*Princess Margaret b. 1930.* Leon Trotsky assass. 1940	233
22	*Saturday*	Claude Debussy b. 1862. Henri Cartier-Bresson b. 1908	234
23	*Sunday*	**12th S. after Pentecost/11th S. after Trinity**	*week* 34 *day* 235
24	*Monday*	**St Bartholomew.** Jorge Luis Borges b. 1899	236
25	*Tuesday*	Faraday b. 1867. First cross-Channel swim by Capt. Webb 1875	237
26	*Wednesday*	Christopher Isherwood b. 1904. Ralph Vaughan-Williams d. 1958	238
27	*Thursday*	Titian d. 1576. C. S. Forester b. 1899	239
28	*Friday*	Leigh Hunt d. 1859. Sir Edward Burne-Jones b. 1833	240
29	*Saturday*	James Hunt b. 1947. First motorcycle patented 1885	241
30	*Sunday*	**13th S. after Pentecost/12th S. after Trinity**	*week* 35 *day* 242
31	*Monday*	*Bank Holiday in England, Wales and Northern Ireland*	243

ASTRONOMICAL PHENOMENA

d	h	
3	07	Uranus at opposition
4	21	Mars in conjunction with Venus. Mars 0°.8 N.
11	00	Jupiter in conjunction with Moon. Jupiter 0°.8 N.
13	13	Saturn in conjunction with Moon. Saturn 2° N.
14	00	Mercury in inferior conjunction
15	19	Saturn at stationary point
16	06	Pluto at stationary point
19	19	Mars in conjunction with Moon. Mars 4° N.
20	12	Venus in conjunction with Moon. Venus 3° N.
21	03	Mercury in conjunction with Moon. Mercury 2° S.
22	02	Annular eclipse of Sun (*see* page 66)
23	08	Sun's longitude 150° ♍
23	23	Mercury at stationary point
26	21	Venus in conjunction with Mercury. Venus 2° N.
31	09	Mercury at greatest elongation W. 18°

MINIMA OF ALGOL

d	h	d	h	d	h
3	17.0	15	04.2	26	15.5
6	13.8	18	01.0	29	12.3
9	10.6	20	21.9		
12	07.4	23	18.7		

CONSTELLATIONS

The following constellations are near the meridian at

	d	h		d	h
July	1	24	August	16	21
July	16	23	September	1	20
August	1	22	September	15	19

Draco, Hercules, Lyra, Cygnus, Sagitta, Ophiuchus, Serpens, Aquila and Sagittarius

THE MOON

Phases, Apsides and Node	d	h	m
○ Full Moon	8	02	10
☾ Last Quarter	14	19	48
● New Moon	22	02	03
☽ First Quarter	30	05	06
Perigee (366,421 km)	11	11	54
Apogee (405,181 km)	27	06	30

Mean longitude of ascending node on August 1, 153°

THE SUN

s.d. 15′.8

Day	Right Ascension	Dec. +	Equation of time	Rise 52°	Rise 56°	Transit	Set 52°	Set 56°	Sidereal time	Transit of First Point of Aries
	h m s	° ′	m s	h m	h m	h m	h m	h m	h m s	h m s
1	8 43 58	18 07	− 6 22	4 21	4 03	12 06	19 50	20 08	20 37 36	3 21 51
2	8 47 51	17 52	− 6 18	4 23	4 05	12 06	19 49	20 06	20 41 33	3 17 55
3	8 51 43	17 37	− 6 14	4 24	4 07	12 06	19 47	20 04	20 45 29	3 13 59
4	8 55 34	17 21	− 6 09	4 26	4 09	12 06	19 45	20 02	20 49 26	3 10 03
5	8 59 25	17 05	− 6 03	4 27	4 11	12 06	19 43	20 00	20 53 22	3 06 07
6	9 03 16	16 49	− 5 57	4 29	4 13	12 06	19 42	19 58	20 57 19	3 02 11
7	9 07 06	16 32	− 5 50	4 31	4 15	12 06	19 40	19 55	21 01 15	2 58 15
8	9 10 55	16 15	− 5 43	4 32	4 17	12 06	19 38	19 53	21 05 12	2 54 19
9	9 14 43	15 58	− 5 35	4 34	4 19	12 06	19 36	19 51	21 09 09	2 50 23
10	9 18 31	15 41	− 5 26	4 35	4 21	12 05	19 34	19 49	21 13 05	2 46 28
11	9 22 19	15 23	− 5 17	4 37	4 22	12 05	19 32	19 47	21 17 02	2 42 32
12	9 26 06	15 06	− 5 07	4 39	4 24	12 05	19 30	19 44	21 20 58	2 38 36
13	9 29 52	14 48	− 4 57	4 40	4 26	12 05	19 28	19 42	21 24 55	2 34 40
14	9 33 38	14 29	− 4 47	4 42	4 28	12 05	19 26	19 40	21 28 51	2 30 44
15	9 37 23	14 11	− 4 35	4 43	4 30	12 04	19 24	19 37	21 32 48	2 26 48
16	9 41 08	13 52	− 4 23	4 45	4 32	12 04	19 22	19 35	21 36 44	2 22 52
17	9 44 52	13 33	− 4 11	4 47	4 34	12 04	19 20	19 33	21 40 41	2 18 56
18	9 48 36	13 14	− 3 58	4 48	4 36	12 04	19 18	19 30	21 44 38	2 15 00
19	9 52 19	12 55	− 3 45	4 50	4 38	12 04	19 16	19 28	21 48 34	2 11 04
20	9 56 02	12 35	− 3 31	4 52	4 40	12 03	19 14	19 25	21 52 31	2 07 08
21	9 59 44	12 15	− 3 17	4 53	4 42	12 03	19 12	19 23	21 56 27	2 03 13
22	10 03 26	11 55	− 3 03	4 55	4 44	12 03	19 10	19 20	22 00 24	1 59 17
23	10 07 08	11 35	− 2 47	4 57	4 46	12 03	19 08	19 18	22 04 20	1 55 21
24	10 10 49	11 15	− 2 32	4 58	4 48	12 02	19 05	19 15	22 08 17	1 51 25
25	10 14 29	10 54	− 2 16	5 00	4 50	12 02	19 03	19 13	22 12 13	1 47 29
26	10 18 09	10 33	− 1 59	5 01	4 52	12 02	19 01	19 10	22 16 10	1 43 33
27	10 21 49	10 13	− 1 42	5 03	4 54	12 02	18 59	19 08	22 20 07	1 39 37
28	10 25 28	9 52	− 1 25	5 05	4 56	12 01	18 57	19 05	22 24 03	1 35 41
29	10 29 07	9 30	− 1 07	5 06	4 58	12 01	18 54	19 03	22 28 00	1 31 45
30	10 32 46	9 09	0 49	5 08	5 00	12 01	18 52	19 00	22 31 56	1 27 49
31	10 36 24	8 48	− 0 31	5 10	5 02	12 00	18 50	18 58	22 35 53	1 23 53

Duration of Twilight (in minutes)

Latitude	52°	56°	52°	56°	52°	56°	52°	56°
	1 August		11 August		21 August		31 August	
Civil	41	48	39	45	37	42	35	40
Nautical	97	120	89	106	83	96	79	89
Astronomical	177	TAN	153	205	138	166	127	147

The Night Sky

Mercury is unsuitably placed for observation for most of August as it passes through inferior conjunction on the 13th. However, for the last few days of the month it is visible as a morning object, magnitude + 1.2 to − 0.2, low above the east-south-eastern horizon, around the beginning of morning civil twilight. Venus, four magnitudes brighter than Mercury, will be in the vicinity, passing 2° north of it late on the 26th; thus Venus, moving slowly in towards the Sun, will be a useful guide to locating Mercury.

Venus, magnitude − 3.9, continues to be visible as a splendid morning object, visible above the east-north-eastern horizon before dawn. On the morning of the 20th the old crescent Moon is about 5° from Venus, having passed Mars on the previous day.

Mars is very gradually becoming a morning object during the month, magnitude + 1.7. It may be seen low above the east-north-eastern horizon by about 03h. During the first part of the month Mars is passing south of Castor and Pollux, in Gemini. Also, during the first part of the month Venus and Mars are quite close, the separation being less than 1 degree on the mornings of the 4th and 5th.

Jupiter is a brilliant object, magnitude − 2.8 in the sky for most of the night, becoming visible low in the eastern sky as early as 20h by the end of the month. The gibbous Moon passes less than 2° south of Jupiter on the night of the 10th to 11th.

Saturn is a morning object, magnitude + 0.3, becoming more visible as it is drawing away from the Sun and also because sunrise is getting later. The Moon, near Last Quarter, is near Saturn on the mornings of the 13th and 14th.

Uranus is at opposition on the 3rd, in Capricornus. It is barely visible to the naked eye as its magnitude is + 5.7 but it is easily located with a small optical aid.

Meteors. The maximum of the famous Perseid meteor shower occurs on the 12th. A gibbous Moon will interfere with observation.

THE MOON

Day	RA h m	Dec. °	Hor. par. '	Semi-diam. '	Sun's co-long. °	PA of Bright Limb °	Phase %	Age d	Rise 52° h m	Rise 56° h m	Transit h m	Set 52° h m	Set 56° h m
1	14 52	−11.3	54.4	14.8	8	287	55	8.4	13 49	14 01	18 49	23 42	23 29
2	15 40	−14.2	54.8	14.9	20	285	64	9.4	14 52	15 07	19 36	—	23 59
3	16 30	−16.5	55.3	15.1	32	282	73	10.4	15 53	16 10	20 25	0 14	—
4	17 21	−18.2	55.9	15.2	45	278	82	11.4	16 51	17 10	21 16	0 53	0 36
5	18 15	−18.9	56.6	15.4	57	274	89	12.4	17 45	18 03	22 09	1 40	1 21
6	19 11	−18.7	57.3	15.6	69	270	95	13.4	18 32	18 50	23 04	2 36	2 17
7	20 07	−17.4	58.1	15.8	81	269	98	14.4	19 14	19 28	23 59	3 40	3 24
8	21 04	−15.1	58.7	16.0	93	306	100	15.4	19 49	20 00	—	4 51	4 38
9	22 01	−11.8	59.3	16.2	106	68	99	16.4	20 21	20 28	0 54	6 07	5 57
10	22 57	− 7.8	59.6	16.2	118	70	95	17.4	20 50	20 53	1 48	7 25	7 20
11	23 52	− 3.3	59.8	16.3	130	69	89	18.4	21 17	21 16	2 41	8 44	8 43
12	0 47	+ 1.4	59.8	16.3	142	70	81	19.4	21 45	21 40	3 34	10 03	10 06
13	1 42	+ 6.0	59.7	16.3	154	71	71	20.4	22 14	22 05	4 26	11 22	11 28
14	2 37	+10.2	59.4	16.2	167	73	60	21.4	22 46	22 34	5 20	12 38	12 49
15	3 33	+13.8	59.0	16.1	179	76	48	22.4	23 24	23 08	6 14	13 52	14 07
16	4 30	+16.5	58.6	16.0	191	80	37	23.4	—	23 50	7 09	15 02	15 19
17	5 27	+18.3	58.2	15.8	203	84	27	24.4	0 07	—	8 04	16 04	16 23
18	6 24	+18.9	57.7	15.7	215	89	17	25.4	0 58	0 40	8 59	16 59	17 17
19	7 20	+18.6	57.2	15.6	228	93	10	26.4	1 56	1 38	9 53	17 45	18 01
20	8 15	+17.2	56.7	15.4	240	97	5	27.4	2 58	2 42	10 45	18 23	18 37
21	9 08	+14.9	56.2	15.3	252	100	1	28.4	4 04	3 50	11 35	18 55	19 06
22	9 59	+11.9	55.7	15.2	264	91	0	29.4	5 10	5 00	12 22	19 22	19 30
23	10 48	+ 8.5	55.2	15.0	277	288	1	0.9	6 17	6 10	13 07	19 47	19 51
24	11 35	+ 4.8	54.8	14.9	289	289	4	1.9	7 22	7 19	13 51	20 09	20 10
25	12 21	+ 0.9	54.5	14.8	301	289	8	2.9	8 27	8 27	14 34	20 31	20 29
26	13 06	− 3.0	54.2	14.8	313	289	14	3.9	9 30	9 34	15 16	20 53	20 48
27	13 52	− 6.7	54.1	14.7	326	288	21	4.9	10 33	10 41	15 59	21 17	21 08
28	14 37	−10.2	54.2	14.8	338	286	30	5.9	11 36	11 46	16 43	21 43	21 31
29	15 24	−13.2	54.4	14.8	350	283	39	6.9	12 38	12 52	17 28	22 13	21 58
30	16 12	−15.8	54.7	14.9	2	280	48	7.9	13 39	13 55	18 15	22 48	22 31
31	17 03	−17.6	55.3	15.1	14	276	58	8.9	14 37	14 56	19 05	23 30	23 12

MERCURY

Day	RA h m	Dec. °	Diam. "	Phase %	Transit h m	5° high 52° h m	5° high 56° h m
1	9 56	+ 8.5	10	18	13 16	19 25	19 29
3	9 55	+ 8.3	11	14	13 06	19 14	19 18
5	9 52	+ 8.2	11	10	12 55	19 03	19 07
7	9 47	+ 8.3	11	7	12 43	18 52	18 55
9	9 42	+ 8.6	11	4	12 30	18 41	18 44
11	9 37	+ 9.1	11	2	12 16	18 30	18 34
13	9 31	+ 9.7	11	1	12 02	18 19	18 24
15	9 25	+10.4	11	1	11 48	5 29	5 23
17	9 19	+11.2	11	2	11 35	5 12	5 06
19	9 15	+12.0	10	5	11 24	4 55	4 49
21	9 12	+12.8	10	9	11 13	4 41	4 33
23	9 11	+13.5	9	13	11 04	4 28	4 20
25	9 11	+14.1	9	19	10 58	4 18	4 10
27	9 14	+14.5	8	26	10 53	4 11	4 03
29	9 19	+14.7	8	34	10 51	4 07	3 58
31	9 26	+14.7	7	43	10 50	4 07	3 58

VENUS

Day	RA h m	Dec. °	Diam. "	Phase %	Transit h m	5° high 52° h m	5° high 56° h m
1	7 05	+22.4	11	91	10 28	2 59	2 42
6	7 31	+21.9	11	92	10 34	3 09	2 53
11	7 57	+21.0	11	93	10 40	3 21	3 05
16	8 22	+19.9	11	94	10 46	3 33	3 19
21	8 48	+18.6	10	95	10 52	3 47	3 34
26	9 13	+17.0	10	96	10 57	4 01	3 49
31	9 37	+15.3	10	96	11 02	4 15	4 06

MARS

Day	RA h m	Dec. °	Diam. "	Phase %	Transit h m	5° high 52° h m	5° high 56° h m
1	7 15	+23.2	4	99	10 37	3 04	2 46
6	7 29	+22.7	4	98	10 31	3 01	2 44
11	7 43	+22.3	4	98	10 25	2 59	2 42
16	7 57	+21.7	4	98	10 19	2 56	2 40
21	8 10	+21.1	4	98	10 13	2 54	2 38
26	8 24	+20.4	4	98	10 07	2 52	2 37
31	8 37	+19.7	4	97	10 00	2 49	2 36

SUNRISE AND SUNSET

	London		Bristol		Birmingham		Manchester		Newcastle		Glasgow		Belfast	
	0°05′	51°30′	2°35′	51°28′	1°55′	52°28′	2°15′	53°28′	1°37′	54°59′	4°14′	55°52′	5°56′	54°35′
	h m	h m	h m	h m	h m	h m	h m	h m	h m	h m	h m	h m	h m	h m
1	4 24	19 49	4 34	19 59	4 27	20 00	4 24	20 05	4 15	20 10	4 21	20 24	4 34	20 25
2	4 25	19 47	4 35	19 57	4 29	19 58	4 26	20 04	4 17	20 08	4 23	20 22	4 36	20 23
3	4 27	19 45	4 37	19 55	4 30	19 56	4 27	20 02	4 18	20 06	4 25	20 20	4 37	20 21
4	4 28	19 44	4 38	19 54	4 32	19 55	4 29	20 00	4 20	20 04	4 27	20 18	4 39	20 19
5	4 30	19 42	4 40	19 52	4 33	19 53	4 31	19 58	4 22	20 02	4 28	20 16	4 41	20 17
6	4 31	19 40	4 41	19 50	4 35	19 51	4 33	19 56	4 24	20 00	4 30	20 14	4 43	20 15
7	4 33	19 38	4 43	19 48	4 37	19 49	4 34	19 54	4 26	19 58	4 32	20 12	4 45	20 13
8	4 34	19 37	4 44	19 46	4 38	19 47	4 36	19 52	4 27	19 56	4 34	20 10	4 46	20 11
9	4 36	19 35	4 46	19 45	4 40	19 45	4 38	19 50	4 29	19 53	4 36	20 07	4 48	20 09
10	4 37	19 33	4 48	19 43	4 42	19 43	4 39	19 48	4 31	19 51	4 38	20 05	4 50	20 07
11	4 39	19 31	4 49	19 41	4 43	19 41	4 41	19 46	4 33	19 49	4 40	20 03	4 52	20 05
12	4 41	19 29	4 51	19 39	4 45	19 39	4 43	19 44	4 35	19 47	4 42	20 01	4 54	20 03
13	4 42	19 27	4 52	19 37	4 46	19 37	4 45	19 42	4 37	19 45	4 44	19 58	4 55	20 01
14	4 44	19 25	4 54	19 35	4 48	19 35	4 46	19 40	4 39	19 42	4 46	19 56	4 57	19 58
15	4 45	19 23	4 55	19 33	4 50	19 33	4 48	19 38	4 40	19 40	4 48	19 54	4 59	19 56
16	4 47	19 21	4 57	19 31	4 51	19 31	4 50	19 36	4 42	19 38	4 50	19 51	5 01	19 54
17	4 48	19 19	4 59	19 29	4 53	19 29	4 51	19 33	4 44	19 36	4 52	19 49	5 03	19 52
18	4 50	19 17	5 00	19 27	4 55	19 27	4 53	19 31	4 46	19 33	4 54	19 47	5 05	19 49
19	4 52	19 15	5 02	19 25	4 56	19 25	4 55	19 29	4 48	19 31	4 56	19 44	5 06	19 47
20	4 53	19 13	5 03	19 23	4 58	19 23	4 57	19 27	4 50	19 29	4 57	19 42	5 08	19 45
21	4 55	19 11	5 05	19 21	5 00	19 21	4 58	19 25	4 52	19 26	4 59	19 39	5 10	19 42
22	4 56	19 09	5 07	19 19	5 01	19 19	5 00	19 22	4 54	19 24	5 01	19 37	5 12	19 40
23	4 58	19 07	5 08	19 17	5 03	19 16	5 02	19 20	4 55	19 22	5 03	19 34	5 14	19 38
24	5 00	19 05	5 10	19 15	5 05	19 14	5 04	19 18	4 57	19 19	5 05	19 32	5 16	19 35
25	5 01	19 03	5 11	19 13	5 06	19 12	5 05	19 16	4 59	19 17	5 07	19 30	5 17	19 33
26	5 03	19 00	5 13	19 10	5 08	19 10	5 07	19 13	5 01	19 14	5 09	19 27	5 19	19 31
27	5 04	18 58	5 15	19 08	5 10	19 08	5 09	19 11	5 03	19 12	5 11	19 25	5 21	19 28
28	5 06	18 56	5 16	19 06	5 11	19 05	5 11	19 09	5 05	19 09	5 13	19 22	5 23	19 26
29	5 08	18 54	5 18	19 04	5 13	19 03	5 12	19 06	5 07	19 07	5 15	19 19	5 25	19 23
30	5 09	18 52	5 19	19 02	5 15	19 01	5 14	19 04	5 08	19 05	5 17	19 17	5 27	19 21
31	5 11	18 49	5 21	18 59	5 16	18 58	5 16	19 02	5 10	19 02	5 19	19 14	5 28	19 18

JUPITER

Day	RA	Dec.	Transit	5° high	
				52°	56°
	h m	° ′	h m	h m	h m
1	23 54.0	− 2 12	3 16	21 57	22 02
11	23 51.8	− 2 29	2 34	21 17	21 22
21	23 48.6	− 2 52	1 52	20 36	20 42
31	23 44.6	− 3 20	1 09	19 55	20 01

Diameters – equatorial 48″ polar 45″

SATURN

Day	RA	Dec.	Transit	5° high	
				52°	56°
	h m	° ′	h m	h m	h m
1	2 08.3	+10 17	5 30	23 07	23 02
11	2 09.0	+10 18	4 51	22 28	22 23
21	2 09.1	+10 16	4 12	21 49	21 44
31	2 08.5	+10 10	3 32	21 09	21 04

Diameters – equatorial 19″ polar 17″
Rings – major axis 42″ minor axis 12″

URANUS

Day	RA	Dec.	Transit	10° high	
				52°	56°
	h m	° ′	h m	h m	h m
1	20 54.0	−18 10	0 16	3 13	2 38
11	20 52.4	−18 16	23 31	2 31	1 56
21	20 50.9	−18 23	22 51	1 49	1 14
31	20 49.4	−18 28	22 10	1 07	0 32

Diameter 4″

NEPTUNE

Day	RA	Dec.	Transit	10° high	
				52°	56°
	h m	° ′	h m	h m	h m
1	20 10.7	−19 41	23 29	2 16	1 35
11	20 09.6	−19 45	22 49	1 35	0 54
21	20 08.6	−19 48	22 08	0 54	0 13
31	20 07.7	19 51	21 28	0 13	23 28

Diameter 2″

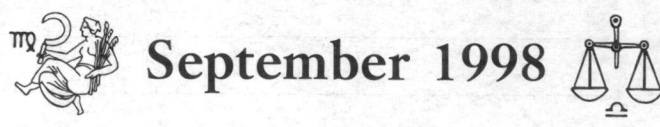

September 1998

NINTH MONTH, 30 DAYS. *Septem* (seven), seventh month of Roman pre-Julian calendar

1	*Tuesday*	Sir Roger Casement b. 1864. Siegfried Sassoon d. 1967	*week 35 day* 244
2	*Wednesday*	Fire of London 1666. Thomas Telford d. 1834	245
3	*Thursday*	Oliver Cromwell d. 1658. Start of Second World War 1939	246
4	*Friday*	French Republic proclaimed 1870. Albert Schweitzer d. 1965	247
5	*Saturday*	John Wisden b. 1826. Jesse James b. 1847	248
6	*Sunday*	**14th S. after Pentecost/13th S. after Trinity**	*week 36 day* 249
7	*Monday*	Catherine Parr d. 1548. Buddy Holly b. 1936	250
8	*Tuesday*	**Blessed Virgin Mary.** Peter Sellers b. 1925	251
9	*Wednesday*	Stéphane Mallarmé d. 1898. End of soap rationing 1950	252
10	*Thursday*	Mary Wollstonecraft Godwin d. 1797. Treaty of St Germain signed 1919	253
11	*Friday*	David Ricardo b. 1823. Jessica Mitford b. 1917	254
12	*Saturday*	Cleopatra's Needle erected 1878. Maurice Chevalier b. 1888	255
13	*Sunday*	**15th S. after Pentecost/14th S. after Trinity**	*week 37 day* 256
14	*Monday*	James Fenimore Cooper d. 1851. Isadora Duncan d. 1927	257
15	*Tuesday*	Prince Henry of Wales b. 1984. Battle of Britain Day	258
16	*Wednesday*	Gabriel Fahrenheit d. 1736. Peter Darrell b. 1929	259
17	*Thursday*	William Fox Talbot d. 1877. Sir Francis Chichester b. 1901	260
18	*Friday*	William Hazlitt d. 1830. Greta Garbo b. 1905	261
19	*Saturday*	George Cadbury b. 1839. Dr Thomas Barnardo d. 1905	262
20	*Sunday*	**16th S. after Pentecost/15th S. after Trinity**	*week 38 day* 263
21	*Monday*	**St Matthew.** JEWISH NEW YEAR (5759)	264
22	*Tuesday*	⚔ Zutphen 1586. Michael Faraday b. 1791	265
23	*Wednesday*	Wilkie Collins d. 1889. Sigmund Freud d. 1939	266
24	*Thursday*	Horace Walpole b. 1717. F. Scott Fitzgerald b. 1896	267
25	*Friday*	William Faulkner b. 1897. Mark Rothko b. 1903	268
26	*Saturday*	George Gershwin b. 1898. James Keir Hardie d. 1915	269
27	*Sunday*	**17th S. after Pentecost/16th S. after Trinity**	*week 39 day* 270
28	*Monday*	W. H. Auden d. 1973. Herman Melville d. 1891	271
29	*Tuesday*	**St Michael and All Angels.** Lord Nelson b. 1758	272
30	*Wednesday*	YOM KIPPUR. Deborah Kerr b. 1921	273

ASTRONOMICAL PHENOMENA

d h
7 05 Jupiter in conjunction with Moon. Jupiter 0°.5 N.
9 19 Saturn in conjunction with Moon. Saturn 2° N.
11 06 Venus in conjunction with Mercury. Venus 0°.3 S.
16 03 Jupiter at opposition
17 11 Mars in conjunction with Moon. Mars 2° N.
19 18 Venus in conjunction with Moon. Venus 0°.03 N.
20 07 Mercury in conjunction with Moon. Mercury 0°.1 S.
23 06 Sun's longitude 180° ♎
25 20 Mercury in superior conjunction

MINIMA OF ALGOL

d	h	d	h	d	h
1	09.1	12	20.3	24	07.6
4	05.9	15	17.1	27	04.4
7	02.7	18	14.0	30	01.2
9	23.5	21	10.8		

CONSTELLATIONS

The following constellations are near the meridian at

	d	h		d	h
August	1	24	September	15	21
August	16	23	October	1	20
September	1	22	October	16	19

Draco, Cepheus, Lyra, Cygnus, Vulpecula, Sagitta, Delphinus, Equuleus, Aquila, Aquarius and Capricornus

THE MOON

Phases, Apsides and Node	d	h	m
○ Full Moon	6	11	21
☾ Last Quarter	13	01	58
● New Moon	20	17	02
☽ First Quarter	28	21	11
Perigee (361,360 km)	8	06	06
Apogee (406,192 km)	23	22	05

Mean longitude of ascending node on September 1, 151°

THE SUN
s.d. 15′.9

Day	Right Ascension	Dec.	Equation of time	Rise 52°	Rise 56°	Transit	Set 52°	Set 56°	Sidereal time	Transit of First Point of Aries
	h m s	° ′	m s	h m	h m	h m	h m	h m	h m s	h m s
1	10 40 02	+ 8 26	− 0 12	5 11	5 04	12 00	18 48	18 55	22 39 49	1 19 58
2	10 43 39	+ 8 04	+ 0 07	5 13	5 06	12 00	18 46	18 53	22 43 46	1 16 02
3	10 47 16	+ 7 42	+ 0 26	5 14	5 08	11 59	18 43	18 50	22 47 42	1 12 06
4	10 50 53	+ 7 20	l 0 46	5 16	5 10	11 59	18 41	18 47	22 51 39	1 08 10
5	10 54 30	+ 6 58	+ 1 06	5 18	5 11	11 59	18 39	18 45	22 55 36	1 04 14
6	10 58 06	+ 6 36	+ 1 26	5 19	5 13	11 58	18 36	18 42	22 59 32	1 00 18
7	11 01 43	+ 6 13	+ 1 46	5 21	5 15	11 58	18 34	18 39	23 03 29	0 56 22
8	11 05 19	+ 5 51	+ 2 07	5 23	5 17	11 58	18 32	18 37	23 07 25	0 52 26
9	11 08 54	+ 5 28	+ 2 27	5 24	5 19	11 57	18 29	18 34	23 11 22	0 48 30
10	11 12 30	+ 5 06	+ 2 48	5 26	5 21	11 57	18 27	18 32	23 15 18	0 44 34
11	11 16 06	+ 4 43	+ 3 09	5 27	5 23	11 57	18 25	18 29	23 19 15	0 40 38
12	11 19 41	+ 4 20	+ 3 30	5 29	5 25	11 56	18 22	18 26	23 23 11	0 36 43
13	11 23 16	+ 3 57	+ 3 51	5 31	5 27	11 56	18 20	18 24	23 27 08	0 32 47
14	11 26 52	+ 3 34	+ 4 13	5 32	5 29	11 56	18 18	18 21	23 31 04	0 28 51
15	11 30 27	+ 3 11	+ 4 34	5 34	5 31	11 55	18 15	18 18	23 35 01	0 24 55
16	11 34 02	+ 2 48	+ 4 55	5 36	5 33	11 55	18 13	18 16	23 38 58	0 20 59
17	11 37 37	+ 2 25	+ 5 17	5 37	5 35	11 55	18 11	18 13	23 42 54	0 17 03
18	11 41 13	+ 2 02	+ 5 38	5 39	5 37	11 54	18 08	18 10	23 46 51	0 13 07
19	11 44 48	+ 1 39	+ 5 59	5 41	5 39	11 54	18 06	18 08	23 50 47	0 09 11
20	11 48 23	+ 1 15	+ 6 21	5 42	5 41	11 53	18 04	18 05	23 54 44	0 05 15
21	11 51 59	+ 0 52	+ 6 42	5 44	5 43	11 53	18 01	18 02	23 58 40	{ 0 01 19 / 23 57 24
22	11 55 34	+ 0 29	+ 7 03	5 45	5 45	11 53	17 59	18 00	0 02 37	23 53 28
23	11 59 09	+ 0 05	+ 7 24	5 47	5 47	11 52	17 57	17 57	0 06 33	23 49 32
24	12 02 45	− 0 18	+ 7 45	5 49	5 49	11 52	17 54	17 54	0 10 30	23 45 36
25	12 06 21	− 0 41	+ 8 06	5 50	5 51	11 52	17 52	17 52	0 14 27	23 41 40
26	12 09 57	− 1 05	+ 8 27	5 52	5 52	11 51	17 50	17 49	0 18 23	23 37 44
27	12 13 33	− 1 28	+ 8 47	5 54	5 54	11 51	17 47	17 47	0 22 20	23 33 48
28	12 17 09	− 1 51	+ 9 07	5 55	5 56	11 51	17 45	17 44	0 26 16	23 29 52
29	12 20 45	− 2 15	+ 9 28	5 57	5 58	11 50	17 43	17 41	0 30 13	23 25 56
30	12 24 22	− 2 38	+ 9 47	5 59	6 00	11 50	17 40	17 39	0 34 09	23 22 00

DURATION OF TWILIGHT (in minutes)

Latitude	52°	56°	52°	56°	52°	56°	52°	56°
	1 September		11 September		21 September		30 September	
Civil	35	39	34	38	34	37	34	37
Nautical	79	89	76	84	74	82	73	80
Astronomical	127	146	120	135	115	129	113	126

THE NIGHT SKY

Mercury, magnitude −0.3 to −1.2, is visible as a morning object for the first ten or 12 days of the month, low above the eastern horizon around the beginning of morning civil twilight. Afterwards Mercury is too close to the Sun for observation as it passes through superior conjunction on the 25th. Venus continues to be in the vicinity of Mercury, passing only 0°.3 south of it on the morning of the 11th. Mercury passes 1° north of Regulus on the 7th.

Venus is a splendid object in the morning skies, magnitude −3.9, visible low above the eastern horizon before dawn. It is getting noticeably closer to the Sun and by the end of the month is only likely to be seen for about ten minutes before being lost in the glare of the rising Sun.

Mars, magnitude +1.6, is a morning object, visible in the eastern sky by 03h. At the beginning of the month Mars is in Cancer but its eastward motion brings it to within about 4° of Regulus, in Leo, by the end of the month.

Jupiter, magnitude −2.9, reaches opposition on the 16th and thus is observable throughout the hours of darkness. The Full Moon passes within 2° south of Jupiter on the morning of the 7th.

Saturn, magnitude +0.1, continues to be visible as a morning object, becoming visible above the eastern horizon earlier each evening. The gibbous Moon is near the planet on the 9th and 10th.

Zodiacal Light. The morning cone may be seen stretching up from the eastern horizon, along the ecliptic, before the beginning of morning twilight, from the beginning of the month to the 4th and again after the 18th.

THE MOON

Day	RA	Dec.	Hor. par.	Semi-diam.	Sun's co-long.	PA of Bright Limb	Phase	Age	Rise 52°	Rise 56°	Transit	Set 52°	Set 56°
	h m	°	′	′	°	°	%	d	h m	h m	h m	h m	h m
1	17 55	−18.7	55.9	15.2	27	272	67	9.9	15 32	15 51	19 56	—	—
2	18 49	−18.9	56.7	15.5	39	268	77	10.9	16 22	16 40	20 50	0 21	0 02
3	19 44	−18.1	57.6	15.7	51	263	85	11.9	17 06	17 22	21 44	1 20	1 03
4	20 41	−16.2	58.5	15.9	63	258	92	12.9	17 44	17 57	22 39	2 28	2 13
5	21 38	−13.3	59.3	16.2	75	253	97	13.9	18 18	18 27	23 34	3 42	3 30
6	22 35	− 9.5	60.0	16.3	88	244	100	14.9	18 49	18 54	—	5 00	4 53
7	23 31	− 5.1	60.5	16.5	100	81	100	15.9	19 17	19 19	0 29	6 21	6 18
8	0 28	− 0.3	60.7	16.5	112	74	97	16.9	19 46	19 43	1 23	7 43	7 44
9	1 24	+ 4.5	60.6	16.5	124	74	91	17.9	20 15	20 08	2 18	9 04	9 09
10	2 21	+ 9.0	60.3	16.4	136	75	83	18.9	20 47	20 37	3 13	10 24	10 34
11	3 18	+12.9	59.8	16.3	148	78	73	19.9	21 24	21 09	4 08	11 41	11 55
12	4 16	+15.9	59.2	16.1	161	81	62	20.9	22 06	21 49	5 04	12 54	13 10
13	5 14	+18.0	58.5	15.9	173	85	51	21.9	22 55	22 36	6 00	13 59	14 18
14	6 11	+18.9	57.9	15.8	185	90	40	22.9	23 50	23 31	6 55	14 56	15 15
15	7 07	+18.8	57.2	15.6	197	95	30	23.9	—	—	7 49	15 44	16 01
16	8 02	+17.6	56.6	15.4	209	100	21	24.9	0 50	0 34	8 41	16 24	16 39
17	8 55	+15.5	56.0	15.3	222	104	13	25.9	1 54	1 40	9 31	16 57	17 09
18	9 46	+12.8	55.5	15.1	234	108	7	26.9	3 00	2 49	10 18	17 26	17 34
19	10 35	+ 9.5	55.1	15.0	246	113	3	27.9	4 06	3 58	11 04	17 51	17 56
20	11 22	+ 5.8	54.7	14.9	258	124	0	28.9	5 11	5 07	11 48	18 13	18 16
21	12 08	+ 2.0	54.4	14.8	271	255	0	0.3	6 16	6 15	12 31	18 35	18 34
22	12 53	− 1.9	54.2	14.8	283	279	2	1.3	7 20	7 22	13 13	18 57	18 53
23	13 38	− 5.7	54.0	14.7	295	282	5	2.3	8 23	8 29	13 56	19 20	19 13
24	14 24	− 9.3	54.0	14.7	307	282	10	3.3	9 26	9 35	14 39	19 45	19 34
25	15 10	−12.5	54.1	14.7	319	281	16	4.3	10 28	10 41	15 23	20 13	19 59
26	15 58	−15.2	54.3	14.8	332	278	24	5.3	11 29	11 44	16 09	20 45	20 29
27	16 47	−17.2	54.6	14.9	344	275	32	6.3	12 28	12 45	16 57	21 24	21 06
28	17 37	−18.6	55.1	15.0	356	271	41	7.3	13 23	13 42	17 47	22 10	21 51
29	18 30	−19.1	55.8	15.2	8	267	51	8.3	14 14	14 32	18 38	23 04	22 45
30	19 23	−18.6	56.6	15.4	20	263	61	9.3	14 59	15 16	19 30	—	23 50

MERCURY

Day	RA	Dec.	Diam.	Phase	Transit	5° high 52°	5° high 56°
	h m	°	″	%	h m	h m	h m
1	9 30	+14.7	7	47	10 51	4 07	3 58
3	9 40	+14.4	7	56	10 53	4 11	4 02
5	9 51	+13.9	6	64	10 56	4 17	4 09
7	10 03	+13.2	6	72	11 01	4 25	4 18
9	10 16	+12.2	6	79	11 06	4 35	4 29
11	10 30	+11.1	6	85	11 12	4 47	4 41
13	10 44	+ 9.9	5	89	11 18	5 00	4 55
15	10 58	+ 8.6	5	93	11 24	5 13	5 09
17	11 12	+ 7.1	5	96	11 31	5 27	5 24
19	11 26	+ 5.6	5	98	11 36	5 40	5 39
21	11 40	+ 4.1	5	99	11 42	5 54	5 54
23	11 53	+ 2.5	5	100	11 48	6 08	6 09
25	12 06	+ 0.9	5	100	11 53	6 21	6 24
27	12 19	− 0.6	5	100	11 58	6 34	6 39
29	12 32	− 2.2	5	100	12 03	17 16	17 11
31	12 44	− 3.7	5	99	12 07	17 13	17 06

VENUS

Day	RA	Dec.	Diam.	Phase	Transit	5° high 52°	5° high 56°
	h m	°	″	%	h m	h m	h m
1	9 42	+14.9	10	96	11 03	4 18	4 09
6	10 06	+12.9	10	97	11 07	4 33	4 26
11	10 30	+10.8	10	98	11 11	4 48	4 43
16	10 53	+ 8.5	10	98	11 15	5 04	5 00
21	11 17	+ 6.2	10	98	11 18	5 19	5 18
26	11 40	+ 3.8	10	99	11 21	5 35	5 35
31	12 02	+ 1.3	10	99	11 25	5 51	5 53

MARS

Day	RA	Dec.	Diam.	Phase	Transit	5° high 52°	5° high 56°
1	8 39	+19.5	4	97	9 59	2 49	2 35
6	8 52	+18.7	4	97	9 52	2 47	2 34
11	9 05	+17.9	4	97	9 46	2 45	2 33
16	9 18	+17.0	4	97	9 38	2 43	2 32
21	9 30	+16.0	4	96	9 31	2 41	2 31
26	9 43	+15.1	4	96	9 24	2 39	2 29
31	9 55	+14.1	4	96	9 16	2 36	2 28

SUNRISE AND SUNSET

	London 0°05' 51°30'		Bristol 2°35' 51°28'		Birmingham 1°55' 52°28'		Manchester 2°15' 53°28'		Newcastle 1°37' 54°59'		Glasgow 4°14' 55°52'		Belfast 5°56' 54°35'	
	h m	h m	h m	h m	h m	h m	h m	h m	h m	h m	h m	h m	h m	h m
1	5 12	18 47	5 22	18 57	5 18	18 56	5 18	18 59	5 12	19 00	5 21	19 12	5 30	19 16
2	5 14	18 45	5 24	18 55	5 20	18 54	5 19	18 57	5 14	18 57	5 23	19 09	5 32	19 14
3	5 16	18 43	5 26	18 53	5 21	18 52	5 21	18 55	5 16	18 55	5 25	19 07	5 34	19 11
4	5 17	18 41	5 27	18 51	5 23	18 49	5 23	18 52	5 18	18 52	5 27	19 04	5 36	19 09
5	5 19	18 38	5 29	18 48	5 25	18 47	5 25	18 50	5 20	18 50	5 29	19 01	5 38	19 06
6	5 20	18 36	5 30	18 46	5 26	18 45	5 26	18 47	5 21	18 47	5 31	18 59	5 39	19 04
7	5 22	18 34	5 32	18 44	5 28	18 42	5 28	18 45	5 23	18 44	5 33	18 56	5 41	19 01
8	5 24	18 31	5 34	18 41	5 30	18 40	5 30	18 42	5 25	18 42	5 34	18 54	5 43	18 59
9	5 25	18 29	5 35	18 39	5 31	18 38	5 32	18 40	5 27	18 39	5 36	18 51	5 45	18 56
10	5 27	18 27	5 37	18 37	5 33	18 35	5 33	18 38	5 29	18 37	5 38	18 48	5 47	18 54
11	5 28	18 25	5 38	18 35	5 35	18 33	5 35	18 35	5 31	18 34	5 40	18 46	5 49	18 51
12	5 30	18 22	5 40	18 32	5 36	18 31	5 37	18 33	5 33	18 32	5 42	18 43	5 50	18 49
13	5 31	18 20	5 42	18 30	5 38	18 28	5 38	18 30	5 35	18 29	5 44	18 40	5 52	18 46
14	5 33	18 18	5 43	18 28	5 40	18 26	5 40	18 28	5 36	18 27	5 46	18 38	5 54	18 43
15	5 35	18 15	5 45	18 25	5 41	18 23	5 42	18 25	5 38	18 24	5 48	18 35	5 56	18 41
16	5 36	18 13	5 46	18 23	5 43	18 21	5 44	18 23	5 40	18 21	5 50	18 33	5 58	18 38
17	5 38	18 11	5 48	18 21	5 45	18 19	5 45	18 21	5 42	18 19	5 52	18 30	6 00	18 36
18	5 39	18 09	5 50	18 19	5 46	18 16	5 47	18 18	5 44	18 16	5 54	18 27	6 01	18 33
19	5 41	18 06	5 51	18 16	5 48	18 14	5 49	18 16	5 46	18 14	5 56	18 25	6 03	18 31
20	5 43	18 04	5 53	18 14	5 50	18 12	5 51	18 13	5 48	18 11	5 58	18 22	6 05	18 28
21	5 44	18 02	5 54	18 12	5 51	18 09	5 52	18 11	5 49	18 09	6 00	18 19	6 07	18 26
22	5 46	17 59	5 56	18 09	5 53	18 07	5 54	18 08	5 51	18 06	6 02	18 17	6 09	18 23
23	5 48	17 57	5 58	18 07	5 55	18 04	5 56	18 06	5 53	18 03	6 04	18 14	6 11	18 21
24	5 49	17 55	5 59	18 05	5 56	18 02	5 58	18 03	5 55	18 01	6 06	18 11	6 12	18 18
25	5 51	17 52	6 01	18 02	5 58	18 00	5 59	18 01	5 57	17 58	6 07	18 09	6 14	18 16
26	5 52	17 50	6 02	18 00	6 00	17 57	6 01	17 59	5 59	17 56	6 09	18 06	6 16	18 13
27	5 54	17 48	6 04	17 58	6 01	17 55	6 03	17 56	6 01	17 53	6 11	18 03	6 18	18 11
28	5 56	17 46	6 06	17 56	6 03	17 53	6 05	17 54	6 03	17 51	6 13	18 01	6 20	18 08
29	5 57	17 43	6 07	17 53	6 05	17 50	6 07	17 51	6 04	17 48	6 15	17 58	6 22	18 05
30	5 59	17 41	6 09	17 51	6 07	17 48	6 08	17 49	6 06	17 46	6 17	17 56	6 24	18 03

JUPITER

Day	RA	Dec.	Transit	5° high 52°	56°
	h m	° '	h m	h m	h m
1	23 44.1	− 3 24	1 04	6 13	6 07
11	23 39.5	− 3 55	0 20	5 26	5 19
21	23 34.6	− 4 27	23 32	4 39	4 32
31	23 29.9	− 4 57	22 48	3 52	3 45

Diameters – equatorial 50″ polar 47″

SATURN

Day	RA	Dec.	Transit	5° high 52°	56°
	h m	° '	h m	h m	h m
1	2 08.4	+10 09	3 28	21 05	21 00
11	2 07.0	+10 00	2 47	20 26	20 21
21	2 05.1	+ 9 48	2 06	19 45	19 41
31	2 02.7	+ 9 33	1 24	19 05	19 00

Diameters – equatorial 19″ polar 18″
Rings – major axis 44″ minor axis 12″

URANUS

Day	RA	Dec.	Transit	10° high 52°	56°
	h m	° '	h m	h m	h m
1	20 49.3	−18 29	22 06	1 03	0 28
11	20 48.0	−18 34	21 25	0 22	23 42
21	20 47.0	−18 37	20 45	23 37	23 01
31	20 46.2	−18 40	20 05	22 57	22 21

Diameter 4″

NEPTUNE

Day	RA	Dec.	Transit	10° high 52°	56°
	h m	° '	h m	h m	h m
1	20 07.6	−19 51	21 24	0 09	23 24
11	20 06.9	−19 54	20 44	23 25	22 43
21	20 06.3	−19 56	20 04	22 45	22 03
31	20 06.0	−19 57	19 25	22 05	21 23

Diameter 2″

October 1998

TENTH MONTH, 31 DAYS. *Octo* (eight), eighth month of Roman pre-Julian calendar

1	*Thursday*	Michaelmas Law Sittings begin. First issue of *News of the World* 1843	*week* 39 *day* 274
2	*Friday*	Graham Greene b. 1904. Dr Marie Stopes d. 1958	275
3	*Saturday*	Francis of Assisi d. 1226. James Herriot b. 1916	276
4	*Sunday*	**18th S. after Pentecost/17th S. after Trinity**	*week* 40 *day* 277
5	*Monday*	FEAST OF TABERNACLES begins. Louis Lumière b. 1864	278
6	*Tuesday*	Jenny Lind b. 1820. Thor Heyerdahl b. 1914	279
7	*Wednesday*	✕ Lepanto 1571. Sir Hubert Parry d. 1918	280
8	*Thursday*	Sir Geoffrey Jellicoe b. 1900. Clement Attlee d. 1967	281
9	*Friday*	John Lennon b. 1940. André Maurois d. 1967	282
10	*Saturday*	Giuseppe Verdi b. 1813. Harold Pinter b. 1930	283
11	*Sunday*	**19th S. after Pentecost/18th S. after Trinity**	*week* 41 *day* 284
12	*Monday*	Elizabeth Fry d. 1845. Edith Cavell exec. 1915	285
13	*Tuesday*	Sir Henry Irving d. 1905. Margaret Thatcher b. 1925	286
14	*Wednesday*	Eamon de Valera b. 1882. Errol Flynn d. 1959	287
15	*Thursday*	P. G. Wodehouse b. 1881. Cole Porter d. 1964	288
16	*Friday*	Houses of Parliament destroyed by fire 1834	289
17	*Saturday*	HINDU DIWALI begins. Arthur Miller b. 1915	290
18	*Sunday*	**St Luke. 20th S. after Pentecost/19th S. after Trinity**	*week* 42 *day* 291
19	*Monday*	Jonathan Swift d. 1745	292
20	*Tuesday*	Grace Darling d. 1842. Dame Anna Neagle b. 1904	293
21	*Wednesday*	✕ Trafalgar 1805. Alfred Nobel b. 1833	294
22	*Thursday*	Franz Liszt b. 1811. Pablo Casals d. 1973	295
23	*Friday*	✕ Leyte Gulf began 1944. Al Jolson d. 1950	296
24	*Saturday*	Jane Seymour d. 1537. Christian Dior d. 1957	297
25	*Sunday*	**9th S. before Christmas/20th S. after Trinity**	*week* 43 *day* 298
26	*Monday*	Founding of Royal Marines 1664. Domenico Scarlatti b. 1685	299
27	*Tuesday*	Dylan Thomas b. 1914. Charles Hawtrey d. 1988	300
28	*Wednesday*	**SS Simon and Jude.** Capt. James Cook b. 1728	301
29	*Thursday*	Sir Walter Raleigh exec. 1618. Wall Street crash 1929	302
30	*Friday*	Ezra Pound b. 1885. Louis Malle b. 1932	303
31	*Saturday*	Hallowmass Eve. Mrs Indira Gandhi assass. 1984	304

ASTRONOMICAL PHENOMENA

d	h	
4	10	Jupiter in conjunction with Moon. Jupiter 0°.2 N.
7	02	Saturn in conjunction with Moon. Saturn 2° N.
11	14	Neptune at stationary point
16	03	Mars in conjunction with Moon. Mars 1° N.
18	21	Uranus at stationary point
20	04	Venus in conjunction with Moon. Venus 3° S.
21	23	Mercury in conjunction with Moon. Mercury 6° S.
23	15	Sun's longitude 210° ♏
23	19	Saturn at opposition
30	04	Venus in superior conjunction
31	16	Jupiter in conjunction with Moon. Jupiter 0°.2 N.

MINIMA OF ALGOL

d	h	d	h	d	h
2	22.0	14	09.3	25	20.5
5	18.8	17	06.1	28	17.3
8	15.6	20	02.9	31	14.1
11	12.4	22	23.7		

CONSTELLATIONS

The following constellations are near the meridian at

	d	h		d	h
September	1	24	October	16	21
September	15	23	November	1	20
October	1	22	November	15	19

Ursa Major (below the Pole), Cepheus, Cassiopeia, Cygnus, Lacerta, Andromeda, Pegasus, Capricornus, Aquarius and Piscis Austrinus

THE MOON

Phases, Apsides and Node	d	h	m
○ Full Moon	5	20	12
☾ Last Quarter	12	11	11
● New Moon	20	10	09
☽ First Quarter	28	11	46
Perigee (357,628 km)	6	13	08
Apogee (406,674 km)	21	05	32

Mean longitude of ascending node on October 1, 149°

THE SUN   s.d. 16'.1

Day	Right Ascension	Dec. −	Equation of time	Rise 52°	Rise 56°	Transit	Set 52°	Set 56°	Sidereal time	Transit of First Point of Aries
	h m s	° '	m s	h m	h m	h m	h m	h m	h m s	h m s
1	12 27 59	3 01	+10 07	6 00	6 02	11 50	17 38	17 36	0 38 06	23 18 04
2	12 31 36	3 25	+10 27	6 02	6 04	11 49	17 36	17 33	0 42 02	23 14 09
3	12 35 13	3 48	+10 46	6 04	6 06	11 49	17 34	17 31	0 45 59	23 10 13
4	12 38 51	4 11	+11 04	6 05	6 08	11 49	17 31	17 28	0 49 56	23 06 17
5	12 42 29	4 34	+11 23	6 07	6 10	11 48	17 29	17 26	0 53 52	23 02 21
6	12 46 08	4 57	+11 41	6 09	6 12	11 48	17 27	17 23	0 57 49	22 58 25
7	12 49 46	5 20	+11 59	6 10	6 14	11 48	17 24	17 20	1 01 45	22 54 29
8	12 53 26	5 43	+12 16	6 12	6 16	11 48	17 22	17 18	1 05 42	22 50 33
9	12 57 05	6 06	+12 33	6 14	6 18	11 47	17 20	17 15	1 09 38	22 46 37
10	13 00 45	6 29	+12 50	6 16	6 20	11 47	17 18	17 13	1 13 35	22 42 41
11	13 04 26	6 52	+13 06	6 17	6 22	11 47	17 15	17 10	1 17 31	22 38 45
12	13 08 07	7 14	+13 21	6 19	6 24	11 47	17 13	17 08	1 21 28	22 34 49
13	13 11 49	7 37	+13 36	6 21	6 27	11 46	17 11	17 05	1 25 25	22 30 54
14	13 15 31	7 59	+13 50	6 22	6 29	11 46	17 09	17 02	1 29 21	22 26 58
15	13 19 13	8 21	+14 04	6 24	6 31	11 46	17 07	17 00	1 33 18	22 23 02
16	13 22 56	8 44	+14 18	6 26	6 33	11 46	17 04	16 57	1 37 14	22 19 06
17	13 26 40	9 06	+14 30	6 28	6 35	11 45	17 02	16 55	1 41 11	22 15 10
18	13 30 25	9 28	+14 43	6 29	6 37	11 45	17 00	16 53	1 45 07	22 11 14
19	13 34 10	9 49	+14 54	6 31	6 39	11 45	16 58	16 50	1 49 04	22 07 18
20	13 37 55	10 11	+15 05	6 33	6 41	11 45	16 56	16 48	1 53 00	22 03 22
21	13 41 42	10 33	+15 15	6 35	6 43	11 45	16 54	16 45	1 56 57	21 59 26
22	13 45 29	10 54	+15 25	6 36	6 45	11 45	16 52	16 43	2 00 53	21 55 30
23	13 49 16	11 15	+15 34	6 38	6 47	11 44	16 50	16 40	2 04 50	21 51 35
24	13 53 04	11 36	+15 42	6 40	6 49	11 44	16 48	16 38	2 08 47	21 47 39
25	13 56 53	11 57	+15 50	6 42	6 51	11 44	16 46	16 36	2 12 43	21 43 43
26	14 00 43	12 18	+15 57	6 44	6 54	11 44	16 44	16 33	2 16 40	21 39 47
27	14 04 33	12 38	+16 03	6 45	6 56	11 44	16 42	16 31	2 20 36	21 35 51
28	14 08 24	12 58	+16 08	6 47	6 58	11 44	16 40	16 29	2 24 33	21 31 55
29	14 12 16	13 18	+16 13	6 49	7 00	11 44	16 38	16 27	2 28 29	21 27 59
30	14 16 09	13 30	+16 17	6 51	7 02	11 44	16 36	16 24	2 32 26	21 24 03
31	14 20 02	13 58	+16 20	6 53	7 04	11 44	16 34	16 22	2 36 22	21 20 07

DURATION OF TWILIGHT (in minutes)

Latitude	52°	56°	52°	56°	52°	56°	52°	56°
	1 October		11 October		21 October		31 October	
Civil	34	37	34	37	34	38	36	40
Nautical	73	80	73	80	74	81	75	83
Astronomical	113	125	112	124	113	124	114	126

THE NIGHT SKY

Mercury remains too close to the Sun for observation.

Venus, magnitude −3.9, is a morning object but only visible for the first week of the month, very low above the east-south-eastern horizon, for a few minutes before sunrise. Thereafter the planet is too close to the Sun for observation.

Mars is a morning object, magnitude +1.5, and visible in the eastern sky for several hours before the morning twilight inhibits observation. The old crescent Moon passes 2° south of the planet on the morning of the 16th. Mars is in Leo and passes 1° north of Regulus on the 6th.

Jupiter is a brilliant object in the southern skies for the greater part of the night, magnitude −2.8. By the end of the month it is lost to view over the western horizon before 02h. The gibbous Moon passes less than 2° south of Jupiter on the 4th and again on the 31st.

Saturn is at opposition on the 23rd, magnitude 0.0, and thus visible throughout the hours of darkness. Saturn is retrograding slowly on the borders of Pisces, Cetus and Aries. The Moon, just past Full, passes about 3° south of the planet on the night of the 6th to 7th. Saturn's largest satellite, Titan, magnitude +8½, is visible in small telescopes.

THE MOON

Day	RA		Dec.	Hor. par.	Semi- diam.	Sun's co- long.	PA of Bright Limb	Phase	Age	Rise		Transit	Set	
										52°	56°		52°	56°
	h	m	°	′	′	°	°	%	d	h m	h m	h m	h m	h m
1	20	18	−17.1	57.5	15.7	33	258	71	10.3	15 39	15 53	20 24	0 06	—
2	21	14	−14.7	58.5	15.9	45	254	81	11.3	16 14	16 25	21 18	1 16	1 02
3	22	10	−11.3	59.5	16.2	57	249	89	12.3	16 45	16 52	22 12	2 31	2 21
4	23	06	− 7.1	60.3	16.4	69	245	95	13.3	17 14	17 18	23 07	3 50	3 45
5	0	03	− 2.4	60.9	16.6	81	235	99	14.3	17 43	17 42	—	5 12	5 11
6	1	00	+ 2.5	61.3	16.7	93	125	100	15.3	18 12	18 07	0 02	6 36	6 39
7	1	58	+ 7.3	61.3	16.7	106	84	98	16.3	18 44	18 35	0 58	7 59	8 07
8	2	57	+11.6	61.0	16.6	118	82	93	17.3	19 20	19 06	1 56	9 21	9 33
9	3	56	+15.2	60.4	16.5	130	83	85	18.3	20 01	19 44	2 54	10 39	10 54
10	4	56	+17.6	59.7	16.3	142	87	76	19.3	20 48	20 30	3 52	11 50	12 08
11	5	56	+18.9	58.8	16.0	154	91	66	20.3	21 43	21 24	4 49	12 52	13 10
12	6	54	+19.0	57.9	15.8	166	96	55	21.3	22 43	22 25	5 45	13 43	14 01
13	7	50	+18.1	57.1	15.6	179	100	44	22.3	23 47	23 31	6 38	14 26	14 42
14	8	43	+16.2	56.3	15.3	191	104	34	23.3	—	—	7 29	15 01	15 14
15	9	34	+13.6	55.7	15.2	203	108	25	24.3	0 52	0 40	8 17	15 30	15 40
16	10	23	+10.4	55.1	15.0	215	112	17	25.3	1 57	1 49	9 03	15 56	16 03
17	11	10	+ 6.8	54.7	14.9	227	115	10	26.3	3 03	2 57	9 46	16 19	16 22
18	11	56	+ 3.0	54.4	14.8	240	118	5	27.3	4 07	4 05	10 29	16 41	16 41
19	12	42	− 0.9	54.1	14.7	252	125	2	28.3	5 11	5 13	11 12	17 02	16 59
20	13	27	− 4.8	54.0	14.7	264	153	0	29.3	6 15	6 20	11 54	17 24	17 18
21	14	12	− 8.4	53.9	14.7	276	254	0	0.6	7 18	7 26	12 37	17 48	17 39
22	14	58	−11.8	53.9	14.7	289	271	2	1.6	8 20	8 32	13 21	18 15	18 02
23	15	45	−14.6	54.1	14.7	301	273	6	2.6	9 22	9 37	14 06	18 45	18 30
24	16	34	−16.9	54.3	14.8	313	272	11	3.6	10 22	10 39	14 53	19 21	19 04
25	17	24	−18.5	54.6	14.9	325	270	18	4.6	11 18	11 37	15 42	20 04	19 45
26	18	15	−19.2	55.1	15.0	337	266	26	5.6	12 10	12 29	16 31	20 54	20 35
27	19	07	−19.0	55.7	15.2	350	262	35	6.6	12 56	13 14	17 22	21 52	21 34
28	20	00	−17.9	56.4	15.4	2	258	45	7.6	13 36	13 52	18 14	22 56	22 41
29	20	54	−15.9	57.3	15.6	14	254	55	8.6	14 12	14 25	19 05	—	23 55
30	21	48	−12.9	58.2	15.9	26	251	66	9.6	14 43	14 53	19 58	0 07	—
31	22	43	− 9.1	59.2	16.1	38	247	76	10.6	15 12	15 18	20 51	1 22	1 14

MERCURY

Day	RA		Dec.	Diam.	Phase	Transit	5° high	
							52°	56°
	h	m	°	″	%	h m	h m	h m
1	12	44	− 3.7	5	99	12 07	17 13	17 06
3	12	57	− 5.3	5	99	12 12	17 09	17 01
5	13	09	− 6.8	5	98	12 16	17 05	16 55
7	13	21	− 8.2	5	97	12 20	17 01	16 50
9	13	33	− 9.6	5	97	12 24	16 57	16 45
11	13	45	−11.0	5	96	12 28	16 53	16 39
13	13	56	−12.3	5	95	12 32	16 49	16 33
15	14	08	−13.6	5	94	12 36	16 45	16 28
17	14	20	−14.8	5	93	12 40	16 41	16 22
19	14	31	−16.0	5	91	12 43	16 37	16 16
21	14	43	−17.2	5	90	12 47	16 33	16 11
23	14	54	−18.2	5	89	12 50	16 29	16 05
25	15	06	−19.2	5	87	12 54	16 25	15 59
27	15	17	−20.2	5	86	12 58	16 22	15 54
29	15	29	−21.0	5	84	13 01	16 19	15 48
31	15	40	−21.9	6	82	13 04	16 15	15 43

VENUS

Day	RA		Dec.	Diam.	Phase	Transit	5° high	
							52°	56°
	h	m	°	″	%	h m	h m	h m
1	12	02	+ 1.3	10	99	11 25	5 51	5 53
6	12	25	− 1.2	10	99	11 28	6 07	6 12
11	12	48	− 3.7	10	100	11 31	6 23	6 30
16	13	11	− 6.2	10	100	11 34	6 40	6 49
21	13	35	− 8.6	10	100	11 38	6 57	7 09
26	13	58	−10.9	10	100	11 42	7 15	7 29
31	14	22	−13.2	10	100	11 46	7 33	7 49

MARS

Day	RA		Dec.	Diam.	Phase	Transit	5° high	
1	9	55	+14.1	4	96	9 16	2 36	2 28
6	10	07	+13.0	4	95	9 08	2 34	2 27
11	10	18	+12.0	4	95	9 00	2 32	2 25
16	10	30	+10.9	4	95	8 52	2 29	2 24
21	10	41	+ 9.8	4	95	8 44	2 27	2 22
26	10	53	+ 8.7	4	94	8 36	2 24	2 20
31	11	04	+ 7.6	5	94	8 27	2 21	2 18

SUNRISE AND SUNSET

	London		Bristol		Birmingham		Manchester		Newcastle		Glasgow		Belfast	
	0°05′	51°30′	2°35′	51°28′	1°55′	52°28′	2°15′	53°28′	1°37′	54°59′	4°14′	55°52′	5°56′	54°35′
	h m	h m	h m	h m	h m	h m	h m	h m	h m	h m	h m	h m	h m	h m
1	6 00	17 39	6 10	17 49	6 08	17 46	6 10	17 46	6 08	17 43	6 19	17 53	6 25	18 00
2	6 02	17 36	6 12	17 46	6 10	17 43	6 12	17 44	6 10	17 40	6 21	17 50	6 27	17 58
3	6 04	17 34	6 14	17 44	6 12	17 41	6 14	17 42	6 12	17 38	6 23	17 48	6 29	17 55
4	6 05	17 32	6 15	17 42	6 13	17 39	6 15	17 39	6 14	17 35	6 25	17 45	6 31	17 53
5	6 07	17 30	6 17	17 40	6 15	17 36	6 17	17 37	6 16	17 33	6 27	17 43	6 33	17 51
6	6 09	17 27	6 19	17 37	6 17	17 34	6 19	17 34	6 18	17 30	6 29	17 40	6 35	17 48
7	6 10	17 25	6 20	17 35	6 19	17 32	6 21	17 32	6 20	17 28	6 31	17 37	6 37	17 46
8	6 12	17 23	6 22	17 33	6 20	17 29	6 23	17 30	6 22	17 25	6 33	17 35	6 39	17 43
9	6 14	17 21	6 24	17 31	6 22	17 27	6 24	17 27	6 24	17 23	6 35	17 32	6 40	17 41
10	6 15	17 19	6 25	17 29	6 24	17 25	6 26	17 25	6 26	17 20	6 37	17 30	6 42	17 38
11	6 17	17 16	6 27	17 26	6 25	17 22	6 28	17 23	6 28	17 18	6 39	17 27	6 44	17 36
12	6 19	17 14	6 29	17 24	6 27	17 20	6 30	17 20	6 29	17 16	6 41	17 25	6 46	17 33
13	6 20	17 12	6 30	17 22	6 29	17 18	6 32	17 18	6 31	17 13	6 43	17 22	6 48	17 31
14	6 22	17 10	6 32	17 20	6 31	17 16	6 34	17 16	6 33	17 11	6 45	17 20	6 50	17 29
15	6 24	17 08	6 34	17 18	6 33	17 14	6 35	17 13	6 35	17 08	6 47	17 17	6 52	17 26
16	6 25	17 06	6 35	17 16	6 34	17 11	6 37	17 11	6 37	17 06	6 49	17 15	6 54	17 24
17	6 27	17 03	6 37	17 13	6 36	17 09	6 39	17 09	6 39	17 03	6 51	17 12	6 56	17 21
18	6 29	17 01	6 39	17 11	6 38	17 07	6 41	17 07	6 41	17 01	6 54	17 10	6 58	17 19
19	6 31	16 59	6 41	17 09	6 40	17 05	6 43	17 04	6 43	16 59	6 56	17 07	7 00	17 17
20	6 32	16 57	6 42	17 07	6 41	17 03	6 45	17 02	6 45	16 56	6 58	17 05	7 02	17 14
21	6 34	16 55	6 44	17 05	6 43	17 01	6 47	17 00	6 47	16 54	7 00	17 02	7 04	17 12
22	6 36	16 53	6 46	17 03	6 45	16 58	6 49	16 58	6 49	16 52	7 02	17 00	7 06	17 10
23	6 38	16 51	6 47	17 01	6 47	16 56	6 50	16 55	6 51	16 49	7 04	16 58	7 08	17 08
24	6 39	16 49	6 49	16 59	6 49	16 54	6 52	16 53	6 53	16 47	7 06	16 55	7 10	17 05
25	6 41	16 47	6 51	16 57	6 50	16 52	6 54	16 51	6 55	16 45	7 08	16 53	7 12	17 03
26	6 43	16 45	6 53	16 55	6 52	16 50	6 56	16 49	6 57	16 43	7 10	16 51	7 14	17 01
27	6 45	16 43	6 54	16 54	6 54	16 48	6 58	16 47	6 59	16 41	7 12	16 48	7 16	16 59
28	6 46	16 41	6 56	16 51	6 56	16 46	7 00	16 45	7 01	16 38	7 14	16 46	7 18	16 57
29	6 48	16 39	6 58	16 49	6 58	16 44	7 02	16 43	7 03	16 36	7 17	16 44	7 20	16 55
30	6 50	16 37	7 00	16 48	7 00	16 42	7 04	16 41	7 05	16 34	7 19	16 42	7 22	16 52
31	6 52	16 36	7 02	16 46	7 01	16 40	7 06	16 39	7 08	16 32	7 21	16 40	7 24	16 50

JUPITER

Day	RA	Dec.	Transit	5° high	
				52°	56°
	h m	° ′	h m	h m	h m
1	23 29.9	− 4 57	22 48	3 52	3 45
11	23 25.7	− 5 23	22 04	3 07	2 59
21	23 22.3	− 5 43	21 22	2 22	2 14
31	23 19.9	− 5 55	20 40	1 39	1 31

Diameters – equatorial 48″ polar 45″

SATURN

Day	RA	Dec.	Transit	5° high	
				52°	56°
	h m	° ′	h m	h m	h m
1	2 02.7	+ 9 33	1 24	19 05	19 00
11	2 00.0	+ 9 17	0 42	18 24	18 20
21	1 57.0	+ 9 01	0 00	17 43	17 39
31	1 54.0	+ 8 44	23 14	17 02	16 59

Diameters – equatorial 20″ polar 18″
Rings – major axis 45″ minor axis 12″

URANUS

Day	RA	Dec.	Transit	10° high	
				52°	56°
	h m	° ′	h m	h m	h m
1	20 46.2	−18 40	20 05	22 57	22 21
11	20 45.8	−18 41	19 25	22 17	21 41
21	20 45.7	−18 41	18 46	21 37	21 01
31	20 45.9	−18 40	18 07	20 59	20 22

Diameter 4″

NEPTUNE

Day	RA	Dec.	Transit	10° high	
				52°	56°
	h m	° ′	h m	h m	h m
1	20 06.0	−19 57	19 25	22 05	21 23
11	20 05.9	−19 58	18 45	21 25	20 44
21	20 06.0	−19 57	18 06	20 46	20 05
31	20 06.3	−19 57	17 27	20 07	19 26

Diameter 2″

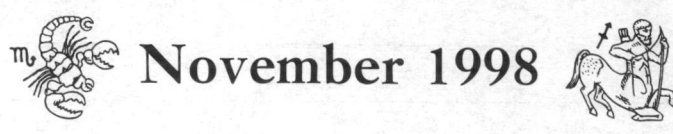

November 1998

ELEVENTH MONTH, 30 DAYS. *Novem* (nine), ninth month of Roman pre-Julian calendar

1	*Sunday*	**All Saints. 8th S. before Christmas/21st S. after Trinity**	*week* 44 *day* 305
2	*Monday*	All Souls. Daniel Boone b. 1734	306
3	*Tuesday*	Vincenzo Bellini b. 1801. Henri Matisse d. 1954	307
4	*Wednesday*	Felix Mendelssohn d. 1847. Wilfred Owen d. 1918	308
5	*Thursday*	✗ Inkerman 1854. Lester Piggott b. 1935	309
6	*Friday*	Piotr Tchaikovsky d. 1893. Kate Greenaway d. 1901	310
7	*Saturday*	Dame Joan Sutherland b. 1926. Gene Tunney d. 1978	311
8	*Sunday*	**7th S. before Christmas/22nd S. after Trinity**	*week* 45 *day* 312
9	*Monday*	Katherine Hepburn b. 1909. Neville Chamberlain d. 1940	313
10	*Tuesday*	Sir Jacob Epstein b. 1880. Anne Shelton b. 1923	314
11	*Wednesday*	Armistice Day 1918. Sir Edward German d. 1936	315
12	*Thursday*	Mrs Elizabeth Gaskell d. 1865. Umberto Giordano d. 1948	316
13	*Friday*	Robert Louis Stevenson b. 1850. Archbishop Carey b. 1935	317
14	*Saturday*	*Prince of Wales b. 1948.* Claude Monet b. 1840	318
15	*Sunday*	**6th S. before Christmas/23rd S. after Trinity**	*week* 46 *day* 319
16	*Monday*	Opening of the Suez Canal 1869. Clark Gable d. 1960	320
17	*Tuesday*	Eric Gill d. 1940. Martin Scorsese b. 1942	321
18	*Wednesday*	Marcel Proust d. 1922. Man Ray d. 1976	322
19	*Thursday*	Thomas Shadwell d. 1692. Gettysberg address 1863	323
20	*Friday*	*Queen's Wedding Day 1947.* Thomas Chatterton b. 1752	324
21	*Saturday*	Henry Purcell d. 1695. André Gide b. 1869	325
22	*Sunday*	**5th S. before Christmas/24th S. after Trinity**	*week* 47 *day* 326
23	*Monday*	Perkin Warbeck d. 1499. Boris Karloff b. 1887	327
24	*Tuesday*	Toulouse Lautrec b. 1864. Erskine Childers exec. 1922	328
25	*Wednesday*	Isaac Watts d. 1748. Lilian Baylis d. 1937	329
26	*Thursday*	William Cowper b. 1731. John McAdam d. 1836	330
27	*Friday*	Anders Celsius b. 1701. Eugene O'Neill d. 1953	331
28	*Saturday*	William Blake b. 1757. Enid Blyton d. 1968	332
29	*Sunday*	**Advent Sunday.** C. S. Lewis b. 1898	*week* 48 *day* 333
30	*Monday*	**St Andrew.** Oscar Wilde d. 1900	334

ASTRONOMICAL PHENOMENA

d	h	
3	10	Saturn in conjunction with Moon. Saturn 2° N.
11	09	Mercury at greatest elongation E.23°
13	13	Jupiter at stationary point
13	18	Mars in conjunction with Moon. Mars 0°.5 S.
19	16	Venus in conjunction with Moon. Venus 5° S.
20	22	Mercury in conjunction with Moon. Mercury 7° S.
21	12	Mercury at stationary point
22	13	Sun's longitude 240° ♐
28	01	Jupiter in conjunction with Moon. Jupiter 0°.6 N.
28	12	Venus in conjunction with Mercury. Venus 0°.3 S.
30	08	Pluto in conjunction
30	18	Saturn in conjunction with Moon. Saturn 2° N.

MINIMA OF ALGOL

d	h	d	h	d	h
3	10.9	14	22.2	26	09.5
6	07.8	17	19.0	29	06.3
9	04.6	20	15.8		
12	01.4	23	12.6		

CONSTELLATIONS

The following constellations are near the meridian at

	d	h		d	h
October	1	24	November	15	21
October	16	23	December	1	20
November	1	22	December	16	19

Ursa Major (below the Pole), Cepheus, Cassiopeia, Andromeda, Pegasus, Pisces, Aquarius and Cetus

THE MOON

Phases, Apsides and Node

	d	h	m
○ Full Moon	4	05	18
☾ Last Quarter	11	00	28
● New Moon	19	04	27
☽ First Quarter	27	00	23

	d	h	m
Perigee (356,616 km)	4	00	45
Apogee (406,478 km)	17	06	38

Mean longitude of ascending node on November 1, 148°

THE SUN
s.d. 16′.2

Day	Right Ascension	Dec.	Equation of time	Rise 52°	Rise 56°	Transit	Set 52°	Set 56°	Sidereal time	Transit of First Point of Aries
	h m s	° ′	m s	h m	h m	h m	h m	h m	h m s	h m s
1	14 23 56	14 17	+16 23	6 54	7 06	11 44	16 32	16 20	2 40 19	21 16 11
2	14 27 51	14 37	+16 25	6 56	7 08	11 44	16 30	16 18	2 44 16	21 12 15
3	14 31 47	14 56	+16 26	6 58	7 11	11 44	16 28	16 16	2 48 12	21 08 20
4	14 35 43	15 14	+16 26	7 00	7 13	11 44	16 27	16 14	2 52 09	21 04 24
5	14 39 40	15 33	+16 25	7 02	7 15	11 44	16 25	16 12	2 56 05	21 00 28
6	14 43 38	15 51	+16 23	7 03	7 17	11 44	16 23	16 09	3 00 02	20 56 32
7	14 47 37	16 09	+16 21	7 05	7 19	11 44	16 22	16 07	3 03 58	20 52 36
8	14 51 37	16 27	+16 18	7 07	7 21	11 44	16 20	16 05	3 07 55	20 48 40
9	14 55 38	16 44	+16 14	7 09	7 23	11 44	16 18	16 04	3 11 51	20 44 44
10	14 59 39	17 01	+16 09	7 11	7 26	11 44	16 17	16 02	3 15 48	20 40 48
11	15 03 42	17 18	+16 03	7 12	7 28	11 44	16 15	16 00	3 19 45	20 36 52
12	15 07 45	17 34	+15 56	7 14	7 30	11 44	16 14	15 58	3 23 41	20 32 56
13	15 11 49	17 51	+15 49	7 16	7 32	11 44	16 12	15 56	3 27 38	20 29 00
14	15 15 54	18 07	+15 40	7 18	7 34	11 44	16 11	15 54	3 31 34	20 25 05
15	15 20 00	18 22	+15 31	7 19	7 36	11 45	16 09	15 53	3 35 31	20 21 09
16	15 24 07	18 38	+15 21	7 21	7 38	11 45	16 08	15 51	3 39 27	20 17 13
17	15 28 14	18 52	+15 10	7 23	7 40	11 45	16 06	15 49	3 43 24	20 13 17
18	15 32 22	19 07	+14 58	7 25	7 42	11 45	16 05	15 48	3 47 20	20 09 21
19	15 36 32	19 21	+14 45	7 26	7 44	11 45	16 04	15 46	3 51 17	20 05 25
20	15 40 42	19 35	+14 32	7 28	7 46	11 46	16 03	15 44	3 55 14	20 01 29
21	15 44 53	19 49	+14 18	7 30	7 48	11 46	16 02	15 43	3 59 10	19 57 33
22	15 49 04	20 02	+14 02	7 31	7 50	11 46	16 00	15 42	4 03 07	19 53 37
23	15 53 17	20 15	+13 46	7 33	7 52	11 46	15 59	15 40	4 07 03	19 49 41
24	15 57 30	20 27	+13 30	7 35	7 54	11 47	15 58	15 39	4 11 00	19 45 45
25	16 01 44	20 40	+13 12	7 36	7 56	11 47	15 57	15 38	4 14 56	19 41 50
26	16 05 59	20 51	+12 54	7 38	7 58	11 47	15 56	15 36	4 18 53	19 37 54
27	16 10 14	21 03	+12 35	7 39	7 59	11 48	15 55	15 35	4 22 49	19 33 58
28	16 14 30	21 14	+12 16	7 41	8 01	11 48	15 55	15 34	4 26 46	19 30 02
29	16 18 47	21 24	+11 55	7 42	8 03	11 48	15 54	15 33	4 30 43	19 26 06
30	16 23 05	21 34	+11 34	7 44	8 05	11 49	15 53	15 32	4 34 39	19 22 10

DURATION OF TWILIGHT (in minutes)

Latitude	52°	56°	52°	56°	52°	56°	52°	56°
	1 November		11 November		21 November		30 November	
Civil	36	40	37	41	38	43	39	45
Nautical	75	84	78	87	80	90	82	93
Astronomical	115	127	117	130	120	134	123	137

THE NIGHT SKY

Mercury is unsuitably placed for observation.

Venus is too close to the Sun for observation.

Mars, magnitude +1.2, is a morning object in the eastern sky, though not suitably placed for observation before 02h. Before the end of the month Mars has moved from Leo into Virgo. Mars has a slightly reddish tinge, which should assist in its identification. The Moon, just after Last Quarter, will be seen approaching the planet during the early hours of the 12th.

Jupiter, magnitude −2.6, is visible as an evening object, in the south and south-western sky. It reaches its second stationary point on the 13th, in Aquarius, close to the border with Pisces. The gibbous Moon, just past First Quarter, passes less than 2° south of Jupiter early on the 28th, shortly after the two bodies have set.

Saturn, magnitude +0.1, just past opposition, is a conspicuous evening object, visible for the greater part of the night. The gibbous Moon passes about 3° south of the planet on the 3rd and again on the evening of the 30th. The rings of Saturn present a beautiful spectacle to the observer with a small telescope. The Earth passed through the ring plane twice in 1995. The rings have been slowly opening up since and the diameter of the minor axis is now 11 arcseconds.

THE MOON

Day	RA	Dec.	Hor. par.	Semi-diam.	Sun's co-long.	PA of Bright Limb	Phase	Age	Rise 52°	Rise 56°	Transit	Set 52°	Set 56°
	h m	°	′	′	°	°	%	d	h m	h m	h m	h m	h m
1	23 38	− 4.7	60.1	16.4	50	245	85	11.6	15 40	15 41	21 44	2 41	2 37
2	0 33	+ 0.2	60.8	16.6	62	242	93	12.6	16 08	16 05	22 39	4 02	4 03
3	1 31	+ 5.1	61.3	16.7	75	236	98	13.6	16 38	16 31	23 36	5 25	5 31
4	2 29	+ 9.8	61.5	16.8	87	196	100	14.6	17 11	17 00	—	6 50	6 59
5	3 30	+13.8	61.3	16.7	99	100	99	15.6	17 50	17 35	0 35	8 12	8 26
6	4 31	+16.9	60.8	16.6	111	92	95	16.6	18 36	18 18	1 35	9 30	9 47
7	5 33	+18.7	60.1	16.4	123	93	89	17.6	19 30	19 10	2 35	10 39	10 58
8	6 34	+19.3	59.2	16.1	135	96	80	18.6	20 30	20 11	3 34	11 37	11 56
9	7 32	+18.7	58.2	15.9	148	100	71	19.6	21 34	21 18	4 30	12 25	12 42
10	8 28	+17.1	57.3	15.6	160	104	61	20.6	22 41	22 27	5 24	13 04	13 18
11	9 21	+14.6	56.4	15.4	172	108	50	21.6	23 48	23 38	6 14	13 35	13 47
12	10 11	+11.5	55.6	15.2	184	111	40	22.6	—	—	7 01	14 02	14 10
13	10 59	+ 7.9	55.0	15.0	196	113	31	23.6	0 54	0 47	7 45	14 26	14 30
14	11 45	+ 4.1	54.6	14.9	208	115	22	24.6	1 59	1 55	8 28	14 47	14 49
15	12 31	+ 0.2	54.2	14.8	221	116	15	25.6	3 03	3 03	9 11	15 08	15 06
16	13 15	− 3.7	54.0	14.7	233	118	9	26.6	4 06	4 10	9 53	15 30	15 25
17	14 00	− 7.5	53.9	14.7	245	120	4	27.6	5 09	5 17	10 35	15 53	15 44
18	14 46	−11.0	54.0	14.7	257	128	1	28.6	6 13	6 23	11 19	16 18	16 06
19	15 33	−14.0	54.1	14.7	269	172	0	29.6	7 15	7 29	12 04	16 47	16 32
20	16 22	−16.5	54.3	14.8	282	251	1	0.8	8 16	8 33	12 51	17 21	17 04
21	17 11	−18.3	54.5	14.9	294	262	3	1.8	9 14	9 33	13 39	18 01	17 42
22	18 03	−19.3	54.9	15.0	306	263	7	2.8	10 08	10 28	14 28	18 49	18 29
23	18 55	−19.4	55.3	15.1	318	261	13	3.8	10 56	11 15	15 19	19 44	19 25
24	19 48	−18.5	55.8	15.2	330	258	21	4.8	11 38	11 55	16 09	20 46	20 29
25	20 40	−16.8	56.5	15.4	342	254	29	5.8	12 14	12 29	17 00	21 53	21 39
26	21 33	−14.1	57.2	15.6	355	251	39	6.8	12 46	12 57	17 51	23 04	22 54
27	22 26	−10.6	57.9	15.8	7	249	50	7.8	13 15	13 22	18 41	—	—
28	23 19	− 6.5	58.7	16.0	19	247	61	8.8	13 41	13 45	19 32	0 18	0 13
29	0 12	− 1.9	59.5	16.2	31	245	72	9.8	14 08	14 07	20 24	1 36	1 34
30	1 07	+ 2.9	60.2	16.4	43	244	81	10.8	14 35	14 30	21 19	2 55	2 58

MERCURY

Day	RA	Dec.	Diam.	Phase	Transit	5° high 52°	5° high 56°
	h m	°	″	%	h m	h m	h m
1	15 45	−22.2	6	81	13 06	16 14	15 41
3	15 56	−22.9	6	78	13 09	16 11	15 36
5	16 07	−23.5	6	75	13 12	16 09	15 31
7	16 18	−24.0	6	72	13 14	16 07	15 27
9	16 27	−24.5	6	68	13 16	16 05	15 23
11	16 37	−24.8	7	64	13 17	16 03	15 20
13	16 45	−25.0	7	59	13 18	16 01	15 18
15	16 53	−25.2	7	54	13 17	16 00	15 15
17	16 59	−25.2	7	48	13 15	15 58	15 14
19	17 03	−25.0	8	41	13 10	15 55	15 12
21	17 05	−24.8	8	33	13 04	15 51	15 10
23	17 04	−24.4	9	24	12 55	15 47	15 07
25	17 01	−23.8	9	16	12 43	15 40	15 03
27	16 54	−23.0	10	9	12 27	15 32	14 58
29	16 45	−22.1	10	3	12 10	15 23	14 51
31	16 35	−21.0	10	0	11 51	8 31	9 00

VENUS

Day	RA	Dec.	Diam.	Phase	Transit	5° high 52°	5° high 56°
	h m	°	″	%	h m	h m	h m
1	14 27	−13.6	10	100	11 47	15 57	15 40
6	14 51	−15.7	10	100	11 52	15 49	15 29
11	15 16	−17.6	10	100	11 57	15 41	15 18
16	15 42	−19.3	10	100	12 03	15 35	15 08
21	16 08	−20.8	10	100	12 09	15 30	15 00
26	16 34	−22.0	10	99	12 16	15 27	14 54
31	17 01	−23.0	10	99	12 23	15 26	14 50

MARS

Day	RA	Dec.	Diam.	Phase	Transit	5° high 52°	5° high 56°
1	11 06	+ 7.4	5	94	8 25	2 20	2 18
6	11 17	+ 6.3	5	94	8 16	2 17	2 16
11	11 28	+ 5.2	5	93	8 08	2 14	2 13
16	11 39	+ 4.0	5	93	7 59	2 11	2 11
21	11 49	+ 2.9	5	93	7 50	2 07	2 08
26	12 00	+ 1.8	5	92	7 40	2 04	2 06
31	12 10	+ 0.8	5	92	7 31	2 00	2 03

SUNRISE AND SUNSET

	London		Bristol		Birmingham		Manchester		Newcastle		Glasgow		Belfast	
	0°05′	51°30′	2°35′	51°28′	1°55′	52°28′	2°15′	53°28′	1°37′	54°59′	4°14′	55°52′	5°56′	54°35′
	h m	h m	h m	h m	h m	h m	h m	h m	h m	h m	h m	h m	h m	h m
1	6 53	16 34	7 03	16 44	7 03	16 38	7 08	16 37	7 10	16 30	7 23	16 37	7 26	16 48
2	6 55	16 32	7 05	16 42	7 05	16 37	7 09	16 35	7 12	16 28	7 25	16 35	7 28	16 46
3	6 57	16 30	7 07	16 40	7 07	16 35	7 11	16 33	7 14	16 26	7 27	16 33	7 30	16 44
4	6 59	16 28	7 09	16 39	7 09	16 33	7 13	16 31	7 16	16 24	7 29	16 31	7 32	16 42
5	7 00	16 27	7 10	16 37	7 11	16 31	7 15	16 29	7 18	16 22	7 31	16 29	7 34	16 40
6	7 02	16 25	7 12	16 35	7 12	16 29	7 17	16 27	7 20	16 20	7 33	16 27	7 36	16 38
7	7 04	16 23	7 14	16 34	7 14	16 28	7 19	16 26	7 22	16 18	7 36	16 25	7 38	16 36
8	7 06	16 22	7 16	16 32	7 16	16 26	7 21	16 24	7 24	16 16	7 38	16 23	7 40	16 35
9	7 07	16 20	7 17	16 30	7 18	16 24	7 23	16 22	7 26	16 14	7 40	16 21	7 42	16 33
10	7 09	16 19	7 19	16 29	7 20	16 23	7 25	16 20	7 28	16 12	7 42	16 19	7 44	16 31
11	7 11	16 17	7 21	16 27	7 22	16 21	7 27	16 19	7 30	16 10	7 44	16 17	7 46	16 29
12	7 13	16 16	7 23	16 26	7 23	16 20	7 28	16 17	7 32	16 09	7 46	16 15	7 48	16 28
13	7 14	16 14	7 24	16 24	7 25	16 18	7 30	16 16	7 34	16 07	7 48	16 14	7 50	16 26
14	7 16	16 13	7 26	16 23	7 27	16 17	7 32	16 14	7 36	16 05	7 50	16 12	7 51	16 24
15	7 18	16 11	7 28	16 21	7 29	16 15	7 34	16 13	7 38	16 04	7 52	16 10	7 53	16 23
16	7 20	16 10	7 29	16 20	7 31	16 14	7 36	16 11	7 40	16 02	7 54	16 08	7 55	16 21
17	7 21	16 09	7 31	16 19	7 32	16 12	7 38	16 10	7 42	16 00	7 56	16 07	7 57	16 19
18	7 23	16 07	7 33	16 18	7 34	16 11	7 40	16 08	7 44	15 59	7 58	16 05	7 59	16 18
19	7 25	16 06	7 35	16 16	7 36	16 10	7 41	16 07	7 46	15 57	8 00	16 04	8 01	16 17
20	7 26	16 05	7 36	16 15	7 38	16 08	7 43	16 05	7 48	15 56	8 02	16 02	8 03	16 15
21	7 28	16 04	7 38	16 14	7 39	16 07	7 45	16 04	7 49	15 55	8 04	16 01	8 05	16 14
22	7 30	16 03	7 39	16 13	7 41	16 06	7 47	16 03	7 51	15 53	8 06	15 59	8 07	16 12
23	7 31	16 02	7 41	16 12	7 43	16 05	7 48	16 02	7 53	15 52	8 08	15 58	8 08	16 11
24	7 33	16 01	7 43	16 11	7 44	16 04	7 50	16 01	7 55	15 51	8 10	15 57	8 10	16 10
25	7 34	16 00	7 44	16 10	7 46	16 03	7 52	16 00	7 57	15 50	8 12	15 55	8 12	16 09
26	7 36	15 59	7 46	16 09	7 48	16 02	7 53	15 59	7 59	15 48	8 14	15 54	8 14	16 08
27	7 37	15 58	7 47	16 08	7 49	16 01	7 55	15 58	8 00	15 47	8 16	15 53	8 15	16 07
28	7 39	15 57	7 49	16 07	7 51	16 00	7 57	15 57	8 02	15 46	8 17	15 52	8 17	16 06
29	7 40	15 56	7 50	16 07	7 52	15 59	7 58	15 56	8 04	15 45	8 19	15 51	8 19	16 05
30	7 42	15 56	7 52	16 06	7 54	15 59	8 00	15 55	8 05	15 44	8 21	15 50	8 20	16 04

JUPITER

Day	RA	Dec.	Transit	5° high	
				52°	56°
	h m	° ′	h m	h m	h m
1	23 19.8	− 5 56	20 36	1 35	1 27
11	23 18.8	− 6 00	19 56	0 55	0 46
21	23 19.0	− 5 56	19 17	0 16	0 07
31	23 20.5	− 5 43	18 39	23 36	23 27

Diameters – equatorial 44″ polar 41″

SATURN

Day	RA	Dec.	Transit	5° high	
				52°	56°
	h m	° ′	h m	h m	h m
1	1 53.7	+ 8 43	23 09	5 25	5 28
11	1 50.8	+ 8 28	22 27	4 41	4 45
21	1 48.2	+ 8 15	21 45	3 58	4 01
31	1 46.0	+ 8 05	21 04	3 16	3 19

Diameters – equatorial 20″ polar 18″
Rings – major axis 45″ minor axis 11″

URANUS

Day	RA	Dec.	Transit	10° high	
				52°	56°
	h m	° ′	h m	h m	h m
1	20 46.0	−18 40	18 03	20 55	20 19
11	20 46.6	−18 37	17 24	20 16	19 41
21	20 47.6	−18 33	16 46	19 39	19 03
31	20 48.8	−18 28	16 08	19 01	18 26

Diameter 4″

NEPTUNE

Day	RA	Dec.	Transit	10° high	
				52°	56°
	h m	° ′	h m	h m	h m
1	20 06.4	−19 57	17 23	20 03	19 22
11	20 07.0	−19 55	16 45	19 25	18 44
21	20 07.8	−19 53	16 06	18 47	18 06
31	20 08.8	−19 50	15 28	18 09	17 28

Diameter 2″

December 1998

TWELFTH MONTH, 31 DAYS. *Decem* (ten), tenth month of Roman pre-Julian calendar

1	*Tuesday*	Woody Allen b. 1935. David Ben-Gurion d. 1973	*week* 48 *day* 335
2	*Wednesday*	St Paul's Cathedral opened 1697. ⚔ Austerlitz 1805	336
3	*Thursday*	Mary Baker Eddy d. 1910. Sir Oswald Mosley d. 1980	337
4	*Friday*	First issue of the *Observer* 1791. Edgar Wallace b. 1875	338
5	*Saturday*	Walt Disney b. 1901. Repeal of Prohibition, USA 1933	339
6	*Sunday*	**2nd S. in Advent.** Anthony Trollope d. 1882	*week* 49 *day* 340
7	*Monday*	Capt. William Bligh d. 1817. ⚔ Pearl Harbor 1941	341
8	*Tuesday*	Thomas de Quincey d. 1859. John Lennon d. 1980	342
9	*Wednesday*	Tip O'Neill b. 1912. Dame Edith Sitwell d. 1964	343
10	*Thursday*	Royal Academy of Arts founded 1768	344
11	*Friday*	Colley Cibber d. 1757. Hector Berlioz b. 1803	345
12	*Saturday*	John Osborne b. 1929. Hovercraft patented 1955	346
13	*Sunday*	**3rd S. in Advent.** Abel Tasman discovered New Zealand 1642	*week* 50 *day* 347
14	*Monday*	CHANUCAH begins. Amundsen reached South Pole 1911	348
15	*Tuesday*	John Paul Getty b. 1892. Grigori Rasputin assass. 1916	349
16	*Wednesday*	Boston Tea Party 1773. Glenn Miller d. 1944	350
17	*Thursday*	Domenico Cimarosa b. 1749. Sir Bernard Spilsbury d. 1947	351
18	*Friday*	Charles Wesley b. 1707. Abolition of slavery, USA 1865	352
19	*Saturday*	Emily Brontë d. 1848. Sir Ralph Richardson b. 1902	353
20	*Sunday*	**4th S. in Advent.** RAMADAN begins	*week* 51 *day* 354
21	*Monday*	*Michaelmas Law Sittings end.* Frank Zappa b. 1940	355
22	*Tuesday*	George Eliot d. 1880. Beatrix Potter d. 1943	356
23	*Wednesday*	Richard Arkwright b. 1732. Thomas Malthus d. 1834	357
24	*Thursday*	Christmas Eve. William Makepeace Thackeray d. 1863	358
25	*Friday*	**Christmas Day.** *Public Holiday in the UK*	359
26	*Saturday*	**St Stephen.** Boxing Day. Radium discovered by the Curies 1898	360
27	*Sunday*	**1st S. after Christmas.** Marlene Dietrich b. 1904	*week* 52 *day* 361
28	*Monday*	**Holy Innocents.** *Bank Holiday in the UK*	362
29	*Tuesday*	**St John the Evangelist.** Christina Rossetti d. 1894	363
30	*Wednesday*	Rudyard Kipling b. 1865. Amelia Bloomer d. 1894	364
31	*Thursday*	Sir Malcolm Campbell d. 1948. The farthing withdrawn 1960	365

ASTRONOMICAL PHENOMENA

d	h	
1	15	Mercury in inferior conjunction
11	07	Mercury at stationary point
12	09	Mars in conjunction with Moon. Mars 2° S.
17	01	Mercury in conjunction with Moon. Mercury 2° S.
20	01	Venus in conjunction with Moon. Venus 4° S.
20	04	Mercury at greatest elongation W.22°
22	02	Sun's longitude 270° ♑
25	11	Jupiter in conjunction with Moon. Jupiter 1° N.
28	01	Saturn in conjunction with Moon. Saturn 2° N.
29	16	Saturn at stationary point

MINIMA OF ALGOL

d	h		d	h		d	h
2	03.1		13	14.4		25	01.6
4	23.9		16	11.2		27	22.5
7	20.7		19	08.0		30	19.3
10	17.6		22	04.8			

CONSTELLATIONS

The following constellations are near the meridian at

	d	h		d	h
November	1	24	December	16	21
November	15	23	January	1	20
December	1	22	January	16	19

Ursa Major (below the Pole), Ursa Minor (below the Pole), Cassiopeia, Andromeda, Perseus, Triangulum, Aries, Taurus, Cetus and Eridanus

THE MOON

Phases, Apsides and Node	d	h	m
○ Full Moon	3	15	19
☾ Last Quarter	10	17	54
● New Moon	18	22	42
☽ First Quarter	26	10	46
Perigee (358,852 km)	2	12	24
Apogee (405,728 km)	14	17	11
Perigee (363,803 km)	30	17	56

Mean longitude of ascending node on December 1, 146°

THE SUN   s.d. 16'.3

Day	Right Ascension	Dec. −	Equation of time	Rise 52°	Rise 56°	Transit	Set 52°	Set 56°	Sidereal time	Transit of First Point of Aries
	h m s	° '	m s	h m	h m	h m	h m	h m	h m s	h m s
1	16 27 23	21 44	+11 13	7 45	8 06	11 49	15 52	15 31	4 38 36	19 18 14
2	16 31 42	21 53	+10 51	7 47	8 08	11 49	15 52	15 30	4 42 32	19 14 18
3	16 36 01	22 02	+10 28	7 48	8 10	11 50	15 51	15 29	4 46 29	19 10 22
4	16 40 21	22 11	+10 04	7 49	8 11	11 50	15 51	15 29	4 50 25	19 06 26
5	16 44 42	22 19	+ 9 40	7 51	8 13	11 51	15 50	15 28	4 54 22	19 02 30
6	16 49 03	22 26	+ 9 15	7 52	8 14	11 51	15 50	15 27	4 58 18	18 58 34
7	16 53 25	22 33	+ 8 50	7 53	8 16	11 51	15 49	15 27	5 02 15	18 54 39
8	16 57 47	22 40	+ 8 24	7 54	8 17	11 52	15 49	15 26	5 06 12	18 50 43
9	17 02 10	22 46	+ 7 58	7 56	8 18	11 52	15 49	15 26	5 10 08	18 46 47
10	17 06 33	22 52	+ 7 31	7 57	8 20	11 53	15 49	15 26	5 14 05	18 42 51
11	17 10 57	22 58	+ 7 04	7 58	8 21	11 53	15 48	15 25	5 18 01	18 38 55
12	17 15 21	23 02	+ 6 37	7 59	8 22	11 54	15 48	15 25	5 21 58	18 34 59
13	17 19 46	23 07	+ 6 09	8 00	8 23	11 54	15 48	15 25	5 25 54	18 31 03
14	17 24 11	23 11	+ 5 40	8 01	8 24	11 55	15 48	15 25	5 29 51	18 27 07
15	17 28 36	23 14	+ 5 12	8 01	8 25	11 55	15 48	15 25	5 33 47	18 23 11
16	17 33 01	23 18	+ 4 43	8 02	8 26	11 56	15 49	15 25	5 37 44	18 19 15
17	17 37 27	23 20	+ 4 14	8 03	8 27	11 56	15 49	15 25	5 41 41	18 15 19
18	17 41 53	23 22	+ 3 44	8 04	8 28	11 57	15 49	15 25	5 45 37	18 11 24
19	17 46 19	23 24	+ 3 15	8 05	8 28	11 57	15 49	15 26	5 49 34	18 07 28
20	17 50 45	23 25	+ 2 45	8 05	8 29	11 57	15 50	15 26	5 53 30	18 03 32
21	17 55 12	23 26	+ 2 15	8 06	8 29	11 58	15 50	15 26	5 57 27	17 59 36
22	17 59 38	23 26	+ 1 45	8 06	8 30	11 59	15 51	15 27	6 01 23	17 55 40
23	18 04 05	23 26	+ 1 15	8 07	8 30	11 59	15 51	15 28	6 05 20	17 51 44
24	18 08 31	23 25	+ 0 45	8 07	8 31	11 59	15 52	15 28	6 09 16	17 47 48
25	18 12 58	23 24	+ 0 15	8 07	8 31	12 00	15 53	15 29	6 13 13	17 43 52
26	18 17 24	23 23	− 0 14	8 08	8 31	12 00	15 53	15 30	6 17 10	17 39 56
27	18 21 50	23 21	− 0 44	8 08	8 32	12 01	15 54	15 30	6 21 06	17 36 00
28	18 26 16	23 18	− 1 13	8 08	8 32	12 01	15 55	15 31	6 25 03	17 32 04
29	18 30 42	23 15	− 1 43	8 08	8 32	12 02	15 56	15 32	6 28 59	17 20 09
30	18 35 08	23 12	− 2 12	8 08	8 32	12 02	15 57	15 33	6 32 56	17 24 13
31	18 39 33	23 08	− 2 41	8 08	8 31	12 03	15 58	15 35	6 36 52	17 20 17

DURATION OF TWILIGHT (in minutes)

Latitude	52°	56°	52°	56°	52°	56°	52°	56°
	1 December		11 December		21 December		31 December	
Civil	40	45	41	47	41	47	41	47
Nautical	82	93	84	96	85	97	84	96
Astronomical	123	138	125	141	126	142	125	141

THE NIGHT SKY

Mercury becomes visible as a morning object after the first ten days of the month and remains so until almost the end of the year. During this period its magnitude ranges from +1.2 to −0.4. Observers should look for it low above the south-eastern horizon around the beginning of morning civil twilight. On the morning of the 17th the crescent Moon, only 1½ days before New, will be seen about 4° to the left of Mercury.

Venus is too close to the Sun for observation at first but gradually becomes visible in the evenings during the last ten days of the month. It will only be seen for a short time after sunset, low above the south-western horizon. Its magnitude is −3.9.

Mars is a morning object, visible in the south-eastern sky and getting perceptibly brighter as its magnitude brightens from +1.4 to +1.0 during the month. Mars is in Virgo and by the end of the month its eastward motion has carried it to a position about 6° north-west of Spica.

Jupiter continues to be visible in the evenings, magnitude −2.4, crossing the meridian about an hour after sunset by the end of the year. The crescent Moon, one day before First Quarter, passes 2° south of Jupiter on the 25th.

Saturn continues to be visible as an evening object, magnitude +0.3, though by the end of the year it is no longer visible after about 01h.

Meteors. The maximum of the well-known Geminid meteor shower occurs on the night of the 13th to 14th. As the old crescent Moon does not rise before 03h there will be little interference with observation.

THE MOON

Day	RA	Dec.	Hor. par.	Semi-diam.	Sun's co-long.	PA of Bright Limb	Phase	Age	Rise 52°	Rise 56°	Transit	Set 52°	Set 56°
	h m	°	'	'	°	°	%	d	h m	h m	h m	h m	h m
1	2 03	+ 7.6	60.8	16.6	55	244	90	11.8	15 05	14 56	22 15	4 17	4 24
2	3 02	+12.0	61.1	16.6	68	242	96	12.8	15 40	15 27	23 14	5 39	5 51
3	4 02	+15.6	61.1	16.6	80	230	99	13.8	16 22	16 05	—	7 00	7 16
4	5 04	+18.1	60.8	16.6	92	127	100	14.8	17 11	16 52	0 14	8 15	8 34
5	6 07	+19.4	60.2	16.4	104	102	97	15.8	18 09	17 50	1 15	9 22	9 41
6	7 08	+19.3	59.4	16.2	116	102	92	16.8	19 14	18 56	2 15	10 17	10 35
7	8 07	+18.1	58.5	15.9	128	104	85	17.8	20 23	20 07	3 12	11 01	11 17
8	9 03	+15.8	57.5	15.7	140	107	77	18.8	21 32	21 20	4 05	11 37	11 50
9	9 56	+12.8	56.6	15.4	152	110	67	19.8	22 40	22 32	4 55	12 06	12 16
10	10 45	+ 9.3	55.8	15.2	165	112	57	20.8	23 47	23 42	5 42	12 31	12 37
11	11 33	+ 5.5	55.1	15.0	177	113	48	21.8	—	—	6 26	12 54	12 56
12	12 18	+ 1.5	54.6	14.9	189	114	38	22.8	0 52	0 51	7 09	13 15	13 14
13	13 03	− 2.5	54.3	14.8	201	114	29	23.8	1 56	1 58	7 51	13 36	13 32
14	13 48	− 6.3	54.1	14.7	213	114	21	24.8	2 59	3 05	8 33	13 58	13 51
15	14 34	− 9.9	54.0	14.7	225	113	14	25.8	4 02	4 12	9 16	14 22	14 11
16	15 20	−13.2	54.1	14.8	238	113	8	26.8	5 06	5 18	10 01	14 49	14 36
17	16 08	−15.9	54.4	14.8	250	113	4	27.8	6 08	6 24	10 47	15 21	15 05
18	16 58	−17.9	54.6	14.9	262	120	1	28.8	7 08	7 26	11 35	15 59	15 41
19	17 49	−19.2	55.0	15.0	274	189	0	0.1	8 04	8 24	12 25	16 45	16 25
20	18 42	−19.6	55.4	15.1	286	250	1	1.1	8 55	9 15	13 15	17 38	17 18
21	19 35	−19.0	55.9	15.2	299	255	4	2.1	9 40	9 58	14 07	18 38	18 20
22	20 28	−17.4	56.3	15.4	311	254	9	3.1	10 18	10 34	14 58	19 44	19 29
23	21 22	−15.0	56.8	15.5	323	252	16	4.1	10 51	11 03	15 48	20 54	20 42
24	22 14	−11.7	57.4	15.6	335	250	25	5.1	11 20	11 29	16 38	22 06	21 59
25	23 06	− 7.8	57.9	15.8	347	248	34	6.1	11 47	11 52	17 28	23 21	23 18
26	23 58	− 3.4	58.5	15.9	359	247	45	7.1	12 12	12 13	18 18	—	—
27	0 51	+ 1.2	59.1	16.1	12	247	56	8.1	12 38	12 35	19 09	0 37	0 38
28	1 44	+ 5.9	59.6	16.2	24	247	67	9.1	13 05	12 58	20 02	1 55	2 00
29	2 40	+10.3	60.0	16.3	36	249	78	10.1	13 36	13 25	20 58	3 14	3 23
30	3 38	+14.1	60.2	16.4	48	251	87	11.1	14 12	13 58	21 56	4 33	4 47
31	4 37	+17.1	60.3	16.4	60	253	94	12.1	14 56	14 39	22 55	5 50	6 07

MERCURY

Day	RA	Dec.	Diam.	Phase	Transit	5° high 52°	5° high 56°
	h m	°	"	%	h m	h m	h m
1	16 35	−21.0	10	0	11 51	8 31	9 00
3	16 23	−20.0	10	1	11 32	8 05	8 31
5	16 13	−19.1	10	5	11 15	7 41	8 06
7	16 06	−18.3	9	12	11 00	7 21	7 44
9	16 01	−17.9	9	21	10 48	7 06	7 29
11	15 59	−17.7	8	29	10 39	6 55	7 18
13	16 00	−17.8	8	38	10 33	6 50	7 12
15	16 03	−18.0	8	46	10 29	6 47	7 11
17	16 09	−18.4	7	54	10 27	6 48	7 12
19	16 16	−18.9	7	60	10 26	6 51	7 16
21	16 24	−19.5	7	66	10 26	6 56	7 22
23	16 33	−20.1	6	70	10 28	7 01	7 29
25	16 43	−20.7	6	74	10 30	7 08	7 37
27	16 53	−21.3	6	78	10 33	7 16	7 46
29	17 05	−21.8	6	81	10 36	7 24	7 56
31	17 16	−22.3	6	83	10 40	7 32	8 05

VENUS

Day	RA	Dec.	Diam.	Phase	Transit	5° high 52°	5° high 56°
	h m	°	"	%	h m	h m	h m
1	17 01	−23.0	10	99	12 23	15 26	14 50
6	17 28	−23.7	10	99	12 31	15 27	14 49
11	17 56	−24.1	10	99	12 39	15 32	14 53
16	18 23	−24.2	10	98	12 46	15 39	15 00
21	18 51	−23.9	10	98	12 54	15 50	15 11
26	19 18	−23.4	10	97	13 02	16 03	15 26
31	19 45	−22.5	10	97	13 09	16 17	15 44

MARS

Day	RA	Dec.	Diam.	Phase	Transit	5° high 52°	5° high 56°
1	12 10	+ 0.8	5	92	7 31	2 00	2 03
6	12 20	− 0.3	5	92	7 21	1 56	2 00
11	12 30	− 1.3	6	91	7 12	1 52	1 56
16	12 40	− 2.4	6	91	7 02	1 47	1 53
21	12 50	− 3.4	6	91	6 52	1 43	1 49
26	12 59	− 4.3	6	91	6 42	1 38	1 45
31	13 09	− 5.3	6	91	6 31	1 32	1 40

SUNRISE AND SUNSET

	London		Bristol		Birmingham		Manchester		Newcastle		Glasgow		Belfast	
	0°05′	51°30′	2°35′	51°28′	1°55′	52°28′	2°15′	53°28′	1°37′	54°59′	4°14′	55°52′	5°56′	54°35′
	h m	h m	h m	h m	h m	h m	h m	h m	h m	h m	h m	h m	h m	h m
1	7 43	15 55	7 53	16 05	7 55	15 58	8 01	15 54	8 07	15 44	8 23	15 49	8 22	16 03
2	7 45	15 54	7 55	16 05	7 57	15 57	8 03	15 53	8 09	15 43	8 24	15 48	8 24	16 02
3	7 46	15 54	7 56	16 04	7 58	15 57	8 04	15 53	8 10	15 42	8 26	15 47	8 25	16 01
4	7 47	15 53	7 57	16 03	7 59	15 56	8 06	15 52	8 12	15 41	8 27	15 46	8 27	16 01
5	7 49	15 53	7 58	16 03	8 01	15 55	8 07	15 52	8 13	15 41	8 29	15 46	8 28	16 00
6	7 50	15 52	8 00	16 03	8 02	15 55	8 08	15 51	8 14	15 40	8 30	15 45	8 29	16 00
7	7 51	15 52	8 01	16 02	8 03	15 55	8 10	15 51	8 16	15 40	8 32	15 45	8 31	15 59
8	7 52	15 52	8 02	16 02	8 04	15 54	8 11	15 50	8 17	15 39	8 33	15 44	8 32	15 59
9	7 53	15 52	8 03	16 02	8 06	15 54	8 12	15 50	8 18	15 39	8 34	15 44	8 33	15 58
10	7 54	15 51	8 04	16 02	8 07	15 54	8 13	15 50	8 20	15 39	8 36	15 43	8 34	15 58
11	7 55	15 51	8 05	16 01	8 08	15 54	8 14	15 50	8 21	15 38	8 37	15 43	8 36	15 58
12	7 57	15 51	8 06	16 01	8 09	15 54	8 16	15 50	8 22	15 38	8 38	15 43	8 37	15 58
13	7 57	15 51	8 07	16 01	8 10	15 54	8 17	15 49	8 23	15 38	8 39	15 43	8 38	15 58
14	7 58	15 51	8 08	16 01	8 11	15 54	8 17	15 49	8 24	15 38	8 40	15 43	8 39	15 58
15	7 59	15 51	8 09	16 02	8 12	15 54	8 18	15 50	8 25	15 38	8 41	15 43	8 40	15 58
16	8 00	15 52	8 10	16 02	8 12	15 54	8 19	15 50	8 26	15 38	8 42	15 43	8 41	15 58
17	8 01	15 52	8 11	16 02	8 13	15 54	8 20	15 50	8 27	15 38	8 43	15 43	8 41	15 58
18	8 02	15 52	8 11	16 02	8 14	15 54	8 21	15 50	8 27	15 39	8 44	15 43	8 42	15 58
19	8 02	15 52	8 12	16 03	8 15	15 55	8 22	15 50	8 28	15 39	8 44	15 44	8 43	15 59
20	8 03	15 53	8 13	16 03	8 15	15 55	8 22	15 51	8 29	15 39	8 45	15 44	8 43	15 59
21	8 03	15 53	8 13	16 03	8 16	15 55	8 23	15 51	8 29	15 40	8 46	15 44	8 44	15 59
22	8 04	15 54	8 14	16 04	8 16	15 56	8 23	15 52	8 30	15 40	8 46	15 45	8 45	16 00
23	8 04	15 54	8 14	16 04	8 17	15 57	8 24	15 52	8 30	15 41	8 47	15 45	8 45	16 00
24	8 05	15 55	8 15	16 05	8 17	15 57	8 24	15 53	8 31	15 41	8 47	15 46	8 45	16 01
25	8 05	15 56	8 15	16 06	8 18	15 58	8 24	15 54	8 31	15 42	8 47	15 47	8 46	16 02
26	8 05	15 56	8 15	16 06	8 18	15 59	8 25	15 54	8 31	15 43	8 47	15 47	8 46	16 03
27	8 06	15 57	8 15	16 07	8 18	15 59	8 25	15 55	8 31	15 44	8 48	15 48	8 46	16 03
28	8 06	15 58	8 16	16 08	8 18	16 00	8 25	15 56	8 31	15 44	8 48	15 49	8 46	16 04
29	8 06	15 59	8 16	16 09	8 18	16 01	8 25	15 57	8 32	15 45	8 48	15 50	8 46	16 05
30	8 06	16 00	8 16	16 10	8 18	16 02	8 25	15 58	8 32	15 46	8 48	15 51	8 46	16 06
31	8 06	16 01	8 16	16 11	8 18	16 03	8 25	15 59	8 31	15 47	8 48	15 52	8 46	16 07

JUPITER

Day	RA	Dec.	Transit	5° high	
				52°	56°
	h m	° ′	h m	h m	h m
1	23 20.5	− 5 43	18 39	23 36	23 27
11	23 23.2	− 5 24	18 03	23 01	22 53
21	23 27.0	− 4 57	17 27	22 28	22 20
31	23 31.8	− 4 24	16 53	21 57	21 50

Diameters – equatorial 40″ polar 38″

SATURN

Day	RA	Dec.	Transit	5° high	
				52°	56°
	h m	° ′	h m	h m	h m
1	1 46.0	+ 8 05	21 04	3 16	3 19
11	1 44.4	+ 7 58	20 23	2 34	2 37
21	1 43.4	+ 7 55	19 43	1 54	1 57
31	1 43.1	+ 7 56	19 03	1 14	1 17

Diameters – equatorial 19″ polar 17″
Rings – major axis 43″ minor axis 11″

URANUS

Day	RA	Dec.	Transit	10° high	
				52°	56°
	h m	° ′	h m	h m	h m
1	20 48.8	−18 28	16 08	19 01	18 26
11	20 50.4	−18 22	15 30	18 25	17 50
21	20 52.2	−18 14	14 52	17 48	17 14
31	20 54.2	−18 06	14 15	17 12	16 38

Diameter 4″

NEPTUNE

Day	RA	Dec.	Transit	10° high	
				52°	56°
	h m	° ′	h m	h m	h m
1	20 08.8	−19 50	15 28	18 09	17 28
11	20 09.9	−19 46	14 50	17 31	16 51
21	20 11.3	−19 43	14 12	16 54	16 14
31	20 12.7	−19 38	13 34	16 17	15 37

Diameter 2″

RISING AND SETTING TIMES

TABLE 1. SEMI-DIURNAL ARCS (HOUR ANGLES AT RISING/SETTING)

Dec.	0° h m	10° h m	20° h m	30° h m	40° h m	45° h m	50° h m	52° h m	54° h m	56° h m	58° h m	60° h m	Dec.
0°	6 00	6 00	6 00	6 00	6 00	6 00	6 00	6 00	6 00	6 00	6 00	6 00	0°
1°	6 00	6 01	6 01	6 02	6 03	6 04	6 05	6 05	6 06	6 06	6 06	6 07	1°
2°	6 00	6 01	6 03	6 05	6 07	6 08	6 10	6 10	6 11	6 12	6 13	6 14	2°
3°	6 00	6 02	6 04	6 07	6 10	6 12	6 14	6 15	6 17	6 18	6 19	6 21	3°
4°	6 00	6 03	6 06	6 09	6 13	6 16	6 19	6 21	6 22	6 24	6 26	6 28	4°
5°	6 00	6 04	6 07	6 12	6 17	6 20	6 24	6 26	6 28	6 30	6 32	6 35	5°
6°	6 00	6 04	6 09	6 14	6 20	6 24	6 29	6 31	6 33	6 36	6 39	6 42	6°
7°	6 00	6 05	6 10	6 16	6 24	6 28	6 34	6 36	6 39	6 42	6 45	6 49	7°
8°	6 00	6 06	6 12	6 19	6 27	6 32	6 39	6 41	6 45	6 48	6 52	6 56	8°
9°	6 00	6 06	6 13	6 21	6 31	6 36	6 44	6 47	6 50	6 54	6 59	7 04	9°
10°	6 00	6 07	6 15	6 23	6 34	6 41	6 49	6 52	6 56	7 01	7 06	7 11	10°
11°	6 00	6 08	6 16	6 26	6 38	6 45	6 54	6 58	7 02	7 07	7 12	7 19	11°
12°	6 00	6 09	6 18	6 28	6 41	6 49	6 59	7 03	7 08	7 13	7 20	7 26	12°
13°	6 00	6 09	6 19	6 31	6 45	6 53	7 04	7 09	7 14	7 20	7 27	7 34	13°
14°	6 00	6 10	6 21	6 33	6 48	6 58	7 09	7 14	7 20	7 27	7 34	7 42	14°
15°	6 00	6 11	6 22	6 36	6 52	7 02	7 14	7 20	7 27	7 34	7 42	7 51	15°
16°	6 00	6 12	6 24	6 38	6 56	7 07	7 20	7 26	7 33	7 41	7 49	7 59	16°
17°	6 00	6 12	6 26	6 41	6 59	7 11	7 25	7 32	7 40	7 48	7 57	8 08	17°
18°	6 00	6 13	6 27	6 43	7 03	7 16	7 31	7 38	7 46	7 55	8 05	8 17	18°
19°	6 00	6 14	6 29	6 46	7 07	7 21	7 37	7 45	7 53	8 03	8 14	8 26	19°
20°	6 00	6 15	6 30	6 49	7 11	7 25	7 43	7 51	8 00	8 11	8 22	8 36	20°
21°	6 00	6 16	6 32	6 51	7 15	7 30	7 49	7 58	8 08	8 19	8 32	8 47	21°
22°	6 00	6 16	6 34	6 54	7 19	7 35	7 55	8 05	8 15	8 27	8 41	8 58	22°
23°	6 00	6 17	6 36	6 57	7 23	7 40	8 02	8 12	8 23	8 36	8 51	9 09	23°
24°	6 00	6 18	6 37	7 00	7 28	7 46	8 08	8 19	8 31	8 45	9 02	9 22	24°
25°	6 00	6 19	6 39	7 02	7 32	7 51	8 15	8 27	8 40	8 55	9 13	9 35	25°
26°	6 00	6 20	6 41	7 05	7 37	7 57	8 22	8 35	8 49	9 05	9 25	9 51	26°
27°	6 00	6 21	6 43	7 08	7 41	8 03	8 30	8 43	8 58	9 16	9 39	10 08	27°
28°	6 00	6 22	6 45	7 12	7 46	8 08	8 37	8 52	9 08	9 28	9 53	10 28	28°
29°	6 00	6 22	6 47	7 15	7 51	8 15	8 45	9 01	9 19	9 41	10 10	10 55	29°
30°	6 00	6 23	6 49	7 18	7 56	8 21	8 54	9 11	9 30	9 55	10 30	12 00	30°
35°	6 00	6 28	6 59	7 35	8 24	8 58	9 46	10 15	10 58	12 00	12 00	12 00	35°
40°	6 00	6 34	7 11	7 56	8 59	9 48	12 00	12 00	12 00	12 00	12 00	12 00	40°
45°	6 00	6 41	7 25	8 21	9 48	12 00	12 00	12 00	12 00	12 00	12 00	12 00	45°
50°	6 00	6 49	7 43	8 54	12 00	12 00	12 00	12 00	12 00	12 00	12 00	12 00	50°
55°	6 00	6 58	8 05	9 42	12 00	12 00	12 00	12 00	12 00	12 00	12 00	12 00	55°
60°	6 00	7 11	8 36	12 00	12 00	12 00	12 00	12 00	12 00	12 00	12 00	12 00	60°
65°	6 00	7 29	9 25	12 00	12 00	12 00	12 00	12 00	12 00	12 00	12 00	12 00	65°
70°	6 00	7 56	12 00	12 00	12 00	12 00	12 00	12 00	12 00	12 00	12 00	12 00	70°
75°	6 00	8 45	12 00	12 00	12 00	12 00	12 00	12 00	12 00	12 00	12 00	12 00	75°
80°	6 00	12 00	12 00	12 00	12 00	12 00	12 00	12 00	12 00	12 00	12 00	12 00	80°

TABLE 2. CORRECTION FOR REFRACTION AND SEMI-DIAMETER

	0° m	10° m	20° m	30° m	40° m	45° m	50° m	52° m	54° m	56° m	58° m	60° m	
0°	3	3	4	4	4	5	5	5	6	6	6	7	0°
10°	3	3	4	4	4	5	5	6	6	6	7	7	10°
20°	4	4	4	5	5	6	7	7	8	8	9		20°
25°	4	4	4	4	5	6	7	8	8	9	11	13	25°
30°	4	4	4	5	6	7	8	9	11	14	21	—	30°

NB: Regarding Table 1. If latitude and declination are of the same sign, take out the respondent directly. If they are of opposite signs, subtract the respondent from 12h.
Example:

Lat.	Dec.	Semi-diurnal arc
+52°	+20°	7h 51m
+52°	−20°	4h 09m

SUNRISE AND SUNSET

The local mean time of sunrise or sunset may be found by obtaining the hour angle from Table 1 and applying it to the time of transit. The hour angle is negative for sunrise and positive for sunset. A small correction to the hour angle, which always has the effect of increasing it numerically, is necessary to allow for the Sun's semi-diameter (16′) and for refraction (34′); it is obtained from Table 2. The resulting local mean time may be converted into the standard time of the country by taking the difference between the longitude of the standard meridian of the country and that of the place, adding it to the local mean time if the place is west of the standard meridian, and subtracting it if the place is east.

Example – Required the New Zealand Mean Time (12h fast on GMT) of sunset on May 23 at Auckland, latitude 36° 50′ S. (or minus), longitude 11h 39m E. Taking the declination as +20°.6 (page 33), we find

	h	m
Tabular entry for Lat. 30° and Dec. 20°, opposite signs	+ 5	11
Proportional part for 6° 50′ of Lat.	−	15
Proportional part for 0°.6 of Dec.	−	2
Correction (Table 2)	+	4
Hour angle	4	58
Sun transits (page 33)	11	57
Longitudinal correction	+	21
New Zealand Mean Time	17	16

MOONRISE AND MOONSET

It is possible to calculate the times of moonrise and moonset using Table 1, though the method is more complicated because the apparent motion of the Moon is much more rapid and also more variable than that of the Sun.

The parallax of the Moon, about 57′, is near to the sum of the semi-diameter and refraction but has the opposite effect on these times. It is thus convenient to neglect all three quantities in the method outlined below.

TABLE 3. LONGITUDE CORRECTION

X A h	40m m	45m m	50m m	55m m	60m m	65m m	70m m
1	2	2	2	2	3	3	3
2	3	4	4	5	5	5	6
3	5	6	6	7	8	8	9
4	7	8	8	9	10	11	12
5	8	9	10	11	13	14	15
6	10	11	13	14	15	16	18
7	12	13	15	16	18	19	20
8	13	15	17	18	20	22	23
9	15	17	19	21	23	24	26
10	17	19	21	23	25	27	29
11	18	21	23	25	28	30	32
12	20	23	25	28	30	33	35
13	22	24	27	30	33	35	38
14	23	26	29	32	35	38	41
15	25	28	31	34	38	41	44
16	27	30	33	37	40	43	47
17	28	32	35	39	43	46	50
18	30	34	38	41	45	49	53
19	32	36	40	44	48	51	55
20	33	38	42	46	50	54	58
21	35	39	44	48	53	57	61
22	37	41	46	50	55	60	64
23	38	43	48	53	58	62	67
24	40	45	50	55	60	65	70

Notation

φ = latitude of observer
λ = longitude of observer (measured positively towards the west)
T_{-1} = time of transit of Moon on previous day
T_0 = time of transit of Moon on day in question
T_1 = time of transit of Moon on following day
δ_0 = approximate declination of Moon
δ_R = declination of Moon at moonrise
δ_S = declination of Moon at moonset
h_0 = approximate hour angle of Moon
h_R = hour angle of Moon at moonrise
h_S = hour angle of Moon at moonset
t_R = time of moonrise
t_S = time of moonset

Method

1. With arguments φ, δ_0 enter Table 1 on page 64 to determine h_0 where h_0 is negative for moonrise and positive for moonset.

2. Form approximate times from
$t_R = T_0 + \lambda + h_0$
$t_S = T_0 + \lambda + h_0$

3. Determine δ_R, δ_S for times t_R, t_S respectively.

4. Re-enter Table 1 on page 64 with
(*a*) arguments φ, δ_R to determine h_R
(*b*) arguments φ, δ_S to determine h_S

5. Form $t_R = T_0 + \lambda + h_R + AX$
$t_S = T_0 + \lambda + h_S + AX$

where $A = (\lambda + h)$

and $X = (T_0 - T_{-1})$ if $(\lambda + h)$ is negative
$X = (T_1 - T_0)$ if $(\lambda + h)$ is positive

AX is the respondent in Table 3.

Example – To find the times of moonrise and moonset at Vancouver ($\varphi = +49°$, $\lambda = +8h 12m$) on 1998 January 27. The starting data (page 18) are

T_{-1} = 10h 30m
T_0 = 11h 27m
T_1 = 12h 24m
δ_0 = −18°

1. h_0 = 4h 32m
2. Approximate values
t_R = 27d 11h 27m + 8h 12m + (−4h 32m)
= 27d 15h 07m
t_S = 27d 11h 27m + 8h 12m + (+4h 32m)
= 28d 00h 11m
3. δ_R = −16°.9
δ_S = −16°.1
4. h_R = −4h 38m
h_S = +4h 43m
5. t_R = 27d 11h 27m + 8h 12m + (−4h 38m) + 8m
= 27d 15h 09m
t_S = 27d 11h 27m + 8h 12m + (+4h 43m) + 31m
= 28d 00h 53m

To get the LMT of the phenomenon the longitude is subtracted from the GMT thus:
Moonrise = 27d 15h 09m − 8h 12m = 27d 06h 57m
Moonset = 28d 00h 53m − 8h 12m = 27d 16h 41m

ECLIPSES AND OCCULTATIONS 1998

ECLIPSES

During 1998 there will be two eclipses of the Sun, but none of the Moon. (Penumbral lunar eclipses are not mentioned in this section as they are too difficult to observe.)

1. A total eclipse of the Sun on February 26 is visible as a partial eclipse from the eastern Pacific Ocean, southern and eastern North America, Central America, the northern part of South America, the North Atlantic Ocean, and the extreme western portions of the Iberian peninsula and West Africa. It begins at 14h and 50m and ends at 20h 06m. The track of totality starts in mid-Pacific and crosses extreme southern Panama, northern Colombia and north-western Venezuela, passes through the Leeward Islands and ends in the eastern North Atlantic Ocean. The total phase begins at 15h 47m and ends at 19h 10m; the maximum duration is 4m 09s.

In the extreme south-west of Ireland the partial phase of the eclipse commences at around 18h 09m, but this is only a few minutes before sunset.

2. An annular eclipse of the Sun on August 21–22 is visible as a partial eclipse from eastern India and south-east Asia in general, Indonesia, Philippines, Australasia, and western and southern parts of the Pacific Ocean. It begins at 21d 23h 10m and ends at 22d 05h 02m. The annular phase commences in the eastern Indian Ocean, crosses northern Sumatra, Malaysia, northern Borneo, New Britain, New Hebrides and Vanuatu, and ends in the South Pacific Ocean. The annular phase begins at 22d 00h 14m and ends at 22d 03h 58m; the maximum duration is 3m 14s.

LUNAR OCCULTATIONS

Observations of the times of occultations are made by both amateur and professional astronomers. Such observations are later analysed to yield accurate positions of the Moon; this is one method of determining the difference between ephemeris time and universal time.

Many of the observations made by amateurs are obtained with the use of a stop-watch which is compared with a time-signal immediately after the observation. Thus an accuracy of about one-fifth of a second is obtainable, though the observer's personal equation may amount to one-third or one-half of a second.

The list on page 67 includes most of the occultations visible under favourable conditions in the British Isles. No occultation is included unless the star is at least 10° above the horizon and the Sun sufficiently far below the horizon to permit the star to be seen with the naked eye or with a small telescope. The altitude limit is reduced from 10° to 2° for stars and planets brighter than magnitude 2.0 and such occultations are also predicted in daylight.

The column Phase shows (i) whether a disappearance (D) or reappearance (R) is to be observed; and (ii) whether it is at the dark limb (D) or bright limb (B). The column headed 'El. of Moon' gives the elongation of the Moon from the Sun, in degrees. The elongation increases from 0° at New Moon to 180° at Full Moon and on to 360° (or 0°) at New Moon again. Times and position angles (P), reckoned from the north point in the direction north, east, south, west, are given for Greenwich (lat. 51° 30′, long. 0°) and Edinburgh (lat. 56° 00′, long. 3° 12′ west).

The coefficients a and b are the variations in the GMT for each degree of longitude (positive to the west) and latitude (positive to the north) respectively; they enable approximate times (to within about 1m generally) to be found for any point in the British Isles. If the point of observation is $\Delta\lambda$ degrees west and $\Delta\phi$ degrees north, the approximate time is found by adding $a.\Delta\lambda + b.\Delta\phi$ to the given GMT.

Example: the disappearance of ZC 692 on December 30 at Coventry, found from both Greenwich and Edinburgh.

	Greenwich	Edinburgh
	°	°
Longitude	0.0	+3.2
Long. of Coventry	+1.5	+1.5
$\Delta\lambda$	+1.5	−1.7
Latitude	+51.5	+56.0
Lat. of Coventry	+52.4	+52.4
$\Delta\phi$	+0.9	−3.6
	h m	h m
GMT	23 17.0	23 12.7
$a.\Delta\lambda$	− 2.1	+ 2.0
$b.\Delta\phi$	− 0.3	− 0.7
	23 14.6	23 14.0

If the occultation is given for one station but not the other, the reason for the suppression is given by the following code:

N = star not occulted

A = star's altitude less than 10° (2° for bright stars and planets)

S = Sun not sufficiently below the horizon

G = occultation is of very short duration

In some cases the coefficients a and b are not given; this is because the occultation is so short that prediction for other places by means of these coefficients would not be reliable.

Observers may like to note that ZC 692 = *Aldebaran* (occulted on April 28, June 22, November 6 and December 30–31).

LUNAR OCCULTATIONS 1998

Date		ZC No.	Mag.	Phase	El. of Moon	Greenwich UT	a	b	P	Edinburgh UT	a	b	P
					°	h m	m	m	°	h m	m	m	°
January	6	322	5.7	D.D.	108	22 44.6	−0.7	0.1	43	22 44.5	−0.6	0.9	26
	9	608	6.0	D.D.	134	1 20.7	−0.5	−1.6	96	1 12.3	−0.6	−1.4	84
	9	741	5.7	D.D.	145	21 40.9	−1.4	1.7	46	21 47.2	−1.0	2.9	26
February	3	426	8.0	D.D.	90	23 6.2	−0.4	−0.1	42	23 5.6	−0.5	0.6	26
	5	699	5.8	D.D.	113	18 55.7	−2.0	−2.0	133	18 45.7	−1.5	−0.3	113
	7	878	5.5	D.D.	129	2 2.9	−0.2	−1.4	86	1 55.9	−0.3	−1.3	78
	8	1029	5.1	D.D.	141	2 12.4	0.0	−2.7	141	2 0.3	−0.2	−2.5	131
	8	1141	5.6	D.D.	152	23 24.7	−1.3	−1.8	125	23 13.9	−1.3	−1.2	113
March	3	508	4.3	D.D.	71	N				21 8.5	−0.3	−3.8	138
	4	661	4.6	D.D.	84	20 30.3	−0.9	−2.5	121	20 17.9	−1.0	−1.7	106
	4	671	3.6	D.D.	84	21 37.2	−0.7	−1.1	79	21 30.6	−0.8	−0.8	67
	4	669	4.0	D.D.	84	21 39.0	−0.8	−0.5	58	21 35.3	−0.8	0.0	44
	4	675	5.7	D.D.	85	22 33.8	G		148	22 18.6	−0.2	−2.8	130
	4	678	5.5	D.D.	85	22 41.2	0.0	−2.8	132	22 29.3	−0.3	−2.3	118
	4	682	6.0	D.D.	85	23 6.8	−0.1	−1.6	98	22 59.1	−0.3	−1.5	88
	5	806	5.1	D.D.	96	21 15.0	−1.1	−1.4	95	21 6.5	−1.1	−0.9	84
	5	820	6.0	D.D.	98	23 14.0	−0.1	−2.7	133	23 1.9	−0.3	−2.3	122
	10	1442	5.0	D.D.	154	20 47.5	−1.6	1.8	71	20 53.0	−1.5	2.9	55
	26	Jupiter	−2.1	D.B.	336	11 17.5	−1.3	0.1	70	11 14.8	−1.1	0.3	60
	26	Jupiter	−2.1	R.D.	337	12 27.8	−1.1	−0.2	243	12 23.0	−1.1	−0.4	255
	31	608	6.0	D.D.	53	21 8.1	−0.3	−0.5	54	21 5.0	−0.4	−0.3	42
April	5	1210	5.9	D.D.	104	1 31.5	G		22	N			
	7	1525	5.9	D.D.	137	22 32.5	−1.8	−0.4	81	22 26.1	−1.7	0.1	73
	28	692	1.1	D.D.	32	18 38.9	−0.8	0.5	34	18 41.8	G		12
	28	692	1.1	R.B.	33	19 16.0	0.1	−2.9	317	18 59.4	G		338
May	4	1486	4.6	D.D.	106	19 48.9	−1.3	−1.6	132	S			
	5	1600	5.1	D.D.	119	23 40.7	−0.9	−1.6	92	23 30.8	−0.9	−1.5	88
	7	1712	3.8	D.D.	131	A				2 20.5	−0.2	−2.1	129
June	4	1866	5.9	D.D.	121	21 26.1	−1.2	−1.6	135	S			
	22	692	1.1	D.B.	339	14 13.1	−0.9	−0.3	55	14 10.2	−0.9	0.3	41
	22	692	1.1	R.D.	339	15 7.9	−0.3	−2.1	293	14 56.4	−0.3	−2.6	306
July	2	1941	4.8	D.D.	103	22 35.7	−0.8	−1.8	109	22 25.0	−0.8	−1.7	105
August	1	2223	4.0	D.D.	106	22 7.1	−1.0	−1.5	96	21 57.3	−1.0	−1.4	91
	25	1821	2.9	D.D.	37	9 10.8	−0.2	0.9	115	A			
	25	1821	2.9	R.B.	38	10 15.7	−0.6	1.1	287	10 18.3	−0.4	0.8	300
September	5	3173	5.3	D.D.	161	N				1 49.7	−1.4	−2.5	126
	12	635	3.9	D.D.	256	0 42.1	G		350	N			
	12	635	3.9	R.D.	256	0 48.1	G		339	N			
October	4	3388	5.6	D.D.	154	0 1.9	−0.1	2.0	8	N			
	16	1547	3.9	D.D.	313	3 57.8	−0.4	0.3	313	3 56.6	−0.4	−0.3	330
	27	2902	6.0	D.D.	83	20 37.3	−1.2	−1.8	108	20 26.7	−1.0	−1.4	97
	29	3173	5.3	D.D.	107	21 7.2	−1.1	−0.5	69	21 2.5	−0.9	−0.2	58
	30	3307	4.9	D.D.	118	18 7.6	−0.7	2.5	10	18 19.3	G		352
November	2	76	5.9	D.D.	149	1 16.7	−1.2	−2.9	122	1 3.6	−1.0	−1.7	101
	5	635	3.9	R.D.	203	18 57.8	0.0	1.1	287	19 2.7	0.0	1.1	296
	5	671	3.6	R.D.	205	22 34.2	−0.5	2.4	217	22 42.3	−0.5	2.0	231
	6	692	1.1	D.B.	207	1 19.3	−1.4	0.6	74	1 19.4	−1.1	1.1	60
	6	692	1.1	R.D.	207	2 31.1	−1.4	−0.2	262	2 25.3	−1.3	−0.5	276
	15	1821	2.9	D.B.	316	4 22.0	0.3	0.2	136	4 23.3	−0.3	0.8	122
	15	1821	2.9	R.D.	317	5 24.7	−0.9	1.6	270	5 28.7	−0.7	1.3	282
	24	2981	5.2	D.D.	63	18 4.2	−1.6	−1.4	109	17 54.5	−1.4	−0.9	98
	24	2987	5.0	D.D.	63	19 9.8	−0.5	−0.1	41	19 8.6	−0.3	0.2	26
	30	270	8.6	D.D.	138	16 51.8	−0.4	1.8	62	16 58.9	−0.3	1.8	56
December	1	405	4.4	D.D.	152	S				16 17.7	G		1
	28	364	4.3	D.D.	120	17 57.3	−1.5	0.5	108	17 56.4	−1.1	1.0	95
	29	405	4.4	D.D.	125	A				2 41.3	−0.1	−0.6	53
	29	508	4.3	D.D.	135	20 44.2	−1.8	−0.8	114	20 37.7	−1.4	0.1	97
	30	661	4.6	D.D.	148	N				18 35.9	G		145
	30	669	4.0	D.D.	148	19 24.7	−1.2	0.7	103	19 25.5	−0.9	1.1	90
	30	671	3.6	D.D.	148	19 34.4	−1.7	−0.6	129	19 30.4	−1.1	0.6	112
	30	667	5.3	D.D.	148	19 50.9	G		6	N			
	30	677	4.8	D.D.	149	20 25.3	−1.3	0.9	83	20 26.7	−1.0	1.3	69
	30	692	1.1	D.D.	150	23 17.0	−1.4	−0.3	82	23 12.7	−1.2	0.2	68
	31	692	1.1	R.B.	151	0 27.2	−1.1	−0.7	258	0 20.0	−1.0	−1.0	271
	31	814	5.3	D.D.	161	18 2.8	−0.4	1.4	90	18 8.7	−0.2	1.6	80
	31	836	5.5	D.D.	163	21 22.5	−0.6	3.7	22	N			

MEAN PLACES OF STARS 1998.5

Name	Mag.	RA (h m)	Dec. (° ')	Spectrum	Name	Mag.	RA (h m)	Dec. (° ')	Spectrum
α And *Alpheratz*	2.1	0 08.3	+29 05	A0p	γ Corvi	2.6	12 15.7	−17 32	B8
β Cassiopeiae *Caph*	2.3	0 09.1	+59 08	F5	α Crucis	1.0	12 26.5	−63 05	B1
γ Pegasi *Algenib*	2.8	0 13.2	+15 11	B2	γ Crucis	1.6	12 31.1	−57 06	M3
β Mensae	2.9	0 25.7	−77 16	G0	γ Centauri	2.2	12 41.4	−48 57	A0
α Phoenicis	2.4	0 26.2	−42 19	K0	γ Virginis	2.7	12 41.6	− 1 26	F0
α Cassiopeiae *Schedar*	2.2	0 40.4	+56 32	K0	β Crucis	1.3	12 47.6	−59 41	B1
β Ceti *Diphda*	2.0	0 43.5	−18 00	K0	ε Ursae Majoris *Alioth*	1.8	12 54.0	+55 58	A0p
γ Cassiopeiae*	Var.	0 56.6	+60 43	B0p	α Canum Venaticorum	2.9	12 56.0	+38 20	A0p
β Andromedae *Mirach*	2.1	1 09.6	+35 37	M0	ζ Ursae Majoris *Mizar*	2.1	13 23.9	+54 56	A2p
δ Cassiopeiae	2.7	1 25.7	+60 14	A5	α Virginis *Spica*	1.0	13 25.1	−11 09	B2
α Eridani *Achernar*	0.5	1 37.7	−57 15	B5	ε Centauri	2.6	13 39.8	−53 28	B1
β Arietis *Sheratan*	2.6	1 54.6	+20 48	A5	η Ursae Majoris *Alkaid*	1.9	13 47.5	+49 19	B3
γ Andromedae *Almak*	2.3	2 03.8	+42 19	K0	β Centauri *Hadar*	0.6	14 03.7	−60 22	B1
α Arietis *Hamal*	2.0	2 07.1	+23 27	K2	θ Centauri	2.1	14 06.6	−36 22	K0
α Ursae Minoris *Polaris*	2.0	2 30.2	+89 15	F8	α Bootis *Arcturus*	0.0	14 15.6	+19 11	K0
β Persei *Algol**	Var.	3 08.1	+40 57	B8	α Centauri *Rigil Kent*	0.1	14 39.5	−60 50	G0
α Persei *Mirfak*	1.8	3 24.2	+49 51	F5	ε Bootis	2.4	14 44.9	+27 05	K0
η Tauri *Alcyone*	2.9	3 47.4	+24 06	B5p	β UMi *Kochab*	2.1	14 50.7	+74 10	K5
α Tauri *Aldebaran*	0.9	4 35.8	+16 30	K5	γ Ursae Minoris	3.1	15 20.7	+71 50	A2
β Orionis *Rigel*	0.1	5 14.5	− 8 12	B8p	α CrB *Alphecca*	2.2	15 34.6	+26 43	A0
α Aurigae *Capella*	0.1	5 16.6	+46 00	G0	β Trianguli Australis	3.0	15 55.0	−63 26	F0
γ Orionis *Bellatrix*	1.6	5 25.1	+ 6 21	B2	δ Scorpii	2.3	16 00.2	−22 37	B0
β Tauri *Elnath*	1.7	5 26.2	+28 36	B8	β Scorpii	2.6	16 05.3	−19 48	B1
δ Orionis	2.2	5 31.9	− 0 18	B0	α Scorpii *Antares*	1.0	16 29.3	−26 26	M0
α Leporis	2.6	5 32.7	−17 49	F0	α Trianguli Australis	1.9	16 48.5	−69 02	K2
ε Orionis	1.7	5 36.1	− 1 12	B0	ε Scorpii	2.3	16 50.1	−34 17	K0
ζ Orionis	1.8	5 40.7	− 1 57	B0	α Herculis†	Var.	17 14.6	+14 24	M3
κ Orionis	2.1	5 47.7	− 9 40	B0	λ Scorpii	1.6	17 33.5	−37 06	B2
α Orionis *Betelgeuse**	Var.	5 55.1	+ 7 24	M0	α Ophiuchi *Rasalhague*	2.1	17 34.9	+12 34	A5
β Aurigae *Menkalinan*	1.9	5 59.4	+44 57	A0p	θ Scorpii	1.9	17 37.2	−43 00	F0
β CMa *Mirzam*	2.0	6 22.6	−17 57	B1	κ Scorpii	2.4	17 42.4	−39 02	B2
α Carinae *Canopus*	−0.7	6 23.9	−52 42	F0	γ Draconis	2.2	17 56.6	+51 29	K5
γ Geminorum *Alhena*	1.9	6 37.6	+16 24	A0	ε Sgr *Kaus Australis*	1.9	18 24.1	−34 23	A0
α Canis Majoris *Sirius*	−1.5	6 45.1	−16 43	A0	α Lyrae *Vega*	0.0	18 36.9	+38 47	A0
ε Canis Majoris	1.5	6 58.6	−28 58	B1	σ Sagittarii	2.0	18 55.2	−26 18	B3
δ Canis Majoris	1.9	7 08.3	−26 23	F8p	β Cygni *Albireo*	3.1	19 30.7	+27 57	K0
α Geminorum *Castor*	1.6	7 34.5	+31 54	A0	α Aquilae *Altair*	0.8	19 50.7	+ 8 52	A5
α CMi *Procyon*	0.4	7 39.2	+ 5 14	F5	α Capricorni	3.8	20 18.0	−12 33	G5
β Geminorum *Pollux*	1.1	7 45.2	+28 02	K0	γ Cygni	2.2	20 22.2	+40 15	F8p
ζ Puppis	2.3	8 03.5	−40 00	Od	α Pavonis	1.9	20 25.5	−56 44	B3
γ Velorum	1.8	8 09.5	−47 20	Oap	α Cygni *Deneb*	1.3	20 41.4	+45 17	A2p
ε Carinae	1.9	8 22.5	−59 30	K0	α Cephei *Alderamin*	2.4	21 18.5	+62 35	A5
δ Velorum	2.0	8 44.7	−54 42	A0	ε Pegasi	2.4	21 44.1	+ 9 52	K0
λ Velorum *Suhail*	2.2	9 07.0	−43 26	K5	δ Capricorni	2.9	21 47.0	−16 08	A5
β Carinae	1.7	9 13.2	−69 43	A0	α Gruis	1.7	22 08.1	−46 58	B5
ι Carinae	2.2	9 17.1	−59 16	F0	δ Cephei†	3.7	22 29.1	+58 24	†
κ Velorum	2.6	9 22.1	−55 00	B3	β Gruis	2.1	22 42.6	−46 54	M3
α Hydrae *Alphard*	2.0	9 27.5	− 8 39	K2	α PsA *Fomalhaut*	1.2	22 57.6	−29 38	A3
α Leonis *Regulus*	1.3	10 08.3	+11 58	B8	β Pegasi *Scheat*	2.4	23 03.7	+28 04	M0
γ Leonis *Algeiba*	1.9	10 19.9	+19 51	K0	α Pegasi *Markab*	2.5	23 04.7	+15 12	A0
β Ursae Majoris *Merak*	2.4	11 01.8	+56 23	A0					
α Ursae Majoris *Dubhe*	1.8	11 03.6	+61 46	K0					
δ Leonis	2.6	11 14.0	+20 32	A3					
β Leonis *Denebola*	2.1	11 49.0	+14 35	A2					
γ Ursae Majoris *Phecda*	2.4	11 53.8	+53 42	A0					

*γ Cassiopeiae, 1997 mag. 2.5. β Persei, mag. 2.1 to 3.4.
α Orionis, mag. 0.1 to 1.2.
†α Herculis, mag. 3.1 to 3.9. δ Cephei, mag. 3.7 to 4.4,
spectrum F5 to G0.

The positions of heavenly bodies on the celestial sphere are defined by two co-ordinates, right ascension and declination, which are analogous to longitude and latitude on the surface of the Earth. If we imagine the plane of the terrestrial equator extended indefinitely, it will cut the celestial sphere in a great circle known as the celestial equator. Similarly the plane of the Earth's orbit, when extended, cuts in the great circle called the ecliptic. The two intersections of these circles are known as the First Point of Aries and the First Point of Libra. If from any star a perpendicular be drawn to the celestial equator, the length of this perpendicular is the star's declination. The arc, measured eastwards along the equator from the First Point of Aries to the foot of this perpendicular, is the right ascension. An alternative definition of right ascension is that it is the angle at the celestial pole (where the Earth's axis, if prolonged, would meet the sphere) between the great circles to the First Point of Aries and to the star.

The plane of the Earth's equator has a slow movement, so that our reference system for right ascension and declination is not fixed. The consequent alteration in these quantities from year to year is called precession. In right ascension it is an increase of about 3 seconds a year for equatorial stars, and larger or smaller changes in either direction for stars near the poles, depending on the right ascension of the star. In declination it varies between $+20''$ and $-20''$ according to the right ascension of the star.

A star or other body crosses the meridian when the sidereal time is equal to its right ascension. The altitude is then a maximum, and may be deduced by remembering that the altitude of the elevated pole is numerically equal to the latitude, while that of the equator at its intersection with the meridian is equal to the co-latitude, or complement of the latitude.

Thus in London (lat. 51° 30′) the meridian altitude of Sirius is found as follows:

	°	′
Altitude of equator	38	30
Declination south	16	43
Difference	21	47

The altitude of Capella (Dec. +46° 00′) at lower transit is:

	°	′
Altitude of pole	51	30
Polar distance of star	44	00
Difference	7	30

The brightness of a heavenly body is denoted by its magnitude. Omitting the exceptionally bright stars Sirius and Canopus, the twenty brightest stars are of the first magnitude, while the faintest stars visible to the naked eye are of the sixth magnitude. The magnitude scale is a precise one, as a difference of five magnitudes represents a ratio of 100 to 1 in brightness. Typical second magnitude stars are Polaris and the stars in the belt of Orion. The scale is most easily fixed in memory by comparing the stars with Norton's *Star Atlas* (*see* page 71). The stars Sirius and Canopus and the planets Venus and Jupiter are so bright that their magnitudes are expressed by negative numbers. A small telescope will show stars down to the ninth or tenth magnitude, while stars fainter than the twentieth magnitude may be photographed by long exposures with the largest telescopes.

MEAN AND SIDEREAL TIME

Acceleration

h	m	s	m	s	s
1	0	10	0	00	
2	0	20	3	02	0
3	0	30	9	07	1
4	0	39	15	13	2
5	0	49	21	18	3
6	0	59	27	23	4
7	1	09	33	28	5
8	1	19	39	34	6
9	1	29	45	39	7
10	1	39	51	44	8
11	1	48	57	49	9
12	1	58	60	00	10
13	2	08			
14	2	18			
15	2	28			
16	2	38			
17	2	48			
18	2	57			
19	3	07			
20	3	17			
21	3	27			
22	3	37			
23	3	47			
24	3	57			

Retardation

h	m	s	m	s	s
1	0	10	0	00	
2	0	20	3	03	0
3	0	29	9	09	1
4	0	39	15	15	2
5	0	49	21	21	3
6	0	59	27	28	4
7	1	09	33	34	5
8	1	19	39	40	6
9	1	28	45	46	7
10	1	38	51	53	8
11	1	48	57	59	9
12	1	58	60	00	10
13	2	08			
14	2	18			
15	2	27			
16	2	37			
17	2	47			
18	2	57			
19	3	07			
20	3	17			
21	3	26			
22	3	36			
23	3	46			
24	3	56			

The length of a sidereal day in mean time is 23h 56m 04s.09. Hence 1h MT = 1h + 9s.86 ST and 1h ST = 1h − 9s.83 MT

To convert an interval of mean time to the corresponding interval of sidereal time, enter the acceleration table with the given mean time (taking the hours and the minutes and seconds separately) and add the acceleration obtained to the given mean time. To convert an interval of sidereal time to the corresponding interval of mean time, take out the retardation for the given sidereal time and subtract.

The columns for the minutes and seconds of the argument are in the form known as critical tables. To use these tables, find in the appropriate left-hand column the two entries between which the given number of minutes and seconds lies; the quantity in the right-hand column between these two entries is the required acceleration or retardation. Thus the acceleration for 11m 26s (which lies between the entries 9m 07s and 15m 13s) is 2s. If the given number of minutes and seconds is a tabular entry, the required acceleration or retardation is the entry in the right-hand column above the given tabular entry, e.g. the retardation for 45m 46s is 7s.

Example – Convert 14h 27m 35s from ST to MT

	h	m	s
Given ST	14	27	35
Retardation for 14h		2	18
Retardation for 27m 35s			5
Corresponding MT	14	25	12

For further explanation, *see* pages 73–4.

ECLIPSES AND SHADOW TRANSITS OF JUPITER'S SATELLITES 1998

GMT (d h m)	Sat.	Phen.
January		
4 18 24	II	Ec.R
6 18 58	I	Sh.I
7 18 23	I	Ec.R
8 18 48	IV	Ec.D
15 17 38	I	Sh.E
June		
15 01 48	I	Sh.I
23 01 00	I	Ec.D
25 00 49	III	Ec.R
26 00 45	II	Sh.I
July		
1 02 18	I	Sh.E
2 01 24	III	Ec.D
8 01 58	I	Sh.I
12 00 04	II	Ec.D
16 01 11	I	Ec.D
17 00 35	I	Sh.E
19 23 33	III	Sh.I
21 00 35	II	Sh.E
23 03 05	I	Ec.D
24 00 14	I	Sh.I
24 02 28	I	Sh.E
28 00 27	II	Sh.I
29 00 41	IV	Ec.R
31 02 08	I	Sh.I
31 23 28	I	Ec.D
August		
1 22 51	I	Sh.E
4 03 03	II	Sh.I
7 00 49	III	Ec.R
8 01 22	I	Ec.D
8 22 30	I	Sh.I
9 00 45	I	Sh.E
12 23 46	II	Ec.D
14 01 29	III	Ec.D
14 21 39	II	Sh.E
15 03 16	I	Ec.D
16 00 24	I	Sh.I
16 02 40	I	Sh.E
16 21 44	I	Ec.D
20 02 23	II	Ec.D
21 21 32	II	Sh.I
22 00 14	II	Sh.E
23 01 02	IV	Sh.I
23 02 19	I	Sh.I
23 03 43	IV	Sh.E
23 04 34	I	Sh.E
23 23 39	I	Ec.D
24 20 47	I	Sh.I
24 22 55	III	Sh.E
24 23 03	I	Sh.E
29 00 07	II	Sh.I
29 02 50	II	Sh.E
30 04 13	I	Sh.I
31 01 33	I	Ec.D
31 22 42	I	Sh.I
31 23 38	III	Sh.I
September		
1 00 57	I	Sh.E

GMT (d h m)	Sat.	Phen.
September		
1 02 55	III	Sh.E
5 02 43	II	Sh.I
6 20 56	II	Ec.D
7 03 27	I	Ec.D
8 00 37	I	Sh.I
8 02 52	I	Sh.E
8 03 39	III	Sh.I
8 21 50	IV	Sh.E
8 21 56	I	Ec.D
9 21 21	I	Sh.E
13 23 33	II	Ec.D
15 02 32	I	Sh.I
15 04 47	I	Sh.E
15 21 18	II	Sh.E
15 23 51	I	Ec.D
16 02 05	I	Sh.I
16 21 00	I	Sh.I
16 23 16	I	Sh.E
17 04 30	IV	Ec.D
17 20 34	I	Ec.R
19 00 51	III	Ec.R
22 21 12	II	Sh.I
22 23 53	II	Sh.E
23 04 00	I	Ec.R
23 22 55	I	Sh.I
24 01 11	I	Sh.E
24 22 29	I	Ec.R
25 19 40	I	Sh.E
29 18 58	III	Sh.E
29 23 48	II	Sh.I
30 02 28	II	Sh.E
October		
1 00 51	I	Sh.I
1 03 06	I	Sh.E
1 20 52	II	Ec.R
2 00 23	I	Ec.R
2 19 20	I	Sh.I
2 21 35	I	Sh.E
3 18 52	I	Ec.R
3 22 51	IV	Ec.D
4 01 01	IV	Ec.R
6 19 48	III	Sh.I
6 23 00	III	Sh.E
7 02 23	II	Sh.I
8 02 46	I	Sh.I
8 23 31	II	Ec.R
9 02 18	I	Ec.R
9 21 15	I	Sh.I
9 23 30	I	Sh.E
10 18 21	II	Sh.E
10 20 47	I	Ec.R
13 23 50	III	Sh.I
14 03 01	III	Sh.E
16 02 09	II	Ec.R
16 23 11	I	Sh.I
17 01 25	I	Sh.E
17 18 17	II	Sh.I
17 20 57	II	Sh.E
17 22 42	I	Ec.R
18 19 54	I	Sh.E
20 19 05	IV	Ec.R
24 01 06	I	Sh.I
24 17 44	III	Ec.D
24 20 53	II	Sh.I

GMT (d h m)	Sat.	Phen.
October		
24 20 55	III	Ec.R
24 23 32	II	Sh.E
25 00 37	I	Ec.R
25 19 35	I	Sh.I
25 21 50	I	Sh.E
26 18 06	II	Ec.R
26 19 05	I	Ec.R
31 21 47	III	Ec.D
31 23 29	II	Sh.I
November		
1 00 57	III	Ec.R
1 21 31	I	Sh.I
1 23 45	I	Sh.E
2 20 45	II	Ec.R
2 21 01	I	Ec.R
3 18 14	I	Sh.E
8 23 27	I	Sh.I
9 22 56	I	Ec.R
9 23 24	II	Ec.R
10 17 56	I	Sh.I
10 20 10	I	Sh.E
11 17 25	I	Ec.R
11 18 01	II	Sh.E
11 19 07	III	Sh.I
14 21 20	IV	Sh.I
14 22 08	IV	Sh.E
17 19 52	I	Sh.I
17 22 06	I	Sh.E
18 17 58	II	Sh.I
18 19 20	I	Ec.R
18 20 03	III	Sh.I
18 20 36	II	Sh.E
18 23 08	III	Sh.E
24 21 48	I	Sh.I
25 00 02	I	Sh.E
25 20 35	II	Sh.I

GMT (d h m)	Sat.	Phen.
November		
25 21 15	I	Ec.R
25 23 12	II	Sh.E
26 00 07	III	Sh.I
26 18 31	I	Sh.E
27 18 02	II	Ec.R
29 17 02	III	Ec.R
December		
1 23 44	I	Sh.I
2 23 11	I	Ec.R
2 23 11	II	Sh.I
3 18 13	I	Sh.I
3 20 27	I	Sh.E
4 17 39	I	Ec.R
4 17 59	II	Ec.D
4 20 40	II	Ec.R
6 17 59	III	Ec.D
6 21 04	III	Ec.R
10 20 10	I	Sh.I
10 22 23	I	Sh.E
11 19 35	I	Ec.R
11 20 38	II	Ec.D
13 17 42	II	Sh.E
13 22 01	III	Ec.D
17 22 06	I	Sh.I
18 21 30	I	Ec.R
19 18 48	I	Sh.E
20 17 41	II	Sh.I
20 20 18	II	Sh.E
24 19 17	III	Sh.E
26 18 31	I	Sh.I
26 20 44	I	Sh.E
27 17 54	I	Ec.R
27 20 18	II	Sh.I
29 17 55	II	Ec.R
31 20 21	III	Sh.I

Jupiter's satellites transit across the disk from east to west, and pass behind the disk from west to east. The shadows that they cast also transit across the disk. With the exception at times of Satellite IV, the satellites also pass through the shadow of the planet, i.e. they are eclipsed. Just before opposition the satellite disappears in the shadow to the west of the planet and reappears from occultation on the east limb. Immediately after opposition the satellite is occulted at the west limb and reappears from eclipse to the east of the planet. At times approximately two to four months before and after opposition, both phases of eclipses of Satellite III may be seen. When Satellite IV is eclipsed, both phases may be seen.

The times given refer to the centre of the satellite. As the satellite is of considerable size, the immersion and emersion phases are not instantaneous. Even when the satellite enters or leaves the shadow along a radius of the shadow, the phase can last for several minutes. With Satellite IV, grazing phenomena can occur so that the light from the satellite may fade and brighten again without a complete eclipse taking place.

The list of phenomena gives most of the eclipses and shadow transits visible in the British Isles under favourable conditions.

Ec. = Eclipse	R. = Reappearance
Sh. = Shadow transit	I. = Ingress
D. = Disappearance	E. = Egress

EXPLANATION OF ASTRONOMICAL DATA

Positions of the heavenly bodies are given only to the degree of accuracy required by amateur astronomers for setting telescopes, or for plotting on celestial globes or star atlases. Where intermediate positions are required, linear interpolation may be employed.

Definitions of the terms used cannot be given here. They must be sought in astronomical literature and textbooks. Probably the best source for the amateur is Norton's *Star Atlas and Reference Handbook* (Longman, 18th edition, 1989, £26.00), which contains an introduction to observational astronomy, and a series of star maps for showing stars visible to the naked eye. Certain more extended ephemerides are available in the British Astronomical Association Handbook, an annual popular among amateur astronomers (Secretary: Burlington House, Piccadilly, London WIV 9AG).

A special feature has been made of the times when the various heavenly bodies are visible in the British Isles. Since two columns, calculated for latitudes 52° and 56°, are devoted to risings and settings, the range 50° to 58° can be covered by interpolation and extrapolation. The times given in these columns are Greenwich Mean Times for the meridian of Greenwich. An observer west of this meridian must add his/her longitude (in time) and vice versa.

In accordance with the usual convention in astronomy, + and − indicate respectively north and south latitudes or declinations.

All data are, unless otherwise stated, for 0h Greenwich Mean Time (GMT), i.e. at the midnight at the beginning of the day named. Allowance must be made for British Summer Time during the period that this is in operation (*see* pages 15 and 75).

PAGE ONE OF EACH MONTH

The calendar for each month is explained on page 15.

Under the heading Astronomical Phenomena will be found particulars of the more important conjunctions of the Sun, Moon and planets with each other, and also the dates of other astronomical phenomena of special interest.

Times of Minima of Algol are approximate times of the middle of the period of diminished light.

The Constellations listed each month are those that are near the meridian at the beginning of the month at 22h local mean time. Allowance must be made for British Summer Time if necessary. The fact that any star crosses the meridian 4m earlier each night or 2h earlier each month may be used, in conjunction with the lists given each month, to find what constellations are favourably placed at any moment. The table preceding the list of constellations may be extended indefinitely at the rate just quoted.

The principal phases of the Moon are the GMTs when the difference between the longitude of the Moon and that of the Sun is 0°, 90°, 180° or 270°. The times of perigee and apogee are those when the Moon is nearest to, and farthest from, the Earth, respectively. The nodes or points of intersection of the Moon's orbit and the ecliptic make a complete retrograde circuit of the ecliptic in about 19 years. From a knowledge of the longitude of the ascending node and the inclination, whose value does not vary much from 5°, the path of the Moon among the stars may be plotted on a celestial globe or star atlas.

PAGE TWO OF EACH MONTH

The Sun's semi-diameter, in arc, is given once a month.

The right ascension and declination (Dec.) is that of the true Sun. The right ascension of the mean Sun is obtained by applying the equation of time, with the sign given, to the right ascension of the true Sun, or, more easily, by applying 12h to the Sidereal Time. The direction in which the equation of time has to be applied in different problems is a frequent source of confusion and error. Apparent Solar Time is equal to the Mean Solar Time plus the Equation of Time. For example at noon on August 8 the Equation of Time is − 5m 39s and thus at 12h Mean Time on that day the Apparent Time is 12h − 5m 39s = 11h 54m 21s.

The Greenwich Sidereal Time at 0h and the Transit of the First Point of Aries (which is really the mean time when the sidereal time is 0h) are used for converting mean time to sidereal time and vice versa.

The GMT of transit of the Sun at Greenwich may also be taken as the local mean time (LMT) of transit in any longitude. It is independent of latitude. The GMT of transit in any longitude is obtained by adding the longitude to the time given if west, and vice versa.

LIGHTING-UP TIME

The legal importance of sunrise and sunset is that the Road Vehicles Lighting Regulations 1989 (SI 1989 No. 1796) make the use of front and rear position lamps on vehicles compulsory during the period between sunset and sunrise. Headlamps on vehicles are required to be used during the hours of darkness on unlit roads or whenever visibility is seriously reduced. The hours of darkness are defined in these regulations as the period between half an hour after sunset and half an hour before sunrise.

In all laws and regulations 'sunset' refers to the local sunset, i.e. the time at which the Sun sets at the place in question. This common-sense interpretation has been upheld by legal tribunals. Thus the necessity for providing for different latitudes and longitudes, as already described, is evident.

SUNRISE AND SUNSET

The times of sunrise and sunset are those when the Sun's upper limb, as affected by refraction, is on the true horizon of an observer at sea-level. Assuming the mean refraction to be 34′, and the Sun's semi-diameter to be 16′, the time given is that when the true zenith distance of the Sun's centre is 90° + 34′ + 16′ or 90° 50′, or, in other words, when the depression of the Sun's centre below the true horizon is 50′. The upper limb is then 34′ below the true horizon, but is brought there by refraction. It is true, of course, that an observer on a ship might see the Sun for a minute or so longer, because of the dip of the horizon, while another viewing the sunset over hills or mountains would record an earlier time. Nevertheless, the moment when the true zenith distance of the Sun's centre is 90° 50′ is a precise time dependent only on the latitude and longitude of the place, and independent of its altitude above sea-level, the contour of its horizon, the vagaries of refraction or the small seasonal change in the Sun's semi-diameter; this moment is suitable in every way as a definition of sunset (or sunrise) for all statutory purposes. (For further information, *see* footnote on page 72.)

TWILIGHT

Light reaches us before sunrise and continues to reach us for some time after sunset. The interval between darkness and sunrise or sunset and darkness is called twilight. Astronomically speaking, twilight is considered to begin or end when the Sun's centre is 18° below the horizon, as no light from the Sun can then reach the observer. As thus defined twilight may last several hours; in high latitudes at the summer solstice the depression of 18° is not reached, and twilight lasts from sunset to sunrise.

The need for some sub-division of twilight is met by dividing the gathering darkness into four stages.

(1) *Sunrise or Sunset*, defined as above
(2) *Civil twilight*, which begins or ends when the Sun's centre is 6° below the horizon. This marks the time when operations requiring daylight may commence or must cease. In England it varies from about 30 to 60 minutes after sunset and the same interval before sunrise
(3) *Nautical twilight*, which begins or ends when the Sun's centre is 12° below the horizon. This marks the time when it is, to all intents and purposes, completely dark
(4) *Astronomical twilight*, which begins or ends when the Sun's centre is 18° below the horizon. This marks theoretical perfect darkness. It is of little practical importance, especially if nautical twilight is tabulated

To assist observers the durations of civil, nautical and astronomical twilights are given at intervals of ten days. The beginning of a particular twilight is found by subtracting the duration from the time of sunrise, while the end is found by adding the duration to the time of sunset. Thus the beginning of astronomical twilight in latitude 52°, on the Greenwich meridian, on March 11 is found as 06h 24m − 113m = 04h 31m and similarly the end of civil twilight as 17h 57m + 34m = 18h 31m. The letters TAN (twilight all night) are printed when twilight lasts all night.

Under the heading The Night Sky will be found notes describing the position and visibility of the planets and other phenomena.

PAGE THREE OF EACH MONTH

The Moon moves so rapidly among the stars that its position is given only to the degree of accuracy that permits linear interpolation. The right ascension (RA) and declination (Dec.) are geocentric, i.e. for an imaginary observer at the centre of the Earth. To an observer on the surface of the Earth the position is always different, as the altitude is always less on account of parallax, which may reach 1°.

The lunar terminator is the line separating the bright from the dark part of the Moon's disk. Apart from irregularities of the lunar surface, the terminator is elliptical, because it is a circle seen in projection. It becomes the full circle forming the limb, or edge, of the Moon at New and Full Moon. The selenographic longitude of the terminator is measured from the mean centre of the visible disk, which may differ from the visible centre by as much as 8°, because of libration.

Instead of the longitude of the terminator the Sun's selenographic co-longitude (Sun's co-long.) is tabulated. It is numerically equal to the selenographic longitude of the morning terminator, measured eastwards from the mean centre of the disk. Thus its value is approximately 270° at New Moon, 360° at First Quarter, 90° at Full Moon and 180° at Last Quarter.

The Position Angle (PA) of the Bright Limb is the position angle of the midpoint of the illuminated limb, measured eastwards from the north point on the disk. The Phase column shows the percentage of the area of the Moon's disk illuminated; this is also the illuminated percentage of the diameter at right angles to the line of cusps. The terminator is a semi-ellipse whose major axis is the line of cusps, and whose semi-minor axis is determined by the tabulated percentage; from New Moon to Full Moon the east limb is dark, and vice versa.

The times given as moonrise and moonset are those when the upper limb of the Moon is on the horizon of an observer at sea-level. The Sun's horizontal parallax (Hor. par.) is about 9″, and is negligible when considering sunrise and sunset, but that of the Moon averages about 57′. Hence the computed time represents the moment when the true zenith distance of the Moon is 90° 50′ (as for the Sun) minus the horizontal parallax. The time required for the Sun or Moon to rise or set is about four minutes (except in high latitudes). *See also* page 65 and footnote below.

The GMT of transit of the Moon over the meridian of Greenwich is given; these times are independent of latitude but must be corrected for longitude. For places in the British Isles it suffices to add the longitude if west, and vice versa. For other places a further correction is necessary because of the rapid movement of the Moon relative to the stars. The entire correction is conveniently determined by first finding the west longitude λ of the place. If the place is in west longitude, λ is the ordinary west longitude; if the place is in east longitude λ is the complement to 24h (or 360°) of the longitude and will be greater than 12h (or 180°). The correction then consists of two positive portions, namely λ and the fraction $\lambda/24$ (or $\lambda°/360$) multiplied by the difference between consecutive transits. Thus for Sydney, New South Wales, the longitude is 10h 05m east, so λ=13h 55m and the fraction $\lambda/24$ is 0.58. The transit on the local date 1998 January 14 is found as follows:

		d	h	m
GMT of transit at Greenwich	Jan.	13	00	20
λ			13	55
0.58×(1h 10m−0h 20m)				29
GMT of transit at Sydney		13	14	44
Corr. to NSW Standard Time			10	00
Local standard time of transit		14	00	44

As is evident, for any given place the quantities λ and the correction to local standard time may be combined permanently, being here 23h 55m.

Positions of Mercury are given for every second day, and those of Venus and Mars for every fifth day; they may be interpolated linearly. The diameter (Diam.) is given in seconds of arc. The phase is the illuminated percentage of the disk. In the case of the inner planets this approaches 100 at superior conjunction and 0 at inferior conjunction. When the phase is less than 50 the planet is crescent-shaped or horned; for greater phases it is gibbous. In the case of the exterior planet Mars, the phase approaches 100 at conjunction and opposition, and is a minimum at the quadratures.

Since the planets cannot be seen when on the horizon, the actual times of rising and setting are not given; instead, the time when the planet has an apparent altitude of 5° has

---

SUNRISE, SUNSET AND MOONRISE, MOONSET
The tables have been constructed for the meridian of Greenwich, and for latitudes 52° and 56°. They give Greenwich Mean Time (GMT) throughout the year. To obtain the GMT of the phenomenon as seen from any other latitude and longitude in the British Isles, first interpolate or extrapolate for latitude by the usual rules of proportion. To the time thus found, the longitude (expressed in time) is to be added if west (as it usually is in Great Britain) or subtracted if east. If the longitude is expressed in degrees and minutes of arc, it must be converted to time at the rate of 1° = 4m and 15′ = 1m.

A method of calculating rise and set times for other places in the world is given on pages 64 and 65

been tabulated. If the time of transit is between 00h and 12h the time refers to an altitude of 5° above the eastern horizon; if between 12h and 24h, to the western horizon. The phenomenon tabulated is the one that occurs between sunset and sunrise. The times given may be interpolated for latitude and corrected for longitude, as in the case of the Sun and Moon.

The GMT at which the planet transits the Greenwich meridian is also given. The times of transit are to be corrected to local meridians in the usual way, as already described.

PAGE FOUR OF EACH MONTH

The GMTs of sunrise and sunset for seven cities, whose adopted positions in longitude (W.) and latitude (N.) are given immediately below the name, may be used not only for these phenomena, but also for lighting-up times (see page 71 for a fuller explanation).

The particulars for the four outer planets resemble those for the planets on Page Three of each month, except that, under Uranus and Neptune, times when the planet is 10° high instead of 5° high are given; this is because of the inferior brightness of these planets. The diameters given for the rings of Saturn are those of the major axis (in the plane of the planet's equator) and the minor axis respectively. The former has a small seasonal change due to the slightly varying distance of the Earth from Saturn, but the latter varies from zero when the Earth passes through the ring plane every 15 years to its maximum opening half-way between these periods. The rings were last open at their widest extent (and Saturn at its brightest) in 1988; this will occur again in 2002. The Earth passed through the ring plane in 1995–6 and will do so again in 2009.

TIME

From the earliest ages, the natural division of time into recurring periods of day and night has provided the practical time-scale for the everyday activities of the human race. Indeed, if any alternative means of time measurement is adopted, it must be capable of adjustment so as to remain in general agreement with the natural time-scale defined by the diurnal rotation of the Earth on its axis. Ideally the rotation should be measured against a fixed frame of reference; in practice it must be measured against the background provided by the celestial bodies. If the Sun is chosen as the reference point, we obtain Apparent Solar Time, which is the time indicated by a sundial. It is not a uniform time but is subject to variations which amount to as much as a quarter of an hour in each direction. Such wide variations cannot be tolerated in a practical time-scale, and this has led to the concept of Mean Solar Time in which all the days are exactly the same length and equal to the average length of the Apparent Solar Day.

The positions of the stars in the sky are specified in relation to a fictitious reference point in the sky known as the First Point of Aries (or the Vernal Equinox). It is therefore convenient to adopt this same reference point when considering the rotation of the Earth against the background of the stars. The time-scale so obtained is known as Apparent Sidereal Time.

GREENWICH MEAN TIME

The daily rotation of the Earth on its axis causes the Sun and the other heavenly bodies to appear to cross the sky from east to west. It is convenient to represent this relative motion as if the Sun really performed a daily circuit around a fixed Earth. Noon in Apparent Solar Time may then be defined as the time at which the Sun transits across the observer's meridian. In Mean Solar Time, noon is similarly defined by the meridian transit of a fictitious Mean Sun moving uniformly in the sky with the same average speed as the true Sun. Mean Solar Time observed on the meridian of the transit circle telescope of the Old Royal Observatory at Greenwich is called Greenwich Mean Time (GMT). The mean solar day is divided into 24 hours and, for astronomical and other scientific purposes, these are numbered 0 to 23, commencing at midnight. Civil time is usually reckoned in two periods of 12 hours, designated a.m. (ante meridiem, i.e. before noon) and p.m. (post meridiem, i.e. after noon).

UNIVERSAL TIME

Before 1925 January 1, GMT was reckoned in 24 hours commencing at noon; since that date it has been reckoned from midnight. To avoid confusion in the use of the designation GMT before and after 1925, since 1928 astronomers have tended to use the term Universal Time (UT) or Weltzeit (WZ) to denote GMT measured from Greenwich Mean Midnight.

In precision work it is necessary to take account of small variations in Universal Time. These arise from small irregularities in the rotation of the Earth. Observed astronomical time is designated UT0. Observed time corrected for the effects of the motion of the poles (giving rise to a 'wandering' in longitude) is designated UT1. There is also a seasonal fluctuation in the rate of rotation of the Earth arising from meteorological causes, often called the annual fluctuation. UT1 corrected for this effect is designated UT2 and provides a time-scale free from short-period fluctuations. It is still subject to small secular and irregular changes.

APPARENT SOLAR TIME

As mentioned above, the time shown by a sundial is called Apparent Solar Time. It differs from Mean Solar Time by an amount known as the Equation of Time, which is the total effect of two causes which make the length of the apparent solar day non uniform. One cause of variation is that the orbit of the Earth is not a circle but an ellipse, having the Sun at one focus. As a consequence, the angular speed of the Earth in its orbit is not constant; it is greatest at the beginning of January when the Earth is nearest the Sun.

The other cause is due to the obliquity of the ecliptic; the plane of the equator (which is at right angles to the axis of rotation of the Earth) does not coincide with the ecliptic (the plane defined by the apparent annual motion of the Sun around the celestial sphere) but is inclined to it at an angle of 23° 26'. As a result, the apparent solar day is shorter than average at the equinoxes and longer at the solstices. From the combined effects of the components due to obliquity and eccentricity, the equation of time reaches its maximum values in February (−14 minutes) and early November (+16 minutes). It has a zero value on four dates during the year, and it is only on these dates (approximately April 15, June 14, September 1, and December 25) that a sundial shows Mean Solar Time.

SIDEREAL TIME

A sidereal day is the duration of a complete rotation of the Earth with reference to the First Point of Aries. The term sidereal (or 'star') time is a little misleading since the time-scale so defined is not exactly the same as that which would be defined by successive transits of a selected star, as there is a small progressive motion between the stars and the First Point of Aries due to the precession of the Earth's axis. This makes the length of the sidereal day shorter than the true period of rotation by 0.008 seconds. Superimposed on this steady precessional motion are small oscillations (nutation), giving rise to fluctuations in apparent sidereal time amounting to as much as 1.2 seconds. It is therefore customary to employ Mean Sidereal Time, from which these fluctuations have been removed. The conversion of GMT to Greenwich sidereal time (GST) may be performed by adding the value of the GST at 0h on the day in question (Page Two of each month) to the GMT converted to sidereal time using the table on page 69.

Example – To find the GST at August 8d 02h 41m 11s GMT

	h	m	s
GST at 0h	21	05	12
GMT	2	41	11
Acceleration for 2h			20
Acceleration for 41m 11s			7
Sum = GST =	23	46	50

If the observer is not on the Greenwich meridian then his/her longitude, measured positively westwards from Greenwich, must be subtracted from the GST to obtain Local Sidereal Time (LST). Thus, in the above example, an observer 5h east of Greenwich, or 19h west, would find the LST as 4h 46m 50s.

EPHEMERIS TIME

An analysis of observations of the positions of the Sun, Moon and planets taken over an extended period is used in preparing ephemerides. (An ephemeris is a table giving the apparent position of a heavenly body at regular intervals of time, e.g. one day or ten days, and may be used to compare current observations with tabulated positions.) Discrepancies between the positions of heavenly bodies observed over a 300-year period and their predicted positions arose because the time-scale to which the observations were related was based on the assumption that the rate of rotation of the Earth is uniform. It is now known that this rate of rotation is variable. A revised time-scale, Ephemeris Time (ET), was devised to bring the ephemerides into agreement with the observations.

The second of ET is defined in terms of the annual motion of the Earth in its orbit around the Sun (1/31556925.9747 of the tropical year for 1900 January 0d 12h ET). The precise determination of ET from astronomical observations is a lengthy process as the requisite standard of accuracy can only be achieved by averaging over a number of years.

In 1976 the International Astronomical Union adopted a new dynamical time-scale for general use whose scale unit is the SI second (*see* Atomic Time). ET is now of little more than historical interest.

TERRESTRIAL DYNAMICAL TIME

The uniform time system used in computing the ephemerides of the solar system is Terrestrial Dynamical Time (TDT), which has replaced ET for this purpose. Except for the most rigorous astronomical calculations, it may be assumed to be the same as ET. During 1998 the estimated difference TDT – UT is about 64 seconds.

ATOMIC TIME

The fundamental standards of time and frequency must be defined in terms of a periodic motion adequately uniform, enduring and measurable. Progress has made it possible to use natural standards, such as atomic or molecular oscillations. Continuous oscillations are generated in an electrical circuit, the frequency of which is then compared or brought into coincidence with the frequency characteristic

of the absorption or emission by the atoms or molecules when they change between two selected energy levels. The National Physical Laboratory (NPL) routinely uses clocks of high stability produced by locking a quartz oscillator to the frequencies defined by caesium or hydrogen atoms.

International Atomic Time (TAI), established through international collaboration, is formed by combining the readings of many caesium clocks and was set close to the astronomically-based Universal Time (UT) near the beginning of 1958. It was formally recognized in 1971 and since 1988 January 1 has been maintained by the International Bureau of Weights and Measures (BIPM). The second markers are generated according to the International System (SI) definition adopted in 1967 at the 13th General Conference of Weights and Measures: 'The second is the duration of 9 192 631 770 periods of the radiation corresponding to the transition between the two hyperfine levels of the ground state of the caesium-133 atom.'

Civil time in almost all countries is now based on Co-ordinated Universal Time (UTC), which was adopted for scientific purposes on 1972 January 1. UTC differs from TAI by an integer number of seconds (determined from studies of the rate of rotation of the Earth) and was designed to make both atomic time and UT accessible with accuracies appropriate for most users. The UTC time-scale is adjusted by the insertion (or, in principle, omission) of leap seconds in order to keep it within ±0.9 s of UT. These leap seconds are introduced, when necessary, at the same instant throughout the world, either at the end of December or at the end of June. So, for example, the 21st leap second occurred at 0h UT on 1997 July 1. All leap seconds so far have been positive, with 61 seconds in the final minute of the UTC month. The time 23h 59m 60s UTC is followed one second later by 0h 0m 00s of the first day of the following month. Notices concerning the insertion of leap seconds are issued by the International Earth Rotation Service (IERS) at the Observatoire de Paris.

RADIO TIME-SIGNALS

UTC is made generally available through time-signals and standard frequency broadcasts such as MSF in the UK, CHU in Canada and WWV and WWVH in the USA. These are based on national time-scales that are maintained in close agreement with UTC and provide traceability to the national time-scale and to UTC. The markers of seconds in the UTC scale coincide with those of TAI.

To disseminate the national time-scale in the UK, special signals are broadcast on behalf of the National Physical Laboratory from the BT (British Telecom) radio station at Rugby (call-sign MSF). The signals are controlled from a caesium beam atomic frequency standard and consist of a precise frequency carrier of 60 kHz which is switched off, after being on for at least half a second, to mark every second. In part of the first second of each minute the carrier may be switched on and off to carry data at 100 bits/second. In the other seconds the carrier is always off for at least one tenth of a second at the start and then it carries an on-off code giving the British clock time and date, together with information identifying the start of the next minute. Changes to and from summer time are made following government announcements. Leap seconds are inserted as announced by the IERS and information provided by them on the difference between UTC and UT is also signalled. Other broadcast signals in the UK include the BBC six pips signal, the BT Timeline (the 'speaking clock'), the NPL Truetime service for computers, and a coded time-signal on the BBC 198 kHz transmitters which is used for timing in the electricity supply industry. From 1972 January 1 the six pips on the BBC have consisted of five short pips from second 55 to second 59 (six pips in the case of a leap second) followed by one lengthened pip, the start of which indicates the exact minute. From 1990 February 5 these signals have been controlled by the BBC with seconds markers referenced to the satellite-based US navigation system GPS (Global Positioning System) and time and day referenced to the MSF transmitter. Formerly they were generated by the Royal Greenwich Observatory. The BT Timeline is compared daily with the National Physical Laboratory caesium beam atomic frequency standard at the Rugby radio station. The NPL Truetime service is directly connected to the national time scale.

Accurate timing may also be obtained from the signals of international navigation systems such as the ground-based Omega, or the satellite-based American GPS or Russian GLONASS systems.

STANDARD TIME

Since 1880 the standard time in Britain has been Greenwich Mean Time (GMT); a statute that year enacted that the word 'time' when used in any legal document relating to Britain meant, unless otherwise specifically stated, the mean time of the Greenwich meridian. Greenwich was adopted as the universal meridian on 13 October 1884. A system of standard time by zones is used world-wide, standard time in each zone differing from that of the Greenwich meridian by an integral number of hours, either fast or slow. The large territories of the USA and Canada are divided into zones approximately 7.5° on either side of central meridians. (For time zones of countries of the world, *see* Index.)

Variations from the standard time of some countries occur during part of the year; they are decided annually and are usually referred to as Summer Time or Daylight Saving Time.

At the 180th meridian the time can be either 12 hours fast on Greenwich Mean Time or 12 hours slow, and a change of date occurs. The internationally-recognized date or calendar line is a modification of the 180th meridian, drawn so as to include islands of any one group on the same side of the line, or for political reasons. The line is indicated by joining up the following co-ordinates:

Lat.	Long.	Lat.	Long.
60° S.	180°	48° N.	180°
51° S.	180°	53° N.	170° E.
45° S.	172.5° W.	65.5° N. 169° W.	
15° S.	172.5° W.	75° N.	180°
5° S.	180°		

BRITISH SUMMER TIME

In 1916 an Act ordained that during a defined period of that year the legal time for general purposes in Great Britain should be one hour in advance of Greenwich Mean Time. The Summer Time Acts 1922 and 1925 defined the period during which Summer Time was to be in force, stabilizing practice until the Second World War.

During the war the duration of Summer Time was extended and in the years 1941 to 1945 and in 1947 Double Summer Time (two hours in advance of Greenwich Mean Time) was in force. After the war, Summer Time was extended each year in 1948–52 and 1961–4 by Order in Council.

Between 1968 October 27 and 1971 October 31 clocks were kept one hour ahead of Greenwich Mean Time throughout the year. This was known as British Standard Time.

The most recent legislation is the Summer Time Act 1972, which enacted that 'the period of summer time for the purposes of this Act is the period beginning at two o'clock, Greenwich mean time, in the morning of the day after the third Saturday in March or, if that day is Easter Day, the day after the second Saturday in March, and ending at two o'clock, Greenwich mean time, in the morning of the day after the fourth Saturday in October.'

The duration of Summer Time can be varied by Order in Council and in recent years alterations have been made to bring the operation of Summer Time in Britain closer to similar provisions in other countries of the European Union; for instance, since 1981 the hour of changeover has been 01h Greenwich Mean Time.

The duration of Summer Time in 1998 is provisionally set to start on 29 March and end on 25 October, but these dates were subject to confirmation at the time of going to press.

MEAN REFRACTION

Alt.	Ref.		Alt.	Ref.		Alt.	Ref.	
° '	'		° '	'		° '	'	
1 20			3 12			7 54		
1 30	21		3 34	13		9 27	6	
1 41	20		4 00	12		11 39	5	
1 52	19		4 30	11		15 00	4	
2 05	18		5 06	10		20 42	3	
2 19	17		5 50	9		32 20	2	
2 35	16		6 44	8		62 17	1	
2 52	15		7 54	7		90 00	0	
3 12	14							

The refraction table is in the form of a critical table (*see* page 69)

ASTRONOMICAL CONSTANTS

Solar parallax	8".794
Astronomical unit	149597870 km
Precession for the year 1998	50".291
Precession in right ascension	3s.075
Precession in declination	20".043
Constant of nutation	9".202
Constant of aberration	20".496
Mean obliquity of ecliptic (1998)	23° 26' 22"
Moon's equatorial hor. parallax	57' 02".70
Velocity of light in vacuo per second	299792.5 km
Solar motion per second	20.0 km
Equatorial radius of the Earth	6378.140 km
Polar radius of the Earth	6356.755 km
North galactic pole (IAU standard)	RA 12h 49m (1950.0). Dec. 27°.4 N.
Solar apex	RA 18h 06m Dec. +30°

Length of year (in mean solar days)

Tropical	365.24219
Sidereal	365.25636
Anomalistic (perihelion to perihelion)	365.25964
Eclipse	346.6200

Length of month (mean values)

	d	h	m	s
New Moon to New	29	12	44	02.9
Sidereal	27	07	43	11.5
Anomalistic (perigee to perigee)	27	13	18	33.2

ELEMENTS OF THE SOLAR SYSTEM

Orb	Mean distance from Sun (Earth = 1)	km 10^6	Sidereal period days	Synodic period days	Incl. of orbit to ecliptic ° '	Diameter km	Mass (Earth = 1)	Period of rotation on axis days
Sun	—	—	—	—	—	1,392,530	332,946	25–35*
Mercury	0.39	58	88.0	116	7 00	4,879	0.0553	58.646
Venus	0.72	108	224.7	584	3 24	12,104	0.8150	243.019r
Earth	1.00	150	365.3	—	—	12,756e	1.0000	0.997
Mars	1.52	228	687.0	780	1 51	6,794e	0.1074	1.026
Jupiter	5.20	778	4,332.6	399	1 18	142,984e / 133,708p	317.89	{ 0.410e
Saturn	9.54	1427	10,759.2	378	2 29	120,536e / 108,728p	95.18	{ 0.426e
Uranus	19.18	2870	30,684.6	370	0 46	51,118e	14.54	0.718r
Neptune	30.06	4497	60,191.0	367	1 46	49,528e	17.15	0.671
Pluto	39.80	5954	91,708.2	367	17 09	2,302	0.002	6.387

e equatorial, p polar, r retrograde, * depending on latitude

THE SATELLITES

Name	Star mag.	Mean distance from primary km	Sidereal period of revolution d	Name	Star mag.	Mean distance from primary km	Sidereal period of revolution d
EARTH				SATURN			
I Moon	—	384,400	27.322	VII Hyperion	14	1,481,100	21.277
MARS				VIII Iapetus	11	3,561,300	79.330
I Phobos	12	9,378	0.319	IX Phoebe	16	12,952,000	550.48r
II Deimos	13	23,459	1.262	URANUS			
JUPITER				VI Cordelia	—	49,770	0.335
XVI Metis	17	127,960	0.295	VII Ophelia	—	53,790	0.376
XV Adrastea	19	128,980	0.298	VIII Bianca	—	59,170	0.435
V Amalthea	14	181,300	0.498	IX Cressida	—	61,780	0.464
XIV Thebe	16	221,900	0.675	X Desdemona	—	62,680	0.474
I Io	5	421,600	1.769	XI Juliet	—	64,350	0.493
II Europa	5	670,900	3.551	XII Portia	—	66,090	0.513
III Ganymede	5	1,070,000	7.155	XIII Rosalind	—	69,940	0.558
IV Callisto	6	1,883,000	16.689	XIV Belinda	—	75,260	0.624
XIII Leda	20	11,094,000	239	XV Puck	—	86,010	0.762
VI Himalia	15	11,480,000	251	V Miranda	17	129,390	1.413
X Lysithea	18	11,720,000	259	I Ariel	14	191,020	2.520
VII Elara	17	11,737,000	260	II Umbriel	15	266,300	4.144
XII Ananke	19	21,200,000	631r	III Titania	14	435,910	8.706
XI Carme	18	22,600,000	692r	IV Oberon	14	583,520	13.463
VIII Pasiphae	17	23,500,000	735r	NEPTUNE			
IX Sinope	18	23,700,000	758r	III Naiad	25	48,230	0.294
SATURN				IV Thalassa	24	50,070	0.311
XVIII Pan	—	133,583	0.575	V Despina	23	52,530	0.335
XV Atlas	18	137,670	0.602	VI Galatea	22	61,950	0.429
XVI Prometheus	16	139,353	0.613	VII Larissa	22	73,550	0.555
XVII Pandora	16	141,700	0.629	VIII Proteus	20	117,650	1.122
XI Epimetheus	15	151,422	0.694	I Triton	13	354,760	5.877
X Janus	14	151,472	0.695	II Nereid	19	5,513,400	360.136
I Mimas	13	185,520	0.942	PLUTO			
II Enceladus	12	238,020	1.370	I Charon	17	19,600	6.387
III Tethys	10	294,660	1.888				
XIII Telesto	19	294,660	1.888				
XIV Calypso	19	294,660	1.888				
IV Dione	10	377,400	2.737				
XII Helene	18	377,400	2.737				
V Rhea	10	527,040	4.518				
VI Titan	8	1,221,830	15.945				

THE EARTH

The shape of the Earth is that of an oblate spheroid or solid of revolution whose meridian sections are ellipses not differing much from circles, whilst the sections at right angles are circles. The length of the equatorial axis is about 12,756 km, and that of the polar axis is 12,714 km. The mean density of the Earth is 5.5 times that of water, although that of the surface layer is less. The Earth and Moon revolve about their common centre of gravity in a lunar month; this centre in turn revolves round the Sun in a plane known as the ecliptic, that passes through the Sun's centre. The Earth's equator is inclined to this plane at an angle of 23.4°. This tilt is the cause of the seasons. In mid-latitudes, and when the Sun is high above the Equator, not only does the high noon altitude make the days longer, but the Sun's rays fall more directly on the Earth's surface; these effects combine to produce summer. In equatorial regions the noon altitude is large throughout the year, and there is little variation in the length of the day. In higher latitudes the noon altitude is lower, and the days in summer are appreciably longer than those in winter.

The average velocity of the Earth in its orbit is 30 km a second. It makes a complete rotation on its axis in about 23h 56m of mean time, which is the sidereal day. Because of its annual revolution round the Sun, the rotation with respect to the Sun, or the solar day, is more than this by about four minutes (see page 73). The extremity of the axis of rotation, or the North Pole of the Earth, is not rigidly fixed, but wanders over an area roughly 20 metres in diameter.

TERRESTRIAL MAGNETISM

A magnetic compass points along the horizontal component of a magnetic line of force. These lines of force converge on the 'magnetic dip-poles', the places where a freely suspended magnetized needle would become vertical. Not only do these poles move with time, but their exact locations are ill-defined, particularly so in the case of the north dip-pole where the lines of force on the north side of it, instead of converging radially, tend to bunch into a channel. Although it is therefore unrealistic to attempt to specify the locations of the dip-poles exactly, the present approximate adopted positions are 79°.2 N., 106°.2 W. and 64°.6 S., 138° 5 E. The two magnetic dip-poles are thus not antipodal, the line joining them passing the centre of the Earth at a distance of about 1,250 km. The distances of the magnetic dip-poles from the north and south geographical poles are about 1,200 km and 2,800 km respectively.

There is also a 'magnetic equator', at all points of which the vertical component of the Earth's magnetic field is zero and a magnetized needle remains horizontal. This line runs between 2° and 10° north of the geographical equator in Asia and Africa, turns sharply south off the west African coast, and crosses South America through Brazil, Bolivia and Peru; it recrosses the geographical equator in mid-Pacific.

Reference has already been made to secular changes in the Earth's field. The following table indicates the changes in magnetic declination (or variation of the compass). Declination is the angle in the horizontal plane between the direction of true north and that in which a magnetic compass points. Similar, though much smaller, changes have occurred in 'dip' or magnetic inclination. Secular changes differ throughout the world. Although the London

observations strongly suggest a cycle with a period of several hundred years, an exact repetition is unlikely.

London		Greenwich	
1580	11° 15' E.	1850	22° 24' W.
1622	5° 56' E.	1900	16° 29' W.
1665	1° 22' W.	1925	13° 10' W.
1730	13° 00' W.	1950	9° 07' W.
1773	21° 09' W.	1975	6° 57' W.

In order that up-to-date information on declination may be available, many governments publish magnetic charts on which there are lines (isogonic lines) passing through all places at which specified values of declination will be found at the date of the chart.

In the British Isles, isogonic lines now run approximately north-east to south-west. Though there are considerable local deviations due to geological causes, a rough value of magnetic declination may be obtained by assuming that at 50° N. on the meridian of Greenwich, the value in 1998 is 2° 57' west and allowing an increase of 15' for each degree of latitude northwards and one of 28' for each degree of longitude westwards. For example, at 53° N., 5° W., declination will be about 2° 57' + 45' + 140', i.e. 6° 02' west. The average annual change at the present time is about 10' decrease.

The number of magnetic observatories is about 200, irregularly distributed over the globe. There are three in Great Britain, run by the British Geological Survey: at Hartland, north Devon; at Eskdalemuir, Dumfriesshire; and at Lerwick, Shetland Islands. The following are some recent annual mean values of the magnetic elements for Hartland.

Year	Declination West	Dip or inclination	Horizontal force	Vertical force
	° '	° '	gauss	gauss
1960	9 59	66 44	0.1871	0.4350
1965	9 30	66 34	0.1887	0.4354
1970	9 06	66 26	0.1903	0.4364
1975	8 32	66 17	0.1921	0.4373
1980	7 44	66 10	0.1933	0.4377
1985	6 56	66 08	0.1938	0.4300
1990	6 15	66 10	0.1939	0.4388
1995	5 33	66 07	0.1946	0.4395
1996	5 24	66 06	0.1948	0.4396

The normal world-wide terrestrial magnetic field corresponds approximately to that of a very strong small bar magnet near the centre of the Earth, but with appreciable smooth spatial departures. The origin and the slow secular change of the normal field are not fully understood but are generally ascribed to electric currents associated with fluid motions in the Earth's core. Superimposed on the normal field are local and regional anomalies whose magnitudes may in places approach that of the normal field, these are due to the influence of mineral deposits in the Earth's crust. A small proportion of the field is of external origin, mostly associated with electric currents in the ionosphere. The configuration of the external field and the ionization of the atmosphere depend on the incident particle and radiation flux from the Sun. There are, therefore, short-term and non-periodic as well as diurnal, 27-day, seasonal and 11-year periodic changes in the magnetic field, dependent upon the position of the Sun and the degree of solar activity.

MAGNETIC STORMS

Occasionally, sometimes with great suddenness, the Earth's magnetic field is subject for several hours to marked disturbance. During a severe storm in 1989 the declination at Lerwick changed by almost 8° in less than an hour. In many instances such disturbances are accompanied by widespread displays of aurorae, marked changes in the incidence of cosmic rays, an increase in the reception of 'noise' from the Sun at radio frequencies, and rapid changes in the ionosphere and induced electric currents within the Earth which adversely affect radio and telegraphic communications. The disturbances are caused by changes in the stream of ionized particles which emanates from the Sun and through which the Earth is continuously passing. Some of these changes are associated with visible eruptions on the Sun, usually in the region of sun-spots. There is a marked tendency for disturbances to recur after intervals of about 27 days, the apparent period of rotation of the Sun on its axis, which is consistent with the sources being located on particular areas of the Sun.

ARTIFICIAL SATELLITES

To consider the orbit of an artificial satellite, it is best to imagine that one is looking at the Earth from a distant point in space. The Earth would then be seen to be rotating about its axis inside the orbit described by the rapidly revolving satellite. The inclination of a satellite orbit to the Earth's equator (which generally remains almost constant throughout the satellite's lifetime) gives at once the maximum range of latitudes over which the satellite passes. Thus a satellite whose orbit has an inclination of 53° will pass overhead all latitudes between 53° S. and 53° N., but would never be seen in the zenith of any place nearer the poles than these latitudes. If we consider a particular place on the earth, whose latitude is less than the inclination of the satellite's orbit, then the Earth's rotation carries this place first under the northbound part of the orbit and then under the southbound portion of the orbit, these two occurrences being always less than 12 hours apart for satellites moving in direct orbits (i.e. to the east). (For satellites in retrograde orbits, the words 'northbound' and 'southbound' should be interchanged in the preceding statement.) As the value of the latitude of the observer increases and approaches the value of the inclination of the orbit, so this interval gets shorter until (when the latitude is equal to the inclination) only one overhead passage occurs each day.

OBSERVATION OF SATELLITES

The regression of the orbit around the Earth causes alternate periods of visibility and invisibility, though this is of little concern to the radio or radar observer. To the visual observer the following cycle of events normally occurs (though the cycle may start in any position): invisibility, morning observations before dawn, invisibility, evening observations after dusk, invisibility, morning observations before dawn, and so on. With reasonably high satellites and for observers in high latitudes around the summer solstice, the evening observations follow the morning observations without interruption as sunlight passing over the polar regions can still illuminate satellites which are passing over temperate latitudes at local midnight. At the moment all satellites rely on sunlight to make them visible, though a satellite with a flashing light has been suggested for a future launching. The observer must be in darkness or twilight in order to make any useful observations and the durations of twilight and the sunrise, sunset times given on Page Two of each month will be a useful guide.

Some of the satellites are visible to the naked eye and much interest has been aroused by the spectacle of a bright satellite disappearing into the Earth's shadow. The event is even more interesting telescopically as the disappearance occurs gradually as the satellite traverses the Earth's penumbral shadow, and during the last few seconds before the eclipse is complete the satellite may change colour (in suitable atmospheric conditions) from yellow to red. This is because the last rays of sunlight are refracted through the denser layers of our atmosphere before striking the satellite.

Some satellites rotate about one or more axes so that a periodic variation in brightness is observed. This was particularly noticeable in several of the Soviet satellites.

Satellite research has provided some interesting results, including a revised value of the Earth's oblateness (1/298.2), and the discovery of the Van Allen radiation belts.

LAUNCHINGS

Apart from their names, e.g. Cosmos 6 Rocket, the satellites are also classified according to their date of launch. Thus 1961 α refers to the first satellite launching of 1961. A number following the Greek letter indicated the relative brightness of the satellites put in orbit. From the beginning of 1963 the Greek letters were replaced by numbers and the numbers by roman letters e.g. 1963–01A. For all satellites successfully injected into orbit the following table gives the designation and names of the main objects, the launch date and some initial orbital data. These are the inclination to the equator (i), the nodal period of revolution (P), the eccentricity (e), and the perigee height.

Although most of the satellites launched are injected into orbits less than 1,000 km high, there are an increasing number of satellites in geostationary orbits, i.e. where the orbital inclination is zero, the eccentricity close to zero, and the period of revolution is 1436.1 minutes. Thus the satellite is permanently situated over the equator at one selected longitude at a mean height of 35,786 km. This geostationary band is crowded. In one case there are four television satellites (Astra 1A, Astra 1B, Astra 1C and Astra 1D) orbiting within a few tens of kilometres of each other. In the sky they appear to be separated by only a few arc minutes.

ARTIFICIAL SATELLITE LAUNCHES 1996–7

Designation	Satellite	Launch date	i	P	e	Perigee height
1996–			°	m		km
021	Astra 1F, rocket	April 8	0.9	1226.4	0.800	27160
022	MSAT M1, Ariane	April 20	3.7	732.1	0.735	5235
023	PRIRODA, rocket	April 23	51.6	91.1	0.036	281
024	MSX, rocket	April 24	99.2	103.0	0.110	897
025	Cosmos, rocket	April 24	82.9	103.6	0.113	294
026	USA 118, rocket	April 24	0.0	1436.0	0.814	35666
027	SAX, Atlas	April 30	3.7	96.0	0.071	590
028	Progress M31, rocket	May 5	51.6	92.5	0.041	366
029	USA 119-124, Titan	May 12	0.0	1436.1	0.800	32768
030	PALAPA C2, Amos Israel, Ariane	May 16	4.0	1436.5	0.814	35666
031	MSTI 3, rocket	May 17	97.0	90.5	0.029	280
032	Shuttle 77, Spartan 207, IAE	May 19	39.0	90.5	0.031	300
033	Galaxy, rocket	May 23	0.0	1436.1	0.800	32768
034	Gorizont, rocket, platform, rocket	May 25	1.5	1436.0	0.814	35666
035	Intelsat 709, Ariane 44P	June 15	1.0	1436.5	0.814	35666
036	Shuttle 78	June 20	39.0	89.6	0.029	275
037	TOMS-EP, Pegasus	July 2	97.4	97.5	0.079	345
038	SDS2, Titan	July 3	55.0	90.6	0.032	294
039	Apstar 1A, rocket	July 3	0.1	1436.5	0.814	35700
040	Arabsat 2A, Turksat Ariane	July 9	0.1	1436.5	0.814	35678
041	GPS Navstar, rocket	July 16	55.0	717.9	0.733	20135
042	UHF FO 7, rocket	July 25	5.0	1425.3	0.814	34598
043	Progress M32, rocket	July 26	51.6	91.0	0.043	377
044	Italsat, Telecom 2D, rocket	August 8	0.2	1413.8	0.813	34911
045	Molniya 1T, rocket, platform, rocket	August 14	62.7	736.0	0.737	458
046	ADIOS, rocket	August 17	98.5	101.1	0.099	801
047	Soyuz TM24, rocket	August 18	51.6	92.1	0.043	375
048	China 7, rocket	August 19	27.3	307.2	0.557	200
049	FAST, rocket	August 21	83.0	133.2	0.246	352
050	Microsat, INTERBOL 2, Magion 5, rocket	August 29	62.7	98.8	0.085	236
051	Cosmos 2333, rocket	September 4	71.0	102.0	0.104	849
052	Cosmos 2334, Unamsat, rocket	September 7	82.9	104.9	0.120	968
053	INMARSAT 3F2, rocket, rocket	September 6	2.7	1461.2	0.816	36242
054	GE 1, rocket	September 8	19.8	1119.9	0.790	2240
055	Echostar 2, Ariane	September 11	6.9	640.0	0.712	223
056	GPS Navstar, rocket, rocket	September 12	54.5	720.0	0.733	20164
057	Shuttle 79	September 16	51.7	92.1	0.043	376
058	Express 12, rocket	September 26	0.2	1418.9	0.816	35843
059	FSW 2-3, rocket	October 20	63.0	89.5	0.025	172
060	Molniya 3-48, rocket, platform, rocket	October 24	62.7	737.8	0.737	625
061	SAC-B, HELE	November 4	38.0	94.9	0.005	486
062	MARS GLOB SV, rocket, ISO engine	November 7	(Heliocentric orbit)			
063	Arabsat 2B, Measat 2, rocket	November 13	1.0	632.3	0.713	252
064	MARS 96	November 16	51.5	86.8	0.004	111
065	Shuttle 80, Orfeus, Wake	November 19	28.5	91.4	0.039	347
066	Progress M33, rocket	November 19	51.7	90.1	0.029	255
067	HOT BIRD 2, Atlas	November 21	23.8	625.5	0.711	168
068	MARS Pathfinder, rocket	December 4	(Heliocentric orbit)			
069	Cosmos 2335, rocket	December 11	65.0	92.8	0.047	404
070	INMARSAT 3F3, rocket	December 18	22.8	647.5	0.717	1027
071	Cosmos 2336, rocket	December 20	82.9	105.1	0.121	979
072	Keyhole, Titan	December 20	97.9	97.8	0.078	273
073	BION 11, rocket	December 24	62.7	90.4	0.031	217

Desig-nation	Satellite	Launch date	*i*	*P*	*e*	Perigee height
1997–						
001	Shuttle 81	January 12	51.6	89.9	0.028	248
002	GE 2, Nahuel 1A, rocket	January 30	7.5	636.5	0.714	245
003	Soyuz TM 25, rocket	February 10	51.6	90.2	0.030	263
004	Shuttle 82	February 11	28.5	96.4	0.071	590
005	Haruka, rocket	February 12	31.3	374.7	0.608	233
006	Cosmos 2337-9, Gonets 4-6	February 14	82.5	114.2	0.167	1410
007	JCSAT 4, rocket	February 17	23.3	2064.6	0.785	223
008	DSP18, USA130, rocket	February 23	—	—	—	—
009	Intelsat 801, rocket	March 1	0.5	1142.3	0.792	23946
010	START ZEYA, rocket	March 4	97.2	93.6	0.052	426
011	TEMPO, rocket	March 8	25.1	369.5	0.605	249
012	DMSP 2-09, rocket	April 4	98.9	102.0	0.103	844
013	Shuttle 83	April 4	28.5	90.4	0.032	300
014	Progress M34, rocket	April 6	51.6	92.2	0.043	378
015	Cosmos 2340, rocket, platform, rocket	April 9	63.0	714.5	0.732	492
016	THAICOM 3, BSAT 1A, rocket	April 16	7.0	630.2	0.712	219
017	Cosmos 2341, rocket	April 17	82.9	105.1	0.121	978
018	Minisat-01, Celestis	April 21	151.0	95.9	0.069	563
019	GOES K, rocket	April 25	27.0	757.7	0.741	144
020	Iridium 1-5, rocket	May 5	86.4	97.5	0.077	627

Astronomers Royal

Instituted in 1675, the title of Astronomer Royal was given to the director of the Royal Greenwich Observatory until 1975. Currently it is an honorary title for an outstanding astronomer, who receives a stipend of approximately £100 a year.

John Flamsteed (1646–1719), appointed 1675
Edmund Halley (1656–1742), appointed 1720
James Bradley (1693–1762), appointed 1742
Nathaniel Bliss (1700–64), appointed 1762
Nevil Maskelyne (1732–1811), appointed 1765

John Pond (1767–1836), appointed 1811
Sir George Airy (1801–92), appointed 1835
Sir William Christie (1845–1922), appointed 1881
Sir Frank Dyson (1868–1939), appointed 1910
Sir Harold Jones (1890–1960), appointed 1933
Sir Richard Woolley (1906–86), appointed 1955
Sir Martin Ryle (1918–84), appointed 1972
Sir Francis Graham-Smith (1923–), appointed 1982
Sir Arnold Wolfendale (1927–), appointed 1991
Sir Martin Rees (1942–), appointed 1995

Time Measurement and Calendars

MEASUREMENTS OF TIME

Measurements of time are based on the time taken by the earth to rotate on its axis (day); by the moon to revolve round the earth (month); and by the earth to revolve round the sun (year). From these, which are not commensurable, certain average or mean intervals have been adopted for ordinary use.

THE DAY

The day begins at midnight and is divided into 24 hours of 60 minutes, each of 60 seconds. The hours are counted from midnight up to 12 noon (when the sun crosses the meridian), and these hours are designated a.m. (*ante meridiem*); and again from noon up to 12 midnight, which hours are designated p.m. (*post meridiem*), except when the 24-hour reckoning is employed. The 24-hour reckoning ignores a.m. and p.m., numbering the hours 0 to 23 from midnight.

Colloquially the 24 hours are divided into day and night, day being the time while the sun is above the horizon (including the four stages of twilight defined on page 72). Day is subdivided into morning, the early part of daytime, ending at noon; afternoon, from noon to about 6 p.m.; and evening, which may be said to extend from 6 p.m. until midnight. Night, the dark period between day and day, begins at the close of astronomical twilight (*see* page 72) and extends beyond midnight to sunrise the next day.

The names of the days are derived from Old English translations or adaptations of the Roman titles.

Sunday	Sun	Sol
Monday	Moon	Luna
Tuesday	Tiw/Tyr (god of war)	Mars
Wednesday	Woden/Odin	Mercury
Thursday	Thor	Jupiter
Friday	Frigga/Freyja	
	(goddess of love)	Venus
Saturday	Saeternes	Saturn

THE MONTH

The month in the ordinary calendar is approximately the twelfth part of a year, but the lengths of the different months vary from 28 (or 29) days to 31.

THE YEAR

The equinoctial or tropical year is the time that the earth takes to revolve round the sun from equinox to equinox, i.e. 365.24219 mean solar days, or 365 days 5 hours 48 minutes and 45 seconds.

The calendar year usually consists of 365 days but a year containing 366 days is called bissextile (*see* Roman calendar, page 89) or leap year, one day being added to the month of February so that a date 'leaps over' a day of the week. In the Roman calendar the day that was repeated was the sixth day before the beginning of March, the equivalent of 24 February.

A year is a leap year if the date of the year is divisible by four without remainder, unless it is the last year of the century. The last year of a century is a leap year only if its number is divisible by 400 without remainder, e.g. the years 1800 and 1900 had only 365 days but the year 2000 will have 366 days.

THE SOLSTICE

A solstice is the point in the tropical year at which the sun attains its greatest distance, north or south, from the Equator. In the northern hemisphere the furthest point north of the Equator marks the summer solstice and the furthest point south the winter solstice.

The date of the solstice varies according to locality. For example, if the summer solstice falls on 21 June late in the day by Greenwich time, that day will be the longest of the year at Greenwich though it may be by only a second, but it will fall on 22 June, local date, in Japan, and so 22 June will be the longest day there. The date of the solstice is also affected by the length of the tropical year, which is 365 days 6 hours less about 11 minutes 15 seconds. If a solstice happens late on 21 June in one year, it will be nearly six hours later in the next (unless the next year is a leap year), i.e. early on 22 June, and that will be the longest day.

This delay of the solstice does not continue because the extra day in leap year brings it back a day in the calendar. However, because of the 11 minutes 15 seconds mentioned above, the additional day in leap year brings the solstice back too far by 45 minutes, and the time of the solstice in the calendar is earlier, in a four-year pattern, as the century progresses. The last year of a century is in most cases not a leap year, and the omission of the extra day puts the date of the solstice later by about six hours too much. Compensation for this is made by the fourth centennial year being a leap year. The solstice has become earlier in date throughout this century and, because the year 2000 is a leap year, the solstice will get earlier still throughout the 21st century.

The date of the winter solstice, the shortest day of the year, is affected by the same factors as the longest day.

At Greenwich the sun sets at its earliest by the clock about ten days before the shortest day. The daily change in the time of sunset is due in the first place to the sun's movement southwards at this time of the year, which diminishes the interval between the sun's transit and its setting. However, the daily decrease of the Equation of Time causes the time of apparent noon to be continuously later day by day, which to some extent counteracts the first effect. The rates of the change of these two quantities are not equal or uniform; their combination causes the date of earliest sunset to be 12 or 13 December at Greenwich. In more southerly latitudes the effect of the movement of the sun is less, and the change in the time of sunset depends on that of the Equation of Time to a greater degree, and the date of earliest sunset is earlier than it is at Greenwich, e.g. on the Equator it is about 1 November.

THE EQUINOX

The equinox is the point at which the sun crosses the Equator and day and night are of equal length all over the world. This occurs in March and September.

DOG DAYS

The days about the heliacal rising of the Dog Star, noted from ancient times as the hottest period of the year in the northern hemisphere, are called the Dog Days. Their incidence has been variously calculated as depending on the Greater or Lesser Dog Star (Sirius or Procyon) and their duration has been reckoned as from 30 to 54 days. A generally accepted period is from 3 July to 15 August.

CHRISTIAN CALENDAR

In the Christian chronological system the years are distinguished by cardinal numbers before or after the birth of Christ, the period being denoted by the letters BC (Before Christ) or, more rarely, AC (*Ante Christum*), and AD (*Anno Domini* – In the Year of Our Lord). The correlative dates of the epoch are the fourth year of the 194th Olympiad, the 753rd year from the foundation of Rome, AM 3761 (Jewish chronology), and the 4714th year of the Julian period. The actual date of the birth of Christ is somewhat uncertain.

The system was introduced into Italy in the sixth century. Though first used in France in the seventh century, it was not universally established there until about the eighth century. It has been said that the system was introduced into England by St Augustine (AD 596), but it was probably not generally used until some centuries later. It was ordered to be used by the Bishops at the Council of Chelsea (AD 816).

The Julian Calendar

In the Julian calendar (adopted by the Roman Empire in 45 BC, *see* page 89) all the centennial years were leap years, and for this reason towards the close of the 16th century there was a difference of ten days between the tropical and calendar years; the equinox fell on 11 March of the calendar, whereas at the time of the Council of Nicaea (AD 325), it had fallen on 21 March. In 1582 Pope Gregory ordained that 5 October should be called 15 October and that of the end-century years only the fourth should be a leap year (*see* page 81).

The Gregorian Calendar

The Gregorian calendar was adopted by Italy, France, Spain and Portugal in 1582, by Prussia, the Roman Catholic German states, Switzerland, Holland and Flanders on 1 January 1583, by Poland in 1586, Hungary in 1587, the Protestant German and Netherland states and Denmark in 1700, and by Great Britain and Dominions (including the North American colonies) in 1752, by the omission of eleven days (3 September being reckoned as 14 September). Sweden omitted the leap day in 1700 but observed leap days in 1704 and 1708, and reverted to the Julian calendar by having two leap days in 1712; the Gregorian calendar was adopted in 1753 by the omission of eleven days (18 February being reckoned as 1 March). Japan adopted the calendar in 1872, China in 1912, Bulgaria in 1915, Turkey and Soviet Russia in 1918, Yugoslavia and Romania in 1919, and Greece in 1923.

In the same year that the change was made in England from the Julian to the Gregorian calendar, the beginning of the new year was also changed from 25 March to 1 January (*see* page 86).

The Orthodox Churches

Some Orthodox Churches still use the Julian reckoning but the majority of Greek Orthodox Churches and the Romanian Orthodox Church have adopted a modified 'New Calendar', observing the Gregorian calendar for fixed feasts and the Julian for movable feasts.

The Orthodox Church year begins on 1 September. There are four fast periods and, in addition to Pascha (Easter), twelve great feasts, as well as numerous commemorations of the saints of the Old and New Testaments throughout the year.

The Dominical Letter

The dominical letter is one of the letters A–G which are used to denote the Sundays in successive years. If the first day of the year is a Sunday the letter is A; if the second, B; the third, C; and so on. A leap year requires two letters, the first for 1 January to 29 February, the second for 1 March to 31 December (*see* page 84).

Epiphany

The feast of the Epiphany, commemorating the manifestation of Christ, later became associated with the offering of gifts by the Magi. The day was of great importance from the time of the Council of Nicaea (AD 325), as the primate of Alexandria was charged at every Epiphany feast with the announcement in a letter to the churches of the date of the forthcoming Easter. The day was also of importance in Britain as it influenced dates, ecclesiastical and lay, e.g. Plough Monday, when work was resumed in the fields, fell on the Monday in the first full week after Epiphany.

Lent

The Teutonic word *Lent*, which denotes the fast preceding Easter, originally meant no more than the spring season; but from Anglo-Saxon times at least it has been used as the equivalent of the more significant Latin term Quadragesima, meaning the 'forty days' or, more literally, the fortieth day. Ash Wednesday is the first day of Lent, which ends at midnight before Easter Day.

Palm Sunday

Palm Sunday, the Sunday before Easter and the beginning of Holy Week, commemorates the triumphal entry of Christ into Jerusalem and is celebrated in Britain (when palm is not available) by branches of willow gathered for use in the decoration of churches on that day.

Maundy Thursday

Maundy Thursday is the day before Good Friday, the name itself being a corruption of *dies mandati* (day of the mandate) when Christ washed the feet of the disciples and gave them the mandate to love one another.

Easter Day

Easter Day is the first Sunday after the full moon which happens on, or next after, the 21st day of March; if the full moon happens on a Sunday, Easter Day is the Sunday after.

This definition is contained in an Act of Parliament (24 Geo. II c. 23) and explanation is given in the preamble to the Act that the day of full moon depends on certain tables that have been prepared. These tables are summarized in the early pages of the Book of Common Prayer. The moon referred to is not the real moon of the heavens, but a hypothetical moon on whose 'full' the date of Easter depends, and the lunations of this 'calendar' moon consist of twenty-nine and thirty days alternately, with certain necessary modifications to make the date of its full agree as nearly as possible with that of the real moon, which is known as the Paschal Full Moon. At present, Easter falls on one of 35 days (22 March to 25 April).

A Fixed Easter

In 1928 the House of Commons agreed to a motion for the third reading of a bill proposing that Easter Day shall, in the calendar year next but one after the commencement of the Act and in all subsequent years, be the first Sunday after the second Saturday in April. Easter would thus fall on the second or third Sunday in April, i.e. between 9 and 15 April (inclusive). A clause in the Bill provided that before it shall come into operation, regard shall be had to any opinion expressed officially by the various Christian churches.

Efforts by the World Council of Churches to secure a unanimous choice of date for Easter by its member churches have so far been unsuccessful.

ROGATION DAYS

Rogation Days are the Monday, Tuesday and Wednesday preceding Ascension Day and from the fifth century were observed as public fasts with solemn processions and supplications. The processions were discontinued as religious observances at the Reformation, but survive in the ceremony known as 'beating the parish bounds'. Rogation Sunday is the Sunday before Ascension Day.

EMBER DAYS

The Ember Days at the four seasons are the Wednesday, Friday and Saturday (*a*) before the third Sunday in Advent,

(*b*) before the second Sunday in Lent, and (*c*) before the Sundays nearest to the festivals of St Peter and of St Michael and All Angels.

TRINITY SUNDAY

Trinity Sunday is eight weeks after Easter Day, on the Sunday following Pentecost (Whit Sunday). Subsequent Sundays are reckoned in the Book of Common Prayer calendar of the Church of England as 'after Trinity'.

Thomas Becket (1118–70) was consecrated Archbishop of Canterbury on the Sunday after Whit Sunday and his first act was to ordain that the day of his consecration should be held as a new festival in honour of the Holy Trinity. This observance spread from Canterbury throughout the whole of Christendom.

MOVABLE FEASTS TO THE YEAR 2030

Year	Ash Wednesday	Easter	Ascension	Pentecost (Whit Sunday)	Sundays after Pentecost	Advent Sunday
1998	25 February	12 April	21 May	31 May	20	29 November
1999	17 February	4 April	13 May	23 May	21	28 November
2000	8 March	23 April	1 June	11 June	19	3 December
2001	28 February	15 April	24 May	3 June	20	2 December
2002	13 February	31 March	9 May	19 May	22	1 December
2003	5 March	20 April	29 May	8 June	19	30 November
2004	25 February	11 April	20 May	30 May	20	28 November
2005	9 February	27 March	5 May	15 May	22	27 November
2006	1 March	16 April	25 May	4 June	20	3 December
2007	21 February	8 April	17 May	27 May	21	2 December
2008	6 February	23 March	1 May	11 May	23	30 November
2009	25 February	12 April	21 May	31 May	20	29 November
2010	17 February	4 April	13 May	23 May	21	28 November
2011	9 March	24 April	2 June	12 June	18	27 November
2012	22 February	8 April	17 May	27 May	21	2 December
2013	13 February	31 March	9 May	19 May	22	1 December
2014	5 March	20 April	29 May	8 June	19	30 November
2015	18 February	5 April	14 May	24 May	21	29 November
2016	10 February	27 March	5 May	15 May	22	27 November
2017	1 March	16 April	25 May	4 June	20	3 December
2018	14 February	1 April	10 May	20 May	22	2 December
2019	6 March	21 April	30 May	9 June	19	1 December
2020	26 February	12 April	21 May	31 May	20	29 November
2021	17 February	4 April	13 May	23 May	21	28 November
2022	2 March	17 April	26 May	5 June	19	27 November
2023	22 February	9 April	18 May	28 May	21	3 December
2024	14 February	31 March	9 May	19 May	22	1 December
2025	5 March	20 April	29 May	8 June	19	30 November
2026	18 February	5 April	14 May	24 May	21	29 November
2027	10 February	28 March	6 May	16 May	22	28 November
2028	1 March	16 April	25 May	4 June	20	3 December
2029	14 February	1 April	10 May	20 May	22	2 December
2030	6 March	21 April	30 May	9 June	19	1 December

NOTES

Ash Wednesday (first day in Lent) can fall at earliest on 4 February and at latest on 10 March

Mothering Sunday (fourth Sunday in Lent) can fall at earliest on 1 March and at latest on 4 April

Easter Day can fall at earliest on 22 March and at latest on 25 April

Ascension Day is forty days after Easter Day and can fall at earliest on 30 April and at latest on 3 June

Pentecost (Whit Sunday) is seven weeks after Easter and can fall at earliest on 10 May and at latest on 13 June

Trinity Sunday is the Sunday after Whit Sunday

Corpus Christi falls on the Thursday after Trinity Sunday

Sundays after Pentecost – there are not less than 18 and not more than 23

Advent Sunday is the Sunday nearest to 30 November

EASTER DAYS AND DOMINICAL LETTERS 1500 to 2033

Dates up to and including 1752 are according to the Julian calendar

	1500–1599	1600–1699	1700–1799	1800–1899	1900–1999	2000–2033
March						
d 22	1573	1668	1761	1818		
e 23	1505/16	1600	1788	1845/56	1913	2008
f 24		1611/95	1706/99		1940	
g 25	1543/54	1627/38/49	1722/33/44	1883/94	1951	
A 26	1559/70/81/92	1654/65/76	1749/58/69/80	1815/26/37	1967/78/89	
b 27	1502/13/24/97	1608/87/92	1785/96	1842/53/64	1910/21/32	2005/16
c 28	1529/35/40	1619/24/30	1703/14/25	1869/75/80	1937/48	2027/32
d 29	1551/62	1635/46/57	1719/30/41/52	1807/12/91	1959/64/70	
e 30	1567/78/89	1651/62/73/84	1746/55/66/77	1823/34	1902/75/86/97	
f 31	1510/21/32/83/94	1605/16/78/89	1700/71/82/93	1839/50/61/72	1907/18/29/91	2002/13/24
April						
g 1	1526/37/48	1621/32	1711/16	1804/66/77/88	1923/34/45/56	2018/29
A 2	1553/64	1643/48	1727/38	1809/20/93/99	1961/72	
b 3	1575/80/86	1659/70/81	1743/63/68/74	1825/31/36	1904/83/88/94	
c 4	1507/18/91	1602/13/75/86/97	1708/79/90	1847/58	1915/20/26/99	2010/21
d 5	1523/34/45/56	1607/18/29/40	1702/13/24/95	1801/63/74/85/96	1931/42/53	2015/26
e 6	1539/50/61/72	1634/45/56	1729/35/40/60	1806/17/28/90	1947/58/69/80	
f 7	1504/77/88	1667/72	1751/65/76	1822/33/44	1901/12/85/96	
g 8	1509/15/20/99	1604/10/83/94	1705/87/92/98	1849/55/60	1917/28	2007/12
A 9	1531/42	1615/26/37/99	1710/21/32	1871/82	1939/44/50	2023
b 10	1547/58/69	1631/42/53/64	1726/37/48/57	1803/14/87/98	1955/66/77	
c 11	1501/12/63/74/85/96	1658/69/80	1762/73/84	1819/30/41/52	1909/71/82/93	2004
d 12	1506/17/28	1601/12/91/96	1789	1846/57/68	1903/14/25/36/98	2009/20
e 13	1533/44	1623/28	1707/18	1800/73/79/84	1941/52	2031
f 14	1555/60/66	1639/50/61	1723/34/45/54	1805/11/16/95	1963/68/74	
g 15	1571/82/93	1655/66/77/88	1750/59/70/81	1827/38	1900/06/79/90	2001
A 16	1503/14/25/36/87/98	1609/20/82/93	1704/75/86/97	1843/54/65/76	1911/22/33/95	2006/17/28
b 17	1530/41/52	1625/36	1715/20	1808/70/81/92	1927/38/49/60	2022/33
c 18	1557/68	1647/52	1731/42/56	1802/13/24/97	1954/65/76	
d 19	1500/79/84/90	1663/74/85	1747/67/72/78	1829/35/40	1908/81/87/92	
e 20	1511/22/95	1606/17/79/90	1701/12/83/94	1851/62	1919/24/30	2003/14/25
f 21	1527/38/49	1622/33/44	1717/28	1867/78/89	1935/46/57	2019/30
g 22	1565/76	1660	1739/53/64	1810/21/32	1962/73/84	
A 23	1508	1671		1848	1905/16	2000
b 24	1519	1603/14/98	1709/91	1859		2011
c 25	1546	1641	1736	1886	1943	

HINDU CALENDAR

The Hindu calendar is a luni-solar calendar of twelve months, each containing 29 days, 12 hours. Each month is divided into a light fortnight (Shukla or Shuddha) and a dark fortnight (Krishna or Vadya) based on the waxing and waning of the moon. In most parts of India the month starts with the light fortnight, i.e. the day after the new moon, although in some regions it begins with the dark fortnight, i.e. the day after the full moon.

The new year begins in the month of Chaitra (March/April) and ends in the month of Phalgun (March). The twelve months, Chaitra, Vaishakh, Jyeshtha, Ashadh, Shravan, Bhadrapad, Ashvin, Kartik, Margashirsh, Paush, Magh and Phalgun, have Sanskrit names derived from twelve asterisms (constellations). There are regional variations to the names of the months but the Sanskrit names are understood throughout India.

Every lunar month must have a solar transit and is termed pure (shuddha). The lunar month without a solar transit is impure (mala) and called an intercalary month. An intercalary month occurs approximately every 32 lunar months, whenever the difference between the Hindu year of 360 lunar days (354 days 8 hours solar time) and the 365 days 6 hours of the solar year reaches the length of one Hindu lunar month (29 days 12 hours).

The leap month may be added at any point in the Hindu year. The name given to the month varies according to when it occurs but is taken from the month immediately following it. Leap months occur in 1996–7 (Ashadh) and 1999–2000 (Jyeshtha).

The days of the week are called Raviwar (Sunday), Somawar (Monday), Mangalwar (Tuesday), Budhawar (Wednesday), Guruwar (Thursday), Shukrawar (Friday) and Shaniwar (Saturday). The names are derived from the Sanskrit names of the Sun, the Moon and five planets, Mars, Mercury, Jupiter, Venus and Saturn.

Most fasts and festivals are based on the lunar calendar but a few are determined by the apparent movement of the Sun, e.g. Sankranti and Pongal (in southern India), which are celebrated on 14/15 January to mark the start of the Sun's apparent journey northwards and a change of season.

Festivals celebrated throughout India are Chaitra (the New Year), Raksha-bandhan (the renewal of the kinship bond between brothers and sisters), Navaratri (a nine-night festival dedicated to the goddess Parvati), Dasara (the victory of Rama over the demon army), Diwali (a festival of lights), Makara Sankranti, Shivaratri (dedicated to Shiva), and Holi (a spring festival).

Regional festivals are Durga-puja (dedicated to the goddess Durga (Parvati)), Sarasvati-puja (dedicated to the goddess Sarasvati), Ganesh Chaturthi (worship of Ganesh on the fourth day (Chaturthi) of the light half of Bhadrapad), Ramanavami (the birth festival of the god Rama) and Janmashtami (the birth festival of the god Krishna).

The main festivals celebrated in Britain are Navaratri, Dasara, Durga-puja, Diwali, Holi, Sarasvati-puja, Ganesh Chaturthi, Raksha-bandhan, Ramanavami and Janmashtami.

For dates of the main festivals in 1998, *see* page 9.

JEWISH CALENDAR

The story of the Flood in the Book of Genesis indicates the use of a calendar of some kind and that the writers recognized thirty days as the length of a lunation. However, after the diaspora, Jewish communities were left in considerable doubt as to the times of fasts and festivals. This led to the formation of the Jewish calendar as used today. It is said that this was done in AD 358 by Rabbi Hillel II, though some assert that it did not happen until much later.

The calendar is luni-solar, and is based on the lengths of the lunation and of the tropical year as found by Hipparchus (c.120 BC), which differ little from those adopted at the present day. The year AM 5758 (1997–8) is the 1st year of the 304th Metonic (Minor or Lunar) cycle of 19 years and the 18th year of the 206th Solar (or Major) cycle of 28 years since the Era of the Creation. Jews hold that the Creation occurred at the time of the autumnal equinox in the year known in the Christian calendar as 3760 BC (954 of the Julian period). The epoch or starting point of Jewish chronology corresponds to 7 October 3761 BC. At the beginning of each solar cycle, the Tekufah of Nisan (the vernal equinox) returns to the same day and to the same hour.

The hour is divided into 1080 minims, and the month between one new moon and the next is reckoned as 29 days, 12 hours, 793 minims. The normal calendar year, called a Regular Common year, consists of 12 months of 30 days and 29 days alternately. Since twelve months such as these comprise only 354 days, in order that each of them shall not diverge greatly from an average place in the solar year, a thirteenth month is occasionally added after the fifth month of the civil year (which commences on the first day of the month Tishri), or as the penultimate month of the ecclesiastical year (which commences on the first day of the month Nisan). The years when this happens are called Embolismic or leap years.

Of the 19 years that form a Metonic cycle, seven are leap years; they occur at places in the cycle indicated by the numbers 3, 6, 8, 11, 14, 17 and 19, these places being chosen so that the accumulated excesses of the solar years should be as small as possible.

A Jewish year is of one of the following six types:

Minimal Common	353 days
Regular Common	354 days
Full Common	355 days
Minimal Leap	383 days
Regular Leap	384 days
Full Leap	385 days.

The Regular year has alternate months of 30 and 29 days. In a Full year, whether common or leap, Marcheshvan, the second month of the civil year, has 30 days instead of 29; in Minimal years Kislev, the third month, has 29 instead of 30. The additional month in leap years is called Adar I and precedes the month called Adar in Common years. Adar II is called Adar Sheni in leap years, and the usual Adar festivals are kept in Adar Sheni. Adar I and Adar II always have 30 days, but neither this, nor the other variations mentioned, is allowed to change the number of days in the other months, which still follow the alternation of the normal twelve.

These are the main features of the Jewish calendar, which must be considered permanent because as a Jewish law it cannot be altered except by a great Sanhedrin.

The Jewish day begins between sunset and nightfall. The time used is that of the meridian of Jerusalem, which is 2h 21m in advance of Greenwich Mean Time. Rules for the beginning of sabbaths and festivals were laid down for the latitude of London in the 18th century and hours for nightfall are now fixed annually by the Chief Rabbi.

JEWISH CALENDAR 5758–9

AM 5758 (758) is a Regular Common year of 12 months, 51 sabbaths and 354 days. AM 5759 (759) is a Full Common year of 12 months, 51 sabbaths and 355 days.

Jewish Month	AM 5758	AM 5759
Tishri 1	2 October 1997	21 September 1998
Marcheshvan 1	1 November	21 October
Kislev 1	30 November	20 November
Tebet 1	30 December	20 December
Shebat 1	28 January 1998	18 January 1999
*Adar 1	27 February	17 February
†*Adar* II		
Nisan 1	28 March	18 March
Iyar 1	27 April	17 April
Sivan 1	26 May	16 May
Tammuz 1	25 June	15 June
Ab 1	24 July	14 July
Elul 1	23 August	13 August

*Known as Adar Rishon in leap years
†Known as Adar Sheni in leap years

JEWISH FASTS AND FESTIVALS

For dates of principal festivals in 1998, *see* page 9

Tishri 1–2	Rosh Hashanah (New Year)
Tishri 3	*Fast of Gedaliah
Tishri 10	Yom Kippur (Day of Atonement)
Tishri 15–21	Succoth (Feast of Tabernacles)
Tishri 21	Hoshana Rabba
Tishri 22	Shemini Atseret (Solemn Assembly)
Tishri 23	Simchat Torah (Rejoicing of the Law)
Kislev 25	Chanucah (Dedication of the Temple) begins
Tebet 10	Fast of Tebet
†*Adar* 13	§Fast of Esther
†*Adar* 14	Purim
†*Adar* 15	Shushan Purim
Nisan 15–22	Pesach (Passover)
Sivan 6–7	Shavuot (Feast of Weeks)
Tammuz 17	*Fast of Tammuz
Ab 9	*Fast of Ab

*If these dates fall on the sabbath the fast is kept on the following day
†Adar Sheni in leap years
§This fast is observed on Adar 11 (or Adar Sheni 11 in leap years) if Adar 13 falls on a sabbath

THE MUSLIM CALENDAR

The Muslim era is dated from the *Hijrah*, or flight of the Prophet Muhammad from Mecca to Medina, the corresponding date of which in the Julian calendar is 16 July AD 622. The lunar *hijri* calendar is used principally in Iran, Egypt, Malaysia, Pakistan, Mauritania, various Arab states and certain parts of India. Iran uses the solar *hijri* calendar as well as the lunar *hijri* calendar. The dating system was adopted about AD 639, commencing with the first day of the month Muharram.

The lunar calendar consists of twelve months containing an alternate sequence of 30 and 29 days, with the intercalation of one day at the end of the twelfth month at stated intervals in each cycle of 30 years. The object of the intercalation is to reconcile the date of the first day of the month with the date of the actual new moon.

Some adherents still take the date of the evening of the first physical sighting of the crescent of the new moon as that of the first of the month. If cloud obscures the moon the present month may be extended to 30 days, after which the new month will begin automatically regardless of whether the moon has been seen. (Under religious law a month must have less than 31 days.) This means that the beginning of a new month and the date of religious festivals can vary from the published calendars.

In each cycle of 30 years, 19 years are common and contain 354 days, and 11 years are intercalary (leap years) of 355 days, the latter being called *kabisah*. The mean length of the Hijrah years is 354 days 8 hours 48 minutes and the period of mean lunation is 29 days 12 hours 44 minutes.

To ascertain if a year is common or kabisah, divide it by 30: the quotient gives the number of completed cycles and the remainder shows the place of the year in the current cycle. If the remainder is 2, 5, 7, 10, 13, 16, 18, 21, 24, 26 or 29, the year is kabisah and consists of 355 days.

MUSLIM CALENDAR 1418–19

Hijrah year 1418 AH (remainder 8) is a common year; 1419 AH (remainder 9) is a common year.

Month (length)	1418 AH	1419 AH
Muharram (30)	9 May 1997	28 April 1998
Safar (29)	8 June	28 May
Rabi' I (30)	7 July	26 June
Rabi' II (29)	6 August	26 July
Jumada I (30)	4 September	24 August
Jumada II (29)	4 October	23 September
Rajab (30)	2 November	22 October
Sha'ban (29)	2 December	21 November
Ramadân (30)	31 December	20 December
Shawwâl (29)	30 January 1998	19 January 1999
Dhû'l-Qa'da (30)	28 February	17 February
Dhû'l-Hijjah (29 or 30)	30 March	19 March

MUSLIM FESTIVALS

Ramadan is a month of fasting for all Muslims because it is the month in which the revelation of the *Qur'an* (Koran) began. During Ramadan Muslims abstain from food, drink and sexual pleasure from dawn until after sunset throughout the month.

The two major festivals are *Id al-Fitr* and *Id al-Adha*. Id al-Fitr marks the end of the Ramadan fast and is celebrated on the day after the sighting of the new moon of the following month. Id al-Adha, the festival of sacrifice (also known as the great festival), celebrates the submission of the Prophet Ibrahim (Abraham) to God. Id al-Adha falls on the tenth day of Dhul-Hijjah, coinciding with the day when those on *hajj* (pilgrimage to Mecca) sacrifice animals.

Other days accorded special recognition are:

Muharram 1	New Year's Day
Muharram 10	Ashura (the day Prophet Noah left the Ark and Prophet Moses was saved from Pharaoh (Sunni), the death of the Prophet's grandson Husain (Shi'ite))
Rabi'u-l-Awwal (Rabi' I) 12	Mawlid al-Nabi (birthday of the Prophet Muhammad)
Rajab 27	Laylat al-Isra' wa'l-Mi'raj (The Night of Journey and Ascension)
Ramadân One of the odd-numbered nights in the last 10 of the month	Laylat al-Qadr (Night of Power)
Dhû'l-Hijjah 10	Id al-Adha (Festival of Sacrifice)

THE SIKH CALENDAR

The Sikh calendar is a lunar calendar of 365 days divided into 12 months. The length of the months varies between 29 and 32 days.

There are no prescribed feast days and no fasting periods. The main celebrations are Baisakhi Mela (the new year and the anniversary of the founding of the Khalsa), Diwali Mela (festival of light), Hola Mohalla Mela (a spring festival held in the Punjab), and the Gurpurbs (anniversaries associated with the ten Gurus).

For dates of the major celebrations in 1998, *see* page 9.

CIVIL AND LEGAL CALENDAR

THE HISTORICAL YEAR

Before 1752, two calendar systems were used in England. The civil or legal year began on 25 March and the historical year on 1 January. Thus the civil or legal date 24 March 1658 was the same day as the historical date 24 March 1659; a date in that portion of the year is written as 24 March 165⅜, the lower figure showing the historical year.

THE NEW YEAR

In England in the seventh century, and as late as the 13th, the year was reckoned from Christmas Day, but in the 12th century the Church in England began the year with the feast of the Annunciation of the Blessed Virgin ('Lady Day') on 25 March and this practice was adopted generally in the 14th century. The civil or legal year in the British Dominions (exclusive of Scotland) began with Lady Day until 1751. But in and since 1752 the civil year has begun with 1 January. New Year's Day in Scotland was changed from 25 March to 1 January in 1600.

Elsewhere in Europe, 1 January was adopted as the first day of the year by Venice in 1522, German states in 1544, Spain, Portugal, and the Roman Catholic Netherlands in 1556, Prussia, Denmark and Sweden in 1559, France in 1564, Lorraine in 1579, the Protestant Netherlands in 1583, Russia in 1725, and Tuscany in 1751.

REGNAL YEARS

Regnal years are the years of a sovereign's reign and each begins on the anniversary of his or her accession, e.g. regnal year 47 of the present Queen begins on 6 February 1998.

The system was used for dating Acts of Parliament until 1962. The Summer Time Act 1925, for example, is quoted as 15 and 16 Geo. V c. 64, because it became law in the parliamentary session which extended over part of both of these regnal years. Acts of a parliamentary session during which a sovereign died were usually given two year numbers, the regnal year of the deceased sovereign and the regnal year of his or her successor, e.g. those passed in 1952 were dated 16 Geo. VI and 1 Elizabeth II. Since 1962 Acts of Parliament have been dated by the calendar year.

QUARTER AND TERM DAYS

Holy days and saints days were the usual means in early times for setting the dates of future and recurrent appointments. The quarter days in England and Wales are the feast of the Nativity (25 December), the feast of the Annunciation (25 March), the feast of St John the Baptist (24 June) and the feast of St Michael and All Angels (29 September).

The term days in Scotland are Candlemas (the feast of the Purification), Whitsunday, Lammas (Loaf Mass), and Martinmas (St Martin's Day). These fell on 2 February, 15 May, 1 August and 11 November respectively. However, by the Term and Quarter Days (Scotland) Act 1990, the dates of the term days were changed to 28 February (Candlemas), 28 May (Whitsunday), 28 August (Lammas) and 28 November (Martinmas).

RED-LETTER DAYS

Red-letter days were originally the holy days and saints days indicated in early ecclesiastical calendars by letters printed in red ink. The days to be distinguished in this way were approved at the Council of Nicaea in AD 325.

These days still have a legal significance, as judges of the Queen's Bench Division wear scarlet robes on red-letter days falling during the law sittings. The days designated as red-letter days for this purpose are:

Holy and saints days
The Conversion of St Paul, the Purification, Ash Wednesday, the Annunciation, the Ascension, the feasts of St Mark, SS Philip and James, St Matthias, St Barnabas, St John the Baptist, St Peter, St Thomas, St James, St Luke, SS Simon and Jude, All Saints, St Andrew

Civil calendar
The anniversaries of The Queen's accession, The Queen's birthday and The Queen's coronation, The Queen's official birthday, the birthday of the Duke of Edinburgh, the birthday of Queen Elizabeth the Queen Mother, the birthday of the Prince of Wales, St David's Day and Lord Mayor's Day

PUBLIC HOLIDAYS

Public holidays are divided into two categories, common law and statutory. Common law holidays are holidays 'by habit and custom'; in England, Wales and Northern Ireland these are Good Friday and Christmas Day.

Statutory public holidays, known as bank holidays, were first established by the Bank Holidays Act 1871. They were, literally, days on which the banks (and other public institutions) were closed and financial obligations due on that day were payable the following day. The legislation currently governing public holidays in the UK, which is the Banking and Financial Dealings Act 1971 stipulates the days that are to be public holidays in England, Wales, Scotland and Northern Ireland.

Certain holidays (indicated by * below) are granted annually by royal proclamation, either throughout the UK or in any place in the UK. The public holidays are:

England and Wales

*New Year's Day
Easter Monday
*The first Monday in May
The last Monday in May
The last Monday in August
26 December, if it is not a Sunday
27 December when 25 or 26 December is a Sunday

Scotland

New Year's Day, or if it is a Sunday, 2 January
2 January, or if it is a Sunday, 3 January
Good Friday
The first Monday in May
*The last Monday in May
The first Monday in August
Christmas Day, or if it is a Sunday, 26 December
*Boxing Day – if Christmas Day falls on a Sunday, 26 December is given in lieu and an alternative day is given for Boxing Day

Northern Ireland

*New Year's Day
17 March, or if it is a Sunday, 18 March
Easter Monday
*The first Monday in May
The last Monday in May
*12 July, or if it is a Sunday, 13 July
The last Monday in August
26 December, if it is not a Sunday
27 December if 25 or 26 December is a Sunday

For dates of public holidays in 1998 and 1999, *see* pages 10–11.

CHRONOLOGICAL CYCLES AND ERAS

SOLAR (OR MAJOR) CYCLE

The solar cycle is a period of twenty-eight years in any corresponding year of which the days of the week recur on the same day of the month.

METONIC (LUNAR, OR MINOR) CYCLE

In 432 BC, Meton, an Athenian astronomer, found that 235 lunations are very nearly, though not exactly, equal in duration to 19 solar years and so after 19 years the phases of the Moon recur on the same days of the month (nearly). The dates of full moon in a cycle of 19 years were inscribed in figures of gold on public monuments in Athens, and the number showing the position of a year in the cycle is called the golden number of that year.

JULIAN PERIOD

The Julian period was proposed by Joseph Scaliger in 1582. The period is 7980 Julian years, and its first year coincides with the year 4713 BC. The figure of 7980 is the product of the number of years in the solar cycle, the Metonic cycle and the cycle of the Roman indiction (28 × 19 × 15).

ROMAN INDICTION

The Roman indiction is a period of fifteen years, instituted for fiscal purposes about AD 300.

EPACT

The epact is the age of the calendar Moon, diminished by one day, on 1 January, in the ecclesiastical lunar calendar.

CHINESE CALENDAR

A lunar calendar was the sole calendar in use in China until 1911, when the government adopted the new (Gregorian) calendar for official and most business activities. The Chinese tend to follow both calendars, the lunar calendar playing an important part in personal life, e.g. birth celebrations, festivals, marriages; and in rural villages the lunar calendar dictates the cycle of activities, denoting the change of weather and farming activities.

The lunar calendar is used in Hong Kong, Singapore, Malaysia, Tibet and elsewhere in south-east Asia. The calendar has a cycle of 60 years. The new year begins at the first new moon after the sun enters the sign of Aquarius, i.e. the new year falls between 21 January and 19 February in the Gregorian calendar.

Each year in the Chinese calendar is associated with one of 12 animals: the rat, the ox, the tiger, the rabbit, the dragon, the snake, the horse, the goat or sheep, the monkey, the chicken or rooster, the dog, and the pig.

The date of the Chinese new year and the astrological sign for the years 1998–2002 are:

1998	28 January	Tiger
1999	16 February	Rabbit
2000	5 February	Dragon
2001	—	Snake
2002	—	Horse

COPTIC CALENDAR

In the Coptic calendar, which is used in parts of Egypt and Ethiopia, the year is made up of 12 months of 30 days each, followed, in general, by five complementary days. Every fourth year is an intercalary or leap year and in these years there are six complementary days. The intercalary year of the Coptic calendar immediately precedes the leap year of the Julian calendar. The era is that of Diocletian or the Martyrs, the origin of which is fixed at 29 August AD 284 (Julian date).

INDIAN ERAS

In addition to the Muslim reckoning, other eras are used in India. The Saka era of southern India, dating from 3 March AD 78, was declared the national calendar of the Republic of India with effect from 22 March 1957, to be used concurrently with the Gregorian calendar. As revised, the year of the new Saka era begins at the spring equinox, with five successive months of 31 days and seven of 30 days in ordinary years, and six months of each length in leap years. The year AD 1998 is 1920 of the revised Saka era.

The year AD 1998 corresponds to the following years in other eras:

Year 2055 of the Vikram Samvat era
Year 1405 of the Bengali San era
Year 1174 of the Kollam era
Vedanga Jyotisa year 4 of the five-yearly cycle (384th cycle of Paitamah Siddhanta)
Year 5099 of the Kaliyuga era
Year 2542 of the Buddha Nirvana era

JAPANESE CALENDAR

The Japanese calendar is essentially the same as the Gregorian calendar, the years, months and weeks being of the same length and beginning on the same days as those of the Gregorian calendar. The numeration of the years is different, based on a system of epochs or periods each of which begins at the accession of an Emperor or other important occurrence. The method is not unlike the British system of regnal years, except that each year of a period closes on 31 December. The Japanese chronology begins about AD 650 and the three latest epochs are defined by the reigns of Emperors, whose actual names are not necessarily used:

Epoch

Taishō	1 August 1912 to 25 December 1926
Shōwa	26 December 1926 to 7 January 1989
Heisei	8 January 1989

The year Heisei 10 begins on 1 January 1998.

The months are known as First Month, Second Month, etc., First Month being equivalent to January. The days of the week are Nichiyōbi (Sun-day), Getsuyōbi (Moon-day), Kayōbi (Fire-day), Suiyōbi (Water-day), Mokuyōbi (Wood-day), Kinyōbi (Metal-day), Doyōbi (Earth-day).

THE MASONIC YEAR

Two dates are quoted in warrants, dispensations, etc., issued by the United Grand Lodge of England, those for the current year being expressed as *Anno Domini* 1998 – *Anno Lucis* 5998. This *Anno Lucis* (year of light) is based on the Book of Genesis 1:3, the 4000-year difference being derived, in modified form, from *Ussher's Notation*, published in 1654, which places the Creation of the World in 4004 BC.

OLYMPIADS

Ancient Greek chronology was reckoned in Olympiads, cycles of four years corresponding with the periodic Olympic Games held on the plain of Olympia in Elis once every four years. The intervening years were the first, second, etc., of the Olympiad, which received the name of the victor at the Games. The first recorded Olympiad is that of Choroebus, 776 BC.

ZOROASTRIAN CALENDAR

Zoroastrians, followers of the Iranian prophet Zarathushtra (known to the Greeks as Zoroaster) are mostly to be found in Iran and in India, where they are known as Parsees.

The Zoroastrian era dates from the coronation of the last Zoroastrian Sasanian king in AD 631. The Zoroastrian calendar is divided into twelve months, each comprising 30 days, followed by five holy days of the Gathas at the end of each year to make the year consist of 365 days.

In order to synchronize the calendar with the solar year of 365 days, an extra month was intercalated once every 120 years. However, this intercalation ceased in the 12th century and the New Year, which had fallen in the spring, slipped back to August. Because intercalation ceased at different times in Iran and India, there was one month's difference between the calendar followed in Iran (Kadmi calendar) and by the Parsees (Shenshai calendar). In 1906 a group of Zoroastrians decided to bring the calendar back in line with the seasons again and restore the New Year to 21 March each year (Fasli calendar).

The Shenshai calendar (New Year in August) is mainly used by Parsees. The Fasli calendar (New Year, 21 March) is mainly used by Zoroastrians living in Iran, in the Indian subcontinent, or away from Iran.

THE ROMAN CALENDAR

Roman historians adopted as an epoch the foundation of Rome, which is believed to have happened in the year 753 BC. The ordinal number of the years in Roman reckoning is followed by the letters AUC (*ab urbe condita*), so that the year 1998 is 2751 AUC (MMDCCLI). The calendar that we know has developed from one said to have been established by Romulus using a year of 304 days divided into ten months, beginning with March. To this Numa added January and February, making the year consist of 12 months of 30 and 29 days alternately, with an additional day so that the total was 355. It is also said that Numa ordered an intercalary month of 22 or 23 days in alternate years, making 90 days in eight years, to be inserted after 23 February.

However, there is some doubt as to the origination and the details of the intercalation in the Roman calendar. It is certain that some scheme of this kind was inaugurated and not fully carried out, for in the year 46 BC Julius Caesar found that the calendar had been allowed to fall into some confusion. He sought the help of the Egyptian astronomer Sosigenes, which led to the construction and adoption (45 BC) of the Julian calendar, and, by a slight alteration, to the Gregorian calendar now in use. The year 46 BC was made to consist of 445 days and is called the Year of Confusion.

In the Roman (Julian) calendar the days of the month were counted backwards from three fixed points, or days, and an intervening day was said to be so many days before the next coming point, the first and last being counted. These three points were the Kalends, the Nones, and the Ides. Their positions in the months and the method of counting from them will be seen in the table below. The year containing 366 days was called *bissextillis annus*, as it had a doubled sixth day (*bissextus dies*) before the March Kalends on 24 February – *ante diem sextum Kalendas Martias*, or a.d. VI Kal. Mart.

Present days of the month	*March, May, July, October have thirty-one days*		*January, August, December have thirty-one days*		*April, June, September, November have thirty days*		*February has twenty-eight days, and in leap year twenty-nine*	
1	Kalendis		Kalendis		Kalendis		Kalendis	
2	VI		IV ⎫ ante		IV ⎫ ante		IV ⎫ ante	
3	V	ante	III ⎭ Nonas		III ⎭ Nonas		III ⎭ Nonas	
4	IV	Nonas	pridie Nonas		pridie Nonas		pridie Nonas	
5	III		Nonis		Nonis		Nonis	
6	pridie Nonas		VIII		VIII		VIII	
7	Nonis		VII		VII		VII	
8	VIII		VI ⎫ ante		VI ⎫ ante		VI ⎫ ante	
9	VII		V ⎭ Idus		V ⎭ Idus		V ⎭ Idus	
10	VI	ante	IV		IV		IV	
11	V	Idus	III		III		III	
12	IV		pridie Idus		pridie Idus		pridie Idus	
13	III		Idibus		Idibus		Idibus	
14	pridie Idus		XIX		XVIII		XVI	
15	Idibus		XVIII		XVII		XV	
16	XVII		XVII		XVI		XIV	
17	XVI		XVI		XV		XIII	
18	XV		XV		XIV		XII	
19	XIV		XIV		XIII		XI	
20	XIII		XIII		XII	ante Kalendas	X	ante Kalendas
21	XII		XII	ante Kalendas	XI	(of the month	IX	Martias
22	XI	ante Kalendas	XI	(of the month	X	following)	VIII	
23	X	(of the month	X	following)	IX		VII	
24	IX	following)	IX		VIII		*VI	
25	VIII		VIII		VII		V	
26	VII		VII		VI		IV	
27	VI		VI		V		III	
28	V		V		IV		pridie Kalendas
29	IV		IV		III		Martias
30	III		III		pridie Kalendas		
31	pridie Kalendas (Aprilis, Iunias, Sextilis, Novembris)		pridie Kalendas (Februarias, Septembris, Ianuarias)		(Maias, Quinctilis, Octobris, Decembris)		* (repeated in leap year)	

Calendar for Any Year 1780–2040

To select the correct calendar for any year between 1780 and 2040, consult the index below
* leap year

Year	Key	Year	Key	Year	Key	Year	Key	Year	Key	Year	Key	Year	Key	Year	Key
1780	N*	1813	K	1846	I	1879	G	1912	D*	1945	C	1978	A	2011	M
1781	C	1814	M	1847	K	1880	J*	1913	G	1946	E	1979	C	2012	B*
1782	E	1815	A	1848	N*	1881	M	1914	I	1947	G	1980	F*	2013	E
1783	G	1816	D*	1849	C	1882	A	1915	K	1948	J*	1981	I	2014	G
1784	J*	1817	G	1850	E	1883	C	1916	N*	1949	M	1982	K	2015	I
1785	M	1818	I	1851	G	1884	F*	1917	C	1950	A	1983	M	2016	L*
1786	A	1819	K	1852	J*	1885	I	1918	E	1951	C	1984	B*	2017	A
1787	C	1820	N*	1853	M	1886	K	1919	G	1952	F*	1985	E	2018	C
1788	F*	1821	C	1854	A	1887	M	1920	J*	1953	I	1986	G	2019	E
1789	I	1822	E	1855	C	1888	B*	1921	M	1954	K	1987	I	2020	H*
1790	K	1823	G	1856	F*	1889	E	1922	A	1955	M	1988	L*	2021	K
1791	M	1824	J*	1857	I	1890	G	1923	C	1956	B*	1989	A	2022	M
1792	B*	1825	M	1858	K	1891	I	1924	F*	1957	E	1990	C	2023	A
1793	E	1826	A	1859	M	1892	L*	1925	I	1958	G	1991	E	2024	D*
1794	G	1827	C	1860	B*	1893	A	1926	K	1959	I	1992	H*	2025	G
1795	I	1828	F*	1861	E	1894	C	1927	M	1960	L*	1993	K	2026	I
1796	L*	1829	I	1862	G	1895	E	1928	B*	1961	A	1994	M	2027	K
1797	A	1830	K	1863	I	1896	H*	1929	E	1962	C	1995	A	2028	N*
1798	C	1831	M	1864	L*	1897	K	1930	G	1963	E	1996	D*	2029	C
1799	E	1832	B*	1865	A	1898	M	1931	I	1964	H*	1997	G	2030	E
1800	G	1833	E	1866	C	1899	A	1932	L*	1965	K	1998	I	2031	G
1801	I	1834	G	1867	E	1900	C	1933	A	1966	M	1999	K	2032	J*
1802	K	1835	I	1868	H*	1901	E	1934	C	1967	A	2000	N*	2033	M
1803	M	1836	L*	1869	K	1902	G	1935	E	1968	D*	2001	C	2034	A
1804	B*	1837	A	1870	M	1903	I	1936	H*	1969	G	2002	E	2035	C
1805	E	1838	C	1871	A	1904	L*	1937	K	1970	I	2003	G	2036	F*
1806	G	1839	E	1872	D*	1905	A	1938	M	1971	K	2004	J*	2037	I
1807	I	1840	H*	1873	G	1906	C	1939	A	1972	N*	2005	M	2038	K
1808	L*	1841	K	1874	I	1907	E	1940	D*	1973	C	2006	A	2039	M
1809	A	1842	M	1875	K	1908	H*	1941	G	1974	E	2007	C	2040	B*
1810	C	1843	A	1876	N*	1909	K	1942	I	1975	G	2008	F*		
1811	E	1844	D*	1877	C	1910	M	1943	K	1976	J*	2009	I		
1812	H*	1845	G	1878	E	1911	A	1944	N*	1977	M	2010	K		

A

	January	February	March
Sun.	1 8 15 22 29	5 12 19 26	5 12 19 26
Mon.	2 9 16 23 30	6 13 20 27	6 13 20 27
Tue.	3 10 17 24 31	7 14 21 28	7 14 21 28
Wed.	4 11 18 25	1 8 15 22	1 8 15 22 29
Thur.	5 12 19 26	2 9 16 23	2 9 16 23 30
Fri.	6 13 20 27	3 10 17 24	3 10 17 24 31
Sat.	7 14 21 28	4 11 18 25	4 11 18 25

	April	May	June
Sun.	2 9 16 23 30	7 14 21 28	4 11 18 25
Mon.	3 10 17 24	1 8 15 22 29	5 12 19 26
Tue.	4 11 18 25	2 9 16 23 30	6 13 20 27
Wed.	5 12 19 26	3 10 17 24 31	7 14 21 28
Thur.	6 13 20 27	4 11 18 25	1 8 15 22 29
Fri.	7 14 21 28	5 12 19 26	2 9 16 23 30
Sat.	1 8 15 22 29	6 13 20 27	3 10 17 24

	July	August	September
Sun.	2 9 16 23 30	6 13 20 27	3 10 17 24
Mon.	3 10 17 24 31	7 14 21 28	4 11 18 25
Tue.	4 11 18 25	1 8 15 22 29	5 12 19 26
Wed.	5 12 19 26	2 9 16 23 30	6 13 20 27
Thur.	6 13 20 27	3 10 17 24 31	7 14 21 28
Fri.	7 14 21 28	4 11 18 25	1 8 15 22 29
Sat.	1 8 15 22 29	5 12 19 26	2 9 16 23 30

	October	November	December
Sun.	1 8 15 22 29	5 12 19 26	3 10 17 24 31
Mon.	2 9 16 23 30	6 13 20 27	4 11 18 25
Tue.	3 10 17 24 31	7 14 21 28	5 12 19 26
Wed.	4 11 18 25	1 8 15 22 29	6 13 20 27
Thur.	5 12 19 26	2 9 16 23 30	7 14 21 28
Fri.	6 13 20 27	3 10 17 24	1 8 15 22 29
Sat.	7 14 21 28	4 11 18 25	2 9 16 23 30

EASTER DAYS

March 26	1815, 1826, 1837, 1967, 1978, 1989
April 2	1809, 1893, 1899, 1961
April 9	1871, 1882, 1939, 1950, 2023, 2034
April 16	1786, 1797, 1843, 1854, 1865, 1911, 1922, 1933, 1995, 2006, 2017
April 23	1905

B (LEAP YEAR)

	January	February	March
Sun.	1 8 15 22 29	5 12 19 26	4 11 18 25
Mon.	2 9 16 23 30	6 13 20 27	5 12 19 26
Tue.	3 10 17 24 31	7 14 21 28	6 13 20 27
Wed.	4 11 18 25	1 8 15 22 29	7 14 21 28
Thur.	5 12 19 26	2 9 16 23	1 8 15 22 29
Fri.	6 13 20 27	3 10 17 24	2 9 16 23 30
Sat.	7 14 21 28	4 11 18 25	3 10 17 24 31

	April	May	June
Sun.	1 8 15 22 29	6 13 20 27	3 10 17 24
Mon.	2 9 16 23 30	7 14 21 28	4 11 18 25
Tue.	3 10 17 24	1 8 15 22 29	5 12 19 26
Wed.	4 11 18 25	2 9 16 23 30	6 13 20 27
Thur.	5 12 19 26	3 10 17 24 31	7 14 21 28
Fri.	6 13 20 27	4 11 18 25	1 8 15 22 29
Sat.	7 14 21 28	5 12 19 26	2 9 16 23 30

	July	August	September
Sun.	1 8 15 22 29	5 12 19 26	2 9 16 23 30
Mon.	2 9 16 23 30	6 13 20 27	3 10 17 24
Tue.	3 10 17 24 31	7 14 21 28	4 11 18 25
Wed.	4 11 18 25	1 8 15 22 29	5 12 19 26
Thur.	5 12 19 26	2 9 16 23 30	6 13 20 27
Fri.	6 13 20 27	3 10 17 24 31	7 14 21 28
Sat.	7 14 21 28	4 11 18 25	1 8 15 22 29

	October	November	December
Sun.	7 14 21 28	4 11 18 25	2 9 16 23 30
Mon.	1 8 15 22 29	5 12 19 26	3 10 17 24 31
Tue.	2 9 16 23 30	6 13 20 27	4 11 18 25
Wed.	3 10 17 24 31	7 14 21 28	5 12 19 26
Thur.	4 11 18 25	1 8 15 22 29	6 13 20 27
Fri.	5 12 19 26	2 9 16 23 30	7 14 21 28
Sat.	6 13 20 27	3 10 17 24	1 8 15 22 29

EASTER DAYS

April 1	1804, 1888, 1956, 2040
April 8	1792, 1860, 1928, 2012
April 22	1832, 1984

C

	January	February	March
Sun.	7 14 21 28	4 11 18 25	4 11 18 25
Mon.	1 8 15 22 29	5 12 19 26	5 12 19 26
Tue.	2 9 16 23 30	6 13 20 27	6 13 20 27
Wed.	3 10 17 24 31	7 14 21 28	7 14 21 28
Thur.	4 11 18 25	1 8 15 22	1 8 15 22 29
Fri.	5 12 19 26	2 9 16 23	2 9 16 23 30
Sat.	6 13 20 27	3 10 17 24	3 10 17 24 31

	April	May	June
Sun.	1 8 15 22 29	6 13 20 27	3 10 17 24
Mon.	2 9 16 23 30	7 14 21 28	4 11 18 25
Tue.	3 10 17 24	1 8 15 22 29	5 12 19 26
Wed.	4 11 18 25	2 9 16 23 30	6 13 20 27
Thur.	5 12 19 26	3 10 17 24 31	7 14 21 28
Fri.	6 13 20 27	4 11 18 25	1 8 15 22 29
Sat.	7 14 21 28	5 12 19 26	2 9 16 23 30

	July	August	September
Sun.	1 8 15 22 29	5 12 19 26	2 9 16 23 30
Mon.	2 9 16 23 30	6 13 20 27	3 10 17 24
Tue.	3 10 17 24 31	7 14 21 28	4 11 18 25
Wed.	4 11 18 25	1 8 15 22 29	5 12 19 26
Thur.	5 12 19 26	2 9 16 23 30	6 13 20 27
Fri.	6 13 20 27	3 10 17 24 31	7 14 21 28
Sat.	7 14 21 28	4 11 18 25	1 8 15 22 29

	October	November	December
Sun.	7 14 21 28	4 11 18 25	2 9 16 23 30
Mon.	1 8 15 22 29	5 12 19 26	3 10 17 24 31
Tue.	2 9 16 23 30	6 13 20 27	4 11 18 25
Wed.	3 10 17 24 31	7 14 21 28	5 12 19 26
Thur.	4 11 18 25	1 8 15 22 29	6 13 20 27
Fri.	5 12 19 26	2 9 16 23 30	7 14 21 28
Sat.	6 13 20 27	3 10 17 24	1 8 15 22 29

EASTER DAYS

March 25	1883, 1894, 1951, 2035
April 1	1866, 1877, 1923, 1934, 1945, 2018, 2029
April 8	1787, 1798, 1849, 1855, 1917, 2007
April 15	1781, 1827, 1838, 1900, 1906, 1979, 1990, 2001
April 22	1810, 1821, 1962, 1973

E

	January	February	March
Sun.	6 13 20 27	3 10 17 24	3 10 17 24 31
Mon.	7 14 21 28	4 11 18 25	4 11 18 25
Tue.	1 8 15 22 29	5 12 19 26	5 12 19 26
Wed.	2 9 16 23 30	6 13 20 27	6 13 20 27
Thur.	3 10 17 24 31	7 14 21 28	7 14 21 28
Fri.	4 11 18 25	1 8 15 22	1 8 15 22 29
Sat.	5 12 19 26	2 9 16 23	2 9 16 23 30

	April	May	June
Sun.	7 14 21 28	5 12 19 26	2 9 16 23 30
Mon.	1 8 15 22 29	6 13 20 27	3 10 17 24
Tue.	2 9 16 23 30	7 14 21 28	4 11 18 25
Wed.	3 10 17 24	1 8 15 22 29	5 12 19 26
Thur.	4 11 18 25	2 9 16 23 30	6 13 20 27
Fri.	5 12 19 26	3 10 17 24 31	7 14 21 28
Sat.	6 13 20 27	4 11 18 25	1 8 15 22 29

	July	August	September
Sun.	7 14 21 28	4 11 18 25	1 8 15 22 29
Mon.	1 8 15 22 29	5 12 19 26	2 9 16 23 30
Tue.	2 9 16 23 30	6 13 20 27	3 10 17 24
Wed.	3 10 17 24 31	7 14 21 28	4 11 18 25
Thur.	4 11 18 25	1 8 15 22 29	5 12 19 26
Fri.	5 12 19 26	2 9 16 23 30	6 13 20 27
Sat.	6 13 20 27	3 10 17 24 31	7 14 21 28

	October	November	December
Sun.	6 13 20 27	3 10 17 24	1 8 15 22 29
Mon.	7 14 21 28	4 11 18 25	2 9 16 23 30
Tue.	1 8 15 22 29	5 12 19 26	3 10 17 24 31
Wed.	2 9 16 23 30	6 13 20 27	4 11 18 25
Thur.	3 10 17 24 31	7 14 21 28	5 12 19 26
Fri.	4 11 18 25	1 8 15 22 29	6 13 20 27
Sat.	5 12 19 26	2 9 16 23 30	7 14 21 28

EASTER DAYS

March 24	1799
March 31	1782, 1793, 1839, 1850, 1861, 1907, 1918, 1929, 1991, 2002, 2013
April 7	1822, 1833, 1901, 1985
April 14	1805, 1811, 1895, 1963, 1974
April 21	1867, 1878, 1889, 1935, 1946, 1957, 2019, 2030

D (LEAP YEAR)

	January	February	March
Sun.	7 14 21 28	4 11 18 25	3 10 17 24 31
Mon.	1 8 15 22 29	5 12 19 26	4 11 18 25
Tue.	2 9 16 23 30	6 13 20 27	5 12 19 26
Wed.	3 10 17 24 31	7 14 21 28	6 13 20 27
Thur.	4 11 18 25	1 8 15 22 29	7 14 21 28
Fri.	5 12 19 26	2 9 16 23	1 8 15 22 29
Sat.	6 13 20 27	3 10 17 24	2 9 16 23 30

	April	May	June
Sun.	7 14 21 28	5 12 19 26	2 9 16 23 30
Mon.	1 8 15 22 29	6 13 20 27	3 10 17 24
Tue.	2 9 16 23 30	7 14 21 28	4 11 18 25
Wed.	3 10 17 24	1 8 15 22 29	5 12 19 26
Thur.	4 11 18 25	2 9 16 23 30	6 13 20 27
Fri.	5 12 19 26	3 10 17 24 31	7 14 21 28
Sat.	6 13 20 27	4 11 18 25	1 8 15 22 29

	July	August	September
Sun.	7 14 21 28	4 11 18 25	1 8 15 22 29
Mon.	1 8 15 22 29	5 12 19 26	2 9 16 23 30
Tue.	2 9 16 23 30	6 13 20 27	3 10 17 24
Wed.	3 10 17 24 31	7 14 21 28	4 11 18 25
Thur.	4 11 18 25	1 8 15 22 29	5 12 19 26
Fri.	5 12 19 26	2 9 16 23 30	6 13 20 27
Sat.	6 13 20 27	3 10 17 24 31	7 14 21 28

	October	November	December
Sun.	6 13 20 27	3 10 17 24	1 8 15 22 29
Mon.	7 14 21 28	4 11 18 25	2 9 16 23 30
Tue.	1 8 15 22 29	5 12 19 26	3 10 17 24 31
Wed.	2 9 16 23 30	6 13 20 27	4 11 18 25
Thur.	3 10 17 24 31	7 14 21 28	5 12 19 26
Fri.	4 11 18 25	1 8 15 22 29	6 13 20 27
Sat.	5 12 19 26	2 9 16 23 30	7 14 21 28

EASTER DAYS

March 24	1940
March 31	1872, 2024
April 7	1844, 1912, 1996
April 14	1816, 1968

F (LEAP YEAR)

	January	February	March
Sun.	6 13 20 27	3 10 17 24	2 9 16 23 30
Mon.	7 14 21 28	4 11 18 25	3 10 17 24 31
Tue.	1 8 15 22 29	5 12 19 26	4 11 18 25
Wed.	2 9 16 23 30	6 13 20 27	5 12 19 26
Thur.	3 10 17 24 31	7 14 21 28	6 13 20 27
Fri.	4 11 18 25	1 8 15 22 29	7 14 21 28
Sat.	5 12 19 26	2 9 16 23	1 8 15 22 29

	April	May	June
Sun.	6 13 20 27	4 11 18 25	1 8 15 22 29
Mon.	7 14 21 28	5 12 19 26	2 9 16 23 30
Tue.	1 8 15 22 29	6 13 20 27	3 10 17 24
Wed.	2 9 16 23 30	7 14 21 28	4 11 18 25
Thur.	3 10 17 24	1 8 15 22 29	5 12 19 26
Fri.	4 11 18 25	2 9 16 23 30	6 13 20 27
Sat.	5 12 19 26	3 10 17 24 31	7 14 21 28

	July	August	September
Sun.	6 13 20 27	3 10 17 24 31	7 14 21 28
Mon.	7 14 21 28	4 11 18 25	1 8 15 22 29
Tue.	1 8 15 22 29	5 12 19 26	2 9 16 23 30
Wed.	2 9 16 23 30	6 13 20 27	3 10 17 24
Thur.	3 10 17 24 31	7 14 21 28	4 11 18 25
Fri.	4 11 18 25	1 8 15 22 29	5 12 19 26
Sat.	5 12 19 26	2 9 16 23 30	6 13 20 27

	October	November	December
Sun.	5 12 19 26	2 9 16 23 30	7 14 21 28
Mon.	6 13 20 27	3 10 17 24	1 8 15 22 29
Tue.	7 14 21 28	4 11 18 25	2 9 16 23 30
Wed.	1 8 15 22 29	5 12 19 26	3 10 17 24 31
Thur.	2 9 16 23 30	6 13 20 27	4 11 18 25
Fri.	3 10 17 24 31	7 14 21 28	5 12 19 26
Sat.	4 11 18 25	1 8 15 22 29	6 13 20 27

EASTER DAYS

March 23	1788, 1856, 2008
April 6	1828, 1980
April 13	1884, 1952, 2036
April 20	1924

G

	January	February	March
Sun.	5 12 19 26	2 9 16 23	2 9 16 23 30
Mon.	6 13 20 27	3 10 17 24	3 10 17 24 31
Tue.	7 14 21 28	4 11 18 25	4 11 18 25
Wed.	1 8 15 22 29	5 12 19 26	5 12 19 26
Thur.	2 9 16 23 30	6 13 20 27	6 13 20 27
Fri.	3 10 17 24 31	7 14 21 28	7 14 21 28
Sat.	4 11 18 25	1 8 15 22	1 8 15 22 29

	April	May	June
Sun.	6 13 20 27	4 11 18 25	1 8 15 22 29
Mon.	7 14 21 28	5 12 19 26	2 9 16 23 30
Tue.	1 8 15 22 29	6 13 20 27	3 10 17 24
Wed.	2 9 16 23 30	7 14 21 28	4 11 18 25
Thur.	3 10 17 24	1 8 15 22 29	5 12 19 26
Fri.	4 11 18 25	2 9 16 23 30	6 13 20 27
Sat.	5 12 19 26	3 10 17 24 31	7 14 21 28

	July	August	September
Sun.	6 13 20 27	3 10 17 24 31	7 14 21 28
Mon.	7 14 21 28	4 11 18 25	1 8 15 22 29
Tue.	1 8 15 22 29	5 12 19 26	2 9 16 23 30
Wed.	2 9 16 23 30	6 13 20 27	3 10 17 24
Thur.	3 10 17 24 31	7 14 21 28	4 11 18 25
Fri.	4 11 18 25	1 8 15 22 29	5 12 19 26
Sat.	5 12 19 26	2 9 16 23 30	6 13 20 27

	October	November	December
Sun.	5 12 19 26	2 9 16 23 30	7 14 21 28
Mon.	6 13 20 27	3 10 17 24	1 8 15 22 29
Tue.	7 14 21 28	4 11 18 25	2 9 16 23 30
Wed.	1 8 15 22 29	5 12 19 26	3 10 17 24 31
Thur.	2 9 16 23 30	6 13 20 27	4 11 18 25
Fri.	3 10 17 24 31	7 14 21 28	5 12 19 26
Sat.	4 11 18 25	1 8 15 22 29	6 13 20 27

EASTER DAYS

March 23	1845, 1913
March 30	1823, 1834, 1902, 1975, 1986, 1997
April 6	1806, 1817, 1890, 1947, 1958, 1969
April 13	1800, 1873, 1879, 1941, 2031
April 20	1783, 1794, 1851, 1862, 1919, 1930, 2003, 2014, 2025

I

	January	February	March
Sun.	4 11 18 25	1 8 15 22	1 8 15 22 29
Mon.	5 12 19 26	2 9 16 23	2 9 16 23 30
Tue.	6 13 20 27	3 10 17 24	3 10 17 24 31
Wed.	7 14 21 28	4 11 18 25	4 11 18 25
Thur.	1 8 15 22 29	5 12 19 26	5 12 19 26
Fri.	2 9 16 23 30	6 13 20 27	6 13 20 27
Sat.	3 10 17 24 31	7 14 21 28	7 14 21 28

	April	May	June
Sun.	5 12 19 26	3 10 17 24 31	7 14 21 28
Mon.	6 13 20 27	4 11 18 25	1 8 15 22 29
Tue.	7 14 21 28	5 12 19 26	2 9 16 23 30
Wed.	1 8 15 22 29	6 13 20 27	3 10 17 24
Thur.	2 9 16 23 30	7 14 21 28	4 11 18 25
Fri.	3 10 17 24	1 8 15 22 29	5 12 19 26
Sat.	4 11 18 25	2 9 16 23 30	6 13 20 27

	July	August	September
Sun.	5 12 19 26	2 9 16 23 30	6 13 20 27
Mon.	6 13 20 27	3 10 17 24 31	7 14 21 28
Tue.	7 14 21 28	4 11 18 25	1 8 15 22 29
Wed.	1 8 15 22 29	5 12 19 26	2 9 16 23 30
Thur.	2 9 16 23 30	6 13 20 27	3 10 17 24
Fri.	3 10 17 24 31	7 14 21 28	4 11 18 25
Sat.	4 11 18 25	1 8 15 22 29	5 12 19 26

	October	November	December
Sun.	4 11 18 25	1 8 15 22 29	6 13 20 27
Mon.	5 12 19 26	2 9 16 23 30	7 14 21 28
Tue.	6 13 20 27	3 10 17 24	1 8 15 22 29
Wed.	7 14 21 28	4 11 18 25	2 9 16 23 30
Thur.	1 8 15 22 29	5 12 19 26	3 10 17 24 31
Fri.	2 9 16 23 30	6 13 20 27	4 11 18 25
Sat.	3 10 17 24 31	7 14 21 28	5 12 19 26

EASTER DAYS

March 22	1818
March 29	1807, 1891, 1959, 1970
April 5	1795, 1801, 1863, 1874, 1885, 1931, 1942, 1953, 2015, 2026, 2037
April 12	1789, 1846, 1857, 1903, 1914, 1925, 1998, 2009
April 19	1829, 1835, 1981, 1987

H (LEAP YEAR)

	January	February	March
Sun.	5 12 19 26	2 9 16 23	1 8 15 22 29
Mon.	6 13 20 27	3 10 17 24	2 9 16 23 30
Tue.	7 14 21 28	4 11 18 25	3 10 17 24 31
Wed.	1 8 15 22 29	5 12 19 26	4 11 18 25
Thur.	2 9 16 23 30	6 13 20 27	5 12 19 26
Fri.	3 10 17 24 31	7 14 21 28	6 13 20 27
Sat.	4 11 18 25	1 8 15 22 29	7 14 21 28

	April	May	June
Sun.	5 12 19 26	3 10 17 24 31	7 14 21 28
Mon.	6 13 20 27	4 11 18 25	1 8 15 22 29
Tue.	7 14 21 28	5 12 19 26	2 9 16 23 30
Wed.	1 8 15 22 29	6 13 20 27	3 10 17 24
Thur.	2 9 16 23 30	7 14 21 28	4 11 18 25
Fri.	3 10 17 24	1 8 15 22 29	5 12 19 26
Sat.	4 11 18 25	2 9 16 23 30	6 13 20 27

	July	August	September
Sun.	5 12 19 26	2 9 16 23 30	6 13 20 27
Mon.	6 13 20 27	3 10 17 24 31	7 14 21 28
Tue.	7 14 21 28	4 11 18 25	1 8 15 22 29
Wed.	1 8 15 22 29	5 12 19 26	2 9 16 23 30
Thur.	2 9 16 23 30	6 13 20 27	3 10 17 24
Fri.	3 10 17 24 31	7 14 21 28	4 11 18 25
Sat.	4 11 18 25	1 8 15 22 29	5 12 19 26

	October	November	December
Sun.	4 11 18 25	1 8 15 22 29	6 13 20 27
Mon.	5 12 19 26	2 9 16 23 30	7 14 21 28
Tue.	6 13 20 27	3 10 17 24	1 8 15 22 29
Wed.	7 14 21 28	4 11 18 25	2 9 16 23 30
Thur.	1 8 15 22 29	5 12 19 26	3 10 17 24 31
Fri.	2 9 16 23 30	6 13 20 27	4 11 18 25
Sat.	3 10 17 24 31	7 14 21 28	5 12 19 26

EASTER DAYS

March 29	1812, 1964
April 5	1896
April 12	1868, 1936, 2020
April 19	1840, 1908, 1992

J (LEAP YEAR)

	January	February	March
Sun.	4 11 18 25	1 8 15 22 29	7 14 21 28
Mon.	5 12 19 26	2 9 16 23	1 8 15 22 29
Tue.	6 13 20 27	3 10 17 24	2 9 16 23 30
Wed.	7 14 21 28	4 11 18 25	3 10 17 24 31
Thur.	1 8 15 22 29	5 12 19 26	4 11 18 25
Fri.	2 9 16 23 30	6 13 20 27	5 12 19 26
Sat.	3 10 17 24 31	7 14 21 28	6 13 20 27

	April	May	June
Sun.	4 11 18 25	2 9 16 23 30	6 13 20 27
Mon.	5 12 19 26	3 10 17 24 31	7 14 21 28
Tue.	6 13 20 27	4 11 18 25	1 8 15 22 29
Wed.	7 14 21 28	5 12 19 26	2 9 16 23 30
Thur.	1 8 15 22 29	6 13 20 27	3 10 17 24
Fri.	2 9 16 23 30	7 14 21 28	4 11 18 25
Sat.	3 10 17 24	1 8 15 22 29	5 12 19 26

	July	August	September
Sun.	4 11 18 25	1 8 15 22 29	5 12 19 26
Mon.	5 12 19 26	2 9 16 23 30	6 13 20 27
Tue.	6 13 20 27	3 10 17 24 31	7 14 21 28
Wed.	7 14 21 28	4 11 18 25	1 8 15 22 29
Thur.	1 8 15 22 29	5 12 19 26	2 9 16 23 30
Fri.	2 9 16 23 30	6 13 20 27	3 10 17 24
Sat.	3 10 17 24 31	7 14 21 28	4 11 18 25

	October	November	December
Sun.	3 10 17 24 31	7 14 21 28	5 12 19 26
Mon.	4 11 18 25	1 8 15 22 29	6 13 20 27
Tue.	5 12 19 26	2 9 16 23 30	7 14 21 28
Wed.	6 13 20 27	3 10 17 24	1 8 15 22 29
Thur.	7 14 21 28	4 11 18 25	2 9 16 23 30
Fri.	1 8 15 22 29	5 12 19 26	3 10 17 24 31
Sat.	2 9 16 23 30	6 13 20 27	4 11 18 25

EASTER DAYS

March 28	1880, 1948, 2032
April 4	1920
April 11	1784, 1852, 2004
April 18	1824, 1976

K

January				February				March			
Sun.	3	10	17	24	31	Sun. 7	14	21	28	Sun. 7	14	21	28

January
- Sun. 3 10 17 24 31
- Mon. 4 11 18 25
- Tue. 5 12 19 26
- Wed. 6 13 20 27
- Thur. 7 14 21 28
- Fri. 1 8 15 22 29
- Sat. 2 9 16 23 30

February
- Sun. 7 14 21 28
- Mon. 1 8 15 22
- Tue. 2 9 16 23
- Wed. 3 10 17 24
- Thur. 4 11 18 25
- Fri. 5 12 19 26
- Sat. 6 13 20 27

March
- Sun. 7 14 21 28
- Mon. 1 8 15 22 29
- Tue. 2 9 16 23 30
- Wed. 3 10 17 24 31
- Thur. 4 11 18 25
- Fri. 5 12 19 26
- Sat. 6 13 20 27

April
- Sun. 4 11 18 25
- Mon. 5 12 19 26
- Tue. 6 13 20 27
- Wed. 7 14 21 28
- Thur. 1 8 15 22 29
- Fri. 2 9 16 23 30
- Sat. 3 10 17 24

May
- Sun. 2 9 16 23 30
- Mon. 3 10 17 24 31
- Tue. 4 11 18 25
- Wed. 5 12 19 26
- Thur. 6 13 20 27
- Fri. 7 14 21 28
- Sat. 1 8 15 22 29

June
- Sun. 6 13 20 27
- Mon. 7 14 21 28
- Tue. 1 8 15 22 29
- Wed. 2 9 16 23 30
- Thur. 3 10 17 24
- Fri. 4 11 18 25
- Sat. 5 12 19 26

July
- Sun. 4 11 18 25
- Mon. 5 12 19 26
- Tue. 6 13 20 27
- Wed. 7 14 21 28
- Thur. 1 8 15 22 29
- Fri. 2 9 16 23 30
- Sat. 3 10 17 24 31

August
- Sun. 1 8 15 22 29
- Mon. 2 9 16 23 30
- Tue. 3 10 17 24 31
- Wed. 4 11 18 25
- Thur. 5 12 19 26
- Fri. 6 13 20 27
- Sat. 7 14 21 28

September
- Sun. 5 12 19 26
- Mon. 6 13 20 27
- Tue. 7 14 21 28
- Wed. 1 8 15 22 29
- Thur. 2 9 16 23 30
- Fri. 3 10 17 24
- Sat. 4 11 18 25

October
- Sun. 3 10 17 24 31
- Mon. 4 11 18 25
- Tue. 5 12 19 26
- Wed. 6 13 20 27
- Thur. 7 14 21 28
- Fri. 1 8 15 22 29
- Sat. 2 9 16 23 30

November
- Sun. 7 14 21 28
- Mon. 1 8 15 22 29
- Tue. 2 9 16 23 30
- Wed. 3 10 17 24
- Thur. 4 11 18 25
- Fri. 5 12 19 26
- Sat. 6 13 20 27

December
- Sun. 5 12 19 26
- Mon. 6 13 20 27
- Tue. 7 14 21 28
- Wed. 1 8 15 22 29
- Thur. 2 9 16 23 30
- Fri. 3 10 17 24 31
- Sat. 4 11 18 25

EASTER DAYS

March 28	1869, 1875, 1937, 2027
April 4	1790, 1847, 1858, 1915, 1926, 1999, 2010, 2021
April 11	1819, 1830, 1841, 1909, 1971, 1982, 1993
April 18	1802, 1813, 1897, 1954, 1965
April 25	1886, 1943, 2038

M

January
- Sun. 2 9 16 23 30
- Mon. 3 10 17 24 31
- Tue. 4 11 18 25
- Wed. 5 12 19 26
- Thur. 6 13 20 27
- Fri. 7 14 21 28
- Sat. 1 8 15 22 29

February
- Sun. 6 13 20 27
- Mon. 7 14 21 28
- Tue. 1 8 15 22
- Wed. 2 9 16 23
- Thur. 3 10 17 24
- Fri. 4 11 18 25
- Sat. 5 12 19 26

March
- Sun. 6 13 20 27
- Mon. 7 14 21 28
- Tue. 1 8 15 22 29
- Wed. 2 9 16 23 30
- Thur. 3 10 17 24 31
- Fri. 4 11 18 25
- Sat. 5 12 19 26

April
- Sun. 3 10 17 24
- Mon. 4 11 18 25
- Tue. 5 12 19 26
- Wed. 6 13 20 27
- Thur. 7 14 21 28
- Fri. 1 8 15 22 29
- Sat. 2 9 16 23 30

May
- Sun. 1 8 15 22 29
- Mon. 2 9 16 23 30
- Tue. 3 10 17 24 31
- Wed. 4 11 18 25
- Thur. 5 12 19 26
- Fri. 6 13 20 27
- Sat. 7 14 21 28

June
- Sun. 5 12 19 26
- Mon. 6 13 20 27
- Tue. 7 14 21 28
- Wed. 1 8 15 22 29
- Thur. 2 9 16 23 30
- Fri. 3 10 17 24
- Sat. 4 11 18 25

July
- Sun. 3 10 17 24 31
- Mon. 4 11 18 25
- Tue. 5 12 19 26
- Wed. 6 13 20 27
- Thur. 7 14 21 28
- Fri. 1 8 15 22 29
- Sat. 2 9 16 23 30

August
- Sun. 7 14 21 28
- Mon. 1 8 15 22 29
- Tue. 2 9 16 23 30
- Wed. 3 10 17 24 31
- Thur. 4 11 18 25
- Fri. 5 12 19 26
- Sat. 6 13 20 27

September
- Sun. 4 11 18 25
- Mon. 5 12 19 26
- Tue. 6 13 20 27
- Wed. 7 14 21 28
- Thur. 1 8 15 22 29
- Fri. 2 9 16 23 30
- Sat. 3 10 17 24

October
- Sun. 2 9 16 23 30
- Mon. 3 10 17 24 31
- Tue. 4 11 18 25
- Wed. 5 12 19 26
- Thur. 6 13 20 27
- Fri. 7 14 21 28
- Sat. 1 8 15 22 29

November
- Sun. 6 13 20 27
- Mon. 7 14 21 28
- Tue. 1 8 15 22 29
- Wed. 2 9 16 23 30
- Thur. 3 10 17 24
- Fri. 4 11 18 25
- Sat. 5 12 19 26

December
- Sun. 4 11 18 25
- Mon. 5 12 19 26
- Tue. 6 13 20 27
- Wed. 7 14 21 28
- Thur. 1 8 15 22 29
- Fri. 2 9 16 23 30
- Sat. 3 10 17 24 31

EASTER DAYS

March 27	1785, 1842, 1853, 1910, 1921, 2005
April 3	1825, 1831, 1983, 1994
April 10	1803, 1814, 1887, 1898, 1955, 1966, 1977, 2039
April 17	1870, 1881, 1927, 1938, 1949, 2022, 2033
April 24	1791, 1859, 2011

L (LEAP YEAR)

January
- Sun. 3 10 17 24 31
- Mon. 4 11 18 25
- Tue. 5 12 19 26
- Wed. 6 13 20 27
- Thur. 7 14 21 28
- Fri. 1 8 15 22 29
- Sat. 2 9 16 23 30

February
- Sun. 7 14 21 28
- Mon. 1 8 15 22 29
- Tue. 2 9 16 23
- Wed. 3 10 17 24
- Thur. 4 11 18 25
- Fri. 5 12 19 26
- Sat. 6 13 20 27

March
- Sun. 6 13 20 27
- Mon. 7 14 21 28
- Tue. 1 8 15 22 29
- Wed. 2 9 16 23 30
- Thur. 3 10 17 24 31
- Fri. 4 11 18 25
- Sat. 5 12 19 26

April
- Sun. 3 10 17 24
- Mon. 4 11 18 25
- Tue. 5 12 19 26
- Wed. 6 13 20 27
- Thur. 7 14 21 28
- Fri. 1 8 15 22 29
- Sat. 2 9 16 23 30

May
- Sun. 1 8 15 22 29
- Mon. 2 9 16 23 30
- Tue. 3 10 17 24 31
- Wed. 4 11 18 25
- Thur. 5 12 19 26
- Fri. 6 13 20 27
- Sat. 7 14 21 28

June
- Sun. 5 12 19 26
- Mon. 6 13 20 27
- Tue. 7 14 21 28
- Wed. 1 8 15 22 29
- Thur. 2 9 16 23 30
- Fri. 3 10 17 24
- Sat. 4 11 18 25

July
- Sun. 3 10 17 24 31
- Mon. 4 11 18 25
- Tue. 5 12 19 26
- Wed. 6 13 20 27
- Thur. 7 14 21 28
- Fri. 1 8 15 22 29
- Sat. 2 9 16 23 30

August
- Sun. 7 14 21 28
- Mon. 1 8 15 22 29
- Tue. 2 9 16 23 30
- Wed. 3 10 17 24 31
- Thur. 4 11 18 25
- Fri. 5 12 19 26
- Sat. 6 13 20 27

September
- Sun. 4 11 18 25
- Mon. 5 12 19 26
- Tue. 6 13 20 27
- Wed. 7 14 21 28
- Thur. 1 8 15 22 29
- Fri. 2 9 16 23 30
- Sat. 3 10 17 24

October
- Sun. 2 9 16 23 30
- Mon. 3 10 17 24 31
- Tue. 4 11 18 25
- Wed. 5 12 19 26
- Thur. 6 13 20 27
- Fri. 7 14 21 28
- Sat. 1 8 15 22 29

November
- Sun. 6 13 20 27
- Mon. 7 14 21 28
- Tue. 1 8 15 22 29
- Wed. 2 9 16 23 30
- Thur. 3 10 17 24
- Fri. 4 11 18 25
- Sat. 5 12 19 26

December
- Sun. 4 11 18 25
- Mon. 5 12 19 26
- Tue. 6 13 20 27
- Wed. 7 14 21 28
- Thur. 1 8 15 22 29
- Fri. 2 9 16 23 30
- Sat. 3 10 17 24 31

EASTER DAYS

March 27	1796, 1864, 1932, 2016
April 3	1836, 1904, 1988
April 17	1808, 1892, 1960

N (LEAP YEAR)

January
- Sun. 2 9 16 23 30
- Mon. 3 10 17 24 31
- Tue. 4 11 18 25
- Wed. 5 12 19 26
- Thur. 6 13 20 27
- Fri. 7 14 21 28
- Sat. 1 8 15 22 29

February
- Sun. 6 13 20 27
- Mon. 7 14 21 28
- Tue. 1 8 15 22 29
- Wed. 2 9 16 23
- Thur. 3 10 17 24
- Fri. 4 11 18 25
- Sat. 5 12 19 26

March
- Sun. 5 12 19 26
- Mon. 6 13 20 27
- Tue. 7 14 21 28
- Wed. 1 8 15 22 29
- Thur. 2 9 16 23 30
- Fri. 3 10 17 24 31
- Sat. 4 11 18 25

April
- Sun. 2 9 16 23 30
- Mon. 3 10 17 24
- Tue. 4 11 18 25
- Wed. 5 12 19 26
- Thur. 6 13 20 27
- Fri. 7 14 21 28
- Sat. 1 8 15 22 29

May
- Sun. 7 14 21 28
- Mon. 1 8 15 22 29
- Tue. 2 9 16 23 30
- Wed. 3 10 17 24 31
- Thur. 4 11 18 25
- Fri. 5 12 19 26
- Sat. 6 13 20 27

June
- Sun. 4 11 18 25
- Mon. 5 12 19 26
- Tue. 6 13 20 27
- Wed. 7 14 21 28
- Thur. 1 8 15 22 29
- Fri. 2 9 16 23 30
- Sat. 3 10 17 24

July
- Sun. 2 9 16 23 30
- Mon. 3 10 17 24 31
- Tue. 4 11 18 25
- Wed. 5 12 19 26
- Thur. 6 13 20 27
- Fri. 7 14 21 28
- Sat. 1 8 15 22 29

August
- Sun. 6 13 20 27
- Mon. 7 14 21 28
- Tue. 1 8 15 22 29
- Wed. 2 9 16 23 30
- Thur. 3 10 17 24 31
- Fri. 4 11 18 25
- Sat. 5 12 19 26

September
- Sun. 3 10 17 24
- Mon. 4 11 18 25
- Tue. 5 12 19 26
- Wed. 6 13 20 27
- Thur. 7 14 21 28
- Fri. 1 8 15 22 29
- Sat. 2 9 16 23 30

October
- Sun. 1 8 15 22 29
- Mon. 2 9 16 23 30
- Tue. 3 10 17 24 31
- Wed. 4 11 18 25
- Thur. 5 12 19 26
- Fri. 6 13 20 27
- Sat. 7 14 21 28

November
- Sun. 5 12 19 26
- Mon. 6 13 20 27
- Tue. 7 14 21 28
- Wed. 1 8 15 22 29
- Thur. 2 9 16 23 30
- Fri. 3 10 17 24
- Sat. 4 11 18 25

December
- Sun. 3 10 17 24 31
- Mon. 4 11 18 25
- Tue. 5 12 19 26
- Wed. 6 13 20 27
- Thur. 7 14 21 28
- Fri. 1 8 15 22 29
- Sat. 2 9 16 23 30

EASTER DAYS

March 26	1780
April 2	1820, 1972
April 9	1944
April 16	2028
April 23	1848, 1916, 2000

GEOLOGICAL TIME

The earth is thought to have come into existence approximately 4,600 million years ago, but for nearly half this time, the Archean era, it was uninhabited. Life is generally believed to have emerged in the succeeding Proterozoic era. The Archean and the Proterozoic eras are often together referred to as the Precambrian.

Although primitive forms of life, e.g. algae and bacteria, existed during the Proterozoic era, it is not until the strata of Palaeozoic rocks is reached that abundant fossilized remains appear.

Since the Precambrian, there have been three great geological eras:

PALAEOZOIC ('ancient life')
*c.*570–*c.*245 million years ago

Cambrian – Mainly sandstones, slate and shales; limestones in Scotland. Shelled fossils and invertebrates, e.g. trilobites and brachiopods appear

Ordovician – Mainly shales and mudstones, e.g. in north Wales; limestones in Scotland. First fishes

Silurian – Shales, mudstones and some limestones, found mostly in Wales and southern Scotland

Devonian – Old red sandstone, shale, limestone and slate, e.g. in south Wales and the West Country

Carboniferous – Coal-bearing rocks, millstone grit, limestone and shale. First traces of land-living life

Permian – Marls, sandstones and clays. First reptile fossils

There were two great phases of mountain building in the Palaeozoic era: the Caledonian, characterized in Britain by NE–SW lines of hills and valleys; and the later Hercyian, widespread in west Germany and adjacent areas, and in Britain exemplified in E.–W. lines of hills and valleys.

The end of the Palaeozoic era was marked by the extensive glaciations of the Permian period in the southern continents and the decline of amphibians. It was succeeded by an era of warm conditions.

MESOZOIC ('middle forms of life')
*c.*245–*c.*65 million years ago

Triassic – Mostly sandstone, e.g. in the West Midlands

Jurassic – Mainly limestones and clays, typically displayed in the Jura mountains, and in England in a NE–SW belt from Lincolnshire and the Wash to the Severn and the Dorset coast

Cretaceous – Mainly chalk, clay and sands, e.g. in Kent and Sussex

Giant reptiles were dominant during the Mesozoic era, but it was at this time that marsupial mammals first appeared, as well as *Archaeopteryx lithographica*, the earliest known species of bird. Coniferous trees and flowering plants also developed during the era and, with the birds and the mammals, were the main species to survive into the Cenozoic era. The giant reptiles became extinct.

CENOZOIC ('recent life')
from *c.*65 million years ago

Palaeocene ⎫ The emergence of new forms of life, includ-
Eocene ⎬ ing existing species
Oligocene – Fossils of a few still existing species
Miocene – Fossil remains show a balance of existing and extinct species
Pliocene – Fossil remains show a majority of still existing species
Pleistocene – The majority of remains are those of still existing species

Holocene – The present, post-glacial period. Existing species only, except for a few exterminated by man

In the last 25 million years, from the Miocene through the Pliocene periods, the Alpine-Himalayan and the circum-Pacific phases of mountain building reached their climax. During the Pleistocene period ice-sheets repeatedly locked up masses of water as land ice; its weight depressed the land, but the locking-up of the water lowered the sea-level by 100–200 metres. The glaciations and interglacials of the Ice Age are difficult to date and classify, but recent scientific opinion considers the Pleistocene period to have begun approximately 1.64 million years ago. The last glacial retreat, merging into the Holocene period, was 10,000 years ago.

HUMAN DEVELOPMENT

Any consideration of the history of mankind must start with the fact that all members of the human race belong to one species of animal, i.e. *Homo sapiens*, the definition of a species being in biological terms that all its members can interbreed. As a species of mammal it is possible to group man with other similar types, known as the primates. Amongst these is found a sub-group, the apes, which includes, in addition to man, the chimpanzees, gorillas, orang-utans and gibbons. All lack a tail, have shoulder blades at the back, and a Y-shaped chewing pattern on the surface of their molars, as well as showing the more general primate characteristics of four incisors, a thumb which is able to touch the fingers of the same hand, and finger and toe nails instead of claws. The factors available to scientific study suggest that human beings have chimpanzees and gorillas as their nearest relatives in the animal world. However, there remains the possibility that there once lived creatures, now extinct, which were closer to modern man than the chimpanzees and gorillas, and which shared with modern man the characteristics of having flat faces (i.e. the absence of a pronounced muzzle), being bipedal, and possessing large brains.

There are two broad groups of extinct apes recognized by specialists. The ramapithecines, the remains of which, mainly jaw fragments, have been found in east Africa, Asia, and Turkey. They lived about 14 to 8 million years ago and from the evidence of their teeth it is thought that the second sub-group, whose geographic spread is limited to south and east Africa and whose geographic spread is limited to 5 million years ago, they were closer relatives of modern man to the extent that they walked upright, did not have an extensive muzzle and had similar types of pre-molars. The first australopithecine remains were recognized at Taung in South Africa in 1924 and subsequent discoveries include those at the Olduvai Gorge in Tanzania. The most impressive discovery was made at Hadar, Ethiopia, in 1974 when about half a skeleton, known as 'Lucy', was found.

Also in east Africa, between 2 million and 1.5 million years ago, lived a hominid group which not only walked upright, had a flat face, and a large brain case, but also made simple pebble and flake stone tools. On present evidence these habilines seem to have been the first people to make tools, however crude. This facility is related to the larger brain size and human beings are the only animals to make implements to be used in other processes. These early pebble tool users, because of their distinctive

GEOLOGICAL TIME

Era	Period	Epoch	Date began*	Evolutionary stages
Cenozoic	Quaternary	Holocene	0.01	Man
		Pleistocene	1.64	
	Tertiary	Pliocene	5.2	
		Miocene	23.3	
		Oligocene	35.4	
		Eocene	56.5	
		Palaeocene	65.0	
Mesozoic	Cretaceous		145.6	
	Jurassic		208.0	First birds
	Triassic		245.0	First mammals
	Permian		290.0	First reptiles
	Carboniferous		362.5	First amphibians and insects
			408.5	
	Ordovician			
	Cambrian		510.0	First fishes
Precambrian			?0.0	First invertebrates
			4,600.0	First primitive life forms, e.g. algae and bacteria

*millions of years ago

characteristics, have been grouped as a separate sub-species, now extinct, of the genus *Homo* and are known as *Homo habilis*.

The use of fire, again a human characteristic, is associated with another group of extinct hominids whose remains, about a million years old, are found in south and east Africa, China, Indonesia, north Africa and Europe. Mastery of the techniques of making fire probably helped the colonization of the colder northern areas and in this respect the site of Vertesszollos in Hungary is of particular importance. *Homo erectus* is the name given to this group of fossils and it includes a number of famous individual discoveries, e.g. Solo Man, Heidelberg Man, and especially Peking Man who lived at the cave site at Choukoutien which has yielded evidence of fire and burnt bone.

The well-known group Neanderthal Man, or *Homo sapiens neandertalensis*, is an extinct form of modern man who lived between about 100,000 and 40,000 years ago, thus spanning the last Ice Age. Indeed, its ability to adapt to the cold climate on the edge of the ice-sheets is one of its characteristic features, the remains being found only in Europe, Asia and the Middle East. Complete neanderthal skeletons were found during excavations at Tabun in Israel, together with evidence of tool-making and the use of fire. Distinguished by very large brains, it seems that neanderthal man was the first to develop recognizable social customs, especially deliberate burial rites. Why the neanderthalers became extinct is not clear but it may be connected with the climatic changes at the end of the Ice Ages, which would have seriously affected their food supplies; possibly they became too specialized for their own good.

The Swanscombe skull is the only known human fossil remains found in England. Some specialists see Swanscombe Man (or, more probably, woman) as a neanderthaler. Others group these remains together with the Steinheim skull from Germany, seeing both as a separate sub-species. There is too little evidence as yet on which to form a final judgement.

Modern Man, *Homo sapiens sapiens*, the surviving sub-species of *Homo sapiens*, had evolved to our present physical condition and had colonized much of the world by about 30,000 years ago. There are many previously distinguished individual specimens, e.g. Cromagnon Man, which may now be grouped together as *Homo sapiens sapiens*. It is modern man who spread to the American continent, crossing the landbridge between Siberia and Alaska, and thence moved south through North America and into South America. Equally it is modern man who over the past 30,000 years has been responsible for the major developments in technology, art and civilization generally.

One of the problems for those studying fossil man is the lack in many cases of sufficient quantities of fossil bone for analysis. It is important that the evidence should be tested against evidence, rather than theories being made to fit the theory. The Piltdown hoax is a well-known example of 'fossils' being forged to fit what was seen in some quarters as the correct theory of man's evolution.

CULTURAL DEVELOPMENT

The Eurocentric bias of early archaeologists meant that the search for a starting point for the development and transmission of cultural ideas, especially by migration, trade and warfare, concentrated unduly on Europe and the Near East. The Three Age system, whereby pre-history was divided into a Stone Age, a Bronze Age and an Iron Age, was devised by Christian Thomsen, curator of the National Museum of Denmark in the early 19th century, to facilitate the classification of the museum's collections.

The descriptive adjectives referred to the materials from which the implements and weapons were made and came to be regarded as the dominant features of the societies to which they related. The refinement of the Three Age system once dominated archaeological thought and remains a generally accepted concept in the popular mind. However, it is now seen by archaeologists as an inadequate model for human development.

Common sense suggests that there were no complete breaks between one so-called Age and another, any more than contemporaries would have regarded 1485 as a complete break between medieval and modern English history. Nor can the Three Age system be applied universally. In some areas it is necessary to insert a Copper Age, while in Africa south of the Sahara there would seem to be no Bronze Age at all; in Australia, Old Stone Age societies survived, while in South America, New Stone Age communities existed into modern times. The civilizations in other parts of the world clearly invalidate a Eurocentric theory of human development.

The concept of the 'Neolithic revolution', associated with the domestication of plants and animals, was a development of particular importance in the human cultural pattern. It reflected change from the primitive hunter/gatherer economies to a more settled agricultural way of life and therefore, so the argument goes, made possible the development of urban civilization. However, it can no longer be argued that this 'revolution' took place only in one area from which all development stemmed. Though it appears that the cultivation of wheat and barley was first undertaken, together with the domestication of cattle and goats/sheep in the Fertile Crescent (the area bounded by the rivers Tigris and Euphrates), there is evidence that rice was first deliberately planted and pigs domesticated in south-east Asia, maize first cultivated in Central America and llamas first domesticated in South America. It has been recognized in recent years that cultural changes can take place independently of each other in different parts of the world at different rates and different times. There is no need for a general diffusionist theory.

Although scholars will continue to study the particular societies which interest them, it may be possible to obtain a reliable chronological framework, in absolute terms of years, against which the cultural development of particular area may be set. The introduction of radiocarbon dating and a number of scientific techniques means that the development of an absolute chronology throughout the world comes closer.

Tidal Tables

CONSTANTS

The constant tidal difference may be used in conjunction with the time of high water at a standard port shown in the predictions data (pages 98–103) to find the time of high water at any of the ports or places listed below.

These tidal differences are very approximate and should be used only as a guide to the time of high water at the places below. More precise local data should be obtained for navigational and other nautical purposes.

All data allow high water time to be found in Greenwich Mean Time; this applies also to data for the months when British Summer Time is in operation and the hour's time difference should be allowed for. Ports marked * are in a different time zone and the standard time zone difference also needs to be added/subtracted to give local time.

EXAMPLE

Required time of high water at Stranraer at 2 January 1998
Appropriate time of high water at Greenock

Morning tide 2 January	0240 hrs
Tidal difference	−0020 hrs
High water at Stranraer	0220 hrs

The columns headed 'Springs' and 'Neaps' show the height, in metres, of the tide above datum for mean high water springs and mean high water neaps respectively.

Port	Diff. h m	Springs m	Neaps m
Aberdeen	Leith −1 19	4.3	3.4
*Antwerp (Prosperpolder)	London +0 50	5.8	4.8
Ardrossan	Greenock −0 15	3.2	2.6
Avonmouth	London −6 45	13.2	9.8
Ayr	Greenock −0 25	3.0	2.5
Barrow (Docks)	Liverpool 0 00	9.3	7.1
Belfast	London −2 47	3.5	3.0
Blackpool	Liverpool −0 10	8.9	7.0
*Boulogne	London −2 44	8.9	7.2
*Calais	London −2 04	7.2	5.9
*Cherbourg	London −6 00	6.4	5.0
Cobh	Liverpool −5 55	4.2	3.2
Cowes	London −2 38	4.2	3.5
Dartmouth	London +4 25	4.9	3.8
*Dieppe	London −3 03	9.3	7.3
Douglas, IOM	Liverpool −0 04	6.9	5.4
Dover	London −2 52	6.7	5.3
Dublin	London −2 05	4.1	3.4
Dun Laoghaire	London −2 10	4.1	3.4
*Dunkirk	London −1 54	6.0	4.9
Fishguard	Liverpool −4 01	4.8	3.4
Fleetwood	Liverpool 0 00	9.2	7.3
*Flushing	London −0 15	4.7	3.9
Folkestone	London −3 04	7.1	5.7
Galway	Liverpool −6 08	5.1	3.9
Glasgow	Greenock +0 26	4.7	4.0
Harwich	London −2 06	4.0	3.4
*Le Havre	London −3 55	7.9	6.6
Heysham	Liverpool +0 05	9.4	7.4
Holyhead	Liverpool −0 50	5.6	4.4
*Hook of Holland	London −0 01	2.1	1.7
Hull (Albert Dock)	London −7 40	7.5	5.8
Immingham	London −8 00	7.3	5.8
Larne	London −2 40	2.8	2.5
Lerwick	Leith −3 48	2.2	1.6
Londonderry	London −5 37	2.7	2.1
Lowestoft	London −4 25	2.4	2.1
Margate	London −1 53	4.8	3.9
Milford Haven	Liverpool −5 08	7.0	5.2
Morecambe	Liverpool +0 07	9.5	7.4
Newhaven	London −2 46	6.7	5.1
Oban	Greenock +5 43	4.0	2.9
*Ostend	London −1 32	5.1	4.2
Plymouth (Devonport)	London +4 05	5.5	4.4
Portland	London +5 09	2.1	1.4
Portsmouth	London −2 38	4.7	3.8
Ramsgate	London −2 32	5.2	4.1
Richmond Lock	London +1 00	4.9	3.7
Rosslare Harbour	Liverpool −5 24	1.9	1.4
Rosyth	Leith +0 09	5.8	4.7
*Rotterdam	London +1 45	2.0	1.7
St Helier	London +4 48	11.0	8.1
St Malo	London +4 27	12.2	9.2
St Peter Port	London +4 54	9.3	7.0
Scrabster	Leith −6 06	5.0	4.0
Sheerness	London −1 19	5.8	4.7
Shoreham	London −2 44	6.3	4.9
Southampton (1st high water)	London −2 54	4.5	3.7
Spurn Head	London −8 25	6.9	5.5
Stornoway	Liverpool −4 16	4.8	3.7
Stranraer	Greenock −0 20	3.0	2.4
Stromness	Leith −5 26	3.6	2.7
Swansea	London −7 35	9.5	7.2
Tees (River Entrance)	Leith +1 09	5.5	4.3
Tilbury	London −0 49	6.4	5.4
Tobermory	Liverpool −5 11	4.4	3.3
Tyne River (North Shields)	London −1030	5.0	3.9
Ullapool	Leith −7 40	5.2	3.9
Walton-on-the-Naze	London −2 10	4.2	3.4
Wick	Leith −3 26	3.5	2.8
*Zeebrugge	London −0 55	4.8	3.9

PREDICTIONS

The data on pages 98–103 are daily predictions of the time and height of high water at London Bridge, Liverpool, Greenock and Leith. The time of the data is Greenwich Mean Time; this applies also to data for the months when British Summer Time is in operation and the hour's time difference should be allowed for. The datum of predictions for each port shows the difference of height, in metres from Ordnance data (Newlyn).

The tidal information for London Bridge, Liverpool, Greenock and Leith is reproduced with the permission of the UK Hydrographic Office and the Controller of HMSO. Crown copyright reserved.

JANUARY 1998   *High water*   GMT

		London Bridge				Liverpool				Greenock				Leith			
		*Datum of predictions 3.20 m below				*Datum of predictions 4.93 m below				*Datum of predictions 1.62 m below				*Datum of predictions 2.90 m below			
		hr	ht m	hr	ht m	hr	ht m	hr	ht m	hr	ht m	hr	ht m	hr	ht m	hr	ht m
1	Thursday	03 15	7.0	15 44	7.2	00 34	9.3	12 56	9.6	01 55	3.4	14 15	3.7	04 09	5.6	16 22	5.6
2	Friday	03 56	7.0	16 28	7.2	01 19	9.3	13 41	9.6	02 40	3.4	14 56	3.7	04 53	5.6	17 05	5.6
3	Saturday	04 38	7.0	17 13	7.1	02 05	9.2	14 28	9.5	03 24	3.4	15 38	3.7	05 39	5.5	17 52	5.5
4	Sunday	05 22	6.8	18 01	6.9	02 54	9.0	15 18	9.2	04 10	3.3	16 24	3.6	06 30	5.3	18 43	5.3
5	Monday	06 08	6.6	18 54	6.6	03 46	8.6	16 13	8.8	05 00	3.2	17 15	3.4	07 26	5.1	19 43	5.1
6	Tuesday	07 03	6.4	19 55	6.3	04 47	8.3	17 16	8.5	05 54	3.1	18 15	3.3	08 28	5.0	20 51	5.0
7	Wednesday	08 12	6.2	21 06	6.2	05 56	8.0	18 27	8.3	06 56	3.1	19 33	3.1	09 36	4.9	22 03	5.0
8	Thursday	09 28	6.1	22 14	6.3	07 10	8.1	19 39	8.3	08 16	3.0	21 04	3.1	10 45	4.9	23 13	5.0
9	Friday	10 38	6.3	23 16	6.5	08 19	8.3	20 46	8.6	09 38	3.1	22 15	3.2	11 51	5.1	——	—
10	Saturday	11 40	6.6	——	—	09 17	8.7	21 42	8.9	10 38	3.3	23 13	3.3	00 18	5.1	12 50	5.2
11	Sunday	00 13	6.7	12 37	6.8	10 07	9.1	22 31	9.2	11 28	3.4	——	—	01 15	5.3	13 41	5.4
12	Monday	01 05	6.9	13 28	7.0	10 52	9.3	23 15	9.3	00 04	3.4	12 12	3.6	02 05	5.4	14 26	5.5
13	Tuesday	01 52	7.0	14 16	7.1	11 33	9.4	23 56	9.3	00 51	3.4	12 53	3.7	02 49	5.5	15 08	5.5
14	Wednesday	02 35	7.0	14 59	7.1	12 12	9.4	——	—	01 35	3.3	13 32	3.7	03 31	5.5	15 48	5.5
15	Thursday	03 13	6.9	15 38	7.0	00 33	9.2	12 49	9.4	02 13	3.3	14 09	3.7	04 10	5.4	16 26	5.4
16	Friday	03 46	6.7	16 14	6.8	01 09	9.0	13 25	9.2	02 49	3.3	14 45	3.7	04 47	5.3	17 02	5.3
17	Saturday	04 16	6.6	16 46	6.7	01 44	8.8	14 00	9.0	03 24	3.3	15 21	3.7	05 24	5.1	17 39	5.2
18	Sunday	04 48	6.6	17 21	6.6	02 20	8.6	14 36	8.7	04 00	3.2	15 57	3.6	06 03	5.0	18 17	5.0
19	Monday	05 25	6.5	17 59	6.5	02 58	8.3	15 16	8.4	04 38	3.2	16 35	3.5	06 44	4.8	19 00	4.8
20	Tuesday	06 06	6.3	18 42	6.3	03 40	7.9	16 01	8.0	05 20	3.1	17 17	3.3	07 29	4.6	19 47	4.6
21	Wednesday	06 53	6.1	19 31	6.1	04 31	7.5	16 55	7.6	06 06	3.0	18 04	3.1	08 19	4.5	20 42	4.5
22	Thursday	07 48	5.9	20 28	6.0	05 34	7.3	18 00	7.4	06 58	2.9	18 59	3.0	09 15	4.4	21 44	4.4
23	Friday	08 53	5.7	21 33	5.9	06 48	7.4	19 12	7.5	08 03	2.8	20 05	2.9	10 17	4.4	22 52	4.5
24	Saturday	10 04	5.8	22 43	6.1	07 58	7.7	20 20	7.8	09 25	2.9	21 21	2.9	11 23	4.6	——	—
25	Sunday	11 15	6.1	23 46	6.4	08 56	8.2	21 16	8.3	10 31	3.0	22 28	3.0	00 00	4.6	12 26	4.8
26	Monday	12 17	6.4	——	—	09 44	8.8	22 05	8.8	11 18	3.2	23 22	3.1	00 59	4.9	13 19	5.1
27	Tuesday	00 42	6.7	13 10	6.8	10 29	9.2	22 51	9.2	11 59	3.4	——	—	01 47	5.2	14 03	5.4
28	Wednesday	01 31	6.9	13 59	7.1	11 13	9.6	23 36	9.5	00 10	3.2	12 40	3.5	02 29	5.5	14 44	5.6
29	Thursday	02 17	7.1	14 45	7.3	11 57	9.9	——	—	00 57	3.3	13 21	3.6	03 11	5.7	15 24	5.8
30	Friday	03 00	7.2	15 30	7.4	00 21	9.7	12 42	10.0	01 43	3.3	14 03	3.7	03 52	5.8	16 04	5.9
31	Saturday	03 43	7.2	16 14	7.4	01 06	9.7	13 27	10.1	02 27	3.4	14 44	3.8	04 35	5.8	16 48	5.9

FEBRUARY 1998   *High water*   GMT

		London Bridge				Liverpool				Greenock				Leith			
1	Sunday	04 25	7.2	16 58	7.3	01 51	9.7	14 13	9.9	03 10	3.4	15 26	3.8	05 21	5.7	17 35	5.7
2	Monday	05 07	7.2	17 43	7.1	02 36	9.4	15 00	9.6	03 51	3.4	16 09	3.7	06 10	5.5	18 25	5.5
3	Tuesday	05 51	6.9	18 31	6.7	03 24	9.0	15 50	9.1	04 35	3.3	16 54	3.5	07 02	5.2	19 21	5.3
4	Wednesday	06 39	6.6	19 24	6.3	04 18	8.4	16 48	8.5	05 21	3.2	17 46	3.3	08 01	5.0	20 27	5.0
5	Thursday	07 39	6.2	20 33	6.0	05 23	7.9	17 59	8.0	06 14	3.1	18 49	3.1	09 08	4.8	21 41	4.8
6	Friday	09 00	6.0	21 48	5.9	06 43	7.7	19 20	7.9	07 20	3.0	20 41	2.9	10 20	4.7	22 57	4.8
7	Saturday	10 18	6.0	22 55	6.1	08 02	7.9	20 33	8.1	09 10	3.0	22 07	3.0	11 34	4.8	——	—
8	Sunday	11 25	6.3	23 54	6.4	09 04	8.4	21 31	8.5	10 21	3.1	23 06	3.1	00 10	4.9	12 40	5.0
9	Monday	12 23	6.7	——	—	09 55	8.8	22 20	8.9	11 13	3.3	23 56	3.2	01 10	5.1	13 33	5.2
10	Tuesday	00 47	6.7	13 15	6.9	10 40	9.2	23 02	9.1	11 58	3.4	——	—	01 59	5.2	14 18	5.4
11	Wednesday	01 36	6.9	14 01	7.1	11 19	9.3	23 40	9.2	00 41	3.2	12 39	3.5	02 39	5.3	14 57	5.4
12	Thursday	02 18	6.9	14 43	7.0	11 56	9.4	——	—	01 21	3.2	13 17	3.6	03 15	5.3	15 32	5.5
13	Friday	02 56	6.8	15 19	6.9	00 14	9.2	12 30	9.4	01 57	3.2	13 51	3.6	03 49	5.3	16 05	5.4
14	Saturday	03 27	6.7	15 50	6.8	00 47	9.1	13 02	9.3	02 28	3.2	14 24	3.6	04 21	5.3	16 37	5.4
15	Sunday	03 54	6.6	16 19	6.7	01 19	9.0	13 34	9.1	02 58	3.2	14 56	3.6	04 54	5.2	17 09	5.3
16	Monday	04 24	6.6	16 51	6.7	01 51	8.8	14 08	8.9	03 29	3.2	15 29	3.5	05 29	5.1	17 44	5.1
17	Tuesday	04 58	6.6	17 27	6.7	02 25	8.6	14 43	8.6	04 01	3.2	16 04	3.4	06 07	4.9	18 21	4.9
18	Wednesday	05 36	6.5	18 07	6.5	03 02	8.3	15 22	8.2	04 37	3.1	16 43	3.3	06 47	4.7	19 02	4.7
19	Thursday	06 19	6.3	18 52	6.3	03 45	7.9	16 10	7.8	05 18	2.9	17 26	3.1	07 32	4.6	19 51	4.5
20	Friday	07 09	6.1	19 44	6.1	04 41	7.5	17 11	7.4	06 07	2.8	18 18	2.9	08 25	4.4	20 52	4.3
21	Saturday	08 08	5.8	20 45	5.9	05 50	7.3	18 22	7.3	07 08	2.7	19 22	2.8	09 27	4.3	22 04	4.3
22	Sunday	09 16	5.8	21 57	5.9	07 09	7.4	19 40	7.5	08 27	2.7	20 41	2.8	10 39	4.4	23 22	4.5
23	Monday	10 35	5.9	23 12	6.2	08 21	8.0	20 49	8.1	09 51	2.9	22 02	2.9	11 51	4.7	——	—
24	Tuesday	11 49	6.3	——	—	09 19	8.6	21 44	8.7	10 49	3.1	23 03	3.0	00 30	4.8	12 51	5.0
25	Wednesday	00 15	6.5	12 48	6.8	10 08	9.2	22 32	9.3	11 36	3.3	23 54	3.2	01 23	5.2	13 39	5.4
26	Thursday	01 09	6.9	13 39	7.1	10 53	9.8	23 18	9.7	12 19	3.5	——	—	02 08	5.5	14 21	5.7
27	Friday	01 56	7.2	14 27	7.4	11 38	10.1	——	—	00 41	3.3	13 04	3.6	02 50	5.8	15 02	5.9
28	Saturday	02 41	7.3	15 12	7.5	00 03	9.9	12 24	10.3	01 27	3.4	13 47	3.7	03 31	5.9	15 44	6.0

MARCH 1998 *High water* GMT

		LONDON BRIDGE *Datum of predictions 3.20 m below*				LIVERPOOL *Datum of predictions 4.93 m below*				GREENOCK *Datum of predictions 1.62 m below*				LEITH *Datum of predictions 2.90 m below*			
		hr	ht m	hr	ht m	hr	ht m	hr	ht m	hr	ht m	hr	ht m	hr	ht m	hr	ht m
1	Sunday	03 24	7.4	15 55	7.6	00 48	10.0	13 09	10.3	02 09	3.4	14 29	3.8	04 15	5.9	16 29	6.0
2	Monday	04 07	7.5	16 38	7.5	01 32	9.9	13 54	10.1	02 49	3.5	15 11	3.8	05 00	5.8	17 16	5.9
3	Tuesday	04 49	7.4	17 21	7.2	02 16	9.6	14 39	9.7	03 28	3.5	15 52	3.7	05 48	5.5	18 07	5.6
4	Wednesday	05 32	7.2	18 05	6.8	03 01	9.1	15 27	9.0	04 08	3.4	16 35	3.5	06 38	5.2	19 02	5.3
5	Thursday	06 17	6.8	18 52	6.3	03 51	8.5	16 23	8.3	04 52	3.3	17 23	3.2	07 35	4.9	20 07	4.9
6	Friday	07 13	6.3	19 56	5.9	04 53	7.8	17 35	7.7	05 41	3.1	18 21	2.9	08 41	4.7	21 20	4.7
7	Saturday	08 35	5.9	21 21	5.7	06 17	7.5	19 02	7.5	06 41	2.9	20 22	2.7	09 54	4.6	22 39	4.6
8	Sunday	10 00	5.9	22 32	5.9	07 41	7.6	20 17	7.7	08 29	2.8	21 57	2.8	11 13	4.6	23 57	4.7
9	Monday	11 07	6.2	23 32	6.2	08 46	8.1	21 15	8.2	10 01	3.0	22 54	3.0	12 24	4.8	——	—
10	Tuesday	12 04	6.6	——	—	09 37	8.6	22 02	8.6	10 54	3.2	23 40	3.1	00 58	4.9	13 19	5.0
11	Wednesday	00 26	6.6	12 56	6.9	10 21	9.0	22 42	8.9	11 39	3.3	——	—	01 45	5.1	14 02	5.2
12	Thursday	01 15	6.8	13 41	7.1	10 59	9.2	23 18	9.1	00 22	3.1	12 20	3.4	02 22	5.2	14 39	5.3
13	Friday	01 58	6.9	14 21	7.0	11 34	9.3	23 51	9.1	01 00	3.1	12 56	3.4	02 54	5.3	15 11	5.4
14	Saturday	02 35	6.8	14 55	6.9	12 06	9.2	——	—	01 34	3.1	13 29	3.4	03 24	5.3	15 41	5.4
15	Sunday	03 05	6.7	15 24	6.8	00 21	9.1	12 37	9.2	02 03	3.1	13 59	3.4	03 54	5.3	16 12	5.4
16	Monday	03 32	6.6	15 51	6.7	00 52	9.0	13 08	9.1	02 29	3.2	14 29	3.4	04 26	5.2	16 43	5.3
17	Tuesday	04 01	6.6	16 22	6.8	01 23	8.9	13 40	8.9	02 56	3.2	15 02	3.4	05 00	5.1	17 16	5.1
18	Wednesday	04 33	6.6	16 57	6.8	01 56	8.8	14 13	8.7	03 26	3.2	15 36	3.3	05 35	5.0	17 51	5.0
19	Thursday	05 10	6.6	17 35	6.7	02 30	8.5	14 50	8.3	04 00	3.1	16 14	3.2	06 12	4.8	18 30	4.8
20	Friday	05 52	6.5	18 19	6.4	03 09	8.1	15 35	7.9	04 37	3.0	16 55	3.0	06 53	4.6	19 17	4.5
21	Saturday	06 40	6.2	19 09	6.1	04 00	7.7	16 34	7.4	05 21	2.8	17 45	2.9	07 43	4.5	20 15	4.4
22	Sunday	07 37	6.0	20 09	5.9	05 09	7.3	17 47	7.2	06 21	2.7	18 49	2.7	08 45	4.3	21 26	4.3
23	Monday	08 44	5.8	21 20	5.9	06 28	7.4	19 07	7.4	07 41	2.6	20 10	2.7	09 59	4.4	22 46	4.5
24	Tuesday	10 03	6.0	22 38	6.1	07 47	7.8	20 22	8.0	09 12	2.8	21 37	2.8	11 16	4.6	23 59	4.8
25	Wednesday	11 22	6.3	23 46	6.5	08 51	8.5	21 20	8.7	10 19	3.0	22 43	3.0	12 20	5.0	——	—
26	Thursday	12 24	6.8	——	—	09 43	9.2	22 10	9.3	11 10	3.3	23 35	3.2	00 56	5.2	13 11	5.3
27	Friday	00 42	6.9	13 17	7.2	10 31	9.8	22 56	9.8	11 57	3.5	——	—	01 43	5.6	13 56	5.7
28	Saturday	01 32	7.2	14 05	7.5	11 17	10.2	23 41	10.0	00 21	3.3	12 43	3.6	02 26	5.8	14 39	6.0
29	Sunday	02 19	7.4	14 50	7.6	12 02	10.3	——	—	01 06	3.4	13 28	3.7	03 09	5.9	15 23	6.1
30	Monday	03 03	7.6	15 34	7.6	00 25	10.1	12 48	10.3	01 47	3.5	14 12	3.8	03 53	5.9	16 10	6.1
31	Tuesday	03 47	7.6	16 16	7.5	01 10	9.9	13 33	10.0	02 26	3.6	14 54	3.8	04 38	5.8	16 58	5.9

APRIL 1998 *High water* GMT

		LONDON BRIDGE				LIVERPOOL				GREENOCK				LEITH			
1	Wednesday	04 30	7.5	16 58	7.2	01 54	9.6	14 19	9.5	03 05	3.6	15 36	3.6	05 26	5.5	17 50	5.6
2	Thursday	05 14	7.3	17 40	6.9	02 38	9.1	15 06	8.8	03 44	3.5	16 19	3.4	06 16	5.2	18 46	5.2
3	Friday	06 00	6.9	18 25	6.4	03 26	8.5	16 00	8.1	04 27	3.4	17 07	3.2	07 11	4.9	19 48	4.8
4	Saturday	06 54	6.3	19 21	5.9	04 26	7.8	17 10	7.5	05 15	3.2	18 05	2.9	08 15	4.6	20 57	4.6
5	Sunday	08 13	5.9	20 50	5.6	05 48	7.4	18 37	7.2	06 13	3.0	19 51	2.7	09 27	4.5	22 12	4.5
6	Monday	09 37	5.9	22 04	5.8	07 12	7.4	19 50	7.5	07 34	2.8	21 36	2.8	10 44	4.5	23 30	4.6
7	Tuesday	10 42	6.2	23 04	6.1	08 17	7.8	20 48	7.9	09 30	2.9	22 31	2.9	11 56	4.7	——	—
8	Wednesday	11 38	6.5	23 58	6.5	09 09	8.3	21 34	8.4	10 27	3.1	23 15	3.0	00 33	4.8	12 52	4.9
9	Thursday	12 29	6.8	——	—	09 54	8.7	22 15	8.7	11 12	3.2	23 55	3.1	01 19	5.0	13 36	5.0
10	Friday	00 47	6.7	13 15	7.0	10 33	8.9	22 51	8.9	11 53	3.2	——	—	01 56	5.1	14 12	5.2
11	Saturday	01 31	6.8	13 54	7.0	11 08	9.0	23 23	9.0	00 32	3.1	12 29	3.2	02 27	5.2	14 45	5.3
12	Sunday	02 09	6.8	14 28	6.9	11 40	9.0	23 54	9.0	01 05	3.1	13 01	3.2	02 56	5.2	15 15	5.3
13	Monday	02 41	6.7	14 57	6.8	12 10	9.0	——	—	01 34	3.1	13 30	3.2	03 27	5.3	15 47	5.3
14	Tuesday	03 09	6.6	15 25	6.8	00 24	9.0	12 42	8.9	01 59	3.2	14 01	3.2	03 59	5.2	16 20	5.2
15	Wednesday	03 39	6.6	15 56	6.8	00 56	8.9	13 14	8.8	02 25	3.2	14 35	3.3	04 33	5.2	16 53	5.1
16	Thursday	04 12	6.6	16 31	6.8	01 29	8.8	13 49	8.6	02 56	3.2	15 12	3.2	05 07	5.0	17 29	5.0
17	Friday	04 49	6.6	17 09	6.7	02 04	8.6	14 27	8.4	03 29	3.2	15 50	3.1	05 43	4.9	18 08	4.8
18	Saturday	05 32	6.5	17 53	6.5	02 44	8.3	15 12	8.0	04 05	3.0	16 33	3.0	06 24	4.7	18 55	4.6
19	Sunday	06 20	6.3	18 43	6.2	03 34	7.9	16 09	7.6	04 46	2.9	17 23	2.8	07 13	4.5	19 52	4.5
20	Monday	07 16	6.1	19 41	6.0	04 40	7.6	17 20	7.4	05 42	2.7	18 27	2.7	08 13	4.4	21 00	4.4
21	Tuesday	08 23	6.0	20 51	5.9	05 56	7.6	18 38	7.5	07 04	2.7	19 46	2.7	09 26	4.4	22 16	4.6
22	Wednesday	09 40	6.1	22 08	6.1	07 14	7.9	19 53	8.0	08 36	2.8	21 10	2.8	10 42	4.6	23 28	4.9
23	Thursday	11 05	6.4	23 16	6.5	08 20	8.6	20 53	8.7	09 48	3.0	22 18	3.0	11 48	5.0	——	—
24	Friday	11 58	6.9	——	—	09 17	9.2	21 45	9.3	10 43	3.2	23 11	3.2	00 27	5.2	12 42	5.3
25	Saturday	00 14	6.9	12 52	7.2	10 07	9.7	22 32	9.7	11 33	3.4	23 59	3.3	01 17	5.5	13 30	5.7
26	Sunday	01 07	7.2	13 41	7.5	10 54	10.0	23 18	9.9	12 20	3.6	——	—	02 02	5.8	14 16	5.9
27	Monday	01 56	7.4	14 28	7.6	11 41	10.1	——	—	00 43	3.4	13 08	3.6	02 46	5.9	15 03	6.0
28	Tuesday	02 42	7.6	15 12	7.5	00 02	10.0	12 28	10.0	01 25	3.5	13 54	3.7	03 31	5.9	15 52	6.0
29	Wednesday	03 28	7.6	15 55	7.4	00 48	9.8	13 14	9.7	02 05	3.6	14 38	3.6	04 18	5.7	16 42	5.8
30	Thursday	04 13	7.5	16 37	7.2	01 32	9.5	13 59	9.3	02 44	3.6	15 21	3.5	05 06	5.5	17 35	5.5

MAY 1998   *High water*   GMT

		LONDON BRIDGE *Datum of predictions 3.20 m below				LIVERPOOL *Datum of predictions 4.93 m below				GREENOCK *Datum of predictions 1.62 m below				LEITH *Datum of predictions 2.90 m below			
		hr	ht m	hr	ht m	hr	ht m	hr	ht m	hr	ht m	hr	ht m	hr	ht m	hr	ht m
1	Friday	04 59	7.3	17 18	6.9	02 17	9.0	14 46	8.7	03 24	3.6	16 06	3.3	05 56	5.2	18 29	5.1
2	Saturday	05 45	6.9	18 01	6.4	03 04	8.5	15 38	8.1	04 06	3.5	16 55	3.1	06 50	4.9	19 27	4.8
3	Sunday	06 38	6.4	18 51	6.0	03 59	7.9	16 41	7.5	04 54	3.3	17 53	2.9	07 50	4.6	20 28	4.6
4	Monday	07 47	6.0	20 10	5.7	05 11	7.5	17 58	7.2	05 50	3.0	19 07	2.7	08 55	4.5	21 34	4.4
5	Tuesday	09 05	5.9	21 28	5.7	06 30	7.4	19 10	7.3	06 57	2.9	20 52	2.7	10 04	4.4	22 45	4.5
6	Wednesday	10 08	6.1	22 29	6.0	07 37	7.6	20 10	7.7	08 33	2.9	21 53	2.8	11 14	4.5	23 50	4.6
7	Thursday	11 04	6.3	23 24	6.2	08 33	8.0	20 59	8.1	09 47	3.0	22 41	3.0	12 13	4.7	——	—
8	Friday	11 55	6.6			09 20	8.3	21 41	8.5	10 37	3.1	23 22	3.0	00 41	4.8	13 01	4.9
9	Saturday	00 14	6.5	12 41	6.8	10 01	8.6	22 18	8.7	11 19	3.1	——		01 21	4.9	13 40	5.0
10	Sunday	00 59	6.6	13 21	6.9	10 37	8.8	22 53	8.9	00 00	3.1	11 57	3.1	01 55	5.1	14 15	5.1
11	Monday	01 39	6.7	13 57	6.9	11 11	8.8	23 25	8.9	00 35	3.1	12 29	3.1	02 27	5.2	14 49	5.2
12	Tuesday	02 14	6.7	14 29	6.8	11 44	8.8	23 58	8.9	01 04	3.1	13 00	3.1	03 01	5.2	15 23	5.2
13	Wednesday	02 47	6.6	15 01	6.8	12 17	8.8	——	—	01 31	3.2	13 34	3.1	03 35	5.2	15 58	5.2
14	Thursday	03 20	6.7	15 35	6.8	00 31	8.9	12 53	8.8	01 59	3.2	14 12	3.1	04 10	5.2	16 33	5.1
15	Friday	03 55	6.7	16 11	6.8	01 07	8.8	13 30	8.7	02 31	3.3	14 51	3.1	04 44	5.1	17 10	5.0
16	Saturday	04 34	6.7	16 50	6.7	01 45	8.7	14 11	8.5	03 06	3.2	15 33	3.1	05 21	5.0	17 51	4.9
17	Sunday	05 18	6.6	17 33	6.5	02 28	8.5	14 57	8.2	03 44	3.1	16 18	3.0	06 03	4.9	18 38	4.8
18	Monday	06 07	6.5	18 22	6.3	03 19	8.2	15 52	7.9	04 26	3.0	17 10	2.9	06 52	4.7	19 34	4.7
19	Tuesday	07 02	6.3	19 20	6.1	04 20	8.0	16 58	7.7	05 21	2.9	18 13	2.8	07 50	4.6	20 38	4.6
20	Wednesday	08 07	6.2	20 29	6.1	05 31	7.9	18 11	7.8	06 36	2.8	19 24	2.8	08 59	4.6	21 48	4.7
21	Thursday	09 20	6.3	21 41	6.0	06 43	8.1	19 22	8.1	08 02	2.9	20 40	2.8	10 11	4.7	22 58	4.9
22	Friday	10 30	6.5	22 48	6.5	07 50	8.6	20 25	8.6	09 17	3.0	21 50	3.0	11 18	5.0	23 59	5.2
23	Saturday	11 32	6.9	23 48	6.8	08 50	9.1	21 20	9.1	10 18	3.2	22 47	3.1	12 16	5.3	——	—
24	Sunday	12 27	7.1	——	—	09 44	9.5	22 09	9.5	11 10	3.4	23 36	3.3	00 52	5.4	13 09	5.5
25	Monday	00 43	7.1	13 19	7.3	10 34	9.7	22 56	9.7	12 00	3.5			01 40	5.6	13 58	5.7
26	Tuesday	01 35	7.3	14 07	7.4	11 22	9.8	23 42	9.7	00 22	3.4	12 50	3.5	02 27	5.7	14 48	5.8
27	Wednesday	02 24	7.4	14 52	7.4	12 09	9.7	——	—	01 05	3.5	13 38	3.5	03 13	5.7	15 37	5.8
28	Thursday	03 12	7.5	15 36	7.3	00 27	9.6	12 56	9.5	01 46	3.6	14 25	3.5	04 00	5.6	16 28	5.6
29	Friday	03 58	7.4	16 18	7.1	01 12	9.3	13 41	9.1	02 27	3.6	15 10	3.4	04 48	5.5	17 18	5.4
30	Saturday	04 44	7.2	16 59	6.8	01 57	9.0	14 26	8.7	03 07	3.6	15 55	3.2	05 37	5.2	18 09	5.1
31	Sunday	05 29	6.9	17 39	6.5	02 42	8.6	15 13	8.2	03 49	3.5	16 42	3.1	06 28	5.0	19 00	4.9

JUNE 1998   *High water*   GMT

		LONDON BRIDGE				LIVERPOOL				GREENOCK				LEITH			
1	Monday	06 17	6.5	18 23	6.2	03 30	8.2	16 04	7.7	04 34	3.4	17 33	2.9	07 21	4.7	19 53	4.6
2	Tuesday	07 11	6.2	19 19	5.9	04 27	7.7	17 06	7.4	05 24	3.2	18 30	2.8	08 18	4.6	20 49	4.5
3	Wednesday	08 16	6.0	20 33	5.8	05 35	7.5	18 16	7.3	06 21	3.0	19 33	2.8	09 18	4.5	21 48	4.4
4	Thursday	09 22	5.9	21 41	5.8	06 45	7.5	19 21	7.4	07 26	2.9	20 50	2.8	10 20	4.4	22 50	4.5
5	Friday	10 19	6.1	22 39	6.0	07 46	7.7	20 16	7.8	08 41	2.9	21 54	2.8	11 21	4.5	23 48	4.6
6	Saturday	11 12	6.3	23 33	6.2	08 39	8.0	21 03	8.2	09 49	2.9	22 44	2.9	12 16	4.7	——	—
7	Sunday	12 01	6.5	——	—	09 24	8.2	21 44	8.5	10 39	3.0	22 36	3.0	00 37	4.8	13 03	4.8
8	Monday	00 21	6.4	12 45	6.7	10 05	8.5	22 22	8.7	11 19	3.0			01 19	4.9	13 44	5.0
9	Tuesday	01 06	6.6	13 26	6.8	10 42	8.6	22 58	8.9	00 03	3.1	11 55	3.0	01 58	5.1	14 22	5.1
10	Wednesday	01 47	6.7	14 04	6.9	11 19	8.7	23 34	9.0	00 36	3.1	12 31	3.0	02 36	5.2	15 00	5.2
11	Thursday	02 25	6.7	14 41	6.9	11 56	8.8	——	—	01 06	3.2	13 10	3.1	03 13	5.3	15 37	5.2
12	Friday	03 03	6.8	15 18	6.9	00 11	9.0	12 35	8.8	01 38	3.3	13 52	3.1	03 49	5.3	16 14	5.2
13	Saturday	03 42	6.8	15 56	6.8	00 50	9.0	13 16	8.8	02 13	3.3	14 35	3.1	04 26	5.2	16 53	5.2
14	Sunday	04 24	6.8	16 36	6.7	01 32	9.0	13 59	8.7	02 51	3.3	15 20	3.1	05 04	5.2	17 36	5.1
15	Monday	05 08	6.8	17 19	6.6	02 17	8.9	14 45	8.6	03 30	3.3	16 07	3.0	05 47	5.1	18 23	5.0
16	Tuesday	05 56	6.6	18 07	6.5	03 06	8.7	15 37	8.3	04 14	3.2	16 58	3.0	06 35	5.0	19 16	4.9
17	Wednesday	06 48	6.5	19 01	6.3	04 02	8.5	16 36	8.1	05 06	3.1	17 54	2.9	07 30	4.9	20 16	4.9
18	Thursday	07 50	6.3	20 05	6.2	05 06	8.3	17 43	8.0	06 10	3.0	18 56	2.9	08 34	4.8	21 22	4.8
19	Friday	08 58	6.3	21 15	6.3	06 14	8.3	18 52	8.1	07 27	2.9	20 05	2.9	09 44	4.9	22 30	4.9
20	Saturday	10 05	6.5	22 22	6.4	07 23	8.5	19 59	8.5	08 48	3.0	21 20	2.9	10 52	5.0	23 34	5.1
21	Sunday	11 08	6.7	23 25	6.7	08 27	8.8	20 58	8.9	09 56	3.1	22 24	3.1	11 55	5.2	——	—
22	Monday	12 06	6.9	——	—	09 25	9.1	21 51	9.2	10 53	3.2	23 17	3.2	00 31	5.3	12 53	5.4
23	Tuesday	00 24	6.9	12 59	7.1	10 18	9.3	22 40	9.4	11 46	3.3	——		01 23	5.4	13 46	5.5
24	Wednesday	01 18	7.2	13 49	7.2	11 07	9.4	23 26	9.5	00 04	3.4	12 38	3.3	02 12	5.6	14 36	5.6
25	Thursday	02 09	7.3	14 35	7.2	11 54	9.4	——	—	00 49	3.5	13 27	3.3	02 59	5.6	15 25	5.6
26	Friday	02 58	7.3	15 19	7.1	00 11	9.4	12 40	9.3	01 31	3.5	14 14	3.3	03 46	5.6	16 13	5.5
27	Saturday	03 44	7.2	16 00	7.0	00 54	9.3	13 23	9.0	02 11	3.6	14 57	3.2	04 32	5.5	16 59	5.4
28	Sunday	04 27	7.1	16 39	6.8	01 36	9.1	14 04	8.8	02 51	3.6	15 39	3.2	05 17	5.3	17 44	5.2
29	Monday	05 09	6.9	17 15	6.6	02 17	8.8	14 44	8.4	03 31	3.5	16 22	3.1	06 02	5.1	18 28	4.9
30	Tuesday	05 49	6.6	17 53	6.4	02 58	8.5	15 26	8.0	04 11	3.4	17 05	3.0	06 48	4.9	19 14	4.7

JULY 1998   *High water*   GMT

		London Bridge				Liverpool				Greenock				Leith			
		Datum of predictions 3.20 m below				*Datum of predictions 4.93 m below*				*Datum of predictions 1.62 m below*				*Datum of predictions 2.90 m below*			
		hr	ht m	hr	ht m	hr	ht m	hr	ht m	hr	ht m	hr	ht m	hr	ht m	hr	ht m
1	Wednesday	06 30	6.3	18 36	6.2	03 43	8.1	16 13	7.7	04 54	3.3	17 51	2.9	07 36	4.7	20 02	4.6
2	Thursday	07 18	6.1	19 28	5.9	04 34	7.7	17 10	7.4	05 41	3.1	18 40	2.8	08 28	4.5	20 54	4.4
3	Friday	08 13	5.9	20 31	5.8	05 36	7.5	18 18	7.3	06 33	2.9	19 34	2.8	09 23	4.4	21 49	4.4
4	Saturday	09 15	5.9	21 38	5.8	06 45	7.4	19 24	7.5	07 32	2.8	20 41	2.8	10 22	4.4	22 48	4.5
5	Sunday	10 17	6.0	22 42	5.9	07 50	7.6	20 21	7.8	08 39	2.8	21 56	2.8	11 25	4.5	23 48	4.6
6	Monday	11 15	6.2	23 41	6.2	08 45	7.9	21 10	8.2	09 47	2.8	22 50	2.9	12 23	4.7	—	—
7	Tuesday	12 08	6.5	—	—	09 33	8.2	21 53	8.6	10 41	2.9	23 33	3.1	00 42	4.8	13 13	4.8
8	Wednesday	00 33	6.4	12 56	6.7	10 16	8.5	22 33	8.9	11 26	3.0	—	—	01 29	5.0	13 57	5.0
9	Thursday	01 21	6.7	13 41	6.9	10 56	8.7	23 13	9.1	00 09	3.2	12 08	3.0	02 12	5.2	14 37	5.2
10	Friday	02 05	6.8	14 23	6.9	11 37	8.9	23 53	9.2	00 45	3.2	12 52	3.1	02 51	5.3	15 16	5.3
11	Saturday	02 47	6.9	15 04	7.0	12 19	9.0	—	—	01 20	3.3	13 37	3.1	03 29	5.4	15 55	5.4
12	Sunday	03 30	7.0	15 44	6.9	00 35	9.3	13 02	9.1	01 58	3.4	14 22	3.1	04 07	5.5	16 36	5.4
13	Monday	04 12	7.0	16 24	6.9	01 19	9.4	13 46	9.1	02 38	3.4	15 07	3.1	04 47	5.5	17 19	5.4
14	Tuesday	04 56	7.0	17 06	6.9	02 04	9.3	14 31	9.0	03 18	3.4	15 52	3.1	05 30	5.4	18 05	5.3
15	Wednesday	05 42	6.9	17 50	6.8	02 51	9.2	15 19	8.8	04 01	3.4	16 39	3.1	06 18	5.3	18 56	5.2
16	Thursday	06 30	6.7	18 39	6.6	03 43	8.9	16 13	8.5	04 48	3.3	17 29	3.0	07 10	5.2	19 53	5.0
17	Friday	07 26	6.4	19 38	6.4	04 41	8.6	17 15	8.2	05 43	3.1	18 23	3.0	08 11	5.0	20 56	4.9
18	Saturday	08 32	6.2	20 48	6.2	05 47	8.3	18 25	8.0	06 51	3.0	19 25	2.9	09 21	4.9	22 04	4.9
19	Sunday	09 41	6.2	22 00	6.2	06 58	8.2	19 37	8.2	08 20	2.9	20 49	2.9	10 33	4.9	23 13	5.0
20	Monday	10 47	6.4	23 08	6.4	08 10	8.4	20 43	8.5	09 42	3.0	22 05	3.0	11 42	5.0	—	—
21	Tuesday	11 47	6.6	—	—	09 13	8.7	21 39	8.9	10 45	3.1	23 02	3.2	00 17	5.1	12 46	5.2
22	Wednesday	00 10	6.7	12 43	6.9	10 08	9.0	22 28	9.2	11 39	3.2	23 51	3.3	01 13	5.3	13 40	5.3
23	Thursday	01 06	7.0	13 33	7.1	10 56	9.2	23 13	9.4	12 30	3.2	—	—	02 03	5.4	14 29	5.5
24	Friday	01 57	7.2	14 20	7.1	11 41	9.2	23 55	9.4	00 35	3.4	13 18	3.2	02 48	5.5	15 13	5.5
25	Saturday	02 44	7.2	15 03	7.1	12 22	9.2	—	—	01 17	3.5	14 02	3.2	03 32	5.5	15 55	5.5
26	Sunday	03 27	7.1	15 41	6.9	00 35	9.3	13 01	9.0	01 56	3.6	14 41	3.2	04 13	5.5	16 36	5.4
27	Monday	04 07	7.0	16 16	6.8	01 13	9.2	13 38	8.8	02 33	3.6	15 17	3.2	04 53	5.4	17 14	5.2
28	Tuesday	04 42	6.8	16 47	6.7	01 49	9.0	14 13	8.6	03 09	3.5	15 53	3.1	05 31	5.2	17 53	5.0
29	Wednesday	05 16	6.6	17 21	6.5	02 25	8.7	14 49	8.3	03 45	3.5	16 30	3.1	06 10	5.0	18 34	4.9
30	Thursday	05 51	6.5	17 59	6.4	03 03	8.4	15 29	8.0	04 22	3.4	17 10	3.0	06 52	4.8	19 17	4.7
31	Friday	06 31	6.3	18 43	6.1	03 46	8.0	16 15	7.6	05 02	3.2	17 52	2.9	07 37	4.6	20 04	4.5

AUGUST 1998   *High water*   GMT

		London Bridge				Liverpool				Greenock				Leith			
1	Saturday	07 17	6.1	19 35	5.9	04 36	7.6	17 12	7.4	05 48	3.0	18 41	2.8	08 29	4.5	20 57	4.4
2	Sunday	08 12	5.9	20 36	5.7	05 38	7.3	18 22	7.3	06 42	2.8	19 37	2.7	09 27	4.4	21 55	4.4
3	Monday	09 17	5.9	21 46	5.7	06 51	7.3	19 35	7.5	07 46	2.8	20 50	2.8	10 32	4.4	22 59	4.5
4	Tuesday	10 27	6.0	22 58	5.9	08 03	7.5	20 36	8.0	08 59	2.8	22 10	2.9	11 41	4.5	—	—
5	Wednesday	11 32	6.3	—	—	09 02	8.0	21 26	8.5	10 10	2.9	23 02	3.0	00 04	4.7	12 42	4.8
6	Thursday	00 01	6.3	12 28	6.6	09 51	8.4	22 10	8.9	11 04	3.0	23 44	3.2	01 00	5.0	13 31	5.0
7	Friday	00 56	6.6	13 18	6.9	10 35	8.8	22 52	9.3	11 51	3.1	—	—	01 47	5.2	14 14	5.3
8	Saturday	01 44	6.9	14 03	7.0	11 18	9.1	23 34	9.6	00 23	3.3	12 37	3.1	02 28	5.5	14 55	5.5
9	Sunday	02 29	7.1	14 46	7.1	12 01	9.3	—	—	01 02	3.4	13 22	3.2	03 07	5.6	15 34	5.7
10	Monday	03 13	7.2	15 27	7.1	00 17	9.7	12 45	9.4	01 43	3.5	14 07	3.2	03 46	5.8	16 15	5.7
11	Tuesday	03 56	7.3	16 07	7.2	01 02	9.8	13 29	9.5	02 23	3.6	14 50	3.3	04 27	5.8	16 59	5.7
12	Wednesday	04 39	7.2	16 48	7.1	01 46	9.7	14 13	9.3	03 04	3.6	15 32	3.3	05 11	5.7	17 45	5.5
13	Thursday	05 22	7.1	17 30	7.0	02 32	9.5	14 59	9.1	03 45	3.6	16 14	3.3	05 58	5.6	18 34	5.3
14	Friday	06 07	6.8	18 16	6.8	03 21	9.1	15 49	8.6	04 24	3.4	16 58	3.2	06 50	5.4	19 29	5.1
15	Saturday	06 58	6.4	19 10	6.4	04 16	8.6	16 48	8.2	05 18	3.2	17 48	3.1	07 52	5.1	20 32	4.9
16	Sunday	08 01	6.1	20 21	6.1	05 23	8.1	18 01	7.8	06 18	3.0	18 47	3.0	09 03	4.9	21 42	4.8
17	Monday	09 17	5.9	21 42	6.0	06 42	7.8	19 22	7.9	07 55	2.8	20 14	2.9	10 19	4.8	22 56	4.8
18	Tuesday	10 28	6.1	22 55	6.2	08 01	8.0	20 33	8.2	09 38	2.9	21 50	3.0	11 35	4.9	—	—
19	Wednesday	11 30	6.4	23 57	6.6	09 05	8.4	21 29	8.7	10 42	3.1	22 49	3.2	00 06	5.0	12 42	5.1
20	Thursday	12 26	6.8	—	—	09 58	8.8	22 17	9.1	11 34	3.2	23 37	3.3	01 06	5.2	13 35	5.3
21	Friday	00 52	7.0	13 17	7.0	10 43	9.0	22 59	9.3	12 21	3.2	—	—	01 54	5.4	14 20	5.4
22	Saturday	01 42	7.2	14 03	7.1	11 24	9.1	23 38	9.4	00 21	3.4	13 05	3.2	02 36	5.5	14 58	5.4
23	Sunday	02 27	7.2	14 44	7.1	12 02	9.1	—	—	01 01	3.5	13 44	3.2	03 15	5.5	15 34	5.4
24	Monday	03 07	7.1	15 20	6.9	00 13	9.3	12 36	9.0	01 37	3.5	14 18	3.2	03 51	5.5	16 09	5.4
25	Tuesday	03 42	6.9	15 50	6.8	00 47	9.2	13 09	8.9	02 11	3.5	14 49	3.2	04 24	5.4	16 42	5.3
26	Wednesday	04 12	6.8	16 18	6.7	01 19	9.0	13 41	8.8	02 43	3.5	15 20	3.2	04 58	5.3	17 18	5.2
27	Thursday	04 41	6.7	16 49	6.6	01 52	8.8	14 14	8.6	03 16	3.5	15 52	3.2	05 33	5.2	17 55	5.0
28	Friday	05 14	6.6	17 25	6.5	02 27	8.5	14 50	8.3	03 50	3.4	16 27	3.1	06 11	5.0	18 35	4.8
29	Saturday	05 51	6.5	18 05	6.3	03 06	8.1	15 31	7.9	04 27	3.3	17 07	3.0	06 53	4.7	19 19	4.6
30	Sunday	06 33	6.3	18 52	6.0	03 52	7.7	16 22	7.5	05 09	3.1	17 53	2.9	07 41	4.5	20 09	4.5
31	Monday	07 23	6.0	19 48	5.8	04 49	7.3	17 27	7.3	06 01	2.9	18 50	2.8	08 38	4.4	21 08	4.4

SEPTEMBER 1998   *High water*   GMT

		LONDON BRIDGE *Datum of predictions 3.20 m below*				LIVERPOOL *Datum of predictions 4.93 m below*				GREENOCK *Datum of predictions 1.62 m below*				LEITH *Datum of predictions 2.90 m below*			
		hr	ht m	hr	ht m	hr	ht m	hr	ht m	hr	ht m	hr	ht m	hr	ht m	hr	ht m
1	Tuesday	08 24	5.8	20 55	5.7	06 00	7.1	18 44	7.3	07 06	2.7	19 58	2.7	09 45	4.3	22 15	4.4
2	Wednesday	09 38	5.8	22 14	5.8	07 20	7.3	20 00	7.8	08 23	2.7	21 23	2.8	11 00	4.4	23 26	4.6
3	Thursday	10 55	6.1	23 30	6.2	08 32	7.8	20 58	8.4	09 44	2.9	22 30	3.0	12 09	4.7	—	—
4	Friday	11 59	6.4	—	—	09 26	8.4	21 45	9.0	10 46	3.0	23 17	3.2	00 29	5.0	13 04	5.1
5	Saturday	00 30	6.6	12 52	6.8	10 13	8.9	22 29	9.5	11 35	3.2	23 59	3.4	01 19	5.3	13 49	5.5
6	Sunday	01 21	7.0	13 39	7.1	10 56	9.4	23 13	9.9	12 20	3.3	—	—	02 01	5.6	14 30	5.7
7	Monday	02 07	7.3	14 23	7.2	11 40	9.6	23 56	10.1	00 41	3.5	13 04	3.3	02 41	5.9	15 11	5.9
8	Tuesday	02 51	7.4	15 05	7.3	12 23	9.8	—	—	01 24	3.6	13 47	3.4	03 22	6.0	15 53	5.9
9	Wednesday	03 34	7.5	15 46	7.4	00 40	10.1	13 07	9.8	02 05	3.7	14 27	3.5	04 04	6.1	16 36	5.9
10	Thursday	04 17	7.4	16 27	7.4	01 26	10.0	13 51	9.6	02 46	3.7	15 07	3.5	04 50	6.0	17 22	5.7
11	Friday	04 59	7.2	17 10	7.2	02 12	9.6	14 36	9.2	03 27	3.7	15 47	3.5	05 39	5.7	18 12	5.4
12	Saturday	05 42	6.9	17 55	6.9	03 00	9.1	15 25	8.7	04 09	3.5	16 29	3.4	06 33	5.4	19 07	5.1
13	Sunday	06 28	6.4	18 46	6.4	03 54	8.4	16 23	8.1	04 56	3.3	17 17	3.2	07 35	5.1	20 10	4.9
14	Monday	07 28	5.9	19 59	6.0	05 03	7.8	17 40	7.6	05 54	3.0	18 14	3.1	08 48	4.8	21 22	4.7
15	Tuesday	08 53	5.7	21 28	5.9	06 30	7.5	19 08	7.7	07 42	2.8	19 36	3.0	10 06	4.7	22 39	4.8
16	Wednesday	10 08	5.9	22 40	6.2	07 50	7.8	20 18	8.1	09 34	2.9	21 32	3.1	11 25	4.8	23 53	5.0
17	Thursday	11 10	6.3	23 41	6.6	08 51	8.2	21 13	8.6	10 34	3.1	22 31	3.3	12 32	5.0	—	—
18	Friday	12 06	6.7	—	—	09 41	8.7	21 59	9.0	11 21	3.2	23 19	3.4	00 52	5.2	13 23	5.2
19	Saturday	00 34	7.0	12 56	7.0	10 24	9.0	22 39	9.3	12 04	3.3	—	—	01 39	5.4	14 03	5.3
20	Sunday	01 22	7.2	13 41	7.1	11 02	9.1	23 16	9.3	00 01	3.5	12 44	3.3	02 18	5.5	14 38	5.4
21	Monday	02 05	7.2	14 21	7.1	11 36	9.1	23 48	9.3	00 39	3.5	13 19	3.3	02 53	5.5	15 09	5.4
22	Tuesday	02 43	7.1	14 55	6.9	12 08	9.1	—	—	01 14	3.5	13 50	3.3	03 24	5.5	15 40	5.4
23	Wednesday	03 14	6.9	15 23	6.7	00 19	9.2	12 38	9.0	01 45	3.5	14 18	3.3	03 55	5.5	16 11	5.4
24	Thursday	03 40	6.8	15 50	6.6	00 50	9.0	13 09	8.9	02 15	3.5	14 46	3.3	04 28	5.4	16 45	5.3
25	Friday	04 08	6.7	16 20	6.6	01 22	8.8	13 41	8.7	02 47	3.5	15 16	3.3	05 02	5.2	17 21	5.1
26	Saturday	04 39	6.7	16 54	6.6	01 55	8.6	14 16	8.4	03 20	3.4	15 49	3.3	05 38	5.0	17 58	4.9
27	Sunday	05 15	6.6	17 34	6.4	02 32	8.2	14 54	8.1	03 57	3.3	16 26	3.2	06 18	4.8	18 39	4.8
28	Monday	05 56	6.4	18 19	6.2	03 15	7.8	15 41	7.7	04 38	3.1	17 10	3.0	07 04	4.6	19 28	4.6
29	Tuesday	06 43	6.1	19 13	5.9	04 11	7.3	16 44	7.3	05 28	2.9	18 06	2.9	07 59	4.4	20 26	4.5
30	Wednesday	07 41	5.8	20 17	5.8	05 22	7.1	18 01	7.3	06 33	2.8	19 17	2.8	09 06	4.4	21 35	4.5

OCTOBER 1998   *High water*   GMT

		LONDON BRIDGE				LIVERPOOL				GREENOCK				LEITH			
1	Thursday	08 51	5.7	21 34	5.8	06 43	7.2	19 20	7.7	07 53	2.8	20 41	2.9	10 22	4.5	22 49	4.7
2	Friday	10 14	5.9	22 56	6.2	08 00	7.8	20 26	8.4	09 18	2.9	21 54	3.1	11 35	4.8	23 55	5.0
3	Saturday	11 25	6.3	—	—	08 59	8.5	21 18	9.1	10 25	3.1	22 48	3.3	12 34	5.2	—	—
4	Sunday	00 00	6.7	12 21	6.8	09 47	9.1	22 04	9.7	11 14	3.3	23 34	3.5	00 48	5.4	13 22	5.6
5	Monday	00 54	7.1	13 10	7.1	10 32	9.6	22 49	10.1	11 59	3.4	—	—	01 33	5.7	14 04	5.8
6	Tuesday	01 41	7.4	13 56	7.3	11 15	9.9	23 34	10.3	00 18	3.7	12 42	3.5	02 15	6.0	14 46	6.0
7	Wednesday	02 26	7.5	14 40	7.5	11 59	10.0	—	—	01 03	3.8	13 24	3.6	02 57	6.2	15 29	6.1
8	Thursday	03 10	7.5	15 24	7.6	00 19	10.2	12 44	9.9	01 46	3.8	14 04	3.7	03 43	6.2	16 13	6.0
9	Friday	03 53	7.5	16 07	7.5	01 05	10.0	13 29	9.7	02 29	3.8	14 43	3.7	04 31	6.0	17 00	5.8
10	Saturday	04 35	7.2	16 51	7.3	01 51	9.6	14 14	9.2	03 10	3.8	15 22	3.7	05 22	5.8	17 50	5.5
11	Sunday	05 18	6.9	17 37	7.0	02 40	9.0	15 03	8.7	03 53	3.6	16 05	3.6	06 17	5.4	18 45	5.1
12	Monday	06 02	6.4	18 30	6.5	03 35	8.3	16 00	8.1	04 41	3.3	16 52	3.4	07 20	5.0	19 49	4.9
13	Tuesday	06 56	6.0	19 41	6.0	04 44	7.7	17 18	7.6	05 40	3.0	17 49	3.2	08 31	4.8	21 01	4.7
14	Wednesday	08 26	5.7	21 08	5.9	06 11	7.4	18 43	7.6	07 27	2.8	19 04	3.1	09 46	4.7	22 16	4.7
15	Thursday	09 43	5.8	22 17	6.1	07 27	7.6	19 53	7.9	09 16	3.0	21 00	3.1	11 03	4.7	23 28	4.9
16	Friday	10 44	6.1	23 15	6.5	08 27	8.0	20 48	8.4	10 13	3.1	22 04	3.3	12 09	4.9	—	—
17	Saturday	11 39	6.5	—	—	09 16	8.5	21 34	8.8	10 58	3.3	22 53	3.4	00 27	5.1	12 59	5.1
18	Sunday	00 08	6.9	12 29	6.9	09 58	8.8	22 14	9.1	11 38	3.4	23 35	3.5	01 14	5.2	13 38	5.3
19	Monday	00 56	7.1	13 14	7.0	10 35	9.0	22 50	9.2	12 15	3.4	—	—	01 53	5.4	14 12	5.4
20	Tuesday	01 38	7.1	13 54	7.0	11 08	9.1	23 22	9.2	00 13	3.5	12 50	3.4	02 27	5.4	14 42	5.4
21	Wednesday	02 14	7.0	14 28	6.8	11 39	9.1	23 52	9.1	00 47	3.5	13 20	3.4	02 58	5.5	15 11	5.4
22	Thursday	02 44	6.9	14 57	6.7	12 09	9.0	—	—	01 18	3.4	13 47	3.4	03 29	5.5	15 43	5.4
23	Friday	03 10	6.8	15 25	6.6	00 22	9.0	12 41	8.9	01 47	3.4	14 14	3.5	04 02	5.4	16 17	5.3
24	Saturday	03 38	6.8	15 55	6.6	00 55	8.8	13 13	8.6	02 20	3.4	14 44	3.5	04 37	5.2	16 51	5.2
25	Sunday	04 09	6.7	16 30	6.6	01 29	8.6	13 47	8.6	02 55	3.4	15 17	3.4	05 13	5.1	17 27	5.0
26	Monday	04 45	6.7	17 10	6.5	02 06	8.3	14 26	8.3	03 32	3.3	15 53	3.3	05 52	4.9	18 07	4.9
27	Tuesday	05 26	6.5	17 56	6.3	02 48	8.0	15 12	7.9	04 14	3.2	16 34	3.2	06 37	4.7	18 54	4.7
28	Wednesday	06 13	6.2	18 48	6.1	03 42	7.6	16 12	7.6	05 02	3.0	17 26	3.0	07 31	4.6	19 50	4.6
29	Thursday	07 08	5.9	19 50	5.9	04 51	7.3	17 25	7.5	06 06	2.9	18 37	2.9	08 35	4.5	20 59	4.6
30	Friday	08 15	5.8	21 03	6.0	06 09	7.4	18 42	7.8	07 24	2.8	20 00	3.0	09 48	4.6	22 13	4.7
31	Saturday	09 35	6.0	22 22	6.3	07 25	7.8	19 51	8.4	08 47	3.0	21 18	3.2	11 00	4.9	23 20	5.0

NOVEMBER 1998 *High water* GMT

		LONDON BRIDGE *Datum of predictions 3.20 m below				LIVERPOOL *Datum of predictions 4.93 m below				GREENOCK *Datum of predictions 1.62 m below				LEITH *Datum of predictions 2.90 m below			
		hr	ht m	hr	ht m	hr	ht m	hr	ht m	hr	ht m	hr	ht m	hr	ht m	hr	ht m
1	Sunday	10 48	6.3	23 28	6.7	08 28	8.5	20 48	9.1	09 56	3.2	22 17	3.4	12 02	5.2	—	—
2	Monday	11 47	6.7	—	—	09 19	9.2	21 38	9.7	10 49	3.4	23 08	3.6	00 16	5.4	12 53	5.6
3	Tuesday	00 24	7.1	12 41	7.1	10 06	9.7	22 26	10.1	11 35	3.5	23 55	3.7	01 05	5.7	13 38	5.8
4	Wednesday	01 15	7.4	13 30	7.4	10 52	10.0	23 12	10.2	12 18	3.6	—	—	01 50	6.0	14 22	6.0
5	Thursday	02 02	7.5	14 17	7.5	11 37	10.1	23 59	10.2	00 42	3.8	13 01	3.8	02 36	6.1	15 06	6.0
6	Friday	02 47	7.5	15 04	7.6	12 22	10.0			01 28	3.8	13 42	3.8	03 24	6.1	15 52	5.9
7	Saturday	03 31	7.4	15 50	7.6	00 45	9.9	13 08	9.7	02 13	3.8	14 22	3.9	04 14	6.0	16 40	5.8
8	Sunday	04 14	7.2	16 36	7.4	01 33	9.5	13 55	9.3	02 57	3.7	15 03	3.9	05 07	5.7	17 30	5.5
9	Monday	04 56	6.9	17 23	7.0	02 22	8.9	14 43	8.8	03 42	3.6	15 46	3.8	06 02	5.4	18 26	5.2
10	Tuesday	05 40	6.5	18 15	6.6	03 15	8.3	15 38	8.2	04 31	3.3	16 33	3.6	07 02	5.1	19 27	4.9
11	Wednesday	06 29	6.1	19 18	6.2	04 18	7.7	16 46	7.8	05 29	3.1	17 27	3.4	08 06	4.8	20 34	4.7
12	Thursday	07 47	5.7	20 37	6.0	05 36	7.4	18 05	7.6	06 48	3.0	18 32	3.2	09 13	4.7	21 42	4.7
13	Friday	09 08	5.7	21 44	6.1	06 50	7.5	19 15	7.8	08 35	3.0	20 00	3.2	10 22	4.7	22 50	4.8
14	Saturday	10 10	6.0	22 42	6.3	07 52	7.8	20 13	8.1	09 38	3.1	21 23	3.2	11 29	4.8	23 51	4.9
15	Sunday	11 05	6.3	23 34	6.6	08 43	8.2	21 02	8.5	10 25	3.3	22 19	3.3	12 23	5.0	—	—
16	Monday	11 56	6.6	—	—	09 27	8.6	21 44	8.7	11 06	3.4	23 04	3.4	00 41	5.1	13 06	5.1
17	Tuesday	00 22	6.8	12 43	6.7	10 05	8.9	22 21	8.9	11 44	3.4	23 43	3.4	01 23	5.2	13 41	5.2
18	Wednesday	01 05	6.9	13 24	6.8	10 39	9.0	22 55	9.0	12 20	3.5			01 59	5.3	14 14	5.3
19	Thursday	01 42	6.9	14 00	6.8	11 12	9.1	23 27	9.0	00 18	3.4	12 52	3.5	02 33	5.3	14 46	5.4
20	Friday	02 14	6.8	14 32	6.7	11 44	9.1	23 59	8.9	00 50	3.4	13 20	3.5	03 06	5.4	15 19	5.4
21	Saturday	02 43	6.8	15 03	6.7	12 17	9.0			01 21	3.4	13 48	3.5	03 41	5.3	15 53	5.3
22	Sunday	03 14	6.8	15 36	6.7	00 32	8.8	12 51	8.9	01 56	3.4	14 19	3.5	04 16	5.3	16 28	5.3
23	Monday	03 47	6.8	16 12	6.7	01 09	8.7	13 27	8.8	02 34	3.3	14 53	3.5	04 53	5.1	17 03	5.1
24	Tuesday	04 23	6.7	16 53	6.6	01 47	8.5	14 07	8.6	03 13	3.3	15 30	3.4	05 32	5.0	17 42	5.0
25	Wednesday	05 04	6.6	17 39	6.5	02 30	8.3	14 53	8.3	03 56	3.2	16 10	3.3	06 16	4.9	18 28	4.9
26	Thursday	05 50	6.4	18 30	6.3	03 21	7.9	15 49	8.1	04 44	3.1	16 58	3.2	07 08	4.8	19 22	4.8
27	Friday	06 42	6.1	19 29	6.2	04 24	7.7	16 55	7.9	05 43	3.0	18 01	3.1	08 08	4.7	20 26	4.7
28	Saturday	07 45	6.0	20 37	6.1	05 36	7.6	18 06	8.1	06 52	2.9	19 18	3.1	09 16	4.7	21 37	4.8
29	Sunday	09 00	6.1	21 50	6.3	06 49	7.9	19 15	8.4	08 08	3.0	20 39	3.2	10 26	4.9	22 46	5.0
30	Monday	10 13	6.3	22 57	6.6	07 55	8.5	20 18	9.0	09 21	3.1	21 47	3.3	11 30	5.2	23 47	5.3

DECEMBER 1998 *High water* GMT

		LONDON BRIDGE				LIVERPOOL				GREENOCK				LEITH			
1	Tuesday	11 16	6.7	23 56	6.9	08 52	9.0	21 14	9.4	10 21	3.3	22 44	3.5	12 25	5.5	—	—
2	Wednesday	12 14	7.0	—	—	09 43	9.5	22 05	9.8	11 11	3.5	23 35	3.6	00 41	5.6	13 15	5.7
3	Thursday	00 49	7.2	13 08	7.3	10 32	9.8	22 54	10.0	11 57	3.7	—	—	01 31	5.8	14 02	5.9
4	Friday	01 39	7.3	13 58	7.5	11 18	9.9	23 42	10.0	00 24	3.7	12 42	3.8	02 21	6.0	14 48	5.9
5	Saturday	02 26	7.4	14 47	7.5	12 05	9.9			01 14	3.7	13 24	3.9	03 10	6.0	15 35	5.9
6	Sunday	03 12	7.3	15 35	7.5	00 30	9.8	12 51	9.7	02 01	3.7	14 06	3.9	04 01	5.9	16 23	5.7
7	Monday	03 55	7.1	16 22	7.3	01 18	9.4	13 38	9.4	02 47	3.6	14 48	3.9	04 52	5.7	17 13	5.5
8	Tuesday	04 38	6.9	17 08	7.1	02 05	9.0	14 24	9.0	03 32	3.5	15 30	3.9	05 45	5.4	18 05	5.3
9	Wednesday	05 19	6.6	17 55	6.7	02 53	8.5	15 12	8.6	04 20	3.4	16 15	3.7	06 38	5.1	19 00	5.0
10	Thursday	06 01	6.3	18 47	6.3	03 44	8.0	16 06	8.1	05 11	3.2	17 04	3.5	07 33	4.8	19 59	4.8
11	Friday	06 53	6.0	19 10	6.0	04 45	7.6	17 10	7.7	06 08	3.1	17 58	3.4	08 31	4.7	20 59	4.7
12	Saturday	08 09	5.7	20 56	5.9	05 55	7.4	18 20	7.6	07 13	3.0	18 59	3.2	09 30	4.6	22 01	4.6
13	Sunday	09 22	5.8	21 59	6.1	07 03	7.5	19 26	7.7	08 33	3.0	20 12	3.1	10 32	4.6	23 03	4.7
14	Monday	10 23	5.9	22 51	6.1	08 02	7.8	20 22	8.0	09 39	3.1	21 30	3.1	11 33	4.7	—	—
15	Tuesday	11 17	6.1	23 42	6.4	08 51	8.2	21 10	8.3	10 30	3.2	22 27	3.2	00 01	4.8	12 25	4.9
16	Wednesday	12 07	6.4	—	—	09 34	8.5	21 52	8.6	11 13	3.3	23 12	3.2	00 50	4.9	13 08	5.0
17	Thursday	00 27	6.6	12 52	6.5	10 12	8.8	22 29	8.7	11 52	3.4	23 50	3.2	01 32	5.1	13 46	5.2
18	Friday	01 09	6.7	13 33	6.7	10 48	9.0	23 05	8.8	12 26	3.5	—	—	02 10	5.2	14 23	5.3
19	Saturday	01 46	6.8	14 10	6.7	11 23	9.1	23 40	8.9	00 24	3.2	13 00	3.5	02 46	5.3	14 58	5.4
20	Sunday	02 22	6.8	14 46	6.7	11 58	9.1			00 59	3.3	13 27	3.5	03 22	5.3	15 34	5.4
21	Monday	02 56	6.8	15 22	6.8	00 16	8.9	12 35	9.1	01 37	3.3	14 00	3.6	03 58	5.3	16 09	5.4
22	Tuesday	03 31	6.8	16 00	6.8	00 54	8.9	13 13	9.1	02 17	3.3	14 35	3.6	04 35	5.3	16 44	5.3
23	Wednesday	04 08	6.7	16 41	6.8	01 34	8.8	13 54	9.0	02 58	3.3	15 13	3.5	05 14	5.2	17 23	5.2
24	Thursday	04 48	6.7	17 25	6.7	02 17	8.7	14 39	8.9	03 41	3.2	15 54	3.4	05 58	5.1	18 07	5.1
25	Friday	05 32	6.6	18 14	6.6	03 04	8.4	15 29	8.7	04 22	3.2	16 38	3.3	06 47	5.0	18 57	5.0
26	Saturday	06 20	6.4	19 08	6.4	03 59	8.2	16 27	8.4	05 17	3.1	17 31	3.2	07 41	4.9	19 55	4.9
27	Sunday	07 18	6.2	20 10	6.3	05 03	8.0	17 33	8.3	06 15	3.0	18 36	3.2	08 44	4.9	21 02	4.9
28	Monday	08 26	6.2	21 20	6.2	06 13	8.0	18 42	8.4	07 21	3.0	19 56	3.1	09 52	4.9	22 14	5.0
29	Tuesday	09 40	6.2	22 29	6.4	07 24	8.2	19 51	8.7	08 40	3.1	21 18	3.2	11 00	5.0	23 22	5.2
30	Wednesday	10 50	6.4	23 32	6.6	08 29	8.7	20 54	9.0	09 53	3.2	22 24	3.3	12 02	5.2	—	—
31	Thursday	11 53	6.7	—	—	09 26	9.2	21 51	9.4	10 51	3.4	23 21	3.4	00 23	5.4	12 57	5.5

World Geographical Statistics

THE EARTH

The shape of the Earth is that of an oblate spheroid or solid of revolution whose meridian sections are ellipses, whilst the sections at right angles are circles.

DIMENSIONS

Equatorial diameter = 12,756.27 km (7,926.38 miles)
Polar diameter = 12,713.50 km (7,899.80 miles)
Equatorial circumference = 40,075.01 km (24,901.46 miles)
Polar circumference = 40,007.86 km (24,859.73 miles)

The equatorial circumference is divided into 360 degrees of longitude, which is measured in degrees, minutes and seconds east or west of the Greenwich meridian (0°) to 180°, the meridian 180° E. coinciding with 180° W. This was internationally ratified in 1884.

Distance north and south of the Equator is measured in degrees, minutes and seconds of latitude. The Equator is 0°, the North Pole is 90° N. and the South Pole is 90° S. The Tropics lie at 23° 26′ N. (Tropic of Cancer) and 23° 26′ S. (Tropic of Capricorn). The Arctic Circle lies at 66° 34′ N. and the Antarctic Circle at 66° 34′ S. (NB The Tropics and the Arctic and Antarctic circles are affected by the slow decrease in obliquity of the ecliptic, of about 0.5 arcseconds per year. The effect of this is to move the Arctic and Antarctic circles nearer to their respective poles by about 14 metres a year, while the Tropics move towards the Equator by the same amount.

AREA, ETC.

The surface area of the Earth is 510,069,120 km² (196,938,800 miles²), of which the water area is 70.92 per cent and the land area is 29.08 per cent.

The velocity of a given point on the Earth's surface at the Equator is 1,674.73 km per hour (1,040.40 m.p.h.). The Earth's mean velocity in its orbit around the Sun is 107,225 km per hour (66,627 m.p.h.). The Earth's mean distance from the Sun is 149,597,870 km (92,955,807 miles).

Source: Royal Greenwich Observatory

OCEANS

AREA

	km²	miles²
Pacific	166,240,000	64,186,300
Atlantic	86,550,000	33,420,000
Indian	73,427,000	28,350,500
Arctic	13,223,700	5,105,700

The division by the Equator of the Pacific into the North and South Pacific and the Atlantic into the North and South Atlantic makes a total of six oceans.

GREATEST DEPTHS

Greatest depth location	metres	feet
Mariana Trench (Pacific)	10,924	35,840
Puerto Rico Trench (Atlantic)	8,605	28,232
Java Trench (Indian)	7,125	23,376
Eurasian Basin (Arctic)	5,450	17,880

SEAS

AREA

	km²	miles²
South China	2,974,600	1,148,500
Caribbean	2,515,900	971,400
Mediterranean	2,509,900	969,100
Bering	2,226,100	873,000
Gulf of Mexico	1,507,600	582,100
Okhotsk	1,392,000	537,500
Japan	1,015,000	391,100
Hudson Bay	730,100	281,900
East China	664,600	256,600
Andaman	564,880	218,100
Black Sea	507,900	196,100
Red Sea	453,000	174,900
North Sea	427,100	164,900
Baltic Sea	382,000	147,500
Yellow Sea	294,000	113,500
Persian Gulf	230,000	88,800

GREATEST DEPTHS

	Maximum depth	
	metres	feet
Caribbean	8,605	28,232
East China	7,507	24,629
South China	7,258	23,812
Mediterranean	5,150	16,896
Andaman	4,267	14,000
Bering	3,936	12,913
Gulf of Mexico	3,504	11,496
Okhotsk	3,365	11,040
Japan	3,053	10,016
Red Sea	2,266	7,434
Black Sea	2,212	7,257
North Sea	439	1,440
Hudson Bay	111	364
Baltic Sea	90	295
Yellow Sea	73	240
Persian Gulf	73	240

THE CONTINENTS

There are six geographic continents, although America is often divided politically into North and Central America, and South America.

AFRICA is surrounded by sea except for the narrow isthmus of Suez in the north-east, through which is cut the Suez Canal. Its extreme longitudes are 17° 20′ W. at Cape Verde, Senegal, and 51° 24′ E. at Ras Hafun, Somalia. The extreme latitudes are 37° 20′ N. at Cape Blanc, Tunisia, and 34° 50′ S. at Cape Agulhas, South Africa, about 4,400 miles apart. The Equator passes through the middle of the continent.

NORTH AMERICA, including Mexico, is surrounded by ocean except in the south, where the isthmian states of CENTRAL AMERICA link North America with South America. Its extreme longitudes are 168° 5′ W. at Cape Prince of Wales, Alaska, and 55° 40′ W. at Cape Charles,

Newfoundland. The extreme continental latitudes are the tip of the Boothia peninsula, NW Territories, Canada (71° 51′ N.) and 14° 22′ N. at Ocós in the south of Mexico.

SOUTH AMERICA lies mostly in the southern hemisphere; the Equator passes through the north of the continent. It is surrounded by ocean except where it is joined to Central America in the north by the narrow isthmus through which is cut the Panama Canal. Its extreme longitudes are 34° 47′ W. at Cape Branco in Brazil and 81° 20′ W. at Punta Pariña, Peru. The extreme continental latitudes are 12° 25′ N. at Punta Gallinas, Colombia, and 53° 54′ S. at the southernmost tip of the Brunswick peninsula, Chile. Cape Horn, on Cape Island, Chile, lies at 55° 59′ S.

ANTARCTICA lies almost entirely within the Antarctic Circle (66° 34′ S.) and is the largest of the world's glaciated areas. The continent has an area of 5.4 million square miles, 99 per cent of which is permanently ice-covered. The ice amounts to some 7.2 million cubic miles and represents more than 90 per cent of the world's fresh water. The environment is too hostile for unsupported human habitation. *See also* pages 781–2

ASIA is the largest continent and occupies 30 per cent of the world's land surface. The extreme longitudes are 26° 05′ E. at Baba Buran, Turkey and 169° 40′ W. at Mys Dežneva (East Cape), Russia, a distance of about 6,000 miles. Its extreme northern latitude is 77° 45′ N. at Cape Čeljuskin, Russia, and it extends over 5,000 miles south to about 1° 15′ N. of the Equator.

AUSTRALIA is the smallest of the continents and lies in the southern hemisphere. It is entirely surrounded by ocean. Its extreme longitudes are 113° 11′ E. at Steep Point and 153° 11′ E. at Cape Byron. The extreme latitudes are 10° 42′ S. at Cape York and 39° S. at South East Point, Tasmania.

EUROPE, including European Russia, is the smallest continent in the northern hemisphere. Its extreme latitudes are 71° 11′ N. at North Cape in Norway, and 36° 23′ N. at Cape Matapan in southern Greece, a distance of about 2,400 miles. Its breadth from Cabo Carvoeiro in Portugal (9° 34′ W.) in the west to the Kara River, north of the Urals (66° 30′ E.) in the east is about 3,300 miles. The division between Europe and Asia is generally regarded as the watershed of the Ural Mountains; down the Ural river to Gur'yev, Kazakhstan; across the Caspian Sea to Apsheronskiy Poluostrov, near Baku; along the watershed of the Caucasus Mountains to Anapa and thence across the Black Sea to the Bosporus in Turkey; across the Sea of Marmara to Çanakkale Boğazi (Dardanelles).

	Area km²	miles²
Asia	43,998,000	16,988,000
*America	41,918,000	16,185,000
Africa	29,800,000	11,506,000
Antarctica	13,980,000	5,400,000
†Europe	9,699,000	3,745,000
Australia	7,618,493	2,941,526

*North and Central America has an area of 24,255,000 km² (9,365,000 miles²)

†Includes 5,571,000 km² (2,151,000 miles²) of former USSR territory, including the Baltic states, Belarus, Moldova, the Ukraine, that part of Russia west of the Ural Mountains and Kazakhstan west of the Ural river. European Turkey (24,378 km²/9,412 miles²) comprises territory to the west and north of the Bosporus and the Dardanelles

GLACIATED AREAS

It is estimated that 15,915,000 km² (6,145,000 miles²) or 10.73 per cent of the world's land surface is permanently covered with ice.

	Area km²	miles²
South Polar regions	13,830,000	5,340,000
North Polar regions (incl. Greenland or Kalaallit Nunaat)	1,965,000	758,500
Alaska-Canada	58,800	22,700
Asia	37,800	14,600
South America	11,900	4,600
Europe	10,700	4,128
New Zealand	984	380
Africa	238	92

PENINSULAS

	Area km²	miles²
Arabian	3,250,000	1,250,000
Southern Indian	2,072,000	800,000
Alaskan	1,500,000	580,000
Labradorian	1,300,000	500,000
Scandinavian	800,300	309,000
Iberian	584,000	225,500

LARGEST ISLANDS

Island (and Ocean)	Area km²	miles²
Greenland (Kalaallit Nunaat) (Arctic)	2,175,500	840,000
New Guinea (Pacific)	792,500	306,000
Borneo (Pacific)	725,450	280,100
Madagascar (Indian)	587,040	226,658
Baffin Island (Arctic)	507,451	195,928
Sumatra (Indian)	427,350	165,000
Honshu (Pacific)	227,413	87,805
*Great Britain (Atlantic)	218,040	84,186
Victoria Island (Arctic)	217,292	83,897
Ellesmere Island (Arctic)	196,236	75,767
Sulawesi (Celebes) (Indian)	178,700	69,000
South Island, NZ (Pacific)	151,010	58,305
Java (Indian)	126,650	48,900
Cuba (Atlantic)	114,525	44,218
North Island, NZ (Pacific)	114,050	44,035
Newfoundland (Atlantic)	108,855	42,030
Luzon (Pacific)	105,880	40,880
Iceland (Atlantic)	103,000	39,770
Mindanao (Pacific)	95,247	36,775
Ireland (Atlantic)	82,462	31,839

*Mainland only

LARGEST DESERTS

	Area (approx.) km²	miles²
The Sahara (N. Africa)	9,000,000	3,500,000
Australian Desert	1,550,000	600,000
*The Gobi (Mongolia/China)	1,300,000	500,000
Arabian Desert	1,200,000	470,000
Kalahari Desert (Botswana/ Namibia/S. Africa)	583,000	225,000
Sonoran Desert (USA/ Mexico)	310,000	120,000
†Kara Kum (Turkmenistan)	310,000	120,000
Namib Desert (Namibia)	285,000	110,000
Thar Desert (India/ Pakistan)	260,000	100,000
Somali Desert (Somalia)	260,000	100,000
†Kyzyl Kum (Kazakhstan/ Uzbekistan)	260,000	100,000
Atacama Desert (Chile)	180,000	70,000
Dasht-e Lut (Iran)	52,000	20,000
Mojave Desert (USA)	35,000	13,500
Desierto de Sechura (Peru)	26,000	10,000

*Including the Takla Makan – 320,000 km² (125,000 miles²)
†Together known as the Turkestan Desert

DEEPEST DEPRESSIONS

	Maximum depth below sea level metres	feet
Dead Sea (Jordan/Israel)	395	1,296
Turfan Depression (Sinkiang, China)	153	505
Qattara Depression (Egypt)	132	436
Mangyshlak peninsula (Kazakhstan)	131	433
Danakil Depression (Ethiopia)	116	383
Death Valley (California, USA)	86	282
Salton Sink (California, USA)	71	235
W. of Ustyurt plateau (Kazakhstan)	70	230
Prikaspiyskaya Nizmennost' (Russia/Kazakhstan)	67	220
Lake Sarykamysh (Uzbekistan/ Turkmenistan)	45	148
El Faiyûm (Egypt)	44	147
Valdies peninsula, Lago Enriquillo (Dominican Republic)	40	131

The world's largest exposed depression is the Prikaspiyskaya Nizmennost' covering the hinterland of the northern third of the Caspian Sea, which is itself 28 m (92 ft) below sea level
Western Antarctica and Central Greenland largely comprise crypto-depressions under ice burdens. The Antarctic Wilkes subglacial basin has a bedrock 2,341 m (7,680 ft) below sea-level. In Greenland (lat. 73° N., long. 39° W.) the bedrock is 365 m (1,197 ft) below sea-level

LONGEST MOUNTAIN RANGES

Range (location)	Length km	miles
Cordillera de Los Andes (W. South America)	7,200	4,500
Rocky Mountains (W. North America)	4,800	3,000
Himalaya-Karakoram-Hindu Kush (S. Central Asia)	3,800	2,400
Great Dividing Range (E. Australia)	3,600	2,250
Trans-Antarctic Mts (Antarctica)	3,500	2,200
Atlantic Coast Range (E. Brazil)	3,000	1,900
West Sumatran-Javan Range (Indonesia)	2,900	1,800
Aleutian Range (Alaska and NW Pacific)	2,650	1,650
Tien Shan (S. Central Asia)	2,250	1,400
Central New Guinea Range (Irian Jaya/Papua New Guinea)	2,000	1,250

HIGHEST MOUNTAINS

The world's 8,000-metre mountains (with six subsidiary peaks) are all in the Himalaya-Karakoram-Hindu Kush range.

Mountain	Height metres	feet
Mt Everest*	8,848	29,028
K2 (Chogori)†	8,607	28,238
Kangchenjunga	8,597	28,208
Lhotse	8,511	27,923
Makalu I	8,481	27,824
Lhotse Shar (II)	8,400	27,560
Dhaulagiri I	8,171	26,810
Manaslu I (Kutang I)	8,156	26,760
Cho Oyu	8,153	26,750
Nanga Parbat (Diamir)	8,125	26,660
Annapurna I	8,078	26,504
Gasherbrum I (Hidden Peak)	8,068	26,470
Broad Peak I	8,046	26,400
Gasherbrum II	8,034	26,360
Shisha Pangma (Gosainthan)	8,012	26,287
Makalu South-East	8,010	26,280
Broad Peak Central	8,000	26,246

*Named after Sir George Everest (1790–1866), Surveyor-General of India 1830–43, in 1863. He pronounced his name Eve-rest
†Formerly Godwin-Austin

The culminating summits in the other major mountain ranges are:

Mountain (by range or country)	Height metres	feet
Pik Pobedy (Tien Shan)	7,439	24,406
Cerro Aconcagua (Cordillera de Los Andes)	6,960	22,834
Mt McKinley, S. Peak (Alaska Range)	6,194	20,320
Kilimanjaro (Kibo) (Tanzania)	5,894	19,340
Hkakabo Razi (Myanmar)	5,881	19,296
Citlaltépetl (Orizaba) (Sierra Madre Oriental, Mexico)	5,699	18,700

Mountain (by range or country)	Height	
	metres	feet
El'brus, W. Peak (Caucasus)	5,641	18,510
Vinson Massif (E. Antarctica)	4,897	16,067
Puncak Jaya (Central New Guinea Range)	4,884	16,023
Mt Blanc (Alps)	4,807	15,771
Klyuchevskaya Sopka (Kamchatka peninsula, Russia)	4,750	15,584
Ras Dashan (Ethiopian Highlands)	4,620	15,158
Zard Kūh (Zagros Mts, Iran)	4,547	14,921
Mt Kirkpatrick (Trans Antarctic)	4,529	14,860
Mt Belukha (Altai Mts, Russia/ Kazakhstan)	4,505	14,783
Mt Elbert (Rocky Mountains)	4,400	14,433
Mt Rainier (Cascade Range, N. America)	4,392	14,410
Nevado de Colima (Sierra Madre Occidental, Mexico)	4,268	14,003
Jebel Toubkal (Atlas Mts, N. Africa)	4,165	13,665
Kinabalu (Crocker Range, Borneo)	4,101	13,455
Kerinci (West Sumatran-Javan Range, Indonesia)	3,800	12,467
Jabal an Nabī Shu'ayb (N. Tihāmat, Yemen)	3,760	12,336
Teotepec (Sierra Madre del Sur, Mexico)	3,703	12,149
Thaban Ntlenyana (Drakensberg, South Africa)	3,482	11,425
Pico de Bandeira (Atlantic Coast Range)	2,890	9,482
Shishaldin (Aleutian Range)	2,861	9,387
Kosciusko (Great Dividing Range)	2,228	7,310

HIGHEST VOLCANOES

Volcano (last major eruption) and location	Height	
	metres	feet
Guallatiri (1993), Andes, Chile	6,060	19,882
Lascar (1995), Andes, Chile	5,990	19,652
Cotopaxi (1975), Andes, Ecuador	5,897	19,347
Tupungatito (1986), Andes, Chile	5,640	18,504
Nevado del Ruiz (1985, 1991), Colombia	5,400	17,716
Sangay (1996), Andes, Ecuador	5,230	17,159
Guagua Pichincha (1993), Andes, Ecuador	4,784	15,696
Purace (1977), Colombia	4,756	15,601
Klyuchevskaya Sopka (1995), Kamchatka peninsula, Russia	4,750	15,584
Nevado de Colima (1991), Mexico	4,268	14,003
Galeras (1993), Colombia	4,266	13,996
Mauna Loa (1987), Hawaii Is.	4,170	13,680
Cameroon (1982), Cameroon	4,070	13,354
Acatenango (1972), Guatemala	3,960	12,992
Fuego (1991), Guatemala	3,835	12,582
Kerinci (1987), Sumatra, Indonesia	3,800	12,467
Erebus (1995), Ross Island, Antarctica	3,794	12,450
Tacana (1988), Guatemala	3,780	12,400
Fuji (1708), Honshu, Japan	3,775	12,388
Santa Maria (1902, 1993), Guatemala	3,768	12,362
Rindjani (1966), Lombok, Indonesia	3,726	12,224
Semeru (1995), Java, Indonesia	3,675	12,060
Nyirgongo (1994), Dem. Rep. of Congo	3,475	11,400

Volcano (last major eruption) and location	Height	
	metres	feet
Koryakskaya (1957), Kamchatka, Russia	3,456	11,339
Irazú (1965, 1992), Costa Rica	3,432	11,260
Slamet (1989), Java, Indonesia	3,428	11,247
Spurr (1953), Alaska, USA	3,374	11,069
Mt Etna (1169, 1669, 1993, 1996), Sicily, Italy	3,369	11,053
Raung (1993), Java, Indonesia	3,322	10,932
Shiveluch (1964), Kamchatka, Russia	3,283	10,771
Turrialba (1866, 1992), Costa Rica	3,246	10,650
Agung (1964), Bali, Indonesia	3,142	10,308
Llaima (1995), Chile	3,128	10,239
Redoubt (1990), Alaska, USA	3,108	10,197
Tjareme (1938), Java, Indonesia	3,078	10,098
On-Take (1980, 1991), Japan	3,063	10,049
Nyamuragira (1994), Dem. Rep. of Congo	3,056	10,028
Iliamna (1953, 1978), Alaska, USA	3,052	10,016

OTHER NOTABLE VOLCANOES

	Height	
	metres	feet
Tambora (1815), Sumbawa, Indonesia	2,850	9,353
Mt St Helens (1980, 1986, 1991), Washington State, USA	2,530	8,300
Pinatubo (1991, 1995), Philippines	1,758	5,770
Hekla (1981, 1991), Iceland	1,491	4,892
Mt Pelée (1902), Martinique	1,397	4,583
Mt Unzen (1792, 1991, 1996), Kyushu, Japan	1,360	4,462
Vesuvius (AD 79, 1631, 1944), Italy	1,280	4,198
Kilauea (1996), Hawaii, USA	1,242	4,077
Soufrière (1979, 1997), St Vincent	1,234	4,048
Stromboli (1996), Lipari Is., Italy	926	3,038
Chances Peak (1997), Montserrat	915	3,002
Krakatau (1883, 1995), Sunda Strait, Indonesia	813	2,667
Santorini (Thíra) (1628 BC, 1950), Aegean Sea, Greece	566	1,857
Vulcano (Monte Aria), Lipari Is., Italy	499	1,637
Tristan da Cunha (1961), South Atlantic	243	800
Surtsey (1963-7), off Iceland	173	568

LARGEST LAKES

The areas of some of these lakes are subject to seasonal variation.

	Area		Length	
	km^2	miles^2	km	miles
Caspian Sea, Iran/ Azerbaijan/Russia/ Turkmenistan/ Kazakhstan	371,000	143,000	1,171	728
*Michigan–Huron, USA/Canada	117,610	45,300	1,010	627
Superior, Canada/ USA	82,100	31,700	563	350

*Lakes Michigan and Huron are regarded as lobes of the same lake. The Michigan lobe has an area of 57,750 km^2 (22,300 miles^2) and the Huron lobe an area of 59,570 km^2 (23,000 miles^2).

	Area km²	miles²	Length km	miles
Victoria, Uganda/ Tanzania/Kenya	69,500	26,828	362	225
Aral Sea, Kazakhstan/ Uzbekistan	40,400	15,600	331	235
Tanganyika, Dem. Rep. of Congo/ Tanzania/Zambia/ Burundi	32,900	12,700	675	420
†Baykal (*Baikal*), Russia	31,500	12,162	635	395
Great Bear, Canada	31,328	12,096	309	192
Malawi (Nyasa), Tanzania/Malawi/ Mozambique	28,880	11,150	580	360
Great Slave, Canada	28,570	11,031	480	298
Erie, Canada/USA	25,670	9,910	388	241
Winnipeg, Canada	24,390	9,417	428	266
Ontario, Canada/USA	19,550	7,550	310	193
Balkhash, Kazakhstan	18,427	7,115	605	376
Ladozhskoye (*Ladoga*), Russia	17,700	6,835	200	124

†World's deepest lake (1,940 m/6,365 ft)

UNITED KINGDOM (BY COUNTRY)

	Area km²	miles²	Length km	miles
Lough Neagh, Northern Ireland	381.73	147.39	28.90	18.00
Loch Lomond, Scotland	71.12	27.46	36.44	22.64
Windermere, England	14.74	5.69	16.90	10.50
Lake Vyrnwy, Wales (artificial)	4.53	1.75	7.56	4.70
Llyn Tegid (*Bala*), Wales (natural)	4.38	1.69	5.80	3.65

LONGEST RIVERS

River (source and outflow)	Length km	miles
Nile (*Bahr-el-Nil*) (R. Luvironza, Burundi – E. Mediterranean Sea)	6,670	4,145
Amazon (*Amazonas*) (Lago Villafro, Peru – S. Atlantic Ocean)	6,448	4,007
Mississippi-Missouri-Red Rock (Montana – Gulf of Mexico)	5,970	3,710
Yenisey-Angara (W. Mongolia – Kara Sea)	5,540	3,442
Yangtze-Kiang (*Chang Jiang*) (Kunlun Mts, W. China – Yellow Sea)	5,530	3,436
Huang He (*Yellow River*) (Bayan Har Shan range, central China – Yellow Sea)	5,463	3,395
Ob'-Irtysh (W. Mongolia – Kara Sea)	5,410	3,362
Zaïre (*Congo*) (R. Lualaba, Dem. Rep. of Congo-Zambia – S. Atlantic Ocean)	4,700	2,920
Amur-Argun (R. Argun, Khingan Mts, N. China – Sea of Okhotsk)	4,670	2,903
Lena-Kirenga (R. Kirenga, W. of Lake Baykal – Arctic Ocean)	4,400	2,734
Mackenzie-Peace (Tatlatui Lake, British Columbia – Beaufort Sea)	4,240	2,635
Mekong (Lants'ang, Tibet – South China Sea)	4,184	2,600
Niger (Loma Mts, Guinea – Gulf of Guinea, E. Atlantic Ocean)	4,168	2,590

River (source and outflow)	Length km	miles
Río de la Plata-Paraná (R. Paranáiba, central Brazil – S. Atlantic Ocean)	4,000	2,485
Murray-Darling (SE Queensland – Lake Alexandrina, S. Australia)	3,750	2,330
Volga (Valdai plateau – Caspian Sea)	3,690	2,293
Zambezi (NW Zambia – S. Indian Ocean)	3,540	2,200

OTHER NOTABLE RIVERS

	Length km	miles
St Lawrence (Minnesota, USA – Gulf of St Lawrence)	3,130	1,945
Ganges-Brahmaputra (R. Matsang, SW Tibet – Bay of Bengal)	2,900	1,800
Indus (R. Sengge, SW Tibet – N. Arabian Sea)	2,880	1,790
Danube (*Donau*) (Black Forest, SW Germany – Black Sea)	2,856	1,775
Tigris-Euphrates (R. Murat, E. Turkey – Persian Gulf)	2,740	1,700
Irrawaddy (R. Mali Hka, Myanmar – Andaman Sea)	2,151	1,337
Don (SE of Novomoskovsk – Sea of Azov)	1,969	1,224

BRITISH ISLES

	Length km	miles
Shannon (Co. Cavan, Rep. of Ireland – Atlantic Ocean)	386	240
Severn (Powys, Wales – Bristol Channel)	354	220
Thames (Gloucestershire, England – North Sea)	346	215
Tay (Perthshire, Scotland – North Sea)	188	117
Clyde (Lanarkshire, Scotland – Firth of Clyde)	158	98½
Tweed (Peeblesshire, Scotland – North Sea)	155	96½
Bann (Upper and Lower) (Co. Down, N. Ireland – Atlantic Ocean)	122	76

GREATEST WATERFALLS – BY HEIGHT

Waterfall (river and location)	Total drop metres	feet	Greatest single leap metres	feet
Angel (Carrao, Venezuela)	979	3,212	807	2,648
Tugela (Tugela, S. Africa)	947	3,110	410	1,350
Utigård (Jostedal Glacier, Norway)	800	2,625	600	1,970
Mongefossen (Monge, Norway)	774	2,540	—	—
Yosemite (Yosemite Creek, USA)	739	2,425	435	1,430
Østre Mardøla Foss (Mardals, Norway)	656	2,154	296	974
Tyssestrengane (Tysso, Norway)	646	2,120	289	948
Cuquenán (Arabopó, Venezuela)	610	2,000	—	—
Sutherland (Arthur, NZ)	580	1,904	248	815
*Kjellfossen (Naeröfjord, Norway)	561	1,841	149	490

*Volume often so low the fall atomizes into a 'bridal veil'

Waterfall (river and location)	Total drop		Greatest single leap	
	metres	feet	metres	feet
BRITISH ISLES (BY COUNTRY)				
Eas a' Chuàl Aluinn (Glas Bheinn, Sutherland, Scotland)	200	658		
Powerscourt Falls (Dargle, Co. Wicklow, Rep. of Ireland)	106	350		
Pistyll-y-Llyn (Powys/ Dyfed border, Wales)	c.73	230– 240	(cascades)	
Pistyll Rhyadr (Clwyd/ Powys border, Wales)	71.5	235	(single leap)	
Caldron Snout (R. Tees, Cumbria/Durham, England)	61	200	(cascades)	

GREATEST WATERFALLS – BY VOLUME

Waterfall (river and location)	Mean annual flow	
	m³/sec	galls/sec
Boyoma (R. Lualaba, Dem. Rep. of Congo)	c.17,000	c.3,750,000
Khône (Mekong, Laos)	11,500	2,530,000
Niagara (Horseshoe) (R. Niagara/Lake Erie–Lake Ontario)	3,000	670,000
Paulo Afonso (R. São Francisco, Brazil)	2,800	625,000
Urubupunga (Alto Paraná, Brazil)	2,800	625,000
Cataratas del Iguazú (R. Iguaçu, Brazil/Argentina)	1,725	380,000
Patos-Maribando (Rio Grande, Brazil)	1,500	330,000
Victoria (Mosi-oa-tunya) (R. Zambezi, Zambia/ Zimbabwe)	1,000	220,000
Churchill (R. Churchill, Canada)	975	215,000
Kaieteur (R. Potaro, Guyana)	660	145,000

TALLEST DAMS

	metres	feet
*Rogun, R. Vakhsh, Tajikistan	335	1,098
Nurek, R. Vakhsh, Tajikistan	300	984
Grande Dixence, Switzerland	285	935
*Longtan, R. Hangshui, China	285	935
Inguri, Georgia	272	892
Chicoasén, Mexico	261	856
Tehri, R. Bhagivathi, India	261	856

*Under construction

The world's most massive dam is the Syncrude Tailings dam in Alberta, Canada, which will have a volume of 540 million cubic metres/706 million cubic yards.

The Three Gorges Chang Jiang (Yangtze) Dam, China, with a crest length of 1,983 m/6,505 ft, is due for completion in 2009.

The Yacyretá-Apipe dam across the River Paraná, Argentina-Paraguay, is being completed to a length of 69,600 m/43.24 miles.

TALLEST INHABITED BUILDINGS

Building and city	Height	
	metres	feet
Chongqing Tower, China	457	1,499
Petronas Towers I and II, Kuala Lumpur	451.9	1,482
Sears Tower, Chicago[1]	443	1,454
Jin Mao, Shanghai, China (1998)	420	1,378
One World Trade Center Tower, New York[2]	417	1,368
Empire State Building, New York[3]	381	1,250
T & C Tower, Kaohsiung, Taiwan	347	1,138
Amoco Building, Chicago	346	1,136
John Hancock Center, Chicago	343	1,127
Shun Hing Square, Shenzhen, China	325	1,066
Chrysler Building, New York	319	1,046
Bank of China, Hong Kong[4]	315	1,033
Nation's Bank Tower, Atlanta	312	1,023
First Interstate World Center, Los Angeles	337	1,107
Vegas World Tower	308	1,012
Central Plaza, Hong Kong[5]	306.5	1,005
Texas Commerce Tower, Houston	305	1,002

[1] With TV antennae 520 m/1,707 ft
[2] With TV antennae, 521.2 m/1,710 ft; Two World Trade Center Tower, 415 m/1,362 ft
[3] With TV tower (added 1950–1), 430.9 m/1,414 ft
[4] With steel mast, 368.5 m/1,209 ft
[5] With steel mast, 374 m/1,227 ft

TALLEST STRUCTURES

Structure and location	Height	
	metres	feet
*Warszawa Radio Mast, Konstantynow, Poland	646	2,120
KTHI-TV Mast, Blanchard, North Dakota (guyed)	629	2,063
CN Tower, Metro Centre, Toronto, Canada	555	1,822
Ostankino Tower, Moscow	537	1,762

*Collapsed during renovation, August 1991

LONGEST BRIDGES – BY SPAN

Bridge and location	Length	
	metres	feet
SUSPENSION SPANS		
*Akashi-Kaikyo, Shikoku, Japan (1998)	1,990	6,528
Store Baelt East Bridge, Denmark	1,624	5,328
Humber Estuary, Humberside, England	1,410	4,626
*Jiangyin (Yangtze), China (1999)	1,385	4,488
Verrazano Narrows, Brooklyn–Staten I, USA	1,298	4,260
Golden Gate, San Francisco Bay, USA	1,280	4,200
Mackinac Straits, Michigan, USA	1,158	3,800
Minami Bisan-Seto, Japan	1,100	3,609
Bosporus I, Istanbul, Turkey	1,089	3,576
Bosporus II, Istanbul, Turkey	1,074	3,524
George Washington, Hudson River, New York City, USA	1,067	3,500
Ponte 25 de Abril (Tagus), Lisbon, Portugal	1,013	3,323

*Under construction

Bridge and location	Length metres	feet
Firth of Forth (road), nr Edinburgh, Scotland	1,006	3,300
Severn River, Severn Estuary, England	988	3,240

The main span of the 5.15 km/3.2 mile long Second Severn bridging opened in 1996 is 456 m/1,496 ft

CANTILEVER SPANS

	Length metres	feet
Pont de Québec (rail-road), St Lawrence, Canada	548.6	1,800
Ravenswood, W. Virginia, USA	525.1	1,723
Firth of Forth (rail), nr Edinburgh, Scotland	521.2	1,710
Nanko, Osaka, Japan	510.0	1,673
Commodore Barry, Chester, Pennsylvania, USA	494.3	1,622
Greater New Orleans, Louisiana, USA	480.0	1,575
Howrah (rail-road), Calcutta, India	457.2	1,500

STEEL ARCH SPANS

	Length metres	feet
New River Gorge, Fayetteville, W. Virginia, USA	553.8	1,817
Bayonne (Kill van Kull), Bayonne, NJ – Staten I, USA	503.5	1,652
Sydney Harbour, Sydney, Australia	502.9	1,650

The 'floating' bridging at Evergreen, Seattle, Washington State, USA, is 3,839 m/12,596 ft long
The longest stretch of bridgings of any kind is that carrying the Interstate 55 and Interstate 10 highways at Manchac on twin concrete trestles over 55.21 km/34.31 miles

LONGEST VEHICULAR TUNNELS

Tunnel and location	Length km	miles
*Seikan (rail), Tsugaru Channel, Japan	53.90	33.49
*Channel Tunnel, Cheriton, Kent – Sangatte, Calais	49.94	31.03
Moscow metro, Belyaevo – Bittsevsky, Moscow, Russia	37.90	23.50
Northern line tube, East Finchley – Morden, London	27.84	17.30
Oshimizu, Honshū, Japan	22.17	13.78
Simplon II (rail), Brigue, Switzerland – Iselle, Italy	19.82	12.31
Simplon I (rail), Brigue, Switzerland – Iselle, Italy	19.80	12.30
*Shin-Kanmon (rail), Kanmon Strait, Japan	18.68	11.61
Great Appennine (rail), Vernio, Italy	18.49	11.49
St Gotthard (road), Göschenen – Airolo, Switzerland	16.32	10.14
Rokko (rail), Ōsaka – Kōbe, Japan	16.09	10.00

*Sub-aqueous

The longest non-vehicular tunnelling in the world is the Delaware Aqueduct in New York State, USA, constructed in 1937–44 to a length of 168.9 km/105 miles

BRITAIN – RAIL TUNNELS

	miles	yards
Severn, Bristol – Newport	4	484
Totley, Manchester – Sheffield	3	950
Standedge, Manchester – Huddersfield	3	66
Sodbury, Swindon – Bristol	2	924
Disley, Stockport – Sheffield	2	346
Ffestiniog, Llandudno – Blaenau Ffestiniog	2	338
Bramhope, Leeds – Harrogate	2	241
Cowburn, Manchester – Sheffield	2	182

The longest road tunnel in Britain is the Mersey Road Tunnel, 2 miles 228 yards long. The longest canal tunnel, at Standedge, W. Yorks, is 3 miles 330 yards long; it was closed in 1944 but is currently being restored

LONGEST SHIP CANALS

Canal (opening date)	Length km	miles	Min. depth metres	feet
White Sea-Baltic (formerly Stalin) (1933) Canalized river; canal 51.5 km/32 miles	227	141.00	5.0	16.5
*Suez (1869) Links Red and Mediterranean Seas	162	100.60	12.9	42.3
V. I. Lenin Volga-Don (1952) Links Black and Caspian Seas	100	62.20	n/a	n/a
Kiel (or North Sea) (1895) Links North and Baltic Seas	98	60.90	13.7	45.0
*Houston (1940) Links inland city with sea	91	56.70	10.4	34.0
Alphonse XIII (1926) Gives Seville access to sea	85	53.00	7.6	25.0
Panama (1914) Links Pacific Ocean and Caribbean Sea; lake chain, 78.9 km/49 miles dug	82	50.71	12.5	41.0
Manchester Ship (1894) Links city with Irish Channel	64	39.70	8.5	28.0
Welland (1932) Circumvents Niagara Falls and Rapids	43	26.70	8.8	29.0
Brussels (Rupel Sea) (1922) Renders Brussels an inland port	32	19.80	6.4	21.0

*Has no locks

The first section of China's Grand Canal, running 1,782 km/1,107 miles from Beijing to Hangzhou, was opened AD 610 and completed in 1283. Today it is limited to 2,000 tonne vessels
The St Lawrence Seaway comprises Beauharnois, Welland and Welland Bypass and Seaway 54–59 canals, and allows access to Duluth, Minnesota, USA via the Great Lakes from the Atlantic end of Canada's Gulf of St Lawrence, a distance of 3,769 km/2,342 miles

Distances from London by Air

The list of the distances in statute miles from London, Heathrow, to various cities (airport) abroad has been supplied by the publishers of *IATA/Serco Aviation Services Air Distances Manual*, Southall, Middx.

To	Miles
Abidjan	3,197
Abu Dhabi (International)	3,425
Addis Ababa	3,675
Adelaide (International)	10,111
Aden	3,670
Algiers	1,035
Amman (Queen Alia)	2,287
Amsterdam	230
Ankara (Esenboga)	1,770
Athens	1,500
Atlanta	4,198
Auckland	11,404
Baghdad (Saddam)	2,551
Bahrain	3,163
Baku	2,485
Bangkok	5,928
Barbados	4,193
Barcelona (Muntadas)	712
Basle	447
Beijing (Capital)	5,063
Beirut	2,161
Belfast (Aldergrove)	325
Belgrade	1,056
Berlin (Tegel)	588
Bermuda	3,428
Berne	476
Bogotá	5,262
Bombay (Mumbai)	4,478
Boston	3,255
Brasilia	5,452
Bratislava	817
Brisbane (Eagle Farm)	10,273
Brussels	217
Bucharest (Otopeni)	1,307
Budapest	923
Buenos Aires	6,915
Cairo (International)	2,194
Calcutta	4,958
Calgary	4,357
Canberra	10,563
Cape Town	6,011
Caracas	4,639
Casablanca (Mohamed V)	1,300
Chicago (O'Hare)	3,941
Cologne	331
Colombo (Katunayake)	5,411
Copenhagen	608
Dakar	2,706
Dallas (Fort Worth)	4,736
Dallas (Lovefield)	4,732
Damascus (International)	2,223
Dar-es-Salaam	4,662
Darwin	8,613
Delhi	4,180
Denver	4,655

To	Miles
Detroit (Metropolitan)	3,754
Dhahran	3,143
Dhaka	4,976
Doha	3,253
Dubai	3,414
Dublin	279
Durban	5,937
Düsseldorf	310
Entebbe	4,033
Frankfurt (Main)	406
Freetown	3,046
Geneva	468
Gibraltar	1,084
Gothenburg (Landvetter)	664
Hamburg	463
Harare	5,156
Havana	4,647
Helsinki (Vantaa)	1,148
Hobart	10,826
Ho Chi Minh City	6,345
Hong Kong	5,990
Honolulu	7,220
Houston (Intercontinental)	4,821
Houston (William P. Hobby)	4,837
Islamabad	3,767
Istanbul	1,560
Jakarta (Halim Perdanakusuma)	7,295
Jeddah	2,947
Johannesburg	5,634
Kabul	3,558
Karachi	3,935
Kathmandu	4,570
Khartoum	3,071
Kiev (Borispol)	1,357
Kiev (Julyany)	1,337
Kingston, Jamaica	4,668
Kuala Lumpur (Subang)	6,557
Kuwait	2,903
Lagos	3,107
Larnaca	2,036
Lima	6,303
Lisbon	972
Lomé	3,129
Los Angeles (International)	5,439
Madras	5,113
Madrid	773
Malta	1,303
Manila	6,685
Marseille	614
Mauritius	6,075
Melbourne (Essendon)	10,504
Melbourne (Tullamarine)	10,499
Mexico City	5,529
Miami	4,414
Milan (Linate)	609
Minsk	1,176
Montego Bay	4,687
Montevideo	6,841
Montreal (Mirabel)	3,241
Moscow (Sheremetievo)	1,557
Munich (Franz Josef Strauss)	584

To	Miles
Muscat	3,621
Nairobi (Jomo Kenyatta)	4,248
Naples	1,011
Nassau	4,333
New York (J. F. Kennedy)	3,440
Nice	645
Oporto	806
Oslo (Fornebu)	722
Ottawa	3,321
Palma, Majorca (Son San Juan)	836
Paris (Charles de Gaulle)	215
Paris (Le Bourget)	215
Paris (Orly)	227
Perth, Australia	9,008
Port of Spain	4,404
Prague	649
Pretoria	5,602
Reykjavik (Domestic)	1,167
Reykjavik (Keflavik)	1,177
Rhodes	1,743
Rio de Janeiro	5,745
Riyadh (King Khaled) International	3,067
Rome (Fiumicino)	895
St John's, Newfoundland	2,308
St Petersburg	1,314
Salzburg	651
San Francisco	5,351
São Paulo	5,892
Sarajevo	1,017
Seoul (Kimpo)	5,507
Shanghai	5,725
Shannon	369
Singapore (Changi)	6,756
Sofia	1,266
Stockholm (Arlanda)	908
Suva	10,119
Sydney (Kingsford Smith)	10,568
Tangier	1,120
Tehran	2,741
Tel Aviv	2,227
Tokyo (Narita)	5,956
Toronto	3,544
Tripoli (International)	1,468
Tunis	1,137
Turin (Caselle)	570
Ulan Bator	4,340
Valencia	826
Vancouver	4,707
Venice (Tessera)	715
Vienna (Schwechat)	790
Vladivostok	5,298
Warsaw	912
Washington (Dulles)	3,665
Wellington	11,692
Yangon/Rangoon	5,582
Yokohama (Aomori)	5,647
Zagreb	848
Zürich	490

The United Kingdom

The United Kingdom comprises Great Britain (England, Wales and Scotland) and Northern Ireland. The Isle of Man and the Channel Islands are Crown dependencies with their own legislative systems, and not a part of the United Kingdom.

AREA AS AT 31 MARCH 1981

	Land miles^2	km^2	*Inland water miles^2	km^2	Total miles^2	km^2
United Kingdom	93,006	240,883	1,242	3,218	94,248	244,101
England	50,058	129,652	293	758	50,351	130,410
Wales	7,965	20,628	50	130	8,015	20,758
Scotland	29,767	77,097	653	1,692	30,420	78,789
†Northern Ireland	5,225	13,532	249	628	5,467	14,160
Isle of Man	221	572	—	—	221	572
Channel Islands	75	194	—	—	75	194

*Excluding tidal water
†Excluding certain tidal waters that are parts of statutory areas in Northern Ireland

POPULATION

The first official census of population in England, Wales and Scotland was taken in 1801 and a census has been taken every ten years since, except in 1941 when there was no census because of war. The last official census in the United Kingdom was taken on 21 April 1991 and the next is due in April 2001.

The first official census of population in Ireland was taken in 1841. However, all figures given below refer only to the area which is now Northern Ireland. Figures for Northern Ireland in 1921 and 1931 are estimates based on the censuses taken in 1926 and 1937 respectively.

Estimates of the population of England before 1801, calculated from the number of baptisms, burials and marriages, are:

1570	4,160,221	1670	5,773,646
1600	4,811,718	1700	6,045,008
1630	5,600,517	1750	6,517,035

	United Kingdom Total	Male	Female	England and Wales Total	Male	Female	Scotland Total	Male	Female	Northern Ireland Total	Male	Female
Thousands												

CENSUS RESULTS 1801–1991

	Total	Male	Female	Total	Male	Female	Total	Male	Female	Total	Male	Female
1801	—	—	—	8,893	4,255	4,638	1,608	739	869	—	—	—
1811	13,368	6,368	7,000	10,165	4,874	5,291	1,806	826	980	—	—	—
1821	15,472	7,498	7,974	12,000	5,850	6,150	2,092	983	1,109	—	—	—
1831	17,835	8,647	9,188	13,897	6,771	7,126	2,364	1,114	1,250	—	—	—
1841	20,183	9,819	10,364	15,914	7,778	8,137	2,620	1,242	1,378	1,649	800	849
1851	22,259	10,855	11,404	17,928	8,781	9,146	2,889	1,376	1,513	1,443	698	745
1861	24,525	11,894	12,631	20,066	9,776	10,290	3,062	1,450	1,612	1,396	668	728
1871	27,431	13,309	14,122	22,712	11,059	11,653	3,360	1,603	1,757	1,359	647	712
1881	31,015	15,060	15,955	25,974	12,640	13,335	3,736	1,799	1,936	1,305	621	684
1891	34,264	16,593	17,671	29,003	14,060	14,942	4,026	1,943	2,083	1,236	590	646
1901	38,237	18,492	19,745	32,528	15,729	16,799	4,472	2,174	2,298	1,237	590	647
1911	42,082	20,357	21,725	36,070	17,446	18,625	4,761	2,309	2,452	1,251	603	648
1921	44,027	21,033	22,994	37,887	18,075	19,811	4,882	2,348	2,535	1,258	610	648
1931	46,038	22,060	23,978	39,952	19,133	20,819	4,843	2,326	2,517	1,243	601	642
1951	50,225	24,118	26,107	43,758	21,016	22,742	5,096	2,434	2,662	1,371	668	703
1961	52,709	25,481	27,228	46,105	22,304	23,801	5,179	2,483	2,697	1,425	694	731
1971	55,515	26,952	28,562	48,750	23,683	25,067	5,229	2,515	2,714	1,536	755	781
1981	55,848	27,104	28,742	49,155	23,873	25,281	5,131	2,466	2,664	*1,533	750	783
1991	56,467	27,344	29,123	49,890	24,182	25,707	4,999	2,392	2,606	1,578	769	809

†RESIDENT POPULATION: PROJECTIONS (MID-YEAR)

	Total	Male	Female	Total	Male	Female	Total	Male	Female	Total	Male	Female
2001	59,472	29,312	30,160	52,661	26,987	26,674	5,135	2,502	2,632	1,676	822	854
2011	60,493	30,011	30,483	53,712	26,680	27,032	5,083	2,493	2,590	1,699	838	861
2021	61,130	30,375	30,754	54,358	27,042	27,316	5,040	2,478	2,562	1,731	856	876
2031	60,720	30,114	30,606	54,036	26,824	27,211	4,934	2,425	2,510	1,750	865	885

*Figures include 44,500 non-enumerated persons
† Projections are 1994 based

Source: The Stationery Office – *Annual Abstract 1997*; ONS – Census reports

ISLANDS: CENSUS RESULTS 1901–91

	Isle of Man Total	Male	Female	Jersey Total	Male	Female	*Guernsey Total	Male	Female
1901	54,752	25,496	29,256	52,576	23,940	28,636	40,446	19,652	20,794
1911	52,016	23,937	28,079	51,898	24,014	27,884	41,858	20,661	21,197
1921	60,284	27,329	32,955	49,701	22,438	27,263	38,315	18,246	20,069
1931	49,308	22,443	26,865	50,462	23,424	27,038	40,643	19,659	20,984
1951	55,123	25,749	29,464	57,296	27,282	30,014	43,652	21,221	22,431
1961	48,151	22,060	26,091	57,200	27,200	30,000	45,068	21,671	23,397
1971	56,289	26,461	29,828	72,532	35,423	37,109	51,458	24,792	26,666
1981	64,679	30,901	33,778	77,000	37,000	40,000	53,313	25,701	27,612
1991	69,788	33,693	36,095	84,082	40,862	43,220	58,867	28,297	30,570

* Population of Guernsey, Herm, Jethou and Lithou. Figures for 1901–71 record all persons present on census night; census figures for 1981 and 1991 record all persons resident in the islands on census night
Source: 1991 Census

RESIDENT POPULATION

MID-YEAR ESTIMATE

	1985	1995
United Kingdom	56,685,000	58,606,000
England	47,180,000	48,903,000
Wales	2,810,000	2,917,000
Scotland	5,137,000	5,137,000
Northern Ireland	1,558,000	1,649,000

Source: The Stationery Office – *Annual Abstract of Statistics 1997*

BY AGE AND SEX 1995

Males	Under 16	65 and over
United Kingdom	6,208,000	3,740,000
England	5,155,000	3,144,000
Wales	310,000	206,000
Scotland	530,000	307,000
Northern Ireland	213,000	84,000

Females	Under 16	60 and over
United Kingdom	5,898,000	6,911,000
England	4,893,000	5,765,000
Wales	295,000	376,000
Scotland	507,000	607,000
Northern Ireland	204,000	163,000

Source: The Stationery Office – *Annual Abstract of Statistics 1997*

BY ETHNIC GROUP (1991 CENSUS (GREAT BRITAIN))

Ethnic group	Estimated population	Percentage
Caribbean	500,000	16.6
African	212,000	7
Other black	178,000	5.9
Indian	840,000	27.9
Pakistani	477,000	15.8
Bangladeshi	163,000	5.4
Chinese	157,000	5.2
Other Asian	198,000	6.6
Other	290,000	9.6
Total ethnic minority groups	3,015,000	100
White	51,874,000	—
All ethnic groups	54,889,000	—

Source: The Stationery Office – *Population Trends 72*

AVERAGE DENSITY *Persons per hectare*

	1981	1991
England	3.55	3.61
Wales	1.34	1.36
Scotland	0.66	0.65
Northern Ireland	1.12	1.11

Sources: ONS – Census reports

IMMIGRATION 1995
Acceptances for settlement in the UK by nationality

Region	Number of persons
Europe: total	4,250
European Economic Area	220
Remainder of Europe	4,030
Americas: total	8,180
USA	3,960
Canada	940
Africa: total	12,000
Asia: total	26,120
Indian sub-continent	14,450
Middle East	2,880
Oceania: total	3,450
British Overseas Citizens	690
Stateless	780
Total	55,480

Source: The Stationery Office – *Annual Abstract of Statistics 1997*

LIVE BIRTHS AND BIRTH RATES 1995

	Live births	Birth rate*
United Kingdom	732,000	12.5
England and Wales	648,000	12.5
Scotland	60,000	11.7
Northern Ireland	24,000	14.5

*Live births per 1,000 population
Source: The Stationery Office – *Annual Abstract of Statistics 1997*

LEGAL ABORTIONS 1995 (ENGLAND AND WALES)

Age group	Number
Under 16	3,370
16–19	26,200
20–34	112,200
35–44	20,200
45 and over	500
Age not stated	—
Total	162,400

Source: The Stationery Office – *Population Trends 87*

BIRTHS OUTSIDE MARRIAGE (UK)

Age group	1981	1995
Under 20	30,000	42,000
20–24	33,000	79,000
25–29	16,000	66,000
Over 30	13,000	60,000
Total	91,000	246,000

Source: The Stationery Office – *Annual Abstract of Statistics 1997*

MARRIAGE AND DIVORCE 1994

	Marriages	Divorces
United Kingdom	331,248p	173,611
England and Wales	291,085p	158,175
Scotland	31,480	13,133
Northern Ireland	8,683	2,303

p provisional
Source: The Stationery Office – *Annual Abstract of Statistics 1997;*
Annual Report of the Registrar-General for Northern Ireland 1995

DEATHS AND DEATH RATES 1995

Males	Deaths	Death rate*
United Kingdom	308,982	10.8
England and Wales	272,709	10.8p
Scotland	28,791	11.6
Northern Ireland	7,482	9.3
Females		
United Kingdom	332,730	11.1
England and Wales	293,193	11.1p
Scotland	31,709	12.0
Northern Ireland	7,828	9.3

* Deaths per 1,000 population
p provisional
Sources: The Stationery Office – *Annual Abstract of Statistics 1997;*
ONS; *Annual Report of the Registrar-General for Scotland 1995; Annual
Report of the Registrar-General for Northern Ireland 1995*

INFANT MORTALITY 1995p
Deaths of infants under 1 year of age per 1,000 live births

	Number
United Kingdom	6.2
England and Wales	6.1
Scotland	6.2
Northern Ireland	7.1

p provisional
Source: The Stationery Office – *Annual Abstract of Statistics 1997*

EXPECTATION OF LIFE LIFE TABLES 1993–95 (INTERIM FIGURES)

	England and Wales		Scotland		Northern Ireland	
Age	Male	Female	Male	Female	Male	Female
0	74.2	79.4	71.9	77.4	72.9	78.4
5	69.8	74.9	67.5	72.9	68.6	74.0
10	64.8	70.0	62.5	67.9	63.6	69.0
15	59.9	65.0	57.6	63.0	58.7	64.1
20	55.0	60.1	52.8	58.1	54.0	59.2
25	50.3	55.2	48.1	53.2	49.3	54.3
30	45.5	50.3	43.4	48.3	44.5	49.4
35	40.7	45.4	38.7	43.5	39.8	44.5
40	35.9	40.6	33.9	38.7	35.0	39.7
45	31.3	35.8	29.3	34.0	30.3	34.9
50	26.7	31.2	24.9	29.4	25.8	30.3
55	22.4	26.7	20.8	25.0	21.5	25.9
60	18.3	22.4	16.9	20.8	17.5	21.6
65	14.6	18.3	13.5	16.9	14.0	17.7
70	11.4	14.6	10.6	13.5	10.9	14.0
75	8.8	11.4	8.1	10.4	8.2	10.8
80	6.6	8.5	6.1	7.8	6.1	7.9
85	4.9	6.2	4.5	5.6	4.3	5.6

Source: The Stationery Office – *Annual Abstract of Statistics 1997*

DEATHS ANALYSED BY CAUSE 1995

	England & Wales	Scotland	N. Ireland
TOTAL DEATHS	565,902	60,500	15,310
Infectious and parasitic diseases	3,590	326	44
Neoplasms	140,791	15,462	3,585
Malignant neoplasm of stomach	7,068	758	170
Malignant neoplasm of colon	10,777	1,144	354
Malignant neoplasm of rectum, rectosigmoid junction and anus	4,916	587	100
Malignant neoplasm of trachea, bronchus and lung	31,486	4,221	752
Malignant neoplasm of female breast	12,509	1,244	327
Leukaemia	3,530	283	83
Endocrine, nutritional and metabolic diseases and immunity disorders	7,839	732	84
Diabetes mellitus	6,204	461	43
Diseases of blood and blood-forming organs	1,922	129	31
Mental disorders	9,030	1,583	78
Diseases of the nervous system and sense organs	9,646	832	224
Meningitis	207	18	3
Diseases of the circulatory system	241,871	27,079	6,929
Chronic rheumatic heart disease	1,698	178	47
Hypertensive disease	2,884	324	94
Ischaemic heart disease	132,993	14,977	4,086
Diseases of pulmonary circulation and other forms of heart disease	26,705	2,351	641
Cerebrovascular disease	59,646	7,748	1,690
Atherosclerosis	2,306	253	41
Diseases of the respiratory system	90,094	7,668	2,656
Pneumonia	54,538	4,021	1,781
Diseases of the digestive system	19,390	2,252	449
Ulcer of stomach and duodenum	3,981	359	87
Chronic liver disease and cirrhosis	3,611	607	71
Diseases of the genitourinary system	7,085	928	251
Complications of pregnancy, childbirth and the puerperium	46	6	—
Diseases of the skin, musculoskeletal system and connective tissue	4,680	383	77
Congenital anomalies	1,288	176	91
Certain conditions originating in the perinatal period	151	178	93
Signs, symptoms and ill-defined conditions	9,672	365	55
All forms of injury and poisoning	16,129	2,395	663
Motor vehicle traffic accidents	3,144	417	131
Suicide and self-inflicted injury	3,547	623	122

Sources: ONS; *Annual Report of the Registrar-General for Scotland 1995; Annual Report of the Registrar-General for Northern Ireland 1995*

The National Flag

The national flag of the United Kingdom is the Union Flag, generally known as the Union Jack. (The name 'Union Jack' derives from the use of the Union Flag on the jack-staff of naval vessels.)

The Union Flag is a combination of the cross of St George, patron saint of England, the cross of St Andrew, patron saint of Scotland, and a cross similar to that of St Patrick, patron saint of Ireland.

Cross of St George: cross Gules in a field Argent (red cross on a white ground).

Cross of St Andrew: saltire Argent in a field Azure (white diagonal cross on a blue ground).

Cross of St Patrick: saltire Gules in a field Argent (red diagonal cross on a white ground).

The Union Flag was first introduced in 1606 after the union of the kingdoms of England and Scotland under one sovereign. The cross of St Patrick was added in 1801 after the union of Great Britain and Ireland.

DAYS FOR FLYING FLAGS

The correct orientation of the Union Flag when flying is with the broader diagonal band of white uppermost in the hoist (i.e. near the pole) and the narrower diagonal band of white uppermost in the fly (i.e. furthest from the pole).

It is the practice to fly the Union Flag daily on some customs houses. In all other cases, flags are flown on government buildings by command of The Queen.

Days for hoisting the Union Flag are notified to the Department of National Heritage by The Queen's command and communicated by the department to the other government departments. On the days appointed, the Union Flag is flown on government buildings in the United Kingdom from 8 a.m. to sunset.

The Queen's Accession	6 February
Birthday of The Duke of York	19 February
*St David's Day (in Wales only)	1 March
Commonwealth Day (1998)	9 March
Birthday of The Prince Edward	10 March
Birthday of The Queen	21 April
*St George's Day (in England only)	23 April
Coronation Day	2 June
Birthday of The Duke of Edinburgh	10 June
The Queen's Official Birthday (1998)	13 June
Birthday of Queen Elizabeth the Queen Mother	4 August
Birthday of The Princess Royal	15 August
Birthday of The Princess Margaret	21 August
Remembrance Sunday (1998)	8 November
Birthday of The Prince of Wales	14 November
The Queen's Wedding Day	20 November
*St Andrew's Day (in Scotland only)	30 November
†The opening of Parliament by The Queen	
†The prorogation of Parliament by The Queen	

*Where a building has two or more flagstaffs, the appropriate national flag may be flown in addition to the Union Flag, but not in a superior position
†Flags are flown whether or not The Queen performs the ceremony in person. Flags are flown only in the Greater London area

FLAGS AT HALF-MAST

Flags are flown at half-mast on the following occasions:

(a) From the announcement of the death up to the funeral of the Sovereign, except on Proclamation Day, when flags are hoisted right up from 11 a.m. to sunset

(b) The funerals of members of the Royal Family, subject to special commands from The Queen in each case

(c) The funerals of foreign rulers, subject to special commands from The Queen in each case

(d) The funerals of Prime Ministers and ex-Prime Ministers of the United Kingdom, subject to special commands from The Queen in each case

(e) Other occasions by special command of The Queen

On occasions when days for flying flags coincide with days for flying flags at half-mast, the following rules are observed. Flags are flown:

(a) although a member of the Royal Family, or a near relative of the Royal Family, may be lying dead, unless special commands be received from The Queen to the contrary

(b) although it may be the day of the funeral of a foreign ruler

If the body of a very distinguished subject is lying at a government office, the flag may fly at half-mast on that office until the body has left (provided it is a day on which the flag would fly) and then the flag is to be hoisted right up. On all other government buildings the flag will fly as usual.

THE ROYAL STANDARD

The Royal Standard is hoisted only when The Queen is actually present in the building, and never when Her Majesty is passing in procession.

The Royal Family

THE SOVEREIGN

ELIZABETH II, by the Grace of God, of the United Kingdom of Great Britain and Northern Ireland and of her other Realms and Territories Queen, Head of the Commonwealth, Defender of the Faith

Her Majesty Elizabeth Alexandra Mary of Windsor, elder daughter of King George VI and of HM Queen Elizabeth the Queen Mother
Born 21 April 1926, at 17 Bruton Street, London W1
Ascended the throne 6 February 1952
Crowned 2 June 1953, at Westminster Abbey
Married 20 November 1947, in Westminster Abbey, HRH The Duke of Edinburgh
Official residences: Buckingham Palace, London SW1; Windsor Castle, Berks; Palace of Holyroodhouse, Edinburgh
Private residences: Sandringham, Norfolk; Balmoral Castle, Aberdeenshire
Office: Buckingham Palace, London SW1A 1AA. Tel: 0171-930 4832

HUSBAND OF HM THE QUEEN

HRH THE PRINCE PHILIP, DUKE OF EDINBURGH, KG, KT, OM, GBE, AC, QSO, PC, Ranger of Windsor Park
Born 10 June 1921, son of Prince and Princess Andrew of Greece and Denmark (*see* page 129), naturalized a British subject 1947, created Duke of Edinburgh, Earl of Merioneth and Baron Greenwich 1947

CHILDREN OF HM THE QUEEN

HRH THE PRINCE OF WALES (Prince Charles Philip Arthur George), KG, KT, GCB and Great Master of the Order of the Bath, AK, QSO, PC, ADC(P)
Born 14 November 1948, created Prince of Wales and Earl of Chester 1958, succeeded as Duke of Cornwall, Duke of Rothesay, Earl of Carrick and Baron Renfrew, Lord of the Isles and Prince and Great Steward of Scotland 1952
Married 29 July 1981 Lady Diana Frances Spencer (Diana, Princess of Wales (1961–97), youngest daughter of the 8th Earl Spencer and the Hon. Mrs Shand Kydd), marriage dissolved 1996
Issue:
(1) HRH Prince William of Wales (Prince William Arthur Philip Louis), *born* 21 June 1982
(2) HRH Prince Henry of Wales (Prince Henry Charles Albert David), *born* 15 September 1984
Residences of the Prince of Wales: St James's Palace, London SW1A 1BS; Highgrove, Doughton, Tetbury, Glos.
Office of the Prince of Wales: St James's Palace, London SW1A 1BS. Tel: 0171-930 4832
Office of Diana, Princess of Wales, Kensington Palace, London W8 4PU. Tel: 0171-930 4832

HRH THE PRINCESS ROYAL (Princess Anne Elizabeth Alice Louise), KG, GCVO
Born 15 August 1950, declared The Princess Royal 1987
Married (1) 14 November 1973 Captain Mark Anthony

Peter Phillips, CVO (*born* 22 September 1948); marriage dissolved 1992; (2) 12 December 1992 Captain Timothy James Hamilton Laurence, MVO, RN (*born* 1 March 1955)
Issue:
(1) Peter Mark Andrew Phillips, *born* 15 November 1977
(2) Zara Anne Elizabeth Phillips, *born* 15 May 1981
Residence: Gatcombe Park, Minchinhampton, Glos.
Office: Buckingham Palace, London SW1A 1AA. Tel: 0171-930 4832

HRH THE DUKE OF YORK (Prince Andrew Albert Christian Edward), CVO, ADC(P)
Born 19 February 1960, created Duke of York, Earl of Inverness and Baron Killyleagh 1986
Married 23 July 1986 Sarah Margaret Ferguson, now Sarah, Duchess of York (*born* 15 October 1959, younger daughter of Major Ronald Ferguson and Mrs Hector Barrantes), marriage dissolved 1996
Issue:
(1) HRH Princess Beatrice of York (Princess Beatrice Elizabeth Mary), *born* 8 August 1988
(2) HRH Princess Eugenie of York (Princess Eugenie Victoria Helena), *born* 23 March 1990
Residences: Buckingham Palace, London SW1; Sunninghill Park, Ascot, Berks.
Office: Buckingham Palace, London SW1 1AA. Tel: 0171-930 4832

HRH THE PRINCE EDWARD (Prince Edward Antony Richard Louis), CVO
Born 10 March 1964
Residence and Office: Buckingham Palace, London SW1A 1AA. Tel: 0171-930 4832

SISTER OF HM THE QUEEN

HRH THE PRINCESS MARGARET, COUNTESS OF SNOWDON, CI, GCVO, Royal Victorian Chain, Dame Grand Cross of the Order of St John of Jerusalem
Born 21 August 1930, younger daughter of King George VI and HM Queen Elizabeth the Queen Mother
Married 6 May 1960 Antony Charles Robert Armstrong-Jones, GCVO (*born* 7 March 1930, created Earl of Snowdon 1961, Constable of Caernarvon Castle); marriage dissolved 1978
Issue:
(1) David Albert Charles, Viscount Linley, *born* 3 November 1961, *married* 8 October 1993 the Hon. Serena Stanhope
(2) Lady Sarah Chatto (Sarah Frances Elizabeth), *born* 1 May 1964, *married* 14 July 1994 Daniel Chatto, and has issue, Samuel David Benedict Chatto, *born* 28 July 1996
Residence and Office: Kensington Palace, London W8 4PU. Tel: 0171-930 3141

MOTHER OF HM THE QUEEN

HM QUEEN ELIZABETH THE QUEEN MOTHER (Elizabeth Angela Marguerite), Lady of the Garter, Lady of the Thistle, CI, GCVO, GBE, Dame Grand Cross of the Order of St John, Royal Victorian Chain, Lord Warden and Admiral of the Cinque Ports and Constable of Dover Castle

Born 4 August 1900, youngest daughter of the 14th Earl of Strathmore and Kinghorne
Married 26 April 1923 (as Lady Elizabeth Bowes-Lyon) Prince Albert, Duke of York, afterwards King George VI (*see* page 128)
Residences: Clarence House, St James's Palace, London sw1; Royal Lodge, Windsor Great Park, Berks; Castle of Mey, Caithness
Office: Clarence House, St James's Palace, London sw1A 1BA. Tel: 0171-930 3141

AUNT OF HM THE QUEEN

HRH Princess Alice, Duchess of Gloucester (Alice Christabel), gcb, ci, gcvo, gbe, Grand Cordon of Al Kamal
Born 25 December 1901, third daughter of the 7th Duke of Buccleuch and Queensberry
Married 6 November 1935 (as Lady Alice Montagu-Douglas-Scott) Prince Henry, Duke of Gloucester, third son of King George V (*see* page 128)
Residence and Office: Kensington Palace, London w8 4pu. Tel: 0171-937 6374

COUSINS OF HM THE QUEEN

HRH The Duke of Gloucester (Prince Richard Alexander Walter George), kg, gcvo, Grand Prior of the Order of St John of Jerusalem
Born 26 August 1944
Married 8 July 1972 Birgitte Eva van Deurs, now HRH The Duchess of Gloucester, gcvo (*born* 20 June 1946, daughter of Asger Henriksen and Vivian van Deurs)
Issue:
(1)   Earl of Ulster (Alexander Patrick Gregers Richard), *born* 24 October 1974
(2)   Lady Davina Windsor (Davina Elizabeth Alice Benedikte), *born* 19 November 1977
(3)   Lady Rose Windsor (Rose Victoria Birgitte Louise), *born* 1 March 1980
Residence and Office: Kensington Palace, London w8 4pu. Tel: 0171-937 6374

HRH The Duke of Kent (Prince Edward George Nicholas Paul Patrick), kg, gcmg, gcvo, adc(p)
Born 9 October 1935
Married 8 June 1961 Katharine Lucy Mary Worsley, now HRH The Duchess of Kent, gcvo (*born* 22 February 1933, daughter of Sir William Worsley, Bt.)
Issue:
(1)   Earl of St Andrews (George Philip Nicholas), *born* 26 June 1962, *married* 9 January 1988 Sylvana Tomaselli, and has issue, Edward Edmund Maximilian George, Baron Downpatrick, *born* 2 December 1988; Lady Marina Charlotte Alexandra Katharine Windsor, *born* 30 September 1992; Lady Amelia Sophia Theodora Mary Margaret Windsor, *born* 24 August 1995
(2)   Lady Helen Taylor (Helen Marina Lucy), *born* 28 April 1964, *married* 18 July 1992 Timothy Taylor, and has issue, Columbus George Donald Taylor, *born* 6 August 1994; Cassius Edward Taylor, *born* 26 December 1996
(3)   Lord Nicholas Windsor (Nicholas Charles Edward Jonathan), *born* 25 July 1970
Residence: Wren House, Palace Green, London w8 4py
Office: York House, St James's Palace, London sw1 1bq. Tel: 0171-930 4872

HRH Princess Alexandra, the Hon. Lady Ogilvy (Princess Alexandra Helen Elizabeth Olga Christabel), gcvo *Born* 25 December 1936
Married 24 April 1963 The Rt. Hon. Sir Angus Ogilvy, kcvo (*born* 14 September 1928, second son of 12th Earl of Airlie)
Issue:
(1)   James Robert Bruce Ogilvy, *born* 29 February 1964, *married* 30 July 1988 Julia Rawlinson, and has issue, Flora Alexandra Ogilvy, *born* 15 December 1994; Alexander Charles Ogilvy, *born* 12 November 1996
(2)   Marina Victoria Alexandra, Mrs Mowatt, *born* 31 July 1966, *married* 2 February 1990 Paul Mowatt (separated 1996), and has issue, Zenouska May Mowatt, *born* 26 May 1990; Christian Alexander Mowatt, *born* 4 June 1993
Residence: Thatched House Lodge, Richmond Park, Surrey
Office: Buckingham Palace, London sw1A 1aa. Tel: 0171-930 1860

HRH Prince Michael of Kent (Prince Michael George Charles Franklin), kcvo
Born 4 July 1942
Married 30 June 1978 Baroness Marie-Christine Agnes Hedwig Ida von Reibnitz, now HRH Princess Michael of Kent (*born* 15 January 1945, daughter of Baron Gunther von Reibnitz)
Issue:
(1)   Lord Frederick Windsor (Frederick Michael George David Louis), *born* 6 April 1979
(2)   Lady Gabriella Windsor (Gabriella Marina Alexandra Ophelia), *born* 23 April 1981
Residences: Kensington Palace, London w8 4pu; Nether Lypiatt Manor, Stroud, Glos.
Office: Kensington Palace, London w8 4pu. Tel: 0171-938 3519

ORDER OF SUCCESSION

1   HRH The Prince of Wales
2   HRH Prince William of Wales
3   HRH Prince Henry of Wales
4   HRH The Duke of York
5   HRH Princess Beatrice of York
6   HRH Princess Eugenie of York
7   HRH The Prince Edward
8   HRH The Princess Royal
9   Peter Phillips
10   Zara Phillips
11   HRH The Princess Margaret, Countess of Snowdon
12   Viscount Linley
13   Lady Sarah Chatto
14   Samuel Chatto
15   HRH The Duke of Gloucester
16   Earl of Ulster
17   Lady Davina Windsor
18   Lady Rose Windsor
19   HRH The Duke of Kent
20   Baron Downpatrick
21   Lady Marina Charlotte Windsor
22   Lady Amelia Windsor
23   Lord Nicholas Windsor
24   Lady Helen Taylor
25   Columbus Taylor
26   Cassius Taylor
27   Lord Frederick Windsor
28   Lady Gabriella Windsor
29   HRH Princess Alexandra, the Hon. Lady Ogilvy
30   James Ogilvy
31   Alexander Ogilvy
32   Flora Ogilvy
33   Marina, Mrs Paul Mowatt

Royal Households

THE QUEEN'S HOUSEHOLD

Lord Chamberlain, The Earl of Airlie, KT, GCVO, PC (The Lord Camoys from 1 January 1998)
Lord Steward, The Viscount Ridley, KG, GCVO, TD
Master of the Horse, The Lord Somerleyton, KCVO
Treasurer of the Household, G. Mudie, MP
Comptroller of the Household, T. McAvoy, MP
Vice-Chamberlain, Mrs J. Anderson, MP

Gold Sticks, Maj.-Gen. Lord Michael Fitzalan-Howard, GCVO, CB, CBE, MC; Gen. Sir Desmond Fitzpatrick, GCB, GCVO, DSO, MBE, MC
Vice-Adm. of the United Kingdom, Adm. Sir John Brigstocke, KCB
Rear-Adm. of the United Kingdom, Adm. Sir Nicholas Hunt, GCB, LVO
First and Principal Naval Aide-de-Camp, Adm. Sir Jock Slater, GCB, LVO
Flag Aide-de-Camp, Adm. Sir Michael Boyce, KCB, OBE
Aides-de-Camp-General, Gen. Sir Charles Guthrie, GCB, LVO, OBE; Gen. Sir Michael Rose, KCB, CBE, DSO, QGM; Gen. Sir Jeremy Mackenzie, KCB, OBE
Air Aides-de-Camp, Air Chief Marshal Sir Richard Johns, GCB, CBE, LVO; Air Chief Marshal Sir John Allison, KCB, CBE

Mistress of the Robes, The Duchess of Grafton, GCVO
Ladies of the Bedchamber, The Countess of Airlie, DCVO; The Lady Farnham
Extra Lady of the Bedchamber, The Marchioness of Abergavenny, DCVO
Women of the Bedchamber, Hon. Mary Morrison, DCVO; Lady Susan Hussey, DCVO; Lady Dugdale, DCVO; The Lady Elton; Mrs Christian Adams (temp.)
Extra Women of the Bedchamber, The Hon. Mrs Van der Woude, CVO; Mrs John Woodroffe, CVO; Mrs Michael Wall, DCVO; Lady Abel Smith, DCVO; Mrs Robert de Pass
Equerries, Lt.-Col. Sir Guy Acland, Bt., MVO; Lt.-Cdr. T. Williamson; Capt. C. Clifton (temp.)
Extra Equerries, Vice-Adm. Sir Peter Ashmore, KCB, KCVO, DSC; Maj. Sir Shane Blewitt, GCVO; Lt.-Col. The Lord Charteris of Amisfield, GCB, GCVO,QSO, OBE, PC; Maj.-Gen. Sir Simon Cooper, KCVO; Air Cdre the Hon. T. Elworthy, CVO, CBE; The Rt Hon. Sir Robert Fellowes, GCVO, KCB; Sir Edward Ford, KCB, KCVO, ERD; Rear-Adm. Sir John Garnier, KCVO, CBE; Rear-Adm. Sir Paul Greening, GCVO; The Rt. Hon. Sir William Heseltine, GCB, GCVO, AC, QSO; Lt.-Col. Sir John Johnston, GCVO, MC; Lt.-Col. A. Mather, OBE; Sir Peter Miles, KCVO; Lt.-Col. Sir John Miller, GCVO, DSO, MC; Air Cdre Sir Dennis Mitchell, KBE, CVO, DFC, AFC; The Lord Moore of Wolvercote, GCB, GCVO, CMG, QSO; Lt.-Gen. Sir John Richards, KCB, KCVO; Lt.-Col. W. H. M. Ross, CVO, OBE; Sir Kenneth Scott, KCVO, CMG; Air Vice-Marshal Sir John Severne, KCVO, OBE, AFC; Lt.-Col. Sir Blair Stewart-Wilson, KCVO; Rear-Adm. Sir Richard Trowbridge, KCVO; Lt.-Col. G. West, CVO; Air Cdre Sir Archie Winskill, KCVO, CBE, DFC, AE; Rear-Adm. Sir Robert Woodard, KCVO

THE PRIVATE SECRETARY'S OFFICE
Buckingham Palace, London SW1A 1AA

Private Secretary to The Queen, The Rt Hon. Sir Robert Fellowes, GCVO, KCB
Deputy Private Secretary, R. B. Janvrin, CB, CVO
Assistant Private Secretary, Mrs M. Francis
Special Assistant to the Private Secretary, S. Gimson
Press Secretary, G. Crawford, LVO
Deputy Press Secretary, Miss P. Russell-Smith
Assistant Press Secretary, D. Tuck
Chief Clerk, Mrs G. Middleburgh
Secretary to the Private Secretary, Miss E. Ash

THE QUEEN'S ARCHIVES
Round Tower, Windsor Castle, Berks
Keeper of The Queen's Archives, The Rt Hon. Sir Robert Fellowes, GCVO, KCB
Assistant Keeper, O. Everett, CVO
Registrar, Lady de Bellaigue, MVO

THE PRIVY PURSE AND TREASURER'S OFFICE
Buckingham Palace, London SW1A 1AA
Keeper of the Privy Purse and Treasurer to The Queen, M. Peat, CVO
Deputy Keeper of the Privy Purse and Deputy Treasurer, J. Parsons, LVO
Chief Accountant and Paymaster, I. McGregor
Personnel Officer, Miss P. Lloyd
Land Agent, Sandringham, J. Major, FRICS
Resident Factor, Balmoral, P. Ord, FRICS
Master of The Queen's Music, M. Williamson, CBE, AO
Poet Laureate, Ted Hughes, OBE
Keeper of the Royal Philatelic Collection, C. Goodwyn

PROPERTY SERVICES
Director of Property Services, J. Tiltman, LVO
Director of Finance, Property Services and Royal Travel, S. Cawley

ROYAL ALMONRY
Lord High Almoner, The Bishop of Wakefield
Hereditary Grand Almoner, The Marquess of Exeter
Sub-Almoner, Revd W. Booth
Secretary, C. Williams, RVM
Assistant Secretary, P. Hartley, LVO

THE LORD CHAMBERLAIN'S OFFICE
Buckingham Palace, London SW1A 1AA
Comptroller, Lt.-Col. W. H. M. Ross, CVO, OBE
Assistant Comptroller, Lt.-Col. A. Mather, OBE
Secretary, J. Spencer, MVO
Assistant Secretary, Miss A. Krysztofiak
State Invitations Assistant, J. O. Hope
Permanent Lords-in-Waiting, Lt.-Col. the Lord Charteris of Amisfield, GCB, GCVO, OBE, QSO, PC; The Lord Moore of Wolvercote, GCB, GCVO, CMG, QSO
Lords-in-Waiting, The Lord Camoys; The Viscount Brookeborough; The Lord Haskell; The Lord Whitty; The Lord Hoyle
Baronesses-in-Waiting, The Baroness Farrington of Ribbleton; The Baroness Gould of Potternewton
Gentlemen Ushers, Capt. M. Barrow, DSO, RN; Capt. M. Fulford-Dobson, RN; Lt.-Gen. Sir Richard Vickers, KCB, LVO, OBE; Air Vice-Marshal B. Newton, CB, OBE; Col. M. Havergal, OBE; Rear Adm. C. H. D. Cooke-Priest, CB; Air Vice-Marshal D. Hawkins, CB, MBE; Maj.-

Gen. B. Pennicott, CVO; Gp Capt. H. Rolfe, CVO, CBE; Lt.-Col. G. Birdwood
Extra Gentlemen Ushers, Maj. T. Harvey, CVO, DSO, ERD; Lt.-Col. Sir John Hugo, KCVO, OBE; Vice-Adm. Sir Ronald Brockman, KCB, CSI, CIE, CVO, CBE; Air Marshal Sir Maurice Heath, KBE, CB, CVO; Sir James Scholtens, KCVO; Sir Patrick O'Dea, KCVO; Adm. Sir David Williams, GCB; H. Davis, CVO, CM; Maj.-Gen. R. Reid, CVO, MC, CM, CD; Lt.-Cdr. J. Holdsworth, CVO, OBE, RN; Col. G. Leigh, CVO, CBE; Lt.-Cdr. Sir Russell Wood, KCVO, VRD; Maj.-Gen. Sir Desmond Rice, KCVO, CBE; Lt.-Col. Sir Julian Paget, Bt., CVO; S. W. F. Martin, CVO; J. Haslam, CVO; Prof. Sir Norman Blacklock, KCVO, OBE, FRCS; Air Marshal Sir Roy Austen-Smith, KBE, CB, CVO, DFC; Vice-Adm. Sir David Loram, KCB, CVO; Sir Carron Greig, KCVO, CBE; Gp Capt J. Slessor, CVO; Maj. N. Chamberlayne-Macdonald, CVO, OBE
Gentleman Usher to the Sword of State, Adm. Sir Michael Layard, KCB, CBE
Gentleman Usher of the Black Rod, Gen. Sir Edward Jones, KCB, CBE
Serjeants-at-Arms, Maj. B. Eastwood, LVO, MBE; M. Jephson, MVO; M. Parker, MVO
Marshal of the Diplomatic Corps, Vice-Adm. Sir James Weatherall, KBE
Vice-Marshal, P. Astley, LVO
Constable and Governor of Windsor Castle, Gen. Sir Patrick Palmer, KBE
Bargemaster, R. Crouch
Swan Warden, Prof. C. Perrins, LVO
Swan Marker, D. Barber
Superintendent of the State Apartments, St James's Palace, B. Andrews, BEM

ECCLESIASTICAL HOUSEHOLD

THE COLLEGE OF CHAPLAINS

Clerk of the Closet, The Bishop of Derby
Deputy Clerk of the Closet, Revd W. Booth
Chaplains to The Queen, Revd Canon J. V. Bean; Revd K. Huxley; Revd Canon D. C. Gray, TD; Revd S. Pedley; Revd Canon M. A. Moxon; Revd Canon G. Murphy, LVO; Revd D. J. Burgess; Revd E. R. Ayerst; Revd R. S. Clarke; Revd Canon K. Pound; Revd J. Haslam; Revd Canon G. Hall; Revd Canon A. C. Hill; Revd J. C. Priestley; Revd Canon J. O. Colling; Revd Canon G. Jones; Revd Canon D. G. Palmer; Revd Canon D. H. Wheaton; Revd Canon P. Boulton; Revd Canon R. A. Bowden; Revd Canon E. Buchanan; Revd J. Robson; Revd Canon J. Stanley; Revd Canon I. Hardaker; Revd Canon L. F. Webber; Ven. F. Bentley; Revd D. Adams; Revd Canon J. Sykes; Revd Canon I. Smith-Cameron; Revd Canon A. Craig; Ven. D. Fleming; Revd Canon R. Gilbert; Ven. D. Bartles-Smith; Revd Canon I. Knox; Revd Canon M. Mingins; Revd Canon R. Chapman; Revd Canon B. Osborne
Extra Chaplains, Preb. S. A. Williams, CVO; Ven. E. J. G. Ward, LVO; Revd J. R W. Stott; Revd Canon A. D. Caesar, CVO; Revd Canon E. James; Revd Canon J. G. M. W. Murphy, LVO

CHAPELS ROYAL

Dean of the Chapels Royal, The Bishop of London
Sub-Dean of Chapels Royal, Revd W. Booth
Priests in Ordinary, Revd S. E. Young; Revd R. Bolton; Revd P. Hunt
Organist, Choirmaster and Composer, R. J. Popplewell, MVO, FRCO, FRCM
Domestic Chaplain, Buckingham Palace, Revd W. Booth

Domestic Chaplain, Windsor Castle, The Dean of Windsor
Domestic Chaplain, Sandringham, Revd Canon G. R. Hall
Chaplain, Royal Chapel, Windsor Great Park, Revd Canon M. Moxon
Chaplain, Hampton Court Palace, Revd Canon M. Moore
Chaplain, Tower of London, Revd P. Abram
Organist and Choirmaster, Hampton Court Palace, C. Jackson

MEDICAL HOUSEHOLD

Head of the Medical Household and Physician to The Queen, R. Thompson, DM, FRCP
Physician, R. W. Davey
Serjeant Surgeon, B. T. Jackson, FRCS
Surgeon Oculist, P. Holmes Sellors, LVO, FRCS, FRCophth.
Surgeon Gynaecologist, M. E. Setchell, FRCS, FRCOG
Surgeon Dentist, N. A. Sturridge, CVO, DDS
Orthopaedic Surgeon, R. H. Vickers, FRCS
Physician to the Household, J. Cunningham, DM, FRCP
Surgeon to the Household, A. A. M. Lewis, FRCS
Surgeon Oculist to the Household, T. J. ffytche, LVO, FRCS, FRCophth.
Apothecary to The Queen and to the Household, N. R. Southward, CVO
Apothecary to the Household at Windsor, J. Holliday
Apothecary to the Household at Sandringham, I. K. Campbell, D.obst., FRCGP
Coroner of The Queen's Household, J. Burton, CBE

CENTRAL CHANCERY OF THE ORDERS OF KNIGHTHOOD
St James's Palace, London SW1A 1BS

Secretary, Lt.-Col. A. Mather, OBE
Assistant Secretary, Miss R. Wells, MVO

THE HONOURABLE CORPS OF GENTLEMEN-AT-ARMS
St James's Palace, London SW1A 1BS

Captain, The Lord Carter
Lieutenant, Col. T. A. Hall, OBE
Standard Bearer, Col. Sir Piers Bengough, KCVO, OBE
Clerk of the Cheque and Adjutant, Lt.-Col. R. Mayfield, DSO
Harbinger, Maj. G. M. B. Colenso-Jones

Gentlemen of the Corps

Colonels, Hon. N. Crossley, TD; T. Wilson; D. Fanshawe, OBE; J. Baker; R. ffrench Blake; Sir William Mahon, Bt.; Sir Brian Barttelot, Bt., OBE; M. J. C. Robertson, MC; R. Broke; Sir Charles Lowther, Bt.
Lieutenant-Colonels, Hon. P. H. Lewis; R. Macfarlane; Hon. G. B. Norrie; J. H. Fisher, OBE; R. Ker, MC; P. Chamberlin
Majors, I. B. Ramsden, MBE; M. J. Drummond-Brady; A. Arkwright; T. Gooch, MBE; J. B. B. Cockcroft; C. J. H. Gurney; P. D. Johnson; R. M. O. Webster; J. Warren; E. Crofton; J. Groves

THE QUEEN'S BODY GUARD OF THE YEOMEN OF THE GUARD
St James's Palace, London SW1A 1BS

Captain, The Lord McIntosh of Haringey
Lieutenant, Col. G. W. Tufnell
Clerk of the Cheque and Adjutant, Col. S. Longsdon
Ensign, Maj. C. Marriott
Exons, Maj. C. Enderby; Maj. M. T. N. H. Wills

MASTER OF THE HOUSEHOLD'S DEPARTMENT

BOARD OF GREEN CLOTH
Buckingham Palace, London SW1A 1AA

Master of the Household, Maj.-Gen. Sir Simon Cooper, KCVO

Deputy Master of the Household, Lt.-Col. Sir Guy Acland, Bt., MVO
Assistants to the Master of the Household, M. T. Parker, MVO; A. Jarman; A. Smith
Chief Clerk, M. C. W. N. Jephson, LVO
Chief Housekeeper, Miss H. Colebrook, MVO
Palace Steward, P. S. Croasdale, RVM
Royal Chef, L. Mann, RVM
Superintendent, Windsor Castle, Maj. B. Eastwood, LVO, MBE
Superintendent, The Palace of Holyroodhouse, Lt.-Col. D. Anderson, OBE

ROYAL MEWS DEPARTMENT
Buckingham Palace, London SW1W 0QH

Crown Equerry, Lt.-Col. S. Gilbart-Denham, CVO
Veterinary Surgeon, P. Scott Dunn, LVO
Superintendent Royal Mews, Buckingham Palace, Maj. A. Smith, MVO, MBE (Maj. I. Kelly from 1 January 1998)

THE ROYAL COLLECTION TRUST
St James's Palace, London SW1A 1BS

Director of Royal Collection and Surveyor of The Queen's Works of Art, H. Roberts, LVO, FSA
Surveyor of The Queen's Pictures, C. Lloyd, LVO
Surveyor Emeritus of The Queen's Pictures, Sir Oliver Millar, GCVO, FBA, FSA
Surveyor Emeritus of The Queen's Works of Art, Sir Geoffrey de Bellaigue, GCVO, FBA, FSA
Librarian, The Royal Library, Windsor Castle, O. Everett, CVO
Deputy Surveyor of The Queen's Works of Art, J. Marsden
Librarian Emeritus, Sir Robin Mackworth-Young, GCVO, FSA
Director of Media Affairs, R. Arbiter, LVO
Curator of the Print Room, The Hon. Mrs Roberts, LVO
Financial Director, M. Stevens
Financial Controller, Mrs G. Johnson
Administrator and Assistant to The Surveyors, D. Rankin-Hunt, MVO, MBE
Senior Picture Restorer, Miss V. Pemberton Pigott, MVO
Chief Restorer, Old Master Drawings, A. Donnithorne
Senior Furniture Restorer, E. Fancourt, MVO, RVM
Armourer, J. Jackson, RVM
Chief Binder, R. Day, MVO, RVM

ROYAL COLLECTION ENTERPRISES LTD

Managing Director, M. E. K. Hewlett, LVO

ASCOT OFFICE
St James's Palace, London SW1A 1BS
Tel 0171-930 9882

Her Majesty's Representative at Ascot, Col. Sir Piers Bengough, KCVO, OBE
Secretary, Miss L. Thompson-Royds, MVO

THE QUEEN'S HOUSEHOLD IN SCOTLAND

Hereditary Lord High Constable, The Earl of Erroll
Hereditary Master of the Household, The Duke of Argyll
Lord Lyon King of Arms, Sir Malcolm Innes of Edingight, KCVO, WS
Hereditary Bearer of the Royal Banner of Scotland, The Earl of Dundee
Hereditary Bearer of the Scottish National Flag, The Earl of Lauderdale
Hereditary Keepers:
  Palace of Holyroodhouse, The Duke of Hamilton and Brandon

Falkland Palace, N. Crichton-Stuart
Stirling Castle, The Earl of Mar and Kellie
Dunstaffnage Castle, The Duke of Argyll
Dunconnel Castle, Sir Charles Maclean, Bt.
Hereditary Carver, Maj. Sir Ralph Anstruther, Bt., GCVO, MC
Keeper of Dumbarton Castle, Brig. D. Hardie, TD
Governor of Edinburgh Castle, Maj.-Gen. J. Hall, OBE
Historiographer, Prof. T. C. Smout, CBE, FBA, FRSE, FSA Scot.
Botanist, Prof. D. Henderson, CBE, FRSE
Painter and Limner, vacant
Sculptor in Ordinary, Prof. Sir Eduardo Paolozzi, CBE, RA
Astronomer, Prof. J. Brown, PH.D., FRSE
Heralds and Pursuivants, see page 282

ECCLESIASTICAL HOUSEHOLD

Dean of the Chapel Royal, Very Revd J. Harkness, CB, OBE
Dean of the Order of the Thistle, Very Revd G. I. Macmillan
Chaplains in Ordinary, Very Revd J. Harkness, CB, OBE; Very Revd G. I. Macmillan; Revd M. D. Craig; Very Revd J. L. Weatherhead, DD; Revd C. Robertson; Very Revd J. A. Simpson; Revd N. W. Drummond; Revd J. Paterson; Revd A. Symington; Revd J. B. Cairns
Extra Chaplains, Very Revd W. R. Sanderson, DD; Revd T. J. T. Nicol, LVO, MBE, MC, TD; Very Revd Prof. J. McIntyre, CVO, DD, FRSE; Revd C. Forrester-Paton; Revd H. W. M. Cant; Very Revd R. A. S. Barbour, KCVO, MC, DD; Revd K. MacVicar, MBE, DFC, TD; Very Revd W. B. Johnston, DD; Revd A. J. C. Macfarlane; Revd M. I. Levison, DD; Revd J. K. Angus, LVO, TD; Revd J. McLeod; Very Revd W. J. Morris, KCVO, DD; Revd A. S. Todd, DD; Very Revd W. B. R. Macmillan, LL.D, DD
Domestic Chaplain, Balmoral, Revd R. P. Sloan

MEDICAL HOUSEHOLD

Physicians in Scotland, P. Brunt, OBE, MD, FRCP; A. Toft, CBE, FRCPE
Surgeon in Scotland, J. Engeset, FRCS
Apothecary to the Household at Balmoral, D. J. A. Glass
Apothecary to the Household at the Palace of Holyroodhouse, Dr J. Cormack, MD, FRCPE, FRCGP

THE QUEEN'S BODY GUARD FOR SCOTLAND

ROYAL COMPANY OF ARCHERS
Archers' Hall, Buccleuch Street, Edinburgh EH8 9LR

Captain-General and Gold Stick for Scotland, Maj. Sir Hew Hamilton-Dalrymple, Bt., KCVO
Captains, The Duke of Buccleuch and Queensberry, KT, VRD; The Earl of Airlie, KT, GCVO; Capt. Sir Iain Tennant, KT; The Marquess of Lothian, KCVO
Lieutenants, Cdre Sir John Clerk of Penicuik, Bt., CBE, VRD; The Earl of Elgin and Kincardine, KT; Col. G. R. Simpson, DSO, LVO, TD; Maj. Sir David Butter, KCVO, MC
Ensigns, The Earl of Minto, OBE; Maj.-Gen. Sir John Swinton, KCVO, OBE; Gen. Sir Michael Gow, GCB; The Hon. Lord Elliott, MC
Brigadiers, Maj. the Hon. Sir Lachlan Maclean, Bt.; The Viscount Younger of Leckie, KT, KCVO, TD, PC; Capt. G. Burnet, LVO; The Duke of Montrose; Lt.-Gen. Sir Norman Arthur, KCB; The Hon. Sir William Macpherson of Cluny, TD; The Lord Nickson, KBE; Maj. the Lord Glenarthur; Earl of Dalkeith; Maj. R. Y. Henderson, TD; Col. H. F. O. Bewsher, LVO, OBE; Lord Ramsay; Brig. C. D. M. Ritchie, CBE
Adjutant, Maj. the Hon. Sir Lachlan Maclean, Bt.
Surgeon, Dr P. A. P. Mackenzie, TD
Chaplain, Very Revd W. K. Morris, KCVO, DD
President of the Council and Silver Stick for Scotland, The Duke of Buccleuch and Queensberry, KT, VRD

Vice-President, Capt. Sir Iain Tennant, KT
Secretary, Capt. J. D. B. Younger
Treasurer, J. M. Haldane of Gleneagles

HOUSEHOLD OF THE PRINCE PHILIP, DUKE OF EDINBURGH

Treasurer, Sir Brian McGrath, KCVO
Private Secretary, Brig. M. G. Hunt-Davis, CBE
Equerry, Lt.-Cdr. R. Tarran
Extra Equerries, J. B. V. Orr, CVO; The Lord Buxton of Alsa, KCVO, MC; Brig. C. Robertson, CVO; Sir Brian McGrath, KCVO
Temporary Equerries, Capt. R. Goodfellow; Lt.-Col. P. Denning; Capt. S. Courtauld
Chief Clerk and Accountant, G. D. Partington

HOUSEHOLD OF QUEEN ELIZABETH THE QUEEN MOTHER

Lord Chamberlain, The Earl of Crawford and Balcarres, KT, PC
Private Secretary, Comptroller and Equerry, Capt. Sir Alastair Aird, GCVO
Assistant Private Secretary and Equerry, Maj. R. Seymour, CVO
Treasurer and Equerry, Maj. Sir Ralph Anstruther, Bt., GCVO, MC
Equerry, Maj. A. C. B. MacEwan (*temp.*)
Extra Equerries, Maj. Sir John Griffin, KCVO; The Lord Sinclair, CVO; Maj. W. Richardson, LVO; Maj. D. McMicking, LVO; Capt. A. Windham, LVO
Apothecary to the Household, Dr N. Southward, CVO
Surgeon-Apothecary to the Household (*Royal Lodge, Windsor*), J. Holliday
Mistress of the Robes, vacant
Ladies of the Bedchamber, The Lady Grimthorpe, DCVO; The Countess of Scarbrough
Women of the Bedchamber, Dame Frances Campbell-Preston, DCVO; Lady Angela Oswald, LVO; The Hon. Mrs Rhodes; Mrs Michael Gordon-Lennox
Extra Women of the Bedchamber, Lady Jean Rankin, DCVO; Miss Jane Walker-Okeover, LVO; Lady Margaret Colville, CVO; Lady Elizabeth Basset, DCVO; Lady Penn
Clerk Comptroller, M. Blanch, CVO
Information Officer, Mrs R. Murphy, LVO
Clerks, Miss F. Fletcher, LVO; Mrs W. Stevens

HOUSEHOLD OF THE PRINCE OF WALES

Private Secretary and Treasurer, S. M. J. Lamport
Assistant Private Secretaries, Dr M. Williams; J. Skan; M. Bolland; N. S. Archer
Press Secretary, Miss S. Henney
Equerry, Lt. Cdr. J. Lavery, RN
Extra Equerries, The Hon. Edward Adeane, CVO; Maj.-Gen. Sir Christopher Airy, KCVO, CBE; Sqn. Ldr. Sir David Checketts, KCVO; Sir David Landale, KCVO; Sir John Riddell, Bt., CVO; G. J. Ward, CBE; Brig. J. Q. Winter, LVO; M. Butler, LVO
Secretary to the Duchy of Cornwall and Keeper of the Records, W. R. A. Ross

HOUSEHOLD OF THE DUKE OF YORK

Private Secretary, Treasurer and Extra Equerry, Capt. R. N. Blair, LVO, RN
Comptroller and Assistant Private Secretary, Cdr. C. Manley, OBE
Equerry, Maj. T. E. D. Allan

HOUSEHOLD OF THE PRINCE EDWARD

Private Secretary, Lt.-Col. S. G. O'Dwyer, LVO
Clerk, Mrs L. Sharp

HOUSEHOLD OF THE PRINCESS ROYAL

Private Secretary, Lt.-Col. P. Gibbs, CVO
Assistant Private Secretary, The Hon. Mrs Louloudis, LVO
Ladies-in-Waiting, Lady Carew Pole, LVO; Mrs Andrew Feilden, LVO; The Hon. Mrs Legge-Bourke, LVO; Mrs William Nunneley; Mrs Timothy Holderness-Roddam; Mrs Charles Ritchie; Mrs David Bowes Lyon
Extra Ladies-in-Waiting, Miss Victoria Legge-Bourke, LVO; Mrs Malcolm Innes, LVO; The Countess of Lichfield, LVO

HOUSEHOLD OF THE PRINCESS MARGARET, COUNTESS OF SNOWDON

Private Secretary and Comptroller, The Lord Napier and Ettrick, KCVO
Lady-in-Waiting, The Hon. Mrs Whitehead, LVO
Extra Ladies-in-Waiting, Lady Elizabeth Cavendish, CVO; Lady Aird, LVO; Mrs Robin Benson, LVO, OBE; Lady Juliet Townsend, LVO; Mrs Jane Stevens, LVO; The Hon. Mrs Wills, LVO; The Lady Glenconner, LVO; The Countess Alexander of Tunis, LVO; Mrs Charles Vyvyan

HOUSEHOLD OF THE DUKE AND DUCHESS OF GLOUCESTER

Private Secretary, Comptroller and Equerry, Maj. N. M. L. Barne, LVO
Assistant Private Secretary to the Duchess of Gloucester, Miss S. Marland, LVO
Extra Equerry, Lt.-Col. Sir Simon Bland, KCVO
Ladies-in-Waiting, Mrs Michael Wigley, CVO; Mrs Euan McCorquodale, LVO; Mrs Howard Page, LVO
Extra Ladies-in-Waiting, Miss Jennifer Thomson; The Lady Camoys

HOUSEHOLD OF PRINCESS ALICE, DUCHESS OF GLOUCESTER

Private Secretary, Comptroller and Equerry, Maj. N. M. L. Barne, LVO
Extra Equerry, Lt.-Col. Sir Simon Bland, KCVO

Ladies-in-Waiting, Dame Jean Maxwell-Scott, DCVO; Mrs Michael Harvey, LVO
Extra Ladies-in-Waiting, Miss Diana Harrison; Miss Jane Egerton-Warburton, LVO

HOUSEHOLD OF THE DUKE AND DUCHESS OF KENT

Private Secretary, N. C. Adamson, OBE
Extra Equerries, Lt. Cdr. Sir Richard Buckley, KCVO; Maj. J. Stewart; A. Palmer, CVO, CMG
Temporary Equerry, Capt. D. Hampshire
Ladies-in-Waiting, Mrs Fiona Henderson, CVO; Mrs Colin Marsh, LVO, Mrs Julian Tomkins; Mrs Peter Troughton; Mrs Richard Beckett

HOUSEHOLD OF PRINCE AND PRINCESS MICHAEL OF KENT

Personal Secretary, Miss C. Jenkins
Ladies-in-Waiting, The Hon. Mrs Sanders; Miss Anne Frost; Mrs J. Fellowes

HOUSEHOLD OF PRINCESS ALEXANDRA, THE HON. LADY OGILVY

Comptroller and Private Secretary, Capt. N. Blair, LVO, RN
Extra Equerry, Maj. Sir Peter Clarke, KCVO
Lady-in-Waiting, Lady Mary Mumford, DCVO
Extra Ladies-in-Waiting, Mrs Peter Afia; Lady Mary Colman; Lady Nicholas Gordon Lennox; The Hon. Lady Rowley; Dame Mona Mitchell, DCVO

Royal Salutes

A salute of 62 guns is fired on the wharf at the Tower of London on the following occasions:
(a) the anniversaries of the birth, accession and coronation of the Sovereign
(b) the anniversary of the birth of HM Queen Elizabeth the Queen Mother
(c) the anniversary of the birth of HRH Prince Philip, Duke of Edinburgh

A salute of 41 guns only is fired on extraordinary and triumphal occasions, e.g. on the occasion of the Sovereign opening, proroguing or dissolving Parliament in person, or when passing through London in procession, except when otherwise ordered.

A salute of 41 guns is fired from the two saluting stations in London (the Tower of London and Hyde Park) on the occasion of the birth of a Royal infant.
Constable of the Royal Palace and Fortress of London, Field Marshal the Lord Inge, GCB
Lieutenant of the Tower of London, Lt.-Gen. Sir Michael Gray, KCB, OBE
Resident Governor and Keeper of the Jewel House, Maj.-Gen. G. Field, CB, OBE

Master Gunner of St James's Park, Field Marshal the Lord Vincent of Coleshill, GBE, KCB, DSO
Master Gunner within the Tower, Col. S. Lalor

SCOTLAND

Royal salutes are authorized at Edinburgh Castle and Stirling Castle, although in practice Edinburgh Castle is the only operating saluting station in Scotland.

A salute of 21 guns is fired on the following occasions:
(a) the anniversaries of the birth, accession and coronation of the Sovereign
(b) the anniversary of the birth of HM Queen Elizabeth the Queen Mother
(c) the anniversary of the birth of HRH Prince Philip, Duke of Edinburgh

A salute of 21 guns is fired in Edinburgh on the occasion of the opening of the General Assembly of the Church of Scotland.

A salute of 21 guns may also be fired in Edinburgh on the arrival of HM The Queen, HM Queen Elizabeth the Queen Mother, or a member of the Royal Family who is a Royal Highness on an official visit.

Royal Finances

FUNDING

The Civil List

The Civil List dates back to the late 17th century. It was originally used by the sovereign to supplement hereditary revenues for paying the salaries of judges, ambassadors and other government officers as well as the expenses of the royal household. In 1760 on the accession of George III it was decided that the Civil List would be provided by Parliament to cover all relevant expenditure in return for the King surrendering the hereditary revenues of the Crown. At that time Parliament undertook to pay the salaries of judges, ambassadors, etc. In 1831 Parliament agreed also to meet the costs of the royal palaces in return for a reduction in the Civil List. Each sovereign has agreed to continue this arrangement.

The Civil List paid to The Queen is charged on the Consolidated Fund. Until 1972, the amount of money allocated annually under the Civil List was set for the duration of a reign. The system was then altered to a fixed annual payment for ten years but from 1975 high inflation made an annual review necessary. The system of payments reverted to the practice of a fixed annual payment for ten years from 1 January 1991.

The Civil List Acts provide for other members of the royal family to receive parliamentary annuities from government funds to meet the expenses of carrying out their official duties. Since 1975 The Queen has reimbursed the Treasury for the annuities paid to the Duke of Gloucester, the Duke of Kent and Princess Alexandra. Since April 1993 The Queen has reimbursed all the annuities except those paid to herself, Queen Elizabeth the Queen Mother and the Duke of Edinburgh.

The Prince of Wales does not receive a parliamentary annuity. He derives his income from the revenues of the Duchy of Cornwall and these monies meet the official and private expenses of the Prince of Wales and his family.

The annual payments for the years 1991–2000 are:

The Queen	£7,900,000
Queen Elizabeth the Queen Mother	643,000
The Duke of Edinburgh	359,000
*The Duke of York	249,000
*The Prince Edward	96,000
*The Princess Royal	228,000
*The Princess Margaret, Countess of Snowdon	219,000
*Princess Alice, Duchess of Gloucester	87,000
*The Duke of Gloucester	175,000
*The Duke of Kent	236,000
*Princess Alexandra	225,000
	10,417,000
*Refunded to the Treasury	1,515,000
Total	8,902,000

Property Services Grant-in-Aid

Grant-in-aid from the Department of National Heritage is voted annually by Parliament to pay for the upkeep of the occupied royal palaces which are used as royal residences and for official or ceremonial purposes.

Royal Travel Grant-in-Aid

From April 1997 a grant-in-aid is provided to the Royal Household by the Department of Transport to meet the cost of official royal travel by aeroplane and train, using mainly aircraft from 32 (The Royal) Squadron and the Royal Train.

The Privy Purse

The funds received by the Privy Purse pay for official expenses incurred by The Queen as head of state and for some of The Queen's private expenditure. The revenues of the Duchy of Lancaster are the principal source of income for the Privy Purse. The revenues of the Duchy were retained by George III in 1760 when the hereditary revenues were surrendered in exchange for the Civil List.

Personal Income

The Queen's personal income derives mostly from investments, and is used to meet private expenditure.

Departmental Votes

Items of expenditure connected with the official duties of the royal family which fall directly on votes of government departments include:

Ministry of Defence – The Royal Yacht (to be decommissioned at the end of 1997); equerries
Foreign and Commonwealth Office – Marshal of the Diplomatic Corps; costs (other than travel costs) associated with overseas visits at the request of government departments
HM Treasury – Central Chancery of the Orders of Knighthood
Central Office of Information – publicity services
The Post Office – postal services

TAXATION

The sovereign is not legally liable to pay income tax, capital gains tax or inheritance tax. After income tax was reintroduced in 1842 some income tax was paid voluntarily by the sovereign but over a long period these payments were phased out. In 1992 The Queen offered to pay tax on a voluntary basis from 6 April 1993, and the Prince of Wales to pay tax on a voluntary basis on his income from the Duchy of Cornwall. (He was already taxed in all other respects.)

The main provisions for The Queen and the Prince of Wales to pay tax, set out in a Memorandum of Understanding on Royal Taxation presented to Parliament on 11 February 1993, are that The Queen will pay income tax and capital gains tax in respect of her private income and assets, and on the proportion of the income and capital gains of the Privy Purse used for private purposes. Inheritance tax will be paid on The Queen's assets, except for those which pass to the next sovereign, whether automatically or by gift or bequest. The Prince of Wales will pay income tax on income from the Duchy of Cornwall used for private purposes.

The Prince of Wales has confirmed that he intends to pay tax on the same basis following his accession to the throne.

Other members of the royal family are subject to tax as for any taxpayer.

Military Ranks and Titles

Lord High Admiral of the United Kingdom

Colonel-in-Chief
The Life Guards; The Blues and Royals (Royal Horse Guards and 1st Dragoons); The Royal Scots Dragoon Guards (Carabiniers and Greys); The Queen's Royal Lancers; Royal Tank Regiment; Corps of Royal Engineers; Grenadier Guards; Coldstream Guards; Scots Guards; Irish Guards; Welsh Guards; The Royal Welch Fusiliers; The Queen's Lancashire Regiment; The Argyll and Sutherland Highlanders (Princess Louise's); The Royal Green Jackets; Adjutant General's Corps; The Royal Mercian and Lancastrian Yeomanry; The Governor General's Horse Guards (of Canada); The King's Own Calgary Regiment; Canadian Forces Military Engineers Branch; Royal 22e Regiment (of Canada); Governor-General's Foot Guards (of Canada); The Canadian Grenadier Guards; Le Regiment de la Chaudiere (of Canada); 2nd Bn Royal New Brunswick Regiment (North Shore); The 48th Highlanders of Canada; The Argyll and Sutherland Highlanders of Canada (Princess Louise's); The Calgary Highlanders; Royal Australian Engineers; Royal Australian Infantry Corps; Royal Australian Army Ordnance Corps; Royal Australian Army Nursing Corps; The Corps of Royal New Zealand Engineers; Royal New Zealand Infantry Regiment; Royal New Zealand Army Ordnance Corps; Royal Malta Artillery; The Malawi Rifles

Affiliated Colonel-in-Chief
The Queen's Gurkha Engineers

Captain-General
Royal Regiment of Artillery; The Honourable Artillery Company; Combined Cadet Force; Royal Regiment of Canadian Artillery; Royal Regiment of Australian Artillery; Royal Regiment of New Zealand Artillery; Royal New Zealand Armoured Corps

Patron
Royal Army Chaplains' Department

Air Commodore-in-Chief
Royal Auxiliary Air Force; Royal Air Force Regiment; Royal Observer Corps; Air Reserve (of Canada); Royal Australian Air Force Reserve; Territorial Air Force (of New Zealand)

Commandant-in-Chief
Royal Air Force College, Cranwell

Hon. Air Commodore
RAF Marham

Admiral of the Fleet
Field Marshal
Marshal of the Royal Air Force

Admiral of the Fleet, Royal Australian Navy
Field Marshal, Australian Military Forces

Marshal of the Royal Australian Air Force
Admiral of the Fleet, Royal New Zealand Navy
Field Marshal, New Zealand Army
Marshal of the Royal New Zealand Air Force

Captain-General, Royal Marines

Admiral
Royal Canadian Sea Cadets

Colonel-in-Chief
The Royal Gloucestershire, Berkshire and Wiltshire Regiment; The Highlanders (Seaforth, Gordons and Camerons); Corps of Royal Electrical and Mechanical Engineers; Intelligence Corps; Army Cadet Force; The Royal Canadian Regiment; The Royal Hamilton Light Infantry (Wentworth Regiment) (of Canada); The Cameron Highlanders of Ottawa; The Queen's Own Cameron Highlanders of Canada; The Seaforth Highlanders of Canada; The Royal Canadian Army Cadets; The Royal Australian Electrical and Mechanical Engineers; The Australian Cadet Corps; The Royal New Zealand Corps of Electrical and Mechanical Engineers

Deputy Colonel-in-Chief
The Queen's Royal Hussars (Queen's Own and Royal Irish)

Colonel
Grenadier Guards

Hon. Colonel
City of Edinburgh Universities Officers' Training Corps; The Trinidad and Tobago Regiment

Air Commodore-in-Chief
Air Training Corps; Royal Canadian Air Cadets

Hon. Air Commodore
RAF Kinloss

Colonel-in-Chief
1st The Queen's Dragoon Guards; The Queen's Royal Hussars (Queen's Own and Royal Irish); 9th/12th Royal Lancers (Prince of Wales's); The King's Regiment; The Royal Anglian Regiment; The Light Infantry; The Black Watch (Royal Highland Regiment); Royal Army Medical Corps; The Black Watch (Royal Highland Regiment) of Canada; The Toronto Scottish Regiment; Canadian Forces Medical Services; Royal Australian Army Medical Corps; Royal New Zealand Army Medical Corps

Hon. Colonel
The Royal Yeomanry; The London Scottish; Inns of Court and City Yeomanry; The King's Own Yorkshire Yeomanry (Light Infantry)

Commandant-in-Chief
Women in the Royal Navy; Women, Royal Air Force; Royal Air Force Central Flying School

HRH THE PRINCE OF WALES

Captain, Royal Navy
Group Captain, Royal Air Force

Colonel-in-Chief
The Royal Dragoon Guards; The Cheshire Regiment;
The Royal Regiment of Wales (24th/41st Foot); The
Parachute Regiment; The Royal Gurkha Rifles; Army
Air Corps; The Royal Canadian Dragoons; Lord
Strathcona's Horse (Royal Canadians); Royal Regiment
of Canada; Royal Winnipeg Rifles; Air Reserve Group
of Air Command (of Canada); Royal Australian
Armoured Corps; The Royal Pacific Islands Regiment

Deputy Colonel-in-Chief
The Highlanders (Seaforth, Gordons and Camerons)

Colonel
Welsh Guards

Air Commodore-in-Chief
Royal New Zealand Air Force

Hon. Air Commodore
RAF Valley

HRH THE DUKE OF YORK

Lieutenant-Commander, Royal Navy

Admiral
Sea Cadet Corps

Colonel-in-Chief
The Staffordshire Regiment (The Prince of Wales's);
The Royal Irish Regiment (27th (Inniskilling), 83rd,
87th and The Ulster Defence Regiment); Royal New
Zealand Army Logistic Regiment; The Queen's York
Rangers (1st American Regiment)

Hon. Air Commodore
RAF Lossiemouth

HRH THE PRINCESS ROYAL

Rear Admiral
Chief Commandant for Women in the Royal Navy

Colonel-in-Chief
The King's Royal Hussars; Royal Corps of Signals; The
Royal Scots (The Royal Regiment); The
Worcestershire and Sherwood Foresters Regiment
(29th/45th Foot); The Royal Logistic Corps; 8th
Canadian Hussars (Princess Louise's); Canadian Forces
Communications and Electronics Branch; The Grey
and Simcoe Foresters; The Royal Regina Rifle
Regiment; Royal Newfoundland Regiment; Royal
Australian Corps of Signals; Royal New Zealand Corps
of Signals; Royal New Zealand Nursing Corps

Affiliated Colonel-in-Chief
The Queen's Gurkha Signals; The Queen's Own
Gurkha Transport Regiment

Hon. Colonel
University of London Officers' Training Corps

Hon. Air Commodore
RAF Lyneham; University of London Air Squadron

Commandant-in-Chief
Women's Transport Service (FANY)

HRH THE PRINCESS MARGARET, COUNTESS OF SNOWDON

Colonel-in-Chief
The Light Dragoons; The Royal Highland Fusiliers
(Princess Margaret's Own Glasgow and Ayrshire
Regiment); Queen Alexandra's Royal Army Nursing
Corps; The Highland Fusiliers of Canada; The Princess
Louise Fusiliers (of Canada); The Bermuda Regiment

Deputy Colonel-in-Chief
The Royal Anglian Regiment

Hon. Air Commodore
RAF Coningsby

HRH PRINCESS ALICE, DUCHESS OF GLOUCESTER

Air Chief Marshal

Colonel-in-Chief
The King's Own Scottish Borderers; Royal Australian
Corps of Transport

Deputy Colonel-in-Chief
The King's Royal Hussars; The Royal Anglian
Regiment

Air Chief Commandant
Women, Royal Air Force

HRH THE DUKE OF GLOUCESTER

Hon. Air Marshal

Deputy Colonel-in-Chief
The Royal Gloucestershire, Berkshire and Wiltshire
Regiment; The Royal Logistic Corps

Hon. Colonel
Royal Monmouthshire Royal Engineers (Militia)

Hon. Air Commodore
RAF Odiham

HRH THE DUCHESS OF GLOUCESTER

Colonel-in-Chief
Royal Australian Army Educational Corps; Royal New
Zealand Army Educational Corps

Deputy Colonel-in-Chief
Adjutant-General's Corps

HRH THE DUKE OF KENT

Field Marshal
Hon. Air Chief Marshal

Colonel-in-Chief
The Royal Regiment of Fusiliers; The Devonshire and Dorset Regiment; The Lorne Scots (Peel, Dufferin and Hamilton Regiment)

Deputy Colonel-in-Chief
The Royal Scots Dragoon Guards (Carabiniers and Greys)

Colonel
Scots Guards

Hon. Air Commodore
RAF Leuchars

HRH THE DUCHESS OF KENT

Hon. Major-General

Colonel-in-Chief
The Prince of Wales's Own Regiment of Yorkshire

Deputy Colonel-in-Chief
The Royal Dragoon Guards; Adjutant-General's Corps; The Royal Logistic Corps

---

HRH PRINCE MICHAEL OF KENT

Major, The Royal Hussars (Prince of Wales's Own)

Hon. Commodore
Royal Naval Reserve

HRH PRINCESS ALEXANDRA, THE HON. LADY OGILVY

Patron
Queen Alexandra's Royal Naval Nursing Service

Colonel-in-Chief
The King's Own Royal Border Regiment; The Queen's Own Rifles of Canada; The Canadian Scottish Regiment (Princess Mary's)

Deputy Colonel-in-Chief
The Queen's Royal Lancers; The Light Infantry

Deputy Hon. Colonel
The Royal Yeomanry

Patron and Air Chief Commandant
Princess Mary's Royal Air Force Nursing Service

The Royal Arms

ENGLAND

1st and 4th quarters (representing England) – Gules, three lions passant guardant in pale Or
2nd quarter (representing Scotland) – Or, a lion rampant within a double tressure flory counterflory Gules
3rd quarter (representing Ireland) – Azure, a harp Or, stringed Argent
The whole shield is encircled with the Garter

SCOTLAND

The Royal Arms shown with the Lion of Scotland in the 1st and 4th quarters, and the Lions of England in the 2nd quarter
The whole shield is encircled with the Thistle

SUPPORTERS (ENGLAND)

Dexter (right) – a lion rampant guardant Or, imperially crowned (shown in Scotland on the sinister)
Sinister (left) – a unicorn Argent, armed, crined, and unguled Or, gorged with a coronet composed of crosses patées and fleurs-de-lis, a chain affixed, passing between the forelegs, and reflexed over the back (shown in Scotland on the dexter and imperially crowned)

CRESTS

England – the Royal Crown Proper thereon a lion statant guardant Or imperially crowned also Proper
Scotland – upon an imperial crown Proper a lion sejant affrontée Gules imperially crowned Or, holding in the dexter paw a sword and in the sinister a sceptre erect, also Proper
Ireland – a tower triple-towered of the First, from the portal a hart springing Argent, attired and hooved Or

BADGES

England – the red and white rose united, slipped and leaved proper
Scotland – a thistle, slipped and leaved proper
Ireland – a shamrock leaf slipped Vert; also a harp Or, stringed Argent
United Kingdom – the rose of England, the thistle of Scotland, and the shamrock of Ireland engrafted on the same stem proper, and an escutcheon charged as the Union Flag (all ensigned with the Royal Crown)
Wales – upon a mount Vert a dragon passant, wings elevated Gules

The House of Windsor

King George V assumed by royal proclamation (17 June 1917) for his House and family, as well as for all descendants in the male line of Queen Victoria who are subjects of these realms, the name of Windsor.

KING GEORGE V (George Frederick Ernest Albert), second son of King Edward VII, *born* 3 June 1865; *married* 6 July 1893 HSH Princess Victoria Mary Augusta Louise Olga Pauline Claudine Agnes of Teck (Queen Mary, *born* 26 May 1867; *died* 24 March 1953); *succeeded* to the throne 6 May 1910; *died* 20 January 1936. *Issue:*

1. HRH PRINCE EDWARD Albert Christian George Andrew Patrick David, *born* 23 June 1894; *succeeded* to the throne as King Edward VIII, 20 January 1936; *abdicated* 11 December 1936; created *Duke of Windsor,* 1937; *married* 3 June 1937, Mrs Wallis Warfield (Her Grace The Duchess of Windsor, *born* 19 June 1896; *died* 24 April 1986), *died* 28 May 1972

2. HRH PRINCE ALBERT Frederick Arthur George, *born* 14 December 1895, *created* Duke of York 1920; *married* 26 April 1923, Lady Elizabeth Bowes-Lyon, youngest daughter of the 14th Earl of Strathmore and Kinghorne (HM Queen Elizabeth the Queen Mother, *see* pages 117–8), *succeeded* to the throne as King George VI, 11 December 1936; *died* 6 February 1952, having had issue (*see* page 117)

3. HRH PRINCESS (Victoria Alexandra Alice) MARY, *born* 25 April 1897, *created* Princess Royal 1932; *married* 28 February 1922, Viscount Lascelles, later the 6th Earl of Harewood (1882–1947), *died* 28 March 1965. *Issue:*
   (1) George Henry Hubert Lascelles, 7th Earl of Harewood, KBE, *born* 7 February 1923; *married* (1) 1949, Maria (Marion) Stein (marriage dissolved 1967); *issue,* (a) David Henry George, Viscount Lascelles, *born* 1950; (b) James Edward, *born* 1953; (c)

(Robert) Jeremy Hugh, *born* 1955; (2) 1967, Mrs Patricia Tuckwell; *issue,* (d) Mark Hubert, *born* 1964
   (2) Gerald David Lascelles, *born* 21 August 1924, *married* (1) 1952, Miss Angela Dowding (marriage dissolved 1978); *issue,* (a) Henry Ulick, *born* 1953; (2) 1978, Mrs Elizabeth Colvin; *issue,* (b) Martin David, *born* 1962

4. HRH PRINCE HENRY William Frederick Albert, *born* 31 March 1900, *created* Duke of Gloucester, Earl of Ulster and Baron Culloden 1928, *married* 6 November 1935, Lady Alice Christabel Montagu-Douglas-Scott, daughter of the 7th Duke of Buccleuch (HRH Princess Alice, Duchess of Gloucester, *see* page 118); *died* 10 June 1974. *Issue:*
   (1) HRH Prince William Henry Andrew Frederick, *born* 18 December 1941; *accidentally killed* 28 August 1972
   (2) HRH Prince Richard Alexander Walter George (HRH The Duke of Gloucester), *see* page 118

5. HRH PRINCE GEORGE Edward Alexander Edmund, *born* 20 December 1902, *created* Duke of Kent, Earl of St Andrews and Baron Downpatrick 1934, *married* 29 November 1934, HRH Princess Marina of Greece and Denmark (*born* 30 November OS, 1906; *died* 27 August 1968; *killed on active service,* 25 August 1942. *Issue:*
   (1) HRH Prince Edward George Nicholas Paul Patrick (HRH The Duke of Kent), *see* page 118
   (2) HRH Princess Alexandra Helen Elizabeth Olga Christabel (HRH Princess Alexandra, the Hon. Lady Ogilvy), *see* page 118
   (3) HRH Prince Michael George Charles Franklin (HRH Prince Michael of Kent), *see* page 118

6. HRH PRINCE JOHN Charles Francis, *born* 12 July 1905; *died* 18 January 1919

Descendants of Queen Victoria

QUEEN VICTORIA (Alexandrina Victoria), *born* 24 May 1819; *succeeded* to the throne 20 June 1837; *married* 10 February 1840 (Francis) Albert Augustus Charles Emmanuel, Duke of Saxony, Prince of Saxe-Coburg and Gotha (HRH Albert, Prince Consort, *born* 26 August 1819, *died* 14 December 1861; *died* 22 January 1901. *Issue:*

1. HRH PRINCESS VICTORIA Adelaide Mary Louisa (Princess Royal) (1840–1901), *m.* 1858, Friedrich III (1831–88), German Emperor March–June 1888. *Issue:*
   (1) HIM Wilhelm II (1859–1941), German Emperor 1888–1918, *m.* (1) 1881 Princess Augusta Victoria of Schleswig-Holstein-Sonderburg-Augustenburg (1858–1921); (2) 1922 Princess Hermine of Reuss (1887–1947). *Issue:*
      (a) Prince Wilhelm (1882–1951), *Crown Prince* 1888–1918, *m.* 1905 Duchess Cecilie of Mecklenburg-Schwerin; *issue:* Prince Wilhelm (1906–40); Prince Louis Ferdinand (1907–94), *m.* 1938 Grand Duchess Kira (*see* page 129); Prince Hubertus (1909–50); Prince Friedrich Georg (1911–66); Princess Alexandrine Irene (1915–80); Princess Cecilie (1917–75)
      (b) Prince Eitel-Friedrich (1883–1942), *m.* 1906 Duchess Sophie of Oldenburg (marriage dissolved 1926)
      (c) Prince Adalbert (1884–1948), *m.* 1914 Duchess Adelheid of Saxe-Meiningen; *issue:* Princess Victoria Marina (1917–81); Prince Wilhelm Victor (1919–89)
      (d) Prince August Wilhelm (1887–1949), *m.* 1908 Princess Alexandra of Schleswig-Holstein-Sonderburg-Glücksburg (marriage dissolved 1920); *issue:* Prince Alexander (1912–85)
      (e) Prince Oskar (1888–1958), *m.* 1914 Countess von Ruppin; *issue:* Prince Oskar (1915–39); Prince Burchard (1917–88); Princess Herzeleide (1918–89); Prince Wilhelm-Karl (b. 1922)

   (f) Prince Joachim (1890–1920), *m.* 1916 Princess Marie of Anhalt; *issue:* Prince (Karl) Franz Joseph (1916–75), and has issue
   (g) Princess Viktoria Luise (1892–1980), *m.* 1913 Ernst, Duke of Brunswick 1913–18 (1887–1953); *issue:* Prince Ernst (1914–87); Prince Georg (b. 1915), *m.* 1946 Princess Sophie of Greece (*see* page 129) and has issue (two sons, one daughter); Princess Frederika (1917–81), *m.* 1938 Paul I, King of the Hellenes (*see* page 129); Prince Christian (1919–81); Prince Welf Heinrich (b. 1923)
   (2) Princess Charlotte (1860–1919), *m.* 1878 Bernhard, Duke of Saxe-Meiningen 1914 (1851–1914). *Issue:*
      Princess Feodora (1879–1945), *m.* 1898 Prince Heinrich XXX of Reuss
   (3) Prince Heinrich (1862–1929), *m.* 1888 Princess Irene of Hesse (*see* page 129). *Issue:*
      (a) Prince Waldemar (1889–1945), *m.* Princess Calixta Agnes of Lippe
      (b) Prince Sigismund (1896–1978), *m.* 1919 Princess Charlotte of Saxe-Altenburg; *issue:* Princess Barbara (1920–94); Prince Alfred (b. 1924)
      (c) Prince Heinrich (1900–4)
   (4) Prince Sigismund (1864–6)
   (5) Princess Victoria (1866–1929), *m.* (1) 1890, Prince Adolf of Schaumburg-Lippe (1859–1916); (2) 1927 Alexander Zubkov
   (6) Prince Waldemar (1868–79)
   (7) Princess Sophie (1870–1932), *m.* 1889 Constantine I (1868–1923), King of the Hellenes 1913–17, 1920–3. *Issue:*
      (a) George II (1890–1947), King of the Hellenes 1923–4 and 1935–47, *m.* 1921 Princess Elisabeth of Roumania (marriage dissolved 1935) (*see* page 129)

(b) Alexander I (1893–1920), King of the Hellenes 1917–20, m. 1919 Aspasia Manos; issue: Princess Alexandra (1921–93), m. 1944 King Petar II of Yugoslavia (see below)

(c) Princess Helena (1896–1982), m. 1921 King Carol of Roumania (see below), (marriage dissolved 1928)

(d) Paul I (1901–64), King of the Hellenes 1947–64, m. 1938 Princess Frederika of Brunswick (see page 128); issue: King Constantine II (b. 1940), m. 1964 Princess Anne-Marie of Denmark (see page 130), and has issue (three sons, two daughters); Princess Sophie (b. 1938), m. 1962 Juan Carlos I of Spain (see page 130); Princess Irene (b. 1942)

(e) Princess Irene (1904–74), m. 1939 4th Duke of Aosta; issue: Prince Amedeo, 5th Duke of Aosta (b. 1943)

(f) Princess Katherine (Lady Katherine Brandram) (b. 1913), m. 1947 Major R. C. A. Brandram, MC, TD; issue: R. Paul G. A. Brandram (b. 1948)

(8) Princess Margarethe (1872–1954), m. 1893 Prince Friedrich Karl of Hesse (1868–1940), Issue:

  (a) Prince Friedrich Wilhelm (1893–1916)

  (b) Prince Maximilian (1894–1914)

  (c) Prince Philipp (1896–1980), m. 1925 Princess Mafalda of Italy; issue: Prince Moritz (b. 1926); Prince Heinrich (b. 1927); Prince Otto (b. 1937); Princess Elisabeth (b. 1940)

  (d) Prince Wolfgang (1896–1989), m. (1) 1924 Princess Marie Alexandra of Baden; (2) 1948 Ottilie Möller

  (e) Prince Richard (1901–69)

  (f) Prince Christoph (1901–43), m. 1930 Princess Sophie of Greece (see below) and has issue (two sons, three daughters)

2. HRH PRINCE ALBERT EDWARD (HM KING EDWARD VII), b. 9 November 1841, m. 1863 HRH Princess Alexandra of Denmark (1844–1925), succeeded to the throne 22 January 1901, d. 6 May 1910. Issue:

  (1) Albert Victor, Duke of Clarence and Avondale (1861–92)

  (2) George (HM KING GEORGE V) (see page 128)

  (3) Louise (1867–1931) Princess Royal 1905–31, m. 1889 1st Duke of Fife (1849–1912). Issue:

    (a) Princess Alexandra, Duchess of Fife (1891–1959), m. 1913 Prince Arthur of Connaught (see page 130)

    (b) Princess Maud (1893–1945), m. 1923 11th Earl of Southesk (1893–1992); issue: The Duke of Fife (b. 1929)

  (4) Victoria (1868–1935)

  (5) Maud (1869–1938), m. 1896 Prince Carl of Denmark (1872–1957), later King Haakon VII of Norway 1905–57. Issue:

    (a) Olav V (1903–91), King of Norway 1957–91, m. 1929 Princess Märtha of Sweden (1901–54); issue: Princess Ragnhild (b. 1930); Princess Astrid (b. 1932); Harald V, King of Norway (b. 1937)

  (6) Alexander (6–7 April 1871)

3. HRH PRINCESS ALICE Maud Mary (1843–78), m. 1862 Prince Ludwig (1837–92), Grand Duke of Hesse 1877–92. Issue:

  (1) Victoria (1863–1950), m. 1884 Admiral of the Fleet Prince Louis of Battenberg (1854–1921), cr. 1st Marquess of Milford Haven 1917. Issue:

    (a) Alice (1885–1969), m. 1903 Prince Andrew of Greece (1882–1944); issue: Princess Margarita (1905–81) m. 1931 Prince Gottfried of Hohenlohe-Langenburg (see below); Princess Theodora (1906–69), m. Prince Berthold of Baden (1906–63) and has issue (two sons, one daughter); Princess Cecilie (1911–37), m. George, Grand Duke of Hesse (see below); Princess Sophie (b. 1914), m. (1) 1930 Prince Christoph of Hesse (see above); (2) 1946 Prince Georg of Hanover (see page 128); Prince Philip, Duke of Edinburgh (b. 1921) (see page 117)

    (b) Louise (1889–1965), m. 1923 Gustaf VI Adolf (1882–1973), King of Sweden 1950–73

    (c) George, 2nd Marquess of Milford Haven (1892–1938), m. 1916 Countess Nadejda, daughter of Grand Duke Michael of Russia; issue: Lady Tatiana (1917–88); David Michael, 3rd Marquess (1919–70)

    (d) Louis, 1st Earl Mountbatten of Burma (1900–79), m. 1922 Edwina Ashley, daughter of Lord Mount Temple; issue: Patricia, Countess Mountbatten of Burma (b. 1924), Pamela (b. 1929)

  (2) Elizabeth (1864–1918), m. 1884 Grand Duke Sergius of Russia (1857–1905)

  (3) Irene (1866–1953), m. 1888 Prince Heinrich of Prussia (see page 128)

  (4) Ernst Ludwig (1868–1937), Grand Duke of Hesse 1892–1918, m. (1) 1894 Princess Victoria Melita of Saxe-Coburg (see below) (marriage dissolved 1901); (2) 1905 Princess Eleonore of Solms-Hohensolmslich. Issue:

    (a) Princess Elizabeth (1895–1903)

    (b) George, Hereditary Grand Duke of Hesse (1906–37), m. Princess Cecilie of Greece (see above), and had issue, two sons, accidentally killed with parents 1937

    (c) Ludwig, Prince of Hesse (1908–68), m. 1937 Margaret, daughter of 1st Lord Geddes

  (5) Frederick William (1870–3)

  (6) Alix (Tsaritsa of Russia) (1872–1918), m. 1894 Nicholas II (1868–1918) Tsar of All the Russias 1894–1917, assassinated 16 July 1918. Issue:

    (a) Grand Duchess Olga (1895–1918)

    (b) Grand Duchess Tatiana (1897–1918)

    (c) Grand Duchess Marie (1899–1918)

    (d) Grand Duchess Anastasia (1901–18)

    (e) Alexis, Tsarevich of Russia (1904–18)

  (7) Marie (1874–8)

4. HRH PRINCE ALFRED Ernest Albert, Duke of Edinburgh, Admiral of the Fleet (1844–1900), m. 1874 Grand Duchess Marie Alexandrovna of Russia (1853–1920); succeeded as Duke of Saxe-Coburg and Gotha 22 August 1893. Issue:

  (1) Alfred, Prince of Saxe-Coburg (1874–99)

  (2) Marie (1875–1938), m. 1893 Ferdinand (1865–1927), King of Roumania 1914–27. Issue:

    (a) Carol II (1893–1953), King of Roumania 1930–40, m. (2) 1921 Princess Helena of Greece (see above) (marriage dissolved 1928); issue: Michael (b. 1921), King of Roumania 1927–30, 1940–7, m. 1948 Princess Anne of Bourbon-Parma, and has issue (five daughters)

    (b) Elisabeth (1894–1956), m. 1921 George II, King of the Hellenes (see page 128)

    (c) Marie (1900–61), m. 1922 Alexander (1888–1934), King of Yugoslavia 1921–34; issue: Petar II (1923–70), King of Yugoslavia 1934–45, m. 1944 Princess Alexandra of Greece (see above) and has issue (Crown Prince Alexander, b. 1945); Prince Tomislav (b. 1928), m. (1) 1957 Princess Margarita of Baden (daughter of Princess Theodora of Greece and Prince Berthold of Baden, see above), (2) 1982 Linda Bonney; and has issue (three sons, one daughter); Prince Andrej (1929–90), m. (1) 1956 Princess Christina of Hesse (daughter of Prince Christoph of Hesse and Princess Sophie of Greece, see above); (2) 1963 Princess Kira Melita of Leiningen (see below); and has issue (three sons, two daughters)

    (d) Prince Nicolas (1903–78)

    (e) Princess Ileana (1909–91), m. (1) 1931 Archduke Anton of Austria; (2) 1954 Dr Stefan Issarescu; issue: Archduke Stefan (b. 1932); Archduchess Maria Ileana (1933–59); Archduchess Alexandra (b. 1935); Archduke Dominic (b. 1937); Archduchess Maria Magdalena (b. 1939); Archduchess Elisabeth (b. 1942)

    (f) Prince Mircea (1913–16)

  (3) Victoria Melita (1876–1936), m. (1) 1894 Grand Duke Ernst Ludwig of Hesse (see above) (marriage dissolved 1901); (2) 1905 the Grand Duke Kirill of Russia (1876–1938). Issue:

    (a) Marie Kirillovna (1907–51), m. 1925 Prince Friedrich Karl of Leiningen, issue: Prince Emich (1926–91); Prince Karl (1928–90); Princess Kira-Melita (b. 1930), m. Prince Andrej of Yugoslavia (see above); Princess Margarita (b. 1932); Princess Mechtilde (b. 1936); Prince Friedrich (b. 1938)

    (b) Kira Kirillovna (1909–67), m. 1938 Prince Louis Ferdinand of Prussia (see page 128); issue: Prince Friedrich Wilhelm (b. 1939); Prince Michael (b. 1940); Princess Marie (b. 1942); Princess Kira (b. 1943); Prince Louis Ferdinand (1944–77); Prince Christian (b. 1946); Princess Xenia (1949–92)

    (c) Vladimir Kirillovich (1917–92), m. 1948 Princess Leonida Bagration-Mukhransky; issue: Grand Duchess Maria (b. 1953), and has issue

  (4) Alexandra (1878–1942), m. 1896 Ernst, Prince of Hohenlohe Langenburg. Issue:

    (a) Gottfried (1897–1960), m. 1931 Princess Margarita of Greece (see above); issue: Prince Kraft (b. 1935), Princess Beatrix (b. 1936), Prince Georg Andreas (b. 1938), Prince Ruprecht (1944–76); Prince Albrecht (1944–92)

(b) Maria (1899–1967), m. 1916 Prince Friedrich of
Schleswig-Holstein-Sonderburg-Glücksburg; issue: Prince
Peter (1922–80); Princess Marie (b. 1927)
(c) Princess Alexandra (1901–63)
(d) Princess Irma (1902–86)
(5) Princess Beatrice (1884–1966), m. 1909 Alfonso of Orleans,
Infante of Spain. Issue:
(a) Prince Alvaro (b. 1910), m. 1937 Carla Parodi-Delfino;
issue: Doña Gerarda (b. 1939); Don Alonso (1941–75); Doña
Beatriz (b. 1943); Don Alvaro (b. 1947)
(b) Prince Alonso (1912–36)
(c) Prince Ataulfo (1913–74)

5. HRH Princess Helena Augusta Victoria (1846–1923), m. 1866
Prince Christian of Schleswig-Holstein-Sonderburg-Augustenburg (1831–1917). Issue:
(1) Prince Christian Victor (1867–1900)
(2) Prince Albert (1869–1931), Duke of Schleswig-Holstein
1921–31
(3) Princess Helena (1870–1948)
(4) Princess Marie Louise (1872–1956), m. 1891 Prince Aribert of
Anhalt (marriage dissolved 1900)
(5) Prince Harold (12–20 May 1876)

6. HRH Princess Louise Caroline Alberta (1848–1939), m. 1871
the Marquess of Lorne, afterwards 9th Duke of Argyll (1845–1914);
without issue

7. HRH Prince Arthur William Patrick Albert, Duke of
Connaught, Field Marshal (1850–1942), m. 1879 Princess Louisa of
Prussia (1860–1917). Issue:
(1) Margaret (1882–1920), m. 1905 Crown Prince Gustaf Adolf
(1882–1973), afterwards King of Sweden 1950–73. Issue:
(a) Gustaf Adolf, Duke of Västerbotten (1906–47), m. 1932
Princess Sibylla of Saxe-Coburg-Gotha (see below); issue:
Princess Margaretha (b. 1934); Princess Birgitta (b. 1937);
Princess Désirée (b. 1938); Princess Christina (b. 1943); Carl
XVI Gustaf, King of Sweden (b. 1946)
(b) Count Sigvard Bernadotte (b. 1907), m.; issue: Count
Michael (b. 1944)
(c) Princess Ingrid (Queen Mother of Denmark) (b. 1910), m.
1935 Frederick IX (1899–72), King of Denmark 1947–72;
issue: Margrethe II, Queen of Denmark (b. 1940); Princess
Benedikte (b. 1944); Princess Anne-Marie (b. 1946), m. 1964
Constantine II of Greece (see page 129)
(d) Prince Bertil, Duke of Halland (1912–97), m. 1976 Mrs
Lilian Craig
(e) Count Carl Bernadotte (b. 1916), m. (1) 1946 Mrs Kerstin
Johnson; (2) 1988 Countess Gunnila Bussler

(2) Arthur (1883–1938), m. 1913 HH the Duchess of Fife (see
page 129). Issue:
Alastair Arthur, 2nd Duke of Connaught (1914–43)
(3) (Victoria) Patricia (1886–1974), m. 1919 Adm. Hon. Sir
Alexander Ramsay. Issue:
Alexander Ramsay of Mar (b. 1919), m. 1956 Hon. Flora
Fraser (Lady Saltoun)

8. HRH Prince Leopold George Duncan Albert, Duke of Albany
(1853–84), m. 1882 Princess Helena of Waldeck (1861–1922). Issue:
(1) Alice (1883–1981), m. 1904 Prince Alexander of Teck
(1874–1957), cr. 1st Earl of Athlone 1917. Issue:
(a) Lady May (1906–94), m. 1931 Sir Henry Abel-Smith,
KCMG, KCVO, DSO; issue: Anne (b. 1932); Richard (b. 1933);
Elizabeth (b. 1936)
(b) Rupert, Viscount Trematon (1907–28)
(c) Prince Maurice (March–September 1910)
(2) Charles Edward (1884–1954), Duke of Albany 1884 until
title suspended 1917, Duke of Saxe-Coburg-Gotha 1900–18, m.
1905 Princess Victoria Adelheid of Schleswig-Holstein-
Sonderburg-Glücksburg. Issue:
(a) Prince Johann Leopold (1906–72), and has issue
(b) Princess Sibylla (1908–72) m. 1932 Prince Gustav Adolf
of Sweden (see above)
(c) Prince Dietmar Hubertus (1909–43)
(d) Princess Caroline (1912–83), and has issue
(e) Prince Friedrich Josias (b. 1918), and has issue

9. HRH Princess Beatrice Mary Victoria Feodore (1857–1944),
m. 1885 Prince Henry of Battenberg (1858–96). Issue:
(1) Alexander, 1st Marquess of Carisbrooke (1886–1960), m.
1917 Lady Irene Denison. Issue:
Lady Iris Mountbatten (1920–82), m.; issue: Robin A. Bryan (b.
1957)
(2) Victoria Eugénie (1887–1969), m. 1906 Alfonso XIII
(1886–1941) King of Spain 1886–1931. Issue:
(a) Prince Alfonso (1907–38)
(b) Prince Jaime (1908–75), and has issue
(c) Princess Beatrice (b. 1909), and has issue
(d) Princess Maria (1911–96), and has issue
(e) Prince Juan (1913–93), Count of Barcelona; issue:
Princess Maria (b. 1936); Juan Carlos I, King of Spain
(b. 1938), m. 1962 Princess Sophie of Greece (see page 129)
and has issue (one son, two daughters); Princess Margarita
(b. 1939)
(f) Prince Gonzalo (1914–34)
(3) Major Lord Leopold Mountbatten (1889–1922)
(4) Maurice (1891–1914), died of wounds received in action

Kings and Queens

HOUSES OF CERDIC AND DENMARK

Reign	
927–939	ÆTHELSTAN
	Son of Edward the Elder, by Ecgwynn, and
	grandson of Alfred
	Acceded to Wessex and Mercia c.924, established
	direct rule over Northumbria 927, effectively
	creating the Kingdom of England
	Reigned 15 years
939–946	EDMUND I
	Born 921, son of Edward the Elder, by Eadgifu
	Married (1) Ælfgifu (2) Æthelflæd
	Killed aged 25, reigned 6 years
946–955	EADRED
	Son of Edward the Elder, by Eadgifu
	Reigned 9 years
955–959	EADWIG
	Born before 943, son of Edmund and Ælfgifu

	Married Ælfgifu
	Reigned 3 years
959–975	EDGAR I
	Born 943, son of Edmund and Ælfgifu
	Married (1) Æthelflæd (2) Wulfthryth
	(3) Ælfthryth
	Died aged 32, reigned 15 years
975–978	EDWARD I (the Martyr)
	Born c.962, son of Edgar and Æthelflæd
	Assassinated aged c.16, reigned 2 years
978–1016	ÆTHELRED (the Unready)
	Born c.968/969, son of Edgar and Ælfthryth
	Married (1) Ælfgifu (2) Emma, daughter of Richard
	I, count of Normandy
	1013–14 dispossessed of kingdom by Swegn
	Forkbeard (king of Denmark 987–1014)
	Died aged c.47, reigned 38 years
1016	EDMUND II (Ironside)
	Born before 993, son of Æthelred and Ælfgifu
	Married Ealdgyth
	Died aged over 23, reigned 7 months
	(April–November)
1016–1035	CNUT (Canute)
	Born c.995, son of Swegn Forkbeard, king of
	Denmark, and Gunhild

Married (1) Ælfgifu (2) Emma, widow of
Æthelred the Unready
Gained submission of West Saxons 1015,
Northumbrians 1016, Mercia 1016, king of all
England after Edmund's death
King of Denmark 1019–35, king of Norway
1028–35
Died aged *c.*40, *reigned* 19 years

1035–1040   HAROLD I (Harefoot)
*Born c.*1016/17, son of Cnut and Ælfgifu
Married Ælfgifu
1035 recognized as regent for himself and his
brother Harthacnut; 1037 recognized as king
Died aged *c.*23, *reigned* 4 years

1040–1042   HARTHACNUT
*Born c.*1018, son of Cnut and Emma
Titular king of Denmark from 1028
Acknowledged king of England 1035–7 with
Harold I as regent; effective king after Harold's
death
Died aged *c.*24, *reigned* 2 years

1042–1066   EDWARD II (the Confessor)
Born between 1002 and 1005, son of Æthelred the
Unready and Emma
Married Eadgyth, daughter of Godwine, earl of
Wessex
Died aged over 60, *reigned* 23 years

1066   HAROLD II (Godwinesson)
*Born c.*1020, son of Godwine, earl of Wessex, and
Gytha
Married (1) Eadgyth (2) Ealdgyth
Killed in battle aged *c.*46, *reigned* 10 months
(January–October)

THE HOUSE OF NORMANDY

1066–1087   WILLIAM I (the Conqueror)
Born 1027/8, son of Robert I, duke of Normandy;
obtained the Crown by conquest
Married Matilda, daughter of Baldwin, count of
Flanders
Died aged *c.*60, *reigned* 20 years

1087–1100   WILLIAM II (Rufus)
Born between 1056 and 1060, third son of
William I, succeeded his father in England only
Killed aged *c.*40, *reigned* 12 years

1100–1135   HENRY I (Beauclerk)
Born 1068, fourth son of William I
Married (1) Edith or Matilda, daughter of
Malcolm III of Scotland (2) Adela, daughter of
Godfrey, count of Louvain
Died aged 67, *reigned* 35 years

1135–1154   STEPHEN
Born not later than 1100, third son of Adela,
daughter of William I, and Stephen, count of Blois
Married Matilda, daughter of Eustace, count of
Boulogne
1141 (February–November) held captive by
adherents of Matilda, daughter of Henry I, who
contested the crown until 1153
Died aged over 53, *reigned* 18 years

THE HOUSE OF ANJOU (PLANTAGENETS)

1154–1189   HENRY II (Curtmantle)
Born 1133, son of Matilda, daughter of Henry I,
and Geoffrey, count of Anjou
Married Eleanor, daughter of William, duke of
Aquitaine, and divorced queen of Louis VII of
France
Died aged 56, *reigned* 34 years

1189–1199   RICHARD I (Coeur de Lion)
Born 1157, third son of Henry II
Married Berengaria, daughter of Sancho VI, king of
Navarre
Died aged 42, *reigned* 9 years

1199–1216   JOHN (Lackland)
Born 1167, fifth son of Henry II

Married (1) Isabella or Avisa, daughter of William,
earl of Gloucester (divorced) (2) Isabella, daughter
of Aymer, count of Angoulême
Died aged 48, *reigned* 17 years

1216–1272   HENRY III
Born 1207, son of John and Isabella of Angoulême
Married Eleanor, daughter of Raymond, count of
Provence
Died aged 65, *reigned* 56 years

1272–1307   EDWARD I (Longshanks)
Born 1239, eldest son of Henry III
Married (1) Eleanor, daughter of Ferdinand III,
king of Castile (2) Margaret, daughter of Philip III
of France
Died aged 68, *reigned* 34 years

1307–1327   EDWARD II
Born 1284, eldest surviving son of Edward I and
Eleanor
Married Isabella, daughter of Philip IV of France
Deposed January 1327, *killed* September 1327 aged
43, *reigned* 19 years

1327–1377   EDWARD III
Born 1312, eldest son of Edward II
Married Philippa, daughter of William, count of
Hainault
Died aged 64, *reigned* 50 years

1377–1399   RICHARD II
Born 1367, son of Edward (the Black Prince), eldest
son of Edward III
Married (1) Anne, daughter of Emperor Charles IV
(2) Isabelle, daughter of Charles VI of France
Deposed September 1399, *killed* February 1400 aged
33, *reigned* 22 years

THE HOUSE OF LANCASTER

1399–1413   HENRY IV
Born 1366, son of John of Gaunt, fourth son of
Edward III, and Blanche, daughter of Henry, duke
of Lancaster
Married (1) Mary, daughter of Humphrey, earl of
Hereford (2) Joan, daughter of Charles, king of
Navarre, and widow of John, duke of Brittany
Died aged *c.*47, *reigned* 13 years

1413–1422   HENRY V
Born 1387, eldest surviving son of Henry IV and
Mary
Married Catherine, daughter of Charles VI of
France
Died aged 34, *reigned* 9 years

1422–1471   HENRY VI
Born 1421, son of Henry V
Married Margaret, daughter of René, duke of
Anjou and count of Provence
Deposed March 1461, *restored* October 1470
Deposed April 1471, *killed* May 1471 aged 49, *reigned*
39 years

THE HOUSE OF YORK

1461–1483   EDWARD IV
Born 1442, eldest son of Richard of York (grandson
of Edmund, fifth son of Edward III, and son of
Anne, great-granddaughter of Lionel, third son of
Edward III)
Married Elizabeth Woodville, daughter of Richard,
Lord Rivers, and widow of Sir John Grey
Acceded March 1461, *deposed* October 1470, *restored*
April 1471
Died aged 40, *reigned* 21 years

1483   EDWARD V
Born 1470, eldest son of Edward IV
Deposed June 1483, *died* probably July–September
1483, aged 12, *reigned* 2 months (April–June)

1483–1485   RICHARD III
Born 1452, fourth son of Richard of York
Married Anne Neville, daughter of Richard, earl of
Warwick, and widow of Edward, Prince of Wales,
son of Henry VI
Killed in battle aged 32, *reigned* 2 years

THE HOUSE OF TUDOR

1485–1509   HENRY VII
Born 1457, son of Margaret Beaufort (great-granddaughter of John of Gaunt, fourth son of Edward III) and Edmund Tudor, earl of Richmond
Married Elizabeth, daughter of Edward IV
Died aged 52, *reigned* 23 years

1509–1547   HENRY VIII
Born 1491, second son of Henry VII
Married (1) Catherine, daughter of Ferdinand II, king of Aragon, and widow of his elder brother Arthur (divorced) (2) Anne, daughter of Sir Thomas Boleyn (executed) (3) Jane, daughter of Sir John Seymour (died in childbirth) (4) Anne, daughter of John, duke of Cleves (divorced) (5) Catherine Howard, niece of the Duke of Norfolk (executed) (6) Catherine, daughter of Sir Thomas Parr and widow of Lord Latimer
Died aged 55, *reigned* 37 years

1547–1553   EDWARD VI
Born 1537, son of Henry VIII and Jane Seymour
Died aged 15, *reigned* 6 years

1553   JANE
Born 1537, daughter of Frances (daughter of Mary Tudor, the younger daughter of Henry VII) and Henry Grey, duke of Suffolk
Married Lord Guildford Dudley, son of the Duke of Northumberland
Deposed July 1553, *executed* February 1554 aged 16, *reigned* 14 days

1553–1558   MARY I
Born 1516, daughter of Henry VIII and Catherine of Aragon
Married Philip II of Spain
Died aged 42, *reigned* 5 years

1558–1603   ELIZABETH I
Born 1533, daughter of Henry VIII and Anne Boleyn
Died aged 69, *reigned* 44 years

BRITISH KINGS AND QUEENS SINCE 1603

THE HOUSE OF STUART

Reign
1603–1625   JAMES I (VI OF SCOTLAND)
Born 1566, son of Mary, queen of Scots (granddaughter of Margaret Tudor, elder daughter of Henry VII), and Henry Stewart, Lord Darnley
Married Anne, daughter of Frederick II of Denmark
Died aged 58, *reigned* 22 years
(*see also* page 134)

1625–1649   CHARLES I
Born 1600, second son of James I
Married Henrietta Maria, daughter of Henry IV of France
Executed 1649 aged 48, *reigned* 23 years

COMMONWEALTH DECLARED 19 May 1649
1649–53 Government by a council of state
1653–8 Oliver Cromwell, *Lord Protector*
1658–9 Richard Cromwell, *Lord Protector*

1660–1685   CHARLES II
Born 1630, eldest son of Charles I
Married Catherine, daughter of John IV of Portugal
Died aged 54, *reigned* 24 years

1685–1688   JAMES II (VII of Scotland)
Born 1633, second son of Charles I
Married (1) Lady Anne Hyde, daughter of Edward, earl of Clarendon (2) Mary, daughter of Alphonso, duke of Modena
Reign ended with flight from kingdom December 1688
Died 1701 aged 67, *reigned* 3 years

INTERREGNUM 11 December 1688 to 12 February 1689

1689–1702   WILLIAM III
Born 1650, son of William II, prince of Orange, and Mary Stuart, daughter of Charles I
Married Mary, elder daughter of James II
Died aged 51, *reigned* 13 years

and
1689–1694   MARY II
Born 1662, elder daughter of James II and Anne
Died aged 32, *reigned* 5 years

1702–1714   ANNE
Born 1665, younger daughter of James II and Anne
Married Prince George of Denmark, son of Frederick III of Denmark
Died aged 49, *reigned* 12 years

THE HOUSE OF HANOVER

1714–1727   GEORGE I (Elector of Hanover)
Born 1660, son of Sophia (daughter of Frederick, elector palatine, and Elizabeth Stuart, daughter of James I) and Ernest Augustus, elector of Hanover
Married Sophia Dorothea, daughter of George William, duke of Lüneburg-Celle
Died aged 67, *reigned* 12 years

1727–1760   GEORGE II
Born 1683, son of George I
Married Caroline, daughter of John Frederick, margrave of Brandenburg-Anspach
Died aged 76, *reigned* 33 years

1760–1820   GEORGE III
Born 1738, son of Frederick, eldest son of George II
Married Charlotte, daughter of Charles Louis, duke of Mecklenburg-Strelitz
Died aged 81, *reigned* 59 years

REGENCY 1811–20
Prince of Wales regent owing to the insanity of George III

1820–1830   GEORGE IV
Born 1762, eldest son of George III
Married Caroline, daughter of Charles, duke of Brunswick-Wolfenbüttel
Died aged 67, *reigned* 10 years

1830–1837   WILLIAM IV
Born 1765, third son of George III
Married Adelaide, daughter of George, duke of Saxe-Meiningen
Died aged 71, *reigned* 7 years

1837–1901   VICTORIA
Born 1819, daughter of Edward, fourth son of George III
Married Prince Albert of Saxe-Coburg and Gotha
Died aged 81, *reigned* 63 years

THE HOUSE OF SAXE-COBURG AND GOTHA

1901–1910   EDWARD VII
Born 1841, eldest son of Victoria and Albert
Married Alexandra, daughter of Christian IX of Denmark
Died aged 68, *reigned* 9 years

THE HOUSE OF WINDSOR

1910–1936   GEORGE V
Born 1865, second son of Edward VII
Married Victoria Mary, daughter of Francis, duke of Teck
Died aged 70, *reigned* 25 years

1936   EDWARD VIII
Born 1894, eldest son of George V
Married (1937) Mrs Wallis Warfield
Abdicated 1936, *died* 1972 aged 77, *reigned* 10 months (20 January to 11 December)

1936–1952   GEORGE VI
Born 1895, second son of George V
Married Lady Elizabeth Bowes-Lyon, daughter of 14th Earl of Strathmore and Kinghorne (*see also* pages 117–8)
Died aged 56, *reigned* 15 years

1952–   ELIZABETH II
Born 1926, elder daughter of George VI
Married Philip, son of Prince Andrew of Greece
(see also page 117)
WHOM GOD PRESERVE

KINGS AND QUEENS OF SCOTS 1016 TO 1603

Reign
1016–1034   MALCOLM II
Born c.954, son of Kenneth II
Acceded to Alba 1005, secured Lothian c.1016,
obtained Strathclyde for his grandson Duncan
c.1016, thus reigning over an area approximately
the same as that governed by later rulers of
Scotland
Died aged c.80, reigned 18 years

THE HOUSE OF ATHOLL

1034–1040   DUNCAN I
Son of Bethoc, daughter of Malcolm II, and
Crinan, mormaer of Atholl
Married a cousin of Siward, earl of Northumbria
Reigned 5 years
1040–1057   MACBETH
Born c.1005, son of a daughter of Malcolm II and
Finlaec, mormaer of Moray
Married Gruoch, granddaughter of Kenneth III
Killed aged c.52, reigned 17 years
1057–1058   LULACH
Born c.1032, son of Gillacomgan, mormaer of
Moray, and Gruoch (and stepson of Macbeth)
Died aged c.26, reigned 7 months (August–March)
1058–1093   MALCOLM III (Canmore)
Born c.1031, elder son of Duncan I
Married (1) Ingibiorg (2) Margaret (St Margaret),
granddaughter of Edmund II of England
Killed in battle aged c.62, reigned 35 years
1093–1097   DONALD III BÁN
Born c. 1033, second son of Duncan I
Deposed May 1094, restored November 1094, deposed
October 1097, reigned 3 years
1094   DUNCAN II
Born c.1060, elder son of Malcolm III and Ingibiorg
Married Octreda of Dunbar
Killed aged c.34, reigned 6 months
(May–November)
1097–1107   EDGAR
Born c.1074, second son of Malcolm III and
Margaret
Died aged c.32, reigned 9 years
1107–1124   ALEXANDER I (The Fierce)
Born c.1077, fifth son of Malcolm III and Margaret
Married Sybilla, illegitimate daughter of Henry I
of England
Died aged c.47, reigned 17 years
1124–1153   DAVID I (The Saint)
Born c.1085, sixth son of Malcolm III and Margaret
Married Matilda, daughter of Waltheof, earl of
Huntingdon
Died aged c.68, reigned 29 years
1153–1165   MALCOLM IV (The Maiden)
Born c.1141, son of Henry, earl of Huntingdon,
second son of David I
Died aged c.24, reigned 12 years
1165–1214   WILLIAM I (The Lion)
Born c.1142, brother of Malcolm IV
Married Ermengarde, daughter of Richard,
viscount of Beaumont
Died aged c.72, reigned 49 years
1214–1249   ALEXANDER II
Born 1198, son of William I
Married (1) Joan, daughter of John, king of
England (2) Marie, daughter of Ingelram de Coucy
Died aged 50, reigned 34 years

1249–1286   ALEXANDER III
Born 1241, son of Alexander II and Marie
Married (1) Margaret, daughter of Henry III of
England (2) Yolande, daughter of the Count of
Dreux
Killed accidentally aged 44, reigned 36 years
1286–1290   MARGARET (The Maid of Norway)
Born 1283, daughter of Margaret (daughter of
Alexander III) and Eric II of Norway
Died aged 7, reigned 4 years

FIRST INTERREGNUM 1290–2
Throne disputed by 13 competitors. Crown
awarded to John Balliol by adjudication of Edward
I of England

THE HOUSE OF BALLIOL

1292–1296   JOHN (Balliol)
Born c.1250, son of Dervorguilla, great-great-
granddaughter of David I, and John de Balliol
Married Isabella, daughter of John, earl of Surrey
Abdicated 1296, died 1313 aged c.63, reigned 3 years

SECOND INTERREGNUM 1296–1306
Edward I of England declared John Balliol to have
forfeited the throne for contumacy in 1296 and
took the government of Scotland into his own
hands

THE HOUSE OF BRUCE

1306–1329   ROBERT I (Bruce)
Born 1274, son of Robert Bruce and Marjorie,
countess of Carrick, and great-grandson of the
second daughter of David, earl of Huntingdon,
brother of William I
Married (1) Isabella, daughter of Donald, earl of
Mar (2) Elizabeth, daughter of Richard, earl of
Ulster
Died aged 54, reigned 23 years
1329–1371   DAVID II
Born 1324, son of Robert I and Elizabeth
Married (1) Joanna, daughter of Edward II of
England (2) Margaret Drummond, widow of Sir
John Logie (divorced)
Died aged 46, reigned 41 years

1332 Edward Balliol, son of John Balliol, crowned
King of Scots September, expelled December
1333–6 Edward Balliol restored as King of Scots

THE HOUSE OF STEWART

1371–1390   ROBERT II (Stewart)
Born 1316, son of Marjorie (daughter of Robert I)
and Walter, High Steward of Scotland
Married (1) Elizabeth, daughter of Sir Robert Mure
of Rowallan (2) Euphemia, daughter of Hugh, earl
of Ross
Died aged 74, reigned 19 years
1390–1406   ROBERT III
Born c.1337, son of Robert II and Elizabeth
Married Annabella, daughter of Sir John
Drummond of Stobhall
Died aged c.69, reigned 16 years
1406–1437   JAMES I
Born 1394, son of Robert III
Married Joan Beaufort, daughter of John, earl of
Somerset
Assassinated aged 42, reigned 30 years
1437–1460   JAMES II
Born 1430, son of James I
Married Mary, daughter of Arnold, duke of
Gueldres
Killed accidentally aged 29, reigned 23 years
1460–1488   JAMES III
Born 1452, son of James II
Married Margaret, daughter of Christian I of
Denmark
Assassinated aged 36, reigned 27 years

1488–1513	**JAMES IV**
	Born 1473, son of James III
	Married Margaret Tudor, daughter of Henry VII of England
	Killed in battle aged 40, *reigned* 25 years
1513–1542	**JAMES V**
	Born 1512, son of James IV
	Married (1) Madeleine, daughter of Francis I of France (2) Mary of Lorraine, daughter of the Duc de Guise
	Died aged 30, *reigned* 29 years
1542–1567	**MARY**
	Born 1542, daughter of James V and Mary
	Married (1) the Dauphin, afterwards Francis II of France (2) Henry Stewart, Lord Darnley (3) James Hepburn, earl of Bothwell
	Abdicated 1567, prisoner in England from 1568, *executed* 1587, *reigned* 24 years
1567–1625	**JAMES VI (and I of England)**
	Born 1566, son of Mary, queen of Scots, and Henry, Lord Darnley
	Acceded 1567 to the Scottish throne, *reigned* 58 years
	Succeeded 1603 to the English throne, so joining the English and Scottish crowns in one person. The two kingdoms remained distinct until 1707 when the parliaments of the kingdoms became conjoined
	For British Kings and Queens since 1603, *see* pages 132–3

WELSH SOVEREIGNS AND PRINCES

Wales was ruled by sovereign princes from the earliest times until the death of Llywelyn in 1282. The first English Prince of Wales was the son of Edward I, who was born in Caernarvon town on 25 April 1284. According to a discredited legend, he was presented to the Welsh chieftains as their prince, in fulfilment of a promise that they should have a prince who 'could not speak a word of English' and should be native born. This son, who afterwards became Edward II, was created 'Prince of Wales and Earl of Chester' at the Lincoln Parliament on 7 February 1301.

The title Prince of Wales is borne after individual conferment and is not inherited at birth, though some Princes have been declared and styled Prince of Wales but never formally so created (*s.*). The title was conferred on Prince Charles by The Queen on 26 July 1958. He was invested at Caernarvon on 1 July 1969.

INDEPENDENT PRINCES AD 844 TO 1282

844–878	Rhodri the Great
878–916	Anarawd, son of Rhodri
916–950	Hywel Dda, the Good
950–979	Iago ab Idwal (or Ieuaf)
979–985	Hywel ab Ieuaf, the Bad
985–986	Cadwallon, his brother
986–999	Maredudd ab Owain ap Hywel Dda
999–1008	Cynan ap Hywel ab Ieuaf
1018–1023	Llywelyn ap Seisyll
1023–1039	Iago ab Idwal ap Meurig
1039–1063	Gruffydd ap Llywelyn ap Seisyll
1063–1075	Bleddyn ap Cynfyn
1075–1081	Trahaern ap Caradog
1081–1137	Gruffydd ap Cynan ab Iago
1137–1170	Owain Gwynedd
1170–1194	Dafydd ab Owain Gwynedd
1194–1240	Llywelyn Fawr, the Great
1240–1246	Dafydd ap Llywelyn
1246–1282	Llywelyn ap Gruffydd ap Llywelyn

ENGLISH PRINCES SINCE 1301

1301	Edward (Edward II)
1343	Edward the Black Prince, s. of Edward III
1376	Richard (Richard II), s. of the Black Prince
1399	Henry of Monmouth (Henry V)
1454	Edward of Westminster, son of Henry VI

1471	Edward of Westminster (Edward V)
1483	Edward, son of Richard III (d. 1484)
1489	Arthur Tudor, son of Henry VII
1504	Henry Tudor (Henry VIII)
1610	Henry Stuart, son of James I (d. 1612)
1616	Charles Stuart (Charles I)
c.1638 (*s.*)	Charles Stuart (Charles II)
1688 (*s.*)	James Francis Edward Stuart (The Old Pretender), son of James II (d. 1766)
1714	George Augustus (George II)
1729	Frederick Lewis, s. of George II (d. 1751)
1751	George William Frederick (George III)
1762	George Augustus Frederick (George IV)
1841	Albert Edward (Edward VII)
1901	George (George V)
1910	Edward (Edward VIII)
1958	Charles Philip Arthur George

PRINCESSES ROYAL

The style Princess Royal is conferred at the Sovereign's discretion on his or her eldest daughter. It is an honorary title, held for life, and cannot be inherited or passed on. It was first conferred on Princess Mary, daughter of Charles I, in approximately 1642.

c.1642	Princess Mary (1631–60), daughter of Charles I
1727	Princess Anne (1709–59), daughter of George II
1766	Princess Charlotte (1766–1828), daughter of George III
1840	Princess Victoria (1840–1901), daughter of Victoria
1905	Princess Louise (1867–1931), daughter of Edward VII
1932	Princess Mary (1897–1965), daughter of George V
1987	Princess Anne (b. 1950), daughter of Elizabeth II

Precedence

ENGLAND AND WALES

The Sovereign
The Prince Philip, Duke of
  Edinburgh
The Prince of Wales
The Sovereign's younger sons
The Sovereign's grandsons
The Sovereign's cousins
Archbishop of Canterbury
Lord High Chancellor
Archbishop of York
The Prime Minister
Lord President of the Council
Speaker of the House of Commons
Lord Privy Seal
Ambassadors and High
  Commissioners
Lord Great Chamberlain
Earl Marshal
Lord Steward of the Household
Lord Chamberlain of the Household
Master of the Horse
Dukes, according to their patent of
  creation:
  (1) of England
  (2) of Scotland
  (3) of Great Britain
  (4) of Ireland
  (5) those created since the Union
Ministers and Envoys
Eldest sons of Dukes of Blood Royal
Marquesses, according to their
  patent of creation:
  (1) of England
  (2) of Scotland
  (3) of Great Britain
  (4) of Ireland
  (5) those created since the Union
Dukes' eldest sons
Earls, according to their patent of
  creation:
  (1) of England
  (2) of Scotland
  (3) of Great Britain
  (4) of Ireland
  (5) those created since the Union
Younger sons of Dukes of Blood
  Royal
Marquesses' eldest sons
Dukes' younger sons
Viscounts, according to their patent
  of creation:
  (1) of England
  (2) of Scotland
  (3) of Great Britain
  (4) of Ireland
  (5) those created since the Union
Earls' eldest sons
Marquesses' younger sons
Bishops of London, Durham and
  Winchester

Other English Diocesan Bishops,
  according to seniority of
  consecration
Suffragan Bishops, according to
  seniority of consecration
Secretaries of State, if of the degree
  of a Baron
Barons, according to their patent of
  creation:
  (1) of England
  (2) of Scotland
  (3) of Great Britain
  (4) of Ireland
  (5) those created since the Union
Treasurer of the Household
Comptroller of the Household
Vice-Chamberlain of the Household
Secretaries of State under the degree
  of Baron
Viscounts' eldest sons
Earls' younger sons
Barons' eldest sons
Knights of the Garter
Privy Counsellors
Chancellor of the Exchequer
Chancellor of the Duchy of
  Lancaster
Lord Chief Justice of England
Master of the Rolls
President of the Family Division
Vice-Chancellor
Lords Justices of Appeal
Judges of the High Court
Viscounts' younger sons
Barons' younger sons
Sons of Life Peers
Baronets, according to date of patent
Knights of the Thistle
Knights Grand Cross of the Bath
Members of the Order of Merit
Knights Grand Commanders of the
  Star of India
Knights Grand Cross of St Michael
  and St George
Knights Grand Commanders of the
  Indian Empire
Knights Grand Cross of the Royal
  Victorian Order
Knights Grand Cross of the British
  Empire
Companions of Honour
Knights Commanders of the Bath
Knights Commanders of the Star of
  India
Knights Commanders of St Michael
  and St George
Knights Commanders of the Indian
  Empire
Knights Commanders of the Royal
  Victorian Order
Knights Commanders of the British
  Empire
Knights Bachelor
Vice-Chancellor of the County
  Palatine of Lancaster

Official Referees of the Supreme
  Court
Circuit judges and judges of the
  Mayor's and City of London
  Court
Companions of the Bath
Companions of the Star of India
Companions of St Michael and St
  George
Companions of the Indian Empire
Commanders of the Royal Victorian
  Order
Commanders of the British Empire
Companions of the Distinguished
  Service Order
Lieutenants of the Royal Victorian
  Order
Officers of the British Empire
Companions of the Imperial Service
  Order
Eldest sons of younger sons of Peers
Baronets' eldest sons
Eldest sons of Knights, in the same
  order as their fathers
Members of the Royal Victorian
  Order
Members of the British Empire
Younger sons of the younger sons of
  Peers
Baronets' younger sons
Younger sons of Knights, in the same
  order as their fathers
Naval, Military, Air, and other
  Esquires by office

WOMEN

Women take the same rank as their
husbands or as their brothers; but the
daughter of a peer marrying a commoner retains her title as Lady or
Honourable. Daughters of peers rank
next immediately after the wives of
their elder brothers, and before their
younger brothers' wives. Daughters
of peers marrying peers of lower
degree take the same order of precedence as that of their husbands;
thus the daughter of a Duke marrying
a Baron becomes of the rank of
Baroness only, while her sisters
married to commoners retain their
rank and take precedence of the
Baroness. Merely official rank on the
husband's part does not give any
similar precedence to the wife.

Peeresses in their own right take
the same precedence as peers of the
same rank, i.e. from their date of
creation.

Forms of address

It is only possible to cover here the forms of address for peers, baronets and knights, their wife and children, and Privy Counsellors. Greater detail should be sought in one of the publications devoted to the subject.

Both formal and social forms of address are given where usage differs; nowadays, the social form is generally preferred to the formal, which increasingly is used only for official documents and on very formal occasions.
F— represents forename
S— represents surname

BARON – *Envelope (formal)*, The Right Hon. Lord —; *(social)*, The Lord —. *Letter (formal)*, My Lord; *(social)*, Dear Lord —. *Spoken*, Lord —.

BARON'S WIFE – *Envelope (formal)*, The Right Hon. Lady —; *(social)*, The Lady —. *Letter (formal)*, My Lady; *(social)*, Dear Lady —. *Spoken*, Lady —.

BARON'S CHILDREN – *Envelope*, The Hon. F— S—. *Letter*, Dear Mr/Miss/Mrs S—. *Spoken*, Mr/Miss/Mrs S—.

BARONESS IN OWN RIGHT – *Envelope*, may be addressed in same way as a Baron's wife or, if she prefers *(formal)*, The Right Hon. the Baroness —; *(social)*, The Baroness —. Otherwise as for a Baron's wife.

BARONET – *Envelope*, Sir F— S—, Bt. *Letter (formal)*, Dear Sir; *(social)*, Dear Sir F—. *Spoken*, Sir F—.

BARONET'S WIFE – *Envelope*, Lady S—. *Letter (formal)*, Dear Madam; *(social)*, Dear Lady S—. *Spoken*, Lady S—.

COUNTESS IN OWN RIGHT – As for an Earl's wife.

COURTESY TITLES – The heir apparent to a Duke, Marquess or Earl uses the highest of his father's other titles as a courtesy title. (For list, *see* pages 165–6.) The holder of a courtesy title is not styled The Most Hon. or The Right Hon., and in correspondence 'The' is omitted before the title. The heir apparent to a Scottish peerage may use the title 'Master' (*see* below).

DAME – *Envelope*, Dame F— S—, followed by appropriate post-nominal letters. *Letter (formal)*, Dear Madam; *(social)*, Dear Dame F—. *Spoken*, Dame F—.

DUKE – *Envelope (formal)*, His Grace the Duke of —; *(social)*, The Duke of —. *Letter (formal)*, My Lord Duke; *(social)*, Dear Duke. *Spoken (formal)*, Your Grace; *(social)*, Duke.

DUKE'S WIFE – *Envelope (formal)*, Her Grace the Duchess of —; *(social)*, The Duchess of —. *Letter (formal)*, Dear Madam; *(social)*, Dear Duchess. *Spoken*, Duchess.

DUKE'S ELDEST SON – *see* Courtesy titles.

DUKE'S YOUNGER SONS – *Envelope*, Lord F— S—. *Letter (formal)*, My Lord; *(social)*, Dear Lord F—. *Spoken (formal)*, My Lord; *(social)*, Lord F—.

DUKE'S DAUGHTER – *Envelope*, Lady F— S—. *Letter (formal)*, Dear Madam; *(social)*, Dear Lady F—. *Spoken*, Lady F—.

EARL – *Envelope (formal)*, The Right Hon. the Earl (of) —; *(social)*, The Earl (of) —. *Letter (formal)*, My Lord; *(social)*, Dear Lord —. *Spoken (formal)*, My Lord; *(social)*, Lord —.

EARL'S WIFE – *Envelope (formal)*, The Right Hon. the Countess (of) —; *(social)*, The Countess (of) —. *Letter (formal)*, Madam; *(social)*, Lady —. *Spoken (formal)*, Madam; *(social)*, Lady —.

EARL'S CHILDREN – *Eldest son, see* Courtesy titles. *Younger sons*, The Hon. F— S— (for forms of address, *see* Baron's children). *Daughters*, Lady F— S— (for forms of address, *see* Duke's daughter).

KNIGHT (BACHELOR) – *Envelope*, Sir F— S—. *Letter (formal)*, Dear Sir; *(social)*, Dear Sir F—. *Spoken*, Sir F—.

KNIGHT (ORDERS OF CHIVALRY) – *Envelope*, Sir F— S—, followed by appropriate post-nominal letters. Otherwise as for Knight Bachelor.

KNIGHT'S WIFE – As for Baronet's wife.

LIFE PEER – As for Baron or for Baroness in own right.

LIFE PEER'S WIFE – As for Baron's wife.

LIFE PEER'S CHILDREN – As for Baron's children.

MARQUESS – *Envelope (formal)*, The Most Hon. the Marquess of —; *(social)*, The Marquess of —. *Letter (formal)*, My Lord; *(social)*, Dear Lord —. *Spoken (formal)*, My Lord; *(social)*, Lord —.

MARQUESS'S WIFE – *Envelope (formal)*, The Most Hon. the Marchioness of —; *(social)*, The Marchioness of —. *Letter (formal)*, Madam; *(social)*, Dear Lady —. *Spoken*, Lady —.

MARQUESS'S CHILDREN – *Eldest son, see* Courtesy titles. *Younger sons*, Lord F— S— (for forms of address, *see* Duke's younger sons). *Daughters*, Lady F— S— (for forms of address, *see* Duke's daughter).

MASTER – The title is used by the heir apparent to a Scottish peerage, though usually the heir apparent to a Duke, Marquess or Earl uses his courtesy title rather than 'Master'. *Envelope*, The Master of —. *Letter (formal)*, Dear Sir; *(social)*, Dear Master of —. *Spoken (formal)*, Master, or Sir; *(social)*, Master, or Mr S—.

MASTER'S WIFE – Addressed as for the wife of the appropriate peerage style, otherwise as Mrs S—.

PRIVY COUNSELLOR – *Envelope*, The Right (or Rt.) Hon. F— S—. *Letter*, Dear Mr/Miss/Mrs S—. *Spoken*, Mr/Miss/Mrs S—. It is incorrect to use the letters PC after the name in conjunction with the prefix The Right Hon., unless the Privy Counsellor is a peer below the rank of Marquess and so is styled The Right Hon. because of his rank. In this case only, the post-nominal letters may be used in conjunction with the prefix The Right Hon.

VISCOUNT – *Envelope (formal)*, The Right Hon. the Viscount —; *(social)*, The Viscount —. *Letter (formal)*, My Lord; *(social)*, Dear Lord —. *Spoken*, Lord —.

VISCOUNT'S WIFE – *Envelope (formal)*, The Right Hon. the Viscountess —; *(social)*, The Viscountess —. *Letter (formal)*, Madam; *(social)*, Dear Lady —. *Spoken*, Lady —.

VISCOUNT'S CHILDREN – As for Baron's children.

The Peerage

and Members of the House of Lords

The rules which govern the creation and succession of peerages are extremely complicated. There are, technically, five separate peerages, the Peerage of England, of Scotland, of Ireland, of Great Britain, and of the United Kingdom. The Peerage of Great Britain dates from 1707 when an Act of Union combined the two kingdoms of England and Scotland and separate peerages were discontinued. The Peerage of the United Kingdom dates from 1801 when Great Britain and Ireland were combined under an Act of Union. Some Scottish peers have received additional peerages of Great Britain or of the United Kingdom since 1707, and some Irish peers additional peerages of the United Kingdom since 1801.

The Peerage of Ireland was not entirely discontinued from 1801 but holders of Irish peerages, whether pre-dating or created subsequent to the Union of 1801, are not entitled to sit in the House of Lords if they have no additional English, Scottish, Great Britain or United Kingdom peerage. However, they are eligible for election to the House of Commons and to vote in parliamentary elections, which other peers are not. An Irish peer holding a peerage of a lower grade which enables him to sit in the House of Lords is introduced there by the title which enables him to sit, though for all other purposes he is known by his higher title.

In the Peerage of Scotland there is no rank of Baron; the equivalent rank is Lord of Parliament, abbreviated to 'Lord' (the female equivalent is 'Lady'). All peers of England, Scotland, Great Britain or the United Kingdom who are 21 years or over, and of British, Irish or Commonwealth nationality are entitled to sit in the House of Lords.

No fees for dignities have been payable since 1937. The House of Lords surrendered the ancient right of peers to be tried for treason or felony by their peers in 1948.

Hereditary Women Peers

Most hereditary peerages pass on death to the nearest male heir, but there are exceptions, and several are held by women (*see* pages 145 and 157).

A woman peer in her own right retains her title after marriage, and if her husband's rank is the superior she is designated by the two titles jointly, the inferior one second. Her hereditary claim still holds good in spite of any marriage whether higher or lower. No rank held by a woman can confer any title or even precedence upon her husband but the rank of a hereditary woman peer in her own right is inherited by her eldest son (or in some cases daughter).

Since the Peerage Act 1963, hereditary women peers in their own right have been entitled to sit in the House of Lords, subject to the same qualifications as men.

Life Peers

Since 1876 non-hereditary or life peerages have been conferred on certain eminent judges to enable the judicial functions of the House of Lords to be carried out. These Lords are known as Lords of Appeal or law lords and, to date, such appointments have all been male.

Since 1958 life peerages have been conferred upon distinguished men and women from all walks of life, giving them seats in the House of Lords in the degree of Baron or Baroness. They are addressed in the same way as hereditary Lords and Barons, and their children have similar courtesy titles.

Peerages Extinct Since the Last Edition

EARLDOMS: Sondes (*cr.* 1880)
BARONIES: Archibald (*cr.* 1949); Calthorpe (*cr.* 1796); Horder (*cr.* 1933); Kinnaird (*cr.* 1682)
LIFE PEERAGES: Amery of Lustleigh (*cr.* 1992); Bancroft (*cr.* 1982); Banks (*cr.* 1974); Birk (*cr.* 1967); Chelmer (*cr.* 1963); Colnbrook (*cr.* 1987); Finsberg (*cr.* 1992); Goold (*cr.* 1987); Harvington (*cr.* 1974); Mayhew (*cr.* 1981); Rippon of Hexham (*cr.* 1987); Roskill (*cr.* 1980); Seear (*cr.* 1971); Taylor of Gosforth (*cr.* 1992); Todd (*cr.* 1962)

Disclaimer of Peerages

The Peerage Act 1963 enables peers to disclaim their peerages for life. Peers alive in 1963 could disclaim within twelve months after the passing of the Act (31 July 1963); a person subsequently succeeding to a peerage may disclaim within 12 months (one month if an MP) after the date of succession, or of reaching 21, if later. The disclaimer is irrevocable but does not affect the descent of the peerage after the disclaimant's death, and children of a disclaimed peer may, if they wish, retain their precedence and any courtesy titles and styles borne as children of a peer. The disclaimer permits the disclaimant to sit in the House of Commons if elected as an MP.

The following peerages are currently disclaimed:

EARLDOMS: Durham (1970); Selkirk (1994)
VISCOUNTCIES: Camrose (1995); Hailsham (1963); Stansgate (1963)
BARONIES: Altrincham (1963); Merthyr (1977); Reith (1972); Sanderson of Ayot (1971); Silkin (1972)

PEERS WHO ARE MINORS (i.e. under 21 years of age)
EARLS: Craven (*b.* 1989)
BARONS: Elphinstone (*b.* 1980); Lovat (*b.* 1977)

Contractions and Symbols

s. Scottish title
I. Irish title
* The peer holds also an Imperial title, specified after the name by Engl., Brit. or UK
o there is no 'of' in the title
b. born
s. succeeded
m. married
w. widower or widow
M. minor
† heir not ascertained at time of going to press

Hereditary Peers

ROYAL DUKES

Style, His Royal Highness The Duke of __
Style of address (formal) May it please your Royal Highness; (*informal*) Sir

Created	Title, order of succession, name, etc.	Heir
1947	*Edinburgh* (1st), The Prince Philip, Duke of Edinburgh, (*see* page 117)	The Prince of Wales
1337	*Cornwall,* Charles, Prince of Wales, *s.* 1952 (*see* page 117)	‡
1398	*Rothesay,* Charles, Prince of Wales, *s.* 1952 (*see* page 117)	‡
1986	*York* (1st), The Prince Andrew, Duke of York (*see* page 117)	None
1928	*Gloucester* (2nd), Prince Richard, Duke of Gloucester, *s.* 1974 (*see* page 118)	Earl of Ulster (*see* page 118)
1934	*Kent* (2nd), Prince Edward, Duke of Kent, *s.* 1942 (*see* page 118)	Earl of St Andrews (*see* page 118)

‡ The title is not hereditary but is held by the Sovereign's eldest son from the moment of his birth or the Sovereign's accession

DUKES

Coronet, Eight strawberry leaves
Style, His Grace the Duke of __
Wife's style, Her Grace the Duchess of __
Eldest son's style, Takes his father's second title as a courtesy title
Younger sons' style, 'Lord' before forename and family name
Daughters' style, 'Lady' before forename and family name
For forms of address, *see* page 136

Created	Title, order of succession, name, etc.	Heir
1868 I.*	*Abercorn* (5th), James Hamilton (6th *Brit. Marq.,* 1790, and 14th *Scott. Earl,* 1606, both *Abercorn*), *b.* 1934, *s.* 1979, *m.*	Marquess of Hamilton, *b.* 1969
1701 S.*	*Argyll* (12th), Ian Campbell (5th *UK Duke Argyll,* 1892), *b.* 1937, *s.* 1973, *m.*	Marquess of Lorne, *b.* 1968
1703 S.	*Atholl* (11th), John Murray, *b.* 1929, *s.* 1996, *m.*	Marquess of Tullibardine, *b.* 1960
1682	*Beaufort* (11th), David Robert Somerset, *b.* 1928, *s.* 1984, *w.*	Marquess of Worcester, *b.* 1952
1694	*Bedford* (13th), John Robert Russell, *b.* 1917, *s.* 1953, *m.*	Marquess of Tavistock, *b.* 1940
1663 S.*	*Buccleuch* (9th) & *Queensberry* (11th) (1684), Walter Francis John Montagu Douglas Scott, KT, VRD (8th *Engl. Earl, Doncaster,* 1662), *b.* 1923, *s.* 1973, *m.*	Earl of Dalkeith, *b.* 1954
1694	*Devonshire* (11th), Andrew Robert Buxton Cavendish, KG, MC, PC, *b.* 1920, *s.* 1950, *m.*	Marquess of Hartington, CBE, *b.* 1944
1900	*Fife* (3rd), James George Alexander Bannerman Carnegie (12th *Scott. Earl, Southesk,* 1633, *s.* 1992), *b.* 1929, *s.* 1959. (*see* page 129)	Earl of Southesk, *b.* 1961
1675	*Grafton* (11th), Hugh Denis Charles FitzRoy, KG, *b.* 1919, *s.* 1970, *m.*	Earl of Euston, *b.* 1947
1643 S.*	*Hamilton* (15th) & *Brandon* (12th) (*Brit.* 1711), Angus Alan Douglas Douglas-Hamilton (*Premier Peer of Scotland*), *b.* 1938, *s.* 1973	Marquess of Douglas and Clydesdale, *b.* 1978
1766 I.*	*Leinster* (8th), Gerald FitzGerald (*Premier Duke and Marquess of Ireland;* 8th *Brit. Visct., Leinster,* 1747), *b.* 1914, *s.* 1976, *m.*	Marquess of Kildare, *b.* 1948
1719	*Manchester* (12th), Angus Charles Drogo Montagu, *b.* 1938, *s.* 1985, *m.*	Viscount Mandeville, *b.* 1962
1702	*Marlborough* (11th), John George Vanderbilt Henry Spencer-Churchill, *b.* 1926, *s.* 1972, *m.*	Marquess of Blandford, *b.* 1955
1707 S.*	*Montrose* (8th), James Graham (6th *Brit. Earl, Graham,* 1722), *b.* 1935, *s.* 1992, *m.*	Marquess of Graham, *b.* 1973
1483	*Norfolk* (17th), Miles Francis Stapleton Fitzalan-Howard, KG, GCVO, CB, CBE, MC (*Premier Duke;* 12th *Engl. Baron Beaumont,* 1309, *s.* 1971; 4th *UK Baron Howard of Glossop,* 1869, *s.* 1972), *b.* 1915, *s.* 1975, *m.* Earl Marshal	Earl of Arundel and Surrey, *b.* 1956
1766	*Northumberland* (12th), Ralph George Algernon Percy, *b.* 1956, *s.* 1995, *m.*	Earl Percy, *b.* 1984
1675	*Richmond* (10th) & *Gordon* (5th) (*UK* 1876), Charles Henry Gordon Lennox (10th *Scott. Duke, Lennox,* 1675), *b.* 1929, *s.* 1989, *m.*	Earl of March and Kinrara, *b.* 1955

Created	Title, order of succession, name, etc.	Heir
1707 s.*	*Roxburghe* (10th), Guy David Innes-Ker (5th *UK Earl, Innes,* 1837), *b.* 1954, *s.* 1974, *m.* (*Premier Baronet of Scotland*)	Marquess of Bowmont and Cessford, *b.* 1981
1703	*Rutland* (10th), Charles John Robert Manners, CBE, *b.* 1919, *s.* 1940, *m.*	Marquess of Granby, *b.* 1959
1684	*St Albans* (14th), Murray de Vere Beauclerk, *b.* 1939, *s.* 1988, *m.*	Earl of Burford, *b.* 1965
1547	*Somerset* (19th), John Michael Edward Seymour, *b.* 1952, *s.* 1984, *m.*	Lord Seymour, *b.* 1982
1833	*Sutherland* (6th), John Sutherland Egerton, TD (5th *UK Earl, Ellesmere,* 1846, *s.* 1944), *b.* 1915, *s.* 1963, *m.*	Francis R. E., *b.* 1940
1814	*Wellington* (8th), Arthur Valerian Wellesley, KG, LVO, OBE, MC (9th *Irish Earl, Mornington,* 1760), *b.* 1915, *s.* 1972, *m.*	Marquess of Douro, *b.* 1945
1874	*Westminster* (6th), Gerald Cavendish Grosvenor, OBE, *b.* 1951, *s.* 1979, *m.*	Earl Grosvenor, *b.* 1991

MARQUESSES

Coronet, Four strawberry leaves alternating with four silver balls
Style, The Most Hon. the Marquess (of) __. In Scotland the spelling 'Marquis' is preferred for pre-Union creations
Wife's style, The Most Hon. the Marchioness (of) __
Eldest son's style, Takes his father's second title as a courtesy title
Younger sons' style, 'Lord' before forename and family name
Daughters' style, 'Lady' before forename and family name
For forms of address, *see* page 136

Created	Title, order of succession, name, etc.	Heir
1916	*Aberdeen and Temair* (6th), Alastair Ninian John Gordon (12th *Scott. Earl, Aberdeen,* 1682), *b.* 1920, *s.* 1984, *m.*	Earl of Haddo, *b.* 1955
1876	*Abergavenny* (5th), John Henry Guy Nevill, KG, OBE, *b.* 1914, *s.* 1954, *m.*	Christopher G. C. N., *b.* 1955
1821	*Ailesbury* (8th), Michael Sidney Cedric Brudenell-Bruce, *b.* 1926, *s.* 1974	Earl of Cardigan, *b.* 1952
1831	*Ailsa* (8th), Archibald Angus Charles Kennedy (20th *Scott. Earl, Cassillis,* 1509), *b.* 1956, *s.* 1994	Lord David Kennedy, *b.* 1958
1815	*Anglesey* (7th), George Charles Henry Victor Paget, *b.* 1922, *s.* 1947, *m.*	Earl of Uxbridge, *b.* 1950
1789	*Bath* (7th), Alexander George Thynn, *b.* 1932, *s.* 1992, *m.*	Viscount Weymouth, *b.* 1974
1826	*Bristol* (7th), (Frederick William) John Augustus Hervey, *b.* 1954, *s.* 1985	Lord F. W. C. Nicholas W. H., *b.* 1961
1796	*Bute* (7th), John Colum Crichton-Stuart (12th *Scott. Earl, Dumfries,* 1633), *b.* 1958, *s.* 1993, *m.*	Earl of Dumfries, *b.* 1989
1812	°*Camden* (6th), David George Edward Henry Pratt, *b.* 1930, *s.* 1983	Earl of Brecknock, *b.* 1965
1815	*Cholmondeley* (7th), David George Philip Cholmondeley (11th *Irish Viscount, Cholmondeley,* 1661), *b.* 1960, *s.* 1990. *Lord Great Chamberlain*	Charles G. C., *b.* 1959
1816 I.*	°*Conyngham* (7th), Frederick William Henry Francis Conyngham (7th *UK Baron, Minster,* 1821), *b.* 1924, *s.* 1974, *m.*	Earl of Mount Charles, *b.* 1951
1791 I.*	*Donegall* (7th), Dermot Richard Claud Chichester, LVO (7th *Brit. Baron, Fisherwick,* 1790, 6th *Brit. Baron, Templemore,* 1831, *s.* 1953), *b.* 1916, *s.* 1975, *m.*	Earl of Belfast, *b.* 1952
1789 I.*	*Downshire* (8th), (Arthur) Robin Ian Hill (8th *Brit. Earl, Hillsborough,* 1772), *b.* 1929, *s.* 1989, *m.*	Earl of Hillsborough, *b.* 1959
1801 I.*	*Ely* (8th) Charles John Tottenham (8th *UK Baron, Loftus,* 1801), *b.* 1913, *s.* 1969, *m.*	Viscount Loftus, *b.* 1943
1801	*Exeter* (8th), (William) Michael Anthony Cecil, *b.* 1935, *s.* 1988, *m.*	Lord Burghley, *b.* 1970
1800 I.*	*Headfort* (6th), Thomas Geoffrey Charles Michael Taylour (4th *UK Baron, Kenlis,* 1831), *b.* 1932, *s.* 1960, *m.*	Earl of Bective, *b.* 1959
1793	*Hertford* (8th), Hugh Edward Conway Seymour (9th *Irish Baron, Conway,* 1712), *b.* 1930, *s.* 1940, *m.*	Earl of Yarmouth, *b.* 1958
1599 s.*	*Huntly* (13th), Granville Charles Gomer Gordon (*Premier Marquess of Scotland*) (5th *UK Baron, Meldrum,* 1815), *b.* 1944, *s.* 1987, *m.*	Earl of Aboyne, *b.* 1973
1784	*Lansdowne* (8th), George John Charles Mercer Nairne Petty-Fitzmaurice, PC (8th *Irish Earl, Kerry,* 1723), *b.* 1912, *s.* 1944, *m.*	Earl of Shelburne, *b.* 1941
1902	*Linlithgow* (4th), Adrian John Charles Hope (10th *Scott. Earl, Hopetoun,* 1703), *b.* 1946, *s.* 1987, *m.*	Earl of Hopetoun, *b.* 1969
1816 I.*	*Londonderry* (9th), Alexander Charles Robert Vane-Tempest-Stewart (6th *UK Earl, Vane,* 1823), *b.* 1937, *s.* 1955, *m.*	Viscount Castlereagh, *b.* 1972
1701 s.*	*Lothian* (12th), Peter Francis Walter Kerr, KCVO (6th *UK Baron, Kerr,* 1821), *b.* 1922, *s.* 1940, *m.*	Earl of Ancram, PC, MP, *b.* 1945

Created	Title, order of succession, name, etc.	Heir
1917	*Milford Haven* (4th), George Ivar Louis Mountbatten, *b.* 1961, *s.* 1970, *m.*	Earl of Medina, *b.* 1991
1838	*Normanby* (5th), Constantine Edmund Walter Phipps, (9th *Irish Baron, Mulgrave,* 1767), *b.* 1954, *s.* 1994, *m.*	Lord Justin, C. P., *b.* 1958
1812	*Northampton* (7th), Spencer Douglas David Compton, *b.* 1946, *s.* 1978, *m.*	Earl Compton, *b.* 1973
1825 I.*	*Ormonde* (7th), James Hubert Theobald Charles Butler, MBE (7th *UK Baron, Ormonde,* 1821), *b.* 1899, *s.* 1971, *w.*	None to Marquessate. To Earldoms of Ormonde and Ossory, Viscount Mountgarret, *b.* 1936 (*see* page 147)
1682 S.	*Queensberry* (12th), David Harrington Angus Douglas, *b.* 1929, *s.* 1954	Viscount Drumlanrig, *b.* 1967
1926	*Reading* (4th), Simon Charles Henry Rufus Isaacs, *b.* 1942, *s.* 1980, *m.*	Viscount Erleigh, *b.* 1986
1789	*Salisbury* (6th), Robert Edward Peter Cecil, *b.* 1916, *s.* 1972, *m.*	Viscount Cranborne, PC, *b.* 1946 (*see also* Baron Cecil, page 150)
1800 I.*	*Sligo* (11th), Jeremy Ulick Browne (11th *UK Baron, Monteagle,* 1806), *b.* 1939, *s.* 1991, *m.*	Sebastian U. B., *b.* 1964
1787	°*Townshend* (7th), George John Patrick Dominic Townshend, *b.* 1916, *s.* 1921, *w.*	Viscount Raynham, *b.* 1945
1694 S.*	*Tweeddale* (13th), Edward Douglas John Hay (4th *UK Baron, Tweeddale,* 1881), *b.* 1947, *s.* 1979	Lord Charles D. M. H., *b.* 1947
1789 I.*	*Waterford* (8th), John Hubert de la Poer Beresford (8th *Brit. Baron, Tyrone,* 1786), *b.* 1933, *s.* 1934, *m.*	Earl of Tyrone, *b.* 1958
1551	*Winchester* (18th), Nigel George Paulet (*Premier Marquess of England*), *b.* 1941, *s.* 1968, *m.*	Earl of Wiltshire, *b.* 1969
1892	*Zetland* (4th), Lawrence Mark Dundas (6th *UK Earl of Zetland,* 1838, 7th *Brit. Baron Dundas,* 1794), *b.* 1937, *s.* 1989, *m.*	Earl of Ronaldshay, *b.* 1965

EARLS

Coronet, Eight silver balls on stalks alternating with eight gold strawberry leaves
Style, The Right Hon. the Earl (of) __
Wife's style, The Right Hon. the Countess (of) __
Eldest son's style, Takes his father's second title as a courtesy title
Younger sons' style, 'The Hon.' before forename and family name
Daughters' style, 'Lady' before forename and family name
For forms of address, *see* page 136

Created	Title, order of succession, name, etc.	Heir
1639 S.	*Airlie* (13th), David George Coke Patrick Ogilvy, KT, GCVO, PC, *b.* 1926, *s.* 1968, *m. Lord Chamberlain (until end* 1997)	Lord Ogilvy, *b.* 1958
1696	*Albemarle* (10th), Rufus Arnold Alexis Keppel, *b.* 1965, *s.* 1979	Crispian W. J. K., *b.* 1948
1952	°*Alexander of Tunis* (2nd), Shane William Desmond Alexander, *b.* 1935, *s.* 1969, *m.*	Hon. Brian J. A., *b.* 1939
1662 S.	*Annandale and Hartfell* (11th), Patrick Andrew Wentworth Hope Johnstone, *b.* 1941, *claim established* 1985, *m.*	Lord Johnstone, *b.* 1971
1789 I.	°*Annesley* (10th), Patrick Annesley, *b.* 1924, *s.* 1979, *m.*	Hon. Philip H. A., *b.* 1927
1785 I.	*Antrim* (9th), Alexander Randal Mark McDonnell, *b.* 1935, *s.* 1977, *m.* (*Viscount Dunluce*)	Hon. Randal A. St J. M., *b.* 1967
1762 I.*	*Arran* (9th), Arthur Desmond Colquhoun Gore (5th *UK Baron, Sudley,* 1884), *b.* 1938, *s.* 1983, *m.*	Paul A. G., CMG, CVO, *b.* 1921
1955	°*Attlee* (3rd), John Richard Attlee, *b.* 1956, *s.* 1991, *m.*	None
1714	*Aylesford* (11th), Charles Ian Finch-Knightley, *b.* 1918, *s.* 1958, *w.*	Lord Guernsey, *b.* 1947
1937	°*Baldwin of Bewdley* (4th), Edward Alfred Alexander Baldwin, *b.* 1938, *s.* 1976, *m.*	Viscount Corvedale, *b.* 1973
1922	*Balfour* (4th), Gerald Arthur James Balfour, *b.* 1925, *s.* 1968, *m.*	Eustace A. G. B., *b.* 1921
1772	°*Bathurst* (8th), Henry Allen John Bathurst, *b.* 1927, *s.* 1943, *m.*	Lord Apsley, *b.* 1961
1919	°*Beatty* (3rd), David Beatty, *b.* 1946, *s.* 1972, *m.*	Viscount Borodale, *b.* 1973
1797 I.	*Belmore* (8th), John Armar Lowry-Corry, *b.* 1951, *s.* 1960, *m.*	Viscount Corry, *b.* 1985
1739 I.*	*Bessborough* (11th), Arthur Mountifort Longfield Ponsonby (8th *UK Baron, Duncannon,* 1834), *b.* 1912, *s.* 1993, *m.*	Hon. Myles F. L. P., *b.* 1941
1815	*Bradford* (7th), Richard Thomas Orlando Bridgeman, *b.* 1947, *s.* 1981, *m.*	Viscount Newport, *b.* 1980
1677 S.	*Breadalbane and Holland* (10th), John Romer Boreland Campbell, *b.* 1919, *s.* 1959	None
1469 S.*	*Buchan* (17th), Malcolm Harry Erskine, (8th *UK Baron, Erskine* 1806), *b.* 1930, *s.* 1984, *m.*	Lord Cardross, *b.* 1960

Created	Title, order of succession, name, etc.	Heir
1746	Buckinghamshire (10th), (George) Miles Hobart-Hampden, b. 1944, s. 1983, m.	Sir John Hobart, Bt., b. 1945
1800	°Cadogan (8th), Charles Gerald John Cadogan, b. 1937, s. 1997, m.	Viscount Chelsea, b. 1966
1878	°Cairns (6th), Simon Dallas Cairns, CBE, b. 1939, s. 1989, m.	Viscount Garmoyle, b. 1965
1455 s.	Caithness (20th), Malcolm Ian Sinclair, PC, b. 1948, s. 1965, w.	Lord Berriedale, b. 1981
1800 I.	Caledon (7th), Nicholas James Alexander, b. 1955, s. 1980, m.	Viscount Alexander, b. 1990
1661	Carlisle (13th), George William Beaumont Howard (13th Scott. Baron, Ruthven of Freeland, 1651), b. 1949, s. 1994	Hon. Philip C. W. H., b. 1963
1793	Carnarvon (7th), Henry George Reginald Molyneux Herbert, KCVO, KBE, b. 1924, s. 1987, m.	Lord Porchester, b. 1956
1748 I.*	Carrick (10th), David James Theobald Somerset Butler (4th UK Baron, Butler, 1912), b. 1953, s. 1992, m.	Viscount Ikerrin, b. 1975
1800 I.	°Castle Stewart (8th), Arthur Patrick Avondale Stuart, b. 1928, s. 1961, m.	Viscount Stuart, b. 1953
1814	°Cathcart (6th), Alan Cathcart, CB, DSO, MC (15th Scott. Baron, Cathcart, 1447), b. 1919, s. 1927, m.	Lord Greenock, b. 1952
1647 I.	Cavan. The 12th Earl died in 1988. Heir had not established his claim to the title at the time of going to press	Roger C. Lambart, b. 1944
1827	°Cawdor (7th), Colin Robert Vaughan Campbell, b. 1962, s. 1993, m.	Hon. Frederick W. C., b. 1965
1801	Chichester (9th), John Nicholas Pelham, b. 1944, s. 1944, m.	Richard A. H. P., b. 1952
1803 I.*	Clancarty (9th), Nicholas Power Richard Le Poer Trench (8th UK Visct., Clancarty, 1823), b. 1952, s. 1995	None
1776 I.*	Clanwilliam (7th), John Herbert Meade (5th UK Baron Clanwilliam, 1828), b. 1919, s. 1989, m.	Lord Gillford, b. 1960
1776	Clarendon (7th), George Frederick Laurence Hyde Villiers, b. 1933, s. 1955, m.	Lord Hyde, b. 1976
1620 I.*	Cork (14th) & Orrery (14th) (I. 1660), John William Boyle, DSC (10th Brit. Baron, Boyle of Marston, 1711), b. 1916, s. 1995, m.	Hon. John R. B., b. 1945
1850	Cottenham (8th), Kenelm Charles Everard Digby Pepys, b. 1948, s. 1968, m.	Viscount Crowhurst, b. 1983
1762 I.*	Courtown (9th), James Patrick Montagu Burgoyne Winthrop Stopford (8th Brit. Baron, Saltersford, 1796), b. 1954, s. 1975, m.	Viscount Stopford, b. 1988
1697	Coventry (11th), George William Coventry, b. 1934, s. 1940, m.	Viscount Deerhurst, b. 1957
1857	°Cowley (7th), Garret Graham Wellesley, b. 1934, s. 1975, m.	Viscount Dangan, b. 1965
1892	Cranbrook (5th), Gathorne Gathorne-Hardy, b. 1933, s. 1978, m.	Lord Medway, b. 1968
1801	Craven (9th), Benjamin Robert Joseph Craven, b. 1989, s. 1990, M.	Rupert J. E. C., b. 1926
1398 s.*	Crawford (29th) & Balcarres (12th) (s. 1651), Robert Alexander Lindsay, KT, PC (Premier Earl on Union Roll, 5th UK Baron, Wigan, 1826, and Baron Balniel (life peerage)), 1974, b. 1927, s 1975, m.	Lord Balniel, b. 1958
1861	Cromartie (5th), John Ruaridh Blunt Grant Mackenzie, b. 1948, s. 1989, m.	Viscount Tarbat, b. 1987
1901	Cromer (4th), Evelyn Rowland Esmond Baring, b. 1946, s. 1991, m.	Viscount Errington, b 1994
1633 s.*	Dalhousie (16th), Simon Ramsay, KT, GCVO, GBE, MC (4th UK Baron, Ramsay, 1875), b. 1914, s. 1950, w.	Lord Ramsay, b. 1948
1725 I.*	Darnley (11th), Adam Ivo Stuart Bligh (20th Engl. Baron, Clifton of Leighton Bromswold, 1608), b. 1941, s. 1980, m.	Lord Clifton, b. 1968
1711	Dartmouth (9th), Gerald Humphry Legge, b. 1924, s. 1962, m.	Viscount Lewisham, b. 1949
1761	°De La Warr (11th), William Herbrand Sackville, b. 1948, s. 1988, m.	Lord Buckhurst, b. 1979
1622	Denbigh (12th) & Desmond (11th) (I. 1622), Alexander Stephen Rudolph Feilding, b. 1970, s. 1995, m.	William D. F, b. 1939
1485	Derby (19th), Edward Richard William Stanley, b. 1962, s. 1994, m.	Hon. Peter H. C. S, b. 1964
1553	Devon (17th), Charles Christopher Courtenay, b. 1916, s. 1935, m.	Lord Courtenay, b. 1942
1800 I.*	Donoughmore (8th), Richard Michael John Hely-Hutchinson (8th UK Visct., Hutchinson, 1821), b. 1927, s. 1981, m.	Viscount Suirdale, b. 1952
1661 I.*	Drogheda (12th), Henry Dermot Ponsonby Moore (3rd UK Baron, Moore, 1954), b. 1937, s. 1989, m.	Viscount Moore, b. 1983
1837	Ducie (7th), David Leslie Moreton, b. 1951, s. 1991, m.	Lord Moreton, b. 1981
1860	Dudley (4th), William Humble David Ward, b. 1920, s. 1969, m.	Viscount Ednam, b. 1947
1660 s.*	Dundee (12th), Alexander Henry Scrymgeour (2nd UK Baron, Glassary, 1954), b. 1949, s. 1983, m.	Lord Scrymgeour, b. 1982
1669 s.	Dundonald (15th), Iain Alexander Douglas Blair Cochrane, b. 1961, s. 1986, m.	Lord Cochrane, b. 1991
1686 s.	Dunmore (12th), Malcolm Kenneth Murray, b. 1946, s. 1995, m.	Hon. Geoffrey C. M., b. 1949
1822 I.	Dunraven and Mount-Earl (7th), Thady Windham Thomas Wyndham-Quin, b. 1939, s. 1965, m.	None
1833	Durham. Disclaimed for life 1970 (Antony Claud Frederick Lambton, b. 1922, s. 1970, m.)	Hon. Edward R. L. (Baron Durham), b. 1961
1837	Effingham (7th), David Mowbray Algernon Howard (17th Engl. Baron, Howard of Effingham, 1554), b. 1939, s. 1996, m.	Lord Howard of Effingham, b. 1971

Created	Title, order of succession, name, etc.	Heir
1507 s.*	*Eglinton* (18th) & *Winton* (9th) (1600), Archibald George Montgomerie (6th *UK Earl, Winton*, 1859), *b.* 1939, *s.* 1966, *m.*	Lord Montgomerie, *b.* 1966
1733 I.*	*Egmont* (11th), Frederick George Moore Perceval (9th *Brit. Baron, Lovel & Holland*, 1762), *b.* 1914, *s.* 1932, *m.*	Viscount Perceval, *b.* 1934
1821	*Eldon* (5th), John Joseph Nicholas Scott, *b.* 1937, *s.* 1976, *m.*	Viscount Encombe, *b.* 1962
1633 s.*	*Elgin* (11th), & *Kincardine* (15th) (s. 1647), Andrew Douglas Alexander Thomas Bruce (4th *UK Baron, Elgin*, 1849), KT, *b.* 1924, *s.* 1968, *m.*	Lord Bruce, *b.* 1961
1789 I.*	*Enniskillen* (7th), Andrew John Galbraith Cole (5th *UK Baron, Grinstead*, 1815) *b.* 1942, *s.* 1989, *m.*	Arthur G. C., *b.* 1920
1789 I.*	*Erne* (6th), Henry George Victor John Crichton (3rd *UK Baron, Fermanagh*, 1876), *b.* 1937, *s.* 1940, *m.*	Viscount Crichton, *b.* 1971
1452 s.	*Erroll* (24th), Merlin Sereld Victor Gilbert Hay, *b.* 1948, *s.* 1978, *m.* *Hereditary Lord High Constable and Knight Marischal of Scotland*	Lord Hay, *b.* 1984
1661	*Essex* (10th), Robert Edward de Vere Capell, *b.* 1920, *s.* 1981, *m.*	Viscount Malden, *b.* 1944
1711	°*Ferrers* (13th), Robert Washington Shirley, PC, *b.* 1929, *s.* 1954, *m.*	Viscount Tamworth, *b.* 1952
1789	°*Fortescue* (8th), Charles Hugh Richard Fortescue, *b.* 1951, *s.* 1993, *m.*	Hon. Martin D. F., *b.* 1924
1841	*Gainsborough* (5th), Anthony Gerard Edward Noel, *b.* 1923, *s.* 1927, *m.*	Viscount Campden, *b.* 1950
1623 s.*	*Galloway* (13th), Randolph Keith Reginald Stewart (6th *Brit. Baron, Stewart of Garlies*, 1796), *b.* 1928, *s.* 1978, *m.*	Andrew C. S., *b.* 1949
1703 s.*	*Glasgow* (10th), Patrick Robin Archibald Boyle (4th *UK Baron, Fairlie*, 1897), *b.* 1939, *s.* 1984, *m.*	Viscount of Kelburn, *b.* 1978
1806 I.*	*Gosford* (7th), Charles David Nicholas Alexander John Sparrow Acheson (5th *UK Baron, Worlingham*, 1835), *b.* 1942, *s.* 1966, *m.*	Hon. Patrick B. V. M. A., *b.* 1915
1945	*Gowrie* (2nd), Alexander Patric Greysteil Hore-Ruthven, PC (3rd *UK Baron, Ruthven of Gowrie*, 1919), *b.* 1939, *s.* 1955, *m.*	Viscount Ruthven of Canberra, *b.* 1964
1684 I.*	*Granard* (10th), Peter Arthur Edward Hastings Forbes, (5th *UK Baron, Granard*, 1806), *b.* 1957, *s.* 1992, *m.*	Viscount Forbes, *b.* 1981
1833	°*Granville* (6th), Granville George Fergus Leveson-Gower, *b.* 1959, *s.* 1996, *m.*	Hon. Niall J. L.-G., *b.* 1963
1806	°*Grey* (6th), Richard Fleming George Charles Grey, *b.* 1939, *s.* 1963, *m.*	Philip K. G., *b.* 1940
1752	*Guilford* (9th), Edward Francis North, *b.* 1933, *s.* 1949, *w.*	Lord North, *b.* 1971
1619 s.	*Haddington* (13th), John George Baillie-Hamilton, *b.* 1941, *s.* 1986, *m.*	Lord Binning, *b.* 1985
1919	°*Haig* (2nd), George Alexander Eugene Douglas Haig, OBE, *b.* 1918, *s.* 1928, *m.*	Viscount Dawick, *b.* 1961
1944	*Halifax* (3rd), Charles Edward Peter Neil Wood (5th *UK Visct., Halifax*, 1866), *b.* 1944, *s.* 1980, *m.*	Lord Irwin, *b.* 1977
1898	*Halsbury* (3rd), John Anthony Hardinge Giffard, FRS, FENG., *b.* 1908, *s.* 1943, *w.*	Adam E. G., *b.* 1934
1754	*Hardwicke* (10th), Joseph Philip Sebastian Yorke, *b.* 1971, *s.* 1974	Richard C. J. Y., *b.* 1916
1812	*Harewood* (7th), George Henry Hubert Lascelles, KBE, *b.* 1923, *s.* 1947, *m.* (*see also* page 128)	Viscount Lascelles, *b.* 1950
1742	*Harrington* (11th), William Henry Leicester Stanhope (8th *Brit. Visct., Stanhope of Mahon*, 1717), *b.* 1922, *s.* 1929, *m.*	Viscount Petersham, *b.* 1945
1809	*Harrowby* (7th), Dudley Danvers Granville Coutts Ryder, TD, *b.* 1922, *s.* 1987, *m.*	Viscount Sandon, *b.* 1951
1605 s.	*Home* (15th) David Alexander Cospatrick Douglas-Home, CVO, *b.* 1943, *s.* 1995, *m.*	Lord Dunglass, *b.* 1987
1821	°*Howe* (7th), Frederick Richard Penn Curzon, *b.* 1951, *s.* 1984, *m.*	Viscount Curzon, *b.* 1994
1529	*Huntingdon* (16th), William Edward Robin Hood Hastings Bass, *b.* 1948, *s.* 1990, *m.*	Hon. Simon A. R. H. H. B., *b.* 1950
1885	*Iddesleigh* (4th), Stafford Henry Northcote, *b.* 1932, *s.* 1970, *m.*	Viscount St Cyres, *b.* 1957
1756	*Ilchester* (9th), Maurice Vivian de Touffreville Fox-Strangways, *b.* 1920, *s.* 1970, *m.*	Hon. Raymond G. F.-S., *b.* 1921
1929	*Inchcape* (4th), (Kenneth) Peter (Lyle) Mackay, *b.* 1943, *s.* 1994, *m.*	Viscount Glenapp, *b.* 1979
1919	*Iveagh* (4th), Arthur Edward Rory Guinness, *b.* 1969, *s.* 1992	Hon. Rory M. B. G., *b.* 1974
1925	°*Jellicoe* (2nd), George Patrick John Rushworth Jellicoe, KBE, DSO, MC, PC, FRS, *b.* 1918, *s.* 1935, *m.*	Viscount Brocas, *b.* 1950
1697	*Jersey* (9th), George Francis Child Villiers (12th *Irish Visct., Grandison*, 1620), *b.* 1910, *s.* 1923, *m.*	Viscount Villiers, *b.* 1948
1822 I.	*Kilmorey* (6th), Richard Francis Needham, Kt., PC, *b.* 1942, *s.* 1977, *m.*	Viscount Newry and Morne, *b.* 1966
1866	*Kimberley* (4th), John Wodehouse, *b.* 1924, *s.* 1941, *m.*	Lord Wodehouse, *b.* 1951
1768 I.	*Kingston* (11th), Barclay Robert Edwin King-Tenison, *b.* 1943, *s.* 1948, *m.*	Viscount Kingsborough, *b.* 1969
1633 s.*	*Kinnoull* (15th), Arthur William George Patrick Hay (9th *Brit. Baron, Hay of Pedwardine*, 1711), *b.* 1935, *s.* 1938, *m.*	Viscount Dupplin, *b.* 1962
1677 s.*	*Kintore* (13th), Michael Canning William John Keith (3rd *UK Visct., Stonehaven*, 1938), *b.* 1939, *s.* 1989, *m.*	Lord Inverurie, *b.* 1976
1914	°*Kitchener of Khartoum* (3rd), Henry Herbert Kitchener, TD, *b.* 1919, *s.* 1937	None

Created	Title, order of succession, name, etc.	Heir
1756 I.	*Lanesborough* (9th), Denis Anthony Brian Butler, TD, *b.* 1918, *s.* 1950, *m.*	None
1624 s.	*Lauderdale* (17th), Patrick Francis Maitland, *b.* 1911, *s.* 1968, *m.*	Viscount Maitland, *b.* 1937
1837	*Leicester* (7th), Edward Douglas Coke, *b.* 1936, *s.* 1994, *m.*	Viscount Coke, *b.* 1965
1641 s.	*Leven* (14th) & *Melville* (13th) (s. 1690), Alexander Robert Leslie Melville, *b.* 1924, *s.* 1947, *m.*	Lord Balgonie, *b.* 1954
1831	*Lichfield* (5th), Thomas Patrick John Anson, *b.* 1939, *s.* 1960	Viscount Anson, *b.* 1978
1803 I.*	*Limerick* (6th), Patrick Edmund Pery, KBE (6th *UK Baron, Foxford,* 1815), *b.* 1930, *s.* 1967, *m.*	Viscount Glentworth, *b.* 1963
1572	*Lincoln* (18th), Edward Horace Fiennes-Clinton, *b.* 1913, *s.* 1988, *m.*	Hon. Edward G. *F.-C.*, *b.* 1943
1633 s.	*Lindsay* (16th), James Randolph Lindesay-Bethune, *b.* 1955, *s.* 1989, *m.*	Viscount Garnock, *b.* 1990
1626	*Lindsey* (14th) *and Abingdon* (9th) (1682), Richard Henry Rupert Bertie, *b.* 1931, *s.* 1963, *m.*	Lord Norreys, *b.* 1958
1776 I.	*Lisburne* (8th), John David Malet Vaughan, *b.* 1918, *s.* 1965, *m.*	Viscount Vaughan, *b.* 1945
1822 I.*	*Listowel* (6th), Francis Michael Hare (4th *UK Baron, Hare,* 1869), *b.* 1964, *s.* 1997, *m.*	Hon. Timothy P. *H.*, *b.* 1966
1905	*Liverpool* (5th), Edward Peter Bertram Savile Foljambe, *b.* 1944, *s.* 1969, *m.*	Viscount Hawkesbury, *b.* 1972
1945	°*Lloyd George of Dwyfor* (3rd), Owen Lloyd George, *b.* 1924, *s.* 1968, *m.*	Viscount Gwynedd, *b.* 1951
1785 I.*	*Longford* (7th), Francis Aungier Pakenham, KG, PC (6th *UK Baron, Silchester,* 1821; 1st *UK Baron, Pakenham,* 1945), *b.* 1905, *s.* 1961, *m.*	Thomas F. D. *P.*, *b.* 1933
1807	*Lonsdale* (7th), James Hugh William Lowther, *b.* 1922, *s.* 1953, *m.*	Viscount Lowther, *b.* 1949
1838	*Lovelace* (5th), Peter Axel William Locke King (12th *Brit. Baron, King,* 1725), *b.* 1951, *s.* 1964, *m.*	None
1795 I.*	*Lucan* (7th), Richard John Bingham (3rd *UK Baron, Bingham,* 1934), *b.* 1934, *s.* 1964, *m.*	Lord Bingham, *b.* 1967
1880	*Lytton* (5th), John Peter Michael Scawen Lytton (18th *Engl. Baron, Wentworth,* 1529), *b.* 1950, *s.* 1985, *m.*	Viscount Knebworth, *b.* 1989
1721	*Macclesfield* (9th), Richard Timothy George Mansfield Parker, *b.* 1943, *s.* 1992, *m.*	Hon. J. David G. *P.*, *b.* 1945
1800	*Malmesbury* (6th), William James Harris, TD, *b.* 1907, *s.* 1950, *w.*	Viscount FitzHarris, *b.* 1946
1776 & 1792	*Mansfield and Mansfield* (8th), William David Mungo James Murray (14th *Scott. Visct., Stormont,* 1621), *b.* 1930, *s.* 1971, *m.*	Viscount Stormont, *b.* 1956
1565 s.	*Mar* (14th) & *Kellie* (16th) (s. 1616), James Thorne Erskine, *b.* 1949, *s.* 1994, *m.*	Hon. Alexander D. *E.*, *b.* 1952
1785 I.	*Mayo* (10th), Terence Patrick Bourke, *b.* 1929, *s.* 1962	Lord Naas, *b.* 1953
1627 I.*	*Meath* (14th), Anthony Windham Normand Brabazon (5th *UK Baron, Chaworth,* 1831), *b.* 1910, *s.* 1949, *m.*	Lord Ardee, *b.* 1941
1766 I.	*Mexborough* (8th), John Christopher George Savile, *b.* 1931, *s.* 1980, *m.*	Viscount Pollington, *b.* 1959
1813	*Minto* (6th), Gilbert Edward George Lariston Elliot-Murray-Kynynmound, OBE, *b.* 1928, *s.* 1975, *m.*	Viscount Melgund, *b.* 1953
1562 s.*	*Moray* (20th) Douglas John Moray Stuart (12th *Brit. Baron, Stuart* of Castle Stuart, 1796), *b.* 1928, *s.* 1974, *m.*	Lord Doune, *b.* 1966
1815	*Morley* (6th), John St Aubyn Parker, *b.* 1923, *s.* 1962, *m.*	Viscount Boringdon, *b.* 1956
1458 s.	*Morton* (22nd), John Charles Sholto Douglas, *b.* 1927, *s.* 1976, *m.*	Lord Aberdour, *b.* 1952
1789	*Mount Edgcumbe* (8th), Robert Charles Edgcumbe, *b.* 1939, *s.* 1982	Piers V. *E.*, *b.* 1946
1831	*Munster* (7th), Anthony Charles FitzClarence, *b.* 1926, *s.* 1983, *m.*	None
1805	°*Nelson* (9th), Peter John Horatio Nelson, *b.* 1941, *s.* 1981, *m.*	Viscount Merton, *b.* 1971
1660 s.	*Newburgh* (12th), Don Filippo Giambattista Camillo Francesco Aldo Maria Rospigliosi, *b.* 1942, *s.* 1986, *m.*	Princess Donna Benedetta F. M. *R.*, *b.* 1974
1827 I.	*Norbury* (6th), Noel Terence Graham Toler, *b.* 1939, *s* 1955, *m.*	Viscount Glandine, *b.* 1967
1006 I.*	*Normanton* (6th), Shaun James Christian Welbore Ellis Agar (9th *Brit. Baron, Mendip,* 1794, 4th *UK Baron, Somerton,* 1873), *b.* 1945, *s.* 1967, *m.*	Viscount Somerton, *b.* 1982
1647 s.	*Northesk* (14th), David John MacRae Carnegie, *b.* 1954, *s.* 1994, *m.*	Lord Rosehill, *b.* 1980
1801	*Onslow* (7th), Michael William Coplestone Dillon Onslow, *b.* 1938, *s.* 1971, *m.*	Viscount Cranley, *b.* 1967
1696 s.	*Orkney* (8th), Cecil O'Bryen Fitz-Maurice, *b.* 1919, *s.* 1951, *w.*	O. Peter *St John*, *b.* 1938
1925	*Oxford and Asquith* (2nd), Julian Edward George Asquith, KCMG, *b.* 1916, *s.* 1928, *m.*	Viscount Asquith, OBE, *b.* 1952
1929	°*Peel* (3rd), William James Robert Peel (4th *UK Visct., Peel,* 1895), *b.* 1947, *s.* 1969, *m.*	Viscount Clanfield, *b.* 1976
1551	*Pembroke* (17th) & *Montgomery* (14th) (1605), Henry George Charles Alexander Herbert, *b.* 1939, *s.* 1969	Lord Herbert, *b.* 1978
1605 s.	*Perth* (17th), John David Drummond, PC, *b.* 1907, *s.* 1951, *w.*	Viscount Strathallan, *b.* 1935
1905	*Plymouth* (3rd), Other Robert Ivor Windsor-Clive (15th *Engl. Baron, Windsor,* 1529), *b.* 1923, *s.* 1943, *m.*	Viscount Windsor, *b.* 1951
1785 I.	*Portarlington* (7th), George Lionel Yuill Seymour Dawson-Damer, *b.* 1938, *s.* 1959, *m.*	Viscount Carlow, *b.* 1965

Created	Title, order of succession, name, etc.	Heir
1689	*Portland* (12th), Count Timothy Charles Robert Noel Bentinck, *b.* 1953, *s.* 1997, *m.*	Viscount Woodstock, *b.* 1984
1743	*Portsmouth* (10th), Quentin Gerard Carew Wallop, *b.* 1954, *s.* 1984, *m.*	Viscount Lymington, *b.* 1981
1804	*Powis* (8th), John George Herbert (9th *Irish Baron, Clive,* 1762), *b.* 1952, *s.* 1993, *m.*	Viscount Clive, *b.* 1979
1765	*Radnor* (8th), Jacob Pleydell-Bouverie, *b.* 1927, *s.* 1968, *m.*	Viscount Folkestone, *b.* 1955
1831 I.*	*Ranfurly* (7th), Gerald Françoys Needham Knox (8th *UK Baron, Ranfurly,* 1826), *b.* 1929, *s.* 1988, *m.*	Edward J. K., *b.* 1957
1771 I.	*Roden* (10th), Robert John Jocelyn, *b.* 1938, *s.* 1993, *m.*	Viscount Jocelyn, *b.* 1989
1801	*Romney* (7th), Michael Henry Marsham, *b.* 1910, *s.* 1975, *m.*	Julian C. M., *b.* 1948
1703 s.*	*Rosebery* (7th), Neil Archibald Primrose (3rd *UK Earl, Midlothian,* 1911), *b.* 1929, *s.* 1974, *m.*	Lord Dalmeny, *b.* 1967
1806 I.	*Rosse* (7th), William Brendan Parsons, *b.* 1936, *s.* 1979, *m.*	Lord Oxmantown, *b.* 1969
1801	*Rosslyn* (7th), Peter St Clair-Erskine, *b.* 1958, *s.* 1977, *m.*	Lord Loughborough, *b.* 1986
1457 s.	*Rothes* (21st), Ian Lionel Malcolm Leslie, *b.* 1932, *s.* 1975, *m.*	Lord Leslie, *b.* 1958
1861	°*Russell* (5th), Conrad Sebastian Robert Russell, FBA, *b.* 1937, *s.* 1987, *m.*	Viscount Amberley, *b.* 1968
1915	°*St Aldwyn* (3rd), Michael Henry Hicks Beach, *b.* 1950, *s.* 1992, *m.*	Hon. David S. H. B., *b.* 1955
1815	*St Germans* (10th), Peregrine Nicholas Eliot, *b.* 1941, *s.* 1988	Lord Eliot, *b.* 1966
1660	*Sandwich* (11th), John Edward Hollister Montagu, *b.* 1943, *s.* 1995, *m.*	Viscount Hinchingbrooke, *b.* 1969
1690	*Scarbrough* (12th), Richard Aldred Lumley (13th *Irish Visct., Lumley,* 1628), *b.* 1932, *s.* 1969, *m.*	Viscount Lumley, *b.* 1973
1701 s.	*Seafield* (13th), Ian Derek Francis Ogilvie-Grant, *b.* 1939, *s.* 1969, *m.*	Viscount Reidhaven, *b.* 1963
1882	*Selborne* (4th), John Roundell Palmer, KBE, FRS, *b.* 1940, *s.* 1971, *m.*	Viscount Wolmer, *b.* 1971
1646 s.	*Selkirk.* Disclaimed for life 1994. (*Rt. Hon. Lord James Douglas-Hamilton, b.* 1942, *succession decided in his favour* 1996, *m.*)	Hon. John A. D.-H., *b.* 1978
1672	*Shaftesbury* (10th), Anthony Ashley-Cooper, *b.* 1938, *s.* 1961, *m.*	Lord Ashley, *b.* 1977
1756 I.*	*Shannon* (9th), Richard Bentinck Boyle (8th *Brit. Baron, Carleton,* 1786), *b.* 1924, *s.* 1963	Viscount Boyle, *b.* 1960
1442	*Shrewsbury* & *Waterford* (22nd), (I. 1446), Charles Henry John Benedict Crofton Chetwynd Chetwynd-Talbot (*Premier Earl of England and Ireland;* 7th *Earl Talbot,* 1784), *b.* 1952, *s.* 1980, *m.*	Viscount Ingestre, *b.* 1978
1961	*Snowdon* (1st), Antony Charles Robert Armstrong-Jones, GCVO, *b.* 1930, *m.* (*see also* page 117)	Viscount Linley, *b.* 1961 (*see also* page 117)
1765	°*Spencer* (9th), Charles Edward Maurice Spencer, *b.* 1964, *s.* 1992, *m.*	Viscount Althorp, *b.* 1994
1703 s.*	*Stair* (14th), John David James Dalrymple (7th *UK Baron, Oxenfoord,* 1841), *b.* 1961, *s.* 1996	Hon. David H. D., *b.* 1963
1984	*Stockton* (2nd), Alexander Daniel Alan Macmillan, *b.* 1943, *s.* 1986, *m.*	Viscount Macmillan of Ovenden, *b.* 1974
1821	*Stradbroke* (6th), Robert Keith Rous, *b.* 1937, *s.* 1983, *m.*	Viscount Dunwich, *b.* 1961
1847	*Strafford* (8th), Thomas Edmund Byng, *b.* 1936, *s.* 1984, *m.*	Viscount Enfield, *b.* 1964
1606 s.*	*Strathmore* & *Kinghorne* (18th), Michael Fergus Bowes Lyon (16th *Scottish Earl, Strathmore,* 1677, & 18th *Kinghorne,* 1606; 5th *UK Earl, Strathmore* & *Kinghorne,* 1937), *b.* 1957, *s.* 1987, *m.*	Lord Glamis, *b.* 1986
1603	*Suffolk* (21st) & *Berkshire* (14th) (1626), Michael John James George Robert Howard, *b.* 1935, *s.* 1941, *m.*	Viscount Andover, *b.* 1974
1955	*Swinton* (2nd), David Yarburgh Cunliffe-Lister, *b.* 1937, *s.* 1972, *m.*	Hon. Nicholas J. C.-L., *b.* 1939
1714	*Tankerville* (10th), Peter Grey Bennet, *b.* 1956, *s.* 1980	Revd the Hon. George A. G. B., *b.* 1925
1822	°*Temple of Stowe* (8th), (Walter) Grenville Algernon Temple-Gore-Langton, *b.* 1924, *s.* 1988, *m.*	Lord Langton, *b.* 1955
1815	*Verulam* (7th), John Duncan Grimston (11th *Irish Visct., Grimston,* 1719; 16th *Scott. Baron, Forrester of Corstorphine,* 1633), *b.* 1951, *s.* 1973, *m.*	Viscount Grimston, *b.* 1978
1729	°*Waldegrave* (13th), James Sherbrooke Waldegrave, *b.* 1940, *s.* 1995, *m.*	Viscount Chewton, *b.* 1986
1759	*Warwick* (9th) & °*Brooke* (9th) (*Brit.* 1746), Guy David Greville, *b.* 1957, *s.* 1996, *m.*	Lord Brooke, *b.* 1982
1633 s.*	*Wemyss* (12th) & *March* (8th) (s. 1697), Francis David Charteris, KT (5th *UK Baron, Wemyss,* 1821), *b.* 1912, *s.* 1937, *m.*	Lord Neidpath, *b.* 1948
1621 I.	*Westmeath* (13th), William Anthony Nugent, *b.* 1928, *s.* 1971, *m.*	Hon. Sean C. W. N., *b.* 1965
1624	*Westmorland* (16th), Anthony David Francis Henry Fane, *b.* 1951, *s.* 1993, *m.*	Hon. Harry St C. F., *b.* 1953
1876	*Wharncliffe* (5th), Richard Alan Montagu Stuart Wortley, *b.* 1953, *s.* 1987, *m.*	Viscount Carlton, *b.* 1980
1801	*Wilton* (7th), Seymour William Arthur John Egerton, *b.* 1921, *s.* 1927, *m.*	Baron Ebury, *b.* 1934 (*see* page 151)
1628	*Winchilsea* (16th) & *Nottingham* (11th) (1681), Christopher Denys Stormont Finch Hatton, *b.* 1936, *s.* 1950, *m.*	Viscount Maidstone, *b.* 1967
1766 I.	°*Winterton* (8th), (Donald) David Turnour, *b.* 1943, *s.* 1991, *m.*	Robert C. T., *b.* 1950

Created	Title, order of succession, name, etc.	Heir
1956	*Woolton* (3rd), Simon Frederick Marquis, *b.* 1958, *s.* 1969, *m.*	None
1837	*Yarborough* (8th), Charles John Pelham, *b.* 1963, *s.* 1991, *m.*	Lord Worsley, *b.* 1990

COUNTESSES IN THEIR OWN RIGHT

Style, The Right Hon. the Countess (of) __
Husband, Untitled
Children's style, As for children of an Earl
For forms of address, *see* page 136

Created	Title, order of succession, name, etc.	Heir
1643 s.	*Dysart* (11th in line), Rosamund Agnes Greaves, *b.* 1914, *s.* 1975	Lady Katherine *Grant of Rothiemurchus*, *b.* 1918
1633 s.	*Loudoun* (13th in line), Barbara Huddleston Abney-Hastings, *b.* 1919, *s.* 1960, *m.*	Lord Mauchline, *b.* 1942
c.1115 s.	*Mar* (31st in line), Margaret of Mar (*Premier Earldom of Scotland*), *b.* 1940, *s.* 1975, *m.*	Mistress of Mar, *b.* 1963
1947	°*Mountbatten of Burma* (2nd in line), Patricia Edwina Victoria Knatchbull, CBE, *b.* 1924, *s.* 1979, *m.*	Lord Romsey, *b.* 1947 (*see also* page 149)
c.1235 s.	*Sutherland* (24th in line), Elizabeth Millicent Sutherland, *b.* 1921, *s.* 1963, *m.*	Lord Strathnaver, *b.* 1947

VISCOUNTS

Coronet, Sixteen silver balls
Style, The Right Hon. the Viscount __
Wife's style, The Right Hon. the Viscountess __
Children's style, 'The Hon.' before forename and family name
In Scotland, the heir apparent to a Viscount may be styled 'The Master of __ (title of peer)'
For forms of address, *see* page 136

Created	Title, order of succession, name, etc.	Heir
1945	*Addison* (4th), William Matthew Wand Addison, *b.* 1945, *s.* 1992, *m.*	Hon. Paul W. *A.*, *b.* 1973
1946	*Alanbrooke* (3rd), Alan Victor Harold Brooke, *b.* 1932, *s.* 1972	None
1919	*Allenby* (3rd), Lt.-Col. Michael Jaffray Hynman Allenby, *b.* 1931, *s.* 1984, *m.*	Hon. Henry J. H. *A.*, *b.* 1968
1911	*Allendale* (3rd), Wentworth Hubert Charles Beaumont, *b.* 1922, *s.* 1956	Hon. Wentworth P. I. *B.*, *b.* 1948
1642 s.	*of Arbuthnott* (16th), John Campbell Arbuthnott, KT, CBE, DSC, FRSE, *b.* 1924, *s.* 1966, *m.*	Master of Arbuthnott, *b.* 1950
1751 I.	*Ashbrook* (11th), Michael Llowarch Warburton Flower, *b.* 1935, *s.* 1995, *m.*	Hon. Rowland F. W. *F.*, *b.* 1975
1917	*Astor* (4th), William Waldorf Astor, *b.* 1951, *s.* 1966, *m.*	Hon. William W. *A.*, *b.* 1979
1781 I.	*Bangor* (8th), William Maxwell David Ward, *b.* 1948, *s.* 1993, *m.*	Hon. E. Nicholas *W.*, *b.* 1953
1925	*Bearsted* (5th), Nicholas Alan Samuel, *b.* 1950, *s.* 1996, *m.*	Hon. Harry R. *S.*, *b.* 1988
1963	*Blakenham* (2nd), Michael John Hare, *b.* 1938, *s.* 1982, *m.*	Hon. Caspar J. *H.*, *b.* 1972
1935	*Bledisloe* (3rd), Christopher Hiley Ludlow Bathurst, QC, *b.* 1934, *s.* 1979	Hon. Rupert E. L. *B.*, *b.* 1964
1712	*Bolingbroke* (7th) & *St John* (8th) (1716), Kenneth Oliver Musgrave St John, *b.* 1927, *s.* 1974	Hon. Henry F. *St J.*, *b.* 1957
1960	*Boyd of Merton* (2nd), Simon Donald Rupert Neville Lennox-Boyd, *b.* 1939, *s.* 1983, *m.*	Hon. Benjamin A. *L.-B.*, *b.* 1964
1717 I.*	*Boyne* (11th), Gustavus Michael Stucley Hamilton-Russell (5th UK *Baron, Brancepeth*, 1866), *b.* 1965, *s.* 1995, *m.*	Hon. Richard G. *H.-R.*, DSO, LVO, *b.* 1909
1929	*Brentford* (4th), Crispin William Joynson-Hicks, *b.* 1933, *s.* 1983, *m.*	Hon. Paul W. *J.-H.*, *b.* 1971
1929	*Bridgeman* (3rd), Robin John Orlando Bridgeman, *b.* 1930, *s.* 1982, *m.*	Hon. William O. C. *B.*, *b.* 1968
1868	*Bridport* (4th), Alexander Nelson Hood (7th *Duke of Brontë in Sicily*, 1799, *and* 6th *Irish Baron, Bridport*, 1794), *b.* 1948, *s.* 1969, *m.*	Hon. Peregrine A. N. *H.*, *b.* 1974

Created	Title, order of succession, name, etc.	Heir
1952	Brookeborough (3rd), Alan Henry Brooke, b. 1952, s. 1987, m.	Hon. Christopher A. B., b. 1954
1933	Buckmaster (3rd), Martin Stanley Buckmaster, OBE, b. 1921, s. 1974	Hon. Colin J. B., b. 1923
1939	Caldecote (2nd), Robert Andrew Inskip, KBE, DSC, FEng., b. 1917, s. 1947, m.	Hon. Piers J. H. I., b. 1947
1941	Camrose. Disclaimed for life 1995 (see Baron Hartwell, page 160)	Hon. Adrian M. Berry, b. 1937
1954	Chandos (3rd), Thomas Orlando Lyttelton, b. 1953, s. 1980, m.	Hon. Oliver A. L., b. 1986
1665 I.	Charlemont (14th), John Day Caulfeild (18th Irish Baron, Caulfeild of Charlemont, 1620), b.1934, s.1985, m.	Hon. John D. C., b. 1966
1921	Chelmsford (3rd), Frederic Jan Thesiger, b. 1931, s.1970, m.	Hon. Frederic C. P. T., b. 1962
1717 I.	Chetwynd (10th), Adam Richard John Casson Chetwynd, b. 1935, s. 1965, m.	Hon. Adam D. C., b. 1969
1911	Chilston (4th), Alastair George Akers-Douglas, b. 1946, s. 1982, m.	Hon. Oliver I. A.-D., b. 1973
1902	Churchill (3rd), Victor George Spencer (5th UK Baron, Churchill, 1815), b. 1934, s. 1973	None to Viscountcy. To Barony, Richard H. R. S., b. 1926
1718	Cobham (11th), John William Leonard Lyttelton (8th Irish Baron, Westcote, 1776), b. 1943, s. 1977, m.	Hon. Christopher C. L., b. 1947
1902	Colville of Culross (4th), John Mark Alexander Colville, QC (13th Scott. Baron, Colville of Culross, 1604), b. 1933, s. 1945, m.	Master of Colville, b. 1959
1826	Combermere (5th), Michael Wellington Stapleton-Cotton, b. 1929, s. 1969, m.	Hon. Thomas R. W. S.-C., b. 1969
1917	Cowdray (4th), Michael Orlando Weetman Pearson (4th UK Baron, Cowdray, 1910), b. 1944, s. 1995, m.	Hon. Charles A. P., b. 1956
1927	Craigavon (3rd), Janric Fraser Craig, b. 1944, s. 1974	None
1886	Cross (3rd), Assheton Henry Cross, b. 1920, s. 1932	None
1943	Daventry (3rd), Francis Humphrey Maurice FitzRoy Newdegate, b. 1921, s. 1986, m.	Hon. James E. F. N., b. 1960
1937	Davidson (2nd), John Andrew Davidson, b. 1928, s. 1970, m.	Hon. Malcolm W. M. D., b. 1934
1956	De L'Isle (2nd), Philip John Algernon Sidney, MBE, (7th Baron De L'Isle and Dudley, 1835), b. 1945, s. 1991, m.	Hon. Philip W. E. S., b. 1985
1776 I.	De Vesci (7th), Thomas Eustace Vesey (8th Irish Baron, Knapton, 1750), b. 1955, s. 1983, m.	Hon. Oliver I. V., b. 1991
1917	Devonport (3rd), Terence Kearley, b. 1944, s. 1973	Chester D. H. K., b. 1932
1964	Dilhorne (2nd), John Mervyn Manningham-Buller, b. 1932, s. 1980, m.	Hon. James E. M.-B., b. 1956
1622 I.	Dillon (22nd), Henry Benedict Charles Dillon, b. 1973, s. 1982	Hon. Richard A. L. D., b. 1948
1785 I.	Doneraile (10th), Richard Allen St Leger, b. 1946, s. 1983, m.	Hon. Nathaniel W. R. St J. St L., b. 1971
1680 I.*	Downe (11th), John Christian George Dawnay (4th UK Baron, Dawnay, 1897), b. 1935, s. 1965, m.	Hon. Richard H. D., b. 1967
1959	Dunrossil (2nd), John William Morrison, CMG, b. 1926, s. 1961, m.	Hon. Andrew W. R. M., b. 1953
1964	Eccles (1st), David McAdam Eccles, CH, KCVO, PC, b. 1904, m.	Hon. John D. E., CBE, b. 1931
1897	Esher (4th), Lionel Gordon Baliol Brett, CBE, b. 1913. s. 1963, m.	Hon. Christopher L. B. B., b. 1936
1816	Exmouth (10th), Paul Edward Pellew, b. 1940, s. 1970, m.	Hon. Edward F. P., b. 1978
1620 S.	Falkland (15th), Lucius Edward William Plantagenet Cary (Premier Scottish Viscount on the Roll), b. 1935, s. 1984, m.	Master of Falkland, b. 1963
1720	Falmouth (9th), George Hugh Boscawen (26th Eng. Baron, Le Despencer, 1264), b. 1919, s. 1962, m.	Hon. Evelyn A. H. B., b. 1955
1720 I.*	Gage (8th), (Henry) Nicolas Gage, (7th Brit. Baron, Gage, 1790), b. 1934, s. 1993, m.	Hon. Henry W. G., b. 1975
1727 I.	Galway (12th), George Rupert Monckton-Arundell, b. 1922, s. 1980, m.	Hon. J. Philip M., b. 1952
1478 I.*	Gormanston (17th), Jenico Nicholas Dudley Preston (Premier Viscount of Ireland; 5th UK Baron, Gormanston, 1868), b. 1939, s. 1940, w.	Hon. Jenico F. T. P., b. 1974
1816 I.	Gort (9th), Foley Robert Standish Prendergast Vereker, b. 1951, s. 1995, m.	Hon. Nicholas L. P. V., b. 1954
1900	Goschen (4th), Giles John Harry Goschen, b. 1965, s. 1977, m.	None
1849	Gough (5th), Shane Hugh Maryon Gough, b. 1941, s. 1951	None
1937	Greenwood (2nd), David Henry Hamar Greenwood, b. 1914, s. 1948	Hon. Michael G. H. G., b. 1923
1929	Hailsham. Disclaimed for life 1963 (see Lord Hailsham of St Marylebone, page160)	Rt. Hon. Douglas M. Hogg, QC, MP, b. 1945
1891	Hambleden (4th), William Herbert Smith, b. 1930, s. 1948, m.	Hon. William H. B. S., b. 1955
1884	Hampden (6th), Anthony David Brand, b. 1937, s. 1975, m.	Hon. Francis A. B., b. 1970
1936	Hanworth (3rd), David Stephen Geoffrey Pollock, b. 1946, s. 1996, m.	Hon. Richard C. S. P., b. 1951
1791 I.	Harberton (10th), Thomas de Vautort Pomeroy, b. 1910, s. 1980, m.	Hon. Robert W. P., b. 1916
1846	Hardinge (6th), Charles Henry Nicholas Hardinge, b. 1956, s. 1984, m.	Hon. Andrew H. H., b. 1960
1791 I.	Hawarden (9th), (Robert) Connan Wyndham Leslie Maude, b. 1961, s. 1991, m.	Hon. Thomas P. C. M., b. 1964
1960	Head (2nd), Richard Antony Head, b. 1937, s. 1983, m.	Hon. Henry J. H., b. 1980

Created	Title, order of succession, name, etc.	Heir
1550	*Hereford* (18th), Robert Milo Leicester Devereux (*Premier Viscount of England*), *b* 1932, *s.* 1952	Hon. Charles R. de B. *D.*, *b.* 1975
1842	*Hill* (8th), Antony Rowland Clegg-Hill, *b.* 1931, *s.* 1974, *m.*	Peter D. R. C. *C. H.*, *b.* 1945
1796	*Hood* (7th), Alexander Lambert Hood (7th *Irish Baron, Hood*, 1782), *b.* 1914, *s.* 1981, *m.*	Hon. Henry L. A. *H.*, *b.* 1958
1956	*Ingleby* (2nd), Martin Raymond Peake, *b.* 1926, *s.* 1966, *w.*	None
1945	*Kemsley* (2nd), (Geoffrey) Lionel Berry, *b.* 1909, *s.* 1968, *m.*	Richard G. *B.*, *b.* 1951
1911	*Knollys* (3rd), David Francis Dudley Knollys, *b.* 1931, *s.* 1966, *m.*	Hon. Patrick N. M. *K.*, *b.* 1962
1895	*Knutsford* (6th), Michael Holland-Hibbert, *b.* 1926, *s.* 1986, *m.*	Hon. Henry T. *H.-H.*, *b.* 1959
1945	*Lambert* (3rd), Michael John Lambert, *b.* 1912, *s.* 1989, *m.*	None
1954	*Leathers* (3rd), Christopher Graeme Leathers, *b.* 1941, *s.* 1996, *m.*	Hon. James F. *L.*, *b.* 1969
1922	*Leverhulme* (3rd), Philip William Bryce Lever, KG, TD, *b.* 1915, *s.* 1949, *w.*	None
1781 I.	*Lifford* (9th), (Edward) James Wingfield Hewitt, *b.* 1949, *s.* 1987, *m.*	Hon. James T. W. *H.*, *b.* 1979
1921	*Long* (4th), Richard Gerard Long, CBE, *b.* 1929, *s.* 1967, *m.*	Hon. James R. *L.*, *b.* 1960
1957	*Mackintosh of Halifax* (3rd), (John) Clive Mackintosh, *b.* 1958, *s.* 1980, *m.*	Hon. Thomas H. G. *M.*, *b.* 1985
1955	*Malvern* (3rd), Ashley Kevin Godfrey Huggins, *b.* 1949, *s.* 1978	Hon. M. James *H*, *b.* 1928
1945	*Marchwood* (3rd), David George Staveley Penny, *b.* 1936, *s.* 1979, *w.*	Hon. Peter G. W. *P.*, *b.* 1965
1942	*Margesson* (2nd), Francis Vere Hampden Margesson, *b.* 1922, *s.* 1965, *m.*	Capt. Hon. Richard F. D. *M.*, *b.* 1960
1660 I.*	*Massereene* (14th) & *Ferrard* (7th) (1797), John David Clotworthy Whyte-Melville Foster Skeffington (7th *UK Baron, Oriel*, 1821), *b.* 1940, *s.* 1992, *m.*	Hon. Charles J. C. W.-M. F. *S.*, *b.* 1973
1802	*Melville* (9th), Robert David Ross Dundas, *b.* 1937, *s.* 1971, *m.*	Hon. Robert H. K. *D.*, *b.* 1984
1916	*Mersey* (4th), Richard Maurice Clive Bigham (13th *Scott. Lord Nairne*, 1681, *s.* 1995), *b.* 1934, *s.* 1979, *m.*	Hon. Edward J. H. *B.*, *b.* 1966
1717 I.*	*Midleton* (12th), Alan Henry Brodrick (9th *Brit. Baron, Brodrick of Peper Harow*, 1796), *b.* 1949, *s.* 1988, *m.*	Hon. Ashley R. *B.*, *b.* 1980
1962	*Mills* (3rd), Christopher Philip Roger Mills, *b.* 1956, *s.* 1988, *m.*	None
1716 I.	*Molesworth* (11th), Richard Gosset Molesworth, *b.* 1907, *s.* 1961, *w.*	Hon. Robert B. K. *M.*, *b.* 1959
1801 I.*	*Monck* (7th), Charles Stanley Monck (4th *UK Baron, Monck*, 1866), *b.* 1953, *s.* 1982 (does not use title)	Hon. George S. *M.*, *b.* 1957
1957	*Monckton of Brenchley* (2nd), Maj.-Gen. Gilbert Walter Riversdale Monckton, CB, OBE, MC, *b.* 1915, *s.* 1965, *m.*	Hon Christopher W *M.*, *b.* 1952
1946	*Montgomery of Alamein* (2nd), David Bernard Montgomery, CBE, *b.* 1928, *s.* 1976, *m.*	Hon. Henry D. *M.*, *b.* 1954
1550 I.*	*Mountgarret* (17th), Richard Henry Piers Butler (4th *UK Baron, Mountgarret*, 1911), *b.* 1936, *s.* 1966, *m.*	Hon. Piers J. R. *B.*, *b.* 1961
1952	*Norwich* (2nd), John Julius Cooper, CVO, *b.* 1929, *s.* 1954, *m.*	Hon. Jason C. D. B. *C.*, *b.* 1959
1651 S.	*of Oxfuird* (13th), George Hubbard Makgill, CBE, *b.* 1934, *s.* 1986, *m.*	Master of Oxfuird, *b.* 1969
1873	*Portman*, (9th), Edward Henry Berkeley Portman, *b.* 1934, *s.* 1967, *m.*	Hon. Christopher E. B. *P.*, *b.* 1958
1743 I.*	*Powerscourt* (10th), Mervyn Niall Wingfield (4th *UK Baron, Powerscourt*, 1885), *b.* 1935, *s.* 1973, *m.*	Hon. Mervyn A. *W.*, *b.* 1963
1900	*Ridley* (4th), Matthew White Ridley, KG, GCVO, TD, *b.* 1925, *s.* 1964, *m.* *Lord Steward*	Hon. Matthew W. *R.*, *b.* 1958
1960	*Rochdale* (2nd), St John Durival Kemp, *b.* 1938, *s.* 1993, *m.*	Hon. Jonathan H. D. *K.*, *b.* 1961
1919	*Rothermere* (3rd), Vere Harold Esmond Harmsworth, *b.* 1925, *s.* 1978, *m.*	Hon. H. Jonathan E. V. *H.*, *b.* 1967
1937	*Runciman of Doxford* (3rd), Walter Garrison Runciman (Garry), CBE, FBA (4th *UK Baron, Runciman*, 1933), *b.* 1934, *s.* 1989, *m.*	Hon. David W. *R.*, *b.* 1967
1918	*St Davids* (3rd), Colwyn Jestyn John Philipps (20th *Engl. Baron Strange of Knokin*, 1299, 8th *Engl. Baron Hungerford*, 1426, and *De Moleyns*, 1445), *b.* 1939, *s.* 1991, *m.*	Hon. Rhodri C. *P.*, *b.* 1966
1801	*St Vincent* (7th), Ronald George James Jervis, *b.* 1905, *s.* 1940, *m.*	Hon. Edward R. J. *J.*, *b.* 1951
1937	*Samuel* (3rd), David Herbert Samuel, OBE, PH.D., *b.* 1922, *s.* 1978, *m.*	Hon. Dan J. *S.*, *b.* 1925
1911	*Scarsdale* (3rd), Francis John Nathaniel Curzon (7th *Brit. Baron, Scarsdale*, 1761), *b.* 1924, *s.* 1977, *m.*	Hon. Peter G. N. *C.*, *b.* 1949
1905	*Selby* (5th), Edward Thomas William Gully, *b.* 1967, *s.* 1997, *m.*	Hon. Christopher R. T. *G.*, *b.* 1993
1805	*Sidmouth* (7th), John Tonge Anthony Pellew Addington, *b.* 1914, *s.* 1976, *m.*	Hon. Jeremy F. *A.*, *b.* 1947
1940	*Simon* (3rd), Jan David Simon, *b.* 1940, *s.* 1993, *m.*	None
1960	*Slim* (2nd), John Douglas Slim, OBE, *b.* 1927, *s.* 1970, *m.*	Hon. Mark W. R. *S.*, *b.* 1960
1954	*Soulbury* (2nd), James Herwald Ramsbotham, *b.* 1915, *s.* 1971, *w.*	Hon. Sir Peter E. *R.*, GCMG, GCVO, *b.* 1919
1776 I.	*Southwell* (7th), Pyers Anthony Joseph Southwell, *b.* 1930, *s.* 1960, *m.*	Hon. Richard A. P. *S.*, *b.* 1956
1942	*Stansgate.* Disclaimed for life 1963 (*Rt. Hon. Anthony Neil Wedgwood Benn*, MP, *b.* 1925, *s.* 1960, *m.*)	Stephen M. W. *B.*, *b.* 1951

Created	Title, order of succession, name, etc.	Heir
1959	*Stuart of Findhorn* (2nd), David Randolph Moray Stuart, *b.* 1924, *s.* 1971, *m.*	Hon. J. Dominic *S., b.* 1948
1957	*Tenby* (3rd), William Lloyd George, *b.* 1927, *s.* 1983, *m.*	Hon. Timothy H. G. *L. G., b.* 1962
1952	*Thurso* (3rd), John Archibald Sinclair, *b.* 1953, *s.* 1995, *m.*	Hon. James A. R. *S., b.* 1984
1983	*Tonypandy* (1st), (Thomas) George Thomas, PC, *b.* 1909	None
1721	*Torrington* (11th), Timothy Howard St George Byng, *b.* 1943, *s.* 1961, *m.*	John L. *B.,* MC, *b.* 1919
1936	*Trenchard* (3rd), Hugh Trenchard, *b.* 1951, *s.* 1987, *m.*	Hon. Alexander T. *T., b.* 1978
1921	*Ullswater* (2nd), Nicholas James Christopher Lowther, PC, *b.* 1942, *s.* 1949, *m.*	Hon. Benjamin J. *L., b.* 1975
1621 I.	*Valentia* (15th), Richard John Dighton Annesley, *b.* 1929, *s.* 1983, *m.*	Hon. Francis W. D. *A., b.* 1959
1952	*Waverley* (3rd), John Desmond Forbes Anderson, *b.* 1949, *s.* 1990	None
1938	*Weir* (3rd), William Kenneth James Weir, *b.* 1933, *s.* 1975, *m.*	Hon. James W. H. *W., b.* 1965
1983	*Whitelaw* (1st), William Stephen Ian Whitelaw, KT, CH, MC, PC, *b.* 1918, *m.*	None
1918	*Wimborne* (4th), Ivor Mervyn Vigors Guest (5th *UK Baron, Wimborne,* 1880), *b.* 1968, *s.* 1993	Hon. Julian J. *G., b.* 1945
1923	*Younger of Leckie* (4th), George Kenneth Hotson Younger, KT, KCVO, TD, PC, (Baron Younger of Prestwick (life peerage)) *b.* 1931, *s.* 1997, *m.*	Hon. James E. G. *Y., b.* 1955

BARONS/LORDS

Coronet, Six silver balls
Style, The Right Hon. the Lord ___ . In the Peerage of Scotland there is no rank of Baron; the equivalent rank is Lord of Parliament (*see* page 137) and Scottish peers should always be styled 'Lord', never 'Baron'
Wife's style, The Right Hon. the Lady ___
Children's style, 'The Hon.' before forename and family name
In Scotland, the heir apparent to a Lord may be styled 'The Master of ___ (title of peer)'
For forms of address, *see* page 136

Created	Title, order of succession, name, etc.	Heir
1911	*Aberconway* (3rd), Charles Melville McLaren, *b.* 1913, *s.* 1953, *m.*	Hon. H. Charles *M., b.* 1948
1873	*Aberdare* (4th), Morys George Lyndhurst Bruce, KBE, PC, *b.* 1919, *s.* 1957, *m.*	Hon. Alastair J. L. *B., b.* 1947
1835	*Abinger* (8th), James Richard Scarlett, *b.* 1914, *s.* 1943, *m.*	Hon. James H. *S., b.* 1959
1869	*Acton* (4th), Richard Gerald Lyon-Dalberg-Acton, *b.* 1941, *s.* 1989, *m.*	Hon. John C. F. H. *L.-D.-A., b.* 1966
1887	*Addington* (6th), Dominic Bryce Hubbard, *b.* 1963, *s.* 1982	Hon. Michael W. L. *H., b.* 1965
1896	*Aldenham* (6th), and *Hunsdon of Hunsdon* (4th) (1923), Vicary Tyser Gibbs, *b.* 1948, *s.* 1986, *m.*	Hon. Humphrey W. F. *G., b.* 1989
1962	*Aldington* (1st), Toby Austin Richard William Low, KCMG, CBE, DSO, TD, PC, b. 1914, *m.*	Hon Charles H. S. *L., b.* 1948
1945	*Altrincham.* Disclaimed for life 1963 (*John Edward Poynder Grigg, b.* 1924, *s.* 1955, *m.*)	Hon. Anthony U. D. D. *G., b.* 1934
1929	*Alvingham* (2nd), Maj.-Gen. Robert Guy Eardley Yerburgh, CBE, *b.* 1926, *s.* 1955, *m.*	Capt. Hon. Robert R. G. *Y., b.* 1956
1892	*Amherst of Hackney* (4th), William Hugh Amherst Cecil, *b.* 1940, *s.* 1980, *m.*	Hon. H. William A. *C., b.* 1968
1881	*Ampthill* (4th), Geoffrey Denis Erskine Russell, CBE, PC, *b.* 1921, *s.* 1973	Hon. David W. E. *R., b.* 1947
1947	*Amwell* (3rd), Keith Norman Montague, *b.* 1943, *s.* 1990, *m.*	Hon. Ian K. *M., b.* 1973
1863	*Annaly* (6th), Luke Richard White, *b.* 1954, *s.* 1990, *m.*	Hon. Luke H. *W., b.* 1990
1885	*Ashbourne* (4th), Edward Barry Greynville Gibson, *b.* 1933, *s.* 1983, *m.*	Hon. Edward C. d'O. *G., b.* 1967
1835	*Ashburton* (7th), John Francis Harcourt Baring, KG, KCVO, *b.* 1928, *s.* 1991, *m.*	Hon. Mark F. R. *B., b.* 1958
1892	*Ashcombe* (4th), Henry Edward Cubitt, *b.* 1924, *s.* 1962, *m.*	Mark E. *C., b.* 1964
1911	*Ashton of Hyde* (3rd), Thomas John Ashton, TD, *b.* 1926, *s.* 1983, *m.*	Hon. Thomas H. *A., b.* 1958
1800 I.	*Ashtown* (7th), Nigel Clive Crosby Trench, KCMG, *b.* 1916, *s.* 1990, *w.*	Hon. Roderick N. G. *T., b.* 1944
1956	*Astor of Hever* (3rd), John Jacob Astor, *b.* 1946, *s.* 1984, *m.*	Hon. Charles G. J. *A., b.* 1990
1789 I.*	*Auckland* (10th), Robert Ian Burnard Eden (10th *Brit. Baron, Auckland,* 1793), *b.* 1962, *s.* 1997, *m.*	†
1313	*Audley.* The 25th Lord Audley died in July 1997, leaving three co-heiresses	
1900	*Avebury* (4th), Eric Reginald Lubbock, *b.* 1928, *s.* 1971, *m.*	Hon. Lyulph A. J. *L., b.* 1954

Created	Title, order of succession, name, etc.	Heir
1718 I.	*Aylmer* (13th), Michael Anthony Aylmer, *b.* 1923, *s.* 1982, *m.*	Hon. A. Julian *A., b.* 1951
1929	*Baden-Powell* (3rd), Robert Crause Baden-Powell, *b.* 1936, *s.* 1962, *m.*	Hon. David M. *B.-P., b.* 1940
1780	*Bagot* (9th), Heneage Charles Bagot, *b.* 1914, *s.* 1979, *m.*	Hon. C. H. Shaun *B., b.* 1944
1953	*Baillieu* (3rd), James William Latham Baillieu, *b.* 1950, *s.* 1973, *m.*	Hon. Robert L. *B., b.* 1979
1607 S.	*Balfour of Burleigh* (8th), Robert Bruce, FRSE, *b.* 1927, *s.* 1967, *m.*	Hon. Victoria B., *b.* 1973
1945	*Balfour of Inchrye* (2nd), Ian Balfour, *b.* 1924, *s.* 1988, *m.*	None
1924	*Banbury of Southam* (3rd), Charles William Banbury, *b.* 1953, *s.* 1981, *m.*	None
1698	*Barnard* (11th), Harry John Neville Vane, TD, *b.* 1923, *s.* 1964	Hon. Henry F. C. *V., b.* 1959
1887	*Basing* (5th), Neil Lutley Sclater-Booth, *b.* 1939, *s.* 1983, *m.*	Hon. Stuart W. *S.-B., b.* 1969
1917	*Beaverbrook* (3rd), Maxwell William Humphrey Aitken, *b.* 1951, *s.* 1985, *m.*	Hon. Maxwell F. *A, b.* 1977
1647 S.	*Belhaven and Stenton* (13th), Robert Anthony Carmichael Hamilton, *b.* 1927, *s.* 1961, *m.*	Master of Belhaven, *b.* 1953
1848 I.	*Bellew* (7th), James Bryan Bellew, *b.* 1920, *s.* 1981, *m.*	Hon. Bryan E. *B., b.* 1943
1856	*Belper* (4th), (Alexander) Ronald George Stuutt, *b.* 1912, *s.* 1956	Hon. Richard H. *S., b.* 1941
1938	*Belstead* (2nd), John Julian Ganzoni, PC, *b.* 1932, *s.* 1958	None
1421	*Berkeley* (18th), Anthony Fitzhardinge Gueterbock, OBE, *b.* 1939, *s.* 1992, *m.*	Hon. Thomas F. *G., b.* 1969
1922	*Bethell* (4th), Nicholas William Bethell, *b.* 1938, *s.* 1967, *m.*	Hon. James N. *B., b.* 1967
1938	*Bicester* (3rd), Angus Edward Vivian Smith, *b.* 1932, *s.* 1968	Hugh C. V. *S., b.* 1934
1903	*Biddulph* (5th), (Anthony) Nicholas Colin Maitland Biddulph, *b.* 1959, *s.* 1988, *m.*	Hon. William I. R. *M. B., b.* 1963
1938	*Birdwood* (3rd), Mark William Ogilvie Birdwood, *b.* 1938, *s.* 1962, *m.*	None
1958	*Birkett* (2nd), Michael Birkett, *b.* 1929, *s.* 1962, *m.*	Hon. Thomas *B., b.* 1982
1907	*Blyth* (4th), Anthony Audley Rupert Blyth, *b.* 1931, *s.* 1977, *m.*	Hon. Riley A. J. *B., b.* 1955
1797	*Bolton* (7th), Richard William Algar Orde-Powlett, *b.* 1929, *s.* 1963, *m.*	Hon. Harry A. N. *O.-P., b.* 1954
1452 S.	*Borthwick* (24th), John Hugh Borthwick, *b.* 1940, *s.* 1997, *m.*	Hon. James H. A. *B. of Glengelt, b.* 1940
1922	*Borwick* (4th), James Hugh Myles Borwick, MC, *b.* 1917, *s.* 1961, *m.*	Hon. George S. *B., b.* 1922
1761	*Boston* (10th), Timothy George Frank Boteler Irby, *b.* 1939, *s.* 1978, *m.*	Hon. George W. E. B. *I., b.* 1971
1942	*Brabazon of Tara* (3rd), Ivon Anthony Moore-Brabazon, *b.* 1946, *s.* 1974, *m.*	Hon. Benjamin R. *M.-B., b.* 1983
1880	*Brabourne* (7th), John Ulick Knatchbull, CBE, *b.* 1924, *s.* 1943, *m.*	Lord Romsey, *b.* 1947 (*see* page 145)
1925	*Bradbury* (3rd), John Bradbury, *b.* 1940, *s.* 1994, *m.*	Hon. John *B., b.* 1973
1962	*Brain* (2nd), Christopher Langdon Brain, *b.* 1926, *s.* 1966, *m.*	Hon. Michael C. *B.,* DM, FRCP, *b.* 1928
1938	*Brassey of Apethorpe* (3rd), David Henry Brassey, OBE, *b.* 1932, *s.* 1967, *m.*	Hon. Edward *B., b.* 1964
1788	*Braybrooke* (10th), Robin Henry Charles Neville, *b.* 1932, *s.* 1990, *m.*	George *N., b.* 1943
1957	*Bridges* (2nd), Thomas Edward Bridges, GCMG, *b.* 1927, *s.* 1969, *m.*	Hon. Mark T. *B., b.* 1954
1945	*Broadbridge* (3rd), Peter Hewett Broadbridge, *b.* 1938, *s.* 1972, *m.*	Martin H. *B., b.* 1929
1933	*Brocket* (3rd), Charles Ronald George Nall-Cain, *b.* 1952, *s.* 1967, *m.*	Hon. Alexander C. C. *N.-C., b.* 1984
1860	*Brougham and Vaux* (5th), Michael John Brougham, CBE, *b.* 1938, *s.* 1967	Hon. Charles W. *B., b.* 1971
1945	*Broughshane* (3rd), (William) Kensington Davison, DSO, DFC, *b.* 1914, *s.* 1995	None
1776	*Brownlow* (7th), Edward John Peregrine Cust, *b.* 1936, *s.* 1978, *m.*	Hon. Peregrine E. Q. *C., b.* 1974
1942	*Bruntisfield* (2nd), John Robert Warrender, OBE, MC, TD, *b.* 1921, *s.* 1993, *m.*	Hon. Michael J. V. *W., b.* 1949
1950	*Burden* (3rd), Andrew Philip Burden, *b.* 1959, *s.* 1995	Hon. Fraser W. E. *B., b.* 1964
1529	*Burgh* (7th), Alexander Peter Willoughby Leith, *b.* 1935, *s.* 1959, *m.*	Hon. A. Gregory D. *L., b.* 1958
1903	*Burnham* (6th), Hugh John Frederick Lawson, *b.* 1931, *s.* 1993, *m.*	Hon. Harry F. A. *L., b.* 1968
1897	*Burton* (3rd), Michael Evan Victor Baillie, *b.* 1924, *s.* 1962, *m.*	Hon. Evan M. R. *B, b.* 1949
1643	*Byron* (13th), Robert James Byron, *b.* 1950, *s.* 1989, *m.*	Hon. Charles R. G. *B., b.* 1990
1937	*Cadman* (3rd), John Anthony Cadman, *b.* 1938, *s.* 1966, *m.*	Hon. Nicholas A. J. *C., b.* 1977
1945	*Calverley* (3rd), Charles Rodney Muff, *b.* 1946, *s.* 1971, *m.*	Hon. Jonathan E. *M., b.* 1975
1383	*Camoys* (7th), (Ralph) Thomas Campion George Sherman Stonor, *b.* 1940, *s.* 1976, *m. Lord Chamberlain (from Jan.1998)*	Hon. R. William R. T. *S., b.* 1974
1715 I.	*Carbery* (11th), Peter Ralfe Harrington Evans-Freke, *b.* 1920, *s.* 1970, *m.*	Hon. Michael P. *E.-F., b.* 1942
1834 I.*	*Carew* (7th), Patrick Thomas Conolly-Carew (7th *UK Baron, Carew,* 1838), *b.* 1938, *s.* 1994, *m.*	Hon. William P. *C.-C., b.* 1973
1916	*Carnock* (4th), David Henry Arthur Nicolson, *b.* 1920, *s.* 1982	Nigel *N.,* MBE, *b.* 1917
1796 I.*	*Carrington* (6th), Peter Alexander Rupert Carington, KG, GCMG, CH, MC, PC (6th *Brit. Baron, Carrington,* 1797), *b.* 1919, *s.* 1938, *m.*	Hon. Rupert F. J. *C., b.* 1948
1812 I.	*Castlemaine* (8th), Roland Thomas John Handcock, MBE, *b.* 1943, *s.* 1973, *m.*	Hon. Ronan M. E. *H., b.* 1989
1936	*Catto* (2nd), Stephen Gordon Catto, *b.* 1923, *s.* 1959, *m.*	Hon. Innes G. *C., b.* 1950
1918	*Cawley* (3rd), Frederick Lee Cawley, *b.* 1913, *s.* 1954, *m.*	Hon. John F. *C., b.* 1946

Created	Title, order of succession, name, etc.	Heir
1603	*Cecil*, a subsidiary title of the Marquess of Salisbury. His heir Viscount Cranborne, PC, was given a Writ in Acceleration in this title to enable him to sit in the House of Lords whilst his father is still alive (*see also* page 140)	
1937	*Chatfield* (2nd), Ernle David Lewis Chatfield, *b.* 1917, *s.* 1967, *m.*	None
1858	*Chesham* (6th), Nicholas Charles Cavendish, *b.* 1941, *s.* 1989, *m.*	Hon. Charles G. C. C., *b.* 1974
1945	*Chetwode* (2nd), Philip Chetwode, *b.* 1937, *s.* 1950, *m.*	Hon. Roger C., *b.* 1968
1945	*Chorley* (2nd), Roger Richard Edward Chorley, *b.* 1930, *s.* 1978, *m.*	Hon. Nicholas R. D. C., *b.* 1966
1858	*Churston* (5th), John Francis Yarde-Buller, *b.* 1934, *s.* 1991, *m.*	Hon. Benjamin F. A. Y.-B., *b.* 1974
1946	*Citrine* (2nd), Norman Arthur Citrine, *b.* 1914, *s.* 1983, *w.*	Hon. Ronald E. C., *b.* 1919
1800 I.	*Clanmorris* (8th), Simon John Ward Bingham, *b.* 1937, *s.* 1988, *m.*	Robert D. de B. B., *b.* 1942
1672	*Clifford of Chudleigh* (14th), Thomas Hugh Clifford, *b.* 1948, *s.* 1988, *m.*	Hon. Alexander T. H. C., *b.* 1985
1299	*Clinton* (22nd), Gerard Nevile Mark Fane Trefusis, *b.* 1934, *title called out of abeyance* 1965, *m.*	Hon. Charles P. R. F. T., *b.* 1962
1955	*Clitheroe* (2nd), Ralph John Assheton, *b.* 1929, *s.* 1984, *m.*	Hon. Ralph C. A., *b.* 1962
1919	*Clwyd* (3rd), (John) Anthony Roberts, *b.* 1935, *s.* 1987, *m.*	Hon. J. Murray R., *b.* 1971
1948	*Clydesmuir* (3rd), David Ronald Colville, *b.* 1949, *s.* 1996, *m.*	Hon. Richard C., *b.* 1980
1960	*Cobbold* (2nd), David Antony Fromanteel Lytton Cobbold, *b.* 1937, *s.* 1987, *m.*	Hon. Henry F. L. C., *b.* 1962
1919	*Cochrane of Cults* (4th), (Ralph Henry) Vere Cochrane, *b.* 1926, *s.* 1990, *m.*	Hon. Thomas H. V. C., *b.* 1957
1954	*Coleraine* (2nd), (James) Martin (Bonar) Law, *b.* 1931, *s.* 1980, *w.*	Hon. James P. B. L., *b.* 1975
1873	*Coleridge* (5th), William Duke Coleridge, *b.* 1937, *s.* 1984, *m.*	Hon. James D. C., *b.* 1967
1946	*Colgrain* (3rd), David Colin Campbell, *b.* 1920, *s.* 1973, *m.*	Hon. Alastair C. L. C., *b.* 1951
1917	*Colwyn* (3rd), (Ian) Anthony Hamilton-Smith, CBE, *b.* 1942, *s.* 1966, *m.*	Hon. Craig P. H.-S., *b.* 1968
1956	*Colyton* (2nd), Alisdair John Munro Hopkinson, *b.* 1958, *s.* 1996, *m.*	Hon. James P. M. H., *b.* 1983
1841	*Congleton* (8th), Christopher Patrick Parnell, *b.* 1930, *s.* 1967, *m.*	Hon. John P. C. P., *b.* 1959
1927	*Cornwallis* (3rd), Fiennes Neil Wykeham Cornwallis, OBE, *b.* 1921, *s.* 1982, *m.*	Hon. F. W. Jeremy C., *b.* 1946
1874	*Cottesloe* (5th), Cdr. John Tapling Fremantle, *b.* 1927, *s.* 1994, *m.*	Hon. Thomas F. H. F., *b.* 1966
1929	*Craigmyle* (3rd), Thomas Donald Mackay Shaw, *b.* 1923, *s.* 1944, *m.*	Hon. Thomas C. S., *b.* 1960
1899	*Cranworth* (3rd), Philip Bertram Gurdon, *b.* 1940, *s.* 1964, *m.*	Hon. Sacha W. R. G., *b.* 1970
1959	*Crathorne* (2nd), Charles James Dugdale, *b.* 1939, *s.* 1977, *m.*	Hon. Thomas A. J. D., *b.* 1977
1892	*Crawshaw* (4th), William Michael Clifton Brooks, *b.* 1933, *s.* 1946	Hon. David G. B., *b.* 1934
1940	*Croft* (3rd), Bernard William Henry Page Croft, *b.* 1949, *s.* 1997, *w.*	None
1797 I.	*Crofton* (7th), Guy Patrick Gilbert Crofton, *b.* 1951, *s.* 1989, *m.*	Hon. E. Harry P. C., *b.* 1988
1375	*Cromwell* (7th), Godfrey John Bewicke-Copley, *b.* 1960, *s.* 1982, *m.*	Hon. Thomas D. B.-C., *b.* 1964
1947	*Crook* (2nd), Douglas Edwin Crook, *b.* 1926, *s* 1989, *m.*	Hon. Robert D. E. C., *b.* 1955
1920	*Cullen of Ashbourne* (2nd), Charles Borlase Marsham Cokayne, MBE, *b.* 1912, *s.* 1932, *w.*	Hon. Edmund W. M. C., *b.* 1916
1914	*Cunliffe* (3rd), Roger Cunliffe, *b.* 1932, *s.* 1963, *m.*	Hon. Henry C., *b.* 1962
1927	*Daresbury* (4th), Peter Gilbert Greenall, *b.* 1953, *s.* 1996, *m.*	Hon. Thomas E. G., *b.* 1984
1924	*Darling* (2nd), Robert Charles Henry Darling, *b.* 1919, *s.* 1936, *m.*	Hon. R. Julian H. D., *b.* 1944
1946	*Darwen* (3rd), Roger Michael Davies, *b.* 1938, *s.* 1988, *m.*	Hon. Paul D., *b.* 1962
1932	*Davies* (3rd), David Davies, *b.* 1940, *s.* 1944, *m.*	Hon. David D. D., *b.* 1975
1812 I.	*Decies* (7th), Marcus Hugh Tristram de la Poer Beresford, *b.* 1948, *s.* 1992, *m.*	Hon. Robert M. D. *de la P. B.*, *b.* 1988
1299	*de Clifford* (27th), John Edward Southwell Russell, *b.* 1928, *s.* 1982, *m.*	Hon. William S. R., *b.* 1930
1851	*De Freyne* (7th), Francis Arthur John French, *b.* 1927, *s.* 1935, *m.*	Hon. Fulke C. A. J. F., *b.* 1957
1821	*Delamere* (5th), Hugh George Cholmondeley, *b.* 1934, *s.* 1979, *m.*	Hon. Thomas P. G. C., *b.* 1968
1838	*de Mauley* (6th), Gerald John Ponsonby, *b.* 1921, *s.* 1962, *m.*	Col. Hon. Thomas M. P., TD, *b.* 1930
1937	*Denham* (2nd), Bertram Stanley Mitford Bowyer, KBE, PC, *b.* 1927, *s.* 1948, *m.*	Hon. Richard G. G. B., *b.* 1959
1834	*Denman* (5th), Charles Spencer Denman, CBE, MC, TD, *b.* 1916, *s.* 1971, *w.*	Hon. Richard T. S. D., *b.* 1946
1885	*Deramore* (6th), Richard Arthur de Yarburgh-Bateson, *b.* 1911, *s.* 1964, *m.*	None
1887	*De Ramsey* (4th), John Ailwyn Fellowes, *b.* 1942, *s.* 1993, *m.*	Hon. Freddie J. F., *b.* 1978
1264	*de Ros* (28th), Peter Trevor Maxwell, *b.* 1958, *s.* 1983, *m.* (*Premier Baron of England*)	Hon. Finbar J. M., *b.* 1988
1881	*Derwent* (5th), Robin Evelyn Leo Vanden-Bempde-Johnstone, LVO, *b.* 1930, *s.* 1986, *m.*	Hon. Francis P. H. V.-B.-J., *b.* 1965
1831	*de Saumarez* (7th), Eric Douglas Saumarez, *b.* 1956, *s.* 1991, *m.*	Hon. Victor T. S., *b.* 1956
1910	*de Villiers* (3rd), Arthur Percy de Villiers, *b.* 1911, *s.* 1934	Hon. Alexander C. *de V.*, *b.* 1940
1930	*Dickinson* (2nd), Richard Clavering Hyett Dickinson, *b.* 1926, *s.* 1943, *m.*	Hon. Martin H. D., *b.* 1961
1620 I.*	*Digby* (12th), Edward Henry Kenelm Digby (6th *Brit. Baron, Digby*, 1765), *b.* 1924, *s.* 1964, *m.*	Hon. Henry N. K. D., *b.* 1954

Created	Title, order of succession, name, etc.	Heir
1615	*Dormer* (17th), Geoffrey Henry Dormer, *b.* 1920, *s.* 1995, *m.*	Hon. William R. *D.*, *b.* 1960
1943	*Dowding* (3rd), Piers Hugh Tremenheere Dowding, *b.* 1948, *s.* 1992	Hon. Mark D. J. *D.*, *b.* 1949
1800 I.	*Dufferin and Clandeboye.* The 10th Baron died in 1991. Heir had not established his claim to the title at the time of going to press	Sir John Blackwood, Bt., *b.* 1944
1929	*Dulverton* (3rd), (Gilbert) Michael Hamilton Wills, *b.* 1944, *s.* 1992, *m.*	Hon. Robert A. H. *W.*, *b.* 1983
1800 I.	*Dunalley* (7th), Henry Francis Cornelius Prittie, *b.* 1948, *s.* 1992, *m.*	Hon. Joel H. *P.*, *b.* 1981
1324 I.	*Dunboyne* (28th), Patrick Theobald Tower Butler, VRD, *b.* 1917, *s.* 1945, *m.*	Hon. John F. *B.*, *b.* 1951
1802	*Dunleath* (5th), Michael Henry Mulholland, *b.* 1915, *s.* 1993, *w.*	Hon. Brian H. *M.*, *b.* 1950
1439 I.	*Dunsany* (19th), Randal Arthur Henry Plunkett, *b.* 1906, *s.* 1957, *m.*	Hon. Edward J. C. *P.*, *b.* 1939
1780	*Dynevor* (9th), Richard Charles Uryan Rhys, *b.* 1935, *s.* 1962	Hon. Hugo G. U. *R.*, *b.* 1966
1857	*Ebury* (6th), Francis Egerton Grosvenor, *b.* 1934, *s.* 1957, *m.*	Hon. Julian F. M. *G.*, *b.* 1959
1963	*Egremont* (2nd), & *Leconfield* (7th) (1859), John Max Henry Scawen Wyndham, *b.* 1948, *s.* 1972, *m.*	Hon. George R. V. *W.*, *b.* 1983
1643	*Elibank* (14th), Alan D'Ardis Erskine-Murray, *b.* 1923, *s.* 1973, *w.*	Master of Elibank, *b.* 1964
1802	*Ellenborough* (8th), Richard Edward Cecil Law, *b.* 1926, *s.* 1945, *m.*	Maj. Hon. Rupert E. H. *L.*, *b.* 1955
1509 s.*	*Elphinstone* (19th), Alexander Mountstuart Elphinstone (5th *UK Baron Elphinstone*, 1885), *b.* 1980, *s.* 1994, *M.*	Hon. Angus J. *E.*, *b.* 1982
1934	*Elton* (2nd), Rodney Elton, TD, *b.* 1930, *s.* 1973, *m.*	Hon. Edward P. *E.*, *b.* 1966
1964	*Erroll of Hale* (1st), Frederick James Erroll, TD, PC, *b.* 1914, *m.*	None
1627 s.	*Fairfax of Cameron* (14th), Nicholas John Albert Fairfax, *b.* 1956, *s.* 1964, *m.*	Hon. Edward N. T. *F.*, *b.* 1984
1961	*Fairhaven* (3rd), Ailwyn Henry George Broughton, *b.* 1936, *s.* 1973, *m.*	Maj. Hon. James H. A. *B.*, *b.* 1963
1916	*Faringdon* (3rd), Charles Michael Henderson, *b.* 1937, *s.* 1977, *m.*	Hon. James H. *H.*, *b.* 1961
1756 I.	*Farnham* (12th), Barry Owen Somerset Maxwell, *b.* 1931, *s.* 1957, *m.*	Hon. Simon K. *M.*, *b.* 1933
1856 I.	*Fermoy* (6th), Patrick Maurice Burke Roche, *b.* 1967, *s.* 1984	Hon. E. Hugh B. *R.*, *b.* 1972
1826	*Feversham* (6th), Charles Antony Peter Duncombe, *b.* 1945, *s.* 1963, *m.*	Hon. Jasper O. S. *D.*, *b.* 1968
1798 I.	*ffrench* (8th), Robuck John Peter Charles Mario ffrench, *b.* 1956, *s.* 1986, *m.*	Hon. John C. M. J. F. *ff.*, *b.* 1928
1909	*Fisher* (3rd), John Vavasseur Fisher, DSC, *b.* 1921, *s.* 1955, *m.*	Hon. Patrick V. *F.*, *b.* 1953
1295	*Fitzwalter* (21st), (Fitzwalter) Brook Plumptre, *b.* 1914, *title called out of abeyance* 1953, *m.*	Hon. Julian B. *P.*, *b.* 1952
1776	*Foley* (8th), Adrian Gerald Foley, *b.* 1923, *s.* 1927, *m.*	Hon. Thomas H. *F.*, *b.* 1961
1445 s.	*Forbes* (22nd), Nigel Ivan Forbes, KBE (*Premier Lord of Scotland*), *b.* 1918, *s.* 1953, *m.*	Master of Forbes, *b.* 1946
1821	*Forester* (8th), (George Cecil) Brooke Weld-Forester, *b.* 1938, *s.* 1977, *m.*	Hon. C. R. George *W.-F.*, *b.* 1975
1922	*Forres* (4th), Alastair Stephen Grant Williamson, *b.* 1946, *s.* 1978, *m.*	Hon. George A. M. *W.*, *b.* 1972
1917	*Forteviot* (4th), John James Evelyn Dewar, *b.* 1938, *s.* 1993, *m.*	Hon. Alexander J. E. *D.*, *b.* 1971
1951	*Freyberg* (3rd), Valerian Bernard Freyberg, *b.* 1970, *s.* 1993	None
1917	*Gainford* (3rd), Joseph Edward Pease, *b.* 1921, *s.* 1971, *m.*	Hon. George *P.*, *b.* 1926
1818 I.	*Garvagh* (5th), (Alexander Leopold Ivor) George Canning, *b.* 1920, *s.* 1956, *m.*	Hon. Spencer G. S. de R. *C.*, *b.* 1953
1942	*Geddes* (3rd), Euan Michael Ross Geddes, *b.* 1937, *s.* 1975, *m.*	Hon. James G. N. *G.*, *b.* 1969
1876	*Gerard* (5th), Anthony Robert Hugo Gerard, *b.* 1949, *s.* 1992, *m.*	Hon. Rupert B. C. *G.*, *b.* 1981
1824	*Gifford* (6th), Anthony Maurice Gifford, QC, *b.* 1940, *s.* 1961, *m.*	Hon. Thomas A. *G.*, *b.* 1967
1917	*Gisborough* (3rd), Thomas Richard John Long Chaloner, *b.* 1927, *s.* 1951, *m.*	Hon. T. Peregrine L. *C.*, *b.* 1961
1960	*Gladwyn* (2nd), Miles Alvery Gladwyn Jebb, *b.* 1930, *s.* 1996	None
1899	*Glanusk* (5th), Christopher Russell Bailey, *b.* 1942, *s.* 1997, *m.*	Hon. C. H. *B.*, *b.* 1976
1918	*Glenarthur* (4th), Simon Mark Arthur, *b.* 1944, *s.* 1976, *m.*	Hon. Edward A. *A.*, *b.* 1973
1911	*Glenconner* (3rd), Colin Christopher Paget Tennant, *b.* 1926, *s.* 1983, *m.*	Hon. Cody *T.*, *b.* 1994
1964	*Glendevon* (2nd), Julian John Somerset Hope, *b.* 1950, *s.* 1996	Hon. Jonathan C. *H.*, *b.* 1952
1922	*Glendyne* (3rd), Robert Nivison, *b.* 1926, *s.* 1967, *m.*	Hon. John *N.*, *b.* 1960
1939	*Glentoran* (3rd), (Thomas) Robin (Valerian) Dixon, CBE, *b.* 1935, *s.* 1995, *m.*	Hon. Daniel G. *D.*, *b.* 1959
1909	*Gorell* (4th), Timothy John Radcliffe Barnes, *b.* 1927, *s.* 1963, *m.*	Hon. Ronald A. H. *B.*, *b.* 1931
1953	*Grantchester* (3rd), Christopher John Suenson-Taylor, *b.* 1951, *s.* 1995, *m.*	Hon. Jesse D. *S.-T.*, *b.* 1977
1782	*Grantley* (8th), Richard William Brinsley Norton, *b.* 1956, *s.* 1995	Hon. Francis J. H. *N.*, *b.* 1960
1794 I.	*Graves* (9th), Evelyn Paget Graves, *b.* 1926, *s.* 1994, *m.*	Hon. Timothy E. *G.*, *b.* 1960
1445 s.	*Gray* (22nd), Angus Diarmid Ian Campbell-Gray, *b.* 1931, *s.* 1946, *m.*	Master of Gray, *b.* 1964
1950	*Greenhill* (3rd), Malcolm Greenhill, *b.* 1924, *s.* 1989	None
1927	*Greenway* (4th), Ambrose Charles Drexel Greenway, *b.* 1941, *s.* 1975, *m.*	Hon. Mervyn S. K. *G.*, *b.* 1942
1902	*Grenfell* (3rd), Julian Pascoe Francis St Leger Grenfell, *b.* 1935, *s.* 1976, *m.*	Francis P. J. *G.*, *b.* 1938
1944	*Gretton* (4th), John Lysander Gretton, *b.* 1975, *s.* 1989	None
1397	*Grey of Codnor* (6th), Richard Henry Cornwall-Legh, *b.* 1936, *s.* 1996, *m.*	Hon. Richard S. C. *C.-L.*, *b.* 1976

Created	Title, order of succession, name, etc.	Heir
1955	*Gridley* (3rd), Richard David Arnold Gridley, *b.* 1956, *s.* 1996, *m.*	Hon. Carl R. *G.*, *b.* 1981
1964	*Grimston of Westbury* (2nd), Robert Walter Sigismund Grimston, *b.* 1925, *s.* 1979, *m.*	Hon. Robert J. S. *G.*, *b.* 1951
1886	*Grimthorpe* (4th), Christopher John Beckett, OBE, *b.* 1915, *s.* 1963, *m.*	Hon. Edward J. *B.*, *b.* 1954
1945	*Hacking* (3rd), Douglas David Hacking, *b.* 1938, *s.* 1971, *m.*	Hon. Douglas F. *H.*, *b.* 1968
1950	*Haden-Guest* (5th), Christopher Haden-Guest, *b.* 1948, *s.* 1996, *m.*	Hon. Nicholas *H.-G.*, *b.* 1951
1886	*Hamilton of Dalzell* (4th), James Leslie Hamilton, *b.* 1938, *s.* 1990, *m.*	Hon. Gavin G. *H.*, *b.* 1968
1874	*Hampton* (6th), Richard Humphrey Russell Pakington, *b.* 1925, *s.* 1974, *m.*	Hon. John H. A. *P.*, *b.* 1964
1939	*Hankey* (3rd), Donald Robin Alers Hankey, *b.* 1938, *s.* 1996, *m.*	Hon. Alexander M. A. *H.*, *b.* 1947
1958	*Harding of Petherton* (2nd), John Charles Harding, *b.* 1928, *s.* 1989, *m.*	Hon. William A. J. *H.*, *b.* 1969
1910	*Hardinge of Penshurst* (4th), Julian Alexander Hardinge, *b.* 1945, *s.* 1997	Hon. Hugh F. *H.*, *b.* 1948
1876	*Harlech* (6th), Francis David Ormsby-Gore, *b.* 1954, *s.* 1985, *m.*	Hon. Jasset D. C. *O.-G.*, *b.* 1986
1939	*Harmsworth* (3rd), Thomas Harold Raymond Harmsworth, *b.* 1939, *s.* 1990, *m.*	Hon. Dominic M. E. *H.*, *b.* 1973
1815	*Harris* (8th), Anthony Harris, *b.* 1942, *s.* 1996, *m.*	Ronald G. T. *H.*, *b.* 1911
1954	*Harvey of Tasburgh* (2nd), Peter Charles Oliver Harvey, *b.* 1921, *s.* 1968, *w.*	Charles J. G. *H.*, *b.* 1951
1295	*Hastings* (22nd), Edward Delaval Henry Astley, *b.* 1912, *s.* 1956, *m.*	Hon. Delaval T. H. *A.*, *b.* 1960
1835	*Hatherton* (8th), Edward Charles Littleton, *b.* 1950, *s.* 1985, *m.*	Hon. Thomas E. *L.*, *b.* 1977
1776	*Hawke* (11th), Edward George Hawke, TD, *b.* 1950, *s.* 1992, *m.*	None
1927	*Hayter* (3rd), George Charles Hayter Chubb, KCVO, CBE, *b.* 1911, *s.* 1967, *m.*	Hon. G. William M. *C.*, *b.* 1943
1945	*Hazlerigg* (2nd), Arthur Grey Hazlerigg, MC, TD, *b.* 1910, *s.* 1949, *w.*	Hon. Arthur G. *H.*, *b.* 1951
1943	*Hemingford* (3rd), (Dennis) Nicholas Herbert, *b.* 1934, *s.* 1982, *m.*	Hon. Christopher D. C. *H.*, *b.* 1973
1906	*Hemphill* (5th), Peter Patrick Fitzroy Martyn Martyn-Hemphill, *b.* 1928, *s.* 1957, *m.*	Hon. Charles A. M. *M.-H.*, *b.* 1954
1799 I.*	*Henley* (8th), Oliver Michael Robert Eden (6th *UK Baron, Northington,* 1885), *b.* 1953, *s.* 1977, *m.*	Hon. John W. O. *E.*, *b.* 1988
1800 I.*	*Henniker* (8th), John Patrick Edward Chandos Henniker-Major, KCMG, CVO, MC (4th *UK Baron, Hartismere,* 1866), *b.* 1916, *s.* 1980, *m.*	Hon. Mark I. P. C. *H.-M.*, *b.* 1947
1886	*Herschell* (3rd), Rognvald Richard Farrer Herschell, *b.* 1923, *s.* 1929, *m.*	None
1935	*Hesketh* (3rd), Thomas Alexander Fermor-Hesketh, KBE, PC, *b.* 1950, *s.* 1955, *m.*	Hon. Frederick H. *F.-H.*, *b.* 1988
1828	*Heytesbury* (6th), Francis William Holmes à Court, *b.* 1931, *s.* 1971, *m.*	Hon. James W. *H. à C.*, *b.* 1967
1886	*Hindlip* (6th), Charles Henry Allsopp, *b.* 1940, *s.* 1993, *m.*	Hon. Henry W. *A.*, *b.* 1973
1950	*Hives* (2nd), John Warwick Hives, CBE, *b.* 1913, *s.* 1965, *m.*	Matthew P. *H.*, *b.* 1971
1912	*Hollenden* (3rd), Gordon Hope Hope-Morley, *b.* 1914, *s.* 1977, *m.*	Hon. Ian H. *H.-M.*, *b.* 1946
1897	*HolmPatrick* (4th), Hans James David Hamilton, *b.* 1955, *s.* 1991, *m.*	Hon. Ion H. J. *H.*, *b.* 1956
1797 I.	*Hotham* (8th), Henry Durand Hotham, *b.* 1940, *s.* 1967, *m.*	Hon. William B. *H.*, *b.* 1972
1881	*Hothfield* (6th), Anthony Charles Sackville Tufton, *b.* 1939, *s.* 1991, *m.*	Hon. William S. *T.*, *b.* 1977
1597	*Howard de Walden* (9th), John Osmael Scott-Ellis, TD (5th *UK Baron, Seaford,* 1826), *b.* 1912, *s.* 1946, *m.*	To Barony of Howard de Walden, four co-heiresses. To Barony of Seaford, Colin H. F. *Ellis*, *b.* 1946
1930	*Howard of Penrith* (2nd), Francis Philip Howard, *b.* 1905, *s.* 1939, *m.*	Hon. Philip E. *H.*, *b.* 1945
1960	*Howick of Glendale* (2nd), Charles Evelyn Baring, *b.* 1937, *s.* 1973, *m.*	Hon. David E. C. *B.*, *b.* 1975
1796 I.	*Huntingfield* (7th), Joshua Charles Vanneck, *b.* 1954, *s.* 1994, *m.*	Hon. Gerard C. A. *V.*, *b.* 1985
1866	*Hylton* (5th), Raymond Hervey Jolliffe, *b.* 1932, *s.* 1967, *m.*	Hon. William H. M. *J.*, *b.* 1967
1933	*Iliffe* (3rd), Robert Peter Richard Iliffe, *b.* 1944, *s.* 1996, *m.*	Hon. Edward R. *I.*, *b.* 1968
1543 I.	*Inchiquin* (18th), Conor Myles John O'Brien, *b.* 1943, *s.* 1982, *m.*	Murrough R. *O'B.*, *b.* 1910
1962	*Inchyra* (2nd), Robert Charles Reneke Hoyer Millar, *b.* 1935, *s.* 1989, *m.*	Hon. C. James C. H. *M.*, *b.* 1962
1964	*Inglewood* (2nd), (William) Richard Fletcher-Vane, *b.* 1951, *s.* 1989, *m.*	Hon. Henry W. F. *F.-V.*, *b.* 1990
1919	*Inverforth* (4th), Andrew Peter Weir, *b.* 1966, *s.* 1982	Hon. John V. *W.*, *b.* 1935
1941	*Ironside* (2nd), Edmund Oslac Ironside, *b.* 1924, *s.* 1959, *m.*	Hon. Charles E. G. *I.*, *b.* 1956
1952	*Jeffreys* (3rd), Christopher Henry Mark Jeffreys, *b.* 1957, *s.* 1986, *m.*	Hon. Arthur M. H. *J.*, *b.* 1989
1906	*Joicey* (5th), James Michael Joicey, *b.* 1953, *s.* 1993, *m.*	Hon. William J. *J.*, *b.* 1990
1937	*Kenilworth* (4th), (John) Randle Siddeley, *b.* 1954, *s.* 1981, *m.*	Hon. William R. J. *S.*, *b.* 1992
1935	*Kennet* (2nd), Wayland Hilton Young, *b.* 1923, *s.* 1960, *m.*	Hon. W. A. Thoby *Y.*, *b.* 1957
1776 I.*	*Kensington* (8th), Hugh Ivor Edwardes (5th *UK Baron, Kensington,* 1886), *b.* 1933, *s.* 1981, *m.*	Hon. W. Owen A. *E.*, *b.* 1964
1951	*Kenswood* (2nd), John Michael Howard Whitfield, *b.* 1930, *s.* 1963, *m.*	Hon. Michael C. *W.*, *b.* 1955
1788	*Kenyon* (6th), Lloyd Tyrell-Kenyon, *b.* 1947, *s.* 1993, *m.*	Hon. Lloyd N. *T.-K.*, *b.* 1972
1947	*Kershaw* (4th), Edward John Kershaw, *b.* 1936, *s.* 1962, *m.*	Hon. John C. E. *K.*, *b.* 1971
1943	*Keyes* (2nd), Roger George Bowlby Keyes, *b.* 1919, *s.* 1945, *m.*	Hon. Charles W. P. *K.*, *b.* 1951
1909	*Kilbracken* (3rd), John Raymond Godley, DSC, *b.* 1920, *s.* 1950	Hon. Christopher J. *G.*, *b.* 1945
1900	*Killanin* (3rd), Michael Morris, MBE, TD, *b.* 1914, *s.* 1927, *m.*	Hon. G. Redmond F. *M.*, *b.* 1947

Created	Title, order of succession, name, etc.	Heir
1943	*Killearn* (3rd), Victor Miles George Aldous Lampson, *b.* 1941, *s.* 1996, *m.*	Hon. Miles H. M. *L.*, *b.* 1977
1789 I.	*Kilmaine* (7th), John David Henry Browne, *b.* 1948, *s.* 1978, *m.*	Hon. John F. S. *B.*, *b.* 1983
1831	*Kilmarnock* (7th), Alastair Ivor Gilbert Boyd, *b.* 1927, *s.* 1975, *m.*	Hon. Robin J. *B.*, *b.* 1941
1941	*Kindersley* (3rd), Robert Hugh Molesworth Kindersley, *b.* 1929, *s.* 1976, *m.*	Hon. Rupert J. M. *K.*, *b.* 1955
1223 I.	*Kingsale* (35th), John de Courcy (*Premier Baron of Ireland*), *b.* 1941, *s.* 1969	Nevinson R. *de C.*, *b.* 1920
1902	*Kinross* (5th), Christopher Patrick Balfour, *b.* 1949, *s.* 1985, *m.*	Hon. Alan I. *B.*, *b.* 1978
1951	*Kirkwood* (3rd), David Harvie Kirkwood, PH.D., *b.* 1931, *s.* 1970, *m.*	Hon. James S. *K.*, *b.* 1937
1800 I.	*Langford* (9th), Col. Geoffrey Alexander Rowley-Conwy, OBE, *b.* 1912, *s.* 1953, *m.*	Hon. Owain G. *R. C.*, *b.* 1958
1942	*Latham* (2nd), Dominic Charles Latham, *b.* 1954, *s.* 1970	Anthony M. *L.*, *b.* 1954
1431	*Latymer* (8th), Hugo Nevill Money-Coutts, *b.* 1926, *s.* 1987, *m.*	Hon. Crispin J. A. N. *M.-C.*, *b.* 1955
1869	*Lawrence* (5th), David John Downer Lawrence, *b.* 1937, *s.* 1968	None
1947	*Layton* (3rd), Geoffrey Michael Layton, *b.* 1947, *s.* 1989, *m.*	Hon. David *L.*, MBE, *b.* 1914
1839	*Leigh* (5th), John Piers Leigh, *b.* 1935, *s.* 1979, *m.*	Hon. Christopher D. P. *L.*, *b.* 1960
1962	*Leighton of St Mellons* (2nd), (John) Leighton Seager, *b.* 1922, *s.* 1963, *m.*	Hon. Robert W. H. L. *S.*, *b.* 1955
1797	*Lilford* (7th), George Vernon Powys, *b.* 1931, *s.* 1949, *m.*	Hon. Mark V. *P.*, *b.* 1975
1945	*Lindsay of Birker* (3rd), James Francis Lindsay, *b.* 1945, *s.* 1994, *m.*	Hon. Thomas M. *L.*, *b.* 1915
1758 I.	*Lisle* (7th), John Nicholas Horace Lysaght, *b.* 1903, *s.* 1919, *m.*	Patrick J. *L.*, *b.* 1931
1850	*Londesborough* (9th), Richard John Denison, *b.* 1959, *s.* 1968, *m.*	Hon. James F. *D.*, *b.* 1990
1541 I.	*Louth* (16th), Otway Michael James Oliver Plunkett, *b.* 1929, *s.* 1950, *m.*	Hon. Jonathan O. *P.*, *b.* 1952
1458 S.*	*Lovat* (16th), Simon Fraser (5th *UK Baron, Lovat*, 1837), *b.* 1977, *s.* 1995, *M.*	Jack *F.*, *b.* 1984
1946	*Lucas of Chilworth* (2nd), Michael William George Lucas, *b.* 1926, *s.* 1967, *m.*	Hon. Simon W. *L.*, *b.* 1957
1663	*Lucas* (11th) & *Dingwall* (8th) (*Scottish Lordship*, 1609), Ralph Matthew Palmer, *b.* 1951, *s.* 1991, *m.*	Hon. Lewis E. *P.*, *b.* 1987
1929	*Luke* (3rd), Arthur Charles St John Lawson-Johnston, *b.* 1933, *s.* 1996, *m.*	Hon. Ian J. St J. *L.-J.*, *b.* 1963
1914	*Lyell* (3rd), Charles Lyell, *b.* 1939, *s.* 1943	None
1859	*Lyveden* (6th), Ronald Cecil Vernon, *b.* 1915, *s.* 1973, *m.*	Hon. Jack L. *V.*, *b.* 1938
1959	*MacAndrew* (3rd), Christopher Anthony Colin MacAndrew, *b.* 1945, *s.* 1989, *m.*	Hon. Oliver C. J. *M.*, *b.* 1983
1776 I.	*Macdonald* (8th), Godfrey James Macdonald of Macdonald, *b.* 1947, *s.* 1970, *m.*	Hon. Godfrey E. H. T. *M.*, *b.* 1982
1949	*Macdonald of Gwaenysgor* (2nd), Gordon Ramsay Macdonald, *b.* 1915, *s.* 1966, *m.*	None
1937	*McGowan* (3rd), Harry Duncan Cory McGowan, *b.* 1938, *s.* 1966, *m.*	Hon. Harry J C. *M.*, *b.* 1971
1922	*Maclay* (3rd), Joseph Paton Maclay, *b.* 1942, *s.* 1969, *m.*	Hon. Joseph P. *M.*, *b.* 1977
1955	*McNair* (3rd), Duncan James McNair, *b.* 1947, *s.* 1989, *m.*	Hon. Thomas J. *M.*, *b.* 1990
1951	*Macpherson of Drumochter* (2nd), (James) Gordon Macpherson, *b.* 1924, *s.* 1965, *m.*	Hon. James A. *M.*, *b.* 1979
1937	*Mancroft* (3rd), Benjamin Lloyd Stormont Mancroft, *b.* 1957, *s.* 1987, *m.*	None
1807	*Manners* (5th), John Robert Cecil Manners, *b.* 1923, *s.* 1972, *m.*	Hon. John H. R. *M.*, *b.* 1956
1922	*Manton* (3rd), Joseph Rupert Eric Robert Watson, *b.* 1924, *s.* 1968, *m.*	Maj. Hon. Miles R. M. *W.*, *b.* 1958
1908	*Marchamley* (4th), William Francis Whiteley, *b.* 1968, *s.* 1994	None
1964	*Margadale* (2nd), James Ian Morrison, TD, *b.* 1930, *s.* 1996, *m.*	Hon. Alastair J. *M.*, *b.* 1958
1961	*Marks of Broughton* (2nd), Michael Marks, *b.* 1920, *s.* 1964, *m.*	Hon. Simon R. *M.*, *b.* 1950
1964	*Martonmere* (2nd), John Stephen Robinson, *b.* 1963, *s.* 1989	David A. *R.*, *b.* 1965
1776 I.	*Massy* (9th), Hugh Hamon John Somerset Massy, *b.* 1921, *s.* 1958, *m.*	Hon. David H. S. *M.*, *b.* 1947
1935	*May* (3rd), Michael St John May, *b.* 1931, *s.* 1950, *m.*	Hon. Jasper B. St J. *M.*, *b.* 1965
1928	*Melchett* (4th), Peter Robert Henry Mond, *b.* 1948, *s.* 1973	None
1925	*Merrivale* (3rd), Jack Henry Edmond Duke, *b.* 1917, *s.* 1951, *m.*	Hon. Derek J. P. *D.*, *b.* 1948
1911	*Merthyr.* Disclaimed for life 1977 (*Trevor Oswin Lewis*, Bt., CBE, *b.* 1935, *s.* 1977, *m.*)	David T. *L.*, *b.* 1977
1919	*Meston* (3rd), James Meston, *b.* 1950, *s.* 1984, *m.*	Hon. Thomas J. D. *M.*, *b.* 1977
1838	*Methuen* (7th), Robert Alexander Holt Methuen, *b.* 1931, *s.* 1994, *m.*	Christopher P. M. C. *Methuen-Campbell*, *b.* 1928
1711	*Middleton* (12th), (Digby) Michael Godfrey John Willoughby, MC, *b.* 1921, *s.* 1970, *m.*	Hon. Michael C. J. *W.*, *b.* 1948
1939	*Milford* (3rd), Hugo John Laurence Philipps, *b.* 1929, *s.* 1993, *m.*	Hon. Guy W. *P.*, *b.* 1961
1933	*Milne* (2nd), George Douglass Milne, TD, *b.* 1909, *s.* 1948, *m.*	Hon. George A. *M.*, *b.* 1941
1951	*Milner of Leeds* (2nd), Arthur James Michael Milner, AE, *b.* 1923, *s.* 1967, *m.*	Hon. Richard J. *M.*, *b.* 1959

Created	Title, order of succession, name, etc.	Heir
1947	*Milverton* (2nd), Revd Fraser Arthur Richard Richards, *b.* 1930, *s.* 1978, *m.*	Hon. Michael H. *R.*, *b.* 1936
1873	*Moncreiff* (5th), Harry Robert Wellwood Moncreiff, *b.* 1915, *s.* 1942, *w.*	Hon. Rhoderick H. W. *M.*, *b.* 1954
1884	*Monk Bretton* (3rd), John Charles Dodson, *b.* 1924, *s.* 1933, *m.*	Hon. Christopher M. *D.*, *b.* 1958
1885	*Monkswell* (5th), Gerard Collier, *b.* 1947, *s.* 1984, *m.*	Hon. James A. *C.*, *b.* 1977
1728	*Monson* (11th), John Monson, *b.* 1932, *s.* 1958, *m.*	Hon. Nicholas J. *M.*, *b.* 1955
1885	*Montagu of Beaulieu* (3rd), Edward John Barrington Douglas-Scott-Montagu, *b.* 1926, *s.* 1929, *m.*	Hon. Ralph *D.-S.-M.*, *b.* 1961
1839	*Monteagle of Brandon* (6th), Gerald Spring Rice, *b.* 1926, *s.* 1946, *m.*	Hon. Charles J. S. *R.*, *b.* 1953
1943	*Moran* (2nd), (Richard) John (McMoran) Wilson, KCMG, *b.* 1924, *s.* 1977, *m.*	Hon. James M. *W.*, *b.* 1952
1918	*Morris* (3rd), Michael David Morris, *b.* 1937, *s.* 1975, *m.*	Hon. Thomas A. S. *M.*, *b.* 1982
1950	*Morris of Kenwood* (2nd), Philip Geoffrey Morris, *b.* 1928, *s.* 1954, *m.*	Hon. Jonathan D. *M.*, *b.* 1968
1945	*Morrison* (2nd), Dennis Morrison, *b.* 1914, *s.* 1953	None
1831	*Mostyn* (5th), Roger Edward Lloyd Lloyd-Mostyn, MC, *b.* 1920, *s.* 1965, *m.*	Hon. Llewellyn R. L. *L.-M.*, *b.* 1948
1933	*Mottistone* (4th), David Peter Seely, CBE, *b.* 1920, *s.* 1966, *m.*	Hon. Peter J. P. *S.*, *b.* 1949
1945	*Mountevans* (3rd), Edward Patrick Broke Evans, *b.* 1943, *s.* 1974, *m.*	Hon. Jeffrey de C. R. *E.*, *b.* 1948
1283	*Mowbray* (26th), *Segrave* (27th) (1283), & *Stourton* (23rd) (1448), Charles Edward Stourton, CBE, *b.* 1923, *s.* 1965, *m.*	Hon. Edward W. S. *S.*, *b.* 1953
1932	*Moyne* (3rd), Jonathan Bryan Guinness, *b.* 1930, *s.* 1992, *m.*	Hon. Jasper J. R. *G.*, *b.* 1954
1929	*Moynihan* (4th), Colin Berkeley Moynihan, *b.* 1955, *s.* 1997, *m.*	Hon. Nicholas E. B. *M.*, *b.* 1994
1781 I.	*Muskerry* (9th), Robert Fitzmaurice Deane, *b.* 1948, *s.* 1988, *m.*	Hon. Jonathan F. *D.*, *b.* 1986
1627 S.	*Napier* (14th) & *Ettrick* (5th) (*UK* 1872), Francis Nigel Napier, KCVO, *b.* 1930, *s.* 1954, *m.*	Master of Napier, *b.* 1962
1868	*Napier of Magdala* (6th), Robert Alan Napier, *b.* 1940, *s.* 1987, *m.*	Hon. James R. *N.*, *b.* 1966
1940	*Nathan* (2nd), Roger Carol Michael Nathan, *b.* 1922, *s.* 1963, *m.*	Hon. Rupert H. B. *N.*, *b.* 1957
1960	*Nelson of Stafford* (3rd), Henry Roy George Nelson, *b.* 1943, *s.* 1995, *m.*	Hon. Alistair W. H. *N.*, *b.* 1973
1959	*Netherthorpe* (3rd), James Frederick Turner, *b.* 1964, *s.* 1982, *m.*	Hon. Andrew J. E. *T.*, *b.* 1993
1946	*Newall* (2nd), Francis Storer Eaton Newall, *b.* 1930, *s.* 1963, *m.*	Hon. Richard H. E. *N.*, *b.* 1961
1776 I.	*Newborough* (7th), Robert Charles Michael Vaughan Wynn, DSC, *b.* 1917, *s.* 1965, *m.*	Hon. Robert V. *W.*, *b.* 1949
1892	*Newton* (5th), Richard Thomas Legh, *b.* 1950, *s.* 1992, *m.*	Hon. Piers R. *L.*, *b.* 1979
1930	*Noel-Buxton* (3rd), Martin Connal Noel-Buxton, *b.* 1940, *s.* 1980, *m.*	Hon. Charles C. *N.-B.*, *b.* 1975
1957	*Norrie* (2nd), (George) Willoughby Moke Norrie, *b.* 1936, *s.* 1977, *m.*	Hon. Mark W. J. *N.*, *b.* 1972
1884	*Northbourne* (5th), Christopher George Walter James, *b.* 1926, *s.* 1982, *m.*	Hon. Charles W. H. *J.*, *b.* 1960
1866	*Northbrook* (6th), Francis Thomas Baring, *b.* 1954, *s.* 1990, *m.*	None
1878	*Norton* (8th), James Nigel Arden Adderley, *b.* 1947, *s.* 1993, *m.*	Hon. Edward J. A. *A.*, *b.* 1982
1906	*Nunburnholme* (4th), Ben Charles Wilson, *b.* 1928, *s.* 1974	Hon. Charles T. *W.*, *b.* 1935
	Oaksey, see *Trevethin and Oaksey*	
1950	*Ogmore* (2nd), Gwilym Rees Rees-Williams, *b.* 1931, *s.* 1976, *m.*	Hon. Morgan *R.-W.*, *b.* 1937
1870	*O'Hagan* (4th), Charles Towneley Strachey, *b.* 1945, *s.* 1961	Hon. Richard T. *S.*, *b.* 1950
1868	*O'Neill* (4th), Raymond Arthur Clanaboy O'Neill, TD, *b.* 1933, *s.* 1944, *m.*	Hon. Shane S. C. *O'N.*, *b.* 1965
1836 I.*	*Oranmore and Browne* (4th), Dominick Geoffrey Edward Browne (2nd *UK Baron Mereworth*, 1926), *b.* 1901, *s.* 1927, *m.*	Hon. Dominick G. T. *B.*, *b.* 1929
1933	*Palmer* (4th), Adrian Bailie Nottage Palmer, *b.* 1951, *s.* 1990, *m.*	Hon. Hugo B. R. *P.*, *b.* 1980
1914	*Parmoor* (4th), (Frederick Alfred) Milo Cripps, *b.* 1929, *s.* 1977	M. Anthony L. *C.*, CBE, DSO, TD, QC, *b.* 1913
1937	*Pender* (3rd), John Willoughby Denison-Pender, *b.* 1933, *s.* 1965, *m.*	Hon. Henry J. R. *D.-P.*, *b.* 1968
1866	*Penrhyn* (6th), Malcolm Frank Douglas-Pennant, DSO, MBE, *b.* 1908, *s.* 1967, *m.*	Hon. Nigel *D.-P.*, *b.* 1909
1603	*Petre* (18th), John Patrick Lionel Petre, *b.* 1942, *s.* 1989, *m.*	Hon. Dominic W. *P.*, *b.* 1966
1918	*Phillimore* (5th), Francis Stephen Phillimore, *b.* 1944, *s.* 1994, *m.*	Hon. Tristan A. S. *P.*, *b.* 1977
1945	*Piercy* (3rd), James William Piercy, *b.* 1946, *s.* 1981	Hon. Mark E. P. *P.*, *b.* 1953
1827	*Plunket* (8th), Robin Rathmore Plunket, *b.* 1925, *s.* 1975, *m.*	Hon. Shaun A. F. S. *P.*, *b.* 1931
1831	*Poltimore* (7th), Mark Coplestone Bampfylde, *b.* 1957, *s.* 1978, *m.*	Hon. Henry A. W. *B.*, *b.* 1985
1690 S.	*Polwarth* (10th), Henry Alexander Hepburne-Scott, TD, *b.* 1916, *s.* 1944, *m.*	Master of Polwarth, *b.* 1947
1930	*Ponsonby of Shulbrede* (4th), Frederick Matthew Thomas Ponsonby, *b.* 1958, *s.* 1990	None
1958	*Poole* (2nd), David Charles Poole, *b.* 1945, *s.* 1993, *m.*	Hon. Oliver J. *P.*, *b.* 1972
1852	*Raglan* (5th), FitzRoy John Somerset, *b.* 1927, *s.* 1964	Hon. Geoffrey *S.*, *b.* 1932
1932	*Rankeillour* (4th), Peter St Thomas More Henry Hope, *b.* 1935, *s.* 1967	Michael R. *H.*, *b.* 1940
1953	*Rathcavan* (3rd), Hugh Detmar Torrens O'Neill, *b.* 1939, *s.* 1994, *m.*	Hon. François H. N. *O'N.*, *b.* 1984
1916	*Rathcreedan* (3rd), Christopher John Norton, *b.* 1949, *s.* 1990, *m.*	Hon. Adam G. *N.*, *b.* 1952

Created	Title, order of succession, name, etc.	Heir
1868 I.	*Rathdonnell* (5th), Thomas Benjamin McClintock-Bunbury, *b.* 1938, *s.* 1959, *m.*	Hon. William L. *M.-B.*, *b.* 1966
1911	*Ravensdale* (3rd), Nicholas Mosley, MC, *b.* 1923, *s.* 1966, *m.*	Hon. Shaun N. *M.*, *b.* 1949
1821	*Ravensworth* (8th), Arthur Waller Liddell, *b.* 1924, *s.* 1950, *m.*	Hon. Thomas A. H. *L.*, *b.* 1954
1821	*Rayleigh* (6th), John Gerald Strutt, *b.* 1960, *s.* 1988, *m.*	Hon. John F. *S.*, *b.* 1993
1937	*Rea* (3rd), John Nicolas Rea, MD, *b.* 1928, *s.* 1981, *m.*	Hon. Matthew J. *R.*, *b.* 1956
1628 S.	*Reay* (14th), Hugh William Mackay, *b.* 1937, *s.* 1963, *m.*	Master of Reay, *b.* 1965
1902	*Redesdale* (6th), Rupert Bertram Mitford, *b.* 1967, *s.* 1991	None
1940	*Reith*. Disclaimed for life 1972 (*Christopher John Reith*, *b.* 1928, *s.* 1971, *m.*)	Hon. James H. J. *R.*, *b.* 1971
1928	*Remnant* (3rd), James Wogan Remnant, CVO, *b.* 1930, *s.* 1967, *m.*	Hon. Philip J. *R.*, *b.* 1954
1806 I.	*Rendlesham* (8th), Charles Anthony Hugh Thellusson, *b.* 1915, *s.* 1943, *w.*	Hon. Charles W. B. *T.*, *b.* 1954
1933	*Rennell* (3rd), (John Adrian) Tremayne Rodd, *b.* 1935, *s.* 1978, *m.*	Hon. James R. D. T. *R.*, *b.* 1978
1964	*Renwick* (2nd), Harry Andrew Renwick, *b.* 1935, *s.* 1973, *m.*	Hon. Robert J. *R.*, *b.* 1966
1885	*Revelstoke* (5th), John Baring, *b.* 1934, *s.* 1994	Hon. James C. *B.*, *b.* 1938
1905	*Ritchie of Dundee* (5th), (Harold) Malcolm Ritchie, *b.* 1919, *s.* 1978, *m.*	Hon. C. Rupert R. *R.*, *b.* 1958
1935	*Riverdale* (2nd), Robert Arthur Balfour, *b.* 1901, *s.* 1957, *w.*	Hon. Mark R. *B.*, *b.* 1927
1961	*Robertson of Oakridge* (2nd), William Ronald Robertson, *b.* 1930, *s.* 1974, *m.*	Hon. William B. E. *R.*, *b.* 1975
1938	*Roborough* (3rd), Henry Massey Lopes, *b.* 1940, *s.* 1992, *m.*	Hon. Massey J. H. *L.*, *b.* 1969
1931	*Rochester* (2nd), Foster Charles Lowry Lamb, *b.* 1916, *s.* 1955, *m.*	Hon. David C. *L.*, *b.* 1944
1934	*Rockley* (3rd), James Hugh Cecil, *b.* 1934, *s.* 1976, *m.*	Hon. Anthony R. *C.*, *b.* 1961
1782	*Rodney* (10th), George Brydges Rodney, *b.* 1953, *s.* 1992, *m.*	Nicholas S. H. *R.*, *b.* 1947
1651 S.*	*Rollo* (13th), Eric John Stapylton Rollo (4th *UK Baron, Dunning*, 1869), *b.* 1915, *s.* 1947, *m.*	Master of Rollo, *b.* 1943
1959	*Rootes* (3rd), Nicholas Geoffrey Rootes, *b.* 1951, *s.* 1992, *m.*	William B. *R.*, *b.* 1944
1796 I.*	*Rossmore* (7th), William Warner Westenra (6th *UK Baron, Rossmore*, 1838), *b.* 1931, *s.* 1958, *m.*	Hon. Benedict W. *W.*, *b.* 1983
1939	*Rotherwick* (3rd), (Herbert) Robin Cayzer, *b.* 1954, *s.* 1996, *m.*	Hon. H. Robin *C.*, *b.* 1989
1885	*Rothschild* (4th), (Nathaniel Charles) Jacob Rothschild, *b.* 1936, *s.* 1990, *m.*	Hon. Nathaniel P. V. J. *R.*, *b.* 1971
1911	*Rowallan* (4rh), John Polson Cameron Corbett, *b.* 1947, *s.* 1993, *m.*	Hon. Jason W. P. C. *C.*, *b.* 1972
1947	*Rugby* (3rd), Robert Charles Maffey, *b.* 1951, *s.* 1990, *m.*	Hon. Timothy J. H. *M.*, *b.* 1975
1919	*Russell of Liverpool* (3rd), Simon Gordon Jared Russell, *b.* 1952, *s.* 1981, *m.*	Hon. Edward C. S. *R.*, *b.* 1985
1876	*Sackville* (6th), Lionel Bertrand Sackville-West, *b.* 1913, *s.* 1965, *m.*	Hugh R. I. *S.-W.*, MC, *b.* 1919
1964	*St Helens* (2nd), Richard Francis Hughes-Young, *b.* 1945, *s.* 1980, *m.*	Hon. Henry T. *H.-Y.*, *b.* 1986
1559	*St John of Bletso* (21st), Anthony Tudor St John, *b.* 1957, *s.* 1978, *m.*	Hon. Oliver B. *St J.*, *b.* 1995
1887	*St Levan* (4th), John Francis Arthur St Aubyn, DSC, *b.* 1919, *s.* 1978, *m.*	Hon. O. Piers *St A.*, MC, *b.* 1920
1885	*St Oswald* (5th), Derek Edward Anthony Winn, *b.* 1919, *s.* 1984, *m.*	Hon. Charles R. A. *W.*, *b.* 1959
1960	*Sanderson of Ayot*. Disclaimed for life 1971 (*Alan Lindsay Sanderson*, *b.* 1931, *s.* 1971, *m.*)	Hon. Michael *S.*, *b.* 1959
1945	*Sandford* (2nd), Revd John Cyril Edmondson, DSC, *b.* 1920, *s.* 1959, *m.*	Hon. James J. M. *E.*, *b.* 1949
1871	*Sandhurst* (5th), (John Edward) Terence Mansfield, DFC, *b.* 1920, *s.* 1964, *m.*	Hon. Guy R. J. *M.*, *b.* 1949
1802	*Sandys* (7th), Richard Michael Oliver Hill, *b.* 1931, *s.* 1961, *m.*	The Marquess of Downshire (*see* page 139)
1888	*Savile* (3rd), George Halifax Lumley-Savile, *b.* 1919, *s.* 1931	Hon. Henry L. T. *L.-S.*, *b.* 1923
1447	*Saye and Sele* (21st), Nathaniel Thomas Allen Fiennes, *b.* 1920, *s.* 1968, *m.*	Hon. Richard I. *F.*, *b.* 1959
1932	*Selsdon* (3rd), Malcolm McEacharn Mitchell-Thomson, *b.* 1937, *s.* 1963, *m.*	Hon. Callum M. M. *M. T.*, *b.* 1969
1489 S.	*Sempill* (21st), James William Stuart Whitemore Sempill, *b.* 1949, *s.* 1995, *m.*	Master of Sempill, *b.* 1979
1916	*Shaughnessy* (3rd), William Graham Shaughnessy, *b.* 1922, *s.* 1938, *m.*	Hon. Michael J. *S.*, *b.* 1946
1946	*Shepherd* (2nd), Malcolm Newton Shepherd, PC, *b.* 1918, *s.* 1954, *m.*	Hon. Graeme G. *S.*, *b.* 1949
1964	*Sherfield* (2nd), Christopher James Makins, *b.* 1942, *s.* 1996, *m.*	†
1902	*Shuttleworth* (5th), Charles Geoffrey Nicholas Kay-Shuttleworth, *b.* 1948, *s.* 1975, *m.*	Hon. Thomas E. *K.-S.*, *b.* 1976
1950	*Silkin*. Disclaimed for life 1972 (*Arthur Silkin*, *b.* 1916, *s.* 1972, *m.*)	Hon. Christopher L. *S.*, *b.* 1947
1963	*Silsoe* (2nd), David Malcolm Trustram Eve, QC, *b.* 1930, *s.* 1976, *m.*	Hon. Simon R. T. *E.*, *b.* 1966
1947	*Simon of Wythenshawe* (2nd), Roger Simon, *b.* 1913, *s.* 1960, *m.*	Hon. Matthew *S.*, *b.* 1955
1449 S.	*Sinclair* (17th), Charles Murray Kennedy St Clair, CVO, *b.* 1914, *s.* 1957, *m.*	Master of Sinclair, *b.* 1968
1957	*Sinclair of Cleeve* (3rd), John Lawrence Robert Sinclair, *b.* 1953, *s.* 1985	None
1919	*Sinha* (5th), Anindo Kumar Sinha, *b.* 1930, *s.* 1992	Hon. Arup K. *S.*, *b.* 1966
1828	*Skelmersdale* (7th), Roger Bootle-Wilbraham, *b.* 1945, *s.* 1973, *m.*	Hon. Andrew *B.-W.*, *b.* 1977

Created	Title, order of succession, name, etc.	Heir
1916	*Somerleyton* (3rd), Savile William Francis Crossley, KCVO, *b.* 1928, *s.* 1959, *m. Master of the Horse*	Hon. Hugh F. S. C., *b.* 1971
1784	*Somers* (9th), Philip Sebastian Somers Cocks, *b.* 1948, *s.* 1995	Alan B. C., *b.* 1930
1780	*Southampton* (6th), Charles James FitzRoy, *b.* 1928, *s.* 1989, *w.*	Hon. Edward C. F., *b.* 1955
1959	*Spens* (3rd), Patrick Michael Rex Spens, *b.* 1942, *s.* 1984, *m.*	Hon. Patrick N. G. S., *b.* 1968
1640	*Stafford* (15th), Francis Melfort William Fitzherbert, *b.* 1954, *s.* 1986, *m.*	Hon. Benjamin J.B. F., *b.* 1983
1938	*Stamp* (4th), Trevor Charles Bosworth Stamp, MD, FRCP, *b.* 1935, *s.* 1987, *m.*	Hon. Nicholas C. T. S., *b.* 1978
1839	*Stanley of Alderley* (8th) & *Sheffield* (8th) (1738 I.), Thomas Henry Oliver Stanley (7th *UK Baron Eddisbury*, 1848), *b.* 1927, *s.* 1971, *m.*	Hon. Richard O. S., *b.* 1956
1318	*Strabolgi* (11th), David Montague de Burgh Kenworthy, *b.* 1914, *s.* 1953, *m.*	Andrew D. W. K., *b.* 1967
1954	*Strang* (2nd), Colin Strang, *b.* 1922, *s.* 1978, *m.*	None
1955	*Strathalmond* (3rd), William Roberton Fraser, *b.* 1947, *s.* 1976, *m.*	Hon. William G. F., *b.* 1976
1936	*Strathcarron* (2nd), David William Anthony Blyth Macpherson, *b.* 1924, *s.* 1937, *m.*	Hon. Ian D. P. M., *b.* 1949
1955	*Strathclyde* (2nd), Thomas Galloway Dunlop du Roy de Blicquy Galbraith, PC, *b.* 1960, *s.* 1985, *m.*	Hon. Charles W. du R. de B. G., *b.* 1962
1900	*Strathcona and Mount Royal* (4th), Donald Euan Palmer Howard, *b.* 1923, *s.* 1959, *m.*	Hon. D. Alexander S. H., *b.* 1961
1836	*Stratheden* (6th) & *Campbell* (6th) (1841), Donald Campbell, *b.* 1934, *s.* 1987, *m.*	Hon. David A. C., *b.* 1963
1884	*Strathspey* (6th), James Patrick Trevor Grant of Grant, *b.* 1943, *s.* 1992, *m.*	Hon. Michael P. F. G., *b.* 1953
1838	*Sudeley* (7th), Merlin Charles Sainthill Hanbury-Tracy, *b.* 1939, *s.* 1941	D. Andrew J. H-T., *b.* 1928
1786	*Suffield* (11th), Anthony Philip Harbord-Hamond, MC, *b.* 1922, *s.* 1951, *m.*	Hon. Charles A. A. H.-H., *b.* 1953
1893	*Swansea* (4th), John Hussey Hamilton Vivian, *b.* 1925, *s.* 1934, *m.*	Hon. Richard A. H. V., *b.* 1957
1907	*Swaythling* (4th), David Charles Samuel Montagu, *b.* 1928, *s.* 1990, *m.*	Hon. Charles E. S. M., *b.* 1954
1919	*Swinfen* (3rd), Roger Mynors Swinfen Eady, *b.* 1938, *s.* 1977, *m.*	Hon. Charles R. P. S. E., *b.* 1971
1935	*Sysonby* (3rd), John Frederick Ponsonby, *b.* 1945, *s.* 1956	None
1831 I.	*Talbot of Malahide* (10th), Reginald John Richard Arundell, *b.* 1931, *s.* 1987, *m.*	Hon. Richard J. T. A., *b.* 1957
1946	*Tedder* (3rd), Robin John Tedder, *b.* 1955, *s.* 1994, *m.*	Hon. Benjamin J. T., *b.* 1985
1884	*Tennyson* (5th), Cdr. Mark Aubrey Tennyson, DSC, *b.* 1920, *s.* 1991, *m.*	Lt.-Cdr. James A. T., DSC, *b.* 1913
1918	*Terrington* (4th), (James Allen) David Woodhouse, *b.* 1915, *s.* 1961, *m.*	Hon. C. Montague W., DSO, OBE, *b.* 1917
1940	*Teviot* (2nd), Charles John Kerr, *b.* 1934, *s.* 1968, *m.*	Hon. Charles R. K., *b.* 1971
1616	*Teynham* (20th), John Christopher Ingham Roper-Curzon, *b.* 1928, *s.* 1972, *m.*	Hon. David J. H. I. R.-C., *b.* 1965
1964	*Thomson of Fleet* (2nd), Kenneth Roy Thomson, *b.* 1923, *s.* 1976, *m.*	Hon. David K. R. T., *b.* 1957
1792	*Thurlow* (8th), Francis Edward Hovell-Thurlow-Cumming-Bruce, KCMG, *b.* 1912, *s.* 1971, *w.*	Hon. Roualeyn R. H.-T.-C.-B., *b.* 1952
1876	*Tollemache* (5th), Timothy John Edward Tollemache, *b.* 1939, *s.* 1975, *m.*	Hon. Edward J. H. T., *b.* 1976
1564 S.	*Torphichen* (15th), James Andrew Douglas Sandilands, *b.* 1946, *s.* 1975, *m.*	Douglas R. A. S., *b.* 1926
1947	*Trefgarne* (2nd), David Garro Trefgarne, PC, *b.* 1941, *s.* 1960, *m.*	Hon. George G. T., *b.* 1970
1921	*Trevethin* (4th), *and Oaksey* (2nd) (1947), John Geoffrey Tristram Lawrence, OBE, *b.* 1929, *s.* 1971, *m.*	Hon. Patrick J. T. L., *b.* 1960
1880	*Trevor* (5th), Marke Charles Hill-Trevor, *b.* 1970, *s.* 1997, *m.*	Hon. Iain R. H.-T., *b.* 1971
1461 I.	*Trimlestown* (21st), Raymond Charles Barnewall, *b.* 1930, *s.* 1997	None
1940	*Tryon* (3rd), Anthony George Merrik Tryon, *b.* 1940, *s.* 1976	Hon. Charles G. B. T., *b.* 1976
1935	*Tweedsmuir* (3rd), William de l'Aigle Buchan, *b.* 1916, *s.* 1996, *m.*	Hon. John W. H. de l'A. B., *b.* 1950
1523	*Vaux of Harrowden* (10th), John Hugh Philip Gilbey, *b.* 1915, *s.* 1977, *m.*	Hon. Anthony W. G., *b.* 1940
1800 I.	*Ventry* (8th), Andrew Wesley Daubeny de Moleyns, *b.* 1943, *s.* 1987, *m.*	Hon. Francis W. D. de M., *b.* 1965
1762	*Vernon* (10th), John Lawrance Vernon, *b.* 1923, *s.* 1963, *m.*	Col. William R. D. *Vernon-Harcourt*, OBE, *b.* 1909
1922	*Vestey* (3rd), Samuel George Armstrong Vestey, *b.* 1941, *s.* 1954, *m.*	Hon. William G. V., *b.* 1983
1841	*Vivian* (6th), Nicholas Crespigny Laurence Vivian, *b.* 1935, *s.* 1991, *m.*	Hon. Charles H. C. V., *b.* 1966
1934	*Wakehurst* (3rd), (John) Christopher Loder, *b.* 1925, *s.* 1970, *m.*	Hon. Timothy W. L., *b.* 1958
1723	*Walpole* (10th), Robert Horatio Walpole (*8th Brit. Baron Walpole of Wolterton*, 1756), *b.* 1938, *s.* 1989, *m.*	Hon. Jonathan R. H. W., *b.* 1967
1780	*Walsingham* (9th), John de Grey, MC, *b.* 1925, *s.* 1965, *m.*	Hon. Robert *de G.*, *b.* 1969
1936	*Wardington* (2nd), Christopher Henry Beaumont Pease, *b.* 1924, *s.* 1950, *m.*	Hon. William S. P., *b.* 1925

Created	Title, order of succession, name, etc.	Heir
1792 I.	*Waterpark* (7th), Frederick Caryll Philip Cavendish, *b.* 1926, *s.* 1948, *m.*	Hon. Roderick A. *C.*, *b.* 1959
1942	*Wedgwood* (4th), Piers Anthony Weymouth Wedgwood, *b.* 1954, *s.* 1970, *m.*	John *W.*, CBE, MD, FRCP, *b.* 1919
1861	*Westbury* (5th), David Alan Bethell, CBE, MC, *b.* 1922, *s.* 1961, *m.*	Hon. Richard N. *B.*, MBE, *b.* 1950
1944	*Westwood* (3rd), (William) Gavin Westwood, *b.* 1944, *s.* 1991, *m.*	Hon. W. Fergus *W.*, *b.* 1972
1935	*Wigram* (2nd), (George) Neville (Clive) Wigram, MC, *b.* 1915, *s.* 1960, *w.*	Maj. Hon. Andrew F. C. *W.*, MVO, *b.* 1949
1491	*Willoughby de Broke* (21st), Leopold David Verney, *b.* 1938, *s.* 1986, *m.*	Hon. Rupert G. *V.*, *b.* 1966
1946	*Wilson* (2nd), Patrick Maitland Wilson, *b.* 1915, *s.* 1964, *w.*	None
1937	*Windlesham* (3rd), David James George Hennessy, CVO, PC, *b.* 1932, *s.* 1962, *w.*	Hon. James R. *H.*, *b.* 1968
1951	*Wise* (2nd), John Clayton Wise, *b.* 1923, *s.* 1968, *m.*	Hon. Christopher J. C. *W.*, PH.D., *b.* 1949
1869	*Wolverton* (7th), Christopher Richard Glyn, *b.* 1938, *s.* 1988	Hon. Andrew J. *G.*, *b.* 1943
1928	*Wraxall* (2nd), George Richard Lawley Gibbs, *b.* 1928, *s.* 1931	Hon. Sir Eustace H. B. *G.*, KCVO, CMG, *b.* 1929
1915	*Wrenbury* (3rd), Revd John Burton Buckley, *b.* 1927, *s.* 1940, *m.*	Hon. William E. *B.*, *b.* 1966
1838	*Wrottesley* (6th), Clifton Hugh Lancelot de Verdon Wrottesley, *b.* 1968, *s.* 1977	Hon. Stephen J. *W.*, *b.* 1955
1919	*Wyfold* (3rd), Hermon Robert Fleming Hermon-Hodge, ERD, *b.* 1915, *s.* 1942	None
1829	*Wynford* (8th), Robert Samuel Best, MBE, *b.* 1917, *s.* 1943, *m.*	Hon. John P. R. *B.*, *b.* 1950
1308	*Zouche* (18th), James Assheton Frankland, *b.* 1943, *s.* 1965, *m.*	Hon. William T. A. *F.*, *b.* 1984

BARONESSES/LADIES IN THEIR OWN RIGHT

Style, The Right Hon. the Lady __ , *or* The Right Hon. the Baroness __ , according to her preference. Either style may be used, except in the case of Scottish titles (indicated by s.), which are not baronies (*see* page 137) and whose holders are always addressed as Lady
Husband, Untitled
Children's style, As for children of a Baron
For forms of address, *see* page 136

Created	Title, order of succession, name, etc.	Heir
1455	*Berners* (16th in line), Pamela Vivien Kirkham, *b.* 1929, *title called out of abeyance* 1995, *m.*	Hon. Rupert W. T. *K.*, *b.* 1953
1529	*Braye* (8th in line), Mary Penelope Aubrey-Fletcher, *b.* 1941, *s.* 1985, *m.*	Two co-heiresses
1321	*Dacre* (27th in line), Rachel Leila Douglas-Home, *b.* 1929, *title called out of abeyance* 1970, *w.*	Hon. James T. A. *D.-H.*, *b.* 1952
1332	*Darcy de Knayth* (18th in line), Davina Marcia Ingrams, DBE, *b.* 1938, *s.* 1943, *w.*	Hon. Caspar D. *I.*, *b.* 1962
1439	*Dudley* (14th in line), Barbara Amy Felicity Hamilton, *b.* 1907, *s.* 1972, *m.*	Hon. Jim A. H. *Wallace*, *b.* 1930
1490 s.	*Herries of Terregles* (14th in line), Anne Elizabeth Fitzalan-Howard, *b.* 1938, *s.* 1975, *m.*	Lady Mary *Mumford*, CVO, *b.* 1940
1602 s.	*Kinloss* (12th in line), Beatrice Mary Grenville Freeman-Grenville, *b.* 1922, *s.* 1944, *m.*	Master of Kinloss, *b.* 1953
1445 s.	*Saltoun* (20th in line), Flora Marjory Fraser, *b.* 1930, *s.* 1979, *m.*	Hon. Katharine I. M. I. *F.*, *b.* 1957
1628	*Strange* (16th in line), (Jean) Cherry Drummond of Megginch, *b.* 1928, *title called out of abeyance* 1986, *m.*	Hon. Adam H. *D.* of *M.*, *b.* 1953
1544/5	*Wharton* (11th in line), Myrtle Olive Felix Robertson, *b.* 1934, *title called out of abeyance* 1990, *m.*	Hon. Myles C. D. *R.*, *b.* 1964
1313	*Willoughby de Eresby* (27th in line), (Nancy) Jane Marie Heathcote-Drummond-Willoughby, *b.* 1934, *s.* 1983	Two co-heiresses

Life Peers

Law Lords: Hon. Lord Clyde; Rt. Hon. Sir Brian Hutton; Sir Mark Savile
New Year's Honours (30 December 1996): Dame Audrey Emerton, DBE; Raj Bagri, CBE; Sir Andrew Lloyd Webber
Dissolution Honours (18 April 1997): David Alton, MP; Rt. Hon. Kenneth Baker, CH, MP; Rt. Hon. John Biffen, MP; Rt. Hon. Paul Channon, MP; Rt. Hon. Donald Dixon, MP; John Evans, MP; Rt. Hon. Roy Hattersley, MP*; Rt. Hon. David Howell, MP; Douglas Hoyle, MP; Rt. Hon. Douglas Hurd, CH, CBE, MP; Sir Russell Johnston, MP; Rt. Hon. Michael Jopling, MP; Miss Joan Lestor, MP; Sir Geoffrey Lofthouse, MP; Rt. Hon. Sir Patrick Mayhew, QC; Rt. Hon. Sir James Molyneaux, KBE, MP; Rt. Hon. John Patten, MP; Rt. Hon. Timothy Renton, MP; Rt. Hon. Richard Ryder, OBE, MP*; Rt. Hon. Peter Shore, MP; Rt. Hon. Sir David Steel, KBE, MP
New Ministers (May 1997): Charles Falconer, QC; Rt. Hon. John Gilbert; Andrew Hardie, QC; Sir David Simon, CBE
Queen's Birthday Honours (13 June 1997): Sir Colin Cowdrey, CBE; Field Marshal Sir Peter Inge, GCB; Sir Peter Levene, KBE
Resignation Honours (1 August 1997): Norman Blackwell*; Dame Janet Fookes, DBE*; Rt. Hon. Roger Freeman*; Rt. Hon. Lord James Douglas-Hamilton*; Rt. Hon. Sir Terence Higgins*; Rt. Hon. David Hunt*; Dame Jill Knight, DBE*; Rt. Hon. Ian Lang*; Rt. Hon. Antony Newton*; Rt. Hon. Sir Cranley Onslow*
Working Peers (1 August 1997): Valerie Amos*; Steven Bassam*; Clive Brooke*; Tom Burlison*; Rt. Hon. Sir John Cope*; Bryan Davies*; David Davies, CBE*; Navnit Dholakia, OBE*; Sir William Goodhart, QC*; James Gordon, CBE*; Peter Hardy*; Norman Hogg*; Robert Hughes*; Roy Hughes*; Philip Hunt, OBE*; Sir Anthony Jacobs*; Greville Janner, QC*; Rt. Hon. Tristan Garel-Jones*; Helena Kennedy, QC*; Michael Levy*; Veronica Linklater*; Sarah Ludford*; Diana Maddock*; Rt. Hon. Sir Hector Monro*; Michael Montague, CBE*; Rt. Hon. Alf Morris*; Rt. Hon. Michael Morris*; Richard Newby, OBE*; Emma Nicholson*; Rt. Hon. Stan Orme*; Jill Pitkeathley, OBE*; Sir David Puttnam, CBE*; Stuart Randall*; Timothy Razzall, CBE*; Ruth Rendell, CBE*; Sir Robin Renwick, KCMG*; Rt. Hon. Sir Wyn Roberts*; David Sainsbury*; Sir Michael Sandberg, CBE*; Patricia Scotland, QC*; Barbara Scott Young*; George Simpson*; Sir Trevor Smith*; Andrew Stone*; Terence Thomas, CBE*; Rt. Hon. Sir Harold Walker*; Michael Watson*

*No title gazetted at time of going to press

CREATED UNDER THE APPELLATE JURISDICTION ACT 1876 (as amended)

BARONS

Created
1986   *Ackner*, Desmond James Conrad Ackner, PC, *b. 1920, m.*
1981   *Brandon of Oakbrook*, Henry Vivian Brandon, MC, PC, *b. 1920, m.*
1980   *Bridge of Harwich*, Nigel Cyprian Bridge, PC, *b. 1917, m.*
1982   *Brightman*, John Anson Brightman, PC, *b. 1911, m.*
1991   *Browne-Wilkinson*, Nicolas Christopher Henry Browne-Wilkinson, PC, *b. 1930, m.* Lord of Appeal in Ordinary
1996   *Clyde*, James John Clyde, *b. 1932, m.* Lord of Appeal in Ordinary
1957   *Denning*, Alfred Thompson Denning, PC, *b. 1899, w.*
1986   *Goff of Chieveley*, Robert Lionel Archibald Goff, PC, *b. 1926, m.* Lord of Appeal in Ordinary
1985   *Griffiths*, (William) Hugh Griffiths, MC, PC, *b. 1923, m.*
1995   *Hoffmann*, Leonard Hubert Hoffmann, PC, *b. 1934, m.*
1997   *Hutton*, (James) Brian (Edward) Hutton, PC, *b. 1931, m.*
1988   *Jauncey of Tullichettle*, Charles Eliot Jauncey, PC, *b. 1925, m.*
1977   *Keith of Kinkel*, Henry Shanks Keith, GBE, PC, *b. 1922, m.*
1979   *Lane*, Geoffrey Dawson Lane, AFC, PC, *b. 1918, m.*
1993   *Lloyd of Berwick*, Anthony John Leslie Lloyd, PC, *b. 1929, m.* Lord of Appeal in Ordinary
1992   *Mustill*, Michael John Mustill, PC, *b. 1931, m.*
1994   *Nicholls of Birkenhead*, Donald James Nicholls, PC, *b. 1933, m.*
1994   *Nolan*, Michael Patrick Nolan, PC, *b. 1928, m.* Lord of Appeal in Ordinary
1986   *Oliver of Aylmerton*, Peter Raymond Oliver, PC, *b. 1921, m.*
1997   *Saville of Newdigate*, Mark Oliver Savile, PC, *b. 1936, m.*
1977   *Scarman*, Leslie George Scarman, OBE, PC, *b. 1911, m.*
1992   *Slynn of Hadley*, Gordon Slynn, PC, *b. 1930, m.* Lord of Appeal in Ordinary
1995   *Steyn*, Johan van Zyl Steyn, PC, *b. 1932, m.*
1982   *Templeman*, Sydney William Templeman, MBE, PC, *b. 1920, m.*
1964   *Wilberforce*, Richard Orme Wilberforce, CMG, OBE, PC, *b. 1907, m.*
1992   *Woolf*, Harry Kenneth Woolf, PC, *b. 1933, m.* Master of the Rolls

CREATED UNDER THE LIFE PEERAGES ACT 1958

BARONS

Created
1996   *Alderdice*, John Thomas Alderdice, *b. 1955, m.*
1988   *Alexander of Weedon*, Robert Scott Alexander, QC, *b. 1936, m.*
1976   *Allen of Abbeydale*, Philip Allen, GCB, *b. 1912, m.*
1961   *Alport*, Cuthbert James McCall Alport, TD, PC, *b. 1912, w.*
1997   *Alton of Liverpool*, David Patrick Paul Alton, *b. 1951, m.*
1965   *Annan*, Noël Gilroy Annan, OBE, *b. 1916, m.*
1992   *Archer of Sandwell*, Peter Kingsley Archer, PC, QC, *b. 1926, m.*
1992   *Archer of Weston-super-Mare*, Jeffrey Howard Archer, *b. 1940, m.*

1988   *Armstrong of Ilminster*, Robert Temple
Armstrong, GCB, CVO, *b.* 1927, *m.*
1992   *Ashley of Stoke*, Jack Ashley, CH, PC, *b.* 1922, *m.*
1993   *Attenborough*, Richard Samuel Attenborough, CBE,
b. 1923, *m.*
1997   *Bagri*, Raj Kumar Bagri, CBE, *b.* 19–
1997   *Baker of Dorking*, Kenneth Wilfred Baker, CH, PC,
b. 1934, *m.*
1974   *Balniel*, The Earl of Crawford and Balcarres, *see*
page 141
1974   *Barber*, Anthony Perrinott Lysberg Barber, TD,
PC, *b.* 1920, *m.*
1992   *Barber of Tewkesbury*, Derek Coates Barber, *b.*
1918, *m.*
1983   *Barnett*, Joel Barnett, PC, *b.* 1923, *m.*
1982   *Bauer*, Prof. Peter Thomas Bauer, D.SC., FBA, *b.*
1915
1967   *Beaumont of Whitley*, Revd Timothy Wentworth
Beaumont, *b.* 1928, *m.*
1979   *Bellwin*, Irwin Norman Bellow, *b.* 1923, *m.*
1981   *Beloff*, Max Beloff, FBA, *b.* 1913, *m.*
1997   *Biffen*, (William) John Biffen, PC, *b.* 1930, *m.*
1996   *Bingham of Cornhill*, Thomas Henry Bingham, PC,
b. 1933, *m., Lord Chief Justice of England*
1971   *Blake*, Robert Norman William Blake, FBA, *b.*
1916, *w.*
1994   *Blaker*, Peter Allan Renshaw Blaker, KCMG, PC, *b.*
1922, *m.*
1978   *Blease*, William John Blease, *b.* 1914, *m.*
1995   *Blyth of Rowington*, James Blyth, *b.* 1940, *m.*
1980   *Boardman*, Thomas Gray Boardman, MC, TD, *b.*
1919, *m.*
1996   *Borrie*, Gordon Johnson Borrie, QC, *b.* 1931, *m.*
1976   *Boston of Faversham*, Terence George Boston, QC,
b. 1930, *m.*
1996   *Bowness*, Peter Spencer Bowness, CBE, *b.* 1943, *m.*
1972   *Boyd-Carpenter*, John Archibald Boyd-Carpenter,
PC, *b.* 1908, *m.*
1992   *Braine of Wheatley*, Bernard Richard Braine, PC, *b.*
1914, *w.*
1987   *Bramall*, Edwin Noel Westby Bramall, KG, GCB,
OBE, MC, *Field Marshal, b.* 1923, *m.*
1976   *Briggs*, Asa Briggs, FBA, *b.* 1921, *m.*
1975   *Brookes*, Raymond Percival Brookes, *b.* 1909, *m.*
1979   *Brooks of Tremorfa*, John Edward Brooks, *b.* 1927,
m.
1974   *Bruce of Donington*, Donald William Trevor
Bruce, *b.* 1912, *m.*
1976   *Bullock*, Alan Louis Charles Bullock, FBA, *b.* 1914,
m.
1988   *Butterfield*, (William) John (Hughes) Butterfield,
OBE, DM, FRCP, *b.* 1920, *m.*
1985   *Butterworth*, John Blackstock Butterworth, CBE, *b.*
1918, *m.*
1978   *Buxton of Alsa*, Aubrey Leland Oakes Buxton,
KCVO, MC, *b.* 1918, *m.*
1987   *Callaghan of Cardiff*, (Leonard) James Callaghan,
KG, PC, *b.* 1912, *m.*
1984   *Cameron of Lochbroom*, Kenneth John Cameron,
PC, *b.* 1931, *m.*
1981   *Campbell of Alloway*, Alan Robertson Campbell,
QC, *b.* 1917, *m.*
1974   *Campbell of Croy*, Gordon Thomas Calthrop
Campbell, MC, PC, *b.* 1921, *m.*
1987   *Carlisle of Bucklow*, Mark Carlisle, QC, PC, *b.* 1929,
m.
1983   *Carmichael of Kelvingrove*, Neil George
Carmichael, *b.* 1921
1975   *Carr of Hadley*, (Leonard) Robert Carr, PC, *b.*
1916, *m.*

1987   *Carter*, Denis Victor Carter, *b.* 1932, *m.*
1977   *Carver*, (Richard) Michael (Power) Carver, GCB,
CBE, DSO, MC, *Field Marshal, b.* 1915, *m.*
1990   *Cavendish of Furness*, (Richard) Hugh Cavendish,
b. 1941, *m.*
1982   *Cayzer*, (William) Nicholas Cayzer, *b.* 1910, *w.*
1996   *Chadlington*, Peter Selwyn Gummer, *b.* 1942, *m.*
1964   *Chalfont*, (Alun) Arthur Gwynne Jones, OBE, MC,
PC, *b.* 1919, *m.*
1985   *Chapple*, Francis (Frank) Joseph Chapple, *b.* 1921,
w.
1978   *Charteris of Amisfield*, Martin Michael Charles
Charteris, GCB, GCVO, OBE, PC, *Royal Victorian
Chain, b.* 1913, *m.*
1987   *Chilver*, (Amos) Henry Chilver, FRS, FENG., *b.*
1926, *m.*
1977   *Chitnis*, Pratap Chidamber Chitnis, *b.* 1936, *m.*
1992   *Clark of Kempston*, William Gibson Haig Clark,
PC, *b.* 1917, *m.*
1979   *Cledwyn of Penrhos*, Cledwyn Hughes, CH, PC, *b.*
1916, *m.*
1990   *Clinton-Davis*, Stanley Clinton Clinton-Davis, *b.*
1928, *m.*
1978   *Cockfield*, (Francis) Arthur Cockfield, PC, *b.* 1916,
w.
1987   *Cocks of Hartcliffe*, Michael Francis Lovell Cocks,
PC, *b.* 1929, *m.*
1980   *Coggan*, Rt. Revd (Frederick) Donald Coggan, PC,
Royal Victorian Chain, b. 1909, *m.*
1981   *Constantine of Stanmore*, Theodore Constantine,
CBE, AE, *b.* 1910, *w.*
1992   *Cooke of Islandreagh*, Victor Alexander Cooke,
OBE, *b.* 1920, *m.*
1996   *Cooke of Thorndon*, Robin Brunskill Cooke, KBE,
PC, PH.D., *b.* 1926, *m.*
1997   *Cowdrey of Tonbridge*, (Michael) Colin Cowdrey,
CBE, *b.* 1932, *m.*
1991   *Craig of Radley*, David Brownrigg Craig, GCB, OBE,
Marshal of the Royal Air Force, b. 1929, *m.*
1987   *Crickhowell*, (Roger) Nicholas Edwards, PC, *b.*
1934, *m.*
1978   *Croham*, Douglas Albert Vivian Allen, GCB, *b.*
1917, *w.*
1995   *Cuckney*, John Graham Cuckney, *b.* 1925, *m.*
1974   *Cudlipp*, Hugh Cudlipp, OBE, *b.* 1913, *m.*
1996   *Currie of Marylebone*, David Anthony Currie, *b.*
1946, *m.*
1979   *Dacre of Glanton*, Hugh Redwald Trevor-Roper,
b. 1914, *w.*
1993   *Dahrendorf*, Ralf Dahrendorf, KBE, PH.D., D.PHIL.,
FBA, *b.* 1929, *m.*
1986   *Dainton*, Frederick Sydney Dainton, PH.D., SC.D.,
FRS, *b.* 1914, *m.*
1983   *Dean of Beswick*, Joseph Jabez Dean, *b.* 1922
1993   *Dean of Harptree*, (Arthur) Paul Dean, PC, *b.* 1924,
m.
1986   *Deedes*, William Francis Deedes, MC, PC, *b.* 1913,
m.
1991   *Desai*, Prof. Meghnad Jagdishchandra Desai,
PH.D., *b.* 1940, *m.*
1970   *Diamond*, John Diamond, PC, *b.* 1907, *m.*
1997   *Dixon*, Donald Dixon, PC, *b.* 1929, *m.*
1993   *Dixon-Smith*, Robert William Dixon-Smith, *b.*
1934, *m.*
1967   *Donaldson of Kingsbridge*, John George Stuart
Donaldson, OBE, *b.* 1907, *w.*
1988   *Donaldson of Lymington*, John Francis Donaldson,
PC, *b.* 1920, *m.*
1985   *Donoughue*, Bernard Donoughue, D.PHIL., *b.* 1934

1987   *Dormand of Easington*, John Donkin Dormand, *b.* 1919, *m.*
1994   *Dubs*, Alfred Dubs, *b.* 1932, *m.*
1995   *Eames*, Robert Henry Alexander Eames, PH.D., *b.* 1937, *m.*
1992   *Eatwell*, John Leonard Eatwell, *b.* 1945, *m.*
1983   *Eden of Winton*, John Benedict Eden, PC, *b.* 1925, *m.*
1992   *Elis-Thomas*, Dafydd Elis Elis-Thomas, *b.* 1946, *m.*
1985   *Elliott of Morpeth*, Robert William Elliott, *b.* 1920, *m.*
1981   *Elystan-Morgan*, Dafydd Elystan Elystan-Morgan, *b.* 1932, *m.*
1980   *Emslie*, George Carlyle Emslie, MBE, PC, FRSE, *b.* 1919, *m.*
1997   *Evans of Parkside*, John Evans, *b.* 1930, *m.*
1992   *Ewing of Kirkford*, Harry Ewing, *b.* 1931, *m.*
1983   *Ezra*, Derek Ezra, MBE, *b.* 1919, *m.*
1997   *Falconer of Thoroton*, Charles Leslie Falconer, QC, *b.* 1951, *m.*
1983   *Fanshawe of Richmond*, Anthony Henry Fanshawe Royle, KCMG, *b.* 1927, *m.*
1996   *Feldman*, Basil Feldman, *b.* 1926, *m.*
1983   *Fitt*, Gerard Fitt, *b.* 1926, *w.*
1979   *Flowers*, Brian Hilton Flowers, FRS, *b.* 1924, *m.*
1967   *Foot*, John Mackintosh Foot, *b.* 1909, *m.*
1982   *Forte*, Charles Forte, *b.* 1908, *m.*
1989   *Fraser of Carmyllie*, Peter Lovat Fraser, PC, QC, *b.* 1945, *m.*
1982   *Gallacher*, John Gallacher, *b.* 1920, *m.*
1992   *Geraint*, Geraint Wyn Howells, *b.* 1925, *m.*
1975   *Gibson*, (Richard) Patrick (Tallentyre) Gibson, *b.* 1916, *m.*
1979   *Gibson-Watt*, (James) David Gibson-Watt, MC, PC, *b.* 1918, *m.*
1997   *Gilbert*, John William Gilbert, PC, PH.D., *b.* 1927, *m.*
1996   *Gillmore of Thamesfield*, David Howe Gillmore, GCMG, *b.* 1934, *m.*
1992   *Gilmour of Craigmillar*, Ian Hedworth John Little Gilmour, PC, *b.* 1926, *m.*
1994   *Gladwin of Clee*, Derek Oliver Gladwin, CBE, *b.* 1930, *m.*
1977   *Glenamara*, Edward Watson Short, CH, PC, *b.* 1912, *m.*
1976   *Grade*, Lew Grade, *b.* 1906, *m.*
1983   *Graham of Edmonton*, (Thomas) Edward Graham, *b.* 1925, *m.*
1967   *Granville of Eye*, Edgar Louis Granville, *b.* 1899, *m.*
1983   *Gray of Contin*, James (Hamish) Hector Northey Gray, PC, *b.* 1927, *m.*
1974   *Greene of Harrow Weald*, Sidney Francis Greene, CBE, *b.* 1910, *m.*
1974   *Greenhill of Harrow*, Denis Arthur Greenhill, GCMG, OBE, *b.* 1913, *m.*
1975   *Gregson*, John Gregson, *b.* 1924
1968   *Grey of Naunton*, Ralph Francis Alnwick Grey, GCMG, GCVO, OBE, *b.* 1910, *w.*
1991   *Griffiths of Fforestfach*, Brian Griffiths, *b.* 1941, *m.*
1995   *Habgood*, Rt. Revd John Stapylton Habgood, PC, PH.D., *b.* 1927, *m.*
1970   *Hailsham of St Marylebone*, Quintin McGarel Hogg, KG, CH, PC, FRS, *b.* 1907, *m.*
1994   *Hambro*, Charles Eric Alexander Hambro, *b.* 1930, *m.*
1983   *Hanson*, James Edward Hanson, *b.* 1922, *m.*
1997   *Hardie*, Andrew Rutherford Hardie, QC, PC, *b.* 1946, *m. Lord Advocate*

1974   *Harmar-Nicholls*, Harmar Harmar-Nicholls, *b.* 1912, *m.*
1974   *Harris of Greenwich*, John Henry Harris, *b.* 1930, *m.*
1979   *Harris of High Cross*, Ralph Harris, *b.* 1924, *m.*
1996   *Harris of Peckham*, Philip Charles Harris, *b.* 1942, *m.*
1968   *Hartwell*, (William) Michael Berry, MBE, TD, *b.* 1911, *w.*
1993   *Haskel*, Simon Haskel, *b.* 1934, *m.*
1990   *Haslam*, Robert Haslam, *b.* 1923, *m.*
1992   *Hayhoe*, Bernard John (Barney) Hayhoe, PC, *b.* 1925, *m.*
1992   *Healey*, Denis Winston Healey, CH, MBE, PC, *b.* 1917, *m.*
1984   *Henderson of Brompton*, Peter Gordon Henderson, KCB, *b.* 1922, *m.*
1979   *Hill-Norton*, Peter John Hill-Norton, GCB, *Admiral of the Fleet, b.* 1915, *m.*
1979   *Holderness*, Richard Frederick Wood, PC, *b.* 1920, *m.*
1991   *Hollick*, Clive Richard Hollick, *b.* 1945, *m.*
1990   *Holme of Cheltenham*, Richard Gordon Holme, CBE, *b.* 1936, *m.*
1979   *Hooson*, (Hugh) Emlyn Hooson, QC, *b.* 1925, *m.*
1995   *Hope of Craighead*, (James Arthur) David Hope, PC, *b.* 1938, *m. Lord of Appeal in Ordinary*
1992   *Howe of Aberavon*, (Richard Edward) Geoffrey Howe, CH, PC, QC, *b.* 1926, *m.*
1992   *Howell*, Denis Herbert Howell, PC, *b.* 1923, *m.*
1997   *Howell of Guildford*, David Arthur Russell Howell, PC, *b.* 1936, *m.*
1978   *Howie of Troon*, William Howie, *b.* 1924, *m.*
1997   *Hoyle*, (Eric) Douglas Harvey Hoyle, *b.* 1930, *w.*
1961   *Hughes*, William Hughes, CBE, PC, *b.* 1911, *w.*
1966   *Hunt*, (Henry Cecil) John Hunt, KG, CBE, DSO, *b.* 1910, *m.*
1980   *Hunt of Tanworth*, John Joseph Benedict Hunt, GCB, *b.* 1919, *m.*
1997   *Hurd of Westwell*, Douglas Richard Hurd, CH, CBE, PC, *b.* 1930, *m.*
1996   *Hussey of North Bradley*, Marmaduke James Hussey, *b.* 1923, *m.*
1978   *Hutchinson of Lullington*, Jeremy Nicolas Hutchinson, QC, *b.* 1915, *m.*
1997   *Inge*, Peter Anthony Inge, GCB, *b.* 1935, *m. Field Marshal*
1982   *Ingrow*, John Aked Taylor, OBE, TD, *b.* 1917, *m.*
1987   *Irvine of Lairg*, Alexander Andrew Mackay Irvine, PC, QC, *b.* 1940, *m. Lord High Chancellor*
1988   *Jakobovits*, Immanuel Jakobovits, *b.* 1921, *m.*
1987   *Jenkin of Roding*, (Charles) Patrick (Fleeming) Jenkin, PC, *b.* 1926, *m.*
1987   *Jenkins of Hillhead*, Roy Harris Jenkins, OM, PC, *b.* 1920, *m.*
1981   *Jenkins of Putney*, Hugh Gater Jenkins, *b.* 1908, *w.*
1987   *Johnston of Rockport*, Charles Collier Johnston, TD, *b.* 1915, *m.*
1997   *Jopling*, (Thomas) Michael Jopling, PC, *b.* 1930, *m.*
1991   *Judd*, Frank Ashcroft Judd, *b.* 1935, *m.*
1980   *Keith of Castleacre*, Kenneth Alexander Keith, *b.* 1916, *m.*
1997   *Kelvedon*, (Henry) Paul Guinness Channon, PC, *b.* 1935, *m.*
1996   *Kilpatrick of Kincraig*, Robert Kilpatrick, CBE, *b.* 1926, *m.*
1985   *Kimball*, Marcus Richard Kimball, *b.* 1928, *m.*
1983   *King of Wartnaby*, John Leonard King, *b.* 1918, *m.*

1993　*Kingsdown*, Robert (Robin) Leigh-Pemberton, KG, PC, *b.* 1927, *m.*

1994　*Kingsland*, Christopher James Prout, TD, PC, QC, *b.* 1942

1965　*Kings Norton*, Harold Roxbee Cox, PH.D., FENG., *b.* 1902, *m.*

1975　*Kirkhill*, John Farquharson Smith, *b.* 1930, *m.*

1974　*Kissin*, Harry Kissin, *b.* 1912, *m.*

1987　*Knights*, Philip Douglas Knights, CBE, QPM, *b.* 1920, *m.*

1991　*Laing of Dunphail*, Hector Laing, *b.* 1923, *m.*

1990　*Lane of Horsell*, Peter Stewart Lane, *b.* 1925, *w.*

1992　*Lawson of Blaby*, Nigel Lawson, PC, *b.* 1932, *m.*

1993　*Lester of Herne Hill*, Anthony Paul Lester, QC, *b.* 1936, *m.*

1997　*Levene of Portsoken*, Peter Keith Levene, KBE, *b.* 1941, *m.*

1982　*Lewin*, Terence Thornton Lewin, KG, GCB, LVO, DSC, Admiral of the Fleet, b. 1920, *m.*

1989　*Lewis of Newnham*, Jack Lewis, FRS, b. 1928, *m.*

1997　*Lloyd-Webber*, Andrew Lloyd Webber, b. 1948, *m.*

1997　*Lofthouse of Pontefract*, Geoffrey Lofthouse, b. 1925, *w.*

1974　*Lovell-Davis*, Peter Lovell Lovell-Davis, b. 1924, *m.*

1979　*Lowry*, Robert Lynd Erskine Lowry, PC, PC (NI), b. 1919, *m.*

1984　*McAlpine of West Green*, (Robert) Alistair McAlpine, b. 1942, *m.*

1988　*Macaulay of Bragar*, Donald Macaulay, QC, b. 1933, *m.*

1975　*McCarthy*, William Edward John McCarthy, D.phil., b. 1925, *m.*

1976　*McCluskey*, John Herbert McCluskey, b. 1929, *m.*

1989　*McColl of Dulwich*, Ian McColl, CBE, FRCS, FRCSE, b. 1933, *m.*

1995　*McConnell*, Robert William Brian McConnell, PC (NI), b 1922, *m.*

1991　*Macfarlane of Bearsden*, Norman Somerville Macfarlane, KT, FRSE, b. 1926, *m.*

1978　*McGregor of Durris*, Oliver Ross McGregor, b. 1921, *m.*

1982　*McIntosh of Haringey*, Andrew Robert McIntosh, b. 1933, *m.*

1991　*Mackay of Ardbrecknish*, John Jackson Mackay, PC, b. 1938, *m.*

1979　*Mackay of Clashfern*, James Peter Hymers Mackay, PC, FRSE, b. 1927, *m.*

1995　*Mackay of Drumadoon*, Donald Sage Mackay, b. 1946, *m.*

1988　*Mackenzie-Stuart*, Alexander John Mackenzie Stuart, b. 1924, *m.*

1974　*Mackie of Benshie*, George Yull Mackie, CBE, DSO, DFC, b. 1919, *m.*

1996　*MacLaurin*, Ian Charter MacLaurin, b. 1937, *m.*

1982　*MacLehose of Beoch*, (Crawford) Murray MacLehose, KT, GBE, KCMG, KCVO, b. 1917, *m.*

1995　*McNally*, Tom McNally, b. 1943, *m.*

1991　*Marlesford*, Mark Shuldham Schreiber, b. 1931, *m.*

1981　*Marsh*, Richard William Marsh, PC, b. 1928, *m.*

1987　*Mason of Barnsley*, Roy Mason, PC, b. 1924, *m.*

1997　*Mayhew of Twysden*, Patrick Barnabas Burke Mayhew, QC, PC, b. 1929, *m.*

1985　*Mellish*, Robert Joseph Mellish, PC, b. 1913, *m.*

1993　*Menuhin*, Yehudi Menuhin, OM, KBE, b. 1916, *m.*

1992　*Merlyn-Rees*, Merlyn Merlyn-Rees, PC, b. 1920, *m.*

1978　*Mishcon*, Victor Mishcon, b. 1915, *m.*

1981　*Molloy*, William John Molloy, b. 1918

1997　*Molyneaux of Killead*, James Henry Molyneaux, KBE, PC, b. 1920

1992　*Moore of Lower Marsh*, John Edward Michael Moore, PC, b. 1937, *m.*

1986　*Moore of Wolvercote*, Philip Brian Cecil Moore, GCB, GCVO, CMG, PC, b. 1921, *m.*

1990　*Morris of Castle Morris*, Brian Robert Morris, D.Phil., b. 1930, *m.*

1971　*Moyola*, James Dawson Chichester-Clark, PC (NI), b. 1923, *m.*

1985　*Murray of Epping Forest*, Lionel Murray, OBE, PC, b. 1922, *m.*

1979　*Murton of Lindisfarne*, (Henry) Oscar Murton, OBE, TD, PC, b. 1914, *m.*

1994　*Nickson*, David Wigley Nickson, KBE, FRSE, b. 1929, *m.*

1975　*Northfield*, (William) Donald Chapman, b. 1923

1976　*Oram*, Albert Edward Oram, b. 1913, *m.*

1971　*Orr-Ewing*, (Charles) Ian Orr-Ewing, OBE, b. 1912, *m.*

1992　*Owen*, David Anthony Llewellyn Owen, CH, PC, b. 1938, *m.*

1991　*Palumbo*, Peter Garth Palumbo, b. 1935, *m.*

1992　*Parkinson*, Cecil Edward Parkinson, PC, b. 1931, *m.*

1975　*Parry*, Gordon Samuel David Parry, b. 1925, *m.*

1997　*Patten*, John Haggitt Charles Patten, PC, b. 1945, *m.*

1996　*Paul*, Swraj Paul, b. 1931, *m.*

1990　*Pearson of Rannoch*, Malcolm Everard MacLaren Pearson, b. 1942, *m.*

1979　*Perry of Walton*, Walter Laing Macdonald Perry, OBE, FRS, FRSE, b. 1921, *m.*

1987　*Peston*, Maurice Harry Peston, b. 1931, *m.*

1983　*Peyton of Yeovil*, John Wynne William Peyton, PC, b. 1919, *m.*

1994　*Phillips of Ellesmere*, Prof. David Chilton Phillips, KBE, FRS, b. 1924, *m.*

1996　*Pilkington of Oxenford*, Revd Canon Peter Pilkington, b. 1933, *m.*

1997　*Plant of Highfield*, Prof. Raymond Plant, PH.D., b. 1945, *m.*

1959　*Plowden*, Edwin Noel Plowden, GBE, KCB, b. 1907, *m.*

1987　*Plumb*, (Charles) Henry Plumb, MEP, b. 1925, *m.*

1981　*Plummer of St Marylebone*, (Arthur) Desmond (Herne) Plummer, TD, b. 1914, *m.*

1990　*Porter of Luddenham*, George Porter, OM, FRS, b. 1920, *m.*

1992　*Prentice*, Reginald Ernest Prentice, PC, b. 1923, *m.*

1987　*Prior*, James Michael Leathes Prior, PC, b. 1927, *m.*

1982　*Prys-Davies*, Gwilym Prys Prys-Davies, b. 1923, *m.*

1987　*Pym*, Francis Leslie Pym, MC, PC, b. 1922, *m.*

1982　*Quinton*, Anthony Meredith Quinton, FBA, b. 1925, *m.*

1994　*Quirk*, Prof. (Charles) Randolph Quirk, CBE, FBA, b. 1920, *m.*

1978　*Rawlinson of Ewell*, Peter Anthony Grayson Rawlinson, PC, QC, b. 1919, *m.*

1976　*Rayne*, Max Rayne, b. 1918, *m.*

1983　*Rayner*, Derek George Rayner, b. 1926

1987　*Rees*, Peter Wynford Innes Rees, PC, QC, b. 1926, *m.*

1988　*Rees-Mogg*, William Rees-Mogg, b. 1928, *m.*

1991　*Renfrew of Kaimsthorn*, (Andrew) Colin Renfrew, FBA, b. 1937, *m.*

1979　*Renton*, David Lockhart-Mure Renton, KBE, TD, PC, QC, b. 1908, *w.*

1997　*Renton of Mount Harry*, (Ronald) Timothy Renton, PC, b. 1932, *m.*

1990   *Richard,* Ivor Seward Richard, PC, QC, *b.* 1932, *m.*
1979   *Richardson,* John Samuel Richardson, LVO, MD, FRCP, *b.* 1910, *w.*
1983   *Richardson of Duntisbourne,* Gordon William Humphreys Richardson, KG, MBE, TD, PC, *b.* 1915, *m.*
1992   *Rix,* Brian Norman Roger Rix, CBE, *b.* 1924, *m.*
1961   *Robens of Woldingham,* Alfred Robens, PC, *b.* 1910, *m.*
1992   *Rodger of Earlsferry,* Alan Ferguson Rodger, PC, QC, FBA, *b.* 1944
1992   *Rodgers of Quarry Bank,* William Thomas Rodgers, PC, *b.* 1928, *m.*
1996   *Rogers of Riverside,* Richard George Rogers, RA, RIBA, *b.* 1933, *m.*
1977   *Roll of Ipsden,* Eric Roll, KCMG, CB, *b.* 1907, *m.*
1991   *Runcie,* Rt Revd Robert Alexander Kennedy Runcie, MC, PC, Royal Victoria Chain, *b.* 1921, *m.*
1997   *Russell-Johnston,* (David) Russell Russell-Johnston, *b.* 1932, *m.*
1975   *Ryder of Eaton Hastings,* Sydney Thomas Franklin (Don) Ryder, *b.* 1916, *m.*
1996   *Saatchi,* Maurice Saatchi, *b.* 1946, *m.*
1962   *Sainsbury,* Alan John Sainsbury, *b.* 1902, *w.*
1989   *Sainsbury of Preston Candover,* John Davan Sainsbury, KG, *b.* 1927, *m.*
1987   *St John of Fawsley,* Norman Antony Francis St John-Stevas, PC, *b.* 1929
1985   *Sanderson of Bowden,* Charles Russell Sanderson, *b.* 1933, *m.*
1979   *Scanlon,* Hugh Parr Scanlon, *b.* 1913, *m.*
1978   *Sefton of Garston,* William Henry Sefton, *b.* 1915, *m.*
1996   *Sewel,* John Buttifant Sewel, CBE, *b.* 19–
1994   *Shaw of Northstead,* Michael Norman Shaw, *b.* 1920, *m.*
1959   *Shawcross,* Hartley William Shawcross, GBE, PC, QC, *b.* 1902, *m.*
1994   *Sheppard of Didgemere,* Allan John George Sheppard, *b.* 1932, *m.*
1997   *Shore of Stepney,* Peter David Shore, PC, *b.* 1924, *m.*
1980   *Sieff of Brimpton,* Marcus Joseph Sieff, OBE, *b.* 1913, *w.*
1971   *Simon of Glaisdale,* Jocelyn Edward Salis Simon, PC, *b.* 1911, *m.*
1997   *Simon of Highbury,* David Alec Gwyn Simon, CBE, *b.* 1939, *m.*
1991   *Skidelsky,* Robert Jacob Alexander Skidelsky, D.Phil., *b.* 1939, *m.*
1978   *Smith,* Rodney Smith, KBE, FRCS, *b.* 1914, *m.*
1965   *Soper,* Revd Donald Oliver Soper, PH.D., *b.* 1903, *m.*
1990   *Soulsby of Swaffham Prior,* Ernest Jackson Lawson Soulsby, PH.D., *b.* 1926, *m.*
1983   *Stallard,* Albert William Stallard, *b.* 1921, *m.*
1997   *Steel of Aikwood,* David Martin Scott Steel, KBE, PC, *b.* 1938, *m.*
1991   *Sterling of Plaistow,* Jeffrey Maurice Sterling, CBE, *b.* 1934, *m.*
1987   *Stevens of Ludgate,* David Robert Stevens, *b.* 1936, *m.*
1992   *Stewartby,* (Bernard Harold) Ian (Halley) Stewart, RD, PC, FBA, FRSE, *b.* 1935, *m.*
1981   *Stodart of Leaston,* James Anthony Stodart, PC, *b.* 1916, *w.*
1983   *Stoddart of Swindon,* David Leonard Stoddart, *b.* 1926, *m.*
1969   *Stokes,* Donald Gresham Stokes, TD, FEng., *b.* 1914, *w.*

1971   *Tanlaw,* Simon Brooke Mackay, *b.* 1934, *m.*
1996   *Taverne,* Dick Taverne, QC, *b.* 1928, *m.*
1978   *Taylor of Blackburn,* Thomas Taylor, CBE, *b.* 1929, *m.*
1968   *Taylor of Gryfe,* Thomas Johnston Taylor, FRSE, *b.* 1912, *m.*
1996   *Taylor of Warwick,* John David Beckett Taylor, *b.* 1952, *m.*
1992   *Tebbit,* Norman Beresford Tebbit, CH, PC, *b.* 1931, *m.*
1996   *Thomas of Gresford,* Donald Martin Thomas, OBE, QC, *b.* 1937, *m.*
1987   *Thomas of Gwydir,* Peter John Mitchell Thomas, PC, QC, *b.* 1920, *w.*
1981   *Thomas of Swynnerton,* Hugh Swynnerton Thomas, *b.* 1931, *m.*
1977   *Thomson of Monifieth,* George Morgan Thomson, KT, PC, *b.* 1921, *m.*
1990   *Tombs,* Francis Leonard Tombs, FEng., *b.* 1924, *m.*
1994   *Tope,* Graham Norman Tope, CBE, *b.* 1943, *m.*
1981   *Tordoff,* Geoffrey Johnson Tordoff, *b.* 1928, *m.*
1993   *Tugendhat,* Christopher Samuel Tugendhat, *b.* 1937, *m.*
1990   *Varley,* Eric Graham Varley, PC, *b.* 1932, *m.*
1996   *Vincent of Coleshill,* Richard Frederick Vincent, GBE, KCB, DSO, *b.* 1931, *m.*
1985   *Vinson,* Nigel Vinson, LVO, *b.* 1931, *m.*
1990   *Waddington,* David Charles Waddington, GCVO, PC, QC, *b.* 1929, *m.*
1990   *Wade of Chorlton,* (William) Oulton Wade, *b.* 1932, *m.*
1992   *Wakeham,* John Wakeham, PC, *b.* 1932, *m.*
1992   *Walker of Worcester,* Peter Edward Walker, MBE, PC, *b.* 1932, *m.*
1974   *Wallace of Campsie,* George Wallace, *b.* 1915, *m.*
1974   *Wallace of Coslany,* George Douglas Wallace, *b.* 1906, *m.*
1995   *Wallace of Saltaire,* William John Lawrence Wallace, PH.D., *b.* 1941, *m.*
1989   *Walton of Detchant,* John Nicholas Walton, TD, FRCP, *b.* 1922, *m.*
1992   *Weatherill,* (Bruce) Bernard Weatherill, PC, *b.* 1920, *m.*
1977   *Wedderburn of Charlton,* (Kenneth) William Wedderburn, FBA, QC, *b.* 1927, *m.*
1976   *Weidenfeld,* (Arthur) George Weidenfeld, *b.* 1919, *m.*
1980   *Weinstock,* Arnold Weinstock, *b.* 1924, *m.*
1978   *Whaddon,* (John) Derek Page, *b.* 1927, *m.*
1996   *Whitty,* John Lawrence (Larry) Whitty, *b.* 1943, *m.*
1974   *Wigoder,* Basil Thomas Wigoder, QC, *b.* 1921, *m.*
1985   *Williams of Elvel,* Charles Cuthbert Powell Williams, CBE, *b.* 1933, *m.*
1992   *Williams of Mostyn,* Gareth Wyn Williams, QC, *b.* 1941, *m.*
1969   *Wilson of Langside,* Henry Stephen Wilson, PC, QC, *b.* 1916, *m.*
1992   *Wilson of Tillyorn,* David Clive Wilson, GCMG, PH.D., *b.* 1935, *m.*
1995   *Winston,* Robert Maurice Lipson Winston, FRCOG, *b.* 1940, *m.*
1985   *Wolfson,* Leonard Gordon Wolfson, *b.* 1927, *m.*
1991   *Wolfson of Sunningdale,* David Wolfson, *b.* 1935, *m.*
1994   *Wright of Richmond,* Patrick Richard Henry Wright, GCMG, *b.* 1931, *m.*
1987   *Wyatt of Weeford,* Woodrow Lyle Wyatt, *b.* 1918, *m.*
1978   *Young of Dartington,* Michael Young, PH.D., *b.* 1915, *m.*

1984	*Young of Graffham*, David Ivor Young, PC, b. 1932, m.
1992	*Younger of Prestwick*, The Viscount Younger of Leckie, *see* page 148

BARONESSES

Created

1996   *Anelay of St Johns*, Joyce Anne Anelay, DBE, b. 1947, m.

1987   *Blackstone*, Tessa Ann Vosper Blackstone, PH.D., b. 1942

1987   *Blatch*, Emily May Blatch, CBE, PC, b. 1937, m.

1990   *Brigstocke*, Heather Renwick Brigstocke, b. 1929, w.

1964   *Brooke of Ystradfellte*, Barbara Muriel Brooke, DBE, b. 1908, w.

1996   *Byford*, Hazel Byford, DBE, b. 1941, m.

1982   *Carnegy of Lour*, Elizabeth Patricia Carnegy of Lour, b. 1925

1990   *Castle of Blackburn*, Barbara Anne Castle, PC, b. 1910, w.

1992   *Chalker of Wallasey*, Lynda Chalker, PC, b. 1942, m.

1982   *Cox*, Caroline Anne Cox, b. 1937, m.

1990   *Cumberlege*, Julia Frances Cumberlege, CBE, b. 1943, m.

1978   *David*, Nora Ratcliff David, b. 1913, w.

1993   *Dean of Thornton-le-Fylde*, Brenda Dean, b. 1943, m.

1974   *Delacourt-Smith of Alteryn*, Margaret Rosalind Delacourt-Smith, b. 1916, m.

1978   *Denington*, Evelyn Joyce Denington, DBE, b. 1907, m.

1991   *Denton of Wakefield*, Jean Denton, CBE, b. 1935

1990   *Dunn*, Lydia Selina Dunn, DBE, b. 1940, m.

1990   *Eccles of Moulton*, Diana Catherine Eccles, b. 1933, m.

1972   *Elles*, Diana Louie Elles, b. 1921, m.

1997   *Emerton*, Audrey Caroline Emerton, DBE, b. 1935

1974   *Falkender*, Marcia Matilda Falkender, CBE, b. 1932

1994   *Farrington of Ribbleton*, Josephine Farrington, b. 1940, m.

1974   *Fisher of Rednal*, Doris Mary Gertrude Fisher, b. 1919, w.

1990   *Flather*, Shreela Flather, b. 19–, m.

1981   *Gardner of Parkes*, (Rachel) Trixie (Anne) Gardner, b. 1927, m.

1993   *Gould of Potternewton*, Joyce Brenda Gould, b. 1932, m.

1991   *Hamwee*, Sally Rachel Hamwee, b. 1947

1996   *Hayman*, Helene Valerie Hayman, b. 1949, m.

1991   *Hilton of Eggardon*, Jennifer Hilton, QPM, b. 1936

1995   *Hogg*, Sarah Elizabeth Mary Hogg, b. 1946, m.

1990   *Hollis of Heigham*, Patricia Lesley Hollis, D.Phil., b. 1941, m.

1985   *Hooper*, Gloria Dorothy Hooper, b. 1939

1965   *Hylton-Foster*, Audrey Pellew Hylton-Foster, DBE, b. 1908, w.

1991   *James of Holland Park*, Phyllis Dorothy White (P. D. James), OBE, b. 1920, w.

1992   *Jay of Paddington*, Margaret Ann Jay, b. 1939

1979   *Jeger*, Lena May Jeger, b. 1915, w.

1997   *Lestor of Eccles*, Joan Lestor, b. 1931

1967   *Llewelyn-Davies of Hastoe*, (Annie) Patricia Llewelyn-Davies, PC, b. 1915, w.

1996   *Lloyd of Highbury*, Prof. June Kathleen Lloyd, DBE, FRCP, FRCPE, FRCGP, b. 1928

1978   *Lockwood*, Betty Lockwood, b. 1924, w.

1979   *McFarlane of Llandaff*, Jean Kennedy McFarlane, b. 1926

1971   *Macleod of Borve*, Evelyn Hester Macleod, b. 1915, w.

1991   *Mallalieu*, Ann Mallalieu, QC, b. 1945, m.

1970   *Masham of Ilton*, Susan Lilian Primrose Cunliffe-Lister, b. 1935, m. (*Countess of Swinton*)

1993   *Miller of Hendon*, Doreen Miller, MBE, b. 1933, m.

1982   *Nicol*, Olive Mary Wendy Nicol, b. 1923, m.

1991   *O'Cathain*, Detta O'Cathain, OBE, b. 1938, m.

1989   *Oppenheim-Barnes*, Sally Oppenheim-Barnes, PC, b. 1930, m.

1990   *Park of Monmouth*, Daphne Margaret Sybil Désirée Park, CMG, OBE, b. 1921

1991   *Perry of Southwark*, Pauline Perry, b. 1931, m.

1974   *Pike*, (Irene) Mervyn (Parnicott) Pike, DBE, b. 1918

1981   *Platt of Writtle*, Beryl Catherine Platt, CBE, FEng., b. 1923, m.

1996   *Ramsay of Cartvale*, Margaret Mildred (Meta) Ramsay, b. 1936

1994   *Rawlings*, Patricia Elizabeth Rawlings, b. 1939

1974   *Robson of Kiddington*, Inga-Stina Robson, b. 1919, w.

1979   *Ryder of Warsaw*, Margaret Susan Cheshire (Sue Ryder), CMG, OBE, b. 1923, w.

1991   *Seccombe*, Joan Anna Dalziel Seccombe, DBE, b. 1930, m.

1967   *Serota*, Beatrice Serota, DBE, b. 1919, m.

1973   *Sharples*, Pamela Sharples, b. 1923, m.

1995   *Smith of Gilmorehill*, Elizabeth Margaret Smith, b. 1940, w.

1996   *Symons of Vernham Dean*, Elizabeth Conway Symons, b. 1951

1992   *Thatcher*, Margaret Hilda Thatcher, KG, OM, PC, FRS, b. 1925, m.

1994   *Thomas of Walliswood*, Susan Petronella Thomas, OBE, b. 1935, m

1980   *Trumpington*, Jean Alys Barker, PC, b. 1922, w.

1985   *Turner of Camden*, Muriel Winifred Turner, b. 1927, m.

1985   *Warnock*, Helen Mary Warnock, DBE, b. 1924, w.

1970   *White*, Eirene Lloyd White, b. 1909, w.

1996   *Wilcox*, Judith Ann Wilcox, b. 19–, w.

1993   *Williams of Crosby*, Shirley Vivien Teresa Brittain Williams, PC, b. 1930, m.

1971   *Young*, Janet Mary Young, PC, b. 1926, m.

Lords Spiritual

The Lords Spiritual are the Archbishops of Canterbury and York and 24 diocesan bishops of the Church of England. The Bishops of London, Durham and Winchester always have seats in the House of Lords; the other 21 seats are filled by the remaining diocesan bishops in order of seniority. The Bishop of Sodor and Man and the Bishop of Gibraltar are not eligible to sit in the House of Lords.

ARCHBISHOPS

Style, The Most Revd and Right Hon. the Lord Archbishop of __
Addressed as Archbishop, *or* Your Grace

Introduced to House of Lords
1991   *Canterbury* (103rd), George Leonard Carey, PC, PH.D., *b.* 1935, *m. Consecrated Bishop of Bath and Wells* 1987, *trans.* 1991
1990   *York* (96th), David Michael Hope, KCVO, PC, D.PHIL., *b.* 1940, *cons.* 1985, *elected* 1985, *trans.* 1991, 1995

BISHOPS

Style, The Right Revd the Lord Bishop of __
Addressed as My Lord
elected date of election as diocesan bishop

Introduced to House of Lords
1996   *London* (132nd), Richard John Carew Chartres, *b.* 1947, *m.*, *cons.* 1992
1994   *Durham* (93rd), (Anthony) Michael (Arnold) Turnbull, *b.* 1935, *m.*, *cons.* 1988, *elected* 1988, *trans.* 1994
1996   *Winchester* (96th), Michael Charles Scott-Joynt, *b.* 1943, *m.*, *cons.* 1987
1979   *Chichester* (102nd), Eric Waldram Kemp, DD, *b.* 1915, *m.*, *cons.* 1974, *elected* 1974
1984   *Ripon* (11th), David Nigel de Lorentz Young, *b.* 1931, *m.*, *cons.* 1977, *elected* 1977
1989   *Lichfield* (97th), Keith Norman Sutton, *b.* 1934, *m.*, *cons.* 1978, *elected* 1984
1990   *Exeter* (69th), (Geoffrey) Hewlett Thompson, *b.* 1929, *m.*, *cons.* 1974, *elected* 1985
1990   *Bristol* (54th), Barry Rogerson, *b.* 1936, *m.*, *cons.* 1979, *elected* 1985
1991   *Norwich* (70th), Peter John Nott, *b.* 1933, *m.*, *cons.* 1977, *elected* 1985
1993   *Lincoln* (70th), Robert Maynard Hardy, *b.* 1936, *m.*, *cons.* 1980, *elected* 1986
1993   *Oxford* (41st), Richard Douglas Harries, *b.* 1936, *m.*, *cons.* 1987, *elected* 1987
1994   *Birmingham* (7th), Mark Santer, *b.* 1936, *w.*, *cons.* 1981, *elected* 1987
1995   *Southwell* (9th), Patrick Burnet Harris, *b.* 1934, *m.*, *cons.* 1973, *elected* 1988
1995   *Blackburn* (7th), Alan David Chesters, *b.* 1937, *m.*, *cons.* 1989, *elected* 1989
1996   *Carlisle* (65th), Ian Harland, *b.* 1932, *m.*, *cons.* 1985, *elected* 1989

1996   *Ely* (67th), Stephen Whitefield Sykes, *b.* 1939, *m.*, *cons.* 1990, *elected* 1990
1996   *Hereford* (103rd), John Keith Oliver, *b.* 1935, *m.*, *cons.* 1990, *elected* 1990
1996   *Leicester* (5th), Thomas Frederick Butler, *b.* 1940, *m.*, *cons.* 1985, *elected* 1991

Bishops awaiting seats, in order of seniority
Bath and Wells (77th), James Lawton Thompson, *b.* 1936, *m.*, *cons.* 1978, *elected* 1991
Wakefield (11th), Nigel Simeon McCulloch, *b.* 1942, *m.*, *cons.* 1986, *elected* 1992
Bradford (8th), David James Smith, *b.* 1935, *m.*, *cons.* 1987, *elected* 1992
Manchester (10th), Christopher John Mayfield, *b.* 1935, *m.*, *cons.* 1985, *elected* 1993
Salisbury (77th), David Staffurth Stancliffe, *b.* 1942, *m.*, *cons.* 1993, *elected* 1993
Gloucester (39th), David Edward Bentley, *b.* 1935, *m.*, *cons.* 1986, *elected* 1993
Rochester (106th), Michael James Nazir-Ali, PH.D., *b.* 1949, *m.*, *cons.* 1984, *elected* 1995
Guildford (8th), John Warren Gladwin, *b.* 1942, *m.*, *cons.* 1994, *elected* 1994
Portsmouth (8th), Kenneth William Stevenson, *b.* 1949, *m.*, *cons.* 1995, *elected* 1995
Derby (6th), Jonathan Sansbury Bailey, *b.* 1940, *m.*, *cons.* 1992, *elected* 1995
St Albans (9th), Christopher William Herbert, *b.* 1944, *m.*, *cons.* 1995, *elected* 1995
Chelmsford (8th), John Freeman Perry, *b.* 1935, *m.*, *cons.* 1989, *elected* 1996
Peterborough (37th), Ian Cundy, *b.* 1945, *m.*, *cons.* 1992, *elected* 1996
Chester (40th), Peter Robert Forster, PH.D., *b.* 1950, *cons.* 1996, *elected* 1996
St Edmundsbury and Ipswich (9th), (John Hubert) Richard Lewis, *b.* 1943, *m.*, *cons.* 1992, *elected* 1997
Worcester (112th), Peter Stephen Maurice Selby, *b.* 1941, *cons.* 1984, *elected* 1997
Newcastle (11th), (John) Martin Wharton, *b.* 1944, *m.*, *cons.* 1992, *elected* 1997
Sheffield (6th), John Nicholls, *b.* 1943, *m.*, *cons.* 1990, *elected* 1997
Truro (14th), William Ind, *b.* 1942, *m.*, *cons.* 1987, *elected* 1997

The sees of Coventry, Liverpool and Southwark were vacant at the time of going to press

COURTESY TITLES

From this list it will be seen that, for example, the Marquess of Blandford is heir to the Dukedom of Marlborough, and Viscount Amberley to the Earldom of Russell. Titles of second heirs are also given, and the courtesy title of the father of a second heir is indicated by *; e.g. Earl of Burlington, eldest son of *Marquess of Hartington

For forms of address, *see* page 136

MARQUESSES

*Blandford – *Marlborough, D.*
Bowmont and Cessford – *Roxburghe, D.*
Douglas and Clydesdale – *Hamilton, D.*
*Douro – *Wellington, D.*
Graham – *Montrose, D.*
Granby – *Rutland, D.*
Hamilton – *Abercorn, D.*
*Hartington – *Devonshire, D.*
*Kildare – *Leinster, D.*
Lorne – *Argyll, D.*
*Tavistock – *Bedford, D.*
Tullibardine – *Atholl, D.*
*Worcester – *Beaufort, D.*

EARLS

Aboyne – *Huntly, M.*
Altamont – *Sligo, M.*
Ancram – *Lothian, M.*
Arundel and Surrey – *Norfolk, D.*
*Bective – *Headfort, M.*
*Belfast – *Donegall, M.*
Brecknock – *Camden, M.*
Burford – *St Albans, D.*
Burlington – **Hartington, M.*
*Cardigan – *Ailesbury, M.*
Compton – *Northampton, M.*
*Dalkeith – *Buccleuch, D.*
Dumfries – *Bute, M.*
*Euston – *Grafton, D.*
Glamorgan – **Worcester, M.*
Grosvenor – *Westminster, D.*
*Haddo – *Aberdeen and Temair, M.*
Hillsborough – *Downshire, M.*
Hopetoun – *Linlithgow, M.*
March and Kinrara – *Richmond, D.*
*Mount Charles – *Conyngham, M.*
Mornington – **Douro, M.*
Percy – *Northumberland, D.*
Ronaldshay – *Zetland, M.*
*St Andrews – *Kent, D.*
*Shelburne – *Lansdowne, M.*
*Southesk – *Fife, D.*
Sunderland – **Blandford, M.*
*Tyrone – *Waterford, M.*

Ulster – *Gloucester, D.*
*Uxbridge – *Anglesey, M.*
Wiltshire – *Winchester, M.*
Yarmouth – *Hertford, M.*

VISCOUNTS

Althorp – *Spencer, E.*
Amberley – *Russell, E.*
Andover – *Suffolk and Berkshire, E.*
Anson – *Lichfield, E.*
Asquith – *Oxford and Asquith, E.*
Boringdon – *Morley, E.*
Borodale – *Beatty, E.*
Boyle – *Shannon, E.*
Brocas – *Jellicoe, E.*
Calne and Calstone – **Shelburne, E.*
Campden – *Gainsborough, E.*
Carlow – *Portarlington, E.*
Carlton – *Wharncliffe, E.*
Castlereagh – *Londonderry, M.*
Chelsea – *Cadogan, E.*
Chewton – *Waldegrave, E.*
Chichester – **Belfast, E.*
Clanfield – *Peel, E.*
Clive – *Powis, E.*
Coke – *Leicester, E.*
Corry – *Belmore, E.*
Corvedale – *Baldwin of Bewdley, E.*
Cranborne – *Salisbury, M.*
Cranley – *Onslow, E.*
Crichton – *Erne, E.*
Crowhurst – *Cottenham, E.*
Curzon – *Howe, E.*
Dangan – *Cowley, E.*
Dawick – *Haig, E.*
Deerhurst – *Coventry, E.*
Drumlanrig – *Queensberry, M.*
Dunwich – *Stradbroke, E.*
Dupplin – *Kinnoull, E.*
Ebrington – *Fortescue, E.*
Ednam – *Dudley, E.*
Emlyn – *Cawdor, E.*
Encombe – *Eldon, E.*
Enfield – *Strafford, E.*
Erleigh – *Reading, M.*
Errington – *Cromer, E.*
FitzHarris – *Malmesbury, E.*
Folkestone – *Radnor, E.*
Forbes – *Granard, E.*
Garmoyle – *Cairns, E.*
Garnock – *Lindsay, E.*

Glandine – *Norbury, E.*
Glenapp – *Inchcape, E.*
Glentworth – *Limerick, E.*
Grimstone – *Verulam, E.*
Gwynedd – *Lloyd George of Dwyfor, E.*
Hawkesbury – *Liverpool, E.*
Hinchingbrooke – *Sandwich, E.*
Ikerrin – *Carrick, E.*
Ingestre – *Shrewsbury, E.*
Ipswich – **Euston, E.*
Jocelyn – *Roden, E.*
Kelburn – *Glasgow, E.*
Kilwarlin – *Hillsborough, E.*
Kingsborough – *Kingston, E.*
Knebworth – *Lytton, E.*
Lascelles – *Harewood, E.*
Lewisham – *Dartmouth, E.*
Linley – *Snowdon, E.*
Loftus – *Ely, M.*
Lowther – *Lonsdale, E.*
Lumley – *Scarbrough, E.*
Lymington – *Portsmouth, E.*
Macmillan of Ovenden – *Stockton, E.*
Maidstone – *Winchilsea and Nottingham, E.*
Maitland – *Lauderdale, E.*
Malden – *Essex, E.*
Mandeville – *Manchester, D.*
Medina – *Milford Haven, M.*
Melgund – *Minto, E.*
Merton – *Nelson, E.*
Moore – *Drogheda, E.*
Newport – *Bradford, E.*
Newry and Mourne – *Kilmorey, E.*
Parker – *Macclesfield, E.*
Perceval – *Egmont, E.*
Petersham – *Harrington, E.*
Pollington – *Mexborough, E.*
Raynham – *Townshend, M.*
Reidhaven – *Seafield, E.*
Ruthven of Canberra – *Gowrie, E.*
St Cyres – *Iddesleigh, E.*
Sandon – *Harrowby, E.*
Savernake – **Cardigan, E.*
Slane – **Mount Charles, E.*
Somerton – *Normanton, E.*
Stopford – *Courtown, E.*
Stormont – *Mansfield, E.*
Strathallan – *Perth, E.*
Stuart – *Castle Stewart, E.*
Suirdale – *Donoughmore, E.*
Tamworth – *Ferrers, E.*

Tarbat – *Cromartie, E.*
Vaughan – *Lisburne, E.*
Villiers – *Jersey, E.*
Weymouth – *Bath, M.*
Windsor – *Plymouth, E.*
Wolmer – *Selborne, E.*
Woodstock – *Portland, E.*

BARONS (LORD —)

Aberdour – *Morton, E.*
Apsley – *Bathurst, E.*
Ardee – *Meath, E.*
Ashley – *Shaftesbury, E.*
Balgonie – *Leven and Melville, E.*
Balniel – *Crawford and Balcarres, E.*
Berriedale – *Caithness, E.*
Bingham – *Lucan, E.*
Binning – *Haddington, E.*
Brooke – *Warwick, E.*
Bruce – *Elgin, E.*
Buckhurst – *De La Warr, E.*
Burghley – *Exeter, M.*
Cardross – *Buchan, E.*
Carnegie – **Southesk, E.*
Clifton – *Darnley, E.*
Cochrane – *Dundonald, E.*
Courtenay – *Devon, E.*
Dalmeny – *Rosebery, E.*
Doune – *Moray, E.*
Downpatrick – **St Andrews, E.*
Dunglass – *Home, E.*
Eliot – *St Germans, E.*
Eskdail – **Dalkeith, E.*
Formartine – **Haddo, E.*
Gillford – *Clanwilliam, E.*
Glamis – *Strathmore, E.*
Greenock – *Cathcart, E.*
Guernsey – *Aylesford, E.*
Hay – *Erroll, E.*
Herbert – *Pembroke, E.*
Howard of Effingham – *Effingham, E.*
Howland – **Tavistock, M.*
Hyde – *Clarendon, E.*
Inverurie – *Kintore, E.*
Irwin – *Halifax, E.*
Johnstone – *Annandale and Hartfell, E.*
Kenlis – **Bective, E.*
Langton – *Temple of Stowe, E.*
La Poer – **Tyrone, E.*
Leslie – *Rothes, E.*
Loughborough – *Rosslyn, E.*
Maltravers – **Arundel and Surrey, E.*
Mauchline – *Loudoun, C.*
Medway – *Cranbrook, E.*
Montgomerie – *Eglinton and Winton, E.*

Moreton – *Ducie, E.*
Naas – *Mayo, E.*
Neidpath – *Wemyss and March, E.*
Norreys – *Lindsey and Abingdon, E.*

North – *Guilford, E.*
Ogilvy – *Airlie, E.*
Oxmantown – *Rosse, E.*
Paget de Beaudesert – *Uxbridge, E.*
Porchester – *Carnarvon, E.*

Ramsay – *Dalhousie, E.*
Romsey – *Mountbatten of Burma, C.*
Rosehill – *Northesk, E.*
Scrymgeour – *Dundee, E.*
Seymour – *Somerset, D.*

Strathnaver – *Sutherland, C.*
Wodehouse – *Kimberley, E.*
Worsley – *Yarborough, E.*

PEERS' SURNAMES WHICH DIFFER FROM THEIR TITLES

The following symbols indicate the rank of the peer holding each title:

C. Countess
D. Duke
E. Earl
M. Marquess
V. Viscount
*   Life Peer

Where no designation is given, the title is that of an hereditary Baron or Baroness

Abney-Hastings – *Loudoun, C.*
Acheson – *Gosford, E.*
Adderley – *Norton*
Addington – *Sidmouth, V.*
Agar – *Normanton, E.*
Aitken – *Beaverbrook*
Akers-Douglas – *Chilston, V.*
Alexander – *A. of Tunis, E.*
Alexander – *A. of Weedon*
Alexander – *Caledon, E.*
Allen – *A. of Abbeydale**
Allen – *Croham**
Allsopp – *Hindlip*
Alton – *A. of Liverpool**
Anderson – *Waverley, V.*
Anelay – *A. of St Johns**
Annesley – *Valentia, V.*
Anson – *Lichfield, E.*
Archer – *A. of Sandwell**
Archer – *A. of Weston-super-Mare**
Armstrong – *A. of Ilminster**
Armstrong-Jones – *Snowdon, E.*
Arthur – *Glenarthur*
Arundell – *Talbot of Malahide*
Ashley – *A. of Stoke**
Ashley-Cooper – *Shaftesbury, E.*
Ashton – *A. of Hyde*
Asquith – *Oxford and Asquith, E.*
Assheton – *Clitheroe*
Astley – *Hastings*
Astor – *A. of Hever*
Aubrey-Fletcher – *Braye*
Bailey – *Glanusk*
Baillie – *Burton*
Baillie Hamilton – *Haddington, E.*
Baker – *B. of Dorking**
Baldwin – *B. of Bewdley, E.*

Balfour – *B. of Inchrye*
Balfour – *Kinross*
Balfour – *Riverdale*
Bampfylde – *Poltimore*
Banbury – *B. of Southam*
Barber – *B. of Tewkesbury**
Baring – *Ashburton*
Baring – *Cromer, E.*
Baring – *Howick of Glendale*
Baring – *Northbrook*
Baring – *Revelstoke*
Barker – *Trumpington**
Barnes – *Gorell*
Barnewall – *Trimlestown*
Bathurst – *Bledisloe, V.*
Beauclerk – *St Albans, D.*
Beaumont – *Allendale, V.*
Beaumont – *B. of Whitley**
Beckett – *Grimthorpe*
Bellow – *Bellwin**
Benn – *Stansgate, V.*
Bennet – *Tankerville, E.*
Bentinck – *Portland, E.*
Beresford – *Decies*
Beresford – *Waterford, M.*
Berry – *Camrose, V.*
Berry – *Hartwell**
Berry – *Kemsley, V.*
Bertie – *Lindsey, E.*
Best – *Wynford*
Bethell – *Westbury*
Bewicke-Copley – *Cromwell*
Bigham – *Mersey, V.*
Bingham – *B. of Cornhill**
Bingham – *Clanmorris*
Bingham – *Lucan, E.*
Blackwood – *Dufferin and Clandeboye*
Bligh – *Darnley, E.*
Blyth – *B. of Rowington**
Bootle-Wilbraham – *Skelmersdale*
Boscawen – *Falmouth, V.*
Boston – *B. of Faversham**
Bourke – *Mayo, E.*
Bowes Lyon – *Strathmore, E.*
Bowyer – *Denham*
Boyd – *Kilmarnock*
Boyle – *Cork and Orrery, E.*
Boyle – *Glasgow, E.*
Boyle – *Shannon, E.*
Brabazon – *Meath, E.*
Braine – *B. of Wheatley**
Brand – *Hampden, V.*
Brandon – *B. of Oakbrook**
Brassey – *B. of Apethorpe*
Brett – *Esher, V.*

Bridge – *B. of Harwich**
Bridgeman – *Bradford, E.*
Brodrick – *Midleton, V.*
Brooke – *Alanbrooke, V.*
Brooke – *Brookeborough, V.*
Brooke – *B. of Ystradfellte**
Brooks – *B. of Tremorfa**
Brooks – *Crawshaw*
Brougham – *Brougham and Vaux*
Broughton – *Fairhaven*
Browne – *Kilmaine*
Browne – *Oranmore and Browne*
Browne – *Sligo, M.*
Bruce – *Aberdare*
Bruce – *Balfour of Burleigh*
Bruce – *B. of Donington**
Bruce – *Elgin and Kincardine, E.*
Brudenell-Bruce – *Ailesbury, M.*
Buchan – *Tweedsmuir*
Buckley – *Wrenbury*
Butler – *Carrick, E.*
Butler – *Dunboyne*
Butler – *Lanesborough, E.*
Butler – *Mountgarret, V.*
Butler – *Ormonde, M.*
Buxton – *B. of Alsa**
Byng – *Strafford, E.*
Byng – *Torrington, V.*
Callaghan – *C. of Cardiff **
Cameron – *C. of Lochbroom**
Campbell – *Argyll, D.*
Campbell – *Breadalbane and Holland, E.*
Campbell – *C. of Alloway**
Campbell – *C. of Croy**
Campbell – *Cawdor, E.*
Campbell – *Colgrain*
Campbell – *Stratheden and Campbell*
Campbell-Gray – *Gray*
Canning – *Garvagh*
Capell – *Essex, E.*
Carington – *Carrington*
Carlisle – *C. of Bucklow**
Carmichael – *C. of Kelvingrove**
Carnegie – *Fife, D.*
Carnegie – *Northesk, E.*
Carr – *C. of Hadley**
Cary – *Falkland, V.*
Castle – *C. of Blackburn**
Caulfeild – *Charlemont, V.*
Cavendish – *C. of Furness**
Cavendish – *Chesham*
Cavendish – *Devonshire, D.*

Cavendish – *Waterpark*
Cayzer – *Rotherwick*
Cecil – *Amherst of Hackney*
Cecil – *Exeter, M.*
Cecil – *Rockley*
Cecil – *Salisbury, M.*
Chalker – *C. of Wallasey**
Chaloner – *Gisborough*
Channon – *Kelvedon**
Chapman – *Northfield**
Charteris – *C. of Amisfield**
Charteris – *Wemyss and March, E.*
Cheshire – *Ryder of Warsaw**
Chetwynd-Talbot – *Shrewsbury, E.*
Chichester – *Donegall, M.*
Chichester-Clark – *Moyola**
Child Villiers – *Jersey, E.*
Cholmondeley – *Delamere*
Chubb – *Hayter*
Clark – *C. of Kempston**
Clegg-Hill – *Hill, V.*
Clifford – *C. of Chudleigh*
Cochrane – *C. of Cults*
Cochrane – *Dundonald, E.*
Cocks – *C. of Hartcliffe**
Cocks – *Somers*
Cokayne – *Cullen of Ashbourne*
Coke – *Leicester, E.*
Cole – *Enniskillen, E.*
Collier – *Monkswell*
Colville – *Clydesmuir*
Colville – *C. of Culross, V.*
Compton – *Northampton, M.*
Conolly-Carew – *Carew*
Constantine – *C. of Stanmore**
Cooke – *C. of Islandreagh**
Cooke – *C. of Thorndon**
Cooper – *Norwich, V.*
Corbett – *Rowallan*
Courtenay – *Devon, E.*
Cowdrey – *C. of Tonbridge**
Cox – *Kings Norton**
Craig – *C. of Radley**
Craig – *Craigavon, V.*
Crichton – *Erne, E.*
Crichton-Stuart – *Bute, M.*
Cripps – *Parmoor*
Crossley – *Somerleyton*
Cubitt – *Ashcombe*
Cunliffe-Lister – *Masham of Ilton**

Cunliffe-Lister – *Swinton, E.*
Currie – *C. of Marylebone**
Curzon – *Howe, E.*
Curzon – *Scarsdale, V.*
Cust – *Brownlow*
Dalrymple – *Stair, E.*
Daubeny de Moleyns – *Ventry*
Davies – *Darwen*
Davison – *Broughshane*
Dawnay – *Downe, V.*
Dawson-Damer – *Portarlington, E.*
Dean – *D. of Beswick**
Dean – *D. of Harptree**
Dean – *D. of Thornton-le-Fylde**
Deane – *Muskerry*
de Courcy – *Kingsale*
de Grey – *Walsingham*
Delacourt-Smith – *Delacourt Smith of Alteryn**
Denison – *Londesborough*
Denison-Pender – *Pender*
Denton – *D. of Wakefield**
Devereux – *Hereford, V.*
Dewar – *Forteviot*
De Yarburgh-Bateson – *Deramore*
Dixon – *Glentoran*
Dodson – *Monk Bretton*
Donaldson – *D. of Kingsbridge**
Donaldson – *D. of Lymington**
Dormand – *D. of Easington**
Douglas – *Morton, E.*
Douglas – *Queensberry, M*
Douglas-Hamilton – *Hamilton, D.*
Douglas-Hamilton – *Selkirk, E.*
Douglas-Home – *Dacre*
Douglas-Home – *Home, E.*
Douglas-Pennant – *Penrhyn*
Douglas-Scott-Montagu – *Montagu of Beaulieu*
Drummond – *Perth, E.*
Drummond of Megginch – *Strange*
Dugdale – *Crathorne*
Duke – *Merrivale*
Duncombe – *Feversham*
Dundas – *Melville, V.*
Dundas – *Zetland, M.*
Eady – *Swinfen*
Eccles – *E. of Moulton**
Eden – *Auckland*
Eden – *E. of Winton**
Eden – *Henley*
Edgcumbe – *Mount Edgcumbe, E.*
Edmondson – *Sandford*
Edwardes – *Kensington*
Edwards – *Crickhowell**
Egerton – *Sutherland, D.*
Egerton – *Wilton, E.*
Eliot – *St Germans, E.*

Elliot-Murray-Kynynmound – *Minto, E.*
Elliott – *E. of Morpeth**
Erroll – *E. of Hale*
Erskine – *Buchan, E.*
Erskine – *Mar and Kellie, E.*
Erskine-Murray – *Elibank*
Evans – *E. of Parkside**
Evans – *Mountevans*
Evans-Freke – *Carbery*
Eve – *Silsoe*
Ewing – *E. of Kirkford**
Fairfax – *F. of Cameron*
Falconer – *F. of Thoroton**
Fane – *Westmorland, E.*
Farrington – *F. of Ribbleton**
Feilding – *Denbigh, E.*
Fellowes – *De Ramsey*
Fermor-Hesketh – *Hesketh*
Fiennes – *Saye and Sele*
Fiennes-Clinton – *Lincoln, E.*
Finch Hatton – *Winchilsea, E.*
Finch-Knightley – *Aylesford, E.*
Fisher – *F. of Rednal**
Fitzalan-Howard – *Herries of Terregles*
Fitzalan-Howard – *Norfolk, D.*
FitzClarence – *Munster, E.*
FitzGerald – *Leinster, D.*
Fitzherbert – *Stafford*
Fitz-Maurice – *Orkney, E.*
FitzRoy – *Grafton, D.*
FitzRoy – *Southampton*
FitzRoy Newdegate – *Daventry, V.*
Fletcher-Vane – *Inglewood*
Flower – *Ashbrook, V.*
Foljambe – *Liverpool, E.*
Forbes – *Granard, E.*
Fox-Strangways – *Ilchester, E.*
Frankland – *Zouche*
Fraser – *F. of Carmyllie**
Fraser – *F. of Kilmorack**
Fraser – *Lovat*
Fraser – *Saltoun*
Fraser – *Strathalmond*
Freeman-Grenville – *Kinloss*
Fremantle – *Cottesloe*
French – *De Freyne*
Galbraith – *Strathclyde*
Ganzoni – *Belstead*
Gardner – *G. of Parkes**
Gathorne-Hardy – *Cranbrook, E.*
Gibbs – *Aldenham*
Gibbs – *Wraxall*
Gibson – *Ashbourne*
Giffard – *Halsbury, E.*
Gilbey – *Vaux of Harrowden*
Gillmore – *G. of Thamesfield**
Gilmour – *G. of Craigmillar**
Gladwin – *G. of Clee**
Glyn – *Wolverton*

Godley – *Kilbracken*
Goff – *G. of Chieveley**
Gordon – *Aberdeen, M.*
Gordon – *Huntly, M.*
Gordon Lennox – *Richmond, D.*
Gore – *Arran, E.*
Gould – *G. of Potternewton**
Graham – *G. of Edmonton**
Graham – *Montrose, D.*
Graham-Toler – *Norbury, E.*
Grant of Grant – *Strathspey*
Granville – *G. of Eye**
Gray – *G. of Contin**
Greaves – *Dysart, C.*
Greenall – *Daresbury*
Greene – *G. of Harrow Weald**
Greenhill – *G. of Harrow**
Greville – *Warwick, E.*
Grey – *G. of Naunton**
Griffiths – *G. of Fforestfach**
Grigg – *Altrincham*
Grimston – *G. of Westbury*
Grimston – *Verulam, E.*
Grosvenor – *Ebury*
Grosvenor – *Westminster, D.*
Gueterbock – *Berkeley*
Guest – *Wimborne, V.*
Guinness – *Iveagh, E.*
Guinness – *Moyne*
Gully – *Selby, V.*
Gummer – *Chadlington**
Gurdon – *Cranworth*
Gwynne Jones – *Chalfont**
Hamilton – *Abercorn, D.*
Hamilton – *Belhaven and Stenton*
Hamilton – *Dudley*
Hamilton – *H. of Dalzell*
Hamilton – *Holm Patrick*
Hamilton-Russell – *Boyne, V.*
Hamilton-Smith – *Colwyn*
Hanbury-Tracy – *Sudeley*
Handcock – *Castlemaine*
Harbord-Hamond – *Suffield*
Harding – *H. of Petherton*
Hardinge – *H. of Penshurst*
Hare – *Blakenham, V.*
Hare – *Listowel, E.*
Harmsworth – *Rothermere, V.*
Harris – *H. of Greenwich**
Harris – *H. of High Cross**
Harris – *H. of Peckham**
Harris – *Malmesbury, E.*
Harvey – *H. of Tasburgh*
Hastings Bass – *Huntingdon, E.*
Hay – *Erroll, E.*
Hay – *Kinnoull, E.*
Hay – *Tweeddale, M.*
Heathcote-Drummond-Willoughby – *Willoughby de Eresby*
Hely Hutchinson – *Donoughmore, E.*

Henderson – *Faringdon*
Henderson – *H. of Brompton**
Hennessy – *Windlesham*
Henniker-Major – *Henniker*
Hepburne-Scott – *Polwarth*
Herbert – *Carnarvon, E.*
Herbert – *Hemingford*
Herbert – *Pembroke, E.*
Herbert – *Powis, E.*
Hermon-Hodge – *Wyfold*
Hervey – *Bristol, M.*
Hewitt – *Lifford, V.*
Hicks Beach – *St Aldwyn, E.*
Hill – *Downshire, M.*
Hill – *Sandys*
Hill-Trevor – *Trevor*
Hilton – *H. of Eggardon**
Hobart-Hampden – *Buckinghamshire, E.*
Hogg – *Hailsham of St Marylebone**
Holland-Hibbert – *Knutsford, V.*
Hollis – *H. of Heigham**
Holme – *H. of Cheltenham**
Holmes à Court – *Heytesbury*
Hood – *Bridport, V.*
Hope – *Glendevon*
Hope – *H. of Craighead**
Hope – *Linlithgow, M.*
Hope – *Rankeillour*
Hope Johnstone – *Annandale and Hartfell, E.*
Hope-Morley – *Hollenden*
Hopkinson – *Colyton*
Hore Ruthven – *Gowrie, E.*
Houghton – *H. of Sowerby**
Hovell-Thurlow-Cumming-Bruce – *Thurlow*
Howard – *Carlisle, E.*
Howard – *Effingham, E.*
Howard – *H. of Penrith*
Howard – *Strathcona*
Howard à *Suffolk and Berkshire, E.*
Howe – *H. of Aberavon**
Howell – *H. of Guildford**
Howells – *Geraint**
Howie – *H. of Troon**
Hubbard – *Addington*
Huggins – *Malvern, V.*
Hughes – *Cledwyn of Penrhos**
Hughes-Young – *St Helens*
Hunt – *H. of Tanworth**
Hurd – *H. of Westwell**
Hussey – *H. of North Bradley**
Hutchinson – *H. of Lullington**
Ingrams – *Darcy de Knayth*
Innes-Ker – *Roxburghe, D.*
Inskip – *Caldecote, V.*
Irby – *Boston*
Irvine – *I. of Lairg**
Isaacs – *Reading, M.*

Orders of Chivalry

THE MOST NOBLE ORDER OF THE GARTER (1348)

KG

Ribbon, Blue
Motto, Honi soit qui mal y pense
(*Shame on him who thinks evil of it*)
The number of Knights Companions is limited to 24

SOVEREIGN OF THE ORDER
The Queen

LADIES OF THE ORDER
HM Queen Elizabeth the Queen
  Mother, 1936
HRH The Princess Royal, 1994

ROYAL KNIGHTS
HRH The Prince Philip, Duke of
  Edinburgh, 1947
HRH The Prince of Wales, 1958
HRH The Duke of Kent, 1985

EXTRA KNIGHTS COMPANIONS AND
LADIES
HRH Princess Juliana of the
  Netherlands, 1958
HRH The Grand Duke of
  Luxembourg, 1972
HM The Queen of Denmark, 1979
HM The King of Sweden, 1983
HM The King of Spain, 1988
HM The Queen of the Netherlands,
  1989
HRH The Duke of Gloucester, 1997

KNIGHTS AND LADY COMPANIONS
The Earl of Longford, 1971
The Marquess of Abergavenny, 1974
The Duke of Grafton, 1976
The Lord Hunt, 1979
The Duke of Norfolk, 1983
The Lord Lewin, 1983
The Lord Richardson of
  Duntisbourne, 1983
The Lord Carrington, 1985
The Lord Callaghan of Cardiff, 1987
The Viscount Leverhulme, 1988
The Lord Hailsham of St
  Marylebone, 1988
The Duke of Wellington, 1990
Field Marshal the Lord Bramall, 1990
Sir Edward Heath, 1992
The Viscount Ridley, 1992
The Lord Sainsbury of Preston
  Candover, 1992
The Lord Ashburton, 1994
The Lord Kingsdown, 1994

Sir Ninian Stephen, 1994
The Baroness Thatcher, 1995
Sir Edmund Hillary, 1995
The Duke of Devonshire, 1996
Sir Timothy Colman, 1996

Prelate, The Bishop of Winchester
Chancellor, The Lord Carrington, KG,
  GCMG, CH, MC
Register, The Dean of Windsor
Garter King of Arms, P. Gwynn-Jones,
  LVO
Gentleman Usher of the Black Rod, Gen.
  Sir Edward Jones, KCB, CBE
Secretary, D. H. B. Chesshyre, LVO

THE MOST ANCIENT AND MOST NOBLE ORDER OF THE THISTLE (REVIVED 1687)

KT

Ribbon, Green
Motto, Nemo me impune lacessit (*No
  one provokes me with impunity*)
The number of Knights is limited to 16

SOVEREIGN OF THE ORDER
The Queen

LADY OF THE THISTLE
HM Queen Elizabeth the Queen
  Mother, 1937

ROYAL KNIGHTS
HRH The Prince Philip, Duke of
  Edinburgh, 1952
HRH The Prince of Wales, Duke of
  Rothesay, 1977

KNIGHTS
The Earl of Wemyss and March, 1966
The Earl of Dalhousie, 1971
Sir Donald Cameron of Lochiel, 1973
The Duke of Buccleuch and
  Queensberry, 1978
The Earl of Elgin and Kincardine,
  1981
The Lord Thomson of Monifieth,
  1981
The Lord MacLehose of Beoch, 1983
The Earl of Airlie, 1985
Capt. Sir Iain Tennant, 1986
The Viscount Whitelaw, 1990
The Viscount Younger of Leckie,
  1995
The Viscount Arbuthnot, 1996
The Earl of Crawford and Balcarres,
  1996
Lady Fraser, 1996

The Lord Macfarlane of Bearsden,
  1996

Chancellor, The Duke of Buccleuch
  and Queensberry, KT, VRD
Dean, The Very Revd G. I. Macmillan
Secretary and Lord Lyon King of Arms, Sir
  Malcolm Innes of Edingight, KCVO,
  WS
Usher of the Green Rod, Rear-Adm. C. H.
  Layman, CB, DSO, LVO

THE MOST HONOURABLE ORDER OF THE BATH (1725)

GCB *Military*   GCB *Civil*

GCB Knight (or Dame) Grand
       Cross
KCB Knight Commander
DCB Dame Commander
CB   Companion

Ribbon, Crimson
Motto, Tria juncta in uno (*Three joined
  in one*)

Remodelled 1815, and enlarged many
times since. The Order is divided into
civil and military divisions. Women
became eligible for the Order from 1
January 1971

THE SOVEREIGN

GREAT MASTER AND FIRST OR
PRINCIPAL KNIGHT GRAND
CROSS
HRH The Prince of Wales, KG, KT,
  GCB

Dean of the Order, The Dean of
  Westminster
Bath King of Arms, Air Chief Marshal
  Sir David Evans, GCB, CBE
Registrar and Secretary, Rear-Adm.
  D. E. Macey, CB
Genealogist, P. Gwynn-Jones, LVO
Gentleman Usher of the Scarlet Rod, Air
  Vice-Marshal Sir Richard Peirse,
  KCVO, CB
Deputy Secretary, The Secretary of the
  Central Chancery of the Orders of
  Knighthood
Chancery, Central Chancery of the
  Orders of Knighthood, St James's
  Palace, London SW1A 1BH

THE ORDER OF MERIT
(1902)

OM *Military*   OM *Civil*

OM

Ribbon, Blue and crimson

This Order is designed as a special distinction for eminent men and women without conferring a knighthood upon them. The Order is limited in numbers to 24, with the addition of foreign honorary members. Membership is of two kinds, military and civil, the badge of the former having crossed swords, and the latter oak leaves

THE SOVEREIGN

HRH The Prince Philip, Duke of Edinburgh, 1968
Sir Isaiah Berlin, 1971
Sir George Edwards, 1971
Sir Alan Hodgkin, 1973
Revd Prof. Owen Chadwick, KBE, 1983
Sir Andrew Huxley, 1983
Sir Michael Tippett, 1983
Frederick Sanger, 1986
The Lord Menuhin, 1987
Prof. Sir Ernst Gombrich, 1988
Dr Max Perutz, 1988
Dame Cicely Saunders, 1989
The Lord Porter of Luddenham, 1989
The Baroness Thatcher, 1990
Dame Joan Sutherland, 1991
Prof. Francis Crick, 1991
Dame Ninette de Valois, 1992
Sir Michael Atiyah, 1992
Lucian Freud, 1993
The Lord Jenkins of Hillhead, 1993
Sir Aaron Klug, 1995
Sir John Gielgud, 1996
Honorary Member, Nelson Mandela, 1995

Secretary and Registrar, Sir Edward Ford, KCB, KCVO, ERD
Chancery, Central Chancery of the Orders of Knighthood, St James's Palace, London SW1A 1BH

THE MOST EXALTED ORDER OF THE STAR OF INDIA (1861)

GCSI   Knight Grand Commander
KCSI   Knight Commander
CSI   Companion
Ribbon, Light blue, with white edges
Motto, Heaven's Light our Guide

THE SOVEREIGN
Registrar, The Secretary of the Central Chancery of the Orders of Knighthood
No conferments have been made since 1947

THE MOST DISTINGUISHED ORDER OF ST MICHAEL AND ST GEORGE (1818)

GCMG   KCMG

GCMG   Knight (or Dame) Grand Cross
KCMG   Knight Commander
DCMG   Dame Commander
CMG   Companion

Ribbon, Saxon blue, with scarlet centre
Motto, Auspicium melioris aevi (*Token of a better age*)

THE SOVEREIGN

GRAND MASTER
HRH The Duke of Kent, KG, GCMG, GCVO, ADC

Prelate, The Rt. Revd Simon Barrington-Ward
Chancellor, Sir Antony Acland, GCMG, GCVO
Secretary, Sir John Coles, GCMG
Registrar, Sir John Graham, Bt., GCMG
King of Arms, Sir Ewen Fergusson, GCMG, GCVO
Gentleman Usher of the Blue Rod, Sir John Margetson, KCMG
Dean, The Dean of St Paul's
Deputy Secretary, The Secretary of the Central Chancery of the Orders of Knighthood
Chancery, Central Chancery of the Orders of Knighthood, St James's Palace, London SW1A 1BH

THE MOST EMINENT ORDER OF THE INDIAN EMPIRE (1868)

GCIE   Knight Grand Commander
KCIE   Knight Commander
CIE   Companion

Ribbon, Imperial purple
Motto, Imperatricis auspiciis (*Under the auspices of the Empress*)

THE SOVEREIGN
Registrar, The Secretary of the Central Chancery of the Orders of Knighthood
No conferments have been made since 1947

THE IMPERIAL ORDER OF THE CROWN OF INDIA (1877) FOR LADIES

CI

Badge, the royal cipher in jewels within an oval, surmounted by an heraldic crown and attached to a bow of light blue watered ribbon, edged white
The honour does not confer any rank or title upon the recipient
No conferments have been made since 1947

HM The Queen, 1947
HM Queen Elizabeth the Queen Mother, 1931
HRH The Princess Margaret, Countess of Snowdon, 1947
HRH Princess Alice, Duchess of Gloucester, 1937

THE ROYAL VICTORIAN ORDER (1896)

GCVO   KCVO

GCVO   Knight or Dame Grand Cross
KCVO   Knight Commander
DCVO   Dame Commander
CVO   Commander
LVO   Lieutenant
MVO   Member

Ribbon, Blue, with red and white edges
Motto, Victoria

THE SOVEREIGN
GRAND MASTER
HM Queen Elizabeth the Queen Mother

Chancellor, The Lord Chamberlain
Secretary, The Keeper of the Privy Purse
Registrar, The Secretary of the Central Chancery of the Orders of Knighthood
Chaplain, The Revd J. Robson
Hon. Genealogist, D. H. B. Chesshyre, LVO

THE MOST EXCELLENT ORDER OF THE BRITISH EMPIRE (1917)

GBE   KBE

The Order was divided into military and civil divisions in December 1918

GBE   Knight or Dame Grand Cross
KBE   Knight Commander
DBE   Dame Commander
CBE   Commander
OBE   Officer
MBE   Member

Ribbon, Rose pink edged with pearl grey with vertical pearl stripe in centre (military division); without vertical pearl stripe (civil division)
Motto, For God and the Empire

THE SOVEREIGN

GRAND MASTER
HRH The Prince Philip, Duke of Edinburgh, KG, KT, OM, GBE, PC, FRS

Prelate, The Bishop of London
King of Arms, Air Chief Marshal Sir Patrick Hine, GCB, GBE
Registrar, The Secretary of the Central Chancery of the Orders of Knighthood
Secretary, Sir Robin Butler, GCB, CVO
Dean, The Dean of St Paul's
Gentleman Usher of the Purple Rod, Sir Robin Gillett, Bt., GBE, RD
Chancery, Central Chancery of the Orders of Knighthood, St James's Palace, London SW1A 1BH

ORDER OF THE COMPANIONS OF HONOUR (1917)

CH

Ribbon, Carmine, with gold edges

This Order consists of one class only and carries with it no title. The number of awards is limited to 65 (excluding honorary members)

Anthony, Rt. Hon. John, 1981
Ashley of Stoke, The Lord, 1975
Astor, Hon. David, 1993
Attenborough, Sir David, 1995
Baker, Dame Janet, 1993
Baker of Dorking, The Lord, 1992
Brenner, Sydney, 1986
Brooke, Rt. Hon. Peter, 1992

Carrington, The Lord, 1983
Casson, Sir Hugh, 1984
Cledwyn of Penrhos, The Lord, 1976
de Valois, Dame Ninette, 1981
Doll, Prof. Sir Richard, 1995
Eccles, The Viscount, 1984
Fraser, Rt. Hon. Malcolm, 1977
Freud, Lucian, 1983
Gielgud, Sir John, 1977
Glenamara, The Lord, 1976
Gorton, Rt. Hon. Sir John, 1971
Guinness, Sir Alec, 1994
Hailsham of St Marylebone, The Lord, 1974
Hawking, Prof. Stephen, 1989
Healey, The Lord, 1979
Heseltine, Rt. Hon. Michael, 1997
Hockney, David, 1997
Howe of Aberavon, The Lord, 1996
Hurd of Westwell, The Lord, 1995
Jones, James, 1977
Jones, Prof. Reginald, 1994
King, Rt. Hon. Tom, 1992
Lange, Rt. Hon. David, 1989
Lasdun, Sir Denys, 1995
Milstein, César, 1994
Owen, The Lord, 1994
Pasmore, Victor, 1980
Perutz, Dr Max, 1975
Powell, Anthony, 1987
Powell, Sir Philip, 1984
Rowse, Alfred, 1996
Runciman, Hon. Sir Steven, 1984
Rylands, George, 1987
Sanger, Frederick, 1981
Sisson, Charles, 1993
Smith, Sir John, 1993
Somare, Rt. Hon. Sir Michael, 1978
Talboys, Rt. Hon. Sir Brian, 1981
Tebbit, The Lord, 1987
Tippett, Sir Michael, 1979
Trudeau, Rt. Hon. Pierre, 1984
Whitelaw, The Viscount, 1974
Widdowson, Dr Elsie, 1993
Honorary Members, Lee Kuan Yew, 1970; Dr Joseph Luns, 1971

Secretary and Registrar, The Secretary of the Central Chancery of the Orders of Knighthood

THE DISTINGUISHED SERVICE ORDER (1886)

DSO

Ribbon, Red, with blue edges

Bestowed in recognition of especial services in action of commissioned officers in the Navy, Army and Royal Air Force and (since 1942) Mercantile Marine. The members are Companions only. A Bar may be awarded for any additional act of service

THE IMPERIAL SERVICE ORDER (1902)

ISO

Ribbon, Crimson, with blue centre

Appointment as Companion of this Order is open to members of the Civil Services whose eligibility is determined by the grade they hold. The Order consists of The Sovereign and Companions to a number not exceeding 1,900, of whom 1,300 may belong to the Home Civil Services and 600 to Overseas Civil Services. The Prime Minister announced in March 1993 that he would make no further recommendations for appointments to the Order.

Secretary, Sir Robin Butler, GCB, CVO
Registrar, The Secretary of the Central Chancery of the Orders of Knighthood, St James's Palace, London SW1A 1BH

THE ROYAL VICTORIAN CHAIN (1902)

It confers no precedence on its holders

HM THE QUEEN
HM Queen Elizabeth the Queen Mother, 1937

HRH Princess Juliana of the Netherlands, 1950
HM The King of Thailand, 1960
HM The King of Jordan, 1966
HM King Zahir Shah of Afghanistan, 1971
HM The Queen of Denmark, 1974
HM The King of Nepal, 1975
HM The King of Sweden, 1975
The Lord Coggan, 1980
HM The Queen of the Netherlands, 1982
Gen. Antonio Eanes, 1985
HM The King of Spain, 1986
HM The King of Saudi Arabia, 1987
HRH The Princess Margaret, Countess of Snowdon, 1990
The Lord Runcie, 1991
The Lord Charteris of Amisfield, 1992
HE Richard von Weizsäcker, 1992
HM The King of Norway, 1994

Baronetage and Knightage

BARONETS

Style, 'Sir' before forename and surname, followed by 'Bt.'
Wife's style, 'Lady' followed by surname
For forms of address, *see* page 136

There are five different creations of baronetcies: Baronets of England (creations dating from 1611); Baronets of Ireland (creations dating from 1619); Baronets of Scotland or Nova Scotia (creations dating from 1625); Baronets of Great Britain (creations after the Act of Union 1707 which combined the kingdoms of England and Scotland); and Baronets of the United Kingdom (creations after the union of Great Britain and Ireland in 1801).

Badge of Baronets of the United Kingdom

Badge of Baronets of Nova Scotia

Badge of Ulster

The patent of creation limits the destination of a baronetcy, usually to male descendants of the first baronet, although special remainders allow the baronetcy to pass, if the male issue of sons fail, to the male issue of daughters of the first baronet. In the case of baronetcies of Scotland or Nova Scotia, a special remainder of 'heirs male and of tailzie' allows the baronetcy to descend to heirs general, including women. There are four existing Scottish baronets with such a remainder, one of whom, the holder of the Dunbar of Hempriggs creation, is a Baroness.

The Official Roll of Baronets is kept at the Home Office by the Registrar of the Baronetage. Anyone who considers that he is entitled to be entered on the Roll may petition the Crown through the Home Secretary. Every person succeeding to a baronetcy must exhibit proofs of succession to the Home Secretary. A person whose name is not entered on the Official Roll will not be addressed or mentioned by the title of baronet in any official document, nor will he be accorded precedence as a baronet.

BARONETCIES EXTINCT SINCE THE LAST EDITION
Gough-Calthorpe (*cr.* 1728), by the death of Lord Calthorpe; Hanson (*cr.* 1887); Harris (*cr.* 1953); Horder (*cr.* 1923), by the death of Lord Horder; Schuster (*cr.* 1906)

Registrar of the Baronetage, Miss C. E. C. Sinclair
Assistant Registrar, Mrs F. G. Bright
Office, Home Office, 50 Queen Anne's Gate, London SW1H 9AT. Tel: 0171-273 3498

KNIGHTS

Style, 'Sir' before forename and surname, followed by appropriate post-nominal initials if a Knight Grand Cross, Knight Grand Commander or Knight Commander
Wife's style, 'Lady' followed by surname
For forms of address, *see* page 136
The prefix 'Sir' is not used by knights who are clerics of the Church of England, who do not receive the accolade. Their wives are entitled to precedence as the wife of a knight but not to the style of 'Lady'.

ORDERS OF KNIGHTHOOD

Knight Grand Cross, Knight Grand Commander, and Knight Commander are the higher classes of the Orders of Chivalry (*see* pages 170–2). Honorary knighthoods of these Orders may be conferred on men who are citizens of countries of which The Queen is not head of state. As a rule, the prefix 'Sir' is not used by honorary knights.

KNIGHTS BACHELOR

The Knights Bachelor do not constitute a Royal Order, but comprise the surviving representation of the ancient State Orders of Knighthood. The Register of Knights Bachelor, instituted by James I in the 17th century, lapsed, and in 1908 a voluntary association under the title of The Society of Knights (now The Imperial Society of Knights Bachelor by Royal Command) was formed with the primary objects of continuing the various registers dating from 1257 and obtaining the uniform registration of every created Knight Bachelor. In 1926 a design for a badge to be worn by Knights Bachelor was approved and adopted; in 1974 a neck badge and miniature were added.

Knight Principal, Sir Conrad Swan, KCVO
Chairman of Council, The Lord Lane of Horsell
Prelate, Rt. Revd and Rt. Hon. The Bishop of London
Hon. Registrar, Sir Kenneth Newman, GBE, QPM
Hon. Treasurer, Sir Douglas Morpeth, TD
Clerk to the Council, R. M. Esden
Office, 21 Old Buildings, Lincoln's Inn, London WC2A 3UJ

LIST OF BARONETS AND KNIGHTS
Revised to 31 August 1997

Peers are not included in this list

†   Not registered on the Official Roll of the Baronetage at the time of going to press
( )   The date of creation of the baronetcy is given in parenthesis
I   Baronet of Ireland
NS   Baronet of Nova Scotia
S   Baronet of Scotland

If a baronet or knight has a double barrelled or hyphenated surname, he is listed under the final element of the name
A full entry in italic type indicates that the recipient of a knighthood died during the year in which the honour was conferred. The name is included for purposes of record

Abal, Sir Tei, Kt., CBE
Abbott, Sir Albert Francis, Kt., CBE
Abbott, *Vice-Adm.* Sir Peter Charles, KCB
Abdy, Sir Valentine Robert Duff, Bt. (1850)
Abel, Sir Seselo (Cecil) Charles Geoffrey, Kt., OBE
Abeles, Sir (Emil Herbert) Peter, Kt.
Abercromby, Sir Ian George, Bt. (s. 1636)
Abraham, Sir Edward Penley, Kt., CBE, FRS
Acheson, *Prof.* Sir (Ernest) Donald, KBE
Ackers, Sir James George, Kt.
Ackroyd, Sir Timothy Robert Whyte, Bt. (1956)
Acland, Sir Antony Arthur, GCMG, GCVO
Acland, *Lt.-Col.* Sir (Christopher) Guy (Dyke), Bt., MVO (1890)
Acland, Sir John Dyke, Bt. (1644)
Acland, *Maj.-Gen.* Sir John Hugh Bevil, KCB, CBE
Adam, Sir Christopher Eric Forbes, Bt. (1917)
Adams, Sir Philip George Doyne, KCMG
Adams, Sir William James, KCMG
Adamson, Sir (William Owen) Campbell, Kt.
Adrien, *Hon.* Sir Maurice Latour-, Kt.
Adye, Sir John Anthony, KCMG
Agnew, Sir Crispin Hamlyn, Bt. (s. 1629)
Agnew, Sir John Keith, Bt. (1895)
Aiken, *Air Chief Marshal* Sir John Alexander Carlisle, KCB
Ainsworth, Sir (Thomas) David, Bt. (1916)
Aird, *Capt.* Sir Alastair Sturgis, GCVO
Aird, Sir (George) John, Bt. (1901)
Airey, Sir Lawrence, KCB
Airy, *Maj.-Gen.* Sir Christopher John, KCVO, CBE
Aitchison, Sir Charles Walter de Lancey, Bt. (1938)
Akehurst, *Gen.* Sir John Bryan, KCB, CBE
Albert, Sir Alexis François, Kt., CMG, VRD
Albu, Sir George, Bt. (1912)
Alcock, *Air Chief Marshal* Sir (Robert James) Michael, GCB, KBE
Aldous, *Rt. Hon.* Sir William, Kt.
Alexander, Sir Charles Gundry, Bt. (1945)
Alexander, Sir Claud Hagart-, Bt. (1886)
Alexander, Sir Douglas, Bt. (1921)
Alexander, Sir (John) Lindsay, Kt.
Alexander, *Prof.* Sir Kenneth John Wilson, Kt.
Alexander, Sir Michael O'Donal Bjarne, GCMG
†Alexander, Sir Patrick Desmond William Cable-, Bt. (1809)
Allan, Sir Anthony James Allan Havelock-, Bt. (1858)

Allen, *Prof.* Sir Geoffrey, Kt., PH.D., FRS
Allen, Sir John Derek, Kt., CBE
Allen, *Hon.* Sir Peter Austin Philip Jermyn, Kt.
Allen, Sir William Guilford, Kt.
Allen, Sir (William) Kenneth (Gwynne), Kt.
Alleyne, Sir George Allanmoore Ogarren, Kt.
Alleyne, *Revd* Sir John Olpherts Campbell, Bt. (1769)
Alliance, Sir David, Kt., CBE
Allinson, Sir (Walter) Leonard, KCVO, CMG
Alliott, *Hon.* Sir John Downes, Kt.
Allison, *Air Chief Marshal* Sir John Shakespeare, KCB, CBE
Alment, Sir (Edward) Anthony John, Kt.
Althaus, Sir Nigel Frederick, Kt.
Ambo, *Rt. Revd* George, KBE
Amet, *Hon.* Sir Arnold Karibone, Kt.
Amies, Sir (Edwin) Hardy, KCVO
Amory, Sir Ian Heathcoat, Bt. (1874)
Anderson, Sir John Anthony, KBE
Anderson, *Maj.-Gen.* Sir John Evelyn, KBE
Anderson, Sir John Muir, Kt., CMG
Anderson, *Hon.* Sir Kevin Victor, Kt.
Anderson, *Vice-Adm.* Sir Neil Dudley, KBE, CB
Anderson, *Prof.* Sir (William) Ferguson, Kt., OBE
Anderton, Sir (Cyril) James, Kt., CBE, QPM
Andrew, Sir Robert John, KCB
Andrews, Sir Derek Henry, KCB, CBE
Andrews, *Hon.* Sir Dormer George, Kt.
Angus, Sir Michael Richardson, Kt.
Annesley, Sir Hugh Norman, Kt., QPM
Anson, *Vice-Adm.* Sir Edward Rosebery, KCB
Anson, Sir John, KCB
Anson, *Rear-Adm.* Sir Peter, Bt., CB (1831)
Anstey, *Brig.* Sir John, Kt., CBE, TD
Anstruther, *Maj.* Sir Ralph Hugo, Bt., GCVO, MC (s. 1694)
Antico, Sir Tristan Venus, Kt.
Antrobus, Sir Charles James, GCMG, OBE
Antrobus, Sir Edward Philip, Bt. (1815)
Appleyard, Sir Leonard Vincent, KCMG
Appleyard, Sir Raymond Kenelm, KBE
Arbuthnot, Sir Keith Robert Charles, Bt. (1823)
Arbuthnot, Sir William Reierson, Bt. (1964)
Archdale, *Capt.* Sir Edward Folmer, Bt., DSC, RN (1928)
Archer, *Gen.* Sir (Arthur) John, KCB, OBE
Arculus, Sir Ronald, KCMG, KCVO

Armitage, *Air Chief Marshal* Sir Michael John, KCB, CBE
Armour, *Prof.* Sir James, Kt., CBE
Armstrong, Sir Andrew Clarence Francis, Bt., CMG (1841)
Armytage, Sir John Martin, Bt. (1738)
Arnold, *Rt. Hon.* Sir John Lewis, Kt.
Arnold, Sir Malcolm Henry, Kt., CBE
Arnold, Sir Thomas Richard, Kt.
Arnott, Sir Alexander John Maxwell, Bt. (1896)
Arnott, *Prof.* Sir (William) Melville, Kt., TD, MD
Arrindell, Sir Clement Athelston, GCMG, GCVO, QC
Arthur, *Lt.-Gen.* Sir (John) Norman Stewart, KCB
Arthur, Sir Stephen John, Bt. (1841)
Ash, *Prof.* Sir Eric Albert, Kt., CBE, FRS, FENG.
Ashburnham, Sir Denny Reginald, Bt. (1661)
Ashe, Sir Derick Rosslyn, KCMG
Ashley, Sir Bernard Albert, Kt.
Ashmore, *Admiral of the Fleet* Sir Edward Beckwith, GCB, DSC
Ashmore, *Vice-Adm.* Sir Peter William Beckwith, KCB, KCVO, DSC
Ashworth, Sir Herbert, Kt.
Aske, *Revd* Sir Conan, Bt. (1922)
Askew, Sir Bryan, Kt.
Asscher, Prof. (Adolf) William, Kt., MD, FRCP
Astill, *Hon.* Sir Michael John, Kt.
Aston, Sir Harold George, Kt., CBE
Aston, *Hon.* Sir William John, KCMG
Astor, *Hon.* Sir John Jacob, Kt., MBE
Astwood, *Hon.* Sir James Rufus, KBE
Astwood, *Lt.-Col.* Sir Jeffrey Carlton, Kt., CBE, ED
Atcherley, Sir Harold Winter, Kt.
Atiyah, Sir Michael Francis, Kt., OM, PH.D., FRS
Atkins, *Rt. Hon.* Sir Robert James, Kt.
Atkinson, *Air Marshal* Sir David William, KBE
Atkinson, Sir Frederick John, KCB
Atkinson, Sir John Alexander, KCB, DFC
Atkinson, Sir Robert, Kt., DSC, FENG.
Attenborough, Sir David Frederick, Kt., CH, CVO, CBE, FRS
Atwell, Sir John William, Kt., CBE, FRSE, FENG.
Atwill, Sir (Milton) John (Napier), Kt.
Audland, Sir Christopher John, KCMG
Audley, Sir George Bernard, Kt.
Augier, *Prof.* Sir Fitz-Roy Richard, Kt.
Auld, *Rt. Hon.* Sir Robin Ernest, Kt.
†Austin, Sir Anthony Leonard, Bt. (1894)
Austin, *Vice-Adm.* Sir Peter Murray, KCB
Austin, *Air Marshal* Sir Roger Mark, KCB, AFC
Axford, Sir William Ian, Kt.

Beldam, *Rt. Hon.* Sir (Alexander) Roy (Asplan), Kt.

Belich, Sir James, Kt.

Bell, Sir Brian Ernest, KBE

Bell, Sir (George) Raymond, KCMG, CB

Bell, Sir John Lowthian, Bt. (1885)

Bell, *Hon.* Sir Rodger, Kt.

Bell, Sir Timothy John Leigh, Kt.

Bell, Sir (William) Ewart, KCB

Bell, Sir William Hollin Dayrell Morrison-, Bt. (1905)

Bellew, Sir Henry Charles Gratton-, Bt. (1838)

Bellinger, Sir Robert Ian, GBE

Bellingham, Sir Noel Peter Roger, Bt. (1796)

Bengough, *Col.* Sir Piers, KCVO, OBE

Benn, Sir (James) Jonathan, Bt. (1914)

Bennett, Sir Charles Moihi Te Arawaka, Kt., DSO

Bennett, *Air Vice-Marshal* Sir Erik Peter, KBE, CB

Bennett, *Rt. Hon.* Sir Frederic Mackarness, Kt.

Bennett, Sir Hubert, Kt.

Bennett, *Hon.* Sir Hugh Peter Derwyn, Kt.

Bennett, Sir John Mokonuiarangi, Kt.

Bennett, *Gen.* Sir Phillip Harvey, KBE, DSO

Bennett, Sir Reginald Frederick Brittain, Kt., VRD

Bennett, Sir Ronald Wilfrid Murdoch, Bt. (1929)

Benson, Sir Christopher John, Kt.

Bentley, Sir William, KCMG

Benyon, Sir William Richard, Kt.

Beresford, Sir (Alexander) Paul, Kt., MP

Berger, *Vice-Adm.* Sir Peter Egerton Capel, KCB, LVO, DSC

Berghuser, *Hon.* Sir Eric, Kt., MBE

Berlin, Sir Isaiah, Kt., OM, CBE

Berman, Sir Franklin Delow, KCMG

Bernard, Sir Dallas Edmund, Bt. (1954)

Berney, Sir Julian Reedham Stuart, Bt. (1620)

Berrill, Sir Kenneth Ernest, GBE, KCB

Berriman, Sir David, Kt.

Berry, *Prof.* Sir Colin Leonard, Kt., FRCpath.

Berry, *Prof.* Sir Michael Victor, Kt., FRS

Berthon, *Vice-Adm.* Sir Stephen Ferrier, KCB

Berthoud, Sir Martin Seymour, KCVO, CMG

Best, Sir Richard Radford, KCVO, CBE

Bethune, Sir Alexander Maitland Sharp, Bt. (s. 1683)

Bethune, *Hon.* Sir (Walter) Angus, Kt.

Bett, Sir Michael, Kt., CBE

Bevan, Sir Martyn Evan Evans, Bt. (1958)

Bevan, Sir Timothy Hugh, Kt.

Beveridge, Sir Gordon Smith Grieve, Kt., FRSE, FEng., FRSA

Beverley, *Lt.-Gen.* Sir Henry York La Roche, KCB, OBE, RM

Bibby, Sir Derek James, Bt., MC (1959)

Bick, *Hon.* Sir Martin James Moore-, Kt.

Bickersteth, *Rt. Revd* John Monier, KCVO

Biddulph, Sir Ian D'Olier, Bt. (1664)

Bide, Sir Austin Ernest, Kt.

Bidwell, Sir Hugh Charles Philip, GBE

Biggam, Sir Robin Adair, Kt.

Biggs, *Vice-Adm.* Sir Geoffrey William Roger, KCB

Biggs, Sir Norman Paris, Kt.

Bilas, Sir Angmai Simon, Kt., OBE

Billière, *Gen.* Sir Peter Edgar de la Cour de la, KCB, KBE, DSO, MC

Bing, Sir Rudolf Franz Josef, KBE

Bingham, *Hon.* Sir Eardley Max, Kt., QC

Birch, Sir John Allan, KCVO, CMG

Birch, Sir Roger, Kt., CBE, QPM

Bird, Sir Richard Geoffrey Chapman, Bt. (1922)

Birkin, Sir John Christian William, Bt. (1905)

Birkin, Sir (John) Derek, Kt., TD

Birkmyre, Sir Archibald, Bt. (1921)

Birley, Sir Derek Sydney, Kt.

Birrell, Sir James Drake, Kt.

Birtwistle, Sir Harrison, Kt.

Bishop, Sir Frederick Arthur, Kt., CB, CVO

Bishop, Sir George Sidney, Kt., CB, OBE

Bishop, Sir Michael David, Kt., CBE

Bisson, *Rt. Hon.* Sir Gordon Ellis, Kt.

Black, *Prof.* Sir Douglas Andrew Kilgour, Kt., MD, FRCP

Black, Sir James Whyte, Kt., FRCP, FRS

Black, *Adm.* Sir (John) Jeremy, GBE, KCB, DSO

Black, Sir Robert Brown, GCMG, OBE

Black, Sir Robert David, Bt. (1922)

Blackburne, *Hon.* Sir William Anthony, Kt.

Blacker, *Gen.* Sir (Anthony Stephen) Jeremy, KCB, CBE

Blacker, *Gen.* Sir Cecil Hugh, GCB, OBE, MC

Blackett, Sir Hugh Francis, Bt. (1673)

Blacklock, *Surgeon Capt. Prof.* Sir Norman James, KCVO, OBE

Blackman, Sir Frank Milton, KCVO, OBE

Blackwell, Sir Basil Davenport, Kt., FEng.

Blackwood, Sir John Francis, Bt. (1814)

Blair, Sir Alastair Campbell, KCVO, TD, WS

Blair, *Lt.-Gen.* Sir Chandos, KCVO, OBE, MC

Blair, Sir Edward Thomas Hunter, Bt. (1786)

Blake, Sir Alfred Lapthorn, KCVO, MC

Blake, Sir Francis Michael, Bt. (1907)

Blake, Sir Peter James, KBE

Blake, Sir (Thomas) Richard (Valentine), Bt. (I. 1622)

Blaker, Sir John, Bt. (1919)

Blakiston, Sir Ferguson Arthur James, Bt. (1763)

Bland, Sir (Francis) Christopher (Buchan), Kt.

Bland, Sir Henry Armand, Kt., CBE

Bland, *Lt.-Col.* Sir Simon Claud Michael, KCVO

Blatherwick, Sir David Elliott Spiby, KCMG, OBE

Blelloch, Sir John Nial Henderson, KCB

Blennerhassett, Sir (Marmaduke) Adrian Francis William, Bt. (1809)

Blewitt, *Maj.* Sir Shane Gabriel Basil, GCVO

Blofeld, *Hon.* Sir John Christopher Calthorpe, Kt.

Blois, Sir Charles Nicholas Gervase, Bt. (1686)

Blomefield, Sir Thomas Charles Peregrine, Bt. (1807)

Bloomfield, Sir Kenneth Percy, KCB

Blosse, *Capt.* Sir Richard Hely Lynch-, Bt. (1622)

Blount, Sir Walter Edward Alpin, Bt., DSC (1642)

Blundell, Sir Thomas Leon, Kt., FRS

Blunden, Sir George, Kt.

†Blunden, Sir Philip Overington, Bt. (I. 1766)

Blunt, Sir David Richard Reginald Harvey, Bt. (1720)

Blyth, Sir Charles (Chay), Kt., CBE, BEM

Boardman, *Prof.* Sir John, Kt., FSA, FBA

Bodmer, Sir Walter Fred, Kt., PH.D., FRS

Body, Sir Richard Bernard Frank Stewart, Kt.

Boevey, Sir Thomas Michael Blake Crawley-, Bt. (1784)

Bogan, Sir Nagora, KBE

Bogarde, Sir Dirk (Derek Niven van den Bogaerde), Kt.

Boileau, Sir Guy (Francis), Bt. (1838)

Boles, Sir Jeremy John Fortescue, Bt. (1922)

Boles, Sir John Dennis, Kt., MBE

Bolland, Sir Edwin, KCMG

Bollers, *Hon.* Sir Harold Brodie Smith, Kt.

Bolton, Sir Frederic Bernard, Kt., MC

Bona, Sir Kina, KBE

Bond, Sir Kenneth Raymond Boyden, Kt.

Bond, *Prof.* Sir Michael Richard, Kt., FRCpsych., FRCPGlas., FRCSE

Bondi, *Prof.* Sir Hermann, KCB, FRS

Bonfield, Sir Peter Leahy, Kt., CBE, FEng.

Bonham, *Maj.* Sir Antony Lionel Thomas, Bt. (1852)

Bonington, Sir Christian John Storey, Kt., CBE

Bonsall, Sir Arthur Wilfred, KCMG, CBE

Bonsor, Sir Nicholas Cosmo, Bt. (1925)

Boolell, Sir Satcam, Kt.

Boord, Sir Nicolas John Charles, Bt. (1896)

Boorman, *Lt.-Gen.* Sir Derek, KCB

Booth, Sir Christopher Charles, Kt., MD, FRCP

Booth, Hon. Sir David Alwyn Gore-, KCMG

Booth, Sir Douglas Allen, Bt. (1916)

Booth, Sir Gordon, KCMG, CVO

Booth, Sir Josslyn Henry Robert Gore-, Bt. (1. 1760)

Booth, Sir Michael Addison John Wheeler-, KCB

Boothby, Sir Brooke Charles, Bt. (1660)

Boreel, Sir Francis David, Bt. (1645)

Boreham, Hon. Sir Leslie Kenneth Edward, Kt.

Bornu, The Waziri of, KCMG, CBE

Borthwick, Sir John Thomas, Bt., MBE (1908)

Bossom, *Hon.* Sir Clive, Bt. (1953)

Boswall, Sir (Thomas) Alford Houstoun-, Bt (1836)

Boswell, *Lt.-Gen.* Sir Alexander Crawford Simpson, KCB, CBE

Bosworth, Sir Neville Bruce Alfred, Kt., CBE

Bottomley, Sir James Reginald Alfred, KCMG

Boughey, Sir John George Fletcher, Bt. (1798)

Boulton, Sir Clifford John, GCB

Boulton, Sir (Harold Hugh) Christian, Bt. (1905)

Boulton, Sir William Whytehead, Bt., CBE, TD (1944)

Bourn, Sir John Bryant, KCB

Bourne, Sir (John) Wilfrid, KCB

Bovell, *Hon.* Sir (William) Stewart, Kt.

Bowater, Sir Euan David Vansittart, Bt. (1939)

Bowater, Sir (John) Vansittart, Bt. (1914)

Bowden, Sir Andrew, Kt., MBE

Bowden, Sir Frank, Bt. (1915)

Bowen, Sir Geoffrey Fraser, Kt.

Bowen, Sir Mark Edward Mortimer, Bt. (1921)

†Bowlby, Sir Richard Peregrine Longstaff, Bt. (1923)

Bowman, Sir Jeffery Haverstock, Kt.

Bowman, Sir Paul Humphrey Armytage, Bt. (1884)

Bowmar, Sir Charles Erskine, Kt.

Bowness, Sir Alan, Kt., CBE

Boxer, *Air Vice-Marshal* Sir Alan Hunter Cachemaille, KCVO, CB, DSO, DFC

Boyce, *Vice-Adm.* Sir Michael Cecil, KCB, OBE

Boyce, Sir Robert Charles Leslie, Bt. (1952)

Boyd, Sir Alexander Walter, Bt. (1916)

Boyd, Sir John Dixon Iklé, KCMG

Boyd, The Hon. Sir Mark Alexander Lennox-, Kt.

Boyd, *Prof.* Sir Robert Lewis Fullarton, Kt., CBE, D.SC., FRS

Boyes, Sir Brian Gerald Barratt-, KBE

Boyle, Sir Stephen Gurney, Bt. (1904)

Boyne, Sir Henry Brian, Kt., CBE

Boynton, Sir John Keyworth, Kt., MC

Boys, *Rt. Hon.* Sir Michael Hardie, GCMG

Boyson, *Rt. Hon.* Sir Rhodes, Kt.

Brabham, Sir John Arthur, Kt., OBE

Bradbeer, Sir John Derek Richardson, Kt., OBE, TD

Bradbury, *Surgeon Vice-Adm.* Sir Eric Blackburn, KBE

Bradford, Sir Edward Alexander Slade, Bt. (1902)

Bradley, Sir Burton Gyrth Burton-, Kt., OBE

Bradman, Sir Donald George, Kt.

Bradshaw, Sir Kenneth Anthony, KCB

Bradshaw, *Lt.-Gen.* Sir Richard Phillip, KBE

Brain, Sir (Henry) Norman, KBE, CMG

Braithwaite, Sir (Joseph) Franklin Madders, Kt.

Braithwaite, *Rt. Hon.* Sir Nicholas Alexander, Kt., OBE

Braithwaite, Sir Rodric Quentin, GCMG

Bramall, Sir (Ernest) Ashley, Kt.

Bramley, *Prof.* Sir Paul Anthony, Kt.

Branigan, Sir Patrick Francis, Kt., QC

Bray, Sir Theodor Charles, Kt., CBE

Brennan, *Hon.* Sir (Francis) Gerard, KBE

Brett, Sir Charles Edward Bainbridge, Kt., CBE

Brickwood, Sir Basil Greame, Bt. (1927)

Bridges, *Hon.* Sir Phillip Rodney, Kt., CMG

Brierley, Sir Ronald Alfred, Kt.

Bright, Sir Graham Frank James, Kt.

Bright, Sir Keith, Kt.

Brigstocke, *Adm.* Sir John Richard, KCB

Brinckman, Sir Theodore George Roderick, Bt. (1831)

†Brisco, Sir Campbell Howard, Bt. (1782)

Briscoe, Sir John Geoffrey James, Bt. (1910)

Brise, Sir John Archibald Ruggles-, Bt., CB, OBE, TD (1935)

Bristow, *Hon.* Sir Peter Henry Rowley, Kt.

Brittan, *Rt. Hon.* Sir Leon, Kt., QC

Brittan, Sir Samuel, Kt.

Britton, Sir Edward Louis, Kt., CBE

Broackes, Sir Nigel, Kt.

†Broadbent, Sir Andrew George, Bt. (1893)

Brocklebank, Sir Aubrey Thomas, Bt. (1885)

Brockman, *Vice-Adm.* Sir Ronald Vernon, KCB, CSI, CIE, CVO, CBE

Brodie, Sir Benjamin David Ross, Bt. (1834)

Bromhead, Sir John Desmond Gonville, Bt. (1806)

Bromley, Sir Rupert Charles, Bt. (1757)

Bromley, Sir Thomas Eardley, KCMG

Brook, Sir Robin, Kt., CMG, OBE

†Brooke, Sir Alistair Weston, Bt. (1919)

Brooke, Sir Francis George Windham, Bt. (1903)

Brooke, *Rt. Hon.* Sir Henry, Kt.

Brooke, Sir Richard Neville, Bt. (1662)

Brookes, Sir Wilfred Deakin, Kt., CBE, DSO

Brooksbank, Sir (Edward) Nicholas, Bt. (1919)

Broom, *Air Marshal* Sir Ivor Gordon, KCB, CBE, DSO, DFC, AFC

Broomfield, Sir Nigel Hugh Robert Allen, KCMG

Broughton, *Air Marshal* Sir Charles, KBE, CB

†Broughton, Sir David Delves, Bt. (1661)

Broun, Sir William Windsor, Bt. (s. 1686)

Brown, Sir Allen Stanley, Kt., CBE

Brown, Sir (Arthur James) Stephen, KBE

Brown, Sir (Austen) Patrick, KCB

Brown, *Adm.* Sir Brian Thomas, KCB, CBE

Brown, Sir (Cyril) Maxwell Palmer, KCB, CMG

Brown, *Vice-Adm.* Sir David Worthington, KCB

Brown, Sir Derrick Holden-, Kt.

Brown, Sir Douglas Denison, Kt.

Brown, *Hon.* Sir Douglas Dunlop, Kt.

|Brown, Sir George Francis Richmond, Bt. (1863)

Brown, Sir George Noel, Kt.

Brown, Sir John Douglas Keith, Kt.

Brown, Sir John Gilbert Newton, Kt., CBE

Brown, Sir Mervyn, KCMG, OBE

Brown, Sir Peter Randolph, Kt.

Brown, *Hon.* Sir Ralph Kilner, Kt., OBE, TD

Brown, Sir Robert Crichton-, KCMG, CBE, TD

Brown, *Rt. Hon.* Sir Simon Denis, Kt.

Brown, *Rt. Hon.* Sir Stephen, Kt.

Brown, Sir Thomas, Kt.

Brown, Sir William Brian Piggott-, Bt. (1903)

Brownrigg, Sir Nicholas (Gawen), Bt. (1816)

Browse, *Prof.* Sir Norman Leslie, Kt., MD, FRCS

Bruce, Sir (Francis) Michael Ian, Bt. (s. 1628)

Bruce, Sir Hervey James Hugh, Bt. (1804)

Bruce, *Rt. Hon.* Sir (James) Roualeyn Hovell-Thurlow-Cumming-, Kt.

Brunner, Sir John Henry Kilian, Bt. (1895)

Brunton, Sir (Edward Francis) Lauder, Bt. (1908)

Brunton, Sir Gordon Charles, Kt.

Bryan, Sir Arthur, Kt.

Bryan, Sir Paul Elmore Oliver, Kt., DSO, MC

Bryce, *Hon.* Sir (William) Gordon, Kt., CBE

Bryson, *Adm.* Sir Lindsay Sutherland, KCB, FEng.

Buchan, Sir John, Kt., CMG

Buchanan, Sir Andrew George, Bt. (1878)

Buchanan, Sir Charles Alexander James Leith-, Bt. (1775)

Buchanan, *Prof.* Sir Colin Douglas, Kt., CBE

Buchanan, *Vice-Adm.* Sir Peter William, KBE

Buchanan, Sir Robert Wilson (Robin), Kt.

Buchanan, Sir (Ranald) Dennis, Kt., MBE

Buck, Sir (Philip) Antony (Fyson), Kt., QC

Buckland, Sir Ross, Kt.

Buckley, *Rt. Hon.* Sir Denys Burton, Kt., MBE

Buckley, Sir John William, Kt.

Buckley, *Lt.-Cdr.* Sir (Peter) Richard, KCVO

Buckley, *Hon.* Sir Roger John, Kt.

Budd, Sir Alan Peter, Kt.

Bulkeley, Sir Richard Thomas Williams-, Bt. (1661)

Bull, Sir Simeon George, Bt. (1922)

Bullard, Sir Julian Leonard, GCMG

Bullus, Sir Eric Edward, Kt.

Bulmer, Sir William Peter, Kt.

Bultin, Sir Bato, Kt., MBE

Bunbury, Sir Michael William, Bt. (1681)

Bunbury, Sir (Richard David) Michael Richardson-, Bt. (I. 1787)

Bunch, Sir Austin Wyeth, Kt., CBE

Bunyard, Sir Robert Sidney, Kt., CBE, QPM

Burbidge, Sir Herbert Dudley, Bt. (1916)

Burdett, Sir Savile Aylmer, Bt. (1665)

Burgen, Sir Arnold Stanley Vincent, Kt., FRS

Burgess, *Gen.* Sir Edward Arthur, KCB, OBE

Burgess, Sir (Joseph) Stuart, Kt., CBE, ph.D., FRSC

Burgh, Sir John Charles, KCMG, CB

Burke, Sir James Stanley Gilbert, Bt. (I. 1797)

Burke, Sir (Thomas) Kerry, Kt.

Burley, Sir Victor George, Kt., CBE

Burman, Sir (John) Charles, Kt.

Burnet, Sir James William Alexander (Sir Alastair Burnet), Kt.

Burnett, *Air Chief Marshal* Sir Brian Kenyon, GCB, DFC, AFC

Burnett, Sir David Humphery, Bt., MBE, TD (1913)

Burnett, Sir John Harrison, Kt.

Burnett, Sir Walter John, Kt.

Burney, Sir Cecil Denniston, Bt. (1921)

Burns, Sir (Robert) Andrew, KCMG

Burns, Sir Terence, GCB

Burrell, Sir John Raymond, Bt. (1774)

Burrenchobay, Sir Dayendranath, KBE, CMG, CVO

Burrows, Sir Bernard Alexander Brocas, GCMG

Burston, Sir Samuel Gerald Wood, Kt., OBE

Burt, *Hon.* Sir Francis Theodore Page, KCMG

Burton, Sir Carlisle Archibald, Kt., OBE

Burton, Sir George Vernon Kennedy, Kt., CBE

Burton, Sir Michael St Edmund, KCVO, CMG

Bush, *Adm.* Sir John Fitzroy Duyland, GCB, DSC

Butler, *Rt. Hon.* Sir Adam Courtauld, Kt.

Butler, *Hon.* Sir Arlington Griffith, KCMG

Butler, Sir Clifford Charles, Kt., ph.D., FRS

Butler, Sir (Frederick) (Edward) Robin, GCB, CVO

Butler, Sir Michael Dacres, GCMG

Butler, Sir (Reginald) Michael (Thomas), Bt. (1922)

Butler, *Hon.* Sir Richard Clive, Kt.

†Butler, Sir Richard Pierce, Bt. (1628)

Butt, Sir (Alfred) Kenneth Dudley, Bt. (1929)

Butter, *Maj.* Sir David Henry, KCVO, MC

Butterfield, *Hon.* Sir Alexander Neil Logie, Kt.

Buxton, Sir Jocelyn Charles Roden, Bt. (1840)

Buxton, *Hon.* Sir Richard Joseph, Kt.

Buzzard, Sir Anthony Farquhar, Bt. (1929)

Byatt, Sir Hugh Campbell, KCVO, CMG

Byers, Sir Maurice Hearne, Kt., CBE, QC

Byford, Sir Lawrence, Kt., CBE, QPM

Cable, Sir James Eric, KCVO, CMG

Cadbury, Sir (George) Adrian (Hayhurst), Kt.

Cadbury, Sir (Nicholas) Dominic, Kt.

Cadell, *Vice-Adm.* Sir John Frederick, KBE

Cadogan, *Prof.* Sir John Ivan George, Kt., CBE, FRS, FRSE

Cahn, Sir Albert Jonas, Bt. (1934)

Cain, Sir Edward Thomas, Kt., CBE

Cain, Sir Henry Edney Conrad, Kt.

Caine, Sir Michael Harris, Kt.

Caines, Sir John, KCB

Cairncross, Sir Alexander Kirkland, KCMG

Calcutt, Sir David Charles, Kt., QC

Calderwood, Sir Robert, Kt.

Caldwell, *Surgeon Vice-Adm.* Sir (Eric) Dick, KBE, CB

Callard, Sir Eric John, Kt., FEng.

Callaway, *Prof.* Sir Frank Adams, Kt., CMG, OBE

Calley, Sir Henry Algernon, Kt., DSO, DFC

Calman, *Prof.* Sir Kenneth Charles, KCB, MD, FRCP, FRCS, FRSE

Calne, *Prof.* Sir Roy Yorke, Kt., FRS

Calthorpe, Sir Euan Hamilton Anstruther-Gough-, Bt. (1929)

Cameron of Lochiel, Sir Donald Hamish, KT, CVO, TD

Cameron, Sir (Eustace) John, Kt., CBE

Cameron, Sir John Watson, Kt., OBE

Campbell, Sir Alan Hugh, GCMG

Campbell, Sir Colin Moffat, Bt., MC (s. 1668)

Campbell, *Prof.* Sir Colin Murray, Kt.

Campbell, *Prof.* Sir Donald, Kt., CBE, FRCS, FRCPGlas.

Campbell, Sir Ian Tofts, Kt., CBE, VRD

Campbell, Sir Ilay Mark, Bt. (1808)

Campbell, Sir Lachlan Philip Kemeys, Bt. (1815)

Campbell, Sir Matthew, KBE, CB, FRSE

Campbell, Sir Niall Alexander Hamilton, Bt. (1831)

Campbell, Sir Robin Auchinbreck, Bt. (s. 1628)

Campbell, Sir Thomas Cockburn-, Bt. (1821)

Campbell, *Hon.* Sir Walter Benjamin, Kt.

Campbell, *Hon.* Sir William Anthony, Kt.

†Carden, Sir Christopher Robert, Bt. (1887)

Carden, Sir John Craven, Bt. (I. 1787)

Carew, Sir Rivers Verain, Bt. (1661)

Carey, Sir Peter Willoughby, GCB

Carlisle, Sir James Beethoven, GCMG

Carlisle, Sir John Michael, Kt.

Carlisle, Sir Kenneth Melville, Kt.

Carmichael, Sir David Peter William Gibson-Craig-, Bt. (s. 1702 and 1831)

Carnac, *Revd Canon* Sir (Thomas) Nicholas Rivett-, Bt. (1836)

Carnegie, *Lt.-Gen.* Sir Robin Macdonald, KCB, OBE

Carnegie, Sir Roderick Howard, Kt.

Carnwath, Sir Robert John Anderson, Kt., CVO

Caro, Sir Anthony Alfred, Kt., CBE

Carpenter, *Very Revd* Edward Frederick, KCVO

Carpenter, *Lt.-Gen.* the Hon. Sir Thomas Patrick John Boyd-, KBE

Carr, Sir (Albert) Raymond (Maillard), Kt.

Carr, *Air Marshal* Sir John Darcy Baker-, KBE, CB, AFC

Carrick, *Hon.* Sir John Leslie, KCMG
Carrick, Sir Roger John, KCMG, LVO
Carsberg, *Prof.* Sir Bryan Victor, Kt.
Carswell, *Rt Hon.* Sir Robert Douglas, Kt.
Carter, Sir Charles Frederick, Kt., FBA
Carter, *Prof.* Sir David Craig, Kt., FRCSE, FRCSGlas., FRCPE
Carter, Sir Derrick Hunton, Kt., TD
Carter, Sir John, Kt., QC
Carter, Sir John Alexander, Kt.
Carter, Sir Philip David, Kt., CBE
Carter, Sir Richard Henry Alwyn, Kt.
Carter, Sir William Oscar, Kt.
Cartland, Sir George Barrington, Kt., CMG
Cartledge, Sir Bryan George, KCMG
Cary, Sir Roger Hugh, Bt. (1955)
Casey, *Rt. Hon.* Sir Maurice Eugene, Kt.
Cash, Sir Gerald Christopher, GCMG, GCVO, OBE
Cass, Sir Geoffrey Arthur, Kt.
Cassel, Sir Harold Felix, Bt., TD, QC (1920)
Cassels, *Field Marshal* Sir (Archibald) James Halkett, GCB, KBE, DSO
Cassels, Sir John Seton, Kt., CB
Cassels, *Adm.* Sir Simon Alastair Cassillis, KCB, CBE
Cassidi, *Adm.* Sir (Arthur) Desmond, GCB
Casson, Sir Hugh Maxwell, CH, KCVO, PPRA, FRIBA
Cater, Sir Jack, KBE
Cater, Sir John Robert, Kt.
Catford, Sir (John) Robin, KCVO, CBE
Catherwood, Sir (Henry) Frederick (Ross), Kt., MEP
Catling, Sir Richard Charles, Kt., CMG, OBE
Cato, *Hon.* Sir Arnott Samuel, KCMG
Cave, Sir Charles Edward Coleridge, Bt. (1896)
Cave, Sir (Charles) Philip Haddon-, KBE, CMG
Cave, Sir Robert Cave-Browne-, Bt. (1641)
Cawley, Sir Charles Mills, Kt., CBE, Ph.D.
Cayley, Sir Digby William David, Bt. (1661)
Cayzer, Sir James Arthur, Bt. (1904)
Cazalet, *Hon.* Sir Edward Stephen, Kt.
Cazalet, Sir Peter Grenville, Kt.
Cecil, *Rear-Adm.* Sir (Oswald) Nigel Amherst, KBE, CB
Chacksfield, *Air Vice-Marshal* Sir Bernard Albert, KBE, CB
Chadwick, *Revd Prof.* Henry, KBE
Chadwick, *Hon.* Sir John Murray, Kt., ED
Chadwick, Sir Joshua Kenneth Burton, Bt. (1935)
Chadwick, *Revd Prof.* (William) Owen, OM, KBE, FBA

Chalstrey, Sir (Leonard) John, Kt., MD, FRCS
Chan, *Rt. Hon.* Sir Julius, GCMG, KBE
Chance, Sir (George) Jeremy ffolliott, Bt. (1900)
Chandler, Sir Colin Michael, Kt.
Chandler, Sir Geoffrey, Kt., CBE
Chaney, *Hon.* Sir Frederick Charles, KBE, AFC
Chantler, *Prof.* Sir Cyril, Kt., MD, FRCP
Chaplin, Sir Malcolm Hilbery, Kt., CBE
Chapman, Sir David Robert Macgowan, Bt. (1958)
Chapman, Sir George Alan, Kt.
Chapman, Sir Sidney Brookes, Kt., MP
Chapple, *Field Marshal* Sir John Lyon, GCB, CBE
Charlton, Sir Robert (Bobby), Kt., CBE
Charnley, Sir (William) John, Kt., CB, FEng.
Chataway, *Rt. Hon.* Sir Christopher, Kt.
Chatfield, Sir John Freeman, Kt., CBE
Chaytor, Sir George Reginald, Bt. (1831)
Checketts, *Sqn. Ldr.* Sir David John, KCVO
Checkland, Sir Michael, Kt.
Cheetham, Sir Nicolas John Alexander, KCMG
Cheshire, *Air Marshal* Sir John Anthony, KBE, CB
Chessells, Sir Arthur David (Tim), Kt.
Chesterman, Sir (Dudley) Ross, Kt., Ph.D.
Chesterton, Sir Oliver Sidney, Kt., MC
Chetwood, Sir Clifford Jack, Kt.
Chetwynd, Sir Arthur Ralph Talbot, Bt. (1795)
Cheung, Sir Oswald Victor, Kt., CBE
Cheyne, Sir Joseph Lister Watson, Bt., OBE (1908)
Chichester, Sir (Edward) John, Bt. (1641)
Chilcot, Sir John Anthony, KCB
Child, Sir (Coles John) Jeremy, Bt. (1919)
Chilton, *Brig.* Sir Frederick Oliver, Kt., CBE, DSO
Chilwell, *Hon.* Sir Muir Fitzherbert, Kt.
Chinn, Sir Trevor Edwin, Kt., CVO
Chipperfield, Sir Geoffrey Howes, KCB
Chitty, Sir Thomas Willes, Bt. (1924)
Cholmeley, Sir Montague John, Bt. (1806)
Christie, Sir George William Langham, Kt.
Christie, Sir William, Kt., MBE
Christopherson, Sir Derman Guy, Kt., OBE, D.phil., FRS, FEng.
Chung, Sir Sze-yuen, GBE, FEng.
Clapham, Sir Michael John Sinclair, KBE

Clark, Sir Francis Drake, Bt. (1886)
Clark, Sir John Allen, Kt.
Clark, Sir John Stewart-, Bt., MEP (1918)
Clark, Sir Jonathan George, Bt. (1917)
Clark, Sir Robert Anthony, Kt., DSC
Clark, Sir Robin Chichester-, Kt.
Clark, Sir Terence Joseph, KBE, CMG, CVO
Clark, Sir Thomas Edwin, Kt.
Clarke, *Hon.* Sir Anthony Peter, Kt.
Clarke, Sir (Charles Mansfield) Tobias, Bt. (1831)
Clarke, *Prof.* Sir Cyril Astley, KBE, MD, SC.D., FRS, FRCP
Clarke, Sir Ellis Emmanuel Innocent, GCMG
Clarke, Sir Jonathan Dennis, Kt.
Clarke, *Maj.* Sir Peter Cecil, KCVO
Clarke, Sir Robert Cyril, Kt.
Clarke, Sir Rupert William John, Bt., MBE (1882)
Clay, Sir Richard Henry, Bt. (1841)
Clayton, Sir David Robert, Bt. (1732)
Clayton, Sir Robert James, Kt., CBE, FEng.
Cleaver, Sir Anthony Brian, Kt.
Cleminson, Sir James Arnold Stacey, KBE, MC
Clerk, Sir John Dutton, Bt., CBE, VRD (s. 1679)
Clerke, Sir John Edward Longueville, Bt. (1660)
Clifford, Sir Roger Joseph, Bt. (1887)
Clothier, Sir Cecil Montacute, KCB, QC
Clucas, Sir Kenneth Henry, KCB
Clutterbuck, *Vice-Adm.* Sir David Granville, KBE, CB
Coates, Sir David Frederick Charlton, Bt. (1921)
Coats, Sir Alastair Francis Stuart, Bt. (1905)
Coats, Sir William David, Kt.
Cobban, Sir James Macdonald, Kt., CBE, TD
Cobham, Sir Michael John, Kt., CBE
Cochrane, Sir (Henry) Marc (Sursock), Bt. (1903)
Cockburn, Sir John Elliot, Bt. (s. 1671)
Cockcroft, Sir Wilfred Halliday, Kt., D.phil.
Cockerell, Sir Christopher Sydney, Kt., CBE, FRS
Cockram, Sir John, Kt.
Cockshaw, Sir Alan, Kt., FEng.
Codrington, Sir Simon Francis Bethell, Bt. (1876)
Codrington, Sir William Alexander, Bt. (1721)
Coghill, Sir Egerton James Nevill Tobias, Bt. (1778)
Coghlin, *Hon.* Sir Patrick, Kt.
Cohen, Sir Edward, Kt.
Cohen, Sir Ivor Harold, Kt., CBE, TD
Cohen, Sir Stephen Harry Waley-, Bt. (1961)

Coldstream, Sir George Phillips, KCB, KCVO, QC

Cole, Sir (Alexander) Colin, KCB, KCVO, TD

Cole, Sir (Robert) William, Kt.

Coleman, Sir Timothy, KG

Coles, Sir (Arthur) John, GCMG

Colfox, Sir (William) John, Bt. (1939)

Collett, Sir Christopher, GBE

Collett, Sir Ian Seymour, Bt. (1934)

Collins, Hon. Sir Andrew David, Kt.

Collins, Sir Arthur James Robert, KCVO

Collins, Sir Bryan Thomas Alfred, Kt., OBE, QFSM

Collins, Sir John Alexander, Kt.

Collyear, Sir John Gowen, Kt., FEng.

Colman, Hon. Sir Anthony David, Kt.

Colman, Sir Michael Jeremiah, Bt. (1907)

Colquhoun of Luss, Sir Ivar Iain, Bt. (1786)

Colt, Sir Edward William Dutton Bt. (1694)

Colthurst, Sir Richard La Touche, Bt. (1744)

Coltman, Sir (Arthur) Leycester Scott, KBE, CMG

Colvin, Sir Howard Montagu, Kt., CVO, CBE, FBA

Compston, Vice-Adm. Sir Peter Maxwell, KCB

Compton, Rt. Hon. Sir John George Melvin, KCMG

Conant, Sir John Ernest Michael, Bt. (1954)

Condon, Sir Paul Leslie, Kt., QPM

Connell, Hon. Sir Michael Bryan, Kt.

Conran, Sir Terence Orby, Kt.

Cons, Hon. Sir Derek, Kt.

Constable, Sir Frederic Strickland-, Bt. (1641)

Constantinou, Sir Georkios, Kt., OBE

Cook, Prof. Sir Alan Hugh, Kt.

Cook, Sir Christopher Wymondham Rayner Herbert, Bt. (1886)

Cooke, Sir Charles Fletcher-, Kt., QC

Cooke, Lt.-Col. Sir David William Perceval, Bt. (1661)

Cooke, Sir Howard Felix Hanlan, GCMG, GCVO

Cooksey, Sir David James Scott, Kt.

Cooley, Sir Alan Sydenham, Kt., CBE

Cooper, Rt. Hon. Sir Frank, GCB, CMG

Cooper, Sir (Frederick Howard) Michael Craig-, Kt., CBE, TD

Cooper, Gen. Sir George Leslie Conroy, GCB, MC

Cooper, Sir Louis Jacques Blom-, Kt., QC

Cooper, Sir Patrick Graham Astley, Bt. (1821)

Cooper, Sir Richard Powell, Bt. (1905)

Cooper, Maj.-Gen. Sir Simon Christie, KCVO

Cooper, Sir William Daniel Charles, Bt. (1863)

Coote, Sir Christopher John, Bt., Premier Baronet of Ireland (I. 1621)

Copas, Most Revd Virgil, KBE, DD

Cope, Rt. Hon. Sir John Ambrose, Kt.

Copisarow, Sir Alcon Charles, Kt.

Corbett, Maj.-Gen. Sir Robert John Swan, KCVO, CB

Corby, Sir (Frederick) Brian, Kt.

Corfield, Rt. Hon. Sir Frederick Vernon, Kt., QC

Corfield, Sir Kenneth George, Kt., FEng.

Cork, Sir Roger William, Kt.

Corley, Sir Kenneth Sholl Ferrand, Kt.

Cormack, Sir Magnus Cameron, KBE

Cormack, Sir Patrick Thomas, Kt., MP

Corness, Sir Colin Ross, Kt.

Cornford, Sir (Edward) Clifford, KCB, FEng.

Cornforth, Sir John Warcup, Kt., CBE, D.Phil., FRS

Corry, Sir William James, Bt. (1885)

Cortazzi, Sir (Henry Arthur) Hugh, GCMG

Cory, Sir (Clinton Charles) Donald, Bt. (1919)

Cossons, Sir Neil, Kt., OBE

Cotter, Lt.-Col. Sir Delaval James Alfred, Bt., DSO (I. 1763)

Cotterell, Sir John Henry Geers, Bt. (1805)

Cotton, Sir John Richard, KCMG, OBE

Cotton, Hon. Sir Robert Carrington, KCMG

Cottrell, Sir Alan Howard, Kt., Ph.D., FRS, FEng.

†Cotts, Sir Richard Crichton Mitchell, Bt. (1921)

Coulson, Sir John Eltringham, KCMG

Couper, Sir (Robert) Nicholas (Oliver), Bt. (1841)

Court, Hon. Sir Charles Walter Michael, KCMG, OBE

Cousins, Air Marshal Sir David, KCB, AFC

Coutts, Sir David Burdett Money-, KCVO

Couzens, Sir Kenneth Edward, KCB

Covacevich, Sir (Anthony) Thomas, Kt., DFC

Cowan, Lt.-Gen. Sir Samuel, KCB, CBE

Coward, Vice-Adm. Sir John Francis, KCB, DSO

Cowen, Rt. Hon. Prof. Sir Zelman, GCMG, GCVO, QC

Cowie, Sir Thomas (Tom), Kt., OBE

Cowperthwaite, Sir John James, KBE, CMG

Cox, Sir Alan George, Kt., CBE

Cox, Prof. Sir David Roxbee, Kt., FRS

Cox, Sir Geoffrey Sandford, Kt., CBE

Cox, Vice-Adm. Sir John Michael Holland, KCB

Cradock, Rt. Hon. Sir Percy, GCMG

Craig, Sir (Albert) James (Macqueen), GCMG

Craufurd, Sir Robert James, Bt. (1781)

Craven, Sir John Anthony, Kt.

Craven, Air Marshal Sir Robert Edward, KBE, CB, DFC

Crawford, Prof. Sir Frederick William, Kt., FEng.

Crawford, Sir (Robert) Stewart, GCMG, CVO

Crawford, Vice-Adm. Sir William Godfrey, KBE, CB, DSC

Creagh, Maj.-Gen. Sir (Kilner) Rupert Brazier-, KBE, CB, DSO

Cresswell, Hon. Sir Peter John, Kt.

Crill, Sir Peter Leslie, KBE

Cripps, Sir Cyril Humphrey, Kt.

Crisp, Sir (John) Peter, Bt. (1913)

Critchett, Sir Ian (George Lorraine), Bt. (1908)

Critchley, Sir Julian Michael Gordon, Kt.

Croft, Sir Owen Glendower, Bt. (1671)

Croft, Sir Thomas Stephen Hutton, Bt. (1818)

†Crofton, Sir Hugh Denis, Bt. (1801)

Crofton, Prof. Sir John Wenman, Kt.

Crofton, Sir Malby Sturges, Bt. (1838)

Croker, Sir Walter Russell, KBE

Crookenden, Lt.-Gen. Sir Napier, KCB, DSO, OBE

Cross, Air Chief Marshal Sir Kenneth Brian Boyd, KCB, CBE, DSO, DFC

Crossland, Prof. Sir Bernard, Kt., CBE, FEng.

Crossland, Sir Leonard, Kt.

Crossley, Sir Nicholas John, Bt. (1909)

Crouch, Sir David Lance, Kt.

Cruthers, Sir James Winter, Kt.

Cubbon, Sir Brian Crossland, GCB

Cubitt, Sir Hugh Guy, Kt., CBE

Cullen, Sir (Edward) John, Kt., F.Eng.

Cumming, Sir William Gordon Gordon-, Bt. (1804)

Cuninghame, Sir John Christopher Foggo Montgomery-, Bt. (NS 1672)

†Cuninghame, Sir William Henry Fairlie-, Bt. (s. 1630)

Cunliffe, Sir David Ellis, Bt. (1759)

Cunningham, Sir Charles Craik, GCB, KBE, CVO

Cunningham, Lt.-Gen. Sir Hugh Patrick, KBE

Cunynghame, Sir Andrew David Francis, Bt. (s. 1702)

Curle, Sir John Noel Ormiston, KCVO, CMG

Curran, Sir Samuel Crowe, Kt., D.SC., Ph.D., FRS, FRSE, FEng.

†Currie, Sir Donald Scott, Bt. (1847)

Currie, Sir Neil Smith, Kt., CBE

Curtis, Sir Barry John, Kt.

Curtis, Sir (Edward) Leo, Kt.

Curtis, Hon. Sir Richard Herbert, Kt.

Curtis, Sir William Peter, Bt. (1802)

Curtiss, Air Marshal Sir John Bagot, KCB, KBE

Curwen, Sir Christopher Keith, KCMG

Cutler, Sir (Arthur) Roden, VC, KCMG, KCVO, CBE

Cutler, Sir Charles Benjamin, KBE, ED

Dacie, *Prof.* Sir John Vivian, Kt., MD, FRS

Dale, Sir William Leonard, KCMG

Dalrymple, *Maj.* Sir Hew Fleetwood Hamilton-, Bt., KCVO (s. 1697)

Dalton, Sir Alan Nugent Goring, Kt., CBE

Dalton, *Vice-Adm.* Sir Geoffrey Thomas James Oliver, KCB

Daly, *Lt.-Gen.* Sir Thomas Joseph, KBE, CB, DSO

Dalyell, Sir Tam (Thomas), Bt., MP (NS 1685)

Daniel, Sir Goronwy Hopkin, KCVO, CB, D.phil.

Daniel, Sir John Sagar, Kt., D.SC.

Daniell, Sir Peter Averell, Kt., TD

Danks, Sir Alan John, KBE

Darby, Sir Peter Howard, Kt., CBE, QFSM

Darell, Sir Jeffrey Lionel, Bt., MC (1795)

Dargie, Sir William Alexander, Kt., CBE

Dark, Sir Anthony Michael Beaumont-, Kt.

Darling, Sir Clifford, GCVO

Darling, *Gen.* Sir Kenneth Thomas, GBE, KCB, DSO

Darlington, *Rear-Adm.* Sir Charles Roy, KBE

Darvall, Sir (Charles) Roger, Kt., CBE

Dashwood, Sir Francis John Vernon Hereward, Bt., *Premier Baronet of Great Britain* (1707)

Dashwood, Sir Richard James, Bt. (1604)

Daunt, Sir Timothy Lewis Achilles, KCMG

David, Sir Jean Marc, Kt., CBE, QC

David, *His Hon.* Sir Robin (Robert) Daniel George, Kt., QC

Davidson, Sir Robert James, Kt., FENG.

†Davie, Sir John Ferguson-, Bt. (1847)

Davies, *Air Marshal* Sir Alan Cyril, KCB, CBE

Davies, *Hon.* Sir (Alfred William) Michael, Kt.

Davies, Sir Alun Talfan, Kt., QC

Davies, Sir (Charles) Noel, Kt.

Davies, *Prof.* Sir David Evan Naughton, Kt., CBE, FRS, FENG.

Davies, Sir David Henry, Kt.

Davies, *Hon.* Sir (David Herbert) Mervyn, Kt., MC, TD

Davies, *Prof.* Sir Graeme John, Kt., FENG.

Davies, *Vice-Adm.* Sir Lancelot Richard Bell, KBE

Davies, Sir Peter Maxwell, Kt., CBE

Davies, Sir Victor Caddy, Kt., OBE

Davis, Sir Charles Sigmund, Kt., CB

Davis, Sir Colin Rex, Kt., CBE

Davis, Sir (Ernest) Howard, Kt., CMG, OBE

Davis, Sir John Gilbert, Bt. (1946)

Davis, Sir Peter John, Kt.

Davis, Sir Rupert Charles Hart-, Kt.

Davis, *Hon.* Sir Thomas Robert Alexander Harries, KBE

Davison, *Rt. Hon.* Sir Ronald Keith, GBE, CMG

Dawbarn, Sir Simon Yelverton, KCVO, CMG

Dawson, Sir Anthony Michael, KCVO, MD, FRCP

Dawson, *Hon.* Sir Daryl Michael, KBE, CB

Dawson, Sir Hugh Michael Trevor, Bt. (1920)

Dawtry, Sir Alan (Graham), Kt., CBE, TD

Day, Sir Derek Malcolm, KCMG

Day, Sir (Judson) Graham, Kt.

Day, Sir Michael John, Kt., OBE

Day, Sir Robin, Kt.

Day, Sir Simon James, Kt.

Deakin, Sir (Frederick) William (Dampier), Kt., DSO

Deane, *Hon.* Sir William Patrick, KBE

Dear, Sir Geoffrey James, Kt., QPM

Dearing, Sir Ronald Ernest, Kt., CB

de Bellaigue, Sir Geoffrey, GCVO

Debenham, Sir Gilbert Ridley, Bt. (1931)

de Deney, Sir Geoffrey Ivor, KCVO

de Hoghton, Sir (Richard) Bernard (Cuthbert), Bt. (1611)

De la Bère, Sir Cameron, Bt. (1953)

de la Rue, Sir Andrew George Ilay, Bt. (1898)

Dellow, Sir John Albert, Kt., CBE

de Montmorency, Sir Arnold Geoffroy, Bt. (I. 1631)

Denholm, Sir John Ferguson (Ian), Kt., CBE

Denman, Sir (George) Roy, KCB, CMG

Denny, Sir Anthony Coningham de Waltham, Bt. (I. 1782)

Denny, Sir Charles Alistair Maurice, Bt. (1913)

Dent, Sir John, Kt., CBE, FENG.

Dent, Sir Robin John, KCVO

Denton, *Prof.* Sir Eric James, Kt., CBE, FRS

Derbyshire, Sir Andrew George, Kt.

Derham, Sir Peter John, Kt.

de Trafford, Sir Dermot Humphrey, Bt. (1841)

Devesi, Sir Baddeley, GCMG, GCVO

De Ville, Sir Harold Godfrey Oscar, Kt., CBE

Devitt, Sir James Hugh Thomas, Bt. (1916)

de Waal, Sir (Constant Henrik) Henry, KCB, QC

Dewey, Sir Anthony Hugh, Bt. (1917)

Dewhurst, *Prof.* Sir (Christopher) John, Kt.

d'Eyncourt, Sir Mark Gervais Tennyson-, Bt. (1930)

Dhenin, *Air Marshal* Sir Geoffrey Howard, KBE, AFC, GM, MD

Dhrangadhra, HH the Maharaja Raj Saheb of, KCIE

Dibela, *Hon.* Sir Kingsford, GCMG

Dick, *Maj.-Gen.* Sir Iain Charles Mackay-, KCVO, MBE

Dickenson, Sir Aubrey Fiennes Trotman-, Kt.

Dickinson, Sir Harold Herbert, Kt.

Dickinson, Sir Samuel Benson, Kt.

Dilbertson, Sir Geoffrey, Kt., CBE

Dilke, Sir John Fisher Wentworth, Bt. (1862)

Dillon, *Rt. Hon.* Sir (George) Brian (Hugh), Kt.

Dixon, Sir Ian Leonard, Kt., CBE

Dixon, Sir Jonathan Mark, Bt. (1919)

Djanogly, Sir Harry Ari Simon, Kt., CBE

Dobbs, *Capt.* Sir Richard Arthur Frederick, KCVO

Dobson, *Vice-Adm.* Sir David Stuart, KBE

Dobson, *Gen.* Sir Patrick John Howard-, GCB

Dodds, Sir Ralph Jordan, Bt. (1964)

Dodson, Sir Derek Sherborne Lindsell, KCMG, MC

Dodsworth, Sir John Christopher Smith-, Bt. (1784)

Doll, *Prof.* Sir (William) Richard (Shaboe), Kt., CH, OBE, FRS, DM, MD, D.SC.

Dollery, Sir Colin Terence, Kt.

Donald, Sir Alan Ewen, KCMG

Donald, *Air Marshal* Sir John George, KBE

Donne, *Hon.* Sir Gaven John, KBE

Donne, Sir John Christopher, Kt.

Dookun, Sir Dewoonarain, Kt.

Dorey, Sir Graham Martyn, Kt.

Dorman, Sir Philip Henry Keppel, Bt. (1923)

Dougherty, *Maj.-Gen.* Sir Ivan Noel, Kt., CBE, DSO, ED

Doughty, Sir William Roland, Kt.

Douglas, Sir (Edward) Sholto, Kt.

Douglas, *Hon.* Sir Roger Owen, Kt.

Douglas, *Rt. Hon.* Sir William Randolph, KCMG

Dover, *Prof.* Sir Kenneth James, Kt., D.Litt., FBA, FRSE

Dowell, Sir Anthony James, Kt., CBE

Down, Sir Alastair Frederick, Kt., OBE, MC, TD

Downes, Sir Edward Thomas, Kt., CBE

Downey, Sir Gordon Stanley, KCB

Downs, Sir Diarmuid, Kt., CBE, FENG.

Downward, Sir William Atkinson, Kt.

Dowson, Sir Philip Manning, Kt., CBE, PRA

Doyle, Sir Reginald Derek Henry, Kt., CBE

D'Oyly, Sir Nigel Hadley Miller, Bt. (1663)

Drake, *Hon.* Sir (Frederick) Maurice, Kt., DFC

Dreyer, *Adm.* Sir Desmond Parry, GCB, CBE, DSC

Drinkwater, Sir John Muir, Kt., QC

Driver, Sir Antony Victor, Kt.

Driver, Sir Eric William, Kt.

Drummond, Sir John Richard Gray, Kt., CBE

Drury, Sir (Victor William) Michael, Kt., OBE

Dryden, Sir John Stephen Gyles, Bt. (1733 and 1795)

du Cann, *Rt. Hon.* Sir Edward Dillon Lott, KBE

Duckworth, *Maj.* Sir Richard Dyce, Bt. (1909)

du Cros, Sir Claude Philip Arthur Mallet, Bt. (1916)

Duff, *Rt. Hon.* Sir (Arthur) Antony, GCMG, CVO, DSO, DSC

Duffell, *Lt.-Gen.* Sir Peter Royson, KCB, CBE, MC

Duffus, *Hon.* Sir William Algernon Holwell, Kt.

Duffy, Sir (Albert) (Edward) Patrick, Kt., PH.D.

Dugdale, Sir William Stratford, Bt., MC (1936)

Dunbar, Sir Archibald Ranulph, Bt. (s. 1700)

Dunbar, Sir David Hope-, Bt. (s. 1664)

Dunbar, Sir Drummond Cospatrick Ninian, Bt., MC (s. 1698)

Dunbar, Sir James Michael, Bt. (s. 1694)

Dunbar of Hempriggs, Dame Maureen Daisy Helen (Lady Dunbar of Hempriggs), Btss. (s. 1706)

Duncan, Sir James Blair, Kt.

Duncombe, Sir Philip Digby Pauncefort-, Bt. (1859)

Dunham, Sir Kingsley Charles, Kt., PH.D., FRS, FRSE, FEng.

Dunlop, Sir Thomas, Bt. (1916)

Dunlop, Sir William Norman Gough, Kt.

Dunn, *Air Marshal* Sir Eric Clive, KBE, CB, BEM

Dunn, *Air Marshal* Sir Patrick Hunter, KBE, CB, DFC

Dunn, *Rt. Hon.* Sir Robin Horace Walford, Kt., MC

Dunne, Sir Thomas Raymond, KCVO

Dunnett, Sir Alastair MacTavish, Kt.

Dunnett, Sir (Ludovic) James, GCB, CMG

Dunning, Sir Simon William Patrick, Bt. (1930)

Dunphie, *Maj.-Gen.* Sir Charles Anderson Lane, Kt., CB, CBE, DSO

Dunstan, *Lt.-Gen.* Sir Donald Beaumont, KBE, CB

†Duntze, Sir Daniel Evans, Bt. (1774)

Dupre, Sir Tumun, Kt., MBE

Dupree, Sir Peter, Bt. (1921)

Durand, Sir Edward Alan Christopher David Percy, Bt. (1892)

Durant, Sir (Robert) Anthony (Bevis), Kt.

Durham, Sir Kenneth, Kt.

Durie, Sir Alexander Charles, Kt., CBE

Durkin, *Air Marshal* Sir Herbert, KBE, CB

Durrant, Sir William Alexander Estridge, Bt. (1784)

Duthie, *Prof.* Sir Herbert Livingston, Kt.

Duthie, Sir Robert Grieve (Robin), Kt., CBE

Dyer, *Prof.* Sir (Henry) Peter (Francis) Swinnerton-, Bt., KBE, FRS (1678)

Dyke, Sir David William Hart, Bt. (1677)

Dyson, *Hon.* Sir John Anthony, Kt.

Eady, *Hon.* Sir David, Kt.

Earle, Sir (Hardman) George (Algernon), Bt. (1869)

East, Sir (Lewis) Ronald, Kt., CBE

Easton, Sir Robert William Simpson, Kt., CBE

Eaton, *Adm.* Sir Kenneth John, GBE, KCB

Eberle, *Adm.* Sir James Henry Fuller, GCB

Ebrahim, Sir (Mahomed) Currimbhoy, Bt. (1910)

Echlin, Sir Norman David Fenton, Bt. (I. 1721)

Eckersley, Sir Donald Payze, Kt., OBE

Edge, *Capt.* Sir (Philip) Malcolm, KCVO

†Edge, Sir William, Bt. (1937)

Edmonstone, Sir Archibald Bruce Charles, Bt. (1774)

Edwardes, Sir Michael Owen, Kt.

Edwards, Sir Christopher John Churchill, Bt. (1866)

Edwards, Sir George Robert, Kt., OM, CBE, FRS, FEng.

Edwards, Sir (John) Clive (Leighton), Bt. (1921)

Edwards, Sir Llewellyn Roy, Kt.

Edwards, *Prof.* Sir Samuel Frederick, Kt., FRS

Egan, Sir John Leopold, Kt.

Egerton, Sir John Alfred Roy, Kt.

Egerton, Sir (Philip) John (Caledon) Grey-, Bt. (1617)

Egerton, Sir Seymour John Louis, GCVO

Egerton, Sir Stephen Loftus, KCMG

Eggleston, *Hon.* Sir Richard Moulton, Kt.

Eichelbaum, *Rt. Hon.* Sir Thomas, GBE

Eliott of Stobs, Sir Charles Joseph Alexander, Bt. (s. 1666)

Ellerton, Sir Geoffrey James, Kt., CMG, MBE

Elliot, Sir Gerald Henry, Kt.

Elliott, Sir Clive Christopher Hugh, Bt. (1917)

Elliott, Sir David Murray, KCMG, CB

Elliott, *Prof.* Sir John Huxtable, Kt., FBA

Elliott, Sir Randal Forbes, KBE

Elliott, *Prof.* Sir Roger James, Kt., FRS

Elliott, Sir Ronald Stuart, Kt.

Ellis, Sir John Rogers, Kt., MBE, MD, FRCP

Ellis, Sir Ronald, Kt., FEng.

Ellison, *Col.* Sir Ralph Harry Carr-, Kt., TD

Elphinstone, Sir John, Bt. (s. 1701)

Elphinstone, Sir John Howard Main, Bt. (1816)

Elton, Sir Arnold, Kt., CBE

Elton, Sir Charles Abraham Grierson, Bt. (1717)

Elwes, Sir Jeremy Vernon, Kt., CBE

Elwood, Sir Brian George Conway, Kt., CBE

Elworthy, Sir Peter Herbert, Kt.

Elyan, Sir (Isadore) Victor, Kt.

Emery, *Rt. Hon.* Sir Peter Frank Hannibal, Kt., MP

Empson, *Adm.* Sir (Leslie) Derek, GBE, KCB

Engineer, Sir Noshirwan Phirozshah, Kt.

Engle, Sir George Lawrence Jose, KCB, QC

English, Sir David, Kt.

English, Sir Terence Alexander Hawthorne, KBE, FRCS

Epstein, *Prof.* Sir (Michael) Anthony, Kt., CBE, FRS

Ereaut, Sir (Herbert) Frank Cobbold, Kt.

Errington, *Col.* Sir Geoffrey Frederick, Bt. (1963)

Errington, Sir Lancelot, KCB

Erskine, Sir (Thomas) David, Bt. (1821)

Esmonde, Sir Thomas Francis Grattan, Bt. (I. 1629)

Espie, Sir Frank Fletcher, Kt., OBE

Esplen, Sir John Graham, Bt. (1921)

Eustace, Sir Joseph Lambert, GCMG, GCVO

Evans, Sir Anthony Adney, Bt. (1920)

Evans, *Rt. Hon.* Sir Anthony Howell Meurig, Kt., RD

Evans, *Air Chief Marshal* Sir David George, GCB, CBE

Evans, *Air Chief Marshal* Sir David Parry-, GCB, CBE

Evans, *Hon.* Sir Haydn Tudor, Kt.

Evans, *Prof.* Sir John Grimley, Kt., FRCP

Evans, Sir Richard Harry, Kt., CBE

Evans, Sir Richard Mark, KCMG, KCVO

Evans, Sir Robert, Kt., CBE, FEng.

Evans, Sir (William) Vincent (John), GCMG, MBE, QC

Eveleigh, *Rt. Hon.* Sir Edward Walter, Kt., ERD

Everard, Sir Robin Charles, Bt. (1911)

Everson, Sir Frederick Charles, KCMG

Every, Sir Henry John Michael, Bt. (1641)

Ewans, Sir Martin Kenneth, KCMG

†Ewart, Sir William Michael, Bt. (1887)

Ewbank, *Hon.* Sir Anthony Bruce, Kt.

Ewin, Sir (David) Ernest Thomas
Floyd, Kt., OBE, LVO
Ewing, Sir Ronald Archibald Orr-,
Bt. (1886)
Eyre, Sir Graham Newman, Kt., QC
Eyre, *Maj.-Gen.* Sir James Ainsworth
Campden Gabriel, KCVO, CBE
Eyre, Sir Reginald Edwin, Kt.
Eyre, Sir Richard Charles Hastings,
Kt., CBE
Faber, Sir Richard Stanley, KCVO,
CMG
Fadahunsi, Sir Joseph Odeleye,
KCMG
Fagge, Sir John William Frederick,
Bt. (1660)
Fairbairn, Sir (James) Brooke, Bt.
(1869)
Fairclough, Sir John Whitaker, Kt.,
FEng.
Fairgrieve, Sir (Thomas) Russell,
Kt., CBE, TD
Fairhall, *Hon.* Sir Allen, KBE
Fairweather, Sir Patrick Stanislaus,
KCMG
Falconer, *Hon.* Sir Douglas William,
Kt., MBE
Falkiner, Sir Edmond Charles, Bt. (I.
1778)
Fall, Sir Brian James Proetel, GCVO,
KCMG
Falle, Sir Samuel, KCMG, KCVO, DSC
Fang, *Prof.* Sir Harry, Kt., CBE
Fareed, Sir Djamil Sheik, Kt.
Farmer, Sir Thomas, Kt., CBE
Farndale, *Gen.* Sir Martin Baker, KCB
Farquhar, Sir Michael Fitzroy
Henry, Bt. (1796)
Farquharson, *Rt. Hon.* Sir Donald
Henry, Kt.
Farquharson, Sir James Robbie, KBE
Farr, Sir John Arnold, Kt.
Farrer, Sir (Charles) Matthew, GCVO
Farrington, Sir Henry Francis
Colden, Bt. (1818)
Fat, Sir (Maxime) Edouard (Lim
Man) Lim, Kt.
Faulkner, Sir (James) Dennis
(Compton), Kt., CBE, VRD
Fawcus, Sir (Robert) Peter, KBE, CMG
Fawkes, Sir Randol Francis, Kt.
Fay, Sir (Humphrey) Michael
Gerard, Kt.
Fayrer, Sir John Lang Macpherson,
Bt. (1896)
Fearn, Sir (Patrick) Robin, KCMG
Feilden, Sir Bernard Melchior, Kt.,
CBE
Feilden, Sir Henry Wemyss, Bt.,
(1846)
Fell, Sir Anthony, Kt.
Fell, Sir David, KCB
Fellowes, *Rt. Hon.* Sir Robert, GCVO,
KCB
Fenn, Sir Nicholas Maxted, GCMG
Fennell, *Hon.* Sir (John) Desmond
Augustine, Kt., OBE
Fennessy, Sir Edward, Kt., CBE
Ferguson, Sir Ian Edward Johnson-,
Bt. (1906)

Fergusson of Kilkerran, Sir Charles,
Bt. (s. 1703)
Fergusson, Sir Ewan Alastair John,
GCMG, GCVO
Fergusson, Sir James Herbert
Hamilton Colyer-, Bt. (1866)
Feroze, Sir Rustam Moolan, Kt., FRCS
Ferris, *Hon.* Sir Francis Mursell, Kt.,
TD
ffolkes, Sir Robert Francis
Alexander, Bt, OBE (1774)
Field, Sir Malcolm David, Kt.
Fielding, Sir Colin Cunningham, Kt.,
CB
Fielding, Sir Leslie, KCMG
Fiennes, Sir Ranulph Twisleton-
Wykcham-, Bt., OBE (1916)
Figg, Sir Leonard Clifford William,
KCMG
Figgis, Sir Anthony St John Howard,
KCVO, CMG
Figures, Sir Colin Frederick, KCMG,
OBE
Fingland, Sir Stanley James Gunn,
KCMG
Finlay, Sir David Ronald James Bell,
Bt. (1964)
Firth, *Prof.* Sir Raymond William,
Kt., ph.D., FBA
Fish, Sir Hugh, Kt., CBE
Fisher, Sir George Read, Kt., CMG
Fisher, *Hon.* Sir Henry Arthur Pears,
Kt.
Fison, Sir (Richard) Guy, Bt., DSC
(1905)
†Fitzgerald, *Revd* (Sir) Daniel
Patrick, Bt. (1903)
FitzGerald, Sir George Peter
Maurice, Bt., MC (*The Knight of
Kerry*) (1880)
FitzHerbert, Sir Richard Ranulph,
Bt. (1784)
Fitzpatrick, *Gen.* Sir (Geoffrey
Richard) Desmond, GCB, GCVO,
DSO, MBE, MC
Fitzpatrick, *Air Marshal* Sir John
Bernard, KBE, CB
Flanagan, Sir James Bernard, Kt., CBE
Fletcher, Sir Henry Egerton
Aubrey-, Bt. (1782)
Fletcher, Sir James Muir Cameron,
Kt.
Fletcher, Sir Leslie, Kt., DSC
Fletcher, *Air Chief Marshal* Sir Peter
Carteret, KCB, OBE, DFC, AFC
Floissac, *Hon.* Sir Vincent Frederick,
Kt., CMG, OBE, QC
Floyd, Sir Giles Henry Charles, Bt.
(1816)
Foley, *Lt.-Gen.* Sir John Paul, KCB,
OBE, MC
Foley, Sir (Thomas John) Noel, Kt.,
CBE
Follett, *Prof.* Sir Brian Keith, Kt., FRS
Foot, Sir Geoffrey James, Kt.
Foots, Sir James William, Kt.
Forbes, *Hon.* Sir Alastair Granville,
Kt.
Forbes, *Maj.* Sir Hamish Stewart, Bt.,
MBE, MC (1823)

Forbes of Craigievar, Sir John
Alexander Cumnock, Bt. (s. 1630)
Forbes, *Vice-Adm.* Sir John Morrison,
KCB
Forbes, *Hon.* Sir Thayne John, Kt.
†Forbes of Pitsligo, Sir William
Daniel Stuart-, Bt. (s. 1626)
Ford, Sir Andrew Russell, Bt. (1929)
Ford, Sir David Robert, KBE, LVO, OBE
Ford, *Maj.* Sir Edward William
Spencer, KCB, KCVO
Ford, *Air Marshal* Sir Geoffrey
Harold, KBE, CB, FEng.
Ford, *Prof.* Sir Hugh, Kt., FRS, FEng.
Ford, Sir James Anson St Clair-, Bt.
(1793)
Ford, Sir John Archibald, KCMG, MC
Ford, Sir Richard Brinsley, Kt., CBE
Ford, *Gen.* Sir Robert Cyril, GCB, CBE
Foreman, Sir Philip Frank, Kt., CBE,
FEng.
Forman, Sir John Denis, Kt., OBE
Forrest, *Prof.* Sir (Andrew) Patrick
(McEwen), Kt.
Forrest, *Rear-Adm.* Sir Ronald
Stephen, KCVO
Forster, Sir Archibald William, Kt.,
FEng.
Forster, Sir Oliver Grantham, KCMG,
LVO
Forsyth, *Rt. Hon.* Sir Michael Bruce,
Kt.
Forte, Hon. Sir Rocco John Vincent,
Kt.
Forwood, Sir Dudley Richard, Bt.
(1895)
Foster, *Prof.* Sir Christopher David,
Kt.
Foster, Sir John Gregory, Bt. (1930)
Foster, Sir Norman Robert, Kt.
Foster, Sir Robert Sidney, GCMG,
KCVO
Foulis, Sir Ian Primrose Liston-, Bt.
(s. 1634)
Foulkes, Sir Nigel Gordon, Kt.
Fountain, *Hon.* Sir Cyril Stanley
Smith, Kt.
Fowden, Sir Leslie, Kt., FRS
Fowke, Sir David Frederick
Gustavus, Bt. (1814)
Fowler, Sir (Edward) Michael
Coulson, Kt.
Fowler, *Rt. Hon.* Sir (Peter) Norman,
Kt., MP
Fox, Sir (Henry) Murray, GBE
Fox, *Rt. Hon.* Sir (John) Marcus, Kt.,
MBE
Fox, *Rt. Hon.* Sir Michael John, Kt.
Fox, Sir Paul Leonard, Kt., CBE
France, Sir Arnold William, GCB
France, Sir Christopher Walter, GCB
France, Sir Joseph Nathaniel, KCMG,
CBE
Francis, Sir Horace William
Alexander, Kt., CBE, FEng.
Frank, Sir Douglas George Horace,
Kt., QC
Frank, Sir (Frederick) Charles, Kt.,
OBE, FRS
Frank, Sir Robert Andrew, Bt. (1920)

Frankel, Sir Otto Herzberg, Kt., D.SC., FRS

Franklin, Sir Michael David Milroy, KCB, CMG

Franks, Sir Arthur Temple, KCMG

Fraser, Sir Angus McKay, KCB, TD

Fraser, Sir Charles Annand, KCVO

Fraser, *Gen.* Sir David William, GCB, OBE

Fraser, *Air Marshal Revd* Sir (Henry) Paterson, KBE, CB, AFC

Fraser, Sir Iain Michael Duncan, Bt. (1943)

Fraser, Sir Ian, Kt., DSO, OBE

Fraser, Sir Ian James, Kt., CBE, MC

Fraser, Sir (James) Campbell, Kt.

Fraser, Sir William Kerr, GCB

Frederick, Sir Charles Boscawen, Bt. (1723)

Freeland, Sir John Redvers, KCMG

Freeman, Sir James Robin, Bt. (1945)

Freeman, Sir Ralph, Kt., CVO, CBE, FEng.

Freer, *Air Chief Marshal* Sir Robert William George, GBE, KCB

Freeth, *Hon.* Sir Gordon, KBE

French, *Hon.* Sir Christopher James Saunders, Kt.

Frere, *Vice-Adm.* Sir Richard Tobias, KCB

Fretwell, Sir (Major) John (Emsley), GCMG

Freud, Sir Clement Raphael, Kt.

Froggatt, Sir Leslie Trevor, Kt.

Froggatt, Sir Peter, Kt.

Frossard, Sir Charles Keith, KBE

Frost, Sir David Paradine, Kt., OBE

Frost, *Hon.* Sir (Thomas) Sydney, Kt.

Fry, Sir Peter Derek, Kt.

Fry, *Hon.* Sir William Gordon, Kt.

Fuchs, Sir Vivian Ernest, Kt., PH.D.

Fuller, *Hon.* Sir John Bryan Munro, Kt.

Fuller, Sir John William Fleetwood, Bt. (1910)

Fung, *Hon.* Sir Kenneth Ping-Fan, Kt., CBE

Furness, Sir Stephen Roberts, Bt. (1913)

Gadsden, Sir Peter Drury Haggerston, GBE, FEng.

Gage, *Hon.* Sir William Marcus, Kt.

Gainsford, Sir Ian Derek, Kt., DDS

Gaius, *Rt. Revd* Saimon, KBE

Gallwey, Sir Philip Frankland Payne-, Bt. (1812)

Gam, *Rt. Revd* Sir Getake, KBE

Gamble, Sir David Hugh Norman, Bt. (1897)

Garden, *Air Marshal* Sir Timothy, KCB

Gardiner, Sir George Arthur, Kt.

Gardner, Sir Douglas Bruce Bruce-, Bt. (1945)

Gardner, Sir Edward Lucas, Kt., QC

Garland, *Hon.* Sir Patrick Neville, Kt.

Garland, *Hon.* Sir Ransley Victor, KBE

Garlick, Sir John, KCB

Garner, Sir Anthony Stuart, Kt.

Garnier, *Rear-Adm.* Sir John, KCVO, CBE

Garrett, Sir Anthony Peter, Kt., CBE

Garrick, Sir Ronald, Kt., CBE, FEng.

Garrioch, Sir (William) Henry, Kt.

Garrod, *Lt.-Gen.* Sir (John) Martin Carruthers, KCB, OBE

Garthwaite, Sir (William) Mark (Charles), Bt. (1919)

Gaskell, Sir Richard Kennedy Harvey, Kt.

Gatehouse, *Hon.* Sir Robert Alexander, Kt.

Geddes, Sir (Anthony) Reay (Mackay), Kt.

George, Sir Arthur Thomas, Kt.

George, Sir Richard William, Kt.

Gerken, *Vice-Adm.* Sir Robert William Frank, KCB, CBE

Gery, Sir Robert Lucian Wade-, KCMG, KCVO

Gethin, Sir Richard Joseph St Lawrence, Bt. (I. 1665)

Ghurburrun, Sir Rabindrah, Kt.

Gibb, Sir Francis Ross (Frank), Kt., CBE, FEng.

Gibbings, Sir Peter Walter, Kt.

Gibbons, Sir (John) David, KBE

Gibbons, Sir William Edward Doran, Bt. (1752)

Gibbs, *Hon.* Sir Eustace Hubert Beilby, KCVO, CMG

Gibbs, *Rt. Hon.* Sir Harry Talbot, GCMG, KBE

Gibbs, Sir Roger Geoffrey, Kt.

Gibbs, *Field Marshal* Sir Roland Christopher, GCB, CBE, DSO, MC

†Gibson, Revd Sir Christopher Herbert, Bt. (1931)

Gibson, *Revd* Sir David, Bt. (1926)

Gibson, *Vice-Adm.* Sir Donald Cameron Ernest Forbes, KCB, DSC

Gibson, *Rt. Hon.* Sir Peter Leslie, Kt.

Gibson, *Rt. Hon.* Sir Ralph Brian, Kt.

Giddings, *Air Marshal* Sir (Kenneth Charles) Michael, KCB, OBE, DFC, AFC

Gielgud, Sir (Arthur) John, Kt., OM, CH

Giffard, Sir (Charles) Sydney (Rycroft), KCMG

Gilbert, *Air Chief Marshal* Sir Joseph Alfred, KCB, CBE

Gilbert, Sir Martin John, Kt., CBE

†Gilbey, Sir Walter Gavin, Bt. (1893)

Giles, *Rear-Adm.* Sir Morgan Charles Morgan-, Kt., DSO, OBE, GM

Gill, Sir Anthony Keith, Kt., FEng.

Gillett, Sir Robin Danvers Penrose, Bt., GBE, RD (1959)

Gilmour, *Col.* Sir Allan Macdonald, KCVO, OBE, MC

Gilmour, Sir John Edward, Bt., DSO, TD (1897)

Gina, Sir Lloyd Maepeza, KBE

Gingell, *Air Chief Marshal* Sir John, GBE, KCB, KCVO

Girolami, Sir Paul, Kt.

Girvan, *Hon.* Sir (Frederick) Paul, Kt.

Gladstone, Sir (Erskine) William, Bt. (1846)

Glasspole, Sir Florizel Augustus, GCMG, GCVO

Glen, Sir Alexander Richard, KBE, DSC

Glenn, Sir (Joseph Robert) Archibald, Kt., OBE

Glidewell, *Rt. Hon.* Sir Iain Derek Laing, Kt.

Glock, Sir William Frederick, Kt., CBE

Glover, *Gen.* Sir James Malcolm, KCB, MBE

Glover, Sir Victor Joseph Patrick, Kt.

Glyn, Sir Alan, Kt., ERD

Glyn, Sir Anthony Geoffrey Leo Simon, Bt. (1927)

Glyn, Sir Richard Lindsay, Bt. (1759 and 1800)

Goad, Sir (Edward) Colin (Viner), KCMG

Godber, Sir George Edward, GCB, DM

Goff, Sir Robert (William) Davis-, Bt. (1905)

Gold, Sir Arthur Abraham, Kt., CBE

Gold, Sir Joseph, Kt.

Goldberg, *Prof.* Sir Abraham, Kt., MD, D.SC., FRCP

Goldberg, *Prof.* Sir David Paul Brandes, Kt.

Goldman, Sir Samuel, KCB

Gombrich, *Prof.* Sir Ernst Hans Josef, Kt., OM, CBE, PH.D., FBA, FSA

Gooch, Sir (Richard) John Sherlock, Bt. (1746)

Gooch, Sir Trevor Sherlock (Sir Peter), Bt. (1866)

Goodall, Sir (Arthur) David Saunders, GCMG

Goodenough, Sir Anthony Michael, KCMG

Goodenough, Sir William McLernon, Bt. (1943)

Goodhart, Sir Philip Carter, Kt.

Goodhart, Sir Robert Anthony Gordon, Bt. (1911)

Goodhart, Sir William Howard, Kt., QC

Goodhew, Sir Victor Henry, Kt.

Goodison, Sir Alan Clowes, KCMG

Goodison, Sir Nicholas Proctor, Kt.

Goodlad, *Rt. Hon.* Sir Alastair Robertson, KCMG, MP

Goodman, Sir Patrick Ledger, Kt., CBE

Goodson, Sir Mark Weston Lassam, Bt. (1922)

Goodwin, Sir Matthew Dean, Kt., CBE

Goold, Sir George Leonard, Bt. (1801)

Gordon, Sir Alexander John, Kt., CBE

Gordon, Sir Andrew Cosmo Lewis Duff-, Bt. (1813)

Gordon, Sir Charles Addison Somerville Snowden, KCB

Gordon, Sir Keith Lyndell, Kt., CMG

Gordon, Sir (Lionel) Eldred (Peter) Smith-, Bt. (1838)

Gordon, Sir Robert James, Bt. (s. 1706)
Gordon, Sir Sidney Samuel, Kt., CBE
Gordon Lennox, Lord Nicholas Charles, KCMG, KCVO
†Gore, Sir Nigel Hugh St George, Bt. (I. 1622)
Gorham, Sir Richard Masters, Kt., CBE, DFC
Goring, Sir William Burton Nigel, Bt. (1627)
Gorst, Sir John Michael, Kt.
Gorton, Rt. Hon. Sir John Grey, GCMG, CH
Goschen, Sir Edward Christian, Bt., DSO (1916)
Gosling, Sir (Frederick) Donald, Kt.
Goswell, Sir Brian Lawrence, Kt.
Goulden, Sir (Peter) John, KCMG
Goulding, Sir (Ernest) Irvine, Kt.
Goulding, Sir Marrack Irvine, KCMG
Goulding, Sir (William) Lingard Walter, Bt. (1904)
Gourlay, Gen. Sir (Basil) Ian (Spencer), KCB, OBE, MC, RM
Gourlay, Sir Simon Alexander, Kt.
Govan, Sir Lawrence Herbert, Kt.
Gow, Gen. Sir (James) Michael, GCB
Gowans, Sir James Learmonth, Kt., CBE, FRCP, FRS
Graaff, Sir de Villiers, Bt., MBE (1911)
Grabham, Sir Anthony Henry, Kt.
Graham, Sir Alexander Michael, GBE
Graham, Sir James Bellingham, Bt. (1662)
†Graham, Sir James Fergus Surtees, Bt. (1783)
Graham, Sir James Thompson, Kt., CMG
Graham, Sir John Alexander Noble, Bt., GCMG (1906)
Graham, Sir John Moodie, Bt. (1964)
Graham, Sir Norman William, Kt., CB
Graham, Sir Peter, KCB, QC
Graham, Sir Peter Alfred, Kt., OBE
Graham, Lt.-Gen. Sir Peter Walter, KCB, CBE
†Graham, Sir Ralph Stuart, Bt. (1629)
Graham, Hon. Sir Samuel Horatio, Kt., CMG, OBE
Grandy, Marshal of the Royal Air Force Sir John, GCB, GCVO, KBE, DSO
Grant, Sir Archibald, Bt. (s. 1705)
Grant, Sir Clifford, Kt.
Grant, Sir (John) Anthony, Kt.
Grant, Sir (Matthew) Alistair, Kt.
Grant, Sir Patrick Alexander Benedict, Bt. (s. 1688)
Gray, Sir John Archibald Browne, Kt., SC.D., FRS
Gray, Vice-Adm. Sir John Michael Dudgeon, KBE, CB
Gray, Sir John Walton David, KBE, CMG
Gray, Lt.-Gen. Sir Michael Stuart, KCB, OBE
Gray, Sir Robert McDowall (Robin), Kt.
Gray, Sir William Hume, Bt. (1917)

Gray, Sir William Stevenson, Kt.
Graydon, Air Chief Marshal Sir Michael James, GCB, CBE
Grayson, Sir Jeremy Brian Vincent Harrington, Bt. (1922)
Green, Sir Allan David, KCB, QC
Green, Hon. Sir Guy Stephen Montague, KBE
Green, Sir Kenneth, Kt.
Green, Sir Owen Whitley, Kt.
†Green, Sir Stephen Lycett, Bt., TD (1886)
Greenaway, Sir John Michael Burdick, Bt. (1933)
Greenborough, Sir John, KBE
Greenbury, Sir Richard, Kt.
Greene, Sir (John) Brian Massy-, Kt.
Greengross, Sir Alan David, Kt.
Greening, Rear-Adm. Sir Paul Woollven, GCVO
Greenwell, Sir Edward Bernard, Bt. (1906)
Gregson, Sir Peter Lewis, GCB
Greig, Sir (Henry Louis) Carron, KCVO, CBE
Grenside, Sir John Peter, Kt., CBE
Grey, Sir Anthony Dysart, Bt. (1814)
Grierson, Sir Michael John Bewes, Bt. (s. 1685)
Grierson, Sir Ronald Hugh, Kt.
Griffin, Maj. Sir (Arthur) John (Stewart), KCVO
Griffin, Sir (Charles) David, Kt., CBE
Griffiths, Sir Eldon Wylie, Kt.
Griffiths, Sir John Norton-, Bt. (1922)
Grimwade, Sir Andrew Sheppard, Kt., CBE
Grindrod, Most Revd John Basil Rowland, KBE
Grinstead, Sir Stanley Gordon, Kt.
Grose, Vice-Adm. Sir Alan, KBE
Grossart, Sir Angus McFarlane McLeod, Kt., CBE
Grotrian, Sir Philip Christian Brent, Bt. (1934)
Grove, Sir Charles Gerald, Bt. (1874)
Grove, Sir Edmund Frank, KCVO
Grugeon, Sir John Drury, Kt.
Grylls, Sir (William) Michael (John), Kt.
Guinness, Sir Alec, Kt., CH, CBE
Guinness, Sir Howard Christian Sheldon, Kt., VRD
Guinness, Sir Kenelm Ernest Lee, Bt. (1867)
Guise, Sir John Grant, Bt. (1783)
Gull, Sir Rupert William Cameron, Bt. (1872)
Gumbs, Sir Emile Rudolph, Kt.
Gunn, Prof. Sir John Currie, Kt., CBE
Gunn, Sir Robert Norman, Kt.
Gunn, Sir William Archer, KBE, CMG
†Gunning, Sir Charles Theodore, Bt. (1778)
Gunston, Sir John Wellesley, Bt. (1938)
Gurdon, Prof. Sir John Bertrand, Kt., D Phil, FRS

Guthrie, Gen. Sir Charles Ronald Llewelyn, GCB, LVO, OBE
Guthrie, Sir Malcolm Connop, Bt., (1936)
Guy, Gen. Sir Roland Kelvin, GCB, CBE, DSO
Habakkuk, Sir John Hrothgar, Kt., FBA
Hackett, Gen. Sir John Winthrop, GCB, CBE, DSO, MC
Hadfield, Sir Ronald, Kt., QPM
Hadlee, Sir Richard John, Kt., MBE
Hadley, Sir Leonard Albert, Kt.
Hague, Prof. Sir Douglas Chalmers, Kt., CBE
Halberg, Sir Murray Gordon, Kt., MBE
Hale, Prof. Sir John Rigby, Kt.
Hall, Sir Arnold Alexander, Kt., FRS, FENG.
Hall, Sir Basil Brodribb, KCB, MC, TD
Hall, Air Marshal Sir Donald Percy, KCB, CBE, AFC
Hall, Sir Douglas Basil, Bt., KCMG (s. 1687)
Hall, Sir Ernest, Kt., OBE
Hall, Sir (Frederick) John (Frank), Bt. (1923)
Hall, Sir John, Kt.
Hall, Sir John Bernard, Bt. (1919)
Hall, Sir Peter Edward, KBE, CMG
Hall, Sir Peter Reginald Frederick, Kt., CBE
Hall, Sir Robert de Zouche, KCMG
Hall, Brig. Sir William Henry, KBE, DSO, ED
Halliday, Vice-Adm. Sir Roy William, KBE, DSC
Hallinan, Sir (Adrian) Lincoln, Kt.
Halpern, Sir Ralph Mark, Kt.
Halsey, Revd Sir John Walter Brooke, Bt. (1920)
Halstead, Sir Ronald, Kt., CBE
Ham, Sir David Kenneth Rowe-, GBE
Hambling, Sir (Herbert) Hugh, Bt. (1924)
Hamburger, Sir Sidney Cyril, Kt., CBE
Hamer, Hon. Sir Rupert James, KCMG, ED
Hamill, Sir Patrick, Kt., QPM
Hamilton, Rt. Hon. Sir Archibald Gavin, Kt., MP
Hamilton, Sir Edward Sydney, Bt. (1776 and 1819)
Hamilton, Sir James Arnot, KCB, MBE, FENG.
Hamilton, Sir Malcolm William Bruce Stirling-, Bt. (s. 1673)
Hamilton, Sir Michael Aubrey, Kt.
Hamilton, Sir (Robert Charles) Richard Caradoc, Bt. (s. 1646)
Hammett, Hon. Sir Clifford James, Kt.
Hammick, Sir Stephen George, Bt. (1834)
Hampel, Sir Ronald Claus, Kt.
Hampshire, Sir Stuart Newton, Kt., FBA

Hancock, Sir David John Stowell, KCB

Hancock, *Air Marshal* Sir Valston Eldridge, KBE, CB, DFC

Hand, *Most Revd* Geoffrey David, KBE

Handley, Sir David John Davenport-, Kt., OBE

Hanham, Sir Michael William, Bt., DFC (1667)

Hanley, *Rt. Hon.* Sir Jeremy James, KCMG

Hanley, Sir Michael Bowen, KCB

Hanmer, Sir John Wyndham Edward, Bt. (1774)

Hann, Sir James, Kt., CBE

Hannam, Sir John Gordon, Kt.

Hannay, Sir David Hugh Alexander, GCMG

Hanson, Sir (Charles) Rupert (Patrick), Bt. (1918)

Hanson, Sir John Gilbert, KCMG, CBE

Hardcastle, Sir Alan John, Kt.

Harders, Sir Clarence Waldemar, Kt., OBE

Hardie, Sir Charles Edgar Mathewes, Kt., CBE

Hardie, Sir Douglas Fleming, Kt., CBE

Harding, Sir Christopher George Francis, Kt.

Harding, Sir George William, KCMG, CVO

Harding, *Marshal of the Royal Air Force* Sir Peter Robin, GCB

Harding, Sir Roy Pollard, Kt., CBE

Hardman, Sir Henry, KCB

Hardy, Sir David William, Kt.

Hardy, Sir James Gilbert, Kt., OBE

†Hardy, Sir Richard Charles Chandos, Bt. (1876)

Hare, Sir Philip Leigh, Bt. (1818)

Harford, Sir (John) Timothy, Bt. (1934)

Hargroves, *Brig.* Sir Robert Louis, Kt., CBE

Harington, *Gen.* Sir Charles Henry Pepys, GCB, CBE, DSO, MC

Harington, Sir Nicholas John, Bt. (1611)

Harland, *Air Marshal* Sir Reginald Edward Wynyard, KBE, CB

Harley, *Lt.-Gen.* Sir Alexander George Hamilton, KBE, CB

Harman, *Gen.* Sir Jack Wentworth, GCB, OBE, MC

Harman, *Hon.* Sir Jeremiah LeRoy, Kt.

Harman, Sir John Andrew, Kt.

Harmsworth, Sir Hildebrand Harold, Bt. (1922)

Harpham, Sir William, KBE, CMG

Harris, *Prof.* Sir Alan James, Kt., CBE, FEng.

Harris, *Prof.* Sir Henry, Kt., FRCP, FRCPath., FRS

Harris, *Lt.-Gen.* Sir Ian Cecil, KBE, CB, DSO

Harris, Sir Jack Wolfred Ashford, Bt. (1932)

Harris, *Air Marshal* Sir John Hulme, KCB, CBE

Harris, Sir William Gordon, KBE, CB, FEng.

Harrison, Sir David, Kt., CBE, FEng.

Harrison, *Prof.* Sir Donald Frederick Norris, Kt., FRCS

Harrison, Sir Ernest Thomas, Kt., OBE

Harrison, Sir Francis Alexander Lyle, Kt., MBE, QC

Harrison, *Surgeon Vice-Adm.* Sir John Albert Bews, KBE

Harrison, *Hon.* Sir (John) Richard, Kt., ED

Harrison, *Hon.* Sir Michael Guy Vicat, Kt.

Harrison, Sir Michael James Harwood, Bt. (1961)

Harrison, *Prof.* Sir Richard John, Kt., FRS

Harrison, Sir (Robert) Colin, Bt. (1922)

Harrison, Sir Terence, Kt., FEng.

Harrop, Sir Peter John, KCB

Hart, Sir Graham Allan, KCB

Hartley, *Air Marshal* Sir Christopher Harold, KCB, CBE, DFC, AFC

Hartopp, *Lt. Cdr* Sir Kenneth Alston Cradock-, Bt., MBE, DSC (1796)

Hartwell, Sir (Francis) Anthony Charles Peter, Bt. (1805)

Harvey, Sir Charles Richard Musgrave, Bt. (1933)

Harvie, Sir John Smith, Kt., CBE

Haselhurst, Sir Alan Gordon Barraclough, Kt., MP

Haskard, Sir Cosmo Dugal Patrick Thomas, KCMG, MBE

Haslam, *Hon.* Sir Alec Leslie, Kt.

Haslam, *Rear-Adm.* Sir David William, KBE, CB

Hassett, *Gen.* Sir Francis George, KBE, CB, DSO, LVO

Hastings, Sir Stephen Lewis Edmonstone, Kt., MC

Hatty, *Hon.* Sir Cyril James, Kt.

Haughton, Sir James, Kt., CBE, QPM

Havelock, Sir Wilfrid Bowen, Kt.

Hawkins, Sir Arthur Ernest, Kt.

†Hawkins, Sir Howard Caesar, Bt. (1778)

Hawkins, Sir Paul Lancelot, Kt., TD

Hawley, Sir Donald Frederick, KCMG, MBE

†Hawley, Sir Henry Nicholas, Bt. (1795)

Haworth, Sir Philip, Bt. (1911)

Hawthorne, *Prof.* Sir William Rede, Kt., CBE, SC.D., FRS, FEng.

Hay, Sir David Osborne, Kt., CBE, DSO

Hay, Sir David Russell, Kt., CBE, FRCP, MD

Hay, Sir Hamish Grenfell, Kt.

Hay, Sir James Brian Dalrymple-, Bt. (1798)

Hay, Sir John Erroll Audley, Bt. (s. 1663)

†Hay, Sir Ronald Frederick Hamilton, Bt. (s. 1703)

Haydon, Sir Walter Robert, KCMG

Hayes, Sir Brian David, GCB

Hayes, *Vice-Adm.* Sir John Osier Chattock, KCB, OBE

Hayr, *Air Marshal* Sir Kenneth William, KCB, KBE, AFC

Hayward, Sir Anthony William Byrd, Kt.

Hayward, Sir Jack Arnold, Kt., OBE

Haywood, Sir Harold, KCVO, OBE

Head, Sir Francis David Somerville, Bt. (1838)

Healey, Sir Charles Edward Chadwyck-, Bt. (1919)

Heap, Sir Desmond, Kt.

Heap, Sir Peter William, KCMG

Heath, *Rt. Hon.* Sir Edward Richard George, KG, MBE, MP

Heath, Sir Mark Evelyn, KCVO, CMG

Heath, *Air Marshal* Sir Maurice Lionel, KBE, CB, CVO

Heathcote, *Brig.* Sir Gilbert Simon, Bt., CBE (1733)

Heathcote, Sir Michael Perryman, Bt. (1733)

Heatley, Sir Peter, Kt., CBE

Heaton, Sir Yvo Robert Henniker-, Bt. (1912)

Heiser, Sir Terence Michael, GCB

Hellaby, Sir (Frederick Reed) Alan, Kt.

Henderson, Sir Denys Hartley, Kt.

Henderson, Sir (John) Nicholas, GCMG, KCVO

Henderson, Sir William MacGregor, Kt., D.SC., FRS

Henley, Sir Douglas Owen, KCB

Henley, *Rear-Adm.* Sir Joseph Charles Cameron, KCVO, CB

Hennessy, Sir James Patrick Ivan, KBE, CMG

†Henniker, Sir Adrian Chandos, Bt. (1813)

Henry, Sir Denis Aynsley, Kt., OBE, QC

Henry, *Rt. Hon.* Sir Denis Robert Maurice, Kt.

Henry, *Hon.* Sir Geoffrey Arama, KBE

Henry, Sir Patrick Denis, Bt. (1923)

Henry, *Hon.* Sir Trevor Ernest, Kt.

Hepburn, Sir John Alastair Trant Kidd Buchan-, Bt. (1815)

Herbecq, Sir John Edward, KCB

Herbert, *Adm.* Sir Peter Geoffrey Marshall, KCB, OBE

Hermon, Sir John Charles, Kt., OBE, QPM

Heron, Sir Conrad Frederick, KCB, OBE

Heron, Sir Michael Gilbert, Kt.

Hervey, Sir Roger Blaise Ramsay, KCVO, CMG

Heseltine, *Rt. Hon.* Sir William Frederick Payne, GCB, GCVO

Hetherington, Sir Arthur Ford, Kt., DSC, FEng.

Hetherington, Sir Thomas Chalmers, KCB, CBE, TD, QC

Hewetson, Sir Christopher Raynor, Kt., TD

Hewett, Sir Peter John Smithson, Bt., MM (1813)

Hewitt, Sir (Cyrus) Lenox (Simson), Kt., OBE

Hewitt, Sir Nicholas Charles Joseph, Bt. (1921)

Heygate, Sir Richard John Gage, Bt. (1831)

Heyman, Sir Horace William, Kt.

Heywood, Sir Peter, Bt. (1838)

Hezlet, *Vice-Adm.* Sir Arthur Richard, KBE, CB, DSO, DSC

Hibbert, Sir Jack, KCB

Hibbert, Sir Reginald Alfred, GCMG

Hickey, Sir Justin, Kt.

Hickman, Sir (Richard) Glenn, Bt. (1903)

Hicks, Sir Robert, Kt.

Hidden, *Hon.* Sir Anthony Brian, Kt.

Hielscher, Sir Leo Arthur, Kt.

Higgins, Sir Christopher Thomas, Kt.

Higgins, *Hon.* Sir Malachy Joseph, Kt.

Higgins, *Rt. Hon.* Sir Terence Langley, KBE

Higginson, Sir Gordon Robert, Kt., ph.D., FEng.

Hill, Sir Alexander Rodger Erskine-, Bt. (1945)

Hill, Sir Arthur Alfred, Kt., CBE

Hill, Sir Brian John, Kt.

Hill, Sir James Frederick, Bt. (1917)

Hill, Sir John McGregor, Kt., ph.D., FEng.

Hill, Sir John Maxwell, Kt., CBE, DFC

|Hill, Sir John Rowley, Bt. (I. 1779)

Hill, *Vice-Adm.* Sir Robert Charles Finch, KBE, FEng.

Hill, Sir (Stanley) James (Allen), Kt.

Hillary, Sir Edmund, KG, KBE

Hillhouse, Sir (Robert) Russell, KCB

Hills, Sir Graham John, Kt.

Hine, *Air Chief Marshal* Sir Patrick Bardon, GCB, GBE

Hines, Sir Colin Joseph, Kt., OBE

Hinsley, *Prof.* Sir Francis Harry, Kt., OBE, FBA

Hirsch, *Prof.* Sir Peter Bernhard, Kt., ph.D., FRS

Hirst, *Rt. Hon.* Sir David Cozens-Hardy, Kt.

Hirst, Sir Michael William, Kt.

Hoare, Sir Peter Richard David, Bt. (1786)

Hoare, Sir Timothy Edward Charles, Bt., OBE (I. 1784)

Hobart, Sir John Vere, Bt. (1914)

Hobday, Sir Gordon Ivan, Kt.

Hobhouse, Sir Charles John Spinney, Bt. (1812)

Hobhouse, *Rt. Hon.* Sir John Stewart, Kt.

Hockaday, Sir Arthur Patrick, KCB, CMG

Hockley, *Gen.* Sir Anthony Heritage Farrar-, GBE, KCB, DSO, MC

†Hodge, Sir Andrew Rowland, Bt. (1921)

Hodge, Sir James William, KCVO, CMG

Hodge, Sir Julian Stephen Alfred, Kt.

Hodges, *Air Chief Marshal* Sir Lewis MacDonald, KCB, CBE, DSO, DFC

Hodgkin, *Prof.* Sir Alan Lloyd, OM, KBE, FRS, SC.D.

Hodgkin, Sir Gordon Howard Eliot, Kt., CBE

Hodgkinson, *Air Chief Marshal* Sir (William) Derek, KCB, CBE, DFC, AFC

Hodgson, Sir Maurice Arthur Eric, Kt., FEng.

Hodgson, *Hon.* Sir (Walter) Derek (Thornley), Kt.

Hodson, Sir Michael Robin Adderley, Bt. (I. 1789)

Hoffenberg, *Prof.* Sir Raymond, KBE

Hogg, Sir Christopher Anthony, Kt.

Hogg, Sir Edward William Lindsay-, Bt. (1905)

Hogg, *Vice-Adm.* Sir Ian Leslie Trower, KCB, DSC

Hogg, Sir John Nicholson, Kt., TD

Hogg, Sir Michael David, Bt. (1846)

Holcroft, Sir Peter George Culcheth, Bt. (1921)

Holden, Sir David Charles Beresford, KBE, CB, ERD

Holden, Sir Edward, Bt. (1893)

Holden, Sir John David, Bt. (1919)

Holder, Sir John Henry, Bt. (1898)

Holder, *Air Marshal* Sir Paul Davie, KBE, CB, DSO, DFC, ph.D.

Holderness, Sir Richard William, Bt. (1920)

Holdgate, Sir Martin Wyatt, Kt., CB, ph.D.

Holland, *Hon.* Sir Alan Douglas, Kt.

Holland, *Hon.* Sir Christopher John, Kt.

Holland, Sir Clifton Vaughan, Kt.

Holland, Sir Geoffrey, KCB

Holland, Sir Guy (Hope), Bt. (1917)

Holland, Sir Kenneth Lawrence, Kt., CBE, QFSM

Holland, Sir Philip Welsby, Kt.

Holliday, *Prof.* Sir Frederick George Thomas, Kt., CBE, FRSE

Hollings, *Hon.* Sir (Alfred) Kenneth, Kt., MC

Hollis, *Hon.* Sir Anthony Barnard, Kt.

Hollom, Sir Jasper Quintus, KBE

Holloway, *Hon.* Sir Barry Blyth, KBE

Holm, Sir Carl Henry, Kt., OBE

Holman, *Hon.* Sir (Edward) James, Kt.

Holmes, *Prof.* Sir Frank Wakefield, Kt.

Holmes, Sir Maurice Andrew, Kt.

Holmes, Sir Peter Fenwick, Kt., MC

Holroyd, *Air Marshal* Sir Frank Martyn, KBE, CB, FEng.

Holt, *Prof.* Sir James Clarke, Kt.

Holt, Sir Michael, Kt., CBE

Home, Sir William Dundas, Bt. (s. 1671)

Honeycombe, *Prof.* Sir Robert William Kerr, Kt., FRS, FEng.

Honywood, Sir Filmer Courtenay William, Bt. (1660)

Hood, Sir Harold Joseph, Bt., TD (1922)

Hookway, Sir Harry Thurston, Kt.

Hoole, Sir Arthur Hugh, Kt.

Hooper, *Hon.* Sir Anthony, Kt.

Hope, Sir (Charles) Peter, KCMG, TD

Hope, Sir Colin Frederick Newton, Kt.

Hope, *Rt. Revd and Rt. Hon.* David Michael, KCVO

Hope, Sir John Carl Alexander, Bt. (s. 1628)

Hopkin, Sir (William Aylsham) Bryan, Kt., CBE

Hopkins, Sir Anthony Philip, Kt., CBE

Hopkins, Sir Michael John, Kt., CBE, RA, RIBA

Hopwood, *Prof.* Sir David Alan, Kt., FRS

Hordern, *Rt. Hon.* Sir Peter Maudslay, Kt.

Horlick, *Vice-Adm.* Sir Edwin John, KBE, FEng.

Horlick, Sir James Cunliffe William, Bt. (1914)

Horlock, *Prof.* Sir John Harold, Kt., FRS, FEng.

Hornby, Sir Derek Peter, Kt.

Hornby, Sir Simon Michael, Kt.

Horne, Sir Alan Gray Antony, Bt. (1929)

Horsfall, Sir John Musgrave, Bt., MC, TD (1909)

Horsley, *Air Marshal* Sir (Beresford) Peter (Torrington), KCB, CBE, LVO, AFC

†Hort, Sir Andrew Edwin Fenton, Bt. (1767)

Horton, Sir Robert Baynes, Kt.

Hosker, Sir Gerald Albery, KCB, QC

Hoskyns, Sir Benedict Leigh, Bt. (1676)

Hoskyns, Sir John Austin Hungerford Leigh, Kt.

Hotung, Sir Joseph Edward, Kt.

Houghton, Sir John Theodore, Kt., CBE, FRS

†Houldsworth, Sir Richard Thomas Reginald, Bt (1887)

Hounsfield, Sir Godfrey Newbold, Kt., CBE

Hourston, Sir Gordon Minto, Kt.

House, *Lt.-Gen.* Sir David George, GCB, KCVO, CBE, MC

Houssemayne du Boulay, Sir Roger William, KCVO, CMG

Howard, Sir (Hamilton) Edward de Coucey, Bt., GBE (1955)

Howard, *Prof.* Sir Michael Eliot, Kt., CBE, MC

Howard, *Maj.-Gen.* Lord Michael Fitzalan-, GCVO, CB, CBE, MC

Howard, Sir Walter Stewart, Kt., MBE

Howell, Sir Ralph Frederic, Kt.

Howells, Sir Eric Waldo Benjamin, Kt., CBE

Howlett, *Gen.* Sir Geoffrey Hugh Whitby, KBE, MC
Hoyle, *Prof.* Sir Fred, Kt., FRS
Hoyos, *Hon.* Sir Fabriciano Alexander, Kt.
Huddie, Sir David Patrick, Kt., FEng.
Hudson, *Lt.-Gen.* Sir Peter, KCB, CBE
Huggins, *Hon.* Sir Alan Armstrong, Kt.
Hughes, Sir David Collingwood, Bt. (1773)
Hughes, *Prof.* Sir Edward Stuart Reginald, Kt., CBE
Hughes, Sir Jack William, Kt.
Hughes, Sir Trevor Denby Lloyd-, Kt.
Hughes, Sir Trevor Poulton, KCB
Hugo, *Lt.-Col.* Sir John Mandeville, KCVO, OBE
Hull, *Prof.* Sir David, Kt.
Hulse, Sir Edward Jeremy Westrow, Bt. (1739)
Hume, Sir Alan Blyth, Kt., CB
Humphreys, Sir (Raymond Evelyn) Myles, Kt.
Hunn, Sir Jack Kent, Kt., CMG
Hunt, Sir David Wathen Stather, KCMG, OBE
Hunt, Sir John Leonard, Kt.
Hunt, *Adm.* Sir Nicholas John Streynsham, GCB, LVO
Hunt, Sir Peter John, Kt., FRICS
Hunt, Sir Rex Masterman, Kt., CMG
Hunt, Sir Robert Frederick, Kt., CBE, FEng.
Hunter, *Hon.* Sir Alexander Albert, KBE
Hunter, Sir Alistair John, KCMG
Hunter, Sir Ian Bruce Hope, Kt., MBE
Hunter, *Prof.* Sir Laurence Colvin, Kt., CBE, FRSE
Hurn, Sir (Francis) Roger, Kt.
Hurrell, Sir Anthony Gerald, KCVO, CMG
Husbands, Sir Clifford Straugh, GCMG
Hutchinson, *Hon.* Sir Ross, Kt., DFC
Hutchison, *Lt.-Cdr.* Sir (George) Ian Clark, Kt., RN
Hutchison, *Rt. Hon.* Sir Michael, Kt.
Hutchison, Sir Peter, Bt., CBE (1939)
Hutchison, Sir Peter Craft, Bt. (1956)
Huxley, *Prof.* Sir Andrew Fielding, Kt., OM, FRS
Huxtable, *Gen.* Sir Charles Richard, KCB, CBE
Hyatali, *Hon.* Sir Isaac Emanuel, Kt.
Hyslop, Sir Robert John (Robin) Maxwell-, Kt.
Ibbs, Sir (John) Robin, KBE
Imbert, Sir Peter Michael, Kt., QPM
Imray, Sir Colin Henry, KBE, CMG
Ingham, Sir Bernard, Kt.
Ingilby, Sir Thomas Colvin William, Bt. (1866)
Inglis, Sir Brian Scott, Kt.
Inglis of Glencorse, Sir Roderick John, Bt. (s. 1703)
Ingram, Sir James Herbert Charles, Bt. (1893)

Ingram, Sir John Henderson, Kt., CBE
Inkin, Sir Geoffrey David, Kt., OBE
†Innes, Sir David Charles Kenneth Gordon, Bt. (NS 1686)
Innes of Edingight, Sir Malcolm Rognvald, KCVO
Innes, Sir Peter Alexander Berowald, Bt. (s. 1628)
Inniss, *Hon.* Sir Clifford de Lisle, Kt.
Irvine, Sir Donald Hamilton, Kt., CBE, MD, FRCGP
Irvine, *Dr* Sir Robin Orlando Hamilton, Kt.
Irving, *Prof.* Sir Miles Horsfall, Kt., MD, FRCS, FRCSE
Isaacs, Sir Jeremy Israel, Kt.
Isham, Sir Ian Vere Gyles, Bt. (1627)
Jack, *Hon.* Sir Alieu Sulayman, Kt.
Jack, Sir David, Kt., CBE, FRS, FRSE
Jack, Sir David Emmanuel, GCMG, MBE
Jackson, *Air Chief Marshal* Sir Brendan James, GCB
Jackson, Sir (John) Edward, KCMG
Jackson, Sir Michael Roland, Bt. (1902)
Jackson, Sir Nicholas Fane St George, Bt. (1913)
Jackson, Sir Robert, Bt. (1815)
Jackson, *Gen.* Sir William Godfrey Fothergill, GBE, KCB, MC
Jackson, Sir William Thomas, Bt. (1869)
Jacob, Sir Isaac Hai, Kt., QC
Jacob, *Hon.* Sir Robert Raphael Hayim (Robin), Kt.
Jacobi, Sir Derek George, Kt., CBE
Jacobi, *Dr* Sir James Edward, Kt., OBE
Jacobs, Sir David Anthony, Kt.
Jacobs, *Hon.* Sir Kenneth Sydney, KBE
Jacobs, Sir Piers, KBE
Jacobs, Sir Wilfred Ebenezer, GCMG, GCVO, OBE, QC
Jacomb, Sir Martin Wakefield, Kt.
Jaffray, Sir William Otho, Bt. (1892)
James, Sir Cynlais Morgan, KCMG
James, Sir Gerard Bowes Kingston, Bt. (1823)
James, Sir John Nigel Courtenay, KCVO, CBE
James, Sir Robert Vidal Rhodes, Kt.
James, Sir Stanislaus Anthony, GCMG, OBE
Jamieson, *Air Marshal* Sir David Ewan, KBE, CB
Jansen, Sir Ross Malcolm, KBE
Jardine, Sir Andrew Colin Douglas, Bt. (1916)
Jardine, *Maj.* Sir (Andrew) Rupert (John) Buchanan-, Bt., MC (1885)
Jardine of Applegirth, Sir Alexander Maule, Bt. (s. 1672)
Jarratt, Sir Alexander Anthony, Kt., CB
Jawara, *Hon.* Sir Dawda Kairaba, Kt.
Jay, Sir Antony Rupert, Kt., CVO
Jeewoolall, Sir Ramesh, Kt.
Jefferson, Sir George Rowland, Kt., CBE, FEng.

Jefferson, Sir Mervyn Stewart Dunnington-, Bt. (1958)
Jeffreys, *Prof.* Sir Alec John, Kt., FRS
Jeffries, *Hon.* Sir John Francis, Kt.
Jehangir, Sir Hirji, Bt. (1908)
Jejeebhoy, Sir Rustom, Bt. (1857)
Jenkins, Sir Brian Garton, GBE
Jenkins, Sir Elgar Spencer, Kt., OBE
Jenkins, Sir Michael Nicholas Howard, Kt., OBE
Jenkins, Sir Michael Romilly Heald, KCMG
Jenkinson, Sir John Banks, Bt. (1661)
†Jenks, Sir Maurice Arthur Brian, Bt. (1932)
Jennings, Sir John Southwood, Kt., CBE, FRSE
Jennings, *Prof.* Sir Robert Yewdall, Kt., QC
Jephcott, Sir (John) Anthony, Bt. (1962)
Jessel, Sir Charles John, Bt. (1883)
Jewkes, Sir Gordon Wesley, KCMG
Joel, *Hon.* Sir Asher Alexander, KBE
Johns, *Air Chief Marshal* Sir Richard Edward, GCB, CBE, LVO
Johnson, *Rt. Hon.* Sir David Powell Croom-, Kt., DSC, VRD
Johnson, *Gen.* Sir Garry Dene, KCB, OBE, MC
Johnson, Sir John Rodney, KCMG
†Johnson, Sir Patrick Eliot, Bt. (1818)
Johnson, Sir Peter Colpoys Paley, Bt. (1755)
Johnson, *Hon.* Sir Robert Lionel, Kt.
Johnson, Sir Vassel Godfrey, Kt., CBE
Johnston, Sir John Baines, GCMG, KCVO
Johnston, *Lt.-Col.* Sir John Frederick Dame, GCVO, MC
Johnston, *Lt.-Gen.* Sir Maurice Robert, KCB, OBE
Johnston, Sir Thomas Alexander, Bt. (s. 1626)
Johnston, Sir William Robert Patrick Knox- (Sir Robin), Kt., CBE, RD
Johnstone, Sir (George) Richard Douglas, Bt. (s. 1700)
Johnstone, Sir (John) Raymond, Kt., CBE
Jolliffe, Sir Anthony Stuart, GBE
Jones, *Gen.* Sir (Charles) Edward Webb, KCB, CBE
Jones, Sir Christopher Lawrence-, Bt. (1831)
Jones, Sir David Akers-, KBE, CMG
Jones, *Air Marshal* Sir Edward Gordon, KCB, CBE, DSO, DFC
Jones, Sir Ewart Ray Herbert, Kt., D.SC., ph.D., FRS
Jones, Sir Francis Avery, Kt., CBE, FRCP
Jones, Sir Gordon Pearce, Kt.
Jones, Sir Harry Ernest, Kt., CBE
Jones, Sir (John) Derek Alun-, Kt.
Jones, Sir John Henry Harvey-, Kt., MBE
Jones, Sir John Lewis, KCB, CMG
Jones, Sir John Prichard-, Bt. (1910)
Jones, Sir Keith Stephen, Kt.

Jones, *Hon.* Sir Kenneth George Illtyd, Kt.

Jones, Sir (Owen) Trevor, Kt.

Jones, Sir (Peter) Hugh (Jefferd) Lloyd-, Kt.

Jones, Sir Richard Anthony Lloyd, KCB

Jones, Sir Robert Edward, Kt.

Jones, Sir Simon Warley Frederick Benton, Bt. (1919)

Jones, Sir (Thomas) Philip, Kt., CB

Jones, Sir (William) Emrys, Kt.

Jones, *Hon.* Sir William Lloyd Mars-, Kt., MBE

Jones, Sir Wynn Normington Hugh-, Kt., LVO

†Joseph, *Hon.* Sir James Samuel, Bt. (1943)

Jowitt, *Hon.* Sir Edwin Frank, Kt.

Joyce, *Lt.-Gen.* Sir Robert John Hayman-, KCB, CBE

Judge, *Rt. Hon.* Sir Igor, Kt.

Judge, Sir Paul Rupert, Kt.

Jugnauth, *Rt. Hon.* Sir Anerood, KCMG, QC

Jungius, *Vice-Adm.* Sir James George, KBE

Jupp, *Hon.* Sir Kenneth Graham, Kt., MC

Kaberry, *Hon.* Sir Christopher Donald, Bt. (1960)

Kalms, Sir (Harold) Stanley, Kt.

Kalo, Sir Kwamala, Kt., MBE

Kan Yuet-Keung, Sir, GBE

Kapi, *Hon.* Sir Mari, Kt., CBE

Kaputin, Sir John Rumet, KBE, CMG

Katsina, The Emir of, KBE, CMG

Katz, Sir Bernard, Kt., FRS

Kausimae, Sir David Nanau, KBE

Kavall, Sir Thomas, Kt., OBE

Kawharu, *Prof.* Sir Ian Hugh, Kt.

Kay, *Prof.* Sir Andrew Watt, Kt.

Kay, *Hon.* Sir John William, Kt.

Kay, *Hon.* Sir Maurice Ralph, Kt.

Kaye, Sir Emmanuel, Kt., CBE

Kaye, Sir John Phillip Lister Lister-, Bt. (1812)

†Kaye, Sir Paul Henry Gordon, Bt. (1923)

Keane, Sir Richard Michael, Bt. (1801)

Keatinge, Sir Edgar Mayne, Kt., CBE

Keeble, Sir (Herbert Ben) Curtis, GCMG

Keene, *Hon.* Sir David Wolfe, Kt.

Keith, *Prof.* Sir James, KBE

Kellett, Sir Stanley Charles, Bt. (1801)

Kelly, Sir David Robert Corbett, Kt., CBE

Kelly, *Rt. Hon.* Sir (John William) Basil, Kt.

Kelly, Sir William Theodore, Kt., OBE

Kemball, *Air Marshal* Sir (Richard) John, KCB, CBE

Kemp, Sir (Edward) Peter, KCB

Kenilorea, *Rt. Hon.* Sir Peter, KBE

Kennard, *Lt.-Col.* Sir George Arnold Ford, Bt. (1891)

Kennaway, Sir John Lawrence, Bt. (1791)

Kennedy, Sir Clyde David Allen, Kt.

Kennedy, Sir Francis, KCMG, CBE

Kennedy, *Hon.* Sir Ian Alexander, Kt.

Kennedy, Sir Ludovic Henry Coverley, Kt.

†Kennedy, Sir Michael Edward, Bt., (1836)

Kennedy, *Rt. Hon.* Sir Paul Joseph Morrow, Kt.

Kennedy, *Air Chief Marshal* Sir Thomas Lawrie, GCB, AFC

Kennedy-Good, Sir John, KBE

Kenny, Sir Anthony John Patrick, Kt., D.phil., D.Litt., FBA

Kenny, *Gen.* Sir Brian Leslie Graham, GCB, CBE

Kent, Sir Harold Simcox, GCB, QC

Kenyon, Sir George Henry, Kt.

Kermode, Sir (John) Frank, Kt., FBA

Kermode, Sir Ronald Graham Quale, KBE

Kerr, *Hon.* Sir Brian Francis, Kt.

Kerr, *Adm.* Sir John Beverley, GCB

Kerr, Sir John Olav, KCMG

Kerr, *Rt. Hon.* Sir Michael Robert Emanuel, Kt.

Kerruish, Sir (Henry) Charles, Kt., OBE

Kerry, Sir Michael James, KCB, QC

Kershaw, Sir (John) Anthony, Kt., MC

Keswick, Sir John Chippendale Lindley, Kt.

Kidd, Sir Robert Hill, KBE, CB

Kikau, *Ratu* Sir Jone Latianara, KBE

Killen, *Hon.* Denis James, KCMG

Killick, Sir John Edward, GCMG

Kimber, Sir Charles Dixon, Bt. (1904)

King, *Gen.* Sir Frank Douglas, GCB, MBE

King, Sir John Christopher, Bt. (1888)

King, *Vice-Adm.* Sir Norman Ross Dutton, KBE

King, Sir Richard Brian Meredith, KCB, MC

King, Sir Wayne Alexander, Bt. (1815)

Kingman, *Prof.* Sir John Frank Charles, Kt., FRS

Kingsland, Sir Richard, Kt., CBE, DFC

Kingsley, Sir Patrick Graham Toler, KCVO

Kinloch, Sir David, Bt. (s. 1686)

Kinloch, Sir David Oliphant, Bt. (1873)

Kipalan, Sir Albert, Kt.

Kirby, *Hon.* Sir Richard Clarence, Kt.

Kirkham, Sir Graham, Kt.

Kirkpatrick, Sir Ivone Elliott, Bt. (s. 1685)

Kirkwood, *Hon.* Sir Andrew Tristram Hammett, Kt.

Kirwan, Sir (Archibald) Laurence Patrick, KCMG, TD

Kitcatt, Sir Peter Julian, Kt., CB

Kitson, *Gen.* Sir Frank Edward, GBE, KCB, MC

Kitson, Sir Timothy Peter Geoffrey, Kt.

Kleinwort, Sir Richard Drake, Bt. (1909)

Klug, Sir Aaron, Kt., OM

Kneller, Sir Alister Arthur, Kt.

Knight, Sir Allan Walton, Kt., CMG

Knight, Sir Arthur William, Kt.

Knight, Sir Harold Murray, KBE, DSC

Knight, *Air Chief Marshal* Sir Michael William Patrick, KCB, AFC

Knill, Sir John Kenelm Stuart, Bt. (1893)

Knill, *Prof.* Sir John Lawrence, Kt., FEng.

Knott, Sir John Laurence, Kt., CBE

Knowles, Sir Charles Francis, Bt. (1765)

Knowles, Sir Durward Randolph, Kt., OBE

Knowles, Sir Leonard Joseph, Kt., CBE

Knowles, Sir Richard Marchant, Kt.

Knox, Sir Bryce Muir, KCVO, MC, TD

Knox, Sir David Laidlaw, Kt.

Knox, *Hon.* Sir John Leonard, Kt.

Knox, *Hon.* Sir William Edward, Kt.

Koraea, Sir Thomas, Kt.

Kornberg, *Prof.* Sir Hans Leo, Kt., D.SC., SC. D., Ph.D., FRS

Korowi, Sir Wiwa, GCMG

Kroto, *Prof.* Sir Harold Walter, Kt., FRS

Krusin, Sir Stanley Marks, Kt., CB

Kulukundis, Sir Elias George (Eddie), Kt., OBE

Kurongku, *Most Revd* Peter, KBE

Labouchere, Sir George Peter, GBE, KCMG

Lacon, Sir Edmund Vere, Bt. (1818)

Lacy, Sir Hugh Maurice Pierce, Bt. (1921)

Lacy, Sir John Trend, Kt., CBE

Laddie, *Hon.* Sir Hugh Ian Lang, Kt.

Laidlaw, Sir Christophor Charles Fraser, Kt.

Laing, Sir (John) Martin (Kirby), Kt., CBE

Laing, Sir (John) Maurice, Kt.

Laing, Sir (William) Kirby, Kt., FEng.

Laird, Sir Gavin Harry, Kt., CBE

Lake, Sir (Atwell) Graham, Bt. (1711)

Laker, Sir Frederick Alfred, Kt.

Lakin, Sir Michael, Bt. (1909)

Laking, Sir George Robert, KCMG

Lamb, Sir Albert (Larry), Kt.

Lamb, Sir Albert Thomas, KBE, CMG, DFC

Lambert, Sir Anthony Edward, KCMG

Lambert, Sir John Henry, KCVO, CMG

†Lambert, Sir Peter John Biddulph, Bt. (1711)

Laming, Sir (William) Herbert, Kt., CBE

Lampl, Sir Frank William, Kt.

Landale, Sir David William Neil, KCVO

Landau, Sir Dennis Marcus, Kt.

Lane, Sir David William Stennis Stuart, Kt.

Lang, *Lt.-Gen.* Sir Derek Boileau, KCB, DSO, MC
Langham, Sir James Michael, Bt. (1660)
Langley, *Hon.* Sir Gordon Julian Hugh, Kt.
Langley, *Maj.-Gen.* Sir Henry Desmond Allen, KCVO, MBE
Langrishe, Sir Hercules Ralph Hume, Bt. (I. 1777)
Lankester, Sir Timothy Patrick, KCB
Lapun, *Hon.* Sir Paul, Kt.
Larcom, Sir (Charles) Christopher Royde, Bt. (1868)
Large, Sir Andrew McLeod Brooks, Kt.
Large, Sir Peter, Kt., CBE
Larmour, Sir Edward Noel, KCMG
Lasdun, Sir Denys Louis, Kt., CH, CBE, FRIBA
Latey, *Rt. Hon.* Sir John Brinsmead, Kt., MBE
Latham, *Hon.* Sir David Nicholas Ramsey, Kt.
Latham, Sir Michael Anthony, Kt.
Latham, Sir Richard Thomas Paul, Bt. (1919)
Latimer, Sir (Courtenay) Robert, Kt., CBE
Latimer, Sir Graham Stanley, KBE
Lauder, Sir Piers Robert Dick-, Bt. (s. 1690)
Laughton, Sir Anthony Seymour, Kt.
Laurantus, Sir Nicholas, Kt., MBE
Laurence, Sir Peter Harold, KCMG, MC
Laurie, Sir Robert Bayley Emilius, Bt. (1834)
Lauti, *Rt. Hon.* Sir Toaripi, GCMG
Lavan, *Hon.* Sir John Martin, Kt.
Law, *Adm.* Sir Horace Rochfort, GCB, OBE, DSC
Lawes, Sir (John) Michael Bennet, Bt. (1882)
Lawler, Sir Peter James, Kt., OBE
Lawrence, Sir David Roland Walter, Bt. (1906)
Lawrence, Sir Guy Kempton, Kt., DSO, OBE, DFC
Lawrence, Sir Ivan John, Kt., QC
Lawrence, Sir John Patrick Grosvenor, Kt., CBE
Lawrence, Sir John Waldemar, Bt., OBE (1858)
Lawrence, Sir William Fettiplace, Bt. (1867)
Laws, *Hon.* Sir John Grant McKenzie, Kt.
Lawson, Sir Christopher Donald, Kt.
Lawson, *Col.* Sir John Charles Arthur Digby, Bt., DSO, MC (1900)
Lawson, Sir John Philip Howard-, Bt. (1841)
Lawson, *Gen.* Sir Richard George, KCB, DSO, OBE
Lawton, *Prof.* Sir Frank Ewart, Kt.
Lawton, *Rt. Hon.* Sir Frederick Horace, Kt.
Layard, *Adm.* Sir Michael Henry Gordon, KCB, CBE

Layfield, Sir Frank Henry Burland Willoughby, Kt., QC
Lea, *Vice-Adm.* Sir John Stuart Crosbie, KBE
Lea, Sir Thomas William, Bt. (1892)
Leach, *Admiral of the Fleet* Sir Henry Conyers, GCB
Leahy, Sir Daniel Joseph, Kt.
Leahy, Sir John Henry Gladstone, KCMG
Learmont, *Gen.* Sir John Hartley, KCB, CBE
Leask, *Lt.-Gen.* Sir Henry Lowther Ewart Clark, KCB, DSO, OBE
Leather, Sir Edwin Hartley Cameron, KCMG, KCVO
Leaver, Sir Christopher, GBE
Le Bailly, *Vice-Adm.* Sir Louis Edward Stewart Holland, KBE, CB
Le Cheminant, *Air Chief Marshal* Sir Peter de Lacey, GBE, KCB, DFC
Lechmere, Sir Berwick Hungerford, Bt. (1818)
Ledwidge, Sir (William) Bernard (John), KCMG
Lee, Sir Arthur James, KBE, MC
Lee, *Air Chief Marshal* Sir David John Pryer, GBE, CB
Lee, *Brig.* Sir Leonard Henry, Kt., CBE
Lee, Sir Quo-wei, Kt., CBE
Leeds, Sir Christopher Anthony, Bt. (1812)
Lees, Sir David Bryan, Kt.
Lees, Sir Thomas Edward, Bt. (1897)
Lees, Sir Thomas Harcourt Ivor, Bt. (1804)
Lees, Sir (William) Antony Clare, Bt. (1937)
Leese, Sir John Henry Vernon, Bt. (1908)
Le Fanu, *Maj.* Sir (George) Victor (Sheridan), KCVO
le Fleming, Sir David Kelland, Bt. (1705)
Legard, Sir Charles Thomas, Bt. (1660)
Legg, Sir Thomas Stuart, KCB, QC
Leggatt, *Rt. Hon.* Sir Andrew Peter, Kt.
Leggatt, Sir Hugh Frank John, Kt.
Leggett, Sir Clarence Arthur Campbell, Kt., MBE
Leigh, Sir Geoffrey Norman, Kt.
Leigh, Sir Richard Henry, Bt. (1918)
Leighton, Sir Michael John Bryan, Bt. (1693)
Leitch, Sir George, KCB, OBE
Leith, Sir Andrew George Forbes-, Bt. (1923)
Le Marchant, Sir Francis Arthur, Bt. (1841)
Lemon, Sir (Richard) Dawnay, Kt., CBE
Leng, *Gen.* Sir Peter John Hall, KCB, MBE, MC
Lennard, *Revd* Sir Hugh Dacre Barrett-, Bt. (1801)
Leon, Sir John Ronald, Bt. (1911)
Leonard, *Rt. Revd and Rt. Hon.* Graham Douglas, KCVO

Leonard, *Hon.* Sir (Hamilton) John, Kt.
Lepping, Sir George Geria Dennis, GCMG, MBE
Le Quesne, Sir (Charles) Martin, KCMG
Le Quesne, Sir (John) Godfray, Kt., QC
Leslie, Sir Colin Alan Bettridge, Kt.
Leslie, Sir John Norman Ide, Bt. (1876)
†Leslie, Sir (Percy) Theodore, Bt. (s. 1625)
Leslie, Sir Peter Evelyn, Kt.
Lester, Sir James Theodore, Kt.
Lethbridge, Sir Thomas Periam Hector Noel, Bt. (1804)
Leupena, Sir Tupua, GCMG, MBE
Lever, Sir (Tresham) Christopher Arthur Lindsay, Bt. (1911)
Levey, Sir Michael Vincent, Kt., LVO
Levine, Sir Montague Bernard, Kt.
Levinge, Sir Richard George Robin, Bt. (I. 1704)
Lewando, Sir Jan Alfred, Kt., CBE
Lewinton, Sir Christopher, Kt.
Lewis, Sir David Courtenay Mansel, KCVO
Lewthwaite, *Brig.* Sir Rainald Gilfrid, Bt., CVO, OBE, MC (1927)
Ley, Sir Ian Francis, Bt. (1905)
Leyland, Sir Philip Vyvyan Naylor-, Bt. (1895)
Lickiss, Sir Michael Gillam, Kt.
Lickley, Sir Robert Lang, Kt., CBE, FEng.
Lidderdale, Sir David William Shuckburgh, KCB
Liggins, *Prof.* Sir Graham Collingwood, Kt., CBE, FRS
Lighthill, Sir (Michael) James, Kt., FRS
Lightman, *Hon.* Sir Gavin Anthony, Kt.
Lighton, Sir Thomas Hamilton, Bt. (I. 1791)
Lim, Sir Han-Hoe, Kt., CBE
Limon, Sir Donald William, KCB
Linacre, Sir (John) Gordon (Seymour), Kt., CBE, AFC, DFM
Lindop, Sir Norman, Kt.
Lindsay, Sir James Harvey Kincaid Stewart, Kt.
Lindsay, *Hon.* Sir John Edmund Frederic, Kt.
Lindsay, Sir Ronald Alexander, Bt. (1962)
Lipworth, Sir (Maurice) Sydney, Kt.
Lithgow, Sir William James, Bt. (1925)
Little, *Most Revd* Thomas Francis, KBE
Littler, Sir (James) Geoffrey, KCB
Livesay, *Adm.* Sir Michael Howard, KCB
Llewellyn, Sir Henry Morton, Bt., CBE (1922)
Llewelyn, Sir John Michael Dillwyn-Venables-, Bt. (1890)

Lloyd, *Prof.* Sir Geoffrey Ernest Richard, Kt., FBA
Lloyd, Sir Ian Stewart, Kt.
Lloyd, Sir Nicholas Markley, Kt.
Lloyd, *Rt. Hon.* Sir Peter Robert Cable, Kt., MP
Lloyd, Sir Richard Ernest Butler, Bt. (1960)
Lloyd, *Hon.* Sir Timothy Andrew Wigram, Kt.
Loader, Sir Leslie Thomas, Kt., CBE
Loane, *Most Revd* Marcus Lawrence, KBE
Lobo, Sir Rogerio Hyndman, Kt., CBE
Lock, *Cdr.* Sir (John) Duncan, Kt.
Lockhart, Sir Simon John Edward Francis Sinclair-, Bt. (s. 1636)
Loder, Sir Giles Rolls, Bt. (1887)
Logan, Sir Donald Arthur, KCMG
Logan, Sir Raymond Douglas, Kt.
Lokoloko, Sir Tore, GCMG, GCVO, OBE
Lombe, *Hon.* Sir Edward Christopher Evans-, Kt.
Longden, Sir Gilbert James Morley, Kt., MBE
Longmore, *Hon.* Sir Andrew Centlivres, Kt.
Loram, *Vice-Adm.* Sir David Anning, KCB, CVO
Lorimer, Sir (Thomas) Desmond, Kt.
Los, *Hon.* Sir Kubulan, Kt., CBE
Lovell, Sir (Alfred Charles) Bernard, Kt., OBE, FRS
Lovelock, Sir Douglas Arthur, KCB
Loveridge, Sir John Warren, Kt.
Lovill, Sir John Roger, Kt., CBE
Low, Sir Alan Roberts, Kt.
Low, Sir James Richard Morrison-, Bt. (1908)
Lowe, *Air Chief Marshal* Sir Douglas Charles, GCB, DFC, AFC
Lowe, Sir Thomas William Gordon, Bt. (1918)
Lowry, Sir John Patrick, Kt., CBE
Lowson, Sir Ian Patrick, Bt. (1951)
Lowther, *Maj.* Sir Charles Douglas, Bt. (1824)
Lowther, Sir John Luke, KCVO, CBE
Loyd, Sir Francis Alfred, KCMG, OBE
Loyd, Sir Julian St John, KCVO
Lu, Sir Tseng Chi, Kt.
Lucas, Sir Cyril Edward, Kt., CMG, FRS
Lucas, Sir Thomas Edward, Bt. (1887)
Luce, *Rt. Hon.* Sir Richard Napier, Kt.
Luckhoo, Sir Lionel Alfred, KCMG, CBE, QC
Lucy, Sir Edmund John William Hugh Cameron-Ramsay-Fairfax, Bt. (1836)
Luddington, Sir Donald Collin Cumyn, KBE, CMG, CVO
Lumsden, Sir David James, Kt.
Lus, *Hon.* Sir Pita, Kt., OBE
Lush, *Hon.* Sir George Hermann, Kt.
Lushington, Sir John Richard Castleman, Bt. (1791)
Luttrell, *Col.* Sir Geoffrey Walter Fownes, KCVO, MC

Lyell, *Rt. Hon.* Sir Nicholas Walter, Kt., QC, MP
Lygo, *Adm.* Sir Raymond Derek, KCB
Lyle, Sir Gavin Archibald, Bt. (1929)
Lyons, Sir Edward Houghton, Kt.
Lyons, Sir James Reginald, Kt.
Lyons, Sir John, Kt.
McAdam, Sir Ian William James, Kt., OBE
McAlpine, Sir William Hepburn, Bt. (1918)
†Macara, Sir Hugh Kenneth, Bt. (1911)
Macartney, Sir John Barrington, Bt. (1. 1799)
McAvoy, Sir (Francis) Joseph, Kt., CBE
McCaffrey, Sir Thomas Daniel, Kt.
McCall, Sir (Charles) Patrick Home, Kt., MBE, TD
McCallum, Sir Donald Murdo, Kt., CBE, FEng.
McCamley, Sir Graham Edward, Kt., MBE
McCarthy, *Rt. Hon.* Sir Thaddeus Pearcey, KBE
McCartney, Sir (James) Paul, Kt., MBE
McClellan, *Col.* Sir Herbert Gerard Thomas, Kt., CBE, TD
McClintock, Sir Eric Paul, Kt.
McColl, Sir Colin Hugh Verel, KCMG
McCollum, *Rt. Hon.* Sir William, Kt.
McConnell, Sir Robert Shean, Bt. (1900)
McCorkell, *Col.* Sir Michael William, KCVO, OBE, TD
McCowan, *Rt. Hon.* Sir Anthony James Denys, Kt.
McCowan, Sir Hew Cargill, Bt. (1934)
McCrea, *Prof.* Sir William Hunter, Kt., FRS
McCrindle, Sir Robert Arthur, Kt.
McCullough, *Hon.* Sir (Iain) Charles (Robert), Kt.
McCusker, Sir James Alexander, Kt.
MacDermott, *Rt. Hon.* Sir John Clarke, Kt.
McDermott, Sir (Lawrence) Emmet, KBE
MacDonald, *Gen.* Sir Arthur Leslie, KBE, CB
Macdonald of Sleat, Sir Ian Godfrey Bosville, Bt. (s. 1625)
Macdonald, Sir Kenneth Carmichael, KCB
Macdonald, *Vice-Adm.* Sir Roderick Douglas, KBE
McDonald, Sir Tom, Kt., OBE
McDonald, *Hon.* Sir William John Farquhar, Kt.
MacDougall, Sir (George) Donald (Alastair), Kt., CBE, FBA
McDowell, Sir Eric Wallace, Kt., CBE
McDowell, Sir Henry McLorinan, KBE
Mace, *Lt.-Gen.* Sir John Airth, KBE, CB
McEwen, Sir John Roderick Hugh, Bt. (1953)

McFarland, Sir John Talbot, Bt. (1914)
Macfarlane, Sir (David) Neil, Kt.
Macfarlane, Sir George Gray, Kt., CB, FEng.
McFarlane, Sir Ian, Kt.
McGeoch, *Vice-Adm.* Sir Ian Lachlan Mackay, KCB, DSO, DSC
McGrath, Sir Brian Henry, KCVO
Macgregor, Sir Edwin Robert, Bt. (1828)
MacGregor of MacGregor, Sir Gregor, Bt. (1795)
McGregor, Sir Ian Alexander, Kt., CBE, FRS
MacGregor, Sir Ian Kinloch, Kt.
McGrigor, *Capt.* Sir Charles Edward, Bt. (1831)
McIntosh, *Vice-Adm.* Sir Ian Stewart, KBE, CB, DSO, DSC
McIntosh, Sir Malcolm Kenneth, Kt., ph.D.
McIntosh, Sir Ronald Robert Duncan, KCB
McIntyre, Sir Donald Conroy, Kt., CBE
McIntyre, Sir Meredith Alister, Kt.
MacKay, *Prof.* Sir Donald Iain, Kt., FRSE
Mackay, Sir (George Patrick) Gordon, Kt., CBE
McKay, Sir John Andrew, Kt., CBE
Mackechnie, Sir Alistair John, Kt.
McKee, *Maj.* Sir (William) Cecil, Kt., ERD
McKellen, Sir Ian Murray, Kt., CBE
McKenzie, Sir Alexander, KBE
Mackenzie, Sir Alexander Alwyne Henry Charles Brinton Muir-, Bt. (1805)
†Mackenzie, Sir (James William) Guy, Bt. (1890)
Mackenzie, *Gen.* Sir Jeremy John George, KCB, OBE
†Mackenzie, Sir Peter Douglas, Bt. (s. 1673)
†Mackenzie, Sir Roderick McQuhae, Bt. (s. 1703)
McKenzie, Sir Roy Allan, KBE
Mackeson, Sir Rupert Henry, Bt. (1954)
MacKinlay, Sir Bruce, Kt., CBE
McKinnon, Sir James, Kt.
McKinnon, *Hon.* Sir Stuart Nell, Kt.
Mackintosh, Sir Cameron Anthony, Kt.
Macklin, Sir Bruce Roy, Kt., OBE
Mackworth, *Cdr.* Sir David Arthur Geoffrey, Bt. (1776)
McLaren, Sir Robin John Taylor, KCMG
Maclean, Sir Donald Og Grant, Kt.
†Maclean of Dunconnell, Sir Charles Edward, Bt. (1957)
McLean, Sir Francis Charles, Kt., CBE
MacLean, *Vice-Adm.* Sir Hector Charles Donald, KBE, CB, DSC
Maclean, Sir Lachlan Hector Charles, Bt. (NS 1631)
Maclean, Sir Robert Alexander, KBE

McLennan, Sir Ian Munro, KCMG, KBE

McLeod, Sir Charles Henry, Bt. (1925)

McLeod, Sir Ian George, Kt.

MacLeod, Sir (John) Maxwell Norman, Bt. (1924)

Macleod, Sir (Nathaniel William) Hamish, KBE

McLintock, Sir Michael William, Bt. (1934)

Maclure, Sir John Robert Spencer, Bt. (1898)

McMahon, Sir Brian Patrick, Bt. (1817)

McMahon, Sir Christopher William, Kt.

Macmillan, Sir (Alexander McGregor) Graham, Kt.

MacMillan, Lt.-Gen. Sir John Richard Alexander, KCB, CBE

McMullin, Rt. Hon. Sir Duncan Wallace, Kt.

Macnaghten, Sir Patrick Alexander, Bt. (1836)

McNamara, Air Chief Marshal Sir Neville Patrick, KBE

Macnaughton, Prof. Sir Malcolm Campbell, Kt.

McNee, Sir David Blackstock, Kt., QPM

McNeice, Sir (Thomas) Percy (Fergus), Kt., CMG, OBE

MacPhail, Sir Bruce Dugald, Kt.

Macpherson, Sir Ronald Thomas Steward (Tommy), CBE, MC, TD

Macpherson of Cluny, Hon. Sir William Alan, Kt., TD

McQuarrie, Sir Albert, Kt.

MacRae, Sir (Alastair) Christopher (Donald Summerhayes), KCMG

Macrae, Col. Sir Robert Andrew Scarth, KCVO, MBE

Macready, Sir Nevil John Wilfrid, Bt. (1923)

Mactaggart, Sir John Auld, Bt. (1938)

Macwhinnie, Sir Gordon Menzies, Kt., CBE

McWilliam, Sir Michael Douglas, KCMG

McWilliams, Sir Francis, GBE, FEng.

Madden, Adm. Sir Charles Edward, Bt., GCB (1919)

Maddocks, Sir Kenneth Phipson, KCMG, KCVO

Maddox, Sir John Royden, Kt.

Madel, Sir (William) David, Kt., MP

Madigan, Sir Russel Tullie, Kt., OBE

Magnus, Sir Laurence Henry Philip, Bt. (1917)

Maguire, Air Marshal Sir Harold John, KCB, DSO, OBE

Mahon, Sir (John) Denis, Kt., CBE

Mahon, Sir William Walter, Bt. (1819)

Maiden, Sir Colin James, Kt., D.Phil.

Main, Sir Peter Tester, Kt., ERD

Maini, Sir Amar Nath, Kt., CBE

Maino, Sir Charles, KBE

†Maitland, Sir Charles Alexander, Bt. (1818)

Maitland, Sir Donald James Dundas, GCMG, OBE

Makins, Sir Paul Vivian, Bt. (1903)

Malcolm, Sir James William Thomas Alexander, Bt. (s. 1665)

Malet, Sir Harry Douglas St Lo, Bt. (1791)

Mallaby, Sir Christopher Leslie George, GCMG, GCVO

†Mallinson, Sir William James, Bt. (1935)

Malone, Hon. Sir Denis Eustace Gilbert, Kt.

Mamo, Sir Anthony Joseph, Kt., OBE

Mance, Hon. Sir Jonathan Hugh, Kt.

Manchester, Sir William Maxwell, KBE

Mander, Sir Charles Marcus, Bt. (1911)

Manduell, Sir John, Kt., CBE

Mann, Rt. Hon. Sir Michael, Kt.

Mann, Rt. Revd Michael Ashley, KCVO

Mann, Sir Rupert Edward, Bt. (1905)

Mansel, Sir Philip, Bt. (1622)

Mansfield, Vice-Adm. Sir (Edward) Gerard (Napier), KBE, CVO

Mansfield, Prof. Sir Peter, Kt., FRS

Mansfield, Sir Philip (Robert Aked), KCMG

Mantell, Hon. Sir Charles Barrie Knight, Kt.

Manton, Sir Edwin Alfred Grenville, Kt.

Manuella, Sir Tulaga, GCMG, MBE

Manzie, Sir (Andrew) Gordon, KCB

Mara, Rt. Hon. Ratu Sir Kamisese Kapaiwai Tuimacilai, GCMG, KBE

Margetson, Sir John William Denys, KCMG

Marjoribanks, Sir James Alexander Milne, KCMG

Mark, Sir Robert, GBE

Markham, Sir Charles John, Bt. (1911)

Marking, Sir Henry Ernest, KCVO, CBE, MC

Marling, Sir Charles William Somerset, Bt. (1882)

Marr, Sir Leslie Lynn, Bt. (1919)

Marriner, Sir Neville, Kt., CBE

Marriott, Sir Hugh Cavendish Smith-, Bt. (1774)

Marriott, Sir John Brook, KCVO

Marsden, Sir Nigel John Denton, Bt. (1924)

Marshall, Sir Arthur Gregory George, Kt., OBE

Marshall, Sir Colin Marsh, Kt.

Marshall, Sir Denis Alfred, Kt.

Marshall, Prof. Sir (Oshley) Roy, Kt., CBE

Marshall, Sir Peter Harold Reginald, KCMG

Marshall, Sir Robert Braithwaite, KCB, MBE

Marshall, Sir (Robert) Michael, Kt.

Martell, Vice-Adm. Sir Hugh Colenso, KBE, CB

Martin, Sir George Henry, Kt., CBE

Martin, Vice-Adm. Sir John Edward Ludgate, KCB, DSC

Martin, Prof. Sir (John) Leslie, Kt., Ph.D.

Martin, Prof. Sir Laurence Woodward, Kt.

Martin, Sir (Robert) Bruce, Kt., QC

Marychurch, Sir Peter Harvey, KCMG

Masefield, Sir Charles Beech Gordon, Kt.

Masefield, Sir Peter Gordon, Kt.

Masire, Sir Ketumile, GCMG

Mason, Hon. Sir Anthony Frank, KBE

Mason, Sir (Basil) John, Kt., CB, D.SC., FRS

Mason, Prof. Sir David Kean, Kt., CBE

Mason, Sir Frederick Cecil, KCVO, CMG

Mason, Sir Gordon Charles, Kt., OBE

Mason, Sir John Charles Moir, KCMG

Mason, Sir John Peter, Kt., CBE

Mason, Prof. Sir Ronald, KCB, FRS

Matane, Sir Paulias Nguna, Kt., CMG, OBE

Mather, Sir (David) Carol (Macdonell), Kt., MC

Mather, Sir William Loris, Kt., CVO, OBE, MC, TD

Mathers, Sir Robert William, Kt.

Matheson, Sir (James Adam) Louis, KBE, CMG, FEng.

Matheson of Matheson, Sir Fergus John, Bt. (1882)

Matthews, Sir Peter Alec, Kt.

Matthews, Sir Peter Jack, Kt., CVO, OBE, QPM

Matthews, Sir Stanley, Kt., CBE

Maud, The Hon. Sir Humphrey John Hamilton, KCMG

Mawhinney, Rt. Hon. Sir Brian Stanley, Kt., MP

†Maxwell, Sir Michael Eustace George, Bt. (s. 1681)

Maxwell, Sir Nigel Mellor Heron-, Bt. (s. 1683)

May, Hon. Sir Anthony Tristram Kenneth, Kt.

May, Sir Kenneth Spencer, Kt., CBE

May, Prof. Sir Robert McCredie, Kt., FRS

Maynard, Hon. Sir Clement Travelyan, Kt.

Maynard, Air Chief Marshal Sir Nigel Martin, KCB, CBE, DFC, AFC

Mayne, Very Revd Michael Clement Otway, KCVO

Meadow, Prof. Sir (Samuel) Roy, Kt., FRCP, FRCPE

Medlycott, Sir Mervyn Tregonwell, Bt. (1808)

Megarry, Rt. Hon. Sir Robert Edgar, Kt., FBA

Megaw, Rt. Hon. Sir John, Kt., CBE, TD

Meinertzhagen, Sir Peter, Kt., CMG

Melhuish, Sir Michael Ramsay, KBE, CMG

Mellon, Sir James, KCMG

Melville, Sir Harry Work, KCB, Ph.D., D.SC., FRS

Melville, Sir Leslie Galfreid, KBE

Melville, Sir Ronald Henry, KCB

Mensforth, Sir Eric, Kt., CBE, F.Eng.

Menter, Sir James Woodham, Kt., ph.D., SC.D., FRS

Menteth, Sir James Wallace Stuart-, Bt. (1838)

Menzies, Sir Peter Thomson, Kt.

Meyer, Sir Anthony John Charles, Bt. (1910)

Meyjes, Sir Richard Anthony, Kt.

Meyrick, Sir David John Charlton, Bt. (1880)

Meyrick, Sir George Christopher Cadafael Tapps-Gervis-, Bt. (1791)

Miakwe, Hon. Sir Akepa, KBE

Michael, Sir Peter Colin, Kt., CBE

Middleton, Sir George Humphrey, KCMG

Middleton, Sir Lawrence Monck, Bt. (1662)

Middleton, Sir Peter Edward, GCB

Miers, Sir (Henry) David Alastair Capel, KBE, CMG

Milbank, Sir Anthony Frederick, Bt. (1882)

Milburn, Sir Anthony Rupert, Bt. (1905)

Miles, Sir Peter Tremayne, KCVO

Miles, Sir William Napier Maurice, Bt. (1859)

Millais, Sir Geoffrey Richard Everett, Bt. (1885)

Millar, Sir Oliver Nicholas, GCVO, FBA

Millar, Sir Ronald Graeme, Kt.

Millard, Sir Guy Elwin, KCMG, CVO

Miller, Sir Donald John, Kt., FRSE, FEng.

Miller, Sir Harry Holmes, Bt. (1705)

Miller, Sir Hilary Duppa (Hal), Kt.

Miller, Lt.-Col. Sir John Mansel, GCVO, DSO, MC

Miller, Sir (Oswald) Bernard, Kt.

Miller, Sir Peter North, Kt.

Miller, Sir Ronald Andrew Baird, Kt., CBE

Miller of Glenlee, Sir Stephen William Macdonald, Bt. (1788)

Millett, Rt. Hon. Sir Peter Julian, Kt.

Millichip, Sir Frederick Albert (Bert), Kt.

Mills, Vice-Adm. Sir Charles Piercy, KCB, CBE, DSC

Mills, Sir Frank, KCVO, CMG

Mills, Sir John Lewis Ernest Watts, Kt., CBE

Mills, Sir Peter Frederick Leighton, Bt. (1921)

Milman, Lt.-Col. Sir Derek, Bt. (1800)

Milne, Sir John Drummond, Kt.

†Milner, Sir Timothy William Lycett, Bt. (1717)

Milnes Coates, Sir Anthony Robert, Bt. (1911)

Mirrlees, Prof. Sir James Alexander, Kt., FBA

Mitchell, Air Cdre Sir (Arthur) Dennis, KBE, CVO, DFC, AFC

Mitchell, Sir David Bower, Kt.

Mitchell, Sir Derek Jack, KCB, CVO

Mitchell, Prof. Sir (Edgar) William John, Kt., CBE, FRS

Mitchell, Rt. Hon. Sir James FitzAllen, KCMG

Mitchell, Hon. Sir Stephen George, Kt.

Moate, Sir Roger Denis, Kt.

Mobbs, Sir (Gerald) Nigel, Kt.

Moberly, Sir John Campbell, KBE, CMG

Moberly, Sir Patrick Hamilton, KCMG

Moffat, Sir Brian Scott, Kt., OBE

Moffat, Lt.-Gen. Sir (William) Cameron, KBE

Mogg, Gen. Sir (Herbert) John, GCB, CBE, DSO

Moir, Sir Ernest Ian Royds, Bt. (1916)

Moller, Hon. Sir Lester Francis, Kt.

†Molony, Sir Thomas Desmond, Bt. (1925)

Monck, Sir Nicholas Jeremy, KCB

Monro, Sir Hector Seymour Peter, Kt.

Montgomery, Sir (Basil Henry) David, Bt. (1801)

Montgomery, Sir (William) Fergus, Kt.

Mookerjee, Sir Birendra Nath, Kt.

Moollan, Sir Abdool Hamid Adam, Kt.

Moollan, Hon. Sir Cassam (Ismael), Kt.

Moon, Sir Peter Wilfred Giles Graham-, Bt. (1855)

†Moon, Sir Roger, Bt. (1887)

Moore, Most Revd Desmond Charles, KBE

Moore, Sir Francis Thomas, Kt.

Moore, Sir Henry Roderick, Kt., CBE

Moore, Hon. Sir John Cochrane, Kt.

Moore, Maj.-Gen. Sir (John) Jeremy, KCB, OBE, MC

Moore, Sir John Michael, KCVO, CB, DSC

Moore, Vice-Adm. Sir Michael Antony Claës, KBE, LVO

Moore, Prof. Sir Norman Winfrid, Bt. (1919)

Moore, Sir Patrick William Eisdell, Kt., OBE

Moore, Sir William Roger Clotworthy, Bt., TD (1932)

Morauta, Sir Mekere, Kt.

Mordaunt, Sir Richard Nigel Charles, Bt. (1611)

Moreton, Sir John Oscar, KCMG, KCVO, MC

Morgan, Vice-Adm. Sir Charles Christopher, KBE

Morgan, Maj.-Gen. Sir David John Hughes-, Bt., CB, CBE (1925)

Morgan, Sir John Albert Leigh, KCMG

Morison, Hon. Sir Thomas Richard Atkin, Kt.

Morland, Hon. Sir Michael, Kt.

Morland, Sir Robert Kenelm, Kt.

Morpeth, Sir Douglas Spottiswoode, Kt., TD

Morris, Air Marshal Sir Arnold Alec, KBE, CB, FEng.

Morris, Sir (James) Richard (Samuel), Kt., CBE, FEng.

Morris, Sir Keith Elliot Hedley, KBE, CMG

Morris, Prof. Sir Peter John, Kt., FRS

Morris, Sir Robert Byng, Bt. (1806)

Morris, Sir Trefor Alfred, Kt., CBE, QPM

Morris, Very Revd Sir William James, KCVO, ph.D.

Morrison, Hon. Sir Charles Andrew, Kt.

Morrison, Sir Howard Leslie, Kt., OBE

Morritt, Hon. Sir (Robert) Andrew, Kt., CVO

Morrow, Sir Ian Thomas, Kt.

Morse, Sir Christopher Jeremy, KCMG

Morton, Adm. Sir Anthony Storrs, GBE, KCB

Morton, Sir (Robert) Alastair (Newton), Kt.

Moseley, Sir George Walker, KCB

Moser, Prof. Sir Claus Adolf, KCB, CBE, FBA

Moses, Hon. Sir Alan George, Kt.

†Moss, Sir David John Edwards-, Bt. (1868)

Mostyn, Gen. Sir (Joseph) David Frederick, KCB, CBE

†Mostyn, Sir William Basil John, Bt. (1670)

Mott, Sir John Harmer, Bt. (1930)

†Mount, Sir (William Robert) Ferdinand, Bt. (1921)

Mountain, Sir Denis Mortimer, Bt. (1922)

Mowbray, Sir John, Kt.

Mowbray, Sir John Robert, Bt. (1880)

Muir, Sir Laurence Macdonald, Kt.

†Muir, Sir Richard James Kay, Bt. (1892)

Muirhead, Sir David Francis, KCMG, CVO

Mulcahy, Sir Geoffrey John, Kt.

Mullens, Lt.-Gen. Sir Anthony Richard Guy, KCB, OBE

Mummery, Hon. Sir John Frank, Kt.

Munn, Sir James, Kt., OBE

Munro, Sir Alan Gordon, KCMG

Munro, Sir Ian Talbot, Bt. (s. 1634)

†Munro, Sir Keith Gordon, Bt. (1825)

Munro, Sir Sydney Douglas Gun-, GCMG, MBE

Muria, Hon. Sir Gilbert John Baptist, Kt.

Murley, Sir Reginald Sydney, KBE, TD, FRCS

Murphy, Sir Leslie Frederick, Kt.

Murray, Rt. Hon. Sir Donald Bruce, Kt.

Murray, Sir Donald Frederick, KCVO, CMG

Murray, Sir James, KCMG

Murray, Sir John Antony Jerningham, Kt., CBE

Murray, *Prof.* Sir Kenneth, Kt., FRCPath., FRS, FRSE

Murray, Sir Nigel Andrew Digby, Bt. (s. 1628)

Murray, Sir Patrick Ian Keith, Bt. (s. 1673)

†Murray, Sir Rowland William Patrick, Bt. (s. 1630)

Mursell, Sir Peter, Kt., MBE

Musgrave, Sir Christopher Patrick Charles, Bt. (1611)

Musgrave, Sir Richard James, Bt. (I. 1782)

Musson, *Gen.* Sir Geoffrey Randolph Dixon, GCB, CBE, DSO

Myers, Sir Kenneth Ben, Kt., MBE

Myers, Sir Philip Alan, Kt., OBE, QPM

Myers, *Prof.* Sir Rupert Horace, KBE

Mynors, Sir Richard Baskerville, Bt. (1964)

Nabarro, Sir John David Nunes, Kt., MD, FRCP

Naipaul, Sir Vidiadhar Surajprasad, Kt.

Nairn, Sir Michael, Bt. (1904)

Nairn, Sir Robert Arnold Spencer-, Bt. (1933)

Nairne, *Rt. Hon.* Sir Patrick Dalmahoy, GCB, MC

Naish, Sir (Charles) David, Kt.

Nall, Sir Michael Joseph, Bt., RN (1954)

Namaliu, *Rt. Hon.* Sir Rabbie Langanai, Kt., CMG

†Napier, Sir Charles Joseph, Bt. (1867)

Napier, Sir John Archibald Lennox, Bt. (s. 1627)

Napier, Sir Oliver John, Kt.

Nasmith, *Prof.* Sir James Duncan Dunbar-, Kt., CBE, RIBA, FRSE

Neal, Sir Eric James, Kt., CVO

Neal, Sir Leonard Francis, Kt., CBE

Neale, Sir Gerrard Anthony, Kt.

Neave, Sir Paul Arundell, Bt. (1795)

Nedd, *Hon.* Sir Robert Archibald, Kt.

Needham, *Rt. Hon.* Sir Richard (The Earl of Kilmorey, *see* page 142)

Neill, *Rt. Hon.* Sir Brian Thomas, Kt.

Neill, Sir Francis Patrick, Kt., QC

Neill, *Rt. Hon.* Sir Ivan, Kt., PC (NI)

Neill, Sir (James) Hugh, KCVO, CBE, TD

†Nelson, Sir Jamie Charles Vernon Hope, Bt. (1912)

Nelson, *Hon.* Sir Robert Franklyn, Kt.

Nelson, *Air Marshal* Sir (Sidney) Richard (Carlyle), KCB, OBE, MD

Nepean, *Lt.-Col.* Sir Evan Yorke, Bt. (1802)

Neuberger, *Hon.* Sir David Edmond, Kt.

Neubert, Sir Michael John, Kt.

Neville, Sir Roger Albert Gartside, Kt., VRD

New, *Maj.-Gen.* Sir Laurence Anthony Wallis, Kt., CB, CBE

Newall, Sir Paul Henry, Kt., TD

Newington, Sir Michael John, KCMG

Newman, Sir Francis Hugh Cecil, Bt. (1912)

Newman, Sir Geoffrey Robert, Bt. (1836)

Newman, *Hon.* Sir George Michael, Kt.

Newman, Sir Jack, Kt., CBE

Newman, Sir Kenneth Leslie, GBE, QPM

Newman, *Vice-Adm.* Sir Roy Thomas, KCB

Newman, *Col.* Sir Stuart Richard, Kt., CBE, TD

Newns, Sir (Alfred) Foley (Francis Polden), KCMG, CVO

Newsam, Sir Peter Anthony, Kt.

Newton, Sir (Charles) Wilfred, Kt., CBE

Newton, Sir (Harry) Michael (Rex), Bt. (1900)

Newton, Sir Kenneth Garnar, Bt., OBE, TD (1924)

Newton, Sir (Leslie) Gordon, Kt.

Ngata, Sir Henare Kohere, KBE

Nichol, Sir Duncan Kirkbride, Kt., CBE

Nicholas, Sir David, Kt., CBE

Nicholas, Sir John William, KCVO, CMG

Nicholls, *Air Marshal* Sir John Moreton, KCB, CBE, DFC, AFC

Nicholson, Sir Bryan Hubert, Kt.

†Nicholson, Sir Charles Christian, Bt. (1912)

Nicholson, *Hon.* Sir David Eric, Kt.

Nicholson, *Rt. Hon.* Sir Michael, Kt.

Nicholson, Sir Paul Douglas, Kt.

Nicholson, Sir Robin Buchanan, Kt., ph.D., FRS, FEng.

Nicoll, Sir William, KCMG

Nightingale, Sir Charles Manners Gamaliel, Bt. (1628)

Nightingale, Sir John Cyprian, Kt., CBE, BEM, QPM

Nimmo, *Hon.* Sir John Angus, Kt., CBE

Nixon, *Maj.* Sir Cecil Dominic Henry Joseph, Bt., MC (1906)

Nixon, Sir Edwin Ronald, Kt., CBE

Noble, Sir David Brunel, Bt. (1902)

Noble, Sir Iain Andrew, Bt., OBE (1923)

Noble, Sir (Thomas Alexander) Fraser, Kt., MBE

Nombri, Sir Joseph Karl, Kt., ISO, BEM

Norman, Sir Arthur Gordon, KBE, DFC

Norman, Sir Mark Annesley, Bt. (1915)

Norman, Sir Robert Henry, Kt., OBE

Norman, Sir Robert Wentworth, Kt.

Norman, Sir Ronald, Kt., OBE

Norrington, Sir Roger Arthur Carver, Kt., CBE

Norris, *Air Chief Marshal* Sir Christopher Neil Foxley-, GCB, DSO, OBE

Norris, Sir Eric George, KCMG

North, Sir Thomas Lindsay, Kt.

North, Sir (William) Jonathan (Frederick), Bt. (1920)

Norton, *Vice-Adm. Hon.* Sir Nicholas John Hill-, KCB

Norwood, Sir Walter Neville, Kt.

Nossal, Sir Gustav Joseph Victor, Kt., CBE

Nott, *Rt. Hon.* Sir John William Frederic, KCB

Nourse, *Rt. Hon.* Sir Martin Charles, Kt.

Nugent, Sir John Edwin Lavallin, Bt. (I. 1795)

Nugent, *Maj.* Sir Peter Walter James, Bt. (1831)

Nugent, Sir Robin George Colborne, Bt. (1806)

Nursaw, Sir James, KCB, QC

Nuttall, Sir Nicholas Keith Lillington, Bt. (1922)

Nutting, *Rt. Hon.* Sir (Harold) Anthony, Bt. (1903)

Oakeley, Sir John Digby Atholl, Bt. (1790)

Oakes, Sir Christopher, Bt. (1939)

Oakshott, Hon. Sir Anthony Hendrie, Bt. (1959)

Oates, Sir Thomas, Kt., CMG, OBE

Obolensky, *Prof.* Sir Dimitri, Kt.

O'Brien, Sir Frederick William Fitzgerald, Kt.

O'Brien, Sir Richard, Kt., DSO, MC

O'Brien, Sir Timothy John, Bt. (1849)

O'Brien, *Adm.* Sir William Donough, KCB, DSC

O'Connell, Sir Maurice James Donagh MacCarthy, Bt. (1869)

O'Connor, *Rt. Hon.* Sir Patrick McCarthy, Kt.

O'Dea, Sir Patrick Jerad, KCVO

Odell, Sir Stanley John, Kt.

Odgers, Sir Graeme David William, Kt.

Ogden, Sir (Edward) Michael, Kt., QC

Ogilvie, Sir Alec Drummond, Kt.

Ogilvy, *Rt. Hon.* Sir Angus James Bruce, KCVO

Ogilvy, Sir Francis Gilbert Arthur, Bt. (s. 1626)

Ognall, *Hon.* Sir Harry Henry, Kt.

Ohlson, Sir Brian Eric Christopher, Bt. (1920)

Okeover, *Capt.* Sir Peter Ralph Leopold Walker-, Bt. (1886)

Olewale, *Hon.* Sir Niwia Ebia, Kt.

Oliphant, Sir Mark (Marcus Laurence Elwin), KBE, FRS

O'Loghlen, Sir Colman Michael, Bt. (1838)

Olver, Sir Stephen John Linley, KBE, CMG

O'Neil, *Hon.* Sir Desmond Henry, Kt.

Ongley, *Hon.* Sir Joseph Augustine, Kt.

Onslow, *Rt. Hon.* Sir Cranley Gordon Douglas, KCMG

Onslow, Sir John Roger Wilmot, Bt. (1797)

Oppenheim, Sir Alexander, Kt., OBE, D.SC., FRSE

Oppenheim, Sir Duncan Morris, Kt.

Oppenheimer, Sir Michael Bernard Grenville, Bt. (1921)

Orde, Sir John Alexander Campbell-, Bt. (1790)

O'Regan, *Dr* Sir Stephen Gerard (Tipene), Kt.

Orlebar, Sir Michael Keith Orlebar Simpson-, KCMG

Orr, Sir David Alexander, Kt., MC

Osborn, Sir John Holbrook, Kt.

Osborn, Sir Richard Henry Danvers, Bt. (1662)

Osborne, Sir Peter George, Bt. (I. 1629)

Osifelo, Sir Frederick Aubarua, Kt., MBE

Osmond, Sir Douglas, Kt., CBE

Osmond, Sir (Stanley) Paul, Kt., CB

O'Sullevan, Sir Peter John, Kt., CBE

Oswald, *Admiral of the Fleet* Sir (John) Julian Robertson, GCB

Otton, Sir Geoffrey John, KCB

Otton, *Rt. Hon.* Sir Philip Howard, Kt.

Oulton, Sir Antony Derek Maxwell, GCB, QC

Ouseley, Sir Herman George, Kt.

Outram, Sir Alan James, Bt. (1858)

Overall, Sir John Wallace, Kt., CBE, MC

Owen, Sir Geoffrey, Kt.

Owen, Sir Hugh Bernard Pilkington, Bt. (1813)

Owen, Sir Hugo Dudley Cunliffe-, Bt. (1920)

Owen, *Hon.* Sir John Arthur Dalziel, Kt.

Owo, The Olowo of, Kt.

Oxburgh, *Prof.* Sir Ernest Ronald, KBE, Ph.D., FRS

Oxford, Sir Kenneth Gordon, Kt., CBE, QPM

Packard, *Lt.-Gen.* Sir (Charles) Douglas, KBE, CB, DSO

Page, Sir (Arthur) John, Kt

Page, Sir Frederick William, Kt., CBE, FEng.

Page, Sir John Joseph Joffre, Kt., OBE

Paget, Sir Julian Tolver, Bt., CVO (1871)

Paget, Sir Richard Herbert, Bt. (1886)

Pain, *Lt.-Gen.* Sir (Horace) Rollo (Squarey), KCB, MC

Pain, *Hon.* Sir Peter Richard, Kt.

Paine, Sir Christopher Hammon, Kt., FRCP, FRCR

Palin, *Air Chief Marshal* Sir Roger Hewlett, KCB, OBE

Palmar, Sir Derek James, Kt.

Palmer, Sir (Charles) Mark, Bt. (1886)

Palmer, *Gen.* Sir (Charles) Patrick (Ralph), KBE

Palmer, Sir Geoffrey Christopher John, Bt. (1660)

Palmer, *Rt. Hon.* Sir Geoffrey Winston Russell, KCMG

Palmer, Sir John Chance, Kt.

Palmer, Sir John Edward Somerset, Bt. (1791)

Palmer, *Maj.-Gen.* Sir (Joseph) Michael, KCVO

Palmer, Sir Reginald Oswald, GCMG, MBE

Pantlin, Sir Dick Hurst, Kt., CBE

Paolozzi, Sir Eduardo Luigi, Kt., CBE, RA

Parbo, Sir Arvi Hillar, Kt.

Parish, Sir David Elmer Woodbine, Kt., CBE

Park, *Hon.* Sir Hugh Eames, Kt.

Parker, Sir (Arthur) Douglas Dodds-, Kt.

Parker, Sir Eric Wilson, Kt.

Parker, *Hon.* Sir Jonathan Frederic, Kt.

Parker, Sir Peter, KBE, LVO

Parker, Sir Richard (William) Hyde, Bt. (1681)

Parker, *Rt. Hon.* Sir Roger Jocelyn, Kt.

Parker, *Vice-Adm.* Sir (Wilfred) John, KBE, CB, DSC

Parker, Sir William Peter Brian, Bt. (1844)

Parkes, Sir Edward Walter, Kt., FEng.

Parkinson, Sir Nicholas Fancourt, Kt.

Parsons, Sir (John) Michael, Kt.

Parsons, Sir Richard Edmund (Clement Fownes), KCMG

Partridge, Sir Michael John Anthony, KCB

Pascoe, *Gen.* Sir Robert Alan, KCB, MBE

Pasley, Sir John Malcolm Sabine, Bt. (1794)

Patel, *Prof.* Sir Narendra Babubhai, Kt.

Paterson, Sir Dennis Craig, Kt.

Paterson, Sir John Valentine Jardine, Kt.

Patnick, Sir (Cyril) Irvine, Kt., OBE

Paton, Sir (Thomas) Angus (Lyall), Kt., CMG, FRS, FEng.

Pattie, *Rt. Hon.* Sir Geoffrey Edwin, Kt.

Pattinson, Sir (William) Derek, Kt.

Pattullo, Sir (David) Bruce, Kt., CBE

Paul, Sir John Warburton, GCMG, OBE, MC

Paul, *Air Marshal* Sir Ronald Ian Stuart-, KBE

Payne, Sir Norman John, Kt., CBE, FEng.

Peach, Sir Leonard Harry, Kt.

Peacock, *Prof.* Sir Alan Turner, Kt., DSC

Pearce, Sir Austin William, Kt., CBE, Ph.D., FEng.

Pearce, Sir (Daniel Norton) Idris, Kt., CBE, TD

Pearce, Sir Eric Herbert, Kt., OBE

Pearse, Sir Brian Gerald, Kt.

Pearson, Sir Francis Nicholas Fraser, Bt. (1964)

Pearson, *Gen.* Sir Thomas Cecil Hook, KCB, CBE, DSO

Peart, *Prof.* Sir William Stanley, Kt., MD, FRS

Pease, Sir (Alfred) Vincent, Bt. (1882)

Pease, Sir Richard Thorn, Bt. (1920)

Peat, Sir Gerrard Charles, KCVO

Peck, Sir Edward Heywood, GCMG

Peckham, *Prof.* Sir Michael John, Kt., FRCP, FRCPGlas., FRCR, FRCPath.

Pedder, *Air Marshal* Sir Ian Maurice, KCB, OBE, DFC

†Peek, Sir William Grenville, Bt. (1874)

Peek, *Vice-Adm.* Sir Richard Innes, KBE, CB, DSC

Peel, Sir John Harold, KCVO

Peel, Sir (William) John, Kt.

Peirse, Sir Henry Grant de la Poer Beresford-, Bt. (1814)

Peirse, *Air Vice-Marshal* Sir Richard Charles Fairfax, KCVO, CB

Pelgen, Sir Harry Friedrich, Kt., MBE

Pelly, Sir Richard John, Bt. (1840)

Pemberton, Sir Francis Wingate William, Kt., CBE

Penrose, *Prof.* Sir Roger, Kt., FRS

Percival, *Rt. Hon.* Sir (Walter) Ian, Kt., QC

Pereira, Sir (Herbert) Charles, Kt., D.SC., FRS

Perring, Sir Ralph Edgar, Bt. (1963)

Perris, Sir David (Arthur), Kt., MBE

Perry, Sir David Howard, KCB

Perry, Sir (David) Norman, Kt., MBE

Perry, Sir Michael Sydney, Kt., CBE

Pestell, Sir John Richard, KCVO

Peterkin, Sir Neville, Kt.

Peters, *Prof.* Sir David Keith, Kt., FRCP

Petersen, Sir Jeffrey Charles, KCMG

Petersen, Sir Johannes Bjelke-, KCMG

Peterson, Sir Christopher Matthew, Kt., CBE, TD

Petit, Sir Dinshaw Manockjee, Bt. (1890)

Peto, Sir Henry George Morton, Bt. (1855)

Peto, Sir Michael Henry Basil, Bt. (1927)

Petrie, Sir Peter Charles, Bt., CMG (1918)

Pettigrew, Sir Russell Hilton, Kt.

Pettit, Sir Daniel Eric Arthur, Kt.

Philips, *Prof.* Sir Cyril Henry, Kt.

Phillips, Sir Fred Albert, Kt., CVO

Phillips, Sir Henry Ellis Isidore, Kt., CMG, MBE

Phillips, Sir Horace, KCMG

Phillips, *Hon.* Sir Nicholas Addison, Kt.

Phillips, Sir Peter John, Kt., OBE

Phillips, Sir Robin Francis, Bt. (1912)

Pickard, Sir (John) Michael, Kt.

Pickering, Sir Edward Davies, Kt.

Pickthorn, Sir James Francis Mann,
Bt. (1959)
Pidgeon, Sir John Allan Stewart, Kt.
†Piers, Sir James Desmond, Bt. (I.
1661)
Pigot, Sir George Hugh, Bt. (1764)
Pigott, Sir Berkeley Henry
Sebastian, Bt. (1808)
Pike, Sir Michael Edmund, KCVO,
CMG
Pike, Sir Philip Ernest Housden, Kt.,
QC
Pilditch, Sir Richard Edward, Bt.
(1929)
Pile, Sir Frederick Devereux, Bt., MC
(1900)
Pilkington, Sir Antony Richard, Kt.
Pilkington, Sir Thomas Henry
Milborne-Swinnerton-, Bt.
(s. 1635)
Pill, Rt. Hon. Sir Malcolm Thomas,
Kt.
Pillar, Adm. Sir William Thomas,
GBE, KCB
Pindling, Rt. Hon. Sir Lynden Oscar,
KCMG
Pinker, Sir George Douglas, KCVO
Pinsent, Sir Christopher Roy, Bt.
(1938)
Pippard, Prof. Sir (Alfred) Brian, Kt.,
FRS
Pirie, Gp Capt Sir Gordon Hamish,
Kt., CVO, CBE
Pitakaka, Sir Moses Puibangara,
GCMG
Pitcher, Sir Desmond Henry, Kt.
Pitman, Sir Brian Ivor, Kt.
Pitoi, Sir Sere, Kt., CBE
Pitt, Sir Harry Raymond, Kt., PH.D.,
FRS
Pitts, Sir Cyril Alfred, Kt.
Plastow, Sir David Arnold Stuart, Kt.
†Platt, Sir (Frank) Lindsey, Bt. (1958)
Platt, Sir Harold Grant, Kt.
Platt, Prof. Hon. Sir Peter, Bt. (1959)
Playfair, Sir Edward Wilder, KCB
Pliatzky, Sir Leo, KCB
Plowman, Hon. Sir John Robin, Kt.,
CBE
Plumb, Prof. Sir John Harold, Kt.
Pohai, Sir Timothy, Kt., MBE
Pole, Sir (John) Richard (Walter
Reginald) Carew, Bt. (1628)
Pole, Sir Peter Van Notten, Bt.
(1791)
Polkinghorne, Revd Canon John
Charlton, KBE, FRS
Pollen, Sir John Michael
Hungerford, Bt. (1795)
Pollock, Sir George Frederick, Bt.
(1866)
Pollock, Sir Giles Hampden
Montagu-, Bt. (1872)
Pollock, Admiral of the Fleet Sir
Michael Patrick, GCB, LVO, DSC
Ponsonby, Sir Ashley Charles Gibbs,
Bt., KCVO, MC (1956)
Pontin, Sir Frederick William, Kt.
Poole, Hon. Sir David Anthony, Kt.

Poore, Sir Herbert Edward, Bt.
(1795)
Pope, Vice-Adm. Sir (John) Ernle,
KCB
Pope, Sir Joseph Albert, Kt., D.SC.,
PH.D.
Popplewell, Hon. Sir Oliver Bury, Kt.
†Porritt, Sir Jonathon Espie, Bt.
(1963)
Portal, Sir Jonathan Francis, Bt.
(1901)
Porter, Sir John Simon Horsbrugh-,
Bt. (1902)
Porter, Sir Leslie, Kt.
Porter, Air Marshal Sir (Melvin)
Kenneth (Drowley), KCB, CBE
Porter, Rt. Hon. Sir Robert Wilson,
Kt., PC (NI), QC
Posnett, Sir Richard Neil, KBE, CMG
Potter, Rt. Hon. Sir Mark Howard, Kt.
Potter, Maj.-Gen. Sir (Wilfrid) John,
KBE, CB
Potts, Hon. Sir Francis Humphrey,
Kt.
Pound, Sir John David, Bt. (1905)
Pountain, Sir Eric John, Kt.
Powell, Sir (Arnold Joseph) Philip,
Kt., CH, OBE, RA, FRIBA
Powell, Sir Charles David, KCMG
Powell, Sir Nicholas Folliott
Douglas, Bt. (1897)
Powell, Sir Raymond, Kt., MP
Powell, Sir Richard Royle, GCB, KBE,
CMG
Power, Sir Alastair John Cecil, Bt.
(1924)
Prance, Prof. Sir Ghillean Tolmie,
Kt., FRS
Prendergast, Sir (Walter) Kieran,
KCVO, CMG
Prentice, Hon. Sir William Thomas,
Kt., MBE
Prescott, Sir Mark, Bt. (1938)
Preston, Sir Ronald Douglas
Hildebrand, Bt. (1815)
Prevost, Sir Christopher Gerald, Bt.
(1805)
Price, Sir Charles Keith Napier
Rugge-, Bt. (1804)
Price, Sir David Ernest Campbell,
Kt.
Price, Sir Francis Caradoc Rose, Bt.
(1815)
Price, Sir Frank Leslie, Kt.
Price, Sir (James) Robert, KBE
Price, Sir Leslie Victor, Kt., OBE
Price, Sir Norman Charles, KCB
Price, Sir Robert John Green-, Bt.
(1874)
Prickett, Air Chief Marshal Sir
Thomas Other, KCB, DSO, DFC
Prideaux, Sir Humphrey Povah
Treverbian, Kt., OBE
†Primrose, Sir John Ure, Bt. (1903)
Pringle, Air Marshal Sir Charles
Norman Seton, KBE, FEng.
Pringle, Hon. Sir John Kenneth, Kt.
Pringle, Lt.-Gen. Sir Steuart (Robert),
Bt., KCB, RM (s. 1683)
Pritchard, Sir Neil, KCMG

Proby, Sir Peter, Bt. (1952)
Prosser, Sir Ian Maurice Gray, Kt.
Proud, Sir John Seymour, Kt.
Pryke, Sir David Dudley, Bt. (1926)
Pugh, Sir Idwal Vaughan, KCB
Pugsley, Prof. Sir Alfred Grenvile,
Kt., OBE, D.SC., FRS, FEng.
Pullinger, Sir (Francis) Alan, Kt., CBE
Pumphrey, Sir (John) Laurence,
KCMG
Purchas, Rt. Hon. Sir Francis Brooks,
Kt.
Purves, Sir William, Kt., CBE, DSO
Purvis, Vice-Adm. Sir Neville, KCB
Puttnam, Sir David Terrance, Kt.,
CBE
Quicke, Sir John Godolphin, Kt., CBE
Quigley, Sir (William) George
(Henry), Kt., CB, PH.D.
Quilliam, Hon. Sir (James) Peter, Kt.
Quilter, Sir Anthony Raymond
Leopold Cuthbert, Bt. (1897)
Quinlan, Sir Michael Edward, GCB
Quinton, Sir James Grand, Kt.
Radcliffe, Sir Sebastian Everard, Bt.
(1813)
Radzinowicz, Prof. Sir Leon, Kt., LLD
Rae, Hon. Sir Wallace Alexander
Ramsay, Kt.
Raeburn, Sir Michael Edward
Norman, Bt. (1923)
Raeburn, Maj.-Gen. Sir (William)
Digby (Manifold), KCVO, CB, DSO,
MBE
Raffray, Sir Piat Joseph Raymond
Andre, Kt.
Raikes, Vice-Adm. Sir Iwan Geoffrey,
KCB, CBE, DSC
Raison, Rt. Hon. Sir Timothy Hugh
Francis, Kt.
Ralli, Sir Godfrey Victor, Bt., TD
(1912)
Ramdanee, Sir Mookteswar
Baboolall Kailash, Kt.
Ramphal, Sir Shridath Surendranath,
GCMG
Ramphul, Sir Baalkhristna, Kt.
Ramphul, Sir Indurduth, Kt.
Ramsay, Sir Alexander William
Burnett, Bt. (1806)
Ramsay, Sir Allan John (Hepple),
KBE, CMG
Ramsbotham, Gen. Sir David John,
GCB, CBE
Ramsbotham, Hon. Sir Peter Edward,
GCMG, GCVO
Ramsden, Sir John Charles Josslyn,
Bt. (1689)
Ramsey, Sir Alfred Ernest, Kt.
Randle, Prof. Sir Philip John, Kt.
Ranger, Sir Douglas, Kt., FRCS
Rank, Sir Benjamin Keith, Kt., CMG
Rankin, Sir Alick Michael, Kt., CBE
Rankin, Sir Ian Niall, Bt. (1898)
Rasch, Sir Simon Anthony Carne, Bt.
(1903)
Rashleigh, Sir Richard Harry, Bt.
(1831)
Ratford, Sir David John Edward,
KCMG, CVO

Rattee, *Hon.* Sir Donald Keith, Kt.

Rattle, Sir Simon Dennis, Kt., CBE

Rault, Sir Louis Joseph Maurice, Kt.

Rawlins, *Surgeon Vice-Adm.* Sir John Stuart Pepys, KBE

Rawlinson, Sir Anthony Henry John, Bt. (1891)

Read, *Air Marshal* Sir Charles Frederick, KBE, CB, DFC, AFC

Read, *Gen.* Sir (John) Antony (Jervis), GCB, CBE, DSO, MC

Read, Sir John Emms, Kt.

†Reade, Sir Kenneth Ray, Bt. (1661)

Reay, *Lt.-Gen.* Sir (Hubert) Alan John, KBE

Redgrave, *Maj.-Gen.* Sir Roy Michael Frederick, KBE, MC

Redmayne, Sir Nicholas, Bt. (1964)

Redmond, Sir James, Kt., FEng.

Redwood, Sir Peter Boverton, Bt. (1911)

Reece, Sir Charles Hugh, Kt.

Reece, Sir James Gordon, Kt.

Reed, *Hon.* Sir Nigel Vernon, Kt., CBE

Rees, Sir (Charles William) Stanley, Kt., TD

Rees, Sir David Allan, Kt., ph.D., D.SC., FRS

Rees, *Prof.* Sir Martin John, Kt., FRS

Reeve, Sir Anthony, KCMG, KCVO

Reeves, *Most Revd* Paul Alfred, GCMG, GCVO

Reffell, *Adm.* Sir Derek Roy, KCB

Refshauge, *Maj.-Gen.* Sir William Dudley, Kt., CBE

Reid, Sir Alexander James, Bt. (1897)

Reid, Sir (Harold) Martin (Smith), KBE, CMG

Reid, Sir Hugh, Bt. (1922)

Reid, Sir Norman Robert, Kt.

Reid, Sir Robert Paul, Kt.

Reid, Sir William Kennedy, KCB

Reiher, Sir Frederick Bernard Carl, KBE, CMG

Reilly, Sir (D'Arcy) Patrick, GCMG, OBE

Reilly, *Lt.-Gen.* Sir Jeremy Calcott, KCB, DSO

Renals, Sir Stanley, Bt. (1895)

Rennie, Sir John Shaw, GCMG, OBE

Renouf, Sir Clement William Bailey, Kt.

Renouf, Sir Francis Henry, Kt.

Renshaw, Sir (Charles) Maurice Bine, Bt. (1903)

Renwick, Sir Richard Eustace, Bt. (1921)

Renwick, Sir Robin William, KCMG

Reporter, Sir Shapoor Ardeshirji, KBE

Reynolds, Sir David James, Bt. (1923)

Reynolds, Sir Peter William John, Kt., CBE

Rhodes, Sir Basil Edward, Kt., CBE, TD

Rhodes, Sir John Christopher Douglas, Bt. (1919)

Rhodes, Sir Peregrine Alexander, KCMG

Rice, *Maj.-Gen.* Sir Desmond Hind Garrett, KCVO, CBE

Rice, Sir Timothy Miles Bindon, Kt.

Richard, Sir Cliff, Kt., OBE

Richards, Sir Brian Mansel, Kt., CBE, ph.D.

Richards, Sir (Francis) Brooks, KCMG, DSC

Richards, *Lt.-Gen.* Sir John Charles Chisholm, KCB, KCVO, RM

Richards, Sir Rex Edward, Kt., D.SC., FRS

Richardson, Sir Anthony Lewis, Bt. (1924)

Richardson, *Rt. Hon.* Sir Ivor Lloyd Morgan, Kt.

Richardson, Sir (John) Eric, Kt., CBE

Richardson, Sir Michael John de Rougemont, Kt.

Richardson, *Lt.-Gen.* Sir Robert Francis, KCB, CVO, OBE

Richardson, Sir Simon Alaisdair Stewart-, Bt. (s. 1630)

Riches, Sir Derek Martin Hurry, KCMG

Richmond, *Rt. Hon.* Sir Clifford Parris, KBE

Richmond, Sir John Frederick, Bt. (1929)

Richmond, *Prof.* Sir Mark Henry, Kt., FRS

Ricketts, Sir Robert Cornwallis Gerald St Leger, Bt. (1828)

Riddell, Sir John Charles Buchanan, Bt., CVO (s. 1628)

Ridley, Sir Adam (Nicholas), Kt.

Ridsdale, Sir Julian Errington, Kt., CBE

Rifkind, *Rt. Hon.* Sir Malcolm Leslie, KCMG, QC

Rigby, *Lt.-Col.* Sir (Hugh) John (Macbeth), Bt. (1929)

Riley, Sir Ralph, Kt., FRS

Rimer, *Hon.* Sir Colin Percy Farquharson, Kt.

Ringadoo, *Hon.* Sir Veerasamy, GCMG

Ripley, Sir Hugh, Bt. (1880)

Risk, Sir Thomas Neilson, Kt.

Ritako, Sir Thomas Baha, Kt., MBE

Rix, *Hon.* Sir Bernard Anthony, Kt.

Rix, Sir John, Kt., MBE, FEng.

Roberts, *Hon.* Sir Denys Tudor Emil, KBE, QC

Roberts, Sir Derek Harry, Kt., CBE, FRS, FEng.

Roberts, Sir (Edward Fergus) Sidney, Kt., CBE

Roberts, Sir Frank Kenyon, GCMG, GCVO

Roberts, *Prof.* Sir Gareth Gwyn, Kt., FRS

Roberts, Sir Gilbert Howland Rookehurst, Bt. (1809)

Roberts, Sir Gordon James, Kt., CBE

Roberts, *Rt. Hon.* Sir (Ieuan) Wyn Pritchard, Kt.

Roberts, Sir Samuel, Bt (1919)

Roberts, Sir Stephen James Leake, Kt.

Roberts, Sir William James Denby, Bt. (1909)

Robertson, Sir John Fraser, KCMG, CBE

Robertson, Sir Lewis, Kt., CBE, FRSE

Robertson, *Prof.* Sir Rutherford Ness, Kt., CMG

Robins, Sir Ralph Harry, Kt., FEng.

Robinson, Sir Albert Edward Phineas, Kt.

†Robinson, Sir Christopher Philipse, Bt. (1854)

†Robinson, Sir Dominick Christopher Lynch-, Bt. (1920)

Robinson, Sir John James Michael Laud, Bt. (1660)

Robinson, Sir Wilfred Henry Frederick, Bt. (1908)

Robotham, *Hon.* Sir Lascelles Lister, Kt.

Robson, *Prof.* Sir James Gordon, Kt., CBE

Robson, Sir John Adam, KCMG

Roch, *Rt. Hon.* Sir John Ormond, Kt.

Roche, Sir David O'Grady, Bt. (1838)

†Rodgers, Sir (Andrew) Piers (Wingate), Bt. (1964)

Rodrigues, Sir Alberto Maria, Kt., CBE, ED

Roe, *Air Chief Marshal* Sir Rex David, GCB, AFC

Rogers, Sir Frank Jarvis, Kt.

Rogers, *Air Chief Marshal* Sir John Robson, Kt.

Roll, *Revd* Sir James William Cecil, Bt. (1921)

Rooke, Sir Denis Eric, Kt., CBE, FRS, FEng.

Ropner, Sir John Bruce Woollacott, Bt. (1952)

Ropner, Sir Robert Douglas, Bt. (1904)

Roscoe, Sir Robert Bell, KBE

Rose, *Rt. Hon.* Sir Christopher Dudley Roger, Kt.

Rose, Sir Clive Martin, GCMG

Rose, Sir David Lancaster, Bt. (1874)

Rose, *Gen.* Sir (Hugh) Michael, KCB, CBE, DSO, QGM

Rose, Sir Julian Day, Bt. (1872 and 1909)

Rosier, *Air Chief Marshal* Sir Frederick Ernest, GCB, CBE, DSO

Ross, Sir (James) Keith, Bt., RD, FRCS (1960)

Ross, *Lt.-Gen.* Sir Robert Jeremy, KCB, OBE

Rosser, Sir Melvyn Wynne, Kt.

Rossi, Sir Hugh Alexis Louis, Kt.

Roth, *Prof.* Sir Martin, Kt., MD, FRCP

Rothschild, Sir Evelyn Robert Adrian de, Kt.

Rougier, *Hon.* Sir Richard George, Kt.

Rous, *Lt.-Gen.* Hon. Sir William Edward, KCB, OBE

Rowell, Sir John Joseph, Kt., CBE

Rowland, *Air Marshal* Sir James Anthony, KBE, DFC, AFC

Rowland, Sir (John) David, Kt.

Rowlands, *Air Marshal* Sir John Samuel, GC, KBE

Rowley, Sir Charles Robert, Bt. (1836) †(1786)

Roxburgh, *Vice-Adm.* Sir John Charles Young, KCB, CBE, DSO, DSC

Royden, Sir Christopher John, Bt. (1905)

Rudd, Sir (Anthony) Nigel (Russell), Kt.

Rumbold, Sir Henry John Sebastian, Bt. (1779)

Rumbold, Sir Jack Seddon, Kt.

Runchorelal, Sir (Udayan) Chinubhai Madhowlal, Bt. (1913)

Runciman, *Hon.* Sir James Cochran Stevenson (Sir Steven), Kt., CH

Rusby, *Vice-Adm.* Sir Cameron, KCB, LVO

†Russell, Sir (Arthur) Mervyn, Bt. (1812)

Russell, Sir Charles Ian, Bt. (1916)

Russell, *Hon.* Sir David Sturrock West-, Kt.

Russell, Sir George, Kt., CBE

Russell, *Prof.* Sir Peter Edward Lionel, Kt., D.L.itt., FBA

Russell, Sir (Robert) Mark, KCMG

Russell, Sir Spencer Thomas, Kt.

Russell, *Rt. Hon.* Sir (Thomas) Patrick, Kt.

Rutter, Sir Frank William Eden, KBE

Rutter, *Prof.* Sir Michael Llewellyn, Kt., CBE, MD, FRS

Ryan, Sir Derek Gerald, Bt. (1919)

Rycroft, Sir Richard Newton, Bt. (1784)

Ryrie, Sir William Sinclair, KCB

Sabola, *Hon.* Sir Joaquim Claudino Gonsalves-, Kt.

Sachs, *Hon.* Sir Michael Alexander Geddes, Kt.

Sainsbury, Sir Robert James, Kt.

Sainsbury, *Rt. Hon.* Sir Timothy Alan Davan, Kt.

St Aubyn, Sir (John) Arscott Molesworth-, Bt. (1689)

St George, Sir George Bligh, Bt. (I. 1766)

St Johnston, Sir Kerry, Kt.

Sainty, Sir John Christopher, KCB

Sakzewski, Sir Albert, Kt.

Salt, Sir Patrick MacDonnell, Bt. (1869)

Salt, Sir (Thomas) Michael John, Bt. (1899)

Sampson, Sir Colin, Kt., CBE, QPM

Samuel, Sir John Michael Glen, Bt. (1898)

Samuelson, Sir (Bernard) Michael (Francis), Bt. (1884)

Samuelson, Sir Sydney Wylie, Kt., CBE

Sandberg, Sir Michael Graham Ruddock, Kt., CBE

Sanders, Sir John Reynolds Mayhew-, Kt.

Sanders, Sir Robert Tait, KBE, CMG

Sanderson, Sir Frank Linton, Bt. (1920)

Sarei, Sir Alexis Holyweek, Kt., CBE

Sarell, Sir Roderick Francis Gisbert, KCMG, KCVO

Sargant, Sir (Henry) Edmund, Kt.

Saunders, *Hon.* Sir John Anthony Holt, Kt., CBE, DSO, MC

Saunders, Sir Peter, Kt.

Sauzier, Sir (André) Guy, Kt., CBE, ED

Savage, Sir Ernest Walter, Kt.

Savile, Sir James Wilson Vincent, Kt., OBE

Say, *Rt. Revd* Richard David, KCVO

Schiemann, *Rt. Hon.* Sir Konrad Hermann Theodor, Kt.

Scholey, Sir David Gerald, Kt., CBE

Scholey, Sir Robert, Kt., CBE, FEng.

Scholtens, Sir James Henry, KCVO

Schubert, Sir Sydney, Kt.

Scipio, Sir Hudson Rupert, Kt.

Scoon, Sir Paul, GCMG, GCVO, OBE

Scott, Sir Anthony Percy, Bt. (1913)

Scott, Sir (Charles) Peter, KBE, CMG

Scott, Sir David Aubrey, GCMG

Scott, Sir Dominic James Maxwell-, Bt. (1642)

Scott, Sir Ian Dixon, KCMG, KCVO, CIE

Scott, Sir James Jervoise, Bt. (1962)

Scott, Sir Kenneth Bertram Adam, KCVO, CMG

Scott, Sir Michael, KCVO, CMG

Scott, *Rt. Hon.* Sir Nicholas Paul, KBE

Scott, Sir Oliver Christopher Anderson, Bt. (1909)

Scott, *Prof.* Sir Philip John, KBE

Scott, *Rt. Hon.* Sir Richard Rashleigh Folliott, Kt.

Scott, Sir Robert David Hillyer, Kt.

Scott, Sir Walter John, Bt. (1907)

Scott, *Rear-Adm.* Sir (William) David (Stewart), KBE, CB

Scowen, Sir Eric Frank, Kt., MD, D.SC., LLD, FRCP, FRCS

Scrivenor, Sir Thomas Vaisey, Kt., CMG

Seale, Sir John Henry, Bt. (1838)

Seaman, Sir Keith Douglas, KCVO, OBE

Sebastian, Sir Cuthbert Montraville, GCMG, OBE

†Sebright, Sir Peter Giles Vivian, Bt. (1626)

Seccombe, Sir (William) Vernon Stephen, Kt.

Secombe, Sir Harry Donald, Kt., CBE

Seconde, Sir Reginald Louis, KCMG, CVO

Sedley, *Hon.* Sir Stephen John, Kt.

Seely, Sir Nigel Edward, Bt. (1896)

Seeto, Sir Ling James, Kt., MBE

Seeyave, Sir Rene Sow Choung, Kt., CBE

Seligman, Sir Peter Wendel, Kt., CBE

Sergeant, Sir Patrick, Kt.

Series, Sir (Joseph Michel) Emile, Kt., CBE

Serpell, Sir David Radford, KCB, CMG, OBE

Seton, Sir Iain Bruce, Bt. (s. 1663)

†Seton, Sir James Christall, Bt. (s. 1683)

Severne, *Air Vice-Marshal* Sir John de Milt, KCVO, OBE, AFC

Seymour, *Cdr.* Sir Michael Culme-, Bt., RN (1809)

Shakerley, Sir Geoffrey Adam, Bt. (1838)

†Shakespeare, Sir Thomas William, Bt. (1942)

Shapland, Sir William Arthur, Kt.

Sharp, Sir Adrian, Bt. (1922)

Sharp, Sir George, Kt., OBE

Sharp, Sir Kenneth Johnston, Kt., TD

Sharp, Sir Leslie, Kt., QPM

Sharp, Sir Richard Lyall, KCVO, CB

†Sharp, Sir Samuel Christopher Reginald, Bt. (1920)

Sharpe, *Hon.* Sir John Henry, Kt., CBE

Sharples, Sir James, Kt., QPM

Shattock, Sir Gordon, Kt.

Shaw, Sir Brian Piers, Kt.

Shaw, Sir (Charles) Barry, Kt., CB, QC

Shaw, Sir (George) Neville Bowan-, Kt.

Shaw, *Prof.* Sir John Calman, Kt., CBE, FRSE

Shaw, Sir (John) Giles (Dunkerley), Kt.

Shaw, Sir John Michael Robert Best-, Bt. (1665)

Shaw, Sir Neil McGowan, Kt.

Shaw, Sir Robert, Bt. (1821)

Shaw, Sir Roy, Kt.

Shaw, Sir Run Run, Kt., CBE

Sheehy, Sir Patrick, Kt.

Sheen, *Hon.* Sir Barry Cross, Kt.

Sheffield, Sir Reginald Adrian Berkeley, Bt. (1755)

Shehadie, Sir Nicholas Michael, Kt., AO

Sheil, *Hon.* Sir John, Kt.

Sheldon, *Hon.* Sir (John) Gervase (Kensington), Kt.

Shelley, Sir John Richard, Bt. (1611)

Shelton, Sir William Jeremy Masefield, Kt.

Shepheard, Sir Peter Faulkner, Kt., CBE

Shepherd, Sir Colin Ryley, Kt.

Shepperd, Sir Alfred Joseph, Kt.

Sherlock, Sir Philip Manderson, KBE

Sherman, Sir Alfred, Kt.

Sherman, Sir Louis, Kt., OBE

Shields, Sir Neil Stanley, Kt., MC

Shields, *Prof.* Sir Robert, Kt., MD

Shiffner, Sir Henry David, Bt. (1818)

Shillington, Sir (Robert Edward) Graham, Kt., CBE

Shinwell, Sir (Maurice) Adrian, Kt.

Shock, Sir Maurice, Kt.

Short, Sir Apenera Pera, KBE

Short, *Brig.* Sir Noel Edward Vivian, Kt., MBE, MC

Shuckburgh, Sir Rupert Charles Gerald, Bt. (1660)

Siaguru, Sir Anthony Michael, KBE

Siddall, Sir Norman, Kt., CBE, FEng.
Sidey, *Air Marshal* Sir Ernest Shaw, KBE, CB, MD
Sie, Sir Banja Tejan-, GCMG
Simeon, Sir John Edmund Barrington, Bt. (1815)
Simmons, *Air Marshal* Sir Michael George, KCB, AFC
Simmons, Sir Stanley Clifford, Kt., FRCS, FRCOG
Simon, Sir David Alec Gwyn, Kt., CBE
Simonet, Sir Louis Marcel Pierre, Kt., CBE
Simpson, *Hon.* Sir Alfred Henry, Kt.
Simpson, Sir William James, Kt.
Sims, Sir Roger Edward, Kt.
Sinclair, Sir Clive Marles, Kt.
Sinclair, Sir George Evelyn, Kt., CMG, OBE
Sinclair, Sir Ian McTaggart, KCMG, QC
Sinclair, *Air Vice-Marshal* Sir Laurence Frank, GC, KCB, CBE, DSO
Sinclair, Sir Patrick Robert Richard, Bt. (s. 1704)
Sinclair, Sir Ronald Ormiston, KBE
Sinden, Sir Donald Alfred, Kt., CBE
Singer, *Prof.* Sir Hans Wolfgang, Kt.
Singer, *Hon.* Sir Jan Peter, Kt.
Singh, *Hon.* Sir Vijay Raghubir, Kt.
Sitwell, Sir (Sacheverell) Reresby, Bt. (1808)
Skeet, Sir Trevor Herbert Harry, Kt.
Skeggs, Sir Clifford George, Kt.
Skehel, Sir John James, Kt., FRS
Skingsley, *Air Chief Marshal* Sir Anthony Gerald, GBE, KCB
Skinner, Sir (Thomas) Keith (Hewitt), Bt. (1912)
Skipwith, Sir Patrick Alexander d'Estoteville, Bt. (1622)
Skyrme, Sir (William) Thomas (Charles), KCVO, CB, CBE, TD
Slack, Sir William Willatt, KCVO, FRCS
Slade, Sir Benjamin Julian Alfred, Bt. (1831)
Slade, *Rt. Hon.* Sir Christopher John, Kt.
Slaney, *Prof.* Sir Geoffrey, KBE
Slater, *Adm.* Sir John (Jock) Cunningham Kirkwood, GCB, LVO
Sleight, Sir Richard, Bt. (1920)
Sloan, Sir Andrew Kirkpatrick, Kt., QPM
Sloman, Sir Albert Edward, Kt., CBE
Smart, *Prof.* Sir George Algernon, Kt., MD, FRCP
Smart, Sir Jack, Kt., CBE
Smedley, *Hon.* Sir (Frank) Brian, Kt.
Smedley, Sir Harold, KCMG, MBE
Smiley, *Lt.-Col.* Sir John Philip, Bt. (1903)
Smith, Sir Alan, Kt., CBE, DFC
Smith, Sir Alexander Mair, Kt., Ph.D.
Smith, Sir Andrew Colin Hugh-, Kt.
Smith, *Lt.-Gen.* Sir Anthony Arthur Denison-, KBE

Smith, Sir Charles Bracewell-, Bt. (1947)
Smith, Sir Christopher Sydney Winwood, Bt. (1809)
Smith, *Prof.* Sir Colin Stansfield, Kt., CBE
Smith, Sir Cyril, Kt., MBE
Smith, *Prof.* Sir David Cecil, Kt., FRS
Smith, *Air Chief Marshal* Sir David Harcourt-, GBE, KCB, DFC
Smith, Sir David Iser, KCVO
Smith, Sir Douglas Boucher, KCB
Smith, Sir Dudley (Gordon), Kt.
Smith, *Maj.-Gen.* Sir (Francis) Brian Wyldbore-, Kt., CB, DSO, OBE
Smith, *Prof.* Sir Francis Graham-, Kt., FRS
Smith, Sir Geoffrey Johnson, Kt., MP
Smith, Sir John Alfred, Kt., QPM
Smith, *Prof.* Sir John Cyril, Kt., CBE, QC, FBA
Smith, Sir John Hamilton-Spencer-, Bt. (1804)
Smith, Sir John Jonah Walker-, Bt. (1960)
Smith, Sir John Kenneth Newson-, Bt. (1944)
Smith, Sir John Lindsay Eric, Kt., CH, CBE
Smith, Sir John Rathbone Vassar-, Bt. (1917)
Smith, Sir Joseph William Grenville, Kt., MD, FRCP
Smith, Sir Leslie Edward George, Kt.
Smith, Sir Michael John Llewellyn, KCVO, CMG
Smith, *Rt. Hon.* Sir Murray Stuart-, Kt.
Smith, Sir Raymond Horace, KBE
Smith, Sir Robert Courtney, Kt., CBE
Smith, Sir Robert Hill, Bt. (1945)
Smith, *Prof.* Sir Roland, Kt.
Smith, *Air Marshal* Sir Roy David Austen-, KBE, CB, CVO, DFC
Smith, *Lt.-Gen.* Sir Rupert Anthony, KCB, DSO, OBE, QGM
Smith, Sir (Thomas) Gilbert, Bt. (1897)
Smith, *Prof.* Sir Trevor Arthur, Kt.
Smith, *Adm.* Sir Victor Alfred Trumper, KBE, CB, DSC
Smith, Sir (William) Antony (John) Reardon-, Bt. (1920)
Smith, Sir (William) Richard Prince-, Bt. (1911)
Smithers, Sir Peter Henry Berry Otway, Kt., VRD, D.Phil.
Smyth, Sir Thomas Weyland Bowyer-, Bt. (1661)
Smyth, Sir Timothy John, Bt. (1955)
Soakimori, Sir Frederick Pa-Nukuanca, KBE, CPM
Soame, Sir Charles John Buckworth-Herne-, Bt. (1697)
Sobers, Sir Garfield St Auburn, Kt.
Solomon, Sir David Arnold, Kt., MBE
Solomon, Sir Harry, Kt.
Solti, Sir Georg, KBE
Somare, *Rt. Hon.* Sir Michael Thomas, GCMG, CH

Somers, *Rt. Hon.* Sir Edward Jonathan, Kt.
Somerville, *Brig.* Sir John Nicholas, Kt., CBE
Somerville, Sir Quentin Charles Somerville Agnew-, Bt. (1957)
Soutar, *Air Marshal* Sir Charles John Williamson, KBE
South, Sir Arthur, Kt.
Southby, Sir John Richard Bilbe, Bt. (1937)
Southern, Sir Richard William, Kt., FBA
Southern, Sir Robert, Kt., CBE
Southey, Sir Robert John, Kt., CMG
Southgate, Sir Colin Grieve, Kt.
Southgate, Sir William David, Kt.
Southward, Sir Leonard Bingley, Kt., OBE
Southward, Sir Ralph, KCVO, FRCP
Southwood, *Prof.* Sir (Thomas) Richard (Edmund), Kt., FRS
Southworth, Sir Frederick, Kt., QC
Souyave, *Hon.* Sir (Louis) Georges, Kt.
Sowrey, *Air Marshal* Sir Frederick Beresford, KCB, CBE, AFC
Sparkes, Sir Robert Lyndley, Kt.
Sparrow, Sir John, Kt.
Spearman, Sir Alexander Young Richard Mainwaring, Bt. (1840)
Spedding, *Prof.* Sir Colin Raymond William, Kt., CBE
Spedding, Sir David Rolland, KCMG, CVO, OBE
Speed, Sir (Herbert) Keith, Kt., RD
Speed, Sir Robert William Arney, Kt., CB, QC
Speelman, Sir Cornelis Jacob, Bt. (1686)
Speight, *Hon.* Sir Graham Davies, Kt.
Speir, Sir Rupert Malise, Kt.
Spencer, Sir Derek Harold, Kt., QC
Spicer, Sir James Wilton, Kt.
Spicer, Sir Nicholas Adrian Albert, Bt., MB (1906)
Spicer, Sir (William) Michael Hardy, Kt., MP
Spiers, Sir Donald Maurice, Kt., CB, TD
Spooner, Sir James Douglas, Kt.
Spotswood, *Marshal of the Royal Air Force* Sir Denis Frank, GCB, CBE, DSO, DFC
Spratt, *Col.* Sir Greville Douglas, GBE, TD
Spring, Sir Dryden Thomas, Kt.
Spry, *Hon.* Sir John Farley, Kt.
Squire, *Air Marshal* Sir Peter Ted, KCB, DFC, AFC
Stabb, *Hon.* Sir William Walter, Kt., QC
Stainton, Sir (John) Ross, Kt., CBE
Stakis, Sir Reo Argiros, Kt.
Stamer, Sir (Lovelace) Anthony, Bt. (1809)
Stanbridge, *Air Vice-Marshal* Sir Brian Gerald Tivy, KCVO, CBE, AFC
Stanier, Sir Beville Douglas, Bt. (1917)

Stanier, *Field Marshal* Sir John Wilfred, GCB, MBE

Stanley, *Rt. Hon.* Sir John Paul, Kt., MP

†Staples, Sir Thomas, Bt. (I. 1628)

Stark, Sir Andrew Alexander Steel, KCMG, CVO

Starkey, Sir John Philip, Bt. (1935)

Starrit, Sir James, KCVO

Statham, Sir Norman, KCMG, CVO

Staughton, *Rt. Hon.* Sir Christopher Stephen Thomas Jonathan Thayer, Kt.

Staveley, Sir John Malfroy, KBE, MC

Staveley, *Admiral of the Fleet* Sir William Doveton Minet, GCB

Stear, *Air Chief Marshal* Sir Michael James Douglas, KCB, CBE

Steel, Sir David Edward Charles, Kt., DSO, MC, TD

Steel, *Maj.* Sir (Fiennes) Michael Strang, Bt. (1938)

Steele, Sir (Philip John) Rupert, Kt.

Steere, Sir Ernest Henry Lee-, KBE

Stenhouse, Sir Nicol, Kt.

Stening, *Col.* Sir George Grafton Lees, Kt., ED

Stephen, *Rt. Hon.* Sir Ninian Martin, KG, GCMG, GCVO, KBE

Stephenson, Sir Henry Upton, Bt. (1936)

Stephenson, *Rt. Hon.* Sir John Frederick Eustace, Kt.

Sternberg, Sir Sigmund, Kt.

Stevens, Sir Jocelyn Edward Greville, Kt., CVO

Stevens, Sir Laurence Houghton, Kt., CBE

Stevenson, *Vice-Adm.* Sir (Hugh) David, KBE

Stevenson, Sir Simpson, Kt.

Stewart, Sir Alan, KBE

Stewart, Sir Alan d'Arcy, Bt. (I. 1623)

Stewart, Sir David James Henderson-, Bt. (1957)

Stewart, Sir David John Christopher, Bt. (1803)

Stewart, Sir Edward Jackson, Kt.

Stewart, *Prof.* Sir Frederick Henry, Kt., PH.D., FRS, FRSE

Stewart, Sir Houston Mark Shaw-, Bt., MC, TD (S. 1667)

Stewart, Sir James Douglas, Kt.

Stewart, Sir James Moray, KCB

Stewart, Sir (John) Simon (Watson), Bt. (1920)

Stewart, Sir Robertson Huntly, Kt., CBE

Stewart, Sir Robin Alastair, Bt. (1960)

Stewart, Sir Ronald Compton, Bt. (1937)

Stewart, *Prof.* Sir William Duncan Paterson, Kt., FRS, FRSE

Stibbon, *Gen.* Sir John James, KCB, OBE

Stirling, Sir Alexander John Dickson, KBE, CMG

Stirling, Sir Angus Duncan Aeneas, Kt.

Stockdale, Sir Arthur Noel, Kt.

Stockdale, Sir Thomas Minshull, Bt. (1960)

Stoddart, *Wg Cdr.* Sir Kenneth Maxwell, KCVO, AE

Stoker, *Prof.* Sir Michael George Parke, Kt., CBE, FRCP, FRS, FRSE

Stokes, Sir John Heydon Romaine, Kt.

Stone, Sir Alexander, Kt., OBE

Stones, Sir William Frederick, Kt., OBE

Stonhouse, *Revd* Sir Michael Philip, Bt. (1628)

Stonor, *Air Marshal* Sir Thomas Henry, KCB

Stoppard, Sir Thomas, Kt., CBE

Storey, *Hon.* Sir Richard, Bt., CBE (1960)

Stormonth Darling, Sir James Carlisle, Kt., CBE, MC, TD

Stott, Sir Adrian George Ellingham, Bt. (1920)

Stow, Sir Christopher Philipson-, Bt., DFC (1907)

Stowe, Sir Kenneth Ronald, GCB, CVO

Stracey, Sir John Simon, Bt. (1818)

Strachan, Sir Curtis Victor, Kt., CVO

Strachey, Sir Charles, Bt. (1801)

Straker, Sir Michael Ian Bowstead, Kt., CBE

Strawson, *Prof.* Sir Peter Frederick, Kt., FBA

Street, *Hon.* Sir Laurence Whistler, KCMG

Streeton, Sir Terence George, KBE, CMG

Stringer, Sir Donald Edgar, Kt., CBE

Strong, Sir Roy Colin, Kt., PH.D., FSA

Stronge, Sir James Anselan Maxwell, Bt. (1803)

Stroud, *Prof.* Sir (Charles) Eric, Kt., FRCP

Strutt, Sir Nigel Edward, Kt., TD

Stuart, Sir James Keith, Kt.

Stuart, Sir Kenneth Lamonte, Kt.

†Stuart, Sir Phillip Luttrell, Bt. (1660)

Stubblefield, Sir (Cyril) James, Kt., D.SC., FRS

Stubbs, Sir James Wilfrid, KCVO, TD

Stubbs, Sir William Hamilton, Kt., PH.D.

Stucley, *Lt.* Sir Hugh George Coplestone Bampfylde, Bt. (1859)

Studd, Sir Edward Fairfax, Bt. (1929)

Studd, Sir Peter Malden, GBE, KCVO

Studholme, Sir Henry William, Bt. (1956)

Stuttaford, Sir William Royden, Kt., CBE

Style, *Lt.-Cdr.* Sir Godfrey William, Kt., CBE, DSC, RN

†Style, Sir William Frederick, Bt. (1627)

Suffield, Sir (Henry John) Lester, Kt.

Sugden, Sir Arthur, Kt.

Sullivan, Sir Desmond John, Kt.

Sullivan, Sir Richard Arthur, Bt. (1804)

Sumner, *Hon.* Sir Christopher John, Kt.

Sutherland, Sir John Brewer, Bt. (1921)

Sutherland, Sir Maurice, Kt.

Sutherland, *Prof.* Sir Stewart Ross, Kt., FBA

Sutherland, Sir William George MacKenzie, Kt.

Suttie, Sir (George) Philip Grant-, Bt. (S. 1702)

Sutton, Sir Frederick Walter, Kt., OBE

Sutton, *Air Marshal* Sir John Matthias Dobson, KCB

Sutton, Sir Richard Lexington, Bt. (1772)

Swaffield, Sir James Chesebrough, Kt., CBE, RD

Swaine, Sir John Joseph, Kt., CBE

Swan, Sir Conrad Marshall John Fisher, KCVO, PH.D.

Swan, Sir John William David, KBE

Swann, Sir Michael Christopher, Bt., TD (1906)

Swanwick, Sir Graham Russell, Kt., MBE

Swartz, *Hon.* Sir Reginald William Colin, KBE, ED

Sweetnam, Sir (David) Rodney, KCVO, CBE, FRCS

Swinburn, *Lt.-Gen.* Sir Richard Hull, KCB

Swinson, Sir John Henry Alan, Kt., OBE

Swinton, *Maj.-Gen.* Sir John, KCVO, OBE

Swire, Sir Adrian Christopher, Kt.

Swire, Sir John Anthony, Kt., CBE

Swynnerton, Sir Roger John Massy, Kt., CMG, OBE, MC

Sykes, Sir Francis John Badcock, Bt. (1781)

Sykes, Sir Hugh Ridley, Kt.

Sykes, Sir John Charles Anthony le Gallais, Bt. (1921)

Sykes, *Prof.* Sir (Malcolm) Keith, Kt.

Sykes, Sir Richard, Kt.

Sykes, Sir Tatton Christopher Mark, Bt. (1783)

Symington, *Prof.* Sir Thomas, Kt., MD, FRSE

Symons, *Vice-Adm.* Sir Patrick Jeremy, KBE

Synge, Sir Robert Carson, Bt. (1801)

Tait, *Adm.* Sir (Allan) Gordon, KCB, DSC

Tait, Sir James Sharp, Kt., D.SC., LLD., PH.D.

Tait, Sir Peter, KBE

Talbot, *Vice-Adm.* Sir (Arthur Allison) FitzRoy, KBE, CB, DSO

Talbot, *Hon.* Sir Hilary Gwynne, Kt.

Talboys, *Rt. Hon.* Sir Brian Edward, CH, KCB

Tancred, Sir Henry Lawson-, Bt. (1662)

Tangaroa, *Hon.* Sir Tangoroa, Kt., MBE

Tange, Sir Arthur Harold, Kt., CBE

Tuck, Sir Bruce Adolph Reginald, Bt. (1910)

Tucker, *Hon.* Sir Richard Howard, Kt.

Tuckey, *Hon.* Sir Simon Lane, Kt.

Tuita, Sir Mariano Kelesimalefo, Kt., OBE

Tuite, Sir Christopher Hugh, Bt., PH.D. (1622)

Tuivaga, Sir Timoci Uluiburotu, Kt.

Tuke, Sir Anthony Favill, Kt.

Tumim, *His Hon.* Sir Stephen, Kt.

Tupper, Sir Charles Hibbert, Bt. (1888)

Turbott, Sir Ian Graham, Kt., CMG, CVO

Turing, Sir John Dermot, Bt. (s. 1638)

Turnberg, *Prof.* Sir Leslie Arnold, Kt., MD, FRCP

Turnbull, Sir Richard Gordon, GCMG

Turner, Sir Colin William Carstairs, Kt., CBE, DFC

Turner, *Hon.* Sir Michael John, Kt.

Turnquest, Sir Orville Alton, GCMG, QC

Tuti, *Revd* Dudley, KBE

Tuzo, *Gen.* Sir Harry Craufurd, GCB, OBE, MC

Tweedie, *Prof.* Sir David Philip, Kt.

Tyree, Sir (Alfred) William, Kt., OBE

Tyrwhitt, Sir Reginald Thomas Newman, Bt. (1919)

Udoma, *Hon.* Sir (Egbert) Udo, Kt.

Unsworth, *Hon.* Sir Edgar Ignatius Godfrey, Kt., CMG

Unwin, Sir (James) Brian, KCB

Ure, Sir John Burns, KCMG, LVO

Urquhart, Sir Brian Edward, KCMG, MBE

Urwick, Sir Alan Bedford, KCVO, CMG

Usher, Sir Leonard Gray, KBE

Usher, Sir (William) John Tevenar, Bt. (1899)

Ustinov, Sir Peter Alexander, Kt., CBE

Utting, Sir William Benjamin, Kt., CB

Vai, Sir Mea, Kt., CBE, ISO

Vallance, Sir Iain David Thomas, Kt.

Vallat, Sir Francis Aimé, GBE, KCMG, QC

Vallings, *Vice-Adm.* Sir George Montague Francis, KCB

Vanderfelt, Sir Robin Victor, KBE

Vane, Sir John Robert, Kt., D.Phil., D.SC., FRS

Vanneck, *Air Cdre Hon.* Sir Peter Beckford Rutgers, GBE, CB, AFC

van Straubenzee, Sir William Radcliffe, Kt., MBE

Vasquez, Sir Alfred Joseph, Kt., CBE, QC

Vaughan, Sir Gerard Folliott, Kt., FRCP

†Vavasour, Sir Eric Michael Joseph Marmaduke, Bt. (1828)

Veale, Sir Alan John Ralph, Kt., FEng.

Verco, Sir Walter John George, KCVO

†Verney, Sir John Sebastian, Bt. (1946)

Verney, *Hon.* Sir Lawrence John, Kt., TD

Verney, Sir Ralph Bruce, Bt., KBE (1818)

Vernon, Sir James, Kt., CBE

Vernon, Sir Nigel John Douglas, Bt. (1914)

Vernon, Sir (William) Michael, Kt.

Vesey, Sir (Nathaniel) Henry (Peniston), Kt., CBE

Vestey, Sir (John) Derek, Bt. (1921)

Vial, Sir Kenneth Harold, Kt., CBE

Vick, Sir (Francis) Arthur, Kt., OBE, PH.D.

Vickers, *Lt.-Gen.* Sir Richard Maurice Hilton, KCB, LVO, OBE

Victoria, Sir (Joseph Aloysius) Donatus, Kt., CBE

Vincent, Sir William Percy Maxwell, Bt. (1936)

Vinelott, *Hon.* Sir John Evelyn, Kt.

Vines, Sir William Joshua, Kt., CMG

†Vyvyan, Sir Ralph Ferrers Alexander, Bt. (1645)

Waddell, Sir Alexander Nicol Anton, KCMG, DSC

Waddell, Sir James Henderson, Kt., CB

Wade, *Prof.* Sir Henry William Rawson, Kt., QC, FBA

Wade, *Air Chief Marshal* Sir Ruthven Lowry, KCB, DFC

Waine, *Rt. Revd* John, KCVO

Waite, *Rt. Hon.* Sir John Douglas, Kt.

Wake, Sir Hereward, Bt., MC (1621)

Wakefield, Sir (Edward) Humphry (Tyrell), Bt. (1962)

Wakefield, Sir Norman Edward, Kt.

Wakefield, Sir Peter George Arthur, KBE, CMG

Wakeford, *Air Marshal* Sir Richard Gordon, KCB, OBE, LVO, AFC

Wakeley, Sir John Cecil Nicholson, Bt., FRCS (1952)

†Wakeman, Sir Edward Offley Bertram, Bt. (1828)

Walford, Sir Christopher Rupert, Kt.

Walker, *Revd* Alan Edgar, Kt., OBE

Walker, *Gen.* Sir Antony Kenneth Frederick, KCB

Walker, Sir Baldwin Patrick, Bt. (1856)

Walker, Sir (Charles) Michael, GCMG

Walker, Sir Colin John Shedlock, Kt., OBE

Walker, Sir David Alan, Kt.

Walker, Sir Gervas George, Kt.

Walker, *Rt. Hon.* Sir Harold, Kt.

Walker, Sir Harold Berners, KCMG

Walker, *Maj.* Sir Hugh Ronald, Bt. (1906)

Walker, Sir James Graham, Kt., MBE

Walker, Sir James Heron, Bt. (1868)

Walker, *Air Marshal* Sir John Robert, KCB, CBE, AFC

Walker, *Lt.-Gen.* Sir Michael John Dawson, KCB, CMG, CBE

Walker, Sir Michael Leolin Forestier-, Bt. (1835)

Walker, Sir Miles Rawstron, Kt., CBE

Walker, Sir Patrick Jeremy, KCB

Walker, *Hon.* Sir Robert, Kt.

Walker, Sir Rodney Myerscough, Kt.

Walker, *Hon.* Sir Timothy Edward, Kt.

Walker, *Gen.* Sir Walter Colyear, KCB, CBE, DSO

Wall, Sir (John) Stephen, KCMG, LVO

Wall, *Hon.* Sir Nicholas Peter Rathbone, Kt.

Wall, Sir Patrick Henry Bligh, Kt., MC, VRD

Wall, Sir Robert William, Kt., OBE

Wallace, *Lt.-Gen.* Sir Christopher Brooke Quentin, KBE

Wallace, Sir Ian James, Kt., CBE

Waller, *Hon.* Sir (George) Mark, Kt.

Waller, *Rt. Hon.* Sir George Stanley, Kt., OBE

Waller, Sir Robert William, Bt. (I. 1780)

Walley, Sir John, KBE, CB

Wallis, Sir Peter Gordon, KCVO

Wallis, Sir Timothy William, Kt.

Walmsley, *Vice-Adm.* Sir Robert, KCB

Walsh, Sir Alan, Kt., D.SC., FRS

Walsh, *Prof.* Sir John Patrick, KBE

†Walsham, Sir Timothy John, Bt. (1831)

Walters, *Prof.* Sir Alan Arthur, Kt.

Walters, Sir Dennis Murray, Kt., MBE

Walters, Sir Frederick Donald, Kt.

Walters, Sir Peter Ingram, Kt.

Walters, Sir Roger Talbot, KBE, FRIBA

Walton, Sir John Robert, Kt.

Wan, Sir Wamp, Kt., MBE

Wanstall, *Hon.* Sir Charles Gray, Kt.

Ward, *Rt. Hon.* Sir Alan Hylton, Kt.

Ward, Sir John Devereux, Kt., CBE

Ward, Sir Joseph James Laffey, Bt. (1911)

Ward, *Maj.-Gen.* Sir Philip John Newling, KCVO, CBE

Ward, Sir Timothy James, Kt.

Wardale, Sir Geoffrey Charles, KCB

Wardlaw, Sir Henry (John), Bt. (s. 1631)

Wardle, Sir Thomas Edward Jewell, Kt.

Waring, Sir (Alfred) Holburt, Bt. (1935)

Warmington, Sir David Marshall, Bt. (1908)

Warner, Sir (Edward Courtenay) Henry, Bt. (1910)

Warner, Sir Edward Redston, KCMG, OBE

Warner, *Prof.* Sir Frederick Edward, Kt., FRS, FEng.

Warner, Sir Gerald Chierici, KCMG

Warner, *Hon.* Sir Jean-Pierre Frank Eugene, Kt.

Warren, Sir (Frederick) Miles, KBE

Warren, Sir Kenneth Robin, Kt.

†Warren, Sir Michael Blackley, Bt. (1784)

Wass, Sir Douglas William Gretton, GCB

Waterhouse, *Hon.* Sir Ronald Gough, Kt.

Waterlow, Sir Christopher Rupert, Bt. (1873)

Waterlow, Sir (James) Gerard, Bt. (1930)

Waters, *Gen.* Sir (Charles) John, GCB, CBE

Waters, Sir (Thomas) Neil (Morris), Kt.

Wates, Sir Christopher Stephen, Kt.

Watkins, *Rt. Hon.* Sir Tasker, VC, GBE

Watson, Sir Bruce Dunstan, Kt.

Watson, Sir Duncan Amos, Kt., CBE

Watson, Sir (James) Andrew, Bt. (1866)

Watson, Sir John Forbes Inglefield-, Bt. (1895)

Watson, Sir Michael Milne-, Bt., CBE (1937)

Watson, Sir (Noel) Duncan, KCMG

Watson, *Vice-Adm.* Sir Philip Alexander, KBE, LVO

Watson, Sir Ronald Matthew, Kt., CBE

Watt, *Surgeon Vice-Adm.* Sir James, KBE, FRCS

Watt, Sir James Harvie-, Bt. (1945)

Watts, Sir Arthur Desmond, KCMG

Watts, *Lt.-Gen.* Sir John Peter Barry Condliffe, KBE, CB, MC

Wauchope, Sir Roger (Hamilton) Don-, Bt. (s. 1667)

Way, Sir Richard George Kitchener, KCB, CBE

Weatherall, *Prof.* Sir David John, Kt., FRS

Weatherall, *Vice-Adm.* Sir James Lamb, KBE

Weatherstone, Sir Dennis, KBE

Weaver, Sir Tobias Rushton, Kt., CB

Webb, Sir Thomas Langley, Kt.

Webster, *Very Revd* Alan Brunskill, KCVO

Webster, *Vice-Adm.* Sir John Morrison, KCB

Webster, *Hon.* Sir Peter Edlin, Kt.

Wedderburn, Sir Andrew John Alexander Ogilvy-, Bt. (1803)

Wedgwood, Sir (Hugo) Martin, Bt. (1942)

Weekes, Sir Everton DeCourcey, KCMG, OBE

Weinberg, Sir Mark Aubrey, Kt.

Weir, Sir Michael Scott, KCMG

Weir, Sir Roderick Bignell, Kt.

Welby, Sir (Richard) Bruno Gregory, Bt. (1801)

Welch, Sir John Reader, Bt. (1957)

Weldon, Sir Anthony William, Bt. (I. 1723)

Wellings, Sir Jack Alfred, Kt., CBE

†Wells, Sir Christopher Charles, Bt. (1944)

Wells, Sir John Julius, Kt.

Wells, Sir William Henry Weston, Kt., FRICS

Westbrook, Sir Neil Gowanloch, Kt., CBE

Westerman, Sir (Wilfred) Alan, Kt., CBE

Weston, Sir Michael Charles Swift, KCMG, CVO

Weston, Sir (Philip) John, KCMG

Whalen, Sir Geoffrey Henry, Kt., CBE

Wheeler, Sir Harry Anthony, Kt., OBE

Wheeler, *Air Chief Marshal* Sir (Henry) Neil (George), GCB, CBE, DSO, DFC, AFC

Wheeler, *Rt. Hon.* Sir John Daniel, Kt.

Wheeler, Sir John Hieron, Bt. (1920)

Wheeler, *Hon.* Sir Kenneth Henry, Kt.

Wheeler, *Lt.-Gen.* Sir Roger Neil, GCB, CBE

Wheler, Sir Edward Woodford, Bt. (1660)

Whent, Sir Gerald Arthur, Kt., CBE

Whishaw, Sir Charles Percival Law, Kt.

Whitaker, *Maj.* Sir James Herbert Ingham, Bt., OBE (1936)

White, Sir Christopher Robert Meadows, Bt. (1937)

White, *Hon.* Sir Christopher Stuart Stuart-, Kt.

White, Sir David Harry, Kt.

White, Sir Frank John, Kt.

White, Sir George Stanley James, Bt. (1904)

White, *Wg Cdr.* Sir Henry Arthur Dalrymple-, Bt., DFC (1926)

White, *Adm.* Sir Hugo Moresby, GCB, CBE

White, *Hon.* Sir John Charles, Kt., MBE

White, Sir John Woolmer, Bt. (1922)

White, Sir Lynton Stuart, Kt., MBE, TD

White, Sir Nicholas Peter Archibald, Bt. (1802)

White, *Adm.* Sir Peter, GBE

Whitehead, Sir John Stainton, GCMG, CVO

Whitehead, Sir Rowland John Rathbone, Bt. (1889)

Whiteley, Sir Hugo Baldwin Huntington-, Bt. (1918)

Whiteley, *Gen.* Sir Peter John Frederick, GCB, OBE, RM

Whitfield, Sir William, Kt., CBE

Whitford, *Hon.* Sir John Norman Keates, Kt.

Whitley, *Air Marshal* Sir John René, KBE, CB, DSO, AFC

Whitmore, Sir Clive Anthony, GCB, CVO

Whitmore, Sir John Henry Douglas, Bt. (1954)

Whitney, Sir Raymond William, Kt., OBE, MP

Whittome, Sir (Leslie) Alan, Kt.

Wickerson, Sir John Michael, Kt.

Wicks, Sir James Albert, Kt.

Wicks, Sir Nigel Leonard, KCB, CVO,

†Wigan, Sir Michael Iain, Bt. (1898)

Wiggin, Sir Alfred William (Jerry), Kt., TD

†Wiggin, Sir Charles Rupert John, Bt. (1892)

Wigram, *Revd Canon* Sir Clifford Woolmore, Bt. (1805)

Wilbraham, Sir Richard Baker, Bt. (1776)

Wilford, Sir (Kenneth) Michael, GCMG

Wilkes, *Gen.* Sir Michael John, KCB, CBE

Wilkins, Sir Graham John, Kt.

Wilkinson, Sir (David) Graham (Brook) Bt. (1941)

Wilkinson, *Prof.* Sir Denys Haigh, Kt., FRS

Wilkinson, Sir Peter Allix, KCMG, DSO, OBE

Wilkinson, Sir Philip William, Kt.

Willcocks, Sir David Valentine, Kt., CBE, MC

Williams, Sir Alastair Edgcumbe James Dudley-, Bt. (1964)

Williams, Sir Alwyn, Kt., Ph.D., FRS

Williams, Sir Arthur Dennis Pitt, Kt.

Williams, Sir (Arthur) Gareth Ludovic Emrys Rhys, Bt. (1918)

Williams, *Prof.* Sir Bruce Rodda, KBE

Williams, Sir Daniel Charles, GCMG, QC

Williams, *Adm.* Sir David, GCB

Williams, *Prof.* Sir David Glyndwr Tudor, Kt.

Williams, Sir David Innes, Kt.

Williams, *Hon.* Sir Denys Ambrose, KCMG

Williams, Sir Donald Mark, Bt. (1866)

Williams, *Prof.* Sir (Edward) Dillwyn, Kt., FRCP

Williams, *Hon.* Sir Edward Stratten, KCMG, KBE

Williams, *Prof.* Sir Glanmor, Kt., CBE, FBA

Williams, Sir Henry Sydney, Kt., OBE

Williams, Sir John Robert, KCMG

Williams, Sir (Lawrence) Hugh, Bt. (1798)

Williams, Sir Leonard, KBE, CB

Williams, Sir Osmond, Bt., MC (1909)

Williams, *Prof.* Sir Robert Evan Owen, Kt., MD, FRCP

Williams, Sir (Robert) Philip Nathaniel, Bt. (1915)

Williams, Sir Robin Philip, Bt. (1953)

Williams, Sir (William) Maxwell (Harries), Kt.

Williamson, *Marshal of the Royal Air Force* Sir Keith Alec, GCB, AFC

Williamson, Sir (Nicholas Frederick) Hedworth, Bt. (1642)

Willink, Sir Charles William, Bt. (1957)

Willis, *Hon.* Sir Eric Archibald, KBE, CMG

Dames Grand Cross and Dames Commanders

Style, 'Dame' before forename and surname, followed by appropriate post-nominal initials. Where such an award is made to a lady already in enjoyment of a higher title, the appropriate initials follow her name
Husband, Untitled
For forms of address, *see* page 136

Dame Grand Cross and Dame Commander are the higher classes for women of the Order of the Bath, the Order of St Michael and St George, the Royal Victorian Order, and the Order of the British Empire. Dames Grand Cross rank after the wives of Baronets and before the wives of Knights Grand Cross. Dames Commanders rank after the wives of Knights Grand Cross and before the wives of Knights Commanders.

Honorary Dames Commanders may be conferred on women who are citizens of countries of which The Queen is not head of state.

LIST OF DAMES *Revised to 31 August 1997*

Women peers in their own right and life peers are not included in this list. Female members of the royal family are not included in this list; details of the orders they hold are given on pages 117–8

If a dame has a double barrelled or hyphenated surname, she is listed under the final element of the name

Abaijah, Dame Josephine, DBE
Abel Smith, Lady, DCVO
Abergavenny, The Marchioness of, DCVO
Airlie, The Countess of, DCVO
Albemarle, The Countess of, DBE
Anderson, *Brig.* Hon. Dame Mary Mackenzie (Mrs Pihl), DBE
Anglesey, The Marchioness of, DBE
Anson, Lady (Elizabeth Audrey), DBE
Anstee, Dame Margaret Joan, DCMG
Arden, *Hon.* Dame Mary Howarth (Mrs Mance), DBE
Baker, Dame Janet Abbott (Mrs Shelley), CH, DBE
Ballin, Dame Reubina Ann, DBE
Barnes, Dame (Alice) Josephine (Mary Taylor), DBE, FRCP, FRCS
Barrow, Dame Jocelyn Anita (Mrs Downer), DBE
Barstow, Dame Josephine Clare (Mrs Anderson), DBE
Basset, Lady Elizabeth, DCVO
Bean, Dame Majorie Louise, DBE
Beaurepaire, Dame Beryl Edith, DBE
Bergquist, *Prof.* Dame Patricia Rose, DBE
Berry, Dame Alice Miriam, DBE
Blaize, Dame Venetia Ursula, DBE
Blaxland, Dame Helen Frances, DBE
Booth, *Hon.* Dame Margaret Myfanwy Wood, DBE
Bottomley, Dame Bessie Ellen, DBE
Bowman, Dame (Mary) Elaine Kellett-, DBE
Bowtell, Dame Ann Elizabeth, DCB
Boyd, Dame Vivienne Myra, DBE
Bracewell, *Hon.* Dame Joyanne Winifred (Mrs Copeland), DBE
Brain, Dame Margaret Anne (Mrs Wheeler), DBE

Brazill, Dame Josephine (Sister Mary Philippa), DBE
Bridges, Dame Mary Patricia, DBE
Brown, Dame Gillian Gerda, DCVO, CMG
Browne, Lady Moyra Blanche Madeleine, DBE
Bryans, Dame Anne Margaret, DBE
Buttfield, Dame Nancy Eileen, DBE
Bynoe, Dame Hilda Louisa, DBE
Caldicott, Dame Fiona, DBE, FRCP, FRCPsych.
Cartland, Dame Barbara Hamilton, DBE
Cartwright, Dame Mary Lucy, DBE, SC.D., D.Phil., FRS
Cartwright, Dame Silvia Rose, DBE
Casey, Dame Stella Katherine, DBE
Cayford, Dame Florence Evelyn, DBE
Charles, Dame (Mary) Eugenia, DBE
Chesterton, Dame Elizabeth Ursula, DBE
Clark, *Prof.* Dame (Margaret) June, DBE, Ph.D.
Clay, Dame Marie Mildred, DBE
Clayton, Dame Barbara Evelyn (Mrs Klyne), DBE
Cleland, Dame Rachel, DBE
Coll, Dame Elizabeth Anne Loosemore Esteve-, DBE
Cookson, Dame Catherine Ann, DBE
Corsar, The Hon. Dame Mary Drummond, DBE
Coulshed, Dame (Mary) Frances, DBE, TD
Daws, Dame Joyce Margaretta, DBE
Dell, Dame Miriam Patricia, DBE
Dench, Dame Judith Olivia (Mrs Williams), DBE
de Valois, Dame Ninette, OM, CH, DBE
Digby, Lady, DBE
Donaldson, Dame (Dorothy) Mary (Lady Donaldson of Lymington), GBE
Doyle, *Air Comdt.* Dame Jean Lena Annette Conan (Lady Bromet), DBE
Drake, *Brig.* Dame Jean Elizabeth Rivett-, DBE
Dugdale, Kathryn, Lady, DCVO
Dumont, Dame Ivy Leona, DCMG

Dyche, Dame Rachael Mary, DBE
Ebsworth, *Hon.* Dame Ann Marian, DBE
Engel, Dame Pauline Frances (Sister Pauline Engel), DBE
Evison, Dame Helen June Patricia, DBE
Fenner, Dame Peggy Edith, DBE
Fitton, Dame Doris Alice (Mrs Mason), DBE
Fookes, Dame Janet Evelyn, DBE
Fraser, Dame Dorothy Rita, DBE
Friend, Dame Phyllis Muriel, DBE
Fritchie, Dame Irene Tordoff (Dame Rennie Fritchie), DBE
Frost, Dame Phyllis Irene, DBE
Fry, Dame Margaret Louise, DBE
Gallagher, Dame Monica Josephine, DBE
Gardiner, Dame Helen Louisa, DBE, MVO
Gibbs, Dame Molly Peel, DBE
Giles, *Air Comdt.* Dame Pauline (Mrs Parsons), DBE, RRC
Goodman, Dame Barbara, DBE
Gordon, Dame Minita Elmira, GCMG, GCVO
Gow, Dame Jane Elizabeth (Mrs Whiteley), DBE
Grafton, The Duchess of, GCVO
Green, Dame Mary Georgina, DBE
Grey, Dame Beryl Elizabeth (Mrs Svenson), DBE
Grimthorpe, The Lady, DCVO
Guilfoyle, Dame Margaret Georgina Constance, DBE
Guthardt, *Revd Dr* Dame Phyllis Myra, DBE
Haig, Dame Mary Alison Glen-, DBE
Hale, *Hon.* Dame Brenda Marjorie (Mrs Farrand), DBE
Harper, Dame Elizabeth Margaret Way, DBE
Heilbron, *Hon.* Dame Rose, DBE
Henderson, Dame Louise Etiennette Sidonie, DBE
Henrison, Dame Anne Elizabeth Rosina, DBE
Herbison, Dame Jean Marjory, DBE, CMG

Hercus, *Hon.* Dame (Margaret) Ann, DCMG

Hetet, Dame Rangimarie, DBE

Higgins, *Prof.* Dame Rosalyn, DBE, QC

Hill, *Air Cdre* Dame Felicity Barbara, DBE

Hiller, Dame Wendy (Mrs Gow), DBE

Hine, Dame Deirdre Joan, DBE, FRCP

Hird, Dame Thora (Mrs Scott), DBE

Hogg, *Hon.* Dame Mary Claire (Mrs Koops), DBE

Howard, Dame (Rosemary) Christian, DBE

Hunter, Dame Pamela, DBE

Hurley, *Prof.* Dame Rosalinde (Mrs Gortvai), DBE

Hussey, Lady Susan Katharine (Lady Hussey of North Bradley), DCVO

Isaacs, Dame Albertha Madeline, DBE

James, Dame Naomi Christine (Mrs Haythorne), DBE

Jenkins, Dame (Mary) Jennifer (Lady Jenkins of Hillhead), DBE

Jones, Dame Gwyneth (Mrs Haberfeld-Jones), DBE

Jones, Dame (Lilian) Pauline Neville-, DCMG

Kekedo, Dame Mary, DBE, BEM

Kekedo, Dame Rosalina Violet, DBE

Kelleher, Dame Joan, DBE

Kettlewell, *Comdt.* Dame Marion Mildred, DBE

Kilroy, Dame Alix Hester Marie (Lady Meynell), DBE

Kirby, Dame Georgina Kamiria, DBE

Kirk, Dame (Lucy) Ruth, DBE

Knight, Dame (Joan Christabel) Jill, DBE

Kramer, *Prof.* Dame Leonie Judith, DBE

Laine, Dame Cleo (Clementine) Dinah (Mrs Dankworth), DBE

Lamb, Dame Dawn Ruth, DBE

Lewis, Dame Edna Leofrida (Lady Lewis), DBE

Lister, Dame Unity Viola, DBE

Litchfield, Dame Ruby Beatrice, DBE

Lott, Dame Felicity Ann Emwhyla (Mrs Woolf), DBE

Lowrey, *Air Comdt.* Dame Alice, DBE, RRC

Lympany, Dame Moura, DBE

Lynn, Dame Vera (Mrs Lewis), DBE

Mackinnon, Dame (Una) Patricia, DBE

Macknight, Dame Ella Annie Noble, DBE, MD

McLaren, Dame Anne Laura, DBE, FRCOG, FRS

Macmillan of Ovenden, Katharine, Viscountess, DBE

Major, Dame Malvina Lorraine (Mrs Fleming), DBE

Mann, Dame Ida Caroline, DBE, D.SC., FRCS

Markova, Dame Alicia, DBE

Martin, Rosamund Mary Holland-, Lady, DBE

Masters, Dame Sheila Valerie (Mrs Noakes), DBE

Metge, *Dr* Dame (Alice) Joan, DBE

Miller, Dame Mabel Flora Hobart, DBE

Miller, Dame Mary Elizabeth Hedley-, DCVO, CB

Mills, Dame Barbara Jean Lyon, DBE, QC

Mitchell, Dame Mona, DCVO

Mitchell, *Hon.* Dame Roma Flinders, DBE

Mitchell, Dame Wendy, DBE

Morrison, *Hon.* Dame Mary Anne, DCVO

Mueller, Dame Anne Elisabeth, DCB

Muldoon, Thea Dale, Lady, DBE, QSO

Mumford, Lady Mary Katharine, DCVO

Munro, Dame Alison, DBE

Murdoch, Dame Elisabeth Joy, DBE

Murdoch, Dame (Jean) Iris (Mrs Bayley), DBE

Murray, Dame (Alice) Rosemary, DBE, D.phil.

Ogilvie, Dame Bridget Margaret, DBE, ph.D., D.SC.

Ollerenshaw, Dame Kathleen Mary, DBE, D.phil.

Oxenbury, Dame Shirley Anne, DBE

Park, Dame Merle Florence (Mrs Bloch), DBE

Paterson, Dame Betty Fraser Ross, DBE

Peake, *Air Cdre* Dame Felicity Hyde, DBE, AE

Penhaligon, Dame Annette (Mrs Egerton), DBE

Plowden, The Lady, DBE

Poole, Dame Avril Anne Barker, DBE

Porter, Dame Shirley (Lady Porter), DBE

Prendergast, Dame Simone Ruth, DBE

Prentice, Dame Winifred Eva, DBE

Preston, Dame Frances Olivia Campbell-, DCVO

Price, Dame Margaret Berenice, DBE

Purves, Dame Daphne Helen, DBE

Pyke, Lady, DBE

Quinn, Dame Sheila Margaret Imelda, DBE

Railton, Dame Ruth (Mrs King), DBE

Rankin, Lady Jean Margaret Florence, DCVO

Raven, Dame Kathleen Annie (Mrs Ingram), DBE

Restieaux, *Dr* Dame Norma Jean, DBE

Riddelsdell, Dame Mildred, DCB, CBE

Ridley, Dame (Mildred) Betty, DBE

Ridsdale, Dame Victoire Evelyn Patricia (Lady Ridsdale), DBE

Rigg, Dame Diana, DBE

Rimington, Dame Stella, DCB

Robertson, *Comdt.* Dame Nancy Margaret, DBE

Roe, Dame Raigh Edith, DBE

Rue, Dame (Elsie) Rosemary, DBE

Rumbold, *Rt. Hon.* Dame Angela Claire Rosemary, DBE

Salas, Dame Margaret Laurence, DBE

Salmond, *Prof.* Dame Mary Anne, DBE

Saunders, Dame Cicely Mary Strode, OM, DBE, FRCP

Sawyer, *Hon.* Dame Joan Augusta, DCMG

Schwarzkopf, Dame Elisabeth Friederike Marie Olga Legge-, DBE

Scott, Dame Catherine Campbell, DBE

Scott, Dame Jean Mary Monica Maxwell-, DCVO

Scott, Dame Margaret, (Dame Catherine Margaret Mary Denton), DBE

Shenfield, Dame Barbara Estelle, DBE

Sherlock, *Prof.* Dame Sheila Patricia Violet, DBE, MD, FRCP

Sibley, Dame Antoinette (Mrs Corbett), DBE

Sloss, *Rt. Hon.* Dame (Ann) Elizabeth (Oldfield) Butler-, DBE

Smieton, Dame Mary Guillan, DBE

Smith, *Hon.* Dame Janet Hilary (Mrs Mathieson), DBE

Smith, Dame Margaret Natalie (Maggie) (Mrs Cross), DBE

Smith, Dame Margot, DBE

Snagge, Dame Nancy Marion, DBE

Soames, Mary, Lady, DBE

Spark, Dame Muriel Sarah, DBE

Steel, *Hon.* Dame (Anne) Heather (Mrs Beattie), DBE

Stephens, *Air Comdt.* Dame Anne, DBE

Stewart, Dame Muriel Acadia, DBE

Sutherland, Dame Joan (Mrs Bonynge), OM, DBE

Szaszy, Dame Miraka Petricevich, DBE

Taylor, Dame Jean Elizabeth, DCVO

Te Atairangikaahu, Te Arikinui, Dame, DBE

Te Kanawa, Dame Kiri Janette (Mrs Park), DBE

Thorneycroft, Carla, Lady, CBE

Tinson, Dame Sue, DBE

Tizard, Dame Catherine Anne, GCMG, GCVO, DBE

Tokiel, Dame Rosa, DBE

Uatioa, Dame Mere, DBE

Uvarov, Dame Olga, DBE

Varley, Dame Joan Fleetwood, DBE

Wagner, Dame Gillian Mary Millicent (Lady Wagner), DBE

Wall, (Alice) Anne, (Mrs Michael Wall), DCVO

Wallace, Dame (Georgina Catriona Pamela) Augusta, DBE

Warburton, Dame Anne Marion, DCVO, CMG

Warwick, Dame Margaret Elizabeth Harvey Turner-, DBE, FRCP, FRCPEd.

Waterhouse, Dame Rachel Elizabeth, DBE, ph.D.

Weir, Dame Gillian Constance (Mrs Phelps), DBE

Weston, Dame Margaret Kate, DBE

Williamson, Dame (Elsie) Marjorie, DBE, ph.D.

Winstone, Dame Dorothy Gertrude, DBE, CMG

Wong Yick-ming, Dame Rosanna, DBE

Decorations and Medals

PRINCIPAL DECORATIONS AND MEDALS
In order of precedence

Victoria Cross (VC), 1856 (*see* page 208)
George Cross (GC), 1940 (*see* page 209)

British Orders of Knighthood, etc.
Baronet's Badge
Knight Bachelor's Badge

Decorations
Conspicuous Gallantry Cross (CGC), 1995
Royal Red Cross Class I (RRC), 1883
Distinguished Service Cross (DSC), 1914. For all ranks for actions at sea
Military Cross (MC), December 1914. For all ranks for actions on land
Distinguished Flying Cross (DFC), 1918. For all ranks for acts of gallantry when flying in active operations against the enemy
Air Force Cross (AFC), 1918. For all ranks for acts of courage when flying, although not in active operations against the enemy
Royal Red Cross Class II (ARRC)
Order of British India
Kaisar-i-Hind Medal
Order of St John

Medals for Gallantry and Distinguished Conduct
Union of South Africa Queen's Medal for Bravery, in Gold
Distinguished Conduct Medal (DCM), 1854
Conspicuous Gallantry Medal (CGM), 1874
Conspicuous Gallantry Medal (Flying)
George Medal (GM), 1940
Queen's Police Medal for Gallantry
Queen's Fire Service Medal for Gallantry
Royal West African Frontier Force Distinguished Conduct Medal
King's African Rifles Distinguished Conduct Medal
Indian Distinguished Service Medal
Union of South Africa Queen's Medal for Bravery, in Silver
Distinguished Service Medal (DSM), 1914
Military Medal (MM), 1916
Distinguished Flying Medal (DFM), 1918
Air Force Medal (AFM)
Constabulary Medal (Ireland)
Medal for Saving Life at Sea
Sea Gallantry Medal
Indian Order of Merit (Civil)
Indian Police Medal for Gallantry
Ceylon Police Medal for Gallantry
Sierra Leone Police Medal for Gallantry
Sierra Leone Fire Brigades Medal for Gallantry
Colonial Police Medal for Gallantry (CPM)
Queen's Gallantry Medal, 1974
Royal Victorian Medal (RVM), Gold, Silver and Bronze

British Empire Medal (BEM), (formerly the Medal of the Order of the British Empire, for Meritorious Service; also includes the Medal of the Order awarded before 29 December 1922)
Canada Medal
Queen's Police (QPM) and Queen's Fire Service Medals (QFSM) for Distinguished Service
Queen's Medal for Chiefs

War Medals and Stars (in order of date)

Polar Medals (in order of date)

Imperial Service Medal

Police Medals for Valuable Service

Badge of Honour

Jubilee, Coronation and Durbar Medals
King George V, King George VI and Queen Elizabeth II Long and Faithful Service Medals

Efficiency and Long Service Decorations and Medals
Medal for Meritorious Service
Accumulated Campaign Service Medal
The Medal for Long Service and Good Conduct (Military)
Naval Long Service and Good Conduct Medal
Royal Marines Meritorious Service Medal
Royal Air Force Meritorious Service Medal
Royal Air Force Long Service and Good Conduct Medal
Medal for Long Service and Good Conduct (Ulster Defence Regiment)
Police Long Service and Good Conduct Medal
Fire Brigade Long Service and Good Conduct Medal
Colonial Police and Fire Brigades Long Service Medals
Colonial Prison Service Medal
Hong Kong Disciplined Services Medal
Army Emergency Reserve Decoration (ERD), 1952
Volunteer Officers' Decoration (VD)
Volunteer Long Service Medal
Volunteer Officers' Decoration for India and the Colonies
Volunteer Long Service Medal for India and the Colonies
Colonial Auxiliary Forces Officers' Decoration
Colonial Auxiliary Forces Long Service Medal
Medal for Good Shooting (Naval)
Militia Long Service Medal
Imperial Yeomanry Long Service Medal
Territorial Decoration (TD), 1908
Efficiency Decoration (ED)
Territorial Efficiency Medal
Efficiency Medal
Special Reserve Long Service and Good Conduct Medal
Decoration for Officers, Royal Navy Reserve (RD), 1910
Decoration for Officers, RNVR (VRD)
Royal Naval Reserve Long Service and Good Conduct Medal
RNVR Long Service and Good Conduct Medal
Royal Naval Auxiliary Sick Berth Reserve Long Service and Good Conduct Medal

Royal Fleet Reserve Long Service and Good Conduct Medal
Royal Naval Wireless Auxiliary Reserve Long Service and Good Conduct Medal
Air Efficiency Award (AE), 1942
Ulster Defence Regiment Medal
Northern Ireland Home Service Medal
The Queen's Medal. For champion shots in the RN, RM, RNZN, Army, RAF
Cadet Forces Medal, 1950
Coastguard Auxiliary Service Long Service Medal (formerly Coast Life Saving Corps Long Service Medal)
Special Constabulary Long Service Medal
Royal Observer Corps Medal
Civil Defence Long Service Medal
Ambulance Service (Emergency Duties) Long Service and Good Conduct Medal
Rhodesia Medal
Royal Ulster Constabulary Service Medal
Service Medal of the Order of St John
Badge of the Order of the League of Mercy
Voluntary Medical Service Medal, 1932
Women's Voluntary Service Medal
Colonial Special Constabulary Medal

Foreign Orders, Decorations and Medals (in order of date)

THE VICTORIA CROSS (1856)
FOR CONSPICUOUS BRAVERY

VC

Ribbon, Crimson, for all Services (until 1918 it was blue for the Royal Navy)

Instituted on 29 January 1856, the Victoria Cross was awarded retrospectively to 1854, the first being held by Lt. C. D. Lucas, RN, for bravery in the Baltic Sea on 21 June 1854 (gazetted 24 February 1857). The first 62 Crosses were presented by Queen Victoria in Hyde Park, London, on 26 June 1857.

The Victoria Cross is worn before all other decorations, on the left breast, and consists of a cross-pattée of bronze, one and a half inches in diameter, with the Royal Crown surmounted by a lion in the centre, and beneath there is the inscription *For Valour*. Holders of the VC receive a tax-free annuity of £1,300, irrespective of need or other conditions. In 1911, the right to receive the Cross was extended to Indian soldiers, and in 1920 to matrons, sisters and nurses, and the staff of the Nursing Services and other services pertaining to hospitals and nursing, and to civilians of either sex regularly or temporarily under the orders, direction or supervision of the naval, military, or air forces of the Crown.

SURVIVING RECIPIENTS OF THE VICTORIA CROSS
as at 31 August 1997

Agansing Rai, *Capt.*, MM (Gurkha Rifles)
 1944 *World War*
Ali Haidar, *Jemadar* (Frontier Force Rifles)
 1945 *World War*
Annand, *Capt.* R. W. (Durham Light Infantry)
 1940 *World War*

Bhan Bhagta Gurung, *Havildar* (2nd Gurkha Rifles)
 1945 *World War*
Bhandari Ram, *Capt.* (Baluch R.)
 1944 *World War*
Chapman, *Sgt.* E. T., BEM (Monmouthshire R.)
 1945 *World War*
Cruickshank, *Flt. Lt.* J. A. (RAFVR)
 1944 *World War*
Cutler, *Capt.* Sir Roden, AK, KCMG, KCVO, CBE (Australia)
 1941 *World War*
Fraser, *Lt.-Cdr.* I. E., DSC (RNR)
 1945 *World War*
Gaje Ghale, *Capt.* (Gurkha Rifles)
 1943 *World War*
Ganju Lama, *Capt.*, MM (Gurkha Rifles)
 1944 *World War*
Gardner, *Capt.* P. J., MC (RTR)
 1941 *World War*
Gould, *Lt.* T. W. (RN)
 1942 *World War*
Jamieson, *Maj.* D. A., CVO (R. Norfolk R.)
 1944 *World War*
Kenna, *Pte.* E. (Australian M. F.)
 1945 *World War*
Kenneally, *Guardsman* J. P. (Irish Guards)
 1943 *World War*
Lachhiman Gurung, *Havildar* (Gurkha Rifles)
 1945 *World War*
Merritt, *Lt.-Col.* C. C. I., CD (S. Saskatchewan R.)
 1942 *World War*
Norton, *Capt.* G. R., MM (SAMF)
 1944 *World War*
Payne, *WO* K. (Australian Army)
 1969 *Vietnam*
Porteous, *Col.* P. A. (RA)
 1942 *World War*
Rambahadur Limbu, *Capt.*, MVO (Gurkha Rifles)
 1965 *Sarawak*
Reid, *Flt. Lt.* W. (RAFVR)
 1943 *World War*
Smith, *Sgt.* E. A., CD (Seaforth Highlanders of Canada)
 1944 *World War*
Smythe, *Capt.* Q. G. M. (SAMF)
 1942 *World War*
Speakman-Pitt, *Sgt.* W. (Black Watch)
 1951 *Korea*
Tulbahadur Pun, *Lt.* (Gurkha Rifles)
 1944 *World War*
Umrao Singh, *Sgt. Major* (IA)
 1944 *World War*
Watkins, *Maj. Rt. Hon.* Sir Tasker, GBE (Welch R.)
 1944 *World War*
Wilson, *Lt.-Col.* E. C. T. (E. Surrey R.)
 1940 *World War*

THE GEORGE CROSS (1940)
FOR GALLANTRY

GC

Ribbon, Dark blue, threaded through a bar adorned with laurel leaves
Instituted 24 September 1940 (with amendments, 3 November 1942).

The George Cross is worn before all other decorations (except the VC) on the left breast (when worn by a woman it may be worn on the left shoulder from a ribbon of the same width and colour fashioned into a bow). It consists of a plain silver cross with four equal limbs, the cross having in the centre a circular medallion bearing a design showing St George and the Dragon. The inscription *For Gallantry* appears round the medallion and in the angle of each limb of the cross is the Royal cypher 'G VI' forming a circle concentric with the medallion. The reverse is plain and bears the name of the recipient and the date of the award. The cross is suspended by a ring from a bar adorned with laurel leaves on dark blue ribbon one and a half inches wide.

The cross is intended primarily for civilians; awards to the fighting services are confined to actions for which purely military honours are not normally granted. It is awarded only for acts of the greatest heroism or of the most conspicuous courage in circumstances of extreme danger. From 1 April 1965, holders of the Cross have received a tax-free annuity, which is now £1,300.

The royal warrant which ordained that the grant of the Empire Gallantry Medal should cease authorized holders of that medal to return it to the Central Chancery of the Orders of Knighthood and to receive in exchange the George Cross. A similar provision applied to posthumous awards of the Empire Gallantry Medal made after the outbreak of war in 1939. In October 1971 all surviving holders of the Albert Medal and the Edward Medal exchanged those decorations for the George Cross.

SURVIVING RECIPIENTS OF THE GEORGE CROSS
as at 31 August 1997

If the recipient originally received the Empire Gallantry Medal (EGM), the Albert Medal (AM) or the Edward Medal (EM), this is indicated by the initials in parenthesis.

Archer, *Col.* B. S. T., GC, OBE, ERD, 1941
Baker, J. T., GC (EM), 1929
Bamford, J., GC, 1952
Beaton, J., GC, CVO, 1974
Biggs, *Maj.* K. A., GC, 1946
Bridge, *Lt.-Cdr.* J., GC, GM*, 1944
Butson, *Lt.-Col.* A. R. C., GC, CD, MD (AM), 1948
Bywater, R. A. S., GC, GM, 1944
Errington, H., GC, 1941
Fairfax, F. W., GC, 1953
Farrow, K., GC (AM), 1948
Flintoff, H. H., GC (EM), 1944
Gledhill, A. J., GC, 1967
Gregson, J. S., GC (AM), 1943
Hawkins, E., GC (AM), 1943
Johnson, *WO1 (SSM)* B., GC, 1990
Kinne, D. G., GC, 1954
Lowe, A. R., GC (AM), 1949

Lynch, J., GC, BEM (AM), 1948
Malta, GC, 1942
Manwaring, T. G., GC (EM), 1949
Moore, R. V., GC, CBE, 1940
Moss, B., GC, 1940
Naughton, F., GC (EGM), 1937
Pearson, Miss J. D. M., GC (EGM), 1940
Pratt, M. K., GC, 1978
Purves, Mrs M., GC (AM), 1949
Raweng, Awang anak, GC, 1951
Riley, G., GC (AM), 1944
Rowlands, *Air Marshal* Sir John, GC, KBE, 1943
Sinclair, *Air Vice-Marshal* Sir Laurence, GC, KCB, CBE, DSO, 1941
Stevens, H. W., GC, 1958
Stronach, *Capt.* G. P., GC, 1943
Styles, *Lt.-Col.* S. G., GC, 1972
Taylor, *Lt.-Cdr.* W. H., GC, MBE, 1941
Walker, C., GC, 1972
Walker, C. H., GC (AM), 1942
Walton, E. W. K., GC (AM), DSO, 1948
Wilcox, C., GC (EM), 1949
Wiltshire, S. N., GC (EGM), 1930
Wooding, E. A., GC (AM), 1945
Yates, P. W., GC (EM), 1932

Chiefs of Clans and Names in Scotland

Only chiefs of whole Names or Clans are included, except certain special instances (marked *) who, though not chiefs of a whole name, were or are for some reason (e.g. the Macdonald forfeiture) independent. Under decision (*Campbell-Gray*, 1950) that a bearer of a 'double or triple-barrelled' surname cannot be held chief of a part of such, several others cannot be included in the list at present.

THE ROYAL HOUSE: HM The Queen

AGNEW: Sir Crispin Agnew of Lochnaw, Bt., QC, 6 Palmerston Road, Edinburgh EH9 1TN

ANSTRUTHER: Sir Ralph Anstruther of that Ilk, Bt., GCVO, MC, Balcaskie, Pittenweem, Fife KY10 2RD

ARBUTHNOTT: The Viscount of Arbuthnott, KT, CBE, DSC, Arbuthnott House, Laurencekirk, Kincardineshire AB30 1PA

BARCLAY: Peter C. Barclay of Towie Barclay and of that Ilk, 28A Gordon Place, London W8 4JE

BORTHWICK: The Lord Borthwick, Crookston, Heriot, Midlothian EH38 5YS

BOYD: The Lord Kilmarnock, 194 Regent's Park Road, London NW1 8XP

BOYLE: The Earl of Glasgow, Kelburn, Fairlie, Ayrshire KA29 OBE

BRODIE: Ninian Brodie of Brodie, Brodie Castle, Forres, Morayshire IV36 OTE

BRUCE: The Earl of Elgin and Kincardine, KT, Broomhall, Dunfermline, Fife KY11 3DU

BUCHAN: David S. Buchan of Auchmacoy, Auchmacoy House, Ellon, Aberdeenshire

BURNETT: J. C. A. Burnett of Leys, Crathes Castle, Banchory, Kincardineshire

CAMERON: Sir Donald Cameron of Lochiel, KT, CVO, TD, Achnacarry, Spean Bridge, Inverness-shire

CAMPBELL: The Duke of Argyll, Inveraray, Argyll PA32 8XF

CARMICHAEL: Richard J. Carmichael of Carmichael, Carmichael, Thankerton, Biggar, Lanarkshire

CARNEGIE: The Duke of Fife, Elsick House, Stonehaven, Kincardineshire AB3 2NT

CATHCART: Maj.-Gen. The Earl Cathcart, CB, DSO, MC, Moor Hatches, West Amesbury, Salisbury SP4 7BH

CHARTERIS: The Earl of Wemyss and March, KT, Gosford House, Longniddry, East Lothian EH32 OPX

CLAN CHATTAN: M. K. Mackintosh of Clan Chattan, Maxwell Park, Gwelo, Zimbabwe

CHISHOLM: Hamish Chisholm of Chisholm (*The Chisholm*), Elmpine, Beck Row, Bury St Edmunds, Suffolk

COCHRANE: The Earl of Dundonald, Lochnell Castle, Ledaig, Argyllshire

COLQUHOUN: Sir Ivar Colquhoun of Luss, Bt., Camstraddan, Luss, Dunbartonshire G83 8NX

CRANSTOUN: David A. S. Cranstoun of that Ilk, Corehouse, Lanark

CRICHTON: vacant

CUMMING: Sir William Cumming of Altyre, Bt., Altyre, Forres, Moray

DARROCH: Capt. Duncan Darroch of Gourock, The Red House, Branksome Park Road, Camberley, Surrey

DAVIDSON: Duncan Davidson of Davidston, Durham Drive, Havelock North, New Zealand

DEWAR: Kenneth Dewar of that Ilk and Vogrie, The Dower House, Grayshott, Nr. Hindhead, Surrey

DRUMMOND: The Earl of Perth, PC, Stobhall, Perth PH2 6DR

DUNBAR: Sir James Dunbar of Mochrum, Bt., Bld 848 C.2, 66877 Flugplatz, Ramstein, Germany

DUNDAS: David D. Dundas of Dundas, 8 Derna Road, Kenwyn 7700, South Africa

DURIE: Raymond V. D. Durie of Durie, Court House, Pewsey, Wilts

ELIOTT: Mrs Margaret Eliott of Redheugh, Redheugh, Newcastleton, Roxburghshire

ERSKINE: The Earl of Mar and Kellie, Erskine House, Kirk Wynd, Clackmannan FK10 4JF

FARQUHARSON: Capt. A. Farquharson of Invercauld, MC, Invercauld, Braemar, Aberdeenshire AB35 5TT

FERGUSSON: Sir Charles Fergusson of Kilkerran, Bt., Kilkerran, Maybole, Ayrshire

FORBES: The Lord Forbes, KBE, Balforbes, Alford, Aberdeenshire AB33 8DR

FORSYTH: Alistair Forsyth of that Ilk, Ethie Castle, by Arbroath, Angus DD11 5SP

FRASER: The Lady Saltoun, Cairnbulg Castle, Fraserburgh, Aberdeenshire AB43 5TN

*FRASER (OF LOVAT): The Lord Lovat, Beaufort Lodge, Beauly, Inverness-shire IV4 7AZ

GAYRE: R. Gayre of Gayre and Nigg, Minard Castle, Minard, Inverary, Argyll PA32 8YB

GORDON: The Marquess of Huntly, Aboyne Castle, Aberdeenshire AB34 5JP

GRAHAM: The Duke of Montrose, Buchanan Auld House, Drymen, Stirlingshire

GRANT: The Lord Strathspey, The House of Lords, London SW1A OPW

GRIERSON: Sir Michael Grierson of Lag, Bt., 40C Palace Road, London SW2 3NJ

HAIG: The Earl Haig, OBE, Bemersyde, Melrose, Roxburghshire TD6 9DP

HALDANE: Martin Haldane of Gleneagles, Gleneagles, Auchterarder, Perthshire

HANNAY: Ramsey Hannay of Kirkdale and of that Ilk, Cardoness House, Gatehouse-of-Fleet, Kirkcudbrightshire

HAY: The Earl of Erroll, Woodbury Hall, Sandy, Beds

HENDERSON: John Henderson of Fordell, 7 Owen Street, Toowoomba, Queensland, Australia

HUNTER: Pauline Hunter of Hunterston, Plovers Ridge, Lon Cecrist, Treaddur Bay, Holyhead, Gwynedd

IRVINE OF DRUM: David C. Irvine of Drum, 20 Enville Road, Bowden, Altrincham, Cheshire WA14 2PQ

JARDINE: Sir Alexander Jardine of Applegirth, Bt., Ash House, Thwaites, Millom, Cumbria LA18 5HY

JOHNSTONE: The Earl of Annandale and Hartfell, Raehills, Lockerbie, Dumfriesshire

KEITH: The Earl of Kintore, The Stables, Keith Hall, Inverurie, Aberdeenshire AB51 OLD

KENNEDY: The Marquess of Ailsa, Cassillis House, Maybole, Ayrshire

KERR: The Marquess of Lothian, KCVO, Ferniehurst Castle, Jedburgh, Roxburghshire TN8 6NX

KINCAID: Mrs Heather V. Kincaid of Kincaid, 4 Watling Street, Leintwardine, Craven Arms, Shropshire

LAMONT: Peter N. Lamont of that Ilk, St Patrick's College, Manly, NSW 2095, Australia

LEASK: Madam Leask of Leask, 1 Vincent Road, Sheringham, Norfolk

LENNOX: Edward J. H. Lennox of that Ilk, Pools Farm, Downton on the Rock, Ludlow, Shropshire

LESLIE: The Earl of Rothes, Tanglewood, West Tytherley, Salisbury, Wilts SP5 ILX

LINDSAY: The Earl of Crawford and Balcarres, KT, PC, Balcarres, Colinsburgh, Fife

LOCKHART: Angus H. Lockhart of the Lee, Newholme, Dunsyre, Lanark

LUMSDEN: Gillem Lumsden of that Ilk and Blanerne, Kinderslegh, Bois Avenue, Chesham Bois, Amersham

MACALESTER: William St J. S. McAlester of Loup and Kennox, 2 Avon Road East, Christchurch, Dorset

McBAIN: J. H. McBain of McBain, 7025 North Finger Rock Place, Tucson, Arizona, USA

MALCOLM (MACCALLUM): Robin N. L. Malcolm of Poltalloch, Duntrune Castle, Lochgilphead, Argyll

MACDONALD: The Lord Macdonald (*The Macdonald of Macdonald*), Kinloch Lodge, Sleat, Isle of Skye

*MACDONALD OF CLANRANALD: Ranald A. Macdonald of Clanranald, Mornish House, Killin, Perthshire FK21 8TX

*MACDONALD OF SLEAT (CLAN HUSTEAIN): Sir Ian Bosville Macdonald of Sleat, Bt., Thorpe Hall, Rudston, Driffield, N. Humberside YO25 OJE

*MACDONELL OF GLENGARRY: Air Cdre Aeneas R. MacDonell of Glengarry, CB, DFC, Elonbank, Castle Street, Fortrose, Ross-shire IV10 8TH

MACDOUGALL: vacant

MACDOWALL: Fergus D. H. Macdowall of Garthland, 9170 Ardmore Drive, North Saanich, British Columbia, Canada

MACGREGOR: Sir Gregor MacGregor of MacGregor, Bt., Bannatyne, Newtyle, Blairgowrie, Perthshire PH12 8TR

MACINTYRE: James W. MacIntyre of Glenoe, 15301 Pine Orchard Drive, Apartment 3H, Silver Spring, Maryland, USA

MACKAY: The Lord Reay, House of Lords, London SW1

MACKENZIE: The Earl of Cromartie, Castle Leod, Strathpeffer, Ross-shire IV14 9AA

MACKINNON: Madam Anne Mackinnon of Mackinnon, 16 Purleigh Road, Bridgwater, Somerset

MACKINTOSH: *The Mackintosh of Mackintosh*, Moy Hall, Inverness IV13 7YQ

MACLACHLAN: vacant

MACLAREN: Donald MacLaren of MacLaren and Achleskine, Achleskine, Kirkton, Balquidder, Lochearnhead

MACLEAN: The Hon. Sir Lachlan Maclean of Duart, Bt., Arngask House, Glenfarg, Perthshire PH2 9QA

MACLENNAN: vacant

MACLEOD: John MacLeod of MacLeod, Dunvegan Castle, Isle of Skye

MACMILLAN: George MacMillan of MacMillan, Finlaystone, Langbank, Renfrewshire

MACNAB: J. C. Macnab of Macnab (*The Macnab*), Leuchars Castle Farmhouse, Leuchars, Fife KY16 OEY

MACNAGHTEN: Sir Patrick Macnaghten of Macnaghten and Dundarave, Bt., Dundarave, Bushmills, Co. Antrim

MACNEACAIL: Iain Macneacail of Macneacail and Scorrybreac, 12 Fox Street, Ballina, NSW, Australia

MACNEIL OF BARRA: Ian R. Macneil of Barra (*The Macneil of Barra*), Kisimul Castle, Barra

MACPHERSON: The Hon. Sir William Macpherson of Cluny, TD, Newtown Castle, Blairgowrie, Perthshire

MACTHOMAS: Andrew P. C. MacThomas of Finegand, c/o The Clan MacThomas Society, 19 Warriston Avenue, Edinburgh

MAITLAND: The Earl of Lauderdale, 12 St Vincent Street, Edinburgh

MAKGILL: The Viscount of Oxfuird, Hill House, St Mary Bourne, Andover, Hants SP11 6BG

MAR: The Countess of Mar, St Michael's Farm, Great Witley, Worcs WR6 6JB

MARJORIBANKS: Andrew Marjoribanks of that Ilk

MATHESON: Maj. Sir Fergus Matheson of Matheson, Bt., Old Rectory, Hedenham, Bungay, Suffolk NR35 2LD

MENZIES: David R. Menzies of Menzies, 20 Nardina Crescent, Dalkeith, Western Australia

MOFFAT: Madam Moffat of that Ilk, St Jasual, Bullocks Farm Lane, Wheeler End Common, High Wycombe

MONCREIFFE: vacant

MONTGOMERIE: The Earl of Eglinton and Winton, The Dutch House, West Green, Hartley Wintney, Hants

MORRISON: Dr Iain M. Morrison of Ruchdi, Magnolia Cottage, The Street, Walberton, Sussex

MUNRO: Hector W. Munro of Foulis, Foulis Castle, Evanton, Ross-shire IV16 9UX

MURRAY: The Duke of Atholl, Blair Castle, Blair Atholl, Perthshire

NESBITT (or NISBET): Robert Nesbitt of that Ilk, Upper Roundhurst Farm, Roundhurst, Haslemere, Surrey

NICOLSON: The Lord Carnock, 90 Whitehall Court, London SW1A 2EL

OGILVY: The Earl of Airlie, KT, GCVO, PC, Cortachy Castle, Kirriemuir, Angus

RAMSAY: The Earl of Dalhousie, KT, GCVO, GBE, MC, Brechin Castle, Brechin, Angus DD7 6SH

RATTRAY: James S. Rattray of Rattray, Craighall, Rattray, Perthshire

ROBERTSON: Alexander G. H. Robertson of Struan (*Struan Robertson*), The Breach Farm, Goudhurst Road, Cranbrook, Kent

ROLLO: The Lord Rollo, Pitcairns, Dunning, Perthshire

ROSE: Miss Elizabeth Rose of Kilravock, Kilravock Castle, Croy, Inverness

ROSS: David C. Ross of that Ilk, The Old Schoolhouse, Fettercairn, Kincardineshire

RUTHVEN: The Earl of Gowrie, PC, Castlemartin, Kilcullen, Co. Kildare, Republic of Ireland

SCOTT: The Duke of Buccleuch and Queensberry, KT, VRD, Bowhill, Selkirk

SCRYMGEOUR: The Earl of Dundee, Birkhill, Cupar, Fife

SEMPILL: The Lord Sempill, 3 Vanburgh Street, Edinburgh

SHAW: John Shaw of Tordarroch, Newhall, Balblair, By Conon Bridge, Ross-shire

SINCLAIR: The Earl of Caithness, Churchill, Chipping Norton, Oxford OX7 5UX

SKENE: Danus Skene of Skene, Nether Pitlour, Strathmiglo, Fife

STIRLING: Fraser J. Stirling of Cader, 44A Oakley Street, London SW3 5HA

STRANGE: Maj. Timothy Strange of Balcaskie, Little Holme, Porton Road, Amesbury, Wilts

SUTHERLAND: The Countess of Sutherland, House of Tongue, Brora, Sutherland

SWINTON: John Swinton of that Ilk, 123 Superior Avenue SW, Calgary, Alberta, Canada

TROTTER: Alexander Trotter of Mortonhall, Charterhall, Duns, Berwickshire

URQUHART: Kenneth T. Urquhart of Urquhart, 507 Jefferson Park Avenue, Jefferson, New Orleans, Louisiana 70121, USA

WALLACE: Ian F. Wallace of that Ilk, 5 Lennox Street, Edinburgh EH4 1QB

WEDDERBURN OF THAT ILK: The Master of Dundee, Birkhill, Cupar, Fife

WEMYSS: David Wemyss of that Ilk, Invermay, Fortevoit, Perthshire

The Privy Council

The Sovereign in Council, or Privy Council, was the chief source of executive power until the system of Cabinet government developed in the 18th century. Now the Privy Council's main functions are to advise the Sovereign and to exercise its own statutory responsibilities independent of the Sovereign in Council (*see also* page 216).

Membership of the Privy Council is automatic upon appointment to certain government and judicial positions in the United Kingdom, e.g. Cabinet ministers must be Privy Counsellors and are sworn in on first assuming office. Membership is also accorded by The Queen to eminent people in the UK and independent countries of the Commonwealth of which Her Majesty is Queen, on the recommendation of the British Prime Minister. Membership of the Council is retained for life, except for very occasional removals.

The administrative functions of the Privy Council are carried out by the Privy Council Office (*see* page 334) under the direction of the President of the Council, who is always a member of the Cabinet.

President of the Council, The Rt. Hon. Ann Taylor, MP
Clerk of the Council, N. H. Nicholls, CBE

MEMBERS *as at 31 August 1997*

HRH The Duke of Edinburgh, 1951
HRH The Prince of Wales, 1977

Aberdare, Lord, 1974
Ackner, Lord, 1980
Airlie, Earl of, 1984
Aldington, Lord, 1954
Aldous, Sir William, 1995
Alebua, Ezekiel, 1988
Alison, Michael, 1981
Alport, Lord, 1960
Ampthill, Lord, 1995
Ancram, Michael, 1996
Anthony, Douglas, 1971
Archer of Sandwell, Lord, 1977
Arnold, Sir John, 1979
Arthur, Hon. Owen, 1995
Ashdown, Paddy, 1989
Ashley of Stoke, Lord, 1979
Atkins, Sir Robert, 1995
Auld, Sir Robin, 1995
Baker of Dorking, Lord, 1984
Balcombe, Sir John, 1985
Barber, Lord, 1963
Barnett, Lord, 1975

Beckett, Margaret, 1993
Beith, Alan, 1992
Beldam, Sir Roy, 1989
Belstead, Lord, 1983
Benn, Anthony, 1964
Bennett, Sir Frederic, 1985
Biffen, Lord, 1979
Bingham of Cornhill, Lord, 1986
Birch, William, 1992
Bird, Vere, 1982
Bisson, Sir Gordon, 1987
Blair, Anthony, 1994
Blaker, Lord, 1983
Blatch, Baroness, 1993
Blunkett, David, 1997
Bolger, James, 1991
Booth, Albert, 1976
Boothroyd, Betty, 1992
Boscawen, Hon. Robert, 1992
Bottomley, Virginia, 1992
Boyd-Carpenter, Lord, 1954
Boyson, Sir Rhodes, 1987
Braine of Wheatley, Lord, 1985
Brandon of Oakbrook, Lord, 1978
Brathwaite, Sir Nicholas, 1991
Bridge of Harwich, Lord, 1975
Brightman, Lord, 1979
Brittan, Sir Leon, 1981
Brooke, Sir Henry, 1996
Brooke, Peter, 1988
Brown, Gordon, 1996
Brown, Nicholas, 1997
Brown, Sir Simon, 1992
Brown, Sir Stephen, 1983
Browne-Wilkinson, Lord, 1983
Buckley, Sir Denys, 1970
Butler, Sir Adam, 1984
Butler-Sloss, Dame Elizabeth, 1988
Caithness, Earl of, 1990
Callaghan of Cardiff, Lord, 1964
Cameron of Lochbroom, Lord, 1984
Campbell of Croy, Lord, 1970
Canterbury, The Archbishop of, 1991
Carlisle of Bucklow, Lord, 1979
Carr of Hadley, Lord, 1963
Carrington, Lord, 1959
Carswell, Sir Robert, 1993
Casey, Sir Maurice, 1986
Castle of Blackburn, Baroness, 1964
Cato, Robert, 1981
Chalfont, Lord, 1964
Chalker of Wallasey, Baroness, 1987
Chan, Sir Julius, 1981
Charteris of Amisfield, Lord, 1972
Chataway, Sir Christopher, 1970
Clark, Alan, 1991
Clark, David, 1997
Clark, Helen, 1990
Clark of Kempston, Lord, 1990
Clarke, Kenneth, 1984
Clarke, Thomas, 1997
Cledwyn of Penrhos, Lord, 1966
Clyde, Lord, 1996

Cockfield, Lord, 1982
Cocks of Hartcliffe, Lord, 1976
Coggan, Lord, 1961
Colman, Fraser, 1986
Compton, Sir John, 1983
Concannon, John, 1978
Cook, Robin, 1996
Cooke of Thorndon, Lord, 1977
Cooper, Sir Frank, 1983
Cope, Sir John, 1988
Corfield, Sir Frederick, 1970
Cowen, Sir Zelman, 1981
Cradock, Sir Percy, 1993
Cranborne, Viscount, 1994
Crawford and Balcarres, Earl of, 1972
Crickhowell, Lord, 1979
Croom-Johnson, Sir David, 1984
Cullen, *Hon.* Lord, 1997
Cumming-Bruce, Sir Roualeyn, 1977
Cunningham, Jack, 1993
Curry, David, 1996
Darling, Alistair, 1997
Davies, Denzil, 1978
Davies, Ronald, 1997
Davis, David, 1997
Davison, Sir Ronald, 1978
Dean of Harptree, Lord, 1991
Deedes, Lord, 1962
Dell, Edmund, 1970
Denham, Lord, 1981
Denning, Lord, 1948
Devonshire, Duke of, 1964
Dewar, Donald, 1996
Diamond, Lord, 1965
Dillon, Sir Brian, 1982
Dixon, Lord, 1996
Dobson, Frank, 1997
Donaldson of Lymington, Lord, 1979
Dorrell, Stephen, 1994
Douglas, Sir William, 1977
Douglas-Hamilton, Lord James, 1996
du Cann, Sir Edward, 1964
Duff, Sir Antony, 1980
Dunn, Sir Robin, 1980
Eccles, Viscount, 1951
Eden of Winton, Lord, 1972
Eggar, Timothy, 1995
Eichelbaum, Sir Thomas, 1989
Emery, Sir Peter, 1993
Emslie, Lord, 1972
Erroll of Hale, Lord, 1960
Esquivel, Manuel, 1986
Evans, Sir Anthony, 1992
Eveleigh, Sir Edward, 1977
Farquharson, Sir Donald, 1989
Fellowes, Sir Robert, 1990
Ferrers, Earl, 1982
Field, Frank, 1997
Floissac, Sir Vincent, 1992
Foot, Michael, 1974
Forsyth, Sir Michael, 1995
Forth, Eric, 1997

Redwood, John, 1993
Rees, Lord, 1983
Renton, Lord, 1962
Renton of Mount Harry, Lord, 1989
Richard, Lord, 1993
Richardson, Sir Ivor, 1978
Richardson of Duntisbourne, Lord, 1976
Rifkind, Sir Malcolm, 1986
Robens of Woldingham, Lord, 1951
Roberts, Sir Wyn, 1991
Robertson, George, 1997
Roch, Sir John, 1993
Rodger of Earlsferry, Lord, 1992
Rodgers of Quarry Bank, Lord, 1975
Rose, Sir Christopher, 1992
Ross, *Hon.* Lord, 1985
Rumbold, Dame Angela, 1991
Runcie, Lord, 1980
Russell, Sir Patrick, 1987
Ryder, Richard, 1990
Sainsbury, Sir Timothy, 1992
St John of Fawsley, Lord, 1979
Sandiford, Erskine, 1989
Saville of Newdigate, Lord, 1994
Scarman, Lord, 1973
Schiemann, Sir Konrad, 1995
Scott, Sir Nicholas, 1989
Scott, Sir Richard, 1991
Seaga, Edward, 1981
Shawcross, Lord, 1946
Shearer, Hugh, 1969
Sheldon, Robert, 1977
Shephard, Gillian, 1992
Shepherd, Lord, 1965
Shore of Stepney, Lord, 1967

Short, Clare, 1997
Simmonds, Kennedy, 1984
Simon of Glaisdale, Lord, 1961
Sinclair, Ian, 1977
Slade, Sir Christopher, 1982
Slynn of Hadley, Lord, 1992
Smith, Andrew, 1997
Smith, Christopher, 1997
Smith, Sir Geoffrey Johnson, 1996
Somare, Sir Michael, 1977
Somers, Sir Edward, 1981
Stanley, Sir John, 1984
Staughton, Sir Christopher, 1988
Steel of Aikwood, Lord, 1977
Stephen, Sir Ninian, 1979
Stephenson, Sir John, 1971
Stewartby, Lord, 1989
Steyn, Lord, 1992
Stodart of Leaston, Lord, 1974
Stott, Lord, 1964
Strang, Gavin, 1997
Strathclyde, Lord, 1995
Straw, Jack, 1997
Stuart-Smith, Sir Murray, 1988
Talboys, Sir Brian, 1977
Taylor, Ann, 1997
Tebbit, Lord, 1981
Templeman, Lord, 1978
Thatcher, Baroness, 1970
Thomas, Edmund, 1996
Thomas of Gwydir, Lord, 1964
Thomas, Sir Swinton, 1994
Thomson, David, 1981
Thomson of Monifieth, Lord, 1966
Thorpe, Jeremy, 1967
Thorpe, Sir Matthew, 1995

Tizard, Robert, 1986
Tonypandy, Viscount, 1968
Trefgarne, Lord, 1989
Trumpington, Baroness, 1992
Ullswater, Viscount, 1994
Varley, Lord, 1974
Waddington, Lord, 1987
Waite, Sir John, 1993
Wakeham, Lord, 1983
Waldegrave, William, 1990
Walker, Sir Harold, 1979
Walker of Worcester, Lord, 1970
Waller, Sir George, 1976
Waller, Sir Mark, 1996
Ward, Sir Alan, 1995
Watkins, Sir Tasker, 1980
Weatherill, Lord, 1980
Wheeler, Sir John, 1993
Whitelaw, Viscount, 1967
Widdecombe, Ann, 1997
Wilberforce, Lord, 1964
Williams, Alan, 1977
Williams of Crosby, Baroness, 1974
Wilson of Langside, Lord, 1967
Windlesham, Lord, 1973
Wingti, Paias, 1987
Withers, Reginald, 1977
Woodhouse, Sir Owen, 1974
Woolf, Lord, 1986
Wylie, *Hon.* Lord, 1970
York, The Archbishop of, 1991
Young, Baroness, 1981
Young, Sir George, 1993
Young of Graffham, Lord, 1984
Younger of Leckie, Viscount, 1979
Zacca, Edward, 1992

The Privy Council of Northern Ireland

The Privy Council of Northern Ireland had responsibilities in Northern Ireland similar to those of the Privy Council in Great Britain until the Northern Ireland Act 1974 instituted direct rule and a UK Cabinet minister became responsible for the functions previously exercised by the Northern Ireland government.

Membership of the Privy Council of Northern Ireland is retained for life. The postnominal initials PC (NI) are used to differentiate its members from those of the Privy Council.

MEMBERS *as at 31 August 1997*

Bailie, Robin, 1971
Bleakley, David, 1971
Bradford, Roy, 1969
Craig, William, 1963
Dobson, John, 1969
Kelly, Sir Basil, 1969

Kirk, Herbert, 1962
Long, William, 1966
Lowry, The Lord, 1971
McConnell, The Lord, 1964
McIvor, Basil, 1971
Morgan, William, 1961
Moyola, The Lord, 1966
Neill, Sir Ivan, 1950
Porter, Sir Robert, 1969
Taylor, John, MP, 1970
West, Henry, 1960

General Election statistics

PRINCIPAL PARTIES IN PARLIAMENT SINCE 1970

	1970	1974 Feb.	1974 Oct.	1979	1983	1987	1992	1997
Conservative	330*	296	276	339	397	375	336	165
Labour	287	301	319	268	209	229	270	418
Liberal/LD	6	14	13	11	17	17	20	46
Social Democrat	—	1	—	—	6	5	—	—
Independent	5†	1	1	2	—	—	—	1
Plaid Cymru	—	2	3	2	2	3	4	4
Scottish Nationalist	1	7	11	2	2	3	3	6
Democratic Unionist	—	—	—	3	3	3	3	2
SDLP	—	1	1	1	1	3	4	3
Sinn Fein	—	—	—	—	1	1	—	2
Ulster Popular Unionist	—	—	—	—	1	1	1	—
Ulster Unionist‡	*	11	10	6	10	9	9	10
UK Unionist	—	—	—	—	—	—	—	1
The Speaker	1	1	1	1	1	1	1	1
Total	630	635	635	635	650	650	651	659

* Including 8 Ulster Unionists
† Comprising: Independent Labour 1, Independent Unity 1, Protestant Unity 1, Republican Labour 1, Unity 1
‡ Comprises:
   1974 (February) United Ulster Unionist Council 11
   1974 (October) United Ulster Unionist 10
   1979 Ulster Unionist 5, United Ulster Unionist 1
   1983 Official Unionist 10

PARLIAMENTS SINCE 1970

		Duration		
Assembled	Dissolved	yr	m.	d.
29 June 1970	8 February 1974	3	7	10
6 March 1974	20 September 1974	0	6	14
22 October 1974	7 April 1979	4	5	16
9 May 1979	13 May 1983	4	0	4
15 June 1983	18 May 1987	3	11	3
17 June 1987	16 March 1992	4	8	28
27 April 1992	8 April 1997	4	11	12
7 May 1997				

MAJORITIES IN THE COMMONS SINCE 1970

Year	Party	Maj.
1970	Conservative	31
1974 Feb.	No majority	
1974 Oct.	Labour	5
1979	Conservative	43
1983	Conservative	144
1987	Conservative	102
1992	Conservative	21
1997	Labour	178

VOTES CAST 1992 AND 1997

	1992	1997
Conservative	14,089,722	9,600,940
Labour	11,567,764	13,517,911
Liberal Democrats	6,027,552	5,243,440
Scottish Nationalist	629,564	622,260
Plaid Cymru	154,390	161,030
N. Ireland parties	740,859	780,920
Others	401,239	1,361,701
Total	33,619,090	31,287,702

DISTRIBUTION OF SEATS BY COUNTRY 1997

	England	Wales	Scotland	N. Ireland
Conservative	165	—	—	—
Labour	328	34	56	—
Lib. Dem.	34	2	10	—
SNP	—	—	6	—
Plaid Cymru	—	4	—	—
Other	2*	—	—	18

* Includes the Speaker

SIZE OF ELECTORATE 1997

England	36,806,557
Wales	2,222,533
Scotland	3,984,406
Northern Ireland	1,190,198
Total	44,203,694

Parliament

The United Kingdom constitution is not contained in any single document but has evolved in the course of time, formed partly by statute, partly by common law and partly by convention. A constitutional monarchy, the United Kingdom is governed by Ministers of the Crown in the name of the Sovereign, who is head both of the state and of the government.

The organs of government are the legislature (Parliament), the executive and the judiciary. The executive consists of HM Government (Cabinet and other Ministers) (*see* pages 276–7), government departments (*see* pages 278–353), local authorities (*see* Local Government), and public corporations operating nationalized industries or social or cultural services (*see* pages 278–353). The judiciary (*see* Law Courts and Offices) pronounces on the law, both written and unwritten, interprets statutes and is responsible for the enforcement of the law; the judiciary is independent of both the legislature and the executive.

THE MONARCHY

The Sovereign personifies the state and is, in law, an integral part of the legislature, head of the executive, head of the judiciary, the commander-in-chief of all armed forces of the Crown and the 'Supreme Governor' of the Church of England. The seat of the monarchy is in the United Kingdom. In the Channel Islands and the Isle of Man, which are Crown dependencies, the Sovereign is represented by a Lieutenant-Governor. In the member states of the Commonwealth of which the Sovereign is head of state, her representative is a Governor-General; in United Kingdom dependencies the Sovereign is usually represented by a Governor, who is responsible to the British Government.

Although the powers of the monarchy are now very limited, restricted mainly to the advisory and ceremonial, there are important acts of government which require the participation of the Sovereign. These include summoning, proroguing and dissolving Parliament, giving royal assent to bills passed by Parliament, appointing important office-holders, e.g. government ministers, judges, bishops and governors, conferring peerages, knighthoods and other honours, and granting pardon to a person wrongly convicted of a crime. An important function is appointing a Prime Minister, by convention the leader of the political party which enjoys, or can secure, a majority of votes in the House of Commons. In international affairs the Sovereign as head of state has the power to declare war and make peace, to recognize foreign states and governments, to conclude treaties and to annex or cede territory. However, as the Sovereign entrusts executive power to Ministers of the Crown and acts on the advice of her Ministers, which she cannot ignore, in practice royal prerogative powers are exercised by Ministers, who are responsible to Parliament.

Ministerial responsibility does not diminish the Sovereign's importance to the smooth working of government. She holds meetings of the Privy Council, gives audiences to her Ministers and other officials at home and overseas, receives accounts of Cabinet decisions, reads dispatches and signs state papers; she must be informed and consulted on every aspect of national life; and she must show complete impartiality.

COUNSELLORS OF STATE

In the event of the Sovereign's absence abroad, it is necessary to appoint Counsellors of State under letters patent to carry out the chief functions of the Monarch, including the holding of Privy Councils and giving royal assent to acts passed by Parliament. The normal procedure is to appoint as Counsellors three or four members of the royal family among those remaining in the United Kingdom.

In the event of the Sovereign on accession being under the age of 18 years, or at any time unavailable or incapacitated by infirmity of mind or body for the performance of the royal functions, provision is made for a regency.

THE PRIVY COUNCIL

The Sovereign in Council, or Privy Council, was the chief source of executive power until the system of Cabinet government developed. Now its main function is to advise the Sovereign to approve Orders in Council and to advise on the issue of royal proclamations. The Council's own statutory responsibilities (independent of the powers of the Sovereign in Council) include powers of supervision over the registering bodies for the medical and allied professions. A full Council is summoned only on the death of the Sovereign or when the Sovereign announces his or her intention to marry. (For full list of Counsellors, *see* pages 212–4)

There are a number of advisory Privy Council committees, whose meetings the Sovereign does not attend. Some are prerogative committees, such as those dealing with legislative matters submitted by the legislatures of the Channel Islands and the Isle of Man or with applications for charters of incorporation; and some are provided for by statute, e.g. those for the universities of Oxford and Cambridge and the Scottish universities.

The Judicial Committee of the Privy Council is the final court of appeal from courts of the United Kingdom dependencies, courts of independent Commonwealth countries which have retained the right of appeal, courts of the Channel Islands and the Isle of Man, some professional and disciplinary committees, and church sources. The Committee is composed of Privy Counsellors who hold, or have held, high judicial office, although usually only three or five hear each case.

Administrative work is carried out by the Privy Council Office under the direction of the President of the Council, a Cabinet Minister.

PARLIAMENT

Parliament is the supreme law-making authority and can legislate for the United Kingdom as a whole or for any parts of it separately (the Channel Islands and the Isle of Man are Crown dependencies and not part of the United Kingdom).

The main functions of Parliament are to pass laws, to provide (by voting taxation) the means of carrying on the work of government and to scrutinize government policy and administration, particularly proposals for expenditure. International treaties and agreements are by custom presented to Parliament before ratification.

Parliament emerged during the late 13th and early 14th centuries. The officers of the King's household and the King's judges were the nucleus of early Parliaments, joined by such ecclesiastical and lay magnates as the King might summon to form a prototype 'House of Lords', and occasionally by the knights of the shires, burgesses and proctors of the lower clergy. By the end of Edward III's reign a 'House of Commons' was beginning to appear; the first known Speaker was elected in 1377.

Parliamentary procedure is based on custom and precedent, partly formulated in the Standing Orders of both Houses (see Standing Orders, page 222), and each House has the right to control its own internal proceedings and to commit for contempt. The system of debate in the two Houses is similar; when a motion has been moved, the Speaker proposes the question as the subject of a debate. Members speak from wherever they have been sitting. Questions are decided by a vote on a simple majority. Draft legislation is introduced, in either House, as a bill. Bills can be introduced by a Government Minister or a private Member, but in practice the majority of bills which become law are introduced by the Government. To become law, a bill must be passed by each House (for parliamentary stages, see Bill, page 220) and then sent to the Sovereign for the royal assent, after which it becomes an Act of Parliament.

Proceedings of both Houses are public, except on extremely rare occasions. The minutes (called Votes and Proceedings in the Commons, and Minutes of Proceedings in the Lords) and the speeches (The Official Report of Parliamentary Debates, Hansard) are published daily. Proceedings are also recorded for transmission on radio and television and stored in the Parliamentary Recording Unit before transfer to the National Sound Archive. Television cameras have been allowed into the House of Lords since 1985 and into the House of Commons since 1989; committee meetings may also be televised.

By the Parliament Act of 1911, the maximum duration of a Parliament is five years (if not previously dissolved), the term being reckoned from the date given on the writs for the new Parliament. The maximum life has been prolonged by legislation in such rare circumstances as the two world wars (31 January 1911 to 25 November 1918; 26 November 1935 to 15 June 1945). Dissolution and writs for a general election are ordered by the Sovereign on the advice of the Prime Minister. The life of a Parliament is divided into sessions, usually of one year in length, beginning and ending most often in October or November.

THE HOUSE OF LORDS
London SW1A 0PW
Tel 0171-219 3000

The House of Lords consists of the Lords Spiritual and Temporal. The Lords Spiritual are the Archbishops of Canterbury and York, the Bishops of London, Durham and Winchester, and the 21 senior diocesan bishops of the Church of England. The Lords Temporal consist of all hereditary peers of England, Scotland, Great Britain and the United Kingdom who have not disclaimed their peerages, life peers created under the Life Peerages Act 1958, and those Lords of Appeal in Ordinary created life peers under the Appellate Jurisdiction Act 1876, as amended (law lords). Disclaimants of a hereditary peerage

lose their right to sit in the House of Lords but gain the right to vote at parliamentary elections and to offer themselves for election to the House of Commons (see also page 137). Those peers disqualified from sitting in the House include:

– aliens, i.e. any peer who is not a British citizen, a Commonwealth citizen (under the British Nationality Act 1981) or a citizen of the Republic of Ireland
– peers under the age of 21
– undischarged bankrupts or, in Scotland, those whose estate is sequestered
– peers convicted of treason

Peers who do not wish to attend sittings of the House of Lords may apply for leave of absence for the duration of a Parliament.

Until the beginning of this century the House of Lords had considerable power, being able to veto any bill submitted to it by the House of Commons, but those powers were greatly reduced by the Parliament Acts of 1911 and 1949 (see page 221).

Combined with its legislative role, the House of Lords has judicial powers as the ultimate Court of Appeal for courts in Great Britain and Northern Ireland, except for criminal cases in Scotland. These powers are exercised by the Lord Chancellor and the law lords.

Members of the House of Lords are unpaid. However, they are entitled to reimbursement of travelling expenses on parliamentary business within the UK and certain other expenses incurred for the purpose of attendance at sittings of the House, within a maximum for each day of £75.50 for overnight subsistence, £33.50 for day subsistence and incidental travel, and £32.50 for secretarial costs, postage and certain additional expenses.

COMPOSITION as at 10 July 1997

Archbishops and Bishops, 26
Peers by succession, 752 (16 women)
Hereditary Peers of first creation (including the Prince of Wales), 10
Life Peers under the Appellate Jurisdiction Act 1876, 25
Life Peers under the Life Peerages Act 1958, 406 (70 women)
Total 1,219
Of whom:
Peers without Writs of Summons, 72 (3 minors)
Peers on leave of absence from the House, 56

STATE OF PARTIES as at 10 July 1997

About half of the members of the House of Lords take the whip of one of the political parties. The other members sit on the cross-benches or as independents.

Conservative, 479
Labour, 126
Liberal Democrats, 55
Cross-bench, 323
Other (including Bishops), 236 (of whom 128 are ineligible to attend)

OFFICERS

The House is presided over by the Lord Chancellor, who is ex officio Speaker of the House. A panel of deputy Speakers is appointed by Royal Commission. The first deputy Speaker is the Chairman of Committees, appointed at the beginning of each session, a salaried officer of the House who takes the chair in committee of the whole House and in some select committees. He is assisted by a panel of deputy chairmen, headed by the salaried Principal Deputy

Chairman of Committees, who is also chairman of the European Communities Committee of the House.

The permanent officers include the Clerk of the Parliaments, who is in charge of the administrative staff collectively known as the Parliament Office; the Gentleman Usher of the Black Rod, who is also Serjeant-at-Arms in attendance upon the Lord Chancellor and is responsible for security and for accommodation and services in the House of Lords; and the Yeoman Usher who is Deputy Serjeant-at-Arms and assists Black Rod in his duties.

Speaker (£19,693), The Lord Irvine of Lairg, PC, QC
  Private Secretary, Ms E. Hutchinson
Chairman of Committees (£51,838), The Lord Boston of
  Faversham, QC
Principal Deputy Chairman of Committees (£47,739), The
  Lord Tordoff
Clerk of the Parliaments (£108,192), J. M. Davies
Clerk Assistant and Clerk of Legislation (£57,020–£91,800),
  P. D. G. Hayter, LVO
Reading Clerk and Principal Finance Officer
  (£57,020–£91,800), M. G. Pownall
Counsel to Chairman of Committees (£57,020–£91,800),
  D. Rippengal, CB, QC; Sir James Nursaw, KCB, QC: Dr C. S.
  Kerse
Principal Clerks (£52,020–£86,700), J. A. Vallance White,
  CB (*Judicial Office and Fourth Clerk at the Table*); B. P. Keith
  (*Clerk of the Journals*); (£47,120–£77,110) D. R. Beamish
  (*Committees and Overseas Office*); R. H. Walters, D.phil.
  (*Establishment Officer*); (£42,740–£68,540) Dr F. Tudor
  (*Private Bills*); E. C. Ollard (*Public Bills*); A. Makower;
  T. V. Mohan (*Select Committees*)
Senior Clerks (£29,689–£44,983), Mrs M. E. Ollard; E. J. J.
  Wells; S. P. Burton (*seconded as Secretary to the Leader of the
  House and Chief Whip*); J. L. Goddard; Mrs M. B. Bloor;
  T. E. Radice; Dr D. Rolt; D. J. Batt; I. Smyth
Clerks (£15,475–£26,892), Dr C. A. Mylne; Miss L. J.
  Mouland; J. A. Vaughan
Clerk of the Records (£42,740–£68,540), D. J. Johnson, FSA
Deputy Clerk of the Records (£33,621–£54,551), S. K. Ellison
Establishment Officer, R. H. Walters, D.phil.
Deputy Establishment Officer (£29,689–£44,983), G.
  Embleton
Accountant (£42,740–£68,540), C. Preece
Deputy Accountant (£22,858–£29,511), A. D. Underwood
Computer Executive (£29,689–£44,983), Ms S. C. White
Internal Auditor (£29,689–£44,983), C. H. Rogers
Staff Adviser (£29,689–£44,983), D. A. W. Dunn, ISO
Senior Information Officer (£29,689–£44,983), Mrs M. L.
  Morgan
Judicial Taxing Clerk (£22,858–£29,511), C. G. Osborne
Librarian (£47,120–£77,110), D. L. Jones
Deputy Librarian (£33,621–£54,511), P. G. Davis, Ph.D.
Senior Library Clerk (£29,689–£44,983), Miss J. L. Victory,
  Ph.D.
Examiners of Petitions for Private Bills, Dr F. P. Tudor; W. J.
  Proctor
Gentleman Usher of the Black Rod and Serjeant-at-Arms
  (£47,120–£77,110), Gen. Sir Edward Jones, KCB, CBE
Yeoman Usher of the Black Rod and Deputy Serjeant-at-Arms
  (£29,689–£44,983), Air Vice-Marshal D. R. Hawkins,
  CB, MBE
Administration Officer (£29,689–£44,983), Brig. A. J. M.
  Clark
Staff Superintendent, Maj. A. M. Charlesworth
Shorthand Writer (fees), Mrs P. J. Woolgar
Editor, Official Report (*Hansard*), (£42,740–£68,540), Mrs
  M. E. Villiers
Deputy Editor, Official Report (£33,621–£54,551), G. R.
  Goodbarne

THE HOUSE OF COMMONS
London SW1A 0AA
Tel 0171-219 3000

The members of the House of Commons are elected by universal adult suffrage. For electoral purposes, the United Kingdom is divided into constituencies, each of which returns one member to the House of Commons, the member being the candidate who obtains the largest number of votes cast in the constituency. To ensure equitable representation the four Boundary Commissions keep constituency boundaries under review and recommend any redistribution of seats which may seem necessary because of population movements, etc. The number of seats was raised to 640 in 1945, reduced to 625 in 1948, and subsequently rose to 630 in 1955, 635 in 1970, 650 in 1983, 651 in 1992 and 659 in 1997. Of the present 659 seats, there are 529 for England, 40 for Wales, 72 for Scotland and 18 for Northern Ireland.

ELECTIONS

Elections are by secret ballot, each elector casting one vote; voting is not compulsory. When a seat becomes vacant between general elections, a by-election is held.

British subjects and citizens of the Irish Republic can stand for election as Members of Parliament (MPs) provided they are 21 or over and not subject to disqualification. Those disqualified from sitting in the House include:

– undischarged bankrupts
– people sentenced to more than one year's imprisonment
– clergy of the Church of England, Church of Scotland,
  Church of Ireland and Roman Catholic Church
– members of the House of Lords
– holders of certain offices listed in the House of Commons
  Disqualification Act 1975, e.g. members of the judiciary,
  Civil Service, regular armed forces, police forces, some
  local government officers and some members of public
  corporations and government commissions

For entitlement to vote in parliamentary elections, *see* Legal Notes section.

A candidate does not require any party backing but his or her nomination for election must be supported by the signatures of ten people registered in the constituency. A candidate must also deposit with the returning officer £500, which is forfeit if the candidate does not receive more than 5 per cent of the votes cast. All election expenses at a general election, except the candidate's personal expenses, are subject to a statutory limit of £4,965, plus 4.2 pence for each elector in a borough constituency or 5.6 pence for each elector in a county constituency.

See pages 226–33 for an alphabetical list of MPs, pages 236–68 for the results of the last General Election, and page 268 for the results of recent by-elections.

STATE OF PARTIES *as at 31 July 1997*

Conservative, 163 (13 women)
Labour, 416 (101 women)
Liberal Democrats, 46 (3 women)
Plaid Cymru, 4
Scottish Nationalist, 6 (2 women)
Sinn Fein, 2
Social Democratic and Labour, 3
Ulster Democratic Unionist, 2
Ulster Unionist, 10
United Kingdom Unionist, 1
Independent, 1
The Speaker and three Deputy Speakers, 4 (1 woman)
Vacant, 1
Total, 659 (120 women)

BUSINESS

The week's business of the House is outlined each Thursday by the Leader of the House, after consultation between the Chief Government Whip and the Chief Opposition Whip. A quarter to a third of the time will be taken up by the Government's legislative programme, and the rest by other business, e.g. question time. As a rule, bills likely to raise political controversy are introduced in the Commons before going on to the Lords, and the Commons claims exclusive control in respect of national taxation and expenditure. Bills such as the Finance Bill, which imposes taxation, and the Consolidated Fund Bills, which authorize expenditure, must begin in the Commons. A bill of which the financial provisions are subsidiary may begin in the Lords; and the Commons may waive its rights in regard to Lords' amendments affecting finance.

The Commons has a public register of MPs' financial and certain other interests; this is published annually as a House of Commons paper. Members must also disclose any relevant financial interest or benefit in a matter before the House when taking part in a debate, in certain other proceedings of the House, or in consultations with other MPs, with Ministers or civil servants.

MEMBERS' PAY AND ALLOWANCES

Since 1911 members of the House of Commons have received salary payments; facilities for free travel were introduced in 1924. Members are entitled to claim income tax relief on expenses incurred in the course of their parliamentary duties. Salary rates since 1911 are as follows:

1911	£400 p.a.	1982 June	£14,510 p.a.
1931	360	1983 June	15,308
1934	380	1984 Jan	16,106
1935	400	1985 Jan	16,904
1937	600	1986 Jan	17,702
1946	1,000	1987 Jan	18,500
1954	1,250	1988 Jan	22,548
1957	1,750	1989 Jan	24,107
1964	3,250	1990 Jan	26,701
1972 Jan	4,500	1991 Jan	28,970
1975 June	5,750	1992 Jan	30,854
1976 June	6,062	1994 Jan	31,687
1977 July	6,270	1995 Jan	33,189
1978 June	6,897	1996 Jan	34,085
1979 June	9,450	1996 July	43,000
1980 June	11,750	1997 April	43,860
1981 June	13,950		

In 1969 MPs were granted an allowance for secretarial and research expenses. In 1987 this became known as the Office Costs Allowance. From April 1997 the allowance is £47,568 a year

Since 1972 MPs can claim reimbursement for the additional cost of staying overnight away from their main residence while on parliamentary business. From April 1997 this has been £12,287 a year and since 1984 has been non-taxable.

From 1980 provision was made enabling each MP in receipt of Office Costs Allowance to contribute sums to an approved pension scheme for the provision of a pension, or other benefits, for or in respect of persons whose salary is met by him/her from the Office Costs Allowance.

MEMBERS' PENSIONS

Pension arrangements for MPs were first introduced in 1964. The arrangements currently provide a pension of one-fiftieth of salary for each year of pensionable service with a maximum of two-thirds of salary at age 65. Pension is payable normally at age 65, for men and women, or on later retirement. Pensions may be paid earlier, e.g. on ill-health retirement. The widow/widower of a former MP receives a pension of five-eighths of the late MP's pension. Pensions are index-linked. Members currently contribute 6 per cent of salary to the pension fund; there is an Exchequer contribution, currently slightly more than the amount contributed by MPs.

The House of Commons Members' Fund provides for annual or lump sum grants to ex-MPs, their widows or widowers, and children whose incomes are below certain limits. Alternatively, payments of £2,116 a year to ex-MPs with at least ten years' service and who left the House of Commons before October 1964, and £1,323 a year to their widows or widowers are made as of right. Members contribute £24 a year and the Exchequer £215,000 a year to the fund.

OFFICERS AND OFFICIALS

The House of Commons is presided over by the Speaker, who has considerable powers to maintain order in the House. A deputy, the Chairman of Ways and Means, and two Deputy Chairmen may preside over sittings of the House of Commons; they are elected by the House, and, like the Speaker, neither speak nor vote other than in their official capacity.

The staff of the House are employed by a Commission chaired by the Speaker. The heads of the six House of Commons departments are permanent officers of the House, not MPs. The Clerk of the House is the principal adviser to the Speaker on the privileges and procedures of the House, the conduct of the business of the House, and committees. The Serjeant-at-Arms is responsible for security, ceremonial, and for accommodation in the Commons part of the Palace of Westminster.

Speaker (£103,860), The Rt. Hon. Betty Boothroyd, MP
  (West Bromwich West)
Chairman of Ways and Means (£74,985), Sir Alan Haselhurst,
  MP (Saffron Walden)
First Deputy Chairman of Ways and Means (£71,215), Michael
  Martin, MP (Glasgow Springburn)
Second Deputy Chairman of Ways and Means (£71,215),
  Michael Lord, MP (Suffolk Central and Ipswich North)

OFFICES OF THE SPEAKER AND CHAIRMAN OF WAYS AND MEANS

Speaker's Secretary (£42,717–£62,391), N. Bevan, CB
Chaplain to the Speaker, The Revd Canon D. Gray, TD
Secretary to the Chairman of Ways and Means,
  (£28,954–£43,802), Ms L. M. Gardner

DEPARTMENT OF THE CLERK OF THE HOUSE

Clerk of the House of Commons (£102,816), Sir Donald Limon,
  KCB
Clerk Assistant (£68,850–£85,950), W. R. McKay, CB
Clerk of Committees (£68,850–£85,950), C. B. Winnifrith
Principal Clerks (£56,100–£69,700)
  Public Bills, R. B. Sands
  Table Office, G. Cubie
  Journals, A. J. Hastings
  Select Committees, D. G. Millar
  Domestic Committees, M. R. Jack, PH.D.
  Overseas Office, R. W. G. Wilson
  Standing Committees and Private Bills, W. A. Proctor
  Second Clerk of Select Committees, Ms H. E. Irwin
  Financial Committees, Mrs J. Sharpe

Deputy Principal Clerks (£42,717–£62,391), S. Panton; Ms A.
Milner-Barry; F. Cranmer; R. Rogers; C. Ward, ph.d.; D.
Doig; D. Natzler; E. Silk; A. Kennon; L. Laurence
Smyth; S. Patrick; D. Gerhold; C. Poyser; D. Harrison; S.
Priestley; A. Doherty; P. Evans; R. Phillips; R. James,
ph.d.; D. Lloyd; Ms P. Helme; B. Hutton; J. Benger,
d.phil.; Ms E. Samson; N. Walker; M. Hamlyn; Mrs E.
Flood; P. Seaward, d.phil.
Senior Clerks (£28,954–£43,802), C. Lee; C. Stanton;
A. Azad; C. Shaw; Ms L. Gardner; K. Brown; F. Reid; M.
Hennessy; G. Devine; P. Moon; M. Clark; Mrs J. Mulley;
T. Healey; Mrs S. Davies; Mrs E. Attridge (*acting*); Ms J.
Eldred (*acting*); Ms E. Hopkins (*acting*)
Examiners of Petitions for Private Bills, W. A. Proctor; Dr F. P.
Tudor
Registrar of Members' Interests, R. J. Willoughby (*seconded to Speaker's Office*)
Taxing Officer, W. A. Proctor

Vote Office

Deliverer of the Vote (£42,717–£62,391), H. Foster
Deputy Deliverers of the Vote (£28,954–£43,802), J. Collins
(*Distribution*); O. Sweeney (*Parliamentary*);
(£34,729–£47,982) F. Hallett (*Production*)

Speaker's Counsel

Speaker's Counsel (£56,100–£69,700), J. Mason, cb
Speaker's Counsel (European legislation) (£56,100–£69,700),
T. Pratt, cb
Speaker's Assistant Counsel (£42,717–£62,391), A. Akbar; J.
Mallinson

DEPARTMENT OF THE SERJEANT-AT-ARMS

Serjeant-at-Arms (£56,100–£69,700), P. Jennings
Deputy Serjeant-at-Arms (£42,717–£62,391), M. Cummings
Assistant Serjeant-at-Arms (£32,791–£53,108), P. Wright
Deputy Assistant Serjeant-at-Arms (£28,954–£43,802), J.
Robertson; M. Harvey

Parliamentary Works Directorate

Director of Works (£55,769–£62,391), H. Webber
Deputy Director of Works (£32,791–£53,108), L.
Brantingham

Communications Directorate

Director of Communications (£42,717–£62,391), C. Gilbert

DEPARTMENT OF THE LIBRARY

Librarian (£56,100–£69,700), Miss J. B. Tanfield
Deputy Librarian (£51,791–£62,391), Miss P. Baines
Service Directors (£42,717–£62,391), K. Cuninghame; Mrs
J. Wainwright
Heads of Sections (£32,791–£53,108), C. Pond, ph.d.;
Mrs C. Andrews; R. Clements; Mrs J. Lourie; R. Ware,
d.phil.; C. Barclay; Mrs J. Fiddick; Mrs C. Gillie; R.
Twigger; Mrs G. Allen
Senior Library Clerks (£28,954–£43,802), Ms F. Poole; T.
Edmonds; R. Cracknell; Miss O. Gay; Miss E. McInnes;
Dr D. Gore; B. Winetrobe; Miss M. Baber; Ms A. Walker;
Mrs H. Holden; Mrs P. Carling; Miss J. Seaton; A.
Crompton; Miss P. Strickland; Miss V. Miller; Ms H.
Jeffs; M. P. Hillyard; Ms J. Roll; Ms W. Wilson; S. Wise;
E. Wood; P. Bowers; T. Dodd; A. Seely; Ms J. Dyson;
Miss N. Chedgey; Miss F. Watson; G. Danby, ph.d.; Miss
P. Hughes, ph.d.; R. Dewdrey

DEPARTMENT OF FINANCE AND ADMINISTRATION

Director of Finance and Administration (£56,100–£69,700), A.
Walker
Accountant (£51,791–£62,391), A. Marskell

Head of Establishments Office (£51,791–£62,391), B. Wilson
Head of Finance Office (£42,717–£62,391), M. Barram

DEPARTMENT OF THE OFFICIAL REPORT

Editor (£51,791–£62,391), I. Church
Deputy Editor (£42,717–£62,391), P. Walker
Principal Assistant Editors (£32,791–£53,108), J. Gourley;
W. Garland; Miss H. Hales; Miss L. Sutherland
Assistant Editors (£32,791–£49,325), Miss V. Grainger; Miss
V. Clarke; S. Hutchinson; Miss C. Fogarty; Miss
V. Widgery; Ms K. Stewart; P. Hadlow

REFRESHMENT DEPARTMENT

Director of Catering Services (£42,717–£62,391), Mrs S.
Harrison
Financial Controller (£28,954–£43,802), Mrs J. Rissen
Operations Manager (£28,954–£43,802), N. Hutson

PARLIAMENTARY INFORMATION

The following is a short glossary of aspects of the work of
Parliament. Unless otherwise stated, references are to
House of Commons procedures.

BILL – Proposed legislation is termed a bill. The stages
of a public bill (for private bills, *see* page 221) in the House
of Commons are as follows:
First Reading: There is no debate at this stage, which
nowadays merely constitutes an order to have the bill
printed
Second Reading: The debate on the principles of the bill
Committee Stage: The detailed examination of a bill, clause
by clause. In most cases this takes place in a standing
committee, or the whole House may act as a committee. A
special standing committee may take evidence before
embarking on detailed scrutiny of the bill. Very rarely, a
bill may be examined by a select committee (*see* page 222)
Report Stage: Detailed review of a bill as amended in
committee
Third Reading: Final debate on a bill
Public bills go through the same stages in the House of
Lords, except that in almost all cases the committee stage is
taken in committee of the whole House.
  A bill may start in either House, and has to pass through
both Houses to become law. Both Houses have to agree the
same text of a bill, so that the amendments made by the
second House are then considered in the originating
House, and if not agreed, sent back or themselves amended,
until agreement is reached.

CHILTERN HUNDREDS – A legal fiction, a nominal office
of profit under the Crown, the acceptance of which
requires an MP to vacate his seat. The Manor of Northstead is similar. These are the only means by which an MP
may resign.

CLOSURE AND GUILLOTINE – To prevent deliberate
waste of time of either House, a motion may be made that
the question be now put. In the House of Commons, if the
Speaker decides that the rights of a minority are not being
prejudiced and 100 members support the closure motion
in a division, if carried, the original motion is put to the
House without further debate.
  The guillotine represents a more rigorous and systematic application of the closure. Under this system, a bill
proceeds in accordance with a rigid timetable and discussion is limited to the time allotted to each group of
clauses. The closure is hardly ever used in the Lords, and
there is no procedure for a guillotine. The completion of

business in the Lords is ensured by agreement from all sides of the House.

CONSOLIDATED FUND BILL – A bill to authorize issue of money to maintain Government services. The bill is dealt with without debate.

DISSOLUTION – Parliament comes to an end either by dissolution by the Sovereign, on the advice of the Prime Minister, or on the expiration of the term of five years for which the House of Commons was elected. Dissolution is normally effected by a royal proclamation.

EARLY DAY MOTION – A motion put on the notice paper by an MP without in general the real prospect of its being debated. Such motions are expressions of back-bench opinion.

EMERGENCY DEBATE – In the Commons a method of obtaining prompt discussion of a matter of urgency is by moving the adjournment under Standing Order No. 24 for the purpose of discussing a specific and important matter that should have urgent consideration. A member may ask leave to make this motion by giving written notice to the Speaker, usually before 12 noon, and if the Speaker considers the matter of sufficient importance and the House agrees, it is discussed usually at 7 p.m. on the following day.

FATHER OF THE HOUSE – The Member whose continuous service in the House of Commons is the longest. The present Father of the House is the Rt. Hon. Sir Edward Heath, KG, MBE, MP, elected first in 1950.

HANSARD – The official report of debates in both Houses (and in standing committees) published by The Stationery Office, normally on the day after the sitting concerned.

HOURS OF MEETING – The House of Commons meets Monday, Tuesday and Thursday at 2.30 p.m., and on Wednesday and Friday at 9.30 a.m.; there are ten Fridays without sittings in each session. The House of Lords normally meets at 2.30 p.m. Monday to Wednesday and at 3 p.m. on Thursday. In the latter part of the session, the House of Lords sometimes sits on Fridays at 11 a.m.

HYBRIDITY – A public bill which is considered to affect specific private or local interests, as distinct from all such interests of a single category, is called a hybrid bill and is subject to a special form of scrutiny to enable people affected to object. In the House of Lords, affirmative instruments may also be treated as hybrid.

LEADER OF THE OPPOSITION – In 1937 the office of Leader of the Opposition was recognized and a salary was assigned to the post. Since May 1997 the salary has been £98,860 (including parliamentary salary of £43,860). The present Leader of the Opposition is the Rt. Hon. William Hague, MP.

THE LORD CHANCELLOR – The Lord High Chancellor of Great Britain is (ex officio) the Speaker of the House of Lords. Unlike the Speaker of the House of Commons, he is a member of the Government, takes part in debates and votes in divisions. He has none of the powers to maintain order that the Speaker in the Commons has, these powers being exercised in the Lords by the House as a whole. The Lord Chancellor sits in the Lords on one of the Woolsacks, couches covered with red cloth and stuffed with wool. If he wishes to address the House in any way except formally as Speaker, he leaves the Woolsack.

NAMING – When a member has been named by the Speaker for a breach of order, i.e. contrary to the practice of the House, called by surname and not addressed as the 'Hon. Member for ... (her/his constituency)', the Leader of the House moves that the offender 'be suspended from the service of the House' for (in the case of a first offence) a period of five sitting days. Should the member offend again, the period of suspension is increased.

OPPOSITION DAY – A day on which the topic for debate is chosen by the Opposition. There are 20 such days in a normal session. On 17 days, subjects are chosen by the Leader of the Opposition; on the remaining three days by the leader of the next largest opposition party.

PARLIAMENT ACTS 1911 AND 1949 – Under these Acts, bills may become law without the consent of the Lords.

Since at least the 18th century the Commons has had the privilege of having bills concerned with supply (i.e. taxation and money matters) passed without amendment by the Lords, though until 1911 the Lords retained the right to reject such bills outright.

By the Parliament Act 1911, a bill which has been endorsed by the Speaker of the House of Commons as a money bill, and has been passed by the Commons and sent up to the Lords at least one month before the end of a session, can become law without the consent of the Lords if it is not passed by them without amendment within a month.

Under the Parliament Acts 1911 and 1949, if the Lords reject any other public bill (except one to prolong the life of a Parliament) which has been passed by the Commons in two successive sessions, then that bill shall (unless the Commons direct to the contrary) become law without the consent of the Lords. The Lords have power, therefore, to delay a public bill for 13 months from its first second reading in the House of Commons.

PRIME MINISTER'S QUESTIONS – The Prime Minister answers questions from 3.00 to 3.30 p.m. on Wednesdays. Nowadays the 'open question' predominates. Members tend to ask the Prime Minister what are his or her official engagements for the day; a supplementary question on virtually any topic can then be put.

PRIVATE BILL – A bill promoted by a body or an individual to give powers additional to, or in conflict with, the general law, and to which a special procedure applies to enable people affected to object.

PRIVATE MEMBER'S BILL – A public bill promoted by a Member who is not a member of the Government.

PRIVATE NOTICE QUESTION – A question adjudged of urgent importance on submission to the Speaker (in the Lords, the Leader of the House), answered at the end of oral questions, usually at 3.30 p.m.

PRIVILEGE – The following are covered by the privilege of Parliament:
(i) freedom from interference in going to, attending at, and going from, Parliament
(ii) freedom of speech in parliamentary proceedings
(iii) the printing and publishing of anything relating to the proceedings of the two Houses is subject to privilege
(iv) each House is the guardian of its dignity and may punish any insult to the House as a whole

PROROGATION – The bringing to an end, by the Sovereign on the advice of the Government, of a session of Parliament. Public bills which have not completed all their stages lapse on prorogation.

QUEEN'S SPEECH – The speech delivered by The Queen at the State Opening of Parliament, in which the Government's programme for the session is set forth. The speech is drafted by civil servants and approved by the Cabinet.

QUESTION TIME – Oral questions are answered by Ministers in the Commons from 2.30 to 3.30 p.m. every day except Friday. They are also taken at the start of the Lords sittings, with a daily limit of four oral questions.

ROYAL ASSENT – The royal assent is signified by letters patent to such bills and measures as have passed both Houses of Parliament (or bills which have been passed under the Parliament Acts 1911 and 1949). The Sovereign has not given royal assent in person since 1854. On occasion, for instance in the prorogation of Parliament, royal assent may be pronounced to the two Houses by Lords Commissioners. More usually royal assent is notified to each House sitting separately in accordance with the Royal Assent Act 1967. The old French formulae for royal assent are then endorsed on the acts by the Clerk of the Parliaments.

The power to withhold assent resides with the Sovereign but has not been exercised in the United Kingdom since 1707, in the reign of Queen Anne.

SCOTTISH GRAND COMMITTEE – Established in its present form in 1957, the committee consists of all 72 MPs representing Scottish constituencies, with a quorum of ten. The functions of the committee are to consider the principle of all public bills relating exclusively to Scotland (constituting in effect the bill's second reading); to consider the Scottish estimates on not less than six days a session; and to consider matters relating exclusively to Scotland on not more than six days a session. From the beginning of the 1994–5 session, the committee's powers were enhanced to allow oral questions, short debates, ministerial statements, and consideration of appropriate statutory instruments. The committee can meet on appointed days at specified places in Scotland.

The Scottish Affairs select committee is empowered to examine the expenditure, administration and policy of the Scottish Office, and the expenditure and administration of the Lord Advocate's Office.

SELECT COMMITTEES – Consisting usually of ten to 15 members of all parties, select committees are a means used by both Houses in order to investigate certain matters.

Most select committees in the House of Commons are now tied to departments; each committee investigates subjects within a government department's remit. There are other House of Commons select committees dealing with public accounts (i.e. the spending by the Government of money voted by Parliament) and European legislation, and also domestic committees dealing, for example, with privilege and procedure. Major select committees usually take evidence in public; their evidence and reports are published by The Stationery Office.

The principal select committee in the House of Lords is that on the European Communities, which has, at present, six sub-committees dealing with all areas of Community policy. The House of Lords also has a select committee on science and technology, which appoints sub-committees to deal with specific subjects. In addition, *ad hoc* select committees have been set up from time to time to investigate specific subjects, e.g. overseas trade, murder and life imprisonment. There are also some joint committees of the two Houses, e.g. the Joint Committee on Statutory Instruments.

Select committees are reconstituted after a general election and the following are the more important of those which had been set up by 31 July 1997:

DEPARTMENTAL COMMITTEES
Agriculture – Chair, Peter Luff, MP; *Clerk*, N. Walker

Culture, Media and Sport – Chair, Rt. Hon. Gerald Kaufman, MP; *Clerk*, C. Lee
Defence – Chair, Bruce George, MP; *Clerk*, A. Kennon
Education and Employment – Chair, not yet known; *Clerk*, M. Hamlyn
Environment, Transport and the Regions – Chairs, Andrew Bennett, MP; Gwyneth Dunwoody, MP; *Clerk*, D. Harrison
  Sub-committees: Environment – Chair, Andrew Bennett, MP; *Clerk*, Ms E. Payne; *Transport* – Chair, Gwyneth Dunwoody, MP; *Clerk*, C. Stanton
Foreign Affairs – Chair, Donald Anderson, MP; *Clerks*, Dr C. Ward, Mrs J. Davies
Health – Chair, David Hinchliffe, MP; *Clerks*, Dr R. James, T. Goldsmith
Home Affairs – Chair, Chris Mullin, MP; *Clerks*, C. Poyser; T. Goldsmith
International Development – Chair, Bowen Wells, MP; *Clerk*, Y. Azad
Northern Ireland – Chair, Rt. Hon. Peter Brooke, CH, MP; *Clerks*, not yet known
Science and Technology – Chair, Dr Michael Clark, MP; *Clerk*, Mrs J. Mulley
Scottish Affairs – Chair, David Marshall, MP; *Clerk*, F. Cranmer
Social Security – Chair, Archy Kirkwood, MP; *Clerk*, L. Lawrence Smyth
Trade and Industry – Chair, Martin O'Neill, MP; *Clerk*, Ms A. Milner-Barry
Treasury – Chair, Giles Radice, MP; *Clerks*, Mrs J. Sharpe; Ms J. Long
Welsh Affairs – Chair, Martyn Jones, MP; *Clerk*, Ms P. Helme

NON-DEPARTMENTAL COMMITTEES
Deregulation – Chair, not yet known; *Clerks*, R. Rogers; Mrs E. Flood
European Legislation – Chair, James Hood, MP; *Clerks*, R. Rogers; D. Lloyd
Modernization – Chair, Rt. Hon. Ann Taylor, MP; *Clerks*, D. Natzler, C. Winnifrith
Public Accounts – Chair, Rt. Hon. David Davis, MP; *Clerk*, K. Brown
Public Administration – Chair, Rhodri Morgan, MP; *Clerk*, Dr P. Seaward
Standards and Privileges – Chair, Rt. Hon. Robert Sheldon, MP; *Clerks*, A. Hastings; F. Reid

THE SPEAKER – The Speaker of the House of Commons is the spokesman and president of the Chamber. He or she is elected by the House at the beginning of each Parliament or when the previous Speaker retires or dies. The Speaker neither speaks in debates nor votes in divisions except when the voting is equal.

STANDING ORDERS – Rules which have from time to time been agreed by each House of Parliament to regulate the conduct of its business. These orders may be amended or repealed, and are from time to time suspended or dispensed with.

STATE OPENING – This marks the start of each new session of Parliament. Parliament is normally opened, in the presence of both Houses, by The Queen in person, who makes the speech from the throne which outlines the Government's policies for the coming session (*see* Queen's Speech). In the absence of The Queen, Parliament is opened by Royal Commission, and The Queen's Speech is read by one of the Lords Commissioners specially appointed by letters patent for the occasion.

STRANGERS – Anyone who is not a Member or Officer of the House is a stranger. Visitors are generally admitted to debates of both Houses but may be excluded if the House so decides; in practice this happens only in time of war. However, the cry of 'I spy strangers' causes the public gallery to be cleared, and occurs often.

VACANT SEATS – When a vacancy occurs in the House of Commons during a session of Parliament, the writ for the by-election is moved by a Whip of the party to which the member whose seat has been vacated belonged. If the House is in recess, the Speaker can issue a warrant for a writ, should two members certify to him that a seat is vacant.

WELSH GRAND COMMITTEE – First appointed in the 1959–60 session, the committee consists of all 40 MPs representing Welsh constituencies plus five other members nominated by the selection committee. The functions of the committee are to consider the principle of all public bills referred to it (constituting in effect the second reading of such a bill); and to consider matters relating exclusively to Wales.

The Welsh Affairs select committee is empowered to examine the expenditure, administration and policy of the Welsh Office.

WHIPS – In order to secure the attendance of Members of a particular party in Parliament on all occasions, and particularly on the occasion of an important vote, Whips (originally known as 'Whippers-in') are appointed. The written appeal or circular letter issued by them is also known as a 'whip', its urgency being denoted by the number of times it is underlined. Failure to respond to a three-line whip, headed 'Most important', is tantamount in the Commons to secession (at any rate temporarily) from the party. Whips are officially recognized by Parliament and are provided with office accommodation in both Houses. In both Houses, Government and some Opposition Whips receive salaries from public funds.

PUBLIC INFORMATION SERVICES

HOUSE OF COMMONS – Public Information Office, House of Commons, London SW1A 0AA. Tel: 0171-219 4272
HOUSE OF LORDS – The Journal and Information Office, House of Lords, London SW1A 0PW. Tel: 0171–219 3107

GOVERNMENT OFFICE

The Government is the body of Ministers responsible for the administration of national affairs, determining policy and introducing into Parliament any legislation necessary to give effect to government policy. The majority of Ministers are members of the House of Commons but members of the House of Lords or of neither House may also hold ministerial responsibility. The Lord Chancellor is always a member of the House of Lords. The Prime Minister is, by current convention, always a member of the House of Commons.

THE PRIME MINISTER

The office of Prime Minister, which had been in existence for nearly 200 years, was officially recognized in 1905 and its holder was granted a place in the table of precedence. The Prime Minister, by tradition also First Lord of the Treasury and Minister for the Civil Service, is appointed by the Sovereign and is usually the leader of the party which enjoys, or can secure, a majority in the House of Commons. Other Ministers are appointed by the Sovereign on the recommendation of the Prime Minister, who also allocates functions amongst Ministers and has the power to obtain their resignation or dismissal individually.

The Prime Minister informs the Sovereign of state and political matters, advises on the dissolution of Parliament, and makes recommendations for important Crown appointments, the award of honours, etc.

As the chairman of Cabinet meetings and leader of a political party, the Prime Minister is responsible for translating party policy into government activity. As leader of the Government, the Prime Minister is responsible to Parliament and to the electorate for the policies and their implementation.

The Prime Minister also represents the nation in international affairs, e.g. summit conferences.

THE CABINET

The Cabinet developed during the 18th century as an inner committee of the Privy Council, which was the chief source of executive power until that time. The Cabinet is composed of about 20 Ministers chosen by the Prime Minister, usually the heads of government departments (generally known as Secretaries of State unless they have a special title, e.g. Chancellor of the Exchequer), the leaders of the two Houses of Parliament, and the holders of various traditional offices.

The Cabinet's functions are the final determination of policy, control of government and co-ordination of government departments. The exercise of its functions is dependent upon enjoying majority support in the House of Commons. Cabinet meetings are held in private, taking place once or twice a week during parliamentary sittings and less often during a recess. Proceedings are confidential, the members being bound by their oath as Privy Counsellors not to disclose information about the proceedings.

The convention of collective responsibility means that the Cabinet acts unanimously even when Cabinet Ministers do not all agree on a subject. The policies of departmental Ministers must be consistent with the policies of the Government as a whole, and once the Government's policy has been decided, each Minister is expected to support it or resign.

The convention of ministerial responsibility holds a Minister, as the political head of his or her department, accountable to Parliament for the department's work. Departmental Ministers usually decide all matters within their responsibility, although on matters of political importance they normally consult their colleagues collectively. A decision by a departmental Minister is binding on the Government as a whole.

POLITICAL PARTIES

Before the reign of William and Mary the principal officers of state were chosen by and were responsible to the Sovereign alone and not to Parliament or the nation at large. Such officers acted sometimes in concert with one another but more often independently, and the fall of one did not, of necessity, involve that of others, although all were liable to be dismissed at any moment.

In 1693 the Earl of Sunderland recommended to William III the advisability of selecting a ministry from the political party which enjoyed a majority in the House of Commons and the first united ministry was drawn in 1696 from the Whigs, to which party the King owed his throne. This group became known as the Junto and was regarded with suspicion as a novelty in the political life of the nation, being a small section meeting in secret apart from the main body of Ministers. It may be regarded as the forerunner of the Cabinet and in course of time it led to the establishment of the principle of joint responsibility of Ministers, so that internal disagreement caused a change of personnel or resignation of the whole body of Ministers.

The accession of George I, who was unfamiliar with the English language, led to a disinclination on the part of the Sovereign to preside at meetings of his Ministers and caused the appearance of a Prime Minister, a position first acquired by Robert Walpole in 1721 and retained without interruption for 20 years and 326 days.

DEVELOPMENT OF PARTIES

In 1828 the Whigs became known as Liberals, a name originally given to it by its opponents to imply laxity of principles, but gradually accepted by the party to indicate its claim to be pioneers and champions of political reform and progressive legislation. In 1861 a Liberal Registration Association was founded and Liberal Associations became widespread. In 1877 a National Liberal Federation was formed, with headquarters in London. The Liberal Party was in power for long periods during the second half of the 19th century and for several years during the first quarter of the 20th century, but after a split in the party the numbers elected were small from 1931. In 1988, a majority of the Liberals agreed on a merger with the Social Democratic Party under the title Social and Liberal Democrats; since 1989 they have been known as the Liberal Democrats. A minority continue separately as the Liberal Party.

Soon after the change from Whig to Liberal the Tory Party became known as Conservative, a name believed to have been invented by John Wilson Croker in 1830 and to have been generally adopted about the time of the passing of the Reform Act of 1832 to indicate that the preservation of national institutions was the leading principle of the party. After the Home Rule crisis of 1886 the dissentient Liberals entered into a compact with the Conservatives, under which the latter undertook not to contest their seats, but a separate Liberal Unionist organization was maintained until 1912, when it was united with the Conservatives.

Labour candidates for Parliament made their first appearance at the general election of 1892, when there were 27 standing as Labour or Liberal-Labour. In 1900 the Labour Representation Committee was set up in order to establish a distinct Labour group in Parliament, with its own whips, its own policy, and a readiness to co-operate with any party which might be engaged in promoting legislation in the direct interest of labour. In 1906 the LRC became known as the Labour Party.

The Council for Social Democracy was announced by four former Labour Cabinet Ministers in January 1981 and on 26 March 1981 the Social Democratic Party was launched. Later that year the SDP and the Liberal Party formed an electoral alliance. In 1988 a majority of the SDP agreed on a merger with the Liberal Party (see above) but a minority continued as a separate party under the SDP title. In 1990 it was decided to wind up the party organization and its three sitting MPs were known as independent social democrats. None were returned at the 1992 general election.

Plaid Cymru was founded in 1926 to provide an independent political voice for Wales and to campaign for self-government in Wales.

The Scottish National Party was founded in 1934 to campaign for independence for Scotland.

The Social Democratic and Labour Party was founded in 1970, emerging from the civil rights movement of the 1960s, with the aim of promoting reform, reconciliation and partnership across the sectarian divide in Northern Ireland and of opposing violence from any quarter.

The Ulster Democratic Unionist Party was founded in 1971 to resist moves by the Official Unionist Party which were considered a threat to the Union. Its aims are to maintain Northern Ireland as an integral part of the United Kingdom; and to express unionist opinion and defend the interest of Ulster unionism.

The Ulster Unionist Council first met formally in 1905. Its objectives are to maintain Northern Ireland as an integral part of the United Kingdom; to express unionist opinion and defend the interests of Ulster unionism; and to promote the aims of the Ulster Unionist Party.

GOVERNMENT AND OPPOSITION

The government of the day is formed by the party which wins the largest number of seats in the House of Commons at a general election, or which has the support of a majority of members in the House of Commons. By tradition, the leader of the majority party is asked by the Sovereign to form a government, while the largest minority party becomes the official Opposition with its own leader and 'Shadow Cabinet'. Leaders of the Government and Opposition sit on the front benches of the Commons with their supporters (the back-benchers) sitting behind them.

FINANCIAL SUPPORT

Financial support to Opposition parties was introduced in 1975 and is commonly known as Short Money, after Edward Short, the Leader of the House at that time, who introduced the scheme. For 1996−7 financial assistance was:

Labour	£1,530,190.51
Liberal Democrats	316,480.54
Plaid Cymru	22,040.36
SNP	36,782.68
SDLP	23,134.12
Democratic Unionists	15,954.37
Ulster Unionsts	46,357.18

PARTIES

The parties included here are those with MPs sitting in the House of Commons in the present Parliament. Addresses of other political parties may be found in the Societies and Institutions section.

CONSERVATIVE AND UNIONIST PARTY

Central Office, 32 Smith Square, London SW1P 3HH
Tel 0171-222 9000
Chairman, The Lord Parkinson, PC
Deputy Chairman, Hon. Michael Trend, CBE, MP
Vice-Chairmen, Alan Duncan, MP; Archie Norman, MP

SHADOW CABINET *as at end July 1997*

Leader of the Opposition, Rt. Hon. William Hague, MP
Agriculture, Fisheries and Food, Rt. Hon. David Curry, MP
Constitutional Affairs, Scotland, Wales, Rt. Hon. Michael Ancram, QC, MP
Culture, Media and Sport, Rt. Hon. Francis Maude, MP
Defence, Rt. Hon. Sir George Young, Bt., MP
Education and Employment, Rt. Hon. Stephen Dorrell, MP
Environment, Transport and the Regions, Rt. Hon. Sir Norman Fowler, MP
Foreign and Commonwealth Affairs, Rt. Hon. Michael Howard, QC, MP
Health, John Maples, MP
Home Affairs, Rt. Hon. Sir Brian Mawhinney, MP
International Development, Rt. Hon. Sir Alastair Goodlad, KCMG, MP
Leader of the House of Commons and Chancellor of the Duchy of Lancaster, Rt. Hon. Gillian Shephard, MP

Leader of the House of Lords, Viscount Cranborne, PC
Lord Chancellor, The Lord Kingsland, QC, PC
Attorney-General, Rt. Hon. Sir Nicholas Lyell, QC, MP
Northern Ireland, Andrew Mackay, MP
Social Security, Iain Duncan-Smith, MP
Trade and Industry, Rt. Hon. John Redwood, MP
Treasury, Rt. Hon. Peter Lilley, MP
Chief Secretary to the Treasury, Rt. Hon. David Heathcoat
   Amory, MP

CONSERVATIVE CHIEF WHIPS
House of Lords, The Lord Strathclyde, PC
House of Commons, James Arbuthnot, MP

SCOTTISH CONSERVATIVE AND UNIONIST CENTRAL
OFFICE
Suite 1/1, 14 Links Place, Leith, Edinburgh EH6 7EZ
Tel 0131-555 2900
Chairman, R. Robertson
Deputy Chairman, J. Carlaw
Vice-Chairman, P. Gallie
Hon. Treasurer, W. Y. Hughes, CBE
Director of the Party in Scotland, R. Pratt, CBE

LABOUR PARTY
John Smith House, 150 Walworth Road, London SE17 1JT
Tel 0171-701 1234
Parliamentary Party Leader, The Rt. Hon. Anthony Blair, MP
Deputy Party Leader, The Rt. Hon. John Prescott, MP
Leader in the Lords, The Lord Richard, PC, QC
Chair, Rt. Hon. Robin Cook, MP
Vice-Chair, R. Rosser
Treasurer, Ms M. Prosser
General Secretary, T. Sawyer

LIBERAL DEMOCRATS
4 Cowley Street, London SW1P 3NB
Tel 0171-222 7999
President, Robert Maclennan, MP
Hon. Treasurer, T. Razzall, CBE
General Secretary, G. Elson
Parliamentary Party Leader, The Rt. Hon. Paddy Ashdown,
   MP
Leader in the Lords, The Lord Jenkins of Hillhead, PC

LIBERAL DEMOCRAT SPOKESMEN *as at end June 1997*
Deputy Leader, Home and Legal Affairs, Alan Beith, MP
Agriculture and Rural Affairs, Charles Kennedy, MP
Culture, Media and Sport, Constitution, Robert Maclennan, MP
Disabled People, Paul Burstow, MP
Education and Employment, Don Foster, MP
Environment, Matthew Taylor, MP
Foreign Affairs, Defence and Europe, Menzies Campbell, MP
Health, Simon Hughes, MP
Local Government and Housing, David Rendel, MP
Social Security and Welfare, Archy Kirkwood, MP
Trade and Industry, Nick Harvey, MP
Transport, David Chidgey, MP
Treasury, Malcolm Bruce, MP
Women, Jackie Ballard, MP
Young People, Lembit Opik, MP
Northern Ireland, The Lord Holme of Cheltenham
Scotland, Jim Wallace, MP
Wales, Richard Livsey, MP

LIBERAL DEMOCRAT WHIPS
House of Lords, The Lord Harris of Greenwich
House of Commons, Paul Tyler, MP (*Chief Whip*); Andrew
   Stunell, MP (*Deputy Whip*)

WELSH LIBERAL DEMOCRATS
57 St Mary Street, Cardiff CF1 1FE
Tel 01222-382210

Party President, The Lord Thomas of Gresford, OBE, QC
Party Leader, Richard Livsey, CBE, MP
Chairman, P. Black
Treasurer, N. Howells
Secretary, J. Burree
Party Manager, Ms J. Lewis, MBE

SCOTTISH LIBERAL DEMOCRATS
4 Clifton Terrace, Edinburgh EH12 5DR
Tel 0131-337 2314
Party President, R. Thomson
Party Leader, Jim Wallace, MP
Chair, Ms M. MacLaren
Hon. Treasurer, D. R. Sullivan
Chief Executive, A. Myles

PLAID CYMRU
18 Park Grove, Cardiff CF1 3BN
Tel 01222-646000
Party President, Dafydd Wigley, MP
Chairman, M. Phillips
Hon. Treasurer, O. Williams
Chief Executive/General Secretary, K. Davies

SCOTTISH NATIONAL PARTY
6 North Charlotte Street, Edinburgh EH2 4JH
Tel 0131-226 3661
Parliamentary Party Leader, Margaret Ewing, MP
Chief Whip, Andrew Welsh, MP
National Convener, Alex Salmond, MP
Senior Vice-Convener, Dr A. Macartney, MEP
National Treasurer, K. MacAskill
National Secretary, A. Morgan, MP

NORTHERN IRELAND

SOCIAL DEMOCRATIC AND LABOUR PARTY
121 Ormeau Road, Belfast BT7 1SU
Tel 01232-247700
Parliamentary Party Leader, John Hume, MP, MEP
Deputy Leader, Seamus Mallon, MP
Chief Whip, Eddie McGrady, MP
Chairman, J. Stephenson
Hon. Treasurer, P. O'Hagan
General Secretary, Mrs G. Cosgrove

ULSTER DEMOCRATIC UNIONIST PARTY
91 Dundela Avenue, Belfast BT4 3BU
Tel 01232-471155
Parliamentary Party Leader, I. Paisley, MP, MEP
Deputy Leader, Peter Robinson, MP
Chairman, W. J. McClure
Hon. Treasurer, G. Campbell
Party Secretary, N. Dodds

ULSTER UNIONIST PARTY
3 Glengall Street, Belfast BT12 5AE
Tel 01232-324601
Party Leader, David Trimble, MP
Chief Whip, Revd Martin Smyth, MP
Ulster Unionist Council
President, J. Cunningham
Chairman, D. Rogan
Hon. Treasurer, J. Allen, OBE
Party Secretary, J. Wilson

MEMBERS OF PARLIAMENT AS AT 2 AUGUST 1997

For abbreviations, *see* page 235
* Member of last Parliament
† Former Member of Parliament
An entire entry in italic indicates that the MP was elected at the general election but has died since; the name is included for the purposes of record

*Abbott, Ms Diane J. (*b.* 1953) *Lab., Hackney North and Stoke Newington,* maj. 15,627

Adams, Gerard (Gerry) (*b.* 1948) *SF, Belfast West,* maj. 7,909

*Adams, Mrs K. Irene (*b.* 1948) *Lab., Paisley North,* maj. 12,814

*Ainger, Nicholas R. (*b.* 1949) *Lab., Carmarthen West and Pembrokeshire South,* maj. 9,621

*Ainsworth, Peter M. (*b.* 1956) *C., Surrey East,* maj. 15,093

*Ainsworth, Robert W. (*b.* 1952) *Lab., Coventry North East,* maj. 22,569

Allan, Richard B. (*b.* 1966) *LD, Sheffield Hallam,* maj. 8,271

*Allen, Graham W. (*b.* 1953) *Lab., Nottingham North,* maj. 18,801

*Amess, David A. A. (*b.* 1952) *C., Southend West,* maj. 2,615

*Ancram, Rt. Hon. Michael A. F. J. K. (Earl of Ancram) (*b.* 1945) *C., Devizes,* maj. 9,782

*Anderson, Donald (*b.* 1939) *Lab., Swansea East,* maj. 25,569

*Anderson, Mrs Janet (*b.* 1949) *Lab., Rossendale and Darwen,* maj. 10,949

*Arbuthnot, James N. (*b.* 1952) *C., Hampshire North East,* maj. 14,398

*Armstrong, Miss Hilary J. (*b.* 1945) *Lab., Durham North West,* maj. 24,754

*Ashdown, Rt. Hon. J. J. D. (Paddy) (*b.* 1941) *LD, Yeovil,* maj. 11,403

*Ashton, Joseph W. (*b.* 1933) *Lab., Bassetlaw,* maj. 17,460

Atherton, Ms Candice K. (*b.* 1955) *Lab., Falmouth and Camborne,* maj. 2,688

Atkins, Ms Charlotte (*b.* 1950) *Lab., Staffordshire Moorlands,* maj. 10,049

*Atkinson, David A. (*b.* 1940) *C., Bournemouth East,* maj. 4,346

*Atkinson, Peter L. (*b.* 1943) *C., Hexham,* maj. 222

*Austin-Walker, John E. (*b.* 1944) *Lab., Erith and Thamesmead,* maj. 17,424

Baker, Norman J. (*b.* 1957) *LD, Lewes,* maj. 1,300

*Baldry, Antony B. (*b.* 1950) *C., Banbury,* maj. 4,737

Ballard, Mrs Jacqueline M. (*b.* 1953) *LD, Taunton,* maj. 2,443

*Banks, Anthony L. (*b.* 1943) *Lab., West Ham,* maj. 19,494

*Barnes, Harold (*b.* 1936) *Lab., Derbyshire North East,* maj. 18,321

*Barron, Kevin J. (*b.* 1946) *Lab., Rother Valley,* maj. 23,485

*Battle, John D. (*b.* 1951) *Lab., Leeds West,* maj. 19,771

*Bayley, Hugh (*b.* 1952) *Lab., City of York,* maj. 20,523

Beard, C. Nigel (*b.* 1936) *Lab., Bexleyheath and Crayford,* maj. 3,415

*Beckett, Rt. Hon. Margaret M. (*b.* 1943) *Lab., Derby South,* maj. 16,106

Begg, Ms Anne (*b.* 1955) *Lab., Aberdeen South,* maj. 3,365

*Beggs, Roy (*b.* 1936) *UUP, Antrim East,* maj. 6,389

*Beith, Rt. Hon. Alan J. (*b.* 1943) *LD, Berwick upon Tweed,* maj. 8,042

Bell, Martin, OBE (*b.* 1938) *Ind., Tatton,* maj. 11,077

*Bell, Stuart (*b.* 1938) *Lab., Middlesbrough,* maj. 25,018

*Benn, Rt. Hon. Anthony N. W. (*b.* 1925) *Lab., Chesterfield,* maj. 5,775

*Bennett, Andrew F. (*b.* 1939) *Lab., Denton and Reddish,* maj. 20,311

*Benton, Joseph E. (*b.* 1933) *Lab., Bootle,* maj. 28,421

Bercow, John S. (*b.* 1963) *C., Buckingham,* maj. 12,386

*Beresford, Sir Paul (*b.* 1946) *C., Mole Valley,* maj. 10,221

*Bermingham, Gerald E. (*b.* 1940) *Lab., St Helens South,* maj. 23,739

*Berry, Roger L., D.phil. (*b.* 1948) *Lab., Kingswood,* maj. 14,253

Best, Harold (*b.* 1939) *Lab., Leeds North West,* maj. 3,844

*Betts, Clive J. C. (*b.* 1950) *Lab., Sheffield Attercliffe,* maj. 21,818

Blackman, Ms Elizabeth M. (*b.* 1949) *Lab., Erewash,* maj. 9,135

*Blair, Rt. Hon. Anthony C. L. (*b.* 1953) *Lab., Sedgefield,* maj. 25,143

Blears, Hazel A. (*b.* 1956) *Lab., Salford,* maj. 17,069

Blizzard, Robert J. (*b.* 1950) *Lab., Waveney,* maj. 12,453

*Blunkett, Rt. Hon. David (*b.* 1947) *Lab., Sheffield Brightside,* maj. 19,954

Blunt, Crispin J. R. (*b.* 1960) *C., Reigate,* maj. 7,741

*Boateng, Paul Y. (*b.* 1951) *Lab., Brent South,* maj. 19,691

*Body, Sir Richard (*b.* 1927) *C., Boston and Skegness,* maj. 647

*Boothroyd, Rt. Hon. Betty (*b.* 1929) *The Speaker, West Bromwich West,* maj. 15,423

Borrow, David S. (*b.* 1952) *Lab., Ribble South,* maj. 5,084

*Boswell, Timothy E. (*b.* 1942) *C., Daventry,* maj. 7,378

*Bottomley, Peter J. (*b.* 1944) *C., Worthing West,* maj. 7,713

*Bottomley, Rt. Hon. Virginia H. B. M. (*b.* 1948) *C., Surrey South West,* maj. 2,694

*Bradley, Keith J. C. (*b.* 1950) *Lab., Manchester Withington,* maj. 18,581

Bradley, Peter C. S. (*b.* 1953) *Lab., Wrekin, The,* maj. 3,025

Bradshaw, Benjamin P. J. (*b.* 1960) *Lab., Exeter,* maj. 11,705

Brady, Graham (*b.* 1967) *C., Altrincham and Sale West,* maj. 1,505

Brake, Thomas A. (*b.* 1962) *LD, Carshalton and Wallington,* maj. 2,267

Brand, Dr Peter (*b.* 1947) *LD, Isle of Wight,* maj. 6,406

*Brazier, Julian W. H., TD (*b.* 1953) *C., Canterbury,* maj. 3,964

Breed, Colin E. (*b.* 1947) *LD, Cornwall South East,* maj. 6,480

Brinton, Ms Helen R. (*b.* 1954) *Lab., Peterborough,* maj. 7,323

*Brooke, Rt. Hon. Peter L., CH (*b.* 1934) *C., Cities of London and Westminster,* maj. 4,881

*Brown, Rt. Hon. J. Gordon, PH.D. (*b.* 1951) *Lab., Dunfermline East,* maj. 18,751

*Brown, Nicholas H. (*b.* 1950) *Lab., Newcastle upon Tyne East and Wallsend,* maj. 23,811

Brown, Russell L. (*b.* 1951) *Lab., Dumfries,* maj. 9,643

Browne, Desmond (*b.* 1952) *Lab., Kilmarnock and Loudoun,* maj. 7,256

*Browning, Mrs Angela F. (*b.* 1946) *C., Tiverton and Honiton,* maj. 1,653

*Bruce, Ian C. (*b.* 1947) *C., Dorset South,* maj. 77

*Bruce, Malcolm G. (*b.* 1944) *LD, Gordon,* maj. 6,997

Buck, Ms Karen P. (*b.* 1958) *Lab., Regent's Park and Kensington North,* maj. 14,657

*Burden, Richard H. (*b.* 1954) *Lab., Birmingham Northfield,* maj. 11,443

Burgon, Colin (*b.* 1948) *Lab., Elmet,* maj. 8,779

Burnett, John P. A. (*b.* 1945) *LD, Devon West and Torridge,* maj. 1,957

*Burns, Simon H. M. (*b.* 1952) *C., Chelmsford West,* maj. 6,691

Burstow, Paul K. (*b.* 1962) *LD, Sutton and Cheam,* maj. 2,097

Butler, Ms Christine M. (*b.* 1943) *Lab., Castle Point,* maj. 1,116

*Liddell, Mrs Helen (b. 1950) Lab., Airdrie and Shotts, maj. 15,412
*Lidington, David R., ph.d. (b. 1956) C., Aylesbury, maj. 8,419
*Lilley, Rt. Hon. Peter B. (b. 1943) C., Hitchin and Harpenden, maj. 6,671
Linton, J. Martin (b. 1944) Lab., Battersea, maj. 5,360
*Livingstone, Kenneth R. (b. 1945) Lab., Brent East, maj. 15,882
†Livsey, Richard A. L., cbe (b. 1935) LD, Brecon and Radnorshire, maj. 5,097
*Lloyd, Anthony J. (b. 1950) Lab., Manchester Central, maj. 19,682
*Lloyd, Rt. Hon. Sir Peter (b. 1937) C., Fareham, maj. 10,358
*Llwyd, Elfyn (b. 1951) PC, Meirionnydd nant Conwy, maj. 6,805
Lock, David A. (b. 1960) Lab., Wyre Forest, maj. 6,946
*Lord, Michael N. (b. 1938) C., Suffolk Central and Ipswich North, maj. 3,538
Loughton, Timothy P. (b. 1962) C., Worthing East and Shoreham, maj. 5,098
Love, Andrew (b. 1949) Lab. Co-op., Edmonton, maj. 13,472
*Luff, Peter J. (b. 1955) C., Worcestershire Mid, maj. 9,412
*Lyell, Rt. Hon. Sir Nicholas, qc (b. 1938) C., Bedfordshire North East, maj. 5,883
*McAllion, John (b. 1948) Lab., Dundee East, maj. 9,961
*McAvoy, Thomas M. (b. 1943) Lab. Co-op., Glasgow Rutherglen, maj. 15,007
McCabe, Stephen J. (b. 1955) Lab., Birmingham Hall Green, maj. 8,420
McCafferty, Ms Christine (b. 1945) Lab., Calder Valley, maj. 6,255
*McCartney, Ian (b. 1951) Lab., Makerfield, maj. 26,177
*McCartney, Robert L., qc(ni) (b. 1936) UKU, Down North, maj. 1,449
McDonagh, Ms Siobhain A. (b. 1960) Lab., Mitcham and Morden, maj. 13,741
*Macdonald, Calum A., ph.d. (b. 1956) Lab., Western Isles, maj. 3,576
McDonnell, John M. (b. 1951) Lab., Hayes and Harlington, maj. 14,291
*McFall, John (b. 1944) Lab. Co-op., Dumbarton, maj. 10,883
*McGrady, Edward K. (b. 1935) SDLP, Down South, maj. 9,933
MacGregor, Rt. Hon. John R. R., obe (b. 1937) C., Norfolk South, maj. 7,378
McGuinness, Martin (b. 1950) SF, Ulster Mid, maj. 1,883
McGuire, Mrs Anne (b. 1949) Lab., Stirling, maj. 6,411
McIntosh, Miss Anne C. B., mep (b. 1954) C., Vale of York, maj. 9,721
McIsaac, Ms Shona (b. 1960) Lab., Cleethorpes, maj. 9,176
*Mackay, Andrew J. (b. 1949) C., Bracknell, maj. 10,387
McKenna, Ms Rosemary (b. 1941) Lab., Cumbernauld and Kilsyth, maj. 11,128
*MacKinlay, Andrew S. (b. 1949) Lab., Thurrock, maj. 17,256
*Maclean, Rt. Hon. David J. (b. 1953) C., Penrith and the Border, maj. 10,233
*McLeish, Henry B. (b. 1948) Lab., Fife Central, maj. 13,713
*Maclennan, Robert A. R. (b. 1936) LD, Caithness, Sutherland and Easter Ross, maj. 2,259
*McLoughlin, Patrick A. (b. 1957) C., Derbyshire West, maj. 4,885
*McMaster, Gordon J. (b. 1960) Lab. Co-op., Paisley South, maj. 12,750
*McNamara, J. Kevin (b. 1934) Lab., Hull North, maj. 19,705
McNulty, Anthony J. (b. 1958) Lab., Harrow East, maj. 9,738
*MacShane, Denis, ph.d. (b. 1948) Lab., Rotherham, maj. 21,469
MacTaggart, Ms Fiona M. (b. 1953) Lab., Slough, maj. 13,071

McWalter, Tony (b. 1945) Lab. Co-op., Hemel Hempstead, maj. 3,636
*McWilliam, John D. (b. 1941) Lab., Blaydon, maj. 16,605
*Madel, Sir David (b. 1938) C., Bedfordshire South West, maj. 132
*Maginnis, Kenneth (b. 1938) UUP, Fermanagh and South Tyrone, maj. 13,688
*Mahon, Mrs Alice (b. 1937) Lab., Halifax, maj. 11,212
*Major, Rt. Hon. John (b. 1943) C., Huntingdon, maj. 18,140
†Malins, Humfrey J., cbe (b. 1945) C., Woking, maj. 5,678
Mallaber, Ms C. Judith (b. 1951) Lab., Amber Valley, maj. 11,613
*Mallon, Seamus (b. 1936) SDLP, Newry and Armagh, maj. 4,889
*Mandelson, Peter B. (b. 1953) Lab., Hartlepool, maj. 17,508
†Maples, John C. (b. 1943) C., Stratford-upon-Avon, maj. 14,106
*Marek, John, ph.d. (b. 1940) Lab., Wrexham, maj. 11,762
Marsden, Gordon (b. 1953) Lab., Blackpool South, maj. 11,616
Marsden, Paul W. B. (b. 1968) Lab., Shrewsbury and Atcham, maj. 1,670
*Marshall, David (b. 1941) Lab., Glasgow Shettleston, maj. 15,868
*Marshall, James, ph.d. (b. 1941) Lab., Leicester South, maj. 16,493
Marshall-Andrews, Robert G., qc (b. 1944) Lab., Medway, maj. 5,354
*Martin, Michael J. (b. 1945) Lab., Glasgow Springburn, maj. 17,326
*Martlew, Eric A. (b. 1949) Lab., Carlisle, maj. 12,390
*Mates, Michael J. (b. 1934) C., Hampshire East, maj. 11,590
†Maude, Rt. Hon. Francis A. A. (b. 1953) C., Horsham, maj. 14,862
*Mawhinney, Rt. Hon. Sir Brian, ph.d. (b. 1940) C., Cambridgeshire North West, maj. 7,754
*Maxton, John A. (b. 1936) Lab., Glasgow Cathcart, maj. 12,245
May, Mrs Theresa M. (b. 1956) C., Maidenhead, maj. 11,981
*Meacher, Rt. Hon. Michael H. (b. 1939) Lab., Oldham West and Royton, maj. 16,201
*Meale, J. Alan (b. 1949) Lab., Mansfield, maj. 20,518
*Merchant, Piers R. G. (b. 1951) C., Beckenham, maj. 4,953
Merron, Ms Gillian J. (b. 1959) Lab., Lincoln, maj. 11,130
*Michael, Alun E. (b. 1943) Lab. Co-op., Cardiff South and Penarth, maj. 13,881
*Michie, Mrs J. Ray (b. 1934) LD, Argyll and Bute, maj. 6,081
*Michie, William (b. 1935) Lab., Sheffield Heeley, maj. 17,078
*Milburn, Alan (b. 1958) Lab., Darlington, maj. 16,025
*Miller, Andrew P. (b. 1949) Lab., Ellesmere Port and Neston, maj. 16,036
*Mitchell, Austin V., d.phil. (b. 1934) Lab., Great Grimsby, maj. 16,244
Moffatt, Mrs Laura J. (b. 1954) Lab., Crawley, maj. 11,707
*Moonie, Dr Lewis G. (b. 1947) Lab. Co-op., Kirkcaldy, maj. 10,710
Moore, Michael K. (b. 1965) LD, Tweeddale, Ettrick and Lauderdale, maj. 1,489
Moran, Ms Margaret (b. 1955) Lab., Luton South, maj. 11,319
Morgan, Alastair N. (b. 1945) SNP, Galloway and Upper Nithsdale, maj. 5,624
*Morgan, H. Rhodri (b. 1939) Lab., Cardiff West, maj. 15,628
Morgan, Ms Julie (b. 1944) Lab., Cardiff North, maj. 8,126
*Morley, Elliot A. (b. 1952) Lab., Scunthorpe, maj. 14,173
*Morris, Ms Estelle (b. 1952) Lab., Birmingham Yardley, maj. 5,315
*Morris, Rt. Hon. John, qc (b. 1931) Lab., Aberavon, maj. 21,571
*Moss, Malcolm D. (b. 1943) C., Cambridgeshire North East, maj. 5,101

*Widdecombe, Rt. Hon. Ann N. (*b.* 1947) *C., Maidstone and the Weald,* maj. 9,603

*Wigley, Dafydd (*b.* 1943) *PC, Caernarfon,* maj. 7,949

*Wilkinson, John A. D. (*b.* 1940) *C., Ruislip–Northwood,* maj. 7,794

*Willetts, David L. (*b.* 1956) *C., Havant,* maj. 3,729

*Williams, Rt. Hon. Alan J. (*b.* 1930) *Lab., Swansea West,* maj. 14,459

*Williams, Dr Alan W. (*b.* 1945) *Lab., Carmarthen East and Dinefwr,* maj. 3,450

Williams, Mrs Betty H. (*b.* 1944) *Lab., Conwy,* maj. 1,596

Willis, G. Philip (*b.* 1941) *LD, Harrogate and Knaresborough,* maj. 6,236

Wills, Michael D. (*b.* 1952) *Lab., Swindon North,* maj. 7,688

*Wilshire, David (*b.* 1943) *C., Spelthorne,* maj. 3,473

*Wilson, Brian D. H. (*b.* 1948) *Lab., Cunninghame North,* maj. 11,039

*Winnick, David J. (*b.* 1933) *Lab., Walsall North,* maj. 12,588

*Winterton, Mrs J. Ann (*b.* 1941) *C., Congleton,* maj. 6,130

*Winterton, Nicholas R. (*b.* 1938) *C., Macclesfield,* maj. 8,654

Winterton, Ms Rosalie (*b.* 1958) *Lab., Doncaster Central,* maj. 17,856

*Wise, Mrs Audrey (*b.* 1935) *Lab., Preston,* maj. 18,680

Wood, Michael R. (*b.* 1946) *Lab., Batley and Spen,* maj. 6,141

Woodward, Shaun A. (*b.* 1958) *C., Witney,* maj. 7,028

Woolas, Philip J. (*b.* 1959) *Lab., Oldham East and Saddleworth,* maj. 3,389

*Worthington, Anthony (*b.* 1941) *Lab., Clydebank and Milngavie,* maj. 13,320

*Wray, James (*b.* 1938) *Lab., Glasgow Bailieston,* maj. 14,840

Wright, Anthony D. (*b.* 1954) *Lab., Great Yarmouth,* maj. 8,668

*Wright, Anthony W., D.phil. (*b.* 1948) *Lab., Cannock Chase,* maj. 14,478

Wyatt, Derek M. (*b.* 1949) *Lab., Sittingbourne and Sheppey,* maj. 1,929

*Yeo, Timothy S. K. (*b.* 1945) *C., Suffolk South,* maj. 4,175

*Young, Rt. Hon. Sir George, Bt. (*b.* 1941) *C., Hampshire North West,* maj. 11,551

MEMBERS WITH SMALL MAJORITIES

The following MPs were returned in May 1997 with majorities of fewer than 1,000 votes
* Denotes membership of last Parliament

	Maj.
Oaten, Mark, *LD, Winchester*	2
Sanders, Adrian, *LD, Torbay*	12
Davey, Edward, *LD, Kingston and Surbiton*	56
*Bruce, Ian, *C., Dorset South*	77
Heath, David, *LD, Somerton and Frome*	130
*Madel, Sir David, *C., Bedfordshire South West*	132
Stinchcombe, Paul, *Lab., Wellingborough*	187
Sawford, Philip, *Lab., Kettering*	189
*Atkinson, Peter, *C., Hexham*	222
*Fabricant, Michael, *C., Lichfield*	238
White, Brian, *Lab., Milton Keynes North East*	240
*Nicholls, Patrick, *C., Teignbridge*	281
Ruffley, David, *C., Bury St Edmunds*	368
King, Andrew, *Lab., Rugby and Kenilworth*	495
*Heathcoat-Amory, Rt. Hon. David, *C., Wells*	528
Spelman, Mrs Caroline, *C., Meriden*	582
*Body, Sir Richard, *C., Boston and Skegness*	647
Gordon, Mrs Eileen, *Lab., Romford*	649
Fraser, Christopher, *C., Dorset Mid and Poole North*	681
*Shersby, Sir Michael, *C., Uxbridge*	724
Clarke, Anthony, *Lab., Northampton South*	744
*Chidgey, David, *LD, Eastleigh*	754
*Cran, James, *C., Beverley and Holderness*	811
*Steen, Sir Anthony, *C., Totnes*	877

RETIRING MPs

The following Members of the last Parliament did not stand for re-election at the 1997 general election:

CONSERVATIVE

Alison, Rt. Hon. Michael, *Selby;* Arnold, Sir Tom, *Hazel Grove;* Aspinwall, Jack, *Wansdyke;* Baker, Rt. Hon. Kenneth, *Mole Valley;* Banks, Robert, *Harrogate;* Biffen, Rt. Hon. John, *Shropshire North;* Booth, Hartley, *Finchley;* Butcher, John, *Coventry South West;* Carlisle, John, *Luton North;* Carlisle, Sir Kenneth, *Lincoln;* Channon, Rt. Hon. Paul, *Southend West;* Churchill, Winston, *Davyhulme;* Critchley, Sir Julian, *Aldershot;* Dicks, Terence, *Hayes and Harlington;* Durant, Sir Anthony, *Reading West;* Eggar, Rt. Hon. Timothy, *Enfield North;* Field, Barry, *Isle of Wight;* Fishburn, Dudley, *Kensington;* Fookes, Dame Janet, *Plymouth, Drake;* Garel-Jones, Rt. Hon. Tristan, *Watford;* Grant, Sir Anthony, *Cambridgeshire South West;* Grylls, Sir Michael, *Surrey North West;* Hannam, Sir John, *Exeter;* Harris, David, *St Ives;* Hicks, Sir Robert, *Cornwall South East;* Higgins, Rt. Hon. Sir Terence, *Worthing;* Hordern, Rt. Hon. Sir Peter, *Horsham;* Howell, Rt. Hon. David, *Guildford;* Howell, Sir Ralph, *Norfolk North;* Hunt, Sir John, *Ravensbourne;* Hurd, Rt. Hon. Douglas, *Witney;* Jopling, Rt. Hon. Michael, *Westmorland and Lonsdale;* Kellett-Bowman, Dame Elaine, *Lancaster;* Knight, Dame Jill, *Birmingham, Edgbaston;* Knox, Sir David, *Staffordshire Moorlands;* McNair-Wilson, Sir Patrick, *New Forest;* Marshall, Sir Michael, *Arundel;* Mayhew, Rt. Hon. Sir Patrick, *Tunbridge Wells;* Mitchell, Sir David, *Hampshire North West;* Monro, Rt. Hon. Sir Hector, *Dumfries;* Montgomery, Sir Fergus, *Altrincham and Sale;* Needham, Rt. Hon. Richard (The Earl of Kilmorey), *Wiltshire North;* Nelson, Anthony, *Chichester;* Norris, Steven, *Epping Forest;* Onslow, Rt. Hon. Sir Cranley, *Woking;* Patten, Rt. Hon. John, *Oxford West and Abingdon;* Pattie, Rt. Hon. Sir Geoffrey, *Chertsey and Walton;* Renton, Rt. Hon. Timothy, *Sussex Mid;* Roberts, Rt. Hon. Sir Wyn, *Conwy;* Ryder, Rt. Hon. Richard, *Norfolk Mid;* Sainsbury, Rt. Hon. Sir Timothy, *Hove;* Shaw, Sir Giles, *Pudsey;* Sims, Sir Roger, *Chislehurst;* Skeet, Sir Trevor, *Bedfordshire North;* Smith, Timothy, *Beaconsfield;* Speed, Sir Keith, *Ashford;* Spicer, Sir James, *Dorset West;* Stephen, Michael, *Shoreham;* Stewart, Allan, *Eastwood;* Thomason, Roy, *Bromsgrove;* Thompson, Patrick, *Norwich North;* Townsend, Sir Cyril, *Bexleyheath;* Trotter, Neville, *Tynemouth;* Vaughan, Sir Gerard, *Reading East;* Walden, George, *Buckingham;* Ward, John, *Poole;* Wheeler, Rt. Hon. Sir John, *Westminster North;* Wiggin, Sir Jerry, *Weston-super-Mare;* Wolfson, Mark, *Sevenoaks*

LABOUR

Boyes, Roland, *Houghton and Washington;* Bray, Jeremy, *Motherwell South;* Callaghan, James, *Heywood and Middleton;* Davies, Bryan, *Oldham Central and Royton;* Dixon, Rt. Hon. Donald, *Jarrow;* Dunnachie, James, *Glasgow, Pollok;* Eastham, Kenneth, *Manchester, Blackley;* Evans, John, *St Helens North;* Faulds, Andrew, *Warley East;* Fraser, John, *Norwood;* Garrett, John, *Norwich South;* Gilbert, Rt. Hon. Dr John, *Dudley East;* Gordon, Mrs Mildred, *Bow and Poplar;* Hardy, Peter, *Wentworth;* Hattersley, Rt. Hon. Roy, *Birmingham, Sparkbrook;* Hogg, Norman, *Cumbernauld and Kilsyth;* Hoyle, Douglas, *Warrington North;* Hughes, Robert, *Aberdeen North;* Hughes, Royston, *Newport East;* Janner, Hon. Greville, *Leicester West;* Lestor, Miss Joan, *Eccles;* Litherland, Robert, *Manchester Central;* Lofthouse, Sir Geoffrey, *Pontefract and Castleford;* Loyden, Edward, *Liverpool, Garston;* McKelvey, William, *Kilmarnock and Loudoun;* Morris, Rt. Hon. Alfred, *Manchester Wythenshawe;* Oakes, Rt. Hon. Gordon, *Halton;* Orme, Rt. Hon. Stanley,

Salford East; Parry, Robert, *Liverpool Riverside;* Randall, Stuart, *Hull West;* Shore, Rt. Hon. Peter, *Bethnal Green and Stepney;* Spearing, Nigel, *Newham South;* Thompson, John, *Wansbeck;* Walker, Rt. Hon. Sir Harold, *Doncaster Central;* Wardell, Gareth, *Gower;* Watson, Michael, *Glasgow Central*

LIBERAL DEMOCRAT

Alton, David, *Liverpool, Mossley Hill;* Carlile, Alex, *Montgomery ;* Johnston, Sir Russell, *Inverness, Nairn and Lochaber;* Nicholson, Emma, *Devon West and Torridge;* Steel, Rt Hon. Sir David, *Tweeddale, Ettrick and Lauderdale;* Thurnham, Peter, *Bolton North East*

OTHERS

Molyneaux, Rt. Hon. Sir James, *UUP, Lagan Valley*

DESELECTED MPs

The following MPs were deselected by their constituency parties before the 1997 general election:

Ashby, David, *C., Leicestershire North West;* Gardiner, Sir George, *C., Reigate* (*see also* Defeated MPs); Madden, Max, *Lab., Bradford West;* Scott, Rt. Hon. Sir Nicholas, *C., Chelsea;* Young, David, *Lab., Bolton South East*

DIED DURING ELECTION CAMPAIGN

Baker, Sir Nicholas, *C., Dorset North*

DEFEATED MEMBERS

The following Members of the last Parliament stood for re-election in 1997 but failed to win a seat:
† Stood in a different constituency, or one affected by boundary changes

CONSERVATIVE

†Aitken, Rt. Hon. Jonathan, *Thanet South;* Alexander, Richard, *Newark;* Allason, Rupert, *Torbay;* †Arnold, Jacques, *Gravesham;* †Atkins, Rt. Hon. Robert, *Ribble South;* Banks, Matthew, *Southport;* †Bates, Michael, *Middlesbrough South and Cleveland East;* Batiste, Spencer, *Elmet;* Bellingham, Henry, *Norfolk North West;* †Bendall, Vivian, *Ilford North;* †Bonsor, Sir Nicholas, *Upminster;* †Bowden, Sir Andrew, *Brighton Kemptown;* †Bowis, John, *Battersea;* †Boyson, Rt. Hon. Sir Rhodes, *Brent North;* †Brandreth, Gyles, *City of Chester;* †Bright, Sir Graham, *Luton South;* †Brown, Michael, *Cleethorpes;* Budgen, Nicholas, *Wolverhampton South West;* Burt, Alistair, *Bury North;* †Butler, Peter, *Milton Keynes North East;* †Carrington, Matthew, *Hammersmith and Fulham;* Carttiss, Michael, *Great Yarmouth;* Coe, Sebastian, *Falmouth and Camborne;* †Congdon, David, *Croydon Central;* Conway, Derek, *Shrewsbury and Atcham;* †Coombs, Anthony, *Wyre Forest;* †Coombs, Simon, *Swindon South;* †Cope, Rt. Hon. Sir John, *Northavon;* †Couchman, James, *Gillingham;* †Currie, Mrs Edwina, *Derbyshire South;* †Deva, Niranjan, *Brentford and Isleworth;* †Devlin, Tim, *Stockton South;* †Douglas-Hamilton, Rt. Hon. Lord James, *Edinburgh West;* †Dover, Densmore, *Chorley;* †Dunn, Robert, *Dartford;* †Dykes, Hugh, *Harrow East;* †Elletson, Harold, *Blackpool North and Fleetwood;* †Evans, David, *Welwyn Hatfield;* Evans, Jonathan, *Brecon and Radnorshire;* Evans, Roger, *Monmouth;* †Evennett, David, *Bexleyheath and Crayford;* Fenner, Dame Peggy, *Medway;* Forman, Nigel, *Carshalton and Wallington;* †Forsyth, Rt. Hon. Michael, *Stirling;* Fox, Rt. Hon. Sir Marcus, *Shipley;* †Freeman, Rt. Hon. Roger, *Kettering;* †French, Douglas, *Gloucester;* Fry, Sir Peter, *Wellingborough;* †Gallie, Philip, *Ayr;* Goodson-Wickes, Dr Charles, *Wimbledon;* †Gorst, Sir John, *Hendon;* †Greenway, Harry, *Ealing North;* †Griffiths, Peter, *Portsmouth North;*

†Hamilton, Neil, *Tatton;* Hampson, Dr Keith, *Leeds North West;* †Hanley, Rt. Hon. Jeremy, *Richmond Park;* Hargreaves, Andrew, *Birmingham, Hall Green;* †Hawksley, Warren, *Stourbridge;* †Hayes, Jerry, *Harlow;* †Hendry, Charles, *High Peak;* †Hill, Sir James, *Southampton Test;* Hughes, Robert, *Harrow West;* Hunt, Rt. Hon. David, *Wirral West;* †Jessel, Toby, *Twickenham;* Jones, Gwilym, *Cardiff North;* †Jones, Robert, *Hemel Hempstead;* Kirkhope, Timothy, *Leeds North East;* †Knapman, Roger, *Stroud;* †Knight, Mrs Angela, *Erewash;* Knight, Rt. Hon. Gregory, *Derby North;* †Kynoch, George, *Aberdeenshire West and Kincardine;* †Lait, Mrs Jacqui, *Hastings and Rye;* †Lamont, Rt. Hon. Norman, *Harrogate and Knaresborough;* †Lang, Rt. Hon. Ian, *Galloway and Upper Nithsdale;* †Lawrence, Sir Ivan, *Burton;* Legg, Barry, *Milton Keynes South West;* †Lennox-Boyd, Hon. Sir Mark, *Morecambe and Lunesdale;* †Lester, Sir James, *Broxtowe;* Maitland, Lady Olga, *Sutton and Cheam;* †Malone, Gerald, *Winchester;* †Mans, Keith, *Lancaster and Wyre;* †Marland, Paul, *Forest of Dean;* †Marlow, Antony, *Northampton North;* †Marshall, John, *Finchley and Golders Green;* Martin, David, *Portsmouth South;* Mellor, Rt. Hon. David, *Putney;* †Mitchell, Andrew, *Gedling;* †Moate, Sir Roger, *Sittingbourne and Sheppey;* †Morris, Rt. Hon. Michael, *Northampton South;* †Neubert, Sir Michael, *Romford;* †Newton, Rt. Hon. Antony, *Braintree;* Nicholson, David, *Taunton;* †Oppenheim, Hon. Phillip, *Amber Valley;* †Patnick, Sir Irvine, *Sheffield Hallam;* †Pawsey, James, *Rugby and Kenilworth;* †Peacock, Mrs Elizabeth, *Batley and Spen;* †Porter, David, *Waveney;* †Portillo, Rt. Hon. Michael, *Enfield Southgate;* Powell, William, *Corby;* †Rathbone, Tim, *Lewes;* Richards, Roderick, *Clwyd West;* Riddick, Graham, *Colne Valley;* †Rifkind, Rt. Hon. Malcolm, *Edinburgh, Pentlands;* †Robertson, Raymond, *Aberdeen South;* †Robinson, Mark, *Somerton and Frome;* Rumbold, Rt. Hon. Dame Angela, *Mitcham and Morden;* †Sackville, Hon. Thomas, *Bolton West;* †Shaw, David, *Dover;* †Shepherd, Sir Colin, *Hereford;* †Smith, Sir Dudley, *Warwick and Leamington;* †Spencer, Sir Derek, *Brighton, Pavilion;* Spink, Dr Robert, *Castle Point;* †Sproat, Iain, *Harwich;* Squire, Robin, *Hornchurch;* †Stern, Michael, *Bristol North West;* †Sumberg, David, *Bury South;* †Sweeney, Walter, *Vale of Glamorgan;* Sykes, John, *Scarborough and Whitby;* Thompson, Sir Donald, *Calder Valley;* †Thornton, Sir Malcolm, *Crosby;* †Tracey, Richard, *Kingston and Surbiton;* Twinn, Dr Ian, *Edmonton;* †Waldegrave, Rt. Hon. William, *Bristol West;* †Walker, William, *Tayside North;* Waller, Gary, *Keighley;* †Watts, John, *Reading East;* †Wood, Timothy, *Stevenage*

LIBERAL DEMOCRAT

†Davies, Christopher, *Oldham East and Saddleworth;* †Lynne, Elizabeth, *Rochdale;* †Maddock, Mrs Diana, *Christchurch*

OTHERS

†Gardiner, Sir George, *Ref., Reigate;* †Hendron, Dr Joseph, *SDLP, Belfast West;* †McCrea, Revd William, *DUP, Ulster Mid*

PARLIAMENTARY CONSTITUENCIES AS AT 1 MAY 1997

The results of voting in each parliamentary division at the general election of 1 May 1997 are given below. The majority in the 1992 general election, and any by-election between 1987 and 1992, is given below the 1992 result where the constituency covers the same area as in 1992. Where the boundaries of a constituency have changed since 1992, a notional result for 1992 is given.

Symbols
E. Total number of electors in the constituency at the 1997 general election
T. Turnout of electors at the 1997 general election
* Member of the last Parliament in unchanged constituency
† Member of the last Parliament in different constituency or one affected by boundary changes

Abbreviations
All.	Alliance Party (NI)
C.	Conservative
DUP	Democratic Unionist Party
Green	Green Party
Ind.	Independent
Lab.	Labour
Lab. Co-op.	Labour Co-operative
LD	Liberal Democrat
PC	Plaid Cymru
SDLP	Social Democratic and Labour Party
SF	Sinn Fein
SNP	Scottish National Party
UKU	United Kingdom Unionist
UUP	Ulster Unionist Party
ACA	Anti-Child Abuse
ACC	Anti-Corruption Candidate
Albion	Albion Party
Alt.	Alternative
ANP	All Night Party
Anti-maj.	Independent Anti-majority Democracy
AS	Anti-sleaze
Barts	Independent Save Barts Candidate
BDP	British Democratic Party
Beanus	Space Age Superhero from Planet Beanus
Beaut.	Independently Beautiful Party
Bert	Berties Party
BFAIR	British Freedom and Individual Rights
BHMBCM	Black Haired Medium Build Caucasian Male
BHR	British Home Rule
B. Ind.	Beaconsfield Independent: Unity Through Electoral Reform
BIPF	British Isles People First Party
BNP	British National Party
Bypass	Newbury Bypass Stop Construction Now
Byro	Lord Byro versus the Scallywag Tories
Care	Care in the Community
CASC	Conservatives Against the Single Currency
CFSS	Country Field and Shooting Sports
Ch. D.	Christian Democrat

Ch. Nat.	Christian Nationalist
Choice	People's Choice
Ch. P.	Christian Party
Ch. U.	Christian Unity
Comm. L.	Communist League
Comm. P.	Communist Party of Britain
Constit.	Constitutionalist
Consult.	Independent Democracy Means Consulting the People
CRP	Community Representative Party
CSSPP	Common Sense Sick of Politicians Party
Cvty	Conservatory
D. Nat.	Democratic Nationalist
Dream	Rainbow Dream Ticket Party
Dynamic	First Dynamic Party
EDP	English Democratic Party
Embryo	Anti-Abortion Euthanasia Embryo Experiments
EUP	European Unity Party
Fair	Building a Fair Society
FDP	Fancy Dress Party
Fellowship	Fellowship Party for Peace and Justice
FEP	Full Employment Party
FP	Freedom Party
Glow	Glow Bowling Party
GRLNSP	Green Referendum Lawless Naturally Street Party
Heart	Heart 106.2 Alien Party
Hemp	Hemp Coalition
HR	Human Rights '97
Hum.	Humanist Party
IAC	Independent Anti-Corruption in Government/TGWU
Ind. AFE	Independent Against a Federal Europe
Ind. BB	Independent Back to Basics
Ind. CRP	Independent Conservative Referendum Party
Ind. Dean	Independent Royal Forest of Dean
Ind. Dem.	Independent Democrat
Ind. ECR	Independent English Conservative and Referendum
Ind. F.	Independent Forester
Ind. Green	Independent Green: Your Children's Future
Ind. Hum.	English Independent Humanist Party
Ind. Is.	Island Independent
Ind. JRP	Justice and Renewal Independent Party
Ind. No	Independent No to Europe
IZB	Islam Zinda Baad Platform
JP	Justice Party
Juice	Juice Party
KBF	Keep Britain Free and Independent Party
Lab. Change	Labour Time for Change Candidate
LC	Loyal Conservative
LCP	Legalize Cannabis Party
LGR	Local Government Reform
Lib.	Liberal
Loc.	Local
Logic	Logic Party Truth Only Allowed
Loony	Monster Raving Loony Party
Mal	Mal Voice of the People Party
Miss M.	Miss Moneypenny's Glamorous One Party
MK	Mebyon Kernow

Mongolian	Mongolian Barbeque Great Place to Party
MRAC	Multi-racial Anti-Corruption Alliance
Nat. Dem.	National Democrat
New Way	New Millennium New Way Hemp Candidate
NF	National Front
NIFT	Former Captain NI Football Team
NIP	Northern Ireland Party
NI Women	Northern Ireland Women's Coalition
NLP	Natural Law Party
NLPC	New Labour Party Candidate
None	None of the Above Parties
NPC	Non-party Conservative
Pacifist	Pacifist for Peace, Justice, Co-operation, Environment
PAYR	Protecting All Your Rights Locally Effectively
PF	Pathfinders
PLP	People's Labour Party
Plymouth	Plymouth First Group
PP	People's Party
PPP	People's Party Party
ProLife	ProLife Alliance
PUP	Progressive Unionist Party
RA	Residents Association
Rain. Is.	Rainbow Connection Your Island Candidate
Rain. Ref.	Rainbow Referendum
R. Alt.	Radical Alternative
Ref.	Referendum Party
Ren. Dem.	Renaissance Democrat
Rep. GB	Republican Party of Great Britain
Rights	Charter for Basic Rights
Ronnie	Ronnie the Rhino Party
Route 66	Route 66 Party Posse Party
Scrapit	Scrapit Stop Avon Ring Road Now
SCU	Scottish Conservative Unofficial
SEP	Socialist Equality Party
SFDC	Stratford First Democratic Conservative
SG	Sub-genus Party
Shields	Pro Interests of South Shields People
SIP	Sheffield Independent Party
SLI	Scottish Labour Independent
Slough	People in Slough Shunning Useless Politicians
SLU	Scottish Labour Unofficial
Soc.	Socialist Party
Soc. Dem.	Social Democrat
Soc. Lab.	Socialist Labour Party
SPGB	Socialist Party of Great Britain
Spts All.	Sportsman's Alliance: Anything but Mellor
SSA	Scottish Socialist Alliance
Stan	Happiness Stan's Freedom to Party Party
Teddy	Teddy Bear Alliance Party
Top	Top Choice Liberal Democrat
21st Cent.	21st Century Independent Foresters
UA	Universal Alliance
UK Ind.	UK Independence Party
UKPP	UK Pensioners Party
WCCC	West Cheshire College in Crisis Party
Wessex	Wessex Regionalist
WP	Workers' Party
WRP	Workers' Revolutionary Party

ENGLAND

ALDERSHOT
E.76,189 T. 71.07%
G. Howarth, C.	23,119
A. Collett, LD	16,498
T. Bridgeman, Lab.	13,057
J. Howe, UK Ind.	794
A. Pendragon, Ind.	361
Dr D. Stevens, BNP	322
C. majority 6,621	

(Boundary change: notional C.)

ALDRIDGE-BROWNHILLS
E.62,441 T. 74.26%
*R. Shepherd, C.	21,856
J. Toth, Lab.	19,330
Ms C. Downie, LD	5,184
C. majority 2,526	

(April 1992, C. maj. 11,024)

ALTRINCHAM AND SALE WEST
E.70,625 T. 73.32%
G. Brady, C.	22,348
Ms J. Baugh, Lab.	20,843
M. Ramsbottom, LD	6,535
A. Landes, Ref.	1,348
J. Stephens, ProLife	313
Dr R. Mrozinski, UK Ind.	270
J. Renwick, NLP	125
C. majority 1,505	

(Boundary change: notional C.)

AMBER VALLEY
E.72,005 T. 76.07%
Ms J. Mallaber, Lab.	29,943
†P. Oppenheim, C.	18,330
R. Shelley, LD	4,219
Mrs I. McGibbon, Ref.	2,283
Lab. majority 11,613	

(Boundary change: notional C.)

ARUNDEL AND SOUTH DOWNS
E.67,641 T. 75.90%
H. Flight, C.	27,251
J. Goss, LD	13,216
R. Black, Lab.	9,376
J. Herbert, UK Ind.	1,494
C. majority 14,035	

(Boundary change: notional C.)

ASHFIELD
E.72,269 T. 70.02%
†G. Hoon, Lab.	32,979
M. Simmonds, C.	10,251
W. Smith, LD	4,882
M. Betts, Ref.	1,896
S. Belshaw, BNP	595
Lab. majority 22,728	

(Boundary change: notional Lab.)

ASHFORD
E.74,149 T. 74.57%
D. Green, C.	22,899
J. Ennals, Lab.	17,544
J. Williams, LD	10,901
C. Cruden, Ref.	3,201
R. Boden, Green	660
S. Tyrell, NLP	89
C. majority 5,355	

(April 1992, C. maj. 17,359)

ASHTON UNDER LYNE
E.72,206 T. 65.48%
†Rt. Hon. R. Sheldon, Lab.	31,919
R. Mayson, C.	8,954
T. Pickstone, LD	4,603
Mrs L. Clapham, Ref.	1,346
Prince Cymbal, Loony	458
Lab. majority 22,965	

(Boundary change: notional Lab.)

AYLESBURY
E.79,047 T. 72.81%
†D. Lidington, C.	25,426
Ms S. Bowles, LD	17,007
R. Langridge, Lab.	12,759
M. John, Ref.	2,196
L. Sheaff, NLP	166
C. majority 8,419	

(Boundary change: notional C.)

BANBURY
E.77,456 T. 75.46%
†A. Baldry, C.	25,076
Ms H. Peperell, Lab.	20,339
Mrs C. Bearder, LD	9,761
J. Ager, Ref.	2,245
Ms B. Cotton, Green	530
Mrs L. King, UK Ind.	364
I. Pearson, NLP	131
C. majority 4,737	

(Boundary change: notional C.)

BARKING
E.53,682 T. 61.41%
†Mrs M. Hodge, Lab.	21,698
K. Langford, C.	5,802
M. Marsh, LD	3,128
C. Taylor, Ref.	1,283
M. Tolman, BNP	894
D. Mearns, ProLife	159
Lab. majority 15,896	

(Boundary change: notional Lab.)

BARNSLEY CENTRAL
E.61,133 T. 59.68%
†E. Illsley, Lab.	28,090
S. Gutteridge, C.	3,589
D. Finlay, LD	3,481
J. Walsh, Ref.	1,325
Lab. majority 24,501	

(Boundary change: notional Lab.)

BARNSLEY EAST AND MEXBOROUGH
E.67,840 T. 63.88%
†J. Ennis, Lab.	31,699
Miss J. Ellison, C.	4,936
D. Willis, LD	4,489
K. Capstick, Soc. Lab.	1,213
A. Miles, Ref.	797
Ms J. Hyland, SEP	201
Lab. majority 26,763	

(Boundary change: notional Lab.)

BARNSLEY WEST AND PENISTONE
E.64,894 T. 65.04%
*M. Clapham, Lab.	25,017
P. Watkins, C.	7,750
Mrs W. Knight, LD	7,613
Mrs J. Miles, Ref.	1,828
Lab. majority 17,267	

(April 1992, Lab. maj. 14,504)

BARROW AND FURNESS
E.66,960 T. 72.03%
*J. Hutton, Lab.	27,630
R. Hunt, C.	13,133
Mrs A. Metcalfe, LD	4,264
J. Hamzeian, PLP	1,995
D. Mitchell, Ref.	1,208
Lab. majority 14,497	

(April 1992, Lab. maj. 3,578)

BASILDON
E.73,989 T. 71.74%
Ms A. Smith, Lab. Co-op.	29,646
J. Baron, C.	16,366
Ms L. Granshaw, LD	4,608
C. Robinson, Ref.	2,462
Lab. Co-op. majority 13,280	

(Boundary change: notional C.)

BASINGSTOKE
E.77,035 T. 74.16%
†A. Hunter, C.	24,751
N. Lickley, Lab.	22,354
M. Rimmer, LD	9,714
E. Selim, Ind.	310
C. majority 2,397	

(Boundary change: notional C.)

BASSETLAW
E.68,101 T. 70.37%
†J. Ashton, Lab.	29,298
M. Cleasby, C.	11,838
M. Kerrigan, LD	4,950
R. Graham, Ref.	1,838
Lab. majority 17,460	

(Boundary change: notional Lab.)

BATH
E.70,815 T. 76.24%
†D. Foster, LD	26,169
Ms A. McNair, C.	16,850
T. Bush, Lab.	8,828
A. Cook, Ref.	1,192
R. Scrase, Green	580
P. Sandell, UK Ind.	315
N. Pullen, NLP	55
LD majority 9,319	

(Boundary change: notional LD)

BATLEY AND SPEN
E.64,209 T. 73.14%
M. Wood, Lab.	23,213
†Mrs E. Peacock, C.	17,072
Mrs K. Pinnock, LD	4,133
E. Wood, Ref.	1,691
R. Smith, BNP	472
C. Lord, Green	384
Lab. majority 6,141	

(Boundary change: notional C.)

BATTERSEA
E.66,928 T. 70.82%
M. Linton, Lab.	24,047
†J. Bowis, C.	18,687
Ms P. Keaveney, LD	3,482
M. Slater, Ref.	804
R. Banks, UK Ind.	250
J. Marshall, Dream	127
Lab. majority 5,360	

(Boundary change: notional C.)

BEACONSFIELD
*E*68,959 *T.* 72.80%

D. Grieve, *C.*	24,709
P. Mapp, *LD*	10,722
A. Hudson, *Lab.*	10,063
H. Lloyd, *Ref.*	2,197
C. Story, *CASC*	1,434
C. Cooke, *UK Ind.*	451
Ms G. Duval, *ProLife*	286
T. Dyball, *NLP*	193
R. Matthews, *B. Ind.*	146

C. majority 13,987
(Boundary change: notional C.)

BECKENHAM
*E.*72,807 *T.* 74.65%

†P. Merchant, *C.*	23,084
R. Hughes, *Lab.*	18,131
Ms R. Vetterlein, *LD*	9,858
L. Mead, *Ref.*	1,663
P. Rimmer, *Lib.*	720
C. Pratt, *UK Ind.*	506
J. Mcauley, *NF*	388

C. majority 4,953
(Boundary change: notional C.)

BEDFORD
*E.*66,560 *T.* 73.53%

P. Hall, *Lab.*	24,774
R. Blackman, *C.*	16,474
C. Noyce, *LD*	6,044
P. Conquest, *Ref.*	1,503
Ms P. Saunders, *NLP*	149

Lab. majority 8,300
(Boundary change: notional C.)

BEDFORDSHIRE MID
*E.*66,979 *T.* 78.41%

J. Sayeed, *C.*	24,176
N. Mallett, *Lab.*	17,086
T. Hill, *LD*	8,823
Mrs S. Marler, *Ref.*	2,257
M. Lorys, *NLP*	174

C. majority 7,090
(Boundary change: notional C.)

BEDFORDSHIRE NORTH EAST
*E.*64,743 *T.* 77.83%

†Rt. Hon. Sir N. Lyell, *C.*	22,311
J. Lehal, *Lab.*	16,428
P. Bristow, *LD*	7,179
J. Taylor, *Ref.*	2,490
L. Foley, *Ind. C.*	1,842
B. Bence, *NLP*	138

C. majority 5,883
(Boundary change: notional C.)

BEDFORDSHIRE SOUTH WEST
*E.*69,781 *T.* 75.76%

†Sir D. Madel, *C.*	21,534
A. Date, *Lab.*	21,402
S. Owen, *LD*	7,559
Ms R. Hill, *Ref.*	1,761
T. Wise, *UK Ind.*	446
A. Le Carpentier, *NLP*	162

C. majority 132
(Boundary change: notional C.)

BERWICK-UPON-TWEED
*E.*56,428 *T.* 74.08%

*A. Beith, *LD*	19,007
P. Brannen, *Lab.*	10,965
N. Herbert, *C.*	10,056

N. Lambton, *Ref.*	1,423
I. Dodds, *UK Ind.*	352

LD majority 8,042
(April 1992, LD maj. 5,043)

BETHNAL GREEN AND BOW
*E.*73,008 *T.* 61.20%

Ms O. King, *Lab.*	20,697
K. Choudhury, *C.*	9,412
S. N. Islam, *LD*	5,361
D. King, *BNP*	3,350
T. Milson, *Lib.*	2,963
S. Osman, *Real Lab.*	1,117
S. Petter, *Green*	812
M. Abdullah, *Ref.*	557
A. Hamid, *Soc. Lab.*	413

Lab. majority 11,285
(Boundary change: notional Lab.)

BEVERLEY AND HOLDERNESS
*E.*71,916 *T.* 73.62%

†J. Cran, *C.*	21,629
N. O'Neill, *Lab.*	20,818
J. Melling, *LD*	9,689
D. Barley, *UK Ind.*	695
S. Withers, *NLP*	111

C. majority 811
(Boundary change: notional C.)

BEXHILL AND BATTLE
*E.*65,584 *T.* 74.70%

†C. Wardle, *C.*	23,570
Mrs K. Field, *LD*	12,470
R. Beckwith, *Lab.*	8,866
Mrs V. Thompson, *Ref.*	3,302
J. Pankhurst, *UK Ind.*	786

C. majority 11,100
(Boundary change: notional C.)

BEXLEYHEATH AND CRAYFORD
*E.*63,334 *T.* 76.14%

N. Beard, *Lab.*	21,942
†D. Evennett, *C.*	18,527
Mrs F. Montford, *LD*	5,391
B. Thomas, *Ref.*	1,551
Ms P. Smith, *BNP*	429
W. Jenner, *UK Ind.*	383

Lab. majority 3,415
(Boundary change: notional C.)

BILLERICAY
*E.*76,550 *T.* 72.40%

†Mrs T. Gorman, *C.*	22,033
P. Richards, *Lab.*	20,677
G. Williams, *LD*	8,763
B. Hughes, *LC*	3,377
J. Buchanan, *ProLife*	570

C. majority 1,356
(Boundary change: notional C.)

BIRKENHEAD
*E.*59,782 *T.* 65.78%

*F. Field, *Lab.*	27,825
J. Crosby, *C.*	5,982
R. Wood, *LD*	3,548
M. Cullen, *Soc. Lab.*	1,168
R. Evans, *Ref.*	800

Lab. majority 21,843
(April 1992, Lab. maj. 17,613)

BIRMINGHAM EDGBASTON
*E.*70,204 *T.* 69.03%

Mrs G. Stuart, *Lab.*	23,554

A. Marshall, *C.*	18,712
J. Gallagher, *LD*	4,691
J. Oakton, *Ref.*	1,065
D. Campbell, *BDP*	443

Lab. majority 4,842
(Boundary change: notional C.)

BIRMINGHAM ERDINGTON
*E.*66,380 *T.* 60.87%

†R. Corbett, *Lab.*	23,764
A. Tompkins, *C.*	11,107
I. Garrett, *LD*	4,112
G. Cable, *Ref.*	1,424

Lab. majority 12,657
(Boundary change: notional Lab.)

BIRMINGHAM HALL GREEN
*E.*58,767 *T.* 71.16%

S. McCabe, *Lab.*	22,372
*A. Hargreaves, *C.*	13,952
A. Dow, *LD*	4,034
P. Bennett, *Ref.*	1,461

Lab. majority 8,420
(April 1992, C. maj. 3,665)

BIRMINGHAM HODGE HILL
*E.*56,066 *T.* 60.91%

*T. Davis, *Lab.*	22,398
E. Grant, *C.*	8,198
H. Thomas, *LD*	2,891
P. Johnson, *UK Ind.*	660

Lab. majority 14,200
(April 1992, Lab. maj. 7,068)

BIRMINGHAM LADYWOOD
*E.*70,013 *T.* 54.24%

†Ms C. Short, *Lab.*	28,134
S. Vara, *C.*	5,052
S. S. Marwa, *LD*	3,020
Mrs R. Gurney, *Ref.*	1,086
A. Carmichael, *Nat. Dem.*	685

Lab. majority 23,082
(Boundary change: notional Lab.)

BIRMINGHAM NORTHFIELD
*E.*56,842 *T.* 68.34%

†R. Burden, *Lab.*	22,316
A. Blumenthal, *C.*	10,873
M. Ashall, *LD*	4,078
D. Gent, *Ref.*	1,243
K. Axon, *BNP*	337

Lab. majority 11,443
(Boundary change: notional Lab.)

BIRMINGHAM PERRY BARR
*E.*71,031 *T.* 64.60%

†J. Rooker, *Lab.*	28,921
A. Dunnett, *C.*	9,964
R. Hassall, *LD*	4,523
S. Mahmood, *Ref.*	843
A. Baxter, *Lib.*	718
L. Windridge, *BNP*	544
A. S. Panesar, *Fourth Party*	374

Lab. majority 18,957
(Boundary change: notional Lab.)

BIRMINGHAM SELLY OAK
*E.*72,049 *T.* 70.16%

*Dr L. Jones, *Lab.*	28,121
G. Greene, *C.*	14,033
D. Osborne, *LD*	6,121
L. Marshall, *Ref.*	1,520
Dr G. Gardner, *ProLife*	417

P. Sherriff-Knowles, *Loony* 253
H. Meads, *NLP* 85
Lab. majority 14,088
(April 1992, Lab. maj. 2,060)

BIRMINGHAM SPARKBROOK AND
SMALL HEATH
*E.*73,130   *T.* 57.11%
†R. Godsiff, *Lab.* 26,841
K. Hardeman, *C.* 7,315
R. Harmer, *LD* 3,889
A. Clawley, *Green* 959
R. Dooley, *Ref.* 737
P. Patel, *Fourth Party* 538
R. M. Syed, *PAYR* 513
Ms S. Bi, *Ind.* 490
C. Wren, *Soc. Lab.* 483
Lab. majority 19,526
(Boundary change: notional Lab.)

BIRMINGHAM YARDLEY
*E.*53,058   *T.* 71.22%
*Ms E. Morris, *Lab.* 17,778
J. Hemming, *LD* 12,463
Mrs A. Jobson, *C.* 6,736
D. Livingston, *Ref.* 646
A. Ware, *UK Ind.* 164
Lab. majority 5,315
(April 1992, Lab. maj. 162)

BISHOP AUCKLAND
*E.*66,754   *T.* 68.88%
†Rt. Hon. D. Foster, *Lab.* 30,359
Mrs J. Fergus, *C.* 9,295
L. Ashworth, *LD* 4,223
D. Blacker, *Ref.* 2,104
Lab. majority 21,064
(Boundary change: notional Lab.)

BLABY
*E.*70,471   *T.* 76.05%
†A. Robathan, *C.* 24,564
R. Willmott, *Lab.* 18,090
G. Welsh, *LD* 8,001
R. Harrison, *Ref.* 2,018
J. Peacock, *BNP* 523
T. Stokes, *Ind.* 397
C. majority 6,474
(Boundary change: notional C.)

BLACKBURN
*E.*73,058   *T.* 65.01%
*J. Straw, *Lab.* 26,141
Ms S. Sidhu, *C.* 11,690
S. Fenn, *LD* 4,990
D. Bradshaw, *Ref.* 1,892
Mrs T. Wingfield, *Nat. Dem.* 671
Mrs H. Drummond, *Soc. Lab.* 637
R. Field, *Green* 608
Mrs M. Carmichael-Grimshaw,
KBF 506
W. Batchelor, *CSSPP* 362
Lab. majority 14,451
(April 1992, Lab. maj. 6,027)

BLACKPOOL NORTH AND
FLEETWOOD
*E.*74,989   *T.* 71.67%
Mrs J. Humble, *Lab.* 28,051
†H. Elletson, *C.* 19,105
Mrs B. Hill, *LD* 4,600
Ms K. Stacey, *Ref.* 1,704
J. Ellis, *BNP* 288

Lab. majority 8,946
(Boundary change: notional C.)

BLACKPOOL SOUTH
*E.*75,720   *T.* 67.80%
G. Marsden, *Lab.* 29,282
R. Booth, *C.* 17,666
Mrs D. Holt, *LD* 4,392
Lab. majority 11,616
(Boundary change: notional C.)

BLAYDON
*E.*64,699   *T.* 70.98%
*J. McWilliam, *Lab.* 27,535
P. Maughan, *LD* 10,930
M. Watson, *C.* 6,048
R. Rook, *Ind. Lab.* 1,412
Lab. majority 16,605
(April 1992, Lab. maj. 13,343)

BLYTH VALLEY
*E.*61,761   *T.* 68.78%
*R. Campbell, *Lab.* 27,276
A. Lamb, *LD* 9,540
Mrs B. Musgrave, *C.* 5,666
Lab. majority 17,736
(April 1992, Lab. maj. 8,044)

BOGNOR REGIS AND
LITTLEHAMPTON
*E.*66,480   *T.* 69.86%
N. Gibb, *C.* 20,537
R. Nash, *Lab.* 13,216
Dr J. Walsh, *LD* 11,153
G. Stride, *UK Ind.* 1,537
C. majority 7,321
(Boundary change: notional C.)

BOLSOVER
*E.*66,476   *T.* 71.32%
†D. Skinner, *Lab.* 35,073
R. Harwood, *C.* 7,924
I. Cox, *LD* 4,417
Lab. majority 27,149
(Boundary change: notional Lab.)

BOLTON NORTH EAST
*E.*67,930   *T.* 72.44%
D. Crausby, *Lab.* 27,621
R. Wilson, *C.* 14,952
Dr E. Critchley, *LD* 4,862
D. Staniforth, *Ref.* 1,096
W. Kelly, *Soc. Lab.* 676
Lab. majority 12,669
(Boundary change: notional Lab.)

BOLTON SOUTH EAST
*E.*66,459   *T.* 65.23%
B. Iddon, *Lab.* 29,856
P. Carter, *C.* 8,545
F. Harasiwka, *LD* 3,805
W. Pickering, *Ref.* 973
L. Walch, *NLP* 170
Lab. majority 21,311
(Boundary change: notional Lab.)

BOLTON WEST
*E.*63,535   *T.* 77.37%
Ms R. Kelly, *Lab.* 24,342
†T. Sackville, *C.* 17,270
Mrs B. Ronson, *LD* 5,309
Mrs D. Kelly, *Soc. Lab.* 1,374
Mrs G. Frankl-Slater, *Ref.* 865

Lab. majority 7,072
(Boundary change: notional C.)

BOOTLE
*E.*57,284   *T.* 66.73%
†J. Benton, *Lab.* 31,668
R. Mathews, *C.* 3,247
K. Reid, *LD* 2,191
J. Elliott, *Ref.* 571
P. Glover, *Soc.* 420
S. Cohen, *NLP* 126
Lab. majority 28,421
(Boundary change: notional Lab.)

BOSTON AND SKEGNESS
*E.*67,623   *T.* 68.87%
†Sir R. Body, *C.* 19,750
P. McCauley, *Lab.* 19,103
J. Dodsworth, *LD* 7,721
C. majority 647
(Boundary change: notional C.)

BOSWORTH
*E.*68,113   *T.* 76.57%
†D. Tredinnick, *C.* 21,189
A. Furlong, *Lab.* 20,162
J. Ellis, *LD* 9,281
S. Halborg, *Ref.* 1,521
C. majority 1,027
(Boundary change: notional C.)

BOURNEMOUTH EAST
*E.*61,862   *T.* 70.20%
†D. Atkinson, *C.* 17,997
D. Eyre, *LD* 13,651
Mrs J. Stevens, *Lab.* 9,181
A. Musgrave-Scott, *Ref.* 1,808
K. Benney, *UK Ind.* 791
C. majority 4,346
(Boundary change: notional C.)

BOURNEMOUTH WEST
*E.*62,028   *T.* 66.22%
†J. Butterfill, *C.* 17,115
Ms J. Dover, *LD* 11,405
D. Gritt, *Lab.* 10,093
R. Mills, *Ref.* 1,910
Mrs L. Tooley, *UK Ind.* 281
J. Morse, *BNP* 165
A. Springham, *NLP* 103
C. majority 5,710
(Boundary change: notional C.)

BRACKNELL
*E.*79,292   *T.* 74.52%
†A. Mackay, *C.* 27,983
Ms A. Snelgrove, *Lab.* 17,596
A. Hilliar, *LD* 9,122
J. Tompkins, *New Lab.* 1,909
W. Cairns, *Ref.* 1,636
L. Boxall, *UK Ind.* 569
Ms D. Roberts, *ProLife* 276
C. majority 10,387
(Boundary change: notional C.)

BRADFORD NORTH
*E.*66,228   *T.* 63.26%
*T. Rooney, *Lab.* 23,493
R. Skinner, *C.* 10,723
T. Browne, *LD* 6,083
H. Wheatley, *Ref.* 1,227
W. Beckett, *Loony* 369

Lab. majority 12,770
(April 1992, Lab. maj. 7,664)

BRADFORD SOUTH
*E.*68,391 *T.* 65.88%

*G. Sutcliffe, *Lab.*	25,558
Mrs A. Hawkesworth, *C.*	12,622
A. Wilson-Fletcher, *LD*	5,093
Mrs M. Kershaw, *Ref.*	1,785

Lab. majority 12,936
(April 1992, Lab. maj. 4,902)
(June 1994, Lab. maj. 9,664)

BRADFORD WEST
*E.*71,961 *T.* 63.32%

M. Singh, *Lab.*	18,932
M. Riaz, *C.*	15,055
Mis H. Wright, *LD*	6,737
A. Khan, *Soc. Lab.*	1,551
C. Royston, *Ref.*	1,348
J. Robinson, *Green*	861
G. Osborn, *BNP*	839
S. Shah, *Soc.*	245

Lab. majority 3,877
(April 1992, Lab. maj. 9,502)

BRAINTREE
*E.*72,772 *T.* 76.37%

A. Hurst, *Lab.*	23,729
†Rt. Hon. A. Newton, *C.*	22,278
T. Ellis, *LD*	6,418
N. Westcott, *Ref.*	2,165
J. Abbott, *Green*	712
M. Nolan, *New Way*	274

Lab. majority 1,451
(Boundary change: notional C.)

BRENT EAST
*E.*53,548 *T.* 65.87%

†K. Livingstone, *Lab.*	23,748
M. Francois, *C.*	7,866
J. Hunter, *LD*	2,751
S. Keable, *Soc. Lab.*	466
A. Shanks, *ProLife*	218
Ms C. Warrilo, *Dream*	120
D. Jenkins, *NLP*	103

Lab. majority 15,882
(Boundary change: notional Lab.)

BRENT NORTH
*E.*54,149 *T.* 70.50%

B. Gardiner, *Lab.*	19,343
†Rt. Hon. Sir R. Boyson, *C.*	15,324
P. Lorber, *LD*	3,104
A. Davids, *NLP*	204
G. Clark, *Dream*	199

Lab. majority 4,019
(Boundary change: notional C.)

BRENT SOUTH
*E.*53,505 *T.* 64.48%

†P. Boateng, *Lab.*	25,180
S. Jackson, *C.*	5,489
J. Brazil, *LD*	2,670
Ms J. Phythian, *Ref.*	497
D. Edler, *Green*	389
C. Howard, *Dream*	175
Ms A. Mahaldar, *NLP*	98

Lab. majority 19,691
(Boundary change: notional Lab.)

BRENTFORD AND ISLEWORTH
*E.*79,058 *T.* 71.00%

Mrs A. Keen, *Lab.*	32,249
†N. Deva, *C.*	17,825
Dr G. Hartwell, *LD*	4,613
J. Bradley, *Green*	687
Mrs B. Simmerson, *UK Ind.*	614
M. Ahmed, *NLP*	147

Lab. majority 14,424
(Boundary change: notional C.)

BRENTWOOD AND ONGAR
*E.*66,005 *T.* 76.85%

†E. Pickles, *C.*	23,031
Mrs E. Bottomley, *LD*	13,341
M. Young, *Lab.*	11,231
Mrs A. Kilmartin, *Ref.*	2,658
Capt. D. Mills, *UK Ind.*	465

C. majority 9,690
(Boundary change: notional C.)

BRIDGWATER
*E.*73,038 *T.* 74.79%

*Rt. Hon. T. King, *C.*	20,174
M. Hoban, *LD*	18,378
R. Lavers, *Lab.*	13,519
Ms F. Evens, *Ref.*	2,551

C. majority 1,796
(April 1992, C. maj. 9,716)

BRIGG AND GOOLE
*E.*63,648 *T.* 73.53%

I. Cawsey, *Lab.*	23,493
D. Stewart, *C.*	17,104
Mrs M.-R. Hardy, *LD*	4,692
D. Rigby, *Ref.*	1,513

Lab. majority 6,389
(Boundary change: notional C.)

BRIGHTON KEMPTOWN
*E.*65,147 *T.* 70.81%

D. Turner, *Lab.*	21,479
†Sir A. Bowden, *C.*	17,945
C. Gray, *LD*	4,478
D. Inman, *Ref.*	1,526
Ms H. Williams, *Soc. Lab.*	316
J. Bowler, *NLP*	172
Ms L. Newman, *Loony*	123
R. Darlow, *Dream*	93

Lab. majority 3,534
(Boundary change: notional C.)

BRIGHTON PAVILION
*E.*66,431 *T.* 73.69%

D. Lepper, *Lab. Co-op.*	26,737
†Sir D. Spencer, *C.*	13,556
K. Blanshard, *LD*	4,644
P. Stocken, *Ref.*	1,304
P. West, *Green*	1,249
R. Huggett, *Ind. C.*	1,098
F. Stevens, *UK Ind.*	179
R. Dobbs, *SG*	125
A. Card, *Dream*	59

Lab. Co-op. majority 13,181
(Boundary change: notional C.)

BRISTOL EAST
*E.*68,990 *T.* 69.87%

†Ms J. Corston, *Lab.*	27,418
E. Vaizey, *C.*	11,259
P. Tyzack, *LD*	7,121
G. Philp, *Ref.*	1,479
P. Williams, *Soc. Lab.*	766

J. McLaggan, *NLP*	158

Lab. majority 16,159
(Boundary change: notional Lab.)

BRISTOL NORTH WEST
*E.*75,009 *T.* 73.65%

D. Naysmith, *Lab. Co-op.*	27,575
†M. Stern, *C.*	16,193
I. Parry, *LD*	7,263
C. Horton, *Ind. Lab.*	1,718
J. Quintanilla, *Ref.*	1,609
G. Shorter, *Soc. Lab.*	482
S. Parnell, *BNP*	265
T. Leighton, *NLP*	140

Lab. Co-op. majority 11,382
(Boundary change: notional Lab.
Co-op.)

BRISTOL SOUTH
*E.*72,393 *T.* 68.87%

†Ms D. Primarolo, *Lab.*	29,890
M. Roe, *C.*	10,562
S. Williams, *LD*	6,691
D. Guy, *Ref.*	1,486
J. Boxall, *Green*	722
I. Marshall, *Soc.*	355
Louis Taylor, *Glow*	153

Lab. majority 19,328
(Boundary change: notional Lab.)

BRISTOL WEST
*E.*84,870 *T.* 73.81%

Ms V. Davey, *Lab.*	22,068
†Rt. Hon. W. Waldegrave, *C.*	20,575
C. Boney, *LD*	17,551
Lady M. Beauchamp, *Ref.*	1,304
J. Quinnell, *Green*	852
R. Nurse, *Soc. Lab.*	244
J. Brierley, *NLP*	47

Lab. majority 1,493
(Boundary change: notional C.)

BROMLEY AND CHISLEHURST
*E.*71,104 *T.* 74.17%

†Rt. Hon. E. Forth, *C.*	24,428
R. Yeldham, *Lab.*	13,310
Dr P. Booth, *LD*	12,530
R. Bryant, *UK Ind.*	1,176
Ms F. Speed, *Green*	640
M. Stoneman, *NF*	369
G. Aitman, *Lib.*	285

C. majority 11,118
(Boundary change: notional C.)

BROMSGROVE
*E.*67,744 *T.* 77.07%

Miss J. Kirkbride, *C.*	24,620
P. McDonald, *Lab.*	19,725
Mrs J. Davy, *LD*	6,200
Mrs D. Winsor, *Ref.*	1,411
Mrs G. Wetton, *UK Ind.*	251

C. majority 4,895
(Boundary change: notional C.)

BROXBOURNE
*E.*66,720 *T.* 70.41%

†Mrs M. Roe, *C.*	22,952
B. Coleman, *Lab.*	16,299
Mrs J. Davies, *LD*	5,310
D. Millward, *Ref.*	1,633
D. Bruce, *BNP*	610
B. Cheetham, *Third Way*	172

C. majority 6,653
(Boundary change: notional C.)

BROXTOWE
*E.*74,144   *T.* 78.41%

N. Palmer, *Lab.*	27,343
†Sir J. Lester, *C.*	21,768
T. Miller, *LD*	6,934
R. Tucker, *Ref.*	2,092

Lab. majority 5,575
(Boundary change: notional C.)

BUCKINGHAM
*E.*62,945   *T.* 78.48%

J. Bercow, *C.*	24,594
R. Lehmann, *Lab.*	12,208
N. Stuart, *LD*	12,175
Dr G. Clements, *NLP*	421

C. majority 12,386
(Boundary change: notional C.)

BURNLEY
*E.*67,582   *T.* 66.95%

*P. Pike, *Lab.*	26,210
W. Wiggin, *C.*	9,148
G. Birtwistle, *LD*	7,877
R. Oakley, *Ref.*	2,010

Lab. majority 17,062
(April 1992, Lab. maj. 11,491)

BURTON
*E.*72,601   *T.* 75.08%

Ms J. Dean, *Lab.*	27,810
†Sir I. Lawrence, *C.*	21,480
D. Fletcher, *LD*	4,617
K. Sharp, *Nat. Dem.*	604

Lab. majority 6,330
(Boundary change: notional C.)

BURY NORTH
*E.*70,515   *T.* 78.07%

D. Chaytor, *Lab.*	28,523
*A. Burt, *C.*	20,657
N. Kenyon, *LD*	4,536
R. Hallewell, *Ref.*	1,337

Lab. majority 7,866
(April 1992, C. maj. 4,764)

BURY SOUTH
*E.*66,568   *T.* 75.60%

I. Lewis, *Lab.*	28,658
†D. Sumberg, *C.*	16,225
V. D'Albert, *LD*	4,227
B. Slater, *Ref.*	1,216

Lab. majority 12,433
(Boundary change: notional C.)

BURY ST EDMUNDS
*E.*74,017   *T.* 75.02%

D. Ruffley, *C.*	21,290
M. Ereira-Guyer, *Lab.*	20,922
D. Cooper, *LD*	10,102
I. McWhirter, *Ref.*	2,939
Mrs J. Lillis, *NLP*	272

C. majority 368
(Boundary change: notional C.)

CALDER VALLEY
*E.*74,901   *T.* 75.39%

Ms C. McCafferty, *Lab.*	26,050
*Sir D. Thompson, *C.*	19,795
S. Pearson, *LD*	8,322
A. Mellor, *Ref.*	1,380
Ms V. Smith, *Green*	488

C. Jackson, *BNP*	431

Lab. majority 6,255
(April 1992, C. maj. 4,878)

CAMBERWELL AND PECKHAM
*E.*50,214   *T.* 56.71%

†Ms H. Harman, *Lab.*	19,734
K. Humphreys, *C.*	3,383
N. Williams, *LD*	3,198
N. China, *Ref.*	692
Ms A. Ruddock, *Soc. Lab.*	685
G. Williams, *Lib.*	443
Ms J. Barker, *Soc.*	233
C. Eames, *WRP*	106

Lab. majority 16,351
(Boundary change: notional Lab.)

CAMBRIDGE
*E.*71,669   *T.* 71.63%

*Mrs A. Campbell, *Lab.*	27,436
D. Platt, *C.*	13,299
G. Heathcock, *LD*	8,287
W. Burrows, *Ref.*	1,262
Ms M. Wright, *Green*	654
Ms A. Johnstone, *ProLife*	191
R. Athow, *WRP*	107
Ms P. Gladwin, *NLP*	103

Lab. majority 14,137
(April 1992, Lab. maj. 580)

CAMBRIDGESHIRE NORTH EAST
*E.*76,056   *T.* 72.87%

†M. Moss, *C.*	23,855
Mrs V. Bucknor, *Lab.*	18,754
A. Nash, *LD*	9,070
M. Bacon, *Ref.*	2,636
C. Bennett, *Soc. Lab.*	851
L. Leighton, *NLP*	259

C. majority 5,101
(Boundary change: notional C.)

CAMBRIDGESHIRE NORTH WEST
*E.*65,791   *T.* 74.20%

†Rt. Hon. Dr B. Mawhinney, *C.*	23,488
L. Steptoe, *Lab.*	15,734
Mrs B. McCoy, *LD*	7,388
A.Watt, *Ref.*	1,939
W. Wyatt, *UK Ind.*	269

C. majority 7,754
(Boundary change: notional C.)

CAMBRIDGESHIRE SOUTH
*E.*69,850   *T.* 76.85%

A. Lansley, *C.*	22,572
J. Quinlan, *LD*	13,860
A. Gray, *Lab.*	13,485
R. Page, *Ref.*	3,300
D. Norman, *UK Ind.*	298
F. Chalmers, *NLP*	168

C. majority 8,712
(Boundary change: notional C.)

CAMBRIDGESHIRE SOUTH EAST
*E.*75,666   *T.* 75.08%

†J. Paice, *C.*	24,397
R. Collinson, *Lab.*	15,048
Ms S. Brinton, *LD*	14,246
J. Howlett, *Ref.*	2,838
K. Lam, *Fair*	167
P. While, *NLP*	111

C. majority 9,349
(Boundary change: notional C.)

CANNOCK CHASE
*E.*72,362   *T.* 72.37%

†Dr A. Wright, *Lab.*	28,705
J. Backhouse, *C.*	14,227
R. Kirby, *LD*	4,537
P. Froggatt, *Ref.*	1,663
W. Hurley, *New Lab.*	1,615
M. Conroy, *Soc. Lab.*	1,120
M. Hartshorn, *Loony*	499

Lab. majority 14,478
(Boundary change: notional Lab.)

CANTERBURY
*E.*74,548   *T.* 72.58%

†J. Brazier, *C.*	20,913
Ms C. Hall, *Lab.*	16,949
M. Vye, *LD*	12,854
J. Osborne, *Ref.*	2,460
G. Meaden, *Green*	588
J. Moore, *UK Ind.*	281
A. Pringle, *NLP*	64

C. majority 3,964
(Boundary change: notional C.)

CARLISLE
*E.*59,917   *T.* 72.78%

†E. Martlew, *Lab.*	25,031
R. Lawrence, *C.*	12,641
C. Mayho, *LD*	4,576
A. Fraser, *Ref.*	1,233
W. Stevens, *NLP*	126

Lab. majority 12,390
(Boundary change: notional Lab.)

CARSHALTON AND WALLINGTON
*E.*66,038   *T.* 73.33%

T. Brake, *LD*	18,490
*N. Forman, *C.*	16,223
A. Theobald, *Lab.*	11,565
J. Storey, *Ref.*	1,289
P. Hickson, *Green*	377
G. Ritchie, *BNP*	261
L. Povey, *UK Ind.*	218

LD majority 2,267
(April 1992, C. maj. 9,943)

CASTLE POINT
*E.*67,146   *T.* 72.34%

Ms C. Butler, *Lab.*	20,605
*Dr R. Spink, *C.*	19,489
D. Baker, *LD*	4,477
H. Maulkin, *Ref.*	2,700
Miss L. Kendall, *Consult.*	1,301

Lab. majority 1,116
(April 1992, C. maj. 16,830)

CHARNWOOD
*E.*72,692   *T.* 77.28%

†Rt. Hon. S. Dorrell, *C.*	26,110
D. Knaggs, *Lab.*	20,210
R. Wilson, *LD*	7,224
H. Meechan, *Ref.*	2,104
M. Palmer, *BNP*	525

C. majority 5,900
(Boundary change: notional C.)

CHATHAM AND AYLESFORD
*E.*69,172   *T.* 71.07%

J. Shaw, *Lab.*	21,191
R. Knox-Johnston, *C.*	18,401
R. Murray, *LD*	7,389
K. Riddle, *Ref.*	1,538
A. Harding, *UK Ind.*	493

T. Martel, *NLP* 149
Lab. majority 2,790
(Boundary change: notional C.)

CHEADLE
*E.*67,627 *T.* 77.58%
†S. Day, *C.* 22,944
Mrs P. Calton, *LD* 19,755
P. Diggett, *Lab.* 8,253
P. Brook, *Ref.* 1,511
C. majority 3,189
(Boundary change: notional C.)

CHELMSFORD WEST
*E.*76,086 *T.* 76.99%
†S. Burns, *C.* 23,781
M. Bracken, *LD* 17,090
Dr R. Chad, *Lab.* 15,436
T. Smith, *Ref.* 1,536
G. Rumens, *Green* 411
M. Levin, *UK Ind.* 323
C. majority 6,691
(Boundary change: notional C.)

CHELTENHAM
*E.*67,950 *T.* 74.03%
†N. Jones, *LD* 24,877
J. Todman, *C.* 18,232
B. Leach, *Lab.* 5,100
Mrs A. Powell, *Ref.* 1,065
K. Hanks, *Loony* 375
G. Cook, *UK Ind.* 302
Ms A. Harriss, *ProLife* 245
Ms S. Brighouse, *NLP* 107
LD majority 6,645
(Boundary change: notional LD)

CHESHAM AND AMERSHAM
*E.*69,244 *T.* 75.38%
|Mrs C. Gillan, *C.* 26,298
M. Brand, *LD* 12,439
P. Farrelly, *Lab.* 10,240
P. Andrews, *Ref.* 2,528
C. Shilson, *UK Ind.* 618
H. Godfrey, *NLP* 74
C. majority 13,859
(Boundary change: notional C.)

CHESTER, CITY OF
*E.*71,730 *T.* 78.43%
Ms C. Russell, *Lab.* 29,806
†G. Brandreth, *C.* 19,253
D. Simpson, *LD* 5,353
R. Mullen, *Ref.* 1,487
I. Sanderson, *Loony* 204
J. Gerrard, *WCCC* 154
Lab. majority 10,553
(Boundary change: notional C.)

CHESTERFIELD
*E.*72,472 *T.* 70.91%
*Rt. Hon. A. Benn, *Lab.* 26,105
A. Rogers, *LD* 20,330
M. Potter, *C.* 4,752
N. Scarth, *Ind. OAP* 202
Lab. majority 5,775
(April 1992, Lab. maj. 6,414)

CHICHESTER
*E.*74,489 *T.* 74.88%
A. Tyrie, *C.* 25,895
Prof. P. Gardiner, *LD* 16,161
C. Smith, *Lab.* 9,605

D. Denny, *Ref.* 3,318
J. Rix, *UK Ind.* 800
C. majority 9,734
(Boundary change: notional C.)

CHINGFORD AND WOODFORD
GREEN
*E.*62,904 *T.* 70.66%
†I. Duncan Smith, *C.* 21,109
T. Hutchinson, *Lab.* 15,395
G. Seeff, *LD* 6,885
A. Gould, *BNP* 1,059
C. majority 5,714
(Boundary change: notional C.)

CHIPPING BARNET
*E.*69,049 *T.* 71.78%
†Sir S. Chapman, *C.* 21,317
G. Cooke, *Lab.* 20,282
S. Hooker, *LD* 6,121
V. Ribekow, *Ref.* 1,190
B. Miskin, *Loony* 253
B. Scallan, *ProLife* 243
Ms D. Dirksen, *NLP* 159
C. majority 1,035
(Boundary change: notional C.)

CHORLEY
*E.*74,387 *T.* 77.58%
L. Hoyle, *Lab.* 30,607
†D. Dover, *C.* 20,737
S. Jones, *LD* 4,900
A. Heaton, *Ref.* 1,319
P. Leadbetter, *NLP* 143
Lab. majority 9,870
(Boundary change: notional C.)

CHRISTCHURCH
*E.*71,488 *T.* 78.61%
C. Chope, *C.* 26,095
†Mrs D. Maddock, *LD* 23,930
C. Mannan, *Lab.* 3,884
R. Spencer, *Ref.* 1,684
R. Dickinson, *UK Ind.* 606
C. majority 2,165
(Boundary change: notional C.)

CITIES OF LONDON AND
WESTMINSTER
*E.*69,047 *T.* 58.16%
†Rt. Hon. P. Brooke, *C.* 18,981
Ms K. Green, *Lab.* 14,100
M. Dumigan, *LD* 4,933
Sir A. Walters, *Ref.* 1,161
Ms P. Wharton, *Barts* 266
C. Merton, *UK Ind.* 215
R. Johnson, *NLP* 176
N. Walsh, *Loony* 138
G. Webster, *Hemp* 112
J. Sadowitz, *Dream* 73
C. majority 4,881
(Boundary change: notional C.)

CLEETHORPES
*E.*68,763 *T.* 73.40%
Ms S. McIsaac, *Lab.* 26,058
†M. Brown, *C.* 16,882
K. Melton, *LD* 5,746
J. Berry, *Ref.* 1,787
Lab. majority 9,176
(Boundary change: notional C.)

COLCHESTER
*E.*74,743 *T.*69.58%
R. Russell, *C.* 17,886
S. Shakespeare, *C.* 16,305
R. Green, *Lab.* 15,891
J. Hazell, *Ref.* 1,776
Ms L. Basker, *NLP* 148
LD majority 1,581
(Boundary change: notional C.)

COLNE VALLEY
*E.*73,338 *T.*76.92%
Ms K. Mountford, *Lab.* 23,285
*G. Riddick, *C.* 18,445
N. Priestley, *LD* 12,755
A. Brooke, *Soc. Lab.* 759
A. Cooper, *Green* 493
J. Nunn, *UK Ind.* 478
Ms M. Staniforth, *Loony* 196
Lab. majority 4,840
(April 1992, C. maj. 7,225)

CONGLETON
*E.*68,873 *T.*77.56%
†Mrs A. Winterton, *C.* 22,012
Mrs J. Walmsley, *LD* 15,882
Ms H. Scholey, *Lab.* 14,714
J. Lockett, *UK Ind.* 811
C. majority 6,130
(Boundary change: notional C.)

COPELAND
*E.*54,263 *T.*76.19%
*Rt. Hon. Dr J. Cunningham,
Lab. 24,025
A. Cumpsty, *C.* 12,081
R. Putnam, *LD* 3,814
C. Johnston, *Ref.* 1,036
G. Hanratty, *ProLife* 389
Lab. majority 11,944
(April 1992, Lab. maj. 2,439)

CORBY
*E.*69,252 *T.*77.91%
P. Hope, *Lab. Co-op.* 29,888
*W. Powell, *C.* 18,028
I. Hankinson, *LD* 4,045
S. Riley-Smith, *Ref.* 1,356
I. Gillman, *UK Ind.* 507
Ms J. Bence, *NLP* 133
Lab. Co-op. majority 11,860
(April 1992, C. maj. 342)

CORNWALL NORTH
*E.*80,076 *T.*73.16%
*P. Tyler, *LD* 31,186
N. Linacre, *C.* 17,253
Ms A. Lindo, *Lab.* 5,523
Ms F. Odam, *Ref.* 3,636
J. Bolitho, *MK* 645
R. Winfield, *Lib.* 186
N. Cresswell, *NLP* 152
LD majority 13,933
(April 1992, LD maj. 1,921)

CORNWALL SOUTH EAST
*E.*75,825 *T.*75.74%
C. Breed, *C.* 27,044
W. Lightfoot, *C.* 20,564
Mrs D. Kirk, *Lab.* 7,358
J. Wonnacott, *UK Ind.* 1,428
P. Dunbar, *MK* 573
W. Weights, *Lib* 268

Ms M. Hartley, *NLP* 197
LD majority 6,480
(April 1992, C. maj. 7,704)

COTSWOLD
*E.*67,333   *T.*75.92%
†G. Clifton-Brown, *C.* 23,698
D. Gayler, *LD* 11,733
D. Elwell, *Lab.* 11,608
R. Lowe, *Ref.* 3,393
Ms V. Michael, *Green* 560
H. Brighouse, *NLP* 129
C. majority 11,965
(Boundary change: notional C.)

COVENTRY NORTH EAST
*E.*74,274   *T.*64.74%
†R. Ainsworth, *Lab.* 31,856
M. Burnett, *C.* 9,287
G. Sewards, *LD* 3,866
N. Brown, *Lib.* 1,181
R. Hurrell, *Ref.* 1,125
H. Khamis, *Soc. Lab.* 597
C. Sidwell, *Dream* 173
Lab. majority 22,569
(Boundary change: notional Lab.)

COVENTRY NORTH WEST
*E.*76,439   *T.*71.07%
†G. Robinson, *Lab.* 30,901
P. Bartlett, *C.* 14,300
Dr N. Penlington, *LD* 5,690
D. Butler, *Ref.* 1,269
D. Spencer, *Soc. Lab.* 940
R. Wheway, *Lib.* 687
P. Mills, *ProLife* 359
L. Francis, *Dream* 176
Lab. majority 16,601
(Boundary change: notional Lab.)

COVENTRY SOUTH
*E.*71,826   *T.*69.79%
†J. Cunningham, *Lab.* 25,511
P. Ivey, *C.* 14,558
G. MacDonald, *LD* 4,617
D. Nellist, *Soc.* 3,262
P. Garratt, *Ref.* 943
R. Jenking, *Lib.* 725
J. Astbury, *BNP* 328
Ms A.-M. Bradshaw, *Dream* 180
Lab. majority 10,953
(Boundary change: notional C.)

CRAWLEY
*E.*69,040   *T.*73.03%
Mrs L. Moffatt, *Lab.* 27,750
Miss J. Crabb, *C.* 16,043
H. de Souza, *LD* 4,141
R. Walters, *Ref.* 1,931
E. Saunders, *UK Ind.* 322
A. Kahn, *JP* 230
Lab. majority 11,707
(Boundary change: notional C.)

CREWE AND NANTWICH
*E.*68,694   *T.*73.67%
†Mrs G. Dunwoody, *Lab.* 29,460
M. Loveridge, *C.* 13,662
D. Cannon, *LD* 5,940
P. Astbury, *Ref.* 1,543
Lab. majority 15,798
(Boundary change: notional Lab.)

CROSBY
*E.*57,190   *T.*77.18%
Ms C. Curtis-Tansley, *Lab.* 22,549
†Sir M. Thornton, *C.* 15,367
P. McVey, *LD* 5,080
J. Gauld, *Ref.* 813
J. Marks, *Lib.* 233
W. Hite, *NLP* 99
Lab. majority 7,182
(Boundary change: notional C.)

CROYDON CENTRAL
*E.*80,152   *T.*69.62%
G. Davies, *Lab.* 25,432
†D. Congdon, *C.* 21,535
G. Schlich, *LD* 6,061
C. Cook, *Ref.* 1,886
M.-S. Barnsley, *Green* 595
J. Woollcott, *UK Ind.* 290
Lab. majority 3,897
(Boundary change: notional C.)

CROYDON NORTH
*E.*77,063   *T.*68.21%
†M. Wicks, *Lab.* 32,672
I. Martin, *C.* 14,274
M. Morris, *LD* 4,066
R. Billis, *Ref.* 1,155
J. Feisenberger, *UK Ind.* 396
Lab. majority 18,398
(Boundary change: notional C.)

CROYDON SOUTH
*E.*73,787   *T.*73.45%
†R. Ottaway, *C.* 25,649
C. Burling, *Lab.* 13,719
S. Gauge, *LD* 11,441
A. Barber, *Ref.* 2,631
P. Ferguson, *BNP* 354
A. Harker, *UK Ind.* 309
M. Samuel, *Choice* 96
C. majority 11,930
(Boundary change: notional C.)

DAGENHAM
*E.*58,573   *T.*61.74%
†Mrs J. Church, *Lab.* 23,759
J. Fairrie, *C.* 6,705
T. Dobrashian, *LD* 2,704
S. Kraft, *Ref.* 1,411
W. Binding, *BNP* 900
R. Dawson, *Ind.* 349
M. Hipperson, *Nat. Dem.* 183
Ms K. Goble, *ProLife* 152
Lab. majority 17,054
(Boundary change: notional Lab.)

DARLINGTON
*E.*65,140   *T.*73.95%
*A. Milburn, *Lab.* 29,658
P. Scrope, *C.* 13,633
L. Boxell, *LD* 3,483
M. Blakey, *Ref.* 1,399
Lab. majority 16,025
(April 1992, Lab. maj. 2,798)

DARTFORD
*E.*69,726   *T.*74.57%
H. Stoate, *Lab.* 25,278
†R. Dunn, *C.* 20,950
Mrs D. Webb, *LD* 4,827
P. McHale, *BNP* 428
P. Homden, *FDP* 287

J. Pollitt, *Ch. D.* 228
Lab. majority 4,328
(Boundary change: notional C.)

DAVENTRY
*E.*80,151   *T.*77.04%
†T. Boswell, *C.* 28,615
K. Ritchie, *Lab.* 21,237
J. Gordon, *LD* 9,233
Mrs B. Russocki, *Ref.* 2,018
B. Mahoney, *UK Ind.* 443
R. France, *NLP* 204
C. majority 7,378
(Boundary change: notional C.)

DENTON AND REDDISH
*E.*68,866   *T.*66.92%
†A. Bennett, *Lab.* 30,137
Ms B. Nutt, *C.* 9,826
I. Donaldson, *LD* 6,121
Lab. majority 20,311
(Boundary change: notional Lab.)

DERBY NORTH
*E.*76,116   *T.*73.76%
R. Laxton, *Lab.* 29,844
*Rt. Hon. G. Knight, *C.* 19,229
R. Charlesworth, *LD* 5,059
P. Reynolds, *Ref.* 1,816
J. Waters, *ProLife* 195
Lab. majority 10,615
(April 1992, C. maj. 4,453)

DERBY SOUTH
*E.*76,386   *T.*67.84%
†Rt. Hon. Mrs M. Beckett, *Lab.* 29,154
J. Arain, *C.* 13,048
J. Beckett, *LD* 7,438
J. Browne, *Ref.* 1,862
R. Evans, *Nat. Dem.* 317
Lab. majority 16,106
(Boundary change: notional Lab.)

DERBYSHIRE NORTH EAST
*E.*71,653   *T.*72.54%
*H. Barnes, *Lab.* 31,425
S. Elliott, *C.* 13,104
S. Hardy, *LD* 7,450
Lab. majority 18,321
(April 1992, Lab. maj. 6,270)

DERBYSHIRE SOUTH
*E.*76,672   *T.*78.21%
M. Todd, *Lab.* 32,709
†Mrs E. Currie, *C.* 18,742
R. Renold, *LD* 5,408
R. North, *Ref.* 2,491
Dr I. Crompton, *UK Ind.* 617
Lab. majority 13,967
(Boundary change: notional C.)

DERBYSHIRE WEST
*E.*72,716   *T.*78.23%
†P. McLoughlin, *C.* 23,945
S. Clamp, *Lab.* 19,060
C. Seeley, *LD* 9,940
J. Gouriet, *Ref.* 2,499
G. Meynell, *Ind. Green* 593
H. Price, *UK Ind.* 484
N. Delves, *Loony* 281
M. Kyslun, *Ind. BB* 81

C. *majority* 4,885
(Boundary change: notional C.)

DEVIZES
E.80,383   T.74.69%
†Rt. Hon. M. Ancram, *C.* 25,710
A. Vickers, *LD* 15,928
F. Jeffrey, *Lab.* 14,551
J. Goldsmith, *Ref.* 3,021
S. Oram, *UK Ind.* 622
S. Haysom, *NLP* 204
C. *majority* 9,782
(Boundary change: notional C.)

DEVON EAST
E.69,094   T.76.06%
†Rt. Hon. Sir P. Emery, *C.* 22,797
Miss R. Trethewey, *LD* 15,308
A. Siantonas, *Lab.* 9,292
W. Dixon, *Ref.* 3,200
G. Halliwell, *Lib.* 1,363
C. Giffard, *UK Ind.* 459
G. Needs, *Nat. Dem.* 131
C. *majority* 7,489
(Boundary change: notional C.)

DEVON NORTH
E.70,350   T.77.94%
†N. Harvey, *LD* 27,824
R. Ashworth, *C.* 21,643
Mrs E. Brenton, *Lab.* 5,367
LD majority 6,181
(Boundary change: notional LD)

DEVON SOUTH WEST
E.69,293   T.76.22%
†G. Streeter, *C.* 22,695
C. Mavin, *Lab.* 15,262
K. Baldry, *LD* 12,542
R. Sadler, *Ref.* 1,668
Mrs H. King, *UK Ind.* 491
J. Hyde, *NLP* 159
C. *majority* 7,433
(Boundary change: notional C.)

DEVON WEST AND TORRIDGE
E.75,919   T.77.91%
J. Burnett, *LD* 24,744
I. Liddell-Grainger, *C.* 22,787
D. Brenton, *Lab.* 7,319
R. Lea, *Ref.* 1,946
M. Jackson, *UK Ind.* 1,841
M. Pithouse, *Lib.* 508
LD majority 1,957
(Boundary change: notional C.)

DEWSBURY
E.61,523   T.70.01%
†Mrs A. Taylor, *Lab.* 21,286
Dr P. McCormick, *C.* 12,963
K. Hill, *LD* 4,422
Ms F. Taylor, *BNP* 2,232
Ms W. Goff, *Ref.* 1,019
D. Daniel, *Ind. Lab.* 770
I. McCourtie, *Green* 383
Lab. majority 8,323
(Boundary change: notional Lab.)

DONCASTER CENTRAL
E.67,965   T.63.92%
Ms R. Winterton, *Lab.* 26,961
D. Turtle, *C.* 9,105
S. Tarry, *LD* 4,091

M. Cliff, *Ref.* 1,273
M. Kenny, *Soc. Lab.* 854
J. Redden, *ProLife* 697
P. Davies, *UK Ind.* 462
Lab. majority 17,856
(April 1992, Lab. maj. 10,682)

DONCASTER NORTH
E.63,019   T.63.30%
†K. Hughes, *Lab.* 27,843
P. Kennerley, *C.* 5,906
M. Cook, *LD* 3,369
R. Thornton, *Ref.* 1,589
M. Swan, *AS Lab.* 1,181
Lab. majority 21,937
(Boundary change: notional Lab.)

DON VALLEY
E.65,643   T.66.35%
Ms C. Flint, *Lab.* 25,376
Mrs C. Gledhill, *C.* 10,717
P. Johnston, *LD* 4,238
P. Davis, *Ref.* 1,379
N. Ball, *Soc. Lab.* 1,024
S. Platt, *Green* 493
Ms C. Johnson, *ProLife* 330
Lab. majority 14,659
(Boundary change: notional Lab.)

DORSET MID AND POOLE NORTH
E.67,049   T.75.67%
C. Fraser, *C.* 20,632
A. Leaman, *LD* 19,951
D. Collis, *Lab.* 8,014
D. Nabarro, *Ref.* 2,136
C. *majority* 681
(Boundary change: notional C.)

DORSET NORTH
E.68,923   T.76.30%
R. Walter, *C.* 23,294
Mrs P. Yates, *LD* 20,548
J. Fitzmaurice, *Lab.* 5,380
Mrs M. Evans, *Ref.* 2,564
Revd D. Wheeler, *UK Ind.* 801
C. *majority* 2,746
(Boundary change: notional C.)

DORSET SOUTH
E.66,318   T.74.16%
†I. Bruce, *C.* 17,755
J. Knight, *Lab.* 17,678
M. Plummer, *LD* 9,936
P. McAndrew, *Ref.* 2,791
Capt. M. Shakesby, *UK Ind.* 861
G. Napper, *NLP* 161
C. *majority* 77
(Boundary change: notional C.)

DORSET WEST
E.70,369   T.76.10%
O. Letwin, *C.* 22,036
R. Legg, *LD* 20,196
R. Bygraves, *Lab.* 9,491
P. Jenkins, *UK Ind.* 1,590
M. Griffiths, *NLP* 239
C. *majority* 1,840
(Boundary change: notional C.)

DOVER
E.68,669   T.78.93%
G. Prosser, *Lab.* 29,535
†D. Shaw, *C.* 17,796

M. Corney, *LD* 4,302
Mrs S. Anderson, *Ref.* 2,124
C. Hyde, *UK Ind.* 443
Lab. majority 11,739
(Boundary change: notional C.)

DUDLEY NORTH
E.68,835   T.69.45%
R. Cranston, *Lab.* 24,471
C. MacNamara, *C.* 15,014
G. Lewis, *LD* 3,939
M. Atherton, *Soc. Lab.* 2,155
S. Bavester, *Ref.* 1,201
G. Cartwright, *NF* 559
S. Darby, *Nat. Dem.* 469
Lab. majority 9,457
(Boundary change: notional Lab.)

DUDLEY SOUTH
E.66,731   T.71.78%
†I. Pearson, *Lab.* 27,124
M. Simpson, *C.* 14,097
R. Burt, *LD* 5,214
C. Birch, *Ref.* 1,467
Lab. majority 13,027
(Boundary change: notional Lab.)

DULWICH AND WEST NORWOOD
E.69,655   T.65.49%
†Ms T. Jowell, *Lab.* 27,807
R. Gough, *C.* 11,038
Mrs S. Kramer, *LD* 4,916
B. Coles, *Ref.* 897
Dr A. Goldie, *Lib.* 587
D. Goodman, *Dream* 173
E. Pike, *UK Ind.* 159
Capt. Rizz, *Rizz Party* 38
Lab. majority 16,769
(Boundary change: notional Lab.)

DURHAM NORTH
E.67,891   T.69.48%
†G. Radice, *Lab.* 33,142
M. Hardy, *C.* 6,843
B. Moore, *LD* 5,225
I. Parkin, *Ref.* 1,958
Lab. majority 26,299
(Boundary change: notional Lab.)

DURHAM NORTH WEST
E.67,156   T.68.97%
†Miss H. Armstrong, *Lab.* 31,855
Mrs L. St J. Howe, *C.* 7,101
A. Gillings, *LD* 4,991
R. Atkinson, *Ref.* 2,372
Lab. majority 24,754
(Boundary change: notional Lab.)

DURHAM, CITY OF
E.69,340   T.70.86%
*G. Steinberg, *Lab.* 31,102
R. Chalk, *C.* 8,598
Dr N. Martin, *LD* 7,499
Ms M. Robson, *Ref.* 1,723
P. Kember, *NLP* 213
Lab. majority 22,504
(April 1992, Lab. maj. 15,058)

EALING ACTON AND SHEPHERD'S BUSH
E.72,078   T.66.68%
†C. Soley, *Lab.* 28,052
Mrs B. Yerolemou, *C.* 12,405

A. Mitchell, *LD* — 5,163
C. Winn, *Ref.* — 637
J. Gilbert, *Soc. Lab.* — 635
J. Gomm, *UK Ind.* — 385
P. Danon, *ProLife* — 265
C. Beasley, *Glow* — 209
W. Edwards, *Ch. P.* — 163
K. Turner, *NLP* — 150
Lab. majority 15,647
(Boundary change: notional Lab.)

EALING NORTH
*E.*78,144   *T.*71.31%
S. Pound, *Lab.* — 29,904
†H. Greenway, *C.* — 20,744
A. Gupta, *LD* — 3,887
G. Slysz, *UK Ind.* — 689
Ms A. Siebe, *Green* — 502
Lab. majority 9,160
(Boundary change: notional C.)

EALING SOUTHALL
*E.*81,704   *T.*66.88%
†P. Khabra, *Lab.* — 32,791
J. Penrose, *C.* — 11,368
Ms N. Thomson, *LD* — 5,687
H. Brar, *Soc. Lab.* — 2,107
N. Goodwin, *Green* — 934
B. Cherry, *Ref.* — 854
Ms K. Klepacka, *ProLife* — 473
Dr R. Mead, *UK Ind.* — 428
Lab. majority 21,423
(Boundary change: notional Lab.)

EASINGTON
*E.*62,518   *T.*67.01%
*J. Cummings, *Lab.* — 33,600
J. Hollands, *C.* — 3,588
J. Heppell, *LD* — 3,025
R. Pulfrey, *Ref.* — 1,179
S. Colborn, *SPGB* — 503
Lab. majority 30,012
(April 1992, Lab. maj. 26,390)

EASTBOURNE
*E.*72,347   *T.*72.80%
†N. Waterson, *C.* — 22,183
C. Berry, *LD* — 20,189
D. Lines, *Lab.* — 6,576
T. Lowe, *Ref.* — 2,724
Mrs T. Williamson, *Lib.* — 741
J. Dawkins, *UK Ind.* — 254
C. majority 1,994
(Boundary change: notional C.)

EAST HAM
*E.*65,591   *T.*60.81%
†S. Timms, *Lab.* — 25,779
Miss A. Bray, *C.* — 6,421
I. Khan, *Soc. Lab.* — 2,697
M. Sole, *LD* — 2,599
C. Smith, *BNP* — 1,258
Mrs J. McCann, *Ref.* — 845
G. Hardy, *Nat. Dem.* — 290
Lab. majority 19,358
(Boundary change: notional Lab.)

EASTLEIGH
*E.*72,155   *T.*76.91%
†D. Chidgey, *LD* — 19,453
S. Reid, *C.* — 18,699
A. Lloyd, *Lab.* — 14,883
V. Eldridge, *Ref.* — 2,013

P. Robinson, *UK Ind.* — 446
LD majority 754
(Boundary change: notional C.)

ECCLES
*E.*69,645   *T.*65.60%
I. Stewart, *Lab.* — 30,468
G. Barker, *C.* — 8,552
R. Boyd, *LD* — 4,905
J. De Roeck, *Ref.* — 1,765
Lab. majority 21,916
(Boundary change: notional Lab.)

EDDISBURY
*E.*65,256   *T.*75.78%
†Rt.. Hon. A. Goodlad, *C.* — 21,027
Ms M. Hanson, *Lab.* — 19,842
D. Reaper, *LD* — 6,540
Ms N. Napier, *Ref.* — 2,041
C. majority 1,185
(Boundary change: notional C.)

EDMONTON
*E.*63,718   *T.*70.37%
A. Love, *Lab. Co-op.* — 27,029
*Dr I. Twinn, *C.* — 13,557
A. Wiseman, *LD* — 2,847
J. Wright, *Ref.* — 708
B. Cowd, *BNP* — 437
Mrs P. Weald, *UK Ind.* — 260
Lab. Co-op. majority 13,472
(April 1992, C. maj. 593)

ELLESMERE PORT AND NESTON
*E.*67,573   *T.*77.79%
†A. Miller, *Lab.* — 31,310
Mrs L. Turnbull, *C.* — 15,274
Ms J. Pemberton, *LD* — 4,673
C. Rodden, *Ref.* — 1,305
Lab. majority 16,036
(Boundary change: notional Lab.)

ELMET
*E.*70,423   *T.*76.81%
C. Burgon, *Lab.* — 28,348
*S. Batiste, *C.* — 19,569
B. Jennings, *LD* — 4,691
C. Zawadski, *Ref.* — 1,487
Lab. majority 8,779
(April 1992, C. maj. 3,261)

ELTHAM
*E.*57,358   *T.*75.71%
C. Efford, *Lab.* — 23,710
C. Blackwood, *C.* — 13,528
Ms A. Taylor, *LD* — 3,701
M. Clark, *Ref.* — 1,414
H. Middleton, *Lib.* — 584
W. Hitches, *BNP* — 491
Lab. majority 10,182
(Boundary change: notional C.)

ENFIELD NORTH
*E.*67,680   *T.*70.43%
Ms J. Ryan, *Lab.* — 24,148
M. Field, *C.* — 17,326
M. Hopkins, *LD* — 4,264
R. Ellingham, *Ref.* — 857
Ms J. Griffin, *BNP* — 590
Mrs J. O'Ware, *UK Ind.* — 484
Lab. majority 6,822
(April 1992, C. maj. 9,430)

ENFIELD SOUTHGATE
*E.*65,796   *T.*70.72%
S. Twigg, *Lab.* — 20,570
†Rt. Hon. M. Portillo, *C.* — 19,137
J. Browne, *LD* — 4,966
N. Luard, *Ref.* — 1,342
A. Storkey, *Ch. D.* — 289
A. Malakouna, *Mal* — 229
Lab. majority 1,433
(Boundary change: notional C.)

EPPING FOREST
*E.*72,795   *T.*72.82%
Mrs E. Laing, *C.* — 24,117
S. Murray, *Lab.* — 18,865
S. Robinson, *LD* — 7,074
J. Berry, *Ref.* — 2,208
P. Henderson, *BNP* — 743
C. majority 5,252
(Boundary change: notional C.)

EPSOM AND EWELL
*E.*73,222   *T.*74.00%
†Rt. Hon. Sir A. Hamilton, *C.* — 24,717
P. Woodford, *Lab.* — 13,192
J. Vincent, *LD* — 12,380
C. Macdonald, *Ref.* — 2,355
H. Green, *UK Ind.* — 544
H. Charlton, *Green* — 527
Ms K. Weeks, *ProLife* — 466
C. majority 11,525
(Boundary change: notional C.)

EREWASH
*E.*77,402   *T.*77.95%
Ms E. Blackman, *Lab.* — 31,196
†Mrs A. Knight, *C.* — 22,061
Dr M. Garnett, *LD* — 5,181
S. Stagg, *Ref.* — 1,404
M. Simmons, *Soc. Lab.* — 496
Lab. majority 9,135
(Boundary change: notional C.)

ERITH AND THAMESMEAD
*E.*62,887   *T.*66.13%
†J. Austin-Walker, *Lab.* — 25,812
N. Zahawi, *C.* — 8,388
A. Grigg, *LD* — 5,001
J. Flunder, *Ref.* — 1,394
V. Dooley, *BNP* — 718
M. Jackson, *UK Ind.* — 274
Lab. majority 17,424
(Boundary change: notional Lab.)

ESHER AND WALTON
*E.*72,382   *T.*74.14%
†I. Taylor, *C.* — 26,747
Ms J. Reay, *Lab.* — 12,219
G. Miles, *LD* — 10,937
A. Cruickshank, *Ref.* — 2,904
B. Collignon, *UK Ind.* — 558
Ms S. Kay, *Dream* — 302
C. majority 14,528
(Boundary change: notional C.)

ESSEX NORTH
*E.*68,008   *T.*75.30%
†B. Jenkin, *C.* — 22,480
T. Young, *Lab.* — 17,004
A. Phillips, *LD* — 10,028
R. Lord, *UK Ind.* — 1,202
Ms S. Ransome, *Green* — 495

C. majority 5,476
(Boundary change: notional C.)

EXETER
E.79,154   T.78.16%
B. Bradshaw, *Lab.*	29,398
Dr A. Rogers, *C.*	17,693
D. Brewer, *LD*	11,148
D. Morrish, *Lib.*	2,062
P. Edwards, *Green*	643
Mrs C. Haynes, *UK Ind.*	638
J. Meakin, *UKPP*	282

Lab. majority 11,705
(Boundary change: notional C.)

FALMOUTH AND CAMBORNE
E.71,383   T.75.13%
Ms C. Atherton, *Lab.*	18,151
*S. Coe, *C.*	15,463
Mrs T. Jones, *LD*	13,512
P. de Savary, *Ref.*	3,534
J. Geach, *Ind. Lab.*	1,691
P. Holmes, *Lib.*	527
R. Smith, *UK Ind.*	355
Ms R. Lewarne, *MK*	238
G. Glitter, *Loony*	161

Lab. majority 2,688
(April 1992, C. maj. 3,267)

FAREHAM
E.68,787   T.75.85%
†Rt. Hon. Sir P. Lloyd, *C.*	24,436
M. Pryor, *Lab.*	14,078
Mrs G. Hill, *LD*	10,234
D. Markham, *Ref.*	2,914
W. O'Brien, *Ind. No*	515

C. majority 10,358
(Boundary change: notional C.)

FAVERSHAM AND KENT MID
E.67,490   T.73.50%
†A. Rowe, *C.*	22,016
A. Stewart, *Lab.*	17,843
B. Parmenter, *LD*	6,138
R. Birley, *Ref.*	2,073
N. Davidson, *Loony*	511
M. Cunningham, *UK Ind.*	431
D. Currer, *Green*	380
Ms C. Morgan, *GRLNSP*	115
N. Pollard, *NLP*	99

C. majority 4,173
(Boundary change: notional C.)

FELTHAM AND HESTON
E.71,093   T.65.58%
†A. Keen, *Lab. Co-op.*	27,836
P. Ground, *C.*	12,563
C. Penning, *LD*	4,264
R. Stubbs, *Ref.*	1,099
R. Church, *BNP*	682
D. Fawcett, *NLP*	177

Lab. Co-op. majority 15,273
(Boundary change: notional Lab. Co-op.)

FINCHLEY AND GOLDERS GREEN
E.72,225   T.69.65%
R. Vis, *Lab.*	23,180
†J. Marshall, *C.*	19,991
J. Davies, *LD*	5,670
G. Shaw, *Ref.*	684
A. Gunstock, *Green*	576
D. Barraclough, *UK Ind.*	205

Lab. majority 3,189
(Boundary change: notional C.)

FOLKESTONE AND HYTHE
E.71,153   T.73.15%
†Rt. Hon. M. Howard, *C.*	20,313
D. Laws, *LD*	13,981
P. Doherty, *Lab.*	12,939
J. Aspinall, *Ref.*	4,188
J. Baker, *UK Ind.*	378
E. Segal, *Soc.*	182
R. Saint, *CFSS*	69

C. majority 6,332
(Boundary change: notional C.)

FOREST OF DEAN
E.63,465   T.79.07%
Ms D. Organ, *Lab.*	24,203
†P. Marland, *C.*	17,860
Dr A. Lynch, *LD*	6,165
J. Hopkins, *Ref.*	1,624
G. Morgan, *Ind. Dean*	218
C. Palmer, *21st Cent.*	80
S. Porter, *Ind. F.*	34

Lab. majority 6,343
(Boundary change: notional Lab.)

FYLDE
E.71,385   T.72.94%
†Rt. Hon. M. Jack, *C.*	25,443
J. Garrett, *Lab.*	16,480
W. Greene, *LD*	7,609
D. Britton, *Ref.*	2,372
T. Kerwin, *NLP*	163

C. majority 8,963
(Boundary change: notional C.)

GAINSBOROUGH
E.64,106   T.74.56%
†E. Leigh, *C.*	20,593
P. Taylor, *Lab.*	13,767
N. Taylor, *LD*	13,436

C. majority 6,826
(Boundary change: notional C.)

GATESHEAD EAST AND
WASHINGTON WEST
E.64,114   T.67.19%
†Miss J. Quin, *Lab.*	31,047
Miss J. Burns, *C.*	6,097
A. Ord, *LD*	4,622
M. Daley, *Ref.*	1,315

Lab. majority 24,950
(Boundary change: notional Lab.)

GEDLING
E.68,820   T.73.80%
V. Coaker, *Lab.*	24,390
*A. Mitchell, *C.*	20,588
R. Poynter, *LD*	5,180
J. Connor, *Ref.*	2,006

Lab. majority 3,802
(April 1992, C. maj. 10,637)

GILLINGHAM
E.70,389   T.72.00%
P. Clark, *Lab.*	20,187
†J. Couchman, *C.*	18,207
R. Sayer, *LD*	9,649
G. Cann, *Ref.*	1,492
C. MacKinlay, *UK Ind.*	590
D. Robinson, *Loony*	305
C. Jury, *BNP*	195

Ms G. Duguay, *NLP*	58

Lab. majority 1,980
(Boundary change: notional C.)

GLOUCESTER
E.78,682   T.73.61%
Ms T. Kingham, *Lab.*	28,943
†D. French, *C.*	20,684
P. Munisamy, *LD*	6,069
A. Reid, *Ref.*	1,482
A. Harris, *UK Ind.*	455
Ms M. Hamilton, *NLP*	281

Lab. majority 8,259
(Boundary change: notional C.)

GOSPORT
E.68,830   T.70.25%
*P. Viggers, *C.*	21,085
I. Gray, *Lab.*	14,827
S. Hogg, *LD*	9,479
A. Blowers, *Ref.*	2,538
P. Ettie, *Ind.*	426

C. majority 6,258
(April 1992, C. maj. 16,318)

GRANTHAM AND STAMFORD
E.72,310   T.73.25%
†Q. Davies, *C.*	22,672
P. Denning, *Lab.*	19,980
J. Sellick, *LD*	6,612
Ms M. Swain, *Ref.*	2,721
M. Charlesworth, *UK Ind.*	556
Ms R. Clark, *ProLife*	314
I. Harper, *NLP*	115

C. majority 2,692
(Boundary change: notional C.)

GRAVESHAM
E.69,234   T.76.92%
C. Pond, *Lab.*	26,460
†J. Arnold, *C.*	20,681
Dr M. Ganet, *LD*	4,128
Mrs P. Curtis, *Ref.*	1,441
A. Leyshon, *Ind.*	414
D. Palmer, *NLP*	129

Lab. majority 5,779
(Boundary change: notional C.)

GREAT GRIMSBY
E.65,043   T.66.26%
*A. Mitchell, *Lab.*	25,765
D. Godson, *C.*	9,521
A. De Freitas, *LD*	7,810

Lab. majority 16,244
(April 1992, Lab. maj. 7,504)

GREAT YARMOUTH
E.68,625   T.71.23%
A. Wright, *Lab.*	26,084
*M. Carttiss, *C.*	17,416
D. Wood, *LD*	5,381

Lab. majority 8,668
(April 1992, C. maj. 5,309)

GREENWICH AND WOOLWICH
E.61,352   T.65.85%
†N. Raynsford, *Lab.*	25,630
M. Mitchell, *C.*	7,502
Mrs C. Luxton, *LD*	5,049
D. Ellison, *Ref.*	1,670
R. Mallone, *Fellowship*	428
D. Martin-Eagle, *Constit.*	124

Lab. majority 18,128
(Boundary change: notional Lab.)

GUILDFORD
E.75,541　T.75.40%
N. St Aubyn, *C.*	24,230
Mrs M. Sharp, *LD*	19,439
J. Burns, *Lab.*	9,945
J. Gore, *Ref.*	2,650
R. McWhirter, *UK Ind.*	400
J. Morris, *Pacifist*	294

C. majority 4,791
(Boundary change: notional C.)

HACKNEY NORTH AND STOKE
NEWINGTON
E.62,045　T.52.95%
*Ms D. Abbott, *Lab.*	21,110
M. Lavender, *C.*	5,483
D. Taylor, *LD*	3,806
Yen Chit Chong, *Green*	1,395
B. Maxwell, *Ref.*	544
D. Tolson, *None*	368
Miss L. Lovebucket, *Rain. Ref.*	146

Lab. majority 15,627
(April 1992, Lab. maj. 10,727)

HACKNEY SOUTH AND
SHOREDITCH
E.61,728　T.54.67%
†B. Sedgemore, *Lab.*	20,048
M. Pantling, *LD*	5,068
C. O'Leary, *C.*	4,494
T. Betts, *New Lab.*	2,436
R. Franklin, *Ref.*	613
G. Callow, *BNP*	531
M. Goldman, *Comm. P.*	298
Ms M. Goldberg, *NLP*	145
W. Rogers, *WRP*	113

Lab. majority 14,980
(Boundary change: notional Lab.)

HALESOWEN AND ROWLEY REGIS
E.66,245　T.73.61%
Mrs S. Heal, *Lab.*	26,366
J. Kennedy, *C.*	16,029
Ms E. Todd, *LD*	4,169
P. White, *Ref.*	1,244
Ms K. Meeds, *Nat. Dem.*	592
T. Weller, *Green*	361

Lab. majority 10,337
(Boundary change: notional C.)

HALIFAX
E.71,701　T.70.51%
*Mrs A. Mahon, *Lab.*	27,465
R. Light, *C.*	16,253
E. Waller, *LD*	6,059
Mrs C. Whitaker, *UK Ind.*	779

Lab. majority 11,212
(April 1992, Lab. maj. 478)

HALTEMPRICE AND HOWDEN
E.65,602　T.75.53%
†Rt. Hon. D. Davis, *C.*	21,809
Ms D. Wallis, *LD*	14,295
G. McManus, *Lab.*	11,701
T. Pearson, *Ref.*	1,370
G. Bloom, *UK Ind.*	301
B. Stevens, *NLP*	74

C. majority 7,514
(Boundary change: notional C.)

HALTON
E.64,987　T.68.38%
D. Twigg, *Lab.*	31,497
P. Balmer, *C.*	7,847
Ms J. Jones, *LD*	3,263
R. Atkins, *Ref.*	1,036
D. Proffitt, *Lib.*	600
J. Alley, *Rep. GB*	196

Lab. majority 23,650
(Boundary change: notional Lab.)

HAMMERSMITH AND FULHAM
E.78,637　T.68.70%
I. Coleman, *Lab.*	25,262
†M. Carrington, *C.*	21,420
Ms A. Sugden, *LD*	4,728
Mrs M. Bremner, *Ref.*	1,023
W. Johnson-Smith, *New Lab.*	695
Ms E. Streeter, *Green*	562
G. Roberts, *UK Ind.*	183
A. Phillips, *NLP*	79
A. Elston, *Care*	74

Lab. majority 3,842
(Boundary change: notional C.)

HAMPSHIRE EAST
E.76,604　T.75.88%
†M. Mates, *C.*	27,927
R. Booker, *LD*	16,337
R. Hoyle, *Lab.*	9,945
J. Hayter, *Ref.*	2,757
I. Foster, *Green*	649
S. Coles, *UK Ind.*	513

C. majority 11,590
(Boundary change: notional C.)

HAMPSHIRE NORTH EAST
E.69,111　T.73.95%
†J. Arbuthnot, *C.*	26,017
I. Mann, *LD*	11,619
P. Dare, *Lab.*	8,203
D. Rees, *Ref.*	2,420
K. Jessavala, *Ind.*	2,400
C. Berry, *UK Ind.*	452

C. majority 14,398
(Boundary change: notional C.)

HAMPSHIRE NORTH WEST
E.73,222　T.74.66%
†Rt. Hon. Sir G. Young, Bt., *C.*
	24,730
C. Fleming, *LD*	13,179
M. Mumford, *Lab.*	12,900
Mrs P. Callaghan, *Ref.*	1,533
T. Rolt, *UK Ind.*	1,383
W. Baxter, *Green*	486
H. Anscomb, *Bypass*	231
R. Dodd, *Ind.*	225

C. majority 11,551
(Boundary change: notional C.)

HAMPSTEAD AND HIGHGATE
E.64,889　T.67.86%
†Ms G. Jackson, *Lab.*	25,275
Miss E. Gibson, *C.*	11,991
Mrs B. Fox, *LD*	5,481
Ms M. Siddique, *Ref.*	667
J. Leslie, *NLP*	147
R. Carroll, *Dream*	141
Miss P. Prince, *UK Ind.*	123
R. J. Harris, *Hum.*	105
Capt. Rizz, *Rizz Party*	101

Lab. majority 13,284
(Boundary change: notional Lab.)

HARBOROUGH
E.70,424　T.75.27%
†E. Garnier, *C.*	22,170
M. Cox, *LD*	15,646
N. Holden, *Lab.*	13,332
N. Wright, *Ref.*	1,859

C. majority 6,524
(Boundary change: notional C.)

HARLOW
E.64,072　T.74.62%
W. Rammell, *Lab.*	25,861
†J. Hayes, *C.*	15,347
Ms L. Spenceley, *LD*	4,523
M. Wells, *Ref.*	1,422
G. Batten, *UK Ind.*	340
J. Bowles, *BNP*	319

Lab. majority 10,514
(Boundary change: notional C.)

HARROGATE AND KNARESBOROUGH
E.65,155　T.73.14%
P. Willis, *LD*	24,558
†Rt. Hon. N. Lamont, *C.*	18,322
Ms B. Boyce, *Lab.*	4,159
J. Blackburn, *LC*	614

LD majority 6,236
(Boundary change: notional C.)

HARROW EAST
E.79,846　T.71.37%
A. McNulty, *Lab.*	29,927
†H. Dykes, *C.*	20,189
B. Sharma, *LD*	4,697
B. Casey, *Ref.*	1,537
A. Scholefield, *UK Ind.*	464
A. Planton, *NLP*	171

Lab. majority 9,738
(Boundary change: notional C.)

HARROW WEST
E.72,005　T.72.92%
G. Thomas, *Lab.*	21,811
*R. Hughes, *C.*	20,571
Mrs P. Nandhra, *LD*	8,127
H. Crossman, *Ref.*	1,997

Lab. majority 1,240
(Boundary change: notional C.)

HARTLEPOOL
E.67,712　T.65.65%
*P. Mandelson, *Lab.*	26,997
M. Horsley, *C.*	9,489
R. Clark, *LD*	6,248
Miss M. Henderson, *Ref.*	1,718

Lab. majority 17,508
(April 1992, Lab. maj. 8,782)

HARWICH
E.75,775　T.70.62%
I. Henderson, *Lab.*	20,740
†I. Sproat, *C.*	19,524
Mrs A. Elvin, *LD*	7,037
J. Titford, *Ref.*	4,923
R. Knight, *CRP*	1,290

Lab. majority 1,216
(Boundary change: notional C.)

HASTINGS AND RYE
E.70,388　T.69.71%
M. Foster, *Lab.*	16,867

*Mrs J. Lait, *C.* 14,307
M. Palmer, *LD* 13,717
C. McGovern, *Ref.* 2,511
Ms J. Amstad, *Lib.* 1,046
W. Andrews, *UK Ind.* 472
D. Howell, *Loony* 149
Lab. majority 2,560
(April 1992, C. maj. 6,634)

HAVANT
*E.*68,420 *T.*70.63%
†D. Willetts, *C.* 19,204
Ms L. Armstrong, *Lab.* 15,475
M. Kooner, *LD* 10,806
A. Green, *Ref.* 2,395
M. Atwal, *BIPF* 442
C. majority 3,729
(Boundary change: notional C.)

HAYES AND HARLINGTON
*E.*56,829 *T.*72.31%
J. McDonnell, *Lab.* 25,458
A. Retter, *C.* 11,167
A. Little, *LD* 3,049
F. Page, *Ref.* 778
J. Hutchins, *NF* 504
D. Farrow, *ANP* 135
Lab. majority 14,291
(Boundary change: notional C.)

HAZEL GROVE
*E.*63,694 *T.*77.46%
A. Stunell, *LD* 26,883
B. Murphy, *C.* 15,069
J. Lewis, *Lab.* 5,882
J. Stanyer, *Ref.* 1,055
G. Black, *UK Ind.* 268
D. Firkin-Flood, *Ind. Hum.* 183
LD majority 11,814
(April 1992, C. maj. 929)

HEMEL HEMPSTEAD
*E.*71,168 *T.*77.09%
A. McWalter, *Lab. Co-op.* 25,175
†R. Jones, *C.* 21,539
Mrs P. Lindsley, *LD* 6,789
P. Such, *Ref.* 1,327
Ms D. Harding, *NLP* 262
Lab. Co-op. majority 3,636
(Boundary change: notional C.)

HEMSWORTH
*E.*66,964 *T.*67.91%
†J. Trickett, *Lab.* 32,088
N. Hazell, *C.* 8,096
Ms J. Kirby, *LD* 4,033
D. Irvine, *Ref.* 1,260
Lab. majority 23,992
(Boundary change: notional Lab.)

HENDON
*E.*76,195 *T.*65.67%
A. Dismore, *Lab.* 24,683
†Sir J. Gorst, *C.* 18,528
W. Casey, *LD* 5,427
S. Rabbow, *Ref.* 978
B. Wright, *UK Ind.* 267
Ms S. Taylor, *WRP* 153
Lab. majority 6,155
(Boundary change: notional C.)

HENLEY
*E.*66,424 *T.*77.60%
†Rt. Hon. M. Heseltine, *C.* 23,908
T. Horton, *LD* 12,741
D. Enright, *Lab.* 11,700
S. Sainsbury, *Ref.* 2,299
Mrs S. Miles, *Green* 514
N. Barlow, *NLP* 221
T. Hibbert, *Whig Party* 160
C. majority 11,167
(Boundary change: notional C.)

HEREFORD
*E.*69,864 *T.*75.22%
P. Keetch, *LD* 25,198
†Sir C. Shepherd, *C.* 18,550
C. Chappell, *Lab.* 6,596
C. Easton, *Ref.* 2,209
LD majority 6,648
(Boundary change: notional C.)

HERTFORD AND STORTFORD
*E.*71,759 *T.*76.03%
†B. Wells, *C.* 24,027
S. Speller, *Lab.* 17,142
M. Wood, *LD* 9,679
H. Page Croft, *Ref.* 2,105
B. Smalley, *UK Ind.* 1,223
M. Franey, *ProLife* 259
D. Molloy, *Logic* 126
C. majority 6,885
(Boundary change: notional C.)

HERTFORDSHIRE NORTH EAST
*E.*67,161 *T.*77.42%
†O. Heald, *C.* 21,712
I. Gibbons, *Lab.* 18,624
S. Jarvis, *LD* 9,493
J. Grose, *Ref.* 2,166
C. majority 3,088
(Boundary change: notional C.)

HERTFORDSHIRE SOUTH WEST
*E.*71,671 *T.*77.31%
†R. Page, *C.* 25,462
M. Wilson, *Lab.* 15,441
Mrs A. Shaw, *LD* 12,381
T. Millward, *Ref.* 1,853
C. Adamson, *NLP* 274
C. majority 10,021
(Boundary change: notional C.)

HERTSMERE
*E.*68,011 *T.*74.03%
†J. Clappison, *C.* 22,305
Ms E. Kelly, *Lab.* 19,230
Mrs A. Gray, *LD* 6,466
J. Marlow, *Ref.* 1,703
R. Saunders, *UK Ind.* 453
N. Kahn, *NLP* 191
C. majority 3,075
(Boundary change: notional C.)

HEXHAM
*E.*58,914 *T.*77.52%
*P. Atkinson, *C.* 17,701
I. McMinn, *Lab.* 17,479
Dr P. Carr, *LD* 7,959
R. Waddell, *Ref.* 1,362
D. Lott, *UK Ind.* 1,170
C. majority 222
(April 1992, C. maj. 13,438)

HEYWOOD AND MIDDLETON
*E.*73,898 *T.*68.41%
J. Dobbin, *Lab. Co-op.* 29,179
S. Grigg, *C.* 11,637
D. Clayton, *LD* 7,908
Mrs C. West, *Ref.* 1,076
P. Burke, *Lib.* 750
Lab. Co-op. majority 17,542
(Boundary change: notional Lab. Co-op.)

HIGH PEAK
*E.*72,315 *T.*79.03%
T. Levitt, *Lab.* 29,052
|C. Hendry, *C.* 20,261
Mrs S. Barber, *LD* 6,420
C. Hanson-Orr, *Ref.* 1,420
Lab. majority 8,791
(Boundary change: notional C.)

HITCHIN AND HARPENDEN
*E.*67,219 *T.*77.99%
†Rt. Hon. P. Lilley, *C.* 24,038
Ms R. Sanderson, *Lab.* 17,367
C. White, *LD* 10,515
D. Cooke, *NLP* 290
J. Horton, *Soc.* 217
C. majority 6,671
(Boundary change: notional C.)

HOLBORN AND ST PANCRAS
*E.*63,037 *T.*60.28%
†F. Dobson, *Lab.* 24,707
J. Smith, *C.* 6,804
Ms J. McGuinness, *LD* 4,750
Mrs J. Carr, *Ref.* 790
T. Bedding, *NLP* 191
S. Smith, *JP* 173
Ms B. Conway, *WRP* 171
M. Rosenthal, *Dream* 157
P. Rice-Evans, *EUP* 140
D. Quintavalle, *ProLife* 114
Lab. majority 17,903
(Boundary change: notional Lab.)

HORNCHURCH
*E.*60,775 *T.*72.30%
J. Cryer, *Lab.* 22,066
*R. Squire, *C.* 16,386
R. Martins, *LD* 3,446
R. Khilkoff-Boulding, *Ref.* 1,595
Miss J. Trueman, *Third Way* 259
J. Sowerby, *ProLife* 189
Lab. majority 5,680
(April 1992, C. maj. 9,165)

HORNSEY AND WOOD GREEN
*E.*74,537 *T.*69.08%
*Mrs B. Roche, *Lab.* 31,792
Mrs H. Hart, *C.* 11,293
Ms L. Featherstone, *LD* 5,794
Ms H. Jago, *Green* 1,214
Ms R. Miller, *Ref.* 808
P. Sikorski, *Soc. Lab.* 586
Lab. majority 20,499
(April 1992, Lab. maj. 5,177)

HORSHAM
*E.*75,432 *T.*75.78%
Rt. Hon. F. Maude, *C.* 29,015
Mrs M. Millson, *LD* 14,153
Ms M. Walsh, *Lab.* 10,691
R. Grant, *Ref.* 2,281

H. Miller, *UK Ind.* 819
M. Corbould, *FEP* 206
C. majority 14,862
(Boundary change: notional C.)

HOUGHTON AND WASHINGTON
EAST
*E.*67,343   *T.*62.10%
F. Kemp, *Lab.* 31,946
P. Booth, *C.* 5,391
K. Miller, *LD* 3,209
J. Joseph, *Ref.* 1,277
Lab. majority 26,555
(Boundary change: notional Lab.)

HOVE
*E.*69,016   *T.*69.72%
I. Caplin, *Lab.* 21,458
R. Guy, *C.* 17,499
T. Pearce, *LD* 4,645
S. Field, *Ref.* 1,931
J. Furness, *Ind. C.* 1,735
P. Mulligan, *Green* 644
J. Vause, *UK Ind.* 209
Lab. majority 3,959
(April 1992, C. maj. 12,268)

HUDDERSFIELD
*E.*65,824   *T.*67.69%
*B. Sheerman, *Lab. Co-op.* 25,171
W. Forrow, *C.* 9,323
G. Beever, *LD* 7,642
P. McNulty, *Ref.* 1,480
J. Phillips, *Green* 938
Lab. Co-op. majority 15,848
(April 1992, *Lab. majority* 7,258)

HULL EAST
*E.*68,733   *T.*58.90%
*Rt. Hon. J. Prescott, *Lab.* 28,870
A. West, *C.* 5,552
J. Wastling, *LD* 3,965
G. Rogers, *Ref.* 1,788
Ms M. Nolan, *ProLife* 190
D. Whitley, *NLP* 121
Lab. majority 23,318
(April 1992, Lab. maj. 18,719)

HULL NORTH
*E.*68,106   *T.*56.96%
*K. McNamara, *Lab.* 25,542
D. Lee, *C.* 5,837
D. Nolan, *LD* 5,667
A. Scott, *Ref.* 1,533
T. Brotheridge, *NLP* 215
Lab. majority 19,705
(April 1992, Lab. maj. 15,384)

HULL WEST AND HESSLE
*E.*65,840   *T.*58.25%
A. Johnson, *Lab.* 22,520
R. Tress, *LD* 6,995
C. Moore, *C.* 6,933
R. Bate, *Ref.* 1,596
B. Franklin, *NLP* 310
Lab. majority 15,525
(Boundary change: notional Lab.)

HUNTINGDON
*E.*76,094   *T.*74.86%
†Rt. Hon. J. Major, *C.* 31,501
J. Reece, *Lab.* 13,361
M. Owen, *LD* 8,390

D. Bellamy, *Ref.* 3,114
C. Coyne, *UK Ind.* 331
Ms V. Hufford, *Ch. D.* 177
D. Robertson, *Ind.* 89
C. majority 18,140
(Boundary change: notional C.)

HYNDBURN
*E.*66,806   *T.*72.26%
†G. Pope, *Lab.* 26,831
P. Britcliffe, *C.* 15,383
L. Jones, *LD* 4,141
P. Congdon, *Ref.* 1,627
J. Brown, *IAC* 290
Lab. majority 11,448
(Boundary change: notional Lab.)

ILFORD NORTH
*E.*68,218   *T.*71.60%
Ms L. Perham, *Lab.* 23,135
†V. Bendall, *C.* 19,911
A. Dean, *LD* 5,049
P. Wilson, *BNP* 750
Lab. majority 3,224
(Boundary change: notional C.)

ILFORD SOUTH
*E.*72,104   *T.*69.37%
†M. Gapes, *Lab. Co-op.* 29,273
Sir N. Thorne, *C.* 15,073
Ms A. Khan, *LD* 3,152
D. Hodges, *Ref.* 1,073
B. Ramsey, *Soc. Lab.* 868
A. Owens, *BNP* 580
Lab. Co-op. majority 14,200
(Boundary change: notional C.)

IPSWICH
*E.*66,947   *T.*72.24%
†J. Cann, *Lab.* 25,484
S. Castle, *C.* 15,045
N. Roberts, *LD* 5,881
T. Agnew, *Ref.* 1,637
W. Vinyard, *UK Ind.* 208
E. Kaplan, *NLP* 107
Lab. majority 10,439
(Boundary change: notional Lab.)

ISLE OF WIGHT
*E.*101,680   *T.*71.95%
Dr P. Brand, *LD* 31,274
A. Turner, *C.* 24,868
Ms D. Gardiner, *Lab.* 9,646
T. Bristow, *Ref.* 4,734
M. Turner, *UK Ind.* 1,072
H. Rees, *Ind. Is.* 848
P. Scivier, *Green* 544
C. Daly, *NLP* 87
J. Eveleigh, *Rain. Is.* 86
LD majority 6,406
(April 1992, C. maj. 1,827)

ISLINGTON NORTH
*E.*57,385   *T.*62.49%
*J. Corbyn, *Lab.* 24,834
J. Kempton, *LD* 4,879
S. Fawthrop, *C.* 4,631
C. Ashby, *Green* 1,516
Lab. majority 19,955
(April 1992, Lab. maj. 12,784)

ISLINGTON SOUTH AND FINSBURY
*E.*55,468   *T.*63.67%
†C. Smith, *Lab.* 22,079
Ms S. Ludford, *LD* 7,516
D. Berens, *C.* 4,587
Miss J. Bryett, *Ref.* 741
A. Laws, *ACA* 171
M. Creese, *NLP* 121
E. Basarik, *Ind.* 101
Lab. majority 14,563
(Boundary change: notional Lab.)

JARROW
*E.*63,828   *T.*68.84%
S. Hepburn, *Lab.* 28,497
M. Allatt, *C.* 6,564
T. Stone, *LD* 4,865
A. LeBlond, *Ind. Lab.* 2,538
P. Mailer, *Ref.* 1,034
J. Bissett, *SPGB* 444
Lab. majority 21,933
(Boundary change: notional Lab.)

KEIGHLEY
*E.*67,231   *T.*76.57%
Mrs A. Cryer, *Lab.* 26,039
*G. Waller, *C.* 18,907
M. Doyle, *LD* 5,064
C. Carpenter, *Ref.* 1,470
Lab. majority 7,132
(April 1992, C. maj. 3,596)

KENSINGTON AND CHELSEA
*E.*67,786   *T.*54.71%
Rt. Hon. A. Clark, *C.* 19,887
R. Atkinson, *Lab.* 10,368
R. Woodthorpe Browne, *LD* 5,668
Ms A. Ellis-Jones, *UK Ind.* 540
E. Bear, *Teddy* 218
G. Oliver, *UKPP* 176
Ms S. Hamza, *NLP* 122
P. Sullivan, *Dream* 65
P. Parliament, *Heart* 44
C. majority 9,519
(Boundary change: notional C.)

KETTERING
*E.*75,153   *T.*75.79%
P. Sawford, *Lab.* 24,650
†Rt. Hon. R. Freeman, *C.* 24,461
R. Aron, *LD* 6,098
A. Smith, *Ref.* 1,551
Mrs R. le Carpentier, *NLP* 197
Lab. majority 189
(Boundary change: notional C.)

KINGSTON AND SURBITON
*E.*73,879   *T.*75.35%
E. Davey, *LD* 20,411
†R. Tracey, *C.* 20,355
Ms S. Griffin, *Lab.* 12,811
Mrs G. Tchiprout, *Ref.* 1,470
Ms P. Burns, *UK Ind.* 418
C. Port, *Dream* 100
M. Leighton, *NLP* 100
LD majority 56
(Boundary change: notional C.)

KINGSWOOD
*E.*77,026   *T.*77.75%
†Dr R. Berry, *Lab.* 32,181
J. Howard, *C.* 17,928
Mrs J. Pinkerton, *LD* 7,672

Ms A. Reather, *Ref.* 1,463
P. Hart, *BNP* 290
A. Harding, *NLP* 238
A. Nicolson, *Scrapit* 115
Lab. majority 14,253
(Boundary change: notional C.)

KNOWSLEY NORTH AND SEFTON
EAST
*E.*70,918   *T.*70.09%
†G. Howarth, *Lab.* 34,747
C. Doran, *C.* 8,600
D. Bamber, *LD* 5,499
C. Jones, *Soc. Lab.* 857
Lab. majority 26,147
(Boundary change: notional Lab.)

KNOWSLEY SOUTH
*E.*70,532   *T.*67.47%
†E. O'Hara, *Lab.* 36,695
G. Robertson, *C.* 5,987
C. Mainey, *LD* 3,954
A. Wright, *Ref.* 954
Lab. majority 30,708
(Boundary change: notional Lab.)

LANCASHIRE WEST
*E.*73,175   *T.*74.79%
†C. Pickthall, *Lab.* 33,022
C. Varley, *C.* 15,903
A. Wood, *LD* 3,938
M. Carter, *Ref.* 1,025
J. Collins, *NLP* 449
D. Hill, *Home Rule* 392
Lab. majority 17,119
(Boundary change: notional Lab.)

LANCASTER AND WYRE
*E.*78,168   *T.*75.30%
H. Dawson, *Lab.* 25,173
†K. Mans, *C.* 23,878
J. Humberstone, *LD* 6,002
Mrs V. Ivell, *Ref.* 1,516
J. Barry, *Green* 795
Dr J. Whittaker, *UK Ind.* 698
Lab. majority 1,295
(Boundary change: notional C.)

LEEDS CENTRAL
*E.*67,664   *T.*54.70%
†D. Fatchett, *Lab.* 25,766
E. Wild, *C.* 5,077
D. Freeman, *LD* 4,164
P. Myers, *Ref.* 1,042
D. Rix, *Soc. Lab.* 656
C. Hill, *Soc.* 304
Lab. majority 20,689
(Boundary change: notional Lab.)

LEEDS EAST
*E.*56,963   *T.*62.83%
*G. Mudie, *Lab.* 24,151
J. Emsley, *C.* 6,685
Mrs M. Kirk, *LD* 3,689
L. Parish, *Ref.* 1,267
Lab. majority 17,466
(April 1992, Lab. maj. 12,697)

LEEDS NORTH EAST
*E.*63,185   *T.*72.03%
F. Hamilton, *Lab.* 22,368
*T. Kirkhope, *C.* 15,409
Dr W. Winlow, *LD* 6,318

I. Rose, *Ref.* 946
Ms J. Egan, *Soc. Lab.* 468
Lab. majority 6,959
(April 1992, C. maj. 4,244)

LEEDS NORTH WEST
*E.*69,972   *T.*70.57%
H. Best, *Lab.* 19,694
*Dr K. Hampson, *C.* 15,850
Mrs B. Pearce, *LD* 11,689
S. Emmett, *Ref.* 1,325
R. Lamb, *Soc. Lab.* 335
R. Toone, *ProLife* 251
D. Duffy, *Ronnie* 232
Lab. majority 3,844
(April 1992, C. maj. 7,671)

LEEDS WEST
*E.*63,965   *T.*62.88%
*J. Battle, *Lab.* 26,819
J. Whelan, *C.* 7,048
N. Amor, *LD* 3,622
W. Finley, *Ref.* 1,210
D. Blackburn, *Green* 896
N. Nowosielski, *Lib.* 625
Lab. majority 19,771
(April 1992, Lab. maj. 13,828)

LEICESTER EAST
*E.*64,012   *T.*69.37%
*K. Vaz, *Lab.* 29,083
S. Milton, *C.* 10,661
J. Matabudul, *LD* 3,105
P. Iwaniw, *Ref.* 1,015
S. Sidhu, *Soc. Lab.* 436
N. Slack, *Glow* 102
Lab. majority 18,422
(April 1992, Lab. maj. 11,316)

LEICESTER SOUTH
*E.*71,750   *T.*67.06%
*J. Marshall, *Lab.* 27,914
C. Heaton-Harris, *C.* 11,421
B. Coles, *LD* 6,654
J. Hancock, *Ref.* 1,184
J. Dooher, *Soc. Lab.* 634
K. Sills, *Nat. Dem.* 307
Lab. majority 16,493
(April 1992, Lab. maj. 9,440)

LEICESTER WEST
*E.*64,570   *T.*63.36%
Ms P. Hewitt, *Lab.* 22,580
R. Thomas, *C.* 9,716
M. Jones, *LD* 5,795
W. Shooter, *Ref.* 970
G. Forse, *Green* 586
D. Roberts, *Soc. Lab.* 452
Ms J. Nicholls, *Soc.* 327
A. Belshaw, *BNP* 302
C. Potter, *Nat. Dem.* 186
Lab. majority 12,864
(April 1992, Lab. maj. 3,978)

LEICESTERSHIRE NORTH WEST
*E.*65,069   *T.*79.95%
D. Taylor, *Lab.* 29,332
R. Goodwill, *C.* 16,113
S. Heptinstall, *LD* 4,492
M. Abney-Hastings, *Ref.* 2,088
Lab. majority 13,219
(Boundary change: notional C.)

LEIGH
*E.*69,908   *T.*65.69%
†L. Cunliffe, *Lab.* 31,652
E. Young, *C.* 7,156
P. Hough, *LD* 5,163
R. Constable, *Ref.* 1,949
Lab. majority 24,496
(Boundary change: notional Lab.)

LEOMINSTER
*E.*65,993   *T.*76.60%
†P. Temple-Morris, *C.* 22,888
T. James, *LD* 14,053
R. Westwood, *Lab.* 8,831
A. Parkin, *Ref.* 2,815
Ms F. Norman, *Green* 1,086
R. Chamings, *UK Ind.* 588
J. Haycock, *BNP* 292
C. majority 8,835
(Boundary change: notional C.)

LEWES
*E.*64,340   *T.*76.42%
N. Baker, *LD* 21,250
†T. Rathbone, *C.* 19,950
Dr M. Patton, *Lab.* 5,232
Mrs L. Butler, *Ref.* 2,481
J. Harvey, *UK Ind.* 256
LD majority 1,300
(Boundary change: notional C.)

LEWISHAM DEPTFORD
*E.*58,141   *T.*57.87%
†Mrs J. Ruddock, *Lab.* 23,827
Mrs I. Kimm, *C.* 4,949
K. Appiah, *LD* 3,004
J. Mulrenan, *Soc. Lab.* 996
Ms S. Shepherd, *Ref.* 868
Lab. majority 18,878
(Boundary change: notional Lab.)

LEWISHAM EAST
*E.*56,333   *T.*66.41%
†Ms B. Prentice, *Lab.* 21,821
P. Hollobone, *C.* 9,694
D. Buxton, *LD* 4,178
S. Drury, *Ref.* 910
R. Croucher, *NF* 431
P. White, *Lib.* 277
Capt. Rizz, *Dream* 97
Lab. majority 12,127
(Boundary change: notional Lab.)

LEWISHAM WEST
*E.*58,659   *T.*64.00%
*J. Dowd, *Lab.* 23,273
Mrs C. Whelan, *C.* 8,936
Miss K. McGrath, *LD* 3,672
A. Leese, *Ref.* 1,098
N. Long, *Soc. Lab.* 398
Ms E. Oram, *Lib.* 167
Lab. majority 14,337
(April 1992, Lab. maj. 1,809)

LEYTON AND WANSTEAD
*E.*62,176   *T.*63.24%
†H. Cohen, *Lab.* 23,922
R. Vaudry, *C.* 8,736
C. Anglin, *LD* 5,920
S. Duffy, *ProLife* 488
A. Mian, *Ind.* 256
Lab. majority 15,186
(Boundary change: notional Lab.)

LICHFIELD
E.62,720   T.77.48%

†M. Fabricant, C.	20,853
Ms S. Woodward, Lab.	20,615
Dr P. Bennion, LD	5,473
G. Seward, Ref.	1,652

C. majority 238
(Boundary change: notional C.)

LINCOLN
E.65,485   T.71.08%

Ms G. Merron, Lab.	25,563
A. Brown, C.	14,433
Ms L. Gabriel, LD	5,048
J. Ivory, Ref.	1,329
A. Myers, NLP	175

Lab. majority 11,130
(Boundary change: notional Lab.)

LIVERPOOL GARSTON
E.66,755   T.65.14%

Ms M. Eagle, Lab.	26,667
Ms F. Clucas, LD	8,250
N. Gordon-Johnson, C.	6,819
F. Dunne, Ref.	833
G. Copeland, Lib.	666
J. Parsons, NLP	127
S. Nolan, SEP	120

Lab. majority 18,417
(Boundary change: notional Lab.)

LIVERPOOL RIVERSIDE
E.73,429   T.51.93%

Ms L. Ellman, Lab. Co-op.	26,858
Ms B. Fraenkel, LD	5,059
D. Sparrow, C.	3,635
Ms C. Wilson, Soc.	776
D. Green, Lib.	594
G. Skelly, Ref.	586
Ms H. Neilson, ProLife	277
D. Braid, MRAC	179
G. Gay, NLP	171

Lab. Co-op. majority 21,799
(Boundary change: notional Lab.
Co-op.)

LIVERPOOL WALTON
E.67,527   T.59.54%

*P. Kilfoyle, Lab.	31,516
R. Roberts, LD	4,478
M. Kotecha, C.	2,551
C. Grundy, Ref.	620
Ms L. Mahmood, Soc.	444
Ms H. Williams, Lib.	352
Ms V. Mearns, ProLife	246

Lab. majority 27,038
(April 1992, Lab. maj. 28,299)

LIVERPOOL WAVERTREE
E.73,063   T.62.85%

†Ms J. Kennedy, Lab.	29,592
R. Kemp, LD	9,891
C. Malthouse, C.	4,944
P. Worthington, Ref.	576
K. McCullough, Lib.	391
Ms R. Kingsley, ProLife	346
Ms C. Corkhill, WRP	178

Lab. majority 19,701
(Boundary change: notional Lab.)

LIVERPOOL WEST DERBY
E.68,682   T.61.38%

†R. Wareing, Lab.	30,002

S. Radford, Lib.	4,037
Ms A. Hines, LD	3,805
N. Morgan, C.	3,656
P. Forrest, Ref.	657

Lab. majority 25,965
(Boundary change: notional Lab.)

LOUGHBOROUGH
E.68,945   T.75.95%

A. Reed, Lab.	25,448
K. Andrew, C.	19,736
Ms D. Brass, LD	6,190
R. Gupta, Ref.	991

Lab. majority 5,712
(Boundary change: notional C.)

LOUTH AND HORNCASTLE
E.68,824   T.72.58%

†Sir P. Tapsell, C.	21,699
J. Hough, Lab.	14,799
Mrs F. Martin, LD	12,207
Ms R. Robinson, Green	1,248

C. majority 6,900
(Boundary change: notional C.)

LUDLOW
E.61,267   T.75.55%

†C. Gill, C.	19,633
I. Huffer, LD	13,724
Ms N. O'Kane, Lab.	11,745
T. Andrewes, Green	798
E. Freeman-Keel, UK Ind.	385

C. majority 5,909
(Boundary change: notional C.)

LUTON NORTH
E.64,618   T.73.25%

K. Hopkins, Lab.	25,860
D. Senior, C.	16,234
Mrs K. Newbound, LD	4,299
C. Brown, UK Ind.	689
A. Custance, NLP	250

Lab. majority 9,626
(Boundary change: notional C.)

LUTON SOUTH
E.68,395   T.70.45%

Ms M. Moran, Lab.	26,428
†Sir G. Bright, C.	15,109
K. Fitchett, LD	4,610
C. Jacobs, Ref.	1,205
C. Lawman, UK Ind.	390
M. Scheimann, Green	356
Ms C. Perrin, NLP	86

Lab. majority 11,319
(Boundary change: notional C.)

MACCLESFIELD
E.72,049   T.75.22%

†N. Winterton, C.	26,888
Ms J. Jackson, Lab.	18,234
M. Flynn, LD	9,075

C. majority 8,654
(Boundary change: notional C.)

MAIDENHEAD
E.67,302   T.75.61%

Mrs T. May, C.	25,344
A. Ketteringham, LD	13,363
Ms D. Robson, Lab.	9,205
C. Taverner, Ref.	1,638
D. Munkley, Lib.	896
N. Spiers, UK Ind.	277

K. Ardley, Glow	166

C. majority 11,981
(Boundary change: notional C.)

MAIDSTONE AND THE WEALD
E.72,466   T.73.98%

†Rt. Hon. Miss A. Widdecombe, C.	23,657
J. Morgan, Lab.	14,054
Mrs J. Nelson, LD	11,986
Ms S. Hopkins, Ref.	1,998
Ms M. Cleator, Soc. Lab.	979
Ms P. Kemp, Green	480
Mrs R. Owen, UK Ind.	339
J. Oldbury, NLP	115

C. majority 9,603
(Boundary change: notional C.)

MAKERFIELD
E.67,358   T.66.83%

†I. McCartney, Lab.	33,119
M. Winstanley, C.	6,942
B. Hubbard, LD	3,743
A. Seed, Ref.	1,210

Lab. majority 26,177
(Boundary change: notional Lab.)

MALDON AND CHELMSFORD EAST
E.66,184   T.76.13%

†J. Whittingdale, C.	24,524
K. Freeman, Lab.	14,485
G. Pooley, LD	9,758
L. Overy-Owen, UK Ind.	935
Ms E. Burgess, Green	685

C. majority 10,039
(Boundary change: notional C.)

MANCHESTER BLACKLEY
E.62,227   T.57.46%

G. Stringer, Lab.	25,042
S. Barclay, C.	5,454
S. Wheale, LD	3,937
P. Stanyer, Ref.	1,323

Lab. majority 19,588
(Boundary change: notional Lab.)

MANCHESTER CENTRAL
E.63,815   T.52.55%

†A. Lloyd, Lab.	23,803
Ms A. Firth, LD	4,121
S. McIlwaine, C.	3,964
F. Rafferty, Soc. Lab.	810
J. Maxwell, Ref.	742
T. Rigby, Comm L.	97

Lab. majority 19,682
(Boundary change: notional Lab.)

MANCHESTER GORTON
E.64,349   T.56.43%

†Rt. Hon. G. Kaufman, Lab.	23,704
Dr J. Pearcey, LD	6,362
G. Senior, C.	4,249
K. Hartley, Ref.	812
Dr S. Fitz-Gibbon, Green	683
T. Wongsam, Soc. Lab.	501

Lab. majority 17,342
(Boundary change: notional Lab.)

MANCHESTER WITHINGTON
E.66,116   T.66.59%

†K. Bradley, Lab.	27,103
J. Smith, C.	8,522
Dr Y. Zalzala, LD	6,000

M. Sheppard, *Ref.* 1,079
S. Caldwell, *ProLife* 614
Ms J. White, *Soc.* 376
S. Kingston, *Dream* 181
M. Gaskell, *NLP* 152
Lab. majority 18,581
(Boundary change: notional Lab.)

MANSFIELD
E.67,057   T.70.72%
*A. Meale, *Lab.* 30,556
T. Frost, *C.* 10,038
P. Smith, *LD* 5,244
W. Bogusz, *Ref.* 1,588
Lab. majority 20,518
(April 1992, Lab. maj. 11,724)

MEDWAY
E.61,736   T.72.47%
R. Marshall-Andrews, *Lab.* 21,858
*Dame P. Fenner, *C.* 16,504
R. Roberts, *LD* 4,555
J. Main, *Ref.* 1,420
Mrs S. Radlett, *UK Ind.* 405
Lab. majority 5,354
(April 1992, C. maj. 8,786)

MERIDEN
E.76,287   T.71.73%
Mrs C. Spelman, *C.* 22,997
B. Seymour-Smith, *Lab.* 22,415
A. Dupont, *LD* 7,098
P. Gilbert, *Ref.* 2,208
C. majority 582
(April 1992, C. maj. 14,699)

MIDDLESBROUGH
E.70,931   T.64.99%
†S. Bell, *Lab.* 32,925
L. Benham, *C.* 7,907
Miss A. Charlesworth, *LD* 3,934
R. Edwards, *Ref.* 1,331
Lab. majority 25,018
(Boundary change: notional Lab.)

MIDDLESBROUGH SOUTH AND
CLEVELAND EAST
E.70,481   T.76.03%
Dr A. Kumar, *Lab.* 29,319
†M. Bates, *C.* 18,712
H. Garrett, *LD* 4,004
R. Batchelor, *Ref.* 1,552
Lab. majority 10,607
(Boundary change: notional C.)

MILTON KEYNES NORTH EAST
E.70,395   T.72.78%
B. White, *Lab.* 20,201
†P. Butler, *C.* 19,961
G. Mabbutt, *LD* 8,907
M. Phillips, *Ref.* 1,492
A. Francis, *Green* 576
M. Simson, *NLP* 99
Lab. majority 240
(Boundary change: notional C.)

MILTON KEYNES SOUTH WEST
E.71,070   T.71.42%
Mrs P. Starkey, *Lab.* 27,298
*B. Legg, *C.* 17,006
P. Jones, *LD* 6,065
H. Kelly, *NLP* 389

Lab. majority 10,292
(April 1992, C. maj. 4,687)

MITCHAM AND MORDEN
E.65,385   T.73.33%
Ms S. McDonagh, *Lab.* 27,984
*Rt. Hon. Dame A. Rumbold, *C.* 14,243
N. Harris, *LD* 3,632
P. Isaacs, *Ref.* 810
Ms L. Miller, *BNP* 521
T. Walsh, *Green* 415
K. Vasan, *Ind.* 144
J. Barrett, *UK Ind.* 117
N. Dixon, *ACC* 80
Lab. majority 13,741
(April 1992, C. maj. 1,734)

MOLE VALLEY
E.69,140   T.78.86%
†Sir P. Beresford, *C.* 26,178
S. Cooksey, *LD* 15,957
C. Payne, *Lab.* 8,057
N. Taber, *Ref.* 2,424
R. Burley, *Ind. CRP* 1,276
Capt. I. Cameron, *UK Ind.* 435
Ms J. Thomas, *NLP* 197
C. majority 10,221
(Boundary change: notional C.)

MORECAMBE AND LUNESDALE
E.68,013   T.72.41%
Ms G. Smith, *Lab.* 24,061
†Sir M. Lennox-Boyd, *C.* 18,096
Mrs J. Greenwell, *LD* 5,614
I. Ogilvie, *Ref.* 1,313
D. Walne, *NLP* 165
Lab. majority 5,965
(Boundary change: notional C.)

MORLEY AND ROTHWELL
E.68,385   T.67.12%
†J. Gunnell, *Lab.* 26,836
A. Barraclough, *C.* 12,086
M. Galdas, *LD* 5,087
D. Mitchell-Innes, *Ref.* 1,359
R. Wood, *BNP* 381
Ms P. Sammon, *ProLife* 148
Lab. majority 14,750
(Boundary change: notional Lab.)

NEW FOREST EAST
E.65,717   T.74.64%
Dr J. Lewis, *C.* 21,053
G. Dawson, *LD* 15,838
A. Goodfellow, *Lab.* 12,161
C. majority 5,215
(Boundary change: notional C.)

NEW FOREST WEST
E.66,522   T.74.79%
D. Swayne, *C.* 25,149
R. Hale, *LD* 13,817
D. Griffiths, *Lab.* 7,092
Mrs M. Elliott, *Ref.* 2,150
M. Holmes, *UK Ind.* 1,542
C. majority 11,332
(Boundary change: notional C.)

NEWARK
E.69,763   T.74.50%
Ms F. Jones, *Lab.* 23,496
*R. Alexander, *C.* 20,480

P. Harris, *LD* 5,960
G. Creedy, *Ref.* 2,035
Lab. majority 3,016
(April 1992, C. maj. 8,229)

NEWBURY
E.73,680   T.76.65%
†D. Rendel, *LD* 29,887
R. Benyon, *C.* 21,370
P. Hannon, *Lab.* 3,107
E. Snook, *Ref.* 992
Ms R. Stark, *Green* 644
R. Tubb, *UK Ind.* 302
Ms K. Howse, *Soc. Lab.* 174
LD majority 8,517
(Boundary change: notional C.)

NEWCASTLE-UNDER LYME
E.66,686   T.73.67%
*Mrs L. Golding, *Lab.* 27,743
M. Hayes, *C.* 10,537
Dr R. Studd, *LD* 6,858
Ms K. Suttle, *Ref.* 1,510
S. Mountford, *Lib.* 1,399
Ms B. Bell, *Soc. Lab.* 1,082
Lab. majority 17,206
(April 1992, Lab. maj. 9,839)

NEWCASTLE UPON TYNE CENTRAL
E.69,781   T.66.05%
†J. Cousins, *Lab.* 27,272
B. Newmark, *C.* 10,792
Ms R. Berry, *LD* 6,911
C. Coxon, *Ref.* 1,113
Lab. majority 16,480
(Boundary change: notional Lab.)

NEWCASTLE UPON TYNE EAST AND
WALLSEND
E.63,272   T.65.73%
†N. Brown, *Lab.* 29,607
J. Middleton, *C.* 5,796
G. Morgan, *LD* 4,415
P. Cossins, *Ref.* 966
Ms B. Carpenter, *Soc. Lab.* 642
M. Levy, *Comm. P.* 163
Lab. majority 23,811
(Boundary change: notional Lab.)

NEWCASTLE UPON TYNE NORTH
E.65,357   T.69.20%
*D. Henderson, *Lab.* 28,125
G. White, *C.* 8,793
P. Allen, *LD* 6,578
Mrs D. Chipchase, *Ref.* 1,733
Lab. majority 19,332
(April 1992, Lab. maj. 8,946)

NORFOLK MID
E.75,311   T.76.29%
K. Simpson, *C.* 22,739
D. Zeichner, *Lab.* 21,403
Mrs S. Frary, *LD* 8,617
N. Holder, *Ref.* 3,229
A. Park, *Green* 1,254
B. Parker, *NLP* 215
C. majority 1,336
(Boundary change: notional C.)

NORFOLK NORTH
E.77,113   T.76.27%
D. Prior, *C.* 21,456
N. Lamb, *LD* 20,163

M. Cullingham, *Lab.* 14,736
J. Allen, *Ref.* 2,458
C. majority 1,293
(April 1992, C. maj. 12,545)

NORFOLK NORTH WEST
*E.*77,083　*T.*74.72%
Dr G. Turner, *Lab.* 25,250
*H. Bellingham, *C.* 23,911
Ms E. Knowles, *LD* 5,513
R. Percival, *Ref.* 2,923
Lab. majority 1,339
(April 1992, C. maj. 11,564)

NORFOLK SOUTH
*E.*79,239　*T.*78.37%
†Rt. Hon. J. MacGregor, *C.* 24,935
Mrs B. Hacker, *LD* 17,557
Ms J. Ross, *Lab.* 16,188
Mrs P. Bateson, *Ref.* 2,533
Mrs S. Ross-Wagenknecht, *Green* 484
A. Boddy, *UK Ind.* 400
C. majority 7,378
(Boundary change: notional C.)

NORFOLK SOUTH WEST
*E.*80,236　*T.*73.28%
†Rt. Hon. Mrs G. Shephard, *C.* 24,694
A. Heffernan, *Lab.* 22,230
D. Buckton, *LD* 8,178
R. Hoare, *Ref.* 3,694
C. majority 2,464
(Boundary change: notional C.)

NORMANTON
*E.*62,980　*T.*68.28%
†W. O'Brien, *Lab.* 26,046
Miss F. Bulmer, *C.* 10,153
D. Ridgway, *LD* 5,347
K. Shuttleworth, *Ref.* 1,458
Lab. majority 15,893
(Boundary change: notional Lab.)

NORTHAMPTON NORTH
*E.*73,664　*T.*70.18%
Ms S. Keeble, *Lab.* 27,247
†A. Marlow, *C.* 17,247
Ms L. Dunbar, *LD* 6,579
D. Torbica, *UK Ind.* 464
B. Spivack, *NLP* 161
Lab. majority 10,000
(Boundary change: notional C.)

NORTHAMPTON SOUTH
*E.*79,384　*T.*71.94%
A. Clarke, *Lab.* 24,214
†Rt. Hon. M. Morris, *C.* 23,470
A. Worgan, *LD* 6,316
C. Petrie, *Ref.* 1,405
D. Clark, *UK Ind.* 1,159
G. Woollcombe, *NLP* 541
Lab. majority 744
(Boundary change: notional C.)

NORTHAVON
*E.*78,943　*T.*79.21%
Prof. S. Webb, *LD* 26,500
†Rt. Hon. Sir J. Cope, *C.* 24,363
R. Stone, *Lab.* 9,767
J. Parfitt, *Ref.* 1,900
LD majority 2,137
(Boundary change: notional C.)

NORWICH NORTH
*E.*72,521　*T.*75.92%
Dr I. Gibson, *Lab.* 27,346
Dr R. Kinghorn, *C.* 17,876
P. Young, *LD* 6,951
A. Bailey-Smith, *Ref.* 1,777
H. Marks, *LCP* 512
J. Hood, *Soc. Lab.* 495
Mrs D. Mills, *NLP* 100
Lab. majority 9,470
(Boundary change: notional C.)

NORWICH SOUTH
*E.*70,009　*T.*72.56%
C. Clarke, *Lab.* 26,267
B. Khanbhai, *C.* 12,028
A. Aalders-Dunthorne, *LD* 9,457
Dr D. Holdsworth, *Ref.* 1,464
H. Marks, *LCP* 765
A. Holmes, *Green* 736
B. Parsons, *NLP* 84
Lab. majority 14,239
(Boundary change: notional Lab.)

NOTTINGHAM EAST
*E.*65,581　*T.*60.60%
*J. Heppell, *Lab.* 24,755
A. Raca, *C.* 9,336
K. Mulloy, *LD* 4,008
B. Brown, *Ref.* 1,645
Lab. majority 15,419
(April 1992, Lab. maj. 7,680)

NOTTINGHAM NORTH
*E.*65,698　*T.*63.02%
*G. Allen, *Lab.* 27,203
Ms G. Shaw, *C.* 8,402
Ms R. Oliver, *LD* 3,301
J. Neal, *Ref.* 1,858
A. Belfield, *Soc.* 637
Lab. majority 18,801
(April 1992, Lab. maj. 10,743)

NOTTINGHAM SOUTH
*E.*72,418　*T.*67.00%
*A. Simpson, *Lab.* 26,825
B. Kirsch, *C.* 13,461
G. Long, *LD* 6,265
K. Thompson, *Ref.* 1,523
Ms S. Edwards, *Nat. Dem.* 446
Lab. majority 13,364
(April 1992, Lab. maj. 3,181)

NUNEATON
*E.*72,032　*T.*74.29%
*W. Olner, *Lab.* 30,080
R. Blunt, *C.* 16,540
R. Cockings, *LD* 4,732
R. English, *Ref.* 1,533
D. Bray, *Loc. Ind.* 390
P. Everitt, *UK Ind.* 238
Lab. majority 13,540
(April 1992, Lab. maj. 1,631)

OLD BEXLEY AND SIDCUP
*E.*68,044　*T.*75.53%
†Rt. Hon. Sir E. Heath, *C.* 21,608
R. Justham, *Lab.* 18,039
I. King, *LD* 8,284
B. Reading, *Ref.* 2,457
C. Bullen, *UK Ind.* 489

Ms V. Tyndall, *BNP* 415
R. Stephens, *NLP* 99
C. majority 3,569
(Boundary change: notional C.)

OLDHAM EAST AND SADDLEWORTH
*E.*73,189　*T.*73.92%
P. Woolas, *Lab.* 22,546
†C. Davies, *LD* 19,157
J. Hudson, *C.* 10,666
D. Findlay, *Ref.* 1,116
J. Smith, *Soc. Lab.* 470
I. Dalling, *NLP* 146
Lab. majority 3,389
(Boundary change: notional C.)

OLDHAM WEST AND ROYTON
*E.*69,203　*T.*66.09%
†M. Meacher, *Lab.* 26,894
J. Lord, *C.* 10,693
H. Cohen, *LD* 5,434
G. Choudhury, *Soc. Lab.* 1,311
P. Etherden, *Ref.* 1,157
Mrs S. Dalling, *NLP* 249
Lab. majority 16,201
(Boundary change: notional Lab.)

ORPINGTON
*E.*78,749　*T.*76.40%
†J. Horam, *C.* 24,417
C. Maines, *LD* 21,465
Ms S. Polydorou, *Lab.* 10,753
D. Clark, *Ref.* 2,316
J. Carver, *UK Ind.* 526
R. Almond, *Lib.* 494
N. Wilton, *ProLife* 191
C. majority 2,952
(Boundary change: notional C.)

OXFORD EAST
*E.*69,339　*T.*69.05%
†A. Smith, *Lab.* 27,205
J. Djanogly, *C.* 10,540
G. Kershaw, *LD* 7,038
M. Young, *Ref.* 1,391
C. Simmons, *Green* 975
W. Harper-Jones, *Embryo* 318
Dr P. Gardner, *UK Ind.* 234
J. Thompson, *NLP* 108
P. Mylvaganam, *Anti-maj.* 68
Lab. majority 16,665
(Boundary change: notional Lab.)

OXFORD WEST AND ABINGDON
*E.*79,329　*T.*77.14%
Dr E. Harris, *LD* 26,268
L. Harris, *C.* 19,983
Ms S. Brown, *Lab.* 12,361
Mrs G. Eustace, *Ref.* 1,258
Dr M. Woodin, *Green* 691
R. Buckton, *UK Ind.* 258
Mrs L. Hodge, *ProLife* 238
Ms A.-M. Wilson, *NLP* 91
J. Rose, *LGR* 48
LD majority 6,285
(Boundary change: notional C.)

PENDLE
*E.*63,049　*T.*74.60%
*G. Prentice, *Lab.* 25,059
J. Midgeley, *C.* 14,235
A. Greaves, *LD* 5,460

D. Hockney, *Ref.* 2,281
Lab. majority 10,824
(April 1992, Lab. maj. 2,113)

PENRITH AND THE BORDER
*E.*66,496   *T.*73.63%
†Rt. Hon. D. Maclean, *C.* 23,300
G. Walker, *LD* 13,067
Mrs M. Meling, *Lab.* 10,576
C. Pope, *Ref.* 2,018
C. majority 10,233
(Boundary change: notional C.)

PETERBOROUGH
*E.*65,926   *T.*73.46%
Ms H. Brinton, *Lab.* 24,365
Mrs J. Foster, *C.* 17,042
D. Howarth, *LD* 5,170
P. Slater, *Ref.* 924
C. Brettell, *NLP* 334
J. Linskey, *UK Ind.* 317
S. Goldspink, *ProLife* 275
Lab. majority 7,323
(Boundary change: notional C.)

PLYMOUTH DEVONPORT
*E.*74,483   *T.*69.76%
†D. Jamieson, *Lab.* 31,629
A. Johnson, *C.* 12,562
R. Copus, *LD* 5,570
C. Norsworthy, *Ref.* 1,486
Mrs C. Farrand, *UK Ind.* 478
S. Ebbs, *Nat. Dem.* 238
Lab. majority 19,067
(Boundary change: notional Lab.)

PLYMOUTH SUTTON
*E.*70,666   *T.*67.43%
Mrs L. Gilroy, *Lab. Co-op.* 23,881
A. Crisp, *C.* 14,441
S. Melia, *LD* 6,613
T. Hanbury, *Ref.* 1,654
R. Bullock, *UK Ind.* 499
K. Kelway, *Plymouth* 396
F. Lyons, *NLP* 168
Lab. Co-op. majority 9,440
(Boundary change: notional C.)

PONTEFRACT AND CASTLEFORD
*E.*62,350   *T.*66.39%
Ms Y. Cooper, *Lab.* 31,339
A. Flook, *C.* 5,614
W. Paxton, *LD* 3,042
R. Wood, *Ref.* 1,401
Lab. majority 25,725
(April 1992, Lab. maj. 23,495)

POOLE
*E.*66,078   *T.*70.84%
R. Syms, *C.* 19,726
A. Tetlow, *LD* 14,428
H. White, *Lab.* 10,100
J. Riddington, *Ref.* 1,932
P. Tyler, *UK Ind.* 487
Mrs J. Rosta, *NLP* 137
C. majority 5,298
(Boundary change: notional C.)

POPLAR AND CANNING TOWN
*E.*67,172   *T.*58.46%
J. Fitzpatrick, *Lab.* 24,807
B. Steinberg, *C.* 5,892
Ms J. Ludlow, *LD* 4,072

J. Tyndall, *BNP* 2,849
I. Hare, *Ref.* 1,091
Ms J. Joseph, *Soc. Lab.* 557
Lab. majority 18,915
(Boundary change: notional Lab.)

PORTSMOUTH NORTH
*E.*64,539   *T.*70.14%
S. Rapson, *Lab.* 21,339
†P. Griffiths, *C.* 17,016
S. Sollitt, *LD* 4,788
S. Evelegh, *Ref.* 1,757
P. Coe, *UK Ind.* 298
C. Bex, *Wessex* 72
Lab. majority 4,323
(Boundary change: notional C.)

PORTSMOUTH SOUTH
*E.*80,514   *T.*64.21%
M. Hancock, *LD* 20,421
*D. Martin, *C.* 16,094
A. Burnett, *Lab.* 13,086
C. Trim, *Ref.* 1,629
J. Thompson, *Lib.* 184
Mrs J. Evans, *UK Ind.* 141
W. Treend, *NLP* 140
LD majority 4,327
(April 1992, C. maj. 242)

PRESTON
*E.*72,933   *T.*65.92%
†Mrs A. Wise, *Lab.* 29,220
P. Gray, *C.* 10,540
W. Chadwick, *LD* 7,045
J. C. Porter, *Ref.* 924
J. Ashforth, *NLP* 345
Lab. majority 18,680
(Boundary change: notional Lab.)

PUDSEY
*E.*70,922   *T.*74.35%
P. Truswell, *Lab.* 25,370
P. Bone, *C.* 19,163
Dr J. Brown, *LD* 7,375
D. Crabtree, *Ref.* 823
Lab. majority 6,207
(April 1992, C. maj. 8,972)

PUTNEY
*E.*60,176   *T.*73.11%
A. Colman, *Lab.* 20,084
*Rt. Hon. D. Mellor, *C.* 17,108
R. Pyne, *LD* 4,739
Sir J. Goldsmith, *Ref.* 1,518
W. Jamieson, *UK Ind.* 233
L. Beige, *Star* 101
M. Yardley, *Spts All.* 90
J. Small, *NLP* 66
Ms A. Poole, *Beaut.* 49
D. Vanbraam, *Ren. Dem.* 7
Lab. majority 2,976
(April 1992, C. maj. 7,526)

RAYLEIGH
*E.*68,737   *T.*74.65%
†Dr M. Clark, *C.* 25,516
R. Ellis, *Lab.* 14,832
S. Cumberland, *LD* 10,137
A. Farmer, *Lib.* 829
C. majority 10,684
(Boundary change: notional C.)

READING EAST
*E.*71,586   *T.*70.15%
Ms J. Griffiths, *Lab.* 21,461
†J. Watts, *C.* 17,666
R. Samuel, *LD* 9,307
D. Harmer, *Ref.* 1,042
J. Buckley, *NLP* 254
Miss A. Thornton, *UK Ind.* 252
Ms B. Packer, *BNP* 238
Lab. majority 3,795
(Boundary change: notional C.)

READING WEST
*E.*69,073   *T.*70.05%
M. Salter, *Lab.* 21,841
N. Bennett, *C.* 18,844
Mrs D. Tomlin, *LD* 6,153
S. Brown, *Ref.* 976
I. Dell, *BNP* 320
D. Black, *UK Ind.* 255
Lab. majority 2,997
(Boundary change: notional C.)

REDCAR
*E.*68,965   *T.*70.99%
†Dr M. Mowlam, *Lab.* 32,972
A. Isaacs, *C.* 11,308
Ms J. Benbow, *LD* 4,679
Lab. majority 21,664
(Boundary change: notional Lab.)

REDDITCH
*E.*60,841   *T.*73.55%
Ms J. Smith, *Lab.* 22,280
Miss A. McIntyre, *C.* 16,155
M. Hall, *LD* 4,935
R. Cox, *Ref.* 1,151
P. Davis, *NLP* 227
Lab. majority 6,125
(Boundary change: notional C.)

REGENT'S PARK AND KENSINGTON NORTH
*E.*73,752   *T.*64.19%
Ms K. Buck, *Lab.* 28,367
P. McGuinness, *C.* 13,710
Miss E. Gasson, *LD* 4,041
Ms S. Dangoor, *Ref.* 867
J. Hinde, *NLP* 192
Ms D. Sadowitz, *Dream* 167
Lab. majority 14,657
(Boundary change: notional Lab.)

REIGATE
*E.*64,750   *T.*74.40%
C. Blunt, *C.* 21,123
A. Howard, *Lab.* 13,382
P. Samuel, *LD* 9,615
†Sir G. Gardiner, *Ref.* 3,352
R. Higgs, *Ind.* 412
S. Smith, *UK Ind.* 290
C. majority 7,741
(Boundary change: notional C.)

RIBBLE SOUTH
*E.*71,670   *T.*77.06%
D. Borrow, *Lab.* 25,856
†Rt. Hon. R. Atkins, *C.* 20,772
T. Farron, *LD* 5,879
G. Adams, *Ref.* 1,475
N. Ashton, *Lib.* 1,127
Ms B. Leadbetter, *NLP* 122

Lab. majority 5,084
(Boundary change: notional C.)

RIBBLE VALLEY
E.72,664   T.78.75%
†N. Evans, *C.*   26,702
M. Carr, *LD*   20,062
M. Johnstone, *Lab.*   9,013
J. Parkinson, *Ref.*   1,297
Miss N. Holmes, *NLP*   147
C. majority 6,640
(Boundary change: notional C.)

RICHMOND (Yorks)
E.65,058   T.73.38%
†Rt. Hon. W. Hague, *C.*   23,326
S. Merritt, *Lab.*   13,275
Mrs J. Harvey, *LD*   8,773
A. Bentley, *Ref.*   2,367
C. majority 10,051
(Boundary change: notional C.)

RICHMOND PARK
E.71,572   T.79.43%
Dr J. Tonge, *LD*   25,393
†Rt. Hon. J. Hanley, *C.*   22,442
Ms S. Jenkins, *Lab.*   7,172
J. Pugh, *Ref.*   1,467
D. Beaupre, *Loony*   204
B. D'Arcy, *NLP*   102
P. Davies, *Dream*   73
LD majority 2,951
(Boundary change: notional C.)

ROCHDALE
E.68,529   T.70.16%
Ms L. Fitzsimons, *Lab.*   23,758
†Miss E. Lynne, *LD*   19,213
M. Turnberg, *C.*   4,237
G. Bergin, *BNP*   653
S. Mohammed, *IZB*   221
Lab. majority 4,545
(Boundary change: notional LD)

ROCHFORD AND SOUTHEND EAST
E.72,848   T.63.97%
†Sir E. Taylor, *C.*   22,683
N. Smith, *Lab.*   18,458
Ms P. Smith, *LD*   4,387
B. Lynch, *Lib.*   1,070
C. majority 4,225
(Boundary change: notional C.)

ROMFORD
E.59,611   T.70.66%
Mrs E. Gordon, *Lab.*   18,187
†Sir M. Neubert, *C.*   17,538
N. Meyer, *LD*   3,341
S. Ward, *Ref.*   1,431
T. Hurlstone, *Lib.*   1,100
M. Carey, *BNP*   522
Lab. majority 649
(Boundary change: notional C.)

ROMSEY
E.67,306   T.76.99%
†M. Colvin, *C.*   23,834
M. Cooper, *LD*   15,249
Ms J. Ford, *Lab.*   9,623
Dr A. Sked, *UK Ind.*   1,824
M. Wigley, *Ref.*   1,291
C. majority 8,585
(Boundary change: notional C.)

ROSSENDALE AND DARWEN
E.69,749   T.73.42%
†Mrs J. Anderson, *Lab.*   27,470
Mrs P. Buzzard, *C.*   16,521
B. Dunning, *LD*   5,435
R. Newstead, *Ref.*   1,108
A. Wearden, *BNP*   674
Lab. majority 10,949
(Boundary change: notional Lab.)

ROTHER VALLEY
E.68,622   T.67.26%
*K. Barron, *Lab.*   31,184
S. Stanbury, *C.*   7,699
S. Burgess, *LD*   5,342
S. Cook, *Ref.*   1,932
Lab. majority 23,485
(April 1992, Lab. maj. 17,222)

ROTHERHAM
E.59,895   T.62.86%
*D. MacShane, *Lab.*   26,852
S. Gordon, *C.*   5,383
D. Wildgoose, *LD*   3,919
R. Hollibone, *Ref.*   1,132
A. Neal, *ProLife*   364
Lab. majority 21,469
(April 1992, Lab. maj. 17,561)

RUGBY AND KENILWORTH
E.79,384   T.77.10%
A. King, *Lab.*   26,356
†J. Pawsey, *C.*   25,861
J. Roodhouse, *LD*   8,737
M. Twite, *NLP*   251
Lab. majority 495
(Boundary change: notional C.)

RUISLIP-NORTHWOOD
E.60,393   T.74.24%
†J. Wilkinson, *C.*   22,526
P. Barker, *Lab.*   14,732
C. Edwards, *LD*   7,279
Ms C. Griffin, *NLP*   296
C. majority 7,794
(Boundary change: notional C.)

RUNNYMEDE AND WEYBRIDGE
E.72,177   T.71.44%
P. Hammond, *C.*   25,051
I. Peacock, *Lab.*   15,176
G. Taylor, *LD*   8,397
P. Rolt, *Ref.*   2,150
S. Slater, *UK Ind.*   625
J. Sleeman, *NLP*   162
C. majority 9,875
(Boundary change: notional C.)

RUSHCLIFFE
E.78,735   T.78.89%
*Rt. Hon. K. Clarke, *C.*   27,558
Ms J. Pettit, *Lab.*   22,503
S. Boote, *LD*   8,851
Miss S. Chadd, *Ref.*   2,682
J. Moore, *UK Ind.*   403
Ms A. Maszwska, *NLP*   115
C. majority 5,055
(April 1992, C. maj. 19,766)

RUTLAND AND MELTON
E.70,150   T.75.02%
†A. Duncan, *C.*   24,107
J. Meads, *Lab.*   15,271

K. Lee, *LD*   10,112
R. King, *Ref.*   2,317
J. Abbott, *UK Ind.*   823
C. majority 8,836
(Boundary change: notional C.)

RYEDALE
E.65,215   T.74.80%
†J. Greenway, *C.*   21,351
J. Orrell, *LD*   16,293
Ms A. Hiles, *Lab.*   8,762
J. Mackfall, *Ref.*   1,460
S. Feaster, *UK Ind.*   917
C. majority 5,058
(Boundary change: notional C.)

SAFFRON WALDEN
E.74,097   T.76.99%
†Sir A. Haselhurst, *C.*   25,871
M. Caton, *LD*   15,298
M. Fincken, *Lab.*   12,275
R. Glover, *Ref.*   2,308
I. Evans, *UK Ind.*   658
B. Tyler, *Ind.*   486
C. Edwards, *NLP*   154
C. majority 10,573
(Boundary change: notional C.)

ST ALBANS
E.65,560   T.77.49%
K. Pollard, *Lab.*   21,338
D. Rutley, *C.*   16,879
A. Rowlands, *LD*   10,692
J. Warrilow, *Ref.*   1,619
Ms S. Craigen, *Dream*   166
I. Docker, *NLP*   111
Lab. majority 4,459
(Boundary change: notional C.)

ST HELENS NORTH
E.71,380   T.68.97%
D. Watts, *Lab.*   31,953
P. Walker, *C.*   8,536
J. Beirne, *LD*   6,270
D. Johnson, *Ref.*   1,276
R. Waugh, *Soc. Lab.*   832
R. Rudin, *UK Ind.*   363
Lab. majority 23,417
(April 1992, Lab. maj. 16,244)

ST HELENS SOUTH
E.66,526   T.66.53%
†G. Bermingham, *Lab.*   30,367
Ms M. Russell, *C.*   6,628
B. Spencer, *LD*   5,919
W. Holdaway, *Ref.*   1,165
Ms H. Jump, *NLP*   179
Lab. majority 23,739
(Boundary change: notional Lab.)

ST IVES
E.71,680   T.75.20%
A. George, *LD*   23,966
W. Rogers, *C.*   16,796
C. Fegan, *Lab.*   8,184
M. Faulkner, *Ref.*   3,714
Mrs P. Garnier, *UK Ind.*   567
G. Stephens, *Lib.*   425
K. Lippiatt, *R. Alt.*   178
W. Hitchins, *BHMBCM*   71
LD majority 7,170
(April 1992, C. maj. 1,645)

SALFORD
E.58,610   T.56.51%

Ms H. Blears, *Lab.*	22,848
E. Bishop, *C.*	5,779
N. Owen, *LD*	3,407
R. Cumpsty, *Ref.*	926
Ms S. Herman, *NLP*	162

Lab. majority 17,069
(Boundary change: notional Lab.)

SALISBURY
E.78,973   T.73.75%

*R. Key, *C.*	25,012
Ms Y. Emmerson-Peirce, *LD*	18,736
R. Rogers, *Lab.*	10,242
N. Farage, *UK Ind.*	3,332
II. Soutar, *Green*	623
W. Holmes, *Ind.*	184
Mrs S. Haysom, *NLP*	110

C. majority 6,276
(April 1992, C. maj. 8,973)

SCARBOROUGH AND WHITBY
E.75,862   T.71.61%

L. Quinn, *Lab.*	24,791
*J. Sykes, *C.*	19,667
M. Allinson, *LD*	7,672
Ms S. Murray, *Ref.*	2,191

Lab. majority 5,124
(April 1992, C. maj. 11,734)

SCUNTHORPE
E.60,393   T.68.84%

†E. Morley, *Lab.*	25,107
M. Fisher, *C.*	10,934
G. Smith, *LD*	3,497
P. Smith, *Ref.*	1,637
B. Hopper, *Soc. Lab.*	399

Lab. majority 14,173
(Boundary change: notional Lab.)

SEDGEFIELD
E.64,923   T.72.57%

†Rt. Hon. A. Blair, *Lab.*	33,526
Mrs E. Pitman, *C.*	8,383
R. Beadle, *LD*	3,050
Miss M. Hall, *Ref.*	1,683
B. Gibson, *Soc. Lab.*	474

Lab. majority 25,143
(Boundary change: notional Lab.)

SELBY
E.75,141   T.74.95%

J. Grogan, *Lab.*	25,838
K. Hind, *C.*	22,002
E. Batty, *LD*	6,778
D. Walker, *Ref.*	1,162
P. Spence, *UK Ind.*	536

Lab. majority 3,836
(Boundary change: notional C.)

SEVENOAKS
E.66,474   T.75.44%

M. Fallon, *C.*	22,776
J. Hayes, *Lab.*	12,315
R. Walshe, *LD*	12,086
N. Large, *Ref.*	2,138
Ms M. Lawrence, *Green*	443
M. Ellis, *PF*	244
A. Hankey, *NLP*	147

C. majority 10,461
(Boundary change: notional C.)

SHEFFIELD ATTERCLIFFE
E.68,548   T.64.65%

*C. Betts, *Lab.*	28,937
B. Doyle, *C.*	7,119
Mrs G. Smith, *LD*	6,973
J. Brown, *Ref.*	1,289

Lab. majority 21,818
(April 1992, Lab. maj. 15,480)

SHEFFIELD BRIGHTSIDE
E.58,930   T.57.47%

*D. Blunkett, *Lab.*	24,901
F. Butler, *LD*	4,947
C. Buckwell, *C.*	2,850
B. Farnsworth, *Ref.*	624
P. Davidson, *Soc. Lab.*	482
R. Scott, *NLP*	61

Lab. majority 19,954
(April 1992, Lab. maj. 22,681)

SHEFFIELD CENTRAL
E.68,667   T.53.04%

†R. Caborn, *Lab.*	23,179
A. Qadar, *LD*	6,273
M. Hess, *C.*	4,341
A. D'Agorne, *Green*	954
A. Brownlow, *Ref.*	863
K. Douglas, *Soc.*	466
Ms M. Aitken, *ProLife*	280
M. Driver, *WRP*	63

Lab. majority 16,906
(Boundary change: notional Lab.)

SHEFFIELD HALLAM
E.62,834   T.72.38%

R. Allan, *LD*	23,345
†Sir I. Patnick, *C.*	15,074
S. Conquest, *Lab.*	6,147
I. Davidson, *Ref.*	788
P. Booler, *SIP*	125

LD majority 8,271
(Boundary change: notional C.)

SHEFFIELD HEELEY
E.66,599   T.64.96%

*W. Michie, *Lab.*	26,274
R. Davison, *LD*	9,196
J. Harthman, *C.*	6,767
D. Mawson, *Ref.*	1,029

Lab. majority 17,078
(April 1992, Lab. maj. 14,954)

SHEFFIELD HILLSBOROUGH
E.74,642   T.71.04%

*Mrs H. Jackson, *Lab.*	30,150
A. Dunworth, *LD*	13,699
D. Nuttall, *C.*	7,707
J. Rusling, *Ref.*	1,468

Lab. majority 16,451
(April 1992, Lab. maj. 7,068)

SHERWOOD
E.74,788   T.75.59%

*P. Tipping, *Lab.*	33,071
R. Spencer, *C.*	16,259
B. Moult, *LD*	4,889
L. Slack, *Ref.*	1,882
P. Ballard, *BNP*	432

Lab. majority 16,812
(April 1992, Lab. maj. 2,910)

SHIPLEY
E.69,281   T.76.32%

C. Leslie, *Lab.*	22,962
*Rt. Hon. Sir M. Fox, *C.*	19,966
J. Cole, *LD*	7,984
Dr S. Ellams, *Ref.*	1,960

Lab. majority 2,996
(April 1992, C. maj. 12,382)

SHREWSBURY AND ATCHAM
E.73,542   T.75.25%

P. Marsden, *Lab.*	20,484
*D. Conway, *C.*	18,814
Mrs A. Woolland, *LD*	13,838
D. Barker, *Ref.*	1,346
D. Rowlands, *UK Ind.*	477
A. Dignan, *CFSS*	257
A. Williams, *PPP*	128

Lab. majority 1,670
(April 1992, C. maj. 10,965)

SHROPSHIRE NORTH
E.70,852   T.72.71%

O. Paterson, *C.*	20,730
I. Lucas, *Lab.*	18,535
J. Stevens, *LD*	10,489
D. Allen, *Ref.*	1,764

C. majority 2,195
(Boundary change: notional C.)

SITTINGBOURNE AND SHEPPEY
E.63,850   T.72.30%

D. Wyatt, *Lab.*	18,723
†Sir R. Moate, *C.*	16,794
R. Truelove, *LD*	8,447
P. Moull, *Ref.*	1,082
C. Driver, *Loony*	644
N. Risi, *UK Ind.*	472

Lab. majority 1,929
(Boundary change: notional C.)

SKIPTON AND RIPON
E.72,042   T.75.44%

†Rt. Hon. D. Curry, *C.*	25,294
T. Mould, *LD*	13,674
R. Marchant, *Lab.*	12,171
Mrs N. Holdsworth, *Ref.*	3,212

C. majority 11,620
(Boundary change: notional C.)

SLEAFORD AND NORTH HYKEHAM
E.71,486   T.74.39%

†Rt. Hon. D. Hogg, *C.*	23,358
S. Harriss, *Lab.*	18,235
J. Marriott, *LD*	8,063
P. Clery, *Ref.*	2,942
R. Overton, *Ind.*	578

C. majority 5,123
(Boundary change: notional C.)

SLOUGH
E.70,283   T.67.91%

Ms F. MacTaggart, *Lab.*	27,029
Mrs P. Buscombe, *C.*	13,958
C. Bushill, *LD*	3,509
Ms A. Bradshaw, *Lib.*	1,835
T. Sharkey, *Ref.*	1,124
P. Whitmore, *Slough*	277

Lab. majority 13,071
(Boundary change: notional Lab.)

SOLIHULL
E.78,898   T.74.66%

†J. Taylor, C.	26,299
M. Southcombe, LD	14,902
Ms R. Harris, Lab.	14,334
M. Nattrass, Ref.	2,748
J. Caffery, ProLife	623

C. majority 11,397
(Boundary change: notional C.)

SOMERTON AND FROME
E.73,988   T.77.58%

D. Heath, LD	22,684
†M. Robinson, C.	22,554
R. Ashford, Lab.	9,385
R. Rodwell, Ref.	2,449
R. Gadd, UK Ind.	331

LD majority 130
(Boundary change: notional C.)

SOUTHAMPTON ITCHEN
E.76,869   T.70.06%

†J. Denham, Lab.	29,498
P. Fleet, C.	15,289
D. Harrison, LD	6,289
J. Clegg, Ref.	1,660
K. Rose, Soc. Lab.	628
C. Hoar, UK Ind.	172
G. Marsh, Soc.	113
Ms R. Barry, NLP	110
F. McDermott, ProLife	99

Lab. majority 14,209
(Boundary change: notional Lab.)

SOUTHAMPTON TEST
E.72,983   T.71.85%

A. Whitehead, Lab.	28,396
†Sir J. Hill, C.	14,712
A. Dowden, LD	7,171
P. Day, Ref.	1,397
H. Marks, LCP	388
A. McCabe, UK Ind.	219
P. Taylor, Glow	81
J. Sinel, NLP	77

Lab. majority 13,684
(Boundary change: notional Lab.)

SOUTHEND WEST
E.66,493   T.69.95%

†D. Amess, C.	18,029
Mrs N. Stimson, LD	15,414
A. Harley, Lab.	10,600
C. Webster, Ref.	1,734
B. Lee, UK Ind.	636
P. Warburton, NLP	101

C. majority 2,615
(April 1992, C. maj. 11,902)

SOUTH HOLLAND AND THE
DEEPINGS
E.69,642   T.71.98%

J. Hayes, C.	24,691
J. Lewis, Lab.	16,700
P. Millen, LD	7,836
G. Erwood, NPC	902

C. majority 7,991
(Boundary change: notional C.)

SOUTHPORT
E.70,194   T.72.08%

R. Fearn, LD	24,346
*M. Banks, C.	18,186
Ms S. Norman, Lab.	6,125

F. Buckle, Ref.	1,368
Ms S. Ashton, Lib.	386
E. Lines, NLP	93
M. Middleton, Nat. Dem.	92

LD majority 6,160
(April 1992, C. maj. 3,063)

SOUTH SHIELDS
E.62,261   T.62.60%

†Dr D. Clark, Lab.	27,834
M. Hoban, C.	5,681
D. Ord, LD	3,429
A. Loraine, Ref.	1,660
I. Wilburn, Shields	374

Lab. majority 22,153
(Boundary change: notional Lab.)

SOUTHWARK NORTH AND
BERMONDSEY
E.65,598   T.62.19%

†S. Hughes, LD	19,831
J. Fraser, Lab.	16,444
G. Shapps, C.	2,835
M. Davidson, BNP	713
W. Newton, Ref.	545
I. Grant, Comm L.	175
J. Munday, Lib.	157
Ms I. Yngvison, Nat. Dem.	95

LD majority 3,387
(Boundary change: notional LD)

SPELTHORNE
E.70,562   T.73.58%

*D. Wilshire, C.	23,306
K. Dibble, Lab.	19,833
E. Glynn, LD	6,821
B. Coleman, Ref.	1,495
J. Fowler, UK Ind.	462

C. majority 3,473
(April 1992, C. maj. 19,843)

STAFFORD
E.67,555   T.76.64%

D. Kidney, Lab.	24,606
D. Cameron, C.	20,292
Mrs P. Hornby, LD	5,480
S. Culley, Ref.	1,146
A. May, Loony	248

Lab. majority 4,314
(Boundary change: notional C.)

STAFFORDSHIRE MOORLANDS
E.66,095   T.77.34%

Ms C. Atkins, Lab.	26,686
Dr A. Ashworth, C.	16,637
Mrs C. Jebb, LD	6,191
D. Stanworth, Ref.	1,603

Lab. majority 10,049
(Boundary change: notional Lab.)

STAFFORDSHIRE SOUTH
E.68,896   T.74.19%

†Sir P. Cormack, C.	25,568
Ms J. LeMaistre, Lab.	17,747
Mrs J. Calder, LD	5,797
P. Carnell, Ref.	2,002

C. majority 7,821
(Boundary change: notional C.)

STALYBRIDGE AND HYDE
E.65,468   T.65.80%

†T. Pendry, Lab.	25,363
N. de Bois, C.	10,557

M. Cross, LD	5,169
R. Clapham, Ref.	1,992

Lab. majority 14,806
(Boundary change: notional Lab.)

STEVENAGE
E.66,889   T.76.82%

Ms B. Follett, Lab.	28,440
†T. Wood, C.	16,858
A. Wilcock, LD	4,588
J. Coburn, Ref.	1,194
D. Bundy, ProLife	196
A. Calcraft, NLP	110

Lab. majority 11,582
(Boundary change: notional C.)

STOCKPORT
E.65,232   T.71.54%

†Ms A. Coffey, Lab.	29,338
S. Fitzsimmons, C.	10,426
Mrs S. Roberts, LD	4,951
W. Morley-Scott, Ref.	1,280
G. Southern, Soc. Lab.	255
C. Newitt, Loony	213
C. Dronfield, Ind.	206

Lab. majority 18,912
(Boundary change: notional Lab.)

STOCKTON NORTH
E.64,380   T.69.08%

†F. Cook, Lab.	29,726
B. Johnston, C.	8,369
Mrs S. Fletcher, LD	4,816
K. McConnell, Ref.	1,563

Lab. majority 21,357
(Boundary change: notional Lab.)

STOCKTON SOUTH
E.68,470   T.76.12%

Ms D. Taylor, Lab.	28,790
†T. Devlin, C.	17,205
P. Monck, LD	4,721
J. Horner, Ref.	1,400

Lab. majority 11,585
(Boundary change: notional C.)

STOKE-ON-TRENT CENTRAL
E.64,113   T.62.77%

*M. Fisher, Lab.	26,662
N. Jones, C.	6,738
E. Fordham, LD	4,809
P. Stanyer, Ref.	1,071
M. Coleman, BNP	606
Ms F. Oborski, Lib.	359

Lab. majority 19,924
(April 1992, Lab. maj. 13,420)

STOKE-ON-TRENT NORTH
E.59,030   T.65.50%

†Ms J. Walley, Lab.	25,190
C. Day, C.	7,798
H. Jebb, LD	4,141
Ms J. Tobin, Ref.	1,537

Lab. majority 17,392
(Boundary change: notional Lab.)

STOKE-ON-TRENT SOUTH
E.69,968   T.66.08%

*G. Stevenson, Lab.	28,645
Mrs S. Scott, C.	10,342
P. Barnett, LD	4,710
R. Adams, Ref.	1,103
Mrs A. Micklem, Lib.	580

S. Batkin, *BNP* 568
B. Lawrence, *Nat. Dem.* 288
Lab. majority 18,303
(April 1992, Lab. maj. 6,909)

STONE
E.68,242 T.77.77%
†W. Cash, *C.* 24,859
J. Wakefield, *Lab.* 21,041
B. Stamp, *LD* 6,392
Ms A. Winfield, *Lib.* 545
Ms D. Grice, *NLP* 237
C. majority 3,818
(Boundary change: notional C.)

STOURBRIDGE
E.64,966 T.76.50%
Ms D. Shipley, *Lab.* 23,452
†W. Hawksley, *C.* 17,807
C. Bramall, *LD* 7,123
P. Quick, *Ref.* 1,319
Lab. majority 5,645
(Boundary change: notional C.)

STRATFORD-ON-AVON
E.81,434 T.76.26%
J. Maples, *C.* 29,967
Dr S. Juned, *LD* 15,861
S. Stacey, *Lab.* 12,754
A. Hilton, *Ref.* 2,064
J. Spilsbury, *UK Ind.* 556
J. Brewster, *NLP* 307
S. Marcus, *SFDC* 306
Ms S. Miller, *ProLife* 284
C. majority 14,106
(Boundary change: notional C.)

STREATHAM
E.74,509 T.60.24%
†K. Hill, *Lab.* 28,181
E. Noad, *C.* 9,758
R. O'Brien, *LD* 6,082
J. Wall, *Ref.* 864
Lab. majority 18,423
(Boundary change: notional Lab.)

STRETFORD AND URMSTON
E.69,913 T.69.65%
Ms B. Hughes, *Lab.* 28,480
J. Gregory, *C.* 14,840
J. Bridges, *LD* 3,978
Ms C. Dore, *Ref.* 1,397
Lab. majority 13,640
(Boundary change: notional Lab.)

STROUD
E.77,494 T.80.45%
D. Drew, *Lab. Co-op.* 26,170
†R. Knapman, *C.* 23,260
P. Hodgkinson, *LD* 9,502
J. Marjoram, *Green* 3,415
Lab. Co-op. majority 2,910
(Boundary change: notional C.)

SUFFOLK CENTRAL AND IPSWICH
NORTH
E.70,222 T.75.22%
†M. Lord, *C.* 22,493
Ms C. Jones, *Lab.* 18,955
Dr M. Goldspink, *LD* 10,886
Ms S. Bennell, *Ind.* 489
C. majority 3,538
(Boundary change: notional C.)

SUFFOLK COASTAL
E.74,219 T.75.80%
†Rt. Hon. J. Gummer, *C.* 21,696
M. Campbell, *Lab.* 18,442
Ms A. Jones, *LD* 12,036
S. Caulfield, *Ref.* 3,416
A. Slade, *Green* 514
Ms F. Kaplan, *NLP* 152
C. majority 3,254
(Boundary change: notional C.)

SUFFOLK SOUTH
E.67,323 T.77.20%
†T. Yeo, *C.* 19,402
P. Bishop, *Lab.* 15,227
Mrs K. Pollard, *LD* 14,395
C. de Chair, *Ref.* 2,740
Mrs A. Holland, *NLP* 211
C. majority 4,175
(Boundary change: notional C.)

SUFFOLK WEST
E.68,638 T.71.51%
†R. Spring, *C.* 20,081
M. Jefferys, *Lab.* 18,214
A. Graves, *LD* 6,892
J. Carver, *Ref.* 3,724
A. Shearer, *NLP* 171
C. majority 1,867
(Boundary change: notional C.)

SUNDERLAND NORTH
E.64,711 T.59.05%
†W. Etherington, *Lab.* 26,067
A. Selous, *C.* 6,370
G. Pryke, *LD* 3,973
M. Nicholson, *Ref.* 1,394
K. Newby, *Loony* 409
Lab. majority 19,697
(Boundary change: notional Lab.)

SUNDERLAND SOUTH
E.67,937 T.58.77%
†C. Mullin, *Lab.* 27,174
T. Schofield, *C.* 7,536
J. Lennox, *LD* 4,606
M. Wilkinson, *UK Ind.* 609
Lab. majority 19,638
(Boundary change: notional Lab.)

SURREY EAST
E.72,852 T.75.02%
†P. Ainsworth, *C.* 27,389
Ms B. Ford, *LD* 12,296
D. Ross, *Lab.* 11,573
M. Sydney, *Ref.* 2,656
A. Stone, *UK Ind.* 569
Ms S. Bartrum, *NLP* 173
C. majority 15,093
(Boundary change: notional C.)

SURREY HEATH
E.73,813 T.74.14%
†N. Hawkins, *C.* 28,231
D. Newman, *LD* 11,944
Ms S. Jones, *Lab.* 11,511
J. Gale, *Ref.* 2,385
R. Squire, *UK Ind.* 653
C. majority 16,287
(Boundary change: notional C.)

SURREY SOUTH WEST
E.72,350 T.78.03%
*Rt. Hon. Mrs V. Bottomley, *C.*
25,165
N. Sherlock, *LD* 22,471
Ms M. Leicester, *Lab.* 5,333
Mrs J. Clementson, *Ref.* 2,830
J. Kirby, *UK Ind.* 401
Ms J. Quintavalle, *ProLife* 258
C. majority 2,694
(April 1992, C. maj. 14,975)

SUSSEX MID
E.68,784 T.77.73%
†N. Soames, *C.* 23,231
Mrs M. Collins, *LD* 16,377
M. Hamilton, *Lab.* 9,969
T. Large, *Ref.* 3,146
J. Barnett, *UK Ind.* 606
E. Tudway, *Ind. JRP* 134
C. majority 6,854
(Boundary change: notional C.)

SUTTON AND CHEAM
E.62,785 T.75.01%
P. Burstow, *LD* 19,919
*Lady O. Maitland, *C.* 17,822
M. Allison, *Lab.* 7,280
P. Atkinson, *Ref.* 1,784
S. McKie, *UK Ind.* 191
Ms D. Wright, *NLP* 96
LD majority 2,097
(April 1992, C. maj. 10,756)

SUTTON COLDFIELD
E.71,864 T.72.92%
*Rt. Hon. Sir N. Fowler, *C.* 27,373
A. York, *Lab.* 12,488
J. Whorwood, *LD* 10,139
D. Hope, *Ref.* 2,401
C. majority 14,885
(April 1992, C. maj. 26,036)

SWINDON NORTH
E.65,535 T.73.66%
M. Wills, *Lab.* 24,029
G. Opperman, *C.* 16,341
M. Evemy, *LD* 6,237
Ms G. Goldsmith, *Ref.* 1,533
A. Fiskin, *NLP* 130
Lab. majority 7,688
(Boundary change: notional Lab.)

SWINDON SOUTH
E.70,207 T.72.87%
Ms J. Drown, *Lab.* 23,943
†S. Coombs, *C.* 18,298
S. Pajak, *LD* 7,371
D. Mackintosh, *Ref.* 1,273
R. Charman, *Route 66* 181
K. Buscombe, *NLP* 96
Lab. majority 5,645
(Boundary change: notional C.)

TAMWORTH
E.67,205 T.74.18%
†B. Jenkins, *Lab.* 25,808
Lady A. Lightbown, *C.* 18,312
Mrs J. Pinkett, *LD* 4,025
Mrs D. Livesey, *Ref.* 1,163
C. Lamb, *UK Ind.* 369
Ms C. Twelvetrees, *Lib.* 177

Lab. majority 7,496
(Boundary change: notional C.)

TATTON
*E.*63,822   *T.*76.45%
M. Bell, *Ind.*	29,354
†N. Hamilton, *C.*	18,277
S. Hill, *Ind.*	295
S. Kinsey, *Ind.*	187
B. Penhaul, *Miss M.*	128
J. Muir, *Albion*	126
M. Kennedy, *NLP*	123
D. Bishop, *Byro*	116
R. Nicholas, *Ind.*	113
J. Price, *Juice*	73

Ind. majority 11,077
(Boundary change: notional C.)

TAUNTON
*E.*79,783   *T.*76.47%
Mrs J. Ballard, *LD*	26,064
*D. Nicholson, *C.*	23,621
Ms E. Lisgo, *Lab.*	8,248
B. Ahern, *Ref.*	2,760
L. Andrews, *BNP*	318

LD majority 2,443
(April 1992, C. maj. 3,336)

TEIGNBRIDGE
*E.*81,667   *T.*77.08%
†P. Nicholls, *C.*	24,679
R. Younger-Ross, *LD*	24,398
Ms S. Dann, *Lab.*	11,311
S. Stokes, *UK Ind.*	1,601
N. Banwell, *Green*	817
Mrs L. Golding, *Dream*	139

C. majority 281
(Boundary change: notional C.)

TELFORD
*E.*56,558   *T.*65.62%
†B. Grocott, *Lab.*	21,456
B. Gentry, *C.*	10,166
N. Green, *LD*	4,371
C. Morris, *Ref.*	1,119

Lab. majority 11,290
(Boundary change: notional Lab.)

TEWKESBURY
*E.*68,208   *T.*76.46%
L. Robertson, *C.*	23,859
J. Sewell, *LD*	14,625
K. Tustin, *Lab.*	13,665

C. majority 9,234
(Boundary change: notional C.)

THANET NORTH
*E.*71,112   *T.*68.84%
*R. Gale, *C.*	21,586
Ms I. Johnston, *Lab.*	18,820
P. Kendrick, *LD*	5,576
M. Chambers, *Ref.*	2,535
Ms J. Haines, *UK Ind.*	438

C. majority 2,766
(April 1992, C. maj. 18,210)

THANET SOUTH
*E.*62,792   *T.*71.65%
Dr S. Ladyman, *Lab.*	20,777
†Rt. Hon. J. Aitken, *C.*	17,899
Ms B. Hewett-Silk, *LD*	5,263
C. Crook, *UK Ind.*	631
D. Wheatley, *Green*	418

Lab. majority 2,878
(Boundary change: notional C.)

THURROCK
*E.*71,600   *T.*65.94%
*A. MacKinlay, *Lab.*	29,896
A. Rosindell, *C.*	12,640
J. White, *LD*	3,843
P. Compobassi, *UK Ind.*	833

Lab. majority 17,256
(April 1992, Lab. maj. 1,172)

TIVERTON AND HONITON
*E.*75,744   *T.*78.06%
†Mrs A. Browning, *C.*	24,438
Dr J. Barnard, *LD*	22,785
J. King, *Lab.*	7,598
S. Lowings, *Ref.*	2,952
Mrs J. Roach, *Lib.*	635
Ms E. McIvor, *Green*	485
D. Charles, *Nat. Dem.*	236

C. majority 1,653
(Boundary change: notional C.)

TONBRIDGE AND MALLING
*E.*64,798   *T.*75.97%
†Rt. Hon. Sir J. Stanley, *C.*	23,640
Mrs B. Withstandley, *Lab.*	13,410
K. Brown, *LD*	9,467
J. Scrivenor, *Ref.*	2,005
Mrs B. Bullen, *UK Ind.*	502
G. Valente, *NLP*	205

C. majority 10,230
(Boundary change: notional C.)

TOOTING
*E.*66,653   *T.*69.17%
*T. Cox, *Lab.*	27,516
J. Hutchings, *C.*	12,505
S. James, *LD*	4,320
Mrs A. Husband, *Ref.*	829
J. Rattray, *Green*	527
P. Boddington, *BFAIR*	161
J. Koene, *Rights*	94
D. Bailey-Bond, *Dream*	83
P. Miller, *NLP*	70

Lab. majority 15,011
(April 1992, Lab. maj. 4,107)

TORBAY
*E.*72,258   *T.*73.79%
A. Sanders, *LD*	21,094
*R. Allason, *C.*	21,082
M. Morey, *Lab.*	7,923
G. Booth, *UK Ind.*	1,962
B. Cowling, *Lib.*	1,161
P. Wild, *Dream*	100

LD majority 12
(April 1992, C. maj. 5,787)

TOTNES
*E.*70,473   *T.*76.30%
†Sir A. Steen, *C.*	19,637
R. Chave, *LD*	18,760
V. Ellery, *Lab.*	8,796
Ms P. Cook, *Ref.*	2,552
C. Venmore, *Loc. C.*	2,369
H. Thomas, *UK Ind.*	999
A. Pratt, *Green*	548
J. Golding, *Dream*	108

C. majority 877
(Boundary change: notional C.)

TOTTENHAM
*E.*66,173   *T.*56.98%
*B. Grant, *Lab.*	26,121
A. Scantlebury, *C.*	5,921
N. Hughes, *LD*	4,064
P. Budge, *Green*	1,059
Ms E. Tay, *ProLife*	210
C. Anglin, *WRP*	181
Ms T. Kent, *SEP*	148

Lab. majority 20,200
(April 1992, Lab. maj. 11,968)

TRURO AND ST AUSTELL
*E.*76,824   *T.*73.87%
*M. Taylor, *LD*	27,502
N. Badcock, *C.*	15,001
M. Dooley, *Lab.*	8,697
C. Hearn, *Ref.*	3,682
A. Haithwaite, *UK Ind.*	576
Mrs D. Robinson, *Green*	482
D. Hicks, *MK*	450
Mrs L. Yelland, *PP*	240
P. Boland, *NLP*	117

LD majority 12,501
(April 1992, LD maj. 7,570)

TUNBRIDGE WELLS
*E.*65,259   *T.*74.10%
A. Norman, *C.*	21,853
A. Clayton, *LD*	14,347
P. Warner, *Lab.*	9,879
T. Macpherson, *Ref.*	1,858
M. Anderson Smart, *UK Ind.*	264
P. Levy, *NLP*	153

C. majority 7,506
(Boundary change: notional C.)

TWICKENHAM
*E.*73,281   *T.*79.34%
Dr V. Cable, *LD*	26,237
†T. Jessel, *C.*	21,956
Ms E. Tutchell, *Lab.*	9,065
Miss J. Harrison, *Ind. ECR*	589
T. Haggar, *Dream*	155
A. Hardy, *NLP*	142

LD majority 4,281
(Boundary change: notional C.)

TYNE BRIDGE
*E.*61,058   *T.*57.08%
†D. Clelland, *Lab.*	26,767
A. Lee, *C.*	3,861
Mrs M. Wallace, *LD*	2,785
G. Oswald, *Ref.*	919
Ms E. Brunskill, *Soc.*	518

Lab. majority 22,906
(Boundary change: notional Lab.)

TYNEMOUTH
*E.*66,341   *T.*77.11%
A. Campbell, *Lab.*	28,318
M. Callanan, *C.*	17,045
A. Duffield, *LD*	4,509
C. Rook, *Ref.*	819
Dr F. Rogers, *UK Ind.*	462

Lab. majority 11,273
(Boundary change: notional C.)

TYNESIDE NORTH
*E.*66,449   *T.*67.90%
†S. Byers, *Lab.*	32,810
M. McIntyre, *C.*	6,167
T. Mulvenna, *LD*	4,762

M. Rollings, *Ref.*   1,382
Lab. majority 26,643
(Boundary change: notional Lab.)

UPMINSTER
*E.*57,149   *T.*72.30%
K. Darvill, *Lab.*   19,085
†Sir N. Bonsor, *C.*   16,315
Mrs P. Peskett, *LD*   3,919
T. Murray, *Ref.*   2,000
Lab. majority 2,770
(Boundary change: notional C.)

UXBRIDGE
*E.*57,497   *T.*72.26%
†Sir M. Shersby, *C.*   18,095
D Williams, *Lab.*   17,371
Dr A. Malyan, *LD*   4,528
G. Aird, *Ref.*   1,153
Ms J. Leonard, *Soc.*   398
C. majority 724
(Boundary change: notional C.)
See also page 268

VALE OF YORK
*E.*70,077   *T.*76.01%
Miss A. McIntosh, *C.*   23,815
M. Carter, *Lab.*   14,094
C. Hall, *LD*   12,656
C. Fairclough, *Ref.*   2,503
A. Pelton, *Soc. Dem.*   197
C. majority 9,721
(Boundary change: notional C.)

VAUXHALL
*E.*70,402   *T.*55.49%
†Ms K. Hoey, *Lab.*   24,920
K. Kerr, *LD*   6,260
R. Bacon, *C.*   5,942
I. Driver, *Soc. Lab.*   983
S. Collins, *Green*   864
R. Headicar, *SPGB*   97
Lab. majority 18,660
(Boundary change: notional Lab.)

WAKEFIELD
*E.*73,210   *T.*68.96%
†D. Hinchliffe, *Lab.*   28,977
J. Peacock, *C.*   14,373
D. Dale, *LD*   5,656
S. Shires, *Ref.*   1,480
Lab. majority 14,604
(Boundary change: notional Lab.)

WALLASEY
*E.*63,714   *T.*73.52%
*Ms A. Eagle, *Lab.*   30,264
Mrs P. Wilcock, *C.*   11,190
P. Reisdorf, *LD*   3,899
R. Hayes, *Ref.*   1,490
Lab. majority 19,074
(April 1992, Lab. maj. 3,809)

WALSALL NORTH
*E.*67,587   *T.*64.07%
*D. Winnick, *Lab.*   24,517
M. Bird, *C.*   11,929
Ms T. O'Brien, *LD*   4,050
D. Bennett, *Ref.*   1,430
M. Pitt, *Ind.*   911
A. Humphries, *NF*   465
Lab. majority 12,588
(April 1992, Lab. maj. 3,824)

WALSALL SOUTH
*E.*64,221   *T.*67.33%
*B. George, *Lab.*   25,024
L. Leek, *C.*   13,712
H. Harris, *LD*   2,698
Dr T. Dent, *Ref.*   1,662
Mrs L. Meads, *NLP*   144
Lab. majority 11,312
(April 1992, Lab. maj. 3,178)

WALTHAMSTOW
*E.*63,818   *T.*62.76%
†N. Gerrard, *Lab.*   25,287
Mrs J. Andrew, *C.*   8,138
Dr J. Jackson, *LD*   5,491
Revd G. Hargreaves, *Ref.*   1,139
Lab. majority 17,149
(Boundary change: notional Lab.)

WANSBECK
*E.*62,998   *T.*71.70%
D. Murphy, *Lab.*   29,569
A. Thompson, *LD*   7,202
P. Green, *C.*   6,299
P. Gompertz, *Ref.*   1,146
Dr N. Best, *Green*   956
Lab. majority 22,367
(April 1992, Lab. maj. 18,174)

WANSDYKE
*E.*69,032   *T.*79.27%
D. Norris, *Lab.*   24,117
M. Prisk, *C.*   19,318
J. Manning, *LD*   9,205
K. Clinton, *Ref.*   1,327
T. Hunt, *UK Ind.*   438
P. House, *Loony*   225
Ms S. Lincoln, *NLP*   92
Lab. majority 4,799
(Boundary change: notional C.)

WANTAGE
*E.*71,657   *T.*78.23%
*R. Jackson, *C.*   22,311
Ms C. Wilson, *Lab.*   16,272
Ms J. Riley, *LD*   14,822
S. Rising, *Ref.*   1,549
Ms M. Kennet, *Green*   640
Count N. Tolstoy-Miloslausky,
    UK Ind.   465
C. majority 6,039
(April 1992, C. maj. 16,473)

WARLEY
*E.*59,758   *T.*65.08%
†J. Spellar, *Lab.*   24,813
C. Pincher, *C.*   9,362
J. Pursehouse, *LD*   3,777
K. Gamre, *Ref.*   941
Lab. majority 15,451
(Boundary change: notional Lab.)

WARRINGTON NORTH
*E.*72,694   *T.*70.50%
Ms H. Jones, *Lab.*   31,827
Ms R. Lacey, *C.*   12,300
I. Greenhalgh, *LD*   5,308
Dr A. Smith, *Ref.*   1,816
Lab. majority 19,527
(Boundary change: notional Lab.)

WARRINGTON SOUTH
*E.*72,262   *T.*76.23%
Ms H. Southworth, *Lab.*   28,721
C. Grayling, *C.*   17,914
P. Walker, *LD*   7,199
G. Kelly, *Ref.*   1,082
S. Ross, *NLP*   166
Lab. majority 10,807
(Boundary change: notional C.)

WARWICK AND LEAMINGTON
*E.*79,374   *T.*75.71%
J. Plaskitt, *Lab.*   26,747
†Sir D. Smith, *C.*   23,349
N. Hicks, *LD*   7,133
Mrs V. Davis, *Ref.*   1,484
P Raprie, *Green*   764
G. Warwick, *UK Ind.*   306
M. Gibbs, *EDP*   183
R. McCarthy, *NLP*   125
Lab. majority 3,398
(Boundary change: notional C.)

WARWICKSHIRE NORTH
*E.*72,602   *T.*74.71%
†M. O'Brien, *Lab.*   31,669
S. Hammond, *C.*   16,902
W. Powell, *LD*   4,040
R. Mole, *Ref.*   917
C. Cooke, *UK Ind.*   533
I. Moorecroft, *Bert.*   178
Lab. majority 14,767
(Boundary change: notional Lab.)

WATFORD
*E.*74,015   *T.*74.63%
Ms C. Ward, *Lab.*   25,019
R. Gordon, *C.*   19,227
A. Canning, *LD*   9,272
Dr P. Roe, *Ref.*   1,484
L. Davis, *NLP*   234
Lab. majority 5,792
(Boundary change: notional C.)

WAVENEY
*E.*75,266   *T.*75.21%
R. Blizzard, *Lab.*   31,846
†D. Porter, *C.*   19,393
C. Thomas, *LD*   5,054
N. Clark, *Ind.*   318
Lab. majority 12,453
(Boundary change: notional C.)

WEALDEN
*E.*79,519   *T.*74.32%
†Rt. Hon. Sir G. Johnson Smith,
    C.   29,417
M. Skinner, *LD*   15,213
N. Levine, *Lab.*   10,185
B. Taplin, *Ref.*   3,527
Mrs M. English, *UK Ind.*   569
P. Cragg, *NLP*   188
C. majority 14,204
(Boundary change: notional C.)

WEAVER VALE
*E.*66,011   *T.*73.17%
†M. Hall, *Lab.*   27,244
J. Byrne, *C.*   13,796
T. Griffiths, *LD*   5,949
R. Cockfield, *Ref.*   1,312
Lab. majority 13,448
(Boundary change: notional Lab.)

WELLINGBOROUGH
E.74,955   *T*.75.10%

P. Stinchcombe, *Lab.*	24,854
*Sir P. Fry, *C.*	24,667
P. Smith, *LD*	5,279
A. Ellwood, *UK Ind.*	1,192
Ms A. Lowrys, *NLP*	297

Lab. majority 187
(April 1992, C. maj. 11,816)

WELLS
E.72,178   *T*.78.11%

*Rt. Hon. D. Heathcoat-Amory, *C.*	22,208
Dr P. Gold, *LD*	21,680
M. Eavis, *Lab.*	10,204
Mrs P. Phelps, *Ref.*	2,196
Ms L. Royse, *NLP*	92

C. majority 528
(April 1992, C. maj. 6,649)

WELWYN HATFIELD
E.67,395   *T*.78.59%

Ms M. Johnson, *Lab.*	24,936
†D. Evans, *C.*	19,341
R. Schwartz, *LD*	7,161
E. Cox, *RA*	1,263
Ms H. Harold, *ProLife*	267

Lab. majority 5,595
(Boundary change: notional C.)

WENTWORTH
E.63,951   *T*.65.33%

J. Healey, *Lab.*	30,225
K. Hamer, *C.*	6,266
J. Charters, *LD*	3,867
A. Battley, *Ref.*	1,423

Lab. majority 23,959
(April 1992, Lab. maj. 22,449)

WEST BROMWICH EAST
E.63,401   *T*.65.44%

†P. Snape, *Lab.*	23,710
B. Matsell, *C.*	10,126
M. Smith, *LD*	6,179
G. Mulley, *Ref.*	1,472

Lab. majority 13,584
(Boundary change: notional Lab.)

WEST BROMWICH WEST
E.67,496   *T*.54.37%

†Rt. Hon. Miss B. Boothroyd, *Speaker*	23,969
R. Silvester, *Lab. Change*	8,546
S. Edwards, *Nat. Dem.*	4,181

Speaker majority 15,423
(Boundary change: notional Lab.)

WESTBURY
E.74,301   *T*.76.38%

†D. Faber, *C.*	23,037
J. Miller, *LD*	16,969
K. Small, *Lab.*	11,969
G. Hawkins, *Lib.*	1,956
N. Hawkings-Byass, *Ref.*	1,909
R. Westbury, *UK Ind.*	771
C. Haysom, *NLP*	140

C. majority 6,068
(Boundary change: notional C.)

WEST HAM
E.57,058   *T*.58.99%

†A. Banks, *Lab.*	24,531

M. MacGregor, *C.*	5,037
Ms S. McDonough, *LD*	2,479
K. Francis, *BNP*	1,198
T. Jug, *Loony*	300
J. Rainbow, *Dream*	116

Lab. majority 19,494
(Boundary change: notional Lab.)

WESTMORLAND AND LONSDALE
E.68,389   *T*.74.29%

T. Collins, *C.*	21,470
S. Collins, *LD*	16,949
J. Harding, *Lab.*	10,459
M. Smith, *Ref.*	1,931

C. majority 4,521
(Boundary change: notional C.)

WESTON-SUPER-MARE
E.72,445   *T*.73.68%

B. Cotter, *LD*	21,407
Mrs M. Daly, *C.*	20,133
D. Kraft, *Lab.*	9,557
T. Sewell, *Ref.*	2,280

LD majority 1,274
(Boundary change: notional C.)

WIGAN
E.64,689   *T*.67.74%

†R. Stott, *Lab.*	30,043
M. Loveday, *C.*	7,400
T. Beswick, *LD*	4,390
A. Bradborne, *Ref.*	1,450
C. Maile, *Green*	442
W. Ayliffe, *NLP*	94

Lab. majority 22,643
(Boundary change: notional Lab.)

WILTSHIRE NORTH
E.77,237   *T*.75.11%

J. Gray, *C.*	25,390
S. Cordon, *LD*	21,915
N. Knowles, *Lab.*	8,261
Ms M. Purves, *Ref.*	1,774
A. Wood, *UK Ind.*	410
Ms J. Forsyth, *NLP*	263

C. majority 3,475
(Boundary change: notional C.)

WIMBLEDON
E.64,070   *T*.75.47%

R. Casale, *Lab.*	20,674
*Dr C. Goodson-Wickes, *C.*	17,694
Ms A. Willott, *LD*	8,014
H. Abid, *Ref.*	993
R. Thacker, *Green*	474
Ms S. Davies, *ProLife*	346
M. Kirby, *Mongolian*	112
G. Stacey, *Dream*	47

Lab. majority 2,980
(April 1992, C. maj. 14,761)

WINCHESTER
E.78,884   *T*.78.66%

M. Oaten, *LD*	26,100
†G. Malone, *C.*	26,098
P. Davies, *Lab.*	6,528
P. Strand, *Ref.*	1,598
R. Huggett, *Top*	640
D. Rumsey, *UK Ind.*	476
J. Browne, *Ind. AFE*	307
P. Stockton, *Loony*	307

LD majority 2
(Boundary change: notional C.)

WINDSOR
E.69,132   *T*.73.46%

†M. Trend, *C.*	24,476
C. Fox, *LD*	14,559
Mrs A. Williams, *Lab.*	9,287
J. McDermott, *Ref.*	1,676
P. Bradshaw, *Lib.*	388
Mrs E. Bigg, *UK Ind.*	302
Mr R. Parr, *Dynamic*	93

C. majority 9,917
(Boundary change: notional C.)

WIRRAL SOUTH
E.59,372   *T*.81.01%

†B. Chapman, *Lab.*	24,499
L. Byrom, *C.*	17,495
P. Gilchrist, *LD*	5,018
D. Wilcox, *Ref.*	768
Ms J. Nielsen, *ProLife*	264
G. Mead, *NLP*	51

Lab. majority 7,004
(Boundary change: notional C.)

WIRRAL WEST
E.60,908   *T*.76.98%

S. Hesford, *Lab.*	21,035
*Rt. Hon. D. Hunt, *C.*	18,297
J. Thornton, *LD*	5,945
D. Wharton, *Ref.*	1,613

Lab. majority 2,738
(April 1992, C. maj. 11,064)

WITNEY
E.73,520   *T*.76.72%

S. Woodward, *C.*	24,282
A. Hollingsworth, *Lab.*	17,254
Mrs A. Lawrence, *LD*	11,202
G. Brown, *Ref.*	2,262
M. Montgomery, *UK Ind.*	765
Ms S. Chapple-Perrie, *Green*	636

C. majority 7,028
(Boundary change: notional C.)

WOKING
E.70,053   *T*.72.68%

H. Malins, *C.*	19,553
P. Goldenberg, *LD*	13,875
Ms K. Hanson, *Lab.*	10,695
H. Bell, *Ind. C.*	3,933
C. Skeate, *Ref.*	2,209
M. Harvey, *UK Ind.*	512
Miss D. Sleeman, *NLP*	137

C. majority 5,678
(Boundary change: notional C.)

WOKINGHAM
E.66,161   *T*.75.74%

†Rt. Hon. J. Redwood, *C.*	25,086
Dr R. Longton, *LD*	15,721
Ms P. Colling, *Lab.*	8,424
P. Owen, *Loony*	877

C. majority 9,365
(Boundary change: notional C.)

WOLVERHAMPTON NORTH EAST
E.61,642   *T*.67.17%

K. Purchase, *Lab. Co-op.*	24,534
D. Harvey, *C.*	11,547
B. Niblett, *LD*	2,214
C. Hallmark, *Lib.*	1,560
A. Muchall, *Ref.*	1,192
M. Wingfield, *Nat. Dem.*	356

Lab. Co-op. majority 12,987

(Boundary change: notional Lab. Co-op.)

Wolverhampton South East
E.54,291 T.64.15%
*D. Turner, *Lab. Co-op.*	22,202
W. Hanbury, *C.*	7,020
R. Whitehouse, *LD*	3,292
T. Stevenson-Platt, *Ref.*	980
N. Worth, *Soc. Lab.*	689
K. Bullman, *Lib.*	647

Lab. Co-op. majority 15,182
(April 1992, Lab. maj. 10,240)

Wolverhampton South West
E.67,482 T.72.49%
Ms J. Jones, *Lab.*	24,657
*N. Budgen, *C.*	19,539
M. Green, *LD*	4,012
M. Hyde, *Lib.*	713

Lab. majority 5,118
(April 1992, C. maj. 4,966)

Woodspring
E.69,964 T.78.51%
†Dr L. Fox, *C.*	24,425
Mrs N. Kirsen, *LD*	16,691
Ms D. Sander, *Lab.*	11,377
R. Hughes, *Ref.*	1,614
Dr R. Lawson, *Green*	667
A. Glover, *Ind.*	101
M. Mears, *NLP*	52

C. majority 7,734
(Boundary change: notional C.)

Worcester
E.69,234 T.74.56%
M. Foster, *Lab.*	25,848
N. Bourne, *C.*	18,423
P. Chandler, *LD*	6,462
Mrs P. Wood, *UK Ind.*	886

Lab. majority 7,425
(Boundary change: notional C.)

Worcestershire Mid
E.68,381 T.74.32%
†P. Luff, *C.*	24,092
Mrs D. Smith, *Lab.*	14,680
D. Barwick, *LD*	9,458
T. Watson, *Ref.*	1,780
D. Ingles, *UK Ind.*	646
A. Dyer, *NLP*	163

C. majority 9,412
(Boundary change: notional C.)

Worcestershire West
E.64,712 T.76.25%
†Sir M. Spicer, *C.*	22,223
M. Hadley, *LD*	18,377

N. Stone, *Lab.* 7,738
Ms S. Cameron, *Green* 1,006
C. majority 3,846
(Boundary change: notional C.)

Workington
E.65,766 T.75.08%
†D. Campbell-Savours, *Lab.*	31,717
R. Blunden, *C.*	12,061
P. Roberts, *LD*	3,967
G. Donnan, *Ref.*	1,412
C. Austin, *UA*	217

Lab. majority 19,656
(Boundary change: notional Lab.)

Worsley
E.68,978 T.67.82%
|T. Lewis, *Lab.*	29,083
D. Garrido, *C.*	11,342
R. Bleakley, *LD*	6,356

Lab. majority 17,741
(Boundary change: notional Lab.)

Worthing East and Shoreham
E.70,771 T.72.87%
T. Loughton, *C.*	20,864
M. King, *LD*	15,766
M. Williams, *Lab.*	12,335
J. McCulloch, *Ref.*	1,683
Mrs R. Jarvis, *UK Ind.*	921

C. majority 5,098
(Boundary change: notional C.)

Worthing West
E.71,329 T.72.12%
†P. Bottomley, *C.*	23,733
C. Hare, *LD*	16,020
J. Adams, *Lab.*	8,347
N. John, *Ref.*	2,313
T. Cross, *UK Ind.*	1,029

C. majority 7,713
(Boundary change: notional C.)

Wrekin, The
E.59,126 T.76.56%
P. Bradley, *Lab.*	21,243
P. Bruinvels, *C.*	18,218
I. Jenkins, *LD*	5,807

Lab. majority 3,025
(Boundary change: notional C.)

Wycombe
E.73,589 T.71.10%
†Sir R. Whitney, *C.*	20,890
C. Bryant, *Lab.*	18,520
P. Bensilum, *LD*	9,678
A. Fulford, *Ref.*	2,394
J. Laker, *Green*	716
M. Heath, *NLP*	121

C. majority 2,370
(Boundary change: notional C.)

Wyre Forest
E.73,063 T.75.35%
D. Lock, *Lab.*	26,843
†A. Coombs, *C.*	19,897
D. Cropp, *LD*	4,377
W. Till, *Ref.*	1,956
C. Harvey, *Lib.*	1,670
J. Millington, *UK Ind.*	312

Lab. majority 6,946
(Boundary change: notional C.)

Wythenshawe and Sale East
E.71,986 T.63.25%
P. Goggins, *Lab.*	26,448
P. Fleming, *C.*	11,429
Ms V. Tucker, *LD*	5,639
B. Stanyer, *Ref.*	1,060
J. Flannery, *Soc. Lab.*	957

Lab. majority 15,019
(Boundary change: notional Lab.)

Yeovil
E.74,165 T.72.88%
†Rt. Hon. J. D. D. Ashdown, *LD*	26,349
N. Cambrook, *C.*	14,946
P. Conway, *Lab.*	8,053
J. Beveridge, *Ref.*	3,574
D. Taylor, *Green*	728
J. Archer, *Musician*	306
C. Hudson, *Dream*	97

LD majority 11,403
(Boundary change: notional LD)

York, City Of
E.79,383 T.73.50%
*H. Bayley, *Lab.*	34,956
S. Mallett, *C.*	14,433
A. Waller, *LD*	6,537
J. Sheppard, *Ref.*	1,083
M. Hill, *Green*	880
E. Wegener, *UK Ind.*	319
A. Lightfoot, *Ch. Nat.*	137

Lab. majority 20,523
(April 1992, Lab. maj. 6,342)

Yorkshire East
E.69,409 T.70.55%
†J. Townend, *C.*	20,904
I. Male, *Lab.*	17,567
D. Leadley, *LD*	9,070
R. Allerston, *Soc. Dem.*	1,049
M. Cooper, *Nat. Dem.*	381

C. majority 3,337
(Boundary change: notional C.)

WALES

Aberavon
E.50,025 T.71.89%
*Rt. Hon. J. Morris, *Lab.*	25,650
R. McConville, *LD*	4,079
P. Harper, *C.*	2,835
P. Cockwell, *PC*	2,088
P. David, *Ref.*	970
Capt. Beany, *Beanus*	341

Lab. majority 21,571
(April 1992, Lab. maj. 21,310)

Alyn and Deeside
E.58,091 T.72.21%
†B. Jones, *Lab.*	25,955
T. Roberts, *C.*	9,552
Mrs E. Burnham, *LD*	4,076
M. Jones, *Ref.*	1,627

Mrs S. Hills, *PC* 738
Lab. majority 16,403
(Boundary change: notional Lab.)

Blaenau Gwent
E.54,800 T.72.32%
*L. Smith, *Lab.*	31,493
Mrs G. Layton, *LD*	3,458
Mrs M. Williams, *C.*	2,607

J. Criddle, *PC* 2,072
Lab. majority 28,035
(April 1992, Lab. maj. 30,067)

BRECON AND RADNORSHIRE
*E.*52,142   *T.*82.24%
R. Livsey, *LD* 17,516
*J. Evans, *C.* 12,419
C. Mann, *Lab.* 11,424
Ms E. Phillips, *Ref.* 900
S. Cornelius, *PC* 622
LD majority 5,097
(April 1992, C. maj. 130)

BRIDGEND
*E.*59,721   *T.*72.44%
*W. Griffiths, *Lab.* 25,115
D. Davies, *C.* 9,867
A. McKinlay, *LD* 4,968
T. Greaves, *Ref.* 1,662
D. Watkins, *PC* 1,649
Lab. majority 15,248
(April 1992, Lab. maj. 7,326)

CAERNARFON
*E.*46,815   *T.*72.65%
*D. Wigley, *PC* 17,616
E. Williams, *Lab.* 9,667
E. Williams, *C.* 4,230
Ms M. McQueen, *LD* 1,686
C. Collins, *Ref.* 811
PC majority 7,949
(April 1992, PC maj. 14,476)

CAERPHILLY
*E.*64,621   *T.*70.05%
*R. Davies, *Lab.* 30,697
R. Harris, *C.* 4,858
L. Whittle, *PC* 4,383
A. Ferguson, *LD* 3,724
M. Morgan, *Ref.* 1,337
Mrs C. Williams, *ProLife* 270
Lab. majority 25,839
(April 1992, Lab. maj. 22,672)

CARDIFF CENTRAL
*E.*60,354   *T.*70.01%
*J. Owen Jones, *Lab. Co-op.* 18,464
Mrs J. Randerson, *LD* 10,541
D. Melding, *C.* 8,470
T. Burns, *Soc. Lab.* 2,230
W. Vernon, *PC* 1,504
N. Lloyd, *Ref.* 760
C. James, *Loony* 204
A. Hobbs, *NLP* 80
Lab. Co-op. majority 7,923
(April 1992, Lab. maj. 3,465)

CARDIFF NORTH
*E.*60,430   *T.*80.24%
Ms J. Morgan, *Lab.* 24,460
*G. Jones, *C.* 16,334
R. Rowland, *LD* 5,294
Dr C. Palfrey, *PC* 1,201
E. Litchfield, *Ref.* 1,199
Lab. majority 8,126
(April 1992, C. maj. 2,969)

CARDIFF SOUTH AND PENARTH
*E.*61,838   *T.*68.57%
*A. Michael, *Lab. Co-op.* 22,647
Mrs C. Roberts, *C.* 8,766
Dr S. Wakefield, *LD* 3,964

J. Foreman, *New Lab.* 3,942
D. Haswell, *PC* 1,356
P. Morgan, *Ref.* 1,211
M. Shepherd, *Soc.* 344
Ms B. Caves, *NLP* 170
Lab. Co-op. majority 13,881
(April 1992, Lab. maj. 10,425)

CARDIFF WEST
*E.*58,198   *T.*69.21%
†R. Morgan, *Lab.* 24,297
S. Hoare, *C.* 8,669
Ms J. Gasson, *LD* 4,366
Ms G. Carr, *PC* 1,949
T. Johns, *Ref.* 996
Lab. majority 15,628
(Boundary change: notional Lab.)

CARMARTHEN EAST AND DINEFWR
*E.*53,079   *T.*78.62%
†Dr A. Wynne Williams, *Lab.* 17,907
R. Thomas, *PC* 14,457
E. Hayward, *C.* 5,022
Mrs J. Hughes, *LD* 3,150
I. Humphreys-Evans, *Ref.* 1,196
Lab. majority 3,450
(Boundary change: notional Lab.)

CARMARTHEN WEST AND
PEMBROKESHIRE SOUTH
*E.*55,724   *T.*76.52%
†N. Ainger, *Lab.* 20,956
O. J. Williams, *C.* 11,335
R. Llewellyn, *PC* 5,402
K. Evans, *LD* 3,516
Mrs J. Poirrier, *Ref.* 1,432
Lab. majority 9,621
(Boundary change: notional Lab.)

CEREDIGION
*E.*54,378   *T.*73.90%
†C. Dafis, *PC* 16,728
R. Harris, *Lab.* 9,767
D. Davies, *LD* 6,616
Dr F. Aubel, *C.* 5,983
J. Leaney, *Ref.* 1,092
PC majority 6,961
(Boundary change: notional PC)

CLWYD SOUTH
*E.*53,495   *T.*73.62%
†M. Jones, *Lab.* 22,901
B. Johnson, *C.* 9,091
A. Chadwick, *LD* 3,684
G. Williams, *PC* 2,500
A. Lewis, *Ref.* 1,207
Lab. majority 13,810
(Boundary change: notional Lab.)

CLWYD WEST
*E.*53,467   *T.*75.29%
G. Thomas, *Lab.* 14,918
†R. Richards, *C.* 13,070
E. Williams, *PC* 5,421
G. Williams, *LD* 5,151
Ms H. Collins, *Ref.* 1,114
D. Neal, *Cvty* 583
Lab. majority 1,848
(Boundary change: notional C.)

CONWY
*E.*55,092   *T.*75.44%
Mrs B. Williams, *Lab.* 14,561

R. Roberts, *LD* 12,965
D. Jones, *C.* 10,085
R. Davies, *PC* 2,844
A. Barham, *Ref.* 760
R. Bradley, *Alt. LD* 250
D. Hughes, *NLP* 95
Lab. majority 1,596
(April 1992, C. maj. 995)

CYNON VALLEY
*E.*48,286   *T.*69.22%
*Mrs A. Clwyd, *Lab.* 23,307
A. Davies, *PC* 3,552
H. Price, *LD* 3,459
A. Smith, *C.* 2,262
G. John, *Ref.* 844
Lab. majority 19,755
(April 1992, Lab. maj. 21,364)

DELYN
*E.*53,693   *T.*74.02%
†D. Hanson, *Lab.* 22,300
Mrs K. Lumley, *C.* 10,607
P. Lloyd, *LD* 4,160
A. Drake, *PC* 1,558
Ms E. Soutter, *Ref.* 1,117
Lab. majority 11,693
(Boundary change: notional Lab.)

GOWER
*E.*57,691   *T.*75.12%
M. Caton, *Lab.* 23,313
A. Cairns, *C.* 10,306
H. Evans, *LD* 5,624
E. Williams, *PC* 2,226
R. Lewis, *Ref.* 1,745
A. Popham, *FP* 122
Lab. majority 13,007
(April 1992, Lab. maj. 7,018)

ISLWYN
*E.*50,540   *T.*72.03%
*D. Touhig, *Lab. Co-op.* 26,995
C. Worker, *LD* 3,064
R. Walters, *C.* 2,864
D. Jones, *PC* 2,272
Mrs S. Monaghan, *Ref.* 1,209
Lab. Co-op. majority 23,931
(April 1992, Lab. maj. 24,728)
(Feb. 1995, Lab. maj. 13,097)

LLANELLI
*E.*58,323   *T.*70.66%
†Rt. Hon. D. Davies, *Lab.* 23,851
M. Phillips, *PC* 7,812
A. Hayes, *C.* 5,003
N. Burree, *LD* 3,788
J. Willock, *Soc. Lab.* 757
Lab. majority 16,039
(Boundary change: notional Lab.)

MEIRIONNYDD NANT CONWY
*E.*32,345   *T.*75.98%
*E. Llwyd, *PC* 12,465
H. Rees, *Lab.* 5,660
J. Quin, *C.* 3,922
Mrs B. Feeley, *LD* 1,719
P. Hodge, *Ref.* 809
PC majority 6,805
(April 1992, PC maj. 4,613)

MERTHYR TYDFIL AND RHYMNEY
*E.*56,507   *T.*69.27%

*T. Rowlands, *Lab.* — 30,012
D. Anstey, *LD* — 2,926
J. Morgan, *C.* — 2,508
A. Cox, *PC* — 2,344
A. Cowdell, *Old Lab.* — 691
R. Hutchings, *Ref.* — 660
Lab. majority 27,086
(April 1992, Lab. maj. 26,713)

MONMOUTH
*E.*60,703   *T.*80.76%
H. Edwards, *Lab.* — 23,404
*R. Evans, *C.* — 19,226
M. Williams, *LD* — 4,689
N. Warry, *Ref.* — 1,190
A. Cotton, *PC* — 516
Lab. majority 4,178
(April 1992, C. maj. 3,204)

MONTGOMERYSHIRE
*E.*42,618   *T.*74.91%
L. Opik, *LD* — 14,647
G. Davies, *C.* — 8,344
Ms A. Davies, *Lab.* — 6,109
Ms H. M. Jones, *PC* — 1,608
J. Bufton, *Ref.* — 879
Ms S. Walker, *Green* — 338
LD majority 6,303
(April 1992, LD maj. 5,209)

NEATH
*E.*55,525   *T.*74.28%
*P. Hain, *Lab.* — 30,324
D. Evans, *C.* — 3,583
T. Jones, *PC* — 3,344
F. Little, *LD* — 2,597
P. Morris, *Ref.* — 975
H. Marks, *LCP* — 420
Lab. majority 26,741
(April 1992, Lab. maj. 23,975)

NEWPORT EAST
*E.*50,997   *T.*73.06%
†A. Howarth, *Lab.* — 21,481
D. Evans, *C.* — 7,958
A. Cameron, *LD* — 3,880
A. Scargill, *Soc. Lab.* — 1,951
G. Davis, *Ref.* — 1,267
C. Holland, *PC* — 721
Lab. majority 13,523
(April 1992, Lab. maj. 9,899)

NEWPORT WEST
*E.*53,914   *T.*74.57%
*P. Flynn, *Lab.* — 24,331
P. Clarke, *C.* — 9,794
S. Wilson, *LD* — 3,907
C. Thompsett, *Ref.* — 1,199
H. Jackson, *PC* — 648
H. Moelwyn Hughes, *UK Ind.* — 323

Lab. majority 14,537
(April 1992, Lab. maj. 7,779)

OGMORE
*E.*52,078   *T.*73.10%
*Sir R. Powell, *Lab.* — 28,163
D. Unwin, *C.* — 3,716
Ms K. Williams, *LD* — 3,510
J. Rogers, *PC* — 2,679
Lab. majority 24,447
(April 1992, Lab. maj. 23,827)

PONTYPRIDD
*E.*64,185   *T.*71.44%
*Dr K. Howells, *Lab.* — 29,290
N. Howells, *LD* — 6,161
J. Cowen, *C.* — 5,910
O. Llewelyn, *PC* — 2,977
J. Wood, *Ref.* — 874
P. Skelly, *Soc. Lab.* — 380
R. Griffiths, *Comm. P.* — 178
A. Moore, *NLP* — 85
Lab. majority 23,129
(April 1992, Lab. maj. 19,797)

PRESELI PEMBROKESHIRE
*E.*54,088   *T.*78.40%
Mrs J. Lawrence, *Lab.* — 20,477
R. Buckland, *C.* — 11,741
J. Clarke, *LD* — 5,527
A. Lloyd Jones, *PC* — 2,683
D. Berry, *Ref.* — 1,574
Ms M. Scott Cato, *Green* — 401
Lab. majority 8,736
(Boundary change: notional C.)

RHONDDA
*E.*57,105   *T.*71.46%
*A. Rogers, *Lab.* — 30,381
Ms L. Wood, *PC* — 5,450
Dr R. Berman, *LD* — 2,307
S. Whiting, *C.* — 1,331
S. Gardiner, *Ref.* — 658
K. Jakeway, *Green* — 460
Lab. majority 24,931
(April 1992, Lab. maj. 28,816)

SWANSEA EAST
*E.*57,373   *T.*67.41%
*D. Anderson, *Lab.* — 29,151
Ms C. Dibble, *C.* — 3,582
E. Jones, *LD* — 3,440
Ms M. Pooley, *PC* — 1,308
Ms C. Maggs, *Ref.* — 904
R. Job, *Soc.* — 289
Lab. majority 25,569
(April 1992, Lab. maj. 23,482)

SWANSEA WEST
*E.*58,703   *T.*68.94%

*Rt. Hon. A. Williams, *Lab.* — 22,748
A. Baker, *C.* — 8,289
J. Newbury, *LD* — 5,872
D. Lloyd, *PC* — 2,675
D. Proctor, *Soc. Lab.* — 885
Lab. majority 14,459
(April 1992, Lab. maj. 9,478)

TORFAEN
*E.*60,343   *T.*71.67%
*P. Murphy, *Lab.* — 29,863
N. Parish, *C.* — 5,327
Ms J. Gray, *LD* — 5,249
Ms D. Holler, *Ref.* — 1,245
R. Gough, *PC* — 1,042
R. Coghill, *Green* — 519
Lab. majority 24,536
(April 1992, Lab. maj. 20,754)

VALE OF CLWYD
*E.*52,418   *T.*74.65%
C. Ruane, *Lab.* — 20,617
D. Edwards, *C.* — 11,662
D. Munford, *LD* — 3,425
Ms G. Kensler, *PC* — 2,301
S. Vickers, *Ref.* — 834
S. Cooke, *UK Ind.* — 293
Lab. majority 8,955
(Boundary change: notional C.)

VALE OF GLAMORGAN
*E.*67,213   *T.*80.21%
J. Smith, *Lab.* — 29,054
†W. Sweeney, *C.* — 18,522
Mrs S. Campbell, *LD* — 4,945
Ms M. Corp, *PC* — 1,393
Lab. majority 10,532
(Boundary change: notional C.)

WREXHAM
*E.*50,741   *T.*71.78%
Dr J. Marek, *Lab.* — 20,450
S. Andrew, *C.* — 8,688
A. Thomas, *LD* — 4,833
J. Cronk, *Ref.* — 1,195
K. Plant, *PC* — 1,170
N. Low, *NLP* — 86
Lab. majority 11,762
(Boundary change: notional Lab.)

YNYS MÔN
*E.*52,952   *T.*75.41%
*I. Wyn Jones, *PC* — 15,756
O. Edwards, *Lab.* — 13,275
G. Owen, *C.* — 8,569
D. Burnham, *LD* — 1,537
H. Gray Morris, *Ref.* — 793
PC majority 2,481
(April 1992, PC maj. 1,106)

SCOTLAND

ABERDEEN CENTRAL
*E.*54,257   *T.*65.64%
F. Doran, *Lab.* — 17,745
Mrs J. Wisely, *C.* — 6,944
B. Topping, *SNP* — 5,767
J. Brown, *LD* — 4,714
J. Farquharson, *Ref.* — 446

Lab. majority 10,801
(Boundary change: notional Lab.)

ABERDEEN NORTH
*E.*54,302   *T.*70.74%
M. Savidge, *Lab.* — 18,389
B. Adam, *SNP* — 8,379
J. Gifford, *C.* — 5,763

M. Rumbles, *LD* — 5,421
A. Mackenzie, *Ref.* — 463
Lab. majority 10,010
(Boundary change: notional Lab.)

ABERDEEN SOUTH
*E.*60,490   *T.*72.84%
Ms A. Begg, *Lab.* — 15,541

N. Stephen, *LD*	12,176	
†R. Robertson, *C.*	11,621	
J. Towers, *SNP*	4,299	
R. Wharton, *Ref.*	425	
Lab. majority 3,365		
(Boundary change: notional C.)		

ABERDEENSHIRE WEST AND KINCARDINE
*E.*59,123   *T.*73.05%

Sir R. Smith, *LD*	17,742
†G. Kynoch, *C.*	15,080
Ms J. Mowatt, *SNP*	5,639
Ms Q. Khan, *Lab.*	3,923
S. Ball, *Ref.*	805
LD majority 2,662	
(Boundary change: notional C.)	

AIRDRIE AND SHOTTS
*E.*57,673   *T.*71.40%

†Mrs H. Liddell, *Lab.*	25,460
K. Robertson, *SNP*	10,048
Dr N. Brook, *C.*	3,660
R. Wolseley, *LD*	1,719
C. Semple, *Ref.*	294
Lab. majority 15,412	
(Boundary change: notional Lab.)	

ANGUS
*E.*59,708   *T.*72.14%

†A. Welsh, *SNP*	20,792
S. Leslie, *C.*	10,603
Ms C. Taylor, *Lab.*	6,733
Dr R. Speirs, *LD*	4,065
B. Taylor, *Ref.*	883
SNP majority 10,189	
(Boundary change: notional SNP)	

ARGYLL AND BUTE
*E.*49,451   *T.*72.23%

*Mrs R. Michie, *LD*	14,359
Prof. N. MacCormick, *SNP*	8,278
R. Leishman, *C.*	6,774
A. Syed, *Lab.*	5,596
M. Stewart, *Ref.*	713
LD majority 6,081	
(April 1992, LD maj. 2,622)	

AYR
*E.*55,829   *T.*80.17%

Mrs S. Osborne, *Lab.*	21,679
†P. Gallie, *C.*	15,136
I. Blackford, *SNP*	5,625
Miss C. Hamblen, *LD*	2,116
J. Enos, *Ref.*	200
Lab. majority 6,543	
(Boundary change: notional Lab.)	

BANFF AND BUCHAN
*E.*58,493   *T.*68.69%

†A. Salmond, *SNP*	22,409
W. Frain-Bell, *C.*	9,564
Ms M. Harris, *Lab.*	4,747
N. Fletcher, *LD*	2,398
A. Buchan, *Ref.*	1,060
SNP majority 12,845	
(Boundary change: notional SNP)	

CAITHNESS, SUTHERLAND AND EASTER ROSS
*E.*41,566   *T.*70.18%

†R. Maclennan, *LD*	10,381
J. Hendry, *Lab.*	8,122

E. Harper, *SNP*	6,710
T. Miers, *C.*	3,148
Ms C. Ryder, *Ref.*	369
J. Martin, *Green*	230
M. Carr, *UK Ind.*	212
LD majority 2,259	
(Boundary change: notional LD)	

CARRICK, CUMNOCK AND DOON VALLEY
*E.*65,593   *T.*74.96%

†G. Foulkes, *Lab. Co-op.*	29,398
A. Marshall, *C.*	8,336
Mrs C. Hutchison, *SNP*	8,190
D. Young, *LD*	2,613
J. Higgins, *Ref.*	634
Lab. Co-op. majority 21,062	
(Boundary change: notional Lab. Co-op.)	

CLYDEBANK AND MILNGAVIE
*E.*52,092   *T.*75.03%

†A. Worthington, *Lab.*	21,583
J. Yuill, *SNP*	8,263
Ms N. Morgan, *C.*	4,885
K. Moody, *LD*	4,086
I. Sanderson, *Ref.*	269
Lab. majority 13,320	
(Boundary change: notional Lab.)	

CLYDESDALE
*E.*63,428   *T.*71.60%

*J. Hood, *Lab.*	23,859
A. Doig, *SNP*	10,050
M. Izatt, *C.*	7,396
Mrs S. Grieve, *LD*	3,796
K. Smith, *BNP*	311
Lab. majority 13,809	
(April 1992, Lab. maj. 10,187)	

COATBRIDGE AND CHRYSTON
*E.*52,024   *T.*72.30%

†T. Clarke, *Lab.*	25,697
B. Nugent, *SNP*	6,402
A. Wauchope, *C.*	3,216
Mrs M. Daly, *LD*	2,048
B. Bowsley, *Ref.*	249
Lab. majority 19,295	
(Boundary change: notional Lab.)	

CUMBERNAULD AND KILSYTH
*E.*48,032   *T.*75.00%

Ms R. McKenna, *Lab.*	21,141
C. Barrie, *SNP*	10,013
I. Sewell, *C.*	2,441
J. Biggam, *LD*	1,368
Ms J Kara, *ProLife*	609
K. McEwan, *SSA*	345
Ms P. Cook, *Ref.*	107
Lab. majority 11,128	
(April 1992, Lab. maj. 9,215)	

CUNNINGHAME NORTH
*E.*55,526   *T.*74.07%

*B. Wilson, *Lab.*	20,686
Mrs M. Mitchell, *C.*	9,647
Ms K. Nicoll, *SNP*	7,584
Ms K. Freel, *LD*	2,271
Ms L. McDaid, *Soc. Lab.*	501
I. Winton, *Ref.*	440
Lab. majority 11,039	
(April 1992, Lab. maj. 2,939)	

CUNNINGHAME SOUTH
*E.*49,543   *T.*71.54%

*B. Donohoe, *Lab.*	22,233
Mrs M. Burgess, *SNP*	7,364
Mrs P. Paterson, *C.*	3,571
E. Watson, *LD*	1,604
K. Edwin, *Soc. Lab.*	494
A. Martlew, *Ref.*	178
Lab. majority 14,869	
(April 1992, Lab. maj. 10,680)	

DUMBARTON
*E.*56,229   *T.*73.39%

*J. McFall, *Lab. Co-op.*	20,470
W. Mackechnie, *SNP*	9,587
P. Ramsay, *C.*	7,283
A. Reid, *LD*	3,144
L. Robertson, *SSA*	283
G. Dempster, *Ref.*	255
D. Lancaster, *UK Ind.*	242
Lab. Co-op. majority 10,883	
(April 1992, Lab. maj. 6,129)	

DUMFRIES
*E.*62,759   *T.*78.92%

R. Brown, *Lab.*	23,528
S. Stevenson, *C.*	13,885
R. Higgins, *SNP*	5,977
N. Wallace, *LD*	5,487
D. Parker, *Ref.*	533
Ms E. Hunter, *NLP*	117
Lab. majority 9,643	
(Boundary change: notional C.)	

DUNDEE EAST
*E.*58,388   *T.*69.41%

†J. McAllion, *Lab.*	20,718
Ms S. Robison, *SNP*	10,757
B. Mackie, *C.*	6,397
Dr G. Saluja, *LD*	1,677
E. Galloway, *Ref.*	601
H. Duke, *SSA*	232
Ms E. MacKenzie, *NLP*	146
Lab. majority 9,961	
(Boundary change: notional Lab.)	

DUNDEE WEST
*E.*57,346   *T.*67.67%

†E. Ross, *Lab.*	20,875
J. Dorward, *SNP*	9,016
N. Powrie, *C.*	5,105
Dr E. Dick, *LD*	2,972
Ms M. Ward, *SSA*	428
J. MacMillan, *Ref.*	411
Lab. majority 11,859	
(Boundary change: notional Lab.)	

DUNFERMLINE EAST
*E.*52,072   *T.*70.25%

†Rt. Hon. G. Brown, *Lab.*	24,441
J. Ramage, *SNP*	5,690
I. Mitchell, *C.*	3,656
J. Tolson, *LD*	2,164
T. Dunsmore, *Ref.*	632
Lab. majority 18,751	
(Boundary change: notional Lab.)	

DUNFERMLINE WEST
*E.*52,467   *T.*69.44%

†Ms R. Squire, *Lab.*	19,338
J. Lloyd, *SNP*	6,984
Mrs E. Harris, *LD*	4,963
K. Newton, *C.*	4,606

J. Bain, *Ref.* 543
Lab. majority 12,354
(Boundary change: notional Lab.)

East Kilbride
*E.*65,229　*T.*74.81%
†A. Ingram, *Lab.* 27,584
G. Gebbie, *SNP* 10,200
C. Herbertson, *C.* 5,863
Mrs K. Philbrick, *LD* 3,527
J. Deighan, *ProLife* 1,170
Ms J. Gray, *Ref.* 306
E. Gilmour, *NLP* 146
Lab. majority 17,384
(Boundary change: notional Lab.)

East Lothian
*E.*57,441　*T.*75.61%
†J. Home Robertson, *Lab.* 22,881
M. Fraser, *C.* 8,660
D. McCarthy, *SNP* 6,825
Ms A. MacAskill, *LD* 4,575
N. Nash, *Ref.* 491
Lab. majority 14,221
(Boundary change: notional Lab.)

Eastwood
*E.*66,697　*T.*78.32%
J. Murphy, *Lab.* 20,766
P. Cullen, *C.* 17,530
D. Yates, *SNP* 6,826
Dr C. Mason, *LD* 6,110
D. Miller, *Ref.* 497
Dr M. Tayan, *ProLife* 393
D. McPherson, *UK Ind.* 113
Lab. majority 3,236
(Boundary change: notional C.)

Edinburgh Central
*E.*63,695　*T.*67.09%
†A. Darling, *Lab.* 20,125
M. Scott-Hayward, *C.* 9,055
Ms F. Hyslop, *SNP* 6,750
Ms K. Utting, *LD* 5,605
Ms L. Hendry, *Green* 607
A. Skinner, *Ref.* 495
M. Benson, *Ind. Dem.* 98
Lab. majority 11,070
(Boundary change: notional Lab.)

Edinburgh East and Musselburgh
*E.*59,648　*T.*70.61%
†Dr G. Strang, *Lab.* 22,564
D. White, *SNP* 8,034
K. Ward, *C.* 6,483
Dr C. MacKellar, *LD* 4,511
J. Sibbet, *Ref.* 526
Lab. majority 14,530
(Boundary change: notional Lab.)

Edinburgh North and Leith
*E.*61,617　*T.*66.45%
†M. Chisholm, *Lab.* 19,209
Ms A. Dana, *SNP* 8,231
E. Stewart, *C.* 7,312
Ms H. Campbell, *LD* 5,335
A. Graham, *Ref.* 441
G. Brown, *SSA* 320
P. Douglas-Reid, *NLP* 97
Lab. majority 10,978
(Boundary change: notional Lab.)

Edinburgh Pentlands
*E.*59,635　*T.*76.70%
Ms L. Clark, *Lab.* 19,675
†Rt. Hon. M. Rifkind, *C.* 14,813
S. Gibb, *SNP* 5,952
Dr J. Dawe, *LD* 4,575
M. McDonald, *Ref.* 422
R. Harper, *Green* 224
A. McConnachie, *UK Ind.* 81
Lab. majority 4,862
(Boundary change: notional C.)

Edinburgh South
*E.*62,467　*T.*71.78%
†N. Griffiths, *Lab.* 20,993
Miss E. Smith, *C.* 9,541
M. Pringle, *LD* 7,911
Dr J. Hargreaves, *SNP* 5,791
I. McLean, *Ref.* 504
B. Dunn, *NLP* 98
Lab. majority 11,452
(Boundary change: notional Lab.)

Edinburgh West
*E.*61,133　*T.*77.91%
D. Gorrie, *LD* 20,578
†Rt. Hon. Lord J. Douglas-Hamilton, *C.* 13,325
Ms L. Hinds, *Lab.* 8,948
G. Sutherland, *SNP* 4,210
Dr S. Elphick, *Ref.* 277
P. Coombes, *Lib.* 263
A. Jack, *AS* 30
LD majority 7,253
(Boundary change: notional C.)

Falkirk East
*E.*56,792　*T.*73.24%
†M. Connarty, *Lab.* 23,344
K. Brown, *SNP* 9,959
M. Nicol, *C.* 5,813
R. Spillane, *LD* 2,153
S. Mowbray, *Ref.* 326
Lab. majority 13,385
(Boundary change: notional Lab.)

Falkirk West
*E.*52,850　*T.*72.60%
†D. Canavan, *Lab.* 22,772
D. Alexander, *SNP* 8,989
Mrs C. Buchanan, *C.* 4,639
D. Houston, *LD* 1,970
Lab. majority 13,783
(Boundary change: notional Lab.)

Fife Central
*E.*58,313　*T.*69.90%
†H. McLeish, *Lab.* 23,912
Mrs P. Marwick, *SNP* 10,199
J. Rees-Mogg, *C.* 3,669
R. Laird, *LD* 2,610
J. Scrymgeour-Wedderburn, *Ref.* 375
Lab. majority 13,713
(Boundary change: notional Lab.)

Fife North East
*E.*58,794　*T.*71.16%
*M. Campbell, *LD* 21,432
A. Bruce, *C.* 11,076
C. Welsh, *SNP* 4,545
C. Milne, *Lab.* 4,301
W. Stewart, *Ref.* 485

LD majority 10,356
(Boundary change: notional LD)

Galloway and Upper Nithsdale
*E.*52,751　*T.*79.65%
A. Morgan, *SNP* 18,449
†Rt. Hon. I. Lang, *C.* 12,825
Ms K. Clark, *Lab.* 6,861
J. McKerchar, *LD* 2,700
R. Wood, *Ind.* 566
A. Kennedy, *Ref.* 428
J. Smith, *UK Ind.* 189
SNP majority 5,624
(Boundary change: notional C.)

Glasgow Anniesland
*E.*52,955　*T.*63.98%
†Rt. Hon. D. Dewar, *Lab.* 20,951
Dr W. Wilson, *SNP* 5,797
A. Brocklehurst, *C.* 3,881
C. McGinty, *LD* 2,453
A. Majid, *ProLife* 374
W. Bonnar, *SSA* 229
A. Milligan, *UK Ind.* 86
Ms G. McKay, *Ref.* 84
T. Pringle, *NLP* 24
Lab. majority 15,154
(Boundary change: notional Lab.)

Glasgow Baillieston
*E.*51,152　*T.*62.27%
†J. Wray, *Lab.* 20,925
Mrs P. Thomson, *SNP* 6,085
M. Kelly, *C.* 2,468
Ms S. Rainger, *LD* 1,217
J. McVicar, *SSA* 970
J. McClafferty, *Ref.* 188
Lab. majority 14,840
(Boundary change: notional Lab.)

Glasgow Cathcart
*E.*49,312　*T.*69.17%
†J. Maxton, *Lab.* 19,158
Ms M. Whitehead, *SNP* 6,913
A. Muir, *C.* 4,248
C. Dick, *LD* 2,302
Ms Z. Indyk, *ProLife* 687
R. Stevenson, *SSA* 458
S. Haldane, *Ref.* 344
Lab. majority 12,245
(Boundary change: notional Lab.)

Glasgow Govan
*E.*49,836　*T.*64.70%
M. Sarwar, *Lab.* 14,216
Ms N. Sturgeon, *SNP* 11,302
W. Thomas, *C.* 2,839
R. Stewart, *LD* 1,915
A. McCombes, *SSA* 755
P. Paton, *SLU* 325
I. Badar, *SLI* 319
Z. J. Abbasi, *SCU* 221
K. MacDonald, *Ref.* 201
J. White, *BNP* 149
Lab. majority 2,914
(Boundary change: notional Lab.)

Glasgow Kelvin
*E.*57,438　*T.*56.85%
†G. Galloway, *Lab.* 16,643
Ms S. White, *SNP* 6,978
Ms E. Buchanan, *LD* 4,629
D. McPhie, *C.* 3,539

A. Green, *SSA* — 386
R. Grigor, *Ref.* — 282
V. Vanni, *SPGB* — 102
G. Stidolph, *NLP* — 95
Lab. majority 9,665
(Boundary change: notional Lab.)

GLASGOW MARYHILL
*E.*52,523   *T.*56.59%
†Ms M. Fyfe, *Lab.* — 19,301
J. Wailes, *SNP* — 5,037
Ms E. Attwooll, *LD* — 2,119
S. Baldwin, *C.* — 1,747
Ms L. Blair, *NLP* — 651
Ms A. Baker, *SSA* — 409
J. Hanif, *ProLife* — 344
R. Paterson, *Ref.* — 77
S. Johnstone, *SEP* — 36
Lab. majority 14,264
(Boundary change: notional Lab.)

GLASGOW POLLOK
*E.*49,284   *T.*66.56%
†I. Davidson, *Lab. Co-op.* — 19,653
D. Logan, *SNP* — 5,862
T. Sheridan, *SSA* — 3,639
E. Hamilton, *C.* — 1,979
D. Jago, *LD* — 1,137
Ms M. Gott, *ProLife* — 380
D. Haldane, *Ref.* — 152
Lab. Co-op. majority 13,791
(Boundary change: notional Lab. Co-op.)

GLASGOW RUTHERGLEN
*E.*50,646   *T.*70.14%
†T. McAvoy, *Lab. Co-op.* — 20,430
I. Gray, *SNP* — 5,423
R. Brown, *LD* — 5,167
D. Campbell Bannerman, *C.* — 3,288
G. Easton, *Ind. Lab.* — 812
Ms R. Kane, *SSA* — 251
Ms J. Kerr, *Ref.* — 150
Lab. Co-op. majority 15,007
(Boundary change: notional Lab. Co-op.)

GLASGOW SHETTLESTON
*E.*47,990   *T.*55.87%
†D. Marshall, *Lab.* — 19,616
H. Hanif, *SNP* — 3,748
C. Simpson, *C.* — 1,484
Ms K. Hiles, *LD* — 1,061
Ms C. McVicar, *SSA* — 482
R. Currie, *BNP* — 191
T. Montguire, *Ref.* — 151
J. Graham, *WRP* — 80
Lab. majority 15,868
(Boundary change: notional Lab.)

GLASGOW SPRINGBURN
*E.*53,473   *T.*59.05%
†M. Martin, *Lab.* — 22,534
J. Brady, *SNP* — 5,208
M.Holdsworth, *C.* — 1,893
J. Alexander, *LD* — 1,349
J. Lawson, *SSA* — 407
A. Keating, *Ref.* — 186
Lab. majority 17,326
(Boundary change: notional Lab.)

GORDON
*E.*58,767   *T.*71.89%
†M. Bruce, *LD* — 17,999
J. Porter, *C.* — 11,002
R. Lochhead, *SNP* — 8,435
Ms L. Kirkhill, *Lab.* — 4,350
F. Pidcock, *Ref.* — 459
LD majority 6,997
(Boundary change: notional C.)

GREENOCK AND INVERCLYDE
*E.*48,818   *T.*71.05%
†Dr N. Godman, *Lab.* — 19,480
B. Goodall, *SNP* — 6,440
R. Ackland, *LD* — 4,791
H. Swire, *C.* — 3,976
Lab. majority 13,040
(Boundary change: notional Lab.)

HAMILTON NORTH AND BELLSHILL
*E.*53,607   *T.*70.88%
†Dr J. Reid, *Lab.* — 24,322
M. Matheson, *SNP* — 7,255
G. McIntosh, *C.* — 3,944
K. Legg, *LD* — 1,924
R. Conn, *Ref.* — 554
Lab. majority 17,067
(Boundary change: notional Lab.)

HAMILTON SOUTH
*E.*46,562   *T.*71.07%
†G. Robertson, *Lab.* — 21,709
I. Black, *SNP* — 5,831
R. Kilgour, *C.* — 2,858
R. Pitts, *LD* — 1,693
C. Gunn, *ProLife* — 684
S. Brown, *Ref.* — 316
Lab. majority 15,878
(Boundary change: notional Lab.)

INVERNESS EAST, NAIRN AND LOCHABER
*E.*65,701   *T.*72.71%
D. Stewart, *Lab.* — 16,187
F. Ewing, *SNP* — 13,848
S. Gallagher, *LD* — 8,364
Mrs M. Scanlon, *C.* — 8,355
Ms W. Wall, *Ref.* — 436
M. Falconer, *Green* — 354
D. Hart, *Ch. U.* — 224
Lab. majority 2,339
(Boundary change: notional LD)

KILMARNOCK AND LOUDOUN
*E.*61,376   *T.*77.24%
D. Browne, *Lab.* — 23,621
A. Neil, *SNP* — 16,365
D. Taylor, *C.* — 5,125
J. Stewart, *LD* — 1,891
W. Sneddon, *Ref.* — 284
W. Gilmour, *NLP* — 123
Lab. majority 7,256
(April 1992, Lab. maj. 6,979)

KIRKCALDY
*E.*52,186   *T.*67.02%
†L. Moonie, *Lab. Co-op.* — 18,730
S. Hosie, *SNP* — 8,020
Miss C. Black, *C.* — 4,779
J. Mainland, *LD* — 3,031
V. Baxter, *Ref.* — 413

Lab. Co-op. majority 10,710
(Boundary change: notional Lab. Co-op.)

LINLITHGOW
*E.*53,706   *T.*73.84%
†T. Dalyell, *Lab.* — 21,469
K. MacAskill, *SNP* — 10,631
T. Kerr, *C.* — 4,964
A. Duncan, *LD* — 2,331
K. Plomer, *Ref.* — 259
Lab. majority 10,838
(Boundary change: notional Lab.)

LIVINGSTON
*E.*60,296   *T.*71.04%
†Rt. Hon. R. Cook, *Lab.* — 23,510
P. Johnston, *SNP* — 11,763
H. Craigie Halkett, *C.* — 4,028
E. Hawthorn, *LD* — 2,876
Ms H. Campbell, *Ref.* — 444
M. Culbert, *SPGB* — 213
Lab. majority 11,747
(Boundary change: notional Lab.)

MIDLOTHIAN
*E.*47,552   *T.*74.13%
†E. Clarke, *Lab.* — 18,861
L. Millar, *SNP* — 8,991
Miss A. Harper, *C.* — 3,842
R. Pinnock, *LD* — 3,235
K. Docking, *Ref.* — 320
Lab. majority 9,870
(Boundary change: notional Lab.)

MORAY
*E.*58,302   *T.*68.21%
†Mrs M. Ewing, *SNP* — 16,529
A. Findlay, *C.* — 10,963
L. Macdonald, *Lab.* — 7,886
Ms D. Storr, *LD* — 3,548
P. Mieklejohn, *Ref.* — 840
SNP majority 5,566
(Boundary change: notional SNP)

MOTHERWELL AND WISHAW
*E.*52,252   *T.*70.08%
F. Roy, *Lab.* — 21,020
J. McGuigan, *SNP* — 8,229
S. Dickson, *C.* — 4,024
A. Mackie, *LD* — 2,331
C. Herriot, *Soc. Lab.* — 797
T. Russell, *Ref.* — 218
Lab. majority 12,791
(Boundary change: notional Lab.)

OCHIL
*E.*56,572   *T.*77.40%
†M. O'Neill, *Lab.* — 19,707
G. Reid, *SNP* — 15,055
A. Hogarth, *C.* — 6,383
Mrs A. Watters, *LD* — 2,262
D. White, *Ref.* — 210
I. McDonald, *D. Nat.* — 104
M. Sullivan, *NLP* — 65
Lab. majority 4,652
(Boundary change: notional Lab.)

ORKNEY AND SHETLAND
*E.*32,291   *T.*64.00%
*J. Wallace, *LD* — 10,743
J. Paton, *Lab.* — 3,775
W. Ross, *SNP* — 2,624

H. Vere Anderson, *C.* 2,527
F. Adamson, *Ref.* 820
Ms C. Wharton, *NLP* 116
A. Robertson, *Ind.* 60
LD majority 6,968
(April 1992, LD maj. 5,033)

PAISLEY NORTH
*E.*49,725 *T.*68.65%
†Mrs I. Adams, *Lab.* 20,295
I. Mackay, *SNP* 7,481
K. Brookes, *C.* 3,267
A. Jelfs, *LD* 2,365
R. Graham, *ProLife* 531
E. Mathew, *Ref.* 196
Lab. majority 12,814
(Boundary change: notional Lab.)

PAISLEY SOUTH
*E.*54,040 *T.*69.12%
†G. McMaster, *Lab. Co-op.* 21,482
W. Martin, *SNP* 8,732
Ms E. McCartin, *LD* 3,500
R. Reid, *C.* 3,237
J. Lardner, *Ref.* 254
S. Clerkin, *SSA* 146
Lab. Co-op. majority 12,750
(Boundary change: notional Lab. Co-op.)
See also page 268

PERTH
*E.*60,313 *T.*73.87%
†Ms R. Cunningham, *SNP* 16,209
J. Godfrey, *C.* 13,068
D. Alexander, *Lab.* 11,036
C. Brodie, *LD* 3,583
R. MacAuley, *Ref.* 366
M. Henderson, *UK Ind.* 289
SNP majority 3,141
(Boundary change: notional C.)

RENFREWSHIRE WEST
*E.*52,348 *T.*76.00%
†T. Graham, *Lab.* 18,525
C. Campbell, *SNP* 10,546
C. Cormack, *C.* 7,387
B. MacPherson, *LD* 3,045
S. Lindsay, *Ref.* 283
Lab. majority 7,979
(Boundary change: notional Lab.)

ROSS, SKYE AND INVERNESS WEST
*E.*55,639 *T.*71.81%
†C. Kennedy, *LD* 15,472
D. Munro, *Lab.* 11,453
Mrs M. Paterson, *SNP* 7,821
Miss M. Macleod, *C.* 4,368
L. Durance, *Ref.* 535
A. Hopkins, *Green* 306
LD majority 4,019
(Boundary change: notional LD)

ROXBURGH AND BERWICKSHIRE
*E.*47,259 *T.*73.91%
†A. Kirkwood, *LD* 16,243
D. Younger, *C.* 8,337
Ms H. Eadie, *Lab.* 5,226
M. Balfour, *SNP* 3,959
J. Curtis, *Ref.* 922
P. Neilson, *UK Ind.* 202
D. Lucas, *NLP* 42
LD majority 7,906
(Boundary change: notional LD)

STIRLING
*E.*52,491 *T.*81.84%
Mrs A. McGuire, *Lab.* 20,382
†Rt. Hon. M. Forsyth, *C.* 13,971
E. Dow, *SNP* 5,752
A. Tough, *LD* 2,675
W. McMurdo, *UK Ind.* 154
Ms E. Olsen, *Value Party* 24
Lab. majority 6,411
(Boundary change: notional C.)

STRATHKELVIN AND BEARSDEN
*E.*62,974 *T.*78.94%
†S. Galbraith, *Lab.* 26,278
D. Sharpe, *C.* 9,986
G. McCormick, *SNP* 8,111
J. Morrison, *LD* 4,843
D. Wilson, *Ref.* 339
Ms J. Fisher, *NLP* 155
Lab. majority 16,292
(Boundary change: notional Lab.)

TAYSIDE NORTH
*E.*61,398 *T.*74.25%
J. Swinney, *SNP* 20,447
†W. Walker, *C.* 16,287
I. McFatridge, *Lab.* 5,141
P. Regent, *LD* 3,716
SNP majority 4,160
(Boundary change: notional C.)

TWEEDDALE, ETTRICK AND LAUDERDALE
*E.*50,891 *T.*76.64%
M. Moore, *LD* 12,178
K. Geddes, *Lab.* 10,689
A. Jack, *C.* 8,623
I. Goldie, *SNP* 6,671
C. Mowbray, *Ref.* 406
J. Hein, *Lib.* 387
D. Paterson, *NLP* 47
LD majority 1,489
(Boundary change: notional LD)

WESTERN ISLES
*E.*22,983 *T.*70.08%
*C. Macdonald, *Lab.* 8,955
Dr A. Lorne Gillies, *SNP* 5,379
J. McGrigor, *C.* 1,071
N. Mitchison, *LD* 495
R. Lionel, *Ref.* 206
Lab. majority 3,576
(April 1992, Lab. maj. 1,703)

NORTHERN IRELAND

ANTRIM EAST
*E.*58,963 *T.*58.26%
†R. Beggs, *UUP* 13,318
S. Neeson, *All.* 6,929
J. McKee, *DUP* 6,682
T. Dick, *C.* 2,334
W. Donaldson, *PUP* 1,757
D. O'Connor, *SDLP* 1,576
R. Mason, *Ind.* 1,145
Ms C. McAuley, *SF* 543
Ms M. McCann, *NLP* 69
UUP majority 6,389
(Boundary change: notional UUP)

ANTRIM NORTH
*E.*72,411 *T.*63.78%
*Revd I. Paisley, *DUP* 21,495
J. Leslie, *UUP* 10,921
S. Farren, *SDLP* 7,333
J. McCarry, *SF* 2,896
Dr D. Alderdice, *All.* 2,845
Ms B. Hinds, *NI Women* 580
J. Wright, *NLP* 116

DUP majority 10,574
(April 1992, DUP maj. 14,936)

ANTRIM SOUTH
*E.*69,414 *T.*57.91%
†C. Forsythe, *UUP* 23,108
D. McClelland, *SDLP* 6,497
D. Ford, *All.* 4,668
H. Smyth, *PUP* 3,490
H. Cushinan, *SF* 2,229
Ms B. Briggs, *NLP* 203
UUP majority 16,611
(Boundary change: notional UUP)

BELFAST EAST
*E.*61,744 *T.*63.21%
†P. Robinson, *DUP* 16,640
R. Empey, *UUP* 9,886
J. Hendron, *All.* 9,288
Miss S. Dines, *C.* 928
D. Corr, *SF* 810
Mrs P. Lewsley, *SDLP* 629
D. Dougan, *NIFT* 541
J. Bell, *WP* 237
D. Collins, *NLP* 70

DUP majority 6,754
(Boundary change: notional DUP)

BELFAST NORTH
*E.*64,577 *T.*64.19%
†C. Walker, *UUP* 21,478
A. Maginness, *SDLP* 8,454
G. Kelly, *SF* 8,375
T. Campbell, *All.* 2,221
P. Emerson, *Green* 539
P. Treanor, *WP* 297
Ms A. Gribben, *NLP* 88
UUP majority 13,024
(Boundary change: notional UUP)

BELFAST SOUTH
*E.*63,439 *T.*62.24%
†Revd M. Smyth, *UUP* 14,201
Dr A. McDonnell, *SDLP* 9,601
D. Ervine, *PUP* 5,687
S. McBride, *All.* 5,112
S. Hayes, *SF* 2,019
Ms A. Campbell, *NI Women* 1,204
Miss M. Boal, *C.* 962
N. Cusack, *Ind. Lab.* 292

P. Lynn, *WP*   286
J. Anderson, *NLP*   120
UUP majority 4,600
(Boundary change: notional UUP)

BELFAST WEST
*E.*61,785   *T.*74.27%
G. Adams, *SF*   25,662
†Dr J. Hendron, *SDLP*   17,753
F. Parkinson, *UUP*   1,556
J. Lowry, *WP*   721
L. Kennedy, *HR*   102
Ms M. Daly, *NLP*   91
SF majority 7,909
(Boundary change: notional SDLP)

DOWN NORTH
*E.*63,010   *T.*58.03%
†R. McCartney, *UKU*   12,817
A. McFarland, *UUP*   11,368
Sir O. Napier, *All.*   7,554
L. Fee, *C.*   1,810
Miss M. Farrell, *SDLP*   1,602
Ms J. Morrice, *NI Women*   1,240
T. Mullins, *NLP*   108
R. Mooney, *NIP*   67
UKU majority 1,449
(Boundary change: notional Popular
Unionist)

DOWN SOUTH
*E.*69,855   *T.*70.84%
†E. McGrady, *SDLP*   26,181
D. Nesbitt, *UUP*   16,248
M. Murphy, *SF*   5,127
J. Crozier, *All.*   1,711
Ms R. McKeon, *NLP*   219
SDLP majority 9,933
(Boundary change: notional SDLP)

FERMANAGH AND SOUTH TYRONE
*E.*64,600   *T.*74.75%
†K. Maginnis, *UUP*   24,862
G. McHugh, *SF*   11,174
T. Gallagher, *SDLP*   11,060
S. Farry, *All.*   977
S. Gillan, *NLP*   217
UUP majority 13,688
(Boundary change: notional UUP)

FOYLE
*E.*67,620   *T.*70.71%
†J. Hume, *SDLP*   25,109
M. McLaughlin, *SF*   11,445
W. Hay, *DUP*   10,290
Mrs H.-M. Bell, *All.*   817
D. Brennan, *NLP*   154
SDLP majority 13,664
(Boundary change: notional SDLP)

LAGAN VALLEY
*E.*71,225   *T.*62.21%
J. Donaldson, *UUP*   24,560
S. Close, *All.*   7,635
E. Poots, *DUP*   6,005
Ms D. Kelly, *SDLP*   3,436
S. Sexton, *C.*   1,212
Ms S. Ramsey, *SF*   1,110
Ms F. McCarthy, *WP*   203
H. Finlay, *NLP*   149
UUP majority 16,925
(Boundary change: notional UUP)

LONDONDERRY EAST
*E.*58,831   *T.*64.77%
†W. Ross, *UUP*   13,558
G. Campbell, *DUP*   9,764
A. Doherty, *SDLP*   8,273
M. O'Kane, *SF*   3,463
Ms Y. Boyle, *All.*   2,427
J. Holmes, *C.*   436
Ms C. Gallen, *NLP*   100
I. Anderson, *Nat. Dem.*   81
UUP majority 3,794
(Boundary change: notional UUP)

NEWRY AND ARMAGH
*E.*70,652   *T.*75.40%
†S. Mallon, *SDLP*   22,904
D. Kennedy, *UUP*   18,015
P. McNamee, *SF*   11,218
P. Whitcroft, *All.*   1,015
D. Evans, *NLP*   123
SDLP majority 4,889
(Boundary change: notional SDLP)

STRANGFORD
*E.*69,980   *T.*59.47%
†Rt. Hon. J. Taylor, *UUP*   18,431
Mrs I. Robinson, *DUP*   12,579
K. McCarthy, *All.*   5,467
P. O'Reilly, *SDLP*   2,775
G. Chalk, *C.*   1,743
G. O Fachtna, *SF*   503
Mrs S. Mullins, *NLP*   121
UUP majority 5,852
(Boundary change: notional UUP)

TYRONE WEST
*E.*58,168   *T.*79.55%
W. Thompson, *UUP*   16,003
J. Byrne, *SDLP*   14,842
P. Doherty, *SF*   14,280
Ms A. Gormley, *All.*   829
T. Owens, *WP*   230
R. Johnstone, *NLP*   91
UUP majority 1,161
(Boundary change: notional DUP)

ULSTER MID
*E.*58,836   *T.*86.12%
M. McGuinness, *SF*   20,294
†Revd W. McCrea, *DUP*   18,411
D. Haughey, *SDLP*   11,205
E. Bogues, *All.*   460
Mrs M. Donnelly, *WP*   238
Ms M. Murray, *NLP*   61
SF majority 1,883
(Boundary change: notional DUP)

UPPER BANN
*E.*70,398   *T.*67.88%
*D. Trimble, *UUP*   20,836
Ms B. Rodgers, *SDLP*   11,584
Ms B. O'Hagan, *SF*   5,773
M. Carrick, *DUP*   5,482
Dr W. Ramsay, *All.*   3,017
T. French, *WP*   554
B. Price, *C.*   433
J. Lyons, *NLP*   108
UUP majority 9,252
(Boundary change: notional UUP)

BY-ELECTIONS SINCE THE
LAST EDITION

BARNSLEY EAST
(12 December 1996)
*E.*54,051 *T.*35.6%
J. Ennis, *Lab.*   13,683
D. Willis, *LD*   1,502
Ms J. Ellison, *C.*   1,299
K. Capstick, *Soc. Lab.*   949
N. Tolstoy, *UK Ind.*   378
Ms J. Hyland, *SEP*   89
Labour majority   12,181

WIRRAL SOUTH
(27 February 1997)
*E.*61,116 *T.*73%
B. Chapman, *Lab.*   22,767
L. Byrom, *C.*   14,879
Ms F. Clucas, *LD*   4,357
R. North, *UK Ind.*   410
H. Bence, *Company
    Director*   184
M. Cullen, *Soc. Lab.*   156
P. Gott, *Disillusioned C.
    Campaign for Change*   148
R. Taylor, *Ind.*   132
S. Anthony, *Stop Tories
    Poncing on Tobacco
    Companies*   124
G. Mead, *NLP*   52
C. Palmer, *21st Century*   44
F. Asbury, *Thalidomide
    Action Group UK*   40
Labour majority   7,888

UXBRIDGE
(31 July 1997)
*E.*57,733 *T.*55.2%
J. Randall, *C.*   16,288
A. Slaughter, *Lab.*   12,522
K. Kerr, *LD*   1,792
'Lord Sutch', *Official
    Monster Raving Loony*   396
Ms J. Leonard, *Soc.*   259
Ms F. Taylor, *BNP*   205
I. Anderson, *Nat. Dem.*   157
J. McCauley, *NF*   110
H. Middleton, *Original
    Lib. Party*   69
J. Feisenberger, *UK Ind.*   39
R. Carroll, *Emerald
    Rainbow Islands Dream
    Ticket*   30
Conservative majority   3,766

VACANT SEATS
At the time of the general election:
Meriden – following the death of
    Iain Mills (*C.*) in January 1997
Don Valley – following the death of
    Martin Redmond (*Lab.*) in January
    1997

At the time of going to press:
Paisley South – following the death
    of Gordon McMaster (*Lab.*) on 28
    July 1997

European Parliament

European Parliament elections take place at five-yearly intervals. In mainland Britain MEPs are elected in all constituencies on a first-past-the-post basis; in Northern Ireland three MEPs are elected by proportional representation. From 1979 to 1994 the number of seats held by the UK in the European Parliament was 81. At the June 1994 election the number of seats increased to 87 (England 71, Wales 5, Scotland 8, Northern Ireland 3).

Since 1994, nationals of member states of the European Union have the right to vote in elections to the European Parliament in the UK. British subjects and citizens of the Irish Republic can stand in the UK for election to the European Parliament provided they are 21 or over and not subject to disqualification.

MEPs receive a salary from the parliaments or governments of their respective member states, set at the level of the national parliamentary salary and subject to national taxation rules (for salary of British MPs, *see* page 219).

UK MEMBERS AS AT END JULY 1997

*Denotes membership of the last European Parliament

*Adam, Gordon J., Ph.D. (*b.* 1934), *Lab., Northumbria,* maj. 66,158
*Balfe, Richard A. (*b.* 1944), *Lab., London South Inner,* maj. 59,220
*Barton, Roger (*b.* 1945), *Lab., Sheffield,* maj. 50,288
Billingham, Mrs Angela T. (*b.* 1939), *Lab., Northamptonshire and Blaby,* maj. 26,085
*Bowe, David R. (*b.* 1955), *Lab., Cleveland and Richmond,* maj. 57,568
*Cassidy, Bryan M. D. (*b.* 1934), *C., Dorset and Devon East,* maj. 2,264
Chichester, Giles B. (*b.* 1946), *C., Devon and Plymouth East,* maj. 700
*Coates, Kenneth S. (*b.* 1930), *Lab., Nottinghamshire North and Chesterfield,* maj. 76,260
*Collins, Kenneth D. (*b.* 1939), *Lab., Strathclyde East,* maj. 52,340
Corbett, Richard (*b.* 1955), *Lab., Merseyside West,* maj. 18,704
Corrie, John A. (*b.* 1935), *C., Worcestershire and Warwickshire South,* maj. 1,204
*Crampton, Peter D. (*b.* 1932), *Lab., Humberside,* maj. 40,618
*Crawley, Mrs Christine M. (*b.* 1950), *Lab., Birmingham East,* maj. 55,170
Cunningham, Thomas A. (Tony) (*b.* 1952), *Lab., Cumbria and Lancashire North,* maj. 22,988
*David, Wayne (*b.* 1957), *Lab., South Wales Central,* maj. 86,082
*Donnelly, Alan J. (*b.* 1957), *Lab., Tyne and Wear,* maj. 88,380
Donnelly, Brendan P. (*b.* 1950), *C., Sussex South and Crawley,* maj. 1,746
*Elles, James E. M. (*b.* 1949), *C., Buckinghamshire and Oxfordshire East,* maj. 30,665
*Elliott, Michael N. (*b.* 1932), *Lab., London West,* maj. 42,275
Evans, Robert J. E. (*b.* 1956), *Lab., London North West,* maj. 17,442
*Ewing, Mrs Winifred M. (*b.* 1929), *SNP, Highlands and Islands,* maj. 54,916
*Falconer, Alexander (*b.* 1940), *Lab., Scotland Mid and Fife,* maj. 31,413

*Ford, J. Glyn (*b.* 1950), *Lab., Greater Manchester East,* maj. 55,986
*Green, Mrs Pauline (*b.* 1948), *Lab., London North,* maj. 48,348
Hallam, David J. A. (*b.* 1948), *Lab., Herefordshire and Shropshire,* maj. 1,850
Hardstaff, Mrs Veronica M. (*b.* 1941), *Lab., Lincolnshire and Humberside South,* maj. 13,745
*Harrison, Lyndon H. A. (*b.* 1947), *Lab., Cheshire West and Wirral,* maj. 47,176
Hendrick, Mark P. (*b.* 1958), *Lab., Lancashire Central,* maj. 12,191
*Hindley, Michael J. (*b.* 1947), *Lab., Lancashire South,* maj. 41,404
Howitt, Richard (*b.* 1961), *Lab., Essex South,* maj. 21,367
*Hughes, Stephen S. (*b.* 1952), *Lab., Durham,* maj. 111,638
*Hume, John, MP (*b.* 1937), *SDLP, Northern Ireland,* polled 161,992 votes
*Jackson, Mrs Caroline F., D.Phil. (*b.* 1946), *C., Wiltshire North and Bath,* maj. 8,787
*Kellett-Bowman, Edward T. (*b.* 1931), *C., Itchen, Test and Avon,* maj. 6,903
Kerr, Hugh (*b.* 1944), *Lab., Essex West and Hertfordshire East,* maj. 3,067
Kinnock, Mrs Glenys E. (*b.* 1944), *Lab., South Wales East,* maj. 120,247
*Lomas, Alfred (*b.* 1928), *Lab., London North East,* maj. 57,085
Macartney, W. J. Allan, Ph.D. (*b.* 1941), *SNP, Scotland North East,* maj. 31,227
McCarthy, Ms Arlene (*b.* 1960), *Lab., Peak District,* maj. 49,307
*McGowan, Michael (*b.* 1940), *Lab., Leeds,* maj. 53,082
*McIntosh, Miss Anne C. B., MP (*b.* 1954), *C., Essex North and Suffolk South,* maj. 3,633
*McMahon, Hugh R. (*b.* 1938), *Lab., Strathclyde West,* maj. 25,023
*McMillan-Scott, Edward H. C. (*b.* 1949), *C., Yorkshire North,* maj. 7,072
McNally, Mrs Eryl M. (*b.* 1942), *Lab., Bedfordshire and Milton Keynes,* maj. 33,209
*Martin, David W. (*b.* 1954), *Lab., Lothians,* maj. 37,207
Mather, Graham C. S. (*b.* 1954), *C., Hampshire North and Oxford,* maj. 9,194
*Megahy, Thomas (*b.* 1929), *Lab., Yorkshire South West,* maj. 59,562
Miller, Bill (*b.* 1954), *Lab., Glasgow,* maj. 13,158
*Moorhouse, C. James O. (*b.* 1924), *C., London South and Surrey East,* maj. 8,739
Morgan, Ms Eluned (*b.* 1967), *Lab., Wales Mid and West,* maj. 29,234
*Morris, Revd David R. (*b.* 1930), *Lab., South Wales West,* maj. 84,970
Murphy, Simon F., Ph.D. (*b.* 1962), *Lab., Midlands West,* maj. 54,823
Needle, Clive (*b.* 1956), *Lab., Norfolk,* maj. 26,287
*Newens, A. Stanley (*b.* 1930), *Lab., London Central,* maj. 25,059
*Newman, Edward (*b.* 1953), *Lab., Greater Manchester Central,* maj. 42,445
*Nicholson, James F. (*b.* 1945), *UUUP, Northern Ireland,* polled 133,459 votes
*Oddy, Ms Christine M. (*b.* 1955), *Lab., Coventry and Warwickshire North,* maj. 43,901
*Paisley, Revd Ian R. K., MP (*b.* 1926), *DUP, Northern Ireland,* polled 163,246 votes

Perry, Roy J. (b. 1943), C., Wight and Hampshire South, maj. 5,101

*Plumb, The Lord (b. 1925), C., Cotswolds, maj. 4,268

*Pollack, Ms Anita J. (b. 1946), Lab., London South West, maj. 30,975

Provan, James L. C. (b. 1936), C., South Downs West, maj. 21,067

*Read, Ms I. M. (Mel) (b. 1939), Lab., Nottingham and Leicestershire North West, maj. 39,668

*Seal, Barry H., PH.D. (b. 1937), Lab., Yorkshire West, maj. 48,197

*Simpson, Brian (b. 1953), Lab., Cheshire East, maj. 39,279

Skinner, Peter W. (b. 1959), Lab., Kent West, maj. 16,777

*Smith, Alexander (b. 1943), Lab., Scotland South, maj. 45,155

*Spencer, Thomas N. B. (b. 1948), C., Surrey, maj. 27,018

Spiers, Shaun M. (b. 1962), Lab., London South East, maj. 8,022

*Stevens, John C. C. (b. 1955), C., Thames Valley, maj. 758

*Stewart-Clark, Sir John, Bt. (b. 1929), C., Sussex East and Kent South, maj. 6,212

Sturdy, Robert W. (b. 1944), C., Cambridgeshire, maj. 3,942

Tappin, Michael (b. 1946), Lab., Staffordshire West and Congleton, maj. 40,277

Teverson, Robin (b. 1952), LD, Cornwall and Plymouth West, maj. 29,498

Thomas, David E. (b. 1955), Lab., Suffolk and Norfolk South West, maj. 12,535

*Titley, Gary (b. 1950), Lab., Greater Manchester West, maj. 58,635

*Tomlinson, John E. (b. 1939), Lab., Birmingham West, maj. 39,350

*Tongue, Ms Carole (b. 1955), Lab., London East, maj. 57,389

Truscott, Peter, PH.D. (b. 1959), Lab., Hertfordshire, maj. 10,304

Waddington, Mrs Susan A. (b. 1944), Lab., Leicester, maj. 20,284

Watson, Graham R. (b. 1956), LD, Somerset and Devon North, maj. 22,509

Watts, Mark F. (b. 1964), Lab., Kent East, maj. 635

*West, Norman, (b. 1935), Lab., Yorkshire South, maj. 88,309

*White, Ian (b. 1947), Lab., Bristol, maj. 29,955

Whitehead, Phillip (b. 1937), Lab., Staffordshire East and Derby, maj. 72,196

*Wilson, A. Joseph (b. 1937), Lab., Wales North, maj. 15,242

*Wynn, Terence (b. 1946), Lab., Merseyside East and Wigan, maj. 74,087

UK CONSTITUENCIES AS AT 9 JUNE 1994

Abbreviations

Anti Fed.	UK Independence Anti-Federal
Anti Fed. C.	Official Anti-Federalist Conservative
Beanus	Eurobean from Planet Beanus
C. Non Fed.	Conservative Non-Federal Party
Capital P.	Restoration of Capital Punishment
Comm.	Communist
Comm. YBG	Communist Y Blaid Gomiwyddol
Const. NI	Constitutional Independence for N. Ireland
Corr.	Corrective Party
CPP	Christian People's Party
ICP	International Communist Party
ICP4	International Communist Party (4th International)
Ind. AES	Independent Anti-European Superstate
Ind. Out	Independent Out of Europe
Judo	European People's Party Judo Christian Alliance
Loony C	Raving Loony Commonsense
Loony CP	Monster Raving Loony Christian Party
Loony X	Monster Raving Loony Project X Party
MCCARTHY	Make Criminals Concerned About Our Response To Hostility and Yobbishness
MK	Mebyon Kernow
NCSA	Network Against Child Support Agency
Neeps	North East Ethnic Party, The Neeps
Rainbow	Rainbow Connection – Oui-Say-Non-Party
Sportsman	Sportsman Anti-Common Market Bureaucracy
UUUP	United Ulster Unionist Party

For other abbreviations, *see* page 235

ENGLAND

BEDFORDSHIRE AND MILTON KEYNES
E. 525,524   *T.* 38.74%

E. McNally, *Lab.*	94,837
Mrs E. Currie, *C.*	61,628
Ms M. Howes, *LD*	27,994
A. Sked, *UK Independence*	7,485
A. Francis, *Green*	6,804
A. Howes, *New Britain*	3,878
L. Sheaff, *NLP*	939
Lab. majority	33,209

(Boundary change since June 1989)

BIRMINGHAM EAST
E. 520,782   *T.* 29.77%

*Mrs C. Crawley, *Lab.*	90,291
A. Turner, *C.*	35,171
Ms C. Cane, *LD*	19,455
P. Simpson, *Green*	6,268
R. Cook, *Soc.*	1,969
M. Brierley, *NLP*	1,885
Lab. majority	55,120

(June 1989, Lab. maj. 46,948)

BIRMINGHAM WEST
E. 509,948   *T.* 28.49%

*J. Tomlinson, *Lab.*	77,957
D. Harman, *C.*	38,607
N. McGeorge, *LD*	14,603
Dr B. Juby, *Anti Fed.*	5,237
M. Abbott, *Green*	4,367
A. Carmichael, *NF*	3,727
H. Meads, *NLP*	789
Lab. majority	39,350

(June 1989, Lab. maj. 30,860)

BRISTOL
E. 503,218   *T.* 40.91%

*I. White, *Lab.*	90,790
The Earl of Stockton, *C.*	60,835
J. Barnard, *LD*	40,394

J. Boxall, *Green*	7,163
T. Whittingham, *UK Independence*	5,798
T. Dyball, *NLP*	876
Lab. majority	29,955

(Boundary change since June 1989)

BUCKINGHAMSHIRE AND OXFORDSHIRE EAST
E. 487,692   *T.* 37.31%

*J. Elles, *C.*	77,037
D. Enright, *Lab.*	46,372
Ms S. Bowles, *LD*	42,836
L. Roach, *Green*	8,433
Ms A. Micklem, *Lib.*	5,111
Dr G. Clements, *NLP*	2,156
C. majority	30,665

(Boundary change since June 1989)

CAMBRIDGESHIRE
E. 495,383   *T.* 35.91%

R. Sturdy, *C.*	66,921
Ms M. Johnson, *Lab.*	62,979
A. Duff, *LD*	36,114
Ms M. Wright, *Green*	5,756
P. Wiggin, *Lib.*	4,051
F. Chalmers, *NLP*	2,077
C. majority	3,942

(Boundary change since June 1989)

CHESHIRE EAST
E. 502,726   *T.* 32.46%

*B. Simpson, *Lab.*	87,586
P. Slater, *C.*	48,307
P. Harris, *LD*	20,552
D. Wild, *Green*	3,671
P. Dixon, *Loony CP*	1,600
P. Leadbetter, *NLP*	1,488
Lab. majority	39,279

(Boundary change since June 1989)

CHESHIRE WEST AND WIRRAL
E. 538,571   T. 36.78%
*L. Harrison, *Lab.* 106,160
D. Senior, *C.* 58,981
I. Mottershaw, *LD* 20,746
D. Carson, *British Home Rule* 6,167
M. Money, *Green* 5,096
A. Wilmot, *NLP* 929
Lab. majority 47,176
(Boundary change since June 1989)

CLEVELAND AND RICHMOND
E. 499,580   T. 35.26%
*D. Bowe, *Lab.* 103,355
R. Goodwill, *C.* 45,787
B. Moore, *LD* 21,574
G. Parr, *Green* 4,375
R. Scott, *NLP* 1,068
Lab. majority 57,568
(Boundary change since June 1989)

CORNWALL AND PLYMOUTH WEST
E. 484,697   T. 44.92%
R. Teverson, *LD* 91,113
*C. Beazley, *C.* 61,615
Mrs D. Kirk, *Lab.* 42,907
Mrs P. Garnier, *UK Independence*
6,466
P. Holmes, *Lib.* 6,414
Ms K. Westbrook, *Green* 4,372
Dr L. Jenkin, *MK* 3,315
F. Lyons, *NLP* 921
M. Fitzgerald, *Subsidiarity* 606
LD majority 29,498
(Boundary change since June 1989)

COTSWOLDS
E. 497,588   T. 39.27%
*The Lord Plumb, *C.* 67,484
Ms T. Kingham, *Lab.* 63,216
J. Thomson, *LD* 11,269
M. Rendell, *New Britain* 11,044
D. McCanlis, *Green* 8,254
H. Brighouse, *NLP* 1,151
C. majority 4,268
(Boundary change since June 1989)

COVENTRY AND WARWICKSHIRE
NORTH
E. 523,448   T. 32.54%
*Ms C. Oddy, *Lab.* 89,500
Ms J. Crabb, *C.* 45,599
G. Sewards, *LD* 17,453
R. Meacham, *Free Trade* 9,432
P. Baptie, *Green* 1,360
R. Wheway, *Lib.* 2,885
R. France, *NLP* 1,098
Lab. majority 43,901
(Boundary change since June 1989)

CUMBRIA AND LANCASHIRE NORTH
E. 498,557   T. 40.78%
A. Cunningham, *Lab.* 97,599
*The Lord Inglewood, *C.* 74,611
R. Putnam, *LD* 24,233
R. Frost, *Green* 5,344
I. Docker, *NLP* 1,500
Lab. majority 22,988
(Boundary change since June 1989)

DEVON AND PLYMOUTH EAST
E. 524,320   T. 45.07%
G. Chichester, *C.* 74,953
A. Sanders, *LD* 74,253
Ms L. Gilroy, *Lab.* 47,596
D. Morrish, *Lib.* 14,621
P. Edwards, *Green* 11,172
R. Huggett, *Literal Democrat* 10,203
J. Everard, *Ind.* 2,629
A. Pringle, *NLP* 908
C. majority 700
(Boundary change since June 1989)

DORSET AND DEVON EAST
E. 531,842   T. 41.21%
*B. Cassidy, *C.* 81,551
P. Goldenberg, *LD* 79,287
A. Gardner, *Lab.* 34,856
M. Floyd, *UK Independence* 10,548
Mrs K. Bradbury, *Green* 8,642
I. Mortimer, *C. Non Fed.* 3,229
M. Griffiths, *NLP* 1,048
C. majority 2,264
(Boundary change since June 1989)

DURHAM
E. 532,051   T. 35.62%
*S. Hughes, *Lab.* 136,671
P. Bradbourn, *C.* 25,033
Dr N. Martin, *LD* 20,935
S. Hope, *Green* 5,670
C. Adamson, *NLP* 1,198
Lab. majority 111,638
(June 1989, Lab. maj. 86,848)

ESSEX NORTH AND SUFFOLK SOUTH
E. 497,098   T. 41.33%
*Ms A. McIntosh, *C.* 68,311
C. Pearson, *Lab.* 64,678
S. Mole, *LD* 52,536
S. de Chair, *Ind. 4FS* 12,409
J. Abbott, *Green* 6,641
N. Pullen, *NLP* 884
C. majority 3,633
(Boundary change since June 1989)

ESSEX SOUTH
E. 487,221   T. 33.08%
R. Howitt, *Lab.* 71,883
L. Stanbrook, *C.* 50,516
G. Williams, *LD* 26,132
B. Lynch, *Lib.* 6,780
G. Rumens, *Green* 4,691
M. Heath, *NLP* 1,177
Lab. majority 21,367
(Boundary change since June 1989)

ESSEX WEST AND HERTFORDSHIRE
EAST
E. 504,095   T. 36.39%
H. Kerr, *Lab.* 66,379
*Ms P. Rawlings, *C.* 63,312
Ms G. James, *LD* 35,695
B. Smalley, *Britain* 10,277
Ms F. Mawson, *Green* 5,632
P. Carter, *Sportsman* 1,127
L. Davis, *NLP* 1,026
Lab. majority 3,067
(Boundary change since June 1989)

GREATER MANCHESTER CENTRAL
E. 481,779   T. 29.11%
*E. Newman, *Lab.* 74,935
Mrs S. Mason, *C.* 32,490
J. Begg, *LD* 22,988
B. Candeland, *Green* 4,952
P. Burke, *Lib.* 3,862
P. Stanley, *NLP* 1,017
Lab. majority 42,445
(Boundary change since June 1989)

GREATER MANCHESTER EAST
E. 501,125   T. 27.17%
*G. Ford, *Lab.* 82,289
J. Pinniger, *C.* 26,303
A. Riley, *LD* 20,545
T. Clarke, *Green* 5,823
W. Stevens, *NLP* 1,183
Lab. majority 55,986
(Boundary change since June 1989)

GREATER MANCHESTER WEST
E. 512,618   T. 29.70%
*G. Titley, *Lab.* 94,129
D. Newns, *C.* 35,494
F. Harasiwka, *LD* 13,650
R. Jackson, *Green* 3,950
G. Harrison, *MCCARTHY* 3,693
T. Brotheridge, *NLP* 1,316
Lab. majority 58,635
(Boundary change since June 1989)

HAMPSHIRE NORTH AND OXFORD
E. 525,982   T. 38.31%
G. Mather, *C.* 72,209
Ms J. Hawkins, *LD* 63,015
J. Tanner, *Lab.* 48,525
D. Wilkinson, *UK Independence* 8,377
Dr M. Woodin, *Green* 7,310
H. Godfrey, *NLP* 1,027
R. Boston, *Boston Tea Party* 1,018
C. majority 9,194
(Boundary change since June 1989)

HEREFORDSHIRE AND SHROPSHIRE
E. 536,470   T. 38.69%
D. Hallam, *Lab.* 76,120
*Sir C. Prout, *C.* 74,270
J. Gallagher, *LD* 44,130
Ms F. Norman, *Green* 11,578
T. Mercer, *NLP* 1,480
Lab. majority 1,850
(Boundary change since June 1989)

HERTFORDSHIRE
E. 522,338   T. 40.11%
Dr P. Truscott, *Lab.* 81,821
P. Jenkinson, *C.* 71,517
D. Griffiths, *LD* 38,995
Ms L. Howitt, *Green* 7,741
M. Biggs, *New Britain* 6,555
J. McAuley, *NF* 1,755
D. Lucas, *NLP* 734
J. Laine, *Century* 369
Lab. majority 10,304
(Boundary change since June 1989)

HUMBERSIDE
E. 519,013   T. 32.38%
*P. Crampton, *Lab.* 87,296
D. Stewart, *C.* 46,678
Ms D. Wallis, *LD* 28,818
Ms S. Mummery, *Green* 4,170

Ms A. Miszewska, *NLP*   1,100
Lab. majority   40,618
(Boundary change since June 1989)

ITCHEN, TEST AND AVON
E. 550,406   *T.* 41.83%
*E. Kellett-Bowman, *C.*   81,456
A. Barron, *LD*   74,553
E. Read, *Lab.*   52,416
N. Farage, *UK Independence*   12,423
Ms F. Hulbert, *Green*   7,998
A. Miller-Smith, *NLP*   1,368
C. majority   6,903
(Boundary change since June 1989)

KENT EAST
E. 499,662   *T.* 40.34%
M. Watts, *Lab.*   69,641
*C. Jackson, *C.*   69,006
J. Macdonald, *LD*   44,549
C. Bullen, *UK Independence*   9,414
S. Dawe, *Green*   7,196
C. Beckley, *NLP*   1,746
Lab. majority   635
(Boundary change since June 1989)

KENT WEST
E. 505,658   *T.* 37.33%
P. Skinner, *Lab.*   77,346
*B. Patterson, *C.*   60,569
J. Daly, *LD*   33,869
C. Mackinlay, *UK Independence*   9,750
Ms P. Kemp, *Green*   5,651
J. Bowler, *NLP*   1,598
Lab. majority   16,777
(Boundary change since June 1989)

LANCASHIRE CENTRAL
E. 505,224   *T.* 33.23%
M. Hendrick, *Lab.*   73,420
*M. Welsh, *C.*   61,229
Ms J. Ross-Mills, *LD*   20,578
D. Hill, *Home Rule*   6,751
C. Maile, *Green*   4,169
Ms J. Ayliffe, *NLP*   1,727
Lab. majority   12,191
(Boundary change since June 1989)

LANCASHIRE SOUTH
E. 514,840   *T.* 33.14%
*M. Hindley, *Lab.*   92,598
R. Topham, *C.*   51,194
J. Ault, *LD*   17,008
J. Gaffney, *Green*   4,774
Mrs E. Rokas, *Ind.*   3,439
J. Renwick, *NLP*   1,605
Lab. majority   41,404
(Boundary change since June 1989)

LEEDS
E. 521,989   *T.* 30.03%
*M. McGowan, *Lab.*   89,160
N. Carmichael, *C.*   36,078
Ms J. Harvey, *LD*   17,575
M. Meadowcroft, *Lib.*   6,617
Ms C. Nash, *Green*   6,283
Ms S. Hayward, *NLP*   1,018
Lab. majority   53,082
(June 1989, Lab. maj. 42,518)

LEICESTER
E. 515,343   *T.* 37.63%
Ms S. Waddington, *Lab.*   87,048
A. Marshall, *C.*   66,764
M. Jones, *LD*   28,890
G. Forse, *Green*   8,941
Ms P. Saunders, *NLP*   2,283
Lab. majority   20,284
(Boundary change since June 1989)

LINCOLNSHIRE AND HUMBERSIDE SOUTH
E. 539,981   *T.* 36.34%
Mrs V. Hardstaff, *Lab.*   83,172
*W. Newton Dunn, *C.*   69,427
K. Melton, *LD*   27,241
Ms R. Robinson, *Green*   8,563
E. Wheeler, *Lib.*   3,434
I. Selby, *NCSA*   2,973
H. Kelly, *NLP*   1,429
Lab. majority   13,745
(Boundary change since June 1989)

LONDON CENTRAL
E. 494,610   *T.* 32.57%
*S. Newens, *Lab.*   75,711
A. Elliott, *C.*   50,652
Ms S. Ludford, *LD*   20,176
Ms N. Kortvelyessy, *Green*   7,043
H. Le Fanu, *UK Independence*   4,157
C. Slapper, *Soc.*   1,593
Ms S. Hamza, *NLP*   1,215
G. Weiss, *Rainbow*   547
Lab. majority   25,059
(June 1989, Lab. maj. 11,542)

LONDON EAST
E. 511,523   *T.* 33.38%
*Ms C. Tongue, *Lab.*   98,759
Ms V. Taylor, *C.*   41,370
K. Montgomery, *LD*   15,566
G. Batten, *UK Independence*   5,974
J. Baguley, *Green*   4,337
O. Tillett, *Third Way Independence*   3,484
N. Kahn, *NLP*   1,272
Lab. majority   57,389
(June 1989, Lab. maj. 27,385)

LONDON NORTH
E. 541,269   *T.* 34.00%
*Mrs P. Green, *Lab.*   102,059
M. Keegan, *C.*   53,711
I. Mann, *LD*   15,739
Ms H. Jago, *Green*   5,666
I. Booth, *UK Independence*   5,099
G. Sabrizi, *Judo*   880
J. Hinde, *NLP*   856
Lab. majority   48,348
(June 1989, Lab. maj. 5,837)

LONDON NORTH EAST
E. 486,016   *T.* 26.60%
*A. Lomas, *Lab.*   80,256
S. Gordon, *C.*   23,171
K. Appiah, *LD*   10,242
Ms J. Lambert, *Green*   8,386
E. Murat, *Lib.*   2,573
P. Compobassi, *UK Independence*   2,015
R. Archer, *NLP*   1,111
M. Fischer, *Comm. GB*   869
A. Hyland, *ICP4*   679

Lab. majority   57,085
(June 1989, Lab. maj. 47,767)

LONDON NORTH WEST
E. 481,272   *T.* 35.13%
R. Evans, *Lab.*   80,192
*The Lord Bethell, *C.*   62,750
Ms H. Leighter, *LD*   18,998
D. Johnson, *Green*   4,743
Ms A. Murphy, *Comm. GB*   858
Ms T. Sullivan, *NLP*   807
C. Palmer, *Century*   740
Lab. majority   17,442
(June 1989, C. maj. 7,400)

LONDON SOUTH AND SURREY EAST
E. 486,358   *T.* 34.38%
*J. Moorhouse, *C.*   64,813
Ms G. Rolles, *Lab.*   56,074
M. Reinisch, *LD*   32,059
J. Cornford, *Green*   7,046
J. Major, *Loony X*   3,339
A. Reeve, *Capital P.*   2,983
P. Levy, *NLP*   887
C. majority   8,739
(Boundary change since June 1989)

LONDON SOUTH EAST
E. 493,178   *T.* 35.38%
S. Spiers, *Lab.*   71,505
*P. Price, *C.*   63,483
J. Fryer, *LD*   25,271
I. Mouland, *Green*   6,399
R. Almond, *Lib.*   3,881
K. Lowne, *NF*   2,926
J. Small, *NLP*   1,025
Lab. majority   8,022
(Boundary change since June 1989)

LONDON SOUTH INNER
E. 510,609   *T.* 27.30%
*R. Balfe, *Lab.*   85,079
A. Boff, *C.*   25,859
A. Graves, *LD*   20,708
S. Collins, *Green*   6,570
M. Leighton, *NLP*   1,179
Lab. majority   59,220
(Boundary change since June 1989)

LONDON SOUTH WEST
E. 479,246   *T.* 34.35%
*Ms A. Pollack, *Lab.*   81,850
Prof. P. Treleaven, *C.*   50,875
G. Blanchard, *LD*   18,697
T. Walsh, *Green*   5,460
A. Scholefield, *UK Independence*   4,912
C. Hopewell, *Capital P.*   1,840
M. Simson, *NLP*   625
J. Quanjer, *Spirit of Europe*   377
Lab. majority   30,975
(Boundary change since June 1989)

LONDON WEST
E. 505,791   *T.* 36.02%
*M. Elliott, *Lab.*   94,562
R. Guy, *C.*   52,287
W. Mallinson, *LD*   21,561
J. Bradley, *Green*   6,134
G. Roberts, *UK Independence*   4,583
W. Binding, *NF*   1,963
R. Johnson, *NLP*   1,105
Lab. majority   42,275
(June 1989, Lab. maj. 14,808)

MERSEYSIDE EAST AND WIGAN
E. 518,196   T. 24.66%

*T. Wynn, *Lab.*	91,986
C. Manson, *C.*	17,899
Ms F. Clucas, *LD*	8,874
J. Melia, *Lib.*	4,765
L. Brown, *Green*	3,280
G. Hutchard, *NLP*	1,009
Lab. majority	74,087
(June 1989, Lab. maj. 76,867)	

MERSEYSIDE WEST
E. 515,909   T. 26.18%

*K. Stewart, *Lab.*	78,819
C. Varley, *C.*	27,008
D. Bamber, *LD*	19,097
S. Radford, *Lib.*	4,714
Ms L. Lever, *Green*	4,573
J. Collins, *NLP*	852
Lab. majority	51,811
(June 1989, Lab. maj. 49,817)	
See also page 275	

MIDLANDS WEST
E. 533,742   T. 31.28%

S. Murphy, *Lab.*	99,242
M. Simpson, *C.*	44,419
G. Baldauf-Good, *LD*	12,195
M. Hyde, *Lib.*	5,050
C. Mattingly, *Green*	4,390
J. Oldbury, *NLP*	1,641
Lab. majority	54,823
(June 1989, Lab. maj. 42,364)	

NORFOLK
E. 513,553   T. 44.25%

C. Needle, *Lab.*	102,711
*P. Howell, *C.*	76,424
P. Burall, *LD*	39,107
A. Holmes, *Green*	7,938
B. Parsons, *NLP*	1,075
Lab. majority	26,287
(Boundary change since June 1989)	

NORTHAMPTONSHIRE AND BLABY
E. 524,916   T. 39.37%

Mrs A. Billingham, *Lab.*	95,317
*A. Simpson, *C.*	69,232
K. Scudder, *LD*	27,616
Ms A. Bryant, *Green*	9,121
I. Whitaker, *Ind.*	4,397
B. Spivack, *NLP*	972
Lab. majority	26,085
(Boundary change since June 1989)	

NORTHUMBRIA
E. 516,680   T. 33.65%

*G. Adam, *Lab.*	103,087
J. Flack, *C.*	36,929
L. Opik, *LD*	20,195
D. Lott, *UK Independence*	7,210
J. Hartshorne, *Green*	5,714
L. Walch, *NLP*	740
Lab. majority	66,158
(June 1989, Lab. maj. 60,040)	

NOTTINGHAM AND LEICESTERSHIRE
NORTH WEST
E. 507,915   T. 37.68%

*Ms M. Read, *Lab.*	95,344
M. Brandon-Bravo, *C.*	55,676
A. Wood, *LD*	23,836
Ms S. Blount, *Green*	7,035

J. Downes, *UK Independence*   5,849
P. Walton, *Ind. Out*   2,710
Mrs J. Christou, *NLP*   927
Lab. majority   39,668
(Boundary change since June 1989)

NOTTINGHAMSHIRE NORTH AND
CHESTERFIELD
E. 490,330   T. 36.95%

*K. Coates, *Lab.*	114,353
D. Hazell, *C.*	38,093
Ms S. Pearce, *LD*	21,936
G. Jones, *Green*	5,159
Ms S. Lincoln, *NLP*	1,632
Lab. majority	76,260
(Boundary change since June 1989)	

PEAK DISTRICT
E. 511,357   T. 39.02%

Ms A. McCarthy, *Lab.*	105,853
R. Fletcher, *C.*	56,546
Ms S. Barber, *LD*	29,979
M. Shipley, *Green*	5,598
D. Collins, *NLP*	1,533
Lab. majority	49,307
(Boundary change since June 1989)	

SHEFFIELD
E. 476,530   T. 27.50%

*R. Barton, *Lab.*	76,397
Ms S. Anginotti, *LD*	26,109
Ms K. Twitchen, *C.*	22,374
B. New, *Green*	4,742
M. England, *Comm.*	834
R. Hurford, *NLP*	577
Lab. majority	50,288
(Boundary change since June 1989)	

SOMERSET AND DEVON NORTH
E. 517,349   T. 47.09%

G. Watson, *LD*	106,187
*Mrs M. Daly, *C.*	83,678
J. Pilgrim, *Lab.*	34,540
D. Taylor, *Green*	10,870
G. Livings, *New Britain*	7,165
M. Lucas, *NLP*	1,200
LD majority	22,509
(Boundary change since June 1989)	

SOUTH DOWNS WEST
E. 486,793   T. 39.45%

J. Provan, *C.*	83,813
Dr J. Walsh, *LD*	62,746
Ms L. Armstrong, *Lab.*	32,344
E. Paine, *Green*	7,703
W. Weights, *Lib.*	3,630
P. Kember, *NLP*	1,794
C. majority	21,067
(Boundary change since June 1989)	

STAFFORDSHIRE EAST AND DERBY
E. 519,553   T. 35.46%

P. Whitehead, *Lab.*	102,393
Ms J. Evans, *C.*	50,197
Ms D. Brass, *LD*	17,469
I. Crompton, *UK Independence*	6,993
R. Clarke, *Green*	4,272
R. Jones, *NF*	2,098
Ms D. Grice, *NLP*	793
Lab. majority	72,196
(Boundary change since June 1989)	

STAFFORDSHIRE WEST AND
CONGLETON
E. 502,395   T. 31.60%

M. Tappin, *Lab.*	84,337
A. Brown, *C.*	44,060
J. Stevens, *LD*	24,430
D. Hoppe, *Green*	4,533
D. Lines, *NLP*	1,403
Lab. majority	40,277
(Boundary change since June 1989)	

SUFFOLK AND NORFOLK SOUTH
WEST
E. 477,668   T. 38.38%

D. Thomas, *Lab.*	74,304
*A. Turner, *C.*	61,769
R. Atkins, *LD*	37,975
A. Slade, *Green*	7,760
E. Kaplan, *NLP*	1,530
Lab. majority	12,535
(Boundary change since June 1989)	

SURREY
E. 514,130   T. 37.51%

*T. Spencer, *C.*	83,405
Mrs S. Thomas, *LD*	56,387
Ms F. Wolf, *Lab.*	30,894
Mrs S. Porter, *UK Independence*	7,717
H. Charlton, *Green*	7,198
J. Walker, *Ind. Britain in Europe*	4,627
Mrs J. Thomas, *NLP*	2,638
C. majority	27,018
(Boundary change since June 1989)	

SUSSEX EAST AND KENT SOUTH
E. 513,550   T. 41.90%

*Sir J. Stewart-Clark, *C.*	83,141
D. Bellotti, *LD*	76,929
N. Palmer, *Lab.*	35,273
A. Burgess, *UK Independence*	9,058
Ms R. Addison, *Green*	7,439
Ms T. Williamson, *Lib.*	2,558
P. Cragg, *NLP*	765
C. majority	6,212
(Boundary change since June 1989)	

SUSSEX SOUTH AND CRAWLEY
E. 492,413   T. 37.64%

B. Donnelly, *C.*	62,860
Ms J. Edmond Smith, *Lab.*	61,114
J. Williams, *LD*	41,410
Ms P. Beever, *Green*	9,348
D. Horner, *Ind. Euro-Sceptic*	7,106
N. Furness, *Anti Fed. C.*	2,618
A. Hankey, *NLP*	901
C. majority	1,746
(Boundary change since June 1989)	

THAMES VALLEY
E. 543,685   T. 34.80%

*J. Stevens, *C.*	70,485
J. Howarth, *Lab.*	69,727
N. Bathurst, *LD*	33,187
P. Unsworth, *Green*	6,120
J. Clark, *Lib.*	5,381
P. Owen, *Loony C*	2,859
M. Grenville, *NLP*	1,453
C. majority	758
(June 1989, C. maj. 26,491)	

TYNE AND WEAR
E. 516,436   T. 28.02%

*A. Donnelly, *Lab.*	107,604
I. Liddell-Grainger, *C.*	19,224
P. Maughan, *LD*	8,706
G. Edwards, *Green*	4,375
Ms W. Lundgren, *Lib.*	4,164
A. Fisken, *NLP*	650
Lab. majority	88,380
(June 1989, Lab. maj. 95,780)	

WIGHT AND HAMPSHIRE SOUTH
E. 488,398   T. 37.16%

R. Perry, *C.*	63,306
M. Hancock, *LD*	58,205
Ms S. Fry, *Lab.*	40,442
J. Browne, *Ind.*	12,140
P. Fuller, *Green*	6,697
W. Treend, *NLP*	722
C. majority	5,101
(Boundary change since June 1989)	

WILTSHIRE NORTH AND BATH
E. 496,591   T. 41.46%

*Mrs C. Jackson, *C.*	71,872
Ms J. Matthew, *LD*	63,085
Ms J. Norris, *Lab.*	50,489
P. Cullen, *Lib.*	6,760
M. Davidson, *Green*	5,974
T. Hedges, *UK Independence*	5,842
D. Cooke, *NLP*	1,148
Dr J. Day, *CPP*	725
C. majority	8,787
(Boundary change since June 1989)	

WORCESTERSHIRE AND
WARWICKSHIRE SOUTH
E. 551,162   T. 37.98%

J. Corrie, *C.*	73,573
Ms G. Gschaider, *Lab.*	72,369
P. Larner, *LD*	44,168
Ms J. Alty, *Green*	9,273
C. Hards, *National Independence*	8,447
J. Brewster, *NLP*	1,510
C. majority	1,204
(Boundary change since June 1989)	

YORKSHIRE NORTH
E. 475,686   T. 38.70%

*E. McMillan-Scott, *C.*	70,036
B. Regan, *Lab.*	62,964
M. Pitts, *LD*	43,171
Dr R. Richardson, *Green*	7,036
S. Withers, *NLP*	891
C. majority	7,072
(Boundary change since June 1989)	

YORKSHIRE SOUTH
E. 523,401   T. 28.64%

*N. West, *Lab.*	109,004
J. Howard, *C.*	20,695
Ms C. Roderick, *LD*	11,798
P. Davies, *UK Independence*	3,948
J. Waters, *Green*	3,775
N. Broome, *NLP*	681
Lab. majority	88,309
(June 1989, Lab. maj. 91,784)	

YORKSHIRE SOUTH WEST
E. 547,469   T. 29.03%

*T. Megahy, *Lab.*	94,025
Mrs C. Adamson, *C.*	34,463
D. Ridgway, *LD*	21,595

A. Cooper, *Green*	7,163
G. Mead, *NLP*	1,674
Lab. majority	59,562
(Boundary change since June 1989)	

YORKSHIRE WEST
E. 490,078   T. 34.61%

*B. Seal, *Lab.*	90,652
R. Booth, *C.*	42,455
C. Bidwell, *LD*	20,452
R. Pearson, *New Britain*	8,027
C. Harris, *Green*	7,154
D. Whitley, *NLP*	894
Lab. majority	48,197
(Boundary change since June 1989)	

WALES

SOUTH WALES CENTRAL
E. 477,182   T. 39.40%

*W. David, *Lab.*	115,396
Ms L. Verity, *C.*	29,314
G. Llywelyn, *PC*	18,857
J. Dixon, *LD*	18,471
C. von Ruhland, *Green*	4,002
R. Griffiths, *Comm. YBG*	1,073
G. Duguay, *NLP*	889
Lab. majority	86,082
(Boundary change since June 1989)	

SOUTH WALES EAST
E. 454,794   T. 43.07%

Mrs G. Kinnock, *Lab.*	144,907
Mrs R. Blomfield-Smith, *C.*	24,660
C. Woolgrove, *LD*	9,963
C. Mann, *PC*	9,550
R. Coghill, *Green*	4,509
Ms S. Williams, *Welsh Soc.*	1,270
Dr R. Brussatis, *NLP*	1,027
Lab. majority	120,247
(Boundary change since June 1989)	

SOUTH WALES WEST
E. 395,131   T. 39.92%

*Revd D. Morris, *Lab.*	104,263
R. Buckland, *C.*	19,293
J. Bushell, *LD*	15,499
Ms C. Adams, *PC*	12,364
Ms J. Evans, *Green*	4,114
Ms H. Evans, *NLP*	1,112
Capt. Beany, *Beanus*	1,106
Lab. majority	84,970
(Boundary change since June 1989)	

WALES MID AND WEST
E. 401,529   T. 48.00%

Ms E. Morgan, *Lab.*	78,092
M. Phillips, *PC*	48,858
P. Bone, *C.*	31,606
Ms J. Hughes, *LD*	23,719
D. Rowlands, *UK Independence*	5,536
Dr C. Busby, *Green*	3,938
T. Griffith-Jones, *NLP*	988
Lab. majority	29,234
(Boundary change since June 1989)	

WALES NORTH
E. 475,829   T. 45.34%

*J. Wilson, *Lab.*	88,091
D. Wigley, *PC*	72,849
G. Mon Hughes, *C.*	33,450

Ms R. Parry, *LD*	14,828
P. Adams, *Green*	2,850
D. Hughes, *NLP*	2,065
M. Cooksey, *Ind.*	1,623
Lab. majority	15,242
(Boundary change since June 1989)	

SCOTLAND

GLASGOW
E. 463,364   T. 34.46%

W. Miller, *Lab.*	83,953
T. Chalmers, *SNP*	40,795
T. Sheridan, *SML*	12,113
R. Wilkinson, *C.*	10,888
J. Money, *LD*	7,291
P. O'Brien, *Green*	2,252
J. Fleming, *Soc.*	1,125
M. Wilkinson, *NLP*	868
C. Marsden, *ICP*	381
Lab. majority	43,158
(June 1989, Lab. maj. 59,232)	

HIGHLANDS AND ISLANDS
E. 328,104   T. 39.09%

*Mrs W. Ewing, *SNP*	74,872
M. Macmillan, *Lab.*	19,956
M. Tennant, *C.*	15,767
H. Morrison, *LD*	12,919
Dr E. Scott, *Green*	3,140
M. Carr, *UK Independence*	1,096
Ms M. Gilmour, *NLP*	522
SNP majority	54,916
(June 1989, SNP maj. 44,695)	

LOTHIANS
E. 520,943   T. 38.69%

*D. Martin, *Lab.*	90,531
K. Brown, *SNP*	53,324
Dr P. McNally, *C.*	33,526
Ms H. Campbell, *LD*	17,883
R. Harper, *Green*	5,149
J. McGregor, *Soc.*	637
M. Siebert, *NLP*	500
Lab. majority	37,207
(June 1989, Lab. maj. 38,826)	

SCOTLAND MID AND FIFE
E. 546,060   T. 38.25%

*A. Falconer, *Lab.*	95,667
R. Douglas, *SNP*	64,254
P. Page, *C.*	28,192
Ms H. Lyall, *LD*	17,192
M. Johnston, *Green*	3,015
T. Pringle, *NLP*	532
Lab. majority	31,413
(June 1989, Lab. maj. 52,157)	

SCOTLAND NORTH EAST
E. 575,748   T. 37.72%

A. Macartney, *SNP*	92,892
*H. McCubbin, *Lab.*	61,665
Dr R. Harris, *C.*	40,372
S. Horner, *LD*	18,008
K. Farnsworth, *Green*	2,569
Ms M. Ward, *Comm. GB*	689
L. Mair, *Neeps*	584
D. Paterson, *NLP*	371
SNP majority	31,227
(June 1989, Lab. maj. 2,613)	

SCOTLAND SOUTH
E. 500,643   *T.* 40.14%

*A. Smith, *Lab.*	90,750
A. Hutton, *C.*	45,595
Mrs C. Creech, *SNP*	45,032
D. Millar, *LD*	13,363
J. Hein, *Lib.*	3,249
Ms L. Hendry, *Green*	2,429
G. Gay, *NLP*	539
Lab. majority	45,155
(June 1989, Lab. maj. 15,693)	

STRATHCLYDE EAST
E. 492,618   *T.* 37.26%

*K. Collins, *Lab.*	106,476
I. Hamilton, *SNP*	54,136
B. Cooklin, *C.*	13,915
R. Stewart, *LD*	6,383
A. Whitelaw, *Green*	1,874
D. Gilmour, *NLP*	787
Lab. majority	52,340
(June 1989, Lab. maj. 60,317)	

STRATHCLYDE WEST
E. 489,129   *T.* 40.05%

*H. McMahon, *Lab.*	86,957
C. Campbell, *SNP*	61,934
J. Godfrey, *C.*	28,414
D. Herbison, *LD*	14,772
Ms K. Allan, *Green*	2,886
Ms S. Gilmour, *NLP*	918
Lab. majority	25,023
(June 1989, Lab. maj. 39,591)	

NORTHERN IRELAND

Northern Ireland forms a three-member seat with a single transferable vote system
E. 1,150,304 *T.* 48.67%

*Revd I. Paisley, *DUP*	163,246
*J. Hume, *SDLP*	161,992
*J. Nicholson, *UUUP*	133,459
Mrs M. Clark-Glass, *All.*	23,157
T. Hartley, *SF*	21,273
Ms D. McGuinness, *SF*	17,195
F. Molloy, *SF*	16,747
Revd H. Ross, *Ulster Independence*	7,858
Miss M. Boal, *C.*	5,583
J. Lowry, *WP*	2,543
N. Cusack, *Ind. Lab.*	2,464
J. Anderson, *NLP*	1,418
Mrs J. Campion, *Peace Coalition*	1,088
D. Kerr, *Independence for Ulster*	571
Ms S. Thompson, *NLP*	454
M. Kennedy, *NLP*	419
R. Mooney, *Const. NI*	400

BY-ELECTIONS SINCE 9 JUNE 1994

MERSEYSIDE WEST
(12 December 1996)
E. 515,549   *T.* 11.4%

R. Corbett, *Lab.*	31,484
J. Myers, *C.*	12,780
K. J. C. Reid, *LD*	8,829
S. R. Radford, *Lib.*	4,050
S. Darby, *Nat. Dem.*	718
J. D. Collins, *NLP*	680
Lab. majority	18,704

COMMONWEALTH PARLIAMENTARY ASSOCIATION (1911)

The Commonwealth Parliamentary Association consists of 142 branches in the national, state, provincial or territorial parliaments in the countries of the Commonwealth. Conferences and general assemblies are held every year in different countries of the Commonwealth.

President (1997–8), Hon. Douglas Kidd, MP, Speaker of the House of Representatives, New Zealand
Vice-President, (1997–8), Hon. Hector McClean, MP, Speaker of the House of Representatives, Trinidad and Tobago
Chairman of the Executive Committee (1996–), Hon. Billie Miller, MP (Barbados)
Secretary-General, A. R. Donahoe, QC, Suite 700, Westminster House, 7 Millbank, London SW1P 3JA

UNITED KINGDOM BRANCH

Hon. Presidents, The Lord Chancellor; Madam Speaker
Chairman of Branch, The Rt. Hon. Tony Blair, MP

Chairman of Executive Committee, Donald Anderson, MP
Secretary, A Pearson, Westminster Hall, Houses of Parliament, London, SW1A 0AA

THE INTER-PARLIAMENTARY UNION (1889)

To facilitate personal contact between members of all Parliaments in the promotion of representative institutions, peace and international co-operation.

Secretary-General, P. Cornillon, Place du Petit-Saconnex. BP 99, 1211 Geneva 19, Switzerland

BRITISH GROUP
Palace of Westminster, London SW1A 0AA

Hon. Presidents, The Lord Chancellor; Madam Speaker
President, The Rt. Hon. Tony Blair, MP
Chairman, David Marshall, MP
Secretary, D. Ramsay

The Government

THE CABINET AS AT 31 JULY 1997

Prime Minister, First Lord of the Treasury and Minister for the Civil Service
The Rt. Hon. Anthony Blair, MP, since May 1997
Deputy Prime Minister and Secretary of State for the Environment, Transport and the Regions
The Rt. Hon. John Prescott, MP, since May 1997
Chancellor of the Exchequer
The Rt. Hon. Gordon Brown, MP, since May 1997
Secretary of State for Foreign and Commonwealth Affairs
The Rt. Hon. Robin Cook, MP, since May 1997
Lord High Chancellor
The Lord Irvine of Lairg, PC, QC, since May 1997
Secretary of State for the Home Department
The Rt. Hon. Jack Straw, MP, since May 1997
Secretary of State for Education and Employment
The Rt. Hon. David Blunkett, MP, since May 1997
President of the Board of Trade and Secretary of State for Trade and Industry
The Rt. Hon. Margaret Beckett, MP, since May 1997
Minister of Agriculture, Fisheries and Food
The Rt. Hon. Dr Jack Cunningham, MP, since May 1997
Secretary of State for Scotland
The Rt. Hon. Donald Dewar, MP, since May 1997
Secretary of State for Defence
The Rt. Hon. George Robertson, MP, since May 1997
Secretary of State for Health
The Rt. Hon. Frank Dobson, MP, since May 1997
President of the Council and Leader of the House of Commons
The Rt. Hon. Ann Taylor, MP, since May 1997
Secretary of State for Culture, Media and Sport
The Rt. Hon. Christopher Smith, MP, since May 1997
Secretary of State for Social Security and Minister for Women
The Rt. Hon. Harriet Harman, MP, since May 1997
Secretary of State for Northern Ireland
The Rt. Hon. Dr Marjorie Mowlam, MP, since May 1997
Secretary of State for International Development
The Rt. Hon. Clare Short, MP, since May 1997
Secretary of State for Wales
The Rt. Hon. Ronald Davies, MP, since May 1997
Lord Privy Seal and Leader of the House of Lords
The Lord Richard, PC, QC, since May 1997
Chancellor of the Duchy of Lancaster
The Rt. Hon. Dr David Clark, MP, since May 1997
Minister for Transport
The Rt. Hon. Dr Gavin Strang, MP, since May 1997
Chief Secretary to the Treasury
The Rt. Hon. Alistair Darling, MP, since May 1997

LAW OFFICERS

Attorney-General
The Rt. Hon. John Morris, QC, MP, since May 1997
Lord Advocate
The Lord Hardie, PC, QC, since May 1995
Solicitor-General
The Lord Falconer of Thoroton, QC, since May 1997

Solicitor-General for Scotland
Colin Boyd, QC

MINISTERS OF STATE

Agriculture, Fisheries and Food
Jeffrey Rooker, MP (*Food Safety*)
Cabinet Office
Peter Mandelson, MP (*Minister Without Portfolio*)
Culture, Media and Sport
The Rt. Hon. Thomas Clarke, CBE, MP (*Film and Tourism*)
Defence
John Reid, MP (*Armed Forces*)
The Lord Gilbert, PC, Ph.D. (*Defence Procurement*)
Education and Employment
The Rt. Hon. Andrew Smith, MP (*Welfare to Work and Equal Opportunities*)
Stephen Byers, MP (*School Standards*)
The Baroness Blackstone, Ph.D.
Environment, Transport and the Regions
The Rt. Hon. Michael Meacher, MP (*Environment*)
Hilary Armstrong, MP (*Local Government and Housing*)
Richard Caborn, MP (*Regions, Regeneration and Planning*)
Foreign and Commonwealth Affairs
Douglas Henderson, MP (*Minister for Europe*)
Derek Fatchett, MP
Tony Lloyd, MP
Health
Alan Milburn, MP (*NHS Structure and Resources*)
Tessa Jowell, MP (*Public Health*)
The Baroness Jay of Paddington (*NHS Services*)
Home Office
Alun Michael, MP (*Criminal Policy*)
Joyce Quin, MP (*Prisons, Probation, Europe*)
Northern Ireland Office
Paul Murphy, MP (*Political Development, Finance, Personnel, Information*)
Adam Ingram, MP (*Security, Criminal Justice, Economic Development*)
Scottish Office
Henry McLeish, MP (*Home Affairs and Devolution*)
Brian Wilson, MP (*Education and Industry*)
Social Security
The Rt. Hon. Frank Field, MP (*Welfare Reform*)
Trade and Industry
The Lord Clinton-Davis (*Trade*)
John Battle, MP (*Science, Energy and Industry*)
Ian McCartney, MP (*Competitiveness*)
The Lord Simon of Highbury, CBE (*Trade and Competitiveness in Europe*)*
Treasury
Geoffrey Robinson, MP (*Paymaster-General*)
Dawn Primarolo, MP (*Financial Secretary*)
Helen Liddell, MP (*Economic Secretary*)
The Lord Simon of Highbury, CBE (*Trade and Competitiveness in Europe*)*
*Joint DTI/Treasury minister

UNDER-SECRETARIES OF STATE

Agriculture, Fisheries and Food
  Elliot Morley, MP (*Fisheries, Countryside*)
  The Lord Donoughue, D.Phil. (*Farming, Food Industry*)
Culture, Media and Sport
  Mark Fisher, MP (*Arts*)
  Tony Banks, MP (*Sport*)
Defence
  John Spellar, MP
Education and Employment
  Alan Howarth, MP (*Employment and Equal Opportunities*)
  Estelle Morris, MP (*School Standards*)
  Kim Howells, MP (*Lifelong Learning*)
Environment, Transport and the Regions
  Nick Raynsford, MP (*London, Construction*)
  Glenda Jackson, MP (*Transport in London*)
  The Baroness Hayman (*Roads*)
  Angela Eagle, MP (*Energy, Environment and the Regions*)
Foreign Office
  The Baroness Symons of Vernham Dean
Health
  Paul Boateng, MP (*Social Care, Mental Health*)
Home Office
  George Howarth, MP (*Prisons, Drugs, Elections*)
  Michael O'Brien, MP (*Immigration, Nationality*)
  The Lord Williams of Mostyn, QC (*Constitution*)
International Development
  George Foulkes, MP
Lord Chancellor's Department
  Geoffrey Hoon, MP
Northern Ireland
  Tony Worthington, MP (*Education, Training and Employment, Health, Community Relations*)
  The Lord Dubs (*Environment, Agriculture*)
Office of Public Service
  Peter Kilfoyle, MP
Scottish Office
  Malcolm Chisholm, MP (*Local Government, Transport*)
  Samuel Galbraith, MP (*Health, Arts*)
  The Lord Sewel, CBE (*Agriculture, Environment, Fisheries*)
Social Security
  Keith Bradley, MP (*Income-related Benefits*)
  The Baroness Hollis of Heigham, D.Phil. (*Child Benefit, Child Support, War Pensions*)
  John Denham, MP (*Pensions*)
  Joan Ruddock, MP (*Women*)
Trade and Industry
  Nigel Griffiths, MP (*Competition, Consumer Affairs*)
  Barbara Roche, MP (*Small Firms, Trade and Industry*)
Treasury
  The Lords Commissioners, *see* Government whips
Welsh Office
  Win Griffiths, MP
  Peter Hain, MP

GOVERNMENT WHIPS

HOUSE OF LORDS

Captain of the Honourable Corps of Gentlemen-at-Arms (Chief Whip)
  The Lord Carter
Captain of The Queen's Bodyguard of the Yeoman of the Guard (Deputy Chief Whip)
  The Lord McIntosh of Haringey
Lords-in-Waiting
  The Lord Haskel; The Lord Whitty; The Lord Hoyle
Baronesses-in-Waiting
  The Baroness Farrington of Ribbleton; The Baroness Gould of Potternewton

HOUSE OF COMMONS

Parliamentary Secretary to the Treasury (Chief Whip)
  The Rt. Hon. Nicholas Brown, MP
Treasurer of HM Household (Deputy Chief Whip)
  George Mudie, MP
Comptroller of HM Household
  Thomas McAvoy, MP
Vice-Chamberlain of HM Household
  Janet Anderson, MP
Lords Commissioners
  Robert Ainsworth, MP; Graham Allen, MP; James Dowd, MP; John McFall, MP; Jon Owen Jones, MP
Assistant Whips
  Clive Betts, MP; David Clelland, MP; Kevin Hughes, MP; David Jamieson, MP; Jane Kennedy, MP; Gregory Pope, MP; Bridget Prentice, MP

Government Departments and Public Offices

For changes notified after 31 August, *see* Stop-press

This section covers central government departments, executive agencies, regulatory bodies, other statutory independent organizations, and bodies which are government-financed or whose head is appointed by a government minister.

THE CIVIL SERVICE

Under the Next Steps programme many semi-autonomous executive agencies have been established with the aim of improving the performance of the Civil Service. Executive agencies operate within a framework set by the responsible minister which specifies policies, objectives and available resources. All executive agencies are set annual performance targets by their minister. Each agency has a chief executive, who is responsible for the day-to-day operations of the agency and who is accountable to the minister for the use of resources and for meeting the agency's targets. The minister accounts to Parliament for the work of the agency. Nearly 60 per cent of civil servants now work in executive agencies. Customs and Excise, the Inland Revenue, the Crown Prosecution Service and the Serious Fraud Office, which employ a further 17 per cent of civil servants, also operate on 'Next Steps' lines. In April 1997 there were about 476,000 permanent civil servants.

Most of the Home Civil Service's senior grades were formerly absorbed into an Open pay and grading structure. The Senior Civil Service came into being on 1 April 1996 and comprises about 3,000 staff from Permanent Secretary to the former Grade 5 level, including all agency chief executives. The former civil service grades have been abolished in the Senior Civil Service in favour of pay banding based on job weight. All government departments and executive agencies are now responsible for their own pay and grading systems for civil servants outside the Senior Civil Service. In practice the grades of the former Open structure are still in use in many organizations. The Open structure represented the following:

Grade	Title
1	Permanent Secretary
1A	Second Permanent Secretary
2	Deputy Secretary
3	Under-Secretary
4	Chief Scientific Officer B, Professional and Technology Directing A
5	Assistant Secretary, Deputy Chief Scientific Officer, Professional and Technology Directing B
6	Senior Principal, Senior Principal Scientific Officer, Professional and Technology Superintending Grade
7	Principal, Principal Scientific Officer, Principal Professional and Technology Officer

SALARIES 1997–8

MINISTERIAL SALARIES *from May 1997*

Ministers who are Members of the House of Commons receive a parliamentary salary (£43,860) in addition to their ministerial salary.

*Prime Minister	£100,000
*Secretary of State (Commons)	£60,000
*Secretary of State (Lords)	£77,963
Minister of State (Commons)	£31,125
Minister of State (Lords)	£51,838
Parliamentary Under-Secretary (Commons)	£23,623
Parliamentary Under-Secretary (Lords)	£43,632

* The Prime Minister and Cabinet ministers have decided not to take the full salaries provided for them for the rest of the financial year 1997–8. They will instead draw ministerial salaries at the rates which were in force before the general election (Prime Minister, £58,557; Cabinet minister (Commons), £43,991; Cabinet minister (Lords), £58,876

SPECIAL ADVISERS' SALARIES

Special advisers to ministers are paid out of public funds; their salaries are negotiated individually, but are usually in the range £24,349 to £73,484.

CIVIL SERVICE SALARIES *from 1 December 1997*

Senior Civil Service (SCS)

Secretary of the Cabinet and Head of the Home Civil Service	£92,480–£158,750
Permanent Secretaries	£92,480–£158,750
Band 9	£82,200–£116,420
Band 8	£75,210–£109,840
Band 7	£68,840–£103,670
Band 6	£62,880–£97,920
Band 5	£57,440–£92,480
Band 4	£52,400–£87,340
Band 3	£47,470–£77,680
Band 2	£43,050–£69,050
Band 1	£39,050–£61,340

Staff are placed in pay bands according to their level of responsibility and taking account of other factors such as experience and marketability. Movement within and between bands is based on performance. A recruitment and retention allowance of up to £3,000 may be paid in certain circumstances in addition to the salary ranges shown for bands 1 to 9.

Other Civil Servants

Following the delegation of responsibility for pay and grading to government departments and agencies from 1 April 1996, it is no longer possible to show the pay rates for staff outside the Senior Civil Service. Individual departments and agencies are in the process of introducing their own pay systems.

ADJUDICATOR'S OFFICE

Haymarket House, 28 Haymarket, London SW1Y 4SP
Tel 0171-930 2292

The Adjudicator's Office opened in 1993 and investigates complaints made about the way the Inland Revenue, Customs and Excise or the Contributions Agency have handled an individual's affairs.
The Adjudicator, Ms E. Filkin
Head of Office, M. Savage

ADVISORY, CONCILIATION AND ARBITRATION SERVICE

Brandon House, 180 Borough High Street, London
SE1 1LW
Tel 0171-210 3613

The Advisory, Conciliation and Arbitration Service (ACAS) was set up under the Employment Protection Act 1975 (the provisions now being found in the Trade Union and Labour Relations (Consolidation) Act 1992). ACAS is directed by a Council consisting of a full-time chairman and part-time employer, trade union and independent members, all appointed by the Secretary of State for Trade and Industry. The functions of the Service are to promote the improvement of industrial relations in general, to provide facilities for conciliation, mediation and arbitration as means of avoiding and resolving industrial disputes, and to provide advisory and information services on industrial relations matters to employers, employees and their representatives.

ACAS also has regional offices in Birmingham, Bristol, Cardiff, Fleet, Glasgow, Leeds, Liverpool, London, Manchester, Newcastle upon Tyne and Nottingham.

Chairman, J. Hougham, CBE
Chief Conciliation Officer (G4), D. Evans

MINISTRY OF AGRICULTURE, FISHERIES AND FOOD

Whitehall Place, London SW1A 2HH
Tel 0171-238 6000; *enquiries* 0645-335577

The Ministry of Agriculture, Fisheries and Food is responsible for government policies on agriculture, horticulture and fisheries in England and for policies relating to the safety and quality of food in the UK as a whole, including composition, labelling, additives, contaminants and new production processes. In association with the Agriculture Departments of the Scottish, Welsh and Northern Ireland Offices and with the Intervention Board (*see* page 316), the Ministry is responsible for negotiations in the EU on the common agricultural and fisheries policies, and for single European market questions relating to its responsibilities. Its remit also includes international agricultural and food trade policy.

The Ministry exercises responsibilities for the protection and enhancement of the countryside and the marine environment, for flood defence and for other rural issues. It is the licensing authority for veterinary medicines and the registration authority for pesticides. It administers policies relating to the control of animal, plant and fish diseases. It provides scientific, technical and professional services and advice to farmers, growers and ancillary industries, and it commissions research to assist in the formulation and assessment of policy and to underpin applied research and development work done by industry. Responsibility for food safety and standards is expected to be transferred to a new non-departmental public body following legislation in 1998–9.

Minister of Agriculture, Fisheries and Food, The Rt. Hon. Dr
   Jack Cunningham, MP
   Principal Private Secretary (G7), W. F. G. Strang
   Private Secretary, N. Witney
   Special Advisers, T. Walker; Ms C. McGlynn
   Parliamentary Private Secretary, J. Home Robertson, MP
Minister of State, Jeffrey Rooker, MP (*Food Safety*)
   Private Secretary, D. Chapman

Parliamentary Private Secretary, R. Burden, MP
Parliamentary Secretaries, Elliot Morley, MP (*Fisheries and the
   Countryside*); The Lord Donoughue, D.phil. (*Farming and
   the Food Industry*)
   Private Secretary to Mr Morley, C. Porro
   Private Secretary to Lord Donoughue, Dr P. Grimley
Parliamentary Clerk, G. Lewis
Permanent Secretary (G1), R. J. Packer
   Private Secretary, A. K. R. Slade

ESTABLISHMENT DEPARTMENT
Director of Establishments (G3), J. W. Hepburn

†ESTABLISHMENTS (GENERAL) AND OFFICE SERVICES DIVISION

Head of Division (G6), Dr J. A. Bailey

WELFARE BRANCH
Whitehall Place (West Block), London SW1A 2HH
Tel 0171-238 6000
Chief Welfare Officer (SEO), D. J. Jones

†PERSONNEL MANAGEMENT AND DEVELOPMENT DIVISION

Head of Division (G5), T. J. Osmond

DEPARTMENTAL HEALTH AND SAFETY UNIT
Government Buildings, Hook Rise South, Tolworth,
Surbiton, Surrey KT6 7NF
Tel 0181-330 4411
Head of Unit (G7), C. R. Bradburn

†TRAINING AND DEVELOPMENT BRANCH
Principal (G7), J. M. Cowley

BUILDING AND ESTATE MANAGEMENT
Eastbury House, 30–34 Albert Embankment,
London SE1 7TL
Tel 0171-238 6000
Head of Division (G5), J. A. S. Nickson

INFORMATION TECHNOLOGY DIRECTORATE
Government Buildings, Epsom Road, Guildford, Surrey
GU1 2LD
Tel 01483-68121
Director (G5), A. G. Matthews
Head of Strategies (G6), D. D. Brown
Head of Applications (G6), P. Barber
Head of Infrastructure (G6), S. V. Soper

INFORMATION DIVISION
Whitehall Place (West Block), London SW1A 2HH
Tel 0171-238 6000
Helpline 0645-335577
Chief Information Officer (G5), G. Blakeway
Chief Press Officer (G7), M. Smith
Chief Publicity Officer (G7), N. Wagstaffe
Principal Librarian (G7), P. McShane

FINANCE DEPARTMENT
19–29 Woburn Place, London WC1H 0LU
Tel 0171-270 8080
Principal Finance Officer (G3), P. Elliott

FINANCIAL POLICY DIVISION
Head of Division (G5), B. J. Harding

---

† At Nobel/Ergon House, 17 Smith Square, London SW1P 3JR. Tel: 0171-238 6000

FINANCIAL MANAGEMENT DIVISION
Head of Division (G5), J. M. Lowi

PROCUREMENT AND CONTRACTS DIVISION
Director of Audit (G5), D. V. Fisher

CAP SCHEMES MANAGEMENT
Head of Division (G5), Miss V. A. Smith

MARKET TESTING AND PROCUREMENT ADVICE
Director (G5), D. B. Rabey

RESOURCE MANAGEMENT STRATEGY UNIT
Head of Division (G5), Mrs J. Flint

LEGAL DEPARTMENT
55 Whitehall, London SW1A 2EY
Tel 0171-238 6000

Legal Adviser and Solicitor (G2), Miss K. M. S. Morton
Principal Assistant Solicitors (G3), D. J. Pearson; Ms C. A.
  Crisham

LEGAL DIVISIONS
Assistant Solicitor, Division A1 (G5), Dr M. R. Parke
Assistant Solicitor, Division A2 (G5), P. Kent
Assistant Solicitor, Division A3 (G5), T. J. Middleton
Assistant Solicitor, Division A4 (G5), P. D. Davis
Assistant Solicitor, Division A5 (G5), P. Hall
Assistant Solicitor, Division B1 (G5), Mrs C. A. Davis
Assistant Solicitor, Division B2 (G4), Ms S. B. Spence
Assistant Solicitor, Division B3 (G5), A. I. Corbett
Assistant Solicitor, Division B4 (G5), Mrs F. C. Nash

INVESTIGATION UNIT
Chief Investigation Officer, Miss J. Panting

ECONOMICS AND STATISTICS
Under-Secretary (G3), Dr J. M. Slater

DIVISIONS
*Senior Economic Adviser, Economics and Statistics (Farm
  Business) (G5)*, H. Fearn
*Senior Economic Adviser, Economics (International and Food)
  (G5)*, N. Atkinson
Senior Economic Adviser, Economics (Resource Use) (G5), J. P.
  Muriel

†CHIEF SCIENTIST'S GROUP
Chief Scientist (G3), Dr D. W. F. Shannon

DIVISIONS
Head, Agriculture and Food Technology (G5),
  Dr J. C. Sherlock
Head, Food and Veterinary Science Division (G5),
  Dr K. J. MacOwan
Head, Environment, Fisheries and International Science (G5),
  Dr M. Parker
Head, Research Policy Co-ordination (G5), A. R. Burne

†FISHERIES DEPARTMENT
Fisheries Secretary (G3), S. Wentworth

DIVISIONS
Head, Fisheries I (G5), A. Kuyk
Head, Fisheries II (G5), C. I. Llewellyn
Head, Fisheries III (G5), J. E. Robbs
Head, Fisheries IV (G6), B. S. Edwards
Chief Inspector, Sea Fisheries Inspectorate (G6), S. G. Ellson

AGRICULTURAL COMMODITIES, TRADE AND FOOD PRODUCTION
Deputy Secretary (G2), Ms V. K. Timms

EUROPEAN UNION AND LIVESTOCK
GROUP
Under-Secretary (G3), D. P. Hunter

DIVISIONS
Head, European Union (G5), A. J. Lebrecht
Head, Beef and Sheep (G5), J. R. Cowan
Head, Milk, Pigs, Eggs and Poultry (G5), P. P. Nash
Head, Livestock Quota Unit (G6), Ms L. Cornish

ARABLE CROPS AND HORTICULTURE
Under-Secretary (G3), D. H. Griffiths

DIVISIONS
Head, Cereals and Set-Aside (G5), R. A. Hathaway
Head, Sugar, Tobacco, Oilseeds and Protein (G5), H. B. Brown
†*Head, Horticulture and Potatoes (G5)*, G. W. Noble

PLANT VARIETY RIGHTS OFFICE AND SEEDS DIVISION
White House Lane, Huntingdon Road, Cambridge
CB3 0LF
Tel 01223-277151
Head of Office (G5), D. A. Boreham

FOOD, DRINK AND MARKETING POLICY
Under-Secretary (G3), N. Thornton

DIVISIONS
Head, Food and Drinks Industry (G5), R. E. Melville
Head, International Relations and Export Promotion (G5),
  D. V. Orchard
Head, Trade Policy and Tropical Foods (G5), Miss S. E. Brown
†*Head, Market Task Force (G5)*, vacant

REGIONAL SERVICES AND DEFENCE
GROUP
Under-Secretary (G3), R. A. Saunderson
Head, Deregulation, Agricultural Training and Resources (G5),
  Mrs A. M. Blackburn
*Head, Plant Health and Plant Health and Seeds Inspectorate
  (G5)*, A. J. Perrins
Head, Flood and Coastal Protection (G5), Dr. J. Park

REGIONAL ORGANIZATION
Head, Regional Support Unit (G7), D. Putley

Regional Service Centres

ANGLIA REGION, Block B, Government Buildings,
  Brooklands Avenue, Cambridge CB2 2DR. Tel: 01223-
  462727. *Regional Director (G5)*, Miss C. J. Rabagliati
EAST MIDLANDS REGION, Government Buildings, Block
  7, Chalfont Drive, Nottingham NG8 3SN. Tel: 0115-929
  1191. *Regional Director (G6)*, G. Norbury
NORTH-EAST REGION, Government Buildings, Crosby
  Road, Northallerton, N. Yorks DL6 1AD. Tel: 01609-
  773751. *Regional Director (G6)*, P. Watson
NORTHERN REGION, Eden Bridge House, Lowther
  Street, Carlisle, Cumbria CA3 8DX. Tel: 01228-23400.
  Regional Director (G5), I. G. Pearson
NORTH MERCIA REGION, Berkeley Towers, Nantwich
  Road, Crewe, Cheshire CW2 6PT. Tel: 01270-
  69211. *Regional Director (G6)*, R. Bettley-Smith
SOUTH-EAST REGION, Block A, Government Buildings,
  Coley Park, Reading, Berks RG1 6DT. Tel: 01734-
  581222. *Regional Director (G6)*, Mrs V. Silvester

---

†At Nobel/Ergon House, 17 Smith Square, London SW1P 3JR. Tel: 0171-
238 6000

SOUTH MERCIA REGION, Block C, Government Buildings, Whittington Road, Worcester WR5 2LQ. Tel: 01905-763355. *Regional Director* (*G6*), B. Davies
SOUTH-WEST REGION, Government Buildings, Alphington Road, Exeter EX2 8NQ. Tel: 01392-77951. *Regional Director* (*G6*), M. R. W. Highman
WESSEX REGION, Block 3, Government Buildings, Burghill Road, Westbury-on-Trym, Bristol BS10 6NJ. Tel: 01272-591000. *Regional Director* (*G6*), Mrs A. J. L. Ould

FOOD SAFETY AND ENVIRONMENT GROUP
Deputy Secretary (*G2*), R. J. D. Carden

ENVIRONMENT GROUP
Under-Secretary (*G3*), D. J. Coates
Head, Conservation and Woodlands Policy (*G5*), Ms J. Allfrey
Head, Conservation Management Division (*G5*), P. M. Boyling
Head, Land Use and Rural Economy (*G5*), R. C. McIvor
Head, Environmental Protection (*G5*), D. E. Jones

†FOOD SAFETY AND SCIENCE GROUP
Under-Secretary (*G3*), G. Podger

DIVISIONS
Head, Additives and Novel Foods (*G5*), Dr J. R. Bell
Head, Food Labelling and Standards (*G5*), G. Meekings
Head, Food Contaminants (*G5*), Dr R. Burt
Head, Consumers and Nutrition (*G5*), Miss E. J. Wordley
Head, Radiological Safety (*G5*), Dr M. G. Segal

ANIMAL HEALTH AND VETERINARY GROUP
Government Buildings, Hook Rise South, Tolworth, Surbiton, Surrey KT6 7NF
Tel 0181-330 4411
Under-Secretary (*G3*), B. H. B. Dickinson
Chief Veterinary Officer (*G3*), J. M. Scudamore

DIVISIONS
Head, Animal Health (*BSE*) (*G5*), T. E. D. Eddy
Head, Animal Health (*Disease Control*) (*G5*), T. D. Rossington
Head, Animal Health (*International Trade*) (*G5*), R. A. Bell
Head, Animal Health (*Food Hygiene*) (*G5*), R. J. Harding
Head, Meat Hygiene (*G5*), C. J. Lawson
Head, Services (*G6*), R. Gurd
Head, Animal Welfare (*G5*), C. J. Ryder

VETERINARY FIELD SERVICE
Government Buildings, Hook Rise South, Tolworth, Surbiton, Surrey KT15 3NB
Tel 0181-330 4411
Director of Veterinary Field Services (*G3*), I. Crawford

STATISTICS DIVISION
Foss House, King's Pool, 1–2 Peasholme Green, York YO1 2PX
Tel 01904-455328

Chief Statistician (*Commodities and Food*) (*G5*), S. Platt
Chief Statistician (*Census and Surveys*) (*G5*), P. F. Helm

EXECUTIVE AGENCIES

CENTRAL SCIENCE LABORATORY
Sand Hutton, York YO4 1LZ
Tel 01904-462000
The agency provides MAFF with technical support and policy advice on the protection and quality of the food supply and on related environmental issues.

Chief Executive (*G3*), Prof. P. I. Stanley
Research Director, Agriculture and Environment (*G5*), Prof. A. R. Hardy
Head of Food Science Laboratory (*G5*), Dr J. Gilbert, Norwich Research Park, Colney Lane, Norwich NR4 7UQ. Tel: 01603-259350

CENTRE FOR ENVIRONMENT, FISHERIES AND AQUACULTURE SCIENCE
Pakefield Road, Lowestoft, Suffolk NR33 0HT
Tel 01502-562244
The Agency, established in April 1997, provides research and consultancy services in fisheries science and management, aquaculture, health and hygiene, environmental impact assessment, and environmental quality assessment. Its main laboratory is in Lowestoft; it has three smaller specialist laboratories in Weymouth, Burnham on Crouch and Conwy and a small unit in Whitehaven.
Chief Executive, Dr P. Greig-Smith

INTERVENTION BOARD
— *see* page 316

MEAT HYGIENE SERVICE
Foss House, King's Pool, 1–2 Peasholme Green, York YO1 2PX
Tel 01904-455500
The Agency was launched in April 1995. It protects public health and animal welfare through veterinary supervision and meat inspection in licensed fresh meat establishments.
Chief Executive (*G4*), J. McNeill

FARMING AND RURAL CONSERVATION AGENCY
17 Smith Square, London SW1P 3JR
Tel 0171-238 6000
The Agency, established in April 1997, is responsible jointly to MAFF and the Welsh Office. It has taken over the responsibilities of the former Agricultural Development and Advisory Service (ADAS) which could not be contracted to non-governmental suppliers when ADAS was privatized in April 1997. The Agency provides professional and scientific advice on policy issues relating to agriculture and the environment, and professional services for the administration of agri-environmental schemes. It also enforces certain aspects of the Dairy Hygiene Regulations.
Chief Executive (*G4*), M. Finnigan

PESTICIDES SAFETY DIRECTORATE
Mallard House, King's Pool, 3 Peasholme Green, York YO1 2PX
Tel 01904-640500
The Pesticides Safety Directorate is responsible for the evaluation and approval of pesticides and the development of policies relating to them, in order to protect consumers, users and the environment.
Chief Executive (*G4*), G. K. Bruce
Director (*Policy*) (*G5*), J. A. Bainton
Director (*Approvals*) (*G5*), Dr A. D. Martin

VETERINARY LABORATORIES AGENCY
Woodham Lane, New Haw, Addlestone, Surrey KT15 3NB
Tel 01932-341111
The Veterinary Laboratories Agency provides scientific and technical expertise in animal and public health.
Chief Executive (*G3*), Dr T. W. A. Little
Director of Research (*G4*), Dr J. A. Morris
Director of Operations (*G5*), J. W. Harkness
Director of Veterinary Investigation Centres (*G5*), W. A. Edwards

VETERINARY MEDICINES DIRECTORATE
Woodham Lane, New Haw, Addlestone, Surrey KT15 3NB
Tel 01932-336911

The Veterinary Medicines Directorate is responsible for all aspects of the authorization and control of veterinary medicines, including post-authorization surveillance of residues in meat and animal products, and the provision of policy advice to ministers.
Chief Executive and Director of Veterinary Medicines (*G4*), Dr J. M. Rutter
Director (*Policy*) (*G5*), R. Anderson
Director (*Licensing*) (*G5*), S. Dean
Secretary and Head of Business Unit (*G6*), J. FitzGerald
Licensing Manager, Pharmaceuticals and Feed Additives (*G6*), J. P. O'Brien
Licensing Manager, Immunologicals (*acting*) (*G6*), Dr D. Fawthrop

COLLEGE OF ARMS OR HERALDS COLLEGE
Queen Victoria Street, London EC4V 4BT
Tel 0171-248 2762

The Sovereign's Officers of Arms (Kings, Heralds and Pursuivants of Arms) were first incorporated by Richard III. The powers vested by the Crown in the Earl Marshal (the Duke of Norfolk) with regard to state ceremonial are largely exercised through the College. The College is also the official repository of the arms and pedigrees of English, Welsh, Northern Irish and Commonwealth (except Canadian) families and their descendants, and its records include official copies of the records of Ulster King of Arms, the originals of which remain in Dublin. The 13 officers of the College specialize in genealogical and heraldic work for their respective clients.

Arms have been and still are granted by letters patent from the Kings of Arms. A right to arms can only be established by the registration in the official records of the College of Arms of a pedigree showing direct male line descent from an ancestor already appearing therein as being entitled to arms, or by making application through the College of Arms for a grant of arms. Grants are made to corporations as well as to individuals.

The College of Arms is open Monday–Friday 10–4.
Earl Marshal, His Grace the Duke of Norfolk, KG, GCVO, CB, CBE, MC

KINGS OF ARMS
Garter, P. L. Gwynn-Jones, LVO
Clarenceux (*and Registrar*), D. H. B. Chesshyre, LVO, FSA
Norroy and Ulster, T. Woodcock, LVO, FSA

HERALDS
Richmond (*and Earl Marshal's Secretary*), P. L. Dickinson
York, H. E. Paston-Bedingfeld
Chester, T. H. S. Duke

PURSUIVANTS
Bluemantle, R. J. B. Noel
Portcullis, W. G. Hunt, TD
Rouge Croix, D. V. White

COURT OF THE LORD LYON
HM New Register House, Edinburgh EH1 3YT
Tel 0131-556 7255

The Court of the Lord Lyon is the Scottish Court of Chivalry (including the genealogical jurisdiction of the *Ri-Sennachie* of Scotland's Celtic Kings). The Lord Lyon King of Arms has jurisdiction, subject to appeal to the Court of Session and the House of Lords, in questions of heraldry and the right to bear arms. The Court also administers the Scottish Public Register of All Arms and Bearings and the Public Register of All Genealogies. Pedigrees are established by decrees of Lyon Court and by letters patent. As Royal Commissioner in Armory, the Lord Lyon grants patents of arms (which constitute the grantee and heirs noble in the Noblesse of Scotland) to 'virtuous and well-deserving' Scotsmen and to petitioners (personal or corporate) in Her Majesty's overseas realms of Scottish connection, and issues birthbrieves.
Lord Lyon King of Arms, Sir Malcolm Innes of Edingight, KCVO, WS

HERALDS
Albany, J. A. Spens, RD, WS
Rothesay, Sir Crispin Agnew of Lochnaw, Bt., QC
Ross, C. J. Burnett, FSA SCOT

PURSUIVANTS
Kintyre, J. C. G. George, FSA SCOT
Unicorn, Alastair Campbell of Airds, FSA SCOT
Carrick, Mrs C. G. W. Roads, MVO, FSA SCOT

Lyon Clerk and Keeper of Records, Mrs C. G. W. Roads, MVO, FSA SCOT
Procurator-Fiscal, D. F. Murby, WS
Herald Painter, Mrs J. Phillips
Macer, A. M. Clark

ARTS COUNCILS

The Arts Council of Great Britain was established as an independent body in 1946 to be the principal channel for the Government's support of the arts. In 1994 the Scottish and Welsh Arts Councils became autonomous and the Arts Council of Great Britain became the Arts Council of England.

The Arts Councils are responsible for the distribution of one-fifth of the proceeds of the National Lottery allocated to 'good causes'. They had made awards to the value of £676 million by the end of April 1997.

ARTS COUNCIL OF ENGLAND
14 Great Peter Street, London SW1P 3NQ
Tel 0171-333 0100

The Arts Council of England's objectives are to develop and improve the understanding and practice of the arts and to increase their accessibility to the public. The Council funds the major arts organizations in England and the ten Regional Arts Boards. It is funded by the Department for Culture, Media and Sport and works closely with the Scottish Arts Council and the Arts Council of Wales. The Council operates at 'arm's length' from Government as regards artistic decision-making, although it is expected to account for such decisions to the Government and the public. The Council also provides advice, information and help to artists and arts organizations. Its members are unpaid.

The Council distributes an annual grant from the Department for Culture, Media and Sport; the grant for 1997–8 is £186.1 million.
Chairman, The Lord Gowrie, PC
Deputy Chairman, D. Reid
Members, R. Cork; Prof. R. Cowell; Prof. B. Cox, CBE; C. Denton; Prof. C. Frayling; Ms M. Guillebaud; Sir Ernest Hall, OBE; Sir David Harrison, CBE, PH.D., FENG.; G. Henderson; Ms T. Holt, CBE; Lady MacMillan; Prof. A. Motion; S. Phillips; T. Phillips; Ms U. Prashar, CBE; R. Reed; Mrs S. Robinson; Ms P. Skene; R. Southgate; J. Spearman
Secretary-General (acting), G. Devlin

REGIONAL ARTS BOARDS

EASTERN ARTS BOARD, Cherry Hinton Hall, Cherry Hinton Road, Cambridge CB1 4DW. Tel: 01223-215355. *Chair*, Sir David Harrison, CBE, PH.D., FENG.
EAST MIDLANDS ARTS BOARD, Mountfields House, Forest Road, Loughborough, Leics LE11 3HU. Tel: 01509-218292. *Chair*, Prof. R. Cowell
LONDON ARTS BOARD, Elme House, 133 Long Acre, London WC2E 9AF. Tel: 0171-240 1313. *Chair*, T. Phillips
NORTHERN ARTS BOARD, 9–10 Osborne Terrace, Newcastle upon Tyne NE2 1NZ. Tel: 0191-281 6334. *Chair*, Mrs S. Robinson
NORTH-WEST ARTS BOARD, Manchester House, 22 Bridge Street, Manchester M3 3AB. Tel: 0161-834 9131. *Chair*, Prof. B. Cox, CBE
SOUTH-EAST ARTS BOARD, 10 Mount Ephraim, Tunbridge Wells, Kent TN4 8AS. Tel: 01892-515210. *Chair*, R. Reed
SOUTHERN ARTS BOARD, 13 St Clement Street, Winchester SO23 9DQ. Tel: 01962-855099. *Chair*, D. Reid
SOUTH-WEST ARTS BOARD, Bradninch Place, Gandy Street, Exeter EX4 3LS. Tel: 01392-218188. *Chair*, Ms M. Guillebaud
WEST MIDLANDS ARTS BOARD, 82 Granville Street, Birmingham B1 2LH. Tel: 0121-631 3121. *Chair*, R. Southgate
YORKSHIRE AND HUMBERSIDE ARTS BOARD, 21 Bond Street, Dewsbury, W. Yorks WF13 1AX. Tel: 01924-455555. *Chair*, Sir Ernest Hall, OBE

SCOTTISH ARTS COUNCIL
12 Manor Place, Edinburgh EH3 7DD
Tel 0131-226 6051

The Scottish Arts Council funds arts organizations in Scotland and is funded directly by the Scottish Office. The grant for 1997–8 is £24.68 million.
Chairman, M. Linklater
Members, Dr Sheila Brock; H. Buchanan; R. Chester, W. English; K. Geddes; P. Hamilton; R. Love; Ms M. Marshall; Ms J. Richardson; Prof. E. Spiller; Ms J. Urquart
Director, Ms S. Reid
Lottery Director, D. Bonnar

ARTS COUNCIL OF WALES
Museum Place, Cardiff CF1 3NX
Tel 01222-394711

The Arts Council of Wales funds arts organizations in Wales and is funded directly by the Welsh Office. The grant for 1997–8 is £14.189 million.
Chairman, Sir Richard Lloyd Jones, KCB

Members, E. Bennett; Ms J. Davidson; A. Davies; R. Davies; K. Evans; Ms K. Gass; G. Jenkins; D. Johnston; G. S. Jones; L. Jones; G. Lewis; A. Lloyd; C. Lyddon; D. Richards; A. Roberts; C. Thomas; Ms M. Vincentellil
Chief Executive, E. Jenkins

ARTS COUNCIL OF NORTHERN IRELAND
185 Stranmillis Road, Belfast BT9 5DU
Tel 01232-381591

The Arts Council of Northern Ireland disburses government funds in support of the arts in Northern Ireland. It is funded by the Department of Education for Northern Ireland, and the grant for 1997–8 is £6.67 million.
Chairman, D. Deeny, QC
Vice-Chairman, Sir Charles Brett
Members, J. Aiken; S. Burnside; F. Cobain; P. Donnelly; Ms R. Duffy; Dr Tess Hurson; Ms K. Ingram; Prof. Edna Longley; W. O'Connell; R. Pierce; Ms C. Poulter; Ms I. Sandford; Prof. R. Welch
Chief Executive, B. Ferran

ART GALLERIES, ETC

ROYAL FINE ART COMMISSION
7 St James's Square, London SW1Y 4JU
Tel 0171-839 6537

Established in 1924, the Commission is an autonomous authority on the aesthetic implications of any project or development, primarily but not exclusively architectural, which affects the visual environment.
Chairman, The Lord St John of Fawsley, PC, FRSL
Commissioners, Miss S. Andreae; Prof. R. D. Carter, CBE; E. Cullinan, CBE, RA; Sir Philip Dowson, CBE, PRA; D. H. Fraser, RA; E. Hollinghurst; Sir Michael Hopkins, CBE, RA; S. A. Lipton; Prof. Margaret MacKeith, PH.D.; H. T. Moggridge, OBE; Mrs J. Nutting; T. Osborne, FRICS; J. Ritchie; Prof. J. R. Steer, FSA; Miss W. Taylor, CBE; Q. Terry, FRIBA; Dr G. Worsley
Secretary, F. Golding

ROYAL FINE ART COMMISSION FOR SCOTLAND
Bakehouse Close, 146 Canongate, Edinburgh EH8 8DD
Tel 0131-556 6699

The Commission was established in 1927 and advises ministers and local authorities on the visual impact and quality of design of construction projects. It is an independent body and gives its opinions impartially.
Chairman, The Lord Cameron of Lochbroom, PC, FRSE
Commissioners, Prof. G. Benson; W. A. Cadell; Mrs K. Dalyell; R. G. Maund; D. Page; B. Rae; Prof. T. Ridley; M. Turnbull; Prof. R. Webster; R. Wedgwood; A. Wright
Secretary, C. Prosser

NATIONAL GALLERY
Trafalgar Square, London WC2N 5DN
Tel 0171-839 3321

The National Gallery, which houses a permanent collection of western painting since the 13th century, was founded in 1824, following a parliamentary grant of £60,000 for the purchase and exhibition of the Angerstein collection of pictures. The present site was first occupied in 1838; an extension to the north of the building with a public entrance in Orange Street was opened in 1975, and the Sainsbury wing was opened in 1991. Total government grant-in-aid for 1997–8 is £18.3 million.

BOARD OF TRUSTEES
Chairman, P. Hughes, CBE
Trustees, Sir Keith Thomas, D. Litt, FBA; The Hon. Simon
  Sainsbury; Lady Bingham; Sir Mark Richmond, SC.D.,
  FRS; A. Bennett; Lady Monck; Mrs P. Ridley; Sir Ewen
  Fergusson, GCMG, GCVO; R. Gavron, CBE; C. Le Brun;
  The Hon. R. G. H. Seitz; Dr D. Landau

OFFICERS
Director, R. N. MacGregor
Chief Curator, Dr C. P. H. Brown
Senior Curator, Dr N. Penny
Chief Restorer, M. H. Wyld, CBE
Head of Exhibitions, M. J. Wilson
Scientific Adviser, Dr A. Roy
Director of Administration, J. MacAuslan
Head of Press and Public Relations, Miss J. Liddiard

NATIONAL PORTRAIT GALLERY
St Martin's Place, London WC2H 0HE
Tel 0171-306 0055

A grant was made in 1856 to form a gallery of the portraits
of the most eminent persons in British history. The present
building was opened in 1896 and an extension in 1933.
There are four outstations displaying portraits in appropriate settings: Montacute House, Gawthorpe Hall, Beningbrough Hall and Bodelwyddan Castle. Total government grant-in-aid for 1997–8 is £4.8 million.

BOARD OF TRUSTEES
Chairman, H. Keswick
Trustees, The Lord President of the Council (*ex officio*);
  The President of the Royal Academy of Arts (*ex officio*);
  J. Roberts, CBE, D.Phil.; The Lord Morris of Castle
  Morris, D.Phil.; Prof. N. Lynton; Sir Eduardo Paolozzi;
  J. Tusa; Sir Antony Acland, GCMG, GCVO; Mrs
  J. E. Benson, LVO, OBE; Mrs W. Tumim, OBE; Sir David
  Scholey, CBE; Mrs C. Tomalin; Baroness Willoughby de
  Eresby; M. Hastings; Prof. The Earl Russell, FBA
Director (G3), C. Saumarez-Smith, PH.D.

TATE GALLERY
Millbank, London SW1P 4RG
Tel 0171-887 8000

The Tate Gallery comprises the national collections of
British painting and 20th-century painting and sculpture.
The Gallery was opened in 1897, the cost of erection
(£80,000) being defrayed by Sir Henry Tate, who also
contributed the nucleus of the present collection. The
Turner wing was opened in 1910, galleries to contain the
collection of modern foreign painting in 1926, and a new
sculpture hall in 1937. In 1979 a further extension was
built, and the Clore Gallery, for the Turner collection, was
opened in 1987. The Tate Gallery Liverpool opened in
1988 and the Tate Gallery St Ives in 1993. Total government grant-in-aid for 1997–8 is £18.7 million.

BOARD OF TRUSTEES
Chairman, D. Stevenson, CBE
Trustees, Prof. Dawn Ades; The Hon. Mrs J. de Botton; Sir
  Richard Carew Pole; Prof. M. Craig-Martin; P. Doig;
  D. Gordon; Sir Christopher Mallaby, GCMG, GCVO; Sir
  Mark Richmond; Mrs P. Ridley, OBE; D. Verey; W.
  Woodrow

OFFICERS
Director (G3), N. Serota
Director of Public and Regional Services (G5), S. Nairne
Keeper of the British Collection (G5), A. Wilton
Keeper of the Modern Collection (G5), R. Morphet
Curator, Tate Gallery Liverpool (G6), L. Biggs
Curator, Tate Gallery St Ives (G6), M. Tooby

WALLACE COLLECTION
Hertford House, Manchester Square, London W1M 6BN
Tel 0171-935 0687

The Wallace Collection was bequeathed to the nation by
the widow of Sir Richard Wallace, Bt. in 1897, and Hertford
House was subsequently acquired by the Government.
Total government grant-in-aid for 1997–8 is £1.9 million.
Director, Miss R. J. Savill
Head of Administration, A. W. Houldershaw

NATIONAL GALLERIES OF SCOTLAND
The Mound, Edinburgh EH2 2EL
Tel 0131-624 6200

The National Galleries of Scotland comprise the National
Gallery of Scotland, the Scottish National Portrait Gallery
and the Scottish National Gallery of Modern Art. There
are also outstations at Paxton House, Berwickshire, and
Duff House, Banffshire. Total government grant-in-aid for
1997–8 is £7.168 million.

TRUSTEES
Chairman of the Trustees, Sir Angus Grossart, CBE
Trustees, Mrs L. W. Gibbs; Lord Macfarlane of Bearsden;
  Prof. A. A. Tait; E. Hagman; Prof. E. Fernie; M. Shea;
  The Countess of Airlie, CVO; Mrs A. McCurley; Prof.
  J. R. Harper, CBE; Prof. Christina Lodder; J. H. Blair

OFFICERS
Director (G4), T. Clifford
Keeper of Conservation (G6), J. P. Dick, OBE
Head of Press and Information (G7), Mrs A. M. Wagener
Keeper of Education (G7), M. Cassin
Registrar (G7), Miss A. Buddle
Secretary (G6), Ms S. Edwards
Buildings (G7), R. Galbraith
Keeper, National Gallery of Scotland (G6), M. Clarke
Keeper, Scottish National Portrait Gallery (G6), D. Thomson,
  PH.D.
  Curator of Photography, Miss S. F. Stevenson
Keeper, Scottish National Gallery of Modern Art (G6),
  R. Calvocoressi

UK ATOMIC ENERGY AUTHORITY
Harwell, Didcot, Oxon OX11 0RA
Tel 01235-820220

The UKAEA was established by the Atomic Energy
Authority Act 1954 and took over responsibility for the
research and development of the civil nuclear power
programme. The Authority increasingly evolved its operations, selling its products and services to the nuclear and
non-nuclear sectors while also continuing with the development of nuclear research and development. The commercial arm, AEA Technology PLC, was privatized in 1996.
UKAEA is responsible for the safe management and
decommissioning of its radioactive plant and for maximiz-
ing the income from its still-operating active facilities,
buildings and land on its six sites. UKAEA also undertakes
special nuclear tasks for the Government, including the
UK's contribution to the international fusion programme.
Chairman, Adm. Sir Kenneth Eaton
Chief Executive, Dr J. McKeown

AUDIT COMMISSIONS

AUDIT COMMISSION FOR LOCAL AUTHORITIES AND THE NATIONAL HEALTH SERVICE IN ENGLAND AND WALES

1 Vincent Square, London SW1P 2PN
Tel 0171-828 1212

The Audit Commission was set up in 1983 with responsibility for the external audit of local authorities. This remit was extended from 1990 to include the audit of the National Health Service bodies in England and Wales. The Commission appoints the auditors, who may be from the District Audit Service or from a private firm of accountants. The Commission is also responsible for promoting value for money in the services provided by local authorities and health bodies.

The Commission has 15–17 members who, though appointed by the Secretary of State for the Environment, Transport and the Regions in consultation with the Secretaries of State for Wales and for Health, are responsible to Parliament.
Chairman, R. Brooke
Deputy Chairman, C. Thompson
Controller of Audit, A. Foster
Chief Executive of District Audit Service, D. Prince

ACCOUNTS COMMISSION FOR SCOTLAND

18 George Street, Edinburgh EH2 2QU
Tel 0131-477 1234

The Commission was set up in 1975. It is responsible for securing the audit of the accounts of Scottish local authorities and certain joint boards and joint committees, and for value-for-money audits of authorities. In 1995 it assumed responsibility for securing the audit of National Health Service bodies in Scotland. The Commission is required to deal with reports made by the Controller of Audit on items of account contrary to law; on incorrect accounting; and on losses due to misconduct, negligence and failure to carry out statutory duties.

Members are appointed by the Secretary of State for Scotland.
Chairman, Prof. J. P. Percy, CBE
Controller of Audit, R. W. Black
Secretary, W. F. Magee

ASSEMBLY OMBUDSMAN FOR NORTHERN IRELAND

— *see* Parliamentary Ombudsman for Northern Ireland

THE BANK OF ENGLAND

Threadneedle Street, London EC2R 8AH
Tel 0171-601 4444

The Bank of England was incorporated in 1694 under royal charter. It is the banker of the Government and manages the note issue. Since May 1997 it has been operationally independent and its new Monetary Policy Committee has had responsibility for setting short-term interest rates to meet the Government's inflation target. The Bank of England is also currently responsible for banking supervision, but the Chancellor of the Exchequer has announced his intention of transferring this responsibility to an enlarged Securities and Investments Board. As the central reserve bank of the country, the Bank keeps the accounts of British banks, who maintain with it a proportion of their cash resources, and of most overseas central banks. The Bank is divided into two divisions, Monetary Stability and Financial Stability. (*See also* pages 609 – 610).
Governor, E. A. J. George
Deputy Governors, D. Clementi; M. King (*from spring 1998*)
Directors, C. J. Allsopp; A. R. F. Buxton; T. A. Clark; Sir David Cooksey; M. D. K. W. Foot; Sir John Hall; Mrs F. A. Heaton; Sir John Keswick; M. A. King; Sir David Lees; Dame Sheila Masters, DBE; J. Neill, CBE, Ph.D.; I. Plenderleith; Sir David Scholey, CBE, FRSA; N. I. Simms; Sir Colin Southgate
Monetary Policy Committee, the Governor; the Deputy Governors; M. A. King; I. Plenderleith; Prof. C. Goodhart; Dr D. Julius; Sir Alan Budd; Prof. W. Buiter
Advisers to the Governor, Sir Peter Petrie; L. Berkowitz; M. Foster
Chief Cashier and Deputy Director, Banking and Market Services, G. E. A. Kentfield
Chief Registrar, P. W. F. Ironmonger
General Manager, Printing Works, A. W. Jarvis
Secretary, P. D. Rodgers
The Auditor, K. Butler

BOUNDARY COMMISSIONS

The Commissions are constituted under the Parliamentary Constituencies Act 1986. The Speaker of the House of Commons is ex-officio chairman of all four commissions in the UK. Each of the four commissions is required by law to keep the parliamentary constituencies in their part of the UK under review. The latest review was completed in April 1995 and its proposals took effect at the general election in May 1997. The next review is due to be completed between 2002 and 2006. Each of the three commissions in Great Britain is required by law to keep the European parliamentary constituencies in their part of Great Britain under review.

ENGLAND
1 Drummond Gate, London SW1V 2QQ
Tel 0171-533 5176
Deputy Chairman, vacant
Joint Secretaries, R. Farrance; S. Limpkin

WALES
1 Drummond Gate, London SW1V 2QQ
Tel 0171-533 5172
Deputy Chairman, The Hon. Mr Justice Kay
Joint Secretaries, R. Farrance; S. Limpkin

SCOTLAND
Saughton House, Edinburgh EH1 3XD
Tel 0131-244 2196/2027
Deputy Chairman, The Hon. Lady Cosgrove
Secretary, Miss K. Barton

NORTHERN IRELAND
REL Division, 11 Millbank, London SW1P 4QE
Tel 0171-210 6569
Deputy Chairman, The Hon. Mr Justice Pringle
Secretary, Ms C. Marson

BRITISH BROADCASTING CORPORATION

Broadcasting House, Portland Place, London W1A 1AA
Tel 0171-580 4468
Television Centre, Wood Lane, London W12 7RJ
Tel 0181-743 8000

The BBC was incorporated under royal charter as successor to the British Broadcasting Company Ltd, whose licence expired in 1926. The current charter came into force on 1 May 1996 and extends to 31 December 2006. The chairman, vice-chairman and other governors are appointed by The Queen-in-Council. The BBC is financed by revenue from receiving licences for the home services and by grant-in-aid from Parliament for the World Service (radio). In June 1996 the BBC announced a restructuring of the corporation into six divisions: Production, Broadcast, News, Worldwide, Resources, and Corporate Centre.

For services, *see* Broadcasting section.

BOARD OF GOVERNORS

Chairman (£65,580), Sir Christopher Bland
Vice-Chairman (£16,830), The Lord Cocks of Hartcliffe, PC
National Governors (*each* £16,830), Sir Kenneth Bloomfield, KCB (*N. Ireland*); R. S. Jones (*Wales*); N. Drummond (*Scotland*)
Chairman, English National Forum (£12,630), Mrs M. Spurr, OBE
Governors (*each* £8,420), W. B. Jordan, CBE; Lord Nicholas Gordon Lennox, KCMG, KCVO; Mrs J. Cohen; Sir David Scholey, CBE; Sir Richard Eyre, CBE; A. White, CBE

BOARD OF MANAGEMENT

EXECUTIVE COMMITTEE
Director-General (£339,000), J. Birt
Chief Executive, BBC Worldwide, vacant
Chief Executives, R. Neil (*BBC Production*); W. Wyatt (*BBC Broadcast*); T. Hall (*BBC News*); R. Lynch (*BBC Resources*)
Directors, Ms M. Salmon (*Personnel*); Ms P. Hodgson (*Policy and Planning*); R. Baker-Bates (*Finance and IT*); C. Browne (*Corporate Affairs*)

OTHER BOARD OF MANAGEMENT MEMBERS
Managing Director, World Service, S. Younger
Directors, A. Yentob (*Television*); M. Bannister (*Radio*); Ms J. Drabble (*Education*); M. Byford (*Regional Broadcasting*)

OTHER SENIOR STAFF

The Secretary, C. Graham
Deputy Director, Regional Broadcasting, M. Stevenson
Director, Continuous News, Ms J. Abramsky
Controller, BBC1, P. Salmon
Controller, BBC2, M. Thompson
Controller, Radio 1, M. Bannister
Controller, Radio 2, J. Moir
Controller, Radio 3, N. Kenyon
Controller, Radio 4, J. Boyle
Controller, Radio 5 Live, R. Mosey
Controller, BBC Scotland, J. McCormick
Controller, BBC Wales, G. Talfan Davies
Controller, BBC N. Ireland, P. Loughrey
Controller, English Regions, N. Chapman
Legal Adviser, G. Roscoe

BRITISH COAL CORPORATION

Charles House, 5–11 Lower Regent Street, London
SW1Y 4LR
Tel 0171-201 4141

The British Coal Corporation (formerly the National Coal Board) was constituted in 1946 and took over the mines on 1 January 1947. The Coal Industry Act 1994 established the statutory framework for the privatization of British Coal's mining operations. British Coal's ownership of coal reserves and responsibility for licensing other coal producers were transferred to the Coal Authority, a non-departmental public body (*see* page 291). The sale of regional coal companies, into which British Coal's operational mining assets had been transferred, was concluded in December 1994. The Act also charged British Coal with the disposal of its non-mining activities. This process is continuing, although the bulk of the assets were disposed of by early 1997. The British Coal Corporation will be wound up when the process is completed.

Chairman, P. L. Hutchinson
Non-Executive Director, D. B. Vaughan

THE BRITISH COUNCIL

10 Spring Gardens, London SW1A 2BN
Tel 0171-930 8466
Bridgewater House, 58 Whitworth Street, Manchester
M15 4AA
Tel 0161-957 7000

The British Council was established in 1934, incorporated by royal charter in 1940 and granted a supplemental charter in 1993. It is an independent, non-political organization which promotes Britain abroad. It is the UK's international network for education, culture and development services. The Council is represented in 230 towns and cities in 109 countries and runs 209 libraries, 95 teaching centres and 29 resource centres around the world.

Total funding in 1996–7, including Foreign and Commonwealth Office grants and contracted money, was £430 million.

Chairman, Sir Martin Jacomb
Deputy Chairman, The Lord Chorley
Director-General, Sir John Hanson, KCMG, CBE

BRITISH FILM COMMISSION

70 Baker Street, London W1M 1DJ
Tel 0171-224 5000

The British Film Commission was set up in 1991 and is funded by the Department for Culture, Media and Sport. The Commission promotes the UK as an international production centre, encourages the use of locations, facilities, services and personnel, and provides, at no charge to the enquirer, comprehensive advice and information relating to the practical aspects of filming in the UK.

Commissioner, Sir Sydney Samuelson, CBE
Chief Executive, vacant

BRITISH FILM INSTITUTE
21 Stephen Street, London W1P 2LN
Tel 0171-255 1444

The British Film Institute was established in 1933 under royal charter. It is the UK agency with responsibility for encouraging the arts of film and television and conserving them in the national interest. Divisions include the National Film and Television Archive, the National Cinema Centre and BFI Films. The BFI also supports a network of regional film theatres and the BFI Library contains the world's largest collection of material relating to film and television. Total government funding for 1997–8 is £16 million.
Chairman, J. Thomas (*until 31 December 1997*); A. Parker (*from 1 January 1998*)
Director, vacant

BRITISH PHARMACOPOEIA COMMISSION
Market Towers, 1 Nine Elms Lane, London SW8 5NQ
Tel 0171-273 0561

The British Pharmacopoeia Commission sets standards for medicinal products used in human and veterinary medicines and is responsible for publication of the British Pharmacopoeia (a publicly-available statement of the standard that a product must meet throughout its shelf-life), the British Pharmacopoeia (Veterinary) and the selection of British Approved Names. It has 13 members who are appointed by the Secretary of State for Health, the Minister for Agriculture, Fisheries and Food, the Secretaries of State for Scotland and Wales, and the relevant Northern Ireland departments.
Chairman, Prof. D. Ganderton, OBE
Vice-Chairman, Dr D. H. Calam, OBE
Secretary and Scientific Director, Dr R. C. Hutton

BRITISH RAILWAYS BOARD
Euston House, 24 Eversholt Street, PO Box 100, London NW1 1DZ
Tel 0171-928 5151

The British Railways Board came into being in 1963 under the terms of the Transport Act 1962. Under the Railways Act 1993, the activities of the Board have been restructured and are gradually being transferred to the private sector. For details of privatization and railway operations, *see* Transport section.
Chairman and Chief Executive (£180,000), J. K. Welsby, CBE
Vice-Chairman, J. J. Jerram, CBE
Personnel, A. P. Watkinson
Executive Members, A. D. Roche (*full-time*); C. J. Campbell, CBE (*part-time*)
Non-executive Members (*part-time*), K. H. M. Dixon; Miss K. T. Kantor
Secretary, P. Trewin

BRITISH STANDARDS INSTITUTION (BSI)
389 Chiswick High Road, London W4 4AL
Tel 0181-996 9000

The British Standards Institution is the recognized authority in the UK for the preparation and publication of national standards for industrial and consumer products. About 90 per cent of its standards work is now internationally linked. British Standards are issued for voluntary adoption, though in a number of cases compliance with a British Standard is required by legislation. Industrial and consumer products certified as complying with the relevant British Standard may carry the Institution's certification trade mark, known as the 'Kitemark'.
Chairman, V. E. Thomas, OBE
Managing Director, K. Tozzi

BRITISH TOURIST AUTHORITY
Thames Tower, Black's Road, London W6 9EL
Tel 0181-846 9000

Established under the Development of Tourism Act 1969, the British Tourist Authority has specific responsibility for promoting tourism to Great Britain from overseas. It also has a general responsibility for the promotion and development of tourism and tourist facilities within Great Britain as a whole, and for advising the Secretary of State for Culture, Media and Sport on tourism matters.
Chairman (*part-time*), D. Quarmby
Chief Executive, A. Sell

BRITISH WATERWAYS
Willow Grange, Church Road, Watford, Herts WD1 3QA
Tel 01923-226422

British Waterways is the navigation authority for over 2,000 miles of canals and rivers in England, Scotland and Wales. It is responsible to the Secretary of State for the Environment, Transport and the Regions. Its responsibilities include maintaining the waterways and structures on and around them; making sure that canals have the right amount of water in them; looking after wildlife and the waterway environment; and ensuring that canals and rivers are safe and enjoyable places to visit.
Chairman (*part-time*), B. Henderson, CBE
Vice-Chairman (*part-time*), Sir Peter Hutchison, Bt., CBE
Members (*part-time*), J. Gordon; D. H. R. Yorke; M. Cairns; Sir Neil Cossons, Ms J. Elvey, Ms J. Lewis-Jones
Chief Executive, D. Fletcher
Director of Corporate Services, R. J. Duffy

BROADCASTING STANDARDS COMMISSION
7 The Sanctuary, London SW1P 3JS
Tel 0171-233 0544

The Commission was established in April 1997 under the Broadcasting Act 1996 by the merger of the Broadcasting Standards Council and the Broadcasting Complaints Commission. It is an independent organization representing the interests of the consumer, and its remit covers all television and radio broadcasting. The Commission considers the portrayal of violence and sexual conduct and matters of taste and decency. It also provides redress for people who believe they have been unfairly treated or subjected to unwarranted infringement of privacy. The Commission conducts research into standards and fairness in broadcasting and produces codes of practice, and it considers and adjudicates on complaints. Members of the Commission are appointed by the Secretary of State for Culture, Media and Sport. The appointments are part-time.

Chair (£43,980), The Lady Howe of Aberavon
Deputy Chairman (£35,010), Ms J. Leighton
Commissioners (*each* £13,000–£14,050), Ms D. Barr; Ms R. Bevan; D. Boulton; Dame Fiona Caldicott, DBE; S. Heppel, CB; R. Kernohan, OBE; the Very Revd J. Lang; Ms S. Lloyd; Ms S. O'Sullivan; M. Parris
Director, S. Whittle

THE BROADS AUTHORITY
Thomas Harvey House, 18 Colegate, Norwich NR3 1BQ
Tel 01603-610734

The Broads Authority is a special statutory authority set up under the Norfolk and Suffolk Broads Act 1988. The functions of the Authority are to conserve and enhance the natural beauty of the Broads; to promote the enjoyment of the Broads by the public; and to protect the interests of navigation. The Authority comprises 35 members, appointed by the local authorities in the area covered, environmental conservation bodies, the Environment Agency, and the Great Yarmouth Port Authority.
Chairman, The Viscountess Knollys
Chief Executive, M. A. Clark

THE CABINET OFFICE

The Cabinet Office comprises the Secretariat, who support Ministers collectively in the conduct of Cabinet business; and the Office of Public Service (OPS) which is responsible for the progress and development of deregulation, the Citizen's Charter programme, the Next Steps programme, policy on open government, Senior Civil Service and public appointments, market testing and efficiency in the Civil Service, and Civil Service recruitment.

The OPS supports the Prime Minister in his capacity as Minister for the Civil Service, with responsibility for day-to-day supervision delegated to the Chancellor of the Duchy of Lancaster.

Prime Minister and Minister for the Civil Service,
The Rt. Hon. Anthony Blair, MP
Minister Without Portfolio, Peter Mandelson, MP
　Special Adviser, B. Wegg-Prosser
　Parliamentary Private Secretary, J. Trickett, MP

PRIME MINISTER'S OFFICE
10 Downing Street, London SW1A 2AA
Tel 0171-270 3000

Principal Private Secretary, J. E. Holmes, CMG
Chief of Staff, J. Powell
Private Secretaries (G5), Ms M. Wallace (*Economic Affairs*); M. Adams (*Parliamentary Affairs*); A. Lapsley (*Home Affairs*); P. Barton (*Overseas Affairs*)
Diary Secretary, Ms K. Garvey
Special Assistant for Presentation and Planning, Ms A. Hunter

Assistants to Mrs Blair (*part-time*), Ms F. Millar; Ms R. Preston
Political Secretary, Ms S. Morgan
Head of Policy Unit, D. Miliband
Policy Unit, G. Mulgan; R. Liddle; D. Scott; Ms E. Lloyd; P. Hyman; J. Rees; J. Purnell; P. McFadden; R. Hill; G. Norris; Ms S. White
Parliamentary Private Secretaries, B. Grocott, MP; Ms A. Coffey, MP
Chief Press Secretary, A. Campbell
Deputy Press Secretary, A. Percival, LVO
Special Advisers, Press Office, T. Allan; Ms H. Coffman
Secretary for Appointments, and Ecclesiastical Secretary to the Lord Chancellor, J. Holroyd, CB
Parliamentary Clerk, R. Stone
Secretary of the Cabinet and Head of Home Civil Service,
　Sir Robin Butler, GCB, CVO (*until January 1998*); Sir Richard Wilson, KCB (*from January 1998*)
　Private Secretary, Ms J. A. Polley

SECRETARIAT
70 Whitehall, London SW1A 2AS
Tel 0171-270 3000

Economic and Domestic Secretariat, R. Young; W. A. Jeffrey
Defence and Overseas Affairs Secretariat, C. R. Budd, CMG; A. J. D. Pawson
Joint Intelligence Organization, J. Alpass; W. R. Fittall
European Secretariat, B. Bender; A. T. Cahn
Constitution Secretariat, K. MacKenzie, CB

OFFICE OF PUBLIC SERVICE (OPS)
*Horse Guards Road, London SW1P 3AL
Tel 0171-270 1234
70 Whitehall, London SW1A 2AS
Tel 0171-270 3000

Chancellor of the Duchy of Lancaster, The Rt. Hon. Dr David Clark, MP
　Principal Private Secretary, Ms J. Lemprière
　Private Secretary, Mrs H. R. M. Paxman
　Special Adviser, A. Lappin
Parliamentary Under-Secretary, Peter Kilfoyle, MP
　Private Secretary, J. B. McLaren
Second Permanent Secretary, R. Mountfield, CB
　Private Secretary, Ms D. Crewe
Parliamentary Clerk, S. Brown
Press Secretary, B. Sutlieff

CITIZEN'S CHARTER UNIT
Tel 0171-270 1826

Director, vacant
Deputy Directors, Mrs G. Craig; Dr C. Sanger

CENTRAL IT UNIT
1st Floor, Hampton House, 20 Albert Embankment, London SE1 7TJ
Tel 0171-238 2015

Director, G. H. B. Jordan

EFFICIENCY AND EFFECTIVENESS GROUP
70 Whitehall, London SW1A 2AS
Tel 0171-270 0273

Director, J. R. C. Oughton
Head of Next Steps Project Team, M. J. Cowper

*Unless otherwise stated, this is the address and telephone number for divisions of the OPS

AGENCIES GROUP
Ashley House, Monck Street, London SW1P 2BQ
Tel 0171-270 1234
Director, Miss E. C. Turton, CB

CIVIL SERVICE EMPLOYER GROUP
Director, vacant
Development and Equal Opportunities Division, Ms A.
  Schofield
Fast Stream and European Staffing Division, Dr J. G. Fuller
International Public Service Unit, C. J. Parry
Personnel Management and Conditions of Service Division,
  vacant
Top Management Programme, Ms H. Dudley (*Course Director*)
Civil Service Pensions Division, D. G. Pain

OFFICE OF THE COMMISSIONER FOR PUBLIC
APPOINTMENTS (OCPA)
Horse Guards Road, London SW1P 3AL
Tel 0171-270 5792
The role of the Commissioner for Public Appointments
(CPA) is to monitor, regulate and approve departmental
appointment procedures for ministerial appointments to
executive non-departmental public bodies and NHS
bodies. The Commissioner is appointed by Order-in-
Council.
Commissioner, Sir Leonard Peach
Head of Office, J. Barron

OFFICE OF THE CIVIL SERVICE COMMISSIONERS
(OCSC)
Horse Guards Road, London SW1P 3AL
Tel 0171-270 5081
First Commissioner, Sir Michael Bett, CBE
Commissioners (part-time), D. J. Burr; Ms S. Forbes; Ms J. A.
  Hunt; H. J. F. McLean, CBE; Sir Leonard Peach; J.
  Shrigley; K. Singh; C. Stevens, CB
Secretary to the Commissioners and Head of the Office, J. Barron

INFORMATION OFFICER MANAGEMENT UNIT
Ashley House, 2 Monck Street, London SW1P 2BQ
Tel 0171-270 1234
Director, C. Skinner

BETTER REGULATION UNIT
Director, vacant

SENIOR CIVIL SERVICE GROUP
Director, B. M. Fox
Deputy Director, J. A. Barker

MACHINERY OF GOVERNMENT AND STANDARDS
GROUP
70 Whitehall, London SW1A 2AS
Tel 0171-270 1234
Director, D. A. Wilkinson
Head of Security Division, Ms E. Chivers
Queen's Printer, Mrs C. Tullo

CEREMONIAL BRANCH
53 Parliament Street, London SW1A 2NG
Tel 0171-210 5056
Honours Nomination Unit: Tel 0171-210 5071
Ceremonial Officer, A. J. Merifield, CB

ESTABLISHMENT OFFICER'S GROUP
Queen Anne's Chambers, 28 Broadway, London SW1H 9JS
Tel 0171-270 3000
Principal Establishment and Finance Officer, Mrs N. A.
  Oppenheimer
Deputy Establishment Officer, Miss E. Chennells
Senior Finance Officer, K. Tolladay

EXECUTIVE AGENCIES

THE BUYING AGENCY
Royal Liver Building, Pier Head, Liverpool L3 1PE
Tel 0151-227 4262
The Agency provides a professional purchasing service to
government departments and other public bodies.
Chief Executive (G5), S. P. Sage

CCTA (CENTRAL COMPUTER AND
TELECOMMUNICATIONS AGENCY)
Rosebery Court, St Andrew's Business Park, Norwich
NR7 0HS
Tel 01603 701807
Hampton House, 20 Albert Embankment, London SE1 7TJ
Tel 0171-238 2250
CCTA's objective is to develop, maintain and make
available expertise about information technology which
public sector organizations can draw on in order to operate
more effectively and efficiently. It became an executive
agency of the OPS in April 1996.
Chief Executive, R. Assirati

CENTRAL OFFICE OF INFORMATION
— *see* page 290

CIVIL SERVICE COLLEGE
Sunningdale Park, Ascot, Berks SL5 0QE
Tel 01344-634000
11 Belgrave Road, London SW1V 1RB
Tel 0171-834 6644
199 Cathedral Street, Glasgow G4 0QU
Tel 0141-553 6021
The College provides training in management and pro-
fessional skills for the public and private sectors.
Chief Executive (G3), Dr S. H. F. Hickey
Business Executives (G5/G6), M. N. Barnes; R. Behrens;
  G. W. Llewellyn; P. Tebby; M. Timmis; Dr A. Wyatt

GOVERNMENT CAR AND DISPATCH AGENCY
46 Ponton Road, London SW8 5AX
Tel 0171-217 3839
The Agency provides secure transport and document
transfers between government departments.
Chief Executive, N. Matheson

PROPERTY ADVISERS TO THE CIVIL ESTATE
6th Floor, Trevelyan House, Great Peter Street, London
SW1P 2BY
Tel 0171-271 2610
The Agency co-ordinates government activity on the civil
estate, and provides general property guidance and sup-
port to government departments. It was established in
April 1996.
Chief Executive, J. G. Locke, FRICS

SECURITY FACILITIES EXECUTIVE
St Christopher House, Southwark Street, London SE1 0TE
Tel 0171-921 4813
The Agency provides security support services, products
and systems for central government, the wider public
sector and other approved customers.
Chief Executive (G5), M. J. D. Farrow

CENTRAL ADJUDICATION SERVICES
Quarry House, Quarry Hill, Leeds LS2 7UB
Tel 0113-232 4000
New Court, 48 Carey Street, London WC2A 2LS
Tel 0171-412 1504

The Chief Adjudication Officer and Chief Child Support Officer are independent statutory authorities under the Social Security Act 1975 (as amended) and the Child Support Act 1991. They are appointed by the Secretary of State for Social Security to give advice to adjudication officers dealing with claims for social security cash benefits and to child support officers, and to keep under review the operation of the systems of adjudication. They report annually to the Secretary of State on adjudication standards.
Chief Adjudication Officer and Chief Child Support Officer, E. W. Hazlewood

CENTRAL OFFICE OF INFORMATION
Hercules Road, London SE1 7DU
Tel 0171-928 2345

The Central Office of Information (COI) is an executive agency which offers consultancy, procurement and project management services to central government for publicity. Though the majority of COI's work is for government departments in the UK, it also procures a range of publicity materials for overseas consumption. Administrative responsibility for the COI rests with the Minister of Public Service within the Cabinet Office.
Chief Executive (G3), A. Douglas
  Senior Personal Secretary, Ms L. Sheasgreen

MANAGEMENT BOARD
Members, K. Williamson; R. Windsor; R. Smith; P. Buchanan; I. Hamilton; R. Haslam; J. Murray; Ms S. Whetton
Secretary, Miss K. Gilding

DIRECTORS
Director, New Business (G6), Ms S. Whetton
Director, Marketing Communications (G6), P. Buchanan
Director, Research (G6), D. Whitehead
Director, Films, Radio and Events (G6), I. Hamilton
Director, Commercial Publicity (G6), V. Rowlands
Director, Publications (G6), J. Murray
Director, Central Services (G5), K. Williamson
Director, Regional Network (G6), R. Haslam

NETWORK OFFICES
EASTERN, Three Crowns House, 72–80 Hills Road, Cambridge CB2 1LL. *Network Director (G7),* P. Powell
MIDLANDS EAST, 1st Floor, Severns House, 20 Middle Pavement, Nottingham NG1 7DW. *Network Director (G7),* P. Smith
MIDLANDS WEST, Five Ways House, Islington Row Middleway, Edgbaston, Birmingham B15 1SH. *Network Director (G6),* B. Garner
NORTH-EAST, Wellbar House, Gallowgate, Newcastle upon Tyne NE1 4TB. *Network Director (G7),* H. Cozens
NORTH-WEST, Sunley Tower, Piccadilly Plaza, Manchester M1 4BD. *Network Director (G7),* Mrs E. Jones
SOUTH-EAST, Hercules Road, London SE1 7DU. *Network Director (G6),* Ms V. Burdon
SOUTH-WEST, The Pithay, Bristol BS1 2NF. *Network Director (G7),* P. Whitbread
YORKSHIRE AND HUMBERSIDE, City House, New Station Street, Leeds LS1 4JG. *Network Director (G7),* Ms W. Miller

CERTIFICATION OFFICE FOR TRADE UNIONS AND EMPLOYERS' ASSOCIATIONS
180 Borough High Street, London SE1 1LW
Tel 0171-210 3734/5

The Certification Office is an independent statutory authority. The Certification Officer is appointed by the Secretary of State for Trade and Industry and is responsible for receiving and scrutinizing annual returns from trade unions and employers' associations; for investigating allegations of financial irregularities in the affairs of a trade union or employers' association; for dealing with complaints concerning trade union elections; for ensuring observance of statutory requirements governing political funds and trade union mergers; and for certifying the independence of trade unions.
Certification Officer, E. G. Whybrew
Assistant Certification Officer, G. S. Osborne

SCOTLAND
58 Frederick Street, Edinburgh EH2 1LN
Tel 0131-226 3224
Assistant Certification Officer for Scotland, J. L. J. Craig

CHARITY COMMISSION
St Alban's House, 57–60 Haymarket, London SW1Y 4QX
Tel 0171-210 4556
2nd Floor, 20 King's Parade, Queen's Dock, Liverpool L3 4DQ
Tel 0151-703 1500
Woodfield House, Tangier, Taunton, Somerset TA1 4BL
Tel 01823-345000

The Charity Commission is established under the Charities Act 1993 with the general function of promoting the effective use of charitable resources in England and Wales. The Commission gives information and advice to charity trustees to make the administration of their charity more effective; investigates misconduct and the abuse of charitable assets, and takes or recommends remedial action; and maintains a public register of charities. The Commission does not have at its disposal any funds which to make grants to organizations or individuals.
At the end of 1996 the total number of registered charities was 181,824.
Chief Commissioner (G3), R. Fries
Commissioner (G3), R. M. C. Venables
Commissioners (part-time) (G4), J. Bonds; Mrs T. Baring; Ms J. Warburton
Heads of Legal Sections (G5), J. A. Dutton; G. S. Goodchild; K. M. Dibble; S. Slack
Executive Director (G4), Ms L. Berry
Head of Policy Division (G5), Ms J. Munday
Establishment Officer (G5), Ms C. Stewart
Information Systems Controller (G5), Ms G. Cruickshank

The offices responsible for charities in Scotland and Northern Ireland are:

SCOTLAND – Scottish Charities Office, Crown Office, 25 Chambers Street, Edinburgh EH1 1LA. Tel: 0131-226 2626

NORTHERN IRELAND – Department of Health and Social Services, Charities Branch, Annexe 3, Castle Buildings, Stormont Estate, Belfast BT4 3RA. Tel: 01232-522 780

CHIEF ADJUDICATION OFFICER AND CHIEF CHILD SUPPORT OFFICER
— *see* Central Adjudication Services

CHILD SUPPORT AGENCY
— *see* page 344

CHURCH COMMISSIONERS
1 Millbank, London SW1P 3JZ
Tel 0171-222 7010

The Church Commissioners were established in 1948 by the amalgamation of Queen Anne's Bounty (established 1704) and the Ecclesiastical Commissioners (established 1836).

The Commissioners are responsible for the management of most of the Church of England's assets, the income from which is predominantly used to pay, house and pension the clergy. The Commissioners own 135,018 acres of agricultural land, a number of residential estates in central London, and commercial property in Great Britain. They also carry out administrative duties in connection with pastoral reorganization and redundant churches, and have been designated by the General Synod as the central stipends authority of the Church of England.

The Commissioners are: the Archbishops of Canterbury and of York; the 41 diocesan bishops; five deans or provosts, ten other clergy and ten lay persons appointed by the General Synod; four lay persons nominated by The Queen; four persons nominated by the Archbishop of Canterbury; the Lord Chancellor; the Lord President of the Council; the First Lord of the Treasury; the Chancellor of the Exchequer; the Secretary of State for the Home Department; the Speaker of the House of Commons; the Lord Chief Justice; the Master of the Rolls; the Attorney-General; the Solicitor-General; the Lord Mayor and two Aldermen of the City of London; the Lord Mayor of York; and one representative from each of the Universities of Oxford and Cambridge.

INCOME AND EXPENDITURE
for year ended 31 December 1996

	£ million
Total income	155.1
Net income	145.9
Investments	87.3
Property	51.5
Interest from loans, etc.	16.3
Total expenditure	136.9
Clergy stipends	32.5
Clergy and widows' pensions	79.6
Clergy houses	0.4
Episcopal and cathedral housing	2.7
Financial provision for resigning clergy	2.9
Commissioners' administration of central church functions	5.4
Episcopal administration and payments to Chapters	10.0
Church buildings	1.1
Administration costs of other bodies	2.3
Surplus for year	9.0

CHURCH ESTATES COMMISSIONERS
First, Sir Michael Colman, Bt.
Second, S. Bell, MP
Third, Mrs M. H. Laird

OFFICERS
Secretary, P. Locke
Deputy Secretary (*Policy and Planning*), R. S. Hopgood
Deputy Secretary (*Finance and Investment*), C. W. Daws
Assistant Secretaries:
  The Accountant, G. C. Baines
  Management Accountant, B. J. Hardy
  Chief Surveyor, A. C. Brown
  Computer Manager, J. W. Ferguson
  Estates, P. H. P. Shaw, LVO
  Investments Manager, A. S. Hardy
  Pastoral, Houses and Redundant Churches, M. D. Elengorn
  Stipends and Allocations, M. G. S. Farrell
  Senior Architect, J. A. Taylor
Official Solicitor, vacant

CIVIL AVIATION AUTHORITY
CAA House, 45–59 Kingsway, London WC2B 6TE
Tel 0171-379 7311

The CAA is responsible for the economic regulation of UK airlines and for the safety regulation of UK civil aviation by the certification of airlines and aircraft and by licensing aerodromes, flight crew and aircraft engineers. Through its subsidiary company, National Air Traffic Services Ltd, it is also responsible for the provision of air traffic control and telecommunications services.

The CAA advises the Government on aviation issues, represents consumer interests, conducts economic and scientific research, produces statistical data and provides specialist services and other training, and consultancy services to clients world-wide.
Chairman (*part-time*), Sir Malcolm Field
Secretary, R. J. Britton

THE COAL AUTHORITY
200 Lichfield Lane, Mansfield, Notts NG18 4RG
Tel 01623-427162

The Coal Authority was established under the Coal Industry Act 1994 to manage certain functions previously undertaken by British Coal, including ownership of unworked coal. It is responsible for licensing coal mining operations and for providing information on coal reserves and past and future coal mining. It settles subsidence claims not falling on coal mining operators. It is also responsible for the management and disposal of property, and for dealing with surface hazards such as abandoned coal mine shafts.
Chairman, Sir David White
Chief Executive, K. J. Fergusson

COMMONWEALTH DEVELOPMENT CORPORATION
1 Bessborough Gardens, London SWIV 2JQ
Tel 0171-828 4488

The Commonwealth Development Corporation (CDC) assists overseas countries in the development of their economies. Its sponsoring department is the Department for International Development. Its main activity is providing long-term finance, as loans and risk capital, for financially viable and developmentally sound business enterprises. CDC's area of operations includes British dependent territories and, with ministerial approval, Commonwealth or other developing countries. At present, CDC is authorized to operate in more than 60 countries and territories. Its investments at the end of 1996 were £1,560 million.

Chairman (part-time), The Earl Cairns, CBE
Deputy Chairman (part-time), Sir William Ryrie, KCB
Chief Executive, Dr R. Reynolds

COMMONWEALTH SECRETARIAT
— *see* Index

COMMONWEALTH WAR GRAVES COMMISSION
2 Marlow Road, Maidenhead, Berks SL6 7DX
Tel 01628-34221

The Commonwealth War Graves Commission (formerly Imperial War Graves Commission) was founded by royal charter in 1917. It is responsible for the commemoration of 1,694,999 members of the forces of the Commonwealth who fell in the two world wars. More than one million graves are maintained in 23,194 burial grounds throughout the world. Over three-quarters of a million men and women who have no known grave or who were cremated are commemorated by name on memorials built by the Commission.

The funds of the Commission are derived from the six participating governments, i.e. the UK, Canada, Australia, India, New Zealand and South Africa.

President, HRH The Duke of Kent, KG, GCMG, GCVO, ADC
Chairman, The Secretary of State for Defence in the UK
Vice-Chairman, Air Chief Marshal Sir Joseph Gilbert, KCB, CBE
Members, The Secretary of State for the Environment, Transport and the Regions in the UK; the High Commissioners in London for India, Australia, South Africa, Canada and New Zealand; Dame Janet Fookes, DBE; Sir Nigel Mobbs; The Viscount Ridley, KG, GCVO, TD; Prof. R. J. O'Neill, AO; Mrs L. Golding, MP; Sir Harold Walker, KCMG; Gen. Sir John Akehurst, KCB, CBE; Adm. Sir John Kerr, GCB
Director-General and Secretary to the Commission, D. Kennedy, CMG
Deputy Director-General, R. J. Dalley
Legal Adviser and Solicitor, G. C. Reddie
Directors, D. R. Parker (*Personnel*); A. Coombe (*Works*); R. D. Wilson (*Finance*); D. C. Parker (*Horticulture*); L. J. Hanna (*Information and Secretariat*)

IMPERIAL WAR GRAVES ENDOWMENT FUND
Trustees, The Lord Remnant, CVO (*Chairman*); A. C. Barker; Air Chief Marshal Sir Joseph Gilbert, KCB, CBE
Secretary to the Trustees, R. D. Wilson

COUNTRYSIDE COMMISSION
John Dower House, Crescent Place, Cheltenham, Glos
GL50 3RA
Tel 01242-521381

The Countryside Commission was set up in 1968 and is an independent agency which promotes the conservation and enhancement of landscape beauty in England. It encourages the provision and improvement of facilities in the countryside, and works to secure access for open air recreation. The Commission is funded by an annual grant from the Department of the Environment, Transport and the Regions and members of the Commission are appointed by the Secretary of State. In 1996 the Commission's Countryside Stewardship initiative was transferred to the Ministry of Agriculture, Fisheries and Food.

Chairman, R. Simmonds, CBE
Commissioners, D. Barker, MBE; the Rt Revd A. Chesters; The Lord Denham, KBE; Dr Susan Owens; Prof. A. Patmore, CBE; W. Rogers-Coltman, OBE; R. Swarbrick, CBE; Mrs S. Ward; D. Woodhall, CBE
Chief Executive (G3), R. G. Wakeford
Directors (G5), R. Clarke (*Programmes*); M. Taylor (*Resources*)
National Heritage Adviser, P. Walshe
Head of Strategic Affairs (G7), D. E. Coleman
Head, Farms and Woodlands Branch (G7), R. Lloyd
Head, National Heritage Unit (G7), P. Walshe
Head, Sustainable Leisure Branch (G7), R. Roberts
Head, Planning for Sustainable Development Branch (G7), J. Worth
Head, Local Identity Branch (G7), T. Robinson
Head, Countryside Around Towns Branch (G7), Dr M. Rawson
Head, Information Services (G7), J. Huntley
Head, Resources Management (G7), V. Ellis
Regional Officers (G7), K. Buchanan (*Northern*); Dr M. Carroll (*Eastern*); Dr S. A. Bucknall (*Yorkshire and Humber*); N. Holliday (*South-West*); Dr Liz Newton (*North-West*); Ms M. Spain (*South-East*); T. Allen (*Midlands*)

COUNTRYSIDE COUNCIL FOR WALES / CYNGOR CEFN GWLAD CYMRU
Plas Penrhos, Fford Penrhos, Bangor LL57 2LQ
Tel 01248-385500

The Countryside Council for Wales is the Government's statutory adviser on wildlife, countryside and maritime conservation matters in Wales, and it is the executive authority for the conservation of habitats and wildlife. It promotes the protection of the Welsh landscape and encourages opportunities for public access and enjoyment of the countryside. It provides grant aid to local authorities, voluntary organizations and individuals to pursue countryside management. It is funded by the Welsh Office and accountable to the Secretary of State for Wales, who appoints its members.

Chairman, E. M. W. Griffith, CBE
Chief Executive, P. E. Loveluck, CBE
Director, Policy and Science, Dr M. E. Smith
Director, Conservation, I. R. Bonner

COVENT GARDEN MARKET AUTHORITY
Covent House, New Covent Garden Market, London
SW8 5NX
Tel 0171-720 2211

The Covent Garden Market Authority is constituted
under the Covent Garden Market Acts 1961 to 1977, the
members being appointed by the Minister of Agriculture,
Fisheries and Food. The Authority owns and operates the
56-acre New Covent Garden Markets (fruit, vegetables,
flowers) which have been trading since 1974.
Chairman (part-time), W. P. Bowman, CBE
General Manager, Dr P. M. Liggins
Secretary, C. Farey

CRIMINAL CASES REVIEW COMMISSION
Alpha Tower, Suffolk Street, Queensway, Birmingham
B1 1TT
Tel 0121-633 1800

The Criminal Cases Review Commission is an independent body set up under the Criminal Appeal Act 1995. It is
a non-departmental public body reporting to Parliament
via the Home Secretary. It is responsible for investigating
suspected miscarriages of justice in England, Wales and
Northern Ireland and deciding whether or not to refer
cases back to an appeal court. Membership of the Commis-
sion is by royal appointment; the senior executive staff are
appointed by the Commission.
Chairman, Sir Frederick Crawford, FEng.
Members, B. Capon; L. Elks; A. Foster; Ms J. Gort; Ms F.
  King; J. Knox; D. Kyle; J. Leckey; Prof. L. Leigh; J.
  MacKeith; K. Singh; B. Skitt; E. Weiss
Chief Executive, Ms G. Stacey
Director of Finance and Personnel, D. Robson
Legal Adviser, J. Wagstaff
Police Adviser, R. Barrington

CRIMINAL INJURIES COMPENSATION
AUTHORITY AND BOARD
Morley House, 26–30 Holborn Viaduct, London EC1A 2JQ
Tel 0171-842 6800
Tay House, 300 Bath Street, Glasgow G2 4JR
Tel 0141-331 2726

All applications for compensation for personal injury
arising from crimes of violence in England, Scotland and
Wales are dealt with at the above locations. (Separate
arrangements apply in Northern Ireland.) Applications
received up to 31 March 1996 were assessed on the basis of
common law damages under the 1990 compensation
scheme by the Criminal Injuries Compensation Board
(CICB), which also hears appeals. Applications received on
or after 1 April 1996 are assessed under a tariff-based
scheme by the Criminal Injuries Compensation Authority
(CICA); there is a separate avenue of appeal to the
Criminal Injuries Compensation Appeals Panel (CICAP).
In 1995–6 total compensation paid was £179,036,888.
  The Board was founded in 1964 by the Home Secretary
and Secretary of State for Scotland under the prerogative
powers of the Crown. The Authority and the Panel are
established by the tariff-based scheme made under the
Criminal Injuries Compensation Act 1995.

*Chairman of the Criminal Injuries Compensation Board (part-
  time)* (£35,306), The Lord Carlisle of Bucklow, PC, QC
*Chief Executive of the Board and of the Criminal Injuries
  Compensation Authority*, P. G. Spurgeon
Head of Legal Services, Mrs A. M. Johnstone
Operations Manager, E. McKeown
Chairman of the Criminal Injuries Compensation Appeals Panel,
  M. Lewer, QC
Secretary to the Panel, Miss V. Jenson

CROFTERS COMMISSION
4–6 Castle Wynd, Inverness IV2 3EQ
Tel 01463-663450

The Crofters Commission was established in 1955. It
advises the Secretary of State for Scotland on all matters
relating to crofting. It controls the letting, subletting and,
in certain circumstances, the assignation or enlargement of
crofts; the removal of land from crofting tenure; and the
regulation of common grazings. It delivers schemes to
develop crofts and crofting townships and for the improvement of crofters' livestock.
Chairman, I. MacAskill
Secretary (G6), M. Grantham

CROWN ESTATE
16 Carlton House Terrace, London SW1Y 5AH
Tel 0171-210 4377

The land revenues of the Crown in England and Wales
have been collected on the public account since 1760, when
George III surrendered them to Parliament and received a
fixed annual payment or Civil List. At the time of the
surrender the gross revenues amounted to about £89,000
and the net return to about £11,000.
  The land revenues in Ireland have been carried to the
Consolidated Fund since 1820; from 1923, as regards the
Republic of Ireland, they have been collected and admi-
nistered by the Irish Government.
  The land revenues in Scotland were transferred to the
predecessors of the Crown Estate Commissioners in 1833.
  In the year ended 31 March 1997, the gross income from
the Crown Estate totalled £154 million. The sum of £103
million was paid to the Exchequer in 1996–7 as surplus
revenue.
First Commissioner and Chairman (part-time), Sir Denys
  Henderson
Second Commissioner and Chief Executive, C. K. Howes, CB,
  CVO
Commissioners (part-time), J. N. C. James, CBE; I. Grant;
  J. H. M. Norris, CBE; The Lord De Ramsey; Mrs H.
  Chapman, CBE, FRICS
Commissioner and Deputy Chief Executive, D. E. G. Griffiths
Legal Adviser, M. L. Davies
Director of Urban Estates, N. Borrett
Urban Estates Managers, M. W. Dillon; A. Bickmore;
  R. Wyatt
Agricultural Estates Manager, C. Bourchier
Marine Estates Manager, F. G. Parrish
Information Systems Manager, D. Kingston-Smith
Valuation and Investment Analysis Manager, P. Shearmur
Internal Audit Manager, J. E. Ford
Finance Manager, J. G. Lelliott
Personnel and Office Services Manager, R. J. Blake
Public Relations and Press Officer, Mrs G. Coates

SCOTLAND
10 Charlotte Square, Edinburgh EH2 4BR
Tel 0131-226 7241

Crown Estate Receiver for Scotland, M. J. Gravestock

WINDSOR ESTATE
The Great Park, Windsor, Berks SL4 2HT
Tel 01753-860222

Deputy Ranger and Surveyor, M. J. O'Lone

CROWN PROSECUTION SERVICE
— see pages 363–4

DEPARTMENT FOR CULTURE, MEDIA AND SPORT
2–4 Cockspur Street, London SW1Y 5DH
Tel 0171-211 6000

The Department for Culture, Media and Sport was established in July 1997 from the former Department of National Heritage. It is responsible for government policy relating to the arts, broadcasting, the press, museums and galleries, libraries, sport and recreation, historic buildings and ancient monuments, tourism, and the music industry. It funds the Arts Councils and other arts bodies, is responsible for policy on the National Lottery and the Millennium, and sponsors the Millennium Commission.
Secretary of State for Culture, Media and Sport, The Rt. Hon.
   Christopher Smith, MP
   Private Secretary, D. Fawsett
   Special Advisers, J. Eccles; J. Newbigin
   Parliamentary Private Secretary, Ms A. Mahon, MP
Minister for Film and Tourism, The Rt. Hon. Thomas
   Clarke, CBE, MP
   Private Secretary, Mrs D. Wells
   Parliamentary Private Secretary, M. Connarty, MP
Parliamentary Under-Secretaries, Mark Fisher, MP (*Arts*);
   Tony Banks, MP (*Sport*)
   Private Secretaries, R. Woollard; Ms J. Buggins
Parliamentary Clerk, T. English
Permanent Secretary (*SCS*), G. H. Phillips, CB
   Private Secretary, J. Priestland

LIBRARIES, GALLERIES AND MUSEUMS GROUP
Head of Group (*SCS*), Miss S. Booth, CBE
Head of Libraries and Information Division (*SCS*), N. Mackay
Head of British Library Project (*SCS*), E. D'Silva
Head of Museums and Galleries Division (*SCS*), H. Corner
Head of Cultural Property Unit (*SCS*), M. Helston

SPORT, TOURISM AND NATIONAL LOTTERY CHARITIES
BOARD GROUP
Head of Group (*SCS*), D. Chesterton
Head of Sport and Recreation Division (*SCS*), S. Broadley
Head of Tourism Division (*SCS*), Ms B. Phillips

ARTS, BUILDING AND MILLENNIUM GROUP
Head of Group (*SCS*), L. P. Wright
Head of Arts Division (*SCS*), Ms M. Leech
Director, Government Art Collection (*SCS*), Ms P. Johnson
Head of Buildings, Monuments and Sites Division (*SCS*), N.
   Pittman

BROADCASTING AND MEDIA GROUP
Head of Group (*SCS*), N. J. Kroll
Head of Broadcasting Policy Division (*SCS*), P. Bolt
Head of Media Division (*SCS*), Ms J. Evans

FINANCE, LOTTERY AND PERSONNEL GROUP
Director (*SCS*), A. Ramsay

Head of Finance Division (*SCS*), Ms A. Stewart
Head of National Lottery Division (*SCS*), A. McLellan
Head of Personnel and Central Services Division (*SCS*), Ms S.
   Nason

INFORMATION
Head of Information Division (*SCS*), A. Marre

EXECUTIVE AGENCIES

HISTORIC ROYAL PALACES
Hampton Court Palace, Surrey KT8 9AU
Tel 0181-781 9750

The Historic Royal Palaces agency manages the Tower of London, Hampton Court Palace, Kensington Palace State Apartments and the Royal Ceremonial Dress Collection, Kew Palace with Queen Charlotte's Cottage, and the Banqueting House, Whitehall.
Chief Executive, D. C. Beeton
Director of Finance and Resources, vacant
Surveyor of the Fabric, vacant
Curator, Historic Royal Palaces, Dr E. Impey
Director, Palaces Group, R. Evans, FRICS
Resident Governor, HM Tower of London, Maj.-Gen.
   M. G. Field
Administrator, Kensington Palace, N. J. Arch

ROYAL PARKS AGENCY
The Old Police House, Hyde Park, London W2 2UH
Tel 0171-298 2000

The Agency is responsible for maintaining and developing the royal parks.
Chief Executive (*G5*), D. Welch

BOARD OF CUSTOMS AND EXCISE
*New King's Beam House, 22 Upper Ground, London
SE1 9PJ
Tel 0171-620 1313

Commissioners of Customs were first appointed in 1671 and housed by the King in London. The Excise Department was formerly under the Inland Revenue Department and was amalgamated with the Customs Department in 1909.

HM Customs and Excise is responsible for collecting and administering customs and excise duties and VAT, and advises the Chancellor of the Exchequer on any matters connected with them. The Department is also responsible for preventing and detecting the evasion of revenue laws and for enforcing a range of prohibitions and restrictions on the importation of certain classes of goods. In addition, the Department undertakes certain agency work on behalf of other departments, including the compilation of UK overseas trade statistics from customs import and export documents.

THE BOARD
Chairman (*G1*), Mrs V. P. M. Strachan, CB
   Private Secretaries, Ms J. Mellon; S. Timewell
Deputy Chairman, A. W. Russell, CB
Commissioners (*G3*), D. F. O. Battle; A. C. Sawyer; Mrs
   E. A. Woods; M. J. Eland; D. R. Howard; A. Paynter;
   M. Brown; R. McAfee
Head of Board's Secretariat, J. Bone

---

*Unless otherwise stated, this is the address and telephone number of
   directorates of the Board

PUBLIC RELATIONS OFFICE
Tel 0171-865 5665
Head of Public Relations, Ms L. J. Sinclair

INFORMATION SYSTEMS DIRECTORATE
Alexander House, 21 Victoria Avenue, Southend-on-Sea
SS99 1AA
Tel 01702-348944
Director, A. Paynter

CUSTOMS POLICY DIRECTORATE
Director, M. Eland

EXCISE AND CENTRAL POLICY DIRECTORATE
Director, D. Howard

VAT POLICY DIRECTORATE
Director, M. Brown

PERSONNEL AND FINANCE DIRECTORATE
Director, D. Battle

CENTRAL OPERATIONS DIRECTORATE
Director, R. McAfee

Tariff and Statistical Office
Portcullis House, 27 Victoria Avenue, Southend-on-Sea
SS2 6AL
Tel 01702-348944
Controller, M. McDowall

Accounting Services Division
Alexander House, 21 Victoria Avenue, Southend-on-Sea
SS99 1AA
Tel 01702-348944
Accountant and Comptroller-General, D. Robinson

OPERATIONS (COMPLIANCE) DIRECTORATE
Director, Mrs E. A. Woods

OPERATIONS (PREVENTION) DIRECTORATE
Director, A. Sawyer

National Investigation Service
Custom House, Lower Thames Street, London EC3R 6EE
Tel 0171-283 5353
Chief Investigation Officer, R. Kellaway

SOLICITOR'S OFFICE
Solicitor, D. Pickup
Deputy Solicitor, G. Fotherby

COLLECTORS OF HM CUSTOMS AND EXCISE (G5)
Anglia, R. C. Shepherd
Central England, A. Bowen
Eastern England, M. D. Patten
London Airports, M. Peach
London Central, J. Maclean
Northern England, H. Peden
Northern Ireland, T. W. Logan
North-west England, A. Allen
Scotland, C. Arnott
South-east England, W. I. Stuttle
South London and Thames, J. Hendry
Southern England, H. Burnard
Thames Valley, J. Barnard
Wales, the West and Borders, B. Flavill

OFFICE OF THE DATA PROTECTION
REGISTRAR
Wycliffe House, Water Lane, Wilmslow, Cheshire
SK9 5AF
Tel 01625-545745

The Office of the Data Protection Registrar was created by
the Data Protection Act 1984. It is the Registrar's duty to
compile and maintain the Register of data users and
computer bureaux and to provide facilities for members of
the public to examine the Register; to promote observance
of data protection principles; to consider complaints made
by data subjects; to disseminate information about the Act;
to encourage the production of codes of practice by trade
associations and other bodies; to guide data users in
complying with data protection principles; to co-operate
with other parties to the Council of Europe Convention
and act as UK authority for the purposes of Article 13 of the
Convention; and to report annually to Parliament on the
performance of her functions.
Registrar, Mrs E. France

DEER COMMISSION FOR SCOTLAND
Knowsley, 82 Fairfield Road, Inverness IV3 5LH
Tel 01463-231751

The Deer Commission for Scotland has the general
functions of furthering the conservation and control of
deer in Scotland. It has the statutory duty, with powers, to
prevent damage to agriculture, forestry and the habitat by
deer. The Commission also has the power to advise in the
interest of conservation any owner of land on questions
relating to the carrying of stocks of deer on that land, and to
carry out research into matters of scientific importance
relating to deer. It is funded by the Scottish Office.
Chairman (part-time), P. Gordon-Duff-Pennington, OBE
Director, A. Rinning
Technical Director, R. W. Youngson

MINISTRY OF DEFENCE
— *see* pages 383–6

DESIGN COUNCIL
1 Oxendon Street, London SW1Y 4EE
Tel 0171-208 2121

The Design Council is incorporated by royal charter and is
a registered charity. It works with government, industry
and academia to generate information and practical tools
for uptake in industry and education which demonstrate
the contribution, value and effectiveness of design. Its
sponsoring department is the Department of Trade and
Industry.
Chairman, J. Sorrell, CBE
Chief Executive, A. Summers

THE DUCHY OF CORNWALL
10 Buckingham Gate, London SW1E 6LA
Tel 0171-834 7346

The Duchy of Cornwall was created by Edward III in 1337
for the support of his eldest son Edward, later known as the

Black Prince. It is the oldest of the English duchies. The duchy is acquired by inheritance by the sovereign's eldest son either at birth or on the accession of his parent to the throne, whichever is the later. The primary purpose of the estate remains to provide an income for the Prince of Wales. The estate is mainly agricultural, consisting of 129,000 acres in 24 counties mainly in the south-west of England. The duchy also has some residential property, a number of shops and offices, and a Stock Exchange portfolio. Prince Charles is the 24th Duke of Cornwall.

THE PRINCE'S COUNCIL
Chairman, HRH The Prince of Wales, KG, KT, GCB
Lord Warden of the Stannaries, The Earl Peel
Receiver-General, The Earl Cairns, CBE
Attorney-General to the Prince of Wales, J. M. Sullivan, QC
Secretary and Keeper of the Records, W. R. A. Ross
Other members, Earl of Shelburne; J. E. Pugsley;
    A. M. J. Galsworthy; C. Howes, CB; W. N. Hood, CBE; S. Lamport

OTHER OFFICERS
Auditors, I. Brindle; H. Hughes
Sheriff (1997–8), C. Edward-Collins

THE DUCHY OF LANCASTER
Lancaster Place, Strand, London WC2E 7ED
Tel 0171-836 8277

The estates and jurisdiction known as the Duchy of Lancaster have belonged to the reigning monarch since 1399 when John of Gaunt's son came to the throne as Henry IV. As the Lancaster Inheritance it goes back as far as 1265 when Henry III granted his youngest son Edmund lands and possessions following the Baron's war. In 1267 Henry gave Edmund the County, Honor and Castle of Lancaster and created him the first Earl of Lancaster. In 1351 Edward III created Lancaster a County Palatine.

The Chancellor of the Duchy of Lancaster is responsible for the administration of the Duchy, the appointment of justices of the peace in Lancashire, Greater Manchester and Merseyside and ecclesiastical patronage in the Duchy gift. The Chancellor is also a member of the Cabinet.
Chancellor of the Duchy of Lancaster, The Rt. Hon. Dr David Clark, MP
Attorney-General, R. G. B. McCombe, QC
Receiver-General, M. C. G. Peat, CVO
Clerk of the Council, M. K. Ridley, CVO
Chief Clerk, Col. F. N. J. Davies

ECGD (EXPORT CREDITS GUARANTEE DEPARTMENT)
PO Box 2200, 2 Exchange Tower, Harbour Exchange Square, London E14 9GS
Tel 0171-512 7000

ECGD (Export Credits Guarantee Department), the official export credit insurer, is a separate government department responsible to the President of the Board of Trade and functions under the Export and Investment Guarantees Act 1991. This enables ECGD to facilitate UK exports by making available export credit insurance to British firms engaged in selling overseas and to guarantee repayment to banks in Britain providing finance for export credit for goods sold on credit terms of two years or more. The Act also empowers ECGD to insure British private

investment overseas against political risks such as war, expropriation and restrictions on remittances.
Chief Executive, vacant
Group Directors (G3), V. P. Lunn-Rockliffe (*Asset Management*); J. R. Weiss (*Underwriting*); T. M. Jaffray (*Resource Management*)

DIVISIONS
Director, Finance (G5), R. J. Healey
Director, Central Services (G5), P. J. Callaghan
Directors, Underwriting Divisions (G5), M. Lemmon
    (*Division 1*); J. C. W. Croall (*Division 2*); M. D. Pentecost
    (*Division 3*); Mrs M. E. Maddox (*Division 4*); S. R.
    Dodgson (*Division 5*); C. J. Leeds (*Division 6*)
Director, Office of the General Counsel (G5), R. G. Elden
Director, International Debt (G5), A. J. T. Steele
Director, Claims (G5), R. F. Lethbridge
Director, Treasury and Export Finance (G5), J. S. Snowdon
Director, Risk Management (G5), P. J. Radford
Director, External Relations (G5), R. Gotts
Director, IT Services (G6), E. J. Walsby
Director, Internal Audit (G6), G. Cassell
Director, Operational Research (G6), Ms R. Kaufman

EXPORT GUARANTEES ADVISORY COUNCIL
Chairman, R. T. Fox, CBE
Other Members, Dr A. K. Banerji; B. P. Dewe Mathews, CBE,
    TD; S. J. Doughty; D. H. A. Harrison; M. S. Jaskel;
    G. W. Lynch; R. H. Maudslay; D. B. Newlands; Sir
    Derek Thomas, KCMG; The Viscount Weir

DEPARTMENT FOR EDUCATION AND EMPLOYMENT
Sanctuary Buildings, Great Smith Street, London SW1P 3BT
Tel 0171-925 5000
Caxton House, Tothill Street, London SW1H 9NF
Tel 0171-273 3000
Moorfoot, Sheffield S1 4PQ
Tel 0114-275 3275
Mowden Hall, Staindrop Road, Darlington DL3 9BG
Tel 01325-460155

The Department for Education and Employment was formed in July 1995, bringing together the functions of the former Department for Education with the training and labour market functions of the former Employment Department Group. It includes an executive agency, the Employment Service. The Department aims to support economic growth and improve the nation's competitiveness and quality of life by raising standards of educational achievement and skill and by promoting an efficient and flexible labour market.
Secretary of State for Education and Employment, The Rt. Hon.
    David Blunkett, MP
    Principal Private Secretary, A. T. Evans
    Special Advisers, C. Ryan; Ms S. Linden; H. Benn; Ms L.
    Barclay
    Parliamentary Private Secretary, Ms J. Corston, MP
Ministers of State, The Rt. Hon. Andrew Smith, MP (*Welfare to Work and Equal Opportunities*); Stephen Byers, MP (*School Standards*); The Baroness Blackstone, PH.D.
    Private Secretaries, Ms K. Driver; Ms C. Maye; Ms P.
    Clarke
    Parliamentary Private Secretary to Mr Smith, S. Timms, MP
    Parliamentary Private Secretary to Mr Byers, Ms R. Squire, MP

Parliamentary Under-Secretaries of State, Alan Howarth, MP (*Employment and Equal Opportunities*); Estelle Morris, MP (*School Standards*) ; Kim Howells, MP (*Lifelong Learning*)
Private Secretaries, J. Kittmer; Ms G. Magliocco; D. McGrath
Permanent Secretary, M. Bichard
Private Secretary, Ms J. Wright

EMPLOYMENT AND LIFELONG LEARNING DIRECTORATE
Director-General, N. Stuart
Heads of Divisions, M. Nicholas (*Learning at Work*); Ms F. Everiss (*Individual Learning*)

EMPLOYMENT AND ADULT TRAINING
Director, D. Grover
Heads of Divisions, I. Berry (*New Deal Policy*); C. Barnham (*Employment and Benefits Policy*); E. Galvin (*Employment and Training Programmes*)

EQUAL OPPORTUNITIES, TECHNOLOGY AND OVERSEAS LABOUR
Director, B. Niven
Heads of Divisions, Mrs J. Anderson, Ms S. Weber (*Sex and Race Equality*); Miss D. Fordham (*Disability Policy*); R. Ritzema (*Education and Training Technology*); N. Atkinson (*Overseas Labour Service*)

FINANCE DIRECTORATE
Director, P. Shaw
Heads of Divisions, D. Sandeman (*Expenditure*); Mrs S. Todd (*Private Finance Initiative*); D. Russell (*Programme Performance and Evaluation*); vacant (*Efficiency*); P. Connor (*Accounting and Systems*); N. Thirtle (*Internal Audit*)

FURTHER AND HIGHER EDUCATION AND YOUTH TRAINING DIRECTORATE
Director-General, R. Dawe

FURTHER EDUCATION AND YOUTH TRAINING
Director, D. Forrester
Heads of Divisions, Ms C. Tyler (*16–19 Policy*); Mrs L. Ammon (*Choice and Careers*); J. Stanyer (*Further Education Support Unit*); A. Shaw (*Further Education*); R. Wye (*Training for Young People*)

HIGHER EDUCATION
Director, A. C. Clark
Heads of Divisions, Mrs I. Wilde (*Higher Education Funding*); Miss C. Macready (*Higher Education Quality*); J. Moore (*Student Support*); T. Fellowes (*Higher Education and Employment*)

QUALIFICATIONS
Director, M. Richardson
Heads of Divisions, M. Waring (*School- and College-Based Qualifications*); J. West (*Qualifications for Work*)

LEGAL ADVISER'S OFFICE
Legal Adviser, F. Croft
Heads of Divisions, F. Clarke; S. Harker; C. House; N. Lambert

OPERATIONS DIRECTORATE
Director, J. Hedger

Heads of Divisions, P. Houten (*TECs and Careers Service Policy*); P. Lauener (*Resources and Budget Management*); Mrs P. Jones (*Financial Control, Operations*); Ms S. Orr (*Quality and Performance Improvement*); H. Sharp (*Regional Development and Government Offices*); J. Fuller (*National Training Organizations*)

PERSONNEL AND SUPPORT SERVICES DIRECTORATE
Director, Mrs H. Douglas
Heads of Divisions, R. Hinchcliffe (*Information Systems*); Ms C. Johnson (*Personnel*); K. Jordan (*Procurement and Contracting*); J. Gordon (*Training and Development*); L. Webb (*Estates and Office Services*); T. Jeffery (*Human Resource Policy*)

SCHOOLS DIRECTORATE
Director-General, P. Owen
Head of Division, S. Kershaw (*Education Bill*)

SCHOOL ORGANIZATION AND PLACES GROUP
Director, P. Makeham
Heads of Divisions, S. Marston (*Schools Framework*); A. Cranston (*Organization of School Places*); Ms A. Jackson (*Specialist Schools and School Governance*); K. Beeton (*Capital and Buildings*); M. Hipkins (*Under-Fives Policy*); C. Wells (*Under-Fives Implementation*); M. Patel (*Architects and Buildings*)

SCHOOL CURRICULUM, FUNDING, AND TEACHERS GROUP
Director, N. Sanders
Heads of Divisions, A. Clarke (*School Recurrent Funding*); J. Street (*LEA Finance*); A. Wye (*School Teachers' Pay and Pensions*); Ms C. Bienkowska (*Teacher Supply, Training and Qualifications*); M. G. Richardson (*Curriculum and Assessment*)

PUPILS, PARENTS AND YOUTH GROUP
Director, R. Smith
Heads of Divisions, A. Sargent (*Admissions and Information for Parents*); R. Green (*Special Educational Needs*); P. Thorpe (*Discipline and Attendance*); G. Holley (*Youth Service and Preparation for Adulthood*); M. Phipps (*Pupil Welfare and Opportunities*); S. Johnson (*Pupil Motivation and Community Links*)

SCHOOL STANDARDS AND EFFECTIVENESS UNIT
Head of Unit, Prof. M. Barber
Heads of Divisions, S. Adamson (*Literacy and Numeracy*); M. Stark (*School Effectiveness*)

STRATEGY, INTERNATIONAL AND ANALYTICAL SERVICES DIRECTORATE
Director-General, D. Normington
Heads of Divisions, J. Dewsbury (*Briefing*); R. Harrison (*Strategy and Board Secretariat*)

ANALYTICAL SERVICES
Director, D. Allnutt
Heads of Divisions, M. Britton (*Qualifications*); J. Elliott (*Youth and Further Education*); J. Temple (*Skills and Training Analysis*); D. Thompson (*Higher Education*); vacant (*Schools, Teachers and General*); B. Butcher (*TECs and Lifelong Learning*); B. Wells (*Labour Market Analysis*); R. Bartholomew (*Social Analysis and Research*); Ms A. Brown (*School Resources and Modelling*)

INTERNATIONAL
Director, C. Tucker, CB

Heads of Divisions, Miss E. Hodkinson (*EC Education and Training*); Ms W. Harris (*European Union*); Ms E. Trewartha (*European Social Fund*); B. Shaw (*International Relations*)

COMMUNICATIONS
Director, J. Haslam
Heads of Divisions, D. Cook (*Media Relations*); J. Ross (*Publicity*)

EXECUTIVE AGENCY

THE EMPLOYMENT SERVICE
St Vincent House, 30 Orange Street, London WC2H 7HT
Tel 0171-839 5600

The aim of the Employment Service is to promote a competitive, efficient and flexible labour market by helping unemployed people into work, while ensuring that they understand and fulfil the conditions for receipt of jobseeker's allowance.
Chief Executive, L. Lewis
Director of Jobcentre Services, J. Turner
Director of Human Resources, K. White
Director of Policy and Process Design, R. Phillips
Director of Finance, Planning and Research, P. Collis
Regional Directors, R. Foster (*London and South-East*); M. Groves (*East Midlands and Eastern*); P. Robson (*Northern*); J. Roberts (*North-West*); K. Pascoe (*South-West*); S. McIntyre (*West Midlands*); R. Lasko (*Yorkshire and Humberside*)
Director for Scotland, A. R. Brown
Director for Wales, Mrs S. Keyes

OFFICE OF ELECTRICITY REGULATION
Hagley House, Hagley Road, Birmingham B16 8QG
Tel 0121-456 2100
SCOTLAND: Regent Court, 70 West Regent Street, Glasgow G2 2QZ
Tel 0141-331 2678

The Office of Electricity Regulation (OFFER) is the regulatory body for the electricity supply industry in England, Scotland and Wales. Its functions are to promote competition in the generation and supply of electricity; to ensure that all reasonable demands for electricity are satisfied; to protect customers' interests in relation to prices, security of supply and quality of services; and to promote the efficient use of electricity. Headed by the Director-General of Electricity Supply, OFFER was set up under the Electricity Act 1989 but is independent of ministerial control.
Director-General of Electricity Supply, Prof. S. C. Littlechild
Deputy Director-General, C. P. Carter
Deputy Director-General for Scotland, G. L. Sims
Director of Regulation and Business Affairs, J. Saunders
Director of Supply Competition, A. J. Boorman
Director of Consumer Affairs, Dr D. P. Hauser
Technical Director, Dr B. Wharmby
Director of Public Affairs, Miss J. D. Luke
Director of Administration, H. P. Jones
Legal Adviser, D. R. B. Bevan
Chief Examiner, J. D. Cooper

OFFICE FOR THE REGULATION OF ELECTRICITY AND GAS
Brookmount Buildings, 42 Fountain Street, Belfast BT1 5EE
Tel 01232-311575 (*Electricity*); 01232-314212 (*Gas*)

The Office for the Regulation of Electricity and Gas (OFREG) is the combined regulatory body for the electricity and gas supply industries in Northern Ireland.
Director-General of Electricity Supply and Director-General of Gas for Northern Ireland, D. B. McIldoon
Deputy Director-General of Electricity and Gas, C. H. Coulthard

ENGLISH HERITAGE
— *see* Historic Buildings and Monuments Commission for England

---

ENGLISH NATURE
Northminster House, Peterborough PE1 1UA
Tel 01733-340345

English Nature (the Nature Conservancy Council for England) was established in 1991 and is responsible for advising the Secretary of State for the Environment, Transport and the Regions on nature conservation in England. It promotes, directly and through others, the conservation of England's wildlife and natural features. It selects, establishes and manages National Nature Reserves and identifies and notifies Sites of Special Scientific Interest. It provides advice and information about nature conservation, and supports and conducts research relevant to these functions. Through the Joint Nature Conservation Committee (*see* page 329), it works with its sister organizations in Scotland and Wales on UK and international nature conservation issues.
Chairman, The Earl of Cranbrook
Chief Executive, Dr D. R. Langslow
Directors, Dr K. L. Duff; E. T. Idle; Miss C. E. M. Wood; Ms S. Collins

---

ENGLISH PARTNERSHIPS
16–18 Old Queen Street, London SW1H 9HP
Tel 0171-976 7070

English Partnerships, in statute the Urban Regeneration Agency, came into full operation in April 1994. Its task is to regenerate derelict, vacant and under-used land and buildings throughout England. Its aim is to deliver regeneration, economic development, job creation and environmental improvement. It works in partnership with the public, private and voluntary sectors. Its sponsoring department is the Department of the Environment, Transport and the Regions.
Chairman, The Lord Walker of Worcester, MBE, PC
Deputy Chairman, Sir Idris Pearce, CBE
Chief Executive, A. Dunnett

DEPARTMENT OF THE ENVIRONMENT, TRANSPORT AND THE REGIONS
Eland House, Bressenden Place, London SW1E 5DU
Tel 0171-890 3000
Great Minster House, 76 Marsham Street, London SW1P 4DR
Tel 0171-271 5000

The Department of the Environment, Transport and the Regions (DETR) was formed in June 1997 by the merger of the Department of the Environment and the Department of Transport, with the aim of integrating the policies of the two departments. It is responsible for policies relating to local government, regional development agencies, and regeneration; housing, construction, planning and countryside affairs; and environmental protection and water. It is the sponsoring department for the Health and Safety Executive and the Health and Safety Commission.

The DETR is also responsible for land, sea and air transport, including sponsorship of the rail and bus industries; airports; domestic and international civil aviation; shipping and the ports industry; navigational lights, pilotage, HM Coastguard and marine pollution; motorways and other trunk roads; oversight of road transport including vehicle standards, registration and licensing, driver testing and licensing, bus and road freight licensing, regulation of taxis and private hire cars and road safety; and oversight of local authorities' transport planning, including payment of Transport Supplementary Grant.

Decisions on the final structure of the merged department will be taken in September 1997. This entry therefore largely reflects the separate structures of the two departments and the locations of divisions before merger. Most of the ministers, including the Deputy Prime Minister, are based at Eland House.

Deputy Prime Minister and Secretary of State for the Environment, Transport and the Regions, The Rt. Hon. John Prescott, MP
  Private Secretary, J. Jacobs
  Special Advisers, J. Irvin; D. Taylor; J. Hammell; Ms K. Davies
  Parliamentary Private Secretary, A. Meale, MP
Minister for Transport, The Rt. Hon. Dr Gavin Strang, MP
  Private Secretary, P. Kirk
  Parliamentary Private Secretary, G. Prentice, MP
Minister for the Environment, The Rt. Hon. Michael Meacher, MP
  Private Secretary, Mrs T. Vokes
  Parliamentary Private Secretary, T. Rooney, MP
Minister for Local Government and Housing, Hilary Armstrong, MP
  Private Secretary, T. Redpath
  Parliamentary Private Secretary, K. Hill, MP
Minister for the Regions, Regeneration and Planning, Richard Caborn, MP
  Private Secretary, C. T. Wood
  Parliamentary Private Secretary, B. Chapman, MP
Parliamentary Under-Secretaries of State, Nick Raynsford, MP (*London and Construction*); Glenda Jackson, MP (*Transport in London*); The Baroness Hayman (*Roads*); Angela Eagle, MP (*Energy, Environment and the Regions*)
  Private Secretaries, K. Willison; D. Calpin; L. Sambrook; P. West
Parliamentary Clerks, Miss A. Moore; Ms P. Gaunt
Permanent Secretary (G1), A. Turnbull, CB, CVO
  Private Secretary, S. Bishop

ORGANIZATION AND ESTABLISHMENTS*
Principal Establishments Officer (G3), R. S. Dudding

PERSONNEL
Grade 5, K. G. Arnold; Mrs M. Winckler; M. A. L. Ross
Chief Welfare Officer (G7), Miss E. T. Haines

ADMINISTRATION RESOURCES
Grade 5, J. J. O'Callaghan; Mrs H. Parker-Brown

RESOURCES†

PERSONNEL AND CHANGE MANAGEMENT
Director of Personnel, Ms J. Cotton
SCS, R. D. Bayly (*Personnel Services*); G. Kemp (*Pay and Senior Staff Management*)
Grade 6, B. Meakins (*Development and Training*)
Head of Counselling and Support Services (G7), Miss E. T. Haines

FINANCE
Director of Finance (SCS), B. Wadsworth
Accounting Adviser, A. R. Allum
Heads of Divisions, R. Bennett; R. Parsons; P. A. Sanders

CENTRAL SERVICES
Ashdown House, Sedlescombe Road North, Hastings, E. Sussex TN37 7GA
Tel 01424-458306
Director, M. R. Newey
Heads of Divisions, I. R. Heawood (*Management Support Services*); G. L. Jones (*Departmental Procurement Unit*)
Grade 6, I. Harris (*Accommodation and Office Services*); P. Waller (*IT Management Unit*)

FINANCE CENTRAL*
Principal Finance Officer (G3), J. F. Ballard
Heads of Divisions (G5), M. J. Bailey; A. C. Allberry; M. R. Haselip; I. C. McBrayne; M. J. Burt; A. Brooks

DIRECTORATE OF COMMUNICATION*
Director (G4), S. Dugdale
Grade 5, K. Kerslake
Deputy Director, Communications (Transport) (G6), D. Plews

GOVERNMENT OFFICES CENTRAL UNIT*
Under-Secretary (G3), Ms L. Bell
Grade 5, Mrs J. Scones; J. Craven

HOUSING CONSTRUCTION, PLANNING AND COUNTRYSIDE GROUP*
Deputy Secretary (G2), Mrs M. McDonald

SECRETARIAT
Grade 7, P. G. Tobia

HOUSING POLICY AND PRIVATE SECTOR
Under-Secretary (G3), Dr C. P. Evans
Grade 5, C. L. L. Braun; Ms B. Campbell; M. Faulkner

HOUSING AND URBAN MONITORING AND ANALYSIS
Under-Secretary (G3), Dr C. P. Evans
Grade 5, J. E. Turner; Mrs J. Littlewood; M. Hughes; S. Aldridge; C. Clark

HOUSING, SOCIAL POLICY AND RESOURCES
Under-Secretary (G3), Mrs D. S. Phillips

*Based at Eland House
†Based at Great Minster House

Grade 5, Mrs H. Chipping; R. S. Horsman; R. J. Dinwiddy;
Mrs S. Bonfanti

CONSTRUCTION SPONSORSHIP
Director (G3), P. Ward
Grade 5, J. P. Channing; R. Job; J. Stambollouian
Grade 6, R. Wood

WILDLIFE AND COUNTRYSIDE DIRECTORATE
Tollgate House, Houlton Street, Bristol BS2 9DJ
Tel 0117-987 8178
Under-Secretary (G3), J. P. Plowman
Grade 5, R. M. Pritchard; R. Hepworth; D. Kahn; Ms S.
Carter

PROPERTY AND BUILDINGS
Director (G4), D. O. McCreadie
Grade 5, P. F. Everall
Grade 6, W. J. Marsh

PLANNING DIRECTORATE
Under-Secretary (G3), N. Rickett
Heads of Divisions (G5), R. Jones; W. E. Chapman;
M. R. Ash; J. Zetter; A. M. Oliver; L. Hicks; J. M. Leigh-
Pollitt

CHIEF ECONOMIST DIRECTORATE*
Chief Economist (G3), C. Riley
Economist (G6), R. Davies

LOCAL DEVELOPMENT GROUP*
Deputy Secretary (G2), C. J. S. Brearley, CB

SECRETARIAT
HEO, E. A. Carter

LOCAL GOVERNMENT FINANCE POLICY DIRECTORATE
Director, Local Government Finance Policy (G3), Mrs J.
Williams
Heads of Divisions (G5), Miss L. F. Bell; R. J. Gibson; Mrs
P. Peneck; Dr C. Myerscough; N. Dorling

LOCAL GOVERNMENT DIRECTORATE
Director (G3), A. Whetnall
Heads of Divisions (G5), P. Rowsell; J. R. Footit; T.
Crossley

REGENERATION DIRECTORATE
Director (G3), P. Evans
Heads of Divisions (G5), D. Liston-Jones; *(G6)*, I. Nicol; G.
Lanfer; A. Riddel

PRIVATE FINANCE UNIT
Head of Unit (G5), M. Brasher

LEGAL*
Solicitor and Legal Adviser (G2), Mrs M. A. Morgan, CB
Deputy Solicitors (G3), A. D. Roberts; Ms S. D. Unerman;
P. J. Szell
Assistant Solicitors (G5), J. L. Comber; I. D. Day; Mrs
P. J. Conlon; Mrs G. Hedley-Dent; Miss
D. C. S. Phillips; N. Lefton; P. J. Brocklebank; Mrs C.
Edwards
Director, Legal Services, M. Thomas
Heads of Branches, R. Lines; N. Thomas; C. Ingram; A.
Jones; D. Aries; D. Pope

OFFICE OF THE CHIEF SCIENTIST*
Chief Scientist (G3), Dr D. J. Fisk
Head of Division (G5), Dr A. J. Apling

ENVIRONMENT PROTECTION
Romney House, 43 Marsham Street, London SW1P 3PY
Tel 0171-890 3000

Senior Director (G2), Miss D. A. Nichols

ENVIRONMENT AND INTERNATIONAL DIRECTORATE
Under-Secretary (G3), Dr D. J. Fisk
Heads of Divisions (G5), Dr P. Hinchcliffe; Dr S. Brown;
P. F. Unwin; Dr B. Hackland; Ms S. McCabe

ENVIRONMENT PROTECTION STRATEGY AND WASTES
DIRECTORATE
Under-Secretary (G3), B. H. Leonard
Heads of Divisions (G5), Mrs L. A. C. Simcock; Mrs H. C.
Hillier; B. Glicksman; J. Stevens; R. Wilson; J. Adams

WATER AND LAND DIRECTORATE
Director (G3), A. H. Davis
Heads of Divisions (G5), A. J. C. Simcock; A. M. Wells; S.
Hoggan
Drinking Water Inspectorate
Grade 5, M. J. Rouse

ENVIRONMENTAL AND ENERGY MANAGEMENT
DIRECTORATE
Under-Secretary (G3), P. Ward
Heads of Divisions (G5), A. K. Galloway; H. Cleary; L.
Packer
Grade 6, Dr A. Vincent

EUROPE, STATISTICS AND RESEARCH
DIRECTORATE
Romney House, 43 Marsham Street, London SW1P 3PY
Tel 0171-276 8513
Director (SCS), W. Billington
Heads of Divisions (SCS), I. Jordan; Dr R. L. Butchart;
P. J. Capell; R. P. Donachie

MOBILITY UNIT
Head of Unit, Miss E. A. Frye
Heads of Branches, Ms S. Sharp; Ms M. Carter; Ms A. Gray;
E. Stait

TRANSPORT STRATEGY DIRECTORATE
Director, Transport Strategy Unit, A. Burchell
Heads of Divisions, D. Instone; D. McMillan; Ms B. Hill

RAILWAYS, LONDON TRANSPORT AND
SHIPPING†
Director, D. Rowlands

RAILWAYS
Director, R. J. Griffins
Heads of Divisions, M. Fuhr (*Channel Tunnel Rail Link*); P.
Cox (*Railways Economics*); P. Thomas (*Railways General*);
B. Linnard (*Railways Sponsorship*); Ms P. Williams
(*International Railways*); S. Connolly (*NAO Studies*)

LONDON'S TRANSPORT
Director, R. Allan
Heads of Divisions, S. Gooding (*London's Transport*); M.
Walsh (*Economics, Local Transport and General*); D. Lord
(*Transport Security*)

SHIPPING
Director, R. E. Clarke
Heads of Divisions, J. F. Wall; G. D. Rowe; D. Cooke; C.
Young; S. Reeves

*Based at Eland House
†Based at Great Minster House

MARINE ACCIDENTS INVESTIGATION BRANCH
5–7 Brunswick Place, Southampton SOI 2AN
Tel 01703-232424
Chief Inspector of Marine Accidents, Rear-Adm. J. Lang

LOCAL TRANSPORT, ROAD SAFETY AND HIGHWAYS†
Director, P. Wood, CB

NATIONAL ROADS POLICY
Director, H. Wenban-Smith
Heads of Divisions, T. Worsley (*Highways Economic and Traffic Appraisal*); N. McDonald (*Highways Policy and Programmes*); Mrs C. M. Dixon (*Tolling and Private Finance*)

URBAN AND LOCAL TRANSPORT
Director, R. Bird
Heads of Divisions, E. C. Neve (*Buses and Taxis*); P. McCarthy (*Local Transport Policy*); A. S. D. Whybrow (*Traffic Policy*); M. F. Talbot (*Driver Information and Traffic Management*); P. Hammond (*Transport Works Act*)

ROAD AND VEHICLE SAFETY
Director, Miss S. J. Lambert
Heads of Divisions, M. Fendick (*Vehicle Standards and Engineering*); R. Peal (*Road Safety*); J. L. Gansler (*Licensing and Roadworthiness Policy*); J. R. Fells (*Road Haulage*); (*G6*), J. Winder (*Traffic Area Network Unit*)
Chief Medical Adviser, Dr P. A. M. Diamond, OBE

TRAFFIC AREA OFFICES AND COMMISSIONERS
Senior Traffic Commissioner, Brig. M. W. Betts

Eastern, Brig. C. M. Boyd
North-Eastern and North-Western, K. R. Waterworth
Scottish, Brig. M. W. Betts
South-Eastern and Metropolitan, Brig. M. H. Turner
Western, C. Heaps
West Midlands and S. Wales, J. Mervyn

GOVERNMENT OFFICES UNIT
Head of Unit, J. Parker

EXECUTIVE AGENCIES DIVISION
Head, A. C. Melville
Heads of Divisions, D. Partridge; K. Deadman; A. Murray

AVIATION GROUP†
Director-General, A. J. Goldman, CB
SCS, M. Fawcett (*Airports Policy*); Ms M. J. Clare (*CAA and Safety Policy*); M. C. Mann (*Economics Aviation, Maritime and International*); Ms E. Duthie (*Aviation Environmental*); M. Smethers (*Multilateral Division*)
UK Representative on ICAO Council, D. Evans

INTERNATIONAL AVIATION NEGOTIATIONS
Director, A. T. Baker
SCS, N. Starling

AIR ACCIDENTS INVESTIGATION BRANCH
Royal Aerospace Establishment, Farnborough, Hants
GUI4 6TD
Tel 01252-510300
Chief Inspector of Air Accidents, K. P. R. Smart, CBE

REGIONAL OFFICES
— see pages 305–6

EXECUTIVE AGENCIES

COASTGUARD AGENCY
Spring Place, 105 Commercial Road, Southampton
SOI5 IEG
Tel 01703-329100
The Agency's role is to minimize loss of life among seafarers and coastal users, and to minimize pollution from ships to sea and coastline.
Chief Executive, C. J. Harris, MBE
Chief Coastguard, J. Astbury

DRIVER AND VEHICLE LICENSING AGENCY
Longview Road, Morriston, Swansea 3A6 7JL
Tel 01792-772151
The Agency issues driving licences, registers and licenses vehicles, and collects excise duty.
Chief Executive, Dr S. J. Ford

DRIVING STANDARDS AGENCY
Stanley House, Talbot Street, Nottingham NGI 5GU
Tel 0115-947 4222
The Agency's role is to carry out driving tests and approve driving instructors.
Chief Executive, B. L. Herdan

HIGHWAYS AGENCY
St Christopher House, Southwark Street, London SEI OTE
Tel 0171-928 3666
The Agency is responsible for the management and maintenance of the motorway and trunk road network and for road construction and improvement.
Chief Executive, L. J. Haynes
Directors, J. Seddon (*Finance Services*); K. A. Wyatt (*Human Resource Services*); P. Nutt (*Network and Customer Services*); D. York (*Project Services*); J. A. Kerman (*Quality Services*)
Head of Public Relations, J. Murphy
Secretary to the Board, S. Barnes

MARINE SAFETY AGENCY
Spring Place, 105 Commercial Road, Southampton
SOI5 IEG
Tel 01703-329100
The Agency's role is to develop, promote and enforce high standards of marine safety and to minimize the risk of pollution of the marine environment from ships.
Chief Executive, R. M. Bradley

ORDNANCE SURVEY
— see page 331

PLANNING INSPECTORATE
Tollgate House, Houlton Street, Bristol BS2 9DJ
Tel 0117-987 8927
The Inspectorate is responsible for casework involving planning, housing, roads, environmental and related legislation. It is a joint executive agency of the Department of the Environment, Transport and the Regions and the Welsh Office.
Chief Executive and Chief Planning Inspector (*G3*), C. Shepley
Deputy Chief Planning Inspector (*G4*), D. J. Hanchet
Directors (*G5*), R. E. Wilson; Mrs S. Bruton; B. Dodd
Director of Planning Appeals (*G5*), G. Saunders
Director of Finance and Management Services (*G5*), M. Brasher

QUEEN ELIZABETH II CONFERENCE CENTRE
Broad Sanctuary, London SWIP 3EE
Tel 0171-798 4010
The Centre provides conference and banqueting facilities for both private sector and government use.
Chief Executive (*G5*), M. C. Buck

VEHICLE CERTIFICATION AGENCY
1 Eastgate Office Centre, Eastgate Road, Bristol BS5 6XX
Tel 0117-951 5151

The Agency tests and certificates vehicles to UK and international standards.
Chief Executive, D. W. Harvey

VEHICLE INSPECTORATE
Berkeley House, Croydon Street, Bristol BS5 0DA
Tel 0117-954 3274

The Agency carries out annual testing and inspection of heavy goods and other vehicles and administers the MOT testing scheme.
Chief Executive, R. J. Oliver

TRAFFIC DIRECTOR FOR LONDON
College House, Great Peter Street, London SW1P 3LN
Tel 0171-222 4545

The Traffic Director for London is a non-departmental public body which is independent from the Department of the Environment, Transport and the Regions but is responsible to the Secretary of State and to Parliament. Its role is to co-ordinate the introduction of the Priority (Red) Route Network in London and monitor its operation.
Traffic Director for London, D. Turner

THE ENVIRONMENT AGENCY
Hampton House, 20 Albert Embankment, London SE1 7TJ
Tel 0171-587 3000
Rio House, Waterside Drive, Aztec West, Almondsbury, Bristol BS12 4UD
Tel 01454-624400

The Environment Agency was established in April 1996 under the Environment Act 1995 and is a non-departmental public body sponsored by the Department of the Environment, Transport and the Regions, MAFF and the Welsh Office. It brings together the work formerly undertaken by the National Rivers Authority, HM Inspectorate of Pollution, the waste regulation authorities and some technical units of the former Department of the Environment. The Agency is responsible for pollution prevention and control in England and Wales, and for the management and use of water resources, including flood defences, fisheries and navigation. It has head offices in London and Bristol and eight regional offices which are mainly concerned with operational activities.

THE BOARD
Chairman, The Lord De Ramsey
Members, P. Burnham; Prof. R. Edwards; I. Farookhi; E. Gallagher; Sir Richard George; N. Haigh, OBE; C. Hampson, CBE; J. Harman; G. Manning; Mrs K. Morgan; D. Osborn; Dr A. Powell; T. Rodgers; Mrs J. Wykes

THE EXECUTIVE
Chief Executive, E. Gallagher
Director of Finance, N. Reader
Director of Personnel, G. Duncan
Director of Pollution Prevention and Control, D. Slater
Director of Water Management, G. Mance
Director of Operations, A. Robertson
Director of Public Affairs, M. Wilson
Director of Legal Services, R. Navarro
Chief Scientist, J. Pentreath

ROYAL COMMISSION ON ENVIRONMENTAL POLLUTION
Church House, Great Smith Street, London SW1P 3BZ
Tel 0171-276 2080

The Commission was set up in 1970 to advise on matters, both national and international, concerning the pollution of the environment; on the adequacy of research in this field; and the future possibilities of danger to the environment.
Chairman, Sir John Houghton, CBE, FRS
Members, Sir Geoffrey Allen, FRS; Revd Prof. M. C. Banner; Prof. G. S. Boulton, FRS, FRSE; Prof. C. E. D. Chilvers; Prof. R. Clift, OBE, FEng.; Dr P. Doyle, CBE, FRSE; J. Flemming; Sir Martin Holdgate, CB; Prof. R. Macrory; Prof. M. G. Marmot, PH.D.; Prof. J. G. Morris, CBE, FRS; Dr Penelope A. Rowlatt; The Earl of Selborne, KBE, FRS
Secretary, D. R. Lewis

EQUAL OPPORTUNITIES COMMISSION
Overseas House, Quay Street, Manchester M3 3HN
Tel 0161-833 9244

Press Office, 36 Broadway, London SW1H 0XH. Tel: 0171-222 1110
Other Offices, Stock Exchange House, 7 Nelson Mandela Place, Glasgow G2 1QW. Tel: 0141-248 5833; Caerwys House, Windsor Place, Cardiff. Tel: 01222-343552

The Commission was set up by Parliament in 1975 as a result of the passing of the Sex Discrimination Act. It works towards the elimination of discrimination on the grounds of sex or marital status and to promote equality of opportunity between men and women generally. It is responsible to the Department for Education and Employment.
Chairwoman, Ms K. Bahl, CBE
Deputy Chairwomen, Mrs E. Hodder; Ms G. James
Members, Ms A. Gibson; P. Smith; Ms M. Berg; R. Grayson; Dr J. Stringer; Prof. T. Rees; R. Penn; Ms J. Rubin; Dr A. Wright; Prof. M. Schofield
Chief Executive (acting), F. Spencer

EQUAL OPPORTUNITIES COMMISSION FOR NORTHERN IRELAND
Chamber of Commerce House, 22 Great Victoria Street, Belfast BT2 7BA
Tel 01232-242752
Chair and Chief Executive, Mrs J. Smyth

EXCHEQUER AND AUDIT DEPARTMENT
— *see* National Audit Office

OFFICE OF FAIR TRADING
Field House, Bream's Buildings, London EC4A 1PR
Tel 0171-242 2858

The Office of Fair Trading is a non-ministerial government department headed by the Director-General of Fair Trading. It keeps commercial activities in the UK under review and seeks to protect consumers against unfair trading practices. The Director-General's consumer protection duties under the Fair Trading Act 1973, together with his responsibilities under the Consumer Credit Act 1974, the Estate Agents Act 1979, the Control of Misleading Advertisements Regulations 1988, and the Unfair Terms in Consumer Contracts Regulations 1994, are administered by the Office's Consumer Affairs Division. The Competition Policy Division is concerned with monopolies and mergers (under the Fair Trading Act 1973), and the Director-General's other responsibilities for competition matters, including those under the Restrictive Trade Practices Act 1976, the Resale Prices Act 1976, the Competition Act 1980, the Financial Services Act 1986 and the Broadcasting Act 1990. The Office is the UK competent authority on the application of the European Commission's competition rules, and also liaises with the Commission on consumer protection initiatives.

Director-General, J. Bridgeman
Deputy Director-General, vacant

CONSUMER AFFAIRS DIVISION
Director (G3), G. Horton
Assistant Directors (G5), Miss C. Banks; R. Watson; M. Graham

COMPETITION POLICY DIVISION
Director (G3), Mrs M. J. Bloom
Assistant Directors (G5), A. J. White; H. L. Emden; E. L. Whitehorn; S. Wood; P. Bamford

LEGAL DIVISION
Director (G3), Miss P. Edwards
Assistant Directors (G5), M. A. Khan; P. T. Rostron
Establishment and Finance Officer (G5), Mrs R. Heyhoe
Chief Information Officer (G6), D. Hill

FOREIGN AND COMMONWEALTH OFFICE
Downing Street, London SW1A 2AL
Tel 0171-270 3000

The Foreign and Commonwealth Office provides, mainly through diplomatic missions, the means of communication between the British Government and other governments and international governmental organizations for the discussion and negotiation of all matters falling within the field of international relations. It is responsible for alerting the British Government to the implications of developments overseas; for protecting British interests overseas; for protecting British citizens abroad; for explaining British policies to, and cultivating friendly relations with, governments overseas; and for the discharge of British responsibilities to the dependent territories. Responsibility for overseas development was transferred to the new Department for International Development (*see* pages 315–6) in May 1997.

Secretary of State for Foreign and Commonwealth Affairs, The Rt. Hon. Robin Cook, MP
  Principal Private Secretary, W. G. Ehrman
  Private Secretaries, D. J. Chilcott; Ms F. Mylchreest
  Special Advisers, A. Hood; D. Clark
  Parliamentary Private Secretary, K. Purchase, MP
Ministers of State, Douglas Henderson, MP (*Minister for Europe*); Derek Fatchett, MP; Tony Lloyd, MP
  Private Secretaries, M. Tatham; J. Slater; T. Barrow
Parliamentary Under-Secretary of State, The Baroness Symons of Vernham Dean
Parliamentary Relations Department, E. Jenkinson (*Head*); P. Bromley (*Deputy Head and Parliamentary Clerk*)
Permanent Under-Secretary of State and Head of the Diplomatic Service, Sir John Kerr, KCMG
  Private Secretary, J. King

Deputy Under-Secretaries, J. R. Young, CMG (*Chief Clerk*); M. H. Jay (*Economic Affairs and EU Director*); J. Q. Greenstock, CMG (*Political Director*); Sir Andrew Burns, KCMG; K. R. Tebbit
Legal Adviser, Sir Franklin Berman, KCMG, QC
Deputy Political Director, P. F. Ricketts
Director of General Services, R. Dibble
Director of Resources and Chief Inspector, M. A. Arthur
Assistant Under-Secretaries, E. Jones Parry; E. Clay; J. R. de Fonblanque; J. Rollo; P. J. Torry; R. H. Smith; F. N. Richards, CVO, CMG; R. Dales; G. Fry; J. A. Shepherd, CMG; D. Broucher; P. J. Westmacott; H. N. H. Synnott; D. Hall; D. Plumbly, CMG
HM Vice-Marshal of the Diplomatic Corps, P. S. Astley, LVO

HEADS OF DEPARTMENTS
*Aid Policy Department, G. Stegmann
Aviation and Maritime Department, R. A. Kealy
British Diplomatic Spouses Association, Mrs S. Burns
Central European Department, H. Pearce
Change Management Unit, D. Broucher
Commonwealth Co-ordination Department, M. Hatfull
Commonwealth Foreign and Security Policy Unit, Ms A. Pringle
Conference Unit, M. Dalton
Consular Division, S. F. Howarth
Counter Terrorism Policy Department, V. Fean
Cultural Relations Department, Ms A. Lewis
Drugs and International Crime, M. Raven
Eastern Department, P. Thomas
Eastern Adriatic Unit, N. K. Darroch
*Economic Advisers Department, J. Rollo
*Economic Relations Department, N. Westcott
Engineering Services, I. Whitehead
Environment, Science and Energy Department, D. E. Lyscom
Equatorial Africa Department, Ms A. Grant
European Community Department (External), R. Stagg
European Community Department (Internal), S. Gass
European Union Department (Presidency), M. Kirk
Far Eastern and Pacific Department, D. Coates
Financial Compliance Unit, M. Mayhew
Financial Policy, M. Brown
Home Estate Department, S. Attwood
Hong Kong Department, S. L. Cowper Coles, CMG
Honours Unit, R. M. Sands
Human Rights Policy Unit, R. P. Nash
Information Department, P. J. Dun
Information Systems Department, P. McDermott
Internal Audit, R. Elias
Joint Assistance Unit (Central Europe), S. Laing
Joint Assistance Unit (Eastern Europe), M. McCulloch
†Joint Export Promotion Directorate, P. Beckingham
Latin America Department, H. Hogger
Library and Records Department, S. I. Soutar
*Management Consultancy and Inspection Department, G. Gillham
Medical and Welfare Unit, Ms E. Kennedy
Middle East Department, E. Chaplin
Migration and Visa Department, M. E. Frost
National Audit Office, B. Burwood
Near East and North Africa Department, P. W. Ford
News Department, N. E. Sheinwald
Non-Proliferation Department, B. Cleghorn
North America Department, P. J. Priestley
OSCE and Council of Europe, S. N. Evans, OBE
Overseas Estate Department, M. H. R. Bertram, CBE

---

*Joint Foreign and Commonwealth Office/Department for International Development department
†Joint Foreign and Commonwealth/Department of Trade and Industry directorate

Permanent Under-Secretary's Department, D. Martin
Personnel Management Department, Ms D. Holt
Personnel Policy Unit, Ms P. Major; Ms N. Brewer
Personnel Services Department, R. Fell
Policy Planning Staff, Miss A. M. Leslie
PROSPER, C. J. Edgerton, OBE
Protocol Department, R. S. Gorham (*First Assistant Marshal of the Diplomatic Corps*)
Purchasing Directorate, M. Gower
Republic of Ireland Department, D. A. Lamont
Research and Analysis Department, S. Jack
Resource and Planning Department, R. Kinchen
Royal Matters Unit, B. W. Money
Security Department, T. Duggin
Security Policy Department, R. H. Gozney
Senior Resident Clerk, B. Lowen
Services, Planning and Resources Department, Mrs J. Link, LVO
South Asian Department, C. Elmes
South Atlantic and Antarctic Department, A. J. Longrigg
South-East Asian Department, N. J. Cox
Southern Africa Department, B. H. Dinwiddy
Southern European Department, H. B. Warren-Gash
Support Services Department, M. Carr
United Nations Department, Ms R. M. Marsden
Western European Department, A. Layden
West Indian and Atlantic Department, C. Drace-Francis
Whitley Council, P. Hadley

EXECUTIVE AGENCY

WILTON PARK CONFERENCE CENTRE
Wiston House, Steyning, W. Sussex BN44 3DZ
Tel 01903-815020

The Centre organizes international affairs conferences and is hired out to government departments and commercial users.
Chief Executive, C. B. Jennings

THE SECRET INTELLIGENCE SERVICE
(MI6)
Vauxhall Cross, PO Box 1300, London SEI IBD

The Secret Intelligence Service produces secret intelligence in support of the Government's security, defence, foreign and economic policies. It was placed on a statutory footing by the Intelligence Services Act 1994. The Act also established an Intelligence Services Tribunal, which hears complaints made against the Service (*see* page 315).
Director-General, Sir David Spedding, KCMG, CVO, OBE

GOVERNMENT COMMUNICATIONS
HEADQUARTERS (GCHQ)
Priors Road, Cheltenham, Glos GL52 5AJ
Tel 01242-221491

GCHQ produces signal intelligence in support of the Government's security, defence, foreign and economic policies. It also provides advice and assistance to government departments and the armed forces on the security of their communications and information technology systems. It was placed on a statutory footing by the Intelligence Services Act 1994. The Act also established an Intelligence Services Tribunal, which hears complaints made against GCHQ (*see* page 315).
Director, D. B. Omand

CORPS OF QUEEN'S MESSENGERS
Support Services Department, Foreign and
Commonwealth Office, London SW1A 2AH
Tel 0171-270 2779

Superintendent of the Corps of Queen's Messengers, B. Garside
Queen's Messengers, P. Allen; Maj. J. E. A. Andre;
   Cdr. D. H. Barraclough; Maj. A. N. D. Bols;
   Lt.-Cdr. K. E. Brown; Lt.-Col. W. P. A. Bush;
   Lt.-Col. M. B. de S. Clayton; Capt. G. Courtauld;
   Maj. P. C. H. Dening-Smitherman;
   Sqn. Ldr. J. S. Frizzell; Capt. N. C. E. Gardner;
   Maj. D. A. Griffiths; Maj. K. J. Rowbottom;
   Maj. M. R. Senior; Cdr. K. M. C. Simmons, AFC;
   Maj. P. M. O. Springfield; Maj. J. S. Steele

FOREIGN COMPENSATION COMMISSION
Room 013, 4 Central Buildings, Matthew Parker Street,
London SW1H 9NL
Tel 0171-210 0400/5

The Commission was set up by the Foreign Compensation Act 1950 primarily to distribute, under Orders in Council, funds received from other governments in accordance with agreements to pay compensation for expropriated British property and other losses sustained by British nationals.
Chairman, A. W. E. Wheeler, CBE
Secretary, A. N. Grant

FORESTRY COMMISSION
231 Corstorphine Road, Edinburgh EH12 7AT
Tel 0131-334 0303

The Forestry Commission is the government department responsible for forestry policy in Great Britain. It reports directly to forestry ministers (i.e. the Secretary of State for Scotland, who takes the lead role, the Minister of Agriculture, Fisheries and Food and the Secretary of State for Wales), to whom it is responsible for advice on forestry policy and for the implementation of that policy.

The Commission's principal objectives are to protect Britain's forests and woodlands; expand Britain's forest area; enhance the economic value of the forest resources; conserve and improve the biodiversity, landscape and cultural heritage of forests and woodlands; develop opportunities for woodland recreation; and increase public understanding of and community participation in forestry. Forest Enterprise, a trading body operating as an executive agency of the Commission, manages its forestry estate on a multi-use basis.
Chairman (*part-time*) (£36,965), Sir Peter Hutchison, Bt., CBE
Director-General and Deputy Chairman (G2), D. J. Bills
Head of the Forestry Authority (G3), D. L. Foot
Secretary to the Commissioners (G5), F. Strong

FOREST ENTERPRISE, 231 Corstorphine Road, Edinburgh EH12 7AT. Tel: 0131-334 0303. *Chief Executive*, Dr B. McIntosh

REGISTRY OF FRIENDLY SOCIETIES
Victory House, 30–34 Kingsway, London WC2B 6ES
Tel 0171-663 5000

The Registry of Friendly Societies is a government department serving three statutory bodies, the Building Societies Commission, the Friendly Societies Commission, and the Central Office of the Registry of Friendly

Societies (together with the Assistant Registrar of Friendly Societies for Scotland).

The Building Societies Commission was established by the Building Societies Act 1986. The Commission is responsible for the supervision of building societies and administers the system of regulation. It also advises the Treasury and other government departments on matters relating to building societies.

The Friendly Societies Commission was established by the Friendly Societies Act 1992. Its responsibilities for the supervision of friendly societies parallel those of the Building Societies Commission for building societies.

The Central Office of the Registry of Friendly Societies provides a public registry for mutual organizations registered under the Building Societies Act 1986, Friendly Societies Acts 1974 and 1992, and the Industrial and Provident Societies Act 1965. It is responsible for the supervision of credit unions, and advises the Government on issues affecting them.

BUILDING SOCIETIES COMMISSION
Chairman, G. E. Fitchew
Deputy Chairman, M. Owen
Commissioners, J. M. Palmer; *T. F. Mathews, CBE;
   *F. E. Worsley; *F. G. Sunderland; *N. Fox Bassett; *Sir
   James Birrell
* part-time

FRIENDLY SOCIETIES COMMISSION
Chairman, *D. W. Lee
Commissioners, F. da Rocha; *B. Richardson; *J. A. Geddes;
   *P. E. Couse
* part-time

CENTRAL OFFICE OF THE REGISTRY
Chief Registrar, G. E. Fitchew
Assistant Registrars, A. J. Perrett; Ms S. Eden; D. A. W.
   Stevens

BUILDING SOCIETIES COMMISSION STAFF
Grade 3, M. Owen
Grade 4, J. M. Palmer
Grade 5, D. A. W. Stevens; W. Champion; E. Engstrom
Grade 6, N. F. Digance; A. G. Tebbutt

FRIENDLY SOCIETIES COMMISSION STAFF
Grade 6, F. da Rocha

CENTRAL SERVICES STAFF
Legal Adviser (G4), A. J. Perrett
Establishment and Finance Officer (G5), J. Stevens
Legal Staff (G5), A. D. Preston; C. J. Gregory; (*G6*), Ms S.
   Bagga

REGISTRY OF FRIENDLY SOCIETIES, SCOTLAND
58 Frederick Street, Edinburgh EH2 1NB
Tel 0131-226 3224
Assistant Registrar (G5), J. L. J. Craig, WS

GAMING BOARD FOR GREAT BRITAIN
Berkshire House, 168–173 High Holborn, London
WC1V 7AA
Tel 0171-306 6200

The Board was established in 1968 and is responsible to the Home Secretary. It is the regulatory body for casinos, bingo clubs, gaming machines and the larger society and all local authority lotteries in Great Britain. Its functions are to ensure that those involved in organizing gaming and lotteries are fit and proper to do so and to keep gaming free from criminal infiltration; to ensure that gaming and

lotteries are run fairly and in accordance with the law; and to advise the Home Secretary on developments in gaming and lotteries.
Chairman (part-time) (£35,393), Lady Littler
Secretary, T. Kavanagh

OFFICE OF GAS SUPPLY
Stockley House, 130 Wilton Road, London SW1V 1LQ
Tel 0171-828 0898

The Office of Gas Supply (Ofgas) is a regulatory body set up under the Gas Act 1986. It is headed by the Director-General of Gas Supply, who is independent of ministerial control. Its main aims are to protect the interests of gas consumers by regulating the prices of British Gas Trading and TransCo and to introduce competition into the domestic gas market (*see also* page 502).
Director-General, Ms C. Spottiswoode
Chief Economic Adviser, Dr Eileen Marshall
Legal Adviser, W. Sprigge
Director, Public Affairs, C. Webb
Director, Administration, R. Field

GOVERNMENT ACTUARY'S DEPARTMENT
22 Kingsway, London WC2B 6LE
Tel 0171-211 2600

The Government Actuary provides a consulting service to government departments, the public sector, and overseas governments. The actuaries advise on social security schemes and superannuation arrangements in the public sector at home and abroad, on population and other statistical studies, and on government supervision of insurance companies, friendly societies and pension funds.
Government Actuary, C. D. Daykin, CB
Directing Actuaries, D. G. Ballantine; D. H. Loades, OD;
   A. G. Young
Chief Actuaries, E. I. Battersby; Ms W. M. Beaver; A. J.
   Chamberlain; T. W. Hewitson; A. I. Johnston; D. Lewis;
   J. C. A. Rathbone

GOVERNMENT HOSPITALITY FUND
8 Cleveland Row, London SW1A 1DH
Tel 0171-210 3000

The Government Hospitality Fund was instituted in 1908 for the purpose of organizing official hospitality on a regular basis with a view to the promotion of international goodwill. It is responsible to the Foreign and Commonwealth Office.
Minister in Charge, The Baroness Symons of Vernham
   Dean
Secretary, Col. T. Earl

GOVERNMENT OFFICES FOR THE
REGIONS

The Government Offices for the Regions were established in April 1994. The regional directors are accountable to the Secretary of State for the Environment, Transport and the Regions, the President of the Board of Trade and the Secretary of State for Education and Employment. The offices' role is to promote a coherent approach to competitiveness, sustainable economic development and regeneration using public and private resources.

Central Unit, 23rd Floor, Portland House, Stag Place, London SW1E 5DF
Tel 0171-890 5157

Head of Central Unit (G3), Miss L. Bell
Grade 5, Mrs J. Scoones

EASTERN
Secretariat: Enterprise House, Vision Park, Histon, Cambridge CB4 4DZ
Tel 01223-202065

Regional Director (G3), J. Lambert
Directors (G5), C. Dunabin (*Housing, Environment and Regeneration*); T. Bird (*Planning, Transport and Europe*); M. Oldham (*Trade and Industry*); Mrs C. Hunter (*Skills and Enterprise*)

EAST MIDLANDS
Secretariat: The Belgrave Centre, Stanley Place, Talbot Street, Nottingham NG1 5GG
Tel 0115-971 2755

Regional Director (G3), M. Lanyon
Directors (G5), Dr S. Kennett (*Environment and Transport*); M. Briggs (*Competitiveness, Trade and Industry*); A. Davies (*Skills and Enterprise*)

LONDON
Secretariat: 10th Floor, Riverwalk House, 157–161 Millbank, London SW1P 4RR
Tel 0171-217 3456

Regional Director (G2), Miss E. C. Turton, CB
Directors (G3), J. A. Owen (*Regeneration*); M. Lambirth (*Planning and Transport*); (*G5*), B. Glickman (*Skills Enterprise and Education*); Mrs J. Bridges (*Planning*); Ms A. Munro (*Transport Assessment*); Mrs L. Meek (*Strategy and Co-ordination Unit*); K. Timmins (*Regeneration North-West*); (*G6*), A. Weeden (*Transport*); (*G7*), Ms H. Ghosh (*Regeneration East*)

MERSEYSIDE
Secretariat: Cunard Building, Pier Head, Liverpool L3 9TN
Tel 0151-224 6300

Regional Director (SCS), D. Morrison
Directors (SCS), P. Holme (*Skills and Enterprise*); S. Dunmore (*Regeneration, Transport and Planning*); Ms P. Jackson (*Competitiveness, Investment and Europe*)

NORTH-EAST
Secretariat: Room 404, Stangate House, 2 Groat Market, Newcastle upon Tyne NE1 1YN
Tel 0191-201 3300

Regional Director (G3), Mrs P. Denham, CB
Directors (G5), J. Darlington (*Planning, Environment and Transport*); Miss D. Caudle (*Regeneration and Housing*); A. Dell (*Competitiveness, Industry and Europe*); S. Geary (*Education Skills and Business Development*); (*G6*), Mrs D. Pearce (*Strategy and Resources*)

NORTH-WEST
Secretariat: 20th Floor, Sunley Tower, Piccadilly Plaza, Manchester M1 4BE
Tel 0161-952 4000

Regional Director (G3), Miss M. Neville-Rolfe
Directors, (G5), B. Isherwood (*Regeneration*); D. Higham (*Competitiveness*); P. Styche (*Infrastructure and Planning*); P. Keen (*Skills and Enterprise*); (*G6*), D. Duff (*TEC Operations and Finance*); D. Stewart (*Europe (Regeneration)*)

SOUTH-EAST
Secretariat: 2nd Floor, Bridge House, 1 Walnut Tree Close, Guildford, Surrey GU1 4GA
Tel 01483-882481

Regional Director (G3), Mrs G. Ashmore
Directors (G5), Ms L. Robinson (*Hants/IOW*); N. Wilson (*Berks/Oxon/Bucks*); J. Vaughan (*Kent*); E. Beston (*Surrey/E. and W. Sussex*); Mrs E. A. Baker (*Regional Strategy Team*)

SOUTH-WEST
Secretariat: 4th Floor, The Pithay, Bristol BS1 2PB
Tel 0117-900 1708

Regional Director (G3) (*acting*), T. Shearer
Directors (G5), S. McQuillin (*Devon and Cornwall*); M. Quinn (*Environment and Transport*); T. Shearer (*Education, Trade and Industry*); (*G6*), D. Way (*Strategy and Resources*)

WEST MIDLANDS
Secretariat: 6th Floor, 77 Paradise Circus, Queensway, Birmingham B1 2DT
Tel 0121-212 5000

Regional Director (G3), D. Ritchie
Directors (G4), Dr H. M. Sutton (*Trade, Industrial Development and Europe*); (*G5*), Mrs P. Holland (*Housing and Regeneration*); P. Langley (*Planning, Transport and Environment*); H. Tollyfield (*Education, Skills and Enterprise*); (*G6*), D. Mahoney (*Resource Management*)

YORKSHIRE AND HUMBERSIDE
Secretariat: PO Box 213, City House, New Station Street, Leeds LS1 4US
Tel 0113-280 0600

Regional Director (G3), J. Walker
Directors (G4), Ms S. Seymour (*Strategy and Europe*); (*G5*), I. Crowther (*Environment, Planning and Transport*); D. Stewart (*Regeneration*); G. Dyche (*Business, Enterprise and Skills*); (*G6*), N. Best (*Personnel and Resources*)

DEPARTMENT OF HEALTH
Richmond House, 79 Whitehall, London SW1A 2NS
Tel 0171-210 3000

The Department of Health is responsible for the provision of the National Health Service in England and for social care, including oversight of personal social services run by local authorities in England for children, the elderly, the infirm, the handicapped and other persons in need. It is responsible for health promotion and has functions relating to public and environmental health, food safety and nutrition. The Department is also responsible for the ambulance and emergency first aid services, under the Civil Defence Act 1948. The Department represents the UK at the European Union and other international organizations including the World Health Organization. It also supports UK-based healthcare and pharmaceutical industries.

Secretary of State for Health, The Rt. Hon. Frank Dobson, MP
    Principal Private Secretary, Ms C. Moriarty
    Private Secretaries, F. Sondell; H. Rogers
    Special Adviser, J. McCrea
    Parliamentary Private Secretary, H. Bayley, MP
Ministers of State, Alan Milburn, MP (*NHS Structure and Resources*); Tessa Jowell, MP (*Public Health*); The Baroness Jay of Paddington (*NHS Services*)
    Private Secretaries, Ms K. Fraser; M. Fahy; Miss S. Casemore

Parliamentary Private Secretary to Ms Jowell, J. Ennis, MP
Parliamentary Under-Secretary of State, Paul Boateng, MP
(*Social Care and Mental Health*)
  Private Secretary, J. Marron
Parliamentary Clerk, G. Wakeman
Permanent Secretary (*G1*), Sir Graham Hart, KCB
  Private Secretary, Mrs H. Steele
Chief Medical Officer (*G1A*), Dr Sir Kenneth Calman, KCB
Chief Executive, NHS Executive (*G1A*), A. Langlands
Deputy Chief Medical Officer (*G2*), Dr J. S. Metters, CB

NATIONAL HEALTH SERVICE POLICY BOARD
Chairman, The Secretary of State for Health
Members, Alan Milburn, MP (*Minister of State*); Tessa
  Jowell, MP (*Minister of State for Public Health*); The
  Baroness Jay of Paddington (*Minister of State*); Paul
  Boateng, MP (*Parliamentary Under-Secretary*); Dr Sir
  Kenneth Calman, KCB (*Chief Medical Officer*);
  A. Langlands (*Chief Executive, NHS Executive*); Sir
  Graham Hart, KCB (*Permanent Secretary*); Mrs Y. Moores;
  Sir Bryan Baker; Sir Stuart Burgess, CBE; K. Ackroyd;
  Miss J. Trotter, OBE; J. Greetham, CBE; I. Mills;
  W. Wells; Prof. A. Breckenridge; A. D. M. Liddell, CBE

PUBLIC HEALTH POLICY GROUP

HEALTH ASPECTS OF ENVIRONMENT AND FOOD
DIVISION
Under-Secretary (*G3*), Dr E. Rubery
Head of Branches, Dr R. Skinner; Dr E. Smales; Mrs M. Fry;
  C. P. Kendall

HEALTH PROMOTION DIVISION
Under-Secretary (*G3*), G. J. F. Podger
Principal Medical Officer (*G4*), Dr D. McInnes
Assistant Secretaries (*G5*), J. F. Sharpe, CBE; Miss
  A. Mithani; Ms L. Lockyer; K. J. Guinness

SOCIAL CARE GROUP
Chief Social Services Inspector, Sir Herbert Laming, CBE
Head of Social Care Policy, T. R. H. Luce, CB
Deputy Chief Inspectors, D. Gilroy; Ms A. Nottage
Assistant Secretaries (*G5*), R. M. Orton; N. F. Duncan;
  D. P. Walden; Mrs E. Hunter-Johnston; R. Tyrrell
Assistant Chief Inspectors (*HQ*), J. Kennedy; F. Tolan; Mrs
  W. Rose
Assistant Chief Inspectors (*Regions*), S. Allard; J. Cypher;
  B. Riddell; A. Jones; D. G. Lambert, CBE; Mrs P. K. Hall;
  C. P. Brearley; J. Fraser; Mrs L. Hoare; Ms J. Owen

NURSING GROUP
Chief Nursing Officer/Director of Nursing (*G3*), Mrs
  Y. Moores
Assistant Chief Nursing Officers (*G4*), Mrs P. Cantrill; Mrs
  G. Stevens; (*G5*), Dr G. Chapman; G. Butler

NHS EXECUTIVE
Quarry House, Quarry Hill, Leeds LS2 7UE
Tel 0113-254 5000

Chief Executive, A. Langlands
Director of Human and Corporate Resources, K. Jarrold, CBE
Director of Finance and Performance, C. Reeves
Medical Director, Dr G. Winyard
Chief Nursing Officer, Mrs Y. Moores
Director of Research and Development, Prof. J. D. Swales
Director of Planning and Performance Management,
  A. D. M. Liddell, CBE

HUMAN RESOURCES DIRECTORATE
Director of Human and Corporate Resources (*G2*), K. Jarrold

CORPORATE AFFAIRS
Under-Secretary (*G3*), M. Staniforth

HUMAN RESOURCES
Under-Secretary (*G3*), M. Deegan

INFORMATION MANAGEMENT
Under-Secretary (*G3*), R. Rogers

RESEARCH AND DEVELOPMENT DIVISION
Director of Research and Development, Prof. J. D. Swales
Deputy Director of Research Management (*G4*), Dr C.
  Henshall
Assistant Secretaries (*G5*), Dr P. Greenaway; J. Ennis; Dr D.
  Gardiner; Ms A. Kander

PLANNING DIRECTORATE
Director (*G2*), A. D. M. Liddell, CBE
Chief Economic Adviser, C. Smee, CB
Head of Planning, L. Bradley
Head of Primary Care, A. McKeon
Head of Communications, Mrs H. McCallum
Director of Statistics, Mrs R. Butler

HEALTH SERVICES DIRECTORATE
Director (*G2*), Dr G. Winyard
Deputy Director (*G3*), Dr S. Adam
Heads of Branches, M. Brown; Mrs L. Wolstenholme; A.
  Doran; Ms J. McKessack; Ms G. Fletcher-Cooke

PRIMARY CARE DIVISION
Head of Division, A. McKeon
Chief Dental Officer, J. R. Wild
Chief Pharmaceutical Officer, B. H. Hartley
Heads of Branches, G. Denham (*Dental and Optical Services*);
  J. Thompson (*Pharmacy and Prescribing*); Miss H. Gwynn
  (*NHS Purchasing*); M. Farrar (*General Medical Services*)

FINANCE AND PERFORMANCE
DIRECTORATE
Director (*G2*), C. L. Reeves
Deputy Directors, P. Garland; R. Douglas
Heads of Branches, B. McCarthy; J. Lawler; Dr S. Peck; M.
  Sturges; A. Angilley; M. Harris; J. Thomlinson; P.
  Coates; J. Havelock

REGIONAL OFFICES

ANGLIA AND OXFORD, 6–12 Capital Drive, Linford
  Wood, Milton Keynes MK14 6QP. *Chairman*, Sir Stuart
  Burgess, CBE, PH.D., FRSC; *Regional Director*, Ms
  B. Stocking
NORTHERN AND YORKSHIRE, John Snow House, Durham
  University Science Park, Durham DHI 3YG. *Chairman*,
  J. Grootham, OBE; *Regional Director*, Prof. L. Donaldson
NORTH THAMES, 40 Eastbourne Terrace, London
  W2 3QR. *Chairman*, I. Mills, *Regional Director*, R. Kett
NORTH WEST, 930–932 Birchwood Boulevard,
  Millennium Park, Birchwood, Warrington WA3 7QN.
  Chairman, Prof. A. Breckenridge; *Regional Director*,
  R. Tinston
SOUTH AND WEST, Westward House, Lime Kiln Close,
  Stoke Gifford, Bristol BS12 6SR. *Chairman*, Miss J.
  Trotter, OBE; *Regional Director*, A. Laurance
SOUTH THAMES, 40 Eastbourne Terrace, London W2 3QR.
  Chairman, Sir William Wells; *Regional Director*, N. Crisp
TRENT, Fulwood House, Old Fulwood Road, Sheffield
  S10 3TH. *Chairman*, K. Ackroyd, CBE; *Regional Director*,
  N. McKay

WEST MIDLANDS, Arthur Thompson House, 146 Hagley Road, Birmingham B16 9PA. *Chairman,* Sir Bryan Baker; *Regional Director,* S. Day

DEPARTMENTAL RESOURCES AND SERVICES GROUP
Deputy Secretary (G2), J. Pilling, CB

STATISTICS DIVISION
Director of Statistics (G3), Mrs R. J. Butler
Chief Statisticians (G5), R. K. Willmer; G. J. O. Phillpotts

PERSONNEL SERVICES
Principal Establishment Officer (G3), D. J. Clark
Assistant Secretaries (G5), P. Allen; C. Muir

INFORMATION SERVICES DIVISION
Head of Division (G4), Dr A. A. Holt
Heads of Branches, Mrs L. Wishart; C. Horsey; M. Rainsford; Mrs J. Dainty; M. Smith; R. Long; P. G. Cobb

RESOURCE MANAGEMENT AND FINANCE
Under-Secretary (G3), A. B. Barton
Heads of Branches, P. Kendall; B. Burleigh; J. Stopes-Roe; A. McNeil

ECONOMICS AND OPERATIONAL RESEARCH DIVISION (HEALTH)
Chief Economic Adviser (G3), C. H. Smee, CB
Heads of Branches, Dr S. Harding; J. W. Hurst; Dr G. Royston; A. Hare; D. Franklin

PRESS AND PUBLICITY DIVISION
Director of Information, Miss R. Christopherson
Deputy Directors, C. P. Wilson *(news);* Mrs A. Rea *(publicity)*

POLICY MANAGEMENT UNIT
Head of Branch, Mrs F. Goldhill

SOLICITOR'S OFFICE
Solicitor (G2), P. K. J. Thompson
Principal Assistant Solicitor (G3), Mrs G. S. Kerrigan

ADVISORY COMMITTEES

ADVISORY COMMITTEE ON THE MICROBIOLOGICAL SAFETY OF FOOD, Room 502A, Skipton House, 80 London Road, London SE1 6LW. Tel: 0171-972 5049. *Chairman,* Prof. D. Georgala, CBE, Ph.D.
CLINICAL STANDARDS ADVISORY GROUP, Wellington House, 133–155 Waterloo Road, London SE1 8UG. Tel: 0171-972 4926. *Chairman,* Prof. M. Harris
COMMITTEE ON THE SAFETY OF MEDICINES, Market Towers, 1 Nine Elms Lane, London SW8 5NQ. Tel: 0171-273 0451. *Chairman,* Prof. M. D. Rawlins
MEDICINES COMMISSION, Market Towers, 1 Nine Elms Lane, London SW8 5NQ. Tel: 0171-273 0365. *Chairman,* Prof. D. Lawson, CBE, MD, FRCPEd., FRCP(Glas.)

EXECUTIVE AGENCIES

MEDICINES CONTROL AGENCY
Market Towers, 1 Nine Elms Lane, London SW8 5NQ
Tel 0171-273 0000
The Agency controls medicines through licensing, monitoring and inspection, and enforces safety standards.
Chief Executive, Dr K. H. Jones, CB

MEDICAL DEVICES AGENCY
Hannibal House, Elephant and Castle, London SE1 6TQ
Tel 0171-972 8000
The Agency safeguards the performance, quality and safety of medical devices.
Chief Executive, A. Kent

NHS ESTATES
1 Trevelyan Square, Boar Lane, Leeds LS1 6AE
Tel 0113-254 7000
The Agency provides advice and support in the area of healthcare estate functions to the NHS and the healthcare industry.
Chief Executive (G3), vacant

NHS PENSIONS
Hesketh House, 200–220 Broadway, Fleetwood, Lancs FY7 8LG
Tel 01253-774774
The Agency administers the NHS occupational pension scheme.
Chief Executive (G4), A. F. Cowan

SPECIAL HEALTH AUTHORITIES

ASHWORTH HOSPITAL, Parkbourn, Maghull, Merseyside L31 1HW. Tel: 0151-473 0303. *Executive Nurse Director,* C. Dale
BROADMOOR HOSPITAL, Crowthorne, Berks RG45 7EG. Tel: 01344-773111. *Chief Executive,* vacant
CENTRE FOR APPLIED MICROBIOLOGY AND RESEARCH, Porton Down, Salisbury, Wilts SP4 0JG. Tel: 01980-612100. *Director,* Dr R. H. Gilmour
HEALTH EDUCATION AUTHORITY, Hamilton House, Mabledon Place, London WC1H 9TX. Tel: 0171-383 3833. *Chairman,* A. Close, CBE; *Chief Executive,* S. Fortescue
NATIONAL BLOOD AUTHORITY, Oak House, Reeds Crescent, Watford, Herts WD1 1QH. Tel: 01923-486800. *Chairman,* Sir Colin Walker, OBE; *Chief Executive,* J. Adey
NHS LITIGATION AUTHORITY, 5 Pemberton Row, London EC4A 3BA. Tel: 0171-936 4400. *Chairman,* Sir Bruce Martin, QC; *Chief Executive,* S. Walker
NHS SUPPLIES AUTHORITY, Apex Plaza, Forbury Road, Reading, Berks RG1 1AX. Tel: 01734-595085. *Chairman,* N. Ward; *Chief Executive,* T. Hunt, CBE
RAMPTON HOSPITAL, Retford, Notts DN22 0PD. Tel: 01777-248321. *Chief Executive,* Mrs S. Foley

---

HEALTH AND SAFETY COMMISSION
Rose Court, 2 Southwark Bridge, London SE1 9HS
Tel 0171-717 6000

The Health and Safety Commission was created under the Health and Safety at Work etc. Act 1974, with duties to reform health and safety law, to propose new regulations, and generally to promote the protection of people at work and of the public from hazards arising from industrial and commercial activity, including major industrial accidents and the transportation of hazardous materials. The Commission can appoint agents, and it works in conjunction with local authorities who enforce the Act in such premises as offices and warehouses. The members of the Commission are appointed by the Secretary of State for the Environment, Transport and the Regions. The Commission is made up of representatives of employers, trades unions and local authorities, and has a full-time chairman.

Chairman, F. J. Davies, CBE
Members, R. Symons, CBE; A. Grant; Ms A. Scully, OBE; Ms C. Atwell; Ms A. Gibson; Dr M. McKiernan; Ms J. Edmond-Smith; D. Coulston; R. Turney
Secretary, T. A. Gates

HEALTH AND SAFETY EXECUTIVE
Rose Court, 2 Southwark Bridge, London SE1 9HS
Tel 0171-717 6000

The Health and Safety Executive is the Health and Safety Commission's major instrument. Through its inspectorates it enforces health and safety law in the majority of industrial premises. The Executive advises the Commission in its major task of laying down safety standards through regulations and practical guidance for many industrial processes. The Executive is also the licensing authority for nuclear installations and the reporting officer on the severity of nuclear incidents in Britain. The Executive acts independently of the Government and is guided only by the Commission as to general health and safety policy.
Director-General (G2), Miss J. H. Bacon, CB (*at G1A*)
Deputy Director-General (G2), D. C. T. Eves, CB (*HM Chief Inspector of Factories*)
Director, Field Operations Division (G3), Dr A. Ellis
Director, Nuclear Safety (G3), Dr S. A. Harbison
Director, Science and Technology (G3), Dr J. McQuaid, CB
Director, Safety Policy (G3), M. E. Addison
Director, Health Division (G3), Dr P. J. Graham
Director, Resources and Planning (G3), R. Hillier
Director, Offshore Safety (G3), R. S. Allison, CB

HIGHLANDS AND ISLANDS ENTERPRISE
Bridge House, 20 Bridge Street, Inverness IV1 1QR
Tel 01463-234171

Highlands and Islands Enterprise (HIE) was set up under the Enterprise and New Towns (Scotland) Act 1991. Its role is to design, direct and deliver enterprise development, training, environmental and social projects and services. HIE is made up of a strategic core body and ten Local Enterprise Companies (LECs) to which many of its individual functions are delegated.
Chairman, A. F. Morrison, CBE
Chief Executive, I. A. Robertson, CBE

HISTORIC BUILDINGS AND MONUMENTS COMMISSION FOR ENGLAND (ENGLISH HERITAGE)
23 Savile Row, London W1X 1AB
Tel 0171-973 3000

Under the National Heritage Act 1983, the duties of the Commission are to secure the preservation of ancient monuments and historic buildings; to promote the preservation and enhancement of conservation areas; and to promote the public's enjoyment of, and advance their knowledge of, ancient monuments and historic buildings and their preservation. The Commission has advisory committees on historic buildings and areas, ancient monuments, cathedrals and churches, parks and gardens, museums and collections, and London. It is funded by the Department for Culture, Media and Sport.
Chairman, Sir Jocelyn Stevens, CVO
Commissioners, HRH The Duke of Gloucester, KG, GCVO;
The Lord Cavendish of Furness; Ms B. Cherry; Mrs C. Lycett-Green; J. Seymour; G. Wilson; A. Fane;
Lady Gass; Prof. E. Fernie, CBE; R. MacCormac, CBE; Ms K. McLeod; Prof. R. Morris, FSA
Chief Executive, Ms P. Alexander

HISTORIC BUILDINGS COUNCIL FOR WALES
Crown Building, Cathays Park, Cardiff CF1 3NQ
Tel 01222-500200

The Council's function is to advise the Secretary of State for Wales on the built heritage through Cadw: Welsh Historic Monuments (*see* page 353), which is an executive agency within the Welsh Office.
Chairman, T. Lloyd, FSA
Members, W. Lindsay Evans; R. Haslam; Dr P. Morgan; Mrs S. Furse; Dr S. Unwin; Dr E. Wiliam
Secretary, R. W. Hughes

HISTORIC BUILDINGS COUNCIL FOR SCOTLAND
Longmore House, Salisbury Place, Edinburgh EH9 1SH
Tel 0131-668 8787

The Historic Buildings Council for Scotland is the advisory body to the Secretary of State for Scotland on matters related to buildings of special architectural or historical interest and in particular to proposals for awards by him of grants for the repair of buildings of outstanding architectural or historical interest or lying within outstanding conservation areas.
Chairman, Sir Raymond Johnstone, CBE
Members, R. Cairns; Sir Ilay Campbell, Bt.; Mrs A. Dundas-Bekker; M. Ellington; Dr J. Frew; Lady Jane Grosvenor; J. Hunter Blair; I. Hutchison, OBE; K. Martin; Revd C. Robertson; Mrs F. Walker
Secretary, Ms S. Adams

ROYAL COMMISSION ON THE HISTORICAL MONUMENTS OF ENGLAND
National Monuments Record Centre, Kemble Drive, Swindon SN2 2GZ
Tel 01793-414700
London Search Room: 55 Blandford Street, London W1H 3AF.
Tel: 0171-208 8200

The Royal Commission on the Historical Monuments of England was established in 1908. It is the national body of architectural and archaeological survey and record and manages England's public archive of heritage information, the National Monuments Record. It is funded by the Department for Culture, Media and Sport.
Chairman, The Lord Faringdon
Commissioners, Prof. R. Bradley, FSA; D. J. Keene, PH.D.; R. D. H. Gem, PH.D., FSA; T. R. M. Longman; R. A. Yorke; Miss A. Riches, FSA; Dr M. Airs, FSA; Prof. M. Fulford, PH.D., FSA; Dr M. Palmer, FSA; Miss A. Arrowsmith; P. Addyman, FSA; Prof. E. Fernie, CBE, FSA, FRSE; Ms H. Maclagan; Dr W. Sudbury
Secretary, T. G. Hassall, FSA

ROYAL COMMISSION ON THE ANCIENT AND HISTORICAL MONUMENTS OF WALES
Crown Building, Plas Crug, Aberystwyth SY23 INJ
Tel 01970-621233

The Royal Commission was established in 1908 and is currently empowered by a royal warrant of 1992 to survey, record, publish and maintain a database of ancient and historical and maritime sites and structures, and landscapes in Wales. The Commission is funded by the Welsh Office and is also responsible for the National Monuments Record of Wales, which is open daily for public reference, for the supply of archaeological information to the Ordnance Survey, for the co-ordination of archaeological aerial photography in Wales, and for sponsorship of the regional Sites and Monuments Records.
Chairman, Prof. J. B. Smith
Commissioners, Prof. R. A. Griffiths, Ph.D., D.Litt.;
D. Gruffyd Jones; R. M. Haslam, FSA; Prof.
G. B. D. Jones, D.phil., FSA; Mrs A. Nicol; Prof.
G. J. Wainwright, MBE, Ph.D., FSA; E. Wiliam, Ph.D., FSA
Secretary, P. R. White, FSA

ROYAL COMMISSION ON THE ANCIENT AND HISTORICAL MONUMENTS OF SCOTLAND
John Sinclair House, 16 Bernard Terrace, Edinburgh EH8 9NX
Tel 0131-662 1456

The Royal Commission was established in 1908 and is appointed to provide for the survey and recording of ancient and historical monuments connected with the culture, civilization and conditions of life of the people in Scotland from the earliest times. It is funded by the Scottish Office. The Commission compiles and maintains the National Monuments Record of Scotland as the national record of the archaeological and historical environment. The National Monuments Record is open for reference Monday–Thursday 9.30–4.30, Friday 9.30–4.
Chairman, Sir William Fraser, GCB, FRSE
Commissioners, Prof. J. M. Coles, Ph.D., FBA; Prof. Rosemary Cramp, CBE, FSA; Prof. T. C. Smout, CBE, FRSE, FBA; The Hon. Lord Cullen; Dr Deborah Howard, FSA; Prof. R. A. Paxton, FRSE; Dr Barbara Crawford, FSA, FSA Scot.; Miss A. Riches; J. Simpson, FSA Scot.
Secretary, R. J. Mercer, FSA, FRSE

ANCIENT MONUMENTS BOARD FOR WALES
Crown Building, Cathays Park, Cardiff CFI 3NQ
Tel 01222-500200

The Ancient Monuments Board for Wales advises the Secretary of State for Wales on his statutory functions in respect of ancient monuments.
Chairman, Prof. R. R. Davies, CBE, D.phil., FBA
Members, R. G. Keen; Mrs F. M. Lynch Llewellyn, FSA; Prof. W. H. Manning, Ph.D., FSA; Prof. J. B. Smith; Prof. W. E. Davies, Ph.D., FBA; M. J. Garner
Secretary, S. Morris

ANCIENT MONUMENTS BOARD FOR SCOTLAND
Longmore House, Salisbury Place, Edinburgh EH9 ISH
Tel 0131-668 8764

The Ancient Monuments Board for Scotland advises the Secretary of State for Scotland on the exercise of his functions, under the Ancient Monuments and Archaeological Areas Act 1979, of providing protection for monuments of national importance.
Chairman, Prof. M. Lynch, Ph.D., FRSE, FSA Scot.
Members, A. Wright, FRSA; Mrs E. V. W. Proudfoot, FSA, FSA Scot.; Mrs K. Dalyell, FSA Scot.; P. Clarke, FSA; Dr A. Ritchie, OBE, FSA, FSA Scot.; R. D. Kernohan, OBE; Dr J. Morgan, FSA Scot.; Prof. C. D. Morris, FRSE, FSA, FSA Scot.; R. J. Mercer, FRSE, FSA, FSA Scot.; W. D. H. Sellar, FSA Scot.; B. Mackie; Miss L. M. Thoms, FSA Scot.; J. Higgitt, FSA; Dr C. Swanson, FSA Scot.
Secretary, R. A. J. Dalziel
Assessor, D. J. Breeze, Ph.D., FRSE, FSA Scot.

HOME-GROWN CEREALS AUTHORITY
Caledonia House, 223 Pentonville Road, London NI 9NG
Tel 0171-263 3391 (*until Nov. 1997*)

Set up under the Cereals Marketing Act 1965, the Authority consists of seven members representing UK cereal growers, seven representing dealers in, or processors of, grain and two independent members. The Authority's functions are to improve the production and marketing of UK-grown cereals and oilseeds through a research and development programme, to provide a market information service, to promote UK cereals in export markets and to support work at Food from Britain. The Authority also undertakes agency work for the Intervention Board in connection with the application in the UK of the Common Agricultural Policy for cereals.
Chairman, G. B. Nelson, CBE
Chief Executive, A. J. Williams

HOME OFFICE
50 Queen Anne's Gate, London SWIH 9AT
Tel 0171-273 4000

The Home Office deals with those internal affairs in England and Wales which have not been assigned to other government departments. The Home Secretary is particularly concerned with the administration of justice; criminal law; the treatment of offenders, including probation and the prison service; the police; immigration and nationality; passport policy matters; community relations; certain public safety matters; and fire and civil emergencies services. The Home Secretary personally is the link between The Queen and the public, and exercises certain powers on her behalf, including that of the Royal Pardon.

Other subjects dealt with include electoral arrangements; ceremonial and formal business connected with honours; scrutiny of local authority byelaws; granting of licences for scientific procedures involving animals; cremations, burials and exhumations; firearms; dangerous drugs and poisons; general policy on laws relating to shops, liquor licensing, gaming and marriage; theatre and cinema licensing; and race relations policy.

The Home Secretary is also the link between the UK government and the governments of the Channel Islands and the Isle of Man.

Secretary of State for the Home Department, The Rt. Hon. Jack Straw, MP
  Principal Private Secretary (SCS), K. D. Sutton
  Private Secretaries, Mrs M. K. Bramwell; C. Harnett; D. Redhouse
  Special Advisers, N. Warner; E. Owen
  Parliamentary Private Secretary, P. Tipping, MP
Ministers of State, Alun Michael, MP (*Criminal Policy*); Joyce Quin, MP (*Prisons, Probation and Europe*)
  Private Secretaries, Miss S. Gooch; A. E. Jones
Parliamentary Under-Secretaries of State, George Howarth, MP (*Prisons, Drugs and Elections*); Michael O'Brien, MP (*Immigration and Nationality*); The Lord Williams of Mostyn, QC (*Constitution*)
  Private Secretaries, Miss C. McCombie; G. Park; J. Sedgwick
Parliamentary Clerk, Mrs R. Robinson
Permanent Under-Secretary of State (G1), Sir Richard Wilson, KCB (*until January 1998*)
  Private Secretary, Ms J. L. Hutcheon
Chief Medical Officer (at Department of Health), Dr Sir Kenneth Calman, KCB

CENTRAL SECRETARIAT
Head of Secretariat (SCS), J. Dilling

COMMUNICATION DIRECTORATE
Director, Communication, and Head of the Government Information Service (SCS), M. Granatt
Deputy Head of Communication (Head of News) (SCS), B. Butler
Head of Publicity and Corporate Services (SCS), Miss A. Nash
Assistant Director, News (G7), B. McBride
Assistant Director and Head of Information and Library Services (G7), P. Griffiths

CONSTITUTIONAL AND COMMUNITY POLICY DIRECTORATE
Director (SCS), Miss C. Sinclair
Heads of Units (SCS), Mrs G. Catto; R. Evans; M. Gillespie; S. B. Hickson

ANIMALS (SCIENTIFIC PROCEDURES) INSPECTORATE
Chief Inspector (SCS), Dr J. Richmond
Superintendent Inspector (SCS), Dr J. Anderson
Inspectors (G6), Dr R. Curtis; Dr V. Navaratnam; Dr C. Wilkins

GAMING BOARD FOR GREAT BRITAIN
— see page 305

CORPORATE RESOURCES DIRECTORATE
Grenadier House, 99–105 Horseferry House, London SWIP 2DD
Tel 0171-273 4000
Clive House, Petty France, London SWIH 9HD
Tel 0171-273 4000

Director (SCS), Miss P. Drew
Heads of Units (SCS), Dr M. Allnutt; Dr S. Atkins; A. R. Edwards; Ms E. Sparrow; S. Wharton
Senior Principals (G6), T. Cobley; R. Creedon; J. G. Jones; R. Jones; T. Lewis; D. Meakin; Ms E. Moody

CRIMINAL POLICY DIRECTORATE
Director (SCS), J. Halliday, CB
Deputy Director (SCS), J. Lyon

Heads of Units (SCS), M. Boyle; R. Childs; I. Chisholm; Mrs F. Clarkson; E. Grant; A. Harding; P. Honour; Ms H. Jackson; N. Varney
Senior Principals (G6), Ms A. Fletcher; H. Marriage; A. Macfarlane

CENTRAL DRUGS PREVENTION UNIT
Horseferry House, Dean Ryle Street, London SWIP 2AW
Tel 0171-273 4000
Head of Unit (G6), Ms L. Rogerson

HOME OFFICE CRIME PREVENTION COLLEGE
The Hawkhills, Easingwold, York YO6 3EG
Tel 01347-825060
Director, J. Acton

HM INSPECTORATE OF PROBATION
Chief Inspector (SCS), G. W. Smith, CBE
Assistant Chief Inspector (G6), G. Childs

CRIMINAL INJURIES COMPENSATION AUTHORITY AND BOARD
— see page 293

FIRE AND EMERGENCY PLANNING DIRECTORATE
Horseferry House, Dean Ryle Street, London SWIP 2AW
Tel 0171-273 4000
50 Queen Anne's Gate, London SWIH 9AT
Tel 0171-273 4000

Director (SCS), Mrs S. Street
Heads of Units (SCS), E. Guy; Mrs V. Harris; Miss S. Paul; Dr D. Peace
Civil Emergencies Adviser, D. Bawtree, CB

HM FIRE SERVICE INSPECTORATE
HM Chief Inspector, Sir Bryan Collins, OBE
HM Territorial Inspectors, P. Morphew, QFSM; N. Musselwhite, CBE; G. P. Reid, QFSM; A. Rule, QFSM
Lay Inspector, vacant
HM Inspectors, W. Ambalino; D. Berry; G. P. Bowles; S. D. Christian; M. T. Franklin; D. Kent; E. G. Pearn, QFSM; K. Phillips; R. M. Simpson, OBE; A. C. Wells, QFSM; D. Wright
Principal (G7), Miss G. Kirton

EMERGENCY PLANNING COLLEGE
The Hawkhills, Easingwold, Yorks YO6 3EG
Tel 01347-821406
Senior Principal (G6), A. R. Blackley
College Secretary (acting) (G7), Miss C. Bacon

IMMIGRATION AND NATIONALITY DIRECTORATE, AND EU AND INTERNATIONAL UNIT
Lunar House, 40 Wellesley Road, Croydon, Surrey CR9 2BY
Tel 0181-686 0333
Apollo House, 36 Wellesley Road, Croydon, Surrey CR9 3RR
Tel 0181-686 0333
50 Queen Anne's Gate, London SWIH 9AT
Tel 0171-273 4000
India Buildings, 3rd Floor, Water Street, Liverpool L2 0QN
Tel 0151-237 5200

Director-General (SCS), T. Walker
Deputy Directors-General (SCS), A. R. Rawsthorne (*Policy*); T. Flesher (*Operations*)
Heads of Directorates (SCS), J. Acton; Miss V. M. Dews; Mrs E. C. L. Pallett; J. Potts; A. Walmsley; R. M. Whalley; R. G. Yates
Senior Principals (G6), P. Dawson; B. Downie; G. Stadlen

IMMIGRATION SERVICE
Director (Ports) (SCS), T. Farrage
Deputy Director (G6), V. Hogg
Director (Enforcement) (SCS), D. Cooke
Deputy Director (G6), C. Harbin

EU AND INTERNATIONAL UNIT
Head of Unit (SCS), P. Edwards

LEGAL ADVISERS'S BRANCH
Legal Adviser (SCS), Miss J. Wheldon, CB
Deputy Legal Advisers (SCS), Mrs S. A. Evans; D. Seymour
Assistant Legal Advisers (SCS), R. J. Clayton; J. R. O'Meara;
   C. M. L. Osborne; S. A. Parker

ORGANIZED AND INTERNATIONAL
CRIME DIRECTORATE
Director (SCS), J. Warne
Heads of Units (SCS), J. Duke-Evans; P. Wrench
Senior Principal (G6), J. Nicholson

NATIONAL CRIMINAL INTELLIGENCE SERVICE
— *see* page 374

PLANNING AND FINANCE DIRECTORATE
50 Queen Anne's Gate, London SW1H 9AT
Tel 0171-273 4000
Horseferry House, Dean Ryle Street, London SW1P 2AW
Tel 0171-273 4000
Director (SCS), R. Fulton
Head of Unit (SCS), L. Haugh
Senior Principals (G6), P. Dare; P. Davies; I. Gaskell; R.
   McBurney

POLICE POLICY DIRECTORATE
Director (SCS), S. Boys Smith
Heads of Units (SCS), N. Benger; Miss D. Loudon; C.
   Pelham
Senior Principals (G6), R. Ginman; Dr G. Laycock

NATIONAL DIRECTORATE OF POLICE TRAINING
National Director of Police Training, P. Hermitage, QPM

Central Administration Unit
Senior Principal (G6), P. Curwen

POLICE STAFF COLLEGE
Bramshill House, Bramshill, Hook, Hants RG27 0JW
Tel 0125-126 2931
Head of Higher Training, I. McDonald

POLICE INFORMATION TECHNOLOGY ORGANIZATION
Horseferry House, Dean Ryle Street, London SW1P 2AW
Tel 0171-273 4000
Chief Executive (SCS), Miss J. MacNaughton
Senior Managers (SCS), B. Buck; M. Goulding
Senior Principals (G6), T. Hamer; D. Rowe; Dr
   G. Turnbull

HENDON DATA CENTRE
Aerodrome Road, Colindale, London NW9 5LN
Tel 0181-200 2424
Head of Unit (G6), J. Ladley

POLICE SCIENTIFIC DEVELOPMENT BRANCH
Woodcock Hill, Sandridge, St Albans, Herts AL4 9HQ
Tel 01727-865051
Director (SCS), B. R. Coleman, OBE
Research Director (G6), Dr P. Young

Langhurst House, Langhurstwood Road, Nr Horsham,
W. Sussex RH12 4WX
Tel 01403-255451
Head of Unit Langhurst (G6), Dr G. Thomas

HM INSPECTORATE OF CONSTABULARY
HM Chief Inspector of Constabulary (SCS), D. J. O'Dowd,
   CBE, QPM
HM Inspectors (SCS), D. Crompton, CBE, QPM; K. Povey,
   QPM; C. Smith, CBE, CVO, QPM; P. J. Winship, QPM; J. A.
   Stevens, QPM
Lay Inspector, P. T. G. Hobbs
Senior Principal (G6), L. Davidoff

METROPOLITAN POLICE COMMITTEE AND
SECRETARIAT
Clive House, Petty France, London SW1H 9HD
Tel 0171-273 4000
Head of Secretariat (SCS), R. Halward

RESEARCH AND STATISTICS
DIRECTORATE
Director (SCS), C. Nuttall
Heads of Units (SCS), C. Lewis; D. Moxon; A. Norbury; P.
   Ward
Senior Principals (G6), G. Barclay; Mrs P. Dowdeswell; Dr
   S. Field; P. Goldblatt; P. Jordan; Mrs C. Lehman; Mrs P.
   Mayhew; R. Taylor; Ms J. Vennard; Mrs M. Wilkinson

PRISON SERVICES MONITORING UNIT
Head of Unit (SCS), R. Weatherill

HM INSPECTORATE OF PRISONS
HM Chief Inspector, Gen. Sir David Ramsbotham, GCB, CBE
HM Deputy Chief Inspector, C. Allen
HM Inspectors (Governor 1), R. Jacques; T. Wood

PRISONS OMBUDSMAN
— *see* page 334

PAROLE BOARD FOR ENGLAND AND
WALES
— *see* page 332

THE SECURITY SERVICE (MI5)
Thames House, PO Box 3255, London SW1P 1AE
Tel 0171-273 3000

The Security Service was placed on a statutory footing by
the Security Service Act 1989 and is headed by a director-
general who is directly accountable to the Home Secretary.
The function of the Service is the protection of national
security, in particular against threats from espionage,
terrorism and sabotage, from the activities of agents of
foreign powers, and from actions intended to overthrow or
undermine parliamentary democracy by political, industrial or violent means. It is also the Service's function to
safeguard the economic well-being of the UK against
threats posed by the actions or intentions of persons
outside the British Islands. Under the Security Service Act
1996 the Service's role was extended to support the police
and customs in the prevention and detection of serious
crime. Under the Intelligence Services Act 1994, the
Intelligence and Security Committee of Parliamentarians
was established to oversee the work of all three intelligence
services. The Security Service Tribunal and Commissioner (*see* page 343) investigate complaints about the
Service from the public.
Director-General, S. Lander

HM PRISON SERVICE
— *see* pages 379–82

FIRE SERVICE COLLEGE
Moreton-in-Marsh, Glos GL56 0RH
Tel 01608-650831

An executive agency of the Home Office.
Chief Executive, N. K. Finlayson
Commandant, T. Glossop, QFSM
Dean, Dr R. Willis-Lee
College Secretary, J. K. Burne

FORENSIC SCIENCE SERVICE HEADQUARTERS
— *see* page 375

UK PASSPORT AGENCY
Clive House, Petty France, London SW1H 9HD
Tel 0171-799 2728

An executive agency of the Home Office.
Chief Executive (SCS), D. Gatenby
Deputy Chief Executive and Director of Operations (G6),
T. Lonsdale
Director of Resources (G6), K. J. Sheehan
Director of Systems (G6), R. G. Le Marechal

HORSERACE TOTALISATOR BOARD
74 Upper Richmond Road, London SW15 2SU
Tel 0181-874 6411

The Horserace Totalisator Board was established by the Betting, Gaming and Lotteries Act 1963, as successor to the Racecourse Betting Control Board. Its function is to operate totalisators on approved racecourses in Great Britain, and it also provides on- and off-course cash and credit offices. Under the Horserace Totalisator and Betting Levy Board Act 1972, it is further empowered to offer bets at starting price (or other bets at fixed odds) on any sporting event. The chairman and members of the Board are appointed by the Home Secretary.
Chairman (£99,861), P. Jones
Chief Executive, W. J. Heaton

HOUSING CORPORATION
149 Tottenham Court Road, London W1P 0BN
Tel 0171-393 2000

Established by Parliament in 1964, the Housing Corporation regulates, funds and promotes the proper performance of registered social landlords, which are non-profit making bodies run by voluntary committees. There are over 2,200 social landlords registered with the Corporation, most of which are housing associations, and they are the major providers of new subsidized homes for those in housing need in England. Registered social landlords now provide homes for more than 1.5 million people. Under the Housing Act 1996 the Corporation's regulatory role has widened to embrace new types of landlords, in particular local housing companies. The Corporation is funded by the Department of the Environment, Transport and the Regions.
Chairman, P. Cooke, CBE
Chief Executive, A. Mayer

HUMAN FERTILIZATION AND EMBRYOLOGY AUTHORITY
Paxton House, 30 Artillery Lane, London E1 7LS
Tel 0171-377 5077

The Authority was established under the Human Fertilization and Embryology Act 1990. Its function is to license persons carrying out any of the following activities: the creation or use of embryos outside the body in the provision of infertility treatment services; the use of donated gametes in infertility treatment; the storage of gametes or embryos; and research on human embryos. The Authority also keeps under review information about embryos and, when requested to do so, gives advice to the Secretary of State for Health.
Chairman, Mrs R. Deech
Deputy Chairman, Lady (Diana) Brittan
Members, Dr G. Bahadur; Dr R. Chambers; Mrs J. Denton; Ms E. Forgan; Prof. C. Gosden; D. Greggains; The Most Revd R. Holloway; Prof. M. Johnson; R. Jones; Prof. S. Lewis; Dr B. Lieberman; Mrs A. Mays; Dr A. McLaren; Prof. A. Nichol; Dr J. Stringer; Prof. A. Templeton; Prof. Revd A. Thiselton; Julia, Lady Tugendhat; J. Williams
Chief Executive, Mrs S. McCarthy

INDEPENDENT COMMISSION FOR POLICE COMPLAINTS FOR NORTHERN IRELAND
Chamber of Commerce House, 22 Great Victoria Street, Belfast BT2 7LP
Tel 01232-244821

The Independent Commission for Police Complaints was established under the Police (Northern Ireland) Order 1987. It has powers to supervise the investigation of certain categories of serious complaints, can direct that disciplinary charges be brought, and has oversight of the informal resolution procedure for less serious complaints.
Chairman, P. A. Donnelly
Chief Executive, B. McClelland

INDEPENDENT REVIEW SERVICE FOR THE SOCIAL FUND
4th Floor, Centre City Podium, 5 Hill Street, Birmingham B5 4UB
Tel 0121-606 2100

The Social Fund Commissioner is appointed by the Secretary of State for Social Security. The Commissioner appoints Social Fund Inspectors, who provide an independent review of decisions made by Social Fund Officers in the Benefits Agency of the Department of Social Security.
Social Fund Commissioner, J. Scampion

INDEPENDENT TELEVISION COMMISSION
33 Foley Street, London W1P 7LB
Tel 0171-255 3000

The Independent Television Commission replaced the Independent Broadcasting Authority in 1991. The Commission is responsible for licensing and regulating all commercially funded television services broadcast from

the UK. Members are appointed by the Secretary of State for Culture, Media and Sport.
Chairman (£65,580), Sir Robin Biggam
Deputy Chairman, Earl of Dalkeith
Members (part-time) (£12,630), R. Goddard; Mrs E. Wynne Jones; Dr J. Beynon, FENG.; Ms J. Goffe; Dr M. Moloney; J. Ranelagh; Dr M. Shea, CVO; Sir Michael Checkland
Chief Executive, P. Rogers
Secretary, M. Redley

INDUSTRIAL INJURIES ADVISORY COUNCIL
6th Floor, The Adelphi, 1–11 John Adam Street, London WC2N 6HT
Tel 0171-962 8066

The Industrial Injuries Advisory Council is a statutory body under the Social Security Administration Act 1992 which considers and advises the Secretary of State for Social Security on regulations and other questions relating to industrial injuries benefits or their administration.
Chairman, Prof. A. J. Newman Taylor, OBE, FRCP
Secretary, R. Wakely

BOARD OF INLAND REVENUE
Somerset House, Strand, London WC2R 1LB
Tel 0171-438 6622

The Board of Inland Revenue was constituted under the Inland Revenue Board Act 1849, by the consolidation of the Board of Excise and the Board of Stamps and Taxes. In 1909 the administration of excise duties was transferred to the Board of Customs. The Board of Inland Revenue administers and collects direct taxes – income tax, corporation tax, capital gains tax, inheritance tax, stamp duty, and petroleum revenue tax – and advises the Chancellor of the Exchequer on policy questions involving them.

The Department is organized into a series of management units. The day-to-day operations in assessing and collecting tax and in providing internal support services are carried out by Executive Offices. The Department's Valuation Office is an executive agency responsible for valuing property for tax purposes. In 1996–7 the Inland Revenue collected £103,898 million (provisional) in tax.

THE BOARD
Chairman (G1), N. Montagu, CB
  Private Secretary, Miss S. Woollard
Deputy Chairmen (G2), S. C. T. Matheson, CB; C. W. Corlett, CB
Director-General (G2), G. H. Bush

DIVISIONS
Director, Human Resources Division (G3), J. Gant
Director, Business and Management Services Division (G3), J. Yard
Head, Departmental Planning Division, Miss M. Hay
Director, Self-Assessment Programme, D. A. Smith
Principal Finance Officer (G3), R. R. Martin
Director, Business Operations Division (G3), M. A. Johns
Director, Statistics and Economics Division (G3), R. G. Ward
Director, Company Tax Division, Financial Institutions Division and Business Management Unit (G3), M. F. Cayley
Director, Customer Service Division (G3), T. Evans
Director, International Division (G3), I. Spence

Director, Business Profits Division and Compliance Division (G3), E. J. Gribbon
Director, Personal Tax Division (G3), E. McGivern, CB
Director, Capital and Valuation Division, and Savings and Investment Division (G3), B. A. Mace

EXECUTIVE OFFICES

ACCOUNTS OFFICE (CUMBERNAULD), St Mungo's Road, Cumbernauld, Glasgow G70 5TR. *Controller*, A. Geddes, OBE
ACCOUNTS OFFICE (SHIPLEY), Shipley, Bradford, W. Yorks BD98 8AA. *Controller*, R. J. Warner
CAPITAL TAXES OFFICE, Ferrers House, PO Box 38, Castle Meadow Road, Nottingham NG2 1BB. *Controller*, B. D. Kent
CAPITAL TAXES OFFICE (SCOTLAND), Mulberry House, 16 Picardy Place, Edinburgh EH1 3NB. *Registrar*, Mrs J. Templeton
COMMUNICATIONS UNITS, North-West Wing, Bush House, London WC2B 4PP. *Head of External Communications Unit*, Mrs T. A. Middleton; *Head of Internal Communications Unit*, Mrs S. M. Walton
ENFORCEMENT OFFICE, Durrington Bridge House, Barrington Road, Worthing, W. Sussex BN12 4SE. *Controller*, Mrs S. F. Walsh
FINANCIAL ACCOUNTING OFFICE, South Block, Barrington Road, Worthing, W. Sussex BN12 4XH. *Controller*, J. D. Easey
FINANCIAL INTERMEDIARIES AND CLAIMS OFFICE, St John's House, Merton Road, Bootle L26 9BB; Fitz Roy House, PO Box 46, Castle Meadow, Nottingham NG2 1BD. *Controller*, S. W. Jones
INTERNAL AUDIT OFFICE, North-West Wing, Bush House, London WC2B 4PP. *Controller*, N. R. Buckley
OIL TAXATION OFFICE, Melbourne House, Aldwych, London WC2B 4LL. *Controller*, R. C. Mountain
PENSION SCHEME OFFICE, Yorke House, PO Box 62, Castle Meadow Road, Nottingham NG2 1BG. *Controller*, S. J. McManus
SOLICITOR'S OFFICE, East Wing, Somerset House, London WC2R 1LB. *Solicitor (G2)*, B. E. Cleave, CB
SOLICITOR'S OFFICE (SCOTLAND), Clarendon House, 114–116 George Street, Edinburgh EH2 4LH. *Solicitor*, I. K. Laing
SPECIAL COMPLIANCE OFFICE, Angel Court, 199 Borough High Street, London SE1 1HZ. *Controller*, F. J. Brannigan
STAMP OFFICE, South-West Wing, Bush House, Strand, London WC2B 4QN. *Controller*, K. S. Hodgson, OBE
TRAINING OFFICE, Lawress Hall, Riseholme Park, Lincoln LN2 2BJ. *Controller*, T. Kuczys

REGIONAL EXECUTIVE OFFICES

INLAND REVENUE EAST, Churchgate, New Road, Peterborough PE1 1TD. *Controller*, M. J. Hodgson
INLAND REVENUE LARGE GROUPS OFFICE, New Court, Carey Street, London WC2A 2JE. *Controller*, Mrs M. E. Williams
INLAND REVENUE LONDON, New Court, Carey Street, London WC2A 2JE. *Controller*, J. F. Carling
INLAND REVENUE NORTH, 100 Russell Street, Middlesbrough, Cleveland TS1 2RZ. *Controller*, R. I. Ford
INLAND REVENUE NORTH-WEST, The Triad, Stanley Road, Bootle, Merseyside L75 2DD. *Controller*, G. W. Lunn
INLAND REVENUE SOUTH-EAST, Dukes Court, Dukes Street, Woking GU21 5XR. *Controller*, D. L. S. Bean

INLAND REVENUE SOUTH-WEST, 3rd Floor, Longbrook House, New North Road, Exeter EX4 4UA. *Controller,* R. S. Hurcombe

INLAND REVENUE SOUTH YORKSHIRE, Concept House, 5 Young Street, Sheffield S1 4LF. *Controller,* A. C. Sleeman

INLAND REVENUE WALES AND MIDLANDS, 1st Floor, Phase II Building, Ty Glas Avenue, Llanishen, Cardiff CF4 5TS; 550 Streetsbrook Road, Solihull, West Midlands B91 1QU. *Controller,* M. W. Kirk

INLAND REVENUE SCOTLAND, Clarendon House, 114–116 George Street, Edinburgh EH2 4LH. *Controller,* I. S. Gerrie

INLAND REVENUE NORTHERN IRELAND, Dorchester House, 52–58 Great Victoria Street, Belfast BT2 7QE. *Controller,* R. S. T. Ewing

VALUATION OFFICE AGENCY

New Court, 48 Carey Street, London WC2A 2JE
Tel 0171-324 1183/1057
Meldrum House, 15 Drumsheugh Gardens, Edinburgh EH3 7UN
Tel 0131-225 4938
Chief Executive, Ms V. Lowe
Chief Valuer, Scotland, A. MacLaren, CBE

ADJUDICATOR'S OFFICE

— *see* page 278

INTELLIGENCE SERVICES TRIBUNAL

PO Box 4823, London SW1A 9XD
Tel 0171-273 4383

The Intelligence Services Act 1994 established a tribunal of three senior members of the legal profession, independent of the Government and appointed by The Queen, to investigate complaints from any person about anything which they believe the Secret Intelligence Service or the Government Communications Headquarters has done to them or to their property.
President, The Rt. Hon. Lord Justice Simon Brown
Vice-President, Sheriff J. McInnes, QC
Member, Sir Richard Gaskell

INTERCEPTION COMMISSIONER

c/o PO Box 12376, London SW1P 1XU

The Commissioner is appointed by the Prime Minister. He keeps under review the issue by the Home Secretary, the Foreign Secretary, and the Secretaries of State for Scotland and for Northern Ireland, of warrants under the Interception of Communications Act 1985 and safeguards made in respect of intercepted material obtained through the use of such warrants. He is also required to give all such assistance as the Interception of Communications Tribunal may require to enable it to carry out its functions, and to submit an annual report to the Prime Minister with respect to the carrying out of his functions.
Commissioner, The Lord Nolan, PC

INTERCEPTION OF COMMUNICATIONS TRIBUNAL

PO Box 12376, London SW1P 1XU
Tel 0171-273 4096

Under the Interception of Communications Act 1985, the Tribunal is required to investigate complaints from any person who believes that communications sent to or by them have been intercepted in the course of their transmission by post or by means of a public telecommunications system. The Tribunal comprises senior members of the legal profession, who are appointed by The Queen.
President, The Hon. Mr Justice Macpherson of Cluny
Vice-President, Sir David Calcutt, QC
Members, P. Scott, QC; R. Seabrook, QC; W. Carmichael

DEPARTMENT FOR INTERNATIONAL DEVELOPMENT

94 Victoria Street, London SW1E 5JL
Tel 0171-917 7000
Abercrombie House, Eaglesham Road, East Kilbride, Glasgow G75 8EA
Tel 01355-844000

The Department for International Development (DFID) was established in May 1997 from the former Overseas Development Administration of the Foreign and Commonwealth Office. It deals with British development assistance to overseas countries. This includes both capital aid on concessional terms and technical assistance (mainly in the form of specialist staff abroad and training facilities in the UK), whether provided directly to developing countries or through the various multilateral aid organizations, including the United Nations and its specialized agencies.
Secretary of State for International Development, The Rt. Hon. Clare Short, MP
Private Secretary (G7), R. Calvert
Special Advisers, D. Harris; Ms J. Crowe
Parliamentary Private Secretary, D. Turner, MP
Parliamentary Under-Secretary, George Foulkes, MP
Permanent Secretary (SCS), J. M. M. Vereker
Private Secretary, B. Mellor

PROGRAMMES

Director-General (SCS), B. R. Ireton
Head of Emergency Aid Department (SCS), P. A. Bearpark

AFRICA
Director (SCS), P. D. M. Freeman
Heads of Departments (SCS), Mrs B. M. Kelly, CBE (*Africa, Greater Horn and Co-ordination*); S. Ray (*West and North Africa*); D. Fish (*British Development Division in East Africa*); J. R. Drummond (*British Development Division in Central Africa*); J. H. S. Chard (*British Development Division in South Africa*)

ASIA
Director (SCS), S. Unsworth
Heads of Departments (SCS), C. Myhill (*East Asia and Pacific*); R. Graham-Harrison (*British Development Co-operation Office*); Ms M. H. Vowles (*Western Asia*); A. K. C. Wood (*South-East Asia Development Division*); K. L. Sparkhall (*Aid Management Office, Bangladesh, Dhaka*)

EASTERN EUROPE AND WESTERN HEMISPHERE
Director (SCS), J. Kerby

Heads of Departments (SCS), M. C. McCulloch (*Joint Assistance Department (Eastern)*); J. S. Laing (*Joint Assistance Department (Central Europe)*); B. P. Thomson (*British Development Division in the Caribbean*); (*G6*), D. R. Curran (*Latin America, Caribbean and Atlantic*); (*G7*), J. D. Moye (*EBRD Unit*)

ECONOMICS AND GOVERNANCE
Director, and Chief Economic Adviser (SCS), J. Goudie
Chief Statistician (SCS), A. B. Williams
Head of Asia, Latin America and Oceans Economics (G6), P. J. Ackroyd
Head of African Economics Department (SCS), M. G. Foster
Head of International Economics Department (SCS), P. D. Grant
Senior Small Enterprise Development Adviser (G6), D. L. Wright
Senior Economic Advisers (G6), Ms R. L. Turner; P. L. Owen; P. J. Dearden; P. J. Landymore; E. Hawthorn; F. C. Clift; J. L. Hoy
Head of Government Institutions Advisory Department (SCS), R. J. Wilson
Senior Government and Institutions Advisers (G6), Dr G. W. Glentworth; D. W. Baker; Mrs A. Newsum; S. Sharples; J. G. Clarke
Senior Police Adviser (G6), L. H. Grundy

HUMAN RESOURCE DEVELOPMENT
Director, and Chief Health and Population Adviser (SCS), Dr D. N. Nabarro
Senior Health and Population Advisers (G6), Dr P. J. Key; J. N. Lambert; T. Martineau; S. Tyson; R. N. Grose; Ms C. M. Sergeant
Chief Social Development Adviser (G6), Dr R. Eyben
Senior Social Development Advisers (G6), Ms P. M. Holden; Dr A. M. Coles
Chief Education Adviser (SCS), Ms M. A. Harrison
Senior Education Advisers (G6), Dr C. Treffgarne; M. E. Seath; M. D. Francis; R. T. Allsop; Dr D. B. Pennycuick; S. E. Packer; Dr K. M. Lillis; Dr G. R. H. Jones
Senior Technical Education Adviser (G6), C. Lewis

PRODUCTIVE CAPACITY AND ENVIRONMENT
Director, and Chief Natural Resources Adviser (SCS), A. J. Bennett
Head of Environment Policy Department (SCS), D. P. Turner
Head of Natural Resources Policy and Advisory Department, and Deputy Chief Natural Resources Adviser (SCS), J. M. Scott
Head of Natural Resources Research Department (SCS), Dr I. H. Haines
Senior Natural Resources Advisers (G6), Ms F. Proctor; R. C. Fox; M. J. Wilson; A. J. Tainsh; J. R. F. Hansell; Dr B. E. Grimwood; J. A. Harvey; A. Hall
Natural Resources Systems Programme Manager (G6), J. C. Barrett
Senior Environment and Research Adviser (G6), Ms L. C. Brown
Senior Fisheries Advisers (G6), R. W. Beales; Dr J. Tarbit
Senior Forestry Advisers (G6), J. M. Hudson; I. A. Napier
Senior Animal Health Advisers (G6), G. G. Freeland; Ms L. M. Bell
Chief Engineering Adviser (SCS), J. W. Hodges
Senior Engineering Advisers (G6), B. Dolton; C. I. Ellis; P. J. Davies; D. F. Gillett; P. W. D. H. Roberts; M. F. Sergeant; R. J. Cadwallader; C. J. Hunt
Senior Water Resources Adviser (G6), A. Wray
Senior Architectural and Physical Planning Adviser (G6), M. W. Parkes
Senior Electrical and Mechanical Adviser (G6), R. P. Jones
Senior Renewable Energy and Research Adviser (G6), A. Gilchrist
Industrial Training Adviser (G7), D. G. Marr

RESOURCES
Director-General (SCS), R. G. Manning
Heads of Departments (SCS), M. J. Dinham (*Personnel*); D. Sands-Smith (*Procurement, Appointments and NGO*); P. Aylett (*Information*); G. M. Stegmann (*Aid Policy and Resources*); A. D. Davis (*Information Systems*); R. A. Elias (*Internal Audit Unit*); C. P. Raleigh (*Evaluation*); (*G6*), R. Plumb (*Overseas Pensions*); K. D. Grimshaw (*Sponsored Organizations Unit*)
Assistant Establishment Officer (G6), J. A. Anning

INTERNATIONAL DEVELOPMENT AFFAIRS
Director (SCS), J. A. L. Faint
Heads of Departments (SCS), D. J. Batt (*European Union*); J. C. Machin (*United Nations and Commonwealth*); M. E. Cund (*International Financial Institutions*)

INTERVENTION BOARD
PO Box 69, Reading RG1 3YD
Tel 0118-958 3626

The Intervention Board was established as a government department in 1972 and became operational in 1973; it became an executive agency in 1990. The Board is responsible for the implementation of European Union regulations covering the market support arrangements of the Common Agricultural Policy. Members are appointed by and are responsible to the Minister of Agriculture, Fisheries and Food and the Secretaries of State for Scotland, Wales and Northern Ireland.
Chairman, A. Marshall
Chief Executive (G3), G. Trevelyan

HEADS OF DIVISIONS
External Trade Division (G5), J. P. Bradbury
Internal Market Division (G5), H. MacKinnon
Corporate Services Division (G5), Mrs A. Parker
Finance Division (G5), G. R. R. Jenkins
Legal Division (G5), J. F. McCleary
Chief Accountant (G6), R. Bryant
Procurement and Supply (G6), P. J. Offer
Information Systems (G7), T. G. Lamberstock
Internal Market Operations (G6), J. A. Sutton

LAND AUTHORITY FOR WALES
The Custom House, Customhouse Street, Cardiff CF1 5AP
Tel 01222-223444

The Authority, established under the Local Government Planning and Land Act 1980, is responsible for identifying and acquiring land suitable for development in Wales and making it available for development by others.
Chairman (part-time) (£34,305), Sir Geoffrey Inkin, OBE
Chief Executive, B. Ryan, FRICS

LAND REGISTRIES

HM LAND REGISTRY
Lincoln's Inn Fields, London WC2A 3PH
Tel 0171-917 8888

The registration of title to land was first introduced in England and Wales by the Land Registry Act 1862; HM Land Registry operates today under the Land Registration Acts 1925 to 1988. The object of registering title to land is to create and maintain a register of landowners whose title is guaranteed by the state and so to simplify the transfer, mortgage and other dealings with real property. Registration on sale is now compulsory throughout England and Wales. The register has been open to inspection by the public since 1990.

HM Land Registry is an executive agency administered under the Lord Chancellor by the Chief Land Registrar. The work is decentralized to a number of regional offices. The Chief Land Registrar is also responsible for the Land Charges Department and the Agricultural Credits Department.

HEADQUARTERS OFFICE
Chief Land Registrar and Chief Executive, Dr S. J. Hill
Solicitor to Land Registry, C. J. West
Director of Corporate Services, E. G. Beardsall
Senior Land Registrar, Mrs J. G. Totty
Director of Operations, G. N. French
Director of Information Technology, P. J. Smith
Director of Management Services, P. R. Laker
Land Registrar, M. L. Wood
Deputy Establishment Officer, J. Hodder
Controller of Operations Development, A. W. Howarth

COMPUTER SERVICES DIVISION
Burrington Way, Plymouth PL5 3LP
Tel 01752-635600
Head of Services Division, P. A. Maycock
Head of Development Division, R. T. Davis
Head of National Land Information Service (NLIS), R. J. Smith

LAND CHARGES AND AGRICULTURAL CREDITS DEPARTMENT
Burrington Way, Plymouth PL5 3LP
Tel 01752-635600
Superintendent of Land Charges, J. Hughes

DISTRICT LAND REGISTRIES
BIRKENHEAD – Old Market House, Hamilton Street, Birkenhead L41 5FL. Tel. 0151-473 1110. *District Land Registrar*, M. G. Garwood
COVENTRY – Leigh Court, Torrington Avenue, Coventry CV4 9XZ. Tel: 01203-860860. *District Land Registrar*, S. P. Kelway
CROYDON – Sunley House, Bedford Park, Croydon CR9 3LE. Tel: 0181-781 9100. *District Land Registrar*, D. M. J. Moss
DURHAM – Southfield House, Southfield Way, Durham DH1 5TR. Tel: 0191-301 3500. *District Land Registrar*, P. J. Timothy
GLOUCESTER – Twyver House, Bruton Way, Gloucester GL1 1DQ. Tel: 01452-511111. *District Land Registrar*, W. W. Budden
HARROW – Lyon House, Lyon Road, Harrow, Middx HA1 2EU. Tel: 0181-235 1181. *District Land Registrar*, J. V. Timothy
KINGSTON UPON HULL – Earle House, Portland Street, Hull HU2 8JN. Tel: 01482-223244. *District Land Registrar*, S. R. Coveney
LEICESTER – Thames Tower, 99 Burleys Way, Leicester LE1 3UB. Tel: 0116-265 4000. *District Land Registrar*, Mrs J. A. Goodfellow
LYTHAM – Birkenhead House, East Beach, Lytham, Lancs FY8 5AB. Tel: 01253-849849. *District Land Registrar*, J. G. Cooper
NOTTINGHAM – Chalfont Drive, Nottingham NG8 3RN. Tel: 0115-935 1166. *District Land Registrar (acting)*, P. A. Brown

PETERBOROUGH – Touthill Close, City Road, Peterborough PE1 1XN. Tel: 01733-288288. *District Land Registrar*, C. W. Martin
PLYMOUTH – Plumer House, Tailyour Road, Crownhill, Plymouth PL6 5HY. Tel: 01752-636000. *District Land Registrar*, A. J. Pain
PORTSMOUTH – St Andrews Court, St Michael's Road, Portsmouth PO1 2JH. Tel: 01705-768888. *District Land Registrar*, S. R. Sehrawat
STEVENAGE – Brickdale House, Swingate, Stevenage, Herts SG1 1XG. Tel: 01438-788888. *District Land Registrar*, C. Tate
SWANSEA – Tŷ Bryn Glas, High Street, Swansea SA1 1PW. Tel: 01792-458877. *District Land Registrar*, G. A. Hughes
TELFORD – Parkside Court, Hall Park Way, Telford TF3 4LR. Tel: 01952-290355. *District Land Registrar*, M. A. Roche
TUNBRIDGE WELLS – Curtis House, Hawkenbury, Tunbridge Wells, Kent TN2 5AQ. Tel: 01892-510015. *District Land Registrar*, G. R. Tooke
WEYMOUTH – Melcombe Court, 1 Cumberland Drive, Weymouth, Dorset DT4 9TT. Tel: 01305-363636. *District Land Registrar*, Mrs P. M. Reeson
YORK – James House, James Street, York YO1 3YZ. Tel: 01904-450000. *District Land Registrar*, Mrs R. F. Lovel

REGISTERS OF SCOTLAND (EXECUTIVE AGENCY)
Meadowbank House, 153 London Road, Edinburgh EH8 7AU
Tel 0131-659 6111

The Registers of Scotland is an executive agency of the Scottish Office. The Registers consist of: General Register of Sasines and Land Register of Scotland; Register of Deeds in the Books of Council and Session; Register of Protests; Register of Judgments; Register of Service of Heirs; Register of the Great Seal; Register of the Quarter Seal; Register of the Prince's Seal; Register of Crown Grants; Register of Sheriffs' Commissions; Register of the Cachet Seal; Register of Inhibitions and Adjudications; Register of Entails; Register of Hornings.

The General Register of Sasines and the Land Register of Scotland form the chief security in Scotland of the rights of land and other heritable (or real) property.

Chief Executive and Keeper of the Registers of Scotland, A. W. Ramage
Deputy Keeper, A. G. Rennie
Managing Director, F. Manson
Directors, Miss J. Kyle (*Human Resources*); Miss M. M. D. Archer (*Land Register, Central Division*); D. McCallum (*Land Register, Glasgow and West Division*); Miss V. Clough (*Sasines*); A. M. Gardiner (*Land Register, North-East Division*); J. Clark (*Finance*); Ms A. Rooney (*Business Management and Communications*); T. Wilson (*Commercial*); Mrs P. Stewart (*Land Register, South-West Division*); B. J. Corr (*IT*); I. A. Davis (*Legal Services*)

LAW COMMISSION
Conquest House, 37–38 John Street, London WC1N 2BQ
Tel 0171-453 1220

The Law Commission was set up in 1965, under the Law Commissions Act 1965, to make proposals to the Government for the examination of the law in England and Wales and for its revision where it is unsuited for modern requirements, obscure, or otherwise unsatisfactory. It recommends to the Lord Chancellor programmes for the examination of different branches of the law and suggests whether the examination should be carried out by the Commission itself or by some other body. The Commission is also responsible for the preparation of Consolidation and Statute Law (Repeals) Bills.

Chairman, The Hon. Mrs Justice Arden, DBE
Commissioners, C. Harpum; A. S. Burrows; Miss D. Faber; S. Silber, QC
Secretary, M. W. Sayers

SCOTTISH LAW COMMISSION
140 Causewayside, Edinburgh EH9 1PR
Tel 0131-668 2131

The Commission keeps the law in Scotland under review and makes proposals for its development and reform. It is responsible to the Scottish Courts Administration (*see* page 365).
Chairman (part-time), The Hon. Lord Gill
Commissioners (full-time), Dr E. M. Clive; N. R. Whitty; (*part-time*) Prof. K. G. C. Reid; P. S. Hodge, QC
Secretary, J. G. S. MacLean

LAW OFFICERS' DEPARTMENTS
Legal Secretariat to the Law Officers, Attorney-General's Chambers, 9 Buckingham Gate, London SW1E 6JP
Tel 0171-828 7155
Attorney-General's Chambers, Royal Courts of Justice, Belfast BT1 3JY
Tel 01232-235111

The Law Officers of the Crown for England and Wales are the Attorney-General and the Solicitor-General. The Attorney-General, assisted by the Solicitor-General, is the chief legal adviser to the Government and is also ultimately responsible for all Crown litigation. He has overall responsibility for the work of the Law Officers' Departments (the Treasury Solicitor's Department, the Crown Prosecution Service, the Serious Fraud Office and the Legal Secretariat to the Law Officers). He has a specific statutory duty to superintend the discharge of their duties by the Director of Public Prosecutions (who heads the Crown Prosecution Service) and the Director of the Serious Fraud Office. The Director of Public Prosecutions for Northern Ireland is also responsible to the Attorney-General for the performance of his functions. The Attorney-General has additional responsibilities in relation to aspects of the civil and criminal law.
Attorney-General (*£63,756), The Rt. Hon. John Morris, QC, MP
  Private Secretary, S. M. Whatton
  Parliamentary Private Secretary, K. Vaz, MP
Solicitor-General (£78,072), The Lord Falconer of Thoroton, QC
  Private Secretary, S. M. Whatton
Legal Secretary (G2), D. Seymour
Deputy Legal Secretary (G3), S. J. Wooler

* In addition to a parliamentary salary of £43,860

LEGAL AID BOARD
85 Gray's Inn Road, London WC1X 8AA
Tel 0171-813 1000

The Legal Aid Board has the general function of ensuring that advice, assistance and representation are available in accordance with the Legal Aid Act 1988. In 1989 it took over from the Law Society responsibility for administering legal aid. The Board is a non-departmental government body whose members are appointed by the Lord Chancellor.
Chairman, Sir Tim Chessells
Deputy Chairman, H. Hodge
Members, S. Orchard (*Chief Executive*); Ms D. Charnock; Ms J. Dunkley; P. Ely; C. George; B. Harvey; Ms K. Markus; Ms D. Payne; Ms P. Pearce; J. Shearer; D. Sinker; K. Winberg

SCOTTISH LEGAL AID BOARD
44 Drumsheugh Gardens, Edinburgh EH3 7SW
Tel 0131-226 7061

The Scottish Legal Aid Board was set up under the Legal Aid (Scotland) Act 1986. It is responsible for ensuring that advice, assistance and representation are available in accordance with the Act. The Board is a non-departmental government body whose members are appointed by the Secretary of State for Scotland.
Chairman, Ms C. A. M. Davis, CBE
Members, Mrs K. Blair; Mrs S. Campbell; Mrs J. Couper; Prof. P. H. Grinyer; Sheriff A. Jessop; N. Kuenssberg; R. J. Livingstone; C. N. McEachran, QC; Mrs Y. Osman; R. Scott; A. F. Wylie, QC
Chief Executive, R. Scott

OFFICE OF THE LEGAL SERVICES OMBUDSMAN
22 Oxford Court, Oxford Street, Manchester M2 3WQ
Tel 0161-236 9532

The Legal Services Ombudsman is appointed by the Lord Chancellor under the Courts and Legal Services Act 1990 to oversee the handling of complaints against solicitors, barristers and licensed conveyancers by their professional bodies. A complainant must first complain to the relevant professional body before raising the matter with the Ombudsman. The Ombudsman is independent of the legal profession and his services are free of charge.
Legal Services Ombudsman, Ms A. Abraham
Secretary, S. Murray

OFFICE OF THE SCOTTISH LEGAL SERVICES OMBUDSMAN
2 Greenside Lane, Edinburgh EH1 3AH
Tel 0131-556 5574
Scottish Legal Services Ombudsman, G. S. Watson

LIBRARIES

LIBRARY AND INFORMATION COMMISSION
2 Sheraton Street, London W1V 4BH
Tel 0171-411 0059

The Commission is an independent body set up by the then Secretary of State for National Heritage in 1995 to advise the Government and others on library and information matters, notably in the areas of research strategy and international links. It also aims to promote co-operation and co-ordination between different types of information services.

Chairman, M. Evans

Commissioners, E. Arram; Sir Charles Chadwyck-Healey; Dr G. Chambers; Prof. M. Collier; Prof. Judith Elkin; Dr B. Lang; D. Law; Dr R. McKee; Rabbi Julia Neuberger; Sir Peter Swinnerton-Dyer; Dr Sandra Ward; M. Wood

Executive Secretary, Ms M. Haines

THE BRITISH LIBRARY
96 Euston Road, London NW1 2DB
Tel 0171-412 7000

The British Library was established in 1973. It is the UK's national library and occupies the central position in the library and information network. The Library aims to serve scholarship, research, industry, commerce and all other major users of information. Its services are based on collections which include over 18 million volumes, 1 million discs, and 55,000 hours of tape recordings, at 18 buildings in London and one complex in West Yorkshire. The British Library's new purpose-built accommodation at St Pancras, London NW1 is scheduled to open to the public in a phased programme starting in late 1997. Government grant-in-aid to the British Library in 1997–8 is £86.9 million; the British Library St Pancras Project receives £7.5 million. The Library's sponsoring department is the Department for Culture, Media and Sport.

Access to the Humanities and Social Sciences reading rooms is limited to holders of a British Library Reader's Pass; information about eligibility is available from the Reader Admissions Office. The reading rooms of the Science Reference and Information Service are open to the general public without charge or formality.

Opening hours of services vary; most services are closed for one week each year. Specific information should be checked by telephone.

BRITISH LIBRARY BOARD
96 Euston Road, London NW1 2DB
Tel 0171-412 7262

Chairman, Dr J. Ashworth
Chief Executive and Deputy Chairman (*G2*), Dr B. Lang
Deputy Chief Executive (*G4*), D. Russon
Director-General, Collections and Services (*G4*), D. Bradbury
Part-time Members, T. J. Rix; The Hon. E. Adeane, CVO; Sir Matthew Farrer, GCVO; Mrs P. M. Lively, OBE; Prof. M. Anderson, FBA, FRSE; A. Bloom; B. Naylor; J. Ritblat; Sir Peter Hordern; P. Scherer; C. G. R. Leach

BRITISH LIBRARY, BOSTON SPA
Boston Spa, Wetherby, W. Yorks LS23 7BQ
Tel 01937-546000

BIBLIOGRAPHIC SERVICES AND DOCUMENT SUPPLY,
Director (*G5*), M. Smith
NATIONAL BIBLIOGRAPHIC SERVICE. Tel: 01937-546585.
Director (*G6*), R. Smith
London Unit, 2 Sheraton Street, London WIV 4BH. Tel: 0171-412 7077
ACQUISITIONS PROCESSING AND CATALOGUING,
Director (*G5*), S. Ede
INFORMATION SYSTEMS. Tel: 01937-546879. *Director* (*G5*), J. R. Mahoney

BRITISH LIBRARY, LONDON
Great Russell Street, London WC1B 3DG
Tel 0171-412 7000

Director of Project Services St Pancras Planning (*G6*), Dr R. Coman

PLANNING AND RESOURCES, 2 Sheraton Street, London WIV 4BH. Tel: 0171-412 7132. *Director* (*G5*), D. Gesua
PRESS AND PUBLIC RELATIONS, 96 Euston Road, London NW1 2DB. Tel: 0171-412 7111. *Head* (*G7*), M. Jackson
PUBLIC AFFAIRS. Tel: 0171-412 7626. *Director* (*G5*), Ms J. Carr
Exhibitions and Education Service. Tel: 0171-412 7595
Reader Admissions. Tel: 0171-412 7677

READER SERVICES AND COLLECTION DEVELOPMENT.
Tel: 0171-412 7676. *Director* (*G5*), M. J. Crump
West European Collections, Slavonic and East European Collections, English Language Collections. Tel: 0171-412 7676
Social Policy Information Service. Tel: 0171-412 7536
Newspaper Library, Colindale Avenue, London NW9 5HE. Tel: 0171-412 7353
National Sound Archive, 29 Exhibition Road, London SW7 2AS. Tel: 0171-412 7440

COLLECTIONS AND PRESERVATION. Tel: 0171-412 7676. *Director* (*G5*), Dr M. Foot
Preservation Service (National Preservation Office). Tel: 0171-412 7612

SPECIAL COLLECTIONS. Tel: 0171-412 7513. *Director* (*G5*), Dr A. Prochaska
Oriental and India Office Collections, 197 Blackfriars Road, London SE1 8NG. Tel: 0171-412 7873
Western Manuscripts. Tel: 0171-412 7513
Map Library. Tel: 0171-412 7700
Music Library. Tel: 0171-412 7528
Philatelic Collections. Tel: 0171-412 7729

SCIENCE REFERENCE AND INFORMATION SERVICE, 25 Southampton Buildings, London WC2A 1AW. Tel: 0171-412 7494; 9 Kean Street, London WC2B 4AT. Tel: 0171-412 7288. *Director* (*G5*), A. Gomersall

RESEARCH AND INNOVATION CENTRE, 2 Sheraton Street, London WIV 4BH. Tel: 0171-412 7055. *Director* (*G6*), N. Macartney

NATIONAL LIBRARY OF SCOTLAND
George IV Bridge, Edinburgh EH1 1EW
Tel 0131-226 4531

The Library, which was founded as the Advocates' Library in 1682, became the National Library of Scotland in 1925. It is funded by the Scottish Office. It contains about six million books and pamphlets, 18,000 current periodicals, 230 newspaper titles and 100,000 manuscripts. It has an unrivalled Scottish collection.

The Reading Room is for reference and research which cannot conveniently be pursued elsewhere. Admission is by ticket issued to an approved applicant. Opening hours: Reading Room, weekdays, 9.30–8.30 (Wednesday, 10–8.30); Saturday 9.30–1. Map Library, weekdays, 9.30–5 (Wednesday, 10–5); Saturday 9.30–1. Exhibition, weekdays, 10–5; Saturday 10–5; Sunday 2–5. Scottish Science Library, weekdays, 9.30–5 (Wednesday, 10–8.30).
Chairman of the Trustees, The Earl of Crawford and Balcarres, PC
Librarian and Secretary to the Trustees (*G4*), I. D. McGowan
Secretary of the Library (*G6*), M. C. Graham
Keeper of Printed Books (*G6*), Ms A. Matheson, PH.D.
Keeper of Manuscripts (*G6*), I. C. Cunningham

Director of Public Services (G6), A. M. Marchbank, PH.D.
Director of Electronic Information (G6), B. Gallivan

NATIONAL LIBRARY OF WALES/ LLYFRGELL GENEDLAETHOL CYMRU
Aberystwyth SY23 3BU
Tel 01970-623816

The National Library of Wales was founded by Royal Charter in 1907, and is maintained by annual grant from the Welsh Office. It contains about four million printed books, 40,000 manuscripts, four million deeds and documents, numerous maps, prints and drawings, and a sound and moving image collection. It specializes in manuscripts and books relating to Wales and the Celtic peoples. It is the repository for pre-1858 Welsh probate records, manorial records and tithe documents, and certain legal records. Readers' room open weekdays, 9.30–6 (Saturday 9.30–5); closed first week of October. Admission by Reader's Ticket.

President, Dr R. Brinley Jones
Librarian (G4), Dr J. L. Madden
Heads of Departments (G6), M. W. Mainwaring (*Administration and Technical Services*); G. Jenkins (*Manuscripts and Records*); Dr W. R. M. Griffiths (*Printed Books*); Dr D. H. Owen (*Pictures and Maps*)

LIGHTHOUSE AUTHORITIES

CORPORATION OF TRINITY HOUSE
Trinity House, Tower Hill, London EC3N 4DH
Tel 0171-480 6601

Trinity House, the first general lighthouse and pilotage authority in the kingdom, was granted its first charter by Henry VIII in 1514. The Corporation is the general lighthouse authority for England, Wales and the Channel Islands and maintains 72 lighthouses (of which four are manned), 13 major floating aids to navigation (e.g. light vessels) and more than 420 buoys. It also has certain statutory jurisdiction over aids to navigation maintained by local harbour authorities and is responsible for dealing with wrecks dangerous to navigation, except those occurring within port limits or wrecks of HM ships.

The Trinity House Lighthouse Service is maintained out of the General Lighthouse Fund which is provided from light dues levied on ships calling at ports of the UK and the Republic of Ireland. The Corporation is also a deep-sea pilotage authority and a charitable organization.

The affairs of the Corporation are controlled by a board of Elder Brethren and the Secretary. A separate board, which comprises Elder Brethren, senior staff and outside representatives, currently controls the Lighthouse Service. The Elder Brethren also act as nautical assessors in marine cases in the Admiralty Division of the High Court of Justice.

ELDER BRETHREN
Master, HRH The Prince Philip, Duke of Edinburgh, KG, KT
Deputy Master, Rear-Adm. P. B. Rowe, CBE, LVO

Elder Brethren, Capt. D. J. Orr; Capt. N. M. Turner, RD; HRH The Prince of Wales, KG, KT; HRH The Duke of York, CVO, ADC; Capt. Sir David Tibbits, DSC, RN; Capt. D. A. G. Dickens; Capt. J. E. Bury; Capt. J. A. N. Bezant, DSC, RD, RNR (retd.); Capt. D. J. Cloke; Capt. Sir Miles Wingate, KCVO; The Rt. Hon. Sir Edward Heath, KG, MBE, MP; Capt. I. R. C. Saunders; Capt. P. F. Mason, CBE; Capt. T. Woodfield, OBE; The Lord Simon of Glaisdale, PC; Admiral of the Fleet the Lord Lewin, KG, GCB, LVO, DSC; Capt. D. T. Smith, RN; Cdr. Sir Robin Gillett, Bt., GBE, RD, RNR; Capt. Sir Malcolm Edge, KCVO; The Lord Cuckney; The Lord Carrington, KG, GCMG, CH, MC, PC; Sir Brian Shaw; The Lord Mackay of Clashfern, PC; Sir Adrian Swire; Capt. P. H. King; The Lord Sterling of Plaistow, CBE, RNR; Cdr. M. J. Rivett-Carnac, RN; Capt. C. M. C. Stewart; Adm. Sir Jock Slater, GCB, LVO, ADC; Capt. J. R. Burton-Hall, RD; Capt. I. Gibb; Cdre P. J. Melson, CBE, RN

OFFICERS
Secretary, R. F. Dobb
Director of Finance, K. W. Clark
Director of Engineering, M. G. B. Wannell
Director of Administration, D. I. Brewer
Human Resources and Communication Manager, N. J. Cutmore
Navigation Manager, Mrs K. Hossain
Legal and Insurance Manager, J. D. Price
General Manager Operations, Capt. J. M. Barnes
Operations Administration Manager, S. J. W. Dunning
Deputy Director of Engineering, P. N. Hyde
Senior Inspector of Shipping, J. R. Dunnett
Media and Communication Officer, H. L. Cooper

COMMISSIONERS OF NORTHERN LIGHTHOUSES
84 George Street, Edinburgh EH2 3DA
Tel 0131-226 7051

The Commissioners of Northern Lighthouses are the general lighthouse authority for Scotland and the Isle of Man. The present board owes its origin to an Act of Parliament passed in 1786. At present the Commissioners operate under the Merchant Shipping Act 1894 and are 19 in number.

The Commissioners control five major manned lighthouses, 78 major automatic lighthouses, 114 minor lights and many lighted and unlighted buoys. They have a fleet of two motor vessels.

COMMISSIONERS
The Lord Advocate; the Solicitor-General for Scotland; the Lord Provosts of Edinburgh, Glasgow and Aberdeen; the Provost of Inverness; the Convener of Argyll and Bute Council; the Sheriffs-Principal of North Strathclyde, Tayside, Central and Fife, Grampian, Highlands and Islands, South Strathclyde, Dumfries and Galloway, Lothians and Borders, and Glasgow and Strathkelvin; A. J. Struthers; W. F. Hay, CBE; Capt. D. M. Cowell; Adm. Sir Michael Livesay, KCB; The Lord Maclay

OFFICERS
Chief Executive, Capt. J. B. Taylor, RN
Director of Finance, D. Gorman
Director of Engineering, W. Paterson
Director of Operations and Navigational Requirements, P. J. Christmas

LOCAL COMMISSIONERS

COMMISSION FOR LOCAL ADMINISTRATION IN ENGLAND
21 Queen Anne's Gate, London SW1H 9BU
Tel 0171-915 3210

Local Commissioners (local government ombudsmen) are responsible for investigating complaints from members of the public against local authorities (but not town and parish councils); police authorities; the Commission for New Towns (housing functions); education appeal committees and certain other authorities. The Commissioners are appointed by the Crown on the recommendation of the Secretary of State for the Environment, Transport and the Regions.

Certain types of action are excluded from investigation, including personnel matters and commercial transactions unless they relate to the purchase or sale of land. Complaints can be sent direct to the Local Government Ombudsman or through a councillor, although the Local Government Ombudsman will not consider a complaint unless the council has had an opportunity to investigate and reply to a complainant.

A free leaflet *Complaint about the council? How to complain to the Local Government Ombudsman* is available from the Commission's office.

Chairman of the Commission and Local Commissioner
(£96,952), E. B. C. Osmotherly, CB
Vice-Chairman and Local Commissioner (£81,766), Mrs P. A. Thomas
Local Commissioner (£80,766), J. R. White
Member (ex officio), The Parliamentary Commissioner for Administration
Secretary (£57,277), N. Karney

COMMISSION FOR LOCAL ADMINISTRATION IN WALES
Derwen House, Court Road, Bridgend CF31 1BN
Tel 01656-661325

The Local Commissioner for Wales has similar powers to the Local Commissioners in England. The Commissioner is appointed by the Crown on the recommendation of the Secretary of State for Wales. A free leaflet *Your Local Ombudsman in Wales* is available from the Commission's office.

Local Commissioner, E. R. Moseley
Secretary, D. Bowen
Member (ex officio), The Parliamentary Commissioner for Administration

COMMISSIONER FOR LOCAL ADMINISTRATION IN SCOTLAND
23 Walker Street, Edinburgh EH3 7HX
Tel 0131-225 5300

The Local Commissioner for Scotland has similar powers to the Local Commissioners in England, and is appointed by the Crown on the recommendation of the Secretary of State for Scotland.

Local Commissioner, F. C. Marks, OBE
Deputy and Secretary, Ms J. H. Renton

LONDON REGIONAL TRANSPORT
55 Broadway, London SW1H 0BD
Tel 0171-222 5600

Subject to the financial objectives and principles approved by the Secretary of State for the Environment, Transport, and the Regions, London Regional Transport has a general duty to provide or secure the provision of public transport services for Greater London.

Chairman (£154,500), P. Ford
Member, and Managing Director of London Transport Buses, C. Hodson, CBE
Member for Finance, A. J. Sheppeck
Member, and Managing Director of London Underground Ltd, D. Tunnicliffe, CBE

LORD ADVOCATE'S DEPARTMENT
2 Carlton Gardens, London SW1Y 5AA
Tel 0171-210 1010

The Law Officers for Scotland are the Lord Advocate and the Solicitor-General for Scotland. The Lord Advocate's Department is responsible for drafting Scottish legislation, for providing legal advice to other departments on Scottish questions and for assistance to the Law Officers for Scotland in certain of their legal duties.

Lord Advocate (£78,072), The Lord Hardie, PC, QC
    Private Secretary, A. G. Maxwell
Solicitor-General for Scotland (£66,811), Colin Boyd, QC
    Private Secretary, A. G. Maxwell
Legal Secretary and First Scottish Parliamentary Counsel (G2), J. C. McCluskie, QC
Assistant Legal Secretaries and Scottish Parliamentary Counsel (G3), G. M. Clark; G. Kowalski; P. J. Layden, TD; C. A. M. Wilson
Assistant Legal Secretary and Depute Scottish Parliamentary Counsel (G5), J. D. Harkness

LORD CHANCELLOR'S DEPARTMENT
Selborne House, 54–60 Victoria Street, London SW1E 6QB
Tel 0171-210 8500

The Lord Chancellor is the principal legal adviser of the Crown, Speaker of the House of Lords, President of the House of Lords as an Appellate Court, of the Court of Appeal, and of the Chancery Division of the High Court of Justice, and acting President of the Judicial Committee of the Privy Council. The Lord Chancellor appoints Justices of the Peace (except in Lancashire) and advises the Crown on the appointment of most members of the higher judiciary. He is responsible for promoting general reforms in the civil law, for the procedure of the civil courts and for legal aid schemes. He is a member of the Cabinet. He also has ministerial responsibility for magistrates' courts, which are administered locally. Administration of the Supreme Court and county courts in England and Wales was taken over by the Court Service, an executive agency of the department, in April 1995.

The Lord Chancellor is also responsible for ensuring that letters patent and other formal documents are passed in the proper form under the Great Seal of the Realm, of which he is the custodian. The work in connection with this is carried out under his direction in the Office of the Clerk of the Crown in Chancery.

Lord Chancellor (£140,665), The Lord Irvine of Lairg, PC, QC
 Private Secretary, Ms E. Hutchinson
 Parliamentary Private Secretary, A. Wright, MP
Parliamentary Secretary, Geoffrey Hoon, MP
 Private Secretary, A. Clegg
Permanent Secretary (*SCS*), Sir Thomas Legg, KCB, QC
 Private Secretary, Ms M. Cale

CROWN OFFICE
House of Lords, London SWIA OPW
Tel 0171-219 4713

Clerk of the Crown in Chancery (*SCS*), Sir Thomas Legg, KCB, QC
Deputy Clerk of the Crown in Chancery (*SCS*), M. Huebner, CB
Clerk of the Chamber, C. I. P. Denyer

JUDICIAL APPOINTMENTS GROUP
Tel 0171-210 8926

Head of Group (*SCS*), R. E. K. Holmes
Heads of Divisions (*SCS*), D. E. Staff (*Policy and Conditions of Service*); Mrs M. Pigott (*Circuit Bench*); Miss J. Killick (*Circuit Bench*); E. Adams (*District Bench and Tribunals*); R. Venne (*Magistrates' Appointments*)

Judicial Studies Board
9th Floor, Millbank Tower, London SWIP 4QW
Tel 0171-925 4762
Secretary (*SCS*), D. Hill

POLICY GROUP
Tel 0171-210 8719

Director-General (*SCS*), I. M. Burns, CB
Heads of Divisions (*SCS*), P. G. Harris (*Legal Aid*); Ms J. Rowe (*Criminal Policy*); D. Gladwell (*Civil Justice*); R. Sams (*Law Reform and Tribunals*); W. Arnold (*Family Policy*); S. Smith (*Review of Civil Justive and Legal Aid*)
Head of Secretariat and Agency Monitoring Unit (*SCS*), Ms A. Jones

LEGAL ADVISER'S GROUP
Tel 0171-210 0711

Legal Adviser (*SCS*), R. H. H. White
Heads of Divisions (*SCS*), M. H. Collon (*Legal Advice and Litigation*); J. Watherston (*International and Common Law Services*); M. Kron (*Drafting Services*)

CORPORATE SERVICES GROUP
Tel 0171-210 8503

Director of Corporate Services and Principal Establishment and Finance Officer (*SCS*), Mrs E. Grimsey
Heads of Divisions (*SCS*), Ms H. Tuffs (*Personnel Management*); A. Cogbill (*Finance*); vacant (*Planning and Communications*); K. Cregeen (*Accommodation and Magistrates' Courts Building*); A. Rummins (*Internal Assurance*); K. Garrett (*Statutory Publications Office*)

MAGISTRATES' COURTS GROUP
Tel 0171-210 8809

Director (*SCS*), L. C. Oates
Heads of Divisions (*SCS*), Ms A. Smith (*Magistrates' Courts*); P. White (*LIBRA Project and Magistrates' Courts IT*)

ECCLESIASTICAL PATRONAGE
10 Downing Street, London SWIA 2AA
Tel 0171-930 4433

Secretary for Ecclesiastical Patronage, J. H. Holroyd, CB
Assistant Secretary for Ecclesiastical Patronage, N. C. Wheeler

MAGISTRATES' COURTS' SERVICE INSPECTORATE
Southside, 105 Victoria Street, London SWIE 6QJ
Tel 0171-210 1655

Chief Inspector (*SCS*), Mrs R. L. Melling
Senior Inspectors (*SCS*), Ms J. Eeles; D. Gear; C. Monson; Ms S. Steel

LORD CHANCELLOR'S ADVISORY COMMITTEE ON STATUTE LAW
67 Tufton Street, London SWIP 3QS
Tel 0171-210 2666

The Advisory Committee advises the Lord Chancellor on all matters relating to the revision, modernization and publication of the statute book.
Chairman, The Lord Chancellor
Deputy Chairman, Sir Thomas Legg, KCB, QC
Members, C. Jenkins, CB, QC; J. C. McCluskie, QC; R. Brodie, CB; R. H. H White; G. Gray; J. M. Davies; Sir Donald Limon, KCB; The Hon. Mrs Justice Arden, DBE; The Hon. Lord Gill; A. H. Hammond, CB; Mrs E. Grimsey; P. Macdonald, CBE; C. Carey; K. Garrett
Secretary (*acting*), Ms J. Teah

EXECUTIVE AGENCIES

THE COURT SERVICE
Southside, 105 Victoria Street, London SWIE 6QT
Tel 0171-210 1775

The Court Service provides administrative support to the Supreme Court of England and Wales, county courts and a number of tribunals.
Chief Executive (*SCS*), M. D. Huebner, CB
Director of Civil and Family Operations (*SCS*), P. L. Jacob
Director of Criminal Operations (*SCS*), N. J. Smedley
Director of Tribunals (*SCS*), P. Stockton

Resources and Support Services Directorate
Director (*SCS*), C. W. V. Everett
SCS, K. Pogson (*Resources and Planning*); Miss B. Kenny (*Personnel and Training*); A. Shaw (*Accommodation, Procurement, Libraries and Records*); I. Hyams (*Information Technology*)

Royal Courts of Justice
Strand, London WC2A 2LL
Tel 0171-936 6000
Administrator, G. E. Calvett

For Supreme Court departments and offices and circuit administrators, *see* Law Courts and Offices section

HM LAND REGISTRY
— *see* pages 316–17

PUBLIC RECORD OFFICE
— *see* page 336

PUBLIC TRUST OFFICE
— *see* page 335

LORD GREAT CHAMBERLAIN'S OFFICE
House of Lords, London SWIA OPW
Tel 0171-219 3100

The Lord Great Chamberlain is a Great Officer of State, the office being hereditary since the grant of Henry I to the family of De Vere, Earls of Oxford. The Lord Great Chamberlain is responsible for the Royal Apartments of the Palace of Westminster, i.e. The Queen's Robing Room, the Royal Gallery and, in conjunction with the Lord Chancellor and Madam Speaker, Westminster Hall. The Lord Great Chamberlain has particular responsibility for the internal administrative arrangements within the House of Lords for State Openings of Parliament.

Lord Great Chamberlain, The Marquess of Cholmondeley
Secretary to the Lord Great Chamberlain, Gen. Sir Edward
Jones, KCB, CBE
Clerks to the Lord Great Chamberlain, Miss C. J. Bostock;
Miss R. M. Wilkinson

LORD PRIVY SEAL'S OFFICE
Privy Council Office, 68 Whitehall, London SW1A 2AT
Tel 0171-270 3000

The Lord Privy Seal is a member of the Cabinet and
Leader of the House of Lords. He has no departmental
portfolio, but is a member of a number of domestic and
economic Cabinet committees. He is responsible to the
Prime Minister for the organization of government busi-
ness in the House and has a responsibility to the House
itself to advise it on procedural matters and other
difficulties which arise.
Lord Privy Seal, and Leader of the House of Lords, The Lord
Richard, PC, QC
Principal Private Secretary, Mrs J. Hope
Private Secretary (House of Lords), S. Burton
Special Advisers, Ms M. Morris; D. Welfare
Parliamentary Private Secretary, J. Heppell, MP

LOTTERY, OFFICE OF THE NATIONAL
— *see* page 328

OFFICE OF MANPOWER ECONOMICS
Oxford House, 76 Oxford Street, London W1N 9FD
Tel 0171-467 7244

The Office of Manpower Economics was set up in 1971. It
is an independent non-statutory organization which is
responsible for servicing independent review bodies which
advise on the pay of various public service groups (*see*
Review Bodies, pages 337–8), the Pharmacists Review
Panel and the Police Negotiating Board. The Office is also
responsible for servicing *ad hoc* bodies of inquiry and for
undertaking research into pay and associated matters as
requested by the Government.
OME Director, M. J. Horsman
Director, Statistics, Office Services and Police Secretariat, G. S.
Charles
Director, Armed Forces and Teachers' Secretariats, A. Hughes
Director, Health Secretariat, and OME Deputy Director, Miss
S. M. Haird
Director, Senior Salaries Secretariat, Mrs C. Haworth
Press Liaison Officer, M. C. Cahill

MENTAL HEALTH ACT COMMISSION
Maid Marian House, 56 Hounds Gate, Nottingham
NG1 6BG
Tel 0115-950 4040

The Mental Health Act Commission was established in
1983. Its functions are to keep under review the operation
of the Mental Health Act 1983; to visit and meet patients
detained under the Act; to investigate complaints falling
within the Commission's remit; to operate the consent to
treatment safeguards in the Mental Health Act; to publish a
biennial report on its activities; to monitor the implementation of the Code of Practice; and to advise ministers.

Commissioners are appointed by the Secretary of State for
Health.
Chairman, The Viscountess Runciman of Doxford, OBE
Vice-Chairman, Dr R. Williams
Chief Executive (G6), W. Bingley

MILLENNIUM COMMISSION
Portland House, Stag Place, London SW1E 5EZ
Tel 0171-880 2001

The Millennium Commission was established in February
1994 and is funded by the Department for Culture, Media
and Sport. It is an independent body which distributes 20
per cent of the money allocated to 'good causes' from
National Lottery proceeds to projects to mark the millennium. The Commission had made grants to 109 capital
projects totalling £896 million by May 1997.
Chairman, The Rt. Hon. Chris Smith, MP
Members, Dr D. Clarke; Prof. Heather Couper, FRAS; Earl
of Dalkeith; The Lord Glentoran, CBE; Sir John Hall;
The Rt. Hon. M. Heseltine, MP; S. Jenkins; Miss
P. Scotland, QC
Chief Executive, E. Sorensen

MONOPOLIES AND MERGERS COMMISSION
New Court, 48 Carey Street, London WC2A 2JT
Tel 0171-324 1407

The Commission was established in 1949 as the Monopolies and Restrictive Practices Commission and became
the Monopolies and Mergers Commission under the Fair
Trading Act 1973. Its role is to investigate and report on
matters which are referred to it by the Secretary of State for
Trade and Industry or the Director-General of Fair
Trading or, in the case of privatized industries, by the
appropriate regulator. Its decisions are determined by the
criteria set out in the legislation covering the different
types of reference. The main types of reference which can
be made are: monopolies; mergers; newspaper mergers;
general, involving general practices in an industry; restrictive labour practices; competition, involving anti-
competitive practices of individual firms; public sector
audits; privatized industries; and Channel 3 (ITV) net-
working arrangements between holders of regional Channel 3 licences. References may be made under the Fair
Trading Act 1973, the Competition Act 1980, the Broadcasting Act or other relevant statutes.
The Commission consists of about 35 members, including a full-time chairman and three part-time deputy
chairmen, all appointed by the Secretary of State for Trade
and Industry. Each inquiry is conducted on behalf of the
Commission by a group of four to six members who are
appointed by the chairman.
The Government has announced plans to reform
competition law and replace the Commission with a
Competition Commission, subject to parliamentary approval.
Chairman (£120,000), Sir Graeme Odgers (*until December
1997*)
Deputy Chairmen (£51,000–£68,000), D. Morris, PH.D.;
P. G. Corbett, CBE; Ms D. Kingsmill

Members (£13,765/*£9,175 each), Prof. J. Beatson; Prof. M. Cave; *A. T. Clothier; R. H. F. Croft, CB; *R. O. Davies; *J. Evans; *N. H. Finney, OBE; *Sir Archibald Forster; *Sir Ronald Halstead, CBE; D. B. Hammond; *Ms J. C. Hanratty; *Ms P. A. Hodgson, CBE; D. J. Jenkins, MBE; R. Lyons; P. Mackay, CB; *N. F. Matthews; Prof. J. S. Metcalfe, CBE; *Mrs K. M. H. Mortimer; *R. J. Munson; *Prof. D. M. G. Newbery; Dr G. F. Owen; Prof. J. F. Pickering; M. R. Prosser; Prof. J. A. Rees; *T. S. Richmond; Dr A. Robinson; *J. K. Roe; *Dr L. Rouse; *C. R. Smallwood; *G. H. Stacy, CBE
Secretary, Miss P. Boys
* Reserve members

MUSEUMS

MUSEUMS AND GALLERIES COMMISSION
16 Queen Anne's Gate, London SWIH 9AA
Tel 0171-233 4200

Established in 1931 as the Standing Commission on Museums and Galleries, the Commission was renamed and took up new functions in 1981. Its sponsor department is the Department for Culture, Media and Sport. The Commission advises the Government, including the Department of Education for Northern Ireland, the Scottish Education Department and the Welsh Office, on museum affairs. Commissioners are appointed by the Prime Minister.

The Commission's executive functions include providing the services of the Museums Security Adviser; allocating grants to the seven Area Museum Councils in England; funding and monitoring the work of the Museum Documentation Association; and administering grant schemes for non-national museums. The Commission administers the arrangements for government indemnities and the acceptance of works of art in lieu of inheritance tax, and its Conservation Unit advises on conservation and environmental standards. A registration scheme for museums in the UK is operated by the Commission.
Chairman, J. Joll
Members, Sir Jack Baer; Prof. P. Bateson, FRS; The Baroness Brigstocke; Prof. R. Buchanan; Penelope, Viscountess Cobham; R. Foster; L. Grossman; R. Hiscox; Adm. Sir John Kerr, GCB; R. H. Smith; A. Warhurst, CBE; Mrs C. Wilson
Director and Secretary, T. Mason

THE BRITISH MUSEUM
Great Russell Street, London WCIB 3DG
Tel 0171-636 1555

The British Museum houses the national collection of antiquities, ethnography, coins and paper money, medals, and prints and drawings. The British Museum may be said to date from 1753, when Parliament approved the holding of a public lottery to raise funds for the purchase of the collections of Sir Hans Sloane and the Harleian manuscripts, and for their proper housing and maintenance. The building (Montagu House) was opened in 1759. The present buildings were erected between 1823 and the present day, and the original collection has increased to its present dimensions by gifts and purchases. Total government grant-in-aid for 1997–8 is £32.062 million.

BOARD OF TRUSTEES
Appointed by the Sovereign, HRH The Duke of Gloucester, KG, GCVO

Appointed by the Prime Minister, N. Barber; Prof. Gillian Beer, FBA; Sir John Boyd; E. J. P. Browne, FEng.; Sir Matthew Farrer, GCVO; Sir Michael Hopkins, CBE, RA, RIBA; Sir Joseph Hotung; Prof. M. Kemp, FBA; S. Keswick; Hon. Mrs M. Marten, OBE; Sir John Morgan, KCMG; The Rt. Hon. Sir Timothy Raison; Sir Martin Rees, FRS; Prof. Sir Gunter Treitel, DCL, FBA, QC
Nominated by the Learned Societies, Prof. Jean Thomas, CBE (*Royal Society*); A. Jones, RA (*Royal Academy*); Sir Claus Moser, KCB, CBE, FBA (*British Academy*); The Lord Renfrew of Kaimsthorn, FBA, FSA (*Society of Antiquaries*)
Appointed by the Trustees of the British Museum, G. C. Greene, CBE (*Chairman*); Sir David Attenborough, CH, CVO, CBE, FRS; Prof. Rosemary Cramp, CBE, FSA; The Lord Egremont; Dr Jennifer Montagu, FBA

OFFICERS
Director, Dr R. G. W. Anderson, FRSC, FSA
Director of Finance and Resources, A. B. Blackstock
Secretary, Mrs C. Nihoul Parker
Head of Public Services, G. A. L. House
Head of Press and Public Relations, A. E. Hamilton
Head of Design, Miss M. Hall, OBE
Head of Education, J. F. Reeve
Head of Administration, C. E. I. Jones
Head of Building Development and Planning, K. T. Stannard
Head of Building Management, T. R. A. Giles
Head of Finance, Miss S. E. Davies
Head of Personnel and Office Services, Miss B. A. Hughes

KEEPERS
Keeper of Prints and Drawings, A. V. Griffiths
Keeper of Coins and Medals, Dr A. M. Burnett
Keeper of Egyptian Antiquities, W. V. Davies
Keeper of Western Asiatic Antiquities, Dr J. E. Curtis
Keeper of Greek and Roman Antiquities, Dr D. J. R. Williams
Keeper of Medieval and Later Antiquities, N. M. Stratford
Keeper of Prehistoric and Romano-British Antiquities, Dr T. M. Potter
Keeper of Japanese Antiquities, vacant
Keeper of Oriental Antiquities, R. J. Knox
Keeper of Ethnography, B. J. Mack
Keeper of Scientific Research, Dr S. G. E. Bowman
Keeper of Conservation, W. A. Oddy

NATURAL HISTORY MUSEUM
Cromwell Road, London SW7 5BD
Tel 0171-938 9123

The Natural History Museum originates from the natural history departments of the British Museum, which grew extensively during the 19th century and in 1860 the natural history collection was moved from Bloomsbury to a new location. Part of the site of the 1862 International Exhibition in South Kensington was acquired for the new museum, and the Museum opened to the public in 1881. In 1963 the Natural History Museum became completely independent with its own body of trustees. The Walter Rothschild Zoological Museum, Tring, bequeathed by the second Lord Rothschild, has formed part of the Museum since 1938. The Geological Museum merged with the Natural History Museum in 1985. Total government grant-in-aid for 1997–8 is £27.7 million.

BOARD OF TRUSTEES
Appointed by the Prime Minister: Sir Robert May, FRS (*Chairman*); Mrs J. M. d'Abo; Sir Denys Henderson; Sir Crispin Tickell, GCMG, KCVO; Prof. Sir Ronald Oxburgh, FRS; Dame Anne McLaren, DBE, FRS; Sir Richard Sykes

Appointed by the Trustees of the Natural History Museum, Prof.
Sir Brian Follett, FRS; The Lord Palumbo; Prof. K.
O'Nions, FRS

SENIOR STAFF
Director, N. R. Chalmers, PH.D.
Director of Science, Prof. P. Henderson, D.Phil.
Science Policy Co-ordinator, Ms N. Donlon
Head of Development and Marketing, Ms T. Burman
Keeper of Zoology, C. R. Curds, D.SC
Director, Tring Zoological Museum, I. R. Bishop, OBE
Keeper of Entomology, Dr R. P. Lane
Keeper of Botany, S. Blackmore, PH.D.
Keeper of Palaeontology, L. R. M. Cocks, D.SC
Keeper of Mineralogy, Dr A. Fleet
Head of Finance, J. Card
Head of Personnel, Mrs P. H. I. Orchard
Head of Library and Information Services, R. Lester
Head of Education and Exhibitions (G5), Dr G. Clarke
Head of Visitor Services, Mrs W. B. Gullick
Head of Estates, G. Pellow

THE SCIENCE MUSEUM
South Kensington, London SW7 2DD
Tel 0171-938 8000

The Science Museum, part of the National Museum of
Science and Industry, houses the national collections of
science, technology, industry and medicine. The Museum
began as the science collection of the South Kensington
Museum and first opened in 1857. In 1883 it acquired the
collections of the Patent Museum and in 1909 the science
collections were transferred to the new Science Museum,
leaving the art collections with the Victoria and Albert
Museum.

Some of the Museum's commercial aircraft, agricultural
machinery, and road and rail transport collections are at
Wroughton, Wilts. The Museum is also responsible for the
National Railway Museum, York; the National Museum of
Photography, Film and Television, Bradford; and the
Concorde Exhibition at the Fleet Air Arm Museum,
Yeovilton.

Total government grant-in-aid for 1997–8 is £21.08
million.

BOARD OF TRUSTEES
Chairman, Dr P. Williams, CBE, FEng.
Members, HRH The Duke of Kent, KG, GCMG, GCVO, ADC;
Dr M. Archer; G. Dyke; Miss M. S. Goldring, OBE, Dr A.
Grocock; Mrs A. Higham, OBE; Mrs J. Kennedy, OBE;
Dame Bridget Ogilvie, DBE; Sir David Puttnam, CBE; Sir
Michael Quinlan, GCB; D. E. Rayner, CBE;
L. de Rothschild, CBE; Sir Christopher Wates

OFFICERS
Director, Sir Neil Cossons, OBE, FSA
Assistant Director and Head of Resource Management
Division, J. J. Defries
Head of Personnel and Legal Services, C. Gosling
Head of Finance and IS, Ms A. Caine
Head of Estates, J. Bevin
Assistant Director and Head of Collections Division, Dr T.
Wright
Head of Physical Sciences and Engineering Group,
Dr D. A. Robinson
Head of Life and Communications Technologies Group,
Dr R. F. Bud
Head of Collections Management Group, Dr S. Keene
Assistant Director and Head of Public Affairs Division,
C. M. Pemberton
Assistant Director and Head of Science Communication Division,
Prof. J. R. Durant

Head of Education and Programmes, Dr R. Jackson
Head of Exhibitions, Dr G. Farmelo
Head of Design, T. Molloy
Head of National Railway Museum, A. Scott
Head of National Museum of Photography, Film and Television,
Ms A. Nevill

VICTORIA AND ALBERT MUSEUM
South Kensington, London SW7 2RL
Tel 0171-938 8500

The Victoria and Albert Museum is the national museum
of fine and applied art and design. It descends directly from
the Museum of Manufactures, which opened in Marlbor
ough House in 1852 after the Great Exhibition of 1851.
The Museum was moved in 1857 to become part of the
South Kensington Museum. It was renamed the Victoria
and Albert Museum in 1899. It also houses the National Art
Library and Print Room.

The Museum administers three branch museums: the
National Museum of Childhood in Bethnal Green, the
Theatre Museum in Covent Garden, and the Wellington
Museum at Apsley House. The museum in Bethnal Green
was opened in 1872 and the building is the most important
surviving example of the type of glass and iron construction used by Paxton for the Great Exhibition. Total
government grant-in-aid for 1997–8 is £29.898 million.

BOARD OF TRUSTEES
Chairman, The Lord Armstrong of Ilminster, GCB, CVO
Deputy Chairman, Sir Michael Butler, GCMG
Members, The Lord Barnett, PC; Miss N. Campbell; Sir
Clifford Chetwood; Penelope, Viscountess Cobham;
Lady Copisarow; R. Fitch, CBE; Prof. C. Frayling, PH.D.;
Sir Terence Heiser, GCB; Mrs A. Heseltine; A. Irby III;
Miss A. Plowden, CBE; J. Scott, CBE, FSA; A. Snow;
Prof. J. Steer, FSA, D.Litt.; A. Wheatley, Prof. C. White,
CVO, FBA
Secretary to the Board of Trustees, P. A. Wilson

OFFICERS
Director (G3), Dr A. C. N. Borg, CBE, FSA
Assistant Directors, T. J. Stevens (Collections); J. W. Close
(Administration)
Head of Buildings and Estate, vacant
Chief Curator, Ceramics and Glass, Dr O. Watson
Head of Conservation, Dr J. Ashley-Smith
Head of Education, D. Anderson
Chief Curator, Far Eastern, Miss R. Kerr
Head of Finance and Central Services, Miss R. M. Sykes
Chief Curator, Furniture and Woodwork, C. Wilk
Chief Curator, Indian and South-East Asian, Dr D. Swallow
Head of Major Projects and Collections Management, Mrs G. F.
Miles
Chief Curator, Metalwork, Silver and Jewellery,
Mrs P. Glanville
Chief Librarian, National Art Library, J. F. van den Wateren
Head of Personnel, Mrs G. Henchley
Chief Curator, Prints, Drawings and Paintings,
Miss S. B. Lambert
Head of Public Services, R. Cole-Hamilton
Head of Research, P. Greenhalgh
Chief Curator, Sculpture, Dr P. E. D. Williamson
Chief Curator, Textiles and Dress, Mrs V. D. Mendes
Managing Director, V. and A. Enterprises Ltd, M. Cass
Director of Development, Ms C. Morley
Head of National Museum of Childhood, vacant
Head of Theatre Museum, Miss M. Benton
Head of Wellington Museum (Apsley House), Miss A. Robinson

MUSEUM OF LONDON
London Wall, London EC2Y 5HN
Tel 0171-600 3699

The Museum of London illustrates the history of London from prehistoric times to the present day. It opened in 1976 and is based on the amalgamation of the former Guildhall Museum and London Museum. The Museum is controlled by a Board of Governors, appointed (nine each) by the Government and the Corporation of London. The Museum is funded jointly by the Department for Culture, Media and Sport and the Corporation of London, each contributing £4.310 million in 1997–8.
Chairman of Board of Governors, P. Revell-Smith, CBE
Director, Dr S. Thurley

COMMONWEALTH INSTITUTE
Kensington High Street, London W8 6NQ
Tel 0171-603 4535

The Commonwealth Institute is the UK centre responsible for promoting the Commonwealth in Britain through exhibitions, educational programmes, publications, resources and information. The Institute houses an Education Centre, a Commonwealth Resource Centre and Literature Library, and a Conference and Events Centre. The Commonwealth Experience reopened to the public in May 1997.

The Institute is an independent statutory body funded by the British government with contributions from other Commonwealth governments. It is controlled by a Board of Governors which includes the High Commissioners of all Commonwealth countries represented in London. Total government grant-in-aid for 1997–8 is £800,000.
Director-General, D. French
Administrative and Commercial Director, P. Kennedy
Projects Director, Dr J. Stevenson

IMPERIAL WAR MUSEUM
Lambeth Road, London SE1 6HZ
Tel 0171-416 5000

The Museum, founded in 1917, illustrates and records all aspects of the two world wars and other military operations involving Britain and the Commonwealth since 1914. It was opened in its present home, formerly Bethlem Hospital or Bedlam, in 1936. The Museum also administers HMS *Belfast* in the Pool of London, Duxford Airfield near Cambridge and the Cabinet War Rooms in Westminster.

Total government grant-in-aid for 1997–8 is £10.971 million.

OFFICERS
Director-General, R. W. K. Crawford
Secretary, J. J. Chadwick, OBE
Assistant Directors, D. A. Needham (*Administration*); Miss K. J. Carmichael (*Collections*); G. Marsh (*Planning and Development*)
Head of Personnel Services, Miss L. Court
Head of Finance, Mrs P. A. Whitfield
Head of Information Systems, J. C. Barrett
Head of Support Systems, G. P. McCartney
Director of Duxford Airfield, E. O. Inman
Director of HMS Belfast, E. J. Wenzel

KEEPERS
Department of Museum Services, C. Dowling, D.Phil.
Department of Documents, R. W. A. Suddaby
Department of Exhibits and Firearms, D. J. Penn
Department of Printed Books, G. M. Bayliss, PH.D.
Department of Art, Miss A. H. Weight

Department of Film, R. B. N. Smither
Department of Photographs, Ms B. Kinally
Department of Sound Records, Mrs M. A. Brooks
Department of Marketing and Trading, Miss A. Godwin
Curator of the Cabinet War Rooms, P. Reed

NATIONAL MARITIME MUSEUM
Greenwich, London SE10 9NF
Tel 0181-858 4422

Established by Act of Parliament in 1934, the National Maritime Museum illustrates the maritime history of Great Britain in the widest sense, underlining the importance of the sea and its influence on the nation's power, wealth, culture, technology and institutions. The Museum is in three groups of buildings in Greenwich Park – the main building, the Queen's House (built by Inigo Jones, 1616–35) and the Old Royal Observatory (including Wren's Flamsteed House). Total government grant-in-aid for 1997–8 is £10.5 million.
Director, R. L. Ormond

NATIONAL ARMY MUSEUM
Royal Hospital Road, London SW3 4HT
Tel 0171-730 0717

The National Army Museum covers the history of five centuries of the British Army. It was established by royal charter in 1960. Total government grant-in-aid for 1997–8 is £3.148 million.
Director, I. G. Robertson
Assistant Directors, D. K. Smurthwaite; A. J. Guy; Maj. P. R. Bateman

ROYAL AIR FORCE MUSEUM
Grahame Park Way, London NW9 5LL
Tel 0181-205 2266

Situated on the former airfield at RAF Hendon, the Museum illustrates the development of aviation from before the Wright brothers to the present-day RAF. Total government grant-in-aid for 1997–8, including funding for the aerospace museum at Cosford, is £4.794 million.
Director, Dr M. A. Fopp
Deputy Director, J. D. Freeborn
Keepers, P. Elliott; H. Hall

NATIONAL MUSEUMS AND GALLERIES ON MERSEYSIDE
William Brown Street, Liverpool L3 8EN
Tel 0151-207 0001

The Board of Trustees of the National Museums and Galleries on Merseyside is responsible for the Liverpool Museum, the Merseyside Maritime Museum (incorporating HM Customs and Excise National Museum), the Museum of Liverpool Life, the Lady Lever Art Gallery, the Walker Art Gallery and Sudley House, and the Conservation Centre. Total government grant-in-aid for 1997–8 is £12.7 million.
Chairman of the Board of Trustees, D. McDonnell
Director, R. Foster
Head of Central Services, P. Sudbury, PH.D.
Keeper of Art Galleries, J. Treuherz
Keeper of Conservation, A. Durham
Keeper, Liverpool Museum, E. Greenwood
Keeper, Merseyside Maritime Museum and Museum of Liverpool Life, M. Stammers

NATIONAL MUSEUMS AND GALLERIES OF WALES/AMGUEDDFEYDD AC ORIELAU CENEDLAETHOL CYMRU

Cathays Park, Cardiff CF1 3NP
Tel 01222-397951

The National Museums and Galleries of Wales comprise the National Museum and Gallery, the Museum of Welsh Life, the Roman Legionary Museum, Turner House Art Gallery, the Welsh Slate Museum, the Segontium Roman Museum, the Museum of the Welsh Woollen Industry and the Welsh Industrial and Maritime Museum. Total funding from the Welsh Office for 1997–8 is £10.452 million.
President, M. C. T. Prichard, CBE
Vice-President, A. Thomas

OFFICERS
Director, C. Ford, CBE
Assistant Directors, T. Arnold (*Resource Management*); C. Thomas (*Public Services*); A. Southall (*Museums Development*); I. Fell (*Education and Interpretation*); Dr E. Williams (*Collections and Research*)
Keeper of Geology, M. G. Bassett, PH.D.
Keeper of Bio-diversity and Systematic Diversity, Dr P. G. Oliver
Keeper of Art, D. Alston
Keeper of Archaeology, R. Brewer
Keeper, Museum of Welsh Life, J. Williams-Davies
Officer in Charge, Roman Legionary Museum (*acting*), D. Dollery
Keeper in Charge, Turner House Art Gallery, D. Alston
Keeper in Charge, Welsh Slate Museum, D. Roberts, PH.D.
Officer in Charge, Segontium Roman Museum, R. J. Brewer
Officer in Charge, Museum of the Welsh Woollen Industry, J. Williams-Davies
Keeper, Welsh Industrial and Maritime Museum, E. S. Owen-Jones, PH.D.

NATIONAL MUSEUMS OF SCOTLAND

Chambers Street, Edinburgh EH1 1JF
Tel 0131-225 7534

The National Museums of Scotland comprise the Royal Museum of Scotland, the Scottish United Services Museum, the Scottish Agricultural Museum, the Museum of Flight and Shambellie House Museum of Costume. Total funding from the Scottish Office for 1997–8 is £24.372 million.

BOARD OF TRUSTEES
Chairman, R. Smith, FSA SCOT.
Members, Countess of Dalkeith; Prof. T. Devine; Dr L. Glasser, FRSE; S. G. Gordon, CBE; Sir Alistair Grant, FRSE; Prof. P. H. Jones; Prof. A. Manning; A. Massie; Prof. J. Murray, Dr A. Ritchie, OBE; The Countess of Rosebery; Sir John Thomson; Dr V. Van Heyingen, FRSE

OFFICERS
Director (*G3*), M. Jones, FSA, FSA SCOT., FRSA
Depute Director (Resources) and Project Director, Museum of Scotland (*G5*), I. Hooper, FSA SCOT.
Depute Director (Collections) and Keeper of History and Applied Art (*G5*), Miss D. Idiens, FRSA, FSA SCOT.
Keeper of Archaeology, D. V. Clarke, PH.D., FSA, FSA SCOT.
Keeper of Geology and Zoology (*G5*), M. Shaw, D.phil.
Keeper of Social and Technological History (*G5*), G. Sprott
Head of Public Affairs (*G6*), Ms M. Bryden
Head of Museum Services (*G6*), S. R. Elson, FSA SCOT.
Head of Administration (*G6*), A. G. Young
Campaign Director, Museum of Scotland, S. Brock, PH.D., FRSA
Keeper, Scottish United Services Museum, S. C. Wood

Curator, Scottish Agricultural Museum, G. Sprott
Curator, Museum of Flight, A. Smith
Keeper, Shambellie House Museum of Costume, Miss N. Tarrant

NATIONAL AUDIT OFFICE

157–197 Buckingham Palace Road, London SW1W 9SP
Tel 0171-798 7000
Audit House, 23–24 Park Place, Cardiff CF1 3BA
Tel 01222-378661
22 Melville Street, Edinburgh EH3 7NS
Tel 0131-244 2736

The National Audit Office came into existence under the National Audit Act 1983 to replace and continue the work of the former Exchequer and Audit Department. The Act reinforced the Office's total financial and operational independence from the Government and brought its head, the Comptroller and Auditor-General, into a closer relationship with Parliament as an officer of the House of Commons.

The National Audit Office provides independent information, advice and assurance to Parliament and the public about all aspects of the financial operations of government departments and many other bodies receiving public funds. It does this by examining and certifying the accounts of these organizations and by regularly publishing reports to Parliament on the results of its value for money investigations of the economy, efficiency and effectiveness with which public resources have been used. The National Audit Office is also the auditor by agreement of the accounts of certain international and other organizations. In addition, the Office authorizes the issue of public funds to government departments.
Comptroller and Auditor-General, Sir John Bourn, KCB
  Private Secretary, F. Grogan
Deputy Comptroller and Auditor-General, R. N. Le Marechal, CB
Assistant Auditors-General, T. Burr; J. A. Higgins; L. H. Hughes, CB; J. Marshall; M. C. Pfleger; Miss C. Mawhood
Directors, Mrs C. Allen; B. Hogg; S. Doughty; J. M. Pearce; A. G. Roberts; R. A. Skeen; A. Fiander; M. Daynes; R. J. Eales; J. Colman; B. Payne; N. Sloan; D. Woodward; Ms W. Kenway-Smith; R. Frith; J. Cavanagh; R. Maggs; M. Sinclair; J. Robertson; M. Whitehouse

NATIONAL CONSUMER COUNCIL

20 Grosvenor Gardens, London SW1W 0DH
Tel 0171 730 3469

The National Consumer Council was set up by the Government in 1975 to give an independent voice to consumers in the UK. Its job is to advocate the consumer interest to decision-makers in national and local government, industry and regulatory bodies, business and the professions. It does this through a combination of research and campaigning. It is largely funded by grant-in-aid from the Department of Trade and Industry.
Chairman, D. Hatch, CBE
Vice-Chairman, Mrs D. Hutton
Director, Ms R. Evans

NATIONAL DEBT OFFICE

— *see* National Investment and Loans Office

NATIONAL HERITAGE, DEPARTMENT OF
— *see* Culture, Media and Sport, Department of

NATIONAL HERITAGE MEMORIAL FUND
7 Holbein Place, London SW1W ONR
Tel 0171-591 6000

The National Heritage Memorial Fund is an independent body established in 1980 as a memorial to those who have died for the UK. The Fund is empowered by the National Heritage Act 1980 to give financial assistance towards the cost of acquiring, maintaining or preserving land, buildings, works of art and other objects of outstanding interest which are also of importance to the national heritage. The Fund is administered by 15 trustees who are appointed by the Prime Minister.

The National Lottery Act 1993 designated the Fund as distributor of the heritage share of proceeds from the National Lottery (one fifth of the proceeds to the 'good causes'). As a result, the Fund now operates two funds: the Heritage Memorial Fund and the Heritage Lottery Fund. The Heritage Memorial Fund receives an annual grant from the Department for Culture, Media and Sport (£5 million in 1997–8). The Heritage Lottery Fund had made awards to the value of £656 million by July 1997.
Chairman, The Lord Rothschild
Trustees, Dr E. Anderson; Sir Richard Carew Pole, Bt.;
   W. L. Evans; Sir Nicholas Goodison; Sir Alistair Grant;
   Sir Martin Holdgate; Mrs C. Hubbard; Sir Martin
   Jacomb; J. Keegan; Ms P. Lankester;
   Prof. P. J. Newbould; Mrs J. Nutting; Mrs C. Porteous;
   Dame Sue Tinson, DBE
Director, Ms A. Case

NATIONAL INSURANCE JOINT AUTHORITY
The Adelphi, 1–11 John Adam Street, London WC2N 6HT
Tel 0171-962 8523

The Authority's function is to co-ordinate the operation of social security legislation in Great Britain and Northern Ireland, including the necessary financial adjustments between the two National Insurance Funds.
Members, The Secretary of State for Social Security; the Head of the Department of Health and Social Services for Northern Ireland.
Secretary, M. Driver

NATIONAL INVESTMENT AND LOANS OFFICE
1 King Charles Street, London SW1A 2AP
Tel 0171-270 3861

The National Investment and Loans Office is a non-ministerial government department which was set up in 1980 by the merger of the National Debt Office and the Public Works Loan Board. The Office provides the staff and administrative support for the National Debt Commissioners, the Public Works Loan Commissioners and the Office of HM Paymaster-General. The National Debt Office is responsible for managing the investment portfolios of certain public funds; the management of some residual operations relating to the national debt; and the facilitation of raising funds by central government follow-ing Article 104 of the Maastricht Treaty, in pursuance of section 211 of the Finance Act 1993. The function of the Public Works Loan Board is to make loans from the National Loans Fund to local authorities and certain other statutory bodies, primarily for capital purposes.

The Office of HM Paymaster-General has continuously existed in its present form since 1836; the Paymaster-General has responsibilities assigned from time to time by the Prime Minister and is currently a Treasury minister. The Assistant Paymaster-General is responsible for the banking and financial information services provided to the Government and public sector bodies by the Office of HM Paymaster-General.
Director, I. H. Peattie
Establishment Officer, A. G. Ladd

NATIONAL DEBT OFFICE
Comptroller-General, I. H. Peattie

PUBLIC WORKS LOAN BOARD
Chairman, A. D. Loehnis, CMG
Deputy Chairman, Miss V. J. Di Palma, OBE
Other Commissioners, G. G. Williams; L. B. Woodhall; Dame
   Sheila Masters, DBE; Mrs R. V. Hale; R. Burton; J. A.
   Parkes, CBE; J. Andrews; B. Tanner; T. Fellowes; Mrs R.
   Terry
Secretary, I. H. Peattie
Assistant Secretary, Miss L. M. Ashcroft

OFFICE OF HM PAYMASTER-GENERAL
Paymaster-General, Geoffrey Robinson, MP
Assistant Paymaster-General, I. H. Peattie
Deputy Paymaster-General, L. Palmer

BANKING OPERATIONS, National Investment and Loans
   Office, Sutherland House, Russell Way, Crawley, W.
   Sussex RH10 1UH. *Banking Manager,* P. Harris

OFFICE OF THE NATIONAL LOTTERY
2 Monck Street, London SW1P 2BQ
Tel 0345-125596

The Office of the National Lottery (OFLOT) was established as a non-ministerial government department under the National Lottery Act 1993. It regulates the National Lottery operations and licenses games promoted as part of the Lottery.

About 28 per cent of national lottery proceeds is currently allocated equally to five 'good causes': the arts, charities, heritage, sport and the Millennium Fund.
Director-General (G2), P. Davis
Deputy Director-General (G5), J. Stoker
Head of Compliance Regulation (G5), K. Jones

NATIONAL LOTTERY CHARITIES BOARD
St Vincent House, 30 Orange Street, London WC2H 7HH
Tel 0171-747 5200

The Board is the independent body set up under the National Lottery Act 1993 to distribute funds from the Lottery to support charitable, benevolent and philanthropic organizations (one-fifth of the 28 per cent allocated to 'good causes'). There are 22 Board members including the chairman. Members are appointed by the Secretary of State for Culture, Media and Sport. The Board's main aim is to help meet the needs of those at greatest disadvantage in society and to improve the quality of life in the community through themed grants programmes in the

UK and an international grants programme for UK-based agencies working abroad. The Board is also piloting a small grants scheme in Wales. By June 1997 the Board had awarded 7,750 grants totalling £504.6 million.
Chairman, The Hon. D. Sieff
Chief Executive, T. Hornsby
Members, Mrs T. Baring; A. Bhatia, OBE; G. Bowie; Mrs J. Churchman; I. Clarke; Ms S. Clarke; Ms P. de Lima; A. Higgins; T. Jones; Ms A. Jordan; Ms J. Kaufmann; W. Kirkpatrick; Ms A. McGinley; Ms M. McWilliams; W. G. Morrison; Ms L. Quinn; Sir Adam Ridley; J. Simpson, OBE; N. Stewart; Prof. Sir Eric Stroud, FRCP; C. Woodcock

NATIONAL PHYSICAL LABORATORY
Queens Road, Teddington, Middx TW11 0LW
Tel 0181-977 3222

The Laboratory is the UK's national standards laboratory. It develops, maintains and disseminates national measurement standards and conducts underpinning research on engineering materials and information technology. It is government-owned but contractor-operated.
Managing Director, Dr J. Rae
Director of Marketing and Communications, D. C. Richardson

NATIONAL RADIOLOGICAL PROTECTION BOARD
Chilton, Didcot, Oxon OX11 0RQ
Tel 01235-831600

The National Radiological Protection Board is an independent statutory body created by the Radiological Protection Act 1970. It is the national point of authoritative reference on radiological protection for both ionizing and non-ionizing radiations, and has issued recommendations on limiting human exposure to electromagnetic fields and radiation from a range of sources, including X-rays, the Sun and power generators. Its sponsoring department is the Department of Health.
Chairman, Prof. Sir Keith Peters
Director, Prof. R. H. Clarke

NATIONAL SAVINGS
Charles House, 375 Kensington High Street, London W14 8SD
Tel 0171-605 9300

National Savings was established as a government department in 1969. It became an executive agency of the Treasury in July 1996 and is responsible for the administration of a wide range of schemes for personal savers.
Chief Executive, P. Bareau
Deputy Chief Executive and Contracting Director, K. Chivers
Operational Services Director, D. H. Monaghan
Personnel Director, D. S. Speedie
Finance Director, M. A. Nicholls
Commercial Director, vacant
Funding Director, M. Corcoran

For details of schemes, *see* National Savings section

OFFICE FOR NATIONAL STATISTICS
1 Drummond Gate, London SW1V 2QQ
Tel 0171-533 6363

The Office for National Statistics was created in April 1996 by the merger of the Central Statistical Office and the Office of Population, Censuses and Surveys. It is an executive agency of the Treasury and is responsible for the full range of functions previously carried out by those offices. This includes responsibility for preparing and interpreting key economic statistics for government policy; collecting and publishing business statistics; publishing annual and monthly statistical digests; providing researchers, analysts and other customers with a statistical service; administration of the marriage laws and local registration of births, marriages and deaths in England and Wales; provision of population estimates and projections and statistics on health and other demographic matters in England and Wales; population censuses in England and Wales; surveys for government departments and public bodies; and promoting these functions within the UK, the European Union and internationally to provide a statistical service to meet European Union and international requirements.
The office for National Statistics is also responsible for establishing and maintaining a central database of key economic and social statistics produced to common classifications, definitions and standards.
Chief Executive, Prof. T. Holt
Directors (*G3*), J. Calder (*Survey and Statistical Services*); J. Fox (*Census, Population and Health*); J. Kidgell (*Macro-Economic Statistics*); L. Mayhew (*Administration and Registration*); M. Pepper (*Business Statistics*); D. Roberts (*Socio-Economic Statistics*)
Principal Establishment Officer (*G5*), E. Williams
Principal Finance Officer (*G5*), B. Smith
Head of Information (*G6*), I. Scott
Parliamentary Clerk, L. Land

JOINT NATURE CONSERVATION COMMITTEE
Monkstone House, City Road, Peterborough PE1 1JY
Tel 01733-62626

The Committee was established under the Environmental Protection Act 1990. It advises the Government and others on UK and international nature conservation issues and disseminates knowledge on these subjects. It establishes common standards for the monitoring of nature conservation and research, and analyses the resulting information. It commissions research relevant to these roles, and provides guidance to English Nature, Scottish Natural Heritage, the Countryside Council for Wales and the Department of the Environment for Northern Ireland.
Chairman, Sir Angus Stirling
Chief Officer, Dr A. E. Brown
Director, Dr M. A. Vincent

NOLAN COMMITTEE
— *see* page 345

NORTHERN IRELAND AUDIT OFFICE
106 University Street, Belfast BT7 1EU
Tel 01232-251000

The primary aim of the Northern Ireland Audit Office is to provide independent assurance, information and advice to Parliament on the proper accounting for Northern Ireland departmental and certain other public expenditure, revenue, assets and liabilities; on regularity and propriety; and on the economy, efficiency and effectiveness of the use of resources.
Comptroller and Auditor-General for Northern Ireland,
   J. M. Dowdall

NORTHERN IRELAND OFFICE
11 Millbank, London SW1P 4QE
Tel 0171-210 3000
Stormont Castle, Belfast BT4 3ST
Tel 01232-520700

The Northern Ireland Office was established in 1972, when the Northern Ireland (Temporary Provisions) Act transferred the legislative and executive powers of the Northern Ireland Parliament and Government to the UK Parliament and a Secretary of State.

The Northern Ireland Office is responsible primarily for security issues, law and order and prisons, and for matters relating to the political and constitutional future of the province. It also deals with international issues as they affect Northern Ireland, including the Anglo-Irish Agreement. The Northern Ireland departments are responsible for the administration of social, industrial and economic policies.

The names of most civil servants are not listed for security reasons.
Secretary of State for Northern Ireland, The Rt. Hon. Dr Marjorie Mowlam, MP
   Special Advisers, N. Warner; Ms A. Healy
   Parliamentary Private Secretary, H. Jackson, MP
Ministers of State, Paul Murphy, MP (*Political Development, Finance, Personnel and Information*); Adam Ingram, MP (*Security, Criminal Justice and Economic Development*)
   Parliamentary Private Secretary to Paul Murphy, M. Gapes, MP
Parliamentary Under-Secretaries of State, The Lord Dubs (*Environment and Agriculture*); Tony Worthington, MP (*Education, Training and Employment, Health and Community Relations*)
Permanent Under-Secretary of State (SCS), Sir John Chilcot, KCB
Second Permanent Under-Secretary of State, Head of the Northern Ireland Civil Service, vacant

LONDON
Deputy Secretary (Political Director)
Under-Secretaries (SCS), (Associate Political Director); (International and Planning; Constitutional and Political; Rights and European); (Personnel and Office Services)
SCS, (Information Services)

BELFAST
Deputy Secretary (Political Director)
Under-Secretaries (Associate Political Director); (Security); (Criminal Justice); (Political); (Personnel and Finance)

EXECUTIVE AGENCIES
COMPENSATION AGENCY, Royston House, Upper Queen Street, Belfast BT1 6FD. Tel: 01232-2499444
FORENSIC SCIENCE AGENCY, Seapark, 151 Belfast Road, Carrickfergus, Co. Antrim BT38 8PL. Tel: 01232-365744
PRISON SERVICE AGENCY, *see* page 382

DEPARTMENT OF AGRICULTURE FOR NORTHERN IRELAND
Dundonald House, Upper Newtownards Road, Belfast BT4 3SB
Tel 01232-520100
Parliamentary Under-Secretary of State, The Lord Dubs
Permanent Secretary (SCS)
Under-Secretaries (SCS), (Central Services and Rural Development); (Food and Farm Policy); (Veterinary); (Science); (Agri-Food Development)

EXECUTIVE AGENCIES
INTERVENTION BOARD
— *see* page 316
RIVERS AGENCY, 4 Hospital Road, Belfast BT8 8JP. Tel: 01232-253355

DEPARTMENT OF ECONOMIC DEVELOPMENT NORTHERN IRELAND
Netherleigh, Massey Avenue, Belfast BT4 2JP
Tel 01232-529900
Minister of State, Adam Ingram, MP
Permanent Secretary (SCS)
Under-Secretaries (SCS), (Resources Group); (Regulatory Services Group)
INDUSTRIAL DEVELOPMENT BOARD, IDB House, 64 Chichester Street, Belfast BT1 4JX. Tel: 01232-233233

EXECUTIVE AGENCIES
INDUSTRIAL RESEARCH AND TECHNOLOGY UNIT, Netherleigh, Massey Avenue, Belfast BT4 2JP. Tel: 01232-529900
TRAINING AND EMPLOYMENT AGENCY (NORTHERN IRELAND), Adelaide Street, Belfast BT2 8FD. Tel: 01232-257777

DEPARTMENT OF EDUCATION FOR NORTHERN IRELAND
Rathgael House, Balloo Road, Bangor, Co. Down BT19 7PR
Tel 01247-279279
Parliamentary Under-Secretary of State, Tony Worthington, MP
Permanent Secretary (SCS)
Under-Secretaries (SCS), (Schools); (Finance and Corporate Services); (Education and Training Inspectorate)

DEPARTMENT OF THE ENVIRONMENT FOR NORTHERN IRELAND
Clarence Court, 10–18 Adelaide Street, Belfast BT2 8GB
Tel 01232-540540
Parliamentary Under-Secretary of State, The Lord Dubs
Permanent Secretary (SCS)
Under-Secretaries (SCS), (Personnel, Finance, Housing and Local Government); (Rural and Urban Affairs); (Roads, Water and Transport); (Planning, Works and Environment)

EXECUTIVE AGENCIES
CONSTRUCTION SERVICE, Churchill House, Victoria Square, Belfast BT1 4QW. Tel: 01232-250284

DRIVER AND VEHICLE LICENSING AGENCY (NORTHERN IRELAND), County Hall, Castlerock Road, Coleraine, Co. Londonderry BT51 3HS. Tel: 01265-41200

DRIVER AND VEHICLE TESTING AGENCY (NORTHERN IRELAND), Balmoral Road, Belfast BT12 6QL. Tel: 01232-681831

ENVIRONMENT AND HERITAGE SERVICE, Commonwealth House, Castle Street, Belfast BT1 1GU. Tel: 01232-251477

LAND REGISTERS OF NORTHERN IRELAND, Lincoln Building, 27–45 Great Victoria Street, Belfast BT2 7SL. Tel: 01232-251515

ORDNANCE SURVEY OF NORTHERN IRELAND, Colby House, Stranmillis Court, Belfast BT9 5BJ. Tel: 01232-255755

PLANNING SERVICE, Clarence Court, 10–18 Adelaide Street, Belfast BT2 8GB. Tel: 01232-540540

PUBLIC RECORD OFFICE (NORTHERN IRELAND) – *see* page 337

RATE COLLECTION AGENCY (NORTHERN IRELAND), Oxford House, 49–55 Chichester Street, Belfast BT1 4HH. Tel: 01232-252252

ROADS SERVICE, Clarence Court, 10–18 Adelaide Street, Belfast BT2 8GB. Tel: 01232-540540

WATER SERVICE, Northland House, 3 Frederick Street, Belfast BT1 2NR. Tel: 01232-244711

ADVISORY BODIES

HISTORIC BUILDINGS COUNCIL FOR NORTHERN IRELAND, c/o Environment and Heritage Service, Historic Monuments and Buildings, Commonwealth House, Castle Street, Belfast BT1 1GU. Tel: 01232-251477

COUNCIL FOR NATURE CONSERVATION AND THE COUNTRYSIDE, c/o Environment and Heritage Service, Commonwealth House, Castle Street, Belfast BT1 1GU. Tel: 01232 251477

DEPARTMENT OF FINANCE AND PERSONNEL

Castle Buildings, Stormont, Upper Newtownards Road, Belfast BT4 3SG
Tel 01232-520400

Minister of State, Paul Murphy, MP
Permanent Secretary (*SCS*)
Under-Secretaries (*SCS*), (Supply Group); (Resources Control and Professional Services Group); (Central Personnel Group); (Government Purchasing Service)

NORTHERN IRELAND CIVIL SERVICE (NICS) Stormont Castle, Belfast BT4 3TT
Tel 01232-520700

Head of Civil Service (*SCS*), vacant
Under-Secretaries (*SCS*), (Central Secretariat); (Legal Services); (Office of the Legislative Council)
GENERAL REGISTER OFFICE (NORTHERN IRELAND), Oxford House, 49–65 Chichester Street, Belfast BT1 4HL. Tel: 01232-252000. *Registrar-General* (*G6*)

EXECUTIVE AGENCIES

BUSINESS DEVELOPMENT SERVICE, Craigantlet Buildings, Stoney Road, Belfast BT4 3SX. Tel: 01232-520400

GOVERNMENT PURCHASING AGENCY, Castle Buildings, Stormont, Upper Newtownards Road, Belfast BT4 3SG. Tel: 01232-520400

NORTHERN IRELAND STATISTICS AND RESEARCH AGENCY, The Arches Centre, 11–13 Bloomfield Avenue, Belfast BT5 5HD. Tel: 01232-526093

VALUATION AND LANDS AGENCY, Queen's Court, 56–66 Upper Queen Street, Belfast BT4 6FD. Tel: 01232-250700

DEPARTMENT OF HEALTH AND SOCIAL SERVICES NORTHERN IRELAND

Castle Buildings, Stormont, Belfast BT4 3PP
Tel 01232-520000

Parliamentary Under-Secretary of State, Tony Worthington, MP
Permanent Secretary (*SCS*)
Chief Medical Officer (*SCS*)
Under-Secretaries (*SCS*), (Health and Social Services Executive); (Health and Social Policy); (Medical and Allied Services); (Central Management and Social Security Policy Group)

EXECUTIVE AGENCIES

NORTHERN IRELAND CHILD SUPPORT AGENCY, Great Northern Tower, 17 Great Victoria Street, Belfast BT2 7AD. Tel: 01232-339000

NORTHERN IRELAND HEALTH AND SOCIAL SERVICES ESTATES AGENCY, Stoney Road, Dundonald, Belfast BT16 0US. Tel: 01232-520025

NORTHERN IRELAND SOCIAL SECURITY AGENCY, Castle Buildings, Stormont, Belfast BT4 3SJ. Tel: 01232-520520

OCCUPATIONAL PENSIONS REGULATORY AUTHORITY

Invicta House, Trafalgar Place, Brighton BN1 4DW
Tel 01273-627600

The Occupational Pensions Regulatory Authority (OPRA) was set up under the Pensions Act 1995 and became fully operational on 6 April 1997. It replaced the Occupational Pensions Board (OPB) as the independent regulator of occupational pension schemes in the UK.
Chairman, J Hayes, CBE
Chief Executive, Ms C. Johnston

OMBUDSMEN

— *see* Local Commissioners *and* Parliamentary Commissioner. For non-statutory Ombudsmen, *see* Index

ORDNANCE SURVEY

Romsey Road, Maybush, Southampton SO16 4GU
Tel 01703-792000

Ordnance Survey is the national mapping agency for Britain. It became an executive agency in 1990 and reports to the Secretary of State for the Environment, Transport and the Regions.
Director-General and Chief Executive, Prof. D. Rhind

OFFICE OF THE PARLIAMENTARY COMMISSIONER FOR ADMINISTRATION AND HEALTH SERVICE COMMISSIONER

Church House, Great Smith Street, London SW1P 3BW
Tel 0171-276 2130 (*Parliamentary Commissioner*); 0171-217 4051 (*Health Service Commissioner*)

The Parliamentary Commissioner for Administration (the Parliamentary Ombudsman) is independent of Govern ment and is an officer of Parliament. He is responsible for investigating complaints referred to him by MPs from members of the public who claim to have sustained injustice in consequence of maladministration by or on behalf of government departments and certain non-departmental public bodies. Certain types of action by government departments or bodies are excluded from investigation. The Parliamentary Commissioner is also responsible for investigating complaints, referred by MPs, alleging that access to official information has been wrongly refused under the Code of Practice on Access to Government Information 1994.

The Health Service Commissioners (the Health Service Ombudsmen) for England, for Scotland and for Wales are responsible for investigating complaints against National Health Service authorities and trusts that are not dealt with by those authorities to the satisfaction of the complainant. Complaints can be referred direct by the member of the public who claims to have sustained injustice or hardship in consequence of the failure in a service provided by a relevant body, failure of that body to provide a service or in consequence of any other action by that body. The Ombudsmens' jurisdiction now covers complaints about family doctors, dentists, pharmacists and opticians, and complaints about actions resulting from clinical judgment. The Health Service Ombudsmen are also responsible for investigating complaints that information has been wrongly refused under the Code of Practice on Openness in the National Health Service 1995. The three offices are presently held by the Parliamentary Commissioner.

Parliamentary Commissioner and Health Service Commissioner (*G1*), M. S. Buckley
Deputy Parliamentary Commissioners (*G3*), J. E. Avery, CB; J. Tate
Deputy Health Service Commissioners (*G3*), C. H. Wilson; Miss M. I. Nisbet
Directors, Parliamentary Commissioner (*G5*), N. Cleary; D. J. Coffey; Mrs S. P. Maunsell; G. Monk; A. Watson
Directors, Health Service Commissioners (*G5*), Miss H. Bainbridge; D. P. Flaherty; N. J. Jordan; R. H. Keynes; D. R. G. Pinchin; R. Tyrrell
Finance and Establishment Officer (*G5*), T. G. Hull

PARLIAMENTARY COMMISSIONER FOR STANDARDS
House of Commons, London SW1A 0AA
Tel 0171-219 0320

Following recommendations of the Committee on Standards in Public Life (the Nolan Committee) the House of Commons agreed to the appointment of an independent Parliamentary Commissioner for Standards. The Commissioner was appointed with effect from November 1995 and has responsibility for maintaining and monitoring the operation of the Register of Members' Interests; advising Members of Parliament and the select committee on standards and privileges on the interpretation of the rules on disclosure and advocacy and on other questions of propriety; and receiving and, if he thinks fit, investigating complaints about the conduct of MPs.
Parliamentary Commissioner for Standards, Sir Gordon Downey, KCB

PARLIAMENTARY COUNSEL
36 Whitehall, London SW1A 2AY
Tel 0171-210 6637

Parliamentary Counsel draft all government bills (i.e. primary legislation) except those relating exclusively to Scotland, the latter being drafted by the Lord Advocate's Department. They also advise on all aspects of parliamentary procedure in connection with such bills and draft government amendments to them as well as any motions (including financial resolutions) necessary to secure their introduction into, and passage through, Parliament.
First Counsel (SCS), J. C. Jenkins, CB, QC
Counsel (SCS), D. W. Saunders, CB; E. G. Caldwell, CB; E. G. Bowman, CB; G. B. Sellers, CB; E. R. Sutherland, CB; P. F. A. Knowles, CB; S. C. Laws, CB; R. S. Parker; Miss C. E. Johnston; P. J. Davies

PARLIAMENTARY OMBUDSMAN FOR NORTHERN IRELAND AND NORTHERN IRELAND COMMISSIONER FOR COMPLAINTS
Progressive House, 33 Wellington Place, Belfast BT1 6HN
Tel 01232-233821

The Ombudsman is appointed under legislation with powers to investigate complaints by people claiming to have sustained injustice in consequence of maladministration arising from action taken by a Northern Ireland government department, or any other public body within his remit. Staff are presently seconded from the Northern Ireland Civil Service.
Ombudsman, G. Burns, MBE
Deputy Ombudsman, J. MacQuarrie
Directors, C. O'Hare; R. Doherty

PAROLE BOARD FOR ENGLAND AND WALES
Abell House, John Islip Street, London SW1P 4LH
Tel 0171-217 5314

The Board was constituted under the Criminal Justice Act 1967 and continued under the Criminal Justice Act 1991. It is a non-departmental public body and its duty is to advise the Home Secretary with respect to matters referred to it by him which are connected with the early release or recall of prisoners. Its functions include giving directions concerning the release on licence of prisoners serving discretionary life sentences and of certain prisoners serving long-term determinate sentences.
Chairman, The Lord Belstead, PC
Vice-Chairman, The Hon. Mr Justice Alliott
Chief Executive, M. S. Todd

PAROLE BOARD FOR SCOTLAND
Saughton House, Broomhouse Drive, Edinburgh EH11 3XD
Tel 0131-244 8755

The Board directs and advises the Secretary of State for Scotland on the release of prisoners on licence, and related matters.
Chairman, I. McNee

Vice-Chairman, Sheriff G. Shiach
Secretary, H. P. Boyle

PASSENGER RAIL FRANCHISING, OFFICE OF
— *see* Transport section

PATENT OFFICE
Cardiff Road, Newport NP9 IRH
Tel 0645-500505

The Patent Office is an executive agency of the Department of Trade and Industry. The duties of the Patent Office are to administer the Patent Acts, the Registered Designs Act and the Trade Marks Act, and to deal with questions relating to the Copyright, Designs and Patents Act 1988. The Search and Advisory Service carries out commercial searches through patent information. In 1995 the Office granted 9,475 patents and registered 8,380 designs and 33,400 trade marks.
Comptroller-General, P. R. S. Hartnack
Director, Intellectual Property Policy Directorate, G. Jenkins
Director, Patents and Designs, R. J. Marchant
Director and Assistant Registrar of Trade Marks, N. Harkness
Director, Administration and Resources and Secretary to the Patent Office, C. Octon
Director, Copyright, J. Startup
Director, Finance, J. Thompson

HM PAYMASTER-GENERAL
— *see* National Investment and Loans Office

OFFICE OF THE PENSIONS OMBUDSMAN
11 Belgrave Road, London SW1V IRB
Tel 0171-834 9144

The Pensions Ombudsman is appointed by the Secretary of State for Social Security under the Pension Schemes Act 1993 to deal with complaints and disputes concerning occupational pension schemes. He is completely independent.
Pensions Ombudsman, Dr J. T. Farrand

POLICE COMPLAINTS AUTHORITY
10 Great George Street, London SW1P 3AE
Tel 0171-273 6450

The Police Complaints Authority was established under the Police and Criminal Evidence Act 1984 to provide an independent system for dealing with serious complaints by members of the public against police officers in England and Wales. It is funded by the Home Office. The authority has powers to supervise the investigation of certain categories of serious complaints and certain statutory functions in relation to the disciplinary aspects of complaints. It does not deal with police operational matters; these are usually dealt with by the Chief Constable of the relevant force.
Chairman, P. Moorhouse
Deputy Chairman (Investigations), J. Cartwright
Members, Mrs L. Allan; N. Dholakia, OBE; Ms J. Dobry; J. Elliott; A. Kelly; M. Meacher; Mrs C. Mitchell; A. Potts; Mrs M. Scorer; Ms L. Whyte; A. Williams

INDEPENDENT COMMISSION FOR POLICE COMPLAINTS FOR NORTHERN IRELAND
— *see* page 313

POLITICAL HONOURS SCRUTINY COMMITTEE
Cabinet Office, 53 Parliament Street, London SW1A 2NG
Tel 0171-210 5058

The function of the Political Honours Scrutiny Committee (a committee of Privy Councillors) was set out in an Order of Council in 1991 and amended by Orders in Council in 1994 and 1997. The Prime Minister submits certain particulars to the Committee about persons proposed to be recommended for honour for their political services. The Committee, after such enquiry as they think fit, report to the Prime Minister whether, so far as they believe, the persons whose names are submitted to them are fit and proper persons to be recommended.
Chairman, The Lord Pym, MC, PC
Members, The Lord Cledwyn of Penrhos, CH, PC; The Lord Thomson of Monifieth, KT, PC
Secretary, A. J. Merifield, CB

PORT OF LONDON AUTHORITY
Devon House, 58 – 60 St Katharine's Way, London E1 9LB
Tel 0171-265 2656

The Port of London Authority is a public trust constituted under the Port of London Act 1908 and subsequent legislation. It is the governing body for the Port of London, covering the tidal portion of the River Thames from Teddington to the seaward limit. The Board comprises a chairman and up to seven but not less than four non-executive members appointed by the Secretary of State for the Environment, Transport and the Regions, and up to four but not less than one executive members appointed by the Board.
Chairman, Sir Brian Shaw
Vice-Chairman, J. H. Kelly, CBE
Chief Executive, D. Jeffery
Secretary, G. E. Ennals

THE POST OFFICE
148 Old Street, London EC1V 9HQ
Tel 0171-490 2888

Crown services for the carriage of government dispatches were set up in about 1516. The conveyance of public correspondence began in 1635 and the mail service was made a parliamentary responsibility with the setting up of a Post Office in 1657. Telegraphs came under Post Office control in 1870 and the Post Office Telephone Service began in 1880. The National Girobank service of the Post Office began in 1968. The Post Office ceased to be a government department in 1969 when responsibility for the running of the postal, telecommunications, giro and remittance services was transferred to a public authority called The Post Office. The 1981 British Telecommunications Act separated the functions of the Post Office, making it solely responsible for postal services and Girobank. Girobank was privatized in 1990.

The chairman, chief executive and members of the Post Office Board are appointed by the President of the Board of

Trade but responsibility for the running of the Post Office as a whole rests with the Board in its corporate capacity.

FINANCIAL RESULTS £m	1995–6	1996–7
Post Office Group		
Turnover	6,210	6,370
Profit before tax	422	577
Royal Mail		
Turnover	4,804	5,019
Profit before tax	354	463
Parcelforce		
Turnover	471	457
Profit (loss) before tax	1	(21)
Post Office Counters		
Turnover	1,195	1,161
Profit before tax	35	34

POST OFFICE BOARD
Chairman, Sir Michael Heron
Chief Executive, J. Roberts, CBE
Members, R. Close (*Managing Director, Finance*); J. Cope (*Managing Director, Strategy and Personnel*)
Secretary, R. Adams

For postal services, *see* pages 514–16

PRIME MINISTER'S OFFICE
— *see* page 288

PRISONS OMBUDSMAN FOR ENGLAND AND WALES
St Vincent House, 30 Orange Street, London WC2H 7HH
Tel 0171-389 1527

The post of Prisons Ombudsman was instituted in 1994. The Ombudsman is appointed by the Home Secretary and is an independent point of appeal for prisoners' grievances about their lives in prison, including disciplinary issues. The Ombudsman cannot investigate grievances relating to issues which are the subject of litigation or criminal proceedings, decisions taken by ministers, or actions of bodies outside the prison service.
Prisons Ombudsman, Sir Peter Woodhead, KCB

For Scotland, *see* Scottish Prisons Complaints Commission

PRIVY COUNCIL OFFICE
Whitehall, London SW1A 2AT
Tel 0171-270 3000

The Office is responsible for the arrangements leading to the making of all royal proclamations and Orders in Council; for certain formalities connected with ministerial changes; for considering applications for the granting (or amendment) of royal charters; for the scrutiny and approval of by-laws and statutes of chartered bodies; and for the appointment of High Sheriffs and many Crown and Privy Council appointments to governing bodies.
President of the Council (and Leader of the House of Commons), The Rt. Hon. Ann Taylor, MP
Private Secretary, P. Cohen
Special Adviser, I. McKenzie
Parliamentary Private Secretary, M. Hall, MP
Clerk of the Council (G3), N. H. Nicholls, CBE
Deputy Clerk of the Council (G5), Miss K. P. Makin, OBE
Senior Clerk, Miss M. A. McCullagh

PROCURATOR FISCAL SERVICE
— *see* pages 366–7

PUBLIC HEALTH LABORATORY SERVICE
61 Colindale Avenue, London NW9 5DF
Tel 0181-200 1295

The Public Health Laboratory Service comprises nine groups of laboratories, the Central Public Health Laboratory and the Communicable Disease Surveillance Centre. The PHLS provides diagnostic microbiological services to hospitals, and has reference facilities that are available nationally. It collates information on the incidence of infection, and when necessary it institutes special inquiries into outbreaks and the epidemiology of infectious disease. It also undertakes bacteriological surveillance of the quality of food and water for local authorities and others.
Chairman (£15,125), Prof. Sir Leslie Turnberg, MD, PRCP
Deputy Chairman, D. Noble, CBE
Director, Dr Diana Walford, FRCP, FRCpath.
Deputy Directors, Prof. B. I. Duerden, MD, FRCpath. (*Programmes*); K. M. Saunders (*Corporate Planning and Resources*)
Board Secretary, K. M. Saunders

CENTRAL PUBLIC HEALTH LABORATORY
Colindale Avenue, London NW9 5HT
Director, Prof. S. P. Borriello

COMMUNICABLE DISEASES SURVEILLANCE CENTRE
Colindale Avenue, NW9 5EQ
Director, Dr C. L. R. Bartlett

PHLS GROUPS OF LABORATORIES AND GROUP DIRECTORS
East, Dr P. M. B. White
Midlands, Dr R. E. Warren
North, Dr N. F. Lightfoot
North-West, Dr P. Morgan-Capner
South Thames, Prof. R. Y. Cartwright
South-West, Dr K. A. V. Cartwright
Trent, Dr P. J. Wilkinson
Wessex, Dr S. A. Rousseau
Wales, Dr A. J. Howard

OTHER SPECIAL LABORATORIES AND UNITS
ANAEROBE REFERENCE UNIT, Public Health Laboratory, Cardiff. *Head,* Prof. B. I. Duerden, MD, FRCpath.
ANTIVIRAL SUSCEPTIBILITY REFERENCE UNIT, Public Health Laboratory, Birmingham. *Head,* Dr D. P. Pillay
CRYPTOSPRORIDIUM REFERENCE UNIT, Public Health Laboratory, Rhyl. *Head,* D. N. Looker
FOOD MICROBIOLOGY RESEARCH UNIT, Public Health Laboratory, Exeter. *Head,* Prof. T. J. Humphrey
GENITO-URINARY INFECTIONS REFERENCE LABORATORY, Public Health Laboratory, Bristol. *Head,* Dr J. Herring
LEPTOSPIRA REFERENCE LABORATORY, Public Health Laboratory, Hereford. *Director,* Dr T. J. Coleman
LYME DISEASE REFERENCE UNIT, Public Health Laboratory, Southampton. *Head,* Dr A. Lowes
MALARIA REFERENCE LABORATORY, London School of Hygiene and Tropical Medicine, London WC1E 7HT. *Directors,* Prof. D. J. Bradley, DM; Dr D. C. Warhurst, FRCpath.
MENINGOCOCCAL REFERENCE LABORATORY, Public Health Laboratory, Manchester. *Director,* Dr B. A. Oppenheim
MYCOBACTERIUM REFERENCE UNIT, Public Health Laboratory, Dulwich, London. *Head,* Dr F. Drobniewski

MYCOLOGY REFERENCE LABORATORY, Public Health Laboratory, Bristol. *Head*, Dr D. Warnock; University of Leeds. *Head*, Prof. E. G. V. Evans

PARASITOLOGY REFERENCE LABORATORY, Hospital for Tropical Diseases, London. *Director*, Dr P. L. Chiodini

TOXOPLASMA REFERENCE LABORATORIES, Public Health Laboratory, Swansea. *Head*, D. H. M. Joynson; Public Health Laboratory, Tooting, London. *Head*, Prof. A. R. M. Coates

WATER AND ENVIRONMENTAL MICROBIOLOGY RESEARCH UNIT, Public Health Laboratory, Nottingham. *Head*, Dr J. V. Lee

---

REGISTRAR OF PUBLIC LENDING RIGHT
Bayheath House, Prince Regent Street,
Stockton-on-Tees TS18 1DF
Tel 01642-604699

Under the Public Lending Right system, in operation since 1983, payment is made from public funds to authors whose books are lent out from public libraries. Payment is made once a year and the amount each author receives is proportionate to the number of times (established from a sample) that each registered book has been lent out during the previous year. The Registrar of PLR, who is appointed by the Secretary of State for Culture, Media and Sport, compiles the register of authors and books. Only living authors resident in the UK or Germany are eligible to apply. (The term 'author' covers writers, illustrators, translators, and some editors/compilers.)

A payment of 2.07 pence was made in 1996–7 for each estimated loan of a registered book, up to a top limit of £6,000 for the books of any one registered author; the money for loans above this level is used to augment the remaining PLR payments. In February 1997, the sum of £4.346 million was made available for distribution to 21,055 registered authors and assignees as the annual payment of PLR.

The PLR Advisory Committee advises the Secretary of State for Culture, Media and Sport and the Registrar of Public Lending Right. Its members are appointed by the Secretary of State.

Chairman of Advisory Committee, vacant
Registrar, Dr J. G. Parker

PUBLIC RECORD OFFICE
— *see* page 336

PUBLIC TRUST OFFICE
Stewart House, 24 Kingsway, London WC2B 6JX
Tel 0171-664 7000
COURT FUNDS OFFICE, 22 Kingsway, London WC2B 6LE
Tel 0171-936 6000

The Public Trust Office became an executive agency of the Lord Chancellor's Department in 1994. The chief executive of the agency holds the statutory titles of Public Trustee and Accountant-General of the Supreme Court.

The Public Trustee is a trust corporation created to undertake the business of executorship and trusteeship; she can act as executor or administrator of the estate of a deceased person, or as trustee of a will or settlement. The Public Trustee is also responsible for the performance of all the administrative, but not the judicial, tasks required of the Court of Protection under Part VII of the Mental Health Act 1983, relating to the management and administration of the property and affairs of persons suffering

from mental disorder. The Public Trustee also acts as Receiver when so directed by the Court, usually where there is no other person willing or able so to act.

The Accountant-General of the Supreme Court, through the Court Funds Office, is responsible for the investment and accounting of funds in court for persons under a disability, monies in court subject to litigation and statutory deposits.

Chief Executive (Public Trustee and Accountant-General), Ms J. C. Lomas
Assistant Public Trustee, Mrs S. Hutcheson
Investment Manager, H. Stevenson
Chief Property Adviser, A. Nightingale

MENTAL HEALTH SECTOR
Head, Mrs H. M. Bratton
Receivership Activity, D. Adams
Protection Activity, P. L. Hales

TRUSTS AND FUNDS SECTOR
Head, F. J. Eddy
Court Funds Activity, R. Anns
Trust Activity, M. Munt

ESTABLISHMENTS AND FINANCE SECTOR
Head, E. A. Bloomfield
Finance, M. Guntrip
Planning, Mrs N. M. Hunt

PUBLIC WORKS LOAN BOARD
— *see* National Investment and Loans Office

COMMISSION FOR RACIAL EQUALITY
Elliot House, 10–12 Allington Street, London SW1E 5EH
Tel 0171-828 7022

The Commission was established in 1977, under the Race Relations Act 1976, to work towards the elimination of discrimination and promote equality of opportunity and good relations between different racial groups. It is funded by the Home Office.

Chairman, Sir Herman Ouseley
Deputy Chairs, Mrs Z. Manzoor; H. Harris
Commissioners, R. Purkiss; Dr D. Neil; Ms M. Cunningham; Dr R. Chandran; M. Hastings; Dr M. Jogee; Ms J. Mellor; Ms B. Cluff; Dame Simone Prendergast, DBE; Dr Z. Khan
Executive Director, D. Sharma

THE RADIO AUTHORITY
Holbrook House, 14 Great Queen Street, London WC2B 5DG
Tel 0171-430 2724

The Radio Authority was established in 1991 under the Broadcasting Act 1990. It is the regulator and licensing authority for all independent radio services. Members of the Authority are appointed by the Secretary of State for Culture, Media and Sport; senior executive staff are appointed by the Authority.

Chairman, Sir Peter Gibbings
Deputy Chairman, M. Moriarty, CB
Members, Ms J. Francis; M. Reupke; Lady Sheil; A. Reid; Mrs H. Tennant
Chief Executive, A. Stoller
Deputy Chief Executive, D. Vick
Secretary to the Authority, J. Norrington

OFFICE OF THE RAIL REGULATOR
1 Waterhouse Square, 138–142 Holborn, London
ECIN 2ST
Tel 0171-282 2000

The Office of the Rail Regulator was set up under the Railways Act 1993. It is headed by the Rail Regulator, who is independent of ministerial control. The Regulator's main functions are the licensing of operators of railway assets; the approval of agreements for access by those operators to track, stations and light maintenance depots; the enforcement of domestic competition law; and consumer protection. The Regulator also sponsors a network of Rail Users' Consultative Committees, which represent the interests of passengers.
Rail Regulator, J. A. Swift, QC
Director, Resources and RUCC Sponsorship, P. D. Murphy
Director, Economic Regulation Group, C. W. Bolt
Director, Railway Network Group, C. J. F. Brown
Director, Passenger Services Group, J. A. Rhodes
Chief Legal Adviser, M. R. Brocklehurst

RECORD OFFICES

ADVISORY COUNCIL ON PUBLIC RECORDS
Secretariat: Public Record Office, Ruskin Avenue, Kew, Richmond, Surrey TW9 4DU
Tel 0181-876 3444

Council members are appointed by the Lord Chancellor, under the Public Records Act 1958, to advise him on matters concerning public records in general and, in particular, on those aspects of the work of the Public Record Office which affect members of the public who make use of it. The Council meets quarterly and produces an annual report which is published alongside the Report of the Keeper of Public Records as a House of Commons sessional paper.
Chairman, The Master of the Rolls
Secretary, T. R. Padfield

THE PUBLIC RECORD OFFICE
Ruskin Avenue, Kew, Richmond, Surrey TW9 4DU
Tel 0181-876 3444

The Public Record Office, originally established in 1838 under the Master of the Rolls, was placed under the direction of the Lord Chancellor in 1958. It became an executive agency in 1992. The Lord Chancellor appoints a Keeper of Public Records, whose duties are to co-ordinate and supervise the selection of records of government departments and the law courts for permanent preservation, to safeguard the records and to make them available to the public. There is a separate record office for Scotland (*see* page 337).
    The Office holds records of central government dating from the Domesday Book (1086) to the present. Under the Public Records Act 1967 they are normally open to inspection when 30 years old, and are then available, without charge, in the reading rooms (Monday, Wednesday, Friday, Saturday, 9.30–5; Tuesday 10–7; Thursday 9.30–7).
Keeper of Public Records (G3), Mrs S. Tyacke
Director, Public Services Division (G5), Dr E. Hallam Smith
Director, Government Services Division (G5), Dr N. G. Cox
Director, Corporate Services Division (G5), Dr D. Simpson

HOUSE OF LORDS RECORD OFFICE
House of Lords, London SW1A 0PW
Tel 0171-219 3074

Since 1497, the records of Parliament have been kept within the Palace of Westminster. They are in the custody of the Clerk of the Parliaments. In 1946 a record department was established to supervise their preservation and their availability to the public. The search room of the office is open to the public Monday–Friday, 9.30–5 (Tuesday to 8, by appointment).
    Some three million documents are preserved, including Acts of Parliament from 1497, journals of the House of Lords from 1510, minutes and committee proceedings from 1610, and papers laid before Parliament from 1531. Amongst the records are the Petition of Right, the Death Warrant of Charles I, the Declaration of Breda, and the Bill of Rights. The House of Lords Record Office also has charge of the journals of the House of Commons (from 1547), and other surviving records of the Commons (from 1572), including documents relating to private bill legislation from 1818. Among other documents are the records of the Lord Great Chamberlain, the political papers of certain members of the two Houses, and documents relating to Parliament acquired on behalf of the nation. A permanent exhibition was established in the Royal Gallery in 1979.
Clerk of the Records (£43,676–£68,976), D. J. Johnson, FSA
Deputy Clerk of the Records (£32,962–£53,481), S. K. Ellison
Assistant Clerk of the Records (£22,410–£28,932), D. L. Prior

ROYAL COMMISSION ON HISTORICAL MANUSCRIPTS
Quality House, Quality Court, Chancery Lane, London
WC2A 1HP
Tel 0171-242 1198

The Commission was set up by royal warrant in 1869 to enquire and report on collections of papers of value for the study of history which were in private hands. In 1959 a new warrant enlarged these terms of reference to include all historical records, wherever situated, outside the Public Records and gave it added responsibilities as a central co-ordinating body to promote, assist and advise on their proper preservation and storage. The Commission, which is responsible to the Department for Culture, Media and Sport, has published over 200 volumes of reports.
    It also maintains the National Register of Archives (NRA), which contains over 40,000 unpublished lists and catalogues of manuscript collections describing the holdings of local record offices, national and university libraries, specialist repositories and others in the UK and overseas. The NRA can be searched using computerized indices which are available in the Commission's search room.
    The Commission also administers the Manorial and Tithe Documents Rules on behalf of the Master of the Rolls.
Chairman, The Lord Bingham of Cornhill, PC
Commissioners, The Lord Blake, FBA; Prof. S. F. C. Milsom, FBA; Sir Patrick Cormack, FSA, MP; D. G. Vaisey, CBE, FSA; The Lord Egremont and Leconfield; Sir Matthew Farrer, GCVO; Miss B. Harvey, FBA, FSA; Sir John Sainty, KCB, FSA; Prof. R. H. Campbell, OBE, Ph.D.; Very Revd H. E. C. Stapleton, FSA; Sir Keith Thomas, PBA; Mrs C. M. Short; The Earl of Scarbrough; Mrs A. Dundas-Bekker; G. E. Aylmer, D.Phil, FBA; Mrs S. J. Davies, Ph.D.
Secretary, C. J. Kitching, Ph.D., FSA

SCOTTISH RECORDS ADVISORY COUNCIL
HM General Register House, Edinburgh EH1 3YY
Tel 0131-535 1314

The Council was established under the Public Records (Scotland) Act 1937. Its members are appointed by the Secretary of State for Scotland and it may submit proposals or make representations to the Secretary of State, the Lord Justice General or the Lord President of the Court of Session on questions relating to the public records of Scotland.
Chairman, Prof. M. A. Crowther
Secretary, D. M. Abbott

SCOTTISH RECORD OFFICE
HM General Register House, Edinburgh EH1 3YY
Tel 0131-535 1314

The history of the national archives of Scotland can be traced back to the 13th century. The Scottish Record Office keeps the administrative records of pre-Union Scotland, the registers of central and local courts of law, the public registers of property rights and legal documents, and many collections of local and church records and private archives. Certain groups of records, mainly the modern records of government departments in Scotland, the Scottish railway records, the plans collection, and private archives of an industrial or commercial nature, are preserved in the branch repository at the West Register House in Charlotte Square. The search rooms in both buildings are open Monday–Friday, 9–4.45. A permanent exhibition at the West Register House and changing exhibitions at the General Register House are open to the public on weekdays, 10–4. The National Register of Archives (Scotland), which is a branch of the Scottish Record Office, is based in the West Register House.

The Scottish Record Office became an executive agency of the Scottish Office in 1993.
Keeper of the Records of Scotland, P. M. Cadell
Deputy Keeper, Dr P. D. Anderson

PUBLIC RECORD OFFICE (NORTHERN IRELAND)
66 Balmoral Avenue, Belfast BT9 6NY
Tel 01232-251318

The Public Record Office (Northern Ireland) is responsible for identifying and preserving Northern Ireland's archival heritage and making it available to the public. It is an executive agency of the Department of the Environment for Northern Ireland. The search room is open on weekdays, 9.15–4.15 (Thursday, 9.15–8.15).
Chief Executive, Dr A. P. W. Malcomson

CORPORATION OF LONDON RECORDS OFFICE
Guildhall, London EC2P 2EJ
Tel 0171-332 1251

The Corporation of London Records Office contains the municipal archives of the City of London which are regarded as the most complete collection of ancient municipal records in existence. The collection includes charters of William the Conqueror, Henry II, and later kings and queens to 1957; ancient custumals: Liber Horn, Dunthorne, Custumarum, Ordinacionum, Memorandorum and Albus, Liber de Antiquis Legibus, and collections of Statutes; continuous series of judicial rolls and books from 1252 and Council minutes from 1275; records of the Old Bailey and Guildhall Sessions from 1603; financial records from the 16th century; the records of London Bridge from the 12th century; and numerous subsidiary series and miscellanea of historical interest. Readers' Room open Monday–Friday, 9.30–4.45.
Keeper of the City Records, The City Secretary

City Archivist, J. R. Sewell
Deputy City Archivist, Mrs J. M. Bankes

RESEARCH COUNCILS
— *see* pages 700–6

REVIEW BODIES

The secretariat for these bodies is provided by the Office of Manpower Economics (*see* page 323)

ARMED FORCES PAY

The Review Body on Armed Forces Pay was appointed in 1971 to advise the Prime Minister on the pay and allowances of members of naval, military and air forces of the Crown and of any women's service administered by the Defence Council.
Chairman, Sir Gordon Hourston
Members, C. M. Bolton; Mrs K. Coleman, OBE; J. C. L. Cox, CBE; J. Crosby; Vice-Adm. Sir Toby Frere, KCB; Sir Gavin Laird; Mrs D. Venables

DOCTORS' AND DENTISTS' REMUNERATION

The Review Body on Doctors' and Dentists' Remuneration was set up in 1971 to advise the Prime Minister on the remuneration of doctors and dentists taking any part in the National Health Service.
Chairman, C. B. Gough
Members, Mrs B. Brewer; Mrs C. Hui; M. Innes; R. Jackson; C. King, CBE; Dr E. Nelson; D. Penton

NURSING STAFF, MIDWIVES, HEALTH VISITORS AND PROFESSIONS ALLIED TO MEDICINE

The Review Body for nursing staff, midwives, health visitors and professions allied to medicine was set up in 1983 to advise the Prime Minister on the remuneration of nursing staff, midwives and health visitors employed in the National Health Service; and also of physiotherapists, radiographers, remedial gymnasts, occupational therapists, orthoptists, chiropodists, dietitians and related grades employed in the National Health Service.
Chairman, B. Rigby
Members, Mrs A. Dean; Mrs S. Gleig; L. Haddon; Ms R. Lea; Miss A. Mackie, OBE; K. Miles; Prof. G. Raab

SCHOOL TEACHERS

The School Teachers' Review Body (STRB) is a statutory body, set up under the School Teachers' Pay and Conditions Act 1991. It is required to examine and report on such matters relating to the statutory conditions of employment of school teachers in England and Wales as may be referred to it by the Secretary of State for Education and Employment. The STRB's reports are submitted to the Prime Minister and the Secretary of State and the latter is required to publish them.
Chairman, A. R. Vineall
Members, Mrs B. Amey; Mrs J. Cuthbertson; P. Gedling; M. Harding; V. Harris; Miss J. Langdon

SENIOR SALARIES

A Top Salaries Review Body was set up in 1971 to advise the Prime Minister on the remuneration of the higher judiciary and other judicial appointments, senior civil servants, and senior officers of the armed forces. In 1993 its name was changed to the Senior Salaries Review Body, and its remit was officially extended to cover the pay, pensions and allowances of MPs, ministers and others whose pay is determined by a Ministerial and Other Salaries Order, and the allowances of peers.

Chairman, Sir Michael Perry, CBE

Members, M. Beloff, QC; D. Clayman; Prof. S. Dawson; Mrs R. Day; Sir Gordon Hourston; Sir Sydney Lipworth, QC; Miss P. Mann; M. Sheldon; Sir Anthony Wilson

ROYAL BOTANIC GARDEN EDINBURGH
20A Inverleith Row, Edinburgh EH3 5LR
Tel 0131-552 7171

The Royal Botanic Garden Edinburgh (RBGE) originated as the Physic Garden, established in 1670 beside the Palace of Holyroodhouse. The Garden moved to its present 28-hectare site at Inverleith, Edinburgh, in 1821. There are also three specialist gardens: Younger Botanic Garden Benmore, near Dunoon, Argyllshire; Logan Botanic Garden, near Stranraer, Wigtownshire; and Dawyck Botanic Garden, near Stobo, Peeblesshire. Since 1986, RBGE has been administered by a Board of Trustees established under the National Heritage (Scotland) Act 1985. It receives an annual grant from the Scottish Office.

RBG Edinburgh is an international centre for scientific research on plant diversity and for education and conservation. It has an extensive library and a herbarium with over two million dried plant specimens. Public opening hours: RBGE, daily (except Christmas Day and New Year's Day) November–January 9.30–4; February and October 9.30–5; March and September 9.30–6; April–June 9.30–7; July–August 9.30–8; specialist gardens, 1 March–31 October 9.30–6. Admission free to RBGE; admission charge to specialist gardens.

Chairman of the Board of Trustees, Prof. M. Wilkins, FRSE
Regius Keeper, Prof. D. S. Ingram, FRSE

ROYAL BOTANIC GARDENS KEW
Richmond, Surrey TW9 3AB
Tel 0181-940 1171
Wakehurst Place, Ardingly, nr Haywards Heath,
W. Sussex RH17 6TN
Tel 01444-894066

The Royal Botanic Gardens (RBG) Kew were originally laid out as a private garden for Kew House for George III's mother, HRH Princess Augusta, in 1759. They were much enlarged in the 19th century, notably by the inclusion of the grounds of the former Richmond Lodge. In 1965 the garden at Wakehurst Place was acquired; it is owned by the National Trust and managed by RBG Kew. Under the National Heritage Act 1983 a Board of Trustees was set up to administer the Gardens which in 1984 became an independent body supported by grant-in-aid from the Ministry of Agriculture, Fisheries and Food.

The functions of RBG Kew are to carry out research into plant sciences, to disseminate knowledge about plants and to provide the public with the opportunity to gain knowledge and enjoyment from the Gardens' collections. There are extensive national reference collections of living and preserved plants and a comprehensive library and archive. The main emphasis is on plant conservation and bio-diversity.

Open daily (except Christmas Day and New Year's Day) from 9.30 a.m. (Wakehurst, 10 a.m.). The closing hour varies from 4 p.m. in mid-winter to 6 p.m. on weekdays and 7.30 p.m. on Sundays and Bank Holidays in mid-summer. Admission (1997, £4.50. Concessionary schemes available. Glasshouses (Kew only), 9.30–4.30 (winter); 9.30–5.30 (summer). No dogs except guide-dogs for the blind.

BOARD OF TRUSTEES
Chairman, R. A. E. Herbert, CBE
Members, R. P. Bauman; The Viscount Blakenham; Sir Jeffery Bowman; Prof. H. Dickinson; Miss A. Ford; S. de Grey; Lady Lennox-Boyd; The Lady Renfrew of Kaimsthorn, PH.D., FSA, FSA SCOT.; The Earl of Selborne, KBE, FRS (*Queen's Trustee*); Prof. M. Crawley; Prof. J. S. Parker
Director, Prof. Sir Ghillean Prance, FRS

ROYAL COMMISSION FOR THE EXHIBITION OF 1851
Sherfield Building, Imperial College of Science, Technology and Medicine, London SW7 2AZ
Tel 0171-594 8790

The Royal Commission was incorporated by supplemental charter as a permanent Commission after winding up the affairs of the Great Exhibition of 1851. Its object is to promote scientific and artistic education by means of funds derived from its Kensington estate, purchased with the surplus left over from the Great Exhibition.

President, HRH The Prince Philip, Duke of Edinburgh, KG, KT, PC
Chairman, Board of Management, Sir Denis Rooke, CBE, FRS, FEng.
Secretary to Commissioners, J. P. W. Middleton, CB

THE ROYAL MINT
Llantrisant, Pontyclun, Mid Glamorgan CF72 8YT
Tel 01443-222111

The prime responsibility of the Royal Mint is the provision of United Kingdom coinage, but it actively competes in world markets for a share of the available circulating coin business and, based on the last ten years, two-thirds of the 18,000 tonnes of coins produced annually is exported. The Mint also manufactures special proof and uncirculated quality coins in gold, silver and other metals; military and civil decorations and medals; commemorative and prize medals; and royal and official seals.

The Royal Mint became an executive agency of the Treasury in 1990.

Master of the Mint, The Chancellor of the Exchequer (*ex officio*)
Deputy Master and Comptroller, R. de L. Holmes

ROYAL NATIONAL THEATRE BOARD
South Bank, London, SE1 9PX
Tel 0171-928 2033

The chairman and members of the Board of the Royal National Theatre are appointed by the Secretary of State for Culture, Media and Sport.

Chairman, Sir Christopher Hogg

Members, The Hon. P. Benson; The Hon. Lady Cazalet; M. Codron, CBE; Lady Greenbury; Ms S. Hall; Sir David Hancock, KCB; G. Hutchings; Ms K. Jones; S. Lipton; D. Nandy; M. Oliver; Sir Tom Stoppard, CBE; P. Wiegand
Company Secretary, Ms A. McGregor
Director, T. Nunn, CBE

RURAL DEVELOPMENT COMMISSION
141 Castle Street, Salisbury, Wilts. SP1 3TP
Tel 01722-336255

The Rural Development Commission is the government agency for economic and social development in rural England. The Commission gives advice to the Government and undertakes activities aimed at stimulating job creation and the provision of essential services in the countryside. Its sponsoring department is the Department of the Environment, Transport and the Regions.
Chairman, The Lord Shuttleworth
Chief Executive, R. Butt

SCOTTISH COURTS ADMINISTRATION
— *see* page 365

SCOTTISH ENTERPRISE
120 Bothwell Street, Glasgow G2 7JP
Tel 0141-248 2700

In 1991 Scottish Enterprise took over the economic development and environmental improvement functions of the Scottish Development Agency and the training functions of the Training Agency in lowland Scotland. It is funded by the Scottish Office and its remit is to further the development of Scotland's economy, to enhance the skills of the Scottish workforce, to promote Scotland's international competitiveness and to improve the environment. Many of its functions are contracted out to a network of 13 local enterprise companies. Through Locate in Scotland (*see* page 341), Scottish Enterprise is also concerned with attracting firms to Scotland.
Chairman (acting), Sir Ian Wood
Chief Executive, C. Beveridge, CBE

SCOTTISH ENVIRONMENT PROTECTION AGENCY
Erskine Court, The Castle Business Park, Stirling FK9 4TR
Tel 01786-457700

The Scottish Environment Protection Agency came into being on 1 April 1996 under the Environment Act 1995. It brings together the work formerly undertaken by HM Industrial Pollution Inspectorate, the river purification authorities, and local councils in respect of waste regulation and some air pollution controls. It has regional offices in East Kilbride, Riccarton and Dingwall, and 17 local offices throughout Scotland. It receives funding from the Scottish Office.
THE BOARD
Chairman, Prof. W. Turmeau, CBE
Members, A. Buchan; B. Fitzgerald; G. Gordon, OBE; D. Hughes Hallett, FRICS; A. Hewat, OBE; Prof. C. Johnston; C. McChord; C. McLatchie; Ms A. Magee; Ms J. Shaw

THE EXECUTIVE
Chief Executive, A. Paton
Director of Corporate Services, W. Halcrow
Director of Environmental Strategy, Ms P. Henton
Director, North Region, Prof. D. Mackay
Director, East Region (acting), Dr T. Leatherland
Director, West Region, J. Beveridge

SCOTTISH HOMES
Thistle House, 91 Haymarket Terrace, Edinburgh
EH12 5HE
Tel 0131-313 0044

Scottish Homes, the national housing agency for Scotland, aims to improve the quality and variety of housing available in Scotland by working in partnership with the public and private sectors. The agency is a major funder of new and improved housing provided by housing associations and private developers. It is currently transferring its own rented houses to alternative landlords. It is also involved in housing research. Board members are appointed by the Secretary of State for Scotland.
Chairman, J. Ward, CBE
Chief Executive, P. McKinlay

SCOTTISH NATURAL HERITAGE
12 Hope Terrace, Edinburgh EH9 2AS
Tel 0131-447 4784

Scottish Natural Heritage came into existence in 1992 under the Natural Heritage (Scotland) Act 1991. It provides advice on nature conservation to all those whose activities affect wildlife, landforms and features of geological interest in Scotland, and seeks to develop and improve facilities for the enjoyment and understanding of the Scottish countryside. It is funded by the Scottish Office.
Chairman, M. Magnusson, KBE
Chief Executive, R. Crofts
Chief Scientific Adviser, M. B. Usher
Director of Operations (West), J. Thomson
Director of Operations (East), I. Jardine
Director of Operations (North), J. Watson
Director of Corporate Services, L. Montgomery

SCOTTISH OFFICE

The Secretary of State for Scotland is responsible in Scotland for a wide range of statutory functions which in England and Wales are the responsibility of a number of departmental ministers. He also works closely with ministers in charge of Great Britain departments on topics of special significance to Scotland within their fields of responsibility. His statutory functions are administered by five main departments collectively known as the Scottish Office. The departments are: the Scottish Office Agriculture, Environment and Fisheries Department; the Scottish Office Development Department; the Scottish Office Education and Industry Department; the Scottish Office Department of Health; and the Scottish Office Home Department.
In addition there are a number of other Scottish departments for which the Secretary of State has some degree of responsibility; these include the Scottish Courts Administration, the General Register Office, the Scottish

Record Office and the Department of the Registers of Scotland. The Secretary of State also bears ministerial responsibility for the activities in Scotland of several statutory bodies, such as the Forestry Commission, whose functions extend throughout Great Britain.

Dover House, Whitehall, London, SWIA 2AU
Tel 0171-270 3000

Secretary of State for Scotland, The Rt. Hon. Donald Dewar, MP
  Private Secretary (G5), C. M. A. Lugton
  Special Advisers, M. Elder; Ms W. Alexander
  Parliamentary Private Secretary, C. MacDonald, MP
Ministers of State, Henry McLeish, MP (*Home Affairs and Devolution*); Brian Wilson, MP (*Education and Industry*)
  Private Secretaries, A. T. F. Johnston; S. Farrell
Parliamentary Under-Secretaries of State, Malcolm Chisholm, MP (*Local Government and Transport*); Samuel Galbraith, MP (*Health and the Arts*); The Lord Sewel, CBE (*Agriculture, the Environment and Fisheries*)
  Private Secretaries, G. Owenson; Ms S. Davidson; Ms J. Goodburn
Parliamentary Clerk, Mrs L. J. Stirling
Permanent Under-Secretary of State (G1), Sir Russell Hillhouse, KCB
  Private Secretary, Miss L. M. Harper

LIAISON DIVISION
Assistant Secretary (G5), E. W. Ferguson

MANAGEMENT GROUP SUPPORT STAFF
Principal (G7), M. Grant

St Andrew's House, Edinburgh EHI 3DG
Tel 0131-556 8400

PERSONNEL GROUP
16 Waterloo Place, Edinburgh EHI 3DN
Tel 0131-556 8400

Principal Establishment Officer (G3), C. C. MacDonald
Assistant Secretary (G5), D. F. Middleton

FINANCE DIVISION
Victoria Quay, Edinburgh EH6 6QQ
Tel 0131-556 8400

Principal Finance Officer (G3), J. S. G. Graham
Assistant Secretaries (G5), M. T. S. Batho; J. G. Henderson; D. G. N. Reid; W. T. Tait
Head of Accountancy Services Unit (G6), I. M. Smith
Assistant Director of Finance Strategy (G6), I. A. McLeod

SOLICITOR'S OFFICE
For the Scottish departments and certain UK services, including HM Treasury, in Scotland
Solicitor (G2), R. Brodie, CB
Deputy Solicitor (G3), R. M. Henderson
Divisional Solicitors (G4), J. L. Jamieson; (*G5*), R. Bland (*seconded to Scottish Law Commission*); G. C. Duke; I. H. Harvie; H. F. Macdiarmid; J. G. S. Maclean; N. Raven; Mrs L. A. Towers

SCOTTISH OFFICE INFORMATION DIRECTORATE
For the Scottish departments and certain UK services
Director (G5), Ms E. S. B. Drummond
Deputy Director (G6), W. A. McNeill

SCOTTISH OFFICE AGRICULTURE, ENVIRONMENT AND FISHERIES DEPARTMENT
Pentland House, 47 Robb's Loan, Edinburgh EHI4 ITY
Tel 0131-556 8400

Secretary (G2), A. M. Russell

Under-Secretaries (G3), T. A. Cameron (*Agriculture*); S. F. Hampson (*Environment*)
Fisheries Secretary (G3), I. W. Gordon
Assistant Secretaries (G5), D. A. Brew; D. R. Dickson; R. A. Grant; A. J. Rushworth; Dr P. Rycroft; G. M. D. Thomson; I. M. Whitelaw; J. R. Wildgoose
Chief Agricultural Officer (G4), W. A. Macgregor
Deputy Chief Agricultural Officer (G5), J. I. Woodrow
Assistant Chief Agricultural Officers (G6), J. Henderson; A. Robb; A. J. Robertson
Chief Agricultural Economist (G6), D. J. Greig
Chief Food and Dairy Officer (G7), S. D. Rooke
Principal Surveyor (G6), vacant
Scientific Adviser (G5), vacant
Senior Principal Scientific Officers (G6), Mrs L. A. D. Turl; Dr R. Waterhouse

FISHERIES RESEARCH SERVICES
Marine Laboratory, PO Box 101, Victoria Road, Torry, Aberdeen AB9 8DB
Tel 01224-876544

Director of Fisheries Research for Scotland (G4), Prof. A. D. Hawkins, PH.D., FRSE
Deputy Director (G5), J. Davies

Freshwater Fisheries Laboratory
Faskally, Pitlochry, Perthshire PH6 5LB
Tel 01796-472060

Senior Principal Scientific Officers (G6), Dr R. M. Cook; Dr J. M. Davies; Dr A. E. Ellis; Dr A. L. S. Munro; R. G. J. Shelton; Dr P. A. Stewart; Dr C. S. Wardle
Inspector of Salmon and Freshwater Fisheries for Scotland (G7), D. A. Dunkley

ENVIRONMENTAL AFFAIRS GROUP
Under-Secretary (G3), S. F. Hampson
Assistant Secretaries (G5), J. D. Calder; J. N. Randall; J. A. Rennie
Chief Water Engineer, P. Wright
Ecological Adviser (G6), Dr J. Miles

CONSTITUTION GROUP
Head of Constitution Group (G3), R. S. B. Gordon
Constitutional Policy (G5), Ms I. M. Low
Referendum and Implementation (G5), P. E. Grice
Functions and Whitehall Negotiations (G5), D. J. Crawley
Legal Support to Constitution Group, J. L. Jamieson

DIRECTORATE OF ADMINISTRATIVE SERVICES
Victoria Quay, Edinburgh EH6 6QQ
Tel 0131-556 8400

Director of Administrative Services (G5), A. M. Brown
Chief Estates Officer (G6), J. A. Andrew

Saughton House, Broomhouse Drive, Edinburgh EHII 3DX
Head of Information Technology (G5), A. M. Brown
Director of Telecommunications (G6), K. Henderson, OBE

James Craig Walk, Edinburgh EHI 3BA
Head of Purchasing and Supplies (G5), N. Bowd

EXECUTIVE AGENCIES

INTERVENTION BOARD
— *see* page 316

SCOTTISH AGRICULTURAL SCIENCE AGENCY
East Craig, Edinburgh EHI2 8NJ

The Agency provides scientific information and advice on agricultural and horticultural crops and the environment, and has various statutory and regulatory functions.
Director (G5), Dr R. K. M. Hay
Deputy Director (G6), S. R. Cooper
Senior Principal Scientific Officer (G6), W. J. Rennie

Scottish Fisheries Protection Agency

Pentland House, 47 Robb's Loan, Edinburgh EH14 1TY
Tel 0131-556 8400

The Agency enforces fisheries law and regulations in Scottish waters and ports.

Chief Executive (G5), Capt. P. Du Vivier, RN
Director of Corporate Strategy and Resources (G6), J. B. Roddin
Director of Operational Enforcement (G6), R. J. Walker
Marine Superintendent, Capt. W. A. Brown

SCOTTISH OFFICE DEVELOPMENT DEPARTMENT

Victoria Quay, Edinburgh EH6 6QQ
Tel 0131-556 8400

Secretary (G2), H. H. Mills, CB
Under-Secretaries (G3), D. J. Belfall; J. W. Elvidge
Assistant Secretaries (G5), M. T. Affolter; E. C. Davidson;
   J. A. Ewing; J. D. Gallacher; W. Howat; Mrs D. Mellon;
   W. J. R. McQueen; C. Smith; R. Tait
Senior Economic Adviser (G5), C. L. Wood

PROFESSIONAL STAFF

Director of Construction and Building Control Group and Chief Architect (G3), J. E. Gibbons, PH.D., FSA SCOT.
Deputy Director of Construction and Building Control Group and Deputy Chief Architect (G5), Dr J. P. Cornish
Deputy Director of Construction and Building Control Group and Chief Quantity Surveyor (G5), A. J. Wyllie
Chief Planner (G4), A. Mackenzie
Chief Statistician (G5), vacant

INQUIRY REPORTERS

Robert Stevenson House, 2 Greenside Lane, Edinburgh
EH1 3AG
Tel 0131-244 5680
Chief Reporter (G3), R. M. Hickman
Deputy Chief Reporter (G5), J. M. McCulloch

NATIONAL ROADS DIRECTORATE

Victoria Quay, Edinburgh EH6 6QQ
Tel 0131-556 8400

Director of Roads (G3), J. Innes
Deputy Chief Engineers (G5), J. A. Howison (*Roads*);
   N. B. MacKenzie (*Bridges*)

EXECUTIVE AGENCY

HISTORIC SCOTLAND

Longmore House, Salisbury Place, Edinburgh EH9 1SH
Tel 0131-668 8600

The agency's role is to protect Scotland's historic monuments, buildings and lands, and to promote public understanding and enjoyment of them.

Chief Executive (G3), G. N. Munro
Directors (G5), F. J. Lawrie; I. Maxwell; B. Naylor
Chief Inspector of Ancient Monuments, Dr D. J. Breeze
Chief Inspector, Building Division, J. R. Hume

SCOTTISH OFFICE EDUCATION AND INDUSTRY DEPARTMENT

Victoria Quay, Edinburgh EH6 6QQ
Tel 0131-556 8400

Secretary (G2), G. R. Wilson, CB
Under-Secretaries (G3), J. S. B. Martin; E. J. Weeple
Assistant Secretaries (G5), G. F. Dickson; A. W. Fraser; D. S.
   Henderson; R. D. Jackson; J. W. L. Lonie; S. Y.
   MacDonald; A. K. MacLeod; Mrs R. Menlowe
Chief Statistician (G5), C. R. Macleans

HM INSPECTORS OF SCHOOLS

Senior Chief Inspector (G3), D. A. Osler

Depute Senior Chief Inspector (G4), G. H. C. Donaldson
Chief Inspectors (G5), P. Banks; J. Boyes; J. T. Donaldson;
   Miss K. M. Fairweather; D. E. Kelso; J. J. McDonald;
   A. S. McGlynn; M. Roebuck; H. M. Stalker
There are 79 Grade 6 Inspectors

INDUSTRIAL EXPANSION

Meridian Court, 5 Cadogan Street, Glasgow G2 6AT
Tel 0141-248 2855

Under-Secretary (G3), G. Robson
Industrial Adviser, D. Blair
Scientific Adviser, Prof. D. J. Tedford
Assistant Secretaries (G5), W. Malone; J. K. Mason; Ms J.
   Morgan; Dr J. Rigg

LOCATE IN SCOTLAND

120 Bothwell Street, Glasgow G2 7JP
Tel 0141-248 2700

Director (G4), M. Togneri

SCOTTISH TRADE INTERNATIONAL

120 Bothwell Street, Glasgow G2 7JP
Tel 0141-248 2700

Director, D. Taylor

EXECUTIVE AGENCIES

STUDENT AWARDS AGENCY FOR SCOTLAND

Gyleview House, 3 Redheughs Rigg, Edinburgh EH12 9HH
Tel 0131-244 5867

Chief Executive, K. MacRae

SCOTTISH OFFICE PENSIONS AGENCY

St Margaret's House, 151 London Road, Edinburgh
EH8 7TG
Tel 0131-556 8400

The Agency is responsible for the pension arrangements of some 300,000 people, mainly NHS and teaching services employees and pensioners.

Chief Executive, N. MacLeod
Directors (G7), G. Mowat (*Policy*); A. M. Small (*Operations*);
   M. J. McDermott (*Resources and Customer Services*)

SCOTTISH OFFICE DEPARTMENT OF HEALTH

St Andrew's House, Edinburgh EH1 3DG
Tel 0131-556 8400

NATIONAL HEALTH SERVICE IN SCOTLAND
MANAGEMENT EXECUTIVE

Chief Executive (G3), G. R. Scaife
Director of Purchasing (G4), Dr K. J. Woods
Director of Primary Care (G5), Mrs A. Robson
Director of Finance (G5), Dr P. Collings
Director of Human Resources (G5), M. Sibbald
Director of Nursing, Miss A. Jarvie
Medical Director (G3), Dr A. B. Young, FRCPE
Director of Trusts (G4), P. Wilson
Director of Information Services, NHS, C. B. Knox
Director of Estates, H. R. McCallum
Chief Pharmacist (G5), W. Scott
Chief Scientist, Prof. I. A. D. Bouchier, CBE, FRCP
Chief Dental Officer, T. R. Watkins

PUBLIC HEALTH POLICY UNIT

Head of Unit and Chief Medical Officer (G2), Prof. Sir David
   Carter, FRCSE, FRCSGlas., FRCPE
Deputy Chief Medical Officer (G3), Dr A. B. Young, FRCPE
Under-Secretary (G3), Mrs N. Munro
Assistant Secretary (G5), J. T. Brown
Principal Medical Officers, Dr J. B. Louden (*part-time*); Dr A.
   MacDonald (*part-time*), Dr R. Skinner; Dr E. Sowler

Senior Medical Officers, Dr Angela Anderson; Dr
P. W. Brooks; Dr K. G. Brotherston; Dr D. Campbell; Dr
D. Colin-Thome (*part-time*); Dr J. Cumming; Dr B.
Davis; Dr D. J. Ewing; Dr D. Jolliffe; Dr A. Keel; Dr
Patricia Madden; Dr H. Whyte

NATIONAL HEALTH SERVICE, SCOTLAND

HEALTH BOARDS

ARGYLL AND CLYDE, Ross House, Hawkhead Road,
Paisley PA2 7BN. *Chairman*, M. D. Jones; *General Manager*,
I. C. Smith
AYRSHIRE AND ARRAN, PO Box 13, Seafield House,
Doonfoot Road, Ayr KA7 4DW. *Chairman*, Dr J. Morrow;
General Manager, J. M. Eckford, OBE
BORDERS, Huntlyburn, Melrose, Roxburghshire TD6 9DB.
Chairman, D. A. C. Kilshaw; *General Manager*,
D. A. Peters, OBE
DUMFRIES AND GALLOWAY, Nithbank, Dumfries DG1 2SD.
Chairman, J. Ross; *General Manager*, D. Banks
FIFE, Springfield House, Cupar KY7 5PR. *Chairman*, Mrs C.
Stewhouse; *General Manager*, Miss P. Frost
FORTH VALLEY, 33 Spittal Street, Stirling FK8 1DX.
Chairman, E. Bell-Scott; *General Manager*, D. Hird
GRAMPIAN, Summerfield House, 2 Eday Road, Aberdeen
AB9 1RE. *Chairman*, C. MacLeod, CBE; *General Manager*,
F. E. L. Hartnett, OBE
GREATER GLASGOW, 112 Ingram Street, Glasgow G1 1ET.
Chairman, Prof. D. Hamblen; *General Manager* (*acting*),
T. A. Divers
HIGHLAND, Reay House, 17 Old Edinburgh Road,
Inverness IV2 3HG. *Chairman*, Mrs C. Thomson; *General
Manager*, Dr G. V. Stone
LANARKSHIRE, 14 Beckford Street, Hamilton,
Lanarkshire ML3 0TA. *Chairman*, I. Livingstone, OBE;
General Manager, Prof. F. Clark, CBE
LOTHIAN, 148 The Pleasance, Edinburgh EH8 9RS.
Chairman, Mrs M. Ford; *General Manager*, J. Lusby
ORKNEY, Balfour Hospital, New Scapa Road, Kirkwall,
Orkney KW15 1BQ. *Chairman*, J. Leslie; *General Manager*,
E. Jackson
SHETLAND, Brevik House, South Road, Lerwick ZW1 0RB.
Chairman, J. Telford; *General Manager*, B. J. Atherton
TAYSIDE, PO Box 75, Vernonholme, Riverside Drive,
Dundee DD1 9NL. *Chairman*, Mrs F. Havenga; *General
Manager*, Miss L. Barrie
WESTERN ISLES, 37 South Beach Street, Stornoway, Isle
of Lewis PA87 2BN. *Chairman*, A. Matheson; *General
Manager*, R. Mullan

HEALTH EDUCATION BOARD FOR SCOTLAND
Woodburn House, Canaan Lane, Edinburgh EH10 4SG
Tel 0131-536 5500

Chairman, D. Campbell
Chief Executive, Prof. A. Tannahill

STATE HOSPITAL
Carstairs Junction, Lanark ML11 8RP
Tel 01555-840293

Chairman, D. N. James
General Manager, R. Manson

COMMON SERVICES AGENCY
Trinity Park House, South Trinity Road, Edinburgh
EH5 3SE
Tel 0131-552 6255

Chairman, G. Scaife
General Manager, Dr F. Gibb

SCOTTISH OFFICE HOME DEPARTMENT
Saughton House, Broomhouse Drive, Edinburgh EH11 3XD
Tel 0131-556 8400

Secretary (*G2*), J. Hamill
Under-Secretaries (*G3*), N. G. Campbell; Mrs G. M. Stewart
Assistant Secretaries (*G5*), C. Baxter; Mrs M. H. Brannan;
Mrs M. B. Gunn; R. S. T. MacEwen; D. Macniven, TD
Chief Research Officer, Dr C. P. A. Levein
Senior Principal Research Officer (*G6*), Dr J. Tombs

SOCIAL WORK SERVICES GROUP
James Craig Walk, Edinburgh EH1 3BA
Tel 0131-556 8400

Under-Secretary (*G3*), N. G. Campbell
Assistant Secretaries (*G5*), G. A. Anderson; Ms L. J. Clare;
J. W. Sinclair, CBE
Chief Inspector of Social Work Services, A. Skinner
Assistant Chief Inspectors, Ms M. L. Hunt; F. A. O'Leary;
Mrs G. Ottley; D. Pia; I. C. Robertson; A. Sabine

OTHER APPOINTMENTS
HM Chief Inspector of Constabulary, J. Boyd, CBE, QPM
HM Chief Inspector of Prisons, C. Fairweather, OBE
Commandant, Scottish Police College, H. I. Watson, OBE, QPM
HM Chief Inspector of Fire Services, N. Morrison, CBE, QFSM
Commandant, Scottish Fire Service Training School, D. Grant,
QFSM

MENTAL WELFARE COMMISSION FOR SCOTLAND
K Floor, Argyle House, 3 Lady Lawson Street, Edinburgh
EH3 9SH
Tel 0131-222 6111

Chairman, Sir William Reid, KCB
Commissioners, Mrs N. Bennie; C. Campbell, QC; Mrs
F. Cotter; Mrs M. Jeffcoat; Dr M. Livingston; Dr
E. McCall-Smith; Dr R. McCreadie; D. J. Macdonald;
C. McKay; Ms L. M. Noble; Dr L. Pollock; I. Ross; Dr E.
M. Thomas; W. Gent; Ms M. Whoriskey; A. Robb

COUNSEL TO THE SECRETARY OF STATE
FOR SCOTLAND UNDER THE PRIVATE
LEGISLATION PROCEDURE (SCOTLAND) ACT 1936
50 Frederick Street, Edinburgh EH2 1EN
Tel 0131-226 6499

Senior Counsel, G. S. Douglas, QC
Junior Counsel, N. M. P. Morrison

EXECUTIVE AGENCIES

REGISTERS OF SCOTLAND
— *see* page 317

SCOTTISH COURT SERVICE
— *see* page 365

SCOTTISH PRISON SERVICE
— *see* page 382

SCOTTISH RECORD OFFICE
— *see* page 337

GENERAL REGISTER OFFICE
New Register House, Edinburgh EH1 3YT
Tel 0131-334 0380

The General Register Office for Scotland is an associated
department of the Scottish Office. It is the office of the
Registrar-General for Scotland, who has responsibility for
civil registration and the taking of censuses in Scotland and

has in his custody the following records: the statutory registers of births, deaths, still births, adoptions, marriages and divorces; the old parish registers (recording births, deaths and marriages, etc., before civil registration began in 1855); and records of censuses of the population in Scotland. Hours of public access: Monday–Friday 9–4.30.

Registrar-General, J. Meldrum
Deputy Registrar-General, B. V. Philp
Senior Principal (G6), D. A. Orr
Principals (G7), D. B. L. Brownlee; R. C. Lawson; F. D. Garvie
Statisticians (G7), J. Arrundale; G. W. L. Jackson; F. G. Thomas

SCOTTISH PRISONS COMPLAINTS COMMISSION
Government Buildings, Broomhouse Drive, Edinburgh EH11 3XD
Tel 0131-244 8423

The Commission was established in 1994. It is an independent body to which prisoners in Scottish prisons can make application in relation to any matter where they have failed to obtain satisfaction from the Prison Service's internal grievance procedures. Clinical judgments made by medical officers, matters which are the subject of legal proceedings and matters relating to sentence, conviction and parole decision-making are excluded from the Commission's jurisdiction. The Commissioner is appointed by the Secretary of State for Scotland.
Commissioner, Dr J. McManus

SEA FISH INDUSTRY AUTHORITY
18 Logie Mill, Logie Green Road, Edinburgh EH7 4HG
Tel 0131-558 3331

Established under the Fisheries Act 1981, the Authority is required to promote the efficiency of the sea fish industry. It carries out research relating to the industry and gives advice on related matters. It provides training, promotes the marketing, consumption and export of sea fish and sea fish products, and may provide financial assistance for the improvement of fishing vessels in respect of essential safety equipment. It is responsible to the Ministry of Agriculture, Fisheries and Food.
Chairman, E. Davey
Chief Executive, A. C. Fairbairn

THE SECURITY SERVICE COMMISSIONER
c/o PO Box 18, London SE1 0TZ

The Commissioner is appointed by the Prime Minister. He keeps under review the issue of warrants by the Home Secretary under the Intelligence Services Act 1994, and is required to help the Security Service Tribunal by investigating complaints which allege interference with property and by offering all such assistance in discharging its functions as it may require. He is also required to submit an annual report on the discharge of his functions to the Prime Minister.
Commissioner, The Rt. Hon. Lord Justice Stuart-Smith

SECURITY SERVICE TRIBUNAL
PO Box 18, London SE1 0TZ
Tel 0171-273 4095

The Security Service Act 1989 established a tribunal of three to five senior members of the legal profession, independent of the Government and appointed by The Queen, to investigate complaints from any person about anything which they believe the Security Service has done to them or to their property.
President, The Rt. Hon. Lord Justice Simon Brown
Vice-President, Sheriff J. McInnes, QC
Member, Sir Richard Gaskell

SERIOUS FRAUD OFFICE
Elm House, 10–16 Elm Street, London WC1X 0BJ
Tel 0171-239 7272

The Serious Fraud Office works under the superintendence of the Attorney-General. Its remit is to investigate and prosecute serious and complex fraud. (Other fraud cases are currently handled by the fraud divisions of the Crown Prosecution Service.) The scope of its powers covers England, Wales and Northern Ireland. The staff includes lawyers, accountants and other support staff; investigating teams work closely with the police.
Director, Mrs R. Wright

DEPARTMENT OF SOCIAL SECURITY
Richmond House, 79 Whitehall, London SW1A 2NS
Tel 0171-238 0800

The Department of Social Security is responsible for the payment of benefits and the collection of contributions under the National Insurance and Industrial Injuries schemes, and for the payment of child benefit, one-parent benefit, income support and family credit. It administers the Social Fund, and is responsible for assessing the means of applicants for legal aid. It is also responsible for the payment of war pensions and the operation of the child maintenance system.
Secretary of State for Social Security and Minister for Women, The Rt. Hon. Harriet Harman, MP
  Principal Private Secretary, S. Czerniawski
  Special Advisers, J. McTernan; Ms E. Kendall
  Parliamentary Private Secretary, G. Sutcliffe, MP
Minister of State, The Rt. Hon. Frank Field, MP (*Welfare Reform*)
  Private Secretary, J. Hope
Parliamentary Under-Secretaries of State, Keith Bradley, MP (*Income-related Benefits*); The Baroness Hollis of Heigham, D.phil. (*Child Benefit, Child Support and War Pensions*); John Denham, MP (*Pensions*); Joan Ruddock, MP (*Women*)
  Private Secretaries, J. Vincent; S. Gallagher; C. Payne; Ms H. McCarthy
Permanent Secretary (G1), Dame Ann Bowtell, DCB
  Private Secretary, B. Hearn

CORPORATE MANAGEMENT GROUP
Director (G2), J. Tross

PERSONNEL AND HQ SUPPORT SERVICES
DIRECTORATE
Director, S. Hewitt
Section Heads (*G5*), T. Perl; (*G7*), R. Yeats; B. Glew;
J. Elliott

*ANALYTICAL SERVICES DIVISION
Director* (*G3*), D. Stanton
Chief Statisticians (*G5*), N. Dyson; M. McDowall
Senior Economic Advisers (*G5*), J. Ball; G. Harris
Deputy Chief Scientific Officer (*G5*), D. Barnbrook
Chief Research Officer (*G5*), Ms S. Duncan

FINANCE DIVISION
Grade 3, S. Lord

INFORMATION DIRECTORATE
Head of Information (*G5*), S. Reardon
Deputy Head of Information (*G6*), J. Bretherton
Chief Press Officer (*G7*), Ms S. Lewis
Chief Publicity Officer (*G7*), Ms A. Martin

SOCIAL SECURITY POLICY GROUP
Head of Policy Group (*G2*), C. Kelly
Policy Directors (*G3*), R. Allen; M. Whippman; Miss
M. Peirson, CB; D. Brereton
Head of Women's Unit (*G5*), Ms P. Barrett
Policy Managers (*G5*), Mrs A. Lingwood; D. Jackson; Ms
S. Graham; B. O'Gorman; Miss J. Moore; M. Street;
J. Groombridge; Mrs C. Rookes; B. Calderwood; Miss
J. Leibling; D. Allsop; C. Evans; J. Hughes; P. Cleasby;
G. Bowen; Ms K. Limm; P. Morgan; Mrs L. Richards;
Ms J. Shersby; (*G6*), B. Layton; I. Williams

SOLICITOR'S OFFICE
Solicitor (*G2*), M. Morgan

SOLICITOR'S DIVISION A
New Court, 48 Carey Street, London WC2A 2LS
Tel 0171-412 1465

Principal Assistant Solicitor (*G3*), J. A. Catlin
Assistant Solicitors (*G5*), R. Powell; J. M. Swainson; Mrs
G. Massiah; Mrs F. A. Logan; S. M. Cooper; D. Jordan

SOLICITOR'S DIVISION B
New Court, 48 Carey Street, London WC2A 2LS
Tel 0171-412 1404

Solicitor (G2), M. Morgan
Assistant Solicitors (*G5*), R. G. S. Aitken; W. H. Connell; Ms
S. Edwards

SOLICITOR'S DIVISION C
New Court, 48 Carey Street, London WC2A 2LS
Tel 0171-412 1341

Principal Assistant Solicitor (*G3*), Mrs G. S. Kerrigan
Assistant Solicitors (*G5*), P. Milledge; R. J. Dormer; Miss
M. E. Trefgarne; Mrs S. Walker; Miss G. E. Parker

BENEFITS FRAUD INSPECTORATE
Berkeley House, 12A North Park Road, Harrogate HG1 5QA
Tel 01423-832925

Director-General (*G2*), I. Stewart

EXECUTIVE AGENCIES

BENEFITS AGENCY
Quarry House, Quarry Hill, Leeds LS2 7UA
Tel 0113-232 4000

The Agency administers claims for and payments of social
security benefits.
Chief Executive, P. Mathison
Private Secretary, Ms E. Clayton
Directors, D. Riggs (*Finance*); P. Murphy (*Personnel and
Communications*); Ms U. Brennan (*Change Management*);
A. Cleveland (*Project Director*); G. McCorkell (*Project
Director*); J. Lutton (*North*); T. Edge (*South*)

Medical Policy
Principal Medical Officers, Dr M. Aylward; Dr P. Dewis; Dr
C. Bolt; Dr P. Sawney; Dr A. Braidwood; Dr P. Stidolph

CHILD SUPPORT AGENCY
Quay House, The Waterfront, Brierley Hill, W. Midlands
DY1 1XZ
Tel 01384-488488

The Agency was set up in April 1993. It is responsible for
the administration of the Child Support Act and for the
assessment, collection and enforcement of maintenance
payments for all new cases.
Chief Executive, Ms F. Boardman
Directors, S. Heminsley; C. Francis; M. Davison; C. Peters;
M. Isaacs
Non-Executive Directors, J. King; D. Thornham

CONTRIBUTIONS AGENCY
DSS Longbenton, Benton Park Road, Newcastle upon
Tyne NE98 1YX
Tel 0191-213 5000

The Agency collects and records National Insurance
contributions, maintains individual records, and provides
an advisory service on National Insurance matters.
Chief Executive (*G3*), G. Bertram
Deputy Chief Executive (*G5*), T. Lord
Management Board, K. Wilson; D. Slater; K. Elliott
Non-Executive Member, S. Banyard

INFORMATION TECHNOLOGY SERVICES AGENCY
4th Floor, Verulam Point, Station Way, St Albans, Herts
AL1 5HE
Tel 01727-815838

The Agency maintains and oversees policies on informa-
tion technology strategy, procurement, technical stan-
dards and security.
Chief Executive, I. Magee
Directors, J. Thomas; G. Hextall; J. Brewood; G. Kemp;
P. Sharkey; G. Brown; T. Edkins
Non-Executive Director, K. Pfotzer

WAR PENSIONS AGENCY
Norcross, Blackpool, Lancs FY5 3WP
Tel 01253-858858

The Agency administers the payment of war disablement
and war widows' pensions and provides welfare services
and support to war disablement pensioners, war widows
and their dependants and carers. It became an executive
agency in 1994.
Chief Executive, K. Caldwell

Central Advisory Committee on War Pensions
6th Floor, The Adelphi, 1–11 John Adam Street, London
WC2N 6HT
Tel 0171-962 8028

Secretary, C. Pike

---

*At the Adelphi, 1–11 John Adam Street, London WC2N 6HT. Tel: 0171-
962 8000

ADVISORY BODIES

NATIONAL DISABILITY COUNCIL, 6th Floor, The Adelphi, 1–11 John Adam Street, London WC2N 6HT. Tel: 0171-712 2099. *Chairman*, D. Grayson; *Secretary*, Ms K. Archer

SOCIAL SECURITY ADVISORY COMMITTEE, New Court, Carey Street, London WC2A 2LS. Tel 0171-412 1508. *Chairman*, Sir Thomas Boyd-Carpenter, KBE; *Secretary*, L. C. Smith

SPORTS COUNCIL
— *see* United Kingdom Sports Council

OFFICE FOR STANDARDS IN EDUCATION (OFSTED)
Alexandra House, 33 Kingsway, London WC2B 6SE
Tel 0171-421 6800

A non-ministerial government department established in 1992 to keep the Secretary of State and the public informed about the standards and management of schools in England, and to establish and monitor an independent inspection system for maintained schools in England. *See also* page 434.

HM Chief Inspector, C. Woodhead
Directors of Inspection, A. J. Rose, CBE; M. J. Tomlinson, CBE

TEAM MANAGERS

Planning and Resource, Miss J. Phillips
Personnel Management, C. Payne
Contracts, C. Bramley
Communications, Media and Public Relations, J. Lawson
Information Systems, M. Childs
Administrative Support and Estates Management, K. Francis
Competition and Compliance, Ms E. Slater
Training and Assessment of Independent Inspectors, B. McCafferty
Inspection Quality, Monitoring and Development, P. Matthews
LEA Reviews, Reorganization Proposals, D. Singleton
School Improvement, Ms E. Passmore
Additional Inspector Project, Ms S. O'Sullivan
Nursery and Primary, K. Lloyd
Secondary, Independent and International, C. Gould
Post-Compulsory, D. West
Special Educational Needs, C. Marshall
Research, Analysis and International, Ms C. Agambar
Teacher Education and Training, D. Taylor
Nursery Education Scheme, D. Bradley
Specialist Advisers, N. Bufton; B. Ponchaud; A. Dobson; M. Ive; J. Hamer; P. Smith; Ms J. Mills; G. Clay; P. Jones; J. Hertrich; Ms B. Wintersgill

There are about 200 HM Inspectors

COMMITTEE ON STANDARDS IN PUBLIC LIFE
Horse Guards Road, London SW1P 3AL
Tel 0171-270 5875

The Committee on Standards in Public Life (known as the Nolan Committee) was set up in October 1994. It is a standing body whose chairman and members are appointed by the Prime Minister. Its remit is to examine concerns about standards of conduct of all holders of public office, including arrangements relating to financial and commercial activities, and to make recommendations as to any changes in current arrangements which might be required to ensure the highest standards of propriety in public life. It has published three reports. The committee does not investigate individual allegations of misconduct.
Chairman, vacant
Members, Sir Martin Jacomb; Prof. A. King; The Rt. Hon. T. King, CH, MP; The Lord Shore of Stepney, PC; The Lord Thomson of Monifieth, PC; Sir William Utting, CB; Dame Anne Warburton, DCVO, CMG; Ms D. Warwick
Secretary (SCS), R. Horsman

OFFICE OF TELECOMMUNICATIONS
50 Ludgate Hill, London EC4M 7JJ
Tel 0171-634 8700

The Office of Telecommunications (Oftel) is a non-ministerial government department which is responsible for supervising telecommunications activities and broadcast transmission in the UK. Its principal functions are to ensure that holders of telecommunications licences comply with their licence conditions; to maintain and promote effective competition in telecommunications; and to promote the interests of purchasers and other users of telecommunication services and apparatus in respect of prices, quality and variety.

The Director-General has powers to deal with anti-competitive practices and monopolies. He also has a duty to consider all reasonable complaints and representations about telecommunication apparatus and services.

Director-General, D. G. Cruickshank
Deputy Director-General, Mrs A. Walker
Director of Network Competition, Mrs A. Taylor
Director of Consumer Affairs, Ms C. Farnish
Director of Licensing, Ms S. Chambers
Director of Licence Enforcement and Fair Trading, C. J. C. Wright
Technical Director, P. Walker
Economic Director, A. Bell
Legal Director, D. H. M. Ingham
Director of Information, N. Gammage
Director of Service Competition and International Affairs, J. Niblett

TOURIST BOARDS
(For British Tourist Authority, *see* page 287)

The English Tourist Board, the Scottish Tourist Board, the Wales Tourist Board and the Northern Ireland Tourist Board are responsible for developing and marketing the tourist industry in their respective countries. The Boards' main objectives are to promote holidays and to encourage the provision and improvement of tourist amenities.

ENGLISH TOURIST BOARD, Thames Tower, Black's Road, London W6 9EL. Tel: 0181-846 9000. *Chief Executive*, T. Bartlett

SCOTTISH TOURIST BOARD, 23 Ravelston Terrace, Edinburgh EH4 3EU. Tel: 0131-332 2433. *Chief Executive*, T. Buncle

WALES TOURIST BOARD, Brunel House, 2 Fitzalan Road, Cardiff CF2 1UY. Tel: 01222-499909. *Chief Executive*, J. French

NORTHERN IRELAND TOURIST BOARD, St Anne's Court, 59 North Street, Belfast BT1 1NB. Tel: 01232-31221. *Chief Executive*, I. Henderson

DEPARTMENT OF TRADE AND INDUSTRY

1 Victoria Street, London SW1H 0ET
Tel 0171-215 5000
Business Link: Tel 0800-500200
Business in Europe: Tel 0117-944 4888
Innovation Enquiry Line: Tel 0171-215 1217

The Department is responsible for international trade policy, including the promotion of UK trade interests in the European Union, GATT, OECD, UNCTAD and other international organizations; the promotion of UK exports and assistance to exporters; policy in relation to industry and commerce, including industrial relations policy; policy towards small firms; regional industrial assistance; legislation and policy in relation to the Post Office; competition policy and consumer protection; the development of national policies in relation to all forms of energy and the development of new sources of energy, including international aspects of energy policy; policy on science and technology research and development; space policy; standards, quality and design; company legislation; and the regulation of insurance industries.

President of the Board of Trade and Secretary of State for Trade and Industry, The Rt. Hon. Margaret Beckett, MP
  Principal Private Secretary, J. Alty
  Private Secretaries, R. Jenkinson; A. Phillipson
  Special Advisers, D. Corry; Ms S. Watson
  Parliamentary Private Secretary, J. Hutton, MP
Minister for Trade, The Lord Clinton-Davis
  Private Secretary, U. Marthaler
Minister for Science, Energy and Industry, John Battle, MP
  Private Secretary, W. Perrin
  Parliamentary Private Secretary, Ms A. Campbell, MP
Minister of State, Ian McCartney, MP (*Competitiveness*)
  Private Secretary, C. Pook
  Parliamentary Private Secretary, F. Doran, MP
Minister for Trade and Competitiveness in Europe, The Lord Simon of Highbury, CBE (*joint DTI/ Treasury minister*)
  Private Secretary, J. Mitchell
Parliamentary Under-Secretary of State for Competition and Consumer Affairs, Nigel Griffiths, MP
  Private Secretary, Ms D. Parr
Parliamentary Under-Secretary of State for Small Firms, Trade and Industry, Barbara Roche, MP
  Private Secretary, C. Henning
British Overseas Trade Board Chairman, M. Laing, CBE
  Private Secretary, Ms S. Brown
Parliamentary Clerk, T. Williams
Permanent Secretary, M. Scholar, CB
  Private Secretary, C. Hannant
Chief Scientific Adviser and Head of Office of Science and Technology, Sir Robert May, FRS
  Private Secretary, R. Clay
Directors-General, Sir John Cadogan, CBE, FRS (*Director-General of the Research Councils*); C. W. Roberts, CB (*Trade Policy and Export Promotion*); D. Durie, CMG (*Regional and Small and Medium-Sized Enterprises*); B. Hilton, CB (*Corporate and Consumer Affairs*); D. Nissen (*The Solicitor*); J. Preston (*Energy*); J. Spencer (*Resources and Services*); A. Macdonald, CB (*Industry*)

DIVISIONAL ORGANIZATION

‡AEROSPACE AND DEFENCE INDUSTRIES DIRECTORATE
Director of Aerospace and Defence Industries, R. Foster
Director, S. I. Charik

‡BRITISH NATIONAL SPACE CENTRE
Director-General, D. R. Davis
Deputy Director-General, D. Leadbeater
Directors, H. Evans; Dr P. Murdin; Dr D. Lumley

BUSINESS LINK DIRECTORATE
Director of Business Link, V. Brown
Directors, J. Reid; P. Bentley; P. Waller

COMPETITIVENESS UNIT
Director, R. Dobbie

‡CHEMICALS AND BIOTECHNOLOGY DIRECTORATE
Director of Chemicals and Biotechnology, M. Baker
Directors, Ms G. Alliston; Dr E. A. M. Baker

COAL DIRECTORATE
Director, M. Atkinson

‡COMMUNICATIONS AND INFORMATION INDUSTRIES DIRECTORATE
Director of Communications and Information Industries, W. MacIntyre
Directors, R. King; N. McMillan, CMG; D. Hendon; N. Worman; S. Pride

COMPANY LAW DIRECTORATE
Director of Company Law, R. Rogers
Directors, N. D. Peace; D. E. Love

CONSUMER AFFAIRS AND COMPETITION POLICY DIRECTORATE
Director of Consumer Affairs and Competition Policy, P. Salvidge
Directors, P. Mason; Miss D. Gane; Dr A. Eggington; G. Boon; A. Brimelow; M. Higson

CONSUMER GOODS, BUSINESS AND POSTAL SERVICES DIRECTORATE
Director of Consumer Goods, Business and Postal Services, M. Baker
Directors, D. Sibbick; B. Hopson

ECONOMICS AND STATISTICS DIRECTORATE
Chief Economic Adviser, D. R. Coates
Directors, K. Warwick; Ms J. Dougharty; M. Bradbury

ELECTRICITY DIRECTORATE
Director of Electricity, J. Green

ENERGY POLICY AND ANALYSIS UNIT
Director of Energy Policy and Analysis, M. Keay
Directors, E. Evans; G. C. White

ENERGY TECHNOLOGIES DIRECTORATE
Director, G. Bevan

‡ENGINEERING, AUTOMOTIVE AND METALS DIRECTORATE
Director of Engineering, Automotive and Metals, M. O'Shea
Directors, H. Brown; J. Grewe; R. Poole; A. Vinall; A. Wilks

ENGINEERING INSPECTORATE
Director of Engineering Inspectorate, Dr P. Fenwick

‡ENVIRONMENT DIRECTORATE
Director of Environment, Dr C. Hicks

‡ESTATES AND FACILITIES MANAGEMENT DIRECTORATE
Director, M. Coolican

EUROPE DIRECTORATE
Kingsgate House, 66–74 Victoria Street, London SW1E 6SW
Director, B. Stow

‡ At 151 Buckingham Palace Road, London SW1W 9SS

EXPORT CONTROL AND NON-PROLIFERATION
DIRECTORATE
Kingsgate House, 66–74 Victoria Street, London
SW1E 6SW

Director of Export Control and Non-Proliferation, Dr R.
Heathcote
Directors, A. J. Mantle, P. H. Agrell

EXPORT PROMOTION DIRECTORATES
Kingsgate House, 66–74 Victoria Street, London
SW1E 6SW

Directors, M. Mowlam (*The Americas*); M. Cohen (*Asia
Pacific*), K. Levinson (*Central and Eastern Europe*); S. Lyle
Smythe (*Business in Europe*); N. Armour (*Middle East,
Near East and North Africa*); N. McInnes (*Sub-Saharan
Africa and South Asia*)

EXPORT SERVICES DIRECTORATE
Kingsgate House, 66–74 Victoria Street, London
SW1E 6SW

Director, A. Reynolds

FINANCE AND RESOURCE MANAGEMENT DIRECTORATE
Director of Finance and Resource Management, M. Roberts
Directors, E. Hosker; Dr S. Sklaroff; K. Hills; N. Nandra

IMPORT POLICY DIRECTORATE
Kingsgate House, 66–74 Victoria Street, London
SW1E 6SW

Director, S. Bowen

INDUSTRIAL RELATIONS DIRECTORATE
Director of Industrial Relations, Ms H. Leiser
Directors, K. Masson; R. Niblett; A. Wright; Mrs
Z. Hornstein

‡INDUSTRY ECONOMICS AND STATISTICS
DIRECTORATE
Director, Dr N. Owen

INFORMATION DIRECTORATE
Director of Information, Ms Z. M. Caines
Director of News, M. Ricketts
Director of Publicity, Miss P. R. A. Freedman

‡INFORMATION MANAGEMENT AND TECHNOLOGY
DIRECTORATE
Director, R. Wheeler

‡INNOVATION UNIT
Director, Dr A. Keddie

INSURANCE DIRECTORATE
Director of Insurance, G. Dart
Directors, R. Allen; K. Long; J. Whitlock, P. Casey

‡INTERNAL AUDIT
Director of Internal Audit, A. C. Elkington

INTERNATIONAL ECONOMICS DIRECTORATE
Kingsgate House, 66–74 Victoria Street, London
SW1E 6SW

Director, C. Moir

INVEST IN BRITAIN BUREAU
Chief Executive, A. Fraser

INVESTIGATIONS AND ENFORCEMENT DIRECTORATE
10 Victoria Street, London SW1H 0NN

Director of Investigations and Enforcement, J. Phillips
Directors, J. Sibley; R. Burns; G. Harp; J. Gardner; Mrs B.
Chase; S. Milligan

JOINT EXPORT PROMOTION DIRECTORATE
(FCO/DTI)
Kingsgate House, 66–74 Victoria Street, London
SW1E 6SW

Director-General of Export Promotion, T. Harris, CMG
Director, JEPD, D. Hall

LEGAL RESOURCE MANAGEMENT AND BUSINESS LAW
UNIT
10 Victoria Street, London SW1H 0NN

The Solicitor and Director-General, D. Nissen
Director, J. Burnett

LEGAL SERVICES DIRECTORATE A
10 Victoria Street, London SW1H 0NN

Director of Legal A, J. Stanley
Legal Directors, I. Mathers, J. Roberts; Miss N. O'Flynn;
S. Hyett; Miss G. Richmond

LEGAL SERVICES DIRECTORATE B
10 Victoria Street, London SW1H 0NN

Director of Legal B, P. Bovey
Legal Directors, R. Baker; T. Susman; B. Welch; A. Woods

LEGAL SERVICES DIRECTORATE C
10 Victoria Street, London SW1H 0NN

Director of Legal C, Ms A. Brett-Holt
Legal Directors, R. Perkins; R. Green; M. Bucknill; C.
Raikes

MANAGEMENT BEST PRACTICE
Director of Management Best Practice, Dr K. Poulter
Directors, Dr I. Harrison; J. Sutton

NEW ISSUES AND DEVELOPING COUNTRIES
Kingsgate House, 66–74 Victoria Street, London
SW1E 6SW

Director, C. Bridge

NUCLEAR INDUSTRIES DIRECTORATE
Director of Nuclear Industries, N. Hirst
Directors, Dr M. Draper; J. Rhodes; Dr E. Drage; Miss S
Killen

OFFICE OF SCIENCE AND TECHNOLOGY: SCIENCE AND
ENGINEERING BASE DIRECTORATE
Albany House, 84–86 Petty France, London SW1H 9ST

Director, Science and Engineering Base, A. Quigley
Directors, Ms F. Price; Dr K. Root

OFFICE OF SCIENCE AND TECHNOLOGY:
TRANSDEPARTMENTAL SCIENCE AND TECHNOLOGY
DIRECTORATE
Albany House, 84–86 Petty France, London SW1H 9ST

Director, Transdepartmental Science and Technology, Ms H.
Williams
Directors, R. Wright; S. Spivey

OIL AND GAS DIRECTORATE
Director of Oil and Gas, M. J. Michell
Directors, J. R. V. Brook; S. Price; A. Wilson
Director of Oil and Gas Royalties Office, A. Cran

Oil and Gas Office (Aberdeen)
Atholl House, 86–88 Guild Street, Aberdeen AB9 1DR
Tel 01224-213557

Director, A. S. Wilson

OIL, GAS AND PETROCHEMICALS SUPPLIES OFFICE
Tay House, 300 Bath Street, Glasgow G2 4DX
Tel 0141-228 3646
151 Buckingham Palace Road, London SW1W 9SS
Tel 0171-215 5000

Chief Executive, Oil Supplies Office, M. Stanley
Directors, P. Dunn; K. Forrest; B. Gallagher

PROJECTS EXPORT PROMOTION DIRECTORATE
Director of Projects Export Promotion, D. Marsh
Director, G. Atkinson

REGIONAL ASSISTANCE DIRECTORATE
Director, D. Miner

REGIONAL DEVOLUTION DIRECTORATE
Director, M. Gibson

REGIONAL EUROPEAN FUNDS DIRECTORATE
Director, Ms R. Anderson

REGIONAL POLICY DIRECTORATE
Director, D. Smith

SENIOR STAFF MANAGEMENT
Director, Ms K. Elliott

SMALL AND MEDIUM-SIZED ENTERPRISES (SME)
POLICY DIRECTORATE
St Mary's House, Level 2, c/o Moorfoot, Sheffield S1 4PQ
Director, J. Thompson

SMALL AND MEDIUM-SIZED ENTERPRISES (SME)
TECHNOLOGY DIRECTORATE
Director, R. Allpress

STAFF PAY AND CONDITIONS
Director, C. Johnston

STAFF PERSONNEL OPERATIONS
Director, I. Cameron

‡TECHNOLOGY AND STANDARDS DIRECTORATE
Director of Technology and Standards, Dr D. Evans
Directors, I. C. Downing; J. M. Barber; G. C. Riggs; J.
   Hobday; G. McGregor

TRADE POLICY DIRECTORATE
Kingsgate House, 66–74 Victoria Street, London
SW1E 6SW
Director, J. Hunt

BRITISH OVERSEAS TRADE BOARD
Kingsgate House, 66–74 Victoria Street, London SW1E
6SW
Tel 0171-215 5000

President, The President of the Board of Trade
Chairman, M. Laing, CBE
Vice-Chairman, HRH The Duke of Kent, KG, GCMG, GCVO
Members, Dr D. Baldwin, CBE; A. Buxton; A. Turner; P.
   Godwin, CBE; R. Burman, CBE; Sir Brian Pearse;
   B. Willott; A. Burns, CMG; A. Hunt, CMG; T. Harris, CMG;
   Sir Gilbert Thompson, OBE; Sir Clive Thompson; R.
   Turner, OBE; B. Willott, CB
Secretary, Dr D. Walker

REGIONAL OFFICES
— *see* pages 305–6

EXECUTIVE AGENCIES

COMPANIES HOUSE
Companies House, Crown Way, Cardiff CF4 3UZ
Tel 01222-388588
London Search Room, 55–71 City Road, London EC1Y 1BB
Tel 0171-253 9393
37 Castle Terrace, Edinburgh EH1 2EB
Tel 0131-535 5800

‡ At 151 Buckingham Palace Road, London SW1W 9SS

Companies House incorporates companies, registers company documents and provides company information.
Registrar of Companies for England and Wales, J. Holden
Registrar for Scotland, J. Henderson

EMPLOYMENT TRIBUNALS SERVICE
19–29 Woburn Place, London WC1H 0LU
Tel 0171-273 8666
The Service became an executive agency in April 1997 and brought together the administrative support for the industrial tribunals and the Employment Appeal Tribunal.
Chief Executive, I. Jones

THE INSOLVENCY SERVICE
PO Box 203, 21 Bloomsbury Street, London WC1B 3QW
Tel 0171-637 1110

The Service administers and investigates the affairs of bankrupts and companies in compulsory liquidation; deals with the disqualification of directors in all corporate failures; regulates insolvency practitioners and their professional bodies; provides banking and investment services for bankruptcy and liquidation estates; and advises ministers on insolvency policy issues.
Inspector-General and Chief Executive, P. R. Joyce
Deputy Inspectors-General, D. J. Flynn; M. C. A. Osborne

NATIONAL WEIGHTS AND MEASURES LABORATORY
Stanton Avenue, Teddington, Middx TW11 0JZ
Tel 0181-943 7272

The Laboratory administers weights and measures legislation, carries out type examination, calibration and testing, and runs courses on metrological topics.
Chief Executive (G5), Dr S. Bennett

PATENT OFFICE
— *see* page 333

RADIOCOMMUNICATIONS AGENCY
New King's Beam House, 22 Upper Ground, London
SE1 9SA
Tel 0171-211 0211

The Agency is responsible for most civil radio matters other than telecommunications policy, broadcasting policy and the radio equipment market.
Chief Executive (G3), J. Norton

THE TREASURY
Parliament Street, London SW1P 3AG
Tel 0171-270 3000

The Office of the Lord High Treasurer has been continuously in commission for well over 200 years. The Lord High Commissioners of HM Treasury are the First Lord of the Treasury (who is also the Prime Minister), the Chancellor of the Exchequer and five junior Lords (who are government whips in the House of Commons). This Board of Commissioners is assisted at present by the Chief Secretary, a Parliamentary Secretary who is also the government Chief Whip, a Financial Secretary, an Economic Secretary, the Paymaster-General, and the Permanent Secretary.

The Prime Minister is not primarily concerned in the day-to-day aspects of Treasury business; the management of the Treasury devolves upon the Chancellor of the Exchequer and the other Treasury ministers.

The Chief Secretary is responsible for the planning and control of public expenditure; value for money in the public services; comprehensive spending reviews; public sector pay; strategic oversight of the financial system and financial services; devolution; and export credit.

The Paymaster-General's responsibilities include enterprise and growth; welfare-to-work issues; competition and deregulation policy; review of corporation tax; and Treasury interest in small firms. The Paymaster-General's Office is part of the National Investment and Loans Office (*see* page 328).

The Financial Secretary has responsibility for parliamentary financial business; oversight of the Inland Revenue, Customs and Excise and the Valuation Office Agency; Inland Revenue taxes (excluding the windfall levy); Customs and Excise duties and taxes; charities; and the environment, including energy efficiency.

The Economic Secretary has responsibility for the financial system and financial services; Economic and Monetary Union; foreign exchange reserves management; debt management policy; international issues; parliamentary questions; low pay and the minimum wage; women's issues; economic briefing; the Royal Mint; National Savings; the Office for National Statistics; the National Investment and Loans Office; and the Government Actuary's Department.

The Minister for Trade and Competitiveness in Europe deals with *ad hoc* projects and is chairman of an interdepartmental task force and a member of the Economic and European Cabinet committees.

All Treasury ministers are concerned in tax matters.

Prime Minister and First Lord of the Treasury, The Rt. Hon. Anthony Blair, MP
Chancellor of the Exchequer, The Rt. Hon. Gordon Brown, MP
  Principal Private Secretary, N. I. MacPherson
  Private Secretary, A. Gibbs
  Special Advisers, E. Balls; C. Whelan; E. Miliband; A. Maugham
  Parliamentary Private Secretary, D. Touhig, MP
Chief Secretary to the Treasury, The Rt. Hon. Alistair Darling, MP
  Private Secretary, P. Raynes
  Parliamentary Private Secretary, D. Hanson, MP
Paymaster-General, Geoffrey Robinson, MP
  Private Secretary, S. Field
  Parliamentary Private Secretary, I. Pearson, MP
Financial Secretary to the Treasury, Dawn Primarolo, MP
  Private Secretary, D. Finch
  Parliamentary Private Secretary, N. Gerrard, MP
Economic Secretary, Helen Liddell, MP
  Private Secretary, Ms S. Tebbutt
Minister of State (for Trade and Competitiveness in Europe), The Lord Simon of Highbury, CBE (*joint Treasury/DTI minister*)
Parliamentary Secretary to the Treasury and Government Chief Whip (*£36,613), The Rt. Hon. Nicholas Brown, MP
  Private Secretary, M. Maclean
Treasurer of HM Household and Deputy Chief Whip (*£31,125), George Mudie, MP
Comptroller of HM Household (*£20,029), Thomas McAvoy, MP
Vice-Chamberlain of HM Household (*20,029), Janet Anderson, MP
Lord Commissioners of the Treasury (*£20,029), R. Ainsworth, MP; G. Allen, MP; J. Dowd, MP; J. McFall, MP; J. Owen Jones, MP
Assistant Whips (*£20,029), C. Betts, MP; D. Clelland, MP; K. Hughes, MP; D. Jamieson, MP; Ms J. Kennedy, MP; G. Pope, MP; Ms B. Prentice, MP
Parliamentary Clerk, D. S. Martin
Council of Economic Advisers, C. Wales; P. Gregg; vacancies

Permanent Secretary to the Treasury (G1), Sir Terence Burns, GCB
  Private Secretary, C. Guest
Head of Government Accountancy Service and Chief Accountancy Adviser to the Treasury, A. Likierman

DIRECTORATES

Leader, Ministerial Support Team, N. Macpherson
Leader, Communications Team, P. Curwen
Leader, Strategy Team, N. Holgate

MACROECONOMIC POLICY AND PROSPECTS
Director, Prof. A. Budd
Deputy Directors, J. Grice; J. S. Cunliffe
Team Leaders, M. Bradbury; D. Deaton; C. M. Kelly; A. Kilpatrick; S. Pickford; D. Savage

INTERNATIONAL FINANCE
Director, Sir Nigel Wicks, KCB, CVO, CBE
Deputy Directors, P. McIntyre; D. L. C. Peretz, CB
Team Leaders, S. Brooks; R. Fellgett; N. J. Ilett; Ms S. Owen; D. Roe

BUDGET AND PUBLIC FINANCES
Director, P. R. C. Gray
Deputy Directors, †E. J. W. Gieve; C. J. Mowl
Team Leaders, D. Deaton; J. Dodds; N. M. Hansford; Ms R. Kosmin; S. N. Matthews; M. Parkinson; A. W. Ritchie; P. Wynn Owen

SPENDING
Director, R. P. Culpin, CB, CVO
Deputy Directors, †N. Glass; Miss G. M. Noble; Ms A. Perkins; P. N. Sedgwick
Team Leaders, P. Brook; S. Chakrabarti; D. Griffiths; J. Halligan; A. Hudson; M. Neale; I. V. W. Taylor; Ms R. Thompson; Ms S. Walker

FINANCIAL MANAGEMENT, REPORTING AND AUDIT
Director (Chief Accountancy Adviser), A. Likierman
Deputy Director, †J. E. Mortimer
Team Leaders, C. Butler; Mrs R. M. Dunn; N. Holgate; Ms A. M. Jones; D. Loweth

FINANCE, REGULATION AND INDUSTRY
Director, S. Robson
Deputy Directors, H. J. Bush; B. Rigby; A. Whiting; M. L. Williams
Team Leaders, J. Colling; Mrs P. C. Diggle; C. Farthing; J. J. Heywood; J. May; C. R. Pickering; A. Sharples; Ms J. Simpson; P. Wanless

PERSONNEL AND SUPPORT
Director, Ms M. O'Mara
Team Leaders, I. Cooper; D. Baker; D. Rayson

EXECUTIVE AGENCIES

NATIONAL SAVINGS
— *see* page 329

ROYAL MINT
— *see* page 338

OFFICE FOR NATIONAL STATISTICS
— *see* page 329

---

* In addition to a parliamentary salary of £43,860

†Combined deputy director and head of team

THE TREASURY SOLICITOR
DEPARTMENT OF HM PROCURATOR-GENERAL AND
TREASURY SOLICITOR
Queen Anne's Chambers, 28 Broadway, London SW1H 9JS
Tel 0171-210 3000

The Treasury Solicitor's Department provides legal
services for many government departments. Those without their own lawyers are provided with legal advice, and
both they and other departments are provided with
litigation services. The Treasury Solicitor is also the
Queen's Proctor, and is responsible for collecting Bona
Vacantia on behalf of the Crown. The Department became
an executive agency in April 1996.
HM Procurator-General and Treasury Solicitor (SCS), A. H.
    Hammond, CB
Deputy Treasury Solicitor (SCS), D. A. Hogg

CENTRAL ADVISORY DIVISION
SCS, Mrs I. G. Letwin

LITIGATION DIVISION
SCS, D. Brummell; Mrs D. Babar; A. D. Lawton;
    A. Leithead; P. R. Messer; Mrs J. B. C. Oliver;
    D. Palmer; R. J. Phillips; A. J. Sandal;
    P. F. O. Whitehurst

QUEEN'S PROCTOR DIVISION
Queen's Proctor (SCS), A. H. Hammond, CB
Assistant Queen's Proctor (SCS), Mrs D. Babar

RESOURCES AND SERVICES DIVISION
Principal Establishment and Finance Officer and Security Officer
    (SCS), A. J. E. Hollis
Deputy Establishment Officer (G7), Ms H. Donnelly
Finance Officer (G7), C. A. Woolley
Information Systems Manager (G7), M. Gabbidon
Business Support Manager (SEO), E. Blishen

BONA VACANTIA DIVISION
SCS, R. A. D. Jackson

EUROPEAN DIVISION
SCS, J. E. G. Vaux; J. E. Collins; D. Macrae

CULTURE, MEDIA AND SPORT DIVISION
SCS, P. C. Jenkins

OFFICE OF PUBLIC SERVICE DIVISION
SCS, M. C. L. Carpenter

MINISTRY OF DEFENCE ADVISORY DIVISION
Metropole Building, Northumberland Avenue, London
WC2N 5BL
Tel 0171-218 4691

SCS, A. M. C. Inglese; Mrs P. A. Dayer; C. P. J.
    Muttukumaru

DEPARTMENT FOR EDUCATION AND EMPLOYMENT
ADVISORY DIVISION
Caxton House, Tothill Street, London SW1H 9NF
Tel 0171-273 3000

SCS, F. L. Croft; C. House; Miss R. Jeffreys;
    N. A. D. Lambert; F. D. W. Clarke; S. T. Harker

DEPARTMENT OF THE ENVIRONMENT, TRANSPORT AND
THE REGIONS ADVISORY DIVISION
Great Minster House, 76 Marsham Street, London
SW1P 4DR
Tel 0171-271 5000

SCS, M. C. P. Thomas; D. J. Aries; C. W. M. Ingram;
    A. G. Jones; R. Lines; N. C. Thomas

HM TREASURY ADVISORY DIVISION
Treasury Chambers, Parliament Street, London SW1P 3AG
Tel 0171-270 3000

SCS, M. A. Blythe; M. J. Hemming; Mrs V. Collett; Miss
    J. V. Stokes; J. R. J. Braggins

GOVERNMENT PROPERTY LAWYERS
Riverside Chambers, Castle Street, Taunton, Somerset
TA1 4AP
Tel 01823-345200

An executive agency of the Treasury Solicitor's Depart-
ment.
Chief Executive (G3), P. Horner
Group Directors (G5), M. Benmayor; M. F. Rawlins;
    A. M. Scarfe
Director of Lands Advisory (G5), R. C. Paddock

COUNCIL ON TRIBUNALS
7th Floor, 22 Kingsway, London WC2B 6LE
Tel 0171-936 7045

The Council on Tribunals is an independent statutory
body. It keeps under review the constitution and working
of the various tribunals which have been placed under its
general supervision, and considers and reports on administrative procedures relating to statutory inquiries. It is
consulted by government departments on proposals for
legislation affecting tribunals and inquiries, and on proposals where the need for an appeals procedure may arise. It
also offers advice on draft primary legislation. Some 70
tribunals are currently under the Council's supervision.
    The Scottish Committee of the Council generally
considers Scottish tribunals and matters relating only to
Scotland.
    Members of the Council are appointed by the Lord
Chancellor and the Lord Advocate. The Scottish Committee is composed partly of members of the Council
designated by the Lord Advocate and partly of others
appointed by him. The Parliamentary Commissioner for
Administration is *ex officio* a member of both the Council
and the Scottish Committee.
Chairman, The Lord Archer of Sandwell, PC, QC
Members, The Parliamentary Commissioner for
    Administration; Mrs A. Anderson;
    T. N. Biggart, CBE, WS (*Chairman of the Scottish Committee*);
    Mrs S. Friend, MBE; R. H. Jones, CVO; Dr C. A. Kaplan;
    I. D. Penman, CB; Prof. M. Partington; S. M. D. Brown;
    S. R. Davie, CB; J. H. Eames; S. Jones, CBE; I. J. Irvine
Secretary, A. Twort

SCOTTISH COMMITTEE OF THE COUNCIL ON
TRIBUNALS
44 Palmerston Place, Edinburgh EH12 5BJ
Tel 0131-220 1236

Chairman, T. N. Biggart, CBE, WS
Members, The Parliamentary Commissioner for
    Administration; Mrs H. Sheerin, OBE; Ms M. Burns;
    Mrs A. Middleton; I. D. Penman, CB; Mrs P. Y. Berry,
    MBE; I. J. Irvine
Secretary, Mrs E. M. MacRae

TRIBUNALS
— *see* pages 370–3

UNITED KINGDOM SPORTS COUNCIL
Walkden House, 10 Melton Street, London NW1 2EB
Tel 0171-380 8000

The UK Sports Council became fully operational on 1 January 1997 and replaced the former Great Britain Sports Council. It promotes the development of sport and fosters the provision of facilities for sport and recreation at a UK level. Funding for 1997–8 from the Department for Culture, Media and Sport is £11.8 million.

Responsibility for distributing the funds allocated to sport from the proceeds of the National Lottery rests with the English, Welsh, Scottish and Northern Ireland Sports Councils (*see* page 707).

Chairman (acting), Sir Rodney Walker
Chief Executive, H. Wells

UNRELATED LIVE TRANSPLANT REGULATORY AUTHORITY
Department of Health, c/o Room LG05, Wellington House, 135–155 Waterloo Road, London SE1 8UG
Tel 0171-972 4824

The Unrelated Live Transplant Regulatory Authority (ULTRA) is a statutory body established in 1990. In every case where the transplant of an organ within the definition of the Human Organ Transplants Act 1989 is proposed between a living donor and a recipient who are not genetically related, the proposal must be referred to ULTRA. Applications must be made by registered medical practitioners.

The Authority comprises a chairman and ten members appointed by the Secretary of State for Health. The secretariat is provided by Department of Health officials.

Chairman, Prof. M. Bobrow, CBE
Members, Mrs J. Callman; Dr J. F. Douglas; Dr H. Draper; Dr P. A. Dyer; Mrs D. Eccles; Miss P. Franklin; A. Hooker; S. G. Macpherson; Prof. N. P. Mallick; Prof. J. R. Salaman
Administrative Secretary, W. Kent
Medical Secretary, Dr P. Doyle

WALES YOUTH AGENCY
Leslie Court, Lon-y-Llyn, Caerphilly CF83 1BQ
Tel 01222-880088

The Wales Youth Agency is an independent organization funded by the Welsh Office. Its functions include the encouragement and development of the partnership between statutory and voluntary agencies relating to young people; the promotion of staff development and training; and the extension of marketing and information services in the relevant fields. The board of directors is appointed by the Secretary of State for Wales. Directors do not receive a salary.

Chairman of the Board of Directors, G. Davies
Vice-Chairman of the Board of Directors, Dr H. Williamson
Executive Director, B. Williams

OFFICE OF WATER SERVICES
Centre City Tower, 7 Hill Street, Birmingham B5 4UA
Tel 0121-625 1300

The Office of Water Services (Ofwat) was set up under the Water Act 1989 and is the independent economic regulator of the water and sewerage companies in England and Wales. Ofwat's main duties are to ensure that the companies can finance and carry out the functions specified in the Water Industry Act 1991 and to protect the interests of water customers. Ofwat is a non-ministerial government department headed by the Director-General of Water Services, who is directly accountable to Parliament. There are ten regional customer service committees which are concerned solely with the interests of water customers. Representation of customer interests at national level is the responsibility of the Ofwat National Customer Council (ONCC).

Director-General of Water Services, I. C. R. Byatt

WELSH DEVELOPMENT AGENCY
Principality House, The Friary, Cardiff CF1 4AE
Tel 0345-775577/66

The Agency was established under the Welsh Development Agency Act 1975. Its remit is to help further the regeneration of the economy and improve the environment in Wales. The Agency's main activities include site assembly, provision of premises, encouraging investment by the private sector in property development, grant-aiding land reclamation, stimulating quality urban and rural development, promoting Wales as a location for inward investment, helping to boost the growth, profitability and competitiveness of indigenous Welsh companies, and providing investment capital for industry. Its sponsoring department is the Welsh Office.

Chairman, D. Rowe-Beddoe
Deputy Chairman, R. Lewis, OBE
Chief Executive, W. B. Willott, CB

WELSH OFFICE

The Welsh Office has responsibility in Wales for ministerial functions relating to health and personal social services; education, except for terms and conditions of service and student awards; training; the Welsh language, arts and culture; the implementation of the Citizen's Charter in Wales; local government, housing, water and sewerage, environmental protection; sport; agriculture and fisheries; forestry; land use, including town and country planning and countryside and nature conservation; new towns; non-departmental public bodies and appointments in Wales; ancient monuments and historic buildings and the Welsh Arts Council; roads; tourism; financial assistance to industry; the Strategic Development Scheme in Wales and the Programme for the Valleys; the operation of the European Regional Development Fund in Wales and other European Community matters; civil emergencies; and all financial aspects of these matters, including Welsh rate support grant.

Gwydyr House, Whitehall, London SW1A 2ER
Tel 0171-270 3000

Secretary of State for Wales, The Rt. Hon. Ronald Davies, MP

Private Secretary, Dr J. Milligan
Special Advisers, J. Adams; H. Roberts
Parliamentary Private Secretary, N. Ainger, MP
Parliamentary Under-Secretaries, Win Griffiths, MP; Peter Hain, MP
Private Secretaries, Ms J. Brown; Ms J. Cole
Special Advisers, J. Adams; H. Roberts
Parliamentary Clerk, A. Green
Permanent Secretary (G1), Mrs R. Lomax
Private Secretary, Ms J. M. Brown

Cathays Park, Cardiff CF1 3NQ
Tel 01222-825111

LEGAL GROUP
Legal Adviser (G3), D. G. Lambert
Deputy Legal Adviser (G5), J. H. Turnbull

INFORMATION DIVISION
Director of News (G7), D. Clifford
Principal Publicity Officer (G7), W. J. Edwards

ESTABLISHMENT GROUP
Principal Establishment Officer (G3), S. H. Martin
Heads of Divisions (G5), Mrs B. Wilson; Dr A. G. Thornton; Ms K. Cassidy
Chief Statistician (G5), W. R. L. Alldritt
Head of Health Statistics and Analysis Unit (G6), P. J. Fullerton
Head of Training and Education Intelligence Unit (G6), Mrs C. Fullerton

FINANCE GROUP
Principal Finance Officer (G3), D. T. Richards
Head of Division (G5), L. A. Pavelin
Senior Economic Adviser (G5), M. G. Phelps
Grade 6, M. G. Horlock
Head of Internal Audit (G6), D. Howarth

ECONOMIC AFFAIRS
Deputy Secretary (G2), J. D. Shortridge

AGRICULTURE DEPARTMENT
Head of Department (G3), L. K. Walford
Heads of Divisions (G5), D. R. Thomas; Mrs A. M. Jackson
Divisional Executive Officers (G7), W. K. Griffiths (*Carmarthen*); E. Hughes (*Caernarfon*); J. C. Alexander (*Llandrindod Wells*)

ECONOMIC DEVELOPMENT GROUP
Head of Group (G3), M. J. Cochlin
Heads of Divisions (G5), B. J. Mitchell; A. D. Lansdown; M. L. Evans

INDUSTRY AND TRAINING DEPARTMENT
Director (G3), D. W. Jones
Industrial Director (G4), J. Cameron
Heads of Divisions (G5), G. T. Evans; R. Keveren; N. E. Thomas; (*G6*), Dr R. J. Loveland

SOCIAL POLICY
Deputy Secretary (G2), J. W. Lloyd, CB

EDUCATION DEPARTMENT
Head of Department (G3), R. J. Davies
Heads of Divisions (G5)°, W. G. Davies; H. Evans; R. Thomas

OFFICE OF HM CHIEF INSPECTOR FOR SCHOOLS IN WALES
Chief Inspector (G4)°, Miss S. Lewis
Staff Inspectors (G5)°, S. J. Adams; J. R. N. Evans; T. E. Parry; G. Thomas; P. Thomas
There are 45 Grade 6 Inspectors.
Head of Administration (G7), J. Roberts

LOCAL GOVERNMENT GROUP
Head of Group (G3), D. A. Pritchard
Heads of Divisions (G5), A. C. Wood; M. J. Clancy; Mrs B. J. M. Wilson; Mrs E. A. Taylor
Chief Inspector, Social Services Inspectorate (Wales) (G5), D. G. Evans
Deputy Chief Inspectors, J. F. Mooney; R. C. Woodward
Social Services Inspectors (G7), D. Barker; D. A. Brushett; G. H. Davies; Miss R. E. Evans; I. Forster; Mrs J. Jenkins; C. D. Vyvyan; Mrs P. White

HEALTH DEPARTMENT
Director (G3), P. R. Gregory
Heads of Divisions (G5), D. H. Jones; D. A. Pritchard; M. D. Chown; B. Wilcox; R. C. Williams; A. G. Thornton

HEALTH PROFESSIONAL GROUP
Chief Medical Officer (G3), Dr R. Hall
Principal Medical Officers (G4), Dr B. Fuge; Dr J. K. Richmond
Senior Medical Officers (G5), Dr J. Ludlow; Dr H. N. Williams; Dr D. Salter; Dr P. Lyne
Medical Adviser (part-time), Dr J. Andrew
Chief Dental Officer (G5), D. M. Heap
Senior Dental Officer (G5), P. Langmaid
Chief Scientific Adviser (G5), Dr J. A. V. Pritchard
Deputy Scientific Adviser (G6), Dr E. O. Crawley
Chief Pharmaceutical Adviser (G5), Miss C. W. Howells
Chief Environmental Health Adviser (G5), R. Alexander
Deputy Environmental Health Adviser (G6), D. Worthington

NURSING DIVISION
Chief Nursing Officer, Miss M. Bull
Deputy Chief Nursing Officer, Mrs B. Melvin
Nursing Officers, Mrs S. M. Drayton; P. Johnson; Mrs J. Sait; M. F. Tonkin

TRANSPORT, PLANNING AND ENVIRONMENT GROUP
Head of Group (G3), G. C. G. Craig
Director of Highways (G4), K. J. Thomas°
Deputy Director of Highways (G5), J. G. Evans*
Head of Division (G5), D. I. Westlake°
Chief Planning Adviser (G5), W. P. Roderick
Superintending Engineers (G6), J. R. Rees*; B. H. Hawker, OBE *
Chief Estates Adviser (G6), G. K. Hoad
Senior Principal (G6), P. R. Marsden
Scientific Adviser (G6), Dr H. Prosser
Principal Planning Officers (G7), L. Owen; J. V. Spear
Principal Research Officers (G7), A. S. Dredge; Ms L. J. Roberts
Principal Estates Officer (G7), R. W. Wilson
Principal Professional and Technology Officers, Highways Directorate° (G7), M. J. Gilbert*; I. A. Grindulis; A. P. Howcroft; A. L. Perry; R. H. Powell; S. C. Shouler; J. Collins; K. J. Alexander; R. H. Hooper*; R. K. Cone; J. Dawkins; T. Dorken; R. Shaw; M. J. A. Parker; V. S. Pownall*

HEALTH AUTHORITIES

BRO TAF, Churchill House, Churchill Way, Cardiff CF1 4TW. *Chair*, Mrs K. Thomas; *Chief Executive*, Mrs G. Todd

DYFED POWYS, St David's Hospital, Carmarthen SA31 3HB. *Chair*, Mrs V. Bourne; *Chief Executive*, Mrs P. Stansbie
GWENT, Mamhilad House, Mamhilad, Pontypool NP4 0YP. *Chair*, Hon. Mrs L. Price; *Chief Executive*, J. Hallett
MORGANNWG, The Oldway Centre, 36 Orchard Street, Swansea SA1 5AQ. *Chair*, H. Thomas; *Chief Executive*, Mrs J. Williams
NORTH WALES, Preswylfa, Hendy Road, Mold CH7 1PZ. *Chair*, Dr A. Kenrick; *Chief Executive*, B. Jones

EXECUTIVE AGENCIES

CADW: WELSH HISTORIC MONUMENTS
Crown Building, Cathays Park, Cardiff CF1 3NQ
Tel 01222-500200

Cadw supports the preservation, conservation, appreciation and enjoyment of the built heritage in Wales.
Chief Executive, T. Cassidy
Director of Policy and Administration, R. W. Hughes
Conservation Architect (G6), J. D. Hogg
Principal Inspector of Ancient Monuments and Historic Buildings, J. R. Avent
Inspectors of Ancient Monuments and Historic Buildings, A. D. McLees; Dr S. E. Rees; R. C. Turner; M. J. Yates

FARMING AND RURAL CONSERVATION AGENCY
— *see* page 281

INTERVENTION BOARD
— *see* page 316

PLANNING INSPECTORATE
Cathays Park, Cardiff CF1 3NQ
Tel 01222-823892

A joint executive agency of the Department of the Environment, Transport and the Regions and the Welsh Office (*see* page 301).
Chief Executive and Chief Planning Inspector (G3), C. Shepley
Director (G5), Mrs S. Bruton

WOMEN'S NATIONAL COMMISSION
6th Floor, The Adelphi, 1–11 John Adam Street, London WC2N 6HT
Tel 0171-712 2443

The Women's National Commission is an independent advisory committee to the Government. Its remit is to ensure that the informed opinions of women are given their due weight in the deliberations of the Government and in public debate on matters of public interest including those of special interest to women. The Commission's sponsoring department is the Department for Education and Employment.
Government Co-Chairman, The Baroness Symons of Vernham Dean
Elected Co-Chairman, Miss V. Evans, CBE
Secretary, Ms J. Bailey

CIVIL SERVICE STAFF

BY MAIN DEPARTMENTS *as at 1 April 1996*

	Total	Of whom in agencies
Agriculture, Fisheries and Food	9,993	3,892
Cabinet Office	3,691	2,629
Customs and Excise	23,186	—
Defence	109,858	45,250
Education and Employment	40,327	35,282
Environment	4,678	1,323
Foreign Office	5,815	28
Health	4,795	1,063
HM Prison Service	38,009	38,009
Home Office	11,938	2,490
Inland Revenue	56,470	4,459
Lord Chancellor's Department	11,227	10,376
National Heritage	1,003	666
Northern Ireland Office	215	—
Scottish Departments	12,826	7,695
Social Security	91,516	88,766
Trade and Industry	9,234	3,550
Transport	11,071	9,100
Treasury	958	—
Welsh Office	2,139	211
Other departments	45,343	20,140
TOTAL	494,292	274,929

Source: The Stationery Office – *Civil Service Yearbook 1997*

Law Courts and Offices

THE JUDICIAL COMMITTEE OF THE PRIVY COUNCIL

The Judicial Committee of the Privy Council is primarily the final court of appeal for the United Kingdom dependent territories and those independent Commonwealth countries which have retained the avenue of appeal upon achieving independence (Antigua and Barbuda, The Bahamas, Barbados, Belize, Brunei, Dominica, The Gambia, Jamaica, Kiribati, Mauritius, New Zealand, St Christopher and Nevis, St Lucia, St Vincent and the Grenadines, Trinidad and Tobago, and Tuvalu). The Committee also hears appeals from the Channel Islands and the Isle of Man and the disciplinary and health committees of the medical and allied professions. It has a limited jurisdiction to hear appeals under the Pastoral Measure 1983. In 1996 the Judicial Committee heard 85 appeals and 99 petitions for special leave to appeal.

The members of the Judicial Committee include the Lord Chancellor, the Lords of Appeal in Ordinary (*see* page 355), other Privy Counsellors who hold or have held high judicial office and certain judges from the Commonwealth.

PRIVY COUNCIL OFFICE (JUDICIAL COMMITTEE), Downing Street, London SW1A 2AJ. Tel: 0171-270 0483. *Registrar of the Privy Council*, D. H. O. Owen; *Chief Clerk*, F. G. Hart

The Judicature of England and Wales

The legal system of England and Wales is separate from those of Scotland and Northern Ireland and differs from them in law, judicial procedure and court structure, although there is a common distinction between civil law (disputes between individuals) and criminal law (acts harmful to the community).

The supreme judicial authority for England and Wales is the House of Lords, which is the ultimate Court of Appeal from all courts in Great Britain and Northern Ireland (except criminal courts in Scotland) for all cases except those concerning the interpretation and application of European Community law, including preliminary rulings requested by British courts and tribunals, which are decided by the European Court of Justice (*see* page 774). (The European Convention on Human Rights has not yet been incorporated into domestic law, although the Government has stated its intention to do so; therefore when all remedies available at national level have been exhausted an applicant must petition the European Commission of Human Rights to investigate an alleged violation of the Convention.) As a Court of Appeal the House of Lords consists of the Lord Chancellor and the Lords of Appeal in Ordinary (law lords).

SUPREME COURT OF JUDICATURE

The Supreme Court of Judicature comprises the Court of Appeal, the High Court of Justice and the Crown Court.

The High Court of Justice is the superior civil court and is divided into three divisions. The Chancery Division is concerned mainly with equity, bankruptcy and contentious probate business. The Queen's Bench Division deals with commercial and maritime law, serious personal injury and medical negligence cases, cases involving a breach of contract and professional negligence actions. The Family Division deals with matters relating to family law. Sittings are held at the Royal Courts of Justice in London or at 126 District Registries outside the capital. High Court judges sit alone to hear cases at first instance. Appeals from lower courts are heard by two or three judges, or by single judges of the appropriate division. The Restrictive Practices Court, set up under the Restrictive Trade Practices Act 1956, and the Official Referees' Courts, which deal almost exclusively with cases concerning the construction industry, are also part of the High Court. Appeals from the High Court are heard in the Court of Appeal (Civil Division), presided over by the Master of the Rolls, and may go on to the House of Lords.

CRIMINAL CASES

In criminal matters the decision to prosecute in the majority of cases rests with the Crown Prosecution Service, the independent prosecuting body in England and Wales (*see* page 363–4). At the head of the service is the Director of Public Prosecutions, who discharges her duties under the superintendence of the Attorney-General. Certain categories of offence continue to require the Attorney-General's consent for prosecution.

The Crown Court sits in about 90 centres, divided into six circuits, and is presided over by High Court judges, full-time circuit judges, and part-time recorders and assistant recorders, sitting with a jury in all trials which are contested. There were 353 assistant recorders at 30 June 1997. The Crown Court deals with trials of the more serious criminal offences, the sentencing of offenders committed for sentence by magistrates' courts (when the magistrates consider their own power of sentence inadequate), and appeals from magistrates' courts. Magistrates usually sit with a circuit judge or recorder to deal with appeals and committals for sentence. Appeals from the Crown Court, either against sentence or conviction, are made to the Court of Appeal (Criminal Division), presided over by the Lord Chief Justice. A further appeal from the Court of Appeal to the House of Lords can be brought if a point of law of general public importance is considered to be involved.

Minor criminal offences (summary offences) are dealt with in magistrates' courts, which usually consist of three unpaid lay magistrates (justices of the peace) sitting without a jury, who are advised on points of law and procedure by a legally-qualified clerk to the justices. There were 30,374 justices of the peace at 1 January 1997. In busier courts a full-time, salaried and legally-qualified stipendiary magistrate presides alone. Cases involving people under 18 are heard in youth courts, specially constituted magistrates' courts which sit apart from other courts. Preliminary proceedings in a serious case to decide whether there is evidence to justify committal for trial in the Crown Court are also dealt with in the magistrates' courts. Appeals from magistrates' courts against sentence or conviction are made to the Crown Court. Appeals upon a point of law are made to the High Court, and may go on to the House of Lords.

CIVIL CASES

Most minor civil cases are dealt with by the county courts, of which there are about 270 (details may be found in the local telephone directory). Cases are heard by circuit judges or district judges. There were 338 district judges at 31 May 1997. For cases involving small claims there are special simplified procedures. Where there are financial limits on county court jurisdiction, claims which exceed those limits may be tried in the county courts with the consent of the parties, or in certain circumstances on transfer from the High Court. Outside London, bankruptcy proceedings can be heard in designated county courts. Magistrates' courts can deal with certain classes of civil case and committees of magistrates license public houses, clubs and betting shops. For the implementation of the Children Act 1989, a new structure of hearing centres was set up in 1991 for family proceedings cases, involving magistrates' courts (family proceedings courts), divorce county courts, family hearing centres and care centres. Appeals in family matters heard in the family proceedings courts go to the Family Division of the High Court; affiliation appeals and appeals from decisions of the licensing committees of magistrates go to the Crown Court. Appeals from county courts are heard in the Court of Appeal (Civil Division), and may go on to the House of Lords.

CORONERS' COURTS

Coroners' courts investigate violent and unnatural deaths or sudden deaths where the cause is unknown. Cases may be brought before a local coroner (a senior lawyer or doctor) by doctors, the police, various public authorities or members of the public. Where a death is sudden and the cause is unknown, the coroner may order a post-mortem examination to determine the cause of death rather than hold an inquest in court.

Judicial appointments are made by The Queen; the most senior appointments are made on the advice of the Prime Minister and other appointments on the advice of the Lord Chancellor.

Under the provisions of the Criminal Appeal Act 1995, a Commission has been set up to direct and supervise investigations into possible miscarriages of justice and to refer cases to the courts on the grounds of conviction and sentence (*see* page 293); these functions were formerly the responsibility of the Home Secretary.

For late changes to this section, *see* Stop-Press

THE HOUSE OF LORDS
AS FINAL COURT OF APPEAL

The Lord High Chancellor (£140,665)
The Rt. Hon. the Lord Irvine of Lairg, *born* 1940, *apptd* 1997

LORDS OF APPEAL IN ORDINARY (each £131,034)
Style, The Rt. Hon. Lord —

Rt. Hon. Lord Goff of Chieveley, *born* 1926, *apptd* 1986
Rt. Hon. Lord Browne-Wilkinson, *born* 1930, *apptd* 1991
Rt. Hon. Lord Slynn of Hadley, *born* 1930, *apptd* 1992
Rt. Hon. Lord Lloyd of Berwick, *born* 1929, *apptd* 1993
Rt. Hon. Lord Nolan, *born* 1928, *apptd* 1994
Rt. Hon. Lord Nicholls of Birkenhead, *born* 1933, *apptd* 1994
Rt. Hon. Lord Steyn, *born* 1932, *apptd* 1995
Rt. Hon. Lord Hoffman, *born* 1934, *apptd* 1995

Rt. Hon. Lord Hope of Craighead, *born* 1938, *apptd* 1996
Rt. Hon. Lord Clyde, *born* 1932, *apptd* 1996
Rt. Hon. Lord Hutton, *born* 1931, *apptd* 1997
Rt. Hon. Lord Saville of Newdigate, *born* 1936, *apptd* 1997
Registrar, The Clerk of the Parliaments (*see* page 218)

SUPREME COURT OF JUDICATURE

COURT OF APPEAL

The Master of the Rolls (£131,034), The Rt. Hon. Lord Woolf, *born* 1933, *apptd* 1996
Secretary, Mrs L. Grace
Clerk, Ms J. Jones

LORDS JUSTICES OF APPEAL (EACH £124,551)
Style, The Rt. Hon. Lord/Lady Justice [surname]

Rt. Hon. Sir Martin Nourse, *born* 1932, *apptd* 1985
Rt. Hon. Dame Elizabeth Butler-Sloss, DBE, *born* 1933, *apptd* 1988
Rt. Hon. Sir Murray Stuart-Smith, *born* 1927, *apptd* 1988
Rt. Hon. Sir Christopher Staughton, *born* 1933, *apptd* 1988
Rt. Hon. Sir Roy Beldam, *born* 1925, *apptd* 1989
Rt. Hon. Sir Paul Kennedy, *born* 1935, *apptd* 1992
Rt. Hon. Sir David Hirst, *born* 1925, *apptd* 1992
Rt. Hon. Sir Simon Brown, *born* 1937, *apptd* 1992
Rt. Hon. Sir Anthony Evans, *born* 1934, *apptd* 1992
Rt. Hon. Sir Christopher Rose, *born* 1937, *apptd* 1992
Rt. Hon. Sir John Roch, *born* 1934, *apptd* 1993
Rt. Hon. Sir Peter Gibson, *born* 1934, *apptd* 1993
Rt. Hon. Sir John Hobhouse, *born* 1932, *apptd* 1993
Rt. Hon. Sir Denis Henry, *born* 1931, *apptd* 1993
Rt. Hon. Sir Peter Millett, *born* 1932, *apptd* 1994
Rt. Hon. Sir Swinton Thomas, *born* 1931, *apptd* 1994
Rt. Hon. Sir Andrew Morritt, CVO, *born* 1938, *apptd* 1994
Rt. Hon. Sir Philip Otton, *born* 1933, *apptd* 1995
Rt. Hon. Sir Robin Auld, *born* 1937, *apptd* 1995
Rt. Hon. Sir Malcolm Pill, *born* 1938, *apptd* 1995
Rt. Hon. Sir William Aldous, *born* 1936, *apptd* 1995
Rt. Hon. Sir Alan Ward, *born* 1938, *apptd* 1995
Rt. Hon. Sir Michael Hutchison, *born* 1933, *apptd* 1995
Rt. Hon. Sir Konrad Schiemann, *born* 1937, *apptd* 1995
Rt. Hon. Sir Nicholas Phillips, *born* 1938, *apptd* 1995
Rt. Hon. Sir Mathew Thorpe, *born* 1938, *apptd* 1995
Rt. Hon. Sir Mark Potter, *born* 1937, *apptd* 1996
Rt. Hon. Sir Henry Brooke, *born* 1936, *apptd* 1996
Rt. Hon. Sir Igor Judge, *born* 1941, *apptd* 1996
Rt. Hon. Sir Mark Waller, *born* 1940, *apptd* 1996
Rt. Hon. Sir John Mummery, *born* 1938, *apptd* 1996
Rt. Hon. Sir Charles Mantell, *born* 1937, *apptd* 1997
Rt. Hon. Sir John Chadwick, ED, *born* 1941, *apptd* 1997
Rt. Hon. Sir Robert Walker, *born* 1938, *apptd* 1997

Ex officio Judges, The Lord High Chancellor; the Lord Chief Justice of England; the Master of the Rolls; the President of the Family Division; and the Vice-Chancellor

COURT OF APPEAL (CRIMINAL DIVISION)
Vice-President, The Rt. Hon. Lord Justice Rose
Judges, The Lord Chief Justice of England; the Master of the Rolls; Lords Justices of Appeal; and Judges of the High Court of Justice

COURTS-MARTIAL APPEAL COURT
Judges, The Lord Chief Justice of England; the Master of the Rolls; Lords Justices of Appeal; and Judges of the High Court of Justice

HIGH COURT OF JUSTICE

CHANCERY DIVISION

President, The Lord High Chancellor
The Vice-Chancellor (£124,551), The Rt. Hon. Sir Richard
Scott, *born* 1934, *apptd* 1994
Clerk, W. Northfield, BEM

JUDGES (each £112,011)
Style, The Hon. Mr/Mrs Justice [surname]

Hon. Sir Jeremiah Harman, *born* 1930, *apptd* 1982
Hon. Sir Donald Rattee, *born* 1937, *apptd* 1989
Hon. Sir Francis Ferris, TD, *born* 1932, *apptd* 1990
Hon. Sir Jonathan Parker, *born* 1937, *apptd* 1991
Hon. Sir John Lindsay, *born* 1935, *apptd* 1992
Hon. Dame Mary Arden, DBE, *born* 1947, *apptd* 1993
Hon. Sir Edward Evans-Lombe, *born* 1937, *apptd* 1993
Hon. Sir Robin Jacob, *born* 1941, *apptd* 1993
Hon. Sir William Blackburne, *born* 1944, *apptd* 1993
Hon. Sir Gavin Lightman, *born* 1939, *apptd* 1994
Hon. Sir Robert Carnwath, *born* 1945, *apptd* 1994
Hon. Sir Colin Rimer, *born* 1944, *apptd* 1994
Hon. Sir Hugh Laddie, *born* 1946, *apptd* 1995
Hon. Sir Timothy Lloyd, *born* 1946, *apptd* 1996
Hon. Sir David Neuberger, *born* 1948, *apptd* 1996

HIGH COURT OF JUSTICE IN BANKRUPTCY

Judges, The Vice-Chancellor and judges of the Chancery
Division of the High Court

COMPANIES COURT

Judges, The Vice Chancellor and judges of the Chancery
Division of the High Court

PATENT COURT (APPELLATE SECTION)
Judge, The Hon. Mr Justice Jacob

QUEEN'S BENCH DIVISION

The Lord Chief Justice of England (£140,008) The Rt. Hon.
the Lord Bingham of Cornhill, *born* 1933, *apptd* 1996
Private Secretary, E. Adams
Clerk, J. Bond
Vice-President, The Rt. Hon. Lord Justice Kennedy

JUDGES (each £112,011)
Style, The Hon. Mr/Mrs Justice [surname]

Hon. Sir Charles McCullough, *born* 1931, *apptd* 1981
Hon. Sir Oliver Popplewell, *born* 1927, *apptd* 1983
Hon. Sir Richard Tucker, *born* 1930, *apptd* 1985
Hon. Sir Patrick Garland, *born* 1929, *apptd* 1985
Hon. Sir Michael Turner, *born* 1931, *apptd* 1985
Hon. Sir John Alliott, *born* 1932, *apptd* 1986
Hon. Sir Harry Ognall, *born* 1934, *apptd* 1986
Hon. Sir John Owen, *born* 1925, *apptd* 1986
Hon. Sir Humphrey Potts, *born* 1931, *apptd* 1986
Hon. Sir Richard Rougier, *born* 1932, *apptd* 1986
Hon. Sir Ian Kennedy, *born* 1930, *apptd* 1986
Hon. Sir Stuart McKinnon, *born* 1938, *apptd* 1988
Hon. Sir Scott Baker, *born* 1937, *apptd* 1988
Hon. Sir Edwin Jowitt, *born* 1929, *apptd* 1988
Hon. Sir Douglas Brown, *born* 1931, *apptd* 1996
Hon. Sir Michael Morland, *born* 1929, *apptd* 1989
Hon. Sir Roger Buckley, *born* 1939, *apptd* 1989
Hon. Sir Anthony Hidden, *born* 1936, *apptd* 1989
Hon. Sir Michael Wright, *born* 1932, *apptd* 1990
Hon. Sir John Blofeld, *born* 1932, *apptd* 1990
Hon. Sir Peter Cresswell, *born* 1944, *apptd* 1991
Hon. Sir Anthony May, *born* 1940, *apptd* 1991
Hon. Sir John Laws, *born* 1945, *apptd* 1992

Hon. Dame Ann Ebsworth, DBE, *born* 1937, *apptd* 1992
Hon. Sir Simon Tuckey, *born* 1941, *apptd* 1992
Hon. Sir David Latham, *born* 1942, *apptd* 1992
Hon. Sir Christopher Holland, *born* 1937, *apptd* 1992
Hon. Sir John Kay, *born* 1943, *apptd* 1992
Hon. Sir Richard Curtis, *born* 1933, *apptd* 1992
Hon. Sir Stephen Sedley, *born* 1939, *apptd* 1992
Hon. Dame Janet Smith, DBE, *born* 1940, *apptd* 1992
Hon. Sir Anthony Colman, *born* 1938, *apptd* 1992
Hon. Sir Anthony Clarke, *born* 1943, *apptd* 1993
Hon. Sir John Dyson, *born* 1943, *apptd* 1993
Hon. Sir Thayne Forbes, *born* 1938, *apptd* 1993
Hon. Sir Michael Sachs, *born* 1932, *apptd* 1993
Hon. Sir Stephen Mitchell, *born* 1941, *apptd* 1993
Hon. Sir Rodger Bell, *born* 1939, *apptd* 1993
Hon. Sir Michael Harrison, *born* 1939, *apptd* 1993
Hon. Sir Bernard Rix, *born* 1944, *apptd* 1993
Hon. Dame Heather Steel, DBE, *born* 1940, *apptd* 1993
Hon. Sir William Gage, *born* 1938, *apptd* 1993
Hon. Sir Jonathan Mance, *born* 1943, *apptd* 1993
Hon. Sir Andrew Longmore, *born* 1944, *apptd* 1993
Hon. Sir Thomas Morison, *born* 1939, *apptd* 1993
Hon. Sir Richard Buxton, *born* 1938, *apptd* 1993
Hon. Sir David Keene, *born* 1941, *apptd* 1994
Hon. Sir Andrew Collins, *born* 1942, *apptd* 1994
Hon. Sir Maurice Kay, *born* 1942, *apptd* 1995
Hon. Sir Brian Smedley, *born* 1934, *apptd* 1995
Hon. Sir Anthony Hooper, *born* 1937, *apptd* 1995
Hon. Sir Alexander Butterfield, *born* 1942, *apptd* 1995
Hon. Sir George Newman, *born* 1941, *apptd* 1995
Hon. Sir David Poole, *born* 1938, *apptd* 1995
Hon. Sir Martin Moore-Bick, *born* 1946, *apptd* 1995
Hon. Sir Gordon Langley, *born* 1943, *apptd* 1995
Hon. Sir Roger Thomas, *born* 1947, *apptd* 1996
Hon. Sir Robert Nelson, *born* 1942, *apptd* 1996
Hon. Sir Roger Toulson, *born* 1946, *apptd* 1996
Hon. Sir Michael Astill, *born* 1938, *apptd* 1996
Hon. Sir Alan Moses, *born* 1945, *apptd* 1996
Hon. Sir Timothy Walker, *born* 1946, *apptd* 1996
Hon. Sir David Eady, *born* 1943, *apptd* 1997

FAMILY DIVISION

President (£124,551) The Rt. Hon. Sir Stephen Brown,
born 1924, *apptd* 1988
Secretary, Mrs S. Leung
Clerk, Mrs S. Bell

JUDGES (each £112,011)
Style, The Hon. Mr/Mrs Justice [surname]

Hon. Sir Anthony Hollis, *born* 1927, *apptd* 1982
Hon. Sir Edward Cazalet, *born* 1936, *apptd* 1988
Hon. Sir Robert Johnson, *born* 1933, *apptd* 1989
Hon. Dame Joyanne Bracewell, DBE, *born* 1934, *apptd* 1990
Hon. Sir Michael Connell, *born* 1939, *apptd* 1991
Hon. Sir Peter Singer, *born* 1944, *apptd* 1993
Hon. Sir Nicholas Wilson, *born* 1945, *apptd* 1993
Hon. Sir Nicholas Wall, *born* 1945, *apptd* 1993
Hon. Sir Andrew Kirkwood, *born* 1944, *apptd* 1993
Hon. Sir Christopher Stuart-White, *born* 1933, *apptd* 1993
Hon. Dame Brenda Hale, DBE, *born* 1945, *apptd* 1994
Hon. Sir Hugh Bennett, *born* 1943, *apptd* 1995
Hon. Sir Edward Holman, *born* 1947, *apptd* 1995
Hon. Dame Mary Hogg, DBE, *born* 1947, *apptd* 1995
Hon. Sir Christopher Sumner, *born* 1939, *apptd* 1996

RESTRICTIVE PRACTICES COURT
Room 410, Thomas More Building, Royal Courts of
Justice, Strand, London WC2A 2LL
Tel 0171-936 6727

President, The Hon. Mr Justice Buckley
Judges, The Hon. Mr Justice Ferris; The Hon. Mr Justice Buxton
Lay Members, B. M. Currie; Sir Lewis Robertson, CBE; R. Garrick, CBE; S. J. Ahearne; J. A. Graham; Mrs D. H. Hatfield; J. A. Scott; B. D. Colgate; J. A. C. King
Clerk of the Court, M. Buckley

OFFICIAL REFEREES' COURTS
St Dunstan's House, 133–137 Fetter Lane, London
EC4A 1HD
Tel 0171-936 7427

JUDGES (each £92,378)

His Hon. Judge Lewis, QC (*Senior Official Referee*)
His Hon. Judge Bowsher, QC
His Hon. Judge Loyd, QC
His Hon. Judge Hicks, QC
His Hon. Judge Havery, QC
His Hon. Judge Lloyd, QC
His Hon. Judge Newman, QC
His Hon. Judge Thornton, QC
His Hon. Judge Wilcox

Chief Clerk, Miss B. Joy

LORD CHANCELLOR'S DEPARTMENT
— *see* Government Departments and Public Offices

SUPREME COURT DEPARTMENTS AND OFFICES
Royal Courts of Justice, London WC2A 2LL
Tel 0171-936 6000

DIRECTOR'S OFFICE

Director, G. E. Calvett
Deputy Director, J. Selch
Group Manager, Family Proceedings and Probate Service, R. P. Knight
Finance and Performance Officer, K. T. Fairweather

ADMIRALTY AND COMMERCIAL REGISTRY AND MARSHAL'S OFFICE

Registrar (£67,354), P. Miller
Admiralty Marshal and Court Manager (*G7*), A. Ferrigno

BANKRUPTCY DEPARTMENT

Chief Registrar (£80,430), M. C. B. Buckley
Bankruptcy Registrars (£67,354), W. S. James; J. A. Simmonds; P. J. S. Rawson; S. Baister
Court Manager (*SEO*), M. A. Brown

CENTRAL OFFICE OF THE SUPREME COURT

Senior Master of the Supreme Court (*QBD*), *and Queen's Remembrancer* (£80,430), R. L. Turner
Masters of the Supreme Court (*QBD*) (£67,354), D. L. Prebble; G. H. Hodgson; J. Trench; M. Tennant; P. Miller; N. O. G. Murray; I. H. Foster; G. H. Rose; P. G. A. Eyre; H. J. Leslie; J. G. G. Ungley
Court Manager (*G7*), P. Emery

CHANCERY DIVISION

Court Manager (*G7*), P. Emery

CHANCERY CHAMBERS

Chief Master of the Supreme Court (£80,430), J. M. Dyson
Masters of the Supreme Court (£67,354), G. A. Barratt; J. I. Winegarten; J. A. Moncaster, R. A. Bowman

Court Manager (*SEO*), G. Robinson
Conveyancing Counsel of the Supreme Court, W. D. Ainger; H. M. Harrod; A. C. Taussig

COMPANIES COURT

Registrar (£67,354), M. Buckley
Court Manager (*SEO*), M. A. Brown

COURT OF APPEAL CIVIL DIVISION

Registrar (£80,430), J. D. R. Adams
Deputy Registrar, I. M. Joseph
Court Manager (*SEO*), Miss H. M. Goddard

COURT OF APPEAL CRIMINAL DIVISION

Registrar (£80,430), M. McKenzie, QC
Deputy Registrar, Mrs L. G. Knapman
Chief Clerk (*G7*), M. Bishop

COURTS-MARTIAL APPEALS OFFICE

Registrar (£80,430), M. McKenzie, QC
Chief Clerk (*G7*), M. Bishop

CROWN OFFICE OF THE SUPREME COURT

Master of the Crown Office, and Queen's Coroner and Attorney (£80,430), M. McKenzie, QC
Head of Crown Office, Mrs L. G. Knapman
Chief Clerk (*G7*), M. Bishop

EXAMINERS OF THE COURT
Empowered to take examination of witnesses in all Divisions of the High Court
R. G. Wood; Mrs G. M. Kenne; R. M. Planterose; Miss V. E. I. Selvaratnam

RESTRICTIVE PRACTICES COURT

Clerk of the Court, M. Buckley
Court Manager (*SEO*), M. A. Brown

SUPREME COURT TAXING OFFICE

Chief Master (£80,430), P. T. Hurst
Masters of the Supreme Court (£67,354), M. Ellis; T. H. Seager Berry; C. C. Wright; P. A. Rogers; G. N. Pollard; J. E. O'Hare; C. D. N. Campbell
Court Manager (*SEO*), Mrs H. Oakey

COURT OF PROTECTION
Stewart House, 24 Kingsway, London WC2B 6HD
Tel 0171-664 7000

Master (£80,430), D. A. Lush

ELECTION PETITIONS OFFICE
Room E218, Royal Courts of Justice, Strand, London
WC2A 2LL
Tel 0171-936 6131
The office accepts petitions and deals with all matters relating to the questioning of parliamentary, European Parliament and local government elections, and with applications for relief under the Representation of the People legislation.
Prescribed Officer, R. L. Turner
Chief Clerk, Miss J. L. Waine

OFFICE OF THE LORD CHANCELLOR'S VISITORS
Stewart House, 24 Kingsway, London WC2B 6HD
Tel 0171-664 7317

Legal Visitor, A. R. Tyrrell
Medical Visitors, K. Khan; W. B. Sprey; E. Mateu; S. E. Mahapatra; A. Bailey; A. Kaeser

OFFICIAL RECEIVERS' DEPARTMENT
21 Bloomsbury Street, London WC1B 3SS
Tel 0171-323 3090

Senior Official Receiver, M. C. A. Osborne
Official Receivers, M. J. Pugh; L. T. Cramp; J. Norris

OFFICIAL SOLICITOR'S DEPARTMENT
81 Chancery Lane, London WC2B 6HD
Tel 0171-911 7105

Official Solicitor to the Supreme Court, P. M. Harris
Deputy Official Solicitor, H. J. Baker
Chief Clerk (G7), R. Lancaster

PRINCIPAL REGISTRY (FAMILY DIVISION)
Somerset House, London WC2R 1LP
Tel 0171-936 6000

Senior District Judge (£80,430), G. B. N. A. Angel
District Judges (£67,354), R. B. Rowe; B. P. F. Kenworthy-
  Browne; Mrs K. T. Moorhouse; M. J. Segal; R. Conn;
  Miss I. M. Plumstead; G. J. Maple; Miss H. C. Bradley;
  K. J. White; A. R. S. Bassett-Cross; N. A. Grove;
  M. C. Berry; Miss S. M. Bowman; C. Million; P. Waller;
  Miss P. Cushing; R. Harper; G. C. Brasse
Group Manager, Family Proceedings and Probate Service, R. P.
  Knight

District Probate Registrars

Birmingham and Stoke-on-Trent, C. Marsh
Brighton and Maidstone, P. Ellwood
Bristol, Exeter and Bodmin, R. H. P. Joyce
Ipswich, Norwich and Peterborough, D. N. Mee
Leeds, Lincoln and Sheffield, A. P. Dawson
Liverpool, Lancaster and Chester, B. J. Thomas
Llandaff, Bangor, Carmarthen and Gloucester, R. F. Yeldam
Manchester and Nottingham, M. A. Moran
Newcastle, Carlisle, York and Middlesbrough, P. Sanderson
Oxford, R. R. Da Costa
Winchester, A. K. Biggs

OFFICE OF THE JUDGE ADVOCATE OF
THE FLEET
c/o Group Manager's Office, The Court Service,
Concorde House, 10–12 London Road, Maidstone ME16
8QA
Tel 01622-200120

Judge Advocate of the Fleet (£83,586), His Hon. Judge
  Sessions

OFFICE OF THE JUDGE ADVOCATE-
GENERAL OF THE FORCES
(*Joint Service for the Army and the Royal Air Force*)
22 Kingsway, London WC2B 6LE
Tel 0171-305 7910

Judge Advocate-General (£83,586), His Hon. Judge J. W.
  Rant, CB, QC
Vice-Judge Advocate-General (£80,430), E. G. Moelwyn-
  Hughes
Assistant Judge Advocates-General (£67,354), D. M. Berkson;
  M. A. Hunter; J. P. Camp; Miss S. E. Woollam;
  R. C. C. Seymour; I. H. Pearson; R. G. Chapple; J. F. T.
  Bayliss

HIGH COURT AND CROWN COURT CENTRES

First-tier centres deal with both civil and criminal cases
and are served by High Court and circuit judges. Second-
tier centres deal with criminal cases only and are served
by High Court and circuit judges. Third-tier centres deal
with criminal cases only and are served only by circuit
judges.

MIDLAND AND OXFORD CIRCUIT

First-tier – Birmingham, Lincoln, Nottingham, Oxford,
  Stafford, Warwick
Second-tier – Leicester, Northampton, Shrewsbury,
  Worcester
Third-tier – Coventry, Derby, Grimsby, Hereford,
  Peterborough, Stoke-on-Trent, Wolverhampton
Circuit Administrator, P. Handcock, The Priory Courts, 6th
  Floor, 33 Bull Street, Birmingham B4 6DS. Tel: 0121-
  681 3000
Group Managers: Birmingham Group, K. Dickerson; *Coventry
  Group*, Mrs D. Ponsonby; *Lincoln Group*, A. Phillips;
  Northampton Group, S. Smith; *Nottingham Group*, Mrs E. A.
  Folman; *Stafford Group*, D. Bennett

NORTH-EASTERN CIRCUIT

First-tier – Leeds, Newcastle upon Tyne, Sheffield,
  Teesside
Second-tier – Bradford, York
Third-tier – Doncaster, Durham, Kingston-upon-Hull
Circuit Administrator, P. J. Farmer, 17th Floor, West Riding
  House, Albion Street, Leeds LS1 5AA. Tel: 0113-251
  1200
Group Managers: Bradford Group, F. Taylor; *Leeds Group*, P.
  M. Norris; *Newcastle upon Tyne Group*, K. Budgen;
  Sheffield Group, G. Bingham; *Teesside Group*, Miss E. Yates

NORTHERN CIRCUIT

First-tier – Carlisle, Liverpool, Manchester, Preston
Third-tier – Barrow-in-Furness, Bolton, Burnley,
  Lancaster
Circuit Administrator, R. A. Vincent, 15 Quay Street,
  Manchester M60 9FD. Tel: 0161-833 1005
Group Managers: Liverpool Group, Ms J. Roche; *Manchester
  Central Group*, Mrs C. A. Mayer; *Outer Manchester Group*,
  Ms B. Handcock; *Preston Group*, B. Wilson

SOUTH-EASTERN CIRCUIT

First-tier – Chelmsford, Lewes, Norwich
Second-tier – Ipswich, London (Central Criminal Court),
  Luton, Maidstone, Reading, St Albans
Third-tier – Aylesbury, Basildon, Brighton, Bury St
  Edmunds, Cambridge, Canterbury, Chichester,
  Guildford, King's Lynn, London (Croydon, Harrow,
  Inner London Sessions House, Isleworth, Kingston
  upon Thames, Knightsbridge, Middlesex Guildhall,
  Snaresbrook, Southwark, Wood Green, Woolwich),
  Southend
Circuit Administrator, R. J. Clark, New Cavendish House,
  18 Maltravers Street, London WC2R 3EU. Tel: 0171-936
  7234
Provincial Administrator, J. Powell, Steeple House, Church
  Lane, Chelmsford CM1 INH. Tel: 01245-257425
Group Managers: Chelmsford Group, M. Littlewood;
  Maidstone Group, Mrs H. Hartwell; *Kingston Group*, Miss
  S. Proudlock; *Lewes Group*, B. Macbeth; *London Group
  (Civil)*, D. Marsh; *London Group (Crime)*, G. F. Addicott;
  Luton Group, M. McIver

The High Court in Greater London sits at the Royal Courts of Justice.

WALES AND CHESTER CIRCUIT

First-tier – Caernarfon, Cardiff, Chester, Mold, Swansea
Second-tier – Carmarthen, Merthyr Tydfil, Newport, Welshpool
Third-tier – Dolgellau, Haverfordwest, Knutsford, Warrington
Circuit Administrator, P. Risk, Churchill House, Churchill Way, Cardiff CF1 4HH. Tel: 01222-396925
Group Managers: Cardiff Group, G. Pickett; *Chester Group*, G. Kenney; *Swansea Group*, Mrs D. Thomas

WESTERN CIRCUIT

First tier – Bristol, Exeter, Truro, Winchester
Second-tier – Dorchester, Gloucester, Plymouth, Weymouth
Third-tier – Barnstaple, Bournemouth, Newport (IOW), Portsmouth, Salisbury, Southampton, Swindon, Taunton
Circuit Administrator, D. Ryan, Bridge House, Clifton Down, Bristol BS8 4BN. Tel: 0117-974 3763
Group Managers: Bristol Group, N. Jeffery; *Exeter Group*, D. Gentry; *Winchester Group*, A. Davison

CIRCUIT JUDGES

Senior Circuit Judges, each £92,378
Circuit Judges at the Central Criminal Court, London (Old Bailey Judges), each £92,378
Circuit Judges, each £83,586
Style, His/Her Hon. Judge [surname]
Senior Presiding Judge, The Rt. Hon. Lord Justice Auld

MIDLAND AND OXFORD CIRCUIT

Presiding Judges, The Hon. Mr Justice Jowitt; The Hon. Mr Justice Latham

F. A. Allen; Miss C. Alton; B. J. Appleby, QC; D. P. Bennett; R. S. A. Benson; J. G. Boggis, QC; R. W. A. Bray; D. W. Brunning; J. J. Cavell; F. A. Chapman; P. N. R. Clark; M. F. Coates; R. R. B. Cole; T. G. E. Corrie; P. F. Crane; *P. J. Crawford, QC (Recorder of Birmingham)*; I. T. R. Davidson, QC; P. N. de Mille; T. M. Dillon, QC; C. H. Durman; B. A. Farrer, QC; Miss E. N. Fisher; J. E. Fletcher; A. C. Geddes; R. J. H. Gibbs, QC; J. Hall; V. E. Hall; D. R. D. Hamilton; S. T. Hammond; G. C. W. Harris, QC; M. K. Harrison-Hall; M. J. Heath; Miss E. J. Hindley, QC; C. R. Hodson; J. E. Hopkin; Mrs H. M. Hughes; R. H. Hutchinson; R. A. G. Inglis; R. P. V. Jenkins; A. W. P. King; M. K. Lee, QC; D. L. McCarthy; A. W. McCreath; A. G. MacDuff, QC; D. D. McEvoy, QC; J. V. Machin; M. H. Mander; L. Marshall; K. Matthewman, QC; W. D. Matthews; H. R. Mayor, QC; N. J. Mitchell; P. R. Morrell; J. I. Morris; A. J. H. Morrison; M. D. Mott; A. J. D. Nicholl; R. T. N. Orme; R. C. C. O'Rorke; J. F. F. Orrell; D. S. Perrett, QC; C. J. Pitchers; R. F. D. Pollard; D. P. Pugsley; J. R. Pyke; R. J. Rubery; J. A. O. Shand; D. P. Stanley; P. J. Stretton; G. C. Styler; A. B. Taylor; H. C. Tayler, QC; R. S. W. F. Tonking; J. J. Wait; J. C. Warner; H. Wilson; J. W. Wilson; K. S. W. Wilson Mellor, QC; C. G. Young

NORTH-EASTERN CIRCUIT

Presiding Judges, The Hon. Mr Justice Hooper; The Hon. Mrs Justice Smith

J. R. S. Adams; J. Altman; T. G. F. Atkinson; P. M. Baker, QC; T. W. Barber; J. E. Barry; G. N. Barr

Young; R. Bartfield; C. O. J. Behrens; D. R. Bentley, QC; P. H. Bowers; A. N. J. Briggs; D. M. A. Bryant; J. W. M. Bullimore; B. Bush; M. C. Carr; M. L. Cartlidge; P. J. Charlesworth; P. J. Cockroft; G. J. K. Coles, QC; J. Crabtree; M. T. Cracknell; W. H. R. Crawford, QC; Mrs J. Davies; I. J. Dobkin; E. J. Faulks; P. J. Fox, QC; A. N. Fricker, QC; M. S. Garner; A. R. Goldsack, QC; R. A. Grant; S. P. Grenfell; G. F. R. Harkins; *T. D. T. Hodson (Recorder of Newcastle upon Tyne)*; P. M. L. Hoffman; D. P. Hunt; R. Hunt; A. E. Hutchinson, QC; N. H. Jones, QC; G. H. Kamil; T. D. Kent Jones, TD; G. M. Lightfoot; R. P. Lowden; A. G. McCallum; A. C. Macdonald; C. J. McGonigal; M. K. Mettyear; R. J. Moore; A. L. Myerson, QC; D. A. Orde; Miss H. E. Paling; P. E. Robertshaw; R. M. Scott; A. Simpson; L. Spittle; J. Stephenson; Mrs L. Sutcliffe; J. A. Swanson; M. J. Taylor; R. C. Taylor; J. D. G. Walford; M. Walker; P. H. C. Walker; *B. Walsh, QC*; C. T. Walton; G. Whitburn, QC; J. S. Wolstenholme; D. R. Wood

NORTHERN CIRCUIT

Presiding Judge, The Hon. Mr Justice Kay *(until Jan. 1998)*; The Hon. Mr Justice Forbes; The Hon. Mr Justice Douglas Brown *(from Jan. 1998)*

M. P. Allweis; H. H. Andrew, QC; J. F. Appleton; A. W. Bell; R. C. W. Bennett; Miss I. Bernstein; M. S. Blackburn; R. Brown; J. K. Burke, QC; I. B. Campbell; F. B. Carter, QC; B. I. Caulfield; D. Clark; *D. C. Clarke, QC (Recorder of Liverpool)*; G. M. Clifton; I. W. Crompton; *R. E. Davies, QC (Recorder of Manchester)*; Miss A. E. Downey; B. R. Duckworth; S. B. Duncan; Miss D. B. Eaglestone; T. K. Earnshaw; G. A. Ensor; D. M. Evans, QC; S. J. D. Fawcus; P. S. Fish; J. R. B. Geake; D. S. Gee; W. George; J. A. D. Gilliland, QC; R. G. Hamilton; J. A. Hammond; F. D. Hart, QC; M. Hedley; T. B. Hegarty, QC; F. R. B. Holloway; R. C. Holman; N. J. G. Howarth; G. W. Humphries; C. E. F. James; P. M. Kershaw, QC *(Commercial Circuit Judge)*; H. L. Lachs; P. M. Lakin; B. W. Lewis; R. J. D. Livesey, QC; R. Lockett; D. Lynch; D. I. Mackay; J. B. Macmillan; D. G. Maddison; B. C. Maddocks; C. J. Mahon; J. A. Morgan; W. P. Morris; T. J. Mort; F. D. Owen, TD; R. E. I. Pickering; J. C. Phipps; D. A. Pirie; A. J. Proctor; J. H. Roberts; Miss G. D. Ruaux; H. S. Singer, E. Slinger; A. C. Smith; W. P. Smith; Miss E. M. Steel; D. R. Swift; C. B. Tetlow; J. P. Townend; J. G. Trigger; P. W. G. Urquhart; K. H. P. Wilkinson; B. Woodward

SOUTH-EASTERN CIRCUIT

Presiding Judges, The Hon. Mr Justice Gage; The Hon. Mr Justice Wright

M. F. Addison, A. R. L. Ansell, S. A. Anwyl, QC; J. A. Baker; M. F. Baker, QC; M. J. D. Baker; A. F. Balston; G. S. Barham; C. J. A. Barnett, QC; W. E. Barnett, QC; K. Bassingthwaighte; *G. A. Bathurst Norman*; P. J. L. Beaumont, QC; N. E. Beddard; M. G. Binning; G. J. Binns; J. E. Bishop; B. M. B. Black; H. O. Blacksell, QC; J. G. Boal, QC; A. V. Bradbury; P. N. Brandt; L. J. Bromley, QC; A. E. Brooks; R. G. Brown; J. M. Bull, QC; *N. M. Butter, QC*; H. J. Byrt, QC; C. V. Callman; J. Q. Campbell; B. E. Capstick, QC; M. J. Carroll; B. E. F. Catlin; B. L. Charles, QC; P. C. L. Clark; P. C. Clegg; S. H. Colgan; P. H. Collins; C. C. Colston, QC; S. S. Coltart; Viscount Colville of Culross, QC; J. S. Colyer, QC; C. D. Compston; T. A. C. Coningsby, QC; J. G. Connor; R. D. Connor; M. J. Cook; R. A. Cooke; G. H. Coombe; M. R. Coombe; A. Cooray; P. E. Copley; Dr E. Cotran; P. R. Cowell; R. C. Cox; J. F. Crocker; D. L. Croft, QC;

H. M. Crush; D. M. Cryan; P. Curl; G. L. Davies;
I. H. Davies, TD; W. L. M. Davies, QC; M. Dean, QC;
W. N. Denison, QC (*Common Serjeant*); J. E. Devaux;
M. N. Devonshire, TD; A. E. J. Diamond, QC; P. H. Downes;
W. H. Dunn, QC; A. H. Durrant; C. M. Edwards; D. F. Elfer;
QC; D. R. Ellis; C. Elwen; F. P. L. Evans; S. J. Evans;
J. D. Farnworth; P. Fingret; J. J. Finney; P. E. J. Focke, QC;
P. Ford; J. J. Fordham; G. C. F. Forrester;
Ms D. A. Freedman; R. Gee; L. Gerber; C. A. H. Gibson;
Miss A. F. Goddard, QC; S. A. Goldstein; M. B. Goodman;
C. G. M. Gordon; J. B. Gosschalk; M. Graham, QC;
B. S. Green, QC; P. B. Greenwood; D. J. Griffiths;
G. D. Grigson; R. B. Groves, TD, VRD; N. T. Hague, QC;
A. B. R. Hallgarten, QC; Miss G. Hallon; J. Hamilton;
C. R. H. Hardy; B. Hargrove, OBE, QC; M. F. Harris;
R. G. Hawkins, QC; J. M. Haworth; R. J. Haworth;
R. M. Hayward; A. N. Hitching; D. Holden;
A. C. W. Hordern, QC; K. A. D. Hornby; M. Hucker;
Sir David Hughes-Morgan, Bt., CB, CBE; J. G. Hull, QC;
M. J. Hyam; D. A. Inman; A. B. Issard-Davies;
Dr P. J. E. Jackson; T. J. C. Joseph; S. S. Katkhuda;
M. Kennedy, QC; A. M. Kenny; T. R. King; L. G. Krikler;
L. H. C. Lait; P. St J. H. Langan, QC;
Capt. J. B. R. Langdon, RN; R. Laurie; T. Lawrence;
D. M. Levy, QC; S. H. Lloyd; F. R. Lockhart; D. B. D. Lowe;
Mrs C. M. Ludlow; Capt. S. Lyons; K. M. McHale;
K. A. Machin, QC; K. C. Macrae; T. Maher;
B. A. Marder, QC; F. J. M. Marr-Johnson;
D. N. N. Martineau; N. A. Medawar, QC; D. B. Meier;
D. J. Mellor; G. D. Mercer; D. Q. Miller; F. I. Mitchell;
H. M. Morgan; D. Morton Jack; R. T. Moss; Miss
M. J. S. Mowat; J. I. Murchie; T. M. E. Nash;
M. H. D. Neligan; Mrs M. F. Norrie; Brig. A. P. Norris,
OBE; P. W. O'Brien; M. A. Oppenheimer; D. C. J. Paget, QC;
D. A. Paiba; D. J. Parry; Mrs N. Pearce; Prof. D. S. Pearl;
Miss V. A. Pearlman; B. P. Pearson; J. R. Peppitt, QC;
N. A. J. Philpot; T. D. Pillay; D. C. Pitman; J. R. Platt;
P. B. Pollock; T. G. Pontius; W. D. C. Poulton;
H. C. Pownall, QC; S. Pratt; R. J. C. V. Prendergast;
J. E. Previté, QC; B. H. Pryor, QC; J. E. Pullinger;
D. W. Radford; J. W. Rant, QC; E. V. P. Reece;
M. P. Reynolds; G. K. Rice; M. S. Rich, QC; N. P. Riddell;
G. Rivlin, QC; S. D. Robbins; D. A. H. Rodwell, QC;
J. W. Rogers, QC; G. H. Rooke, TD, QC; P. C. R. Rountree;
J. H. Rucker; T. R. G. Ryland; J. E. A. Samuels, QC;
R. B. Sanders; A. R. G. Scott-Gall; J. S. Sennitt;
J. L. Sessions; J. D. Sheerin; D. R. A. Sich; A. G. Simmons;
K. T. Simpson; P. R. Simpson; M. Singh, QC;
J. K. E. Slack, TD; S. P. Sleeman; P. M. J. Slot;
C. M. Smith, QC; A. R. Smith; R. J. Southan; S. B. Spence;
W. F. C. Thomas; A. G. Y. Thorpe; A. H. Tibber;
C. H. Tilling; J. T. Turner; C. J. M. Tyrer;
Mrs A. P. Uziell-Hamilton; J. E. van der Werff;
Sir Lawrence Verney, TD (*Recorder of London*);
A. O. R. Vick, QC; T. L. Viljoen; Miss M. S. Viner, CBE, QC;
R. Wakefield; R. Walker; S. P. Waller; D. B. Watling, QC;
V. B. Watts; *Sir Frank White; A. F. Wilkie, QC;
S. R. Wilkinson; R. J. Winstanley; E. G. Wrintmore;
K. H. Zucker, QC

WALES AND CHESTER CIRCUIT

Presiding Judges, The Hon. Mr Justice Curtis (*until Jan.
1998*); The Hon. Mr Justice Maurice Kay; The Hon.
Mr Justice Connell; The Hon. Mr Justice Thomas
(*from Jan. 1998*)

K. E. Barnett; M. R. Burr; S. P. Clarke; T. R. Crowther, QC;
J. T. Curran; Miss J. M. P. Daley; G. H. M. Daniel;
D. T. A. Davies; J. B. S. Diehl, QC; R. T. Dutton;
D. E. H. Edwards; G. O. Edwards, QC; The Lord Elystan-
Morgan; D. R. Evans, QC; T. M. Evans, QC; J. W. Gaskell;
*M. Gibbon, QC; D. R. Halbert; D. J. Hale; D. M. Hughes;
P. J. Jacobs; G. J. Jones; H. D. H. Jones; G. E. Kilfoil;
T. E. I. Lewis-Bowen; C. G. Masterman; D. G. Morgan;
D. G. Morris; D. C. Morton; T. H. Moseley, QC;
P. J. Price, QC; E. J. Prosser, QC; H. E. P. Roberts, QC;
S. M. Stephens, QC; H. V. Williams, QC

WESTERN CIRCUIT

Presiding Judges, The Hon. Mr Justice Butterfield; The
Hon. Mr Justice Toulson

P. T. S. Batterbury; J. F. Beashel; R. H. Bond; Miss
J. A. M. Bonvin; C. L. Boothman; M. J. L. Brodrick;
J. M. J. Burford, QC; R. D. H. Bursell, QC; J. R. Chalkley;
M. G. Cotterill; G. W. A. Cottle; K. C. Cutler;
P. M. Darlow; S. C. Darwall Smith; Mrs S. P. Darwall
Smith; Mrs L. H. Davies; *M. Dyer; J. D. Foley;
D. L. Griffiths; J. D. Griggs; Mrs C. M. A. Hagen;
P. J. C. R. Hooton; G. B. Hutton; R. E. Jack, QC;
A. G. H. Jones; T. N. Mackean; Miss S. M. D. McKinney;
I. S. McKintosh; J. G. McNaught; T. J. Milligan;
J. Neligan; E. G. Neville; S. K. O'Malley; S. K. Overend;
R. Price; R. C. Pryor, QC; J. N. P. Rudd; A. Rutherford;
Miss A. O. H. Sander; D. H. D. Selwood; R. M. Shawcross;
D. A. Smith, QC; W. E. M. Taylor; P. M. Thomas;
A. A. R. Thompson, QC; H. J. M. Tucker, QC;
D. M. Webster, QC; J. H. Weeks, QC; J. S. Wiggs;
J. A. J. Wigmore; J. C. Willis

RECORDERS (each £380 per day)

F. A. Abbott; R. D. I. Adam; J. D. R. Adams; P. C. Ader;
R. J. P. Aikens, QC; J. F. Akast; D. J. Ake; R. Akenhead, QC;
I. D. G. Alexander, QC; C. D. Allan, QC; C. J. Alldis;
J. H. Allen, QC; D. M. Altaras; A. J. Anderson, QC;
W. P. Andreae-Jones, QC; P. J. Andrews, QC;
R. A. Anelay, QC; M. G. Anthony; Miss L. E. Appleby, QC;
J. F. A. Archer, QC; The Lord Archer of Sandwell, PC, QC;
A. J. Arlidge, QC; E. K. Armitage, QC; P. J. B. Armstrong;
G. K. Arran; R. Ashton; J. M. Aspinall, QC; E. G. Aspley;
N. J. Atkinson, QC; D. S. Aubrey; M. G. Austin-Smith, QC;
M. J. S. Axtell; W. S. Aylen, QC; P. D. Babb;
J. F. Badenoch, QC; P. G. N. Badge; Miss P. H. Badley;
E. H. Bailey; A. B. Baillie; N. R. J. Baker, QC; S. W. Baker;
C. G. Ball, QC; P. R. Barclay; A. Barker, QC; B. J. Barker, QC;
D. Barker, QC; G. E. Barling, QC; D. N. Barnard;
D. M. W. Barnes, QC; H. J. Barnes; T. P. Barnes, QC;
A. J. Barnett; R. A. Barratt, QC; R. Bartfield; D. A. Bartlett;
G. R. Bartlett, QC; J. C. T. Barton, QC; D. C. Bate, QC;
S. D. Batten; P. D. Batty, QC; J. J. Baughan, QC;
R. A. Bayliss; D. M. Bean; J. Beatson; C. H. Beaumont;
R. V. M. E. Behar; R. W. Belben; P. Bennett, QC;
J. K. Benson; P. C. Benson; R. A. Benson, QC;
H. L. Bentham; D. M. Berkson; C. R. Berry;
M. Bethel, QC; J. P. V. Bevan; Mrs C. V. Bevington;
Mrs M. O. Bickford-Smith; N. Bidder; I. G. Bing;
P. V. Birkett, QC; M. I. Birnbaum; W. J. Birtles;
P. W. Birts, QC; B. G. D. Blair, QC; J. A. Blair-Gould;
A. N. H. Blake; P. E. Bleasdale; C. Bloom, QC;
D. J. Blunt, QC; O. S. P. Blunt, QC; D. R. L. Bodey, QC;
G. T. K. Boney, QC; J. J. Boothby; D. J. Boulton;
S. N. Bourne-Arton, QC; Ms M. R. Bowron; W. Boyce;
S. C. Boyd, QC; J. J. Boyle; D. L. Bradshaw;
W. T. S. Braithwaite, QC; N. D. Bratza, QC; G. B. Breen;
D. J. Brennan, QC; M. L. Brent, QC; G. J. B. G. Brice, QC;
J. N. W. Bridges-Adams; A. J. Brigden; P. J. Briggs;
D. R. Bright; R. P. Brittain; R. A. Britton; J. Bromley-
Davenport; L. F. M. Brown; S. C. Brown, QC;
D. J. M. Browne, QC; J. N. Browne; A. J. N. Brunner, QC;
R. V. Bryan; Miss B. M. Bucknall, QC; A. Bueno, QC;

J. E. Bullen; P. E. Bullock; J. P. Burke, QC;
H. W. Burnett, QC; R. H. Burns; S. J. Burnton, QC;
G. Burrell, QC; M. J. Burton, QC; K. Bush; A. J. Butcher, QC;
Miss J. Butler; C. W. Byers; M. D. Byrne; D. Calvert-
Smith; R. Camden Pratt, QC; Miss S. M. C. Cameron, QC;
A. N. Campbell, QC; J. M. Caplan, QC; G. M. C. Carey, QC;
A. C. Carlile, QC, MP; H. B. H. Carlisle, QC; The Lord
Carlisle of Bucklow, PC, QC; J. J. Carter-Manning, QC;
R. Carus, QC; Mrs J. R. Case; P. D. Cattan;
Miss M. T. Catterson; J. A. Chadwin, QC; R. M. Challinor;
N. M. Chambers, QC; Miss D. C. Champion;
V. R. Chapman; J. M. Cherry, QC; J. R. Cherryman, QC;
C. F. Chruszcz, QC; A. V. Chubb; C. H. Clark, QC;
C. S. C. S. Clarke, QC; P. W. Clarke; P. R. J. Clarkson, QC;
T. Clayson; A. S. L. Cleary; W. Clegg, QC; P. Clements;
T. A. Clover; Miss S. Coates; W. P. Coates; D. J. Cocks, QC;
J. J. Coffey, QC; T. A. Coghlan, QC; J. L. Cohen;
W. J. Coker, QC; J. R. Cole; A. J. S. Coleman; N. J. Coleman;
P. J. D. Coleridge, QC; N. B. C. Coles, QC;
A. R. Collender, QC; P. N. Collier, QC; J. M. Collins;
M. G. Collins, QC; I. Collis; Ms M. Colton;
Mrs J. R. Comyns; A. D. Conrad; C. S. Cook; N. O. Cooke;
K. B. Coonan, QC; A. E. M. Cooper; Miss B. P. Cooper, QC;
P. J. Cooper, QC; Miss S. M. Corkhill; C. J. Cornwall;
P. J. Cosgrove, QC; Miss D. R. Cotton, QC; J. S. Coward, QC;
Mrs L. M. Cox, QC; P. Crampin, QC; R. F. Cranston;
L. S. Crawford; N. Crichton; D. I. Crigman, QC;
M. L. S. Cripps; C. A. Critchlow; D. R. Crome;
Mrs J. Crowley; J. D. Crowley, QC; T. S. Culver;
Miss E. A. M. Curnow, QC; P. D. Curran;
J. W. O. Curtis, QC; M. J. Curwen; A. J. G. Dalziel;
Mrs P. M. T. Dangor; A. M. Darroch; G. W. Davey;
C. P. M. Davidson; A. M. Davies; A. R. M. Davies;
J. T. L. Davies; R. L. Davies, QC; W. E. Davis;
A. W. Dawson; D. H. Day, QC; J. J. Deave; J. B. Deby, QC;
P. G. Dedman; Mrs P. A. Deeley; C. F. Dehn, QC; P. A. de la
Piquerie; M. A. de Navarro, QC; R. L. Denyer, QC;
S. C. Desch, QC; H. A. D. de Silva; P. N. Digney;
C. E. Dines; A. D. Dinkin, QC; D. R. Dobbin; P. Dodgson;
R. A. M. Doggett; Ms B. Dohmann, QC;
D. T. Donaldson, QC; A. M. Donne, QC; A. F. S. Donovan;
A. K. Dooley; J. Dowse; J. R. Duggan; P. R. Dunkels, QC;
J. D. Durham Hall, QC; J. M. Dyson; H. W. P. Eccles, QC;
C. N. Edelman, QC; A. H. Edwards;
Miss S. M. Edwards, QC; A. J. C. Edwards-Stuart, QC;
G. Elias, QC; E. A. Elliott; R. C. Elly; J. A. Elvidge;
R. M. Englehart, QC; T. M. English; D. A. Evans, QC;
D. H. Evans, QC; F. W. H. Evans, QC; G. W. R. Evans, QC;
M. Evans, QC; M. J. Evans; M. A. Everall, QC;
Sir Graham Eyre, QC; T. M. Faber; W. D. Fairclough;
R. B. Farley, QC; P. M. Farmer, QC; D. J. Farrer, QC;
P. E. Feinberg, QC; R. Fernyhough, QC; M. C. Field;
J. E. Finestein; J. E. P. Finnigan; D. T. Fish;
D. P. Fisher, QC; G. D. Flather, CBE, QC; R. A. Fordham, QC;
B. C. Forster; M. D. P. Fortune, D. R. Foskett, QC;
J. R. Foster, QC; Miss R. M. Foster; M. Furness;
M. Gale, QC; C. J. E. Gardner, QC; P. R. Garlick, QC;
C. R. Garside, QC; R. C. Gaskell; S. A. G. L. Gault;
A. H. Gee, QC; I. W. Geering; D. S. Geey;
C. R. George, QC; D. C. Gerrey; J. S. Gibbons, QC;
A. J. Gilbart, QC; F. H. S. Gilbert; N. J. Gilchrist;
K. Gillance; N. B. D. Gilmour, QC; L. Giovene;
A. T. Glass, QC; H. B. Globe, QC; Miss E. Gloster, QC;
H. K. Goddard, QC; H. A. Godfrey, QC;
Ms L. S. Godfrey, QC; J. J. Goldberg, QC; J. B. Goldring, QC;
P. H. Goldsmith, QC; L. C. Goldstone, QC;
I. F. Goldsworthy, QC; A. J. J. Gompertz, QC; Miss
R. M. Goode; A. A. Gordon; J. R. W. Goss;
T. J. C. Goudie, QC; A. A. Goymer; G. Gozem;
A. S. Grabiner, QC; C. A. St J. Gray, QC; G. Gray, QC;

H. Green, QC; Miss J. E. G. Greenberg, QC;
A. E. Greenwood; J. C. Greenwood; J. G. Grenfell, QC;
R. D. Grey, QC; D. E. Griffith-Jones; R. H. Griffith-Jones;
J. P. G. Griffiths, QC; M. G. Grills; M. S. E. Grime, QC;
P. Grobel; P. H. Gross, QC; M. A. W. Grundy; S. J. Gullick;
A. S. Hacking, QC; M. F. Haigh; J. W. Haines; N. J. Hall;
S. J. Hall; J. P. N. Hallam; D. T. Hallchurch;
Miss H. C. Hallett, QC; G. M. Hamilton, TD, QC;
I. M. Hamilton; Miss S. Hamilton, QC; P. L. Hamlin;
J. Hampton; J. L. Hand, QC; Miss R. S. A. Hare, QC;
R. D. Harman, QC; G. T. Harrap; R. J. Harrington, QC;
D. M. Harris, QC; R. D. Harrison; R. M. Harrison, QC;
H. M. Harrod; J. M. Harrow; C. P. Hart-Leverton, QC;
B. Harvey; J. G. Harvey; M. L. T. Harvey, QC;
D. W. Hatton, QC; A. M. D. Havelock-Allan, QC;
The Hon. P. N. Havers, QC; T. S. A. Hawkesworth, QC;
W. G. Hawkesworth; R. W. P. Hay; Prof. D. J. Hayton;
Miss J. E. Hayward; R. Hayward-Smith, QC;
A. T. Hedworth, QC; G. E. Heggs; R. A. Henderson, QC;
R. H. Q. Henriques, QC; M. J. Henshell;
P. J. M. Heppel, QC; R. C. Herman; M. S. Heslop QC;
T. Hewitt; B. J. Higgs, QC; E. M. Hill, QC; J. W. Hillyer;
A. J. H. Hilton, QC; Ms E. J. Hindley, QC; J. W. Hirst, QC;
W. T. J. Hirst; J. D. Hitchen; S. A. Hockman, QC;
H. E. G. Hodge, OBE; A. J. C. Hoggett, QC;
D. A. Hollis, VRD, QC; C. J. Holmes; T. V. Holroyde, QC;
J. F. Holt; R. M. Hone; A. T. Hoolahan, QC; A. D. Hope;
S. Hopkins; M. A. P. Hopmeier; M. Horowitz, QC; Miss
R. Horwood-Smart; C. P. Hotten, QC; B. F. Houlder, QC;
M. N. Howard, QC; C. I. Howells; M. J. Hubbard, QC;
A. P. G. Hughes, QC; Miss J. C. A. Hughes, QC;
P. T. Hughes, QC; R. P. Hughes; T. M. Hughes, QC;
L. D. Hull; Capt. D. R. Humphrey, RN;
W. G. B. Hungerford; D. R. N. Hunt, QC; P. J. Hunt, QC;
I. G. A. Hunter, QC; M. A. Hunter; M. Hussain, QC;
J. G. K. Hyland; B. A. Hytner, QC; P. R. Isaacs;
S. L. Isaacs, QC; S. Jack; D. G. A. Jackson; M. R. Jackson;
R. M. Jackson, QC; I. E. Jacob; N. F. B. Jarman, QC;
J. M. Jarvis, QC; J. R. Jarvis; A. H. Jeffreys;
D. A. Jeffreys, QC; J. Jeffs, QC; J. D. Jenkins, QC;
D. B. Johnson, QC; D. A. F. Jones; D. L. Jones; N. G. Jones;
P. H. F. Jones; R. A. Jones, QC; S. E. Jones, QC; T. G. Jones;
W. J. Jones; W. H. Joss; H. M. Joy; P. S. L. Joyce, QC;
R. W. S. Juckes; M. D. L. Kalisher, QC; M. L. Kallipetis, QC;
Miss L. N. R. Kamill; I. G. F. Karsten, QC; R. G. Kaye, QC;
C. B. Kealy; M. L. Keane; K. R. Keen, QC; Mrs S. M. Keen;
B. R. Keith, QC; C. L. Kelly; C. J. B. Kemp;
D. Kennett Brown; D. M. Kerr; L. D. Kershen, QC;
M. I. Khan; G. M. Khayat, QC; R. I. Kidwell, QC;
T. R. A. King, QC; W. M. Kingston, QC; R. C. Klevan, QC;
B. J. Knight, QC; M. S. Knott; Miss P. E. Knowles; C. Knox;
Miss J. C. M. Korner, QC; S. E. Kramer, QC;
Miss L. J. Kushner, QC; P. E. Kyte, QC; C. A. Lamb;
N. R. W. Lambert; D. A. Landau; D. G. Lane, QC;
T. J. Langdale, QC; B. F. J. Langstaff, QC; D. H. Latham;
R. B. Latham, QC; S. W. Lawler, QC; Sir Ivan Lawrence, QC;
M. H. Lawson, QC; G. S. Lawson-Rogers, QC;
P. L. O. Leaver, QC; D. Lederman; B. W. T. Leech;
I. Leeming, QC; C. H. de V. Leigh, QC; Sir Godfrey Le
Quesne, QC; H. B. G. Lett; B. L. Lever; B. H. Leveson, QC;
S. Levine; A. E. Levy, QC; M. E. Lewer, QC;
A. K. Lewis, QC; J. A. Lewis; M. ap G. Lewis, QC;
R. S. Lewis; K. M. J. Lewison; C. C. D. Lindsay, QC;
S. J. Linehan, QC; J. S. Lipton; B. J. E. Livesey, QC;
C. G. Llewellyn-Jones, QC; C. J. Lockhart-Mummery, QC;
A. J. C. Lodge, QC; T. Longbotham; D. C. Lovell-Pank, QC;
A. C. Lowcock; G. W. Lowe; N. H. Lowe; J. A. M. Lowen;
G. W. Lowther; A. P. Lyon; E. Lyons, QC; P. G. McCahill,
QC; R. G. B. McCombe, QC; A. G. McDowall;
K. M. P. Macgill; R. J. McGregor-Johnson;

R. D. Machell, QC; B. M. McIntyre; C. C. Mackay, QC;
D. L. Mackie; R. G. McKinnon; W. N. McKinnon;
N. A. McKittrick; I. A. B. McLaren, QC; I. McLeod;
N. R. B. Macleod, QC; N. J. C. McLusky; A. G. Mainds;
A. H. R. Maitland; A. R. Malcolm; H. J. Malins;
M. E. Mann, QC; The Hon. G. R. J. Mansfield;
A. C. B. Markham-David; R. L. Marks; J. W. Marrin, QC;
G. M. Marriott; A. S. Marron, QC; P. Marsh;
R. G. Marshall-Andrews, QC; G. C. Marson;
H. R. A. Martineau; S. A. Maskrey, QC; C. P. Mather;
D. Matheson, QC; P. R. Matthews; Mrs S. P. Matthews, QC;
P. B. Mauleverer, QC; R. B. Mawrey, QC; J. F. M. Maxwell;
R. Maxwell, QC; Mrs P. R. May; M. Meggeson;
N. F. Merriman, QC; The Lord Meston, QC;
C. S. J. Metcalf; J. T. Milford, QC; K. S. H. Miller;
R. A. Miller; S. M. Miller, QC; C. J. Millington;
J. B. M. Milmo, QC; D. C. Milne, QC; Miss C. M. Miskin;
Miss A. E. Mitchell; A. P. Mitchell; C. R. Mitchell;
D. C. Mitchell; J. R. Mitchell; J. E. Mitting, QC; F. R. Moat;
E. G. Moelwyn-Hughes; C. R. D. Moger, QC;
Mrs J. P. Moir; D. R. P. Mole, QC; H. J. Montlake;
M. G. C. Moorhouse; A. G. Moran, QC; D. W. Morgan;
P. B. Morgan; G. E. Moriarty, QC; A. P. Morris, QC; The
Rt. Hon. J. Morris, QC, MP; C. Morris-Coole;
H. A. C. Morrison, OBE; G. E. Morrow; C. J. Moss, QC;
P. C. Mott, QC; R. W. Moxon-Browne, QC; J. H. Muir;
F. J. Muller, QC; G. S. Murdoch, QC; I. P. Murphy, QC;
M. J. A. Murphy, QC; N. O. G. Murray; N. J. Mylne, QC;
H. G. Narayan; R. E. Newbold; A. R. H. Newman, QC;
G. Nice, QC; C. A. A. Nicholls, QC; C. V. Nicholls, QC;
A. S. T. E. Nicol; A. E. R. Noble; B. Nolan, QC;
M. C. Norman; J. M. Norris; P. H. Norris; G. Nuttall;
J. G. Nutting, QC; D. P. O'Brien, QC; E. M. Ogden, QC; Mrs
F. M. Oldham, QC; S. Oliver-Jones, QC; R. W. Onions;
C. P. L. Openshaw, QC; M. N. O'Sullivan;
D. B. W. Ouseley, QC; R. M. Owen, QC; T. W. Owen;
N. D. Padfield, QC; S. R. Page; A. O. Palmer, QC;
A. W. Palmer, QC; D. P. Pannick, QC; A. D. W. Pardoe, QC;
S. A. B. Parish; G. C. Parkins, QC; G. E. Parkinson;
M. P. Parroy, QC; E. O. Parry; M. A. Parry Evans;
N. S. K. Pascoe, QC; A. Patience, QC; J. G. Paulusz;
W. E. Pawlak; R. J. Pearse Wheatley;
The Hon. I. J. C. Peddie, QC; J. V. Pegden; D. H. Penry-
Davey, QC; J. Perry, QC; M. Pert, QC; B. J. Phelvin;
J. A. Phillips; W. B. Phillips; M. A. Pickering, QC;
J. K. Pickup; C. J. Pitchford, QC; The Hon. B. M. D. Pitt;
Miss E. F. Platt, QC; R. Platts; J. R. Playford, QC;
A. G. S. Pollock, QC; A. R. Porten, QC; L. R. Portnoy; Mrs
R. M. Poulet, QC; S. R. Powles; T. W. Preston, QC;
D. Price; G. A. L. Price, QC; J. A. Price, QC; J. C. Price;
N. P. L. Price, QC; H. W. Prosser; A. C. Pugh, QC;
G. V. Pugh, QC; G. F. Pulman, QC; C. P. B. Purchas, QC;
R. M. Purchas, QC; N. R. Purnell, QC; P. O. Purnell, QC;
Q. C. W. Querelle; D. A. Radcliffe; Mrs N. P. Radford, QC;
Ms A. J. Rafferty, QC; T. W. H. Raggatt, QC;
A. D. Rawley, QC; P. R. Raynor, QC; L. F. Read, QC;
J. H. Reddihough; A. R. F. Redgrave; P. Rees;
C. E. Reese, QC; J. R. Reid, QC; P. C. Reid; D. J. Rennie;
P. C. Rhodes; R. E. Rhodes, QC; D. G. Rice; D. W. Richards;
S. P. Richards; D. J. Richardson; T. Rigby;
S. V. Riordan, QC; G. Risius; Miss J. H. Ritchie, QC;
M. W. Roach; J. A. Roberts, QC; J. M. Roberts;
J. M. G. Roberts, QC; T. D. Roberts; A. J. Robertson;
V. Robinson, QC; D. E. H. Robson, QC; Miss M. B. Roddy;
G. W. Roddick, QC; Miss D. J. Rodgers; J. M. T. Rogers, QC;
P. F. G. Rook, QC; W. M. Rose; J. G. Ross;
J. G. Ross Martyn; P. C. Rouch; J. J. Rowe, QC;
R. J. Royce, QC; M. W. Rudland; P. E. B. M. Rueff;
A. A. Rumbelow, QC; N. J. Rumfitt, QC; R. J. Rundell;
R. R. Russell; G. C. Ryan, QC; J. R. T. Rylance;

C. R. A. Sallon, QC; C. N. Salmon; D. A. Salter;
A. T. Sander; G. R. Sankey, QC; N. L. Sarony;
J. H. B. Saunders, QC; M. P. Sayers, QC; R. J. Scholes, QC;
Miss P. Scriven, QC; R. J. Seabrook, QC; C. Seagroatt, QC;
M. R. Selfe; W. P. L. Sellick; O. M. Sells, QC; D. Serota, QC;
R. W. Seymour, QC; A. J. Seys-Llewellyn; A. R. F. Sharp;
P. P. Shears; S. J. Sher, QC; Miss J. Shipley;
J. M. Shorrock, QC; S. R. Silber, QC; P. F. Singer, QC;
J. C. N. Slater, QC; A. C. Smith, QC; A. T. Smith, QC;
P. W. Smith, QC; R. D. H. Smith, QC; R. S. Smith, QC;
Ms Z. P. Smith; C. J. Smyth; S. M. Solley, QC; R. F. Solman;
E. Somerset Jones, QC; R. C. Southwell, QC,
R. C. E. Southwell; M. H. Spence, QC; J. Spencer, QC;
M. G. Spencer, QC; S. M. Spencer, QC;
R. V. Spencer Bernard; D. P. Spens, QC; R. W. Spon-Smith;
D. W. Steel, QC; D. Steer, QC; M. T. Steiger, QC;
D. H. Stembridge, QC; Mrs L. J. Stern, QC;
A. W. Stevenson, TD; J. S. H. Stewart, QC; N. A. Stewart;
R. M. Stewart, QC; W. R. Stewart Smith; A. C. Steynor;
G. J. C. Still; D. A. Stockdale, QC; Mrs D. M. Stocken;
D. M. A. Stokes, QC; M. G. T. Stokes, QC;
E. D. R. Stone, QC; J. B. Storey, QC; P. L. Storr;
T. M. F. Stow, QC; D. M. A. Strachan, QC; M. Stuart-
Moore, QC; F. R. C. Such; A. B. Suckling, QC;
J. M. Sullivan, QC; Ms L. E. Sullivan, QC; D. M. Sumner;
J. P. C. Sumption, QC; M. A. Supperstone, QC; P. J. Susman;
R. P. Sutton, QC; C. J. Sutton-Mattocks; N. H. Sweeney;
Miss C. J. Swift, QC; L. Swift, QC; M. R. Swift, QC;
Miss H. H. Swindells, QC; C. J. M. Symons, QC;
J. P. Tabor, QC; J. A. Tackaberry, QC; P. J. Talbot, QC;
R. K. K. Talbot; R. B. Tansey, QC; G. F. Tattersall, QC;
E. Taylor; E. T. H. Teague; J. J. Teare; N. J. M. Teare, QC;
R. H. Tedd, QC; A. D. Temple, QC; V. B. A. Temple, QC;
M. H. Tennant; D. O. Thomas, QC; P. A. Thomas;
R. L. Thomas, QC; R. M. Thomas; R. U. Thomas, QC; Miss
S. M. Thomas; C. F. J. Thompson; P. J. Thompson;
A. R. Thornhill, QC; P. R. Thornton, QC;
D. K. Ticehurst, QC; A. C. Tickle; J. Tiley;
M. B. Tillett, QC; J. W. Tinnion; R. N. Titheridge, QC;
S. M. Tomlinson, QC; J. K. Toulmin, CMG, QC;
P. J. H. Towler; J. B. S. Townend, QC; C. M. Treacy, QC;
H. B. Trethowan; A. D. H. Trollope, QC;
M. G. Tugendhat, QC; H. W. Turcan; D. A. Turner, QC;
P. A. Twigg, QC; A. R. Tyrrell, QC; N. E. Underhill, QC;
J. G. G. Ungley; N. P. Valios, QC; N. C. van der Bijl;
A. R. Vandermeer, QC; D. A. J. Vaughan, QC; M. J. D. Vere-
Hodge, QC; J. P. Wadsworth, QC; S. P. Waine; Miss
A. P. Wakefield; R. M. Wakerley, QC; W. H. Waldron, QC;
Mrs E. A. Walker; R. A. Walker, QC; R. J. Walker, QC;
Sir Jonah Walker-Smith, Bt.; T. M. Walsh; J. J. Wardlow;
J. Warren, QC; N. J. Warren; D. E. B. Waters; Miss
B. J. Watson; Sir James Watson, Bt.; B. J. Waylen;
A. R. Webb; R. S. Webb, QC; A. S. Webster, QC;
M. Weisman; P. Weitzman, QC; C. S. Welchman;
C. P. C. Whelon; C. H. Whitby, QC; G. B. N. White;
W. J. M. White; D. R. B. Whitehouse, QC; R. P. Whitehurst;
P. G. Whiteman, QC; P. J. M. Whiteman, TD;
A. Whitfield, QC; D. G. Widdicombe, QC; C. T. Wide, QC;
R. Wigglesworth; A. D. F. Wilcken; N. V. M. Wilkinson;
Miss E. Willers; G. H. G. Williams, QC; Miss
J. A. Williams; J. G. Williams, QC; J. L. Williams, QC;
M. J. Williams; W. L. Williams, QC; The Lord Williams of
Mostyn, QC; Miss H. E. Williamson, QC;
S. W. Williamson, QC; A. J. D. Wilson, QC;
A. M. Wilson, QC; I. K. R. Wilson; C. Wilson-Smith, QC;
G. W. Wingate-Saul, QC; M. E. Wolff; H. Wolton, QC;
D. A. Wood, QC; N. A. Wood; R. L. J. Wood, QC;
W. R. Wood; L. G. Woodley, QC; Miss S. Woodley;
J. T. Woods; W. C. Woodward, QC; A. P. L. Woolman;
T. H. Workman; Miss A. M. Worrall, QC; D. Worsley;

P. F. Worsley, QC; J. J. Wright; M. P. Yelton;
D. E. M. Young, QC

STIPENDIARY MAGISTRATES

PROVINCIAL (each £67,354)

Cheshire, P. K. Dodd, OBE, apptd 1991
Devon, P. H. Wassall, apptd 1994
East and West Sussex, P. C. Tain, apptd 1992
Essex, K. A. Gray, apptd 1995
Greater Manchester, W. D. Fairclough, apptd 1982;
    Miss J. E. Hayward, apptd 1991; A. Berg, apptd 1994;
    C. R. Darnton, apptd 1994
Hampshire, T. G. Cowling, apptd 1989
Humberside, N. H. White, apptd 1985
Lancashire/Merseyside, J. Finestein, apptd 1992
Leicestershire, D. M. Meredith, apptd 1995
Merseyside, D. R. G. Tapp, apptd 1992; P. S. Ward, apptd
    1994; P. J. Firth, apptd 1994
Middlesex, N. A. McKittrick, apptd 1989; S. N. Day, apptd
    1991; C. S. Wiles, apptd 1996
Mid Glamorgan, Miss P. J. Watkins, apptd 1995
Norfolk, N. P. Heley, apptd 1994
North-East London, G. E. Cawdron, apptd 1993
Nottinghamshire, P. F. Nuttall, apptd 1991; M. L. R. Harris,
    apptd 1991
Shropshire, P. H. R. Browning, apptd 1994
South Glamorgan, G. R. Watkins, apptd 1993
South Wales and Gwent, D. V. Manning-Davies, apptd 1996
South Yorkshire, J. A. Browne, apptd 1992; W. D. Thomas,
    apptd 1989; M. A. Rosenberg, apptd 1993; P. H. F. Jones,
    apptd 1995; Mrs S. E. Driver, apptd 1995
Staffordshire, P. G. G. Richards, apptd 1991
West Midlands, W. M. Probert, apptd 1983; B. Morgan, apptd
    1989; I. Gillespie, apptd 1991; M. F. James, apptd 1991;
    C. M. McColl, apptd 1994
West Yorkshire, F. D. L. Löy, apptd 1972; Mrs P. A. Hewitt,
    apptd 1990; G. A. K. Hodgson, apptd 1993

METROPOLITAN

*Chief Metropolitan Stipendiary Magistrate and Chairman of
Magistrates' Courts Committee for Inner London Area*
(£83,586), G. E. Parkinson, apptd 1997 (*Bow Street*)

Magistrates (each £67,354)

Bow Street, The Chief Magistrate; R. D. Bartle, apptd 1972;
    H. N. Evans, apptd 1994; Mrs L. Morgan, apptd 1995
Camberwell Green, C. P. M. Davidson, apptd 1984;
    B. Loosley, apptd 1989; H. Gott, apptd 1992;
    Miss F. Roscoe, apptd 1994; R. House, apptd 1995;
    Miss C. S. R. Tubbs, apptd 1996
Clerkenwell, M. A. Johnstone, apptd 1980; J. M. Baker, apptd
    1990
Greenwich, D. A. Cooper, apptd 1991; P. S. Wallis, apptd
    1993; H. C. F. Riddle, apptd 1995
Highbury Corner, Miss D. Quick, apptd 1986; A. T. Evans,
    apptd 1990; C. S. F. Black, apptd 1993; Miss D. Lachhar,
    apptd 1996; P. A. M. Clark, apptd 1996
Horseferry Road, A. R. Davies, apptd 1985; G. Breen, apptd
    1986; Mrs K. R. Keating, apptd 1987; Mrs E. Rees, apptd
    1994
Inner London and City Family Proceedings Court, N. Crichton,
    apptd 1987
Marlborough Street, T. H. Workman, apptd 1986;
    Miss D. Wickham, apptd 1989

Marylebone, D. Kennett-Brown, apptd 1982; K. Maitland-
    Davies, apptd 1984; A. C. Baldwin, apptd 1990; C. L.
    Pratt, apptd 1990
South-Western, S. G. Clixby, apptd 1981; C. D. Voelcker,
    apptd 1982; A. W. Ormerod, apptd 1988
Thames, S. E. Dawson, apptd 1984; I. G. Bing, apptd 1989;
    W. A. Kennedy, apptd 1991; M. J. Read, apptd 1993
Tower Bridge, Mrs J. R. Comyns, apptd 1982; J. R. D. Philips,
    apptd 1989; M. Kelly, apptd 1992
West London Magistrates' Court, Miss A. Jennings, apptd
    1972; T. English, apptd 1986; D. L. Thomas, apptd 1990;
    Ms G. B. Babington-Browne, apptd 1991; S. Somjee,
    apptd 1995
West London Youth Court, G. L. Wicks, apptd 1987; D.
    Simpson, apptd 1993; J. B. Coleman, apptd 1995

MAGISTRATES' COURTS COMMITTEE FOR THE INNER
LONDON AREA
65 Romney Street, London SW1P 3RD
Tel 0171-799 3332

Justices' Chief Executive and Clerk to the Committee (*£80,000),
    Miss C. Glenn
Justices' Clerk (Training) (£*51,443), Miss C. Lewis

* 1996–7 figure

CROWN PROSECUTION SERVICE
50 Ludgate Hill, London EC4M 7EX
Tel 0171-273 8000

The Crown Prosecution Service (CPS) is responsible for
the independent review and conduct of criminal proceedings instituted by police forces in England and Wales,
with the exception of cases conducted by the Serious
Fraud Office (*see* page 343) and certain minor offences.

The Director of Public Prosecutions is the head of the
Service and discharges her statutory functions under the
superintendence of the Attorney-General.

The Service comprises a headquarters office and 14
Areas covering England and Wales. Each of the CPS Areas
is supervised by a Chief Crown Prosecutor. The Service
is to be reorganized into 42 areas, corresponding to the
police forces in England and Wales, by spring 1998.

For salary information, *see* page 278

Director of Public Prosecutions (*G1*), Dame
    Barbara Mills, DBE, QC
Director of Corporate Services (*G3*), D. Nooney
Director of Casework Evaluation (*G3*), C. Newell
Director of Casework Services (*G3*), G. Duff

CPS AREAS

CPS ANGLIA, Queen's House, 58 Victoria Street, St
    Albans AL1 3HZ. Tel: 01727-818100. *Chief Crown Prosecutor*
    (*G4*), R. J. Chronnell
CPS CENTRAL CASEWORK, 50 Ludgate Hill, London
    EC4M 7EX. Tel: 0171-273 8000. *Chief Crown Prosecutor*
    (*G4*), D. Sharpling
CPS EAST MIDLANDS, 2 King Edward Court, King
    Edward Street, Nottingham NG1 1EL. Tel: 0115-948 0480.
    Chief Crown Prosecutor (*G4*), B. T. McArdle
CPS HUMBER, Greenfield House, Scotland Street,
    Sheffield S3 7DQ. Tel: 0114-291 2164. *Chief Crown
    Prosecutor* (*G4*), D. Adams, CBE
CPS LONDON, Portland House, Stag Place, London SW1E
    5BH. Tel: 0171-915 5700. *Chief Crown Prosecutor* (*G3*),
    G. D. Etherington

CPS MERSEY/LANCASHIRE, 7th Floor (South), Royal Liver Building, Pier Head, Liverpool L3 1HN. Tel: 0151-236 7575. *Chief Crown Prosecutor (G4)*, G. Brown

CPS MIDLANDS, 14th Floor, Colmore Gate, 2 Colmore Row, Birmingham B3 2QA. Tel: 0121-629 7202. *Chief Crown Prosecutor (G4)*, D. Blundell

CPS NORTH, 1st Floor, Benton House, 136 Sandyford Road, Newcastle upon Tyne NE2 1QE. Tel: 0191-201 2390. *Chief Crown Prosecutor (G4)*, M. Graham

CPS NORTH-WEST, PO Box 237, 8th Floor, Sunlight House, Quay Street, Manchester M60 3PS. Tel: 0161-908 2771. *Chief Crown Prosecutor (G4)*, A. R. Taylor

CPS SEVERN/THAMES, Artillery House, Heritage Way, Droitwich, Worcester WR9 8YB. Tel: 01905-795477. *Chief Crown Prosecutor (G4)*, N. Franklin

CPS SOUTH-EAST, 1 Onslow Street, Guildford, Surrey GU1 4YA. Tel: 01483-882600. *Chief Crown Prosecutor (G4)*, C. Nicholls

CPS SOUTH-WEST, 8 Kew Court, Pynes Hill, Rydon Lane, Exeter EX2 5SS. Tel: 01392-422555. *Chief Crown Prosecutor (G4)*, P. Boeuf

CPS WALES, Tudor House, 16 Cathedral Road, Cardiff CF1 9LJ. Tel: 01222-783000. *Chief Crown Prosecutor (G4)*, R. A. Prickett

CPS YORKSHIRE, 6th Floor, Ryedale Building, 60 Piccadilly, York YO1 1NS. Tel: 01904-610726. *Chief Crown Prosecutor (G4)*, D. V. Dickenson

The Scottish Judicature

Scotland has a legal system separate from and differing greatly from the English legal system in enacted law, judicial procedure and the structure of courts.

In Scotland the system of public prosecution is headed by the Lord Advocate and is independent of the police, who have no say in the decision to prosecute. The Lord Advocate, discharging his functions through the Crown Office in Edinburgh, is responsible for prosecutions in the High Court, sheriff courts and district courts. Prosecutions in the High Court are prepared by the Crown Office and conducted in court by one of the law officers, by an advocate-depute, or by a solicitor advocate. In the inferior courts the decision to prosecute is made and prosecution is preferred by procurators fiscal, who are lawyers and full-time civil servants subject to the directions of the Crown Office. A permanent legally-qualified civil servant known as the Crown Agent is responsible for the running of the Crown Office and the organization of the Procurator Fiscal Service, of which he is the head.

Scotland is divided into six sheriffdoms, each with a full-time Sheriff Principal. The sheriffdoms are further divided into sheriff court districts, each of which has a legally-qualified resident sheriff or sheriffs, who are the judges of the court.

In criminal cases sheriffs principal and sheriffs have the same powers; sitting with a jury of 15 members, they may try more serious cases on indictment, or, sitting alone, may try lesser cases under summary procedure. Minor summary offences are dealt with in district courts which are administered by the district and the islands local government authorities and presided over by lay justices of the peace (of whom there are about 4,000) and, in Glasgow only, by stipendiary magistrates. Juvenile offenders (children under 16) may be brought before an informal children's hearing comprising three local lay people. The superior criminal court is the High Court of Justiciary which is both a trial and an appeal court. Cases on indictment are tried by a High Court judge, sitting with a jury of 15, in Edinburgh and on circuit in other towns. Appeals from the lower courts against conviction or sentence are heard also by the High Court, which sits as an appeal court only in Edinburgh. There is no further appeal to the House of Lords in criminal cases.

In civil cases the jurisdiction of the sheriff court extends to most kinds of action. Appeal against decisions of the sheriff may be made to the Sheriff Principal and thence to the Court of Session, or direct to the Court of Session, which sits only in Edinburgh. The Court of Session is divided into the Inner and the Outer House. The Outer House is a court of first instance in which cases are heard by judges sitting singly, sometimes with a jury of 12. The Inner House, itself subdivided into two divisions of equal status, is mainly an appeal court. Appeals may be made to the Inner House from the Outer House as well as from the sheriff court. An appeal may be made from the Inner House to the House of Lords.

The judges of the Court of Session are the same as those of the High Court of Justiciary, the Lord President of the Court of Session also holding the office of Lord Justice General in the High Court. Senators of the College of Justice are Lords Commissioners of Justiciary as well as judges of the Court of Session. On appointment, a Senator takes a judicial title, which is retained for life. Although styled 'The Hon./Rt. Hon. Lord —', the Senator is not a peer.

The office of coroner does not exist in Scotland. The local procurator fiscal inquires privately into sudden or suspicious deaths and may report findings to the Crown Agent. In some cases a fatal accident inquiry may be held before the sheriff.

COURT OF SESSION AND HIGH COURT OF JUSTICIARY

The Lord President and Lord Justice General (£131,034)
   The Rt. Hon. the Lord Rodger of Earlsferry, *born* 1944, *apptd* 1996
   Secretary, vacant

INNER HOUSE

Lords of Session (each £124,551)

FIRST DIVISION
The Lord President
Hon. Lord Sutherland (Ranald Sutherland), *born* 1932, *apptd* 1985
Hon. Lord Prosser (William Prosser), *born* 1934, *apptd* 1986
Hon. Lord Caplan (Philip Caplan), *born* 1929, *apptd* 1989

SECOND DIVISION
Lord Justice Clerk (£124,551), The Rt. Hon. Lord Cullen (William Cullen), *born* 1935, *apptd* 1997
Rt. Hon. The Lord McCluskey, *born* 1929, *apptd* 1984
Hon. Lord Kirkwood (Ian Kirkwood), *born* 1932, *apptd* 1987
Hon. Lord Coulsfield (John Cameron), *born* 1934, *apptd* 1987

OUTER HOUSE

Lords of Session (each £112,011)

Hon. Lord Milligan (James Milligan), *born* 1934, *apptd* 1988
Rt. Hon. The Lord Cameron of Lochbroom, *born* 1931, *apptd* 1989
Hon. Lord Marnoch (Michael Bruce), *born* 1938, *apptd* 1990

Hon. Lord MacLean (Ranald MacLean), *born* 1938, *apptd* 1990

Hon. Lord Penrose (George Penrose), *born* 1938, *apptd* 1990

Hon. Lord Osborne (Kenneth Osborne), *born* 1937, *apptd* 1990

Hon. Lord Abernethy (Alistair Cameron), *born* 1938, *apptd* 1992

Hon. Lord Johnston (Alan Johnston), *born* 1942, *apptd* 1994

Hon. Lord Gill (Brian Gill), *born* 1942, *apptd* 1994

Hon. Lord Hamilton (Arthur Hamilton), *born* 1942, *apptd* 1995

Hon. Lord Dawson (Thomas Dawson), *born* 1948, *apptd* 1995

Hon. Lord Macfadyen (Donald Macfadyen), *born* 1945, *apptd* 1995

Hon. Lady Cosgrove (Hazel Aronson), *born* 1946, *apptd* 1996

Hon. Lord Nimmo Smith (William Nimmo Smith), *born* 1942, *apptd* 1996

Hon. Lord Philip (Alexander Philip), *born* 1942, *apptd* 1996

Hon. Lord Kingarth (Derek Emslie), *born* 1949, *apptd* 1997

Hon. Lord Bonomy (Fain Bonomy), *born* 1946, *apptd* 1997

Hon. Lord Eassie (Ronald Mackay), *born* 1945, *apptd* 1997

COURT OF SESSION AND HIGH COURT OF JUSTICIARY
Parliament House, Parliament Square, Edinburgh EH1 1RQ
Tel 0131-225 2595

Principal Clerk of Session and Justiciary (£29,902–£49,860), J. L. Anderson

Deputy Principal Clerk of Justiciary and Administration (£26,205–£40,582), T. Fyffe

Deputy Principal Clerk of Session and Principal Extractor (£26,205–£40,582), G. McKeand

Deputy Principal Clerk (Keeper of the Rolls) (£26,205–£40,582), T. M. Thomson

Depute Clerks of Session and Justiciary (£19,830–£26,098), N. J. Dowie; I. F. Smith; T. Higgins; T. B. Cruickshank; Q. A. Oliver; F. Shannly; A. S. Moffat; D. J. Shand; G. G. Ellis; D. G. Lynn; W. Dunn; A. M. Finlayson; C. C. Armstrong; P. Crow; G. M. Prentice; R. Jenkins; J. O. McLean; M. Weir; C. D. Cockburn; R. M. Sinclair; E. G. Appelbe; B. Watson; D. W. Cullen; D. J. Cullum

SCOTTISH COURTS ADMINISTRATION
Hayweight House, 23 Lauriston Street, Edinburgh EH3 9DQ
Tel 0131-229 9200

The Scottish Courts Administration is responsible to the Secretary of State for Scotland for the performance of the Scottish Court Service and central administration pertaining to the judiciary in the Supreme and Sheriff Courts; and to the Lord Advocate for certain aspects of court procedures, jurisdiction and legislation, law reform and other matters.

Director (G2), J. Hamill

Deputy Director (Legal Policy) (Assistant Solicitor) (G5), P. M. Beaton

Deputy Director (Resources and Liaison) (G6), D. Stewart

SCOTTISH COURT SERVICE
Hayweight House, 23 Lauriston Street, Edinburgh EH3 9DQ
Tel 0131-229 9200

The Scottish Court Service became an executive agency within the Scottish Courts Administration in 1995. It is responsible to the Secretary of State for Scotland for the provision of staff, court houses and associated services for the Supreme and Sheriff Courts.

Chief Executive, M. Ewart

SHERIFF COURT OF CHANCERY
27 Chambers Street, Edinburgh EH1 1LB
Tel 0131-225 2525

The Court deals with service of heirs and completion of title in relation to heritable property.

Sheriff of Chancery, C. G. B. Nicholson, QC

HM COMMISSARY OFFICE
27 Chambers Street, Edinburgh EH1 1LB
Tel 0131-225 2525

The Office is responsible for issuing confirmation, a legal document entitling a person to execute a deceased person's will, and other related matters.

Commissary Clerk, J. M. Ross

SCOTTISH LAND COURT
1 Grosvenor Crescent, Edinburgh EH12 5ER
Tel 0131-225 3595

The court deals with disputes relating to agricultural and crofting land in Scotland.

Chairman (£92,378), The Hon. Lord McGhie (James McGhie), QC

Members, D. J. Hanston; D. M. Macdonald; J. Kinloch (*part-time*)

Principal Clerk, K. H. R. Graham, WS

SHERIFFDOMS

SALARIES

Sheriff Principal	£92,378
Sheriff	£83,586
Regional Sheriff Clerk	£29,902–£58,096
Sheriff Clerk	£11,567–£40,582

*Floating Sheriff

GRAMPIAN, HIGHLANDS AND ISLANDS

Sheriff Principal, D. J. Risk
Regional Sheriff Clerk, J. Robertson

SHERIFFS AND SHERIFF CLERKS

Aberdeen and Stonehaven, D. W. Bogie; G. C. Warner; D. Kelbic; L. A. S. Jessop; A. Pollock; *Mrs A. M. Cowan; *Sheriff Clerks*, Mrs E. Laing (*Aberdeen*); I. Smith (*Stonehaven*)

Peterhead and Banff, K. A. McLernan; *Sheriff Clerk*, A. Hempseed (*Peterhead*); *Sheriff Clerk Depute*, Mrs F. L. MacPherson (*Banff*)

Elgin, N. McPartlin; *Sheriff Clerk*, M. McBey

Inverness, Lochmaddy, Portree, Stornoway, Dingwall, Tain, Wick und Dornoch, W. J. Fulton; D. Booker Milburn; J. O. A. Fraser; I. A. Cameron; *Sheriff Clerks*, J. Robertson (*Inverness*); W. Cochrane (*Dingwall*); *Sheriff Clerks Depute*, Miss M. Campbell (*Lochmaddy and Portree*); Mrs M. Macdonald (*Stornoway*); L. MacLachlan (*Tain*); Mrs J. McEwan (*Wick*); K. Kerr (*Dornoch*)

Kirkwall and Lerwick, C. S. Mackenzie; *Sheriff Clerks Depute*, P. Cushen (*Kirkwall*); A. C. Norris (*Lerwick*)

Fort William, C. G. McKay (also *Oban*); *Sheriff Clerk Depute*, D. Hood

TAYSIDE, CENTRAL AND FIFE

Sheriff Principal, J. J. Maguire, QC
Regional Sheriff Clerk, J. S. Doig

SHERIFFS AND SHERIFF CLERKS

Arbroath and Forfar, K. A. Veal; *C. N. R. Stein; *Sheriff Clerks*, M. Herbertson (*Arbroath*); S. Munro (*Forfar*)
Dundee, R. A. Davidson; A. L. Stewart, QC; *J. N. Young; vacant (also *Cupar*); *Sheriff Clerk*, J. S. Doig
Perth, J. F. Wheatley; J. C. McInnes, QC; *Mrs P. M. M. Bowman; *Sheriff Clerk*, W. Jones
Falkirk, A. V. Sheehan; A. J. Murphy; *Sheriff Clerk*, D. Forrester
Stirling, The Hon. R. E. G. Younger; *Sheriff Clerk*, J. Clark
Alloa, W. M. Reid; *Sheriff Clerk*, R. G. McKeand
Cupar, vacant (also *Dundee*); *Sheriff Clerk*, R. Hughes
Dunfermline, J. S. Forbes; C. W. Palmer; *Sheriff Clerk*, W. McCulloch
Kirkcaldy, W. J. Christie; Mrs L. G. Patrick; *Sheriff Clerk*, I. Hay

LOTHIAN AND BORDERS

Sheriff Principal, C. G. B. Nicholson, QC
Regional Sheriff Clerk (*acting*), J. Ross

SHERIFFS AND SHERIFF CLERKS

Edinburgh, vacant (also *Peebles*); R. G. Craik, QC; Miss I. A. Poole; R. J. D. Scott; A. M. Bell; J. M. S. Horsburgh, QC; G. W. S. Presslie (also *Haddington*); J. A. Farrell; *A. Lothian; *F. J. Keane; I. D. Macphail, QC; C. N. Stoddart; A. B. Wilkinson, QC; Mrs D. J. B. Robertson; N. M. P. Morrison, QC; *Miss M. M. Stephen; Mrs M. L. E. Jarvie, QC; *Sheriff Clerk*, J. Anderson
Peebles, vacant (also *Edinburgh*); *Sheriff Clerk Depute*, R. McArthur
Linlithgow, H. R. MacLean; G. R. Fleming; *K. A. Ross; *Sheriff Clerk*, R. Sinclair
Haddington, G. W. S. Presslie (also *Edinburgh*); *Sheriff Clerk*, J. O'Donnell
Jedburgh and Duns, J. V. Paterson; *Sheriff Clerk*, I. W. Williamson
Selkirk, J. V. Paterson; *Sheriff Clerk Depute*, L. McFarlane

NORTH STRATHCLYDE

Sheriff Principal, R. C. Hay, CBE
Regional Sheriff Clerk, I. Scott

SHERIFFS AND SHERIFF CLERKS

Oban, C. G. McKay (also *Fort William*); *Sheriff Clerk Depute*, G. Whitelaw
Dumbarton, J. T. Fitzsimons; T. Scott; S. W. H. Fraser; *Sheriff Clerk*, P. Corcoran
Paisley, R. G. Smith; J. Spy; C. K. Higgins; N. Douglas; *D. J. Pender; *W. Dunlop (also *Campbeltown*); *Sheriff Clerk* (*acting*), R. McMillan
Greenock, J. Herald (also *Rothesay*); Sir Stephen Young; *Sheriff Clerk*, J. Tannahill
Kilmarnock, T. M. Croan; D. B. Smith; T. F. Russell; *Sheriff Clerk*, N. R. Weir
Dunoon, A. W. Noble; *Sheriff Clerk Depute*, Mrs C. Carson
Campbeltown, *W. Dunlop (also *Paisley*); *Sheriff Clerk Depute*, P. G. Hay
Rothesay, J. Herald (also *Greenock*); *Sheriff Clerk Depute*, Mrs C. K. McCormick

GLASGOW AND STRATHKELVIN

Sheriff Principal, vacant
Regional Sheriff Clerk, I. Scott

SHERIFFS AND SHERIFF CLERKS

Glasgow, A. C. Horsfall, QC (*seconded to Scottish Lands Tribunal*); B. Kearney; G. H. Gordon, CBE, PH.D., QC;

B. A. Lockhart; I. G. Pirie; Mrs A. L. A. Duncan; G. J. Evans; E. H. Galt; A. C. Henry; J. K. Mitchell; A. G. Johnston; J. P. Murphy; Miss S. A. O. Raeburn, QC; D. Convery; J. McGowan; B. A. Kerr, QC; Mrs C. M. A. F. Gimblett; I. A. S. Peebles, QC; C. W. McFarlane, QC; K. M. Maciver; H. Matthews, QC; J. D. Lowe, CB; *J. A. Baird; *Sheriff Clerk*, I. Scott

SOUTH STRATHCLYDE, DUMFRIES AND GALLOWAY

Sheriff Principal, G. L. Cox, QC
Regional Sheriff Clerk, M. Bonar

SHERIFFS AND SHERIFF CLERKS

Hamilton, L. Cameron; A. C. MacPherson; W. F. Lunny; D. C. Russell; V. J. Canavan (also *Airdrie*); W. E. Gibson; H. Stirling; J. H. Stewart; *H. S. Neilson; *Sheriff Clerk*, P. Feeney
Lanark, J. D. Allan; *Sheriff Clerk*, A. Whyte
Ayr, N. Gow, QC; R. G. McEwan, QC; *C. B. Miller; *Sheriff Clerk*, G. W. Waddell
Stranraer and Kirkcudbright, J. R. Smith (also *Dumfries*); *Sheriff Clerks*, W. McIntosh (*Stranraer*); B. Lindsay (*Kirkcudbright*)
Dumfries, K. G. Barr; M. J. Fletcher; J. R. Smith (also *Stranraer and Kirkcudbright*); *Sheriff Clerk*, P. McGonigle
Airdrie, V. J. Canavan (also *Hamilton*); R. H. Dickson; I. C. Simpson; *Sheriff Clerk*, M. Bonar

STIPENDIARY MAGISTRATES

GLASGOW

R. Hamilton, *apptd* 1984; J. B. C. Nisbet, *apptd* 1984; R. B. Christie, *apptd* 1985; Mrs J. A. M. MacLean, *apptd* 1990

PROCURATOR FISCAL SERVICE

CROWN OFFICE

25 Chambers Street, Edinburgh EH1 1LA
Tel 0131-226 2626
Crown Agent (£74,660–£109,040), A. C. Normand
Deputy Crown Agent (£52,020–£86,700), N. McFadyen

PROCURATORS FISCAL

SALARIES

Regional Procurator Fiscal–grade 3	£57,020–£91,800
Regional Procurator Fiscal–grade 4	£52,020–£86,700
Procurator Fiscal–upper level	£38,760–£60,890
Procurator Fiscal–lower level	£27,945–£46,295

GRAMPIAN, HIGHLANDS AND ISLANDS REGION

Regional Procurator Fiscal, L. A. Higson (*Aberdeen*)
Procurators Fiscal, E. K. Barbour (*Stonehaven*); A. J. M. Colley (*Banff*); Mrs D. Wilson (*Peterhead*); J. F. MacKay (*Elgin*); A. N. MacDonald (*Wick*); J. Bamber (*Portree, Lochmaddy*); F. Redman (*Stornoway*); G. K. Buchanan (*Inverness*); D. K. Adam (*Kirkwall, Lerwick*); Mrs A. Neizer (*Fort William*); D. R. Hingston (*Dingwall, Dornoch, Tain*)

TAYSIDE, CENTRAL AND FIFE REGION

Regional Procurator Fiscal, B. K. Heywood (*Dundee*)

Procurators Fiscal, I. C. Walker (*Forfar*); I. A. McLeod (*Perth*); J. J. Miller (*Falkirk*); C. Ritchie (*Stirling*); I. D. Douglas (*Alloa*); E. B. Russell (*Cupar*); R. G. Stott (*Dunfermline*); Miss E. C. Munro (*Kirkcaldy*)

LOTHIAN AND BORDERS REGION
Regional Procurator Fiscal, R. F. Lees (*Edinburgh*)
Procurators Fiscal, D. McNeill (*Peebles*); Miss L. M. Ruxton (*Linlithgow*); A. J. P. Reith (*Haddington*); A. R. G. Fraser (*Duns, Jedburgh*); D. McNeill (*Selkirk*)

NORTH STRATHCLYDE REGION
Regional Procurator Fiscal, J. D. Friel (*Paisley*)
Procurators Fiscal, I. Henderson (*Campbeltown*); C. C. Donnelly (*Dumbarton*); W. S. Carnegie (*Greenock, Rothesay*); D. L. Webster (*Dunoon*); J. G. MacGlennan (*Kilmarnock*); B. R. Maguire (*Oban*)

GLASGOW AND STRATHKELVIN REGION
Regional Procurator Fiscal, A. D. Vannet (*Glasgow*)

SOUTH STRATHCLYDE, DUMFRIES AND GALLOWAY REGION
Regional Procurator Fiscal, F. R. Crowe (*Hamilton*)
Procurators Fiscal, S. R. Houston (*Lanark*); J. T. O'Donnell (*Ayr*); F. Walkingshaw (*Stranraer*); D. J. Howdle (*Dumfries, Stranraer, Kirkcudbright*); D. Spiers (*Airdrie*)

Northern Ireland Judicature

In Northern Ireland the legal system and the structure of courts closely resemble those of England and Wales; there are, however, often differences in enacted law.

The Supreme Court of Judicature of Northern Ireland comprises the Court of Appeal, the High Court of Justice and the Crown Court. The practice and procedure of these courts is similar to that in England. The superior civil court is the High Court of Justice, from which an appeal lies to the Northern Ireland Court of Appeal; the House of Lords is the final civil appeal court.

The Crown Court, served by High Court and county court judges, deals with criminal trials on indictment. Cases are heard before a judge and, except those involving offences specified under emergency legislation, a jury. Appeals from the Crown Court against conviction or sentence are heard by the Northern Ireland Court of Appeal; the House of Lords is the final court of appeal.

The decision to prosecute in cases tried on indictment and in summary cases of a serious nature rests in Northern Ireland with the Director of Public Prosecutions, who is responsible to the Attorney General. Minor summary offences are prosecuted by the police.

Minor criminal offences are dealt with in magistrates' courts by a legally qualified resident magistrate and, where an offender is under 17, by juvenile courts each consisting of a resident magistrate and two lay members specially qualified to deal with juveniles (at least one of whom must be a woman). In July 1997 there were 945 justices of the peace in Northern Ireland. Appeals from magistrates' courts are heard by the county court, or by the Court of Appeal on a point of law or an issue as to jurisdiction.

Magistrates' courts in Northern Ireland can deal with certain classes of civil case but most minor civil cases are dealt with in county courts. Judgments of all civil courts

are enforceable through a centralized procedure administered by the Enforcement of Judgments Office.

SUPREME COURT OF JUDICATURE
The Royal Courts of Justice, Belfast BT1 3JF
Tel 01232-235111

Lord Chief Justice of Northern Ireland (£131,034)
The Rt. Hon. Sir Robert Carswell, *born* 1934, *apptd* 1997
Principal Secretary, G. W. Johnston

LORDS JUSTICES OF APPEAL (each £124,551)
Style, The Rt. Hon. Lord Justice [surname]
Rt. Hon. Sir John MacDermott, *born* 1927, *apptd* 1987
Rt. Hon. Sir Michael Nicholson, *born* 1933, *apptd* 1995
Rt. Hon. Sir William McCollum, *born* 1933, *apptd* 1997

PUISNE JUDGES (each £ 112,011)
Style, The Hon. Mr Justice [surname]
Hon. Sir Anthony Campbell, *born* 1936, *apptd* 1988
Hon. Sir John Sheil, *born* 1938, *apptd* 1989
Hon. Sir Brian Kerr, *born* 1948, *apptd* 1993
Hon. Sir John Pringle, *born* 1929, *apptd* 1993
Hon. Sir Malachy Higgins, *born* 1944, *apptd* 1993
Hon. Sir Paul Girvan, *born* 1948, *apptd* 1995
Hon. Sir Patrick Coghlin, *born* 1945, *apptd* 1997

MASTERS OF THE SUPREME COURT (each £67,354)
Master, Queen's Bench and Appeals and Clerk of the Crown, J. W. Wilson, QC
Master, High Court, Mrs D. M. Kennedy
Master, Office of Care and Protection, F. B. Hall
Master, Chancery Office, R. A. Ellison
Master, Bankruptcy and Companies Office, J. B. C. Glass
Master, Probate and Matrimonial Office, vacant
Master, Taxing Office, J. C. Napier

OFFICIAL SOLICITOR
Official Solicitor to the Supreme Court of Northern Ireland, C. W. G. Redpath

COUNTY COURTS
JUDGES (each £83,586–£92,378)
Style, His Hon. Judge [surname]
Judge Curran, QC; Judge McKee, QC; Judge Gibson, QC; Judge Petrie, QC; Judge Smyth, QC; Judge Markey, QC; Judge McKay, QC; vacant (*Chief Social Security and Child Support Commissioner*); Judge Martin, QC; Judge Brady, QC; Judge Rodgers, Judge Foote, QC

RECORDERS (each £92,378)
Belfast, Judge Hart, QC
Londonderry, Judge Burgess

MAGISTRATES' COURTS
RESIDENT MAGISTRATES (each £67,354)
There are 17 resident magistrates in Northern Ireland.

CROWN SOLICITOR'S OFFICE
PO Box 410, Royal Courts of Justice, Belfast BT1 3JY
Tel 01232-542555

Crown Solicitor, N. P. Roberts

DEPARTMENT OF THE DIRECTOR OF
PUBLIC PROSECUTIONS
Royal Courts of Justice, Belfast BT1 3NX
Tel 01232-542444

Director of Public Prosecutions, A. Fraser, CB, QC
Deputy Director of Public Prosecutions, D. Magill

NORTHERN IRELAND COURT SERVICE
Windsor House, Bedford Street, Belfast BT2 7LT
Tel 01232–328594

Director (G3)

Ecclesiastical Courts

Original jurisdiction is exercised by the consistory court of each diocese in England, presided over by the Chancellor of that diocese. Appellate jurisdiction is exercised by the provincial courts detailed below, by the Court for Ecclesiastical Causes Reserved, and by commissions of review (the membership of these being newly constituted for each case).

COURT OF ARCHES (PROVINCE OF CANTERBURY)
Registry, 16 Beaumont Street, Oxford OX1 2LZ
Tel 01865-241974

Dean of the Arches, The Rt. Worshipful Sir John Owen

COURT OF THE VICAR-GENERAL OF THE PROVINCE OF
CANTERBURY
Registry, 16 Beaumont Street, Oxford OX1 2LZ
Tel 01865-241974

Vicar-General, The Rt. Worshipful Miss S. Cameron, QC

CHANCERY COURT OF YORK
Registry, 1 Peckitt Street, York YO1 1SG
Tel 01904-623487

Auditor, The Rt. Worshipful Sir John Owen

THE VICAR-GENERAL OF THE PROVINCE OF YORK
Registry, 1 Peckitt Street, York YO1 1SG
Tel 01904-623487

Vicar-General, His Honour the Worshipful Judge
  T. A. C. Coningsby, QC

COURT OF FACULTIES
Registry, 1 The Sanctuary, London SW1P 3JT
Tel 0171-222 5381

Office for the issue of special and common marriage licences, appointment of notaries public, etc. Office hours, Monday–Friday, 10–4.
Master of the Faculties, The Rt. Worshipful Sir John Owen

The Probation Service

ENGLAND AND WALES

The Probation Service is employed in each area (54 in total) by an independent committee and it provides a professional social work agency in the courts, with responsibility for a wide range of duties which include:
(a) a pre-sentence report service for the criminal courts
(b) provision of a range of non-custodial measures involving the supervision of offenders in the community
(c) supervisory aftercare for offenders released from custody, together with social work in penal establishments and help for the families of those serving sentences
(d) an enquiry, conciliation and supervision service in the divorce and domestic courts
(e) support for and promotion of preventive and containment measures in the community designed to reduce the level of crime and domestic breakdown
It is a direct grant service funded 80 per cent from the Home Office and 20 per cent from the relevant local authority.
  Its national representative bodies are:
THE CENTRAL PROBATION COUNCIL, 4th Floor, 8–9 Grosvenor Place, London SW1X 7SH. Tel: 0171-245 9364. *Director,* I. Miles
THE ASSOCIATION OF CHIEF OFFICERS OF PROBATION, 212 Whitechapel Road, London E1 1BJ. Tel: 0171-377 9141. *General Secretary,* Ms M. Honeyball

THE NATIONAL ASSOCIATION OF PROBATION OFFICERS, 3 Chivalry Road, London SW11 1HT. Tel: 0171-223 4887. *General Secretary,* Ms J. McKnight

SCOTLAND

The probation service in Scotland is a statutory duty of local authorities under section 27 of the Social Work (Scotland) Act 1968. Social workers supervise and provide advice, guidance and assistance to those persons living in their area who are subject to a court's supervision order. This is done by social workers as part of their normal duties and not by a separate probation staff.

NORTHERN IRELAND

The Probation Board for Northern Ireland provides a probation service throughout Northern Ireland. Its function and range of duties is similar to that of the Probation Service in England and Wales (*see* above), except that in Northern Ireland work in divorce and domestic courts is the responsibility of the social services and not the Probation Board. The Probation Board is a statutory body whose 15 members are appointed by the Secretary of State for Northern Ireland and it receives its funding from the Northern Ireland Office.

Crime Statistics

ENGLAND AND WALES

NOTIFIABLE OFFENCES RECORDED 1995

Violence against the person	212,600
Sexual offences	30,300
Burglary	1,239,500
Robbery	68,100
Theft and handling stolen goods	2,452,100
Fraud and forgery	133,000
Criminal damage	914,000
Other offences	50,700
Total offences	5,100,200

Source: The Stationery Office – *Annual Abstract of Statistics 1997*

CRIMINAL JUSTICE STATISTICS 1995

Number of arrests	1,700,000
Notifiable offences cleared up	1,277,000
Clear-up rate	26%
*Number of offenders cautioned	291,000
Defendants proceeded against	
at magistrates' courts	1,928,000
Defendants found guilty at magistrates' courts	1,359,000
Defendants tried at Crown Courts	89,000
Defendants found guilty at Crown Courts	70,000
Defendants sentenced at Crown Courts	
after summary conviction	4,000
Total offenders found guilty at both courts	1,430,000
*Total offenders found guilty or cautioned	1,721,000

*Excludes motoring offences

OFFENDERS SENTENCED BY TYPE OF SENTENCE OR ORDER 1995

Absolute discharge	20,200
Conditional discharge	105,600
Fine	996,700
Probation order	49,400
Supervision order	10,100
Community service order	48,300
Attendance sentence order	7,500
Combination order	14,600
Young offender institution	18,800
Imprisonment:	
Suspended	3,200
Unsuspended	60,300
Otherwise dealt with	19,500
All sentences or orders: total	1,354,300

AVERAGE LENGTH OF SENTENCE 1995 *in months*

	Males aged 21 and over	Females aged 21 and over
Magistrates' courts	2.8	2.4
Crown court	22.0	17.7

Source: The Stationery Office – *Criminal Statistics England and Wales 1995*

SCOTLAND

CRIMES AND OFFENCES RECORDED 1995

Non-sexual crimes of violence against the person	21,100
Crimes involving indecency	5,500
Crimes involving dishonesty	321,200
Fire-raising, vandalism, etc	86,500
Other crimes	68,400
Miscellaneous offences	134,400
Motor vehicle offences	317,500
Total crimes and offences	954,700

Source: The Stationery Office – *Annual Abstract of Statistics 1997*

CRIMINAL JUSTICE STATISTICS 1995

Number of persons proceeded against	177,168
Persons with charge proved	156,707

PERSONS WITH CHARGE PROVED *by main penalty* 1995

Absolute discharge	682
Remit to children's hearing	172
Admonition or caution	15,854
Compensation order	1,671
Fine	110,346
Probation	6,071
Community service order	5,506
Insanity or hospital order	136
Detention of child	48
Young offender institution	4,650
Prison	11,571
All penalties: total	156,707

Source: Scottish Office – *Annual Abstract of Statistics 1996*

POLICE STRENGTHS 1997

	Male	Female	Total
ENGLAND AND WALESp			
Total officers	106,271	18,780	125,051
Ethnic minority officers	1,655	495	2,150
Special constables	12,864	6,972	19,836
Civilians	20,767	32,243	53,010
SCOTLAND			
Officers	12,752	2,037	14,789
Special constables	1,336	450	1,786
Civilians	1,642	2,648	4,290
NORTHERN IRELAND			
Officers	7,559	913	8,472
Special constables	913	496	1,409
Civilians	627	1,853	2,480

p provisional
Sources: Home Office; Scottish Office; RUC

Tribunals

AGRICULTURAL LAND TRIBUNALS
c/o Land Use and Rural Economy Division, Ministry of Agriculture, Fisheries and Food, Nobel House, 17 Smith Square, London SW1P 3JR
Tel 0171-238 6991

Agricultural Land Tribunals were set up under the Agriculture Act 1947 and settle disputes and other issues between agricultural landlords and tenants. They also settle drainage disputes between neighbours.

There are seven tribunals covering England and one covering Wales. For each tribunal the Lord Chancellor appoints a chairman and one or more deputies, who must be barristers or solicitors of at least seven years standing. The Lord Chancellor also appoints lay members to three statutory panels of members: the 'landowners' panel, the 'farmers' panel and the 'drainage' panel.

Each of the eight tribunals is an independent statutory body with jurisdiction only within its own area. A separate tribunal is constituted for each case, and consists of a chairman (who may be the chairman or one of the deputy chairmen) and two lay members nominated by the chairman.
Chairmen (England) (£239 a day), W. D. Greenwood; K. J. Fisher; P. A. de la Piquerie; C. H. Beaumont; His Hon. Judge Lee; G. L. Newsom; His Hon. Judge Robert Taylor
Chairman (Wales) (£239 a day), W. J. Owen

COMMONS COMMISSIONERS
4th Floor, 35 Old Queen Street, London SW1H 9JA
Tel 0171-222 0038

The Commons Commissioners are responsible for deciding disputes arising under the Commons Registration Act 1965 and the Common Land (Rectification of Registers) Act 1989. They also enquire into the ownership of unclaimed common land. Commissioners are appointed by the Lord Chancellor.
Chief Commons Commissioner (part-time) (£40,358), D. M. Burton
Commissioner, I. L. R. Romer
Clerk, Miss S. Hargreaves

COPYRIGHT TRIBUNAL
25 Southampton Buildings, London WC2A 1AY
Tel 0171- 438 4776

The Copyright Tribunal, which replaced the Performing Right Tribunal, was established by the Copyright, Designs and Patents Act 1988 to resolve disputes over copyright licences, principally where there is collective licensing. Its jurisdiction has been extended by the Broadcasting Acts 1990 and 1996, the Duration of Copyright and Rights in Performances Regulations 1995 and the Copyright and Related Rights Regulations 1996.

The chairman and two deputy chairmen are appointed by the Lord Chancellor. Up to eight ordinary members are appointed by the Secretary of State for Trade and Industry.
Chairman (£316 a day), vacant
Secretary, Miss J. E. M. Durdin

DATA PROTECTION TRIBUNAL
c/o The Home Office, Queen Anne's Gate, London SW1H 9AT
Tel 0171-273 3386

The Data Protection Tribunal was established under the Data Protection Act 1984 to determine appeals against decisions of the Data Protection Registrar (*see* page 295). The chairman and two deputy chairmen are appointed by the Lord Chancellor and must be legally qualified. Lay members are appointed by the Home Secretary to represent the interests of data users or data subjects.

A tribunal consists of a legally-qualified chairman sitting with equal numbers of the lay members appointed to represent the interests of data users and data subjects.
Chairman (£359 a day), J. A. C. Spokes, QC
Secretary, D. Anderson

EMPLOYMENT APPEAL TRIBUNAL
Central Office, Audit House, 58 Victoria Embankment, London EC4Y 0DS
Tel 0171-273 1041
Divisional Office, 52 Melville Street, Edinburgh EH3 7HF
Tel 0131-225 3963

The Employment Appeal Tribunal was established as a superior court of record under the provisions of the Employment Protection Act 1975, hearing appeals on a question of law arising from any decision of an industrial tribunal. A tribunal consists of a high court judge and two lay members, one from each side of industry. They are appointed by The Queen on the recommendation of the Lord Chancellor and the Secretary of State for Trade and Industry. Administrative support is provided by the Employment Tribunal Service (*see* page 348).
President, The Hon. Mr Justice Morison
Scottish Chairman, The Hon. Lord Johnston
Registrar, Miss V. J. Selio

IMMIGRATION APPELLATE AUTHORITIES
Thanet House, 231 Strand, London WC2R 1DA
Tel 0171-353 8060

The Immigration Appeal Adjudicators hear appeals from immigration decisions concerning the need for, and refusal of, leave to enter or remain in the UK, refusals to grant asylum, decisions to make deportation orders and directions to remove persons subject to immigration control from the UK. The Immigration Appeal Tribunal hears appeals direct from decisions to make deportation orders in matters concerning conduct contrary to the public good and refusals to grant asylum. Its principal jurisdiction is, however, the hearing of appeals from adjudicators by the party (Home Office or individual) who is aggrieved by the decision. Appeals are subject to leave being granted by the tribunal.

An adjudicator sits alone. The tribunal sits in divisions of three, normally a legally qualified member and two lay members. Members of the tribunal and adjudicators are appointed by the Lord Chancellor.

IMMIGRATION APPEAL TRIBUNAL
President, His Hon. Judge Pearl
Vice-Presidents, Mrs J. Chatwani; A. F. Hatt; M. Rapinet; A. O'Brien-Quinn

IMMIGRATION APPEAL ADJUDICATORS
Chief Adjudicator, vacant
Deputy Chief Adjudicator, vacant

INDEPENDENT TRIBUNAL SERVICE
Whittington House, 19–30 Alfred Place, London
WC1E 7LW
Tel 0171-814 6500

The service is the judicial authority which exercises judicial and administrative control over the independent social security and child support appeal tribunals, medical and disability appeal tribunals, and vaccine damage tribunals.
President, His Hon. Judge Bassingthwaighte
Chief Executive, S. Williams

INDUSTRIAL TRIBUNALS

CENTRAL OFFICE (ENGLAND AND WALES)
19–29 Woburn Place, London WC1H 0LU
Tel 0171-273 8659

Industrial Tribunals for England and Wales sit in 11 regions. The tribunals deal with matters of employment law, redundancy, dismissal, contract disputes, sexual, racial and disability discrimination, and related areas of dispute which may arise in the workplace. A central registration unit records all applications and maintains a public register at Southgate Street, Bury St Edmunds, 1P33 2AQ. The tribunals are funded by the Department of Trade and Industry; administrative support is provided by the Employment Tribunal Service (*see* page 348).
Chairmen, who may be full-time or part-time, are legally qualified. They are appointed by the Lord Chancellor. Tribunal members are nominated by specified employer and employee groups and appointed by the Secretary of State for Trade and Industry.
President, His Hon. Judge Lawrence

CENTRAL OFFICE (SCOTLAND)
Eagle Building, 215 Bothwell Street, Glasgow G2 7TS
Tel 0141-204 0730

Tribunals in Scotland have the same remit as those in England and Wales. Chairmen are appointed by the Lord President of the Court of Session and lay members by the Secretary of State for Trade and Industry.
President (£92,378), Mrs D. Littlejohn

INDUSTRIAL TRIBUNALS AND THE FAIR EMPLOYMENT TRIBUNAL (NORTHERN IRELAND)
Long Bridge House, 20–24 Waring Street, Belfast BT1 2EB
Tel 01232-327666

The industrial tribunal system in Northern Ireland was set up in 1965 and is similar to the system operating in the rest of the UK. The main legislation in Northern Ireland giving jurisdiction to industrial tribunals to hear complaints relating to employment matters corresponds to legislation enacted in Great Britain, except that there is no equivalent legislation to the Race Relations Act.

Since 1990 there has been a separate Fair Employment Tribunal in Northern Ireland. The Fair Employment Tribunal hears and determines individual cases of alleged religious or political discrimination in employment. Employers can also appeal to the Fair Employment Tribunal if they consider the directions of the Fair Employment Commission to be unreasonable, inappropriate or unnecessary, and the Fair Employment Commission can make application to the Tribunal for the enforcement of undertakings or directions with which an employer has not complied.

The president, vice-president and part-time chairmen of the Fair Employment Tribunal are appointed by the Lord Chancellor. The full-time chairman and the part-time chairmen of the industrial tribunals and the panel members to both the industrial tribunals and the Fair Employment Tribunal are appointed by the Department of Economic Development Northern Ireland.
President of the Industrial Tribunals and the Fair Employment Tribunal (£83,586), J. Maguire, CBE
Vice-President of the Industrial Tribunals and the Fair Employment Tribunal, Mrs M. P. Price
Secretary, Mrs P. McVeigh

LANDS TRIBUNAL
48–49 Chancery Lane, London WC2A 1JR
Tel 0171-936 7200

The Lands Tribunal is an independent judicial body constituted by the Lands Tribunal Act 1949 to determine questions relating to the valuation of land, rating appeals from valuation tribunals, the discharge or modification of restrictive covenants, and compulsory purchase compensation. The Act also empowers the tribunal to accept the function of arbitration under references by consent. The tribunal consists of a president and a number of other members, who are appointed by the Lord Chancellor.
President, His Hon. Judge Marder, QC
Members (£80,430), M. St J. Hopper, FRICS; P. H. Clarke, FRICS
Member (part-time), His Hon. Judge Rich, QC
Members (part-time) (£349 a day), J. C. Hill, TD; A. P. Musto, FRICS
Registrar, C. A. McMullan

LANDS TRIBUNAL FOR SCOTLAND
1 Grosvenor Crescent, Edinburgh EH12 5ER
Tel 0131-225 7996

The Lands Tribunal for Scotland was constituted by the Lands Tribunal Act 1949. Its remit is the same as the tribunal for England and Wales but also covers questions relating to tenants' rights. The president is appointed by the Lord President of the Court of Session.
President, The Hon. Lord McGhie, QC
Members (£80,430), Sheriff A. C. Horsfall, QC; A. R. MacLeary; J. Devine
Member (part-time) (£31,867), R. A. Edwards, CBE, WS
Clerk, N. M. Tainsh

MENTAL HEALTH REVIEW TRIBUNALS

The Mental Health Review Tribunals are independent judicial bodies which operate under the Mental Health Act 1983. They are responsible for reviewing the cases of patients compulsorily detained under the Act's provisions. They have the power to discharge the patient, to recommend leave of absence, delayed discharge, transfer to another hospital or that a guardianship order be made, and to reclassify both restricted and unrestricted patients. They also now have powers to recommend consideration of a supervision application. There are eight tribunals in England, each headed by a regional chairman who is appointed by the Lord Chancellor's Department on a part-time basis. Each tribunal is made up of at least three members, and must include a lawyer, who acts as president (£239 a day), a medical member (£226 a day) and a lay member (£97 a day).

The Mental Health Review Tribunals' secretariat is based in five regional offices:

LIVERPOOL, 3rd Floor, Cressington House, 249 St Mary's Road, Garston, Liverpool L19 0NF. Tel: 0151-494 0095. *Clerk*, Mrs B. Foot

LONDON (NORTH), Spur 3, Block 1, Government Buildings, Honeypot Lane, Stanmore, Middx HA7 1AY. Tel: 0171-972 3734. *Clerk*, Ms K. Vale

LONDON (SOUTH), Block 3, Crown Offices, Kingston Bypass Road, Surbiton, Surrey KT6 5QN. Tel: 0181-268 4520. *Clerk*, C. Lilly

NOTTINGHAM, Spur A, Block 5, Government Buildings, Chalfont Drive, Western Boulevard, Nottingham NG8 3RZ. Tel: 0115-929 4222. *Clerk*, M. Chapman

WALES, 4th Floor, Crown Buildings, Cathays Park, Cardiff CF1 3NQ. Tel: 01222-825328. *Clerk*, Mrs C. Thomas

NATIONAL HEALTH SERVICE TRIBUNAL

The NHS Tribunal was set up under the National Health Service Act 1977 and considers representations that the continued inclusion of a doctor, dentist, pharmacist or optician on a health authority's list would be prejudicial to the efficiency of the service concerned. The tribunal sits when required, about eight times a year, and usually in London. The chairman is appointed by the Lord Chancellor and members are appointed by the Secretary of State for Health.
Chairman (£259 a day), A. Whitfield, QC
Deputy Chairmen, Miss E. Platt, QC; Dr R. N. Ough
Clerk, I. D. Keith, East Hookers, Twineham, nr Haywards Heath, W. Sussex RH17 5NN. Tel: 01444-881345

NATIONAL HEALTH SERVICE TRIBUNAL (SCOTLAND)
66 Queen Street, Edinburgh EH2 4NE
Tel 0131-226 4771

The tribunal was set up under the National Health Service (Scotland) Act 1978, and considers representations that the continued inclusion of a registered doctor, dentist, optometrist or pharmacist on a health board's list would be prejudicial to the continuing efficiency of the service concerned.

The tribunal meets when required and is composed of a chairman, one lay member, and one practitioner member drawn from a representative professional panel. The chairman is appointed by the Lord President of the Court of Session, and the lay member and the members of the professional panel are appointed by the Secretary of State for Scotland.
Chairman (£259 a day), M. G. Thomson, QC
Lay member, J. D. M. Robertson
Clerk to the Tribunal, D. G. Brash, WS

PENSIONS APPEAL TRIBUNALS

CENTRAL OFFICE (ENGLAND AND WALES)
48–49 Chancery Lane, London WC2A 1JR
Tel 0171-936 7034

The Pensions Appeal Tribunals are responsible for hearing appeals from ex-servicemen or women and widows who have had their claims for a war pension rejected by the Secretary of State for Social Security. The Entitlement Appeal Tribunals hear appeals in cases where the Secretary of State has refused to grant a war pension. The Assessment Appeal Tribunals hear appeals against the Secretary of State's assessment of the degree of disablement caused by an accepted condition. The tribunal members are appointed by the Lord Chancellor.
President (£67,354), J. R. T. Holt
Secretary, W. Thomas

PENSIONS APPEAL TRIBUNALS FOR SCOTLAND
20 Walker Street, Edinburgh EH3 7HS
Tel 0131-220 1404
President (£285 a day), C. N. McEachran, QC

OFFICE OF THE SOCIAL SECURITY AND CHILD SUPPORT COMMISSIONERS
5th Floor, Newspaper House, 8–16 Great New Street, London EC4A 3BN
Tel 0171-353 5145
23 Melville Street, Edinburgh EH3 7PW
Tel 0131-225 2201

The Social Security Commissioners are the final statutory authority to decide appeals relating to entitlement to social security benefits. The Child Support Commissioners are the final statutory authority to decide appeals relating to child support. Appeals may be made in relation to both matters only on a point of law. The Commissioners' jurisdiction covers England, Wales and Scotland. There are 17 commissioners; they are all qualified lawyers.
Chief Social Security Commissioner and Chief Child Support Commissioner, His Hon. Judge Machin, QC
Secretary, S. Hill (*London*); E. Barschtschyk (*Edinburgh*)

OFFICE OF THE SOCIAL SECURITY AND CHILD SUPPORT COMMISSIONERS FOR NORTHERN IRELAND
Lancashire House, 5 Linenhall Street, Belfast BT2 8AA
Tel 01232-332344

The role of Northern Ireland Social Security and Child Support Commissioners is similar to that of the Commissioners in Great Britain. There are two commissioners for Northern Ireland.
Chief Commissioner, His Hon. Judge Martin, QC
Registrar of Appeals, W. D. Pollock

THE SOLICITORS' DISCIPLINARY TRIBUNAL

50   52 Chancery Lane, London WC2A 1SX
Tel 0171-242 0219

The Solicitors' Disciplinary Tribunal was constituted under the provisions of the Solicitors Act 1974. It is an independent statutory body whose members are appointed by the Master of the Rolls. The tribunal considers applications made to it alleging either professional misconduct and/or a breach of the statutory rules by which solicitors are bound against an individually named solicitor, former solicitor, or registered foreign lawyer. The tribunal's jurisdiction extends to solicitor's clerks, in respect of whom they may make an order restricting that clerk's employment by solicitors. The president and solicitor members do not receive remuneration.
President, G. B. Marsh
Clerk, Mrs S. C. Elson

SPECIAL COMMISSIONERS OF INCOME TAX

15–19 Bedford Avenue, London WC1B 3AS
Tel 0171-631 4242

The Special Commissioners are an independent body appointed by the Lord Chancellor to hear complex appeals against decisions of the Board of Inland Revenue and its officials. In addition to the Presiding Special Commissioner there are two full-time and 13 deputy special commissioners; all are legally qualified.
Presiding Special Commissioner, His Hon. Stephen Oliver, QC
Special Commissioners (£80,430), T. H. K. Everett;
D. A. Shirley
Clerk, R. P. Lester

TRAFFIC COMMISSIONERS

c/o Scottish Traffic Area, Argyle House, 3 Lady Lawson Street, Edinburgh EH3 9SE
Tel 0131-529 8500

The Traffic Commissioners are responsible for the licensing of operators of heavy goods and public service vehicles. They also have responsibility for appeals relating to the licensing of operators and for disciplinary cases involving the conduct of drivers of these vehicles. There are six Commissioners in the eight traffic areas covering Great Britain. Each Traffic Commissioner constitutes a tribunal for the purposes of the Tribunals and Inquiries Act 1971. For Traffic Area Offices and Commissioners, *see* page 301.
Senior Traffic Commissioner (£54,029), M. Betts

TRANSPORT TRIBUNAL

48–49 Chancery Lane, London WC2A 1JR
Tel 0171-936 7493

The Transport Tribunal was set up in 1947 and hears appeals against decisions made by Traffic Commissioners at public inquiries. The tribunal consists of a legally-qualified president, two legal members who may sit as chairmen, and five lay members. The president and legal members are appointed by the Lord Chancellor and the lay

members are appointed by the Secretary of State for the Environment, Transport and the Regions.
President (part-time), His Hon. Judge Main, QC
Legal members (£257 a day), His Hon. Judge Brodrick (*part-time*); R. Owen, QC
Lay members (£206 a day), T. W. Hall; J. W. Whitworth; G. Simms; Miss E. B. Haran; P. Rogers
Secretary, P. J. Fisher

VALUATION TRIBUNALS

c/o Warwickshire Valuation Tribunal, 2nd Floor, Walton House, 11 Parade, Leamington Spa, Warks CV32 4DG
Tel 01926-421875

The Valuation Tribunals hear appeals concerning the council tax, non-domestic rating and land drainage rates in England and Wales. They also have residual jurisdiction to hear appeals concerning the community charge, the pre-1990 rating list, disabled rating and mixed hereditaments. There are 56 tribunals in England, and eight in Wales. Each tribunal is a separate independent body; those in England are funded by the Department of the Environment and those in Wales by the Welsh Office. A separate tribunal is constituted for each hearing, and normally consists of a chairman and two other members. Members are appointed by the local authority/authorities, and serve on a voluntary basis. A National Committee of Valuation Tribunals considers all matters affecting valuations tribunals in England, and the Council of Wales Valuation Tribunals performs the same function in Wales.
President, National Committee of Valuation Tribunals, P. Wood
Secretary, National Committee of Valuation Tribunals,
B. P. Massen
President, Council of Wales Valuation Tribunals, P. J. Law

VAT AND DUTIES TRIBUNALS

15–19 Bedford Avenue, London WC1B 3AS
Tel 0171-631 4242

VAT and Duties Tribunals are administered by the Lord Chancellor's Department in England and Wales, and by the Secretary of State in Scotland. They are independent, and decide disputes between taxpayers and the Commissioners of Customs and Excise. In England and Wales, the president and chairmen are appointed by the Lord Chancellor and members are appointed by the Treasury. Chairmen in Scotland are appointed by the Lord President of the Court of Session.
President, His Hon. Stephen Oliver, QC
Vice-President, England and Wales (£80,430), A. W. Simpson
Vice-President, Scotland (£80,430), T. G. Coutts, QC
Vice-President, Northern Ireland (£80,430), D. C. Morgan, QC
Registrar, R. P. Lester

TRIBUNAL CENTRES

EDINBURGH, 44 Palmerston Place, Edinburgh EH12 5BJ.
Tel: 0131-226 3551
LONDON (including Belfast), 15–19 Bedford Avenue, London WC1B 3AS. Tel: 0171-631 4242
MANCHESTER, Warwickgate House, Warwick Road, Old Trafford, Manchester M16 0GP. Tel: 0161-872 6471

The Police Service

There are 52 police forces in the United Kingdom, each responsible for policing in its area. Most forces' area is conterminous with one or more local authority areas. Policing in London is carried out by the Metropolitan Police and the City of London Police; in Northern Ireland by the Royal Ulster Constabulary; and by the Isle of Man, States of Jersey, and Guernsey forces in their respective islands and bailiwicks. National services include the National Criminal Intelligence Service and the National Missing Persons Bureau (*see* below); the National Crime Squad is being established and is expected to start operating in April 1998.

Police authorities are responsible for maintaining an effective and efficient police force in their areas. The authorities of English and Welsh forces comprise local councillors, magistrates and independent members. In Scotland, there are six joint police boards made up of local councillors; the other two police authorities are councils. In London the authority for the Metropolitan Police is the Home Secretary, advised by the Metropolitan Police Committee; for the City of London Police the authority is a committee of the Corporation of London and includes councillors and magistrates. In Northern Ireland the Secretary of State appoints the police authority.

Police authorities are financed by central and local government grants and a precept on the council tax. Subject to the approval of the Home Secretary and to regulations, they appoint the chief constable. In England and Wales they are responsible for publishing annual policing plans and annual reports, setting local objectives and a budget, and levying the precept. The police authorities in Scotland are responsible for setting a budget, providing the resources necessary to police the area adequately, appointing officers of the rank of Assistant Chief Constable and above, and determining the number of officers and civilian staff in the force. The structure and responsibilities of the police authority in Northern Ireland are under review.

The Home Secretary and the Secretaries of State for Scotland and Northern Ireland are responsible for the organization, administration and operation of the police service. They make regulations covering matters such as police ranks, discipline, hours of duty, and pay and allowances. All police forces are subject to inspection by HM Inspectors of Constabulary, who report to the respective Secretary of State.

COMPLAINTS

The investigation and resolution of a serious complaint against a police officer in England and Wales is subject to the scrutiny of the Police Complaints Authority. An officer who is disciplined by his chief constable, whether as a result of a complaint or not, may appeal to the Home Secretary. In Scotland, chief constables are obliged to investigate a complaint against one of their officers; if there is a suggestion of criminal activity, the complaint is investigated by an independent public prosecutor. In Northern Ireland complaints are investigated by the Independent Commission for Police Complaints.

BASIC RATES OF PAY *from 1 September 1997*

Chief Constable	
No fixed term	£68,325–£101,241
Fixed term appointment	£71,745–£106,182
Assistant Chief Constable-designate	80% of their Chief Constable's pay
Assistant Chief Constable	
No fixed term	£57,012–£65,445
Fixed term appointment	£59,865–£68,718
Superintendent	£41,484–£51,495
Chief Inspector	£33,189–£35,499
Inspector	£30,498–£32,295
Sergeant	£23,583–£27,504
Constable	£15,438–£24,432
Metropolitan Police	
Metropolitan Commissioner	£133,212
Deputy Commissioner	£95,739–£108,183
Assistant Commissioner	£86,574–£95,316
Commander	£57,012–£68,718

The rank of Chief Superintendent was abolished in April 1995. Existing appointments continue and receive the higher ranges of the pay scale for Superintendents
*These pay scales apply from 1 September 1996. Other pay scales apply from 1 September 1995; pay negotiations still in progress at time of going to press

THE SPECIAL CONSTABULARY

Each police force has its own special constabulary, made up of volunteers who work in their spare time. Special Constables have full police powers within their force and adjoining force areas, and assist regular officers with routine policing duties.

NATIONAL CRIMINAL INTELLIGENCE SERVICE

The National Criminal Intelligence Service (NCIS) provides intelligence about serious and organized crime to law enforcement, government and other relevant agencies nationally and internationally. From 1 April 1998, NCIS will be placed on a statutory footing. It will be accountable to a newly created Service Authority.
Headquarters: Spring Gardens, 2 Citadel Place, London SE11 5EF. Tel: 0171-238 8000
Strength, 570
Director-General, new appointment awaited
Deputy Director-General (Director (Intelligence)), J. Abbott, QPM
Director, International Division, N. Bailly
Director, UK Division, P. L. Clay
Director, Resources Division, J. Bamfield

NATIONAL MISSING PERSONS BUREAU

The Police National Missing Persons Bureau (PNMPB) acts as a central clearing house of information, receiving reports about vulnerable missing persons that are still outstanding after 28 days and details of unidentified persons or remains within 48 hours of being found from all forces in England and Wales. Reports are also received from Scottish police forces, the RUC, and foreign police forces via Interpol.
Headquarters: New Scotland Yard, Broadway, London SW1H 0BG. Tel: 0171-230 1212
Director, C. J. Coombes

POLICE INFORMATION TECHNOLOGY ORGANIZATION

The Police Information Technology Organization (PITO) is responsible for promoting the delivery of national police information technology services, such as

the Police National Computer, and for co-ordinating the development of local information technology systems where common standards and systems are needed.
Headquarters: Horseferry House, Dean Ryle Street, London SW1P 2AW. Tel: 0171-217 8661
Chief Executive, Miss J. MacNaughton

FORENSIC SCIENCE SERVICE
The Forensic Science Service (FSS) provides forensic science support to the police forces in England and Wales for the investigation of scenes of crime, scientific analysis of material, and interpretation of scientific results. The FSS is organized into serious crime, volume crime, drugs and specialist services, supported by intelligence and consultancy services. Laboratories are located at London, Huntingdon, Chorley, Wetherby, Chepstow and Birmingham.
Headquarters: Priory House, Gooch Street North, Birmingham B5 6QQ. Tel: 0121-607 6800
Chief Executive, Dr J. Thompson

POLICE FORCES AND AUTHORITIES

Strength: actual strength of force as at mid 1997
Chair: chairman/convener of the police authority/police committee/joint police board

ENGLAND

AVON AND SOMERSET CONSTABULARY, *HQ,* PO Box 37, Valley Road, Portishead, Bristol BS20 8QJ. Tel: 01275-818181. *Strength,* 2,984; *Chief Constable,* D. J. Shattock, CBE, QPM; *Chair,* I. Hoddell

BEDFORDSHIRE POLICE, *HQ,* Woburn Road, Kempston, Bedford MK43 9AX. Tel: 01234-841212. *Strength,* 1,120; *Chief Constable,* M. O'Byrne, QPM; *Chair,* A. P. Hendry, CBE

CAMBRIDGESHIRE CONSTABULARY, *HQ,* Hinchingbrooke Park, Huntingdon, Cambs PE18 8NP. Tel: 01480-456111. *Strength,* 1,298; *Chief Constable,* D. G. Gunn, QPM; *Chair,* J. Reynolds

CHESHIRE CONSTABULARY, *HQ,* Nuns Road, Chester CH1 2PP. Tel: 01244-350000. *Strength,* 2,046; *Chief Constable,* J. M. Jones, QPM; *Chair,* R. Tilling

CLEVELAND POLICE, *HQ,* PO Box 70, Ladgate Lane, Middlesbrough TS8 9EH. Tel: 01642-326326. *Strength,* 1,494; *Chief Constable,* B. D. D. Shaw, QPM; *Chair,* K. Walker

CUMBRIA CONSTABULARY, *HQ,* Carleton Hall, Penrith, Cumbria CA10 2AU. Tel: 01768-891999. *Strength,* 1,145; *Chief Constable,* C. Phillips; *Chair,* R. Watson

DERBYSHIRE CONSTABULARY, *HQ,* Butterley Hall, Ripley, Derbyshire DE5 3RS. Tel: 01773-570100. *Strength,* 1,792; *Chief Constable,* J. F. Newing, QPM; *Chair,* K. Wilkinson

DEVON AND CORNWALL CONSTABULARY, *HQ,* Middlemoor, Exeter EX2 7HQ. Tel: 0990-777444. *Strength,* 2,959; *Chief Constable,* J. S. Evans, QPM; *Chair,* B. Homer, OBE

DORSET POLICE FORCE, *HQ,* Winfrith, Dorchester, Dorset DT2 8DZ. Tel: 01929-462727. *Strength,* 1,285; *Chief Constable,* D. W. Aldous, QPM; *Chair,* P. I. Jones

DURHAM CONSTABULARY, *HQ,* Aykley Heads, Durham DH1 5TT. Tel: 0191-386 4929. *Strength,* 1,466; *Chief Constable,* F. W. Taylor, CBE, QPM; *Chair,* A. Barker

ESSEX POLICE, *HQ,* PO Box 2, Springfield, Chelmsford CM2 6DA. Tel: 01245-491491. *Strength,* 2,944; *Chief Constable,* J. H. Burrow, CBE; *Chair,* E. Peel

GLOUCESTERSHIRE CONSTABULARY, *HQ,* Holland House, Lansdown Road, Cheltenham, Glos GL51 6QH. Tel:

01242-521321. *Strength,* 1,147; *Chief Constable,* A. J. P. Butler, QPM; *Chair,* Brig. M. A. Browne, CBE

GREATER MANCHESTER POLICE, *HQ,* PO Box 22 (S. West PDO), Chester House, Boyer Street, Manchester M16 0RE. Tel: 0161-872 5050. *Strength,* 6,895; *Chief Constable,* D. Wilmot, QPM; *Chair,* S. Murphy

HAMPSHIRE CONSTABULARY, *HQ,* West Hill, Winchester, Hants SO22 5DB. Tel: 01962-841500. *Strength,* 3,489; *Chief Constable,* J. C. Hoddinott, CBE, QPM; *Chair,* M. J. Clark

HERTFORDSHIRE CONSTABULARY, *HQ,* Stanborough Road, Welwyn Garden City, Herts AL8 6XF. Tel: 01707-354200. *Strength,* 1,800; *Chief Constable,* P. Sharpe, QPM; *Chair,* P. Holland

HUMBERSIDE POLICE, *HQ,* Queens Gardens, Kingston upon Hull HU1 3DJ. Tel: 01482-326111. *Strength,* 2,870; *Chief Constable,* D. A. Leonard, QPM; *Chair,* S. Bayes

KENT CONSTABULARY, *HQ,* Sutton Road, Maidstone, Kent ME15 9BZ. Tel: 01622-690690. *Strength,* 4,894; *Chief Constable,* J. D. Phillips, QPM; *Chair,* Sir John Grugeon

LANCASHIRE CONSTABULARY, *HQ,* PO Box 77, Hutton, Preston, Lancs PR4 5SB. Tel: 01772-614444. *Strength,* 3,351; *Chief Constable,* Mrs P. A. Clare, QPM; *Chair,* Mrs R. B. Henig

LEICESTERSHIRE CONSTABULARY, *HQ,* St John's, Narborough, Leicester LE9 5BX. Tel: 0116-222 2222. *Strength,* 1,957; *Chief Constable,* D. J. Wyrko, QPM; *Chair,* D. Saville

LINCOLNSHIRE POLICE, *HQ,* PO Box 999, Lincoln LN5 7PH. Tel: 01522-532222. *Strength,* 1,192; *Chief Constable,* J. P. Bensley, QPM; *Chair,* M. Kennedy

MERSEYSIDE POLICE, *HQ,* PO Box 59, Canning Place, Liverpool L69 1JD. Tel: 0151-709 6010. *Strength,* 4,314; *Chief Constable,* Sir James Sharples, QPM; *Chair,* Ms C. Gustafason

NORFOLK CONSTABULARY, *HQ,* Martineau Lane, Norwich NR1 2DJ. Tel: 01603-768769. *Strength,* 1,402; *Chief Constable,* K. R. Williams, QPM; *Chair,* B. J. Landale

NORTHAMPTONSHIRE POLICE, *HQ,* Wootton Hall, Northampton NN4 0JQ. Tel: 01604-700700. *Strength,* 1,195; *Chief Constable,* C. Fox, QPM; *Chair,* Dr M. Dickie

NORTHUMBRIA POLICE, *HQ,* Ponteland, Newcastle upon Tyne NE20 0BL. Tel: 01661-872555. *Strength,* 3,752; *Chief Constable (acting),* D. Mellish, QPM, *Chair,* G. Gill

NORTH YORKSHIRE POLICE, *HQ,* Newby Wiske Hall, Newby Wiske, Northallerton, N. Yorks DL7 9HA. Tel: 01609-783131. *Strength,* 1,361; *Chief Constable,* D. M. Burke, QPM; *Chair,* Mrs A. F. Harris

NOTTINGHAMSHIRE CONSTABULARY, *HQ,* Sherwood Lodge, Arnold, Nottingham NG5 8PP. Tel: 0115-967 0999. *Strength,* 2,376; *Chief Constable,* C. F. Bailey, QPM; *Chair,* C. P. Winterton

SOUTH YORKSHIRE POLICE, *HQ,* Snig Hill, Sheffield S3 8LY. Tel: 0114-220 2020. *Strength,* 3,554; *Chief Constable,* R. Wells, QPM; *Chair,* C. Swindells

STAFFORDSHIRE POLICE, *HQ,* Cannock Road, Stafford ST17 0QG. Tel: 01785-257717. *Strength,* 2,289; *Chief Constable,* J. W. Giffard, QPM; *Chair,* J. T. Meir

SUFFOLK CONSTABULARY, *HQ,* Martlesham Heath, Ipswich IP5 3QS. Tel: 01473-613500. *Strength,* 1,184; *Chief Constable,* A. T. Coe, QPM; *Chair,* M. N. Smith

SURREY POLICE, *HQ,* Mount Browne, Sandy Lane, Guildford, Surrey GU3 1HG. Tel: 01483-571212. *Strength,* 1,636; *Chief Constable,* D. J. Williams, QPM; *Chair,* A. Peirce

SUSSEX POLICE, *HQ,* Malling House, Church Lane, Lewes, E. Sussex BN7 2DZ. Tel: 01273-475432. *Strength,* 3,103; *Chief Constable,* P. Whitehouse, QPM; *Chair,* K. Bodfish

THAMES VALLEY POLICE, *HQ,* Oxford Road, Kidlington, Oxon OX5 2NX. Tel: 01865-846000. *Strength,* 3,800; *Chief Constable,* C. Pollard, QPM; *Chair,* Mrs D. J. Priestley, OBE

WARWICKSHIRE CONSTABULARY, *HQ*, PO Box 4, Leek Wootton, Warwick CV35 7QB. Tel: 01926-415000. *Strength*, 932; *Chief Constable*, P. D. Joslin, QPM; *Chair*, M. Singh

WEST MERCIA CONSTABULARY, *HQ*, PO Box 55, Hindlip Hall, Hindlip, Worcester WR3 8SP. Tel: 01905-723000. *Strength*, 2,038; *Chief Constable*, D. C. Blakey, QPM; *Chair*, G. Raxster

WEST MIDLANDS POLICE, *HQ*, PO Box 52, Lloyd House, Colmore Circus, Queensway, Birmingham B4 6NQ. Tel: 0121-626 5000. *Strength*, 7,200; *Chief Constable*, E. Crew, QPM; *Chair*, R. Jones

WEST YORKSHIRE POLICE, *HQ*, PO Box 9, Laburnum Road, Wakefield, W. Yorks WF1 3QP. Tel: 01924-375222. *Strength*, 5,221; *Chief Constable*, K. Hellawell, QPM; *Chair*, T. Brennan

WILTSHIRE CONSTABULARY, *HQ*, London Road, Devizes, Wilts SN10 2DN. Tel: 01380-722341. *Strength*, 1,186; *Chief Constable*, Miss E. Neville, QPM, PH.D.; *Chair*, H. A. Woolnough

WALES

DYFED–POWYS POLICE, *HQ*, PO Box 99, Llangunnor, Carmarthen SA31 2PF. Tel: 01267-222020. *Strength*, 1,007; *Chief Constable*, R. White, CBE, QPM; *Chair*, Ms M. Roberts

GWENT CONSTABULARY, *HQ*, Croesyceiliog, Cwmbran NP44 2XJ. Tel: 01633-838111. *Strength*, 1,241; *Chief Constable*, F. J. Wilkinson; *Chair*, D. Turnbull

NORTH WALES POLICE, *HQ*, Glan-y-don, Colwyn Bay, Conwy LL29 8AW. Tel: 01492-517171. *Strength*, 1,382; *Chief Constable*, M. J. Argent, QPM; *Chair*, E. Williams

SOUTH WALES CONSTABULARY, *HQ*, Cowbridge Road, Bridgend CF31 3SU. Tel: 01656-655555. *Strength*, 2,994; *Chief Constable*, A. T. Burden, QPM; *Chair*, B. P. Murray

SCOTLAND

CENTRAL SCOTLAND POLICE, *HQ*, Randolphfield, Stirling FK8 2HD. Tel: 01786-456000. *Strength*, 682; *Chief Constable*, W. J. M. Wilson, QPM; *Convener*, Mrs J. Burness

DUMFRIES AND GALLOWAY CONSTABULARY, *HQ*, Cornwall Mount, Dumfries DG1 1PZ. Tel: 01387-252112. *Strength*, 405; *Chief Constable*, W. Rae, QPM; *Chair*, K. Cameron

FIFE CONSTABULARY, *HQ*, Detroit Road, Glenrothes, Fife KY6 2RJ. Tel: 01592-418888. *Strength*, 835; *Chief Constable*, J. P. Hamilton, QPM; *Chair*, A. Keddie

GRAMPIAN POLICE, *HQ*, Queen Street, Aberdeen AB10 1ZA. Tel: 01224-639111. *Strength*, 1,147; *Chief Constable*, I. T. Oliver, PH.D.; *Chair*, Prof. J. Thomaneck

LOTHIAN AND BORDERS POLICE, *HQ*, Fettes Avenue, Edinburgh EH4 1RB. Tel: 0131-311 3131. *Strength*, 2,667; *Chief Constable*, R. Cameron, QPM; *Convenor*, E. Drummond

NORTHERN CONSTABULARY, *HQ*, Old Perth Road, Inverness IV2 3SY. Tel: 01463-715555. *Strength*, 649; *Chief Constable*, W. A. Robertson, QPM; *Chair*, Maj. N. Graham

STRATHCLYDE POLICE, *HQ*, 173 Pitt Street, Glasgow G2 4JS. Tel: 0141-532 2000. *Strength*, 7,548; *Chief Constable*, J. Orr, OBE, QPM; *Chair*, W. Timoney

TAYSIDE POLICE, *HQ*, PO Box 59, West Bell Street, Dundee DD1 9JU. Tel: 01382-223200. *Strength*, 1,116; *Chief Constable*, W. A. Spence, QPM; *Chair*, A. Shand

NORTHERN IRELAND

ROYAL ULSTER CONSTABULARY, *HQ*, Brooklyn, Knock Road, Belfast BT5 6LE. Tel: 01232-650222. *Strength*, 8,472; *Chief Constable*, R. Flanagan, OBE; *Chair*, P. Armstrong

ISLANDS

ISLAND POLICE FORCE, *HQ*, Hospital Lane, St Peter Port, Guernsey GY1 2QN. Tel: 01481-725111. *Strength*, 144; *Chief Officer*, M. H. Wyeth; *President, States Committee for Home Affairs*, M. Torode

STATES OF JERSEY POLICE, *HQ*, Rouge Bouillon, PO Box 789, St Helier, Jersey JE2 3ZA. Tel: 01534-612612. *Strength*, 242; *Chief Officer*, R. H. Le Breton; *Chair*, M. Wavell

ISLE OF MAN CONSTABULARY, *HQ*, Glencrutchery Road, Douglas, Isle of Man IM2 4RG. Tel: 01624-631212. *Strength*, 213; *Chief Constable*, R. E. N. Oake, QPM; *Chairman, Police Committee*, Hon. A. R. Bell

METROPOLITAN POLICE SERVICE
New Scotland Yard, Broadway, London SW1H 0BG
Tel 0171-230 1212

Establishment, 27,406

Commissioner, Sir Paul Condon, QPM
Deputy Commissioner, B. Hayes, CBE, QPM
Receiver, P. Fletcher

OPERATIONAL AREAS
Assistant Commissioners, A. J. Speed, QPM (*Central*); A. Dunn, QPM (*North-East*); P. A. Manning, QPM (*North-West*); W. I. R. Johnston, QPM (*South-East*); D. F. O'Connor, QPM (*South-West*)
Deputy Assistant Commissioner, D. Flanders, QPM
Commanders, D. M. T. Kendrick, QPM; J. F. Purnell, GM, QPM; T. D. Laidlaw, LVO, QPM; A. L. Rowe, QPM; M. Briggs, QPM; M. R. Campbell; W. I. Griffiths, BEM, QPM; S. C. Pilkington; D. A. Ray, QPM; R. Gaspar; D. Gilbertson; Mrs J. Stichbury; J. Townsend, QPM; A. S. Trotter; C. A. Howlett; Mrs S. E. Becks

SPECIALIST OPERATIONS DEPARTMENT
Assistant Commissioner, D. C. Veness, QPM
Deputy Assistant Commissioner, A. G. Fry, QPM
Commanders, R. C. Marsh, CVO, QPM; B. G. Moss, QPM; J. G. D. Grieve, QPM; N. G. Mulvihill

COMPLAINTS INVESTIGATION BUREAU
Commander, I. G. Quinn, QPM

INSPECTORATE
Commander, B. J. Luckhurst, QPM

OTHER DEPARTMENTS
Director, Strategic Co-ordination, Commander T. C. Lloyd
Director, Personnel, Mrs P. Woods
Director, Consultancy and Information Services, Mrs S. Merchant
Director, Public Affairs (acting), C. Dodsworth
Solicitor, D. Hamilton
Director, Technology, N. Boothman
Director, Property Services, T. G. Lawrence

CITY OF LONDON POLICE
26 Old Jewry, London EC2R 8DJ
Tel 0171-601 2222

Strength, 858

The City of London Police is responsible for policing the City of London. Though small, the area includes one of the most important financial centres in the world and the force has particular expertise in areas such as fraud investigation as well as the areas required of any police force.

The force has a wholly elected police authority, the police committee of the Corporation of London, which appoints the Commissioner.

Commissioner (£94,173), W. Taylor, QPM
Assistant Commissioner (£73,986), P. Nove, QPM
Commander (£63,600), J. Davison
Chairman of Police Committee, L. St J. Jackson

BRITISH TRANSPORT POLICE

15 Tavistock Place, London WC1H 9SJ
Tel 0171-388 7541

Strength (March 1997), 2,132

British Transport Police is the national police force for the railways in England, Wales and Scotland, including the London Underground system and the Docklands Light Railway. The Chief Constable reports to the British Transport Police Committee. The members of the Committee are appointed by the British Railways Board and include representatives of Railtrack and London Underground Ltd as well as independent members.

Chief Constable, D. O'Brien, OBE, QPM
Deputy Chief Constable, A. Parker, QPM

MINISTRY OF DEFENCE POLICE

MDP Wethersfield, Braintree, Essex CM7 4AZ
Tel 01371-854000

Strength (April 1997), 3,823

The Ministry of Defence Police is an agency of the Ministry of Defence. It is a national civilian police force whose officers are appointed by the Secretary of State for Defence. It is responsible for the policing of all military land, stations and establishments in the United Kingdom. The agency also has certain responsibilities for the civilian Ministry of Defence Guard Service.

Chief Constable, W. E. E. Boreham, OBE
Deputy Chief Constable, A. V. Comben
Head of Secretariat, M. J. A. Smallwood

ROYAL PARKS CONSTABULARY

The Old Police House, Hyde Park, London W2 2UH
Tel 0171-298 2000

Strength (June 1997), 162

The Royal Parks Constabulary is maintained by the Royal Parks Agency, an executive agency of the Department of National Heritage, and is responsible for the policing of eight royal parks in and around London. These comprise an area in excess of 6,300 acres. Officers of the force are appointed under the Parks Regulations Act 1872 as amended.

Chief Officer, W. Ross
Deputy Chief Officer, A. McLean

UK ATOMIC ENERGY AUTHORITY CONSTABULARY

Building E6, Culham Laboratory, Abingdon,
Oxon OX14 3DB
Tel 01235-463760

Strength (March 1997), 473

The Constabulary is responsible for policing UK Atomic Energy Authority and British Nuclear Fuels PLC establishments and for escorting nuclear material between establishments. The Chief Constable is responsible, through the Atomic Energy Authority Police Authority, to the President of the Board of Trade.

Chief Constable, A. J. Pointer, QPM
Assistant Chief Constable, W. F. Pryke

STAFF ASSOCIATIONS

ASSOCIATION OF CHIEF POLICE OFFICERS OF ENGLAND, WALES AND NORTHERN IRELAND, 7th Floor, 25 Victoria Street, London SW1H 0EX. Tel: 0171-227 3434. Represents Chief Constables, Deputy and Assistant Chief Constables in England, Wales and Northern Ireland; officers of the rank of Commander and above in the Metropolitan and City of London Police and senior civilian members of these forces. *General Secretary*, Miss M. C. E. Barton

THE POLICE SUPERINTENDENTS' ASSOCIATION OF ENGLAND AND WALES, 67A Reading Road, Pangbourne, Reading RG8 7JD. Tel: 01189-844005. Represents officers of the rank of Superintendent. *Secretary*, Chief Supt. D. C. Parkinson

THE POLICE FEDERATION OF ENGLAND AND WALES, 15–17 Langley Road, Surbiton, Surrey KT6 6LP. Tel: 0181-399 2224. Represents officers up to and including the rank of Chief Inspector. *General Secretary*, J. Moseley

ASSOCIATION OF CHIEF POLICE OFFICERS IN SCOTLAND, Police Headquarters, Fettes Avenue, Edinburgh EH4 1RB. Tel: 0131-311 3051. Represents the Chief Constables, Deputy and Assistant Chief Constables of the Scottish police forces. *Hon. Secretary*, H. R. Cameron, QPM

THE ASSOCIATION OF SCOTTISH POLICE SUPERINTENDENTS, Secretariat, 173 Pitt Street, Glasgow G2 4JS. Tel: 0141-221 5796. Represents officers of the rank of Superintendent. *Hon. Secretary*, Chief Supt. A. Forrest

THE SCOTTISH POLICE FEDERATION, 5 Woodside Place, Glasgow G3 7QF. Tel: 0141-332 5234. Represents officers up to and including the rank of Chief Inspector. *General Secretary*, D J Keil, QPM

THE SUPERINTENDENTS' ASSOCIATION OF NORTHERN IRELAND, RUC Training Centre, Garnerville Road, Belfast BT4 2NX. Tel: 01232-700500. Represents Superintendents and Chief Superintendents in the RUC. *Hon. Secretary*, Supt. W. T. Brown

THE POLICE FEDERATION FOR NORTHERN IRELAND, Royal Ulster Constabulary, Garnerville, Garnerville Road, Belfast BT4 2NX. Tel: 01232-760831. Represents officers up to and including the rank of Chief Inspector. *Secretary*, D. A. McClurg

The Prison Service

The prison services in the United Kingdom are the responsibility of the Home Secretary, the Secretary of State for Scotland and the Secretary of State for Northern Ireland. The chief executives of the Prison Service, the Scottish Prison Service and the Northern Ireland Prison Service are responsible for the day-to-day running of the system.

There are 134 prison establishments in England and Wales, 22 in Scotland and five in Northern Ireland. Convicted prisoners are classified according to their perceived security risk and are housed in establishments appropriate to that level of security. There are no open prisons in Northern Ireland. Female prisoners are housed in women's establishments or in separate wings of mixed prisons. Remand prisoners are, where possible, housed separately from convicted prisoners. Offenders under the age of 21 are usually detained in a young offenders' institution, which may be a separate establishment or part of a prison.

Four prisons are now run by the private sector, and in England and Wales all escort services have been contracted out to private companies. Six prisons are being built and financed under the Private Finance Initiative and will also be run by private contractors.

There are independent prison inspectorates in England and Wales (see page 312) and Scotland (see page 342) which report annually to the Secretary of State on prison conditions and the treatment of prisoners. HM Chief Inspector of Prisons for England and Wales also performs an inspectorate role for prisons in Northern Ireland. Every prison establishment also has an independent board of visitors or visiting committee made up of local volunteers appointed by the Secretary of State. Any prisoner whose complaint is not satisfied by the internal complaints procedures may complain to the Prisons Ombudsman for England and Wales (see page 334) or the Scottish Prisons Complaints Commission (see page 343). There is no Prisons Ombudsman for Northern Ireland, but complaints by prisoners regarding maladministration may be made to the Parliamentary Commissioner for Administration (see pages 331–2).

*Average Prison Population 1995 (UK)

	Remand	Sentenced	Other
England and Wales			
Male	10,884	37,593	591
Female	491	1,464	24
Total	11,375	39,057	615
Scotland			
Male	949	4,499	3
Female	49	125	—
Total	998	4,624	3
†N. Ireland			
Male	292	1,343	35
Female	4	28	1
Total	296	1,371	36
UK total	12,669	45,052	654

*Average daily population
†1995–6 figures

The projected prison population for 2005 in England and Wales is 74,500

Sources: Home Office – *Statistical Bulletins 14/96 and 7/97*; Scottish Office – *Statistical Bulletin 1996/5*; Northern Ireland Prison Service – *Annual Report 1995–6*

Sentenced Prison Population by Sex and Offence (England and Wales) *as at June* 1995

	Male	Female
Violence against the person	8,515	290
Sexual offences	3,658	12
Burglary	5,938	57
Robbery	5,267	108
Theft, handling, fraud and forgery	4,613	379
Drugs offences	3,863	398
Other offences	4,421	145
Offence not known	1,622	93
Total	37,897	1,482

Source: HMSO – *Annual Abstract of Statistics 1997*

Average Sentenced Population By Length Of Sentence 1995 (England and Wales)

	Adults	Young Offenders
Up to 18 months	8,845	2,911
18 months–4 years	10,184	2,159
Over 4 years	13,855	682
Total	32,884	5,752

Source: HMSO – *Annual Abstract of Statistics 1997*

Average Daily Sentenced Population By Length Of Sentence 1995 (Scotland)

	Adults	Young Offenders
Less than 6 months	646	249
6 months–less than 18 months	579	178
18 months–less than 2 years	161	50
2 years–less than 4 years	614	114
4 years or over (excluding life)	1,390	98
Life/Section 205 or 206	433	30
Total	3,823	719

Source: Scottish Office – *Statistical Bulletin 1996/5*

Deaths of Prisoners 1994–5 (England and Wales)

Self-inflicted deaths (adults)	57
Self-inflicted deaths (young prisoners)	8
Other deaths	57
Total	122

Source: HM Prison Service – *Annual Report 1994–5*

Average Number of Prison Service Staff 1995–6 (Great Britain)

	England and Wales*	Scotland
No. of prison officers	24,039	n/a
Other staff	14,568	n/a
Total	38,607	4,390

*1994–5 figures

Sources: HM Prison Service – *Annual Report 1994–5*; Scottish Prison Service – *Annual Report 1995–6*

Net Operating Costs in England and Wales 1994–5 in cash terms

	£ million
Establishments' operating costs	1,091.2
Capital items under £1,750	25.4
Capital receipts	1.4
HQ operating costs	172.7
Exceptional items	16.0
Net operating costs	1,306.7
Average net operating costs per prisoner per annum	22,128

Source: HM Prison Service – *Annual Report 1994–5*

COST OF OPERATIONS OF SCOTTISH PRISON SERVICE
1995–6

	£
Income from sales, rentals, etc.,	2,462,000
Total expenditure	178,126,000
Staff costs	116,327,000
Running costs	50,179,000
Other current expenditure	11,620,000
Operating deficit	175,664,000
Interest on capital	21,624,000
Interest payable and similar charges	9,000
Net cost of operations	197,297,000
Average annual cost per prisoner per place	25,786

Source: Scottish Prison Service – *Annual Report 1995–6*

OPERATING COSTS OF NORTHERN IRELAND PRISON
SERVICE 1995–6

	£
Custodial	126,050,088
Non-custodial	5,985,290
Headquarters	5,679,900
Total	137,715,278
Average annual cost per prisoner	71,762

Source: Northern Ireland Prison Service – *Annual Report 1995–6*

THE PRISON SERVICES

HM PRISON SERVICE

Cleland House, Page Street, London SW1P 4LN
Tel 0171-217 6000

SALARIES 1997–8

Governor 1	£49,058–£50,703
Governor 2	£44,298–£45,615
Governor 3	£38,256–£39,300
Governor 4	£31,479–£33,756
Governor 5	£27,761–£30,236

For civil service salaries, *see* page 278

THE PRISONS BOARD

Director-General (SCS), R. R. Tilt
  Private Secretary, R. Hughs
  Staff Officer, J. Heavens
Director of Personnel (SCS), D. Scott
Director of Finance (SCS), S. Norris
Director of Security and Programmes (SCS), A. J. Pearson
Directors of Operations (SCS), A. Papps (*North*); A. Walker
  (*South*)
Director of Dispersals, P. Wheatley
Director of Services (SCS), H. Taylor
Director of Health Care (SCS), Dr M. Longfield
Non-Executive Members, F. W. Bentley; Sir Duncan Nichol,
  CBE; Mrs R. Thomson, CBE
Board Secretary, N. Newcomen

Chaplain-General and Archdeacon of the Prison Service,
  Ven. D. Fleming
Senior Roman Catholic Chaplain, Mgr J. Branson

AREA MANAGERS (*SCS*)

Directorate of Operations (North)
East Midlands, J. Blakey; *Mercia*, D. Curtis; *Mersey and
  Manchester*, A. Fitzpatrick; *North-East*, R. Mitchell; *North-
  West*, D. I. Lockwood; *Yorkshire*, J. Staples

Directorate of Operations (South)
Central, J. Dring; *Kent*, T. Murtagh, OBE; London North and
  East Anglia, I. Ward; *London South*, P. J. Kitteridge; *South
  Coast*, J. Perriss; *Wales and the West*, J. May

PRISONS

CNA Average number of in use certified normal
  accommodation places 1994–5
Prisoners/ Young Offenders Average number of prisoners/
  young offenders 1994–5

ACKLINGTON, Morpeth, Northumberland NE65 9XF. *CNA,*
  658. *Prisoners,* 613. *Governor*, J. Woods
ALBANY, Newport, Isle of Wight PO30 5RS. *CNA,* 436.
  Prisoners, 415. *Governor*, S. Moore
ALDINGTON, Ashford, Kent TN25 7BQ. *CNA,* 127. *Prisoners,*
  118. *Governor*, L. Cruttenden
ASHWELL, Oakham, Leics LE15 7LS. *CNA,* 404. *Prisoners,* 384.
  Governor, C. Bushell
*ASKHAM GRANGE, Askham Richard, York YO2 3PT. *CNA,*
  136. *Prisoners,* 114. *Governor*, H. E. Crew
BEDFORD, St Loyes Street, Bedford MK40 1HG. *CNA,* 303.
  Prisoners, 296. *Governor*, E. Willets
BELMARSH, Western Way, Thamesmead, London SE28 0EB.
  CNA, 817. *Prisoners,* 724. *Governor*, W. S. Duff
BIRMINGHAM, Winson Green Road, Birmingham B18 4AS.
  CNA, 565. *Prisoners,* 778. *Governor*, G. Gregory-Smith
BLAKENHURST (private prison), Hewell Lane, Redditch,
  Worcs B97 6QS. *CNA,* 649. *Prisoners,* 629. *Monitor*,
  P. J. Hanglin
BLANTYRE HOUSE, Goudhurst, Cranbrook, Kent TN17 2NH.
  CNA, 95. *Prisoners,* 94. *Governor*, E. McLennan-Murray
BLUNDESTON, Lowestoft, Suffolk NR32 5BG. *CNA,* 408.
  Prisoners, 381. *Governor*, S. Robinson
BRISTOL, Cambridge Road, Bristol BS7 8PS. *CNA,* 443.
  Prisoners, 456. *Governor*, R. D. Dixon
BRIXTON, PO Box 369, Jebb Avenue, London SW2 5XF.
  CNA, 484. *Prisoners,* 605. *Governor*, M. O'Sullivan
*BROCKHILL, Redditch, Worcs B97 6RD. *CNA,* 115. *Prisoners,*
  117. *Governor*, N. Croft
BUCKLEY HALL (private prison), Buckley Road, Rochdale,
  Lancs OL12 9DP. *CNA,* 75. *Prisoners,* 71. *Monitor*, Miss
  V. Bird
BULLINGDON, Padrick Haugh Road, Arncott, Bicester,
  Oxon OX6 0PZ. *CNA,* 329. *Prisoners,* 354. *Governor*, J. Cann
*BULLWOOD HALL, High Road, Hockley, Essex SS5 4TE.
  CNA, 81. *Prisoners,* 87. *Governor*, Ms K. Cawley
CAMP HILL, Newport, Isle of Wight PO30 5PB. *CNA,* 378.
  Prisoners, 389. *Governor*, S. Moore
CANTERBURY, Longport, Canterbury CT1 1PJ. *CNA,* 184.
  Prisoners, 259. *Governor*, G. Davies
CARDIFF, Knox Road, Cardiff CF2 1UG. *CNA,* 251. *Prisoners,*
  323. *Governor*, R. Walker
CHANNINGS WOOD, Denbury, Newton Abbott, Devon
  TQ12 6DW. *CNA,* 538. *Prisoners,* 568. *Governor*, J. K.
  Petherick
CHELMSFORD, Springfield Road, Chelmsford, Essex
  CM2 6LQ. *CNA,* 244. *Prisoners,* 371. *Governor*, Ms A.
  Gomme
COLDINGLEY, Bisley, Woking, Surrey GU24 9EX. *CNA,* 292.
  Prisoners, 283. *Governor*, J. Smith
*COOKHAM WOOD, Cookham Wood, Rochester, Kent
  ME1 3LU. *CNA,* 120. *Prisoners,* 129. *Governor*, Ms C.
  Kershaw
DARTMOOR, Princetown, Yelverton, Devon PL20 6RR. *CNA,*
  538. *Prisoners,* 532. *Governor*, J. Lawrence

* Women's establishments/establishments with units for women

DONCASTER (private prison), Off North Bridge, Marshgate, Doncaster DN5 8UX. *CNA,* 706. *Prisoners,* 669. *Director,* K. Rogers

DORCHESTER, North Square, Dorchester DT1 1JD. *CNA,* 120. *Prisoners,* 174. *Governor,* Ms D. Calvert

DOWNVIEW, Sutton Lane, Sutton, Surrey SM2 5PD. *CNA,* 287. *Prisoners,* 277. *Governor,* C. Lambert

*DRAKE HALL, Eccleshall, Staffs ST21 6LQ. *CNA,* 213. *Prisoners,* 199. *Governor,* P. Tidball

*DURHAM, Old Elvet, Durham DH1 3HU. *CNA,* 411. *Prisoners,* 613. *Governor,* N. Clifford

*EAST SUTTON PARK, Sutton Valence, Maidstone, Kent ME17 3DF. *CNA,* 82. *Prisoners,* 86. *Governor,* Mrs C. J. Galbally

*EASTWOOD PARK, Falfield, Wotton-under-Edge, Glos GL12 8DB. *Governor,* P. Winkley

ELMLEY, Church Road, Eastchurch, Sheerness, Kent ME12 4DZ. *CNA,* 634. *Prisoners,* 609. *Governor,* A. Smith

ERLESTOKE HOUSE, Devizes, Wilts SN10 5TU. *CNA,* 258. *Prisoners,* 250. *Governor,* M. Cook

EVERTHORPE, Brough, E. Yorks HU15 1RB. *CNA,* 247. *Prisoners,* 217. *Governor,* R. Smith

EXETER, New North Road, Exeter EX4 4EX. *CNA,* 223. *Prisoners,* 339. *Governor,* N. Evans

FEATHERSTONE, New Road, Featherstone, Wolverhampton WV10 7PU. *CNA,* 599. *Prisoners,* 574. *Governor,* C. Scott

FORD, Arundel, W. Sussex BN18 0BX. *CNA,* 536. *Prisoners,* 440. *Governor,* R. Brandon

*FOSTON HALL, Ashbourne, Derby DE6 5HW. *Governor,* Ms P. Scriven

FRANKLAND, PO Box 40, Frankland, Brasside, Durham, DH1 5YD. *CNA,* 447. *Prisoners,* 418. *Governor,* P. J. Leonard

FULL SUTTON, Full Sutton, York YO4 1PS. *CNA,* 582. *Prisoners,* 543. *Governor,* R. Tasker

GARTH, Ulnes Walton Lane, Leyland, Preston PR5 3NE. *CNA,* 512. *Prisoners,* 505. *Governor,* W. Rose-Quirie

GARTREE, Leicester Road, Market Harborough, Leics LE16 7RP. *CNA,* 277. *Prisoners,* 275. *Governor,* R. J. Perry

GLOUCESTER, Barrack Square, Gloucester GL1 2JN. *CNA,* 126. *Prisoners,* 152. *Governor,* R. Dempsey

GRENDON, Grendon Underwood, Aylesbury, Bucks HP18 0TL. *CNA,* 400. *Prisoners,* 390. *Governor,* T. C. Newell

GUYS MARSH, Shaftesbury, Dorset SP7 0AH. *CNA,* 120. *Prisoners,* 107. *Governor,* R. Gaines

HASLAR, Dolphin Way, Gosport, Hants PO12 2AW. *CNA,* 130. *Prisoners,* 126. *Governor,* I. Truffet

HAVERIGG, Haverigg Camp, Millom, Cumbria LA18 4NA. *CNA,* 392. *Prisoners,* 344. *Governor,* B. Wilson

HEWELL GRANGE, Redditch, Worcs B97 6QQ. *CNA,* 165. *Prisoners,* 164. *Governor,* D. W. Bamber

HIGH DOWN, Sutton Lane, Sutton, Surrey SM2 5PJ. *CNA,* 602. *Prisoners,* 584. *Governor,* D. Wilson

*HIGHPOINT, Stradishall, Newmarket, Suffolk CB8 9YG. *CNA,* 679. *Prisoners,* 602. *Governor,* R. Woolford

HOLLESLEY BAY, Hollesley, Woodbridge, Suffolk IP12 3JS. *CNA,* 180. *Prisoners,* 158. *Governor,* J. Forster

*HOLLOWAY, Parkhurst Road, London N7 0NU. *CNA,* 517. *Prisoners,* 503. *Governor,* M. Sheldrick

HOLME HOUSE, Holme House Road, Stockton-on-Tees TS18 2QU. *CNA,* 649. *Prisoners,* 613. *Governor,* D. Roberts

HULL, Hedon Road, Hull HU9 5LS. *CNA,* 328. *Prisoners,* 394. *Governor,* M. Newell

KINGSTON, Milton Road, Portsmouth PO3 6AS. *CNA,* 154. *Prisoners,* 135. *Governor,* S. McLean

KIRKHAM, Preston PR4 2RA. *CNA,* 644. *Prisoners,* 521. *Governor,* A. F. Jennings

KIRKLEVINGTON GRANGE, Yarm, Cleveland TS15 9PA. *CNA,* 81. *Prisoners,* 76. *Governor,* Mrs P. Midgley

LANCASTER, The Castle, Lancaster LA1 1YL. *CNA,* 256. *Prisoners,* 243. *Governor,* D. G. McNaughton

LATCHMERE HOUSE, Church Road, Ham Common, Richmond, Surrey TW10 5HH. *CNA,* 149. *Prisoners,* 139. *Governor,* E. Butt

LEEDS, Armley, Leeds LS12 2TJ. *CNA,* 815. *Prisoners,* 1,042. *Governor,* R. Daly

LEICESTER, Welford Road, Leicester LE2 7AJ. *CNA,* 192. *Prisoners,* 339. *Governor,* M. Egan

LEWES, Brighton Road, Lewes, E. Sussex BN7 1EA. *CNA,* 290. *Prisoners,* 325. *Governor,* J. F. Dixon

LEYHILL, Wotton-under-Edge, Glos GL12 8HL. *CNA,* 410. *Prisoners,* 387. *Governor,* D. T. Williams

LINCOLN, Greetwell Road, Lincoln LN2 4BD. *CNA,* 444. *Prisoners,* 609. *Governor,* D. Shaw

LINDHOLME, Bawtry Road, Hatfield Woodhouse, Doncaster DN7 6EE. *CNA,* 567. *Prisoners,* 545. *Governor,* M. Shann

LITTLEHEY, Perry, Huntingdon PE18 0SR. *CNA,* 593. *Prisoners,* 555. *Governor,* M. L. Knight

LIVERPOOL, 68 Hornby Road, Liverpool L9 3DF. *CNA,* 1,015. *Prisoners,* 1,222. *Governor,* W. Abbott

LONG LARTIN, South Littleton, Evesham, Worcs WR11 5TZ. *CNA,* 362. *Prisoners,* 355. *Governor,* J. Mullen

*LOW NEWTON, Brasside, Durham DH1 5SD. *CNA,* 36. *Prisoners,* 52. *Governor,* M. Kirby

MAIDSTONE, County Road, Maidstone ME14 1UZ. *CNA,* 488. *Prisoners,* 459. *Governor,* S. O'Neill

MANCHESTER, Southall Street, Manchester M60 9AH. *CNA,* 783. *Prisoners,* 843. *Governor,* P. Earnshaw

MOORLAND, Hatfield Woodhouse, Doncaster DN7 6BW. *CNA,* 308. *Prisoners,* 200. *Governor,* D. Waplington

MORTON HALL, Swinderby, Lincoln LN6 9PS. *CNA,* 168. *Prisoners,* 161. *Governor,* S. G. Wagstaffe

THE MOUNT, Molyneaux Avenue, Bovingdon, Hemel Hempstead HP3 0NZ. *CNA,* 484. *Prisoners,* 476. *Governor,* P. Wailen

*NEW HALL, Dial Wood, Flockton, Wakefield WF4 4AX. *CNA,* 169. *Prisoners,* 178. *Governor,* M. Goodwin

NORTH SEA CAMP, Freiston, Boston, Lincs PE22 0QX. *CNA,* 201. *Prisoners,* 204. *Governor,* M. A. Lewis

NORWICH, Mousehold, Norwich NR1 4LU. *CNA,* 402. *Prisoners,* 384. *Governor,* N. Wall

NOTTINGHAM, Perry Road, Sherwood, Nottingham NG5 3AG. *CNA,* 222. *Prisoners,* 207. *Governor,* P. J. Bennett

PARKHURST, Newport, Isle of Wight PO30 5NX. *CNA,* 267. *Prisoners,* 226. *Governor,* D. M. Morrison

PENTONVILLE, Caledonian Road, London N7 8TT. *CNA,* 559. *Prisoners,* 720. *Governor,* B. Duncan

PRESCOED, Coed-y-Paen, Pontypool NP4 0TD. *CNA,* 60. *Prisoners,* 56. *Governor,* R. Comber

PRESTON, 2 Ribbleton Lane, Preston PR1 5AB. *CNA,* 355. *Prisoners,* 492. *Governor,* R. J. Crouch

RANBY, Ranby, Retford, Notts DN22 8EU. *CNA,* 347. *Prisoners,* 335. *Governor,* J. Slater

*RISLEY, Warrington Road, Risley, Warrington WA3 6BP. *CNA,* 773. *Prisoners,* 724. *Governor,* J. Harrison

ROCHESTER, Rochester, Kent ME1 3QS. *CNA,* 115. *Prisoners,* 167. *Governor,* R. A. Chapman

SEND, Ripley Road, Send, Woking, Surrey GU23 7LJ. *CNA,* 113. *Prisoners,* 119. *Governor,* S. Guy-Gibbons

SHEPTON MALLET, Cornhill, Shepton Mallet, Somerset BA4 5LU. *CNA,* 158. *Prisoners,* 189. *Governor,* J. Shergold

SHREWSBURY, The Dana, Shrewsbury SY1 2HR. *CNA,* 168. *Prisoners,* 276. *Governor,* K. Beaumont

STAFFORD, 54 Gaol Road, Stafford ST16 3AW. *CNA,* 373. *Prisoners,* 516. *Governor,* R. Feeney

STANDFORD HILL, Church Road, Eastchurch, Sheerness, Kent ME12 4AA. *CNA,* 384. *Prisoners,* 361. *Governor,* D. M. Twiner

STOCKEN, Stocken Hall Road, Stretton, Nr Oakham, Leics LE15 7RD. *CNA*, 396. *Prisoners*, 392. *Governor*, R. Curtis

*STYAL, Wilmslow, Cheshire SK9 4HR. *CNA*, 177. *Prisoners*, 200. *Governor*, Ms M. Moulden

SUDBURY, Sudbury, Derbys DE6 5HW. *CNA*, 482. *Prisoners*, 422. *Governor*, P. E. Salter

SWALESIDE, Eastchurch, Isle of Sheppey, Kent ME12 4AX. *CNA*, 512. *Prisoners*, 502. *Governor*, J. Podmore

SWANSEA, Oystermouth Road, Swansea SA1 2SR. *CNA*, 153. *Prisoners*, 211. *Governor*, M. Bolton

USK, 29 Maryport Street, Usk, Gwent NP5 1XP. *CNA*, 122. *Prisoners*, 124. *Governor*, R. Comber

THE VERNE, Portland, Dorset DT5 1EQ. *CNA*, 552. *Prisoners*, 533. *Governor*, T. M. Turner

WAKEFIELD, Love Lane, Wakefield WF2 9AG. *CNA*, 723. *Prisoners*, 696. *Governor*, D. Shaw

WANDSWORTH, PO Box 757, Heathfield Road, London SW18 3HS. *CNA*, 874. *Prisoners*, 907. *Governor*, B. Ritchie

WAYLAND, Griston, Thetford, Norfolk IP25 6RL. *CNA*, 580. *Prisoners*, 542. *Governor*, M. Spurr

WEARE, Portland Harbour, Dorset DT5 1PZ. *Governor*, P. O'Sullivan

WELLINGBOROUGH, Millers Park, Doddington Road, Wellingborough, Northants NN8 2NH. *CNA*, 342. *Prisoners*, 306. *Governor*, J. Whetton

WETHERBY, York Road, Wetherby, W. Yorks LS23 7AZ. *CNA*, 453. *Prisoners*, 425. *Governor*, S. Mitson

WHATTON, Whatton, Notts NG13 9FQ. *CNA*, 216. *Prisoners*, 213. *Governor*, D. Walmsley

WHITEMOOR, Longhill Road, March, Cambs PE15 0PR. *CNA*, 534. *Prisoners*, 474. *Governor*, T. Williams

*WINCHESTER, Romsey Road, Winchester SO22 5DF. *CNA*, 418. *Prisoners*, 408. *Governor*, M. K. Pascoe

THE WOLDS (private prison), Everthorpe, Brough, E. Yorks HU15 2JZ. *CNA*, 322. *Prisoners*, 320. *Director*, J. McDonnell

WOODHILL, Tattenhoe Street, Milton Keynes MK4 4DA. *CNA*, 506. *Prisoners*, 452. *Governor*, Ms M. Gorman

WORMWOOD SCRUBBS, PO Box 757, Du Cane Road, London W12 0AE. *CNA*, 714. *Prisoners*, 804. *Governor*, J. Mullens

WYMOTT, Moss Lane, Ulnes Walton, Leyland, Preston PR5 3LW. *CNA*, 432. *Prisoners*, 389. *Governor*, R. Doughty

Young Offender Institutions

AYLESBURY, Bierton Road, Aylesbury, Bucks HP20 1EH. *CNA*, 237. *Young Offenders*, 219. *Governor*, N. Pascoe

BRINSFORD, New Road, Featherstone, Wolverhampton WV10 7PY. *CNA*, 110. *Young Offenders*, 79. *Governor*, B. Payling

*BULLWOOD HALL, High Road, Hockley, Essex SS5 4TE. *CNA*, 44. *Young Offenders*, 34. *Governor*, Ms K. Cawley

CASTINGTON, Morpeth, Northumberland NE65 9XF. *CNA*, 300. *Young Offenders*, 275. *Governor*, C. Harder

COLCHESTER, Berechurch Park, Colchester CO2 9NU. *Governor*, J. Crowe

DEERBOLT, Bowes Road, Barnard Castle, Co. Durham DL12 9BG. *CNA*, 430. *Young Offenders*, 387. *Governor*, P. Atkinson

DOVER, The Citadel, Western Heights, Dover CT17 9DR. *CNA*, 316. *Young Offenders*, 272. *Governor*, B. Pollett

*DRAKE HALL, Eccleshall, Staffs ST21 6LQ. *CNA*, 42. *Young Offenders*, 25. *Governor*, P. Tidball

*EAST SUTTON PARK, Sutton Valence, Maidstone, Kent ME17 3DF. *CNA*, 11. *Young Offenders*, 3. *Governor*, Mrs C. J. Galbally

*EASTWOOD PARK, Falfield, Wotton-under-Edge, Glos GL12 8DB. *Governor*, P. Winkley

FELTHAM, Bedfont Road, Feltham, Middx TW13 4ND. *CNA*, 440. *Young Offenders*, 434. *Governor*, C. Welsh

GLEN PARVA, Tigers Road, Wigston, Leics LE8 2TN. *CNA*, 447. *Young Offenders*, 381. *Governor*, R. Sherrington

GUYS MARSH, Shaftesbury, Dorset SP7 0AH. *CNA*, 180. *Young Offenders*, 161. *Governor*, R. Gaines

HATFIELD, Hatfield, Doncaster DN7 6EL. *CNA*, 180. *Young Offenders*, 161. *Governor*, Ms C. Davies

HOLLESLEY BAY, Hollesley, Woodbridge, Suffolk IP12 3JS. *CNA*, 185. *Young Offenders*, 163. *Governor*, J. Forster

HUNTERCOMBE, Huntercombe Place, Nuffield, Henley-on-Thames RG9 5SB. *CNA*, 360. *Young Offenders*, 267. *Governor*, P. Manwaring

LANCASTER FARMS, Stone Row Head, Off Quernmore Road, Lancaster LA1 3QZ. *CNA*, 100. *Young Offenders*, 112. *Governor*, D. J. Waplington

MOORLAND, Hatfield Woodhouse, Doncaster DN7 6BW. *CNA*, 245. *Young Offenders*, 198. *Governor*, D. Waplington

*NEW HALL, Dial Wood, Flockton, Wakefield WF4 4AX. *Governor*, D. England

ONLEY, Willoughby, Rugby, Warks CV23 8AP. *CNA*, 521. *Young Offenders*, 476. *Governor*, J. N. Brooke

PORTLAND, Easton, Portland, Dorset DT5 1DL. *CNA*, 428. *Young Offenders*, 405. *Governor*, Ms S. McCormick

PRESCOED, Coed-y-Paen, Pontypool NP4 0TD. *CNA*, 60. *Young Offenders*, 48. *Governor*, R. Comber

STOKE HEATH, Market Drayton, Salop TF9 2JL. *CNA*, 180. *Young Offenders*, 212. *Governor*, J. Aldridge

*STYAL, Wilmslow, Cheshire, SK9 4HR. *CNA*, 35. *Young Offenders*, 34. *Governor*, Ms M. Moulden

SWINFEN HALL, Lichfield, Staffs WS14 9QS. *CNA*, 182. *Young Offenders*, 182. *Governor*, J. P. Francis

THORN CROSS, Arley Road, Appleton Thorn, Warrington WA4 4RL. *CNA*, 217. *Young Offenders*, 143. *Governor*, I. Windebank

WERRINGTON HOUSE, Stoke-on-Trent ST9 0DX. *CNA*, 113. *Young Offenders*, 107. *Governor*, B. Stanhope

WETHERBY, York Road, Wetherby, W. Yorks LS22 5ED. *CNA*, 178. *Young Offenders*, 138. *Governor*, S. Mitson

Remand Centres

BRINSFORD, New Road, Featherstone, Wolverhampton WV10 7PY. *CNA*, 354. *Prisoners*, 379. *Governor*, B. Payling

CARDIFF, Knox Road, Cardiff CF2 1UG. *CNA*, 77. *Prisoners*, 98. *Governor*, R. Walker

DORCHESTER, North Square, Dorchester DT1 1JD. *CNA*, 20. *Prisoners*, 28. *Governor*, Ms D. Calvert

EXETER, New North Road, Exeter EX4 4EX. *CNA*, 42. *Prisoners*, 51. *Governor*, N. Evans

FELTHAM, Bedfont Road, Feltham, Middx TW13 4ND. *CNA*, 403. *Prisoners*, 371. *Governor*, I. Ward

GLEN PARVA, Tigers Road, Wigston, Leics LE8 2TN. *CNA*, 320. *Prisoners*, 388. *Governor*, R. Sherrington

GLOUCESTER, Barrack Square, Gloucester GL1 2JN. *CNA*, 81. *Prisoners*, 96. *Governor*, R. Dempsey

HINDLEY, Gibson Street, Bickershaw, Hindley, Wigan, Lancs WN2 5TH. *CNA*, 288. *Prisoners*, 268. *Governor*, C. Sheffield

LANCASTER FARMS, Stone Rowe Head, Off Quernmore Road, Lancaster LA1 3QZ. *CNA*, 264. *Prisoners*, 233. *Governor*, D. J. Waplington

LOW NEWTON, Brasside, Durham DH1 5SD. *CNA*, 162. *Prisoners*, 196. *Governor*, M. Kirby

NORTHALLERTON, East Road, Northallerton, N. Yorks DL6 1NW. *CNA*, 150. *Prisoners*, 170. *Governor*, D. P. G. Appleton

NORWICH, Mousehold, Norwich NR1 4LU. *CNA*, 59. *Prisoners*, 46. *Governor*, N. Wall

---

*Women's establishments/establishments with units for women

READING, Forbury Road, Reading, Berks RG1 3HY. *CNA,* 182. *Prisoners,* 177. *Governor,* W. Payne

ROCHESTER, Rochester, Kent ME1 3QS. *CNA,* 179. *Prisoners,* 148. *Governor,* R. A. Chapman

STOKE HEATH, Market Drayton, Salop TF9 2JL. *CNA,* 120. *Prisoners,* 66. *Governor,* J. Aldridge

WOODHILL, Tattenhoe Street, Milton Keynes MK4 4DA. *CNA,* 60. *Prisoners,* 66. *Governor,* Ms M. Gorman

SCOTTISH PRISON SERVICE

Calton House, 5 Redheughs Rigg, Edinburgh EH12 9HW
Tel 0131-556 8400

SALARIES 1996–7

Senior managers in the Scottish Prison Service, including governors and deputy governors of prisons, are paid across three pay bands in the range £23,500–£52,100.

Chief Executive of Scottish Prison Service (G3), E. W. Frizzell
Director of Custody, P. Withers
Director, Human Resources, Ms A. Mitchell
Director, Finance and Information Systems, W. Pretswell
Director, Strategy and Corporate Affairs, D. A. Stewart
Deputy Director, Regime Services and Supplies, J. McNeill
Deputy Director, Estates and Buildings, B. Paterson
Area Director, South and West, J. Pearce
Area Director, North and East, P. Russell
Head of Training, Scottish Prison Service College, J. Matthews

PRISONS

Prisoners/Young Offenders Average number of prisoners/ young offenders 1995–6

*ABERDEEN, Craiginches, Aberdeen AB9 2HN. *Prisoners,* 169. *Governor,* J. Bywalec

BARLINNIE, Barlinnie, Glasgow G33 2QX. *Prisoners,* 1,143. *Governor,* R. L. Houchin

CASTLE HUNTLY, Castle Huntly, Longforgan, nr Dundee DD2 5HL. *Prisoners,* 69. *Governor,* K. Rennie

*CORNTON VALE, Cornton Road, Stirling FK9 5NY. *Prisoners,* 144. *Governor,* Mrs K. Donegan

DUNGAVEL, Dungavel House, Strathaven, Lanarkshire ML10 6RF. *Prisoners,* 104. *Governor,* Ms M. Wood

EDINBURGH, 33 Stenhouse Road, Edinburgh EH1 3LN. *Prisoners,* 642. *Governor,* A. Spencer

FRIARTON, Friarton, Perth PH2 8DW. *Prisoners,* 63. *Governor,* E. A. Gordon

GLENOCHIL, King O'Muir Road, Tullibody, Clackmannanshire FK10 3AD. *Prisoners,* 361. *Governor,* L. McBain

GREENOCK, Gateside, Greenock PA16 9AH. *Prisoners,* 238. *Governor,* R. MacCowan

*INVERNESS, Porterfield, Inverness IV2 3HH. *Prisoners,* 116. *Governor,* H. Ross

LONGRIGGEND, Longriggend, nr Airdrie, Lanarkshire ML6 7TL. *Prisoners,* 177. *Governor,* vacant

LOW MOSS, Low Moss, Bishopbriggs, Glasgow G64 2QB. *Prisoners,* 348. *Governor,* W. Middleton

NORANSIDE, Noranside, Fern, by Forfar, Angus DD8 3QY. *Prisoners,* 127. *Governor,* A. MacDonald

PENNINGHAME, Penninghame, Newton Stewart DG8 6RG. *Prisoners,* 59. *Governor,* S. Swan

PERTH, 3 Edinburgh Road, Perth PH2 8AT. *Prisoners,* 473. *Governor,* M. Duffy

PETERHEAD, Salthouse Head, Peterhead, Aberdeenshire AB4 6YY. *Prisoners,* 200. *Governor,* W. Rattray; *Head of Peterhead Unit,* Ms R. Kite

SHOTTS, Shotts ML7 4LF. *Prisoners,* 450. *Governor,* W. McKinlay; *Governor, Special Unit,* A. MacVicar

SHOTTS NATIONAL INDUCTION UNIT, Shotts ML7 4LE. *Prisoners,* 14. *Governor,* J. Gerrie

YOUNG OFFENDER INSTITUTIONS

*CORNTON VALE, Cornton Road, Stirling FK9 5NY. *Young Offenders,* 25. *Governor,* Mrs K. Donegan

*DUMFRIES, Terregles Street, Dumfries DG2 9AX. *Young Offenders,* 134. *Governor,* G. Taylor

GLENOCHIL, King O'Muir Road, Tullibody, Clackmannanshire FK10 3AD. *Young Offenders,* 156. *Governor,* L. McBain

POLMONT, Brightons, Falkirk, Stirlingshire FK2 0AB. *Young Offenders,* 419. *Governor,* D. Gunn

NORTHERN IRELAND PRISON SERVICE

Dundonald House, Upper Newtownards Road, Belfast BT4 3SU
Tel 01232-520700

‡SALARIES 1996–7

Governor 1	£49,058
Governor 2	£44,298
Governor 3	£38,258
Governor 4	£31,479–£32,900
Governor 5	£27,761–£29,533

‡ A Northern Ireland allowance is also payable

PRISONS

Prisoners/Young Offenders Average number of prisoners/ young offenders 1996–7

†BELFAST, Crumlin Road, Belfast BT14 6AE

MAGHABERRY, Old Road, Ballinderry Upper, Lisburn, Co. Antrim BT28 2NF. *Prisoners and Young Offenders,* 534

MAGILLIGAN, Point Road, Magilligan, Co. Londonderry BT49 0LR. *Prisoners,* 357

MAZE, Halftown Road, Maze, Lisburn, Co. Antrim BT27 5RF. *Prisoners,* 549

YOUNG OFFENDER CENTRES

HYDEBANK WOOD, Hospital Road, Belfast BT8 8NA. *Young Offenders,* 171

*MAGHABERRY, Old Road, Ballinderry Upper, Lisburn, Co. Antrim BT28 2NF

† Closed April 1996

---

*Women's establishments/establishments with units for women

Defence

The armed forces of the United Kingdom comprise the Royal Navy, the Army and the Royal Air Force. The Queen is commander-in-chief of all the armed forces. The Ministry of Defence, headed by a Secretary of State, provides the support structure for the armed forces. Within the Ministry of Defence, the Defence Council has overall responsibility for running the armed forces. The Chief of Staff of each service reports through the Chief of the Defence Staff to the Secretary of State on matters relating to the running of his service. The Chief of Staff also chairs the executive committee of the appropriate service board, which manages the service in accordance with centrally-determined objectives and budgets. The military-civilian Central Staffs, headed by the Vice-Chief of the Defence Staff and the Second Permanent Under-Secretary of State, are responsible for policy, operational requirements, commitments, financial management, resource planning and civilian personnel management. The Procurement Executive is responsible for purchasing equipment. The Defence Scientific Staff and the Defence Intelligence staff also form part of the Ministry of Defence; the latter are not listed for security reasons.

A permanent Joint Headquarters for the conduct of joint operations was set up at Northwood in April 1996. The Joint Headquarters connects the policy and strategic functions of the MoD Head Office with the conduct of operations and is intended to strengthen the policy/executive division. A Joint Rapid Deployment Force was established in August 1996.

Britain pursues its defence and security policies through its membership of NATO (to which most of its armed forces are committed), the Western European Union, the European Union, the Organization for Security and Co-operation in Europe and the UN (*see* International Organizations section). The UK pays nearly 6.6 per cent of the costs of UN peacekeeping operations (£137 million in 1995).

The new Government has announced a fundamental review of Britain's defence needs and the role of the armed forces, to be completed by about the end of 1997.

ARMED FORCES STRENGTHS *as at 1 April 1997*

All Services	210,823
Men	195,992
Women	14,831
Royal Naval Services	45,146
Men	41,895
Women	3,251
Army	108,810
Men	102,125
Women	6,685
Royal Air Force	56,867
Men	51,972
Women	4,895

DEPLOYMENT

At 1 January 1997 there were 215,326 members of the UK regular forces. Of these, 170,222 were deployed in the UK, 31,430 in mainland European states, 4,047 in Cyprus, 499 in Gibraltar, 707 elsewhere in the Mediterranean/Near and Middle East, 1,173 in Hong Kong, 284 elsewhere in the Far East, 855 in Canada, 404 in the USA, and 5,705 elsewhere. There were also 4,724 locally entered personnel, of whom 2,082 were deployed in the UK, 162 in Gibraltar and 2,480 in the Far East.

At 1 August 1996 there were 11,750 US forces based in the UK (9,800 Air Force and 1,950 Navy).

NUCLEAR FORCES

Britain's nuclear forces comprise two ballistic missile submarines carrying Trident missiles and equipped with nuclear warheads, and free-fall nuclear bombs carried by Tornado aircraft. Two more Trident submarines are due to enter service, one in 1998 and one in about 2000. All nuclear free-fall bombs are to be taken out of service by the end of 1998.

ARMS CONTROL

The 1990 Conventional Armed Forces in Europe Treaty (the CFE Treaty) commits all NATO and former Warsaw Pact members to limiting five major classes of conventional weapons. In 1968 Britain signed the Nuclear Non-Proliferation Treaty, which was indefinitely and unconditionally extended in 1995. In September 1996 it signed a Comprehensive Nuclear Test Ban Treaty. Britain was a party to the 1972 Biological and Toxin Weapons Convention, which provides for a world-wide ban on biological weapons, and the 1993 Chemical Weapons Convention, which came into force in April 1997 and provides for a world-wide ban on chemical weapons.

DEFENCE CUTS

DEFENCE BUDGET

	£ million
1991−2 outturn	22,913
1995−6 outturn	21,517
1996−7 estimated outturn	22,130
1997−8 plans	21,810

Source: The Stationery Office: *Financial Statement and Budget Report 1997−8*

SERVICE PERSONNEL

	Royal Navy	Army	RAF
1975 strength	76,200	167,100	95,000
1990 strength	63,200	152,800	89,700
1997 strength	45,146	108,810	56,867

CIVILIAN PERSONNEL

1975 level	317,300
1990 level	173,800
1997 level	109,200

MINISTRY OF DEFENCE
Main Building, Whitehall, London SW1A 2HB
Tel 0171-218 9000

For ministerial and civil service salaries, *see* page 278
For Services salaries, *see* pages 392−3
Officers promoted in an acting capacity to a more senior rank are listed under that rank. Promotion to five-star rank is no longer usual in peacetime.
For changes after 31 August 1997, *see* Stop-press
Secretary of State for Defence, The Rt. Hon. George Robertson, MP
  Private Secretary, T. C. McKane

Special Adviser, A. McGowan; B. Gray
Parliamentary Private Secretary, Ms S. Heal, MP
Minister of State for the Armed Forces, Dr John Reid, MP
 Private Secretary, D. King
 Parliamentary Private Secretary, J. Smith, MP
Minister of State for Defence Procurement, The Lord Gilbert,
 PC, Ph.D.
 Private Secretary, R. Keen
Parliamentary Under-Secretary of State, John Spellar, MP
 Private Secretary, Dr S. Cholerton
Permanent Under-Secretary of State (G1), R. C. Mottram
Chief of the Defence Staff, Gen. Sir Charles Guthrie, GCB,
 LVO, OBE, ADC (*Gen.*)

THE DEFENCE COUNCIL
The Defence Council is responsible for running the
Armed Forces. It is chaired by the Secretary of State for
Defence and consists of: the Ministers of State; the
Parliamentary Under-Secretary of State; the Permanent
Under-Secretary of State; the Chief of the Defence Staff;
the Chief of the Naval Staff; the Chief of the General Staff;
the Chief of the Air Staff; the Vice-Chief of the Defence
Staff; the Chief Scientific Adviser; the Chief of Defence
Procurement; and the Second Permanent Under-
Secretary of State.

CHIEFS OF STAFF

CHIEF OF THE NAVAL STAFF
Chief of the Naval Staff and First Sea Lord, Adm. Sir Jock
 Slater, GCB, LVO, ADC
Asst Chief of the Naval Staff, Rear-Adm. J. Band

CHIEF OF THE GENERAL STAFF
Chief of the General Staff, Gen. Sir Roger Wheeler, GCB, CBE,
 ADC (*Gen.*)
Asst Chief of the General Staff, Maj.-Gen. M. A. Willcocks, CB
Director-General, Development and Doctrine, Maj.-Gen. A. D.
 Pigott, CBE

CHIEF OF THE AIR STAFF
Chief of the Air Staff, Air Chief Marshal Sir Richard Johns,
 GCB, CBE, LVO, ADC
Asst Chief of the Air Staff, Air Vice-Marshal T. I. Jenner, CB
British-American Community Relations Co-ordinator, Air
 Marshal Sir John Kemball, KCB, CBE, RAF (retd)
Chief Executive, National Air Traffic Services (G2),
 D. J. McLauchlan

CENTRAL STAFFS
Vice-Chief of the Defence Staff, Adm. Sir Peter Abbott, KCB
Second Permanent Under-Secretary of State (G2), R. T.
 Jackling, CB, CBE
Deputy CDS (Systems), Lt.-Gen. E. F. G. Burton, OBE
Asst CDS, Operational Requirements (Sea Systems), Rear-Adm.
 R. T. R. Phillips
Asst CDS, Operational Requirements (Land Systems), Maj.-
 Gen. P. J. Russell-Jones, OBE
Asst CDS, Operational Requirements (Air Systems), Air Vice-
 Marshal C. C. C. Coville, CB
Deputy CDS (Programmes and Personnel), Air Marshal Sir
 Peter Squire, KCB, DFC, AFC
Asst CDS (Programmes), Rear-Adm. N. R. Essenhigh
Defence Services Secretary, Air Vice-Marshal P. J. Harding,
 CB, CBE, AFC
Deputy CDS (Commitments), Air Marshal J. R. Day, OBE
Asst Under-Secretary (Home and Overseas) (G3), E. V. Buckley
Asst CDS (Operations), Rear-Adm. S. Moore
Asst CDS (Logistics), Maj.-Gen. G. A. Ewer, CBE

Director-General, Information and Communications Services,
 Maj.-Gen. W. J. P. Robins, OBE
Surgeon-General, Air Marshal J. A. Baird, QHP
Director, Defence Nursing Services, Brig. J. Arigho, QHNS
Director-General, Defence Medical Training, Maj.-Gen. C. G.
 Callow, OBE, QHP
Deputy Under-Secretary (Policy) (G2), R. P. Hatfield, CBE
Asst Under-Secretary (Policy) (G3), G. W. Hopkinson
Asst CDS (Policy), Air Vice-Marshal J. C. French, CBE

DEFENCE INFORMATION STAFF
Press Secretary and Chief of Information (G4), Ms G. Samuel
*Deputy Press Secretary and Director of Information (Policy and
 Procurement) (G5)*, A. Boardman
Director, Public Relations (Navy), Cdre B. Leighton
Director, Public Relations (Army), Brig. R. D. S. Gordon, CBE
Director, Public Relations (RAF), Air Cdre G. L. McRobbie

MANAGEMENT AND FINANCE
Deputy Under-Secretaries (G2), J. Howe (*Civilian
 Management*); C. V. Balmer (*Resources, Finance and
 Programmes*)
Defence Housing Executive (G3), C. J. I. James
Asst Under-Secretaries (G3), D. C. R. Heyhoe (*General
 Finance*); I. D. Fauset (*Civilian Management: Personnel*);
 B. A. E. Taylor (*Civilian Management: Policy*); D. G. Jones
 (*Financial Management*); Miss A. Walker (*Service
 Personnel*); vacant (*Director-General of Management and
 Organization*); D. J. Seammen (*Programmes*); D. Fisher
 (*Systems*); A. Inglese (*Legal Adviser*)
Defence Estate Organization (G4), J. Mustow (*Works*); S. A.
 Smith (*Land*)

DEFENCE SCIENTIFIC STAFF
Chief Scientific Adviser (G1A), Prof. Sir David Davies, KBE
Chief Scientist (G2), vacant
Nuclear Weapon Safety Adviser (G2), Dr A. Ferguson
Deputy Chief Scientists (G3), P. M. Sutcliffe (*Research and
 Technology*); M. Earwicker (*Scrutiny and Analysis*)
Asst Chief Scientific Adviser (Nuclear) (G4), P. W. Roper

SECOND SEA LORD/COMMANDER-IN-
CHIEF NAVAL HOME COMMAND
Second Sea Lord and C.-in-C. Naval Home Command, Adm. Sir
 John Brigstocke, KCB
*Director-General, Naval Personnel (Strategy and Plans) and
 Chief of Staff to Second Sea Lord*, Rear-Adm. R. B. Lees
Asst Under-Secretary (Naval Personnel) (G3), B. Miller
*Flag Officer Training and Recruiting and Chief Executive,
 Naval Recruiting and Training Agency*, Rear-Adm. J. H. S.
 McAnally, LVO
Naval Secretary and Chief Executive, Naval Manning Agency,
 Rear-Adm. F. M. Malbon
Director-General, Naval Medical Services, Surgeon Rear-
 Adm. M. P. W. H. Paine
Director-General, Naval Chaplaincy Services, Revd Dr C.
 Stewart

NAVAL SUPPORT COMMAND
Chief of Fleet Support, Vice-Adm. J. H. Dunt
Director-General, Fleet Support (Operations and Plans), Rear-
 Adm. B. B. Perowne
Asst Under-Secretary (Fleet Support) (G3), D. J. Gould
Director-General, Fleet Support (Ships) (G3), R. V. Babington
*Chief Executive, Naval Bases and Supply Agency, and Chief
 Naval Engineering Officer*, Rear-Adm. J. A. Trewby
*Deputy Chief Executive, Naval Bases and Supply Agency, and
 Chief Inspector of Explosives (G4)*, D. J. Stevens

Director-General, Aircraft (Navy), Rear-Adm. D. J. Wood
Flag Officer Scotland, N. England and N. Ireland, Rear-Adm.
A. M. Gregory, OBE

COMMANDER-IN-CHIEF FLEET

C.-in-C. Fleet, Adm. Sir Michael Boyce, KCB, OBE, ADC
Deputy Commander Fleet, Vice-Adm. J. J. Blackham
Chief of Staff (Operations) and Flag Officer Submarines, Rear-
Adm. J. F. Perowne, OBE
Flag Officer Surface Flotilla, Rear-Adm. P. M. Franklyn, MVO
Flag Officer Sea Training and Commander, UK Task Group,
Rear-Adm. R. J. Lippiett, MBE
Flag Officer Naval Aviation, Rear Adm. T. W. Loughran, CB
Commandant-General, Royal Marines, Maj.-Gen. D. A. S.
Pennefather, CB, OBE

QUARTERMASTER-GENERAL'S DEPARTMENT

Quartermaster-General, Lt.-Gen. Sir Samuel Cowan, KCB,
CBE
Chief of Staff, Maj.-Gen. K. O'Donoghue, CBE
Asst Under-Secretary (Quartermaster) (G3), N. H. R. Evans
Director-General, Logistic Support (Army), Maj.-Gen.
M. S. White, CBE
Director-General, Equipment Support (Army), Maj.-Gen. P. V.
R. Besgrove, CBE

ADJUTANT-GENERAL'S DEPARTMENT

Adjutant-General, Gen. Sir Alexander Harley, KCB, CB
Chief of Staff to the Adjutant-General, Maj-Gen. R. A. Oliver,
OBE
Head, Command Secretariat (G4), W. A. Perry
Chaplain-General, Revd Dr V. Dobbins
Director-General, Army Medical Services, Maj.-Gen. W. R.
Short, QHP
Director, Army Legal Services, Maj.-Gen. G. Risius
Military Secretary and Chief Executive, Army Personnel Centre,
Maj. Gen. D. L. Burden, OBE
Director-General, Individual Training, and Chief Executive,
Army Individual Training Organization, Maj.-Gen. C. L.
Elliott, MBE
Commandant, Royal Military Academy, Sandhurst, Maj.-Gen.
J. F. Deverell, OBE
Commandant, Royal Military College of Science, Maj.-Gen. A. S.
H. Irwin, CBE

COMMANDER-IN-CHIEF LAND COMMAND

C. -in-C., Land Command, Gen. Sir Michael Walker, KCB,
CMG, CBE
Deputy C. -in-C., Land Command, and Inspector-General,
Territorial Army, Lt. Gen. Sir How Pike, KCB, DSO, MBE
Chief of Staff, HQ Land Command, Maj.-Gen. P. C. C.
Trousdell
Deputy Chief of Staff, HQ Land Command, Maj.-Gen. J. D.
Stokoe
Head, Command Secretariat (G3), J. S. Pitt-Brooke

HQ STRIKE COMMAND

Air Officer Commanding-in-Chief, Air Chief Marshal Sir
John Allison, KCB, CBE, ADC
Chief of Staff and Deputy C. -in-C., Air Marshal G. A.
Robertson, CBE
*Senior Air Staff Officer and Air Officer Commanding, No. 38
Group,* Air Vice-Marshal D. A. Hurrell, AFC
Air Officer Engineering and Supply, Air Vice-Marshal
D. J. Saunders, CBE

Air Officer Administration, Air Vice-Marshal I. M. Stewart,
AFC
Air Officer Commanding, No. 1 Group, Air Vice-Marshal G. E.
Stirrup, AFC
Air Officer Commanding, No. 11/18 Group, Air Vice-Marshal
C. R. Spink, CBE
Head, Command Secretariat (G5), J. P. Thatcher

HQ LOGISTIC COMMAND

*Air Officer Commanding-in-Chief, Air Member for Logistics and
Chief Engineer (RAF),* Air Marshal C. G. Terry, CB, OBE
Chief of Staff, Air Vice-Marshal M. D. Pledger, OBE, AFC
*Air Officer Communications Information Systems and Air Officer
Commanding Signals Units,* Air Vice-Marshal B. C.
McCandless, CBE
Director-General, Support Management (RAF), Air Vice-
Marshal P. D. Markey, OBE
Command Secretary (G3), H. Griffiths
Chief Executive, RAF Maintenance Group Agency, Cdre K. J.
Proctor

HQ PERSONNEL AND TRAINING COMMAND

*Air Member for Personnel and Air Officer Commanding-in-
Chief,* Air Chief Marshal Sir David Cousins, KCB, AFC
Chief of Staff, Air Vice-Marshal M. D. Smart
*Air Officer Training and Chief Executive, RAF Training Group
Agency,* Air Vice-Marshal A. J. Stables, CBE
*Air Secretary and Chief Executive, RAF Personnel Management
Agency,* Air Vice-Marshal R. P. O'Brien, CB, OBE
Commandant, RAF College, Cranwell, Air Vice-Marshal J. H.
Thompson
Director-General, Medical Services (RAF), Air Vice-Marshal
C. J. Sharples, QHP
Director, Legal Services (RAF), Air Vice-Marshal J. Weeden
Command Secretary (G5), L. D. Kyle
Chaplain-in-Chief (RAF), Ven. P. R. Turner

PROCUREMENT EXECUTIVE

EXECUTIVE

Chief of Defence Procurement, Vice-Adm. Sir Robert
Walmsley, KCB
Director-General, Land Systems, Maj.-Gen. D. J. M. Jenkins,
CBE
*Deputy Chief of Defence Procurement (Operations) and Master-
General of the Ordnance,* Lt.-Gen. Sir Robert Hayman-
Joyce, KCB, CBE
Deputy Chief of Defence Procurement (Support) (G3), J. F.
Howe, CB, OBE

BUSINESS UNITS

Director-General, Business Strategy (G3), J. A. Gulvin, CB
Director-General, Finance (G3), S. Webb
*Director-General, Technical Services and President of the
Ordnance Board,* Air Vice-Marshal P. J. O'Reilly
Director-General, Commercial Directorate (G3), A. T. Phipps
Principal Director, Pricing and Quality Services (G4), N. J.
Bennett
Director-General, Submarines (G3), C. V. Betts
Director-General, Surface Ships, and Controller of the Navy,
Rear-Adm. P. Spencer
Director-General, Surface Weapons (Naval) (G4), A. M. Stagg
Chief, Strategic Systems Executive, Rear-Adm.
P. A. M. Thomas
Director-General (Nuclear) (G4), A. M. Stagg
Director, Nuclear Projects (G4), R. A. Russell
Director-General, Command Information Systems (G3), J. D.
Maines

Controller, Aircraft and Director-General, Air Systems 1, Air Vice-Marshal P. C. Norriss, CB, AFC

Director-General, Air Systems 2 (G3), G. E. Roe

Director-General, Weapons and Electronic Systems (G3), G. N. Beaven

Head of Defence Export Services (G2), C. B. G. Masefield

Military Deputy to Head of DES, Rear-Adm. J. F. T. G. Salt (retd)

Asst Under-Secretary (Export Policy and Finance) (G4), Dr A. M. Fox

Director-General, Saudi Armed Forces Project, Air Marshal I. D. Macfadyen, CB, OBE

Director-General, Marketing (G3), D. J. Bowen

Principal Directors of Contracts (G4), P. A. Gerard *(Navy);* A. V. Carey *(Ordnance);* S. L. Porter *(Air)*

DEFENCE AGENCIES

ARMY BASE REPAIR ORGANIZATION, Monxton Road, Andover, Hants SP11 8HT. Tel: 01264-383295. *Chief Executive,* J. R. Drew, CBE

ARMY BASE STORAGE AND DISTRIBUTION AGENCY, Monxton Road, Andover, Hants SP11 8HT. Tel: 01264-383332. *Chief Executive,* Brig. P. D. Foxton

ARMY INDIVIDUAL TRAINING ORGANIZATION, Trenchard Lines, Upavon, Pewsey, Wilts SN9 6BE. Tel: 01980-615024. *Chief Executive,* Maj.-Gen. C. L. Elliott, MBE

ARMY PERSONNEL CENTRE, Kentigern House, 65 Brown Street, Glasgow G2 8EX. Tel: 0141-248 7890. *Chief Executive,* Maj.-Gen. D. L. Burden, CB, CBE

ARMY TECHNICAL SUPPORT AGENCY, Room 60/1, Portway, Monxton Road, Andover, Hants SP11 8HT. Tel: 01264-383161. *Chief Executive,* Brig. A. D. Ball, OBE

DEFENCE ANALYTICAL SERVICES AGENCY, Northumberland House, Northumberland Avenue, London WC2N 5BP. Tel: 0171-218 0729. *Chief Executive,* P. Altobell

DEFENCE ANIMAL CENTRE, Welby Lane, Melton Mowbray, Leics LE13 0SL. Tel: 01664-410694. *Chief Executive,* Col. A. H. Roache

DEFENCE BILLS AGENCY, Room 410, Mersey House, Drury Lane, Liverpool L2 7PX. Tel: 0151-242 2234. *Chief Executive,* I. S. Elrick

DEFENCE CLOTHING AND TEXTILES AGENCY, Skimmingdish Lane, Caversfield, Oxon OX6 9TS. Tel: 01869-875501. *Chief Executive,* Brig. M. J. Roycroft

DEFENCE CODIFICATION AGENCY, Kentigern House, 65 Brown Street, Glasgow G2 8EX. Tel: 0141-224 2066. *Chief Executive,* K. A. Bradshaw

DEFENCE DENTAL AGENCY, RAF Halton, Aylesbury, Bucks HP22 5PG. Tel: 01296-623535. *Chief Executive,* Air Vice-Marshal I. G. McIntyre, QHDS

DEFENCE EVALUATION AND RESEARCH AGENCY, Ively Road, Farnborough, Hants GU14 0LX. Tel: 01252-392000. *Chief Executive,* J. A. R. Chisholm

DEFENCE INTELLIGENCE AND SECURITY CENTRE, Chicksands, Shefford, Beds SG17 5PR. Tel: 01462-852228. *Chief Executive,* Brig. M. Laurie

DEFENCE POSTAL AND COURIER SERVICES AGENCY, Inglis Barracks, Mill Hill, London NW7 1PX. Tel: 0181-818 6417. *Director and Chief Executive,* Brig. T. M. Brown, OBE

DEFENCE SECONDARY CARE AGENCY, Room 564, St Giles Court, 1–13 St Giles High Street, London WC2H 8LD. Tel: 0171-305 6190. *Chief Executive,* R. Smith

DEFENCE TRANSPORT AND MOVEMENTS EXECUTIVE, Monxton Road, Andover, Hants SP11 8HT. Tel: 01264-382537. *Chief Executive,* Brig. R. E. Ratazzi, CBE

DISPOSAL SALES AGENCY, 7th Floor, 6 Hercules Road, London SE 1 7DJ. Tel: 0171-261 8853. *Chief Executive,* M. Westgate

HYDROGRAPHIC OFFICE, Admiralty Way, Taunton, Somerset TA1 2DN. Tel: 01823-337900. *Chief Executive, and Hydrographer of the Royal Navy,* Rear-Adm. J. P. Clarke, CB, LVO, MBE

JOINT AIR RECONNAISSANCE INTELLIGENCE CENTRE, RAF Brampton, Huntingdon, Cambs PE18 8QL. Tel: 01480-52151. *Chief Executive,* Gp Capt N. J. Pearson

LOGISTIC INFORMATION SYSTEMS AGENCY, Monxton Road, Andover, Hants SP11 8HT. Tel: 01264-382025. *Chief Executive,* Brig. A. W. Pollard

MEDICAL SUPPLIES AGENCY, Drummond Barracks, Ludgershall, Andover, Hants SP11 9RU. Tel: 01980-608606. *Chief Executive,* B. Nimick

METEOROLOGICAL OFFICE, London Road, Bracknell, Berks RG12 2SZ. Tel: 01344-420242. *Chief Executive,* P. D. Ewins, CB, FEng.

MILITARY SURVEY, Elmwood Avenue, Feltham, Middx TW13 7AH. Tel: 0181-818 2181. *Chief Executive,* Brig. P. R. Wildman, OBE

MINISTRY OF DEFENCE POLICE, Wethersfield, Braintree, Essex CM7 4AZ. Tel: 01371-854000. *Chief Executive,* Chief Constable W. E. E. Boreham, OBE

NAVAL AIRCRAFT REPAIR ORGANIZATION, Fareham Road, Gosport, Hants PO13 0AA. Tel: 01705-544910. *Chief Executive,* S. R. Hill

NAVAL BASES AND SUPPLY AGENCY, Room 3A, C Block, Ensleigh, Bath BA1 5AB. Tel: 01225-467156. *Chief Executive,* Rear-Adm. J. A. Trewby

NAVAL MANNING AGENCY, Victory Building, HM Naval Base, Portsmouth PO1 3LS. Tel: 01705-727340. *Chief Executive,* Rear-Adm. F. M. Malbon

NAVAL RECRUITING AND TRAINING AGENCY, Victory Building, HM Naval Base, Portsmouth PO1 3LS. Tel: 01705-727602. *Chief Executive,* Rear-Adm. J. H. S. McAnally, LVO

PAY AND PERSONNEL AGENCY, Warminster Road, Bath BA1 5AA. Tel: 01225-828105. *Chief Executive,* M. A. Rowe

RAF MAINTENANCE GROUP AGENCY, RAF Brampton, Huntingdon, Cambs PE18 8QL. Tel: 01480-52151 ext. 6300. *Chief Executive,* Air Cdre K. J. Proctor

RAF PERSONNEL MANAGEMENT AGENCY, RAF Innsworth, Gloucester GL3 1EZ. Tel: 01452-712612 ext. 7810. *Chief Executive,* Air Vice-Marshal R. P. O'Brien, CB, OBE

RAF SIGNALS ENGINEERING ESTABLISHMENT, RAF Henlow, Beds SG16 6DN. Tel: 01462-851515 ext. 7625. *Chief Executive,* Air Cdre G. Jones, MBE

RAF TRAINING GROUP AGENCY, RAF Innsworth, Gloucester GL3 1EZ. Tel: 01452-712612 ext. 5302. *Chief Executive,* Air Vice-Marshal A. J. Stables, CBE

SERVICE CHILDREN'S EDUCATION, HQ SCE, Building 5, Wegberg Military Complex, BFPO 40. Tel: 00-49 2161 9082372. *Chief Executive,* D. G. Wadsworth

SHIPS SUPPORT AGENCY, B Block, Foxhill, Bath BA5 5AB. Tel: 01225-883935. *Chief Executive,* R. Babington

The Royal Navy

LORD HIGH ADMIRAL OF THE UNITED KINGDOM
HM THE QUEEN

ADMIRALS OF THE FLEET
HRH The Prince Philip, Duke of Edinburgh, KG, KT, OM, GBE, AC, QSO, PC, *apptd* 1953

The Lord Hill-Norton, GCB, *apptd* 1971
Sir Michael Pollock, GCB, LVO, DSC, *apptd* 1974
Sir Edward Ashmore, GCB, DSC, *apptd* 1977
The Lord Lewin, KG, GCB, LVO, DSC, *apptd* 1979
Sir Henry Leach, GCB, *apptd* 1982
Sir William Staveley, GCB, *apptd* 1989
Sir Julian Oswald, GCB, *apptd* 1993
Sir Benjamin Bathurst, GCB, *apptd* 1995

ADMIRALS

Slater, Sir Jock, GCB, LVO, ADC (*Chief of the Naval Staff and First Sea Lord*)
Boyce, Sir Michael, KCB, OBE, ADC (*C.-in-C. Fleet, C.-in-C. Eastern Atlantic Area and Commander Allied Forces North-Western Europe*)
Abbott, Sir Peter, KCB (*Vice Chief of the Defence Staff*)
Brigstocke, Sir John, KCB (*C.-in-C. Naval Home Command and Second Sea Lord*)

VICE-ADMIRALS

Moore, Sir Michael, KBE, LVO (*retires Jan. 1998*)
Gretton, M. P. (*retires Dec. 1997*)
Dunt, J. H. (*Chief of Fleet Support*)
Garnett, I. D. G. (*Military Assistant, Supreme Allied Commander Atlantic*)
Blackham, J. J. (*Deputy Comd. Fleet*)
Haddacks, P. K. (*UK Military Rep. at NATO HQ*)
West, A. W. J., DSC (*Chief of Defence Intelligence*)
Blackburn, D. A. J., LVO (*Chief of Staff to Commander, Allied Naval Forces Southern Europe*)

REAR-ADMIRALS

Wilkinson, N. J., CB (*retires Jan. 1998*)
Tolhurst, J. G., CB (*retires Dec. 1997*)
Essenhigh, N. R. (*Asst CDS (Programmes)*)
Trewby, J. A. (*Chief Executive, Naval Bases and Supply Agency and Chief Naval Engineering Officer*)
Clarke, J. P., CB, LVO, MBE (*Hydrographer of the Navy and Chief Executive, Hydrographic Office Defence Support Agency*)
Franklyn, P. M., MVO (*Flag Officer Surface Flotilla*)
Perowne, J. F., OBE (*Chief of Staff (Operations), Flag Officer Submarines, COMSUBEASTLANT and COMSUBNORTHWEST*)
Wood, D. J. (*Director-General, Aircraft (Navy)*)
Lees, R. B. (*Director-General, Naval Personnel (Strategy and Plans) and Chief of Staff to Second Sea Lord*)
Spencer, P. (*Director-General, Surface Ships, and Controller of the Navy*)
Loughran, T. W., CB (*Flag Officer Naval Aviation*)
Thomas, P. A. M. (*Chief, Strategic Systems Executive*)
Armstrong, J. H. A. J. (*Senior Naval Member, Royal College of Defence Studies*)
McAnally, J. H. S., LVO (*Flag Officer Training and Recruiting and Chief Executive, Naval Recruiting and Training Agency*)
Malbon, F. M. (*Naval Secretary and Chief Executive, Naval Manning Agency*)
Phillips, R. T. R. (*Asst CDS Operational Requirements (Sea Systems)*)
Ross, A. B., CBE (*Asst Director Operations Divn International Military Staff*)
Perowne, B. B. (*Director-General, Fleet Support (Operations and Plans)*)
Gough, A. B. (*Asst CDS (Policy and Requirements) to Supreme Allied Commander Europe*)
Moore, S. (*Asst CDS (Operations)*)
Paine, M. P. W. H. (*Director-General, Naval Medical Services*)
Band, J. (*Asst Chief of Naval Staff*)
Lippiett, R. J., MBE (*Flag Officer Sea Training and Commander, UK Task Group*)
Forbes, I. A. (*Commander, UK Task Force*)

Gregory, A. M., OBE (*Flag Officer Scotland, N. England and N. Ireland*)

HM FLEET *as at 1 April 1997*

SUBMARINES

Trident	Vanguard, Victorious, Vigilant*
Fleet	Sceptre, Sovereign†, Spartan, Splendid, Superb†, Talent, Tireless†, Torbay, Trafalgar, Trenchant, Triumph, Turbulent†

ANTI-SUBMARINE WARFARE CARRIERS	Ark Royal†, Illustrious, Invincible†
ASSAULT SHIPS	Fearless, Intrepid†
LANDING PLATFORM HELICOPTER	Ocean†

DESTROYERS

Type 42	Birmingham, Cardiff†, Edinburgh, Exeter, Glasgow†, Gloucester, Liverpool, Manchester, Newcastle, Nottingham, Southampton, York

FRIGATES

Type 23	Argyll, Grafton*, Iron Duke, Lancaster, Marlborough†, Monmouth, Montrose, Norfolk, Northumberland, Richmond, Somerset, Sutherland*, Westminster
Type 22	Beaver, Boxer, Brave†, Campbeltown, Chatham, Cornwall, Coventry, Cumberland†, London, Sheffield†

OFFSHORE PATROL

Castle Class	Dumbarton Castle†, Leeds Castle
Island Class	Alderney, Anglesey, Guernsey, Lindisfarne†, Orkney, Shetland

MINEHUNTERS

Hunt Class	Atherstone, Berkeley, Bicester, Brecon, Brocklesby, Cattistock, Chiddingfold, Cottesmore†, Dulverton, Hurworth, Ledbury, Middleton, Quorn†
Sandown Class	Bridport, Cromer, Inverness, Penzance†, Sandown†, Walney

PATROL CRAFT

Peacock Class	Peacock, Plover, Starling
River Class	Arun, Blackwater, Itchen, Orwell, Spey
Coastal Training Craft‡	Archer, Biter, Blazer, Charger, Dasher, Example, Exploit, Explorer, Express, Loyal Chancellor, Loyal Watcher, Puncher, Pursuer, Raider†, Smiter, Tracker†

---

* Engaged in trials or training
† Refitting/standby
‡ Operated by the University Royal Naval Units

Gibralter Search and Rescue Craft	Ranger, Trumpeter
ROYAL YACHT	Britannia
ICE PATROL SHIP	Endurance
SURVEY SHIPS	Beagle, Bulldog, Gleaner, Hecla, Herald, Roebuck, Scott†
SOLD/DECOMMISSIONED 1996–7	Battleaxe, Brazen, Brilliant, Repulse

---

OTHER PARTS OF THE NAVAL SERVICE

ROYAL MARINES

The Royal Marines were formed in 1664 and are part of the Naval Service. Their primary purpose is to conduct amphibious and land warfare. The principal operational units are 3 Commando Brigade Royal Marines, an amphibious all-arms brigade trained to operate in arduous environments, which is a core element of the UK's Joint Rapid Reaction Force; Comacchio Group Royal Marines, which is responsible for the security of nuclear weapon facilities; and Special Boat Service Royal Marines, the maritime special forces. The Royal Marines also provide detachments for warships and land-based naval parties as required. The Royal Marines Band Service provides military musical support for the Naval Service. The headquarters of the Royal Marines is at Portsmouth, along with the Royal Marines School of Music, and principal bases are at Plymouth, Arbroath, Poole, Taunton and Chivenor. The Corps of Royal Marines is about 6,500 strong.
Commandant-General, Royal Marines, Maj.-Gen. D. A. S. Pennefather, CB, OBE

ROYAL MARINES RESERVE (RMR)

The Royal Marines Reserve is a commando-trained volunteer force with the principal role, when mobilized, of supporting the Royal Marines. There are RMR centres in London, Glasgow, Bristol, Liverpool and Newcastle. The current strength of the RMR is about 1,000.
Director, RMR, Lt.-Col. R. M. Rundle

ROYAL FLEET AUXILIARY (RFA)

The Royal Fleet Auxiliary supplies ships of the fleet with fuel, food, water, spares and ammunition while at sea. Its ships are manned by merchant seamen. In April 1997 there were 22 ships in the RFA.

FLEET AIR ARM

The Fleet Air Arm was established in 1937 and operates aircraft (including helicopters) for the Royal Navy. In April 1997 there were 203 aircraft in the Fleet Air Arm.

ROYAL NAVAL RESERVE (RNR)

The Royal Naval Reserve is an integrated part of the Naval Service. It comprises up to 3,500 men and women nationwide who volunteer to train in their spare time to enable the Royal Navy to meet its operational commitments, at sea and ashore, in crisis or war.
Director, Naval Reserves, Capt N. R. Hodgson, RN

QUEEN ALEXANDRA'S ROYAL NAVAL NURSING SERVICE

The first nursing sisters were appointed to naval hospitals in 1884 and the Queen Alexandra's Royal Naval Nursing Service (QARNNS) gained its current title in 1902. Nursing ratings were introduced in 1960 and men were integrated into the Service in 1982; both men and women serve as officers and ratings. Female medical assistants were introduced in 1987.
Patron, HRH Princess Alexandra, the Hon. Lady Ogilvy, GCVO
Matron-in-Chief, Capt. P. M. Hambling, QHNS

The Army

THE QUEEN

FIELD MARSHALS

HRH The Prince Philip, Duke of Edinburgh, KG, KT, OM, GBE, AC, QSO, PC, *apptd* 1953
Sir James Cassels, GCB, KBE, DSO, *apptd* 1968
The Lord Carver, GCB, CBE, DSO, MC, *apptd* 1973
Sir Roland Gibbs, GCB, CBE, DSO, MC, *apptd* 1979
The Lord Bramall, KG, GCB, OBE, MC, *apptd* 1982
Sir John Stanier, GCB, MBE, *apptd* 1985
Sir Nigel Bagnall, GCB, CVO, MC, *apptd* 1988
The Lord Vincent of Coleshill, GBE, KCB, DSO (Col. Cmdt. RA, Col. Cmdt. RHA), *apptd* 1991
Sir John Chapple, GCB, CBE, *apptd* 1992
HRH The Duke of Kent, KG, GCMG, GCVO, ADC, *apptd* 1993
The Lord Inge, GCB (Col. Green Howards), *apptd* 1994

GENERALS

Guthrie, Sir Charles, GCB, LVO, OBE, ADC (*Gen.*) (*Chief of the Defence Staff*)
Mackenzie, Sir Jeremy, KCB, OBE, ADC (*Gen.*), Col. Cmdt. AG Corps, Col. Cmdt. APTC, Col. The Highlanders (*D. SACEUR*)
Wheeler, Sir Roger, GCB, CBE, ADC (*Gen.*) Col. Cmdt. Int. Corps, Col. R. Irish (*Chief of the General Staff*)
Walker, Sir Michael, KCB, CMG, CBE, Col. Cmdt. The Queen's Division, Col. Cmdt. AAC (*C.-in-C., Land*)
Harley, Sir Alexander, KBE, CB (*Adjutant-General*)

LIEUTENANT-GENERALS

Foley, Sir John, KCB, OBE, MC, Col. Cmdt. LI
Smith, Sir Rupert, KCB, DSO, OBE, QGM, Col. Cmdt. Parachute Regiment, Col. Cmdt. Corps of REME (*GOC Northern Ireland*)
Cowan, Sir Samuel, KCB, CBE, Col. Bde of Gurkhas (*Quartermaster-General*)
Hayman-Joyce, Sir Robert, KCB, CBE, Col. Cmdt. RAC (*Deputy Chief of Defence Procurement (Operations) and Master-General of the Ordnance*)
Pike, Sir Hew, KCB, DSO, MBE, Col. Cmdt. SASC (*Deputy C.-in-C., Land, and Inspector-General, Territorial Army*)
Grant, S. C., CB, Col. QLR, Col. Cmdt. King's Division (*Commandant, Royal College of Defence Studies*)
Wallace, Sir Christopher, KBE, Col. Cmdt. 2 RGJ (*Comd. Permanent Joint HQ*)
Jackson, M. D., CB, CBE (*Comd. ACE Rapid Reaction Corps*)
Cordy-Simpson, R. A. (*Deputy Force Commander Operations, Operation Joint Endeavour Phase V*)
Burton, E. F. G., OBE (*Deputy CDS (Systems)*)

MAJOR-GENERALS

Dutton, B. H., CB, CBE, Col. Cmdt. POW Division

Robins, W. J. P., OBE, Col. Cmdt. R. Signals (*Director-General, Information and Communications Services*)

Burden, D. L., CB, CBE (*Military Secretary and Chief Executive, Army Personnel Centre*)

Cordingley, P. A. J., DSO (*Senior British Loan Service Officer, Oman*)

Willcocks, M. A., CB (*Asst Chief of the General Staff*)

Deverell, J. F., OBE, Col. LI (*Commandant RMAS*)

Pigott, A. D., CBE, Col. Cmdt. The Queen's Gurkha Engineers (*Director-General, Development and Doctrine*)

Hall, J. M. F. C., OBE, Col. Cmdt. The Scottish Division, Col. Cmdt. RAVC (*GOC Scotland*)

McAfee, R. W. M., Col. Cmdt. RTR (*Comd. Multinational Divn Central (Airmobile)*)

Richards, N. W. F., OBE (*GOC HQ 4 Divn*)

Vyvyan, C. G. C., CBE (*Head of British Defence Staff, Washington*)

White, M. S., CBE (*Director-General, Logistic Support (Army)*)

Jenkins, D. J. M., CBE (*Director-General, Land Systems*)

Granville-Chapman, T. J., CBE (*Commandant Joint Services Command and Staff College*)

Drewienkiewicz, K. J. (*Chief of Staff HQ LANDCENT on Operation Joint Endeavour Phase V*)

Oliver, R. A., OBE (*Chief of Staff to Adjutant-General*)

Sulivan, T. J., CBE (*Chief of Staff HQ ACE Rapid Reaction Corps*)

Drewry, C. F., CBE (*GOC UK Support Command (Germany)*)

Elliott, C. L., MBE (*Director-General, Individual Training and Chief Executive, Army Individual Training Organization*)

Kiszely, J. P., MC (*GOC 1 (UK) Armd Division*)

O'Donoghue, K., CBE (*Chief of Staff, HQ Quartermaster-General*)

Ewer, G. A., CBE (*Asst CDS (Logistics)*)

Short, W. R., QHP (*Director-General, Army Medical Services*)

Callow, C. G., OBE, QHP (*Director-General, Defence Medical Training*)

Searby, R. V. (*GOC 5 Divn*)

Trousdell, P. C. C. (*Chief of Staff, HQ Land Command*)

Besgrove, P. V. R., CBE (*Director-General, Equipment Support (Army)*)

Denaro, A. G., CBE (*Chief Combat Support ACE Rapid Reaction Corps*)

Chambers, P. A., MBE (*Senior Army Member, Royal College of Defence Studies*)

Irwin, A. S. H., CBE (*Commandant, RMCS*)

Stokoe, J. D. (*Deputy Chief of Staff, HQ Land Command*)

Russell-Jones, P. J., OBE (*Asst CDS, Operational Requirements (Land Systems)*)

Risius, G. (*Director, Army Legal Services*)

Ramsay, A. I., CBE (*Commander, Multi-National Sector South-West Bosnia-Hercegovina*)

Reith, J. G., CBE (*Commander Allied Command Europe Mobile Force*)

Webb-Carter, E. J., OBE (*GOC London District*)

Pringle, A. R. D., CBE (*Stabilization Force, Bosnia-Hercegovina*)

CONSTITUTION OF THE ARMY

The regular forces include the following arms, branches and corps. They are listed in accordance with the order of precedence within the British Army. All enquiries with regard to records of officers and soldiers should be directed to Relations with the Public, Army Personnel Office, Kentigern House, 65 Brown Street, Glasgow G2 8EX Tel· 0141-224 3508/3509/3510.

THE ARMS

HOUSEHOLD CAVALRY – The Household Cavalry Regiment (The Life Guards and The Blues and Royals)

ROYAL ARMOURED CORPS – Cavalry Regiments: 1st The Queen's Dragoon Guards; The Royal Scots Dragoon Guards (Carabiniers and Greys); The Royal Dragoon Guards; The Queen's Royal Hussars (The Queen's Own and Royal Irish); 9th/12th Royal Lancers (Prince of Wales's); The King's Royal Hussars; The Light Dragoons; The Queen's Royal Lancers; Royal Tank Regiment, comprising two regular regiments

ARTILLERY – Royal Regiment of Artillery

ENGINEERS – Corps of Royal Engineers

SIGNALS – Royal Corps of Signals

THE INFANTRY

The Foot Guards and regiments of Infantry of the Line are grouped in divisions as follows:

GUARDS DIVISION – Grenadier, Coldstream, Scots, Irish and Welsh Guards. *Divisional Office*, HQ Infantry, Imber Road, Warminster, Wilts. *Training Centre*, Infantry Training Centre, Vimy Barracks, Catterick, N. Yorks

SCOTTISH DIVISION – The Royal Scots (The Royal Regiment); The Royal Highland Fusiliers (Princess Margaret's Own Glasgow and Ayrshire Regiment); The King's Own Scottish Borderers; The Black Watch (Royal Highland Regiment); The Highlanders (Seaforth, Gordons and Camerons); The Argyll and Sutherland Highlanders (Princess Louise's). *Divisional Office*, HQ Infantry, Imber Road, Warminster, Wilts. *Training Centre*, Infantry Training Centre, Vimy Barracks, Catterick, N. Yorks

QUEEN'S DIVISION – The Princess of Wales's Royal Regiment (Queen's and Royal Hampshire's); The Royal Regiment of Fusiliers; The Royal Anglian Regiment. *Divisional Office*, HQ Infantry, Imber Road, Warminster, Wilts. *Training Centre*, Infantry Training Centre, Vimy Barracks, Catterick, N. Yorks

KING'S DIVISION – The King's Own Royal Border Regiment; The King's Regiment; The Prince of Wales's Own Regiment of Yorkshire; The Green Howards (Alexandra, Princess of Wales's Own Yorkshire Regiment); The Queen's Lancashire Regiment; The Duke of Wellington's Regiment (West Riding). *Divisional Office*, HQ Infantry, Imber Road, Warminster, Wilts. *Training Centre*, Infantry Training Centre, Vimy Barracks, Catterick, N. Yorks

THE ROYAL IRISH REGIMENT (one general service and six home service battalions) – 27th (Inniskilling), 83rd, 87th and the Ulster Defence Regiment. *Regimental HQ and Training Centre*, St Patrick's Barracks, BFPO 808

PRINCE OF WALES'S DIVISION – The Devonshire and Dorset Regiment; The Cheshire Regiment; The Royal Welch Fusiliers; The Royal Regiment of Wales (24th/41st Foot); The Royal Gloucestershire, Berkshire and Wiltshire Regiment; The Worcestershire and Sherwood Foresters Regiment (29th/45th Foot); The Staffordshire Regiment (The Prince of Wales's). *Divisional Office*, HQ Infantry, Imber Road, Warminster, Wilts. *Training Centre*, Infantry Training Centre, Vimy Barracks, Catterick, N. Yorks

LIGHT DIVISION – The Light Infantry; The Royal Green Jackets. *Divisional Office*, HQ Infantry, Imber Road, Warminster, Wilts. *Training Centre*, Infantry Training Centre, Vimy Barracks, Catterick, N. Yorks

BRIGADE OF GURKHAS – The Royal Gurkha Rifles; The Queen's Gurkha Engineers; Queen's Gurkha Signals; The Queen's Own Gurkha Transport Regiment

Regimental HQ and *Training Centre,* Queen Elizabeth Barracks, Church Crookham, Fleet, Aldershot, Hants

THE PARACHUTE REGIMENT (three regular battalions) – *Regimental HQ,* Browning Barracks, Aldershot, Hants. *Training Centre,* Infantry Training Centre, Vimy Barracks, Catterick, N. Yorks

SPECIAL AIR SERVICE REGIMENT – *Regimental HQ* and *Training Centre,* Stirling Lines, Hereford

ARMY AIR CORPS – *Regimental HQ* and *Training Centre,* Middle Wallop, Stockbridge, Hants

SERVICES/ARMS*

Royal Army Chaplains' Department – *Regimental HQ* and *Training Centre,* Netheravon House, Netheravon, Wilts SP 4 9NF

The Royal Logistic Corps – *Regimental HQ,* Blackdown Barracks, Deepcut, Camberley, Surrey. *Training Centre,* Princess Royal Barracks, Deepcut, Camberley, Surrey

Royal Army Medical Corps – *Regimental HQ* and *Training Centre,* Keogh Barracks, Ashvale, Aldershot, Hants

Corps of Royal Electrical and Mechanical Engineers – *Regimental HQ* and *Training Centre,* Hazebrouck Barracks, Isaac Newton Road, Arborfield, Reading, Berks

Adjutant-General's Corps – *Corps HQ* and *Training Centre,* Worthy Down, Winchester, Hants

Royal Army Veterinary Corps – *Corps HQ,* Galloway Road, Aldershot, Hants. *Regimental HQ and Training Centre,* Welby Lane Camp, Elmhurst Avenue, Melton Mowbray, Leics

Small Arms School Corps – *Corps HQ* and *Training Centre,* School of Infantry, Imber Road, Warminster, Wilts

Royal Army Dental Corps – *Regimental HQ,* Evelyn Woods Road, Aldershot, Hants. *Training Centre,* Keogh Barracks, Ashvale, Aldershot, Hants

*Intelligence Corps – *Corps HQ* and *Training Centre,* Templer Barracks, Ashford, Kent

Army Physical Training Corps – *Regimental HQ* and *Training Centre,* Queen's Avenue, Aldershot, Hants

General Service Corps

Queen Alexandra's Royal Army Nursing Corps – *Regimental HQ* and *Training Centre,* Keogh Barracks, Ashvale, Aldershot, Hants

Corps of Army Music – *Corps HQ* and *Training Centre,* Army School of Music, Netherhall, Kneller Road, Twickenham, Middx

ARMY EQUIPMENT HOLDINGS *as at December 1996*

Tanks	523
Armoured combat vehicles or ACV lookalikes	3,388
Artillery pieces	410
Landing craft	49
Helicopters	222

THE TERRITORIAL ARMY (TA)

The Territorial Army is designed to be a General Reserve to the Army. It exists to reinforce the regular Army as and when required, with individuals, sub-units or units either in the UK or overseas, and to provide the framework and basis for regeneration and reconstitution in times of national emergency. The TA also provides an essential link between the military and civilian communities. Its peacetime establishment is 59,000.

Inspector-General, Lt.-Gen. Sir Hew Pike, KCB, DSO, MBE

QUEEN ALEXANDRA'S ROYAL ARMY NURSING CORPS

The Queen Alexandra's Royal Army Nursing Corps (QARANC) was founded in 1902 as Queen Alexandra's Imperial Military Nursing Service (QAIMNS) and gained its present title in 1949. The QARANC has trained nurses for the register since 1950 and also trains and employs health care assistants. Qualified Registered General Nurses are also recruited. Since 1992 men have been eligible to join the QARANC. Members of the Corps serve in military hospitals in the UK and abroad and in MOD hospital units in the UK.

Colonel-in-Chief, HRH The Princess Margaret, Countess of Snowdon, GCVO, CI

Matron-in-Chief (Army) and Director, Army Nursing Services, Brig. J. Arigho, QHNS

The Royal Air Force

THE QUEEN

MARSHALS OF THE ROYAL AIR FORCE

HRH The Prince Philip, Duke of Edinburgh, KG, KT, OM, GBE, AC, QSO, PC, *apptd* 1953

Sir John Grandy, GCB, GCVO, KBE, DSO, *apptd* 1971

Sir Denis Spotswood, GCB, CBE, DSO, DFC, *apptd* 1974

Sir Michael Beetham, GCB, CBE, DFC, AFC, *apptd* 1982

Sir Keith Williamson, GCB, AFC, *apptd* 1985

The Lord Craig of Radley, GCB, OBE, *apptd* 1988

AIR CHIEF MARSHALS

Johns, Sir Richard, GCB, CBE, LVO, ADC (*Chief of the Air Staff*)

Allison, Sir John, KCB, CBE, ADC (*Air Officer Commanding-in-Chief Strike Command and Comd. Allied Air Forces North-Western Europe*)

Cheshire, Sir John, KBE, CB (*C.-in-C. Allied Forces North-Western Europe*)

Cousins, Sir David, KCB, AFC (*Air Member for Personnel and Air Officer Commanding-in-Chief*)

AIR MARSHALS

Macfadyen, I. D., CB, OBE (*Director-General, Saudi Armed Forces Project*)

Squire, Sir Peter, KCB, DFC, AFC (*Deputy CDS (Programmes and Personnel)*)

Robertson, G. A., CBE (*Chief of Staff and Deputy C.-in-C. Strike Command*)

Bagnall, A. J. C., CB, OBE (*Deputy C.-in-C. Allied Air Forces Central Europe*)

Baird, J. A., QHP (*Surgeon-General*)

Day, J. R., OBE (*Deputy CDS (Commitments)*)

Terry, C. G., CB, OBE (*Air Officer C.-in-C., Logistics Command, Air Member for Logistics and Chief Engineer (RAF)*)

AIR VICE-MARSHALS

Harding, P. J., CB, CBE, AFC (*Defence Services Secretary*)

Saunders, D. J., CBE (*Air Officer Engineering and Supply*)

Norriss, P. C., CB, AFC (*Controller, Aircraft and Director-General, Air Systems 1*)

Kyle, R. H., CB, MBE

Coville, C. C. C., CB (*Asst CDS Operational Requirements (Air Systems)*)

O'Brien, R. P., CB, OBE (*Air Secretary and Chief Executive, RAF Personnel Management Agency*)

Feesey, J. D. L., AFC (*Deputy Commander ICAOC 4, Messtetten*)

Goddard, P. J., AFC (*Senior Directing Staff (Air), Royal College of Defence Studies*)

Goodall, R. H., CBE, AFC (*Chief of Staff, Permanent Joint HQ*)

Jenner, T. I., CB (*Asst Chief of the Air Staff*)

Harrison, A. J., CB, CBE

Millar, P. (*Comd. British Forces Cyprus*)

Stables, A. J., CBE (*Air Officer Training and Chief Executive, RAF Training Group Agency*)

Hurrell, D. A., AFC (*Senior Air Staff Officer and AOC No. 38 Group*)

Markey, P. D., OBE (*Director-General, Support Management (RAF)*)

French, J. C., CBE (*Asst CDS (Policy)*)

McCandless, B. C., CBE (*Air Officer Communications Information Systems and Air Officer Commanding Signals Units*)

Smart, M. D. (*Chief of Staff, Personnel and Training Command*)

Elder, R. D., CBE (*Director, Air Space Policy, Joint Air Navigation Services Council*)

Jackson, M. R. (*Director-General, Intelligence (Geographical Resources)*)

Spink, C. R., CBE (*AOC No. 11/18 Group*)

Thompson, J. H. (*Commandant, RAF College, Cranwell*)

O'Reilly, P. J. (*Director-General, Technical Services (Procurement Executive) and President of the Ordnance Board*)

Stewart, I. M., AFC (*Air Officer Administration, Strike Command*)

Weeden, J. (*Director, Legal Services (RAF)*)

Stirrup, G. E., AFC (*AOC No. 1 Group*)

McIntyre, I. G., QHDS (*Chief Executive, Defence Dental Agency*)

Pledger, M. D., OBE, AFC (*Chief of Staff, HQ Logistic Command*)

Sharples, C. J., QHP (*Director-General, Medical Services (RAF)*)

Wright, R. A., AFC (*Military Assistant to the High Representative, Sarajevo*)

CONSTITUTION OF THE ROYAL AIR FORCE

The RAF consists of three commands: Strike Command, Personnel and Training Command and Logistics Command. Strike Command is responsible for all the RAF's front-line forces. Its roles include strike/attack, air defence, reconnaissance, maritime patrol, strategic air transport, air-to-air refuelling, search and rescue, and aero-medical facilities. Personnel and Training Command is responsible for personnel administration and training in the RAF. Logistics Command is responsible for all logistics, engineering and materiel support.

RAF EQUIPMENT *as at 1 July 1997*

AIRCRAFT

Tornado ADV	107
Tornado IDS	142
Harrier	70
Jaguar	54
Canberra	9
Nimrod	28
VC10	26
Tristar	9
Hercules	55
BAe 125	8
BAe 146	3

Sentry	7
Hawk	98
Bulldog	106
Domenie	10
Islander	2
Jetstream	11
Tucano	73

HELICOPTERS

Chinook	34
Puma	39
Sea King	25
Wessex	17
Gazelle	1

ROYAL AUXILIARY AIR FORCE (RAUXAF)

Formed in 1924, the Auxiliary Air Force received the prefix 'Royal' in 1947 in recognition of its war record. The RAUXAF merged with the Royal Air Force Volunteer Reserve in April 1997. The RAUXAF supports the RAF in maritime air operations, air and ground defence of airfields, air movements and aero-medical evacuation.

Air Commodore-in-Chief, HM The Queen

Controller of Reserve Forces (RAF), Air Cdre C. Davison

PRINCESS MARY'S ROYAL AIR FORCE NURSING SERVICE

The Princess Mary's Royal Air Force Nursing Service (PMRAFNS) offers commissions to Registered General Nurses (RGN) with a minimum of two years experience after obtaining RGN and normally with a second qualification. RGNs with no additional experience or qualification are recruited as non-commissioned officers in the grade of Staff Nurse.

Air Chief Commandant, HRH Princess Alexandra, the Hon. Lady Ogilvy, GCVO

Matron-in-Chief, Gp Capt R. H. Williams, QHNS

SERVICE SALARIES

The following rates of pay apply from 1 December 1997 to 31 March 1998. The increasing integration of women in the armed services is reflected in equal pay for equal work and the X factor addition is now the same for men and women (12 per cent).

Annual salaries are derived from daily rates in whole pence and rounded to the nearest £.

The pay rates shown are for Army personnel. The rates apply also to personnel of equivalent rank and pay band in the other services.

OFFICERS' SALARIES

MAIN SCALE

Rank	Daily	Annual
Second Lieutenant	£40.08	£14,629
Lieutenant		
On appointment	52.99	19,341
After 1 year in the rank	54.38	19,849
After 2 years in the rank	55.77	20,356
After 3 years in the rank	57.16	20,863
After 4 years in the rank	58.55	21,371
Captain		
On appointment	67.56	24,659
After 1 year in the rank	69.39	25,327
After 2 years in the rank	71.22	25,995
After 3 years in the rank	73.05	26,663
After 4 years in the rank	74.88	27,331
After 5 years in the rank	76.71	27,999
After 6 years in the rank	78.54	28,667
Major		
On appointment	85.67	31,270
After 1 year in the rank	87.79	32,043
After 2 years in the rank	89.91	32,817
After 3 years in the rank	92.03	33,591
After 4 years in the rank	94.15	34,365
After 5 years in the rank	96.27	35,139
After 6 years in the rank	98.39	35,912
After 7 years in the rank	100.51	36,686
After 8 years in the rank	102.63	37,460
Special List Lieutenant-Colonel	118.49	43,249
Lieutenant-Colonel		
On appointment with less than 19 years service	120.86	44,114
After 2 years in the rank or with 19 years service	124.04	45,275

Rank	Daily	Annual
Lieutenant-Colonel contd.		
After 4 years in the rank or with 21 years service	£127.22	£46,435
After 6 years in the rank or with 23 years service	130.40	47,596
After 8 years in the rank or with 25 years service	133.58	48,757
Colonel		
On appointment	140.47	51,272
After 2 years in the rank	144.17	52,622
After 4 years in the rank	147.87	53,973
After 6 years in the rank	151.57	55,323
After 8 years in the rank	155.27	56,674
Brigadier	172.41	62,930
Major-General		
Level 1	186.62	68,116
Level 2	187.98	68,613
Level 3	190.70	69,606
Lieutenant-General		
Level 1	211.14	77,066
Level 2	212.68	77,628
Level 3	217.81	79,501
General		
Level 1	284.98	104,018
Level 2	293.99	107,306
Level 3	356.17	130,002

Field Marshal – this rank is being phased out. The salary for existing holders of the rank is equivalent to the salary of a level 3 General

---

SALARIES OF OFFICERS COMMISSIONED FROM THE RANKS (LIEUTENANTS AND CAPTAINS ONLY)

YEARS OF COMMISSIONED SERVICE	YEARS OF NON-COMMISSIONED SERVICE FROM AGE 18					
	Less than 12 years		12 years but less than 15 years		15 years or more	
	Daily	Annual	Daily	Annual	Daily	Annual
On commissioning	£74.53	£27,203	£78.38	£28,609	£82.22	£30,010
After 1 year service	76.45	27,904	80.30	29,310	83.49	30,474
After 2 years service	78.38	28,609	82.22	30,010	84.73	30,926
After 3 years service	80.30	29,310	83.49	30,474	85.97	31,379
After 4 years service	82.22	30,010	84.73	30,926	87.21	31,832
After 5 years service	83.49	30,474	85.97	31,379	88.45	32,284
After 6 years service	84.73	30,926	87.21	31,832	89.69	32,737
After 8 years service	85.97	31,379	88.45	32,284	90.93	33,189
After 10 years service	87.21	31,832	89.69	32,737	90.93	33,189
After 12 years service	88.45	32,284	90.93	33,189	90.93	33,189
After 14 years service	89.69	32,737	90.93	33,189	90.93	33,189
After 16 years service	90.93	33,189	90.93	33,189	90.93	33,189

SOLDIERS' SALARIES

The pay structure below officer level is divided into pay bands. Jobs at each rank are allocated to bands according to their score in the job evaluation system. Length of service is from age 18.

Scale A: committed to serve/have completed less than 6 years, or those with less than 9 years' service who are serving on Open Engagement

Scale B: committed to serve/have completed 6 years but less than 9 years

Scale C: committed to serve/have completed more than 9 years, or those with more than 9 years' service who are serving on Open Engagement

Daily rates of pay effective from 1 December 1997 are:

SCALE A

RANK	Band 1	Band 2	Band 3	
Private				
Class 4	£25.15	£ —	£ —	
Class 3	28.17	32.70	37.73	
Class 2	31.49	36.06	41.09	
Class 1	34.25	38.81	43.83	
Lance Corporal				
Class 3	34.25	38.81	43.83	
Class 2	36.62	41.19	46.64	
Class 1	39.39	43.97	49.41	
Corporal				
Class 2	42.13	46.69	52.13	
Class 1	45.23	49.77	55.21	
	Band 4	Band 5	Band 6	Band 7
Sergeant	£49.74	£54.69	£60.09	£ —
Staff Sergeant	52.60	57.53	62.96	69.48
Warrant Officer				
Class 2	56.24	61.19	67.85	74.52
Class 1	59.97	64.91	71.67	78.32

SCALE B

	Band 1	Band 2	Band 3
Private			
Class 4	£25.45	£ —	£ —
Class 3	28.47	33.00	38.03
Class 2	31.79	36.36	41.39
Class 1	34.55	39.11	44.13

SCALE B

	Band 1	Band 2	Band 3	
Lance Corporal				
Class 3	£34.55	£39.11	£44.13	
Class 2	36.92	41.49	46.94	
Class 1	39.69	44.27	49.71	
Corporal				
Class 2	42.43	46.99	52.43	
Class 1	45.53	50.07	55.51	
	Band 4	Band 5	Band 6	Band 7
Sergeant	£50.04	£54.99	£60.39	£ —
Staff Sergeant	52.90	57.83	63.26	69.78
Warrant Officer				
Class 2	56.54	61.49	68.15	74.82
Class 1	60.27	65.21	71.97	78.62

SCALE C

	Band 1	Band 2	Band 3	
Private				
Class 4	£25.90	£ —	£ —	
Class 3	28.92	33.45	38.48	
Class 2	32.24	36.81	41.84	
Class 1	35.00	39.56	44.58	
Lance Corporal				
Class 3	35.00	39.56	44.58	
Class 2	37.37	41.94	47.39	
Class 1	40.14	44.72	50.16	
Corporal				
Class 2	42.88	47.44	52.88	
Class 1	45.98	50.52	55.96	
	Band 4	Band 5	Band 6	Band 7
Sergeant	£50.49	£55.44	£60.44	£ —
Staff Sergeant	53.35	58.28	63.71	70.23
Warrant Officer				
Class 2	56.99	61.94	68.60	75.27
Class 1	60.72	65.66	72.42	79.07

RELATIVE RANK – ARMED FORCES

	Royal Navy		Army		Royal Air Force
1	Admiral of the Fleet	1	Field Marshal	1	Marshal of the RAF
2	Admiral (Adm.)	2	General (Gen.)	2	Air Chief Marshal
3	Vice-Admiral (Vice-Adm.)	3	Lieutenant-General (Lt.-Gen.)	3	Air Marshal
4	Rear-Admiral (Rear-Adm.)	4	Major-General (Maj.-Gen.)	4	Air Vice-Marshal
5	Commodore (Cdre)	5	Brigadier (Brig.)	5	Air Commodore (Air Cdre)
6	Captain (Capt.)	6	Colonel (Col.)	6	Group Captain (Gp Capt)
7	Commander (Cdr.)	7	Lieutenant-Colonel (Lt.-Col.)	7	Wing Commander (Wg Cdr.)
8	Lieutenant-Commander (Lt.-Cdr.)	8	Major (Maj.)	8	Squadron Leader (Sqn. Ldr.)
9	Lieutenant (Lt.)	9	Captain (Capt.)	9	Flight Lieutenant (Flt. Lt.)
10	Sub-Lieutenant (Sub-Lt.)	10	Lieutenant (Lt.)	10	Flying Officer (FO)
11	Acting Sub-Lieutenant (Acting Sub-Lt.)	11	Second Lieutenant (2nd Lt.)	11	Pilot Officer (PO)

SERVICE RETIRED PAY ON COMPULSORY RETIREMENT

Those who leave the services having served at least five years, but not long enough to qualify for the appropriate immediate pension, now qualify for a preserved pension and terminal grant, both of which are payable at age 60. The tax-free resettlement grants shown below are payable on release to those who qualify for a preserved pension and who have completed nine years service from age 21 (officers) or 12 years from age 18 (other ranks).

The annual rates for army personnel are given. The rates apply also to personnel of equivalent rank in the other services, including the nursing services.

OFFICERS

Applicable to officers up to the rank of Brigadier who give full pay service on the active list on or after 30 November 1997. For more senior officers (*) the rates are for those giving full pay service on the active list on or after 31 March 1997, as their pension arrangements are under review.

No. of years reckonable service over age 21	Capt. and below	Major	Lt.-Col.	Colonel	Brigadier	Major-General*	Lieutenant-General*	General*
16	£ 8,170	£ 9,794	£12,903	£ —	£ —	£ —	£ —	£ —
17	8,549	10,259	13,500	—	—	—	—	—
18	8,929	10,724	14,097	16,385	—	—	—	—
19	9,308	11,190	14,694	17,079	—	—	—	—
20	9,688	11,655	15,291	17,773	—	—	—	—
21	10,067	12,120	15,887	18,466	—	—	—	—
22	10,447	12,585	16,484	19,160	22,130	—	—	—
23	10,826	13,051	17,081	19,854	22,830	—	—	—
24	11,206	13,516	17,678	20,548	23,529	25,281	—	—
25	11,585	13,981	18,275	21,242	24,228	26,033	—	—
26	11,964	14,446	18,872	21,936	24,927	26,785	—	—
27	12,344	14,911	19,469	22,630	25,626	27,537	31,152	—
28	12,723	15,377	20,066	23,324	26,326	28,289	32,003	—
29	13,103	15,842	20,663	24,018	27,025	29,041	32,854	—
30	13,482	16,307	21,259	24,711	27,724	29,793	33,705	45,492
31	13,862	16,772	21,856	25,405	28,423	30,545	34,556	46,640
32	14,241	17,238	22,453	26,099	29,123	31,297	35,407	47,788
33	14,621	17,703	23,050	26,793	29,822	32,049	36,258	48,936
34	15,000	18,168	23,647	27,487	30,521	32,794	37,103	50,080

Field Marshal* – active list retired pay at the rate of £64,186 a year

WARRANT OFFICERS, NCOS AND PRIVATES

Applicable to soldiers who give full pay service on or after 30 November 1997

No. of years reckonable service	Below Corporal	Corporal	Sergeant	Staff Sergeant	Warrant Officer Class II	Warrant Officer Class I
22	£4,736	£6,038	£ 6,689	£ 7,614	£ 7,870	£ 8,700
23	4,901	6,249	6,922	7,880	8,149	9,013
24	5,067	6,460	7,156	8,145	8,428	9,326
25	5,232	6,670	7,389	8,411	8,706	9,638
26	5,397	6,881	7,623	8,677	8,985	9,951
27	5,563	7,092	7,856	8,943	9,264	10,264
28	5,728	7,303	8,090	9,208	9,543	10,577
29	5,893	7,514	8,323	9,474	9,822	10,890
30	6,059	7,724	8,557	9,740	10,100	11,202
31	6,224	7,935	8,790	10,006	10,379	11,515
32	6,389	8,146	9,024	10,271	10,658	11,828
33	6,555	8,357	9,257	10,537	10,937	12,141
34	6,720	8,568	9,491	10,803	11,216	12,454
35	6,885	8,778	9,724	11,069	11,494	12,766
36	7,051	8,989	9,958	11,334	11,773	13,079
37	7,216	9,200	10,191	11,600	12,052	13,392

RESETTLEMENT GRANTS

Terminal grants are in each case three times the rate of retired pay or pension. There are special rates of retired pay for certain other ranks not shown above. Lower rates are payable in cases of voluntary retirement.

A gratuity of £2,780 is payable for officers with short service commissions for each year completed. Resettlement grants are: officers £9,556; non-commissioned ranks £6,293.

Archbishops of Canterbury since 1414

Henry Chichele (1362–1443), translated 1414
John Stafford (?–1452), translated 1443
John Kemp (c.1380–1454), translated 1452
Thomas Bourchier (c.1410–86), translated 1454
John Morton (c.1420–1500), translated 1486
Henry Deane (?–1503), translated 1501
William Warham (1450–1532), translated 1503
Thomas Cranmer (1489–1556), consecrated 1533
Reginald Pole (1500–58), consecrated 1556
Matthew Parker (1504–75), consecrated 1559
Edmund Grindal (c. 1519–83), translated 1576
John Whitgift (c.1530–1604), translated 1583
Richard Bancroft (1544–1610), translated 1604
George Abbot (1562–1633), translated 1611
William Laud (1573–1645), translated 1633
William Juxon (1582–1663), translated 1660
Gilbert Sheldon (1598–1677), translated 1663
William Sancroft (1617–93), consecrated 1678
John Tillotson (1630–94), consecrated 1691
Thomas Tenison (1636–1715), translated 1695
William Wake (1657–1737), translated 1716

John Potter (c.1674–1747), translated 1737
Thomas Herring (1693–1757), translated 1747
Matthew Hutton (1693–1758), translated 1757
Thomas Secker (1693–1768), translated 1758
Hon. Frederick Cornwallis (1713–83), translated 1768
John Moore (1730–1805), translated 1783
Charles Manners-Sutton (1755–1828), translated 1805
William Howley (1766–1848), translated 1828
John Bird Sumner (1780–1862), translated 1848
Charles Longley (1794–1868), translated 1862
Archibald Campbell Tait (1811–82), translated 1868
Edward White Benson (1829–96), translated 1883
Frederick Temple (1821–1902), translated 1896
Randall Davidson (1848–1930), translated 1903
Cosmo Lang (1864–1945), translated 1928
William Temple (1881–1944), translated 1942
Geoffrey Fisher (1887–1972), translated 1945
Michael Ramsey (1904–88), translated 1961
Donald Coggan (1909–), translated 1974
Robert Runcie (1921–), translated 1980
George Carey (1935–), translated 1991

Archbishops of York since 1606

Tobias Matthew (1546–1628), translated 1606
George Montaigne (1569–1628), translated 1628
Samuel Harsnett (1561–1631), translated 1629
Richard Neile (1562–1640), translated 1632
John Williams (1582–1650), translated 1641
Accepted Frewen (1588–1664), translated 1660
Richard Sterne (1596–1683), translated 1664
John Dolben (1625–86), translated 1683
Thomas Lamplugh (1615–91), translated 1688
John Sharp (1645–1714), consecrated 1691
William Dawes (1671–1724), translated 1714
Launcelot Blackburn (1658–1743), translated 1724
Thomas Herring (1693–1757), translated 1743
Matthew Hutton (1693–1758), translated 1747
John Gilbert (1693–1761), translated 1757
Robert Hay Drummond (1711–76), translated 1761

William Markham (1719–1807), translated 1777
Edward Vernon Harcourt (1757–1847), translated 1808
Thomas Musgrave (1788–1860), translated 1847
Charles Longley (1794–1868), translated 1860
William Thomson (1819–90), translated 1862
William Connor Magee (1821–91), translated 1891
William Maclagan (1826–1910), translated 1891
Cosmo Lang (1864–1945), translated 1909
William Temple (1881–1944), translated 1929
Cyril Garbett (1875–1955), translated 1942
Michael Ramsey (1904–88), translated 1956
Donald Coggan (1909–), translated 1961
Stuart Blanch (1918–94), translated 1975
John Habgood (1927–), translated 1983
David Hope (1940–), translated 1995

Popes since 1800

The family name is in italics

Pius VII, *Chiaramonti*, elected 1800
Leo XII, *della Genga*, elected 1823
Pius VIII, *Castiglioni*, elected 1829
Gregory XVI, *Cappellari*, elected 1831
Pius IX, *Mastai-Ferretti*, elected 1846
Leo XIII, *Pecci*, elected 1878
Pius X, *Sarto*, elected 1903
Benedict XV, *della Chiesa*, elected 1914

Pius XI, *Ratti*, elected 1922
Pius XII, *Pacelli*, elected 1939
John XXIII, *Roncalli*, elected 1958
Paul VI, *Montini*, elected 1963
John Paul I, *Luciani*, elected 1978
John Paul II, *Wojtyla*, elected 1978

Adrian IV is the only Englishman to be elected pope. He was born Nicholas Breakspear at Langley, near St Albans, and was elected Pope in 1154 on the death of Anastasius IV. He died in 1159.

The Churches

For changes notified after 31 August, *see* Stop-press

The Church of England

The Church of England is the established (i.e. state) church in England and the mother church of the Anglican Communion. A Church of England already existed when Pope Gregory sent Augustine to evangelise the English in AD 596. During the Middle Ages conflicts between Church and State culminated in the Act of Supremacy in 1534. This repudiated papal supremacy and declared Henry VIII to be the supreme head of the Church in England. Since 1559 the English monarch has been termed the Supreme Governor of the Church of England. The Thirty-Nine Articles, a set of doctrinal statements which, together with the Book of Common Prayer of 1662 and the Ordinal, define the position of the Church of England, were adopted in their final form in 1571 and include the emphasis on personal faith and the authority of the scriptures common to the Protestant Reformation throughout Europe.

STRUCTURE

The Church of England is divided into the two provinces of Canterbury and York, each under an archbishop. The two provinces are subdivided into 44 dioceses. Decisions on matters concerning the Church of England are made by the General Synod, established in 1970. It also discusses and expresses opinion on any other matter of religious or public interest. The General Synod has 574 members in total, divided between three houses: the House of Bishops, the House of Clergy and the House of Laity. It is presided over jointly by the Archbishops of Canterbury and York and normally meets twice a year. The Synod has the power, delegated by Parliament, to frame statute law (known as a Measure) on any matter concerning the Church of England. A Measure must be laid before both Houses of Parliament, who may accept or reject it but cannot amend it. Once accepted the Measure is submitted for royal assent and then has the full force of law. The Synod appoints a number of committees, boards and councils which deal with, or advise on, a wide range of matters. In addition to the General Synod, there are synods of clergy and laity at diocesan level.

A report of a commission headed by the Bishop of Durham recommending changes to the national structures of the Church of England was accepted by the General Synod in November 1995; a draft Measure to implement the recommendations has been generally approved by the Synod and is now with a revision committee. If the Measure is finally approved by the Synod and accepted by Parliament, it is envisaged that the changes, which include the creation of an Archbishops' Council, will be implemented in 1998.

In 1995 the Church of England had an electoral roll membership of 1.5 million, of whom about 1 million regularly attended Sunday services. There are (1996 figures) two archbishops, 107 diocesan, suffragan and (stipendiary) assistant bishops, 9,037 other male and 859 female full-time stipendiary clergy, and over 16,000 churches and places of worship. (The Diocese in Europe is not included in these figures.)

THE ORDINATION OF WOMEN

The canon making it possible for women to be ordained to the priesthood was promulged in the General Synod in February 1994 and the first 32 women priests were ordained on 12 March 1994. The Priests (Ordination of Women) Measure 1993 contains provisions safeguarding the position of bishops and parishes who are opposed to the priestly ministry of women. The General Synod agreed to the appointment of up to three 'provincial episcopal visitors' to work with those who are unable to accept the ministry of bishops ordaining women priests. The provincial episcopal visitors, who are suffragan bishops in the newly created sees of Ebbsfleet and Richborough (Province of Canterbury) and Beverley (Province of York) are allowed to carry out confirmations and ordinations in parishes opposed to women priests, as long as they have the permission of the diocesan bishop. Clergy who feel compelled to leave the ministry are entitled to financial assistance.

PORVOO DECLARATION

The Porvoo Declaration was drawn up by representatives of the British and Irish Anglican churches and the Nordic and Baltic Lutheran churches and was approved by the General Synod of the Church of England in July 1995. Churches that approve the Declaration regard baptized members of each other's churches as members of their own, and allow free interchange of episcopally ordained ministers within the rules of each church.

GENERAL SYNOD OF THE CHURCH OF ENGLAND, Church House, Great Smith Street, London SWIP 3NZ. Tel: 0171-222 9011. *Secretary-General*, P. Mawer

HOUSE OF BISHOPS: *Chairman*, The Archbishop of Canterbury; *Vice-Chairman*, The Archbishop of York

HOUSE OF CLERGY: *Chairman*, Canon J. Stanley

HOUSE OF LAITY: *Chairman*, Dr Christina Baxter; *Vice-Chairman*, Dr P. Giddings

STIPENDS 1997–8

Archbishop of Canterbury	£48,825
Archbishop of York	£42,780
Bishop of London	£39,870
Other diocesan bishops	£26,470
Suffragan bishops	£21,760
Deans and provosts	£21,760
Residentiary canons	£17,800
Incumbents and clergy of similar status	£14,520*

*national average, provisional estimate

STIPENDIARY CLERGY 1996 AND ELECTORAL ROLL MEMBERSHIP 1995

	Clergy		Membership
	Male	Female	
Bath and Wells	232	21	48,500
Birmingham	179	29	21,000
Blackburn	259	7	46,100
Bradford	122	7	14,800
Bristol	139	19	23,300
Canterbury	174	12	21,900
Carlisle	154	13	27,800
Chelmsford	395	34	57,600
Chester	273	18	57,000
Chichester	340	7	66,600
Coventry	144	15	19,700
Derby	180	14	23,700
Durham	228	26	32,200

	Clergy		Membership
	Male	Female	
Ely	147	25	24,200
Exeter	271	10	38,000
Gloucester	157	14	29,700
Guildford	183	25	34,300
Hereford	108	12	20,000
Leicester	155	14	19,000
Lichfield	343	37	58,400
Lincoln	204	29	36,300
Liverpool	240	31	38,800
London	500	41	50,300
Manchester	302	28	42,700
Newcastle	151	8	20,100
Norwich	189	18	30,500
Oxford	395	54	66,600
Peterborough	150	13	21,600
Portsmouth	112	9	21,100
Ripon	144	25	25,400
Rochester	220	20	36,400
St Albans	260	32	51,300
St Edmundsbury			
and Ipswich	165	13	27,900
Salisbury	234	17	50,500
Sheffield	188	17	24,400
Sodor and Man	17	0	3,200
Southwark	346	53	51,100
Southwell	181	25	21,300
Truro	122	3	20,900
Wakefield	170	16	27,400
Winchester	241	11	48,800
Worcester	149	15	24,400
York	282	22	42,900
TOTAL	9,145	859	1,467,900

Province of Canterbury

CANTERBURY

103RD ARCHBISHOP AND PRIMATE OF ALL ENGLAND
Most Revd and Rt. Hon. George L. Carey, PH.D., *cons*. 1987,
trans. 1991, *apptd* 1991; Lambeth Palace, London SE1 7JU.
Signs George Cantuar:

BISHOPS SUFFRAGAN
Dover, Rt. Revd J. Richard A. Llewellin, *cons*. 1985, *apptd*
1992; Upway, St Martin's Hill, Canterbury, CT1 1PR
Maidstone, Rt. Revd Gavin H. Reid, *cons*. 1992, *apptd* 1992;
Bishop's House, Pett Lane, Charing, Ashford TN27 0DL
Ebbsfleet, Rt. Revd John Richards, *cons*. 1994, *apptd* 1994
(provincial episcopal visitor); The Rectory, Church
Leigh, Stoke-on-Trent, Staffs ST10 4PT
Richborough, Rt. Revd Edwin Barnes, *cons*. 1995, *apptd* 1995
(provincial episcopal visitor); 14 Hall Place Gardens, St
Albans, Herts AL1 3SP

DEAN
Very Revd John Arthur Simpson, *apptd* 1986

CANONS RESIDENTIARY
P. Brett, *apptd* 1983; R. H. C. Symon, *apptd* 1994; Dr M.
Chandler, *apptd* 1995; Ven. J. Pritchard, *apptd* 1996
Organist, D. Flood, FRCO, *apptd* 1988

ARCHDEACONS
Canterbury, Ven. J. Pritchard, *apptd* 1996
Maidstone, Ven. P. Evans, *apptd* 1989

Vicar-General of Province and Diocese, Chancellor
S. Cameron, QC
Commissary-General, His Hon. Judge Richard Walker
Joint Registrars of the Province, F. E. Robson, OBE; B. J. T.
Hanson, CBE
Diocesan Registrar and Legal Adviser, R. H. B. Sturt
Diocesan Secretary, D. Kemp, Diocesan House, Lady
Wootton's Green, Canterbury CT1 1NQ. Tel: 01227-
459401

LONDON

132ND BISHOP
Rt. Revd Richard C. Chartres; The Old Deanery, Dean's
Court, London EC4V 5AA. *Signs* Richard Londin:

AREA BISHOPS
Edmonton, Rt. Revd Brian J. Masters, *cons*. 1982, *apptd* 1984;
1 Regent's Park Terrace, London NW1 7EE
Kensington, Rt. Revd Michael Colclough, *cons*. 1996, *apptd*
1996; 19 Campden Hill Square, London W8 7JY
Stepney, Rt. Revd Dr John M. Sentamu, *cons*. 1996, *apptd*
1996; 63 Coborn Road, London E3 2DB
Willesden, Rt. Revd Graham G. Dow, *cons*. 1992, *apptd* 1992;
173 Willesden Lane, London NW6 7YN

BISHOP SUFFRAGAN
Fulham, Rt. Revd John Broadhurst, *cons*. 1996, *apptd* 1996;
26 Canonbury Park South, London N1 2FN

DEAN OF ST PAUL'S
Very Revd John H. Moses, PH.D., *apptd* 1996

CANONS RESIDENTIARY
Ven. G. Cassidy, *apptd* 1987; R. J. Halliburton, *apptd* 1990;
M. J. Saward, *apptd* 1991; S. J. Oliver, *apptd* 1997
Registrar and Receiver of St Paul's, Brig. R. W. Acworth, CBE
Organist, J. Scott, FRCO, *apptd* 1990

ARCHDEACONS
Charing Cross, Ven. Dr W. Jacob, *apptd* 1996
Hackney, Ven. C. Young, *apptd* 1992
Hampstead, Ven. P. Wheatley, *apptd* 1995
London, Ven. G. Cassidy, *apptd* 1987
Middlesex, Ven. M. Colmer, *apptd* 1996
Northolt, Ven. P. Broadbent, *apptd* 1995

Chancellor, MISS S. Cameron, QC, *apptd* 1992
Registrar and Legal Secretary, P. C. E. Morris
Diocesan Secretary, C. J. A. Smith, 36 Causton Street,
London SW1P 4AU. Tel: 0171-932 1100

WINCHESTER

96TH BISHOP
Rt. Revd Michael C. Scott-Joynt, *cons*. 1987, *trans*. 1995,
apptd 1995; Wolvesey, Winchester SO23 9ND. *Signs*
Michael Winton:

BISHOPS SUFFRAGAN
Basingstoke, Rt. Revd D. Geoffrey Rowell, *cons*. 1994, *apptd*
1994; Little Acorns, Boynes Wood Road, Medstead
GU34 5EA
Southampton, Rt. Revd Jonathan M. Gledhill, *cons*. 1996,
apptd 1996; Ham House, The Crescent, Romsey
SO51 7NG

DEAN
Very Revd Michael Till, *apptd* 1996

Dean of Jersey (A Peculiar), Very Revd John Seaford, *apptd* 1993
Dean of Guernsey (A Peculiar), Very Revd Marc Trickey, *apptd* 1995

CANONS RESIDENTIARY
A. K. Walker, *apptd* 1987; Ven. A. F. Knight, *apptd* 1991;
P. B. Morgan, *apptd* 1994; C. Stewart, *apptd* 1997

Organist, D. Hill, FRCO, *apptd* 1988

ARCHDEACONS
Basingstoke, Ven. A. F. Knight, *apptd* 1990
Winchester, Ven. A. G. Clarkson, *apptd* 1984

Chancellor, C. Clark, *apptd* 1993
Registrar and Legal Secretary, P. M. White
Diocesan Secretary, R. Anderton, Church House, 9 The Close, Winchester, Hants SO23 9LS. Tel: 01962-844644

BATH AND WELLS

76TH BISHOP
Rt. Revd James L. Thompson, *cons.* 1978, *apptd* 1991; The Palace, Wells BA5 2PD. *Signs* James Bath & Wells

BISHOP SUFFRAGAN
Taunton, Rt. Revd William A. Stewart, *cons.* 1997, *apptd* 1997; Sherford Farm House, Sherford, Taunton TA1 3RF

DEAN
Very Revd Richard Lewis, *apptd* 1990

CANONS RESIDENTIARY
P. de N. Lucas, *apptd* 1988; R. Acworth, *apptd* 1993;
P. G. Walker, *apptd* 1994; M. W. Matthews, *apptd* 1997

Organist, M. Archer, *apptd* 1996

ARCHDEACONS
Bath, Ven. R. J. S. Evens, *apptd* 1996
Taunton, Ven. R. M. C. Frith, *apptd* 1992
Wells, Ven. R. Acworth, *apptd* 1993

Chancellor, T. Briden, *apptd* 1993
Registrar and Legal Secretary, T. Berry
Diocesan Secretary, N. Denison, The Old Deanery, Wells, Somerset BA5 2UG. Tel: 01749-670777

BIRMINGHAM

7TH BISHOP
Rt. Revd Mark Santer, *cons.* 1981, *apptd* 1987; Bishop's Croft, Harborne, Birmingham B17 0BG. *Signs* Mark Birmingham

BISHOP SUFFRAGAN
Aston, Rt. Revd John Austin, *cons.* 1992, *apptd* 1992; Strensham House, 8 Strensham Hill, Moseley, Birmingham B13 8AG

PROVOST
Very Revd Peter A. Berry, *apptd* 1986

CANONS RESIDENTIARY
Ven. C. J. G. Barton, *apptd* 1990; Revd D. Lee, *apptd* 1996;
Revd G. O'Neill, *apptd* 1997

Organist, M. Huxley, FRCO, *apptd* 1986

ARCHDEACONS
Aston, Ven. C. J. G. Barton, *apptd* 1990
Birmingham, Ven. J. F. Duncan, *apptd* 1985

Chancellor, His Honour Judge Aglionby, *apptd* 1970

Registrar and Legal Secretary, H. Carslake
Diocesan Secretary, J. Drennan, 175 Harborne Park Road, Harborne, Birmingham B17 0BH. Tel: 0121-427 5141

BRISTOL

54TH BISHOP
Rt. Revd Barry Rogerson, *cons.* 1979, *apptd* 1985; Bishop's House, Clifton Hill, Bristol BS8 1BW. *Signs* Barry Bristol

BISHOP SUFFRAGAN
Swindon, Rt. Revd Michael Doe, *cons.* 1994, *apptd* 1994; Mark House, Field Rise, Old Town, Swindon SN1 4HP

DEAN
Very Revd Robert W. Grimley, *apptd* 1997

CANONS RESIDENTIARY
A. L. J. Redfern, *apptd* 1987; J. L. Simpson, *apptd* 1989;
P. F. Johnson, *apptd* 1990

Organist, C. Brayne, *apptd* 1990

ARCHDEACONS
Bristol, Ven. D. J. Banfield, *apptd* 1990
Swindon, vacant

Chancellor, Sir David Calcutt, QC, *apptd* 1971
Registrar and Legal Secretary, T. Berry
Diocesan Secretary, Mrs L. Farrall, Diocesan Church House, 23 Great George Street, Bristol, Avon BS1 5QZ. Tel: 0117-921 4411

CHELMSFORD

8TH BISHOP
Rt. Revd John F. Perry, *cons.* 1989, *apptd* 1996; Bishopscourt, Margaretting, Ingatestone CM4 0HD. *Signs* John Chelmsford

BISHOPS SUFFRAGAN
Barking, Rt. Revd Roger F. Sainsbury, *cons.* 1991, *apptd* 1991; 110 Capel Road, Forest Gate, London E7 0JS
Bradwell, Rt. Revd Laurence Green, *cons.* 1993, *apptd* 1993; The Vicarage, Orsett Road, Horndon-on-the-Hill, Stanford-le-Hope, Essex SS17 8NS
Colchester, Rt. Revd Edward Holland, *cons.* 1986, *apptd* 1995; 1 Fitzwalter Road, Lexden, Colchester CO3 3SS

PROVOST
Very Revd Peter S. M. Judd, *apptd* 1997

CANONS RESIDENTIARY
T. Thompson, *apptd* 1988; B. P. Thompson, *apptd* 1988;
D. Knight, *apptd* 1991

Organist, Dr G. Elliott, PH.D., FRCO, *apptd* 1981

ARCHDEACONS
Colchester, Ven. M. W. Wallace, *apptd* 1997
Harlow, Ven. P. F. Taylor, *apptd* 1996
Southend, Ven. D. Jennings, *apptd* 1992
West Ham, Ven. M. J. Fox, *apptd* 1996

Chancellor, Miss S. M. Cameron, QC, *apptd* 1970
Registrar and Legal Secretary, B. Hood
Diocesan Secretary, D. Phillips, 53 New Street, Chelmsford, Essex CM1 1AT. Tel: 01245-266731

CHICHESTER

102ND BISHOP
Rt. Revd Eric W. Kemp, DD, *cons.* 1974, *apptd* 1974; The Palace, Chichester PO19 1PY. *Signs* Eric Cicestr:

BISHOPS SUFFRAGAN
Horsham, Rt. Revd Lindsay G. Urwin, *cons.* 1993, *apptd* 1993; Bishop's House, 21 Guildford Road, Horsham, W. Sussex RH12 1LU
Lewes, Rt. Revd Wallace P. Benn, *cons.* 1997, *apptd* 1997; 16A Prideaux Road, Eastbourne, E. Sussex BN21 2NB

DEAN
Very Revd John D. Treadgold, LVO, *apptd* 1989

CANONS RESIDENTIARY
R. T. Greenacre, *apptd* 1975; F. J. Hawkins, *apptd* 1981; P. G. Atkinson, *apptd* 1997
Organist, A. J. Thurlow, FRCO, *apptd* 1980

ARCHDEACONS
Chichester, Ven. M. Brotherton, *apptd* 1991
Horsham, Ven. W. C. L. Filby, *apptd* 1983
Lewes and Hastings, Ven. N. S. Reade, *apptd* 1997

Chancellor, His Honour Judge Q. T. Edwards, QC, *apptd* 1978
Registrar and Legal Secretary, C. L. Hodgetts
Diocesan Secretary, J. Prichard, Diocesan Church House, 211 New Church Road, Hove, E. Sussex BN3 4ED. Tel. 01273-421021

COVENTRY

BISHOP
vacant; The Bishop's House, 23 Davenport Road, Coventry CV5 6PW. *Signs* — Coventry

BISHOP SUFFRAGAN
Warwick, Rt. Revd Anthony M. Priddis, *cons.* 1996, *apptd* 1996; 139 Kenilworth Road, Coventry CV4 7AF

PROVOST
Very Revd John F. Petty, *apptd* 1987

CANONS RESIDENTIARY
P. Oestreicher, *apptd* 1986; V. Faull, *apptd* 1994; J. C. Burch, *apptd* 1995
Director of Music, R. Jeffcoat, *apptd* 1997

ARCHDEACONS
Coventry, Ven. H. I. L. Russell, *apptd* 1989
Warwick, Ven. M. J. J. Paget-Wilkes, *apptd* 1990

Chancellor, Sir William Gage, *apptd* 1980
Registrar and Legal Secretary, D. J. Dumbleton
Diocesan Secretary, Mrs I. Chapman, Church House, Palmerston Road, Coventry CV5 6FJ. Tel: 01203-674328

DERBY

6TH BISHOP
Rt. Revd Jonathan S. Bailey, *cons.* 1992, *apptd* 1995; Derby Church House, Full Street, Derby DE1 3DR. *Signs* Jonathan Derby

BISHOP SUFFRAGAN
Repton, Rt. Revd F. Henry A. Richmond, *cons.* 1986, *apptd* 1986; Repton House, Lea, Matlock DE4 5JP

PROVOST
Very Revd Benjamin H. Lewers, *apptd* 1981

CANONS RESIDENTIARY
G. A. Chesterman, *apptd* 1989; Ven. I. Gatford, *apptd* 1992; G. O. Marshall, *apptd* 1992; R. M. Parsons, *apptd* 1993
Organist, P. Gould, *apptd* 1982

ARCHDEACONS
Chesterfield, Ven. D. C. Garnett, *apptd* 1996
Derby, Ven. I. Gatford, *apptd* 1992

Chancellor, J. W. M. Bullimore, *apptd* 1981
Registrar and Legal Secretary, J. S. Battie
Diocesan Secretary, R. J. Carey, Derby Church House, Full Street, Derby DE1 3DR. Tel: 01332-382233

ELY

67TH BISHOP
Rt. Revd Stephen W. Sykes, *cons.* 1990, *apptd* 1990; The Bishop's House, Ely, Cambs CB7 4DW. *Signs* Stephen Ely

BISHOP SUFFRAGAN
Huntingdon, Rt. Revd John R. Flack, *cons.* 1997, *apptd* 1996; 14 Lynn Road, Ely, Cambs CB6 1DA

DEAN
Very Revd Michael Higgins, *apptd* 1991

CANONS RESIDENTIARY
D. J. Green, *apptd* 1980; J. Inge, *apptd* 1996
Organist, P. Trepte, FRCO, *apptd* 1991

ARCHDEACONS
Ely, Ven. J. Watson, *apptd* 1993
Huntingdon, Ven. J. Beer, *apptd* 1997
Wisbech, Ven. J. Rone, *apptd* 1995

Chancellor, W. Gage, QC
Joint Registrars, W. H. Godfrey; P. F. B. Beesley (*Legal Secretary*)
Diocesan Secretary, Dr M. Lavis, Bishop Woodford House, Barton Road, Ely, Cambs CB7 4DX. Tel: 01353-663579

EXETER

69TH BISHOP
Rt. Revd G. Hewlett Thompson, *cons.* 1974, *apptd* 1985; The Palace, Exeter EX1 1HY. *Signs* Hewlett Exon:

BISHOPS SUFFRAGAN
Crediton, Rt. Revd Richard S. Hawkins, *cons.* 1988, *apptd* 1996; 10 The Close, Exeter EX1 1EZ
Plymouth, Rt. Revd John H. Garton, *cons.* 1996, *apptd* 1996; 31 Riverside Walk, Tamerton Foliot, Plymouth PL5 4AQ

DEAN
Very Revd Keith B. Jones, *apptd* 1996

CANONS RESIDENTIARY
A. C. Mawson, *apptd* 1979; K. C. Parry, *apptd* 1991
Organist, L. A. Nethsingha, FRCO, *apptd* 1973

ARCHDEACONS
Barnstaple, Ven. T. Lloyd, *apptd* 1989
Exeter, Ven. A. F. Tremlett, *apptd* 1994
Plymouth, Ven. R. G. Ellis, *apptd* 1982
Totnes, Preb. R. T. Gilpin, *apptd* 1996

Chancellor, Sir David Calcutt, QC, *apptd* 1971
Registrar and Legal Secretary, R. K. Wheeler

Diocesan Secretary, M. Beedell, Diocesan House, Palace Gate, Exeter, Devon EX1 1HX. Tel: 01392-72686

GIBRALTAR IN EUROPE

BISHOP
Rt. Revd John Hind, *cons.* 1991, *apptd* 1993; 14 Tufton Street, London SW1P 3QZ

BISHOP SUFFRAGAN
In Europe Rt. Revd Henry Scriven, *cons.* 1995, *apptd* 1994; 14 Tufton Street, London SW1P 3QZ

Vicar-General, Ven. W. G. Reid
Dean, Cathedral Church of the Holy Trinity, Gibraltar, Very Revd B. W. Horlock, OBE
Chancellor, Pro-Cathedral of St Paul, Valletta, Malta, Canon A. Woods
Chancellor, Pro-Cathedral of the Holy Trinity, Brussels, Belgium, Canon N. Walker

ARCHDEACONS
Eastern, Ven. S. J. B. Peake
North-West Europe, Ven. G. G. Allen
France, Ven. M. Draper
Gibraltar, Ven. K. Robinson
Italy, vacant
Scandinavia and Germany, Ven. D. Ratcliff
Switzerland, Ven. P. J. Hawker, OBE

Chancellor, Sir David Calcutt, QC
Registrar and Legal Secretary, J. G. Underwood
Diocesan Secretary, Ven. W. G. Reid, 14 Tufton Street, London SW1P 3QZ. Tel: 0171-976 8001

GLOUCESTER

39TH BISHOP
Rt. Revd David Bentley, *cons.* 1986, *apptd* 1993; Bishopscourt, Gloucester GL1 2BQ. *Signs* David Gloucestr

BISHOP SUFFRAGAN
Tewkesbury, Rt. Revd John S. Went, *cons.* 1995, *apptd* 1995; Green Acre, Hempsted, Gloucester GL2 6LG

DEAN
Very Revd Nicholas A. S. Bury, *apptd* 1996

CANONS RESIDENTIARY
R. D. M. Grey, *apptd* 1982; N. Chatfield, *apptd* 1992; N. Heavisides, *apptd* 1993; C. H. Morgan, *apptd* 1996

Organist, D. Briggs, FRCO, *apptd* 1994

ARCHDEACONS
Cheltenham, Ven. J. A. Lewis, *apptd* 1988
Gloucester, Ven. C. J. H. Wagstaff, *apptd* 1982

Chancellor and Vicar-General, Ms D. J. Rodgers, *apptd* 1990
Registrar and Legal Secretary, C. G. Peak
Diocesan Secretary, M. Williams, Church House, College Green, Gloucester GL1 2LY. Tel: 01452-410022

GUILDFORD

8TH BISHOP
Rt. Revd John W. Gladwin, *cons.* 1994, *apptd* 1994; Willow Grange, Woking Road, Guildford GU4 7QS. *Signs* John Guildford

BISHOP SUFFRAGAN
Dorking, Rt. Revd Ian Brackley, *cons.* 1996, *apptd* 1995; 13 Pilgrims Way, Guildford GU4 8AD

DEAN
Very Revd Alexander G. Wedderspoon, *apptd* 1987

CANONS RESIDENTIARY
J. Schofield, *apptd* 1995; Dr Maureen Palmer
Organist, A. Millington, FRCO, *apptd* 1982

ARCHDEACONS
Dorking, Ven. M. Wilson, *apptd* 1995
Surrey, Ven. R. Reiss, *apptd* 1995

Chancellor, His Hon. Judge Goodman
Registrar and Legal Secretary, P. F. B. Beesley
Diocesan Secretary, Mrs K. Ingate, Diocesan House, Quarry Street, Guildford GU1 3XG. Tel: 01483-571826

HEREFORD

103RD BISHOP
Rt. Revd John Oliver, *cons.* 1990, *apptd* 1990; The Palace, Hereford HR4 9BN. *Signs* John Hereford

BISHOP SUFFRAGAN
Ludlow, Rt. Revd Dr John Saxbee, *cons.* 1994, *apptd* 1994; Bishop's House, Halford, Craven Arms, Shropshire SY7 9BT

DEAN
Very Revd Robert A. Willis, *apptd* 1992

CANONS RESIDENTIARY
P. Iles, *apptd* 1983; J. Tiller, *apptd* 1984; J. Butterworth, *apptd* 1994

Organist, Dr R. Massey, FRCO, *apptd* 1974

ARCHDEACONS
Hereford, Ven. M. W. Hooper, *apptd* 1997
Ludlow, Rt. Revd J. C. Saxbee, *apptd* 1992

Chancellor, J. M. Henty
Joint Registrars and Legal Secretaries, V. T. Jordan; P. F. B. Beesley
Diocesan Secretary, Miss S. Green, The Palace, Hereford HR4 9BL. Tel: 01432-353863

LEICESTER

5TH BISHOP
Rt. Revd Thomas F. Butler, PH.D., LL D, *cons.* 1985, *apptd* 1991; Bishop's Lodge, 10 Springfield Road, Leicester LE2 3BD. *Signs* Thomas Leicester

STIPENDIARY ASSISTANT BISHOP
Rt. Revd William Down, *cons.* 1990, *apptd* 1995

PROVOST
Very Revd Derek Hole, *apptd* 1992

CANONS RESIDENTIARY
M. T. H. Banks, *apptd* 1988; M. Wilson, *apptd* 1988
Organist, J. T. Gregory, *apptd* 1994

ARCHDEACONS
Leicester, Ven. M. Edson, *apptd* 1994
Loughborough, Ven. I. Stanes, *apptd* 1992

Chancellor, N. Seed, *apptd* 1989
Registrars and Legal Secretaries, P. C. E. Morris; R. H. Bloor

Diocesan Secretary, J. Cryer, Church House, 3–5 St Martin's East, Leicester LEI 5FX. Tel: 0116-262 7445

LICHFIELD

97TH BISHOP
Rt. Revd Keith N. Sutton, *cons.* 1978, *apptd* 1984; Bishop's House, The Close, Lichfield WS13 7LG. *Signs* Keith Lichfield

BISHOPS SUFFRAGAN
Shrewsbury, Rt. Revd David M. Hallatt, *cons.* 1994, *apptd* 1994; 68 London Road, Shrewsbury SY2 6PG
Stafford, Rt. Revd Christopher J. Hill, *cons.* 1996, *apptd* 1996; Ash Garth, Broughton Crescent, Barlaston, Staffs ST12 9DD
Wolverhampton, Rt. Revd Michael G. Bourke, *cons.* 1993, *apptd* 1993; 61 Richmond Road, Wolverhampton WV3 9JH

DEAN
Very Revd Tom Wright, *apptd* 1993

CANONS RESIDENTIARY
Ven. R. B. Ninis, *apptd* 1974; A. N. Barnard, *apptd* 1977; C. W. Taylor, *apptd* 1995
Organist, A. Lumsden, *apptd* 1992

ARCHDEACONS
Lichfield, Ven. R. B. Ninis, *apptd* 1974
Salop, Ven. G. Frost, *apptd* 1997
Stoke-on-Trent, Ven. A. G. C. Smith, *apptd* 1997
Walsall, Ven. A. G. Sadler, *apptd* 1997

Chancellor, His Honour Judge Shand
Registrar and Legal Secretary, J. P. Thorneycroft
Diocesan Secretary, D. R. Taylor, St Mary's House, The Close, Lichfield, Staffs WS13 7LD. Tel: 01543-414551

LINCOLN

70TH BISHOP
Rt. Revd Robert M. Hardy, *cons.* 1980, *apptd* 1987; Bishop's House, Eastgate, Lincoln LN2 1QQ. *Signs* Robert Lincoln

BISHOPS SUFFRAGAN
Grantham, vacant
Grimsby, Rt. Revd David Tustin, *cons.* 1979, *apptd* 1979; Bishop's House, Church Lane, Irby-upon-Humber, Grimsby DN37 7JR

DEAN
vacant

CANONS RESIDENTIARY
B. R. Davis, *apptd* 1977; A. J. Stokes, *apptd* 1992; V. White, *apptd* 1994
Organist, C. S. Walsh, FRCO, *apptd* 1988

ARCHDEACONS
Lincoln, Ven. A. Hawes, *apptd* 1995
Lindsey, vacant
Stow, Ven. R. J. Wells, *apptd* 1989

Chancellor, His Honour Judge Goodman, *apptd* 1971
Registrar and Legal Secretary, D. M. Wellman
Diocesan Secretary, P. Hamlyn Williams, The Old Palace, Lincoln LN2 1PU. Tel: 01522-529241

NORWICH

70TH BISHOP
Rt. Revd Peter J. Nott, *cons.* 1977, *apptd* 1985; Bishop's House, Norwich NR3 1SB. *Signs* Peter Norvic:

BISHOPS SUFFRAGAN
Lynn, Rt. Revd David Conner, *cons.* 1994, *apptd* 1994; The Old Vicarage, Castle Acre, King's Lynn PE32 2AA
Thetford, Rt. Revd Hugo F. de Waal, *cons.* 1992, *apptd* 1992; Rectory Meadow, Bramerton, Norwich NR14 7DW

DEAN
Very Revd Stephen Platten, *apptd* 1995

CANONS RESIDENTIARY
M. F. Perham, *apptd* 1992; Ven. C. J. Offer, *apptd* 1994; R. J. Hanmer, *apptd* 1994
Organist, D. Dunnett, *apptd* 1996

ARCHDEACONS
Lynn, Ven. A. C. Foottit, *apptd* 1987
Norfolk, Ven. A. M. Handley, *apptd* 1993
Norwich, Ven. C. J. Offer, *apptd* 1994

Chancellor, His Honour J. H. Ellison, VRD, *apptd* 1955
Registrar and Legal Secretary, J. W. F. Herring
Diocesan Secretary, D. Adeney, Diocesan House, 109 Dereham Road, Easton, Norwich, Norfolk NR9 5ES. Tel: 01603-880853

OXFORD

41ST BISHOP
Rt. Revd Richard D. Harries, *cons.* 1987, *apptd* 1987; Diocesan Church House, North Hinksey, Oxford OX2 0NB. *Signs* Richard Oxon:

AREA BISHOPS
Buckingham, Rt. Revd Colin J. Bennetts, *cons.* 1994, *apptd* 1994; Sheridan, Grimms Hill, Great Missenden HP16 9BD
Dorchester, Rt. Revd Anthony J. Russell, *cons.* 1988, *apptd* 1988; Holmby House, Sibford Ferris, Banbury, Oxon OX15 5RG
Reading, Rt. Revd Edward W. M. (Dominic) Walker, *cons.* 1997, *apptd* 1997; Bishop's House, Tidmarsh Lane, Tidmarsh, Reading RG8 8HA

DEAN OF CHRIST CHURCH
Very Revd John H. Drury, *apptd* 1991

CANONS RESIDENTIARY
Ven. F. V. Weston, *apptd* 1982; O. M. T. O'Donovan, D.Phil., *apptd* 1982; J. M. Pierce, *apptd* 1987; J. S. K. Ward, *apptd* 1991; R. Jeffery, *apptd* 1996; Prof. J. Webster, *apptd* 1996
Organist, S. Darlington, FRCO, *apptd* 1985

ARCHDEACONS
Berkshire, Ven. M. A. Hill, *apptd* 1992
Buckingham, Ven. J. A. Morrison, *apptd* 1989
Oxford, Ven. F. V. Weston, *apptd* 1982

Chancellor, P. T. S. Boydell, QC, *apptd* 1958
Registrar and Legal Secretary, Dr F. E. Robson
Secretary to the Diocesan Board of Finance, T. Landsbert, Diocesan Church House, North Hinksey, Oxford OX2 0NB. Tel: 01865-244566

PETERBOROUGH

37TH BISHOP
Rt. Revd Ian P. M. Cundy, *cons.* 1992, *apptd* 1996; The Palace, Peterborough PEI IYA. *Signs* Ian Petriburg:

BISHOP SUFFRAGAN
Brixworth, Rt. Revd Paul E. Barber, *cons.* 1989, *apptd* 1989; 4 The Avenue, Dallington, Northampton NN1 4RZ

DEAN
Very Revd Michael Bunker, *apptd* 1992

CANONS RESIDENTIARY
T. R. Christie, *apptd* 1980; J. Higham, *apptd* 1983
Organist, C. S. Gower, FRCO, *apptd* 1977

ARCHDEACONS
Northampton, Ven. M. R. Chapman, *apptd* 1991
Oakham, Ven. B. Fernyhough, *apptd* 1977

Chancellor, T. A. C. Coningsby, QC, *apptd* 1989
Registrar and Legal Secretary, R. Hemingray
Diocesan Secretary, K. H. Hope-Jones, The Palace, Peterborough, Cambs PEI 1YB. Tel: 01733-64448

PORTSMOUTH

8TH BISHOP
Rt. Revd Dr Kenneth W. Stevenson, *cons.* 1995, *apptd* 1995; Bishopswood, 23 The Avenue, Fareham, Hants PO14 1NT. *Signs* Kenneth Portsmouth

PROVOST
Very Revd Michael L. Yorke, *apptd* 1994

CANONS RESIDENTIARY
C. J. Bradley, *apptd* 1990; D. T. Isaac, *apptd* 1990; Jane B. Hedges, *apptd* 1993

Organist, D. J. C. Price, *apptd* 1996

ARCHDEACONS
Isle of Wight, Ven. K. M. L. H. Banting, *apptd* 1996
Portsmouth, Ven. G. P. Knowles, *apptd* 1993

Chancellor, His Honour Judge Aglionby, *apptd* 1978
Registrar and Legal Secretary, Miss H. A. G. Tyler
Diocesan Secretary, M. F. Jordan, Cathedral House, St Thomas's Street, Portsmouth, Hants PO1 2HA. Tel: 01705-825731

ROCHESTER

106TH BISHOP
Rt. Revd Dr Michael Nazir-Ali, *cons.* 1984, *apptd* 1994; Bishopscourt, Rochester MEI ITS. *Signs* Michael Roffen:

BISHOP SUFFRAGAN
Tonbridge, Rt. Revd Brian A. Smith, *cons.* 1993, *apptd* 1993; Bishop's Lodge, St Botolph's Road, Sevenoaks TN13 3AG

DEAN
Very Revd Edward F. Shotter, *apptd* 1990

CANONS RESIDENTIARY
E. R. Turner, *apptd* 1981; R. J. R. Lea, *apptd* 1988; J. Armson, *apptd* 1989; N. Warren, *apptd* 1989

Organist, R. Sayer, FRCO, *apptd* 1995

ARCHDEACONS
Bromley, Ven. G. Norman, *apptd* 1994
Rochester, Ven. N. L. Warren, *apptd* 1989
Tonbridge, Ven. Judith Rose, *apptd* 1996

Chancellor, His Honour Judge M. B. Goodman, *apptd* 1971
Registrar and Legal Secretary, M. Thatcher
Diocesan Secretary, P. Law, St Nicholas Church, Boley Hill, Rochester MEI ISL. Tel: 01634-830333

ST ALBANS

9TH BISHOP
Rt. Revd Christopher W. Herbert, *cons.* 1995, *apptd* 1995; Abbey Gate House, St Albans AL3 4HD. *Signs* Christopher St Albans

BISHOPS SUFFRAGAN
Bedford, Rt. Revd John H. Richardson, *cons.* 1994, *apptd* 1994; 168 Kimbolton Road, Bedford MK41 8DN
Hertford, Rt. Revd Robin J. N. Smith, *cons.* 1990, *apptd* 1990; Hertford House, Abbey Mill Lane, St Albans AL3 4HE

DEAN
Very Revd Christopher Lewis, *apptd* 1993

CANONS RESIDENTIARY
C. Garner, *apptd* 1984; G. R. S. Ritson, *apptd* 1987; M. Sansom, *apptd* 1988; C. R. J. Foster, *apptd* 1994

Organist, A. Lucas, *apptd* 1998

ARCHDEACONS
Bedford, Ven. M. L. Lesiter, *apptd* 1993
Hertford, T. P. Jones, *apptd* 1997
St Albans, Ven. P. B. Davies, *apptd* 1987

Chancellor, His Honour Judge Bursell, QC, *apptd* 1992
Registrar and Legal Secretary, D. N. Cheetham
Diocesan Secretary, L. Nicholls, Holywell Lodge, 41 Holywell Hill, St Albans AL1 IHE. Tel: 01727-854532

ST EDMUNDSBURY AND IPSWICH

9TH BISHOP
Rt. Revd J. H. Richard Lewis, *cons.* 1992, *apptd* 1997; Bishop's House, 4 Park Road, Ipswich IP1 3ST. *Signs* Richard St Edmundsbury and Ipswich

BISHOP SUFFRAGAN
Dunwich, Rt. Revd Timothy J. Stevens, *cons.* 1995, *apptd* 1995; The Old Vicarage, Stowupland, Stowmarket IP14 4BQ

PROVOST
Very Revd J. Atwell, *apptd* 1995

CANONS RESIDENTIARY
A. M. Shaw, *apptd* 1989; M. E. Mingins, *apptd* 1993

Organist, J. Thomas, *apptd* 1997

ARCHDEACONS
Ipswich, Ven. T. A. Gibson, *apptd* 1987
Sudbury, Ven. J. Cox, *apptd* 1995
Suffolk, Ven. G. Arrand, *apptd* 1994

Chancellor, His Honour Sir John Blofeld, QC, *apptd* 1974
Registrar and Legal Secretary, Revd J. D. Mitson
Diocesan Secretary, N. Edgell, 13–15 Tower Street, Ipswich IP1 3BG. Tel: 01473-211028

SALISBURY

77TH BISHOP
Rt. Revd David S. Stancliffe, *cons.* 1993, *apptd* 1993; South
Canonry, The Close, Salisbury SP1 2ER. *Signs* David
Sarum

BISHOPS SUFFRAGAN
Ramsbury, Rt. Revd Peter St G. Vaughan, *cons.* 1989, *apptd*
1989; Bishop's House, Urchfont, Devizes, Wilts SN10
4QH
Sherborne, Rt. Revd John D. G. Kirkham, *cons.* 1976, *apptd*
1976; Little Bailie, Sturminster Marshall, Wimborne
BH21 4AD

DEAN
Very Revd Derek Watson, *apptd* 1996

CANONS RESIDENTIARY
D. J. C. Davies, *apptd* 1985; D. M. K. Durston, *apptd* 1992;
June Osborne, *apptd* 1995

Organist, R. G. Seal, FRCO, *apptd* 1968

ARCHDEACONS
Dorset, Ven. G. E. Walton, *apptd* 1982
Sarum, Ven. B. J. Hopkinson, *apptd* 1986
Sherborne, Ven. P. C. Wheatley, *apptd* 1991
Wilts, Ven. B. J. Smith, *apptd* 1980

Chancellor, His Honour J. S. Wiggs, *apptd* 1997
Registrar and Legal Secretary, F. M. Broadbent
Diocesan Secretary, Revd Karen Curnock, Church House,
Crane Street, Salisbury SP1 2QB. Tel: 01722-411922

SOUTHWARK

BISHOP
vacant; Bishop's House, 38 Tooting Bec Gardens, London
SW16 1QZ. *Signs* — Southwark

AREA BISHOPS
Croydon, Rt. Revd Dr Wilfred D. Wood, DD, *cons.* 1985, *apptd*
1985; St Matthew's House, George Street, Croydon CR0
1PE
Kingston upon Thames, vacant; *Kingston Episcopal Area Office*,
Whitelands College, West Hill, London SW15 3SN
Woolwich, Rt. Revd Colin O. Buchanan, *cons.* 1985, *apptd*
1996; 37 South Road, Forest Hill, London SE23 2UJ

PROVOST
Very Revd Colin B. Slee, *apptd* 1994

CANONS RESIDENTIARY
D. Painter, *apptd* 1991; Helen Cunliffe, *apptd* 1995

Organist, P. Wright, FRCO, *apptd* 1989

ARCHDEACONS
Croydon, Ven. V. A. Davies, *apptd* 1994
Lambeth, Ven. C. R. B. Bird, *apptd* 1988
Lewisham, Ven. D. J. Atkinson, *apptd* 1996
Reigate, Ven. M. Baddeley, *apptd* 1996
Southwark, Ven. D. L. Bartles-Smith, *apptd* 1985
Wandsworth, Ven. D. Gerrard, *apptd* 1989

Chancellor, C. George, QC
Registrar and Legal Secretary, P. Morris
Diocesan Secretary, M. Cawte, Trinity House, 4 Chapel
Court, Borough High Street, London SE1 1HW. Tel: 0171-
403 8686

TRURO

14TH BISHOP
Rt. Revd William Ind, *cons.* 1987, *apptd* 1997; Lis Escop,
Truro TR3 6QQ. *Signs* William Truro

BISHOP SUFFRAGAN
St Germans, Rt. Revd Graham R. James, *cons.* 1993, *apptd*
1993; 32 Falmouth Road, Truro TR1 2HX

DEAN
vacant

CANONS RESIDENTIARY
P. R. Gay, *apptd* 1994; K. P. Mellor, *apptd* 1994; P. D.
Goodridge, *apptd* 1996

Organist, A. Nethsingha, FRCO, *apptd* 1994

ARCHDEACONS
Cornwall, Ven. J. T. McCabe, *apptd* 1996
Bodmin, Ven. R. D. C. Whiteman, *apptd* 1989

Chancellor, P. T. S. Boydell, QC, *apptd* 1957
Registrar and Legal Secretary, M. J. Follett
Diocesan Secretary, C. B. Gorton, Diocesan House, Kenwyn,
Truro TR1 3DU. Tel: 01872-74351

WORCESTER

112TH BISHOP
Rt. Revd Dr Peter S. M. Selby, *cons.* 1984, *apptd* 1997; The
Bishop's House, Hartlebury Castle, Kidderminster DY11
7XX. *Signs* Peter Worcester

BISHOP SUFFRAGAN
Dudley, Rt. Revd Dr Rupert Hoare, *cons.* 1993, *apptd* 1993;
The Bishop's House, Brooklands, Halesowen Road,
Cradley Heath B64 7JF

DEAN
Very Revd Peter J. Marshall, *apptd* 1997

CANONS RESIDENTIARY
Ven. F. Bentley, *apptd* 1984; D. G. Thomas, *apptd* 1987;
I. M. MacKenzie, *apptd* 1989

Organist, A. Lucas, *apptd* 1996

ARCHDEACONS
Dudley, Ven. J. Gathercole, *apptd* 1987
Worcester, Ven. F. Bentley, *apptd* 1984

Chancellor, P. T. S. Boydell, QC, *apptd* 1959
Registrar and Legal Secretary, M. Huskinson
Diocesan Secretary, J. Stanbury, The Old Palace, Deansway,
Worcester WR1 2JE. Tel: 01905-20537

ROYAL PECULIARS

WESTMINSTER
The Collegiate Church of St Peter
Dean, Very Revd Dr A. W. Carr, *apptd* 1997
Sub Dean and Archdeacon, A. E. Harvey, *apptd* 1987
Canons of Westminster, A. E. Harvey, *apptd* 1982; D. C. Gray,
apptd 1987; D. H. Hutt, *apptd* 1995; M. J. Middleton, *apptd*
1997
Chapter Clerk and Receiver-General, Rear-Adm. K. A. Snow,
CB, *apptd* 1987
Organist, M. Neary, FRCO, *apptd* 1988

Registrar, S. J. Holmes, MVO, 20 Dean's Yard, London SWIP 3PA
Legal Secretary, C. L. Hodgetts

WINDSOR

The Queen's Free Chapel of St George within Her Castle of Windsor

Dean, Very Revd Patrick R. Mitchell, FSA, *apptd* 1989
Canons Residentiary, J. A. White, *apptd* 1982; M. A. Moxon, *apptd* 1990; L. F. P. Gunner, *apptd* 1996
Chapter Clerk, Lt.-Col. N. J. Newman, *apptd* 1990, Chapter Office, The Cloisters, Windsor Castle, Windsor, Berks SL4 INJ
Organist, J. Rees-Williams, FRCO, *apptd* 1991

Province of York

YORK

96TH ARCHBISHOP AND PRIMATE OF ENGLAND
Most Revd and Rt. Hon. David M. Hope, KCVO, D.Phil., LL D, *cons.* 1985, *trans.* 1995, *apptd* 1995; Bishopthorpe, York YO2 1QE. *Signs* David Ebor:

BISHOPS SUFFRAGAN
Hull, Rt. Revd James S. Jones, *cons.* 1994, *apptd* 1994; Hullen House, Woodfield Lane, Hessle, Hull HU13 0ES
Selby, Rt. Revd Humphrey V. Taylor, *cons.* 1991, *apptd* 1991; 10 Precentor's Court, York YO1 2ES
Whitby, Rt. Revd Gordon Bates, *cons.* 1983, *apptd* 1983; 60 West Green, Stokesley, Middlesbrough TS9 5BD
Beverley, Rt. Revd John Gaisford, *cons.* 1994, *apptd* 1994 (provincial episcopal visitor); 3 North Lane, Roundhay, Leeds LS8 2QJ

DEAN
Very Revd Raymond Furnell, *apptd* 1994

CANONS RESIDENTIARY
J. Toy, Ph.D., *apptd* 1983; R. Metcalfe, *apptd* 1988; P. J. Ferguson, *apptd* 1995; E. R. Norman, Ph.D., DD, *apptd* 1995
Organist, P. Moore, FRCO, *apptd* 1983

ARCHDEACONS
Cleveland, Ven. C. J. Hawthorn, *apptd* 1991
East Riding, Ven. H. F. Buckingham, *apptd* 1988
York, Ven. G. B. Austin, *apptd* 1988

Official Principal and Auditor of the Chancery Court, J. A. D. Owen, QC
Chancellor of the Diocese, His Honour Judge Coningsby, QC, *apptd* 1977
Vicar-General of the Province and Official Principal of the Consistory Court, His Honour Judge Coningsby, QC
Registrar and Legal Secretary, L. P. M. Lennox
Diocesan Secretary, K. W. Dodgson, Church House, Ogleforth, York YO1 2JE. Tel: 01904-611696

DURHAM

92ND BISHOP
Rt. Revd A. Michael A. Turnbull, *cons.* 1988, *apptd* 1994; Auckland Castle, Bishop Auckland DL14 7NR. *Signs* Michael Dunelm:

BISHOP SUFFRAGAN
Jarrow, Rt. Revd Alan Smithson, *cons.* 1990, *apptd* 1990; The Old Vicarage, Hallgarth, Pittington, Durham DH6 1AB

DEAN
Very Revd John R. Arnold, *apptd* 1989

CANONS RESIDENTIARY
M. C. Perry, *apptd* 1970; D. W. Brown, *apptd* 1990; G. S. Pedley, *apptd* 1993; T. Willmott, *apptd* 1997; M. Kitchen, *apptd* 1997
Organist, J. B. Lancelot, FRCO, *apptd* 1985

ARCHDEACONS
Auckland, Ven. G. G. Gibson, *apptd* 1993
Durham, Ven. T. Willmott, *apptd* 1997
Sunderland, Ven. F. White, *apptd* 1997

Chancellor, His Honour Judge Bursell, QC, *apptd* 1989
Registrar and Legal Secretary, A. N. Fairclough
Diocesan Secretary, W. Hurworth, Auckland Castle, Bishop Auckland, Co. Durham DL14 7QJ. Tel: 01388-604515

BLACKBURN

7TH BISHOP
Rt. Revd Alan D. Chesters, *cons.* 1989, *apptd* 1989; Bishop's House, Ribchester Road, Blackburn BB1 9EF. *Signs* Alan Blackburn

BISHOPS SUFFRAGAN
Burnley, Rt. Revd Martyn W. Jarrett, *cons.* 1994, *apptd* 1994; Dean House, 449 Padiham Road, Burnley BB12 6TE
Lancaster, vacant

PROVOST
Very Revd David Frayne, *apptd* 1992

CANONS RESIDENTIARY
J. R. Hall, *apptd* 1994; D. M. Galilee, *apptd* 1995; A. D. Hindley, *apptd* 1996
Organist, G. Stewart, *apptd* 1995

ARCHDEACONS
Blackburn, Ven. F. J. Marsh, *apptd* 1996
Lancaster, vacant

Chancellor, J. W. M. Bullimore, *apptd* 1990
Registrar and Legal Secretary, T. A. Hoyle
Diocesan Secretary, Revd M. J. Wedgeworth, Diocesan Office, Cathedral Close, Blackburn BB1 5AA. Tel: 01254-54421

BRADFORD

8TH BISHOP
Rt. Revd David J. Smith, *cons.* 1987, *apptd* 1992; Bishopscroft, Ashwell Road, Heaton, Bradford BD9 4AU. *Signs* David Bradford

PROVOST
Very Revd John S. Richardson, *apptd* 1990

CANONS RESIDENTIARY
C. G. Lewis, *apptd* 1993; G. Smith, *apptd* 1996
Organist, A. Horsey, FRCO, *apptd* 1986

ARCHDEACONS
Bradford, Ven. D. H. Shreeve, *apptd* 1984
Craven, Ven. M. L. Grundy, *apptd* 1994

Chancellor, D. M. Savill, QC, *apptd* 1976
Registrar and Legal Secretary, J. G. H. Mackrell
Diocesan Secretary, M. Halliday, Cathedral Hall, Stott Hill, Bradford BD1 4ET. Tel: 01274-725958

CARLISLE

65TH BISHOP
Rt. Revd Ian Harland, *cons.* 1985, *apptd* 1989; Rose Castle, Dalston, Carlisle CA5 7BZ. *Signs* Ian Carliol:

BISHOP SUFFRAGAN
Penrith, Rt. Revd Richard Garrard, *cons.* 1994, *apptd* 1994; Holm Croft, Castle Road, Kendal, Cumbria LA9 7AU

DEAN
Very Revd Henry E. C. Stapleton, *apptd* 1988

CANONS RESIDENTIARY
R. A. Chapman, *apptd* 1978; Ven. D. C. Turnbull, *apptd* 1993; D. W. V. Weston, *apptd* 1994; C. Hill, *apptd* 1996

Organist, J. Suter, FRCO, *apptd* 1991

ARCHDEACONS
Carlisle, Ven. D. C. Turnbull, *apptd* 1993
West Cumberland, Ven. A. N. Davis, *apptd* 1996
Westmorland and Furness, Ven. D. T. I. Jenkins, *apptd* 1995

Chancellor, His Honour Judge Aglionby, *apptd* 1991
Registrar and Legal Secretary, Mrs S. Holmes
Diocesan Secretary, Canon C. Hill, Church House, West Walls, Carlisle CA3 8UE. Tel· 01228-22573

CHESTER

40TH BISHOP
Rt. Revd Peter R. Forster, PH.D., *cons.* 1996, *apptd* 1996; Bishop's House, Chester CH1 2JD. *Signs* Peter Cestr:

BISHOPS SUFFRAGAN
Birkenhead, Rt. Revd Michael L. Langrish, *cons.* 1993, *apptd* 1993; 67 Bidston Road, Oxton, Birkenhead L43 6TR
Stockport, Rt. Revd Geoffrey M. Turner, *cons.* 1994, *apptd* 1994; Bishop's Lodge, Back Lane, Dunham Town, Altrincham, Cheshire WA14 4SG

DEAN
Very Revd Dr Stephen S. Smalley, *apptd* 1986

CANONS RESIDENTIARY
R. M. Rees, *apptd* 1990; O. A. Conway, *apptd* 1991; Dr T. J. Dennis, *apptd* 1994; J. W. S. Newcome, *apptd* 1994

Organist, D. G. Poulter, FRCO, *apptd* 1997

ARCHDEACONS
Chester, Ven. C. Hewetson, *apptd* 1994
Macclesfield, Ven. R. J. Gillings, *apptd* 1994

Chancellor, H. H. Lomas, *apptd* 1977
Registrar and Legal Secretary, A. K. McAllester
Diocesan Secretary, S. P. A. Marriott, Diocesan House, Raymond Street, Chester CH1 4PN. Tel: 01244-379222

LIVERPOOL

BISHOP
vacant; Bishop's Lodge, Woolton Park, Liverpool L25 6DT. *Signs* — Liverpool

BISHOP SUFFRAGAN
Warrington, Rt. Revd John Packer, *cons.* 1996, *apptd* 1996; 34 Central Avenue, Eccleston Park, Prescot, Merseyside L34 2QP

DEAN
Very Revd Rhys D. C. Walters, OBE, *apptd* 1983

CANONS RESIDENTIARY
D. J. Hutton, *apptd* 1983; M. C. Boyling, *apptd* 1994; N. T. Vincent, *apptd* 1995

Organist, Prof. I. Tracey, *apptd* 1980

ARCHDEACONS
Liverpool, Ven. R. L. Metcalf, *apptd* 1994
Warrington, Ven. C. D. S. Woodhouse, *apptd* 1981

Chancellor, R. G. Hamilton
Registrar and Legal Secretary, R. H. Arden
Diocesan Secretary, K. Cawdron, Church House, 1 Hanover Street, Liverpool L1 3DW. Tel: 0151-709 9722

MANCHESTER

10TH BISHOP
Rt. Revd Christopher J. Mayfield, *cons.* 1985, *apptd* 1993; Bishopscourt, Bury New Road, Manchester M7 4LE. *Signs* Christopher Manchester

BISHOPS SUFFRAGAN
Bolton, Rt. Revd David Bonser, *cons.* 1991, *apptd* 1991; 4 Sandfield Drive, Lostock, Bolton BL6 4DU
Hulme, Rt. Revd Colin J. F. Scott, *cons.* 1984, *apptd* 1984; 1 Raynham Avenue, Didsbury, Manchester M20 0BW
Middleton, Rt. Revd Stephen Venner, *cons.* 1994, *apptd* 1994; The Hollies, Manchester Road, Rochdale OL11 3QY

DEAN
Very Revd Kenneth Riley, *apptd* 1993

CANONS RESIDENTIARY
Ven. R. B. Harris, *apptd* 1980; J. R. Atherton, PH.D., *apptd* 1984; A. E. Radcliffe, *apptd* 1991; P. Denby, *apptd* 1995

Organist, C. Stokes, *apptd* 1992

ARCHDEACONS
Bolton, Ven. L. M. Davies, *apptd* 1992
Manchester, Ven. R. B. Harris, *apptd* 1980
Rochdale, Ven. J. M. M. Dalby, *apptd* 1991

Chancellor, J. Holden, *apptd* 1997
Registrar and Legal Secretary, M. Darlington
Diocesan Secretary, Mrs J. Park, Diocesan Church House, 90 Deansgate, Manchester M3 2GH. Tel: 0161-833 9521

NEWCASTLE

11TH BISHOP
Rt. Revd J. Martin Wharton, *cons.* 1992, *apptd* 1997; Bishop's House, 29 Moor Road South, Gosforth, Newcastle upon Tyne NE3 1PA. *Signs* Martin Newcastle

STIPENDIARY ASSISTANT BISHOP
Rt. Revd Kenneth Gill, *cons.* 1972, *apptd* 1980

PROVOST
Very Revd Nicholas G. Coulton, *apptd* 1990

CANONS RESIDENTIARY
R. Langley, *apptd* 1985; P. R. Strange, *apptd* 1986;
I. F. Bennett, *apptd* 1988; Ven. P. Elliott, *apptd* 1993
Organist, T. G. Hone, FRCO, *apptd* 1987

ARCHDEACONS
Lindisfarne, Ven. M. E. Bowering, *apptd* 1987
Northumberland, Ven. P. Elliott, *apptd* 1993

Chancellor, His Honour A. J. Blackett-Ord, CVO, *apptd* 1971
Registrar and Legal Secretary, Mrs B. J. Lowdon
Diocesan Secretary, J. M. Craster, Church House, Grainger
Park Road, Newcastle upon Tyne NE4 8SX. Tel: 0191-
226 0622

RIPON

11TH BISHOP
Rt. Revd David N. de L. Young, *cons.* 1977, *apptd* 1977;
Bishop Mount, Ripon HG4 5DP. *Signs* David Ripon

BISHOP SUFFRAGAN
Knaresborough, vacant

DEAN
Very Revd John Methuen, *apptd* 1995

CANONS RESIDENTIARY
M. R. Glanville-Smith, *apptd* 1990; K. Punshon, *apptd* 1996;
J. Bell, *apptd* 1997
Organist, K. Beaumont, FRCO, *apptd* 1994

ARCHDEACONS
Leeds, Ven. J. M. Oliver, *apptd* 1992
Richmond, Ven. K. Good, *apptd* 1993

Chancellor, His Honour Judge Grenfell, *apptd* 1992
Registrar and Legal Secretary, J. R. Balmforth
Diocesan Secretary, P. M. Arundel, Diocesan Office, St
Mary's Street, Leeds LS9 7DP. Tel: 0113-248 7487

SHEFFIELD

6TH BISHOP
Rt. Revd John Nicholls, *cons.* 1990, *apptd* 1997;
Bishopscroft, Snaithing Lane, Sheffield S10 3LG. *Signs*
John Sheffield

BISHOP SUFFRAGAN
Doncaster, Rt. Revd. Michael F. Gear, *cons.* 1993, *apptd* 1993;
Bishops Lodge, Hooton Roberts, Rotherham S65 4PF

PROVOST
Very Revd Michael Sadgrove, *apptd* 1995

CANONS RESIDENTIARY
T. M. Page, *apptd* 1982; Ven. S. R. Lowe, *apptd* 1988;
C. M. Smith, *apptd* 1991; Jane E. M. Sinclair, *apptd* 1993
Organist, N. Taylor, *apptd* 1997

ARCHDEACONS
Doncaster, Ven. B. L. Holdridge, *apptd* 1994
Sheffield, Ven. S. R. Lowe, *apptd* 1988

Chancellor, Prof. J. D. McClean, *apptd* 1992
Registrar and Legal Secretary, C. P. Rothwell
Diocesan Secretary, C. A. Beck, FCIS, Diocesan Church
House, 95–99 Effingham Street, Rotherham S65 1BL.
Tel: 0114-283 7547

SODOR AND MAN

79TH BISHOP
Rt. Revd Noel D. Jones, CB, *cons.* 1989, *apptd* 1989; The
Bishop's House, Quarterbridge Road, Douglas, Isle of
Man IM2 3RF. *Signs* Noel Sodor and Man

CANONS
B. H. Kelly, *apptd* 1980; J. Sheen, *apptd* 1991; F. H. Bird, *apptd*
1993; D. Whitworth, *apptd* 1996

ARCHDEACON
Isle of Man, Ven. B. H. Partington, *apptd* 1996

Vicar-General and Chancellor, Ms C. Faulds
Registrar and Legal Secretary, C. J. Callow
Diocesan Secretary, The Hon. C. Murphy, c/o 1 Kelly Close,
Ramsey, Isle of Man IM8 2AR. Tel: 01624-816545

SOUTHWELL

9TH BISHOP
Rt. Revd Patrick B. Harris, *cons.* 1973, *apptd* 1988; Bishop's
Manor, Southwell NG25 0JR. *Signs* Patrick Southwell

BISHOP SUFFRAGAN
Sherwood, Rt. Revd Alan W. Morgan, *cons.* 1989, *apptd* 1989;
Sherwood House, High Oakham Road, Mansfield
NG18 5AJ

PROVOST
Very Revd David Leaning, *apptd* 1991

CANONS RESIDENTIARY
I. G. Collins, *apptd* 1985; M. R. Austin, *apptd* 1988
Organist, P. Hale, *apptd* 1989

ARCHDEACONS
Newark, Ven. D. C. Hawtin, *apptd* 1992
Nottingham, Ven. G. Ogilvie, *apptd* 1996

Chancellor, J. Shand, *apptd* 1981
Registrar and Legal Secretary, C. C. Hodson
Diocesan Secretary, B. Noake, Dunham House, Westgate,
Southwell, Notts NG25 0JL. Tel: 01636-814331

WAKEFIELD

11TH BISHOP
Rt. Revd Nigel S. McCulloch, *cons.* 1986, *apptd* 1992;
Bishop's Lodge, Woodthorpe Lane, Wakefield WF2 6JL.
Signs Nigel Wakefield

BISHOP SUFFRAGAN
Pontefract, Rt. Revd John Finney, *cons.* 1993, *apptd* 1993;
Pontefract House, 181A Manygates Lane, Wakefield
WF2 7DR

PROVOST
vacant

CANONS RESIDENTIARY
G. Nairn-Briggs, *apptd* 1992; R. Capper, *apptd* 1997; R. Gage,
apptd 1997
Organist, J. Bielby, FRCO, *apptd* 1972

ARCHDEACONS
Halifax, Ven. R. Inwood, *apptd* 1995
Pontefract, Ven. A. Robinson, *apptd* 1997

Chancellor, P. Collier, QC, apptd 1992
Registrar and Legal Secretary, L. Box
Diocesan Secretary, vacant; Church House, 1 South Parade,
Wakefield WF1 ILP. Tel: 01924-371802

The Anglican Communion

The Anglican Communion consists of 36 independent provincial or national Christian churches throughout the world, many of which are in Commonwealth countries and originated from missionary activity by the Church of England. There is no single world authority linking the Communion, but all recognize the leadership of the Archbishop of Canterbury and have strong ecclesiastical and historical links with the Church of England. Every ten years all the bishops in the Communion meet at the Lambeth Conference, convened by the Archbishop of Canterbury. The Conference has no policy-making authority but is an important forum for the discussion of issues of common concern. The Anglican Consultative Council was set up in 1968 to function between conferences and the meeting of the Primates every two years.

There are about 70 million Anglicans and 800 archbishops and bishops world-wide.

THE CHURCH IN WALES

The Anglican Church was the established church in Wales from the 16th century until 1920, when the estrangement of the majority of Welsh people from Anglicanism resulted in disestablishment. Since then the Church in Wales has been an autonomous province consisting of six sees, with one of the diocesan bishops being elected Archbishop of Wales by an electoral college comprising elected lay and clerical members.

The legislative body of the Church in Wales is the Governing Body, which has 356 members in total, divided between the three orders of bishops, clergy and laity. It is presided over by the Archbishop of Wales and meets twice annually. Its decisions are binding upon all members of the Church. There are about 96,000 members of the Church in Wales, with six bishops, about 700 stipendiary clergy and 1,142 parishes.

THE GOVERNING BODY OF THE CHURCH IN WALES,
    39 Cathedral Road, Cardiff CF1 9XF. Tel: 01222–231638.
    Secretary-General, J. W. D. McIntyre

10TH ARCHBISHOP OF WALES, Most Revd Alwyn R. Jones
    (Bishop of St Asaph), elected 1991

BISHOPS
Bangor (79th), Rt. Revd Dr Barry C. Morgan, b. 1947, cons.
    1993, elected 1992; Tŷ'r Esgob, Bangor LL57 2SS. Signs
    Barry Bangor. Stipendiary clergy, 67
Llandaff (101st), Rt. Revd Roy T. Davies, b. 1934, cons. 1985,
    elected 1985; Llys Esgob, The Cathedral Green, Llandaff,
    Cardiff CF5 2YE. Signs Roy Landav. Stipendiary clergy, 167
Monmouth (8th), Rt. Revd Rowan D. Williams, b 1950, cons.
    1992, elected 1992; Bishopstow, Stow Hill, Newport NP9
    4EA. Signs Rowan Monmouth. Stipendiary clergy, 120
St Asaph (74th), Most Revd Alwyn R. Jones, b. 1934, cons.
    1982, elected 1982; Esgobty, St Asaph, Clwyd LL17 0TW.
    Signs Alwyn Cambrensis. Stipendiary clergy, 112

St David's (126th), Rt. Revd D. Huw Jones, b. 1934, cons.
    1993, elected 1995; Llys Esgob, Abergwili, Carmarthen
    SA31 2JG. Signs Huw St Davids. Stipendiary clergy, 138
Swansea and Brecon (7th), Rt. Revd Dewi M. Bridges, b. 1933,
    cons. 1988, elected 1988; Ely Tower, Brecon, Powys LD3
    9DE. Signs Dewi Swansea & Brecon. Stipendiary clergy, 100

The stipend of a diocesan bishop of the Church in Wales is £25,773 a year from 1997

THE SCOTTISH EPISCOPAL CHURCH

The Scottish Episcopal Church was founded after the Act of Settlement (1690) established the presbyterian nature of the Church of Scotland. The Scottish Episcopal Church is in full communion with the Church of England but is autonomous. The governing authority is the General Synod, an elected body of 180 members which meets once a year. The diocesan bishop who convenes and presides at meetings of the General Synod is called the Primus and is elected by his fellow bishops.

There are 54,382 members of the Scottish Episcopal Church, of whom 33,795 are communicants. There are seven bishops, 210 stipendiary clergy, and 320 churches and places of worship.

THE GENERAL SYNOD OF THE SCOTTISH EPISCOPAL
    CHURCH, 21 Grosvenor Crescent, Edinburgh EH12 5EE.
    Tel: 0131-225 6357. Secretary-General, J. F. Stuart

PRIMUS OF THE SCOTTISH EPISCOPAL CHURCH, Most
    Revd Richard F. Holloway (Bishop of Edinburgh),
    elected 1992

BISHOPS
Aberdeen and Orkney, A. Bruce Cameron, b. 1941, cons. 1992,
    elected 1992. Clergy, 19
Argyll and the Isles, Douglas M. Cameron, b. 1935, cons. 1993,
    elected 1992. Clergy, 9
Brechin, Neville Chamberlain, b. 1939, cons. 1997, elected
    1997. Clergy, 19
Edinburgh, Richard F. Holloway, b. 1933, cons. 1986, elected
    1986. Clergy, 53
Glasgow and Galloway, John M. Taylor, b. 1932, cons. 1991,
    elected 1991. Clergy, 48
Moray, Ross and Caithness, Gregor Macgregor, b. 1933, cons.
    1994, elected 1994. Clergy, 13
St Andrews, Dunkeld and Dunblane, Michael H. G. Henley, b.
    1938, cons. 1995, elected 1995. Clergy, 30

The minimum stipend of a diocesan bishop of the Scottish Episcopal Church was £20,646 in 1997 (i.e. 1.5 × the minimum clergy stipend of £13,764)

THE CHURCH OF IRELAND

The Anglican Church was the established church in Ireland from the 16th century but never secured the allegiance of a majority of the Irish and was disestablished in 1871. The Church in Ireland is divided into the provinces of Armagh and Dublin, each under an archbishop. The provinces are subdivided into 12 dioceses.

The legislative body is the General Synod, which has 660 members in total, divided between the House of Bishops and the House of Representatives. The Archbishop of Armagh is elected by the House of Bishops; other episcopal elections are made by an electoral college.

There are about 375,000 members of the Church of Ireland, with two archbishops, ten bishops, about 600 clergy and about 1,000 churches and places of worship.

CENTRAL OFFICE, Church of Ireland House, Church Avenue, Rathmines, Dublin 6. Tel: 00-353-1-4978422. *Chief Officer and Secretary of the Representative Church Body*, R. H. Sherwood; *Assistant Secretary of the General Synod*, D. G. Meredith

PROVINCE OF ARMAGH

ARCHBISHOP OF ARMAGH AND PRIMATE OF ALL IRELAND, Most Revd Robert H. A. Eames, PH.D., *b.* 1937, *cons.* 1975, *trans.* 1986. *Clergy*, 51

BISHOPS
Clogher, Brian D. A. Hannon, *b.* 1936, *cons.* 1986, *apptd* 1986. *Clergy*, 32
Connor, James E. Moore, *b.* 1933, *cons.* 1995, *apptd.* 1995. *Clergy*, 106
Derry and Raphoe, James Mehaffey, PH.D., *b.* 1931, *cons.* 1980, *apptd* 1980. *Clergy*, 50
Down and Dromore, Harold C. Miller, *b.* 1950, *cons.* 1997, *apptd* 1997. *Clergy*, 109
Kilmore, Elphin and Ardagh, Michael H. G. Mayes, *b.* 1941, *cons.* 1993, *apptd* 1993. *Clergy*, 24
Tuam, Killala and Achonry, vacant. *Clergy*, 12

PROVINCE OF DUBLIN

ARCHBISHOP OF DUBLIN, BISHOP OF GLENDALOUGH, AND PRIMATE OF IRELAND, Most Revd Walton N. F. Empey, *b.* 1934, *cons.* 1981, *trans.* 1985, 1996. *Clergy*, 90

BISHOPS
Cashel and Ossory, John R. W. Neill, *b.* 1945, *cons.* 1986, *trans.* 1997. *Clergy*, 37
Cork, Cloyne and Ross, Robert A. Warke, *b.* 1930, *cons.* 1988, *apptd* 1988. *Clergy*, 28
Limerick and Killaloe, Edward F. Darling, *b.* 1933, *cons.* 1985, *apptd* 1985. *Clergy*, 23
Meath and Kildare, Most Revd Robert L. Clarke, PH.D., *b.* 1949, *cons.* 1996, *apptd* 1996. *Clergy*, 23

Anglican Communion Overseas

ANGLICAN CHURCH OF AOTEAROA, NEW ZEALAND AND POLYNESIA

PRIMATE AND ARCHBISHOP OF AOTEAROA, NEW ZEALAND AND POLYNESIA, vacant

BISHOPS
Aotearoa, Whakahuhui Vercoe, *cons.* 1981, *apptd* 1981
Auckland, John Paterson, *cons.* 1995, *apptd* 1995
Christchurch, David Coles, *cons.* 1990, *apptd* 1990
Dunedin, Penelope Jamieson, *cons.* 1990, *apptd* 1990
Nelson, Derek Eaton, *cons.* 1990, *apptd* 1990
Polynesia, Jabez Bryce, *cons.* 1975, *apptd* 1975
Waiapu, Murray Mills, *cons.* 1991, *apptd* 1991
Waikato, David Moxon, *cons.* 1993, *apptd* 1993
Wellington, vacant

ANGLICAN CHURCH OF AUSTRALIA

PRIMATE OF AUSTRALIA, The Most Revd Keith Rayner (Archbishop of Melbourne), *cons.* 1969, *apptd* 1991

PROVINCE OF NEW SOUTH WALES

METROPOLITAN
Archbishop of Sydney, The Most Revd R. Harry Goodhew, *cons.* 1982, *apptd* 1993

BISHOPS
Armidale, Peter Chiswell, *cons.* 1976, *apptd* 1976
Bathurst, Bruce W. Wilson, *cons.* 1984, *apptd* 1989
Canberra and Goulburn, George V. Browning, *cons.* 1985, *apptd* 1993
Grafton, Bruce A. Schultz, *cons.* 1983, *apptd* 1985
Newcastle, Roger A. Herft, *cons.* 1986, *apptd* 1993
Riverina, Bruce Q. Clark, *cons.* 1993, *apptd* 1993

PROVINCE OF QUEENSLAND

METROPOLITAN
Archbishop of Brisbane, The Most Revd Peter Hollingworth, *cons.* 1985, *apptd* 1990

BISHOPS
North Queensland, Clyde M. Wood, *cons.* 1983, *apptd* 1996
Northern Territory, Richard F. Appleby, *cons.* 1992, *apptd* 1992
Rockhampton, Ronald F. Stone, *cons.* 1992, *apptd* 1996

PROVINCE OF SOUTH AUSTRALIA

METROPOLITAN
Archbishop of Adelaide, The Most Revd Ian G. C. George, *cons.* 1989, *apptd* 1991

BISHOPS
The Murray, Graham H. Walden, *cons.* 1981, *apptd* 1989
Willochra, W. David H. McCall, *cons.* 1987, *apptd* 1987

PROVINCE OF VICTORIA

METROPOLITAN
Archbishop of Melbourne, The Most Revd Keith Rayner, *cons.* 1969, *apptd* 1990 (*see* above)

BISHOPS
Ballarat, R. David Silk, *cons.* 1994, *apptd* 1994
Bendigo, R. David Bowden, *cons.* 1995, *apptd* 1995
Gippsland, Arthur L. V. Jones, *cons.* 1994, *apptd* 1994
Wangaratta, Paul Richardson, *cons.* 1987, *apptd* 1995

PROVINCE OF WESTERN AUSTRALIA

METROPOLITAN
Archbishop of Perth, The Most Revd Peter F. Carnley, PH.D., *cons.* 1981, *apptd* 1981

BISHOPS
Bunbury, Hamish J. U. Jamieson, *cons.* 1974, *apptd* 1984
North-West Australia, Anthony Nicholls, *cons.* 1992, *apptd* 1992

EXTRA-PROVINCIAL DIOCESE

Bishop of Tasmania, Rt. Revd Phillip K. Newell, AO, *cons.* 1982, *apptd* 1982

EPISCOPAL ANGLICAN CHURCH OF BRAZIL
Igreja Episcopal Anglicana Do Brasil

PRIMATE, The Most Revd Glauco Soares de Lima (Bishop of São Paulo), *cons.* 1989, *apptd* 1994

BISHOPS
Brasilia, Almir dos Santos, *cons.* 1989, *apptd* 1989
Central Brazil, Sydney A. Ruiz, *cons.* 1985, *apptd* 1985
Northern Brazil, Clovis E. Rodrigues, *cons.* 1985, *apptd* 1986
Pelotas, Luiz O. P. Prado, *cons.* 1987, *apptd* 1989
São Paulo, see above, *apptd* 1989
Southern Brazil, Claudio V. S. Gastal, *cons.* 1984, *apptd* 1984
South-Western Brazil, Jubal P. Neves, *cons.* 1993, *apptd* 1993

CHURCH OF THE PROVINCE OF BURUNDI

ARCHBISHOP OF PROVINCE, The Most Revd Samuel Sindamuka (Bishop of Matana), *cons.* 1975, *apptd* 1989

BISHOPS
Bujumbura, Pie Ntukamazina, *cons.* 1990, *apptd* 1990
Buye, Samuel Ndayisenga, *apptd* 1979
Gitega, Jean Nduwayo, *apptd* 1985
Matana, see above

ANGLICAN CHURCH OF CANADA

ARCHBISHOP AND PRIMATE, The Most Revd Michael G. Peers, *cons.* 1977, *elected* 1986

PROVINCE OF BRITISH COLUMBIA
METROPOLITAN
Archbishop of Kootenay, The Most Revd David Crawley, *cons.* 1990, *elected* 1994

BISHOPS
British Columbia, Barry Jenks, *cons.* 1992, *elected* 1992
Caledonia, John Hannen, *cons.* 1981, *elected* 1981
Cariboo, James Cruickshank, *cons.* 1992, *elected* 1992
Kootenay, see above, *elected* 1990
New Westminster, Michael Ingham, *cons.* 1994, *elected* 1993
Yukon, Terrence O. Buckle, *cons.* 1993, *elected* 1995

PROVINCE OF CANADA
METROPOLITAN
Archbishop of Western Newfoundland, vacant

BISHOPS
Central Newfoundland, Edward Marsh, *cons.* 1990, *elected* 1990
Eastern Newfoundland and Labrador, Donald Harvey, *cons.* 1993, *elected* 1992
Fredericton, George Lemmon, *cons.* 1989, *elected* 1989
Montreal, Andrew Hutchison, *cons.* 1990, *elected* 1990
Nova Scotia, Arthur Peters, *cons.* 1982, *elected* 1982
Quebec, Bruce Stavert, *cons.* 1991, *elected* 1991
Western Newfoundland, vacant

PROVINCE OF ONTARIO
METROPOLITAN
Archbishop of Huron, The Most Revd Percival O'Driscoll, *cons.* 1987, *elected* 1993

BISHOPS
Algoma, Ronald Ferris, *cons.* 1981, *elected* 1995
Huron, see above
Moosonee, Caleb Lawrence, *cons.* 1980, *elected* 1980
Niagara, D. Ralph Spence, *cons.* 1997, *elected* 1997
Ontario, Peter Mason, *cons.* 1992, *elected* 1992
Ottawa, John Baycroft, *cons.* 1985, *elected* 1993
Toronto, Terence Finlay, *cons.* 1986, *elected* 1990

PROVINCE OF RUPERT'S LAND
METROPOLITAN
Archbishop of Calgary, The Most Revd Barry Curtis, *cons.* 1983, *elected* 1994

BISHOPS
Arctic, J. Christopher Williams, *cons.* 1987, *elected* 1991
Athabasca, John Clarke, *cons.* 1992, *elected* 1992
Brandon, Malcolm Harding, *cons.* 1992, *elected* 1992
Calgary, see above, *elected* 1983
Edmonton, Victoria Matthews, *cons.* 1994, *elected* 1997
Keewatin, Gordon Beardy, *cons.* 1993, *elected* 1997
Qu' Appelle, vacant
Rupert's Land, Patrick Lee, *cons.* 1994, *elected* 1994
Saskatchewan, Anthony Burton, *cons.* 1993, *elected* 1993
Saskatoon, Thomas Morgan, *cons.* 1985, *elected* 1993

CHURCH OF THE PROVINCE OF CENTRAL AFRICA

ARCHBISHOP OF PROVINCE, The Most Revd Walter P. K. Makhulu (Bishop of Botswana), *cons.* 1979, *apptd* 1980

BISHOPS
Botswana, see above
Central Zambia, Clement Shaba
Central Zimbabwe, Titus Zhinje
Eastern Zambia, John R. Osmers
Harare, Jonathan Siyachitema, *cons.* 1981
Lake Malawi, Peter Nyanja, *cons.* 1978, *apptd* 1978
Lusaka, Stephen Mumba, *cons.* 1981, *apptd* 1981
Manicaland, Elijah Masuko, *cons.* 1981, *apptd* 1981
Matabeleland, Theophilus Naledi, *cons.* 1987, *apptd* 1987
Northern Malawi, Jackson C. Biggers
Northern Zambia, Bernard Malango, *cons.* 1988, *apptd* 1988
Southern Malawi, vacant

CHURCH OF THE PROVINCE OF THE INDIAN OCEAN

ARCHBISHOP OF PROVINCE, The Most Revd Remi Rabenirina (Bishop of Atananarivo), *cons.* 1984, *apptd* 1995

BISHOPS
Antananarivo, see above, *apptd* 1984
Antsiranana, Keith Benzies, OBE, *cons.* 1982, *apptd* 1982
Mahajanga, Jean-Claude Andrianjafimanana, *cons.* 1994, *apptd* 1994
Mauritius, Rex Donat, *cons.* 1984, *apptd* 1984
Seychelles, French Chang-Him, *cons.* 1979, *apptd* 1979
Toamasina, Donald Smith, *cons.* 1990, *apptd* 1990

HOLY CATHOLIC CHURCH IN JAPAN
Nippon Sei Ko Kai

PRIMATE (acting), The Bishop of Kyushu

BISHOPS
Chubu, vacant
Hokkaido, Nathaniel M. Uematsu
Kita Kanto, vacant
Kobe, John J. Furumoto, *cons.* 1992, *apptd* 1992
Kyoto, Barnabas M. Muto, *cons.* 1995, *apptd* 1995
Kyushu, Joseph N. Iida, *cons.* 1982, *apptd* 1982
Okinawa, vacant
Osaka, Augustine K. Takano, *cons.* 1995, *apptd* 1995
Tohoku, John T. Sato, *cons.* 1996, *apptd* 1996
Tokyo, John M. Takeda, *cons.* 1988, *apptd* 1988
Yokohama, Raphael S. Kajiwara, *cons.* 1984, *apptd* 1984

EPISCOPAL CHURCH IN JERUSALEM AND THE MIDDLE EAST

PRESIDENT-BISHOP, Rt. Revd Ghais A. Malik, *apptd* 1996

BISHOPS
Jerusalem, Samir Kafity, *cons.* 1984, *apptd* 1986
Iran, Iraj Mottahedeh, *cons.* 1990, *apptd* 1990
Egypt, Ghais A. Malik, *cons.* 1984, *apptd* 1984
Cyprus and the Gulf, Clive Handford, *cons.* 1990, *apptd* 1996

CHURCH OF THE PROVINCE OF KENYA

ARCHBISHOP OF PROVINCE The Most Revd Dr David Gitari (Bishop of Nairobi), *cons.* 1975, *apptd* 1996

BISHOPS
Bungoma, Eliud Wabukala
Butere, Horace Etemesi, *cons.* 1993, *apptd* 1993
Eldoret, Stephen Kewasis, *cons.* 1992, *apptd* 1992
Embu, Moses Njue, *cons.* 1990, *apptd* 1990
Kajiado, vacant
Katakwa, Eliud Okiring, *cons.* 1991, *apptd* 1991
Kirinyaga, vacant
Kitui, Benjamin Nzimbi, *cons.* 1985, *apptd* 1995
Machakos, Joseph M. Kanuku
Maseno North, Simon M. Oketch
Maseno South, Francis Mwayi-Abiero, *cons.* 1994, *apptd* 1994
Maseno West, Joseph Wasonga, *cons.* 1991, *apptd* 1991
Mombasa, Julius Kalu, *cons.* 1994, *apptd* 1994
Mount Kenya Central, Julius G. Gachuche, *cons.* 1993, *apptd* 1993
Mount Kenya South, Peter Njenga Kariuki
Mount Kenya West, Alfred Chipman, *cons.* 1993, *apptd* 1993
Mumias, William Wesa
Nairobi, *see* above
Nakuru, Stephen M. Njihia, *cons.* 1990, *apptd* 1990
Nambale, Josiah M. Were, *cons.* 1993, *apptd* 1993
Southern Nyanza, Haggai Nyang', *cons.* 1990, *apptd* 1993
Taita/Taveta, Samson M. Mwaluda, *cons.* 1993, *apptd* 1993

CHURCH OF THE PROVINCE OF KOREA

ARCHBISHOP OF PROVINCE, The Most Revd Bundo C. H. Kim (Bishop of Pusan), *cons.* 1988, *apptd* 1995

BISHOPS
Pusan, *see* above
Seoul, Matthew C. B. Chung, *cons.* 1995, *apptd* 1995
Taejon, Paul Hwan Yoon, *cons.* 1987, *apptd* 1988

CHURCH OF THE PROVINCE OF MELANESIA

ARCHBISHOP OF PROVINCE, The Most Revd Ellison L. Pogo (Bishop of Central Melanesia), *cons.* 1981, *apptd* 1994

BISHOPS
Banks and Torres, Charles W. Ling, *cons.* 1996, *apptd* 1996
Central Melanesia, *see* above
Hanuato'o, James Mason, *cons.* 1991, *apptd* 1991
Malaita, Terry M. Brown, *cons.* 1996, *apptd* 1996
Temotu, Lazarus Munamua, *cons.* 1987, *apptd* 1987
Vanuatu, Michael Tavoa, *cons.* 1990, *apptd* 1990
Ysabel, Walter Siba, *cons.* 1990, *apptd* 1994

EPISCOPAL CHURCH OF MEXICO

ARCHBISHOP OF PROVINCE, The Most Revd José G. Saucedo (Bishop of Cuernavaca), *cons.* 1958, *elected* 1995

BISHOPS
Cuernavaca, *see* above, *apptd* 1989
Mexico, Sergio Carrauza-Gomez, *cons.* 1989, *apptd* 1989
Northern Mexico, German Martinez-Marquez, *cons.* 1987, *apptd* 1987
South-East Mexico, Claro Huerta-Ramos, *cons.* 1980, *apptd* 1989
Western Mexico, Samuel Espinoza-Venegas, *cons.* 1981, *apptd* 1983

CHURCH OF THE PROVINCE OF MYANMAR

ARCHBISHOP OF PROVINCE, The Most Revd Andrew Mya Han (Bishop of Yangon), *cons.* 1988, *apptd* 1988

BISHOPS
Hpa'an, Daniel Hoi Kyin, *cons.* 1992, *apptd* 1992
Mandalay, Andrew Hla Aung, *cons.* 1988, *apptd* 1988
Myitkyina, John Shan Lum, *cons.* 1994, *apptd* 1994
Sittwe, Barnabas Theaung Hawi, *cons.* 1978, *apptd* 1980
Toungoo, Saw (John) Wilme, *cons.* 1994, *apptd* 1994
Yangon (Rangoon), *see* above

CHURCH OF THE PROVINCE OF NIGERIA

ARCHBISHOP OF PROVINCE, The Most Revd Joseph Adetiloye (Bishop of Lagos), *apptd* 1991

BISHOPS
Aba, A. O. Iwuagwu, *apptd* 1985
Abuja, Peter J. Akinola, *apptd* 1989
Akoko, J. O. K. Olowokure, *apptd* 1986
Akure, Emmanuel B. Gbonigi, *apptd* 1983
Asaba, Roland N. C. Nwosu, *apptd* 1977
Awka, Maxwell S. C. Anikwenwa, *apptd* 1987
Bauchi, Emmanuel O. Chukwuma, *apptd* 1990
Benin, Peter Onekpe

Calabar, W. G. Ekprikpo
Damaturu, Daniel Abu Yisa
Egba-Abeokuta, Matthew O. Owadayo
Egbado, Timothy I. O. Bolaji
Egbu, Emmanuel Iheagwam
Ekiti, C. A. Akinbola, *apptd* 1986
Enugu, Gideon N. Otubelu, *apptd* 1969
Ibadan, Gideon I. Olajide, *apptd* 1988
Ife, Gabriel B. Oloniyo
Ijebu, Abraham O. Olowoyo, *apptd* 1990
Ijebu Remo, E. O. I. Ogundana, *apptd* 1984
Ikale-Ilaje, J. Akin Omoyajowo
Ilesa, E. A. Ademowo, *apptd* 1989
Jalingo, Tanimu Samari
Jos, B. A. Kwashi
Kabba, S. O. Oyelade
Kaduna, Titus Ogbonyomi, *apptd* 1975
Kafanchan, William Diya, *apptd* 1990
Kano, B. O. Omosebi, *apptd* 1990
Katsina, J. S. Kwasu, *apptd* 1990
Kebbi, Edmund E. Akanya
Kwara, Jeremiah O. A. Fabuluje
Lagos, see above, *apptd* 1985
Lokoja, George Bako
Maiduguri, E. K. Mani, *apptd* 1990
Makurdi, Nathan N. Nyom
Mbaise, Cyril Chukwka Anyanwu
Minna, Nathaniel Yisa, *apptd* 1990
The Niger, Jonathan A. Onyemelukwe, *apptd* 1975
Niger Delta, Gabriel H. Pepple
Nnewi, G. I. N. Okpala
Nsukka, Jonah Ilonuba
Oke-Osun, Abraham O. Awoson
Okigwe North, Alfred Nwaizuzu
Okigwe South, Bennett Okoro
Ondo, Samuel O. Aderin, *apptd* 1981
Orlu, Samuel C. N. Ebo, *apptd* 1984
Osun, Seth O. Fagbemi, *apptd* 1987
Oturkpo, Ityobee Ugede
Owerri, Benjamin C. Nwankiti, *apptd* 1968
Owo, Peter A. Adebiyi
Sabongida Ora, Albert A. Agbaje
Sokoto, J. A. Idowu-Fearon, *apptd* 1990
Ukwa, Uju Obinya
Umuahia, Ngochukwe U. Ezuoke
Uyo, Ebenezar E. Nglass
Warri, Nathaniel Enuku
Yola, Chris O. Efobi, *apptd* 1990

ANGLICAN CHURCH OF PAPUA NEW GUINEA

ARCHBISHOP OF PROVINCE, The Most Revd James Ayong (Bishop of Aipo Rongo), *cons.* 1995, *elected* 1996

BISHOPS
Aipo Rongo, see above, *elected* 1995
Dogura, Tevita Talanoa, *cons.* 1992, *elected* 1992
New Guinea Islands, Michael Hough, *cons.* 1996, *elected* 1996
Popondota, Reuben Tariambari, *cons.* 1995, *elected* 1994
Port Moresby, vacant

EPISCOPAL CHURCH IN THE PHILIPPINES

PRIME BISHOP, The Most Revd Ignacio C. Soliba, *cons.* 1990, *apptd* 1997

BISHOPS
Central Philippines, Benjamin G. Botengan, *cons.* 1996, *apptd* 1996
North Central Philippines, Joel A. Pachao, *cons.* 1993, *apptd* 1993
Northern Luzon, Renato M. Abibico, *cons.* 1997, *apptd* 1997
Northern Philippines, Miguel P. Yamoyam (*Suffragan Bishop-in-Charge*), *cons.* 1994
Southern Philippines, James B. Manguramas, *cons.* 1993, *apptd* 1993

CHURCH OF THE PROVINCE OF RWANDA

ARCHBISHOP OF PROVINCE, vacant

BISHOPS
Butare, Venuste Mutiganda
Byumba, Onesphore Rwaje
Cyangugu, Kennedy Barham
Kibungo, Prudence Ngarambe
Kigali, Kolini Mboni
Kigeme, Norman Kayumba
Shyira, John Rucyahana
Shyogwe, Jered Kalimba

CHURCH OF THE PROVINCE OF SOUTHERN AFRICA

Metropolitan
Archbishop of Cape Town, The Most Revd Winston H. N. Ndungane, *cons.* 1991, *trans.* 1996

BISHOPS
Bloemfontein, Patrick Glover, *cons.* 1994, *elected* 1997
Christ the King, Peter J. Lee, *cons.* 1990, *elected* 1990
George, Derek G. Damant, *cons.* 1985, *elected* 1985
Grahamstown, David P. H. Russell, *cons.* 1986, *trans.* 1987
Johannesburg, Duncan Buchanan, *cons.* 1986, *elected* 1986
Kimberley and Kuruman, Itumeleng B. Moseki, *cons.* 1996, *elected* 1996
Klerksdorp, David Nkwe, *cons.* 1990, *elected* 1990
Lebombo, Dinis S. Sengulane, *cons.* 1976, *elected* 1976
Lesotho, vacant
Namibia, James H. Kauluma, *cons.* 1978, *elected* 1981
Natal, Michael Nuttall, *cons.* 1975, *trans.* 1982
Niassa, Paulino T. Manhique, *cons.* 1986, *elected* 1986
Port Elizabeth, Eric Pike, *cons.* 1989, *trans.* 1993
Pretoria, Richard A. Kraft, *cons.* 1982, *elected* 1982
St Helena, John H. G. Ruston, *cons.* 1985, *trans.* 1991
St John's, Jacob Z. Dlamini, *cons.* 1980, *elected* 1985
St Mark the Evangelist, Rollo P. J. Le Feuvre, *cons.* 1987, *elected* 1987
South-Eastern Transvaal, David A. Beetge, *cons.* 1990, *elected* 1990
Swaziland, Lawrence Zulu, *cons.* 1975, *trans.* 1993
Umzimvubu, Geoffrey F. Davies, *cons.* 1987, *elected* 1991
Zululand, Anthony Mdletshe, *cons.* 1993, *elected* 1997

Order of Ethiopia, Sigqibo Dwane, *cons.* 1983, *apptd* 1983

ANGLICAN CHURCH OF THE SOUTHERN CONE OF AMERICA

PRESIDING BISHOP, Rt. Revd Maurice Sinclair (Bishop of Northern Argentina), *cons.* 1990

BISHOPS
Argentina, David Leake, *cons.* 1969, *apptd* 1990
Bolivia, Gregory Venables, *cons.* 1993
Chile, Colin Bazley, *cons.* 1969, *apptd* 1977
Northern Argentina, see above, *apptd* 1990
Paraguay, John Ellison, *cons.* 1988, *apptd* 1988
Peru and Bolivia, vacant
Uruguay, Harold Godfrey, *cons.* 1986, *apptd* 1986

PROVINCE OF THE EPISCOPAL CHURCH OF THE SUDAN

ARCHBISHOP OF PROVINCE, The Most Revd Benjamin W. Yugusuk (Bishop of Juba)

BISHOPS
Bor, Nathaniel Garang
Cueibet, Ruben M. Makoi
El Obeil, vacant
Juba, see above
Kaduguli, Peter El Birish
Kajo-keji, Manaseh B. Dawidi
Khartoum, Bulus Idris Tia
Lainya, Eliaba L. Menasona
Lui, Ephraim Natana
Malakal, Kedekia Mabior
Maridi, Joseph Marona
Mundri, Dr Eluzai G. Munda
Port Sudan, vacant
Rajaf, Michael S. Lugor
Renk, Daniel Deng
Rokon, Francis Loyo
Rumbek, Gabriel R. Jur
Torit, Wilson A. Ogwok
Wau, Henery Riak
Yambio, Daniel Zindo, *cons.* 1984, *apptd* 1984
Yei, Seme L. Solomone
Yirol, Benjamin Mangar

CHURCH OF THE PROVINCE OF TANZANIA

ARCHBISHOP OF PROVINCE, The Most Revd John A. Ramadhani (Bishop of Zanzibar and Tanga), *cons.* 1980, *apptd* 1984

BISHOPS
Central Tanganyika, Godfrey Mhogolo, *cons.* 1989, *apptd* 1989
Dar es Salaam, Basil Sambano, *cons.* 1992, *apptd* 1992
Kagera, Edwin Nyamubi, *cons.* 1993, *apptd* 1993
Mara, Hilkia Omindo, *cons.* 1994, *apptd* 1994
Masasi, Patrick Mwachiko, *cons.* 1996, *apptd* 1996
Morogoro, Dudley Mageni, *cons.* 1987, *apptd* 1987
Mount Kilimanjaro, Simon Makundi, *cons.* 1991, *apptd* 1991
Mpwapwa, Simon Chiwanga, *cons.* 1991, *apptd* 1991
Rift Valley, Alpha Mohamed, *cons.* 1982, *apptd* 1991
Ruaha, Donald Mtetemela, *cons.* 1982, *apptd* 1990
Ruvuma, Stanford Shauri, *cons.* 1989, *apptd* 1989
South-West Tanganyika, vacant

Tabora, Francis Ntiruka, *cons.* 1989, *apptd* 1989
Victoria Nyanza, John Changae, *cons.* 1993, *apptd* 1993
Western Tanganyika, Gerard Mpango, *cons.* 1983, *apptd* 1983
Zanzibar and Tanga, see above

CHURCH OF THE PROVINCE OF UGANDA

ARCHBISHOP OF PROVINCE, The Most Revd Livingstone Mpalanyi-Nkoyoyo (Bishop of Kampala)

BISHOPS
Bukedi, Dr Nicodemus Okille, *apptd* 1984
Bunyoro-Kitara, Wilson N. Turumanya
Busoga, vacant
Central Buganda, George Sinabulya
East Ankole, Elisha Kyamugambi, *cons.* 1992, *apptd* 1992
Kampala, see above
Karamoja, Peter L. Lomongin, *apptd* 1987
Kigezi, George Katwesigye
Kinkizi, John Ntegyereize
Kitgum, Macleord B. Ochola II
Lango, Melchizedek Otim, *apptd* 1976
Luwero, Evans Kisekka
Madi and West Nile, Dr Enoch Drati
Mbale, Israel W. Koboyi, *cons.* 1992, *apptd* 1992
Mityana, Wilson Mutebi, *apptd* 1977
Muhabura, Ernest M. Shalita, *cons.* 1990, *apptd* 1990
Mukono, Dr Michael Senyimba
Namirembe, Samuel B. Sekkadde
Nebbi, Henry L. Orombi, *cons.* 1993, *apptd* 1993
North Kigezi, John Kahigwa
North Mbale, Peter B. Mudonyi, *cons.* 1992, *apptd* 1992
Northern Uganda, vacant
Ruwenzori, Dr Eustace Kamanyire, *apptd* 1981
Soroti, Geresom Ilukor, *apptd* 1976
South Ruwenzori, Zebidee K. Masereka
West Ankole, William Magambo
West Buganda, vacant

EPISCOPAL CHURCH IN THE USA

PRESIDING BISHOP AND PRIMATE, Most Revd Edmond Lee Browning, DD, *cons.* 1968, *apptd* 1986

BISHOPS
Province I
Connecticut, Clarence Coleridge, *cons.* 1981, *apptd* 1994
Maine, Edward C. Chalfant
Massachusetts, Thomas Shaw, *cons.* 1994, *apptd* 1995
New Hampshire, Douglas E. Theuner, *cons.* 1986, *apptd* 1986
Rhode Island, Geralyn Wolfe, *cons.* 1996, *apptd* 1996
Vermont, Mary A. Mcleod, *cons.* 1993, *apptd* 1993
Western Massachusetts, Gordon P. Scruton

Province II
Albany, David S. Ball, *cons.* 1984, *apptd* 1984
Central New York, David B. Joslin, *cons.* 1991, *apptd* 1992
Europe, Convocation of American Churches in, Jeffery Rowthorn, *cons.* 1987
*Haiti, Zaché Duracin, *cons.* 1993, *apptd* 1994
Long Island, Orris Walker, *cons.* 1988, *apptd* 1991
New Jersey, Joe M. Doss, *cons.* 1993, *apptd* 1993
New York, Richard Grein, *cons.* 1981, *apptd* 1989

---

*missionary diocese

Newark, John S. Spong, *cons.* 1976, *apptd* 1979
Rochester, William G. Burrill, *cons.* 1984, *apptd* 1984
*Virgin Islands, Telésforo Isaac (*Bishop-in-charge*), *cons.* 1972
Western New York, David C. Bowman, *cons.* 1986, *apptd* 1987

Province III

Bethlehem, vacant
Central Pennsylvania, Michael W. Creighton, *cons.* 1995
Delaware, C. Cabell Tennis, *cons.* 1986, *apptd* 1986
Easton, Martin G. Townsend, *cons.* 1992, *apptd* 1993
Maryland, Robert W. Ihloff, *cons.* 1995
North-Western Pennsylvania, Robert D. Rowley jun., *cons.* 1989, *apptd* 1991
Pennsylvania, Charles E. Bennison
Pittsburgh, Alden M. Hathaway, *cons.* 1981, *apptd* 1983
Southern Virginia, Frank Vest jun., *cons.* 1985, *apptd* 1991
South-Western Virginia, A. Heath Light, *cons.* 1979, *apptd* 1979
Virginia, Peter J. Lee, *cons.* 1984, *apptd* 1985
Washington, Ronald Haines, *cons.* 1986, *apptd* 1990
West Virginia, John H. Smith, *cons.* 1989, *apptd* 1989

Province IV

Alabama, Robert O. Miller, *cons.* 1988, *apptd* 1988
Atlanta, Frank K. Allen, *cons.* 1988, *apptd* 1989
Central Florida, John Howe, *cons.* 1989, *apptd* 1990
Central Gulf Coast, Charles F. Duvall, *cons.* 1981, *apptd* 1981
East Carolina, Sidney Saunders, *cons.* 1979, *apptd* 1983
East Tennessee, Robert G. Tharp, *cons.* 1991, *apptd* 1992
Florida, Stephen H. Jecko, *cons.* 1994, *apptd* 1994
Georgia, Henry Louttit, *cons.* 1994, *apptd* 1994
Kentucky, Edwin F. Gulick, *cons.* 1964
Lexington, Don A. Wimberley, *cons.* 1984, *apptd* 1985
Louisiana, James B. Brown, *cons.* 1976, *apptd* 1976
Mississippi, Alfred C. Marble jun., *cons.* 1991, *apptd* 1993
North Carolina, James G. Gloster, *apptd* 1996
South Carolina, Edward L. Salmon jun., *cons.* 1990, *apptd* 1990
South-East Florida, Calvin O. Schofield jun., *cons.* 1979, *apptd* 1980
South-West Florida, Roger Harris, *cons.* 1989, *apptd* 1989
Tennessee, Bertram N. Herlong, *cons.* 1993, *apptd* 1993
Upper South Carolina, Dorsey F. Henderson, *cons.* 1995
West Tennessee, James Coleman, *cons.* 1993
Western North Carolina, Robert Johnson, *cons* 1989, *apptd* 1990

Province V

Chicago, Frank T. Griswold III, *cons.* 1985, *apptd* 1987
Eastern Michigan, Edwin M. Leidel jun., *cons.* 1996, *apptd* 1996
Eau Claire, William C. Wantland, *cons.* 1980, *apptd* 1980
Fond Du Lac, Russell E. Jacobus, *cons.* 1994, *apptd* 1994
Indianapolis, Edward W. Jones, *cons.* 1977, *apptd* 1977
Michigan, R. Stewart Wood, *cons.* 1990, *apptd* 1990
Milwaukee, Roger J. White, *cons.* 1984, *apptd* 1985
Missouri, Hays Rockwell, *cons.* 1991, *apptd* 1993
Northern Indiana, Francis C. Gray, *cons.* 1986, *apptd* 1987
Northern Michigan, Thomas K. Ray, *cons.* 1982, *apptd* 1982
Ohio, J. Clark Grew II, *cons.* 1994, *apptd* 1994
Quincy, Keith L. Ackerman, *cons.* 1994, *apptd* 1994
Southern Ohio, Herbert Thompson jun., *cons.* 1988, *apptd* 1992
Springfield, Peter H. Beckwith, *cons.* 1991
Western Michigan, Edward L. Lee jun., *cons.* 1989, *apptd* 1989

Province VI

Colorado, William Winterrowd, *cons.* 1991, *apptd* 1991
Iowa, C. Christopher Epting, *cons.* 1988, *apptd* 1988
Minnesota, James L. Jelinek, *cons.* 1993, *apptd* 1993
Montana, Charles I. Jones, *cons.* 1986, *apptd* 1986

Nebraska, James E. Krotz, *cons.* 1989, *apptd* 1989
*North Dakota, Andrew H. Fairfield, *cons.* 1990, *apptd* 1990
South Dakota, Creighton Robertson, *cons.* 1994, *apptd* 1994
Wyoming, vacant

Province VII

Arkansas, Larry Maze, *cons.* 1994, *apptd* 1994
Dallas, James H. Stanton, *cons.* 1993, *apptd* 1993
Fort Worth, Jack L. Iker, *cons.* 1993, *apptd* 1994
Kansas, William E. Smalley, *cons.* 1989, *apptd* 1989
North-West Texas, Sam B. Hulsey, *cons.* 1980, *apptd* 1980
Oklahoma, Robert M. Moody, *cons.* 1988, *apptd* 1989
Rio Grande, Terence Kelshaw, *cons.* 1989, *apptd* 1989
Texas, Claude E. Payne, *cons.* 1994
West Missouri, John C. Buchanan, *cons.* 1989, *apptd* 1989
West Texas, James E. Folts, *cons.* 1996, *apptd* 1996
Western Kansas, Vernon E. Strickland, *cons.* 1995
Western Louisiana, Robert Hargrove jun., *cons.* 1989, *apptd* 1990

Province VIII

Alaska, vacant
Arizona, Robert R. Shahan, *cons.* 1992, *apptd* 1993
California, William E. Swing, *cons.* 1979, *apptd* 1980
El Camino Real, Richard L. Shimpfy, *cons.* 1990, *apptd* 1990
Eastern Oregon, Rustin R. Kimsey, *cons.* 1980, *apptd* 1980
Hawaii, vacant
Idaho, John S. Thornton, *cons.* 1990, *apptd* 1990
Los Angeles, Frederick L. Borsch, *cons.* 1988, *apptd* 1988
*Navajoland Area Mission, Steven T. Plummer, *cons.* 1989, *apptd* 1989
Nevada, Stewart C. Zabriskie, *cons.* 1986, *apptd* 1986
Northern California, Jerry A. Lamb, *cons.* 1991, *apptd* 1992
Olympia, Vincent W. Warner jun., *cons.* 1989, *apptd* 1990
Oregon, Robert L. Ladehoff, *cons.* 1985, *apptd* 1986
San Diego, Gethin B. Hughes, *cons.* 1992, *apptd* 1992
San Joaquin, John-David Schofield, *cons.* 1988, *apptd* 1989
Spokane, Frank J. Terry, *cons.* 1990, *apptd* 1991
*Taiwan, John C. T. Chien, *cons.* 1988, *apptd* 1988
Utah, George E. Bates, *cons.* 1986, *apptd* 1986

Province IX

*Central Ecuador, Neptali L. Moreno, *cons.* 1990, *apptd* 1990
*Colombia, Bernardo Merino-Botero, *cons.* 1979, *apptd* 1979
*Dominican Republic, Julio C. Holguin, *apptd* 1991
*Guatemala, Armando Guerra-Soria, *cons.* 1982, *apptd* 1982
*Honduras, Leopold Frade, *cons.* 1984, *apptd* 1984
*Nicaragua, Sturdie W. Downs, *cons.* 1985, *apptd* 1985
*Panama, Clarence W. Hayes-Dewar, *cons.* 1995
*El Salvador, Martin Barahona, *cons.* 1992, *apptd* 1992

Extra-Provincial

Costa Rica, Cornelius J. Wilson, *cons.* 1978, *apptd* 1978
Puerto Rico, David Alvarez, *cons.* 1987, *apptd* 1987
Venezuela, Orlando Guerrero, *cons.* 1995

CHURCH OF THE PROVINCE OF WEST AFRICA

ARCHBISHOP OF PROVINCE, The Most Revd Robert Okine (Bishop of Koforidua), *cons.* 1981, *apptd* 1993

BISHOPS
Accra, Justice O. Akrofi
Bo, Samuel S. Gbonda, *cons.* 1994, *apptd* 1994
Cape Coast, Kobina Quashie, *apptd* 1992
Freetown, Julius O. P. Lynch
Gambia, Solomon T. Johnson, *cons* 1990, *apptd* 1990

Guinea, vacant
Koforidua, see above, *apptd* 1981
Kumasi, Edmund Yeboah, *cons.* 1985, *apptd* 1985
Liberia, Edward Neufville
Sekondi, Theophilus Annobil, *cons.* 1981, *apptd* 1981
Sunyani/Tamale, Joseph K. Dadson, *cons.* 1981, *apptd* 1981

CHURCH IN THE PROVINCE OF THE WEST INDIES

ARCHBISHOP OF PROVINCE, The Most Revd Orland Lindsay (Bishop of North-Eastern Caribbean and Aruba), *cons.* 1970, *apptd* 1986

BISHOPS
Barbados, Rufus Broome
Belize, Sylvestre D. Romero-Palma
Guyana, Randolph George, *cons.* 1976, *apptd* 1980
Jamaica, Neville de Souza, *cons.* 1973, *apptd* 1979
Nassau and the Bahamas, Michael Eldon, CMG, *cons.* 1971, *apptd* 1972
North-Eastern Caribbean and Aruba, see above
Trinidad and Tobago, Rawle Douglin
Windward Islands, Sehon Goodridge

CHURCH OF THE PROVINCE OF CONGO (ZAÏRE)

ARCHBISHOP OF PROVINCE, The Most Revd Byankya Njojo (Bishop of Boga-Congo), *cons.* 1980, *apptd* 1992

BISHOPS
Boga-Congo, see above, *apptd* 1980
Bukavu, Balufuga Dirokpa, *cons.* 1982, *apptd* 1982
Kisangani, Sylvestre Tibafa Mugera, *cons.* 1980, *apptd* 1980
Maniema, Massimango Katanda, *apptd* 1997
Nord-Kivu, Methusela Munzenda, *cons.* 1992, *apptd* 1992
Shaba, vacant

OTHER CHURCHES AND EXTRA-PROVINCIAL DIOCESES

ANGLICAN CHURCH OF BERMUDA, The Rt. Revd Ewen Ratteray, *apptd* 1996
EPISCOPAL CHURCH OF CUBA, The Rt. Revd Jorge Perera Hurtado, *apptd* 1995
HONG KONG AND MACAO, The Rt. Revd Peter Kwong
KUCHING, The Rt. Revd Made Katib, *apptd* 1995
LUSITANIAN CHURCH (*Portuguese Episcopal Church*), The Rt. Revd Fernando da Luz Soares, *apptd* 1971
SPANISH REFORMED EPISCOPAL CHURCH, The Rt. Revd Carlos Lozano Lopez, *apptd* 1995

The Church of Scotland

The Church of Scotland is the established (i.e. state) church of Scotland. The Church is Reformed and evangelical in doctrine, and presbyterian in constitution. In 1560 the jurisdiction of the Roman Catholic Church in Scotland was abolished and the first assembly of the Church of Scotland ratified the Confession of Faith, drawn up by a committee including John Knox. In 1592 Parliament passed an Act guaranteeing the liberties of the Church and its presbyterian government. James VI (James I of England) and later Stuart monarchs attempted to restore episcopacy, but a presbyterian church was finally restored in 1690 and secured by the Act of Settlement (1690) and the Act of Union (1707). The Free Church of Scotland was formed in 1843 in a dispute over patronage and state interference; in 1900 most of its ministers joined with the United Presbyterian Church (formed in 1847) to form the United Free Church of Scotland. In 1929 most of this body rejoined the Church of Scotland to form the united Church of Scotland.

The Church of Scotland is presbyterian in its organization, i.e. based on a hierarchy of councils of ministers and elders and, since 1990, of members of a diaconate. At local level the kirk session consists of the parish minister and ruling elders. At district level the presbyteries, of which there are 47, consist of all the ministers in the district, one ruling elder from each congregation, and those members of the diaconate who qualify for membership. The General Assembly is the supreme authority, and is presided over by a Moderator chosen annually by the Assembly. The Sovereign, if not present in person, is represented by a Lord High Commissioner who is appointed each year by the Crown.

The Church of Scotland has about 700,000 members, 1,200 ministers and 1,600 churches. There are about 100 ministers and other personnel working overseas.

Lord High Commissioner (1997), The Lord Macfarlane of Bearsden
Moderator of the General Assembly (1997), The Rt. Revd A. McDonald
Principal Clerk, Revd F. A. J. Macdonald
Depute Clerk, Revd M. A. MacLean
Procurator, A. Dunlop, QC
Law Agent and Solicitor of the Church, Mrs J. S. Wilson
Parliamentary Agent, I. McCulloch (*London*)
General Treasurer, D. F. Ross
CHURCH OFFICE, 121 George Street, Edinburgh EH2 4YN. Tel: 0131-225 5722

PRESBYTERIES AND CLERKS
Edinburgh, Revd W. P. Graham
West Lothian, Revd D. Shaw
Lothian, J. D. McCulloch
Melrose and Peebles, Revd J. H. Brown
Duns, Revd A. C. D. Cartwright
Jedburgh, Revd A. D. Reid
Annandale and Eskdale, Revd C. B. Haston
Dumfries and Kirkcudbright, Revd G. M. A. Savage
Wigtown and Stranraer, Revd D. Dutton
Ayr, Revd J. Crichton
Irvine and Kilmarnock, Revd C. G. F. Brockie
Ardrossan, Revd D. Broster
Lanark, Revd I. D. Cunningham
Paisley, Revd D. Kay
Greenock, Revd D. Mill
Glasgow, Revd A. Cunningham
Hamilton, Revd J. H. Wilson
Dumbarton, Revd D. P. Munro
South Argyll, M. A. J. Gossip
Dunoon, Revd R. Samuel
Lorn and Mull, Revd W. Hogg
Falkirk, Revd D. E. McClements
Stirling, Revd B. W. Dunsmore
Dunfermline, Revd W. E. Farquhar
Kirkcaldy, Revd B. L. Tomlinson
St Andrews, Revd J. W. Patterson
Dunkeld and Meigle, Revd A. F. Chisholm
Perth, Revd M. Ward

Dundee, Revd J. A. Roy
Angus, Revd R. J. Ramsay
Aberdeen, Revd A. Douglas
Kincardine and Deeside, Revd J. W. S. Brown
Gordon, Revd I. U. Thomson
Buchan, Revd R. Neilson
Moray, Revd D. J. Ferguson
Abernethy, Revd J. A. I. MacEwan
Inverness, Revd A. S. Younger
Lochaber, Revd A. Ramsay
Ross, Revd R. M. MacKinnon
Sutherland, Revd J. L. Goskirk
Caithness, Revd M. G. Mappin
Lochcarron/Skye, Revd A. I. Macarthur
Uist, Revd A. P. J. Varwell
Lewis, Revd T. S. Sinclair
Orkney (Finstown), Revd T. Hunt
Shetland (Lerwick), Revd N. R. Whyte
England (London), Revd W. A. Cairns
Europe (Portugal), Revd J. W. McLeod

The minimum stipend of a minister in the Church of Scotland in 1997 was £15,816

The Roman Catholic Church

The Roman Catholic Church is one world-wide Christian Church acknowledging as its head the Bishop of Rome, known as the Pope (Father). The Pope is held to be the successor of St Peter and thus invested with the power which was entrusted to St Peter by Jesus Christ. A direct line of succession is therefore claimed from the earliest Christian communities. Papal authority over the doctrine and jurisdiction of the Church in western Europe developed early and was unrivalled after the split with the Eastern Orthodox Church until the Protestant Reformation in the 16th century. With the fall of the Roman Empire the Pope also became an important political leader. His temporal power is now limited to the 107 acres of the Vatican City State.

The Pope exercises spiritual authority over the Church with the advice and assistance of the Sacred College of Cardinals, the supreme council of the Church. He is also advised about the concerns of the Church locally by his ambassadors, who liaise with the Bishops' Conference in each country.

In addition to advising the Pope, those members of the Sacred College of Cardinals who are under the age of 80 also elect a successor following the death of a Pope. The assembly of the Cardinals at the Vatican for the election of a new Pope is known as the Conclave in which, in complete seclusion, the Cardinals elect by a secret ballot; a two-thirds majority is necessary before the vote can be accepted as final. When a Cardinal receives the necessary votes, the Dean of the Sacred College formally asks him if he will accept election and the name by which he wishes to be known. On his acceptance of the office the Conclave is dissolved and the First Cardinal Deacon announces the election to the assembled crowd in St Peter's Square. On the first Sunday or Holyday following the election, the new Pope assumes the pontificate at High Mass in St Peter's Square. A new pontificate is dated from the assumption of the pontificate.

The number of cardinals was fixed at 70 by Pope Sixtus V in 1586, but has been steadily increased since the pontificate of John XXIII and now stands at 150 (as at end June 1997).

The Roman Catholic Church universally and the Vatican City State are run by the Curia, which is made up of the Secretariat of State, the Sacred Council for the Public Affairs of the Church, and various congregations, secretariats and tribunals assisted by commissions and offices. The congregations are permanent commissions for conducting the affairs of the Church and are made up of cardinals, one of whom occupies the office of prefect. Below the Secretariat of State and the congregations are the secretariats and tribunals, all of which are headed by cardinals. (The Curial cardinals are analagous to ministers in charge of government departments.)

The Vatican State has its own diplomatic service, with representatives known as nuncios. Papal nuncios with full diplomatic recognition are given precedence over all other ambassadors to the country to which they are appointed; where precedence is not recognized the Papal representative is known as a pro-nuncio. Where the representation is only to the local churches and not to the government of a country, the Papal representative is known as an apostolic delegate. The Roman Catholic Church has an estimated 890.9 million adherents world-wide.

SOVEREIGN PONTIFF

His Holiness Pope John Paul II (Karol Wojtyla), *born* Wadowice, Poland, 18 May 1920; *ordained priest* 1946; *appointed Archbishop* of Krakow 1964; *created Cardinal* 1967; *assumed pontificate* 16 October 1978

SECRETARIAT OF STATE

Secretary of State, HE Cardinal Angelo Sodano
First Section (General Affairs), Mgr G. Re (Archbishop of Vescovio)
Second Section (Relations with other states), Mgr J. L. Tauran (Archbishop of Telepte)

BISHOPS' CONFERENCE

The Roman Catholic Church in England and Wales is governed by the Bishops' Conference, membership of which includes the Diocesan Bishops, the Apostolic Exarch of the Ukrainians, the Bishop of the Forces and the Auxiliary Bishops. The Conference is headed by the President (Cardinal Basil Hume, Archbishop of Westminster) and Vice-President. There are five departments, each with an episcopal chairman: the Department for Christian Life and Worship (the Archbishop of Southwark), the Department for Mission and Unity (the Bishop of Arundel and Brighton), the Department for Catholic Education and Formation (the Bishop of Leeds), the Department for Christian Responsibility and Citizenship (the Bishop of Plymouth), and the Department for International Affairs.

The Bishops' Standing Committee, made up of all the Archbishops and the chairman of each of the above departments, has general responsibility for continuity and policy between the plenary sessions of the Conference. It prepares the Conference agenda and implements its decisions. It is serviced by a General Secretariat. There are also agencies and consultative bodies affiliated to the Conference.

The Bishops' Conference of Scotland has as its president Archbishop Winning of Glasgow and is the permanently constituted assembly of the Bishops of Scotland. To promote its work, the Conference establishes various agencies which have an advisory function in relation to the Conference. The more important of these agencies are called Commissions and each one has a Bishop President who, with the other members of the Commissions, are appointed by the Conference.

The Irish Episcopal Conference has as its acting president Archbishop Connell of Dublin. Its membership comprises all the Archbishops and Bishops of Ireland and it appoints various Commissions to assist it in its work. There are three types of Commissions: (a) those made up of lay and clerical members chosen for their skills and experience, and staffed by full-time expert secretariats; (b) Commissions whose members are selected from existing institutions and whose services are supplied on a part-time basis; and (c) Commissions of Bishops only.

The Roman Catholic Church in Britain and Ireland has an estimated 8,992,000 members, 11 archbishops, 67 bishops, 11,260 priests, and 8,588 churches and chapels open to the public.

Bishops' Conferences secretariats:

ENGLAND AND WALES, 39 Eccleston Square, London SW1V 1PD. Tel: 0171-630 8220. *General Secretary*, The Rt. Revd Arthur Roche

SCOTLAND, Candida Casa, 8 Corsehill Road, Ayr, Scotland KA7 2ST. Tel: 01292-256750. *General Secretary*, The Rt. Revd Maurice Taylor, Bishop of Galloway

IRELAND, Iona, 65 Newry Road, Dundalk, Co. Louth. *Executive Secretary*, Revd Hugh G. Connelly

---

GREAT BRITAIN

APOSTOLIC NUNCIO TO GREAT BRITAIN
The Most Revd Pablo Puente, 54 Parkside, London SW19 5NE. Tel: 0181-946 1410

ENGLAND AND WALES

THE MOST REVD ARCHBISHOPS
Westminster, HE Cardinal Basil Hume, *cons.* 1976
  Auxiliaries, Victor Guazzelli, *cons.* 1970; Vincent Nichols, *cons.* 1992; James J. O'Brien, *cons.* 1977; Patrick O'Donoghue, *cons.* 1993
  Clergy, 862
  Archbishop's Residence, Archbishop's House, Ambrosden Avenue, London SW1P 1QJ. Tel: 0171-834 4717
Birmingham, Maurice Couve de Murville, *cons.* 1982, *apptd* 1982
  Auxiliaries, Terence Brain, *cons.* 1991; Philip Pargeter, *cons.* 1989
  Clergy, 527
  Diocesan Curia, Cathedral House, St Chad's Queensway, Birmingham B4 6EX. Tel: 0121-236 5535
Cardiff, John A. Ward, *cons.* 1981, *apptd* 1983
  Clergy, 146
  Diocesan Curia, Archbishop's House, 41–43 Cathedral Road, Cardiff CF1 9HD. Tel: 01222-220411
Liverpool, Patrick Kelly, *cons.* 1984, *apptd* 1996
  Auxiliary, Vincent Malone, *cons.* 1989
  Clergy, 591
  Diocesan Curia, 152 Brownlow Hill, Liverpool L3 5RQ. Tel: 0151-709 4801
Southwark, Michael Bowen, *cons.* 1970, *apptd* 1977
  Auxiliaries, Charles Henderson, *cons.* 1972; Howard Tripp, *cons.* 1980; John Jukes, *cons.* 1980
  Clergy, 577
  Diocesan Curia, Archbishop's House, 150 St George's Road, London SE1 6HX. Tel: 0171-928 5592

THE RT. REVD BISHOPS
Arundel and Brighton, Cormac Murphy-O'Connor, *cons.* 1977. *Clergy,* 324. *Diocesan Curia,* Bishop's House, The Upper Drive, Hove, E. Sussex BN3 6NE. Tel: 01273-506387
Brentwood, Thomas McMahon, *cons.* 1980, *apptd* 1980. *Clergy,* 184. *Bishop's Office,* Cathedral House, Ingrave Road, Brentwood, Essex CM15 8AT. Tel: 01277-232266
Clifton, Mervyn Alexander, *cons.* 1972, *apptd* 1975. *Clergy,* 278. *Diocesan Curia,* Egerton Road, Bishopston, Bristol BS7 8HU. Tel: 0117-924 1378
East Anglia, Peter Smith, *cons.* 1995, *apptd* 1995. *Clergy,* 168. *Diocesan Curia,* The White House, 21 Upgate, Poringland, Norwich NR14 7SH. Tel: 01508-492202
Hallam, John Rawsthorne, *cons.* 1981, *apptd* 1997. *Clergy,* 105. *Bishop's Residence,* 'Quarters', Carsick Hill Way, Sheffield S10 3LT. Tel: 0114-230 9101
Hexham and Newcastle, Michael Ambrose Griffiths, *cons.* 1992. *Clergy,* 296. *Diocesan Curia,* Bishop's House, East Denton Hall, 800 West Road, Newcastle upon Tyne NE5 2BJ. Tel: 0191-228 0003
Lancaster, John Brewer, *cons.* 1971, *apptd* 1985. *Clergy,* 274. *Bishop's Residence,* Bishop's House, Cannon Hill, Lancaster LA1 5NG. Tel: 01524-32231
Leeds, David Konstant, *cons.* 1977, *apptd* 1985. *Clergy,* 275. *Diocesan Curia,* 7 St Marks Avenue, Leeds LS2 9BN. Tel: 0113-244 4788
Menevia (*Wales*), Daniel Mullins, *cons.* 1970, *apptd* 1987. *Clergy,* 68. *Diocesan Curia,* 115 Walter Road, Swansea SA1 5RE. Tel: 01792-644017
Middlesbrough, John Crowley, *cons.* 1986, *apptd* 1992. *Clergy,* 218. *Diocesan Curia,* 50A The Avenue, Linthorpe, Middlesbrough, Cleveland TS5 6QT. Tel: 01642-850505
  Auxiliary, Thomas O'Brien, *cons.* 1981
Northampton, Patrick Leo McCartie, *cons.* 1977, *apptd* 1990. *Clergy,* 170. *Diocesan Curia,* Bishop's House, Marriott Street, Northampton NN2 6AW. Tel: 01604-715635
Nottingham, James McGuinness, *cons.* 1972, *apptd* 1975. *Clergy,* 233. *Diocesan Curia,* Willson House, Derby Road, Nottingham NG1 5AW. Tel: 0115-953 9800
Plymouth, Christopher Budd, *cons.* 1986. *Clergy,* 186. *Diocesan Curia,* Vescourt, Hartley Road, Plymouth PL3 5LR. Tel: 01752-772950
Portsmouth, F. Crispian Hollis, *cons.* 1987, *apptd* 1989. *Clergy,* 285. *Bishop's Residence,* Bishop's House, Edinburgh Road, Portsmouth, Hants PO1 3HG. Tel: 01705-820894
Salford, vacant. *Clergy,* 432. *Diocesan Curia,* Cathedral House, 250 Chapel Street, Salford M3 5LL. Tel: 0161-834 9052
Shrewsbury, Brian Noble, *cons.* 1995, *apptd* 1995. *Clergy,* 237. *Diocesan Curia,* 2 Park Road South, Birkenhead, Merseyside L43 4UX. Tel: 0151-652 9855
Wrexham (*Wales*), Edwin Regan, *apptd* 1994. *Clergy,* 90. *Diocesan Curia,* Bishop's House, Sontley Road, Wrexham, Clwyd LL13 7EW. Tel: 01978-262726

SCOTLAND

THE MOST REVD ARCHBISHOPS
St Andrews and Edinburgh, Keith Patrick O'Brien, *cons.* 1985
  Clergy, 201
  Diocesan Curia, 106 Whitehouse Loan, Edinburgh EH9 1BD. Tel: 0131-452 8244
Glasgow, HE Cardinal Thomas Winning, *cons.* 1971, *apptd* 1974
  Clergy, 303
  Diocesan Curia, 196 Clyde Street, Glasgow G1 4JY. Tel: 0141-226 5898

The Rt. Revd Bishops
Aberdeen, Mario Conti, *cons.* 1977. *Clergy*, 58. *Bishop's Residence*, 156 King's Gate, Aberdeen AB2 6BR. Tel: 01224-319154
Argyll and the Isles, vacant. *Clergy*, 32. *Diocesan Curia*, St Mary's, Belford Road, Fort William, Inverness-shire PH33 6BT. Tel: 01397-706046
Dunkeld, Vincent Logan, *cons.* 1981. *Clergy*, 55. *Diocesan Curia*, 26 Roseangle, Dundee DD1 4LR. Tel: 01382-25453
Galloway, Maurice Taylor, *cons.* 1981. *Clergy*, 66. *Diocesan Curia*, 8 Corsehill Road, Ayr KA7 2ST. Tel: 01292-266750
Motherwell, Joseph Devine, *cons.* 1977, *apptd* 1983. *Clergy*, 180. *Diocesan Curia*, Coursington Road, Motherwell ML1 1PW. Tel: 01698-269114
Paisley, John A. Mone, *cons.* 1984, *apptd* 1988. *Clergy*, 95. *Diocesan Curia*, Cathedral House, 8 East Buchanan Street, Paisley, Renfrewshire PA1 1HS. Tel: 0141-889 3601

IRELAND

There is one hierarchy for the whole of Ireland. Several of the dioceses have territory partly in the Republic of Ireland and partly in Northern Ireland.

Apostolic Nuncio to Ireland
The Most Revd Giovanni Ceirano (titular Archbishop of Tigimma), 183 Navan Road, Dublin 7. Tel: 00 353 1-380577

The Most Revd Archbishops
Armagh, HE Cardinal Sean Brady, *cons.* 1993, *apptd* 1996
  Auxiliary, Gerard Clifford, *cons.* 1991
  Clergy, 183
  Diocesan Curia, Ara Coeli, Armagh BT61 7QY. Tel: 01861-522045
Cashel, Dermot Clifford, *cons.* 1986
  Clergy, 136
  Archbishop's Residence, Archbishop's House, Thurles, Co. Tipperary. Tel: 00 353 504-21512
Dublin, Desmond Connell, *cons.* 1988, *apptd* 1988
  Auxiliaries, Donal Murray, *cons.* 1982; Dermot O'Mahony, *cons.* 1975; James Moriarty, *cons.* 1992; Eamonn Walsh, *cons.* 1990; Desmond Williams, *cons.* 1985; Fiachra O'Ceallaigh, *cons* 1994; James Kavanagh, *cons.* 1996
  Clergy, 994
  Archbishop's Residence, Archbishop's House, Drumcondra, Dublin 9. Tel: 00 353 1-8373732
Tuam, Michael Neary, *cons.* 1992
  Clergy, 180
  Archbishop's Residence, Archbishop's House, Tuam, Co. Galway. Tel: 00 353 93-24166

The Most Revd Bishops
Achonry, Thomas Flynn, *cons.* 1975. *Clergy*, 62. *Bishop's Residence*, Bishop's House, Ballaghadaderreen, Co. Roscommon. Tel: 00 353 907-60021
Ardagh and Clonmacnois, Colm O'Reilly, *cons.* 1983. *Clergy*, 100. *Diocesan Office*, Bishop's House, St Michael's, Longford, Co. Longford. Tel: 00 353 43-46432
Clogher, Joseph Duffy, *cons.* 1979. *Clergy*, 108. *Bishop's Residence*, Bishop's House, Monaghan. Tel: 00 353 47-81019
Clonfert, Joseph Kirby, *cons.* 1988. *Clergy*, 71. *Bishop's Residence*, St Brendan's, Coorheen, Loughrea, Co. Galway. Tel: 00 353 91-41560
Cloyne, John Magee, *cons.* 1987. *Clergy*, 158. *Diocesan Centre*, Cobh, Co. Cork. Tel: 00 353 21-811430

Cork and Ross, vacant. *Clergy*, 338. *Diocesan Office*, Bishop's House, Redemption Road, Cork. Tel: 00 353 21-301717
  Auxiliary, John Buckley, *cons.* 1984
Derry, Seamus Hegarty, *cons.* 1984, *apptd* 1994. *Clergy*, 157. *Bishop's Residence*, Bishop's House, St Eugene's Cathedral, Derry BT48 9AP. Tel: 01504-262302
  Auxiliary, Francis Lagan, *cons.* 1988
Down and Connor, Patrick J. Walsh, *cons.* 1991. *Clergy*, 248. *Bishop's Residence*, Lisbreen, 73 Somerton Road, Belfast, Co. Antrim DT15 4DE. Tel: 01232-776185
  Auxiliaries, Anthony Farquhar, *cons.* 1983; Michael Dallat, *cons.* 1994
Dromore, Francis Brooks, *cons.* 1976. *Clergy*, 78. *Bishop's Residence*, Bishop's House, Violet Hill, Newry, Co. Down BT35 6PN. Tel: 01693-62444
Elphin, Christopher Jones, *cons.* 1994. *Clergy*, 101. *Bishop's Residence*, St Mary's, Sligo. Tel: 00 353 71-62670
Ferns, Brendon Comiskey, *cons.* 1980. *Clergy*, 161. *Bishop's Office*, Bishop's House, Summerhill, Wexford. Tel: 00 353 53-22177
Galway and Kilmacduagh, James McLoughlin, *cons.* 1993. *Clergy*, 90. *Diocesan Office*, The Cathedral, Galway. Tel: 00 353 91-63566
Kerry, William Murphy, *cons.* 1995. *Clergy*, 149. *Bishop's Residence*, Bishop's House, Killarney, Co. Kerry. Tel: 00 353 64-31168
Kildare and Leighlin, Laurence Ryan, *cons.* 1984. *Clergy*, 136. *Bishop's Residence*, Bishop's House, Carlow. Tel: 00 353 503-31102
Killala, Thomas Finnegan, *cons.* 1970. *Clergy*, 62. *Bishop's Residence*, Bishop's House, Ballina, Co. Mayo. Tel: 00 353 96-21518
Killaloe, William Walsh, *cons.* 1994. *Clergy*, 149. *Bishop's Residence*, Westbourne, Ennis, Co. Clare. Tel: 00 353 65-28638
Kilmore, Francis McKiernan, *cons.* 1972. *Coadjutor*, Leo O'Reilly. *Clergy*, 115. *Bishop's Residence*, Bishop's House, Cullies, Co. Cavan. Tel: 00 353 49-31496
Limerick, Donal Murray, *cons.* 1996. *Clergy*, 152. *Diocesan Offices*, 66 O'Connell Street, Limerick. Tel: 00 353 61-315856
Meath, Michael Smith, *cons.* 1984, *apptd* 1990. *Clergy*, 141. *Bishop's Residence*, Bishop's House, Dublin Road, Mullingar, Co. Westmeath. Tel: 00 353 44-48841
Ossory, Laurence Forristal, *cons.* 1980. *Clergy*, 111. *Bishop's Residence*, Sion House, Kilkenny. Tel: 00 353 56-62448
Raphoe, Philip Boyce, *cons.* 1994. *Clergy*, 96. *Bishop's Residence*, Ard Adhamhnáin, Letterkenny, Co. Donegal. Tel: 00 353 74-21208
Waterford and Lismore, William Lee, *cons.* 1993. *Clergy*, 130. *Bishop's Residence*, Woodleigh, Summerville Avenue, Waterford. Tel: 00 353 51-71432

RESIDENTIAL ARCHBISHOPRICS THROUGHOUT THE WORLD

Albania
Durrës-Tirana, Brok K. Mirdita
Shkodër, Frano Illia

Algeria
Algiers, Henri Teissier

Angola
Huambo, Francisco Viti
Luanda, HE Cardinal Alexandre do Nascimento
Lubango, Manuel Franklin da Costa
  Coadjutor, Zacarias Kamwenho

ARGENTINA
Bahia Blanca, Romulo Garcia
Buenos Aires, HE Cardinal Antonio Quarracino
Córdoba, HE Cardinal Raúl Francisco Primatesta
Corrientes, Domingo S. Castagna
La Plata, Carlos Galán
Mendoza, José M. Arancibia
Paraná, Estanislao Esteban Karlic
Resistencia, Carmelo J. Giaquinta
Rosario, Eduardo Vicente Miras
Salta, Moises J. Blanchoud
San Juan de Cuyo, Italo Severino Di Stefano
Santa Fe, Edgardo Gabriel Storni
Tucumán, Arsenio R. Casado

AUSTRALIA
Adelaide, Leonard Anthony Faulkner
Brisbane, John A. Bathersby
Canberra, Francis P. Carroll
Hobart, Joseph E. D'Arcy
Melbourne, George Pell
Perth, Barry J. Hickey
Sydney, HE Cardinal Edward B. Clancy

AUSTRIA
Salzburg, Georg Eder
Vienna, Christoph Schoenborn

BANGLADESH
Dhaka, Michael Rozario

BELARUS
Minsk-Mohilev Archdiocese, HE Cardinal Kazimierz Swiatek

BELGIUM
Malines-Bruxelles, HE Cardinal Godfried Danneels

BENIN
Cotonou, Isidore de Souzá

BOLIVIA
Cochabamba, Rene Fernandez Apaza
La Paz, Edmundo Abastoflor Montero
Santa Cruz de la Sierra, Julio T. Sandoval
Sucre, Jesus G. Pérez Rodriguez

BOSNIA-HERCEGOVINA
Vrhbosna, Sarajevo, HE Cardinal Vinko Puljić

BRAZIL
Aparacida, HE Cardinal Aloisio Lorscheider
Aracaju, Luciano José Cabral Duarte
Bélem do Pará, Vicente Joaquim Zico
Belo Horizonte, Serafim Fernandes de Araújo
Botucatu, Antonio M. Mucciolo
Brasilia, HE Cardinal Jose Freire Falcao
Campinas, Gilberto Pereira Lopes
Campo Grande, Vitorio Pavanello
Cascavel, Lucio I. Baumgaertner
Cuiaba, Bonifacio Piccinini
Curitiba, Pedro Antonio Fedalto
Diamantina, Geraldo Majelo Reis
Florianópolis, Eusebio Oscar Scheid
Fortaleza, Claudio Hummes
Goiania, Antonio Ribeiro de Oliveira
Juiz de Fora, Clovis Frainer
Londrina, Albano Bortoletto Cavallin
Maceió, Edvaldo G. Amaral
Manaus, Luiz S. Vieira
Mariana, Luciano Mendes de Almeida
Maringá, Jaime Luis Coelho
Natal, Heitor de Araujo Sales
Niteroi, Carlos A. Navarro
Olinda and Recife, José Cardoso Sobrinho

Palmas, Alberto T. Corrèa
Paraiba, Marcello Pinto Carvalheira
Porto Alegre, Altamiro Rossato
Porto Velho, José Martins da Silva
Pouso Alegre, Ricardo Pinto Filho
Ribeirão Preto, Arnaldo Ribeiro
São Luis do Maranhão, Paulo Eduardo de Andrade Ponte
São Paulo, HE Cardinal Paulo Evaristo Arns
São Salvador da Bahia, HE Cardinal Lucas Moreira Neves
São Sebastião do Rio de Janeiro, HE Cardinal Eugenio de Araújo Sales
Sorocaba, José Lambert
Teresina, Miguel F. Camara Filho
Uberaba, Aloisio R. Oppermann
Vitória, Silvestre L. Scandian

BURKINA FASO
Ouagadougou, Jean-Marie Untaani Compaore

BURUNDI
Gitega, vacant

CAMEROON
Bamenda, Paul Verdzekov
Douala, HE Cardinal Christian W. Tumi
Garoua, Antoine Ntalou
Yaoundé, Jean Zoa

CANADA
Edmonton, Joseph N. MacNeil
Gatineau-Hull, Roger Ebacher
Grouard-McLennon, Henri Goudreault
Halifax, Austin-Emile Burke
Keewatin-Le Pas, Peter Alfred Sutton
Kingston, Francis John Spence
Moncton, Ernest Leger
Montreal, HE Cardinal Jean-Claude Turcotte
Ottawa, Marcel A. Gervais
Quebec, Maurice Couture
Regina, Peter Mallon
Rimouski, Bertrand Blanchet
St Boniface, Antoine Hacault
St Johns, Newfoundland, James H. MacDonald
Sherbrooke, Andre Gaumond
Toronto, Aloysius Matthew Ambrosic
Vancouver, Adam J. Exner
Winnipeg, Leonard J. Wall; (Ukrainian rite), Michael Bzdel

CAUCASIA
Caucasia Apostolic Administrator, Giuseppe Pasotto

CENTRAL AFRICAN REPUBLIC
Bangui, Joachim N'Dayen

CHAD
Ndjamena, Charles Vandame

CHILE
Antofagasta, Patricio Infante Alfonso
Concepción, Antonio M. Casamitjana
La Serena, Francisco J. Cox Huneeus
Puerto Montt, Savino B. Cazzaro Bertollo
Santiago de Chile, HE Cardinal Carlos Oviedo Cavada

CHINA
Anking, Huai-Ning, vacant
Canton, vacant
Changsha, vacant
Chungking, vacant
Foochow, Min-Hou, vacant
Hangchow, vacant
Hankow, vacant
Hong Kong, HE Cardinal J. B. Wu Cheng Chung
    Coadjutor, Joseph Zeng

Kaifeng, vacant
Kunming, vacant
Kweyang, vacant
Lanchow, vacant
Mukden, vacant
Nanchang, vacant
Nanking, vacant
Nanning, vacant
Peking (Beijing), vacant
Sian, vacant
Suiyüan, Francis Wang Hsueh-Ming
Taiyuan, vacant
Tsinan, vacant

COLOMBIA
Barranquilla, Felix Maria Torres Parra
Bogotá, Pedro Rubiano Sáenz
Bucaramanga, vacant
Cali, Isaias Duarte Cancino
Cartagena, Carlos José Ruiseco Vieira
Ibague, Juan S. Jaramillo
Manizales, Fabio Betancur Tirado
Medellin, Hector Rueda Hernández
Nueva Pamplona, Victor M. Lopez Forero
Popayán, Alberto G. Jaramillo
Santa Fe de Antioquia, Ignacio Gomez Aristizabal
Tunja, Augusto Trujillo Arango

CONGO, DEMOCRATIC REPUBLIC OF
Bukavu, vacant
Kananga, Bakole wa Ilunga
Kinshasa, HE Cardinal Frederick Etsou-Nzabi-
  Bamungwabi
Kisangani, Laurent Monsengwo Pasinya
Lubumbashi, Kabanga Songasonga
Mbandaka-Bikoro, Joseph Kumuondala Mbimba

CONGO, REPUBLIC OF
Brazzaville, Barthélémy Batantu

COSTA RICA
San José, Román Arrieta Villalobos

CÔTE D'IVOIRE
Abidjan, Bernard Agre
Bouake, Vital Komenan Yao
Gagnoa, Noel Kokora-Tekry
Korhogo, Auguste Nobou

CROATIA
Rijeka-Senj, Anton Tamarut
Split-Makarska, Ante Juric
Zadar, Ivan Prendja
Zagreb, HE Cardinal Franjo Kuharić

CUBA
San Cristobal de la Habana, HE Cardinal Jaime Lucas Ortega
  y Alamino
Santiago de Cuba, Pedro Meurice Estiu

CYPRUS
Cyprus (Maronite seat at Nicosia), Boutros Gemayel

CZECH REPUBLIC
Olomouc, Jan Graubner
Prague, HE Cardinal Miloslav Vlk

DOMINICAN REPUBLIC
Santiago de los Caballeros, Juan A. F. Santana
Santo Domingo, HE Cardinal Nicolás de Jesús López
  Rodriguez

ECUADOR
Cuenca, Alberto Luna Tobar
Guayaquil, Ignacio Larrea Holguin

Quito, Antonio J. González Zumárraga

EQUATORIAL GUINEA
Malabo, Idlefonso Obama Obono

ETHIOPIA
Addis Ababa, HE Cardinal Paul Tzadua

FRANCE
Aix, Louis-Marie Bille
Albi, Roger Meindre
Auch, Maurice Frechard
Avignon, Raymond Bouchex
Besançon, Lucien Daloz
Bordeaux, HE Cardinal Pierre Eyt
Bourges, Pierre Plateau
Cambrai, Jacques Delaporte
Chambéry, Claude Feidt
Lyon, Jean Balland
Marseilles, Bernard Panafieu
Paris, HE Cardinal J. M. Lustiger
Reims, Gerard Defois
Rennes, Jacques Jullien
Rouen, Joseph Duval
Sens, Georges E. R. Gilson
Strasbourg, Charles Amarin Brand
Toulouse, Emile Marcus
Tours, Jean Honoré

FRENCH POLYNESIA
Papeete, Michel Coppenrath

GABON
Libreville, André Fernand Anguilé

GERMANY
Bamberg, Karl Braun
Berlin, HE Cardinal George M. Sterzinsky
Cologne, HE Cardinal Joachim Meisner
Freiburg im Breisgau, Oskar Saier
Munich and Freising, HE Cardinal Friedrich Wetter
Paderborn, Johannes Joachim Degenhardt

GHANA
Accra, Dominic K. Andoh
Cape Coast, Peter Kodwo A. Turkson
Tamale, Gregory E. Kpiebaya

GREECE
Athens, Nicholaos Foscolos
Corfu, Antonio Varthalitis
Naxos, Nicolaos Printesis
Rhodes, vacant (Apostolic Administrator, Nicholaos
  Foscolos)

GUATEMALA
Guatemala, Prospero Penados del Barrio

GUINEA
Conakry, Robert Sarah

HAITI
Cap-Haitien, François Gayot
Port au Prince, François-Wolff Ligondé

HONDURAS
Tegucigalpa, Oscar A. Maradiaga

HUNGARY
Eger, Istvan Seregely
Esztergom, HE Cardinal Laslo Paskai
Kalocsa, Laszlo Danko

INDIA
Agra, Cecil de Sa
Bangalore, Alphonsus Mathias
Bhopal, Paschal Topno

Bombay, Ivan Dias
Calcutta, Henry Sebastian D'Souza
Changanacherry, Joseph Powathil
Cuttack-Bhubaneswar, Raphael Cheenath
Delhi, Alan de Lastic
Ernakulam, vacant
Goa and Daman, Raul Nicolau Gonsalves
Hyderabad, Saminini Arulappa
Madras and Mylapore, James M. Arul Das
Madurai, Marianus Arokiasamy
Nagpur, Leobard D'Souza
Pondicherry and Cuddalore, Michael Augustine
Ranchi, Telesphore P. Toppo
Shillong-Gauhati, Tarcisius Resto Phanrang
Trivandrum (Syrian Melekite rite), Cyril Baselios
    Malancharuvil
Verapoly, Daniel Acharuparambil

INDONESIA
Ende, Longinus da Cunha
Jakarta, HE Cardinal Julius R. Darmaatmadja
Kupang, Gregorius Manteiro
Medan, Alfred Gonti Pius Datubara
Merauke, Jacobus Duivenvoorde
Pontianak, Hieronymus Herculanus Bumbun
Semarang, vacant
Ujung Pandang, Johannes Liku Ada'

IRAN
Ahvāz, Hanna Zora
Tehran, Youhannan Semaan Issayi
Urmyā, Thomas Meram

IRAQ
Arbil, vacant
Baghdad (Latin rite), Paul Dahdah; (Syrian rite), Athanase
    M. S. Matoka; (Armenian rite), Paul Coussa; (Chaldean
    rite), Raphaël Bidawid
Basra, Djibrail Kassab
Kirkuk, André Sana
Mosul (Chaldean rite), Georges Garmo; (Syrian rite),
    Cyrille E. Benni

ISRAEL (*see also* Patriarchs, page 423)
Akka (Greek Melekite Catholic rite), Maximos Salloum

ITALY
Acerenza, Michele Scandiffio
Amalfi, Beniamino De Palma
Ancona, Franco Festorazzi
Bari, Mariano Magrassi
Benevento, Serafino Sprovieri
Bologna, HE Cardinal Giacomo Biffi
Brindisi, Settimio Todisco
Cagliari, Otterino Pietro Alberti
Camerino, vacant
Campobasso-Boiano, Ettore Di Filippo
Capua, Luigi Diligenza
Catania, Luigi Bommarito
Catanzaro, Antonio Cantisani
Chieti, Edoardo Menichelli
Conza, Mario Milano
Cosenza, Dino Trabalzini
Crotone-Santa Severina, Giuseppe Agostino
Fermo, Cleto Bellucci
Ferrara, Carlo Caffarra
Florence, HE Cardinal Silvano Piovanelli
Foggia, Giuseppe Casale
Gaeta, Vincenzo Farano
Genoa, Dionigi Tettamanzi
Gorizia and Gradisca, Antonio Vitale Bommarco
Lanciano, Enzio d'Antonio

L'Aquila, Mario Peressin
Lecce, Cosmo F. Ruppi
Lucca, Bruno Tommasi
Manfredonia, Vincenzo D'Addario
Matera, Antonio Ciliberti
Messina, Ignazio Cannavó
Milan, HE Cardinal Carlo Maria Martini
Modena, Benito Cocchi
Monreale, Salvatore Cassisa
Naples, HE Cardinal Michele Giordano
Oristano, Pier Luigi Tiddia
Otranto, Francesco Cacucci
Palermo, Salvatore De Giorgi
Perugia, Giuseppe Chiaretti
Pescara-Penne, Francesco Cuccarese
Pisa, Alessandro Plotti
Potenza, Ennio Appignanesi
Ravenna, Luigi Amaducci
Reggio Calabria, Vittorio L. Mondello
Rossano-Cariati, Andrea Cassone
Salerno, Gerardo Pierro
Sassari, Salvatore Isgrò
Siena, Gaetano Bonicelli
Siracusa, Giuseppe Costanzo
Sorrento, Felice Cece
Spoleto, Riccardo Fontana
Taranto, Luigi Papa
Trani and Barletta, Carmelo Cassati
Trento, Giovanni Sartori
Turin, HE Cardinal Giovanni Saldarini
Udine, Alfredo Battisti
Urbino, Donato U. Bianchi
Vercelli, Enrico Masseroni

JAMAICA
Kingston, Edgerton R. Clarke

JAPAN
Nagasaki, Francis Xavier Shimamoto
Osaka, Paul Hisao Yasuda
Tokyo, HE Cardinal Peter Seiichi Shirayanagi

JORDAN
Petra and Filadelfia (Greek Melekite Catholic rite), George
    El-Murr

KAZAKHSTAN
Karaganda Apostolic Administration (Latin rite), Apostolic
    Administrator, Mgr Jan Lenga (titular Bishop of Arba)

KENYA
Kisumu, Zacchaeus Okoth
Mombasa, John Njenga
Nairobi, HE Cardinal Maurice Otunga
Nyeri, Nicodemus Kirima

KOREA
Kwang Ju, Victorinus Kong-Hi Youn
Seoul, HE Cardinal Stephen Sou Hwan Kim
Tae Gu, Paul Moun-Hi Ri

LATVIA
Riga, Jānis Pujats

LEBANON
Antelias (Maronite rite), Joseph Mohsen Bechara
Baalbek, Eliopoli (Greek Melekite Catholic rite), Salim
    Bustros
Baniyas (Greek Melekite Catholic rite), Antoine Hayek
Beirut (Greek Melekite Catholic rite), Habib Bacha;
    (Maronite rite), Paul Youssef Matar; (Armenian rite),
    Jean P. Kasparian
Saïda (Greek Melekite Catholic rite), Georges Kwaiter

Tripoli (Maronite rite), Gabriel Toubia; (Greek Melekite
  Catholic rite), George Riashi
Tyre (Greek Melekite Catholic rite), Jean A. Haddad;
  (Maronite rite), Maroun Sader
Zahle and Furzol (Greek Melekite Catholic rite), Andre
  Haddad

LESOTHO
Maseru, Bernard Mohlalisi

LIBERIA
Monrovia, Michael Kpakala Francis

LITHUANIA
Kaunas, Sigitas Tamkevicius
Vilnius, Audris J. Bačkis

LUXEMBOURG
Luxembourg, Fernand Franck

MADAGASCAR
Antananarive, HE Cardinal Armand G. Razafindratandra
Antsiranana, Albert Joseph Tsiahoana
Fianarantsoa, Philibert Randriambololona

MALAWI
Blantyre, James Chiona

MALAYSIA
Kuala Lumpur, Anthony S. Fernandez
Kuching, Peter Chung Hoan Ting

MALI
Bamako, Luc Auguste Sangaré

MALTA
Malta, Joseph Mercieca

MARTINIQUE
Fort de France, Maurice Marie-Sainte

MEXICO
Acapulco, Rafael Bello Ruiz
Antequera, Hector G. Martínez
Chihuahua, José Fernández Arteaga
Durango, José M. Perez
Guadalajara, HE Cardinal Juan Sandoval Iniguez
Hermosillo, Macias Salcedo
Jalapa, Sergio Obeso Rivera
Mexico City, Norberto R. Carrera
Monterrey, HE Cardinal Adolfo Suarez Rivera
Morelia, Alberto S. Inda
Puebla de los Angeles, Rosendo Huesca Pacheco
San Luis Potosi, Arturo A. Szymanski Ramirez
Tlalnepantla, Ricardo G. Diaz
Yucatán, Emilio C. B. Belaunzaran

MONACO
Monaco, Joseph Marie Sardou

MOROCCO
Rabat, Hubert Michon
Tangier, Antonio J. Peteiro Freire

MOZAMBIQUE
Beira, Jaime P. Goncalves
Maputo, HE Cardinal Alexandre José Maria dos Santos
Nampula, Manuel Vieira Pinto

MYANMAR (BURMA)
Mandalay, Alphonse U. Than Aung
Yangon (Rangoon), Gabriel Thohey Mahn Gaby

NAMIBIA
Windhoek, Bonifatius Haushiku

NETHERLANDS
Utrecht, HE Cardinal Adrianus J. Simonis

NEW ZEALAND
Wellington, HE Cardinal Thomas Stafford Williams

NICARAGUA
Managua, HE Cardinal Miguel Obando Bravo

NIGERIA
Jos, Gabriel G. Ganaka
Kaduna, Peter Yariyok Jatau
Lagos, Anthony Okogie
Onitsha, Albert K. Obiefuna

OCEANIA
Agaña, Anthony Sablan Apuron
Honiara, Adrian Thomas Smith
Nouméa, Michel-Marie-Bernard Calvet
Papeete, Michel-Gaspard Copenrath
Samoa, Apia and Tokelau, HE Cardinal Pio Taofino'u
Suva, Petero Mataca

PAKISTAN
Karachi, Simeon Pereira

PANAMA
Panama, Jose Dimas C. Delgado

PAPUA NEW GUINEA
Madang, Benedict To Varpin
Mount Hagen, Michael Meier
Port Moresby, vacant
Rabaul, Karl Hesse

PARAGUAY
Asunción, Felipe Santiago B. Avalos

PERU
Arequipa, Luis Sanchez-Moreno Lira
Ayacucho o Huamanga, Juan L. C. Thorne
Cuzco, Alcides Mendoza Castro
Huancayo, Jose P. Rios Reynoso
Lima, HE Cardinal Augusto Vargas Alzamora
Piura, Oscar Rolando Cantuarias Pastor
Trujillo, Manuel Prado Pérez-Rosas

PHILIPPINES
Caceres, Leonardo Legazpi
Cagayan de Oro, Jesus B. Tuquib
Capiz, Onesimo C. Gordoncillo
Cebu, HE Cardinal Ricardo Vidal
Cotabato, Philip Francis Smith
Davao, Fernando R. Capalla
Jaro, Alberto J. Piamonte
Lingayen-Dagupan, Oscar V. Cruz
Lipa, Gaudencio B. Rosales
Manila, HE Cardinal Jaime L. Sin
Nueva Segovia, Orlando Quevedo
Ozamiz, Jesus Dosado
Palo, Pedro R. Dean
San Fernando, Paciano Aniceto
Tuguegarao, Diosdado A. Talamayan
Zamboanga, Carmelo D. F. Morelos

POLAND
Bialystok, Stanislaw Szymecki
Czestochowa, Stanislaw Nowak
Gdańsk, Tadeusz Goclowski
Gniezno, Henryk Muszyński
Katowice, Damian Zimoń
Kraków, HE Cardinal Franciszek Macharski
Lodz, Wladyslaw Ziolek
Lublin, Boleslaw Pylak
Poznań, Juliusz Paetz
Przemyśl of the Latins, Jozef Michalik
Szczecin-Kamień, Marian Przykucki
Warmia, Edmund Piszcz

Warsaw, HE Cardinal Józef Glemp
Wroclaw, HE Cardinal Henryk Roman Gulbinowicz

PORTUGAL
Braga, Eurico Dias Nogueira
Evora, Maurilio Jorge Quintal de Gouveia

PUERTO RICO
San Juan, HE Cardinal Luis Aponte Martinez

ROMANIA
Alba Julia (Latin rite), Gyorgy-Miklos Jakubinyi
Bucaręsti, Ioan Robu
Fagaras and Alba Julia (Romanian Byzantine rite), Lucian
    Muresan

RUSSIA
Moscow Apostolic Administration (covering European
    Russia), Apostolic Administrator, Archbishop Tadeusz
    Kondrusiewicz
Novosibirsk Apostolic Administration (covering Siberia),
    Apostolic Administrator, Mgr Joseph Werth, SJ (titular
    Bishop of Bulna)

RWANDA
Kigali, Thaddée Ntihinyurwa

ST LUCIA
Castries, Kelvin E. Felix, OBE

EL SALVADOR
San Salvador, Fernando S. Lacalle

SENEGAL
Dakar, HE Cardinal Hyacinthe Thiandoum

SIERRA LEONE
Freetown and Bo, Joseph Ganda

SINGAPORE
Singapore, Gregory Yong Sooi Ngean

SLOVAKIA
Trnava, Jan Sokol

SLOVENIA
Ljubljana, Alojzij Suštar

SOUTH AFRICA
Bloemfontein, Peter John Butelezi
Cape Town, Lawrence Patrick Henry
Durban, Wilfrid Fox Napier
Pretoria, George Francis Daniel

SPAIN
Barcelona, HE Cardinal Ricardo Maria Carles Gordó
Burgos, Santiago Martinez Acebes
Granada, Antonio C. Lovera
Madrid, Antonio M. Rouco Varela
Oviedo, Gabino Diaz Merchán
Pamplona, Fernando S. Aquilar
Santiago de Compostela, Julian Barrio Barrio
Sevilla, Carlos Amigo Vallejo
Tarragona, Ramon Torrella Cascante
Toledo, Francisco A. Martinez
Valencia, Agustin Garcia-Gasco Vicente
Valladolid, José Delicado Baeza
Zaragoza, Elíaz Yanez Alvarez

SRI LANKA
Colombo, Nicholas Marcus Fernando

SUDAN
Juba, Paulino Lukudu Loro
Khartoum, Gabriel Zubeir Wako

SYRIA
Alep, Beroea, Halab (Greek Melekite Catholic rite), Jean-
    Clement Jeanbart; (Syrian rite), Raboula A. Beylouni;
    (Maronite rite), Pierre Callaos; (Armenian rite), Boutros
    Marayati
Baniyas (Greek Melekite Catholic rite), Antoine Hayek
Bosra, Bostra, Boulos Nassif Borkhoche
Damascus (Greek Melekite Catholic rite), S. B. Maximos
    V. Hakim; (Syrian rite), Eustache J. Mounayer;
    (Maronite rite), Hamid A. Mourany
Hassaké-Nisibi, Georges Habib Hafouri
Homs, Emesa (Greek Melekite Catholic rite), Abraham
    Nehmé; (Syrian Catholic rite), Basile Daoud
Laodicea (Greek Melekite Catholic rite), Fares Maakaroun

TAIWAN
Taipei, Joseph Ti-Kang

TANZANIA
Dar es Salaam, Polycarp Pengo
Mwanza, Antony Mayala
Songea, Norbert W. Mtega
Tabora, Mario E. A. Mgulunde

THAILAND
Bangkok, HE Cardinal Michael Michai Kitbunchu
Tharé and Nonseng, Lawrence Khai Saen-Phon-On

TOGO
Lomé, Philippe F. K. Kpodzro

TRINIDAD
Port of Spain, Gordon Anthony Pantin

TURKEY
Diarbekir, Paul Karatas
Istanbul (Constantinople), Jean Tcholakian
Izmir, Giuseppe G. Bernardini

UGANDA
Kampala, HE Cardinal Emmanuel Wamala

UKRAINE
Lvov (Latin rite), Marian Jaworski (Archbishop of Lvov of
    the Latins); (Ukrainian rite), HE Cardinal Myroslav
    I. Lubachivsky (Major Archbishop of Lvov of the
    Ukrainians)
Zakarpattia, Apostolic Administrator, Antonio Franco

URUGUAY
Montevideo, José Gottardi Cristelli

USA
Anchorage, Francis Thomas Hurley
Atlanta, John F. Donoghue
Baltimore, HE Cardinal William Henry Keeler
Boston, HE Cardinal Bernard F. Law
Chicago, vacant
Cincinnati, Daniel E. Pilarczyk
Denver, vacant
Detroit, HE Cardinal Adam J. Maida
Dubuque, Jerome G. Hanus
Hartford, Daniel A. Cronin
Indianapolis, Daniel Mark Buechlein
Kansas City, James P. Keleher
Los Angeles, HE Cardinal Roger M. Mahony
Louisville, Thomas C. Kelly
Miami, John C. Favalora
Milwaukee, Rembert G. Weakland
Mobile, Oscar H. Lipscomb
Newark, Theodore E. McCarrick
New Orleans, Francis B. Schulte
New York, HE Cardinal John J. O'Connor
Oklahoma City, Eusebius Joseph Beltran
Omaha, Elden Curtiss

Philadelphia, HE Cardinal Anthony J. Bevilacqua;
(Ukrainian rite), Stephen Sulyk
Pittsburgh (Byzantine rite), Judson M. Procyk
Portland (*Oregon*), Francis E. George
St Louis (*Missouri*), Justin F. Rigali
St Paul and Minneapolis, Harry J. Flynn
San Antonio, Patrick F. Flores
San Francisco, William J. Levada
Santa Fe, Michael Sheehan
Seattle, Thomas J. Murphy
Washington, HE Cardinal James A. Hickey

VENEZUELA
Barquisimeto, Julio Manuel Chirivella Varela
Calabozo, Helimenas de J. R. Paredes
Caracas, Ignacio A. V. Garcia
Ciudad Bolívar, Medardo Luzardo Romero
Cumana, Alfredo J. R. Figueroa
Maracaibo, Ramon O. Perez Morales
Mérida, Baltazar P. Cardozo
Valencia, Jorge Liberato Urosa Savino

VIETNAM
Hanoi, HE Cardinal Paul Joseph Pham Dinh Tung
Hue, Apostolic Administrator, Etienne N. N. Thê
Thanh-Phô Hôchiminh, Apostolic Administrator, Mgr
Nicolas Huynh Van Nghi

YUGOSLAVIA, FEDERAL REPUBLIC OF
Bar, Petar Perkolić
Belgrade, Franc Perko

ZAMBIA
Kasama, James Spaita
Lusaka, Medardo J. Mazombwe

ZIMBABWE
Harare, Patrick Chakaipa

PATRIARCHS IN COMMUNION WITH THE ROMAN CATHOLIC CHURCH

Alexandria, HB Stephanos II Ghattas (Patriarch for
Catholic Copts)
Antioch, HB Ignace Antoine II Hayek (Patriarch for Syrian
rite Catholics); HB Maximos V. Hakim (Patriarch for
Greek Melekite rite Catholics); HE Cardinal Nasrallah
Pierre Sfeir (Patriarch for Maronite rite Catholics)
Jerusalem, HB Michel Sabbah (Patriarch for Latin rite
Catholics); HB Maximos V. Hakim (Patriarch for Greek
Melekite rite Catholics)
Babilonia of the Chaldeans, HB Raphael I Bidawid
Cilicia of the Armenians, HB Jean Pierre XVIII Kasparian
(Patriarch for Armenian rite Catholics)
Oriental India, Archbishop Raul Nicolau Gonsalves
Lisbon, HE Cardinal Antonio Ribeiro
Venice, HE Cardinal Marco Ce

Other Churches in the UK

AFRICAN AND AFRO-CARIBBEAN CHURCHES

There are more than 160 Christian churches or groups of
African or Afro-Caribbean origin in the UK. These include
the Apostolic Faith Church, the Cherubim and Seraphim
Church, the New Testament Church Assembly, the New

Testament Church of God, the Wesleyan Holiness Church
and the Aladura Churches.

The Afro-West Indian United Council of Churches and
the Council of African and Afro-Caribbean Churches UK
(which was initiated as the Council of African and Allied
Churches in 1979 to give one voice to the various Christian
churches of African origin in the UK) are the media
through which the member churches can work jointly to
provide services they cannot easily provide individually.

There are about 70,000 adherents of African and Afro-
Caribbean churches in the UK, and about 1,000 congregations. The Afro-West Indian United Council of
Churches has about 30,000 individual members, 135
ministers and 65 places of worship. The Council of African
and Afro-Caribbean Churches UK has about 17,000
members, 250 ministers and 75 congregations.

AFRO-WEST INDIAN UNITED COUNCIL OF CHURCHES,
c/o New Testament Church of God, Arcadian Gardens,
High Road, London N22 5AA. Tel: 0181-888 9427.
Secretary, Revd E. Brown
COUNCIL OF AFRICAN AND AFRO-CARIBBEAN
CHURCHES UK, 31 Norton House, Sidney Road,
London SW9 0UJ. Tel: 0171-274 5589. *Chairman*, His
Grace The Most Revd Father Olu A. Abiola

ASSOCIATED PRESBYTERIAN CHURCHES OF SCOTLAND

The Associated Presbyterian Churches came into being in
1989 as a result of a division within the Free Presbyterian
Church of Scotland. Following two controversial disciplinary cases, the culmination of deepening differences
within the Church, a presbytery was formed calling itself
the Associated Presbyterian Churches (APC). The Associated Presbyterian Churches has about 1,000 members, 15
ministers and 20 churches.
Clerk of the Scottish Presbytery, Revd Dr M. MacInnes,
Drumlin, 16 Drummond Road, Inverness IV2 4NB. Tel:
01463-223983

THE BAPTIST CHURCH

Baptists trace their origins to John Smyth, who in 1609 in
Amsterdam reinstituted the baptism of conscious believers
as the basis of the fellowship of a gathered church.
Members of Smyth's church established the first Baptist
church in England in 1612. They came to be known as
'General' Baptists and their theology was Arminian,
whereas a later group of Calvinists who adopted the
baptism of believers came to be known as 'Particular'
Baptists. The two sections of the Baptists were united into
one body, the Baptist Union of Great Britain and Ireland, in
1891. In 1988 the title was changed to the Baptist Union of
Great Britain.

Baptists emphasize the complete autonomy of the local
church, although individual churches are linked in various
kinds of associations. There are international bodies (such
as the Baptist World Alliance) and national bodies, but
some Baptist churches belong to neither. However, in
Great Britain the majority of churches and associations
belong to the Baptist Union of Great Britain. There are also
Baptist Unions in Wales, Scotland and Ireland which are
much smaller than the Baptist Union of Great Britain, and
there is some overlap of membership.

There are over 40 million Baptist church members
world-wide; in the Baptist Union of Great Britain there are

157,000 members, 1,864 pastors and 2,130 churches. In the Baptist Union of Scotland there are 14,328 members, 140 pastors and 171 churches. In the Baptist Union of Wales there are 24,178 members, 118 pastors and 537 churches. In the Baptist Union of Ireland there are 8,454 members, 83 pastors and 109 churches.

President of the Baptist Union of Great Britain (1997–8), Revd Frederick George

General Secretary, Revd D. R. Coffey, Baptist House, PO Box 44, 129 Broadway, Didcot, Oxon OX11 8RT. Tel: 01235-512077

THE CHURCH OF CHRIST, SCIENTIST

The Church of Christ, Scientist was founded by Mary Baker Eddy in the USA in 1879 to 'reinstate primitive Christianity and its lost element of healing'. Christian Science teaches the need for spiritual regeneration and salvation from sin, but is best known for its reliance on prayer alone in the healing of sickness. Adherents believe that such healing is a law, or Science, and is in direct line with that practised by Jesus Christ (revered, not as God, but as the Son of God) and by the early Christian Church.

The denomination consists of The First Church of Christ, Scientist, in Boston, Massachusetts, USA (the Mother Church) and its branch churches in over 60 countries world-wide. Branch churches are democratically governed by their members, while a five-member Board of Directors, based in Boston, is authorized to transact the business of the Mother Church. The Bible and Mary Baker Eddy's book, *Science and Health with Key to the Scriptures*, are used at services; there are no clergy. Those engaged in full-time healing are called practitioners, of whom there are 3,500 world-wide.

No membership figures are available, since Mary Baker Eddy felt that numbers are no measure of spiritual vitality and ruled that such statistics should not be published. There are over 2,400 branch churches world-wide, including nearly 200 in the UK.

CHRISTIAN SCIENCE COMMITTEE ON PUBLICATION, 2 Elysium Gate, 126 New Kings Road, London SW6 4LZ. Tel: 0171-371 0600. *District Manager for Great Britain and Ireland*, A. Grayson

THE CHURCH OF JESUS CHRIST OF LATTER-DAY SAINTS

The Church (often referred to as 'the Mormons') was founded in New York State, USA, in 1830, and came to Britain in 1837. The oldest continuous branch in the world is to be found in Preston, Lancs. Mormons are Christians who claim to belong to the 'Restored Church' of Jesus Christ. They believe that true Christianity died when the last original apostle died, but that it was given back to the world by God and Christ through Joseph Smith, the Church's founder and first president. They accept and use the Bible as scripture, but believe in continuing revelation from God and use additional scriptures, including *The Book of Mormon: Another Testament of Jesus Christ*. The importance of the family is central to the Church's beliefs and practices. Church members set aside Monday evenings as Family Home Evenings when Christian family values are taught. Polygamy was formally discontinued in 1890.

The Church has no paid ministry; local congregations are headed by a leader chosen from amongst their number. The world governing body, based in Utah, USA, is the three-man First Presidency, assisted by the Quorum of the Twelve Apostles.

There are more than 9 million members world-wide, with about 170,000 adherents in Britain in over 350 congregations.

President of the Europe North Area (including Britain), Elder C. O. Samuelson, jun.

BRITISH HEADQUARTERS, Church Offices, 751 Warwick Road, Solihull, W. Midlands B91 3DQ. Tel: 0121-712 1202

THE CONGREGATIONAL FEDERATION

The Congregational Federation was founded by members of Congregational churches in England and Wales who did not join the United Reformed Church (q.v.) in 1972. There are also churches in Scotland and Australia affiliated to the Federation. The Federation exists to encourage congregations of believers to worship in free assembly, but it has no authority over them and emphasizes their right to independence and self-government.

The Federation has 11,923 members, 71 recognized ministers and 313 churches in England, Wales and Scotland.

President of the Federation (1997–8), Revd. C. Gillham

General Secretary, G. M. Adams, The Congregational Centre, 4 Castle Gate, Nottingham NG1 7AS. Tel: 0115-941 3801

THE FREE CHURCH OF ENGLAND

The Free Church of England is a union of two bodies in the Anglican tradition, the Free Church of England, founded in 1844 as a protest against the Oxford Movement in the established Church, and the Reformed Episcopal Church, founded in America in 1873 but which also had congregations in England. As both Churches sought to maintain the historic faith, tradition and practice of the Anglican Church since the Reformation, they decided to unite as one body in England in 1927. The historic episcopate was conferred on the English Church in 1876 through the line of the American bishops, who had pioneered an open table Communion policy towards members of other denominations.

The Free Church of England has 1,500 members, 42 ministers and 25 churches in England. It also has three house churches and three ministers in New Zealand, and one church and one minister in St Petersburg, Russia.

General Secretary, Revd W. J. Lawler, 45 Broughton Road, Wallasey, Merseyside L44 4DT. Tel: 0151-638 2564

THE FREE CHURCH OF SCOTLAND

The Free Church of Scotland was formed in 1843 when over 400 ministers withdrew from the Church of Scotland as a result of interference in the internal affairs of the church by the civil authorities. In 1900, all but 26 ministers joined with others to form the United Free Church (most of which rejoined the Church of Scotland in 1929). In 1904 the remaining 26 ministers were recognized by the House of Lords as continuing the Free Church of Scotland.

The Church maintains strict adherence to the Westminster Confession of Faith (1648) and accepts the Bible as the sole rule of faith and conduct. Its General Assembly meets annually. It also has links with Reformed Churches overseas. The Free Church of Scotland has 6,000 members, 110 ministers and 140 churches.

General Treasurer, I. D. Gill, The Mound, Edinburgh
EH1 2LS. Tel: 0131-226 5286

THE FREE PRESBYTERIAN CHURCH OF SCOTLAND

The Free Presbyterian Church of Scotland was formed in 1893 by two ministers of the Free Church of Scotland who refused to accept a Declaratory Act passed by the Free Church General Assembly in 1892. The Free Presbyterian Church of Scotland is Calvinistic in doctrine and emphasizes observance of the Sabbath. It adheres strictly to the Westminster Confession of Faith of 1648.

The Church has about 3,000 members in Scotland and about 7,000 in overseas congregations. It has 26 ministers and 50 churches.

Moderator, Revd D. M. Boyd, 11 Auldcastle Road, Inverness
IV2 3PZ. Tel: 01463-712872

Clerk of Synod, Revd J. MacLeod, 16 Matheson Road, Stornoway, Isle of Lewis HS1 2LA. Tel: 01851-702755

THE INDEPENDENT METHODIST CHURCHES

The Independent Methodist Churches seceded from the Wesleyan Methodist Church in 1805 and remained independent when the Methodist Church in Great Britain was formed in 1932. They are mainly concentrated in the industrial areas of the north of England.

The churches are Methodist in doctrine but their organization is congregational. All the churches are members of the Independent Methodist Connexion of Churches. The controlling body of the Connexion is the Annual Meeting, to which churches send delegates. The Connexional President is elected annually. Between annual meetings the affairs of the Connexion are handled by departmental committees. Ministers are appointed by the churches and trained through the Connexion. The ministry is open to both men and women and is unpaid.

There are 3,050 members, 106 ministers and 100 churches in Great Britain.

Connexional President (1997−8), J. S. Cheers

General Secretary, J. M. Day, The Old Police House, Croxton, Stafford ST21 6PE. Tel: 0163-062 0671

JEHOVAH'S WITNESSES

The movement now known as Jehovah's Witnesses grew from a Bible study group formed by Charles Taze Russell in 1872 in Pennsylvania, USA. In 1896 it adopted the name of the Watch Tower Bible and Tract Society, and in 1931 its members became known as Jehovah's Witnesses. Jehovah's (God's) Witnesses believe in the Bible as the word of God, and consider it to be inspired and historically accurate. They take the scriptures literally, except where there are obvious indications that they are figurative or symbolic, and reject the doctrine of the Trinity. Witnesses also believe that the earth will remain for ever and that all those approved of by Jehovah will have eternal life on a cleansed and beautified earth; only 144,000 will go to heaven to rule with Christ. They believe that the second coming of Christ and his thousand-year reign on earth

have been imminent since 1914, and that Armageddon (a final battle in which evil will be defeated) will precede Christ's rule of peace. They refuse to take part in military service, and do not accept stimulants or blood transfusions. They publish a magazine, *The Watchtower.*

The 12-member world governing body is based in New York, USA. Witnesses world-wide are divided into branches, countries or areas, districts, circuits and congregations. There are overseers at each level, and two assemblies are held annually for each circuit. There is no paid ministry, but each congregation has elders assigned to look after various duties and every Witness is assigned homes to visit in their congregation.

There are over 5 million Jehovah's Witnesses world-wide, with 130,000 Witnesses in the UK organized into over 1,400 congregations.

BRITISH ISLES HEADQUARTERS, Watch Tower House, The Ridgeway, London NW7 1RN. Tel: 0181-906 2211

THE LUTHERAN CHURCH

Lutheranism is based on the teachings of Martin Luther, the German leader of the Protestant Reformation. The authority of the scriptures is held to be supreme over Church tradition and creeds, and the key doctrine is that of justification by faith alone.

Lutheranism is one of the largest Protestant denominations and it is particularly strong in northern Europe and the USA. Some Lutheran churches are episcopal, while others have a synodal form of organization; unity is based on doctrine rather than structure. Most Lutheran churches are members of the Lutheran World Federation, based in Geneva.

Lutheran services in Great Britain are held in many languages to serve members of different nationalities. English-language congregations are members either of the Lutheran Church in Great Britain−United Synod, or of the Evangelical Lutheran Church of England. The United Synod and most of the various national congregations are members of the Lutheran Council of Great Britain.

There are over 70 million Lutherans world-wide; in Great Britain there are 27,000 members, 45 ministers and 100 churches.

Chairman of the Lutheran Council of Great Britain, Very Revd R. J. Patkai, 5 Kingscroft Road, London NW2 3QE. Tel: 0181-452 9363

THE METHODIST CHURCH

The Methodist movement started in England in 1729 when the Revd John Wesley, an Anglican priest, and his brother Charles met with others in Oxford and resolved to conduct their lives and study by 'rule and method'. In 1739 the Wesleys began evangelistic preaching and the first Methodist chapel was founded in Bristol in the same year. In 1744 the first annual conference was held, at which the Articles of Religion were drawn up. Doctrinal emphases included repentance, faith, the assurance of salvation, social concern and the priesthood of all believers. After John Wesley's death in 1791 the Methodists withdrew from the established Church to form the Methodist Church. Methodists gradually drifted into many groups, but in 1932 the Wesleyan Methodist Church, the United Methodist Church and the Primitive Methodist Church united to form the Methodist Church in Great Britain as it now exists.

The governing body and supreme authority of the Methodist Church is the Conference, but there are also 33 district synods, consisting of all the ministers and selected lay people in each district, and circuit meetings of the ministers and lay people of each circuit.

There are over 60 million Methodists world-wide; in Great Britain (1995 figures) there are 380,269 members, 3,660 ministers, 12,611 lay preachers and 6,678 churches.

President of the Conference in Great Britain (1997–8), Revd J. B. Taylor

Vice-President of the Conference (1997–8), Sir Michael Checkland

Secretary of the Conference, Revd B. E. Beck, Methodist Church, Conference Office, 25 Marylebone Road, London NW1 5JR. Tel: 0171-486 5502

THE METHODIST CHURCH IN IRELAND

The Methodist Church in Ireland is closely linked to British Methodism but is autonomous. It has 17,636 members, 196 ministers, 316 lay preachers and 232 churches.

President of the Methodist Church in Ireland (1997–8), Revd N. W. Taggart, PH.D., 33 Grange Road, Coleraine, Co. Londonderry BT52 1NG. Tel: 01265-43158

Secretary of the Methodist Church in Ireland, Revd E. T. I. Mawhinney, 1 Fountainville Avenue, Belfast BT9 6AN. Tel: 01232-324554

THE ORTHODOX CHURCHES

The Eastern (or Byzantine) Orthodox Church is a communion of self-governing Christian churches recognizing the honorary primacy of the Oecumenical Patriarch of Constantinople.

In the first millennium of the Christian era the faith was slowly formulated. Between AD 325 and 787 there were seven Oecumenical Councils at which bishops from the entire Christian world assembled to resolve various doctrinal disputes which had arisen. The estrangement between East and West began after Constantine moved the centre of the Roman Empire from Rome to Constantinople, and it gained momentum after the temporal administration was divided. Linguistic and cultural differences between Greek East and Latin West served to encourage separate ecclesiastical developments which became pronounced in the tenth and early 11th centuries.

The administration of the church was divided between five ancient patriarchates: Rome and all the West, Constantinople (the imperial city – the 'New Rome'), Jerusalem and all Palestine, Antioch and all the East, and Alexandria and all Africa. Of these, only Rome was in the Latin West and after the Great Schism in 1054, Rome developed a structure of authority centralized on one source, the Papacy, while the Orthodox East maintained the style of localized administration.

To the older patriarchates were later added the Patriarchates of Russia, Serbia, Romania, Bulgaria and Georgia. The Eastern Orthodox Church also includes autocephalous (self-governing) national churches in Cyprus, Greece, Poland and Albania, and autonomous national churches in the Czech and Slovak Republics, Finland and Estonia. The Latvian and part of the Estonian Orthodox Churches are in practice part of the Moscow Patriarchate. The Belorussians and Ukrainians have recently been given greater autonomy by Moscow, but some Ukrainians have broken away to establish an independent Ukrainian Patriarchate. In Macedonia the local hierarchy has declared itself independent of the Serbian Patriarchate. The Russian dioceses in the diaspora fall into four groups: those under the direct control of the Moscow Patriarchate; the Russian Orthodox Church Outside Russia, sometimes known as the Synod in Exile; the Russian Archdiocese centred at the cathedral in rue Daru, Paris, which is part of the Patriarchate in Constantinople; and the Orthodox Church in America, which was granted autocephalous status by Moscow in 1970.

The term 'Oriental Orthodox Churches' is now generally used to describe a group of six ancient eastern churches which reject the Christological definition of the Council of Chalcedon (AD 451) and use Christological terms in different ways from the Eastern Orthodox Church.

The position of Orthodox Christians is that the faith was fully defined during the period of the Oecumenical Councils. In doctrine it is strongly trinitarian, and stresses the mystery and importance of the sacraments. It is episcopal in government. The structure of the Orthodox Christian year differs from that of western Churches (*see* page 82).

Orthodox Christians throughout the world are estimated to number about 300 million, of whom about 34 million are members of the Oriental Orthodox Churches.

PATRIARCHS OF THE EASTERN ORTHODOX CHURCH

Archbishop of Constantinople, New Rome and Oecumenical Patriarch, Bartholomew, *elected* 1991

Pope and Patriarch of Alexandria and All Africa, Petros VII, *elected* 1997

Patriarch of Antioch and All the East, Ignatios IV, *elected* 1979

Patriarch of Jerusalem and All Palestine, Diodoros, *elected* 1981

Patriarch of Moscow and All Russia, Alexei II, *elected* 1990

Archbishop of Pec, Metropolitan of Belgrade and Karlovci, Patriarch of Serbia, Paul, *elected* 1990

Archbishop of Bucharest and Patriarch of Romania, Teoctist, *elected* 1986

Metropolitan of Sofia and Patriarch of Bulgaria, Maxim, *elected* 1971

Archbishop of Tbilisi and Mtskheta, Catholicos-Patriarch of All Georgia, Ilia II, *elected* 1977

PATRIARCHS OF THE ORIENTAL ORTHODOX CHURCHES

ARMENIAN ORTHODOX CHURCH – *Supreme Patriarch Catholicos of All Armenians (Etchmiadzin)*, Karekin I, *elected* 1995; *Catholicos of Cilicia*, Aram I, *elected* 1995; *Patriarch of Jerusalem*, Torkom, *elected* 1994; *Patriarch of Constantinople*, Karekin II, *elected* 1990

COPTIC ORTHODOX CHURCH – *Pope of Alexandria and Patriarch of the See of St Mark*, Shenouda III, *elected* 1971

ERITREAN ORTHODOX CHURCH – *Patriarch of Eritrea*, vacant

ETHIOPIAN ORTHODOX CHURCH – *Patriarch of Ethopia*, Paulos, *elected* 1992

MALANKARA ORTHODOX SYRIAN CHURCH – *Catholicos of the East*, Basilios Mar Thoma Mathews II, *elected* 1991

SYRIAN ORTHODOX CHURCH – *Patriarch of Antioch and All the East*, Ignatius Zakka I, *elected* 1980

EASTERN ORTHODOX CHURCHES IN THE UK

THE PATRIARCHATE OF ANTIOCH

There are ten parishes served by 11 clergy. In Great Britain the Patriarchate is represented by the Revd Fr Samir Gholam, 1A Redhill Street, London NW1 4BG. Tel: 0171-383 0403.

THE GREEK ORTHODOX CHURCH (PATRIARCHATE OF CONSTANTINOPLE)

The presence of Greek Orthodox Christians in Britain dates back at least to 1677 when Archbishop Joseph Geogirenes of Samos fled from Turkish persecution and came to London. The present Greek cathedral in Moscow Road, Bayswater, was opened for public worship in 1879 and the Diocese of Thyateira and Great Britain was established in 1922. There are now 112 parishes and other communities (including monasteries) in Great Britain, served by six bishops, 96 clergy and 101 churches.

In Great Britain the Patriarchate of Constantinople is represented by Archbishop Gregorios of Thyateira and Great Britain, 5 Craven Hill, London W2 3EN. Tel: 0171-723 4787.

THE RUSSIAN ORTHODOX CHURCH (PATRIARCHATE OF MOSCOW) AND THE RUSSIAN ORTHODOX CHURCH OUTSIDE RUSSIA

The records of Russian Orthodox Church activities in Britain date from the visit to England of Tsar Peter I in the early 18th century. Clergy were sent from Russia to serve the chapel established to minister to the staff of the Imperial Russian Embassy in London.

In Great Britain the Patriarchate of Moscow is represented by Metropolitan Anthony of Sourozh, 67 Ennismore Gardens, London SW7 1NH. Fax only: 0171-584 9864. He is assisted by one archbishop, one vicar bishop and 24 clergy. There are 27 parishes and smaller communities.

The Russian Orthodox Church Outside Russia is represented by Archbishop Mark of Berlin, Germany and Great Britain, c/o 57 Harvard Road, London W4 4ED. Tel: 0181-742 3493. There are eight communities, including two monasteries, served by five clergy.

THE SERBIAN ORTHODOX CHURCH (PATRIARCHATE OF SERBIA)

There are 33 parishes and smaller communities in Great Britain served by nine clergy. The Patriarchate of Serbia is represented by the Episcopal Vicar, the Very Revd Milenko Zebic, 131 Cob Lane, Bournville, Birmingham B30 1QE. Tel: 0121 458 5273.

OTHER NATIONALITIES

Most of the Ukrainian parishes in Britain have joined the Patriarchate of Constantinople, leaving five Ukrainian parish in Britain under the care of the Patriarch of Kiev. The Latvian, Polish and some Belorussian parishes are also under the care of the Patriarchate of Constantinople. The Patriarchate of Romania has one parish served by two priests. The Patriarchate of Bulgaria has one parish served by one priest. The Belorussian Autocephalous Orthodox Church has five parishes served by two priests.

ST GEORGE ORTHODOX INFORMATION SERVICE, The White House, Mettingham, Suffolk NR35 1TP. Tel: 01986-896708. *Secretary*, A. Bond

ORIENTAL ORTHODOX CHURCHES IN THE UK

THE ARMENIAN ORTHODOX CHURCH (PATRIARCHATE OF ETCHMIADZIN)

The Armenian Orthodox Church is the longest-established Oriental Orthodox community in Great Britain. It is represented by Archbishop Yeghishe Gizirian, Armenian Primate of Great Britain, Armenian Vicarage, Iverna Gardens, London W8 6TP. Tel: 0171-937 0152.

THE COPTIC ORTHODOX CHURCH

The Coptic Orthodox Church is the largest Oriental Orthodox community in Great Britain. It has four dioceses (Birmingham, Scotland, Ireland and North East England; the British Orthodox Church; and churches directly under Pope Shenouda III). The representative in Great Britain of Pope Shenouda III is Fr Antonious Thabit Shenouda, 14 Newton Mansions, Queen's Club Gardens, London W14 9RR. Tel: 0171-385 1991.

THE ERITREAN ORTHODOX CHURCH

In Great Britain the Eritrean Orthodox Church is represented by Bishop Markos, 11 Anfield Close, Weir Road, London SW12 0NT. Tel: 0181-675 5115.

THE ETHIOPIAN ORTHODOX CHURCH

The Ethiopian Primate for Europe is Archbishop Yohannes, 33 Jupiter Crescent, London NW1 8HA. Tel: 0956-513700.

THE MALANKARA ORTHODOX SYRIAN CHURCH

The Malankara Orthodox Syrian Church is part of the Diocese of Europe under Metropolitan Thomas Mar Makarios. His representative in Great Britain is Fr M. S. Skariah, Paramula House, 44 Newbury Road, Newbury Park, Ilford, Essex IG2 7HD. Tel: 0181-599 3836.

THE SYRIAN ORTHODOX CHURCH

The Syrian Orthodox Church in Great Britain comes under the Patriarchal Vicar, whose representative is Fr Thomas H. Dawood, Antiochian, 5 Canning Road, Croydon CRO 6QA. Tel: 0181-654 7531. The Indian congregation under the Syrian Patriarch of Antioch is represented by Fr Eldhose Koungampillil, 1 Roslyn Court, Roslyn Avenue, East Barnet, Herts EN4 8DJ. Tel: 0181-368 2794.

THE COUNCIL OF ORIENTAL ORTHODOX CHURCHES, 34 Chertsey Road, Church Square, Shepperton, Middx TW17 9LF. Tel: 0181-368 8447. *Secretary*, Deacon Aziz M. A Nour

PENTECOSTAL CHURCHES

Pentecostalism is inspired by the descent of the Holy Spirit upon the apostles at Pentecost. The movement began in Los Angeles, USA, in 1906 and is characterized by baptism with the Holy Spirit, divine healing, speaking in tongues (glossolalia), and a literal interpretation of the scriptures. The Pentecostal movement in Britain dates from 1907. Initially, groups of Pentecostalists were led by laymen and did not organize formally. However, in 1915 the Elim Foursquare Gospel Alliance (more usually called the Elim Pentecostal Church) was founded in Ireland by George Jeffreys and in 1924 about 70 independent assemblies formed a fellowship, the Assemblies of God in Great Britain and Ireland. The Apostolic Church grew out of the 1904–5 revivals in South Wales and was established in 1916, and the New Testament Church of God was established in England in 1953. In recent years many aspects of Pentecostalism have been adopted by the growing charismatic movement within the Roman Catholic, Protestant and Eastern Orthodox churches.

There are about 105 million Pentecostalists world-wide, with about 200,000 adult adherents in Great Britain and Ireland.

The Apostolic Church, International Administration Offices, PO Box 389, 24–27 St Helens Road, Swansea sa1 1zh. Tel: 01792-473992. *President*, Pastor P. Cawthorne; *Administrator*, Pastor M. Davies. The Apostolic Church has about 130 churches, 5,500 adherents and 83 ministers

The Assemblies of God in Great Britain and Ireland, General Offices, 16 Bridgford Road, West Bridgford, Nottingham ng2 6af. Tel: 0115-981 1188. *General Superintendent*, P. Weaver; *General Administrator*, B. D. Varnam. The Assemblies of God has 653 churches, about 75,000 adherents (including children) and 880 accredited ministers

The Elim Pentecostal Church, PO Box 38, Cheltenham, Glos gl50 3hn. Tel: 01242-519904. *General Superintendent*, Pastor I. W. Lewis; *Administrator*, Pastor B. Hunter. The Elim Pentecostal Church has 596 churches, 68,500 adherents and 650 accredited ministers

The New Testament Church of God, Main House, Overstone Park, Overstone, Northampton nn6 0ad. Tel: 01604-645944. *National Overseer*, Revd Dr R. O. Brown. The New Testament Church of God has 110 organized congregations, 7,500 baptized members, about 20,000 adherents and 242 accredited ministers

THE PRESBYTERIAN CHURCH IN IRELAND

The Presbyterian Church in Ireland is Calvinistic in doctrine and presbyterian in constitution. Presbyterianism was established in Ireland as a result of the Ulster plantation in the early 17th century, when English and Scottish Protestants settled in the north of Ireland.

There are 21 presbyteries and five regional synods under the chief court known as the General Assembly. The General Assembly meets annually and is presided over by a Moderator who is elected for one year. The ongoing work of the Church is undertaken by 18 boards under which there are a number of specialist committees.

There are about 297,000 Presbyterians in Ireland, mainly in the north, in 562 congregations and with 400 ministers.

Moderator (1997–8), Rt. Revd Dr S. Hutchinson
Clerk of Assembly and General Secretary (acting), Revd R. F. S. Poots, Church House, Belfast bt1 6dw. Tel: 01232-322284

THE PRESBYTERIAN CHURCH OF WALES

The Presbyterian Church of Wales or Calvinistic Methodist Church of Wales is Calvinistic in doctrine and presbyterian in constitution. It was formed in 1811 when Welsh Calvinists severed the relationship with the established church by ordaining their own ministers. It secured its own confession of faith in 1823 and a Constitutional Deed in 1826, and since 1864 the General Assembly has met annually, presided over by a Moderator elected for a year. The doctrine and constitutional structure of the Presbyterian Church of Wales was confirmed by Act of Parliament in 1931–2.

The Church has 51,720 members, 136 ministers and 939 churches.

Moderator (1997–8), Revd H. Owain Jones
General Secretary, Revd D. H. Owen, 53 Richmond Road, Cardiff cf2 3up. Tel: 01222-494913

THE RELIGIOUS SOCIETY OF FRIENDS (QUAKERS)

Quakerism is a movement, not a church, which was founded in the 17th century by George Fox and others in an attempt to revive what they saw as 'primitive Christianity'. The movement was based originally in the Midlands, Yorkshire and north-west England, but there are now Quakers in 36 countries around the world. The colony of Pennsylvania, founded by William Penn, was originally Quaker.

Emphasis is placed on the experience of God in daily life rather than on sacraments or religious occasions. There is no church calendar. Worship is largely silent and there are no appointed ministers; the responsibility for conducting a meeting is shared equally among those present. Social reform and religious tolerance have always been important to Quakers, together with a commitment to non-violence in resolving disputes.

There are 213,800 Quakers world-wide, with over 19,000 in Great Britain and Ireland. There are about 490 meeting houses in Great Britain.

Central Offices: (Great Britain) Friends House, Euston Road, London nw1 2bj. Tel: 0171-387 3601; (Ireland) Swanbrook House, Morehampton Road, Dublin 4. Tel: 00 353 1-683684

THE SALVATION ARMY

The Salvation Army was founded by a Methodist minister, William Booth, in the east end of London in 1865, and has since become established in 103 countries world-wide. It was first known as the Christian Mission, and took its present name in 1878 when it adopted a quasi-military command structure intended to inspire and regulate its endeavours and to reflect its view that the Church was engaged in spiritual warfare. Salvationists emphasize evangelism, social work and the relief of poverty.

The world leader, known as the General, is elected by a High Council composed of the Chief of the Staff and senior ranking officers known as commissioners.

There are about 1.5 million members, 17,389 active officers (full-time ordained ministers) and 16,080 worship centres and outposts world-wide. In Great Britain and Ireland there are 65,168 members, 1,732 active officers and 986 worship centres.

General, P. A. Rader
UK Territorial Commander, Commissioner J. Gowans
Territorial Headquarters, 101 Queen Victoria Street, London ec4p 4ep. Tel: 0171-236 5222

THE SEVENTH-DAY ADVENTIST CHURCH

The Seventh-day Adventist Church was founded in 1863 in the USA. Its members look forward to the second coming of Christ and observe the Sabbath (the seventh day) as a day of rest, worship and ministry. The Church bases its faith and practice wholly on the Bible and has developed 27 fundamental beliefs.

The World Church is divided into 14 divisions, each made up of unions of churches. The Seventh-day Adventist Church in the British Isles is known as the British Union of Seventh-day Adventists and is a member of the Trans-European Division. In the British Isles the administrative organization of the church is arranged in three tiers: the local churches; the regional conferences for south England, north England, Wales, Scotland and Ireland; and the national 'union' conference.

There are about 9 million Adventists and 39,403 churches in 208 countries world-wide. In the UK and Ireland there are 18,806 members, 145 ministers and 238 churches.

President of the British Union Conference, Pastor C. R. Perry
BRITISH ISLES HEADQUARTERS, Stanborough Park, Watford WD2 6JP. Tel: 01923-672251

UNDEB YR ANNIBYNWYR CYMRAEG
The Union of Welsh Independents

The Union of Welsh Independents was formed in 1872 and is a voluntary association of Welsh Congregational Churches and personal members. It is entirely Welsh-speaking. Congregationalism in Wales dates back to 1639 when the first Welsh Congregational Church was opened in Gwent. Member churches are Calvinistic in doctrine and congregationalist in organization. Each church has complete independence in the government and administration of its affairs.

The Union has 42,442 members, 150 ministers and 555 member churches.

President of the Union (1997–8), Revd F. M. Jones
General Secretary, Revd D. Morris Jones, Tŷ John Penry, 11 Heol Sant Helen, Swansea SA1 4AL. Tel: 01792-652542

UNITARIAN AND FREE CHRISTIAN CHURCHES

Unitarianism has its historical roots in the Judaeo-Christian tradition but rejects the deity of Christ and the doctrine of the trinity. It allows the individual to embrace insights from all the world's faiths and philosophies, as there is no formal creed. It is accepted that beliefs may evolve in the light of personal experience.

Unitarian communities first became established in Poland and Transylvania in the 16th century. The first avowedly Unitarian place of worship in the British Isles opened in London in 1774. The General Assembly of Unitarian and Free Christian Churches came into existence in 1928 as the result of the amalgamation of two earlier organizations.

There are about 7,000 Unitarians in Great Britain and Ireland, and 150 Unitarian ministers. About 200 self-governing congregations and fellowship groups, including a small number overseas, are members of the General Assembly.

GENERAL ASSEMBLY OF UNITARIAN AND FREE CHRISTIAN CHURCHES, Essex Hall, 1–6 Essex Street, Strand, London WC2R 3HY. Tel: 0171-240 2384. *General Secretary*, J. J. Teagle

THE UNITED REFORMED CHURCH

The United Reformed Church was formed by the union of most of the Congregational churches in England and Wales with the Presbyterian Church of England in 1972.

Congregationalism dates from the mid 16th century. It is Calvinistic in doctrine, and its followers form independent self-governing congregations bound under God by covenant, a principle laid down in the writings of Robert Browne (1550–1633). From the late 16th century the movement was driven underground by persecution, but the cause was defended at the Westminster Assembly in 1643 and the Savoy Declaration of 1658 laid down its principles. Congregational churches formed county associations for mutual support and in 1832 these associations merged to form the Congregational Union of England and Wales.

The Presbyterian Church in England also dates from the mid 16th century, and was Calvinistic and evangelical in its doctrine. It was governed by a hierarchy of courts.

In the 1960s there was close co-operation locally and nationally between Congregational and Presbyterian Churches. This led to union negotiations and a Scheme of Union, supported by Act of Parliament in 1972. In 1981 a further unification took place, with the Reformed Association of Churches of Christ becoming part of the URC. In its basis the United Reformed Church reflects local church initiative and responsibility with a conciliar pattern of oversight. The General Assembly is the central body, and is made up of equal numbers of ministers and lay members.

The United Reformed Church is divided into 12 Provinces, each with a Provincial Moderator who chairs the Synod, and 75 Districts. There are 100,192 members, 741 full-time stipendiary ministers, 204 non-stipendiary ministers and 1,752 local churches.

General Secretary, Revd A. G. Burnham, 86 Tavistock Place, London WC1H 9RT. Tel: 0171-916 2020

THE WESLEYAN REFORM UNION

The Wesleyan Reform Union was founded by Methodists who left or were expelled from Wesleyan Methodism in 1849 following a period of internal conflict. Its doctrine is conservative evangelical and its organization is congregational, each church having complete independence in the government and administration of its affairs. The main concentration of churches is in Yorkshire.

The Union has 2,401 members, 20 ministers, 137 lay preachers and 115 churches.

President (1997–8), P. Busby
General Secretary, Revd E. W. Downing, Wesleyan Reform Church House, 123 Queen Street, Sheffield S1 2DU. Tel: 0114-272 1938

Non-Christian Faiths

BUDDHISM

Buddhism originated in northern India, in the teachings of Siddharta Gautama, who was born near Kapilavastu about 560 BC. After a long spiritual quest he experienced enlightenment beneath a tree at the place now known as Bodhgaya, and began missionary work.

Fundamental to Buddhism is the concept that there is no such thing as a permanent soul or self; when someone dies, consciousness is the only one of the elements of which they were composed which is lost. All the other elements regroup in a new body and carry with them the consequences of the conduct of the earlier life (known as the law of *karma*). This cycle of death and rebirth is broken only when the state of *nirvana* has been reached. Buddhism steers a middle path between belief in personal immortality and belief in death as the final end.

The Four Noble Truths of Buddhism (*dukkha*, suffering; *tanha*, a thirst or desire for continued existence which causes dukkha; *nirvana*, the final liberation from desire and ignorance; and *ariya*, the path to nirvana) are all held to be universal and to sum up the *dhamma* or true nature of life. Necessary qualities to promote spiritual development are *sila* (morality), *samadhi* (meditation) and *panna* (wisdom).

There are two main schools of Buddhism: *Theravada* Buddhism, the earliest extant school, which is more traditional, and *Mahayana* Buddhism, which began to develop about 100 years after the Buddha's death and is more liberal; it teaches that all people may attain Buddahood. Important schools which have developed within Mahayana Buddhism are *Zen* Buddhism, *Nichiren* Buddhism and Pure Land Buddhism or *Amidism*. There are also distinctive Tibetan forms of Buddhism. Buddhism began to establish itself in the West in the early 20th century.

The scripture of Theravada Buddhism is the *Pali Canon*, which dates from the first century BC. Mahayana Buddhism uses a Sanskrit version of the Pali Canon but also has many other works of scripture.

There is no set time for Buddhist worship, which may take place in a temple or in the home. Worship centres around *paritta* (chanting), acts of devotion centering on the image of the Buddha, and, where possible, offerings to a relic of the Buddha. Buddhist festivals vary according to local traditions and within Theravada and Mahayana Buddhism. For religious purposes Buddhists use solar and lunar calendars, the New Year being celebrated in April. Other festivals mark events in the life of the Buddha.

There is no supreme governing authority in Buddhism. In the United Kingdom communities representing all schools of Buddhism have developed and operate independently. The Buddhist Society was established in 1924; it runs courses and lectures, and publishes books about Buddhism. It represents no one school of Buddhism.

There are estimated to be at least 300 million Buddhists world-wide, and more than 500 groups and centres, an estimated 25,000 adherents and up to 20 temples or monasteries in the UK.

THE BUDDHIST SOCIETY, 58 Eccleston Square, London swiv iph. Tel: 0171-834 5858. *General Secretary*, R. C. Maddox

HINDUISM

Hinduism has no historical founder but had become highly developed in India by about 1200 BC. Its adherents originally called themselves Aryans; Muslim invaders first called the Aryans 'Hindus' (derived from 'Sindhu', the name of the river Indus) in the eighth century.

Hinduism's evolution has been complex and it embraces many different religious beliefs, mythologies and practices. Most Hindus hold that *satya* (truthfulness), *ahimsa* (non-violence), honesty, physical labour and tolerance of other faiths are essential for good living. They believe in one supreme spirit (*Brahman*), and in the transmigration of *atman* (the soul). Most Hindus accept the doctrine of *karma* (consequences of actions), the concept of *samsara* (successive lives) and the possibility of all atmans achieving *moksha* (liberation from samsara) through *jnana* (knowledge), *yoga* (meditation), *karma* (work or action) and *bhakti* (devotion).

Most Hindus offer worship to *murtis* (images or statues) representing different aspects of Brahman, and follow their *dharma* (religious and social duty) according to the traditions of their *varna* (social class), *ashrama* (stage in life), *jati* (caste) and *kula* (family).

Hinduism's sacred texts are divided into *shruti* ('heard' or divinely inspired), including the *Vedas*, or *smriti* ('remembered' tradition), including the *Ramayana*, the *Mahabharata*, the *Puranas* (ancient myths), and the sacred law books. Most Hindus recognize the authority of the *Vedas*, the oldest holy books, and accept the philosophical teachings of the *Upanishads*, the *Vedanta Sutras* and the *Bhagavad-Gita*.

Brahman is formless, limitless and all-pervading, and is represented in worship by murtis which may be male or female and in the form of a human, animal or bird. Brahma, Vishnu and Shiva are the most important gods worshipped by Hindus; their respective consorts are Saraswati, Lakshmi and Durga or Parvati, also known as Shakti. There are held to have been ten *avatars* (incarnations) of Vishnu, of whom the most important are Rama and Krishna. Other popular gods are Ganesha, Hanuman and Subrahmanyam. All gods are seen as aspects of the supreme God, not as competing deities.

Orthodox Hindus revere all gods and goddesses equally, but there are many sects, including the Hare-Krishna movement (ISKCon), the Arya Samaj, the Swami Narayan Hindu mission and the Satya Sai-Baba movement. Worship in the sects is concentrated on one deity to the exclusion of others. In some sects a human *guru* (spiritual teacher) is revered more than the deity, while in other sects the guru is seen as the source of spiritual guidance.

Hinduism does not have a centrally-trained and ordained priesthood. The pronouncements of the *shankaracharyas* (heads of monasteries) of Shringeri, Puri, Dwarka and Badrinath are heeded by the orthodox but may be ignored by the various sects.

The commonest form of worship is a *puja*, in which offerings of red and yellow powders, rice grains, water, flowers, food, fruit, incense and light are made to the *murti* (image) of a deity. Puja may be done either in a home shrine or a *mandir* (temple). Many British Hindus celebrate life-cycle rituals with Sanskrit mantras for naming a baby, the sacred thread (an initiation ceremony), marriage and cremation. For details of the Hindu calendar, main festivals etc, *see* pages 84–5.

The largest communities of Hindus in Britain are in Leicester, London, Birmingham and Bradford, and developed as a result of immigration from India, east Africa and Sri Lanka. Many Hindus now are British by birth, with English as their first language; the main ethnic languages are Gujarati, Hindi, Punjabi, Tamil, Bengali and Marathi.

There are an estimated 800 million Hindus world-wide; there are about 360,000 adherents and over 150 temples in the UK.

ARYA PRATINIDHI SABHA (UK) AND ARYA SAMAJ
    LONDON, 69A Argyle Road, London W13 0LY. Tel: 0181-
    991 1732. *President*, Prof. S. N. Bharadwaj
BHARATIYA VIDYA BHAVAN , Old Church Building, 4A
    Castletown Road, London W14 9HQ. Tel: 0171-381 3086.
    Executive Director, Dr M. N. Nandakumara
INTERNATIONAL SOCIETY FOR KRISHNA
    CONSCIOUSNESS (ISKCon), Bhaktivedanta Manor,
    Dharam Marg, Hilfield Lane, Aldenham, Watford, Herts
    WD2 8EZ. Tel: 01923-857244. *Governing Body
    Commissioner*, H. H. Sivarama Swami
NATIONAL COUNCIL OF HINDU TEMPLES (UK), c/o
    Shree Sanatan Mandir, Weymouth Street, off Catherine
    Street, Leicester LE4 6FP. Tel: 0116-266 1402. *Secretary*,
    V. Aery
SWAMINARAYAN HINDU MISSION, 105-119 Brentfield
    Road, London NW10 8JB. Tel: 0181-965 2651. *Head of
    Mission*, Sadhu Atmaswarupdas
VISHWA HINDU PARISHAD (UK), 48 Wharfedale
    Gardens, Thornton Heath, Surrey CR7 6LB. Tel: 0181-
    684 9716. *General Secretary*, K. Ruparelia

ISLAM

Islam (which means 'peace arising from submission to the will of Allah' in Arabic) is a monotheistic religion which originated in Arabia through the Prophet Muhammad, who was born in Mecca (Makkah) in AD 570. Islam spread to Egypt, North Africa, Spain and the borders of China in the century following the prophet's death, and is now the predominant religion in Indonesia, the Near and Middle East, North and parts of West Africa, Pakistan, Bangladesh, Malaysia and some of the former Soviet republics. There are also large Muslim communities in other countries.

For Muslims (adherents of Islam), God (*Allah*) is one and holds absolute power. His commands were revealed to mankind through the prophets, who include Abraham, Moses and Jesus, but his message was gradually corrupted until revealed finally and in perfect form to Muhammad through the angel *Jibril* (Gabriel) over a period of 23 years. This last, incorruptible message has been recorded in the *Qur'an* (Koran), which contains 114 divisions called *surahs*, each made up of *ayahs*, and is held to be the essence of all previous scriptures. The *Ahadith* are the records of the Prophet Muhammad's deeds and sayings (the *Sunnah*) as recounted by his immediate followers. A culture and a system of law and theology gradually developed to form a distinctive Islamic civilization. Islam makes no distinction between sacred and worldly affairs and provides rules for every aspect of human life. The *Shari'ah* is the sacred law of Islam based upon prescriptions derived from the Qur'an and the Sunnah of the Prophet.

The 'five pillars of Islam' are *shahadah* (a declaration of faith in the oneness and supremacy of Allah and the messengership of Muhammad); *salat* (formal prayer, to be performed five times a day facing the Ka'bah (sacred house)

in the holy city of Mecca); *zakat* (welfare due); *saum* (fasting during the month of Ramadan); and *hajj* (pilgrimage to Mecca); some Muslims would add *jihad* (striving for the cause of good and resistance to evil).

Two main groups developed among Muslims. *Sunni* Muslims accept the legitimacy of Muhammad's first four *caliphs* (successors as head of the Muslim community) and of the authority of the Muslim community as a whole. About 90 per cent of Muslims are *Sunni* Muslims. *Shi'ites* recognize only Muhammad's son-in-law Ali as his rightful successor and the *Imams* (descendants of Ali, not to be confused with *imams* (prayer leaders or religious teachers)) as the principal legitimate religious authority. The largest group within *Shi'ism* is *Twelver Shi'ism*, which has been the official school of law and theology in Iran since the 16th century; other subsects include the *Ismailis* and the *Druze*, the latter being an offshoot of the Ismailis and differing considerably from the main body of Muslims.

There is no organized priesthood, but learned men such as *ulama*, *imams* and *ayatollahs* are accorded great respect. The *Sufis* are the mystics of Islam. Mosques are centres for worship and teaching and also for social and welfare activities. For details of the Muslim calendar and festivals, *see* page 86.

Islam was first known in western Europe in the eighth century AD when 800 years of Muslim rule began in Spain. Later, Islam spread to eastern Europe. More recently, Muslims came to Europe from Africa, the Middle East and Asia in the late 19th century. Both the Sunni and Shi'ah traditions are represented in Britain, but the majority of Muslims in Britain adhere to Sunni Islam.

The largest communities are in London, Liverpool, Manchester, Birmingham, Bradford, Cardiff, Edinburgh and Glasgow. There is no central organization, but the Islamic Cultural Centre, which is the London Central Mosque, and the Imams and Mosques Council are influential bodies; there are many other Muslim organizations in Britain.

There are about 1,000 million Muslims world-wide, with more than one million adherents and about 900 mosques in Britain.

IMAMS AND MOSQUES COUNCIL, 20–22 Creffield Road,
    London W5 3RP. Tel: 0181-992 6636. *Director of the Council
    and Principal of the Muslim College*, Dr M. A. Z. Badawi
ISLAMIC CULTURAL CENTRE, 146 Park Road, London
    NW8 7RG. Tel: 0171-724 3363. *Director*, H. Al-Majed
MUSLIM WORLD LEAGUE, 46 Goodge Street, London W1P
    1FJ. Tel: 0171-636 7568. *Director*, U. A. Baidulmaal
UNION OF MUSLIM ORGANIZATIONS OF THE UK AND
    EIRE, 109 Campden Hill Road, London W8 7TL. Tel:
    0171-229 0538. *General Secretary*, Dr S. A. Pasha

JUDAISM

Judaism is the oldest monotheistic faith. The primary authority of Judaism is the Hebrew Bible or *Tanakh*, which records how the descendants of Abraham were led by Moses out of their slavery in Egypt to Mount Sinai where God's law (*Torah*) was revealed to them as the chosen people. The *Talmud*, which consists of commentaries on the *Mishnah* (the first text of rabbinical Judaism), is also held to be authoritative, and may be divided into two main categories: the *halakah* (dealing with legal and ritual matters) and the *Aggadah* (dealing with theological and ethical matters not directly concerned with the regulation of conduct). The *Midrash* comprises rabbinic writings containing biblical interpretations in the spirit of the

Aggadah. The *halakah* has become a source of division; Orthodox Jews regard Jewish law as derived from God and therefore unalterable; Reform and Liberal Jews seek to interpret it in the light of contemporary considerations; and Conservative Jews aim to maintain most of the traditional rituals but to allow changes in accordance with tradition. Reconstructionist Judaism, a 20th-century movement, regards Judaism as a culture rather than a theological system and accepts all forms of Jewish practice.

The family is the basic unit of Jewish ritual, with the synagogue playing an important role as the centre for public worship and religious study. A synagogue is led by a group of laymen who are elected to office. The Rabbi is primarily a teacher and spiritual guide. The Sabbath is the central religious observance. For details of the Jewish calendar, fasts and festivals, *see* page 85. Most British Jews are descendants of either the *Ashkenazim* of central and eastern Europe or the *Sephardim* of Spain and Portugal.

The Chief Rabbi of the United Hebrew Congregations of the Commonwealth is appointed by a Chief Rabbinate Conference, and is the rabbinical authority of the Orthodox sector of the Ashkenazi Jewish community. His authority is not recognized by the Reform Synagogues of Great Britain (the largest progressive group), the Union of Liberal and Progressive Synagogues, the Union of Orthodox Hebrew Congregations, the Federation of Synagogues, the Sephardi community, or the Assembly of Masorti Synagogues. He is, however, generally recognized both outside the Jewish community and within it as the public religious representative of the totality of British Jewry.

The *Beth Din* (Court of Judgment) is the rabbinic court. The *Dayanim* (Assessors) adjudicate in disputes or on matters of Jewish law and tradition; they also oversee dietary law administration. The Chief Rabbi is President of the *Beth Din* of the United Synagogue.

The Board of Deputies of British Jews, established in 1760, is the representative body of British Jewry. The basis of representation is mainly synagogal, but communal organizations are also represented. It watches over the interests of British Jewry and seeks to counter anti-Jewish discrimination and anti-Semitic activities.

There are over 12.5 million Jews world-wide; in Great Britain and Ireland there are an estimated 285,000 adherents and about 365 synagogues. Of these, 191 congregations and about 150 rabbis and ministers are under the jurisdiction of the Chief Rabbi; 99 orthodox congregations have a more independent status; and 75 congregations do not recognize the authority of the Chief Rabbi.

CHIEF RABBINATE, 735 High Road, London N12 0US. Tel: 0181-343 6301. *Chief Rabbi*, Dr Jonathan Sacks; *Executive Director*, Mrs S. Weinberg

BETH DIN (COURT OF THE CHIEF RABBI), 735 High Road, London N12 0US. Tel: 0181-343 6280. *Registrar*, vacant; *Dayanim*, Rabbi C. Ehrentreu; Rabbi I. Binstock; Rabbi C. D. Kaplin; Rabbi M. Gelley

BOARD OF DEPUTIES OF BRITISH JEWS, Commonwealth House, 1–19 New Oxford Street, London WC1A 1NF. Tel: 0171-543 5400. *President*, E. Tabachnik, QC; *Director-General*, N. A. Nagler

ASSEMBLY OF MASORTI SYNAGOGUES, 1097 Finchley Road, London NW11 0PU. Tel: 0181-201 8772. *Director*, H. Freedman

FEDERATION OF SYNAGOGUES, 65 Watford Way, London NW4 3AQ. Tel: 0181-202 2263. *Administrator*, G. Kushner

REFORM SYNAGOGUES OF GREAT BRITAIN, The Sternberg Centre for Judaism, 80 East End Road, London N3 2SY. Tel: 0181-349 4731. *Chief Executive*, Rabbi T. Bayfield

SPANISH AND PORTUGUESE JEWS' CONGREGATION, 2 Ashworth Road, London W9 1JY. Tel: 0171-289 2573. *Chief Administrator and Secretary*, H. Miller

UNION OF LIBERAL AND PROGRESSIVE SYNAGOGUES, The Montagu Centre, 21 Maple Street, London W1P 6DS. Tel: 0171-580 1663. *Director*, Mrs R. Rosenberg

UNION OF ORTHODOX HEBREW CONGREGATIONS, 140 Stamford Hill, London N16 6QT. Tel: 0181-802 6226. *Executive Director*, Rabbi A. Klein

UNITED SYNAGOGUE HEAD OFFICE, 735 High Road, London N12 0US. Tel: 0181-343 8989. *Chief Executive*, J. M. Lew

SIKHISM

The Sikh religion dates from the birth of Guru Nanak in the Punjab in 1469. 'Guru' means teacher but in Sikh tradition has come to represent the divine presence of God giving inner spiritual guidance. Nanak's role as the human vessel of the divine guru was passed on to nine successors, the last of whom (Guru Gobind Singh) died in 1708. The immortal guru is now held to reside in the sacred scripture, *Guru Granth Sahib*, and so to be present in all Sikh gatherings.

Guru Nanak taught that there is one God and that different religions are like different roads leading to the same destination. He condemned religious conflict, ritualism and caste prejudices. The fifth Guru, Guru Arjan, largely compiled the Sikh Holy Book, a collection of hymns (*gurbani*) known as the *Adi Granth*. It includes the writings of the first five Gurus and the ninth Guru, and selected writings of Hindu and Muslim saints whose views are in accord with the Gurus' teachings. Guru Arjan also built the Golden Temple at Amritsar, the centre of Sikhism. The tenth Guru, Guru Gobind Singh, passed on the guruship to the sacred scripture, Guru Granth Sahib. He also founded the *Khalsa*, an order intended to fight against tyranny and injustice. Male initiates to the order added 'Singh' to their given names and women added 'Kaur'. Guru Gobind Singh also made five symbols obligatory: *kaccha* (a special undergarment), *kara* (a steel bangle), *kirpan* (a small sword), *kesh* (long unshorn hair, and consequently the wearing of a turban), and *kangha* (a comb). These practices are still compulsory for those Sikhs who are initiated into the *Khalsa* (the *Amritdharis*). Those who do not seek initiation are known as *Sehajdharis*.

There are no professional priests in Sikhism; anyone with a reasonable proficiency in the Punjabi language can conduct a service. Worship can be offered individually or communally, and in a private house or a *gurdwara* (temple). Sikhs are forbidden to eat meat prepared by ritual slaughter; they are also asked to abstain from smoking, alcohol and other intoxicants. For details of the Sikh calendar and main celebrations, *see* page 86.

There are about 20 million Sikhs world-wide and about 400,000 adherents and 250 gurdwaras in Great Britain. The largest communities are in London, Bradford, Leeds, Huddersfield, Birmingham, Coventry and Wolverhampton. Every gurdwara manages its own affairs and there is no central body in the UK. The Sikh Missionary Society provides an information service.

SIKH MISSIONARY SOCIETY UK, 10 Featherstone Road, Southall, Middx UB2 5AA. Tel: 0181-574 1902. *Hon. General Secretary*, M. Singh

WORLD SIKH FOUNDATION, 88 Mollison Way, Edgware, Middx HA8 5QW. Tel: 0181-952 1215. *Secretary*, Mrs. H. Bharara

Education

For addresses of national education departments, *see* Government Departments and Public Offices. For other addresses, *see* Education Directory

Responsibility for education in the United Kingdom is largely decentralized. Overall responsibility for all aspects of education in England lies with the Secretary of State for Education and Employment; in Wales with the Secretary of State for Wales, in Scotland with the Secretary of State for Scotland acting through the Scottish Office Education and Industry Department; and in Northern Ireland with the Secretary of State for Northern Ireland.

The main concerns of the education departments (the Department for Education and Employment (DFEE), the Welsh Office, the Scottish Office Education and Industry Department (SOEID), and the Department of Education for Northern Ireland (DENI)) are the formulation of national policies for education and the maintenance of consistency in educational standards. They are responsible for the broad allocation of resources for education, for the rate and distribution of educational building and for the supply, training and superannuation of teachers.

EXPENDITURE

In the UK in 1994–5, provisional expenditure on education was (£ million):

Schools	20,537.8
Further and higher education	9,005.0
Other education and related expenditure	3,651.6

Most of this expenditure is incurred by local authorities, which make their own expenditure decisions according to their local situations and needs. Expenditure on education by central government departments, in real terms, was (£ million).

	1996–7 estimated outturn	1997–8 planned
DFEE	10,814	11,651
Welsh Office	524.4	562.5
SOEID	1,313	1,215
DENI	1,267	1,242

The bulk of direct expenditure by the DFEE, the Welsh Office and SOEID is directed towards supporting higher education in universities and colleges through the Higher Education Funding Councils (HEFCs) and further education and sixth form colleges through the Further Education Funding Councils (FEFCs) in England and Wales and directly from central government in Scotland. In addition, the DFEE funds the City Technology Colleges (CTCs), the City College for the Technology of the Arts, and pays grants under the specialist schools programme.

The Welsh Office also funds grants for higher and further education, educational services and research, and supports bilingual education and the Welsh language.

In Scotland the main elements of central government expenditure, in addition to those outlined above, are grant-aided special schools, student awards and bursaries (through the Student Award Agency for Scotland), curriculum development, special educational needs and community education.

The Department of Education for Northern Ireland directly funds higher education, teacher education,

teacher salaries and superannuation, student awards, further education, grant-maintained integrated schools, and voluntary grammar schools.

Current net expenditure on education by local education authorities in England, Wales, and Scotland, and education and library boards in Northern Ireland is (£ million):

	1996–7 estimated outturn	1997–8 planned
England	20.5	18.0
Wales	1.25	1.23
Scotland	2.5	2.52
Northern Ireland	0.97	0.94

LOCAL EDUCATION ADMINISTRATION

The education service at present is a national service in which the provision of most school education is locally administered; its administration is still largely decentralized.

In England and Wales the education service is administered by local education authorities (LEAs), which carry the day-to-day responsibility for providing most state primary and secondary education in their areas. They share with the FEFCs the duty to provide adult education to meet the needs of their areas.

The LEAs own and maintain schools and colleges, build new ones and provide equipment. Most of the public money spent on education is disbursed by the local authorities. LEAs are financed largely from the council tax and aggregate external finance (AEF) from the Department for the Environment, Transport and the Regions in England and the Welsh Office in Wales.

The powers of local education authorities as regards the control of schools have been modified in recent years and all LEA-maintained schools manage their own budgets. The LEA allocates funds to the school, largely on the basis of pupil numbers, and the school governing body is responsible for overseeing spending and for most aspects of staffing, including appointments and dismissals. It is proposed to give LEAs greater powers to monitor, maintain and improve standards. An Education Association can be set up to take over the management of failing schools where both the LEA and the governing body have not brought about improvements identified as necessary by inspection.

The duty of providing education locally in Scotland rests with the education authorities. They are responsible for the construction of buildings, the employment of teachers and other staff, and the provision of equipment and materials. Devolved School Management (DSM) is in place for all primary, secondary and special schools except those primary schools with headteachers who teach full-time, where it will be introduced by April 1998.

The powers of local authorities over educational institutions under their control have been reduced also in Scotland. Education authorities are required to establish school boards consisting of parents and teachers as well as co-opted members, responsible among other things for the appointment of staff.

Education is administered locally in Northern Ireland by five education and library boards, whose costs are met in full by DENI. All grant-aided schools include elected parents and teachers on their boards of governors. Provision has been made for schools wishing to provide integrated education to have grant-maintained integrated status from the outset. All schools and colleges of further education have full responsibility for their own budgets, including staffing costs. The Council for Catholic Maintained Schools forms an upper tier of management for Catholic schools and provides advice on matters relating to management and administration.

THE INSPECTORATE

The Office for Standards in Education (OFSTED) is a non-ministerial government department in England headed by HM Chief Inspector of Schools (HMCI). OFSTED's remit is regularly to inspect all maintained schools and report on and thereby improve standards of achievement. All state schools are inspected by teams of independent inspectors on contract to OFSTED, including educationalists and lay people and headed by registered inspectors. HM Inspectors (HMI) within OFSTED report on good practice in schools and other educational issues based on inspection evidence. From 1997 for secondary and from 1998 for primary, schools will be inspected once every six years or more frequently if there is cause. A summary of the inspection report must be sent to the parents of each pupil by the school, followed by a copy of the governors' action plan thereon. OFSTED's counterpart in Wales is the Office of HM Chief Inspector of Schools in Wales (OHMCI Wales), where inspection of maintained schools is carried out on a five-year cycle. The inspection of further and higher education in England and Wales is the responsibility of inspectors appointed to the respective funding councils.

HM Inspectorate in Scotland carries out the inspection of schools and further education institutions in Scotland, using teams which include lay people, and in addition requires schools to produce a document setting out their educational targets for two years ahead and a report on progress over the previous two years. The inspection of higher education is the responsibility of inspectors appointed to the Higher Education Funding Council for Scotland.

Inspection is carried out in Northern Ireland by the Department of Education's Education and Training Inspectorate, using teams which include lay people. The Inspectorate also performs an advisory function to the Secretary of State for Northern Ireland. From September 1992 a five-year cycle of inspection was introduced.

There were, in 1997–8, 200 HMIs on OFSTED's permanent staff, 1,500 trained registered inspectors, 6,500 team inspectors in England, 38 HMIs and about 900 registered inspectors and team members in Wales, 75 HMIs and eight team inspectors in Scotland and 60 members of the Inspectorate in Northern Ireland.

SCHOOLS AND PUPILS

Schooling is compulsory in Great Britain for all children between five and 16 years and between four and 16 years in Northern Ireland. Increasing provision is made for children under five and many pupils remain at school after the minimum leaving age. No fees are charged in any publicly maintained school in England, Wales and Scotland. In Northern Ireland, fees are paid by pupils in preparatory departments of grammar schools, but pupils admitted to the secondary departments of grammar schools do not pay fees.

In the UK, parents have a right to express a preference for a particular school and have a right to appeal if dissatisfied. The policy, known as more open enrolment, requires schools to admit children up to the limit of their capacity if there is a demand for places, and to publish their criteria for selection if they are over-subscribed, in which case parents have a right of appeal.

The 'Parents' Charter', available free from education departments, is a booklet which tells parents about the education system. Schools are now required to make available information about themselves, their public examination and national test results, truancy rates, and destination of leavers. Corporal punishment is no longer legal in publicly maintained schools in the UK.

FALL AND RISE IN NUMBERS

In primary education, and increasingly in secondary education, pupil numbers in the UK declined through the 1980s. In maintained nursery and primary schools pupil numbers reached their lowest figure of 4.6 million in 1986. They stood at 5.2 million in 1996 and are expected to increase gradually year by year until by 2001 they reach about 5.25 million. In secondary schools pupil numbers peaked at 4.6 million in 1981. They stood at 3.7 million in 1996 and are projected to rise to about 4 million in 2006.

ENGLAND AND WALES

There are two main types of school in England and Wales: publicly maintained schools, which charge no fees; and independent schools, which charge fees (*see* pages 437–8). Publicly maintained schools are maintained by local education authorities except for City Technology Colleges.

The number of schools by category in 1996 was:

Maintained schools	22,893
County	15,758
Voluntary	7,135
controlled	2,970
aided	4,124
special agreement*	41
Grant-maintained	1,090
Wales	16
CTCs and CCTAs	15
Independent schools	2,326
TOTAL	26,340

* There are no special agreement schools in Wales

County schools are owned by LEAs and wholly funded by them. They are non-denominational and provide primary and secondary education. Voluntary schools also provide primary and secondary education. Although the buildings are in many cases provided by the voluntary bodies (mainly religious denominations), they are financially maintained by an LEA. In controlled schools the LEA bears all costs. In aided schools the building is usually provided by the voluntary body. The managers or governors are responsible for repairs to the school building and for improvements and alterations to it, though the DFEE may reimburse part of approved capital expenditure, while the LEA pays for internal maintenance and other running costs. Special agreement schools are those where the LEA may, by special agreement, pay between one-half and three-quarters of the cost of building a new, or extending an existing, voluntary school, almost always a secondary school. The Government plans to legislate for a new structure of community, aided and foundation schools in the 1997–8 session of Parliament.

Under the Local Management of Schools (LMS) initiative, LEAs are required to delegate at least 85 per cent of school budgets, including staffing costs, directly to schools. LEAs continue to retain responsibility for various services, including transport and school meals.

Governing bodies – All publicly maintained schools have a governing body, usually made up of a number of parent representatives, governors appointed by the LEA if the school is LEA maintained, the headteacher (unless he or she chooses otherwise), and serving teachers. Schools can appoint up to four sponsor governors from business who will be expected to provide financial and managerial assistance. Governors are responsible for the overall policies of schools and their academic aims and objectives; they also control matters of school discipline and the appointment and dismissal of staff. Governing bodies select inspectors for their schools, are responsible for action as a result of inspection reports and are required to make those reports and their action plans thereon available to parents.

The Specialist Schools Programme – The programme is open to all state secondary schools wishing to specialize in the teaching of technology, mathematics and science (technology colleges), modern foreign languages (language colleges), sports colleges and arts colleges. In addition to the normal funding arrangements, the colleges receive business sponsorship (up to four sponsor governors may sit on governing bodies) and complementary capital grants up to £100,000 from central government, together with extra annual funding of £100 a pupil to assist the delivery of an enhanced curriculum. By September 1997, there were 206 technology colleges, 47 language colleges, six sports colleges and three arts colleges. In Wales the Technology Schools Initiative provides grants to enhance technology teaching to those schools successful in attracting funding through open competition.

Grant-maintained (GM) schools – Under the Conservative government, all secondary and primary schools, whether maintained or independent, were eligible to apply for grant-maintained status, subject to a ballot of parents. GM schools were maintained directly by the Secretary of State and the Welsh Office, not the LEA, and were wholly run by their own governing body. They also had the freedom to borrow commercially to fund capital projects. Legislation is to be introduced to change the position of GM schools and to enable them to be absorbed into the mainstream. The role of the Funding Agency for Schools, which paid grants to GM schools in England is under review. As of September 1996 about 60 per cent of grant-maintained schools were secondary schools.

City Technology Colleges (CTCs) and *City Colleges for the Technology of the Arts (CCTAs)* are state-aided but independent of LEAs. Their aim is to widen the choice of secondary education in disadvantaged urban areas and to teach a broad curriculum with an emphasis on science, technology, business understanding and arts technologies. Capital costs are shared by government and sponsors from industry and commerce, and running costs are covered by a per capita grant from the DFEE in line with comparable costs in an LEA maintained school. The first city technology college opened in 1988 in Solihull. The first CCTA, known as Britschool, opened in Croydon in 1991.

SCOTLAND

The number of schools by category in 1996 was:

Publicly maintained schools:
Education authority	3,704
Self-governing	2
Independent schools	115
TOTAL	3,821

Education authority schools (known as public schools) are financed jointly by the authorities and central government. A small number of grant-aided schools, mainly in the special sector, are conducted by voluntary managers and receive grants direct from the SOEID. Independent schools receive no direct grant and charge fees, but are subject to inspection and registration. Under the previous government, an additional category existed of self-governing schools opting to be managed entirely by a board of management. These schools remained in the public sector and were funded by direct government grant set to match the resources the school would have received under education authority management. Two were established, but legislation during the 1997–8 session of Parliament will provide for them to be returned to the education authority framework.

Education authorities are required to establish school boards to participate in the administration and management of schools. These boards consist of elected parents and staff members as well as co-opted members.

NORTHERN IRELAND

The number of schools by category in 1996 was:

Grant-aided schools:	
Controlled	660
Voluntary maintained	550
Voluntary grammar	53
Integrated schools	28
Independent schools	21
TOTAL	1,312

Controlled schools are controlled by the education and library boards with all costs paid from public funds. Voluntary maintained schools, mainly under Roman Catholic management, receive grants towards capital costs and running costs in whole or in part. Voluntary grammar schools may be under Roman Catholic or non-denominational management and receive grants from DENI. All grant-aided schools include elected parents and teachers on their boards of governors, whose responsibilities also include financial management under the Local Management of Schools (LMS) initiative. All secondary schools now have fully delegated budgets and as of 1995–6 77 per cent of primary schools. Voluntary maintained and voluntary grammar schools can apply for designation as a new category of voluntary school, which is eligible for a 100 per cent as opposed to 85 per cent grant. Such schools are managed by a board of governors on which no single interest group has a majority of nominees.

The majority of children in Northern Ireland are educated in schools which in practice are segregated on religious lines. Integrated schools exist to educate Protestant and Roman Catholic children together. There are two types: grant-maintained integrated schools which are funded by DENI; and controlled integrated schools funded by the education and library boards. Procedures are in place for balloting parents in existing segregated schools to determine whether they want instead to have integrated schools. By September 1998, 34 integrated schools will have been established, 12 of them secondary.

THE STATE SYSTEM

NURSERY EDUCATION – Nursery education is for children from two to five years and is not compulsory. It takes place in nursery schools or nursery classes in primary schools.

The number of children receiving nursery education in the UK in 1995–6 was:

In maintained nursery schools	84,000
In primary schools	986,500
In non-maintained nursery schools	66,500
In special schools	8,200
TOTAL	1,145,200
% of total three- and four-year-old population	72%

Many children also attend pre-school playgroups organized by parents and voluntary bodies such as the Pre-School Learning Alliance. The nursery voucher scheme, whereby every parent of a four-year-old was to be given a voucher worth £1,100 exchangeable for up to three terms of pre-school education, was introduced in England and Wales in April 1997. It was discontinued by the new Labour government in summer 1997, before it had begun in Northern Ireland. Education authorities are instead responsible for funding nursery education in their areas using a range of providers. By April 1998 all education authorities are expected to have Early Years Development Plans in place after reviewing and consulting on under-fives services in their areas. Transitional arrangements exist where necessary in the form of a certificate equal in value to that of a voucher for each four-year-old. In Scotland vouchers will remain in place until August 1998 while consultation on future plans takes place.

PRIMARY EDUCATION – Primary education begins at five years in Great Britain and four years in Northern Ireland, and is almost always co-educational. In England, Wales and Northern Ireland the transfer to secondary school is generally made at 11 years. In Scotland, the primary school course lasts for seven years and pupils transfer to secondary courses at about the age of 12.

Primary schools consist mainly of infants' schools for children aged five to seven, junior schools for those aged seven to 11, and combined junior and infant schools for both age groups. First schools in some parts of England cater for ages five to ten as the first stage of a three-tier system: first, middle and secondary. Many primary schools provide nursery classes for children under five (see above).

Primary schools (UK) 1995–6

No. of primary schools	23,426
No. of pupils	5,142,500
Pupils under five years	986,500

Pupil-teacher ratios in maintained primary schools were:

	1994–5	1995–6
England	22.9	23.2
Wales	22.5	22.5
Scotland	19.5	19.6
Northern Ireland	20.8	19.5
UK	21.4	21.2

The average size of classes 'as taught' was 25.8 in 1994 but fell to 25.5 in 1996.

MIDDLE SCHOOLS – Middle schools (which take children from first schools), mostly in England, cover varying age ranges between eight and 14 and usually lead on to comprehensive upper schools.

SECONDARY EDUCATION – Secondary schools are for children aged 11 to 16 and for those who choose to stay on to 18. At 16, many students prefer to move on to tertiary or sixth form colleges (see page 441). Most secondary schools in England, Wales and Scotland are co-educational. The largest secondary schools have over 1,500 pupils but only 29.5 per cent of the schools take over 1,000 pupils.

Secondary schools 1996

	England and Wales	Scotland	N. Ireland
No. of pupils	3,209,000	316,000	152,000
% over 16 years	37.3%	63.2%	53.6%
Average class size	21.9	19.5	n/a
Pupil-teacher ratio	14.3	13.0	14.5

In England and Wales the main types of secondary schools are: comprehensive schools (86.8 per cent of pupils in England, 100 in Wales), whose admission arrangements are without reference to ability or aptitude; middle deemed secondary schools for children aged variously between eight and 14 years who then move on to senior comprehensive schools at 12, 13 or 14 (5.2 per cent of pupils in England); secondary modern schools (2.6 per cent of pupils in England) providing a general education with a practical bias; secondary grammar schools (4.2 per cent of pupils in England) with selective intake providing an academic course from 11 to 16–18 years; and technical schools (0.1 per cent in England), providing an integrated academic and technical education.

In Scotland all pupils in education authority secondary schools attend schools with a comprehensive intake. Most of these schools provide a full range of courses appropriate to all levels of ability from first to sixth year.

In most areas of Northern Ireland there is a selective system of secondary education with pupils transferring either to grammar schools (40.3 per cent of pupils in 1996) or secondary schools (59.7 per cent of pupils in 1996) at 11–12 years of age. Parents can choose the school they would like their children to attend and all those who apply must be admitted if they meet the criteria. If a school is over-subscribed beyond its statutory admissions number, selection is on the basis of published criteria, which, for most grammar schools, place emphasis on performance in the transfer procedure tests which are set and administered by the Northern Ireland Council for the Curriculum, Examinations and Assessment. When parents consider that a school has not applied its criteria fairly they have access to independent appeals tribunals. Grammar schools provide an academic type of secondary education with A-levels at the end of the seventh year, while secondary non-grammar schools follow a curriculum suited to a wider range of aptitudes and abilities.

SPECIAL EDUCATION – Special education is provided for children with special educational needs, usually because they have a disability which either prevents or hinders them from making use of educational facilities of a kind generally provided for children of their age in schools within the area of the local authority concerned. Wherever possible, such children are educated in ordinary schools, taking the parents' wishes into account, and schools are required to publish their policy for pupils with special educational needs. LEAs in England and Wales are required to identify and secure provision for the needs of children with learning difficulties, to involve the parents in any decision and draw up a formal statement of the child's special educational needs and how they intend to meet them, all within statutory time limits. Parents have a right to appeal to a Special Educational Needs (SEN) Tribunal if they disagree with the statement. A code of practice similar to that in England and Wales is to be introduced in Northern Ireland with effect from 1998–9.

Maintained special schools are run by education authorities which pay all the costs of maintenance, but under the terms of Local Management of Schools (LMS), those able and wishing to manage their own budgets may choose to do so. Non-maintained special schools are run by voluntary bodies; they may receive some grant from central government for capital expenditure and for equipment but their current expenditure is met primarily from the fees charged to education authorities for pupils placed in the schools. Some independent schools provide education wholly or mainly for children with special educational needs and are required to meet similar standards to those for maintained and non-maintained special schools. It is intended that pupils with special education needs should have access to as much of the national curriculum as possible, but there is provision for them to be exempt from it or for it to be modified to suit their capabilities.

The number of full-time pupils with special needs in January 1996 was:

Special schools: total	109,700
England	93,500
Wales	3,400
Scotland	8,200
N. Ireland	4,600
Hospital schools: total	200
Public sector primary and secondary schools: total	149,400
England	126,800
Wales	11,600
Scotland	7,700
N. Ireland	3,300

In Scotland, school placing is a matter of agreement between education authorities and parents. Parents have the right to say which school they want their child to attend, and a right of appeal where their wishes are not being met. Whenever possible, children with special needs are integrated into ordinary schools. However, for those who require a different environment or specialized facilities, there are special schools, both grant-aided by central government and independent, and special classes within ordinary schools. Education authorities are required to respond to reasonable requests for independent special schools and to send children with special needs to schools outside Scotland if appropriate provision is not available within the country.

ALTERNATIVE PROVISION

There is no legal obligation on parents in the UK to educate their children at school provided that the local education authority is satisfied that the child is receiving full-time education suited to its age, abilities and aptitudes. The education authority need not be informed that a child is being educated at home unless the child is already registered at a state school. In this case the parents must arrange for the child's name to be removed from the school's register (by writing to the headteacher) before education at home can begin. Failure to do so leaves the parents liable to prosecution for condoning non-attendance.

In most cases an initial visit is made by an education adviser or education welfare officer, and sometimes subsequent inspections are made, but practice varies according to the individual education authority. There is no requirement for parents educating their children at home to be in possession of a teaching qualification.

Information and support on all aspects of home education can be obtained from Education Otherwise (see page 451).

INDEPENDENT SCHOOLS

Independent schools receive no grants from public funds. They charge fees, and are owned and managed under special trusts, with profits being used for the benefit of the schools concerned. There is a wide variety of provision,

from kindergartens to large day and boarding schools, and from experimental schools to traditional institutions. A number of independent schools have been instituted by religious and ethnic minorities.

All independent schools in the UK are open to inspection by approved inspectors (see page 434) and must register with the appropriate government education department. The education departments lay down certain minimum standards and can make schools remedy any unacceptable features of their building or instruction and exclude any unsuitable teacher or proprietor. Most independent schools offer a similar range of courses to state schools and enter pupils for the same public examinations. Introduction of the national curriculum and the associated education targets and assessment procedures is not obligatory in the independent sector.

The term public schools is often applied to those independent schools in membership of the Headmasters' and Headmistresses' Conference, the Governing Bodies Association or the Governing Bodies of Girls' Schools Association. Most public schools are single-sex but there are some mixed schools and an increasing number of schools have mixed sixth forms.

Preparatory schools are so-called because they prepare pupils for the common entrance examination to senior independent schools. Most cater for pupils from about seven to 13 years. The common entrance examination is set by the Common Entrance Examination Board, but marked by the independent school to which the pupil intends to go. It is taken at 13 by boys, and between 11 and 13 by girls.

The number of schools and pupils in 1995–6 was:

	No. of schools	No. of pupils	Pupil-teacher ratio
England	2,251	559,400	10.0
Wales	62	10,043	10.1
Scotland	87	32,200	11.0
N. Ireland	21	1,100	9.8

Most independent schools in Scotland follow the English examination system, i.e. GCSE followed by A-levels, although some take the Scottish Education Certificate at Standard grade followed by Highers or Advanced Highers.

ASSISTED PLACES SCHEME

The Assisted Places Scheme is to be phased out after the September 1997 entry. It enabled children to attend independent secondary schools which their parents could not otherwise afford. The scheme provides help with tuition fees and other expenses, except boarding costs, on a sliding scale depending on the family's income. The proportion of pupils receiving full fee remission is about 46 per cent. In the 1997–8 academic year, about 38,900 places were offered at the 494 participating schools in England and Wales. The 54 participating schools in Scotland admitted about 3,500 pupils on the scheme in 1996–7, which, unlike that in England and Wales, is cash-limited. The proportion of pupils receiving full fee remission was about 47 per cent. Pupils in secondary education holding their places at the beginning of the 1997–8 school year will keep them until they have completed their education at their current school. Those at the primary stage will hold them until they have completed that phase of their education, although some may exceptionally be allowed to hold their places for a further period to complete their secondary education.

The scheme is administered and funded in England by the DFEE, in Wales by the Welsh Office, and in Scotland by the SOEID. The scheme does not operate in Northern Ireland as the independent sector admits non-fee-paying pupils. There is, however, a similar scheme known as the Talented Children's Scheme to help pupils gifted in music and dance.

Further information can be obtained from the Independent Schools Information Service (*see* page 451).

THE CURRICULUM

ENGLAND AND WALES

The national curriculum was introduced in primary and secondary schools between autumn 1989 and autumn 1996, for the period of compulsory schooling from five to 16. It is mandatory in all maintained schools. As originally proposed, it was widely criticized for being too prescriptive and time-consuming. Following revision in 1994 its requirements were substantially reduced; the revisions were implemented in August 1995 for key stages one to three and from August 1996 for key stage four.

The statutory subjects at key stages one and two (five–11-year olds) are:

Core subjects	*Foundation subjects*
English	Design and technology
Welsh, for Welsh-speaking schools in Wales	Information technology
	History
Mathematics	Geography
Science	Welsh, in Wales
	Art
	Music
	PE

At key stage three (11- to 14-year olds) all pupils must study a modern foreign language. At key stage four (14- to 16-year olds) pupils are required to take GCSEs in the core subjects and at least a GCSE short course in a modern foreign language and design and technology (optional subjects in Wales); they must also continue to study, although they are not required to take examinations in, information technology and PE. Other foundation subjects are optional. Religious education must be taught across all key stages, following a locally agreed syllabus; parents have the right to remove their children if they wish.

National tests and tasks in English and mathematics at key stage one, with the addition of science at key stages two and three, are in place. Teachers make their own assessments of their pupils' progress to set alongside the test results. At key stage four the GCSE and vocational equivalents will be the main form of assessment.

For several years the DFEE and the Welsh Office have published tables showing pupils' performance in A-level, AS-level, GCSE and GNVQ examinations by school. Local education authorities will be required to publish similar information showing the results of the 1997 national curriculum tests and teacher assessments for seven-, 11- and 14-year-olds in January 1998 and thereafter in November each year. Approximately 600,000 pupils in each of the age groups take the tests each year in England and Wales.

In Wales in 1995–6 the Welsh language was in use as the main or secondary medium of instruction or taught as a second language in 99.4 per cent of primary schools. In secondary schools Welsh was taught as a first or second language in 99.1 per cent of schools. It constitutes a core subject of the national curriculum in schools in which Welsh is taught as a first language and a foundation subject in the others, although there is provision for exemptions to be made; by September 1999 all pupils will be taught Welsh throughout the period of compulsory schooling. A two-

year review of assessment arrangements for the national curriculum is taking place.

In October 1997 the School Curriculum and Assessment Authority (SCAA) and the National Council for Vocational Qualifications (NCVQ) (*see* page 442) merged to form the Qualifications and Curriculum Authority (QCA). An independent government agency funded by the DFEE, its remit ranges from the under-fives to higher level vocational qualifications. It is responsible for ensuring that the curriculum and qualifications available to young people and adults are of high quality, coherent and flexible. In Wales its functions are performed by the Qualifications, Curriculum and Assessment Authority for Wales, funded by the Welsh Office.

SCOTLAND

The content and management of the curriculum in Scotland are not prescribed by statute but are the responsibility of education authorities and individual headteachers. Advice and guidance is provided by the SOEID and the Scottish Consultative Council on the Curriculum. SOEID has produced guidelines on the structure and balance of the curriculum for the five–14 age group as well as for each of the curriculum areas. There are also guidelines on assessment across the whole curriculum, on reporting to parents, and on standardized national tests for English language and mathematics at five levels for this age group. A major programme to extend modern language teaching to primary schools is in progress. The curriculum for 14- to 16-year-olds includes study within each of eight modes: language and communication, mathematical studies, science, technology, social studies, creative activities, physical education, and religious and moral education. There is a recommended percentage of class time to be devoted to each area over the two years. Provision is made for teaching in Gaelic in Gaelic-speaking areas.

For 16- to 18-year-olds, there is available a modular system of vocational courses, certificated by the Scottish Qualifications Authority (SQA), in addition to academic courses. A new unified framework of courses and awards is to be introduced in 1999–2000.

The Scottish Consultative Council on the Curriculum has responsibility for development and advisory work on the curriculum in Scottish schools.

NORTHERN IRELAND

A curriculum common to all grant-aided schools exists. Pupils are required to study religious education and, depending on which key stage they have reached, certain subjects from six broad areas of study: English, mathematics, science and technology; the environment and society; creative and expressive studies and, in key stages three and four, language studies. The statutory curriculum requirements at key stages one to three have been revised and new programmes of study were introduced in September 1996. Six cross-curricular educational themes, which include information technology and education for mutual understanding, are woven through the main subjects of the curriculum. Irish is a foundation subject in schools that use it as a medium of instruction.

The assessment of pupils is broadly in line with practice in England and Wales and takes place at the ages of eight, 11, 14 and 16. The GCSE is used to assess 16-year-olds.

The Northern Ireland Council for the Curriculum, Examinations and Assessment (NICCEA) monitors and advises the department and teachers on all matters relating to the curriculum, assessment arrangements and examinations in grant-aided schools. It conducts GCSE, A- and AS-level examinations, pupil assessment at key stages one, two and three and administers the transfer procedure tests.

RECORDS OF ACHIEVEMENT

The National Record of Achievement (NRA) is being reviewed and will be relaunched from September 1998. It sets down the range of a school-leaver's achievements and activities both inside and outside the classroom, including those not tested by examination. It is issued to all those leaving school in England, Wales and Northern Ireland and its use is to be extended within further and higher education, training and employment. It is not compulsory in Scotland but is available to all education authorities for issue to school leavers. Parents in England and Wales must receive a written yearly progress report on all aspects of their child's achievements. There is a similar commitment for Northern Ireland. In Scotland the school report card gives parents information on their child's progress.

THE PUBLIC EXAMINATION SYSTEM

ENGLAND, WALES AND NORTHERN IRELAND

Until the end of 1987, secondary school pupils at the end of compulsory schooling around the age of 16, and others, took the General Certificate of Education (GCE) Ordinary-level or the Certificate of Secondary Education (CSE). From 1988 these were replaced by a single system of examinations, the General Certificate of Secondary Education (GCSE), which is usually taken after five years of secondary education. The GCSE is the main method of assessing the performance of pupils at age 16 in all national curriculum subjects required to be assessed at the end of compulsory schooling. The structure of the examination is being adapted in accordance with national curriculum requirements; new subject criteria were published in 1995 to govern GCSE syllabuses introduced in 1996 for first examination in 1998. From September 1996 GCSE short-course qualifications in a wide range of subjects were introduced. As a rule the syllabus will take half the time of a GCSE course.

The GCSE differs from its predecessors in that there are syllabuses based on national criteria covering course objectives, content and assessment methods; differentiated assessment (i.e. different papers or questions for different ranges of ability); and grade-related criteria (i.e. grades awarded on absolute rather than relative performance). The GCSE certificates are awarded on a seven-point scale, A to G. From 1994 there has been an additional 'starred' A grade (A*), to recognize the achievement of the highest attainers at GCSE. Grades A to C are the equivalent of the corresponding O-level grades A to C or CSE grade 1. Grades D, E, F and G record achievement at least as high as that represented by CSE grades 2 to 5. All GCSE syllabuses, assessments and grading procedures are monitored by the Qualifications and Curriculum Authority (see page 438) to ensure that they conform to the national criteria.

In the UK in 1994–5, 94 per cent of all pupils achieved one or more graded GCSE, SCE Standard grade, or equivalent results.

In Wales the Certificate of Education is intended for 16-year-olds for whom no suitable examination exists. In 1996, 24,524 candidates took the examination, of whom 93.4 per cent obtained pass or better.

Many maintained schools offer BTEC Firsts (see page 441) and an increasing number offer BTEC Nationals. National Vocational Qualifications in the form of General NVQs are also available to students in schools (see page 441). The Part 1 GNVQ has been piloted from 1995 and will be available in all schools from September 1998. It is a two-year course at foundation and intermediate levels, broadly equivalent to two GCSEs.

The General Diploma was introduced in 1995 for 16- to 18-year-olds achieving GCSE at grades A* to C in English, mathematics and science, plus two other GCSEs at the same grades or their vocational equivalent.

Advanced (A-level) examinations are taken by those who choose to continue their education after GCSE. A-level courses last two years and have traditionally provided the foundation for entry to higher education. A-levels are marked on a seven-point scale, from A to E, N (narrow failure) and U (unclassified), which latter grade will not be certificated.

Advanced Supplementary level (AS-level) examinations were introduced in 1987 as an alternative to, and to complement, A-level examinations. AS-levels are for full-time A-level students but are also open to other students. An AS-level syllabus covers not less than half the amount of ground covered by the corresponding A-level syllabus and, where possible, is related to it. An AS-level course lasts two years and requires not less than half the teaching time of the corresponding A-level course, and two AS-levels are equivalent to one A-level. AS-level passes are graded A to E, with grade standards related to A-level grades.

In the UK in 1994–5, 194,000 school pupils (47 per cent boys, 53 per cent girls) achieved one or more passes at A-level or SCE H-grade, an increase of 2.1 per cent on the previous year. Of those in Great Britain who entered for at least one A-level, or at least two SCE H-grades, 38.5 per cent studied sciences (52.3 per cent boys, 47.7 per cent girls) and 61.5 per cent studied arts/social studies (48.4 per cent of boys, 51.6 per cent of girls).

Most examining boards allow the option of an additional paper of greater difficulty to be taken by A-level candidates to obtain what is known as a Special-level or Scholarship-level qualification. S-level papers are available in most of the traditional academic subjects and are marked on a three-point scale.

The City & Guilds Diploma of Vocational Education is intended for a wide ability range. The Diploma provides recognition of achievement at two levels: foundation at pre-16 and intermediate at post-16. The intermediate level is being phased out in favour of the corresponding GNVQs. Within guidelines and to meet specified criteria, schools and colleges design their own courses, which stress activity-based learning, core skills which include application of number, communication and information technology, and work experience. The Diploma is of value to those who want to find out what aptitudes they may have and to prepare themselves for work, but who may not yet be committed to a particular occupation. According to level, it can be taken alongside other courses such as GCSEs, A- or AS-levels. At foundation level it can provide a context for the introduction of GNVQ units into the key stage four curriculum.

SCOTLAND

Scotland has its own system of public examinations. At the end of the fourth year of secondary education, at about the age of 16, pupils take the Standard grade (which has replaced the Ordinary grade) of the Scottish Certificate of Education. Standard grade courses and examinations have been designed to suit every level of ability, with assessment against nationally determined standards of performance.

For most courses there are three separate examination papers at the end of the two-year Standard grade course. They are set at Credit (leading to awards at grade 1 or 2), General (leading to awards at grade 3 or 4) and Foundation (leading to awards at grade 5 or 6) levels. Grade 7 is available to those who, although they have completed the course, have not attained any of these levels. Normally pupils will take examinations covering two pairs of grades, either grades 1–4 or grades 3–6. Most candidates take seven or eight Standard grade examinations.

The Higher grade of the Scottish Certificate of Education is normally taken one year after Standard grade, at the age of 17 or thereabouts. It is common for pupils to be presented for four or more Higher grades at a single diet of the examination.

The Certificate of Sixth Year Studies (CSYS) is designed to give direction and purpose to sixth-year work by encouraging pupils who have completed their main subjects at Higher grade to study a maximum of three of these subjects in depth. Pupils may also use the sixth year to gain improved or additional Higher grades or Standard grades. National Certificates provide an alternative to, and complement Highers and CSYS. They are awarded to pupils normally over the age of 16 who have successfully completed a programme of vocational courses based on modular study units, and the assessment system is based on national criteria. National Certificates are awarded by the Scottish Qualifications Authority (SQA) (*see also* page 442).

A programme of reform, 'Higher Still', is afoot which will draw all upper secondary qualifications into a single framework by 1999–2000. There will be five levels of attainment, the first three corresponding to Standard grade levels, plus Higher and Advanced Higher (which will replace CSYS). Students will study individual units (of 40 or 80 hours) which will be internally assessed, and may combine these into courses (with external assessment) or group awards.

On 1 April 1997 the Scottish Qualifications Authority (SQA) assumed the functions of its predecessors, the Scottish Examinations Board (SEB) and the Scottish Vocational Education Council (SCOTVEC). SQA has responsibility for all aspects of public examinations and will administer the new 'Higher Still' qualifications.

THE INTERNATIONAL BACCALAUREATE

The International Baccalaureate is an internationally recognized two-year pre-university course and examination designed to facilitate the mobility of students and to promote international understanding. Candidates must offer one subject from each of six subject groups, at least three at higher level and the remainder at subsidiary level. Single subjects can be offered, for which a certificate is received. There are 33 schools and colleges in the UK which offer the International Baccalaureate diploma.

TEACHERS

ENGLAND AND WALES

Teachers are appointed by local education authorities, school governing bodies, or school managers. Those in publicly maintained schools must be approved as qualified by the Secretary of State. To obtain Qualified Teacher Status (QTS) it is necessary to have successfully completed a course of initial teacher training, traditionally either a Bachelor of Education (B.Ed.) degree or the Postgraduate Certificate of Education (PGCE) at an accredited institution. In recent years various employment-based routes to teaching have been developed. The Graduate Teacher Programme allows graduates with teaching experience to undergo between one term's and one year's school-based training. The Registered Teacher Scheme, which replaces the Licensed Teacher Scheme, is designed to attract into the teaching profession entrants over 24 years of age without formal teaching qualifications but with relevant training and experience; licensees are paid a salary and undertake one to two years higher education depending on whether they possess relevant teaching experience. With

certain exceptions the profession at present has an all-graduate entry. A one-year course is being considered which will qualify certain non-graduates to teach at nursery and infant level. Teachers in further education are not required to have Qualified Teacher Status, though roughly half have a teaching qualification and most have industrial, commercial or professional experience. A mandatory qualification for aspiring head-teachers is to be introduced. The National Professional Qualification for Headship (NPQH) was introduced in September 1997.

Teacher training is now largely school-based, with student teachers on secondary PGCE courses spending two-thirds of their training in the classroom. Changes have also been made to primary phase teacher training to make it more school-based and to give schools a role in course design and delivery. Individual schools or consortia of schools and CTCs can bid for funds from the DFEE to carry out their own teacher training, including recruitment of students, subject to approval of their proposed training programme by the Teacher Training Agency (TTA) and monitoring and evaluation by the Office for Standards in Education (OFSTED). Funds are given to schools to meet the costs of designing and delivering the courses, and students receive flat-rate bursaries.

The TTA accredits institutions in England providing initial teacher training for school teachers which meet both criteria published by the Secretary of State and appropriate quality standards. The TTA funds all types of teacher training in England, whether run by universities, colleges or schools, and some educational research. An independent professional council, the General Teaching Council, is to be established to advise the Secretary of State and the TTA.

The Higher Funding Council for Wales exercises similar functions to the TTA in respect of Wales. The TTA also acts as a central source of information and advice for both England and Wales about entry to teaching, and has responsibilities relating to the continuing professional development of teachers.

The Specialist Teacher Assistant (STA) scheme was introduced in September 1994 to provide trained support to qualified teachers in the teaching of reading, writing and arithmetic to young pupils.

SCOTLAND

All teachers in maintained schools must be registered with the General Teaching Council for Scotland. They are registered provisionally for a two-year probationary period which can be extended if necessary. Only graduates are accepted as entrants to the profession; primary school teachers undertake either a four-year vocational degree course or a one-year postgraduate course, while teachers of academic subjects in secondary schools undertake the latter. As a result of a review of initial teacher training instituted in 1992 a greater proportion of training is now classroom-based. The colleges of education provide both in-service and pre-service training for teachers and are funded by the Scottish Higher Education Funding Council.

NORTHERN IRELAND

Teacher training in Northern Ireland is provided by the two universities and two colleges of education. The colleges are concerned with teacher education mainly for the primary school sector. They also provide B.Ed. courses for intending secondary school teachers of religious education, commercial studies, and craft, design and technology. With these exceptions, the training of teachers for secondary schools is provided in the education departments of the universities. A professional qualification is not mandatory to teach in secondary schools. A review of primary and secondary teacher training has taken place as a result of which all student teachers spend more time in the classroom. All newly qualified teachers undertake a two-year induction period.

ACCREDITATION OF TRAINING INSTITUTIONS

Advice to central government on the accreditation, content and quality of initial teacher training courses is given in England by the TTA, in Wales by the HEFCW, in Northern Ireland by validating bodies. These bodies also monitor and disseminate good practice, assisted in Northern Ireland by the Teacher Education Committee. In Scotland all training courses in colleges of education must be approved by the SOEID and a validating body.

NEWLY-TRAINED TEACHERS

Of teachers who in 1995 had successfully completed initial training courses in the UK, 20,400 had completed a postgraduate course and 11,700 a course for non-graduates (provisional figures).

Because of a shortage of teachers in certain secondary subjects, providers of initial teacher training can apply for funds from the TTA to provide enhanced courses, and scholarships and bursaries to attract trainee teachers onto one- or two-year full-time courses in priority subjects. The subjects are: science; mathematics; modern languages (including Welsh in Wales); design and technology; information technology, religious education and music (from September 1998).

SERVING TEACHERS 1994–5 *(full-time and part-time)* (thousands)

Public sector schools	451
Primary	211
Secondary	223
Special	17
FE and HE establishments	151
TOTAL	602

SALARIES

Qualified teachers in England, Wales and Northern Ireland, other than heads and deputy heads, are paid on an 18-point scale. Entry points and placement depend on qualifications, experience, responsibilities, excellence, and recruitment and retention factors as calculated by the relevant body, i.e. the governing body or the LEA. There is a statutory superannuation scheme in maintained schools.

Teachers in Scotland are paid on a ten-point scale. The entry point depends on type of qualification, and additional allowances are payable under certain circumstances.

Salaries from 1 December 1997

	England, Wales and N. Ireland	Scotland
Head	£26,208–£57,399	£27,036–£50,079
Deputy head	£25,374–£41,739	£27,036–£37,473
Teacher	£12,873–£34,476	£12,822–£21,315

FURTHER EDUCATION

Further education is defined as all provision outside schools to people aged over 16 of education up to and including A-level and its equivalent. The Further Education Funding Councils for England and Wales, the Scottish Office Education and Industry Department and the Education and Library Boards in Northern Ireland (until 1 April 1998, thereafter DENI) have a duty to secure provision of adequate facilities for further education in their areas.

ENGLAND AND WALES

Further education and sixth form colleges are funded directly by central government through the Further Education Funding Council for England (FEFCE) and the Further Education Funding Council for Wales (FEFCW). These councils are also responsible for the assessment of quality, in which the Councils' inspectorates play a key role. The colleges are controlled by autonomous further education corporations, which include substantial representation from industry and commerce, and which own their own assets and employ their own staff. Their funding is determined in part by the number of students enrolled.

In England and Wales further education courses are taught at a variety of institutions. These include universities which were formerly polytechnics, colleges of higher education, colleges of further education (some of which also offer higher education courses), and tertiary colleges and sixth form colleges, which concentrate on the provision of normal sixth form school courses as well as a range of vocational courses. A number of institutions specific to a particular form of training, e.g. the Royal College of Music, are also involved.

Teaching staff in further education establishments are not necessarily required to have teaching qualifications although many do so, but they are subject to regular appraisal of teaching performance.

Further education tends to be broadly vocational in purpose and employers are often involved in designing courses. It ranges from lower-level technical and commercial courses through courses for those aiming at higher-level posts in industry, commerce and administration, to professional courses. Facilities exist for GCE A and AS levels, GCSEs, GNVQs and a full range of vocational qualifications (*see* pages 439–40). These courses can form the foundation for progress to higher education qualifications.

The main courses and examinations in the vocational field, all of which link in with the National Vocational Qualification (NVQ) framework (*see* below), are offered by the following bodies, but there are also many others:

The Edexcel Foundation was formed by the merger of the Business and Technology Education Council (BTEC) and London Examinations. Existing Edexcel courses and qualifications will continue to be known by their original names. They provide programmes of study across a wide range of subject areas. The main qualifications are a complete range of GNVQs at foundation, intermediate and advanced levels; entry certificates; NVQs; BTEC National Certificates and Diplomas and BTEC Higher National Diplomas and Certificates.

City & Guilds specializes in developing qualifications and assessments for work-related and leisure qualifications. It awards nationally recognized certificates in over 500 qualifications, many of which are NVQs, SVQs and GNVQs. Its progressive structure of awards spans seven levels, from foundation to the highest level of professional competence.

RSA Examinations Board schemes cover a wide range of vocational qualifications, including accounting, business administration, customer service, management, language schemes, information technology and teaching qualifications. A wide range of NVQs and GNVQs are offered and a policy operates of credit accumulation, so that candidates can take a single unit or complete qualifications.

There are 480 further education establishments and sixth form colleges in England and Wales. In 1996–7 there were 743,000 full-time and sandwich-course students and 840,922 part-time day students on further education courses.

Scotland

Further education comprises non-advanced courses up to SCE Highers grade, GCE A-level and work-based awards. Further education colleges are funded directly by central government. Courses are taught mainly at colleges of further education, including technical colleges, and in some schools.

Further education colleges are incorporated bodies, with boards of management which run them and employ staff. The boards include the principal and staff and student representatives among their ten to 16 members, and at least half the members must have experience of commerce, industry or the practice of a profession.

The Scottish Qualifications Authority, which assumed the functions of the Scottish Examinations Board and the Scottish Vocational Education Council on 1 April 1997, awards qualifications for most occupations. It awards at non-advanced level the National Certificate which is available in over 4,000 individual modules and covers the whole range of non-advanced further education provision in Scotland. Students may study for the National Certificate on a full-time, part-time, open learning or work-based learning basis. National Certificate modules can be taken in further education colleges, secondary schools and other centres, normally from the age of 16 onwards. SQA also offers modular advanced-level HNC/HND qualifications and a few post-graduate or post-experience qualifications which are available in further education colleges and higher education institutions. SQA accredits and awards Scottish Vocational Qualifications (SVQs) which have mutual recognition with the NVQs available in the rest of the UK. SVQs are work-place assessed but can also be taken in further education colleges and other centres where work-place conditions can be simulated.

The Record of Education and Training (RET) has been introduced to provide a single certificate recording SQA achievements; an updated version is provided as and when necessary. SQA also administers the National Record of Achievement in Scotland on behalf of the Scottish Office.

In the academic year 1995–6 there were 30,916 full-time and sandwich-course students and 194,544 part-time students on non-advanced vocational courses of further education in the 43 further education colleges and two local authority colleges.

Northern Ireland

The Education and Library Boards currently plan the further education provision to be made by colleges under their management subject to approval by the Department of Education for Northern Ireland. From 1 April 1998 all colleges will become free-standing corporate bodies like their counterparts in the rest of the UK and planning will transfer to DENI, which will also fund the colleges directly. The colleges will own their own property, be responsible for their own services and employ their own staff.

The boards of governors of the colleges must include at least 50 per cent membership from the professions, local business or industry, or other fields of employment relevant to the activities of the college.

On reaching school-leaving age, pupils may attend colleges of further education to pursue the same type of vocational courses as are provided in colleges in England and Wales, administered by the same examining bodies.

In 1995–6 Northern Ireland had 17 institutions of further education, and there were 21,096 full-time students and 51,885 part-time students on non-advanced vocational courses of further education.

Course Information

Applications for further education courses are generally made directly to the colleges concerned. Information on further education courses in the UK and addresses of colleges can be found in the *Directory of Further Education* published annually by the Careers Research and Advisory Centre.

National Vocational Qualifications

The National Council for Vocational Qualifications (NCVQ) was set up by the Government in 1986 to achieve a coherent national framework for vocational qualifications in England, Wales and Northern Ireland. In October 1997 it merged with the School Curriculum and Assessment Authority (SCAA) to form the Qualifications and Curriculum Authority (QCA). Bodies responsible for the regulation of GNVQs and NVQs in the UK are as follows: in England, the QCA; in Wales, the Curriculum and Assessment Authority; in Northern Ireland, the Council for the Curriculum, Examinations and Assessment (NICCEA); and in Scotland, the Scottish Qualifications Authority (SQA). Those bodies do not award qualifications (except for the SQA) but accredit National Vocational Qualifications (NVQs), General National Vocational Qualifications (GNVQs) and core skills. Candidates are assessed through awarding bodies who bestow the qualifications where candidates reach the required standards.

National Vocational Qualifications (NVQs) are work-place based occupational qualifications. In September 1992 General National Vocational Qualifications (GNVQs) were introduced into colleges and schools as a vocational alternative to academic qualifications. They cover broad categories in the NVQ framework and are aimed at those wishing to familiarize themselves with a range of opportunities. Advanced GNVQ or the vocational A-level is designed to be equivalent to two A-levels; intermediate is equivalent to four or five good GCSEs. Foundation GNVQs became available in September 1994.

HIGHER EDUCATION

The term higher education is used to describe education above A-level, Advanced Higher grade and their equivalent, which is provided in universities and colleges of higher education and in some further education colleges.

The Further and Higher Education Act 1992 and parallel legislation in Scotland removed the distinction between higher education provided by the universities, which were funded by the Universities Funding Council (UFC), and that provided in England and Wales by the former polytechnics and colleges of higher education, funded by the Polytechnics and Colleges Funding Council (PCFC), and in Scotland by the former central institutions and other institutions funded by central government. All are now funded by the Higher Education Funding Councils for England, Wales and Scotland. Other provisions brought the non-university sector in line with the universities, allowing all polytechnics, and other higher education institutions which satisfy the necessary criteria, to award their own taught course and research degrees and to adopt the title of university. All the polytechnics and art colleges have since adopted the title of university. The change of name does not affect the legal constitution of the institutions.

The number of students in higher education in the UK in 1995–6 was (thousands):

	Universities	Other	Total
Full-time, sandwich	830	206	1,036
% female	48.9%	57.3%	
Part-time	314	160	474
% female	55.4%	50%	
Overseas	134.2	11.9	146
TOTAL	1,278	377.9	1,656

The proportion of 16- to 24-year-olds undertaking full-time and sandwich courses in higher education in the UK rose from 23.8 per cent in 1985–6 to 47.3 per cent in 1995–6. The number of mature entrants (those aged 21 and over when starting an undergraduate course and 25 and over when starting a postgraduate course) to higher education in Great Britain in 1995–6 (excluding those at the Open University) was 884,000. The number of full-time and part-time home students on science courses in 1995–6 was 558,100, of whom 48.9 per cent were female.

UNIVERSITIES AND COLLEGES

The universities are self-governing institutions established in most cases by royal charter or Act of Parliament. They have academic freedom and are responsible for their own academic appointments, curricula and student admissions and award their own degrees.

Responsibility for universities in England rests with the Secretary of State for Education and Employment, and in their territories with the Secretaries of State for Scotland, Wales and Northern Ireland. Advice to the Government on matters relating to the universities is provided by the Higher Education Funding Councils for England, Wales and Scotland, and by the Northern Ireland Higher Education Council. The HEFCs receive a block grant from central government which they allocate to the universities and colleges. The grant is allocated directly by central government in Northern Ireland.

There are now 88 universities in the UK, where only 47 existed prior to the Further and Higher Education Acts 1992. Of the 88, 71 are in England (including one federal university), two (one a federal institution) in Wales, 13 in Scotland and two in Northern Ireland.

The pre-1992 universities each have their own system of internal government but broad similarities exist. Most are run by two main bodies: the senate, which deals primarily with academic issues and consists of members elected from within the university; and the council, which is the supreme body and is responsible for all appointments and promotions, and bidding for and allocation of financial resources. At least half the members of the council are drawn from outside the university. Joint committees of senate and council are becoming increasingly common.

Those universities which were formerly polytechnics (38) or other higher education institutions (three) and the colleges of higher education (47) are run by higher education corporations (HECs), which are controlled by boards of governors whose members were initially appointed by the Secretaries of State but which will subsequently make their own appointments. At least half the members of each board must be drawn from industry, business, commerce and the professions.

In 1995–6 full-time and sandwich-course student enrolments in England and Wales were (thousands):

England	Universities	Other
Undergraduates	682.7	150.4
% overseas	12.1%	5.2%
Postgraduates	100.9	9.8
% overseas	55.5%	22.5%
Wales		
Undergraduates	40.7	16.4
% overseas	13.7%	8%
Postgraduates	5.9	0.9
% overseas	47.5%	12.5%

Higher education courses funded by the respective HEFCs are also taught in some further education colleges in England and Wales. In England in 1995–6 there were over 37,000 students (2.7 per cent of total higher education student numbers) on such courses and 534 (0.8 per cent of higher education student numbers) in Wales.

The non-residential Open University provides courses nationally leading to degrees. Teaching is through a combination of television and radio programmes, correspondence, tutorials, short residential courses and local audio-visual centres. No qualifications are needed for entry. The Open University offers a modular programme of undergraduate courses by credit accumulation and post-experience and postgraduate courses, including a programme of higher degrees which comprises B.Phil., M.Phil. and Ph.D. through research, and MA, MBA and M.Sc. through taught courses. The Open University throughout the UK is funded by the Higher Education Funding Council for England. Its recurrent grant for 1995–6 was £114.1 million. In 1997, about 116,000 undergraduates were registered at the Open University, of whom about 52 per cent were women. Estimated cost (1997) of a six-credit degree was around £3,300 including course fees of about £2,000.

The independent University of Buckingham provides a two-year course leading to a bachelor's degree and its tuition fees were £9,744 for 1997. It receives no capital or recurrent income from the Government but its students are eligible for mandatory awards from local education authorities. Its academic year consists of four terms of ten weeks each.

ACADEMIC STAFF

Each university and college appoints its own academic staff on its own conditions. However, there is a common salary structure and, except for Oxford and Cambridge, a common career structure in those universities formerly funded by the UFC and a common salary structure for the former PCFC sector. The Universities and Colleges Employers Association (UCEA) acts as a pay agency for universities and colleges.

Teaching staff in higher education require no formal teaching qualification, but teacher trainers are required to spend a certain amount of time in schools to ensure that they have sufficient recent practical experience.

In 1995–6, there were 62,521 full-time and part-time teaching and research staff (UK nationals) in institutions of higher education in the UK.

Salary scales for staff in the former UFC sector differ from those in the former polytechnics and colleges; it is hoped eventually to amalgamate them. The 1996–7 salary scales for non-clinical academic staff in universities formerly funded by the UFC are:

Professor	from £32,927
Senior lecturer	£28,522–£32,266
Lecturer grade B	£21,227–£27,196
Lecturer grade A	£15,593 –£20,424

The salaries of clinical academic staff are kept broadly comparable to those of doctors and dentists in the National Health Service.

Salary scales for lecturers in the former polytechnics, now universities, and colleges of higher education in England, Wales and Northern Ireland are (September 1997):

Head of Department	from £26,304
Principal lecturer	£26,973–£33,915
Senior lecturer	£21,580–£28,516
Lecturer	£13,871–£23,123

The salary scales for staff in Scotland are determined at individual college level.

FINANCE

Although universities and colleges are expected to look to a wider range of funding sources than before, and to generate additional revenue in collaboration with industry, they are still largely financed, directly or indirectly, from government resources.

In 1995–6 the total income of institutions of higher education in the UK was £10.7 million (£10 million in 1994–5). Grants from the funding councils amounted to £4.5 million (£4.4 million in 1994–5), forming 41.6 per cent of total income (43.6 per cent in 1994–5). Income from research grants and contracts was £1.5 million, an increase of 0.1 per cent on the previous year.

In the academic year 1995–6 the HEFCs' recurrent grant to institutions outside their sector and to LEAs for the provision of higher education courses was £85 million.

COURSES

In the UK all universities, including the Open University, and some colleges award their own degrees and other qualifications and can act as awarding and validating bodies for neighbouring colleges which are not yet accredited. The Quality Assurance Agency for Higher Education, funded by institutional contributions, advises the Secretaries of State on applications for degree-awarding powers.

Higher education courses last full-time for at least four weeks or, if part-time, involve more than 60 hours of instruction. Facilities exist for full-time and part-time study, day release, sandwich or block release. Credit accumulation and transfer (CATS) is a system of study which is becoming widely available. It allows a student to achieve a final qualification by accumulating credits for courses of study successfully achieved, or even professional experience, over a period. Credit transfer information and values are carried on an electronic database called ECCTIS 2000, which is available in most careers offices and many schools and colleges.

Higher education courses include: first degree and postgraduate (including research); Diploma in Higher Education (Dip.HE); Higher National Diploma (HND) and Higher National Certificate (HNC); and preparation for professional examinations. The in-service training of teachers is also included, but from September 1994 has been funded in England by the TTA (see page 440), not the HEFC.

The Diploma of Higher Education (Dip.HE) is a two-year diploma usually intended to serve as a stepping-stone to a degree course or other further study. The Dip.HE is awarded by the institution itself if it is accredited; by an accredited institution of its choice if not. The BTEC Higher National Certificate (HNC) is awarded after two years part-time study. The BTEC Higher National Diploma (HND) is awarded after two years full-time, or three years sandwich-course or part-time study.

With the exception of certain Scottish universities where master is sometimes used for a first degree in arts subjects, undergraduate courses lead to the title of Bachelor, Bachelor of Arts (BA) and Bachelor of Science (B.Sc.) being the most common. For a higher degree the titles are: Master of Arts (MA), Master of Science (M.Sc.) (usually taught courses) and the research degrees of Master of Philosophy (M.Phil.) and Doctor of Philosophy (Ph.D. or, at a few universities, D.Phil.).

Most undergraduate courses at British universities and colleges of higher education run for three years, except in Scotland and at the University of Keele where they may take four years. Professional courses in subjects such as medicine, dentistry and veterinary science take longer. Details of courses on offer and of predicted entry requirements for the following year's intake are provided in *University and College Entrance: Official Guide*, published annually by the Universities and Colleges Admissions Service (UCAS), which includes degree, Dip.HE and HND courses at all universities (excluding the Open University) and most colleges of HE; it is available from bookshops.

Postgraduate studies vary in length. Taught courses which lead to certificates, diplomas or master's degrees usually take one year full-time or two years part-time. Research degrees take from two to three years full-time and much longer if completed on a part-time basis. Details of taught courses and research degree opportunities can be found in *Graduate Studies*, published annually for the Careers Research and Advisory Centre (CRAC) by Hobsons Publishing plc (for address, *see* page 453).

Post-experience short courses are forming an increasing part of higher education provision, reflecting the need to update professional and technical training. Most of these courses fund themselves.

ADMISSIONS

The target number of students entering full-time higher education has been set at 30 to 31 per cent of the 18- to 19-year-old age group. Institutions suffer financial penalties if the number of students laid down for them by the funding councils is exceeded, but the individual university or college decides which students to accept. The formal entry requirements to most degree courses are two A-levels at grade E or above (or equivalent), and to HND courses one A-level (or equivalent). In practice, most offers of places require qualifications in excess of this, higher requirements usually reflecting the popularity of a course. These requirements do not, however, exclude applications from students with a variety of non-GCSE qualifications or unquantified experience and skills.

For admission to a degree, Dip.HE or HND, potential students apply through a central clearing house. All universities and most colleges providing higher education courses in the UK are members of the Universities and Colleges Admission Service (UCAS). Applicants are supplied with an application form and a *UCAS Handbook*, available from schools, colleges and careers offices or direct from UCAS, and may apply to a maximum of six institutions/courses on the UCAS form. The only exception among universities is the Open University, which conducts its own admissions.

Applications for undergraduate teacher training courses are made through UCAS. Details of initial teacher training courses in Scotland can be obtained from colleges of education and those universities offering such courses, and from the Committee of Scottish Higher Education Principals (COSHEP).

For admission as a postgraduate student, universities and colleges normally require a good first degree in a subject related to the proposed course of study or research, but other experience and qualifications will be considered on merit. Most applications are made to individual institutions but there are two clearing houses of relevance. Postgraduate teacher training courses in England and Wales utilize the Graduate Teacher Training Registry (*see* page 453). Applications to postgraduate teacher training courses in Scotland are made through the Teacher Education Admissions Clearing House (TEACH) (*see* page 453). Applications for PGCE courses at institutions in Northern Ireland are made to the Department of Education for Northern Ireland. For social work the Social Work Admissions System operates (*see* page 453).

SCOTLAND

The Scottish Higher Education Funding Council (SHEFC) funds 21 institutions of higher education, including 13 universities. The universities are broadly managed as described above and each institution of higher education is managed by an independent governing body which includes representatives of industrial, commercial, professional and educational interests. Most of the courses outside the universities have a vocational orientation and a substantial number are sandwich courses.

Full-time higher education student enrolments in 1995–6 in universities and other higher education institutions were (thousands):

	Universities	Other
Undergraduates	93.8	36.1
% overseas	9%	2.5%
Postgraduates	13.2	1.7
% overseas	34%	17.6%

There were 31,700 students on higher education courses in further education colleges, 19.6 per cent of total higher education students.

NORTHERN IRELAND

In Northern Ireland advanced courses are provided by 17 institutions of further education, the two universities and the two colleges of education. As well as offering first and postgraduate degrees, the University of Ulster offers courses leading to the BTEC Higher National Diploma and professional qualifications. Applications to undertake courses of higher education other than degree courses are made to the institutions direct. Full-time higher education student enrolments in 1995–6 were (thousands):

	Universities	Other
Undergraduates	22.3	4.0
% overseas	16%	9.8%
Postgraduates	3.0	0.08
% overseas	24.2%	10.4%

There were 6,832 students enrolled on advanced courses of higher education in the institutions of further education, 15.4 per cent of higher education student numbers.

FEES

At present, the tuition fees for students with mandatory awards (*see* below) are paid by the grant-awarding body. It is proposed that, from September 1998, students should pay an annual contribution to their fees of up to £1,000, depending on parental income, to be repaid over a period once their earnings reach a certain level. Students from member states of the European Union pay fees at home student rates. Since 1980–1 students from outside the EU have paid fees that are meant to cover the cost of their education, but financial help is available under a number of

schemes. Information about these schemes is available from British Council offices world-wide.

Universities and colleges are free to set their own charges for students from non-EU countries. Undergraduate fees for the academic year 1997–8 for home and EU students are £750 for arts courses (band one), £1,600 for laboratory or workshop based courses, mainly science (band two), and £2,800 for clinical courses (band three).

For postgraduate students, the maximum tuition fee that will be reimbursed through the awards system is £2,540 in 1997–8.

GRANTS FOR STUDENTS

Students in the UK who plan to take a full-time or sandwich course of further study after leaving school may currently be eligible for a grant. A parental contribution is deductible on a sliding scale dependent on income. For married students this may be deducted from their spouse's income instead. However, parental contribution is not deducted from the grant to students over 25 years of age who have been self-supporting for at least three years. The main rates of mandatory grant have been frozen since 1991–2 as it is envisaged that students will increasingly support themselves by loans; the mandatory grant is to be abolished altogether in the near future. Tuition fees are paid in full for all students in receipt of a grant (but *see* Fees above) and they are usually paid direct to the university or college by the education authority.

Grants are paid by local education authorities in England, Wales and Northern Ireland, of which 100 per cent of the cost is reimbursed by central government, and by the SOEID in Scotland through the Student Awards Agency. Applications are made to the authority in the area in which the student normally lives. Applications should not, however, be made earlier than the January preceding the start of the course.

TYPES OF GRANT

Grants are of two kinds: mandatory and discretionary. Mandatory grants are those which awarding authorities must pay to students who are attending designated courses and who can satisfy certain other conditions. Such a grant is awarded normally to enable the student to attend only one designated course and there is no general entitlement to an award for any particular number of years. Discretionary grants are those for which each awarding authority has discretion to decide its own policy.

Designated courses are those full-time or sandwich courses leading to: a degree; the Diploma of Higher Education; the Higher National Diploma; initial teacher-training courses, including those for the postgraduate certificate of education and the art teachers' certificate or diploma; a university certificate or diploma course lasting at least three years and other qualifications which are specifically designated as being comparable to first degree courses. The local education authority should be consulted for advice about eligibility for a grant.

A means-tested maintenance grant, usually paid once a term, covers periods of attendance during term as well as the Christmas and Easter vacations, but not the summer vacation. The basic grant rates for 1997–8 are:

Living in	Grant	Grant to Scottish students
College/lodgings in London area	2,160	2,085
College/lodgings outside London area	1,755	1,685
Parental home	1,435	1,290

Additional allowances are available if, for example, the course requires a period of study abroad.

LEA and SOEID expenditure on student fees and maintenance in 1995–6 was £2,842.5 million; 930,671 mandatory awards were made.

STUDENT LOANS

The Education (Student Loans) Act 1990 legislated for interest-free but indexed top-up loans of up to £2,085 in 1997–8 to be made available to eligible students in the UK. The Government expects that at least £928.8 million will be taken up in loans in 1997–8.

Students apply direct to the Student Loans Company Ltd (*see* page 453), which will require a certificate of eligibility from their place of study. Loans are available to students on designated courses within the scope of mandatory awards and the same residency conditions apply. Repayment is normally over five to seven years, although it can be deferred if income is at or below 85 per cent of national average earnings (about £15,700 a year).

ACCESS FUNDS

Access funds are allocated by education departments to the appropriate funding councils in England, Wales and Scotland and administered by further and higher education institutions. In Northern Ireland they are allocated by central government to the institutions direct. They are available to students whose access to education might otherwise be inhibited by financial considerations or where real financial difficulties are faced. For the academic year 1997–8, provision in the UK will be £35 million.

POSTGRADUATE AWARDS

Unlike funding for undergraduates, which is currently mandatory for most degree and equivalent level courses, grants for postgraduate study, except for teacher training, are usually discretionary. Grants are also often dependent on the class of first degree, especially for research degrees.

An increasing number of scholarships are available from research charities, endowments, and particular industries or companies. For residents in England and Wales, several schemes of postgraduate bursaries or studentships are funded by the DFEE (administered by the British Academy), the government research councils, the Ministry of Agriculture, Fisheries and Food, and the British Academy, which awards grants for study in the humanities.

In Scotland postgraduate funding is provided by the SOEID, the Scottish Office Agriculture and Fisheries Department, and the research councils as in England and Wales.

Awards in Northern Ireland are made by DENI, the Department of Agriculture for Northern Ireland, and the Medical Research Council.

In the UK in 1994–5, 23,600 30-week bursaries for professional and vocational training were awarded . The national rates in 1997–8 are:

Living in	30-week bursary
College/lodgings in London area	3,545
College/lodgings outside London area	2,805
Parental home	2,115

ADULT AND CONTINUING EDUCATION

The term adult education covers a broad spectrum of educational activities ranging from non-vocational courses of general interest, through the acquiring of special vocational skills needed in industry or commerce, to study for a degree at the Open University.

The responsibility for securing adult and continuing education in England and Wales is statutory and shared between the Further Education Funding Councils, which are responsible for and fund those courses which take place in their sector and lead to academic and vocational qualifications, prepare students to undertake further or higher education courses, or confer basic skills; the Higher Education Funding Councils, which fund advanced courses of continuing education; and LEAs, which are responsible for those courses which do not fall within the remit of the funding councils. Funding in Northern Ireland is through the education and library boards and in Scotland by the Scottish Office Education and Industry Department.

PROVIDERS

Courses specifically for adults are provided by many bodies. They include, in the statutory sector: local education authorities in England and Wales; in Scotland the education authorities and the SOEID; education and library boards in Northern Ireland; further education colleges; higher education colleges; universities, especially the Open University and Birkbeck College of the University of London; residential colleges; the BBC, independent television and local radio stations. There are also a number of voluntary bodies.

The LEAs in England and Wales operate through 'area' adult education centres, institutes or colleges, and the adult studies departments of colleges of further education. The SOEID funds adult education, including that provided by the universities and the Workers' Educational Association, at vocational further education colleges (47 in 1996) and evening centres (126 in 1996). In addition, SOEID provides grants to a number of voluntary organizations. Provision in the statutory sector in Northern Ireland is the responsibility of the universities and the education and library boards, which operate 17 further education colleges (until they become incorporated in April 1998) and a number of community schools.

The involvement of universities in adult education and continuing education has diversified considerably and is supported by a variety of administrative structures ranging from dedicated departments to a devolved approach. Birkbeck College in the University of London caters solely for part-time students. Those institutions and colleges formerly in the PCFC sector in England and Wales, because of their range of courses and flexible patterns of student attendance, provide opportunities in the field of adult and continuing education. The Forum for the Advancement of Continuing Education (FACE) promotes collaboration between institutions of higher education active in this area. The Open University, in partnership with the BBC, provides distance teaching leading to first degrees, and also offers post-experience and higher degree courses (*see* page 461).

Of the voluntary bodies, the biggest is the Workers' Educational Association (WEA) which operates throughout the UK, reaching about 150,000 adult students annually. The FEFC for England, the SOEID, and LEAs make grants towards provision.

The National Institute of Adult Continuing Education (England and Wales) (NIACE) provides information and advice to organizations and providers on all aspects of adult continuing education. NIACE conducts research, project and development work, and is funded by the DFEE, the LEAs and other funding bodies. The Welsh committee, NIACE Cymru, receives financial support from the Welsh

Office, support in kind from the Welsh Joint Education Committee, and advises government, voluntary bodies and education providers on adult continuing education and training matters in Wales. In Scotland advice on adult and community education, and promotion thereof, is provided by the Scottish Community Education Council. The Northern Ireland Council for Adult Education has an advisory role. Its membership includes representatives of the education and library boards and of most organizations involved in the field, together with an assessor appointed by DENI.

Membership of the Universities Association for Continuing Education is open to any university or university college in the UK. It promotes university continuing education, facilitates the interchange of information, and supports research and development work in continuing education.

Courses

Although lengths vary, most courses are part-time. Long-term residential colleges in England and Wales are grant-aided by the FEFCs and provide full-time courses lasting one or two years. Some colleges and centres offer short-term residential courses, lasting from a few days to a few weeks, in a wide range of subjects. Local education authorities directly sponsor many of the colleges, while others are sponsored by universities or voluntary organizations. A directory of learning holidays, *Time to Learn*, is published by NIACE.

Grants

Although full-time courses at degree level attract mandatory awards, for courses below that level all students over the age of 19 must pay a fee. However, discretionary grants may be available. Adult education bursaries for students at the long-term residential colleges of adult education are the responsibility of the colleges themselves. The awards are administered for the colleges by the Awards Officer of the Residential Colleges Committee for students resident in England and are funded by the FEFC for England in English colleges; for colleges in Wales they are funded and administered by the FEFC for Wales; and for colleges in Scotland and Northern Ireland they are funded by central government and administered by the education authorities. A booklet, *Adult Education Bursaries*, can be obtained from the Awards Officer, Adult Education Bursaries, c/o Ruskin College (*see* page 463).

Numbers

There are no comprehensive statistics covering all aspects of adult education. However, enrolments on evening courses in the UK numbered 1,510,000 in 1995–6 (65.9 per cent women). This number included 724,000 students at adult education centres.

Education Directory

LOCAL EDUCATION AUTHORITIES

ENGLAND

County Councils

BEDFORDSHIRE, County Hall, Cauldwell Street, Bedford MK42 9AP. Tel: 01234-363222. *Director*, P. Brett

BERKSHIRE, Shire Hall, Shinfield Park, Reading RG2 9XD. Tel: 0118-987 5444. *Chief Education Officer*, A. Dakin

BUCKINGHAMSHIRE, County Hall, Aylesbury HP20 1UA. Tel: 01296-383204. *Director*, D. McGahey

CAMBRIDGESHIRE, Castle Court, Castle Hill, Cambridge CB3 0AP. Tel: 01223-717611. *Director*, A. Baxter

CHESHIRE, County Hall, Chester CH1 1SQ. Tel: 01244-602201. *Director*, D. Cracknell

CORNWALL, County Hall, Truro TR1 3AY. Tel: 01872-322000. *Director*, J. Harris

CUMBRIA, 5 Portland Square, Carlisle CA1 1PU. Tel: 01228-606060. *Director*, J. Nellist

DERBYSHIRE, County Offices, Matlock DE4 3AG. Tel: 01629-580000. *Director*, Ms V. Hannon

DEVON, County Hall, Topsham Road, Exeter EX2 4QD. Tel: 01392-382039. *Director*, S. Jenkin

DORSET, County Hall, Colliton Park, Dorchester DT1 1XJ. Tel: 01305-224171. *Director*, R. Ely

DURHAM, County Hall, Durham DH1 5UJ. Tel: 0191-386 4411. *Director*, K. Mitchell

EAST SUSSEX, PO Box 4, County Hall, St. Anne's Crescent, Lewes BN7 1SG. Tel: 01273-481000. *Director*, D. Mallen

ESSEX, A Block, County Hall, Victoria Road South, Chelmsford CM1 1LD. Tel: 01245-436231. *Director*, P. A. Lincoln

GLOUCESTERSHIRE, Shire Hall, Westgate Street, Gloucester GL1 2TG. Tel: 01452-425006. *Director*, R. Crouch

HAMPSHIRE, The Castle, Winchester SO23 8UG. Tel: 01962-841841. *Director*, P. J. Coles

HEREFORD AND WORCESTER, County Hall, Spetchley Road, Worcester WR5 2NP. Tel: 01905-763763. *Director*, D. A. J. Stanley

HERTFORDSHIRE, County Hall, Pegs Lane, Hertford SG13 8DE. Tel: 01992-555827. *Director*, R. Shostak

ISLE OF WIGHT, County Hall, Newport PO30 1UD. Tel: 01983-821000. *Director*, A. Kaye

KENT, Springfield, Maidstone ME14 2LJ. Tel: 01622-671411. *Director*, R. Pryke

LANCASHIRE, PO Box 78, County Hall, Preston PR1 8XJ. Tel: 01772-254868. *Chief Education Officer*, C. J. Trinick

LEICESTERSHIRE, County Hall, Glenfield, Leicester LE3 8RA. Tel: 0116-232 3232. *Director*, Mrs J. A. M. Strong

LINCOLNSHIRE, County Offices, Newland, Lincoln LN1 1YL. Tel: 01522-552222. *Director*, N. J. Riches

NORFOLK, County Hall, Martineau Lane, Norwich NR1 2DH. Tel: 01603-222146. *Director*, Dr B. Slater

NORTHAMPTONSHIRE, PO Box 149, County Hall, Northampton NN1 1AV. Tel: 01604-236252. *Director*, J. R. Atkinson

NORTHUMBERLAND, County Hall, Morpeth NE61 2EF. Tel: 01670-533601. *Director*, C. C. Tipple

NORTH YORKSHIRE, County Hall, Northallerton DL7 8AE. Tel: 01609-780780. *Director*, Miss C. Welbourn

NOTTINGHAMSHIRE, County Hall, West Bridgford, Nottingham NG2 7QP. Tel: 0115-982 3823. *Director*, R. Valentine

OXFORDSHIRE, Macclesfield House, New Road, Oxford OX1 1NA. Tel: 01865-815449. *Director*, G. Badman

SHROPSHIRE, The Shirehall, Abbey Foregate, Shrewsbury SY2 6ND. Tel: 01743-254302. *Director*, Mrs C. Adams

SOMERSET, County Hall, Taunton TA1 4DY. Tel: 01823-333451. *Chief Education Officer*, N. Henswood

STAFFORDSHIRE, Education Offices, Tipping Street, Stafford ST16 2DH. Tel: 01785-223121. *County Education Officer*, Dr P. J. Hunter

SUFFOLK, St Andrew House, County Hall, Ipswich IP4 1LJ. Tel: 01473-584800. *County Education Officer*, D. J. Peachey

SURREY, County Hall, Kingston upon Thames KT1 2DN. Tel: 0181-541 9501. *County Education Officer*, Dr P. Gray

WARWICKSHIRE, 22 Northgate Street, Warwick CV34 4SR. Tel: 01926-410410. *Director*, E. Wood

WEST SUSSEX, County Hall, Chichester PO19 1RQ. Tel: 01243-777100. *Director*, R. D. C. Bunker

WILTSHIRE, County Hall, Trowbridge BA14 8JN. Tel: 01225-713000. *Chief Education Officer*, Dr L. Davies

Unitary Councils

BARNSLEY, Berneslai Close, Barnsley S70 2HS. Tel: 01226-773500. *Director*, J. Gaskin

BATH AND NORTH-EAST SOMERSET, Northgate House, Upper Borough Walls, Bath BA1 1RG. Tel: 01225-396400. *Director*, R. Jones

BIRMINGHAM, Council House, Margaret Street, Birmingham B3 3BU. Tel: 0121-235 2550. *Chief Education Officer*, Prof. T. Brighouse

BOLTON, Paderborn House, Civic Centre, Bolton BL1 1JW. Tel: 01204-522311. *Director*, Mrs M. Blenkinsop

BOURNEMOUTH, Dorset House, Christchurch Road, Bournemouth BH1 3NL. Tel: 01202-451451. *Director*, K. Shaikh

BRADFORD, Flockton House, Flockton Road, Bradford BD4 7RY. Tel: 01274-751700. *Director*, Mrs D. Cavanagh

BRIGHTON AND HOVE, PO Box 2503, Kings House, Grand Avenue, Hove BN3 2SU. Tel: 01273-291053. *Director*, Ms D. Stokoe

BRISTOL, Avon House, The Haymarket, Bristol BS99 7EB. Tel: 0117-903 7961. *Director*, R. Riddell

BURY, Athenaeum House, Market Street, Bury BL9 0BN. Tel: 0161-253 5652. *Chief Education Officer*, vacant

CALDERDALE, Northgate House, Halifax HX1 1UN. Tel: 01422-392567. *Director*, I. Jennings

COVENTRY, Council House, Earl Street, Coventry CV1 5RR. Tel: 01203-833333. *Chief Education Officer*, Ms C. Goodwin

DARLINGTON, Town Hall, Darlington DL1 5QT. Tel: 01325-388802. *Director*, G. Pennington

DERBY, Middleton House, 27 St Marys Gate, Derby DE1 3NN. Tel: 01332-293111. *Director*, D. O'Hooghe

DONCASTER, PO Box 266, The Council House, College Road, Doncaster DN1 3AD. Tel: 01302-737102. *Director (acting)*, M. Simpson

DUDLEY, Westox House, 1 Trinity Road, Dudley DY1 1JB. Tel: 01384-818181. *Chief Education Officer*, D. Colligan

EAST RIDING OF YORKSHIRE, County Hall, Beverley HU17 9BA. Tel: 01482-887700. *Director*, J. Ginnever

GATESHEAD, Civic Centre, Regent Street, Gateshead NE8 1HH. Tel: 0191-477 1011. *Director*, D. Arbon

HARTLEPOOL, Civic Centre, Victoria Road, Hartlepool TS24 8AY. Tel: 01429-266522. *Director*, J. Fitt

KINGSTON UPON HULL, Essex House, Manor Street, Kingston upon Hull HU1 1YD. Tel: 01482-610610. *Director*, Miss J. E. Taylor

KIRKLEES, Oldgate House, 2 Oldgate, Huddersfield HD1 6QW. Tel: 01484-225242. *Chief Education Officer*, R. Vincent

KNOWSLEY, Huyton Hey Road, Huyton, Knowsley L36 5YH. Tel: 0151-443 3220. *Director*, P. Wylie

LEEDS, Merrion House, Merrion Street, Leeds LS2 8DT. Tel: 0113-247 5575. *Director (acting)*, Ms J. Potter

LEICESTER, Marlborough House, 38 Welford Place, Leicester LE2 7AA. Tel: 0116-252 7710. *Director*, T. Warren

LIVERPOOL, 14 Sir Thomas Street, Liverpool L1 6BJ. Tel: 0151-225 2799. *Director*, M. F. Cogley

LUTON, Unity House, 111 Stuart Street, Luton LU1 5NP. Tel: 01582-548000. *Director*, T. Dessent

MANCHESTER, Cumberland House, Crown Square, Manchester M60 3BB. Tel: 0161-234 5000. *Chief Education Officer*, R. Jobson

MIDDLESBROUGH, PO Box 191, Civic Centre, Middlesbrough TS1 2XS. Tel: 01642-245432. *Director*, M. Stanley

MILTON KEYNES, Saxon Court, 502 Avebury Boulevard, Central Milton Keynes MK9 3HS. Tel: 01908-253325. *Director*, A. Flack

NEWCASTLE UPON TYNE, Civic Centre, Newcastle upon Tyne NE1 8PU. Tel: 0191-232 8520. *Chief Education Officer*, D. Bell

NORTH EAST LINCOLNSHIRE, 7 Eleanor Street, Grimsby DN32 9DU. Tel: 01472-313131. *Head of Education*, G. Hill

NORTH LINCOLNSHIRE, Hewson House, PO Box 35, Station Road, Brigg DN20 8XJ. Tel: 01724-297240. *Director*, T. Thomas

NORTH SOMERSET, PO Box 137, Town Hall, Weston super-Mare BS23 1AE. Tel: 01934-888888. *Director*, Ms J. Wreford

NORTH TYNESIDE, Stephenson House, Stephenson Street, North Shields NE30 1QA. Tel: 0191-200 5009. *Director*, Mrs P. Jefferson

OLDHAM, Chadderton Town Hall, Middleton Road, Chadderton, Oldham OL9 6PP. Tel: 0161-911 4260. *Director*, M. Willis

POOLE, Civic Centre, Poole, Dorset BH15 2RU. Tel: 01202-633633. *Policy Director*, Dr S. Goodwin

PORTSMOUTH, Civic Offices, Guildhall Square, Portsmouth PO1 2AL. Tel: 01705-841200. *City Education Officer*, Ms A. Lawson

REDCAR AND CLEVELAND, Council Offices, Kirkleatham Street, Redcar TS10 1RT. Tel: 01642-444000. *Chief Education Officer*, K. Burton

ROCHDALE, PO Box 70, Municipal Offices, Smith Street, Rochdale OL16 1YD. Tel: 01706-47474. *Director*, B. Atkinson

ROTHERHAM, Norfolk House, Walker Place, Rotherham S60 1QT. Tel: 01709-382121. *Education Officer*, H. C. Bower

RUTLAND, Catmose, Oakham LE15 6HP. Tel: 01572-722458. *Director of Education*, K. Bartley

ST HELENS, Rivington Centre, Rivington Road, St Helens WA10 4ND. Tel: 01744-456000. *Director of Education*, C. Hilton

SALFORD, Chapel Street, Salford M3 5TL. Tel: 0161-832 9751. *Chief Education Officer*, D. C. Johnston

SANDWELL, Shaftesbury House, High Street, West Bromwich B70 9LT. Tel: 0121-525 7366. *Director*, S. Gallacher

SEFTON, Town Hall, Oriel Road, Bootle, Merseyside L20 7AE. Tel: 0151-922 4040. *Education Officer*, J. A. Marsden

SHEFFIELD, Leopold Street, Sheffield S1 1RJ. Tel: 0114-272 6444. *Director*, J. Crossley-Holland

SOLIHULL, PO Box 20, Council House, Solihull B91 3QR. Tel: 0121-704 6000. *Director*, D. Nixon

SOUTHAMPTON, 5th Floor, Frobisher House, Commercial Road, Southampton SO15 1GX. Tel: 01703-223855. *Executive Director*, B. Hogg

SOUTH GLOUCESTERSHIRE, Bowling Hill, Chipping Sodbury BS17 6JX. Tel: 01454-868686. *Director of Education*, Ms T. Gillespie

SOUTH TYNESIDE, Town Hall and Civic Offices, Westoe Road, South Shields NE33 2RL. Tel: 0191-427 1717. *Director*, I. Reid

STOCKPORT, Stopford House, Piccadilly, Stockport SK1 3XE. Tel: 0161-474 3813. *Chief Education Officer*, M. Hunt

STOCKTON-ON-TEES, PO Box 11, Municipal Buildings, Church Road, Stockton-on-Tees TS18 1LD. Tel: 01642-393939. *Director*, S. T. Bradford

STOKE-ON-TRENT, Swann House, Boothen Road, Stoke-on-Trent ST4 4SY. Tel: 01782-234567. *Director of Education*, N. Rigby

SUNDERLAND, Civic Centre, Sunderland SR2 7DN. Tel: 0191-553 1355. *Director*, J. A. Williams, PH.D.

SWINDON, Sanford Street, Swindon SN1 1QH. Tel: 01793-463902. *Director*, M. Lusty

TAMESIDE, Council Offices, Wellington Road, Ashton under Lyne OL6 6DL. Tel: 0161-342 8355. *Director*, A. Webster

TRAFFORD, Sale Town Hall, Tatton Road, Sale M33 7RY. Tel: 0161-912 1212. *Director*, K. August

WAKEFIELD, County Hall, Wakefield WF1 2QL. Tel: 01924-306090. *Education Officer*, J. McLeod

WALSALL, Civic Centre, Darwall Street, Walsall WS1 1TP. Tel: 01922-650000. *Director*, T. Howard

WIGAN, Gateway House, Standishgate, Wigan WN1 1AE. Tel: 01942-828000. *Education Officer*, P. Clark

WIRRAL, Hamilton Building, Conway Street, Birkenhead L41 4FD. Tel: 0151-666 2121. *Director*, D. Rigby

WOLVERHAMPTON, Civic Centre, St Peter's Square, Wolverhampton WV1 1RR. Tel: 01902-554108. *Director*, R. Lockwood

YORK, George Hudson Street, York YO1 1ZG. Tel: 01904-613161. *Director*, M. Peters

London

*Inner London borough

BARKING AND DAGENHAM, Town Hall, Barking, Essex IG11 7LU. Tel: 0181-592 4500. *Education Officer*, A. Larbalestier

BARNET, Frien Barnet Lane, London N11 3DL. Tel: 0181-359 2000. *Director (acting)*, M. Kempson

BEXLEY, Hill View, Hill View Drive, Welling, Kent DA16 3RY. Tel: 0181-303 7777. *Director*, P. McGee

BRENT, Gwenneth Rickus Building, Brentfield Road, London NW10 8HB. Tel: 0181-937 1234. *Chief Education Officer*, J. Simpson

BROMLEY, Civic Centre, Stockwell Close, Bromley BR1 3UH. Tel: 0181-464 3333. *Director*, K. Davis

*CAMDEN, Crowndale Centre, 218–220 Eversholt Street, London NW1 1BD. Tel: 0171-911 1525. *Education Officer*, R. Litchfield

*CITY OF LONDON, Education Department, Corporation of London, PO Box 270, Guildhall, London EC2P 2EJ. Tel: 0171-332 1750. *Director*, Mrs D. McGrath

*City of Westminster, PO Box 240, City Hall, Victoria Street, London SW1E 6QP. Tel: 0171-641 6000. *Director*, Ms D. McGrath

Croydon, Taberner House, Park Lane, Croydon CR9 1TP. Tel: 0181-686 4433. *Director (acting)*, D. Sands

Ealing, Perceval House, 14–16 Uxbridge Road, London W5 2HL. Tel: 0181-579 2424. *Director*, A. Parker

Enfield, PO Box 56, Civic Centre, Silver Street, Enfield EN1 3XQ. Tel: 0181-366 6565. *Director*, Ms L. Graham

*Greenwich, Riverside House, Woolwich High Street, London SE18 6DN. Tel: 0181-854 8888. *Director*, J. Kramer

*Hackney, Edith Cavell Building, Enfield Road, London N1 5BA. Tel: 0171-214 8400. *Executive Director*, Ms S. Ebanja

*Hammersmith, Cambridge House, Cambridge Grove, London W6 0LE. Tel: 0181-748 3020. *Director*, Ms C. Whatford

Haringey, 48 Station Road, Wood Green, London N22 4TY. Tel: 0181-975 9700. *Director of Education Services*, Ms J. Tonge

Harrow, Civic Centre, Station Road, Harrow HA1 2UJ. Tel: 0181-424 1183. *Director (acting)*, P. Osburn

Havering, The Broxhill Centre, Broxhill Road, Harold Hill, Romford RM4 1XN. Tel: 01708-772222. *Director*, C. Hardy

Hillingdon, Civic Centre, High Street, Uxbridge UB8 1UW. Tel: 01895-250111. *Director (acting)*, G. Moss

Hounslow, Civic Centre, Lampton Road, Hounslow TW3 4DN. Tel: 0181-570 7728. *Director*, J. D. Trickett

*Islington, Laycock Street, London N1 1TH. Tel: 0171-477 5753. *Education Officer*, Ms H. Nicolle

*Kensington and Chelsea, Town Hall, Hornton Street, London W8 7NX. Tel: 0171-937 5464. *Executive Director*, R. Wood

Kingston upon Thames, Guildhall 2, Kingston Upon Thames KT1 1EU. Tel: 0181-547 5220. *Director*, J. Braithwaite

*Lambeth, Bluestar House, 234–244 Stockwell Road, London SW9 9SP. Tel: 0171-926 1000. *Executive Director*, Ms H. DuQuesnay

*Lewisham, Lawrence House, Catford, London SE6 4RU. Tel: 0181-314 6301. *Director*, Ms A. Efunshile

Merton, Civic Centre, London Road, Morden, Surrey SM4 5DX. Tel: 0181-543 2222. *Director*, Ms J. Cairns

Newham, Broadway House, 322 High Street, Stratford, London E15 1AJ. Tel: 0181-472 1430. *Director*, I. Harrison

Redbridge, Lynton House, 255–259 High Road, Ilford IG1 1NN. Tel: 0181-478 9130. *Director*, D. Capper

Richmond upon Thames, Regal House, London Road, Twickenham TW1 3QS. Tel: 0181-891 1411. *Director*, G. Alexander

*Southwark, 1 Bradenham Close, London SE17 2BA. Tel: 0171-525 5050. *Director*, G. Mott

Sutton, The Grove, Carshalton, Surrey SM5 3AL. Tel: 0181-770 6500. *Director*, Dr I. Birnbaum

*Tower Hamlets, Mulberry Place, 5 Clove Crescent, London E14 2BG. Tel: 0171-364 5000. *Education Officer*, Ms C. Gilbert

Waltham Forest, Municipal Offices, High Road, Leyton, London E10 5QJ. Tel: 0181-527 5544. *Chief Education Officer*, A. Lockhart

*Wandsworth, Town Hall, Wandsworth High Street, London SW18 2PU. Tel: 0181-871 6000. *Director*, P. Robinson

WALES

Anglesey, Park Mount, Glanhfwa Road, Llangefni LL77 7EY. Tel: 01248-752903. *Director*, R. P. Jones

Blaenau Gwent, Festival House, Festival Park, Ebbw Vale. Tel: 01495-355337. *Director*, B. Mawby

Bridgend, Sunnyside, Sunnyside Road, Bridgend CF31 4AR. Tel: 01656-642200. *Director*, D. Matthews

Caerphilly, Council Offices, Caerphilly Road, Ystrad Mynach, Hengoed CF82 7SF. Tel: 01443-815588. *Director*, N. Harries

Cardiff, County Hall, Atlantic Wharf, Cardiff CF1 5UW. Tel: 01222-872000. *Director*, T. Davies

Carmarthenshire, Pibwrlwyd, Carmarthen SA31 2NH. Tel: 01267-234567. *Director*, K. Price Davies

Ceredigion, Swyddfa'r Sir, Marine Terrace, Aberystwyth SY23 2DE. Tel: 01970-633600. *Director*, D. Lloyd Evans

Conwy, Government Buildings, Dinerth Road, Colwyn Bay LL28 4UL. Tel: 01492-544261. *Director*, R. E. Williams

Denbighshire, County Hall, Mold CH7 6GR. Tel: 01824-706700. *Director*, E. Lewis

Flintshire, County Hall, Mold CH7 6ND. Tel: 01352-704010. *Director*, K. McDonogh

Gwynedd, Council Offices, Caernarfon LL55 1SH. Tel: 01248-672255. *Director*, D. Whittall

Merthyr Tydfil, Ty Keir Hardie, Riverside Court, Avenue De Clichy, Merthyr Tydfil CF47 8XO. Tel: 01685-725000. *Director*, D. Jones

Monmouthshire, County Hall, Cwmbran NP44 2XH. Tel: 01633-644644. *Director*, D. Young

Neath and Port Talbot, Civic Centre, Port Talbot SA13 1PJ. Tel: 01639-763333. *Director*, V. Thomas

Newport, Civic Centre, Newport NP9 4UR. Tel: 01633-244491. *Director*, G. Bingham

Pembrokeshire, Cambria House, Haverfordwest SA61 1TP. Tel: 01437-764551. *Director*, G. Davies

Powys, County Hall, Llandrindod Wells LD1 5LG. Tel: 01597-826422. *Director*, M. Barker

Rhondda, Cynon, Taff, Education Centre, Grawen Street, Porth CF39 0BU. Tel: 01443-687666. *Director*, K. Ryley

Swansea, County Hall, Oystermouth Road, Swansea SA1 3SN. Tel: 01792-636350. *Director*, M. Brunt

Torfaen, County Hall, Cwmbran NP44 2WN. Tel: 01633-648610. *Director*, M. de Val

Vale of Glamorgan, Civic Offices, Holton Road, Barry CF63 4RU. Tel: 01446-700111. *Director*, A. Davies

Wrexham, Roxburgh House, Hill Street, Wrexham LL11 1SN. Tel: 01978-297450. *Director*, T. Garner

SCOTLAND

Aberdeen City, Summerhill, Stronsay Drive, Aberdeen AB15 6JA. Tel: 01224-208626. *Director*, J. Stodter

Aberdeenshire, Woodhill House, Westburn Road, Aberdeen AB16 5GB. Tel: 01224-665427. *Director*, M. White

Angus, County Buildings, Market Street, Forfar DD8 3LG. Tel: 01307-461460. *Director*, J. Anderson

Argyll and Bute, Argyll House, Alexandra Parade, Dunoon PA23 8AG. Tel: 01369-704000. *Director*, A. C. Morton

City of Edinburgh, Council Headquarters, George IV Bridge, Edinburgh EH1 1UQ. Tel: 0131-469 3322. *Director*, Mrs E. Reid

Clackmannanshire, Lime Tree House, Alloa FK10 2EX. Tel: 01259-450000. *Director*, K. Bloomer

Dumfries and Galloway, Education Department, 30 Edinburgh Road, Dumfries DG1 1JG. Tel: 01387-260000. *Director*, K. A. MacLeod

DUNDEE CITY, 8th Floor, Tayside House, 28 Crichton Street, Dundee DD1 3RJ. Tel: 01382-434000. *Director,* Ms A. Wilson

EAST AYRSHIRE, Council Headquarters, London Road, Kilmarnock KA3 7BU. Tel: 01563-576003. *Director,* J. Mulgrew

EAST DUMBARTONSHIRE, Boclair House, 100 Milngavie Road, Bearsden, Glasgow G61 2TQ. Tel: 0141-776 9000. *Director,* I. Mills

EAST LOTHIAN, Council Buildings, 25 Court Street, Haddington EH41 3HA. Tel: 01620-827588. *Director,* A. Blackie

EAST RENFREWSHIRE, Abbey House, Seedhill Road, Paisley PA1 1JS. Tel: 0141-577 3000. *Director,* Ms E. J. Currie

FALKIRK, McLaren House, Marchmont Avenue, Polmont, Falkirk FK2 0NZ. Tel: 01324-506600. *Director,* Dr G. Young

FIFE, Rothesay House, North Street, Glenrothes KY7 5PN. Tel: 01592-414141. *Director,* A. Mackay

GLASGOW CITY, Strathclyde House, Charing Cross Complex, 20 India Street, Glasgow G2 4PF. Tel: 0141-287 2000. *Director,* K. Corsar

HIGHLAND, Glenurquhart Road, Inverness IV3 5NX. Tel: 01463-702802. *Director,* A. Gilchrist

INVERCLYDE, 105 Dalrymple Street, Greenock PA15 1HT. Tel: 01475-882824. *Director,* B. McLeary

MIDLOTHIAN, Greenhall Centre, Gowkshill, Gorebridge EH23 4PE. Tel: 01875-823699. *Director,* D. MacKay

MORAY, Council Offices, High Street, Elgin IV30 1BX. Tel: 01343-543451. *Director,* K. Gavin

NORTH AYRSHIRE, Cunninghame House, Irvine KA12 8EE. Tel: 01294-324100. *Director,* J. Travers

NORTH LANARKSHIRE, Municipal Buildings, Kildonan Street, Coatbridge ML5 3LF. Tel: 01236-812336. *Director,* M. O'Neill

ORKNEY ISLANDS, Council Offices, School Place, Kirkwall KW15 1NY. Tel: 01856-873535. *Director (acting),* M. J. F. Dicver

PERTH AND KINROSS, Blackfriars, Perth PH1 5LT. Tel: 01738-476200. *Director,* R. McKay

RENFREWSHIRE, South Building, Cotton Street, Paisley PA1 1LE. Tel: 0141-842 5601. *Director,* Ms S. Rae

SCOTTISH BORDERS, Council Headquarters, Newtown St Boswells, Melrose TD6 0SA. Tel: 01835-824000. *Director,* J. Christie

SHETLAND ISLANDS, Schlumberger, Gremista Industrial Estate, Lerwick ZE1 0PX. Tel: 01595-744300. *Director,* J. Halcrow

SOUTH AYRSHIRE, County Buildings, Wellington Square, Ayr KA7 1DR. Tel: 01292-612201. *Director,* M. McCabe

SOUTH LANARKSHIRE, Council Headquarters, Almada Street, Hamilton ML3 0AA. Tel: 01698-454477. *Director,* Ms M. Allan

STIRLING, Viewforth, Stirling FK8 2ET. Tel: 01786-442680. *Director,* G. Jeyes

WEST DUMBARTONSHIRE, Garshake Road, Dumbarton G82 3PU. Tel: 01389-737000. *Director,* I. McMurdo

WESTERN ISLES, Council Offices, Sandwick Road, Stornoway HS1 2BW. Tel: 01851-703773. *Director,* N. R. Galbraith

WEST LOTHIAN, Lindsay House, South Bridge Street, Bathgate EH48 1TS. Tel: 01506-776135. *Corporate Manager,* R. Stewart

NORTHERN IRELAND

EDUCATION AND LIBRARY BOARDS

BELFAST, 40 Academy Street, Belfast BT1 2NQ. Tel: 01232-564000. *Chief Executive,* T. G. J. Moag, OBE

NORTH EASTERN, County Hall, 182 Galgorm Road, Ballymena, Co. Antrim BT42 1HN. Tel: 01266-653333. *Chief Executive,* G. Topping

SOUTH EASTERN, 18 Windsor Avenue, Belfast BT9 6EF. Tel: 01232-381188. *Chief Executive,* J. B. Fitzsimons

SOUTHERN, 3 Charlemont Place, The Mall, Armagh BT61 9AX. Tel: 01861-512200. *Chief Executive,* J. G. Kelly

WESTERN, 1 Hospital Road, Omagh, Co. Tyrone BT79 0AW. Tel: 01662-411411. *Chief Executive,* J. Martin

ISLANDS

GUERNSEY, Grange Road, St Peter Port GY1 1RQ. Tel: 01481-710821. *Director,* D. T. Neale

JERSEY, PO Box 142, JE4 8QJ. Tel: 01534-509500. *Director,* B. Grady

ISLE OF MAN, Department of Education, Murray House, 5–11 Mount Havelock, Douglas IM1 2SG. Tel: 01624-685820. *Director,* G. A. Baker

ISLES OF SCILLY, Town Hall, St Mary's TR21 0LW. Tel: 01720-422537. *Secretary for Education,* P. S. Hygate

ADVISORY BODIES

SCHOOLS

EDUCATION OTHERWISE, PO Box 7420, London N9 9SG. *Helpline,* tel: 0891-518303

INTERNATIONAL BACCALAUREATE, Peterson House, Fortran Road, St Mellons, Cardiff CF3 0LT. Tel: 01222-774000. *Director of Academic Affairs,* Dr H. Drennan

NATIONAL ADVISORY COUNCIL FOR EDUCATION AND TRAINING TARGETS, 7th Floor, 222 Grays Inn Road, London WC1X 8HL. Tel: 0171-211 5012. *Chairman,* D Wanless; *Director,* P. Chorley

NATIONAL COUNCIL FOR EDUCATIONAL TECHNOLOGY, Milburn Hill Road, Science Park, Coventry CV4 7JJ. Tel: 01203-416994. *Chief Executive (acting),* M. Littlewood

SPECIAL EDUCATIONAL NEEDS TRIBUNAL, 6th Floor, 71 Victoria Street, London SW1H 0HW. Tel: 0171-925 6925. *President,* T. Aldridge, QC; *Secretary,* Ms J. Saraga

INDEPENDENT SCHOOLS

GOVERNING BODIES ASSOCIATION, The Coach House, Pickforde Lane, Ticehurst, E. Sussex TN5 7BJ. Tel: 01580-200855. *Secretary,* D. G. Banwell

GOVERNING BODIES OF GIRLS' SCHOOLS ASSOCIATION, The Coach House, Pickforde Lane, Ticehurst, E. Sussex TN5 7BJ. Tel: 01580-200855. *Secretary,* D. G. Banwell

INDEPENDENT SCHOOLS EXAMINATIONS BOARD, Jordan House, Christchurch Road, New Milton, Hants BH25 6QJ. Tel: 01425-621111. *Administrator,* Mrs J. Williams

INDEPENDENT SCHOOLS INFORMATION SERVICE, 56 Buckingham Gate, London SW1E 6AG. Tel: 0171-630 8793. *National Director,* D. J. Woodhead

THE ISJC ASSISTED PLACES COMMITTEE, 100 Rochester Row, London SW1P 1JP. Tel: 0171-393 6666. *Secretary,* P. F. V. Waters

FURTHER EDUCATION

FURTHER EDUCATION DEVELOPMENT AGENCY, Dumbarton House, 68 Oxford Street, London W1N 0DA. Tel: 0171-436 0020. *Chief Executive,* S. Crowne

Regional Advisory Councils

ASSOCIATION OF COLLEGES IN THE EASTERN REGION ,
Merlin Place, Milton Road, Cambridge CB4 4DP. Tel:
01223-424022. *Chief Executive*, J. Graystone

CENTRA (EDUCATION AND TRAINING SERVICES) LTD,
Duxbury Park, Duxbury Hall Road, Chorley, Lancs
PR7 4AT. Tel: 01257-241428. *Chief Executive*, P. Wren

EMFEC (EAST MIDLAND FURTHER EDUCATION
COUNCIL), Robins Wood House, Robins Wood Road,
Aspley, Nottingham NG8 3NH. Tel: 0115-929 3291. *Chief
Executive*, R. Ainscough

NCFE (NORTHERN COUNCIL FOR FURTHER
EDUCATION), Portland House, 2nd Floor, Block D,
Newbridge Street, Newcastle upon Tyne NE1 8AL. Tel:
0191-201 3100. *Chief Executive*, J. F. Pearce

SOUTHERN REGIONAL COUNCIL FOR FURTHER
EDUCATION AND TRAINING, Building 33, The
University of Reading, London Road, Reading RG1 5AQ.
Tel: 0118-931 6320. *Chief Executive*, B. J. Knowles

SOUTH WEST ASSOCIATION FOR FURTHER EDUCATION
AND TRAINING, Bishops Hull House, Bishops Hull,
Taunton, Somerset TA1 5RA. Tel: 01823-335491. *Chief
Executive*, S. Fisher

WELSH JOINT EDUCATION COMMITTEE, 245 Western
Avenue, Cardiff CF5 2YX. Tel: 01222-265000. *Secretary*, I.
Hume

YORKSHIRE AND HUMBERSIDE ASSOCIATION FOR
FURTHER AND HIGHER EDUCATION, 13 Wellington
Road East, Dewsbury, W. Yorks WF13 1XG. Tel: 01924-
450900. *Director (acting)*, C. Daniel

Higher Education

ASSOCIATION OF COMMONWEALTH UNIVERSITIES, John
Foster House, 36 Gordon Square, London WC1H 0PF.
Tel: 0171–387 8572. *Secretary-General*, Prof. M. G.
Gibbons

COMMITTEE OF SCOTTISH HIGHER EDUCATION
PRINCIPALS (COSHEP), St Andrews House, 141 West
Nile Street, Glasgow G1 2RN. Tel: 0141-353 1880.
Secretary, Dr R. L. Crawford

COMMITTEE OF VICE-CHANCELLORS AND PRINCIPALS
OF THE UNIVERSITIES OF THE UNITED KINGDOM,
Woburn House, 20 Tavistock Square, London
WC1H 9HQ. Tel: 0171-419 4111. *Chairman*, Prof. M.
Harris; *Chief Executive*, Ms D. Warwick

NORTHERN IRELAND HIGHER EDUCATION COUNCIL,
Rathgael House, Balloo Road, Bangor BT19 7PR. Tel:
01247-279333. *Chairman*, Sir Kenneth Bloomfield, KCB;
Secretary, J. Coote

QUALITY ASSURANCE AGENCY FOR HIGHER
EDUCATION, 344–354 Gray's Inn Road, London
WC1X 8BP. Tel: 0171-837 2223

CURRICULUM COUNCILS

AWDURDOD CYMWYSTERAU, CWRICWLWM ACASESU
CYMRU / QUALIFICATIONS, CURRICULUM AND
ASSESSMENT AUTHORITY FOR WALES, Castle
Buildings, Womanby Street, Cardiff CF1 9SX. Tel:
01222-344946. *Chief Executive*, J. V. Williams

NORTHERN IRELAND COUNCIL FOR THE CURRICULUM,
EXAMINATIONS AND ASSESSMENT, Clarendon Dock,
29 Clarendon Road, Belfast BT1 3BG. Tel: 01232-261200.
Chief Executive, Mrs C. Coxhead

QUALIFICATIONS AND CURRICULUM AUTHORITY,
Newcombe House, 45 Notting Hill Gate, London
W11 3JB. Tel: 0171-229 1234. *Chairman*, Sir William
Stubbs, PH.D.; *Chief Executive*, N. Tate, PH.D.

SCOTTISH CONSULTATIVE COUNCIL ON THE
CURRICULUM, Gardyne Road, Broughty Ferry,
Dundee DD5 1NY. Tel: 01382-455053. *Chief Executive*,
C. E. Harrison

EXAMINING BODIES

GCSE

THE EDEXCEL FOUNDATION (London Examinations),
Stewart House, 32 Russell Square, London WC1B 5DN.
Tel: 0171-331 4000. *Chief Executive*, Ms C. Townsend,
PH.D.

MIDLAND EXAMINING GROUP, 1 Hills Road, Cambridge
CB1 2EU. Tel: 01223-553311. *Chief Executive*, Dr M.
Halstead (Part of UCLES)

NORTHERN EXAMINATIONS AND ASSESSMENT BOARD,
Devas Street, Manchester M15 6EX. Tel: 0161-953 1180.
Chief Executive, Mrs K. Tattersall

NORTHERN IRELAND COUNCIL FOR THE CURRICULUM,
EXAMINATIONS AND ASSESSMENT, Clarendon Dock,
29 Clarendon Road, Belfast BT1 3BG. Tel: 01232-261200.
Chief Executive, Mrs C. Coxhead

SEG (SOUTHERN EXAMINING GROUP), Stag Hill House,
Guildford, Surrey GU2 5XJ. Tel: 01483-506506.
Secretary-General, Dr C. P. Hughes

WELSH JOINT EDUCATION COMMITTEE, 245 Western
Avenue, Cardiff CF5 2YX. Tel: 01222-265000. *Chief
Executive*, I. Hume

A-LEVEL

ASSOCIATED EXAMINING BOARD, Stag Hill House,
Guildford, Surrey GU2 5XJ. Tel: 01483-506506.
Secretary-General, J. A. Day

THE EDEXCEL FOUNDATION (London Examinations),
Stewart House, 32 Russell Square, London WC1B 5DN.
Tel: 0171-331 4000. *Chief Executive*, Ms C. Townsend,
PH.D.

NORTHERN EXAMINATIONS AND ASSESSMENT BOARD,
Devas Street, Manchester M15 6EX. Tel: 0161-953 1180.
Chief Executive, Mrs K. Tattersall

NORTHERN IRELAND COUNCIL FOR THE CURRICULUM,
EXAMINATIONS AND ASSESSMENT, Clarendon Dock,
29 Clarendon Road, Belfast BT1 3BG. Tel: 01232-261200.
Chief Executive, Mrs C. Coxhead

OXFORD AND CAMBRIDGE EXAMINATIONS AND
ASSESSMENT COUNCIL (OCEAC), Syndicate
Buildings, 1 Hills Road, Cambridge CB1 2EU. Tel:
01223-553311 (OCEAC is part of UCLES)

OXFORD AND CAMBRIDGE SCHOOLS EXAMINATION
BOARD, *see* OCEAC

UNIVERSITY OF CAMBRIDGE LOCAL EXAMINATIONS
SYNDICATE (UCLES), *see* OCEAC

UNIVERSITY OF OXFORD DELEGACY OF LOCAL
EXAMINATIONS, *see* OCEAC

WELSH JOINT EDUCATION COMMITTEE, 245 Western
Avenue, Cardiff CF5 2YX. Tel: 01222-265000. *Chief
Executive*, I. Hume

SCOTLAND

SCOTTISH QUALIFICATIONS AUTHORITY, Hanover House, 24 Douglas Street, Glasgow G2 7NQ. Tel: 0141-248 7900; Ironmills Road, Dalkeith EH12 1LE. Tel: 0131-663 6601. *Chief Executive*, R. Tuck

FURTHER EDUCATION

CITY & GUILDS, 1 Giltspur Street, London ECIA 9DD. Tel: 0171-294 2468. *Director-General*, N. Carey, PH.D.
THE EDEXCEL FOUNDATION (BTEC and London Examinations), Stewart House, 32 Russell Square, London WCIB 5DN Tel: 0171-331 4000. *Chief Executive*, Ms C. Townsend, PH.D.
RSA EXAMINATIONS BOARD, Progress House, Westwood Way, Coventry CV4 8HS. Tel: 01203-470033. *Chief Executive*, M. F. Cross

FUNDING COUNCILS

SCHOOLS

FUNDING AGENCY FOR SCHOOLS, Albion Wharf, 25 Skeldergate, York YOI 2XL. Tel: 01904-661661. *Chairman*, Sir Christopher Benson; *Chief Executive*, M. Collier

FURTHER EDUCATION

FURTHER EDUCATION FUNDING COUNCIL FOR ENGLAND, Cheylesmore House, Quinton Road, Coventry CVI 2WT. Tel: 01203-863000. *Chief Executive*, Prof. D. Melville
FURTHER EDUCATION FUNDING COUNCIL FOR WALES, Lambourne House, Cardiff Business Park, Llanishen, Cardiff CF4 5GL. Tel: 01222-761861. *Head of Division*, Mrs L. Gainsbury
SCOTTISH FURTHER EDUCATION FUNDING DIVISION, Scottish Office Education and Industry Department, First Floor West, Victoria Quay, Edinburgh EH6 6QQ Tel: 0131-244 0286. *Head of Division*, C. Reeves

HIGHER EDUCATION

HIGHER EDUCATION FUNDING COUNCIL FOR ENGLAND, Northavon House, Coldharbour Lane, Bristol BSI6 IQD. Tel: 0117-931 7317. *Chief Executive*, Prof. B. Fender
HIGHER EDUCATION FUNDING COUNCIL FOR WALES, Linden Court, The Orchards, Tŷ Glas Avenue, Llanishen, Cardiff CF4 5DZ. Tel: 01222-761861. *Chief Executive*, Prof. J. A. Andrews
SCOTTISH HIGHER EDUCATION FUNDING COUNCIL, Donaldson House, 97 Haymarket Terrace, Edinburgh EHI2 5HD. Tel: 0131-313 6500. *Chief Executive*, Prof. J. Sizer, CBE
STUDENT AWARDS AGENCY FOR SCOTLAND, Gyleview House, 3 Redheughs Rigg, Edinburgh EHI2 9HH. Tel: 0131-244 5823. *Chief Executive*, K. MacRae
STUDENT LOANS COMPANY LTD, 100 Bothwell Street, Glasgow G2 7JD. Tel: 0141-306 2000. *Chief Executive*, C. Ward
TEACHER TRAINING AGENCY, Portland House, Stag Place, London SWIE 5TT. Tel: 0171-925 3700. *Chairman*, C. Booth; *Chief Executive*, Ms A. Millett

ADMISSIONS AND COURSE INFORMATION

CAREERS RESEARCH AND ADVISORY CENTRE (CRAC), Sheraton House, Castle Park, Cambridge CB3 0AX. Tel: 01223-460277. *Director*, D. McGregor. *Publishers*, Hobsons Publishing PLC, Bateman Street, Cambridge CB2 1LZ
COMMITTEE OF SCOTTISH HIGHER EDUCATION PRINCIPALS (COSHEP), St Andrew House, 141 West Nile Street, Glasgow GI 2RN. Tel: 0141-353 1880. *Secretary*, Dr R. L. Crawford
GRADUATE TEACHER TRAINING REGISTRY, Fulton House, Jessop Avenue, Cheltenham, Glos GL50 3SH. Tel: 01242-225868. *Registrar*, Mrs M. Griffiths
SOCIAL WORK ADMISSIONS SYSTEM, Fulton House, Jessop Avenue, Cheltenham, Glos GL50 3SH. Tel: 01242-225977. *Admissions Officer*, Mrs M. Griffiths
TEACHER EDUCATION ADMISSIONS CLEARING HOUSE (TEACH) (Scottish postgraduate only), PO Box 165, Holyrood Road, Edinburgh EH8 8AT. Tel: 0131-558 6169/70. *Office Manager*, Ms J. Wright
UNIVERSITIES AND COLLEGES ADMISSIONS SERVICE, Fulton House, Jessop Avenue, Cheltenham, Glos GL50 3SH. Tel: 01242-222444. *Chief Executive*, M. A. Higgins, PH.D.

UNIVERSITIES

THE UNIVERSITY OF ABERDEEN (1495)
Regent Walk, Aberdeen AB9 1FX
Tel 01224-272000
Full-time students (1996–7), 11,292
Chancellor, The Lord Wilson of Tillyorn, GCMG (1997)
Vice-Chancellor, Prof. C. D. Rice
Registrar, Dr P J Murray
Secretary, N. R. D. Begg
Rector, Dr W. J. A. Macartney, QC (1996–9)

THE UNIVERSITY OF ABERTAY DUNDEE (1994)
Bell Street, Dundee DDI IHG
Tel 01382-308000
Full-time students (1996–7), 4,141
Chancellor, The Earl of Airlie, KT, GCVO, PC
Principal/Vice-Chancellor, Prof. B. King
Vice-Principal, Prof. J. McGoldrick
Assistant Principal, D. Hogarth

ANGLIA POLYTECHNIC UNIVERSITY (1992)
Bishop Hall Lane, Chelmsford, Essex CMI ISQ
Tel 01245-493131
Full-time students (1996–7), 9,839
Chancellor, The Lord Prior, PC (1992)
Vice-Chancellor, M. Malone-Lee, CB
Head of Student Administration, D. Davies
Secretary, S. G. Bennett

ASTON UNIVERSITY (1966)
Aston Triangle, Birmingham B4 7ET
Tel 0121-359 3611
Full-time students (1996–7), 5,153
Chancellor, Sir Adrian Cadbury (1979)
Vice-Chancellor, Prof. M. Wright
Registrar and Secretary, R. D. A. Packham

THE UNIVERSITY OF BATH (1966)
Claverton Down, Bath BA2 7AY
Tel 01225-826826
Full-time students (1996–7), 6,110
Chancellor, Sir Denys Henderson (1993)
Vice-Chancellor, Prof. V. D. VandeLinde, PH.D.
Registrar, J. A. Bursey

THE UNIVERSITY OF BIRMINGHAM (1900)
Edgbaston, Birmingham B15 2TT
Tel 0121-414 3344
Full-time students (1996–7), 16,020
Chancellor, Sir Alexander Jarratt, CB (1983)
Vice-Chancellor, Prof. M. Irvine, PH.D.
Registrar and Secretary, D. R. Holmes

BOURNEMOUTH UNIVERSITY (1992)
Poole House, Talbot Campus, Fern Barrow,
Dorset BH12 5BB
Tel 01202-524111
Full-time students (1996–7), 7,633
Chancellor, The Baroness Cox (1992)
Vice-Chancellor, Prof. G. Slater
Registrar, N. Richardson

THE UNIVERSITY OF BRADFORD (1966)
Bradford BD7 1DP
Tel 01274-733466/232323
Full-time students (1996–7), 7,509
Chancellor, The Baroness Lockwood (1997)
Vice-Chancellor, Prof. D. J. Johns, PH.D., D.SC. (1989)
Registrar and Secretary, N. J. Andrew

THE UNIVERSITY OF BRIGHTON (1992)
Mithras House, Lewes Road, Brighton BN2 4AT
Tel 01273-600900
Full-time students (1996–7), 9,616
Chairman of the Board, M. J. Aldrich
Director, Prof. D. J. Watson
Deputy Director, D. E. House

THE UNIVERSITY OF BRISTOL (1909)
Senate House, Tyndall Avenue, Bristol BS8 1TH
Tel 0117-928 9000
Full-time students (1996–7), 9,676
Chancellor, Sir Jeremy Morse, KCMG (1989)
Vice-Chancellor, Sir John Kingman, FRS
Registrar, J. H. M. Parry
Secretary, Ms K. E. McKenzie, D.phil.

BRUNEL UNIVERSITY (1966)
Uxbridge, Middx UB8 3PH
Tel 01895-274000
Full-time students (1996–7), 12,214
Chancellor, The Earl of Halsbury, FRS (1966)
Vice-Chancellor, Prof. M. J. H. Sterling
Secretary-General and Registrar, D. Neave

THE UNIVERSITY OF BUCKINGHAM (1983)
(Founded 1976 as University College at Buckingham)
Buckingham MK18 1EG
Tel 01280-814080
Full-time students (1996–7), 798
Chancellor, The Baroness Thatcher, KG, OM, PC, FRS (1992)
Vice-Chancellor, Prof. R. H. Taylor
Director of Administration, J. P. Elder

THE UNIVERSITY OF CAMBRIDGE
University Offices, The Old Schools, Cambridge CB2 1TN
Tel 01223-337733
Undergraduates in residence (1996–7), 11,223

UNIVERSITY OFFICERS, ETC.
Chancellor, HRH The Prince Philip, Duke of Edinburgh,
   KG, KT, OM, GBE, PC (1977)
Vice-Chancellor, Prof. A. N. Broers, PH.D., FRS (1996)
High Steward, The Lord Runcie, PC, DD (1991)
Deputy High Steward, The Lord Richardson of
   Duntisbourne, PC, MBE, TD (1983)
Commissary, The Lord Oliver of Aylmerton, PC (*Trinity
   Hall*) (1989)
Proctors, M. A. Message, PH.D. (*St Catherine's*); E. J. Clark-
   King (*Sidney Sussex*) (1997)
Orator, A. J. Bowen (*Jesus*) (1993)
Registrary, T. J. Mead, PH.D. (*Wolfson*) (1997)
Deputy Registrary, N. J. B. A. Branson, PH.D. (*Darwin*) (1993)
Librarian, P. K. Fox (*Selwyn*) (1994)
Treasurer, Mrs J. Womack (*Trinity Hall*) (1993)
Secretary-General of the Faculties, D. A. Livesey,
   PH.D. (*Emmanuel*) (1992)
Director of the Fitzwilliam Museum, D. D. Robinson (*Clare*)
   (1995)

COLLEGES AND HALLS, ETC.
with dates of foundation

CHRIST'S (1505), *Master*, A. J. Munro, PH.D. (1995)
CHURCHILL (1960), *Master*, Sir John Boyd, KCMG (1996)
CLARE (1326), *Master*, Prof. B. A. Hepple, LLD (1993)
CLARE HALL (1966), *President*, Prof. G. P. K. Beer, Litt.D.,
   FBA (1994)
CORPUS CHRISTI (1352), *Master*, Prof. Sir Tony Wrigley,
   PH.D. (1994)
DARWIN (1964), *Master*, Prof. Sir Geoffrey Lloyd, PH.D.,
   FBA (1989)
DOWNING (1800), *Master*, Prof. D. A. King, FRS (1995)
EMMANUEL (1584), *Master*, Prof. J. E. Ffowcs-Williams,
   SC.D. (1996)
FITZWILLIAM (1966), *Master*, Prof. A. W. Cuthbert, PH.D.,
   FRS (1991)
GIRTON (1869), *Mistress*, Mrs J. J. d'A. Campbell, CMG
   (1992)
GONVILLE AND CAIUS (1348), *Master*, N. McKendrick
   (1996)
HOMERTON (1824) (for B.Ed. students), *Principal*,
   Mrs K. B. Pretty, PH.D. (1991)
HUGHES HALL (1885) (for post-graduate students),
   President, J. T. Dingle, D.SC. (1993)
JESUS (1496), *Master*, Prof. D. G. Crighton, SC.D., FRS (1997)
KING'S (1441), *Provost*, Prof. P. P. G. Bateson, SC.D., FRS
   (1987)
*LUCY CAVENDISH COLLEGE (1965) (for women research
   students and mature and affiliated undergraduates),
   President, The Baroness Perry of Southwark (1994)
MAGDALENE (1542), *Master*, Prof. Sir John Gurdon,
   D.phil., FRS (1995)
*NEW HALL (1954), *President*, Mrs A. Lonsdale (1996)
*NEWNHAM (1871), *Principal*, Ms O. S. O'Neill, CBE
   (1992)
PEMBROKE (1347), *Master*, Sir Roger Tomkys, KCMG
   (1992)
PETERHOUSE (1284), *Master*, Prof. Sir John Meurig
   Thomas, FRS (1993)
QUEENS' (1448), *President*, The Lord Eatwell
ROBINSON (1977), *Warden*, Prof. the Lord Lewis of
   Newnham, SC.D., FRS (1977)
ST CATHARINE'S (1473), *Master*, Prof. Sir Terence
   English (1993)

St Edmund's (1896), *Master,* Prof. R. B. Heap, sc.d. (1996)
St John's (1511), *Master,* Prof. P. Goddard, ph.d., frs (1994)
Selwyn (1882), *Master,* Sir David Harrison, cbe, sc.d., f.eng. (1993)
Sidney Sussex (1596), *Master,* Prof. G. Horn, sc.d., frs (1992)
Trinity (1546), *Master,* Prof. A. K. Sen (from Jan. 1998)
Trinity Hall (1350), *Master,* Sir John Lyons, ph.d. (1984)
Wolfson (1965), *President,* G. Johnson ph.d. (1994)

*College for women only

THE UNIVERSITY OF CENTRAL ENGLAND IN BIRMINGHAM (1992)
Perry Barr, Birmingham b42 2su
Tel 0121-331 5000
Full-time students (1995–6), 11,000
Chancellor, The Lord Mayor of Birmingham
Vice-Chancellor, Dr P. C. Knight, cbe
Secretary and Registrar, Ms M. Penlington

THE UNIVERSITY OF CENTRAL LANCASHIRE (1992)
Preston pr1 2he
Tel 01772-201201
Full-time students (1995–6), 13,856
Chancellor, Sir Francis Kennedy, kcmg, cbe
Vice-Chancellor, B. G. Booth
Academic Registrar, L. Munro
Secretary, Ms P. M. Ackroyd

THE CITY UNIVERSITY (1966)
Northampton Square, London ec1v 0hb
Tel 0171-477 8020
Full-time students (1996–7), 8,000
Chancellor, The Rt. Hon. the Lord Mayor of London
Vice-Chancellor, Prof. R. N. Franklin, cbe, d.phil., d.sc.
Academic Registrar, A. H. Seville, ph.d.
Secretary, M. M. O'Hara

COVENTRY UNIVERSITY (1992)
Priory Street, Coventry cv1 5fb
Tel 01203-631313
Full-time students (1996–7), 16,000
Chancellor, The Lord Plumb, mep
Vice-Chancellor, M. Goldstein, cbe, ph.d., d.sc.
Academic Registrar, J. Gledhill, ph.d.
Secretary, Ms L. Arlidge

CRANFIELD UNIVERSITY (1969)
(Founded as Cranfield Institute of Technology)
Cranfield, Beds mk43 0al
Tel 01234-750111
Full-time students (1996–7), 2,319
Chancellor, vacant
Vice-Chancellor, Prof. F. R. Hartley, d.sc.
Secretary and Registrar, J. K. Pettifer

DE MONTFORT UNIVERSITY (1992)
The Gateway, Leicester le1 9bh
Tel 0116-255 1551
Full-time students (1996–7), 28,000
Chancellor, Sir Clive Whitmore, gcb, cvo
Vice-Chancellor, Prof. K. Barker, cbe
Academic Registrar, V. E. Critchlow

THE UNIVERSITY OF DERBY (1993)
(formerly Derbyshire College of Higher Education)
Kedleston Road, Derby de22 1gb
Tel 01332-622222
Full-time students (1996–7), 9,000
Chancellor, Sir Christopher Ball
Vice-Chancellor, Prof. R. Waterhouse
Registrar, Mrs J. Fry
Secretary, R. Gillis

THE UNIVERSITY OF DUNDEE (1967)
Dundee dd1 4hn
Tel 01382-344000
Full-time students (1996–7), 8,900
Chancellor, Sir James Black, frcp, frs (1992)
Vice-Chancellor, Dr I. J. Graham-Bryce
Secretary, R. Seaton
Rector, S. Fry (1995–8)

THE UNIVERSITY OF DURHAM
(Founded 1832; re-organized 1908, 1937 and 1963)
Old Shire Hall, Durham dh1 3hp
Tel 0191-374 2000
Full-time students (1996–7), 9,812
Chancellor, Sir Peter Ustinov, cbe, frsl
Vice-Chancellor, Prof. E. A. V. Ebsworth, cbe, ph.d., sc.d., frse
Registrar and Secretary, J. C. F. Hayward

COLLEGES
Collingwood, *Principal,* Prof. G. H. Blake, ph.d.
Graduate Society, *Principal,* M. Richardson, ph.d.
Grey, *Master,* V. E. Watts
Hatfield, *Master,* Prof. T. P. Burt, ph.d.
St Aidan's, *Principal,* A. Yarwood, ph.d. (*acting*)
St Chad's, *Principal,* J. P. M. Cassidy, ph.d.
St Cuthbert's Society, *Principal,* S. G. C. Stoker
St Hild and St Bede, *Principal,* Prof. D. J. Davies, ph.d.
St John's, *Principal,* D. V. Day
St Mary's, *Principal,* Miss J. M. Kenworthy
Trevelyan, *Principal,* Prof. M. Todd, d.litt
University (Durham), *Master,* E. C. Salthouse, ph.d.
University (Stockton), *Principal,* J. C. F. Hayward
Ushaw, *President,* Revd J. O'Keefe
Van Mildert, *Principal,* Ms J. Turner, ph.d.

THE UNIVERSITY OF EAST ANGLIA (1963)
Norwich nr4 7tj
Tel 01603-456161
Full-time students (1996–7), 7,200
Chancellor, Sir Geoffrey Allen, feng, frs (1994)
Vice-Chancellor, V. Watts
Registrar and Secretary, M. G. E. Paulson-Ellis, obe

THE UNIVERSITY OF EAST LONDON (1992)
Longbridge Road, Dagenham, Essex rm8 2as
Tel 0181-590 7000
Full-time students (1996–7), 10,000
Chancellor, The Lord Rix, cbe
Vice-Chancellor, Prof. F. W. Gould
Secretary and Registrar, A. Ingle

THE UNIVERSITY OF EDINBURGH (1583)
7–11 Nicolson Street, Edinburgh eh8 9be
Tel 0131-650 1000
Full-time students (1996–7), 13,774
Chancellor, HRH The Prince Philip, Duke of Edinburgh, kg, kt, om, gbe, pc, frs (1952)
Vice-Chancellor, Prof. Sir Stewart Sutherland, fba, frse

Registrar, D. Cattenach
Secretary, M. J. B. Lowe, PH.D.
Rector, J. Colquhoun (1997–2000)

THE UNIVERSITY OF ESSEX (1964)
Wivenhoe Park, Colchester CO4 3SQ
Tel 01206-873333
Full-time students (1995–6), 5,645
Chancellor, The Lord Nolan, PC (1997)
Vice-Chancellor, I. Crewe
Registrar and Secretary, A. F. Woodburn

THE UNIVERSITY OF EXETER (1955)
Northcote House, The Queen's Drive, Exeter EX4 4QJ
Tel 01392-263263
Full-time students (1996–7), 8,883
Chancellor, Sir Rex Richards, D.SC., FRS (1981)
Vice-Chancellor, Sir Geoffrey Holland, KCB
Registrar and Secretary, I. H. C. Powell

GLAMORGAN UNIVERSITY (1992)
Treforest, Pontypridd CF37 1DL
Tel 01443-480480
Full-time students (1996–7), 10,137
Chancellor, The Lord Rees, PC, QC
Vice-Chancellor, Prof. A. L. Webb
Academic Registrar, J. O'Shea
Secretary, J. L. Bracegirdle

THE UNIVERSITY OF GLASGOW (1451)
Glasgow G12 8QQ
Tel 0141-339 8855
Full-time students (1996–7), 17,369
Chancellor, Sir William Kerr Fraser
Vice-Chancellor, Prof. Sir Graeme Davies, PH.D., FEng.
Registrar, Mrs C. Lowther
Secretary, D. Mackie
Rector, R. Wilson (1996–9)

GLASGOW CALEDONIAN UNIVERSITY (1993)
Cowcaddens Road, Glasgow G4 0BA
Tel 0141-331 3000
Full-time students (1996–7), 13,500
Chancellor, The Lord Nickson, KBE
Principal (acting), B. Laurie
Secretary, B. M. Murphy

THE UNIVERSITY OF GREENWICH (1992)
Bexley Road, Eltham, London SE9 2PQ
Tel 0181-331 8000
Full-time students (1996–7), 15,130
Chancellor, The Baroness Young
Vice-Chancellor, Dr D. E. Fussey
Academic Registrar, Ms C. H. Rose
Secretary, J. M. Charles

HERIOT-WATT UNIVERSITY (1966)
Riccarton, Edinburgh EH14 4AS
Tel 0131-449 5111
Full-time students (1995–6), 5,121
Chancellor, The Lord Mackay of Clashfern, PC, QC, FRSE (1979)
Vice-Chancellor, Prof. J. S. Archer, FEng.
Secretary, P. L. Wilson

THE UNIVERSITY OF HERTFORDSHIRE (1992)
College Lane, Hatfield, Herts AL10 9AB
Tel 01707-284000
Full-time students (1996–7), 18,000
Chancellor, The Lord MacLaurin
Vice-Chancellor, Prof. N. K. Buxton
Registrar and Secretary, P. G. Jeffreys

THE UNIVERSITY OF HUDDERSFIELD (1992)
Queensgate, Huddersfield HD1 3DH
Tel 01484-422288
Full-time students (1996–7), 12,319
Chancellor, Sir Ernest Hall, OBE
Vice-Chancellor, Prof. J. R. Tarrant, PH.D.
Registrar and Secretary, Mrs M. H. Andrew

THE UNIVERSITY OF HULL (1954)
Cottingham Road, Hull HU6 7RX
Tel 01482-346311
Full-time students (1996–7), 11,500
Chancellor, The Lord Armstrong of Ilminster, GCB, CVO
Vice-Chancellor, Prof. D. N. Dilks, FRSL
Registrar and Secretary, D. J. Lock

KEELE UNIVERSITY (1962)
Newcastle under Lyme, Staffs ST5 5BG
Tel 01782-621111
Full-time students (1996–7), 5,374
Chancellor, Sir Claus Moser, KCB, CBE, FBA (1986)
Vice-Chancellor, Prof. J. V. Finch
Registrar, S. Morris

THE UNIVERSITY OF KENT AT CANTERBURY (1965)
Canterbury CT2 7NZ
Tel 01227-764000
Full-time students (1996–7), 7,239
Chancellor, Sir Crispin Tickell, GCMG, KCVO
Vice-Chancellor, Prof. R. Sibson, PH.D.
Secretary and Registrar, N. A. McHard

KINGSTON UNIVERSITY (1992)
Penrhyn Road, Kingston upon Thames, Surrey KT1 2EE
Tel 0181-547 2000
Full-time students (1996–7), 11,146
Chancellor, Sir Frank Lampl
Vice-Chancellor, Prof. P. Scott (from Jan. 1998)
Secretary, R. Abdulla

THE UNIVERSITY OF LANCASTER (1964)
Bailrigg, Lancaster LA1 4YW
Tel 01524-65201
Full-time students (1996–7), 8,646
Chancellor, HRH Princess Alexandra, the Hon. Lady Ogilvy, GCVO (1964)
Vice-Chancellor, Prof. W. Ritchie, OBE
Secretary, S. A. C. Lamley

THE UNIVERSITY OF LEEDS (1904)
Leeds LS2 9JT
Tel 0113-243 1751
Full-time students (1996–7), 20,768
Chancellor, HRH The Duchess of Kent, GCVO (1966)
Vice-Chancellor, Prof. A. G. Wilson
Secretary and Registrar, D. S. Robinson, PH.D.

LEEDS METROPOLITAN UNIVERSITY (1992)
Calverley Street, Leeds LS1 3HE
Tel 0113-283 2600
Full-time students (1996–7), 14,066
Chairman of the Board of Governors, L. Silver
Vice-Chancellor, Prof. L. Wagner
Academic Registrar, Ms C. Orange
Secretary, M. Wilkinson

THE UNIVERSITY OF LEICESTER (1957)
University Road, Leicester LE1 7RH
Tel 0116-252 2522
Full-time students (1996–7), 8,321
Chancellor, Sir Michael Atiyah, OM, PH.D., D.SC. (1995)
Vice-Chancellor, K. J. R. Edwards, PH.D.
Registrar and Secretary, K. J. Julian

THE UNIVERSITY OF LINCOLNSHIRE AND
HUMBERSIDE
(University of Humberside founded 1992; re-organized
1996)
Humberside Campus: Cottingham Road, Hull HU6 7RT
Tel 01482-440550
Lincoln Campus: Lincoln LN2 4YF
Tel 01522-882000
Full-time students (1996–7), 14,000
Chancellor, Dr J. H. Hooper, CBE
Vice-Chancellor, Prof. R. P. King
Registrar, F. S. Marks
Secretary, Ms M. Harries-Jenkins

THE UNIVERSITY OF LIVERPOOL (1903)
Senate House, Abercromby Square, Liverpool L69 3BX
Tel 0151-794 2000
Full-time students (1996–7), 12,995
Chancellor, The Lord Owen, CH, PC
Vice-Chancellor, Prof. P. N. Love, CBE
Registrar and Secretary, M. D. Carr

LIVERPOOL JOHN MOORES UNIVERSITY
(1992)
Rodney House, 70 Mount Pleasant, Liverpool L3 5UX
Tel 0151-231 2121
Full-time students (1996–7), 19,959
Chancellor, J. Moores, CBE
Vice-Chancellor, Prof. P. Toyne
Registrar and Secretary, Ms A. Wild

THE UNIVERSITY OF LONDON (1836)
Senate House, Malet Street, London WC1E 7HU
Tel 0171-636 8000
Internal students (1996–7), 82,262, External students,
24,500
Visitor, HM The Queen in Council
Chancellor, HRH The Princess Royal, KG, GCVO, FRS (1981)
Vice-Chancellor, Prof. G. Zellick, PH.D.
Chairman of the Council, The Lord Woolf, PC
Chairman of Convocation, D. Leslie

COLLEGES OF THE UNIVERSITY
BIRKBECK COLLEGE, Malet Street, London
WC1E 7HX. *Master (acting),* Prof. R. Evans
CHARING CROSS AND WESTMINSTER MEDICAL SCHOOL,
see Imperial College of Science, Technology and
Medicine
GOLDSMITHS COLLEGE, Lewisham Way, New Cross,
London SE14 6NW. *Warden,* Prof. K. J. Gregory, PH.D.
HEYTHROP COLLEGE, Kensington Square, London
W8 5HQ. *Principal,* C. J. Moss, D.phil.

IMPERIAL COLLEGE OF SCIENCE, TECHNOLOGY AND
MEDICINE (includes Imperial College Schools of
Medicine at Charing Cross, Hammersmith and St
Mary's hospitals and at the National Heart and Lung
Institute), South Kensington, London SW7 2AZ. *Rector,*
Prof. Sir Ronald Oxburgh, KBE, FRS
INSTITUTE OF CANCER RESEARCH, Royal Cancer
Hospital, Chester Beatty Laboratories, 17A Onslow
Gardens, London SW7 3AL. *Chief Executive,* Prof.
P. B. Garland, PH.D., FRSE
INSTITUTE OF EDUCATION, 20 Bedford Way, London
WC1H 0AL. *Director,* Prof. P. Mortimore, OBE
KING'S COLLEGE LONDON (includes King's College
School of Medicine and Dentistry), Strand, London
WC2R 2LS. *Principal,* Prof. A. Lucas, PH.D.
Associated Institute:
Institute of Psychiatry, De Crespigny Park, Denmark Hill,
London SE5 8AF. *Dean,* Prof. S. Checkley
LONDON BUSINESS SCHOOL, Sussex Place, Regent's Park,
London NW1 4SA. *Principal,* Prof. G. S. Bain, D.phil.
THE LONDON HOSPITAL MEDICAL COLLEGE, *see* Queen
Mary and Westfield College.
LONDON SCHOOL OF ECONOMICS AND POLITICAL
SCIENCE, Houghton Street, London WC2A 2AE. *Director,*
Prof. A. Giddens
LONDON SCHOOL OF HYGIENE AND TROPICAL
MEDICINE, Keppel Street, London WC1E 7HT. *Dean,*
Prof. H. Spencer
QUEEN MARY AND WESTFIELD COLLEGE (incorporating
St Bartholomew's and the Royal London School of
Medicine and Dentistry and the London Hospital
Medical College), Mile End Road, London
E1 4NS. *Principal,* Prof. G. Zellick, PH.D.
ROYAL FREE HOSPITAL SCHOOL OF MEDICINE, Rowland
Hill Street, London NW3 2PF. *Dean,* Prof. A. J.
Zuckerman, MD, FRCP
ROYAL HOLLOWAY, Egham Hill, Egham, Surrey TW20
0EX. *Principal,* Prof. N. Gowar, M.phil.
ROYAL POSTGRADUATE MEDICAL SCHOOL, *see* Imperial
College of Science, Technology and Medicine
ROYAL VETERINARY COLLEGE, Royal College Street,
London NW1 0TU. *Principal and Dean,* Prof.
L. E. Lanyon, PH.D.
ST BARTHOLOMEW'S AND THE ROYAL LONDON SCHOOL
OF MEDICINE AND DENTISTRY, *see* Queen Mary and
Westfield College
ST GEORGE'S HOSPITAL MEDICAL SCHOOL, Cranmer
Terrace, London SW17 0RE. *Dean,* Prof. R. Boyd, FRCP
SCHOOL OF ORIENTAL AND AFRICAN STUDIES,
Thornhaugh Street, Russell Square, London
WC1H 0XG. *Director,* Sir Tim Lankester, KCB
SCHOOL OF PHARMACY, 29–39 Brunswick Square,
London WC1N 1AX. *Dean,* Prof. A. T. Florence, CBE, PH.D.,
FRSE
SCHOOL OF SLAVONIC AND EAST EUROPEAN STUDIES,
Senate House, Malet Street, London WC1E 7HU. *Director,*
Prof. M. A. Branch, PH.D.
UNITED MEDICAL AND DENTAL SCHOOLS OF GUY'S AND
ST THOMAS' HOSPITALS, Guy's, London Bridge,
London SE1 9RT; St Thomas', Lambeth Palace Road,
London SE1 7EH. *Principal,* Prof. Sir Cyril Chantler, FRCP
UNIVERSITY COLLEGE LONDON (including UCL
Medical School), Gower Street, London
WC1E 6BT. *Provost,* Sir Derek Roberts, CBE, FRS, FENG.
WYE COLLEGE, Wye, Near Ashford, Kent
TN25 5AH. *Principal,* Prof. J. H. D. Prescott, PH.D.

SCHOOL OF ADVANCED STUDY
Senate House, Malet Street, London WC1E 7HU. *Dean,* Prof.
T. C. Daintith

Comprises:

INSTITUTE OF ADVANCED LEGAL STUDIES, Charles Clore House, 17 Russell Square, London WCIB 5DR. *Director*, Prof. B. A. K. Rider

INSTITUTE OF CLASSICAL STUDIES, Senate House, Malet Street, London WCIE 7HU. *Director*, Prof. G. B. Waywell, FSA

INSTITUTE OF COMMONWEALTH STUDIES, 27–28 Russell Square, London WCIB 5DS. *Director*, Prof. J. Manor

INSTITUTE OF GERMANIC STUDIES, 29 Russell Square, London WCIB 5DP. *Hon. Director*, E. M. Batley

INSTITUTE OF HISTORICAL RESEARCH, Senate House, Malet Street, London WCIE 7HU. *Director*, Prof. P. K. O'Brien, D.phil.

INSTITUTE OF LATIN AMERICAN STUDIES, 31 Tavistock Square, London WCIH 9HA. *Director*, Prof. V. G. Bulmer-Thomas, D.phil.

INSTITUTE OF ROMANCE STUDIES, Senate House, Malet Street, London WCIE 7HU. *Hon. Director*, Prof. A. Lavers, ph.D.

INSTITUTE OF UNITED STATES STUDIES, Senate House, Malet Street, London WCIE 7HU. *Director*, Prof. G. L. McDowell, ph.D.

WARBURG INSTITUTE, Woburn Square, London WCIH OAB. *Director*, Prof. C. N. J. Mann, ph.D.

INSTITUTES AND ASSOCIATE INSTITUTIONS

BRITISH INSTITUTE IN PARIS, 9–11 rue de Constantine, 75340 Paris, Cedex 07, France. *Director*, Prof. C. L. Campos, CBE, ph.D. *London office:* Senate House, Malet Street, London WCIE 7HU

CENTRE FOR DEFENCE STUDIES, King's College London, Strand, London WC2R 2LS. *Director*, Prof. L. Freedman, CBE, FBA

CENTRE FOR ENGLISH STUDIES, Senate House, Malet Street, London WCIE 7HU. *Director*, Dr W. Gould

COURTAULD INSTITUTE OF ART, North Block, Somerset House, Strand, London WC2R ORN. *Director*, Prof. E. C. Fernie, CBE, FSA, FRSE

INSTITUTE OF ZOOLOGY, Royal Zoological Society, Regent's Park, London NWI 4RY. *Director*, Prof. M. Gosling.

JEWS' COLLEGE, 44A Albert Road, London NW4 2SJ. *Principal*, Rabbi Dr D. Sinclair

ROYAL ACADEMY OF MUSIC, Marylebone Road, London NWI 5HT. *Principal*, Prof. C. Price

ROYAL COLLEGE OF MUSIC, Prince Consort Road, London SW7 2BS. *Director*, Ms J. Ritterman, ph.D.

TRINITY COLLEGE OF MUSIC, 11–13 Mandeville Place, London WIM 6AQ. *Principal*, G. Henderson

UNIVERSITY MARINE BIOLOGICAL STATION MILLPORT, Isle of Cumbrae, Scotland KA28 OEG. *Director*, Prof. J. Davenport, ph.D., D.SC., FRSE

LONDON GUILDHALL UNIVERSITY (1993)
31 Jewry Street, London EC3N 2EY
Tel 0171-320 1000
Full-time students (1996–7), 7,541
Provost, Prof. R. Floud, D.phil.
Academic Registrar, Ms J. Grinstead
Secretary, M. Weaver

LOUGHBOROUGH UNIVERSITY (1966)
Loughborough, Leics LEII 3TU
Tel 01509-263771
Full-time students (1996–7), 10,506
Chancellor, Sir Denis Rooke, CBE, FRS, FEng (1989)
Vice-Chancellor, Prof. D.Wallace, ph.D., FRS, FRSE
Registrar, D. E. Fletcher, ph.D.

THE UNIVERSITY OF LUTON (1993)
(formerly Luton College of Higher Education)
Park Square, Luton LUI 3JU
Tel 01582-734111
Full-time students (1996–7), 10,719
Chancellor, Sir David Plastow
Vice-Chancellor, Dr A. Wood

THE UNIVERSITY OF MANCHESTER
(Founded 1851; re-organized 1880 and 1903)
Oxford Road, Manchester MI3 9PL
Tel: 0161-275 2000
Full-time students (1995–6), 17,797
Chancellor, The Lord Flowers, FRS
Vice-Chancellor, Prof. M. B. Harris, CBE, ph.D.
Registrar and Secretary, E. Newcomb
Academic Registrar, A. McMenemy

UNIVERSITY OF MANCHESTER
INSTITUTE OF SCIENCE AND
TECHNOLOGY (1824)
PO Box 88, Manchester M6O IQD
Tel 0161-236 3311
Full-time students (1995–6), 6,000
Chancellor, Prof. Sir Roland Smith, ph.D. (1995)
Vice-Chancellor, Prof. R. F. Boucher, FEng.
Registrar and Secretary, P. C. C. Stephenson

MANCHESTER METROPOLITAN
UNIVERSITY (1992)
All Saints, Manchester MI5 6BH
Tel 0161-247 2000
Full-time students (1995–6), 22,000
Chancellor, The Duke of Westminster, OBE, TD
Vice-Chancellor, A. V. Burslem, OBE, JP
Academic Registrar, J. Karczewski-Slowikowski
Secretary, T. A. Hendley

MIDDLESEX UNIVERSITY (1992)
White Hart Lane, London NI7 8HR
Tel 0181-362 5000
Full-time students (1996–7), 19,696
Chancellor, The Baroness Platt of Writtle
Vice-Chancellor, Prof. M. Driscoll
Registrar and Secretary, G. Jones

NAPIER UNIVERSITY (1992)
219 Colinton Road, Edinburgh EHI4 IDJ
Tel 0131-444 2266
Full-time students (1996–7), 8,945
Chancellor, The Viscount Younger of Leckie, KCVO, TD, PC, FRSE
Vice-Chancellor, Prof. J. Mavor
Secretary and Registrar, I. J. Miller

THE UNIVERSITY OF NEWCASTLE UPON
TYNE
(Founded 1852; re-organized 1908, 1937 and 1963)
6 Kensington Terrace, Newcastle upon Tyne NEI 7RU
Tel 0191-222 6000
Full-time students (1996–7), 11,673
Chancellor, The Viscount Ridley, KG, GCVO, TD (1989)
Vice-Chancellor, J. R. G. Wright
Registrar, D. E. T. Nicholson

THE UNIVERSITY OF NORTH LONDON
(1992)
166–220 Holloway Road, London N7 8DB
Tel 0171-607 2789
Full-time students (1996–7), 11,389

Vice-Chancellor, B. Roper
Academic Registrar, Dr M. Storey

THE UNIVERSITY OF NORTHUMBRIA AT NEWCASTLE (1992)
Ellison Place, Newcastle upon Tyne NEI 8ST
Tel 0191-232 6002
Full-time students (1996–7), 18,416
Chancellor, The Lord Glenamara, CH, PC (1984)
Vice-Chancellor, Prof. G. Smith
Registrar, Mrs C. Penna
Secretary, R. A. Bott

THE UNIVERSITY OF NOTTINGHAM (1948)
University Park, Nottingham NG7 2RD
Tel 0115-951 5151
Full-time students (1996–7), 15,500
Chancellor, Sir Ron Dearing, CB, FEng. (1993)
Vice-Chancellor, Prof. Sir Colin Campbell
Registrar, D. J. Allen

NOTTINGHAM TRENT UNIVERSITY (1992)
Burton Street, Nottingham NGI 4BU
Tel 0115-941 8418
Full-time students (1995–6), 18,213
Vice-Chancellor, Prof. R. Cowell, PH.D.
Academic Registrar, D. W. Samson
Secretary, S. Smith

THE UNIVERSITY OF OXFORD
University Offices, Wellington Square, Oxford OXI 2JD
Tel 01865-270001
Students in residence (1996–7), 15,641

UNIVERSITY OFFICERS, ETC.

Chancellor, The Lord Jenkins of Hillhead, OM, PC (*Balliol*), *elected* 1987
High Steward, The Lord Goff of Chieveley, PC (*Lincoln* and *New College*), *elected* 1990
Vice-Chancellor, Dr C. R. Lucas (*Balliol*), *elected* 1997
Proctors, Dr M. E. Ceadel (*New College*); Dr A. M. Volfing (*Oriel*), *elected* 1997
Assessor, Dr R. J. Goodman (*St Antonys*), *elected* 1997
Public Orator, J. Griffin (*Balliol*), *elected* 1992
Bodley's Librarian, R. P. Carr (*Balliol*), *elected* 1997
Keeper of Archives, D. G. Vaisey (*Exeter*), *elected* 1995
Director of the Ashmolean Museum, vacant
Registrar of the University, A. J. Dorey, D.PHIL. (*Linacre*), *elected* 1979
Surveyor to the University, P. M. R. Hill, *elected* 1993
Secretary of Faculties, A. P. Weale (*Worcester*), *elected* 1984
Secretary of the Chest, J. R. Clements, *elected* 1995
Deputy Registrar (Administration), P. W. Jones (*Green*), *elected* 1991

OXFORD COLLEGES AND HALLS
with dates of foundation

ALL SOULS (1438), *Warden,* Prof. J. Davis (1994)
BALLIOL (1263), *Master (acting),* A. Graham (from Jan. 1998)
BRASENOSE (1509), *Principal,* The Lord Windlesham, CVO, PC (1989)
CHRIST CHURCH (1546), *Dean,* Very Revd J. H. Drury (1991)
CORPUS CHRISTI (1517), *President,* Prof. Sir Keith Thomas, FBA (1986)

EXETER (1314), *Rector,* Prof. M. Butler (1994)
GREEN (1979), *Warden,* Sir John Hanson, KCMG, CBE (1997)
HARRIS MANCHESTER (1786), *Principal,* Revd R. Waller, PH.D. (1990)
HERTFORD (1874), *Principal,* Sir Walter Bodmer, FRS (1996)
JESUS (1571), *Principal,* Dr P. M. North, CBE, FBA (1984)
KEBLE (1868), *Warden,* A. Cameron, FBA, FSA (1994)
KELLOG (1990), *President,* G. P. Thomas, PH.D. (1990)
LADY MARGARET HALL (1878), *Principal,* Sir Brian Fall, KCMG (1995)
LINACRE (1962), *Principal,* Dr P. A. Slack (1996)
LINCOLN (1427), *Rector,* E. K. Anderson, FRSE (1994)
MAGDALEN (1458), *President,* A. D. Smith, CBE (1988)
MANSFIELD (1886), *Principal,* D. J. Marquand (1996)
MERTON (1264), *Warden,* Dr. J Rawson, FBA (1994)
NEW COLLEGE (1379), *Warden,* Prof. A. J. Ryan (1996)
NUFFIELD (1937), *Warden,* Prof. A. Atkinson, FBA (1994)
ORIEL (1326), *Provost,* E. W. Nicholson, DD, FBA (1990)
PEMBROKE (1624), *Master,* Prof. R. Stevens, DCL (1993)
QUEEN'S (1340), *Provost,* G. Marshall (1993)
ST ANNE'S (1952) (originally Society of Oxford Home-Students (1879)), *Principal,* Mrs R. L. Deech (1991)
ST ANTONY'S (1950), *Warden,* M. I. Goulding (1997)
ST CATHERINE'S (1962), *Master,* The Lord Plant of Highfield (1994)
ST CROSS (1965), *Master,* R. C. Repp, D.PHIL. (1987)
ST EDMUND HALL (c.1278), *Principal,* His Hon. Sir Stephen Tumim (1996)
*ST HILDA'S (1893), *Principal,* Miss E. Llewellyn-Smith, CB (1990)
ST HUGH'S (1886), *Principal,* D. Wood, QC (1991)
ST JOHN'S (1555), *President,* W. Hayes, D.PHIL. (1987)
ST PETER'S (1929), *Master,* J. P. Barron, D.PHIL. (1991)
SOMERVILLE (1879), *Principal,* Dame Fiona Caldicott, DBE, FRCP (1996)
TEMPLETON (1965), *President,* Dr M. van Clemm (1996)
TRINITY (1554), *President,* The Hon. Michael J. Beloff, QC (1996)
UNIVERSITY (1249), *Master,* Sir Robin Butler, GCB, CVO (from Jan. 1998)
WADHAM (1612), *Warden,* J. S. Flemming (1993)
WOLFSON (1966), *President,* Sir David Smith, D.PHIL. (1994)
WORCESTER (1714), *Provost,* R. G. Smethurst (1991)

BLACKFRIARS (1921), *Regent,* Very Revd P. Merrill (1996)
CAMPION HALL (1896), *Master,* Revd J. A. Munitiz (1989)
GREYFRIARS (1910), *Warden,* Revd T. G. Weinandy, (1996)
REGENT'S PARK (1810), *Principal,* Revd P. S. Fiddes, D PHIL (1989)
ST BENET'S HALL (1897), *Master,* Revd H. Wansbrough, OSB (1991)
WYCLIFFE HALL (1877), *Principal,* Revd A. E. McGrath

OXFORD BROOKES UNIVERSITY (1993)
Headington, Oxford OX3 0BP
Tel 01865-741111
Full-time students (1995–6), 8,000
Chancellor, Ms H. Kennedy, QC (created a life peer, August 1997)
Vice-Chancellor, Prof. G. Upton
Deputy Vice-Chancellor, Corporate Services, B. Summers
Academic Secretary, Ms L. Winders

THE UNIVERSITY OF PAISLEY (1992)
(formerly Paisley College of Technology)
Paisley PAI 2BE
Tel 0141-848 3000
Full-time students (1996–7), 6,000

---

* College for women only

Chancellor, Sir Robert Easton, CBE
Vice-Chancellor, Prof. R. W. Shaw, CBE
Registrar, D. Rigg
Secretary, J. Fraser

THE UNIVERSITY OF PLYMOUTH (1992)
Drake Circus, Plymouth PL4 8AA
Tel 01752-600600
Full-time students (1995–6), 15,426
Vice-Chancellor, Prof. J. Bull
Registrar, Dr C. J. Sparrow

THE UNIVERSITY OF PORTSMOUTH (1992)
University House, Winston Churchill Avenue,
Portsmouth PO1 2UP
Tel 01705-876543
Full-time students (1996–7), 11,500
Chancellor, The Lord Palumbo
Vice-Chancellor, Prof. J. Craven
Academic Registrar, A. Rees
Secretary, R. Moore

THE QUEEN'S UNIVERSITY OF BELFAST (1908)
Belfast BT7 1NN
Tel 01232-245133
Full-time students (1995–6), 11,444
Chancellor, Sir David Orr, MC
Vice-Chancellor, Prof. G. Bain (from Jan. 1998)
Academic Secretary, Dr G. Baird
Administrative Secretary, D. H. Wilson

THE UNIVERSITY OF READING (1926)
Whiteknights, PO Box 217, Reading RG6 2AH
Tel 0118-987 5123
Full-time students (1996–7), 9,626
Chancellor, The Lord Carrington, KG, GCMG, CH, MC, PC (1992)
Vice-Chancellor, Prof. R. Williams
Secretary and Registrar, D. C. R. Frampton

THE ROBERT GORDON UNIVERSITY (1992)
Schoolhill, Aberdeen AB10 1FR
Tel 01224-262210
Full-time students (1996–7), 8,000
Chancellor, Sir Bob Reid (1993)
Vice-Chancellor, Prof. B. Stevely
Secretary, D. Caldwell

THE UNIVERSITY OF ST ANDREWS (1411)
College Gate, St Andrews KY16 9AJ
Tel 01334-476161
Full-time students (1996–7), 5,631
Chancellor, Sir Kenneth Dover, D.Litt., FRSE, FBA (1981)
Vice-Chancellor, Prof. S. Arnott, CBE, Ph.D., SC .D., FRS, FRSE
Secretary, D. J. Corner
Rector, D. Findlay, QC (1997–2000)

THE UNIVERSITY OF SALFORD (1967)
Salford M5 4WT
Tel 0161-745 5000
Full-time students (1996–7), 13,000
Chancellor, Sir Walter Bodmer, Ph.D., FRS
Vice-Chancellor, Prof. M. Harloe
Registrar, M. D. Winton, Ph.D.

THE UNIVERSITY OF SHEFFIELD (1905)
8 Palmerston Road, Sheffield S10 2TE
Tel 0114-276 8555
Full-time students (1996–7), 16,488

Chancellor, The Lord Dainton, Ph.D., SC.D., FRS (1979)
Vice-Chancellor, Prof. Sir Gareth Roberts, Ph.D., D.SC., FRS
Registrar and Secretary, J. S. Padley, Ph.D.

SHEFFIELD HALLAM UNIVERSITY (1992)
Pond Street, Sheffield S1 1WB
Tel 0114-272 0911
Full-time students (1995–6), 20,000
Chancellor, Sir Bryan Nicholson
Vice-Chancellor, J. Stoddart, CBE
Registrar, Ms J. Tory
Secretary, Ms S. Neocosmos

THE UNIVERSITY OF SOUTHAMPTON (1952)
Highfield, Southampton SO17 1BJ
Tel 01703-595000
Full-time students (1996–7), 13,279
Chancellor, The Earl of Selbourne, KBE, FRS
Vice-Chancellor, Prof. H. Newby, CBE, Ph.D.
Secretary and Registrar, J. F. D. Lauwerys
Academic Registrar, R. Knight

SOUTH BANK UNIVERSITY (1992)
103 Borough Road, London SE1 0AA
Tel 0171-928 8989
Full-time students (1996–7), 15,000
Chancellor, C. McLaren
Vice-Chancellor, Prof. G. Bernbaum
Registrar, R. Phillips
Secretary, Mrs L. Gander

STAFFORDSHIRE UNIVERSITY (1992)
College Road, Stoke-on-Trent ST4 2DE
Tel 01782-294000
Full-time students (1996–7), 11,730
Chancellor, The Lord Ashley of Stoke, CH, PC
Vice-Chancellor, Prof. C. E. King, Ph.D.
Academic Registrar, Miss F. Francis
Secretary, K. Sproston

THE UNIVERSITY OF STIRLING (1967)
Stirling FK9 4LA
Tel 01786-473171
Full-time students (1996–7), 5,950
Chancellor, The Lord Balfour of Burleigh, FRSE (1988)
Vice-Chancellor, Prof. A. Miller, Ph.D., FRSE
Academic Registrar, D. G. Wood
Secretary, K. J. Clarke

THE UNIVERSITY OF STRATHCLYDE (1964)
McCance Building, John Anderson Campus, Glasgow G1 1XQ
Tel 0141-552 4400
Full-time students (1996–7), 14,100
Chancellor, The Lord Tombs, LL D, D.SC., FEng. (1990)
Vice-Chancellor, Prof. J. P. Arbuthnott, SC.D., FRSE
Secretary, P. W. A. West

THE UNIVERSITY OF SUNDERLAND (1992)
Langham Tower, Ryhope Road, Sunderland SR2 7EE
Tel 0191-515 2000
Full-time students (1995–6), 12,612
Vice-Chancellor, Ms A. Wright, CBE, Ph.D.
Academic Registrar, S. Porteous
Secretary, J. D. Pacey

THE UNIVERSITY OF SURREY (1966)
Guildford, Surrey GU2 5XH
Tel 01483-300800
Full-time students (1996–7), 8,406
Chancellor, HRH The Duke of Kent, KG, GCMG, GCVO (1977)
Vice-Chancellor, Prof. P. J. Dowling, PH.D., FEng.
Secretary and Registrar, H. W. B. Davies

THE UNIVERSITY OF SUSSEX (1961)
Falmer, Brighton BN1 9RH
Tel 01273-606755
Full-time students (1996–7), 9,122
Chancellor, The Duke of Richmond and Gordon (1985)
Vice-Chancellor, Prof. G. Conway, PH.D.
Registrar and Secretary, B. Gooch

THE UNIVERSITY OF TEESSIDE (1992)
Middlesbrough TS1 3BA
Tel 01642-218121
Full-time students (1996–7), 8,235
Chancellor, Sir Leon Brittan
Vice-Chancellor, Prof. D. Fraser
University Secretary, J. M. McClintock

THAMES VALLEY UNIVERSITY (1992)
St Mary's Road, Ealing, London W5 5RF
Tel 0181-579 5000
Full-time students (1995–6), 11,500
Chancellor, P. Hamlyn, CBE
Vice-Chancellor, M. Fitzgerald, PH.D.
Head of Registry, P. Head

THE UNIVERSITY OF ULSTER (1984)
(Amalgamation of New University of Ulster and Ulster
Polytechnic)
Cromore Road, Coleraine BT52 1SA
Tel 01265-44141
Full-time students (1996–7), 20,000
Chancellor, Rabbi J. Neuberger
Vice-Chancellor, Prof. Sir Trevor Smith
Academic Registrar, K. Miller, PH.D.

THE UNIVERSITY OF WALES (1893)
King Edward VII Avenue, Cathays Park, Cardiff CF1 3NS
Tel 01222-382656
Full-time students (1996–7), 45,000
Chancellor, HRH The Prince of Wales, KG, KT, GCB, PC
(1976)
Senior Vice-Chancellor, Prof. K. Robbins, D.Litt., D.Phil., FRSE
Secretary-General, J. D. Pritchard

MEMBER INSTITUTIONS

UNIVERSITY OF WALES, BANGOR, Bangor LL57 2DG. Tel.
01248-351151. *Vice-Chancellor*, Prof. H. R. Evans, PH.D.,
FEng. (1995)
UNIVERSITY OF WALES, ABERYSTWYTH, Old College,
King Street, Aberystwyth SY23 2AX. Tel: 01970-623111.
Vice-Chancellor, Prof. D. Llwyd Morgan, D.phil. (1995)
UNIVERSITY OF WALES, CARDIFF, PO Box 920, Cardiff
CF1 3XP. Tel: 01222-874000. *Vice-Chancellor*, Prof.
E. B. Smith, PH.D., D.SC. (1993)
UNIVERSITY OF WALES COLLEGE, NEWPORT, Caerleon
Campus, PO Box 179, Newport NP6 1YG. Tel: 01633-
430088. *Principal*, Prof. K. J. Overshott, PH.D.
UNIVERSITY OF WALES COLLEGE OF MEDICINE, Heath
Park, Cardiff CF4 4XN. Tel: 01222-747747. *Vice-
Chancellor*, Prof. I. R. Cameron, FRCP (1994)
UNIVERSITY OF WALES INSTITUTE, CARDIFF, Llandaff
Centre, Western Avenue, Cardiff CF5 2SG. Tel. 01222-
506070. *Principal*, J. D. Winslow

UNIVERSITY OF WALES, LAMPETER, Lampeter SA48 7ED.
Tel: 01570-422351. *Vice-Chancellor*, Prof. K. Robbins,
D.Litt., D.Phil., FRSE (1992)
UNIVERSITY OF WALES SWANSEA, Singleton Park,
Swansea SA2 8PP. Tel: 01792-205678. *Vice-Chancellor*,
Prof. R. H. Williams, PH.D., D.SC, FRS (1994)

THE UNIVERSITY OF WARWICK (1965)
Coventry CV4 7AL
Tel 01203-523523
Full-time students (1996–7), 13,400
Chancellor, Sir Shridath Surendranath Ramphal, GCMG, QC
(1989)
Vice-Chancellor, Prof. Sir Brian Follett, FRS, D.SC.
Registrar, M. L. Shattock, OBE

THE UNIVERSITY OF WESTMINSTER (1992)
309 Regent Street, London W1R 8AL
Tel 0171-911 5000
Full-time students (1996–7), 9,198
Vice-Chancellor and Rector, Dr G. M. Copland
Registrar, Ms J. Hopkinson

THE UNIVERSITY OF THE WEST OF
ENGLAND, BRISTOL (BRISTOL UWE) (1992)
Coldharbour Lane, Bristol BS16 1QY
Tel 0117-965 6261
Full-time students (1996–7), 15,042
Chancellor, Dame Elizabeth Butler-Sloss, DBE
Vice-Chancellor, A. C. Morris
Academic Registrar, Ms M. J. Carter

THE UNIVERSITY OF WOLVERHAMPTON
(1992)
Wulfruna Street, Wolverhampton WV1 1SB
Tel 01902 321000
Full-time students (1996–7), 21,815
Chancellor, The Earl of Shrewsbury and Talbot
Vice-Chancellor, Prof. M. J. Harrison
Registrar, J. Baldwin
Secretary, A. W. Lee

THE UNIVERSITY OF YORK (1963)
Heslington, York YO1 5DD
Tel 01904-430000
Full-time students (1996–7), 7,200
Chancellor, Dame Janet Baker, CH, DBE
Vice-Chancellor, Prof. R. U. Cooke, PH.D.
Registrar, D. J. Foster

THE OPEN UNIVERSITY (1969)
Walton Hall, Milton Keynes MK7 6AA
Tel 01908-274066
Students and clients (1997), *c*.200,000
Tuition by correspondence linked with special radio and
television programmes, video and audio cassettes, computing, residential schools and a locally-based tutorial and
counselling service. The University awards degrees of BA,
B.Sc, B.Phil., MA, MBA, MBA (Technology), M.Eng.,
M.Sc., M.Phil., Ph.D., D.Ed., D.Sc. and D.Litt. There are
faculties and schools of arts; education; health and social
welfare; law; management; mathematics and computing;
modern languages; science; social sciences; technology;
and a wide range of qualification courses and study packs.
Chancellor, The Rt. Hon. Betty Boothroyd, MP
Vice-Chancellor, Sir John Daniel
Secretary, D. J. Clinch, OBE

THE ROYAL COLLEGE OF ART (1837)

Kensington Gore, London SW7 2EU
Tel 0171-590 4444
Under royal charter (1967) the Royal College of Art grants
the degrees of Doctor, Doctor of Philosophy, Master of
Philosophy and Master of Arts.
Students (1996–7), 800 (all postgraduate)
Provost, The Earl of Snowdon, GCVO
Rector and Vice-Provost, Prof. C. Frayling
Registrar, A. Selby

COLLEGES

It is not possible to name here all the colleges offering
courses of higher or further education. The list does not
include colleges forming part of a polytechnic or a university. The English colleges that follow are confined to those
in the Higher Education Funding Council for England
sector; there are many more colleges in England providing
higher education courses, some with HEFCFE funding.

The list of colleges in Wales, Scotland and Northern
Ireland includes institutions providing at least one full-
time course leading to a first degree granted by an
accredited validating body.

ENGLAND

BATH SPA UNIVERSITY COLLEGE, Newton Park, Newton
St Loe, Bath BA2 9BN. Tel: 01225-875875. *Director*, F.
Morgan
BISHOP GROSSETESTE COLLEGE, Lincoln LN1 3DY. Tel:
01522-527347. *Principal*, Ms E. Baker
BOLTON INSTITUTE OF HIGHER EDUCATION, Deane
Road, Bolton BL3 5AB. Tel: 01204-528851. *Principal*,
Prof. R. Oxtoby, PH.D.
BRETTON HALL, West Bretton, Wakefield, W. Yorks
WF4 4LG. Tel: 01924-830261. *Principal*, Prof. G. H. Bell
BUCKINGHAMSHIRE UNIVERSITY COLLEGE, Queen
Alexandra Road, High Wycombe, Bucks HP11 2JZ. Tel:
01494-522141. *Director*, Prof. P. B. Mogford
CANTERBURY CHRIST CHURCH COLLEGE, North
Holmes Road, Canterbury, Kent CT1 1QU. Tel: 01227-
767700. *Principal*, Prof. M. Wright
THE CENTRAL SCHOOL OF SPEECH AND DRAMA,
Embassy Theatre, 64 Eton Avenue, London NW3 3HY.
Tel: 0171-722 8183. *Principal*, Prof. R. S. Fowler, FRSA
CHELTENHAM AND GLOUCESTER COLLEGE OF HIGHER
EDUCATION, PO Box 220, The Park, Cheltenham, Glos
GL50 2QF. Tel: 01242-532700. *Director*, Miss J. O.
Trotter, OBE
CHICHESTER INSTITUTE OF HIGHER EDUCATION,
College Lane, Chichester, West Sussex PO19 4PE. Tel:
01243-816000. *Director*, P. E. D. Robinson
DARTINGTON COLLEGE OF ARTS, Totnes, Devon
TQ9 6EJ. Tel: 01803-862224. *Principal*, Prof.
K. Thompson
EDGE HILL UNIVERSITY COLLEGE, St Helens Road,
Ormskirk, Lancs L39 4QP. Tel: 01695-575171. *Director*,
Dr. J. Cater
FALMOUTH COLLEGE OF ARTS, Woodlane, Falmouth,
Cornwall TR11 4RA. Tel: 01326-211077. *Principal*,
Prof. A. G. Livingston
HARPER ADAMS AGRICULTURAL COLLEGE, Newport,
Shropshire TF10 8NB. Tel: 01952-820280. *Principal*, Dr
E. W. Jones
HOMERTON COLLEGE, Cambridge CB2 2PH. Tel: 01223-
507111. *Principal*, Mrs K. Pretty, PH.D.

KENT INSTITUTE OF ART AND DESIGN, Oakwood Park,
Maidstone ME16 8AG (*also* New Dover Road,
Canterbury CT1 3AN; and Fort Pitt, Rochester ME1 1DZ).
Tel: 01622-757286. *Director*, Prof. V. Grylls
KING ALFRED'S COLLEGE OF HIGHER EDUCATION,
Winchester SO22 4NR. Tel: 01962-841515. *Principal*,
Prof. J. P. Dickinson
LIVERPOOL HOPE UNIVERSITY COLLEGE, Hope Park,
Liverpool L16 9JD. Tel: 0151-291 3477. *Rector*, Prof. S.
Lee
THE LONDON INSTITUTE, 65 Davies Street, London
W1Y 2DA. Tel: 0171-514 6000. *Rector*, Sir William Stubbs
Comprising:
Camberwell College of Arts, Peckham Road, London SE5 8UF
Central St Martins College of Art and Design, Southampton
Row, London WC1B 4AP
Chelsea College of Art and Design, Manresa Road, London
SW3 6LS
London College of Fashion, 20 John Prince's Street, London
W1M 0BJ
London College of Printing and Distributive Trades, Elephant
and Castle, London SE1 6SB
LOUGHBOROUGH COLLEGE OF ART AND DESIGN, Epinal
Way, Loughborough, Leics LE11 3GE. Tel: 01509-
261515. *Principal*, T. Kavanagh
LSU COLLEGE OF HIGHER EDUCATION, The Avenue,
Southampton SO17 1BG. Tel: 01703-216200. *Principal*
(*acting*), J. Layman
NENE COLLEGE, Park Campus, Boughton Green Road,
Northampton NN2 7AL. Tel: 01604-735500. *Director*,
S. M. Gaskell, PH.D.
NEWMAN COLLEGE, Genners Lane, Bartley Green,
Birmingham B32 3NT. Tel: 0121-476 1181. *Principal*,
Prof. B. Ray
RCN INSTITUTE, Royal College of Nursing, 20
Cavendish Square, London W1M 0AB. Tel: 0171-409
3333. *Director*, Prof. A. Kitson
ROEHAMPTON INSTITUTE LONDON, Whitelands College,
West Hill, London SW15 3SN. Comprises Digby Stuart
College, Froebel Institute College, Southlands College
and Whitelands College. Tel: 0181-392 3000. *Rector*,
Prof. S. C. Holt, PH.D.
ROSE BRUFORD COLLEGE, Lamorbey Park, Sidcup, Kent
DA15 9DF. Tel: 0181-300 3024. *Principal*, R. Ely
ROYAL NORTHERN COLLEGE OF MUSIC, 124 Oxford
Road, Manchester M13 9RD. Tel: 0161-907 5200.
Principal, Prof. E. Gregson
SOUTHAMPTON INSTITUTE, East Park Terrace,
Southampton SO14 0YN. Tel: 01703-319000. *Director*
(*acting*), Prof. T. J. Wheeler
SURREY INSTITUTE OF ART AND DESIGN, Falkner Road,
Farnham, Surrey GU9 7DS. Tel: 01252-722441. *Director*,
Prof. N. J. Taylor
TRINITY AND ALL SAINTS' COLLEGE, Brownberrie Lane,
Horsforth, Leeds LS18 5HD. Tel: 0113-283 7100.
Principal, Dr G. L. Turnbull
UNIVERSITY COLLEGE CHESTER, Cheyney Road,
Chester CH1 4BJ. Tel: 01244-375444. *Principal*, Canon
E. V. Binks
UNIVERSITY COLLEGE OF RIPON AND YORK ST JOHN,
Lord Mayor's Walk, York YO3 7EX. Tel: 01904-656771.
Principal, Prof. R. A. Butlin
UNIVERSITY COLLEGE OF ST MARK AND ST JOHN,
Derriford Road, Plymouth PL6 8BH. Tel: 01752-636700.
Principal, Dr W. J. Rea
UNIVERSITY COLLEGE OF S. MARTIN, Lancaster LA1 3JD.
Tel: 01524-384384. *Principal*, Prof. C. J. Carr
UNIVERSITY COLLEGE SCARBOROUGH, Filey Road,
Scarborough YO11 3AZ. Tel: 01723-362392. *Principal*,
R. A. Withers, PH.D.

WESTHILL COLLEGE, Weoley Park Road, Selly Oak, Birmingham B29 6LL. Tel: 0121-472 7245. *Principal,* J. Briggs

WESTMINSTER COLLEGE, Oxford OX2 9AT. Tel: 01865-247644. *Principal,* Revd Dr R. Ralph

WINCHESTER SCHOOL OF ART, Park Avenue, Winchester, Hants SO23 8DL. Tel: 01962-842500. *Head of School,* Prof. K. Crouan

WORCESTER COLLEGE OF HIGHER EDUCATION, Henwick Grove, Worcester WR2 6AJ. Tel: 01905-855000. *Principal,* Ms D. Urwin

WALES

THE NORTH-EAST WALES INSTITUTE OF HIGHER EDUCATION, Plas Coch, Mold Road, Wrexham LL11 2AW. Tel: 01978-290666. *Principal,* Prof. J. O. Williams, PH.D, D.SC.

SWANSEA INSTITUTE OF HIGHER EDUCATION, Mount Pleasant, Swansea SA1 6ED. Tel: 01792-481000. *Principal,* Dr A. Davies

TRINITY COLLEGE, Carmarthen SA31 3EP. Tel: 01267-237971. *Principal,* D. C. Jones-Davies, OBE

WELSH COLLEGE OF MUSIC AND DRAMA, Castle Grounds, Cathays Park, Cardiff CF1 3ER. Tel: 01222-342854. *Principal,* E. Fivet

SCOTLAND

BELL COLLEGE OF TECHNOLOGY, Almada Street, Hamilton ML3 0JB. Tel: 01698-283100. *Principal,* Dr K. MacCallum

DUMFRIES AND GALLOWAY COLLEGE, Heathhall, Dumfries DG1 3QZ. Tel: 01387-261261. *Principal,* J. W. M. Neil

FIFE COLLEGE OF FURTHER AND HIGHER EDUCATION, St Brycedale Avenue, Kirkcaldy, Fife KY1 1EX. Tel: 01592-268591. *Principal,* Mrs J. S. R. Johnston

GLASGOW SCHOOL OF ART, 167 Renfrew Street, Glasgow G3 6RQ. Tel: 0141-353 4500. *Director,* Prof. D. Cameron

INVERNESS COLLEGE, 3 Longman Road, Inverness IV1 1SA. Tel: 01463-236681. *Principal,* Ms J. Price

NORTHERN COLLEGE OF EDUCATION, Hilton Place, Aberdeen AB24 4FA. Tel: 01224-283500; Gardyne Road, Dundee DD5 1NY. Tel: 01382-464000. *Principal,* D. A. Adams

QUEEN MARGARET COLLEGE, Clerwood Terrace, Edinburgh EH12 8TS. Tel: 0131-317 3000; Duke Street, Edinburgh EH6 8HF. Tel: 0131-317 3355. *Principal,* Dr J. Stringer

ROYAL SCOTTISH ACADEMY OF MUSIC AND DRAMA, 100 Renfrew Street, Glasgow G2 3DB. Tel: 0141-332 4101. *Principal,* Dr P. Ledger, CBE, FRCO

SAC (SCOTTISH AGRICULTURAL COLLEGE), Central Office, West Mains Road, Edinburgh EH9 3JG. Tel: 0131-535 4000. Campuses at Aberdeen, Auchincruive, Ayr, and Edinburgh. *Principal,* Prof. P. C. Thomas

ST ANDREW'S COLLEGE OF EDUCATION, Duntocher Road, Bearsden, Glasgow G61 4QA. Tel: 0141-943 3400. *Principal,* Prof. B. J. McGettrick, OBE

NORTHERN IRELAND

EAST DOWN INSTITUTE OF FURTHER AND HIGHER EDUCATION, Market Street, Downpatrick, Co. Down BT30 6ND. Tel: 01396-615815. *Principal,* T. L. Place

ST MARY'S COLLEGE, 191 Falls Road, Belfast BT12 6FE. Tel: 01232-327678. *Principal,* Revd M. O'Callaghan

STRANMILLIS COLLEGE, Stranmillis Road, Belfast BT9 5DY. Tel: 01232-381271. *Principal,* Dr J. R. McMinn

ADULT AND CONTINUING EDUCATION

FORUM FOR THE ADVANCEMENT OF CONTINUING EDUCATION (FACE), Centre for Innovation and External Developments, University of Plymouth, Plymouth PL4 8AA. Tel: 01752-232374. *Chair,* C. Bell

NATIONAL INSTITUTE OF ADULT CONTINUING EDUCATION, 21 De Montfort Street, Leicester LE1 7GE. Tel: 0116-255 1451. *Director,* A. Tuckett

NIACE CYMRU, 245 Western Avenue, Cardiff CF5 2YX. Tel: 01222-265001. *Associate Director,* Ms A. Poole

NORTHERN IRELAND COUNCIL FOR ADULT EDUCATION, c/o Western Education and Library Board, 1 Hospital Road, Omagh, Co. Tyrone BT79 0AW. Tel: 01662-240240. *Chairman,* J. Martin; *Education Officer,* M. Clarke

THE RESIDENTIAL COLLEGES COMMITTEE, c/o Ruskin College, Oxford OX1 2HE. Tel: 01865-556360. *Awards Officer,* Mrs F. A. Bagchi

SCOTTISH COMMUNITY EDUCATION COUNCIL, Rosebery House, 9 Haymarket Terrace, Edinburgh EH12 5EZ. Tel: 0131-313 2488. *Chief Executive,* C. McConnell

THE UNIVERSITIES ASSOCIATION FOR CONTINUING EDUCATION, School of Adult Continuing Education, University of Leeds, Leeds LS2 9JT. Tel: 0113-233 3184. *Secretary,* Prof. R. Taylor

THE WORKERS' EDUCATIONAL ASSOCIATION, Temple House, 17 Victoria Park Square, London E2 9PB. Tel: 0181-983 1515. *General Secretary,* R. Lochrie

LONG-TERM RESIDENTIAL COLLEGES FOR ADULT EDUCATION

COLEG HARLECH, Harlech, Gwynedd LL46 2PU. Tel: 01766-780363. *Warden,* J. W. England

CO-OPERATIVE COLLEGE, Stanford Hall, Loughborough, Leics LE12 5QP. Tel: 01509-852333. *Chief Executive,* R. Wildgusp

FIRCROFT COLLEGE, 1018 Bristol Road, Selly Oak, Birmingham B29 6LH. Tel: 0121-472 0116. *Principal,* K. Jackson

HILLCROFT COLLEGE, South Bank, Surbiton, Surrey KT6 6DF. Tel: 0181-399 2688. For women only. *Principal,* Ms J. Ireton

NEWBATTLE ABBEY COLLEGE, Dalkeith, Midlothian EH22 3LL. Tel: 0131-663 1921. *Principal,* W. M. Conboy

NORTHERN COLLEGE, Wentworth Castle, Stainborough, Barnsley, S. Yorks S75 3ET. Tel: 01226-776000. *Principal,* Prof. R. H. Fryer

PLATER COLLEGE, Pullens Lane, Oxford OX3 0DT. Tel: 01865-740500. *Principal,* M. Blades

RUSKIN COLLEGE, Walton Street, Oxford OX1 2HE. Tel: 01865-554331. *Principal (acting),* Mrs E. Barnes

PROFESSIONAL EDUCATION
Excluding postgraduate study

The organizations listed below are those which, by providing specialist training or conducting examinations, control entry into a profession, or organizations responsible for maintaining a register of those with professional qualifications in their sector.

Many professions now have a largely graduate entry, and possession of a first degree can exempt entrants from certain of the professional examinations. Enquiries about obtaining professional qualifications should be made to the relevant professional organization(s). Details of higher education providers of first degrees may be found in *University and College Entrance: Official Guide* (available from UCAS, *see* page 453).

EC RECOGNITION

It is now possible for those with professional qualifications obtained in the UK to have these recognized in other European Community countries. This applies to certain professions where access is in some way regulated by the state and where at least three years undergraduate education and relevant work experience are necessary to qualify. Further information can be obtained from:
DEPARTMENT OF TRADE AND INDUSTRY, Bay 212 Kingsgate House, Victoria Street, London SW1E 6SW. Tel: 0171-215 4648. *Contact,* Ms A. Wilson

ACCOUNTANCY

The main bodies granting membership on examination after a period of practical work are:
ASSOCIATION OF CHARTERED CERTIFIED ACCOUNTANTS, 29 Lincoln's Inn Fields, London WC2A 3EE. Tel: 0171-242 6855. *Chief Executive,* Mrs A. L. Rose
CHARTERED INSTITUTE OF MANAGEMENT ACCOUNTANTS, 63 Portland Place, London WIN 4AB. Tel: 0171-637 2311. *Secretary,* J. S. Chester, OBE
CHARTERED INSTITUTE OF PUBLIC FINANCE AND ACCOUNTANCY, 3 Robert Street, London WC2N 6BH. Tel: 0171-543 5600. *Chief Executive,* D. Adams
INSTITUTE OF CHARTERED ACCOUNTANTS IN ENGLAND AND WALES, Chartered Accountants' Hall, PO Box 433, Moorgate Place, London EC2P 2BJ. Tel: 0171-920 8100. *Secretary and Chief Executive,* A. J. Colquhoun
INSTITUTE OF CHARTERED ACCOUNTANTS OF SCOTLAND, 27 Queen Street, Edinburgh EH2 1LA. Tel: 0131-225 5673. *Chief Executive,* P. W. Johnston

ACTUARIAL SCIENCE

Two professional organizations grant qualifications after examination:
INSTITUTE OF ACTUARIES, Staple Inn Hall, High Holborn, London WC1V 7QJ. Tel: 0171-242 0106. *Secretary-General,* G. B. L. Campbell. Enquiries to Napier House, 4 Worcester Street, Oxford OX1 2AW. Tel: 01865-794144
FACULTY OF ACTUARIES, 17 Thistle Street, Edinburgh EH2 1DF. Tel: 0131-220 4555. *Secretary,* W. W. Mair

ARCHITECTURE

The Education and Professional Development Board of the Royal Institute of British Architects sets standards and guides the whole system of architectural education throughout the UK. The RIBA recognizes courses at 35 schools of architecture in the UK for exemption from their own examinations.
ARCHITECTS REGISTRATION BOARD, 73 Hallam Street, London WIN 6EE. Tel: 0171-580 5861. *Chief Officer and Registrar,* A. Finch
THE ROYAL INSTITUTE OF BRITISH ARCHITECTS, 66 Portland Place, London WIN 4AD. Tel: 0171-580 5533. *President,* D. Rock; *Director-General,* A. Reid, PH.D.

Schools of architecture outside the universities include:
THE ARCHITECTURAL ASSOCIATION, 34–36 Bedford Square, London WC1B 3ES. *Secretary,* E. A. Le Maistre
PRINCE OF WALES'S INSTITUTE OF ARCHITECTURE, 14–15 Gloucester Gate, London NW1 4HG. Tel: 0171-916 7380. *Director,* Prof. R. Hodges, OBE, PH.D., FSA

BANKING

Professional organizations granting qualifications after examination are:
CHARTERED INSTITUTE OF BANKERS, 90 Bishopsgate, London EC2N 4AS. Tel: 0171-444 7111. *Chief Executive,* G. Shreeve
CHARTERED INSTITUTE OF BANKERS IN SCOTLAND, 19 Rutland Square, Edinburgh EH1 2DE. Tel: 0131-229 9869. *Chief Executive,* Dr C. W. Munn

BIOLOGY, CHEMISTRY, PHYSICS

Professional qualifications are awarded by:
INSTITUTE OF BIOLOGY, 20–22 Queensberry Place, London SW7 2DZ. Tel: 0171-581 8333. *President,* Prof. R. B. Heap; *General Secretary,* Dr R. H. Priestley
INSTITUTE OF PHYSICS, 76 Portland Place, London WIN 3DH. Tel: 0171-470 4800. *Chief Executive,* Dr A. D. W. Jones
ROYAL SOCIETY OF CHEMISTRY, Burlington House, Piccadilly, London W1V 0BN. Tel: 0171-437 8656. *President,* E. Abel, CBE; *Secretary-General,* T. D. Inch, PH.D., D.SC.

BUILDING

Examinations are conducted by:
CHARTERED INSTITUTE OF BUILDING, Englemere, King's Ride, Ascot, Berks SL5 7TB. Tel: 01344-630700. *Chief Executive,* K. Banbury
INSTITUTE OF BUILDING CONTROL, 92–104 East Street, Epsom, Surrey KT17 1EB. Tel: 01372-745577. *Chief Executive,* Ms R. Raywood
INSTITUTE OF CLERKS OF WORKS OF GREAT BRITAIN, 41 The Mall, London W5 3TJ. Tel: 0181-579 2917/8. *Secretary,* A. P. Macnamara

BUSINESS, MANAGEMENT AND ADMINISTRATION

Professional bodies conducting training and/or examinations in business, administration, management or commerce include:
AMETS (ASSOCIATION FOR MANAGEMENT EDUCATION AND TRAINING IN SCOTLAND), c/o University of Stirling, Stirling FK9 4LA. Tel: 01786-450906. *Chairman,* N. Kuenssberg
THE ASSOCIATION OF MBAs, 15 Duncan Terrace, London N1 8BZ. Tel: 0171-837 3375. Publishes a directory giving details of MBA courses provided at UK institutions. *Director,* M. Jones
CAM FOUNDATION (COMMUNICATIONS, ADVERTISING AND MARKETING EDUCATION FOUNDATION), Abford House, 15 Wilton Road, London SW1V 1NJ. Tel: 0171-828 7506. *General Secretary,* J. Knight
CHARTERED INSTITUTE OF HOUSING, Octavia House, Westwood Business Park, Westwood Way, Coventry CV4 8JP. Tel: 01203-694966. *Chief Executive,* Ms C. Laird
CHARTERED INSTITUTE OF MARKETING, Moor Hall, Cookham, Maidenhead, Berks SL6 9QH. Tel: 01628-427500. *Director-General,* S. Cuthbert

CHARTERED INSTITUTE OF PURCHASING AND SUPPLY, Easton House, Easton on the Hill, Stamford, Lincs PE9 3NZ. Tel: 01780-756777. *Director-General*, P. Thomson

CHARTERED INSTITUTE OF TRANSPORT, 80 Portland Place, London WIN 4DP. Tel: 0171-467 9425. *Director*, Mrs S. Gross

HENLEY MANAGEMENT COLLEGE, Greenlands, Henley-on-Thames, Oxon RG9 3AU. Tel: 01491-571454. *Principal*, Prof. R. Wild, PH.D., D.SC.

INSTITUTE OF ADMINISTRATIVE MANAGEMENT, 40 Chatsworth Parade, Petts Wood, Orpington, Kent BR5 IRW. Tel: 01689-875555. *Chief Executive*, Prof. G. Robinson

INSTITUTE OF CHARTERED SECRETARIES AND ADMINISTRATORS, 16 Park Crescent, London WIN 4AH. Tel: 0171-580 4741. *Chief Executive*, M. J. Ainsworth

INSTITUTE OF CHARTERED SHIPBROKERS, 3 St Helen's Place, London EC3A 6EJ. Tel: 0171-628 5559. *Director*, Mrs B. Fletcher

INSTITUTE OF EXPORT, Export House, 64 Clifton Street, London EC2A 4HB. Tel: 0171-247 9812. *Director-General*, I. J. Campbell

INSTITUTE OF HEALTH SERVICES MANAGEMENT, 39 Chalton Street, London NWI IJD. Tel: 0171-388 2626. *Director*, Ms K. Caines

INSTITUTE OF MANAGEMENT, Management House, Cottingham Road, Corby, Northants NN17 ITT. Tel: 01536-204222. *Director-General*, R. Young

INSTITUTE OF PERSONNEL AND DEVELOPMENT, IPD House, Camp Road, London SWI9 4UX. Tel: 0181-971 9000. *Director-General*, G. Armstrong

INSTITUTE OF PRACTITIONERS IN ADVERTISING, 44 Belgrave Square, London SWIX 8QS. Tel: 0171-235 7020. *Secretary*, J. Raad

CHIROPRACTIC

Chiropractic is accorded statutory regulation by the Chiropractic Act 1994. There are currently four bodies operating voluntary registration schemes. These are to be replaced by a General Chiropractic Council when it opens a new register, probably in 1998. Once the register is in place it will be illegal for anyone to call themselves a chiropractor unless they have undertaken a recognized course of training and are registered with the General Chiropractic Council.

There are currently three training centres for chiropractic. Two of these provide four-year part-time training programmes leading to internal academic awards and one provides a five-year full-time training programme leading to a B.Sc. and M.Sc. in chiropractic. Chiropractic will, however, become an all-graduate profession with students in the future having to complete a degree and postgraduate diploma at one of the recognized institutes in order to qualify for registration.

BRITISH CHIROPRACTIC ASSOCIATION, 29 Whitley Street, Reading, Berks RG2 0EG. Tel: 01734-757557. *Executive Director*, Ms S. A. Wakefield

SCOTTISH CHIROPRACTIC ASSOCIATION, St Boswells Chiropractic Clinic, Main Street, St Boswells, Melrose TD6 0AP. Tel: 01835-823645. *Secretary*, Dr C. How

DANCE

IMPERIAL SOCIETY OF TEACHERS OF DANCING, Imperial House, 22–26 Paul Street, London EC2A 4QE. Tel: 0171-377 1577. *Chief Executive*, M. J. Browne

INTERNATIONAL DANCE TEACHERS' ASSOCIATION, International House, 76 Bennett Road, Brighton BN2 5JL. Tel: 01273-685652. *Company Secretary*, J. Dearling

ROYAL ACADEMY OF DANCING, 36 Battersea Square, London SWII 3RA. Tel: 0171-223 0091. *Chief Executive*, D. Watchman; *Artistic Director*, Miss L. Wallis

ROYAL BALLET SCHOOL, 155 Talgarth Road, London WI4 9DE. Tel: 0181-748 6335. Also at White Lodge, Richmond Park, Surrey TWIO 5HR. Tel: 0181-876 5547. *Director*, Dame Merle Park, DBE

DEFENCE

ROYAL COLLEGE OF DEFENCE STUDIES, Seaford House, 37 Belgrave Square, London SWIX 8NS. Tel: 0171-915 4800. Prepares selected senior officers and officials for responsibilities in the direction and management of defence and security. *Commandant*, Lt.-Gen. S. C. Grant, CB

JOINT SERVICES COMMAND AND STAFF COLLEGE, Bracknell, Berks RG12 9DD. Tel: 01344-54593. *Commandant*, Maj.-Gen. T. Granville-Chapman; *Dean of Academic Studies*, Prof. G. Till, PH.D.

ROYAL NAVAL COLLEGES

BRITANNIA ROYAL NAVAL COLLEGE, Dartmouth, Devon TQ6 0HJ. Tel: 01803-832141. Provides professional training and vocational education for all new entry officers. *Commodore*, Cdre R. A. G. Clare (from Jan. 1998)

MILITARY COLLEGES

DIRECTORATE OF EDUCATIONAL AND TRAINING SERVICES, HQ Adjutant General's Corp, Worthy Down, Winchester, Hants SO21 2RG. Tel: 01962-887660. *Director*, Brig. C. F. P. Horsfall

ROYAL MILITARY ACADEMY SANDHURST, Camberley, Surrey GU15 4PQ. Tel: 01276-63344. *Commandant*, Maj.-Gen. J. F. Deverell, OBE

ROYAL MILITARY COLLEGE OF SCIENCE, Shrivenham, Swindon, Wilts SN6 8LA. Tel: 01793-785435. Students from UK and overseas study from degree to postgraduate levels in management, science and technology. The College is a faculty of Cranfield University. *Commandant*, Maj.-Gen. A. S. H. Irwin, CBE; *Principal*, Prof. P. Hutchinson

ROYAL AIR FORCE COLLEGES

ROYAL AIR FORCE COLLEGE, Cranwell, Sleaford, Lincs. NG34 8HB. Selects all officer and aircrew entrants to the RAF and provides initial training for all officer entrants to the RAF. Also provides specialist training for junior officers of some ground branches and supervision of elementary flying training, general service training for University Air Squadrons, and supervision of the Air Cadet Organization. *Air Officer Commanding and Commandant*, Air Vice-Marshal J. H. Thompson

ROYAL AIR FORCE TRAINING, DEVELOPMENT AND SUPPORT UNIT, RAF Halton, Aylesbury, Bucks HP22 5PG. Tel: 01296-623535. *Commanding Officer*, Gp Capt. K. L. Sherit

DENTISTRY

To be entitled to be registered in the Dentists Register, a person must hold the degree or diploma in dental surgery of a university in the UK or the diploma of any of the licensing authorities (the Royal Colleges of Surgeons of England and of Edinburgh, and the Royal College of Physicians and Surgeons of Glasgow). Nationals of an EU member state holding an appropriate European diploma, and holders of certain overseas diplomas, may also be registered. The Dentists Register is maintained by:

THE GENERAL DENTAL COUNCIL, 37 Wimpole Street,
London WIM 8DQ. Tel: 0171-486 2171. *Chief Executive
and Registrar*, Mrs R. M. J. Hepplewhite

DIETETICS
See also FOOD AND NUTRITION SCIENCE

The professional association is the British Dietetic
Association. Full membership is open to dietitians holding
a recognized qualification, who may also become State
Registered Dietitians through the Council for Professions
Supplementary to Medicine (*see* Medicine)

THE BRITISH DIETETIC ASSOCIATION, 7th Floor,
Elizabeth House, 22 Suffolk Street, Queensway,
Birmingham BI ILS. Tel: 0121-643 5483. *Secretary*,
J. Grigg

DRAMA

The national validating body for courses providing train-
ing in drama for the professional theatre is the National
Council for Drama Training. It currently has accredited
courses at the following: Academy of Live and Recorded
Arts; Arts Educational Schools; Birmingham School of
Speech Training and Dramatic Art; Bristol Old Vic
Theatre School; Central School of Speech and Drama;
Drama Centre, London; Drama Studio, London; Guild-
ford School of Acting; Guildhall School of Music and
Drama, London; London Academy of Music and Dramatic
Art; Manchester Metropolitan University School of
Theatre; Mountview Theatre School; Oxford School of
Drama, Woodstock; Queen Margaret College, Edinburgh;
Rose Bruford College, Sidcup; Royal Academy of
Dramatic Art, London; Royal Scottish Academy of Music
and Drama; Webber Douglas Academy of Dramatic Art;
Welsh College of Music and Drama.

The accreditation of a course in a school does not
necessarily imply that other courses of different type or
duration in the same school are also accredited.

THE NATIONAL COUNCIL FOR DRAMA TRAINING, 5
Tavistock Place, London WCIH 9SN. *Executive Secretary*,
Ms A. Bailey

ENGINEERING

The Engineering Council supervises the engineering
profession through the 39 nominated engineering institutions who are represented on its Board for Engineers'
Regulation. Working with and through the institutions, the
Council sets the standards for the registration of individuals, and also the accreditation for academic courses in
universities and colleges and the practical training in
industry.

THE ENGINEERING COUNCIL, 10 Maltravers Street,
London WC2R 3ER. Tel: 0171-240 7891. *Director-General*,
M. Heath

The principal qualifying bodies are:

BRITISH COMPUTER SOCIETY, 1 Sanford Street, Swindon
SNI 1HJ. Tel: 01793-417417. *Chief Executive*, Ms J. Scott

CHARTERED INSTITUTION OF BUILDING SERVICES
ENGINEERS, 222 Balham High Road, London SWI2 9BS.
Tel: 0181-675 5211. *Secretary*, A. V. Ramsay

INSTITUTION OF CHEMICAL ENGINEERS, Davis Building,
165–189 Railway Terrace, Rugby, Warks CV2I 3HQ. Tel:
01788-578214. *Chief Executive*, Dr T. J. Evans

INSTITUTION OF CIVIL ENGINEERS, 1 Great George
Street, London SWIP 3AA. Tel: 0171-222 7722. *Director-
General*, R. S. Dobson, OBE, FEng.

INSTITUTION OF ELECTRICAL ENGINEERS, Savoy Place,
London WC2R OBL. Tel: 0171-240 1871. *Secretary*, Dr
J. C. Williams, OBE, FEng.

INSTITUTE OF ENERGY, 18 Devonshire Street, London
WIN 2AU. Tel: 0171-580 7124. *Secretary* (*acting*),
Ms L. Evans

INSTITUTION OF GAS ENGINEERS, 21 Portland Place,
London WIN 3AF. Tel: 0171-636 6603. *Secretary*, Mrs
S. M. Raine

INSTITUTE OF MARINE ENGINEERS, The Memorial
Building, 76 Mark Lane, London EC3R 7JN. Tel: 0171-
481 8493. *Secretary*, J. E. Sloggett, OBE

INSTITUTE OF MATERIALS, 1 Carlton House Terrace,
London SWIY 5DB. Tel: 0171-839 4071. *Chief Executive*,
Dr B. A. Rickinson

INSTITUTE OF MEASUREMENT AND CONTROL, 87 Gower
Street, London WCIE 6AA. Tel: 0171-387 4949. *Secretary*,
M. J. Yates

INSTITUTION OF MECHANICAL ENGINEERS, 1 Birdcage
Walk, London SWIH 9JJ. Tel: 0171-222 7899. *Director-
General*, Dr R. Pike

INSTITUTION OF MINING AND METALLURGY, 44
Portland Place, London WIN 4BR. Tel: 0171-580 3802.
Secretary, M. J. Jones

INSTITUTION OF MINING ENGINEERS, Danum House, 6A
South Parade, Doncaster DNI 2DY. Tel: 01302-320486.
Secretary, Dr G. J. M. Woodrow

INSTITUTE OF PHYSICS, 76 Portland Place, London WIN
3DH. Tel: 0171-470 4800. *Chief Executive*, Dr A. D. W.
Jones

INSTITUTION OF STRUCTURAL ENGINEERS, 11 Upper
Belgrave Street, London SWIX 8BH. Tel: 0171-235 4535.
Chief Executive, Dr J. W. Dougill, FEng.

ROYAL AERONAUTICAL SOCIETY, 4 Hamilton Place,
London WIV OBQ. Tel: 0171-499 3515. *Director*,
R. J. Kennett

ROYAL INSTITUTION OF NAVAL ARCHITECTS, 10 Upper
Belgrave Street, London SWIX 8BQ. Tel: 0171-235 4622.
Secretary, T. Blakeley

FILM AND TELEVISION

Postgraduate training for those intending to make a career
in film and television production is provided by the
National Film and Television School, which provides
courses in production, direction, animation, screenwrit-
ing, editing, cinematography, camera work and other
specialisms. Short post-experience courses to enable
professionals to update or expand their skills are also
provided.

NATIONAL FILM AND TELEVISION SCHOOL, Station
Road, Beaconsfield, Bucks HP9 ILJ. Tel: 01494-671234.
Director, H. Camre

FOOD AND NUTRITION SCIENCE
See also DIETETICS

Scientific and professional bodies include:

INSTITUTE OF FOOD SCIENCE & TECHNOLOGY, 5
Cambridge Court, 210 Shepherd's Bush Road, London
W6 7NJ. Tel: 0171-603 6316. *Chief Executive*, Ms H. G.
Wild

FORESTRY AND TIMBER STUDIES

Professional organizations include:

COMMONWEALTH FORESTRY ASSOCIATION, c/o Oxford
Forestry Institute, South Parks Road, Oxford OXI 3RB.
Tel: 01865-275072. *Chairman*, Dr J. S. Maini

INSTITUTE OF CHARTERED FORESTERS, 7 A St Colme
Street, Edinburgh EH3 6AA. Tel: 0131-225 2705.
Secretary, Mrs M. W. Dick

ROYAL FORESTRY SOCIETY OF ENGLAND, WALES AND NORTHERN IRELAND, 102 High Street, Tring, Herts HP23 4AF. Tel: 01442-822028. *Director*, J. E. Jackson, PH.D.
ROYAL SCOTTISH FORESTRY SOCIETY, The Stables, Dalkeith Country Park, Dalkeith, Midlothian EH22 2NA. Tel: 0131-660 9480. *Director*, M. Osborne

FUEL AND ENERGY SCIENCE

The principal professional bodies are:
INSTITUTE OF ENERGY, 18 Devonshire Street, London WIN 2AU. Tel: 0171-580 7124. *Secretary (acting)*, Ms L. Evans
INSTITUTION OF GAS ENGINEERS, 21 Portland Place, London WIN 3AF. Tel: 0171-636 6603. *Secretary*, Mrs S. M. Raine
INSTITUTE OF PETROLEUM, 61 New Cavendish Street, London WIM 8AR. Tel: 0171-467 7100. *Director-General*, I. Ward

HOTELKEEPING, CATERING AND INSTITUTIONAL MANAGEMENT
See also DIETETICS, and FOOD AND NUTRITION SCIENCE

The qualifying professional body in these areas is:
HOTEL AND CATERING INTERNATIONAL MANAGEMENT ASSOCIATION, 191 Trinity Road, London SW17 7HN. Tel: 0181-672 4251. *Chief Executive*, D. Wood

INDUSTRIAL AND VOCATIONAL TRAINING

The NTO National Council represents national training organizations (NTOs), a new network of sector training bodies established in 1997. NTOs are independent, employer-owned bodies which represent the education and training interests of their respective sectors to government and ensure the development and adoption of occupational standards, particularly through National and Scottish Vocational Qualifications.
NTO NATIONAL COUNCIL, 10 Meadowcourt, Amos Road, Sheffield S9 1BX. Tel: 0114-261 9926. *Chair*, Ms L. Millington; *Administrator*, Miss J. Maisari

INSURANCE

Organizations conducting examinations and awarding diplomas are:
ASSOCIATION OF AVERAGE ADJUSTERS, 200 Aldersgate Street, London EC1A 4JJ. Tel: 0171-956 0099. *Hon. Secretary*, D. W. Taylor
CHARTERED INSTITUTE OF LOSS ADJUSTERS, Manfield House, 1 Southampton Street, London WC2R 0LR. Tel: 0171-240 1496. *Director*, A. F. Clack
CHARTERED INSURANCE INSTITUTE, 20 Aldermanbury, London EC2V 7HY. Tel: 0171-606 3835. *Director-General*, Prof. D. E. Bland

JOURNALISM

Courses for trainee newspaper journalists are available at 26 centres. One-year full-time courses are available for selected students and 18-week courses for graduates. Particulars of all these courses are available from the National Council for the Training of Journalists. Short courses for mid-career development can be arranged, as can various distance learning courses. The NCTJ also offers Assessor, Internal Verifier (IV) and Accreditation of Prior Achievement (APA) training, and NVQs.
For periodical journalists, there are ten centres running courses approved by the Periodicals Training Council.

THE NATIONAL COUNCIL FOR TRAINING OF JOURNALISTS, Latton Bush Centre, Southern Way, Harlow, Essex CM18 7BL. Tel: 01279-430009. *Chief Executive*, R. Selwood
THE PERIODICALS TRAINING COUNCIL, Queen's House, 55–56 Lincoln's Inn Field, London WC2A 3LJ. Tel: 0171-404 4168. *Executive Director*, Ms J. Butcher

LAW

THE BAR

Admission to the Bar of England and Wales is controlled by the Inns of Court, admission to the Bar of Northern Ireland by the Honorable Society of the Inn of Court of Northern Ireland and admission as an Advocate of the Scottish Bar is controlled by the Faculty of Advocates. The governing body of the barristers' branch of the legal profession in England and Wales is the General Council of the Bar. The governing body in Northern Ireland is the Honorable Society of the Inn of Court of Northern Ireland, and the Faculty of Advocates is the governing body of the Scottish Bar. The education and examination of students training for the Bar of England and Wales is regulated by the General Council of the Bar. The Inns of Court School of Law was the sole provider of the Bar's vocational course but from September 1997 six other institutions have been validated to provide the course. Those who intend to practise at the Bar of England and Wales must pass the Bar's vocational course.
FACULTY OF ADVOCATES, Advocates Library, Parliament House, Edinburgh EH1 1RF. Tel: 0131-226 5071. *Dean*, G. N. H. Emslie, QC; *Clerk*, I. G. Armstrong
THE GENERAL COUNCIL OF THE BAR, 3 Bedford Row, London WC1R 4DB. Tel: 0171-242 0082. *Chairman*, R. Owen, QC; *Chief Executive*, N. Morison
THE HONORABLE SOCIETY OF THE INN OF COURT OF NORTHERN IRELAND, Royal Courts of Justice, Belfast BT1 3JF. Tel: 01232-235111. *Treasurer* (1997), The Hon. Mr Justice Sheil; *Under-Treasurer*, J. W. Wilson, QC

The Inns of Court

GRAY'S INN, 8 South Square, London WC1R 5EU. Tel: 0171-405 8164. *Treasurer*, His Hon. Judge Lewis, QC; *Under-Treasurer*, D. Machin
THE INNER TEMPLE, London EC4Y 7HL. Tel: 0171-797 8250. *Treasurer*, The Rt. Hon. Lord Justice Staughton; *Sub-Treasurer*, Brig. P. A. Little, CBE
INNS OF COURT SCHOOL OF LAW, 4 Gray's Inn Place, Gray's Inn, London WC1R 5DX. Tel: 0171-404 5787. *Chairman*, The Hon. Mr Justice Hooper; *Principal*, R. Stone
LINCOLN'S INN, London WC2A 3TL. Tel: 0171-405 1393. *Treasurer*, Sir Michael Ogden, QC; *Under-Treasurer*, Col. D. H. Hills, MBE
THE MIDDLE TEMPLE, London EC4Y 9AT. Tel: 0171-427 4800. *Treasurer*, The Rt. Hon. Lord Nicholls; *Deputy Treasurer*, Sir David Calcutt, QC

SOLICITORS

Qualifications for solicitor are obtainable only from one of the Law Societies, which control the education and examination of trainee solicitors and the admission of solicitors.
THE COLLEGE OF LAW provides courses for the Common Professional Examination and Legal Practice Course at Braboeuf Manor, St Catherines, Guildford, Surrey GU3 1HA; 14 Store Street, London WC1E 7DE; Christleton Hall, Chester CH3 7AB; Bishopthorpe Road, York YO2 1QA. The college also provides the Bar's vocational course at its London branch.

LAW SOCIETY OF ENGLAND AND WALES, 113 Chancery
Lane, London WC2A 1PL. Tel: 0171-242 1222. *President*
(1997–8), P. Sycamore; *Vice-President* (1997–8),
M. Mathews; *Secretary-General,* Mrs J. M. Betts
LAW SOCIETY OF NORTHERN IRELAND, Law Society
House, 98 Victoria Street, Belfast BT1 3JZ. Tel: 01232-
231614. *Chief Executive,* J. Bailie
LAW SOCIETY OF SCOTLAND, Law Society's Hall, 26
Drumsheugh Gardens, Edinburgh EH3 7YR. Tel: 0131-
226 7411. *President* (1997–8), J. Elliot; *Secretary,*
D. R. Hill
OFFICE FOR THE SUPERVISION OF SOLICITORS, Victoria
Court, 8 Dormer Place, Leamington Spa, Warks
CV32 5AE. Tel: 01926-820082. The Office is an
establishment of the Law Society set up to handle
complaints about solicitors and regulate solicitors'
practices

LIBRARIANSHIP AND INFORMATION SCIENCE/MANAGEMENT

The Library Association accredits degree and postgraduate courses in library and information science which
are offered by 18 universities in the UK. A full list of
accredited degree and postgraduate courses is available
from its Information Services. The Association also maintains a professional register of Chartered Members open to
graduate ordinary members of the Association.
THE LIBRARY ASSOCIATION, 7 Ridgmount Street,
London WC1E 7AE. Tel: 0171-636 7543. *Chief Executive,*
R. Shimmon

MATERIALS STUDIES

The qualifying body is:
INSTITUTE OF MATERIALS, 1 Carlton House Terrace,
London SW1Y 5DB. Tel: 0171-839 4071. *Chief Executive,*
Dr B. A. Rickinson

MEDICINE

All doctors must be registered with the General Medical
Council. In order to register, medical students must
complete a five-year undergraduate degree at one of the
19 universities with medical schools, followed by a year of
general clinical training. Once registered, doctors undertake general professional and basic specialist training as
senior house officers. Further specialist training is provided by the royal colleges, faculties and societies listed
below. The General Medical Council keeps a register of
those doctors who have been awarded Certificates of
Completion of Specialist Training.
The United Examining Board holds qualifying examinations for candidates who have trained overseas. These
candidates must also have spent a period at a UK medical
school.
GENERAL MEDICAL COUNCIL, 178 Great Portland
Street, London W1N 6JE. Tel: 0171-580 7642. *President,*
Sir Donald Irvine, CBE, MD, FRGCP; *Chief Executive,*
F. Scott
UNITED EXAMINING BOARD, Apothecaries Hall, Black
Friars Lane, London EC4V 6EJ. Tel: 0171-236 1180.
Chairman, H. B. Devlin; *Registrar,* A. M. Wallington-
Smith

COLLEGES/SOCIETIES HOLDING POSTGRADUATE
MEMBERSHIP AND DIPLOMA EXAMINATIONS

FACULTY OF ACCIDENT AND EMERGENCY MEDICINE,
Royal College of Surgeons of England, 35–43 Lincoln's
Inn Fields, London WC2A 3PN. Tel: 0171-405 7071

FACULTY OF OCCUPATIONAL MEDICINE, 6 St Andrews
Place, London NW1 4LB. Tel: 0171-487 3414
FACULTY OF PHARMACEUTICAL MEDICINE, 1 St Andrews
Place, London NW1 4LB. Tel: 0171-224 0343
FACULTY OF PUBLIC HEALTH MEDICINE, 4 St Andrews
Place, London NW1 4LB. Tel: 0171-935 0243
ROYAL COLLEGE OF ANAESTHETISTS, 48–49 Russell
Square, London WC1B 4JY. Tel: 0171-813 1900. *President,*
Prof. L. Strunin; *Chief Executive,* Ms W. Cogger
ROYAL COLLEGE OF GENERAL PRACTITIONERS, 14
Princes Gate, London SW7 1PU. Tel: 0171-581 3232. *Hon.
President,* Prof. D. P. Gray; *Hon. Secretary,* Dr W. Reith
ROYAL COLLEGE OF OBSTETRICIANS AND
GYNAECOLOGISTS, 27 Sussex Place, London NW1 4RG.
Tel: 0171-262 5425. *President,* Dr Sir Narendra Patel;
Secretary, P. A. Barnett
ROYAL COLLEGE OF PAEDIATRICS AND CHILD HEALTH,
5 St Andrews Place, London NW1 4LB. Tel: 0171-486
6151. *President,* Prof. J. D. Baum; *Secretary,* J. Kempton
ROYAL COLLEGE OF PATHOLOGISTS, 2 Carlton House
Terrace, London SW1Y 5AF. Tel: 0171-930 5861.
President, Prof. R. N. M. MacSween; *Secretary,*
K. Lockyer
ROYAL COLLEGE OF PHYSICIANS, 11 St Andrews Place,
London NW1 4LE. Tel: 0171-935 1174. *President,* Prof.
K. G. M. M. Alberti, FRCP; *Secretary,* D. B. Lloyd
ROYAL COLLEGE OF PHYSICIANS AND SURGEONS OF
GLASGOW, 232–242 St Vincent Street, Glasgow G2 5RJ.
Tel: 0141-221 6072. *President,* Prof. N. McKay, CBE;
Hon. Secretary, Dr S. Slater
ROYAL COLLEGE OF PHYSICIANS OF EDINBURGH,
9 Queen Street, Edinburgh EH2 1JQ. Tel: 0131-225 7324.
President, Dr J. D. Cash; *Secretary,* Dr J. Thomas
ROYAL COLLEGE OF PSYCHIATRISTS, 17 Belgrave Square,
London SW1X 8PG. Tel: 0171-235 2351. *President,* Dr R.
Kendell; *Secretary,* Mrs V. Cameron
ROYAL COLLEGE OF RADIOLOGISTS, 38 Portland Place,
London W1N 4QJ. Tel: 0171-636 4432. *President,* Dr M. J.
Brindle; *Secretary,* A. J. Cowles
ROYAL COLLEGE OF SURGEONS OF EDINBURGH,
Nicolson Street, Edinburgh EH8 9DW. Tel: 0131-527
1600. *President,* Prof. A. G. D. Maran; *Secretary,* Ms A.
Campbell
ROYAL COLLEGE OF SURGEONS OF ENGLAND, 35–43
Lincoln's Inn Fields, London WC2A 3PN. Tel: 0171-405
3474. *President,* Sir Rodney Sweetnam, KCVO, CBE;
Secretary, C. Duncan
SOCIETY OF APOTHECARIES OF LONDON, 14 Black Friars
Lane, London EC4V 6EJ. Tel: 0171-236 1189. *Clerk,*
R. J. Stringer

PROFESSIONS SUPPLEMENTARY TO MEDICINE

The standard of professional education in biomedical
sciences, chiropody, dietetics, occupational therapy,
orthoptics, physiotherapy and radiography is the responsibility of seven professional boards, which also publish an
annual register of qualified practitioners. The work of the
boards is co-ordinated by the Council for Professions
Supplementary to Medicine.
In 1997 permission was given for two new boards to be
set up, one for prosthetists and orthotists and one for art
therapists. These will set up registers of qualified practitioners over the next two years.
THE COUNCIL FOR PROFESSIONS SUPPLEMENTARY TO
MEDICINE, Park House, 184 Kennington Park Road,
London SE11 4BU. Tel: 0171-582 0866. *Registrar,* M. D.
Hall

BIOMEDICAL SCIENCES

Qualifications from higher education establishments and training in medical laboratories are required for membership of the Institute of Biomedical Science.

INSTITUTE OF BIOMEDICAL SCIENCE, 12 Coldbath Square, London ECIR 5HL. Tel: 0171-636 8192. *Chief Executive*, A. Potter

CHIROPODY

Professional recognition is granted by the Society of Chiropodists and Podiatrists to students who are awarded B.Sc. degrees in Podiatry or Podiatric Medicine after attending a course of full-time training for three or four years at one of the 14 recognized schools in the UK (11 in England and Wales, two in Scotland and one in Northern Ireland). Qualifications granted and degrees recognized by the Society are approved by the Chiropodists Board for the purpose of State Registration, which is a condition of employment within the National Health Service.

THE SOCIETY OF CHIROPODISTS AND PODIATRISTS, 53 Welbeck Street, London WIM 7HE. Tel: 0171-486 3381. *General Secretary*, J. G. C. Trouncer

See also DIETETICS

OCCUPATIONAL THERAPY

The professional qualification may be obtained upon successful completion of a validated course in any of the 28 institutions approved by the College of Occupational Therapists. The courses are normally degree-level courses based in higher education institutions.

COLLEGE OF OCCUPATIONAL THERAPISTS, 6–8 Marshalsea Road, London SEI IHL. Tel: 0171-357 6480. *Secretary*, J. Thompson

ORTHOPTICS

Orthoptists undertake the diagnosis and treatment of all types of squint and other anomalies of binocular vision, working in close collaboration with ophthalmologists. The training and maintenance of professional standards are the responsibility of the Orthoptists Board of the Council for the Professions Supplementary to Medicine. The professional body is the British Orthoptic Society. Training is at degree level.

THE BRITISH ORTHOPTIC SOCIETY, Tavistock House North, Tavistock Square, London WCIH 9HX. *Hon. Secretary*, Mrs A. Charnock

PHYSIOTHERAPY

Full-time three- or four-year degree courses are available at 28 recognized schools in the UK. Information about courses leading to eligibility for Membership of the Chartered Society of Physiotherapy and to State Registration is available from the Chartered Society of Physiotherapy.

THE CHARTERED SOCIETY OF PHYSIOTHERAPY, 14 Bedford Row, London WCIR 4ED. Tel: 0171-306 6666. *Chief Executive*, P. Lambden

RADIOGRAPHY AND RADIOTHERAPY

In order to practise both diagnostic and therapeutic radiography in the UK, it is necessary to have successfully completed a course of education and training recognized by the Privy Council. Such courses are offered by universities throughout the UK and lead to the award of a degree in radiography. Further information is available from the college.

THE COLLEGE OF RADIOGRAPHERS, 2 Carriage Row, 183 Eversholt Street, London NWI IBU. Tel: 0171 391 4500. *Chief Executive*, S. Evans

COMPLEMENTARY MEDICINE

Professional courses are validated by:

INSTITUTE FOR COMPLEMENTARY MEDICINE, PO Box 194, London SE16 IQZ. Tel: 0171-237 5165

MERCHANT NAVY TRAINING SCHOOLS

OFFICERS

WARSASH MARITIME CENTRE, Southampton Institute, Newtown Road, Warsash, Southampton SO31 9ZL. Tel: 01489-576161. *Dean*, Capt. G. B. Angas

SEAFARERS

NATIONAL SEA TRAINING CENTRE, North West Kent College, Dering Way, Gravesend, Kent DAI2 2JJ. Tel: 01474-363656. *Director of Faculty*, R. MacDonald

MUSIC

ASSOCIATED BOARD OF THE ROYAL SCHOOLS OF MUSIC, 14 Bedford Square, London WCIB 3JG. Tel: 0171-636 5400. The Board conducts graded music examinations in over 80 countries and provides other services to music education through its professional development department and publishing company. *Chief Executive*, R. Morris

GUILDHALL SCHOOL OF MUSIC AND DRAMA, Silk Street, London EC2Y 8DT. Tel: 0171-628 2571. *Principal*, I. Horsbrugh

LONDON COLLEGE OF MUSIC, Thames Valley University, St Mary's Road, London W5 5RF. Tel: 0181-231 2304. *Director*, A. Creamer

ROYAL ACADEMY OF MUSIC, Marylebone Road, London NWI 5HT. Tel: 0171-873 7373. *Principal*, Prof. C. Price

ROYAL COLLEGE OF MUSIC, Prince Consort Road, London SW7 2BS. Tel: 0171-589 3643. *Director*, Ms J. Ritterman, PH.D.

ROYAL COLLEGE OF ORGANISTS, 7 St Andrew Street, London EC4A 3LQ. Tel: 0171-936 3606. *Senior Executive*, A. Dear

ROYAL NORTHERN COLLEGE OF MUSIC, 124 Oxford Road, Manchester MI3 9RD. Tel: 0161-273 6283. *Principal*, Prof. E. Gregson

ROYAL SCOTTISH ACADEMY OF MUSIC AND DRAMA, 100 Renfrew Street, Glasgow G2 3DB. Tel: 0141-332 4101. *Principal*, Dr P. Ledger, CBE, FRSE

TRINITY COLLEGE OF MUSIC, 11–13 Mandeville Place, London WIM 6AQ. Tel: 0171-935 5773. *Principal*, G. Henderson

NURSING

All nurses must be registered with the UK Central Council for Nursing, Midwifery and Health Visiting. Courses leading to registration as a nurse are at least three years in length. There are also some programmes which are combined with degrees. Students study in colleges of nursing or in institutions of higher education. Courses offer a combination of theoretical and practical experience in a variety of settings. Different courses lead to different types of registration, including: Registered General Nurse (RGN) or Registered Nurse (RN), Registered Mental Nurse (RMN), Registered Mental Handicap Nurse (RMHN), Registered Sick Children's Nurse (RSCN), Registered Midwife (RM) and Registered Health Visitor (RHV). The various national boards, listed below, are responsible for validating courses in nursing.

The Royal College of Nursing is the professional union representing nurses and provides higher education through its Institute.

ENGLISH NATIONAL BOARD FOR NURSING, MIDWIFERY AND HEALTH VISITING, Victory House, 170 Tottenham Court Road, London WIP OHA. Tel: 0171-388 3131. *Chief Executive*, A. P. Smith

NATIONAL BOARD FOR NURSING, MIDWIFERY AND HEALTH VISITING FOR NORTHERN IRELAND, Centre House, 79 Chichester Street, Belfast BT1 4JE. Tel: 01232-238152. *Chief Executive*, Dr O. D'A. Slevin, PH.D.

NATIONAL BOARD FOR NURSING, MIDWIFERY AND HEALTH VISITING FOR SCOTLAND, 22 Queen Street, Edinburgh EH2 INT. Tel: 0131-226 7371. *Chief Executive*, Mrs L. Mitchell

THE ROYAL COLLEGE OF NURSING OF THE UNITED KINGDOM, 20 Cavendish Square, London WIM OAB. Tel: 0171-409 3333. *General Secretary*, Miss C. Hancock; *Director of the RCN Institute*, Prof. A. Kitson

WELSH NATIONAL BOARD FOR NURSING, MIDWIFERY AND HEALTH VISITING, 2nd Floor, Golate House, 101 St Mary Street, Cardiff CF1 IDX. Tel: 01222-261400. *Chief Executive*, D. A. Ravey

UK CENTRAL COUNCIL FOR NURSING, MIDWIFERY AND HEALTH VISITING, 23 Portland Place, London WIN 4JT. Tel: 0171-637 7181. *Chief Executive and Registrar*, Ms S. Norman

OPHTHALMIC AND DISPENSING OPTICS

Professional bodies are:

THE ASSOCIATION OF BRITISH DISPENSING OPTICIANS, 6 Hurlingham Business Park, Sulivan Road, London SW6 3DU. Tel: 0171-736 0088. Grants qualifications as a dispensing optician. *Registrar*, D. G. Baker

THE COLLEGE OF OPTOMETRISTS, 10 Knaresborough Place, London SW5 OTG. Tel: 0171-373 7765. Grants qualifications as an optometrist. *General Secretary*, P. D. Leigh

OSTEOPATHY

Osteopathy is accorded statutory regulation by the Osteopaths Act 1993. There are currently four bodies that operate voluntary registration schemes. These are to be replaced by a General Osteopathic Council when it opens a new register in early 1998. After this, osteopaths will have two years to register. From 2000 it will be an offence for anyone who is not on the statutory register to call themselves an osteopath. Osteopathy is becoming an all-graduate profession. Courses vary in length from three to five years, granting various qualifications from diploma to honours degree. Shorter courses are available for qualified doctors. Details of accrediting institutions and courses can be obtained from the Osteopathic Information Service.

OSTEOPATHIC INFORMATION SERVICE, PO Box 2074, Reading, Berks RG1 4YR. Tel: 01734-512051. *Public Relations Manager*, B. Daniels

PHARMACY

Information may be obtained from the Secretary and Registrar of the Royal Pharmaceutical Society of Great Britain.

ROYAL PHARMACEUTICAL SOCIETY OF GREAT BRITAIN, 1 Lambeth High Street, London SE1 7JN. Tel: 0171-735 9141. *Secretary and Registrar*, J. Ferguson, OBE

PHOTOGRAPHY

The professional body is:

BRITISH INSTITUTE OF PROFESSIONAL PHOTOGRAPHY, Fox Talbot House, Amwell End, Ware, Herts SG12 9HN. Tel: 01920-464011. *Chief Executive*, A. Mair

PRINTING

Details of training courses in printing can be obtained from the Institute of Printing and the British Printing Industries Federation. In addition to these examining and organizing bodies, examinations are held by various independent regional examining boards in further education.

BRITISH PRINTING INDUSTRIES FEDERATION, 11 Bedford Row, London 4DX. Tel: 0171-242 6904. *Chief Executive*, T. P. E. Machin

INSTITUTE OF PRINTING, 8A Lonsdale Gardens, Tunbridge Wells, Kent TN1 1NU. Tel: 01892-538118. *Secretary-General*, D. Freeland

SOCIAL WORK

The Central Council for Education and Training in Social Work promotes education and training for social work and social care in the UK. It approves education and training programmes, including those leading to its qualifying award, the Diploma in Social Work.

THE CENTRAL COUNCIL FOR EDUCATION AND TRAINING IN SOCIAL WORK, Derbyshire House, St Chad's Street, London WC1H 8AD. Tel: 0171-278 2455. *Chairman*, J. Greenwood; *Chief Executive*, J. Bernard

SPEECH AND LANGUAGE THERAPY

The Royal College of Speech and Language Therapists provides details of courses leading to qualification as a speech and language therapist. Other professionals may become Associates of the College. A directory of registered members is published annually.

THE ROYAL COLLEGE OF SPEECH AND LANGUAGE THERAPISTS, 7 Bath Place, Rivington Street, London EC2A 3DR. Tel: 0171-613 3855. *Director*, Mrs P. Evans

SURVEYING

The qualifying professional bodies include:

ARCHITECTS AND SURVEYORS INSTITUTE, St Mary House, 15 St Mary Street, Chippenham, Wilts SN15 3WD. Tel: 01249-444505. *Chief Executive*, C. G. A. Nash, OBE

ASSOCIATION OF BUILDING ENGINEERS, Jubilee House, Billing Brook Road, Weston Favell, Northampton NN3 8NW. Tel: 01604-404121. *Chief Executive*, B. D. Hughes

INCORPORATED SOCIETY OF VALUERS AND AUCTIONEERS (1968), 3 Cadogan Gate, London SW1X 0AS. Tel: 0171-235 2282. *Chief Executive*, H. Whitty

INSTITUTE OF REVENUES, RATING AND VALUATION, 41 Doughty Street, London WC1N 2LF. Tel: 0171-831 3505. *Director*, C. Farrington

ROYAL INSTITUTION OF CHARTERED SURVEYORS (incorporating The Institute of Quantity Surveyors), 12 Great George Street, London SW1P 3AD. Tel: 0171-222 7000. *Chief Executive*, Ms C. Makin

TEACHING

Teachers in maintained schools must have Qualified Teacher Status (QTS). Teaching is rapidly becoming an all-graduate profession, and QTS may be gained by a number of different routes. Those without a first degree may take a Bachelor of Education (B.Ed) or a Bachelor of Arts/Science (BA/BSc) with QTS, full-time for three or four years, depending on the programme followed. These degrees combine subject and professional studies with teaching practice. Shortened courses of these degrees are available for those who have successfully completed one or two years of higher education. The Licensed Teacher Scheme is also available to those with two years higher education who wish to be employed as teachers at the same time as they train for QTS. (This will become the Registered Teacher Programme in 1998.) For those who already have a first degree, the most common route is through a one-year Postgraduate Certificate of Education (PGCE). This may be taken full-time or part-time, or as a distance learning programme. Postgraduates may also gain QTS through training in a school (School-Centred Initial Teacher Training). Starting in January 1998, graduates may join the Graduate Teacher Programme which provides teaching and training for one year (*see also* pages 440–1).

Details of courses in England and Wales are contained in the *Handbook of Degree and Advanced Courses* published annually by the National Association of Teachers in Further and Higher Education. Further information about teaching in England and Wales is available from the Teaching Information Line, 01245-454454. Details of courses in Scotland can be obtained from colleges of education, universities, from COSHEP, and from TEACH (*see* page 453). Details of courses in Northern Ireland can be obtained from the Department of Education for Northern Ireland. Applications for teacher training courses in Northern Ireland are made to the institutions direct. For applications, *see* pages 444–5.

TEXTILES

THE TEXTILE INSTITUTE, International Headquarters, 10 Blackfriars Street, Manchester M3 5DR. Tel: 0161-834 8457. *Operations Manager*, P. Daniels

THEOLOGICAL COLLEGES

The number of students training for the ministry in the academic year 1996–7 is shown in parenthesis. Those marked * show figures for 1995–6.

ANGLICAN

COLLEGE OF THE RESURRECTION, Mirfield, W. Yorks WF14 0BW. Tel: 01924-490441. (19). *Principal (acting)*, Fr G. Guiver

CRANMER HALL, St John's College, Durham DH1 3RJ. Tel: 0191-374 3579. (56). *Principal*, D. V. Day

OAK HILL COLLEGE, Chase Side, London N14 4PS. Tel: 0181-449 0467. (55). *Principal*, Revd Dr D. Peterson

RIDLEY HALL, Cambridge CB3 9HG. Tel: 01223-741080. (50). *Principal*, Revd G. A. Cray

RIPON COLLEGE, Cuddesdon, Oxford OX44 9EX. Tel: 01865-874404. (75). *Principal*, Revd J. Clarke

ST JOHN'S COLLEGE, Chilwell Lane, Bramcote, Nottingham NG9 3DS. Tel: 0115-925 1114. (70). *Principal*, Revd Dr C. Baxter

ST MICHAEL'S THEOLOGICAL COLLEGE, Llandaff, Cardiff CF5 2YJ. Tel: 01222-563379/116. (28). *Warden*, Revd Dr J. I. Holdsworth

ST STEPHEN'S HOUSE, 16 Marston Street, Oxford OX4 1JX. Tel: 01865-247874. (45). *Principal*, Revd Dr J. Sheehy

THEOLOGICAL INSTITUTE OF THE SCOTTISH EPISCOPAL CHURCH, 21 Inverleith Terrace, Edinburgh EH3 5NS. Tel: 0131-343 2038. (18). *Principal*, Revd Canon R. A. Nixon

TRINITY COLLEGE, Stoke Hill, Bristol BS9 1JP. Tel: 0117-968 2803. (60). *Principal*, Revd Canon D. Gillett

WESTCOTT HOUSE, Jesus Lane, Cambridge CB5 8BP. Tel: 01223-741000. (55). *Principal*, Revd M. G. V. Roberts

WYCLIFFE HALL, 54 Banbury Road, Oxford OX2 6PW. Tel: 01865-274200. (67). *Principal*, Revd Dr A. McGrath

BAPTIST

BRISTOL BAPTIST COLLEGE, Woodland Road, Bristol BS8 1UN. Tel: 0117-926 0248. (20). *Principal*, Revd Dr B. Haymes

NORTHERN BAPTIST COLLEGE, Luther King House, Brighton Grove, Rusholme, Manchester M14 5JP. Tel: 0161-224 2214. (20). *Principal*, Revd Dr R. L. Kidd

NORTH WALES BAPTIST COLLEGE, Ffordd Ffriddoedd, Bangor LL57 2EH. Tel: 01248-362608. (*2). *Warden*, Revd Dr D. D. Morgan

REGENT'S PARK COLLEGE, Oxford OX1 2LB. Tel: 01865-288120. (21). *Principal*, Revd Dr P. S. Fiddes

THE SCOTTISH BAPTIST COLLEGE, 12 Aytoun Road, Glasgow G41 5RN. Tel: 0141-424 0747. (15). *Principal*, Revd K. B. E. Roxburgh

SOUTH WALES BAPTIST COLLEGE, 54 Richmond Road, Cardiff CF2 3UR. Tel: 01222-256066. (27). *Principal*, Revd D. H. Matthews

CHURCH OF SCOTLAND

NEW COLLEGE, Mound Place, Edinburgh EH1 2LU. Tel: 0131-650 8900. (*33). *Principal*, Revd Dr R. Page

TRINITY COLLEGE, 4 The Square, University of Glasgow, Glasgow G12 8QQ. Tel: 0141-339 8855. (30). *Principal*, Revd Dr D. M. Murray

CONGREGATIONAL

SCOTTISH CONGREGATIONAL COLLEGE, St Colm's, 20 Inverleith Terrace, Edinburgh EH3 5NS. Tel: 0131-315 3595. (*1). *Principal*, Revd Dr J. W. S. Clark

ECUMENICAL

QUEEN'S COLLEGE, Somerset Road, Edgbaston, Birmingham B15 2QH. Tel: 0121-454 1527. (105). *Principal*, Revd P. Fisher

METHODIST

EDGHILL THEOLOGICAL COLLEGE, 9 Lennoxvale, Belfast BT9 5BY. Tel: 01232-665870. (20). *Principal*, Revd Dr W. D. D. Cooke, PH.D.

HARTLEY VICTORIA COLLEGE, Luther King House, Brighton Grove, Manchester M14 5JP. Tel: 0161-224 2215. (25). *Principal*, Revd Dr J. A. Harrod

WESLEY COLLEGE, College Park Drive, Henbury Road, Bristol BS10 7QD. Tel: 0117-959 1200. (60). *Principal*, Revd Dr N. Richardson

WESLEY HOUSE, Jesus Lane, Cambridge CB5 8BJ. Tel: 01223-741033. (32). *Principal*, Revd Dr I. H. Jones

WESLEY STUDY CENTRE, 55 The Avenue, Durham DH1 4EB. Tel: 0191-386 1833. (24). *Director*, Revd P. Luscombe, PH.D.

NON-DENOMINATIONAL

CHRIST'S COLLEGE, 25 High Street, Old Aberdeen AB24 3EE. Tel: 01224-272138. (30). *Master*, Revd Prof. A. Main, TD, PH.D.

ST MARY'S COLLEGE, The University, St Andrews, Fife KY16 9JU. Tel: 01334-462851. (7). *Principal*, Dr R. A. Piper

SPURGEON'S COLLEGE, South Norwood Hill, London SE25 6DJ. Tel: 0181-653 0850. (250). *Principal*, Revd M. Quicke

PRESBYTERIAN

UNION THEOLOGICAL COLLEGE, 108 Botanic Avenue, Belfast BT7 1JT. Tel: 01232-205080. (40). *Principal*, Revd Prof. T. S. Reid

PRESBYTERIAN CHURCH OF WALES

UNITED THEOLOGICAL COLLEGE, Aberystwyth SY23 2LT. Tel: 01970-624574. (20). *Principal*, Revd Prof. E. N. Roberts

ROMAN CATHOLIC

ALLEN HALL, 28 Beaufort Street, London SW3 5AA. Tel: 0171-351 1296. (45). *Principal*, Revd K. Barltrop, STL

CAMPION HOUSE COLLEGE, 112 Thornbury Road, Isleworth, Middx TW7 4NN. Tel: 0181-560 1924. (13). *Principal*, Revd C. C. Dykehoff, SJ

OSCOTT COLLEGE, Chester Road, Sutton Coldfield, W. Midlands B73 5AA. Tel: 0121-354 7117. (50). *Rector*, Rt. Revd P. McKinney, STL

ST JOHN'S SEMINARY, Wonersh, Guildford, Surrey GU5 0QX. Tel: 01483-892217. (60). *Rector*, Revd K. Haggerty, STL

SCOTUS COLLEGE, 2 Chesters Road, Bearsden, Glasgow G61 4AG. Tel: 0141-942 8384. (35). *Rector*, Rt Revd M. J. Conway

USHAW COLLEGE, Durham DH7 9RH. Tel: 0191-373 1366. (50). *President*, Revd J. P. O'Keefe

UNITARIAN

UNITARIAN COLLEGE, Luther King House, Brighton Grove, Rusholme, Manchester M14 5JP. Tel: 0161-224 2849. (5). *Principal*, Revd L. Smith, PH.D.

UNITED REFORMED

MANSFIELD COLLEGE, Mansfield Road, Oxford OX1 3TF. Tel: 01865-270999. (25). *Director*, Revd J. C. Brock

NORTHERN COLLEGE, Luther King House, Brighton Grove, Rusholme, Manchester M14 5JP. Tel: 0161-224 4381. (25). *Principal*, Revd Dr D. R. Peel

WESTMINSTER COLLEGE, Madingley Road, Cambridge CB3 0AA. Tel: 01223-271084. (30). *Principal*, Revd D. G. Cornick, PH.D.

JEWISH

JEWS' COLLEGE, Albert Road, London NW4 2SJ. Tel: 0181-203 6427. (10). *Principal*, Rabbi Dr S. Stern

LEO BAECK COLLEGE, Sternberg Centre for Judaism, 80 East End Road, London N3 2SY. Tel: 0181-349 4525. (15). *Principal*, Rabbi Prof. J. Magonet

TOWN AND COUNTRY PLANNING

Degree and diploma courses in town planning are accredited by the Royal Town Planning Institute.

THE ROYAL TOWN PLANNING INSTITUTE, 26 Portland Place, London W1N 4BE. Tel: 0171-636 9107. *Secretary-General*, R. Upton

TRANSPORT

Qualifying examinations in transport management and logistics leading to chartered professional status are conducted by the Chartered Institute of Transport.

THE CHARTERED INSTITUTE OF TRANSPORT, 80 Portland Place, London W1N 4DP. Tel: 0171-467 9425. *Director*, Mrs S. Gross

VETERINARY MEDICINE

The regulatory body for veterinary medicine is the Royal College of Veterinary Surgeons, which keeps the register of those entitled to practise veterinary medicine. In order to be registered, a person must complete a five-year undergraduate degree (BVetMed or BVSc.) at one of the six authorized institutions.

The British Veterinary Association is the professional body representing veterinary surgeons. The British Veterinary Nursing Association is the professional body representing veterinary nurses who are also registered with the Royal College of Veterinary Surgeons.

BRITISH VETERINARY ASSOCIATION, 7 Mansfield Street, London W1M 0AT. Tel: 0171-636 6541. *Chief Executive*, J. Baird

BRITISH VETERINARY NURSING ASSOCIATION, Unit D12, The Seedbed Centre, Coldharbour Road, Harlow, Essex CM19 5AF. Tel: 01279-450567. *Chairman*, Ms J. Costello

ROYAL COLLEGE OF VETERINARY SURGEONS, Belgravia House, 62–64 Horseferry Road, London SW1P 2AF. Tel: 0171-222 2001. *President*, Dr N. Gorman; *Registrar*, Ms J. Hern

Independent Schools

The following pages list those independent schools whose Head is a member of the Headmasters' and Headmistress' Conference, the Society of Headmasters and Headmistresses of Independent Schools or the Girls' Schools Association

THE HEADMASTERS' AND HEADMISTRESS' CONFERENCE

Chairman (1998), P. J. F. Tobin (Daniel Stewart's and Melville College)
Secretary, V. S. Anthony, 130 Regent Road, Leicester LEI 7PG. Tel: 0116-285 4810
Membership Secretary, D. E. Prince
The annual meeting is, as a rule, held at the end of September or early in October

* Woodard Corporation School, 1 The Sanctuary, London SW1P 3JT. Tel: 0171-222 5381
† Girls in VI form
‡ Co-educational
° 1996 figures

Name of School	Foun-ded	No. of pupils	Annual fees £ Boarding	Day	Head (with date of appointment)
ENGLAND AND WALES			Boarding	Day	
Abbotsholme School, Rocester	1889	230‡	12,513	8,355	I. M. Allison (1984)
Abingdon School, Oxon	1256	788	10,962	5,946	M. St J. Parker (1975)
Ackworth School, W. Yorks	1779	365‡	10,200	5,805	M. J. Dickinson (1995)
Aldenham School, Elstree, Herts	1597	390†	11,910	8,580	S. R. Borthwick (1994)
Alleyn's School, London SE22	1619	919‡	—	6,255	Dr C. H. R. Niven (1992)
Ampleforth College (*RC*), N. Yorks	1802	500	13,305	6,870	Revd G. F. L. Chamberlain, OSB (1993)
*Ardingly College, Haywards Heath	1858	453‡	12,810	9,930	J. W. Flecker (1980)
Arnold School, Blackpool	1896	820‡	—	4,140	W. T. Gillen (1993)
Ashville College, Harrogate	1877	570‡	9,698	5,185	M. H. Crosby (1987)
Bablake School, Coventry	1560	850‡	—	4,215	Dr S. Nuttall (1991)
Bancroft's School, Woodford Green, Essex	1727	754‡	—	6,384	Dr P. R. Scott (1996)
Barnard Castle School, Co. Durham	1883	521‡	9,477	5,610	M. D. Featherstone (1997)
Batley Grammar School, W. Yorks	1612	559‡	—	4,191	W. M. Duggan (1995)
Bedales School, Petersfield	1893	410‡	14,328	10,851	Mrs A. A. Willcocks (1995)
Bedford Modern School	1566	659	9,846	5,235	S. Smith (1996)
Bedford School	1552	730	12,120	7,635	Dr I. P. Evans (1990)
Berkhamsted Collegiate School, Herts	1541	900‡	11,946	7,317	Dr P. Chadwick (1996)
Birkdale School, Sheffield	1904	523	—	4,797	Revd M. D. A. Hepworth (1983)
Birkenhead School, Merseyside	1860	677	—	4,155	S. J. Haggett (1988)
Bishop's Stortford College, Herts	1868	320‡	11,160	8,040	J. G. Trotman (1997)
*Bloxham School, Banbury	1860	345†	13,125	10,290	D. K. Exham (1991)
Blundell's School, Tiverton	1604	444‡	12,135	7,410	J. Leigh (1992)
Bolton School	1524	850	—	4,779	A. W. Wright (1983)
Bootham School, York	1823	364↓	10,995	7,155	I. M. Small (1988)
Bradfield College, Reading	1850	600†	13,425	10,070	P. B. Smith (1985)
Bradford Grammar School	1662	910†	—	4,510	S. R. Davidson (1996)
Brentwood School, Essex	1557	1,079‡	11,298	6,486	J. A. B. Kelsall (1993)
Brighton College, E. Sussex	1845	485‡	13,575	8,760	Dr A. F. Seldon (1997)
Bristol Cathedral School	1140	470†	—	4,362	K. J. Riley (1993)
Bristol Grammar School	1532	1,040‡	—	4,293	C. E. Martin (1986)
Bromsgrove School, Worcs	1553	692‡	10,725	6,720	T. M. Taylor (1986)
Bryanston School, Blandford Forum	1928	626‡	14,295	9,531	T. D. Wheare (1983)
Bury Grammar School, Lancs	1634	680	—	4,014	K. Richards (1990)
Canford School, Wimborne	1923	550‡	13,000	9,750	J. D. Lever (1992)
Caterham School, Surrey	1811	710‡	11,799	6,396	R. A. E. Davey (1995)
Charterhouse, Godalming	1611	700†	13,941	11,520	Revd J. S. Witheridge (1996)
Cheadle Hulme School, Cheshire	1855	985‡	—	4,530	D. J. Wilkinson (1990)
Cheltenham College, Glos	1841	565†	13,200	9,975	P. C. Chamberlain (1990)
Chetham's School of Music, Manchester	1653	259‡	16,425	12,714	Revd Canon P. F. Hullah (1992)
Chigwell School, Essex	1629	380†	9,933	6,903	D. F. Gibbs (1996)

Name of School	Foun-ded	No. of pupils	Annual fees £		Head (with date of appointment)
			Boarding	Day	
Christ College, Brecon	1541	354‡	10,671	8,268	D. P. Jones (1996)
Christ's Hospital, Horsham	1553	792‡	varies	—	Dr P. C. D. Southern (1996)
Churcher's College, Petersfield	1722	562‡	—	5,520	G. W. Buttle (1988)
City of London Freemen's School, Ashtead	1854	420‡	10,200	6,600	D. C. Haywood (1987)
City of London, London EC4	1442	880	—	6,426	R. M. Dancey (1995)
Clifton College, Bristol	1862	630‡	13,245	9,105	A. H. Monro (1991)
Colfe's School, London SE12	1652	720†	—	5,694	Dr D. J. Richardson (1990)
Colston's Collegiate School, Bristol	1710	450‡	11,118	6,030	D. G. Crawford (1995)
Cranleigh School, Surrey	1863	485†	13,710	10,140	G. de W. Waller (1997)
Culford School, Bury St Edmunds	1881	380‡	11,577	7,533	J. S. Richardson (1992)
Dame Allan's Boys' School, Newcastle upon Tyne	1705	450†	—	4,011	D. W. Welsh (*Principal*) (1996)
Dauntsey's School, Devizes	1543	670‡	11,622	7,155	S. B. Roberts (1997)
Dean Close School, Cheltenham	1884	455‡	13,350	9,300	C. J. Bacon (1979)
*Denstone College, Uttoxeter	1873	302‡	11,668	4,500	D. M. Derbyshire (1997)
Douai School (*RC*), Upper Woolhampton, Reading	1903	206‡	11,520	7,440	Dr P. McLaughlin (1997)
Dover College, Kent	1871	270‡	11,985	6,780	M. P. G. Wright (1991)
Downside School (*RC*), Somerset	1607	300	12,180	6,180	Revd Dom. A. Sutch (*Master*) (1995)
Dulwich College, London SE21	1619	941	13,236	6,618	G. G. Able (*Master*) (1997)
Durham School	1414	306†	11,883	7,779	N. G. Kern (1997)
Eastbourne College	1867	499‡	12,690	9,000	C. M. P. Bush (1993)
*Ellesmere College, Shropshire	1884	286‡	11,650	7,716	B. J. Wignall (1996)
Eltham College, London SE9	1842	580†	12,081	6,000	D. M. Green (1990)
Emanuel School, London SW11	1594	760‡	—	5,310	T. Jones-Parry (1994)
Epsom College, Surrey	1855	655‡	12,825	9,525	A. H. Beadles (1993)
Eton College, Windsor	1440	1,281	13,410	—	J. E. Lewis (1994)
Exeter School	1633	690‡	8,895	4,695	N. W. Gamble (1992)
Felsted School, Dunmow, Essex	1564	372‡	13,620	10,740	S. C. Roberts (1993)
Forest School, London E17	1834	830†	9,633	6,138	A. G. Boggis (*Warden*) (1992)
Framlingham College, Woodbridge, Suffolk	1864	456‡	10,680	6,855	Mrs. G. M. Randall (1994)
Frensham Heights, Farnham	1925	290‡	13,125	7,700	P. M. de Voil (1993)
Giggleswick School, Settle	1512	320‡	12,750	8,460	A. P. Millard (1993)
The Grange School, Northwich, Cheshire	1978	550‡	—	3,855	Mrs J. E. Stephens (1997)
Gresham's School, Holt, Norfolk	1555	520‡	13,305	9,480	J. H. Arkell (1991)
Haberdashers' Aske's School, Elstree, Herts	1690	1,109	—	6,378	J. W. R. Goulding (1996)
Haileybury, Hertford	1862	605†	13,980	10,140	S. A. Westley (*Master*) (1996)
Hampton School, Middx	1557	940	—	5,760	B. R. Martin (1997)
Harrow School, Middx	1571	785	14,295	—	N. R. Bomford (1991)
Hereford Cathedral School	1384	623‡	9,015	5,040	Dr H. C. Tomlinson (1987)
Highgate School, London N6	1565	605	—	7,875	R. P. Kennedy (1989)
Hulme Grammar School, Oldham	1611	700	—	3,912	T. J. Turvey (1995)
*Hurstpierpoint College, Hassocks, W. Sussex	1849	349‡	12,540	9,720	S. D. A. Meek (1995)
Hymers College, Hull	1889	721‡	—	4,032	J. C. Morris (1990)
Ipswich School	1390	580†	9,606	5,598	I. G. Galbraith (1993)
John Lyon School, Harrow	1876	525	—	6,075	Revd T. J. Wright (1986)
Kelly College, Tavistock	1877	310‡	11,670	6,510	M. Turner (1995)
Kent College, Canterbury	1885	490‡	11,418	6,411	E. B. Halse (1995)
Kimbolton School, Huntingdon	1600	560‡	9,969	5,859	R. V. Peel (1987)
King Edward VI School, Southampton	1553	950‡	—	5,367	P. B. Hamilton (1996)
King Edward VII School, Lytham St Annes	1908	495	—	4,062	P. J. Wilde (1993)
King Edward's School, Bath	1552	660†	—	4,992	P. J. Winter (1994)
King Edward's School, Birmingham	1552	890	—	4,914	H. R. Wright (*Chief Master*) (1991)
King Edward's School, Witley, Surrey	1553	475‡	9,945	6,870	R. J. Fox (1988)
King Henry VIII School, Coventry	1545	820‡	—	4,215	T. J. Vardon (1994)
*King's College, Taunton	1880	450‡	12,600	8,298	R. S. Funnell (1988)
King's College School, London SW19	1829	710	—	7,350	A. C. V. Evans (1997)
King's School, Bruton, Somerset	1519	339‡	11,790	8,355	R. I. Smyth (1993)
King's School, Canterbury	600	750‡	14,115	9,750	Revd K. H. Wilkinson (1996)
King's School, Chester	1541	515	—	4,494	A. R. D. Wickson (1981)
King's School, Ely	970	379‡	12,666	8,511	R. H. Youdale (1992)
King's School, Gloucester	1541	300‡	9,400	6,200	P. Lacey (1992)
King's School, Macclesfield	1502	1,170‡	—	4,575	A. G. Silcock (1987)

Name of School	Founded	No. of pupils	Annual fees £ Boarding	Day	Head (with date of appointment)
King's School, Rochester, Kent	604	331‡	13,170	7,590	Dr I. R. Walker (1986)
*King's School, Tynemouth	1860	640‡	—	4,158	Dr D. Younger (1993)
King's School, Worcester	1541	800‡	9,600	5,538	Dr J. M. Moore (1983)
Kingston Grammar School, Surrey	1561	600‡	—	6,180	C. D. Baxter (1991)
Kingswood School, Bath	1748	470‡	12,540	6,720	G. M. Best (1987)
*Lancing College, W. Sussex	1848	500‡	13,335	10,020	C. J. Saunders (1993)
Latymer Upper School, London w6	1624	921†	—	6,540	C. Diggory (1991)
Leeds Grammar School	1552	1,104	—	5,316	B. W. Collins (1986)
Leicester Grammar School	1981	640‡	—	4,650	J. B. Sugden (1989)
Leighton Park School, Reading	1890	360‡	12,185	9,153	J. Dunston (1996)
The Leys School, Cambridge	1875	429‡	12,780	8,379	Revd Dr J. C. A. Barrett (1990)
Liverpool College	1840	617‡	—	4,290	J. P. Siviter (*Principal*) (1997)
Llandovery College, Carmarthenshire	1848	235‡	10,467	6,951	Dr C. E. Evans (*Warden*) (1988)
Lord Wandsworth College, Long Sutton, Hants	1912	475‡	10,764	8,376	I. Power (1997)
Loughborough Grammar School	1495	960	8,973	4,896	D. N. Ireland (1984)
Magdalen College School, Oxford	1480	520	—	5,394	P. M. Tinniswood (*Master*) (1991)
Malvern College, Worcs	1865	615‡	13,350	9,705	H. C. K. Carson (1997)
Manchester Grammar School	1515	1430	—	4,560	G. M. Stephen, ph.d (*High Master*) (1994)
Marlborough College, Wilts	1843	800‡	14,100	10,140	E. J. H. Gould (*Master*) (1993)
Merchant Taylors' School, Liverpool	1620	730	—	4,122	S. J. R. Dawkins (1985)
Merchant Taylors' School, Northwood, Middx	1561	752	12,050	7,200	J. R. Gabitass (1991)
Millfield, Street, Somerset	1935	1,242‡	14,385	9,315	C. S. Martin (1990)
Mill Hill School, London nw7	1807	530‡	12,648	8,205	W. R. Winfield (1996)
Monkton Combe School, Bath	1868	340‡	12,905	8,865	M. J. Cuthbertson (1990)
Monmouth School	1614	575	9,141	5,487	T. H. P. Haynes (1995)
Mount St Mary's College (*RC*), Sheffield	1842	290‡	9,891	6,150	P. B. Fisher (1991)
Newcastle-under-Lyme School	1874	1,104‡	—	3,939	Dr R. M. Reynolds (*Principal*) (1990)
Norwich School	1250	630†	—	5,088	C. D. Brown (1984)
Nottingham High School	1513	834	—	4,923	C. S. Parker (1995)
Oakham School, Rutland	1584	1,000‡	12,780	7,440	A. R. M. Little (1996)
The Oratory School (*RC*), Woodcote, Berks	1859	413	12,015	9,030	S. W. Barrow (1991)
Oundle School, Northants	1556	840‡	13,920	—	D. B. McMurray (1984)
Pangbourne College, Berks	1917	380‡	12,480	8,730	A. B. E. Hudson (1988)
Perse School, Cambridge	1615	570†	—	5,250	N. P. V. Richardson (1994)
Plymouth College	1877	575‡	10,212	5,322	A. J. Morsley (1992)
Pocklington School, York	1514	620‡	9,615	5,568	J. N. D. Gray (1992)
Portsmouth Grammar School	1732	795‡	—	4,890	T. R. Hands, d.phil. (1997)
Prior Park College (*RC*), Bath	1830	515‡	11,499	6,360	R. G. G. Mercer, d.phil. (1996)
Queen Elizabeth GS, Wakefield	1591	727	—	4,674	R. P. Mardling (1985)
Queen Elizabeth's GS, Blackburn	1567	980†	—	4,389	Dr D. S. Hempsall (1995)
Queen Elizabeth's Hospital, Bristol	1590	533	7,899	4,335	Dr R. Gliddon (1985)
Queen's College, Taunton	1843	483‡	10,080	6,606	C. T. Bradnock (1991)
Radley College, Abingdon	1847	620	13,650	—	R. M. Morgan (*Warden*) (1991)
Ratcliffe College (*RC*), Leicester	1844	490‡	9,837	6,561	T. A. Kilbride (1996)
Reading Blue Coat School	1646	590†	10,050	5,514	S. J. W. McArthur (1997)
Reed's School, Cobham, Surrey	1813	360	11,292	8,535	D. W. Jarrett (1997)
Reigate Grammar School, Surrey	1675	810‡	—	5,472	P. V. Dixon (1996)
Rendcomb College, Cirencester	1920	242‡	11,340	8,970	J. Tolputt (1987)
Repton School, Derby	1557	550‡	12,720	9,555	G. E. Jones (1987)
RNIB New College, Worcester	1987	110‡	varies	varies	Mrs H. Williams (*Principal*) (1995)
Rossall School, Fleetwood, Lancs	1844	370‡	12,090	4,545	R. D. W. Rhodes (1988)
Royal Grammar School, Guildford	1552	850	—	6,255	T. M. S. Young (1992)
Royal Hospital School, Ipswich	1712	660‡	9,048	4,965	N. K. D. Ward (1995)
Royal Grammar School, Newcastle upon Tyne	1545	950	—	4,215	J. F. X. Miller (1994)
Royal Grammar School, Worcester	1291	762	—	4,842	W. A. Jones (1993)
Rugby School	1567	750‡	13,815	8,205	M. B. Mavor, cvo (1990)
Rydal Penrhos School, Colwyn Bay	1880	395‡	10,860	7,758	N. W. Thorne (1991)
Ryde School, Isle of Wight	1921	480‡	9,231	4,524	Dr N. J. England (1997)
St Albans School	1570	680†	—	6,213	A. R. Grant (1993)
St Bede's College (*RC*), Manchester	1876	1,002‡	—	4,170	J. Byrne (1983)

Name of School	Foun-ded	No. of pupils	Annual fees £		Head (with date of appointment)
			Boarding	Day	
St Bees School, Cumbria	1583	290‡	11,622	7,995	Mrs J. D. Pickering (from January 1998)
St Benedict's School (RC), London w5	1902	578†	—	5,460	Dr A. J. Dachs (1987)
St Dunstan's College, London se6	1888	650‡	—	6,105	To be appointed
°St Edmund's College (RC), Ware, Herts	1568	450‡	10,320	6,480	D. J. J. McEwen (1984)
St Edmund's School, Canterbury	1749	270‡	13,260	8,589	A. N. Ridley (1994)
St Edward's School, Oxford	1863	555‡	13,425	9,600	D. Christie (Warden) (1988)
St George's College (RC), Addlestone, Surrey	1869	550†	—	6,990	J. A. Peake (1995)
St John's School, Leatherhead, Surrey	1851	395‡	11,700	8,100	C. H. Tongue (1993)
St Lawrence College in Thanet, Ramsgate	1879	355‡	12,600	8,400	M. Slater (1996)
St Mary's College (RC), Liverpool	1919	624‡	—	4,050	W. Hammond (1991)
St Paul's School, London sw13	1509	777	13,560	8,985	R. S. Baldock (High Master) (1992)
St Peter's School, York	627	488‡	10,698	6,369	A. F. Trotman (1995)
Sedbergh School, Cumbria	1525	350	12,945	9,060	C. H. Hirst (1995)
Sevenoaks School, Kent	1418	950‡	12,798	7,794	T. R. Cookson (1996)
Sherborne School, Dorset	1550	576	13,770	10,350	P. H. Lapping (1988)
Shrewsbury School	1552	690	13,650	9,600	F. E. Maidment (1988)
Silcoates School, Wakefield	1820	421‡	—	5,760	A. P. Spillane (1991)
Solihull School	1560	794†	—	4,530	P. S. J. Derham (1996)
Stamford School, Lincs	1532	550	9,048	4,524	J. Hale (1997)
Stockport Grammar School	1487	990‡	—	4,266	I. Mellor (1996)
Stonyhurst College (RC), Clitheroe	1593	395†	12,045	7,500	A. J. F. Aylward (1996)
Stowe School, Bucks	1923	558†	14,175	9,930	J. G. L. Nichols (1989)
Sutton Valence School, Kent	1576	375‡	12,360	7,920	N. A. Sampson (1994)
Taunton School	1847	460‡	12,150	7,785	J. P. Whiteley (1997)
Tettenhall College, Wolverhampton	1863	220‡	9,798	6,039	Dr P. C. Bodkin (1994)
Tonbridge School, Kent	1553	700	14,400	10,170	J. M. Hammond (1990)
Trent College, Nottingham	1868	700‡	11,445	7,026	J. S. Lee (1989)
Trinity School, Croydon	1596	850	—	5,950	B. J. Lenon (1995)
Truro School	1879	800‡	9,495	5,052	G. A. G. Dodd (1993)
University College School, London nw3	1830	700	—	7,626	K. J. Durham (1996)
Uppingham School, Oakham, Rutland	1584	635†	13,320	7,995	Dr S. C. Winkley (1991)
Warwick School	914	823	10,980	5,145	Dr P. J. Cheshire (1988)
Wellingborough School, Northants	1595	400‡	10,350	5,880	F. R. Ullmann (1993)
Wellington College, Crowthorne, Berks	1856	800†	13,350	9,735	C. J. Driver (Master) (1989)
Wellington School, Somerset	1837	775‡	8,856	4,848	A. J. Rogers (1990)
Wells Cathedral School, Somerset	1180	610‡	10,725	6,369	J. S. Baxter (1986)
West Buckland School, Barnstaple, Devon	1858	475‡	9,888	5,595	J. Vick (1997)
Westminster School, London sw1	1560	679†	14,400	9,930	D. M. Summerscale (1986)
Whitgift School, South Croydon	1596	1,074	—	6,147	C. A. Barnett, d.phil. (1991)
William Hulme's GS, Manchester	1887	745‡	—	4,614	B. J. Purvis (1997)
Winchester College	1382	680	14,544	10,908	J. P. Sabben-Clare (1985)
Wisbech Grammar School, Cambs	1379	640‡	—	5,160	R. S. Repper (1988)
Wolverhampton Grammar School	1512	780‡	—	5,400	Dr B. Trafford (1990)
Woodbridge School, Suffolk	1662	542‡	9,789	5,958	S. H. Cole (1994)
Woodhouse Grove School, Bradford	1812	550‡	9,990	5,835	D. C. Humphreys (1996)
*Worksop College, Notts	1895	350‡	11,835	8,145	R. A. Collard (1994)
Worth School (RC), Crawley	1959	300	12,552	8,595	Fr C. Jamison (1994)
Wrekin College, Telford	1880	300‡	12,450	7,350	P. M. Johnson (1991)
Wycliffe College, Stonehouse, Glos	1882	400‡	12,750	9,000	D. C. M. Prichard (1994)
Yarm School, Stockton-on-Tees	1978	560†	—	5,220	R. N. Tate (1978)

SCOTLAND

Name of School	Foun-ded	No. of pupils	Annual fees £		Head (with date of appointment)
Daniel Stewart's and Melville College, Edinburgh	1832	806†	9,342	4,812	P. J. F. Tobin (Principal) (1989)
Dollar Academy, Clackmannanshire	1818	760‡	10,188	4,599	J. S. Robertson (Rector) (1994)
Dundee High School	1239	750‡	—	4,398	A. M. Duncan (1997)
The Edinburgh Academy	1824	488†	11,706	5,490	J. V. Light (Rector) (1995)
Fettes College, Edinburgh	1870	397‡	13,455	9,090	M. T. Thyne, frse (1988)
George Heriot's School, Edinburgh	1659	947‡	—	4,131	A. G. Hector (1997)
George Watson's College, Edinburgh	1741	1,258‡	9,186	4,512	F. E. Gerstenberg (Principal) (1985)
Glasgow Academy	1845	576‡	—	4,665	D. Comins (Rector) (1994)
Glenalmond College, Perth	1841	334‡	13,185	8,790	I. G. Templeton (Warden) (1992)

Name of School	Foun-ded	No. of pupils	Annual fees £		Head (with date of appointment)
			Boarding	Day	
Gordonstoun School, Elgin	1934	450‡	12,918	8,337	M. C. S.-R. Pyper (1990)
High School of Glasgow	1124	640‡	—	4,743	R. G. Easton (1983)
Hutcheson's Grammar School, Glasgow	1641	1,236‡	—	4,221	D. R. Ward (*Rector*) (1987)
Kelvinside Academy, Glasgow	1878	400	—	4,950	J. H. Duff (*Rector*) (1980)
Loretto School, Musselburgh	1827	319‡	12,195	8,130	K. J. Budge (1995)
Merchiston Castle School, Edinburgh	1833	390	12,765	8,490	D. M. Spawforth (1980)
Morrison's Academy, Crieff	1860	416‡	11,700	4,110	G. H. Edwards (*Rector*) (1996)
Robert Gordon's College, Aberdeen	1729	930‡	—	4,475	B. R. W. Lockhart (1996)
St Aloysius' College, Glasgow	1859	811‡	—	3,500	Revd A. Porter, SJ (1995)
St Columba's School, Kilmacolm	1897	360‡	—	4,206	A. H. Livingstone (1987)
Strathallan School, Perth	1913	490‡	12,600	8,790	A. W. McPhail (1993)
NORTHERN IRELAND					
Bangor Grammar School	1856	913	—	450	T. W. Patton (1979)
Belfast Royal Academy	1785	1,358‡	—	80	W. M. Sillery (1980)
Campbell College, Belfast	1894	740	5,559	1,044	Dr R. J. I. Pollock (1987)
Coleraine Academical Institution	1856	860	4,200	3,000	R. S. Forsythe (1984)
Methodist College, Belfast	1868	1,864‡	3,449	244	T. W. Mulryne (*Principal*) (1988)
Portora Royal School, Enniskillen	1618	130	—	42	R. L. Bennett (1983)
Royal Belfast Academical Institution	1810	1,040	—	450	R. M. Ridley (*Principal*) (1990)
CHANNEL ISLANDS AND ISLE OF MAN					
Elizabeth College, Guernsey	1563	520†	6,930	2,730	J. H. F. Doulton (1988)
King William's College, Isle of Man	1668	320‡	12,285	8,745	P. K. Fulton-Peebles (*Principal*) (1996)
Victoria College, Jersey	1852	620†	—	1,842	J. Hydes (1992)
EUROPE					
Aiglon College, Switzerland	1949	223‡	Fr.57,000	Fr.37,400	R. McDonald (1994)
British School in the Netherlands	1935	510†	—	Gld.21,300	J. Hollis (1996)
British School of Brussels	1970	508†	—	Fr.664,000	Ms J. M. Bray (*Principal*) (1992)
British School of Paris	1954	325‡	Fr.115,000	Fr.85,000	M. Honour (*Principal*) (1992)
The International School of Geneva	1924	1,400‡	Fr.41,690	Fr.19,240	G. Walker, OBE (*Director-General*) (1991)
The International School of Paris	1964	180‡	—	Fr.84,000	G. Jones (1997)
King's College, Madrid	1969	580‡	Pesetas 2.02m	Pesetas 1.12m	C. T. G. Leech (1997)
St Columba's College, Dublin	1843	310‡	Ir£6,315	Ir£3,645	T. E. Macey (*Warden*) (1988)
St Edward's College, Malta	1929	400†	—	LM.780	G. Briscoe (1989)
St George's English School, Rome	1958	320‡	—	L.18m	Mrs B. Gardner (1994)

OTHER OVERSEAS MEMBERS

AFRICA

DIOCESAN COLLEGE, Rondebosch, SA. *Head*, C. N. Watson

FALCON COLLEGE, PO Esigodini, Zimbabwe. *Head*, P. N. Todd

HILTON COLLEGE, Kwazulu-Natal, SA. *Head*, M. J. Nicholson

MICHAELHOUSE, Balgowan, SA. *Head*, J. H. Pluke

PETERHOUSE, Marondera, Zimbabwe. *Head*, M. A. Bawden

ST GEORGE'S COLLEGE, Harare, Zimbabwe. *Head*, K. F. Brennan

ST JOHN'S COLLEGE, Johannesburg, SA. *Head*, R. J. D. Clarence

ST STITHIAN'S COLLEGE, Randburg, SA. *Head*, D. B. Wylde

AUSTRALIA

ANGLICAN CHURCH GRAMMAR SCHOOL, Brisbane, Queensland. *Head*, C. V. Ellis

BRIGHTON GRAMMAR SCHOOL, Brighton, Victoria. *Head*, R. L. Rolfe

BRISBANE BOYS' COLLEGE, Toowong, Queensland. *Head*, G. M. Cujes

CAMBERWELL GRAMMAR SCHOOL, Balwyn, Victoria. *Head*, C. F. Black

CANBERRA GRAMMAR SCHOOL, Red Hill, ACT. *Head*, T. C. Murray

CAULFIELD GRAMMAR SCHOOL, Elsternwick, Victoria. *Head*, S. H. Newton

CHRIST CHURCH GRAMMAR SCHOOL, Claremont, W. Australia. *Head*, J. J. S. Madin

CRANBROOK SCHOOL, Sydney, NSW. *Head*, Dr B. N. Carter

THE GEELONG COLLEGE, Geelong, Victoria. *Head*, Ms P. Turner

GEELONG GRAMMAR SCHOOL, Corio, Victoria. *Head*, L. Hannah

GUILDFORD GRAMMAR SCHOOL, Guildford, W. Australia. *Head*, J. M. Moody

HAILEYBURY COLLEGE, Keysborough, Victoria. *Head*, A. H. M. Aikman

THE HALE SCHOOL, Wembley Downs, W. Australia. *Head*, R. J. Inverarity

THE ILLAWARRA GRAMMAR SCHOOL, Wollongong, NSW. *Head*, Revd P. J. R. Smart

THE KING'S SCHOOL, Parramatta, NSW. *Head*, J. A. Wickham

KINROSS WOLAROI SCHOOL, Orange, NSW. *Head*, A. E. S. Anderson

KNOX GRAMMAR SCHOOL, Wahroonga, NSW. *Head*, Dr I. Paterson

MELBOURNE GRAMMAR SCHOOL, South Yarra, Victoria. *Head*, A. P. Sheahan

MENTONE GRAMMAR SCHOOL, Mentone, Victoria. *Head*, N. Clark

NEWINGTON COLLEGE, Stanmore, NSW. *Head*, M. E. Smee

ST PETER'S COLLEGE, St Peter's, S. Australia. *Head*, R. L. Burchnall

SCOTCH COLLEGE, Adelaide, S. Australia. *Head*, K. Webb

SCOTCH COLLEGE, Melbourne, Victoria. *Head*, Dr F. G. Donaldson

SCOTCH COLLEGE, Claremont, W. Australia. *Head*, W. R. Dickinson

THE SCOTS COLLEGE, Sydney, NSW. *Head*, Dr R. L. Iles

THE SCOTS SCHOOL, Bathurst, NSW. *Head*, R. D. Fraser

THE SOUTHPORT SCHOOL, Southport, Queensland. *Head*, B. A. Cook

SYDNEY CHURCH OF ENGLAND GRAMMAR SCHOOL, Sydney, NSW. *Head*, R. A. I. Grant

SYDNEY GRAMMAR SCHOOL, Darlinghurst, NSW. *Head*, Dr R. D. Townsend

WESLEY COLLEGE, Melbourne, Victoria. *Head*, D. G. McArthur

WESTBOURNE AND WILLIAMSTOWN GRAMMAR SCHOOLS, Hoppers Crossing, Victoria. *Head*, G. G. Ryan

CANADA

BRENTWOOD COLLEGE SCHOOL, Mill Bay, BC. *Head*, W. T. Ross

GLENLYON-NORFOLK SCHOOL, Victoria, BC. *Head*, D. Brooks

HILLFIELD STRATHALLAN COLLEGE, Hamilton, Ontario. *Head*, W. S. Boyer

PICKERING COLLEGE, Newmarket, Ontario. *Head*, acting head

ST ANDREW'S COLLEGE, Aurora, Ontario. *Head*, R. P. Bedard

TRINITY COLLEGE SCHOOL, Port Hope, Ontario. *Head*, R. C. N. Wright

UPPER CANADA COLLEGE, Toronto, Ontario. *Head*, J. D. Blakey

HONG KONG

ISLAND SCHOOL, Borrett Road. *Head*, D. J. James

KING GEORGE V SCHOOL, Kowloon. *Head*, M. J. Behennah

INDIA

BISHOP COTTON SCHOOL, Shimla. *Head*, K. Mustafi

THE CATHEDRAL AND JOHN CONNON SCHOOL, Bombay. *Head*, D. E. W. Shaw

THE LAWRENCE SCHOOL, Sanawar. *Head*, Dr H. S. Dhillon

THE SCINDIA SCHOOL, Gwalior. *Head*, A. N. Dar

MALAYSIA

KOLEJ TUANKU JA'AFAR, Negeri Sembilan. *Head*, S. Morris

NEW ZEALAND

CHRIST'S COLLEGE, Christchurch. *Head*, Dr M. J. Rosser

KING'S COLLEGE, Auckland. *Head*, J. S. Taylor

ST ANDREW'S COLLEGE, Christchurch. *Head*, B. Maister

THE COLLEGIATE SCHOOL, Wanganui. *Head*, T. S. McKinley

WAITAKI BOYS' HIGH SCHOOL, Oamaru. *Head*, B. R. Gollop

PAKISTAN

AITCHISON COLLEGE, Lahore. *Head*, S. Khan

SOUTH AMERICA

ACADEMIA BRITANICA CUSCATLECA, Santa Tecla, El Salvador. *Head*, R. Braund

THE BRITISH SCHOOLS, Montevideo, Uruguay. *Head*, C. D. T. Smith

MARKHAM COLLEGE, Lima, Peru. *Head*, W. J. Baker

ST ANDREW'S SCOTS SCHOOL, Buenos Aires, Argentina. *Head*, A. G. F. Fisher

ST GEORGE'S COLLEGE, Buenos Aires, Argentina. *Head*, N. P. O. Green

ST PAULS' SCHOOL, São Paulo, Brazil. *Head*, M. T. M. C. McCann

USA

ST MARK'S COLLEGE, Southborough, Massachusetts. *Head*, A. J. de V. Hill

ADDITIONAL MEMBERS

The headteachers of some maintained schools are by invitation Additional Members of the HMC. They include the following:

BISHOP WORDSWORTH'S SCHOOL, Salisbury. *Head*, C. D. Barnett

DURHAM JOHNSTON COMPREHENSIVE SCHOOL, Durham. *Head*, J. Dunford, OBE

EGGBUCKLAND COMMUNITY COLLEGE, Plymouth. *Head*, H. E. Green

HABERDASHERS' ASKE'S HATCHAM COLLEGE, London SE14. *Head*, Dr E. M. Sidwell

HAYWARDS HEATH SIXTH FORM COLLEGE, W. Sussex. *Head*, B. W. Derbyshire

HINCHINGBROOKE SCHOOL, Huntington, Cambs. *Head*, P. J. Downes

THE JUDD SCHOOL, Tonbridge, Kent. *Head*, K. A. Starling

THE LONDON ORATORY SCHOOL, London SW6. *Head*, J. C. McIntosh, OBE

PRESCOT SCHOOL, Prescot, Merseyside. *Head*, P. A. Barlow

PRINCE HENRY'S GRAMMAR SCHOOL, Otley, W Yorks. *Head*, M. Franklin

PRINCE WILLIAM SCHOOL, Oundle, Cambs. *Head*, C. J. Lowe

THE ROYAL GRAMMAR SCHOOL, Lancaster. *Head*, P. J. Mawby

ROYAL GRAMMAR SCHOOL, High Wycombe, Bucks. *Head*, D. R. Levin

ST AMBROSE COLLEGE, Altrincham, Cheshire. *Head*, G. E. Hester

ST ANSELM'S COLLEGE, Birkenhead, Merseyside. *Head*, C. J. Cleugh

ST OLAVE'S GRAMMAR SCHOOL, Orpington, Kent. *Head*, T. Jarvis

SOCIETY OF HEADMASTERS AND HEADMISTRESSES OF INDEPENDENT SCHOOLS

The Society was founded in 1961 and, in general, represents smaller boarding schools.

Secretary, I. D. Cleland, Celedston, Rhosesmor Road, Halkyn, Holywell CH8 8DL. Tel: 01352-781102

Headmasters/mistresses of the following schools are members of both HMC and SHMIS; details of these schools appear in the HMC list: Abbotsholme School, Bedales School, Churcher's College, Colston's Collegiate School, King's School, Gloucester, King's School, Tynemouth, Lord Wandsworth College, Pangbourne College, Reading Blue Coat School, Reed's School, Rendcomb College, Ryde School, St George's College, Silcoates School, Tettenhall College, Wisbech Grammar School, Yarm School

CSC Church Schools Company, Church Schools House, Chapel Street, Titchmarsh, Kettering, Northants NN14 3DA. Tel: 01832-735105

* Woodard Corporation School
† Girls in VI form
‡ Co-educational
° 1996 figures

Name of School	Foun-ded	No. of pupils	Annual fees £		Head (with date of appointment)
			Boarding	Day	
Abbey Gate College, Saighton, Chester	1977	271‡	—	4,440	E. W. Mitchell (1991)
Austin Friars School (RC), Carlisle	1951	307‡	8,748	4,995	Revd D. Middleton (1996)
Battle Abbey School, E. Sussex	1912	120‡	9,900	6,150	D. J. A. Teall (1982)
Bearwood College, Wokingham	1827	225‡	11,100	6,225	Dr R. J. Belcher (1993)
Bedstone College, Bucknell, Shropshire	1948	175‡	11,100	6,006	M. S. Symonds (1990)
Bentham School, N. Yorks	1726	200‡	9,500	4,800	T. Halliwell (1995)
Bethany School, Cranbrook, Kent	1866	298‡	10,458	6,690	N. Dorey (from January 1998)
Birkdale School, Sheffield	1904	530†	—	4,797	Revd M. D. A. Hepworth (1983)
Box Hill School, Dorking	1959	260‡	11,070	6,540	Dr R. A. S. Atwood (1987)
Claremont Fan Court School, Esher	1932	343‡	9,915	6,270	Mrs. P. B. Farrar (*Principal*) (1994)
Clayesmore School, Blandford Forum	1896	296‡	12,105	8,475	D. J. Beeby (1986)
Cokethorpe School, Witney, Oxon	1957	250‡	12,420	8,130	P. J. S. Cantwell (1995)
Duke of York's Royal Military School, Dover	1803	500‡	825	—	Col. G. H. Wilson (1992)
Elmhurst Ballet School, Camberley	1903	80‡	10,470	7,680	J. McNamara (*Principal*) (1995)
Embley Park School, Romsey, Hants	1946	250‡	10,395	6,330	D. F. Chapman (1987)
°Ewell Castle School, Epsom	1926	320†	—	4,635	R. A. Fewtrell (1983)
Friends' School, Saffron Walden	1702	225‡	11,145	6,687	Ms J. Laing (1996)
Fulneck School (Boys), Pudsey, W. Yorks	1753	313	9,540	5,085	Mrs H. Gordon, (*Principal*) (1996)
*Grenville College, Bideford	1954	275‡	11,184	5,484	Dr M. C. V. Cane (1992)
Halliford School, Shepperton, Middx	1956	281†	—	4,950	J. R. Crook (1984)
Hipperholme Grammar School, Halifax	1648	330‡	—	4,020	C. C. Robinson (1988)
Keil School, Dumbarton	1915	168‡	10,509	5,892	J. A. Cummings (1993)
Kingham Hill School, Chipping Norton	1886	225‡	10,440	6,720	M. H. Payne (1990)
Kirkham Grammar School, Preston	1549	570‡	7,995	4,095	B. Stacey (1991)
Langley School, Norwich	1910	247‡	11,235	5,835	J. Malcolm (1997)
Leighton Park School, Reading	1890	380‡	12,195	9,153	J. Dunston (1996)
Lincoln Minster School (CSC)	1905	220‡	7,500	4,800	Mrs M. Bradley (1996)
Lomond School, Helensburgh, Argyll and Bute	1977	300‡	10,305	4,770	A. D. Macdonald (1986)
Milton Abbey School, Blandford Forum	1954	83	12,090	8,070	W. J. Hughes D'Aeth (1995)
Oswestry School, Shropshire	1407	370‡	10,449	6,225	P. K. Smith (1995)
The Purcell School (music), Harrow	1962	144‡	17,988	11,700	K. J. Bain (1983)
Rannoch School, Pitlochry	1959	210‡	11,205	5,880	Dr J. D. Halliday (1997)
Rishworth School, W. Yorks	1724	400‡	10,050	5,190	M. J. Elford (1992)
Royal Russell School, Croydon	1853	500‡	11,040	5,820	Dr J. R. Jennings (1996)
Royal School, Dungannon, N. Ireland	1614	400‡	6,400	3,000	P. D. Hewitt (1986)
Royal Wolverhampton School	1850	305‡	11,073	5,574	Mrs B. A. Evans (1995)
Ruthin School, Denbighshire	1574	161‡	10,785	6,855	J. S. Rowlands (1993)
St Bede's School, Hailsham	1979	480‡	12,450	7,500	R. A. Perrin (1978)
St Christopher School, Letchworth	1915	325‡	11,910	6,750	C. Reid (1981)
St David's College, Llandudno	1965	210	10,884	7,077	W. Seymour (1991)
Scarborough College, N. Yorks	1898	372‡	10,143	5,499	T. L. Kirkup (1996)
Seaford College, Petworth, W. Sussex	1884	310‡	10,830	7,125	T. J. Mullins (1997)
Shebbear College, Devon	1841	230‡	10,290	5,520	L. Clark (1997)
Shiplake College, Henley-on-Thames	1959	290	12,300	8,280	N. V. Bevan (1988)
Sibford School, Banbury	1842	250‡	10,485	5,580	Ms S. Freestone (1997)
Sidcot School, North Somerset	1808	410‡	10,650	6,150	A. Slesser (1997)

Name of School	Foun-ded	No. of pupils	Annual fees £ Boarding	Day	Head (with date of appointment)
°Stafford Grammar School	1982	300‡	—	4,080	M. S. James (1992)
Stanbridge Earls School, Romsey, Hants	1952	190‡	12,660	9,495	H. Moxon (1984)
Sunderland High School (CSC)	1887	263‡	—	4,095	Ms C. Rendle-Short (1994)
Thetford Grammar School, Norfolk	1119	230‡	—	4,596	J. R. Weeks (1990)
°Warminster School, Wilts	1707	290‡	9,690	5,610	T. D. Holgate (1990)
Yehudi Menuhin School (music), Surrey	1963	46‡	varies	—	N. Chisholm (1988)

GIRLS' SCHOOLS ASSOCIATION

THE GIRLS' SCHOOLS ASSOCIATION, 130 Regent Road, Leicester LEI 7PG. Tel: 0116-254 1619
President (from Jan. 1998), Mrs J. Anderson
Secretary, Ms S. Cooper

Headmasters/mistresses of the following schools are members of both HMC and GSA; details of these schools appear in the HMC list: Berkhamsted Collegiate School, Ryde School

CSC Church Schools Company
§ Girls Public Day School Trust, 26 Queen Anne's Gate, London SWIH 9AN. Tel: 0171-222 9595
* Woodard Corporation School
† Boys in VI form
‡ Co-educational
° 1996 figures

Name of School	Foun-ded	No. of pupils	Annual fees £ Boarding	Day	Head (with date of appointment)
ENGLAND AND WALES					
Abbey School, Reading	1887	686	—	4,620	Miss B. C. L. Sheldon (1991)
Abbot's Hill, Hemel Hempstead	1912	153	11,250	6,645	Mrs K. Lewis (1997)
Adcote School for Girls, Shrewsbury	1907	82	10,200	5,850	Mrs A. Read (1997)
Alice Ottley School, Worcester	1883	561	—	5,406	Miss C. Sibbit (1986)
Amberfield School, Ipswich	1952	180	—	3,990	Mrs L. A. Lewis (1992)
Ashford School, Kent	1910	373	12,168	7,002	Mrs J. Burnett (1997)
Atherley School, Southampton (CSC)	1926	250	—	4,707	Miss A. Burrows (1997)
Badminton School, Bristol	1858	300	12,525	6,975	Mrs J. A. Scarrow (1997)
§Bath High School	1875	455	—	4,152	Miss M. A. Winfield (1985)
Bedford High School	1882	730	10,170	5,400	Mrs B. E. Stanley (1995)
Bedgebury School, Goudhurst, Kent	1860	216	11,994	7,449	Mrs L. J. Griffin (1995)
Beechwood Sacred Heart (RC), Tunbridge Wells	1915	138	11,700	7,020	Dr S. Price-Cabrera (1997)
§Belvedere School, Liverpool	1880	480	—	4,152	Mrs G. Richards (1997)
Benenden School, Cranbrook, Kent	1923	440	14,205	—	Mrs G. duCharme (1985)
§Birkenhead High School	1901	671	—	4,152	Mrs C. H. Evans (1997)
§Blackheath High School, London SE3	1880	369	—	4,968	Miss R. K. Musgrave (1989)
Bolton School	1877	801	—	4,626	Miss E. J. Panton (1994)
Bradford Girls' Grammar School	1875	670	—	4,461	Mrs L. J. Warrington (1987)
§Brighton and Hove High School	1876	501	—	4,152	Miss R. A. Woodbridge (1989)
Brigidine School, Windsor	1948	203	—	4,950	Mrs M. B. Cairns (1986)
§Bromley High School, Kent	1883	559	—	4,968	Mrs E. J. Hancock (1989)
Bruton School, Somerset	1900	500	8,265	4,272	Mrs J. M. Wade (1987)
Burgess Hill School, W. Sussex	1906	360	10,125	5,985	Mrs R. F. Lewis (1992)
Bury Grammar School, Lancs	1884	786	—	4,014	Miss J. M. Lawley (1987)
Casterton School, Carnforth, Lancs	1823	315	10,098	6,336	A. F. Thomas (1990)
§Central Newcastle High School	1895	606	—	4,152	Mrs A. M. Chapman (1985)
Channing School, London N6	1885	322	—	6,210	Mrs I. R. Raphael (1984)
Cheltenham Ladies' College, Glos	1853	845	13,545	8,595	Mrs A. V. Tuck (*Principal*) (1996)
City of London School for Girls, London EC2	1894	550	—	5,886	Mrs Y. A. Burne, PH.D. (1995)
Clifton High School, Bristol	1877	387	8,985	4,710	Mrs E. A. Anderson (*acting*) (1997)
Cobham Hall, Kent	1962	200	12,300	8,550	Mrs R. J. McCarthy (1989)
Colston's Girls' School, Bristol	1891	480	—	4,080	Mrs J. P. Franklin (1989)
Combe Bank School, Sevenoaks	1868	190	—	6,390	Miss N. Spurr (1993)
Commonweal Lodge School, Purley, Surrey	1916	120	—	4,815	Mrs S. C. Law (1995)
Cranford House School, Moulsford, Oxon	1931	82	—	5,520	Mrs A. B. Gray (1992)
Croham Hurst School, South Croydon	1899	314	—	5,175	Miss S. C. Budgen (1994)
§Croydon High School	1874	695	—	4,968	Mrs P. E. Davies (1990)
Dame Alice Harpur School, Bedford	1882	730	—	4,992	Mrs R. Randle (1990)

Name of School	Foun-ded	No. of pupils	Annual fees £ Boarding	Day	Head (with date of appointment)
Dame Allan's Girls' School, Newcastle upon Tyne	1705	380†	—	4,011	D. W. Welsh (*Principal*) (1996)
Derby High School for Girls	1892	313	—	4,680	G. H. Goddard, ph.d. (1983)
Downe House, Newbury	1907	630	13,500	9,786	Mrs M. McKendrick (1997)
Dunottar School, Reigate	1926	274	—	5,340	Ms M. J. Skinner (1997)
Durham High School for Girls	1884	260	—	5,460	Miss M. L. Walters (1992)
Edgbaston Church of England College, Birmingham	1886	249	—	4,785	Mrs A. Varley-Tipton (1992)
Edgbaston High School for Girls, Birmingham	1876	512	—	4,620	Miss E. Mullenger (from January 1998)
Edgehill College, Bideford	1884	308‡	10,740	5,880	Mrs E. M. Burton (1987)
Elmslie Girls' School, Blackpool	1918	155	—	4,620	Miss S J Woodward (1997)
Farlington School, Horsham	1896	243	10,455	6,450	Mrs P. M. Mawer (1992)
Farnborough Hill, Hants	1889	527	—	5,163	Miss R. McGeoch (1996)
Farringtons and Stratford House, Chislehurst	1911	300	10,914	5,595	Mrs B. J. Stock (1987)
Francis Holland School, London NW1	1878	380	—	5,955	Mrs P. H. Parsonson (1988)
Francis Holland School, London SW1	1881	205	—	6,675	Miss S. Pattenden (1997)
Gateways School, Harewood, W. Yorks	1941	200	—	3,870	Mrs D. Davidson (1997)
Godolphin and Latymer School, London W6	1905	700	—	6,630	Miss M. Rudland (1986)
Godolphin School, Salisbury	1726	400	11,886	7,119	Miss J. Horsburgh (1996)
Greenacre School, Banstead	1933	226	—	5,475	Mrs P. M. Wood (1990)
Guildford High School (*CSC*)	1888	540	—	5,685	Mrs S. H. Singer (1991)
Haberdashers' Aske's School for Girls, Elstree, Herts	1873	830	—	4,674	Mrs P. Penney (1991)
Haberdashers' Monmouth School	1891	563	9,192	4,881	Dr B. Despontin (1997)
Harrogate Ladies' College	1893	350	10,170	6,570	Dr M. J. Hustler (1996)
Headington School, Oxford	1915	517	10,338	5,415	Mrs H. A. Fender (1996)
Heathfield School, Ascot, Berks	1900	220	13,800	—	Mrs J. M. Benammar (1992)
§Heathfield School, Pinner, Middx	1900	309	—	4,968	Miss C. M. Juett (1997)
Hethersett Old Hall School, Norwich	1928	201	9,975	5,025	Mrs V. M. Redington (1983)
Highclare School, Birmingham	1932	170†	—	4,650	Mrs C. A. Hanson (1974)
Hollygirt School, Nottingham	1877	230	—	3,945	Mrs M. I. Connolly (1997)
Holy Child School, Birmingham	1933	149	—	4,914	Mrs J. M. C. Hill (1994)
Holy Trinity College, Bromley	1886	256	—	4,695	Mrs D. A. Bradshaw (1994)
Holy Trinity School, Kidderminster	1903	168	—	4,020	Mrs S. M. Bell (1990)
Howell's School, Denbigh	1859	193	10,485	7,185	Mrs M. Steel (1991)
§Howell's School, Llandaff, Cardiff	1860	566	—	4,152	Mrs C. J. Fitz (1991)
Hull High School (*CSC*)	1890	146	—	4,311	Mrs M. A. Benson (1994)
Hulme Grammar School, Oldham	1895	529	—	3,912	Miss M. S. Smolenski (1992)
Ilford Ursuline High School, Essex	1903	360	—	4,896	Miss J. Reddington (1990)
§Ipswich High School	1878	448	—	4,152	Miss V. C. MacCuish (1993)
James Allen's Girls' School, London SE22	1741	740	—	6,111	Mrs M. Gibbs (1994)
Kent College, Tunbridge Wells	1885	239	12,120	7,200	Miss B. J. Crompton (1990)
King Edward VI High School for Girls, Birmingham	1883	550	—	4,725	Ms S. H. Evans (1996)
King's High School for Girls, Warwick	1879	550	—	4,620	Mrs J. M. Anderson (1987)
Kingsley School, Leamington Spa	1884	460	—	4,725	Mrs Mannion Watson (1997)
Lady Eleanor Holles School, Hampton, Middx	1711	710	—	5,850	Miss E. M. Candy (1981)
°La Retraite School, Salisbury	1953	120	—	4,815	Mrs R. A. Simmons (1994)
La Sagesse Convent High School, Newcastle upon Tyne	1906	350	—	4,149	Miss L. Clark (1994)
Lavant House Rosemead School, Chichester	1919	110	10,950	6,135	Mrs S. E. Watkins (1996)
Leeds Girls' High School	1876	610	—	4,836	Mrs S. Fishburn (1997)
Leicester High School	1906	303	—	4,725	Mrs P. A. Watson (1992)
Loughborough High School	1850	540	—	4,428	Miss J. E. L. Harvatt (1978)
°Luckley-Oakfield School, Wokingham	1895	240	8,349	5,175	R. C. Blake (1984)
Malvern Girls' College, Worcs	1893	460	13,815	9,480	Mrs P. Leggate (1996)
Manchester High School	1874	733‡	—	4,395	Miss E. M. Diggory (1994)
Manor House School, Little Bookham, Surrey	1927	130	8,190	5,640	Mrs L. Mendes (1989)
Marymount International School, Kingston upon Thames	1955	210	14,800	8,600	Sr R. Sheridan (1990)
Maynard School, Exeter	1877	484	—	4,680	Miss F. Murdin (1980)
Merchant Taylors' School, Liverpool	1888	660	—	4,122	Mrs J. I. Mills (1994)
Moira House School, Eastbourne	1875	230	12,090	7,800	Mrs A. Harris (*Principal*) (1997)
More House School, London SW1	1953	200	—	5,910	Miss M. Connell (1991)

Name of School	Foun-ded	No. of pupils	Annual fees £		Head (with date of appointment)
			Boarding	Day	
Moreton Hall, Oswestry	1913	280	12,600	8,700	J. Forster (1992)
Mount School, York	1831	260	10,794	6,645	Miss B. J. Windle (1986)
Newcastle upon Tyne Church High School	1885	379	—	4,185	Mrs L. G. Smith (1996)
New Hall School, Chelmsford	1642	430	11,370	7,275	Sr Anne-Marie (1996)
Northampton High School	1878	595	—	4,425	Mrs L. A. Mayne (1988)
North Foreland Lodge, Hook	1909	150	11,550	7,050	Miss S. Cameron (1996)
North London Collegiate School, Edgware	1850	760	—	5,424	Mrs B. McCabe (1997)
Northwood College, Middx	1878	447	—	5,172	Mrs J. A. Mayou (1991)
§Norwich High School	1875	657	—	4,152	Mrs V. C. Bidwell (1985)
Notre Dame Senior School, Cobham, Surrey	1937	300	—	5,025	Sr F. Ede (1987)
§Nottingham High School for Girls	1875	843	—	4,152	Mrs A. C. Rees (1996)
§Notting Hill and Ealing High School, London W13	1873	562	—	4,968	Mrs S. M. Whitfield (1991)
Ockbrook School, Derby	1799	470	7,755	4,200	Miss D. P. Bolland (1995)
Old Palace School, Croydon	1887	599	—	4,572	Miss K. L. Hilton (1974)
§Oxford High School	1875	557	—	4,152	Miss F. Lusk (1997)
Palmers Green High School, London N21	1905	136	—	4,950	Mrs S. Grant (1989)
Parsons Mead, Ashtead, Surrey	1897	230	9,270	5,280	Miss E. B. Plant (1990)
Perse School for Girls, Cambridge	1881	540	—	5,172	Miss H. S. Smith (1989)
*Peterborough High School	1939	200	9,279	4,620	Mrs A. J. V. Storey (1977)
°Pipers Corner School, High Wycombe	1930	300	9,702	5,808	Mrs V. M. Staltensfield (1996)
Polam Hall School, Darlington	1848	320	9,618	4,704	Mrs H. C. Hamilton (1986)
§Portsmouth High School	1882	473	—	4,152	Mrs J. M. Dawtrey (1984)
Princess Helena College, Hitchin, Herts	1820	145	10,935	7,605	Mrs A. M. Hodgkiss (acting) (1997)
Prior's Field, Godalming	1902	230	10,905	7,290	Mrs J. M. McCallum (1987)
§Putney High School, London SW15	1893	552	—	4,968	Mrs E. Merchant (1991)
Queen Anne's School, Reading	1698	320	12,465	8,160	Mrs D. Forbes (1993)
Queen Ethelburga's College, York	1912	200	11,997	7,797	Mrs E. I. E. Taylor (1997)
Queen Margaret's School, York	1901	365	11,316	7,170	Dr G. A. H. Chapman (1992)
Queen Mary School, Lytham St Anne's	1930	470	—	4,062	Miss M. C. Ritchie (1981)
Queen's College, London W1	1848	385	—	6,600	Lady Goodhart (1991)
Queen's Gate School, London SW7	1891	240	—	5,625	Mrs A. M. Holyoak (Principal) (1989)
Queen's School, Chester	1878	470	—	4,725	Miss D. M. Skilbeck (1989)
Queenswood, Hatfield, Herts	1894	420	11,985	7,392	Ms C. Farr (Principal) (1996)
Redland High School for Girls, Bristol	1882	478	—	4,431	Mrs C. Lear (1989)
Red Maids' School, Bristol	1634	505	8,160	4,080	Miss S. Hampton (1987)
Roedean School, Brighton	1885	404	14,325	8,700	Mrs P. Metham (1997)
Royal Masonic School, Herts	1788	530	9,030	5,496	Mrs I. M. Andrews (1992)
§The Royal School, Bath	1864	203	11,001	5,886	Mrs C. Edmundson (1997)
Rydal Penrhos School (Girls), Colwyn Bay	1880	220	10,205	6,993	C. M. J. Allen (1993)
Rye St Antony School (RC), Oxford	1930	330	9,150	5,460	Miss A. M. Jones (1990)
St Albans High School	1889	558	—	5,370	Mrs C. Y. Daly (1994)
St Andrew's School, Bedford	1897	150	—	4,290	Mrs J. M. Mark (1995)
St Anne's School, Windermere	1863	220	10,020	6,810	R. D. Hunter (1996)
St Antony's-Leweston School (RC), Sherborne	1891	285	11,700	7,638	Miss B. A. King (1996)
St Catherine's School, Guildford	1885	481	10,350	6,300	Mrs C. M. Oulton (1994)
St David's School, Ashford, Middx	1716	250	10,110	5,694	Mrs J. G. Osborne (1985)
°St Dunstan's Abbey School, Plymouth	1850	180	8,652	4,860	R. A. Bye (1990)
St Elphin's School, Matlock	1844	170	10,545	6,141	Mrs V. E. Fisher (1994)
St Felix School, Southwold, Suffolk	1897	200	11,550	7,650	Mrs S. Roberts (acting) (1997)
St Francis' College (RC), Letchworth	1933	180	10,965	5,625	Miss M. Hegarty (1993)
St Gabriel's School, Newbury	1929	152	—	5,385	D. J. Cobb (1990)
St George's School, Ascot, Berks	1923	286	12,750	7,350	Mrs A. M. Griggs (1989)
School of St Helen and St Katharine, Abingdon	1903	520	—	4,962	Mrs C. L. Hall (1993)
St Helen's School, Northwood, Middx	1899	620	10,101	5,361	Mrs D. M. Jefkins (1995)
*St Hilary's School, Alderley Edge	1880	120	—	4,410	Ms P. Bristow (1997)
St James' and the Abbey, West Malvern	1896	170	12,366	7,722	Mrs S. Kershaw (from January 1998)
St Joseph's Convent School (RC), Reading	1909	378	—	4,350	Mrs V. Brookes (1990)
St Leonards-Mayfield School, Mayfield	1850	505	11,511	7,674	Sr J. Sinclair (1980)
St Margaret's School, Bushey, Herts	1749	360	9,885	5,925	Miss M. de Villiers (1992)
*St Margaret's School, Exeter	1904	380	—	4,542	Mrs M. D'Albertanson (1993)
St Martin's School, Solihull	1941	235	—	4,935	Mrs S. J. Williams (1988)

Name of School	Foun-ded	No. of pupils	Annual fees £		Head (with date of appointment)
			Boarding	Day	
°*School of S. Mary and S. Anne, Abbots Bromley, Staffs	1874	227	11,205	7,485	A. J. Grigg (1989)
°St Mary's Convent School, Worcester	1934	220	—	3,780	Miss G. Morrissey (1995)
St Mary's Hall, Brighton	1836	241	9,315	5,958	Mrs S. M. Meek (1997)
°St Mary's School (RC), Ascot, Berks	1885	338	12,246	7,705	Sr M. F. Orchard (1982)
St Mary's School, Calne, Wilts	1872	290	12,840	7,635	Mrs C. Shaw (1996)
St Mary's School, Cambridge	1898	520	8,025	4,485	Ms M. Conway (1989)
Sr Mary's School, Colchester	1908	197	—	4,185	Mrs G. M. G. Mouser (1981)
°St Mary's School, Gerrards Cross	1872	160	—	5,615	Mrs F. Balcombe (1995)
St Mary's School (RC), Shaftesbury	1945	313	10,590	6,870	Sr M. Campion Livesey (1985)
St Mary's School, Wantage, Oxon	1873	225	12,300	8,200	Mrs S. Bodinham (1994)
St Maur's Senior School, Weybridge	1898	372	—	4,800	Mrs M. F. Dodds (1991)
St Nicholas' School, Fleet, Hants	1935	161	—	4,290	Mrs A. V. Whatmough (1995)
St Paul's Girls' School, London w6	1904	640	—	6,993	Miss J. Gough (High Mistress) (1992)
St Swithun's School, Winchester	1884	460	12,075	7,290	Dr H. Harvey (1995)
St Teresa's School, Dorking	1928	330	10,800	6,000	Mrs M. E. Prescott (1997)
§Sheffield High School	1878	563	—	4,152	Mrs M. A. Houston (1989)
Sherborne School for Girls, Dorset	1899	414	12,960	9,060	Miss J. M. Taylor (1985)
§Shrewsbury High School	1885	386	—	4,152	Miss S. Gardner (1990)
Sir William Perkins's School, Chertsey, Surrey	1725	580	—	4,530	Miss S. Ross (1994)
§South Hampstead High School, London NW3	1876	612	—	4,968	Mrs J. G. Scott (1993)
Stamford High School, Lincs	1876	704	9,048	4,524	Mrs P. J. Clark (1997)
Stonar School, Melksham, Wilts	1921	428	10,260	5,685	Mrs C. Homan (1997)
Stover School, Newton Abbot	1932	190	9,300	4,785	P. E. Bujak (1994)
§Streatham Hill and Clapham High School, London sw2	1887	419	—	4,968	Miss G. M. Ellis (1979)
Surbiton High School, Kingston-upon-Thames (CSC)	1884	612	—	5,115	Miss M. G. Perry (1993)
§Sutton High School, Surrey	1884	510	—	4,968	Mrs A. J. Coutts (1995)
§Sydenham High School, London se26	1887	471	—	4,968	Mrs G. Baker (1988)
Talbot Heath, Bournemouth	1886	420	9,630	5,520	Mrs C. Dipple (1991)
Teesside High School, Stockton-on Tees	1970	370	—	4,032	Miss J. F. Hamilton (1995)
Tormead School, Guildford	1905	503	—	5,670	Mrs H. E. M. Alleyne (1992)
Truro High School	1880	341	8,817	4,797	J. Graham-Brown (1992)
Tudor Hall School, Banbury	1850	264	11,280	7,032	Miss N. Godfrey (1984)
Wakefield Girls' High School	1878	713†	—	4,674	Mrs P. A. Langham (1987)
Walthamstow Hall, Sevenoaks	1838	300	13,290	7,170	Mrs J. S. Lang (1984)
Wentworth College, Bournemouth	1871	245	9,750	6,114	Miss S. D. Coe (1990)
Westfield School, Newcastle upon Tyne	1962	220	—	4,698	Mrs M. Farndale (1990)
West Heath, Sevenoaks	1867	105	12,600	7,200	Mrs A. Williamson (Principal) (1994)
Westholme School, Blackburn	1923	660	—	3,690	Mrs L. Croston (Principal) (1988)
Westonbirt School, Tetbury, Glos	1928	220	11,991	7,878	Mrs G. Hylson-Smith (1986)
§Wimbledon High School, London sw19	1880	578	—	4,968	Dr J. L. Clough (1995)
°Wispers School, Haslemere, Surrey	1946	120	9,507	6,117	L. H. Beltran (1980)
Withington Girls' School, Manchester	1890	525	—	4,125	Mrs M. Kenyon (1986)
Woldingham School, Surrey	1842	550	12,009	7,263	Mrs M. M. Ribbins (1997)
Wychwood School, Oxford	1897	160	7,470	4,710	Mrs S. Wingfield Digby (1997)
Wycombe Abbey School, High Wycombe	1896	523	13,500	10,125	Mrs J. M. Goodland (1989)
Wykeham House School, Fareham, Hants	1913	150	—	4,266	Mrs R. M. Kamaryc (1995)

SCOTLAND

Name of School	Foun-ded	No. of pupils	Annual fees £		Head (with date of appointment)
Kilgraston School, Bridge of Earn, Perth	1930	190	10,965	6,315	Mrs J. L. Austin (1993)
Mary Erskine School, Edinburgh	1694	668	9,060	4,530	P. F. J. Tobin (Principal) (1989)
St Denis and Cranley School, Edinburgh	1858	100	9,600	4,800	Mrs S. Duncanson (1996)
St George's School, Edinburgh	1888	560	9,225	4,725	Dr J. McClure (1994)
St Leonards School, St Andrews	1877	270‡	13,110	6,930	Mrs M. James (1988)
St Margaret's School, Aberdeen	1846	220	—	4,200	Miss L. M. Ogilvie (1989)
St Margaret's School, Edinburgh	1890	350	9,240	4,515	Miss A. Mitchell (1994)

CHANNEL ISLANDS

Name of School	Foun-ded	No. of pupils	Annual fees £		Head (with date of appointment)
The Ladies' College, Guernsey	1872	350	—	2,340	Miss M. E. Macdonald (Principal) (1992)

Social Welfare

National Health Service
and Local Authority Personal Social Services

The National Health Service came into being on 5 July 1948 as a result of the National Health Service Act 1946, covering England and Wales, and separate legislation for Scotland and Northern Ireland. The Acts placed a duty on the relevant Secretaries of State to promote the establishment of a comprehensive health service designed to secure improvement in the mental and physical health of the people and the prevention, diagnosis and treatment of illness. The National Health Service is administered in England by the Secretary of State for Health, and in Wales, Scotland and Northern Ireland by the Secretaries of State for Wales, Scotland and Northern Ireland.

The National Health Service covers a comprehensive range of hospital, specialist, family practitioner (medical, dental, ophthalmic and pharmaceutical), artificial limb and appliance, ambulance, and community health services. Everyone normally resident in the UK is entitled to use any of these services without charge, except where charges are specifically provided for by statute, e.g. prescriptions.

In addition, the Secretary of State for Health is responsible under the Local Authority Social Services Act 1970 for the provision by local authorities of social services for the elderly, the disabled, those with mental disorders and for families and children.

The NHS is financed mainly from taxation and the cost met from moneys voted by Parliament. The estimated level of expenditure in 1997–8 is £44,200 million.

STRUCTURE

The National Health Service and Community Care Act 1990 reformed management and patient care. The Act provided for more streamlined Regional and District Health Authorities and Family Health Services Authorities, and for the establishment of NHS Trusts, which operate as self-governing health care providers. One result of the Act is that health care is provided through NHS contracts, where one body (the purchaser) is responsible for obtaining the appropriate health care for its population from another body (the provider). From 1 April 1993, the Community Care Reforms introduced changes in the way care is administered for the elderly, the mentally ill, the physically handicapped and people with learning disabilities.

The eight Regional Health Authorities were abolished from 1 April 1996 and replaced by eight regional offices which, together with the headquarters in Leeds, form the NHS Executive. The regional offices are part of the Civil Service, and their functions include financial and performance monitoring of local purchasers and providers, public health, and regional research and development and education programmes.

From April 1996, 100 new Health Authorities (HAs) replaced the previous structure of 105 District Health Authorities and 90 Family Health Service Authorities. The new HAs are responsible for health and health services in their areas. They are also responsible for assessing the health care needs of the local population and developing integrated strategies for meeting these needs in partnership with GPs and in consultation with the public, hospitals and others. HAs' resources are allocated by the NHS

Executive headquarters, to which they are also accountable for their performance.

The new Labour Government has said that it intends to replace the NHS internal market and will issue a white paper in autumn 1997.

HEALTH SERVICES

FAMILY DOCTOR SERVICE

In England and Wales the Family Doctor Service (or General Medical Services) was managed by 90 Family Health Services Authorities (FHSAs) which also organized the general dental, pharmaceutical and ophthalmic services for their areas. These functions are now the responsibility of the Health Authorities (HAs). In England the chairman is appointed by the Secretary of State and the non-executive members by the regional offices of the NHS Executive. In Wales the chairman and non-executive members are appointed by the Secretary of State.

Any doctor may take part in the Family Doctor Service (provided the area in which he/she wishes to practise has not already an adequate number of doctors) and about 28,000 general practitioners in England and Wales do so. They may at the same time have private fee-paying patients. Family doctors are paid for their NHS work in accordance with a scheme of remuneration which includes a basic practice allowance, capitation fees, reimbursement of certain practice expenses and payments for out-of-hours work.

The National Health Service and Community Care Act 1990 enables general practitioner practices to apply for fundholding status. This makes the practice responsible for its own NHS budget for a specified range of goods and services. Since 1 April 1996 there have been two types of general practitioner fundholding: Standard fundholders, for practices with at least 5,000 patients, who purchase a full range of in- and out-patient services; and Community fundholders, for whom there is no minimum list size, who purchase only community nursing services and diagnostic tests. There are currently 3,481 fundholding units, comprising 4,243 practices. Fundholding practices are monitored by the HAs on behalf of the NHS Executive regional offices.

Everyone aged 16 or over can choose their doctor (parents or guardians choose for children under 16) and the doctor is also free to accept a person or not as he or she chooses. Should a patient have difficulty in registering with a doctor, HAs have powers to assign the patient to a general practitioner. A person may change their doctor if they wish, by going to the surgery of a general practioner of their choice who is willing to accept them, and either handing in their medical card to register or filling in a form. When people are away from home they can still use the Family Doctor Service if they ask to be treated as temporary residents, and in an emergency, if a person's own doctor is not available, any doctor in the service will give treatment and advice.

Patients are treated either in the doctor's surgery, primary care emergency centres or, when necessary, at home. Doctors may prescribe for their patients all drugs and medicines which are medically necessary for their treatment and also a certain number of surgical appliances (the more elaborate being provided through hospitals).

DENTAL SERVICE

Dentists, like doctors, may take part in the NHS and also have private patients. About 16,000 dentists in England provide NHS general dental services. They are responsible to the HAs in whose areas they provide services.

Patients are free to go to any dentist who is taking part in the NHS and willing to accept them. Dentists receive payment for items of treatment for individual adult patients and, in addition, a continuing care payment for those registered with them.

Patients are asked to pay 80 per cent of the cost of NHS dental treatment. The maximum charge for a course of treatment is £330. There is no charge for arrest of bleeding, repairs to dentures, home visits by the dentist or re-opening a surgery in an emergency (in these two cases, payment will be for treatment given in the normal way). The following are exempt from dental charges/have charges remitted:

(i)   young people under 18
(ii)   full-time students under 19
(iii)   women who were pregnant when accepted for treatment
(iv)   women who have had a child in the previous 12 months
(v)   people or the partners of people who receive income support, family credit, disability working allowance or income-based jobseeker's allowance

Leaflet HC11 available from post offices and local social security offices explains how other people on a low income can, depending on their financial circumstances, get free treatment or help with charges.

PHARMACEUTICAL SERVICE

Patients may obtain medicines, appliances and oral contraceptives prescribed under the NHS from any pharmacy whose owner has entered into arrangements with the HA to provide this service. Almost all pharmacy owners have done so and display notices that they dispense under the NHS; the number of these pharmacies in England and Wales in September 1996 was about 10,500. There are also some appliance suppliers who only provide special appliances. In rural areas where access to a pharmacy may be difficult, patients may be able to obtain medicines, etc., from their doctor.

Except for contraceptives (for which there is no charge), a charge of £5.65 is payable for each item supplied unless the patient is exempt and the declaration on the back of the prescription form is completed. Exemptions cover:

(i)   children under 16
(ii)   those under 19 and in full-time education
(iii)   men and women aged 60 and over
(iv)   pregnant women
(v)   women who have had a baby within the last 12 months
(vi)   people suffering from certain medical conditions
(vii)   people who receive income support or family credit and their dependants
(viii)   people who receive disability working allowance and their partners
(ix)   people who receive income-based jobseeker's allowance, and their partners
(x)   people who hold an HC2 certificate issued by the Health Benefits Division, and their dependants
(xi)   war pensioners (for their accepted disablements)

Prepayment certificates (£29.30 valid for four months, £80.50 valid for a year) may be purchased by those patients not entitled to exemption who require frequent prescriptions. Further information about the exemption and prepayment arrangements is given in leaflet HC11.

GENERAL OPHTHALMIC SERVICES

General Ophthalmic Services, which are administered by HAs, form part of the ophthalmic services available under the NHS. The NHS sight test is available free to:

(i)   children under 16
(ii)   full-time students under the age of 19
(iii)   people in receipt of income support, income-based jobseeker's allowance or family credit, and their partners
(iv)   people in receipt of disability working allowance and their partners
(v)   people prescribed complex lenses
(vi)   the registered blind and partially sighted
(vii)   diagnosed diabetic and glaucoma patients
(viii)   close relatives aged 40 or over of diagnosed glaucoma patients

Those on a low income may qualify for help with the cost.

Certain groups are automatically entitled to help with the purchase of glasses under an NHS voucher scheme:

(i)   children under 16
(ii)   full-time students under 19
(iii)   people in receipt of income support, income-based jobseeker's allowance or family credit, and their partners
(iv)   people in receipt of disability working allowance and their partners
(v)   people wearing certain complex lenses
(vi)   people whose spectacles are lost or damaged as a result of their disability, injury or illness

The value of the voucher depends on the lenses required. Vouchers may be used to help pay for the glasses or contact lenses of the patient's choice. People with a low income may claim help on form HC1. Glasses or contact lenses should not be purchased until the result of a claim is known as no refunds can be given. Booklet HC11 gives further details.

Diagnosis and specialist treatment of eye conditions is available through the Hospital Eye Service as well as the provision of glasses of a special type.

Testing of sight may be carried out by any ophthalmic medical practitioner or ophthalmic optician. The optician must give the prescription, and a voucher if eligible, to the patient who can take this to any supplier of glasses of his/her choice to have dispensed. However, only registered opticians can supply glasses to children and to people registered as blind or partially sighted.

PRIMARY HEALTH CARE SERVICES

Primary health care services include the general medical, dental, ophthalmic and pharmaceutical services. They also include community services run by HAs, health centres and clinics, family planning outside the hospital service, and preventive activities in the community including vaccination, immunization and fluoridation.

The district nursing and health visiting services include community psychiatric nursing for mentally ill people living outside hospital, and school nursing for the health surveillance of schoolchildren of all ages. Ante- and postnatal care and chiropody are also an integral part of the primary health care service.

COMMUNITY CHILD HEALTH SERVICES

Pre-school services at GP surgeries or child health clinics provide regular surveillance of children's physical, mental and emotional health and development, and advice to parents on their children's health and welfare.

The School Health Service provides for the medical and dental examination of schoolchildren, and advises the local education authority, the school, the parents and the pupil of any health factors which may require special consideration during the pupil's school life. GPs are increasingly undertaking child health surveillance to improve the preventive health care of children.

Hospitals and Other Services

The Secretary of State for Health has a duty to provide, to such extent as he/she considers necessary to meet all reasonable requirements, hospital and other accommodation; medical, dental, nursing and ambulance services; other facilities for the care of expectant and nursing mothers and young children; facilities for the prevention of illness and the care and after-care of persons suffering from illness; and such other services as are required for the diagnosis and treatment of illness. Rehabilitation services (occupational therapy, physiotherapy and speech therapy) may also be provided for those who need it and surgical and medical appliances are supplied in appropriate cases. NHS services and equipment should be free of charge unless current legislation on prescriptions states otherwise.

Specialists and consultants who work in the NHS can engage in private practice, including the treatment of their private patients in NHS hospitals. Any private work a consultant does is additional to NHS duties.

Trusts

The National Health Service and Community Care Act 1990 enables hospitals and other providers of health care to become independent of health authority control as self-governing NHS Trusts run by boards of directors. The Trusts derive their income principally from contracts to provide health services to health authorities and fund-holding general practitioners. As at April 1996 there were 429 trusts, representing the majority of hospitals in England.

Charges

In a number of hospitals, accommodation is available for the treatment of private in-patients who undertake to pay the full costs of hospital accommodation and services and (usually) separate medical fees to a specialist as well. The amount of the medical fees is a matter for agreement between doctor and patient. Hospital charges for private in-patients are set locally at a commercial rate.

Certain hospitals have accommodation in single rooms or small wards which, if not required for patients who need privacy for medical reasons, may be made available to patients who desire it as an amenity for a small charge. These patients are still NHS patients and are treated as such.

There is no charge for drugs supplied to NHS hospital in-patients but out-patients pay £5.65 an item unless they are exempt.

With certain exceptions, hospital out-patients have to pay fixed charges for dentures, contact lenses and certain appliances. Glasses may be obtained either from the hospital or an optician and the charge will be related to the type of lens prescribed and the choice of frame.

PERSONAL SOCIAL SERVICES

Local authorities are responsible for personal social services within their area. Each authority has a Director of Social Services and a Social Services Committee responsible for the social services functions placed upon them by the Local Authority Social Services Act 1970.

FINANCE

ENGLAND

Cost of National Health and Personal Social Services 1995

	£ million
All services	41,839
Central government services: total	33,266
Central administration	217
Health Authorities, current	24,176
Health Authorities, capital	409
Family Health Services Authorities:	
Administration and related services	82
General medical	1,902
Pharmaceutical	2,953
General dental	1,281
General ophthalmic	213
Other	2,032
Personal social services	8,573

Source: The Stationery Office – *Health and Personal Social Services Statistics for England 1996*

WALES

Central Government Support for Health and Personal Social Services 1994–5[*]

	£ thousand
Total	2,341,254
District Health Authorities	1,326,096
NHS Trusts	136,084
General medical	117,863
Pharmaceutical	218,468
General dental	70,424
General ophthalmic	15,910
Welfare foods	13,983
Other	435,101

[*] Excludes local authority expenditure on personal social services funded through general grants
Source: Welsh Office – *Digest of Welsh Statistics 1996*

SCOTLAND

Net Costs of the National Health Service 1995–6

	£ thousand
Total cost	4,391,825
Central administration	7,651
Total NHS cost	4,384,174
NHS contributions	452,536
Net costs to Exchequer	3,931,638
Health Board administration	95,274
Hospital and community health services	3,160,044
Family practitioner services	914,012
Central health services	145,943
State hospital	21,563
Training	3,243
Research	10,234
Disabled services	2,247
Welfare foods	14,434
Miscellaneous health services	17,180

Source: Scottish Office – *Annual Abstract of Statistics 1996*

EMPLOYEES

Health and Personal Social Services Workforce 1995 (*Great Britain*)

General medical practitioners	34,421*
General dental practitioners	18,736
Ophthalmic medical practitioners	752
Ophthalmic opticians	7,445
Medical staff	60,172
Dental staff	3,070
Nursing and midwifery staff	421,648
Professional and technical staff	114,720
Administrative and clerical staff	190,529
Ancillary, works and maintenance staff	102,669
Ambulance staff	21,619
Other Health Service staff	3,518
†Personal social services staff	233,861

*1994 figure
†England only
Source: The Stationery Office – *Annual Abstract of Statistics 1997*

NUMBER OF BEDS AND PATIENT ACTIVITY

ENGLAND AND WALES 1994

	England	*Wales*
In-patients:		
Average daily available beds	212,000	16,800
Average daily occupation of beds	n/a	12,900
Persons waiting for admission at 31 March	1,065,000	61,000
Day-case admissions	2,474,000	240,000
Ordinary admissions	8,065,000	513,400
Out-patient attendances:		
New patients	10,363,000	638,300
Total attendances	39,306,000	2,587,700
Accident and emergency:		
New patients	11,943,000	763,300
Total attendances	13,812,000	960,600
Family Health Services:		
Number of patients per doctor	1,900	1,739
Prescriptions dispensed	422,600,000	35,800,000
NHS sight tests conducted	6,383,000	421,000
Pairs of glasses paid for by FHSAs	3,741,000	268,000
Number of adult courses of dental treatment	24,913,000	1,369,000

n/a not available

SCOTLAND 1994

In-patients:	
Average available staffed beds	44,200
Average occupied beds	35,900
Out-patient attendances:	
New patients	2,503,000
Total attendances	6,145,000
Primary care services:	
Average number of patients per principal doctor	1,524
Prescriptions dispensed	49,270,000
NHS sight tests conducted	614,000
Pairs of glasses supplied	473,000
Number of courses of dental treatment completed	2,723,000

Source: The Stationery Office – *Annual Abstract of Statistics 1997*

National Insurance and Related Cash Benefits

NB All leaflets referred to in this section can be obtained from local social security offices unless an alternative source is given

The state insurance and assistance schemes, comprising schemes of national insurance and industrial injuries insurance, national assistance, and non-contributory old age pensions, came into force from 5 July 1948. The Ministry of Social Security Act 1966 replaced national assistance and non-contributory old age pensions with a scheme of non-contributory benefits. These and sub-sequent measures relating to social security provision in Great Britain were consolidated by the Social Security Act 1975, the Social Security (Consequential Provisions) Act 1975, and the Industrial Injuries and Diseases (Old Cases) Act 1975. Corresponding measures were passed for Northern Ireland. The Social Security Pensions Act 1975 introduced a new state pensions scheme in 1978, and the graduated pension scheme 1961 to 1975 has been wound up, existing rights being preserved. Under the Pensions Act 1995 the age of retirement is to be 65 for both men and women, this being phased in between 2010 and 6 April 2020. The Pensioners' Payments and Social Security Act 1979 provided for a Christmas bonus for pensioners in 1979 and in succeeding years. The Child Benefit Act 1975 replaced family allowances (introduced 1946) with child benefit and one-parent benefit. Some of this legislation has been superseded by the provisions of the Social Security Acts 1969 to 1992.

NATIONAL INSURANCE SCHEME

The National Insurance (NI) scheme operates under the Social Security Contributions and Benefits Act 1992 and the Social Security Administration Act 1992, and orders and regulations made thereunder. The scheme is financed by contributions payable by earners, employers and others (*see* below) and by a Treasury grant. Money collected under the scheme is used to finance the National Insurance Fund (from which contributory benefits are paid) and to contribute to the cost of the National Health Service.

NATIONAL INSURANCE FUND

Approximate receipts and payments of the National Insurance Fund for the year ended 31 March 1996 were:

Receipts	£'000
Balance, 1 April 1995	6,827,599
Contributions under the Social Security Acts (net of SSP and SMP)	40,008,370
Treasury grant	3,575,000
Compensation from Consolidated Fund for SSP and SMP recoveries	458,000
Income from investments	444,434
Other receipts	96,912
	51,410,315

Payments	£'000	£'000
Unemployment benefit	1,101,827	
Sickness benefit	12,000	
Invalidity benefit	271,000	
Incapacity benefit	7,622,940	
Maternity allowance	28,557	
Widow's benefit	1,016,385	
Guardian's allowance and child's special allowance	1,721	
Retirement pension	29,962,569	
Pensioners' lump sum payments	124,179	40,141,178
Personal pensions		1,960,996
Transfers to Northern Ireland		125,000
Administration		1,179,841
Other payments		14,174
Redundancy payments		153,297
Balance, 31 March 1996		7,835,829
		51,410,315

CONTRIBUTIONS

There are five classes of NI contributions:

Class 1   paid by employees and their employers
Class 1A paid by employers who provide employees with cars/fuel for private use
Class 2   paid by self-employed people
Class 3   voluntary contributions paid to protect entitle-ment to certain benefits
Class 4   paid by the self-employed on their taxable profits over a set limit

The lower and upper earnings limits and the percentage rates referred to below apply from 6 April 1997 to 5 April 1998.

CLASS 1

Class 1 contributions are paid where a person:
– is an employed earner (employee) or office holder (e.g. company director)
– is 16 or over and under state pension age
– earns at or above the lower earning limit of £62.00 per week (including overtime pay, bonus, commission, etc., without deduction of superannuation contributions)
Class 1 contributions are not paid where a person earns less than the lower earnings limit.

Class 1 contributions are made up of primary and secondary contributions. Primary contributions are those paid by the employee and these are deducted from earnings by the employer. The percentage rates paid by the employee are as follows:
– 2 per cent on all earnings up to and including the lower earnings limit of £62.00
– 10 per cent on earnings between the lower earnings limit and the upper earnings limit of £465.00 per week (8.4 per cent for contracted-out employment, *see* page 489)
Some married women or widows pay a reduced rate of 3.85 per cent on all earnings up to and including the upper earnings limit. It is no longer possible to elect to pay the reduced rate but those who had reduced liability before 12 May 1977 may retain it so long as certain conditions are met. *See* leaflet CA09 (widows) or leaflet CA13 (married women).

Secondary contributions are paid by employers of employed earners on all earnings at or above the lower earnings limit. There is no upper earnings limit for employers' contributions, which are as follows:

Weekly earnings	Percentage of reckonable income		
	Not contracted out	Contracted-out schemes COSR*	COMP*
£62.00–109.99	3.0	0	1.5
110.00–154.99	5.0	2.0	3.5
155.00–209.99	7.0	4.0	5.5
210.00–465.00	10.0	7.0	8.5
over 465.00	10.0	10.0	10.0

* For explanation of COSR and COMP schemes, *see* page 490

The contracted-out rate applies only to that portion of earnings between the lower and upper earnings limits. Employers' contributions below and above those respective limits are assessed at the appropriate not contracted-out rate.

Class 2

Class 2 contributions are paid where a person is self-employed and is 16 or over and under state pension age. Contributions are paid at a flat rate of £6.15 per week regardless of the amount earned. However, those with earnings of less than £3,480 a year can apply for Small Earnings Exception, i.e. exemption from liability to pay Class 2 contributions. Those granted exemption from Class 2 contributions may pay Class 2 or Class 3 contributions voluntarily. Self-employed earners (whether or not they pay Class 2 contributions) may also be liable to pay Class 4 contributions based on profits. There are special rules for those who are concurrently employed and self-employed.

Married women and widows can no longer choose not to pay Class 2 contributions but those who elected not to pay Class 2 contributions before 12 May 1977 may retain the right so long as certain conditions are met.

Class 2 contributions are collected by the Contributions Agency, an executive agency of the Department of Social Security, by direct debit or quarterly bills. *See* leaflets CA03 and CA02.

Class 3

Class 3 contributions are voluntary flat-rate contributions of £6.05 per week payable by persons over the age of 16 who would otherwise be unable to qualify for retirement pension and certain other benefits because they have an insufficient record of Class 1 or Class 2 contributions. This may include those who are not working, those not liable for Class 1 or Class 2 contributions or those excepted from Class 2 contributions. Married women and widows who on or before 11 May 1977 elected not to pay Class 1 (full rate) or Class 2 contributions cannot pay Class 3 contributions while they retain this right.

Class 3 contributions are collected by the Contributions Agency by quarterly bills or direct debit. *See* leaflet CA08.

Class 4

Self-employed people whose profits and gains are over £7,010 a year pay Class 4 contributions in addition to Class 2 contributions. This applies to self-employed earners over 16 and under the state pension age. Class 4 contributions are calculated at 6 per cent of annual profits or gains between £7,010 and £24,180. The maximum Class 4 contribution payable on £24,180 or more is £1,030.20.

Class 4 contributions are assessed and collected by the Inland Revenue together with Schedule D tax. It is possible, in some circumstances, to apply for exceptions from liability to pay Class 4 contributions or to have the amount of contribution reduced (where Class 1 contributions are payable on earnings assessed for Class 4 contributions). *See* leaflet CA03.

PENSIONS

The Social Security Pensions Act came into force in 1978. It aimed to:
- reduce reliance on means-tested benefit in old age, widowhood and chronic ill-health
- ensure that occupational pension schemes which are contracted out of the state scheme fulfil the conditions of a good scheme
- ensure that pensions are adequately protected against inflation
- ensure that men and women are treated equally in state and occupational schemes

Legislation and regulations introduced since 1978 go further towards fulfilling these aims and more changes came into effect in April 1997 (*see* below). One of the changes is to equalize the state pension age for men (currently 65 years) and women (currently 60 years) from 6 April 2020. The change will be phased in over the ten years leading up to 6 April 2020. As a result the state pension age is as follows:
- the pension age for men remains at 65
- the pension age for women born on or before 5 April 1950 remains at 60
- the pension age for women born on or after 6 April 1955 is now 65
- for women born after 5 April 1950 and before 6 April 1955, the pension age is 60 plus one month for every month, or part of a month, that their date of birth fell after 5 April 1950

State Pension Scheme (SERPS)

The state pension scheme consists of the basic flat-rate pension and the state earnings-related pension scheme, also known as additional pension.

The amount of basic pension paid is dependent on the number of 'qualifying years' a person has in their 'working life'. A 'qualifying year' is a tax year in which a person pays Class 1 (at the standard rate), 2 or 3 NI contributions for the whole year (*see* above). Those in receipt of invalid care allowance, disability working allowance, jobseeker's allowance, incapacity benefit, severe disablement allowance or approved training have contributions credited to them for each week they receive benefit or fulfil certain other conditions. For those reaching pensionable age on or after 6 April 1999, a Class 3 credit of earnings will be awarded for each week from 6 April 1995 that family credit has been received. 'Working life' is counted from the start of the tax year in which a person reaches 16 to the end of the tax year before the one in which they reach pensionable age: for men this is normally 49 years and for women this varies between 44 and 49 years because the pension ages vary (*see* above). To get the full rate (100 per cent) basic pension a person must have qualifying years for about 90 per cent of their working life. To get the minimum basic pension (25 per cent) a person will need nine or ten qualifying years. Married women who are not entitled to a pension on their own contributions may get a pension on their husband's contributions. It is possible for people who are unable to work because they care for children or a sick or disabled person at home to reduce the number of qualifying years required. This is called home responsibilities protection (HRP) and can be given for any tax year since April 1978; the number of years for which HRP is given is deducted from the number of qualifying years needed. At present HRP only covers basic pensions but there are plans to extend it to SERPS.

The amount of additional pension paid depends on the amount of earnings a person has between the lower and upper earnings limits (*see* page 489) for each complete tax year between 6 April 1978 (when the scheme started) and the tax year before they reach state pension age. The right to additional pension does not depend on the person's right to basic pension. The amount of additional pension paid also depends on when a person reaches retirement; changes being phased in from 6 April 1999 mean that pensions will be calculated differently from that date. Women widowed before 6 April 2000 will inherit all their late husband's additional pension and women widowed on or after this date will inherit half of the husband's additional pension.

There are four categories of state pension provided under the Social Security Contributions and Benefits Act 1992:

- Category A, a contributory pension made up of basic and additional elements, payable to those of pensionable age who satisfy the entitlement conditions described above (*see* pages 491–2)
- Category B, a contributory pension made up of basic and additional elements, payable to married women and widows and based on their husband's contributions. This category of pension is to be extended to men from 6 April 2010 (*see* pages 491–2)
- Category C, a non-contributory pension payable to those who reached pensionable age before 5 July 1948 (*see* page 493)
- Category D, a non-contributory pension for those over 80 (*see* page 493)

Graduated retirement benefit is also available to those who paid graduated NI contributions into the scheme when it existed between April 1961 and April 1975 (*see* page 492).

It is possible to find out how much basic and additional pension a person might receive by filling in form BR19, available from local social security offices.

CONTRACTED-OUT AND PERSONAL PENSION SCHEMES

Under the Pensions Schemes Act 1993, an employer can contract out of SERPS those employees who are members of an occupational scheme, so long as the occupational scheme satisfies certain conditions. The occupational pension takes the place of the additional pension from April 1997 (previously it took the place of part of the additional pension); the state remains responsible for the basic pension. Until April 1997 members of contracted-out occupational and personal pension schemes accrued additional pension in the same way as someone who is not contracted-out but the rate payable was reduced by contracted-out deductions. Since 5 April 1997, it has not been possible to accrue any SERPS while being a member of a contracted-out occupational or personal pension scheme. Members of a COSR, COMP or personal pension scheme can no longer earn additional pension but they are still entitled to those rights earned before April 1997. From April 1997 there are age-related NI contribution rebates for people who leave SERPS and become members of a COMP or personal pension scheme; these will be lower for younger people and higher for older people.

There are two types of contracted-out occupational schemes.

Contracted-Out Salary Related Scheme (COSR)

- this scheme must provide a pension related to earnings
- the pension provided must not be less than a person's guaranteed minimum pension (GMP), i.e. worth about the same as the additional pension provided by the state scheme

- any additional pension earned from 6 April 1978 to 5 April 1997 will be reduced by the amount of GMP earned during that period
- from 6 April 1997 these schemes no longer have to provide a GMP but do have to satisfy a new scheme-based test in order to be issued with a contracting-out certificate

Contracted-Out Money Purchase Scheme (COMP)

- this scheme must provide a pension based on the value of the fund built up, i.e. the money paid in, along with returns from investment
- part of the pension, known as protected rights, takes the place of the additional pension. A contracted-out deduction, which may be more or less than the pension provided by the scheme, will be made from any additional pension earned from 6 April 1987 to 5 April 1997

In contracted-out occupational pension schemes, both the employee and employer pay lower NI contribution rates in recognition that SERPS will not be paid.

Personal Pension Schemes

The option of a personal pension scheme is open to all employees, even if their employer has an occupational pension scheme. A personal pension scheme must provide a pension based on the value of the fund built up, i.e. the money paid in, along with returns from investment. Part of the pension, known as protected rights, takes the place of the additional pension. A contracted-out deduction, which may be more or less than the pension provided by the scheme, will be made from any additional pension earned from 6 April 1987 to 5 April 1997.

Employees who are members of a personal pension plan and their employers pay NI contributions at the full rate and the DSS pays the difference between the full rate and the contracted-out rate into the personal pension scheme.

A Pensions Ombudsman deals with complaints about maladministration of pensions schemes. The Occupational Pensions Board, which supervised contracting-out and approved personal pension schemes, was abolished in April 1997 and replaced by the Occupational Pensions Regulatory Authority. *See* leaflet NP46.

BENEFITS

Leaflets relating to the various benefits and contribution conditions for different benefits are available from local social security offices; leaflets NI196 *Social Security Benefit Rates*, FB2 *Which Benefit?* and MG1 *A Guide to Benefits* are general guides to benefits, benefit rates and contributions.

The benefits payable under the Social Security Acts are:

CONTRIBUTORY BENEFITS
Jobseeker's allowance (contribution-based)
Incapacity benefit
Maternity allowance
Widow's benefit (comprising widow's payment, widowed mother's allowance and widow's pension)
Retirement pensions, categories A and B

NON-CONTRIBUTORY BENEFITS
Child benefit
Guardian's allowance
Jobseeker's allowance (income-based)
Invalid care allowance
Severe disablement allowance
Attendance allowance
Disability living allowance
Disability working allowance

Retirement pensions, categories C and D
Income support
Family credit
Housing benefit
Council tax benefit
Social fund

BENEFITS FOR INDUSTRIAL INJURIES AND
DISABLEMENT

OTHER
Statutory sick pay
Statutory maternity pay

CONTRIBUTORY BENEFITS

Entitlement to contributory benefits depends on contribution conditions being satisfied either by the claimant or by some other person (depending on the kind of benefit). The class or classes of contribution which for this purpose are relevant to each benefit are:

Jobseeker's allowance (contribution-based) Class 1
Incapacity benefit   Class 1 or 2
Maternity allowance   Class 1 or 2
Widow's benefits   Class 1, 2 or 3
Retirement pensions, categories A and B   Class 1, 2 or 3

The system of contribution conditions relates to yearly levels of earnings on which contributions have been paid.

JOBSEEKER'S ALLOWANCE

Jobseeker's allowance (JSA) replaced unemployment benefit and income support for unemployed people under pension age from 7 October 1996. There are two routes of entitlement. Contribution-based JSA is paid as a personal rate (i.e. additional benefit for dependants is not paid) to those who have made sufficient NI contributions. Savings and partner's earnings are not taken into account and payment can be made for up to six months. Those who do not qualify for contribution-based JSA, those who have exhausted their entitlement to contribution-based JSA or those for whom contribution-based JSA provides insufficient income may qualify for income-based JSA. The amount paid depends on age and number of dependants, and income and savings are taken into account. This is payable for the claimant and their dependants for as long as they satisfy the rules. Rates of jobseeker's allowance correspond to income support rates.

Claims for this benefit are made through job centres/employment offices. A person wishing to claim jobseeker's allowance must be unemployed, capable of work and available for any work which they can reasonably be expected to do, usually for at least 40 hours per week. They must agree and sign a 'jobseeker's agreement', which will set out each claimant's plans to find work, and must actively seek work.

A person will be disqualified from jobseeker's allowance if they have left a job voluntarily or through misconduct, if they refuse to take up an offer of employment or if they fail to attend a training scheme or employment programme. In these circumstances, it may be possible to receive hardship payments, particularly where the claimant or their family is vulnerable, e.g. if sick or pregnant, or for those with children or caring responsibilities. See leaflet JSAL5.

INCAPACITY BENEFIT

Incapacity benefit is available to those who are unemployed, self-employed and to those who work but cannot get statutory sick pay from their employer. It is not payable to those over state pension age. However, people who are already in receipt of short-term incapacity benefit when they reach state pension age may continue to receive this benefit for 52 weeks. There are three rates of incapacity benefit:
– short-term lower rate for the first 28 weeks of sickness
– short-term higher rate from weeks 29-52
– long-term rate after week 52
The terminally ill and those entitled to the highest rate care component of disability living allowance are paid the long-term rate after 28 weeks. Incapacity benefit is taxable after 28 weeks.

Two rates of age addition are paid with long-term benefit based on the claimant's age when incapacity started. The higher rate is payable where incapacity for work commenced before the age of 35; and the lower rate where incapacity commenced before the age of 45. Increases for dependents are also payable with short and long-term incapacity benefit.

There are two medical tests of incapacity: the 'own occupation' test and the 'all work' test. Those who worked before becoming incapable of working will be assessed, for the first 28 weeks of incapacity, on their ability to do their own job. After 28 weeks (or from the start of incapacity for those who were not working) claimants are assessed on their ability to carry out a range of work-related activities. The 'all work' test applies to most former sickness and invalidity benefit claimants. See leaflets IB202 and FB28.

MATERNITY ALLOWANCE

The maternity allowance (MA) scheme covers women who are self-employed or otherwise do not qualify for statutory maternity pay (see page 496). In order to qualify the woman must have been working and paying standard rate NI contributions for at least 26 weeks in the 66-week period which ends with the week before the week in which the baby is due. MA may be paid from 11 weeks before the week in which the baby is due or when the woman stops working and is paid for a period of up to 18 weeks. MA is only paid while the woman is not working. See leaflet NI17A.

WIDOW'S BENEFITS

Only the late husband's contributions of any class count for widow's benefit in any of its three forms:
Widow's payment – may be received by a woman who at her husband's death is under 60, or whose husband was not entitled to a Category A retirement pension when he died. It is a single tax-free lump sum payable immediately the woman becomes a widow
Widowed mother's allowance – a taxable benefit payable to a widow if she is entitled or treated as entitled to child benefit, or if she is expecting her husband's baby
Widow's pension – a widow may receive this pension if aged 45 or over at the time of her husband's death (40 or over if widowed before 11 April 1988) or when her widowed mother's allowance ends. If aged 55 or over (50 or over if widowed before 11 April 1988) she will receive the full widow's pension rate
It is not possible to receive widowed mother's allowance and widow's pension at the same time, and widow's benefit in any form ceases upon remarriage or during a period in which a widow lives with a man as his wife. Different rules and conditions (other than those mentioned) apply to women widowed before 11 April 1988. See leaflet NP45.

RETIREMENT PENSION: CATEGORIES A AND B

A Category A pension is payable for life to men and women who reach state pension age and who satisfy the contributions conditions (see page 489). A Category B pension is payable for life to a woman and is based on her husband's contributions. It becomes payable only when the husband has claimed his pension and the woman has reached state pension age. It is also payable on widowhood after 60 regardless of whether the late husband had qualified for his pension. There are special rules for those who are widowed before reaching pensionable age.

A person may defer claiming their pension for five years after state pension age. In doing so they may earn increments which will increase the weekly amount paid when they claim their pension. If a married man defers his Category A pension, his wife cannot claim a Category B pension on his contributions but she may earn increments on her pension during this time. A woman can defer her Category B pension, and earn increments, even if her husband is claiming his Category A pension.

The basic state pension is £62.45 per week plus any additional (earnings-related) pension the person may be entitled to (see page 490). An increase of £37.35 is paid for an adult dependent, providing the dependent's earnings do not exceed the rate of jobseeker's allowance for a single person (see below). It is also possible to get an increase of Category A and B pensions for a child or children. An age addition of 25p per week is payable if a retirement pensioner is aged 80 or over.

Since 1989 pensioners have been allowed to have unlimited earnings without affecting their retirement pension. Income support is payable on top of a pension where a pension does not give the person enough to live on and to those who are entitled to retirement pension but who have not claimed it. Pensioners may also be entitled to housing and council tax benefits.

GRADUATED RETIREMENT BENEFIT

Graduated NI contributions were first payable from 1961 and were calculated as a percentage of earnings between certain bands. They were discontinued in 1975. Any graduated pension which an employed person over 18 and under 70 (65 for a woman) had earned by paying graduated contributions will be paid when the contributor claims retirement pension or at 70 (65 for a woman), in addition to any retirement pension for which he or she qualifies. A wife can get a graduated pension in return for her own graduated contributions, but not for her husband's.

Graduated retirement benefit is at the rate of 8.11p per week (April 1997) for each 'unit' of graduated contributions paid by the employee (half a unit or more counts as a whole unit). A unit of graduated pension can be calculated by adding together all graduated contributions and dividing by 7.5 (men) or 9.0 (women). If a person defers making a claim beyond 65 (60 for a woman), entitlement may be increased by one seventh of a penny per £1 of its weekly rate for each complete week of deferred retirement, as long as the retirement is deferred for a minimum of seven weeks.

WEEKLY RATES OF BENEFIT
from April 1997

Jobseeker's allowance (contribution-based)

Person under 18	£29.60
Person aged 18–24	38.90
Person over 25	49.15

Short-term incapacity benefit

Person under pension age – lower rate	47.10
*Person under pension age – higher rate	55.70
Increase for adult dependant	29.15
*Person over pension age	59.90
Increase for adult dependant	33.85

Long-term incapacity benefit

Person (under or over pension age)	62.45
Increase for adult dependant	37.35
Age addition – lower rate	6.60
Age addition – higher rate	13.15

Invalidity allowance: maximum amount payable

Higher rate	13.15
Middle rate	8.30
Lower rate	4.15

Maternity allowance

Employed	55.70
Self-employed or unemployed	48.35

Widow's benefits

Widow's payment (lump sum)	1,000.00
*Widowed mother's allowance	62.45
*Widow's pension	62.45

Retirement pension: categories A and B

Single person	62.45
Increase for wife/other adult dependant	37.35

*These benefits attract an increase for each dependent child (in addition to child benefit) of £9.90 for the first or only child and £11.20 for each subsequent child

NON-CONTRIBUTORY BENEFITS

These benefits are paid from general taxation and are not dependent on NI contributions. Unless otherwise stated, a benefit is tax-free and is not means tested.

CHILD BENEFIT

Child benefit is payable for virtually all children aged under 16, and for those aged 16 to 18 who are studying full-time up to and including A-level or equivalent standard. It is also payable for a short period if the child has left school recently and is registered for work or youth training at a careers office.

A higher rate of benefit (lone parent) may be paid to a person who is responsible for bringing up one or more children on his/her own. It is a flat rate benefit payable for the eldest child only. See leaflets CH1 and CH11.

GUARDIAN'S ALLOWANCE

Where the parents of a child are dead, the person who has the child in his/her family may claim a guardian's allowance in addition to child benefit. In exceptional circumstances the allowance is payable on the death of only one parent. See leaflet NI14.

INVALID CARE ALLOWANCE

Invalid care allowance (ICA) is a taxable benefit payable to people of working age who are not gainfully employed because they are regularly and substantially engaged (spending at least 35 hours per week as a carer) in caring for a severely disabled person. To qualify for ICA a person must be caring for someone in receipt of one of the following benefits:
– the middle or highest rate of disability living allowance care component
– either rate of attendance allowance
– constant attendance allowance, paid at not less than the normal maximum rate, under the industrial injuries or war pension schemes
See leaflets FB31 and FB28.

SEVERE DISABLEMENT ALLOWANCE

Persons who have been incapable of work for a continuous period of at least 28 weeks but who do not qualify for contributory incapacity benefit may be entitled to severe disablement allowance (SDA). This benefit is available to people over 16 and under 65. Those who are over 65 can only get SDA if they were entitled to it on the day before their 65th birthday. People who became incapable of work on or before their 20th birthday do not have to have their disability assessed but those who became incapable after their 20th birthday must be assessed as at least 80 per cent disabled. *See* leaflet NI252.

ATTENDANCE ALLOWANCE

This is payable to disabled people over 65 who need a lot of care or supervision because of physical or mental disability for a period of at least six months. People not expected to live for six months because of an illness do not have to wait six months. The allowance has two rates: the lower rate is for day or night care, and the higher rate is for day and night care. *See* leaflets DS702 and FB28.

DISABILITY LIVING ALLOWANCE

This is payable to disabled people over 65 who have personal care and mobility needs because of an illness or disability for a period of at least three months and are likely to have those needs for a further six months or more. People not expected to live for six months because of an illness do not have to wait three months. The allowance has two components: the care component, which has three rates, and the mobility component, which has two rates. The rates depend on the care and mobility needs of the claimant. The mobility component is payable only to those aged five or over. *See* leaflet DS704.

DISABILITY WORKING ALLOWANCE

This is an income-related benefit for people who are working 16 hours per week or more but have an illness or disability which puts them at a disadvantage in getting a job. To qualify a person must be aged 16 or over and must, at the date of the claim, have one of the 'qualifying benefits', such as disability living allowance. The amount payable depends on the size of the family and weekly income. The allowance is not payable if any savings exceed £16,000. *See* leaflet DS703.

RETIREMENT PENSION: CATEGORIES C AND D

A Category C pension is provided, subject to a residence test, for persons who were over pensionable age on 5 July 1948, and for the wives and widows of men who qualified if they are over pension age. A Category D pension is provided for people aged 80 and over if they are not entitled to another category of pension or are entitled to less than the Category D rate.

WEEKLY RATES OF BENEFIT
from April 1997

Child benefit

Eldest child	£11.05
Eldest child of certain lone parents	17.10
Each subsequent child	9.00

Guardian's allowance

Eldest child	9.85
Each subsequent child	11.05

* Invalid care allowance

	37.35
Increase for wife/other adult dependant	22.35

* Severe disablement allowance

†Basic rate	37.75
Under 40	13.15
40–49	8.30
50–59	4.15
Increase for wife/other adult dependant	22.40

Attendance allowance

Higher rate	49.50
Lower rate	33.10

Disability living allowance

Care component

Higher rate	49.50
Middle rate	33.10
Lower rate	13.15

Mobility component

Higher rate	34.60
Lower rate	13.15

Disability working allowance

Single person	49.55
Couple or single parent	77.75
Child aged under 11	12.05
aged 11–15	19.95
aged 16–17	24.80
aged 18	34.70
Disabled child allowance	20.95
Thirty hours allowance	10.55

‡Applicable amount (income threshold)

Single person	57.85
Couple or single parent	77.15

Retirement pension: categories *C and D

Single person	37.35
Increase for wife/other adult dependant	22.35
(not payable with Category D pension)	

*These benefits attract an increase for each dependent child (in addition to child benefit) of £9.90 for the first or only child and £11.20 for each subsequent child
†The age addition applies to the age when incapacity began
‡70 pence is deducted from the maximum DWA payable (this is obtained by adding up the appropriate allowance for each person in the family) for every £ coming in each week over the appropriate applicable amount. Where weekly income is below the applicable amount, maximum DWA is payable

INCOME SUPPORT

Income support is a benefit for those aged 16 and over whose income is below a certain level. It can be paid to people who are not expected to sign on as unemployed (income support for unemployed people was replaced by jobseeker's allowance in October 1996) and who are:

– incapable of work due to sickness or disability
– bringing up children alone
– 60 or over
– looking after a person who has a disability
– registered blind

Some people who are not in these categories may also be able to claim income support.

Income support is also payable to people who work for less than 16 hours a week on average (or 24 hours for a partner). Some people can claim income support if they work longer hours.

Income support is not payable if the claimant, or claimant and partner, have capital or savings in excess of £8,000. For capital and savings in excess of £3,000 a deduction of £1 is made for every £250, or part of £250, held.

Sums payable depend on fixed allowances laid down by law for people in different circumstances. If both partners are entitled to income support, either may claim it for the couple. People receiving income support may be able to receive housing benefit, help with mortgage or home loan interest and help with health care. They may also be eligible for help with exceptional expenses from the Social Fund. Special rates may apply to some people living in residential care or nursing homes. Leaflet IS20 gives a detailed explanation of income support.

INCOME SUPPORT PREMIUMS

Income support premiums are additional weekly payments for those with special needs. People qualifying for more than one premium will normally only receive the highest single premium for which they qualify. However, family premium, disabled child premium, severe disability premium and carer premium are payable in addition to other premiums.

People with children may qualify for:
- the family premium if they have at least one child (a higher rate is paid to lone parents)
- the disabled child premium if they have a child who receives disability living allowance or is registered blind

Carers may qualify for:
- the carer premium if they or their partner are in receipt of invalid care allowance

Long-term sick or disabled people may qualify for:
- the disability premium if they or their partner are receiving certain benefits because they are disabled or cannot work; are registered blind; or if the claimant has been incapable of work or receiving statutory sick pay for at least 364 days (196 days if the person is terminally ill), including periods of incapacity separated by eight weeks or less
- the severe disability premium if the person lives alone and receives attendance allowance or the middle or higher rate of disability living allowance care component and no one receives invalid care allowance for caring for that person. This premium is also available to couples where both partners meet the above conditions

People aged 60 and over may qualify for:
- the pensioner premium if they or their partner are aged 60 to 74
- the enhanced pensioner premium if they or their partner are aged 75 to 79
- the higher pensioner premium if they or their partner are aged 80 or over. This is also available to people over 60 who receive attendance allowance, disability living allowance, long-term incapacity benefit or severe disablement allowance, or who are registered blind

WEEKLY RATES OF BENEFIT
from April 1997

Income support

Single person

under 18	£29.60
under 18 (higher)	38.90
aged 18–24	38.90
aged 25 and over	49.15
aged 18 and over and a single parent	49.15

Couples*

both under 18	58.70
one or both aged 18 or over	77.15

For each child in a family	
until September following 11th birthday	16.90
from September following 11th birthday to September following 16th birthday	24.75
†from September following 16th birthday to day before 19th birthday	29.60

Premiums

Family premium	10.80
Family (lone parent) premium	15.75
Disabled child premium	20.95
Carer premium	13.35
Disability premium	
Single	20.95
Couple	29.90
Severe disability premium	
Single	37.15
Couple (one person qualified)	37.15
Couple (both qualified)	74.30
Pensioner premium	
Single	19.65
Couple	29.65
Higher pensioner premium	
Single	26.55
Couple	38.00

Enhanced pensioner premium	
Single	21.85
Couple	32.75

*Where one or both partners are aged under 18, their personal allowance will depend on their situation

†If in full-time education up to A-level or equivalent standard

FAMILY CREDIT

Family credit is a tax-free benefit for working families with children. To qualify, a family must include at least one child under 16 (under 19 if in full-time education up to A-level or equivalent standard) and the claimant, or partner if there is one, must be working for at least 16 hours per week. It does not matter which partner is working and they may be employed or self-employed. Family credit is not payable if the claimant, or claimant and partner, have capital or savings in excess of £8,000. The rate of benefit is affected if capital or savings in excess of £3,000 are held.

Family credit is usually paid at the same rate for 26 weeks, after which a new claim can be made. The rate of family credit depends on:
- the family's net income, excluding child benefit, child benefit (lone-parent) and the first £15.00 of any maintenance in payment
- the number of children and the children's ages
- the number of hours the claimant or their partner work
- in certain circumstances, the amount of childcare charges paid for children under 11

Family credit is claimed by post and in two-parent families the woman should claim. A claim pack, FC1, is available from social security offices or the Family Credit Helpline on 01253-500050. *See* leaflet NI261.

WEEKLY RATES OF BENEFIT
from 8 April 1997

The maximum amount of family credit is payable where income is less than £77.15 per week. For every pound earned over £77.15, 70 pence will be deducted from the maximum amount of family credit that can be paid. The maximum rate consists of:

Adult credit (amount is the same for lone parents and couples)	£47.65
30-hour credit (where one parent works at least 30 hours per week)	10.55

Child credit	
each child under 11	12.05
each child aged 11–15	19.95
each child aged 16–17	24.80
each child aged 18	34.70

HOUSING BENEFIT

Housing benefit is designed to help people with rent (including rent for accommodation in guest houses, lodgings or hostels). It does not cover mortgage payments. The amount of benefit paid depends on:
- the income of the claimant, and partner if there is one, including earned income, unearned income (any other income including some other benefits) and savings
- number of dependents
- number of people sharing the home who are not dependent on the claimant
- how much rent is paid

Housing benefit is not payable if the claimant, or claimant and partner, have savings of over £16,000. The amount of benefit is affected if savings held exceed £3,000. Housing benefit is not paid for meals, fuel or certain service charges that may be included in the rent. Deductions are also made for most non-dependents who live in the same accommodation as the claimant (and their partner).

The maximum amount of benefit (which is not necessarily the same as the amount of rent paid) may be paid where the claimant is in receipt of income support or income-based jobseeker's allowance or where the claimant's income is less than the amount allowed for their needs. Any income over that allowed for their needs will mean that their benefit is reduced.

Claims for housing benefit are made to the local council. Those who are also claiming income support or income-based jobseeker's allowance may claim housing benefit at the local benefits or employment services office. *See* leaflets RR1 and RR2.

COUNCIL TAX BENEFIT

Nearly all the rules which apply to housing benefit apply to council tax benefit, which helps people on low incomes to pay council tax bills. The amount payable depends on how much council tax is paid and who lives with the claimant.

The maximum amount that is payable is 100 per cent of the claimant's council tax liability. This may be available to those receiving income support or income-based jobseeker's allowance or to those whose income is less than that allowed for their needs. Any income over that allowed for their needs will mean that their council tax benefit is reduced. Deductions are made for non-dependents.

If a person shares a home with one or more adults (not their partner) who are on a low income, it may be possible to claim a second adult rebate. Those who are entitled to both council tax benefit and second adult rebate will be awarded whichever is the greater. Second adult rebate may be claimed by those not in receipt of council tax benefit.

THE SOCIAL FUND

The Social Fund helps people with expenses which are difficult to meet from regular income. Regulated maternity and funeral payments are decided by Adjudication Officers and cold weather payments are made automatically. These payments are not limited by the district's Social Fund budget. Discretionary community care grants, and budgeting and crisis loans are decided by Social Fund Officers and come out of a yearly budget which is allocated to each district (1997–8, grants £97 million; loans £370.5 million; £0.5 million set aside as a contingency reserve). *See* leaflet SB16.

Regulated Payments
Maternity Payments

A payment of up to £100 for each baby expected, born, adopted, or the subject of a parental order. It is payable to people on income support, income-based jobseeker's allowance, disability working allowance and family credit and does not have to be repaid.

Funeral Payments

Payable for specified funeral director's charges, including the necessary cost of all burial or cremation expenses and other funeral expenses reasonably incurred by people receiving income support, income-based jobseeker's allowance, disability working allowance, family credit, council tax benefit or housing benefit. These payments are recoverable from the estate of the deceased.

Cold-Weather Payments

£8.50 for any consecutive seven days when the average temperature is 0°C or below in their area. Payments are made to people on income support or income-based jobseeker's allowance who are pensioners, disabled or

parents with a child under the age of five. They do not have to be repaid.

Discretionary Payments
Community Care Grants

These are intended to help people on income support or income-based jobseeker's allowance to move into the community or avoid institutional or residential care; ease exceptional pressures on families; care for a prisoner on release on temporary licence; and/or meet certain essential travelling expenses. They do not have to be repaid.

Budgeting Loans

These are interest free loans to people who have been receiving income support or income-based jobseeker's allowance for at least 26 weeks, for intermittent expenses that may be difficult to budget for.

Crisis Loans

These are interest-free loans to anyone, whether receiving benefit or not, who is without resources in an emergency, where there is no other means of preventing serious damage or serious risk to their health or safety.

Savings

Savings over £500 (£1,000 for people aged 60 or over) are taken into account for maternity and funeral payments, community care grants and budgeting loans. All savings are taken into account for crisis loans. Savings are not taken into account for cold-weather payments.

INDUSTRIAL INJURIES AND DISABLEMENT BENEFITS

The industrial injuries scheme, administered under the Social Security Contributions and Benefits Act 1992, provides a range of benefits designed to compensate for disablement resulting from an industrial accident (i.e. an accident arising out of and in the course of an employed earner's employment) or from a prescribed disease due to the nature of a person's employment. Those who are self-employed are not covered by this scheme.

Industrial Injuries Disablement Benefit

A person must be at least 14 per cent disabled (except for certain respiratory diseases) in order to qualify for this benefit. The amount paid depends on the degree of disablement:

- those assessed as 14–19 per cent disabled are paid at the 20 per cent rate
- those with disablement of over 20 per cent will have the percentage rounded up or down to the nearest 10 per cent, e.g. a disablement of 44 per cent will be paid at the 40 per cent rate while a disablement of 45 per cent will be paid at the 50 per cent rate

Benefit is payable 15 weeks (90 days) after the date of the accident or onset of the disease and may be payable for a limited period or for life. The benefit is payable whether the person works or not and those who are incapable of work are entitled to draw statutory sick pay or incapacity benefit in addition to industrial injuries disablement benefit. It may also be possible to claim the following allowances:

- reduced earnings allowance for those who are unable to return to their regular work or work of the same standard and who had their accident (or whose disease started) before 1 October 1990

- retirement allowance for those who were entitled to reduced earnings allowance who have reached state pension age
- constant attendance allowance for those with a disablement of 95 per cent or more who need constant care. There are four rates of allowance depending on how much care the person needs
- exceptionally severe disablement allowance for those who are entitled to constant care attendance allowance at one of the higher rates and who need constant care permanently

See leaflets NI6 and N12.

OTHER BENEFITS

People who are disabled because of an accident or disease that was the result of work that they did before 5 July 1948 are not entitled to industrial injuries disablement benefit. They may, however, be entitled to payment under the workmen's compensation scheme or the pneumoconiosis, byssinosis and miscellaneous diseases benefit scheme. *See* leaflets WS1 and PN1.

WEEKLY RATES OF BENEFIT
from April 1997

*Disablement benefit/pension
Degree of disablement

100 per cent	£101.10
90	90.99
80	80.88
70	70.77
60	60.66
50	50.55
40	40.44
30	30.33
20	20.22
†Unemployability supplement	62.45
Addition for adult dependant (subject to earnings rule)	37.35
Reduced earnings allowance (maximum)	40.44
Retirement allowance (maximum)	10.11
Constant attendance allowance (normal maximum rate)	40.50
Exceptionally severe disablement allowance	40.50

*There is a weekly benefit for those under 18 with no dependants which is set at a lower rate
†This benefit attracts an increase for each dependent child (in addition to child benefit) of £10.11 for the first child and £11.20 for each subsequent child

CLAIMS AND QUESTIONS

With a few exceptions, claims and questions relating to social security benefits are decided by statutory authorities who act independently of the Department of Social Security and Department for Education and Employment. *See* leaflets NI246 and NI260.

Entitlement to benefit and regulated Social Fund payments is determined by the Adjudication Officer. A claimant who is dissatisfied with that decision has the right of appeal to an independent Social Security Appeal Tribunal. There is a further right of appeal to a Social Security Commissioner against the tribunal's decision but leave to appeal must first be obtained. Appeals to the Commissioner must be on a point of law. Provision is also made for the determination of certain questions by the Secretary of State for Social Security.

Disablement questions are decided by adjudicating medical authorities or medical appeal tribunals. Appeal to the Commissioner against a tribunal's decision is with leave and on a point of law only.

Decisions on applications to the discretionary Social Fund are made by Social Fund Officers. Applicants can ask for a review within 28 days of the date on the decision letter. The Social Fund Review Officer will review the case and there is a further right of review to an independent Social Fund Inspector.

Reviews of housing and council tax benefit decisions are dealt with initially by the council. The claimant must ask for a review within six weeks of being told how much benefit they will receive. Further reviews are dealt with by an independent review board.

OTHER BENEFITS

STATUTORY SICK PAY

Employers usually pay statutory sick pay (SSP) to their employees for up to 28 weeks of sickness in any period of incapacity for work that lasts longer than four days. SSP is paid at £55.70 per week and is subject to PAYE tax and NI deductions. Employees who cannot obtain SSP may be able to claim incapacity benefit. Employers can recover some SSP costs. See leaflets NI244 and NI245.

STATUTORY MATERNITY PAY

In general, employers pay statutory maternity pay (SMP) to pregnant women who have been employed by them full or part-time for at least 26 weeks before the end of the 'qualifying week', which is 15 weeks before the week the baby is due, and whose earnings are on average at least at the lower earnings limit for the payment of NI contributions. All women who meet these conditions receive payment of 90 per cent of their average earnings for six weeks, followed by a maximum of 12 weeks at £55.70. SMP can be paid from the beginning of the 11th week before the week in which the baby is due but women can decide to begin maternity leave later than this. SMP is not payable for any week in which the woman works. Employers are reimbursed for 92 per cent of the SMP they pay (106.5 per cent for those whose annual NI liability is £20,000 or less). *See* Leaflet NI17A.

War Pensions

The War Pensions Agency, an executive agency of the Department of Social Security (DSS), awards war pensions under The Naval, Military and Air Forces, Etc. (Disablement and Death) Service Pensions Order 1983 to members of the armed forces in respect of the periods 4 August 1914 to 30 September 1921 and subsequent to 3 September 1939 (including present members of the armed forces). War pensions for the period 1 October 1921 to 2 September 1939 were dealt with by the Ministry of Defence until July 1996 when responsibility passed to the DSS. There is also a scheme for civilians and civil defence workers in respect of the 1939–45 war, and other schemes for groups such as merchant seamen and Polish armed forces who served under British command.

PENSIONS

War disablement pension is awarded for the disabling effects of any injury, wound or disease which is the result of, or has been aggravated by, conditions of service in the armed forces. It can only be paid once the person has left the armed forces. The amount of pension paid depends on the severity of disablement, which is assessed by comparing the health of the claimant with that of a healthy person of the same age and sex. The person's earning capacity or occupation are not taken into account in this assessment. A pension is awarded if the person has a disablement of 20 per cent or more and a lump sum is usually payable to those with a disablement of less than 20 per cent. No award is made for noise-induced sensorineural hearing loss where the assessment of disablement is less than 20 per cent.

War widow's pension is payable where the husband's death was due to, or hastened by, his service in the armed forces or where the husband was in receipt of a war disablement pension constant attendance allowance (or would have been had he not been in hospital). Since April 1997 a war widow's pension is also payable if the husband was getting unemployability supplement at the time of his death and his pensionable disablement was at least 80 per cent. Most war widows receive a standard rank-related rate but a lower weekly rate is payable to war widows of men below the rank of Lieutenant-Colonel who are under the age of 40, without children and capable of maintaining themselves. This is increased to the standard rate at age 40. Allowances are paid for children (in addition to child benefit) and adult dependents. An age allowance may also be given when the woman reaches 65 and increased at age 70 and age 80.

A war widower's pension may be payable to a man whose wife died because of service in the armed forces, if he was dependent on his wife before her death and cannot support himself.

All war pensions and war widow's pensions are tax-free and pensioners living overseas receive the same amount as those resident in the UK.

SUPPLEMENTARY ALLOWANCES

A number of supplementary allowances may be awarded to a war pensioner which are intended to meet various needs which may result from disablement or death and take account of its particular effect on the pensioner or spouse. The principal supplementary allowances are unemployability supplement, allowance for lowered standard of occupation and constant attendance allowance. Others include exceptionally severe disablement allowance, severe disablement occupational allowance, treatment allowance, mobility supplement, comforts allowance, clothing allowance, age allowance and widow's age allowance. There is a rent allowance available on a war widow's pension.

SOCIAL SECURITY BENEFITS

Most social security benefits are paid in addition to the basic war disablement pension or war widow's pension. Any retirement pension for which a war widow qualifies on her own NI contribution record can be paid in addition to her war widow's pension.

A war pensioner or war widow who claims income support, family credit or disability working allowance has the first £10 of pension disregarded. A similar provision operates for housing benefit and council tax benefit; but the local authority may, at its discretion, disregard any or all of the balance.

CLAIMS AND QUESTIONS

To claim a war pension it is necessary to contact the nearest war pensioners' welfare service office, the address of which is available from local social security offices, or to write to the War Pensions Agency, Norcross, Blackpool FY5 3WP. The war pensioners' welfare service advises and assists

war pensioners and war widows on any matters affecting their welfare.

Independent pensions appeal tribunals hear appeals against decisions, made by the DSS, on entitlement and on the assessment of disability with respect to the 1939–45 war and subsequent service cases. War widows from the 1914 war may appeal against decisions about entitlement but there are now no rights of appeal in disablement cases from the 1914 war. Decisions on supplementary allowances are made on a discretionary basis and there is no provision for a statutory right of appeal against them. The DSS send information about how to appeal and the time limits that exist for appeals when they notify claimants of their decision. See leaflet WPA1.

WEEKLY RATES OF PENSIONS AND ALLOWANCES
from week commencing 7 April 1997

War disablement pension
Degree of disablement

100 per cent	£107.20
90	96.48
80	85.76
70	75.04
60	64.32
50	53.60
40	42.88
30	32.16
20	21.44

Unemployability supplement

Personal allowance	66.25
Increase for wife/other adult dependant	37.35
Increase for first child	9.90
Increase for other children	11.20
Allowance for lowered standard of occupation (maximum)	40.44

Constant attendance allowance

Half day rate	20.25
Full day rate	40.50
Intermediate rate	60.75
Exceptional rate	81.00

Widow's pension
(widow of Private or equivalent rank)

Standard rate	81.00
Increase for first child	14.15
Increase for other children	15.45
Childless widow under 40	18.74

Widow's age allowance

aged 65–69	9.25
aged 70–79	17.75
aged 80 and over	26.45

The rates for officers and widows of officers differ from those given above. See leaflet WPA9.

The Water Industry

ENGLAND AND WALES

In England and Wales the Secretary of State for the Environment, Transport and the Regions and the Secretary of State for Wales have overall responsibility for water policy and set the environmental and health and safety standards for the water industry. The Director-General of Water Services, as the independent economic regulator, is responsible for ensuring that the private water companies are able to fulfil their statutory obligation to provide water supply and sewerage services, and for protecting the interests of consumers.

The Minister of Agriculture, Fisheries and Food and the Secretary of State for Wales are responsible for policy relating to land drainage, flood protection, sea defences and the protection and development of fisheries.

The Environment Agency is responsible for water quality and the control of pollution, the management of water resources and nature conservation. The Drinking Water Inspectorate and local authorities are responsible for the quality of drinking water.

THE WATER COMPANIES

Until 1989 nine regional water authorities in England and the Welsh Water Authority in Wales were responsible for water supply and the development of water resources, sewerage and sewage disposal, pollution control, freshwater fisheries, flood protection, water recreation, and environmental conservation. The Water Act 1989 provided for the creation of a privatized water industry under public regulation, and the functions of the regional water authorities were taken over by ten holding companies and the regulatory bodies.

Of the 99 per cent of the population of England and Wales who are connected to a public water supply, 75 per cent are supplied by the water companies (through their principal operating subsidiaries, the water service companies). The remaining 25 per cent are supplied by statutory water companies which were already in the private sector. Most of these have public limited company (PLC) status and many are now French-owned. They are represented by the Water Companies Association. The ten water service companies are also responsible for sewerage and sewage disposal in England and Wales. The Water Services Association is the trade association for all the water service companies except Wessex Water Services.

WATER COMPANIES ASSOCIATION, 1 Queen Anne's Gate, London SW1H 9BT. Tel: 0171-222 0644. *Chief Executive*, Ms P. Taylor

WATER SERVICES ASSOCIATION, 1 Queen Anne's Gate, London SW1H 9BT. Tel: 0171-957 4567. *Chief Executive*, Miss J. Langdon

Water Service Companies

ANGLIAN WATER SERVICES LTD, Anglian House, Ambury Road, Huntingdon, Cambs PE18 6NZ

DWR CYMRU (WELSH WATER), Cambrian Way, Brecon, Powys LD3 7HP

NORTHUMBRIAN WATER LTD, Abbey Road, Pity Me, Durham DH1 5FJ

NORTH WEST WATER LTD, Dawson House, Liverpool Road, Great Sankey, Warrington WA5 3LW

SEVERN TRENT WATER LTD, 2297 Coventry Road, Sheldon, Birmingham B26 3PU

SOUTHERN WATER SERVICES LTD, Southern House, Yeoman Road, Worthing, W. Sussex BN13 3NX

SOUTH WEST WATER SERVICES LTD, Peninsula House, Rydon Lane, Exeter EX2 7HR

THAMES WATER UTILITIES LTD, Nugent House, Vastern Road, Reading RG1 8DB

WESSEX WATER SERVICES LTD, Wessex House, Passage Street, Bristol BS2 0JQ

YORKSHIRE WATER SERVICES LTD, West Riding House, 67 Albion Street, Leeds LS1 5AA

WATER SUPPLY AND CONSUMPTION 1995–6

	Supply		Consumption			
	Supply from treatment works (*Ml/day*)	Total leakage (*Ml/day*)	Household (*l/head/day*) Unmetered	Metered	Non-household (*l/prop/day*) Unmetered	Metered
WATER SERVICE COMPANIES						
Anglian	1,175.6	235.9	174.3	140.5	1,435.6	3,628.8
Dwr Cymru (Welsh)	1,088.5	412.9	184.3	164.7	986.1	3,093.3
Northumbrian	802.9	189.8	170.5	141.2	595.5	5,361.4
North West	2,355.2	789.0	168.7	120.7	707.4	3,484.0
Severn Trent	2,202.0	632.1	162.3	142.1	750.0	3,047.6
Southern	643.2	120.0	179.6	141.6	913.4	3,174.3
South West	505.4	142.0	185.7	142.6	1,098.5	1,839.3
Thames	2,872.3	1,108.7	198.8	167.6	876.6	4,214.1
Wessex	433.0	132.6	173.0	133.5	1,885.3	2,883.5
Yorkshire	1,450.1	485.0	160.3	135.2	698.2	3,286.3
Total	13,528.1	4,248.0	—	—	—	—
Average	—	—	175.3	141.2	879.3	3,400.0
WATER COMPANIES						
Total	3,498.6	731.6	—	—	—	—
Average	—	—	189.5	156.7	918.9	3,403.5

REGULATORY BODIES

The Office of Water Services (Ofwat) (*see* page 351) was set up under the Water Act 1989 and is the independent economic regulator of the water and sewerage companies in England and Wales. Ofwat's main duty is to ensure that the companies can finance and carry out their statutory functions and to protect the interests of water customers. Ofwat is a non-ministerial government department headed by the Director-General of Water Services, who is appointed by the Secretary of State for the Environment, Transport and the Regions and the Secretary of State for Wales.

An independent national body, the National Rivers Authority, took over the regulatory and river management functions of the regional water authorities. It had statutory duties and powers in relation to water resources, pollution control, flood defence, fisheries, recreation, conservation and navigation in England and Wales. In 1996 the statutory duties, powers and functions of the National Rivers Authority were transferred to the new Environment Agency (*see* page 302).

The Drinking Water Inspectorate (*see* page 300) is responsible for assessing the quality of the drinking water supplied by the water companies, inspecting the companies themselves and investigating any accidents affecting drinking water quality. The Chief Inspector presents an annual report to the Secretary of State for the Environment, Transport and the Regions and the Secretary of State for Wales.

METHODS OF CHARGING

In England and Wales, most domestic customers still pay for domestic water supply and sewerage services through charges based on the old rateable value of their property, although about 10 per cent of householders are now charged according to consumption, which is recorded by meter. Industrial and most commercial customers are charged according to consumption.

Under the Water Industry Act 1991, water companies must discontinue basing their charges on the old rateable value of property after 31 March 2000. In May 1997 the Government announced a review of the system of charging for water. Among other issues, the review will consider alternative bases of charging, including the future use of rateable values, the use of council tax bands and metering policy.

SCOTLAND

Overall responsibility for national water policy in Scotland rests with the Secretary of State for Scotland. Most aspects of water policy are administered through the Scottish Office Agriculture, Environment and Fisheries Department.

Water supply and sewerage services were formerly local authority responsibilities and the Central Scotland Water Development Board had the function of developing new sources of water supply for the purpose of providing water in bulk to water authorities whose limits of supply were within the board's area. The Local Government etc. (Scotland) Act 1994 provided for three new public water authorities, covering the north, east and west of Scotland respectively, to be established to take over the provision of water and sewerage services from April 1996. From that date the Central Scotland Water Development Board was abolished. The new authorities are accountable to Parliament through the Secretary of State for Scotland. The Act also provided for a Scottish Water and Sewerage Customers Council to be established to represent consumer

interests. It monitors the performance of the authorities; approves charges schemes; investigates complaints; and keeps the Secretary of State advised on standards of service and customer relations.

The Scottish Environment Protection Agency (SEPA) (*see* page 339) is responsible for promoting the cleanliness of Scotland's rivers, lochs and coastal waters. SEPA is also responsible for controlling pollution.

WATER RESOURCES 1995

	No.	Yield (Ml/day)
Reservoirs and lochs	308	2,990
Feeder intakes	26	—
River intakes	233	424
Bore-holes	37	55
Underground springs	106	32
Total	*728	3,501

* Including compensation reservoirs

WATER CONSUMPTION 1995

TOTAL (*Ml/day*)	2,322
Potable	2,306
Unmetered	1,748
Metered	558
Non-potable†	16
TOTAL (*l/head/day*)	452
Unmetered	340
Metered and non-potable†	112

† 'Non-potable' supplied for industrial purposes. Metered supplies in general relate to commercial and industrial use and unmetered to domestic use

EAST OF SCOTLAND WATER AUTHORITY, Pentland Gait, 597 Calder Road, Edinburgh EH11 4HJ. Tel: 0131-453 7500. *Chief Executive*, R. Rennet

NORTH OF SCOTLAND WATER AUTHORITY, Cairngorm House, Beechwood Park North, Inverness IV2 3ED. Tel: 01463-245400. *Chief Executive*, A. Findlay

SCOTTISH WATER AND SEWERAGE CUSTOMERS COUNCIL, Suite 4, Ochil House, Springkerse Business Park, Stirling FK7 7XE. Tel: 01786-430200. *Director*, Dr V. Nash

WEST OF SCOTLAND WATER AUTHORITY, 419 Balmore Road, Glasgow G22 6NU. Tel: 0141-355 3555. *Chief Executive*, E. Chambers

METHODS OF CHARGING

The water authorities set charges for domestic and non-domestic water and sewerage provision through charges schemes which have to be approved by the Scottish Water and Sewerage Customers Council. The authorities must publish a summary of their charges schemes.

NORTHERN IRELAND

In Northern Ireland ministerial responsibility for water services lies with the Secretary of State for Northern Ireland. The Water Service, which is an executive agency of the Department of the Environment for Northern Ireland, is responsible for policy and co-ordination with regard to supply, distribution and cleanliness of water, and the provision and maintenance of sewerage services.

The Water Service (*see* page 331) is divided into four regions, the Eastern, Northern, Western and Southern Divisions. These are based in Belfast, Ballymena, Londonderry and Craigavon respectively.

On major issues the Department of the Environment for Northern Ireland seeks the views of the Northern Ireland Water Council, a body appointed to advise the Department on the exercise of its water and sewerage functions. The Council includes representatives from agriculture, angling, industry, commerce, tourism, trade unions and local government.

METHODS OF CHARGING

Usually householders do not pay separately for water and sewerage services; the costs of these services are allowed for in the Northern Ireland regional rate. Water consumed by industry, commerce and agriculture in excess of 100 cubic metres (22,000 gallons) per half year is charged through meters. Traders operating from industrially derated premises are required to pay for the treatment and disposal of the trade effluent which they discharge into the public sewerage system.

HM Coastguard

Founded in 1822, originally to guard the coasts against smuggling, HM Coastguard's role today is the very different one of guarding and saving life at sea. The Service is responsible for co-ordinating all civil maritime search and rescue operations around the 10,500 mile coastline of Great Britain and Northern Ireland and 1,000 miles into the Atlantic. In addition, it co-operates with search and rescue organizations of neighbouring countries in western Europe and around the Atlantic seaboard. The Service maintains a 24-hour radar watch on the Dover Strait, providing a Channel navigation information service for all shipping in one of the busiest sea lanes in the world. It also liaises very closely with the off-shore oil and gas industry and with merchant shipping companies.

Since 1997 HM Coastguard has been organized into five regions, each with a Regional Controller. Each region is subdivided into districts under District Controllers, operating from Maritime Rescue Co-ordination Centres or Sub-Centres. In all there are 21 of these centres. They are on 24-hour watch and are fitted with a comprehensive range of communications equipment. They are supported by smaller stations staffed by part-time Auxiliary Coastguards under the direction of Regulars, each of which keeps its parent centre fully informed of day-to-day casualty risk, particularly on the more remote danger spots around the coast.

Between 1 January and 31 December 1996, HM Coastguard co-ordinated 11,291 incidents requiring search and rescue facilities, resulting in assistance being given to 19,235 persons. All distress telephone and radio calls are centralized on the 21 centres, which are on the alert for people or vessels in distress, shipping hazards and pollution incidents. Using telecommunications equipment, including satellite, they can alert and co-ordinate the most appropriate rescue facilities; RNLI lifeboats, Royal Navy, RAF or Coastguard helicopters, fixed-wing aircraft, vessels in the vicinity, or Coastguard shore and cliff rescue teams.

For those who regularly sail in local waters or make longer passages, the Coastguard Yacht and Boat Safety Scheme provides a valuable free service. Its aim is to give the Coastguard a record of the details of craft, their equipment fit and normal operating areas. Yacht and Boat Safety Scheme cards are available from all Coastguard stations, harbourmasters' offices, and most yacht clubs and marinas as well as Coastguard Headquarters.

Members of the public who see an accident or a potentially dangerous incident on or around the coast should dial 999 and ask for the Coastguard.

In 1994 HM Coastguard and the Marine Pollution Control Unit together formed the Coastguard Agency, an executive agency of the Department of Transport. In April 1998 the Coastguard Agency and the Marine Safety Agency are to merge.

Coastguard Headquarters and Office of the Chief Coastguard, Spring Place, 105 Commercial Road, Southampton SO15 1EG. Tel: 01703-329100

Energy

The main primary sources of energy in Britain are oil, natural gas, coal, nuclear power and water power. The main secondary sources (i.e. sources derived from the primary sources) are electricity, coke and smokeless fuels, and petroleum products. The Department of the Environment, Transport and the Regions is responsible for promoting energy efficiency.

INDIGENOUS PRODUCTION OF PRIMARY FUELS
Million tonnes of oil equivalent

	1995	1996
Coal	33.3	31.9
Petroleum	143.6	144.7
Natural gas	71.1	84.0
Primary electricity:		
Nuclear	21.4	22.7
Natural flow hydro	0.5	0.3
Total	269.9	283.7

INLAND ENERGY CONSUMPTION BY PRIMARY FUEL
Million tonnes of oil equivalent, seasonally adjusted

	1995	1996
Coal	50.1	45.9
Petroleum	77.3	77.2
Natural gas	72.7	81.9
Primary electricity:		
Nuclear	21.4	22.7
Natural flow hydro	0.5	0.3
Net imports	1.4	1.4
Total	223.3	229.5

TRADE IN FUELS AND RELATED MATERIALS 1995p

	Quantity*	Value†
IMPORTS		
Coal and other solid fuel	11.5	601
Crude petroleum	44.1	3,237
Petroleum products	16.9	1,543
Natural gas	1.3	105
Electricity	1.4	408
Total	75.2	5,894
Total (fob)‡	—	5,606
EXPORTS		
Coal and other solid fuel	0.9	74
Crude petroleum	87.3	6,497
Petroleum products	26.2	2,676
Natural gas	0.9	54
Electricity	—	—
Total	115.4	9,301
Total (fob)‡	—	9,301

p provisional
* Million tonnes of oil equivalent
† £ million
‡ Adjusted to exclude estimated costs of insurance, freight etc.
Source: Department of Trade and Industry

OIL

Until the 1960s Britain imported almost all its oil supplies. In 1969 oil was discovered in the Arbroath field of the UK Continental Shelf (UKCS), and since the mid-1970s Britain has been a major producer of crude oil.

Licences for exploration and production are granted to companies by the Department of Trade and Industry; the leading British oil companies are British Petroleum (BP) and Shell Transport and Trading. At the end of 1995, 144 onshore licences were in force, and at March 1997 there were 96 offshore oilfields. In 1996 there were 11 oil refineries and four smaller refining units processing crude and process oils. There are estimated to be 3,400 million tonnes of proven or probable recoverable reserves of oil in the UKCS. Royalties are payable on fields approved before April 1982 and petroleum revenue tax is levied on fields approved between 1975 and March 1993.

DRILLING ACTIVITY 1995 p

Number of wells started	Offshore	Onshore
Exploration and appraisal	98	2
Exploration	60	—
Appraisal	38	—
Development	244	19

p provisional

VALUE OF UKCS OIL AND GAS PRODUCTION AND INVESTMENT
£ million

	1994	1995
Total income	15,942	17,828
Operating costs	3,876	3,919
Exploration expenditure	939	1,085
Gross trading profits*	9,708	10,949
Percentage contribution to GDP	2.0	2.1
Capital investment	3,547	4,228
Percentage contribution to industrial investment	16	18

* Net of stock appreciation

PRODUCTION AND REFINERY RECEIPTS

	1995	1996
Indigenous production (million tonnes)	130.2	131.4
Crude oil	121.9	123.2
NGLs*	8.4	8.1
Refinery receipts (thousand tonnes)		
Indigenous	43,444	47,282
Other†	1,110	997
Net foreign arrivals	47,591	49,779

* Natural gas liquids: condensates and petroleum gases derived at onshore treatment plants
† Mainly recycled products

DELIVERIES OF PETROLEUM PRODUCTS FOR INLAND CONSUMPTION BY ENERGY USE
Thousand tonnes

	1994	1995
Electricity generators	3,831	3,686
Gas works	50	47
Iron and steel industry	887	876
Other industries	7,470	6,501
Transport	44,830	44,843
Domestic	2,701	2,701
Other	4,010	3,751
Total	63,780	62,405

Source: Department of Trade and Industry

GAS

From the late 18th century gas in Britain was produced from coal. In the 1960s town gas began to be produced from oil-based feedstocks using imported oil. In 1965 gas was discovered in the West Sole field in the North Sea, and from the late 1960s natural gas began to replace town gas. Britain is now the world's fifth largest producer of gas and in 1996 only 2.1 per cent of gas available for consumption in the UK was imported.

The gas industry in Britain was nationalized in 1949 and operated as the Gas Council. The Gas Council was replaced by the British Gas Corporation in 1972 and the industry became more centralized. The British Gas Corporation was privatized in 1986 as British Gas PLC and is still the main supplier of gas in Great Britain, although competition is being introduced into the industry (*see* below). The Office of Gas Supply (*see* page 305) is the regulatory body for the gas industry.

In 1993 the Monopolies and Mergers Commission found that British Gas's integrated business in Great Britain as a gas trader and the owner of the gas transportation system could be expected to operate against the public interest. In February 1997 British Gas demerged. Two separate companies were formed: BG PLC, which runs the Transco pipeline business and oil and gas exploration and production; and Centrica, which runs the trading and service operation.

In early 1997 there were 67 offshore gasfields producing natural gas and associated gas (mainly methane). There are estimated to be between 760,000 million and 1.96 million million cubic metres of recoverable gas reserves in existing discoveries. There are about 8,450 km of major submarine pipelines for transporting hydrocarbons, and onshore pipelines for carrying refined products and chemicals. Natural gas is transported around Britain by about 267,300 km of pipelines supplied by five pipeline terminals. This pipeline system is owned by Transco but BG's competitors are allowed access under a network code.

Competition was gradually introduced into the industrial gas market from 1986. Supply of gas to the domestic market was opened to companies other than British Gas in April 1996 when a pilot project involving 500,000 customers in Cornwall, Devon and Wales was implemented. In February and March 1997 competition was extended to Dorset, the former county of Avon, Kent, and East and West Sussex. Competition is due to be introduced in Scotland and north-east England in late 1997, and in the rest of England and Wales by April 1998.

BG PLC, The Adelphi, 1–11 John Adam Street, London WC2N 6HT. Tel: 0171-321 2880. *Chairman*, R. V. Giordano; *Chief Executive*, D. Varney

CENTRICA PLC, Charter Court, 50 Windsor Road, Slough, Berks SL1 2HA. Tel: 01753-758000. *Chief Executive*, R. Gardner

NATURAL GAS PRODUCTION AND SUPPLY
GWh

	1995	1996
Gross gas production	821,904	971,815
Exports	11,234	14,943
Imports	19,457	19,804
Gas available	776,645	917,206
Gas transmitted‡	777,483	907,789

‡ Figures differ from gas available mainly because of stock changes

NATURAL GAS CONSUMPTION
GWh

	1994	1995
Electricity generators	114,574	145,790
Iron and steel industry	20,327	20,689
Other industries	146,843	148,207
Domestic	329,710	326,010
Public administration, commerce and agriculture	99,976	113,831
Total	711,432	754,527

Source: Department of Trade and Industry

COAL

Coal has been mined in Britain for centuries and the availability of coal was crucial to the industrial revolution of the 18th and 19th centuries. Mines were in private ownership until 1947 when they were nationalized and came under the management of the National Coal Board, later the British Coal Corporation. In addition to producing coal at its own deep-mine and opencast sites, of which there were 850 in 1955, British Coal was responsible for licensing private operators.

Under the Coal Industry Act 1994, the Coal Authority (*see* page 291) was established to take over ownership of coal reserves and to issue licences to private mining companies as part of the privatization of British Coal. The Coal Authority also deals with the physical legacy of mining, e.g. subsidence damage claims, and is responsible for holding and making available all existing records. The mines were sold as five separate businesses in 1994 and coal production in the UK is now undertaken entirely in the private sector. At the end of 1996 there were 27 large deep mines in operation.

The main UK customer for coal is the electricity supply industry, but the latter's demand for coal has declined as it turns increasingly to alternative fuels. National Power (*see* page 503) has announced that it expects to close ten of its 18 coal-fired power stations by 2000.

BRITISH GAS FINANCE 1996*
£ million

	BG	Centrica	Adjustments†	British Gas Group
Turnover	4,383	8,125	(3,055)	9,453
Operating costs excluding exceptional charges	(3,052)	(8,057)	3,087	(8,022)
Exceptional charges	(316)	(822)	—	(1,138)
Total operating costs	(3,368)	(8,879)	3,087	(9,160)
Operating profit/(loss)	1,015	(754)	32	293
Profit/(loss) for the financial period	379	(1,060)	503	(178)

* The approximate pro-forma financial position of the demerged businesses if the demerger had taken place on 31 December 1996
† Consolidation and demerger adjustments

Coal Production and Foreign Trade
Thousand tonnes

	1992	1996p
Total production	84,493	50,515
Deep-mined	65,800	33,139
Opencast	18,187	16,167
Imports	20,339	17,572
Exports	973	953

p provisional

Inland Coal Use
Thousand tonnes

	1992	1996
Fuel producers		
Collieries	79	8
Electricity generators	78,509	54,837
Coke ovens	9,031	8,635
Other conversion industries	1,319	946
Total	100,620	71,111
Final users		
Industry	6,581	3,509
Domestic	4,156	2,934
Public administration, commerce and agriculture	945	242

Source: Department of Trade and Industry

ELECTRICITY

The first power station in Britain generating electricity for public supply began operating in 1882. In the 1930s a national transmission grid was developed, and it was reconstructed and extended in the 1950s and 1960s. Power stations were operated by the Central Electricity Generating Board.

Under the Electricity Act 1989, 12 regional electricity companies (RECs), which are responsible for the distribution of electricity from the national grid to consumers, were formed from the former area electricity boards in England and Wales. Four companies were formed from the Central Electricity Generating Board: three generating companies (National Power PLC, Nuclear Electric PLC and PowerGen PLC) and the National Grid Company PLC, which owns and operates the transmission system. National Power and PowerGen were floated on the stock market in 1991. Nuclear Electric was split into two parts in 1995; the part comprising the more modern nuclear stations was incorporated into a new company, British Energy, which was floated on the stock market in 1996. Ownership of the National Grid Company was transferred to the RECs and subsequently floated in 1995. There are now 27 electricity generating companies in Britain. The RECs currently have a monopoly on sales of 100 kW or less to consumers in their regions; over this limit competition has been introduced. Competition is due to be introduced into the domestic electricity market in April 1998.

In Scotland, three new companies were formed under the Electricity Act 1989: Scottish Power PLC and Scottish Hydro-Electric PLC, which are responsible for generation, transmission, distribution and supply; and Scottish Nuclear Ltd. Scottish Power and Scottish Hydro-Electric were floated on the stock market in 1991; Scottish Nuclear was incorporated into British Energy in 1995.

In Northern Ireland, Northern Ireland Electricity PLC was set up in 1993 under a 1991 Order in Council. It is responsible for transmission, distribution and supply and has been floated on the stock market. Three private companies are responsible for electricity generation.

The Electricity Association is the electricity industry's main trade association. Electricity Association Services Ltd, the Association's principal subsidiary, provides representational and professional services for the electricity companies. EA Technology Ltd provides distribution and utilization research, development and technology transfer. The Offices of Electricity Regulation (*see* page 298) are the regulatory bodies for the electricity industry.

Nuclear Power

Nuclear power began to supply electricity to the national grid in 1956. It is generated at six Magnox reactors, seven Advanced Gas-cooled Reactors (AGRs) and one Pressurized Water Reactor (PWR), Sizewell 'B' in Suffolk. Nuclear stations now generate about 27 per cent of Britain's electricity.

In preparation for privatization, the nuclear industry was restructured in December 1995. A holding company, British Energy PLC, was formed with two operational subsidiaries, Nuclear Electric Ltd and Scottish Nuclear Ltd. Nuclear Electric operates the five AGRs and the PWR in England and Wales; Scottish Nuclear operates the two AGRs in Scotland. British Energy was floated on the stock market in 1996. The Magnox reactors were transferred to Magnox Electric PLC, which remains in public ownership. British Nuclear Fuels Ltd (BNFL), which is also in public ownership, provides reprocessing, waste management and effluent treatment services. Work is currently under way on the integration of Magnox Electric and BNFL into one company. The UK Atomic Energy Authority (*see* page 284) is responsible for the maintenance and decommissioning of redundant nuclear facilities used in research and development, and for fusion research. Nirex, which is owned by the nuclear generating companies and the Government, is responsible for the disposal of nuclear waste. The Nuclear Installations Inspectorate of the Health and Safety Executive (*see* page 309) is the nuclear industry's regulator.

Supply Companies

British Energy PLC, 10 Lochside Place, Edinburgh EH12 9DF. Tel: 0131-527 2000. *Chief Executive (acting)*, J. Robb

Magnox Electric PLC, Berkeley Centre, Berkeley, Glos GL13 9PB. Tel: 01453-810451. *Chief Executive*, R. Hall

The National Grid Company PLC, National Grid House, Kirby Corner Road, Coventry CV4 8JY. Tel: 01203-423000. *Chief Executive*, D. Jones

National Power PLC, Windmill Hill Business Park, Whitehill Way, Swindon, Wilts SN5 6PB. Tel: 01793-877777. *Chief Executive*, K. Henry

PowerGen PLC, Westwood Way, Westwood Business Park, Coventry CV4 8LG. Tel: 01203-424000. *Chairman*, E. Wallis

Regional Electricity Companies

Eastern Electricity PLC, PO Box 40, Wherstead, Ipswich IP9 2AQ

East Midlands Electricity PLC, PO Box 444, Wollaton, Nottingham NG8 1EZ

London Electricity PLC, Templar House, 81–87 High Holborn, London WC1V 6NU

Manweb PLC, Manweb House, Kingsfield Court, Chester Business Park, Chester CH4 9RF

Midlands Electricity PLC, Mucklow Hill, Halesowen, W. Midlands B62 8BP

Northern Electric PLC, Carliol House, Market Street, Newcastle upon Tyne NE1 6NE

Norweb PLC, Talbot Road, Manchester M16 0HQ

SEEBOARD PLC, Forest Gate, Brighton Road, Crawley, W. Sussex RH11 9BH

SOUTHERN ELECTRIC PLC, Southern Electric House, Westacott Way, Littlewick Green, Maidenhead, Berks SL6 3QB

SWALEC PLC, Newport Road, St Mellons, Cardiff CF3 9XW

SOUTH WESTERN ELECTRICITY PLC, 800 Park Avenue, Aztec West, Almondsbury, Bristol BS12 4SE

YORKSHIRE ELECTRICITY GROUP PLC, Wetherby Road, Scarcroft, Leeds LS14 3HS

SCOTLAND

SCOTTISH HYDRO-ELECTRIC PLC, Dunkeld Road, Perth PH1 5WA. Tel: 01738-455040. *Chief Executive,* R. Young

SCOTTISH POWER PLC, 1 Atlantic Quay, Glasgow G2 8SP. Tel: 0141-248 8200. *Chief Executive,* I. Robinson

NORTHERN IRELAND

NORTHERN IRELAND ELECTRICITY PLC, 120 Malone Road, Belfast BT9 5HT. Tel: 01232-661100. *Chief Executive,* Dr P. Haren

ELECTRICITY ASSOCIATION SERVICES LTD, 30 Millbank, London SW1P 4RD. Tel: 0171-963 5700. *Chief Executive,* P. E. G. Daubeney

EA TECHNOLOGY LTD, Capenhurst, Chester CH1 6ES. Tel: 0151-339 4181. *Managing Director,* Dr S. F. Exell

ELECTRICITY GENERATION, SUPPLY AND CONSUMPTION

GWh	1994	1995
Electricity generated		
Major power producers: total	302,807	310,292
Conventional steam stations	175,362	169,866
Nuclear stations	83,944	85,298
Gas turbines and oil engines	244	190
Combined cycle gas turbine stations	36,971	48,720
Hydro-electric stations:		
Natural flow	4,317	4,096
Pumped storage	1,463	1,552
Renewables other than hydro	506	570
Electricity used on works: total	17,504	17,391
Major generating companies	15,921	15,799
Other generators	1,583	1,592
Electricity supplied (gross)		
Major power producers: total	286,886	294,493
Conventional steam stations	167,289	162,084
Nuclear stations	76,412	77,643
Gas turbines and oil engines	233	181
Combined cycle gas turbine stations	36,815	48,525
Hydro-electric stations:		
Natural flow	4,265	4,051
Pumped storage	1,417	1,502
Renewables other than hydro	455	506
Electricity used in pumping		
Major power producers	2,051	2,282
Electricity supplied (net): total	305,846	314,781
Major power producers	284,835	292,211
Other generators	21,011	22,570
Net imports	16,887	16,313
Electricity available	322,733	331,094
Losses in transmission, etc.	30,951	24,922
Electricity consumption: total	291,782	306,172
Fuel industries	7,518	8,393
Final users: total	284,264	297,779
Industrial sector	95,067	102,507
Domestic sector	101,407	101,648
Other sectors	87,790	93,624

Source: The Stationery Office – Annual Abstract of Statistics 1997

RENEWABLE SOURCES

Renewable sources of energy principally include biofuels, hydro, wind, waste and solar heating. Renewable sources accounted for 1.7 million tonnes of oil equivalent of primary energy use in 1996; of this, about 1.2 million tonnes was used to generate electricity and about 0.5 million tonnes to generate heat.

The Non-Fossil Fuel Obligation (NFFO) Renewables Orders are the Government's principal mechanism for developing renewable energy sources. NFFO Renewables Orders require the regional electricity companies to buy specified amounts of electricity from specified non-fossil fuel sources.

The Government will be conducting a review to consider what measures would be necessary and practicable to achieve 10 per cent of the UK's electricity needs from renewables by 2010, and how renewables can contribute to meeting requirements for future reductions in greenhouse gases.

RENEWABLE ENERGY SOURCES 1995

	Percentages
Biofuels	71.1
Landfill gas	12.0
Sewage gas	10.1
Wood combustion	10.2
Straw combustion	4.2
Refuse combustion	20.4
Other biofuels	14.2
Hydro	26.5
Large-scale	25.5
Small-scale	1.0
Wind	1.8
Active solar heating	0.6
Total	100

Source: Department of Trade and Industry

Transport

GOODS TRANSPORT 1995

TOTAL TONNE KILOMETRES (*millions*)	n/a
Road	149,600
Rail (British Rail only)	n/a
Water: coastwise oil products*	31,400
Water: other*	21,200
Pipelines (except gases)	12,200
TOTAL (*million tonnes*)	n/a
Road	1,701
Rail (British Rail only)	n/a
Water: coastwise oil products*	47
Water: other*	98
Pipelines (except gases)	181

*'Coastwise' includes all sea traffic within the UK, Isle of Man and
Channel Islands. 'Other' means other coastwise plus inland water-
way traffic and one port traffic
Source: The Stationery Office – *Annual Abstract of Statistics 1997*

PASSENGER TRANSPORT 1995p
Million passenger kilometres (estimated)

TOTAL	688,000
Air	6,000
Rail*	36,900
Road: Public service vehicles	43,000
Cars, vans and taxis	594,000
Motorcycles	4,000
Pedal cycles	5,000

p provisional
*Including London Underground and other urban railway systems
Source: The Stationery Office – *Annual Abstract of Statistics 1997*

AIR PASSENGERS 1996*

ALL UK AIRPORTS: TOTAL	137,505,506
LONDON AREA AIRPORTS: TOTAL	88,409,670
Battersea Heliport	5,130
Gatwick	24,323,812
Heathrow	56,049,806
London City	725,888
Luton	2,435,101
Southend	5,748
Stansted	4,864,185
OTHER UK AIRPORTS: TOTAL	49,095,836
Aberdeen	2,387,692
Barra	8,203
Barrow-in-Furness	155
Belfast City	1,366,339
Belfast International	2,392,557
Benbecula	37,589
Biggin Hill	6,373
Birmingham	5,468,100
Blackpool	86,282
Bournemouth	162,770
Bristol	1,424,499
Cambridge	28,948
Campbeltown	9,228
Cardiff	1,038,145
Carlisle	762
Coventry	3,007
Dundee	15,750
East Midlands	1,831,846
Edinburgh	3,898,228
Exeter	213,564
Glasgow	5,593,523
Gloucestershire	2,482
Hawarden	170
Humberside	285,527
Inverness	300,669
Islay	20,936
Isle of Man	622,533
Isles of Scilly–St Mary's	125,260
–Tresco	27,588
Kent International	2,447
Kirkwall	102,751
Leeds/Bradford	1,064,231
Lerwick (Tingwall)	4,382
Liverpool	623,630
Londonderry	63,945
Lydd	303
Manchester	14,659,803
Newcastle	2,475,741
Norwich	265,511
Penzance Heliport	105,571
Plymouth	121,593
Prestwick	537,160
Scatsta	78,807
Shoreham	3,030
Southampton	562,156
Stornoway	94,468
Sumburgh	423,439
Teesside	482,440
Tiree	5,497
Unst	17,848
Wick	42,358
CHANNEL IS. AIRPORTS: TOTAL	2,665,280
Alderney	84,012
Guernsey	890,545
Jersey	1,690,723

*Total terminal, transit, scheduled and charter passengers
Source: Civil Aviation Authority

AERODROMES/AIRPORTS

The following aerodromes in the UK, the Isle of Man and the Channel Islands are either state owned or licensed for use by civil aircraft. A number of unlicensed aerodromes not included in this list are also available for private use by special permission. Aerodromes designated as Customs airports are printed in small capitals. Customs facilities are available at certain other aerodromes by special arrangement.

BAA   Owned by BAA PLC
H   Licensed for helicopters
HIAL Operated by Highland and Islands Airports Ltd
L   Owned by municipal authority
M   Military aerodromes – civil availability by prior permission
P   Private ownership
S   Government owned and operated

ENGLAND AND WALES

Aberporth, Ceredigion   M
Andrewsfield, Essex
Barrow (Walney Island), Cumbria
Bembridge, IOW
Benson, Oxon   M
Beverley/Linley Hill, E. Yorks
BIGGIN HILL, Kent   P
BIRMINGHAM   P
Blackbushe, Hants
BLACKPOOL, Lancs   P
Bodmin, Cornwall
Boscombe Down, Wilts   M
Bourn, Cambridge
BOURNEMOUTH, Dorset   P
BRISTOL   P
Brize Norton, Oxford   M
Brough, E. Yorks
Caernarfon
CAMBRIDGE   P
CARDIFF   P
Carlisle, Cumbria   L
Chichester (Goodwood), Sussex
Chivenor, Devon   H, M
Church Fenton, N. Yorks   M
Clacton, Essex
Compton Abbas, Dorset
Cosford, Wolverhampton   M
COVENTRY, W. Midlands   L
Cranfield, Beds
Cranwell, Lincs   M
Crowfield, Suffolk
Culdrose, Cornwall   M
Denham, Bucks
Derby
Dishforth, N. Yorks   M
Dunkeswell, Devon
Dunsfold, Surrey   L
Duxford, Cambs   L
Eaglescott, Devon
Earls Colne, Halstead

EAST MIDLANDS, Derbys   P
Elstree, Herts
EXETER, Devon
Fairoaks, Surrey
Farnborough, Hants   S
Fenland, Lincs
Filton, Bristol
Fowlmere, Cambs
Full Sutton, N. Yorks
Gloucestershire (Staverton)   P
Great Yarmouth (North Denes), Norfolk   H
Halfpenny Green, Staffs
Halton, Bucks   M
Haverfordwest, Pembrokeshire   L
Hawarden, Flintshire
Hucknall, Notts
HUMBERSIDE, Lincs   P
Isle of Wight/Sandown
Land's End (St Just), Cornwall
Lashenden, Headcorn, Kent
LEEDS/BRADFORD   P
Leicester
Linton-on-Ouse, Yorks   M
Little Gransden, Beds
LIVERPOOL   P
Llanbedr, Caernarfonshire   M
LONDON/CITY
LONDON/GATWICK   BAA
LONDON/HEATHROW   BAA
LONDON/LUTON   P
LONDON/STANSTED   BAA
London/Westland Heliport   H
LYDD, Kent
Lyneham, Wilts   M
MANCHESTER   P
Manchester (Barton)
MANSTON (M)/KENT INTERNATIONAL
Mona, Anglesey   M
Netherthorpe, S. Yorks
NEWCASTLE UPON TYNE   P
Newton, Notts   M
Northampton (Sywell)
Northolt, Middx   M
NORWICH, Norfolk   L
Nottingham
Old Sarum, Wilts
Oxford (Kidlington)
Penzance, Cornwall   H
Perranporth, Cornwall
Peterborough (Conington)
Peterborough (Sibson)
PLYMOUTH (ROBOROUGH), Devon
Portland Naval, Dorset   H, M
Redhill, Surrey
Retford/Gamston, Notts
Rochester, Kent
St Mawgan, Cornwall   M
Sandtoft, Lincs
Scilly Isles (St Mary's)   L
Seething, Norfolk
Shawbury, Shropshire   M
SHEFFIELD CITY
Sherburn-in-Elmet, N. Yorks
Shipdham, Norfolk
Shobdon, Herefordshire
SHOREHAM, W. Sussex
Silverstone, Northants   H
Sleap, Shropshire
SOUTHAMPTON   P

SOUTHEND, Essex   P
Stapleford, Essex
Sturgate, Lincs
Swansea   L
TEESSIDE   P
Thruxton, Hants
Tresco, Isles of Scilly   H
Turweston, Northants
Valley, Anglesey   M
Warton, Lancs
Wattisham, Suffolk   M
Wellesbourne Mountford, Warwick
Welshpool, Powys
Weston, Somerset   H
White Waltham, Berks
Wickenby, Lincs
Woodford, Gtr Manchester
Woodvale, Merseyside   M
Wycombe Air Park (Booker), Bucks
Yeovil, Somerset
Yeovilton, Somerset   M

SCOTLAND

ABERDEEN (DYCE)   BAA
Barra, Hebrides
Benbecula, Hebrides   HIAL
Campbeltown   HIAL
Cumbernauld, Strathclyde
Dundee   L
Eday, Orkneys   L
EDINBURGH   BAA
Fair Isle, Shetlands
Fife   L
Flotta, Orkneys
GLASGOW   BAA
Inverness (Dalcross)   HIAL
Islay (Port Ellen), Hebrides   HIAL
Kirkwall, Orkneys   HIAL
Lerwick (Tingwall), Shetlands   L
Leuchars, Fife   M
North Ronaldsay, Orkneys   L
Papa Westray, Orkneys   L
Perth (Scone)
PRESTWICK, Ayrshire   BAA
Sanday, Orkneys   L
Scatsta, Shetlands
Stornoway, Hebrides   HIAL
Stronsay, Orkneys   L
SUMBURGH, Shetlands   HIAL
Tiree, Hebrides   HIAL
Unst, Shetlands   L
West Freugh, Dumfries   S
Westray, Orkneys   L
Whalsay, Shetlands
Wick, Caithness   HIAL

NORTHERN IRELAND

BELFAST (ALDERGROVE)
Belfast (City)
Enniskillen (St Angelo), Co. Fermanagh   P
Londonderry (Eglinton)   L
Newtownards, Co. Down

ISLANDS

ALDERNEY, CI   S
GUERNSEY, CI   S
ISLE OF MAN   S
JERSEY, CI   S

RAILWAYS

Britain pioneered railways and a railway network was developed across Britain by private companies in the course of the 19th century. In 1948 the main railway companies were nationalized and were run by a public authority, the British Transport Commission. The Commission was replaced by the British Railways Board in 1963, operating as British Rail. On 1 April 1994, under the Railways Act 1993, responsibility for managing the railway infrastructure passed to a newly-formed company, Railtrack; the British Railways Board continued as operator of all train services until they were sold or franchised to the private sector. All passenger activities have now been franchised. British Rail continues to operate Railfreight Distribution (international freight) pending EC approval of a sale agreement. All other freight activities have been sold.

Prior to privatization, management of the railways had been organized into the business sectors of InterCity, Network SouthEast, Regional Railways, Trainload Freight and Railfreight Distribution. These businesses have ceased to exist corporately but some of the names will continue to be used for trading purposes in the short term. European Passenger Services Ltd (now Eurostar UK Ltd) was set up to manage international passenger rail services through the Channel Tunnel. Ownership was transferred to the Government in May 1994 and the company was subsequently sold to London and Continental Railways.

PRIVATIZATION

Since 1 April 1994, ownership of operational track and land has been vested in Railtrack, which was floated on the Stock Exchange in 1996. Railtrack manages the track and charges for access to it and is responsible for signalling and timetabling. It does not operate train services. It owns the stations, and leases most of them out to the train operating companies. Initially, Railtrack's infrastructure support functions were provided by British Rail service companies; these companies have now been sold into the private sector. Railtrack invests in infrastructure principally using finance raised by track charges, and takes investment decisions in consultation with rail operators. Railtrack is also responsible for overall safety on the railways.

Domestic passenger services were divided into 25 train-operating units, which have been franchised to private sector operators via a competitive tendering process overseen by the Director of the Office of Passenger Rail Franchising. The private sector will eventually also be able to run completely new services with a right of open access to the track. The Government will continue to subsidize loss making but socially necessary rail services. The franchising director is responsible for monitoring the performance of the franchisees and allocating and administering government subsidy payments.

British Rail's passenger rolling stock was divided between three subsidiary companies which lease rolling stock to franchisees. The three companies were transferred to government ownership in 1995 and sold to the private sector in 1996. The bulk freight haulage companies and Rail Express Systems, which carries Royal Mail traffic, were sold to English, Welsh and Scottish Railways. The domestic and deep-sea container business (Freightliner) and British Rail's technical support and specialist function businesses have also been sold.

The independent Rail Regulator is responsible for the licensing of new railway operators, approving access agreements, promoting the use and development of the network, and protecting the interests of rail users.

BRITISH RAILWAYS BOARD, *see* page 287
RAILTRACK, Railtrack House, Euston Square, London NW1 3EE. Tel: 0171-557 8000. *Chairman,* Sir Robert Horton. *Chief Executive,* J. Edmonds, CBE (*until March 1998*)
ASSOCIATION OF TRAIN OPERATING COMPANIES, 3rd Floor, The Podium, 1 Eversholt Street, London NW1 1DN. Tel: 0171-214 9143. *Chairman,* C. Tibbetts
OFFICE OF PASSENGER RAIL FRANCHISING (OPRAF), Golding's House, 2 Hay's Lane, London SE1 2HR. Tel: 0171-940 4200. *Franchising Director,* J. O'Brien
OFFICE OF THE RAIL REGULATOR (ORR), 1 Waterhouse Square, Holborn Bars, 138–142 Holborn, London EC1N 2SU. Tel: 0171-282 2000. *Rail Regulator,* J. Swift, QC

RAIL OPERATIONS

At 31 March 1997, Railtrack had about 20,000 miles of standard gauge lines and sidings in use, representing over 10,000 miles of route of which about 3,000 miles were electrified. Standard rail on main line has a weight of 110 lb per yard. Railtrack owns about 2,500 stations, 90 light maintenance depots, about 40,000 bridges, viaducts and tunnels, and over 9,000 level crossings.

Passenger journeys made in 1996–7 totalled 808.1 million, including 345.6 million made by holders of season tickets. The average distance of each passenger journey on ordinary fare was 24.8 miles; and on season ticket, 15.72 miles. Passenger stations in use numbered 2,514.

On 31 March 1997 Railtrack employed 10,937 staff (11,516 at 31 March 1996). On 31 March 1996 British Rail employed 63,982 staff (94,344 at 31 March 1995).

FINANCIAL RESULTS

Railtrack

In 1996–7 Railtrack showed an operating profit of £339 million and a pre-tax profit of £346 million.

	£ million
Income	
Passenger	2,119
Freight	159
Property rental	120
Other	39
Total	2,437
Costs	
Production and management	507
Infrastructure maintenance	732
Asset maintenance plan charge	515
Joint industry costs	220
Depreciation	124
Total	2,098

British Rail

British Rail's profit and loss account for 1995–6 showed a profit of £58 million after interest and extraordinary items, compared with a profit of £362 million in 1994–5. The railway operating surplus was £13.7 million (including a write-off of £500 million against Channel Tunnel freight services) compared with a surplus of £571 million for the previous year.

	£ million
*Income	
Passenger	4,394
Freight and Parcels	444
Railfreight Distribution	47
Others	165
Infrastructure services	1,019
Group Services	317
Total	6,386

Operating expenditure	
Staff costs	1,919
Railtrack access charges	2,155
Rolling stock leasing	487
Materials, supplies and services	1,162
Depreciation	102
Amortization of deferred grant	(27)
Own work capitalized	(1)
Total	5,797
Operating profit	589
Profit on disposals	176
Restructuring costs	(52)
Exceptional items	(575)
Profit before interest	139
Interest	(81)
Group profit	58

*Income includes government grants totalling £2,010 million

ACCIDENTS ON RAILWAYS

	1994–5	1995–6
Train accidents: total	907	989
Persons killed: total	12	7
Passengers	3	1
Railway staff	5	1
Others	4	5
Persons injured: total	296	166
Passengers	190	62
Railway staff	83	75
Others	23	29
Other accidents through movement of railway vehicles		
Persons killed	27	15
Persons injured	2,417	2,517
Other accidents on railway premises		
Persons killed	3	4
Persons injured	7,933	6,401
Trespassers and suicides		
Persons killed	254	244
Persons injured	85	82

THE CHANNEL TUNNEL

The earliest recorded scheme for a submarine transport connection between Britain and France was in 1802. Tunnelling has begun simultaneously on both sides of the Channel three times: in 1881, in the early 1970s, and on 1 December 1987, when construction workers began to bore the first of the three tunnels which form the current project. They 'holed through' the first tunnel (the service tunnel) on 1 December 1990 and tunnelling was completed in June 1991. The tunnel was officially inaugurated by The Queen and President Mitterrand of France on 6 May 1994.

In 1986 the concession for construction and operation of the tunnel and its services was awarded to a paired Anglo-French private-sector company, CTG-FM, wholly owned by Eurotunnel. Eurotunnel's costs from establishment in 1986 to the first commercial service in 1994 were about £8,700 million. The funds available to Eurotunnel amount to £10,535 million, raised through equity and loans. In September 1995 Eurotunnel suspended interest payments on its 'junior' debt (i.e. all money raised before the rights issue in 1994) in line with its credit agreement. This gives Eurotunnel an interest payment moratorium until December 1997. In May 1997 Eurotunnel announced its final proposals for restructuring its debt, and these were approved by shareholders on 10 July 1997.

Passenger services (Eurostar) run from Waterloo station in London to Paris and Brussels. Connecting services from Edinburgh and Manchester via London began in January 1997 and through services from these cities, not stopping in London, are scheduled to begin by the end of 1997. Vehicle shuttle services (Le Shuttle) operate between Folkestone and Calais.

The submarine link comprises three tunnels. There are two rail tunnels, each carrying trains in one direction, which measure 24.93 ft (7.6 m) in diameter. Between them lies a smaller service tunnel, measuring 15.75 ft (4.8 m) in diameter. The service tunnel is linked to the rail tunnels by 130 cross-passages for maintenance and safety purposes. The tunnels are 31 miles (50 km) long, 24 miles (38 km) of which is under the sea-bed at an average depth of 132 ft (40 m). The rail terminals are situated at Folkestone and Calais, and the tunnels go underground at Shakespeare Cliff, Dover, and Sangatte, west of Calais.

RAIL LINKS

The route for the British Channel Tunnel rail link was confirmed by the Government in 1994 and authorized by the Channel Tunnel Rail Link Act 1996. The rail link will run from Folkestone to a new terminal at St Pancras station, London, with new intermediate stations at Ebbsfleet, Kent, and Stratford, east London; at present services run into a terminal at Waterloo station, London.

Construction of the rail link will be financed by the private sector with a substantial government contribution. A private sector consortium, London and Continental Railways Ltd, is responsible for the design, construction and ownership of the rail link, and has taken over Union Railways and European Passenger Services Ltd, the UK operator of Eurostar (now renamed Eurostar (UK) Ltd). Construction is expected to be completed in 2003.

Infrastructure developments in France have been completed and high-speed trains run from Calais to Paris, linking the Channel tunnel with the high-speed European network.

ROADS

HIGHWAY AUTHORITIES

The powers and responsibilities of highway authorities in England and Wales are set out in the Highways Acts 1980; for Scotland there is separate legislation.

Responsibility for trunk road motorways and other trunk roads in Great Britain rests in England with the Secretary of State for the Environment, Transport and the Regions, in Scotland with the Secretary of State for Scotland, and in Wales with the Secretary of State for Wales. The costs of construction, improvement and maintenance are paid for by central government. The highway authority for non-trunk roads in England, Wales and Scotland is, in general, the unitary authority, county council or London borough council in whose area the roads lie. In Northern Ireland the Department of the Environment for Northern Ireland is the statutory road authority responsible for public roads and their maintenance and construction; the Roads Service executive agency (*see* page 331) carries out these functions on behalf of the Department.

FINANCE

The Government contributes towards capital expenditure through Transport Supplementary Grant (TSG) in England and Transport Grant (TG) in Wales. Grant rates are determined by the respective Secretaries of State; at present, grant is paid at 50 per cent of expenditure accepted for grant in England and Wales.

In England TSG is paid towards capital spending on highways and the regulation of traffic; current expenditure is funded by revenue support grant (i.e. central government grants to local authorities for non-specific services). TSG is also paid towards capital spending on bridge assessment and strengthening; towards structural maintenance on the primary route network; and towards all principal 'A' roads. In Wales TG is paid towards capital expenditure only; current expenditure is funded by revenue support grant.

For the financial year 1997–8 local authorities in England will receive £195 million in TSG. Total estimated expenditure on building and maintaining motorways and trunk roads in England in 1996–7 was £1,584 million; estimated outturn for 1997–8 is £1,491 million.

For the financial year 1997–8 local authorities in Wales will receive up to £28 million in TG. Total expenditure on roads in Wales in 1995–6 was £277 million.

The Scottish Office receives a block vote from Parliament and the Secretary of State for Scotland determines how much is allocated towards roads. Total expenditure on building and maintaining trunk roads in Scotland was estimated at £206 million in 1996–7.

In Northern Ireland expenditure on roads in 1996–7 was £157.4 million, and estimated expenditure for 1997–8 is £151.3 million.

PRIVATE FINANCE

Contracts have been let which allow greater involvement by the private sector in the design, finance, construction and operation of roads. A research programme is under way to assess the technology necessary for the introduction of electronic motorway tolls.

ROAD BUILDING PROGRAMME

In November 1996 the Conservative Government announced that its road programme would consist of 24 schemes then under construction, 112 conventionally-funded schemes in preparation and 44 schemes in the Design, Build, Finance and Operate programme, part of the Private Finance Initiative. Most of the schemes in the longer-term programme were withdrawn to remove blight and uncertainty.

In June 1997 the Labour Government launched a roads review. The object of the review is to determine the role which roads should play in an integrated transport policy and to establish a forward investment programme for the road network in England. Public consultation was launched in July 1997, inviting responses by the end of October. The Government hopes to announce the conclusions of the review in spring 1998. Schemes which were already under construction have continued, as has work on developer-funded schemes. Twelve cases with urgent decisions pending were subject to accelerated review. In the remainder of cases, work continued to the end of the stage reached in June 1997 and was then put on hold until the results of the review are known.

ROAD LENGTHS (in miles) as at April 1996

	Total roads	Trunk roads† (including motorways)	Motorways*
England	175,048	6,538	1,704
Wales	21,143	1,061	78
Scotland	32,698	2,032	200
N. Ireland	15,131	1,463	70
UK	244,020	11,094	2,052

*There were in addition 43.9 miles of local authority motorway in England
†'A' roads in N. Ireland, where there are no designated trunk roads

MOTORWAYS

England and Wales:

M1	London to Yorkshire
M2	London to Faversham
M3	London to Southampton
M4	London to South Wales
M5	Birmingham to Exeter
M6	Catthorpe to Carlisle
M10	St Albans spur
M11	London to Cambridge
M18	Rotherham to Goole
M20	London to Folkestone
M23	London to Gatwick
M25	London orbital
M26	M20 to M25 spur
M27	Southampton bypass
M32	M4 to Bristol spur
M40	London to Birmingham
M41	London to West Cross
M42	South-west of Birmingham to Measham
M45	Dunchurch spur
M50	Ross spur
M53	Chester to Birkenhead
M54	M6 to Telford
M55	Preston to Blackpool
M56	Manchester to Chester
M57	Liverpool outer ring
M58	Liverpool to Wigan
M61	Manchester to Preston
M62	Liverpool to Hull
M63	Manchester southern ring road
M65	Calder Valley
M66	Manchester eastern ring road to Rochdale
M67	Manchester Hyde to Denton
M69	Coventry to Leicester
M180	South Humberside

Scotland:

M8	Edinburgh-Newhouse, Baillieston-West Ferry Interchange
M9	Edinburgh to Dunblane
M73	Maryville to Mollinsburn
M74	Glasgow-Paddy's Rickle Bridge, Cleuchbrae-Gretna
M77	Ayr Road Route
M80	Stirling to Haggs/Glasgow (M8) to Stepps
M90	Inverkeithing to Perth
M876	Dennyloanhead (M80) to Kincardine Bridge

Northern Ireland:

M1	Belfast to Dungannon
M2	Belfast to Antrim
M2	Ballymena bypass
M3	Belfast Cross Harbour Bridge
M5	M2 to Greencastle
M12	M1 to Craigavon
M22	Antrim to Randalstown

ROAD USE

ESTIMATED TRAFFIC ON ALL ROADS (GREAT BRITAIN) 1996

Million vehicle kilometres

All motor vehicles	442,500
Cars and taxis	362,400
Two-wheeled motor vehicles	4,200
Buses and coaches	4,800
Light vans	40,400
Other goods vehicles	30,700
Total goods vehicles	71,100
Pedal cycles	4,300

BUSES AND COACHES (GREAT BRITAIN) 1995–6

Number of vehicles (31 March 1996)	75,700
Vehicle kilometres (millions)	4,105
Local bus passenger journeys (millions)	4,383
Passenger receipts (£ million)	3,431

ROAD GOODS TRANSPORT (GREAT BRITAIN) 1996

Analysis by mode of working and by gross weight of vehicle

Estimated tonne kilometres (thousand million)	146.8
Own account	37.7
Public haulage	109.1
By gross weight of vehicle (billion tonne kilometres)	
Not over 25 tonnes	25.3
Over 25 tonnes	121.5
Estimated tonnes carried (millions)	1,628.0
Own account	618.0
Public haulage	1,011.0
By gross weight of vehicle (million tonnes)	
Not over 25 tonnes	447.0
Over 25 tonnes	1,181.0

ROAD ACCIDENTS 1996

Road accidents	235,939
Vehicles involved:	
Pedal cycles	25,051
Motor vehicles	401,625
Total casualties	320,302
Pedestrians	46,381
Vehicle users	273,921
Killed*	3,598
Pedestrians	997
Pedal cycles	203
All two-wheeled motor vehicles	440
Cars and taxis	1,806
Others	152

*Died within 30 days of accident

	Killed	Injured
1965	7,952	389,986
1970	7,499	355,869
1975	6,366	318,584
1980	6,010	323,000
1985	5,165	312,359
1990	5,217	335,924
1994	3,650	311,539
1995	3,621	306,885
1996	3,598	316,704

Source: Department of the Environment, Transport and the Regions

DRIVING LICENCES

It is necessary to hold a valid full licence in order to drive on public roads in the UK. Learner drivers obtain a provisional driving licence before starting to learn to drive and must then pass a test to obtain a full driving licence. Application forms for a driving licence (form D1) are available from post offices. There are separate tests for driving motor cycles, cars, passenger-carrying vehicles (PCVs) and large goods vehicles (LGVs). Drivers must hold full car entitlement before they can apply for PCV or LGV entitlements. In 1996, 36.4 million people in the UK held a valid driving licence (full or provisional). The minimum age for driving motor cars, light goods vehicles up to 3.5 tonnes and motor cycles is 17 (moped, 16). Since June 1997, drivers who collect six or more penalty points within two years of qualifying lose their licence and are required to take another test. A leaflet, *What You Need to Know About Driving Licences*, (form D100) is available from post offices.

The Driver and Vehicle Licensing Agency is responsible for issuing driving licences, registering and licensing vehicles, and collecting excise duty in Great Britain. In Northern Ireland the Driver and Vehicle Licensing Agency (Northern Ireland) has similar responsibilities.

DRIVING LICENCE FEES *as at June 1997*

First provisional licence	£21.00
Changing a provisional to a full licence after passing a driving test	free
Renewal of licence	£6.00
Renewal of licence including PCV or LGV entitlements	£21
Medical renewal	free
Medical renewal (over 70)	£6.00
Duplicate Licence	£6.00
Exchange Licence	£6.00
Removing endorsements	£6.00
New licence after a period of disqualification	£12.00
New licence after disqualification for some drinking and driving offences	£20

DRIVING TESTS

The Driving Standards Agency is responsible for carrying out driving tests and approving driving instructors in Great Britain. In Northern Ireland the Driver and Vehicle Testing Agency (Northern Ireland) is responsible for testing drivers and vehicles.

More than 1.5 million car driving tests were conducted in Great Britain in 1996–7 of which 44.7 per cent resulted in a pass. In addition over 66,000 lorry tests were undertaken, of which 48.1 per cent were successful. There were more than 15,000 bus tests, with a pass rate of 48.7 per cent. Over 136,000 motorcycle tests were undertaken, of which 67.5 per cent were successful.

Since 1 March 1997 driving test candidates have been required to produce photographic confirmation of their identity.

*DRIVING TEST FEES (weekday rate/evening and Saturday rate) *as at 1 April 1997*

For cars	£31/£41
†For motor cycles	£38/£50
For lorries, buses	£65/£83
For invalid carriages	free

*Since 1 July 1996 most candidates for car and motor cycle tests have also been required to take a written driving theory test, for which there is a separate fee of £15. Theory tests for lorry and bus drivers were introduced on 1 January 1997
†Before riding on public roads, learner motor cyclists and learner moped riders are required to have completed Compulsory Basic Training, provided by DSA-approved training bodies. Prices vary. All exemptions from CBT were removed on 1 January 1997

An extended driving test was introduced in 1992 for those convicted of dangerous driving. The fee is £62/£82 (car) or £76/£100 (motorcycle).

MOTOR VEHICLES

Vehicles must be licensed by the DVLA or the DVLA (Northern Ireland) before they can be driven on public roads. They must also be approved as roadworthy by the Vehicle Certification Agency. The Vehicle Inspectorate carries out annual testing and inspection of goods vehicles, buses and coaches.

There were 37.4 million vehicles registered at the DVLA at March 1996, of which 25.6 million were licensed:

Private and light goods	23,068,000
Motor cycles, scooters, mopeds	590,000
Coaches and buses	77,000
Large goods vehicles	416,000
Electric vehicles	17,000
Others	1,425,000
Total	25,593,000

VEHICLE LICENCES

Registration and first licensing of vehicles is through local offices (known as Vehicle Registration Offices) of the Driver and Vehicle Licensing Agency in Swansea (*see* page 301). Local facilities for relicensing are available as follows:

(i) with a licence reminder (form V11) in person at any post office which deals with vehicle licensing, or post it to the post office shown on the form

(ii) with a vehicle licence renewal (form V10). Applicants may normally apply in person at any licensing post office. They will need to take their vehicle registration document; if this is not available the applicant must complete form V62 which is held at post offices. Postal applications can be made to the post offices shown on form V100, available at any post office. This form also provides guidance on registering and licensing vehicles.

Details of the present duties chargeable on motor vehicles are available at post offices and Vehicle Registration Offices. The Vehicle Excise and Registration Act 1994 provides *inter alia* that any vehicle kept on a public road but not used on roads is chargeable to excise duty as if it were in use. All non-commercial vehicles over 25 years old are exempt from vehicle excise duty.

VEHICLE EXCISE DUTY RATES *from 15 November 1997*

	12 months £	6 months £
Motor Cars		
Light vans, cars, taxis, etc.	150.00	82.50
Motor Cycles		
With or without sidecar, not over 150 cc	15.00	—
With or without sidecar, 150–250 cc	40.00	—
Others	60.00	33.00
Electric motorcycles (including tricycles)	15.00	—
Tricycles (not over 450 kg)		
Not over 150 cc	15.00	—
Others	60.00	33.00
Buses		
Seating 9–16 persons	160.00	82.50
Seating 17–35 persons	210.00	115.50
Seating 36–60 persons	320.00	176.00
Seating over 60 persons	480.00	264.00

MoT TESTING

Cars, motor cycles, motor caravans, light goods and dual-purpose vehicles more than three years old must be covered by a current MoT test certificate. The certificate must be renewed annually. Copies of the legislation governing MoT testing can be obtained from any bookshop which stocks HMSO publications. The legislation comprises the Road Traffic Act 1988 (Sections 45 and 46), the Motor Vehicles (Test) Regulations 1981, and subsequent amendments. The MoT testing scheme is administered by the Vehicle Inspectorate.

A fee is payable to MoT testing stations, which must be authorized to carry out tests. The maximum fees, which are prescribed by regulations, are:

For cars and light vans	£29.42
For solo motor cycles	£12.33
For motor cycle combinations	£20.64
For three-wheeled vehicles	£24.12
For non-public service vehicle buses	£36.15
For light goods vehicles	£31.60
For goods vehicles up to 3,500 kg	£31.60

SHIPPING

PRINCIPAL MERCHANT FLEETS 1996

Flag	No	Gross tonnage
Panama	6,105	82,130,668
Liberia	1,684	59,988,908
Greece	1,743	27,507,109
Bahamas	1,186	24,408,787
Cyprus	1,652	23,798,904
Malta	1,247	19,479,431
Japan	9,399	19,200,927
Norway (NIS)	685	18,948,844
China	3,121	16,992,863
Singapore	1,480	16,448,536
Russia	4,866	13,755,374
*United States of America	5,289	12,024,644
Philippines	1,617	9,033,849
Hong Kong	398	7,862,964
Korea (South)	2,327	7,557,931
St Vincent	1,168	7,134,236
India	920	7,127,246
Italy	1,348	6,594,302
Turkey	1,114	6,425,682
Taiwan	681	6,174,535
Germany	1,101	5,842,091
Denmark (DIS)	433	5,200,332
Marshall Islands	130	4,897,062
Brazil	539	4,530,039
Malaysia	755	4,175,303
Netherlands	1,115	3,994,632
United Kingdom	1,429	3,871,768
Ukraine	1,061	3,825,390
Iran	414	3,566,819
Bermuda	91	3,462,210
Isle of Man	177	3,140,113
Sweden	618	3,001,719
Indonesia	2,348	2,972,579
Norway	1,542	2,856,943
Australia	625	2,717,870
Romania	420	2,567,509
French Antarctic Territory	84	2,534,242
Canada	872	2,406,161
Poland	507	2,292,646
Antigua and Barbuda	520	2,176,204
WORLD TOTAL	84,264	507,873,011

DIS   Danish International Register of Shipping – offshore registry
NIS   Norwegian International Ship Register – offshore registry
*Excluding ships of United States Reserve Fleet

Source: Lloyd's Register of Shipping

MERCHANT SHIPS COMPLETED 1996

Country of Build	No.	Gross tonnage
Japan	617	10,182,465
Korea (South)	188	7,374,474
Germany	80	1,202,137
*China	97	1,148,066
Italy	30	666,750
Taiwan	13	651,504
Poland	45	629,423
Spain	74	616,437
Denmark	26	491,648
Finland	7	453,666
Croatia	14	365,006
Romania	18	237,379
Netherlands	82	232,320
France	17	213,067
Singapore	64	192,325
*Ukraine	10	189,380
United Kingdom	21	187,398
Norway	43	173,082
Brazil	7	162,634
*Russia	29	109,557
Bulgaria	9	91,868
Turkey	16	48,472
Australia	28	33,645
Indonesia	17	31,546
Slovakia	12	28,633
Other countries	181	168,313
For Registration in		
Panama	306	8,035,152
Liberia	72	3,196,821
Germany	109	1,588,511
Singapore	125	1,458,806
Greece	25	1,158,356
Bahamas	34	1,142,508
Iran	10	850,407
Norway (NIS)	15	707,846
Japan	296	690,652
Hong Kong	17	620,369
Philippines	28	575,797
Marshall Islands	6	525,091
Korea (South)	42	505,928
Cyprus	25	453,494
Italy	22	363,453
Denmark (DIS)	13	360,855
Netherlands	57	341,116
Luxembourg	4	257,170
Isle of Man	8	255,442
Taiwan	5	243,971
Malaysia	27	181,631
Brazil	12	163,234
French Antarctic Territory	4	148,958
Sweden	10	135,465
Denmark	11	124,856
Other countries	462	1,795,306
WORLD TOTAL	1,745	25,881,195

DIS   Danish International Register of Shipping – offshore registry
NIS   Norwegian International Ship Register – offshore registry
*Information incomplete

Source: Lloyd's Register of Shipping

BRITISH-REGISTERED* TRADING VESSELS
OF 500 GROSS TONS AND OVER *as at end 1995*

Type of vessel	No.	Gross tonnage
Tankers[1]	113	2,346,000
Bulk carriers[2]	18	485,000
Specialized carriers[3]	12	52,000
Container (fully cellular)	37	1,326,000
Ro-Ro[4]	83	910,000
Other general cargo	90	282,000
Passenger[5]	12	360,000
TOTAL	365	5,761,000

* Registered in the UK and British Crown dependencies
1 Includes oil, gas, chemical and other specialized tankers
2 Includes combination bulk carriers: ore/oil and ore bulk/oil carriers
3 Includes livestock, car and chemical carriers
4 Roll-on, roll-off passenger and cargo vessels
5 Cruise liner and other passenger vessels

Source: The Stationery Office – *Annual Abstract of Statistics 1997*

SEAPORT TRAFFIC OF GREAT BRITAIN 1995
BY MODE OF APPEARANCE

	Million gross tonnes
FOREIGN TRAFFIC: *Imports*	174.9
Bulk fuel traffic	66.0
Other bulk traffic	45.0
Container and roll-on traffic	50.2
Semi-bulk traffic	12.2
Conventional traffic	1.4
FOREIGN TRAFFIC: *Exports*	170.4
Bulk fuel traffic	109.0
Other bulk traffic	15.8
Container and roll-on traffic	40.4
Semi-bulk traffic	4.5
Conventional traffic	0.9
DOMESTIC TRAFFIC*	148.1
Bulk fuel traffic	108.1
Other bulk traffic	30.7
Container and roll-on traffic	5.8
Semi-bulk traffic	0.1
Conventional traffic	0.3
Non-oil traffic with UK offshore installations	3.0
TRAFFIC THROUGH MINOR PORTS†	34.3
TOTAL FOREIGN AND DOMESTIC TRAFFIC	527.9

* Domestic traffic refers to traffic through the ports of Great Britain only, to all parts of the UK, Isle of Man and the Channel Islands. Traffic to and from offshore installations, landing of sea-dredged aggregates and material shipped for dumping at sea included
† Ports with less than 2 million tonnes of traffic

Source: The Stationery Office – *Annual Abstract of Statistics 1997*

SEABORNE TRADE OF THE UK 1995
EXPORTS (INCLUDING RE-EXPORTS) PLUS IMPORTS BY SEA

	Million tonnes	% carried by UK-registered vessels*
By weight		
All cargo	354.1	11
Dry bulk cargo	87.7	8
Other dry cargo	112.2	17
Tanker cargo	154.2	11
	£ million	
By value		
All cargo	2,457,000	26
Dry bulk cargo	84,800	11
Other dry cargo	2,233,500	28
Tanker cargo	138,800	11

* Relates to trade with countries outside the EU
Source: The Stationery Office – *Annual Abstract of Statistics 1997*

PASSENGER MOVEMENT BY SEA 1995

*Arrivals plus departures at UK seaports by place of embarkation or landing**

All passenger movements	34,595,000
Irish Republic	3,632,000
Belgium	2,480,000
France†	25,164,000
Netherlands	1,837,000
Other EU countries	1,056,000
Other European and Mediterranean countries‡	188,000
USA	29,900
Rest of the world	2,700
Pleasure cruises beginning and/or ending at UK seaports	207,000

* Passengers are included at both departure and arrival if their journeys begin and end at a UK seaport
† Includes hovercraft passengers
‡ Includes North Africa and Middle East Mediterranean countries

Source: The Stationery Office – *Annual Abstract of Statistics 1997*

Communications

Postal Services

Responsibility for running postal services rests in the UK with a public authority, the Post Office (*see* pages 333–4). The Secretary of State for Trade and Industry has powers to suspend the letter monopoly of the Post Office in certain areas and to issue licences to other bodies to provide an alternative service. Non-Post Office bodies are permitted to transfer mail between document exchanges and to deliver letters, provided that a minimum fee of £1 per letter is charged. Charitable organizations are allowed to carry and deliver Christmas and New Year cards.

INLAND POSTAL SERVICES AND REGULATIONS

INLAND LETTER POST RATES*

Not over	1st class†	2nd class†
60 g	26p	20p
100 g	39p	31p
150 g	49p	38p
200 g	60p	45p
250 g	70p	55p
300 g	80p	64p
350 g	92p	73p
400 g	£1.04	83p
450 g	£1.17	93p
500 g	£1.30	£1.05
600 g	£1.60	£1.25
700 g	£2.00	£1.45
750 g	£2.15	£1.55 (not
800 g	£2.30	admissible
900 g	£2.55	over 750 g)
1,000 g	£2.50	
Each extra 250 g or part thereof	70p	

UK PARCEL RATES

Not over		Not over	
1 kg	£2.70	8 kg	£6.40
2 kg	£4.60	10 kg	£7.30
4 kg	£5.15	30 kg	£8.55
6 kg	£5.80		

*Postcards travel at the same rates as letter post
†There is a two-tier postal delivery system in the UK with first class letters normally being delivered the following day and second class post within three days

OVERSEAS POSTAL SERVICES AND REGULATIONS

OVERSEAS SURFACE MAIL RATES

Letters

Not over		Not over	
20 g	31p	450 g	£2.88
60 g	52p	500 g	£3.18
100 g	75p	750 g	£4.70
150 g	£1.06	1,000 g	£6.21
200 g	£1.36	1,250 g	£7.71
250 g	£1.66	1,500 g	£9.21
300 g	£1.97	1,750 g	£10.71
350 g	£2.27	2,000 g	£12.21
400 g	£2.57		

AIRMAIL LETTER RATES

Europe: Letters

Not over		Not over	
20 g	26p	260 g	£1.82
20 g non EC	31p	280 g	£1.95
40 g	44p	300 g	£2.07
60 g	56p	320 g	£2.20
80 g	69p	340 g	£2.32
100 g	82p	360 g	£2.45
120 g	94p	380 g	£2.57
140 g	£1.07	400 g	£2.70
160 g	£1.19	420 g	£2.82
180 g	£1.32	440 g	£2.95
200 g	£1.44	460 g	£3.08
220 g	£1.57	480 g	£3.20
240 g	£1.69	*500 g	£3.33

* Max. 2 kg

Outside Europe: Letters

	Not over 10 g	Not over 20 g	Over 20 g
Zone 1	43p	63p	varies
Zone 2	43p	63p	varies

For airmail letter zones outside Europe, *see* pages 520–1

STAMPS

Postage stamps are sold in values of 1p, 2p, 4p, 5p, 6p, 10p, 19p, 20p, 25p, 26p, 29p, 30p, 31p, 35p, 36p, 37p, 38p, 39p, 41p, 43p, 50p, 63p, £1, £1.50, £2.00, £5.00, and £10.00. Books or rolls of first and second class stamps are also available. Stamps are sold at Post Offices and some other outlets, including stationers and newsagents.

PREPAID STATIONERY

Aerogrammes to all destinations are 36p. Forces Aerogrammes are free to certain destinations.

Prepaid envelopes:
Standard services (DL size)

	1st class	2nd class
single	31p	25p
packet of 10	£2.85	£2.25

Guaranteed services	Special Delivery	Registered	Registered Plus
C4, 500g	£4.00	£4.30	£4.90
C5, 250g	3.30	3.60	4.20

Printed postage stamps cut from envelopes, postcards, newspaper wrappers, etc., may be used as stamps in payment of postage, provided that they are not imperfect or defaced.

POSTAL ORDERS

Postal orders (British pattern) are issued and paid at nearly all post offices in the UK and in many other countries.

Postal orders are printed with a counterfoil for denominations of 50p and £1, followed by £1 steps to £10, £15 and £20. Postage stamps may be affixed in the space provided to increase the value of the postal order by up to 49p. Charges (in addition to the value of the postal order): Up to £1, 25p; £2–£4, 45p; £5–£7, 65p; £8–£10, 80p; £15, 90p; £20, 95p.

The name of the payee must be inserted on the postal order. If not presented within six months of the last day of the month of issue, orders must be sent to the local customer services manager of Post Office Counters Ltd (listed in the telephone directory) to ascertain whether the order may still be paid. If the counterfoil has been retained postal orders not more than four years out of date may be paid when presented with the counterfoil at a post office.

RESTRICTIONS

Articles which may not be sent in the post include offensive or dangerous articles (such as articles containing batteries, aerosol products), packets likely to impede Post Office sorters, and certain kinds of advertisement. Certain other articles may be posted only if packed correctly. Advice is available from Royal Mail (tel: 0345-740740) for letters and small packets; Parcelforce (tel: 0800-224466) for parcels; or local post office counter staff.

The exportation of some goods by post is prohibited except under Department of Trade licence. Enquiries should be addressed to the Export Data Branch, Overseas Trade Divisions, Department of Trade and Industry, 1 Victoria Street, London SW1H 0ET. Tel: 0171-215 5000.

SPECIAL DELIVERY SERVICES

DATAPOST

A guaranteed service for the delivery of documents and packages: (i) Datapost Sameday offers same working day collection and delivery in many areas; (ii) Datapost 10 (for delivery before 10 a.m.) and Datapost 12 (for delivery before noon) offer next working day delivery nationwide and are available only to certain destinations. Items may be collected or handed in at post offices. There are also Datapost links with a number of overseas countries. Parcelforce 24 (next working day delivery) and 48 (delivery in two working days) offer a similar guaranteed service.

ROYAL MAIL SPECIAL DELIVERY

A guaranteed next-day delivery service by 12.30 p.m. to most UK destinations for first class letters and packets. The fee of £2.70 plus first class postage is refunded if next working day delivery is not achieved, provided that items are posted before latest recommended posting times.

SWIFTAIR

Express delivery of airmail letters and packets up to 2 kg anywhere in the world. Items normally arrive at least one day in advance of normal air mail. Charge (in addition to postage), £2.70.

OTHER SERVICES

ADVICE OF DELIVERY

Written confirmation of delivery from the post office at the stated destination. Charge: 33p (inland); 40p (international); plus postage.

CERTIFICATE OF POSTING

Issued free on request at time of posting.

COMPENSATION (INLAND AND INTERNATIONAL)

Inland: compensation up to a maximum of £26 may be paid where it can be shown that a letter was damaged or lost in the post due to the fault of the Post Office, its employees or agents. The Post Office does not accept responsibility for loss or damage arising from faulty packing. Charges: Parcelforce – compensation up to £20 per parcel for loss or damage if a certificate of posting has been obtained. Compensation Fee Certificate of Posting – 75p, up to £150 compensation; £1.30, up to £500 compensation.

International: if a certificate of posting is produced, compensation up to a maximum of £26 may be given for loss or damage in the UK to uninsured parcels to or from most overseas countries. No compensation will be paid for any loss or damage due to the action of the Queen's Enemies.

INTERNATIONAL REPLY COUPONS

Coupons used to prepay replies to letters, exchangeable abroad for stamps representing the minimum surface mail letter rate from the country concerned to the UK. Charge: 60p each.

NEWSPAPER POST

Copies of newspapers registered at the Post Office may be posted only by the publisher or their agents in open-ended wrappers or unsealed envelopes approved by the Post Office, or tied with string removable without cutting. Wrappers and envelopes must be prominently marked 'newspaper post' in the top left-hand corner. The only additional writing or printing permitted is 'with compliments', the name and address of sender, request for return if undeliverable, and a page reference. Items receive first class letter service.

POSTE RESTANTE

Poste Restante is solely for travellers and is for three months in any one town. A packet may be addressed to any post office, except town sub-offices, and should state 'Poste Restante' or 'to be called for' in the address. Redirection from a Poste Restante is undertaken for up to three months. Letters for an expected ship at a port are kept for two months, otherwise letters are kept for two weeks, or one month if from abroad. At the end of this period mail is treated as undeliverable or is returned.

PRIVATE BOX

Provides an alternative address (e.g. PO Box 123) and mail is held at the local delivery office for collection. Charge: £42 (six months); £52 (12 months).

RECORDED DELIVERY (INLAND)

Provides a record of posting and delivery of letters and ensures a signature on delivery. This service is recommended for items of little or no monetary value. Charge: 60p plus postage.

REDIRECTION

By agent of addressee: mail other than parcels, business reply and freepost items may be reposted free not later than the day after delivery (not counting Sundays and public holidays) if unopened and if original addressee's name is unobscured. Parcels may be redirected free within the same time limits only if the original and substituted address are in the same local parcel delivery area (or the London postal area). Registered packets must be taken to a post office and are re-registered free up to the day after delivery.

By the Post Office: a printed form obtainable from the Post Office must be signed by the person to whom the letters are to be addressed. A fee is payable for each different surname on the application form. Charges: up to 1 calendar month, £6.00 (abroad, £12.00); up to 3 calendar months, £13.00 (£26.00); up to 12 calendar months, £30.00 (£60.00).

REGISTERED MAIL (INLAND AND INTERNATIONAL)

Inland: all packets must be handed to the post office and a certificate of posting obtained. Charges (plus postage): up to £500 compensation, £3.00; Registered Plus for compensation between £500 and £1,500, £3.30; up to £2,200 compensation, £3.60. Consequential Loss Insurance provides cover up to £10,000:

Compensation up to	Standard fee in addition to registered fee and postage
£1,000	45p
£2,500	60p
£5,000	85p
£7,500	£1.10
£10,000	£1.35

Compensation in respect of currency or other forms of monetary worth is given only if money is sent by registered letter post. Compensation cannot be paid in the case of any packet containing prohibited articles (see Restrictions). Compensation is only paid for well-packed fragile articles and not for exceptionally fragile or perishable articles.

International: packets containing valuable papers, documents or articles can be insured as letters, or as parcels if the country of destination does not accept dutiable goods in the letter post. For HM ships abroad and members of the Army and RAF overseas using BFPO numbers, parcels only are insurable up to £140 at a fee of £1.20. Charges (plus airmail postage): compensation up to £500, £3.00; up to £1,000, £4.00.

SMALL PACKETS POST (INTERNATIONAL)

Permits the transmission of goods up to 2 kg to all countries, in the same mails as printed papers (NB: to Myanmar (Burma) and Papua New Guinea there is a limit of 500 g). Packets can be sealed and can contain personal correspondence relating to the contents. Registration is allowed as insurance as long as the item is packed in a way complying with any insurance regulations. A customs declaration is required and the packet must be marked with 'small packet' and a return address. Instructions for the disposal of undelivered packets must be given at the time of posting. An undeliverable packet will be returned to the sender at his/her expense.

Surface Mail: World-wide

Not over		Not over	
100 g	50p	450 g	£1.67
150 g	67p	500 g	£1.84
200 g	84p	750 g	£2.68
250 g	£1.00	1,000 g	£3.51
300 g	£1.17	1,500 g	£5.21
350 g	£1.34	2,000 g	£6.91
400 g	£1.51		

UNDELIVERED AND UNPAID MAIL

Undelivered mail is returned to the sender provided the return address is indicated either on the outside of the envelope or inside. If the sender's address is not available items not containing property are destroyed. If the packet contains something of value it is retained for up to three months. Undeliverable second class mail containing newspapers, magazines or commercial advertising is destroyed.

All unpaid or underpaid letters are treated as second class mail. The recipient is charged the amount of underpayment plus 15p per item. Parcels over 750 g are charged at first class rates plus 15p.

Public Telecommunications Services

Under the British Telecommunications Act 1981 British Telecom (now BT) was created to provide a national public telecommunications service. The Telecommunications Act 1984 removed BT's monopoly on running the public telecommunications system and BT was privatized in 1984.

The Telecommunications Act 1984 also established the Office of Telecommunications (Oftel) as the independent regulatory body for the telecommunications industry (see also Government Departments and Public Offices).

PUBLIC TELECOMMUNICATIONS OPERATORS

Until 1991 the three licensed fixed-link public telecommunications operators (PTOs) in the UK were BT, Mercury Communications Ltd, and Kingston Communications (Hull) PLC. In March 1991 the Government announced that it was opening up the existing duopoly of the two major fixed-link operators, BT and Mercury, and would be encouraging applications for telecommunications licences. The Department of Trade and Industry has granted over 200 PTO licences.

BT's obligations under its operating licence continue to include the provision of a universal telecommunications service; a service in rural areas; and essential services, such as public call boxes and emergency services.

Mercury Communications (which merged with other communications companies in 1997 to form Cable and Wireless Communications PLC) is licensed to provide national and international public telecommunications services for residential and business customers. These services utilize the digital network created by Mercury. Cable and Wireless can also provide the following services: public and private telephone services; national and international switched voice and data services; electronic messaging (private circuits and networks (national and international), integrated voice and data); data network services; customer equipment; and mobile communications services.

In December 1996 the Government liberalized international facilities licensing in the UK. The end of the BT/Mercury duopoly means that other operators are now able to apply for licences to own and operate their own international telecommunications networks. By June

1997, 50 operators had been granted international facilities licences.

PRIVATE TELEPHONE SERVICES

There are over 260 private telephone companies which offer information on a variety of subjects such as the weather, stock market analysis, horoscopes, etc., on the BT, Cable and Wireless and Vodafone networks.

The lines and equipment are provided by BT under condition that services adhere to the codes of practice of the Independent Committee for the Supervision of Standards of Telephone Information Services. Services are charged at different rates from 10p to £1.50 per minute.

MOBILE TELEPHONE SYSTEMS

Cellular telephone network systems allow calls to be made to and from mobile telephones. The four companies licensed by the Department of Trade and Industry to provide competing cellular telephone systems are Cellnet, jointly owned by BT and Securicor; One-2-One, jointly owned by Cable and Wireless and US West; Orange and Vodafone.

INLAND TELEPHONES

An individual customer can install an extension telephone socket or apparatus in their own home without the need to buy the items from any of the licensed public telecommunications operators. However, it is necessary to possess a special style of master-socket which must be supplied by the public network operator. Although an individual need not buy or rent an apparatus from a PTO, a telephone bought from a retail outlet must be of an approved standard compatible with the public network (indicated by a green disc on the label).

BT EXCHANGE LINE RENTALS (including VAT)

	Per quarter
Residential, exclusive	£26.62
Light user scheme	from £9.24
Business, exclusive	£42.12

BT TELEPHONE APPARATUS RENTAL Per quarter

Residential	from £4.47
Business	from £5.53
Private payphone	from £35.00

EXCHANGE LINE CONNECTION AND TAKE-OVER CHARGES (including VAT)

BT

New line	£116.33
Removing customer	£0.00
Take-over of existing lines:	
Simultaneous (same day)	£0.00
Non-simultaneous	£9.99

Cable and Wireless

Initial and quarterly administration charge (UK Call)	£4.50

RATES

BT and Cable and Wireless local and dialled national calls are charged by the second. Calls made from payphones are charged in 10p units. There is a 5p minimum charge on all BT calls and a 3.5p minimum charge on Cable and Wireless calls. All charges are subject to VAT, except those from payphones which are VAT inclusive. VAT charges on ordinary lines are calculated as a percentage of the total quarterly (BT)/monthly (Cable and Wireless) bill.

The charge per second depends on the time of day and the distance of the call.

BT	Cable and Wireless	
Daytime	Daytime	Monday to Friday 8 a.m. to 6 p.m.
Cheap	Evening	Monday to Friday 6 p.m. to 8 a.m.
Weekend	Weekend	Midnight Friday to midnight Sunday

Local rate
Regional rate – up to 35 miles (56 km)
National rate – over 35 miles (56 km) (including Channel Islands and Isle of Man)
Calls to mobile phones

DIALLED CALL TIME pence per minute charges (including VAT)

	BT	Cable and Wireless
Local rate		
Daytime	4.00	3.75
Cheap/Evening	1.70	0.98
Weekend	1.00	0.75
Regional rate		
Daytime	7.91	6.58
Cheap/Evening	4.00	2.40
Weekend	3.30	1.88
National rate		
Daytime	7.91	6.58
Cheap/Evening	4.65	2.40
Weekend	3.30	1.88
Calls to Cellnet and Vodafone mobile phones		
Daytime	37.50	32.40
Cheap/Evening	20.00	19.20
Weekend	10.00	9.01
Calls to Orange and One-2-One mobile phones		
Daytime	30.00	27.21
Cheap/Evening	20.00	19.20
Weekend	10.00	7.51

OPERATOR-CONNECTED CALLS

Operator-connected calls from ordinary lines are generally subject to a one-minute minimum charge (and thereafter by the minute) which varies with distance and time of day. Operator-connected calls from payphones are charged in three-minute periods at the payphone tariff. There is also a £1.80 handling charge for operator-connected calls. For calls that have to be placed through the operator because a dialled call has failed, the charge is equivalent to the dialled rate, subject normally to the one-minute minimum.

Higher charges apply to other operator-connected calls, including special services calls and those to mobile phones, the Irish Republic and the Channel Islands.

PHONECARDS

BT phonecards to the value of £2, £5, £10 and £20 are available from post offices and other outlets for use in specially designated public telephone boxes. Each phonecard unit is equivalent to a 10p coin in a payphone. Special public payphones at major railway stations and airports also accept commercial credit cards.

INTERNATIONAL TELEPHONES

All UK customers have access to International Direct Dialling (IDD) and can dial direct to numbers on most exchanges in over 230 countries world-wide. Details about how to make calls are given in dialling code information and in the International Telephone Guide.

For countries without IDD, calls have to be made through the International Operator. All operator-connected calls are subject to a £1.80 handling charge. Thereafter the call is charged by the minute.

Countries which can be called on IDD fall into one of 14 international charge bands depending on location. Charges in each band also vary according to the time of day; cheap rate dialled calls are available to all countries at certain times, but there is no reduced rate for operator-connected calls. Details of current international telephone charges can be obtained from the International Operator.

For International Dialling Codes, *see* pages 520–1

OTHER TELECOMMUNICATIONS SERVICES

TELEX SERVICE

There are now 208 countries that can be reached by the BT telex service from the UK, over 200 of them by direct dialling. For most customers, direct dialled calls to international destinations are charged by the second. Calls via the BT operator are charged in one-minute steps with a three-minute minimum, plus a surcharge of £1.30 a call. Operator-connected calls are charged at between 39p and £1.60 a minute depending upon the country called.

Calls made via BT's Telex Plus store and forward facility attract normal telex charges and a handling charge of 13p for inland delivered messages and 30p for international delivered messages.

TELEMESSAGE

Telemessages can be sent by telephone or telex within the UK for 'hard copy' delivery the next working day, including Saturdays. To achieve this, a telemessage must be telephoned/telexed before 10 p.m. Monday to Saturday (7 p.m. Sundays and Bank Holidays). Dial 100 (190 in London, Birmingham and Glasgow) and ask for the Telemessage Service or see the telex directory for codes.

A telemessage costs £5 for the first 50 words and £2.75 for each subsequent group of 50 words – the name and address are free. A sender's copy costs 85p. A selection of cards is available for special occasions at 80p per card. All prices are subject to VAT.

INTERNATIONAL TELEMESSAGE

Telemessage is also available to the USA. For next working day delivery a telemessage must be filed by 10 p.m. UK time Monday to Saturday (7 p.m. Sundays and Bank Holidays). US addresses must include the ZIP code. Charges are £7.25 for the first 50 words and £3.60 for each subsequent group of 50 words. The name and address are free but all charges are subject to VAT.

BT SERVICES

OPERATOR SERVICES – 100
   For difficulties
   For the following call services: alarm calls (booking charge £2.70); advice of duration and charge (charge £1.80); charge card calls (charge £1.50); freephone calls; international personal calls (charge £2.15–£4.30); transferred charge calls (charge £1.80); subscriber controlled transfer (All charges exclude VAT)
INTERNATIONAL OPERATOR – 155
DIRECTORY ENQUIRIES – 192 (25p charge per call)
INTERNATIONAL DIRECTORY ENQUIRIES – 153
EMERGENCY SERVICES – 999
   Services include fire service; police service; ambulance service; coastguard; lifeboat; cave rescue; mountain rescue
FAULTS – 151
TELEMESSAGE – 100 (190 in London, Birmingham and Glasgow)
INTERNATIONAL TELEMESSAGE – 100 (190 in London, Birmingham and Glasgow). The service is only available to the USA
INTERNATIONAL TELEGRAMS – 100 (190 in London, Birmingham and Glasgow). The service is available world-wide
MARITIME SERVICES – 100
   Includes Ship's Telegram Service and Ship's Telephone Service
BT INMARSAT SATELLITE SERVICE – 155
ALL OTHER CALL ENQUIRIES – 191

The Internet

The Internet is a rapidly-growing world-wide network of computer networks which use the same protocols (agreed methods of communication). It has its origins in the Advanced Research Projects Agency Network (ARPA-NET), a government-funded defence network in the USA, and other research and academic networks, such as the UK Joint Academic Network (JANET), a network linking universities and higher education institutions in the UK. JANET has extensive links to international and other national academic networks, and also to commercial and public network services. It is funded by the higher education funding agencies in the UK.

The main protocol used by the networks is Transmission Control Protocol/Internet Protocol (TCP/IP). Other protocols include:

- file transfer protocol (ftp), which allows files to be transferred between computers
- simple mail transfer protocol (smtp), which allows electronic mail (e-mail) to be sent
- hypertext transfer protocol (http), which allows hypertext facilities to be provided
- telnet, a facility which allows users to log on to other computers on the Internet

The most common uses of the Internet include:

- sending and receiving e-mail; text can be sent directly to another computer linked to the Internet
- playing computer games
- commercial transactions
- mailing lists, which enable users to send and receive information on specialist interests
- 'newsgroups' or bulletin boards, where messages on specialist interests can be left for users to read
- the publication of information

The World-Wide Web (WWW or the Web) is a vast collection of computers able to support multi-media formats and accessible via Web 'browsers' (search and navigation tools). Data stored on these computers (servers) is organized into pages with hypertext links; each page has a unique address. For practical purposes the WWW and the Internet are now almost synonymous. Web browsers include Netscape Navigator, Internet Explorer and Mosaic. Web browsers can also be used to access information in other formats on the Internet, e.g. gophers (see below).

The Internet is increasingly used by commercial organizations for the conduct of electronic business. Policies and standards are being developed by users to ensure an appropriate level of privacy; tools include access control mechanisms, data labelling and cryptography standards. There is no central body to develop standards or guarantee the reliability or currency of information on the Internet.

The speed of access to Internet sources and of downloading information depends on the number of users on the system (which varies according to the time of day), the location of the information, and the amount of information being downloaded.

CONNECTIONS

Connection to the Internet requires access to a computer, a modem and a telephone line. Commercial access providers/service providers supply an Internet address and password, an electronic mailbox and some or all of the necessary software. Most providers provide only a connection to the Internet, but a few also offer more sophisticated on-line services which are usually easier to

use but more expensive than direct Internet access. Details of providers are available in computer magazines and specialist Internet publications, and from British Telecom.

The main methods of connecting to the Internet are by a dial-up connection or a leased-line connection. A dial-up connection may be made over standard telephone lines or over ISDN lines. There are two types of dial-up connection: an online account, which allows the user to log on to an account on a remote computer which is connected to the Internet; and a dial-up IP connection, where a full Internet connection is made from the user's computer. The latter requires more complicated software. A permanent leased-line connection (a data line requiring no modem) is likely to be used where there are a large number of potential users, e.g. where all the users on a local area network (LAN) are to be connected.

TERMS

Archie – a tool for searching indexes of files on ftp sites on the Internet; now largely being superseded by Web browsers

Gophers – menu-based systems which facilitate browsing on the Internet; now largely being superseded by Web sites

Home page – the introductory section of a site on the Web

Hypertext mark-up language (HTML) – a standard document mark-up language used on the Web

Server – a computer storing data and software which can be used by other computers on a network

Uniform/Universal resource locators (URLs) – the address system for the Web

Users' network (USENET) – a large bulletin board system on the Internet

Veronica – a tool for searching gopher menus for keywords; now largely being superseded by Web browsers

Wide area information server (WAIS) – a tool for searching the content of files on the Internet; now largely being superseded by Web browsers

Airmail and IDD Codes

AIRMAIL ZONES (AZ)
The table includes airmail letter zones for countries outside Europe, and destinations to which European and European Union airmail letter rates apply (*see also* page 514).

(*Source: Post Office*)

1	airmail zone 1
2	airmail zone 2
e	Europe
eu	European Union

INTERNATIONAL DIRECT DIALLING (IDD)
International dialling codes are composed of four elements which are dialled in sequence:

(i)   the international code
(ii) the country code (*see* below)
(iii) the area code
(iv) the customer's telephone number

Calls to some countries must be made via the international operator. (*Source: BT*)

†	Calls must be made via the international operator
p	A pause in dialling is necessary whilst waiting for a second tone
*	Varies in some areas
**	Varies depending on carrier

Country	AZ	IDD from UK	IDD to UK
Afghanistan	1	00 93	†
Albania	e	00 355	00 44
Algeria	1	00 213	00p44
Andorra	eu	00 376	00 44
Angola	1	00 244	00 44
Anguilla	1	00 1 264	00 11 44
Antigua and Barbuda	1	00 1 268	011 44
Argentina	1	00 54	00 44
Armenia	e	00 374	810 44
Aruba	1	00 297	00 44
Ascension Island	1	00 247	01 44
Australia	2	00 61	00 11 44
Austria	eu	00 43	00 44
Azerbaijan	e	00 994	810 44
Azores	eu	00 351	00 44
Bahamas	1	00 1 242	011 44
Bahrain	1	00 973	0 44
Bangladesh	1	00 880	00 44
Barbados	1	00 1 246	011 44
Belarus	e	00 375	810 44
Belgium	eu	00 32	00 44
Belize	1	00 501	011 44
Benin	1	00 229	00p44
Bermuda	1	00 1 441	011 44
Bhutan	1	00 975	00 44
Bolivia	1	00 591	00 44
Bosnia-Hercegovina	e	00 396	99 44
Botswana	1	00 267	00 44
Brazil	1	00 55	00 44
British Virgin Islands	1	00 1 809	011 44
Brunei	1	00 673	01 44
Bulgaria	e	00 359	00 44
Burkina Faso	1	00 226	00 44
Burundi	1	00 257	90 44
Cambodia	1	00 855	00 44
Cameroon	1	00 237	00 44
Canada	1	00 1	011 44

Country	AZ	IDD from UK	IDD to UK
Canary Islands	eu	00 34	07p44
Cape Verde	1	00 238	0 44
Cayman Islands	1	00 1 345	0 44
Central African Republic	1	00 236	00p44
Chad	1	00 235	†
Chile	1	00 56	00 44
China	2	00 86	00 44
Hong Kong	1	00 852	001 44
Colombia	1	00 57	90 44
Comoros	1	00 269	10 44
Congo, Dem. Rep. of	1	00 243	00 44
Congo, Republic of	1	00 242	00 44
Cook Islands	2	00 682	00 44
Costa Rica	1	00 506	00 44
Côte d'Ivoire	1	00 225	00 44
Croatia	e	00 385	99 44
Cuba	1	00 53	119 44
Cyprus	e	00 357	00 44
Czech Republic	e	00 420	00 44
Denmark	eu	00 45	00 44
Djibouti	1	00 253	00 44
Dominica	1	00 1 809	011 44
Dominican Republic	1	00 1 809	011 44
Ecuador	1	00 593	01 44
Egypt	1	00 20	00 44
Equatorial Guinea	1	00 240	19 44
Eritrea	1	00 291	†
Estonia	e	00 372	800 44
Ethiopia	1	00 251	00 44
Falkland Islands	1	00 500	01 44
Faroe Islands	e	00 298	009 44
Fiji	2	00 679	05 44
Finland	eu	00 358	990 44**
France	eu	00 33	00 44
French Guiana	1	00 594	†
French Polynesia	2	00 689	00 44
Gabon	1	00 241	00 44
The Gambia	1	00 220	00 44
Georgia	e	00 995	810 44
Germany	eu	00 49	00 44
Ghana	1	00 233	00 44
Gibraltar	eu	00 350	00 44
Greece	eu	00 30	00 44
Greenland	e	00 299	009 44
Grenada	1	00 1 809	011 44
Guadeloupe	1	00 590	19 44
Guam	2	00 671	001 44
Guatemala	1	00 502	00 44
Guinea	1	00 224	00 44
Guinea-Bissau	1	00 245	†
Guyana	1	00 592	001 44
Haiti	1	00 509	†
Honduras	1	00 504	00 44
Hungary	e	00 36	00 44
Iceland	e	00 354	00 44
India	1	00 91	00 44
Indonesia	1	00 62	001p44
Iran	1	00 98	00 44
Iraq	1	00 964	00 44
Ireland, Republic of	eu	00 353	00 44
Israel	1	00 972	00 44
Italy	eu	00 39	00 44
Jamaica	1	00 1 879	011 44
Japan	2	00 81	001 44
Jordan	1	00 962	00 44*
Kazakhstan	e	00 7	810 44
Kenya	1	00 254	000 44

Country	AZ	IDD from UK	IDD to UK	Country	AZ	IDD from UK	IDD to UK
Kiribati	2	00 686	0 44	Russia	e	00 7	810 44
Korea, North	2	00 850	010 44	Rwanda	1	00 250	00 44
Korea, South	2	00 82	001 44	St Helena	1	00 290	01 44
Kuwait	1	00 965	00 44	St Kitts and Nevis	1	00 1 869	†
Kyrgystan	e	00 996	810 44	St Lucia	1	00 1 758	0 44
Laos	1	00 856	†	St Pierre and			
Latvia	e	00 371	810 44	Miquelon	1	00 508	19p44
Lebanon	1	00 961	00 44	St Vincent and the			
Lesotho	1	00 266	00 44	Grenadines	1	00 1 809	00 44
Liberia	1	00 231	00 44	El Salvador	1	00 503	00 44
Libya	1	00 218	00 44	Samoa, American	1	00 684	144
Liechtenstein	e	00 41	00 44	San Marino	eu	00 378	00 44
Lithuania	e	00 370	810 44	São Tomé and			
Luxembourg	eu	00 352	00 44	Príncipe	1	00 239	00 44
Macao	1	00 853	00 44	Saudi Arabia	1	00 966	00 44
Macedonia	e	00 389	99 44	Senegal	1	00 221	00p44
Madagascar	1	00 261	16p44	Serbia	e	00 381	99 44
Madeira	eu	00 351 91	00 44*	Seychelles	1	00 248	0 44
Malawi	1	00 265	101 44	Sierra Leone	1	00 232	0 44
Malaysia	1	00 60	00 44	Singapore	1	00 65	005 44
Maldives	1	00 960	00 44	Slovak Republic	e	00 42	00 44
Mali	1	00 223	00 44	Slovenia	e	00 386	00 44
Malta	e	00 356	00 44	Solomon Islands	2	00 677	00 44
Mariana Islands,				Somalia	1	00 252	†
Northern	2	00 1 670	011 44	South Africa	1	00 27	09 44
Marshall Islands	2	00 692	012 44	Spain	eu	00 34	07p44
Martinique	1	00 596	19p44	Sri Lanka	1	00 94	00 44
Mauritania	1	00 222	00 44	Sudan	1	00 249	00 44
Mauritius	1	00 230	00 44	Suriname	1	00 597	001 44
Mayotte	1	00 269	19p44	Swaziland	1	00 268	00 44
Mexico	1	00 52	98 44	Sweden	eu	00 46	007 44**
Micronesia, Federated				Switzerland	e	00 41	00 44
States of	2	00 691	011 44	Syria	1	00 963	00 44
Moldova	e	00 373	810 44	Taiwan	2	00 886	002 44
Monaco	eu	00 377 93	00 44	Tajikistan	e	00 7	810 44
Mongolia	2	00 976	†	Tanzania	1	00 255	00 44
Montenegro	e	00 381	99 44	Thailand	1	00 66	001 44
Montserrat	1	00 1 664	†	Tibet	1	00 86	00 44
Morocco	1	00 212	00p44	Togo	1	00 228	00 44
Mozambique	1	00 258	00 44	Tonga	2	00 676	00 44
Myanmar	1	00 95	0 44	Trinidad and Tobago	1	00 1 868	011 44
Namibia	1	00 264	09 44	Tristan da Cunha	1	00 2 897	†
Nauru	2	00 674	00 44	Tunisia	1	00 216	00 44
Nepal	1	00 977	00 44	Turkey	e	00 90	00 44
Netherlands	eu	00 31	00 44	Turkmenistan	e	00 993	810 44
Netherlands Antilles	1	00 599	00 44	Turks and Caicos			
New Caledonia	2	00 687	00 44	Islands	1	00 1 649	0 44
New Zealand	2	00 64	00 44	Tuvalu	2	00 688	00 44
Nicaragua	1	00 505	00 44	Uganda	1	00 256	00 44
Niger	1	00 227	00 44	Ukraine	e	00 380	810 44
Nigeria	1	00 234	009 44	United Arab Emirates	1	00 971	00 44
Niue	2	00 683	†	Uruguay	1	00 598	00 44
Norfolk Island	2	00 672	00 44	USA	1	00 1	011 44
Norway	e	00 47	095 44	Alaska		00 1 907	011 44
Oman	1	00 968	00 44	Hawaii		00 1 808	011 44
Pakistan	1	00 92	00 44	Uzbekistan	e	00 7	810 44
Palau	2	00 680	†	Vanuatu	2	00 678	00 44
Panama	1	00 507	00 44	Vatican City State	eu	00 39 66982	00 44
Papua New Guinea	2	00 675	05 44	Venezuela	1	00 58	00 44
Paraguay	1	00 595	002 44	Vietnam	1	00 84	00 44
			003 44	Virgin Islands (US)	1	00 1 340	011 44
Peru	1	00 51	00 44	Western Samoa	2	00 685	0 44
Philippines	2	00 63	00 44	Yemen	1	00 967	00 44
Poland	e	00 48	0p044	Yugoslav Fed. Rep.	e	00 381	99 44
Portugal	eu	00 351	00 44	Zambia	1	00 260	00 44
Puerto Rico	1	00 1 787	011 44	Zimbabwe	1	00 263	110 44
Qatar	1	00 974	044				
Réunion	1	00 262	19p44				
Romania	e	00 40	00 44				

Development Corporations

NEW TOWNS

COMMISSION FOR THE NEW TOWNS
Glen House, Stag Place, London SW1E 5AJ
Tel 0171-828 7722

The Commission was established under the New Towns Act 1959. Its remit is to hold, manage and turn to account the property of development corporations transferred to the Commission; and to dispose of property so transferred and any other property held by it, as soon as it considers it expedient to do so. In carrying out its remit the Commission must have due regard to the convenience and welfare of persons residing, working or carrying on business there and, until disposal, the maintenance and enhancement of the value of the land held and return obtained from it.

The Commission has such responsibilities in Basildon, Bracknell, Central Lancashire, Corby, Crawley, Harlow, Hatfield, Hemel Hempstead, Milton Keynes, Northampton, Peterborough, Redditch, Skelmersdale, Stevenage, Telford, Warrington and Runcorn, Washington, and Welwyn Garden City. The Commission has minimal responsibilities (principally financial and litigation) in Aycliffe and Peterlee, and Cwmbran following the wind-up of their development corporations in 1988.

From April 1998 the Commission will take on responsibility for any assets and liabilities remaining when urban development corporations and housing action trusts are wound up. In preparation for its new role the Commission is being reorganized and from April 1998 its main office will be at the Milton Keynes address given below.

Chairman, Dr J. R. G. Bradfield, CBE
Deputy Chairman, M. H. Mallinson, CBE
Members, R. B. Caws, CBE; F. C. Graves, OBE; Sir Brian Jenkins, GBE; Lady Marsh; J. Trustram Eve
Chief Executive, N. J. Walker

REGIONAL OFFICES
NORTH (Central Lancashire, Skelmersdale, Warrington and Runcorn, Washington, Aycliffe and Peterlee), New Town House, Buttermarket Street, Warrington WA1 2LF. Tel: 01925-651144. *Director*, C. Mackrell

CENTRAL (Milton Keynes, Corby, Northampton), Central Business Exchange, 414–428 Midsummer Boulevard, Central Milton Keynes MK9 2EA. Tel: 01908-692692. *Director*, J. Napleton

WEST MIDLANDS (Redditch, Telford), Jordan House West, Hall Court, Hall Park Way, Telford TF3 4NN. Tel: 01952-293131. *Director*, C. Mackrell

SOUTH (Basildon, Bracknell, Crawley, Harlow, Hatfield, Hemel Hempstead, Peterborough, Stevenage, Welwyn Garden City), Glen House, Stag Place, London SW1E 5AJ. Tel: 0171-828 7722. *Director*, G. D. Johnston

DEVELOPMENT CORPORATIONS

WALES
DEVELOPMENT BOARD FOR RURAL WALES (1977), Ladywell House, Newtown, Powys SY16 1JB. Tel: 01686-626965. *Chairman*, D. Rowe-Beddoe; *Chief Executive*, J. Taylor

SCOTLAND
CUMBERNAULD (1956), wound up 31 December 1996
EAST KILBRIDE (1947), wound up 31 December 1995
GLENROTHES (1948), wound up 31 December 1995
IRVINE (1966), wound up 31 March 1997
LIVINGSTON (1962), wound up 31 March 1997

URBAN DEVELOPMENT CORPORATIONS

Urban development corporations were established under the Local Government, Planning and Land Act 1980, as short-life public bodies. Their objectives are to bring land and buildings back into effective use; to develop existing and new industry and commerce; to improve the environment; and to ensure that housing and social facilities are available in the area.

BIRMINGHAM HEARTLANDS (1992), Waterlinks House, Richard Street, Birmingham, B7 4AA. Tel: 0121-333 3060. *Chairman*, Sir Reginald Eyre; *Chief Executive*, J. Beeston. Area, 1,000 hectares. To be wound up March 1998

BLACK COUNTRY (1987), Black Country House, Rounds Green Road, Oldbury B69 2RD. Tel: 0121-511 2000. *Chairman*, G. Carter, CBE; *Chief Executive*, D. Morgan. Area, 2,600 hectares. To be wound up March 1998

CARDIFF BAY (1987), Baltic House, Mount Stuart Square, Cardiff CF1 6DH. Tel: 01222-823958. *Chairman*, Sir Geoffrey Inkin, OBE; *Chief Executive*, M. Boyce. Area, 1,094 hectares

LAGANSIDE (1989), Clarendon Building, 15 Clarendon Road, Belfast BT1 3BG. Tel: 01232-328507. *Chairman*, The Duke of Abercorn; *Chief Executive*, G. Mackey. Area, 122 hectares

LONDON DOCKLANDS (1981), Thames Quay, 191 Marsh Wall, London E14 9TJ. Tel: 0171-512 3000. *Chairman*, M. Pickard; *Chief Executive*, E. Sorensen. Area, 2,226 hectares. To be wound up March 1998

MERSEYSIDE (1981), Royal Liver Buildings, Pier Head, Liverpool L3 1JH. Tel: 0151-236 6090. *Chairman*, Sir Desmond Pitcher; *Chief Executive*, C. Farrow. Area, 960 hectares. To be wound up March 1998

PLYMOUTH (1993), Royal William Yard, Plymouth PL1 3RP. Tel: 01752-256132. *Chairman*, Lord Chilver, FRS; *Chief Executive*, G. Timbrell. Area, 67 hectares. To be wound up March 1998

TEESSIDE (1987), Dunedin House, Riverside Quay, Stockton-on-Tees TS17 6BJ. Tel: 01642-677123. *Chairman*, Sir Ronald Norman, OBE; *Chief Executive*, D. Hall. Area, 4,600 hectares. To be wound up March 1998

TRAFFORD PARK (1987), Waterside, Trafford Wharf Road, Trafford Park, Manchester M17 1EX. Tel: 0161-848 8000. *Chairman*, W. Morgan; *Chief Executive*, M. Shields. Area, 1,270 hectares. To be wound up March 1998

TYNE AND WEAR (1987), Scotswood House, Newcastle Business Park, Newcastle upon Tyne NE4 7YL. Tel: 0191-226 1234. *Chairman*, Sir Paul Nicholson; *Chief Executive*, A. Balls, CB. Area, 2,400 hectares. To be wound up March 1998

Local Government

The Local Government Acts of 1972, 1985 and 1992, the Local Government (Wales) Act 1994, the Local Government (Scotland) Act 1973 and the London Government Act 1963 are the main Acts which have brought about the present structure of local government in Great Britain. This structure has been in effect in England and Wales since 1974, with alterations in 1986, 1995 and 1996; and in Scotland since 1975.

The structure in England is based on two tiers of local authorities (county councils and district councils) in the non-metropolitan areas; and a single tier of metropolitan and London borough councils in the six metropolitan areas of England and in London respectively.

Following recent reviews of the structure of local government in England by the Local Government Commission, 46 unitary (all-purpose) authorities have been or are being created to cover certain areas in the non-metropolitan counties. The remaining county areas will continue to have two tiers of local authorities. The county and district councils in the Isle of Wight were replaced by a single unitary authority on 1 April 1995; the former counties of Avon, Cleveland and Humberside were replaced by unitary authorities on 1 April 1996; York became a unitary authority at the same date; 14 district councils were replaced by 13 unitary authorities on 1 April 1997. Changes in other areas will take effect in April 1998.

Legislation passed in 1994 abolished the two-tier structure in Wales and Scotland with effect from 1 April 1996 and replaced it with a single tier of unitary authorities.

Local authorities are empowered or required by various Acts of Parliament to carry out functions in their areas. The legislation concerned comprises public general Acts and 'local' Acts which local authorities have promoted as private bills.

ELECTIONS

Local elections are normally held on the first Thursday in May. Generally, all British subjects and citizens of the Republic of Ireland of 18 years or over who are resident on the qualifying date in the area for which the election is being held, are entitled to vote at local government elections. A register of electors is prepared and published annually by local electoral registration officers.

A returning officer has the overall responsibility for an election. Voting takes place at polling stations, arranged by the local authority and under the supervision of a presiding officer specially appointed for the purpose. Candidates, who are subject to various statutory qualifications and disqualifications designed to ensure that they are suitable persons to hold office, must be nominated by electors for the electoral area concerned.

In England, the Local Government Commission is responsible for carrying out periodic reviews of electoral arrangements and making proposals to the Secretary of State for changes found necessary. In Wales and Scotland these matters are the responsibility of the Local Government Boundary Commission for Wales and the Local Boundary Commission for Scotland respectively.

LOCAL GOVERNMENT COMMISSION FOR ENGLAND, Dolphyn Court, 10–11 Great Turnstile, Lincoln's Inn Fields, London WC1V 7JU. Tel: 0171-430 8400
LOCAL GOVERNMENT BOUNDARY COMMISSION FOR WALES, 1–6 St Andrew's Place, Cardiff CF1 3BE. Tel: 01222-395031

INTERNAL ORGANIZATION

The council as a whole is the final decision-making body within any authority. Councils are free to a great extent to make their own internal organizational arrangements.

Normally, questions of policy are settled by the full council, while the administration of the various services is the responsibility of committees of councillors. Day-to-day decisions are delegated to the council's officers, who act within the policies laid down by the councillors.

FINANCE

Local government in England, Wales and Scotland is financed from four sources: the council tax, non-domestic rates, government grants, and income from fees and charges for services. (For arrangements in Northern Ireland, *see* page 527.)

COUNCIL TAX

Under the Local Government Finance Act 1992, from 1 April 1993 the council tax replaced the community charge (which had been introduced in April 1989 in Scotland and April 1990 in England and Wales in place of domestic rates).

The council tax is a local tax levied by each local council. Liability for the council tax bill usually falls on the owner-occupier or tenant of a dwelling which is their sole or main residence. Council tax bills may be reduced because of the personal circumstances of people resident in a property, and there are discounts in the case of dwellings occupied by fewer than two adults.

In England, each county council, each district council and each police authority sets its own council tax rate. The district councils collect the combined council tax, and the county councils and police authorities claim their share from the district councils' collection funds. In Wales, each unitary authority and each police authority sets its own council tax rate. The unitary authorities collect the combined council tax and the police authorities claim their share from the funds. In Scotland each island council and unitary authority sets its own rate of council tax.

The tax relates to the value of the dwelling. Each dwelling is placed in one of eight valuation bands, ranging from A to H, based on the property's estimated market value as at 1 April 1991.

The valuation bands and ranges of values in England, Wales and Scotland are:

England

A	Up to £40,000	E	£88,001–£120,000
B	£40,001–£52,000	F	£120,001–£160,000
C	£52,001–£68,000	G	£160,001–£320,000
D	£68,001–£88,000	H	Over £320,000

Wales

A	Up to £30,000	E	£66,001–£90,000
B	£30,001–£39,000	F	£90,001–£120,000
C	£39,001–£51,000	G	£120,001–£240,000
D	£51,001–£66,000	H	Over £240,000

Scotland

A	Up to £27,000	E	£58,001–£80,000
B	£27,001–£35,000	F	£80,001–£106,000
C	£35,001–£45,000	G	£106,001–£212,000
D	£45,001–£58,000	H	Over £212,000

The council tax within a local area varies between the different bands according to proportions laid down by law. The charge attributable to each band as a proportion of the Band D charge set by the council is approximately:

A	67%	E	122%
B	78%	F	144%
C	89%	G	167%
D	100%	H	200%

The band D rate is given in the tables on pages 544–49 (England), 556 (London), 559 (Wales), and 564 (Scotland). There may be variations from the given figure within each district council area because of different parish or community precepts being levied.

Non-Domestic Rates

Non-domestic (business) rates are collected by billing authorities; these are the district councils in those areas of England with two tiers of local government and unitary authorities in other parts of England, in Wales and in Scotland. In respect of England and Wales, the Local Government Finance Act 1988 provides for liability for rates to be assessed on the basis of a poundage (multiplier) tax on the rateable value of property (hereditaments). Separate multipliers are set by the appropriate Secretaries of State in England, Wales and Scotland, and rates are collected by the billing authority for the area where a property is located. Rate income collected by billing authorities is paid into a national non-domestic rating (NNDR) pool and redistributed to individual authorities on the basis of the adult population figure as prescribed by the appropriate Secretary of State. The rates pools are maintained separately in England, Wales and Scotland. For the years 1995–6 to 2000–1 actual payment of rates in certain cases are subject to transitional arrangements, to phase in the larger increases and reductions in rates resulting from the effects of the 1995 revaluation.

Rates are levied in Scotland in accordance with the Local Government (Scotland) Act 1975. For 1995–6, the Secretary of State for Scotland prescribed a single non-domestic rates poundage to apply throughout the country at the same level as the uniform business rate (UBR) in England. Rate income is pooled and redistributed to local authorities on a per capita basis. For the year 1995–6 payment of rates was subject to transitional arrangements to phase in the effect of the 1995 revaluation.

Rateable values for the rating lists came into force on 1 April 1995. They are derived from the rental value of property as at 1 April 1993 and determined on certain statutory assumptions by the Valuation Office Agency in England and Wales, and by Regional Assessors in Scotland. New property which is added to the list, and significant changes to existing property, necessitate amendments to the rateable value on the same basis. Rating lists (valuation rolls in Scotland) remain in force until the next general revaluation. Such revaluations take place every five years, the next being in 2000.

Certain types of property are exempt from rates, e.g. agricultural land and buildings, and places of public religious worship. Charities and other non-profit-making organizations may receive full or partial relief. Empty property is liable to pay rates at 50 per cent, except for certain specified classes which are exempt entirely.

Government Grants

In addition to specific grants in support of revenue expenditure on particular services, central government pays revenue support grant to local authorities. This grant is paid to each local authority so that if each authority spends at a level sufficient to provide a standard level of service, all authorities in the same class can set broadly the same council tax.

COMPLAINTS

Commissioners for Local Administration in England, Wales and Scotland (*see* page 321) are responsible for investigating complaints from members of the public who claim to have suffered injustice as a consequence of maladministration in local government or in certain local bodies.

The Northern Ireland Commissioner for Complaints fulfils a similar function in Northern Ireland, investigating complaints about local authorities and certain public bodies.

THE QUEEN'S REPRESENTATIVES

The Lord-Lieutenant of a county is the permanent local representative of the Crown in that county. The appointment of Lord-Lieutenants is now regulated by the Lieutenancies Act 1997. They are appointed by the Sovereign on the recommendation of the Prime Minister. The retirement age is 75. The office of Lord-Lieutenant dates from 1557, and its holder was originally responsible for the maintenance of order and for local defence in the county. The duties of the post include attending on royalty during official visits to the county, performing certain duties in connection with armed forces of the Crown (and in particular the reserve forces), and making presentations of honours and awards on behalf of the Crown. In England, Wales and Northern Ireland, the Lord-Lieutenant usually also holds the office of *Custos Rotulorum*. As such, he or she acts as head of the county's commission of the peace (which recommends the appointment of magistrates).

The office of Sheriff (from the Old English shire-reeve) of a county was created in the tenth century. The Sheriff was the special nominee of the Sovereign, and the office reached the peak of its influence under the Norman kings. The Provisions of Oxford (1258) laid down a yearly tenure of office. Since the mid-16th century the office has been purely civil, with military duties taken over by the Lord-Lieutenant of the county. The Sheriff (commonly known as 'High Sheriff') attends on royalty during official visits to the county, acts as the returning officer during parliamentary elections in county constituencies, attends the opening ceremony when a High Court judge goes on circuit, executes High Court writs, and appoints under-sheriffs to act as deputies. The appointments and duties of the High Sheriffs in England and Wales are laid down by the Sheriffs Act 1887.

The serving High Sheriff submits a list of names of possible future sheriffs to a tribunal which chooses three names to put to the Sovereign. The tribunal nominates the High Sheriff annually on 12 November and the Sovereign pricks the name of the Sheriff to succeed in the following year. The term of office runs from 25 March to the following 24 March (the civil and legal year before 1752). No person may be chosen twice in three years if there is any other suitable person in the county.

CIVIC DIGNITIES

District councils in England may petition for a royal charter granting borough or 'city' status to the district. Local councils in Wales may petition for a royal charter granting county borough or 'city' status to the council.

In England and Wales the chairman of a borough or county borough council may be called a mayor, and the chairman of a city council a Lord Mayor. Parish councils in

England and Wales may call themselves 'town councils', in which case their chairman is the town mayor.

In Scotland the chairman of a local council may be known as a convenor; a provost is the equivalent of a mayor. The chairmen of the councils for the cities of Aberdeen, Dundee, Edinburgh and Glasgow are Lord Provosts.

ENGLAND
(For London, *see* below)

There are currently 36 non-metropolitan counties; all (apart from the Isle of Wight) are divided into non-metropolitan districts. In addition, there are 26 unitary authorities (13 created in April 1996 and 13 created in April 1997). A further 19 unitary authorities will come into being in April 1998. At present there are 260 non-metropolitan districts. The populations of most of the new unitary authorities are in the range of 100,000 to 300,000. The non-metropolitan districts have populations broadly in the range of 60,000 to 100,000; some, however, have larger populations, because of the need to avoid dividing large towns, and some in mainly rural areas have smaller populations.

Six metropolitan counties cover the main conurbations outside Greater London: Tyne and Wear, West Midlands, Merseyside, Greater Manchester, West Yorkshire and South Yorkshire. They are divided into 36 metropolitan districts, most of which have a population of over 200,000.

There are also about 10,000 parishes, in 219 of the non-metropolitan and 18 of the metropolitan districts.

ELECTIONS

For districts, non-metropolitan counties and for about 8,000 parishes, there are elected councils, consisting of directly elected councillors. The councillors elect annually one of their number as chairman.

Generally, councillors serve four years and there are no elections of district and parish councillors in county election years. In metropolitan districts, one-third of the councillors for each ward are elected each year except in the year when county elections take place elsewhere. Non-metropolitan districts can choose whether to have elections by thirds or whole council elections. In the former case, one-third of the council, as nearly as may be, is elected in each year of metropolitan district elections. If whole council elections are chosen, these are held in the year midway between county elections.

FUNCTIONS

In non-metropolitan areas, functions are divided between the districts and counties, those requiring the larger area or population for their efficient performance going to the county. The metropolitan district councils, with the larger population in their areas, already had wider functions than non-metropolitan councils, and following abolition of the metropolitan county councils were given most of their functions also. A few functions continue to be exercised over the larger area by joint bodies, made up of councillors from each district.

The allocation of functions is as follows:

County councils: education; strategic planning; traffic, transport and highways; fire service; consumer protection; refuse disposal; smallholdings; social services; libraries

Non-metropolitan district councils: local planning; housing; highways (maintenance of certain urban roads and off-street car parks); building regulations; environmental health; refuse collection; cemeteries and crematoria

Non-metropolitan unitary councils: their functions are all those listed above, except that the fire service is exercised by a joint body

Concurrently by county and district councils: recreation (parks, playing fields, swimming pools); museums; encouragement of the arts, tourism and industry

The Police and Magistrates Court Act 1994 set up police authorities in England and Wales separate from the local authorities.

PARISH COUNCILS

Parishes with 200 or more electors must generally have parish councils, which means that over three-quarters of the parishes have councils. A parish council comprises at least five members, the number being fixed by the district council. Elections are held every four years, at the time of the election of the district councillor for the ward including the parish. All parishes have parish meetings, comprising the electors of the parish. Where there is no council, the meeting must be held at least twice a year.

Parish council functions include: allotments; encouragement of arts and crafts; community halls, recreational facilities (e.g. open spaces, swimming pools), cemeteries and crematoria; and many minor functions. They must also be given an opportunity to comment on planning applications. They may, like county and district councils, spend limited sums for the general benefit of the parish. They levy a precept on the district councils for their funds.

The Local Government and Rating Act 1997 gave additional powers to parish councils to spend money on community transport initiatives and crime prevention equipment.

FINANCE

Aggregate external finance for 1997–8 was originally determined at £35,767 million. Of this, specific and special grants were estimated at £4,921 million. £18,675 million was in respect of revenue support grant and £12,027 million was support from the national non-domestic rate pool. Total standard spending by local authorities considered for grant purposes was £45,665 million.

The average council taxes, expressed in terms of Band C, two-adult properties for 1997–8, were: inner London boroughs and the City of London £647; outer London boroughs £654; metropolitan districts £779; shire areas £671. The average for England was £689.

National non-domestic rate (or uniform business rate) for 1997–8 is 45.8p. The provisional amount estimated to be raised from central, local and Crown lists is £12.5 billion. Total rateable value held on draft local authority lists at 31 December 1996 was £29.9 billion. The amount to be redistributed to authorities from the pool in 1997–8 is £12 billion.

Under the Local Government and Housing Act 1989, local authorities have four main ways of paying for capital expenditure: borrowing and other forms of extended credit; capital grants from central government towards some types of capital expenditure; 'usable' capital receipts from the sale of land, houses and other assets; and revenue.

The amount of capital expenditure which a local authority can finance by borrowing (or other forms of credit) is effectively limited by the credit approvals issued to it by central government. Most credit approvals can be used for any local authority service; these are known as basic credit approvals. Others (supplementary credit approvals) are for particular projects or services.

Generally, the 'usable' part of a local authority's capital receipts consists of 25 per cent of receipts from the sale of council houses and 50 per cent of most other receipts. The balance has to be set aside as provision for repaying debt and meeting other credit liabilities.

EXPENDITURE

Local authority budgeted net revenue expenditure for 1997–8 was (1997–8 cash prices):

Service	£m
Education	18,816
Personal social services	8,411
Police	6,539
Highway maintenance	1,694
Fire	1,347
Civil defence and other Home Office services	540
Magistrates courts	309
Public transport and parking	693
Housing benefit administration	5,694
Non-housing revenue account housing	366
Libraries, museums and art galleries	759
Swimming pools and recreation	488
Local environmental services	5,500
Other services	376
Net current expenditure	51,532
Capital charges	2,188
Capital charged to revenue	772
Other non-current expenditure	3,880
Interest receipts	−723
Gross revenue expenditure	57,649
Specific and special grants outside AEF	−9,363
Other income	−96
Revenue expenditure	48,190
Specific and special grants inside AEF	−1,696
Net revenue expenditure	46,494

AEF = aggregate external finance

LONDON

Since the abolition of the Greater London Council in 1986, the Greater London area has not had a single local government body. The area is divided into 32 borough councils, which have a status similar to the metropolitan district councils in the rest of England, and the Corporation of the City of London.

LONDON BOROUGH COUNCILS

The London boroughs have whole council elections every four years, in the year immediately following the county council election year. The next elections will be in 1998.

The borough councils have responsibility for the following functions: building regulations; cemeteries and crematoria; consumer protection; education; youth employment; environmental health; electoral registration; food; drugs; housing; leisure services; libraries; local planning; local roads; museums; parking; recreation (parks, playing fields, swimming pools); refuse collection and street cleansing; social services; town planning; and traffic management.

THE CORPORATION OF LONDON

(*see also* pages 551–3)

The Corporation of London is the local authority for the City of London. Its legal definition is 'The Mayor and Commonalty and Citizens of the City of London'. It is governed by the Court of Common Council, which consists of the Lord Mayor, 24 other aldermen, and 130 common councilmen. The Lord Mayor and two sheriffs are nominated annually by the City guilds (the livery companies) and elected by the Court of Aldermen. Alder-

men and councilmen are elected by businesses in the 25 wards into which the City is divided; councilmen must stand for re-election annually. The Council is a legislative assembly, and there are no political parties.

The Corporation has the same functions as the London borough councils. In addition, it runs the City of London Police; is the health authority for the Port of London; has health control of animal imports throughout Greater London, including at Heathrow airport; owns and manages public open spaces throughout Greater London; runs the Central Criminal Court; and runs Billingsgate, Smithfield and Spitalfields markets.

THE CITY GUILDS (LIVERY COMPANIES)

The livery companies of the City of London grew out of early medieval religious fraternities and began to emerge as trade and craft guilds, retaining their religious aspect, in the 12th century. From the early 14th century, only members of the trade and craft guilds could call themselves citizens of the City of London. The guilds began to be called livery companies, because of the distinctive livery worn by the most prosperous guild members on ceremonial occasions, in the late 15th century.

By the early 19th century the power of the companies within their trades had begun to wane, but those wearing the livery of a company continued to play an important role in the government of the City of London. Liverymen still have the right to nominate the Lord Mayor and sheriffs, and most members of the Court of Common Council are liverymen (*see also* page 553).

GREATER LONDON SERVICES

After the abolition of the Greater London Council (GLC) in 1986, the London boroughs took over most of its functions. Successor bodies have also been set up for certain functions. The London Residuary Body (LRB) was set up in 1986 to deal with residual matters of the GLC. It completed its work and was wound up in 1995.

WALES

The Local Government (Wales) Act 1994 abolished the two-tier structure of eight county and 37 district councils which had existed since 1974, and replaced it, from 1 April 1996, with 22 unitary authorities. The new authorities were elected in May 1995. Each unitary authority has inherited all the functions of the previous county and district councils, except fire services (which are provided by three combined fire authorities, composed of representatives of the unitary authorities) and National Parks (which are the responsibility of three independent National Park authorities).

The Police and Magistrates Courts Act 1994 set up four police authorities with effect from 1 April 1995: Dyfed-Powys, Gwent, North Wales, and South Wales.

COMMUNITY COUNCILS

In Wales parishes are known as communities. Unlike England, where many areas are not in any parish, communities have been established for the whole of Wales, approximately 865 communities in all. Community meetings may be convened as and when desired.

Community councils exist in 735 communities and further councils may be established at the request of a community meeting. Community councils have broadly the same range of powers as English parish councils. Community councillors are elected at the same time as a unitary authority election and for a term of four years.

FINANCE

Aggregate external finance for 1997–8 is £2,577.9 million. This comprises revenue support grant of £1,732.7 million, specific grants of £241.5 million, support from the national non-domestic rate pool of £584 million, and £16.7 million in council tax reduction grants. Total standard spending by local authorities considered for grant purposes is £2,931.3 million.

The average council tax levied in Wales for 1997–8 is £495, comprising unitary authorities £446 and police authorities £49.

National non-domestic rates (or uniform business rate) in Wales for 1997–8 is 41.4p. The amount estimated to be raised is £584 million. Total rateable value held on local authority lists at 31 December 1996 was £1,340 million.

SCOTLAND

The Local Government etc. (Scotland) Act abolished the two-tier structure of nine regional and 53 district councils which had existed since 1975 and replaced it, from 1 April 1996, with 29 unitary authorities on the mainland; the three islands councils remain. The new authorities were elected in April 1995. Each unitary authority has inherited all the functions of the regional and district councils, except water and sewerage (now provided by three public bodies whose members are appointed by the Secretary of State for Scotland) and reporters panels (now a national agency).

ELECTIONS

The unitary authorities consist of directly elected councillors. Elections take place every three years; the next elections are in 1999. In 1997 the register showed 3,995,923 electors in Scotland.

FUNCTIONS

The functions of the councils and islands councils are: education; social work; strategic planning; the provision of infrastructure such as roads; consumer protection; flood prevention; coast protection; valuation and rating; police and fire services; civil defence; electoral registration; public transport; registration of births, deaths and marriages; housing; leisure and recreation; development control and building control; environmental health; licensing; allotments; public conveniences; and the administration of district courts.

COMMUNITY COUNCILS

Unlike the parish councils and community councils in England and Wales, Scottish community councils are not local authorities. Their purpose as defined in statute is to ascertain and express the views of the communities which they represent, and to take in the interests of their communities such action as appears to be expedient or practicable. Over 1,000 community councils have been established under schemes drawn up by district and islands councils in Scotland.

Since April 1996 community councils have had an enhanced role, becoming statutory consultees on local planning issues and on the decentralization schemes which the new councils have to draw up for delivery of services.

FINANCE

Figures for 1996–7 show total receipts from non-domestic rates of £1,241 million and £975.1 million from the council tax. The unified business rate for 1996–7 was 44.9p and the average Band D council tax payable was £708. The average Band D council water charge payable was £66.62.

NORTHERN IRELAND

For the purpose of local government Northern Ireland has a system of 26 single-tier district councils.

ELECTIONS

There are 582 members of the councils, elected for periods of four years at a time on the principle of proportional representation.

FUNCTIONS

The district councils have three main roles. These are:
Executive: responsibility for a wide range of local services including building regulations; community services; consumer protection; cultural facilities; environmental health; miscellaneous licensing and registration provisions, including dog control; litter prevention; recreational and social facilities; refuse collection and disposal; street cleansing; and tourist development
Representative: nominating representatives to sit as members of the various statutory bodies responsible for the administration of regional services such as drainage, education, fire, health and personal social services, housing, and libraries
Consultative: acting as the medium through which the views of local people are expressed on the operation in their area of other regional services, notably conservation (including water supply and sewerage services), planning, and roads, provided by those departments of central government which have an obligation, statutory or otherwise, to consult the district councils about proposals affecting their areas

FINANCE

Local government in Northern Ireland is funded by a system of rates (a local property tax calculated by using the rateable value of a property multiplied by an amount per pound of rateable value). Rates are collected by the Rate Collection Agency, an executive agency within the Department of the Environment for Northern Ireland. A general revaluation of non-domestic properties became effective on 1 April 1997. As a result of this, separate regional rates are now made at standard uniform amounts by the Department of Finance and Personnel for both domestic and non-domestic sectors. District councils now make their individual district rates on the same basis.

In 1996–7 approximately £463 million was raised in rates and the total rateable value was £229.85 million (net). The average domestic poundage levied was 179.49p and the average non-domestic rate poundage was 251.49p.

Political Composition of Local Councils

AS AT END MAY 1997

Abbreviations:

C.	Conservative
Com.	Communist
Dem.	Democrat
Green	Green
Ind.	Independent
Lab.	Labour
Lib.	Liberal
LD	Liberal Democrat
MK	Mebyon Kernow
NP	Non-political/Non-party
PC	Plaid Cymru
RA	Ratepayers'/Residents' Associations
SD	Social Democrat
SNP	Scottish National Party

ENGLAND

COUNTY COUNCILS

*Unitary council

Bedfordshire	C. 25, Lab. 14, LD 10
Berkshire	LD 32, Lab. 24, C. 16, Ind. 2, Lib. 1, Ind. Lab. 1
Buckinghamshire	C. 38, LD 9, Lab. 5, Ind. 1, Lib. 1
Cambridgeshire	C. 40, Lab. 19, LD 17, Lib. 1
Cheshire	Lab. 37, C. 22, LD 12
Cornwall	LD 39, Ind. 23, Lab. 8, C. 7, Lib. 1, MK 1
Cumbria	Lab. 44, C. 23, LD 12, Ind. 4
Derbyshire	Lab. 45, C. 12, LD 6, Ind. 1
Devon	LD 37, C. 21, Lab. 19, Ind. 4, Lib. 3, vacant 1
Dorset	LD 21, C. 15, Lab. 5, Ind. 1
Durham	Lab. 53, Ind. 4, C. 2, LD 2
East Sussex	C. 21, LD 16, Lab. 7
Essex	C. 44, Lab. 33, LD 20, Ind. 1
Gloucestershire	LD 22, C. 21, Lab. 18, Ind. 1, others 1
Hampshire	C. 43, LD 21, Lab. 8, Ind. 2
Hereford and Worcester	C. 25, Lab. 24, LD 21, Ind. 6
Hertfordshire	C. 38, Lab. 30, LD 9
Isle of Wight	LD 32, C. 6, Ind. 6, Lab. 3, others 1
Kent	C. 50, Lab. 30, LD 19
Lancashire	Lab. 60, C. 29, LD 8, Ind. Lab. 1, vacant 1
Leicestershire	C. 25, Lab. 17, LD 11, Ind. C. 1
Lincolnshire	C. 43, Lab. 19, LD 11, Ind. 3
Norfolk	C. 36, Lab. 34, LD 13, Ind. 1
Northamptonshire	Lab. 37, C. 27, LD 4
Northumberland	Lab. 43, C. 14, LD 8, Ind. 1
North Yorkshire	C. 35, LD 21, Lab. 12, Ind. 6
Nottinghamshire	Lab. 61, C. 18, LD 5, Ind. 1, vacant 3
Oxfordshire	Lab. 22, C. 27, LD 19, Green 2
Shropshire	C. 25, Lab. 23, LD 13, Ind. 1, Ind. LD 1, others 3
Somerset	LD 37, C. 17, Lab. 3
Staffordshire	Lab. 40, C. 20, LD 2
Suffolk	Lab. 33, C. 31, LD 15, Ind. 1
Surrey	C. 47, LD 17, Lab. 6, RA 5, Ind. 1
Warwickshire	Lab. 31, C. 22, LD 8, Ind. 1
West Sussex	C. 37, LD 24, Lab. 9, Ind. 1
Wiltshire	C. 22, LD 20, Lab. 4, Ind. 1

UNITARY COUNCILS

Barnsley	Lab. 63, Ind. 2, C. 1
Bath and North-East Somerset	LD 28, Lab. 21, C. 16
Birmingham	Lab. 85, LD 17, C. 13, vacant 2
Bolton	Lab. 48, C. 6, LD 6
Bournemouth	LD 27, C. 20, Lab. 6, Ind. 4
Bradford	Lab. 70, C. 14, LD 6
Brighton and Hove	Lab. 54, C. 23, Green 1
Bristol	Lab. 50, LD 12, C. 5, vacant 1
Bury	Lab. 41, C. 4, LD 3
Calderdale	Lab. 36, LD 9, C. 8, Ind. 1
Coventry	Lab. 50, C. 3, vacant 1
Darlington	Lab. 36, C. 13, LD 2, Ind. 1
Derby	Lab. 37, C. 3, LD 2, vacant 2
Doncaster	Lab. 58, C. 3, Lib. 2
Dudley	Lab. 60, C. 8, LD 4
East Riding of Yorkshire	Lab. 23, C. 19, LD 18, Ind. 5, SDP 1, vacant 1
Gateshead	Lab. 51, LD 14, Lib. 1
Hartlepool	Lab. 40, LD 4, C. 2, Ind. C. 1
Kingston upon Hull	Lab. 58, LD 1, Ind. Lab. 1
Kirklees	Lab. 46, LD 18, C. 6, Ind. 1, Green 1
Knowsley	Lab. 64, LD 2
Leeds	Lab. 80, LD 9, C. 8, vacant 2
Leicester	Lab. 40, LD 9, C. 7
Liverpool	Lab. 51, LD 41, Lib. 2, C. 1, Ind. 1, others 3
Luton	Lab. 36, C. 3, LD 9
Manchester	Lab. 84, LD 15
Middlesbrough	Lab. 44, LD 4, C. 2, Ind. Lab. 1, vacant 2
Milton Keynes	Lab. 30, LD 18, C. 2, Ind. 1
Newcastle upon Tyne	Lab. 64, LD 12, vacant 2
North-East Lincolnshire	Lab. 32, LD 7, C. 2, Ind. 1
North Lincolnshire	Lab. 35, C. 7
North Somerset	LD 30, C. 17, Ind. 5, Lab. 5, Green 1, Lib. 1
North Tyneside	Lab. 45, C. 7, LD 6, Ind. 2
Oldham	Lab. 35, LD 24, Ind. Lab. 1
Poole	LD 23, C. 13, Lab. 3,
Portsmouth	Lab. 21, LD 12, C. 6
Redcar and Cleveland	Lab. 47, LD 8, Ind. Lab. 2, C. 1, vacant 1
Rochdale	Lab. 36, LD 18, C. 6
Rotherham	Lab. 64, C. 1, vacant 1
Rutland	Ind. 10, LD 6, C. 2, Lab. 2
St Helens	Lab. 44, LD 9, C. 1
Salford	Lab. 57, LD 3,
Sandwell	Lab. 59, LD 9, C. 2, Ind. Lab. 1, vacant 1
Sefton	Lab. 31, LD 24, C. 13, Ind. Lab. 1
Sheffield	Lab. 55, LD 31, C. 1
Solihull	C. 17, Lab. 16, LD 12, Ind. 6
Southampton	Lab. 29, LD 13, C. 3
South Gloucestershire	Lab. 31, LD 30, C. 8, others 1
South Tyneside	Lab. 52, LD 6, others 2
Stockport	LD 31, Lab. 27, Ind. 3, C. 2

Stockton-on-Tees	*Lab.* 43, *C.* 7, *LD* 4, *Ind. Lab.* 1
Stoke-on-Trent	*Lab.* 60
Sunderland	*Lab.* 65, *C.* 4, *LD* 2, *Ind.* 1, *Lib.* 1, *vacant* 2
Swindon	*Lab.* 41, *LD* 9, *C.* 3, *Ind.* 1
Tameside	*Lab.* 54, *LD* 1, *others* 2
Trafford	*Lab.* 35, *C.* 22, *LD* 5, *Ind. C.* 1
Wakefield	*Lab.* 61, *C.* 2
Walsall	*Lab.* 26, *C.* 13, *LD* 5, *Ind.* 1, *others* 15
Wigan	*Lab.* 69, *LD* 2, *Ind. Lab.* 1
Wirral	*Lab.* 41, *C.* 16, *LD* 8, *Ind. LD* 1
Wolverhampton	*Lab.* 45, *C.* 11, *LD* 2, *vacant* 2
York	*Lab.* 30, *LD* 18, *C.* 3, *Ind.* 2

DISTRICT COUNCILS

*Denotes councils where one-third of councillors retire each year except in the year of county council elections

*Adur	*LD* 28, *Lab.* 6, *C.* 3, *RA* 2
Allerdale	*Lab.* 36, *C.* 7, *Ind.* 7, *LD* 4, *vacant* 1
Alnwick	*LD* 12, *Lab.* 6, *NP* 3, *others* 8
Amber Valley	*Lab.* 37, *C.* 5, *vacant* 1
Arun	*C.* 29, *LD* 14, *Lab.* 10, *Ind.* 3
Ashfield	*Lab.* 33
Ashford	*C.* 19, *LD* 14, *Lab.* 13, *Ind.* 3
Aylesbury Vale	*LD* 32, *C.* 12, *Ind.* 9, *Lab.* 5
Babergh	*Lab.* 12, *Ind.* 11, *C.* 9, *LD* 8, *NP* 2
*Barrow-in-Furness	*Lab.* 31, *C.* 4, *others* 3
*Basildon	*Lab.* 24, *LD* 17, *C.* 1
*Basingstoke and Deane	*C.* 22, *LD* 17, *Lab.* 13, *Ind.* 4, *vacant* 1
*Bassetlaw	*Lab.* 35, *C.* 6, *LD* 3, *Ind.* 2, *others* 4
*Bedford	*Lab.* 22, *LD* 14, *C.* 10, *Ind.* 7
Berwick-upon-Tweed	*LD* 11, *Ind.* 11, *Lab.* 2, *C.* 2, *Ind. Lib.* 1, *others* 1
Blaby	*Lab.* 17, *C.* 11, *LD* 9, *Ind.* 1, *Ind. C.* 1
*Blackburn with Darwen	*Lab.* 46, *C.* 12, *LD* 4
Blackpool	*Lab.* 34, *C.* 7, *LD* 3
Blyth Valley	*Lab.* 39, *LD* 7, *Ind. Lab.* 1
Bolsover	*Lab.* 35, *Ind.* 2
Boston	*Lab.* 14, *Ind.* 8, *LD* 7, *C.* 5
Bracknell Forest	*C.* 23, *Lab.* 17
Braintree	*Lab.* 37, *C.* 10, *LD* 6, *Ind.* 7
Breckland	*Lab.* 24, *C.* 18, *Ind.* 8, *LD* 2, *Green* 1
*Brentwood	*LD* 24, *C.* 12, *Lab.* 2, *Lib.* 1
Bridgnorth	*Ind.* 9, *Lab.* 6, *NP* 5, *Ind. C.* 4, *LD* 4, *C.* 3, *Ind. Lab.* 1, *vacant* 1
Broadland	*Lab.* 19, *C.* 12, *LD* 12, *Ind.* 6
Bromsgrove	*Lab.* 24, *C.* 12, *LD* 1, *others* 2
*Broxbourne	*C.* 26, *Lab.* 14, *LD* 2
Broxtowe	*Lab.* 36, *C.* 7, *LD* 5, *Ind.* 1
*Burnley	*Lab.* 38, *LD* 7, *C.* 1, *Ind.* 1, *vacant* 1
*Cambridge	*Lab.* 23, *LD* 17, *C.* 1, *Ind.* 1
*Cannock Chase	*Lab.* 40, *LD* 2
Canterbury	*LD* 22, *Lab.* 15, *C.* 11, *Ind.* 1
Caradon	*Ind. Lab.* 18, *LD* 18, *RA* 2, *Lab.* 2, *C.* 1
*Carlisle	*Lab.* 33, *C.* 14, *LD* 3, *Ind.* 1
Carrick	*LD* 19, *Lab.* 8, *Ind.* 8, *C.* 6, *MK* 1, *others* 2, *vacant* 1
Castle Morpeth	*Lab.* 12, *Ind.* 10, *C.* 6, *LD* 6

Castle Point	*Lab.* 34, *C.* 5
Charnwood	*Lab.* 30, *C.* 15, *LD* 5, *Ind.* 2
Chelmsford	*LD* 32, *C.* 13, *Lab.* 7, *Ind.* 4
*Cheltenham	*LD* 33, *Ind.* 4, *C.* 3, *Lab.* 1
*Cherwell	*Lab.* 27, *C.* 14, *LD* 6, *Ind.* 4, *others* 1
*Chester	*Lab.* 27, *LD* 18, *C.* 12, *Ind.* 2, *vacant* 1
Chesterfield	*Lab.* 37, *LD* 10
Chester-le-Street	*Lab.* 30, *C.* 1, *Ind.* 1, *LD* 1
Chichester	*LD* 24, *C.* 21, *Ind.* 4, *Lab.* 1
Chiltern	*LD* 24, *C.* 22, *RA* 2, *Ind.* 1, *Lab.* 1
*Chorley	*Lab.* 35, *LD* 7, *C.* 5, *Ind.* 1
Christchurch	*LD* 9, *C.* 8, *Ind.* 8
*Colchester	*LD* 33, *Lab.* 14, *C.* 11, *Ind.* 2
*Congleton	*LD* 28, *Lab.* 11, *C.* 5, *Ind. LD* 1
Copeland	*Lab.* 33, *C.* 11, *Ind.* 2, *Ind. Lab.* 1, *vacant* 4
Corby	*Lab.* 23, *LD* 2, *C.* 1, *Ind. Lab.* 1
Cotswold	*Ind.* 17, *LD* 8, *Lab.* 4, *Ind. C.* 4, *C.* 3, *others* 9
*Craven	*LD* 19, *C.* 7, *Lab.* 5, *Ind.* 3
*Crawley	*Lab.* 28, *LD* 2, *C.* 2
*Crewe and Nantwich	*Lab.* 38, *C.* 15, *LD* 3, *Ind.* 1
Dacorum	*Lab.* 32, *C.* 19, *LD* 4, *Ind.* 2, *vacant* 1
Dartford	*Lab.* 34, *C.* 10, *Ind.* 2, *Ind. Lab.* 1
*Daventry	*C.* 15, *Lab.* 15, *Ind.* 3, *LD* 2
Derbyshire Dales	*LD* 16, *Ind. C.* 15, *Lab.* 8
Derwentside	*Lab.* 49, *Ind.* 5, *vacant* 1
Dover	*Lab.* 35, *C.* 14, *LD* 4, *vacant* 3
Durham	*Lab.* 39, *LD* 7, *Ind.* 3
Easington	*Lab.* 44, *Lib.* 3, *Ind.* 2, *Ind. Lab.* 2
*Eastbourne	*LD* 21, *C.* 9
East Cambridgeshire	*LD* 13, *Ind.* 13, *NP* 5, *Lab.* 4, *C.* 1, *Ind. C.* 1
East Devon	*C.* 32, *LD* 17, *Ind.* 8, *Lib.* 1, *vacant* 2
East Dorset	*LD* 23, *C.* 12, *Ind.* 1
East Hampshire	*LD* 26, *C.* 13, *Ind.* 3
East Hertfordshire	*C.* 23, *LD* 16, *Lab.* 8, *Ind.* 2, *RA* 1
*Eastleigh	*LD* 30, *Lab.* 7, *C.* 7
East Lindsey	*NP* 34, *Lab.* 13, *LD* 7, *Green* 3, *others* 2, *vacant* 1
East Northamptonshire	*Lab.* 25, *C.* 9, *LD* 2
East Staffordshire	*Lab.* 36, *C.* 4, *Ind. C.* 3, *LD* 3
Eden	*Ind.* 31, *LD* 4, *Lab.* 2
*Ellesmere Port and Neston	*Lab.* 36, *C.* 5
*Elmbridge	*C.* 21, *RA* 21, *LD* 9, *Lab.* 8, *Ind.* 1
*Epping Forest	*Lab.* 17, *LD* 15, *C.* 15, *RA* 9, *Ind.* 2, *vacant* 1
Epsom and Ewell	*RA* 32, *LD* 3, *Lab.* 2, *vacant* 2
Erewash	*Lab.* 39, *C.* 10, *LD* 1, *Ind.* 1, *vacant* 1
*Exeter	*Lab.* 24, *LD* 7, *Lib.* 3, *C.* 2
*Fareham	*LD* 21, *C.* 9, *Lab.* 8, *Ind. C.* 4
Fenland	*Lab.* 15, *C.* 15, *Ind.* 3, *LD* 2, *others* 3, *vacant* 2
Forest Heath	*C.* 10, *Ind.* 6, *LD* 5, *Lab.* 4
Forest of Dean	*Lab.* 29, *Ind.* 8, *LD* 5, *C.* 1, *others* 6
Fylde	*C.* 14, *Ind.* 12, *Lab.* 5, *LD* 4, *others* 10
Gedling	*Lab.* 29, *C.* 20, *LD* 7, *Ind.* 1

*Gillingham	LD 30, Lab. 10, C. 1, vacant 1
*Gloucester	Lab. 25, LD 8, C. 2
*Gosport	LD 13, Lab. 7, C. 5, Ind. LD 3, others 2
Gravesham	Lab. 33, C. 10, Ind. Lab. 1
*Great Yarmouth	Lab. 37, C. 9, LD 1, vacant 1
Guildford	LD 19, C. 14, Lab. 6, Ind. Lib. 2, Ind. 1, others 3
*Halton	Lab. 47, LD 8, C. 1
Hambleton	C. 23, Ind. 15, Lab. 4, LD 3, Ind. C. 2
Harborough	LD 15, C. 12, Lab. 8, Ind. 2
*Harlow	Lab. 40, LD 2
*Harrogate	LD 41, C. 10, Lab. 4, Ind. 1, vacant 3
*Hart	LD 15, C. 12, Ind. 7, vacant 1
*Hastings	Lab. 15, LD 16, vacant 1
*Havant	LD 18, C. 10, Lab. 7, Ind. 3, Ind. Lab. 3, others 1
*Hereford	LD 22, Lab. 5
*Hertsmere	Lab. 22, C. 8, LD 8, Ind. 1
High Peak	Lab. 30, LD 6, C. 5, Ind. 3
Hinckley and Bosworth	LD 16, Lab. 13, C. 5
Horsham	LD 22, C. 18, Ind. 3
*Huntingdonshire	C. 33, LD 13, Lab. 5, Ind. 2
*Hyndburn	Lab. 44, C. 3
*Ipswich	Lab. 41, C. 6, LD 1
Kennet	Ind. 14, Lab. 9, C. 9, LD 8
Kerrier	Lab. 15, Ind. 13, LD 12, others 4
Kettering	Lab. 33, LD 3, C. 6, Ind. 3
King's Lynn and West Norfolk	Lab. 38, Ind. C. 15, LD 6, Ind. 1
Lancaster	Lab. 34, C. 11, Ind. 9, LD 4, Ind. C. 1, NP 1
*Leominster	Ind. 16, LD 7, Lab. 6, C. 3, Ind. C. 3, Green 1
Lewes	LD 28, C. 16, Lab. 2, Ind. 1, RA 1
Lichfield	Lab. 33, C. 19, LD 2, Ind. 1, Ind. Lab. 1
*Lincoln	Lab. 33
*Macclesfield	C. 33, Lab. 12, LD 12, RA 3
*Maidstone	LD 20, Lab. 18, C. 11, Ind. 5, vacant 1
Maldon	C. 12, Lab. 7, Ind. 6, LD 1, others 4
Malvern Hills	Ind. 19, LD 19, C. 6, Lab. 3, Green 3, Ind. C. 1
Mansfield	Lab. 45, C. 1
Melton	C. 8, Lab. 6, LD 4, Ind. 4, Ind. LD 2, vacant 2
Mendip	LD 20, Lab. 9, C. 8, Ind. 3, RA 2, others 1
Mid Bedfordshire	C. 23, Lab. 20, LD 5, Ind. 5
Mid Devon	Ind. 19, LD 19, Lab. 1, Lib. 1
Mid Suffolk	Lab. 17, LD 11, C. 7, Ind. 4, others 1
*Mid Sussex	LD 27, C. 19, Lab. 4, Ind. 4
*Mole Valley	LD 18, C. 12, Ind. 9, Lab. 2
Newark and Sherwood	Lab. 36, C. 11, LD 4, Ind. 2, vacant 1
Newbury	LD 38, C. 15, Ind. 1
*Newcastle under Lyme	Lab. 42, LD 10, C. 4
New Forest	LD 32, C. 23, Ind. 3
Northampton	Lab. 34, LD 8, C. 1
North Cornwall	Ind. 27, LD 10, C. 1
North Devon	LD 31, Ind. 11, C. 1, NP 1
North Dorset	LD 18, Ind. 11, others 4
North East Derbyshire	Lab. 43, C. 4, LD 3, Ind. 1, others 2
*North Hertfordshire	Lab. 26, C. 16, LD 7, Ind. 1
North Kesteven	Lab. 17, LD 8, C. 6, Ind. 4, others 4
North Norfolk	Lab. 19, LD 12, Ind. 8, C. 7
North Shropshire	NP 22, Lab. 6, Ind. 6, LD 4, C. 2
North Warwickshire	Lab. 29, C. 4, Ind. 1
North West Leicestershire	Lab. 35, C. 3, Ind. 2
North Wiltshire	LD 29, C. 12, Lab. 6, Ind. 4, vacant 1
*Norwich	Lab. 37, LD 11
Nottingham	Lab. 50, C. 3, LD 2
*Nuneaton and Bedworth	Lab. 42, C. 3
*Oadby and Wigston	LD 25, C. 1
Oswestry	Lab. 10, C. 5, LD 5, others 9
*Oxford	Lab. 39, LD 9, Green 3
*Pendle	LD 29, Lab. 19, C. 3
*Penwith	LD 10, Lab. 8, Ind. 8, C. 4, MK 2, others 2
*Peterborough	Lab. 27, C. 24, LD 1, others 5
Plymouth	Lab. 45, C. 13, vacant 2
*Preston	Lab. 32, C. 13, LD 12
*Purbeck	LD 11, Ind. 4, C. 3, Lab. 3, vacant 1
*Reading	Lab. 35, LD 6, C. 3, Ind. 1
*Redditch	Lab. 22, C. 4, LD 1, vacant 2
*Reigate and Banstead	C. 15, Lab. 14, LD 14, RA 4, Ind. 2
Restormel	LD 30, Ind. 9, Lab. 4, C. 1
Ribble Valley	LD 19, C. 18, Lab. 1, Ind. C. 1
Richmondshire	Ind. 22, LD 6, C. 2, Ind. C. 1, Ind. LD 1, others 1
Rochester upon Medway	Lab. 44, LD 5, C. 1
*Rochford	LD 23, Lab. 11, RA 3, C. 2, Ind. 1
*Rossendale	Lab. 31, C. 5
Rother	LD 19, C. 15, Ind. 6, Lab. 5
*Rugby	Lab. 22, C. 11, LD 5, others 10
*Runnymede	C. 21, Lab. 14, Ind. 6, LD 1
Rushcliffe	C. 24, Lab. 17, LD 8, Ind. 5
*Rushmoor	LD 18, Lab. 14, C. 13
Ryedale	Ind. 10, LD 8, C. 4, Lab. 1
*St Albans	LD 39, Lab. 12, C. 6
St Edmundsbury	Lab. 22, C. 14, LD 5, Ind. 2, vacant 1
Salisbury	LD 30, Lab. 11, C. 9, Ind. 7, NP 1
Scarborough	Lab. 24, C. 13, Ind. 8, LD 4
Sedgefield	Lab. 47, Ind. 2
Sedgemoor	C. 22, Lab. 13, LD 12, Ind. 2
Selby	Lab. 26, C. 9, Ind. 5, LD 1
Sevenoaks	LD 20, C. 17, Lab. 11, Ind. 5
Shepway	LD 19, C. 19, Lab. 14, Ind. 3, vacant 1
*Shrewsbury and Atcham	Lab. 22, LD 12, C. 9, Ind. 5
*Slough	Lab. 34, C. 4, Lib. 3
*South Bedfordshire	Lab. 24, LD 15, C. 11, Ind. 3
South Bucks	C. 20, Ind. 16, LD 4
*South Cambridgeshire	Ind. 22, C. 13, Lab. 10, LD 10
South Derbyshire	Lab. 27, C. 5, vacant 2
*Southend-on-Sea	C. 18, LD 14, Lab. 7
South Hams	C. 18, Ind. 12, LD 9, Lab. 1, others 4
*South Herefordshire	Ind. 24, LD 12, Lab. 1, others 2
South Holland	Ind. 16, Lab. 8, C. 8, others 5, vacant 1
South Kesteven	Lab. 14, C. 13, Ind. 12, LD 8, Ind. Lab. 3, Lib. 2, Ind. C. 1, NP 1, vacant 3

*South Lakeland — LD 20, C. 11, Ind. 10, Lab. 6, vacant 5

South Norfolk — LD 30, C. 12, Lab. 3, Ind. 2

South Northamptonshire — C. 16, Lab. 10, Ind. 8, LD 6

South Oxfordshire — LD 21, Lab. 13, C. 9, Ind. 5, others 2

South Ribble — Lab. 27, C. 16, LD 9, others 2

South Shropshire — NP 8, Ind. 8, LD 7, Green 2, Lab. 1, others 14

South Somerset — LD 45, C. 8, Ind. 6, Lab. 1

South Staffordshire — C. 28, Lab. 15, LD 4, RA 2, Ind. 1

Speldhurst — C. 21, Lab. 16, LD 3

Stafford — Lab. 33, C. 16, LD 10, Ind. 1

*Staffordshire Moorlands — Lab. 27, Ind. C. 11, LD 7, Ind. 3, others 8

*Stevenage — Lab. 38, LD 1

*Stratford-on-Avon — LD 24, C. 17, Ind. 9, Lab. 5

*Stroud — Lab. 28, LD 10, C. 7, Ind. 6, Green 4

Suffolk Coastal — C. 20, Lab. 15, LD 15, Ind. 5

Surrey Heath — C. 24, LD 8, Lab. 4

*Swale — LD 23, Lab. 19, C. 6, Ind. 1

*Tamworth — Lab. 27, Ind. 3

*Tandridge — LD 19, C. 16, Lab. 7

Taunton Deane — LD 29, C. 14, Lab. 6, Ind. 4

Teesdale — Ind. 12, Lab. 10, NP 6, C. 2, vacant 1

Teignbridge — LD 25, Ind. 22, C. 6, Lab. 5

Tendring — Lab. 37, Ind. 10, C. 7, LD 5, others 1

Test Valley — LD 23, C. 21

Tewkesbury — Ind. 23, LD 7, Lab. 6

Thanet — Lab. 44, C. 4, LD 4, Ind. 2

*Three Rivers — LD 23, C. 17, Lab. 3

*Thurrock — Lab. 46, C. 3

*Tonbridge and Malling — C. 23, LD 21, Lab. 11

*Torbay — LD 22, C. 11, Lab. 2, others 1

Torridge — LD 13, Ind. 9, Lab. 5, NP 3, C. 2, Green 1, others 3

*Tunbridge Wells — LD 27, C. 14, Lab. 6, Ind. 1

Tynedale — Lab. 19, LD 13, C. 11, Ind. 4

Uttlesford — LD 17, C. 12, Ind. 7, Lab. 4, vacant 2

Vale of White Horse — LD 34, C. 11, Lab. 5, Ind. 1

Vale Royal — Lab. 41, C. 15, LD 4

Wansbeck — Lab. 46

Warrington — Lab. 45, LD 11, C. 4

Warwick — Lab. 17, C. 12, LD 11, Ind. 4, others 1

*Watford — Lab. 21, LD 9, C. 6

*Waveney — Lab. 44, Ind. 2, C. 2

Waverley — LD 36, C. 18, Lab. 2, Ind. 1

Wealden — C. 29, LD 24, Ind. 5

Wear Valley — Lab. 35, Ind. 3, LD 2

Wellingborough — Lab. 16, C. 15, Ind. 3

*Welwyn Hatfield — Lab. 32, C. 15

West Devon — LD 15, Ind. 15

West Dorset — Ind. 20, C. 18, LD 11, Lab. 5, vacant 1

*West Lancashire — Lab. 34, C. 20, vacant 1

*West Lindsey — LD 19, Ind. 10, Lab. 3, C. 1, others 3, vacant 1

*West Oxfordshire — Ind. 15, LD 14, Lab. 11, C. 9

West Somerset — Ind. 13, C. 8, Lab. 8, LD 2, vacant 1

West Wiltshire — LD 26, C. 7, Lab. 6, Ind. 4

*Weymouth and Portland — Lab. 15, Ind. Lab. 13, Ind. 7

*Winchester — LD 36, C. 9, Lab. 6, Ind. 4

Windsor and Maidenhead — LD 29, C. 22, RA 6, Ind. 1

*Woking — LD 19, C. 9, Lab. 7

*Wokingham — C. 31, LD 23

*Worcester — Lab. 23, C. 9, LD 3, Ind. 1

*Worthing — LD 24, C. 11, vacant 1

Wrekin — Lab. 38, C. 8, LD 4, Ind. 1, Ind. C. 1, Ind. Lab. 1, RA 1

Wychavon — C. 19, LD 16, Lab. 9, Ind. 4, vacant 1

Wycombe — C. 24, LD 19, Lab. 15, Ind. 2

Wyre — Lab. 30, C. 18, LD 4, RA 2, Ind. 1, vacant 1

*Wyre Forest — Lab 26, LD 8, C. 3, Lib. 3, Ind. 2

GREATER LONDON BOROUGHS

Barking and Dagenham — Lab. 47, Ind. 3, LD 1

Barnet — C. 29, Lab. 25, LD 6

Bexley — Lab. 24, C. 24, LD 14

Brent — C. 33, Lab. 26, LD 5

Bromley — C. 32, LD 21, Lab. 7

Camden — Lab. 47, C. 7, LD 4, Ind. 1

City of Westminster — C. 45, Lab. 15

Croydon — Lab. 40, C. 30

Ealing — Lab. 49, C. 19, LD 3

Enfield — Lab. 41, C. 24, Ind. C. 1

Greenwich — Lab. 46, C. 9, LD 3, SD 2, Ind. 1, vacant 1

Hackney — Lab. 25, LD 9, C. 8, Ind. 1, others 17

Hammersmith and Fulham — Lab. 33, C. 14, LD 2, vacant 1

Haringey — Lab. 57, C. 2

Harrow — LD 29, C. 16, Lab. 14, RA 2, Ind. 1, vacant 1

Havering — Lab. 28, RA 17, C. 12, LD 2, others 4

Hillingdon — Lab. 40, C. 25, Ind. Lab. 1, others 3

Hounslow — Lab. 49, C. 6, LD 4, vacant 1

Islington — Lab. 34, LD 13, Ind. 2, C. 1, vacant 2

Kensington and Chelsea — C. 39, Lab. 15

Kingston upon Thames — LD 27, C. 17, Lab. 6

Lambeth — LD 25, Lab. 24, C. 14, Ind. 1

Lewisham — Lab. 61, LD 2, C. 1, others 2, vacant 1

Merton — Lab. 40, C. 10, RA 4, LD 3

Newham — Lab. 60

Redbridge — Lab. 29, C. 24, LD 9

Richmond upon Thames — LD 43, C. 7, Lab. 2

Southwark — Lab. 35, LD 24, C. 3, Ind. Lib. 1, others 1

Sutton — LD 47, Lab. 5, C. 4

Tower Hamlets — Lab. 42, LD 7, Ind. Lab. 1

Waltham Forest — Lab. 26, C. 16, LD 13, Ind. 2

Wandsworth — C. 45, Lab. 16

WALES

Anglesey — Ind. 26, PC 7, Lab. 5, C. 1, vacant 1,

Blaenau Gwent — Lab. 33, Ind. 3, C. 1, Lib. 1, PC 1, others 2, vacant 1

Bridgend — Lab. 43, Ind. 2, C. 2, Ind. Lab. 1

Caerphilly — Lab. 56, PC 9, Ind. 3

Cardiff — Lab. 56, LD 9, C. 1, PC 1

Carmarthenshire	*Lab.* 37, *Ind.* 28, *PC* 8, *LD* 3, *Ind. Lab* 2, *C.* 1, *others* 2
Ceredigion	*Ind.* 23, *LD* 11, *PC* 8, *Lab.* 1, *others* 1
Conwy	*Lab.* 18, *LD* 16, *C.* 10, *Ind.* 10, *PC* 4, *others* 1, *vacant* 1
Denbighshire	*Ind.* 18, *Lab.* 17, *PC* 7, *Ind. Lab.* 3, *LD* 3
Flintshire	*Lab.* 45, *Ind.* 15, *LD* 7, *C.* 3, *others* 2
Gwynedd	*PC* 46, *Ind.* 20, *Lab.* 11, *LD* 4, *others* 2
Merthyr Tydfil	*Lab.* 29, *Ind.* 4
Monmouthshire	*Lab.* 26, *C.* 11, *Ind.* 4, *LD* 1
Neath and Port Talbot	*Lab.* 50, *PC* 3, *RA* 3, *Ind.* 2, *LD* 2, *SD* 1, *Ind. Lab.* 1, *others* 2
Newport	*Lab.* 46, *C.* 1
Pembrokeshire	*Ind.* 41, *Lab.* 11, *PC* 4, *LD* 3, *vacant* 1
Powys	*Ind.* 60, *LD* 10, *Lab.* 9, *C.* 3, *PC* 1
Rhondda, Cynon, Taff	*Lab.* 57, *PC* 13, *Ind.* 3, *Ind. Lab.* 1, *RA* 1
Swansea	*Lab.* 55, *Ind.* 7, *LD* 7, *Ind. Lab.* 2, *C.* 1, *vacant* 1
Torfaen	*Lab.* 41, *Ind.* 1, *LD* 1, *C.* 1
Vale of Glamorgan	*Lab.* 36, *C.* 6, *PC* 5
Wrexham	*Lab.* 35, *Ind. C.* 6, *Ind. Lab.* 2, *others* 9
Shetland Islands	*NP* 11, *Ind.* 6, *LD* 3, *Lab.* 2, *Ind. Lab.* 1, *others* 3
South Ayrshire	*Lab.* 21, *C.* 4
South Lanarkshire	*Lab.* 62, *SNP* 8, *LD* 2, *C.* 2
Stirling	*Lab.* 13, *C.* 7, *SNP* 2
West Dumbartonshire	*Lab.* 14, *SNP* 8
Western Isles	*NP* 25, *Lab.* 5
West Lothian	*Lab.* 15, *SNP* 10, *Ind.* 1, *C.* 1

SCOTLAND

Aberdeen City	*Lab.* 30, *LD* 10, *C.* 9, *SNP* 1
Aberdeenshire	*LD* 16, *SNP* 15, *Ind.* 12, *C.* 4
Angus	*SNP* 21, *C.* 2, *LD* 2, *Ind.* 1
Argyll and Bute	*Ind.* 19, *LD* 4, *SNP* 4, *C.* 3, *Lab.* 2, *vacant* 1
City of Edinburgh	*Lab.* 33, *C.* 14, *LD* 10, *SNP* 1
Clackmannanshire	*Lab.* 8, *SNP* 3, *C.* 1
Dumfries and Galloway	*Ind.* 25, *Lab.* 20, *LD* 10, *SNP* 9, *C.* 2, *others* 4
Dundee City	*Lab.* 28, *C.* 4, *SNP* 3, *Ind. Lab.* 1
East Ayrshire	*Lab.* 22, *SNP* 8
East Dumbartonshire	*Lab.* 15, *LD* 9, *C.* 2
East Lothian	*Lab.* 15, *C.* 3
East Renfrewshire	*C.* 9, *Lab.* 8, *LD* 2, *RA* 1
Falkirk	*Lab.* 23, *SNP* 8, *C.* 2, *Ind.* 2, *NP* 1
Fife	*Lab.* 54, *LD* 25, *SNP* 9, *Ind.* 2, *Com.* 1, *others* 1
Glasgow City	*Lab.* 77, *C.* 3, *LD* 1, *SNP* 1, *others* 1
Highland	*Ind.* 48, *SNP* 9, *Lab.* 7, *LD* 6, *C.* 1, *vacant* 1
Inverclyde	*Lab.* 13, *LD* 6, *C.* 1
Midlothian	*Lab.* 13, *SNP* 2
Moray	*SNP* 13, *Lab.* 3, *Ind.* 2
North Ayrshire	*Lab.* 27, *C.* 1, *Ind.* 1, *SNP* 1
North Lanarkshire	*Lab.* 60, *SNP* 7, *Ind.* 2
Orkney Islands	*Ind.* 28
Perth and Kinross	*SNP* 18, *Lab.* 6, *LD* 5, *C.* 2, *Ind.* 1
Renfrewshire	*Lab.* 20, *SNP* 13, *LD* 3, *C.* 2, *Ind.* 2
Scottish Borders	*Ind.* 22, *LD* 17, *NP* 6, *SNP* 6, *Lab.* 4, *C.* 3

England

The Kingdom of England lies between 55° 46' and 49° 57' 30″ N. latitude (from a few miles north of the mouth of the Tweed to the Lizard), and between 1° 46' E. and 5° 43' W. (from Lowestoft to Land's End). England is bounded on the north by the Cheviot Hills; on the south by the English Channel; on the east by the Straits of Dover (Pas de Calais) and the North Sea; and on the west by the Atlantic Ocean, Wales and the Irish Sea. It has a total area of 50,351 sq. miles (130,410 sq. km): land 50,058 sq. miles (129,652 sq. km); inland water 293 sq. miles (758 sq. km).

POPULATION

The population at the 1991 census was 46,382,050 (males 22,469,707; females 23,912,343). The average density of the population in 1991 was 3.6 persons per hectare.

FLAG

The flag of England is the cross of St George, a red cross on a white field (cross gules in a field argent). The cross of St George, the patron saint of England, has been used since the 13th century.

RELIEF

There is a marked division between the upland and lowland areas of England. In the extreme north the Cheviot Hills (highest point, The Cheviot, 2,674 ft) form a natural boundary with Scotland. Running south from the Cheviots, though divided from them by the Tyne Gap, is the Pennine range (highest point, Cross Fell, 2,930 ft), the main orological feature of the country. The Pennines culminate in the Peak District of Derbyshire (Kinder Scout, 2,088 ft). West of the Pennines are the Cumbrian mountains, which include Scafell Pike (3,210 ft), the highest peak in England, and to the east are the Yorkshire Moors, their highest point being Urra Moor (1,490 ft).

In the west, the foothills of the Welsh mountains extend into the bordering English counties of Shropshire (the Wrekin, 1,334 ft; Long Mynd, 1,694 ft) and Hereford and Worcester (the Malvern Hills – Worcestershire Beacon, 1,394 ft). Extensive areas of high land and moorland are also to be found in the south-western peninsula formed by Somerset, Devon and Cornwall: principally Exmoor (Dunkery Beacon, 1,704 ft), Dartmoor (High Willhays, 2,038 ft) and Bodmin Moor (Brown Willy, 1,377 ft). Ranges of low, undulating hills run across the south of the country, including the Cotswolds in the Midlands and south-west, the Chilterns to the north of London, and the North (Kent) and South (Sussex) Downs of the south-east coastal areas.

The lowlands of England lie in the Vale of York, East Anglia and the area around the Wash. The lowest-lying are the Cambridgeshire Fens in the valleys of the Great Ouse and the River Nene, which are below sea-level in places. Since the 17th century extensive drainage has brought much of the Fens under cultivation. The North Sea coast between the Thames and the Humber, low-lying and formed of sand and shingle for the most part, is subject to erosion and defences against further incursion have been built along many stretches.

HYDROGRAPHY

The Severn is the longest river in Great Britain, rising in the north-eastern slopes of Plynlimon (Wales) and entering England in Shropshire with a total length of 220 miles (354 km) from its source into its outflow into the Bristol Channel, where it receives on the east the Bristol Avon, and on the west the Wye, its other tributaries being the Vyrnwy, Tern, Stour, Teme and Upper (or Warwickshire) Avon. The Severn is tidal below Gloucester, and a high bore or tidal wave sometimes reverses the flow as high as Tewkesbury (13½ miles above Gloucester). The scenery of the greater part of the river is very picturesque and beautiful, and the Severn is a noted salmon river, some of its tributaries being famous for trout. Navigation is assisted by the Gloucester and Berkeley Ship Canal (16½ miles), which admits vessels of 350 tons to Gloucester. The Severn Tunnel was begun in 1873 and completed in 1886 at a cost of £2 million and after many difficulties from flooding. It is 4 miles 628 yards in length (of which 2¼ miles are under the river). The Severn road bridge between Haysgate, Gwent, and Almondsbury, Glos, with a centre span of 3,240 ft, was opened in 1966.

The longest river wholly in England is the Thames, with a total length of 215 miles (346 km) from its source in the Cotswold hills to the Nore, and is navigable by ocean-going ships to London Bridge. The Thames is tidal to Teddington (69 miles from its mouth) and forms county boundaries almost throughout its course; on its banks are situated London, Windsor Castle, the oldest royal residence still in regular use, Eton College and Oxford, the oldest university in the kingdom.

Of the remaining English rivers, those flowing into the North Sea are the Tyne, Wear, Tees, Ouse and Trent from the Pennine Range, the Great Ouse (160 miles), which rises in Northamptonshire, and the Orwell and Stour from the hills of East Anglia. Flowing into the English Channel are the Sussex Ouse from the Weald, the Itchen from the Hampshire Hills, and the Axe, Teign, Dart, Tamar and Exe from the Devonian hills. Flowing into the Irish Sea are the Mersey, Ribble and Eden from the western slopes of the Pennines and the Derwent from the Cumbrian mountains.

The English Lakes, noteworthy for their picturesque scenery and poetic associations, lie in Cumbria, the largest being Windermere (10 miles long), Ullswater and Derwent Water.

ISLANDS

The Isle of Wight is separated from Hampshire by the Solent. The capital, Newport, stands at the head of the estuary of the Medina, Cowes (at the mouth) being the chief port. Other centres are Ryde, Sandown, Shanklin, Ventnor, Freshwater, Yarmouth, Totland Bay, Seaview and Bembridge.

Lundy (the name means Puffin Island), 11 miles north-west of Hartland Point, Devon, is about two miles long and about half a mile wide on average, with a total area of about 1,116 acres, and a population of about 20. It became the property of the National Trust in 1969 and is now principally a bird sanctuary.

The Isles of Scilly consist of about 140 islands and skerries (total area, 6 sq. miles/10 sq. km) situated 28 miles south-west of Land's End. Only five are inhabited: St Mary's, St Agnes, Bryher, Tresco and St Martin's. The population is 1,978. The entire group has been designated a Conservation Area, a Heritage Coast, and an Area of Outstanding Natural Beauty, and has been given National Nature Reserve status by the Nature Conservancy Council because of its unique flora and fauna. Tourism and the winter/spring flower trade for the home market form the basis of the economy of the Isles. The island group is a recognized rural development area.

EARLY HISTORY

Archaeological evidence suggests that England has been inhabited since at least the Palaeolithic period, though the extent of the various Palaeolithic cultures was dependent upon the degree of glaciation. The succeeding Neolithic and Bronze Age cultures have left abundant remains throughout the country, the best-known of these being the henges and stone circles of Stonehenge (ten miles north of Salisbury, Wilts) and Avebury (Wilts), both of which are believed to have been of religious significance. In the latter part of the Bronze Age the Goidels, a people of Celtic race, and in the Iron Age other Celtic races of Brythons and Belgae, invaded the country and brought with them Celtic civilization and dialects, place names in England bearing witness to the spread of the invasion over the whole kingdom.

THE ROMAN CONQUEST

The Roman conquest of Gaul (57–50 BC) brought Britain into close contact with Roman civilization, but although Julius Caesar raided the south of Britain in 55 BC and 54 BC, conquest was not undertaken until nearly 100 years later. In AD 43 the Emperor Claudius dispatched Aulus Plautius, with a well-equipped force of 40,000, and himself followed with reinforcements in the same year. Success was delayed by the resistance of Caratacus (Caractacus), the British leader from AD 48–51, who was finally captured and sent to Rome, and by a great revolt in AD 61 led by Boudicca (Boadicea), Queen of the Iceni; but the south of Britain was secured by AD 70, and Wales and the area north to the Tyne by about AD 80.

In AD 122, the Emperor Hadrian visited Britain and built a continuous rampart, since known as Hadrian's Wall, from Wallsend to Bowness (Tyne to Solway). The work was entrusted by the Emperor Hadrian to Aulus Platorius Nepos, legate of Britain from AD 122 to 126, and it was intended to form the northern frontier of the Roman Empire.

The Romans administered Britain as a province under a Governor, with a well-defined system of local government, each Roman municipality ruling itself and its surrounding territory, while London was the centre of the road system and the seat of the financial officials of the Province of Britain. Colchester, Lincoln, York, Gloucester and St Albans stand on the sites of five Roman municipalities, and Wroxeter, Caerleon, Chester, Lincoln and York were at various times the sites of legionary fortresses. Well-preserved Roman towns have been uncovered at or near Silchester (*Calleva Atrebatum*), ten miles south of Reading, Wroxeter (*Viroconium Cornoviorum*), near Shrewsbury, and St Albans (*Verulamium*) in Hertfordshire.

Four main groups of roads radiated from London, and a fifth (the Fosse) ran obliquely from Lincoln through Leicester, Cirencester and Bath to Exeter. Of the four groups radiating from London, one ran south-east to Canterbury and the coast of Kent, a second to Silchester and thence to parts of western Britain and south Wales, a third (later known as Watling Street) ran through Verulamium to Chester, with various branches, and the fourth reached Colchester, Lincoln, York and the eastern counties.

In the fourth century Britain was subject to raids along the east coast by Saxon pirates, which led to the establishment of a system of coast defence from the Wash to Southampton Water, with forts at Brancaster, Burgh Castle (Yarmouth), Walton (Felixstowe), Bradwell, Reculver, Richborough, Dover, Lympne, Pevensey and Porchester (Portsmouth). The Irish (Scoti) and Picts in the north were also becoming more aggressive; from about AD 350

incursions became more frequent and more formidable. As the Roman Empire came under attack increasingly towards the end of the fourth century, many troops were removed from Britain for service in other parts of the empire. The island was eventually cut off from Rome by the Teutonic conquest of Gaul, and with the withdrawal of the last Roman garrison early in the fifth century, the Romano-British were left to themselves.

SAXON SETTLEMENT

According to legend, the British King Vortigern called in the Saxons to defend him against the Picts, the Saxon chieftains being Hengist and Horsa, who landed at Ebbsfleet, Kent, and established themselves in the Isle of Thanet; but the events during the one and a half centuries between the final break with Rome and the re-establishment of Christianity are unclear. However, it would appear that in the course of this period the raids turned into large-scale settlement by invaders traditionally known as Angles (England north of the Wash and East Anglia), Saxons (Essex and southern England) and Jutes (Kent and the Weald), which pushed the Romano-British into the mountainous areas of the north and west, Celtic culture outside Wales and Cornwall surviving only in topographical names. Various kingdoms were established at this time which attempted to claim overlordship of the whole country, hegemony finally being achieved by Wessex (capital, Winchester) in the ninth century. This century also saw the beginning of raids by the Vikings (Danes), which were resisted by Alfred the Great (871–899), who fixed a limit to the advance of Danish settlement by the Treaty of Wedmore (878), giving them the area north and east of Watling Street, on condition that they adopt Christianity.

In the tenth century the kings of Wessex recovered the whole of England from the Danes, but subsequent rulers were unable to resist a second wave of invaders. England paid tribute (*Danegeld*) for many years, and was invaded in 1013 by the Danes and ruled by Danish kings from 1016 until 1042, when Edward the Confessor was recalled from exile in Normandy. On Edward's death in 1066 Harold Godwinson (brother-in-law of Edward and son of Earl Godwin of Wessex) was chosen King of England. After defeating (at Stamford Bridge, Yorkshire, 25 September) an invading army under Harald Hadraada, King of Norway (aided by the outlawed Earl Tostig of Northumbria, Harold's brother), Harold was himself defeated at the Battle of Hastings on 14 October 1066, and the Norman conquest secured the throne of England for Duke William of Normandy, a cousin of Edward the Confessor.

CHRISTIANITY

Christianity reached the Roman province of Britain from Gaul in the third century (or possibly earlier); Alban, traditionally Britain's first martyr, was put to death as a Christian during the persecution of Diocletian (22 June 303), at his native town Verulamium; and the Bishops of Londinium, Eboracum (York), and Lindum (Lincoln) attended the Council of Arles in 314. However, the Anglo-Saxon invasions submerged the Christian religion in England until the sixth century when conversion was undertaken in the north from 563 by Celtic missionaries from Ireland led by St Columba, and in the south by a mission sent from Rome in 597 which was led by St Augustine, who became the first archbishop of Canterbury. England appears to have been converted again by the end of the seventh century and followed, after the Council of Whitby in 663, the practices of the Roman Church, which brought the kingdom into the mainstream of European thought and culture.

PRINCIPAL CITIES

BIRMINGHAM

Birmingham is Britain's second city. It is a focal point in national communications networks with a rapidly expanding International Airport. The generally accepted derivation of 'Birmingham' is the *ham* (dwelling-place) of the *ing* (family) of *Beorma*, presumed to have been Saxon. During the Industrial Revolution the town grew into a major manufacturing centre and in 1889 was granted city status.

Despite the decline in manufacturing, Birmingham is still a major hardware trade and motor component industry centre. As well as the National Exhibition Centre and the Aston Science Park, recent developments include the International Convention Centre and the National Indoor Arena.

The principal buildings are the Town Hall (1834–50); the Council House (1879); Victoria Law Courts (1891); Birmingham University (1906–9); the 13th-century Church of St Martin-in-the-Bull-Ring (rebuilt 1873); the Cathedral (formerly St Philip's Church) (1711) and the Roman Catholic Cathedral of St Chad (1839–41).

BRADFORD

Bradford lies on the southern edge of the Yorkshire Dales National Park, including within its boundaries the village of Haworth, home of the Brontë sisters, and Ilkley Moor.

Originally a Saxon township, Bradford received a market charter in 1251 but developed only slowly until the industrialization of the textile industry brought rapid growth during the 19th century; it was granted its city charter in 1897. The prosperity of that period is reflected in much of the city's architecture, particularly the public buildings: City Hall (1873), Wool Exchange (1867), St George's Hall (Concert Hall, 1853), Cartwright Hall (Art Gallery, 1904) and the Technical College (1882). Other chief buildings are the Cathedral (15th century) and Bolling Hall (14th century).

Textiles still play an important part in the city's economy but industry is now more broadly based, including engineering, micro-electronics, printing and chemicals. The city has a strong financial services sector, and a growing tourism industry.

BRISTOL

Bristol was a Royal Borough before the Norman Conquest. The earliest form of the name is *Bricgstow*. In 1373 it received from Edward III a charter granting it county status.

The chief buildings include the 12th-century Cathedral (with later additions), with Norman chapter house and gateway, the 14th-century Church of St Mary Redcliffe, Wesley's Chapel, Broadmead, the Merchant Venturers' Almshouses, the Council House (1956), Guildhall, Exchange (erected from the designs of John Wood in 1743), Cabot Tower, the University and Clifton College. The Roman Catholic Cathedral at Clifton was opened in 1973.

The Clifton Suspension Bridge, with a span of 702 feet over the Avon, was projected by Brunel in 1836 but was not completed until 1864. Brunel's SS *Great Britain*, the first ocean-going propeller-driven ship, is now being restored in the City Docks from where she was launched in 1843. The docks themselves have been extensively restored and redeveloped.

CAMBRIDGE

Cambridge, a settlement far older than its ancient University, lies on the River Cam or Granta. The city is a county town and regional headquarters. Its industries include electronics, high technology research and development, and biotechnology. Among its open spaces are Jesus Green, Sheep's Green, Coe Fen, Parker's Piece, Christ's Pieces, the University Botanic Garden, and the Backs, or lawns and gardens through which the Cam winds behind the principal line of college buildings. East of the Cam, King's Parade, upon which stand Great St Mary's Church, Gibbs' Senate House and King's College Chapel with Wilkins' screen, joins Trumpington Street to form one of the most beautiful throughfares in Europe.

University and college buildings provide the outstanding features of Cambridge architecture but several churches (especially St Benet's, the oldest building in the city, and St Sepulchre's, the Round Church) are also notable. The Guildhall (1939) stands on a site of which at least part has held municipal buildings since 1224.

CANTERBURY

Canterbury, the Metropolitan City of the Anglican Communion, has a history going back to prehistoric times. It was the Roman *Durovernum Cantiacorum* and the Saxon *Cant-wara-byrig* (stronghold of the men of Kent). Here in 597 St Augustine began the conversion of the English to Christianity, when Ethelbert, King of Kent, was baptized.

Of the Benedictine St Augustine's Abbey, burial place of the Jutish Kings of Kent (whose capital Canterbury was), only ruins remain. St Martin's Church, on the eastern outskirts of the city, is stated by Bede to have been the place of worship of Queen Bertha, the Christian wife of King Ethelbert, before the advent of St Augustine.

In 1170 the rivalry of Church and State culminated in the murder in Canterbury Cathedral, by Henry II's knights, of Archbishop Thomas Becket, whose shrine became a great centre of pilgrimage, as described by Chaucer in his *Canterbury Tales*. After the Reformation pilgrimages ceased, but the prosperity of the city was strengthened by an influx of Huguenot refugees, who introduced weaving. The poet and playwright Christopher Marlowe was born and reared in Canterbury, and there are also literary associations with Defoe, Dickens, Joseph Conrad and Somerset Maugham.

The Cathedral, with architecture ranging from the 11th to the 15th centuries, is world famous. Modern pilgrims are attracted particularly to the Martyrdom, the Black Prince's Tomb, the Warriors' Chapel and the many examples of medieval stained glass.

The medieval city walls are built on Roman foundations and the 14th-century West Gate is one of the finest buildings of its kind in the country.

The 1,000 seat Marlowe Theatre is a centre for the Canterbury Arts Festival each autumn.

CARLISLE

Carlisle is situated at the confluence of the River Eden and River Caldew, 309 miles north-west of London and about ten miles from the Scottish border. It was granted a charter in 1158.

The city stands at the western end of Hadrian's Wall and dates from the original Roman settlement of *Luguvalium*. Granted to Scotland in the tenth century, Carlisle is not included in the Domesday Book. William Rufus reclaimed the area in 1092 and the castle and city walls were built to guard Carlisle and the western border; the citadel is a Tudor addition to protect the south of the city. Border disputes were common until the problem of the Debateable Lands was settled in 1552. During the Civil War the city remained Royalist; in 1745 Carlisle was besieged for the last time by the Young Pretender.

The Cathedral, originally a 12th-century Augustinian priory, was enlarged in the 13th and 14th centuries after the diocese was created in 1133. To the south is a restored Tithe Barn and nearby the 18th-century church of St Cuthbert, the third to stand on a site dating from the seventh century.

Carlisle is the major shopping, commercial and agricultural centre for the area, and industries include the manufacture of metal goods, biscuits and textiles. However, the largest employer is the services sector, notably in central and local government, retailing and transport. The city has an important communications position at the centre of a network of major roads, as a stage on the main west coast rail services, and with its own airport at Crosby-on-Eden.

CHESTER

Chester is situated on the River Dee, and was granted borough and city status in 1974. Its recorded history dates from the first century when the Romans founded the fortress of *Deva*. The city's name is derived from the Latin *castra* (a camp or encampment). During the Middle Ages, Chester was the principal port of north-west England but declined with the silting of the Dee estuary and competition from Liverpool. The city was also an important military centre, notably during Edward I's Welsh campaigns and the Elizabethan Irish campaigns. During the Civil War, Chester supported the King and was besieged from 1643 to 1646. Chester's first charter was granted *c*.1175 and the city was incorporated in 1506. The office of Sheriff is the earliest created in the country (*c*.1120s), and in 1992 the Mayor was granted the title of Lord Mayor. He/she also enjoys the title 'Admiral of the Dee'.

The city's architectural features include the city walls (an almost complete two-mile circuit), the unique 13th-century Rows (covered galleries above the street-level shops), the Victorian Gothic Town Hall (1869), the Castle (rebuilt 1788 and 1822) and numerous half-timbered buildings. The Cathedral was a Benedictine abbey until the Dissolution. Remaining monastic buildings include the chapter house, refectory and cloisters and there is a modern free-standing bell tower. The Norman church of St John the Baptist was a cathedral church in the early Middle Ages.

Chester is a thriving retail, business and tourist centre.

COVENTRY

Coventry is an important industrial centre, producing vehicles, machine tools, agricultural machinery, man-made fibres, aerospace components and telecommunications equipment. New investment has come from financial services, power transmission, professional services and education.

The city owes its beginning to Leofric, Earl of Mercia, and his wife Godiva who, in 1043, founded a Benedictine monastery. The guildhall of St Mary dates from the 14th century, three of the city's churches date from the 14th and 15th centuries, and 16th-century almshouses may still be seen. Coventry's first cathedral was destroyed at the Reformation, its second in the 1940 blitz (the walls and spire remain) and the new cathedral designed by Sir Basil Spence, consecrated in 1962, now draws innumerable visitors.

Coventry is the home of the University of Warwick and its Science Park, Coventry University, the Westwood Business Park, the Cable and Wireless College, and the Museum of British Road Transport.

DERBY

Derby stands on the banks of the River Derwent, and its name dates back to 880 when the Danes settled in the locality and changed the original Saxon name of *Northworthy* to *Deoraby*.

Derby has a wide range of industries: its products include aero engines, cars, pipework, specialized mechanical engineering equipment, textiles, chemicals, plastics and the Royal Crown Derby porcelain. The city is an established railway centre with rail research, engineering, safety testing, infrastructure and train-operating companies.

Buildings of interest include St Peter's Church and the Old Abbey Building (14th century), the Cathedral (1525), St Mary's Roman Catholic Church (1839) and the Industrial Museum, formerly the Old Silk Mill (1721). The traditional city centre is complemented by the Eagle Centre and 'out-of-centre' retail developments. In addition to the Derby Playhouse, the Assembly Rooms are a multi-purpose venue.

The first charter granting a Mayor and Aldermen was that of Charles I in 1637. Previous charters date back to 1154. It was granted city status in 1977.

DURHAM

The city of Durham is a district in the county of Durham and a major tourist attraction because of its prominent Norman Cathedral and Castle set high on a wooded peninsula overlooking the River Wear. The Cathedral was founded as a shrine for the body of St Cuthbert in 995. The present building dates from 1093 and among its many treasures is the tomb of the Venerable Bede (673–735). Durham's Prince Bishops had unique powers up to 1836, being lay rulers as well as religious leaders. As a palatinate Durham could have its own army, nobility, coinage and courts. The Castle was the main seat of the Prince Bishops for nearly 800 years; it is now used as a college by the University. The University, founded on the initiative of Bishop William Van Mildert, is England's third oldest.

Among other buildings of interest is the Guildhall in the Market Place which dates originally from the 14th century. Work has been carried out to conserve this area as part of the city's contribution to the Council of Europe's Urban Renaissance Campaign. Annual events include Durham's Regatta in June (claimed to be the oldest rowing event in Britain) and the Annual Gala (formerly Durham Miners' Gala) in July.

The economy has undergone a significant change with the replacement of mining as the dominant industry by 'white collar' employment. Although still a predominantly rural area, the industrial and commercial sector is growing and a wide range of manufacturing and service industries are based on industrial estates in and around the city. A research and development centre, linked to the University, also plays an important role in the local economy.

EXETER

Exeter lies on the River Exe ten miles from the sea. It was granted a charter by Henry II. The Romans founded *Isca Dumnoniorum* in the first century AD, and in the third century a stone wall (much of which remains) was built, providing protection against Saxon, and then Danish invasions. After the Conquest, the city led resistance to William in the west until reduced by siege. The Normans built the ringwork castle of Rougemont, the gatehouse and one tower of which remain, although the rest was pulled down in 1784. The first bridge across the Exe was built in the early 13th century. The city's main port was situated downstream at Topsham until the construction in the 1560s of the first true canal in England, the redevelopment of which in 1700 brought seaborne trade direct to the city. Exeter was the Royalist headquarters in the west during the Civil War.

The diocese of Exeter was established by Edward the Confessor in 1050, although a minster existed near the Cathedral site from the late seventh century. A new cathedral was built in the 12th century but the present building was begun c.1275, although incorporating the Norman towers, and completed about a century later. The Guildhall dates from the 12th century and there are many other medieval buildings in the city, as well as architecture in the Georgian and Regency styles, and the Custom House (1680). Damage suffered by bombing in 1942 led to the redevelopment of the city centre.

Exeter's prosperity from medieval times was based on trade in wool and woollen cloth (commemorated by Tuckers Hall), which remained at its height until the late 18th century when export trade was hit by the French wars. Subsequently Exeter has developed as an administrative and commercial centre, notably in the distributive trades, light manufacturing industries and tourism.

KINGSTON UPON HULL

Hull (officially Kingston upon Hull) lies at the junction of the River Hull with the Humber, 22 miles from the North Sea. It is one of the major seaports of the United Kingdom, comprising 2,000 acres in four main dock installations. The port provides a wide range of cargo services, including ro-ro and container traffic, and handles a million passengers annually on daily sailings to Rotterdam and Zeebrugge. There is a variety of industry and service industries, as well as increasing tourism and conference business.

The city, restored after heavy air raid damage during the Second World War, has good office and administrative buildings, its municipal centre being the Guildhall, its educational centres the University of Hull and the University of Lincolnshire and Humberside and its religious centre the Parish Church of the Holy Trinity. The old town area has been renovated and includes a marina and shopping complex. Just west of the city is the Humber Bridge, the world's longest single-span suspension bridge.

Kingston upon Hull was so named by Edward I. City status was accorded in 1897 and the office of Mayor raised to the dignity of Lord Mayor in 1914.

LEEDS

Leeds, situated in the lower Aire Valley, is a junction for road, rail, canal and air services and an important manufacturing and commercial centre. Seventy-three per cent of employment is in services, notably the distributive trades, public administration, medical services and business services. The main manufacturing industries are mechanical engineering, printing and publishing, metal goods and furniture.

The principal buildings are the Civic Hall (1933), the Town Hall (1858), the Municipal Buildings and Art Gallery (1884) with the Henry Moore Gallery (1982), the Corn Exchange (1863) and the University. The Parish Church (St Peter's) was rebuilt in 1841; the 17th-century St John's Church has a fine interior with a famous English Renaissance screen; the last remaining 18th-century church in the city is Holy Trinity in Boar Lane (1727). Kirkstall Abbey (about three miles from the centre of the

city), founded by Henry de Lacy in 1152, is one of the most complete examples of Cistercian houses now remaining. Temple Newsam, birthplace of Lord Darnley, was acquired by the Council in 1922. The present house was largely rebuilt by Sir Arthur Ingram in about 1620. Adel Church, about five miles from the centre of the city, is a fine Norman structure. The new Royal Armouries Museum houses the collection of antique arms and armour formerly held at the Tower of London.

Leeds was first incorporated by Charles I in 1626. The earliest forms of the name are *Loidis* or *Ledes*, the origins of which are obscure.

LEICESTER

Leicester is situated geographically in the centre of England. It dates back to pre-Roman times and was one of the five Danish *Burghs*. In 1589 Queen Elizabeth I granted a charter to the city and the ancient title was confirmed by letters patent in 1919.

The principal industries are hosiery, knitwear, footwear manufacturing and engineering. The growth of Leicester as a hosiery centre increased rapidly from the introduction there of the first stocking frame in 1670 and today it has some of the largest hosiery factories in the world.

The principal buildings are the Town Hall, the New Walk Centre, the University of Leicester, De Montfort University, De Montfort Hall, one of the finest concert halls in the provinces seating over 2,750 people, and the Granby Halls, an indoor sports facility. The ancient churches of St Martin (now Leicester Cathedral), St Nicholas, St Margaret, All Saints, St Mary de Castro, and buildings such as the Guildhall, the 14th-century Newarke Gate, the Castle and the Jewry Wall Roman site still exist. The Haymarket Theatre was opened in 1973 and The Shires shopping centre in 1992.

LINCOLN

Situated 40 miles inland on the River Witham, Lincoln derives its name from a contraction of *Lindum Colonia*, the settlement founded in AD 48 by the Romans to command the crossing of Ermine Street and Fosse Way. Sections of the third-century Roman city wall can be seen, including an extant gateway (Newport Arch), and excavations have discovered traces of a sewerage system unique in Britain. The Romans also drained the surrounding fenland and created a canal system, laying the foundations of Lincoln's agricultural prosperity and also of the city's importance in the medieval wool trade as a port and Staple town.

As one of the Five Boroughs of the Danelaw, Lincoln was an important trading centre in the ninth and tenth centuries and medieval prosperity from the wool trade lasted until the 14th century, enabling local merchants to build parish churches (of which three survive), and attracting in the 12th century a Jewish community (Jew's House and Court, Aaron's House). However, the removal of the Staple to Boston in 1369 heralded a decline from which the city only recovered fully in the 19th century when improved fen drainage made Lincoln agriculturally important and improved canal and rail links led to industrial development, mainly in the manufacture of machinery, components and engineering products.

The castle was built shortly after the Conquest and is unusual in having two mounds; on one motte stands a Keep (Lucy's Tower) added in the 12th century. It currently houses one of the four surviving copies of the Magna Carta. The Cathedral was begun c.1073 when the first Norman bishop moved the see of Lindsey to Lincoln, but was mostly destroyed by fire and earthquake in the 12th century. Rebuilding was begun by St Hugh and completed over a century later. Other notable architectural features are the 12th-century High Bridge, the oldest in Britain still to carry buildings, and the Guildhall situated above the 15th–16th-century Stonebow gateway.

LIVERPOOL

Liverpool, on the right bank of the River Mersey, three miles from the Irish Sea, is the United Kingdom's foremost port for the Atlantic trade. Tunnels link Liverpool with Birkenhead and Wallasey.

There are 2,100 acres of dockland on both sides of the river and the Gladstone and Royal Seaforth Docks can accommodate the largest vessels afloat. Annual tonnage of cargo handled is approximately 27.8 million tonnes. The main imports are crude oil, grain, ores, edible oils, timber, containers and break-bulk cargo. Liverpool Free Port, Britain's largest, was opened in 1984.

Liverpool was created a free borough in 1207 and a city in 1880. From the early 18th century it expanded rapidly with the growth of industrialization and the Atlantic trade. Surviving buildings from this date include the Bluecoat Chambers (1717, formerly the Bluecoat School), the Town Hall (1754, rebuilt to the original design 1795), and buildings in Rodney Street, Canning Street and the suburbs. Notable from the 19th and 20th centuries are the Anglican Cathedral, built from the designs of Sir Giles Gilbert Scott (the foundation stone was laid in 1904, and the building was completed only in 1980), the Catholic Metropolitan Cathedral (designed by Sir Frederick Gibberd, consecrated 1967) and St George's Hall (1838–54), regarded as one of the finest modern examples of classical architecture. The refurbished Albert Dock (designed by Jesse Hartley) contains the Merseyside Maritime Museum and Tate Gallery, Liverpool.

In 1852 an Act was obtained for establishing a public library, museum and art gallery; as a result Liverpool had one of the first public libraries in the country. The Brown, Picton and Hornby libraries now form one of the country's major libraries. The Victoria Building of Liverpool University, the Royal Liver, Cunard and Mersey Docks & Harbour Company buildings at the Pier Head, the Municipal Buildings and the Philharmonic Hall are other examples of the city's fine buildings.

MANCHESTER

Manchester (the *Mamucium* of the Romans, who occupied it in AD 79) is a commercial and industrial centre with a population engaged in the engineering, chemical, clothing, food processing and textile industries and in education. Banking, insurance and a growing leisure industry are among the prime commercial activities. The city is connected with the sea by the Manchester Ship Canal, opened in 1894, $35\frac{1}{2}$ miles long, and accommodating ships up to 15,000 tons. Manchester Airport handles 15 million passengers yearly.

The principal buildings are the Town Hall, erected in 1877 from the designs of Alfred Waterhouse, together with a large extension of 1938; the Royal Exchange (1869, enlarged 1921); the Central Library (1934); Heaton Hall; the 17th-century Chetham Library; the Rylands Library (1900), which includes the Althorp collection; the University precinct; the 15th-century Cathedral (formerly the parish church); G-MEX exhibition centre and the Free Trade Hall. Recent developments include the Manchester Arena, the largest indoor arena in Europe, and the Bridgewater Hall. Manchester is the home of the Hallé Orchestra, the Royal Northern College of Music, the Royal Exchange Theatre and seven public art galleries. Metrolink, the new light rail system, opened in 1992.

The Commonwealth Games are to be held in Manchester in 2002 and new sports facilities include a stadium, a swimming pool complex and the National Cycling Centre.

The town received its first charter of incorporation in 1838 and was created a city in 1853.

NEWCASTLE UPON TYNE

Newcastle upon Tyne, on the north bank of the River Tyne, is eight miles from the North Sea. A cathedral and university city, it is the administrative, commercial and cultural centre for north-east England and the principal port. It is an important manufacturing centre with a wide variety of industries.

The principal buildings include the Castle Keep (12th century), Black Gate (13th century), Blackfriars (13th century), West Walls (13th century), St Nicholas's Cathedral (15th century, fine lantern tower), St Andrew's Church (12th–14th century), St John's (14th–15th century), All Saints (1786 by Stephenson), St Mary's Roman Catholic Cathedral (1844), Trinity House (17th century), Sandhill (16th-century houses), Guildhall (Georgian), Grey Street (1834–9), Central Station (1846–50), Laing Art Gallery (1904), University of Newcastle Physics Building (1962) and Medical Building (1985), Civic Centre (1963), Central Library (1969) and Eldon Square Shopping Development (1976). Open spaces include the Town Moor (927 acres) and Jesmond Dene. Nine bridges span the Tyne at Newcastle.

The city derives its name from the 'new castle' (1080) erected as a defence against the Scots. In 1400 it was made a county, and in 1882 a city.

NORWICH

Norwich grew from an early Anglo-Saxon settlement near the confluence of the Rivers Yare and Wensum, and now serves as provincial capital for the predominantly agricultural region of East Anglia. The name is thought to relate to the most northerly of a group of Anglo-Saxon villages or *wics*. The city's first known charter was granted in 1158 by Henry II.

Norwich serves its surrounding area as a market town and commercial centre, banking and insurance being prominent among the city's businesses. From the 14th century until the Industrial Revolution, Norwich was the regional centre of the woollen industry, but now the biggest single industry is financial services and principal trades are engineering, printing, shoemaking, double glazing, the production of chemicals and clothing, food processing and technology. Norwich is accessible to seagoing vessels by means of the River Yare, entered at Great Yarmouth, 20 miles to the east.

Among many historic buildings are the Cathedral (completed in the 12th century and surmounted by a 15th-century spire 315 feet in height), the keep of the Norman castle (now a museum and art gallery), the 15th-century flint-walled Guildhall (now a tourist information centre), some thirty medieval parish churches, St Andrew's and Blackfriars' Halls, the Tudor houses preserved in Elm Hill and the Georgian Assembly House. The University of East Anglia is on the city's western boundary.

NOTTINGHAM

Nottingham stands on the River Trent and is connected by canal with the Atlantic Ocean and the North Sea. *Snotingaham* or *Notingeham*, literally the homestead of the people of Snot, is the Anglo-Saxon name for the Celtic settlement of *Tigguocobauc*, or the house of caves. In 878, Nottingham became one of the Five Boroughs of the Danelaw. William the Conqueror ordered the construction of Nottingham Castle, while the town itself developed rapidly under Norman rule. Its laws and rights were later formally recognized by Henry II's charter in 1155. The Castle became a favoured residence of King John. In 1642 King Charles I raised his personal standard at Nottingham Castle at the start of the Civil War.

Nottingham is a major sporting centre, home to Nottingham Forest FC, Notts County FC (the world's oldest Football league side), Nottingham Racecourse and the National Watersports Centre. The principal industries include textiles, pharmaceuticals, food manufacturing, engineering and telecommunications. There are two universities within the city boundaries.

Architecturally, Nottingham has a wealth of notable buildings, particularly those designed in the Victorian era by T. C. Hine and Watson Fothergill. The City Council owns the Castle, of Norman origin but restored in 1878, Wollaton Hall (1580–8), Newstead Abbey (home of Lord Byron), the Guildhall (1888) and Council House (1929). St Mary's, St Peter's and St Nicholas's Churches are of interest, as is the Roman Catholic Cathedral (Pugin, 1842–4).

Nottingham was granted city status in 1897.

OXFORD

Oxford is a university city, an important industrial centre, and a market town. Industry played a minor part in Oxford until the motor industry was established in 1912.

It is for its architecture that Oxford is of most interest to the visitor, its oldest specimens being the reputedly Saxon tower of St Michael's church, the remains of the Norman castle and city walls, and the Norman church at Iffley. It is chiefly famous, however, for its Gothic buildings, such as the Divinity Schools, the Old Library at Merton College, William of Wykeham's New College, Magdalen College and Christ Church and many other college buildings. Later centuries are represented by the Laudian quadrangle at St John's College, the Renaissance Sheldonian Theatre by Wren, Trinity College Chapel, and All Saints Church; Hawksmoor's mock-Gothic at All Souls College, and the 18th-century Queen's College. In addition to individual buildings, High Street and Radcliffe Square, just off it, both form architectural compositions of great beauty. Most of the Colleges have gardens, those of Magdalen, New College, St John's and Worcester being the largest.

PLYMOUTH

Plymouth is situated on the borders of Devon and Cornwall at the confluence of the Rivers Tamar and Plym. The city has a long maritime history; it was the home port of Sir Francis Drake and the starting point for his circumnavigation of the world, as well as the last port of call for the *Mayflower* when the Pilgrim Fathers sailed for the New World in 1620. Today Plymouth is host to many international yacht races. The Barbican harbour area has many Elizabethan buildings and on Plymouth Hoe stands Smeaton's lighthouse, the third to be built on the Eddystone Rocks 13 miles offshore.

The city centre was rebuilt following extensive war damage, and comprises a large shopping centre, municipal offices, law courts and public buildings. The main employment is provided at the naval base, though many industrial firms and service industries have become established in the post-war period and the city is a growing tourism centre. In 1982 the Theatre Royal was opened. In conjunction with the Cornwall County Council, the Tamar Bridge was constructed linking the city by road with Cornwall.

PORTSMOUTH

Portsmouth occupies Portsea Island, Hampshire, with boundaries extending to the mainland. It is a centre of industry and commerce, including many high technology and manufacturing industries. It is the British headquarters of several major international companies. The Royal Navy base still has a substantial work-force, although this has decreased in recent years. The commercial port and continental ferry port is owned and run by the City Council, and carries passengers and vehicles to France and northern Spain.

A major port since the 16th century, Portsmouth is also a thriving seaside resort catering for thousands of visitors annually. Among many historic attractions are Lord Nelson's flagship, HMS *Victory*, the Tudor warship *Mary Rose*, Britain's first 'ironclad' warship, HMS *Warrior*, the D-Day Museum, Charles Dickens' birthplace at 393 Old Commercial Road, the Royal Naval and Royal Marine museums, Southsea Castle (built by Henry VIII), the Round Tower and Point Battery, which for hundreds of years have guarded the entrance to Portsmouth Harbour, Fort Nelson on Portsdown Hill and the Sealife Centre.

ST ALBANS

The origins of St Albans, situated on the River Ver, stem from the Roman town of *Verulamium*. Named after the first Christian martyr in Britain, who was executed here, St Albans has developed around the Norman Abbey and Cathedral Church (consecrated 1115), built partly of materials from the old Roman city. The museums house Iron Age and Roman artefacts and the Roman Theatre, unique in Britain, has a stage as opposed to an amphitheatre. Archaeological excavations in the city centre have revealed evidence of pre-Roman, Saxon and medieval occupation.

The town's significance grew to the extent that it was a signatory and venue for the drafting of the Magna Carta. It was also the scene of riots during the Peasants' Revolt, the French King John was imprisoned there after the Battle of Poitiers, and heavy fighting took place there during the Wars of the Roses.

Previously controlled by the Abbot, the town achieved a charter in 1553 and city status in 1877. The street market, first established in 1553, is still an important feature of the city, as are many hotels and inns which survive from the days when St Albans was an important coach stop. Tourist attractions include historic churches and houses, and a 15th-century clock tower.

The city now contains a wide range of firms, with special emphasis on information and legal services. In addition, it is the home of the Royal National Rose Society, and of Rothamsted Park, the agricultural research centre.

SHEFFIELD

Sheffield, the centre of the special steel and cutlery trades, is situated at the junction of the Sheaf, Porter, Rivelin and Loxley valleys with the River Don. Though its cutlery, silverware and plate have long been famous, Sheffield has other and now more important industries: special and alloy steels, engineering, tool-making, medical equipment and media-related industries (in its new Cultural Industries Quarter). Sheffield has two universities and is an important research centre.

The parish church of St Peter and St Paul, founded in the 12th century, became the Cathedral Church of the Diocese of Sheffield in 1914. The Roman Catholic Cathedral Church of St Marie (founded 1847) was created Cathedral for the new diocese of Hallam in 1980. Parts of the present building date from c.1435. The principal buildings are the Town Hall (1897), the Cutlers' Hall (1832), City Hall (1932), Graves Art Gallery (1934), Mappin Art Gallery, the Crucible Theatre and the restored 19th-century Lyceum theatre, which dates from 1897 and was reopened in 1990. Three major sports venues were opened in 1990 to 1991.

Sheffield was created a city in 1893.

Master Cutler of the Company of Cutlers in Hallamshire 1996–7, R. Field

SOUTHAMPTON

Southampton is the leading British deep-sea port on the Channel and is situated on one of the finest natural harbours in the world. The first charter was granted by Henry II and Southampton was created a county of itself in 1447. In 1964 it was granted city status.

There were Roman and Saxon settlements on the site of the city, which has been an important port since the time of the Conquest due to its natural deep-water harbour. The oldest church is St Michael's (1070) which has an unusually tall spire built in the 18th century as a landmark for navigators of Southampton Water. Other buildings and monuments within the city walls are the Tudor House Museum, God's House Tower, the Bargate museum, the Tudor Merchants Hall, the Weigh-house, West Gate, King John's House, Long House, Wool House, the ruins of Holy Rood Church, St Julien's Church and the Mayflower Memorial. The medieval town walls, built for artillery, are among the most complete in Europe. Public open spaces total over 1,000 acres and comprise 9 per cent of the city's area. The Common covers an area of 328 acres in the central district of the city and is mostly natural parkland. Two recent additions to work in marine technology in Southampton are Europe's leading oceanographic research centre (part of the University) and the marine science and technology business park.

STOKE-ON-TRENT

Stoke-on-Trent, standing on the River Trent and familiarly known as The Potteries, is the main centre of employment for the population of North Staffordshire. The city is the largest clayware producer in the world (china, earthenware, sanitary goods, refractories, bricks and tiles) and also has a wide range of other manufacturing industry, including steel, chemicals, engineering and tyres. Extensive reconstruction has been carried out in recent years.

The city was formed by the federation of the separate municipal authorities of Tunstall, Burslem, Hanley, Stoke, Fenton, and Longton in 1910 and received its city status in 1925.

WINCHESTER

Winchester, the ancient capital of England, is situated on the River Itchen. The city is rich in architecture of all types but the Cathedral takes pride of place. The longest Gothic cathedral in the world, it was built in 1079–93 and exhibits examples of Norman, Early English and Perpendicular styles. Winchester College, founded in 1382, is one of the most famous public schools, the original building (1393) remaining largely unaltered. St Cross Hospital, another great medieval foundation, lies one mile south of the city. The almshouses were founded in 1136 by Bishop Henry de Blois, and Cardinal Henry Beaufort added a new almshouse of 'Noble Poverty' in 1446. The chapel and dwellings are of great architectural interest, and visitors may still receive the 'Wayfarer's Dole' of bread and ale.

Excavations have done much to clarify the origins and development of Winchester. Part of the forum and several of the streets of the Roman town have been discovered; excavations in the Cathedral Close have uncovered the entire site of the Anglo-Saxon cathedral (known as the Old Minster) and parts of the New Minster which was built by Alfred's son Edward the Elder and is the burial place of the Alfredian dynasty. The original burial place of St Swithun, before his remains were translated to a site in the present cathedral, was also uncovered.

Excavations in other parts of the city have thrown much light on Norman Winchester, notably on the site of the Royal Castle (adjacent to which the new Law Courts have been built) and in the grounds of Wolvesey Castle, where the great house built by Bishops Giffard and Henry de Blois in the 12th century has been uncovered. The Great Hall, built by Henry III between 1222 and 1236 survives and houses the Arthurian Round Table.

YORK

The city of York is an archiepiscopal seat. Its recorded history dates from AD 71, when the Roman Ninth Legion established a base under Petilius Cerealis which later became the fortress of *Eburacum.* In Anglo-Saxon times the city was the royal and ecclesiastical centre of Northumbria, and after capture by a Viking army in AD 866 it became the capital of the Viking kingdom of Jorvik. By the 14th century the city had become a great mercantile centre, mainly because of its control of the wool trade, and was used as the chief base against the Scots. Under the Tudors its fortunes declined, though Henry VIII made it the headquarters of the Council of the North. Excavations on many sites, including Coppergate, have greatly expanded knowledge of Roman, Viking and medieval urban life.

With its development as a railway centre in the 19th century the commercial life of York expanded. The principal industries are the manufacture of chocolate, scientific instruments and sugar. It is the location of several government departments.

The city is rich in examples of architecture of all periods. The earliest church was built in AD 627 and, in the 12th to 15th centuries, the present Minster was built in a succession of styles. Other examples within the city are the medieval city walls and gateways, churches and guildhalls. Domestic architecture includes the Georgian mansions of The Mount, Micklegate and Bootham.

English Counties and Shires

LORD-LIEUTENANTS AND HIGH SHERIFFS

County/Shire	Lord-Lieutenant	High Sheriff, 1997–8
Bedfordshire	S. C. Whitbread	C. T. Lousada
Berkshire	P. L. Wroughton	Maj. J. R. Trustram Eve
Bristol	J. Tidmarsh, MBE	R. A. Lalonde
Buckinghamshire	Sir Nigel Mobbs	D. J. Burrell, CBE
Cambridgeshire	J. G. P. Crowden	D. T. Rampley
Cheshire	W. A. Bromley-Davenport	E. S. Tudor Evans
Cornwall	Lady Holborow	Maj. C. F. T. Edward-Collins
Cumbria	J. A. Cropper	J. H. Fryer-Spedding, OBE
Derbyshire	J. K. Bather	R. H. A. Perkins
Devon	Lt.-Col. the Earl of Morley	N. F. A. Page-Turner
Dorset	The Lord Digby	R. W. Fielding
Durham	Sir Paul Nicholson	M. P. Weston
East Riding of Yorkshire	R. Marriott, TD	P. W. J. Carver
East Sussex	Admiral Sir Lindsay Bryson, KCB, FRSE, FENG.	J. Whitmore
Essex	The Lord Braybrooke	R. F. Erith, TD
Gloucestershire	H. W. G. Elwes	W. G. F. Meath-Baker
Greater London	Field Marshal the Lord Bramall, KG, GCB, OBE, MC	W. R. Harrison
Greater Manchester	Col. J. B. Timmins, OBE, TD	W. J. Smith
Hampshire	Mrs F. M. Fagan	Mrs L. G. Fox
Hereford and Worcester	Sir Thomas Dunne, KCVO	M. E. Howard
Hertfordshire	S. A. Bowes Lyon	R. Walduck
Isle of Wight	*C. D. J. Bland	R. L. Bradbeer
Kent	The Lord Kingsdown, KG, PC	E. R. P. Boorman
Lancashire	The Lord Shuttleworth	Col. Sir David Trippier, RD
Leicestershire	T. G. M. Brooks	D. C. Samworth, CBE
Lincolnshire	Mrs B. K. Cracroft-Eley	Sarah, Lady Bruce-Gardyne
Merseyside	A. W. Waterworth	B. Thaxter, OBE
Norfolk	Sir Timothy Colman, KG	Lady Evans-Lombe
Northamptonshire	Sir John Lowther, KCVO, CBE	A. R. Heygate
Northumberland	The Viscount Ridley, KG, GCVO, TD	A. G. P. Ramsey
North Yorkshire	Sir Marcus Worsley, Bt.	A. G. S. Chisenhale-Marsh
Nottinghamshire	Sir Andrew Buchanan, Bt.	H. P. Matheson
Oxfordshire	H. L. J. Brunner	Lady French
Rutland	Air Chief Marshal Sir Thomas Kennedy, GCB, AFC	D. B. Owen
Shropshire	A. E. H. Heber-Percy	The Lady Forester
Somerset	Sir John Wills, Bt., TD	R. S. R. Sheldon
South Yorkshire	The Earl of Scarbrough	M. J. Mallett
Staffordshire	J. A. Hawley, TD	G. R. Tams
Suffolk	The Lord Belstead, PC	J. M Paul
Surrey	Mrs S. Goad	J. D. M. Robertson
Tyne and Wear	Sir Ralph Carr-Ellison, TD	Mrs S. M. Murray, CBE
Warwickshire	M. Dunne	The Hon. Lady Butler
West Midlands	R. R. Taylor, OBE	E. M. Worley
West Sussex	Maj.-Gen. Sir Philip Ward, KCVO, CBE	Col. Sir Brian Barttelot, Bt., OBE
West Yorkshire	J. Lyles, CBE	F. T. B. Jowitt
Wiltshire	Lt.-Gen. Sir Maurice Johnston, KCB, OBE	J. B. Bush

* Lord-Lieutenant and Governor

COUNTY COUNCILS: AREA, POPULATION, FINANCE

Council	Administrative headquarters	Area (hectares)	Population 1995	Total demand upon collection fund 1997–8
Bedfordshire	County Hall, Bedford	123,468	364,300	£79,285,000
Berkshire	Shire Hall, Shinfield Park, Reading	125,901	783,200	146,200,000
Buckinghamshire	County Hall, Aylesbury	188,279	473,000	96,000,000
Cambridgeshire	Shire Hall, Cambridge	340,181	693,900	108,041,309
Cheshire	County Hall, Chester	233,325	978,100	187,144,363
Cornwall	County Hall, Truro	356,442†	482,700†	79,970,099
Cumbria	The Courts, Carlisle	682,451	490,300	92,289,000
Derbyshire	County Offices, Matlock	263,098	726,000	133,800,000
Devon	County Hall, Exeter	671,096	1,058,800	174,752,000
Dorset	County Hall, Dorchester	265,433	378,900	83,948,630
Durham	County Hall, Durham	243,369	507,100	77,247,684
East Sussex	Pelham House, St Andrew's Lane, Lewes	179,530	482,800	97,722,000
Essex	County Hall, Chelmsford	367,167	1,577,500	283,000,000
Gloucestershire	Shire Hall, Gloucester	264,270	552,700	95,329,000
Hampshire	The Castle, Winchester	378,022	1,213,400	227,455,000
Hereford and Worcester	County Hall, Worcester	392,650	694,300	117,238,000
Hertfordshire	County Hall, Hertford	163,601	1,011,200	194,600,000
§Isle of Wight	County Hall, Newport	38,063	125,100	29,642,000
Kent	County Hall, Maidstone	373,063	1,551,300	273,900,000
Lancashire	County Hall, Preston	306,957	1,426,000	252,365,000
Leicestershire	County Hall, Glenfield, Leicester	255,297	592,700	107,393,810
Lincolnshire	County Offices, Newland, Lincoln	591,791	611,800	96,588,000
Norfolk	County Hall, Norwich	537,482	772,400	127,689,068
Northamptonshire	County Hall, Northampton	236,721	599,300	94,025,000
Northumberland	County Hall, Morpeth	503,165	307,300	54,511,000
North Yorkshire	County Hall, Northallerton	803,741	556,200	94,482,000
Nottinghamshire	County Hall, Nottingham	216,090	1,031,900	181,966,837
Oxfordshire	County Hall, Oxford	260,798	598,400	110,621,000
Shropshire	The Shirehall, Shrewsbury	349,013	419,900	68,700,000
Somerset	County Hall, Taunton	345,233	481,000	90,000,000
Staffordshire	County Buildings, Stafford	271,616	802,100	123,845,000
Suffolk	County Hall, Ipswich	379,664	656,800	107,835,058
Surrey	County Hall, Kingston upon Thames	167,924	1,044,400	224,500,000
Warwickshire	Shire Hall, Warwick	198,052	498,700	96,955,980
West Sussex	County Hall, Chichester	198,935	731,500	143,524,000
Wiltshire	County Hall, Trowbridge	347,883	416,800	76,346,000

Source for population figures: ONS Monitor PP1 96/2, 29 August 1996
† Including Isles of Scilly
§ Unitary authority since April 1995

THE ISLES OF SCILLY

The five inhabited islands of the Scillies group, St Mary's, Tresco, Bryher, St Agnes and St Martin's, are administered by the Council of the Isles of Scilly, a 21-member non-political body which combines the powers and duties of a county council and a district council under the Local Government Act 1972 and the Isles of Scilly Order 1978. Legislation is specifically applied to the Isles of Scilly by Special Order. The Council is responsible for education, fire services, highways, planning, social services, tourism, coastal defence, water and the airport. The Isles of Scilly have their own separate Community Health Council which meets and is administered on St Mary's. The police service is administered by the Devon and Cornwall Police Authority, of which the Council is a constituent member. The Isles are part of the St Ives electoral division.

Administrative Headquarters, Town Hall, St Mary's, Isles of Scilly TR21 0LW
Chairman of the Council, C. Daly
Clerk and Chief Executive, P. S. Hygate
Chief Technical Officer, B. M. Lowen

COUNTY COUNCILS: Officers and Chairman

Council	Chief Executive	County Treasurer	Chairman of County Council
Bedfordshire	D. Cleggett	°B. Dodds	J. Hawksby
Berkshire	¶S. R. Goodchild, CBE	*I. Hyson	Mrs A. Risman
Buckinghamshire	I. Crookall	§§S. Nolan	K. Ross
Cambridgeshire	A. G. Lister	D. T. Earle	J. McKay
Cheshire	M. E. Pitt	A. Cope	J. M. Clarke
Cornwall	J. Mills	F. Twyning	W. Hosking
Cumbria	J. E. Burnet	R. F. Mather	Mrs M. Dinning
Derbyshire	A. R. N. Hodgson	P. Swaby	L. G. Cannon
Devon	P. Jenkinson	J. Glasby	J. Glanvill
Dorset	P. K. Harvey	A. P. Peel	Mrs P. Hymers
Durham	K. W. Smith	J. Kirkby	M. Nicholls
East Sussex	Ms C. Miller	J. Davies	D. Norcross
Essex	K. W. S. Ashurst	K. D. Neale	R. J. Kennedy
Gloucestershire	††R. Cockroft	**J. R. Cockroft	F. Thompson
Hampshire	P. C. B. Robertson	J. C. Pittam	Capt. M. P. R. Boyle
Hereford and Worcester	††D. A. J. Stanley	P. Middlebrough	J. T. O'Reilly
Hertfordshire	W. D. Ogley	*C. Sweeney	Sir Norman Lindop
Isle of Wight	††F. Hetherington	J. Pulsford	J. A. Bowker
Kent	P. R. Sabin	§D. Lewis	Sir John Grugeon
Lancashire	G. A. Johnson	B. G. Aldred	Mrs H. Harding
Leicestershire	J. B. Sinnott	A. Youd	A. Kind
Lincolnshire	Ms J. Barrow	‡‡M. Spink	D. C. Hoyes
Norfolk	T. J. Byles	R. D. Summers	Mrs D. M. Hockaday
Northamptonshire	J. V. Picking	*R. Paver	A. T. Allen
Northumberland	°°K. Morris	*K. Morris	Mrs L. M. E. Camsell
North Yorkshire	J. A. Ransford	†J. S. Moore	J. Marshall
Nottinghamshire	P. Housden	R. Latham	A. Davison
Oxfordshire	J. Harwood	C. Gray	D. Buckle
Shropshire	A. J. Barnish	N. T. Pursey	G. Raxster
Somerset	Dr D. Radford	C. N. Bilsland	R. B. Clark
Staffordshire	B. A. Price, CBE	R. G. Tettenborn, OBE	T. R. Wright
Suffolk	P. F. Bye	‡‡P. B. Atkinson	D. F. Smith
Surrey	P. Coen	‡P. Derrick	Mrs H. Hawker
Warwickshire	I. G. Caulfield	S. R. Freer	L. Reynolds
West Sussex	D. P. Rigg	Mrs H. Kilpatrick	I. R. W. Elliott
Wiltshire	Dr K. Robinson	D. Chalker	Mrs G. Hill

* Director of Finance
° Corporate Financial Adviser
† Chief Financial Services Officer
‡ Director of Finance and Corporate Services
§§ Head of Finance
¶ Senior Director
** Director of Corporate Services
°° Managing Director
†† Head of Paid Service
‡‡ Director of Finance and Resources
§ Director of Corporate Finance

Unitary Councils

SMALL CAPITALS denote CITY status
§ Denotes Metropolitan council

Council	Population 1995†	Band D charge 1997*	Chief Executive	Mayor (a) Lord Mayor (b) Chairman 1997–8
§Barnsley	226,700	£690.89	J. Edwards	C. Wraith
Bath and North-East Somerset	164,600	708.48	J. Everitt	(b) D. Hawkins
§BIRMINGHAM	1,017,500	793.62	M. Lyons	(a) Ms S. Spence
§Bolton	265,400	786.56	B. Knight	P. Birch
Bournemouth	160,900	612.39	D. Newell	P. Brushett
§BRADFORD	482,700	714.46	R. Penn	(a) T. Cairns
Brighton and Hove	248,100	598.94	G. Jones	Ms B. Walshe
BRISTOL	400,700	914.91	Ms L. de Groot	(a) J. Fisk
§Bury	181,900	710.78	D. Taylor (acting)	R. E. Walker
§Calderdale	193,200	776.41	P. Sheehan	Ms S. Tucker
§COVENTRY	303,600	838.52	I. Roxburgh	(a) J. R. Mutton
Darlington	100,600	597.57	B. Keel	Mrs H. Straiton
DERBY	231,900	671.76	R. Cowlishaw	J. Fuller
§Doncaster	292,900	674.10	A. M. Taylor (acting)	A. S. Mitchinson
§Dudley	312,500	696.76	A. V. Astling	Mrs M. K. Hill
East Riding of Yorkshire	308,400	898.06	D. Stephenson	(b) Mrs D. Engall
§Gateshead	201,800	859.50	L. N. Elton	F. J. Donovan
Hartlepool	92,200	885.61	B. J. Dinsdale	Mrs M. Doyle
KINGSTON UPON HULL	268,600	683.01	I. Crookham	(a) G. B. Caselton
§Kirklees	387,700	798.39	R. V. Hughes	Ms R. Briggs
§Knowsley	154,000	841.71	D. G. Henshaw	G. W. Howard
§LEEDS	725,000	674.49	‡J. P. Smith	(a) Ms L. R. Middleton
LEICESTER	295,700	610.42	R. Green	(a) R. A. Flint
§LIVERPOOL	470,800	1,110.66	P. Bounds	(a) Ms M. Clarke
Luton	181,400	602.27	Mrs K. Jones	M. Akhtar
§MANCHESTER	432,600	897.98	A. Sandford	(a) G. Carroll
Middlesbrough	147,500	711.85	D. W. Ashton	O. Johnson
Milton Keynes	192,900	633.61	H. Miller	Ms V. Squires
§NEWCASTLE UPON TYNE	283,100	830.09	K. Lavery	(a) Ms I. M. Nixon
North-East Lincolnshire	160,100	786.35	R. Bennett	T. P. Walker
North Lincolnshire	152,100	879.62	Dr M. Garnett	P. Kirk
North Somerset	183,800	622.90	P. May	Mrs V. McGann
§North Tyneside	193,900	809.00	Executive Directorate	E. N. Darke
§Oldham	220,000	815.00	C. Smith	(a) P. Dean
Poole	138,900	610.47	J. Brooks	Mrs A. L. Brooke
PORTSMOUTH	189,900	603.09	N. Gurney	(a) A. J. Golds
Redcar and Cleveland	141,400	908.53	A. W. Kilburn	(b) Mrs K. McBride
§Rochdale	207,600	707.03	Mrs F. W. Done	Ms J. Gartside
§Rotherham	255,800	703.80	J. Bell	G. Smith
Rutland	34,600	743.28	Dr J. Morphet	(b) Col. J. Weir
§St Helens	179,900	878.10	Ms C. Hudson	J. Mealor
§SALFORD	230,500	874.25	J. C. Willis	R. B. Carter
§Sandwell	293,700	745.79	F. N. Summers	B. Melia
§Sefton	291,000	832.22	G. J. Haywood	J. A. Hayes
§SHEFFIELD	528,500	765.19	B. Kerslake	(a) T. Arber
§Solihull	202,900	651.59	Dr N. H. Perry	P. Hogarth
SOUTHAMPTON	213,400	602.96	J. Cairns	K. Street
South Gloucestershire	233,200	705.75	M. Robinson	(b) Ms S. Hope
§South Tyneside	156,300	763.20	‡‡P. J. Haigh	Ms C. Brown
§Stockport	290,600	839.18	J. Schultz	M. Lowe
Stockton-on-Tees	178,100	806.35	G. Garlick	B. Woodhouse
STOKE-ON-TRENT	254,300	644.64	B. Smith	(a) D. A. Brown
§SUNDERLAND	295,800	704.15	Dr C. W. Sinclair	G. J. Scott
Swindon	173,800	609.21	P. Doherty	M. Fanning
§Tameside	221,500	814.50	M. J. Greenwood	Ms E. Shorrock
§Trafford	218,300	620.37	W. Allan Lewis	D. Merrell

Council	Population 1995†	Band D charge 1997*	Chief Executive	Mayor (a) Lord Mayor (b) Chairman 1997–8
§WAKEFIELD	317,100	£649.77	R. Mather	(a) C. Oldroyd
§Walsall	262,800	662.17	D. C. Winchurch	N. Matthews
§Wigan	309,800	699.60	S. M. Jones	K. Pye
§Wirral	331,500	857.93	A. White	B. Gilfoyle
§Wolverhampton	244,300	867.24	D. B. Anderson	F. Docherty
YORK	174,400	607.96	D. Clark	(a) M. Bradley

Source of 1995 population figures: ONS Monitor PP1 96/2, 29 August 1996 and PP1 96/3, 17 September 1996
† 1996 figures given for new unitary authorities
* For explanation of council tax, see pages 523–4
‡ The Chief Officer
‡‡ Director of Corporate Services

District Councils

SMALL CAPITALS denote CITY status
§ Denotes Borough status
Source of population figures: ONS Monitor PP1 96/2, 29 August 1996, Monitor PP1 96/3, 17 September 1996
For explanation of council tax, see pages 523–4
* Executive Director
† General Manager
‡ Head of Paid Service
¶ Managing Director

Council	Population 1995	Band D charge 1997	Chief Executive	Chairman 1997–8 (a) Mayor (b) Lord Mayor
Adur, W. Sussex	58,500	£687.14	F. M. G. Staden	D. Hancock
§Allerdale, Cumbria	95,900	747.68	C. J. Hart	(a) M. Rourke
Alnwick, Northumberland	30,900	734.18	L. A. B. St Ruth	J. Hinson
§Amber Valley, Derbys	114,900	728.28	P. M. Carney	(a) P. J. Hook
Arun, W Sussex	136,200	658.77	J. Sumnall	D. Hill
Ashfield, Notts	109,200	761.94	¶E. N. Bernasconi	Ms M. Barsby
§Ashford, Kent	96,300	616.41	D. Lambert	(a) Ms C. M. Rosson
Aylesbury Vale, Bucks	153,600	643.55	B. Hurley	Mrs F. Roberts, MBE
Babergh, Suffolk	78,900	652.30	D. Bishop	R. Kemp
§Barrow-in-Furness, Cumbria	71,800	793.54	T. Campbell	(a) Mrs M. L. Martindale
Basildon, Essex	162,800	676.71	J. Robb	Mrs A. Bruce
§Basingstoke and Deane, Hants	147,400	635.41	Mrs K. Sporle	(a) R. Morris
Bassetlaw, Notts	106,600	753.51	M. S. Havenhand	W. T. Walters
§Bedford	137,000	721.00	L. W. Gould	(a) F. Garrick
§Berwick-upon-Tweed, Northumberland	26,400	729.69	E. O. Cawthorn, TD	(a) D. McClymont
Blaby, Leics	85,200	706.36	E. Hemsley	R. S. Dixon
§Blackburn with Darwen, Lancs	140,300	840.25	P. S. Watson	(a) P. Greenwood
§Blackpool, Lancs	153,600	729.14	G. E. Essex-Crosby	(a) F. Jackson
§Blyth Valley, Northumberland	80,300	714.97	D. Crawford	(a) Mrs T. Heslop
Bolsover, Derbys	70,800	766.73	J. R. Holmes	Mrs P. Richardson
§Boston, Lincs	54,100	661.75	M. James (acting)	(a) F. E. Gilchrist
§Bracknell Forest, Berks	107,700	583.58	G. Mitchell	(a) J. G. Finnie
Braintree, Essex	125,100	622.08	Ms A. F. Ralph	M. J. Allard
Breckland, Norfolk	112,000	602.00	R. Garnett	Mrs T. Paines
Brentwood, Essex	71,700	629.82	C. P. Sivell	(a) Ms A. Long
Bridgnorth, Shrops	50,500	640.76	Mrs T. M. Elliott	D. Beechey
Broadland, Norfolk	112,500	601.92	J. Bryant	G. E. Debbage
Bromsgrove, Hereford and Worcs	85,100	595.75	R. P. Bradshaw	P. J. Baker
§Broxbourne, Herts	82,200	591.26	M. J. Walker	(a) G. R. Morris
§Broxtowe, Notts	112,100	752.45	M. Brown	(a) Ms M. I. Tewson
§Burnley, Lancs	89,800	791.17	R. Ellis	(a) Mrs E. Tate
CAMBRIDGE	114,800	634.33	R. Hammond	(a) Ms D. Roper
Cannock Chase, Staffs	90,700	671.81	M. G. Kemp	D. Dixon

Council	Population 1995	Band D charge 1997	Chief Executive	Chairman 1997–8 (a) Mayor (b) Lord Mayor
CANTERBURY, Kent	135,000	£633.42	C. Carmichael	(b) D. Linfoot, OBE
Caradon, Cornwall	79,400	636.93	J. Neal	B. G. Wilson, TD
CARLISLE, Cumbria	103,500	776.80	R. S. Brackley	(a) J. Metcalfe
Carrick, Cornwall	84,600	652.55	P. M. Kidwell-Talbot	P. Tregunna
§Castle Morpeth, Northumberland	49,700	716.48	P. Wilson	(a) Ms S. Campbell
§Castle Point, Essex	85,400	667.71	B. Rollinson	(a) A. N. Wright
§Charnwood, Leics	154,400	713.91	S. M. Peatfield	(a) Ms J. A. Tyrrell
§Chelmsford, Essex	156,500	641.17	M. Easteal	(a) B. Hurslen
§Cheltenham, Glos	106,600	637.43	L. Davison	(a) L. G. Godwin
Cherwell, Oxon	131,300	645.00	G. J. Handley	Mrs W. Humphries
CHESTER, Cheshire	120,100	699.23	P. F. Durham	(b) D. J. Evans
§Chesterfield, Derbys	100,900	715.73	D. R. Shaw	(a) Ms M. A. Higgins
Chester-le-Street, Co. Durham	55,300	706.07	J. A. Greensmith	J. R. Johnson
Chichester, W. Sussex	104,100	639.19	J. S. Marsland	A. J. French
Chiltern, Bucks	92,400	650.35	A. Goodrum	S. W. James
§Chorley, Lancs	97,000	737.00	J. W. Davies	(a) L. Hoyle
§Christchurch, Dorset	43,100	697.31	M. A. Turvey	(a) C. Bungey
§Colchester, Essex	151,200	629.61	J. Cobley	(a) Ms J. Stevens
§Congleton, Cheshire	85,700	710.00	¶P. Cooper	(a) B. Edwards
§Copeland, Cumbria	70,700	752.62	†Dr J. Stanforth	(a) C. Carter
Corby, Northants	52,300	661.12	F. A. Dobson (acting)	(a) J. Noble
Cotswold, Glos	81,400	637.63	C. Abbott	Mrs S. M. H. Herdman
Craven, N. Yorks	51,000	618.50	Dr G. Taylor	Ms B. Graham
§Crawley, W. Sussex	91,900	651.87	M. D. Sander	(a) M. E. Mayne
§Crewe and Nantwich, Cheshire	113,600	697.19	A. Wenham	(a) D. N. Butterill
§Dacorum, Herts	134,500	593.82	K. Hunt	(a) D. Dennison
§Dartford, Kent	83,600	658.00	C. R. Shepherd	(a) D. Baker
Daventry, Northants	64,800	637.68	P. Cook	Mrs J. Hewitt
Derbyshire Dales	69,300	734.14	D. Wheatcroft	A. Hodkinson
Derwentside, Co. Durham	87,500	794.16	Executive Directorate	A. Donaghy
Dover, Kent	107,300	640.99	J. P. Moir, TD	W. V. Newman
DURHAM	89,700	726.34	C. G. Firmin	(a) N. Griffin
Easington, Co. Durham	96,600	784.00	†P. Innes	J. Johnson
§Eastbourne, E. Sussex	88,600	685.20	Mrs S. E. Conway	(a) Mrs B. Healy
East Cambridgeshire	64,900	569.65	R. C. Carr	H. J. L. Fitch
East Devon	123,600	607.08	F. J. Vallender	Miss S. M. Randall Johnson
East Dorset	81,600	710.75	A. Breakwell	D. J. C. Ryan
East Hampshire	109,800	669.18	Miss J. Hunter	Ms J. Walker
East Hertfordshire	122,600	579.32	R. J. Bailey	Mrs J. Geall
§Eastleigh, Hants	111,300	675.17	C. Tapp	(a) G. Olson
East Lindsey, Lincs	122,400	647.58	P. Haigh	J. V. Ranyard
East Northamptonshire	70,500	666.00	R. K. Heath	I. J. Byrnes
East Staffordshire	100,400	650.58	F. W. Saunders	(a) C. B. Cornell
Eden, Cumbria	47,900	746.71	I. W. Bruce	J. B. Thornborrow
§Ellesmere Port and Neston, Cheshire	81,000	733.91	S. Ewbank	(a) D. W. Davies
§Elmbridge, Surrey	122,200	646.64	D. W. L. Jenkins	(a) H. G. Chubb
Epping Forest, Essex	118,800	642.83	J. Burgess	J. D. Hadfield
§Epsom and Ewell, Surrey	69,200	621.14	D. J. Smith	(a) D. Youell
§Erewash, Derbys	106,700	723.84	G. A. Pook	(a) Mrs G. A. Stevenson
EXETER, Devon	106,600	595.41	P. Bostock	(a) J. Holman
§Fareham, Hants	102,500	645.93	A. A. Davies	(a) I. C. Emery
Fenland, Cambs	78,900	614.24	N. R. Topliss	B. E. A. Diggle
Forest Heath, Suffolk	67,400	612.15	D. W. Burnip	C. A. Duncan
Forest of Dean, Glos	75,400	650.00	R. A. Willis	B. W. Hobman
§Fylde, Lancs	74,500	775.16	J. R. Wilkinson	(a) Mrs D. S. Prestwich
§Gedling, Notts	111,300	742.11	D. Kennedy	(a) T. Lee
§Gillingham, Kent	95,800	616.68	J. A. McBride	(a) G. Smith
GLOUCESTER	105,800	637.74	G. Garbutt	(a) D. Dobbins
§Gosport, Hants	74,800	658.46	M. Crocker	(a) P. R. Edgar
§Gravesham, Kent	92,400	591.10	E. C. Anderson	(a) M. Singh
§Great Yarmouth, Norfolk	88,900	611.12	R. W. Packham	P. Dye
§Guildford, Surrey	125,100	622.54	D. T. Watts	(a) Ms L. Strudwick
§Halton, Cheshire	123,200	685.70	M. H. Cuff	(a) I. Evans

Council	Population 1995	Band D charge 1997	Chief Executive	Chairman 1997–8 (a) Mayor (b) Lord Mayor
Hambleton, N. Yorks	83,900	£543.40	P. Simpson	R. I. Andrew
Harborough, Leics	72,100	700.23	M. C. Wilson	K. Day
Harlow, Essex	73,000	704.74	†D. F. Byrne	J. Young
§Harrogate, N. Yorks	145,600	655.12	P. M. Walsh	(a) S. P. Fawcett
Hart, Hants	84,100	652.61	G. R. Jelbart	C. Lynch
§Hastings, E. Sussex	82,600	703.81	R. A. Carrier	(a) G. White
§Havant, Hants	118,100	664.94	R. G. Smith	(a) A. Emerson
HEREFORD	49,500	607.38	C. E. S. Willis	(a) C. A. Tudge
§Hertsmere, Herts	94,800	624.81	P. H. Copland	(a) T. Gadsden
§High Peak, Derbys	87,900	721.68	R. P. H. Brady	(a) Ms M. Williams
§Hinckley and Bosworth, Leics	97,500	673.99	S. W. Catchpole	(a) D. B. Everitt
Horsham, W. Sussex	116,200	624.26	M. J. Pearson	L. H. Walker
Huntingdonshire, Cambs	149,600	578.87	D. Monks	J. G. Rignall
§Hyndburn, Lancs	80,200	806.63	M. J. Chambers	(a) M. S. Cowell
§Ipswich, Suffolk	114,100	718.92	J. D. Hehir	(a) Mrs J. E. Macartney
Kennet, Wilts	74,700	631.32	P. L. Owens	D. L. Parker
Kerrier, Cornwall	88,800	652.47	G. G. Fox	Mrs S. Swift
§Kettering, Northants	79,900	663.75	P. Walker	(a) R. Wright
§King's Lynn and West Norfolk	131,100	619.90	A. E. Pask	(a) C. Walters
Lancaster, Lancs	136,200	731.32	J. Burrows	(a) Mrs H. M. Shuttleworth
Leominster, Hereford and Worcs	41,200	605.41	Mrs M. L. Holborow	R. Farmer
Lewes, E. Sussex	88,000	686.73	J. N. Crawford	Ms R. F. Collict
Lichfield, Staffs	93,300	631.85	J. T. Thompson	J. J. Brown
LINCOLN	84,300	656.01	A. Sparke	(a) L. Wells
§Macclesfield, Cheshire	151,800	699.13	B. W. Longden	(a) D. Page
§Maidstone, Kent	139,300	670.80	J. D. Makepeace	(a) Mrs J. Gibson
Maldon, Essex	54,300	621.61	E. A. P. Plumridge	J. H. Smith
Malvern Hills, Hereford and Worcs	91,700	635.09	C. Bocock	D. Rule
Mansfield, Notts	101,600	756.85	R. P. Goad	Ms S. Higgins
§Melton, Leics	46,500	616.25	P. M. Murphy	(a) Ms E. Holmes
Mendip, Somerset	98,600	686.25	G. Jeffs	Mrs H. Milroy
Mid Bedfordshire	116,400	763.22	C. A. Tucker	Mrs P. Cook
Mid Devon	66,000	640.28	M. I. R. Bull	Mrs J. Palk
Mid Suffolk	79,600	651.15	G. R. Chilton	Mrs W. Marchant
Mid Sussex	126,100	645.39	W. I. H. Hatton	T. Davies
Mole Valley, Surrey	79,400	601.01	Mrs H. Kerswell	Mrs W. K. Oliver
Newark and Sherwood, Notts	104,100	807.99	¶R. G. Dix	Mrs G. Dawn
Newbury, Berks	142,600	649.40	Ms S. Manzie	Mrs J. Gardner
§Newcastle under Lyme, Staffs	123,100	639.79	J. Nixon	(a) A. A. Clarke
New Forest, Hants	168,800	677.00	¶I. B. Mackintosh	J. A. G. Hutchins
§Northampton	189,700	677.88	R. J. B. Morris	(a) R. W. Church
North Cornwall	77,800	658.95	D. Brown	A. D. Hirst
North Devon	85,600	610.13	D. T. Cunliffe	E. L. G. Nightingale
North Dorset	56,900	670.80	Ms E. Peters	M. F. Lane
North East Derbyshire	99,300	785.05	‡Ms C. A. Gilby	Ms D. Ward
North Hertfordshire	114,900	620.04	S. Philp	Mrs L. Kercher
North Kesteven, Lincs	84,900	664.11	S. Lamb	Mrs P. Woodman
North Norfolk	95,700	621.24	B. A. Barrell	D. E. Russell
North Shropshire	54,100	672.09	D. Pearce	A. Boughey
§North Warwickshire	61,500	756.94	J. Hutchinson	(a) R. Robinson
North West Leicestershire	83,800	716.30	M. J. Diaper	C. A. Stanley
North Wiltshire	121,600	664.95	R. Marshall	A. S. R. Jackson
NORWICH, Norfolk	126,700	663.75	J. R. Packer	(b) H. Watson
NOTTINGHAM	283,800	808.72	E. F. Cantle	(b) R. E. W. Greensmith
§Nuneaton and Bedworth, Warwickshire	119,000	745.69	vacant	(a) D. Ensor
§Oadby and Wigston, Leics	53,200	702.17	Mrs R. E. Hyde	(a) D. Vann
§Oswestry, Shrops	34,800	656.59	D. A. Towers	(a) Mrs B. J. Willis
OXFORD	134,800	733.33	R. S. Block	(b) W. J. Baker
§Pendle, Lancs	85,300	800.74	S. Barnes	(a) Mrs J. M. Belbin
Penwith, Cornwall	60,000	641.71	‡D. H. Hosken	W. T. Trevorrow
PETERBOROUGH, Cambs	159,300	616.00	W. E. Samuel	(a) Ms Y. Lowndes
PLYMOUTH, Devon	257,500	678.68	Mrs A. Stone	(b) Mrs J. I. Stopporton
§Preston, Lancs	134,300	783.89	J. E. Carr	(a) H. R. Evans
Purbeck, Dorset	44,900	692.18	P. B. Croft	D. A. Budd

Council	Population 1995	Band D charge 1997	Chief Executive	Chairman 1997–8 (a) Mayor (b) Lord Mayor
§Reading, Berks	141,500	£706.40	Ms J. Markham	(a) Ms R. Williams
§Redditch, Hereford and Worcs	77,900	647.33	Ms K. Kerswell	(a) Mrs I. Beech
§Reigate and Banstead, Surrey	118,700	631.82	M. Bacon	(a) Ms M. Wallar
§Restormel, Cornwall	90,200	625.51	Mrs P. Crowson	(a) A. Parkyn
§Ribble Valley, Lancs	52,100	735.91	D. Morris	(a) Mrs J. Grimes
Richmondshire, N. Yorks	46,300	620.17	H. Tabiner	P. Cullen
ROCHESTER UPON MEDWAY, Kent	144,200	540.09	R. I. Gregory	(a) Mrs L. Robson
Rochford, Essex	76,100	630.81	R. A. Lovell	Revd J. Stanton
§Rossendale, Lancs	65,400	812.37	J. S. Hartley	(a) P. N. Heyworth
Rother, E. Sussex	87,200	674.94	D. F. Powell	(a) W. H. Clements
§Rugby, Warwickshire	87,000	734.33	Mrs D. M. Colley	(a) J. F. Wells
§Runnymede, Surrey	75,600	559.53	T. N. Williams	(a) Mrs H. Drake
§Rushcliffe, Notts	103,200	714.14	K. Beaumont	(a) J. G. Kelk
§Rushmoor, Hants	86,300	651.23	A. Lloyd	(a) J. Hiscock
Ryedale, N. Yorks	48,000	659.30	H. W. Mosley	Mrs J. E. Taylor
ST ALBANS, Herts	129,600	628.88	E. A. Hackford	(a) Ms P. Harris
§St Edmundsbury, Suffolk	93,100	636.47	G. R. N. Toft	(a) M. J. Ames
Salisbury, Wilts	110,800	643.57	R. Sheard	Miss M. A. Tomlinson
§Scarborough, N. Yorks	108,900	617.69	J. M. Trebble	(a) B. G. Wormald
Sedgefield, Co. Durham	90,800	777.67	N. Vaulks	(a) B. Avery
Sedgemoor, Somerset	101,100	680.00	A. G. Lovell	C. A. Buchanan
Selby, N. Yorks	72,500	630.00	M. Connor	B. Thorne
Sevenoaks, Kent	109,700	640.00	N. Howells	Dr Wilfred Harding, CBE
Shepway, Kent	97,000	658.61	R. J. Thompson	K. Hudson
§Shrewsbury and Atcham, Shrops	95,800	642.69	D. Bradbury	(a) P. E. Dunham
§Slough, Berks	109,300	589.27	Ms C. Coppell	(a) L. S. Minhas
South Bedfordshire	110,900	770.00	T. D. Rix	B. Stevens
South Bucks	62,900	600.44	C. R. Furness	K. M. Dolan
South Cambridgeshire	126,300	549.01	J. S. Ballantyne	Mrs S. Saunders
South Derbyshire	76,200	713.38	D. J. Dugdale	W. Dunn
§Southend-on-Sea, Essex	171,200	621.23	G. Krawiec	(a) Mrs J. E. Dunn
South Hams, Devon	79,100	622.35	M. S. Carpenter	D. W. S. Thorning
South Herefordshire	54,700	607.52	A. Hughes	Mrs R. F. Lincoln
South Holland, Lincs	71,100	522.60	C. J. Simpkins	J. R. Pearl
South Kesteven, Lincs	117,500	631.50	K. R. Cann	K. M. Joynson
South Lakeland, Cumbria	100,400	739.49	A. F. Winstanley	J. Studholme
South Norfolk	105,400	622.88	A. G. T. Kellett	T. East
South Northamptonshire	73,900	685.37	K. Whitehead	S. Troup
South Oxfordshire	123,300	672.94	R. Watson	K. C. H. Hall
§South Ribble, Lancs	103,100	731.41	P. Halsall	(a) Mrs B. J. Wilson
South Shropshire	39,800	647.14	G. C. Biggs, MBE	R. D. Phillips
South Somerset	150,400	669.93	M. Usher	Ms G. Coleshill
South Staffordshire	104,300	565.84	L. T. Barnfield	R. A. Wright
§Spelthorne, Surrey	89,400	630.77	M. B. Taylor	(a) Mrs M. Hartley
§Stafford	123,300	624.81	J. K. M. Krawiec	(a) Mrs J. Dalgarno
Staffordshire Moorlands	94,800	653.92	B. J. Preedy	Mrs J. A. Finn
§Stevenage, Herts	76,100	654.82	I. Paske	(a) K. Vale
Stratford-on-Avon, Warwickshire	110,500	677.19	I. B. Prosser	J. Holder
Stroud, Glos	107,300	691.35	R. M. Ollin	Mrs M. E. A. Nolder
Suffolk Coastal	116,000	642.37	T. K. Griffin	A. C. Healey
§Surrey Heath, Surrey	82,100	617.08	B. R. Catchpole	(a) D. Franklin
§Swale, Kent	117,900	609.09	J. C. Edwards	(a) D. Sargent
§Tamworth, Staffs	72,200	606.96	C. Moore	(a) S. Peaple
Tandridge, Surrey	77,000	628.46	P. J. D. Thomas	I. Pavely
§Taunton Deane, Somerset	98,700	652.27	†Mrs S. Douglas	(a) A. Paul
Teesdale, Co. Durham	24,200	719.53	C. M. Anderson	A. Smith
Teignbridge, Devon	114,700	611.94	B. T. Jones	F. Symons
Tendring, Essex	131,600	634.57	J. Hawkins	F. A. Baker
§Test Valley, Hants	105,900	636.92	A. Jones	(a) R. J. Bailey
§Tewkesbury, Glos	76,200	571.89	H. Davis	(a) B. Jones
Thanet, Kent	125,300	658.30	D. Ralls, CBE, DFC	Mrs M. Davies
Three Rivers, Herts	84,000	640.16	A. Robertson	P. Brading
§Thurrock, Essex	131,600	641.88	K. Barnes	(a) M. Jones
§Tonbridge and Malling, Kent	104,100	644.99	T. Thompson	(a) G. Chapman
§Torbay, Devon	123,900	600.63	T. Hodgkiss	(a) J. Davies
Torridge, Devon	55,000	613.23	R. K. Brasington	D. Rowe

Council	Population 1995	Band D charge 1997	Chief Executive	Chairman 1997–8 (a) Mayor (b) Lord Mayor
§Tunbridge Wells, Kent	103,300	£615.00	R. J. Stone	(a) D. Mills
Tynedale, Northumberland	57,700	733.00	A. Baty	Mrs D. Ewell
Uttlesford, Essex	68,300	612.85	K. Ivory	R. Green
Vale of White Horse, Oxon	113,100	642.11	T. Stock	Mrs J. Hutchinson
§Vale Royal, Cheshire	114,700	718.79	W. R. T. Woods	(a) J. Beech
Wansbeck, Northumberland	62,200	764.74	A. G. White	Miss P. Dixon
§Warrington, Cheshire	188,000	724.13	S. Broomhead	(a) R. Humphreys
Warwick	120,700	694.83	Miss J. Barrett	Mrs M. Begg
§Watford, Herts	77,200	700.73	Ms C. Hassan	(a) Ms S. Rosser
Waveney, Suffolk	107,700	623.01	M. Berridge	Ms I. Turrell
§Waverley, Surrey	115,300	639.99	Miss C. L. Pointer	(a) M. H. W. Biddiscombe
Wealden, E. Sussex	136,300	703.60	D. R. Holness	R. I. F. Parsons
Wear Valley, Co. Durham	63,000	790.02	*Mrs C. Hughes	Mrs B. Bousfield
§Wellingborough, Northants	68,200	584.82	M. Jones (acting)	(a) E. Coleman
Welwyn Hatfield, Herts	95,200	632.73	M. Saminaden (acting)	J. C. Lonergan
§West Devon	46,600	656.38	D. Incoll	(a) Ms A. Clish-Green
West Dorset	89,700	667.00	R. C. Rennison	T. M. Frost
West Lancashire	110,200	751.57	‡T. L. Abernethy	J. Draper
West Lindsey, Lincs	77,600	670.28	R. W. Nelsey	R. Rainsforth
West Oxfordshire, Oxon	95,800	620.72	G. Bonner	C. D. James
West Somerset	32,400	681.07	C. W. Rockall	Mrs S. Pearce
West Wiltshire	109,700	636.20	J. Ligo	P. Bryant
§Weymouth and Portland, Dorset	62,900	705.89	M. N. Ashby	(a) R. E. H. Beare
WINCHESTER, Hants	104,400	664.45	D. H. Cowan	(a) N. Hibdige
§Windsor and Maidenhead, Berks	140,200	627.79	D. Lunn	(a) E. Wiles
§Woking, Surrey	90,300	629.02	P. Russell	(a) Mrs I. K. Matthews
Wokingham, Berks	142,000	665.15	Ms G. C. Norton	J. Green
WORCESTER	91,100	607.05	D. Wareing	(a) Mrs M. Leyland
§Worthing, W. Sussex	98,500	654.48	M. J. Ball	(a) Mrs G. Lissenburg
Wrekin, Shrops	144,600	700.00	D. G. Hutchinson	J. S. Uppal
Wychavon, Hereford and Worcs	106,000	606.68	W. S. Nott	S. Selby
Wycombe, Bucks	164,100	640.00	R. J. Cummins	(a) Mrs E. Hall
§Wyre, Lancs	104,300	738.75	M. Brown	(a) L. M. Jolley
Wyre Forest, Hereford and Worcs	97,000	635.33	W. S. Baldwin	J. R. Cooper

---

LOCAL GOVERNMENT CHANGES FROM 1 APRIL 1998

UA Unitary Authority

Present county (no. of DCs at present)

Berkshire (6)	UAs in Bracknell Forest, Newbury, Reading, Slough, Windsor and Maidenhead, Wokingham
Cambridgeshire (6)	UA in Peterborough; rest remain two-tier
Cheshire (8)	UAs in Halton, Warrington; rest remain two-tier
Devon (10)	UAs in Plymouth, Torbay; rest remain two-tier
Essex (14)	UAs in Southend, Thurrock; rest remain two-tier
Hereford and Worcester (9)	UA in Herefordshire (pre-1974 boundary); Worcestershire retains two tiers
Kent (14)	UA in Rochester and Gillingham; rest remain two-tier
Lancashire (14)	UAs in Blackburn with Darwen, Blackpool; rest remain two-tier
Nottinghamshire (8)	UA in Nottingham; rest remain two-tier
Shropshire (6)	UA in The Wrekin; rest remain two-tier

No changes are proposed in the following:
Cornwall; Cumbria; Gloucestershire; Hertfordshire; Lincolnshire; Norfolk; Northamptonshire; Northumberland; Oxfordshire; Somerset; Suffolk; Surrey; Warwickshire; West Sussex

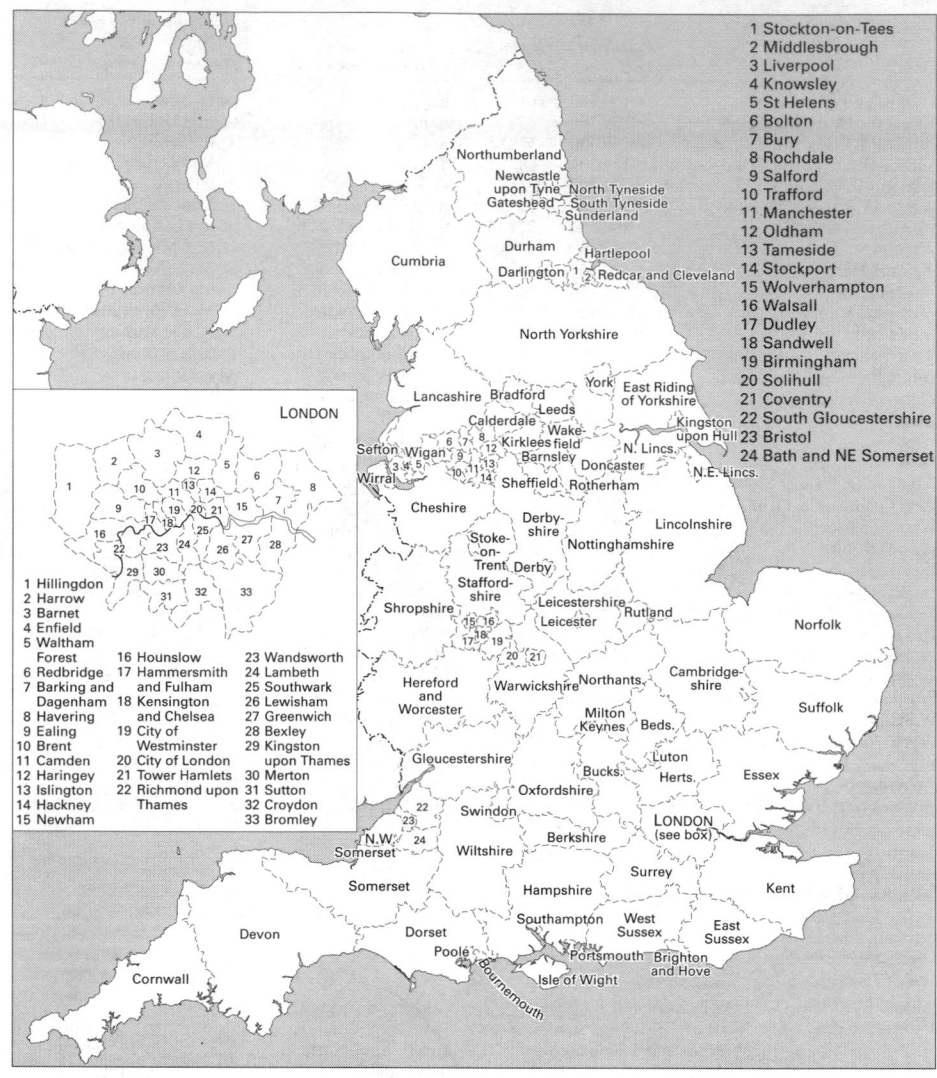

1 Stockton-on-Tees
2 Middlesbrough
3 Liverpool
4 Knowsley
5 St Helens
6 Bolton
7 Bury
8 Rochdale
9 Salford
10 Trafford
11 Manchester
12 Oldham
13 Tameside
14 Stockport
15 Wolverhampton
16 Walsall
17 Dudley
18 Sandwell
19 Birmingham
20 Solihull
21 Coventry
22 South Gloucestershire
23 Bristol
24 Bath and NE Somerset

LONDON

1 Hillingdon	16 Hounslow
2 Harrow	17 Hammersmith
3 Barnet	and Fulham
4 Enfield	18 Kensington
5 Waltham	and Chelsea
Forest	19 City of
6 Redbridge	Westminster
7 Barking and	20 City of London
Dagenham	21 Tower Hamlets
8 Havering	22 Richmond upon
9 Ealing	Thames
10 Brent	
11 Camden	23 Wandsworth
12 Haringey	24 Lambeth
13 Islington	25 Southwark
14 Hackney	26 Lewisham
15 Newham	27 Greenwich
	28 Bexley
	29 Kingston
	upon Thames
	30 Merton
	31 Sutton
	32 Croydon
	33 Bromley

London

THE CORPORATION OF LONDON
(*see also* page 526)

The City of London is the historic centre at the heart of London known as 'the square mile' around which the vast metropolis has grown over the centuries. The City's residential population is 5,500. The civic government is carried on by the Corporation of London through the Court of Common Council.

The City is an international financial centre, generating over £20 billion a year for the British economy. It includes the head offices of the principal banks, insurance companies and mercantile houses, in addition to buildings ranging from the historic Roman Wall and the 15th-century Guildhall, to the massive splendour of St Paul's Cathedral and the architectural beauty of Wren's spires.

The City of London was described by Tacitus in AD 62 as 'a busy emporium for trade and traders'. Under the Romans it became an important administration centre and hub of the road system. Little is known of London in Saxon times, when it formed part of the kingdom of the East Saxons. In 886 Alfred recovered London from the Danes and reconstituted it a burgh under his son-in-law. In 1066 the citizens submitted to William the Conqueror who in 1067 granted them a charter, which is still preserved, establishing them in the rights and privileges they had hitherto enjoyed.

THE MAYORALTY

The Mayoralty was probably established about 1189, the first Mayor being Henry Fitz Ailwyn who filled the office for 23 years and was succeeded by Fitz Alan (1212–14). A new charter was granted by King John in 1215, directing the Mayor to be chosen annually, which has ever since been done, though in early times the same individual often held the office more than once. A familiar instance is that of 'Whittington, thrice Lord Mayor of London' (in reality four times, 1397, 1398, 1406, 1419); and many modern cases have occurred. The earliest instance of the phrase 'Lord Mayor' in English is in 1414. It was used more generally in the latter part of the 15th century and became invariable from 1535 onwards. At Michaelmas the liverymen in Common Hall choose two Aldermen who have served the office of Sheriff for presentation to the Court of Aldermen, and one is chosen to be Lord Mayor for the following mayoral year.

LORD MAYOR'S DAY

The Lord Mayor of London was previously elected on the feast of St Simon and St Jude (28 October), and from the time of Edward I, at least, was presented to the King or to the Barons of the Exchequer on the following day, unless that day was a Sunday. The day of election was altered to 16 October in 1346, and after some further changes was fixed for Michaelmas Day in 1546, but the ceremonies of admittance and swearing-in of the Lord Mayor continued to take place on 28 and 29 October respectively until 1751. In 1752, at the reform of the calendar, the Lord Mayor was continued in office until 8 November, the 'New Style' equivalent of 28 October. The Lord Mayor is now presented to the Lord Chief Justice at the Royal Courts of Justice on the second Saturday in November to make the final declaration of office, having been sworn in at Guildhall on the preceding day. The procession to the Royal Courts of Justice is popularly known as the Lord Mayor's Show.

REPRESENTATIVES

Aldermen are mentioned in the 11th century and their office is of Saxon origin. They were elected annually between 1377 and 1394, when an Act of Parliament of Richard II directed them to be chosen for life.

The Common Council, elected annually on the first Friday in December, was, at an early date, substituted for a popular assembly called the *Folkmote*. At first only two representatives were sent from each ward, but the number has since been greatly increased.

OFFICERS

Sheriffs were Saxon officers; their predecessors were the *wic-reeves* and *portreeves* of London and Middlesex. At first they were officers of the Crown, and were named by the Barons of the Exchequer; but Henry I (in 1132) gave the citizens permission to choose their own Sheriffs, and the annual election of Sheriffs became fully operative under King John's charter of 1199. The citizens lost this privilege, as far as the election of the Sheriff of Middlesex was concerned, by the Local Government Act 1888; but the liverymen continue to choose two Sheriffs of the City of London, who are appointed on Midsummer Day and take office at Michaelmas.

The office of Chamberlain is an ancient one, the first contemporary record of which is 1237. The Town Clerk (or Common Clerk) is mentioned in 1274.

ACTIVITIES

The work of the Corporation is assigned to a number of committees which present reports to the Court of Common Council. These Committees are: City Lands and Bridge House Estates, Policy and Resources, Finance, Planning and Transportation, Central Markets, Billingsgate and Leadenhall Markets, Spitalfields Market, Police, Port and City of London Health and Social Services, Libraries, Art Galleries and Records, Boards of Governors of Schools, Music and Drama (Guildhall School of Music and Drama), Establishment, Housing and Sports Development, Gresham (City side), Hampstead Heath Management, Epping Forest and Open Spaces, West Ham Park, Privileges, Barbican Residential and Barbican Centre (Barbican Arts and Conference Centre).

The City's estate, in the possession of which the Corporation of London differs from other municipalities, is managed by the City Lands and Bridge House Estates Committee, the chairmanship of which carries with it the title of Chief Commoner.

The Honourable the Irish Society, which manages the Corporation's estates in Ulster, consists of a Governor and five other Aldermen, the Recorder, and 19 Common Councilmen, of whom one is elected Deputy Governor.

THE LORD MAYOR 1996–7*

The Rt. Hon. the Lord Mayor, Sir Roger Cork
  Secretary, Air Vice-Marshal M. Dicken, CB

THE SHERIFFS 1997–8

D. H. S. Howard (*Alderman, Cornhill*) and J. M. Y. Oliver (*Alderman, Bishopsgate*); *elected*, 24 June 1997; *assumed office*, 26 September 1997

---

* The Lord Mayor for 1997–8 was elected on Michaelmas Day. *See* Stop-press

OFFICERS, ETC

Town Clerk and Chamberlain, B. P. Harty
Chief Commoner (1997), F. M. Bramwell
Clerk, The Honourable the Irish Society, S. Waley, The Irish
  Chamber, 1st Floor, 75 Watling Street, London EC4M 9BJ

THE ALDERMEN

Name and Ward	CC	Ald.	Shff.	Lord Mayor
Sir Peter Gadsden, GBE,				
Farringdon Wt.	1969	1971	1970	1979
Sir Christopher Leaver, GBE,				
Dowgate	1973	1974	1979	1981
Sir Alan Traill, GBE,				
Langbourn	1970	1975	1982	1984
Sir David Rowe-Ham, GBE,				
Bridge and *Bridge Wt.*	—	1976	1984	1986
Sir Christopher Collett, GBE,				
Broad Street	1973	1979	1985	1988
Sir Alexander Graham, GBE,				
Queenhithe	1978	1979	1986	1990
Sir Brian Jenkins, GBE,				
Cordwainer	—	1980	1987	1991
Sir Paul Newall, TD, *Walbrook*	1980	1981	1989	1993
Sir Christopher Walford,				
Farringdon Wn.	—	1982	1990	1994
Sir John Chalstrey, *Vintry*	1981	1984	1993	1995
Sir Roger Cork, *Tower*	1978	1983	1992	1996

All the above have passed the Civic Chair

Richard Nichols, *Candlewick*	1983	1984	1994
Lord Levene of Portsoken,			
KBE, *Portsoken*	1983	1984	1995
Clive Martin, OBE, TD, *Aldgate*	—	1985	1996
David Howard, *Cornhill*	1972	1986	1997
James Oliver, *Bishopsgate*	1980	1987	1997
Peter Bull, *Cheap*	1968	1984	
Gavyn Arthur, *Cripplegate*	1988	1991	
Robert Finch, *Coleman Street*	—	1992	
Richard Agutter, *Castle Baynard*	—	1995	
Michael Savory, *Bread Street*	1980	1996	
David Brewer, *Bassishaw*	1992	1996	
Nicholas Anstee, *Aldersgate*	1987	1996	
Michael Everard, CBE, *Lime Street*	—	1996	
John Hughesdon, *Billingsgate*	1991	1997	

THE COMMON COUNCIL

Deputy: Each Common Councilman so described serves as
deputy to the Alderman of her/his ward

Absalom, J. D. (1994)	*Farringdon Wt.*
Altman, L. P. (1996)	*Cripplegate Wn.*
Angell, E. H. (1991)	*Cripplegate Wt.*
Archibald, *Deputy* W. W. (1986)	*Cornhill*
Ayers, K. E. (1996)	*Bassishaw*
Bailey, J. (1993)	*Cripplegate Wt.*
Ballard, K. A., MC (1969)	*Castle Baynard*
Balls, H. D. (1970)	*Castle Baynard*
Barker, *Deputy* J. A. (1981)	*Cripplegate Wn.*
Barnes-Yallowley, H. M. F. (1986)	*Coleman Street*
Beale, *Deputy* M. J. (1979)	*Lime Street*
Bird, J. L. (1977)	*Bridge*
Biroum-Smith, P. L. (1988)	*Dowgate*
Block, S. A. A. (1983)	*Cheap*
Bowman, J. C. R. (1995)	*Aldgate*
Bradshaw, D. J. (1991)	*Cripplegate Wn.*
Bramwell, F. M. (1983)	*Langbourn*
Branson, N. A. C. (1996)	*Bassishaw*
Brewster, J. W., OBE (1994)	*Bassishaw*
Brighton, R. L. (1984)	*Portsoken*
Brooks, W. I. B. (1988)	*Billingsgate*
Brown, *Deputy* D. T. (1971)	*Walbrook*
Caspi, D. R. (1994)	*Bridge*
Cassidy, *Deputy* M. J. (1989)	*Coleman Street*
Catt, B. F. (1982)	*Farringdon Wn.*
Chadwick, R. A. H. (1994)	*Tower*
Challis, G. H., CBE (1978)	*Langbourn*
Charkham, J. P. (1996)	*Farringdon Wt.*
Cohen, Mrs C. M. (1986)	*Lime Street*
Cole, Lt.-Col. Sir Colin, KCB, KCVO, TD (1964)	*Castle Baynard*
Cotgrove, D. (1991)	*Lime Street*
Coven, *Deputy* Mrs E. O., CBE (1972)	*Dowgate*
Currie, *Deputy* Miss S. E. M. (1985)	*Cripplegate Wt.*
Daily-Hunt, R. B. (1989)	*Cripplegate Wt.*
Darwin, G. E. (1995)	*Farringdon Wt.*
Davis, C. B. (1991)	*Bread Street*
Davis, D. R. (1996)	*Cheap*
Delderfield, *Deputy* D. W. (1995)	*Farringdon Wt.*
Dove, W. H., MBE (1993)	*Bishopsgate*
Dunitz, A. A. (1984)	*Portsoken*
Eskenzi, A. N. (1970)	*Farringdon Wn.*
Eve, R. A. (1980)	*Cheap*
Everett, K. M. (1984)	*Candlewick*
Falk, F. A., TD (1997)	*Broad Street*
Farrow, M. W. W. (1996)	*Farringdon Wt.*
Farthing, R. B. C. (1981)	*Aldgate*
Fell, J. A. (1982)	*Queenhithe*
FitzGerald, *Deputy* R. C. A. (1981)	*Bread Street*
Forbes, G. B. (1993)	*Bishopsgate*
Fraser, S. J. (1993)	*Coleman Street*
Fraser, W. B. (1981)	*Vintry*
Galloway, A. D. (1981)	*Broad Street*
Gillon, G. M. F. (1995)	*Cordwainer*
Ginsburg, S. (1990)	*Bishopsgate*
Gowman, Miss A. (1991)	*Dowgate*
Graves, A. C. (1985)	*Bishopsgate*
Green, C. (1994)	*Aldersgate*
Griffiths, Mrs R. M. (1996)	*Cripplegate Wt.*
Hall, B. R. H. (1995)	*Farringdon Wn.*
Halliday, Mrs P. (1992)	*Walbrook*
Hardwick, Dr P. B. (1987)	*Aldgate*
Harries, R. E. (1995)	*Cripplegate Wt.*
Harris, B. N. (1996)	*Broad Street*
Hart, *Deputy* M. G. (1970)	*Bridge*
Haynes, J. E. H. (1986)	*Cornhill*
Henderson, *Deputy* J. S., OBE (1975)	*Langbourn*
Henderson-Begg, M. (1977)	*Coleman Street*
Holland, *Deputy* J., CBE (1972)	*Aldgate*
Holliday, Mrs E. H. L. (1987)	*Vintry*
Horlock, *Deputy* H. W. S. (1969)	*Farringdon Wn.*
Jackson, L. St J. T. (1978)	*Bread Street*
Kellett, Mrs M. W. F. (1986)	*Tower*
Kemp, D. L. (1984)	*Coleman Street*
Knowles, S. K. (1984)	*Candlewick*
Lawrence, G. A. (1994)	*Farringdon Wt.*
Lawson, G. C. H. (1971)	*Portsoken*
Littlestone, N. (1993)	*Aldersgate*
MacLellan, A. P. W. (1989)	*Walbrook*
McNeil, I. D. (1977)	*Lime Street*
Malins, J. H., QC (1981)	*Farringdon Wt.*
Martin, R. C. (1986)	*Queenhithe*
Martinelli, *Deputy* P. J. (1994)	*Bassishaw*
Mayhew, Miss J. (1986)	*Queenhithe*
Mayhew, J. P. (1996)	*Aldersgate*

Mitchell, *Deputy* C. R. (1971)	*Castle Baynard*
Mizen, *Deputy* D. H. (1979)	*Broad Street*
Mobsby, *Deputy* D. J. L. (1985)	*Billingsgate*
Morgan, *Deputy* B. L., CBE (1963)	*Bishopsgate*
Moss, A. D. (1989)	*Tower*
Nash, *Deputy* Mrs J. C. (1983)	*Aldersgate*
Newman, Mrs P. B. (1989)	*Aldersgate*
Northall-Laurie, P. D. (1975)	*Walbrook*
O'Ferrall, P. C. K., OBE (1996)	*Aldgate*
Owen, Mrs J. (1975)	*Langbourn*
Owen-Ward, J. R. (1983)	*Bridge*
Parmley, A. C. (1992)	*Vintry*
Pembroke, *Deputy* Mrs A. M. F. (1978)	*Cheap*
Platts-Mills, J. F. F., QC	*Farringdon Wt.*
Ponsonby of Shulbrede, *Deputy* Lady (1981)	*Farringdon Wt.*
Price, E. E. (1996)	*Farringdon Wt.*
Pulman, *Deputy* G. A. G. (1983)	*Tower*
Punter, C. (1993)	*Cripplegate Wn.*
Reed, *Deputy* J. L., MBE (1967)	*Farringdon Wn.*
Revell-Smith, *Deputy* P. A., CBE (1959)	*Vintry*
Rigby, P. P., CBE (1972)	*Farringdon Wn.*
Robinson, Mrs D. C. (1989)	*Bishopsgate*
Roney, *Deputy* E. P. T., CBE (1974)	*Bishopsgate*
Samuel, *Deputy* Mrs I., MBE (1971)	*Portsoken*
Sargant, K. A. (1991)	*Cornhill*
Saunders, *Deputy* R. (1975)	*Candlewick*
Scriven, R. G. (1984)	*Candlewick*
Sellon, S. A., OBE, TD (1990)	*Cordwainer*
Shalit, D. M. (1972)	*Farringdon Wn.*
Sharp, *Deputy* Mrs I. M. (1974)	*Queenhithe*
Sherlock, M. R. C. (1992)	*Dowgate*
Simpson, A. S. J. (1987)	*Aldersgate*
Smith, Miss A. M. (1995)	*Farringdon Wt.*
Snyder, *Deputy* M. J. (1986)	*Cordwainer*
Spanner, J. H., TD (1984)	*Broad Street*
Stevenson, F. P. (1994)	*Cripplegate Wn.*
Taylor, J. A. F., TD (1991)	*Bread Street*
Thorp, C. P. (1996)	*Billingsgate*
Trotter, J. (1993)	*Billingsgate*
Walsh, S. (1989)	*Farringdon Wt.*
Warner, D. W. (1994)	*Cripplegate Wn.*
White, Dr J. W. (1986)	*Cornhill*
Willoughby, P. J. (1985)	*Bishopsgate*
Wilmot, R. T. D. (1973)	*Cordwainer*
Wixley, G. R. A., CBE, TD (1964)	*Coleman Street*
Wooldridge, F. D. (1988)	*Farringdon Wn.*

The City Guilds (Livery Companies)

The constitution of the livery companies has been unchanged for centuries. There are three ranks of membership: freemen, liverymen and assistants. A person can become a freeman by patrimony (through a parent having been a freeman); by servitude (through having served an apprenticeship to a freeman); or by redemption (by purchase).

Election to the livery is the prerogative of the company, who can elect any of its freemen as liverymen. Assistants are usually elected from the livery and form a Court of Assistants which is the governing body of the company. The Master (in some companies called the Prime Warden) is elected annually from the assistants.

As at June 1997, 23,809 liverymen of the guilds were entitled to vote at elections at Common Hall.

The order of precedence, omitting extinct companies, is given in parenthesis after the name of each company in the list below. In certain companies the election of Master or Prime Warden for the year does not take place till the autumn. In such cases the Master or Prime Warden for 1996–7 is given.

THE TWELVE GREAT COMPANIES
In order of civic precedence

MERCERS (1). *Hall*, Ironmonger Lane, London EC2V 8HE. *Livery*, 251. *Clerk*, G. M. M. Wakeford, OBE. *Master*, D. A. Tate

GROCERS (2). *Hall*, Princes Street, London EC2R 8AD. *Livery*, 318. *Clerk*, C. G. Mattingley, CBE. *Master*, The Hon. S. Fortescue

DRAPERS (3). *Hall*, Throgmorton Avenue, London EC2N 2DQ. *Livery*, 238. *Clerk*, A. J. Lang, MBE. *Master*, Sir Michael Craig-Cooper, CBE, TD

FISHMONGERS (4). *Hall*, London Bridge, London EC4R 9EL. *Livery*, 300. *Clerk*, K. S. Waters. *Prime Warden*, J. Bennett

GOLDSMITHS (5). *Hall*, Foster Lane, London EC2V 6BN. *Livery*, 275. *Clerk*, R. D. Buchanan-Dunlop, CBE. *Prime Warden*, The Lord Cunliffe

MERCHANT TAYLORS (6/7). *Hall*, 30 Threadneedle Street, London EC2R 8AY. *Livery* 310. *Clerk*, D. A. Peck. *Master*, M. C. Clarke

SKINNERS (6/7). *Hall*, 8 Dowgate Hill, London EC4R 2SP. *Livery*, 370. *Clerk*, Capt. D. Hart-Dyke, CBE, LVO, RN. *Master*, D. Kemp

HABERDASHERS (8). *Livery*, 320. *Clerk*, Capt. R. J. Fisher, RN, 39–40 Bartholomew Close, London EC1A 7JN. *Master*, N. K. S. Wills

SALTERS (9). *Hall*, 4 Fore Street, London EC2Y 5DE. *Livery*, 160. *Clerk*, Col. M. P. Barneby. *Master*, L. V. Stell

IRONMONGERS (10). *Hall*, Shaftesbury Place, Barbican, London EC2Y 8AA. *Livery*, 225. *Clerk*, J. A. Oliver. *Master*, A. H. Boddy

VINTNERS (11). *Hall*, Upper Thames Street, London EC4V 3BJ. *Livery*, 306. *Clerk*, Brig. M. Smythe, OBE. *Master* F. C. D. Berry Green, TD

CLOTHWORKERS (12). *Hall*, Dunster Court, Mincing Lane, London EC3R 7AH. *Livery*, 200. *Clerk*, M. G. T. Harris. *Master*, A. A. M. Mays-Smith

OTHER CITY GUILDS
In alphabetical order

ACTUARIES (*91*). *Livery*, 190. *Clerk*, P. D. Esslemont, 16A Cadogan Square, London SW1X 0JU. *Master*, C. R. C. Hawkes

AIR PILOTS AND AIR NAVIGATORS, GUILD OF (*81*). *Livery*, 416. *Grand Master*, HRH The Prince Philip, Duke of Edinburgh, KG, KT, OM, GBE, PC. *Clerk*, Gp Capt. W. M. Watkins, OBE, Cobham House, 291 Gray's Inn Road, London WC1X 8QF. *Master*, R. W. Bridge

APOTHECARIES, SOCIETY OF (*58*). *Hall*, 14 Black Friars Lane, London EC4V 6EJ. *Livery*, 1,250. *Clerk*, Lt.-Col. R. J. Stringer. *Master*, M. A. Pugh

ARBITRATORS (*93*). *Livery*, 224. *Clerk*, Lt.-Col. I. R. P. Green, 2 Bolts Hill, Castle Camps, Cambs CB1 6TL. *Master*, I. W. Menzies

ARMOURERS AND BRASIERS (*22*). *Hall*, 81 Coleman Street, London EC2R 5BJ. *Livery*, 122. *Clerk*, Cdr. T. J. K. Sloane, OBE. *Master*, P. J. Fenton, FRCS

BAKERS (*19*). *Hall*, Harp Lane, London EC3R 6DP. *Livery*, 390. *Clerk*, J. W. Tompkins. *Master*, C. Gilford

BARBERS (*17*). *Hall*, Monkwell Square, Wood Street, London EC2Y 5BL. *Livery*, 200. *Clerk*, Brig. A. F. Eastburn. *Master*, A. J. B. Missen, MD, FRCS

BASKETMAKERS (*52*). *Livery*, 335. *Clerk*, Maj. G. J. Flint-Shipman, TD, 48 Seymour Walk, London SW10 9NF. *Prime Warden*, D. W. Imrie-Brown, OBE

BLACKSMITHS (*40*). *Livery*, 237. *Clerk*, R. C. Jorden, 27 Cheyne Walk, Grange Park, London N21 1DB. *Prime Warden*, T. S. Herring

BOWYERS (*38*). *Livery*, 110. *Clerk*, J. R. Owen-Ward, 261 Green Lanes, London N13 4XE. *Master*, P. J. Begent

BREWERS (*14*). *Hall*, Aldermanbury Square, London EC2V 7HR. *Livery*, 115. *Clerk*, C. W. Dallmeyer. *Master*, S. H. Wingfield Digby

BRODERERS (*48*). *Livery*, 161. *Clerk*, P. J. C. Crouch, 11 Bridge Road, East Molesey, Surrey KT8 9EU. *Master*, S. G. Errington, CBE

BUILDERS MERCHANTS (*88*). *Livery*, 180. *Clerk*, Miss S. M. Robinson, TD, 4 College Hill, London EC2R 2RA. *Master*, J. Hauxwell

BUTCHERS (*24*). *Hall*, 87 Bartholomew Close, London EC1A 7EB. *Livery*, 650. *Clerk*, G. Sharp. *Master*, G. C. Adams

CARMEN (*77*). *Livery*, 440. *Clerk*, Cdr. R. M. H. Bawtree, OBE, 35–37 Ludgate Hill, London EC4M 7JN. *Master*, J. E. Ratcliff

CARPENTERS (*26*). *Hall*, 1 Throgmorton Avenue, London EC2N 2JJ. *Livery*, 150. *Clerk*, Maj.-Gen. P. T. Stevenson, OBE. *Master*, H. M. Neal, CBE

CHARTERED ACCOUNTANTS (*86*). *Livery*, 340. *Clerk*, C. Bygrave, The Rustlings, Valley Close, Studham, Dunstable, Beds LU6 2QN. *Master*, G. H. Kingsmill

CHARTERED ARCHITECTS (*98*). *Livery*, 105. *Clerk*, J. Griffiths, 28 Palace Road, East Molesey, Surrey KT8 9DL. *Master*, J. R. Richardson

CHARTERED SECRETARIES AND ADMINISTRATORS (*87*). *Livery*, 210. *Hon. Clerk*, W. C. Hammond, MBE, Saddlers' Hall, 3rd Floor, 40 Gutter Lane, London EC2V 6BR. *Master*, Rear-Adm. J. Carine

CHARTERED SURVEYORS (*85*). *Livery*, 350. *Clerk*, Mrs A. L. Jackson, 16 St Mary-at-Hill, London EC3R 8EE. *Master*, R. S. Broadhurst

CLOCKMAKERS (*61*). *Livery*, 235. *Clerk*, Gp Capt P. H. Gibson, MBE, Room 66–67 Albert Buildings, 49 Queen Victoria Street, London EC4N 4SE. *Master*, M. B. Savory

COACHMAKERS AND COACH-HARNESS MAKERS (*72*). *Livery*, 400. *Clerk*, Gp Capt. G. Bunn, CBE, Charlcote

House, Burfield Road, Chorleywood, Herts WD3 5NS. *Master*, R. G. Croall

CONSTRUCTORS (*99*). *Livery*, 116. *Clerk*, L. L. Brace, 181 Fentiman Road, London SW8 1JY. *Master*, R. V. Wharton

COOKS (*35*). *Livery*, 75. *Clerk*, M. C. Thatcher, 35 Great Peter Street, London SW1P 3LR. *Master*, J. G. V. Price

COOPERS (*36*). *Hall*, 13 Devonshire Square, London EC2M 4TH. *Livery*, 260. *Clerk*, J. A. Newton. *Master*, D. L. Jones

CORDWAINERS (*27*). *Livery* 154. *Clerk*, Lt.-Col. J. R. Blundell, RM, Eldon Chambers, 30 Fleet Street, London EC4Y 1AA. *Master*, R. P. B. Skinner

CURRIERS (*29*). *Livery*, 95. *Clerk*, Gp Capt F. J. Hamilton, Kestrel Cottage, East Knoyle, Salisbury SP3 6AD. *Master*, C. S. Heaps

CUTLERS (*18*). *Hall*, Warwick Lane, London EC4M 7BR. *Livery*, 100. *Clerk*, K. S. G. Hinde, TD. *Master*, C. J. Osborn-Jones

DISTILLERS (*69*). *Livery*, 300. *Clerk*, C. V. Hughes, 71 Lincoln's Inn Fields, London WC2A 3JF. *Master*, C. Mitchell

DYERS (*13*). *Hall*, 10 Dowgate Hill, London EC4R 2ST. *Livery*, 117. *Clerk*, J. R. Chambers. *Prime Warden*, J. R. Vaizey

ENGINEERS (*94*). *Livery*, 280. *Clerk*, Cdr. B. D. Gibson, Kiln Bank, Bodle Street Green, Hailsham, E. Sussex BN27 4UA. *Master*, Dr J. C. Smith, CBE, FEng., FRSE

ENVIRONMENTAL CLEANERS (*97*). *Livery*, 220. *Clerk*, S. J. Holt, Whitethorns, Rannoch Road, Crowborough, E. Sussex TN6 1RA. *Master*, T. D. King

FAN MAKERS (*76*). *Livery*, 202. *Clerk*, Lt.-Col. I. R. P. Green, 2 Bolts Hill, Castle Camps, Cambs CB1 6TL. *Master*, N. G. Crispin

FARMERS (*80*). *Hall*, 3 Cloth Street, London EC1A 7LD. *Livery*, 300. *Clerk*, Miss M. L. Winter. *Master*, The Hon. Sir Richard Butler

FARRIERS (*55*). *Livery*, 350. *Clerk*, H. W. H. Ellis, 37 The Uplands, Loughton, Essex IG10 1NQ. *Master*, Mrs D. H. Pagan

FELTMAKERS (*63*). *Livery*, 170. *Clerk*, Lt.-Col. C. J. Holroyd, Providence Cottage, Chute Cadley, Andover, Hants SP11 9EB. *Master*, P. A. Grant

FLETCHERS (*39*). *Hall*, 3 Cloth Street, London EC1A 7LD. *Livery*, 110. *Clerk*, J. R. Owen-Ward. *Master*, A. P. W. MacLellan, CB, CVO, MBE

FOUNDERS (*33*). *Hall*, 1 Cloth Fair, London EC1A 7HT. *Livery*, 170. *Clerk*, A. J. Gillett. *Master*, W. G. Fossick

FRAMEWORK KNITTERS (*64*). *Livery*, 208. *Clerk*, H. W. H. Ellis, Whitegarth Chambers, 37 The Uplands, Loughton, Essex IG10 1NQ. *Master*, R. B. Osborne

FRUITERERS (*45*). *Livery*, 250. *Clerk*, Lt.-Col. L. G. French, Chapelstones, 84 High Street, Codford St Mary, Warminster, Wilts BA12 0ND. *Master*, D. Tullett, CBE

FUELLERS (*95*). *Livery*, 60. *Clerk*, S. J. Lee, Fords, 134 Ockford Road, Godalming, Surrey GU7 1RG. *Master*, C. J. MacLeod

FURNITURE MAKERS (*83*). *Livery*, 229. *Clerk*, Mrs J. A. Wright, 9 Little Trinity Lane, London EC4V 2AD. *Master*, C. E. F. Brett

GARDENERS (*66*). *Livery*, 250. *Clerk*, Col. N. G. S. Gray, 25 Luke Street, London EC2A 4AR. *Master*, R. P. Franklin

GIRDLERS (*23*). *Hall*, Basinghall Avenue, London EC2V 5DD. *Livery*, 80. *Clerk*, Lt.-Col. R. Sullivan. *Master*, D. R. L. James

GLASS-SELLERS (*71*). *Livery*, 165. *Hon. Clerk*, B. J. Rawles, 43 Aragon Avenue, Thames Ditton, Surrey KT7 0PY. *Master*, J. R. Hitch

GLAZIERS AND PAINTERS OF GLASS (*53*). *Hall*, 9 Montague Close, London SE1 9DD. *Livery*, 275. *Clerk*, P. R. Batchelor. *Master*, G. C. Bond

GLOVERS (62). *Livery*, 280. *Clerk*, Mrs M. Hood, 71 Ifield Road, London SW10 9AU. *Master*, M. Silverman

GOLD AND SILVER WYRE DRAWERS (74). *Livery*, 320. *Clerk*, J. R. Williams, 50 Cheyne Avenue, London E18 2DR. *Master*, P. H. E. Padley-Smith

GUNMAKERS (73). *Livery*, 275. *Clerk*, J. M. Riches, The Proof House, 48–50 Commercial Road, London E1 1LP. *Master*, R. T. Gallyon

HORNERS (54). *Livery*, 260. *Clerk*, S. J. Holt, Whitethorns, Rannoch Road, Crowborough, E. Sussex TN6 1RA. *Master*, C. K. Howe

INFORMATION TECHNOLOGISTS (100). *Livery*, 260. *Clerk*, Mrs G. Davies, 30 Aylesbury Street, London EC1R 0ER. *Master*, D. W. Mann

INNHOLDERS (32). *Hall*, College Street, London EC4R 2RH. *Livery*, 138. *Clerk*, J. R. Edwardes Jones. *Master*, C. H. G. Brann

INSURERS (92). *Hall*, 20 Aldermanbury, London EC2V 7HY. *Livery*, 383. *Clerk*, L. J. Walters. *Master*, J. E. Phillips

JOINERS AND CEILERS (41). *Livery*, 130. *Clerk*, Mrs A. L. Jackson, 75 Meadway Drive, Horsell, Woking, Surrey GU21 4TF. *Master*, C. Capel

LAUNDERERS (89). *Hall*, 9 Montague Close, London SE1 9DD. *Livery*, 225. *Clerk*, Mrs J. Polek. *Master*, R. C. L. Orford

LEATHERSELLERS (15). *Hall*, 15 St Helen's Place, London EC3A 6DQ. *Livery*, 150. *Clerk*, Capt. J. G. F. Cooke, OBE, RN. *Master*, B. D. Carter

LIGHTMONGERS (96). *Livery*, 132. *Clerk*, D. B. Wheatley, Crown Wharf, 11A Coldharbour, Blackwall Reach, London E14 9NS. *Master*, D. Rowden

LORINERS (57). *Livery*, 440. *Clerk*, J. R. Williams, 50 Cheyne Avenue, London E18 2DR. *Master*, G. B. Forbes

MAKERS OF PLAYING CARDS (75). *Livery*, 149. *Clerk*, M. J. Smyth, 6 The Priory, Godstone, Surrey RH9 8NL. *Master*, P. D. Crabbe

MARKETORS (90). *Livery*, 231. *Clerk*, Mrs G. Duffy, 4 College Hill, London EC4R 2RA. *Master*, D. Thomas

MASONS (30). *Livery*, 125. *Clerk*, T. F. Ackland, 261 Green Lanes, London N13 4XE. *Master*, P. A. Copland

MASTER MARINERS, HONOURABLE COMPANY OF (78). HQS *Wellington*, Temple Stairs, Victoria Embankment, London WC2R 2PN. *Livery*, 220. *Clerk*, J. A. V. Maddock. *Admiral*, HRH The Prince Philip, Duke of Edinburgh, KG, KT, OM, GBE, PC. *Master*, Capt. R. Clucas

MUSICIANS (50). *Livery*, 332. *Clerk*, S. F. N. Waley, 75 Watling Street, London EC4M 9BJ. *Master*, F. N. Fowler

NEEDLEMAKERS (65). *Livery*, 240. *Clerk*, M. G. Cook, 5 Staple Inn, London WC1V 7QH. *Master*, D. A. Culling

PAINTER-STAINERS (28). *Hall*, 9 Little Trinity Lane, London EC4V 2AD. *Livery*, 320. *Clerk*, Col. W. J. Chesshyre. *Master*, G. F. Jacobs

PATTENMAKERS (70). *Livery*, 167. *Clerk*, C. L. K. Ledger, 17 Orchard Close, The Rutts, Bushey Heath, Herts WD2 1LW. *Master*, I. Scarr Hall

PAVIORS (56). *Livery*, 245. *Clerk*, R. F. Coe, 154 Dukes Avenue, New Malden, Surrey KT3 4HR. *Master*, J. W. A. Clugston

PEWTERERS (16). *Hall*, Oat Lane, London EC2V 7DE. *Livery*, 116. *Clerk*, Cdr. A. St John Steiner, OBE. *Master*, Dr G. M. Pearl

PLAISTERERS (46). *Hall*, 1 London Wall, London EC4Y 5JU. *Livery*, 208. *Clerk*, R. Vickers. *Master*, R. Faulkner

PLUMBERS (31). *Livery*, 350. *Clerk*, Lt.-Col. R. J. A. Paterson-Fox, 49 Queen Victoria Street, London EC4N 4SA. *Master*, P. Brunner

POULTERS (34). *Livery*, 173. *Clerk*, A. W. Scott, 23 Orchard Drive, Chorleywood, Herts WD3 5QN. *Master*, T. G. Harris

SADDLERS (25). *Hall*, 40 Gutter Lane, London EC2V 6BR. *Livery*, 70. *Clerk*, Gp Capt W. S. Brereton Martin, CBE. *Master*, E. J. Pearson

SCIENTIFIC INSTRUMENT MAKERS (84). *Hall*, 9 Montague Close, London SE1 9DD. *Livery*, 237. *Clerk*, F. G. Everard. *Master*, Sir Ivor Cohen, CBE, TD

SCRIVENERS (44). *Livery*, 215. *Clerk*, P. C. Stevens, HQS *Wellington*, Temple Stairs, Victoria Embankment, London WC2R 2PN. *Master*, D. Jackson

SHIPWRIGHTS (59). *Livery*, 396. *Clerk*, Capt. R. F. Channon, RN, Ironmongers' Hall, Barbican, London EC2Y 8AA. *Permanent Master*, HRH The Prince Philip, Duke of Edinburgh, KG, KT, OM, GBE, PC. *Prime Warden*, J Freeland

SOLICITORS (79). *Livery*, 394. *Clerk*, Miss S. M. Robinson, TD, 14 Charterhouse Square, London EC1M 6AX. *Master*, Dr J. Avery Jones, CBE

SPECTACLE MAKERS (60). *Livery*, 293. *Clerk*, C. J. Eldridge, Apothecaries' Hall, Black Friars Lane, London EC4V 6EL. *Master*, P. Mills

STATIONERS AND NEWSPAPER MAKERS (47). *Hall*, Ave Maria Lane, London EC4M 7DD. *Livery*, 458. *Clerk*, Brig. D. G. Sharp. *Master*, C. H. Martin, OBE, TD

TALLOW CHANDLERS (21). *Hall*, 4 Dowgate Hill, London EC4R 2SH. *Livery*, 180. *Clerk*, Brig. W. K. L. Prosser, CBE, MC. *Master*, J. B. N. Kurkjian

TIN PLATE WORKERS alias WIRE WORKERS (67). *Livery*, 180. *Clerk*, S. J. Holt, Whitethorns, Rannoch Road, Crowborough, E. Sussex TN6 1RA. *Master*, H. G. Mutkin

TOBACCO PIPE MAKERS AND TOBACCO BLENDERS (82). *Livery*, 161. *Clerk*, N. J. Hallings-Pott, Hackhurst Farm, Lower Dicker, Hailsham, E. Sussex BN27 4BP. *Master*, R. Vanderpump

TURNERS (51). *Livery*, 159. *Clerk*, Maj.-Gen. D. Shaw, CB, CBE, c/o Apothecaries' Hall, Black Friars Lane, London EC4V 6EL. *Master*, P. F. Worlidge

TYLERS AND BRICKLAYERS (37). *Livery*, 125. *Clerk*, J. Griffiths, 28 Palace Road, East Molesey, Surrey KT8 9DL. *Master*, G. E. N. Mason Elliott, TD

UPHOLDERS (49). *Livery*, 200. *Clerk*, G. J. K. Darby, Kirstone, Beckenham Place Park, Beckenham, Kent BR3 2BN. *Master*, D. S. Austin

WAX CHANDLERS (20). *Hall*, Gresham Street, London EC2V 7AD. *Livery*, 95. *Clerk*, Cdr J. Stevens. *Master*, M. Harvey

WEAVERS (42). *Livery*, 127. *Clerk*, Mrs F. Newcombe, Saddlers' House, Gutter Lane, London EC2V 6BR. *Upper Bailiff*, N. R. Winterton, MP

WHEELWRIGHTS (68). *Livery*, 243. *Clerk*, P. J. C. Crouch, 11 Bridge Road, East Molesey, Surrey KT8 9EU. *Master*, W. N. Bolt

WOOLMEN (43). *Livery*, 130. *Clerk*, F. Allen, Hollands, Hedsor Road, Bourne End, Bucks SL8 5EC. *Master*, R. S. Johnson

FIREFIGHTERS (*No livery*), *Freemen*, 110 *Clerk*, G. P. Ellis, 20 Aldermanbury, London EC2V 7GF. *Master*, F. David

PARISH CLERKS (*No livery*). *Members*, 90. *Clerk*, B. J. N. Coombes, 1 Dean Trench Street, London SW1P 3HB. *Master*, O. W. H. Clark, CBE

WATER CONSERVATORS (*No livery*). *Hall*, 16 St Mary-at-Hill, London EC2R 8EE. *Freemen*, 180. *Hon. Clerk*, H. B. Berridge, MBE. *Master*, B. A. O. Hewett

WATERMEN AND LIGHTERMEN (*No livery*). *Hall*, 16 St Mary-at-Hill, London EC3R 8EE. *Craft Owning Freemen*, 369. *Clerk*, C. Middlemas. *Master*, J. Jenkinson

WORLD TRADERS (*No livery*). *Freemen*, 116. *Clerk*, J. T. Norman, 13 Pinewood Road, Branksome Park, Poole, Dorset BH13 6JP. *Master*, D. Watt

LONDON BOROUGH COUNCILS

Council	Municipal offices	Population 1995	Band D charge 1997	Chief Executive (*Managing Director)	Mayor (a) Lord Mayor 1997–8
Barking and Dagenham	°Dagenham, RM10 7BN	154,800	£635.00	W. C. Smith	J. P. Wainwright
Barnet	†The Burroughs, Hendon, NW4 4BG	312,400	665.14	M. Caller	Ms A. Slocombe
Bexley	‡Bexleyheath, Kent DA6 7LB	220,300	623.80	C. Duffield	Ms R. Sams
Brent	†Forty Lane, Wembley, HA9 9EZ	245,300	553.70	G. Benham	M. Cummins
Bromley	°Bromley, BRI 3UH	293,400	580.50	M. Blanch	Mrs I. Buckley
§Camden	†Judd Street, WC1H 9JE	184,900	799.95	S. Bundred	R. Adamson
§CITY OF WESTMINSTER	City Hall, Victoria Street, SW1E 6QP	195,300	304.00	W. Roots	(a) R. Raymond-Cox
Croydon	Taberner House, Park Lane, Croydon, CR9 3JS	330,900	624.70	D. Wechsler	T. Letts
Ealing	†Uxbridge Road, W5 2HL	292,100	585.00	Ms G. Guy	Ms J. Clements-Elliott
Enfield	°Enfield, EN1 3XA	261,300	637.88	D. Plank	J. Connew
§Greenwich	†Wellington Street, SE18 6PW	211,400	820.92	D. Brooks (acting)	B. Strong
§Hackney	†Mare Street, E8 1EA	194,200	796.00	T. Elliston	J. Lobenstein, MBE
§Hammersmith and Fulham	†King Street, W6 9JU	156,100	790.00	*N. Newton	V. Barker
Haringey	°Wood Green, N22 4LE	213,300	827.30	G. Singh	D. Basu
Harrow	°Harrow, HA1 2UJ	210,100	668.70	T. Redmond	K. Toms
Havering	†Romford, RM1 3BD	231,000	654.00	H. W. Tinworth	D. Smith
Hillingdon	°Uxbridge, UB8 1UW	245,300	627.41	Ms G. Andrews (acting)	S. Panayi
Hounslow	°Lampton Road, Hounslow, TW3 4DN	204,000	691.01	D. Myers (acting)	P. Dodkins
§Islington	†Upper Street, N1 2UD	174,500	879.00	L. Fullick	R. Perry
§Kensington and Chelsea (RB)	†Hornton Street, W8 7NX	153,900	425.27	A. Taylor	E. Hess
Kingston upon Thames (RB)	Guildhall, Kingston upon Thames, KT1 1EU	140,100	640.45	B. Quoroll	Ms C. Hitchcock
§Lambeth	†Brixton Hill, SW2 1RW	261,700	665.00	Ms H. Rabbatts	N. Cattermole
§Lewisham	†Catford, SE6 4RU	239,700	657.71	Dr B. Quirk	Ms J. Addison
Merton	°London Road, Morden, SM4 5DX	179,200	695.37	Ms S. Charteris	Ms S. Knights
Newham	†East Ham, E6 2RP	228,400	648.00	Dr W. Thomson	V. Turner
Redbridge	†Ilford, IG1 1DD	227,300	581.00	M. Frater	R. Golding
Richmond upon Thames	°Richmond Road, Twickenham, TW1 3AA	175,600	745.00	R. L. Harbord	Ms M. Woodriff
§Southwark	†Peckham Road, SE5 8UB	232,000	747.71	B. Coomber	W. Skelly
Sutton	‡St Nicholas Way, Sutton, SM1 1EA	174,400	633.51	Mrs P. Hughes	Ms M. Woodley
§Tower Hamlets	107A Commercial Street, E1 6BG	172,800	645.91	Ms S. Pierce	J. Ramanoop
Waltham Forest	†Forest Road, Walthamstow, E17 4JF	221,100	826.65	A. Tobias	S. A. Poulson
§Wandsworth	†Wandsworth, SW18 2PU	265,100	419.33	G. Jones	Ms C. Thompson

§ Inner London Borough
RB Royal Borough
° Civic Centre
† Town Hall
‡ Civic Offices
Source of population statistics: ONS Monitor PP1 96/2, 29 August 1996
For explanation of council tax, *see* pages 523–4

Wales

The Principality of Wales (Cymru) occupies the extreme west of the central southern portion of the island of Great Britain, with a total area of 8,015 sq. miles (20,758 sq. km): land 7,965 sq. miles (20,628 sq. km); inland water 50 sq. miles (130 sq. km). It is bounded on the north by the Irish Sea, on the south by the Bristol Channel, on the east by the English counties of Cheshire, Shropshire, Hereford and Worcester, and Gloucestershire, and on the west by St George's Channel.

Across the Menai Straits is the island of Anglesey (Ynys Môn) (276 sq. miles), communication with which is facilitated by the Menai Suspension Bridge (1,000 ft long) built by Telford in 1826, and by the tubular railway bridge (1,100 ft long) built by Stephenson in 1850. Holyhead harbour, on Holy Isle (north-west of Anglesey), provides accommodation for ferry services to Dublin (70 miles).

POPULATION

The population at the 1991 census was 2,811,865 (males 1,356,886; females 1,454,979). The average density of population in 1991 was 1.36 persons per hectare.

RELIEF

Wales is a country of extensive tracts of high plateau and shorter stretches of mountain ranges deeply dissected by river valleys. Lower-lying ground is largely confined to the coastal belt and the lower parts of the valleys. The highest mountains are those of Snowdonia in the north-west (Snowdon, 3,559 ft), Berwyn (Aran Fawddwy, 2,971 ft), Cader Idris (Pen y Gadair, 2,928 ft), Dyfed (Plynlimon, 2,467 ft), and the Black Mountain, Brecon Beacons and Black Forest ranges in the south-east (Carmarthen Van, 2,630 ft, Pen y Fan, 2,906 ft, Waun Fâch, 2,660 ft).

HYDROGRAPHY

The principal river rising in Wales is the Severn (*see also page 333*), which flows from the slopes of Plynlimon to the English border. The Wye (130 miles) also rises in the slopes of Plynlimon. The Usk (56 miles) flows into the Bristol Channel, through Gwent. The Dee (70 miles) rises in Bala Lake and flows through the Vale of Llangollen, where an aqueduct (built by Telford in 1805) carries the Pontcysyllte branch of the Shropshire Union Canal across the valley. The estuary of the Dee is the navigable portion, 14 miles in length and about five miles in breadth, and the tide rushes in with dangerous speed over the 'Sands of Dee'. The Towy (68 miles), Teifi (50 miles), Taff (40 miles), Dovey (30 miles), Taf (25 miles) and Conway (24 miles), the last named broad and navigable, are wholly Welsh rivers.

The largest natural lake is Bala (Llyn Tegid) in Gwynedd, nearly four miles long and about one mile wide. Lake Vyrnwy is an artificial reservoir, about the size of Bala, and forms the water supply of Liverpool; Birmingham is supplied from reservoirs in the Elan and Claerwen valleys.

WELSH LANGUAGE

According to the 1991 census results, the percentage of persons of three years and over able to speak Welsh was:

Clwyd	18.2	Powys	20.2
Dyfed	43.7	S. Glamorgan	6.5
Gwent	2.4	W. Glamorgan	15.0
Gwynedd	61.0		
Mid Glamorgan	8.5	Wales	18.7

The 1991 figure represents a slight decline from 18.9 per cent in 1981 (1971, 20.8 per cent; 1961, 26 per cent).

FLAG

The flag of Wales, the Red Dragon (Y Ddraig Goch), is a red dragon on a field divided white over green (per fess argent and vert a dragon passant gules). The flag was augmented in 1953 by a royal badge on a shield encircled with a riband bearing the words *Ddraig Goch Ddyry Cychwyn* and imperially crowned, but this augmented flag is rarely used.

EARLY HISTORY

The earliest inhabitants of whom there is any record appear to have been subdued or exterminated by the Goidels (a people of Celtic race) in the Bronze Age. A further invasion of Celtic Brythons and Belgae followed in the ensuing Iron Age. The Roman conquest of southern Britain and Wales was for some time successfully opposed by Caratacus (Caractacus or Caradog), chieftain of the Catuvellauni and son of Cunobelinus (Cymbeline). South-east Wales was subjugated and the legionary fortress at Caerleon-on-Usk established by about AD 75–77; the conquest of Wales was completed by Agricola about AD 78. Communications were opened up by the construction of military roads from Chester to Caerleon-on-Usk and Caerwent, and from Chester to Conwy (and thence to Carmarthen and Neath). Christianity was introduced during the Roman occupation, in the fourth century.

ANGLO-SAXON ATTACKS

The Anglo-Saxon invaders of southern Britain drove the Celts into the mountain stronghold of Wales, and into Strathclyde (Cumberland and south-west Scotland) and Cornwall, giving them the name of *Waelisc* (Welsh), meaning 'foreign'. The West Saxons' victory of Deorham (AD 577) isolated Wales from Cornwall and the battle of Chester (AD 613) cut off communication with Strathclyde and northern Britain. In the eighth century the boundaries of the Welsh were further restricted by the annexations of Offa, King of Mercia, and counter-attacks were largely prevented by the construction of an artificial boundary from the Dee to the Wye (Offa's Dyke).

In the ninth century Rhodri Mawr (844–878) united the country and successfully resisted further incursions of the Saxons by land and raids of Norse and Danish pirates by sea, but at his death his three provinces of Gwynedd (north), Powys (mid) and Dcheubarth (south) were divided among his three sons, Anarawd, Mervyn and Cadell. Cadell's son Hywel Dda ruled a large part of Wales and codified its laws but the provinces were not united again until the rule of Llewelyn ap Seisyllt (husband of the heiress of Gwynedd) from 1018 to 1023.

THE NORMAN CONQUEST

After the Norman conquest of England, William I created palatine counties along the Welsh frontier, and the Norman barons began to make encroachments into Welsh territory. The Welsh princes recovered many of their losses during the civil wars of Stephen's reign and in the early 13th century Owen Gruffydd, prince of Gwynedd, was the dominant figure in Wales. Under Llywelyn ap Iorwerth (1194–1240) the Welsh united in powerful resistance to English incursions and Llywelyn's privileges and *de facto* independence were recognized in Magna Carta.

His grandson, Llywelyn ap Gruffydd, was the last native prince; he was killed in 1282 during hostilities between the Welsh and English, allowing Edward I of England to establish his authority over the country. On 7 February 1301, Edward of Caernarvon, son of Edward I, was created Prince of Wales, a title which has subsequently been borne by the eldest son of the sovereign.

Strong Welsh national feeling continued, expressed in the early 15th century in the rising led by Owain Glyndŵr, but the situation was altered by the accession to the English throne in 1485 of Henry VII of the Welsh House of Tudor. Wales was politically assimilated to England under the Act of Union of 1535, which extended English laws to the Principality and gave it parliamentary representation for the first time.

EISTEDDFOD

The Welsh are a distinct nation, with a language and literature of their own, and the national bardic festival (Eisteddfod), instituted by Prince Rhys ap Griffith in 1176, is still held annually (for date, *see* page 12). These *Eisteddfodau* (sessions) form part of the *Gorsedd* (assembly), which is believed to date from the time of Prydian, a ruling prince in an age many centuries before the Christian era.

PRINCIPAL CITIES

CARDIFF

Cardiff, at the mouth of the Rivers Taff, Rhymney and Ely, is the capital city of Wales and a major administrative, commercial and business centre. It has many industries, including steel and cigars, and its flourishing port is within the Cardiff Bay area, subject of a major redevelopment until the year 2000.

The many fine buildings include the City Hall, the National Museum of Wales, University Buildings, Law Courts, Welsh Office, County Hall, Police Headquarters, the Temple of Peace and Health, Llandaff Cathedral, the Welsh National Folk Museum at St Fagans, Cardiff Castle, the New Theatre, the Sherman Theatre and the Welsh College of Music and Drama. More recent buildings include St David's Hall, Cardiff International Arena and World Trade Centre, and the Welsh National Ice Rink. The Millennium Stadium is to be completed for the 1999 rugby World Cup.

SWANSEA

Swansea (*Abertawe*) is a city and a seaport. The Gower peninsula was brought within the city boundary under local government reform in 1974. The trade of the port includes coal, steel products, containerized goods and the import and export of petroleum products and petrochemicals.

The principal buildings are the Norman Castle (rebuilt *c*.1330), the Royal Institution of South Wales, founded in 1835 (including Library), the University College at Singleton, and the Guildhall, containing the Brangwyn panels. More recent buildings include the Industrial and Maritime Museum, the new Maritime Quarter and Marina and the leisure centre.

Swansea was chartered by the Earl of Warwick, *c*.1158–84, and further charters were granted by King John, Henry III, Edward II, Edward III and James II, Cromwell (two) and the Marcher Lord William de Breos.

LOCAL COUNCILS

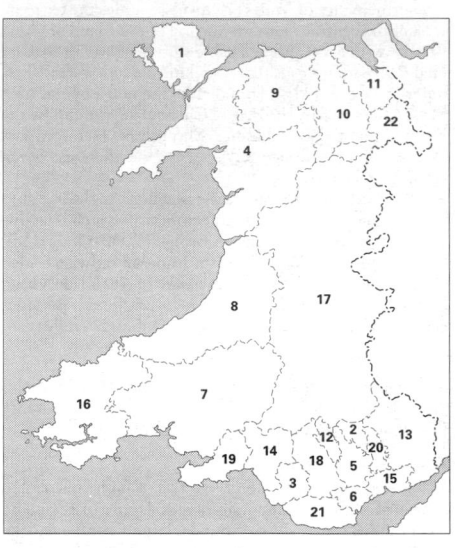

Key	County
1	Anglesey
2	Blaenau Gwent
3	Bridgend
4	Gwynedd
5	Caerphilly
6	Cardiff
7	Carmarthenshire
8	Ceredigion
9	Conwy
10	Denbighshire
11	Flintshire
12	Merthyr Tydfil
13	Monmouthshire
14	Neath and Port Talbot
15	Newport
16	Pembrokeshire
17	Powys
18	Rhondda, Cynon, Taff
19	Swansea
20	Torfaen
21	The Vale of Glamorgan
22	Wrexham

LORD-LIEUTENANTS AND HIGH SHERIFFS

County	Lord-Lieutenant	High Sheriff, 1997–8
Clwyd	Sir William Gladstone, Bt.	Col. Sir Charles Lowther, Bt.
Dyfed	Sir David Mansel Lewis, KCVO	Cdr. H. C. Lloyd-Williams
Gwent	Sir Richard Hanbury Tenison, KCVO	A. M. Kerr
Gwynedd	R. E. Meuric Rees, CBE	Mrs E. W. Jones
Mid Glamorgan	M. A. McLaggan	R. W. Martin
Powys	M. L. Bourdillon	The Hon. Mrs Rosalind H. P. Price, CBE
South Glamorgan	Capt. N. Lloyd-Edwards	J. W. Phillips, CBE
West Glamorgan	R. C. Hastie, CBE	P. J. Hodges

LOCAL COUNCILS

SMALL CAPITALS denote CITY status
§ Denotes Borough status

Council	Administrative headquarters	Population 1995	Band D charge 1997	Chief Executive	Chairman 1997–8 (a) Mayor (b) Lord Mayor
Anglesey	Llangefni	67,200	£307.79	L. Gibson	G. Roberts
§Blaenau Gwent	Ebbw Vale	73,200	430.39	R. Leadbetter, OBE	(a) C. Jones
§Bridgend	Bridgend	130,700	539.52	I. K. Lewis	(a) G. Walters
§Caerphilly	Hengoed	169,900	505.04	M. Davies	(a) Ms C. Sadler
CARDIFF	Cardiff	309,400	484.45	B. Davies	(b) M. J. Phillips
Carmarthenshire	Carmarthen	169,500	535.00	B. Roynon	H. Jones
Ceredigion	Aberaeron	70,200	584.45	O. Watkin	T. A. Thomas
§Conwy	Conwy	111,200	402.71	C. D. Barker	W. R. Jones
Denbighshire	Ruthin	91,600	528.00	H. V. Thomas	E. Williams
Flintshire	Mold	145,700	510.78	P. McGreevy	H. Clarke
Gwynedd	Caernarfon	118,000	513.07	G R. Jones	Mrs P. G. Larsen
§Merthyr Tydfil	Merthyr Tydfil	58,700	584.95	G. Meredith	(a) T. C. Lewis
Monmouthshire	Cwmbran	85,600	387.59	Ms J. Redfearn	J. G. Nelmes
§Neath and Port Talbot	Port Talbot	139,600	600.78	K. R. Sawyers	(a) T. D. M. John
§Newport	Newport	137,200	410.78	R. D. Blair	(a) R. Bright
Pembrokeshire	Haverfordwest	113,500	378.95	B. Parry-Jones	P. Stock
Powys	Llandrindod Wells	122,300	426.28	N. M. Pringle	E. T. Morgan
§Rhondda, Cynon, Taff	Tonypandy	239,900	544.00	G. R. Thomas	(a) Mrs K. Rees
SWANSEA	Swansea	230,600	472.10	Ms V. Sugar	(b) G. Williams
§Torfaen	Pontypool	90,400	478.70	Dr C. Grace	(a) S. J. Brooks
§Vale of Glamorgan	Barry	118,800	447.35	D. Foster	F. Johnson
§Wrexham	Wrexham	123,400	520.00	D. Griffin	(a) D. Broderick

For explanation of council tax, *see* pages 523–4
Source of 1995 population figures: ONS Monitor PP1 96/3, 17 September 1996

Scotland

The Kingdom of Scotland occupies the northern portion of the main island of Great Britain and includes the Inner and Outer Hebrides, and the Orkney, Shetland, and many other islands. It lies between 60° 51′ 30″ and 54° 38′ N. latitude and between 1° 45′ 32″ and 6° 14′ W. longitude, with England to the south, the Atlantic Ocean on the north and west, and the North Sea on the east.

The greatest length of the mainland (Cape Wrath to the Mull of Galloway) is 274 miles, and the greatest breadth (Buchan Ness to Applecross) is 154 miles. The customary measurement of the island of Great Britain is from the site of John o' Groats house, near Duncansby Head, Caithness, to Land's End, Cornwall, a total distance of 603 miles in a straight line and approximately 900 miles by road.

The total area of Scotland is 30,420 sq. miles (78,789 sq. km); land 29,767 sq. miles (77,097 sq. km), inland water 653 sq. miles (1,692 sq. km).

POPULATION

The population at the 1991 census was 4,998,567 (males 2,391,961; females 2,606,606). The average density of the population in 1991 was 0.65 persons per hectare.

RELIEF

There are three natural orographic divisions of Scotland. The southern uplands have their highest points in Merrick (2,766 ft), Rhinns of Kells (2,669 ft), and Cairnsmuir of Carsphairn (2,614 ft), in the west; and the Tweedsmuir Hills in the east (Hartfell 2,651 ft, Dollar Law 2,682 ft, Broad Law 2,756 ft).

The central lowlands, formed by the valleys of the Clyde, Forth and Tay, divide the southern uplands from the northern Highlands, which extend almost from the extreme north of the mainland to the central lowlands, and are divided into a northern and a southern system by the Great Glen.

The Grampian Mountains, which entirely cover the southern Highland area, include in the west Ben Nevis (4,406 ft), the highest point in the British Isles, and in the east the Cairngorm Mountains (Cairn Gorm 4,084 ft, Braeriach 4,248 ft, Ben Macdui 4,296 ft). The north-western Highland area contains the mountains of Wester and Easter Ross (Carn Eige 3,880 ft, Sgurr na Lapaich 3,775 ft).

Created, like the central lowlands, by a major geological fault, the Great Glen (60 miles long) runs between Inverness and Fort William, and contains Loch Ness, Loch Oich and Loch Lochy. These are linked to each other and to the north-east and south-west coasts of Scotland by the Caledonian Canal, providing a navigable passage between the Moray Firth and the Inner Hebrides.

HYDROGRAPHY

The western coast is fragmented by peninsulas and islands, and indented by fjords (sea-lochs), the longest of which is Loch Fyne (42 miles long) in Argyll. Although the east coast tends to be less fractured and lower, there are several great drowned inlets (firths), e.g. Firth of Forth, Firth of Tay, Moray Firth, as well as the Firth of Clyde in the west.

The lochs are the principal hydrographic feature. The largest in Scotland and in Britain is Loch Lomond (27 sq. miles), in the Grampian valleys; the longest and deepest is Loch Ness (24 miles long and 800 feet deep), in the Great Glen; and Loch Shin (20 miles long) and Loch Maree in the Highlands.

The longest river is the Tay (117 miles), noted for its salmon. It flows into the North Sea, with Dundee on the estuary, which is spanned by the Tay Bridge (10,289 ft) opened in 1887 and the Tay Road Bridge (7,365 ft) opened in 1966. Other noted salmon rivers are the Dee (90 miles) which flows into the North Sea at Aberdeen, and the Spey (110 miles), the swiftest flowing river in the British Isles, which flows into Moray Firth. The Tweed, which gave its name to the woollen cloth produced along its banks, marks in the lower stretches of its 96-mile course the border between Scotland and England.

The most important river commercially is the Clyde (106 miles), formed by the junction of the Daer and Portrail water, which flows through the city of Glasgow to the Firth of Clyde. During its course it passes over the picturesque Falls of Clyde, Bonnington Linn (30 ft), Corra Linn (84 ft), Dundaff Linn (10 ft) and Stonebyres Linn (80 ft), above and below Lanark. The Forth (66 miles), upon which stands Edinburgh, the capital, is spanned by the Forth (Railway) Bridge (1890), which is 5,330 feet long, and the Forth (Road) Bridge (1964), which has a total length of 6,156 feet (over water) and a single span of 3,000 feet.

The highest waterfall in Scotland, and the British Isles, is Eas a'Chùal Aluinn with a total height of 658 feet (200 m), which falls from Glas Bheinn in Sutherland. The Falls of Glomach, on a head-stream of the Elchaig in Wester Ross, have a drop of 370 feet.

GAELIC LANGUAGE

According to the 1991 census, 1.4 per cent of the population of Scotland, mainly in the Highlands and western coastal regions, were able to speak the Scottish form of Gaelic.

FLAG

The flag of Scotland is known as the Saltire. It is a white diagonal cross on a blue field (saltire argent in a field azure) and represents St Andrew, the patron saint of Scotland.

THE SCOTTISH ISLANDS

ORKNEY

The Orkney Islands (total area 375½ sq. miles) lie about six miles north of the mainland, separated from it by the Pentland Firth. Of the 90 islands and islets (holms and skerries) in the group, about one-third are inhabited.

The total population at the 1991 census was 19,612; the 1991 populations of the islands shown here include those of smaller islands forming part of the same civil parish.

Mainland, 15,128	Rousay, 291
Burray, 363	Sanday, 533
Eday, 166	Shapinsay, 322
Flotta and Fara, 126	South Ronaldsay, 943
Graemsay and Hoy, 477	Stronsay, 382
North Ronaldsay, 92	Westray, 704
Papa Westray, 85	

The islands are rich in prehistoric and Scandinavian remains, the most notable being the Stone Age village of Skara Brae, the burial chamber of Maeshowe, the many brochs (towers) and the 12th-century St Magnus Cathedral. Scapa Flow, between the Mainland and Hoy, was the war station of the British Grand Fleet from 1914 to 1919 and the scene of the scuttling of the surrendered German High Seas Fleet (21 June 1919).

Most of the islands are low-lying and fertile, and farming (principally beef cattle) is the main industry. Flotta, to the south of Scapa Flow, is the site of the oil terminal for the Piper, Claymore and Tartan fields in the North Sea.

The capital is Kirkwall (population 6,881) on Mainland.

SHETLAND

The Shetland Islands have a total area of 551 sq. miles and a population at the 1991 census of 22,522. They lie about 50 miles north of the Orkneys, with Fair Isle about half-way between the two groups. Out Stack, off Muckle Flugga, one mile north of Unst, is the most northerly part of the British Isles (60° 51′ 30″ N. lat.).

There are over 100 islands, of which 16 are inhabited. Populations at the 1991 census were:

Mainland, 17,596	Muckle Roe, 115
Bressay, 352	Trondra, 117
East Burra, 72	Unst, 1,055
Fair Isle, 67	West Burra, 857
Fetlar, 90	Whalsay, 1,041
Housay, 85	Yell, 1,075

Shetland's many archaeological sites include Jarlshof, Mousa and Clickhimin, and its long connection with Scandinavia has resulted in a strong Norse influence on its place-names and dialect.

Industries include fishing, knitwear and farming. In addition to the fishing fleet there are fish processing factories, while the traditional handknitting of Fair Isle and Unst is supplemented now with machine-knitted garments. Farming is mainly crofting, with sheep being raised on the moorland and hills of the islands. Latterly the islands have become a centre of the North Sea oil industry, with pipelines from the Brent and Ninian fields running to the terminal at Sullom Voe, the largest of its kind in Europe. Lerwick is the main centre for supply services for offshore oil exploration and development.

The capital is Lerwick (population 7,901) on Mainland.

THE HEBRIDES

Until the late 13th century the Hebrides included other Scottish islands in the Firth of Clyde, the peninsula of Kintyre (Argyll), the Isle of Man, and the (Irish) Isle of Rathlin. The origin of the name is stated to be the Greek *Eboudai*, latinized as *Hebudes* by Pliny, and corrupted to its present form. The Norwegian name *Sudreyjar* (Southern Islands) was latinized as *Sodorenses*, a name that survives in the Anglican bishopric of Sodor and Man.

There are over 500 islands and islets, of which about 100 are inhabited, though mountainous terrain and extensive peat bogs mean that only a fraction of the total area is under cultivation. Stone, Bronze and Iron Age settlement has left many remains, including those at Callanish on Lewis, and Norse colonization influenced language, customs and place-names. Occupations include farming (mostly crofting and stock-raising), fishing and the manufacture of tweeds and other woollens. Tourism is also an important factor in the economy.

The Inner Hebrides lie off the west coast of Scotland and relatively close to the mainland. The largest and best-known is Skye (area 643 sq. miles; pop. 8,868; chief town, Portree), which contains the Cuillin Hills (Sgurr Alasdair 3,257 ft), the Red Hills (Beinn na Caillich 2,403 ft), Bla Bheinn (3,046 ft) and The Storr (2,358 ft). Skye is also famous as the refuge of the Young Pretender in 1746. Other islands in the Highland council area include Raasay (pop. 163), Rum, Eigg and Muck.

Further south the Inner Hebridean islands include Arran (pop. 4,474) containing Goat Fell (2,868 ft); Coll and Tiree (pop. 940); Colonsay and Oronsay (pop. 106); Islay (area 235 sq. miles, pop. 3,538); Jura (area 160 sq miles; pop. 196) with a range of hills culminating in the

Paps of Jura (Beinn-an-Oir, 2,576 ft, and Beinn Chaolais, 2,477 ft); and Mull (area 367 sq. miles; pop. 2,708; chief town Tobermory) containing Ben More (3,171 ft).

The Outer Hebrides, separated from the mainland by the Minch, now form the Western Isles Islands Council area (area 1,119 sq. miles; population at the 1991 census 29,600). The main islands are Lewis with Harris (area 770 sq. miles, pop. 21,737), whose chief town, Stornoway, is the administrative headquarters; North Uist (pop. 1,404); South Uist (pop. 2,106); Baleshare (55); Benbecula (pop. 1,803) and Barra (pop. 1,244). Other inhabited islands include Bernera (262), Berneray (141), Eriskay (179), Grimsay (215), Scalpay (382) and Vatersay (72).

EARLY HISTORY

There is evidence of human settlement in Scotland dating from the third millennium BC, the earliest settlers being Middle Stone Age hunters and fishermen. Early in the second millennium BC, New Stone Age farmers began to cultivate crops and rear livestock; their settlements were on the west coast and in the north, and included Skara Brae and Maeshowe (Orkney). Settlement by the Early Bronze Age 'Beaker folk', so-called from the shape of their drinking vessels, in eastern Scotland dates from about 1800 BC. Further settlement is believed to have occurred from 700 BC onwards, as tribes were displaced from further south by new incursions from the Continent and the Roman invasions from AD 43.

Julius Agricola, the Roman governor of Britain AD 77–84, extended the Roman conquests in Britain by advancing into Caledonia, culminating with a victory at Mons Graupius, probably in AD 84; he was recalled to Rome shortly afterwards and his forward policy was not pursued. Hadrian's Wall, mostly completed by AD 30, marked the northern frontier of the Roman empire except for the period between about AD 144 and 190 when the frontier moved north to the Forth–Clyde isthmus and a turf wall, the Antonine Wall, was manned.

After the Roman withdrawal from Britain, there were centuries of warfare between the Picts, Scots, Britons, Angles and Vikings. The Picts, believed to be a non-Indo-European race, occupied the area north of the Forth. The Scots, a Gaelic-speaking people of northern Ireland, colonized the area of Argyll and Bute (the kingdom of Dalriada) in the fifth century AD and then expanded eastwards and northwards. The Britons, speaking a Brythonic Celtic language, colonized Scotland from the south from the first century BC; they lost control of south-eastern Scotland (incorporated into the kingdom of Northumbria) to the Angles in the early seventh century but retained Strathclyde (south-western Scotland and Cumbria). Viking raids from the late eighth century were followed by Norse settlement in the western and northern isles, Argyll, Caithness and Sutherland from the mid-ninth century onwards.

UNIFICATION

The union of the areas which now comprise Scotland began in AD 843 when Kenneth mac Alpin, king of the Scots from c.834, became also king of the Picts, joining the two lands to form the kingdom of Alba (comprising Scotland north of a line between the Forth and Clyde rivers). Lothian, the eastern part of the area between the Forth and the Tweed, seems to have been leased to Kenneth II of Alba (reigned 971–995) by Edgar of England c.973/4, and Scottish possession was confirmed by Malcolm II's victory over a Northumbrian army at Carham c.1016. At about this time Malcolm II (reigned 1005–34) placed his grandson Duncan on the throne of the British kingdom of Strathclyde, bringing under Scots rule virtually all of what is now Scotland.

The Norse possessions were incorporated into the kingdom of Scotland from the 12th century onwards. An uprising in the mid-12th century drove the Norse from most of mainland Argyll. The Hebrides were ceded to Scotland by the Treaty of Perth in 1266 after a Norwegian expedition in 1263 failed to maintain Norse authority over the islands. Orkney and Shetland fell to Scotland in 1468–9 as a pledge for the unpaid dowry of Margaret of Denmark, wife of James III, though Danish claims of suzerainty were relinquished only with the marriage of Anne of Denmark to James VI in 1590.

From the 11th century, there were frequent wars between Scotland and England over territory and the extent of England's political influence. The failure of the Scottish royal line with the death of Margaret of Norway in 1290 led to disputes over the throne which were resolved by the adjudication of Edward I of England. He awarded the throne to John Balliol in 1292 but Balliol's refusal to be a puppet king led to war. Balliol surrendered to Edward I in 1296 and Edward attempted to rule Scotland himself. Resistance to Scotland's loss of independence was led by William Wallace, who defeated the English at Stirling Bridge (1297), and Robert Bruce, crowned in 1306, who held most of Scotland by 1311 and routed Edward II's army at Bannockburn (1314). England recognized the independence of Scotland in the Treaty of Northampton in 1328. Subsequent clashes include the disastrous battle of Flodden (1513) in which James IV and many of his nobles fell.

THE UNION

In 1603 James VI of Scotland succeeded Elizabeth I on the throne of England (his mother, Mary Queen of Scots, was the great-granddaughter of Henry VII), his successors reigning as sovereigns of Great Britain. Political union of the two countries did not occur until 1707.

THE JACOBITE REVOLTS

After the abdication (by flight) in 1688 of James VII and II, the crown devolved upon William III (grandson of Charles I) and Mary II (elder daughter of James VII and II). In 1689 Graham of Claverhouse roused the Highlands on behalf of James VII and II, but died after a military success at Killiecrankie.

After the death of Anne (younger daughter of James VII and II), the throne devolved upon George I (great-grandson of James VI and I). In 1715, armed risings on behalf of James Stuart (the Old Pretender, son of James VII and II) led to the indecisive battle of Sheriffmuir, and the Jacobite movement died down until 1745, when Charles Stuart (the Young Pretender) defeated the Royalist troops at Prestonpans and advanced to Derby (1746). From Derby, the adherents of 'James VIII and III' (the title claimed for his father by Charles Stuart) fell back on the defensive and were finally crushed at Culloden (16 April 1746).

PRINCIPAL CITIES

ABERDEEN

Aberdeen, 130 miles north-east of Edinburgh, received its charter as a Royal Burgh in 1179. Scotland's third largest city, Aberdeen is the second largest Scottish fishing port and the main centre for offshore oil exploration and production. It is also an ancient university town and distinguished research centre. Other industries include engineering, food processing, textiles, paper manufacturing and chemicals.

Places of interest include King's College, St Machar's Cathedral, Brig o' Balgownie, Duthie Park and Winter Gardens, Hazlehead Park, the Kirk of St Nicholas, Mercat Cross, Marischal College and Marischal Museum, Provost Skene's House, Art Gallery, James Dun's House, Satrosphere Hands-On Discovery Centre, and Aberdeen Maritime Museum in Provost Ross's House.

DUNDEE

Dundee, a Royal Burgh, is situated on the north bank of the Tay estuary. The city's port and dock installations are important to the offshore oil industry and the airport also provides servicing facilities. Principal industries include textiles, computers and other electronic industries, lasers, printing, tyre manufacture, food processing, carpets, engineering, clothing manufacture and tourism.

The unique City Churches – three churches under one roof, together with the 15th-century St Mary's Tower – are the most prominent architectural feature. Dundee has two historic ships: the Dundee-built RRS *Discovery* which took Capt. Scott to the Antarctic lies alongside Discovery Quay, and the frigate *Unicorn*, the only British-built wooden warship still afloat, is moored in Victoria Dock. Places of interest include Mills Public Observatory, the Tay road and rail bridges, McManus Galleries, Barrack Street Museum, Claypotts Castle, Broughty Castle and Verdant Works (Textile Heritage Centre).

EDINBURGH

Edinburgh is the capital of and seat of government in Scotland. The city is built on a group of hills and contains in Princes Street one of the most beautiful thoroughfares in the world.

The principal buildings are the Castle, which now houses the Stone of Scone and also includes St Margaret's Chapel, the oldest building in Edinburgh, and near it, the Scottish National War Memorial; the Palace of Holyroodhouse; Parliament House, the present seat of the judicature; three universities (Edinburgh, Heriot-Watt, Napier); St Giles' Cathedral; St Mary's (Scottish Episcopal) Cathedral (Sir George Gilbert Scott); the General Register House (Robert Adam); the National and the Signet Libraries; the National Gallery; the Royal Scottish Academy; the National Portrait Gallery; and the Edinburgh International Conference Centre, opened in 1995.

GLASGOW

Glasgow, a Royal Burgh, is the principal commercial and industrial centre in Scotland. The city occupies the north and south banks of the Clyde, formerly one of the chief commercial estuaries in the world. The principal industries include engineering, electronics, finance, chemicals and printing. The city has also developed recently as a tourism and conference centre.

The chief buildings are the 13th-century Gothic Cathedral, the University (Sir Gilbert Scott), the City Chambers, the Royal Concert Hall, St Mungo Museum of Religious Life and Art, Pollok House, the School of Art (Mackintosh), Kelvingrove Art Galleries, the Gallery of Modern Art, the Burrell Collection museum and the Mitchell Library. The city is home to the Scottish National Orchestra, Scottish Opera and Scottish Ballet.

LORD-LIEUTENANTS

Title	Name
Aberdeenshire	Capt. C. A. Farquharson
Angus	The Earl of Airlie, KT, GCVO, PC
Argyll and Bute	The Duke of Argyll
Ayrshire and Arran	Maj. R. Y. Henderson, TD
Banffshire	J. A. S. McPherson, CBE
Berwickshire	Maj.-Gen. Sir John Swinton, KCVO, OBE
Caithness	Maj. G. T. Dunnett, TD
Clackmannan	Lt.-Col. R. C. Stewart, CBE, TD
Dumfries	Capt. R. C. Cunningham-Jardine
Dumbartonshire	Brig. D. D. G. Hardie, TD
East Lothian	Sir Hew Hamilton-Dalrymple, Bt., KCVO
Fife	The Earl of Elgin and Kincardine, KT
Inverness	The Lord Gray of Contin, PC
Kincardineshire	The Viscount of Arbuthnott, CBE, DSC, FRSE
Lanarkshire	H. B. Sneddon, CBE
Midlothian	Capt. G. W. Burnet, LVO
Moray	Air Vice-Marshal G. A. Chesworth, CB, OBE, DFC
Nairn	The Earl of Leven and Melville
Orkney	G. R. Marwick
Perth and Kinross	Sir David Montgomery, Bt.
Renfrewshire	The Lord Goold
Ross and Cromarty	Capt. R. W. K. Stirling of Fairburn, TD
Roxburgh, Ettrick and Lauderdale	The Duke of Buccleugh and Queensberry, KT, VRD
Shetland	J. H. Scott
Stirling and Falkirk	Lt.-Col. J. Stirling of Garden, CBE, TD, FRICS
Sutherland	Maj.-Gen. D. Houston, CBE
The Stewartry of Kirkcudbright	Lt.-Gen. Sir Norman Arthur, KCB
Tweeddale	Capt. J. D. B. Younger
West Lothian	The Earl of Morton
Western Isles	The Viscount Dunrossil, CMG
Wigtown	Maj. E. S. Orr-Ewing

The Lord Provosts of the four city districts of Aberdeen, Dundee, Edinburgh and Glasgow are Lord-Lieutenants for those districts *ex officio*

LOCAL COUNCILS

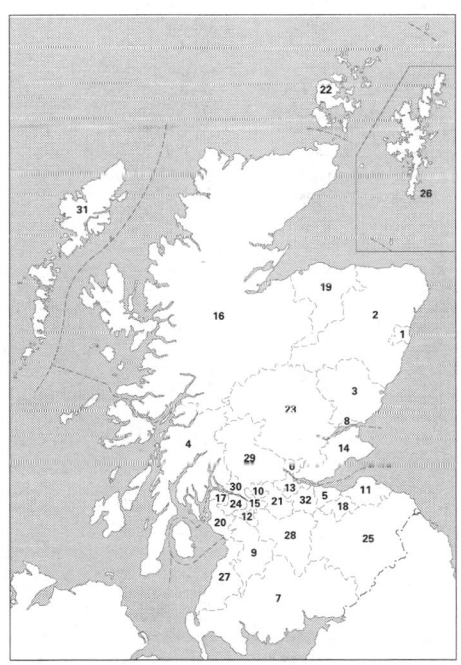

Key	Council
1	Aberdeen City
2	Aberdeenshire
3	Angus
4	Argyll and Bute
5	City of Edinburgh
6	Clackmannanshire
7	Dumfries and Galloway
8	Dundee City
9	East Ayrshire
10	East Dumbartonshire
11	East Lothian
12	East Renfrewshire
13	Falkirk
14	Fife
15	Glasgow City
16	Highland
17	Inverclyde
18	Midlothian
19	Moray
20	North Ayrshire
21	North Lanarkshire
22	Orkney
23	Perth and Kinross
24	Renfrewshire
25	Scottish Borders
26	Shetland
27	South Ayrshire
28	South Lanarkshire
29	Stirling
30	West Dumbartonshire
31	Western Isles
32	West Lothian

LOCAL COUNCILS

Council	Administrative headquarters	Population (latest estimate)	Band D charge 1997	Chief Executive	Chairman (a) Convener (b) Provost (c) Lord Provost
Aberdeen City	Aberdeen	217,260	£712.00	D. Paterson	(c) Ms M. Farquhar
Aberdeenshire	Aberdeen	227,000	643.00	A. G. Campbell	(a) Dr C. S. Millar
Angus	Forfar	111,750	679.00	A. B. Watson	(b) Mrs F. E. Duncan
Argyll and Bute	Lochgilphead	92,058	919.43	J. McLellan	(a) J. Wilson
City of Edinburgh	Edinburgh	447,550	837.00	T. N. Aitchison	(c) E. Milligan
Clackmannanshire	Alloa	48,820	833.79	R. Allan	(b) R. Elder
Dumfries and Galloway	Dumfries	144,856	706.38	I. F. Smith	(a) A. T. Baldwick
Dundee City	Dundee	150,250	1033.76	A. Stephen	(c) M. Rolfe
East Ayrshire	Kilmarnock	122,455	894.31	D. Montgomery	(b) R. Stirling
East Dumbartonshire	Glasgow	111,130	924.70	C. Mallon	(b) J. Dempsey
East Lothian	Haddington	88,140	845.79	J. Lindsay	(a) P. O'Brien
East Renfrewshire	Glasgow	89,417	682.00	P. Daniels	(b) A. Steele
Falkirk	Falkirk	142,800	680.00	W. Weir	(b) A. H. Fowler
Fife	Glenrothes	351,600	694.00	J. Markland	(a) J. MacDougal
Glasgow City	Glasgow	616,430	1,100.43	J. F. Anderson	(c) P. J. Lally
Highland	Inverness	208,300	845.47	A. D. McCourt	(a) P. J. Peacock
Inverclyde	Greenock	89,990	831.00	G. H. Bettison	(b) Mrs C. Allan
Midlothian	Dalkeith	80,000	858.00	T. Muir	(b) D. Molloy
Moray	Elgin	87,600	652.00	A. Connell	(a) G. McDonald
North Ayrshire	Irvine	139,000	836.43	B. Devine	(a) G. Steven
North Lanarkshire	Motherwell	326,700	699.56	A. Cowe	(b) V. Mathieson
Orkney Islands	Kirkwall	19,870	515.00	A. Buchan	(a) H. Halcro-Johnston
Perth and Kinross	Perth	133,000	732.00	H. Robertson	(b) J. Culliven
Renfrewshire	Paisley	178,550	901.43	T. Scholes	(b) Ms N. Allison
Scottish Borders	Melrose	105,300	612.00	A. M. Croall	(a) A. L Tulley
Shetland Islands	Lerwick	22,522	563.71	M. Green	(a) Canon L. Smith
South Ayrshire	Ayr	114,000	883.43	G. W. F. Thorley	(b) R. Campbell
South Lanarkshire	Hamilton	307,100	793.00	A. MacNish	(b) S. Casserly
Stirling	Stirling	82,114	856.79	K. Yates	(b) J. Paterson
West Dumbartonshire	Dumbarton	96,290	978.00	M. Waters	(b) P. O'Neill
Western Isles	Stornoway	28,880	599.00	B. W. Stewart	(a) D. M. Mackay
West Lothian	Livingston	147,870	708.00	A. M. Linkston	(b) J. Thomas

For explanation of council tax, *see* pages 523–4

Northern Ireland

Northern Ireland has a total area of 5,461 sq. miles (14,144 sq. km): land, 5,215 sq. miles (13,506 sq. km); inland water and tideways, 246 sq. miles (638 sq. km).

The population of Northern Ireland at the 1991 census was 1,577,836 (males, 769,071; females, 808,765). The average density of population in 1991 was 1.11 persons per hectare.

In 1991 the number of persons in the various religious denominations (expressed as percentages of the total population) were: Roman Catholic, 38.4; Presbyterian, 21.4; Church of Ireland, 17.7; Methodist, 3.8; others 7.7; none, 3.7; not stated, 7.3.

PRINCIPAL CITIES

BELFAST

Belfast, the administrative centre of Northern Ireland, is situated at the mouth of the River Lagan at its entrance to Belfast Lough. The city grew, owing to its easy access by sea to Scottish coal and iron, to be a great industrial centre.

The principal buildings are of a relatively recent date and include the Parliament Buildings at Stormont, the City Hall, the Law Courts, the Public Library and the Museum and Art Gallery.

Belfast received its first charter of incorporation in 1613 and was created a city in 1888; the title of Lord Mayor was conferred in 1892.

LONDONDERRY

Londonderry (originally Derry) is situated on the River Foyle, and has important associations with the City of London. The Irish Society was created by the City of London in 1610, and under its royal charter of 1613 it fortified the city and was for long closely associated with its administration. Because of this connection the city was incorporated in 1613 under the new name of Londonderry.

The city is famous for the great siege of 1688–9, when for 105 days the town held out against the forces of James II until relieved by sea. The city walls are still intact and form a circuit of almost a mile around the old city.

Interesting buildings are the Protestant Cathedral of St Columb's (1633) and the Guildhall, reconstructed in 1912 and containing a number of beautiful stained glass windows, many of which were presented by the livery companies of London.

CONSTITUTION AND GOVERNMENT

As part of the United Kingdom, Northern Ireland is subject to the same fundamental constitutional provisions which apply to the rest of the United Kingdom. It had its own parliament and government from 1921 to 1972, but after increasing civil unrest the Northern Ireland (Temporary Provisions) Act 1972 transferred the legislative and executive powers of the Northern Ireland parliament and government to the UK Parliament and a Secretary of State. The Northern Ireland Constitution Act 1973 provided for devolution in Northern Ireland through an assembly and executive, and in January 1974 a power-sharing executive was formed by the Northern Ireland political parties. This collapsed in May 1974 and since then Northern Ireland has been governed by direct rule under the provisions of the

Northern Ireland Act 1974. This allows Parliament to approve all laws for Northern Ireland and places the Northern Ireland department under the direction and control of the Secretary of State for Northern Ireland.

Attempts have been made by successive governments to find a means of restoring a widely acceptable form of devolved government to Northern Ireland. A 78-member Assembly was elected by proportional representation in 1982 but was dissolved four years later after it failed to discharge its responsibilities of making proposals for the resumption of devolved government and of monitoring the work of the Northern Ireland departments.

In 1985 the governments of the United Kingdom and the Republic of Ireland signed the Anglo-Irish Agreement, establishing an intergovernmental conference in which the Irish government may put forward views and proposals on certain aspects of Northern Ireland affairs.

Discussions between the British and Irish governments and the main Northern Ireland parties began in 1991. It was agreed that any political settlement would need to address three key relationships: those within Northern Ireland; those within the island of Ireland (north/south); and those between the British and Irish governments (east/west). Although round table talks ended in 1992 the process continued from September 1993 as separate bilateral discussions with three of the Northern Ireland parties (the DUP declined to participate).

In December 1993 the British and Irish governments published the Joint Declaration complementing the political talks, and making clear that any settlement would need to be founded on principles of democracy and consent. The declaration also stated that all democratically mandated parties could be involved in political talks as long as they permanently renounced paramilitary violence.

The provisional IRA and loyalist paramilitary groups announced cease-fires on 31 August and 13 October 1994 respectively. The Government initiated a series of separate exploratory meetings with Sinn Fein and loyalist representatives in December 1994. The purposes of these were to explore the basis upon which Sinn Fein and the loyalist representatives would be admitted to an inclusive political talks process; to exchange views on how they would be able to play the same role as the current constitutional parties in the public life of Northern Ireland; and to examine the practical consequences of the ending of violence.

In February 1995 the Prime Minister launched *A Framework for Accountable Government in Northern Ireland* and, with the Irish Prime Minister, *A New Framework for Agreement*. These outlined what a comprehensive political settlement might look like. The ideas were intended to facilitate multilateral dialogue involving the Northern Ireland parties and the British government. To this end the Secretary of State for Northern Ireland (Sir Patrick Mayhew) initiated separate bilateral meetings with the leaders of the main parties. The Government had previously given an undertaking to submit the final outcome of political talks to the electorate of Northern Ireland for approval in a referendum.

In the autumn of 1995 the Prime Minister said that Sinn Fein would not be invited to all-party talks until the IRA had decommissioned its arms; the IRA ruled out any decommissioning of weapons in advance of a political settlement. In November 1995 the Prime Minister and the Irish Prime Minister agreed to set up a three-member international body chaired by a former US senator, George

Mitchell, to advise both governments on suitable methods of decommissioning arms. The international body reported in January 1996 that no weapons would be decommissioned before the start of all-party talks and that a compromise agreement was necessary under which weapons would be decommissioned during negotiations. The Prime Minister accepted the report and proposed that elections should be held to provide a pool of representatives to conduct all-party talks. On 9 February 1996 the IRA called off its cease-fire.

The elections were held on 30 May 1996 and all-party talks opened at Stormont Castle on 10 June 1996 which included nine of the ten parties returned at the election; Sinn Fein were turned away because the IRA had failed to reinstate its cease-fire. Delegates returned at the election also constituted a peace forum, independent of the negotiations, concerned with the promotion of dialogue and understanding. The peace forum met for the first time on 14 June 1997; it was boycotted by Sinn Fein members and the Social Democratic and Labour Party withdrew from it in July 1996.

The participants of the all-party talks agreed the rules of procedure and set up a business committee. On 29 July 1996 the all-party talks were suspended after disagreements over the issue of decommissioning arms. From September 1996 discussion focused on the issue of decommissioning arms, and an opening agenda for the talks was agreed in October 1996. The talks were suspended on 5 March 1997 (the peace forum was suspended a week later) in advance of the UK general election and local government elections in Northern Ireland.

The talks resumed on 3 June 1997. On 25 June 1997 the newly-elected Labour Government said that substantive negotiations should begin in September 1997 with a view to reaching conclusions by May 1998. The British and Irish Governments issued a joint paper outlining their proposals for resolving the decommissioning issue. The Government also indicated that if the IRA were to call a cease-fire, it would assess whether it was genuine over a period of six weeks, and if satisfied that it was so, would then invite Sinn Fein to the talks. The Government said that it was willing to organize meetings between its officials and Sinn Fein; two meetings were held. An IRA cease-fire was declared on 20 July 1997.

FLAG

The official national flag of Northern Ireland is now the Union Flag. The flag formerly in use (a white, six-pointed star in the centre of a red cross on a white field, enclosing a red hand and surmounted by a crown) has not been used since the imposition of direct rule.

ECONOMY

FINANCE

Taxation in Northern Ireland is largely imposed and collected by the United Kingdom government. After deducting the cost of collection and of Northern Ireland's contributions to the European Community the balance, known as the Attributed Share of Taxation, is paid over to the Northern Ireland Consolidated Fund. Northern Ireland's revenue is insufficient to meet its expenditure and is supplemented by a grant-in-aid.

	1996–7*	1997–8**
Public income	£6,728,752,128	£6,954,316,000
Public expenditure	6,698,130,391	6,954,316,000

* Outturn
** Estimate

PRODUCTION

The products of the engineering and allied industries, which employed 26,500 persons in 1994, were valued at £1,848 million. The textiles industry, employing about 11,500 persons, produced products valued at approximately £584 million. The food products, beverages and tobacco industry, employing about 22,500 persons, produced goods valued at £3,478 million.

In 1996 1,460 persons were employed in mining and quarrying operations in Northern Ireland and the minerals raised (25,113,409 tonnes) were valued at £63,325,000.

COMMUNICATIONS

The total tonnage handled by Northern Ireland ports in 1996 was 20 million. Regular ferry, freight and container services operate to ports in Great Britain and Europe from a number of ports, with most trade passing through Belfast (60 per cent of the total), Larne and Warrenpoint.

The Northern Ireland Transport Holding Company is largely responsible for the supervision of the subsidiary companies, Ulsterbus and Citybus (which operate the public road passenger services) and Northern Ireland Railways (collectively known as Translink). Road freight services are also provided by a large number of hauliers operating competitively under licence.

Belfast International Airport was privatized in July 1994. It has substantial passenger and freight handling facilities and provides scheduled and chartered services on domestic and international routes.

Scheduled services also operate from Belfast City Airport (BCA) to 20 UK destinations and from City of Derry Airport (Londonderry) to Glasgow, Manchester, Birmingham and to Belfast, providing links to many of the locations serviced by BCA.

Northern Ireland Counties

County	Area* (sq. miles)	Lord-Lieutenant	High Sheriff, 1997
Antrim	1,093	The Lord O'Neill, TD	R. F. A. Dobbs
Armagh	484	The Earl of Caledon	Dr J. O. Woods
‡Belfast City	25	Col. J. E. Wilson, OBE	N. McCausland
Down	945	Maj. W. J. Hall	Mrs L. M. L. Blakiston Houston
Fermanagh	647	The Earl of Erne	P. M. C. Little
†Londonderry	798	Sir Michael McCorkell, KCVO, OBE, TD	T. M. McIlwaine
‡Londonderry City	3.4	J. T. Eaton, CBE, TD	S. C. Keys
Tyrone	1,211	The Duke of Abercorn	P. A. Black

* Excluding inland waters and tideways
‡ Denotes County Borough
† Excluding the City of Londonderry

District Councils

Council	Population (30 June 1995)	Net Annual Value	Council Clerk	Chairman †Mayor 1997
§Antrim, Co. Antrim	46,400	£7,583,073	S. J. Magee	†F. R. H. Marks
§Ards, Co. Down	66,700	8,614,136	D. J. Fallows	†R. Ferguson
§ARMAGH, Co. Armagh	52,400	5,571,964	D. R. D. Mitchall	†P. Brannigan
§Ballymena, Co. Antrim	57,400	9,095,910	M. G. Rankin	†J. Currie
§Ballymoney, Co. Antrim	24,600	2,800,383	J. C. Alderdice	†F. Campbell
Banbridge, Co. Down	37,300	4,528,828	R. Gilmore	Mrs J. Baird
BELFAST, Co. Antrim and Co. Down	296,300	57,837,592	B. Hanna	A. Maginnis
§Carrickfergus, Co. Antrim	34,900	4,916,621	R. Boyd	|D. W. Hilditch
§Castlereagh, Co. Down	63,400	8,910,942	C. Sneddon	†J. Norris
§Coleraine, Co. Londonderry	54,100	8,354,863	W. Moore	†J. McClure
Cookstown, Co. Tyrone	31,300	3,396,329	M. J. McGuckin	S. Begley
§Craigavon, Co. Armagh	77,900	11,669,017	T. Reaney	†K. Twyble
DERRY, Co. Londonderry	101,700	14,336,834	T. J. Keanie	†M. Bradley
Down, Co. Down	60,000	6,706,885	O. O'Connor	P. Toman
Dungannon, Co. Tyrone	46,100	5,320,672	W. J. Beattie	P. Daly
				D. Irwin
Fermanagh, Co. Fermanagh	54,700	6,549,877	Mrs A. McGinley	P. McCaffrey
§Larne, Co. Antrim	30,000	4,383,112	T. Clark (acting)	†Mrs J. Drummond
§Limavady, Co. Londonderry	30,100	3,196,468	J. K. Stevenson	†G. Lynch
§Lisburn, Co. Antrim and Co. Down	103,600	15,037,406	N. Davidson	†G. Morrison
Magherafelt, Co. Londonderry	37,000	3,983,988	J. A. McLaughlin	P. Groogan
Moyle, Co. Antrim	14,800	1,654,686	R. G. Lewis	R. Kerr
Newry and Mourne, Co. Down and Co. Armagh	83,500	9,026,544	K. O'Neill	C. Smyth
§Newtownabbey, Co. Antrim	78,600	12,109,090	N. Dunn	†N. Crilly
§North Down, Co. Down	73,000	10,623,630	A. McDowell	†Mrs R. Cooling
Omagh, Co. Tyrone	46,200	5,200,205	J. P. McKinney	J. Byrne
Strabane, Co. Tyrone	36,100	3,507,621	Dr V. R. Eakin	E. Mullen

The Isle of Man

Ellan Vannin

The Isle of Man is an island situated in the Irish Sea, in latitude 54° 3'–54° 25' N. and longitude 4° 18'–4° 47' W., nearly equidistant from England, Scotland and Ireland. Although the early inhabitants were of Celtic origin, the Isle of Man was part of the Norwegian Kingdom of the Hebrides until 1266, when this was ceded to Scotland. Subsequently granted to the Stanleys (Earls of Derby) in the 15th century and later to the Dukes of Atholl, it was brought under the administration of the Crown in 1765. The island forms the bishopric of Sodor and Man.

The total land area is 221 sq. miles (572 sq. km). The report on the 1991 census showed a resident population of 69,788 (males, 33,693; females, 36,095). The main language in use is English. There are no remaining native speakers of Manx Gaelic but 643 people are able to speak the language. CAPITAL – ΨDouglas; population (1991), 22,214. ΨCastletown (3,152) is the ancient capital; the other towns are ΨPeel (3,829) and ΨRamsey (6,496)

FLAG – A red flag charged with three conjoined armoured legs in white and gold

TYNWALD DAY – 5 July.

GOVERNMENT

The Isle of Man is a self-governing Crown dependency, having its own parliamentary, legal and administrative system. The British Government is responsible for international relations and defence. Under the UK Act of Accession, Protocol 3, the island's relationship with the European Community is limited to trade alone and does not extend to financial aid. The Lieutenant-Governor is The Queen's personal representative in the island.

The legislature, Tynwald, is the oldest parliament in the world in continuous existence. It has two branches: the Legislative Council and the House of Keys. The Council consists of the President of Tynwald, the Bishop of Sodor and Man, the Attorney-General (who does not have a vote) and eight members elected by the House of Keys. The House of Keys has 24 members, elected by universal adult suffrage. The branches sit separately to consider legislation and sit together, as Tynwald Court, for most other parliamentary purposes.

The presiding officer in Tynwald Court is the President of Tynwald, elected by the members, who also presides over sittings of the Legislative Council. The presiding officer of the House of Keys is Mr Speaker, who is elected by members of the House.

The principal members of the Manx Government are the Chief Minister and nine departmental ministers, who comprise the Council of Ministers.

Lieutenant-Governor, HE Sir Timothy Daunt, KCMG
  ADC to the Lieutenant-Governor, M. M. Wood
President of Tynwald, The Hon. Sir Charles Kerruish, OBE
Speaker, House of Keys, The Hon. N. Q. Cringle
The First Deemster and Clerk of the Rolls, His Honour J. W. Corrin, CBE
Clerk of Tynwald, Secretary to the House of Keys and Counsel to the Speaker, Prof. T. St J. N. Bates
Clerk of Legislative Council and Clerk Assistant of Tynwald, T. A. Bawden
Attorney-General, J. M. Kerruish, QC
Chief Minister, The Hon. D. J. Gelling
Chief Secretary, J. F. Kissack
Chief Financial Officer, J. A. Cashen

ECONOMY

Most of the income generated in the island is earned in the services sector with financial and professional services accounting for just over half of the national income. Tourism and manufacturing are also major generators of income whilst the island's other traditional industries of agriculture and fishing now play a smaller role in the economy.

Under the terms of Protocol 3, the island has tariff-free access to EU markets for its goods.

The island's unemployment rate is approximately 2 per cent and price inflation is around 2 per cent per annum.

FINANCE

The budget for 1997–8 provided for gross expenditure of £383 million. The principal sources of government revenue are taxes on income and expenditure. Income tax is payable at a rate of 15 per cent on the first £9,270 of taxable income for single resident individuals and 20 per cent on the balance, after personal allowances of £6,800. These bands are doubled for married couples. The rate of income tax is 20 per cent on the whole taxable income of non-residents and companies. By agreement with the British Government, the island keeps most of its rates of indirect taxation (VAT and duties) the same as those in the United Kingdom, but this agreement may be terminated by either party. However, VAT on tourist accommodation is charged at 5 per cent. A reciprocal agreement on national insurance benefits and pensions exists between the Governments of the Isle of Man and the United Kingdom. Taxes are also charged on property (rates), but these are comparatively low.

The major government expenditure items are health, social security and education, which account for 61 per cent of the government budget. The island makes a voluntary annual contribution to the United Kingdom for defence and other external services.

The island has a special relationship with the European Union and neither contributes money to nor receives funds from the EU budget.

The Channel Islands

The Channel Islands, situated off the north-west coast of France (at distances of from ten to 30 miles), are the only portions of the Dukedom of Normandy still belonging to the Crown, to which they have been attached since the Conquest. They were the only British territory to come under German occupation during the Second World War, following invasion on 30 June to 1 July 1940. The islands were relieved by British forces on 9 May 1945, and 9 May (Liberation Day) is now observed as a bank and public holiday.

The islands consist of Jersey (28,717 acres/11,630 ha), Guernsey (15,654 acres/6,340 ha), and the dependencies of Guernsey: Alderney (1,962 acres/795 ha), Brechou (74/30), Great Sark (1,035/419), Little Sark (239/97), Herm (320/130), Jethou (44/18) and Lihou (38/15) – a total of 48,083 acres/19,474 ha, or 75 sq. miles/194 sq. km. In 1991 the population of Jersey was 84,082; and of Guernsey, 58,867; Alderney, 2,297 and Sark, 575. The official languages are English and French but French is being supplanted by English, which is the language in daily use. In country districts of Jersey and Guernsey and throughout Sark a Norman-French *patois* is also in use, though to a declining extent.

GOVERNMENT

The islands are Crown dependencies with their own legislative assemblies (the States in Jersey, Guernsey and Alderney, and the Court of Chief Pleas in Sark), and systems of local administration and of law, and their own courts. Acts passed by the States require the sanction of The Queen-in-Council. The British Government is responsible for defence and international relations. The Channel Islands have trading rights alone within the European Union; these rights do not include financial aid.

In both Bailiwicks the Lieutenant-Governor and Commander-in-Chief, who is appointed by the Crown, is the personal representative of The Queen and the channel of communication between the Crown (via the Privy Council) and the island's government.

The government of each Bailiwick is conducted by committees appointed by the States. Justice is administered by the Royal Courts of Jersey and Guernsey, each consisting of the Bailiff and 12 elected Jurats. The Bailiffs of Jersey and Guernsey, appointed by the Crown, are President of the States and of the Royal Courts of their respective islands.

Each Bailiwick constitutes a deanery under the jurisdiction of the Bishop of Winchester (*see* Index).

ECONOMY

A mild climate and good soil have led to the development of intensive systems of agriculture and horticulture, which form a significant part of the economy. Equally important are invisible earnings, principally from tourism and banking and finance, the low rate of income tax (20p in the £ in Jersey and Guernsey; no tax of any kind in Sark) and the absence of super-tax and death duties making the islands a popular tax-haven.

Principal exports are agricultural produce and flowers; imports are chiefly machinery, manufactured goods, food, fuel and chemicals. Trade with the UK is regarded as internal.

British currency is legal tender in the Channel Islands but each Bailiwick issues its own coins and notes (*see* page 607). They also issue their own postage stamps; UK stamps are not valid.

JERSEY

Lieutenant-Governor and Commander-in-Chief of Jersey, HE Gen. Sir Michael Wilkes, KCB, CBE, *apptd* 1995
   Secretary and ADC, Lt.-Col. A. J. C. Woodrow, OBE, MC
Bailiff of Jersey, Sir Philip Bailhache, Kt.
Deputy Bailiff, F. C. Hamon
Attorney-General, M. C. St J. Burt, QC
Receiver-General, Gp Capt R. Green, OBE
Solicitor-General, Miss S. C. Nicolle, QC
Greffier of the States, G. H. C. Coppock
States Treasurer, G. M. Baird

FINANCE

Year to 31 Dec.	1995	1996
Revenue income	£417,271,388	£427,619,424
Revenue expenditure	376,752,850	395,666,525
Capital expenditure	72,823,770	83,413,237
Public debt	0	0

CHIEF TOWN – ΨSt Helier, on the south coast of Jersey
FLAG – A white field charged with a red saltire cross, and the arms of Jersey in the upper centre

GUERNSEY AND DEPENDENCIES

Lieutenant-Governor and Commander-in-Chief of the Bailiwick of Guernsey and its Dependencies, HE Vice-Adm. Sir John Coward, KCB, DSO, *apptd* 1994
   Secretary and ADC, Capt. D. P. L. Hodgetts
Bailiff of Guernsey, Sir Graham Dorey
Deputy Bailiff, de V. G. Carey
HM Procureur and Receiver-General, A. C. K. Day, QC
HM Comptroller, G. R. Rowland, QC
States Supervisor, M. J. Brown

FINANCE

Year to 31 Dec.	1995	1996
Revenue	£171,506,000	£182,016,695
Expenditure	152,222,000	166,817,571

CHIEF TOWNS – ΨSt Peter Port, on the east coast of Guernsey; St Anne on Alderney
FLAG – White, bearing a red cross of St George, with a gold cross overall in the centre

ALDERNEY

President of the States, J. Kay-Mouat, OBE
Clerk of the States, D. V. Jenkins
Clerk of the Court, A. Johnson

SARK

Seigneur of Sark, J. M. Beaumont
The Seneschal, L. P. de Carteret
The Greffier, J. P. Hamon

OTHER DEPENDENCIES

Brechou, Lihou and Jethou are leased by the Crown. Herm is leased by the States of Guernsey.

Conservation and Heritage

Countryside Conservation

NATIONAL PARKS

ENGLAND AND WALES

The ten National Parks of England and Wales were set up under the provisions of the National Parks and Access to the Countryside Act 1949 to conserve and protect scenic landscapes from inappropriate development and to provide access to the land for public enjoyment.

The Countryside Commission is the statutory body which has the power to designate National Parks in England, and the Countryside Council for Wales is responsible for National Parks in Wales. Designations in England are confirmed by the Secretary of State for the Environment, and those in Wales by the Secretary of State for Wales. The designation of a National Park does not affect the ownership of the land or remove the rights of the local community. The majority of the land in the National Parks is owned by private landowners (74 per cent) or by bodies such as the National Trust (7 per cent) and the Forestry Commission (7 per cent). The National Park Authorities own only 2.3 per cent of the land.

The Environment Act 1995 replaced the existing National Park boards and committees with free-standing National Park Authorities (NPAs). NPAs are the sole local planning authorities for their areas and as such influence land use and development, and deal with planning applications. Their duties include conserving and enhancing the natural beauty, wildlife and cultural heritage of the National Parks; promoting opportunities for public understanding and enjoyment of the National Parks; and fostering the economic and social well-being of the communities within National Parks. The NPAs publish management plans as statements of their policies and appoint their own officers and staff.

Membership of the NPAs differs slightly between England and Wales. In England membership is split between representatives of the constituent local authorities and members appointed by the Secretary of State (of whom one half minus one are nominated by the parish councils in the park), with the local authority representatives in a majority of one. The Countryside Commission advises the Secretary of State on appointments not nominated by the parish councils. In Wales two-thirds of NPA members are appointed by the constituent local authorities and one-third are appointed by the Secretary of State for Wales, advised by the Countryside Council for Wales.

Central government provides 75 per cent of the funding for the parks through the National Park Grant. The remaining 25 per cent is supplied by the local authorities concerned. Approved net expenditure for all National Parks in England and Wales in 1997–8 was £28,998,667.

The Countryside Commission has stated that other areas are regarded as being worthy of National Parks status. Two areas considered as having equivalent status are the Broads and the New Forest (*see* page 571).

The National Parks (with date designation confirmed) are:

BRECON BEACONS (1957), 1,351 sq. km/522 sq. miles – The park lies in Powys (66 per cent), Carmarthenshire, Rhondda, Cynon and Taff, Merthyr Tydfil, Blaenau Gwent and Monmouthshire. The park is centred on the Beacons, Pen y Fan, Corn Du and Cribyn, but also includes the valley of the Usk, the Black Mountains to the east and the Black Mountain to the west. There are information centres at Brecon, Craig-y-nos Country Park, Abergavenny and Llandovery, a study centre at Danywenallt and a day visitor centre near Libanus. *Information Office*, 7 Glamorgan Street, Brecon, Powys LD3 7DP. Tel: 01874-624437. *National Park Officer*, M. Fitton

DARTMOOR (1951 and 1994), 954 sq. km/368 sq. miles – The park lies wholly in Devon. It consists of moorland and rocky granite tors, and is rich in prehistoric remains. There are information centres at Newbridge, Tavistock, Bovey Tracey, Steps Bridge, Princetown and Postbridge. *Information Office*, Parke, Haytor Road, Bovey Tracey, Devon TQ13 9JQ. Tel: 01626-832093. *National Park Officer*, N. Atkinson

EXMOOR (1954), 693 sq. km/268 sq. miles – The park lies in Somerset (71 per cent) and Devon. Exmoor is a moorland plateau inhabited by wild ponies and red deer. There are many ancient remains and burial mounds. There are information centres at Lynmouth, County Gate, Dulverton and Combe Martin. *Information Office*, Exmoor House, Dulverton, Somerset TA22 9HL. Tel: 01398-23665. *National Park Officer*, K. Bungay

LAKE DISTRICT (1951), 2,292 sq. km/885 sq. miles – The park lies wholly in Cumbria. The Lake District includes England's highest mountains (Scafell Pike, Helvellyn and Skiddaw) but it is most famous for its glaciated lakes. There are information centres at Keswick, Waterhead, Hawkshead, Seatoller, Bowness, Grasmere, Coniston, Glenridding and Pooley Bridge, an information van at Gosforth and a park centre at Brockhole, Windermere. *Information Office*, Brockhole, Windermere, Cumbria LA23 1LJ. Tel: 01539-446601. *National Park Officer*, J. Toothill

NORTHUMBERLAND (1956), 1,049 sq. km/405 sq. miles – The park lies wholly in Northumberland. It is an area of hill country stretching from Hadrian's Wall to the Scottish Border. There are information centres at Ingram, Once Brewed, Rothbury, Housesteads, Harbottle and Kielder, and an information caravan at Cawfields. *Information Office*, Eastburn, South Park, Hexham, Northumberland NE46 1BS. Tel: 01434-605555. *National Park Officer*, G. Taylor

NORTH YORK MOORS (1952), 1,436 sq. km/554 sq. miles – The park lies in North Yorkshire (96 per cent) and Redcar and Cleveland. It consists of woodland and moorland, and includes the Hambleton Hills and the Cleveland Way. There are information centres at Danby, Pickering, Sutton Bank, Ravenscar, Helmsley and Hutton-le-Hole, and a day study centre at Danby.

Information Office, The Old Vicarage, Bondgate, Helmsley, York YO6 5BP. Tel: 01439-70657. *National Park Officer*, D. Arnold-Forster

PEAK DISTRICT (1951), 1,438 sq. km/555 sq. miles – The park lies in Derbyshire (64 per cent), Staffordshire, South Yorkshire, Cheshire, West Yorkshire and Greater Manchester. The Peak District includes the gritstone moors of the 'Dark Peak' and the limestone dales of the 'White Peak'. There are information centres at Bakewell, Edale, Fairholmes and Castleton, and information points at Torside (in the Longdendale Valley) and at Hartington (former station).
Information Office, Aldern House, Baslow Road, Bakewell, Derbyshire DE45 1AE. Tel. 01629-814321. *National Park Officer*, C. Harrison

PEMBROKESHIRE COAST (1952 and 1995), 584 sq. km/225 sq. miles – The park lies wholly in Pembrokeshire. It includes cliffs, moorland and Skomer Island. There are information centres at Tenby, St David's, Pembroke, Newport, Kilgetty, Haverfordwest and Broad Haven.
Information Office, Winch Lane, Haverfordwest, Pembrokeshire SA61 1PY. Tel: 01437-764636. *National Park Officer*, N. Wheeler

SNOWDONIA (1951), 2,142 sq. km/827 sq. miles – Snowdonia lies in Gwynedd and Conwy. It is an area of deep valleys and rugged mountains. There are information centres at Aberdyfi, Bala, Betws y Coed, Blaenau Ffestiniog, Conwy, Harlech, Dolgellau and Llanberis.
Information Office, Penrhyndeudraeth, Gwynedd LL48 6LF. Tel: 01766-770274. *National Park Officer*, I. Huws.

YORKSHIRE DALES (1954), 1,769 sq. km/683 sq. miles – The park lies in North Yorkshire (88 per cent) and Cumbria. The Yorkshire Dales are composed primarily of limestone overlaid in places by millstone grit. The three peaks of Ingleborough, Whernside and Pen-y-Ghent are within the park. There are information centres at Clapham, Grassington, Hawes, Aysgarth Falls, Malham and Sedbergh.
Information Office, Yorebridge House, Bainbridge, Leyburn, N. Yorks DL8 3BP. Tel: 01969-50456. *National Park Officer*, G. Hallas

Two other areas considered to have equivalent status to national parks are the Broads and the New Forest. The Broads Authority, a special statutory authority, was established in 1989 to develop, conserve and manage the Norfolk and Suffolk Broads (*see also* Government Departments and Public Offices). The Government declared in 1992 its intention of giving the New Forest a status equivalent to that of a National Park by declaring it an 'area of national significance'.

THE BROADS (1989), 303 sq. km/117 sq. miles – The Broads are located between Norwich and Great Yarmouth on the flood plains of the five rivers flowing through the area to the sea. The area is one of fens, winding waterways, woodland and marsh. The 40 or so broads are man-made, and are connected to the rivers by dykes, providing over 200 km of navigable waterways. There are information centres at Beccles, Hoveton, North-west Tower (Yarmouth), Ranworth and Toad Hole.
Broads Authority, Thomas Harvey House, 18 Colegate, Norwich NR3 1BQ. Tel: 01603-610734. *Chief Executive*, A. Clark

THE NEW FOREST, 376 sq. km/145 sq. miles – The forest has been protected since 1079 when it was declared a royal hunting forest. The area consists of forest, ancient woodland and heathland. Much of the Forest is managed by the Forestry Commission, which provides several camp-sites. The main villages are Brockenhurst, Burley and Lyndhurst, which has a visitor centre.
The Forestry Commission, Office of the Deputy Surveyor of the New Forest and the New Forest Committee, The Queen's House, Lyndhurst, Hants SO43 7NH. Tel: 01703-284149

SCOTLAND AND NORTHERN IRELAND

The National Parks and Access to the Countryside Act 1949 dealt only with England and Wales and made no provision for Scotland or Northern Ireland. Although there are no national parks in these two countries, there is power to designate them in Northern Ireland under the Amenity Lands Act 1965 and the Nature Conservation and Amenity Lands Order (Northern Ireland) 1985. In 1989 the Scottish Office asked Scottish Natural Heritage to report on whether national parks should be designated in Scotland.

AREAS OF OUTSTANDING NATURAL BEAUTY

ENGLAND AND WALES

Under the National Parks and Access to the Countryside Act 1949, provision was made for the designation of Areas of Outstanding Natural Beauty (AONBs) by the Countryside Commission. The Countryside Act 1968 further defines the role of AONBs, suggesting that they should show due regard for the interests of other land users, such as agriculture and forestry groups. The Countryside Commission continues to be responsible for AONBs in England but since April 1991 the Countryside Council for Wales has been responsible for the Welsh AONBs. Designations in England are confirmed by the Secretary of State for the Environment and those in Wales by the Secretary of State for Wales.

Although less emphasis is placed upon the provision of open-air enjoyment for the public than in the national parks, AONBs are areas which are no less beautiful and require the same degree of protection to conserve and enhance the natural beauty of the countryside. This includes protecting flora and fauna, geological and other landscape features. In AONBs planning and management responsibilities are split between county and district councils; where Unitary Authorities exist they have sole responsibility for planning and management. Several AONBs cross local authority boundaries. Finance for the AONBs is provided by grant-aid.

The 41 Areas of Outstanding Natural Beauty (with date designation confirmed) are:

ANGLESEY (1967), Anglesey, 221 sq. km/85 sq. miles
ARNSIDE AND SILVERDALE (1972), Cumbria/Lancashire, 75 sq. km/29 sq. miles
BLACKDOWN HILLS (1991), Devon/Somerset, 370 sq. km/143 sq. miles.
CANNOCK CHASE (1958), Staffordshire, 68 sq. km/26 sq. miles
CHICHESTER HARBOUR (1964), Hampshire/West Sussex, 74 sq. km/29 sq. miles
CHILTERNS (1965; extended 1990), Bedfordshire/Hertfordshire/Buckinghamshire/Oxfordshire, 833 sq. km/322 sq. miles
CLWYDIAN RANGE (1985), Denbighshire/Flintshire, 157 sq. km/60 sq. miles
CORNWALL (1959; Camel estuary 1983), 958 sq. km/370 sq. miles

COTSWOLDS (1966; extended 1990), Gloucestershire/ Wiltshire/Warwickshire/Hereford and Worcester/ Somerset, 2,038 sq. km/787 sq. miles

CRANBORNE CHASE AND WEST WILTSHIRE DOWNS (1983), Dorset/Hampshire/Somerset/Wiltshire, 983 sq. km/379 sq. miles

DEDHAM VALE (1970; extended 1978, 1991), Essex/ Suffolk, 90 sq. km/35 sq. miles

EAST DEVON (1963), 268 sq. km/103 sq. miles

NORTH DEVON (1960), 171 sq. km/66 sq. miles

SOUTH DEVON (1960), 337 sq. km/130 sq. miles

DORSET (1959), 1,129 sq. km/436 sq. miles

FOREST OF BOWLAND (1964), Lancashire/North Yorkshire, 802 sq. km/310 sq. miles

GOWER (1956), Swansea, 189 sq. km/73 sq. miles

EAST HAMPSHIRE (1962), 383 sq. km/148 sq. miles

SOUTH HAMPSHIRE COAST (1967), 77 sq. km/30 sq. miles

HIGH WEALD (1983), Kent/Surrey/East Sussex/West Sussex, 1,460 sq. km/564 sq. miles

HOWARDIAN HILLS (1987), North Yorkshire, 204 sq. km/ 79 sq. miles

KENT DOWNS (1968), 878 sq. km/339 sq. miles

LINCOLNSHIRE WOLDS (1973), 558 sq. km/215 sq. miles

LLŶN (1957), Gwynedd, 161 sq. km/62 sq. miles

MALVERN HILLS (1959), Hereford and Worcester/ Gloucestershire, 105 sq. km/40 sq. miles

MENDIP HILLS (1972; extended 1989), Somerset, 198 sq. km/76 sq. miles

NIDDERDALE (1994), North Yorkshire, 603 sq. km/233 sq. miles

NORFOLK COAST (1968), 451 sq. km/174 sq. miles

NORTH PENNINES (1988), Cumbria/Durham/ Northumberland, 1,983 sq. km/766 sq. miles

NORTHUMBERLAND COAST (1958), 135 sq. km/52 sq. miles

QUANTOCK HILLS (1957), Somerset, 99 sq. km/38 sq. miles

ISLES OF SCILLY (1976), 16 sq. km/6 sq. miles

SHROPSHIRE HILLS (1959), 804 sq. km/310 sq. miles

SOLWAY COAST (1964), Cumbria, 115 sq. km/44 sq. miles

SUFFOLK COAST AND HEATHS (1970), 403 sq. km/156 sq. miles

SURREY HILLS (1958), 419 sq. km/162 sq. miles

SUSSEX DOWNS (1966), 983 sq. km/379 sq. miles

TAMAR VALLEY (1995), Cornwall/Devon, 195 sq. km/115 sq. miles

NORTH WESSEX DOWNS (1972), Berkshire/Hampshire/ Oxfordshire/Wiltshire, 1,730 sq. km/668 sq. miles

ISLE OF WIGHT (1963), 189 sq. km/73 sq. miles

WYE VALLEY (1971), Monmouthshire/Gloucestershire/ Hereford and Worcester, 326 sq. km/126 sq. miles

NORTHERN IRELAND

The Department of the Environment for Northern Ireland, with advice from the Council for Nature Conservation and the Countryside, designates Areas of Outstanding Natural Beauty in Northern Ireland. At present there are nine and these cover a total area of approximately 284,948 hectares (704,121 acres).

ANTRIM COAST AND GLENS, Co. Antrim, 70,600 ha/ 174,452 acres

CAUSEWAY COAST, Co. Antrim, 4,200 ha/10,378 acres

LAGAN VALLEY, Co. Down, 2,072 ha/5,119 acres

LECALE COAST, Co. Down, 3,108 ha/7,679 acres

MOURNE, Co. Down, 57,012 ha/140,876 acres

NORTH DERRY, Co. Londonderry, 12,950 ha/31,999 acres

RING OF GULLION, Co. Armagh, 15,353 ha/37,938 acres

SPERRIN, Co. Tyrone/Co. Londonderry, 101,006 ha/ 249,585 acres

STRANGFORD LOUGH, Co. Down, 18,647 ha/46,077 acres

NATIONAL SCENIC AREAS

No Areas of Outstanding Natural Beauty are designated in Scotland. However, National Scenic Areas have a broadly equivalent status. Scottish Natural Heritage recognizes areas of national scenic significance. At mid 1997 there were 40, covering a total area of 1,001,800 hectares (2,475,448 acres).

Development within National Scenic Areas is dealt with by the local planning authority, who are required to consult Scottish Natural Heritage concerning certain categories of development. Land management uses can also be modified in the interest of scenic conservation. The Secretary of State for Scotland has limited powers of intervention should a planning authority and Scottish Natural Heritage disagree.

ASSYNT-COIGACH, Highland, 90,200 ha/222,884 acres

BEN NEVIS AND GLEN COE, Highland/Argyll and Bute/ Perthshire and Kinross, 101,600 ha/251,053 acres

CAIRNGORM MOUNTAINS, Highland/Aberdeenshire/ Moray, 67,200 ha/166,051 acres

CUILLIN HILLS, Highland, 21,900 ha/54,115 acres

DEESIDE AND LOCHNAGAR, Aberdeenshire/Angus, 40,000 ha/98,840 acres

DORNOCH FIRTH, Highland, 7,500 ha/18,532 acres

EAST STEWARTRY COAST, Dumfries and Galloway, 4,500 ha/11,119 acres

EILDON AND LEADERFOOT, Borders, 3,600 ha/8,896 acres

FLEET VALLEY, Dumfries and Galloway, 5,300 ha/13,096 acres

GLEN AFFRIC, Highland, 19,300 ha/47,690 acres

GLEN STRATHFARRAR, Highland, 3,800 ha/9,390 acres

HOY AND WEST MAINLAND, Orkney Islands, 14,800 ha/ 36,571 acres

JURA, Argyll and Bute, 21,800 ha/53,868 acres

KINTAIL, Highland, 15,500 ha/38,300 acres

KNAPDALE, Argyll and Bute, 19,800 ha/48,926 acres

KNOYDART, Highland, 39,500 ha/97,604 acres

KYLE OF TONGUE, Highland, 18,500 ha/45,713 acres

KYLES OF BUTE, Argyll and Bute, 4,400 ha/10,872 acres

LOCHNA KEAL, MULL, Argyll and Bute, 12,700 ha/31,382 acres

LOCH LOMOND, Argyll and Bute/Stirling/West Dumbartonshire, 27,400 ha/67,705 acres

LOCH RANNOCH AND GLEN LYON, Perthshire and Kinross/Stirling, 48,400 ha/119,596 acres

LOCH SHIEL, Highland, 13,400 ha/33,111 acres

LOCH TUMMEL, Perthshire and Kinross, 9,200 ha/22,733 acres

LYNN OF LORN, Argyll and Bute, 4,800 ha/11,861 acres

MORAR, MOIDART AND ARDNAMURCHAN, Highland, 13,500 ha/33,358 acres

NORTH-WEST SUTHERLAND, Highland, 20,500 ha/50,655 acres

NITH ESTUARY, Dumfries and Galloway, 9,300 ha/ 22,980 acres

NORTH ARRAN, North Ayrshire, 23,800 ha/58,810 acres

RIVER EARN, Perthshire and Kinross, 3,000 ha/7,413 acres

RIVER TAY, Perthshire and Kinross, 5,600 ha/13,838 acres

ST KILDA, Western Isles, 900 ha/2,224 acres

SCARBA, LUNGA AND THE GARVELLACHS, Argyll and
 Bute, 1,900 ha/4,695 acres
SHETLAND, Shetland Islands, 11,600 ha/28,664 acres
SMALL ISLES, Highland, 15,500 ha/38,300 acres
SOUTH LEWIS, HARRIS AND NORTH UIST, Western Isles,
 109,600 ha/270,822 acres
SOUTH UIST MACHAIR, Western Isles, 6,100 ha/15,073
 acres
THE TROSSACHS, Stirling, 4,600 ha/11,367 acres
TROTTERNISH, Highland, 5,000 ha/12,355 acres
UPPER TWEEDDALE, Borders, 10,500 ha/25,945 acres
WESTER ROSS, Highland, 145,300 ha/359,036 acres

THE NATIONAL FOREST

The National Forest will be planted in about 200 square
miles of Derbyshire, Leicestershire and Staffordshire.
About 30 million trees, of mixed species but mainly
broadleaved, will be planted over the next 20 years and
beyond, and will eventually cover about one-third of the
designated area. The project is funded by the Department
of the Environment. It was developed in 1992–5 by the
Countryside Commission and is now run by the National
Forest Company. Competitive bids for woodland creation
projects are submitted to the National Forest Company by
anybody who wishes to undertake a project, and are
considered under the National Forest tender scheme.
Sixteen tenders were approved in the first round of the
scheme in 1995. Approval of tenders in the second round of
the scheme was given in autumn 1996 and the results of the
third round were announced in autumn 1997.
NATIONAL FOREST COMPANY, Enterprise Glade, Bath
 Lane, Moira, Swadlincote, Derbys DE12 6BD. Tel:
 01283-551211. *Chief Executive*, Miss S Bell

Nature Conservation Areas

SITES OF SPECIAL SCIENTIFIC INTEREST

Site of Special Scientific Interest (SSSI) is a legal notification applied to land in England, Scotland or Wales which
English Nature (EN), Scottish Natural Heritage (SNH), or
the Countryside Council for Wales (CCW) identifies as
being of special interest because of its flora, fauna,
geological or physiographical features. In some cases,
SSSIs are managed as nature reserves.
 EN, SNH and CCW must notify the designation of a
SSSI to the local planning authority, every owner/
occupier of the land, and the relevant Secretary of State.
Forestry and agricultural departments and a number of
other bodies are also informed of this notification.
 Objections to the notification of a SSSI can be made and
ultimately considered at a full meeting of the Council of
EN or CCW. In Scotland an objection will be dealt with by
the appropriate regional board or the main board of SNH,
depending on the nature of the objection. Unresolved
objections on scientific grounds must be referred to the
Advisory Committee for SSSI.
 The protection of these sites depends on the co-
operation of individual landowners and occupiers.
Owner/occupiers must consult EN, SNH or CCW and
gain written consent before they can undertake certain
listed activities on the site. Funds are available through

management agreements and grants to assist owners and
occupiers in conserving sites' interests. As a last resort a site
can be purchased.
 The number and area of SSSIs in Britain as at 31 March
1997 was:

	no.	hectares	acres
England	3,912	951,680	2,351,653
Scotland	1,429	912,212	2,280,530
Wales	919	218,173	696,150

NORTHERN IRELAND
In Northern Ireland 122 Areas of Special Scientific Interest
(ASSIs) have been established by the Department of the
Environment for Northern Ireland. These cover a total
area of 79,153.8 hectares (195,506 acres).

NATIONAL NATURE RESERVES

National Nature Reserves are defined in the National
Parks and Access to the Countryside Act 1949 as land
designated for the study and preservation of flora and
fauna, or of geological or physiographical features.
 English Nature (EN), Scottish Natural Heritage (SNH)
or the Countryside Council for Wales (CCW) can
designate as a National Nature Reserve land which is
being managed as a nature reserve under an agreement
with one of the statutory nature conservation agencies;
land held and managed by EN, SNH or CCW; or land held
and managed as a nature reserve by another approved
body. EN, SNH or CCW can make by-laws to protect
reserves from undesirable activities; these are subject to
confirmation by the relevant Secretary of State.
 The number and area of National Nature Reserves in
Britain as at 31 March 1997 was:

	no.	hectares	acres
England	185	70,561	174,360
Scotland	70	113,238	279,609
Wales	62	18,592	45,922

NORTHERN IRELAND
National Nature Reserves are established and managed by
the Department of the Environment for Northern Ireland,
with advice from the Council for Nature Conservation and
the Countryside. There are 45 National Nature Reserves
covering 4,322.1 hectares (10,676 acres).

LOCAL NATURE RESERVES

Local Nature Reserves are defined in the National Parks
and Access to the Countryside Act 1949 as land designated
for the study and preservation of flora and fauna, or of
geological or physiographical features. The Act gives local
authorities in England, Scotland and Wales the power to
acquire, declare and manage local nature reserves in
consultation with English Nature, Scottish Natural Heritage and the Countryside Council for Wales. Conservation
trusts can also own and manage non-statutory local nature
reserves.
 The number and area of designated Local Nature
Reserves in Britain as at 31 March 1997 was:

	no.	hectares	acres
England	566	20,428	50,479
Scotland	23	7,456	18,416
Wales	38	5,078	12,548

An additional 38 km of linear trails are designated as Local Nature Reserves.

FOREST NATURE RESERVES

Forest Enterprise (an executive agency of the Forestry Commission) is responsible for the management of the Commission's forests. It has created 46 Forest Nature Reserves with the aim of protecting and conserving special forms of natural habitat, flora and fauna. There are about 300 SSSIs on the estates, some of which are also Nature Reserves.

Forest Nature Reserves extend in size from under 50 hectares (124 acres) to over 500 hectares (1,236 acres). The largest include the Black Wood of Rannoch, by Loch Rannoch; Cannop Valley Oakwoods, Forest of Dean; Culbin Forest, near Forres; Glen Affric, near Fort Augustus; Kylerhea, Skye; Pembrey, Carmarthen Bay; Starr Forest, in Galloway Forest Park; and Wyre Forest, near Kidderminster.

Northern Ireland

There are 36 Forest Nature Reserves in Northern Ireland, covering 1,759 hectares (4,346 acres). They are designated and administered by the Forest Service, a division of the Department of Agriculture for Northern Ireland. There are also 15 National Nature Reserves on Forest Service-owned property.

MARINE NATURE RESERVES

The Wildlife and Countryside Act 1981 gives the Secretary of State for the Environment (and the Secretaries of State for Wales and for Scotland where appropriate) power to designate Marine Nature Reserves, and English Nature, Scottish Natural Heritage and the Countryside Council for Wales powers to select and manage these reserves.

Marine Nature Reserves provide protection for marine flora and fauna, and geological and physiographical features on land covered by tidal waters or parts of the sea in or adjacent to Great Britain. Reserves also provide opportunities for study and research.

The three statutory Marine Nature Reserves are:

Lundy (1986), Bristol Channel
Skomer (1990), Dyfed
Strangford Lough (1995), Northern Ireland

Two other areas proposed for designation as reserves are: the Menai Strait, and Bardsey Island and part of the Llŷn peninsula, both in Wales.

A number of non-statutory marine reserves have been set up by conservation groups.

Wildlife Conservation

The Wildlife and Countryside Act 1981 gives legal protection to a wide range of wild animals and plants. Subject to parliamentary approval, the Secretary of State for the Environment may vary the animals and plants given legal protection. The most recent variation of Schedules 5 and 8 came into effect in October 1992. A review of protected species is currently in progress, the results of which are to be announced in autumn 1997.

ANIMALS, ETC.

Under Section 9 and Schedule 5 of the Act it is illegal without a licence to kill, injure, take, possess or sell any of the animals mentioned below (whether alive or dead) and to disturb its place of shelter and protection or to destroy that place.

‡Adder (*Vipera berus*)
§Allis shad (*alosa alosa*)
Anemone, Ivell's Sea (*Edwardsia ivelli*)
Anemone, Startlet Sea (*Nematosella vectensis*)
Apus (*Triops cancriformis*)
Bat, Horseshoe (*Rhinolophidae*, all species)
Bat, Typical (*Vespertilionidae*, all species)
Beetle (*Hypebaeus flavipes*)
Beetle, Lesser Silver Water (*Hydrochara caraboides*)
§§Beetle, Mire Pill (*Curimopsis nigrita*)
Beetle, Rainbow Leaf (*Chrysolina cerealis*)
Beetle, Violet Click (*Limoniscus violaceus*)
Beetle, Water (*Graphoderus zonatus*)
Beetle, Water (*Paracymus aeneus*)
Burbot (*Lota lota*)
*Butterfly, Adonis Blue (*Lysandra bellargus*)
*Butterfly, Black Hairstreak (*Strymonidia pruni*)
*Butterfly, Brown Hairstreak (*Thecla betulae*)
*Butterfly, Chalkhill Blue (*Lysandra coridon*)
*Butterfly, Chequered Skipper (*Carterocephalus palaemon*)
*Butterfly, Duke of Burgundy Fritillary (*Hamearis lucina*)
*Butterfly, Glanville Fritillary (*Melitaea cinxia*)
Butterfly, Heath Fritillary (*Mellicta athalia* (or *Melitaea athalia*))
Butterfly, High Brown Fritillary (*Argynnis adippe*)
Butterfly, Large Blue (*Maculinea arion*)
*Butterfly, Large Copper (*Lycaena dispar*)
*Butterfly, Large Heath (*Coenonympha tullia*)
*Butterfly, Large Tortoiseshell (*Nymphalis polychloros*)
*Butterfly, Lulworth Skipper (*Thymelicus acteon*)
*Butterfly, Marsh Fritillary (*Eurodryas aurinia*)
*Butterfly, Mountain Ringlet (*Erebia epiphron*)
*Butterfly, Northern Brown Argus (*Aricia artaxerxes*)
*Butterfly, Pearl-bordered Fritillary (*Boloria euphrosyne*)
*Butterfly, Purple Emperor (*Apatura iris*)
*Butterfly, Silver Spotted Skipper (*Hesperia comma*)
*Butterfly, Silver-studded Blue (*Plebejus argus*)

*Butterfly, Small Blue (*Cupido minimus*)
Butterfly, Swallowtail (*Papilio machaon*)
*Butterfly, White Letter Hairstreak (*Stymonida w-album*)
*Butterfly, Wood White (*Leptidea sinapis*)
Cat, Wild (*Felis silvestris*)
Cicada, New Forest (*Cicadetta montana*)
**Crayfish, Atlantic Stream (*Austropotamobius pallipes*)
Cricket, Field (*Gryllus campestris*)
Cricket, Mole (*Gryllotulpa gryllotulpa*)
Dolphin (*Cetacea*)
Dormouse (*Muscardinus avellanarius*)
Dragonfly, Norfolk Aeshna (*Aeshna isosceles*)
*Frog, Common (*Rana temporaria*)
Grasshopper, Wart-biter (*Decticus verrucivorus*)
Hatchet Shell, Northern (*Thyasira gouldi*)
Lagoon Snail (*Paludinella littorina*)
Lagoon Snail, De Folin's (*Caecum armoricum*)
Lagoon Worm, Tentacled (*Alkmaria romijni*)
Leech, Medicinal (*Hirudo medicinalis*)
Lizard, Sand (*Lacerta agilis*)
‡Lizard, Viviparous (*Lacerta vivipara*)
Marten, Pine (*Martes martes*)
Moth, Barberry Carpet (*Pareulype berberata*)
Moth, Black-veined (*Siona lineata* (or *Idaea lineata*))
Moth, Essex Emerald (*Thetidia smaragdaria*)
Moth, New Forest Burnet (*Zygaena viciae*)
Moth, Reddish Buff (*Acosmetia caliginosa*)
Moth, Sussex Emerald (*Thalera fimbrialis*)
Moth, Viper's Bugloss (*Hadena irregularis*)
†Mussel, Freshwater Pearl (*Margaritifera margaritifera*)
Newt, Great Crested (or Warty) (*Triturus cristatus*)
*Newt, Palmate (*Triturus helveticus*)
*Newt, Smooth (*Triturus vulgaris*)
Otter, Common (*Lutra lutra*)
Porpoise (*Cetacea*)
Sandworm, Lagoon (*Armandia cirrhosa*)
††Sea Fan, Pink (*Eunicella verrucosa*)
Sea-Mat, Trembling (*Victorella pavida*)
Sea Slug, Lagoon (*Tenellia adspersa*)
Shrimp, Fairy (*Chirocephalus diaphanus*)
Shrimp, Lagoon Sand (*Gammarus insensibilis*)
‡Slow-worm (*Anguis fragilis*)
Snail, Glutinous (*Myxas glutinosa*)
Snail, Sandbowl (*Catinella arenaria*)
‡Snake, Grass (*Natrix natrix* (*Natrix helvetica*))
Snake, Smooth (*Coronella austriaca*)
Spider, Fen Raft (*Dolomedes plantarius*)
Spider, Ladybird (*Eresus niger*)
Squirrel, Red (*Sciurus vulgaris*)
Sturgeon (*Acipenser sturio*)
*Toad, Common (*Bufo bufo*)
Toad, Natterjack (*Bufo calamita*)
Turtle, Marine (*Dermochelyidae* and *Cheloniidae*, all species)
Vendace (*Coregonus albula*)
Walrus (*Odobenus rosmarus*)
Whale (*Cetacea*)
Whitefish (*Coregonus lavaretus*)

* the offence relates to 'sale' only
** the offence relates to 'taking' and 'sale' only
† the offence relates to 'killing and injuring' only
‡ the offence relates to 'killing, injuring and sale'
§ the offence relates to 'killing, injuring and taking'
§§ the offence relates only to damaging, destroying or obstructing access
   to a shelter or protection
†† the offence relates to killing, injuring, taking, possession and sale

PLANTS

Under Section 13 and Schedule 8 of the Wildlife and Countryside Act 1981, it is illegal without a licence to pick, uproot, sell or destroy any of the plants mentioned below and, unless authorized, to uproot any wild plant.

Adder's tongue, Least (*Ophioglossum lusitanicum*)
Alison, Small (*Alyssum alyssoides*)

Blackwort (*Southbya nigrella*)
Broomrape, Bedstraw (*Orobanche caryophyllacea*)
Broomrape, Oxtongue (*Orobanche loricata*)
Broomrape, Thistle (*Orobanche reticulata*)
Cabbage, Lundy (*Rhynchosinapis wrightii*)
Calamint, Wood (*Calamintha sylvatica*)
Caloplaca, Snow (*Caloplaca nivalis*)
Catapyrenium, Tree (*Catapyrenium psoromoides*)
Catchfly, Alpine (*Lychnis alpina*)
Catillaria, Laurer's (*Catellaria laureri*)
Centaury, Slender (*Centaurium tenuiflorum*)
Cinquefoil, Rock (*Potentilla rupestris*)
Cladonia, Upright Mountain (*Cladonia stricta*)
Clary, Meadow (*Salvia pratensis*)
Club-rush, Triangular (*Scirpus triquetrus*)
Colt's-foot, Purple (*Homogyne alpina*)
Cotoneaster, Wild (*Cotoneaster integerrimus*)
Cottongrass, Slender (*Eriophorum gracile*)
Cow-wheat, Field (*Melampyrum arvense*)
Crocus, Sand (*Romulea columnae*)
Crystalwort, Lizard (*Riccia bifurca*)
Cudweed, Broad-leaved (*Filago pyramidata*)
Cudweed, Jersey (*Gnaphalium luteoalbum*)
Cudweed, Red-tipped (*Filago lutescens*)
Diapensia (*Diapensia lapponica*)
Dock, Shore (*Rumex rupestris*)
Earwort, Marsh (*Jamesoniella undulifolia*)
Eryngo, Field (*Eryngium campestre*)
Fern, Dickie's Bladder (*Cystopteris dickieana*)
Fern, Killarney (*Trichomanes speciosum*)
Flapwort, Norfolk (*Leiocolea rutheana*)
Fleabane, Alpine (*Erigeron borealis*)
Fleabane, Small (*Pulicaria vulgaris*)
Frostwort, Pointed (*Gymnomitrion apiculatum*)
Galingale, Brown (*Cyperus fuscus*)
Gentian, Alpine (*Gentiana nivalis*)
Gentian, Dune (*Gentianella uliginosa*)
Gentian, Early (*Gentianella anglica*)
Gentian, Fringed (*Gentianella ciliata*)
Gentian, Spring (*Gentiana verna*)
Germander, Cut-leaved (*Teucrium botrys*)
Germander, Water (*Teucrium scordium*)
Gladiolus, Wild (*Gladiolus illyricus*)
Goosefoot, Stinking (*Chenopodium vulvaria*)
Grass-poly (*Lythrum hyssopifolia*)
Grimmia, Blunt-leaved (*Grimmia unicolor*)
Gyalecta, Elm (*Gyalecta ulmi*)
Hare's-ear, Sickle-leaved (*Bupleurum falcatum*)
Hare's-ear, Small (*Bupleurum baldense*)
Hawk's-beard, Stinking (*Crepis foetida*)
Hawkweed, Northroe (*Hieracium northroense*)
Hawkweed, Shetland (*Hieracium zetlandicum*)
Hawkweed, Weak-leaved (*Hieracium attenuatifolium*)
Heath, Blue (*Phyllodoce caerulea*)
Helleborine, Red (*Cephalanthera rubra*)
Helleborine, Young's (*Epipactis youngiana*)
Horsetail, Branched (*Equisetum ramosissimum*)
Hound's-tongue, Green (*Cynoglossum germanicum*)
Knawel, Perennial (*Scleranthus perennis*)
Knotgrass, Sea (*Polygonum maritimum*)
Lady's-slipper (*Cypripedium calceolus*)
Lecanactis, Churchyard (*Lecanactis hemisphaerica*)
Lecanora, Tarn (*Lecanora archariana*)
Lecidea, Copper (*Lecidea inops*)
Leek, Round-headed (*Allium sphaerocephalon*)
Lettuce, Least (*Lactuca saligna*)
Lichen, Arctic Kidney (*Nephroma arcticum*)
Lichen, Ciliate Strap (*Heterodermia leucomelos*)
Lichen, Coralloid Rosette (*Heterodermia propagulifera*)
Lichen, Ear-lobed Dog (*Peltigera lepidophora*)

Lichen, Forked Hair (*Bryoria furcellata*)
Lichen, Golden Hair (*Teloschistes flavicans*)
Lichen, Orange Fruited Elm (*Caloplaca luteoalba*)
Lichen, River Jelly (*Collema dichotomum*)
Lichen, Scaly Breck (*Squamarina lentigera*)
Lichen, Starry Breck (*Buellia asterella*)
Lily, Snowdon (*Lloydia serotina*)
Liverwort (*Petallophyllum ralfsi*)
Liverwort, Lindenberg's Leafy (*Adelanthus lindenbergianus*)
Marsh-mallow, Rough (*Althaea hirsuta*)
Marshwort, Creeping (*Apium repens*)
Milk-parsley, Cambridge (*Selinum carvifolia*)
Moss (*Drepanocladius vernicosus*)
Moss, Alpine Copper (*Mielichoferia mielichoferi*)
Moss, Baltic Bog (*Sphagnum balticum*)
Moss, Blue Dew (*Saelania glaucescens*)
Moss, Blunt-leaved Bristle (*Orthotrichum obtusifolium*)
Moss, Bright Green Cave (*Cyclodictyon laetevirens*)
Moss, Cordate Beard (*Barbula cordata*)
Moss, Cornish Path (*Ditrichum cornubicum*)
Moss, Derbyshire Feather (*Thamnobryum angustifolium*)
Moss, Dune Thread (*Bryum mamillatum*)
Moss, Glaucous Beard (*Barbula glauca*)
Moss, Green Shield (*Buxbaumia viridis*)
Moss, Hair Silk (*Plagiothecium piliferum*)
Moss, Knothole (*Zygodon forsteri*)
Moss, Large Yellow Feather (*Scorpidium turgescens*)
Moss, Millimetre (*Micromitrium tenerum*)
Moss, Multifruited River (*Cryphaea lamyana*)
Moss, Nowell's Limestone (*Zygodon gracilis*)
Moss, Rigid Apple (*Bartramia stricta*)
Moss, Round-leaved Feather (*Rhyncostegium rotundifolium*)
Moss, Schleicher's Thread (*Bryum schleicheri*)
Moss, Triangular Pygmy (*Acaulon triquetrum*)
Moss, Vaucher's Feather (*Hypnum vaucheri*)
Mudwort, Welsh (*Limosella australis*)
Naiad, Holly-leaved (*Najas marina*)
Naiad, Slender (*Najas flexilis*)
Orache, Stalked (*Halimione pedunculata*)
Orchid, Early Spider (*Ophrys sphegodes*)
Orchid, Fen (*Liparis loeselii*)
Orchid, Ghost (*Epipogium aphyllum*)
Orchid, Lapland Marsh (*Dactylorhiza lapponica*)
Orchid, Late Spider (*Ophrys fuciflora*)
Orchid, Lizard (*Himantoglossum hircinum*)
Orchid, Military (*Orchis militaris*)
Orchid, Monkey (*Orchis simia*)
Pannaria, Caledonia (*Pannaria ignobilis*)
Parmelia, New Forest (*Parmelia minarum*)
Parmentaria, Oil Stain (*Parmentaria chilensis*)
Pear, Plymouth (*Pyrus cordata*)
Penny-cress, Perfoliate (*Thlaspi perfoliatum*)
Pennyroyal (*Mentha pulegium*)
Pertusaria, Alpine Moss (*Pertusaria bryontha*)
Physcia, Southern Grey (*Physcia tribacioides*)
Pigmyweed (*Crassula aquatica*)
Pine, Ground (*Ajuga chamaepitys*)
Pink, Cheddar (*Dianthus gratianopolitanus*)
Pink, Childling (*Petroraghia nanteuilii*)
Plantain, Floating Water (*Luronium natans*)
Pseudocyphellaria, Ragged (*Pseudocyphellaria lacerata*)
Psora, Rusty Alpine (*Psora rubiformis*)
Ragwort, Fen (*Senecio paludosus*)
Ramping-fumitory, Martin's (*Fumaria martinii*)
Rampion, Spiked (*Phyteuma spicatum*)
Restharrow, Small (*Ononis reclinata*)
Rock-cress, Alpine (*Arabis alpina*)
Rock-cress, Bristol (*Arabis stricta*)
Rustwort, Western (*Marsupella profunda*)
Sandwort, Norwegian (*Arenaria norvegica*)

Sandwort, Teesdale (*Minuartia stricta*)
Saxifrage, Drooping (*Saxifraga cernua*)
Saxifrage, Marsh (*Saxifrage hirulus*)
Saxifrage, Tufted (*Saxifraga cespitosa*)
Solenopsora, Serpentine (*Solenopsora liparina*)
Solomon's-seal, Whorled (*Polygonatum verticillatum*)
Sow-thistle, Alpine (*Cicerbita alpina*)
Spearwort, Adder's-tongue (*Ranunculus ophioglossifolius*)
Speedwell, Fingered (*Veronica triphyllos*)
Speedwell, Spiked (*Veronica spicata*)
Star-of-Bethlehem, Early (*Gagea bohemica*)
Starfruit (*Damasonium alisma*)
Stonewort, Bearded (*Chara canescens*)
Stonewort, Foxtail (*Lamprothamnium papulosum*)
Strapwort (*Corrigiola litoralis*)
Turpswort (*Geocalyx graveolens*)
Violet, Fen (*Viola persicifolia*)
Viper's-grass (*Scorzonera humilis*)
Water-plantain, Ribbon-leaved (*Alisma gramineum*)
Wood-sedge, Starved (*Carex depauperata*)
Woodsia, Alpine (*Woodsia alpina*)
Woodsia, Oblong (*Woodsia ilvensis*)
Wormwood, Field (*Artemisia campestris*)
Woundwort, Downy (*Stachys germanica*)
Woundwort, Limestone (*Stachys alpina*)
Yellow-rattle, Greater (*Rhinanthus serotinus*)

WILD BIRDS

The Wildlife and Countryside Act 1981 lays down a close season for wild birds (other than game birds) from 1 February to 31 August inclusive, each year. Exceptions to these dates are made for:

Capercaillie and (except Scotland) *Woodcock* – 1 February to 30 September

Snipe – 1 February to 11 August

Wild Duck and *Wild Goose* (below high water mark) – 21 February to 31 August

Birds which may be killed or taken outside the close season (except on Sundays and on Christmas Day in Scotland, and on Sundays in prescribed areas of England and Wales) are the above-named, plus coot, certain wild duck (gadwall, goldeneye, mallard, pintail, pochard, shoveler, teal, tufted duck, wigeon), certain wild geese (Canada, greylag, pinkfooted, white-fronted (in England and Wales only)), moorhen, golden plover and woodcock.

Certain wild birds may be killed or taken subject to the conditions of a general licence at any time by authorized persons: crow, collared dove, gull (great and lesser blackbacked or herring), jackdaw, jay, magpie, pigeon (feral or wood), rook, sparrow (house), and starling. Conditions usually apply where the birds pose a threat to agriculture, public health, air safety, other bird species, and to prevent the spread of disease.

All other British birds are fully protected by law throughout the year.

CLOSE SEASONS AND TIMES

GAME BIRDS

In each case the dates are inclusive:

Black game – 11 December to 19 August (31 August in Somerset, Devon and New Forest)

*Grouse – 11 December to 11 August

*Partridge – 2 February to 31 August

*Pheasant – 2 February to 30 September

*Ptarmigan – (Scotland only) 11 December to 11 August

*It is also unlawful in England and Wales to kill this game on a Sunday or Christmas Day

HUNTING AND GROUND GAME

There is no statutory close time for fox-hunting or rabbit-shooting, nor for hares. However, by an Act passed in 1892 the sale of hares or leverets in Great Britain is prohibited from 1 March to 31 July inclusive. The recognized date for the opening of the fox-hunting season is 1 November, and it continues till the following April.

DEER

The statutory close seasons for deer (all dates inclusive) are:

	England and Wales	Scotland
Fallow deer		
Male	1 May–31 July	1 May–31 July
Female	1 Mar.–31 Oct.	16 Feb.–20 Oct.
Red deer		
Male	1 May–31 July	21 Oct.–30 June
Female	1 Mar.–31 Oct.	16 Feb.–20 Oct.
Roe deer		
Male	1 Nov.–31 Mar.	21 Oct.–31 Mar.
Female	1 Mar.–31 Oct.	1 April–20 Oct.
Sika deer		
Male	1 May–31 July	21 Oct.–30 June
Female	1 Mar.–31 Oct.	16 Feb.–20 Oct.
Red/Sika hybrids		
Male	—	21 Oct.–30 June
Female	—	16 Feb.–20 Oct.

ANGLING

Game Fishing

Where local by-laws neither specify nor dispense with an annual close season, the statutory close times for game fishing are: Trout, 1 October to end February; Salmon, 1 November to 31 January.

Coarse Fishing

Responsibility for the fisheries function of the National Rivers Authority, including licensing and regulation, passed to the Environment Agency on 1 April 1996. The statutory close season for coarse fish in England and Wales runs from 15 March to 15 June on all rivers, streams and drains. Close season arrangements for canals vary from region to region. The close season on all lakes, ponds and reservoirs is at the discretion of the fishery owner, except on the Norfolk Broads and certain Sites of Special Scientific Interest where the statutory close season still applies. It is necessary in all cases to check with the Environment Agency regional office concerning the area (details can be found in the local telephone directory).

Licences

Purchase of a national rod fishing licence is legally required of anglers wishing to fish with rod and line in all waters within the area of the Environment Agency.

	Salmon and sea trout	Non-migratory trout and coarse fish
Full	£55.00	£16.00
Concessionary	27.50	8.00
Eight-day	13.50	6.00
One-day	4.50	2.00

Concessionary licences are available for juniors (12–16 years), for senior citizens (65 years and over), and disabled who are in receipt of long-term incapacity benefit, short-term incapacity benefit (at the higher rate) or severe disablement allowance. Those in receipt of a war pension which includes unemployability supplements are also eligible.

Historic Buildings and Monuments

LISTING

Under the Planning (Listed Buildings and Conservation Areas) Act 1990, the Secretary of State for National Heritage has a statutory duty to compile lists of buildings or groups of buildings in England which are of special architectural or historic interest. Under the Ancient Monuments and Archaeological Areas Act 1979 as amended by the National Heritage Act 1983, the Secretary of State is also responsible for compiling a schedule of ancient monuments. Decisions are taken on the advice of English Heritage (*see* page 309).

Listed buildings are classified into Grade I, Grade II* and Grade II. There are currently about 500,000 individual listed buildings in England, of which about 95 per cent are Grade II listed. Almost all pre-1700 buildings are listed, and most buildings of 1700 to 1840. English Heritage is carrying out thematic surveys of particular types of buildings with a view to making recommendations for listing, and members of the public may propose a building for consideration. The main purpose of listing is to ensure that care is taken in deciding the future of a building. No changes which affect the architectural or historic character of a listed building can be made without listed building consent (in addition to planning permission where relevant). Applications for listed building consent are normally dealt with by the local planning authority, although English Heritage is always consulted about proposals affecting Grade I and Grade II* properties. It is a criminal offence to demolish a listed building, or alter it in such a way as to affect its character, without consent.

There are currently about 22,500 scheduled monuments in England. English Heritage is carrying out a Monuments Protection Programme assessing archaeological sites with a view to making recommendations for scheduling, and members of the public may propose a monument for consideration. All monuments proposed for scheduling are considered to be of national importance. Where buildings are both scheduled and listed, ancient monuments legislation takes precedence. The main purpose of scheduling a monument is to preserve it for the future and to protect it from damage, destruction or any unnecessary interference. Once a monument has been scheduled, scheduled monument consent is required before any works are carried out which would damage or alter the monument in any way. The scope of the control is more extensive and more detailed than that applied to listed buildings, but certain minor works, as detailed in the Ancient Monuments Class Consents Order 1994, may be carried out without consent. It is a criminal offence to carry out unauthorized work to scheduled monuments.

Under the Planning (Listed Buildings and Conservation Areas) Act 1990 and the Ancient Monuments and Archaeological Areas Act 1979, the Secretary of State for Wales is responsible for listing buildings and scheduling monuments in Wales on the advice of Cadw (*see* page 353), the Historic Buildings Council for Wales (*see* page 309) and the Ancient Monuments Board for Wales (*see* page 310). The criteria for evaluating buildings are similar to those in England and the same listing system is used. In April 1997 there were 19,161 listed buildings and 2,999 scheduled monuments in Wales.

Under the Town and Country Planning (Scotland) Act 1972 and the Ancient Monuments and Archaeological Areas Act 1979, the Secretary of State for Scotland is responsible for listing buildings and scheduling monuments in Scotland on the advice of Historic Scotland (*see* page 341), the Historic Buildings Council for Scotland (*see* page 309) and the Ancient Monuments Board for Scotland (*see* page 310). The criteria for evaluating buildings are similar to those in England but an A, B, C grading system is used. There are about 43,286 listed buildings and about 6,508 scheduled monuments in Scotland.

Under the Planning (Northern Ireland) Order 1991 and the Historic Monuments and Archaeological Objects (Northern Ireland) Order 1995, the Department of the Environment for Northern Ireland (*see* page 330) is responsible for listing buildings and scheduling monuments in Northern Ireland on the advice of the Historic Buildings Council for Northern Ireland and the Historic Monuments Council for Northern Ireland. The criteria for evaluating buildings are similar to those in England but no official grading system is used. In June 1997 there were 8,579 listed buildings and 1,225 scheduled monuments in Northern Ireland.

OPENING TO THE PUBLIC

The following is a selection of the many historic buildings and monuments open to the public. The admission charges given are the standard charges for 1997–8; many properties have concessionary rates for children, etc. Opening hours vary. Many properties are closed in winter and some are also closed in the mornings. Most properties are closed on Christmas Eve, Christmas Day, Boxing Day and New Year's Day, and many are closed on Good Friday. During the winter season, most English Heritage monuments are closed on Mondays and Tuesdays and monuments in the care of Cadw are closed on Sunday mornings. Information about a specific property should be checked by telephone.

*Closed in winter (usually November-March)
†Closed in winter, and in mornings in summer

ENGLAND

EH English Heritage property
NT National Trust property

*A LA RONDE (NT), Exmouth, Devon. Tel: 01395-265514. Closed Fri. and Sat. Adm. £3.20. Unique 16-sided house completed *c*.1796

†ALNWICK CASTLE, Northumberland. Tel: 01665-510777. Closed Fri. Adm. charge. Seat of the Dukes of Northumberland since 1309; Italian Renaissance-style interior

ALTHORP, Northants. Tel: 01604-770107. Opening times and prices subject to change. House originally built in early 16th century. Fine art collection

†ANGLESEY ABBEY (NT), Cambs. Tel: 01223-811200. Closed Mon. (except Bank Holidays) and Tues. Gardens open daily July to Sept. Adm. £5.60 (£6.60 Sun. and Bank Holidays); gardens only, £3.30. House built *c*.1600; bought by Lord Fairhaven in early 20th century. Outstanding grounds with unique statuary

APSLEY HOUSE, London W1. Tel: 0171-499 5676. Closed Mon. Adm. £4.00. Built by Robert Adam 1771-8, home of the Dukes of Wellington since 1817 and known as 'No. 1 London'. Collection of fine and decorative arts

†ARUNDEL CASTLE, W. Sussex. Tel: 01903-883136. Closed Sat. Adm. charge. Castle dating from the Norman Conquest. Seat of the Dukes of Norfolk

AVEBURY (NT), Wilts. Adm. free. Remains of stone circles constructed 4,000 years ago surrounding the later village of Avebury. Also *Alexander Keiller Museum*. Tel: 01672-539250. Adm. £1.50

BANQUETING HOUSE, Whitehall, London SW1. Tel: 0171-839 8919. Closed Sun. and Bank Holidays. Adm. £3.25. Designed by Inigo Jones; ceiling paintings by Rubens. Site of the execution of Charles I

†BASILDON PARK (NT), Berks. Tel: 0118-984 3040. Closed Mon. (except Bank Holidays), Tues., some Wed. and Good Friday. Adm. £3.80; grounds only, £1.50. Palladian house built in 1776

BATTLE ABBEY (EH), E. Sussex. Tel: 01424-773792. Adm. £3.50. Remains of the abbey founded by William the Conqueror on the site of the Battle of Hastings

BEAULIEU, Hants. Tel: 01590-612345. Adm. charge. House and gardens, Beaulieu Abbey and exhibition of monastic life, National Motor Museum (*see also* page 585)

BEESTON CASTLE (EH), Cheshire. Tel: 01829-260464. Adm. £2.50. Thirteenth-century inner ward with gatehouse and towers, and remains of large outer ward

†BELTON HOUSE (NT), Grantham, Lincs. Tel: 01476-566116. Closed Mon. (except Bank Holidays), Tues. and Good Friday. Adm. £4.80. Fine 17th-century house in landscaped park

*BELVOIR CASTLE, nr Grantham, Lincs. Tel: 01476-870262. Closed Mon. and Fri. except Bank Holidays; also closed Mon.-Sat. in Oct. Adm. £4.25. Seat of the Dukes of Rutland; 19th-century Gothic-style castle

*BERKELEY CASTLE, Glos. Tel: 01453-810332. Opening times vary. Adm. £4.80. Completed 1153; site of the murder of Edward II (1327)

*BLENHEIM PALACE, Woodstock, Oxon. Tel: 01993 811325. Adm. charge. Seat of the Dukes of Marlborough and Winston Churchill's birthplace; designed by Vanbrugh

†BLICKLING HALL (NT), Norfolk. Tel: 01263-733084. Opening times vary. Adm. £5.50 (£6.50 Sun. and Bank Holidays), garden only, £3.20 and £3.50. Jacobean house with state rooms, temple and 18th-century orangery

BODIAM CASTLE (NT), E. Sussex. Tel: 01580-830436. Closed Mon. in winter. Adm. £3.00. Well-preserved medieval moated castle

BOLSOVER CASTLE (EH), Derbys. Tel: 01246-823349. Closed Mon. and Tues. in winter. Adm. £2.80. Notable for its 17th-century buildings

BOSCOBEL HOUSE (EH), Shropshire. Tel: 01902-850244. Closed Mon. and Tues. in winter; also closed in Jan. Adm. £3.75. Timber-framed 17th-century hunting lodge, refuge of fugitive Charles II

†BOUGHTON HOUSE, Northants. Tel: 01536-515731. House open Aug. only; grounds May to Sept. except Fri.; state rooms by prior booking. Adm. £4.00; grounds, £1.50. A 17th-century house with French-style additions

*BOWOOD HOUSE, Wilts. Tel: 01249-812102. Adm. £5.00. An 18th-century house in Capability Brown park, with lake, temple and arboretum

†BROADLANDS, Hants. Tel: 01794-517888. Open June-Sept. Adm. £5.00. Palladian mansion in Capability Brown parkland. Mountbatten exhibition

BRONTË PARSONAGE, Haworth, W. Yorks. Tel: 01535-642323. Closed Jan.-Feb. Adm. £3.80. Home of the Brontë sisters; museum and memorabilia

BUCKFAST ABBEY, Devon. Tel: 01364-642519. Adm. free. Benedictine monastery on medieval foundations

*BUCKINGHAM PALACE, London SW1. Tel: 0171-839 1377. Open daily for eight weeks from early Aug. each year.

Adm. £9.00. Purchased by George III in 1762, it has been the Sovereign's official London residence since 1837. Eighteen state rooms, including the Throne Room; also the Picture Gallery

BUCKLAND ABBEY (NT), Devon. Tel: 01822-853607. Closed Thurs; in winter open only weekend afternoons. Adm. £4.30. A 13th-century Cistercian monastery. Home of Sir Francis Drake

BURGHLEY HOUSE, Stamford, Lincs. Tel: 01780-52451. Adm. £5.60. Late Elizabethan house; vast state apartments

†CALKE ABBEY (NT), Derbys. Tel: 01332-863822. Closed Thurs. and Fri. Adm. £4.85, by timed ticket. Baroque 18th-century mansion

CARISBROOKE CASTLE (EH), Isle of Wight. Tel: 01983-522107. Adm. £4.00. Norman castle; prison of Charles I 1647-8

CARLISLE CASTLE (EH), Cumbria. Tel: 01228-591922. Adm. £2.70. Medieval castle, prison of Mary Queen of Scots

*CARLYLE'S HOUSE (NT), Cheyne Row, London SW3. Tel: 0171-352 7087. Closed Mon. (except Bank Holidays), Tues. and Good Friday. Adm. £3.00. Home of Thomas Carlyle

CASTLE ACRE PRIORY (EH), Norfolk. Tel: 01760-755394. Closed Mon. and Tues. in winter. Adm. £2.75. Remains include 12th-century church and prior's lodgings

*CASTLE DROGO (NT), Devon. Tel: 01647-433306. Castle closed Fri. (except Good Friday). Adm. £4.90; grounds only, £2.30. Granite castle designed by Lutyens

*CASTLE HOWARD, N. Yorks. Tel: 01653-648444. Adm. £6.50; grounds only, £4.00. Designed by Vanbrugh 1699-1726; mausoleum designed by Hawksmoor

CASTLE RISING CASTLE (EH), Norfolk. Tel: 01553-631330. Closed Mon. and Tues. in winter. Adm. £2.10. A 12th-century keep in a massive earthwork with gatehouse and bridge

†CHARTWELL (NT), Kent. Tel: 01732-866368. Closed Mon. and Tues.; also open weekends and Wed. in March and Nov. Adm. £5.00 by timed ticket; grounds only, £2.50. Home of Sir Winston Churchill

*CHATSWORTH, Derbys. Tel: 01246-582204. Adm. £5.90. Tudor mansion in magnificent parkland

CHESTERS ROMAN FORT (EH), Northumberland. Tel: 01434-681379. Adm. £2.50. Roman cavalry fort

*CHYSAUSTER ANCIENT VILLAGE (EH), Cornwall. Tel: 0831-757934. Adm. £1.50. Romano-Cornish village, 2nd and 3rd century AD, on a probably late Iron Age site

CLIFFORD'S TOWER (EH), York. Tel: 01904-646940. Adm. £1.60. A 13th-century tower built on a mound

†CLIVEDEN (NT), Berks. Tel: 01628-605069. House open Thurs. and Sun. only, gardens daily. Adm. £4.50; £1.00 extra for house. Former home of the Astors, now an hotel set in garden and woodland

CORBRIDGE ROMAN SITE (EH), Northumberland. Tel: 01434-632349. Closed Mon. and Tues. in winter. Adm. £2.50. Excavated central area of a Roman town and successive military bases

CORFE CASTLE (NT), Dorset. Tel: 01929-481294. Adm. £3.50. Ruined former royal castle dating from 11th century

†CROFT CASTLE (NT), Herefordshire. Tel: 01568-780246. Closed Mon. (except Bank Holidays) and Tues.; April and Oct. open weekends only. Adm. £3.20. Pre-Conquest border castle with Georgian-Gothic interior

DEAL CASTLE (EH), Kent. Tel: 01304-372762. Closed Mon. and Tues. in winter. Adm. £2.80. Largest of the coastal defence forts built by Henry VIII

DICKENS HOUSE, Doughty Street, London WC1. Tel: 0171-405 2127. Closed Sun. Adm. £3.50. House occupied by Dickens 1837-9; manuscripts, furniture and portraits

DR JOHNSON'S HOUSE, 17 Gough Square, London EC4. Tel: 0171-353 3745. Closed Sun. and Bank Holidays. Adm. £3.00. Home of Samuel Johnson

DOVE COTTAGE, Grasmere, Cumbria. Tel: 01539-435544. Closed Jan. and early Feb. Adm. £4.25. Wordsworth's home 1799-1808; museum

DOVER CASTLE (EH), Kent. Tel: 01304-201628. Adm. £6.00. Castle with Roman, Saxon and Norman features; wartime operations rooms

DUNSTANBURGH CASTLE (EH), Northumberland. Tel: 01665-576231. Closed Mon. and Tues. in winter. Adm. £1.60. A 14th-century castle on a cliff, with a substantial gatehouse-keep

FARLEIGH HUNGERFORD CASTLE (EH), Somerset. Tel: 01225-754026. Closed Mon. and Tues. in winter. Adm. £2.00. Late 14th-century castle with two courts; chapel with tomb of Sir Thomas Hungerford

*FARNHAM CASTLE KEEP (EH), Surrey. Tel: 01252-713393. Adm. £2.00. Large 12th-century shell-keep

FOUNTAINS ABBEY (NT), nr Ripon, N. Yorks. Tel: 01765-608888. Closed Fri. Nov.-Jan. Adm. £4.20. Ruined Cistercian monastery; 18th-century landscaped gardens of Studley Royal estate

FRAMLINGHAM CASTLE (EH), Suffolk. Tel: 01728-724189. Adm. £2.60. Castle (c.1200) with high curtain walls enclosing an almshouse (1639)

FURNESS ABBEY (EH), Cumbria. Tel: 01229-823420. Closed Mon. and Tues. in winter. Adm. £2.50. Remains of church and conventual buildings founded in 1123

GLASTONBURY ABBEY, Somerset. Tel: 01458-832267. Adm. £2.50. Ruins of a 12th-century abbey rebuilt after fire. Site of an early Christian settlement

GOODRICH CASTLE (EH), Herefordshire. Tel: 01600-890538. Adm. £2.30. Remains of 13th- and 14th-century castle with 12th-century keep

GREENWICH, London SE10. Royal Observatory. Closed Sun. mornings. Adm. charge. Former Royal Observatory (founded 1675) where the time ball and zero meridian of longitude can be seen. The Queen's House. Tel: 0181-858 4422. Closed Sun. mornings. Adm. charge. Designed for Queen Anne, wife of James I, by Inigo Jones. Painted Hall and Chapel (Royal Naval College). Closed mornings. Visitors admitted to Sunday service (11 a.m.) in the chapel during college term

GRIMES GRAVES (EH), Norfolk. Tel: 01842-810656. Closed Mon. and Tues. in winter. Adm. £1.60. Neolithic flint mines. One shaft can be descended

GUILDHALL, London EC2. Tel: 0171-332 1460. Closed Sun. in winter. Adm. free. Centre of civic government of the City. Built c.1440; facade built 1788-9

*HADDON HALL, Derbys. Tel: 01629-812855. Closed Sun. in Aug. except Bank Holiday weekend. Adm. £4.75. Well-preserved 12th-century manor house

HAILES ABBEY (EH), Glos. Tel: 01242-602398. Closed Mon. and Tues. in winter. Adm. £2.40. Ruins of a 13th-century Cistercian monastery

†HAM HOUSE (NT), Richmond, Surrey. Tel: 0181-940 1950. Closed Thurs. and Fri. Adm. £4.50. Garden open all year except Fri. Adm. free. Stuart house with fine interiors

HAMPTON COURT PALACE, East Molesey, Surrey. Tel: 0181-781 9500. Adm. £8.50. A 16th-century palace with additions by Wren. Gardens with maze; Tudor tennis court (summer only)

†HARDWICK HALL (NT), Derbys. Tel: 01246-850430. Closed Mon. (except Bank Holidays), Tues. and Fri.; grounds open daily, all year. Adm £5.80; grounds only £2.50. Built 1591-7 for Bess of Hardwick; notable furnishings

*HARDY'S COTTAGE (NT), Higher Bockhampton, Dorset. Tel: 01305-262366. Closed Fri. (except Good Friday) and Sat. Adm. £2.50. Garden open daily, adm. free. Birthplace of Thomas Hardy

*HAREWOOD HOUSE, W. Yorks. Tel: 0113-288 6331. Adm. £6.50. An 18th-century house designed by John Carr and Robert Adam; park by Capability Brown

†HATFIELD HOUSE, Herts. Tel: 01707-262823. Closed Mon. (except Bank Holidays). Adm. charge. Jacobean house built by Robert Cecil; surviving wing of royal Palace of Hatfield (1497)

HELMSLEY CASTLE (EH), N. Yorks. Tel: 01439-770442. Closed Mon. and Tues. in winter. Adm. £2.00. A 12th-century keep and curtain wall with 16th-century buildings. Spectacular earthwork defences

†HEVER CASTLE, Kent. Tel: 01732-865224. Adm. charge. A 13th-century double-moated castle, childhood home of Anne Boleyn

*HOLKER HALL, Cumbria. Tel: 01539-558328. Closed Sat. Adm. charge. Former home of the Dukes of Devonshire; award-winning gardens

†HOLKHAM HALL, Norfolk. Tel: 01328-710227. Closed Fri. and Sat. Adm. £4.00. Fine Palladian mansion

HOUSESTEADS ROMAN FORT (EH), Northumberland. Tel: 01434-344363. Adm. £2.50. Excavated infantry fort on Hadrian's Wall with extra-mural civilian settlement

†HUGHENDEN MANOR (NT), High Wycombe. Tel: 01494-532580. Closed Mon. (except Bank Holidays) and Tues.; open weekends only in March. Adm. £3.80. Home of Disraeli; small formal garden

JANE AUSTEN'S HOUSE, Chawton, Hants. Tel: 01420-83262. Closed Mon.-Fri. in Jan. and Feb. Adm. £2.00. Jane Austen's home 1809-17

KEATS HOUSE, Keats Grove, London NW3. Tel: 0171-435 2062. Closed Sun. mornings in summer; also closed mornings (except Sat.) in winter. Adm. free. Home of John Keats 1818-20

*KELMSCOTT MANOR, nr Lechlade, Oxon. Tel: 01367-252486. Open Wed. and afternoon of third Sat. in every month. Adm. £6.00. Summer home of William Morris, with products of Morris and Co.

KENILWORTH CASTLE (EH), Warks. Tel: 01926-852078. Adm. £2.75. Castle showing many styles of building from 1155 to 1649

*KENSINGTON PALACE, London W8. Tel: 0171-376 2452. Adm. £6.00. Built in 1605 and enlarged by Wren; bought by William and Mary in 1689. Birthplace of Queen Victoria

KENWOOD (EH), Hampstead Lane, London NW3. Tel: 0181-348 1286. Adm. free. Adam villa housing the Iveagh bequest of paintings and furniture. Open-air concerts in summer

*KEW PALACE, Surrey. Tel: 0181-332 5189. Closed for refurbishment until spring 1998. Also Queen Charlotte's Cottage, weekends and Bank Holidays in May-Sept. Adm. free (but £4.50 adm. to Kew Gardens)

†KINGSTON LACY HOUSE (NT), Dorset. Tel: 01202-883402. Closed Thurs. and Fri. Adm. £5.50; grounds only, £2.20. A 17th-century house with 19th-century alterations; important collection of paintings

†KNEBWORTH HOUSE, Herts. Tel: 01438-812661. Opening times vary. Adm. charge. Tudor manor house concealed by 19th-century Gothic decoration; Lutyens gardens

*KNOLE (NT), Kent. Tel: 01732-450608. Closed Mon. (except Bank Holidays), Tues. and Thurs. morning. Adm. £5.00; grounds free to pedestrians. House dating from 1456 set in parkland; fine art treasures

LAMBETH PALACE, London SE1. Tel: 0171-928 8282. Visits by written application. Official residence of the Archbishop of Canterbury. A 19th-century house with parts dating from the 12th century

*LANERCOST PRIORY (EH), Cumbria. Tel: 01697-73030. Adm. £1.20. The nave of the Augustinian priory church, c.1166, is still used; remains of other claustral buildings

*LANHYDROCK (NT), Cornwall. Tel: 01208-73320. Closed Mon. (except Bank Holidays) Garden open all year. Adm. £6.00; garden and grounds only, £3.00. House dating from the 17th century; 45 rooms, including kitchen and nursery

LEEDS CASTLE, Kent. Tel: 01622-765400. Adm. £8.50; park only, £6.50. Castle dating from the 9th century, on two islands in a lake

*LEVENS HALL, Cumbria. Tel: 01539-560321. Closed Fri. and Sat. Adm. charge. Elizabethan house with unique topiary garden (1694). Steam engine collection

LINCOLN CASTLE. Tel: 01522-511068. Adm. £2.00. Built by William the Conqueror in 1068

LINDISFARNE PRIORY (EH), Northumberland. Tel: 01289-389200. Open all year, subject to tide times. Adm. £2.50. Bishopric of the Northumbrian kingdom destroyed by the Danes; re-established in the 11th century as a Benedictine priory, now ruined

†LITTLE MORETON HALL (NT), Cheshire. Tel: 01260-272018. Closed Mon. (except Bank Holidays) and Tues. Adm. £3.80. Timber-framed moated manor house with knot garden

LONGLEAT HOUSE, Warminster. Tel: 01985-844400. Open daily; safari park closed winter. Adm. charge. Elizabethan house in Italian Renaissance style

LULLINGSTONE ROMAN VILLA (EH), Kent. Tel: 01322-863467. Adm. £2.00. Large villa occupied for much of the Roman period; fine mosaics

†LUTON HOO, Beds. Tel: 01582-722955. Open Fri.-Sun. and Bank Holiday Mon. Adm. £5.75. Houses the Wernher collection of china, glass, pictures and other objets d'art

MANSION HOUSE, London EC4. Tel: 0171-626 2500. Group visits only, by prior arrangement. Adm. free. The official residence of the Lord Mayor of London

MARBLE HILL HOUSE (EH), Twickenham, Middx. Tel: 0181-892 5115. Closed Mon. and Tues. in winter. Adm. £2.50. English Palladian villa with Georgian paintings and furniture

*MICHELHAM PRIORY, E. Sussex. Tel: 01323-844224. Adm. £4.00. Tudor house built onto an Augustinian priory

MIDDLEHAM CASTLE (EH), N. Yorks. Tel: 01969-623899. Closed Mon. and Tues. in winter. Adm. £1.60. A 12th-century keep with later fortifications. Childhood home of Richard III

†MONTACUTE HOUSE (NT), Somerset. Tel: 01935-823289. Closed Tues; grounds open all year. Adm. £5.00; grounds only, £2.80. Elizabethan house with National Portrait Gallery portraits from period

MOUNT GRACE PRIORY (EH), N. Yorks. Tel: 01609-883494. Closed Mon. and Tues. in winter. Adm. £2.50. Carthusian monastery, with remains of monastic buildings

NETLEY ABBEY (EH), Hants. Tel: 01705-378091. Adm. free. Remains of Cistercian abbey, used as house in Tudor period

OLD SARUM (EH), Wilts. Tel: 01722-335398. Adm. £1.90. Earthworks enclosing remains of the castle and the 11th-century cathedral

ORFORD CASTLE (EH), Suffolk. Tel: 01394-450472. Closed Mon. and Tues. in winter. Adm. £2.10. Circular keep of c.1170 and remains of coastal defence castle built by Henry II

*OSBORNE HOUSE (EH), Isle of Wight. Tel: 01983-200022. Adm. £6.00. Queen Victoria's seaside residence

†OSTERLEY PARK HOUSE (NT), Isleworth, Middx. Tel: 0181-560 3918. Closed Mon. (except Bank Holidays), Tues. and Good Friday; grounds open all year. Adm. £3.80; grounds free. Elizabethan mansion set in parkland

PENDENNIS CASTLE (EH), Cornwall. Tel: 01326-316594. Adm. £2.70. Well-preserved coastal defence castle built by Henry VIII

†PENSHURST PLACE, Kent. Tel: 01892-870307. Closed Mon.-Fri. in Mar. and Oct. Adm. charge. House with medieval Baron's Hall and 14th-century gardens

†PETWORTH (NT), W. Sussex. Tel: 01798-342207. Closed Thur. and Fri. (except Good Friday). Adm. £4.50; grounds free. Late 17th-century house set in deer park

PEVENSEY CASTLE (EH), E. Sussex. Tel: 01323-762604. Closed Mon. and Tues. in winter. Adm. £2.00. Walls of a 4th-century Roman fort; remains of an 11th-century castle

PEVERIL CASTLE (EH), Derbys. Tel: 01433-620613. Closed Mon. and Tues. in winter. Adm. £1.60. A 12th-century castle defended on two sides by precipitous rocks

†POLESDEN LACY (NT), Surrey. Tel: 01372-458203. Closed Mon. (except Bank Holidays) and Tues.; open weekends in March and Good Friday; grounds open daily all year. Adm. £6.00; grounds only £3.00. Regency villa remodelled in the Edwardian era. Fine paintings and furnishings

PORTCHESTER CASTLE (EH), Hants. Tel: 01705-378291. Adm. £2.50. Walls of a late Roman fort enclosing a Norman keep and an Augustinian priory church

*POWDERHAM CASTLE, Devon. Tel: 01626-890243. Closed Sat. Adm. £4.95. Medieval castle with 18th- and 19th-century alterations

†RABY CASTLE, Co. Durham. Tel: 01833-660202. Closed Sat. (except Bank Holiday weekends); open Wed. and Sun. only in May and June. Adm. £4.00; grounds only, £1.50. A 14th-century castle with walled gardens

*RAGLEY HALL, Warks. Tel: 01789-762090. Closed Mon.-Wed.; grounds open daily in July and Aug. Adm. £4.50; grounds only, £3.50. A 17th-century house with gardens, park and lake

*RICHBOROUGH CASTLE (EH), Kent. Tel: 01304-612013. Adm. £2.00. Landing-site of the Claudian invasion in AD 43, with 3rd-century stone walls

RICHMOND CASTLE (EH), N. Yorks. Tel: 01748-822493. Adm. £1.80. A 12th-century keep with 11th-century curtain wall and domestic buildings

RIEVAULX ABBEY (EH), N. Yorks. Tel: 01439-798228. Adm. £2.70. Remains of a Cistercian abbey founded c.1131

ROCHESTER CASTLE (EH), Kent. Tel: 01634-402276. Adm. £2.60. An 11th-century castle partly on the Roman city wall, with a square keep of c.1130

†ROCKINGHAM CASTLE, Northants. Tel: 01536-770240. Open Sun. and Thurs. only (and Bank Holiday Mon. and Tues., and Tues. in Aug.). Adm. £3.90; gardens only, £2.50. Built by William the Conqueror

ROYAL PAVILION, Brighton. Tel: 01273-290900. Adm. charge. Palace of George IV, in Chinese style with Indian exterior and Regency gardens

†RUFFORD OLD HALL (NT), Lancs. Tel: 01704-821254. Closed Thurs. and Fri. Adm. £3.30; garden only, £1.70. A 16th-century hall with unique screen

ST AUGUSTINE'S ABBEY (EH), Canterbury, Kent. Tel: 01227-767345. Adm. £2.00. Remains of Benedictine monastery, with Norman church, on site of abbey founded AD 598 by St Augustine

ST MAWES CASTLE (EH), Cornwall. Tel: 01326-270526. Closed Mon. and Tues. in winter. Adm. £2.20. Coastal defence castle built by Henry VIII comprising central tower and three bastions

ST MICHAEL'S MOUNT (NT), Cornwall. Tel: 01736-710507. Opening times vary. Adm. £3.90. A 14th-century castle with later additions and alterations, off the coast at Marazion

*SANDRINGHAM, Norfolk. Tel: 01553-772675. Closed for three weeks in summer and when the Royal Family is in residence. Adm. £4.50; grounds only, £3.50. The Queen's private residence; a neo-Jacobean house built in 1870

SCARBOROUGH CASTLE (EH), N. Yorks. Tel: 01723-372451. Closed Mon. and Tues. in winter. Adm. £1.80. Remains of 12th-century keep and curtain walls

†SHERBORNE CASTLE, Dorset. Tel: 01935-813182. Open Thurs., Sat., Sun. and Bank Holiday Mon. Adm. charge. Sixteenth-century castle built by Sir Walter Raleigh

*SHUGBOROUGH (NT), Staffs. Tel: 01889-881388. Open Sun. only in October; open for booked parties in winter. Adm. house, county museum and farm, £8.00; each site alone, £3.50. House set in 18th-century park with monuments, temples and pavilions in the Greek Revival style

SKIPTON CASTLE, N. Yorks. Tel: 01756-792442. Closed Sun. mornings. Adm. £3.60. D-shaped castle with six round towers and beautiful inner courtyard

†SMALLHYTHE PLACE (NT), Kent. Tel: 01580-762334. Closed Thurs. and Fri. (except Good Friday). Adm. £2.80. Half-timbered 16th-century house; home of Ellen Terry 1899-1928

†STANFORD HALL, Leics. Tel: 01788-860250. Open Sat.-Sun.; also Bank Holiday Mon. and Tues. Adm. £3.70; grounds only, £2.00. William and Mary house with Stuart portraits. Motorcycle museum

STONEHENGE (EH), Wilts. Tel: 01980-624715. Adm. £3.70. Prehistoric monument consisting of a series of concentric stone circles surrounded by a ditch and bank

†STONOR PARK, Oxon. Tel: 01491-638587. Opening days vary. Adm. £4.00. Medieval house with Georgian facade. Centre of Roman Catholicism after the Reformation

†STOURHEAD (NT), Wilts. Tel: 01747-841152. Closed Thurs.-Fri. Gardens open daily all year. Adm. £4.30; gardens, £4.30; combined ticket £7.70. English Palladian mansion with famous gardens

*STRATFIELD SAYE HOUSE, Hants. Tel: 01256-882882. Closed Fri.; May and Sept. open weekends and Bank Holidays only. Adm. charge. House built 1630-40; home of the Dukes of Wellington since 1817

STRATFORD-UPON-AVON, Warks. *Shakespeare's Birthplace* with Shakespeare Centre; *Anne Hathaway's Cottage*, home of Shakespeare's wife; *Mary Arden's House*, home of Shakespeare's mother; *New Place*, where Shakespeare died; and *Hall's Croft*, home of Shakespeare's daughter. Tel: 01789-204016. Adm. charges. Also *Grammar School* attended by Shakespeare, *Holy Trinity Church*, where Shakespeare is buried, *Royal Shakespeare Theatre* (burnt down 1926, rebuilt 1932) and *Swan Theatre* (opened 1986)

*SUDELEY CASTLE, Glos. Tel: 01242-602308. Adm. £5.50; grounds only, £4.00. Castle built in 1442; restored in the 19th century

SYON HOUSE, Brentford, Middx. Tel: 0181-560 0881. Opening times vary. Adm. £5.50; grounds only, £2.50. Built on the site of a former monastery; Adam interior

TILBURY FORT (EH), Essex. Tel: 01375-858489. Closed Mon. and Tues. in winter. Adm. £2.20. A 17th-century coastal fort

TINTAGEL CASTLE (EH), Cornwall. Tel: 01840-770328. Adm. £2.70. A 12th-century cliff-top castle and Dark Age settlement site

TOWER OF LONDON, London EC3. Tel: 0171-709 0765. Adm. charge. Royal palace and fortress begun by William the Conqueror in 1078. Houses the Crown Jewels

*TRERICE (NT), Cornwall. Tel: 01637-875404. Closed Tues. and Sat. (except in Aug.). Adm. £3.80. Elizabethan manor house

TYNEMOUTH PRIORY AND CASTLE (EH), Tyne and Wear. Tel: 0191-257 1090. Closed Mon.-Tues. in winter. Adm. £1.60. Remains of a Benedictine priory, founded *c*.1090, on Saxon monastic site

†UPPARK (NT), W. Sussex. Tel: 01730-825415. Closed Fri. and Sat. Adm. £5.00 by timed ticket. Late 17th-century house, completely restored after fire. Fetherstonhaugh art collection

WALMER CASTLE (EH), Kent. Tel: 01304-364288. Closed Mon. and Tues. in winter; closed Jan.-Feb. and when the Lord Warden is in residence. Adm. £4.00. One of Henry VIII's coastal defence castles, now the residence of the Lord Warden of the Cinque Ports

WALTHAM ABBEY (EH), Essex. Adm. free. Ruined abbey including the nave of the abbey church, 'Harold's Bridge' and late 14th-century gatehouse. Traditionally the burial place of Harold II (1066)

WARKWORTH CASTLE (EH), Northumberland. Tel: 01665-711423. Adm. £2.20. A 15th-century keep amidst earlier ruins, with 14th-century hermitage (open Wed., Sun. and Bank Holidays in summer) upstream

WARWICK CASTLE. Tel: 01926-406600. Adm. £8.95. Medieval castle with Madame Tussaud's waxworks, in Capability Brown parkland

WHITBY ABBEY (EH), N. Yorks. Tel: 01947-603568. Adm. £1.60. Remains of Norman church on the site of a monastery founded in AD 657

*WILTON HOUSE, Wilts. Tel: 01722-746729. Adm. £6.50. A 17th-century house on the site of a Tudor house and Saxon abbey

WINDSOR CASTLE, Berks. Tel: 01753-831118 for recorded information on opening times. Adm. £9.50, including the Castle precincts. Official residence of The Queen; oldest royal residence still in regular use. Restoration of fire-damaged state rooms to be completed by Dec. 1997. Also *St George's Chapel*

WOBURN ABBEY, Beds. Tel: 01525-290666. Closed Nov. and Dec.; also Mon.-Fri. in Jan. and Feb. Adm. £7.00. Built on the site of a Cistercian abbey; seat of the Dukes of Bedford. Important art collection; antiques centre

WROXETER ROMAN CITY (EH), Shropshire. Tel: 01743-761330. Closed Mon. and Tues. in winter. Adm. £2.75. Second-century public baths and part of the forum of the Roman town of Viroconium

WALES

c Property of Cadw: Welsh Historic Monuments
NT National Trust property

BEAUMARIS CASTLE (C), Anglesey. Tel: 01222-500200.
Adm. £2.20. Fine concentrically-planned castle, still
almost intact

CAERLEON ROMAN BATHS AND AMPHITHEATRE (C), nr
Newport. Tel: 01633-422518. Closed Sun. morning in
winter. Adm. £1.70, joint ticket with Legionary
Museum £2.85. Rare example of a legionary bath-
house and late 1st-century arena surrounded by bank
for spectators

CAERNARFON CASTLE (C). Tel: 01222-500200. Adm.
£3.80. Important Edwardian castle built, with the town
wall, between 1283 and 1330

CAERPHILLY CASTLE (C). Tel: 01222-500200. Adm. £2.20.
Concentrically-planned castle (c.1270) notable for its
scale and use of water defences

CARDIFF CASTLE. Tel: 01222-878100. Adm. charge.
Castle built on the site of a Roman fort; spectacular
towers and rich interior

CASTELL COCH (C), nr Cardiff. Tel: 01222-500200. Adm.
£2.20. Rebuilt 1875-90 on medieval foundations

CHEPSTOW CASTLE (C). Tel: 01222-500200. Adm. £3.00.
Rectangular keep amid extensive fortifications

CONWY CASTLE (C). Tel: 01222-500200. Adm. £3.00.
Built by Edward I, 1283-7

*CRICCIETH CASTLE (C). Tel: 01222-500200. Adm. £2.20.
Native Welsh 13th-century castle, altered by Edward I

DENBIGH CASTLE (C). Tel: 01222-500200. Adm. free.
Remains of the castle (begun 1282), including triple-
towered gatehouse

HARLECH CASTLE (C). Tel: 01222-500200. Adm. £3.00.
Well-preserved Edwardian castle, constructed 1283-
90, on an outcrop above the former shore-line

PEMBROKE CASTLE. Tel: 01646-681510. Adm. £2.95.
Castle founded in 1093, with a Great Tower 75 feet tall;
birthplace of King Henry VII

†PENRHYN CASTLE (NT), Bangor. Tel: 01248-353084.
Closed Tues. Adm. £4.60; grounds only, £3.00. Neo-
Norman castle built in the 19th century. Industrial
railway museum

PORTMEIRION, Penrhyndeudraeth. Tel: 01766-770228.
Adm. £3.75. Village in Italianate style

†POWIS CASTLE (NT), nr Welshpool. Tel: 01938-554338.
Closed Mon. (except Bank Holidays) and Tues. (except
June-Aug.). Adm. £6.00; garden only, £4.00. Medieval
castle with interior in variety of styles; 17th-century
gardens and Clive of India museum

RAGLAN CASTLE (C). Tel: 01222-500200. Adm. £2.20.
Remains of 15th-century castle with moated hexagonal
keep

ST DAVIDS BISHOP'S PALACE (C), St Davids. Tel: 01222-
500200. Closed Sun. mornings in winter. Adm. £1.70.
Remains of residence of Bishops of St Davids built
1328-47

TINTERN ABBEY (C), nr Chepstow. Tel: 01222-500200.
Adm. £2.20. Remains of 13th-century church and
conventual buildings of a Cistercian monastery

*TRETOWER COURT AND CASTLE (C), nr Crickhowell.
Tel: 01222-500200. Adm. £2.20. Medieval house with
remains of 12th-century castle nearby

SCOTLAND

HS Historic Scotland property
NTS National Trust for Scotland property

ANTONINE WALL (HS), between the Clyde and the Forth.
Adm. free. Built about AD 142, consists of ditch, turf
rampart and road, with forts every two miles

BALMORAL CASTLE, nr Braemar. Tel: 013397-42334.
Open Easter-July; closed Sun. Adm. £3.50. Mid 19th-
century Baronial-style castle built for Victoria and
Albert. The Queen's private residence

BLACK HOUSE, Arnol (HS), Lewis, Western Isles. Tel:
01851-710395. Closed Sun.; also Fri. in winter. Adm.
£1.50. Traditional Lewis thatched house

*BLAIR CASTLE, Blair Atholl. Tel: 01796-481207. Adm.
£5.50. Mid 18th-century mansion with 13th-century
tower; seat of the Dukes of Atholl

*BONAWE IRON FURNACE (HS), Argyll and Bute. Tel:
01866-822432. Closed Sun. mornings. Adm. £2.30.
Charcoal-fuelled ironworks founded in 1753

†BOWHILL, Selkirk. Tel: 01750-22204. House open July
only; grounds open April-Aug. except Fri. Adm. £4.00;
grounds only, £1.00. Seat of the Dukes of Buccleuch
and Queensberry; fine collection of paintings,
including portrait miniatures

BROUGH OF BIRSAY (HS), Orkney. Adm. free. Remains of
Norse church and village on the tidal island of Birsay

CAERLAVEROCK CASTLE (HS), nr Dumfries. Tel: 01387
770244. Closed Sun. mornings. Adm. £2.30. Fine early
classical Renaissance building

CALLANISH STANDING STONES (HS), Lewis, Western
Isles. Adm. free. Standing stones in a cross-shaped
setting, dating from 3000 BC

CATHERTUNS (BROWN AND WHITE) (HS), nr Brechin.
Adm. free. Two large Iron Age hill forts

*CAWDOR CASTLE, Inverness. Tel: 01667-404615. Adm.
£5.00; grounds only, £2.70. A 14th-century keep with
15th- and 17th-century additions

CLAVA CAIRNS (HS), Highland. Adm. free. Late Neolithic
or early Bronze Age cairns

*CRATHES CASTLE (NTS), nr Banchory. Tel: 01330-
844525. Garden and grounds open all year. Adm. castle,
garden and grounds, £4.50; each site, £1.80. A 16th-
century baronial castle in woodland, fields and gardens

*CULZEAN CASTLE (NTS), S. Ayrshire. Tel: 01655-760274.
Country park open all year. Adm. £6.00; country park
only, £3.00; castle only £4.00. An 18th-century Adam
castle with oval staircase and circular saloon

DRYBURGH ABBEY (HS), Scottish Borders. Tel: 01835-
822381. Closed Sun. mornings. Adm. £2.30. A 12th-
century abbey containing tomb of Sir Walter Scott

*DUNVEGAN CASTLE, Skye. Tel: 01470-521206. Closed
Sun. mornings. Adm. £4.80; gardens only, £3.50. A
13th-century castle with later additions; home of the
chiefs of the Clan MacLeod; trips to seal colony

EDINBURGH CASTLE (HS). Tel: 0131-225 9846. Adm.
£5.50; war memorial free. Includes the Scottish
National War Memorial, Scottish United Services
Museum and historic apartments

EDZELL CASTLE (HS), nr Brechin. Tel: 01356-648631.
Closed Sun. mornings; also Thurs. afternoons and Fri.
in winter. Adm. £2.30. Medieval tower house; unique
walled garden

*EILEAN DONAN CASTLE, Wester Ross. Tel: 01599-
555202. Adm. £3.00. A 13th-century castle with
Jacobite relics

ELGIN CATHEDRAL (HS), Moray. Tel: 01343-547171.
Closed Sun. mornings; also Thurs. afternoons and Fri.
in winter. Adm. £1.20. A 13th-century cathedral with
fine chapterhouse

*FLOORS CASTLE, Kelso. Tel: 01573-223333. Closed
Mon.-Tues. and Thurs.-Sat. in Oct. Adm. £4.50.
Largest inhabited castle in Scotland; seat of the Dukes
of Roxburghe

FORT GEORGE (HS), Highland. Tel: 01667-462777. Closed
Sunday mornings. Adm. £2.80. An 18th-century fort

*GLAMIS CASTLE, Angus. Tel: 01307-840393. Adm.
£5.00; grounds only, £2.30. Seat of the Lyon family
(later Earls of Strathmore and Kinghorne) since 1372

GLASGOW CATHEDRAL (HS). Tel: 0141-552 6891. Closed
Sun. mornings. Adm. free. Medieval cathedral with
elaborately vaulted crypt

GLENELG BROCH (HS), Highland. Adm. free. Two broch
towers with well-preserved structural features

*HOPETOUN HOUSE, nr Edinburgh. Tel: 0131-331 2451.
Adm. £4.50; grounds only, £2.50. House designed by
Sir William Bruce, enlarged by William Adam

HUNTLY CASTLE (HS). Tel: 01466-793191. Closed Sun.
mornings; also Thurs. afternoons and Fri. in winter.
Adm. £2.30. Ruin of a 16th- and 17th-century house

*INVERARAY CASTLE, Argyll. Tel: 01499-302203. Closed
Fri. (except July-Aug.) and Sun. mornings; woods open
all year. Adm. charge. Gothic-style 18th-century castle;
seat of the Dukes of Argyll

IONA ABBEY, Inner Hebrides. Tel: 01681-700404. Adm.
£2.00. Monastery founded by St Columba in AD 563

*JARLSHOF (HS), Shetland. Tel: 01950-460112. Closed
Sun. mornings. Adm. £2.30. Remains from Stone Age

JEDBURGH ABBEY (HS), Scottish Borders. Tel: 01835-
863925. Closed Sun. mornings. Adm. £2.80.
Romanesque and early Gothic church founded c.1138

KELSO ABBEY (HS), Scottish Borders. Adm. free. Remains
of great abbey church founded 1128

LINLITHGOW PALACE (HS). Tel: 01506-842896. Closed
Sun. mornings. Adm. £2.30. Ruin of royal palace in park
setting. Birthplace of Mary, Queen of Scots

MAES HOWE (HS), Orkney. Tel: 01856-761606. Closed
Sun. mornings; also Thurs. afternoons and Fri. in
winter. Adm. £2.30. Neolithic tomb

*MEIGLE SCULPTURED STONE (HS), Angus. Tel: 01828-
640612. Closed Sun. mornings. Adm. £1.50. Celtic
Christian stones

MELROSE ABBEY (HS), Scottish Borders. Tel: 01896-
822562. Closed Sun. mornings. Adm. £2.80. Ruin of
Cistercian abbey founded c.1136

MOUSA BROCH (HS), Shetland. Adm. free. Finest surviving
Iron Age broch tower

NETHER LARGIE CAIRNS (HS), Argyll and Bute. Adm. free.
Bronze Age and Neolithic cairns

NEW ABBEY CORN MILL (HS), nr Dumfries. Tel: 01387-
850260. Closed Sun. mornings; also Thurs. afternoons
and Fri. in winter. Adm. £2.30. Water-powered mill

PALACE OF HOLYROODHOUSE, Edinburgh. Tel: 0131-556
7371. Closed when The Queen is in residence. Adm.
£5.30. The Queen's official Scottish residence. Main
part of the palace built 1671-9

RING OF BROGAR (HS), Orkney. Adm. free. Neolithic
circle of upright stones with an enclosing ditch

RUTHWELL CROSS (HS), Dumfries and Galloway. Adm.
free. Seventh-century Anglian cross

ST ANDREWS CASTLE AND CATHEDRAL (HS), Fife. Tel:
01334-477196 (castle); 01334-472563 (cathedral). Adm.
£2.30 (castle); £1.50 (cathedral); £3.30 (combined
ticket). Closed Sun. mornings. Ruins of 13th-century
castle and remains of the largest cathedral in Scotland

*SCONE PALACE, Perth. Tel: 01738-552300. Adm. £5.00;
grounds only, £2.50. House built 1802-13 on the site of
a medieval palace

SKARA BRAE (HS), Orkney. Tel: 01856-841815. Closed
Sun. mornings. Adm. £2.80. Stone-Age village

*SMAILHOLM TOWER (HS), Scottish Borders. Tel: 01573-
460365. Closed Sun. mornings. Adm. £1.50. Well-
preserved tower-house

STIRLING CASTLE (HS). Tel: 01786-450000. Adm. £4.00.
Great Hall and gatehouse of James IV, palace of James
V, Chapel Royal remodelled by James VI

TANTALLON CASTLE (HS), E. Lothian. Tel: 01620-892727.
Closed Sun. mornings; also Thurs. afternoons and Fri.
in winter. Adm. £2.30. Fortification with earthwork
defences and a 14th-century curtain wall with towers

*THREAVE CASTLE (HS), Dumfries and Galloway. Tel:
0831-168512. Closed Sun. mornings. Adm. £1.50,
including ferry trip. Late 14th-century tower on an
island; reached by boat, long walk to castle

URQUHART CASTLE (HS), Loch Ness. Tel: 01456-450551.
Adm. £3.20. Castle remains with well-preserved tower

NORTHERN IRELAND

DE Property in the care of the Northern Ireland Department
of the Environment

NT National Trust property

CARRICKFERGUS CASTLE (DE), Co. Antrim. Tel: 01960-
351273. Closed Sun. mornings. Adm. £2.70. Castle
begun in 1180 and garrisoned until 1928

†CASTLE COOLE (NT), Enniskillen. Tel: 01365-322690.
Closed Thurs; also closed Mon.-Fri. in April and Sept.
Adm. house, £2.80; estate, £2.00 per car. An 18th-
century mansion by James Wyatt in parkland

†CASTLE WARD (NT), Co. Down. Tel: 01396-881204.
Closed Thurs; also closed Mon.-Fri., April, Sept. and
Oct.; grounds open all year. Adm. £2.60. An 18th-
century house with Classical and Gothic facades

DOWNHILL CASTLE (NT), Co. Londonderry. Tel: 01265-
848728. Adm. free. Ruins of palatial house in
landscaped estate including Mussenden Temple.
Opening times of temple vary

DUNLUCE CASTLE (DE), Co. Antrim. Tel: 012657-31938.
Closed Sun. morning (except July and Aug.) Adm.
£1.50. Ruins of 16th-century stronghold

†FLORENCE COURT (NT), Co. Fermanagh. Tel: 01365-
348249. Closed Tues.; also closed Mon.-Fri. (except
Bank Holidays) in April and Sept.; grounds open all
year. Adm. £2.80; estate £2.00 per car. Mid 18th-
century house with rococo plasterwork

*GREY ABBEY (DE), Co. Down. Tel: 01247-788585. Closed
Sun. morning and Mon. Adm £1.00. Substantial
remains of a Cistercian abbey founded in 1193

HILLSBOROUGH FORT (DE), Co. Down. Closed Sun.
mornings and Mon. Adm. free. Built in 1650

†MOUNT STEWART (NT), Co. Down. Tel: 01247-788387.
Closed Tues.; also closed Mon.-Fri. in April and Oct.
Adm. £3.50; garden only, £3.00. An 18th-century
house, childhood home of Lord Castlereagh

NENDRUM MONASTERY (DE), Mahee Island, Co. Down.
Closed Sun. mornings and Mon.; also Mon.-Fri. in
winter. Adm 75p. Founded in the 5th century

*TULLY CASTLE (DE), Co. Fermanagh. Closed Sun.
mornings and Mon. Adm. £1.00. Fortified house and
bawn built in 1613

*WHITE ISLAND (DE), Co. Fermanagh. Closed Sun.
mornings and Mon. Adm. £2.25. Tenth-century
monastery and 12th-century church. Access by ferry

Museums and Galleries

There are more than 2,500 museums and galleries in the United Kingdom. Over 1,700 are registered with the Museums and Galleries Commission (*see* page 324), which indicates that they have an appropriate constitution, are soundly financed, have adequate collection management standards and public services, and have access to professional curatorial advice. Museums must achieve full or provisional registration status in order to be eligible for grants from the Museums and Galleries Commission and from Area Museums Councils. Over 700 of the registered museums are run by a local authority.

The national museums and galleries (i.e. the British Museum, the Imperial War Museum, the National Army Museum, the National Galleries of Scotland, the National Gallery, the National Maritime Museum, the National Museums and Galleries on Merseyside, the National Museum of Wales, the National Museums of Scotland, the National Portrait Gallery, the Natural History Museum, the RAF Museum, the Royal Armouries, the Science Museum, the Tate Gallery, the Ulster Folk and Transport Museum, the Ulster Museum, the Victoria and Albert Museum, and the Wallace Collection) receive direct government grant-in-aid. Local authority museums are funded by the local authority and may also receive grants from the Museums and Galleries Commission. Independent museums and galleries mainly rely on their own resources but are also eligible for grants from the Museums and Galleries Commission.

Ten Area Museum Councils in the United Kingdom, which are independent charities that receive an annual grant from the Museums and Galleries Commission, give advice and support to the museums in their area and may offer improvement grants. They also circulate exhibitions and assist with training and marketing.

OPENING TO THE PUBLIC

The following is a selection of the museums and art galleries in the United Kingdom. The admission charges given are the standard charges for 1997-8, where a charge is made; many museums have concessionary rates for children, etc. Opening hours vary. Most museums are closed on Christmas Eve, Christmas Day, Boxing Day and New Year's Day, many are closed on Good Friday, and some are closed on May Day Bank Holiday. Some smaller museums close at lunchtimes. Information about a specific museum or gallery should be checked by telephone.

* Local authority museum/gallery

ENGLAND

BARNARD CASTLE, Co. Durham – *The Bowes Museum*, Westwick Road. Tel: 01833-690606. Closed Sun. mornings. Adm. £3.50. European art from the late medieval period to the 19th century; music and costume galleries; English period rooms from Elizabeth I to Victoria; local archaeology

BATH – *American Museum in Britain*, Claverton Manor. Tel: 01225-460503. Closed mornings and Mon. (except Bank Holidays); also closed in winter (except on application). Adm. £5.00 (including house); grounds and galleries only, £2.50. American decorative arts from the 17th to 19th century

Museum of Costume, Bennett Street. Tel: 01225-477752. Adm. £3.60. Fashion from the 16th century to the present day

Roman Baths Museum, Abbey Church Yard. Tel: 01225-477774. Adm. (including 18th-century Pump Room) £6.00. Museum adjoins the remains of a Roman baths and temple complex

Victoria Art Gallery, Bridge Street. Tel: 01225-477772. Closed Bank Holidays. Adm. free. European Old Masters and British art since the 18th century

BEAMISH, Co. Durham – *Beamish, The North of England Open Air Museum*. Tel: 01207-231811. Closed Mon. and Fri. in winter. Adm. charge. Recreated northern town *c.*1900, with rebuilt and furnished local buildings, colliery village, farm, railway station, tramway, Pockerley Manor and horse-yard (set *c.*1800)

BEAULIEU, Hants – *National Motor Museum*. Tel: 01590-612345. Adm. charge. Displays of over 250 vehicles dating from 1895 to the present day

BIRMINGHAM – *Aston Hall*, Albert Road. Tel: 0121-327 0062. Closed mornings and in winter. Adm. free. Jacobean house containing paintings, furniture and tapestries from 17th to 19th century

Birmingham Nature Centre, Edgbaston. Tel: 0121-472 7775. Closed Mon.-Sat. in winter. Adm. £1.50. Indoor and outdoor enclosures displaying British wildlife

City Museum and Art Gallery, Chamberlain Square. Tel: 0121-235 2834. Closed Sun. mornings. Adm. free (except Gas Hall). Includes notable collection of Pre-Raphaelites

Museum of Science and Industry, Newhall Street. Tel: 0121-235 1661. Closed Sun. mornings. Adm. free. Vehicles and industrial machinery from the Industrial Revolution to the present; interactive science centre and mechanical musical instrument collection

BRADFORD – *Cartwright Hall Art Gallery*, Lister Park. Tel: 01274-493313. Closed Mon. (except Bank Holidays). Adm. free. British 19th- and 20th-century fine art

Industrial Museum and Horses at Work, Moorside Road. Tel: 01274-631756. Closed Mon. (except Bank Holidays). Adm. charge. Engineering, textiles, transport and social history exhibits, including recreated back-to-back cottages, shire horses and horse tram-rides

National Museum of Photography, Film and Television, Pictureville. Tel: 01274-727488. Closed Mon. (except school and Bank Holidays). Adm. free. Photography, film and television equipment and materials, including the only IMAX cinema in the UK and the only public Cinerama theatre in the world

BRIGHTON – *Brighton Museum and Art Gallery*, Church Street. Tel: 01273 290900. Closed Sun. mornings and Wed. Adm. free. Includes fine art, design, fashion, archaeology, Brighton history

BRISTOL – *Arnolfini Gallery*, Narrow Quay. Tel: 0117-929 9191. Adm. free; charge for cinema and events. Contemporary visual arts, dance, theatre, film and music

Blaise Castle House Museum, Henbury. Tel: 0117-950 6789. Closed Thurs. and Fri.; also closed in winter. Adm. free. Agricultural and social history collections in an 18th-century mansion

Bristol Industrial Museum, Prince Street. Tel: 0117-925 1470. Closed Thurs. and Fri.; closed Mon.-Fri. in winter. Adm. charge. Industrial, maritime and transport collections

City Museum and Art Gallery, Queen's Road. Tel: 0117-922 3571. Adm. charge. Includes fine and decorative art, oriental art, Egyptology and Bristol ceramics and paintings

CAMBRIDGE – *Duxford Airfield*, Duxford. Tel: 01223-835000. Adm. £5.95. Displays of military and civil aircraft, tanks, guns and naval exhibits

Fitzwilliam Museum, Trumpington Street. Tel: 01223-332900. Closed Mon. (except some Bank Holidays) and Sun. mornings. Adm. free. Antiquities, fine and applied arts, clocks, ceramics, manuscripts, furniture, sculpture, coins and medals, temporary exhibitions

University Museum of Archaeology and Anthropology, Downing Street. Tel: 01223-333516. Closed mornings Mon.-Fri. and Sun. Adm. free. Archaeology and anthropology from all parts of the world

Whipple Museum of the History of Science, Free School Lane. Tel: 01223-334540. Closed mornings and weekends. Adm. free. Scientific instruments from the 14th century to the present day

CARLISLE – *Tullie House Museum and Art Gallery*, Castle Street. Tel: 01228-34781. Closed Sun. mornings. Adm. charge to Border galleries only; ground floor, Old Tullie House and Jacobean galleries, adm. free. Prehistoric archaeology, Hadrian's Wall, Viking and medieval Cumbria, and the social history of Carlisle; also British 19th- and 20th-century art and English porcelain

CHATHAM – *Lifeboat!, the Royal National Lifeboat Collection*, The Historic Dockyard. Tel: 01634-812551. Closed Mon., Tues. and Fri. in winter; also closed Dec.-Jan. Adm. £5.60 (for all attractions in the Historic Dockyard). Lifeboats from the 170-year history of the RNLI

CHESTER – *Grosvenor Museum*, Grosvenor Street. Tel: 01244-321616. Closed Sun. mornings. Adm. free. Roman collections, natural history, art, Chester silver, local history and costume

CHICHESTER – *Weald and Downland Open Air Museum*, Singleton. Tel: 01243-811348. Closed Mon.,Tues., Thurs., Fri. in winter. Adm. £4.90. Rebuilt vernacular buildings from south-east England; includes medieval houses, agricultural and rural craft buildings and a working watermill

COLCHESTER – *Colchester Castle Museum*, Castle Park. Tel: 01206-282939. Closed Sun. mornings. Adm. £3.50. Local archaeological antiquities and displays on Roman Colchester; tours of the Roman vaults, castle walls and chapel with medieval and prison displays

COVENTRY – *Herbert Art Gallery and Museum*, Jordan Well. Tel: 01203-832381. Closed Sun. mornings. Local history, archaeology and industry, oriental ceramics, and fine and decorative art

Museum of British Road Transport, Hales Street. Tel: 01203-832425. Adm. £3.30. Hundreds of motor vehicles and bicycles

CRICH, nr Matlock, Derbys – *National Tramway Museum*. Tel: 01773-852565. Closed some Fri. and Jan.-Feb. Adm. £5.70. Open-air working museum with tram rides

DERBY – *Derby Museum and Art Gallery*, The Strand. Tel: 01332-716659. Closed Sun. mornings and Bank Holiday mornings. Adm. free. Includes paintings by Joseph Wright of Derby and Derby porcelain

Industrial Museum, off Full Street. Tel: 01332-255308. Closed Sun. mornings and Bank Holiday mornings. Adm. free. Rolls-Royce aero engine collection and a railway engineering gallery

DORCHESTER – *Dorset County Museum*, High West Street. Tel: 01305-262735. Closed Sun. (except July and Aug.) Adm. charge. Includes a collection of Thomas Hardy's manuscripts, books, notebooks and drawings

EXETER – *Royal Albert Memorial Museum*, Queen Street. Tel: 01392-265858. Closed Sun. Adm. free. Natural history, archaeology, and fine and decorative art including Exeter silver

GAYDON, Warwick – *British Motor Industry Heritage Trust*, Banbury Road. Tel: 019626-641188. Adm. charge. History of British motor industry from 1895 to present; classic vehicles; engineering gallery; Corgi and Lucas collections

GLOUCESTER, – *National Waterways Museum*, Llanthony Warehouse, The Docks. Tel: 01452-318054. Adm. £4.50. Two-hundred-year history of Britain's canals and inland waterways

GOSPORT, Hants. – *Royal Navy Submarine Museum*, Haslar Jetty Road. Tel: 01705-529217. Adm. £3.50. Underwater warfare, including the submarine *Alliance*; historical and nuclear galleries; and first Royal Navy submarine

HALIFAX – *Eureka! The Museum for Children*, Discovery Road. Tel: 01426-983191. Adm. £4.75 (over age 12), £3.75 (ages 3-12), free (under age 3). Saver ticket £14.75. Hands-on museum designed for children up to age 12

HULL – *Ferens Art Gallery*, Queen Victoria Square. Tel: 01482-613902. Closed Sun. mornings. Adm.: non-residents £1.00; residents free. European art, especially Dutch 17th-century paintings, British portraits from 17th to 20th century, and marine paintings

Town Docks Museum, Queen Victoria Square. Tel: 01482-613902. Closed Sun. mornings. Adm.: non-residents £1.00; residents free. Whaling, fishing and navigation exhibits

HUNTINGDON – *Cromwell Museum*, Grammar School Walk. T¯ ¯: 01480-425830. Closed Mon., and mornings (except Sat.) in winter. Adm. free. Portraits and memorabilia relating to Oliver Cromwell

IPSWICH – *Christchurch Mansion and Wolsey Art Gallery*, Christchurch Park. Tel: 01473-253246. Closed Sun. mornings and Mon. (except Bank Holidays). Adm. free. Tudor house with paintings by Gainsborough, Constable and other Suffolk artists; furniture and 18th-century ceramics. Art gallery for temporary exhibitions

LEEDS – *Abbey House Museum*, Kirkstall. Tel: 0113-275 5821. Closed Sun. mornings and Mon. Adm. charge. Toys, games, dolls, and three full-sized period streets

City Art Gallery, The Headrow. Tel: 0113-247 8248. Closed Sun. mornings. Adm. free. British and European paintings including English watercolours, modern sculpture, Henry Moore gallery, print room

City Museum, Calverley Street. Tel: 0113-247 8275. Closed Sun. and Mon. Adm. free. Natural history, archaeology, ethnography and coin collections

Lotherton Hall, Aberford. Tel: 0113-281 3259. Closed Sun. mornings and Mon.; also closed Jan.-Feb. Adm. charge. Costume and oriental collections in furnished Edwardian house; deer park and bird garden

Royal Armouries Museum, Armouries Drive. Tel: 0990-106666. Adm. £6.95. National collection of arms and armour from BC to present; demonstrations of foot combat in museum's five galleries; falconry and mounted combat in the tiltyard

Temple Newsam House. Tel: 0113-264 7321. Closed Sun. mornings and Mon.; also closed Jan.-Feb. Adm. charge. Old Masters and 17th- and 18th-century decorative art in furnished Jacobean/Tudor house

LEICESTER – *Jewry Wall Museum*, St Nicholas Circle. Tel: 0116-247 3021. Closed Sun. mornings. Adm. free. Archaeology, Roman Jewry Wall and baths, and mosaics

Leicestershire Museum and Art Gallery, New Walk. Tel: 0116-255 4100. Closed Sun. mornings. Adm. free. Natural history, geology, ancient Egypt gallery, European art and decorative arts

*Snibston Discovery Park, Coalville. Tel: 01530-510851. Adm. £4.00. Open-air science and industry museum on site of a coal mine; country park with nature trail

LINCOLN – *Museum of Lincolnshire Life, Burton Road. Tel: 01522-528448. Closed Sun. mornings in winter. Adm. charge. Social history and agricultural collection

*Usher Gallery, Lindum Road. Tel: 01522-527980. Closed Sun. mornings. Adm. £1.00. Watches, miniatures, porcelain, silver; collection of Peter de Wint works; Lincolnshire topography; Tennyson memorabilia

LIVERPOOL – Lady Lever Art Gallery, Wirral. Tel: 0151-478 4136. Closed Sun. mornings. Adm. £3.00 for an 'Eight Pass' which is valid for 12 months and for all National Museums and Galleries on Merseyside. Paintings, furniture and porcelain

Liverpool Museum, William Brown Street. Tel: 0151-478 4399. Closed Sun. mornings. Adm. 'Eight Pass' as above. Includes Egyptian mummies, weapons and classical sculpture; planetarium, aquarium, vivarium and natural history centre

Merseyside Maritime Museum, Albert Dock. Tel: 0151-478 4499. Adm. 'Eight Pass' as above. Floating exhibits, working displays and craft demonstrations; incorporates HM Customs and Excise National Museum

Museum of Liverpool Life, Mann Island. Tel: 0151-478 4080. Adm. 'Eight Pass' as above. The history of Liverpool

Sudley House, Mossley Hill Road. Tel: 0151-724 3245. Closed Sun. mornings. Adm. 'Eight Pass' as above. Late 18th- and 19th-century British paintings in former shipowner's home

Tate Gallery Liverpool, Albert Dock. Tel: 0151-709 3223. Closed until May 1998 for refurbishment. Twentieth-century painting and sculpture

Walker Art Gallery, William Brown Street. Tel: 0151-478 4199. Closed Sun. mornings. Adm. 'Eight Pass' as above. Paintings from the 14th to 20th century

LONDON: GALLERIES – *Barbican Art Gallery, Barbican Centre, EC2. Tel: 0171-382 7105. Temporary exhibitions

Dulwich Picture Gallery, College Road, SE21. Tel: 0181-693 5254. Closed Sun. mornings and Mon. (except Bank Holidays). Adm. £3.00 (free on Fri.). Built by Sir John Soane to house 17th- and 18th-century paintings

Hayward Gallery, South Bank, SE1. Tel: 0171-928 3144. Adm. £5.00. Temporary exhibitions

National Gallery, Trafalgar Square, WC2. Tel: 0171-839 3321. Closed Sun. mornings. Adm. free. Western painting from the 13th to 20th century; early Renaissance collection in the Sainsbury wing

National Portrait Gallery, St Martin's Place, WC2. Tel: 0171-306 0055. Closed Sun. mornings and some Bank Holidays. Adm. free (except for some special exhibitions). Portraits of eminent people in British history

Percival David Foundation of Chinese Art, Gordon Square, WC1. Tel: 0171-387 3909. Closed weekends and Bank Holidays. Adm. free (charge for use of reference library). Chinese ceramics from tenth to 18th century

Photographers Gallery, Great Newport Street, WC2. Tel: 0171-831 1772. Closed Sun. Adm. free. Temporary exhibitions

The Queen's Gallery, Buckingham Palace, SW1. Tel: 0171-839 1377. Adm. £3.50. Art from the Royal Collection

Royal Academy of Arts, Piccadilly, W1. Tel: 0171-439 7438. Adm. charge. British art since 1750 and temporary exhibitions; annual Summer Exhibition

Saatchi Gallery, Boundary Road, NW8. Tel: 0171-624 8299. Closed mornings and Mon.-Wed. Adm. £3.50 (free on Thurs.). Contemporary art including paintings, photographs, sculpture and installations

Serpentine Gallery, Kensington Gardens, W2. Tel: 0171-402 6075. Adm. free. Temporary exhibitions of British and international contemporary art

Tate Gallery, Millbank, SW1. Tel: 0171-887 8000. Adm. free (charge for special exhibitions). British painting and 20th-century painting and sculpture

Wallace Collection, Manchester Square, W1. Tel: 0171-935 0687. Closed Sun. mornings. Adm. free. Paintings and drawings, French 18th-century furniture, armour, porcelain and clocks

Whitechapel Art Gallery, Whitechapel High Street, E1. Tel: 0171-522 7878. Closed Mon. Adm. free to most exhibitions. Temporary exhibitions of modern art

LONDON: MUSEUMS – Bank of England Museum, Threadneedle Street, EC2. Tel: 0171-601 5545. Closed weekends and Bank Holidays. Adm. free. History of the Bank since 1694

Bethnal Green Museum of Childhood, Cambridge Heath Road, E2. Tel: 0181-983 5200. Closed Sun. mornings and Fri. Adm. free but donations invited. Toys, games and exhibits relating to the social history of childhood

British Museum, Great Russell Street, WC1. Tel: 0171-636 1555. Closed Sun. mornings. Adm. free. Antiquities, coins, medals, prints and drawings

Cabinet War Rooms, King Charles Street, SW1. Tel: 0171-930 6961. Adm. £4.40. Underground rooms used by Churchill and the Government during the Second World War

Commonwealth Experience, Kensington High Street, W8. Tel: 0171-603 4535. Exhibitions on Commonwealth nations, visual arts and crafts; Interactive World

Cutty Sark, Greenwich, SE10. Tel: 0181-858 3445. Adm. £3.50. Restored and rerigged tea clipper with exhibits on board. Sir Francis Chichester's round-the-world yacht, Gipsy Moth IV, can also be seen

Design Museum, Shad Thames, SE1. Tel: 0171-378 6055. Adm. £5.00. The development of design and the mass-production of consumer objects

Geffrye Museum, Kingsland Road, E2. Tel: 0171-739 9893. Closed Mon.; also Sun. and Bank Holiday mornings. Adm. free. English urban domestic interiors from 1600-1950s; also paintings, furniture, decorative arts, walled herb garden and knot garden

HMS Belfast, Morgans Lane, Tooley Street, SE1. Tel: 0171-407 6434. Adm £4.40. Life on a warship, illustrated on World War II warship

Horniman Museum and Gardens, London Road, SE23. Tel: 0181-699 1872. Closed Sun. mornings. Adm. free. Museum of ethnography, musical instruments, natural history and aquarium; reference library; sunken, water and rose gardens

Imperial War Museum, Lambeth Road, SE1. Tel: 0171-416 5000. Reference departments closed Sat. (except by appointment) and Sun. Adm. £4.70 (free after 4.30 p.m. daily). All aspects of the two world wars and other military operations involving Britain and the Commonwealth since 1914

Jewish Museum, Albert Street, NW1. Tel: 0171-284 1997. Closed Fri., Sat., public and Jewish holidays. Adm. £3.00. Jewish life, history and religion

London Transport Museum, Covent Garden, WC2. Tel: 0171-379 6344. Adm. charge. Vehicles, photographs and graphic art relating to the history of transport in London

MCC Museum, Lord's, NW8. Tel: 0171-289 1611. Open match days (closed most Sun. mornings); also conducted tours by appointment with Tours Manager. Adm. charge. Cricket museum

Museum of Garden History, Lambeth Palace Road SE1. Tel: 0171-401 8865. Closed Sat. and Dec.-Feb. Adm. free.

Exhibition of aspects of garden history and re-created 17th-century garden

Museum of London, London Wall, EC2. Tel: 0171-600 3699. Closed Sun. mornings and Mon. Adm. £4.00 (ticket valid for three months); free after 4.30 p.m. History of London from prehistoric times to present day

Museum of the Moving Image, South Bank, SE1. Tel: 0171-401 2636. Adm. £5.95. History of the moving image in cinema and television

National Army Museum, Royal Hospital Road, SW3. Tel: 0171-730 0717. Adm. free. Five-hundred-year history of the British soldier; exhibits include model of the Battle of Waterloo and special *Soldiers of the Raj* exhibition

National Maritime Museum, Greenwich. Tel: 0181-858 4422. Reference library closed Sat. (except by appointment) and Sun. Adm. £5.50. Comprises the main building, the Old Royal Observatory and the Queen's House (*see page* 580). Maritime history of Britain; collections include globes, clocks, telescopes and paintings

Natural History Museum, Cromwell Road, SW7. Tel: 0171-938 9123. Adm. £6.00. Natural history collections

Royal Air Force Museum, Colindale, NW9. Tel: 0181-205 2266. Adm. £5.85. National museum of aviation with over 70 full-size aircraft; aviation from before the Wright brothers to the present-day RAF; flight simulator

Royal Mews, Buckingham Palace, SW1. Tel: 0171-839 1377. Open Tues.-Thurs. afternoons in summer, Wed. only in winter. Adm. £3.70. Carriages, coaches, stables and horses

Science Museum, Exhibition Road, SW7. Tel: 0171-938 8000. Adm. charge. Science, technology, industry and medicine collections

Shakespeare Globe Exhibition, Bankside, SE1. Tel: 0171-902 5000. Adm. £5.00. Recreation of Elizabethan theatre using 16th-century techniques

Sherlock Holmes Museum, Baker Street, NW1. Tel: 0171-935 8866. Adm. £5.00. Recreated rooms of the fictional detective

Sir John Soane's Museum, Lincoln's Inn Fields, WC2. Tel: 0171-430 0175. Closed Sun. and Mon. Adm. free (groups by appointment only). Art and antiques

Theatre Museum, Russell Street, WC2. Tel: 0171-836 2330. Closed Mon. Adm. £3.50. History of the performing arts

*Tower Bridge Experience, SE1. Tel: 0171-378 1928. Adm. £5.70. History of the bridge and display of Victorian steam machinery; panoramic views from walkways

Victoria and Albert Museum, Cromwell Road, SW7. Tel: 0171-938 8500. Closed Mon. mornings. Adm. £5.00. Includes National Art Library and Print Room (closed Sun. and Mon.). Fine and applied art and design, including furniture, glass, textiles, dress collections

Wellington Museum, Apsley House, W1 (*see* page 578)

Wimbledon Lawn Tennis Museum, Church Road, SW19. Tel: 0181-946 6131. Closed Sun. mornings and Mon. (except Bank Holidays). Adm. £2.50. Tennis trophies, fashion and memorabilia; access to view Centre Court

MANCHESTER – *City Art Galleries*, Mosley Street and Princess Street. Tel: 0161-236 5244. Closed Sun. mornings. Adm. free. Old Masters, Turner, Gainsborough, Stubbs, the Pre-Raphaelites and 20th-century art

Gallery of English Costume, Rusholme. Tel: 0161-224 5217. Closed Sun., Mon. Adm. free. Exhibits from the 16th to 20th century

Manchester Museum, Oxford Road. Tel: 0161-275 2634. Closed Sun. Adm. free. Archaeology, archery, botany, Egyptology, entomology, ethnography, geology,

natural history, numismatics, oriental and zoology collections

Museum of Science and Industry, Castlefield. Tel: 0161-832 1830. Adm. £5.00. On site of world's oldest passenger railway station; galleries relating to space, energy, power, transport, aviation and social history; interactive science centre

Whitworth Art Gallery, Oxford Road. Tel: 0161-275 7450. Closed Sun. mornings. Adm. free. Watercolours, drawings, prints, textiles, wallpapers and 20th-century British art

NEWCASTLE UPON TYNE – *Laing Art Gallery*, Higham Place. Tel: 0191-232 7734. Closed Sun. mornings. Adm. free. British and European art, ceramics, glass, silver, textiles and costume; local arts and crafts

Newcastle Discovery Museum, West Blandford Square. Tel: 0191-232 6789. Closed Sun. mornings. Adm. free. Local history, fashion, power, and Tyneside's maritime history; hands-on science centre; Turbinia gallery

NEWMARKET – *National Horseracing Museum*, High Street. Tel: 01638-667333. Closed Mon. (except July, Aug. and Bank Holidays), Sun. mornings and Jan.-March. Adm. £3.30. Paintings, trophies and exhibits relating to horseracing

NORWICH – *Castle Museum*. Tel: 01603-223624. Closed Sun. mornings. Adm. £3.10 (£2.30 in winter). Art (including Norwich school), archaeology, natural history, teapot collection; guided tours of battlements and dungeons

NOTTINGHAM – *Brewhouse Yard Museum*, Castle Boulevard. Tel: 0115-915 3600. Adm. free (except weekends and Bank Holidays). Daily life from the 17th to 20th century

Castle Museum. Tel: 0115-915 3700. Adm. free (except weekends and Bank Holidays). Paintings, ceramics, silver and glass; history of Nottingham

Industrial Museum, Wollaton Park. Tel: 0115-915 3910. Closed Sun. mornings, and Mon.-Wed. in winter. Adm. free (except weekends and Bank Holidays). Lacemaking machinery, steam engines and transport exhibits

Museum of Costume and Textiles, Castle Gate. Tel: 0115-915 3500. Adm. free. Costume displays from 1790 to the mid-20th century in period rooms

Natural History Museum, Wollaton Park. Tel: 0115-915 3900. Closed Sun. mornings. Adm. free (except weekends and Bank Holidays). Local natural history and wildlife dioramas

OXFORD – *Ashmolean Museum*, Beaumont Street. Tel: 01865-278000. Closed Mon. (except Bank Holidays) and Sun. mornings. Adm. free. European and Oriental fine and applied arts, archaeology, Egyptology and numismatics

Museum of Modern Art, Pembroke Street. Tel: 01865-722733. Closed Mon. Adm. £2.50. Temporary exhibitions

Museum of the History of Science, Broad Street. Tel: 01865-277280. Closed mornings and Sun.-Mon. Adm. free. Displays include early scientific instruments, chemical apparatus, clocks and watches

Oxford University Museum of Natural History, Parks Road. Tel: 01865-272950. Closed mornings (except for school parties by appointment) and Sun. Adm. free. Entomology, geology, mineralogy and zoology

Pitt Rivers Museum, South Parks Road. Tel: 01865-270927. Closed mornings (except by appointment) and Sun. Adm. free. Ethnological and archaeological artefacts

PLYMOUTH – *City Museum and Art Gallery*, Drake Circus. Tel: 01752-264878. Closed Mon. (except Bank

Holidays) and Sun. Adm. free. Local and natural history, ceramics, silver, Old Masters, temporary exhibitions
*The Dome, The Hoe. Tel: 01752-603300. Adm. charge. Maritime history museum

PORTSMOUTH – *Charles Dickens Birthplace Museum, Old Commercial Road. Tel: 01705-827261. Closed in winter. Adm. charge. Dickens memorabilia
*D-Day Museum, Clarence Esplanade. Tel: 01705-827261. Adm. charge. Includes the Overlord Embroidery
Naval Heritage Area, HM Naval Base. Incorporates the Royal Naval Museum (tel: 01705-727562), HMS Victory (tel: 01705-822034), HMS Warrior (tel: 01705-291379), the Mary Rose (tel: 01705-750521) and the Dockyard Museum. Adm. charge to each (combined ticket available). History of the Royal Navy and of the dockyard and the trades in it

PRESTON – *Harris Museum and Art Gallery, Market Square. Tel: 01772-258248. Closed Sun. and Bank Holidays. Adm. free. British art since the 18th century, ceramics, glass, costume and local history; also contemporary exhibitions

ST ALBANS – *Verulamium Museum, St Michael's. Tel: 01727-819339. Closed Sun. mornings. Adm. £2.80. Iron Age and Roman Verulamium, including wall plasters, jewellery, mosaics and room reconstructions

ST IVES, Cornwall – Tate Gallery St Ives, Porthmeor Beach. Tel: 01736-796226. Closed Mon. Oct.–March. Adm. £3.50. Painting and sculpture by artists associated with St Ives

SHEFFIELD – *City Museum and Mappin Art Gallery, Weston Park. Tel: 0114-276 8588. Closed Mon. and Tues. Adm. free. Includes applied arts, natural history, archaeology and ethnography, 19th- and 20th-century art
*Graves Art Gallery, Surrey Street. Tel: 0114-273 5858. Closed Sun. and Mon. Adm. free. British art from the 16th to 20th century. Old Masters and non-European art
*Kelham Island Industrial Museum, off Alma Street. Tel: 0114-272 2106. Closed Fri. and Sat. Adm. charge. Local industrial and social history

STOKE ON TRENT *City Museum and Art Gallery, Hanley Tel: 01782-232323. Closed Sun. mornings. Adm. free. Pottery, china and porcelain collections
*Etruria Industrial Museum, Etruria. Tel: 01782-287557. Closed Mon. and Tues. Adm. free. Britain's sole surviving steam-powered potter's mill
Gladstone Pottery Museum, Longton. Tel: 01782-319232. Adm. charge. A working Victorian pottery. Pottery factory tours are available by arrangement Mon.–Fri., except during factory holidays, at the following: Royal Doulton, Burslem; Spode, Stoke; John Beswick, Longton; Wedgwood, Barlaston; W. Moorcroft, Cobridge; H & R Johnson Tiles, Tunstall; Moorland Pottery, Burslem; Peggy Davies Ceramics, Stoke; Staffordshire Enamels, Longton; St George's Fine Bone China, Hanley

STYAL, Cheshire – Quarry Bank Mill. Tel: 01625-527468. Closed Mon. in winter. Adm. charge. Working mill illustrating history of cotton industry; costumed guides at restored Apprentice House

TELFORD – *Ironbridge Gorge Museums. Tel: 01952-433522. Smaller sites closed in winter. Adm. charge for each site; £9.00 for all sites (ticket valid until all sites have been visited). Includes first iron bridge; Blists Hill (late Victorian working town); Museum of Iron; Jackfield Tile Museum; Coalport China Museum; Tar Tunnel

TRING, Herts – Tring Zoological Museum, Akeman Street. Tel: 01442-824181. Closed Sun. mornings. Adm. £2.50. Display of more than 4,000 animal species

WAKEFIELD – Yorkshire Sculpture Park, West Bretton. Tel: 01924-830302. Adm. free. Open-air sculpture gallery including works by Moore, Hepworth, Frink and others

WORCESTER – *City Museum and Art Gallery, Foregate Street. Tel: 01905-25371. Closed Thurs. and Sun. Adm. free. Includes a military museum, 19th-century chemist's shop and changing art exhibitions
Dyson Perrins Museum of Worcester Porcelain and Royal Worcester Factory, Severn Street. Tel: 01905-23221. Museum closed for refurbishment until spring 1998; factory tours on weekdays

WROUGHTON, nr Swindon, Wilts – Science Museum, Wroughton Airfield. Tel: 01793-814466. Open selected summer weekends only. Adm. charge. Aircraft displays and some of the Science Museum's transport and agricultural collection

YEOVIL, Somerset – Fleet Air Arm Museum, Royal Naval Air Station, Yeovilton. Tel: 01935-840565. Adm. charge. History of naval aviation; historic aircraft, including Concorde 002
Montacute House, Montacute. (see page 581). Elizabethan and Jacobean portraits from the National Portrait Gallery

YORK – Beningbrough Hall, Shipton-by-Beningbrough. Tel: 01904-470666. Closed Thurs. and Fri. (except Good Friday and July-Aug.); also closed in winter. Adm. £4.50. Portraits from the National Portrait Gallery
*Castle Museum. Tel: 01904-653611. Adm. £4.50. Reconstructed streets; costume and military collections
*City Art Gallery, Exhibition Square. Tel: 01904-551861. Closed Sun. mornings. Adm. free. European and British painting spanning seven centuries; modern pottery
Jorvik Viking Centre, Coppergate. Tel: 01904-653000. Adm. £4.95. Reconstruction of Viking York
National Railway Museum, Leeman Road. Tel: 01904-621261. Adm. £4.80. Includes locomotives, rolling stock and carriages
*Yorkshire Museum, Museum Gardens. Tel: 01904-629745. Adm. £3.50. Yorkshire life from Roman to medieval times; geology gallery

WALES

BODELWYDDAN, Denbighshire – Bodelwyddan Castle. Tel: 01745-584060. Opening times vary. Adm. charge. Portraits from the National Portrait Gallery, furniture from the Victoria and Albert Museum and sculptures from the Royal Academy

CAERLEON – Roman Legionary Museum. Tel: 01633-423134. Closed Sun. mornings. Adm. charge. Material from the site of the Roman fortress of Isca and its suburbs

CARDIFF – National Museum and Gallery Cardiff, Cathays Park. Tel: 01222-397951. Closed Mon. (except Bank Holidays). Adm. charge. Includes natural sciences, archaeology and Impressionist paintings
Museum of Welsh Life, St Fagans. Tel: 01222-569441. Adm. charge. Open-air museum with re-erected buildings, agricultural equipment and costume
Welsh Industrial and Maritime Museum, Bute Street. Tel: 01222-481919. Closed Mon. (except Bank Holidays). Adm. charge. Power, railways, locomotives and shipping exhibitions; miniature railway

DRE-FACH FELINDRE, nr Llandysul – Museum of the Welsh Woollen Industry. Tel: 01559-370929. Closed Sun., and Sat. in winter. Adm. charge. Exhibitions, a working woollen mill and craft workshops

LLANBERIS, nr Caernarfon – Welsh Slate Museum. Tel: 01286-870630. Closed in winter (except by appointment). Adm. charge. Former slate quarry with original machinery and plant; slate crafts demonstrations

SWANSEA – *Glyn Vivian Art Gallery and Museum*, Alexandra Road. Tel: 01792-655006. Closed Mon. (except Bank Holidays). Adm. free. Paintings, ceramics, Swansea pottery and porcelain, clocks, glass and Welsh art
Swansea Maritime and Industrial Museum, Museum Square. Tel: 01792-650351. Closed Mon. (except Bank Holidays). Adm. free. Includes a working woollen mill and historic boats afloat

SCOTLAND

ABERDEEN – *Aberdeen Art Gallery*, Schoolhill. Tel: 01224-646333. Closed Sun. mornings. Adm. free. Art from the 18th to 20th century
Aberdeen Maritime Museum, Shiprow. Tel: 01224-337700. Adm. free. Maritime history, including shipbuilding and North Sea oil
EDINBURGH – *City Art Centre*, Market Street. Tel: 0131-529 3993. Closed Sun. Adm. free. Late 19th- and 20th-century art and temporary exhibitions
Huntly House Museum, Canongate. Tel: 0131-529 4143. Closed Sun. Adm. free. Local history, silver, glass and Scottish pottery
Museum of Childhood, High Street. Tel: 0131-529 4142. Closed Sun. Adm. free. Toys, games, clothes and exhibits relating to the social history of childhood
Museum of Flight, East Fortune Airfield, nr North Berwick. Tel: 01620-880308. Closed in winter. Adm. charge. Display of aircraft
National Gallery of Scotland, The Mound. Tel: 0131-624 6200. Closed Sun. mornings. Adm. free. Paintings, drawings and prints from the 16th to 20th century, and the national collection of Scottish art
The People's Story, Canongate. Tel: 0131-529 4057. Closed Sun. Adm. free. Edinburgh life since the 18th century
Royal Museum of Scotland, Chambers Street. Tel: 0131-225 7534. Closed Sun. mornings. Adm. free. Scottish and international collections from prehistoric times to the present
Scottish Agricultural Museum, Ingliston. Tel: 0131-225 7534. Closed in winter and on Sun.; also on Sat. in May and Sept. Adm. free. History of agriculture in Scotland
Scottish National Portrait Gallery, Queen Street. Tel: 0131-624 6200. Closed Sun. mornings. Adm. free. Portraits of eminent people in Scottish history, and the national collection of photography
Scottish National Gallery of Modern Art, Belford Road. Tel: 0131-624 6200. Closed Sun. mornings. Adm. free. Twentieth-century painting, sculpture and graphic art
Scottish United Services Museum, Edinburgh Castle. Tel: 0131-225 7534. Closed Sun. mornings in winter. Adm. free. History of the armed forces of Scotland
The Writer's Museum, Lawnmarket. Tel: 0131-529 4901. Closed Sun. Adm. free. Robert Louis Stevenson, Walter Scott and Robert Burns exhibits
FORT WILLIAM – *West Highland Museum*, Cameron Square. Tel: 01397-702169. Closed Sun. Adm. £2.00. Includes tartan collections and exhibits relating to 1745 uprising
GLASGOW – *Burrell Collection*, Pollokshaws Road. Tel: 0141-649 7151. Adm. free. Paintings, textiles, furniture, ceramics, stained glass and silver from classical times to the 19th century
Gallery of Modern Art, Queen Street. Tel: 0141-229 1996. Adm. free. Collection of contemporary Scottish and world art
Glasgow Art Gallery and Museum, Kelvingrove. Tel: 0141-287 2699. Adm. free. Includes Old Masters, 19th-century French paintings and armour collection

Hunterian Art Gallery, Hillhead Street. Tel: 0141-330 5431. Closed Sun. Adm. free. Rennie Mackintosh and Whistler collections; Old Masters, Scottish paintings and modern paintings, sculpture and prints
McLellan Galleries, Sauchiehall Street. Tel: 0141-331 1854. Adm. charge. Temporary exhibitions
Museum of Transport, Bunhouse Road. Tel: 0141-287 2720. Adm. free. Includes a reproduction of a 1938 Glasgow street, cars since the 1930s, trams and a Glasgow subway station
People's Palace Museum, Glasgow Green. Tel: 0141-554 0223. Adm. free. History of Glasgow since 1175
Pollok House, Pollokshaws Road. Tel: 0141-649 7151. Adm. free. Spanish paintings, furniture, silver and ceramics
St Mungo Museum of Religious Life and Art, Castle Street. Tel: 0141-553 2557. Adm. free. Explores universal themes through objects of all the main world religions

NORTHERN IRELAND

BELFAST – *Ulster Museum*, Botanic Gardens. Tel: 01232-383000. Closed weekend mornings. Adm. free (£3.00 charge for dinosaur exhibition). Irish antiquities, natural and local history, fine and applied arts
HOLYWOOD, Co. Down – *Ulster Folk and Transport Museum*, Cultra. Tel: 01232-428428. Closed Sun. mornings. Adm. £4.00. Open-air museum with original buildings from Ulster town and rural life c. 1900; indoor galleries including Irish rail and road transport and Titanic exhibitions
LONDONDERRY – *The Tower Museum*, Union Hall Place. Tel: 01504-372411. Closed Sun. and Mon. Adm. £3.25. Tells the story of Ireland through the history of Londonderry
OMAGH, Co. Tyrone – *Ulster American Folk Park*, Castletown. Tel: 01662-243292. Closed weekends in winter. Adm. £3.50. Open-air museum telling the story of Ulster's emigrants to America; restored or recreated dwellings and workshops; ship and dockside gallery

Sights of London

For historic buildings and museums and galleries in London, *see* pages 578–84 and 587–8

ALEXANDRA PALACE, Wood Green, London N22 4AY. Tel: 0181-365 2121. The Victorian Palace was severely damaged by fire in 1980 but was restored, and reopened in 1988. Alexandra Palace now provides modern facilities for exhibitions, conferences, banquets and leisure activities. There is an ice rink, open daily, and a boating lake.

BARBICAN CENTRE, Silk Street, London EC2Y 8DS. Tel: 0171-638 4141. Owned, funded and managed by the Corporation of London, the Barbican Centre opened in 1982 and houses the 1,156-seat Barbican Theatre, a 200-seat studio theatre (The Pit), and the 1,989-seat Barbican Hall. There are also three cinemas, two art galleries, a sculpture court, a lending library, conference, trade and banqueting facilities, conservatory, shops, restaurants, cafés and bars.

BRIDGES. The bridges over the Thames (from east to west) are:

The Queen Elizabeth II Bridge, opened 1991, from Dartford to Thurrock

Tower Bridge, opened 1894 (*see also* page 588)

London Bridge, opened after rebuilding by Rennie, 1831; the new London Bridge opened 1973

Alexandra Bridge (railway bridge), built 1863–6

Southwark Bridge (Rennie), built 1814–19; rebuilt 1912–21

Blackfriars Railway Bridge, completed 1864

Blackfriars Bridge, built 1760–9; rebuilt 1860–9; widened 1907–10

Waterloo Bridge (Rennie), opened 1817; rebuilt 1937–42

Hungerford Railway Bridge (Brunel), suspension bridge built 1841–5; replaced by present railway and footbridge 1863

Westminster Bridge (width 84 ft), opened 1750; rebuilt 1854–62

Lambeth Bridge, built 1862; rebuilt 1929–32

Vauxhall Bridge, built 1811–16; rebuilt 1895–1906

Grosvenor Bridge (railway bridge), built 1859–60; rebuilt 1963–7

Chelsea Bridge, built 1851–8; replaced by suspension bridge 1934; widened 1937

Albert Bridge, opened 1873; restructured (Bazalgette) 1884; strengthened 1971–3

Battersea Bridge (Holland), opened 1772; rebuilt (Bazalgette) 1890

Battersea Railway Bridge, opened 1863

Wandsworth Bridge, opened 1873; rebuilt 1940

Putney Railway Bridge, opened 1889

Putney Bridge, built 1727–9; rebuilt (Bazalgette) 1882–6; starting point of Oxford and Cambridge Boat Race

Hammersmith Bridge, built 1824–7; rebuilt (Bazalgette) 1883–7; closed in 1997 for safety work

Barnes Railway Bridge (also pedestrian), built 1846–9; restructured 1893

Chiswick Bridge, opened 1933

Kew Railway Bridge, opened 1869

Kew Bridge, built 1758–9; rebuilt and renamed King Edward VII Bridge 1903

Richmond Lock; lock, weir and footbridge opened 1894

Twickenham Bridge, opened 1933

Richmond Railway Bridge, opened 1848; restructured 1906–8

Richmond Bridge, built 1774–7; widened 1937

Teddington Lock, footbridge opened 1889; marks the end of the tidal reach of the Thames

Kingston Bridge, built 1825–8; widened 1914

Hampton Court Bridge, built 1753; replaced by iron bridge 1865; present bridge built 1933

CEMETERIES. *Abney Park*, Stamford Hill, N16 (35 acres), tomb of General Booth, founder of the Salvation Army, and memorials to many Nonconformist divines. *Brompton*, Old Brompton Road, SW10 (40 acres), graves of Sir Henry Cole, Emmeline Pankhurst, John Wisden. *City of London Cemetery and Crematorium*, Aldersbrook Road, E12 (200 acres). *Golders Green Crematorium*, Hoop Lane, NW11 (12 acres), with Garden of Rest and memorials to many famous men and women. *Hampstead*, Fortune Green Road, NW6 (36 acres), graves of Kate Greenaway, Lord Lister, Marie Lloyd. *Highgate*, Swains Lane, N6 (38 acres), tombs of George Eliot, Faraday and Marx; guided tours only, west side, £3.00. *Kensal Green*, Harrow Road, W10 (70 acres), tombs of Thackeray, Trollope, Sydney Smith, Wilkie Collins, Tom Hood, George Cruikshank, Leigh Hunt, I. K. Brunel and Charles Kemble. Churchyard of the former *Marylebone Chapel*, Marylebone High Street, W1, Charles Wesley and his son Samuel Wesley buried; chapel demolished in 1949, now Garden of Rest. *Nunhead*, Linden Grove, SE15 (52 acres), closed in 1969, recently restored and opened for burials. *St Marylebone Cemetery and Crematorium*, East End Road, N2 (47 acres). *West Norwood Cemetery and Crematorium*, Norwood High Street, SE27 (42 acres), tombs of Sir Henry Bessemer, Mrs Beeton, Sir Henry Tate and Joseph Whitaker (*Whitaker's Almanack*).

CENOTAPH, Whitehall, London SW1. The word 'cenotaph' means 'empty tomb'. The monument, erected 'To the Glorious Dead', is a memorial to all ranks of the sea, land and air forces who gave their lives in the service of the Empire during the First World War. Designed by Sir Edwin Lutyens and erected as a temporary memorial in 1919, it was replaced by a permanent structure unveiled by George V on Armistice Day 1920. An additional inscription was made after the Second World War to commemorate those who gave their lives in that conflict.

CHARTERHOUSE, Sutton's Hospital, Charterhouse Square, London EC1M 6AN. Tel: 0171-253 9503. A Carthusian monastery from 1371 to 1537, purchased in 1611 by Thomas Sutton, who endowed it as a hospital for aged men 'of gentle birth' and a school for poor scholars (removed to Godalming in 1872). Open to visitors on Wednesdays at 2.15 (April–July). Admission £3.00. *Registrar and Clerk to the Governors*, Lt.-Col. J. Macdonald

CHELSEA PHYSIC GARDEN, 66 Royal Hospital Road, London SW3 4HS. Tel: 0171-352 5646. A garden of general botanical research, maintaining a wide range of rare and unusual plants. The garden was established in 1673 by the Society of Apothecaries. Open Wednesday and Sunday p.m. during summer months. All enquiries to the Curator.

DOWNING STREET, London SW1. Number 10 Downing Street is the official town residence of the Prime Minister, No. 11 of the Chancellor of the Exchequer and No. 12 is the office of the Government Whips. The street was named after Sir George Downing, Bt., soldier and diplomatist, who was MP for Morpeth from 1660 to 1684.

Chequers, a Tudor mansion in the Chilterns near Princes Risborough, was presented by Lord and Lady Lee of

Fareham in 1917 to serve, from 1921, as a country residence for the Prime Minister of the day.

GEORGE INN, Borough High Street, London SE1. The last galleried inn in London, built in 1677. Now run as an ordinary public house.

GREENWICH, London SE10. *The Royal Naval College* was until 1873 the Greenwich Hospital. It was built by Charles II, largely from designs by John Webb, and by Queen Anne and William III, from designs by Wren. It stands on the site of an ancient royal palace and of the more recent Palace of Placentia constructed by Humphrey, Duke of Gloucester (1391–1447), son of Henry IV. Henry VIII, Mary I and Elizabeth I were born in the royal palace (which reverted to the Crown in 1447) and Edward VI died there. *Greenwich Park* (196½ acres) was enclosed by Humphrey, Duke of Gloucester, and laid out by Charles II from the designs of Le Nôtre. On a hill in Greenwich Park is the former Royal Observatory (founded 1675). Its buildings are now managed by the National Maritime Museum (*see* page 588) and the first observatory is named Flamsteed House, after John Flamsteed (1646–1719), the first Astronomer Royal (*see* page 580). *The Cutty Sark*, the last of the famous tea clippers, has been preserved as a memorial to ships and men of a past era. The yacht *Gipsy Moth IV* is preserved alongside the *Cutty Sark*.

HORSE GUARDS, Whitehall, London SW1. Archway and offices built about 1753. The mounting of the guard takes place at 11 a.m. (10 a.m. on Sundays) and the dismounted inspection at 4 p.m. Only those on the Lord Chamberlain's list may drive through the gates and archway into *Horse Guards' Parade* (230,000 sq. ft), where the Colour is 'trooped' on The Queen's official birthday.

THE HOUSES OF PARLIAMENT, Westminster, London SW1. The royal palace of Westminster, originally built by Edward the Confessor, was the normal meeting place of Parliament from about 1340. St Stephen's Chapel was used from about 1550 for the meetings of the House of Commons, which had previously been held in the Chapter House or Refectory of Westminster Abbey. The House of Lords met in an apartment of the royal palace.

The fire of 1834 destroyed much of the palace and the present Houses of Parliament were erected on the site from the designs of Sir Charles Barry and Augustus Welby Pugin between 1840 and 1867. The chamber of the House of Commons was destroyed by bombing in 1941 and a new Chamber designed by Sir Giles Gilbert Scott was used for the first time in 1950.

Westminster Hall was the only part of the old palace of Westminster to survive the fire of 1834. It was built by William Rufus (1097–9) and altered by Richard II (1394–9). The hammerbeam roof of carved oak dates from 1396–8. The Hall was the scene of the trial of Charles I.

The Victoria Tower of the House of Lords is about 330 ft high, and when Parliament is sitting the Union flag flies by day from its flagstaff. *The Clock Tower* of the House of Commons is about 320 ft high and contains 'Big Ben', the hour bell said to be named after Sir Benjamin Hall, First Commissioner of Works when the original bell was cast in 1856. This bell, which weighed 16 tons 11 cwt, was found to be cracked in 1857. The present bell (13½ tons) is a recasting of the original and was first brought into use in 1859. The dials of the clock are 23 ft in diameter, the hands being 9 ft and 14 ft long (including balance piece). A light is displayed from the Clock Tower at night when Parliament is sitting.

For security reasons tours of the Houses of Parliament are available only to those who have made advance arrangements through an MP or peer.

Admission to the Strangers' Gallery of the House of Lords is arranged by a peer or by queue via St Stephen's Entrance. Admission to the Strangers' Gallery of the House of Commons is by Members' order (Members' orders should be sought several weeks in advance), or by queue via St Stephen's Entrance. Queues are usually shorter after 6 p.m. Monday–Thursday and on Wednesday morning. Overseas visitors may write to the Public Information Office to obtain a permit to tour the Houses of Parliament, or obtain cards of introduction from their Embassy or High Commission to attend the public gallery.

INNS OF COURT. The *Inner* and *Middle Temple*, Fleet Street/Victoria Embankment, London EC4, have occupied since the early 14th century the site of the buildings of the Order of Knights Templars. *Inner Temple Hall* is open by appointment on application to the Treasurer's Office. *Middle Temple Hall* (1562–70) is open when not in use, Monday–Friday 10–11.30 and 3–4; closed on public holidays. In Middle Temple Gardens (open to the public Monday–Friday 12–3) Shakespeare (*Henry VI, Part I*) places the incident which led to the 'Wars of the Roses' (1455–85).

Temple Church, London EC4, has a nave which forms one of five remaining round churches in England. Open Wednesday–Friday 10–4. Services: 8.30 and 11.15 a.m. except in August and September. *Master of the Temple*, Revd Canon J. Robinson.

Lincoln's Inn, Chancery Lane/Lincoln's Inn Fields, London WC2, occupies the site of the palace of a former Bishop of Chichester and of a Black Friars monastery. The hall and library buildings are of 1845, although the library is first mentioned in 1474; the old hall (late 15th century) and the chapel were rebuilt *c.*1619–23. Halls open by appointment, chapel and gardens, Monday–Friday 12–2.30. Chapel services Sunday 11.30 a.m. during law terms. *Lincoln's Inn Fields* (7 acres). The square was laid out by Inigo Jones.

Gray's Inn, Holborn/Gray's Inn Road, London WC1. Early 14th century; Hall 1556–8. Matins 11.15 a.m. (during dining term only). Holy Communion first Sunday in every month except January, August and September. Gardens open Monday–Friday 12–2.30 (except Public Holidays). Tel: 0171-405 8164.

No other 'Inns' are active, but there are remains of *Staple Inn*, a gabled front on Holborn (opposite Gray's Inn Road). *Clement's Inn* (near St Clement Danes Church), *Clifford's Inn*, Fleet Street, and *Thavies Inn*, Holborn Circus, are all rebuilt. *Serjeants' Inn*, Fleet Street, and another (demolished 1910) of the same name in Chancery Lane, were composed of Serjeants-at-Law, the last of whom died in 1922.

LLOYD'S, Lime Street, London EC3M 7HA. Society of private underwriters which evolved during the 18th century from Lloyds Coffee House. The present building was opened for business in May 1986, and houses the Lutine Bell. Underwriting is on four floors with a total area of 114,000 sq. feet.

LONDON PARKS, ETC.

Royal Parks

Bushy Park (1,099 acres), Surrey. Adjoining Hampton Court, contains avenue of horse-chestnuts enclosed in a fourfold avenue of limes planted by William III. 'Chestnut Sunday' (when the trees are in full bloom with their 'candles') is usually about 1 to 15 May

Green Park (49 acres), London W1. Between Piccadilly and St James's Park, with Constitution Hill leading to Hyde Park Corner

Greenwich Park (196½ acres), London SE10

Hampton Court Gardens (54 acres), Surrey

Hampton Court Green (17 acres), Surrey

Hampton Court Park (622 acres), Surrey

Hyde Park (341 acres), London W1/W2. From Park Lane to Kensington Gardens, containing the Serpentine. Fine gateway at Hyde Park Corner, with Apsley House, the Achilles Statue, Rotten Row and the Ladies' Mile. To the north-east is the Marble Arch, originally erected by George IV at the entrance to Buckingham Palace and re-erected in the present position in 1851

Kensington Gardens (275 acres), London W2/W8. From the western boundary of Hyde Park to Kensington Palace, containing the Albert Memorial and Peter Pan statue

Kew, Royal Botanic Gardens, see page 338

Regent's Park (464 acres), London NW1. From Marylebone Road to Primrose Hill surrounded by the Outer Circle and divided by the Broad Walk leading to the Zoological Gardens

Richmond Park (2,469 acres), Surrey

St James's Park (93 acres), London SW1. From Whitehall to Buckingham Palace. Ornamental lake of 12 acres. The original suspension bridge built in 1857 was replaced in 1957. The Mall leads from the Admiralty Arch to Buckingham Palace, Birdcage Walk from Storey's Gate to Buckingham Palace

Maintained by the Corporation of London

Ashtead Common (500 acres), Surrey

Burnham Beeches and *Fleet Wood* (540 acres), Bucks. Purchased by the Corporation for the benefit of the public in 1880, Fleet Wood (65 acres) being presented in 1921

Coulsdon Common (133 acres), Surrey

Epping Forest (6,000 acres), Essex. Purchased by the Corporation and opened to the public in 1882. The present forest is 12 miles long by 1 to 2 miles wide, about one-tenth of its original area

Farthing Downs (121 acres), Surrey

Hampstead Heath (789 acres), London NW3. Including Golders Hill (36 acres) and Parliament Hill (271 acres)

Highgate Wood (70 acres), London N6/N10

Kenley Common (138 acres), Surrey

Queen's Park (30 acres), London NW6

Riddlesdown (90 acres), Surrey

Spring Park (51 acres), Kent

West Ham Park (77 acres), London E15

West Wickham Common (25 acres), Kent

Woodredon and Warlies Park Estate (740 acres), Waltham Abbey

Also smaller open spaces within the City of London, including *Finsbury Circus Gardens*

LONDON PLANETARIUM, Marylebone Road, London NW1 5LR. Tel: 0171-935 6861. Open daily (except Christmas Day), star show and interactive exhibits 12.20–5.00. Admission charge.

LONDON ZOO, Regent's Park, London NW1. Tel: 0171-722 3333. Opened in 1828. Open daily (except Christmas Day) 10–5.30 March–September, 10–4 in winter. Admission £8.00.

MADAME TUSSAUD'S, Marylebone Road, London NW1 5LR. Tel: 0171-935 6861. Waxwork exhibition. Open daily (except Christmas Day) 10–5.30 (earlier at weekends and during school holidays). Admission charge.

MARKETS. The London markets are mostly administered by the Corporation of London. *Billingsgate* (fish), Thames Street site dating from 1875, a market site for over 1,000 years, moved to the Isle of Dogs in 1982. *Borough*, SE1 (vegetables, fruit, flowers, etc.), established

on present site 1756, privately owned and run. *Covent Garden* (vegetables, fruit, flowers, etc.), established in 1661 under a charter of Charles II, moved in 1973 to Nine Elms. *Leadenhall*, EC3 (meat, poultry, fish, etc.), built 1881, part recently demolished. *London Fruit Exchange*, Brushfield Street, built by Corporation of London 1928–9 as buildings for Spitalfields market; not connected with the market since it moved in 1991. *Petticoat Lane*, Middlesex Street, E1, a market has existed on the site for over 500 years, now a Sunday morning market selling almost anything. *Portobello Road*, W11, originally for herbs and horse-trading from 1870; became famous for antiques after the closure of the Caledonian Market in 1948; Saturdays. *Smithfield, Central Meat, Fish, Fruit, Vegetable and Poultry Markets*, built 1851–66, the site of St Bartholomew's Fair from 12th to 19th century, new hall built 1963, market refurbished 1993–4. *Spitalfields*, E1 (vegetables, fruit, etc.), established 1682, modernized 1928, moved to Leyton in 1991.

MARLBOROUGH HOUSE, Pall Mall, London SW1A 5HX. Built by Wren for the first Duke of Marlborough and completed in 1711, the house reverted to the Crown in 1835. In 1863 it became the London house of the Prince of Wales and was the London home of Queen Mary until her death in 1953. In 1959 Marlborough House was given by The Queen as a centre for Commonwealth government conferences and it was opened as such in 1962. The Queen's Chapel, Marlborough Gate, begun in 1623 from the designs of Inigo Jones for the Infanta Maria of Spain, and completed for Queen Henrietta Maria, is open to the public for services on Sundays at 8.30 a.m. and 11.15 a.m. between Easter Day and end July (*see* St James's Palace for winter services in The Chapel Royal).

LONDON MONUMENT (commonly called The Monument), Monument Street, London EC3. Built from designs of Wren, 1671–7, to commemorate the Great Fire of London, which broke out in Pudding Lane on 2 September 1666. The fluted Doric column is 120 ft high; the moulded cylinder above the balcony supporting a flaming vase of gilt bronze is an additional 42 ft; and the column is based on a square plinth 40 ft high (with fine carvings on the west face) making a total height of 202 ft. Splendid views of London from gallery at top of column (311 steps).

MONUMENTS (sculptor's name in parenthesis). *Albert Memorial* (Durham), Kensington Gore; *Royal Air Force* (Blomfield), Victoria Embankment; *Viscount Alanbrooke,* Whitehall; *Beaconsfield,* Parliament Square; *Beatty* (Macmillan), Trafalgar Square; *Belgian Gratitude* (setting by Blomfield, statue by Rousseau), Victoria Embankment; *Boadicea* (or Boudicca), Queen of the Iceni (Thornycroft), Westminster Bridge; *Brunel* (Marochetti), Victoria Embankment; *Burghers of Calais* (Rodin), Victoria Tower Gardens, Westminster; *Burns* (Steel), Embankment Gardens; *Canada Memorial* (Granche), Green Park; *Carlyle* (Boehm), Chelsea Embankment; *Cavalry* (Jones), Hyde Park; *Edith Cavell* (Frampton), St Martin's Place; *Cenotaph* (Lutyens), Whitehall; *Charles I* (Le Sueur), Trafalgar Square; *Charles II* (Gibbons), South Court, Chelsea Hospital; *Churchill* (Roberts-Jones), Parliament Square; *Cleopatra's Needle* (68½ ft high, c.1500 BC, erected on the Thames Embankment in 1877–8; the sphinxes are Victorian); *Clive* (Tweed), King Charles Street; *Captain Cook* (Brock), The Mall; *Crimean,* Broad Sanctuary; *Oliver Cromwell* (Thornycroft), outside Westminster Hall; *Cunningham* (Belsky), Trafalgar Square; *Gen. Charles de Gaulle,* Carlton Gardens; *Lord Dowding* (Faith Winter), Strand; *Duke of Cambridge* (Jones), Whitehall; *Duke of York* (124 ft), Carlton House Terrace;

Edward VII (Mackennal), Waterloo Place; *Elizabeth I* (1586, oldest outdoor statue in London; from Ludgate), Fleet Street; *Eros* (Shaftesbury Memorial) (Gilbert), Piccadilly Circus; *Marechal Foch* (Mallisard, copy of one in Cassel, France), Grosvenor Gardens; *Charles James Fox* (Westmacott), Bloomsbury Square; *George III* (Cotes Wyatt), Cockspur Street; *George IV* (Chantrey), riding without stirrups, Trafalgar Square; *George V* (Reid Dick), Old Palace Yard; *George VI* (Macmillan), Carlton Gardens; *Gladstone* (Thornycroft), Strand; *Guards'* (Crimea) (Bell), Waterloo Place; (Great War) (Ledward, figures, Bradshaw, cenotaph), Horse Guards' Parade; *Haig* (Hardiman), Whitehall; *Sir Arthur (Bomber) Harris* (Faith Winter), Strand; *Irving* (Brock), north side of National Portrait Gallery; *James II* (Gibbons and/or pupils), Trafalgar Square; *Jellicoe* (Wheeler), Trafalgar Square; *Samuel Johnson* (Fitzgerald), opposite St Clement Danes; *Kitchener* (Tweed), Horse Guards' Parade; *Abraham Lincoln* (Saint-Gaudens, copy of one in Chicago), Parliament Square; *Milton* (Montford), St Giles, Cripplegate; *The Monument* (*see* above); *Mountbatten*, Foreign Office Green; *Nelson* (170 ft 2 in), Trafalgar Square, with Landseer's lions (cast from guns recovered from the wreck of the *Royal George*); *Florence Nightingale* (Walker), Waterloo Place; *Palmerston* (Woolner), Parliament Square; *Peel* (Noble), Parliament Square; *Pitt* (Chantrey), Hanover Square; *Portal* (Nemon), Embankment Gardens; *Prince Consort* (Bacon), Holborn Circus; *Queen Elizabeth Gate*, Hyde Park Corner; *Raleigh* (Macmillan), Whitehall; *Richard I (Coeur de Lion)* (Marochetti), Old Palace Yard; *Roberts* (Bates), Horse Guards' Parade; *Franklin D. Roosevelt* (Reid Dick), Grosvenor Square; *Royal Artillery* (South Africa) (Colton), The Mall; (Great War), Hyde Park Corner; *Captain Scott* (Lady Scott), Waterloo Place; *Shackleton* (Sarjeant Jagger), Kensington Gore; *Shakespeare* (Fontana, copy of one by Scheemakers in Westminster Abbey), Leicester Square; *Smuts* (Epstein), Parliament Square; *Sullivan* (Goscombe John), Victoria Embankment; *Trenchard* (Macmillan), Victoria Embankment; *Victoria Memorial*, in front of Buckingham Palace; *Raoul Wallenberg* (Phillip Jackson), Great Cumberland Place; *George Washington* (Houdon copy), Trafalgar Square; *Wellington* (Boehm), Hyde Park Corner; (Chantrey) riding without stirrups, outside Royal Exchange; *John Wesley* (Adams Acton), City Road; *William III* (Bacon), St James's Square; *Wolseley* (Goscombe John), Horse Guards' Parade.

PORT OF LONDON. The Port of London covers the tidal section of the River Thames from Teddington to the seaward limit (the outer Tongue buoy and the Sunk light vessel), a distance of 150 km. The governing body is the Port of London Authority (PLA). Eighty-eight per cent of the total port traffic is handled at privately operated riverside terminals between Fulham and Canvey Island, the rest at the enclosed dock at Tilbury, 40 km below London Bridge. Passenger vessels and cruise liners can be handled at moorings at Greenwich, Tower Bridge and Tilbury.

ROMAN REMAINS. The city wall of Roman *Londinium* was largely rebuilt during the medieval period but sections may be seen near the White Tower in the Tower of London; at Tower Hill; at Coopers' Row; at All Hallows, London Wall, its vestry being built on the remains of a semi-circular Roman bastion; at St Alphage, London Wall, showing a succession of building repairs from the Roman until the late medieval period; and at St Giles, Cripplegate. Sections of the great forum and basilica, more than 165 metres square, have been encountered during excavations in the area of Leadenhall, Grace-

church Street and Lombard Street. Traces of Roman activity along the river include a massive riverside wall built in the late Roman period, and a succession of Roman timber quays along Lower and Upper Thames Street. Finds from these sites can be seen at the Museum of London (*see* page 588).

Other major buildings are the amphitheatre at Guildhall; remains of bath-buildings in Upper and Lower Thames Street; and the temple of Mithras in Walbrook.

ROYAL ALBERT HALL, Kensington Gore, London SW7 2AP. Tel: 0171-589 3203. The elliptical hall, one of the largest in the world, was completed in 1871, and since 1941 has been the venue each summer for the Promenade Concerts founded in 1895 by Sir Henry Wood. Other events include pop and classical music concerts, dance, opera, sporting events, conferences and banquets.

ROYAL HOSPITAL, CHELSEA, Royal Hospital Road, London SW3 4SR. Tel: 0171-730 0161. Founded by Charles II in 1682, and built by Wren; opened in 1692 for old and disabled soldiers. Open Monday–Saturday 10–12, daily 2–4. The extensive grounds include the former Ranelagh Gardens and are the venue for the Chelsea Flower Show each May. *Governor*, Gen. Sir Brian Kenny, GCB, CBE.

ROYAL OPERA HOUSE, Covent Garden, London WC2E 9DD. Home of The Royal Ballet (1931) and The Royal Opera (1946). The Royal Opera House is the third theatre to be built on the site, opening 1858; the first was opened in 1732. The theatre is closed for redevelopment until autumn 1999.

ST JAMES'S PALACE, Pall Mall, London SW1. Built by Henry VIII; the Gatehouse and Presence Chamber remain; later alterations were made by Wren and Kent. The Chapel Royal is open for services on Sundays at 8.30 a.m. and 11.15 a.m. between the beginning of October and Good Friday (*see* Marlborough House for summer services in The Queen's Chapel). Representatives of foreign powers are still accredited 'to the Court of St James's'. *Clarence House* (1825) in the palace precinct is the home of The Queen Mother.

ST PAUL'S CATHEDRAL, London EC4M 8AD. Built 1675–1710, cost £747,660. The cross on the dome is 365 ft above the ground level, the inner cupola 218 ft above the floor. 'Great Paul' in the south-west tower weighs nearly 17 tons. The organ by Father Smith (enlarged by Willis and rebuilt by Mander) is in a case carved by Grinling Gibbons, who also carved the choir stalls. Open for sightseeing Monday–Saturday 8.30–4.00. Admission to cathedral and crypt: £3.50, children £2.00; Galleries £3.00/£1.50. Services: Sundays, 8, 10, 11, 3.15 and 6.00. Weekdays, 7.30, 8, 12.30 and 5 (Saturday Matins 8.30 a.m.).

SOMERSET HOUSE, Strand and Victoria Embankment, London WC2. The river façade (600 ft. long) was built in 1776–86 from the designs of Sir William Chambers; the eastern extension, which houses part of King's College, was built by Smirke in 1829. Somerset House was the property of Lord Protector Somerset, at whose attainder in 1552 the palace passed to the Crown, and it was a royal residence until 1692.

SOUTH BANK, London SE1. The arts complex on the south bank of the River Thames includes the South Bank Centre, which consists of the 2,903-seat *Royal Festival Hall* (opened in 1951 for the Festival of Britain), the adjacent 1,056-seat *Queen Elizabeth Hall*, the 368-seat *Purcell Room*, and the 77-seat Voice Box. Tel: 0171-960 4242.

The *National Film Theatre* (opened 1952), administered by the British Film Institute, has three auditoria showing over 2,000 films a year. The London Film Festival is held here every November. Tel: 0171-928 3232.

The *Royal National Theatre* opened in 1976 and stages classical, modern, new and neglected plays in its three auditoria: the 1,160-seat Olivier theatre, the 890-seat Lyttelton theatre and the Cottesloe theatre which seats up to 400. Tel: 0171-928 2252.

SOUTHWARK CATHEDRAL, London SE1 9DA. Mainly 13th century, but the nave is largely rebuilt. The tomb of John Gower (1330–1408) is between the Bunyan and Chaucer memorial windows in the north aisle; Shakespeare's effigy backed by a view of Southwark and the Globe Theatre in the south aisle; the tomb of Bishop Andrewes (died 1626) is near the nave. The lady chapel was the scene of the consistory courts of the reign of Mary (Gardiner and Bonner) and is still used as a consistory court. John Harvard, after whom Harvard University is named, was baptized here in 1607, and the chapel by the north choir aisle is his memorial chapel. Open 9–6, admission free (suggested donation £2). Services: Sundays, 9, 11, 3. Weekdays, 8, 12.45, 5.30 (sung on Tuesdays and Fridays), Saturdays, 9, 4.

THAMES EMBANKMENTS. The *Victoria Embankment*, on the north side from Westminster to Blackfriars, was constructed by Sir Joseph Bazalgette (1819–91) for the Metropolitan Board of Works, 1864–70; the seats, of which the supports of some are a kneeling camel, laden with spicery, and of others a winged sphinx, were presented by the Grocers' Company and by W. H. Smith, MP, in 1874; the *Albert Embankment*, on the south side from Westminster Bridge to Vauxhall, 1866–9; the *Chelsea Embankment*, 1871–4. The total cost exceeded £2,000,000. Bazalgette also inaugurated the London main drainage system, 1858–65. A medallion (*Flumini vincula posuit*) has been placed on a pier of the Victoria Embankment to commemorate the engineer.

THAMES FLOOD BARRIER. Officially opened in May 1984, though first used in February 1983, the barrier consists of ten rising sector gates which span 570 yards from bank to bank of the Thames at Woolwich Reach. When not in use the gates lie horizontally, allowing shipping to navigate the river normally; when the barrier is closed, the gates turn through 90 degrees to stand vertically more than 50 feet above the river bed. The barrier took eight years to complete and can be raised within about 30 minutes.

THAMES TUNNELS. The *Rotherhithe Tunnel*, opened 1908, connects Commercial Road, London E14, with Lower Road, Rotherhithe; it is 1 mile 332 yards long, of which 525 yards are under the river. The first *Blackwall Tunnel* (northbound vehicles only), opened 1897, connects East India Dock Road, Poplar, with Blackwall Lane, East Greenwich. The height restriction on the northbound tunnel is 13ft 4in. A second tunnel (for southbound vehicles only) opened 1967. The lengths of the tunnels measured from East India Dock Road to the Gate House on the south side are 6,215 ft (old tunnel) and 6,152 ft. *Greenwich Tunnel* (pedestrians only), opened 1902, connects the Isle of Dogs, Poplar, with Greenwich; it is 406 yards long. The *Woolwich Tunnel* (pedestrians only), opened 1912, connects North and South Woolwich below the passenger and vehicular ferry from North Woolwich Station, London E16, to High Street, Woolwich, London SE18; it is 552 yards long.

WALTHAM CROSS, Herts. At Waltham Cross is one of the crosses (partly restored) erected by Edward I to mark a resting place of the corpse of Queen Eleanor on its way to Westminster Abbey. Ten crosses were erected, but only those at Geddington, Northampton and Waltham

survive; 'Charing' Cross originally stood near the spot now occupied by the statue of Charles I at Whitehall.

WESTMINSTER ABBEY, London SW1. Built between 1050 and 1745; contains the chapel of Henry VII, chapter house and cloisters, Edward the Confessor's shrine, tombs of kings and queens and many other monuments, including the grave of 'The Unknown Warrior' and Poets' Corner. The Coronation Chair formerly enclosed the Stone of Scone, removed from Scotland by Edward I in 1296 and returned to Scotland in 1996. Open on weekdays 9.20–6. Admission to the Royal Chapels, Poets' Corner, Quire and Statesmen's Aisle £4.00, con. £2.00/£1.00. Last admission Monday–Friday 3.45 p.m., Saturday 4.45 p.m. Nave open on Sundays between services. Services: Sundays, 8, 10, 11.15, 3, 6.30 (generally preceded by an organ recital). Monday–Friday, 7.30, 8, 12.30, 5. Saturdays, 8, 9.20, 3.

WESTMINSTER CATHEDRAL, Ashley Place, London SW1P 1QW. Roman Catholic cathedral built 1895–1903 from the designs of J. F. Bentley. The campanile is 283 feet high. Cathedral open 6.50 a.m.–7 p.m. Masses: Sundays, 7, 8, 9, 10.30 (sung), 12, 5.30 and 7; Solemn Vespers and Benediction 3.30. Monday–Friday, 7, 8, 8.30, 9, 10.30, 12.30, 1.05 and 5.30 (sung), Morning Prayer 7.40, Vespers 5. Saturdays 8, 8.30, 9, 10.30 (sung), 12.30 and 6, Morning Prayer 10.00, Rosary, Benediction 7.00. Holy days of obligation, Low Masses 7, 8, 8.30, 9, 10.30, 12.30, 1.05, 5.30 (sung) and 7.

LONDON TOURISM BOARD AND CONVENTION BUREAU, 26 Grosvenor Gardens, London SW1W 0DU. Tourist information: 0171-730 3450

Hallmarks

Hallmarks are the symbols stamped on gold, silver or platinum articles to indicate that they have been tested at an official Assay Office and that they conform to one of the legal standards. With certain exceptions, all gold, silver or platinum articles are required by law to be hallmarked before they are offered for sale. Hallmarking was instituted in England in 1300 under a statute of Edward I.

MODERN HALLMARKS

Normally a complete modern hallmark consists of four symbols – the sponsor's mark, the assay office mark, the standard mark and the date letter. Additional marks have been authorized from time to time.

SPONSOR'S MARK

Instituted in England in 1363, the sponsor's mark was originally a device such as a bird or fleur-de-lis. Now it consists of the initial letters of the name or names of the manufacturer or firm. Where two or more sponsors have the same initials, there is a variation in the surrounding shield or style of letters.

STANDARD MARK

The standard mark indicates that the content of the precious metal in the alloy from which the article is made, is not less than the legal standard. The legal standard is the minimum content of precious metal by weight in parts per thousand, and the standards are:

Gold	916.6	(22 carat)
	750	(18 carat)
	585	(14 carat)
	375	(9 carat)
Silver	958.4	(Britannia)
	925	(sterling)
Platinum	950	

The metals are marked as follows, if they are manufactured in the United Kingdom:

GOLD – a crown followed by the millesimal figure for the standard, e.g. 916 for 22 carat (see table above)

SILVER – Britannia silver: a full-length figure of Britannia. Sterling silver: a lion passant (England) or a lion rampant (Scotland)

 Britannia Silver

 Sterling Silver (England)

 Sterling Silver (Scotland)

PLATINUM – an orb

ASSAY OFFICE MARK

This mark identifies the particular assay office at which the article was tested and marked. The British assay offices are:

LONDON, Goldsmiths' Hall, London EC2V 8AQ. Tel: 0171-606 8975

BIRMINGHAM, Newhall Street, Birmingham B3 1SB. Tel: 0121-236 6951

 Gold and platinum

 Silver

SHEFFIELD, 137 Portobello Street, Sheffield S1 4DS. Tel: 0114–275 5111

EDINBURGH, 39 Manor Place, Edinburgh EH3 7EB. Tel: 0131-226 1122

Assay offices formerly existed in other towns, e.g. Chester, Exeter, Glasgow, Newcastle, Norwich and York, each having its own distinguishing mark.

DATE LETTER

The date letter shows the year in which an article was assayed and hallmarked. Each alphabetical cycle has a distinctive style of lettering or shape of shield. The date letters were different at the various assay offices and the particular office must be established from the assay office mark before reference is made to tables of date letters.

The table on page 597 shows specimen shields and letters used by the London Assay Office on silver articles in each period from 1498. The same letters are found on gold articles but the surrounding shield may differ. Since 1 January 1975, each office has used the same style of date letter and shield for all articles.

OTHER MARKS

FOREIGN GOODS

Since 1842 foreign goods imported into Britain have been required to be hallmarked before sale. The marks consist of the importer's mark, a special assay office mark, the figure denoting fineness (fineness mark) and the annual date letter.

The following are the assay office marks for gold imported articles. For silver and platinum the symbols remain the same but the shields differ in shape.

 London

 Birmingham

 Sheffield

 Edinburgh

Convention Hallmarks

Special marks at authorized assay offices of the signatory countries of the International Convention (Austria, Denmark, Finland, Ireland, Norway, Portugal, Sweden, Switzerland and the UK) are legally recognized in the United Kingdom as approved hallmarks. These consist of a sponsor's mark, a common control mark, a fineness mark (arabic numerals showing the standard in parts per thousand), and an assay office mark. There is no date letter.

The fineness marks are:

Gold	750	(18 carat)
	585	(14 carat)
	375	(9 carat)
Silver	925	(sterling)
Platinum	950	

The common control marks are:

Gold (18 carat)

Silver

Platinum

Duty Marks

In 1784 an additional mark of the reigning sovereign's head was introduced to signify that the excise duty had been paid. The mark became obsolete on the abolition of the duty in 1890.

Commemorative Marks

There are three other marks to commemorate special events: the silver jubilee of King George V and Queen Mary in 1935, the coronation of Queen Elizabeth II in 1953, and her silver jubilee in 1977.

LONDON (GOLDSMITHS' HALL) DATE LETTERS FROM 1498

	from	to
Black letter, small	1498–9	1517–8
Lombardic	1518–9	1537–8
Roman and other capitals	1538–9	1557–8
Black letter, small	1558–9	1577–8
Roman letter, capitals	1578–9	1597–8
Lombardic, external cusps	1598–9	1617–8
Italic letter, small	1618–9	1637–8
Court hand	1638–9	1657–8

	from	to
Black letter, capitals	1658–9	1677–8
Black letter, small	1678–9	1696–7
Court hand	1697	1715–6
Roman letter, capitals	1716–7	1735–6
Roman letter, small	1736–7	1738–9
Roman letter, small	1739–40	1755–6
Old English, capitals	1756–7	1775–6
Roman letter, small	1776–7	1795–6
Roman letter, capitals	1796–7	1815–6
Roman letter, small	1816–7	1835–6
Old English, capitals	1836–7	1855–6
Old English, small	1856–7	1875–6
Roman letter, capitals [A to M *square* shield N to Z as shown]	1876–7	1895–6
Roman letter, small	1896–7	1915–6
Black letter, small	1916–7	1935–6
Roman letter, capitals	1936–7	1955–6
Italic letter, small	1956–7	1974
Italic letter, capitals	1975	

Economic Statistics

The Budget 1997

GENERAL GOVERNMENT RECEIPTS £ billion

	Outturn 1996–7	Forecast 1997–8	Forecast 1998–9
Income tax	69.5	76.5	83.7
Corporation tax	27.7	30.1	32.0
Windfall tax	—	2.6	2.6
Value added tax	46.7	50.0	52.5
Excise duties*	30.6	33.4	35.4
Other taxes and royalties†	49.7	50.9	53.8
Social security contributions	47.4	49.5	52.0
Other receipts	14.8	15.3	15.2
General government receipts	286.3	308.3	327.2

* Fuel, alcohol and tobacco duties
† Includes council tax and money paid into the National Lottery Distribution Fund, as well as other central government taxes

GENERAL GOVERNMENT EXPENDITURE £ billion

	Outturn 1996–7	Forecast 1997–8	Forecast 1998–9
Control Total	260.4	266.4	273.6
Welfare to Work spending	—	0.2	1.2
Local authority spending under the capital receipts initiative	—	0.2	0.7
Cyclical social security	14.3	13.7	14.0
Central government debt interest	22.3	24.6	24.4
Accounting adjustments	11.4	10.1	10.7
GGE(X)*	308.4	315.3	324.7
Privatization proceeds	−4.4	−2.0	0.0
Other adjustments	5.1	6.2	6.6
GGE	309.0	319.4	331.3
GGE(X) as a percentage of GDP	41%	39½%	38¾%

* Excluding privatization proceeds and lottery financed spending and net of interest and dividend receipts

PUBLIC SECTOR FINANCES £ billion

	Estimated Outturn 1996–7	Forecast 1997–8	Forecast 1998–9
Receipts[1]	285.4	310.9	329.6
Current expenditure[2]	306.6	316.4	325.2
Current balance	−21.2	−5.5	4.4
excluding windfall tax[3]	−21.2	−8.0	2.7
Net capital spending[4]	8.1	7.5	7.9
Financial deficit	29.2	13.0	3.5
Privatization proceeds and other financial transactions	6.5	2.0	−0.5
PSBR	22.7	10.9	4.0
excluding windfall tax[3]	22.7	13.3	5.4
General government financial deficit[5]	30.4	11.2	1.6
per cent of GDP[5]	4%	1½%	¼%
Money GDP	752.2	797.6	838.0

[1] On a national accounts accruals basis. Includes capital taxes
[2] Includes depreciation of fixed capital
[3] Excluding windfall tax receipts and associated spending
[4] Net of depreciation, less capital transfer receipts and including capital grants
[5] Definitions on a Maastricht basis

CONTROL TOTAL AND RESERVE 1998–9

	£ billion
Reserve set in 1996 Budget	5.0
Allocation to NHS	1.2
Allocation to schools	1.0
New reserve	2.8
Control Total unchanged at:	273.6

The Budget 1996

GOVERNMENT RECEIPTS £ billion

	Outturn 1995−6	Forecast 1996−7	Forecast 1997−8
Inland Revenue	96.9	100.8	106.0
Income tax	68.0	68.1	71.8
Corporation tax	23.6	26.1	27.2
Petroleum revenue tax	1.0	1.7	1.6
Capital gains tax	0.8	0.9	1.1
Inheritance tax	1.5	1.6	1.6
Stamp duties	2.0	2.4	2.7
Customs and Excise	76.5	83.3	91.2
Value added tax	43.1	47.5	50.7
Fuel duties	15.4	17.4	19.6
Tobacco duties	7.3	7.8	8.4
Spirits duties	1.7	1.7	1.8
Wine duties	1.2	1.2	1.3
Beer and cider duties	2.8	2.8	3.0
Betting and gaming duties	1.6	1.5	1.6
Air passenger duty	0.3	0.4	0.8
Insurance premium tax	0.6	0.6	1.2
Landfill tax	—	0.1	0.4
Customs duties and levies	2.5	2.2	2.4
Vehicle excise duties	4.0	4.3	4.5
Oil royalties	0.6	0.7	0.6
Business rates	13.6	14.2	14.6
Social security contributions	44.5	46.7	49.1
Council tax	9.6	9.9	10.6
Other taxes and royalties	6.2	5.8	5.5
Interest and dividends	5.6	5.0	5.1
Gross trading surpluses and rent	5.0	5.1	4.9
Other receipts	6.8	5.2	7.2
Total general government receipts	269.2	280.9	299.4
North Sea revenues	2.4	3.5	4.1

Source: HM Treasury − Financial Statement and Budget Report 1997−8 (Nov. 1996)

GOVERNMENT EXPENDITURE

THE CONTROL TOTAL AND GENERAL GOVERNMENT EXPENDITURE
(excluding privatization proceeds) £ million

	Estimated outturn 1996−7	Plans/ projections 1997−8
Central government expenditure	185,900	187,200
Local authority expenditure	75,800	76,100
Financing requirements of nationalized industries	−500	740
Reserve	—	2,500
Allowance for shortfall	−600	—
Control total	260,600	266,500
Cyclical social security	14,300	14,100
Central government debt interest	22,200	24,800
Accounting adjustments	10,300	9,200
General government expenditure excluding privatization proceeds	307,400	314,700
GGE excluding privatization proceeds as a percentage of GDP	41¼%	40%

Source: HM Treasury − Financial Statement and Budget Report 1997−8 (Nov. 1996)

CONTROL TOTAL EXPENDITURE BY DEPARTMENT
£ million

	Estimated outturn 1996−7	New plans 1997−8
Defence	21,190	21,110
Foreign Office	1,100	1,080
Overseas Development	2,340	2,220
Agriculture, Fisheries and Food*	4,410	3,610
Trade and Industry − programmes	3,250	3,070
Trade and Industry − nationalized industries	−520	−20
ECGD	30	10
Transport	4,870	5,190
DoE − Local government	31,320	31,380
DoE − other	8,380	7,600
Home Office	6,550	6,780
Legal departments	2,730	2,710
Education and Employment	14,810	13,950
National Heritage	1,020	920
Health	33,970	34,940
Social security	76,920	79,740
Scotland	14,590	14,330
Wales	6,820	6,900
Northern Ireland	8,190	8,220
Chancellor of the Exchequer's departments	3,270	3,170
Cabinet Office	1,330	1,080
European Communities	1,400	2,250

CONTROL TOTAL EXPENDITURE BY DEPARTMENT *contd.*
£ million

	Estimated outturn 1996−7	New plans 1997−8
Local authority self-financed expenditure	13,300	13,700
Allowance for shortfall	−600	—
Reserve	—	2,500
Control total	260,600	266,500

* Includes expenditure due to BSE
Source: HM Treasury − *Financial Statement and Budget Report 1997−8*
(Nov. 1996)

FINANCING REQUIREMENTS OF NATIONALIZED
INDUSTRIES   *£ million*

Department and industry	Estimated outturn 1996−7	Plans 1997−8
Trade and Industry	−520	−20
British Coal	30	70
Nuclear Electric/Magnox Electric	−170	310
Post Office	−270	−330
British Nuclear Fuels	−110	−70
Transport	−40	690
Railways*	−980	70
Civil Aviation Authority	−10	−30
London Transport	950	650
DoE − Environment	50	50
British Waterways Board	50	50
Scotland	20	20
Caledonian MacBrayne Ltd	10	10
Highlands and Islands Airports	10	10
Total	−500	740

* Includes British Rail, Railtrack, Union Railways and European
Passenger Services
Source: HM Treasury − *Financial Statement and Budget Report 1997−8*
(Nov. 1996)

LOCAL AUTHORITY EXPENDITURE   *£ million*

	Estimated outturn 1996−7	Plans 1997−8
CURRENT		
Aggregate External Finance		
England	35,760	35,770
Scotland	5,390	5,340
Wales	2,520	2,580
Total Aggregate External Finance	43,670	43,690
Other current grants	14,050	14,320
TOTAL CURRENT	57,720	58,010
CAPITAL		
Capital grants	1,710	1,590
Credit approvals	3,150	2,790
TOTAL CAPITAL SUPPORT	4,860	4,380
Total central government support to local authorities	62,600	62,400
Local authority self-financed expenditure	13,300	13,700
TOTAL LOCAL AUTHORITY EXPENDITURE	75,800	76,100

Source: HM Treasury − *Financial Statement and Budget Report 1997−8*
(Nov. 1996)

PUBLIC SECTOR BORROWING
REQUIREMENT 1995−6
£ million

CENTRAL GOVERNMENT BORROWING	
REQUIREMENT	35,463
of which: own account	35,646
Local authorities	
Direct borrowing from central government	473
Net borrowing from other sources	−1,616
less transactions in other public sector debt:	
Central government	4
Public corporations	−3
Borrowing requirement	−1,144
GENERAL GOVERNMENT BORROWING	
REQUIREMENT	33,846
Public corporations	
Direct borrowing from central government	−656
Net borrowing from other sources	−418
less transactions in other public sector debt:	
Central government	2,379
Local authorities	−696
Borrowing requirement	−2,757
PUBLIC SECTOR BORROWING	
REQUIREMENT	31,745
PSBR excluding privatization proceeds	34,180
PSBR as % of GDP	4½

Sources: The Stationery Office − *Annual Abstract of Statistics 1997*; HM
Treasury − *Financial Statement and Budget Report 1997−8* (Nov. 1996)

GDP BY INDUSTRY 1995 BEFORE DEPRECIATION
BUT AFTER STOCK APPRECIATION
£ million

Agriculture, hunting, forestry and fishing	11,896
Mining and quarrying, including gas and oil extraction	14,575
Manufacturing	131,658
Electricity, gas and water supply	15,787
Construction	31,815
Wholesale and retail trade; repairs; hotels and restaurants	84,706
Transport, storage and communication	50,835
Financial intermediation; real estate; renting and business activities	158,224
Public administration, national defence and compulsory social security	39,510
Education; health; social work	72,972
Other services, including sewerage and refuse disposal	23,255
TOTAL	634,402
less adjustment for financial services	30,794
Statistical discrepancy (income adjustment)	−113
GROSS DOMESTIC PRODUCT	603,495

Source: The Stationery Office − *Annual Abstract of Statistics 1997*

BALANCE OF PAYMENTS 1995 £ million

CURRENT ACCOUNT

Trade in goods	
Exports (fob)	152,346
Imports (fob)	163,974
Trade in goods balance	−11,628
Services balance	6,142
Investment income	9,572
Transfers balance	−6,978
CURRENT BALANCE	−2,892

*TRANSACTIONS IN EXTERNAL ASSETS AND LIABILITIES

Investment overseas by UK residents	
Direct	−25,546
Portfolio	−40,327
Total UK investment overseas	−65,873
Investment in the UK by overseas residents	
Direct	20,480
Portfolio	16,859
Total overseas investment in UK	37,339
Foreign currency lending abroad by UK banks	−24,145
Foreign currency borrowing abroad by UK banks	28,797
Net foreign currency transactions of UK banks	4,652
Sterling lending abroad by UK banks	−2,733
Sterling borrowing and deposit liabilities abroad of UK banks	7,542
Net sterling transactions of UK banks	4,809
Deposits with and lending to banks abroad by UK non-bank private sector	−11,096
Borrowing from banks abroad by:	
UK non-bank private sector	18,932
Public corporations	−151
General government	−97
Official reserves (additions to −, drawings on +)	704
Other external assets of:	
UK non-bank private sector and public corporations	−19,761
General government	−637
Other external liabilities of:	
UK non-bank private sector and public corporations	30,316
General government	1,812
NET TRANSACTIONS IN ASSETS AND LIABILITIES	446
BALANCING ITEM	2,446

* Assets: increase −/decrease +
Liabilities: increase +/decrease−
Source: The Stationery Office – *Annual Abstract of Statistics 1997*

UK TRADE ON A BALANCE OF PAYMENTS BASIS
£ million

	Exports	Imports	Balance
1986	72,627	82,186	−9,559
1987	79,153	90,735	−11,582
1988	80,346	101,826	−21,480
1989	92,154	116,837	−24,683
1990	101,718	120,527	−18,809
1991	103,413	113,697	−10,284
1992	107,343	120,447	−13,104
1993	121,398	134,858	−13,460
1994	134,666	145,497	−10,831
1995	152,346	163,974	−11,628

Source: The Stationery Office – *Annual Abstract of Statistics 1997*

VALUE OF UK EXPORTS 1996
BY DESTINATION £ million

European Community	95,431.4
Other western Europe	7,381.2
Eastern Europe	4,685.6
North America	22,436.9
Other America	2,716.7
Middle East and North Africa	9,001.6
Sub-Saharan Africa	3,860.9
Asia and Oceania	21,644.8
Low-value exports	574.9
Total non-EC exports	72,302.6
Total exports	167,734.0

Source: HM Customs and Excise

VALUE OF UK IMPORTS 1996
BY SOURCE £ million

European Community	99,465.1
Other western Europe	11,845.6
Eastern Europe	3,932.8
North America	25,944.8
Other America	3,168.0
Middle East and North Africa	3,802.5
Sub-Saharan Africa	2,887.4
Asia and Oceania	32,651.4
Low-value imports	415.0
Total non-EC imports	84,647.5
Total imports	184,112.6

Source: HM Customs and Excise

EMPLOYMENT

LABOUR FORCE BY AGE 1996 (GREAT BRITAIN)

Age	
16–24	4,400,000
25–44	14,100,000
45–59	8,000,000
60–64	900,000
65 and over	500,000
Total	27,900,000

ECONOMIC STATUS OF PEOPLE OF WORKING AGE (UK)
AS AT SPRING 1996

	Male	Female
Working full-time	13,000,000	6,300,000
Working part-time	1,000,000	4,900,000
Others in employment	200,000	200,000
Unemployed	1,500,000	800,000
Inactive	2,900,000	4,900,000
Total	18,600,000	17,000,000

Source: The Stationery Office – *Social Trends* 27

THE WORKFORCE IN EMPLOYMENT (UK)
SEASONALLY ADJUSTED, AT DECEMBER 1996

Employees in employment	22,363,000
Self-employed	3,369,000
*HM Forces	216,000
*Work-related government-supported training	199,000
Total workforce in employment	26,147,000

* not seasonally adjusted

EMPLOYEES IN EMPLOYMENT, BY MAIN SECTOR (UK)
SEASONALLY ADJUSTED, AT DECEMBER 1996

Service industries	17,024,000
Manufacturing industries	4,033,000
Mining, energy and water supply	190,000
Other industries	1,116,000
Total employees in employment	22,363,000

Source: Office for National Statistics

AVERAGE GROSS WEEKLY EARNINGS OF FULL-TIME EMPLOYEES (GREAT BRITAIN)
AS AT APRIL 1996

	£
All adults	351.7
All men	391.6
Men, manual	301.3
Men, non-manual	464.5
All women	283.0
Women, manual	195.2
Women, non-manual	302.4

Source: The Stationery Office – *Annual Abstract of Statistics 1997*

UNEMPLOYMENT BY REGIONS
SEASONALLY ADJUSTED, AT 10 APRIL 1997*

	Total	% of workforce
United Kingdom	1,651,400	5.9
England:		
Eastern	109,000	4.5
East Midlands	101,400	5.2
London	282,500	7.0
Merseyside	63,300	11.0
North East	94,700	8.5
North West	137,200	5.4
South East	142,800	3.9
South West	111,300	4.7
West Midlands	146,300	5.8
Yorkshire and the Humber	153,500	6.4
Wales	82,400	6.6
Scotland	162,000	6.6
Northern Ireland	64,800	8.4

Note: Percentages calculated using mid-1995 estimates of total employees in employment, unemployed claimants, self-employed and HM Forces, and participants in work-related government training schemes
* provisional
Source: Office for National Statistics

UNEMPLOYMENT RATES BY AGE 1996 (UK)
Percentages

Age	Male	Female
16–19	20.6	14.6
20–24	16.2	8.9
25–44	8.7	6.3
45–54	6.4	4.1
55–59	9.9	4.2
60–64	8.9	—
60 and over	—	n/a
65 and over	4.1	—
All ages	9.7	6.3

Source: The Stationery Office – *Social Trends* 27

INDUSTRIAL STOPPAGES 1995 (UK)

Duration	
Not more than 5 days	199
6–10 days	12
11–20 days	9
21–30 days	6
31–50 days	2
More than 50 days	7
Total number of stoppages	235

Source: The Stationery Office – *Annual Abstract of Statistics 1997*

TRADE UNIONS (UK)

Year	No. of unions at end of year	Total membership at end of year
1970	543	11,187,000
1975	470	12,026,000
1980	438	12,947,000
1985	370	10,821,000
1990	287	9,947,000
1995	238	8,089,000

Source: Office for National Statistics

HOUSEHOLDS AND THEIR EXPENDITURE 1995–6[1]

NUMBER OF HOUSEHOLDS
SUPPLYING DATA	6,797
Total number of persons	16,586
Total number of adults[2]	12,219

DISTRIBUTION BY TENURE
Rented unfurnished	28.9%
Rented furnished	3.7%
Rent-free	1.2%
Owner-occupied	66.1%

AVERAGE NUMBER OF PERSONS
PER HOUSEHOLD
All persons	2.440
Males	1.172
Females	1.268
Adults[2]	1.798
Persons under 65	1.433
Persons 65 and over	0.365
Children[2]	0.642
Children under 2	0.076
Children 2 and under 5	0.108
Children 5 and under 18	0.458
Persons economically active	1.134
Persons not economically active	1.306
Men 65 and over, women 60 and over	0.390
Others	0.915

HOUSEHOLD EXPENDITURE ON COMMODITIES AND
SERVICES – WEEKLY AVERAGE

	£	As % of total
Housing[3]	48.25	16.6
Fuel and power	12.92	4.5
Food	52.88	18.2
Alcoholic drink	11.41	3.9
Tobacco	5.81	2.0
Clothing and footwear	17.15	5.9
Household goods	23.45	8.1
Household services	15.13	5.2
Personal goods and services	11.55	4.0
Motoring expenditure	36.99	12.8
Fares and other travel costs	6.17	2.1
Leisure goods	13.23	4.7
Leisure services	32.05	11.1
Miscellaneous	2.37	0.8
Total	289.86	100.0

[1]Information derived from the Family Expenditure Survey; relates
to the UK
[2]Adults = all persons 18 and over and married persons under 18
Children = all unmarried persons under 18
[3]Excludes mortgage payments but includes imputed expenditure
(i.e. the weekly equivalent of rateable value)
Source: The Stationery Office – *Annual Abstract of Statistics 1997*

SOURCES OF HOUSEHOLD INCOME 1995–6*

AVERAGE WEEKLY INCOME BY SOURCE (£)
Wages and salaries	245.01
Self-employment	32.90
Investments	18.11
Annuities and pensions (other than social security benefits)	25.95
Social security benefits	52.36
Other sources	6.56
Total	380.89

SOURCES AS A PERCENTAGE OF TOTAL HOUSEHOLD
INCOME (%)
Wages and salaries	64.3
Self-employment	8.6
Investments	4.8
Annuities and pensions (other than social security benefits)	6.8
Social security benefits	13.7
Other sources	1.7
Total	100.0

* Information derived from the Family Expenditure Survey; relates
to the UK. Number of households supplying data, 6,797
Source: The Stationery Office – *Annual Abstract of Statistics 1997*

AVAILABILITY OF CERTAIN DURABLE GOODS 1995–6*
PERCENTAGE OF HOUSEHOLDS

Car	69.7
One	46.8
Two	19.2
Three or more	3.7
Central heating, full or partial	85.3
Washing machine	90.9
Refrigerator or fridge/freezer	98.8
Freezer or fridge/freezer	86.8
Television	98.3†
Telephone	92.4
Home computer	19.1†
Video recorder	79.2

* Information derived from the Family Expenditure Survey; relates
to the UK. Number of households supplying data, 6,797
† 1992 figure
Source: The Stationery Office – *Annual Abstract of Statistics 1997*

Cost of Living and Inflation Rates

The first cost of living index to be calculated took July 1914 as 100 and was based on the pattern of expenditure of working-class families in 1914. The cost of living index was superseded in 1947 by the general index of retail prices (RPI), although the older term is still popularly applied to it.

GENERAL INDEX OF RETAIL PRICES

The general index of retail prices measures the changes month by month in the average level of prices of goods and services purchased by most households in the United Kingdom. The spending pattern on which the index is based is revised each year, mainly using information from the Family Expenditure Survey. The expenditure of certain higher income households and of households mainly dependent on state pensions is excluded.

The index is compiled using a selection of over 600 goods and services and the prices charged for these items are collected at regular intervals in about 146 locations throughout the country. For the index, the price changes are weighted in accordance with the pattern of consumption of the average family.

INFLATION RATE

The twelve-monthly percentage change in the 'all items' index of the RPI is usually referred to as the rate of inflation. The percentage change in prices between any two months/years can be obtained using the following formula:

$$\frac{\text{Later date RPI} - \text{Earlier date RPI}}{\text{Earlier date RPI}} \times 100$$

e.g. to find the rate of inflation for 1988, using the annual averages for 1987 and 1988:

$$\frac{106.9 - 101.9}{101.9} \times 100 = 4.9\%$$

PURCHASING POWER OF THE POUND

Changes in the internal purchasing power of the pound may be defined as the 'inverse' of changes in the level of prices; when prices go up, the amount which can be purchased with a given sum of money goes down. To find the purchasing power of the pound in one month or year, given that it was 100p in a previous month or year, the calculation would be:

$$100p \times \frac{\text{Earlier month/year RPI}}{\text{Later month/year RPI}}$$

Thus, if the purchasing power of the pound is taken to be 100p in 1975, the comparable purchasing power in 1996 would be:

$$100p \times \frac{34.2}{152.7} = 22.40p$$

For longer term comparisons, it has been the practice to use an index which has been constructed by linking together the RPI for the period 1962 to date; an index derived from the consumers expenditure deflator for the period from 1938 to 1962; and the prewar 'cost of living' index for the period 1914 to 1938. This long-term index enables the internal purchasing power of the pound to be calculated for any year from 1914 onwards. It should be noted that these figures can only be approximate.

	Long-term index of consumer goods and services (Jan. 1987 = 100)	Comparable purchasing power of £1 in 1996	Rate of inflation (annual average)
1914	2.8	54.54	
1915	3.5	43.63	
1920	7.0	21.81	
1925	5.0	30.54	
1930	4.5	33.93	
1935	4.0	38.18	
1938	4.4	34.70	
There are no official figures for 1939–45			
1946	7.4	20.64	
1950	9.0	16.97	
1955	11.2	13.63	
1960	12.6	12.12	
1965	14.8	10.32	
1970	18.5	8.25	
1975	34.2	4.46	
1980	66.8	2.29	18.0
1981	74.8	2.04	11.9
1982	81.2	1.88	8.6
1983	84.9	1.80	4.6
1984	89.2	1.71	5.0
1985	94.6	1.61	6.1
1986	97.8	1.56	3.4
1987	101.9	1.50	4.2
1988	106.9	1.43	4.9
1989	115.2	1.33	7.8
1990	126.1	1.21	9.5
1991	133.5	1.14	5.9
1992	138.5	1.10	3.7
1993	140.7	1.09	1.6
1994	144.1	1.06	2.4
1995	149.1	1.02	3.5
1996	152.7	1.00	2.4

Gaming and Lotteries

Gaming and lotteries in the UK are officially regulated and may only be run by licensed operators or in licensed premises. Responsibility for policy and the laws on gaming and lotteries rests with the Home Secretary. Supervision of gaming and lottery operations is mostly the responsibility of the Gaming Board of Great Britain, although the National Lottery (*see* below) is regulated by the Director-General of the National Lottery through the Office of the National Lottery.

Most betting is on horseracing and greyhound racing, and may take place at racecourses and greyhound tracks, or at off-course betting offices. The amount spent on on-course betting cannot be calculated precisely since no duty is payable on it and therefore no returns are made; however, it is estimated to be about 10 per cent of the figures for off-course betting.

OFF-COURSE BETTING (UK)

	£ million
1994–5	6,562
1995–6	6,313
1996–7	6,636p

p provisional
Source: Horserace Totalisator Board

Other forms of gaming and lotteries include the following (for National Lottery, *see* below):

Number of casinos operating	119
Drop	£2,548m
Bingo clubs holding gaming licences	906
Amount staked (£ million)	£906m
Gaming machines licensed	271,272*
Society lottery schemes registered	530
Local authority lottery schemes registered	21
Number of lotteries held under registered schemes	1,862
Total ticket sales (£ million)	£78.96m

* 1993–4 figure
Source: Annual Report of the Gaming Board of Great Britain 1995–6

THE NATIONAL LOTTERY

The National Lottery is currently run by a private company, Camelot Group PLC. The Office of the National Lottery (Oflot) regulates the National Lottery operations and licenses games promoted as part of the lottery. The seven-year licence granted to Camelot expires in 2001 and the Government has announced its intention to reform the system for operating the National Lottery.

The first National Lottery tickets draw was made on 19 November 1994 and Instants (scratchcards) were introduced on 25 March 1995. A second weekly draw was introduced on Wednesday 5 February 1997. Tickets for the main lottery game cost £1. If the jackpot prize is not won, it is 'rolled over' to the following week. The highest win on a single ticket to date was £22,590,000 on 10 June 1995.

SALES 1996–7

Average number of tickets sold per week	c.85m
Average sales of Instants sold per week	c.£17m
Average number of people playing weekly	c.30m
% of adult population buying tickets regularly	c.70%
% of adult population buying Instants regularly	c.10%
Amount raised by ticket sales	£3,847m
Amount raised by Instants sales	£4,724m

Sources: Camelot, Oflot

DISTRIBUTION OF PROCEEDS
over the seven-year licence period

Allocated to:	%
Prize money	50
Tax	12
Retailer commission	5
Camelot (operating costs and profit)	5
Good causes	28

The cumulative amount allocated to the good causes from November 1994 to March 1997 was £3,210 million.

AWARDS 1996–7

A total of 9,753 awards were made in 1996–7, with 222 awards being for £1 million or more. Most awards are conditional on partnership funding being obtained from other sources. Awards were initially given only to capital projects, but since April 1996 it has been possible to obtain lottery funding for projects aimed at developing individuals' talents and potential and increasing access to the arts, and in late 1997 lottery funding will be made available for supporting access, education and youth initiatives in the heritage field.

The Government has announced plans to create a sixth 'good cause', the New Opportunities Fund, to fund health, education and environmental initiatives, and to create a National Endowment for Science, Technology and the Arts (NESTA), an independent body with a particular focus on multimedia work.

	Number	Total value £
Total	9,752	1,802,656,563
Arts, total	3,289	390,113,494
Arts Council of England	2,714	338,840,216
Arts Council of Wales	228	14,072,420
Scottish Arts Council	187	30,749,096
Arts Council of Northern Ireland	160	6,451,762
Millennium Commission	59	367,574,302
National Heritage Memorial Fund	563	442,304,896
National Lottery Charities Board	4,616	319,299,478
Sport, total	1,226	283,364,393
Sports Council	901	255,709,163
Sports Council for Wales	109	10,253,779
Scottish Sports Council	124	12,153,156
Sports Council for Northern Ireland	92	5,248,295

NOTABLE AWARDS

	£
Millennium Point, Birmingham	50,000,000
Bristol 2000	41,300,000
University of the Highlands and Islands	33,354,000
Millennium Link, Forth and Clyde Canal and Union Canal	32,214,310
Royal National Theatre	31,590,000
International Centre for Life, Tyne and Wear	27,000,000
National Discovery Park, Liverpool	27,000,000
Kennet and Avon Canal	25,000,000
Science Museum	23,000,000
Royal Academy of Dramatic Art	22,752,283
Nottingham Ice Arena	22,496,600
Royal Albert Hall	20,180,000
Manchester 50 m swimming pool	19,100,000
Tate Gallery	18,750,000
Action with the Communities in Rural England	10,000,000
National Trust for Scotland	8,000,000
Scottish Council for Voluntary Organizations	7,800,000
Grand Theatre, Wolverhampton	5,885,000
Kirklees Stadium development	5,445,000
Dundee Arts Centre	5,380,756
Rural Community Network Northern Ireland	4,617,000
National Playing Fields Association	4,033,265
Central Council of Church Bell Ringers	3,000,000
National Sports Medicine Institute	2,702,738
Canterbury Cathedral	2,250,000
Stiwt Arts and Leisure Community Association	2,237,792
Cleveland Riding for the Disabled Centre	1,160,000
Verbal Arts Centre, Londonderry	1,151,310
Richard House Trust	616,318
Age Concern Liverpool	592,580
Mental Health Foundation	542,772
Leonard Cheshire Foundation	492,203

Sources: Department of Culture, Media and Sport; Oflot; National Lottery Charities Board

Finance

British Currency

COIN

Gold Coins
*One hundred pounds £100
*Fifty pounds £50
*Twenty-five pounds £25
*Ten pounds £10
Five pounds £5
Two pounds £2
Sovereign £1
Half-Sovereign 50p

† *Silver Coins*
(Maundy Money)
Fourpence 4p
Threepence 3p
Twopence 2p
Penny 1p

‡ *Bi-colour Coins*
Two pounds £2

Nickel-Brass Coins
§Two pounds £2
One pound £1

Cupro-Nickel Coins
Crown £5 (since 1990)
¶50 pence 50p
Crown 25p (pre-1990)
20 pence 20p
10 pence 10p
5 pence 5p

Bronze Coins
2 pence 2p
1 penny 1p

Copper-plated Steel Coins
2 penny 2p
1 penny 1p

*Britannia gold bullion coins, introduced in October 1987
†Gifts of special money distributed by the Sovereign annually on Maundy Thursday to the number of aged poor men and women corresponding to the Sovereign's own age
‡Cupro-nickel and nickel-brass
§Commemorative coins; not intended for general circulation
¶New 50p coin introduced on 1 September 1997

GOLD COIN

Gold ceased to circulate during the First World War. Since then controls on buying, selling and holding gold coin have been imposed at various times but subsequently have been revoked. Under the Exchange Control (Gold Coins Exemption) Order 1979 gold coins may now be imported and exported without restriction, except gold coins which are more than 50 years old and valued at a sum in excess of £8,000; these cannot be exported without specific authorization from the Department of Trade and Industry.

In 1982 the Government introduced VAT on sales of all gold coin.

SILVER COIN

Prior to 1920 silver coins were struck from sterling silver, an alloy of which 925 parts in 1,000 were silver. In 1920 the proportion of silver was reduced to 500 parts. From 1 January 1947 all 'silver' coins, except Maundy money, have been struck from cupro-nickel, an alloy of copper 75 parts and nickel 25 parts, except for the 20p, composed of copper 84 parts, nickel 16 parts. Maundy coins continue to be struck from sterling silver.

BRONZE COIN

Bronze, introduced in 1860 to replace copper, is an alloy of copper 97 parts, zinc 2.5 parts and tin 0.5 part. These proportions have been subject to slight variations in the past. Bronze was replaced by copper-plated steel in September 1992.

LEGAL TENDER

Gold, dated 1838 onwards, if not below least current weight, is legal tender to any amount. £5 (Crown since 1990), £2 and £1 coins are legal tender to any amount; 50p, 25p (Crown pre-1990) and 20p coins are legal tender up to £10; 10p and 5p coins are legal tender up to £5, and 2p and 1p coins are legal tender for amounts up to 20p.

Farthings ceased to be legal tender on 31 December 1960, the halfpenny on 1 August 1969, the halfcrown on 1 January 1970, the threepence and penny on 31 August 1971, the sixpence on 30 June 1980, the decimal halfpenny on 31 December 1984, the old 5p on 31 December 1990, the old 10p on 30 June 1993, and the old 50p on 28 February 1998.

The decimal system was introduced on 15 February 1971. Since 1982 the word 'new' in 'new pence' displayed on decimal coins has been dropped.

The Channel Islands and the Isle of Man issue their own coinage, which are legal tender only in the island of issue. For denominations, *see* page 608.

	Metal	Standard weight (g)	Standard diameter (cm)
Penny	bronze	3.564	2.032
Penny	copper-plated steel	3.564	2.032
2 pence	bronze	7.128	2.591
2 pence	copper-plated steel	7.128	2.591
5p	cupro-nickel	3.25	1.80
10p	cupro-nickel	6.5	2.45
20p	cupro-nickel	5.0	2.14
25p Crown	cupro-nickel	28.276	3.861
50p	cupro-nickel	13.5	3.0
¶50p	cupro-nickel	8.00	2.73
£1	nickel-brass	9.5	2.25
£2	nickel-brass	15.98	2.84
‡£2	cupro-nickel, nickel-brass	12.00	2.84
£5 Crown	cupro-nickel	28.28	3.861

The 'remedy' is the amount of variation from standard permitted in weight and fineness of coins when first issued from the Mint.

The Trial of the Pyx is the examination by a jury to ascertain that coins made by the Royal Mint, which have been set aside in the pyx (or box), are of the proper weight, diameter and composition required by law. The trial is held annually, presided over by the Queen's Remembrancer (the Senior Master of the Supreme Court), with a jury of freemen of the Company of Goldsmiths.

BANKNOTES

Bank of England notes are currently issued in denominations of £5, £10, £20 and £50 for the amount of the fiduciary note issue, and are legal tender in England and Wales. Banknotes which are no longer legal tender are payable when presented at the head office of the Bank of England in London.

The white notes for £10, £20, £50, £100, £500 and £1,000, which were issued until April 1943, ceased to be legal tender in May 1945, and the old white £5 note in March 1946.

The white £5 note issued between October 1945 and September 1956, the £5 notes issued between 1957 and 1963, (bearing a portrait of Britannia) and the first series to bear a portrait of The Queen, issued between 1963 and 1971, ceased to be legal tender in March 1961, June 1967 and September 1973 respectively.

The series of £1 notes issued during the years 1928 to 1960 and the 10 shilling notes issued from 1928 to 1961 (those without the royal portrait) ceased to be legal tender in May and October 1962 respectively. The £1 note first issued in March 1960 (bearing on the back a representation of Britannia) and the £10 note first issued in February 1964 (bearing a lion on the back), both bearing a portrait of The Queen on the front, ceased to be legal tender in June 1979. The £1 note first issued in 1978 ceased to be legal tender on 11 March 1988. The 10 shilling note was replaced by the 50p coin in October 1969, and ceased to be legal tender on 21 November 1970.

The D series of banknotes was introduced from 1970 and ceased to be legal tender from the dates shown below. The predominant identifying feature of each note was the portrayal on the back of a prominent figure from British history:

£1	Feb. 1978–March 1988	Sir Isaac Newton
£5	Nov. 1971–Nov. 1991	The Duke of Wellington
£10	Feb. 1975–May 1994	Florence Nightingale
£20	July 1970–March 1993	William Shakespeare
£50	March 1981–Sept. 1996	Sir Christopher Wren

The £1 coin was introduced on 21 April 1983 to replace the £1 note.

The current E series of notes was introduced from June 1990, replacing the D series. The historical figures portrayed in this series are:

£5	June 1990–	George Stephenson
£10	April 1992–	Charles Dickens
£20	June 1991–	Michael Faraday
£50	April 1994–	Sir John Houblon

NOTE CIRCULATION

Note circulation is highest at the two peak spending periods of the year, around Christmas and during the summer holiday period. The total value of notes in circulation at 18 December 1996 was £22,407 million, compared to £21,270 million at 20 December 1995.

The value of notes in circulation at end February 1996 and 1997 was:

	1996	1997
£1*	£56m	£56m
£5	£1,067m	£1,047m
£10	£5,688m	£5,915m
£20	£8,579m	£9,559m
£50	£3,104m	£3,273m
Other notes†	£1,154m	£2,161m
Total	£19,648m	£22,011m

* No £1 notes have been issued since 1984
† Includes higher value notes used internally in the Bank of England, e.g. as cover for the note issues of banks of issue in Scotland and Northern Ireland in excess of their permitted issue

OTHER BANKNOTES

SCOTLAND – Banknotes are issued by three Scottish banks. The Royal Bank of Scotland issues notes for £1, £5, £10, £20 and £100. The Bank of Scotland and the Clydesdale Bank issue notes for £5, £10, £20, £50 and £100. Scottish notes are not legal tender in Scotland but they are an authorized currency and enjoy there a status comparable to that of the Bank of England note.

NORTHERN IRELAND – Banknotes are issued by four banks in Northern Ireland. The Bank of Ireland, the Northern Bank and the Ulster Bank issue notes for £5, £10, £20, £50 and £100. The First Trust Bank issues notes for £10, £20, £50 and £100. Northern Ireland notes are not legal tender in Northern Ireland but they circulate widely and enjoy a status comparable to that of Bank of England notes.

CHANNEL ISLANDS – The States of Guernsey issues its own currency notes and coinage. The notes are for £1, £5, £10, £20 and £50, and the coins are for 1p, 2p, 5p, 10p, 20p, 50p, £1, £2 and £5. The States of Jersey issues its own currency notes and coinage. The notes are for £1, £5, £10, £20 and £50, and the coins are for 1p, 2p, 5p, 10p, 20p, 50p, £1 and £2.

THE ISLE OF MAN – The Isle of Man Government issues notes for £1, £5, £10, £20 and £50. Although these notes are only legal tender in the Isle of Man, they are accepted at face value in branches of the clearing banks in the UK. The Isle of Man issues coins for 1p, 2p, 5p, 10p, 20p, 50p, £1, £2 and £5.

Although none of the series of notes specified above is legal tender in the UK, they are generally accepted by the banks irrespective of their place of issue. At one time the banks made a commission charge for handling Scottish and Irish notes but this was abolished some years ago.

Banking

Deposit-taking institutions may be broadly divided into two sectors: the monetary sector, which is predominantly banks, which are supervised by the Bank of England; and those institutions outside the monetary sector, of which the most important are the building societies and the National Savings Bank. As a result of the conversion of several building societies into banks in recent years, the size of the banking sector, which was already substantially greater than the non-bank deposit taking sector, has increased further.

The main institutions within the British banking system are the Bank of England (the central bank), the retail banks, the merchant banks and the overseas banks. In its role as the central bank, the Bank of England acts as banker to the Government and as a note-issuing authority; it also oversees the efficient functioning of payment and settlement systems.

Since May 1997, the Bank of England has had operational responsibility for monetary policy. At monthly meetings of its monetary policy committee the Bank sets the interest rate at which it will lend to the money markets.

OFFICIAL INTEREST RATES 1996–7

30 October 1996	6.00%	10 July 1997	6.75%
6 May 1997	6.25%	7 August 1997	7.00%
6 June 1997	6.50%		

RETAIL BANKS

The major retail banks are Abbey National, Bank of Scotland, Barclays, Halifax, Lloyds/TSB, Midland, National Westminster and the Royal Bank of Scotland.

Retail banks offer a wide variety of financial services to companies and individuals, including current and deposit accounts, loan and overdraft facilities, automated teller (cashpoint) machines, cheque guarantee cards, credit cards and debit cards.

The Banking Ombudsman scheme provides independent and impartial arbitration in disputes between a bank and its customer (*see also* page 631).

Banking hours differ throughout Great Britain. Many banks now open longer hours and Saturday mornings, and hours vary from branch to branch. Current core opening hours are:

ENGLAND AND WALES: Monday–Friday 9.30–4.30
SCOTLAND: Monday–Friday, 9.00–5.00
NORTHERN IRELAND: Monday–Friday 9.30–4.30
(Wednesdays 10–4.30, except Ulster Bank Ltd);
Northern Bank, 10–3.30, Saturdays 9.30–12.30

PAYMENT CLEARINGS

The Association for Payment Clearing Services (APACS) is an umbrella organization for payment clearings in the UK. It operates three clearing companies:
– BACS Ltd is the UK's automated clearing house for bulk clearing of electronic debits and credits (e.g. direct debits and salary credits)
– the Cheque and Credit Clearing Company Ltd operates bulk clearing systems for inter-bank cheques and paper credit items in Great Britain
– CHAPS Clearing Company Ltd provides same-day clearing for high-value electronic funds transfers throughout the UK

Membership of APACS and the clearing companies is open to any appropriately regulated financial institution providing payment services and meeting the relevant membership criteria. As at June 1997, APACS had 22 members, comprising the major banks and building societies.

ASSOCIATION FOR PAYMENT CLEARING SERVICES (APACS), Mercury House, Triton Court, 14 Finsbury Square, London EC2A 1BR. Tel: 0171-711 6200. *Head of Public Affairs*, R. Tyson-Davies

BACS LTD, De Havilland Road, Edgware, Middx HA8 5QA. *Chief Executive*, G. Younger

CHEQUE AND CREDIT CLEARING COMPANY LTD, Mercury House, Triton Court, 14 Finsbury Square, London EC2A 1BR

CHAPS CLEARING COMPANY LTD, Mercury House, Triton Court, 14 Finsbury Square, London EC2A 1BR

AUTHORIZED INSTITUTIONS

Banking in the UK is regulated by the Banking Act 1987 as amended by the European Community's Second Banking Co-ordination Directive, which came into effect on 1 January 1993. The Banking Act 1987 established a single category of banks eligible to carry out banking business; these are known as authorized institutions. Authorization under the Act is granted by the Bank of England; it is an offence for anyone not on the Bank's list of authorized institutions to conduct deposit-taking business, unless they are exempted from the requirements of the Act (e.g. building societies).

The implementation of the Second Banking Co-ordination Directive permits banks incorporated in one EU member state to carry on certain banking activities in

MAJOR RETAIL BANKS: FINANCIAL RESULTS 1996

Bank Group	Profit before taxation £m	Profit after taxation £m	Total assets £m	Number of UK branches
Abbey National	1,228	764	124,011	870
Bank of Scotland	664.1	427.9	47,275	325
Barclays	2,356	1,686	186,002	c.2,000
Halifax	892.7	539.5	115,539	970
Lloyds/TSB	2,505	1,719	147,367	3,000
Midland	1,272	864	96,200	1,720
NatWest Group	1,122	469	185,336	1,921
Royal Bank of Scotland Group	695	504	61,116	c.680

another member state without the need for authorization by that state. Consequently, the Bank of England no longer authorizes banks incorporated in other EU states with branches in the UK; the authorization of their home state supervisor is sufficient provided that certain notification requirements are met.

In May 1997, the Chancellor of the Exchequer announced that he planned to amend the Banking Act 1987 to transfer responsibility for banking supervision from the Bank of England to a new supervisory body. This new body will combine and restructure the existing supervisory structure for the financial services industry, combining banking supervision, the Securities and Investments Board (SIB) and self-regulating organizations such as the Securities and Futures Authority. Legislation to create the new supervisory body is not expected until 1998–9; legislation to transfer responsibility for banking supervision to the SIB for an interim period is expected in 1997–8.

As at end February 1997, a total of 554 institutions were authorized to carry out banking business in the UK, 361 authorized under the Banking Act 1987 and 193 recognized under the Second Banking Co-ordination Directive as European authorized institutions (EAIs):

UK-incorporated	212
Incorporated outside the UK	342
Of which:	
Incorporated outside the EEA	105
EAIs with UK branches entitled to accept deposits in UK	50
Other EAIs	38

The following institutions were authorized or entitled to accept deposits through presences in the UK as at 18 September 1997.

AUTHORIZED BY THE BANK OF ENGLAND

UK-INCORPORATED
(Including partnerships formed under the law of any part of the UK)

ABC International Bank PLC
AMC Bank Ltd
AY Bank Ltd
Abbey National PLC
Abbey National Treasury Services PLC
Adam & Company PLC
Afghan National Credit & Finance Ltd
Airdrie Savings Bank
Alexanders Discount PLC
Alliance and Leicester PLC
Alliance and Leicester Group Treasury PLC
Alliance Trust (Finance) Ltd
Allied Bank Philippines (UK) PLC
Allied Irish Bank (GB)/First Trust Bank - (AIB Group (UK) PLC)
Alpha Bank London Ltd
Anglo-Romanian Bank Ltd
Henry Ansbacher & Co. Ltd
Arbuthnot Latham & Co. Ltd
Assemblies of God Property Trust
Associates Capital Corporation Ltd
Avco Trust PLC

Bank Leumi (UK) PLC
Bank of America International Ltd
Bank of China International (UK) Ltd
Bank of Cyprus (London) Ltd
Bank of Montreal Europe Ltd
Bank of Scotland
Bank of Scotland Treasury Services PLC
Bank of Tokyo-Mitsubishi (UK) Ltd

Bank of Wales PLC
Bankers Trust International PLC
Bankgesellschaft Berlin (UK) PLC
Banque Nationale de Paris PLC
Baptist Union Corporation Ltd
Barclays Bank PLC
Barclays Bank Trust Company Ltd
Barclays de Zoete Wedd Ltd
Barclays Private Bank Ltd
Baring Brothers Ltd
Beneficial Bank PLC
Bristol and West PLC
British Arab Commercial Bank Ltd
British Bank of the Middle East
British Linen Bank Ltd
Brown, Shipley & Co. Ltd

CIBC Wood Gundy Bank PLC
CLF Municipal Bank PLC
Cafcash Ltd
Capital Bank PLC
Cater Allen Ltd
Chartered Trust PLC
Charterhouse Bank Ltd
Chase Manhattan PLC
Chase Manhattan International Ltd
Cheltenham and Gloucester PLC
Citibank International PLC
Clive Discount Company Ltd
Close Brothers Ltd
Clydesdale Bank PLC
Consolidated Credits Bank Ltd
Co-operative Bank PLC
Coutts & Co.
Crédit Agricole Lazard Financial Products Bank
Credit Suisse Financial Products
Crown Agents Financial Services Ltd
Daiwa Europe Bank PLC
Dalbeattie Finance Co. Ltd
Dao Heng Bank (London) PLC
Direct Line Financial Services Ltd
Dorset, Somerset & Wilts Investment Society Ltd
Dryfield Trust PLC
Dunbar Bank PLC
Duncan Lawrie Ltd

EFG Private Bank Ltd
Eccles Savings and Loans Ltd
Exeter Bank Ltd

FIBI Bank (UK) PLC
Fairmount Capital Management Ltd
Financial & General Bank PLC
First National Bank PLC
First National Commercial Bank PLC
Robert Fleming & Co. Ltd
Ford Credit Europe PLC
Forward Trust Group Ltd
Frizzell Bank Ltd

Gartmore Money Management Ltd
GE Capital Bank Ltd
Gerrard & King Ltd
Girobank PLC
Goldman Sachs International Bank
Granville Bank Ltd
Gresham Trust PLC
Guinness Mahon & Co. Ltd

HFC Bank PLC
HSBC Equator Bank PLC
HSBC Investment Bank PLC
Habibsons Bank Ltd

Halifax PLC
Hambros Bank Ltd
Hampshire Trust PLC
Hardware Federation Finance Co. Ltd
Harrods Bank Ltd
Harton Securities Ltd
Havana International Bank Ltd
Heritable and General Investment Bank Ltd
Hill Samuel Bank Ltd
C. Hoare & Co.
Julian Hodge Bank Ltd
Humberclyde Finance Group Ltd

3i PLC
3i Group PLC
IBJ International PLC
Investec Bank (UK) Ltd
Iran Overseas Investment Bank Ltd
Italian International Bank PLC

Jordan International Bank PLC
Leopold Joseph & Sons Ltd

KDB Bank (UK) Ltd
KEXIM Bank (UK) Ltd
Kleinwort Benson Ltd
Kleinwort Benson Investment Management Ltd
Korea Long Term Credit Bank International Ltd

LTCB International Ltd
Lazard Brothers & Co. Ltd
Legal and General Bank Ltd
Lloyds Bank PLC
Lloyds Bank (BLSA) Ltd
Lloyds Bowmaker Ltd
Lloyds Private Banking Ltd
Lombard & Ulster Ltd
Lombard Bank Ltd
Lombard North Central PLC
London Scottish Bank PLC
London Trust Bank PLC

MBNA International Bank Ltd
W. M. Mann & Co. (Investments) Ltd
Marks and Spencer Financial Services Ltd
Matheson Bank Ltd
Matlock Bank Ltd
Meghraj Bank Ltd
Merrill Lynch International Bank Ltd
Methodist Chapel Aid Association Ltd
Midland Bank PLC
Midland Bank Trust Company Ltd
Minster Trust Ltd
Samuel Montagu & Co. Ltd
Morgan Grenfell & Co. Ltd
Moscow Narodny Bank Ltd
Mutual Trust and Savings Ltd

NIIB Group Ltd
National Bank of Egypt International Ltd
National Bank of Kuwait (International) PLC
National Westminster Bank PLC
NationsBank Europe Ltd
Nikko Bank (UK) PLC
Noble Grossart Ltd
Nomura Bank International PLC
Northern Bank Ltd
Northern Bank Executor & Trustee Company Ltd
PaineWebber International Bank Ltd
Philippine National Bank (Europe) PLC
Pointon York Ltd
Prudential-Bache International Bank Ltd
Prudential Banking PLC
RBS Trust Bank Ltd
R. Raphael & Sons PLC

Rathbone Bros & Co. Ltd
Rea Brothers Ltd
Reliance Bank Ltd
Riggs Bank Europe Ltd
Riyad Bank Europe Ltd
N. M. Rothschild & Sons Ltd
Royal Bank of Canada Europe Ltd
Royal Bank of Scotland PLC
RoyScot Trust PLC
Ruffler Bank PLC

SBI European Bank PLC
Sabanci Bank PLC
Sainsbury's Bank PLC
Sanwa International PLC
Saudi American Bank (UK) Ltd
Saudi International Bank (Al-Bank Al-Saudi Al-Alami Ltd)
Schroder Leasing Ltd
J. Henry Schroder & Co. Ltd
Scotiabank (UK) Ltd
Scottish Amicable Money Managers Ltd
Scottish Widows Bank PLC
Seccombe Marshall & Campion PLC
Secure Trust Bank PLC
Singer & Friedlander Ltd
Smith & Williamson Securities
Southsea Mortgage & Investment Co. Ltd
Standard Bank London Ltd
Standard Chartered Bank
Sun Banking Corporation Ltd

TSB Bank PLC
TSB Bank Scotland PLC
Tokai Bank Europe PLC
Toronto Dominion Bank Europe Ltd
Turkish Bank (UK) Ltd

UCB Bank PLC
Ulster Bank Ltd
Union Discount Company Ltd
United Bank of Kuwait PLC
United Dominions Trust Ltd
United Trust Bank Ltd
Unity Trust Bank PLC

S. G. Warburg & Co. Ltd
Weatherbys & Co. Ltd
Wesleyan Savings Bank Ltd
West Merchant Bank Ltd
Whiteaway Laidlaw Bank Ltd
Wintrust Securities Ltd
Woodchester Credit Lyonnais PLC
Woolwich PLC

Yamaichi Bank (UK) PLC
Yorkshire Bank PLC

INCORPORATED OUTSIDE THE EUROPEAN ECONOMIC
AREA
(Including partnerships or other unincorporated associations formed under the law of any member state of the European Union other than the UK)
†Provisional liquidator appointed

ABSA Bank Ltd
Allied Bank of Pakistan Ltd
American Express Bank Ltd
Arab African International Bank
Arab Bank PLC
Arab Banking Corporation BSC
Arab National Bank
Asahi Bank Ltd
Ashikaga Bank Ltd
Australia & New Zealand Banking Group Ltd

BSI – Banca della Svizzera Italiana
Banca Serfin SA
Banco de la Nación Argentina
Banco do Brasil SA
Banco do Estado de São Paulo SA
Banco Mercantil de São Paulo SA-Finasa
Banco Nacional de Mexico SA
Banco Real SA
Bancomer SA
Bangkok Bank Public Company Ltd
Bank Julius Baer & Co. Ltd
BankBoston NA
Bank Bumiputra Malaysia Berhad
PT Bank Ekspor Impor Indonesia (Persero)
Bank Handlowy w Warszawie SA
Bank Hapoalim BM
Bank Mellat
Bank Melli Iran
PT Bank Negara Indonesia (Persero) Tbk
Bank of America NT & SA
Bank of Baroda
Bank of N. T. Butterfield & Son Ltd
Bank of Ceylon
Bank of China
Bank of Cyprus Ltd
Bank of East Asia Ltd
Bank of Fukuoka Ltd
Bank of India
Bank of Montreal
Bank of New York
Bank of Nova Scotia
Bank of Tokyo-Mitsubishi Ltd
Bank of Yokohama Ltd
Bank Saderat Iran
Bank Sepah-Iran
Bank Tejarat
Bankers Trust Company
Beirut Riyad Bank SAL

Canadian Imperial Bank of Commerce
Canara Bank
Capital One Bank
Chang Hwa Commercial Bank Ltd
Chase Manhattan Bank
Chiba Bank Ltd
Cho Hung Bank
Chuo Trust & Banking Co. Ltd
Citibank NA
Commercial Bank of Korea Ltd
Commonwealth Bank of Australia
CoreStates Bank NA
Crédit Suisse First Boston
Cyprus Popular Bank Ltd

Dai-Ichi Kangyo Bank Ltd
Daiwa Bank Ltd
Development Bank of Singapore Ltd
Discount Bank and Trust Company

Emirates Bank International PJSC

First Bank of Nigeria PLC
First Commercial Bank
First National Bank of Chicago
First Union National Bank
Fuji Bank Ltd

Ghana Commercial Bank
Gulf International Bank BSC

Habib Bank AG Zurich
Habib Bank Ltd
Hanil Bank

Hiroshima Bank Ltd
Hokkaido Takushoku Bank Ltd
Hokuriku Bank Ltd
Hongkong and Shanghai Banking Corporation Ltd

Industrial Bank of Japan Ltd

Joyo Bank Ltd

KorAm Bank
Korea Development Bank
Korea Exchange Bank
Korea First Bank

Long-Term Credit Bank of Japan Ltd

Macquarie Bank Ltd
Malayan Banking Berhad
Mashreq Bank PSC
Mellon Bank NA
Mitsubishi Trust and Banking Corporation
Mitsui Trust & Banking Co. Ltd
Morgan Guaranty Trust Company of New York

Nacional Financiera SNC
National Australia Bank Ltd
National Bank of Abu Dhabi
National Bank of Canada
National Bank of Dubai Public Joint Stock Company
National Bank of Pakistan
NationsBank NA
NationsBank of Texas NA
Nedcor Bank Ltd
Nippon Credit Bank Ltd
Norinchukin Bank
Northern Trust Company

Oversea-Chinese Banking Corporation Ltd
Overseas Trust Bank Ltd
Overseas Union Bank Ltd

People's Bank
Philippine National Bank

Qatar National Bank SAQ

†Rafidain Bank
Republic National Bank of New York
Riggs Bank NA
Riyad Bank
Royal Bank of Canada

Sakura Bank Ltd
Sanwa Bank Ltd
Saudi American Bank
Saudi British Bank
Seoulbank
Shanghai Commercial Bank Ltd
Shinhan Bank
Siam Commercial Bank Public Company Ltd
Sonali Bank
State Bank of India
State Street Bank and Trust Company
Sumitomo Bank Ltd
Sumitomo Trust & Banking Co. Ltd
Swiss Bank Corporation
Syndicate Bank

TC Ziraat Bankasi
Thai Farmers Bank Public Company Ltd
Tokai Bank Ltd
Toronto-Dominion Bank
Toyo Trust & Banking Company Ltd
Türkiye İş Bankası AŞ

Uco Bank
Union Bancaire Privée CBI-TDB

Union Bank of Nigeria PLC
Union Bank of Switzerland
United Bank Ltd
United Mizrahi Bank Ltd
United Overseas Bank Ltd

Westpac Banking Corporation

Yasuda Trust & Banking Co. Ltd

Zambia National Commercial Bank Ltd
Zivnostenská Banka AS

EUROPEAN AUTHORIZED INSTITUTIONS ENTITLED TO ESTABLISH UK BRANCHES

The following are entitled to establish branches in the UK for the purpose of accepting deposits in the UK. The country of the home state supervisory authority is in parenthesis.

ABN AMRO Bank NV (Netherlands)
Allied Irish Banks PLC (Republic of Ireland)
Alpha Credit Bank AE (Greece)
Anglo Irish Bank Corporation PLC (Republic of Ireland)

BfG Bank AG (Germany)
BHF Bank AG (Germany)
Banca Cassa di Risparmio di Torino SpA (Italy)
Banca Commerciale Italiana (Italy)
Banca di Roma SpA (Italy)
Banca March SA (Spain)
Banca Monte dei Paschi di Siena SpA (Italy)
Banca Nazionale dell'Agricoltura SpA (Italy)
Banca Nazionale del Lavoro SpA (Italy)
Banca Popolare di Milano (Italy)
Banca Popolare di Novara (Italy)
Banco Ambrosiano Veneto SpA (Italy)
Banco Bilbao-Vizcaya (Spain)
Banco Central Hispanoamericano SA (Spain)
Banco de Sabadell (Spain)
Banco di Napoli SpA (Italy)
Banco di Sicilia SpA (Italy)
Banco Español de Crédito SA (Spain)
Banco Espirito Santo e Comercial de Lisboa (Portugal)
Banco Exterior de España SA (Spain)
Banco Nacional Ultramarino SA (Portugal)
Banco Português do Atlântico (Portugal)
Banco Santander (Spain)
Banco Santander de Negocios SA (Spain)
Banco Totta & Açores SA (Portugal)
Bank Austria AG (Austria)
Bank Brussels Lambert (Belgium)
Bankgesellschaft Berlin AG (Germany)
Bank of Ireland (Republic of Ireland)
Banque AIG (France)
Banque Arabe et Internationale d'Investissement (France)
Banque Banorabe (France)
Banque Française de l'Orient (France)
Banque Internationale à Luxembourg SA (Luxembourg)
Banque Nationale de Paris (France)
Banque Paribas (France)
Bayerische Hypotheken-und Wechsel-Bank AG (Germany)
Bayerische Landesbank Girozentrale (Germany)
Bayerische Vereinsbank AG (Germany)
Belgolaise SA (Belgium)
Berliner Bank AG (Germany)
Byblos Bank Belgium SA (Belgium)

CARIPLO (Cassa di Risparmio delle Provincie Lombarde SpA) (Italy)
CETELEM (France)

Caisse Nationale de Crédit Agricole (France)
Cariverona Banca SpA (Italy)
Christiania Bank og Kreditkasse (Norway)
Commerzbank AG (Germany)
Compagnie Financière de CIC et de l'Union Européenne (France)
Confederación Española de Cajas de Ahorros (Spain)
Creditanstalt-Bankverein (Austria)
Crédit Agricole Indo Suez (France)
Crédit Commercial de France (France)
Crédit du Nord (France)
Crédit Lyonnais (France)
Credito Italiano (Italy)

De Nationale Investeringsbank NV (Netherlands)
Den Danske Bank Aktieselskab (Denmark)
Den norske Bank ASA (Norway)
Deutsche Bank AG (Germany)
Deutsche Bau- und Bodenbank AG (Germany)
Deutsche Genossenschaftsbank (Germany)
Dresdner Bank AG (Germany)

Equity Bank Ltd (Republic of Ireland)
Ergobank SA (Greece)

FIMAT International Banque (France)
First National Building Society (Republic of Ireland)

Generale Bank (Belgium)
GiroCredit Bank Aktiengesellschaft der Sparkassen (Austria)

Hamburgische Landesbank Girozentrale (Germany)

ICC Bank PLC (Republic of Ireland)
ING Bank NV (Netherlands)
Industrial Bank of Korea Europe SA (Luxembourg)
Ionian and Popular Bank of Greece SA (Greece)
Irish Nationwide Building Society (Republic of Ireland)
Irish Permanent PLC (Republic of Ireland)
Istituto Bancario San Paolo di Torino SpA (Italy)

Jyske Bank (Denmark)

Kas-Associatie NV (Netherlands)
Kredietbank NV (Belgium)

Landesbank Berlin Girozentrale (Germany)
Landesbank Hessen-Thüringen Girozentrale (Germany)
Lehman Brothers Bankhaus AG (Germany)

MeesPierson NV (Netherlands)
Merita Bank Ltd (Finland)

Natexis Banque (France)
National Bank of Greece SA (Greece)
Norddeutsche Landesbank Girozentrale (Germany)

Postipankki Ltd (Finland)

Rabobank International (Coöperatieve Centrale Raiffeisen-Boerenleenbank BA) (Netherlands)
Raiffeisen Zentralbank Osterreich AG (Austria)

Skandinaviska Enskilda Banken AB (publ) (Sweden)
Société Générale (France)
Südwestdeutsche Landesbank Girozentrale (Germany)
Svenska Handelsbanken AB (publ) (Sweden)
SwedBank (Sparbanken Sverige AB (publ)) (Sweden)

Triodosbank NV (Netherlands)

Ulster Bank Markets Ltd (Republic of Ireland)
Unibank AS (Denmark)

Westdeutsche Landesbank Girozentrale (Germany)

Mutual Societies

On 23 July 1997 the Economic Secretary to the Treasury announced that regulatory responsibility for mutual societies, currently exercised by the Registry of Friendly Societies, the Friendly Societies Commission and the Building Societies Commission, would be transferred to a single new regulatory organization. The proposed changes, made under the Government's policy for reform of financial regulation, include the responsibilities in respect of all the mutual societies referred to on the following pages. It is anticipated that the transfer of the work of the current organizations to the new regulatory authority will take place in stages during 1998 and 1999.

FRIENDLY SOCIETIES IN BRITAIN

Friendly societies are voluntary mutual organizations, the main purposes of which are the provision of relief or maintenance during sickness, unemployment or retirement, and the provision of life assurance. Many of the older traditional societies complement their business activities by social activity and a general care for individual members in ways normally outside the scope of a purely commercial organization. There are three main categories of friendly societies: societies with separately registered branches, commonly called orders; centralized societies, which conduct business directly with members (having no separately registered branches); and collecting societies. Collecting societies conduct industrial assurance business and are subject to the requirements of the Industrial Assurance Acts in addition to the Friendly Societies Acts. Industrial assurance is life assurance for which the premiums are payable at intervals of less than two months and are received by means of collectors who make house-to-house visits for the purpose.

The Friendly Societies Act 1974 allowed three other main classes of society to be registered: benevolent societies, working men's clubs and specially authorized societies. Benevolent societies are established for any charitable or benevolent purpose, to provide the same type of benefits as would be permissible for a friendly society, but in contrast the benefits must be for persons who are not members instead of, or in addition to, members. Working men's clubs provide social and recreational facilities for members. Specially authorized societies are registered for any purpose authorized by the Treasury as a purpose to which some or all of the provisions of the 1974 Act ought to be extended. Examples are societies for the promotion of science, literature and the fine arts, or to enable members to pursue an interest in sports and games.

The most recent legislation, the Friendly Societies Act 1992, created a new legislative framework for friendly societies, enabling them to provide a wider range of services to their members and allowing them to compete on more equal terms with other financial institutions. At the same time it provided for more flexible prudential supervision to safeguard members of societies.

The Act enables friendly societies to incorporate and establish subsidiaries to provide various financial and other services to their members and the public. The activities which subsidiaries are able to conduct include those to establish and manage unit trust schemes and personal equity plans; to arrange for the provision of credit, whether as agents or providers; to carry on long-term or general insurance business; to provide insurance intermediary services; to provide fund management services for trustees of pension funds; to administer estates and execute trusts of wills; and to establish and manage sheltered housing, residential homes for the elderly, hospitals and nursing homes.

The Act established a new framework to oversee friendly societies, including a Friendly Societies Commission, whose principal functions are to regulate the activities of friendly societies, promote their financial stability and protect members' funds. All friendly societies carrying on insurance or non-insurance business require authorization by the Commission, which has a broad range of prudential powers. Friendly societies were also to be brought within the scope of the Policyholders Protection Act 1975, the statutory investor protection scheme covering insurance policyholders.

By the end of May 1997, there were 119 societies authorized to write new business. Thirty of the larger societies had taken advantage of the Friendly Societies Act 1992 to incorporate and 17 of them had established subsidiary companies which can provide a wider range of services to both members and non-members as set out in Schedule 7 of the 1992 Act.

The Friendly Societies (Activities of a Subsidiary) Order 1996 came into force on 6 January 1997. The Order extended the range of activities which a subsidiary of an incorporated society may undertake, by allowing them to:

– establish and manage open ended investment companies (OEICs)
– convert unit trusts into OEICs
– establish and manage investment trusts
– provide fund management services to other bodies in addition to the trustees of pension funds

OEICs are collective investment schemes, similar to unit trusts, but in a corporate form.

The new activities are subject to the provisions of the Financial Services Act 1986 and thus to authorization and supervision by the appropriate regulatory authorities, such as the Investment Management Regulatory Organization (IMRO) or the Personal Investment Authority (PIA).

The principal statistics at the end of 1995 are given in the table below.

	No. of societies	No. of members 000s	Benefits paid £000s	Total funds £000s
Orders and branches	1,013*	259	7,757	225,328
Collecting societies	18	6,099†	301,420	5,155,872
Other centralized societies	294	2,692	462,526	4,355,274
Benevolent societies	72	333	9,165	33,320
Working men's clubs	2,271	1,427	n/a	239,524
Specially authorized societies				
Loans	5	15	n/a	167
Others	126	82	169	11,856

* 17 orders, 996 branches
† Includes 4.5 million policies rather than members in the case of seven collecting societies

INDUSTRIAL AND PROVIDENT SOCIETIES IN BRITAIN

The familiar 'Co-op' societies are amongst the wide variety which are registered under the Industrial and Provident Societies Act 1965. This consolidating Act, which is administered by the Chief Registrar of Friendly Societies, provides for the registration of societies and lays down the broad framework within which they must operate. Internal relations of societies are governed by their registered rules.

Registration under the Act confers upon a society corporate status by its registered name with perpetual succession and a common seal, and limited liability. A society qualifies for registration if it is carrying on an industry, business or trade, and it satisfies the Registrar either (a) that it is a bona fide co-operative society, or (b) that in view of the fact that its business is being, or is intended to be, conducted for the benefit of the community, there are special reasons why it should be registered under the Act rather than as a company under the Companies Act.

The Credit Unions Act 1979 added a new class of society registerable under the 1965 Act. It also made provision for the supervision of these savings and loan bodies. Unlike other classes, where the role of the Registry is solely that of a registration authority, it is for credit unions the prudential supervisor, seeking to encourage the prudent safe-keeping of investors' money.

During 1995 the number of registered societies of all classes decreased by 82 to 10,656 but the number of credit unions increased by 56 to 531. Assets of industrial and provident societies totalled £37,611 million, almost half of which is held in the 4,041 housing societies. The principal statistics at the end of 1995 are given in the table below.

	No. of socie-ties	No. of mem-bers 000s	Funds of members £000s	Total assets £000s
Retail	127	5,872	630,321	1,577,068
Wholesale and productive	139	45	634,473	1,397,498
Agricultural	980	262	243,693	684,493
Fishing	83	4	7,508	16,159
Clubs	3,667	2,590	330,062	519,209
General service	1,088	544	1,519,309	15,283,108
Housing	4,041	173	7,496,179	18,053,247
Credit unions	531	162	75,910	79,945
TOTAL	10,656	9,652	10,937,455	37,610,727

BUILDING SOCIETIES IN THE UK

The Building Societies Act 1997, which received royal assent on 21 March 1997, makes substantive amendments to, but does not replace, the Building Societies Act 1986. It substantially liberalizes the statutory regime for building societies and extends the principal purpose of building societies to cover lending for all forms of housing, rented as well as owner-occupied. Outside the principal purpose, a society will, with few exceptions, be able to carry on any type of business it wishes within the terms of its own memorandum.

The Building Societies Act 1986 gave building societies a completely new legal framework for the first time since the initial comprehensive building society legislation in 1874. The 1986 Act sets out detailed provisions in relation to:

- the constitution of building societies
- building societies' powers in relation to raising funds, advances, loans, other assets and the provision of services
- the powers of control of the Building Societies Commission
- protection of investors, and complaints and disputes
- management of building societies, accounts and audit
- mergers and transfers of business

The 1986 Act is prescriptive in respect of building societies' powers and the way in which they are exercised. However, the 1986 Act gives numerous powers to the Building Societies Commission and/or the Treasury to make statutory instruments which, subject to parliamentary approval, can amend, extend and supplement the provisions of the Act. Since it came into force on 1 January 1987 the Act has been amended and extended considerably, especially in respect of building societies' powers.

The Government began a two-stage review of the 1986 Act in 1994. As a result of the first stage of that review, a number of further changes in relation to building societies' powers were made in 1995, some by the Deregulation and Contracting Out Act 1994. Following the second stage of the review, the Building Societies Act 1997 was passed.

The Building Societies Act 1997 makes a number of substantive amendments to the 1986 Act. Its main purposes are:

- to remove the prescriptive powers' regime relating to building societies and to replace it with a permissive regime with appropriately revised balance-sheet 'nature limits', thus increasing the commercial freedom of societies and allowing increased competiton and wider choice for customers
- to enhance the powers of control of the Building Societies Commission
- to introduce a package of measures to enhance the accountability of building societies' boards to their members
- to make changes to the provisions relating to the transfer of a building society's business to a company

The Act comes fully into force by 21 October 1997. Under it a building society may pursue any activities set out in its memorandum, subject only to:

- principal purpose: its purpose or principal purpose must be that of making loans which are secured on residential properties and are funded substantially by its members
- lending limit: at least 75 per cent of its business assets must be loans fully secured on residential property funding limit: at least 50 per cent of its funds must be raised in the form of shares held by individual members
- restrictions: subject to certain exceptions, it must not act as a market maker in securities, commodities or currencies; trade in commodities or currencies; enter into transactions involving derivatives, except in relation to hedging; nor create a floating charge over its assets
- prudential: it must comply with the criteria of prudential management

CONVERSIONS AND TAKE-OVERS

The Alliance and Leicester, Halifax and Woolwich building societies completed their conversions to PLC status on 21 April, 2 June and 7 July 1997 respectively. In April 1997, members of the Bristol and West Building Society approved the proposed take-over by the Bank of Ireland,

and members of the Northern Rock Building Society approved the proposal to convert to a company. On completion of the conversion process of these two societies, the continuing building society sector will control assets of about £120 billion and have around 17 million individual members.

OMBUDSMAN SCHEME

Societies must belong to an ombudsman scheme for the investigation of complaints. Matters to be covered by the scheme include operation of share and deposit accounts, loans (but not the making of new loans), money transmission services, foreign exchange services, agency payments and receipts, and the provision of credit. Grounds for complaint include breach of the Act or contract, unfair treatment or maladministration, and where the complainant has suffered pecuniary loss or expense or inconvenience. A society must agree to be bound by decisions of the adjudicator unless it agrees to give notice to its members and the public of its reasons for not doing so. For address of the Building Societies Ombudsman scheme, see page 631.

BUILDING SOCIETIES 1995-6

	1995	1996
No. of societies – total	94	88
– authorized	80	77
No. of shareholders (000s)	38,998	37,768
No. of depositors (000s)	6,307	6,889
No. of borrowers (000s)	7,178	6,859
Share balances (£m)	200,826	196,546
Deposit balances (£m)	69,220	76,231
Mortgage balances (£m)	233,358	236,930
Total assets (£m)	299,921	318,392
Advances during year		
No. (000s)	1,047	1,115
Amount (£m)	39,200	43,881

MORTGAGE ARREARS AND REPOSSESSIONS

The recession resulted in a sharp rise in mortgage arrears and repossessions, with more than 75,000 properties repossessed in 1991. That total fell by 7,000 in 1992 as a result of a greater willingness by societies to enter into arrangements with borrowers. The number continued to decline in the following two years. Just over 42,000 properties were taken into possession in 1996, the lowest figure since 1989. Details of loans outstanding and properties repossessed for recent years are shown below.

	1989	1990	1991	1992	1993	1994	1995	1996
No. of loans at end year (000s)	9,125	9,415	9,815	9,922	10,137	10,410	10,521	10,637
Properties repossessed in year								
Number	15,810	43,890	75,540	68,540	58,540	49,190	49,410	42,560
%	0.17	0.47	0.77	0.70	0.58	0.47	0.47	0.40

INTEREST RATES: MORTGAGE AND SHARE 1992-7

The interest rates prevailing on mortgage lending and share investment vary from society to society and in relation to the type or amount of loan or investment.

The interval between the payments or compounding of interest is crucial in determining the competitiveness of particular societies' accounts. In order to make a true comparison of interest rates, the annual percentage rate or APR, which should appear in all advertisements and leaflets, must be used.

	1992	1993	1994	1995	1996	1997 1st quarter
Average bank base rate	9.56	6.01	5.46	6.70	5.96	6.00
Building societies average mortgage rate	10.65	8.09	7.68	7.84	6.72	6.66
Building societies average share rate	8.45	5.78	5.36	5.62	4.54	4.60

SOCIETIES WITH TOTAL ASSETS EXCEEDING £1 MILLION AT END OF FINANCIAL YEAR 1996

Name of Society* and head office address	Share investors	Total assets £'000
Alliance and Leicester, 49 Park Lane, London WIY 4EQ	3,260,435	22,846,100
Barnsley, Regent Street, Barnsley, South Yorks S70 2EH	41,939	201,853
Bath Investment, 20 Charles Street, Bath BA1 1HY	17,483	61,762
Beverley, 57 Market Place, Beverley, E. Yorks HU17 8AA	7,693	44,458
Birmingham Midshires, PO Box 81, Pendeford Business Park, Wobaston Road, Wolverhampton, WV9 5HZ	848,563	6,837,600
Bradford and Bingley, Crossflatts, Bingley, West Yorks BD16 2UA	1,701,988	17,038,094
Bristol and West, Broad Quay, Bristol BS99 7AX	1,263,530	9,451,700
Britannia, Britannia House, Cheadle Road, Leek, Staffs ST13 5RG	1,332,373	16,060,400
Buckinghamshire, High Street, Chalfont St Giles, Bucks HP8 4QB	9,000	77,434
Cambridge, 51 Newmarket Road, Cambridge CB5 8EG	52,585	392,028
Catholic, 7 Strutton Ground, London SW1P 2HY	3,555	27,275
Century, 21 Albany Street, Edinburgh EH1 3QW	2,806	13,167
Chelsea, Thirlestaine Hall, Thirlestaine Road, Cheltenham, Glos GL53 7AL	214,955	3,016,466
Chesham, 12 Market Square, Chesham, Bucks HP5 1ER	17,549	115,516
Cheshire, Castle Street, Macclesfield, Cheshire SK11 6AF	247,984	1,641,305
Chorley and District, Key House, Foxhole Road, Chorley, Lancs PR7 1NZ	13,501	73,850
Clay Cross, Eyre Street, Clay Cross, Chesterfield S45 9NS	3,475	16,918
Coventry, PO Box 9, High Street, Coventry CV1 5QN	568,403	3,741,271
Cumberland, Cumberland House, Castle Street, Carlisle CA3 8RX	168,442	673,347
Darlington, Sentinel House, Lingfield Way, Darlington, Co. Durham DL1 4PR	51,022	315,698
Derbyshire, Duffield Hall, Duffield, Derby DE56 1AG	301,471	2,016,952
Dudley, Dudley House, Stone Street, Dudley DY1 1NP	23,613	91,557
Dunfermline, Caledonia House, Carnegie Avenue, Dunfermline, Fife KY11 5PJ	177,400	1,126,138
Earl Shilton, 22 The Hollow, Earl Shilton, Leicester LE9 7NB	11,736	60,512
Ecology, 18 Station Road, Cross Hills, Keighley, West Yorks BD20 7EH	4,525	19,492
Furness, 51–55 Duke Street, Barrow-in-Furness LA14 1RT	66,685	360,870
Gainsborough, 9 Lord Street, Gainsborough, Lincs DN21 2DD	7,027	30,012
Greenwich, 279–283 Greenwich High Road, London SE10 8NL	23,197	187,823
Halifax, Trinity Road, Halifax, West Yorks HX1 2RG	11,600,000	115,539,100
Hanley Economic, Granville House, Festival Park, Hanley, Stoke-on-Trent, Staffs ST1 5TB	28,418	184,929
Harpenden, 14 Station Road, Harpenden, Herts AL5 4SE	10,961	50,451
Hinckley and Rugby, Upper Bond Street, Hinckley, Leics LE10 1DG	69,466	333,689
Holmesdale, 43 Church Street, Reigate, Surrey RH2 0AE	6,743	73,498
Ilkeston Permanent, 24–26 South Street, Ilkeston, Derby DE7 5HQ	3,750	16,260
Ipswich, 44 Upper Brook Street, Ipswich IP4 1DP	44,307	201,617
Kent Reliance, Reliance House, Manor Road, Chatham, Kent ME4 6AF	45,823	271,081
Lambeth, 118–120 Westminster Bridge Road, London SE1 7XE	48,364	592,888
Leeds and Holbeck, 105 Albion Street, Leeds LS1 5AS	318,524	2,647,884
Leek United, 50 St Edward Street, Leek, Staffs ST13 5DH	54,782	379,177
Londonderry Provident, 31A Carlisle Road, Londonderry BT48 6JJ	1,166	9,515
Loughborough, 6 High Street, Loughborough, Leics LE11 2QB	15,500	121,071
Manchester, 24 Queen Street, Manchester M2 5AH	14,638	127,552
Mansfield, Regent House, Regent Street, Mansfield, Notts NG18 1SS	19,051	116,431
Market Harborough, Welland House, The Square, Market Harborough, Leics LE16 7PD	39,442	238,128
Marsden, 6–20 Russell Street, Nelson, Lancs BB9 7NJ	61,856	264,689
Melton Mowbray, 39 Nottingham Street, Melton Mowbray, Leics LE13 1NR	36,010	203,547
Mercantile, Mercantile House, The Silverlink Business Park, Wallsend, Tyne and Wear NE28 9NY	28,762	140,185
Monmouthshire, John Frost Square, Newport, Gwent NP9 1PX	32,617	210,635
National Counties, National Counties House, Church Street, Epsom, Surrey KT17 4NL	16,318	454,427
Nationwide, Nationwide House, Pipers Way, Swindon SN38 1NW	6,213,972	40,453,321
Newbury, 17–20 Bartholomew Street, Newbury, Berks RG14 5LY	33,759	258,090
Newcastle, Portland House, New Bridge Street, Newcastle upon Tyne NE1 8AL	206,190	1,560,451
Northern Rock, Northern Rock House, Gosforth, Newcastle upon Tyne NE3 4PL	1,023,668	13,717,854
Norwich and Peterborough, Peterborough Business Park, Lynchwood, Peterborough PE2 6WZ	203,778	1,667,901
Nottingham, 5–13 Upper Parliament Street, Nottingham NG1 2BX	149,300	1,048,755
Nottingham Imperial, Imperial House, 72 Bridgford Road, West Bridgford, Nottingham NG2 6AP	9,121	52,007
Penrith, 7 King Street, Penrith, Cumbria CA11 7AR	6,106	50,656
Portman, Portman House, Richmond Hill, Bournemouth, Dorset BH2 6EP	768,184	4,011,146
Principality, PO Box 89, Principality Buildings, Queen Street, Cardiff CF1 1UA	250,566	1,563,867

Name of Society* and head office address	Share investors	Total assets £'000
Progressive, 33–37 Wellington Place, Belfast BTI 6HH	57,161	442,616
Saffron Walden, Herts and Essex, 1A Market Street, Saffron Walden, Essex CBIO IHX	49,239	252,820
Scottish, 23 Manor Place, Edinburgh EH3 7XE	22,982	125,260
Shepshed, Bull Ring, Shepshed, Loughborough, Leics LEI2 9QD	6,966	35,737
Skipton, The Bailey, Skipton, North Yorks BD23 IDN	278,625	3,258,908
Stafford Railway, 4 Market Square, Stafford STI6 2JH	9,639	53,551
Staffordshire, Jubilee House, PO Box 66, 84 Salop Street, Wolverhampton WV3 OSA	203,569	1,060,038
Standard, 64 Church Way, North Shields, Tyne and Wear NE29 OAF	2,369	14,959
Stroud and Swindon, Rowcroft, Stroud, Glos GL5 3BG	139,980	935,262
Swansea, 11 Cradock Street, Swansea SAI 3EW	3,647	30,591
Teachers, Allenview House, Hanham Road, Wimborne, Dorset BH2I IAG	13,717	131,752
Tipton and Coseley, 70 Owen Street, Tipton, West Midlands DY4 8HG	22,529	118,219
Universal, Universal House, Kings Manor, Newcastle upon Tyne NEI 6PA	36,600	265,100
Vernon, 19 St Petersgate, Stockport, Cheshire SKI IHF	31,215	127,960
West Bromwich, 374 High Street, West Bromwich, West Midlands B70 8LR	363,294	1,850,038
Woolwich, Watling Street, Bexleyheath, Kent DA6 7RR	3,631,000	30,701,300
Yorkshire, Yorkshire House, Yorkshire Drive, Bradford BD5 8LJ	977,114	7,143,501

* 'Building Society' are the last words in every society's name

National Savings

INVESTMENT AND ORDINARY ACCOUNTS

On 31 May 1997, there were about 16,063,066 active accounts with the sum of approximately £1,376.8 million due to depositors in ordinary accounts and about 4,469,767 active accounts with the sum of approximately £8,440.7 million due to depositors in investment accounts.

Interest is earned at 2.5 per cent per year on each ordinary account for every complete calendar month in which the balance is £500 or more, provided the account is kept open for the whole of 1997 (31 December 1996 to 1 January 1998); and at 1.5 per cent per year for other months or for accounts opened or closed during 1997. The minimum deposit is £10; maximum balance £10,000 plus interest credited. On 31 May 1997 the average amount held in ordinary accounts was approximately £85.

The investment account pays a higher rate of interest depending on the account balance (the current rate can be found at any post office). The minimum deposit is £20; maximum balance £100,000 plus interest credited. On 31 May 1997 the average amount held in investment accounts was approximately £1,888.

PREMIUM BONDS

Premium Bonds are a government security which were first introduced in 1956. Premium Bonds enable savers to enter a regular draw for tax-free prizes, while retaining the right to get their money back. A sum equivalent to interest on each bond is put into a prize fund and distributed by monthly prize draws. (The rate of interest is 4.75 per cent a year from 1 May 1996.) The prizes are drawn by ERNIE (electronic random number indicator equipment) and are free of all UK income tax and capital gains tax.

Bonds are in units of £1, with a minimum purchase of £100; above this, purchases must be in multiples of £10, up to a maximum holding limit of £20,000 per person. The scheme offers a facility to reinvest prize wins automatically. Upon completion of an automatic prize reinvestment mandate, holders receive new bonds which are immediately eligible for future prize draws. Bonds can only be held in the name of an individual and not by organizations.

Bonds become eligible for prizes once they have been held for one clear calendar month following the month of purchase. Each £1 unit can win only one prize per draw, but it will be awarded the highest for which it is drawn. Bonds remain eligible for prizes until they are repaid. When a holder dies, bonds remain eligible for prizes up to and including the twelfth monthly draw after the month in which the holder dies.

By April 1997 bonds to the value of £13,058 million had been sold. Of these £4,884 million had been cashed, leaving £8,174 million still invested. By the April 1997 prize draw, 56.6 million prizes totalling £3,500 million had been distributed since the first prize draw in June 1957.

INCOME BONDS

National Savings Income Bonds were introduced in 1982. They are suitable for those who want to receive regular monthly payments of interest while preserving the full cash value of their capital. The bonds are sold in multiples of £1,000. The minimum holding is £2,000 and the maximum £250,000 (sole or joint holding).

Interest is calculated on a day-to-day basis and paid monthly. Interest is taxable but is paid without deduction of tax at source. The bonds have a guaranteed life of ten years, but may be repaid at par before maturity on giving three months' notice. Repayment is also possible without

giving notice but incurs a penalty. If the sole or sole surviving holder dies, however, no fixed period of notice is required and there is no loss of interest for repayment made within the first year.

Net investment in National Savings Income Bonds was £10,319 million at the end of April 1997.

PENSIONERS GUARANTEED INCOME BONDS

Pensioners Guaranteed Income Bonds were introduced in January 1994 and are designed for people aged 60 and over who wish to receive regular monthly payments with a rate of interest that is fixed for a five-year period whilst preserving the full cash value of their investment.

The minimum limit for each purchase is £500. The maximum holding is £50,000 (£100,000 for a joint holding); within those limits bonds can be bought for any amount in pounds and pence. The rate of interest is fixed and guaranteed for the first five years. Interest is taxable but is paid without deduction of tax at source.

Holders can apply for repayment (or part repayment of a bond subject to the minimum holding limits) by giving 60 days notice (if repayment is before the fifth anniversary date). No interest is earned during the notice period. If repayment is requested within two weeks of any fifth anniversary of purchase, there is no formal period of notice. Repayment is possible without giving notice but a penalty is incurred. On the death of a holder or sole surviving investor in a joint holding, repayment will be made without notice. Interest will be paid in full up to the date of repayment.

Net investment in Pensioners Guaranteed Income Bonds was £4,249 million at the end of March 1997.

CHILDREN'S BONUS BONDS

Children's Bonus Bonds were introduced in 1991. The latest issue, Issue H, was introduced in January 1996. They can be bought for any child under 16 and will go on growing in value until he or she is 21. The bonds are sold in multiples of £25. The minimum holding is £25. The maximum holding in Issue H is £1,000 per child. This is in addition to holdings of earlier issues of the bond (excluding interest and bonuses). Bonds for children under 16 must be held by a parent or guardian.

Children's Bonus Bonds (Issue H) earn 5 per cent a year over five years. A bonus (11.00 per cent) of the purchase price is added at the fifth anniversary. This is equal to 6.75 per cent a year compound. All returns are totally exempt from UK income tax. No interest is earned on bonds cashed in before the first anniversary of purchase. Bonuses are only payable if the bond is held until the next bonus date. Bonds over five years old continue to earn interest and bonuses until the holder is 21, when they should be cashed in. If bonds are not cashed in on the holder's 21st birthday, they earn no interest after that birthday.

FIRST OPTION BONDS

FIRST (Fixed Interest Rate Savings Tax-paid) Option Bonds were introduced in 1992. They offer guaranteed rates without the need for long-term commitment for personal savers over 16. They may be held indefinitely and will continue to grow in value at rates of interest fixed for 12 months at a time. Tax is deducted from the interest at source. The minimum purchase is £1,000 and the maximum holding is £250,000. Withdrawals can be made without penalty at any anniversary date and there is no formal notice period for repayment. No interest is earned on repayments before the first anniversary.

Capital Bonds

National Savings Capital Bonds were introduced in 1989. The latest series, Series J, was introduced in January 1996. Capital Bonds offer capital growth over five years with guaranteed returns at fixed rates. The interest is taxable each year (for those who pay income tax) but is not deducted at source. The minimum purchase is £100. There is a maximum holding limit of £250,000 from Series B onwards.

Capital Bonds will be repaid in full with all interest gained at the end of five years. No interest is earned on bonds repaid in the first year. Reinvestment or extension terms may also be available.

Gilts on the National Savings Stock Register

Government stock or 'gilts' are Stock Exchange securities issued by the Government. They usually have a life of between five and 15 years and most pay a guaranteed fixed rate of interest twice a year throughout this period. When they reach the end of this period they are 'redeemed' (which means repaid) at their face value.

The National Savings Stock Register (NSSR) enables investors to buy and sell gilts by post. It is now possible to have most new issues of gilts registered on the NSSR. Interest on gilts held on the NSSR, although taxable, is paid in full without deduction of tax at source.

National Savings Treasurer's Account

The Treasurer's Account, introduced in September 1996, offers attractive rates and security to non-profit making organizations such as charities, friendly societies, clubs, etc. The minimum holding is £10,000 and the maximum is £2 million. Interest is paid at the rate of 5.25 per cent a year on holdings of £10,000 to £24,999, 5.5 per cent a year on holdings of £25,000 to £99,999, and 5.75 per cent a year on holdings of £100,000 and above.

NATIONAL SAVINGS CERTIFICATES

Recent Issues

The amount, including accrued interest, index-linked increase or bonus remaining to the credit of investors in National Savings Certificates on 30 April 1997 was approximately £20,145.5 million. In 1996–7, approximately £3,677.7 million was subscribed and £3,271.5 million (excluding interest, index-linked increase or bonus) was repaid. Interest, index-linked increase, bonus or other sum payable is free of UK income tax (including investment income surcharge) and capital gains tax.

From June 1982, savings certificates of the 7th to 37th Issues will be extended on general extension rates as they reach the end of their existing extension periods. The percentage interest rate is determined by the Treasury and any change in this general extension rate will be applicable from the first of the month following its announcement. Under the system, a certificate earns interest for each complete period of three months beyond the expiry of the previous extension terms. Within each three-month period, interest is calculated separately for each month at the rate applicable from the beginning of that month. The interest for each month is one-twelfth of the annual rate (i.e. it does not vary with the number of days in the month) and is capitalized annually on the anniversary of the date of purchase. The current rate of interest under the general extension rate is given in leaflets available at post offices.

Fifth Index-linked Issue
2 July 1990–12 November 1992
Maximum holding: 400 units, plus special facilities to hold up to a further 400 units
Unit cost: £25

Interest per unit: the repayment value, subject to their being held for one year, is related to the movement of the UK General Index of Retail Prices. In addition, there is guaranteed extra interest which is paid from the date of purchase for each full year the certificates are held. After the first year the return is the Retail Price Index (RPI) only. Certificates repaid before the first anniversary date earn RPI for each complete month held from the purchase date. For the second year, the RPI plus 0.5 per cent; for the third, the RPI plus 1 per cent; for the fourth, the RPI plus 2 per cent; and at the fifth anniversary, RPI plus 4.5 per cent. Certificates held beyond the fifth anniversary earn the index-linked return only

Thirty-sixth Issue
2 April 1991–2 May 1992
Maximum holding: 400 units, plus special facilities to hold up to a further 400
Unit cost: £25
Value after five years: £37.59
Interest per unit: after one year the repayment value increases by 5.5 per cent for ordinarily held 36th Issue. However, reinvestment certificates earn interest during the first year at a rate of 5.5 per cent a year. Thereafter, all 36th Issue earn 6 per cent after two years; 6.75 per cent after three years; 7.5 per cent after four years; and 8.5 per cent after five years

Thirty-seventh Issue
13 May 1992–5 August 1992
Maximum holding: 300 units, plus special facilities to hold up to a further 400
Unit cost: £25
Value after five years: £36.74
Interest per unit: after one year the repayment value increases by 5.5 per cent for ordinarily held 37th Issue. However, reinvestment certificates earn interest during the first year at a rate of 5.5 per cent a year. After one year, £1.38 is added; during the second year, 41 pence per completed three months; during the third year, 56 pence per completed three months; during the fourth year, 71 pence per completed three months; and during the fifth year, 91 pence per completed three months

Thirty-eighth Issue
24 August 1992–22 September 1992
Maximum holding: 200 units, plus special facilities to hold up to a further 400
Unit cost: £25
Value after five years: £35.89
Interest per unit: after one year the repayment value increases by 5.25 per cent for ordinarily held 38th Issue. However, reinvestment certificates earn interest during the first year at a rate of 5.25 per cent a year. After one year, £1.31 is added; during the second year, 41 pence per completed three months; during the third year, 50 pence per completed three months; during the fourth year, 63 pence per completed three months; and during the fifth year, 86 pence per completed three months

Thirty-ninth Issue
5 October 1992–12 November 1992
Maximum holding: 50 units, plus special facilities to hold up to a further 100
Unit cost: £100
Value after five years: £138.63
Interest per unit: after one year the repayment value increases by 4.6 per cent for ordinarily held 39th Issue. However, reinvestment certificates earn interest during the first year at a rate of 4.6 per cent a year. After one year, £4.60 is added; during the second year, £1.37 per completed three months; during the third year, £1.86 per completed three months; during the fourth year, £2.32 per completed three months; and during the fifth year, £2.96 per completed three months

Fortieth Issue
7 December 1992–16 December 1993
Maximum holding: 400 units, plus special facilities to hold up to a further 800
Unit cost: £100; reinvestment certificates £25
Value after five years: £132.25
Interest per unit: after one year the repayment value increases by 4 per cent for ordinarily held 40th Issue. However, reinvestment certificates earn interest during the first year at a rate of 4 per cent a year. On a £100 unit after one year, £4 is added; during the second year, £1.15 per completed three months; during the third year, £1.56 per completed three months; during the fourth year,

£1.54 per completed three months; and during the fifth year, £2.42 per completed three months

Sixth Index-linked Issue
7 December 1992–16 December 1993

Maximum holding: 400 units, plus special facilities to hold up to a further 800

Unit cost: £100; reinvestment certificates £25

Interest per unit: the repayment value, subject to their being held for one year, is related to the movement of the UK General Index of Retail Prices. In addition, there is a guaranteed extra interest of 1.5 per cent for the first year; 2 per cent for the second year; 2.75 per cent for the third year; 3.75 per cent for the fourth year; and 6.32 per cent for the fifth year. This is worth 3.25 per cent compound over the full five years. Reinvestment certificates repaid before the first anniversary date earn RPI plus extra interest of 1.5 per cent a year for each complete month

Seventh Index-linked Issue
17 December 1993–19 September 1994

Maximum holding: 400 units, plus special facilities to hold up to a further 800

Unit cost: £100; reinvestment certificates £25

Interest per unit: the repayment value, subject to their being held for one year, is related to the movement of the UK General Index of Retail Prices. In addition, there is a guaranteed extra interest of 1.25 per cent for the first year; 1.75 per cent for the second year; 2.5 per cent for the third year; 3.5 per cent for the fourth year and 6.07 per cent for the fifth year. This is worth 3 per cent compound over the full five years. Reinvestment certificates repaid before the first anniversary date will earn RPI plus extra interest of 1.25 per cent a year for each complete month

Forty-first Issue
17 December 1993–19 December 1994

Maximum holding: 400 units, plus special facilities to hold up to a further 800

Unit cost: £100; reinvestment certificates £25

Value after five years: £130.08

Interest per unit: after one year the repayment value increased by 3.65 per cent for ordinarily held 41st Issue. However, reinvestment certificates if encashed before the first anniversary earn interest at 3.65 per cent for each complete period of three months. On a £100 unit after one year, £3.65 is added; during the second year, £1.05 per completed three months; during the third year, £1.45 per completed three months; during the fourth year, £1.82 per completed three months; and during the fifth year, £2.20 per completed three months

Forty-second Issue
20 September 1994–25 January 1996

Maximum holding: £10,000, plus special facilities to hold up to a further £20,000

Unit cost: certificates may be purchased for any amount, subject to a minimum purchase at any time of £100; reinvestment certificates are available for any amount and are not subject to a minimum purchase requirement

Value after five years: £132.88

Interest: after one year the repayment value increases by 4 per cent for ordinarily held 42nd Issue. However, reinvestment certificates if encashed before the first anniversary earn interest at 4 per cent for each complete period of three months. On a £100 certificate after one year £4.00 is added; during the second year £1.19 per completed three months; during the third year, £1.49 per completed three months; during the fourth year, £1.93 per completed three months; and during the fifth year, £2.59 per completed three months

Eighth Index-linked Issue
20 September 1994–25 January 1996

Maximum holding: £10,000, plus special facilities to hold up to a further £20,000

Unit cost: certificates may be purchased for any amount, subject to a minimum purchase at any time of £100; reinvestment certificates are available for any amount and are not subject to a minimum purchase requirement

Interest: the repayment value, subject to their being held for one year, is related to the movement of the UK General Index of Retail Prices. In addition, there is a guaranteed extra interest of 1.25 per cent for the first year, 1.75 per cent for the second year, 2.5 per cent for the third year, 3.5 per cent for the fourth year and 6.07 per cent for the fifth year. This is worth 3 per cent compound over the

full five years. Reinvestment certificates repaid before the first anniversary date will earn RPI plus extra interest of 1.25 per cent a year for each complete month

Forty-third Issue
26 January 1996–31 March 1997

Maximum holding: £10,000, plus special facilities to hold up to a further £20,000

Unit cost: certificates may be purchased for any amount, subject to a minimum purchase at any time of £100; reinvestment certificates are available for any amount and are not subject to a minimum purchase requirement

Value after five years: £129.77

Interest: after one year the repayment value increases by 3.75 per cent for ordinarily held 43rd Issue. However, reinvestment certificates if encashed before the first anniversary earn interest at 3.75 per cent a year for each complete period of three months. On a £100 unit after one year, £3.75 is added; during the second year, £1.07 per completed three months; during the third year, £1.35 per completed three months; during the fourth year, £1.71 per completed three months; and during the fifth year, £2.33 per completed three months

Ninth Index-linked Issue
26 January 1996–31 March 1997

Maximum holding: £10,000, plus special facilities to hold up to a further £20,000

Unit cost: certificates may be purchased for any amount, subject to a minimum purchase at any time of £100; reinvestment certificates are available for any amount and are not subject to a minimum purchase requirement

Interest: the repayment value, subject to their being held for one year, is related to the movement of the UK General Index of Retail Prices. In addition, there is a guaranteed extra interest of 1 per cent for the first year, 1.25 per cent for the second year, 2 per cent for the third year, 3 per cent for the fourth year and 5.31 per cent for the fifth year. This is worth 2.5 per cent a year compound over the full five years. Reinvestment certificates repaid before the first anniversary date will earn RPI plus extra interest of 1 per cent a year for each complete month

Forty-fourth Issue
1 April 1997–

Maximum holding: £10,000, plus special facility to reinvest an unlimited amount

Unit cost: certificates may be purchased for any amount, subject to a minimum purchase at any time of £100; reinvestment certificates are available for any amount and are not subject to a minimum or maximum requirement

Interest: after one year the repayment value increases by 3.75 per cent for ordinarily held 44th Issue. However, reinvestment certificates if encashed before the first anniversary earn interest at 3.75 per cent a year for each complete period of three months. On a £100 certificate after one year £3.75 is added; during the second year £1.07 per completed three months; during the third year, £1.35 per completed three months; during the fourth year, £1.74 per completed three months; and during the fifth year, £2.33 per completed three months

Tenth Index-linked Issue
1 April 1997–

Maximum holding: £10,000, plus special facility to reinvest an unlimited amount

Unit cost: certificates may be purchased for any amount, subject to a minimum purchase at any time of £100; reinvestment certificates are available for any amount and are not subject to a minimum or maximum requirement

Interest: the repayment value, subject to their being held for one year, is related to the movement of the UK General Index of Retail Prices. In addition, there is a guaranteed extra interest of 1 per cent for the first year, 1.25 per cent for the second year, 2 per cent for the third year, 3 per cent for the fourth year and 5.31 per cent for the fifth year. This is worth 2.5 per cent a year compound over the full five years. Reinvestment certificates repaid before the first anniversary date will earn RPI plus extra interest of 1 per cent a year for each complete month.

Insurance

AUTHORIZATION

The Insurance Companies Act 1982 empowers the Department of Trade and Industry to authorize corporate bodies to transact insurance in the United Kingdom provided they comply with the financial and other regulations detailed in the Act. At the end of 1996 there were 826 insurance companies with authorization from the DTI to transact one or more classes of insurance business. However, with the establishment of the single European insurance market on 1 July 1994 an insurer authorized in any of the European Union (EU) countries can now transact insurance in the UK without further formality; this creates a potential market of about 5,000 insurance companies.

REGULATION

Under the Financial Services Act 1986, the Securities and Investments Board (SIB) is empowered to make, monitor and enforce rules about the conduct of investment business. Insurance companies offering investment contracts like life insurance, pensions, unit trusts and annuities can either obtain authorization direct from SIB or from one of the self-regulating organizations (SROs). For life insurance the SRO is currently the Personal Investment Authority (PIA) (see page 631). Following the change of government in May 1997, the new Chancellor announced the reform of financial services regulation. The three SROs, including the PIA, will be wound up and their functions passed to an enlarged and enhanced version of the Securities and Investments Board.

Disputes between policy holders and insurers may be referred to the Insurance Ombudsman or, if appropriate, the PIA Ombudsman or the Pensions Ombudsman (see page 631).

ASSOCIATION OF BRITISH INSURERS

Over 90 per cent of the world-wide business of insurance companies is transacted by the 456 members of the Association of British Insurers (ABI) (51 Gresham Street, London EC2V 7HQ), a trade association which represents both life and general insurers. On general insurance (motor, household, holiday, etc.), ABI acts as a regulatory organization for insurance intermediaries who do not qualify to be registered brokers.

INSURANCE BROKERS

The Insurance Brokers Registration Act 1977 empowers the Insurance Brokers Registration Council (IBRC) (63 St Mary Axe, London EC3A 8NB) as the statutory body responsible for the registration of insurance brokers. The Council is responsible for the registration and training of insurance brokers, conduct of business, and discipline, and it lays down rules relating to such matters as accounting practice, staff qualifications, advertising, etc.

It is possible to act as an insurance intermediary without being registered with the IBRC but unregistered intermediaries are forbidden to use the words 'Insurance Broker' as a title.

IBRC Registered Brokers 1996

Registered individuals	16,579
Limited companies registered	2,178
Sole traders and partnerships	1,022
(containing 1,807 partners and directors)	

BALANCE OF PAYMENTS

The insurance industry's contribution to the balance of payments (export of services) in 1995 was £1,900 million of services and £3,400 million of interest profit and dividends, producing total insurance invisible earnings of £5,300 million.

GENERAL INSURANCE

After four years of improving trading results, 1996 proved to be a turning point. The world-wide general insurance trading profit for UK insurers fell in 1996 to £3,047 million. Despite being a significant (29 per cent) fall on 1995, it was still the third best result in the last decade. The reason for the decline was a sharp increase in the loss made on underwriting. The 1995 loss of £0.6 billion grew to £1.9 billion. The biggest factor in this decline was the UK underwriting result where one-year business saw a profit of £304 million in 1995 become an underwriting loss of £775 million in 1996.

In the UK, the motor insurance market has remained very competitive with companies reluctant to increase premiums, as evidenced by the virtually static premium income figure of £5,917 million (£5,930 million in 1995). However, increases in claims costs caused the overall underwriting loss to increase from £80 million to £633 million. As a result insurers are likely to be looking at premium levels again.

Non-motor business remained in profit but the cold weather in the winter of 1995–6 and a continued high level of subsidence claims contributed to a 59 per cent fall in profits to £173 million.

Overseas general business again recorded losses with the worst motor results being in the US market which saw a loss of £12 million rise to £67 million. The USA also recorded the greatest losses (£424 million) on non-motor business because of increased property claims after an exceptional period of storms and hurricanes.

LONDON INSURANCE MARKET

The London Insurance Market is a distinct, separate part of the UK insurance and reinsurance industry. It is the world's leading market for internationally traded insurances and reinsurance, its business comprising mainly overseas non-life large and high-exposure risks. It is based in the City of London with participating insurers having an underwriting room either within the Lloyd's building or situated nearby. Currently there are 140 Lloyd's syndicates, about 120 insurance companies and 40 Marine Protection and Indemnity Clubs active in the market. In 1994 the market had a written gross premium income of £15,100 million.

The trade association for the international insurance and reinsurance companies writing primarily non-marine insurance and all classes of reinsurance business in the London Market is the London International Insurance and Reinsurance Market Association (LIRMA), Lower Ground Floor, London Underwriting Centre, 3 Minster Court, Mincing Lane, London EC3R 7DD.

BRITISH INSURANCE COMPANIES

The following insurance company figures refer to members and certain non-members of the ABI.

CLAIMS STATISTICS (£ million)

	1995	1996
Domestic claims		
Theft	566	551
Fire	209	223
Weather	267	525
Subsidence	326	554
Business interruption	n/a	n/a
Total	1,368	1,853
Commercial claims		
Theft	206	191
Fire	492	494
Weather	94	201
Subsidence	n/a	n/a
Business interruption	175	203
Total	967	1,089

WORLD-WIDE GENERAL BUSINESS TRADING RESULT

	1995 £m	1996 £m
Net written premiums	35,983	35,274
Underwriting profit (loss) for one year account business	(406)	(1,719)
Transfer to profit and loss account for other business		
Marine, Aviation, Transport	(100)	(58)
Other	(118)	(88)
Total underwriting result	(624)	(1,865)
Net investment income	4,926	4,912
Overall trading profit	4,302	3,047
Profit as % of premium income	12.0	8.6

LLOYD'S OF LONDON

Lloyd's of London is an international market for almost all types of insurance. Lloyd's currently earns a gross premium income of around £8,500 million for underwriters each year. Much of this business comes from outside Great Britain and makes a valuable contribution to the balance of payments.

A policy is underwritten at Lloyd's by a mixture of private and corporate members, corporate members having been admitted for the first time in 1992. Specialist underwriters accept insurance risks at Lloyd's on behalf of members (referred to as 'names') grouped in syndicates. There are currently around 180 syndicates of varying sizes, some with over 2,000 names, each managed by an underwriting agent approved by the Council of Lloyd's.

Individual members are still in the majority at Lloyd's with a total of just under 10,000 individuals as opposed to 202 corporate members. However, the market capacity each sector represents is far more equal with individuals representing £5,800 million of capacity and corporate members £4,500 million.

Lloyd's is incorporated by an Act of Parliament (Lloyd's Acts 1971 onwards) and is governed by a council of 18 members. Market management is handled by a Market Board of 16 members (comprising six working members and one external member of the Council, the chief executive officer, four further working members, two external members and two Corporation executives). Regulation is supervised by a Board of 16 members (comprising four nominated members of the Council, five external members of the Council, four working members, two other appointed members and the Director, Regulatory Services).

The Corporation is a non-profit making body chiefly financed by its members' subscriptions. It provides the premises, administrative staff and services enabling Lloyd's underwriting syndicates to conduct their business. It does not, however, assume corporate liability for the risks accepted by its members, who remain responsible to

WORLD-WIDE GENERAL BUSINESS UNDERWRITING RESULT

	1995					1996				
	UK	Other EU	USA	Other	Total	UK	Other EU	USA	Other	Total
Motor										
Premiums: £m	5,930	1,865	1,637	1,725	11,157	5,917	1,813	1,585	1,768	11,083
Profit (loss): £m	80	178	12	99	369	633	170	67	49	919
% of premiums	1.4	9.6	0.7	5.7	3.31	10.7	9.4	4.2	2.8	8.29
Non-motor										
Premiums: £m	12,238	2,435	2,292	2,152	19,117	12,655	2,445	2,003	2,167	19,270
Profit (loss): £m	421	108	281	91	59	173	99	424	161	511
% of premiums	3.4	4.4	12.2	4.2	0.31	1.4	4.1	21.2	7.4	2.65

NET PREMIUM INCOME BY TERRITORY 1996

	UK £m	Other EU £m	USA £m	Other £m	Total £m
Motor	5,917	1,813	1,585	1,768	11,083
Non-motor	12,655	2,445	2,003	2,167	19,271
Marine, Aviation and Transport	1,330	225	257	188	1,999
Non-MAT reinsurance	1,503	679	11	200	2,393
Other funded business	514	8	0	5	527
Total general business	21,919	5,169	3,856	4,329	35,274
Ordinary long-term	51,509	5,710	3,829	4,162	65,210
Industrial long-term	1,145				1,145
Total long-term business	52,654	5,710	3,829	4,162	66,355

the full extent of their personal means for their under-writing affairs.

Lloyd's syndicates have no direct contact with the public. All business is transacted through insurance brokers accredited by the Corporation of Lloyd's. In addition, non-Lloyd's brokers in the United Kingdom, when guaranteed by Lloyd's brokers, are able to deal directly with Lloyd's motor syndicates, a facility which has made the Lloyd's market more accessible to the insuring public.

Lloyd's also provides the most comprehensive shipping intelligence service in the world. The shipping and other information received from Lloyd's agents, shipowners, news agencies and other sources throughout the world is collated and distributed to the media as well as to the maritime and commercial sectors in general. *Lloyd's List* is London's oldest daily newspaper and contains news of general commercial interest as well as shipping information. *Lloyd's Shipping Index*, also published daily, lists some 25,000 ocean-going vessels in alphabetical order and gives the latest known report of each.

DEVELOPMENTS IN 1996

After a year when pundits and the press predicted every-thing from a severely depleted market to total collapse, the £1,000 million profit for the 1994 year of account provided some welcome news for Lloyd's. However, the pressure on premium rates means that these profit figures are likely to reduce considerably in 1995 and 1996.

The future of the market was all but assured in 1996 by Lloyd's rescue and renewal plan which included a £3,200 million settlement offer to names who had suffered during the lean years. Not all names have accepted the package and some legal actions remain outstanding but the rescue plan is seen as a success. For those names who have accepted the offer, payments have begun to be made.

In addition to the cash settlement, the rescue plan also enabled names to opt to move away from the unlimited liability policy which had been compulsory in the market since it was formed. It is this requirement which has been the cause of hardship for some names. Corporate member-ship is now also possible.

Regulation of the market is also likely to face a shake-up, as it is suggested that the new all-embracing regulator proposed by the Government could include Lloyd's within its remit.

History was made during the year with the introduction of the first female active underwriter.

Chairman, Sir David Rowland
Chief Executive, R. Sandler

LLOYD'S MEMBERSHIP

	1994	1995	1996
Total no. of underwriting members participating			
Individuals	17,526	14,744	12,798
Corporate	95	140	162

TOTAL MARKET CAPACITY

	1994 £m	1995 £m	1996 £m
Individual	9,289	7,835	6,985
Corporate	1,609	2,360	3,009
Total	10,898	10,195	9,994

LLOYD'S GLOBAL ACCOUNTS
as at 31 December 1996

	1993 and prior years of account £m	1994 pure year result £m
Gross premiums written (net of brokerage)	8,492	7,657
Outward reinsurance premiums	2,575	1,969
Net premiums	5,917	5,688
Reinsurance to close premiums received from earlier years of account	3,551	1,385
Amounts retained to meet all known and unknown outstanding liabilities brought forward	9,992	223
	19,460	7,296
Gross claims paid	8,802	3,667
Reinsurers' share	3,350	847
Net claims	5,452	2,820
Reinsurance premiums paid to close the year of account into Equitas	11,626	—
Other reinsurance premiums paid to close the year of account	1,474	2,558
Amounts retained to meet all known and unknown outstanding liabilities carried forward	238	256
	18,790	5,634
Underwriting result	670	1,662
Other profit (loss) on exchange	(12)	14
Syndicate operating expenses	(712)	(426)
Balance on technical account	(54)	1,250
Investment income	848	515
Investment expenses and charges	(13)	(10)
Investment gains less losses	110	(6)
Result before personal expenses	891	1,749
Personal expenses	(666)	(654)
Result after personal expenses	225	1,095

LLOYD'S RESULTS 1994

	Marine 1993 £m	Marine 1994 £m	Non-marine 1993 £m	Non-marine 1994 £m	Aviation 1993 £m	Aviation 1994 £m	Motor 1993 £m	Motor 1994 £m
Net premiums	1,400	1,293	3,047	2,926	457	498	988	973
Pure year result	526	565	881	837	138	138	175	117

LIFE INSURANCE AND PENSIONS

After a drop in 1995, the increased demand for life insurance and pension products in 1996 mirrored the rising consumer confidence in the UK economy. Total world-wide long-term premium income rose by 18 per cent to £66,400 million with premiums increasing by 17 per cent. Single premium life business fared even better with premium income up by 37 per cent. Sales of pensions rose by 16 per cent to £25,600 million, with single premium pensions up 29 per cent to £15,300 million.

REVIEW OF PENSIONS SELLING

Throughout 1996 the review of the selling of personal pensions has continued. The pensions concerned were contracts sold in the late 1980s and early 1990s to up to 1,500,000 people who were advised to opt out of company pension schemes and take out a personal pension plan. The pensions industry has been instructed by its regulators to review each case to check that the advice was correct.

Progress has been slow. Half a million cases have been identified as needing compensation but less than 15,000 have been settled. The pensions industry claims much of the delay has been caused by problems in obtaining the necessary information from company pension schemes but the incoming Labour Government is unimpressed by this argument and has promised to 'get tough' on pension providers who cause unnecessary delay.

PREMIUM INCOME FOR WORLD-WIDE LONG-TERM INSURANCE BUSINESS

	1995 £m	1996 £m
Ordinary Branch		
Business written in UK		
Annual premiums		
Life	11,728	11,961
Annuities	49	51
Pensions	10,144	10,302
Single premiums		
Life	9,056	12,415
Annuities	331	797
Pensions	11,929	15,347
PHI	531	635
Business written overseas		
Annual premiums	5,539	5,485
Single premiums	5,774	8,216
Industrial Business	1,217	1,145
Total	56,298	66,355

PAYMENTS TO POLICYHOLDERS

	1995 £m	1996 £m
Payments to UK policyholders	31,300	39,800
Payments to overseas policyholders	8,400	8,900
Total	39,700	48,700

INVESTMENTS OF INSURANCE COMPANIES 1996

Investment of funds	Long-term business £m	General business £m
Index-linked British Government securities	11,027	1,303
Non-index-linked British Government securities	79,799	13,565
Other UK public sector debt securities	2,355	326
Overseas government, provincial and municipal securities	24,639	14,617
Debentures, loan shares, preference and guaranteed stocks and shares		
UK	37,901	5,981
Overseas	28,064	3,925
Ordinary stocks and shares		
UK	225,983	13,487
Overseas	61,571	7,937
Unit trusts		
Equities	47,014	421
Fixed interest	3,850	25
Loans secured on property	13,254	2,134
Real property and ground rents	39,054	4,333
Other invested assets	34,782	11,643
Total invested assets	609,293	79,699
Net current assets	3,626	9,819
Total	612,918	89,518
Net investment income	34,139	4,912

INDIVIDUAL PENSIONS: NEW BUSINESS 1995–6

	Annual premium policies		Single premium policies	
	No. new policies	New premiums £m	No. new policies	New premiums £m
1995				
1st quarter	211,000	209	70,000	596
2nd quarter	234,000	251	96,000	695
3rd quarter	196,000	212	63,000	565
4th quarter	190,000	232	71,000	632
1996				
1st quarter	210,000	246	71,000	730
2nd quarter	238,000	300	96,000	1,022
3rd quarter	203,000	257	67,000	701
4th quarter	213,000	279	63,000	746

DIRECTORY OF INSURANCE COMPANIES

Classes of insurance undertaken
G   General
L   Life
M   Marine
Re   Reinsurance

Group membership
(CU)   Commercial Union
(ES)   Eagle Star
(GA)   General Accident
(GRE) Guardian Royal Exchange
(NU)   Norwich Union
(RSA) Royal and Sun Alliance

Nature of business	*Name of company*	*Head Office address*
GLM Re	AGF	41 Botolph Lane, London EC3R 8DL
L	AIG Life (UK)	Alico House, 22 Addiscombe Road, Croydon CR9 5AZ
GM Re	Albion	9–13 Fenchurch Buildings, London EC3M 5HR
L	Alico	Alico House, 22 Addiscombe Road, Croydon CR9 5AZ
GLM	Alliance Assurance (RSA)	1 Bartholomew Lane, London EC2N 2AB
L	Allied Dunbar	Allied Dunbar Centre, Swindon SN1 1EL
G	Ansvar	31 St Leonards Road, Eastbourne BN21 3UR
GM	Atlas (GRE)	Royal Exchange, London EC3V 3LS
L	Australian Mutual Provident	100 Temple Street, Bristol BS1 6EA
L	Axa Equity and Law	Amersham Road, High Wycombe HP13 5AL
G	Baptist	1 Merchant Street, London E3 4LY
L	Barclays Life	94 St Paul's Churchyard, London EC4M 8EH
GLM Re	Black Sea and Baltic	65 Fenchurch Street, London EC3M 4EV
M	Bradford (RSA)	Bowling Mill, Dean Clough, Halifax HX3 5WA
L	Britannia Life	Britannia Court, 50 Bothwell Street, Glasgow G2 6HR
GL	Britannic	Moor Green, Moseley, Birmingham B13 8QF
M	British & Foreign Marine (RSA)	New Hall Place, Liverpool
Engineering	British Engine (RSA)	Longridge House, Manchester M60 4DT
GLM	British Equitable (GRE)	Royal Exchange, London EC3V 3LS
L	British Life Office	Reliance House, Mount Ephraim, Tunbridge Wells, Kent TN4 8BL
G	British Oak (GRE)	Royal Exchange, London EC3V 3LS
L	Caledonian (GRE)	Royal Exchange, London EC3V 3LS
GM	Cambrian (GRE)	Royal Exchange, London EC3V 3LS
L	Canada Life	Canada Life House, Potters Bar, Herts EN6 5BA
GM	Car & General (GRE)	Royal Exchange, London EC3V 3LS
L	Century Life	Century House, 5 Old Bailey, London EC4M 7BA
GL	Cigna	PO Box 42, Greenock, Renfrewshire PA15 1AB
L	Citibank Life	21–23 Perrymount Road, Haywards Heath, W. Sussex RH16 3TP
L	Clerical, Medical Group	Narrow Plain, Bristol BS2 0JH
L	Colonial Mutual	Colonial Mutual House, Chatham Maritime, Kent ME14 4YY
GLM Re	Commercial Union	St Helen's, 1 Undershaft, London EC3P 3DQ
L	Commercial Union Life	St Helen's, 1 Undershaft, London EC3P 3DQ
L	Confederation Life	Lytton Way, Stevenage, Herts SG1 2NN
G	Congregational and General	Currer House, Currer Street, Bradford BD1 5BA
GLM Re	Co-operative	Miller Street, Manchester M60 0AL
GLM Re	Cornhill	57 Ladymead, Guildford GU1 1DB
L	Crown Financial Management	Crown House, Crown Square, Woking GU21 1XW
GL	Direct Line Insurance	3 Edridge Road, Croydon CR9 1AG
GM	Dominion	52–54 Leadenhall Street, London EC3A 2AQ
GLM Re	Eagle Star (ES)	60 St Mary Axe, London EC3A 8JQ
GL Re	Ecclesiastical	Beaufort House, Brunswick Road, Gloucester GL1 1JZ
G	Equine and Livestock	PO Box 100, York YO5 9SZ
L	Equitable Life	Walton Street, Aylesbury HP21 7QW
G	Federation General	PO Box 196, Redhill, Surrey RH1 1FG
L	Friends' Provident	United Kingdom House, Castle Street, Salisbury SP1 3SH
GM Re	Gan	Gan House, 12 Arthur Street, London EC4R 9BT
GM Re	General Accident	Pitheavlis, Perth, Scotland PH2 0NH
L	General Accident Life	2 Rougier Street, York YO1 1HR
G	Gresham Fire & Accident	11 Queen Victoria Street, London EC4N 4XP
GM	Guarantee Society (GA)	42–47 Minories, London EC3N 1BX
L	Guardian Insurance (GRE)	Civic Drive, Ipswich IP1 2AN
GLM Re	Guardian Royal Exchange	Civic Drive, Ipswich IP1 2AN
GLM Re	Hibernian	Haddington Road, Dublin 4
L	Hill Samuel Life	NLA Tower, Addiscombe Road, Croydon CR9 2DR
G	Hiscox Insurance Co.	52 Leadenhall Street, London EC3A 2BJ

Nature of business	Name of company	Head Office address
GL	Ideal	Pitmaston, Moseley, Birmingham B13 8NG
L	Irish Life	Irish Life Centre, Victoria Street, St Albans AL1 5TS
GF	Iron Trades	Iron Trades House, 21–24 Grosvenor Place, London SW1X 7JA
GLM Re	Legal and General	Temple Court, 11 Queen Victoria Street, London EC4N 4TP
L	Liberty Life	Liberty House, Station Road, New Barnet EN5 1PA
GF	Licenses & General (GRE)	Royal Exchange, London EC3V 3LS
L	Lincoln	The Quays, 101–105 Oxford Road, Uxbridge, UB8 1LZ
GM	Liverpool Marine & General (RSA)	1 Bartholomew Lane, London EC2N 2AB
GL	Liverpool Victoria Friendly	Victoria House, 135 Poole Road, Bournemouth, Dorset BH4 9BG
GM	Local Government Guarantee (GRE)	Royal Exchange, London EC3V 3LS
GM Re	Lombard General	Lombard House, 182 High Street, Tonbridge TN9 1BY
GM	London & Edinburgh	The Warren, Worthing, W. Sussex BN14 9QD
L	London & Manchester	Winslade Park, Exeter, Devon EX5 1DS
L	M & G Assurance	Three Quays, Tower Hill, London EC3R 6BQ
L	Manulife	St George's Way, Stevenage SG1 1HP
M	Marine (RSA)	34–36 Lime Street, London EC3M 7JE
M Re	Maritime (NU)	Surrey Street, Norwich NR1 3NS
L	Medical, Sickness, Annuity and Life	Pynes Hill House, Rydon Lane, Exeter EX2 5SP
Re	Mercantile & General	Moorfields House, Moorfields, London EC4R 9BJ
L	Merchant Investors (MI Group)	St Bartholomew's House, Lewins Mead, Bristol BS1 2NH
GF	Methodist	Brazennose House, Brazennose Street, Manchester M2 5AS
L	MGM Assurance	MGM House, Heene Road, Worthing BN11 2DY
G	Motor Union (GRE)	Royal Exchange, London EC3V 3LS
L	NPI	NPI House, Tunbridge Wells, Kent TN1 2UE
GL	Nalgo Insurance Association	137 Euston Road, London NW1 2AU
L	National Mutual Life	The Priory, Hitchin, Herts SG5 2DW
Engineering	National Vulcan Eng. Ins. Group (RSA)	St Mary's Parsonage, Manchester M60 9AP
GM	Navigators & General (ES)	Lanchester House, Trafalgar Place, Trafalgar Street, Brighton BN1 4DA
GL Re	NFU Avon	Tiddington Road, Stratford-upon-Avon CV37 7BJ
G	NIG Skandia	Crown House, 145 City Road, London EC1V 1LP
L	NM Financial Management	Enterprise House, Isambard Brunel Road, Portsmouth PO1 2AW
GM	Norwich Union Fire	PO Box 6, Surrey Street, Norwich NR1 3NS
L	Norwich Union Life	PO Box 4, Surrey Street, Norwich NR1 3NG
GLM Re	Pearl	The Pearl Centre, Lynchwood, Peterborough PE2 6FY
GL Sickness	Permanent	Pynes Hill House, Pynes Hill, Rydon Lane, Exeter EX2 5SP
GLM	Phoenix (RSA)	1 Bartholomew Lane, London EC2N 2AB
L	Property Growth	Phoenix House, Redcliff Hill, Bristol BS1 6SX
L	Provident Mutual Life	Six Hills Way, Stevenage, Herts SG1 2ST
F	Provincial	Stramongate, Kendal, Cumbria LA9 4BE
GLM Re	Prudential	142 Holborn Bars, London EC1N 2NH
GL	Refuge	Refuge House, Alderley Road, Wilmslow, Cheshire SK9 1PF
GM	Reliance Marine (GRE)	Royal Exchange, London EC3V 3LS
L	Reliance Mutual	Reliance House, Mount Ephraim, Tunbridge Wells, Kent TN4 8BL
G	Road Transport & General (GA)	Pitheavlis, Perth PH2 0NH
G	Royal Exchange	Royal Exchange, London EC3V 3LS
L	Royal Heritage Life	Royal Insurance House, Business Park, Peterborough PE2 6GG
GL Re M	Royal and Sun Alliance	1 Cornhill, London EC3V 3QR
L	Royal Liver	Royal Liver Building, Pier Head, Liverpool L3 1HT
GL	Royal London	Royal London House, Middleborough, Colchester CO1 1RA
L	Royal National Pension Fund for Nurses	Burdett House, 15 Buckingham Street, Strand, London WC2N 6ED
F	Salvation Army	117–121 Judd Street, London WC1H 9NN
L	Save & Prosper	1 Finsbury Avenue, London EC2M 2QY
L	Scottish Amicable	Craigforth, PO Box 25, Stirling FK9 4UE
Engineering	Scottish Boiler (GA)	PO Box 131, 825 Wilmslow Road, Didsbury, Manchester M20 8GS
L	Scottish Equitable	Edinburgh Park, Edinburgh EH12 9SE
L	Scottish Friendly	16 Blythswood Square, Glasgow G2 6HJ
M	Scottish General (GA)	PO Box 896, 103 Westerhill Road, Bishopbriggs, Glasgow G64 2QX
L	Scottish Legal Life	95 Bothwell Street, Glasgow G2 7HY
L	Scottish Life	19 St Andrew Square, Edinburgh EH2 1YE
L	Scottish Mutual	109 St Vincent Street, Glasgow G2 5HN
L	Scottish Provident Institution	6 St Andrew Square, Edinburgh EH2 2YA

Nature of business	Name of company	Head Office address
GLM	Scottish Union & National (NU)	Surrey Street, Norwich NR1 3NS
L	Scottish Widows'	15 Dalkeith Road, Edinburgh EH16 5BU
GM	Sea (RSA)	1 Bartholomew Lane, London EC2N 2AB
L	Stalwart Assurance	Stalwart House, 142 South Street, Dorking RH4 2EV
L	Standard Life	30 Lothian Road, Edinburgh EH1 2DH
GM	State Assurance (GRE)	Royal Exchange, London EC3V 3LS
GLM	Sun Alliance (RSA)	1 Bartholomew Lane, London EC2N 2AB
GM	Sun Insurance Office (RSA)	1 Bartholomew Lane, London EC2N 2AB
L	Sun Life Assurance	Sun Life Centre, PO Box 1810, Bristol BS99 5SN
L Re	Sun Life of Canada	Basing View, Basingstoke, Hants RG21 2DZ
L	Swiss Life	Swiss Life House, South Park, Sevenoaks TN13 1BG
GL	Teacher's Assurance	Tringham House, Wessex Fields, Deansleigh Road, Bournemouth BH7 7DT
L	Tunstall Assurance	Station Chambers, Tunstall, Stoke-on-Trent ST6 6DU
G Re	UAP Provincial Insurance	Stramongate, Kendal, Cumbria LA9 4BE
M	Ulster Marine (GA)	Pitheavlis, Perth PH2 0NH
L	UIA Insurance Ltd	Kings Court, London Road, Stevenage SG1 2TP
GM	Union Insurance Society of Canton (GRE)	Royal Exchange, London EC3V 3LS
GL	United Friendly	42 Southwark Bridge Road, London SE1 9HE
GL Re	Wesleyan Assurance	Colmore Circus, Birmingham B4 6AR
L	Winterthur Life	Winterthur Way, Basingstoke RG21 6SZ
L	Windsor Life	Windsor House, Telford TF3 4NB
GM Re	Zurich	Zurich House, Stanhope Road, Portsmouth PO1 1DU
L	Zurich Life	Hippodrome House, 11 Guildhall Walk, Portsmouth PO1 2RL

The London Stock Exchange

The London Stock Exchange Ltd serves the needs of government, industry and investors by providing facilities for raising capital and a central market-place for securities trading. This market-place covers government stocks (called gilts), UK and overseas company shares (called equities and fixed interest stocks), and traditional options.

PRIMARY MARKETS

The Exchange enables companies to raise capital for development and growth through the issue of securities. For a company entering the market for the first time there is a choice of Exchange markets, depending upon the size, history and requirements of the company. The first is the Official List, which exists for well-established companies, which must comply with stringent criteria relating to all aspects of their operations. At present, companies coming to this market require a minimum market capitalization of £700,000 and a three-year trading record with a minimum of 25 per cent of the shares held in public hands. The Alternative Investment Market (AIM) began trading in June 1995. It enables small, young and growing companies to raise capital, widen their investor base and have their shares traded on a regulated market without the expense of a full Exchange listing.

Once admitted to the Exchange, all companies are obliged to keep their shareholders informed of their progress, making announcements of a price-sensitive nature through the Exchange's company announcements department.

At the end of 1996 there were 2,423 UK companies listed on the London Stock Exchange; their equity capital had a total market value of £1,016,971 million. Also, 533 foreign companies were listed, with a total equity market value of £2,388,349.2 million. By the end of 1996 the Alternative Investment Market had attracted 252 companies, with a total capitalization of over £5,000 million.

UK equity turnover in 1996 was £741,619.1 million, with an average 43,159 bargains and £2,919 million value a day. Foreign equity turnover averaged 18,087 bargains and £4,091 million value a day. The fastest growing company sectors in 1996 included South Africa (£11,000 million), Thailand (£8,000 million), Malaysia (£7,300 million) and India (£6,500 million).

BIG BANG

During 1986 the London Stock Exchange went through the greatest period of change in its 200-year history. In March 1986 it opened its doors for the first time to overseas and corporate membership of the Exchange, allowing banks, insurance companies and overseas securities houses to become members of the Exchange and to buy existing member firms. On 27 October 1986, three major reforms took place, changes which became known as 'Big Bang':

- the abolition of scales of minimum commissions, allowing clients to negotiate freely with their brokers about the charge for their services
- the abolition of the separation of member firms into brokers and jobbers: firms are now broker/dealers, able to act as agents on behalf of clients; to act as principals buying and selling shares for their own account; and to become registered market makers, making continuous buying and selling prices in specific securities
- the introduction of the Stock Exchange automated quotations (SEAQ) system

Of all these changes, the implementation of SEAQ has had the most visible effect. Dealing in stocks and shares now takes place via the telephone in the firms' own dealing rooms, rather than face to face on the floor of the Exchange. The new systems also provide increased investor protection. All deals taking place via the Exchange's SEAQ system are recorded on a database which can be used to resolve disputes or to carry out investigations.

Members of the London Stock Exchange buy and sell shares on behalf of the public, as well as institutions such as pension funds or insurance companies. In return for transacting the deal, the broker will charge a commission, which is usually based upon the value of the transaction. The market makers, or wholesalers, in each security do not charge a commission for their services, but will quote the broker two prices, a price at which they will buy and a price at which they will sell. It is the middle of these two prices which is published in lists of Stock Exchange prices in newspapers.

REGULATORY BODIES

The London Stock Exchange Ltd and the Securities and Futures Authority are the two regulatory bodies (*see* page 630). They were formed under the provisions of the Financial Services Act 1986, which requires investment businesses to be authorized and regulated by a self-regulating organization (SRO), of which the Securities and Futures Authority is one. The Act also requires business to be conducted through a recognized investment exchange (RIE). The London Stock Exchange is an RIE, regulating three main markets: UK equities, international equities and gilts.

THE GOVERNING BOARD

The London Stock Exchange has its headquarters in London, and representative offices around the UK. At present there are about 318 member firms.

The governing board is responsible for overall policy and the strategic direction of the Exchange. The board consists of representatives drawn from listed companies, investors and other major users, elected at the annual general meeting, and the Government Broker, the Chief Executive and up to five senior executives of the Stock Exchange.

LONDON STOCK EXCHANGE, Old Broad Street, London
    EC2N 1HP. Tel: 0171-797 1000
Chairman, J. Kemp-Welch
Chief Executive, G. Casey
Government Broker, I. Plenderleith (*Deputy Chairman*)
Other Board members, G. Allen, CBE; G. Allen; R. Barfield;
    J. Bond; D. Brydon, OBE; S. Cooke; Ms C. Dann;
    M. Kaneko; R. Kilsby; M. Marks; R. Metzler;
    M. Radcliffe; I. Salter; N. Sherlock; B. Solomons;
    G. Vardey; N. Verey; Ms F. Wicker-Miurin

Investor Protection

The present supervisory framework of Britain's financial services industry was established under the Financial Services Act 1986 which came into force in 1988. Since that date, it has been a criminal offence to conduct investment business without authorization, unless specifically exempt from the authorization requirement.

The Securities and Investments Board (SIB) is the designated agency under the Financial Services Act 1986 for regulating the activities of investment businesses in the UK. Although not a statutory body, the SIB has statutory powers under the Act to recognize self-regulating organizations, professional bodies, investment exchanges and clearing houses, and directly to authorize firms to undertake investment business in the UK.

The SIB oversees the regulation of all investment business in the UK. It is not responsible for areas involving public issues, takeovers and mergers, and insider dealing investigation. Its area of authority currently overlaps with that of the Bank of England, the Department of Trade and Industry (for insurance companies) and the Building Societies Commission where their respective member bodies are carrying out investment business.

The Government announced in May 1997 plans to make supervision and regulation of retail banking, building societies, financial services companies and markets the direct responsibility of an enhanced Securities and Investments Board. The single regulatory framework is expected to come into effect in 1999 or 2000, following legislation in 1998–9.

The regulatory sanctions of the SIB are as follows:

1 It may issue public or private reprimands
2 It may restrict business
3 It may suspend authorization
4 It may withdraw authorization
5 In certain cases it may take out a civil injunction
6 It may petition the courts for the winding up of companies
7 It may ban persons from the industry for life

CENTRAL REGISTER

The SIB maintains the Central Register of all firms who are authorized to carry on investment business. The entry for each firm gives its name, address and telephone number; an SIB reference number; its authorization status; its appropriate regulatory body; and whether it can handle client money.

INVESTORS COMPENSATION SCHEME

The Investors Compensation Scheme, run by a management company as part of the overall investor protection offered by the SIB, comes into play when authorized firms become insolvent owing money to private investors. It is funded by means of a levy on all member firms, according to their size and category. The maximum compensation that the scheme can pay to an investor is £48,000.

SECURITIES AND INVESTMENTS BOARD LTD, Gavrelle House, 2–14 Bunhill Row, London EC1Y 8RA. Tel: 0171-638 1240. *Chairman*, H. Davies; *Chief Executive*, A. Winckler
CENTRAL REGISTER CHECKLINE: 0171-929 3652

SELF-REGULATING ORGANIZATIONS

The SIB recognizes self-regulating organizations (SROs), which are responsible to the SIB for ensuring financial supervision in their respective sectors of investment business. Most members of the financial services industry obtain their authorization by being members of an SRO.

The following are recognized by the SIB as being able to provide proper regulation of the investment business carried out by their members, and the necessary standard of investor protection:

IMRO (Investment Management Regulatory Organization), 5th Floor, Lloyd's Chambers, Portsoken Street, London E1 8BT. Tel: 0171-390 5000
*PIA (Personal Investment Authority), 1 Canada Square, Canary Wharf, London E14 5AZ. Tel: 0171-538 8860
SFA (Securities and Futures Authority Ltd), Cottons Centre, Cottons Lane, London SE1 2QB. Tel: 0171-378 9000
* PIA also regulates the activities of friendly societies

RECOGNIZED PROFESSIONAL BODIES

The SIB is empowered to recognize professional bodies (RPBs) who, as a result, can authorize their members for investment business. Such business must not form the whole or main part of the total business undertaken by the firm.

INSTITUTE OF CHARTERED ACCOUNTANTS IN ENGLAND AND WALES, Chartered Accountants' Hall, PO Box 433, Moorgate Place, London EC2P 2BJ. Tel: 0171-920 8100
INSTITUTE OF CHARTERED ACCOUNTANTS OF SCOTLAND, 27 Queen Street, Edinburgh EH2 1LA. Tel: 0131-225 5673
THE ULSTER SOCIETY OF THE INSTITUTE OF CHARTERED ACCOUNTANTS IN IRELAND, 11 Donegall Square South, Belfast BT1 5JE. Tel: 01232-321600
ASSOCIATION OF CHARTERED CERTIFIED ACCOUNTANTS, 29 Lincoln's Inn Fields, London WC2A 3EE. Tel: 0171-242 6855
INSTITUTE OF ACTUARIES, Staple Inn Hall, High Holborn, London WC1V 7QJ. Tel: 0171-242 0106
INSURANCE BROKERS REGISTRATION COUNCIL, 63 St Mary Axe, London EC3A 8MB. Tel: 0171-621 1061
THE LAW SOCIETY, 113 Chancery Lane, London WC2A 1PL. Tel: 0171-242 1222
LAW SOCIETY OF SCOTLAND, Law Society's Hall, 26 Drumsheugh Gardens, Edinburgh EH3 7YR. Tel: 0131-226 7411
LAW SOCIETY OF NORTHERN IRELAND, Law Society House, 98 Victoria Street, Belfast BT1 3JZ. Tel: 01232-231614

RECOGNIZED INVESTMENT EXCHANGES

Investment exchanges are exempt from needing authorization from the SIB as an investment business. However, to be a recognized investment exchange (RIE), each must fulfil the following requirements: adequate financial resources; proper conduct of business rules; a proper market in its products; procedures for recording transactions; effective monitoring and enforcement of rules; proper arrangements for the clearing and performance of contracts.

INTERNATIONAL PETROLEUM EXCHANGE (IPE), International House, 1 St Katharine's Way, London E1 9UN. Tel: 0171-481 0643
LONDON STOCK EXCHANGE (LSE), Old Broad Street, London EC2N 1HP. Tel: 0171-797 1000

LONDON COMMODITY EXCHANGE LTD, 1 Commodity Quay, St Katharine Dock, London EI 9AX. Tel: 0171-481 2080

LONDON INTERNATIONAL FINANCIAL FUTURES AND OPTIONS EXCHANGE (LIFFE), Cannon Bridge, London EC4R 3XX. Tel: 0171-623 0444

LONDON METAL EXCHANGE LTD (LME), 56 Leadenhall Street, London EC3A 2BJ. Tel: 0171-264 5555

THE LONDON SECURITIES AND DERIVATIVES EXCHANGE LTD (OMLX), Milestone House, 107 Cannon Street, London EC4N 5AD. Tel: 0171-283 0678

TRADEPOINT FINANCIAL NETWORKS PLC, 35 King Street, London WC2E 8JD. Tel: 0171-240 8000

The following overseas exchanges are recognized by the Treasury as offering adequate investor protection:

CHICAGO BOARD OF TRADE (CBOT), European Office, 52–54 Gracechurch Street, London EC3V OEH. Tel: 0171-929 0021

CHICAGO MERCANTILE EXCHANGE (CME), Pinnacle House, 23–26 St Dunstan's Hill, London EC3R 8HL. Tel: 0171-623 2550

DELTA GOVERNMENT OPTIONS CORPORATION, c/o Sullivan and Cromwell, 125 Broad Street, New York 10004-2498, USA. Tel: 00-1-212-558 4675

NATIONAL ASSOCIATION OF SECURITIES DEALERS AUTOMATED QUOTATIONS (NASDAQ), 43 London Wall, London EC2M 5TB. Tel: 0171-374 6969

NEW YORK MERCANTILE EXCHANGE (NYMEX), 35 Piccadilly, London W1V 9PB. Tel: 0171-734 1280

SYDNEY FUTURES EXCHANGE LTD, 30–32 Grosvenor Street, Sydney, NSW 2000, Australia. Tel: 00-612-256 0555

Following the implementation of the EC Investment Services Directive, recognition by the UK authorities is no longer required by exchanges within the European Economic Area (with certain exceptions).

RECOGNIZED CLEARING HOUSES

A recognized clearing house (RCH) must satisfy the same kind of criteria to obtain recognition as the RIEs. There is one RCH which acts as a clearing house for some of the above RIEs:

LONDON CLEARING HOUSE LTD (LCH), Roman Wall House, 1–2 Crutched Friars, London EC3N 2AN. Tel: 0171-265 2000

DESIGNATED INVESTMENT EXCHANGES

The SIB has drawn up a list of 51 overseas exchanges (known as DIEs) whose operations are set in a regulatory context which provides investor protection equivalent to that available from RIEs. Designation does not allow an overseas investment exchange to do business in the UK and, while showing that an exchange meets certain basic criteria, it carries no guarantee for the investor.

OMBUDSMAN SCHEMES

Independent ombudsman schemes have been set up for banks, building societies, insurance companies, financial institutions and independent financial advisers. They provide an independent and impartial method of resolving disputes that arise between a company and a customer. In most ombudsman schemes there is a council which appoints and supervises the Ombudsman. The Ombudsman Council is composed of people representing public and consumer interests and member companies. The schemes are funded in various ways: annual subscription from member companies, a levy on member companies according to the size of their assets, a charge for each complaint handled against a particular company, or a combination of these.

The Investment Ombudsman is responsible for resolving disputes that arise between a customer and a company regulated by IMRO. The Personal Investment Authority (PIA) Ombudsman is primarily responsible for resolving complaints against PIA members about personal investments.

The Pensions Ombudsman is appointed and operates under the Pension Schemes Act 1993 as amended by the Pensions Act 1995; he is responsible to Parliament. He investigates and decides complaints and disputes concerning occupational pension schemes, primarily alleged maladministration by the persons responsible for managing an occupational pension scheme. Personal pension complaints are normally dealt with only if outside the jurisdiction of the Personal Investment Authority.

THE OFFICE OF THE BANKING OMBUDSMAN, 70 Gray's Inn Road, London WC1X 8NB. Tel: 0171-404 9944. *Banking Ombudsman,* D. Thomas

THE OFFICE OF THE BUILDING SOCIETIES OMBUDSMAN, Millbank Tower, Millbank, London SW1P 4XS. Tel: 0171-931 0044. *Building Societies Ombudsman,* B. Murphy

THE INSURANCE OMBUDSMAN BUREAU, City Gate One, 135 Park Street, London SE1 9EA. Tel: 0171-928 4488. *Insurance Ombudsman,* W. Merricks

THE OFFICE OF THE INVESTMENT OMBUDSMAN, 6 Frederick's Place, London EC2R 8BT. Tel: 0171-796 3065. *Investment Ombudsman,* P. Dean, CBE

THE PENSIONS OMBUDSMAN, 6th Floor, 11 Belgrave Road, London SW1V 1RB. Tel: 0171-834 9144. *Pensions Ombudsman,* Dr J T Farrand

THE PIA OMBUDSMAN BUREAU, Hertsmere House, Hertsmere Road, London E14 4AB. Tel: 0171-216 0016. *Principal Ombudsman,* A. J. Holland; *Ombudsmen,* R. Prior; M. Thomas

THE TAKEOVER PANEL

The Takeover Panel was set up in 1968 in response to concern about practices unfair to shareholders in take-over bids for public and certain private companies. Its principal objective is to ensure equality of treatment, and fair opportunity for all shareholders to consider on its merits an offer that would result in the change of control of a company. It is a non-statutory body that operates the City code on take-overs and mergers.

The chairman, deputy chairmen and three lay members of the panel are appointed by the Bank of England. The remainder are representatives of the banking, insurance, investment, pension fund and accountancy professional bodies, the CBI, IMRO and the Stock Exchange.

THE TAKEOVER PANEL, PO Box 226, The Stock Exchange Building, London, EC2P 2JX. Tel: 0171-382 9026. *Chairman,* Sir David Calcutt, QC

Stamp Duties

Stamp duty is a tax on documents. There are a number of separate duties, under different heads of charge.

A stampable instrument may, subject to exceptions, be stamped without penalty if presented for stamping within 30 days after its date of first execution. Where wholly executed abroad, the period begins to run from the date of arrival in the UK.

Instruments presented after the proper time (subject in special provisions in some cases and subject to the Commissioner's power to mitigate) are subject to a penalty equal to the unpaid duty (and interest thereon if duty exceeds £10) plus £10.

AGREEMENT FOR LEASE, *see* LEASES

AGREEMENT FOR SALE OF PROPERTY

Charged with *ad valorem* duty as if an actual conveyance on sale, with certain exceptions, e.g. agreements for the sale of land, stocks and shares, goods, wares or merchandise, or a ship (*see* S. 59 (1), Stamp Act 1891). If *ad valorem* duty is paid on an agreement in accordance with this provision, the subsequent conveyance or transfer is not chargeable with any *ad valorem* duty and the Commissioners will upon application either place a denoting stamp on such conveyance or transfer or will transfer the *ad valorem* duty thereto. Further, if such an agreement is rescinded, not performed, etc., the Commissioners will return the *ad valorem* duty paid.

ASSIGNMENT

By way of sale, *see* CONVEYANCE
By way of gift, *see* VOLUNTARY DISPOSITION

BEARER INSTRUMENT

Inland bearer instrument, i.e. share warrant, stock certificate to bearer or any other instrument to bearer by which stock can be transferred, issued by a company or body formed or established in the UK, 1.5 per cent

Overseas bearer instrument, i.e. such an instrument issued in Great Britain by a company formed out of the UK, 1.5 per cent

BILL OF SALE, ABSOLUTE, *see* CONVEYANCE ON SALE

CONTRACT, *see* AGREEMENT

CONVEYANCE OR TRANSFER ON SALE
(In the case of a Voluntary Disposition, *see* below)

Conveyance or transfer on sale of any property (except stock or marketable securities), where the conveyance or transfer contains a certificate of value certifying that the transaction does not form part of a larger transaction or a series of transactions in respect of which the aggregate amount or value of the consideration exceeds £60,000, *nil*

Value of £60,001–£250,000 (for every £100 or fraction of £100), £1
Value of £250,001–£500,000 (for every £100 or fraction of £100), £1.50
Value exceeds £500,000 (for every £100 or fraction of £100), £2

Conveyances to charities are exempt from duty under this head provided the instrument is stamped with a denoting stamp.

CONVEYANCE OR TRANSFER OF ANY OTHER KIND
Fixed duty, 50p

However, under the Stamp Duty (Exempt Instruments) Regulations 1987, instruments which would otherwise fall under this head are exempt from stamp duty provided that the document is duly certified. The certificate must contain a sufficient description of the category into which the instrument falls, and must be signed by the transferor, his solicitor or agent: 'I/We hereby certify that this instrument falls within category … in the Schedule to the Stamp Duty (Exempt Instruments) Regulations 1987.'

COVENANT, for original creation and sale of any annuity, *see* CONVEYANCE

DECLARATION OF TRUST
Not being a will or settlement, 50p

DEMISE, *see* LEASES

DUPLICATE OR COUNTERPART
Same duty as original, but not to exceed 50p

GIFT, *see* VOLUNTARY DISPOSITION

LEASES (INCLUDING AGREEMENTS FOR LEASES)
Lease or tack for any definite term less than a year of any furnished dwelling-house or apartments where the rent for such term exceeds £500, £1

Of any lands, tenements, etc., in consideration of any rent, according to the following:

Annual rent not exceeding	† Term not exceeding 7 yrs	35 yrs	100 yrs	Exceeding 100 yrs
£	£ p	£ p	£ p	£ p
5	nil	0.10	0.60	1.20
10	nil	0.20	1.20	2.40
15	nil	0.30	1.80	3.60
20	nil	0.40	2.40	4.80
25	nil	0.50	3.00	6.00
50	nil	1.00	6.00	12.00
75	nil	1.50	9.00	18.00
100	nil	2.00	12.00	24.00
150	nil	3.00	18.00	36.00
200	nil	4.00	24.00	48.00
250	nil	5.00	30.00	60.00
300	nil	6.00	36.00	72.00
350	nil	7.00	42.00	84.00
400	nil	8.00	48.00	96.00
450	nil	9.00	54.00	108.00
500	nil	10.00	60.00	120.00
Exceeding £500, *for every* £50 *or fraction thereof*	0.50	1.00	6.00	12.00

†If the term is indefinite the same duty is payable as if the term did not exceed seven years.

Where a consideration other than rent is payable, the same rule applies where the consideration does not exceed £60,000 as under conveyance or transfer on sale (except stock or marketable securities), provided that any rent payable does not exceed £600 a year and a certificate of value is included in the conveyance or transfer.

Where a lease is granted pursuant to a prior agreement for lease, the agreement itself is liable to duty. Credit for any duty paid on the agreement will be given against the duty payable on the lease and the Commissioners will place a denoting stamp on the lease. Where there is no prior agreement for lease, the lease must contain a certificate that it has not been made in pursuance of an agreement.

Leases to charities are exempt from duty under this head provided the instrument is stamped with a denoting stamp.

MORTGAGES, exempt

TRANSFER OF STOCK AND SHARES BY SALE, 0.5 per cent

UNIT TRUST INSTRUMENT

Unit Trust Instrument duty was abolished in the Finance Act 1988. Transfer of property to a unit trust or agreement to transfer units is generally subject to Conveyance on Sale duty.

By the Finance Act 1989, the transfer of units in certain authorized unit trusts is no longer subject to duty.

VOLUNTARY DISPOSITION, *inter vivos*

Fixed duty, 50p

However, under the Stamp Duty (Exempt Intruments) Regulations 1987, instruments which would otherwise fall under this head are exempt from stamp duty provided that the document is certified as falling within category L in the schedule to the Regulations. *See* Conveyance or Transfer of Any Other Kind, above.

Taxation

INCOME TAX

Income tax is charged on the income of individuals for a year of assessment commencing on 6 April and ending on the following 5 April. The rates of tax and the calculation of liability frequently differ as between one year of assessment and another. The following information is confined to the year of assessment 1997–8, ending on 5 April 1998; it has only limited application to earlier years because the basis used for calculating liability to United Kingdom income tax and the steps which must be taken to discharge that liability have been significantly affected by the introduction of self-assessment.

Liability to income tax is determined by establishing the taxable income for a year of assessment. That income will be reduced by an individual's personal allowance and perhaps by some other allowances or reliefs. The first £4,100 of taxable income remaining is assessable to income tax at the lower rate of 20 per cent. Disregarding income from 'savings', the next £22,000 is taxed at the basic rate of 23 per cent. Should any excess over £26,100 (£4,100 plus £22,000) remain, this will be taxable at the higher rate of 40 per cent.

Company dividends, interest and other forms of 'savings income' do not incur liability at the basic rate of 23 per cent. Income of this nature is taxable at 20 per cent unless the individual's taxable income exceeds £26,100, when liability may arise at 40 per cent on the excess.

Certain allowances and reliefs are given at the rate of 15 or 20 per cent as a deduction from income tax payable. These adjustments can only be made once the full amount of tax otherwise due has been calculated.

The tables below show the income tax payable for 1997–8 by an individual on the amount of income specified, after deducting the personal allowance and providing relief for the married couple's allowance, where appropriate. Persons over the age of 74 years may pay less tax, unless their income is substantial. Some taxpayers may be entitled to transitional allowances following the introduction of independent taxation in 1990, together with other reliefs which reduce the tax payable below the amount shown by the tables. These tables have been structured on the assumption that none of the income arises from savings. Should income of this nature be received, less tax may be due.

Trustees administering settled property are chargeable to income tax at the basic rate of 23 per cent. Where the trustees retain discretionary powers or income is accumulated, liability may be increased to 34 per cent. Companies residing in the UK are not liable to income tax but suffer corporation tax on income, profits and gains.

The charge to income tax arises on all taxable income accruing from sources in the UK. Individuals who are resident in this territory may also become liable on income arising overseas. An individual is resident in the UK if he or she normally resides here. Persons not normally residing in the UK may be treated as resident if they visit this territory for periods which average three months or more throughout a period of years, or are present for at least 183 days in a particular year.

Income arising overseas will often incur liability to foreign taxation. If that income is also chargeable to UK income tax, excessive liability could arise. The UK has concluded double taxation agreements with many overseas territories and these ensure that the same slice of income is not doubly taxed. In the absence of such an

Single Persons and Married Women					Married Men				
Income	Persons under 65		Persons 65 or over*		Income	Couples under 65		Couples 65 or over†	
£	Income tax £	Average rate %	Income tax £	Average rate %	£	Income tax £	Average rate %	Income tax £	Average rate %
4,500	91	2.0	—	—	4,500	—	—	—	—
5,000	191	3.8	—	—	5,000	—	—	—	—
6,000	391	6.6	156	2.6	6,000	117	2.0	—	—
7,000	591	8.4	356	5.1	7,000	317	4.5	—	—
8,000	791	9.9	556	7.0	8,000	517	6.5	78	1.0
9,000	1,017	11.3	756	8.4	9,000	742	8.2	278	3.1
10,000	1,247	12.5	976	9.8	10,000	972	9.7	499	5.0
12,000	1,707	14.2	1,436	12.0	12,000	1,432	11.9	959	8.0
14,000	2,167	15.5	1,896	13.5	14,000	1,892	12.2	1,419	10.1
16,000	2,627	16.4	2,402	15.0	16,000	2,352	14.7	1,925	12.0
18,000	3,087	17.2	3,087	17.1	18,000	2,812	15.6	2,613	14.5
20,000	3,547	17.7	3,547	17.7	20,000	3,272	16.4	3,223	16.1
25,000	4,697	18.8	4,697	18.8	25,000	4,422	17.7	4,422	17.7
30,000	5,847	19.5	5,847	19.5	30,000	5,572	18.6	5,572	18.6
40,000	9,822	24.6	9,822	24.6	40,000	9,548	23.9	9,548	23.9
50,000	13,822	27.6	13,822	27.6	50,000	13,548	27.1	13,548	27.1
60,000	17,822	29.7	17,822	29.7	60,000	17,548	29.2	17,548	29.2
100,000	33,822	33.8	33,822	33.8	100,000	33,548	33.5	33,548	33.5

* Persons aged 75 or over suffer less tax on income falling below £18,000 on this table

† Persons aged 75 or over suffer less tax on income falling below £25,000 on this table

agreement, foreign tax suffered can usually be relieved when calculating liability to UK income tax.

HUSBAND AND WIFE

A husband and wife are separately taxed, with each entitled to his or her personal allowance. A married man 'living with' his wife can obtain a married couple's allowance. In the absence of any claim, this allowance must be used by the husband but where any balance remains the surplus may be transferred to the wife. It is possible for a married woman to claim half the basic married couple's allowance as of right. In addition, the entire basic allowance may be claimed by the wife, if her husband so agrees.

Each spouse may obtain other allowances and reliefs where the required conditions are satisfied. Income must be accurately allocated between the couple by reference to the individual beneficially entitled to that income. Where income arises from jointly-held assets, this must be apportioned equally between husband and wife. However, in those cases where the beneficial interests in jointly-held assets are not equal, a special declaration can be made to apportion income by reference to the actual interests in that income.

SELF-ASSESSMENT

A fundamental change in the structure of UK taxation was introduced on 6 April 1996 and applies for 1996–7 and future years. This structural change, known as self-assessment, had no effect on the amount of income tax payable but altered the compliance requirements which many individuals must discharge.

The self-assessment system requires the taxpayer to deliver a completed tax return. This must normally be submitted by 31 January following the end of the year of assessment to which the return relates. In addition to completing the return, the taxpayer must calculate the amount of income tax due. If a taxpayer does not wish to calculate the tax due, the return must be forwarded to the Inland Revenue not later than the previous 30 September; an Inland Revenue representative will then calculate the amount of tax, using the information disclosed by the return, and advise the taxpayer. This is the only advantage of providing a completed return not later than 30 September, as it remains the responsibility of the taxpayer to submit payments of income tax on time.

There may be three different payment dates when discharging income tax due for a year of assessment:
(a) an interim payment due on 31 January in the year of assessment itself
(b) a second interim payment due on the following 31 July
(c) a balancing payment, or possibly a repayment, on the following 31 January
The two interim payments will be based on tax payable for the previous year of assessment but liability may be reduced where income has fallen or even avoided entirely where the amounts are not substantial.

Although all individuals could be affected by self-assessment, its impact will largely be restricted to fewer than nine million persons receiving tax returns and comprising self-employed individuals, those receiving income from the exploitation of land in the UK, company directors, and others with investment income liable to higher rate income tax. Individuals whose only source of income is earnings from an employment where the PAYE system applies are largely unaffected. Separate tax return forms are issued to a husband and wife, where such forms are needed.

Failure to submit completed tax returns by 31 January or to discharge payments of income tax on time will incur a liability to interest, surcharges and penalties.

Self-assessment extends also to capital gains tax. However, there is no requirement to make interim payments on account of capital gains tax as the entire amount due for disposals taking place in a year of assessment must be discharged on the following 31 January.

INCOME TAXABLE

Income tax is assessed under several Schedules. Each Schedule determines the extent of liability and establishes the amount to be included in taxable income. In some instances the actual income arising in a year of assessment will be charged to income tax for that year.

A different basis of assessment may be used for income taxable under Cases I to V of Schedule D. For many years income was assessed under these Cases on a 'preceding year' basis. This involved measuring income for the year by reference to that arising in a previous year or period but there were special rules where a new source was acquired or an existing source discontinued. The 'preceding year' basis has been replaced by a 'current year' basis of assessment. This requires that business profits assessable under Case I or Case II of Schedule D will be those for the accounting period ending in the year of assessment, with special adjustments for the opening and closing years of a business. Other income assessable under Schedule D will be that which arises in the actual year of assessment.

The current year basis applied from the outset for new sources commenced on and after 6 April 1994. Sources existing before that date became fully subject to the current year basis in 1997–8, although special rules had to be introduced to achieve a smooth transition from the old basis to the new. These rules required that a form of averaging was often used to establish the profits or income for 1996–7.

Following the withdrawal of income tax liability for most commercial woodlands in the UK, Schedule B no longer applies. Schedule C has also been withdrawn as the result of further changes. The contents of the remaining schedules are shown below.

Schedule A

Tax is charged under Schedule A on the annual profits or gains arising from any business carried on for the exploitation of land in the UK. As the result of recent amendments, the determination of profits from a Schedule A business adopts principles identical to those used when establishing the profits or gains of a trade, profession or vocation. Rents and other income from the exploitation of land are included in the calculation, and outgoings incurred wholly and exclusively for the purposes of the Schedule A business may be deducted from income.

Schedule A does not extend to profits from farming, market gardening or woodlands, nor does it apply to mineral rents and royalties. Premiums arising on the grant of a lease for a period not exceeding 50 years in duration are treated as rents. However, the amount of the taxable premium may be reduced by 2 per cent for each complete year, after the first 12 months, of the leasing period. Income arising from the provision of certain furnished holiday accommodation attracts a number of tax advantages not otherwise available for most income chargeable under Schedule A.

Receipts not exceeding £4,250 annually and accruing to an individual from letting property furnished in his or her own home are usually excluded from liability to income tax.

Schedule D

This Schedule is divided into six Cases:

Cases I and II – profits arising from trades, professions and vocations, including farming and market gardening. Capital expenditure incurred on assets used for business purposes will often produce an entitlement to capital allowances which reduce the profits chargeable. These profits may also be reduced by claims for loss relief and other matters.

Case III – interest on government stocks not taxed at source, interest on National Savings Bank deposits and discounts. Interest up to £70 on ordinary National Savings Bank deposits is exempt from income tax. The exemption applies to both husband and wife separately. Interest on National Savings Bank special investment accounts is not exempt. Interest and other items of savings income incur no liability at the basic rate.

Cases IV and V – interest from overseas securities, rents, dividends and all other income accruing outside the UK. Assessment is based on the full amount of income arising, whether remitted to the UK or retained overseas, but individuals who are either not domiciled in the UK or who are ordinarily resident overseas may be taxed on a remittance basis. Overseas pensions are taxable but the amount arising may be reduced by 10 per cent for assessment purposes. Dividends and interest on most overseas investments are chargeable only at the lower rate of 20 per cent and the higher rate of 40 per cent.

Case VI – sundry profits and annual receipts not assessed under any other Case or Schedule. These may include insurance commissions, post-cessation receipts and numerous other receipts specifically charged under Case VI.

Schedule E

All earnings from an office or employment are assessable under this Schedule. There are three Cases:

Case I – applies to all earnings of an individual resident and ordinarily resident in the UK.

Case II – of application where the individual is not resident or not ordinarily resident and extends to earnings for duties undertaken in the UK.

Case III – applies in rare situations to other earnings remitted to the UK.

Although earnings for duties performed overseas may be assessable under Case I where the employee is resident and ordinarily resident in the UK, a foreign earnings deduction of 100 per cent may be available, which reduces the overseas assessable earnings to nil. This deduction can be obtained where duties are performed overseas for a continuous period reaching or exceeding 365 days and is confined to earnings from the overseas activity.

A 'receipts basis' applies for determining the year of assessment in which earnings must be taxed. Where earnings are assessable under Case I or Case II, the date of receipt will comprise the earlier of the date of payment, or the date entitlement arises. In the case of company directors it is the earlier of these two dates, with the addition of the following three which establish the time of receipt: the date earnings are credited in the company's books; where earnings for a period are determined after the end of that period, the date of determination; where earnings for a period are determined in that period, the last day of that period.

The earnings assessable under Schedule E include all salaries, wages, director's fees and other money sums. In addition, there is a wide range of benefits which must be added to taxable earnings. These include the provision of living accommodation on advantageous terms and advantages arising from the use of vouchers.

Further taxable benefits accrue to directors and also to employees receiving earnings of £8,500 or more in the year of assessment. These benefits include the reimbursement of expenses, the availability of motor cars for private motoring, the provision of petrol or other fuel for private motoring, the use of vans, the provision of interest-free loans, and other benefits provided at the employer's expense. The cost of providing a limited range of child care facilities may be excluded.

In arriving at the amount to be assessed under Schedule E, all expenses incurred wholly, exclusively and necessarily in the performance of the duties may be deducted. This includes fees and subscriptions paid to certain professional bodies and learned societies. Fees paid to managers by entertainers, actors and others assessable under Schedule E may be deducted, up to a maximum of 17.5 per cent of earnings. From 6 April 1998 some costs of travelling between home and a business location may be set against earnings, but this must not include the cost of commuting.

Compensation for loss of office and other sums received on the termination of an office or employment are assessable to tax. However, the first £30,000 may be excluded with only the balance remaining chargeable, unless the compensatory payment is linked with the retirement of the recipient.

For several years earnings received from an approved profit-related pay scheme have been exempt from income tax. However, this exemption is being phased out and will cease to apply entirely after 31 December 1999.

Schedule F

This Schedule is concerned with company dividends and distributions. A UK resident company paying a dividend or making a distribution must account to the Inland Revenue for advance corporation tax. A shareholder residing in the UK obtains the dividend or distribution together with a tax credit equal to one-quarter of the sum received for 1997–8. The gross dividend or distribution (sum received plus tax credit) is regarded as having suffered income tax, equal to the tax credit, at the lower rate of 20 per cent. Where the shareholder is not liable, or not fully liable, at that rate a repayment can be obtained. Dividends and distributions comprise income from savings and incur no liability to income tax at the basic rate of 23 per cent (*see* below). It is anticipated that the existing tax credit will be substantially reduced from 6 April 1999, with no part of that credit qualifying for repayment. Pension funds have been unable to recover the tax credit for dividends paid after 2 July 1997.

Some payments made by an unquoted trading company to redeem or purchase its own shares are not treated as distributions.

Building society and bank interest

Many payments of interest by building societies and banks are received after the deduction of income tax at the lower rate of 20 per cent. However, investors not liable to income tax may arrange to receive interest gross, with no tax being deducted on payment. Others who suffer income tax by deduction can obtain a repayment in whole or in part if they are not fully liable at the lower rate. This income also comprises income from savings, which is taxable as outlined below.

INCOME FROM SAVINGS

Some forms of investment income attract a reduced rate of income tax for 1997–8. This is limited to 'income from savings', which includes interest on bank and building society accounts, government securities, the income element of life annuities, and dividends from UK companies. In addition, 'income from savings' may extend to dividends and other income of a similar nature arising outside the UK. Not all forms of investment income are included in the list; a notable exception is income from letting property.

A great deal of interest will be received after deduction of income tax at the lower rate of 20 per cent. Dividends have a tax credit attached which effectively represents tax at the rate of 20 per cent on the grossed-up equivalent. The significance of these rates is that income from savings will be taxed at 20 per cent where the income of the recipient is sufficiently substantial. There is no liability at the basic rate of 23 per cent but where taxable income exceeds £26,100, the excess is liable at the higher rate of 40 per cent. As tax will usually have been deducted at source at 20 per cent, higher rate liability arises at a further 20 per cent (40 per cent less 20 per cent). When calculating liability, income from savings is treated as the 'top slice' of the taxpayer's income.

INCOME NOT TAXABLE

Income which is not taxable includes interest on National Savings certificates, most scholarship income, bounty payments to members of the armed services and annuities payable to the holders of certain awards. Dividend income arising from investments in personal equity plans and venture capital trusts may be exempt from tax. Income received under most maintenance agreements and court orders made after 30 June 1988 will not be liable to tax. Nor will payments made under many deeds of covenant be recognized for tax purposes, unless the recipient is a charity. Interest arising on a tax exempt special savings account (TESSA) opened with a building society or bank will be exempt from tax if the account is maintained throughout a five-year period.

SOCIAL SECURITY BENEFITS

Many social security benefits are not liable to income tax. These include income support, family credit, maternity allowance, child benefit, war widow's pension and disability living allowance. The benefits which are taxable include the retirement pension, widow's pension, widowed mother's allowance and jobseeker's allowance. Short-term sick pay and maternity pay payable by an employer are also chargeable to tax. Incapacity benefit is chargeable to tax but no liability arises for the first 28 weeks of receiving benefit.

PAY AS YOU EARN

The Pay As You Earn (PAYE) system is not an independent form of taxation but is designed to collect income tax by deduction from most earnings. When paying earnings to employees, an employer is usually required to deduct income tax and account for that tax to the Inland Revenue. In many cases this deduction procedure will fully exhaust the individual's liability to income tax, unless there is other income. The date of 'receipt' used for assessment purposes (*see* above) also identifies the date of 'payment' when establishing liability for PAYE.

The PAYE system is used to collect tax on certain payments made 'in kind'. This includes payment in the form of gold bullion, diamonds and marketable securities.

ALLOWANCES

The allowances available to individuals for 1997–8 are:

Personal allowance

Each individual receives a basic personal allowance of £4,045. This is increased to £5,220 for individuals over the age of 64 on 5 April 1998, and further increased to £5,400 for those over the age of 74 on the same date. The increased allowance is available for those who died during the year of assessment but who would otherwise have achieved the appropriate age not later than 5 April 1998.

The amount of the increased personal allowance for older taxpayers will be reduced by one-half of total income in excess of £15,600. This reduction in the allowance will continue until it has been reduced to the basic personal allowance of £4,045.

Apart from limited transitional matters mentioned below, any unused part of the personal allowance of one spouse cannot be transferred to the other.

The personal allowance is given as a deduction in calculating taxable income and may therefore produce relief at the rate of 20, 23 or 40 per cent, as appropriate.

Married couple's allowance

A married man who was 'living with' his wife at any time in the year ending on 5 April 1998 is entitled to a married couple's allowance. The basic allowance is £1,830. This may be increased to £3,185 if either the husband or the wife is 65 years or over at any time in the year ending on 5 April 1998. A further increase to £3,225 can be obtained where either party to the marriage was 75 or over on 5 April 1998. Where an individual would otherwise have reached either age by 5 April 1998, but who died earlier in the year, the increased allowance is given.

The amount of the increased married couple's allowance may be reduced where the income of the husband (excluding the income of the wife) exceeds £15,600. The reduction will comprise:
(a) one-half of the husband's total income in excess of £15,600, less
(b) the amount of any reduction made when calculating the husband's increased personal allowance

This reduction in the married couple's allowance cannot reduce that allowance below the basic amount of £1,830.

If husband and wife were married during 1997–8 the married couple's allowance of £1,830, or any increased sum, must be reduced by one-twelfth for each complete month commencing on 6 April 1997 and preceding the date of marriage.

Unlike the personal allowance, the married couple's allowance does not reduce taxable income. Relief is granted by reducing the tax payable by 15 per cent of the allowance. Should the allowance exceed taxable income, no tax will be due, nor will any repayment arise.

In the absence of any further action the married couple's allowance will be given to the husband. If he is unable to utilize all or any part of that allowance due to an absence of income, the husband may transfer the unused portion to his wife. The decision whether or not to transfer remains at the discretion of the husband.

However, a wife may file an election to obtain one-half of the basic married couple's allowance as of right, leaving the husband with the balance of that allowance. Alternatively, the couple may jointly elect that the entire basic allowance should be allocated to the wife only. Should either spouse be unable to utilize his or her share of the married couple's allowance the unused part may be transferred to the other spouse.

Additional personal allowance

An allowance of £1,830 is available to a single person who has a qualifying child resident with him or her in 1997–8. The allowance can also be obtained by a married man whose wife is totally incapacitated by physical or mental infirmity throughout the year.

A 'qualifying child' for 1997–8 must be born during the year, be under the age of 16 years at the commencement of the year, or be over the age of 16 at the commencement of the year and either receiving full-time instruction at a university, college, school or other educational establishment or undergoing training for a trade, profession or vocation throughout a minimum period of two years. It is also necessary that the child is the claimant's own, a stepchild of the claimant, an illegitimate child if the parents married after the child's birth, or an adopted child under the age of 18 at the time of adoption. Alternatively it must be shown that the child was either born during 1997–8 or under the age of 18 at the commencement of the year and maintained by the claimant at his or her own expense during the whole of the succeeding 12-month period.

Only one additional personal allowance of £1,830 can be obtained by an individual notwithstanding the number of children involved. Where an unmarried couple are living together as husband and wife, it is not possible for both to obtain the additional personal allowance. The allowance is given by reducing tax payable at the rate of 15 per cent of £1,830.

Widow's bereavement allowance

For the year of assessment in which a husband dies his surviving widow may obtain a widow's bereavement allowance, which is £1,830 for 1997–8. It is a requirement that the parties were 'living together' immediately before the husband's death. A similar allowance will be available in the year following death, unless the widow remarried in the year of death. No widow's bereavement allowance can be obtained for future years. Relief is granted by reducing tax payable at the rate of 15 per cent of £1,830.

Blind person's allowance

An allowance of £1,280 is available to an individual if at any time during the year ending on 5 April 1998, he or she was registered as blind on a register maintained by a local authority. If the individual is 'living with' a wife or husband, any unused part of the blind person's allowance can be transferred to the other spouse. The allowance reduces taxable income and may therefore give rise to relief at the taxpayer's highest rate of tax suffered.

Transitional allowances

There are three transitional allowances which are intended to ensure that the independent taxation of husband and wife, introduced on 6 April 1990, did not increase liability to income tax for subsequent years. These allowances comprise:

(a) an increased personal allowance available to a wife where the husband cannot fully use that allowance in 1997–8

(b) a special personal allowance available to a husband where his wife falls into a higher age group, namely over 64 or over 74

(c) a married couple's allowance available to a separated husband not 'living with' his wife if the separation occurred before 6 April 1990

Recent increases in tax allowances require that heading (b) has become obsolete. With the passage of time, the two remaining headings are of limited application.

LIFE ASSURANCE RELIEF

Life assurance deduction relief is now restricted to premiums paid on policies made before 14 March 1984. No relief is available for policies issued after this date. Where the terms of a policy made before 14 March 1984 are subsequently varied or extended to produce increased benefits, future premiums paid may no longer qualify for relief.

When paying premiums under a qualifying policy made before 14 March 1984, the payer will deduct and retain income tax at the rate of 12.5 per cent. The ability to retain deductions made in this manner is not affected by the payer's liability to income tax on taxable income. No restriction to the deduction procedure arises if aggregate premiums paid during a year of assessment do not exceed £1,500 (calculated before deducting tax). Should premiums exceed this amount, relief will be confined to £1,500 or one-sixth of total income, whichever is the greater.

INTEREST

In addition to personal and blind person's allowances, which reduce taxable income, and other allowances which reduce tax payable, further reliefs may be available to an individual. These include payments of interest.

In some instances, interest paid by a business proprietor may be included when calculating profits chargeable to income tax under Case I or Case II of Schedule D. In addition, relief for interest paid on a loan applied to acquire or develop land and buildings may be obtained by including the outlay in the calculation of income chargeable under Schedule A. However, many private individuals cannot obtain relief in this manner and must satisfy stringent requirements before relief will be forthcoming. In general terms it is a requirement that before interest can qualify for relief it must be paid for a qualifying purpose. Relief will not be available to the extent that interest exceeds a reasonable commercial rate and no relief is forthcoming for interest on an overdraft.

For 1997–8 relief will be available on the following payments:

(a) Interest on a loan to purchase, develop or improve an interest in land owned by the individual and used as the only or main residence of that individual. 'Land' includes large houseboats and also caravans used for residential purposes. No relief is available for interest on loans applied after 5 April 1988 for the development or improvement of land, unless the work involves the construction of a new building. Relief is available for interest paid on a loan applied to acquire a property which is the only or main residence of a dependent relative, a separated spouse or a divorced former spouse, but only where that person occupied the property before 6 April 1988. Relief may also be forthcoming for interest on a loan used to acquire some other property, perhaps to be used as the only or main residence on retirement, by an individual who is compelled to occupy property by reason of his or her work. If the loan, or aggregate of several loans, exceeds £30,000, relief is restricted to interest on that amount. Where two or more persons apply loans after 31 July 1988 to acquire interests in a single building, those persons cannot, collectively, obtain relief for interest on more than £30,000 in relation to that building. Relief is given by reducing the income tax payable by 15 per cent of the qualifying interest. The rate is being reduced to 10 per cent for interest paid after 5 April 1998

(b) Interest on a loan made to acquire an interest in a close company or in a partnership, or to advance money to such a person

(c) Interest on a loan to a member of a partnership to acquire machinery or plant for use in the partnership business

(d) Interest on a loan to an employed person to acquire machinery or plant for the purposes of his/her employment

(e) Interest on a loan made for the purpose of contributing capital to an industrial co-operative

(f) Interest on a loan applied for investment in an employee-controlled company

(g) Interest on a loan made to elderly persons for the purchase of an annuity where the loan is secured on land. If the loan exceeds £30,000, relief is limited to interest on this amount. This relief is restricted to income tax at the basic rate of 23 per cent

(h) Interest on a loan to personal representatives to provide funds for the payment of inheritance tax

Relief for many payments of mortgage interest is obtained through a special scheme known as MIRAS (mortgage interest relief at source). This applies to interest paid to a building society, bank, insurance company and certain other approved persons. When making payments of this nature in 1997–8 the payer will deduct and retain income tax at the rate of 15 per cent. This will provide the payer with full relief at that rate and no other relief will be necessary. Qualifying payments of interest outside the MIRAS scheme continue to produce relief by reducing tax payable at the rate of 15 per cent. The rate of deduction, or relief, is reduced to 10 per cent from 6 April 1998.

Other relief under headings (b) to (h) (but not (g)) are given by deducting interest from taxable income. This enables the taxpayer to obtain relief at his or her top rate suffered.

OTHER OUTGOINGS

Many employees pay contributions to an approved occupational pension scheme. The amount of their contributions may be deducted when calculating earnings assessable under Schedule E. Relief should also be available for any additional voluntary contributions paid.

Self-employed individuals and those receiving earnings not covered by an occupational pension scheme may contribute under personal pension scheme arrangements. These individuals may also pay premiums under retirement annuity schemes if the arrangements were concluded before 1 July 1988. Contributions paid under both headings and which do not exceed upper limits may obtain income tax relief by deduction from taxable income.

Subject to a maximum of £100,000 in any one year, the cost of subscribing for shares in an unquoted trading company may qualify for relief under the Enterprise Investment Scheme. Many requirements must be satisfied before this relief can be obtained, but husband and wife may each take advantage of the £100,000 annual maximum. Relief is given by reducing tax payable at the rate of 20 per cent of the share subscription cost. Further relief, also to a maximum of £100,000 and given at the rate of 20 per cent, is available for a subscription of shares in a venture capital trust company.

CAPITAL GAINS TAX

An individual is chargeable to capital gains tax on chargeable gains which accrue to him or her during a year of assessment ending on 5 April. The application of the tax has been amended substantially in recent years and the following information is confined to the year of assessment 1997–8, ending on 5 April 1998.

Liability extends to individuals who are either resident or ordinarily resident for the year but special rules apply where a person permanently leaves the UK or comes to this territory for the purpose of acquiring residence. Non-residents are not liable to capital gains tax unless, exceptionally, they carry on a business in the UK through a branch or agency.

Trustees residing in the UK are chargeable to capital gains tax but chargeable gains accruing to companies are assessable to corporation tax.

Capital gains tax is chargeable on the total of chargeable gains which accrue to a person in a year of assessment, after subtracting allowable losses arising in the same year. Unused allowable losses brought forward from some earlier year may be offset against current chargeable gains but in the case of individuals this must not reduce the net chargeable gains for 1997–8 below £6,500. It is possible to utilize trading losses against chargeable gains where those losses have not been offset against income.

RATE OF TAX

Where the net chargeable gains accruing to an individual during 1997–8 do not exceed £6,500 there will be no liability to capital gains tax. If the net gains exceed £6,500 the excess is chargeable at the taxpayer's marginal rate of income tax. This is achieved by adding the excess net chargeable gains to the amount of income chargeable to income tax. The rate attributable to this top slice will disclose the rate of capital gains tax payable, which may be at 20 per cent, 23 per cent, 40 per cent or a combination of the three. Although income tax rates are used, capital gains tax remains a separate tax.

Capital gains tax for 1997–8 falls due for payment in full on 31 January 1999. If payment is delayed beyond this date, interest or surcharges may be imposed.

HUSBAND AND WIFE

Independent taxation requires that a husband and wife 'living together' are separately assessed to capital gains tax. Each spouse must independently calculate his or her gains and losses, with each entitled to the annual exemption of £6,500. No liability to capital gains tax arises from the transfer of assets between husband and wife 'living together'.

DISPOSAL OF ASSETS

Before liability to capital gains tax can arise a disposal, or deemed disposal, of an asset must take place. This occurs not only where assets are sold or exchanged but applies on the making of a gift. There is also a disposal of assets where any capital sum is derived from assets, for example, where compensation is received for loss or damage to an asset.

The date on which a disposal must be treated as having taken place will determine the year of assessment into which the chargeable gain or allowable loss falls. In those cases where a disposal is made under an unconditional contract, the time of disposal will be that when the contract was entered into and not the subsequent date of conveyance or transfer. A disposal under a conditional contract or option is treated as taking place when the contract becomes unconditional or the option is exercised. Disposals by way of gift are undertaken when the gift becomes effective.

VALUATION OF ASSETS

The amount actually received as consideration for the disposal of an asset will be the sum from which very limited outgoings must be deducted for the purpose of establishing the gain or loss. In some cases, however, the consideration passing will not accurately reflect the value of the asset and a different basis must be used. This applies, in particular, where an asset is transferred by way of gift or otherwise than by a bargain made at arm's length. Such transactions are deemed to take place for a consideration representing market value, which will determine both the disposal proceeds accruing to the transferor and the cost of acquisition to the transferee.

Market value represents the price which an asset might reasonably be expected to fetch on a sale in the open market. In the case of unquoted shares or securities, it is to be assumed that the hypothetical purchaser in the open market would have available all the information which a prudent prospective purchaser of shares or securities might reasonably require if he were proposing to purchase them from a willing vendor by private treaty and at arm's length. This is an important consideration as the amount of information deemed to be available to a hypothetical purchaser may materially affect the price 'reasonably' offered in an open market situation. The market value of unquoted shares or securities will usually be established following negotiations with the Shares Valuation Division of the Capital Taxes Office. The valuation of land and interests in land in the UK will be dealt with by the District Valuer.

Special rules apply to determine the market value of shares quoted on the Stock Exchange.

DEDUCTION FOR OUTGOINGS

Once the actual or notional disposal proceeds have been determined, it only remains to subtract eligible outgoings for the purpose of computing the gain or loss. There is the general rule that any outgoings deducted, or which are available to be deducted, when calculating income tax liability must be ignored. Subject to this, deductions will usually be limited to:

(a) the cost of acquiring the asset, together with incidental costs wholly and exclusively incurred in connection with the acquisition

(b) expenditure incurred wholly and exclusively on the asset in enhancing its value, being expenditure reflected in the state or nature of the asset at the time of the disposal, and any other expenditure wholly and exclusively incurred in establishing, preserving or defending title to, or a right over, the asset

(c) the incidental costs of making the disposal

Where the disposal concerns a leasehold interest having less than 50 years to run, any expenditure falling under (a) and (b) must be written off throughout the duration of the lease.

ASSETS HELD ON 31 MARCH 1982

Where the disposal relates to assets held on 31 March 1982, the actual cost of acquisition will not usually enter into the calculation of gain. It is to be assumed that such assets were acquired on 31 March 1982 for a consideration representing market value on that date. The increase in value, if any, occurring before 31 March 1982 will not be assessable to capital gains tax.

INDEXATION ALLOWANCE

An indexation allowance may be available when calculating any gain on the disposal of an asset. This allowance is based on percentage increases in the retail prices index between the month of March 1982 or the month in which expenditure is incurred, if later, and the month of disposal. The increase is applied to the items of expenditure in (a) and (b) above to determine the amount of the indexation allowance. However, if the asset was acquired before 31 March 1982, the allowance will be based on market value at 31 March 1982.

Previously the indexation allowance could be subtracted from the gain, added to the loss or used to convert a gain into a loss. However, for more recent disposals the indexation allowance may only be applied to reduce a gain. It cannot increase the amount of a loss, and where the allowance exceeds the amount of a gain it only remains necessary to reduce the gain to nil.

EXEMPTIONS

There is a general exemption from liability to capital gains tax where the net gains of an individual for 1997–8 do not exceed £6,500. This general exemption applies separately to a husband and wife where the parties are 'living together'.

The disposal of many assets will not give rise to chargeable gains or allowable losses and these assets include:

(a) private motor cars
(b) government securities
(c) loan stock and other securities (but not shares)
(d) options and contracts relating to securities within (b) and (c)
(e) National Savings Certificates, Premium Bonds, Defence Bonds and National Development Bonds
(f) currency of any description acquired for personal expenditure outside the UK
(g) decorations awarded for valour
(h) betting wins and pools, lottery or games prizes
(i) compensation or damages for any wrong or injury suffered by an individual in his/her person, profession or vocation
(j) life assurance and deferred annuity contracts where the person making the disposal is the original beneficial owner
(k) dwelling-houses and land enjoyed with the residence which is an individual's only or main residence
(l) tangible movable property, the consideration for the disposal of which does not exceed £6,000
(m) certain tangible movable property which is a wasting asset having a life not exceeding 50 years
(n) assets transferred to charities and other bodies
(o) works of art, historic buildings and similar assets
(p) assets used to provide maintenance funds for historic buildings
(q) assets transferred to trustees for the benefit of employees

DWELLING-HOUSES

Exemption from capital gains tax will usually be available for any gain which accrues to an individual from the disposal of, or of an interest in, a dwelling-house or part of a dwelling-house which has been his/her only or main residence. The exemption extends to land which has been occupied and enjoyed with the residence as its garden or grounds. Some restriction may be necessary where the land exceeds half a hectare.

The gain will not be chargeable to capital gains tax if the dwelling-house, or part, has been the individual's only or main residence throughout the period of ownership, or throughout the entire period except for all or any part of the last three years. A proportionate part of the gain will be exempt in other cases if the dwelling-house has been the individual's only or main residence for part only of the period of ownership. In the case of property acquired before 31 March 1982, the period of ownership is treated as commencing on this date.

Where part of the dwelling-house has been used exclusively for business purposes, that part of the gain attributable to business use will not be exempt.

In those cases where part of a qualifying dwelling-house has been used to provide rented residential accommodation this non-personal use may frequently be ignored when calculating exemption from capital gains tax, unless relatively substantial sums are involved.

Dwellings occupied by dependent relatives, separated spouses or divorced former spouses, may also qualify for the exemption, but only where occupation commenced before 6 April 1988.

ROLL-OVER RELIEF – BUSINESS ASSETS

Persons carrying on business will often undertake the disposal of an asset and use the proceeds to finance the acquisition of a replacement asset. Where this situation arises a claim for roll-over relief may be available. The broad effect of such a claim is that all or part of the gain arising on the disposal of the old asset may be disregarded. The gain or part is then subtracted from the cost of acquiring the replacement asset. As this cost is reduced, any gain arising from the future disposal of the replacement asset will be correspondingly increased, unless a further roll-over situation then develops.

It remains a requirement that both the old and the replacement asset must be used for the purpose of the taxpayer's business. Relief will only be available if the acquisition of the replacement asset takes place within a period commencing twelve months before, and ending three years after, the disposal of the old asset, although the Inland Revenue retain a discretion to extend this period where the circumstances were such that it was impossible for the taxpayer to acquire the replacement asset before the expiration of the normal time limit.

Whilst many business assets qualify for roll-over relief there are exceptions.

REINVESTMENT RELIEF – SHARES

An additional form of roll-over relief, usually referred to as 'reinvestment relief', is available where the disposal of an asset can be matched with the acquisition of shares in unquoted companies. The conditions governing this relief now enable an individual, and some trustees, to roll-over gains arising on the disposal of virtually any asset. It is a necessary requirement that the individual or trustee making the disposal acquires shares in a qualifying unquoted trading company. Most shareholdings in trading companies will qualify unless the company also undertakes non-trading activities. An unusual feature of reinvestment relief is that, subject to upper limits, the individual or trustee can roll-over any part of the chargeable gain arising on the disposal of assets. The ability to select the amount to be rolled over enables the claimant to leave undisturbed the remaining gain, which can be offset against available losses or perhaps used to absorb the annual exemption of £6,500.

DEFERRAL RELIEF

A novel form of roll-over relief enables gains arising on the disposal of an asset to be matched, in whole or in part, with an investment in shares under the Enterprise Investment Scheme. To the extent that the investment qualifies for income tax relief, any part of the gain arising on disposal, not exceeding the investment qualifying for relief, may become the subject of a claim. Unlike the more usual form of roll-over relief, this claim does not eliminate or reduce the chargeable gain. It has the effect of deferring that gain until the time of some future event, which will usually be identified by the disposal of the newly acquired shares.

A similar form of deferral relief is available for gains arising on other disposals. It is a necessary requirement that the individual undertaking the disposal makes a qualifying investment in a venture capital trust company. To the extent of the gain arising, which must not exceed the amount of the investment qualifying for income tax relief, that gain is deferred until the time of a future event, which

will normally comprise the disposal of shares in the venture capital trust.

HOLD-OVER RELIEF – GIFTS

The gift of an asset is treated as a disposal made for a consideration equal to market value, with a corresponding acquisition by the transferee at an identical value. In the case of gifts made by individuals and a limited range of trustees to a transferee resident in the UK, a form of hold-over relief may be available. Relief is limited to the transfer of certain assets, including the following:

(a) assets used for the purposes of a trade or similar activity carried on by the transferor or his/her personal company

(b) shares or securities of a trading company which is not listed on a stock exchange

(c) shares or securities of a trading company which is listed but which is the transferor's personal company

(d) many interests in agricultural property qualifying for agricultural property relief for inheritance tax purposes

(e) assets involved in transactions which are lifetime transfers for inheritance tax purposes, other than potentially exempt transfers

The effect of the claim is similar to that following a claim for roll-over relief on the disposal of business assets, but adjustments will be necessary where some consideration is given for the transfer, the asset has not been used for business purposes throughout the period of ownership, or not all assets of a company are used for business purposes.

RETIREMENT RELIEF

Retirement relief is available to an individual who disposes by way of sale or gift of the whole or part of a business. It does not necessarily follow that the isolated disposal of assets used for the purpose of a business will represent the disposal of the whole or part of a business. The main condition for granting this relief is that throughout a period of at least one year the business has been owned either by the individual or by a trading company in which the individual retained a sufficient shareholding interest. The relief extends also to cases where an individual disposes by way of sale or gift of shares or securities of a company. It must be demonstrated that the company was a trading company, that the individual retained a sufficient shareholding interest, and that he/she was engaged as a full-time working officer or employee.

An individual who has attained the age of 50 years at the time of a disposal may now obtain retirement relief up to a maximum of £625,000. The amount of this relief must be reduced if the underlying conditions have not been satisfied throughout a ten-year period. With a single exception no retirement relief can be obtained if the disposal occurs before the individual's 50th birthday. This exception arises where an individual is compelled to retire early on the grounds of ill-health. The normal retirement relief may then be obtained. Any retirement relief must be subtracted from the net gains arising on disposal, leaving the balance remaining, if any, chargeable to capital gains tax in the normal manner.

DEATH

No capital gains tax is chargeable on the value of assets retained at the time of death. However, the personal representatives administering the deceased's estate are deemed to acquire those assets for a consideration representing market value on death. This ensures that any increase in value occurring before the date of death will not be chargeable to capital gains tax. If a legatee or other person acquires an asset under a will or intestacy no chargeable gain will accrue to the personal representatives, and the person taking the asset will also be treated as having acquired it at the time of death for its then market value.

INHERITANCE TAX

Liability to inheritance tax may arise on a limited range of lifetime gifts and other dispositions and also on the value of assets retained, or deemed to be retained, at the time of death. An individual's domicile at the time of any gift or on death is an important matter. Domicile will generally be determined by applying normal rules, although special considerations may be necessary where an individual was previously domiciled in the UK but subsequently acquired a domicile of choice overseas. In addition, individuals who have been resident in the UK for at least 17 of the previous 20 years at the time of an event are treated as domiciled in the UK.

Where a person was domiciled, or treated as domiciled, in the UK at the time of a disposition or on death the location of assets is immaterial and full liability to inheritance tax arises. Individuals domiciled outside the UK are, however, chargeable to inheritance tax only on transactions affecting assets located in the UK.

The assets of husband and wife are not merged for inheritance tax purposes. Each spouse is treated as a separate individual entitled to receive the benefit of his or her exemptions, reliefs and rates of tax. Where husband and wife retain similar assets, e.g. shares in the same family company, special 'related property' provisions may require the merger of those assets for valuation purposes only.

Lifetime Gifts and Dispositions

Gifts and dispositions made during lifetime fall under four broad headings, namely:
(a) dispositions which are not transfers of value
(b) exempt transfers
(c) potentially exempt transfers
(d) chargeable transfers

Dispositions which are not transfers of value

Several lifetime transactions are not treated as transfers of value and may be entirely disregarded for inheritance tax purposes. These include transactions not intended to confer gratuitous benefit, the provision of family maintenance, the waiver of the right to receive remuneration or dividends, and the grant of agricultural tenancies for full consideration.

Exempt transfers

Certain transfers are treated as exempt transfers and incur no liability to inheritance tax. The main exempt transfers are listed below:

Transfers between spouses – Transfers between husband and wife are usually exempt. However, if the transferor is, but the transferee spouse is not, domiciled in the UK, transfers will be exempt only to the extent that the total does not exceed £55,000. Unlike the requirement used for income tax and capital gains tax purposes, it is immaterial whether husband and wife are living together.

Annual exemption – The first £3,000 of gifts and other dispositions made in a year ending on 5 April is exempt. If the exemption is not used, or not wholly used, in any year the balance may be carried forward to the following year only. The annual exemption will only be available for a potentially exempt transfer if that transfer becomes chargeable by reason of the donor's subsequent death.

Small gifts – Outright gifts of £250 or less to any person in one year ending 5 April are exempt.

Normal expenditure – A transfer made during lifetime and comprising normal expenditure is exempt. To obtain this exemption it must be shown that:
(a) the transfer was made as part of the normal expenditure of the transferor
(b) taking one year with another, the transfer was made out of income
(c) after allowing for all transfers of value forming part of normal expenditure the transferor was left with sufficient income to maintain his or her usual standard of living

Gifts in consideration of marriage – These are exempt if they satisfy certain requirements. The amount allowed will be governed by the relationship between the donor and a party to the marriage. The allowable amounts comprise:
(a) gifts by a parent, £5,000
(b) gifts by a grandparent, £2,500
(c) gifts by a party to the marriage, £2,500
(d) gifts by other persons, £1,000

Gifts to charities – These are exempt from liability.

Gifts to political parties – Gifts which satisfy certain requirements are generally exempt.

Gifts for national purposes – Gifts made to an extensive list of bodies are exempt from liability. These include, among others, the National Gallery, the British Museum, the National Trust, the National Art Collections Fund, the National Heritage Memorial Fund, the Historic Buildings and Monuments Commission for England (English Heritage), any local authority, any university or university college in the UK.

A number of other gifts made for the public benefit are also exempt.

Potentially exempt transfers

Lifetime gifts and dispositions which are neither to be ignored nor comprise exempt transfers incur possible liability to inheritance tax. However, relief is available for a range of potentially exempt transfers. These comprise gifts made by an individual to:
(a) a second individual
(b) trustees administering an accumulation and maintenance trust
(c) trustees administering a disabled person's trust

The accumulation and maintenance trust mentioned in (b) must provide that on reaching a specified age, not exceeding 25 years, a beneficiary will become absolutely entitled to trust assets or obtain an interest in possession in the income from those assets.

Additions to the above list affect settled property administered by trustees where an individual, or individuals, retain an interest in possession. The transfer of assets to, the removal of assets from, or the rearrangement of interests in such property comprise potentially exempt transfers if the person transferring an interest and the person benefiting from the transfer are both individuals.

No immediate liability to inheritance tax will arise on the making of a potentially exempt transfer. Should the donor survive for a period of seven years, immunity from liability will be confirmed. However, the donor's death within the seven-year *inter vivos* period produces liability if the amounts involved are sufficiently substantial (*see* below).

Chargeable transfers

Any remaining lifetime gifts or dispositions which are neither to be ignored nor represent exempt transfers or potentially exempt transfers, incur liability to inheritance tax. The range of such chargeable transfers is severely limited and is broadly confined to transfers made to or affecting discretionary trusts, transfers to non-individuals and transfers involving companies.

GIFTS WITH RESERVATION

A lifetime gift of assets made at any time after 17 March 1986 may incur additional liability to inheritance tax if the donor retains some interest in the subject matter of the gift. This may arise, for example, where a parent transfers a dwelling-house to a son or daughter and continues to occupy the property or to enjoy some benefit from that property. The retention of a benefit may be ignored where it is enjoyed in return for full consideration, perhaps a commercial rent, or where the benefit arises from changed circumstances which could not have been foreseen at the time of the original gift. The gift with reservation provisions will not usually apply to most exempt transfers.

There are three possibilities which may arise where the donor reserves or enjoys some benefit from the subject matter of a previous gift and subsequently dies, namely:
(a) if no benefit is enjoyed within a period of seven years before death there can be no further liability
(b) if the benefit ceased to be enjoyed within a period of seven years before the date of death, the original donor is deemed to have made a potentially exempt transfer representing the value of the asset at the time of cessation
(c) if the benefit is enjoyed at the time of death, the value of the asset must be included in the value of the deceased's estate on death

It must be emphasized that the existence of a benefit enjoyed at any time within a period of seven years before death will establish liability to tax on gifts with reservation, notwithstanding that the gift may have been made many years earlier, providing it was undertaken after 17 March 1986.

DEATH

Immediately before the time of death an individual is deemed to make a transfer of value. This transfer will comprise the value of assets forming part of the deceased's estate after subtracting most liabilities. Any exempt transfers may, however, be excluded. These include transfers for the benefit of a surviving spouse, a charity and a qualifying political party, together with bequests to approved bodies and for national purposes.

Death may also trigger three additional liabilities, namely:
(a) A potentially exempt transfer made within the period of seven years ending on death loses its potential status and becomes chargeable to inheritance tax
(b) The value of gifts made with reservation may incur liability if any benefit was enjoyed within a period of seven years preceding death
(c) Additional tax may become payable for chargeable lifetime transfers made within seven years before death

VALUATIONS

The valuation of assets is an important matter as this will establish the value transferred for lifetime dispositions and also the value of a person's estate at the time of death. The value of property will represent the price which might reasonably be expected from a sale in the open market. This price cannot be reduced on the grounds that, should the whole property be placed on the market simultaneously, values would be depressed.

In some cases it may be necessary to incorporate the value of 'related property'. This will include property comprised in the estate of the transferor's spouse and certain property previously transferred to charities. The purpose of the related property valuation rules is not to add the value of the property to the estate of the transferor. Related property must be merged to establish the aggregate value of the respective interests and this value is then apportioned, usually on a *pro rata* basis, to the separate interests.

The value of shares and securities listed on the Stock Exchange will be determined by extracting figures from the daily list of official prices.

Where quoted shares and securities are sold or the quotation is suspended within a period of 12 months following the date of death, a claim may be made to substitute the proceeds or subsequent value for the value on death. This claim will only be beneficial if the gross proceeds realized are lower or the value has fallen below market value at the time of death. A similar claim may be available for interests in land sold within a period of four years following death.

RELIEF FOR SELECTED ASSETS

Special relief is made available for certain assets, notably:

Woodlands

Where woodlands pass on death the value will usually be included in the deceased's estate. However, an election may be made in respect of land in the UK on which trees or underwood is growing to delete the value of those assets. Relief is confined to the value of trees or underwood and does not extend to the land on which they are growing. Liability to inheritance tax will arise if and when the trees or underwood are sold.

Agricultural property

Relief is available for the agricultural value of agricultural property. Such property must be occupied and used for agricultural purposes and relief is confined to the agricultural value only.

The value transferred, either on a lifetime gift or on death, must be determined. This value may then be reduced by a percentage. The percentage has changed from time to time but for events taking place after 9 March 1992 a 100 per cent deduction will be available if the transferor retained vacant possession or could have obtained that possession within a period of 12 months following the transfer. In other cases, notably including land let to tenants, a lower deduction of 50 per cent is usually available. However, this lower deduction was increased to 100 per cent if the letting was made after 31 August 1995.

It remains a requirement that the agricultural property was either occupied by the transferor for the purposes of agriculture throughout a two-year period ending on the date of the transfer, or was owned by him/her throughout a period of seven years ending on that date and also occupied for agricultural purposes.

Business property

Where the value transferred is attributable to relevant business property, that value may be reduced by a percentage. The reduction in value applies to:
(a) property consisting of a business or an interest in a business (i.e. a partnership)

(b) shares or securities of an unquoted company which provided the transferor with more than 25 per cent of voting rights

(c) other unquoted shares or securities not falling within (b)

(d) shares or securities of a quoted company which provided the transferor with control

(e) any land, building, machinery or plant which, immediately before the transfer, was used wholly or mainly for the purposes of a business carried on by a company of which the transferor had control

(f) any land, building, machinery or plant which, immediately before the transfer, was used wholly or mainly for the purposes of a business carried on by a partnership of which the transferor was a partner

(g) any land, building, machinery or plant which, immediately before the transfer, was used wholly or mainly for the purposes of a business carried on by the transferor and was then settled property in which he or she retained an interest in possession

The percentage deductions have changed from time to time. For events occurring after 9 March 1992 a deduction of 100 per cent is available for assets falling within (a) and (b). The deductions for unquoted shares in (c) was 50 per cent but this increased to 100 per cent for events taking place after 5 April 1996. A deduction of 50 per cent remains for assets within (d) to (g).

It is a general requirement that the property must have been retained for a period of two years before the transfer or death and restrictions may be necessary if the property has not been used wholly for business purposes. The same property cannot obtain both business property relief and the relief available for agricultural property.

Calculation of Tax Payable

The calculation of inheritance tax payable adopts the use of a cumulative total. Each chargeable lifetime transfer is added to the total with a final addition made on death. The top slice added to the total for the current event determines the rate at which inheritance tax must be paid. However, the cumulative total will only include transfers made within a period of seven years before the current event and those undertaken outside this period must be excluded.

Lifetime chargeable transfers

The value transferred by the limited range of lifetime chargeable transfers must be added to the seven-year cumulative total to calculate whether any inheritance tax is due. Should the nil rate band be exceeded, tax will be imposed on the excess at one-half of the rate shown below, i.e. at the rate of 20 per cent. However, if the donor dies within a period of seven years from the date of the chargeable lifetime transfer, additional tax may be due. This is calculated by applying tax at the full rate (in substitution for the one-half rate previously used). The amount of tax is then reduced to a percentage by applying tapering relief. This percentage is governed by the number of years from the date of the lifetime gift to the date of death and is as follows:

Period of years before death

Not more than 3	100%
More than 3 but not more than 4	80%
More than 4 but not more than 5	60%
More than 5 but not more than 6	40%
More than 6 but not more than 7	20%

Should this exercise produce liability greater than that previously paid at the one-half rate on the lifetime transfer, additional tax, representing the difference, must be discharged. Where the calculation shows an amount falling below tax paid on the lifetime transfer, no additional liability can arise nor will the shortfall become repayable.

Tapering relief will, of course, only be available if the calculation discloses a liability to inheritance tax. There can be no liability to the extent that the lifetime transfer falls within the nil rate band.

Potentially exempt transfers

Where a potentially exempt transfer loses immunity from liability due to the donor's death within the seven-year *inter vivos* period, the value transferred by that transfer enters into the cumulative total. Any liability to inheritance tax will be calculated by applying the full rate shown below, reduced to the percentage governed by tapering relief if the original transfer occurred more than three years before death. Liability can only arise to the extent, if any, that the nil rate band is exceeded.

Death

The final addition to the seven-year cumulative total will comprise the value of an estate on death. Inheritance tax will be calculated by applying the full rate shown below to the extent the nil rate band is exceeded. No tapering relief can be obtained.

Rates of Tax

In earlier times there were several rates of inheritance tax which progressively increased as the value transferred grew in size. However, for events taking place after 5 April 1997, a nil rate applies to the first £215,000. Any excess is charged at the single positive rate of 40 per cent.

Only one-half of the 40 per cent rate (namely 20 per cent) will be applicable for chargeable lifetime transfers.

Payment of Tax

Inheritance tax usually falls due for payment six months after the end of the month in which the chargeable transaction takes place. Where a transfer other than that made on death occurs after 5 April and before the following 1 October, tax falls due on the following 30 April, although there are some exceptions to this general rule.

Inheritance tax attributable to the transfer of certain land, controlling shareholding interests, unquoted shares, businesses and interests in businesses, together with agricultural property, may usually be satisfied by instalments spread over ten years. Except in the case of non-agricultural land, where interest is charged on outstanding instalments, no liability to interest arises where tax is paid on the due date. In all cases, delay in the payment of tax may incur liability to interest.

Settled Property

Complex rules apply to establish inheritance tax liability on settled property. Where a person is beneficially entitled to an interest in possession, that person is effectively deemed to own the property in which the interest subsists. It follows that where the interest comes to an end during the beneficiary's lifetime and some other person becomes entitled to the property or interest, the beneficiary is treated as having made a transfer of value. However, this will usually comprise a potentially exempt transfer. In addition, no liability will arise where the property vests in the absolute ownership of the previous beneficiary. The death of a person entitled to an interest in possession will require the value of the underlying property to be added to the value of the deceased's estate.

In the case of other settled property where there is no interest in possession (e.g. discretionary trusts), liability to tax will arise on each ten-year anniversary of the trust. There will also be liability if property ceases to be held on discretionary trusts before the first ten-year anniversary date is reached or between anniversaries. The rate of tax suffered will be governed by several considerations, including previous dispositions made by the settlor of the trust, transactions concluded by the trustees, and the period throughout which property has been held in trust.

Accumulation and maintenance settlements which require assets to be distributed, or interests in income to be created, not later than a beneficiary's 25th birthday may be exempt from any liability to inheritance tax.

CORPORATION TAX

Profits, gains and income accruing to companies resident in the UK incur liability to corporation tax. Non-resident companies are immune from this tax unless they carry on a trade in the UK through a permanent establishment, branch or office. Companies residing outside the UK may be liable to income tax at the basic rate on other income arising in the UK, perhaps from letting property. The following comments are confined to companies resident in the UK and have little application to those residing overseas.

Liability to corporation tax is governed by the profits, gains or income for an accounting period. This is usually the period for which financial accounts are made up, and in the case of companies preparing accounts to the same accounting date annually will comprise successive periods of 12 months.

RATE OF TAX

The amount of profits or income for an accounting period must be determined on normal taxation principles. The special rules which apply to individuals where a source of income is acquired or discontinued are ignored and consideration is confined to the actual profits or income for an accounting period.

The rate of corporation tax is fixed for a financial year ending on 31 March. Where the accounting period of a company overlaps this date and there is a change in the rate of corporation tax, profits and income must be apportioned.

In recent years the full rate of corporation tax has been as follows:

Financial year
Ending 31 March 1992, 1993, 1994, 1995, 1996, 1997   33%
       31 March 1998   31%

SMALL COMPANIES RATE

Where the profits of a company do not exceed stated limits, corporation tax becomes payable at the small companies rate. It is the amount of profits and not the size of the company which governs the application of this rate.

In recent years the small companies rate has been as follows:

Financial year
Ending 31 March 1992, 1993, 1994, 1995, 1996   25%
       31 March 1997   24%
       31 March 1998   21%

The level of profits which a company may derive without losing the benefit of the small companies rate is frequently changed. For each year ending on 31 March 1995, 31 March 1996, 31 March 1997 and 31 March 1998 the limit is £300,000. However, if profits exceed £300,000 but fall below £1,500,000 marginal small companies rate relief applies. The effect of marginal relief is that the average rate of corporation tax imposed on all profits steadily increases from the lower small companies rate to the full rate of 33 or 31 per cent, with tax being imposed on profits in the margin at an increased rate.

Different upper limits and marginal rates applied for earlier years. Where the accounting period of a company overlaps 31 March, profits must be apportioned to establish the appropriate rate for each part of those profits.

The lower limit of £300,000 and the upper limit of £1,500,000 apply to a period of 12 months and must be proportionately reduced for shorter periods. Some restriction in the small companies rate and the marginal rate may be necessary if there are two or more associated companies, namely companies under common control.

The small companies rate is not available for close investment-holding companies.

CAPITAL GAINS

Chargeable gains arising to a company are calculated in a manner similar to that used for individuals. However, companies cannot obtain the annual exemption of £6,500. Nor are they assessed to capital gains tax. In place of this tax companies suffer liability to corporation tax on chargeable gains. Tax is suffered on the full chargeable gain, after subtracting relief for losses, if any.

DISTRIBUTIONS

Dividends and other qualifying distributions made by a UK resident company are not satisfied after deduction of income tax. However, when making a distribution a company is required to account to the Inland Revenue for advance corporation tax. The amount of this tax is based on the distribution and changes in the rate have been introduced in recent years as follows:

Distribution	Rate
Year ending 5 April 1993	one third
Year ending 5 April 1994	nine thirty firsts
Year ending 5 April 1995, 1996, 1997, 1998	one quarter

Advance corporation tax accounted for in this manner in relation to distributions made in an accounting period may usually be set against a company's corporation tax liability for the same period. Some restrictions are imposed on the amount which can be offset but any surplus may be carried forward, or perhaps carried backwards, and set against corporation tax paid or due for other accounting periods.

A UK resident shareholder receiving a qualifying distribution also obtains a tax credit based on the distribution made. Over the same six-year period the tax credit will be calculated as follows:

Distribution	Rate
Year ending 5 April 1993	one third
Year ending 5 April 1994, 1995, 1996, 1997, 1998	one quarter

The total income of the individual therefore comprises the aggregate of the distribution and the tax credit, with that credit representing income tax at the rate of 20 per cent on the total amount in the more recent years. If the individual is not liable or not fully liable to income tax at this rate, all or part of the tax credit can be refunded by the Inland Revenue. There is no liability on distributions at the basic rate but individuals with substantial income incur liability to income tax at the higher rate of 40 per cent on the aggregate of the distribution and the tax credit. With tax deemed to have been suffered at the lower rate of 20 per cent the additional liability will be limited to the excess over this rate, which is also 20 per cent.

The amount of the tax credit will be reduced for distributions made after 5 April 1999 and it will no longer be possible to obtain any repayment of those credits. The ability of pension funds to obtain such repayments was withdrawn for distributions taking place after 2 July 1997.

The above comments have only limited application to foreign income dividends paid out of foreign income by some UK companies.

INTEREST

On making many payments of interest after 5 April 1996 a company is required to deduct income tax at the lower rate of 20 per cent and account for the tax deducted to the Inland Revenue. The gross amount of interest paid will usually be included in the calculation of profits on which corporation tax becomes payable.

GROUPS OF COMPANIES

Each company within a group is separately charged to corporation tax on profits, gains and income. However, where one group member realizes a loss, other than a capital loss, a claim may be made to offset the deficiency against profits of some other member of the same group.

Claims are also available to avoid the payment of advance corporation tax on distributions, or the deduction of income tax on the payment of interest, for transactions between members of a group of companies. The transfer of capital assets from one member of a group to a fellow member will incur no liability to tax on chargeable gains.

PAY AND FILE

A 'pay and file' system now affects all companies. Under this system tax is payable nine months following the end of the accounting period involved, with accounts and returns being submitted three months later. Failure to satisfy corporation tax or to submit documents within these time limits will result in a liability to discharge interest and penalties.

Although the pay and file system retains some similarity with self-assessment, there are differences. These are likely to be removed shortly when full self-assessment is extended to companies.

VALUE ADDED TAX

Value added tax (VAT) is charged on the value of the supplies made by a registered trader and extends to both the supply of goods and the supply of services. It is administered by Customs and Excise.

Liability to account for VAT arises on the value of goods imported into the UK from sources outside the European Community. In contrast goods imported by a trader from a second trader in a member state of the European Community attract no VAT on importation. Instead there is an acquisition tax whereby a trader who acquires goods must include the acquisition in his normal VAT return and account for the tax due. A UK trader who exports goods to a member state will not be required to account for VAT on the supply, if that trader observes the requirements laid down by regulations.

REGISTRATION

All traders, including professional men and women and companies, making taxable supplies of a value exceeding stated limits are required to register for VAT purposes. Taxable supplies represent the supply of goods and services potentially chargeable with VAT. The limits which govern mandatory registration are amended annually but from 1 December 1997 an unregistered trader must register:

(a) at any time, if there are reasonable grounds for believing that the value of taxable supplies in the next 30 days will exceed £49,000

(b) at the end of any month if the value of taxable supplies in the 12 months then ending has exceeded £49,000.

Liability to register under (b) may be avoided if it can be shown that the value of supplies in the period of 12 months then beginning will not exceed £47,000. There may, however, be liability to register immediately where a business is taken over from another trader as a 'going concern'.

Similar limits apply from 1 January 1998 where goods are acquired from within the European Community.

Where the limits governing mandatory registration have been exceeded, the trader must notify Customs and Excise. In the event of failure to provide prompt notification, the person concerned will be required to account for VAT from the proper registration date.

A trader whose taxable supplies do not reach the mandatory registration limits may apply for voluntary registration. This step may be thought advisable to recover input tax or to compete with other registered traders.

A registered trader may submit an application for deregistration if the value of taxable supplies subsequently falls. From 1 December 1997, an application for deregistration can be made if the value of taxable supplies for the year beginning on the application date is not expected to exceed £47,000.

INPUT TAX

A registered trader will both suffer tax (input tax) when obtaining goods or services for the purposes of his business and also become liable to account for tax (output tax) on the value of goods and services which he supplies. Relief can usually be obtained for input tax suffered, either by setting that tax against output tax due or by repayment. Most items of input tax can be relieved in this manner but there are exceptions, including the prohibition of relief for the cost of business entertaining. Where a registered trader makes both exempt supplies and also taxable supplies to his customers or clients, there may be some restriction in the amount of input tax which can be recovered.

OUTPUT TAX

When making a taxable supply of goods or services a registered trader must account for output tax, if any, on the value of the supply. Usually the price charged by the registered trader will be increased by adding VAT but failure to make the required addition will not remove liability to account for output tax.

The application of output tax, and also input tax, may be affected where a trader is using the special second-hand goods scheme.

EXEMPT SUPPLIES

No VAT is chargeable on the supply of goods or services which are treated as exempt supplies. These include the provision of burial and cremation facilities, insurance, finance and education. The granting of a lease to occupy land or the sale of land will usually comprise an exempt supply, but there are numerous exceptions. In particular, the sale of new non-domestic buildings or certain buildings used by charities cannot be treated as exempt supplies.

A taxable person may elect to tax rents and other supplies of buildings and agricultural land not used for residential or charitable purposes.

Exempt supplies do not enter into the calculation of taxable supplies which governs liability to mandatory registration. Such supplies made by a registered trader may, however, limit the amount of input tax which can be relieved. It is for this reason that the election may be useful.

RATES OF TAX

Two rates of VAT have applied since 1 April 1991, namely:
(a) a zero, or nil, rate
(b) a standard rate of 17.5 per cent

In addition, a special reduced rate of 8 per cent applied to supplies of domestic fuel since March 1994. This rate was further reduced to 5 per cent for supplies made after 1 September 1997.

ZERO-RATING

A large number of supplies are zero-rated. The following list is not exhaustive but indicates the wide range of supplies which may be included under this heading:

(a) the supply of many items of food and drink for human consumption. This does not include ice creams, chocolates, sweets, potato crisps and alcoholic drinks. Nor does it extend to supplies made in the course of catering or to items supplied for consumption in a restaurant or café. Whilst the supply of cold items, e.g. sandwiches, for consumption away from the supplier's premises, is zero-rated, the supply of hot food, for example fish and chips, is not
(b) animal feeding stuffs
(c) sewerage and water, unless supplied for industrial purposes
(d) books, brochures, pamphlets, leaflets, newspapers, maps and charts
(e) talking books for the blind and handicapped, and wireless sets for the blind
(f) supplies of services, other than professional services, when constructing a new domestic building or a building to be used by a charity. The supply of materials for such a building is also zero-rated, together with the sale or the grant of a long lease for these buildings. Alterations to some protected buildings are also zero-rated
(g) the transportation of persons in a vehicle, ship or aircraft designed to carry not less than 12 persons
(h) supplies of drugs, medicines and other aids for the handicapped
(i) supplies of clothing and footwear for young persons
(j) exports

Although no tax is due on a zero-rated supply, this does comprise a taxable supply which must be included in the calculation which governs liability to register.

COLLECTION OF TAX

Registered traders submit VAT returns for accounting periods usually of three months duration but arrangements can be made to submit returns on a monthly basis. Very large traders must account for tax on a monthly basis but this does not affect the three-monthly return. The return will show both the output tax due for supplies made by the trader in the accounting period and also the input tax for which relief is claimed. If the output tax exceeds input tax the balance must be remitted with the VAT return. Where input tax suffered exceeds the output tax due the registered trader may claim recovery of the excess from Customs and Excise.

This basis for collecting tax explains the structure of VAT. Where supplies are made between registered traders the supplier will account for an amount of tax which will usually be identical to the tax recovered by the person to whom the supply is made. However, where the supply is made to a person who is not a registered trader there can be no recovery of input tax and it is on this person that the final burden of VAT eventually falls.

In those cases where goods are acquired by a UK trader from a supplier within a member state of the European Community the trader must also account for the tax due on acquisition.

An optional scheme is available for registered traders having an annual turnover of taxable supplies not exceeding £300,000. Such traders may, if they wish, render returns annually. Nine interim payments of VAT will be paid on account, with a final balancing payment accompanying submission of the return. The number of interim payments may be reduced if turnover does not exceed £100,000.

BAD DEBTS

Many retailers operate special retail schemes for calculating the amount of VAT due. These schemes are based on the volume of consideration received in an accounting period. Should a customer fail to pay for goods or services supplied, there will be no consideration on which VAT falls to be calculated.

To avoid the problem of bad debts incurred by traders not operating a special retail scheme, an optional system of cash accounting is available. This scheme, confined to traders with annual taxable supplies not exceeding £350,000, enables returns to be made on a cash basis, in substitution for the normal supply basis. Traders using such a scheme will not, of course, include bad debts in the calculation of cash receipts.

Where neither the cash accounting arrangements nor the special retail scheme applies, output tax falls due on the value of the supply and liability is not affected by failure to receive consideration. However, where a debt is more than six months old, relief for bad debts will be forthcoming. The calculation of the six-month period now commences from the date on which payment for the supply falls due.

In those cases where a supplier obtains relief for a bad debt, the person to whom the supply has been made must refund to Customs and Excise any input tax relief which may have been granted.

OTHER SPECIAL SCHEMES

In addition to the schemes for retailers, there are several special schemes applied to calculate the amount of VAT due and which also limit the ability to recover input tax. Before 1 January 1995 these schemes were confined to a limited range of goods, but on and after this date virtually all second-hand goods have been brought within special margin schemes.

FARMERS

Farmers may elect to apply a special flat rate scheme. This scheme is available to farmers who are not registered traders. Under the scheme a flat-rate addition of 4 per cent may be made on sales, with the amount of the addition being retained by the farmer. Registered traders to whom such a supply is made may treat the 4 per cent addition as recoverable input tax.

Legal Notes

IMPORTANT

These notes outline certain aspects of the law as they might affect the average person. They are intended only as a broad guideline and are by no means definitive. The information is believed to be correct at the time of going to press but the law is constantly changing so expert advice should always be taken. In some cases, sources of further information are given in these notes.

It is always advisable to consult a solicitor without delay; timely advice will set your mind at rest but sitting on your rights can mean that you lose them. Anyone who does not have a solicitor already can contact the Citizens' Advice Bureau (addresses in the telephone directory or at any post office or town hall), the Law Society of England and Wales (113 Chancery Lane, London WC2A 1PL) or the Law Society of Scotland (26 Drumsheugh Gardens, Edinburgh EH3 7YR) for assistance in finding one.

The legal aid and legal aid and assistance schemes exist to make the help of a lawyer available to those who would not otherwise be able to afford one. Entitlement depends upon an individual's means (*see* pages 659–60) but a solicitor or Citizens' Advice Bureau will be able to advise about entitlement.

ADOPTION OF CHILDREN

In England and Wales the adoption of children is mainly governed by the Adoption Act 1976 and the Children Act 1989.

Anyone over 21, whether married, single, widowed or divorced, can legally adopt a child. Married couples must adopt 'jointly', unless one partner cannot be found, is incapable of making an application, or if a separation is likely to be permanent. Unmarried couples may not adopt 'jointly' although one partner in that couple may adopt. The only organizations allowed to arrange adoptions are the social services departments of local authorities or voluntary agencies such as Barnardo's which are registered as adoption agencies with the local authorities.

Once an adoption has been arranged, a court order is necessary to make it legal. These are obtained from the High Court (Family Division) or from a county or family proceedings court. The child's natural parents (or guardians) must consent to the adoption, unless the court dispenses with the consent, e.g. where the natural parent has neglected the child or is incapable of giving consent. Once adopted, the child has the same status as a child born to the adoptive parents and the natural parents cease to have any rights or responsibilities where the child is concerned. The adopted child will be treated as the natural child of the adoptive parents for the purposes of intestate succession, national insurance, family allowances, etc. The adopted child ceases to have any rights to the estates of his/her natural parents.

REGISTRATION AND CERTIFICATES

All adoptions in England and Wales are registered in the Adopted Children Register kept by the Office of National Statistics, and by the General Register Office for adoptions in Scotland. Certificates from the registers can be obtained in a similar way to birth certificates (*see* page 649).

TRACING NATURAL PARENTS OR CHILDREN WHO HAVE BEEN ADOPTED

An adult adopted person may apply to the Registrar-General for information to enable him/her to obtain a full birth certificate. For those adopted before 12 November 1975 it is obligatory to receive counselling services before this information is given; for those adopted after that date counselling services are optional. There is also an Adoption Contact Register (created after the 1989 Act) in which details of adult adopted people and of their relatives may be recorded. The BAAF (*see* below) can provide addresses of organizations which offer advice, information and counselling to adopted people, adoptive parents and people who have had their children adopted.

SCOTLAND

The relevant legislation is the Adoption (Scotland) Act 1978 (as amended by the Children Act 1995) and the provisions are similar to those described above. In Scotland, petitions for adoption are made to the Sheriff Court or the Court of Session.

Further information can be obtained from:
BRITISH AGENCIES FOR ADOPTION AND FOSTERING (BAAF), Skyline House, 200 Union Street, London SE1 0LX. Tel: 0171-593 2000

BIRTHS (REGISTRATION)

The birth of a child must be registered within 42 days of birth at the register office of the district in which the baby was born. In England and Wales it is possible to give the particulars to be registered at any other register office. Responsibility for registering the birth rests with the parents, except in the case of an illegitimate child, when the mother is responsible for registration. Responsibility rests firstly with the parents but if they fail, particulars may be given to the registrar by:
– a relative of either parent (in Scotland only)
– the occupier of the house in which the baby was born
– a person present at the birth
– the person having charge of the child
Failure to register the birth within 42 days without reasonable cause may leave the parents liable to a penalty.

If the parents were married at the time of the birth, either parent may register the birth and details about both parents will be entered on the register. If the parents were unmarried at the time of the birth, the father's details are entered only if both parents attend or if the parents have made a statutory declaration confirming the identity of the father. Copies of the forms necessary to make such a declaration are available at the register offices. A short birth certificate is issued free when the birth is registered.

STILL BIRTHS

If a baby is stillborn, i.e. born dead after the 24th week of pregnancy, the birth must be registered. The doctor or midwife who attends the birth or afterwards examines the body of the child will issue a Medical Certificate of Stillbirth and this must be presented at the register office.

RE-REGISTRATION

In certain circumstances it may be necessary to re-register a birth, e.g. where the birth of an illegitimate child is legitimated by the subsequent marriage of the parents. It is also possible to re-register the birth of an illegitimate child so that the father's name is entered on the register.

BIRTH AT SEA

The master of a British ship must record any birth on board and send particulars to the Registrar-General of Shipping.

BIRTH ABROAD

Births of British subjects occurring abroad are registered with consular officers and certificates of birth are subsequently available from the Registrar-General. The registration of births among members of the armed forces that occur abroad or on military ships or aircraft is governed by the Registration of Births, Deaths and Marriages (Special Provisions) Act 1957.

SCOTLAND

In Scotland the birth of a child must be registered within 21 days at the register office of either the district in which the baby was born or the district in which the mother was resident at the time of the birth.

If the child is born, either in or out of Scotland, on a ship, aircraft or land vehicle that ends its journey at any place in Scotland, the child, in most cases, will be registered as if born in that place.

CERTIFICATES OF BIRTHS, DEATHS OR MARRIAGES

Certificates of births, deaths or marriages that have taken place in England and Wales since 1837 can be obtained from the Office of National Statistics (General Register Office). Applications can be made:
– by a personal visit to the Family Records Centre, London (for opening hours, *see* below)
– by postal application to the General Register Office, Southport
Certificates are also available from the Superintendent Registrar for the district in which the event took place or, in the case of marriage certificates, from the minister of the church in which the marriage took place. Any register office can advise about the best way to obtain certificates.

There is no charge for the short birth certificate issued when a birth is registered. The fees for other certificates (from 1 April 1997) are:

Obtained from Registrar who registered the birth, death or marriage
Standard certificate, £3.00
Special certificate for certain statutory purposes, £2.50
Short certificate of birth, £3.00

Obtained from Superintendent Registrar
Standard certificate, £6.00
Special certificate for certain statutory purposes, £2.50
Short certificate of birth, £4.00

From the clergyman or other authorized person who registered the marriage
Standard marriage certificate, at time of marriage, £3.00
Standard marriage certificate, subsequent to time of marriage, £6.00
Special certificate of marriage for certain statutory purposes, £2.50

From the Family Records Centre, London/by post from the General Register Office, Southport
Standard certificate of birth, death or marriage
Personal application, £6.00
Postal application, £15.00
Postal application and information from ONS Index supplied, £12.00
Standard certificate of adoption
Personal application, £10.00
Postal application, £10.00
Short certificate of birth
Personal application, £5.00
Postal application, £14.00
Postal application and information from ONS Index supplied, £11.00
Short certificate of adoption
Personal application, £8.00
Postal application, £8.00

Indexes prepared from the registers are available for searching by the public at the Family Records Centre in London or at a Superintendent Registrar's Office; indexes at the latter relate only to births, deaths and marriages which occurred in that registration district. There is no charge for searching the indexes in the Public Search Room at the Family Records Centre but a general search fee is charged for searches at a Superintendent Registrar's Office. A fee is charged for verifying index references against the records.

The Society of Genealogists has many records of baptisms, marriages and deaths prior to 1837.

SCOTLAND

Certificates of births, deaths or marriages that have taken place in Scotland since 1855 can be obtained from the General Register Office or from the appropriate local registrar. The General Register Office also keeps the Register of Divorces (including decrees of declaration of nullity of marriage), and holds parish registers dating from before 1855.

Fees for certificates (from 1 April 1997) are:

Certificates (full or abbreviated) of birth, death, marriage or adoption
Personal application, £11
Postal application, £13

Extract marriage certificate
In the month following the ceremony, £8
More than one month after the ceremony, £11

Extract from the Register of Divorces
Personal application, £11
Postal application, £13

Extract of entries in parish records prior to 1855, £13

Further information can be obtained from:
THE GENERAL REGISTER OFFICE, Office for National Statistics, Smedley Hydro, Trafalgar Road, Birkdale, Southport, Merseyside PR8 2HH. Tel: 01704-569824
FAMILY RECORDS CENTRE, 1 Myddelton Street, London EC1R 1UW. Opens 9 a.m. on Monday, Wednesday, Thursday, Friday, 10 a.m. Tuesday, 9.30 a.m. Saturday. Closes 5 p.m. Monday, Wednesday, Friday, Saturday, 7 p.m. Tuesday, Thursday
THE GENERAL REGISTER OFFICE, New Register House, Edinburgh EH1 3YT. Tel: 0131-334 0380
THE SOCIETY OF GENEALOGISTS, 14 Charterhouse Buildings, Goswell Road, London EC1M 7BA. Tel: 0171-251 8799

BRITISH CITIZENSHIP

The British Nationality Act 1981 which came into force on 1 January 1983 established three types of citizenship to replace the single form of Citizenship of the UK and Colonies created by the British Nationality Act 1948. The three forms of citizenship are: British Citizenship; British Dependent Territories Citizenship; and British Overseas Citizenship. Three residual categories were created: British Subjects; British Protected Persons; and British Nationals (Overseas).

BRITISH CITIZENSHIP

Almost everyone who was a citizen of the UK and colonies and had a right of abode in the UK prior to the 1981 Act became British citizens when the Act came into force. British citizens have the right to live permanently in the UK and are free to leave and re-enter the UK at any time.

A person born on or after 1 January 1983 in the UK (including, for this purpose, the Channel Islands and the Isle of Man) is entitled to British citizenship if he/she falls into one of the following categories:

– he/she has a parent who is a British citizen
– he/she has a parent who is settled in the UK
– he/she is a newborn infant found abandoned in the UK
– his/her parents subsequently settle in the UK
– he/she lives in the UK for the first ten years of his/her life and is not absent for more than 90 days in each of those years
– he/she is adopted in the UK and one of the adopters is a British Citizen

A person born outside the UK may acquire British citizenship if he/she falls into one of the following categories:

– he/she has a parent who is a British citizen otherwise than by descent, e.g. a parent who was born in the UK
– he/she has a parent who is a British citizen serving the Crown overseas
– the Home Secretary consents to his/her registration while he/she is a minor
– he/she is a British Dependent Territories citizen, a British Overseas citizen, a British subject or a British protected person and has been lawfully resident in the UK for five years
– he/she is a British Dependent Territories citizen who acquired that citizenship from a connection with Gibraltar
– he/she is adopted (see above) or naturalized (see below)

Where parents are married, the status of either may confer citizenship on their child. If a child is illegitimate, the status of the mother determines the child's citizenship.

Under the 1981 Act, Commonwealth citizens and citizens of the Republic of Ireland were entitled to registration as British citizens before 1 January 1988. In 1985 citizens of the Falkland Islands were granted British citizenship.

Renunciation of British citizenship must be registered with the Home Secretary and will be revoked if no new citizenship or nationality is acquired within six months. If the renunciation was required in order to retain or acquire another citizenship or nationality, the citizenship may be reacquired once.

BRITISH DEPENDENT TERRITORIES CITIZENSHIP

Under the 1981 Act, this type of citizenship was conferred on citizens of the UK and colonies by birth, naturalization or registration in British Dependent Territories. British Dependent Territories citizens may be entitled to regis-

tration as British citizens on completion of five years' legal residence in the UK.

On 1 July 1997 citizens of Hong Kong who did not qualify to register as British citizens under the British Nationality (Hong Kong) Act 1990 lost their British Dependent Territories citizenship on the handover of sovereignty to China; they could, however, apply to register as British Nationals (Overseas).

Eligibility for British Dependent Territories citizenship is determined by similar rules to those for acquiring British citizenship, except that the connection is with the dependent territory rather than with the UK.

BRITISH OVERSEAS CITIZENSHIP

Under the 1981 Act, this type of citizenship was conferred on any UK and colonies citizens who did not qualify for British citizenship or citizenship of the British Dependent Territories. British Overseas citizenship may be acquired by the wife and minor children of a British Overseas citizen in certain circumstances. British Overseas citizens may be entitled to registration as British citizens on completion of five years' legal residence in the UK.

RESIDUAL CATEGORIES

British subjects, British protected persons and British Nationals (Overseas) may be entitled to registration as British citizens on completion of five years' legal residence in the UK.

Citizens of the Republic of Ireland who were also British subjects before 1 January 1949 can retain that status if they fulfill certain conditions.

EUROPEAN UNION CITIZENSHIP

British citizens (including Gibraltarians who are registered as such) are also EU citizens and are entitled to travel freely to other EU countries to work, study, reside and set up a business. EU citizens have the same rights with respect to the United Kingdom.

NATURALIZATION

Naturalization is granted at the discretion of the Home Secretary. The basic requirements are five years' residence (three years if the applicant is married to a British citizen), good character, adequate knowledge of the English, Welsh or Scottish Gaelic language, and an intention to reside permanently in the UK.

STATUS OF ALIENS

Aliens may not hold public office or vote in Britain and they may not own a British ship or aircraft. Citizens of the Republic of Ireland are not deemed to be aliens.

Further information can be obtained from the Home Office, Immigration and Nationality Directorate, 3rd Floor, India Buildings, Water Street, Liverpool L2 0QN. Tel: 0151-237 5200

CONSUMER LAW

SALE OF GOODS

A sale of goods contract is the most common type of contract. It is governed by the Sale of Goods Act 1979 (as amended by the Sale and Supply of Goods Act 1994). The Act provides protection for buyers by implying terms into every sale of goods contract. These terms are:

– a condition that the seller will pass good title to the buyer (unless the seller agrees to transfer only such title as he has)

– where the seller sells goods by reference to a description, a condition that the goods will match that description and, where the sale is by sample and description, a condition that the bulk of the goods will correspond with such sample and description
– where goods are sold by a business seller, a condition that the goods will be of satisfactory quality if they meet the standard that a reasonable person would regard as satisfactory taking into account any description of the goods, the price, and all other relevant circumstances. The quality of the goods includes their state and condition, relevant aspects being whether they are suitable for their common purpose, their appearance and finish, freedom from minor defects and their safety and durability. This term will not be implied, however, if a buyer has examined the goods and should have noticed the defect or if the seller specifically drew the buyer's attention to the defect
– where goods are sold by a business seller, a condition that the goods are reasonably fit for any purpose made known to the seller by the buyer, unless the buyer does not rely on the seller's judgement, or it is not reasonable for him/her to do so
– where goods are sold by sample, conditions that the bulk of the sample will correspond with the sample in quality, that the buyer will have a reasonable opportunity of comparing the two and that the goods are free from any defect rendering them unsatisfactory which would not be obvious from the sample

Some of the above terms can be excluded from contracts by the seller. The seller's right to do this is, however, restricted by the Unfair Contract Terms Act 1977. The Act offers more protection to a buyer who 'deals as a consumer', that is where the sale is a business sale, the goods are of a type ordinarily bought for private use and the goods are bought by a buyer who is not a business buyer. In a sale by auction or competitive tender, a buyer never deals as consumer. Also, a seller can never exclude the implied term as to title mentioned above.

Hire-purchase Agreements

Terms similar to those implied in contracts of sales of goods are implied into contracts of hire-purchase, under the Supply of Goods (Implied Terms) Act 1973. The 1977 Act limits the exclusion of these implied terms as before.

Supply of Goods and Services

Under the Supply of Goods and Services Act 1982, similar terms are also implied in other types of contract under which ownership of goods passes, e.g. a contract for 'work and materials' such as supplying new parts while servicing a car, and contracts for the hire of goods. These types of contracts have additional implied terms:
– that the supplier will use reasonable care and skill
– that the supplier will carry out the service in a reasonable time (unless the time has been agreed)
– that the supplier will make a reasonable charge (unless the charge has already been agreed)
The 1977 Act limits the exclusion of these implied terms in a similar manner as before.

Unfair Terms

The Unfair Terms in Consumer Contracts Regulations 1994 apply to contracts between business sellers (or suppliers of goods and services) and consumers, where the terms have not been individually negotiated, i.e. where the terms were drafted in advance so that the consumer was unable to influence those terms. An unfair term is one which operates to the detriment of the consumer. An unfair term does not bind the consumer but the contract will continue to bind the parties if it is capable of existing without the unfair term. The regulations contain a non-exhaustive list of terms which are regarded as unfair. Whether a term is regarded as fair or not will depend on many factors, including the nature of the goods or services, the surrounding circumstances (such as the bargaining strength of both parties) and the other terms in the contract.

Trade Descriptions

It is a criminal offence under the Trade Descriptions Act 1968 for a business seller to apply a false trade description of goods or to supply or offer to supply any goods to which a false description has been applied. A 'trade description' includes descriptions of quality, size, composition, fitness for purpose and method, and place and date of manufacture of the goods. It is also an offence to give a false indication of the price of goods. Prosecutions are brought by trading standards inspectors.

Fair Trading

The Fair Trading Act 1973 is designed to protect the consumer. It provides for the appointment of a Director-General of Fair Trading, one of whose duties is to review commercial activities in the UK relating to the supply of goods and services to consumers. An example of a practice which has been prohibited by a reference made under this Act is that of business sellers posing in advertisements as private sellers.

Consumer Protection

Under the Consumer Protection Act 1987, producers of goods are liable for any injury or for any damage exceeding £275 caused by a defect in their product (subject to certain defences).

The Consumer Protection (Cancellation of Contracts Concluded Away from Business Premises) Regulations 1987 allow consumers a seven-day period in which to cancel contracts for the supply of goods and services, where the contracts were made during an unsolicited visit to the consumer's home or workplace. This only applies to contracts where the cost exceeds £35.

Consumer Credit

In matters relating to the provision of credit (or the supply of goods on hire or hire-purchase), consumers are also protected by the Consumer Credit Act 1974. Under this Act a licence, issued by the Director-General of Fair Trading, is required to conduct a consumer credit or consumer hire business or to deal in credit brokerage, debt adjusting, counselling or collecting. Any 'fit' person may apply to the Director-General of Fair Trading for a licence, which is normally renewable after ten years. A licence is not necessary if such types of business are only transacted occasionally, or if only exempt agreements are involved. The provisions of the Act only apply to 'regulated' agreements, i.e. those that are with individuals or partnerships, those that are not exempt (such as certain local authority and building society loans), and those where the total credit does not exceed £15,000. Provisions include:
– the terms of the regulated agreement can be altered by the creditor provided the agreement gives him/her the right to do so; in such cases the debtor must be given proper notice of this
– in order for a creditor to enforce a regulated agreement, the agreement must comply with certain formalities and must be properly executed. The debtor must also be given specified information by the creditor or his/her broker or agent during the negotiations which take place before the signing of the agreement. The agreement must

state certain information such as the amount of credit, the annual percentage rate of interest and the amount and timing of repayments
– if an agreement is signed other than at the creditor's (or credit broker's or negotiator's) place of business and oral representations were made in the debtor's presence during discussions pre-agreement, the debtor has a right to cancel the agreement. Time for cancellation expires five clear days after the debtor receives a second copy of the agreement. The agreement must inform the debtor of his right to cancel and how to cancel
– if the debtor is in arrears (or otherwise in breach of the agreement), the creditor must serve a default notice before taking any action such as repossessing the goods
– if the agreement is a hire-purchase or conditional sale agreement, the creditor cannot repossess the goods without a court order if the debtor has paid one-third of the total price of the goods
– in agreements where the debtor is required to make grossly exorbitant payments or where the agreement grossly contravenes the ordinary principles of fair trading, the debtor may request that the court alter or set aside some of the terms of the agreement. The agreement can also be reopened during enforcement proceedings by the court itself

Where a credit reference agency has been used to check the debtor's financial standing, the creditor must give the agency's name to the debtor, who is entitled to see the agency's file on him. A fee of £1 is payable to the agency.

SCOTLAND

The legislation governing the sale and supply of goods applies to Scotland as follows:
– the Sale of Goods Act 1979 applies with some modifications and it has been amended by the Sale and Supply of Goods Act 1994
– the Supply of Goods (Implied Terms) Act 1973 applies
– the Supply of Goods and Services Act 1982 does not extend to Scotland but some of its provisions were introduced by the Sale and Supply of Goods Act 1994
– only Parts II and III of the Unfair Contract Terms Act 1977 apply
– the Trade Descriptions Act 1968 applies with minor modifications
– the Consumer Credit Act 1974 applies

PROCEEDINGS AGAINST THE CROWN

Until 1947, proceedings against the Crown were generally possible only by a procedure known as a petition of right, which put the litigant at a considerable disadvantage. The Crown Proceedings Act 1947 placed the Crown (not the Sovereign in his/her private capacity, but as the embodiment of the State) largely in the same position as a private individual. The Act did not, however, extinguish or limit the Crown's prerogative or statutory powers, and it granted immunity to HM ships and aircraft. It also left certain Crown privileges unaffected. The Act largely abolished the special procedures which previously applied to civil proceedings by and against the Crown. Civil proceedings may be instituted against the appropriate government department or against the Attorney-General.

In Scotland proceedings against the Crown founded on breach of contract could be taken before the 1947 Act and no special procedures applied. The Crown could, however, claim certain special pleas. The 1947 Act applies in part to Scotland and brings the practice of the two countries as

closely together as the different legal systems permit. Civil proceedings may be instituted against the Lord Advocate representing the appropriate government department.

DEATHS

WHEN A DEATH OCCURS

If the death was expected, the doctor who attended the deceased during their final illness should be contacted. If the death was sudden or unexpected, the family doctor (if known) and police should be contacted. For stillbirths, *see* pages 648–9.

If the cause of death is quite clear the doctor will provide:
– a medical certificate that shows the cause of death (this will be in a sealed envelope, addressed to the registrar)
– a formal notice that states that the doctor has signed the medical certificate and that explains how to get the death registered

If the death was known to be caused by a natural illness but the doctor wishes to know more about the cause of death, he/she may ask the relatives for permission to carry out a post-mortem examination. This should not delay the funeral.

In England and Wales a coroner is responsible for investigating deaths occurring in the following circumstances:
– when no doctor has treated the deceased during his or her last illness or when the doctor attending the patient did not see him or her within 14 days before death, or after death; or
– when the death occured during an operation or before recovery from the effect of an anaesthetic; or
– when the death was sudden and unexplained or attended by suspicious circumstances; or
– when the death might be due to an industrial injury or disease, or to accident, violence, neglect or abortion, or to any kind of poisoning; or
– the death occurred in prison or in police custody

The doctor will write on the formal notice that the death has been referred to the coroner; if the post mortem shows that death was due to natural causes, the coroner may issue a notification which gives the cause of death so that the death can be registered. If the cause of death was violent or unnatural, the coroner is obliged to hold an inquest.

In Scotland the office of coroner does not exist. The local procurator fiscal inquires into sudden or suspicious deaths. A fatal accident inquiry will be held before the sheriff where the death has resulted from an accident during the course of the employment of the person who has died, or where the person who has died was in legal custody, or where the Lord Advocate deems it in the public interest that an inquiry be held.

REGISTERING A DEATH

In England and Wales the death must be registered by the registrar of births and deaths for the district in which it occurred; details can be obtained from the telephone directory (under registration of births and deaths and marriages), from the doctor or local council, or at a post office or police station. From April 1997, information concerning a death can be given before any registrar of births and deaths in England and Wales. The registrar will pass the relevant details to the registrar for the district where the death occurred, who will then register the death. In Scotland a death may be registered in any registration district in which the deceased was ordinarily resident immediately before his/her death.

In England and Wales the death must normally be registered within five days; in Scotland it must be registered within eight days. If the death has been referred to the coroner it cannot be registered until the registrar has received authority from the coroner to do so. Failure to register a death involves a penalty.

If the death occurred at a house, the death may be registered by:
- any relative of the deceased present at the death or in attendance during the last illness
- any relative of the deceased residing or being in the sub-district where the death occurred
- any person present at the death
- the occupier or any inmate of the house if he/she knew of the occurrence of the death
- any person causing the disposal of the body

The person registering the death should take the medical certificate of the cause of death with them; it is also useful, though not essential, to take the deceased's birth and marriage certificates, medical card (if possible), pension documents and life assurance details. The registrar will issue a certificate for burial or cremation and a certificate of registration of death; both are free of charge. A death certificate is a certified copy of the entry in the death register; these can be provided on payment of a fee and may be required for the following purposes:
- the will
- bank and building society accounts
- savings bank certificates and premium bonds
- insurance policies
- pension claims

If the death occurred abroad or on a foreign ship or aircraft, the death should be registered according to the local regulations of the relevant country and a death certificate should be obtained. The death can also be registered with the British Consul in that country and a record will be kept at the General Register Office. This avoids the expense of bringing the body back.

After 12 months of death or the finding of a dead body, no death can be registered without the consent of the Registrar-General.

BURIAL AND CREMATION

In most circumstances in England and Wales a certificate for burial or cremation must be obtained from the registrar before the burial or cremation can take place. If the death has been referred to the coroner, an order for burial or a certificate for cremation must be obtained. In Scotland a body may be buried (but not cremated) before the death is registered.

Most funerals are arranged by a funeral director. The funeral costs can normally be repaid out of the deceased's estate and will be given priority over any other claims. If the deceased has left a will it may contain directions concerning the funeral; however, these directions need not be followed by the executor.

The deceased's papers should also indicate whether a grave space had already been arranged. Most town churchyards and many suburban churchyards are no longer open for burial because they are full. Most cemeteries are non-denominational and may be owned by local authorities or private companies; fees vary.

If the body is to be cremated, an application form, two cremation certificates (for which there is a charge) or a certificate for cremation if the death was referred to the coroner, and a certificate signed by the medical referee must be completed in addition to the certificate for burial or cremation (the form is not required if the coroner has issued a certificate for cremation). All the forms are available from the funeral director or crematorium. Most crematoria are run by local authorities; the fees usually include the medical referee's fee and the use of the chapel. Ashes may be scattered, buried in a churchyard or cemetery, or kept.

The registrar must be notified of the date, place and means of disposal of the body within 96 hours (England and Wales) or three days (Scotland).

If the death occurred abroad or on a foreign ship or aircraft, a local burial or cremation may be arranged. If the body is to be brought back to England or Wales, a death certificate from the relevant country or an authorization for the removal of the body from the country of death from the coroner or relevant authority will be required. To arrange a funeral in England or Wales an authenticated translation of a foreign death certificate or a death certificate issued in Scotland or Northern Ireland which must show the cause of death, is needed, together with a certificate of no liability to register from the registrar in England and Wales in whose sub-district it is intended to bury or cremate the body. If it is intended to cremate the body a cremation order will be required from the Home Office or a certificate for cremation.

Further information can be obtained from:

THE GENERAL REGISTER OFFICE, Office for National Statistics, Smedley Hydro, Trafalgar Road, Birkdale, Southport, Merseyside PR8 2HH. Tel: 01704-569824

THE GENERAL REGISTER OFFICE, New Register House, Edinburgh EH1 3YT. Tel: 0131-334 0380

DIVORCE AND RELATED MATTERS

ENGLAND AND WALES

There are two types of matrimonial suit: those seeking the annulment of a marriage, and those seeking a judicial separation or divorce. To obtain an annulment, judicial separation or divorce in England and Wales, one or both of the parties must have their permanent home in England and Wales when the petition is started, or have been living in England and Wales for at least a year on the day the petition is started. All cases are commenced in divorce county courts or in the Divorce Registry in London. If a suit is defended it may be transferred to the High Court.

NULLITY OF MARRIAGE

A marriage is invalid from the beginning if:
- the parties were within the prohibited degrees of consanguinity, affinity or adoption (*see* page 661)
- the parties were not male and female
- either of the parties was already married (if the polygamous marriage was entered into outside England and Wales, it is invalid if either of the parties lived in England or Wales at the time of the marriage)
- either of the parties was under the age of 16
- the formalities of the marriage were defective, e.g. the marriage did not take place in an authorized building, and both parties knew of the defect

In the case of those aged 16 to 17, absence of parental consent does not invalidate the marriage.

A marriage may be voidable (i.e. a decree of nullity may be obtained but in the meantime the marriage remains valid) on the following grounds:
- either party was unable to consummate the marriage
- the respondent wilfully refused to consummate the marriage (insistence on the use of contraceptives does not constitute wilful refusal to consummate, but may constitute unreasonable behaviour for the purpose of

divorce and may be allowed as a defence to a charge of desertion)
- either party did not validly consent to the marriage, in consequence of duress, mistake, unsoundness of mind, or otherwise
- either party was suffering from a mental disorder at the time of the marriage
- the respondent was suffering from a communicable venereal disease at the time of the marriage, and the petitioner did not know this
- the respondent was pregnant by another man at the time of the marriage, and the petitioner did not know this

In the last four circumstances, proceedings must generally be instituted within three years of the date of the marriage.

A decree of nullity only annuls the marriage from the date of the decree, and any children of the marriage are legitimate. Children of a void marriage are illegitimate unless the father lived in England and Wales at the time of the birth (or father's death, if earlier) and at the time of conception (or marriage, if later) both or either of the parents reasonably believed the marriage was valid.

When a marriage has been annulled, both parties are free to marry again.

SEPARATION

A couple may enter into an agreement to separate by consent but for the agreement to be valid it must be followed by an immediate separation; a solicitor should be contacted.

Judicial separation does not dissolve a marriage and it is not necessary to prove that the marriage has irretrievably broken down. Either party can petition for a judicial separation at any time; the grounds listed below as grounds for divorce are also grounds for judicial separation.

DIVORCE

Divorce dissolves the marriage and leaves both parties at liberty to marry again. Neither party can petition for divorce until at least one year after the date of the marriage. The fee for starting a divorce petition is £150. The sole ground for divorce is the irretrievable breakdown of the marriage; this must be proved on one or more of the following grounds:
- the respondent has committed adultery and the petitioner finds it intolerable to live with him/her; however the petitioner cannot rely on an act of adultery by the other party if they have lived together for more than six months after the discovery that adultery had been committed
- the respondent has behaved in such a way that the petitioner cannot reasonably be expected to continue living with him/her
- the respondent deserted the petitioner for two years immediately before the petition. Desertion may be defined as a voluntary withdrawal from cohabitation by the respondent without just cause and against the wishes of the petitioner; where one party is guilty of serious misconduct which forces the other party to leave, the party at fault is said to be guilty of constructive desertion
- the respondent and the petitioner have lived separately for two years immediately before the petition and the respondent consents to the decree
- the respondent and the petitioner have lived separately for five years immediately before the petition

A total period of less than six months during which the parties have resumed living together is disregarded in determining whether the prescribed period of separation or desertion has been continuous (but cannot be included as part of the period of separation).

The Matrimonial Causes Act 1973 requires the solicitor for the petitioner in certain cases to certify whether the possibility of a reconciliation has been discussed with the petitioner.

THE DECREE NISI

A decree nisi does not dissolve or annul the marriage but must be obtained before a divorce or annulment can take place.

Where the suit is undefended, the evidence normally takes the form of a sworn written statement made by the petitioner which is considered by a district judge. If the judge is satisfied that the petitioner has proved the contents of the petition, he/she will set a date for the pronouncement of the decree nisi in open court; neither party need attend.

If the judge is not satisfied that the petitioner has proved the contents of the petition, or if the suit is defended, the petition will be heard in open court with the parties giving oral evidence.

THE DECREE ABSOLUTE

The decree nisi is usually made absolute after six weeks and on the application of the petitioner. The fee for applying for a decree absolute is £20. If the judge thinks it may be necessary to exercise any of his/her powers under the Children Act 1989, he/she can in exceptional circumstances delay the granting of the decree absolute. The decree absolute dissolves or annuls the marriage.

CHILDREN

Neither parent is now awarded 'custody' of any children of the marriage in England and Wales. The term 'parent with care' is used to describe the parent who lives with the child or children; the parent who does not normally live with the child or children is termed the 'absent parent'. The courts will deal with issues of contact and residence involving children; in all court cases concerning children, whether connected to a matrimonial suit or not, the welfare of the child is the paramount consideration.

MAINTENANCE, ETC.

Either party may be liable to pay maintenance to their former spouse. If there were any children of the marriage, both parents have a legal responsibility to support them financially if they can afford to do so. These so-called ancillary matters, including any property settlements, may be settled before the divorce goes through but currently can go on long after the marriage is dissolved.

The courts are responsible for assessing maintenance for the former spouse, taking into account each party's income and essential outgoings and other aspects of the case. The court also deals with any maintenance for a child which has been treated by the spouses as a 'child of the family', e.g. a stepchild, and any property settlements.

The Child Support Agency (CSA) was set up under the Child Support Act 1991 and is now responsible for assessing the maintenance that absent parents should pay for their natural or adopted children (whether or not a marriage has taken place). The CSA accepts applications only when all the people involved are habitually resident in the UK; the courts will continue to deal with cases where one of the people involved lives abroad. The CSA deals with all new cases, and is gradually taking on cases where the parent with care (or his/her new partner) was already receiving income support, family credit or disability working allowance before 5 April 1993. People with existing court orders or written maintenance agreements made before 5 April 1993 should continue to use the courts. Where it is already collecting child maintenance, the CSA has the power to offer a collection and enforcement service for certain other payments of maintenance.

A formula is used to work out how much child maintenance is payable. The formula ensures that after the payment of child maintenance the absent parent's income, and that of any second family he/she may now have, remains significantly above basic income support rates. Also, no absent parent will normally be assessed to pay more than 30 per cent of his/her net income in current child maintenance, or more than 33 per cent if he/she is also liable for any arrears. Absent parents are normally expected to pay at least a minimum amount of child maintenance (currently about £2.50 a week).

A scheme has begun to be introduced since the end of 1996 which allows departures from the formula in certain tightly defined circumstances, e.g. the high costs of travel to maintain contact with a child, or to have a property and capital transfer ('clean break' settlement) entered into before April 1993 taken into account; there will also be some additional grounds which may result in liability being increased.

Some cases involving unusual circumstances are treated as special cases and the assessment is modified. Where there is financial need (e.g. because of disability or continuing education), maintenance may be ordered by the court for children even beyond the age of 18.

The level of maintenance is reviewed automatically every two years. Either parent can report a change of circumstances and request a review at any time. An independent complaints examiner for the CSA is to be appointed in early 1997.

If the absent parent does not pay the child maintenance, the CSA may make an order for payments to be deducted directly from his/her salary or wages; if all other methods fail, the CSA may take court action to enforce the payment.

COURT ORDERS

Magistrates' courts used for domestic proceedings are now called family proceedings courts. A spouse can apply to the family proceedings court for a court order on the ground that the other spouse:
- has failed to pay reasonable maintenance for the applicant
- has failed to make a proper contribution towards the reasonable maintenance of a 'child of the family'
- has deserted the applicant
- has behaved in such a way that the applicant cannot reasonably be expected to live with the respondent
  If the case is proved, the court can order:
- periodical payments for the applicant and/or a 'child of the family'
- a lump sum payment (not exceeding £1,000) to the applicant and/or a 'child of the family'

In deciding what orders (if any) to make, the court must consider guidelines which are similar to those governing financial orders in divorce cases. There are also special provisions relating to consent orders and separation by agreement. An order may be enforceable even if the parties are living together, but in some cases it will cease to have effect if they continue to do so for six months.

DOMESTIC VIOLENCE

If one spouse has been subjected to violence at the hands of the other, it is now possible to obtain a court order very quickly to restrain further violence and if necessary to have the other spouse excluded from the home. Such orders may also relate to unmarried couples. A person disobeying such a court order is liable to be imprisoned for contempt of court.

IMPENDING LEGISLATION

A recent Act of Parliament provides that irretrievable breakdown would be the sole ground for divorce; the partner initiating the divorce would be required to attend an information session about the nature of divorce and the options available; and divorce would be granted after one year, or 18 months if the couple have children, during which time the couple would have the chance to take part in mediation sessions to make arrangements concerning children, property and money. These changes are unlikely to be effective until 1999 at the earliest.

SCOTLAND

Although there is separate legislation for Scotland covering nullity of marriage, judicial separation, divorce and ancillary matters, the provisions are in most respects the same as those for England and Wales. The following is confined to those points on which the law in Scotland differs.

A suit for judicial separation or divorce may be raised in the Court of Session; it may also be raised in the Sheriff Court if either party was resident in the sheriffdom for 40 days immediately before the date of the action or for 40 days ending not more than 40 days before the date of the action. The fee for starting a divorce petition is £70 in the Sheriff Court.

When adultery is cited as proof that the marriage has broken down irretrievably, it is not necessary in Scotland to prove also that it is intolerable for the petitioner to live with the respondent. In the case of desertion, irretrievable breakdown is not established if cohabitation is resumed for a period of more than three months after the two-year desertion period has expired.

The court is responsible for seeking to promote a reconciliation between the spouses. Where a divorce action has been raised, it may be postponed by the court to enable the parties to seek to effect a reconciliation if the court feels that there may be a reasonable prospect of such reconciliation. If the parties do cohabit during such postponement, no account is taken of the cohabitation if the action later proceeds.

In actions for divorce and separation, the court has the power to award custody of any children of the marriage. The welfare of the children is of paramount importance, and the fact that a spouse has caused the breakdown of the marriage does not in itself preclude him or her from being awarded custody.

A simplified procedure for 'do-it-yourself' divorce was introduced in 1983 for certain divorces. If the action is based on two or five years' separation and will not be opposed, and if there are no children under 16 and no financial claims, the applicant can write directly to the local sheriff court or to the Court of Session for the appropriate forms to enable him or her to proceed. The fee is £55, unless the applicant receives income support, family credit or legal advice and assistance, in which case there is no fee.

The decree absolute is known in Scotland as the extract decree. The fee for applying for an extract decree is £14.

Further information can be obtained from any divorce county court, solicitor or Citizens' Advice Bureau, the Lord Chancellor's Department or the Lord Advocate's Department (for entries, see Index), or the following:

THE PRINCIPAL REGISTRY, Somerset House, London WC2R 1LP. Tel: 0171-936 6000

THE COURT OF SESSION, Divorce Section (SP), Parliament House, Parliament Square, Edinburgh EH1 1RQ. Tel: 0131-225 2595

THE CHILD SUPPORT AGENCY, 2 Western Road, Crewe CW98 1BD. Tel: 0345-131000

EMPLOYMENT LAW

PAY AND CONDITIONS

The Employment Rights Act 1996 consolidates the statutory provisions relating to employees' rights. Employers must give each employee based in Great Britain and employed for more than one month a written statement containing the following information:
– names of employer and employee
– date when employment began
– remuneration and intervals at which it will be paid
– job title or description of job
– hours and place(s) of work
– holiday entitlement and holiday pay
– entitlement to sick leave and sick pay
– details of pension scheme(s)
– length of notice period that employer and employee need to give to terminate employment, or the end date for a fixed-term contract
– details of any collective agreement which affects the terms of employment
– details of disciplinary and grievance procedures
– if the employee is to work outside the UK for more than one month, the period of such work and the currency in which payment is made
This must be given to the employee within two months of the start of their employment.

SICK PAY

Employees absent from work through illness or injury are entitled to receive Statutory Sick Pay (SSP) from the employer for a maximum period of 28 weeks in any three-year period. This applies to all employees, both men and women, up to the age of 65.

DEDUCTIONS FROM PAY

Employers may not make deductions from an employee's wages without the employee's prior written consent or unless authorized by statute (e.g. deductions for national insurance or tax).

PART-TIME EMPLOYEES

The rights of part-time workers are in most circumstances in line with the treatment of full-time workers.

SUNDAY TRADING

The Sunday Trading Act 1994 gave new rights to shop workers. They have the right not to be dismissed, selected for redundancy or to suffer any detriment (such as the denial of overtime, promotion or training) if they refuse to work on Sundays. This does not apply to those who, under their contracts, are employed to work on Sundays.

TRADE UNION MEMBERSHIP

Under employment legislation, employees or potential employees may not be penalized because they are or are not a member of a trade union.

DISPUTES

Where it has not been possible to settle a dispute in the workplace, it may be possible for employees to make a complaint to an industrial tribunal. ACAS (the Advisory, Conciliation and Arbitration Service; for entry, see Index) offers advice and conciliation in employment disputes.

TERMINATION OF EMPLOYMENT

An employee may be dismissed without notice if guilty of gross misconduct but in other cases a period of notice must be given by the employer. The minimum periods of notice specified in the Employment Rights Act 1996 are:
– at least one week if the employee has been continuously employed for one month or more but for less than two years
– at least two weeks if the employee has been continuously employed for two years or more. A week is added for every complete year of continuous employment up to 12 years
– at least 12 weeks for those who have been continuously employed for 12 years or more
– longer periods apply if these are specified in the contract of employment
If an employee is dismissed with less notice than he/she is entitled to, the employer is generally liable to pay wages for the period of proper notice (or for the period of the contract for those on fixed-term contracts). Generally, no notice needs to be given of the expiry of a fixed-term contract.

REDUNDANCY

An employee dismissed because of redundancy may be entitled to a lump sum. This applies if:
– the employee has at least two years' continuous service (qualified as for unfair dismissal, below)
– the employee is actually dismissed by the employer (even in cases of voluntary redundancy)
– dismissal is due to a reduction in the work force
An employee may not be entitled to a redundancy payment if offered a new job by the same employer. The amount of payment depends on the length of service, the salary and the age of the employee.

UNFAIR DISMISSAL

Complaints about unfair dismissal are dealt with by an industrial tribunal. Any employee, with two years' continuous service (although this requirement has been referred by the House of Lords to the European Court of Justice) subject to exceptions, regardless of their hours of work, can make a complaint to the tribunal. At the tribunal the employer must prove that he/she acted reasonably in dismissing the employee and that the dismissal was due to one or more of the following reasons:
– the employee's capability for the job
– the employee's conduct
– redundancy
– a legal restriction preventing the continuation of the employee's contract
– some other substantial reason
If the employee is found to have been unfairly dismissed, the tribunal can order that he/she be reinstated or compensated.

DISCRIMINATION

Discrimination in employment on the grounds of sex, race or (subject to wide exceptions) disability is unlawful. The following legislation applies to those employed in Great Britain but not to employees in Northern Ireland or to those who work mainly abroad:
– The Equal Pay Act 1970 (as amended) entitles men and women to equality in matters related to their contracts of employment. Those doing like work for the same employer are entitled to the same pay and conditions regardless of their sex

- The Sex Discrimination Act 1975 (as amended by the Sex Discrimination Act 1986) makes it unlawful to discriminate on grounds of sex or marital status. This covers all aspects of employment, including advertising for recruits, terms offered, opportunities for promotion and training, and dismissal procedures
- The Race Relations Act 1976 gives individuals the right not to be discriminated against in employment matters on the grounds of race, colour, nationality, or ethnic or national origins. It applies to all aspects of employment
- The Disability Discrimination Act 1995 makes discrimination against a disabled person in all aspects of employment unlawful. Unlike sex and race discrimination, an employer may show that the treatment is justified and that the employer acted reasonably. Employers with 20 or fewer employees are exempt

The Equal Opportunities Commission and the Commission for Racial Equality (for entries, *see* Index) have the function of eliminating such discriminations in the workplace and can provide further information and assistance.

In Northern Ireland like provisions exist but are constituted in separate legislation. The Fair Employment (Northern Ireland) Act 1989 adds specific provisions aimed at preventing religious discrimination.

ILLEGITIMACY AND LEGITIMATION

The Children Act 1989 gives the mother parental responsibility for the child when she is not married to the father. The father can acquire parental responsibility either by agreement with her (in prescribed form) or by applying to the court. If an illegitimate child is to be adopted, the father's consent is required only where he has been awarded parental rights by the court.

Every child born to a married woman during marriage is presumed to be legitimate, unless the couple are separated under court order when the child is conceived, in which case the child is presumed not to be the husband's child. It is possible to challenge the presumption of legitimacy or illegitimacy through civil proceedings.

LEGITIMATION

Under the Legitimacy Act 1976, an illegitimate person automatically becomes legitimate when his/her parents marry. This applies even where one of the parents was married to a third person at the time of the birth. In such cases it is necessary to re-register the birth of the child. In Scotland, the relevant legislation is the Legitimation (Scotland) Act 1968 which came into operation on 8 June 1968, on which date thousands of existing illegitimate children were regarded as legitimate.

RIGHTS OF ILLEGITIMATE PEOPLE

For the purposes of most legislation, illegitimate and legitimate people have the same rights and responsibilities. In particular, under the Family Law Reform Acts 1969 and 1987, legitimate and illegitimate children have broadly the same rights on an intestacy. Furthermore, in any will made after 31 December 1969, it is assumed that any reference to children or relatives will include those who are illegitimate and those related through another person who is illegitimate. In Scotland, illegitimate and legitimate people are given equal status under the Law Reform (Parent and Child) Scotland Act 1986.

In Scotland, the father of an illegitimate child has a responsibility to provide for that child until he/she is 16. The mother of the child can take action in court if this is not done. The court will also decide on custody and access issues.

JURY SERVICE

A person charged with any but the most minor offences is entitled to be tried by jury, although jury trials are now unusual in civil cases. There are 12 members of a jury in England and Wales. In Scotland there are 12 members of a jury in a civil case in the Court of Session, seven in the Sheriff Court, and 15 in a criminal trial. Jurors are normally asked to serve for ten working days, although jurors selected for longer cases are expected to sit for the duration of the trial.

Every parliamentary or local elector between the ages of 18 and 70 who has lived in the UK (including, for this purpose, the Channel Islands and the Isle of Man) for any period of at least five years since reaching the age of 13 is qualified to serve on a jury unless he/she is ineligible or disqualified.

ENGLAND AND WALES

Those ineligible for jury service include:
- those who have at any time been judges, magistrates or senior court officials
- those who have within the previous ten years been concerned with the adminstration of justice (e.g. barristers, solicitors and their clerks, court officials, coroners, police officers, prison officers and probation officers)
- priests of any religion and vowed members of religious communities
- certain sufferers from mental illness

Those disqualified from jury service include:
- those who have at any time been sentenced by a court in the UK (including, for this purpose, the Channel Islands and the Isle of Man) to a term of imprisonment or custody of five years or more
- those who have within the previous ten years served any part of a sentence of imprisonment, youth custody or detention, been detained in a young offenders' institution, received a suspended sentence of imprisonment or order for detention, or received a community service order
- those who have within the previous five years been placed on probation

Those who may be excused as of right from jury service include:
- persons over the age of 65
- members and officers of the Houses of Parliament
- full-time serving members of the armed forces
- registered and practising members of the medical, dental, nursing, veterinary and pharmaceutical professions
- those who have served on a jury in the previous two years

The court has the discretion to excuse a juror from service, or defer the date of service, if the service would be a hardship to the juror. If a person serves on a jury knowing himself/herself to be ineligible or disqualified, he/she is liable to be fined up to £1,000 or £5,000 respectively. Jurors failing to attend without good cause are liable to be fined up to £1,000. The defendant can object to any juror if he/she can show that the juror is ineligible, disqualified, or biased against him/her.

A juror may claim travelling expenses, a subsistence allowance and an allowance for other financial loss (e.g. loss of earnings or benefits, fees paid to carers or child-minders) up to a stated limit.

It is an offence for a juror to discuss a case with anyone who is not a member of the jury, even after the trial is over. A jury's verdict must normally be unanimous, but if no verdict has been reached after two hours' consideration (or such longer period as the court deems to be reasonable) a majority verdict is acceptable if ten jurors agree to it.

It is an offence to intimidate, threaten or harm a juror.

SCOTLAND

Qualification criteria for jury service in Scotland are similar to those in England and Wales, except that the maximum age for a juror is 65, and those who have within the previous five years been concerned with the administration of justice are ineligible for service. Ministers of religion, persons in holy orders and those who have served on a jury in the previous five years are excusable as of right.

The maximum fine for a person serving on a jury knowing himself/herself to be ineligible is £1,000. The maximum fine for failing to attend without good cause is £400.

Further information can obtained from:

THE COURT SERVICE, Southside, 105 Victoria Street, London SW1E 6QT. Tel: 0171-210 1775

THE CLERK OF JUSTICIARY, High Court of Justiciary, Parliament House, Parliament Square, Edinburgh EH1 1RQ. Tel: 0131-225 2595

LANDLORD AND TENANT

When a property is rented to a tenant, the rights and responsibilities of the landlord and the tenant are determined largely by the tenancy agreement but also by statutory provisions. Some of the main provisions are outlined below but it is advisable to contact the Citizens' Advice Bureau or the local authority housing department for further information.

RESIDENTIAL LETTINGS

The provisions outlined here apply only where the tenant lives in a separate dwelling from the landlord and where the dwelling is the tenant's only or main home. It does not apply to licensees such as lodgers, guests or service occupiers.

The 1996 Housing Act radically changes certain aspects of the legislation referred to below, in particular the grant of assured and assured shorthold tenancies under the Housing Act 1988. It is advisable to check whether the new legislation has come into force before relying on the provisions set out below.

ASSURED SHORTHOLD TENANCIES

If a tenancy was granted on or after 15 January 1989 and before 28 February 1997, the tenant may have an assured tenancy giving that tenant greater rights. The tenant could, for example, stay in possession of the dwelling for as long as the tenant observed the terms of the tenancy. The landlord cannot obtain possession from such a tenant unless the landlord can establish a specific ground for possession (set out in the Housing Act 1988) and obtains a court order. The rent payable is that agreed with the landlord unless the rent has been fixed by the rent assessment committee of the local authority. The tenant or the landlord may request that the committee set the rent in line with open market rents for that type of property. Any rent increases that are to take place should be written into the agreement but failing that, the landlord must give advance notice of the increase.

Under the Housing Act 1996, most new lettings entered into on or after 28 February 1997 will be assured shorthold tenancies. This means that tenants are given limited rights. The landlord must obtain a court order, however, to obtain possession if the tenant refuses to vacate at the end of the tenancy.

REGULATED TENANCIES

Before the Housing Act 1988 came into force (15 January 1989) there were regulated tenancies; some are still in existence and are protected by the Rent Act 1977. Under this Act it is possible for the landlord or the tenant to apply to the local rent officer to have a 'fair' rent registered. The fair rent is then the maximum rent payable.

SECURE TENANCIES

Secure tenancies are generally given to tenants of local authorities, housing associations and certain other bodies. This gives the tenant lifelong tenure unless the terms of the agreement are broken by the tenant. In certain circumstances those with secure tenancies may have the right to buy their property. In practice this right is generally only available to council tenants.

AGRICULTURAL PROPERTY

Tenancies in agricultural properties are governed by the Agricultural Holdings Act 1986 and the Rent (Agricultural) Act 1976, which give similar protections to those described above, e.g. security of tenure, right to compensation for disturbance, etc. The Agricultural Holdings (Scotland) Act 1991 applies similar provisions to Scotland.

EVICTION

Under the Protection from Eviction Act 1977 (as amended by the Housing Act 1988), a landlord must give reasonable notice that he/she is to evict the tenant, and in most cases a possession order, granted in court, is necessary. Notice is generally to be at least four weeks and in prescribed statutory form (notices are available from law stationers). It is illegal for a landlord to evict a person by putting their belongings onto the street, by changing the locks and so on. It is also illegal for a landlord to harass a tenant in any way in order to persuade him/her to give up the tenancy.

LANDLORD RESPONSIBILITIES

Under the Landlord and Tenant Act 1985, where the term of the lease is less than seven years the landlord is responsible for maintaining the structure and exterior of the property and all installations for the supply of water, gas and electricity, for sanitation, and for heating and hot water.

LEASEHOLDERS

Legally leaseholders have bought a long lease rather than a property and in certain limited circumstances the landlord can end the tenancy. Under the Leasehold Reform Act 1967 (as amended by the Housing Acts 1969, 1974 and 1980), leaseholders of houses may have the right to buy the freehold or to take an extended lease for a term of 50 years. This applies to leases where the term of the lease is over 21 years and where the leaseholder has occupied the house as his/her main residence for the last three years, or for a total of three years over the last ten.

The Leasehold Reform, Housing and Urban Development Act came into force in 1993 and allows the leaseholders of flats in certain circumstances to buy the freehold of the building in which they live.

Responsibility for maintenance of the structure, exterior and interior of the building should be set out in the lease. Usually the upkeep of the interior of his/her part of the property is the responsibility of the leaseholder, and responsibility for the structure, exterior and common interior areas is shared between the freeholder and the leaseholder(s).

BUSINESS LETTINGS

The Landlord and Tenant Acts 1927 and 1954 (as amended) give security of tenure to the tenants of most business premises. The landlord can only evict the tenant on one of the grounds laid down in the 1954 Act, and in some cases where the landlord repossesses the property the tenant may be entitled to compensation.

SCOTLAND

In Scotland assured and short assured tenancies exist for lettings after 2 January 1989 and are similar to assured tenancies in England and Wales. The relevant legislation is the Housing (Scotland) Act 1988.

Most tenancies created before 2 January 1989 were regulated tenancies and the Rent Act 1984 still applies where these exist. The Act defines, among other things, the circumstances in which a landlord can increase the rent when improvements are made to the property. The provisions of the Rent Act do not apply to tenancies where the landlord is the Crown, a local authority, the development corporation of a new town or a housing corporation.

The Housing (Scotland) Act 1987 and its provisions relate to local authority responsibilities for housing, the right to buy, and local authority secured tenancies. The provisions are broadly similar to England and Wales.

In Scotland, business premises are not controlled by statute to the same extent as in England and Wales, although the Shops (Scotland) Act 1949 gives some security to tenants of shops. Tenants of shops can apply to the sheriff for a renewal of tenancy if threatened with eviction. This application may be dismissed if the landlord has offered to sell the property to the tenant at an agreed price. The Act extends to properties where the Crown or government departments are the landlords or the tenants.

Under the Leases Act 1449 the landlord's successors (either purchasers or creditors) are bound by the agreement made with any tenants so long as the following conditions are met:
– the lease, if for more than one year, must be in writing
– there must be a rent
– there must be a term of expiry
– the tenant must have entered into possession
Many leases contain references to term and quarter days. The statutory dates of these are listed on page 9.

LEGAL AID

Under the Legal Aid Act 1988 (as amended) and the Legal Aid (Scotland) Act 1986, people on low or moderate incomes may qualify for help with the costs of legal advice or representation. The scheme is administered in England and Wales by the Legal Aid Board and in Scotland by the Scottish Legal Aid Board (for entries, *see* Index). There are three types of legal aid: civil legal aid, legal advice and assistance, and criminal legal aid.

CIVIL LEGAL AID

Applications for legal aid are made through a solicitor; the Citizens' Advice Bureau will have addresses for local solicitors. Franchised solicitors are those approved by the Legal Aid Boards, which can provide details.

Civil legal aid is available for proceedings in the following:
– the House of Lords
– the High Court
– the Court of Appeal
– county courts
– lands tribunals
– the Employment Appeal Tribunal
– the Restrictive Practices Court
– the Commons Commissioners
– civil proceedings in magistrates' courts
– family proceedings courts

It is not available for the following:
– tribunals other than those mentioned above
– defamation proceedings
– obtaining the decree in undefended divorce and judicial separation
– court cases outside England and Wales

ELIGIBILITY

The Legal Aid Board will only grant a civil legal aid certificate where:
– the applicant qualifies financially, and
– the applicant has reasonable grounds for taking or defending the action, and
– it is reasonable to grant legal aid in the circumstances of the case. For example, civil legal aid will not be granted where it appears that the applicant will gain only trivial advantage from the proceedings

In order to qualify for civil legal aid, a person's disposable income must be £7,595 a year or less and their disposable capital must be £6,750 or less. (The financial limits are different for pensioners and in personal injury claims). Disposable income is the total income, less outgoings such as tax and national insurance contributions, rent, council tax, mortgage payments, etc., with allowances made for dependants. The income of a spouse or cohabitee is taken into account unless they are living apart or have a contrary interest in the proceedings. Disposable capital includes savings, insurances, any personal possessions of substantial value and property owned. For applications from 1 June 1996, the applicant's dwelling house is treated as follows:
– the capital value of the property (i.e. market value, less amount outstanding on any mortgage) will be taken into account in so far as it exceeds £100,000
– the capital amount allowed in respect of mortgage debt or charge over the property cannot exceed £100,000
– if the mortgage debt exceeds £100,000, the amount allowed against income for mortgage payments will be reduced in proportion
– the total amount of mortgage debt allowed for all properties (including second and subsequent dwellings) cannot exceed £100,000

CONTRIBUTIONS

Some of those who qualify for legal aid will have to contribute towards their legal costs:
– if in receipt of income support, no contributions are due
– if annual disposable income is between £2,565 and £7,595, a contribution must be made from disposable income
– if disposable capital is over £3,000, all disposable capital in excess of £3,000 must be paid as a contribution
Contributions from disposable income are paid monthly for as long as the person has legal aid. The amount of the contribution depends on the amount of disposable income

in excess of £2,565; the greater the excess income, the greater the contribution. Contributions from capital are payable immediately.

STATUTORY CHARGES

A statutory charge is made if a person receives money or property in a case for which they have received legal aid. This means that the amount paid by the Legal Aid Fund on their behalf is deducted from the amount that the person receives. This does not apply if the court has ordered that the costs be paid by the other party or if the payments are for maintenance. In family proceedings cases, the first £2,500 is exempt and the statutory charge is taken from anything in excess of that.

In urgent cases, e.g. domestic violence, legal aid may be granted without the means test. This will be carried out later and the person will have to reimburse the Legal Aid Fund for any aid that they received which exceeded their entitlement.

SCOTLAND

Civil legal aid is available for cases in the following:
– the House of Lords
– the Court of Session
– the Lands Valuation Appeal Court
– the Scottish Land Court
– sheriff courts
– the Lands Tribunal for Scotland
– the Employment Appeal Tribunals
– the Restrictive Practices Court

Eligibility for civil legal aid is assessed in a similar way to that in England and Wales, though the financial limits differ in some respects and are as follows:
– a person is eligible if disposable income is £8,158 or less and disposable capital is £6,750 or less
– if disposable income is between £2,498 and £8,158, contributions are payable
– if disposable capital exceeds £3,000, contributions are payable

LEGAL ADVICE AND ASSISTANCE

The legal aid and assistance scheme (commonly referred to as the green form scheme) covers the costs of getting advice and help from a solicitor, and, in some cases, representation in court under the 'assistance by way of representation' scheme (*see* below).

A person is eligible for legal advice and assistance if:
– they have a disposable income of £77 a week or less and disposable capital of £1,000 or less
– they are eligible for income support or family credit (unless they have disposable capital of more than £1,000)
There are no contributions under this scheme.

If a person is eligible, the Legal Aid Board will pay for up to two hours' work by a solicitor on behalf of the person (three hours where drafting a petition for divorce). The solicitor must seek the approval of the Legal Aid Board to claim for longer periods of time. The work the solicitor does may include giving advice, writing letters, making an application for civil/criminal legal aid, seeking the advice of a barrister, etc. The scheme does not cover any form of proceedings before a court or tribunal.

Any money or property recovered with the help of legal advice and assistance will be subject to a 'solicitor's charge', which is similar to a statutory charge in civil legal aid but with some differences.

ASSISTANCE BY WAY OF REPRESENTATION

This type of assistance is available for most cases in a family proceedings court and to patients before a mental health review tribunal. It covers the cost of preparing a case and of legal representation in the court.

Under this scheme the two-hour limit does not apply and the approval of the Legal Aid Board is needed in all cases. The income and capital limits are different to legal advice and assistance. In order to qualify, a person's disposable income must be £162 a week or less and their savings must not exceed £3,000. There is no means test for patients due before a mental health review tribunal. Contributions may have to be made and a solicitor's charge will apply to money or property recovered (as with legal advice and assistance).

DUTY SOLICITORS

The Legal Aid Act 1988 also provides free advice and assistance to anyone questioned by the police (whether under arrest or helping the police with their enquiries). No means test or contributions are required for this. The advice or assistance can be from the duty solicitor at the police station, from a person's own solicitor or from any local solicitor (a list is available at police stations).

Duty solicitors are usually available at the magistrates' court, in criminal cases, for advice and/or representation on first appearances. This assistance is not means-tested.

The Legal Aid Fund also covers the costs of a solicitor present in the buildings of family proceedings or county courts who may be requested by the court to advise or represent someone in need of help.

SCOTLAND

Legal advice and assistance operates in a similar way in Scotland. A person is eligible:
– if disposable income does not exceed £162 a week. If disposable income is between £67 and £162 a week, contributions are payable
– if disposable capital does not exceed £1,000 (£1,335 if the person has one dependant, £1,535 if two dependants). There are no contributions from capital

CRIMINAL LEGAL AID

It is up to the criminal court in which proceedings are to take place to grant criminal legal aid. The court will do this if it is desirable in the interests of justice (e.g. if there are important questions of law to be argued or the case is so serious that if found guilty the person may go to prison) and the person needs help to pay their legal costs.

Criminal legal aid covers the cost of preparing a case and legal representation (including the cost of a barrister) in criminal proceedings. It is also available for appeals against verdicts or sentences in magistrates' courts, the Crown Court or the Court of Appeal. It is not available for bringing a private prosecution in a criminal court.

If granted criminal legal aid, either the person may choose their own solicitor or the court will assign one. Contributions to the legal costs must be paid by anyone who has a disposable income of over £49 a week or disposable capital of over £3,000. These contributions are payable each month and will probably be returned to the person if they are acquitted. If the payments are not made, the legal aid order may be revoked.

SCOTLAND

The procedure for application for criminal legal aid depends on the circumstances of each case. In solemn cases (more serious cases, e.g. homicide) heard before a jury, it is for the court to decide whether to grant legal aid. In summary cases (less serious) the procedure depends on whether the person is in custody:

- anyone taken into custody has the right to free legal aid from the duty solicitor up to and including the first court appearance
- if the person is not in custody and wishes to plead guilty, they are not entitled to criminal legal aid but may be entitled to legal advice and assistance, including assistance by way of representation
- if the person is not in custody and wishes to plead not guilty, they can apply for criminal legal aid. This must be done within 14 days of the first court appearance at which they made the plea

The criteria used to assess whether or not criminal legal aid should be granted is similar to the criteria for England and Wales.

MARRIAGE

Any two persons may marry provided that:
- they are at least 16 years old on the day of the marriage (in England and Wales persons under the age of 18 must generally obtain the consent of their parents; if consent is refused an appeal may be made to the High Court, the county court or a court of summary jurisdiction)
- they are not related to one another in a way which would prevent their marrying (see below)
- they are unmarried (a person who has already been married must produce documentary evidence that the previous marriage has been ended by death, divorce or annulment)
- they are not of the same sex
- they are capable of understanding the nature of a marriage ceremony and of consenting to marriage
- the marriage would be regarded as valid in any foreign country of which either party is a citizen

DEGREES OF RELATIONSHIP

A marriage between persons within the prohibited degrees of consanguinity, affinity or adoption is void.

A man may not marry his mother, daughter, grandmother, granddaughter, sister, aunt, niece, great-grandmother, great-granddaughter, adoptive mother, former adoptive mother, adopted daughter or former adopted daughter. In some circumstances he may now be allowed to marry his former wife's daughter, former wife's granddaughter, father's former wife or grandfather's former wife.

A woman may not marry her father, son, grandfather, grandson, brother, uncle, nephew, great-grandfather, great-grandson, adoptive father, former adoptive father, adopted son or former adopted son. In some circumstances she may now be allowed to marry her former husband's son, former husband's grandson, mother's former husband or grandmother's former husband.

ENGLAND AND WALES

TYPES OF MARRIAGE CEREMONY

It is possible to marry by either religious or civil ceremony. A religious ceremony can take place at a church or chapel of the Church of England or the Church in Wales, or at any other place of worship which has been formally registered by the Registrar-General.

A civil ceremony can take place at a register office, a registered building or any other premises approved by the local authority. A list of approved premises for the area can be obtained from the local authority.

An application for an approved premises licence must be made by the owners or trustees of the building concerned;

it cannot be made by the prospective marriage couple. Approved premises must be regularly open to the public so that the marriage can be witnessed; the venue must be deemed to be a permanent and immovable structure. Open-air ceremonies are prohibited.

Non-Anglican marriages may also be solemnized following the issue of a Registrar-General's licence in unregistered premises where one of the parties is seriously ill, is not expected to recover, and cannot be moved to registered premises. Detained and housebound persons may be married at their place of residence.

MARRIAGE IN THE CHURCH OF ENGLAND OR THE CHURCH IN WALES

Marriage by banns

The marriage must take place in a parish in which one of the parties lives, or in a church in another parish if it is the usual place of worship of either or both of the parties. The banns must be called in the parish in which the marriage is to take place on three Sundays before the day of the ceremony; if either or both of the parties lives in a different parish the banns must also be called there. After three months the banns are no longer valid.

Marriage by common licence

The vicar who is to conduct the marriage will arrange for a common licence to be issued by the diocesan bishop; this dispenses with the necessity for banns. One of the parties must have lived in the parish for 15 days immediately before the issuing of the licence or must usually worship at the church. Affidavits are prepared from the personal instructions of one of the parties and the licence will be given to the applicant in person.

Marriage by special licence

A special licence is granted by the Archbishop of Canterbury in special circumstances for the marriage to take place at any place, with or without previous residence in the parish, or at any time. Application must be made to the Faculty Office of the Archbishop of Canterbury, 1 The Sanctuary, London SW1P 3JT. Tel: 0171-222 5381.

Marriage by certificate

The marriage can be conducted on the authority of the superintendent registrar's certificate, provided that the vicar's consent is obtained. One of the parties must live in the parish or must usually worship at the church.

MARRIAGE BY OTHER RELIGIOUS CEREMONY

One of the parties must normally live in the registration district where the marriage is to take place. In addition to giving notice to the superintendent registrar (see below), it may also be necessary to book a registrar to be present at the ceremony.

CIVIL MARRIAGE

A marriage may be solemnized at any register office, registered building or approved premises in England and Wales. The superintendent registrar of the district should be contacted, and, if the marriage is to take place at approved premises, the necessary arrangements at the venue must also be made.

NOTICE OF MARRIAGE

Unless it is to take place by banns or under common or special licence in the Church of England or the Church in Wales, a notice of the marriage must be given in person to the superintendent registrar. Notice of marriage may be given in the following ways:

– by certificate. Both parties must have lived in a registration district in England or Wales for at least seven days immediately before giving notice at the local register office. If they live in different registration districts, notice must be given in both districts. The marriage can take place in any register office in England and Wales 21 days after notice has been given

– by licence (often known as 'special licence'). One of the parties must have lived in a registration district in England or Wales for at least 15 days before giving notice at the register office; the other party need only be a resident of, or be physically in, England and Wales on the day notice is given. The marriage can take place one clear day (other than a Sunday, Christmas Day or Good Friday) after notice has been given

A notice of marriage is valid for 12 months. It is not therefore possible to give formal notice of a marriage more than three months before it is to take place, but it should be possible to make an advance (provisional) booking 12 months before the ceremony. In this case it is still necessary to give formal notice three months before the marriage. When giving notice of the marriage it is necessary to produce official proof, if relevant, that any previous marriage has ended in divorce or death; it is also useful, but not necessary, to take birth certificates or passports as proof of age and identity.

SOLEMNIZATION OF THE MARRIAGE

On the day of the wedding there must be at least two other people present who are prepared to act as witnesses and sign the marriage register. A registrar of marriages must be present at a marriage in a register office or at approved premises, but an authorized person may act in the capacity of registrar in a registered building.

If the marriage takes place at approved premises, the room must be separate from any other activity on the premises at the time of the ceremony, and no food or drink can be sold or consumed in the room during the ceremony or for one hour beforehand.

The marriage must be solemnized between 8 a.m. and 6 p.m., with open doors. At some time during the ceremony the parties must make a declaration that they know of no legal impediment to the marriage and they must also say the contracting words; the declaratory and contracting words may vary according to the form of service in use but the most basic forms are:

– (*declaratory words*) 'I declare that I know of no legal reason why I, A. B., may not be joined in marriage to C. D.' Alternatively, the couple may answer 'I am' to the question 'Are you, A. B., free lawfully to marry C. D.?'

– (*contracting words*) 'I, A. B., take you, C. D., to be my wedded wife [or husband]'

A civil marriage cannot contain any religious aspects, but it may be possible for non-religious music and/or poetry readings to be included. It may also be possible to embellish the marriage vows taken by the couple.

If both parties are Jews, they may be married in a synagogue, in a private house or elsewhere. The wedding may take place at any time of day and must be registered by the secretary of the synagogue of which the man is a member. The presence of a registrar of marriages is not necessary.

If both parties are members of the Society of Friends (Quakers), they may be married in a Friends' meeting-house. The marriage must be registered by the registering officer of the Society appointed to act for the district in which the meeting-house is situated. The presence of a registrar of marriages is not necessary.

CIVIL FEES *from 1 April 1997*

Marriage at a register office or registered building
By certificate, where both parties live in the same district, £47
By certificate, where the parties live in different districts, £67
By licence, £92
These amounts include the fee of £27 for the registrar's attendance on the day of the wedding.

Marriage on approved premises
By certificate, where both parties live in the same district, £20
By certificate, where the parties live in different districts, £40
By licence, £65
Additional fees must be paid for the attendance of the superintendent registrar or the registrar on the day of the wedding; these fees are set by the local authority. A further charge is likely to be made by the owners of the building for the use of the premises.

Marriage in a religious building
(other than in the Church of England or the Church in Wales)
By certificate, where both parties live in the same district, £20
By certificate, where the parties live in different districts, £40
By licence, £65
An additional fee of £35 must be paid for the registrar's attendance on the day of the wedding unless an authorized person appointed by the trustees of the building is to register the marriage. Additional fees may also be charged by the trustees of the building and by the person who performs the ceremony.

Marriage certificate on day of marriage, £3.00

ECCLESIASTICAL FEES *from 1 January 1997*

(Church of England and Church in Wales*)
Marriage by banns
For publication of banns, £13
For certificate of banns issued at time of publication, £7
For marriage service, £117
Marriage by common licence
Fee for licence, £53
Marriage by special licence
Fee for licence, £120
Further fees may be payable for additional facilities at the marriage, e.g. the organist's fee.

*Some of these fees may not apply to the Church in Wales

SCOTLAND

REGULAR MARRIAGES

A regular marriage is one which is celebrated by a minister of religion or authorized registrar or other celebrant. Proclamation of banns is not required in Scotland. Each of the parties must complete a marriage notice form and return it to the district registrar for the area in which they are to be married, irrespective of where they live, at least 15 days before the ceremony is due to take place.

A marriage schedule, which is prepared by the registrar, will be issued to one or both of the parties in person up to seven days before a religious marriage; for a civil marriage the schedule will be available at the ceremony. The schedule must be handed to the celebrant before the ceremony starts; it must be signed immediately after the wedding and the marriage must be registered within three days.

The authority to conduct a marriage is deemed to be vested in the person conducting the ceremony rather than the building in which it takes place; open-air ceremonies are therefore permissable in Scotland.

MARRIAGE BY HABIT AND REPUTE

If two people live together constantly as husband and wife and are generally held to be such by the neighbourhood and among their friends and relations, there may arise a presumption from which marriage can be inferred. Before such a marriage can be registered, however, a decree of declarator of marriage must be obtained from the Deputy Principal Clerk of the Court of Session.

CIVIL FEES *from 1 April 1997*

Fee for a statutory notice of intention to marry, £11 per person
Fee for solemnization of marriage in a register office, £40

Further information can be obtained from:
THE GENERAL REGISTER OFFICE, Office for National Statistics, Smedley Hydro, Trafalgar Road, Birkdale, Southport, Merseyside PR8 2HH. Tel: 01704-569824
THE GENERAL REGISTER OFFICE FOR SCOTLAND, New Register House, Edinburgh EH1 3YT. Tel: 0131-334 0380

TOWN AND COUNTRY PLANNING

The principal legislation governing the development of land and buildings in England and Wales is the Town and Country Planning Act 1990 (as amended by the Planning and Compensation Act 1991). The equivalent legislation in Scotland is the Town and Country Planning (Scotland) Act 1972. The uses of buildings are classified by the Town and Country Planning (Use Classes) Order 1987 (as amended) in England and Wales, and in Scotland by the Town and Country Planning (Use Classes) (Scotland) Order 1989. It is advisable in all cases to contact the planning department of the local authority to check whether planning or other permission is needed.

PLANNING PERMISSION

Planning permission is needed if the work involves:
– making a material change in use, such as dividing off part of the house so that it can be used as a separate home or dividing off part of the house for commercial use, e.g. for a workshop
– going against the terms of the original planning permission, e.g. there may be a restriction on fences in front gardens on an open-plan estate
– obstructing the view of road users
– new or wider access to a main road
– additions or extensions to flats or maisonettes, even if they were originally converted from a house
Planning permission is not needed to carry out internal alterations or work which does not affect the external appearance of the building.
    There are certain types of development for which the Secretary of State for the Environment has granted general permissions. These include:
– house extensions and additions (including conservatories, loft conversions, garages and dormer windows). Up to 10 per cent or up to 50 cubic metres (whichever is the greater) can be added to the original house for terraced houses. Up to 15 per cent or 70 cubic metres (whichever is the greater) to other kinds of houses. The maximum that can be added to any house is 115 cubic metres

– buildings such as garden sheds and greenhouses so long as they are no more than 3 metres high (or 4 metres if the roof is ridged), are no nearer to a highway than the house, and at least half the ground around the house remains uncovered by buildings
– adding a porch with a ground area of less than 3 square metres and that is less than 3 metres in height
– putting up fences, walls and gates of under 1 metre in height if next to a road and under 2 metres elsewhere
– laying patios, paths or driveways for domestic use

OTHER RESTRICTIONS

It may be necessary to obtain other types of permissions before carrying out any development. These permissions are separate from planning permission and apply regardless of whether or not planning permission is needed, e.g.:
– building regulations will probably apply if a new building is to be erected, if an existing one is to be altered or extended, or if the work involves building over a drain or sewer. The building control department of the local authority will advise on this
– any alterations to a listed building or the grounds of a listed building must be approved by the local authority
– local authority approval is necessary if a building (or, in some circumstances, gates, walls, fences or railings) in a conservation area is to be demolished; each local authority keeps a register of all local buildings that are in conservation areas
– many trees are protected by tree preservation orders and must not be pruned or taken down without local authority consent
– bats and other species are protected and English Nature, the Countryside Council for Wales or Scottish Natural Heritage (for entries, *see* Index) must be notified before any work is carried out that will affect the habitat of protected species, e.g. timber treatment, renovation or extensions of lofts
– any development in areas designated as a National Park, an Area of Outstanding Natural Beauty, a National Scenic Area or in the Norfolk or Suffolk Broads is subject to greater restrictions. The local planning authority will advise or refer enquirers to the relevant authority

VOTERS' QUALIFICATIONS

Those entitled to vote at parliamentary, European Union (EU) and local government elections are those who are:
– resident in the constituency or ward on the qualifying date i.e. 10 October in the year before the electoral register (*see* below) comes into effect; in Northern Ireland the qualifying date is 15 September and voters must have been resident in Northern Ireland for the three months leading up to that date
– over 18 years old
– Commonwealth (which includes British) citizens or citizens of the Republic of Ireland
    British citizens resident abroad are entitled to vote, for 20 years after leaving Britain, as overseas electors in parliamentary and EU elections in the constituency in which they were last resident. Members of the armed forces, Crown servants and employees of the British Council who are overseas and their spouses are entitled to vote regardless of how long they have been abroad.
    European Union citizens resident in the UK may vote in EU and local government elections.

The following people are not entitled to vote:
- peers, and peeresses in their own right, who are members of the House of Lords (except that they may vote in EU and local government elections)
- patients detained under mental health legislation
- voluntary mental patients (unless they make a prescribed declaration)
- those serving prison sentences
- those convicted within the previous five years of corrupt or illegal election practices

REGISTERING TO VOTE

Voters must be entered on an electoral register, which runs from 16 February in one year to 15 February in the following year. The registration officer for each constituency is responsible for preparing and publishing the register. A registration form is sent to all households in the autumn of each year and the householder is required to provide details of all occupants who are eligible to vote, including ones who will reach their 18th birthday in the year covered by the register. Those who fail to give the required information or who give false information are liable to be fined. A draft register is usually published at the end of November. Any person whose name has been omitted may ask to be registered and should contact the registration officer. Anyone on the register may object to the inclusion of another person's name, in which case he/she should notify the registration officer, who will investigate that person's eligibility. Supplementary electors lists are published throughout the duration of the register.

VOTING

Voting is not compulsory in the UK. Those who wish to vote must generally vote in person at the allotted polling station. Those who will be away at the time of the election, those who will not be able to attend in person due to physical incapacity or the nature of their occupation, and those who have changed address during the period for which the register is valid, may apply for a postal vote or nominate a proxy to vote for them. Overseas electors who wish to vote must do so by proxy.

Further information can be obtained from the local authority's electoral registration officer in England and Wales or the regional valuation assessor in Scotland (details in local telephone directories), or the Chief Electoral Officer in Northern Ireland (3rd Floor, St Anne's House, 15 Church Street, Belfast BTI IER. Tel: 01232-245353).

WILLS AND INTESTACY

In a will a person leaves instructions as to the disposal of their property after they die. A will is also used to appoint executors (who will administer the estate), give directions as to the disposal of the body, appoint guardians for children and, for larger estates, can operate to reduce the level of inheritance tax. It is best to have a will drawn up by a solicitor but if a solicitor is not employed, the following points must be taken into account:
- if possible the will must not be prepared on behalf of another person by someone who is to benefit from it or who is a close relative of a major beneficiary
- the language used must be clear and unambiguous and it is better to avoid the use of legal terms where the same thing can be expressed in plain language
- it is better to rewrite the whole document if a mistake is made. If necessary, alterations can be made by striking through the words with a pen, and the signature or initials

of the testator and the witnesses must be put in the margin opposite the alteration. No alteration of any kind should be made after the will has been executed
- if the person later wishes to change the will or part of it, it is better to write a new will revoking the old. The use of codicils (documents written as supplements or containing modifications to the will) should be left to a solicitor
- the will should be typed or printed, or if handwritten be legible and preferably in ink. Commercial will forms can be obtained from some stationers

The form of a will varies to suit different cases; the following is an example of how a will might be written. The notes after this example explain the terms used and procedures that need to be followed in drawing up a will.

This is the last will and testament of me [*Thomas Smith*] of [*Heather Cottage, Prospero Road, Manchester* MI 4DK] which I make this [*seventeenth*] day of [*May* 1998] and I revoke all previous wills and testamentary dispositions.
1. I appoint as my executors and trustees [*Ann Green of _____ and Richard Brown of _____*]. In my will the expression 'my Trustees' means any executors and trustees for the time being of my will and of any trust arising under it.
2. I give all my property to [*such of my children as shall survive me by 28 days and if more than one in equal shares* or as the case may be].
or
2. I give to [*Pamela Henderson of _____*] the sum of [£_____] and to [*Michael Broadbent of _____*] the sum of [£_____] and to [*Ruth Walker of _____*] all of my [*jewellery, books* or as the case may be]
and
3. I give everything not otherwise disposed of to [*Richard Black of _____*]
Signed by the testator in our joint presence and then by us in his.

Thomas Smith
[*Signature of the person making the will*]
Elizabeth Wall
[*Signature of witness*] of 67 Beatrice Lane, Manchester MI 4DK, journalist
William Jones
[*Signature of witness*] of 17 Paris Road, Manchester MI 4EN, tailor

TERMS TO AVOID USING

Keep the will as simple as possible. Try to avoid using the following terms, as they have specific legal meaning:
- real property
- personal property
- goods and chattels
- my money

SPECIFIC GIFTS AND LEGACIES

Gifts of specific items usually fail if the property is not owned by the person making the will on their death. This problem can be avoided by making a gift of any property fulfilling a particular description, e.g. a car, which is owned at the date of death. It is better in all cases where such gifts are made, to insert a clause which reads 'I give everything not otherwise disposed of to [Richard Black of _____], even if it seems that all property has already been disposed of in the will.

LAPSED LEGATEES

If a person who has been left property in a will dies before the person who made the will, the gift fails and will pass to the person entitled to everything not otherwise disposed of (the residuary estate).

If the person left the residuary estate dies before the person who made the will, their share will generally pass to the closest relative(s) of the person who made the will unless the will names a beneficiary such as a charity who will take as a 'long stop' if this gift is unable to take effect for any reason.

It is always better to draw up a new will if a beneficiary predeceases the person who made the will.

EXECUTORS

It is usual to appoint two executors, although one is sufficient. No more than four persons can deal with the estate of the person who has died. The name and address of each executor should be given in full (the addresses are not essential but including them adds clarity to the document).

Executors should be 18 years of age or over. An executor may be a beneficiary of the will.

WITNESSES

Someone who is a beneficiary of a will, or the spouse of a beneficiary at the time the will is signed, ought not to act as a witness or else they will be unable to take their gift. Husband and wife can both act as witnesses provided neither benefits from the will. A blind person cannot witness a will.

It is better that a person does not act as an executor and as a witness, as he/she can take no benefit under a will to which he/she is witness. The identity of the witnesses should be made as explicit as possible.

EXECUTION OF A WILL

The person making the will should sign his/her name at the foot of the document, in the presence of the two witnesses. The witnesses must then sign their names while the person making the will looks on. If this procedure is not adhered to, the will will be considered invalid. There are certain exceptional circumstances where these rules are relaxed, e g where the person may be too ill to sign, and in these cases the attestation clause which normally reads 'signed by the testator in our joint presence and then by us in his/hers' should be reworded as follows:

The will was read over to Thomas Smith in our presence when he stated that he understood it. It was then signed on his behalf by Thomas Brown in the presence of the testator and by his direction in our joint presence and then by us in his.

CAPACITY TO MAKE A WILL

Anyone aged 18 or over can make a will. However, if there is any suspicion that the person making the will is not, through reasons of infirmity or age, fully in command of his/her faculties, it is advisable to arrange for a medical practitioner to examine the person making the will at the time it is to be executed to verify his/her mental capacity and to record that medical opinion in writing, and to ask the examining practitioner to act as a witness. If a person is not mentally able to make a will, the Court may do this for him/her under provisions contained in the Mental Health Act 1983.

REVOCATION

A will may be revoked or cancelled in a number of ways:
- a later will revokes an earlier one if it says so; otherwise the earlier will is impliedly revoked by the later one to the extent that it contradicts or repeats the earlier one
- a will is also revoked if the physical document on which it is written is destroyed by the person whose will it is.

There must be an intention to revoke the will. It may not be sufficient to obliterate the will with a pen
- a will is revoked when the person marries, unless it is clear from the will that the person intended the will to stand after the marriage
- where a marriage ends in divorce or is annulled or declared void, gifts to the spouse and the appointment of the spouse as executor fail unless the will says that this is not to happen. A separation does not change the effect of a married person's will.

PROBATE AND LETTERS OF ADMINISTRATION

Probate is granted to the executors named in a will and once granted, the executors are obliged to carry out the instructions of the will. Letters of administration are granted where no executor is named in a will or is willing or able to act or where there is no will or no valid will; this gives a person, often the next of kin, similar powers and duties to those of an executor.

Applications for probate or for letters of administration can be made to the Principal Registry of the Family Division, to a district probate registry or to a probate sub-registry. Applicants will need the following documents: the original will (if any); a certificate of death; particulars of all property and assets left by the deceased; a list of debts and funeral expenses. Certain property, up to the value of £5,000, may be disposed of without a grant of probate or letters of administration.

WHERE TO FIND A PROVED WILL

Since 1858 wills which have been proved, that is wills on which probate or letters of administration have been granted, must have been proved at the Principal Registry of the Family Division or at district probate registry. The Lord Chancellor has power to direct where the original documents are kept but most are filed where they were proved and may be inspected there and a copy obtained. The Principal Registry also holds copies of all wills proved at district probate registries and these may be inspected at Somerset House. An index of all grants, both of probate and of letters of administration, is compiled by the Principal Registry and may be seen either at the Principal Registry or at a district probate registry.

It is also possible to discover when a grant of probate or letters of administration is issued by requesting a standing search. In response to a request and for a small fee, a district probate registry will supply the names and addresses of executors or administrators and the registry in which the grant was made, of any grant in the estate of a specified person made in the previous 12 months or following six months. This is useful for applicants under the Inheritance (Provision for Family and Dependants) Act 1975 (*see* Intestacy, page 666) and for creditors of the deceased.

SCOTLAND

In Scotland any person over 12 and of sound mind can make a will. The person making the will can only freely dispose of what is known as the 'dead's part' of the estate because:
- the spouse has the right to inherit one-third of the moveable estate if there are children or other descendants, and one-half of it if there are not
- children are entitled to one-third of the moveable estate if there is a surviving spouse, and one-half of it if there is not

The remaining portion is the dead's part, and legacies and bequests are payable from this. Debts are payable out of the whole estate before any division.

From August 1995, wills no longer needed to be 'holographed' and it is now only necessary to have one witness. The person making the will still needs to sign each page. It is better that the will is not witnessed by a beneficiary although the attestation would still be sound and the beneficiary would not have to relinquish the gift (as is the case in England and Wales).

Subsequent marriage does not revoke a will but the birth of a child who is not provided for may do so. A will may be revoked by a subsequent will, either expressly or by implication, but in so far as the two can be read together both have effect. If a subsequent will is revoked, the earlier will is revived.

Wills may be registered in the Books of the Sheriffdom in which the deceased lived or in the Books of Council and Session at the Registers of Scotland. The original will can be inspected and a copy obtained for small fee.

CONFIRMATION

Confirmation (probate) is obtained in the sheriff court of the sheriffdom in which the deceased was resident at the time of death. Executors are either 'nominate' (named by the deceased in the will) or 'dative' (appointed by the court in cases where no executor is named in a will or in cases of intestacy). Applicants for confirmation must first provide an inventory of the deceased's estate and a schedule of debts, with an affidavit. In estates under £17,000 gross, confirmation can be obtained under a simplified procedure at reduced fees. The local sheriff clerk's office can provide assistance.

Further information can be obtained from:

PRINCIPAL REGISTRY (FAMILY DIVISION), Somerset
    House, London, WC2R 1LP. Tel: 0171-936 6000
REGISTERS OF SCOTLAND, Meadowbank House, 153
    London Road, Edinburgh, EH8 7AU. Tel: 0131-659 6111

INTESTACY

Intestacy occurs when someone dies without leaving a will or leaves a will which is invalid or which does not take effect for some reason. In such cases the person's estate (property, possessions, other assets following the payment of debts) passes to certain members of the family. The relevant legislation is the Administration of Estates Act 1925, as amended by various legislation including the Intestates Estates Act 1952, the Law Reform (Succession) Act 1995, and the Trusts of Land and Appointment of Trustees Act 1996 and Orders made thereunder. Some of the provisions of this legislation are described below. If a will has been written that disposes of only part of a person's property, these rules apply to the part which is undisposed of.

If the person (intestate) leaves a spouse who survives for 28 days and children (legitimate, illegitimate and adopted children and other descendants), the estate is divided as follows:
- the spouse takes the 'personal chattels' (household articles, including cars, but nothing used for business purposes), £125,000 free of tax (with interest payable at 6 per cent from the time of the death until payment) and a life interest in half of the rest of the estate (which can be capitalized by the spouse if he/she wishes)
- the rest of the estate goes to the children*

If the person leaves a spouse who survives for 28 days but no children:
- the spouse takes the personal chattels, £200,000 free of tax (interest payable as before) and full ownership of half of the rest of the estate

- the other half of the rest of the estate goes to the parents (equally, if both alive) or, if none, to the brothers and sisters of the whole blood*
- if there are no parents or brothers or sisters of the whole blood or their children, the spouse takes the whole estate

If there is no surviving spouse, the estate is distributed among those who survive the intestate as follows:
- to surviving children*, but if none to
- parents (equally, if both alive), but if none to
- brothers and sisters of the whole blood*, but if none to
- brothers and sisters of the half blood*, but if none to
- grandparents (equally, if more than one), but if none to
- aunts and uncles of the whole blood*, but if none to
- aunts and uncles of the half blood*, but if none to
- the Crown, Duchy of Lancaster or the Duke of Cornwall (*bona vacantia*)

* To inherit, a member of these groups must survive the intestate and attain 18, or marry under that age. If they die under 18 (unless married under that age), their share goes to others, if any, in the same group. If any member of these groups predeceases the intestate leaving children, their share is divided equally among their children.

In England and Wales the provisions of the Inheritance (Provision for Family and Dependants) Act 1975 may allow other people to claim provision from the deceased's assets. This Act also applies to cases where a will has been made and allows a person to apply to the Court if they feel that the will or rules of intestacy or both do not make adequate provision for them. The Court can order payment from the deceased's assets or the transfer of property from them if the applicant's claim is accepted. The application must be made within six months of the grant of probate or letters of administration and the following people can make an application:
- the spouse
- a former spouse who has not remarried
- a child of the deceased
- someone treated as a child of the deceased's family
- someone maintained by the deceased
- someone who has cohabited for two years before the death in the same household as the deceased and as the husband or wife of the deceased

SCOTLAND

Under the Succession (Scotland) Act 1964, no distinction is made between 'moveable' and 'heritable' property in intestacy cases.

A surviving spouse is entitled to 'prior rights'. This means that the spouse has the right to inherit:
- the matrimonial home up to a value of £110,000, or one matrimonial home if there is more than one, or, in certain circumstances, the value of the matrimonial home
- the furnishings and contents of that home, up to the value of £20,000
- £30,000 if the deceased left children or other descendants, or £50,000 if not

These figures are increased from time to time by order of the Secretary of State.

Once prior rights have been satisfied, what remains of the estate is generally divided between the surviving spouse and children (legitimate and illegitimate) according to 'legal' rights. Legal rights are:

Jus relicti(ae) – the right of a surviving spouse to one-half of the net moveable estate, after satisfaction of prior rights, if there are no surviving children; if there are surviving children, the spouse is entitled to one-third of the net moveable estate

Legitim – the right of surviving children to one-half of the net moveable estate if there is no surviving spouse; if there is a surviving spouse, the children are entitled to one-third of the net moveable estate after the satisfaction of prior rights

Where there is no surviving spouse or children, half of the estate is taken by the parents and half by the brothers and sisters. Failing that, the lines of succession, in general, are:
– to descendants
– if no descendants, then to collaterals (i.e. brothers and sisters) and parents
– surviving spouse
– if no collaterals or parents or spouse, then to ascendants collaterals (i.e. aunts and uncles), and so on in an ascending scale
– if all lines of succession fail, then to the Crown

Relatives of the whole blood are preferred to relatives of the half blood. The right of representation, i.e. the right of the issue of a person who would have succeeded if he/she had survived the intestate, also applies.

Wedding Anniversaries

First	*Cotton*	Fourteenth	*Ivory*
Second	*Paper*	Fifteenth	*Crystal*
Third	*Leather*	Twentieth	*China*
Fourth	*Fruit and Flower*	Twenty-fifth	*Silver*
Fifth	*Wood*	Thirtieth	*Pearl*
Sixth	*Sugar/Iron*	Thirty-fifth	*Coral*
Seventh	*Wool*	Fortieth	*Ruby*
Eighth	*Bronze/Electrical appliances*	Forty-fifth	*Sapphire*
Ninth	*Copper/Pottery*	Fiftieth	*Gold*
Tenth	*Tin*	Fifty-fifth	*Emerald*
Eleventh	*Steel*	Sixtieth	*Diamond*
Twelfth	*Silk and Fine Linen*	Seventieth	*Platinum*
Thirteenth	*Lace*		

Intellectual Property

COPYRIGHT

Copyright protects all original literary, dramatic, musical and artistic works (including photographs, maps and plans), published editions of works, computer programs, sound recordings, films (including video), broadcasts (including satellite broadcasts) and cable programmes (including on-line information services). Under copyright the creators of these works can control the various ways in which their material may be exploited, the rights broadly covering copying, adapting, issuing (including renting and lending) copies to the public, performing in public, and broadcasting the material.

Copyright protection in the United Kingdom is automatic and there is no registration system. The main legislation is the Copyright, Designs and Patents Act 1988, which has been amended by Statutory Instrument to take account of EC Directives. As a result of an EC Directive effective from January 1996, the term of copyright protection for literary, dramatic, musical and artistic works lasts until 70 years after the death of the author, and for film now lasts for 70 years after the death of the last surviving author, i.e. director, author of the screenplay, scriptwriter, or composer of the music. Sound recordings are protected for 50 years after their publication, and broadcasts and cable programmes for 50 years from the end of the year in which the first broadcast/transmission is made. Published editions remain under copyright protection for 25 years from the end of the year in which the edition was published.

The main international treaties protecting copyright are the Berne Convention for the Protection of Literary and Artistic Works, the Rome Convention for the Protection of Performers, Producers of Phonograms and Broadcasting Organizations, and the Universal Copyright Convention (UCC); the UK is a signatory to these conventions. Copyright material created by UK nationals or residents is protected in each country which is a member of the conventions by the national law of that country. A list of participating countries may be obtained from the Patent Office.

Two new treaties were agreed in December 1996, but have yet to enter into force. These are the WIPO (World Intellectual Property Organization) Copyright Treaty, and the WIPO Performance and Phonograms Treaty, which strengthen and update international standards of protection, particularly in relation to new technologies.

Licensing

Reproduction of copyright material without seeking permission in each instance may be permitted under licence. (For a list of licensing agencies, *see* page 669.) The International Federation of Reproduction Rights Organizations facilitates agreements between its member licensing agencies and on behalf of its members with organizations such as the WIPO, UNESCO, the European Union and the Council of Europe.

Legal Deposit

Publishers are legally obliged to send one copy of a new publication to each of the copyright deposit libraries within one month of publication. The aim of legal deposit is to keep a complete national archive of published works as a current reference and information source. The copyright deposit libraries are the British Library, the Bodleian Library in Oxford, Cambridge University Library, the National Library of Scotland, the National Library of Wales, and Trinity College Library in Dublin.

The British Library's Legal Deposit Office is split between two locations; books and other publications are deposited at Boston Spa, and newspapers and periodicals at the Newspaper Legal Deposit Office in London. All publications for the other four copyright libraries in the UK are dealt with by the Agent for Copyright Libraries.

PATENTS

A patent is a document issued by the Patent Office relating to an invention and giving the proprietor monopoly rights, effective within the United Kingdom (including the Isle of Man). In return the patentee pays a fee to cover the costs of processing the patent and publicly discloses details of the invention.

To qualify for a patent an invention must be new, must exhibit an inventive step, and must be capable of industrial application. The patent is valid for a maximum of 20 years from the date on which the application was filed, subject to payment of annual fees from the end of the fourth year.

The Patent Office, established in 1852, is responsible for ensuring that all stages of an application comply with the Patents Act 1977, and that the invention meets the criteria for a patent. Patent Office Examiners check that the invention is new and innovative by searching previously published documents on the Patent Office databank, which contains details of some two million British patents, together with published international and European applications. The contents of the databank and of the Science Reference Library, which developed from the library established at the Patent Office, are available to the public.

The World Intellectual Property Organization (WIPO), a United Nations body, is responsible for administering many of the international conventions on intellectual property. The Patent Co-operation Treaty allows inventors to file a single application for patent rights in some or all of the 92 contracting states. This application is searched by an International Searching Authority and published by the International Bureau of WIPO. It may also be the subject of an (optional) international preliminary examination. Applicants must then deal directly with the patent offices in the countries where they are seeking patent rights.

The European Patent Convention, linked to the Patent Co-operation Treaty, allows inventors to obtain patent rights in all 18 contracting states by filing a single European patent application which is processed by the European Patent Office (EPO). Once granted, the patent is subject to national laws in each signatory country. To comply with security requirements, an applicant resident in the UK must file a European patent application with the UK Patent Office unless the Patent Office gives permission for it to be filed directly with the EPO. The EPO office for international patent documentation acts as an information, collection and reference centre for patent offices around the world.

TRADE MARKS

Trade marks are a means of identification, whether a word or device or a combination of both, a logo, or the shape of goods or their packaging, which enable traders to make their goods or services readily distinguishable from those supplied by other traders. Registration prevents other traders using the same or a similar trade mark for similar products or services for which the mark is registered.

In the UK trade marks are registered at the Trade Marks Registry in the Patent Office. In order to qualify for registration a mark must be capable of distinguishing its proprietor's goods or services from those of other undertakings. It should be non-deceptive and not easily confused with a mark that has already been registered for the same or similar goods or services. The relevant current legislation is the Trade Marks Act 1994.

It is possible to obtain an international trade mark registration in 53 countries, under the Madrid Agreement. UK companies cannot take advantage of this because the UK is not a party to this agreement. Following revision of UK trade marks law, however, the UK has ratified the protocol to the Madrid Agreement, and British companies can now obtain international trade mark registration through a single application to WIPO in those countries party to the protocol.

EC trade mark regulation is now in force and is administered by the Office for Harmonization in the Internal Market (trade marks and designs) in Alicante, Spain. The office registers EC trade marks, which are a unitary right valid throughout the European Union. The national registration of trade marks in member states is continuing in parallel with the EC trade mark.

DESIGN PROTECTION

Design protection covers the outward appearance of an article and takes two forms in the UK, registered design and design right, which are not mutually exclusive. Registered design protects the aesthetic appearance of an article, including shape, configuration, pattern or ornament, although artistic works such as sculptures are excluded, being generally protected by copyright. In order to qualify for protection, a design must be new and materially different from earlier UK published designs. The owner of the design must apply to the Designs Registry at the Patent Office. Initial registration lasts for five years and is extendible in five-yearly steps to a maximum of 25 years. The current legislation is the Registered Designs Act 1949 (as amended).

There is no international design registry currently available to UK applicants; in general, separate applications must be made in each country in which protection is sought. Proposals for an EC design regulation are being discussed. If adopted, these would result in a unitary design right valid throughout the European Union, obtainable via a single application.

Design right is an automatic right which applies to the shape or configuration of articles and does not require registration. Unlike registered design, two-dimensional designs do not qualify for protection but designs of semiconductor chips (topographies) are protected by design right. Designs must be original and non-commonplace. The term of design right is ten years from first marketing of the design and the right is effective only in the UK. The current legislation is Part 3 of the Copyright, Designs and Patents Act 1988.

INTELLECTUAL PROPERTY ORGANIZATIONS

AGENT FOR THE COPYRIGHT LIBRARIES, 100 Euston Street, London NW1 2HQ. Tel: 0171-380 0240. *Agent*, A. T. Smail

CHARTERED INSTITUTE OF PATENT AGENTS, Staple Inn Buildings, London WC1V 7PZ. Tel: 0171-405 9450

DESIGNS REGISTRY, The Patent Office, Cardiff Road, Newport NP9 1RH. Tel: 0645-500505

EUROPEAN PATENT OFFICE, *Headquarters*, Erhardtstrasse 27, D-80331 Munich, Germany. Tel: Munich 23990

INTERNATIONAL FEDERATION OF REPRODUCTION RIGHTS ORGANIZATIONS (IFRRO), Goethestrasse 49, D-80336 Munich, Germany. Tel: Munich 514120

LEGAL DEPOSIT OFFICE, The British Library, Boston Spa, Wetherby, West Yorkshire LS23 7BY. Tel: 01937-546267

NEWSPAPER LEGAL DEPOSIT OFFICE, The British Library Newspaper Library, 120 Colindale Avenue, London NW9 5LF. Tel: 0171-412 7378

OFFICE FOR HARMONIZATION IN THE INTERNAL MARKET (TRADE MARKS AND DESIGNS), 20 Avenida de la Aguilera, 03080 Alicante, Spain. Tel: Alicante 513 9100

THE PATENT OFFICE, Cardiff Road, Newport NP9 1RH. Tel: 0645-500505

REGISTRY OF COPYRIGHT AT STATIONERS' HALL, The Registrar, Stationers' Hall, Ave Maria Lane, London EC4M 7DD. Tel: 0171-248 2934

SCIENCE REFERENCE LIBRARY, 25 Southampton Buildings, London WC2A 1AW. Tel: 0171-412 7494

TRADE MARKS REGISTRY, The Patent Office, Cardiff Road, Newport NP9 1RH. Tel: 0645-500505

WORLD INTELLECTUAL PROPERTY ORGANIZATION (WIPO), 34 chemin des Colombettes, 1211 Geneva 20, Switzerland. Tel: Geneva 338 9111

COPYRIGHT LICENSING/COLLECTING AGENCIES

AUTHORS' LICENSING AND COLLECTING SOCIETY, Marlborough Court, 14–18 Holborn, London EC1N 2LE. Tel: 0171-395 0600

CHRISTIAN COPYRIGHT LICENSING (EUROPE) LTD, PO Box 1339, Eastbourne, E. Sussex BN21 4YF. Tel: 01323-417711

COPYRIGHT LICENSING AGENCY LTD, 90 Tottenham Court Road, London W1P 0LP. Tel: 0171-436 5931

DESIGN AND ARTISTS COPYRIGHT AGENCY, Parchment House, 13 Northburgh Street, London EC1V 0AH. Tel: 0171-336 8811

EDUCATIONAL RECORDING AGENCY LTD, New Premier House, 150 Southampton Row, London WC1B 5AL. Tel: 0171-837 3222

INTERNATIONAL FEDERATION OF THE PHONOGRAPHIC INDUSTRIES, 54 Regent Street, London W1R 5PJ. Tel: 0171-878 7900

MECHANICAL COPYRIGHT PROTECTION SOCIETY, Elgar House, 41 Streatham High Road, London SW16 1ER. Tel: 0181-664 4400

NEWSPAPER LICENSING AGENCY, Lonsdale Gate, Lonsdale Gardens, Tunbridge Wells, Kent TN1 1NL. Tel: 01892-525274

PERFORMING RIGHT SOCIETY, 29–33 Berners Street, London W1P 4AA. Tel: 0171-580 5544

PHONOGRAPHIC PERFORMANCE LTD, Ganton House, 14–22 Ganton Street, London W1V 1LB. Tel: 0171-437 0311

PUBLISHERS LICENSING SOCIETY, 5 Dryden Street, London WC2E 9NW. Tel: 0171-829 8486

VIDEO PERFORMANCE LTD, Ganton House, 14–22 Ganton Street, London W1V 1LB. Tel: 0171-437 0311

The Media

Broadcasting

The British Broadcasting Corporation (*see* page 286) is responsible for public service broadcasting in the UK. Its role is to provide high-quality programmes with wide-ranging appeal that educate, inform and entertain. Its constitution and finances are governed by royal charter and agreement. On 1 May 1996 a new royal charter came into force, establishing the framework for the BBC's activities until 2006.

The Independent Television Commission (*see* pages 313–4) and the Radio Authority (*see* page 335) were set up under the terms of the Broadcasting Act 1990. The ITC is the regulator and licensing authority for all commercially-funded television services, including cable and satellite services. The Radio Authority is the regulator and licensing authority for all independent radio services.

There are rules on cross-media ownership to prevent undue concentration of ownership. These were amended by the Broadcasting Act 1996. Radio companies are now permitted to own one AM, one FM and one other (AM or FM) service; ownership of the third licence is subject to a public interest test. Local newspapers with a circulation under 20 per cent in an area are also allowed to own one AM, one FM and one other service, and may control a regional Channel 3 television service subject to a public interest test. Local newspapers with a circulation between 20 and 50 per cent in an area may own one AM and one FM service, subject to a public interest test, but may not control a regional Channel 3 service. Those with a circulation over 50 per cent may own one radio service in the area (provided that more than one independent local radio service serves the area) subject to a public interest test.

Ownership controls on the number of television or radio licences have been removed; holdings are now restricted to 15 per cent of the total television audience or 15 per cent of the total points available in the radio points scheme. Ownership controls on cable operators have also been removed. National newspapers with less than 20 per cent of national circulation may apply to control any broadcasting licences, subject to a public interest test. National news-papers with more than 20 per cent of national circulation may not have more than a 20 per cent interest in a licence to provide a Channel 3 service, Channel 5 or national and local analogue radio services.

COMPLAINTS

The Broadcasting Standards Commisson was set up in April 1997 under the Broadcasting Act 1996 and was formed from the merger of the Broadcasting Complaints Commission and the Broadcasting Standards Council. The Commission considers and adjudicates upon complaints of unfair treatment or unwarranted infringement of privacy in all broadcast programmes and advertisements on tele-vision, radio, cable, satellite and digital services. It also monitors the portrayal of violence and sex, and matters of taste and decency.

BROADCASTING STANDARDS COMMISSION, 7 The Sanctuary, London SW1P 3JS. Tel: 0171-233 0544. *Chairman*, The Lady Howe of Aberavon; *Deputy Chairman*, Ms J. Leighton; *Director*, S. Whittle

TELEVISION

All channels are broadcast in colour on 625 lines UHF from a network of transmitting stations. The BBC's transmission network was sold to the Castle Tower Consortium in February 1997; ITV transmission services are owned and operated by National Transcommunications Ltd. Trans-missions are available to more than 99 per cent of the population.

The total number of receiving television licences in the UK at end May 1997 was 21,329,626, of which 443,864 were for monochrome receivers and 20,885,762 for colour receivers. Annual television licence fees are: monochrome £30.50; colour £91.50.

No overall statistics are available for subscriptions in the UK to satellite television services; British Sky Broadcast-ing had 6.2 million subscribers at March 1997, though an increasing number of these view through cable. At April 1997 there were 1,968,342 subscribers to cable television.

DIGITAL TELEVISION

Digital television broadcasting is a new technique for improving the quality of the current reception of television programmes. It uses digital modulation to provide a consistently high quality of reception and digital compres-sion to make more effective use of the frequency channels available than PAL, the analogue system currently used.

The Broadcasting Act 1996 provided for the licensing of 20 or more digital terrestrial television channels (on six frequency channels or 'multiplexes'). Three multiplexes have been allocated to existing national television broad-casters (one to the BBC, one to ITV and Channel 4, and one to Channel 5 and S4C), and all programmes broadcast on existing analogue channels will have to be broadcast on the equivalent digital service. In June 1997 the licences to run the remaining digital multiplexes were awarded by the ITC to British Digital Broadcasting, a consortium led by Carlton Communications and Granada. The first digital services are due to be on air by mid-1998. Until digital television sets are on the market it will be necessary to purchase a set-top box to convert the digital signals into analogue sound and picture waves in order to watch the digital channels. Digital television services will also be offered by cable and satellite companies.

BBC TELEVISION
Television Centre, Wood Lane, London W12 7RJ
Tel 0181-743 8000

The BBC's experiments in television broadcasting started in 1929 and in 1936 the BBC began the world's first public service of high-definition television from Alexandra Palace. The BBC broadcasts two UK-wide television services, BBC 1 and BBC 2; outside England these services are designated BBC Scotland on 1, BBC Scotland on 2, BBC 1 Northern Ireland, BBC 2 Northern Ireland, BBC Wales on 1 and BBC Wales on 2.

BBC WORLDWIDE LTD
Woodlands, 80 Wood Lane, London W12 0TT
Tel 0181-576 2000

BBC Worldwide was formed in May 1994 to develop a co-ordinated approach to the BBC's international and com-mercial activities. The World Service broadcasts in 46 languages to a weekly audience of 143 million. Worldwide Ltd provides commercial products and services in a range of media including television channels.

INDEPENDENT TELEVISION

The ITV franchises for the 15 regional companies and for breakfast television were allocated new ten-year licences from January 1993. A new independent national television channel was due to be established by autumn 1993, but the ITC decided not to award the licence to Channel Five Holdings Ltd, the only applicant. The ITC received a further four bids for the licence in May 1995. The winner was Channel 5 Broadcasting Ltd and the new channel was launched on 30 March 1997.

ITV NETWORK CENTRE/ITV ASSOCIATION
200 Gray's Inn Road, London WC1X 8HF
Tel 0171-843 8000

The ITV Network Centre is wholly owned by the ITV companies and undertakes the commissioning and scheduling of those television programmes which are shown across the ITV network. Through its sister organization, the ITV Association, it also provides a range of services to the ITV companies where a common approach is required.
Network Director, R. Eyre
Director, ITV Association, B. Cox

INDEPENDENT TELEVISION NETWORK COMPANIES
ANGLIA TELEVISION LTD (owned by MAI) (*eastern England*), Anglia House, Norwich NR1 3JG. Tel: 01603-615151
BORDER TELEVISION PLC (*the Borders*), The Television Centre, Carlisle CA1 3NT. Tel: 01228-25101
CARLTON UK TELEVISION (*London (weekdays)*), 101 St Martin's Lane, London WC2N 4AZ. Tel: 0171-240 4000
CENTRAL INDEPENDENT TELEVISION LTD (owned by Carlton Communications) (*the Midlands*), Central Court, Gas Street, Birmingham B1 2JT. Tel: 0121-643 9898
CHANNEL TELEVISION LTD (*Channel Islands*), The Television Centre, St Helier, Jersey JE2 3ZD. Tel: 01534-816816
GMTV LTD (*breakfast television*), The London Television Centre, Upper Ground, London SE1 9TT. Tel: 0171-827 7000
GRAMPIAN TELEVISION PLC (owned by Scottish Media) (*northern Scotland*), Queen's Cross, Aberdeen AB15 2XJ. Tel: 01224-846846
GRANADA TELEVISION LTD (owned by Granada Media) (*north-west England*), Quay Street, Manchester M60 9EA. Tel: 0161-832 7211
HTV GROUP PLC (*Wales and western England*), HTV Wales, The Television Centre, Culverhouse Cross, Cardiff CF5 6XJ. Tel: 01222-590590; HTV West, The Television Centre, Bath Road, Bristol BS4 3HG. Tel: 0117-977 8366
LONDON WEEKEND TELEVISION LTD (owned by Granada Media) (*London (weekends)*), The London Television Centre, Upper Ground, London SE1 9LT. Tel: 0171-620 1620
MERIDIAN BROADCASTING LTD (owned by MAI) (*south and south-east England*), The Television Centre, Southampton SO14 0PZ. Tel: 01703-222555
SCOTTISH TELEVISION PLC (owned by Scottish Media) (*central Scotland*), Cowcaddens, Glasgow G2 3PR. Tel: 0141-300 3000

TYNE TEES TELEVISION LTD (owned by Granada Media) (*north-east England*), The Television Centre, City Road, Newcastle upon Tyne NE1 2AL. Tel: 0191-261 0181
ULSTER TELEVISION PLC (*Northern Ireland*), Havelock House, Ormeau Road, Belfast BT7 1EB. Tel: 01232-328122
WESTCOUNTRY TELEVISION LTD (owned by Carlton Communications) (*south-west England*), Langage Science Park, Plymouth PL7 5BG. Tel: 01752-333333
YORKSHIRE TELEVISION LTD (owned by Granada Media) (*Yorkshire*), The Television Centre, Leeds LS3 1JS. Tel: 0113-243 8283

OTHER INDEPENDENT TELEVISION COMPANIES
CHANNEL 5 BROADCASTING LTD, 22 Long Acre, London WC2E 9LY. Tel: 0171-550 5555
CHANNEL FOUR TELEVISION CORPORATION, 124 Horseferry Road, London SW1P 2TX. Tel: 0171-396 4444. Provides a service to the UK except Wales, and is charged to cater for interests under-represented by the ITV network companies. Channel 4 sells its own advertising. The ITV companies are currently required to provide some financial support for Channel 4 if Channel 4's income falls below a certain point; they benefit financially if Channel 4's revenues are higher. The Government has announced plans to phase out this arrangement by 1999. In 1996 Channel 4 gave the ITV companies £87.1 million. In return ITV promotes Channel 4 programmes.
INDEPENDENT TELEVISION NEWS LTD, 200 Gray's Inn Road, London WC1X 8XZ. Tel: 0171-833 3000
TELETEXT LTD, 101 Farm Lane, London SW6 1QJ. Tel: 0171-386 5000. Provides teletext services for the ITV companies and Channel 4
WELSH FOURTH CHANNEL AUTHORITY (Sianel Pedwar Cymru), Parc Ty Glas, Llanishen, Cardiff CF4 5DU. Tel: 01222-747444. S4C schedules Welsh language programmes and relays most Channel 4 programmes

DIRECT BROADCASTING BY SATELLITE TELEVISION

BRITISH SKY BROADCASTING LTD, Grant Way, Isleworth, Middx TW7 5QD. Tel: 0171-705 3000. Broadcasts 11 channels which are wholly owned by Sky (Sky One, Sky News, Sky Sports 1, Sky Sports 2, Sky Sports 3, Sky Movies, The Movie Channel, Sky Movies Gold, Sky Soap, Sky Travel and The Computer Channel). Sky also co-operates with 14 joint venture channels and distributes 16 multi-channels for third parties.

RADIO

UK domestic radio services are broadcast across three wavebands: FM (or VHF), medium wave (also referred to as AM) and long wave (used by BBC Radio 4). In the UK the FM waveband extends in frequency from 87.5 MHz to 108 MHz and the medium wave band extends from 531 kHz to 1602 kHz. Some radios are still calibrated in wavelengths rather than frequency. To convert frequency to wavelength, divide 300,000 by the frequency in kHz.

DIGITAL RADIO

Digital audio broadcasting (DAB) is a new technique for improving the robustness of high fidelity radio services, especially compared with current FM and AM radio transmissions. It was developed in a collaborative research project under the pan-European EUREKA initiative and has been adopted as a world standard for new digital radio systems. DAB allows more services to be broadcast to a higher technical quality in a given amount of radio spectrum, and provides the data facility for text or pictures associated with sound programmes. The frequencies allocated for terrestrial DAB in the UK are 217.5 to 230 MHz.

The Broadcasting Act 1996 provided for the licensing of up to 42 digital radio services (on seven frequency channels or 'multiplexes'). The BBC has been allocated a multiplex capable of broadcasting six to eight national stereo services; BBC DAB broadcasts began in the London area in September 1995. A national DAB multiplex has also been made available, and local and regional services will use the remaining five multiplexes. The Radio Authority will be responsible for awarding licences for capacity on the non-BBC multiplexes; the first licences will be advertised in spring 1998 and awarded in late summer 1998, with the first independent digital services due to be broadcast in 1999. Analogue services will eventually be withdrawn.

BBC RADIO

Broadcasting House, Portland Place, London WIA IAA
Tel 0171-580 4468

BBC Radio broadcasts five national services to the UK, Isle of Man and the Channel Islands. There is also a tier of national regional services in Wales, Scotland and Northern Ireland and 39 local radio stations in England and the Channel Islands. In Wales there are two national regional services based on the Welsh and English languages respectively.

BBC NATIONAL SERVICES

RADIO 1 (Contemporary pop music, social action campaigns and entertainment news) – 24 hours a day. *Frequencies:* FM 97.6–99.8 MHz, coverage 99%
RADIO 2 (Popular music, entertainment, comedy and the arts) – 24 hours a day. *Frequencies:* FM 88–90.2 MHz, coverage 99%
RADIO 3 (Classical music, classic drama, documentaries and features) – 24 hours a day. *Frequencies:* FM 90.2–92.4 MHz, coverage 99%
RADIO 4 (News, documentaries, drama, entertainment, and cricket on long wave in season) – 5.55 a.m.–1.00 a.m. daily, with BBC World Service overnight. *Frequencies:* FM in England 94.6–96.1 MHz and 103.5–105 MHz, coverage 99%; LW 198 kHz/1449m, plus eight local fillers on MW
RADIO 5 LIVE (News and sport) – 24 hours a day. *Frequencies:* MW 693 kHz and 909 kHz, plus one local filler

BBC NATIONAL REGIONAL SERVICES

RADIO SCOTLAND *Frequencies:* MW 810 kHz plus two local fillers; FM 92.4–94.7 MHz, coverage 99%. Local programmes on FM as above: HIGHLANDS; NORTH-EAST BORDERS; SOUTH-WEST (also MW 585 kHz); ORKNEY; SHETLAND. RADIO NAN GAIDHEAL (Gaelic service) (FM 103.5–105 MHz) available in Western Highlands and Islands, Moray Firth and central Scotland; also available on MW 990 kHz in Aberdeen
RADIO ULSTER *Frequencies:* MW 1341 kHz, plus two local fillers; FM 92.4–96.1 MHz, coverage 96%. Local programmes on RADIO FOYLE *Frequencies:* MW 792 kHz; FM 93.1 MHz
RADIO WALES *Frequencies:* MW 882 kHz plus two local fillers; FM 95.1, 95.9 MHz (*Gwent*), coverage 96%

RADIO CYMRU (Welsh-language) *Frequencies:* FM 92.4–94.6, 95.7 (*Llanfyllin*), 96.1 (*Llandinam*), 96.8 and 103.5–105 MHz, coverage 96%

BBC LOCAL RADIO STATIONS

There are 39 local stations serving England and the Channel Islands:

ASIAN NETWORK, Epic House, Charles Street, Leicester LEI 3SH. Tel: 0116-251 6688. *Frequencies:* MW 828/837/1458 kHz
BRISTOL, PO Box 194, Bristol BS99 7QT. Tel: 0117-974 1111; 14–15 Paul Street, Taunton TAI 3PF. Tel: 01823-252437. *Frequencies:* MW 1548 kHz, 1323 kHz (*Somerset Sound*), 94.9/95.5/104.6 FM
CAMBRIDGESHIRE, Broadcasting House, 104 Hills Road, Cambridge CB2 ILD. Tel: 01223-259696. *Frequencies:* MW 1026/1449 kHz, 96.0/95.7 FM
CLEVELAND, PO Box 95 FM, Newport Road, Middlesbrough TSI 5DG. Tel: 01642-225211. *Frequencies:* 95.0/95.8 FM
CORNWALL, Phoenix Wharf, Truro, Cornwall TRI IUA. Tel: 01872-75421. *Frequencies:* MW 630/657 kHz, 95.2/96.0/103.9 FM
CUMBRIA, Annetwell Street, Carlisle CA3 8BB. Tel: 01228-592444. *Frequencies:* MW 756/837/1458 kHz, 95.2/95.6/96.1/104.1 FM
DERBY, PO Box 269, Derby DEI 3HL. Tel: 01332-361111. *Frequencies:* MW 1116 kHz, 94.2/95.3/104.5 FM
DEVON, PO Box 5, Broadcasting House, Seymour Road, Plymouth PL3 3BD. Tel: 01752-260323. *Frequencies:* MW 801/990/1458/855 kHz, 103.4/96.0/95.8/94.8 FM
ESSEX, 198 New London Road, Chelmsford CM2 9XB. Tel: 01245-262393. *Frequencies:* MW 765/729/1530 kHz, 103.5/95.3 FM
GLOUCESTERSHIRE, London Road, Gloucester GLI ISW. Tel: 01452-308585. *Frequencies:* 95.0/104.7/95.8 FM
GLR (GREATER LONDON RADIO), 35c Marylebone High Street, London WIA 4LG. Tel: 0171-224 2424. *Frequency:* 94.9 FM
GMR TALK (GREATER MANCHESTER RADIO), PO Box 951, Oxford Road, Manchester M6O ISD. Tel: 0161-244 3002. *Frequencies:* 95.1/104.6 FM
GUERNSEY, Commerce House, Les Banques, St Peter Port, Guernsey GYI 2HS. Tel: 01481-728977. *Frequencies:* MW 1116 kHz, 93.2 FM
HEREFORD AND WORCESTERSHIRE, Hylton Road, Worcester WR2 5WW. Tel: 01905-748485. *Frequencies:* MW 738/819 kHz, 104.6/104.0/94.7 FM
HUMBERSIDE, 9 Chapel Street, Hull HUI 3NU. Tel: 01482-323232. *Frequencies:* MW 1485 kHz, 95.9 FM
JERSEY, 18 Parade Road, St Helier, Jersey JE2 3PL. Tel: 01534-870000. *Frequencies:* MW 1026 kHz, 88.8 FM
KENT, Sun Pier, Chatham, Kent ME4 4EZ. Tel: 01634-830505. *Frequencies:* MW 774/1602 kHz, 96.7/97.6/104.2 FM
LANCASHIRE, 26 Darwen Street, Blackburn BB2 2EA. Tel: 01254-262411. *Frequencies:* MW 855/1557 kHz, 95.5/104.5/103.9 FM
LEEDS, Broadcasting House, Woodhouse Lane, Leeds LS2 9PN. Tel: 0113-244 2131. *Frequencies:* MW 774 kHz, 92.4/95.3/103.9 FM
LEICESTER, Epic House, Charles Street, Leicester LEI 3SH. Tel: 0116-251 6688. *Frequency:* 104.9 FM
LINCOLNSHIRE, PO Box 219, Newport, Lincoln LNI 3XY. Tel: 01522-511411. *Frequencies:* MW 1368 kHz, 94.9 FM
MERSEYSIDE, 55 Paradise Street, Liverpool LI 3BP. Tel: 0151-708 5500. *Frequencies:* MW 1485 kHz, 95.8 FM

NEWCASTLE, Broadcasting Centre, Barrack Road, Newcastle upon Tyne NE99 1RN. Tel: 0191-232 4141. *Frequencies:* MW 206 kHz, 95.4/104.4/96.0/103.7 FM

NORFOLK, Norfolk Tower, Surrey Street, Norwich NR1 3PA. Tel: 01603-617411. *Frequencies:* MW 855/873 kHz, 95.1/104.4 FM

NORTHAMPTON, Broadcasting House, Abington Street, Northampton NN1 2BE. Tel: 01604-239100. *Frequencies:* MW 1107 kHz, 104.2/103.6 FM

NOTTINGHAM, York House, Mansfield Road, Nottingham NG1 3JB. Tel: 0115-955 0500. *Frequencies:* MW 1584 kHz, 103.8/95.5 FM

SHEFFIELD, Ashdell Grove, 60 Westbourne Road, Sheffield S10 2QU. Tel: 0114-268 6185. *Frequencies:* MW 1035 kHz, 94.7/104.1/88.6 FM

SHROPSHIRE, 2–4 Boscobel Drive, Shrewsbury SY1 3TT. Tel: 01743-248484. *Frequencies:* MW 1584 kHz, 95.0/96.0 FM

SOLENT, Broadcasting House, Havelock Road, Southampton SO14 7PW. Tel: 01703-631311. *Frequencies:* MW 999/1359 kHz, 96.1/103.8 FM

SOUTHERN COUNTIES, Broadcasting Centre, Guildford GU2 5AP. Tel: 01483-306306. *Frequencies:* 95–95.3/104–104.8 FM

STOKE, Cheapside, Hanley, Stoke-on-Trent ST1 1JJ. Tel: 01782-208080. *Frequencies:* MW 1503 kHz, 94.6/104.1 FM

SUFFOLK, Broadcasting House, St Matthew's Street, Ipswich IP1 3EP. Tel: 01473-250000. *Frequencies:* 103.9/104.6/95.5 FM

THAMES VALLEY FM, 269 Banbury Road, Oxford OX2 7DW. Tel: 01865-311444. *Frequencies:* 95.2/104.1/95.4/94.6 FM

THREE COUNTIES RADIO, PO Box 3CR, Luton, Beds LU1 5XL. Tel: 01582-441000. *Frequencies:* MW 1161/630 kHz, 104.5/95.5/103.8 FM

WILTSHIRE SOUND, Broadcasting House, Prospect Place, Swindon SN1 3RW. Tel: 01793-513626. *Frequencies:* MW 1332/1368 kHz, 103.6/103.4/103.5/104.9 FM

WM (WEST MIDLANDS), Pebble Mill Road, Birmingham B5 7SD. Tel: 0121-414 8484; 25 Warwick Road, Coventry CV1 2WR. Tel: 01203-559911. *Frequencies:* 95.6 FM; 94.8/103.7/104.0 FM (Coventry and Warwickshire)

YORK, 20 Bootham Row, York YO3 7BR. Tel: 01904-641351. *Frequencies:* MW 666/1260 kHz, 103.7/104.3/95.5 FM

BBC WORLD SERVICE
Bush House, Strand, London WC2B 4PH
Tel 0171-240 3456

The BBC World Service broadcasts over 1,000 hours of programmes a week in 45 languages including English. Of the 111 transmitters in use, 40 are in the UK and 71 overseas.

The World Service is organized into five world regions, each responsible for programmes in English as well as regional languages.

AFRICA AND THE MIDDLE EAST, Arabic, French, Hausa, Kinyarwanda/Kirundi, Portuguese, Somali and Swahili; English programmes including *Network Africa* and *Focus on Africa.*

ASIA AND THE PACIFIC, Bengali, Burmese, Cantonese, Hindi, Indonesian, Mandarin, Nepali, Sinhala, Tamil, Thai, Urdu and Vietnamese; English programmes including *East Asia Today* and *South Asia Report.*

EUROPE, Albanian, Bulgarian, Croatian, Czech, Finnish, German, Greek, Hungarian, Macedonian, Polish, Romanian, Serbian, Slovak and Slovene; English programmes including *Europe Today.*

FORMER SOVIET UNION AND SOUTH-WEST ASIA, Azeri, Kazakh, Kyrgyz, Pashto, Persian, Russian, Turkish, Ukrainian and Uzbek.

THE AMERICAS, Portuguese for Brazil, Spanish; English programmes including *The World* (a global news magazine for American listeners), *Caribbean Report* and *Calling the Falklands.*

BBC ENGLISH teaches English world-wide through radio, television and a wide range of published courses

BBC INTERNATIONAL BROADCASTING AND AUDIENCE RESEARCH carries out audience research and sells printed publications and data

BBC MONITORING supplies news and information from the output of overseas radio and television stations and news agency sources

BBC MPM (Marshall Plan of the Mind) makes programmes about business, democracy and management for countries of the former Soviet Union

BBC WORLD SERVICE TRAINING runs journalism, management and skills training courses for overseas broadcasters

INDEPENDENT RADIO

The Radio Authority began advertising new licences for the development of commercial radio in January 1991. Since then it has awarded three national licences, 77 new local radio licences (including eight regional licences) and one additional channel service licence (to use the spare capacity in an existing channel which is not used by the programme service). The Authority has also issued about 1,600 restricted service licences (for temporary low-powered radio services). In February 1997 it issued a consultation document which examined the possibility of advertising a fourth national radio service which would utilize the long-wave frequency 225 kHz. A decision has not yet been made as to whether the Authority will proceed with the advertisment of this licence.

The Authority will award regional licences for the Solent area and north-west England and other local licences by the end of 1997. It will continue to advertise about two local licences a month in 1997–8, including regional licences for north-east England and central Scotland.

COMMERCIAL RADIO COMPANIES ASSOCIATION, 77 Shaftesbury Avenue, London W1V 7AD. Tel: 0171-306 2603. *Chief Executive,* P. Brown

INDEPENDENT NATIONAL RADIO STATIONS

CLASSIC FM, Academic House, 24–28 Oval Road, London NW1 7DQ. Tel: 0171-284 3000. 24 hours a day. *Frequencies:* FM 99.9–101.9 MHz

TALK RADIO UK, PO Box 1089, London W1A 1PP. Tel: 0171-636 1089. 24 hours a day. *Frequencies:* MW 1053/1089 kHz

VIRGIN RADIO, 1 Golden Square, London W1R 4DJ. Tel: 0171-434 1215. 24 hours a day. *Frequencies:* MW 1215/1197/1233/1242/1260 kHz

INDEPENDENT REGIONAL LOCAL RADIO STATIONS

100.7 HEART FM (*West Midlands*), 1 The Square, 111 Broad Street, Birmingham B15 1AS. Tel: 0121-626 1007. *Frequency:* 100.7 FM

CENTURY RADIO (*North-East*), Century House, PO Box 100, Gateshead NE8 2YX. Tel: 0191-477 6666. *Frequencies:* 100.7/101.8/96.2/96.4 FM

GALAXY 101 (*Severn Estuary*), PO Box 1010, Bristol or Cardiff. Tel: 0117-924 0111. *Frequencies:* 101.0/97.2 FM (Bristol)

JAZZ FM 100.4 (*North-West*), The World Trade Centre, Exchange Quay, Manchester M5 3EJ. Tel: 0161-877 1004. *Frequency,* 100.4 FM

KISS 105 (*Yorkshire*), Kiss House, 2A Joseph's Well, West Gate, Leeds LS3 1AB. Tel: 0113-246 0105. *Frequencies:* 105.1 FM (Leeds); 105.6 FM (Bradford and Sheffield); 105.8 FM (Hull)

RADIO 106 FM (*East Midlands*), Manor Farm, Main Street, Upton, Notts NG23 5ST. Tel: 0115-955 5106. *Frequency:* 106.0 FM

SCOT FM (*Central Scotland*), 1 Albert Quay, Leith EH6 7DN. Tel: 0131-554 6677. *Frequencies:* 100.3/101.1 FM

VIBE FM (*Eastern Counties*), Radio House, 19–20 Clifftown Road, Southend-on-Sea, Essex SS1 1SX. Tel: 01245-493131 ext. 3235

INDEPENDENT LOCAL RADIO STATIONS

England

2-TEN FM, PO Box 2020, Reading RG31 7FG. Tel: 0118-925 4400. *Frequencies:* 97.0/102.9 FM

2CR FM, 5 Southcote Road, Bournemouth BH1 3LR. Tel: 01202-294881. *Frequency:* 102.3 FM

96.3 AIRE FM, PO Box 2000, 51 Burley Road, Leeds LS3 1LR. Tel: 0113-245 2299. *Frequency:* 96.3 FM

96.4 FM BRMB, Radio House, Aston Road North, Birmingham B6 4BX. Tel: 0121-359 4481. *Frequency:* 96.4 FM

96.4 THE EAGLE, Dolphin House, North Street, Guildford, Surrey GU1 4AA. Tel: 01483-300964. *Frequency:* 96.4 FM

96.6 FM CLASSIC HITS, 7 Hatfield Road, St Albans, Herts AL1 3RS. Tel: 01727-831966. *Frequency:* 96.6 FM

96.9 VIKING FM, Commercial Road, Hull HU1 2SG. Tel: 01482-325141. *Frequency:* 96.9 FM

97.2 STRAY FM, PO Box 972, Station Parade, Harrogate HG1 5YF. Tel: 01423-522972. *Frequency:* 97.2 FM

97.4 Gold Radio, Longmead, Shaftesbury, Dorset SP7 8QQ. Tel: 01747-855711. *Frequency:* 97.4 FM

102.7 HEREWARD FM, PO Box 225, Queensgate Centre, Peterborough PE1 1XJ. Tel: 01733-460460. *Frequency:* 102.7 FM

107.7 The Wolf, 10th Floor, Mander House, Wolverhampton WV1 3NB. Tel: 01902-319112. *Frequency:* 107.7 FM

963 Liberty Radio, 26–27 Castlereagh Street, London W1H 6DJ. Tel: 0171-706 9963. *Frequency:* MW 963 kHz

1152 XTRA AM, Radio House, Aston Road North, Birmingham B6 4BX. Tel: 0121-359 4481. *Frequency:* MW 1152 kHz

1458 LITE AM, PO Box 1458, Quay West, Trafford Park, Manchester M17 1FL. Tel: 0161-872 1458. *Frequency:* MW 1458 kHz

ALPHA 103.2, Radio House, 11 Woodland Road, Darlington DL3 7BJ. Tel: 01325-255552. *Frequency:* 103.2 FM

AMBER RADIO, St George's Plain, 47–49 Colegate, Norwich NR3 1DB. Tel: 01603-630621; Radio House, Alpha Business Park, White House Road, Ipswich IP1 5LT. Tel: 01473-461000. *Frequencies:* MW 1152 kHz (Norfolk); 1170/1251 kHz (Suffolk)

ASIAN SOUND RADIO, Globe House, Southall Street, Manchester M3 1LG. Tel: 0161-288 1000. *Frequencies:* MW 1377/963 kHz

B97, 55 Goldington Road, Bedford MK40 3LS. Tel: 01234-272400. *Frequency:* 97.6 FM

THE BAY, PO Box 969, St George's Quay, Lancaster LA1 3LD. Tel: 01524-848747. *Frequencies:* 96.9/102.3/103.2 FM

THE BEACH, PO Box 103.4, Lowestoft, Suffolk NR32 2TL. Tel: 07000-001035. *Frequency:* 103.4 FM

BEACON RADIO, 267 Tettenhall Road, Wolverhampton WV6 0DQ. Tel: 01902-838383. *Frequencies:* 97.2 FM (Wolverhampton and Black Country); 103.1 FM (Shrewsbury and Telford)

THE BREEZE, Radio House, Clifftown Road, Southend-on-Sea, Essex SS1 1SX. Tel: 01702-333711. *Frequency:* MW 1359 kHz (Chelmsford); 1431 kHz (Southend)

BROADLAND 102, St George's Plain, 47–49 Colegate, Norwich NR3 1DB. Tel: 01603-630621. *Frequency:* 102.4 FM

BRUNEL CLASSIC GOLD, PO Box 2020, Lime Kiln, Wootton Bassett, Wilts SN4 7EX. Tel: 01793-440301. *Frequency:* MW 1260 kHz

CAMBRIDGE COMMUNITY RADIO 107.9 FM, East View, Coles Lane, Oakington, Cambs CB8 5BA. Tel: 01223-237700. *Frequency:* 107.9 FM

CAPITAL FM AND GOLD, 29–30 Leicester Square, London WC2H 7LA. Tel: 0171-766 6000. *Frequencies:* MW 1548 kHz (*Gold*), 95.8 FM

CFM, PO Box 964, Carlisle, Cumbria CA1 3NG. Tel: 01228-818964. *Frequencies:* 96.4/102.5 FM (Penrith); 102.2 FM (Workington); 103.4 FM (Whitehaven)

CHANNEL TRAVEL RADIO, Main Control Building, PO Box 2000, Eurotunnel UK Terminal, Folkestone, Kent CT18 8XY. Tel: 01303-283873. *Frequency:* 107.6 FM

CHELTENHAM RADIO, Regent Arcade, Cheltenham, Glos GL50 1JZ. Tel: 01242-699555. *Frequency:* MW 603 kHz

CHILTERN FM, Chiltern Road, Dunstable, Beds LU6 1HQ. Tel: 01582-666001. *Frequency:* 97.6 FM

CHOICE FM BIRMINGHAM, 95 Broad Street, Birmingham B15 1AU. Tel: 0121-616 1000. *Frequency:* 102.2 FM

CHOICE FM LONDON, 16–18 Trinity Gardens, London SW9 8DP. Tel: 0171-738 7969. *Frequency:* 96.9 FM

CITY FM, 8–10 Stanley Street, Liverpool L1 6AF. Tel: 0151-227 5100. *Frequency:* 96.7 FM

CLASSIC GOLD 774, Old Talbot House, Southgate Street, Gloucester GL1 2DQ. Tel: 01452-423791. *Frequency:* MW 774 kHz

CLASSIC GOLD 792/828, Chiltern Road, Dunstable, Beds LU6 1HQ. Tel: 01582-676200. *Frequencies:* MW 792 kHz (Bedford); 828 kHz (Luton)

CLASSIC GOLD 828, 5 Southcote Road, Bournemouth, Dorset BH1 3LR. Tel: 01202-294881. *Frequency:* MW 828 kHz

CLASSIC GOLD 1278/1530, Pennine House, Forster Square, Bradford BD1 5NE. Tel: 01274-203040. *Frequencies:* MW 1278/1530 kHz

CLASSIC GOLD 1332 AM, PO Box 2020, Queensgate Centre, Peterborough PE1 1LL. Tel: 01733-460460. *Frequency:* MW 1332 kHz

CLASSIC GOLD 1359, Hertford Place, Coventry CV1 3TT. Tel: 01203-868200. *Frequency:* MW 1359 kHz

CLASSIC GOLD 1431/1485, PO Box 2020, Reading RG31 7FG. Tel: 0118-925 4400. *Frequencies:* MW 1431/1485 kHz

CLASSIC GOLD 1557, 19–21 St Edmunds Road, Northampton NN1 5DY. Tel: 01604-795600. *Frequency:* MW 1557 kHz

COUNTY SOUND RADIO 1476 AM, Dolphin House, North Street, Guildford GU1 4AA. Tel: 01483-300964. *Frequency:* MW 1476 kHz

CRASH FM, Room 156, The Liverpool Palace, 9 Slater Street, Liverpool L1 4BW. Tel: 0151-709 3357

CTFM, PO Box 440, Canterbury, Kent CT1 2GX. Tel: 01227-789106. *Frequency:* 106.0 FM

DELTA RADIO 97.1 FM, 65 Weyhill, Haslemere, Surrey GU27 1HN. Tel: 01428-651971. *Frequency:* 97.1 FM

DUNE FM, 12 Chandley Close, Ainsdale, Southport PR8 2SJ. Tel: 01704-533866

ELEVEN SEVENTY, PO Box 1170, High Wycombe, Bucks HP13 6YT. Tel: 01494-446611. *Frequency:* MW 1170 kHz

ESSEX FM, Radio House, Clifftown Road, Southend-on-Sea, Essex SS1 1SX. Tel: 01702-333711. *Frequencies:* 96.3 FM (Southend); 102.8 FM (Chelmsford)

FAME 1521, Broadfield House, Brighton Road, Crawley, W. Sussex RH11 9TT. Tel: 01293-519161. *Frequency:* MW 1521 kHz

FM 102 – THE BEAR, The Guard House Studios, Banbury Road, Stratford-upon-Avon, Warks CV37 7HX. Tel: 01789-262636. *Frequency:* 102.0 FM

FM 103 HORIZON, The Broadcast Centre, Vincent Avenue, Crownhill, Milton Keynes MK8 0AB. Tel: 01908-269111. *Frequency:* 103.3 FM

FOX FM, Brush House, Pony Road, Oxford OX4 2XR. Tel: 01865-871000. *Frequencies:* 102.6/97.4 FM

GEM-AM, 29–31 Castle Gate, Nottingham NG1 7AP. Tel: 0115-952 7000. *Frequencies:* MW 999/945 kHz

GEMINI AM AND FM, Hawthorne House, Exeter Business Park, Exeter EX1 3QS. Tel: 01392-444444. *Frequencies:* MW 666/954 kHz, 97.0/96.4/103.0 FM

GNR (GREAT NORTH RADIO), Swalwell, Newcastle upon Tyne NE99 1BB. Tel: 0191-420 3040. *Frequencies:* MW 1152 kHz (Northumberland, Tyne and Wear, Durham); 1170 kHz (Durham, Teesside, N. Yorks)

GWR FM (BRISTOL AND BATH), PO Box 2000, Watershed, Canon's Road, Bristol BS99 7SN. Tel: 0117-984 3200. *Frequencies:* 96.3 FM (Bristol); 103.0 FM (Bath)

GWR FM (SWINDON AND WEST WILTSHIRE), PO Box 2000, Swindon SN4 7EX. Tel: 01793-440300. *Frequencies:* 97.2 FM (Swindon); 102.2 FM (West Wilts)

HALLAM FM, Radio House, 900 Herries Road, Sheffield S6 1RH. Tel: 0114-285 3333. *Frequencies:* 97.4 FM (Sheffield); 102.9/103.4 FM (Rotherham); 102.9 FM (Barnsley); 103.4 FM (Doncaster)

HEART 106.2, The Chrysalis Building, Bramley Road, London W10 6SP. Tel: 0171-468 1062. *Frequency:* 106.2 FM

INVICTA FM AND SUPERGOLD, Radio House, John Wilson Business Park, Whitstable, Kent CT5 3QX. Tel: 01227-772004. *Frequencies:* MW 1242 kHz (West Kent), 603 kHz (East Kent); 103.1 FM (Maidstone and Medway), 102.8 FM (Canterbury), 95.9 FM (Thanet), 97.0 FM (Dover), 96.1 FM (Ashford)

ISLE OF WIGHT RADIO, Dodnor Park, Newport, Isle of Wight PO30 5XE. Tel: 01983-822557. *Frequency:* MW 1242 kHz

JAZZ FM 102.2, 26–27 Castlereagh Street, London W1H 6DJ. Tel: 0171-706 4100. *Frequency:* 102.2 FM

KCBC 1584 AM, Unit 1, Centre 2000, Robinson Close, Telford Way Industrial Estate, Kettering, Northants NN16 8PU. Tel: 01536-412413. *Frequency:* MW 1584 kHz

KEY 103, Castle Quay, Castlefield, Manchester M1 4AW. Tel: 0161-288 5000. *Frequency:* 103.0 FM

KFM, 1 East Street, Tonbridge, Kent TN9 1AR. Tel: 01732-369200. *Frequencies:* 96.2/101.6 FM

KISS 100 FM, Kiss House, 80 Holloway Road, London N7 8JG. Tel: 0171-700 6100. *Frequency:* 100.0 FM

KISS 102, Kiss House, PO Box 102, Manchester M60 1GJ. Tel: 0161-228 0102. *Frequency:* 102 FM

KIX 96, St Mark's Church Annexe, Bird Street, Stoney Stanton Road, Coventry CV1 4FH. Tel: 01203-525656. *Frequency:* 96.2 FM

KL.FM 96.7, PO Box 77, 18 Blackfriars Street, King's Lynn, Norfolk PE30 1NN. Tel: 01553-772777. *Frequency:* 96.7 FM

LANTERN FM, The Light House, 17 Market Place, Bideford, N. Devon EX39 2DR. Tel: 01237-424444. *Frequency:* 96.2 FM

LBC 1152, 200 Gray's Inn Road, London WC1X 8XZ. Tel: 0171-973 1152. *Frequency:* MW 1152 kHz

LEICESTER SOUND, Granville House, Granville Road, Leicester LE1 7RW. Tel: 0116-256 1300. *Frequency:* 103.2 FM

LINCS FM, Witham Park, Waterside South, Lincoln LN5 7JN. Tel: 01522-549900. *Frequency:* 102.2 FM/96.7 FM (Grantham Relay)

LONDON GREEK RADIO, Florentia Village, Vale Road, London N4 1TD. Tel: 0181-800 8001. *Frequency:* 103.3 FM

LONDON TURKISH RADIO LTR, 185B High Road, Wood Green, London N22 6BA. Tel: 0181-881 0606 *Frequency:* MW 1584 kHz

MAGIC, Radio House, 900 Herries Road, Sheffield S6 1RH. Tel: 0114-285 3333. *Frequencies:* MW 1161 kHz (Humberside); 990/1305/1548 kHz (South Yorks)

MAGIC 828, PO Box 2000, 51 Burley Road, Leeds LS3 1LR. Tel: 0113-245 2299. *Frequency:* MW 828 kHz

MAGIC 1548 AM, 8–10 Stanley Street, Liverpool L1 6AF. Tel: 0151-227 5100. *Frequency:* MW 1548 kHz

MARCHER GOLD, The Studios, Mold Road, Gwersyllt, Nr Wrexham LL11 4AF. Tel: 01978-752202. *Frequency:* MW 1260 kHz

MEDWAY FM, Berkeley House, 186 High Street, Rochester ME1 1EY. Tel: 01634-841111. *Frequencies:* 107.9/100.4 FM

MELLOW 1557, Media Centre, 2 St Johns Wynd, Culver Square, Colchester CO1 1WG. Tel: 01206-764466. *Frequency:* MW 1557 kHz

MELODY FM, 180 Brompton Road, London SW3 1HF. Tel: 0171-581 1054. *Frequency:* 105.4 FM

MERCIA FM, Hertford Place, Coventry CV1 3TT. Tel: 01203-868200. *Frequencies:* 97.0/102.9 FM

MERCURY FM, Broadfield House, Brighton Road, Crawley, W. Sussex RH11 9TT. Tel: 01293-519161. *Frequency:* 102.7 FM

METRO FM, Newcastle upon Tyne NE99 1BB. Tel: 0191-420 0971. *Frequencies:* 97.1 FM (Northumberland, Tyne and Wear, Durham); 103.0/103.2 FM (Tyne Valley), 102.6 FM (North Northumberland)

MFM, The Studios, Mold Road, Gwersyllt, Nr Wrexham LL11 4AF. Tel: 01978-752202. *Frequencies:* 103.4/97.1 FM

MILLENNIUM RADIO, Harrow Manor Way, Thamesmead South, London SE2 9XH. Tel: 0181-311 3112. *Frequency:* 103.8 FM

MINSTER FM, PO Box 123, Dunnington, York YO1 5ZX. Tel: 01904-488888. *Frequency:* 104.7 FM

MIX 96, Friars Square Studios, 11 Bourbon Street, Aylesbury, Bucks HP20 2PZ. Tel: 01296-399396. *Frequency:* 96.2 FM

NEWS DIRECT 97.3 FM, 200 Gray's Inn Road, London WC1X 8XZ. Tel: 0171-973 1152. *Frequency:* 97.3 FM

NORTHANTS 96, 19–21 St Edmunds Road, Northampton NN1 5DY. Tel: 01604-795600. *Frequency:* 96.6 FM

OCEAN FM, Radio House, Whittle Avenue, Fareham, Hants PO15 5SH. Tel: 01489-589911. *Frequencies:* 97.5/96.7 FM

ORCHARD FM, Haygrove House, Taunton TA3 7BT. Tel: 01823-338448. *Frequencies:* 102.6/97.1 FM

OXYGEN 107.9, Suite 41, Westgate Centre, Oxford OX1 1PD. Tel: 01865-724442. *Frequency:* 107.9 FM

PICCADILLY RADIO 1152 AM, Castle Quay, Castlefield, Manchester M5 4PR. Tel: 0161-288 5000. *Frequency:* MW 1152 kHz

PIRATE FM 102, 102 Wilson Way, Redruth, Cornwall TR15 3XX. Tel: 01209-314400; Foot and Bowden Building, 19 The Crescent, Plymouth PL1 3AO. Tel: 01752-675179. *Frequencies:* 102.2 FM (East Cornwall and West Devon); 102.8 FM (West Cornwall and Isles of Scilly)

PLYMOUTH SOUND AM AND FM, Earl's Acre, Plymouth PL3 4HX. Tel: 01752-227272. *Frequencies:* MW 1152 kHz; 97.0/96.6 FM

POWER FM, Radio House, Whittle Avenue, Fareham, Hants PO15 5SH. Tel: 01489-589911. *Frequency:* 103.2 FM.

PREMIER RADIO, Glen House, Stag Place, London SW1E 5AG. Tel: 0171-233 6705. *Frequencies:* MW 1305/1332/1413 kHz

THE PULSE, Pennine House, Forster Square, Bradford BD1 5NE. Tel: 01274-203040. *Frequencies:* 97.5 FM (Bradford); 102.5 FM (Huddersfield and Halifax)

Q103 FM, Enterprise House, The Vision Park, Chivers Way, Histon, Cambridge CB4 4WW. Tel: 01223-235255. *Frequencies:* 103.0 FM (Cambridge); 97.4 FM (Newmarket)

RADIO WAVE, 965 Mowbray Drive, Blackpool FY3 7JR. Tel: 01253-304965. *Frequency:* 96.5 FM

RADIO XL 1296 AM, KMS House, Bradford Street, Birmingham B12 0JD. Tel: 0121-753 5353. *Frequency:* MW 1296 kHz

RAM FM, The Market Place, Derby DE1 3AA. Tel: 01332-292945. *Frequency:* 102.8 FM

RED ROSE 999, PO Box 999, St Paul's Square, Preston PR1 1XR. Tel: 01772-556301. *Frequency:* MW 999 kHz

ROCK FM, PO Box 974, St Paul's Square, Preston PR1 1YE. Tel: 01772-556301. *Frequency:* 97.4 FM

RTL COUNTRY 1035 AM, PO Box 1035, London SW6 3QQ. Tel: 0171-546 1000. *Frequency:* MW 1035 kHz

SABRAS SOUND, Radio House, 63 Melton Road, Leicester LE4 6PN. Tel: 0116-261 0666. *Frequency:* MW 1260 kHz

SEVERN SOUND FM, Old Talbot House, Southgate Street, Gloucester GL1 2DQ. Tel: 01452-423791. *Frequencies:* 103.0/102.4 FM

SGR COLCHESTER, Abbeygate Two, 9 Whitewell Road, Colchester CO2 7DE. Tel: 01206-575859. *Frequency:* 96.1 FM

SGR-FM, Radio House, Alpha Business Park, White House Road, Ipswich IP1 5LT. Tel: 01473-461000. *Frequencies:* 97.1 FM (Ipswich); 96.4 FM (Bury St Edmunds)

SIGNAL 105, Regent House, Heaton Lane, Stockport SK4 1BX. Tel: 0161-285 4545. *Frequencies:* 104.9 FM (South Manchester); 96.4 FM (Cheshire)

SIGNAL ONE (FM) AND TWO (MW), Stoke Road, Stoke-on-Trent ST4 2SR. Tel: 01782-747047. *Frequencies:* MW 1170 kHz, 102.6/96.9 FM

THE SOUND, PO Box 1068, Dover, Kent CT16 1GB. Tel: 01304-240402; PO Box 964, Folkestone, Kent CT18 8GG. Tel: 01304-240402. *Frequencies:* 106.8 FM (Dover); 96.4 FM (Folkestone)

SOUTH COAST RADIO, Radio House, Whittle Avenue, Fareham, Hants PO15 5SH. Tel: 01489-589911; Radio House, PO Box 2000, Brighton BN14 2SS. Tel: 01273-430111. *Frequencies:* MW 1170/1557/945 kHz (South Hants); 945/1323 kHz (East Sussex)

SOUTHERN FM, Radio House, PO Box 2000, Brighton BN41 2SS. Tel: 01273-430111. *Frequencies:* 102.4/103.4 FM

SPECTRUM INTERNATIONAL RADIO, 80 Silverthorne Road, London SW8 3XA. Tel: 0171-627 4433. *Frequency:* MW 558 kHz

SPIRE FM, City Hall Studios, Malthouse Lane, Salisbury, Wilts SP2 7QQ. Tel: 01722-416644. *Frequency:* 102.0 FM

SPIRIT FM, Dukes Court, Bognor Road, Chichester, W. Sussex PO19 2FX. Tel: 01243-773600. *Frequencies:* 96.6/102.3 FM

STAR FM, The Observatory Shopping Centre, Slough, Berks SL1 1LH. Tel: 01753-551066. *Frequency:* 106.6 FM

SUN FM, PO Box 1034, Sunderland SR1 3YZ. Tel: 0191-567 3333. *Frequency:* 103.4 FM

SUNRISE RADIO (BRADFORD), Sunrise House, 30 Chapel Street, Little Germany, Bradford BD1 5DN. Tel: 01274-735043. *Frequency:* 103.2 FM

SUNRISE RADIO (GREATER LONDON), Sunrise House, Sunrise Road, Southall, Middx UB2 4AU. Tel: 0181-574 6666. *Frequency:* MW 1458 kHz

SUNSHINE 855, Sunshine House, Waterside, Ludlow, Shropshire SY8 1GS. Tel: 01584-873795. *Frequency:* MW 855 kHz

TEN 17, Latton Bush Centre, Southern Way, Harlow, Essex CM18 7BU. Tel: 01279-432415. *Frequency:* 101.7 FM

TFM, Radio House, Yale Crescent, Thornaby, Stockton-on-Tees TS17 6AA. Tel: 01642-888222. *Frequency:* 96.6 FM

THAMES FM, Brentham House, 45C High Street, Hampton Wick, Kingston upon Thames KT1 4DG. Tel: 0181-288 1300. *Frequency:* 107.8 FM

THANET LOCAL RADIO, IMPERIAL HOUSE, 2–14 High Street, Margate, Kent CT9 1DH. Tel: 01843-220222. *Frequency:* 107.2 FM

TRENT -FM, 29–31 Castle Gate, Nottingham NG1 7AP. Tel: 0115-952 7000. *Frequencies:* 96.2/96.5 FM

VIRGIN RADIO LONDON, 1 Golden Square, London W1R 4DJ. Tel: 0171-434 1215. *Frequency:* 105.8 FM

WABC CLASSIC GOLD, 267 Tettenhall Road, Wolverhampton WV6 0DQ. Tel: 01902-838383. *Frequencies:* MW 990 kHz (Wolverhampton); 1017 kHz (Shrewsbury and Telford)

WESSEX FM, Radio House, Trinity Street, Dorchester DT1 1DJ. Tel: 01305-250333. *Frequencies:* 97.2/96.0 FM

WEY VALLEY RADIO, Prospect Place, Mill Lane, Alton, Hants GU34 2SY. Tel: 01420-544444. *Frequencies:* 102.0/101.6 FM

WISH 102.4 FM, Orrell Lodge, Orrell Road, Orrell, Wigan WN5 8HJ. Tel: 01942-761024. *Frequency:* 102.4 FM

WYVERN AM and FM, 5 Barbourne Terrace, Worcester WR1 3JZ. Tel: 01905-612212. *Frequencies:* MW 954 kHz, 97.6 FM (Hereford); 1530 kHz, 102.8 FM (Worcester); 96.7 FM (Kidderminster)

XFM, 97 Charlotte Street, London W1P 1LB. Tel: 0171-580 7577. *Frequency:* 104.9 FM

YORKSHIRE COAST RADIO, PO Box 962, Scarborough, N. Yorks YO12 5YX. Tel: 01723-500962. *Frequencies:* 96.2/103.1 FM

YORKSHIRE DALES RADIO LTD, YDR House, Gargrave Road, Skipton, N. Yorks BD23 1YD. Tel: 01756-799991. *Frequencies:* MW 936 kHz (Hawes); 1413 kHz (Skipton).

Wales

COAST FM, The Studios, 41 Conwy Road, Colwyn Bay LL28 5AB. Tel: 01492-534555. *Frequency:* 96.3 FM

RADIO CEREDIGION, Yr Hen Ysgol Gymraeg, Ffordd Alexandra, Aberystwyth SY23 1LF. Tel: 01970-627999. *Frequencies:* 103.3/96.6 FM

RADIO MALDWYN, The Studios, The Park, Newtown, Powys SY16 2NZ. Tel: 01686-623555. *Frequency:* MW 756 kHz

RED DRAGON FM, Radio House, West Canal Wharf, Cardiff CF1 5XJ. Tel: 01222-384041. *Frequencies:* 103.2 FM (Cardiff); 97.4 FM (Newport)

SOUND WAVE, PO Box 964, Victoria Road, Gowerton, Swansea SA4 3AB. Tel: 01792-511964. *Frequency:* 96.4 FM

SWANSEA SOUND, PO Box 1170, Victoria Road, Gowerton, Swansea SA4 3AB. Tel: 01792-511170. *Frequency:* MW 1170 kHz

TOUCH RADIO, West Canal Wharf, Cardiff CF1 5XJ. Tel: 01222-237878. *Frequencies:* MW 1359 kHz (Cardiff); 1305 kHz (Newport)

VALLEYS RADIO, Festival Park, Victoria, Ebbw Vale NP3 6XW. Tel: 01495-301116. *Frequencies:* MW 999/1116 kHz

Scotland

96.3 QFM, 26 Lady Lane, Paisley PA1 2NS. Tel: 0141-887 9630. *Frequency:* 96.3 FM

CENTRAL FM, John Player Building, Stirling Enterprise Park, Stirling FK7 7YJ. Tel: 01786-451188. *Frequency:* 103.1 FM

CLYDE 1 (FM) AND 2 (MW), Clydebank Business Park, Clydebank, Glasgow G81 2RX. Tel: 0141-306 2200. *Frequencies:* 102.5 FM; 97.0 FM (Vale of Leven); 103.3 FM (Firth of Clyde), MW 1152 kHz

FORTH AM AND FM, Forth House, Forth Street, Edinburgh EH1 3LF. Tel: 0131-556 9255. *Frequencies:* MW 1548 kHz, 97.3/97.6 FM

HEARTLAND FM, Atholl Curling Rink, Lower Oakfield, Pitlochry, Perthshire PH16 5HQ. Tel: 01796-474040. *Frequency:* 97.5 FM

ISLES FM, PO Box 333, Stornoway, Isle of Lewis HS1 2PT. Licence awarded conditional upon confirmation of funding

LOCHBROOM FM, 24 Argyle Street, Ullapool, Wester Ross IV26 2UB. Tel: 01854-613131. *Frequency:* 102.2 FM

MORAY FIRTH RADIO, Scorguie Place, Inverness IV3 6SF. Tel: 01463-224433. *Frequency:* 97.4 FM

NECR (NORTH-EAST COMMUNITY RADIO), Town House, Kintore, Inverurie, Aberdeenshire AB51 0US. Tel: 01467-632909. *Frequency:* 102.1 FM

NEVIS RADIO, Inverlochy, Fort William, Inverness-shire PH33 6LU. Tel: 01397-700007. *Frequency:* 96.6 FM

NORTHSOUND ONE (FM) AND TWO (MW), 45 Kings Gate, Aberdeen AB15 4EL. Tel: 01224-632234 *Frequencies:* MW 1035 kHz, 96.9/97.6/103.0 FM

OBAN FM, McLeod Units, Lochavullin Estate, Oban, Argyll. Tel: 01631-570057. *Frequency:* 103.3 FM

RADIO BORDERS, Tweedside Park, Galashiels TD1 3TD. Tel: 01896-759444. *Frequencies:* 96.8/97.5/103.1/103.4 FM

RADIO TAY AM AND TAY FM, 6 North Isla Street, Dundee DD3 7JQ. Tel: 01382-200800. *Frequencies:* MW 1161 kHz, 102.8 FM (Dundee); MW 1584 kHz, 96.4 FM (Perth)

SIBC, Market Street, Lerwick, Shetland ZE1 0JN. Tel: 01595-695299. *Frequency:* 96.2 FM

SOUTH WEST SOUND, Campbell House, Bankend Road, Dumfries DG1 4TH. Tel: 01387-250999. *Frequencies:* 97.0/96.5/103.0 FM

WEST SOUND AM AND FM, Radio House, 54A Holmston Road, Ayr KA7 3BE. Tel: 01292-283662. *Frequencies:* MW 1035 kHz, 96.7 FM (Ayr); 97.5 FM (Girvan)

Northern Ireland

CITY BEAT 96.7, Lamont Buildings, Stranmillis Embankment, Belfast BT9 5FN. Tel: 01232-205967. *Frequency:* 96.7 FM

COOL FM, PO Box 974, Belfast BT1 1RT. Tel: 01247-817181. *Frequency:* 97.4 FM

DOWNTOWN RADIO, Newtownards, Co. Down BT23 4ES. Tel: 01247-815555. *Frequencies:* MW 1026 kHz (Belfast); 102.4 FM (Londonderry); 96.4 FM (Limavady); 96.6 FM (Enniskillen)

Q 102.9, The Riverside Suite, The Old Waterside Railway Station, Duke Street, Waterside, Londonderry BT47 1DH. Tel: 01504-44449. *Frequency:* 102.9 FM

RADIO 1521, Carn Business Park, Craigavon, Co. Armagh BT63 5RH. Tel: 01762-330033. *Frequency:* MW 1521 kHz

TOWNLAND RADIO, 2c Park Avenue, Cookstown, Co. Tyrone BT80 8AH. Tel: 016487-64828. *Frequency:* MW 828 kHz

Channel Islands

CHANNEL 103 FM, 6 Tunnel Street, St Helier, Jersey JE2 4LU. Tel: 01543-888103. *Frequency:* 103.7 FM

ISLAND FM, 12 Westerbrook, St Sampsons, Guernsey GY2 4QQ. Tel: 01481-42000. *Frequencies:* 104.7 FM (Guernsey); 93.7 FM (Alderney)

SERVICES BROADCASTING

The British Forces Broadcasting Service (BFBS) and Teleport London International (TLI), both part of the Services Sound and Vision Corporation (SSVC) group of companies, provide HM Forces and their families with radio and television broadcasting. The broadcasting service covers Britain and Northern Ireland, Cyprus, Germany, Gibraltar, the Falkland Islands, Belize, Bosnia and Brunei.

SSVC, Chalfont Grove, Gerrards Cross, Bucks SL9 8TN. Tel: 01494-874461. *Managing Director,* D. O. Crwys-Williams, CB

The Press

The newspaper and periodical press in the UK is large and diverse, catering for a wide variety of views and interests. There is no state control or censorship of the press, though it is subject to the laws on publication and the Press Complaints Commission (*see* below) was set up by the industry as a means of self-regulation.

The press is not state-subsidized and receives few tax concessions. The income of most newspapers and periodicals is derived largely from sales and from advertising; the press is the largest advertising medium in Britain.

Self-Regulation

The report of the Committee on Privacy and Related Matters, chaired by David Calcutt, QC, was published in June 1990 and led to the setting up of a non-statutory Press Complaints Commission. The performance of the Press Complaints Commission was reviewed after 18 months of operation (the *Calcutt Review of Press Self-Regulation*, presented to Parliament in January 1993) to determine whether statutory measures were required. No proposals for replacing the self-regulation system have been made to date.

Complaints

The Press Complaints Commission was founded by the newspaper and magazine industry in January 1991 to replace the Press Council (established in 1953). It is a voluntary, non-statutory body set up to operate the press's self-regulation system, and funded by the industry through the Press Standards Board of Finance.

The Commission's objects are to consider, adjudicate, conciliate, and resolve complaints of unfair treatment by the press; and to ensure that the press maintains the highest professional standards with respect for generally recognized freedoms, including freedom of expression, the public's right to know, and the right of the press to operate free from improper pressure. The Commission judges newspaper and magazine conduct by a code of practice drafted by editors, agreed by the industry and ratified by the Commission.

Seven of the Commission's members are editors of national, regional and local newspapers and magazines, and nine, including the chairman, are drawn from other fields. One member has been appointed Privacy Commissioner with special powers to investigate complaints about invasion of privacy.

PRESS COMPLAINTS COMMISSION, 1 Salisbury Square, London EC4Y 8AE. Tel: 0171-353 1248. *Chairman*, Lord Wakeham, PC; *Director*, G. Black

---

NEWSPAPERS

Newspapers are usually financially independent of any political party, though most adopt a political stance in their editorial comments, usually reflecting proprietorial influence. Ownership of the national and regional daily newspapers is concentrated in the hands of large corporations whose interests cover publishing and communications. The rules on cross-media ownership, as amended by the Broadcasting Act 1996, limit the extent to which newspaper organizations with over 20 per cent of national circulation may become involved in broadcasting (*see* page 670).

There are 17 daily and about 14 Sunday national papers, about 80 regional daily papers, and several hundred local papers that are published weekly or twice-weekly. Scotland, Wales and Northern Ireland all have at least one daily and one Sunday national paper.

Newspapers are usually published in either broadsheet or tabloid format. The 'quality' daily papers, i.e. those providing detailed coverage of a wide range of public matters, have a broadsheet format. The tabloid papers take a more popular approach and are more illustrated.

NATIONAL DAILY NEWSPAPERS

DAILY EXPRESS, Ludgate House, 245 Blackfriars Road, London SE1 9UX. Tel: 0171-928 8000. Fax: 0171-633 0244

DAILY MAIL, Northcliffe House, 2 Derry Street, London W8 5TT. Tel: 0171-938 6000. Fax: 0171-606 1234

DAILY SPORT, 19 Great Ancoats Street, Manchester M60 4BT. Tel: 0161-236 4466. Fax: 0161-236 4535

DAILY STAR, Ludgate House, 245 Blackfriars Road, London SE1 9UX. Tel: 0171-928 8000. Fax: 0171-633 0244

DAILY TELEGRAPH, 1 Canada Square, Canary Wharf, London E14 5DT. Tel: 0171-538 5000. Fax: 0171-538 6242

THE EUROPEAN, 200 Gray's Inn Road, London WC1X 8NE. Tel: 0171-418 7777. Fax: 0171-713 1840

FINANCIAL TIMES, 1 Southwark Bridge, London SE1 9HL. Tel: 0171-873 3000. Fax: 0171-407 5700

THE GUARDIAN, 119 Farringdon Road, London EC1R 3ER. Tel: 0171-278 2332. Fax: 0171-713 1449

THE HERALD, 195 Albion Street, Glasgow G1 1QP. Tel: 0141-552 6255. Fax: 0141-552 1344

THE INDEPENDENT, 1 Canada Square, Canary Wharf, London E14 5DL. Tel: 0171-293 2000. Fax: 0171-293 2435

THE MIRROR, 1 Canada Square, Canary Wharf, London E14 5AP. Tel: 0171-293 3000. Fax: 0171-293 3405

MORNING STAR, 1–3 Ardleigh Road, London N1 4HS. Tel: 0171-254 0033. Fax: 0171-254 5950

RACING POST, 112–120 Coombe Lane, London SW20 0BA. Tel: 0181-879 3377. Fax: 0181-879 3722

THE SCOTSMAN, 20 North Bridge, Edinburgh EH1 1YT. Tel: 0131-225 2468. Fax: 0131-226 7420

THE SPORTING LIFE, 1 Canada Square, Canary Wharf, London E14 5AP. Tel: 0171-293 3000. Fax: 0171-293 3405

THE SUN, 1 Virginia Street, London E1 9XN. Tel: 0171-782 4000. Fax: 0171-583 9504

THE TIMES, 1 Pennington Street, London E1 9XN. Tel: 0171-782 5000. Fax: 0171-782 5658

REGIONAL DAILY NEWSPAPERS

BERKSHIRE

EVENING POST, 8 Tessa Road, Reading RG1 8NS

CAMBRIDGESHIRE

CAMBRIDGE EVENING NEWS, Winship Road, Milton, Cambridge CB4 6PP

PETERBOROUGH EVENING TELEGRAPH, New Priestgate House, 57 Priestgate, Peterborough PE1 1JW

CUMBRIA

NEWS AND STAR, Newspaper House, Dalston Road, Carlisle CA2 5UA

NORTH-WEST EVENING MAIL, Newspaper House, Abbey Road, Barrow-in-Furness LA14 5QS

DERBYSHIRE

DERBY EVENING TELEGRAPH, Northcliffe House, Meadow Road, Derby DEI 2DW

DEVON

EVENING HERALD, 17 Brest Road, Derriford Business Park, Plymouth PL6 5AA
EXPRESS AND ECHO, Heron Road, Sowton, Exeter EX2 7NF
HERALD EXPRESS, Harmsworth House, Barton Hill Road, Torquay TQ2 8JN
WESTERN MORNING NEWS, 17 Brest Road, Derriford Business Park, Plymouth PL6 5AA

DORSET

DORSET EVENING ECHO, 57 St Thomas Street, Weymouth DT4 8EU
EVENING ECHO, Richmond Hill, Bournemouth BH2 6HH

DURHAM

NORTHERN ECHO, Priestgate, Darlington DLI INF

EAST SUSSEX

THE ARGUS/EVENING ARGUS, Argus House, Crowhurst Road, Hollingbury, Brighton BNI 8AR

ESSEX

ESSEX CHRONICLE, Westway, Chelmsford CMI 3BE
EVENING ECHO, Newspaper House, Chester Hall Lane, Basildon SS14 3BL
EVENING GAZETTE, Oriel House, 43–44 North Hill, Colchester COI ITZ

GLOUCESTERSHIRE

THE GLOUCESTERSHIRE CITIZEN, St John's Lane, Gloucester GLI 2AY
GLOUCESTERSHIRE ECHO, 1 Clarence Parade, Cheltenham GL50 3NZ

HAMPSHIRE

THE NEWS, The News Centre, Hilsea, Portsmouth PO2 9SX
SOUTHERN DAILY ECHO, Newspaper House, Test Lane, Southampton SO16 9JX

HEREFORD AND WORCESTER

WORCESTER EVENING NEWS, Hylton Road, Worcester WR2 5JX

KENT

KENT TODAY, Messenger House, New Hythe Lane, Larkfield, Aylesford ME20 6SG

LANCASHIRE

BOLTON EVENING NEWS, Churchgate, Bolton BLI IDE
EVENING CHRONICLE, 172 Union Street, Oldham OLI IEQ
THE GAZETTE, PO Box 20, Preston New Road, Blackpool FY4 4AU
LANCASHIRE EVENING POST, Oliver's Place, Fulwood, Preston PR2 9ZA
LANCASHIRE EVENING TELEGRAPH, Newspaper House, High Street, Blackburn BBI IHT
MANCHESTER EVENING NEWS, 164 Deansgate, Manchester M60 2RR
WIGAN EVENING POST, Martland Mill, Martland Mill Lane, Wigan WN5 OLX

LEICESTERSHIRE

LEICESTER MERCURY, St George Street, Leicester LEI 9FQ

LINCOLNSHIRE

GRIMSBY EVENING TELEGRAPH, 80 Cleethorpe Road, Grimsby DN31 3EH
LINCOLNSHIRE ECHO, Brayford Wharf East, Lincoln LN5 7AT
SCUNTHORPE EVENING TELEGRAPH, Telegraph House, Doncaster Road, Scunthorpe DN15 7RE

LONDON

THE EVENING STANDARD, Northcliffe House, 2 Derry Street, London W8 5TT

MERSEYSIDE

DAILY POST, and LIVERPOOL ECHO, PO Box 48, Old Hall Street, Liverpool L69 3EB

NORFOLK

EASTERN DAILY PRESS, and EVENING NEWS, Prospect House, Rouen Road, NRI IRE

NORTHAMPTONSHIRE

CHRONICLE AND ECHO, Upper Mounts, Northampton NNI 3HR
NORTHAMPTONSHIRE EVENING TELEGRAPH, Northfield Avenue, Kettering NN16 9TT

NOTTINGHAMSHIRE

NOTTINGHAM EVENING POST, Forman Street, Nottingham NGI 4AB

OXFORDSHIRE

THE OXFORD MAIL, Newspaper House, Osney Mead, Oxford OX2 OEJ

SHROPSHIRE

SHROPSHIRE STAR, Ketley, Telford TFI 4HU

SOMERSET

THE BATH CHRONICLE, Newspaper House, 100 Victoria Road, Swindon SNI 3BE
BRISTOL EVENING POST, AND WESTERN DAILY PRESS, Temple Way, Bristol BS99 7HD

STAFFORDSHIRE

BURTON MAIL, 65–68 High Street, Burton-on-Trent DE14 ILE
THE SENTINEL, Sentinel House, Etruria, Stoke-on-Trent STI 5SS

SUFFOLK

EAST ANGLIAN DAILY TIMES, and EVENING STAR, 30 Lower Brook Street, Ipswich IP4 IAN

TYNE AND WEAR

EVENING CHRONICLE, and THE JOURNAL, Thomson House, Groat Market, Newcastle upon Tyne NEI IED
SHIELDS GAZETTE, Chapter Row, South Shields NE33 IBL
SUNDERLAND ECHO, Echo House, Pennywell, Sunderland SR4 9ER

WARWICKSHIRE

HEARTLAND EVENING NEWS, Newspaper House, 11–15 Newtown Road, Nuneaton CVII 4HR

WEST MIDLANDS

THE BIRMINGHAM POST, and BIRMINGHAM EVENING MAIL, 28 Colmore Circus, Queensway, Birmingham B4 6AX
COVENTRY EVENING TELEGRAPH, Corporation Street, Coventry CVI IFP

EXPRESS AND STAR, 51–53 Queen Street, Wolverhampton WV1 1ES

WILTSHIRE
EVENING ADVERTISER, Newspaper House, 100 Victoria Road, Swindon SN1 3BE

YORKSHIRE
BARNSLEY STAR, York Street, Sheffield S1 1PU
THE DONCASTER STAR, York Street, Sheffield S1 1PU
EVENING GAZETTE, Gazette Buildings, Borough Road, Middlesbrough TS1 3AZ
HALIFAX EVENING COURIER, PO Box 19, Courier Buildings, King Cross Street, Halifax HX1 2SF
HUDDERSFIELD DAILY EXAMINER, PO Box A26, Queen Street South, Huddersfield HD1 2TD
HULL DAILY MAIL, Blundell's Corner, Beverley Road, Hull HU3 1XS
ROTHERHAM STAR, York Street, Sheffield S1 1PU
SCARBOROUGH EVENING NEWS, 17–23 Aberdeen Walk, Scarborough YO11 1BB
THE STAR, York Street, Sheffield S1 1PU
TELEGRAPH AND ARGUS, Hall Ings, Bradford BD1 1JR
YORKSHIRE EVENING POST, PO Box 168, Wellington Street, Leeds LS1 1RF
YORKSHIRE EVENING PRESS, PO Box 29, 76–86 Walmgate, York YO1 1YN
YORKSHIRE POST, PO Box 168, Wellington Street, Leeds LS1 1RF

WALES
EVENING LEADER, Mold Business Park, Wrexham Road, Mold CH7 1XY
SOUTH WALES ARGUS, Cardiff Road, Maesglas, Newport NP9 1QW
SOUTH WALES ECHO, Thomson House, Havelock Street, Cardiff CF1 1XR
SOUTH WALES EVENING POST, Adelaide Street, Swansea SA1 1QT
WESTERN MAIL, Thomson House, Havelock Street, Cardiff CF1 1XR

SCOTLAND
COURIER AND ADVERTISER, 2 Albert Square, Dundee DD1 9QJ
DAILY RECORD, 40 Anderston Quay, Glasgow G3 8DA
EDINBURGH EVENING NEWS, 20 North Bridge, Edinburgh EH1 1YT
EVENING EXPRESS, PO Box 43, Lang Stracht, Mastrick, Aberdeen AB15 6DF
EVENING TELEGRAPH AND POST, 2 Albert Square, Dundee DD1 9QJ
EVENING TIMES, 195 Albion Street, Glasgow G1 1QP
GREENOCK TELEGRAPH, Pitreavie Business Park, Dunfermline KY11 5QS
PAISLEY DAILY EXPRESS, 1 Woodside Terrace, Glasgow G3 7UY
PRESS AND JOURNAL, PO Box 43, Lang Stracht, Mastrick, Aberdeen AB15 6DF

NORTHERN IRELAND
BELFAST TELEGRAPH, 124–144 Royal Avenue, Belfast BT1 1EB

CHANNEL ISLANDS
GUERNSEY EVENING PRESS AND STAR, PO Box 57, Braye Road, Vale, Guernsey GY1 3BW
JERSEY EVENING POST, PO Box 582, Five Oaks, St Saviour, Jersey JE4 8XQ

WEEKLY NEWSPAPERS
THE EXPRESS ON SUNDAY, Ludgate House, 245 Blackfriars Road, London SE1 9UX. Tel: 0171-928 8000. Fax: 0171-633 0244
INDEPENDENT ON SUNDAY, 1 Canada Square, Canary Wharf, London E14 5DL. Tel: 0171-293 2000. Fax: 0171-293 2435
INDIA TIMES, Global House, 90 Ascot Gardens, Southall, Middx UB1 2SB. Tel: 0181-575 0151. Fax: 0181-575 5661
THE MAIL ON SUNDAY, Northcliffe House, 2 Derry Street, London W8 5TS. Tel: 0171-938 6000. Fax: 0171-937 7896
NEWS OF THE WORLD, 1 Virginia Street, London E1 9XR. Tel: 0171-782 4000. Fax: 0171-583 9504
THE OBSERVER, 119 Farringdon Road, London EC1 3ER. Tel: 0171-278 2332. Fax: 0171-713 1449
THE PEOPLE, 1 Canada Square, Canary Wharf, London E14 5AP. Tel: 0171-293 3000. Fax: 0171-293 3404
SCOTLAND ON SUNDAY, 20 North Bridge, Edinburgh EH1 1YT. Tel: 0131-225 2468. Fax: 0131-220 2443
SUNDAY MAIL, 40 Anderston Quay, Glasgow G3 8DA. Tel: 0141-248 7000. Fax: 0141-242 3340
SUNDAY MIRROR, 1 Canada Square, Canary Wharf, London E14 5AP. Tel: 0171-293 3000. Fax: 0171-293 3404
SUNDAY POST, Courier Place, Dundee DD1 9QJ. Tel: 01382-223131. Fax: 01382-201664
SUNDAY SPORT, 848B Melton Road, Thurmaston, Leicester LE4 8BJ. Tel: 0116-269 4892. Fax: 0116-264 0948
THE SUNDAY TELEGRAPH, 1 Canada Square, Canary Wharf, London E14 5AR. Tel: 0171-538 5000. Fax: 0171-538 1330
THE SUNDAY TIMES, 1 Pennington Street, London E1 9XN. Tel: 0171-782 5000. Fax: 0171-782 5658
WALES ON SUNDAY, Thomson House, Havelock Street, Cardiff CF1 1XR. Tel: 01222-583583. Fax: 01222-583725
WEEKLY NEWS, Courier Place, Dundee DD1 9QJ. Tel: 01382-223131. Fax: 01382-201390

RELIGIOUS PAPERS

Alt. = Alternate; *M.* = Monthly; *Q.* = Quarterly; *W.* = Weekly

BAPTIST TIMES, PO Box 54, 129 The Broadway, Didcot, Oxon OX11 8XB. *W.*
CATHOLIC HERALD, Herald House, Lamb's Passage, Bunhill Row, London EC1Y 8TQ. *W.*
CHALLENGE - THE GOOD NEWS PAPER, PO Box 300, Kingstown Broadway, Carlisle CA3 0QS. *M.*
THE CHURCH OF ENGLAND NEWSPAPER, 10 Little College Street, London SW1P 3SH. *W.*
CHURCH OF IRELAND GAZETTE, 36 Bachelor's Walk, Lisburn, Co. Antrim, BT28 1XN. *W.*
CHURCH TIMES, 33 Upper Street, London N1 6PN. *W.*
ENGLISH CHURCHMAN, 22 Lesley Avenue, Canterbury, Kent CT1 3LF. *Alt. W.*
THE FRIEND, Drayton House, 30 Gordon Street, London WC1H 0BQ. *W.*
JEWISH CHRONICLE, 25 Furnival Street, London EC4A 1JT. *W.*
JEWISH TELEGRAPH, Telegraph House, 11 Park Hill, Bury Old Road, Prestwich, Manchester M25 0HH. *W.*
LIFE AND WORK, Church of Scotland, 121 George Street, Edinburgh EH2 4YN. *M.*
METHODIST RECORDER, 122 Golden Lane, London EC1Y 0TL. *W.*
MIDDLE WAY, Buddhist Society, 58 Eccleston Square, London SW1V 1PH. *Q.*

ORTHODOX OUTLOOK, 42 Withen's Lane, Wallasey, Wirral, Merseyside L43 7NN. *Alt. M.*

PRESBYTERIAN HERALD, Church House, Fisherwick Place, Belfast BT1 6DW. *Ten times a year*

QUAKER MONTHLY, Friends House, Euston Road, London NW1 2BJ. *M.*

REFORM, United Reformed Church, 86 Tavistock Place, London WC1H 9RT. *Eleven times a year*

THE SIKH COURIER INTERNATIONAL, The Sikh Cultural Society of Great Britain, 88 Mollison Way, Edgware, Middx HA8 5QW. *Q.*

THE SIKH MESSENGER, 43 Dorset Road, London SW19 3EZ. *Q.*

THE TABLET, 1 King Street Cloisters, Clifton Walk, London W6 0QZ. *W.*

THE UNIVERSE, 1st Floor, St James Building, Oxford Street, Manchester M1 6FP. *W.*

THE WAR CRY, 101 Queen Victoria Street, London EC4P 4EP. *W.*

PERIODICALS

There are about 6,500 periodicals published in Britain. These are classified as consumer, i.e. general interest, or as trade, professional or academic.

CONSUMER PERIODICALS

Alt. = Alternate; *M.* = Monthly; *Q.* = Quarterly; *W.* = Weekly

AL MAJALLA, Arab Press House, 184 High Holborn, London WC1V 7AP. *W.*

AMATEUR PHOTOGRAPHER, King's Reach Tower, Stamford Street, London SE1 9LS. *W.*

ANGLING TIMES, Bretton Court, Bretton, Peterborough PE3 8DZ. *W.*

ANTIQUE, 10–11 Lower John Street, London W1R 3PE. *Q.*

APOLLO, 1 Castle Lane, London SW1D 6DR. *M.*

ARENA, 3rd Floor, Block A, Exmouth House, Pine Street, London EC1R 0JL. *M.*

ART MONTHLY, Suite 17, 26 Charing Cross Road, London WC2H 0DG. *M.*

ASIAN TIMES, 3rd Floor, Tower House, 141–149 Fonthill Road, London N4 3HF. *W.*

ASTRONOMY NOW, PO Box 175, Tonbridge, Kent TN10 4ZY. *M.*

ATHLETICS WEEKLY, Bretton Court, Bretton, Peterborough PE3 8DZ. *W.*

AUTOCAR, 38–42 Hampton Road, Teddington, Middx TW11 0JE. *W.*

BBC GARDENER'S WORLD, Woodlands, 80 Wood Lane, London W12 0TT. *M.*

BBC GOOD FOOD, Woodlands, 80 Wood Lane, London W12 0TT. *M.*

BBC VEGETARIAN GOOD FOOD, Woodlands, 80 Wood Lane, London W12 0TT. *M.*

BBC WILDLIFE MAGAZINE, Woodlands, 80 Wood Lane, London W12 0TT. *M.*

BELFAST GAZETTE (*Official*), 64 Chichester Street, Belfast BT1 4PS. *W.*

BELLA, 2nd Floor, Shirley House, 25–27 Camden Road, London NW1 9LL. *W.*

BEST, 10th Floor, Portland House, Stag Place, London SW1E 5AU. *W.*

THE BIG ISSUE, Fleet House, 57–61 Clerkenwell Road, London EC1M 5NP. *W.*

BIKE, Bushfield House, Orton Centre, Peterborough PE2 5UW. *M.*

BIRDS, RSPB, The Lodge, Sandy, Beds SG19 2DL. *Q.*

BIRD WATCHING, Bretton Court, Bretton, Peterborough PE3 8DZ. *M.*

BOXING MONTHLY, 24 Notting Hill Gate, London W11 3JE. *M.*

BRIDES & SETTING UP HOME, Vogue House, Hanover Square, London W1R 0AD. *Alt. M.*

BRITISH PHILATELIC BULLETIN, 20 Brandon Street, Edinburgh EH3 5TT. *M.*

THE BURLINGTON MAGAZINE, 6 Bloomsbury Square, London WC1A 2LP. *M.*

CAMPING & CARAVANNING, Greenfields House, Westwood Way, Coventry CV4 8JH. *M.*

CAR, Abbots Court, 34 Farringdon Lane, London EC1R 3AU. *M.*

CARIBBEAN TIMES, 3rd Floor, Tower House, 141–149 Fonthill Road, London N4 3HF. *W.*

CAT WORLD, 10 Western Road, Shoreham-by-Sea, W. Sussex BN43 5WD. *M.*

CHAT, King's Reach Tower, Stamford Street, London SE1 9LS. *W.*

CLASSIC AND SPORTSCAR, 38–42 Hampton Road, Teddington, Middx TW11 0JE. *M.*

CLASSIC CARS, Abbots Court, 34 Farringdon Lane, London EC1R 3AU. *M.*

CLASSIC CD, Beauford Court, 30 Monmouth Street, Bath BA1 2BW. *M.*

CLOTHES SHOW MAGAZINE, Woodlands, 80 Wood Lane, London W12 0TT. *M.*

COARSE FISHERMAN, 67 Tyrell Street, Leicester LE3 5SB. *M.*

COIN NEWS, PO Box 14, Honiton, Devon EX14 9YP. *M.*

COMPANY, National Magazine House, 72 Broadwick Street, London W1V 2BP. *M.*

COMPUTER AND VIDEO GAMES, Priory Court, 30–32 Farringdon Road, London EC1R 3AU. *M.*

COMPUTER SHOPPER, 19 Bolsover Street, London W1P 7HJ. *M.*

COSMOPOLITAN, National Magazine House, 72 Broadwick Street, London W1V 2BP. *M.*

COUNTRY HOMES AND INTERIORS, King's Reach Tower, Stamford Street, London SE1 9LS. *M.*

COUNTRY LIFE, King's Reach Tower, Stamford Street, London SE1 9LS. *W.*

COUNTRY LIVING MAGAZINE, National Magazine House, 72 Broadwick Street, London W1V 2BP. *M.*

THE COUNTRYMAN, Link House, Dingwall Avenue, Croydon, Surrey CR9 2TA. *Alt. M.*

COUNTRY WALKING, Bretton Court, Bretton, Peterborough PE3 8DZ. *M.*

THE CRICKETER INTERNATIONAL, Beech Hanger, Ashurst, Tunbridge Wells, Kent TN3 9ST. *M.*

CYCLING WEEKLY, King's Reach Tower, Stamford Street, London SE1 9LS. *W.*

THE DALESMAN, Stable Courtyard, Broughton Hall, Skipton, N. Yorks BD23 3AE. *M.*

DALTONS WEEKLY, CI Tower, St George's Square, New Malden, Surrey KT3 4JA. *W.*

DANCE THEATRE JOURNAL, Laban Centre for Movement and Dance, Laurie Grove, London SE14 6NH. *Three times a year*

DANCING TIMES, Clerkenwell House, 45–47 Clerkenwell Green, London EC1R 0EB. *M.*

DOGS TODAY, Pankhurst Farm, Bagshot Road, West End, Woking, Surrey GU24 9QR. *Once a year*

DOG WORLD, 9 Tufton Street, Ashford, Kent TN23 1QN. *W.*

THE ECOLOGIST, Agriculture House, Bath Road, Sturminster Newton, Dorset DT10 1DU. *Alt. M.*

THE ECONOMIST, 25 St James's Street, London SW1A 1HG. *W.*

EDINBURGH GAZETTE (*Official*), The Stationery Office, PO Box 276, London sw8 5DT. *Alt. W.*

ELLE, Victory House, 14 Leicester Place, London wc2h 7BP. *M.*

EMPIRE, 4 Winsley Street, London win 7AR. *M.*

ESQUIRE, National Magazine House, 72 Broadwick Street, London wiv 2BP. *M.*

ESSENTIALS, King's Reach Tower, Stamford Street, London sei 9ls. *M.*

EXCHANGE AND MART, Link House, 25 West Street, Poole, Dorset bh15 ill. *W.*

THE FACE, 3rd Floor, Block A, Exmouth House, Pine Street, London ecir 0jl. *M.*

FAMILY CIRCLE, King's Reach Tower, Stamford Street, London sei 9ls. *M.*

FHM, Mappin House, 4 Winsley Street, London win 7ar. *M.*

THE FIELD, King's Reach Tower, Stamford Street, London sei 9ls. *M.*

FILM REVIEW, 9 Blades Court, Deodar Road, London sw15 2nu. *M.*

FORE!, Bretton Court, Bretton, Peterborough pe3 8dz. *M.*

GARDEN NEWS, Apex House, Oundle Road, Peterborough pe2 9np. *W.*

GAY TIMES, Ground Floor, Worldwide House, 116–134 Bayham Street, London nw1 0ba. *M.*

GEOGRAPHICAL JOURNAL, Royal Geographical Society, 1 Kensington Gore, London sw7 7ar. *Three times a year*

GOLF WORLD, Mappin House, 4 Winsley Street, London win 7ar. *M.*

GOOD HOLIDAY MAGAZINE, 91 High Street, Esher, Surrey kt10 9qd. *Q.*

GOOD HOUSEKEEPING, National Magazine House, 72 Broadwick Street, London wiv 2bp. *M.*

THE GOOD SKI GUIDE, 91 High Street, Esher, Surrey kt10 9qa. *Five times a year*

GQ, Vogue House, Hanover Square, London wir 0ad. *M.*

GRAMOPHONE, 135 Greenford Road, Harrow, Middx ha1 3yd. *M.*

GRANTA, 2–3 Hanover Yard, Noel Road, London ni 8be. *Q.*

THE GUARDIAN WEEKLY, 119 Farringdon Road, London ecir 3er. *W.*

GUIDING, 17–19 Buckingham Palace Road, London swiw 0pt. *M.*

HANSARD, *see* Parliamentary Debates

HARPERS AND QUEEN, National Magazine House, 72 Broadwick Street, London wiv 2bp. *M.*

HEALTH AND FITNESS MAGAZINE, Nexus House, Azalea Drive, Swanley, Kent br8 8hy. *M.*

HELLO!, 69–71 Upper Ground, London sei 9pq. *W.*

HOMES AND GARDENS, King's Reach Tower, Stamford Street, London sei 9ls. *M.*

HORSE AND HOUND, King's Reach Tower, Stamford Street, London sei 9ls. *W.*

HOUSE AND GARDEN, Vogue House, Hanover Square, London wir 0ad. *M.*

HOUSE BEAUTIFUL, National Magazine House, 72 Broadwick Street, London wiv 2bp. *Eleven times a year*

i-D MAGAZINE, 44 Earlham Street, London wc2h 9la. *M.*

IDEAL HOME, King's Reach Tower, Stamford Street, London sei 9ls. *M.*

ILLUSTRATED LONDON NEWS, 20 Upper Ground, London sei 9pf. *Twice a year*

IN BRITAIN, Haymarket House, 1 Oxendon Street, London swiy 4ee. *M.*

INVESTORS CHRONICLE, Greystoke Place, Fetter Lane, London ec4a ind. *W.*

IRISH POST, Uxbridge House, 464 Uxbridge Road, Hayes, Middx ub4 0sp. *W.*

JAZZ JOURNAL INTERNATIONAL, 1–5 Clerkenwell Road, London ecim 5pa. *M.*

JUST SEVENTEEN, Victory House, 14 Leicester Place, London wc2h 7bp. *W.*

LABOUR RESEARCH, 78 Blackfriars Road, London sei 8hf. *M.*

THE LADY, 39–40 Bedford Street, London wc2e 9er. *W.*

LAND AND LIBERTY, 177 Vauxhall Bridge Road, London swiv ieu. *Q.*

LITERARY REVIEW, 44 Lexington Street, London wir 3lh. *M.*

LONDON GAZETTE (*Official*), The Stationery Office, 51 Nine Elms Lane, London sw8 5dr. *Five times a week*

LONDON REVIEW OF BOOKS, 28–30 Little Russell Street, London wcia 2hn. *Alt. W.*

MAJESTY, 26–28 Hallam Street, London win 6np. *M.*

MARIE CLAIRE, 2 Hatfields, London sei 9pg. *M.*

MAX POWER, Bushfield House, Orton Centre, Peterborough pe2 5uw. M.

MELODY MAKER (MM), King's Reach Tower, Stamford Street, London sei 9ls. *W.*

METEOROLOGICAL MAGAZINE, The Stationery Office, PO Box 276, London sw8 5dt. *M.*

MIZZ, King's Reach Tower, Stamford Street, London sei 9ls. *Alt. W.*

MODEL BOATS, Nexus House, Boundary Way, Hemel Hempstead, Herts hp2 7st. *M.*

MONEYWISE, Berkeley Square House, Berkeley Square, London wix 6ab. *M.*

MORE!, Victory House, 14 Leicester Place, London wc2h 7bp. *Alt. W.*

MOTHER AND BABY, Victory House, 14 Leicester Place, London wc2h 7bp. *M.*

MY WEEKLY, 80 Kingsway East, Dundee dd4 8sl. *W.*

NATURE, Porters South, Crinan Street, London ni 9xw. *W.*

NEEDLECRAFT, Beauford Court, 30 Monmouth Street, Bath bai 2bw. *Thirteen times a year*

NEW INTERNATIONALIST, 55 Rectory Road, Oxford ox4 1bw. *M.*

NEW MUSICAL EXPRESS (NME), King's Reach Tower, Stamford Street, London sei 9ls. *W.*

NEW SCIENTIST, King's Reach Tower, Stamford Street, London sei 9ls. *W.*

NEW STATESMAN AND SOCIETY, 7th Floor, Victoria Station House, 191 Victoria Street, London swie 5ne. *W.*

NEWSWEEK, 18 Park Street, London wiy 4hh. *W.*

NEW WOMAN, Victory House, 14 Leicester Place, London wc2h 7bp. *M.*

19, King's Reach Tower, Stamford Street, London sei 9ls. *M.*

OK!, Northern and Shell Tower, City Harbour, London ei4 9gl. *W.*

THE OLDIE, 45–46 Poland Street, London wiv 4au. *M.*

OPERA, 1a Mountgrove Road, London n5 2lu. *M.*

OPERA NOW, 241 Shaftesbury Avenue, London wc2h 8eh. *Alt. M.*

OPTIONS, King's Reach Tower, Stamford Street, London sei 9ls. *M.*

OUR DOGS, 5 Oxford Road, Station Approach, Manchester m60 isx. *W.*

PARENTS, Victory House, 14 Leicester Place, London wc2h 7bp. *M.*

PARLIAMENTARY DEBATES (COMMONS) (Hansard), The Stationery Office, PO Box 276, London sw8 5dt. *Daily or weekly during parliamentary session*

PARLIAMENTARY DEBATES (LORDS) (Hansard), The Stationery Office, PO Box 276, London sw8 5dt. *Daily or weekly during parliamentary session*

PC USER, Greater London House, Hampstead Road, London nw1 7qz. *Alt. W.*

PEOPLE'S FRIEND, 80 Kingsway East, Dundee DD4 8SL. *W.*

PHILOSOPHY NOW, 226 Bramford Road, Ipswich IP1 4AS. *Q.*

POETRY REVIEW, 22 Betterton Street, London WC2H 9BU. *Q.*

PONY, Haslemere House, Lower Street, Haslemere, Surrey GU27 2PE. *M.*

PRACTICAL BOAT OWNER, Westover House, West Quay Road, Poole, Dorset BH15 1JG. *M.*

PRACTICAL CARAVAN, 60 Waldegrave Road, Teddington, Middx TW11 8LG. *M.*

PRACTICAL GARDENING, Apex House, Oundle Road, Peterborough PE2 9NP. *M.*

PRACTICAL HOUSEHOLDER, Nexus House, Azalea Drive, Swanley, Kent BR8 8HY. *M.*

PRACTICAL PARENTING, King's Reach Tower, Stamford Street, London SE1 9LS. *M.*

PRACTICAL PHOTOGRAPHY, Apex House, Oundle Road, Peterborough PE2 9NP. *M.*

PRIMA, 9th Floor, Portland House, Stag Place, London SW1E 5AU. *M.*

PRIVATE EYE, 6 Carlisle Street, London W1V 5RG. *Alt. W.*

PROGRESS (*Braille type*), RNIB, Technical Consumer Services Division, Orton Southgate, Peterborough PE2 0XU. *M.*

PROSPECT, 4 Bedford Square, London WC1B 3RA. *M.*

THE PUZZLER, Glenthorne House, Hammersmith Grove, London W6 0LG. *M.*

Q, Mappin House, 4 Winsley Street, London W1N 7AR. *M.*

THE RACING CALENDAR, British Horseracing Board Publications, c/o Weatherbys Group Ltd, Sanders Road, Wellingborough, Northants NN8 4BX. *W.*

RADIO TIMES, Woodlands, 80 Wood Lane, London W12 0TT. *W.*

RAILWAY MAGAZINE, King's Reach Tower, Stamford Street, London SE1 9LS. *M.*

RAILWAY MODELLER, Peco Publications and Publicity Ltd, Beer, Seaton, Devon EX12 3NA. *M.*

READER'S DIGEST, Berkeley Square House, Berkeley Square, London W1X 6AB. *M.*

RIDE, Abbots Court, 31 Farringdon Lane, London EC1N 3AU. *M.*

RIDING, 2 West Street, Bourne, Lincs PE10 9NE. *M.*

RUGBY LEAGUER, Martland Mill, Martland Mill Lane, Wigan, Lancs WN5 0LX. *W.*

SCOTS MAGAZINE, 2 Albert Square, Dundee DD1 9QJ. *M.*

SCOTTISH FIELD, PO Box 1, Oban, Argyll PA34 5PY. *M.*

SCOUTING, Baden-Powell House, Queen's Gate, London SW7 5JS. *M.*

SEA ANGLER, Bretton Court, Bretton, Peterborough PE3 8DZ. *M.*

SHE, National Magazine House, 72 Broadwick Street, London W1V 2BP. *M.*

SHOOT, King's Reach Tower, Stamford Street, London SE1 9LS. *W.*

SHOOTING TIMES AND COUNTRY MAGAZINE, King's Reach Tower, Stamford Street, London SE1 9LS. *W.*

SKY MAGAZINE, 5th Floor, Mappin House, 4 Winsley Street, London W1N 7AR. *M.*

SLIMMING MAGAZINE, Victory House, 14 Leicester Place, London WC2H 7BP. *Ten times a year*

SMASH HITS, 5th Floor, Mappin House, 4 Winsley Street, London W1N 7AR. *Alt. W.*

THE SPECTATOR, 56 Doughty Street, London WC1N 2LL. *W.*

THE STRAD, 7 St John's Road, Harrow, Middx HA1 2EE. *M.*

TATLER, Vogue House, Hanover Square, London W1R 0AD. *Ten times a year*

TENNIS WORLD, The Spendlove Centre, Enstone Road, Charlbury, Oxford OX7 3PQ. *M.*

THIS ENGLAND, Alma House, 73 Rodney Road, Cheltenham, Glos GL50 1YQ. *Q.*

TIME INTERNATIONAL, Brettenham House, Lancaster Place, London WC2E 7TL. *W.*

TIME OUT, Universal House, 251 Tottenham Court Road, London W1P 0AB. *W.*

THE TIMES EDUCATIONAL SUPPLEMENT, Admiral House, 66–68 East Smithfield, London E1 9XY. *W.*

THE TIMES HIGHER EDUCATION SUPPLEMENT, Admiral House, 66–68 East Smithfield, London E1 9XY. *W.*

THE TIMES LITERARY SUPPLEMENT, Admiral House, 66–68 East Smithfield, London E1 9XY. *W.*

TOP GEAR, Woodlands, 80 Wood Lane, London W12 0TT. *M.*

TRIBUNE, 308 Gray's Inn Road, London WC1X 8DY. *W.*

TROUT AND SALMON, Bretton Court, Bretton, Peterborough PE3 8DZ. *M.*

TV TIMES, King's Reach Tower, Stamford Street, London SE1 9LS. *W.*

VACHER'S PARLIAMENTARY COMPANION, 113 High Street, Berkhamsted, Herts HP4 2DJ. *Q.*

VANITY FAIR, Vogue House, Hanover Square, London W1R 0AD. *M.*

VIZ MAGAZINE, The Boat House, Crabtree Lane, London SW6 6LU. *Alt. M.*

VOGUE, Vogue House, Hanover Square, London W1R 0AD. *M.*

THE VOICE, 370 Coldharbour Lane, London SW9 8PL. *W.*

VOX, King's Reach Tower, Stamford Street, London SE1 9LS. *M.*

WEATHER, 104 Oxford Road, Reading RG1 7LJ. *M.*

THE WEEKLY TELEGRAPH, 1 Canada Square, Canary Wharf, London E14 5DT. *W.*

WELSH NATION, 51 Cathedral Road, Cardiff CF1 9HD. *Twice a year*

WHAT CAR?, 38–42 Hampton Road, Teddington, Middx TW11 0JE. *M.*

WHICH?, 2 Marylebone Road, London NW1 4DX. *M.*

WOMAN, King's Reach Tower, Stamford Street, London SE1 9LS. *W.*

WOMAN AND HOME, King's Reach Tower, Stamford Street, London SE1 9LS. *M.*

WOMAN'S JOURNAL, King's Reach Tower, Stamford Street, London SE1 9LS. *M.*

WOMAN'S OWN, King's Reach Tower, Stamford Street, London SE1 9LS. *W.*

WOMAN'S REALM, King's Reach Tower, Stamford Street, London SE1 9LS. *W.*

WOMAN'S WEEKLY, King's Reach Tower, Stamford Street, London SE1 9LS. *W.*

THE WORLD OF INTERIORS, Vogue House, Hanover Square, London W1R 0AD. *Eleven times a year*

YACHTING MONTHLY, King's Reach Tower, Stamford Street, London SE1 9LS. *M.*

TRADE, PROFESSIONAL AND ACADEMIC PERIODICALS

Alt. = Alternate; *M.* = Monthly; *Q.* = Quarterly; *W.* = Weekly

ACCOUNTANCY, Institute of Chartered Accountants, 40 Bernard Street, London WC1N 1LD. *M.*

ACCOUNTANCY AGE, VNU House, 32–34 Broadwick Street, London W1A 2HG. *W.*

ACCOUNTANTS' MAGAZINE, Institute of Chartered Accountants of Scotland, 27 Queen Street, Edinburgh EH2 1LA. *Alt. M.*

THE ACTUARY, 7th Floor, The Plaza Tower, East Kilbride, Glasgow G74 1LW. *M.*

AGRICULTURE AND EQUIPMENT INTERNATIONAL, 222 Maylands Avenue, Hemel Hempstead, Herts RH6 9JP. *Alt. M.*

ANTIQUARIAN BOOK MONTHLY (ABM), 1 Park Parade, Park Road, Farnham Royal, Slough SL2 3AU. *M.*

ANTIQUE DEALER AND COLLECTORS' GUIDE, PO Box 805, London SE10 8TD. *M.*

ANTIQUES TRADE GAZETTE, 17 Whitcomb Street, London WC2H 7PL. *W.*

THE ARCHITECTS' JOURNAL, 151 Rosebery Avenue, London EC1R 4QX. *W.*

THE ARCHITECTURAL REVIEW, 151 Rosebery Avenue, London EC1R 4QX. *M.*

THE AUTHOR, Society of Authors, 84 Drayton Gardens, London SW10 9SB. *Q.*

BANKING WORLD (Chartered Institute of Bankers), Haymarket House, 1 Oxendon Street, London SW1Y 4EE. *M.*

THE BIOCHEMIST, The Biochemical Society, 59 Portland Place, London W1N 3AJ. *Alt. M.*

BIOLOGIST, Institute of Biology, 20–22 Queensberry Place, London SW7 2DZ. *Five times a year*

THE BOOKSELLER, 12 Dyott Street, London WC1A 1DF. *W.*

BRAIN, Osney Mead, Oxford OX2 0EL. *Alt. M.*

BREWING AND DISTILLING INTERNATIONAL, Southbound House, 163 Burton Road, Burton-on-Trent, Staffs DE14 3DP. *M.*

BRITISH BAKER, Maclaren House, 19 Scarbrook Road, Croydon CR9 1QH. *W.*

BRITISH DENTAL JOURNAL, BMA House, Tavistock Square, London WC1H 9JR. *Alt. W.*

BRITISH FOOD JOURNAL, 60–62 Toller Lane, Bradford, W. Yorks BD8 9BY. *Eleven times a year*

BRITISH JEWELLER, 67 Clerkenwell Road, London EC1R 5BH. *Eleven times a year*

BRITISH JOURNAL OF PHOTOGRAPHY, 39 Earlham Street, London WC2H 9LD. *W.*

BRITISH JOURNAL OF PSYCHIATRY, Royal College of Psychiatrists, 17 Belgrave Square, London SW1X 8PG. *M.*

BRITISH JOURNAL OF PSYCHOLOGY, British Psychological Society, 13A Church Lane, London N2 8DX. *Q.*

BRITISH MEDICAL JOURNAL, British Medical Association, BMA House, Tavistock Square, London WC1H 9JR. *W.*

BRITISH PRINTER, Miller Freeman House, Sovereign Way, Tonbridge, Kent TN9 1RW. *M.*

BRITISH TAX REVIEW, 100 Avenue Road, London NW3 3PF. *Alt. M.*

BUILDING, 40 Marsh Wall, London E14 9TP. *W.*

BUILDING TRADE & INDUSTRY, 131–133 Duckmoor Road, Ashton Gate, Bristol BS3 2BH. *M.*

BUSINESS CONNECTIONS, Node Court, Drivers End, Hitchin, Herts SG4 8TR. *Q.*

BUSINESS EDUCATION TODAY, 128 Long Acre, London WC2E 9AN. *Alt. M.*

CABINET MAKER, Miller Freeman House, Sovereign Way, Tonbridge, Kent TN9 1RW. *W.*

CAMPAIGN, 174 Hammersmith Road, London W6 7JP. *W.*

CARPET AND FLOORCOVERINGS REVIEW, Miller Freeman House, Sovereign Way, Tonbridge, Kent TN9 1RW. *Alt. W.*

CATERER AND HOTELKEEPER, Quadrant House, The Quadrant, Sutton, Surrey SM2 5AS. *W.*

CHEMIST AND DRUGGIST, Miller Freeman House, Sovereign Way, Tonbridge, Kent TN9 1RW. *W.*

CHEMISTRY AND INDUSTRY, 15 Belgrave Square, London SW1X 8PS. *Alt. W.*

CHEMISTRY IN BRITAIN, Royal Society of Chemistry, Burlington House, Piccadilly, London W1V 0BN. *M.*

CHILD EDUCATION, Villiers House, Clarendon Avenue, Leamington Spa, Warks CV32 5PR. *M.*

CLASSICAL MUSIC, 241 Shaftesbury Avenue, London WC2H 8EH. *Alt. W.*

COMMUNITY CARE, Quadrant House, The Quadrant, Sutton, Surrey SM2 5AS. *W.*

COMPUTER WEEKLY, Quadrant House, The Quadrant, Sutton, Surrey SM2 5AS. *W.*

COMPUTING, VNU House, 32–34 Broadwick Street, London W1A 2HG. *W.*

CONSTRUCTION NEWS, 151 Rosebery Avenue, London EC1R 4QX. *W.*

CONTAINER MANAGEMENT, 4th Floor, Regal House, 70 London Road, Twickenham, Middx TW1 3QS. *M.*

CONTRACT JOURNAL, Quadrant House, The Quadrant, Sutton, Surrey SM2 5AS. *W.*

CONTROL AND INSTRUMENTATION, Miller Freeman House, 30 Calderwood Street, London SE18 6QH. *M.*

COUNTRYSIDE, The Countryside Commission, John Dower House, Crescent Place, Cheltenham GL50 3RA. *Alt. M.*

CRAFTS MAGAZINE, Crafts Council, 44A Pentonville Road, London N1 9BY. *Alt. M.*

CRIMINOLOGIST, East Row, Little London, Chichester, W. Sussex PO19 1PG. *Q.*

DAIRY FARMER AND DAIRY BEEF PRODUCER, Fenton House, 2 Wharfedale Road, Ipswich IP1 4LG. *M.*

DAIRY INDUSTRIES INTERNATIONAL, Wilmington House, Church Hill, Wilmington, Dartford, Kent DA2 7EF. *M.*

THE DENTIST, Unit 2, Riverview Business Park, Walnut Tree Close, Guildford, Surrey GU1 4QT. *M.*

DESIGN WEEK, St Giles House, 49–50 Poland Street, London W1V 4AX. *W.*

THE DIRECTOR, Institute of Directors, Mountbarrow House, 6–20 Elizabeth Street, London SW1W 9RB. *M.*

THE DRAPERS RECORD, 67 Clerkenwell Road, London EC1R 5BH. *W.*

THE ECONOMIC JOURNAL, 108 Cowley Road, Oxford OX4 1JF. *Alt. M.*

EDUCATION AND TRAINING NEWS, Bradford and Ilkley Community College, Great Horton Road, Bradford BD7 1AY. *Q.*

EDUCATION TODAY, Datateam House, Tovil Hill, Maidstone, Kent ME15 6QS. *Nine times a year*

ELECTRICAL AND RADIO TRADING, Quadrant House, The Quadrant, Sutton, Surrey SM2 5AS. *W.*

ELECTRICAL REVIEW, Quadrant House, The Quadrant, Sutton, Surrey SM2 5AS. *Alt. W.*

ELECTRICAL TIMES, Quadrant House, The Quadrant, Sutton, Surrey SM2 5AS. *M.*

ELECTRONIC ENGINEERING, Miller Freeman House, 30 Calderwood Street, London SE18 6QH. *M.*

ENERGY MANAGEMENT, 19 Scarbrook Road, Croydon, Surrey CR9 1QH. *Alt. M.*

THE ENGINEER, Miller Freeman House, 30 Calderwood Street, London SE18 6QH. *W.*

ENGINEERING, Chester Court, High Street, Knowle, Solihull, W. Midlands B93 0LL. *Eleven times a year*

THE ENGLISH HISTORICAL REVIEW, Addison Wesley Longman, Edinburgh Gate, Harlow, Essex CM20 2JE. *Five times a year*

ENGLISH TODAY, Cambridge University Press, The Edinburgh Building, Shaftesbury Road, Cambridge CB2 2RU. *Q.*

EQUITY JOURNAL, Guild House, Upper St Martin's Lane, London WC2H 9EG. *Q.*

ESTATES GAZETTE, 151 Wardour Street, London W1V 4BN. *W.*

FAIRPLAY INTERNATIONAL SHIPPING WEEKLY, 20 Ullswater Crescent, Ullswater Business Park, Coulsdon, Surrey CR5 2HR. *W.*

FARMERS WEEKLY, Quadrant House, The Quadrant, Sutton, Surrey SM2 5AS. *W.*

FIRE, Queensway House, 2 Queensway, Redhill, Surrey RH1 1QS. *M.*

FIRE PREVENTION, Fire Protection Association, Melrose Avenue, Borehamwood, Herts WD6 2BJ. *Ten times a year*

FISHING NEWS INTERNATIONAL, Meed House, 21 John Street, London WC1N 2BP. *M.*

FISH TRADER, Queensway House, 2 Queensway, Redhill, Surrey RH1 1QS. *M.*

FLIGHT INTERNATIONAL, Quadrant House, The Quadrant, Sutton, Surrey SM2 5AS. *W.*

FOOD TRADE REVIEW, Station House, Hortons Way, Westerham, Kent TN16 1BZ. *M.*

FORESTRY AND BRITISH TIMBER, Miller Freeman House, Sovereign Way, Tonbridge, Kent TN9 1RW. *M.*

FOUNDRY TRADE JOURNAL, Queensway House, 2 Queensway, Redhill, Surrey RH1 1QS. *Alt. W.*

FROZEN AND CHILLED FOODS, Queensway House, 2 Queensway, Redhill, Surrey RH1 1QS. *M.*

FUEL, The Boulevard, Langford Lane, Kidlington, Oxford OX5 1GB. *M.*

GARDEN TRADE NEWS, Apex House, Oundle Road, Peterborough PE2 9NP. *M.*

GAS ENGINEERING AND MANAGEMENT, Institute of Gas Engineers, 21 Portland Place, London W1N 3AF. *Ten times a year*

GEOGRAPHY, Geographical Association, 343 Fulwood Road, Sheffield S10 3BP. *Q.*

GEOLOGICAL MAGAZINE, Cambridge University Press, The Edinburgh Building, Shaftesbury Road, Cambridge CB2 2RU. *Alt. M.*

GLASS AND GLAZING PRODUCTS, Maclaren House, 19 Scarbrook Road, Croydon CR9 1QH. *M.*

THE GROCER, Broadfield Park, Crawley, W. Sussex RH11 9RT. *W.*

GROWER, Nexus House, Azalea Drive, Swanley, Kent BR8 8HY. *W.*

HAIRDRESSERS' JOURNAL INTERNATIONAL, Quadrant House, The Quadrant, Sutton, Surrey SM2 5AS. *W.*

THE HEALTH SERVICE JOURNAL, Porters South, 4–6 Crinan Street, London N1 9SQ. *W.*

HEALTH VISITOR, BMA House, Tavistock Square, London WC1H 9JR. *M.*

HEATING, VENTILATING AND PLUMBING, Hereford House, Bridle Path, Croydon, Surrey CR9 4NL. *M.*

HISTORY, 108 Cowley Road, Oxford OX4 1JF. *Q.*

HISTORY TODAY, 20 Old Compton Street, London W1V 5PE. *M.*

INDEPENDENT RETAILER, Alliance House, Bank Chambers, Worcester WR1 1UW. *M.*

INDEX ON CENSORSHIP, 35 Islington High Street, London N1 9LH. *Ten times a year*

INDUSTRIAL EXCHANGE AND MART, Link House, West Street, Poole, Dorset BH1 5LL. *W.*

INDUSTRIAL RELATIONS JOURNAL, 108 Cowley Road, Oxford OX4 1JF. *Alt. M.*

INTERNATIONAL AFFAIRS, Cambridge University Press, The Edinburgh Building, Shaftesbury Road, Cambridge CB2 2RU. *Q.*

JANE'S DEFENCE WEEKLY, Sentinel House, 163 Brighton Road, Coulsdon, Surrey CR5 2NH. *W.*

THE JOURNALIST, National Union of Journalists, Acorn House, 314 Gray's Inn Road, London WC1X 8DP. *Alt. M.*

JOURNAL OF ALTERNATIVE AND COMPLEMENTARY MEDICINE, 9 Rickett Street, London SW6 1RU. *M.*

JOURNAL OF THE BRITISH ASTRONOMICAL ASSOCIATION, Burlington House, Piccadilly, London W1V 9AG. *Alt. M.*

JOURNAL OF THE CHEMICAL SOCIETY, Thomas Graham House, Science Park, Milton Road, Cambridge CB4 4WF. *Irregular*

JUSTICE OF THE PEACE REPORTS, East Row, Little London, Chichester, W. Sussex PO19 1PG. *Alt. W.*

THE LANCET, 42 Bedford Square, London WC1B 3SL. *W.*

LAW QUARTERLY REVIEW, 100 Avenue Road, London NW3 3PF. *Q.*

THE LAW REPORTS, 3 Stone Buildings, Lincoln's Inn, London WC2A 3XN. *M.*

LAW SOCIETY'S GAZETTE, 50 Chancery Lane, London WC2A 1SX. *W.*

LEATHER: THE INTERNATIONAL JOURNAL, Miller Freeman House, Sovereign Way, Tonbridge, Kent TN9 1RW. *M.*

LEISURE WEEK, St Giles House, 49–50 Poland Street, London W1V 4AX. *Alt. W.*

LIBRARY ASSOCIATION RECORD, 7 Ridgmount Street, London WC1E 7AE. *M.*

LLOYD'S LOADING LIST, Sheepen Place, Colchester, Essex CO3 3LP. *W.*

LLOYD'S SHIPPING INDEX, Sheepen Place, Colchester, Essex CO3 3LP. *W.*

LOCAL GOVERNMENT CHRONICLE, 33–39 Bowling Green Lane, London EC1 0DA. *W.*

MACHINERY AND PRODUCTION ENGINEERING, Franks Hall, Franks Lane, Horton Kirby, Dartford, Kent DA4 9LL. *Alt. W.*

MACHINERY MARKET, 6 Blyth Road, Bromley, Kent BR1 3RX. *W.*

MANAGEMENT ACCOUNTING, Chartered Institute of Management Accountants, 63 Portland Place, London W1N 4AB. *M.*

MANAGEMENT TODAY, 174 Hammersmith Road, London W6 7JP. *M.*

MANAGING INFORMATION, Aslib, Information House, 20–24 Old Street, London EC1V 9AP. *M.*

MANUFACTURING CHEMIST, Miller Freeman House, 30 Calderwood Street, London SE18 6QH. *M.*

MARKETING, 174 Hammersmith Road, London W6 7JP. *W.*

MARKETING WEEK, St Giles House, 49–50 Poland Street, London W1V 4AX. *W.*

MATERIALS RECYCLING WEEKLY, Maclaren House, 19 Scarbrook Road, Croydon, Surrey CR9 1QH. *W.*

MATERIALS WORLD, Institute of Materials, 1 Carlton House Terrace, London SW1 5DB. *M.*

MEAT TRADES' JOURNAL, Maclaren House, 19 Scarbrook Road, Croydon, Surrey CR9 1QH. *W.*

MEDIA WEEK, 33–39 Bowling Green Lane, London EC1 0DA. *W.*

METALS INDUSTRY NEWS, Queensway House, 2 Queensway, Redhill, Surrey RH1 1QS. *Q.*

MINING JOURNAL, 60 Worship Street, London EC2A 2HD. *W.*

MOTOR TRANSPORT, Quadrant House, The Quadrant, Sutton, Surrey SM2 5AS. *W.*

MUNICIPAL JOURNAL, 32 Vauxhall Bridge Road, London SW1 2SS. *W.*

MUSEUMS JOURNAL, Museums Association, 42 Clerkenwell Close, London EC1R 0PA. *M.*

MUSICIAN, 241 Shaftesbury Avenue, London WC2H 8EH. *Q.*

MUSIC JOURNAL, Incorporated Society of Musicians, 10 Stratford Place, London W1N 9AE. *M.*

MUSIC WEEK, 8th Floor, Ludgate House, 245 Blackfriars Road, London SE1 9UR. *W.*

NUCLEAR ENGINEERING INTERNATIONAL, Wilmington House, Church Street, Dartford, Kent DA1 7AS. *M.*

NURSING TIMES, Porters South, Crinan Street, London N1 9XW. *W.*

OFF-LICENCE NEWS, Broadfield Park, Crawley, W. Sussex RH11 9RT. *W.*

OPERA NOW, 241 Shaftesbury Avenue, London WC2H 8EH. *Alt. W.*

OPTICIAN, Quadrant House, The Quadrant, Sutton, Surrey SM2 5AS. *W.*

OPTOMETRY TODAY, Association of Optometrists, 233–234 Blackfriars Road, London SE1 8NW. *Alt. W.*

PACKAGING WEEK, Miller Freeman House, Sovereign Way, Tonbridge, Kent TN9 1RW. *W.*

PATENT WORLD, 3rd Floor, Brigade House, London SW6 4TH. *Ten times a year*

PC PLUS, Kingsgate House, 536 Kings Road, London SW10 0TE. *M.*

PERSONAL COMPUTER WORLD, VNU House, 32–34 Broadwick Street, London W1A 2HG. *M.*

PERSONNEL MANAGEMENT, Institute of Personnel Management, 17 Britton Street, London EC1M 5NQ. *M.*

PHARMACEUTICAL JOURNAL, Royal Pharmaceutical Society of Great Britain, 1 Lambeth High Street, London SE1 7JN. *W.*

PHILOSOPHY, (Royal Institute of Philosophy), Cambridge University Press, The Edinburgh Building, Shaftesbury Road, Cambridge CB2 2RU. *Q.*

THE PHOTOGRAPHER, British Institute of Professional Photography, Fox Talbot House, Amwell End, Ware, Herts SG12 9HN. *M.*

PHYSICS WORLD, Techno House, Redcliffe Way, Bristol BS1 6NX. *M.*

PLUMBING AND HEATING NEWS, Peterson House, Northbank, Berryhill Industrial Estate, Droitwich, Worcs WR9 9BL. *M.*

POLICE REVIEW, 5th Floor, Celcon House, 289–293 High Holborn, London WC1V 7AU. *W.*

THE PRACTITIONER, Miller Freeman House, 30 Calderwood Street, London SE18 6QH. *M.*

PRESS GAZETTE, 33–39 Bowling Green Lane, London EC1R 0DA. *W.*

PRINTING WORLD, Miller Freeman House, Sovereign Way, Tonbridge, Kent TN9 1RW. *W.*

PROBATION JOURNAL, National Association of Probation Officers, 3–4 Chivalry Road, London SW11 1HT. *Q.*

PROFESSIONAL CARE OF MOTHER AND CHILD, PO Box 100, Chichester, W. Sussex PO18 8HD. *Eight times a year*

THE PSYCHOLOGIST, The British Psychological Society, St Andrews House, 48 Princess Road East, Leicester LE1 7DR. *M.*

QUARRY MANAGEMENT, 7 Regent Street, Nottingham NG1 5BS. *M.*

RAILWAY GAZETTE INTERNATIONAL, Quadrant House, The Quadrant, Sutton, Surrey SM2 5AS. *M.*

RATING & VALUATION REPORTER, 4 Breams Buildings, London EC4A 1AQ. *M.*

RETAIL NEWSAGENT, Robert Taylor House, 11 Angel Gate, City Road, London EC1V 2PT. *W.*

RETAIL WEEK, Maclaren House, PO Box 109, Croydon CR9 1QH. *W.*

RUSI JOURNAL, Royal United Services Institute for Defence Studies, Whitehall, London SW1A 2ET. *Alt. M.*

SCREEN INTERNATIONAL, 33–39 Bowling Green Lane, London EC1R 0DA. *W.*

SHIPPING WORLD & SHIPBUILDER, 4 Hubbard Road, Houndsmill, Basingstoke, Hants RG21 6UH. *M.*

SHOE & LEATHER NEWS, 67 Clerkenwell Road, London EC1R 5BH. *M.*

SMALLHOLDER, High Street, Stoke Ferry, King's Lynn, Norfolk PE33 9SF. *M.*

SOCIOLOGICAL REVIEW, 108 Cowley Road, Oxford OX4 1JF. *Q.*

SOLICITORS' JOURNAL, 21–27 Lamb's Conduit Street, London WC1N 3NJ. *W.*

THE STAGE, Stage House, 47 Bermondsey Street, London SE1 3XT. *W.*

THE STRUCTURAL ENGINEER, (Institution of Structural Engineers), 11 Upper Belgrave Street, London SW1X 8BH. *Alt. W.*

THE SURVEYOR, 32 Vauxhall Bridge Road, London SW1V 2SS. *W.*

TAXATION PRACTITIONER, (Chartered Institute of Taxation), 12 Upper Belgrave Street, London SW1X 8BB. *M.*

TAXI, Licensed Taxi Drivers' Association, Taxi House, 7–11 Woodfield Road, London W9 2BA. *Alt. W.*

THE TEACHER, National Union of Teachers, Hamilton House, Mabledon Place, London WC1H 9BD. *Eight times a year*

TEACHING HISTORY, 59A Kennington Park Road, London SE11 4JH. *Q.*

TELEVISION, Royal Television Society, Holborn Hall, 100 Gray's Inn Road, London WC1X 8AL. *Eight times a year*

TEXTILE HORIZONS, 8 De Montfort Street, Leicester LE1 7GA. *M.*

TEXTILE MONTH, Perkin House, 1 Longlands Street, Bradford, W. Yorks BD1 2TB. *M.*

TOBACCO, Queensway House, 2 Queensway, Redhill, Surrey RH1 1QS. *Alt. M.*

TOWN AND COUNTRY PLANNING, Town and Country Planning Association, 17 Carlton House Terrace, London SW1Y 5AS. *M.*

TOWN PLANNING REVIEW, Liverpool University Press, Senate House, Liverpool L69 3BX. *Q.*

TRADE MARKS JOURNAL, Patent Office, Cardiff Road, Newport NP9 1RH. *W.*

THE TRADER, Link House, West Street, Poole, Dorset BH15 1LL. *M.*

TRAVEL TRADE GAZETTE (UK & IRELAND), Miller Freeman House, 30 Calderwood Street, London SE18 6QH. *W.*

TTJ – TIMBER TRADES JOURNAL, Miller Freeman House, Sovereign Way, Tonbridge, Kent TN9 1RW. *W.*

VETERINARY RECORD, British Veterinary Association, 7 Mansfield Street, London W1M 0AT. *W.*

WEEKLY LAW REPORTS, 3 Stone Buildings, Lincoln's Inn, London WC2A 3XN. *W.*

WOODCARVING, Castle Place, 166 High Street, Lewes, E. Sussex BN7 1XU. *Ten times a year*

WORLD'S FAIR, 2 Daltry Street, Oldham, Lancs OL1 4BB. *W.*

NEWS AGENCIES IN LONDON

THE ASSOCIATED PRESS LTD (AP), 12 Norwich Street, London EC4A 4BP. Tel: 0171-353 1515

CENTRAL PRESS FEATURES LTD, 20 Spectrum House, 32–34 Gordon House Road, London NW5 1LP. Tel: 0171-284 1433

EXTEL FINANCIAL LTD, Fitzroy House, 13–17 Epworth Street, London EC2A 4DL. Tel: 0171-825 8000

HAYTERS, 146–148 Clerkenwell Road, London EC1R 5DP. Tel: 0171-837 7171

PARLIAMENTARY AND EEC NEWS SERVICE, 19 Douglas Street, London SW1P 4PA. Tel: 0171-233 8283

THE PRESS ASSOCIATION, 292 Vauxhall Bridge Road, London SW1V 1AE. Tel: 0171-963 7000

REUTERS LTD, 85 Fleet Street, London EC4P 4AJ. Tel: 0171-250 1122

TWO-TEN COMMUNICATIONS LTD, Communications House, 210 Old Street, London EC1V 9UN. Tel: 0171-490 8111

UNITED PRESS INTERNATIONAL (UK) LTD, 2 Greenwich View, Millharbour, London E14 9NN. Tel: 0171-333 1690

Book Publishers

More than 15,000 firms, individuals and societies have published one or more books in recent years. The list which follows is a selective one comprising those firms whose names are most familiar to the general public. A fuller list, *Whitaker Directory of Publishers*, containing some 3,400 names and addresses is published annually in March by J. Whitaker.

ADDISON-WESLEY PUBLISHERS, Finchampstead Road, Wokingham, Berks RG11 2NZ. Tel: 0118-979 4000

ALLAN (IAN), Coombelands House, Coombelands Lane, Addlestone, Surrey KT15 1HY. Tel: 01932-855909

ALLEN (J.A.), 1 Lower Grosvenor Place, London SW1W 0EL. Tel: 0171-834 0090

ALLISON & BUSBY, 114 New Cavendish Street, London W1M 7FD. Tel: 0171-636 2942

APPLE PRESS, Fitzpatrick Building, 188–194 York Way, London N7 9QR. Tel: 0171-700 8521/7

ARMADA BOOKS, 77 Fulham Palace Road, London W6 8JB. Tel: 0181-741 7070

ARMS & ARMOUR PRESS, 125 Strand, London WC2R 0BB. Tel: 0171-420 5555

ARNOLD, 338 Euston Road, London NW1 3BH. Tel: 0171-873 6000

ARROW BOOKS, 20 Vauxhall Bridge Road, London SW1V 2SA. Tel: 0171-973 9700

ATHLONE PRESS, 1 Park Drive, London NW11 7SG. Tel: 0181-458 0888

AURUM PRESS, 25 Bedford Avenue, London WC1B 3AT. Tel: 0171-637 3225

AUTOMOBILE ASSOCIATION, Norfolk House, Priestly Road, Basingstoke, Hants RG24 9NY. Tel: 01256-491524

BAILLIÈRE TINDALL, 24 Oval Road, London NW1 7DX. Tel: 0171-267 4466

BANTAM BOOKS, 61 Uxbridge Road, London W5 5SA. Tel: 0181-579 2652

BARRIE & JENKINS, 20 Vauxhall Bridge Road, London SW1V 2SA. Tel: 0171-973 9690

BARTHOLOMEW, 77 Fulham Palace Road, London W6 8JB. Tel: 0181-741 7070

BATSFORD (B.T.), 583 Fulham Road, London SW6 5UA. Tel: 0171-471 1100

BBC BOOKS, 80 Wood Lane, London W12 0TT. Tel: 0181-576 2570

BLACK (A. & C.), 35 Bedford Row, London WC1R 4JH. Tel: 0171-242 0946

BLACKIE CHILDREN'S BOOKS, 27 Wrights Lane, London W8 5TZ. Tel: 0171-416 3000

BLACKWELL PUBLISHERS, 108 Cowley Road, Oxford OX4 1JF. Tel: 01865-791100

BLANDFORD PRESS, 125 Strand, London WC2R 0BB. Tel: 0171-420 5555

BLOOMSBURY PUBLISHING, 38 Soho Square, London W1V 5DF. Tel: 0171-494 2111

BODLEY HEAD, 20 Vauxhall Bridge Road, London SW1V 2SA. Tel: 0171-973 9730

BOXTREE, 25 Eccleston Place, London SW1W 9NF. Tel: 0171-881 8000

BOYARS (MARION), 24 Lacy Road, London SW15 1NL. Tel: 0181-788 9522

BRIMAX BOOKS, 4 Studlands Park Industrial Estate, Exning Road, Newmarket, Suffolk CB8 7AU. Tel: 01638-664611

BRITISH MUSEUM PRESS, 46 Bloomsbury Street, London WC1B 3QQ. Tel: 0171-323 1234

BUTTERWORTH & Co., 35 Chancery Lane, London WC2A 1ER. Tel: 0171-400 2500

CADOGAN BOOKS, 3rd Floor, 27-29 Berwick Street, London W1V 3RF. Tel: 0171-287 6555

CALDER PUBLICATIONS, 126 Cornwall Road, London SE1 8TQ. Tel: 0171-633 0599

CAMBRIDGE UNIVERSITY PRESS, The Edinburgh Building, Cambridge CB2 2RU. Tel: 01223-312393

CANONGATE BOOKS, 14 High Street, Edinburgh EH1 1TE. Tel: 0131-557 5111

CAPE (JONATHAN), 20 Vauxhall Bridge Road, London SW1V 2SA. Tel: 0171-973 9730

CASSELL, 125 Strand, London WC2R 0BB. Tel: 0171-420 5555

CAVENDISH PUBLISHING, The Glass House, Wharton Street, London WC1X 9PX. Tel: 0171-278 8000

CENTURY PUBLISHING Co., *see* Random House UK

CHAMBERS, New Penderel House, 283–288 High Holborn, London WC1V 7HZ. Tel: 0171-903 9999

CHANCELLOR PRESS, 81 Fulham Road, London SW3 6RB. Tel: 0171-581 9393

CHAPMAN & HALL, 2 Boundary Row, London SE1 8HN. Tel: 0171-865 0066

CHAPMAN (GEOFFREY), 125 Strand, London WC2R 0BB. Tel: 0171-420 5555

CHAPMANS PUBLISHERS, 5 Upper St Martin's Lane, London WC2H 9EA. Tel: 0171-240 3444

CHATTO & WINDUS, 20 Vauxhall Bridge Road, London SW1V 2SA. Tel: 0171-973 9740

CHIVERS PRESS, Windsor Bridge Road, Bath BA2 3AX. Tel: 01225-335336

CHURCH HOUSE PUBLISHING, Church House, Great Smith Street, London SW1P 3NZ. Tel: 0171-222 9011

CHURCHILL LIVINGSTONE, 1–3 Baxter's Place, Leith Walk, Edinburgh EH1 3AF. Tel: 0131-556 2424

COLLINS (WILLIAM), *see* HarperCollins Publishers

CONSTABLE & Co., 3 The Lanchesters, 162 Fulham Palace Road, London W6 9ER. Tel: 0181-741 3663

CONSUMERS' ASSOCIATION, see Which? Books

CORGI BOOKS, 61 Uxbridge Road, London W5 5SA. Tel: 0181-579 2652

CROWOOD PRESS, The Stable Block, Crowood Lane, Ramsbury, Marlborough, Wilts SN8 2HR. Tel: 01672-520320

DARTON, LONGMAN & TODD, 1 Spencer Court, 140 Wandsworth High Street, London SW18 4JJ. Tel: 0181-875 0134

DAVID & CHARLES, Brunel House, Newton Abbot, Devon TQ12 4PU. Tel: 01626-61121

DEAN & SON, 81 Fulham Road, London SW3 6RB. Tel: 0171-581 9393

DENT (J.M.) & SONS, 5 Upper St Martin's Lane, London WC2H 9EA. Tel: 0171-240 3444

DEUTSCH (ANDRE), 106 Great Russell Street, London WC1B 3LJ. Tel: 0171-580 2746

DORLING KINDERSLEY, 9 Henrietta Street, London WC2E 8PS. Tel: 0171-836 5411

DOUBLEDAY, 61 Uxbridge Road, London W5 5SA. Tel: 0181-579 2652

DUCKWORTH & Co., 48 Hoxton Square, London N1 6PB. Tel: 0171-729 5986

EBURY PRESS, 20 Vauxhall Bridge Road, London SW1V 2SA. Tel: 0171-973 9690

ELEMENT BOOKS, The Old School House, The Courtyard, Bell Street, Shaftesbury, Dorset SP7 8BP. Tel: 01747-851448

ELLIOT RIGHT WAY BOOKS, Kingswood Building, Kingswood, Tadworth, Surrey KT20 6TD. Tel: 01737-832202

ELSEVIER SCIENCE, The Boulevard, Langford Lane, Kidlington, Oxon OX5 1GB. Tel: 01865-843000

ENCYCLOPAEDIA BRITANNICA INTERNATIONAL, Chancery House, St Nicholas Way, Sutton SM1 1JB. Tel: 0181-770 7766

EPWORTH PRESS, c/o SCM Press, 9-17 St Albans Place, London N1 ONX. Tel: 0171-359 8033

EVANS BROS, 2A Portman Mansions, Chiltern Street, London W1M 1LE. Tel: 0171-935 7160

EVERYMAN, see Orion Publishing Group

EVERYMAN'S LIBRARY, 79 Berwick Street, London W1V 3PF. Tel: 0171-287 0035

FABER & FABER, 3 Queen Square, London WC1N 3AU. Tel: 0171-465 0045

FLAMINGO, see HarperCollins Publishers

FONTANA, 77 Fulham Palace Road, London W6 8JB. Tel: 0181-741 7070

FOULIS (G. T.), Sparkford, Yeovil, Somerset BA22 7JJ. Tel: 01963-440635

FOULSHAM (W.) & Co., Bennetts Close, Cippenham, Slough SL1 5AP. Tel: 01753-526769

FOURTH ESTATE, 6 Salem Road, London W2 4BU. Tel: 0171-727 8993

FRENCH (SAMUEL), 52 Fitzroy Street, London W1P 6JR. Tel: 0171-387 9373

GAIA BOOKS, 20 High Street, Stroud GL5 1AS. Tel: 01453-752985

GIBBONS (STANLEY), 5 Parkside, Christchurch Road, Ringwood, Hants BH24 3SH. Tel: 01425-472363

GINN & Co., Prebendal House, Parson's Fee, Aylesbury, Bucks HP20 2QZ. Tel: 01296-394442

GOLLANCZ (VICTOR), 125 Strand, London WC2R 0BB. Tel: 0171-420 5555

GOWER PUBLISHING Co., Croft Road, Aldershot, Hants GU11 3HR. Tel: 01252-331551

GRANTA BOOKS, 2 Hanover Yard, London N1 8BE. Tel: 0171-704 9776

GUINNESS PUBLISHING, 338 Euston Road, London NW1 3BD. Tel: 0171-891 4567

HALE (ROBERT), 45 Clerkenwell Green, London EC1R OHT. Tel: 0171-251 2661

HAMILTON (HAMISH), 27 Wrights Lane, London W8 5TZ. Tel: 0171-416 3000

HAMLYN (PAUL), 81 Fulham Road, London SW3 6RB. Tel: 0171-581 9393

HARCOURT BRACE, 24 Oval Road, London NW1 7DX. Tel: 0171-267 4466

HARPERCOLLINS PUBLISHERS, 77 Fulham Palace Road, London W6 8JB. Tel: 0181-741 7070

HARRAP, New Penderel House, 283–288 High Holborn, London WC1V 7HZ. Tel: 0171-903 9999

HAYNES (J. H.), Sparkford, Yeovil, Somerset BA22 7JJ. Tel: 01963-440635

HEADLINE BOOK PUBLISHING, see Hodder Headline

HEINEMANN (WILLIAM), (Adults' books), see Random House

HEINEMANN (WILLIAM), (Children's books), 81 Fulham Road, London SW3 6RB. Tel: 0171-581 9393

HERBERT PRESS, 35 Bedford Row, London WC1R 4JH. Tel: 0171-242 0946

HIPPO BOOKS, 1-19 New Oxford Street, London WC1A 1NU. Tel: 0171-421 9000

HMSO, see Stationery Office Books

HODDER & STOUGHTON, see Hodder Headline

HODDER HEADLINE, 338 Euston Road, London NW1 3BH. Tel: 0171-873 6000

HOGARTH PRESS, 20 Vauxhall Bridge Road, London SW1V 2SA. Tel: 0171-973 9740

HUTCHINSON, see Random House UK

JARROLD PUBLISHING, Whitefriars, Norwich NR3 1TR. Tel: 01603-763300

JORDAN PUBLISHING, 21 St Thomas Street, Bristol BS1 6JS. Tel: 0117-923 0600

JOSEPH (MICHAEL), 27 Wrights Lane, London W8 5TZ. Tel: 0171-416 3000

KEGAN PAUL INTERNATIONAL, PO Box 256, London WC1B 3SW. Tel: 0171-580 5511

KINGFISHER BOOKS, New Penderel House, 283–288 High Holborn, London WC1V 7HZ. Tel: 0171-903 9999

KINGSWAY PUBLICATIONS, Lottbridge Drive, Eastbourne BN23 6NT. Tel: 01323-410930

KOGAN PAGE, 120 Pentonville Road, London N1 9JN. Tel: 0171-278 0433

LADYBIRD BOOKS, Beeches Road, Loughborough LE11 2NQ. Tel: 01509-268021

LAROUSSE, New Penderel House, 283–288 High Holborn, London WC1V 7HZ. Tel: 0171-903 9999

LASCELLES (ROGER), 47 York Road, Brentford, Middx TW8 0QP. Tel: 0181-847 0935

LAWRENCE & WISHART, 99A Wallis Road, London E9 5LN. Tel: 0181-533 2506

LENNARD PUBLISHING, Windmill Cottage, Mackerye End, Harpenden, Herts AL5 5DR. Tel: 01582-715866

LETTS OF LONDON, 24 Nutford Place, London W1H 6DQ. Tel: 0171-724 7773

LINCOLN (FRANCES), 4 Torriano Mews, Torriano Avenue, London NW5 2RZ. Tel: 0171-284 4009

LION PUBLISHING, Sandy Lane West, Oxford OX4 5HG. Tel: 01865-747550

LITTLE, BROWN & Co., Brettenham House, Lancaster Place, London WC2E 7EN. Tel: 0171-911 8000

LONGMAN, Edinburgh Gate, Harlow, Essex CM20 2JE. Tel: 01279-623623

LUND HUMPHRIES, 1 Russell Gardens, London NW11 9NN. Tel: 0181-458 6314

LUTTERWORTH PRESS, PO Box 60, Cambridge CB1 2NT. Tel: 01223-350865

MACDONALD & EVANS, 128 Long Acre, London WC2E 9AN. Tel: 0171-447 2000

MACDONALD YOUNG BOOKS, 61 Western Road, Hove, E. Sussex BN3 1JD. Tel: 01273-722561

McGRAW-HILL, Shoppenhangers Road, Maidenhead, Berks SL6 2QL. Tel: 01628-23432

MACMILLAN PUBLISHERS, 25 Eccleston Place, London SW1W 9NF. Tel: 0171-881 8000

MACRAE (JULIA), 20 Vauxhall Bridge Road, London SW1V 2SA. Tel: 0171-973 9750

MAINSTREAM PUBLISHING Co. (EDINBURGH), 7 Albany Street, Edinburgh EH1 3UG. Tel: 0131-557 2959

MAMMOTH, 81 Fulham Road, London SW3 6RB. Tel: 0171-581 9393

MANDALA, see HarperCollins Publishers

MANDARIN, 20 Vauxhall Bridge Road, London SW1V 2SA. Tel: 0171-973 9000

METHUEN LONDON, 20 Vauxhall Bridge Road, London SW1V 2SA. Tel: 0171-973 9000

MILLS & BOON, 18 Paradise Road, Richmond, Surrey TW9 1SR. Tel: 0181-948 0444

MINERVA PRESS, 195 Knightsbridge, London SW7 1RE. Tel: 0171-225 3113

MITCHELL BEAZLEY, 81 Fulham Road, London SW3 6RB. Tel: 0171-581 9393

MOWBRAY, 125 Strand, London WC2R 0BB. Tel: 0171-420 5555

MURRAY (JOHN), 50 Albemarle Street, London W1X 4BD. Tel: 0171-493 4361

NATIONAL CHRISTIAN EDUCATION COUNCIL, 1020 Bristol Road, Selly Oak, Birmingham B29 6LB. Tel: 0121-472 4242

NELSON (THOMAS), Mayfield Road, Walton-on-Thames KT12 5PL. Tel: 01932-252211

NEW ENGLISH LIBRARY, see Hodder Headline

NEXUS SPECIAL INTEREST, Nexus House, Boundary Way, Hemel Hempstead, Herts HP2 7ST. Tel: 01442-66551

NISBET & Co., 78 Tilehouse Street, Hitchin, Herts SG5 2DY. Tel: 01462-438331

NOVELLO & Co., 8 Frith Street, London W1V 5TZ. Tel: 0171-434 0066

OCTOPUS BOOKS, 81 Fulham Road, London SW3 6RB. Tel: 0171-581 9393

OLIVER & BOYD, Edinburgh Gate, Harlow, Essex CM20 2JE. Tel: 01279-623623

O'MARA (MICHAEL) BOOKS, 9 Lion Yard, Tremadoc Road, London SW4 7NQ. Tel: 0171-720 8643

ORCHARD BOOKS, 96 Leonard Street, London EC2A 4RH. Tel: 0171-739 2929

ORION PUBLISHING GROUP, 5 Upper St Martin's Lane, London WC2H 9EA. Tel: 0171-240 3444

OWEN (PETER), 73 Kenway Road, London SW5 0RE. Tel: 0171-373 5628

OXFORD UNIVERSITY PRESS, Walton Street, Oxford OX2 6DP. Tel: 01865-56767

PAN BOOKS, 25 Eccleston Place, London SW1W 9NF. Tel: 0171-881 8000

PAVILION BOOKS, 26 Upper Ground, London SE1 9PD. Tel: 0171-620 1666

PELHAM BOOKS, 27 Wrights Lane, London W8 5TZ. Tel: 0171-416 3000

PENGUIN BOOKS, 27 Wrights Lane, London W8 5TZ. Tel: 0171-416 3000

PERGAMON PRESS, The Boulevard, Langford Lane, Kidlington, Oxon OX5 1GB. Tel: 01865-843000

PHAIDON PRESS, Regent's Wharf, All Saints Street, London N1 9PA. Tel: 0171-843 1234

PHILIP (GEORGE), 81 Fulham Road, London SW3 6RB. Tel: 0171-581 9393

PIATKUS BOOKS, 5 Windmill Street, London W1P 1HF. Tel: 0171-631 0710

PICADOR, see Pan Books

PICCADILLY PRESS, 5 Castle Road, London NW1 8PR. Tel: 0171-267 4492

PINTER PUBLISHERS, 125 Strand, London WC2R 0BB. Tel: 0171-420 5555

PITKIN GUIDES, Healey House, Dene Road, Andover, Hants SP10 2AA. Tel: 01264-334303

PITMAN PUBLISHING, 128 Long Acre, London WC2E 9AN. Tel: 0171-447 2000

QUARTET BOOKS, 27 Goodge Street, London W1P 2LD. Tel: 0171-636 3992

QUILLER PRESS, 46 Lillie Road, London SW6 1TN. Tel: 0171-499 6529

RANDOM HOUSE UK, 20 Vauxhall Bridge Road, London SW1V 2SA. Tel: 0171-973 9000

READER'S DIGEST, 11 West Ferry Circus, London E14 4AG. Tel: 0171-715 8000

RELIGIOUS & MORAL EDUCATION PRESS, St Mary's Works, St Mary's Plain, Norwich NR3 3BH. Tel: 01603-615995

ROUGH GUIDES, 1 Mercer Street, London WC2H 9QJ. Tel: 0171-379 3329

ROUTLEDGE, 11 New Fetter Lane, London EC4P 4EE. Tel: 0171-583 9855

ST ANDREW PRESS, 121 George Street, Edinburgh EH2 4YN. Tel: 0131-225 5722

SCM PRESS, 9-17 St Albans Place, London N1 0NX. Tel: 0171-359 8033

SCRIPTURE UNION, 207-209 Queensway, Bletchley, Milton Keynes, MK2 2EB. Tel: 01908-856000

SECKER & WARBURG, 20 Vauxhall Bridge Road, London SW1V 2SA. Tel: 0171-973 9000

SERPENT'S TAIL PUBLISHING, 4 Blackstock Mews, London N4 2BT. Tel: 0171-354 1949

SEVERN HOUSE, 9 Sutton High Street, Sutton SM1 1DF. Tel: 0181-770 3930

SHELDON PRESS, Holy Trinity Church, Marylebone Road, London NW1 4DU. Tel: 0171-387 5282

SIDGWICK & JACKSON, 25 Eccleston Place, London SW1W 9NF. Tel: 0171-881 8000

SIMON & SCHUSTER, Campus 400, Maylands Avenue, Hemel Hempstead, Herts HP2 7EZ. Tel: 01442-881900

SINCLAIR-STEVENSON, 20 Vauxhall Bridge Road, London SW1V 2SA. Tel: 0171-973 9000

SOUVENIR PRESS, 43 Great Russell Street, London WC1B 3PA. Tel: 0171-580 9307

SPCK, Holy Trinity Church, Marylebone Road, London NW1 4DU. Tel: 0171-387 5282

SPON (E. & F. N.), 2 Boundary Row, London SE1 8HN. Tel: 0171-865 0066

STATIONERY OFFICE BOOKS, PO Box 276, London SW8 5DT. Tel: 0171-873 0011

STEPHENS (PATRICK), Sparkford, Yeovil BA22 7JJ. Tel: 01963-440635

SUTTON PUBLISHING, Phoenix Mill, Far Thrupp, Stroud, Glos GL5 2BU. Tel: 01453-731114

SWEET & MAXWELL, 100 Avenue Road, London NW3 3PS. Tel: 0171-393 7000

THAMES & HUDSON, 30 Bloomsbury Street, London WC1B 3QP. Tel: 0171-636 5488

THORNES (STANLEY) (PUBLISHERS), Ellenborough House, Wellington Street, Cheltenham, Glos GL50 1YW. Tel: 01242-228888

THORSONS, 77 Fulham Palace Road, London W6 8JB. Tel: 0181-741 7070

TIMES BOOKS, 77 Fulham Palace Road, London W6 8JB. Tel: 0181-741 7070

UNIVERSITY OF WALES PRESS, 6 Gwennyth Street, Cardiff CF2 4YD. Tel: 01222-231919

USBORNE PUBLISHING, Usborne House, 83-85 Saffron Hill, London EC1N 8RT. Tel: 0171-430 2800

VIKING, 27 Wrights Lane, London W8 5TZ. Tel: 0171-416 3000

VIRAGO PRESS, Brettenham House, Lancaster Place, London WC2E 7EN. Tel: 0171-911 8000

VIRGIN PUBLISHING, 33-34 Grand Union Centre, 332 Ladbroke Grove, London W10 5AH. Tel: 0181-968 7554

WALKER BOOKS, 87 Vauxhall Walk, London SE11 5HJ. Tel: 0171-793 0909

WARD LOCK, 125 Strand, London WC2R 0BB. Tel: 0171-420 5555

WARD LOCK EDUCATIONAL CO., 1 Christopher Road, East Grinstead, W. Sussex RH19 3BT. Tel: 01342-318980

WARNE (FREDERICK), see Penguin Books

WATTS (FRANKLIN), 96 Leonard Street, London EC2A 4RH. Tel: 0171-739 2929

WAYLAND (PUBLISHERS), 61 Western Road, Hove, E. Sussex BN3 1JD. Tel: 01273-722561

WEIDENFELD & NICOLSON, 5 Upper St Martin's Lane, London WC2H 9EA. Tel: 0171-240 3444

WHICH? BOOKS, Consumer's Association, 2 Marylebone Road, London NW1 4DF. Tel: 0171-830 6000

WHITAKER (J.), 12 Dyott Street, London WC1A 1DF. Tel: 0171-420 6000

WILEY (JOHN) & SONS, Baffins Lane, Chichester, W. Sussex PO19 1UD. Tel: 01243-779777

WISDEN (JOHN), 25 Down Road, Merrow, Guildford GU1 2PY. Tel: 01483-570358

Annual Reference Books

If the address of the editorial office of a publication differs from the address to which orders should be sent, the address given is usually the one for orders

AA HOTEL GUIDE, Christchurch House, Sir Thomas Longley Road, Medway City Estate, Rochester, Kent ME2 4FX. (Oct.) £13.99

ADVERTISER'S ANNUAL, Harlequin House, 7 High Street, Teddington, Middx TW11 8EL. £185.00

AEROSPACE EUROPE, Riverbank House, Angel Lane, Tonbridge, Kent TN9 1SE. £83.00

ALLIED DUNBAR INVESTMENT AND SAVINGS HANDBOOK, 12–14 Slaidburn Crescent, Southport, Merseyside PR9 9YF. £25.99

ALLIED DUNBAR TAX HANDBOOK, 12–14 Slaidburn Crescent, Southport, Merseyside PR9 9YF. £25.99

ANNUAL ABSTRACT OF STATISTICS, PO Box 276, London SW8 5DT. (Feb.) £37.50

ANNUAL REGISTER: A RECORD OF WORLD EVENTS, 12–14 Slaidburn Crescent, Southport, Merseyside PR9 9YF. £99.00

ANTIQUE SHOPS OF BRITAIN, GUIDE TO THE, 5 Church Street, Woodbridge, Suffolk IP12 1DS. £14.95

ART SALES INDEX, 1 Thames Street, Weybridge, Surrey KT13 8JG. 2 vol. £105.00

ART YEAR REVIEW, 1 Stewarts Court, 220 Stewarts Road, London SW8 4UO. (Jan.) £9.99

ASSOCIATION OF CONSULTING ENGINEERS DIRECTORY OF MEMBERS FIRMS, Alliance House, 12 Caxton Street, London SW1H 0QL. £10.00

ASTRONOMICAL ALMANAC, PO Box 276, London SW8 5DT. (Dec.) £25.00

ATHLETICS: ASSOCIATION OF TRACK AND FIELD STATISTICIANS YEAR BOOK, Waldenbury, North Common, North Chailey, Lewes, E. Sussex BN8 4DR. (May) £14.95

AUTOMOBILE YEAR, Star Road, Partridge Green, Horsham, W. Sussex RH13 8LD. £29.95

BAILY'S HUNTING DIRECTORY, Chesterton Mill, French's Road, Cambridge CB4 3NP. (Nov.) £29.95

BANKER'S ALMANAC, East Grinstead House, East Grinstead, W. Sussex RH19 1XE. (Feb.) 5 vol. £365.00

BENEDICTINE AND CISTERCIAN MONASTIC YEAR BOOK, Ampleforth Abbey, York YO6 4EN. (Dec.) £2.25

BENN'S MEDIA, Riverbank House, Angel Lane, Tonbridge, Kent TN9 1SE. 3 vol. £290.00

BIRMINGHAM POST AND MAIL YEAR BOOK AND WHO'S WHO, 137 Newhall Street, Birmingham B3 1SF. (Sept.) £30.00

BPIF SERVICES AND LIST OF MEMBERS, 11 Bedford Row, London WC1R 4DX. £90.00

BRASSEY'S DEFENCE YEAR BOOK, PO Box 269, Abingdon, Oxon OX14 4YN. £37.50

BRITAIN: AN OFFICIAL HANDBOOK, PO Box 276, London SW8 5DT. (Jan.) £30.00

BRITANNICA BOOK OF THE YEAR, Chancery House, St Nicholas Way, Sutton SM1 1JB. (May) £57.50

BRITISH CLOTHING INDUSTRY YEAR BOOK, 11 The Swan Courtyard, Charles Edward Road, Yardley, Birmingham B26 1BU. £50.00

BRITISH EXPORTS, East Grinstead House, East Grinstead, W. Sussex RH19 1XA. £160.00

BRITISH MUSIC YEARBOOK, 241 Shaftesbury Avenue, London WC2H 8EH. £19.95

BRITISH PERFORMING ARTS YEAR BOOK, 241 Shaftesbury Avenue, London WC2H 8EH. (Jan.) £18.95

BRITISH PLASTICS AND RUBBER DIRECTORY, Catalyst House, 159 Clapham High Street, London SW4 7SS. £10.00

BROWN'S NAUTICAL ALMANAC DAILY TIDE TABLES, 4–10 Darnley Street, Glasgow G41 2SD. (Sept.) £38.00

BUILDING AND CONSTRUCTION INDEX, Riverbank House, Angel Lane, Tonbridge, Kent TN9 1SE. (Jan.) £62.00

BUILDING SOCIETIES YEAR BOOK, 100 Avenue Road, London NW3 3PS. £72.50

BUSES YEARBOOK, 10–14 Eldon Way, Lineside Industrial Estate, Littlehampton, W. Sussex BN17 7HE. £12.99

BUTTERWORTHS LAW DIRECTORY AND LEGAL SERVICES DIRECTORY, Maypole House, Maypole Road, East Grinstead, W. Sussex RH19 1HH. (Feb.) 2 vol. £54.00

CATHOLIC DIRECTORY OF ENGLAND AND WALES, St James's Buildings, Oxford Street, Manchester M1 6FP. £23.50

CHARITIES DIGEST, Paulton House, 8 Shepherdess Walk, London N1 7LB. £19.95

CHEMICAL INDUSTRY EUROPE, Riverbank House, Angel Lane, Tonbridge, Kent TN9 1SE. £89.00

CHEMIST AND DRUGGIST DIRECTORY, Riverbank House, Angel Lane, Tonbridge, Kent TN9 1SE. £102.00

CHRISTIES' REVIEW OF THE SEASON, 1 Stewart's Court, 220 Stewart's Road, London SW8 4UD. (Nov.) £35.00

CHURCH OF ENGLAND YEAR BOOK, S t Mary's Works, St Mary's Plain, Norwich NR3 3BH. (Jan.) £21.00

CHURCH OF SCOTLAND YEAR BOOK, 121 George Street, Edinburgh EH2 4YN. (Sept.) £10.00

CITY OF LONDON DIRECTORY AND LIVERY COMPANIES GUIDE, Seatrade House, 42–48 North Station Road, Colchester, Essex CO1 1RB. £21.00, £19.00

CIVIL SERVICE YEAR BOOK, PO Box 276, London SW8 5DT. (Feb.) £25.00

COMMONWEALTH UNIVERSITIES YEAR BOOK, 36 Gordon Square, London WC1H 0PF. (July) 2 vol. £130.00

COMMONWEALTH YEAR BOOK, Jordan House, 47 Brunswick Place, London N1 6EB (May) £50.00

COMPUTER USERS' YEAR BOOK, Woodside, Hinksey Hill, Oxford OX1 5BE. 3 vol. £275.00

CONCRETE YEAR BOOK, Thomas Telford House, 1 Heron Quay, London E14 4JD. £64.00

CURRENT LAW YEAR BOOK, Cheriton House, North Way, Andover, Hants SP10 5BE. £150.00

DIPLOMATIC SERVICE LIST, PO Box 276, London SW8 5DT. (April) £21.00

DIRECTORY OF DIRECTORS, East Grinstead House, East Grinstead, W. Sussex RH19 1XA. (Jan.) 2 vol. £220.00

DIRECTORY OF FURTHER EDUCATION, Star Road, Partridge Green, Horsham, W. Sussex RH13 8LD. (June) £66.50

DIY TRADE BUYERS GUIDE, Riverbank House, Angel Lane, Tonbridge, Kent TN9 1SE. £75.00

DOD'S PARLIAMENTARY COMPANION, Hurst Green, Etchingham, E. Sussex TN19 7PX. £90.00

EDUCATION AUTHORITIES' DIRECTORY AND ANNUAL, Derby House, Bletchingley Road, Merstham, Surrey RH1 3DN. (Jan.) £68.00, £58.00

EDUCATION YEAR BOOK, 12–14 Slaidburn Crescent, Southport, Merseyside PR9 9YF. £85.00

ELECTRICAL AND ELECTRONIC TRADES DIRECTORY, Michael Faraday House, Six Hills Way, Stevenage, Herts SG1 2AY. (Feb.) £80.00

ELECTRICITY SUPPLY HANDBOOK, PO Box 935, Finchingfield, Braintree, Essex CM7 4LN. (Feb.) £75.00

EUROPA WORLD YEAR BOOK, 18 Bedford Square, London WC1B 3JN. 2 vol. £370.00

EUROPEAN FOOD TRADES DIRECTORY, 32 Vauxhall Bridge Road, London SW1V 2SS. 2 vol. £140.00

EUROPEAN GLASS DIRECTORY AND BUYER'S GUIDE, 2 Queensway, Redhill, Surrey RH1 1QS. £138.50

FLIGHT INTERNATIONAL DIRECTORY, PO Box 1315, Potters Bar, Herts EN6 1PU. 2 vol. £64.00, £60.00

FROZEN AND CHILLED FOODS YEAR BOOK, Queensway House, 2 Queensway, Redhill, Surrey RH1 1QS. £114.75

FURNITURE AND FURNISHINGS INDUSTRY, DIRECTORY OF THE, Riverbank House, Angel Lane, Tonbridge, Kent TN9 1SE. £98.00

GAS INDUSTRY DIRECTORY, Riverbank House, Angel Lane, Tonbridge, Kent TN9 1SE. (Oct.) £89.00

GIBBONS' SIMPLIFIED CATALOGUE OF STAMPS OF THE WORLD, 5 Parkside, Christchurch Road, Ringwood, Hants BH24 3SH. (Oct.) 3 vol. £24.95, £24.95, £22.95

GOOD FOOD GUIDE, Bath Road, Harmondsworth, West Drayton, Middx UB7 0DA. £14.99

GOOD GUIDE TO BRITAIN, Church Road, Tiptree, Colchester CO5 0SR. (Nov.) £14.99

GOOD HOTEL GUIDE, Church Road, Tiptree, Colchester CO5 0SR. 14.99

GOVERNMENT AND MUNICIPAL BUYERS GUIDE, Riverbank House, Angel Lane, Tonbridge, Kent TN9 1SE. (Jan.) £90.00

GRADUATE STUDIES, Star Road, Partridge Green, Horsham, W. Sussex RH13 8LD. (July) £99.99

GUINNESS BOOK OF KNOWLEDGE, Brunel Road, Houndmills, Basingstoke, Hants RG21 2XS. (Oct.) £20.00

GUINNESS BOOK OF RECORDS, Brunel Road, Houndmills, Basingstoke, Hants RG21 2XS. (Oct.) £17.00

HEALTH AND SOCIAL SERVICES YEARBOOK, 12–14 Slaidburn Crescent, Southport, Merseyside PR9 9YF. £120.00

HEALTH CARE BUYERS GUIDE, Riverbank House, Angel Lane, Tonbridge, Kent TN9 1SE. £82.00

HISTORIC HOUSES, CASTLES AND GARDENS, Star Road, Partridge Green, Horsham, W. Sussex RH13 8LD. (March) £6.95

HOLLIS UK PRESS AND PR ANNUAL, Harlequin House, 7 High Street, Teddington TW11 8EY. (Oct.) £80.00

HOUSING AND PLANNING YEARBOOK, 12–14 Slaidburn Crescent, Southport, Merseyside PR9 9YF. £92.00

HUTCHINS' PRICED SCHEDULES, Halley Court, Jordan Hill, Oxford OX2 8EJ. £69.99

INDEPENDENT SCHOOLS YEAR BOOK, PO Box 19, Huntingdon, Cambs PE19 3SF. £25.00

INSURANCE DIRECTORY, 39 Earlham Street, London WC2H 9LD. (Feb.) £204.00

INTERNATIONAL PAPER DIRECTORY, PHILLIPS', Riverbank House, Angel Lane, Tonbridge, Kent TN9 1SE. £120.00

INTERNATIONAL WHO'S WHO, 18 Bedford Square, London WC1R 4JH. (July) £215.00

INTERNATIONAL YEARBOOK AND STATESMEN'S WHO'S WHO, Maypole House, Maypole Road, East Grinstead, W. Sussex RH19 1HU. (April) £175.00

JANE'S ALL THE WORLD'S AIRCRAFT, Sentinel House, 163 Brighton Road, Coulsdon, Surrey CR5 2NH. (Oct.) £250.00

JANE'S ARMOUR AND ARTILLERY, Sentinel House, 163 Brighton Road, Coulsdon, Surrey CR5 2NH. (Nov.) £250.00

JANE'S FIGHTING SHIPS, Sentinel House, 163 Brighton Road, Coulsdon, Surrey CR5 2NH. £250.00

JANE'S HIGH SPEED MARINE TRANSPORTATION, Sentinel House, 163 Brighton Road, Coulsdon, Surrey CR5 2NH. £235.00

JANE'S INFANTRY WEAPONS, Sentinel House, 163 Brighton Road, Coulsdon, Surrey CR5 2NH. (Aug.) £215.00

JANE'S NAVAL WEAPON SYSTEMS, Sentinel House, 163 Brighton Road, Coulsdon, Surrey CR5 2NH. £365.00

JANE'S WORLD RAILWAYS, Sentinel House, 163 Brighton Road, Coulsdon, Surrey CR5 2NH. £260.00

JEWISH YEAR BOOK, Star Road, Partridge Green, Horsham, W. Sussex RH13 8LD. (Feb.) £24.00

KELLY'S BUSINESS DIRECTORY, East Grinstead House, East Grinstead, W. Sussex RH19 1XA. £175.00

KEMPE'S ENGINEERS YEAR BOOK, Riverbank House, Angel Lane, Tonbridge, Kent TN9 1SE. £110.00

KIME'S INTERNATIONAL LAW DIRECTORY, 12–14 Slaidburn Crescent, Southport, Merseyside PR9 9YF. (Dec.) £77.00

LAXTON'S BUILDING PRICE BOOK, Halley Court, Jordan Hill, Oxford OX2 8EJ. 2 vol. £94.00

LIBRARY ASSOCIATION YEARBOOK, 39 Milton Park, Abingdon, Oxon OX14 4TD. (June) £37.50

LLOYD'S LIST OF SHIPOWNERS, 100 Leadenhall Street, London EC3A 3BP (Sept.) £115.00

LLOYD'S MARITIME DIRECTORY, Sheepen Place, Colchester CO3 3LP. (Jan.) £225.00

LLOYD'S NAUTICAL YEAR BOOK, Sheepen Place, Colchester CO3 3LP. (Sept.) £49.50

LLOYD'S REGISTER OF SHIPS, 100 Leadenhall Street, London EC3A 3BP. (July) 3 vol. £495.00

LYLE OFFICIAL ANTIQUES PRICE GUIDE, Glenmayne, Galashiels TD1 3NR. £19.95

MACMILLAN NAUTICAL ALMANACK, Brunel Road, Houndmills, Basingstoke, Hants RG21 2XS. £29.95

MAGISTRATES' COURT GUIDE, Halsbury House, 35 Chancery Lane, London WC2A 1EL. £23.95

MEDICAL DIRECTORY, 12–14 Slaidburn Crescent, Southport, Merseyside PR9 9YF. (June) 3 vol. £170.00

MEDICAL REGISTER, 178 Great Portland Street, London W1N 6JE. (March) 4 vol. £110.00

MIDDLE EAST AND NORTH AFRICA, 18 Bedford Square, London WC1B 3JN. (Oct.) £200.00

MILLER'S ANTIQUES PRICE GUIDE, The Cellars, 5 High Street, Tenterden, Kent TN30 6BN. £21.99

MINING ANNUAL REVIEW AND METALS AND MINERALS ANNUAL REVIEW, PO Box 10, Edenbridge, Kent TN8 5NE. £80.00

MINING INTERNATIONAL YEAR BOOK, 12–14 Slaidburn Crescent, Southport, Merseyside PR9 9YF. (June) £165.00

MOTOR INDUSTRY OF GREAT BRITAIN WORLD AUTOMOTIVE STATISTICS, Forbes House, Halkin Street, London SW1X 7DS. (Oct.) £75.00

MOTOR SHIP DIRECTORY, PO Box 935, Finchingfield, Braintree, Essex CM7 4LN. £107.00

MUNICIPAL YEARBOOK AND PUBLIC SERVICES DIRECTORY, 32 Vauxhall Bridge Road, London SW1V 2SS. (Dec.) 2 vol. £165.00

MUSEUMS AND GALLERIES IN GREAT BRITAIN AND IRELAND, Star Road, Partridge Green, Horsham, W. Sussex RH13 8LD. (Oct.) £8.95

NAUTICAL ALMANAC, PO Box 276, London SW8 5DT. (Oct.) £21.00

PACKAGING INDUSTRY DIRECTORY, Riverbank House, Angel Lane, Tonbridge, Kent TN9 1SE. £87.00

PEARS CYCLOPEDIA, 27 Wright's Lane, London W8 5TZ. £15.99

PEOPLE OF TODAY, 39 Milton Park, Abingdon, Oxon OX14 4TD. (April) £97.50

PHOTOGRAPHY YEAR BOOK, Fountain House, 2 Gladstone Road, Kingston-upon-Thames, Surrey KT1 3HD. £24.95

POLYMERS, PAINT AND COLOUR YEAR BOOK, Queensway House, 2 Queensway, Redhill, Surrey RH1 1QS. £112.70

PORTS OF THE WORLD, Sheepen Place, Colchester, Essex CO3 3LP. £185.00

PRINTING TRADES DIRECTORY, Riverbank House, Angel Lane, Tonbridge, Kent TN9 1SE. £102.00

PUBLIC AUTHORITIES DIRECTORY, Lansdowne Mews, 196 High Street, Tonbridge, Kent TN9 1EF. (Jan.) £98.00

PUBLIC SERVICES YEARBOOK, 12–14 Slaidburn Crescent, Southport, Merseyside PR9 9YF. (April) £27.00

PUBLISHING, DIRECTORY OF, Stanley House, 3 Fleets Lane, Poole, Dorset BH15 3AJ. (Oct.) £57.50

RAC EUROPEAN HOTEL GUIDE, 39 Milton Park, Abingdon, Oxon OX14 4TD. £8.99

RAC HOTEL GUIDE, 39 Milton Park, Abingdon, Oxon OX14 4TD. £9.99

RAILWAY DIRECTORY, PO Box 935, Finchingfield, Braintree, Essex CM7 4LN. (Dec.) £95.00

REGIONAL TRENDS, PO Box 276, London SW8 5DT. (July) £35.95

RETAIL DIRECTORY OF THE UNITED KINGDOM, 32 Vauxhall Bridge Road, London SW1V 2SS. £155.00

RIBA DIRECTORY OF PRACTICES, 39 Moreland Street, London EC1V 8BB. (Oct.) £57.75

ROTHMAN'S FOOTBALL YEAR BOOK, 39 Milton Park, Abingdon, Oxon OX14 4TD. (Aug.) £30.00, £17.99

ROTHMAN'S RUGBY LEAGUE YEAR BOOK, 39 Milton Park, Abingdon, Oxon OX14 4TD. (Sept.) £16.99

ROTHMAN'S RUGBY UNION YEAR BOOK, 39 Milton Park, Abingdon, Oxon OX14 4TD. (Sept.) £16.99

ROYAL AND ANCIENT GOLFER'S HANDBOOK, Brunel Road, Houndmills, Basingstoke, Hants RG21 2XS. (April) £49.99, £19.99

ROYAL SOCIETY YEAR BOOK, 6 Carlton House Terrace, London SW1Y 5AG. (Feb.) £20.00

SALVATION ARMY YEAR BOOK, 117–121 Judd Street, London WC1H 9NN. (April) £5.50

SCOTTISH CURRENT LAW YEAR BOOK, 21 Alva Street, Edinburgh EH2 4PS. 2 vol. £98.00

SCOTTISH LAW DIRECTORY, 59 George Street, Edinburgh EH2 2LQ. £34.00

SEABY STANDARD CATALOGUE OF BRITISH COINAGE, 5–7 King Street, London SW1Y 6QS. (Sept.) £14.99

SELL'S PRODUCTS AND SERVICES DIRECTORY, Riverbank House, Angel Lane, Tonbridge, Kent TN9 1SE. (June) £90.00

SHEET METAL INDUSTRIES YEAR BOOK, Queensway House, 2 Queensway, Redhill, Surrey RH1 1QS. £78.00

SHOWCASE INTERNATIONAL MUSIC BOOK, 38C The Broadway, London N8 9SU. £35.00

SOCIAL SERVICES YEAR BOOK, 12–14 Slaidburn Crescent, Southport, Merseyside PR9 9YF. (April) £99.00

SOCIAL TRENDS, PO Box 276, London SW8 5DT. (Jan.) £37.50

SOLICITORS AND BARRISTERS, DIRECTORY OF, Cheriton House, North Way, Andover, Hants SP10 5BE. £55.00

SPON'S ARCHITECTS' AND BUILDERS' PRICE BOOK, Cheriton House, North Way, Andover, Hants SP10 5BE. £72.50

SPON'S MECHANICAL AND ELECTRICAL SERVICES PRICE BOOK, Cheriton House, North Way, Andover, Hants SP10 5BE. £72.50

STATESMAN'S YEARBOOK, Brunel Road, Houndmills, Basingstoke, Hants RG21 2XS. (Aug.) £50.00

STOCK EXCHANGE YEARBOOK, Brunel Road, Houndmills, Basingstoke, Hants RG21 2XS. £245.00

STONE'S JUSTICES' MANUAL, PO Box 3000, Halsbury House, 35 Chancery Lane, London WC2A 1EL. 3 vol. (May) £250.00

STUDENT BOOK, 12 Hill Rise, Richmond, Surrey TW10 6UA. (June) £9.99

TANKER REGISTER, 12 Camomile Street, London EC3A 7BP. (April) £155.00

TIMBER TRADES ADDRESS BOOK, Riverbank House, Angel Lane, Tonbridge, Kent TN9 1SE. £69.00

TRAINING AND ENTERPRISE DIRECTORY, 120 Pentonville Road, London N1 9JN. £27.50

TRAVEL TRADE DIRECTORY, Riverbank House, Angel Lane, Tonbridge, Kent TN9 1SE. (April) £50.00

UK KOMPASS REGISTER, East Grinstead House, East Grinstead, W. Sussex RH19 1XD. 2 vol. £299.00

UNITED KINGDOM MINERALS YEARBOOK, British Geological Survey, Keyworth, Nottingham NG12 5GG. £30.00

UNITED REFORMED CHURCH YEAR BOOK, 86 Tavistock Place, London WC1H 9RT. (Sept.) £17.50

UNIT TRUST YEAR BOOK, Maple House, 149 Tottenham Court Road, London W1P 9LL. £295.00

UNIVERSITY AND COLLEGE ENTRANCE, 14 Cooper's Row, London EC3N 2BH. (June) £18.95

VETERINARY ANNUAL, PO Box 269, Abingdon, Oxon. OX14 4YN. £59.50

WATER SERVICES YEAR BOOK, Queensway House, 2 Queensway, Redhill, Surrey RH1 1QS. (Oct.) £80.00

WHITAKER DIRECTORY OF PUBLISHERS, 12 Dyott Street, London WC1A 1DF. (March) £20.00

WHITAKER'S ALMANACK, PO Box 276, London SW8 5DT. (Oct.) £60.00, £35.00

WHITAKER'S BOOKS IN PRINT, 12 Dyott Street, London WC1A 1DF. (Jan.) 5 vol. £375.00

WHITAKER'S CONCISE ALMANACK, PO Box 276, London SW8 5DT. (Oct.) £12.99

WHO OWNS WHOM?, Holmers Farm Way, High Wycombe, Bucks HP12 4UL. 2 vol. £338.00

WHO'S WHO, PO Box 19, Huntingdon, Cambs PE19 3SF. £105.00

WILLING'S PRESS GUIDE, Harlequin House, 7 High Street, Teddington, Middx TW11 8EY. (Feb.) 2 vol. £179.00

WISDEN CRICKETERS' ALMANACK, Bath Road, Harmondsworth, West Drayton, Middx UB7 0DA. (April) £26.00

WORLD HOTEL DIRECTORY, 12–14 Slaidburn Crescent, Southport, Merseyside PR9 9YF. £135.00

WORLD INSURANCE, 12–14 Slaidburn Crescent, Southport, Merseyside PR9 9YF. £195.00

WORLD MINERAL STATISTICS, British Geological Survey, Keyworth, Notts NG12 5GG. (Sept.) 2 vol. £80.00

WORLD OF LEARNING, 18 Bedford Square, London WC1B 3JN. (Jan.) 2 vol. £225.00

WORLD SHIPPING DIRECTORY, PO Box 96, Coulsdon, Surrey CR5 2TE. £99.00

WRITERS' AND ARTISTS' YEAR BOOK, PO Box 19, Huntingdon, Cambs PE19 3SF. (Sept.) £11.99

Employers' and Trade Associations

At 31 December 1996 there were 110 employers' associations listed by the Certification Officer (*see* page 290) and 115 which had not sought to be listed. Most national employers' associations are members of the Confederation of British Industry (CBI). For ACAS, the Certification Office, the Commission for Racial Equality, the Equal Opportunities Commission, the Health and Safety Commission, the Industrial Tribunals and Review Bodies, *see* Index.

CONFEDERATION OF BRITISH INDUSTRY
Centre Point, 103 New Oxford Street, London WC1A 1DU
Tel 0171-379 7400

The Confederation of British Industry was founded in 1965 and is an independent non-party political body financed by industry and commerce. It exists primarily to ensure that the Government understands the intentions, needs and problems of British business. It is the recognized spokesman for the business viewpoint and is consulted as such by the Government.

The CBI represents, directly and indirectly, some 250,000 companies, large and small, from all sectors.

The governing body of the CBI is the 400-strong Council, which meets four times a year in London under the chairmanship of the President. It is assisted by some 27 expert standing committees which advise on the main aspects of policy. There are 13 regional councils and offices covering the administrative regions of England, Wales, Scotland and Northern Ireland. There is also an office in Brussels.

President, Sir Colin Marshall
Director-General, J. Adair Turner
Secretary, P. Forder

ASSOCIATIONS

ADVERTISING ASSOCIATION, Abford House, 15 Wilton Road, London SW1V 1NJ. Tel: 0171-828 2771. *Director-General,* A. Brown
AEROSPACE COMPANIES LTD, SOCIETY OF BRITISH, 60 Petty France, London SW1H 9EU. Tel: 0171-227 1000. *Director-General,* D. Marshall
APPAREL AND TEXTILE CONFEDERATION LTD, BRITISH, 5 Portland Place, London WIN 3AA. Tel: 0171-636 7788. *Director-General,* J. R. Wilson
BAKERS, FEDERATION OF, 20 Bedford Square, London WC1B 3HF. Tel: 0171-580 4252. *Director,* A. Casdagli, CBE
BANKERS' ASSOCIATION, BRITISH, 105–108 Old Broad Street, London EC2N 1EX. Tel: 0171-216 8800. *Director-General,* T. P. Sweeney
BLC (BRITISH LEATHER CONFEDERATION) - THE LEATHER TECHNOLOGY CENTRE, Leather Trade House, Kings Park Road, Moulton Park, Northampton NN3 6JD. Tel: 01604-494131. *Chief Executive,* K. T. W. Alexander, PH.D,
BREWERS' AND LICENSED RETAILERS' ASSOCIATION, 42 Portman Square, London WIH 0BB. Tel: 0171-486 4831. *Director,* R. W. Simpson

BUILDING MATERIAL PRODUCERS, NATIONAL COUNCIL OF, 26 Store Street, London WC1E 7BT. Tel: 0171-323 3770. *Director-General,* N. M. Chaldecott, OBE
CHAMBER OF SHIPPING LTD, Carthusian Court, 12 Carthusian Street, London EC1M 6EB. Tel: 0171-417 8400. *Director-General,* Adm. Sir Nicholas Hunt, GCB, LVO
CHEMICAL INDUSTRIES ASSOCIATION LTD, Kings Buildings, Smith Square, London SW1P 3JJ. Tel: 0171-834 3399. *Director-General,* Dr E. G. Finer
CLOTHING INDUSTRY ASSOCIATION LTD, BRITISH, 5 Portland Place, London WIN 3AA. Tel: 0171-636 7788. *Director,* J. R. Wilson
CONSTRUCTION CONFEDERATION, 82 New Cavendish Street, London WIM 8AD. Tel: 0171-580 5588. *Chief Executive,* I. A. Deslandes
DAIRY INDUSTRY FEDERATION, 19 Cornwall Terrace, London NW1 4QP. Tel: 0171-486 7244. *Director-General,* J. P. Price
ELECTROTECHNICAL AND ALLIED MANUFACTURERS' ASSOCIATIONS, FEDERATION OF BRITISH (BEAMA), Westminster Tower, 3 Albert Embankment, London SE1 7SL. Tel: 0171-793 3000. *Director-General,* J. G. Gaddes
ENGINEERING EMPLOYERS' FEDERATION, Broadway House, Tothill Street, London SW1H 9NQ. Tel: 0171-222 7777. *Director-General,* G. R. Mackenzie, OBE, F.ENG.
FARMERS' UNION, NATIONAL (NFU), 164 Shaftesbury Avenue, London WC2H 8HL. Tel: 0171-331 7200. *Director-General,* R. Macdonald
FARMERS' UNION OF SCOTLAND, NATIONAL, Rural Centre-West Mains, Ingliston, Newbridge, Midlothian EH28 8LT. Tel: 0131-472 4000. *Chief Executive,* T. J. Brady
FARMERS' UNION, ULSTER, 475 Antrim Road, Belfast BT15 3DA. Tel: 01232-370222. *Director-General,* A. MacLaughlin
FINANCE AND LEASING ASSOCIATION, 15–19 Imperial House, London WC2B 6UN. Tel: 0171-836 6511. *Director-General,* M. A. Hall, MVO
FOOD AND DRINK FEDERATION, 6 Catherine Street, London WC2B 5JJ. Tel: 0171-836 2460. *Director-General,* M. P. Mackenzie
FOREST PRODUCTS ASSOCIATION, UNITED KINGDOM, Office 14, John Player Building, Stirling Enterprise Park, Springbank Road, Stirling FK7 7RP. Tel: 01786-449029. *Executive Director,* D. J. Sulman
FREIGHT TRANSPORT ASSOCIATION LTD, Hermes House, 157 St John's Road, Tunbridge Wells, Kent TN4 9UZ. Tel: 01892-526171. *Director-General,* D. C. Green
INSURERS, ASSOCIATION OF BRITISH, 51 Gresham Street, London EC2V 7HQ. Tel: 0171-600 3333. *Director-General,* M. Boléat
KNITTING INDUSTRIES' FEDERATION LTD, 53 Oxford Street, Leicester LE1 5XY. Tel: 0116-254 1608. *Director,* J. P. Harrison
LEATHER PRODUCERS' ASSOCIATION, Leather Trade House, Kings Park Road, Moulton Park, Northampton NN3 6JD. Tel: 01604-494131. *National Secretary,* J. Purvis
MANAGEMENT CONSULTANCIES ASSOCIATION, 11 West Halkin Street, London SW1X 8JL. Tel: 0171-235 3897. *Executive Director,* B. O'Rorke

MARINE INDUSTRIES FEDERATION, BRITISH, Meadlake Place, Thorpe Lea Road, Egham, Surrey TW20 8HE. Tel: 01784-473377. *Executive Chairman*, A. V. Beechey

MARKET TRADERS' FEDERATION, NATIONAL, Hampton House, Hawshaw Lane, Hoyland, Barnsley S74 0HA. Tel: 01226-749021. *General Secretary*, D. E. Feeny

MASTER BUILDERS, FEDERATION OF, Gordon Fisher House, 14–15 Great James Street, London WC1N 3DP. Tel: 0171-242 7583. *Director-General*, I. Davis

MOTOR MANUFACTURERS AND TRADERS LTD, SOCIETY OF, Forbes House, Halkin Street, London SW1X 7DS. Tel: 0171-235 7000. *Chief Executive*, R. E. Thompson

NEWSPAPER PUBLISHERS ASSOCIATION LTD, 34 Southwark Bridge Road, London SE1 9EU. Tel: 0171-207 2200. *Director*, S. Oram

NEWSPAPER SOCIETY, Bloomsbury House, 74–77 Great Russell Street, London WC1B 3DA. Tel: 0171-636 7014. *Director*, D. Newell

OFFICE SYSTEMS AND STATIONERY FEDERATION, BRITISH, 6 Wimpole Street, London W1M 8AS. Tel: 0171-637 7692. *Chief Executive*, K. Davies

PAPER FEDERATION OF GREAT BRITAIN LTD, Papermakers House, Rivenhall Road, Swindon SN5 7BD. Tel: 01793-886086. *Director-General*, W. J. Bartlett

PASSENGER TRANSPORT UK, CONFEDERATION OF, Imperial House, 15–19 Kingsway, London WC2B 6UN. Tel: 0171-240 3131. *Director-General*, Mrs V. Palmer, OBE

PLASTICS FEDERATION, BRITISH, 6 Bath Place, Rivington Street, London EC2A 3JE. Tel: 0171-457 5000. *Director-General*, D. R. Jones

PORTS ASSOCIATION, BRITISH, Africa House, 64–78 Kingsway, London WC2B 6AH. Tel: 0171-242 1200. *Director*, D. Whitehead

PRINTING INDUSTRIES FEDERATION, BRITISH, 11 Bedford Row, London WC1R 4DX. Tel: 0171-242 6904. *Chief Executive*, T. P. E. Machin

PRIVATE MARKET OPERATORS, ASSOCIATION OF, 4 Worrygoose Lane, Whiston, Rotherham S60 4AD. Tel: 01709-700072. *Secretary*, D. J. Glasby

PROPERTY FEDERATION, BRITISH, 35 Catherine Place, London SW1E 6DY. Tel: 0171-828 0111. *Director-General*, W. A. McKee

PUBLISHERS ASSOCIATION, THE, 1 Kingsway, London WC2B 6XF. Tel: 0171-565 7474. *Chief Executive*, C. Bradley, CBE

RADIO COMPANIES ASSOCIATION, COMMERCIAL, 77 Shaftesbury Avenue, London W1V 7AD. Tel: 0171-306 2603. *Chief Executive*, P. Brown

RETAIL CONSORTIUM, BRITISH, 5 Grafton Street, London W1X 3LB. Tel: 0171-647 1500. *Director-General*, Ms A. Robinson

RETAIL NEWSAGENTS, NATIONAL FEDERATION OF, Yeoman House, Sekforde Street, London EC1R 0HD. Tel: 0171-253 4225. *Chief Executive*, R. Clarke

ROAD FEDERATION, BRITISH, Pillar House, 194–202 Old Kent Road, London SE1 5TG. Tel: 0171-703 9769. *Director*, R. Diment

ROAD HAULAGE ASSOCIATION LTD, Roadway House, 35 Monument Hill, Weybridge, Surrey KT13 8RN. Tel: 01932-841515. *Director-General*, S. J. Norris

RUBBER MANUFACTURERS' ASSOCIATION LTD, BRITISH, 90 Tottenham Court Road, London W1P 0BR. Tel: 0171-580 2794. *Director*, A. J. Dorken

SPORT AND ALLIED INDUSTRIES FEDERATION LTD, BRITISH, Federation House, National Agricultural Centre, Stoneleigh Park, Kenilworth, Warks CV8 2RF. Tel: 01203-414999. *Chief Executive*, M. Johnson

TIMBER GROWERS ASSOCIATION LTD, 5 Dublin Street Lane South, Edinburgh EH1 3PX. Tel: 0131-538 7111. *Chief Executive*, P. H. Wilson

TIMBER TRADE FEDERATION, Clareville House, 26–27 Oxendon Street, London SW1Y 4EL. Tel: 0171-839 1891. *Director-General*, P. G. Harris

UK OFFSHORE OPERATORS ASSOCIATION LTD, 3 Hans Crescent, London SW1X 0LN. Tel: 0171-589 5255. *Director-General*, Dr H. W. D. Hughes, OBE

UK PETROLEUM INDUSTRY ASSOCIATION LTD, 9 Kingsway, London WC2B 6XF. Tel: 0171-240 0289. *Director-General*, Dr M. A. Frend

Trade Unions

At 31 December 1996 there were 245 trade unions listed by the Certification Officer (*see* page 290). In 1995 8,031,326 people were members of listed trade unions, compared with 8,230,545 in 1994. Nearly 80 per cent of trade union members belong to unions affiliated to the TUC (*see* below).

The Central Arbitration Committee arbitrates in industrial disputes between trade unions and employers, and determines disclosure of information complaints. The Commissioner for the Rights of Trade Union Members provides assistance to individuals taking action against their trade union when they have not been afforded their statutory rights or when specific union rules have been breached. The Commissioner for Protection Against Unlawful Industrial Action assists individuals who have been, or are likely to be, deprived of goods or services because of industrial action unlawfully organized by a trade union.

For ACAS, the Certification Office, the Commission for Racial Equality, the Equal Opportunities Commission, the Health and Safety Commission, the Industrial Tribunals and Review Bodies, *see* Index.

THE CENTRAL ARBITRATION COMMITTEE, Brandon House, 180 Borough High Street, London SE1 1LW. Tel: 0171-210 3737/8. *Chairman*, Prof. Sir John Wood, CBE; *Secretary*, S. Gouldstone

THE COMMISSIONER FOR THE RIGHTS OF TRADE UNION MEMBERS, 1st Floor, Bank Chambers, 2A Rylands Street, Warrington, Cheshire WA1 1EN. Tel: 01925-415771. *Commissioner*, G. Corless

THE COMMISSIONER FOR PROTECTION AGAINST UNLAWFUL INDUSTRIAL ACTION, 2nd Floor, Bank Chambers, 2A Rylands Street, Warrington, Cheshire WA1 1EN. Tel: 01925-414128. *Commissioner*, G. Corless

TUC-AFFILIATED TRADE UNIONS

TRADES UNION CONGRESS (TUC)
Congress House, 23–28 Great Russell Street, London WC1B 3LS
Tel 0171-636 4030

The Trades Union Congress, founded in 1868, is an independent association of trade unions. The TUC promotes the rights and welfare of those in work and helps the unemployed. It helps its member unions promote membership in new areas and industries, and campaigns for rights at work for all employees, including part-time and temporary workers, whether union members or not. TUC representatives sit on many public bodies at national and international level. It makes representations to government, political parties, employers and international bodies such as the European Union.

The governing body of the TUC is the annual Congress. Between Congresses, business is conducted by a General Council, which meets five times a year, and an Executive Committee, which meets monthly. The full-time staff is headed by the General Secretary who is elected by Congress and is a permanent member of the General Council.

Affiliated unions (in 1996–7) totalled 75 with a total membership of nearly 6,800,000.

President (1996–7), A. Dubbins (GPMU). (The President for 1997–8 was elected in September 1997. *See* Stoppress)
General Secretary, J. Monks, *elected* 1993

SCOTTISH TRADES UNION CONGRESS
Middleton House, 16 Woodlands Terrace, Glasgow G3 6DF
Tel 0141-332 4946

The Congress was formed in 1897 and acts as a national centre for the trade union movement in Scotland. In 1997 it consisted of 47 unions with a membership of 659,871 and 28 directly affiliated Trades Councils.

The Annual Congress in April elects a 37-member General Council on the basis of eight industrial sections.
Chairperson, P. Kelly
General Secretary, C. Christie, CBE

AFFILIATED UNIONS AS AT 1 SEPTEMBER 1997
(Number of members in parenthesis)

AMALGAMATED ENGINEERING AND ELECTRICAL UNION (AEEU) (700,000), Hayes Court, West Common Road, Bromley, Kent BR2 7AU. Tel: 0181-462 7755. *General Secretary*, K. Jackson

ASSOCIATED METALWORKERS UNION (AMU) (1,000), 92 Worsley Road North, Worsley, Manchester M28 5QW. Tel: 01204-793245. *General Secretary*, R. Marron

ASSOCIATED SOCIETY OF LOCOMOTIVE ENGINEERS AND FIREMEN (ASLEF) (15,400), 9 Arkwright Road, London NW3 6AB. Tel: 0171-317 8600 *General Secretary*, L. Adams

ASSOCIATION OF FIRST DIVISION CIVIL SERVANTS (10,137), 2 Caxton Street, London SW1H 0QH. Tel: 0171-222 6242. *General Secretary*, J. Baume

ASSOCIATION OF FLIGHT ATTENDANTS – COUNCIL 07, LONDON, United Airlines Cargo Centre, Shoreham Road East, Heathrow Airport, Hounslow TW6 3RD. Tel: 0181-750 9723. *President*, K. Creighan

ASSOCIATION OF MAGISTERIAL OFFICERS (5,280), 231 Vauxhall Bridge Road, London SW1V 1EG. Tel: 0171-630 5455. *General Secretary*, Ms R. Eagleson

ASSOCIATION OF UNIVERSITY TEACHERS (38,000), United House, 9 Pembridge Road, London W11 3JY. Tel: 0171-221 4370. *General Secretary*, D. Triesman

BAKERS, FOOD AND ALLIED WORKERS' UNION (27,934), Stanborough House, Great North Road, Stanborough, Welwyn Garden City, Herts AL8 7TA. Tel: 01707-260150. *General Secretary*, J. R. Marino

BANKING, INSURANCE AND FINANCE UNION (116,000), Sheffield House, 1B Amity Grove, London SW20 0LG. Tel: 0181-946 9151. *General Secretary*, E. Sweeney

BRITISH ACTORS' EQUITY ASSOCIATION (43,000), Guild House, Upper St Martin's Lane, London WC2H 9EG. Tel: 0171-379 6000. *General Secretary*, I. McGarry

BRITISH AIR LINE PILOTS ASSOCIATION (BALPA) (5,824), 81 New Road, Harlington, Hayes, Middx UB3 5BG. Tel: 0181-476 4000. *General Secretary*, C. Darke

BRITISH ASSOCIATION OF COLLIERY MANAGEMENT (4,600), 17 South Parade, Doncaster, S. Yorks DN1 2DN. Tel: 01302-815551. *General Secretary*, P. M. Carragher

BRITISH DIETETIC ASSOCIATION (4,300), 7th Floor, Elizabeth House, 22 Suffolk Street, Queensway, Birmingham B1 1LS. Tel: 0121-643 5483. *Secretary*, J. Grigg

BRITISH ORTHOPTIC SOCIETY (888), Tavistock House North, Tavistock Square, London wc1H 9HX. Tel: 0171-387 7992. *Executive Secretary*, Ms J. Brown

BROADCASTING, ENTERTAINMENT, CINEMATOGRAPH AND THEATRE UNION (BECTU) (30,600), 111 Wardour Street, London w1V 4AY. Tel: 0171-437 8506. *General Secretary*, R. Bolton

CARD SETTING MACHINE TENTERS' SOCIETY (88), 48 Scar End Lane, Staincliffe, Dewsbury, W. Yorks wF12 4NY. Tel: 01924-400206. *Secretary*, A. Moorhouse

CERAMIC AND ALLIED TRADES UNION (21,849), Hillcrest House, Garth Street, Hanley, Stoke-on-Trent sT1 2AB. Tel: 01782-272755. *General Secretary*, G. Bagnall

THE CHARTERED SOCIETY OF PHYSIOTHERAPY (23,000), 14 Bedford Row, London wc1R 4ED. Tel: 0171-306 6666. *Secretary*, P. Lambden

CIVIL AND PUBLIC SERVICES ASSOCIATION (110,000), 160 Falcon Road, London sw11 2LN. Tel: 0171-924 2727. *General Secretary*, B. Reamsbottom

COMMUNICATION MANAGERS' ASSOCIATION (15,000), CMA House, Ruscombe Road, Twyford, Reading rg10 9JD. Tel: 0118-934 2300. *General Secretary*, T. L. Deegan

COMMUNICATION WORKERS UNION (275,000), CWU House, Crescent Lane, London sw4 9RN. Tel: 0171-622 9977. *Joint General Secretaries*, A. I. Young, D. Hodgson

COMMUNITY AND DISTRICT NURSING ASSOCIATION (5,500), Thames Valley University, 8 University House, Ealing Green, London w5 5ED. Tel: 0181-231 2776. *General Secretary*, Ms A. Keen

COMMUNITY AND YOUTH WORKERS UNION (2,500), Unit 302, The Argent Centre, 60 Frederick Street, Birmingham b1 3HS. Tel: 0121-244 3344. *General Secretary*, D. Nicholls

THE EDUCATIONAL INSTITUTE OF SCOTLAND (50,185), 46 Moray Place, Edinburgh eH3 6BH. Tel: 0131-225 6244. *General Secretary*, R. A. Smith

ENGINEERING AND FASTENER TRADE UNION (241), 42 Galton Road, Warley, West Midlands b67 5JU. Tel: 0121-429 2594. *General Secretary*, J. Burdis

ENGINEERS' AND MANAGERS' ASSOCIATION (30,000), Flaxman House, Gogmore Lane, Chertsey, Surrey kT16 9JS. Tel: 01932-577007. *General Secretary*, D. A. Cooper

THE FIRE BRIGADES UNION (48,000), Bradley House, 68 Coombe Road, Kingston upon Thames, Surrey kT2 7AE. Tel: 0181-541 1765. *General Secretary*, K. Cameron

GENERAL UNION OF LOOM OVERLOOKERS (380), 9 Wellington Street, St Johns, Blackburn, Lancs bb1 8AF. Tel: 01254-51760. *General Secretary*, D. J. Rishton

GMB (formerly General, Municipal, Boilermakers and Allied Trades Union) (730,000), 22–24 Worple Road, London sw19 4DD. Tel: 0181-947 3131. *General Secretary*, J. Edmonds

GRAPHICAL, PAPER AND MEDIA UNION (216,991), 63–67 Bromham Road, Bedford mK40 2AG. Tel: 01234-351521. *General Secretary*, A. D. Dubbins

HOSPITAL CONSULTANTS AND SPECIALISTS ASSOCIATION (2,302), 1 Kingsclere Road, Overton, Basingstoke, Hants rG25 3JA. Tel: 01256-771777. *Chief Executive*, S. J. Charkham

INDEPENDENT UNION OF HALIFAX STAFF (25,000), Simmons House, 46 Old Bath Road, Charvil, Reading rg10 9QR. Tel: 0118-934 1808. *General Secretary*, G. Nichols

INSTITUTION OF PROFESSIONALS, MANAGERS AND SPECIALISTS (77,500), 75–79 York Road, London se1 7AQ. Tel: 0171-902 6600. *General Secretary*, W. Brett

IRON AND STEEL TRADES CONFEDERATION (50,100), Swinton House, 324 Gray's Inn Road, London wc1X 8DD. Tel: 0171-837 6691. *General Secretary*, D. K. Brookman

MANAGERIAL AND PROFESSIONAL OFFICERS UNION (12,000), Terminus House, The High, Harlow, Essex cm20 1TZ. Tel: 01279-434444. *General Secretary*, G. Corless

MANUFACTURING, SCIENCE AND FINANCE UNION (MSF) (425,000), MSF Centre, 33–37 Moreland Street, London ec1V 8BB. Tel: 0171-505 3000. *General Secretary*, R. Lyons

MILITARY AND ORCHESTRAL MUSICAL INSTRUMENT MAKERS TRADE SOCIETY (62), 2 Whitehouse Avenue, Borehamwood, Herts wD6 1HD. *General Secretary*, F. McKenzie

MUSICIANS' UNION (30,000), 60–62 Clapham Road, London sw9 0JJ. Tel: 0171-582 5566. *General Secretary*, D. Scard

NASUWT (NATIONAL ASSOCIATION OF SCHOOLMASTERS/UNION OF WOMEN TEACHERS) (165,000), 5 King Street, London wc2E 8HN. Tel: 0171-379 9499. *General Secretary*, N. de Gruchy

NATFHE (THE UNIVERSITY AND COLLEGE LECTURERS UNION) (70,000), 27 Britannia Street, London wc1X 9JP. Tel: 0171-837 3636. *General Secretary*, D.Betts (acting)

NATIONAL ASSOCIATION OF COLLIERY OVERMEN, DEPUTIES AND SHOTFIRERS (1,000), Simpson House, 48 Nether Hall Road, Doncaster dN1 2PZ. Tel: 01302-368015. *Secretary*, P. McNestry

NATIONAL ASSOCIATION OF CO-OPERATIVE OFFICIALS (3,232), Coronation House, Arndale Centre, Manchester m4 2HW. Tel: 0161-834 6029. *General Secretary*, L. W. Ewing

NATIONAL ASSOCIATION OF LICENSED HOUSE MANAGERS (6,000), Carlton House, 7 Wilson Patten Street, Warrington, Cheshire wa1 1PG. Tel: 01925-244888. *General Secretary*, P. Love

NATIONAL ASSOCIATION OF PROBATION OFFICERS (7,500), 3–4 Chivalry Road, London sw11 1HT. Tel: 0171-223 4887. *General Secretary*, Ms J. McKnight

NATIONAL LEAGUE OF THE BLIND AND DISABLED (2,200), 2 Tenterden Road, London n17 8BE. Tel: 0181-808 6030. *General Secretary*, J. Mann

NATIONAL UNION OF DOMESTIC APPLIANCES AND GENERAL OPERATIVES (2,400), 6–8 Imperial Buildings, Corporation Street, Rotherham, S. Yorks s60 1PB. Tel: 01709-382820. *General Secretary*, A. McCarthy

NATIONAL UNION OF INSURANCE WORKERS (10,200), 27 Old Gloucester Street, London wc1N 3AF. Tel: 0171-405 6798. *General Secretary*, K. Perry

NATIONAL UNION OF JOURNALISTS (NUJ) (27,000), Acorn House, 314–320 Gray's Inn Road, London wc1X 8DP. Tel: 0171-278 7916. *General Secretary*, J. Foster

NATIONAL UNION OF KNITWEAR, FOOTWEAR AND APPAREL TRADES (40,000), 55 New Walk, Leicester le1 7EB. Tel: 0116-255 6703. *General Secretary*, P. Gates

NATIONAL UNION OF LOCK AND METAL WORKERS (4,916), Bellamy House, Wilkes Street, Willenhall, W. Midlands wv13 2BS. Tel: 01902-366651. *General Secretary*, R. Ward

NATIONAL UNION OF MARINE, AVIATION AND SHIPPING TRANSPORT OFFICERS (18,000), Oceanair House, 750–760 High Road, London e11 3BB. Tel: 0181-989 6677. *General Secretary*, B. Orrell

NATIONAL UNION OF MINEWORKERS (NUM) (9,187), Miners' Offices, 2 Huddersfield Road, Barnsley, S. Yorks s70 2LS. Tel: 01226-215555. *President*, A. Scargill

NATIONAL UNION OF RAIL, MARITIME AND TRANSPORT WORKERS (RMT) (65,000), Unity House, Euston Road, London NW1 2BL. Tel: 0171-387 4771. *General Secretary*, J. Knapp

NATIONAL UNION OF TEACHERS (NUT) (188,213), Hamilton House, Mabledon Place, London WC1H 9BD. Tel: 0171-388 6191. *General Secretary*, D. McAvoy

NORTHERN CARPET TRADES' UNION (670), 22 Clare Road, Halifax HX1 2HX. Tel: 01422-360492. *General Secretary*, K. Edmondson

POWER LOOM CARPET WEAVERS' AND TEXTILE WORKERS' UNION (1,500), 148 Hurcott Road, Kidderminster, Worcs DY10 2RL. Tel: 01562-823192. *General Secretary*, G. Rudd

PRISON OFFICERS' ASSOCIATION (27,664), Cronin House, 245 Church Street, London N9 9HW. Tel: 0181-803 0255. *General Secretary*, D. Evans

PROFESSIONAL FOOTBALLERS ASSOCIATION (3,329), 2 Oxford Court, Bishopsgate, Manchester M2 3WQ. Tel: 0161-236 0575. *Chief Executive*, G. Taylor

PUBLIC SERVICES, TAX AND COMMERCE UNION (150,000), New Bridgewater House, 5–13 Great Suffolk Street, London SE1 0NS. Tel: 0171-960 3000. *Joint General Secretaries*, C. Brooke; J. Sheldon

SCOTTISH PRISON OFFICERS' ASSOCIATION (3,174), 21 Calder Road, Edinburgh EH11 3PF. Tel: 0131-443 8105. *General Secretary*, D. Turner

SCOTTISH UNION OF POWER-LOOM OVERLOOKERS (42), 3 Napier Terrace, Dundee DD2 2SL. Tel: 01382-612196. *Secretary*, J. D. Reilly

SHEFFIELD WOOL SHEAR WORKERS' UNION (11), 5 Collin Avenue, Sheffield S6 4ES. Tel: 0114-220 6748. *Secretary*, B. Bell

SOCIETY OF CHIROPODISTS AND PODIATRISTS (6,458), 53 Welbeck Street, London W1M 7HE. Tel: 0171-486 3381. *General Secretary*, J. G. C. Trouncer

THE SOCIETY OF RADIOGRAPHERS (13,000), 2 Carriage Row, 183 Eversholt Street, London NW1 1BU. Tel: 0171 391 4500. *General Secretary*, S. Evans

SOCIETY OF TELECOM EXECUTIVES (17,000), 1 Park Road, Teddington, Middx TW11 0AR. Tel: 0181-943 5181. *General Secretary*, S. Petch

TRANSPORT AND GENERAL WORKERS' UNION (TGWU) (882,392), 16 Palace Street, London SW1E 5JD. Tel: 0171-828 7788. *General Secretary*, W. Morris

TRANSPORT SALARIED STAFFS' ASSOCIATION (33,000), Walkden House, 10 Melton Street, London NW1 2EJ. Tel: 0171-387 2101. *General Secretary*, R. A. Rosser

UNDEB CENEDLAETHOL ATHRAWON CYMRU (NATIONAL ASSOCIATION OF TEACHERS OF WALES) (4,200), Pen Roc, Rhodfa'r Môr, Aberystwyth, Ceredigion SY23 2AZ. Tel: 01970-615577. *General Secretary*, G. W. James

UNIFI (47,000), Oathall House, Oathall Road, Haywards Heath, W. Sussex RH16 3DG. Tel: 01444-458811. *General Secretary*, J. P. S. Snowball

UNION OF CONSTRUCTION, ALLIED TRADES AND TECHNICIANS (UCATT) (117,000), UCATT House, 177 Abbeville Road, London SW4 9RL. Tel: 0171-622 2442. *Secretary*, G. Brumwell

UNION OF SHOP, DISTRIBUTIVE AND ALLIED WORKERS (USDAW) (292,872), Oakley, 188 Wilmslow Road, Fallowfield, Manchester M14 6LJ. Tel: 0161-224 2804. *Secretary*, D. G. Davies, CBE

UNION OF TEXTILE WORKERS (1,600), 18 West Street, Leek, Staffs ST13 8AA. Tel: 01538-382068. *General Secretary*, A. Hitchmough

UNISON (1,300,000), 1 Mabledon Place, London WC1H 9AJ. Tel: 0171-388 2366. *General Secretary*, R. Bickerstaffe

UNITED ROAD TRANSPORT UNION (17,000), 76 High Lane, Chorlton-cum-Hardy, Manchester M21 9EF. Tel: 0161-881 6245. *General Secretary*, D. Higginbottom

WRITERS' GUILD OF GREAT BRITAIN (2,400), 430 Edgware Road, London W2 1EH. Tel: 0171 723 8074. *General Secretary*, Ms A. Gray

MERGERS

In 1996–7 the Rossendale Union of Boot, Shoe and Slipper Operatives merged with the National Union of Knitwear, Footwear and Apparel Trades.

NON-AFFILIATED TRADE UNIONS

ASSOCIATION OF TEACHERS AND LECTURERS (160,000), 7 Northumberland Street, London WC2N 5DA. Tel: 0171-930 6441. *General Secretary*, P. Smith

BRITISH DENTAL ASSOCIATION (16,000), 64 Wimpole Street, London W1M 8AL. Tel: 0171-935 0875. *Chief Executive*, J. M. G. Hunt

CHARTERED INSTITUTE OF JOURNALISTS (1,200), 2 Dock Offices, Surrey Quays Road, London SE16 2XU. Tel: 0171-252 1187. *General Secretary*, C. Underwood

GOVERNMENT COMMUNICATIONS STAFF FEDERATION (2,200), Room A0904A, Priors Road, Cheltenham, Glos GL52 5AJ. Tel: 01242-573906. *Chairman*, B. Moore

NATIONAL ASSOCIATION OF HEAD TEACHERS (NAHT) (32,000), 1 Heath Square, Boltro Road, Haywards Heath, W. Sussex RH16 1BL. Tel: 01444-472472. *General Secretary*, D. Hart, OBE

NATIONAL SOCIETY FOR EDUCATION IN ART AND DESIGN (2,500), The Gatehouse, Corsham Court, Corsham, Wilts SN13 0BZ. Tel: 01249-714825. *General Secretary*, Dr J. H. M. Steers

PATTERN WEAVERS SOCIETY (48), 20 Hayfield Avenue, Oakes, Huddersfield HD3 4FZ. Tel: 01484-656886. *Secretary*, D. Mellor

PRISON GOVERNORS ASSOCIATION (1,000), Room 409, Horseferry House, Dean Ryle Street, London SW1P 2AW. Tel: 0171-217 8591. *General Secretary*, D. Roddan

RETAIL BOOK, STATIONERY AND ALLIED TRADES EMPLOYEES' ASSOCIATION (6,000), 8-9 Commercial Road, Swindon SN1 5RB. Tel: 01793-615811. *President*, A. Willmott

ROYAL COLLEGE OF MIDWIVES (37,000), 15 Mansfield Street, London W1M 0BE. Tel: 0171-872 5100. *General Secretary*, Mrs K. Davis

SCOTTISH SECONDARY TEACHERS' ASSOCIATION (7,116), 15 Dundas Street, Edinburgh EH3 6QG. Tel: 0131-556 5919. *General Secretary*, D. H. Eaglesham

SECONDARY HEADS ASSOCIATION (8,758), 130 Regent Road, Leicester LE1 7PG. Tel: 0116 247 1797. *General Secretary*, J. Sutton, CBE

SOCIETY OF AUTHORS (6,200), 84 Drayton Gardens, London SW10 9SB. Tel: 0171-373 6642. *General Secretary*, M. Le Fanu, OBE

National Academies of Scholarship

THE BRITISH ACADEMY (1901)
20–21 Cornwall Terrace, London NW1 4QP
Tel 0171-487 5966
(10 Carlton House Terrace, London SW1Y 5AH, from late 1997)

The British Academy is an independent, self-governing learned society for the promotion of historical, philosophical and philological studies. It supports advanced academic research in the humanities and social sciences, and is a channel for the Government's support of research in those disciplines. The Humanities Research Board is responsible for the administration of the majority of the Academy's grant programmes.

The Fellows are scholars who have attained distinction in one of the branches of study that the Academy exists to promote. Candidates must be nominated by existing Fellows. At 1 June 1997 there were 650 Fellows, 14 Honorary Fellows, and 312 Corresponding Fellows overseas.

President, Sir Tony Wrigley, PBA
Vice-Presidents and Honorary Officers, Prof. R. R. Davies, FBA; J. S. Flemming, FBA; Prof. M. M. McGowan, FBA; Prof. F. G. B. Millar, FBA; Prof. B. E. Supple, FBA
Chairman, Humanities Research Board, Prof. J. D. M. H. Laver, FBA
Secretary, P. W. H. Brown, CBE

THE ROYAL ACADEMY (1768)
Burlington House, London W1V 0DS
Tel 0171-439 7438

The Royal Academy of Arts is an independent, self-governing society devoted to the encouragement and promotion of the fine arts.

Membership of the Academy is limited to 80 Royal Academicians, all being painters, engravers, sculptors or architects. Candidates are nominated and elected by the existing Academicians. There is also a limited class of honorary membership and there were 14 honorary members as at mid-1997.

President, Sir Philip Dowson, CBE, PRA
Treasurer, M. Kenny, RA
Keeper, L. McComb, RA
Secretary, D. Gordon

THE ROYAL ACADEMY OF ENGINEERING (1976)
29 Great Peter Street, London SW1P 3LW
Tel 0171-222 2688

The Royal Academy of Engineering was established as the Fellowship of Engineering in 1976. It was granted a Royal Charter in 1983 and its present title in 1992. It is an independent, self-governing body whose object is the pursuit, encouragement and maintenance of excellence in the whole field of engineering, in order to promote the advancement of the science, art and practice of engineering for the benefit of the public.

Election to the Fellowship is by invitation only from nominations supported by the body of Fellows. Fellows are chosen from among chartered engineers of all disciplines. At July 1997 there were 1,062 Fellows, 17 Honorary Fellows and 71 Foreign Members. The Duke of Edinburgh is the Senior Fellow and the Duke of Kent is a Royal Fellow.

President, Sir David Davies, CBE, FRS, F.Eng
Senior Vice-President, B. R. R. Butler, CBE, F.Eng
Vice-Presidents, Dr J. R. Forrest, F.Eng; Sir Gordon Higginson, F.Eng; S. N. Mustow, CBE, F.Eng
Hon. Treasurer, J. W. Herbert, F.Eng
Hon. Secretaries, P. N. Paul, F.Eng (*Civil Engineering*); Prof. J. M. Brady FRS, F.Eng (*Electrical Engineering*); Prof. P. Braiden, F.Eng (*Mechanical Engineering*); J. R. Darley, F.Eng (*Process Engineering*); B. R. R. Butler, CBE, F.Eng (*International Activities*); Dr J. R. Forrest, F.Eng (*Education, Training and Competence to Practise*)
Executive Secretary, J. R. Appleton

THE ROYAL SCOTTISH ACADEMY (1838)
The Mound, Edinburgh EH2 2EL
Tel 0131-225 6671

The Scottish Academy was founded in 1826 to arrange exhibitions for contemporary paintings and to establish a society of fine art in Scotland. The Academy was granted a Royal Charter in 1838.

Members are elected from the disciplines of painting, sculpture, architecture and printmaking. Elections are from nominations put forward by the existing membership. At mid-1997 there were eight Senior Academicians, four Senior Associates, 36 Academicians, 44 Associates, three non-resident Associates and 23 Honorary Members.

President, W. J. L. Baillie, PRSA
Secretary, I. McKenzie Smith, RSA
Treasurer, J. Morris, RSA
Librarian, P. Collins, RSA
Administrative Secretary, B. Laidlaw

ROYAL SOCIETY (1660)
6 Carlton House Terrace, London SW1Y 5AG
Tel 0171-839 5561

The Royal Society is the United Kingdom academy of science. It is an independent, self-governing body under a Royal Charter, promoting and advancing all fields of physical and biological sciences, of mathematics and engineering, medical and agricultural sciences, their applications and place in society.

Election to Fellowship of the Royal Society is limited to those distinguished for original scientific work. Each year up to 40 new Fellows and six Foreign Members are elected from the most distinguished scientists. In addition, the Council can recommend for election members of the Royal family and, on average, one person each year for conspicuous service to the cause of science. At June 1997, there were 1,152 Fellows, 108 Foreign Members and six Royal Fellows or Patrons.

President, Sir Aaron Klug, OM, PRS
Treasurer, Sir John Horlock, FRS, F.Eng

Biological Secretary, Prof. P. J. Lachmann, FRS
Physical Secretary, Prof. J. S. Rowlinson, FRS, F.Eng
Foreign Secretary, Prof. R. B. Heap, CBE, FRS
Executive Secretary, S. Cox

THE ROYAL SOCIETY OF EDINBURGH
(1783)
22–24 George Street, Edinburgh EH2 2PQ
Tel 0131-225 6057

The Royal Society of Edinburgh is Scotland's premier learned society. The Society was founded by Royal Charter in 1783 for 'the advancement of learning and useful knowledge', and its principal role is the promotion of scholarship in all its branches. It provides a forum for broadly-based interdisciplinary activity in Scotland, including organizing public lectures, conferences and specialist research seminars; providing advice to Parliament and government; administering a range of research fellowships held in Scotland; and publishing learned journals.

Fellows are elected by ballot after being nominated by at least four existing Fellows. At 30 April 1997 there were 1,137 Ordinary Fellows and 67 Honorary Fellows.

President, Prof. M. A. Jeeves, CBE
Treasurer, Sir Lewis Robertson, CBE, FRSE
General Secretary, Prof. P. N. Wilson, CBE
Executive Secretary, Dr W. Duncan

Royal Academicians

*Senior Academician

1989 Abrahams, Ivor	1990 Draper, Kenneth	1975 Levene, Ben
1988 Ackroyd, Prof. Norman	1959 *Dunstan, Bernard	1987 McComb, Leonard
1967 Adams, Norman	1994 Durrant, Jennifer	1993 MacCormac, Richard, CBE
1978 Aitchison, Craigie	1976 Eyton, Anthony	1947 *Machin, Arnold, OBE
1989 *Armfield, Diana	1992 *Fedden, Mary	1995 Maine, John
1994 *Armitage, Kenneth	1987 Flanagan, Barry, OBE	1976 *Manasseh, Leonard, OBE
1982 Ayres, Gillian, OBE	1983 Foster, Sir Norman	1994 Manser, Michael
1986 Bellany, John, CBE	1975 Fraser, Donald Hamilton	1985 *Martin, Sir Leslie
1992 Berg, Adrian	1990 Freeth, Peter	1991 Mistry, Dhruva
1971 Blackadder, Elizabeth, OBE	1992 *Frost, Terry	1994 Moon, Mick
1974 Blake, Peter, CBE	1964 *Gore, Frederick, CBE	1992 Neiland, Prof. Brendan
1970 *Blamey, Norman	1971 Green, Anthony	1995 Orr, Christopher
1971 Blow, Sandra	1994 Grimshaw, Nicholas	1979 Paolozzi, Sir Eduardo, CBE
1970 Bowey, Olwyn	1963 *Hayes, Colin	1980 Partridge, John, CBE
1974 Bowyer, William	1990 *Herman, Josef, OBE	1983 *Pasmore, Victor, CH, CBE
1968 Brown, Ralph	1985 Hockney, David	1984 Phillips, Tom
1964 Butler, James	1974 *Hogarth, Paul, OBE	1972 *Powell, Sir Philip, CH, OBE
1971 *Cadbury-Brown, Prof. H. T., OBE	1992 Hopkins, Sir Michael, CBE	1996 Procktor, Patrick
	1983 Howard, Ken	1978 Rogers, Sir Richard
1974 Camp, Jeffery	1983 Hoyland, John	1990 Rooney, Michael
1962 *Casson, Sir Hugh, CH, KCVO	1987 Huxley, Prof. Paul	1960 *Rosoman, Leonard, OBE
1993 Caulfield, Patrick, CBE	1996 *Irwin, Flavia	1982 Sandle, Prof. Michael*
1980 Christopher, Ann	1989 Jacklin, Bill	1975 Stephenson, Ian
1970 Clarke, Geoffrey	1997 Jiricna, Eva	1977 Sutton, Philip
1968 Clatworthy, Robert	1981 Jones, Allen	1985 Tilson, Joe
1965 Coker, Peter	1976 Kenny, Michael	1973 Tindle, David
1965 Cooke, Jean	1996 *Kestelman, Morris	1986 Titchell, John
1994 Cragg, Prof. Tony	1989 Kiff, Ken	1992 Tucker, William
1993 Craxton, John	1977 King, Prof. Phillip, CBE	1956 *Ward, John, CBE
1989 Cullinan, Edward, CBE	1984 Kitaj, R. B.	1900 Whishaw, Anthony
1969 Cuming, Frederick	1970 Kneale, Bryan	1970 *Williams, Kyffin, OBE
1992 Cummins, Gus	1986 Koralek, Paul, CBE	1990 Wilson, Colin St J.
1977 *Dannatt, Prof. Trevor	1991 *Lasdun, Sir Dennis, CBE	1983 Wragg, John
1970 Dickson, Jennifer	1982 Lawson, Sonia	*Resigned Sept 1997
1979 Dowson, Sir Philip, CBE	1996 Le Brun, Christopher	

The Research Councils

The Government funds basic and applied civil science research, mostly through the seven research councils, which are supported by the Department of Trade and Industry. The councils support research and training in universities and other higher education establishments. They also receive income for research commissioned by government departments and the private sector.

The Government science budget for 1997–8 was £1,330.327 million in total and included the following allocations:

	£m
BBSRC	183.30
CCLRC	1.45
ESRC	64.89
EPSRC	386.37
MRC	289.07
NERC	165.11
PPARC	191.85
Royal Society	22.27
Royal Academy of Engineering	3.37
OST initiatives	2.30

BIOTECHNOLOGY AND BIOLOGICAL SCIENCES RESEARCH COUNCIL (BBSRC)
Polaris House, North Star Avenue, Swindon SN2 1UH Tel 01793-413200

The BBSRC promotes and supports research and postgraduate training relating to the understanding and exploitation of biological systems; advances knowledge and technology, and provides trained scientists to meet the needs of biotechnological-related industries; and provides advice, disseminates knowledge, and promotes public understanding of biotechnology and the biological sciences.
Chairman, Sir Alistair Grant, FRSE
Chief Executive, Prof. R. Baker, FRS

INSTITUTES

BABRAHAM INSTITUTE
Director, Dr R. G. Dyer, Babraham Hall, Babraham, Cambridge CB2 4AT. Tel: 01223-832312

INSTITUTE FOR ANIMAL HEALTH
Director, Dr C. J. Bostock, Compton, Newbury, Berks RG20 7NN. Tel: 01635-577237

BBSRC AND MRC NEUROPATHOGENESIS UNIT, Ogston Building, West Mains Road, Edinburgh EH9 3JF. Tel: 0131-667 5204/5. *Head*, Dr C. J. Bostock
COMPTON LABORATORY, Compton, Newbury, Berks RG20 7NN. Tel: 01635-578411. *Divisional Head in Charge*, Dr P. W. Jones
PIRBRIGHT LABORATORY, Ash Road, Pirbright, Woking, Surrey GU24 0NF. Tel: 01483-232441. *Head*, Dr A. I. Donaldson

INSTITUTE OF ARABLE CROPS RESEARCH
Director, Prof. B. J. Miflin, Rothamsted, Harpenden, Herts AL5 2JQ. Tel: 01582-763133
IACR – BROOM'S BARN, Higham, Bury St Edmunds, Suffolk IP28 6NP. Tel: 01284-810363. *Head*, Dr J. D. Pidgeon

IACR – LONG ASHTON RESEARCH STATION, Department of Agricultural Sciences, University of Bristol, Long Ashton, Bristol BS18 9AF. Tel: 01275-392181. *Head*, Prof. P. R. Shewry
IACR – ROTHAMSTED, Harpenden, Herts AL5 2JQ. Tel: 01582-763133. *Head*, Prof. B. J. Miflin.

INSTITUTE OF FOOD RESEARCH
Director, Prof. A. D. B. Malcolm, Earley Gate, Whiteknights Road, Reading RG6 6BZ. Tel: 01189-357055
NORWICH LABORATORY, Norwich Research Park, Colney Lane, Norwich NR4 7UA. Tel: 01603-255000. *Deputy Director and Head of Laboratory*, Prof. P. S. Belton
READING LABORATORY, Earley Gate, Whiteknights Road, Reading RG6 6BZ. Tel: 01189-357000. *Deputy Director and Head of Laboratory*, Prof. H. J. H. MacFie

INSTITUTE OF GRASSLAND AND ENVIRONMENTAL RESEARCH
Director, Prof. C. J. Pollock, Plas Gogerddan, Aberystwyth, Ceredigion SY23 3EB. Tel: 01970-828255
ABERYSTWYTH RESEARCH CENTRE, Plas Gogerddan, Aberystwyth, Ceredigion SY23 3EB. Tel: 01970-828255
NORTH WYKE RESEARCH STATION, Okehampton, Devon EX20 2SB. Tel: 01837-82558. *Head*, Prof. R. J. Wilkins

JOHN INNES CENTRE
Director, Prof. R. B. Flavell, Norwich Research Park, Colney, Norwich NR4 7UH. Tel: 01603-452571

ROSLIN INSTITUTE
Director, Prof. G. Bulfield, Roslin, Midlothian EH25 9PS. Tel: 0131-527 4200

SILSOE RESEARCH INSTITUTE
Director, Prof. B. J. Legg, Wrest Park, Silsoe, Bedford MK45 4HS. Tel: 01525-860000

INTERDISCIPLINARY RESEARCH CENTRES

ADVANCED CENTRE FOR BIOCHEMICAL ENGINEERING
Director, Prof. P. Dunnill, FEng., University College London, Torrington Place, London WC1E 7JE. Tel: 0171-380 7031
CENTRE FOR GENOME RESEARCH
Director (acting), Dr A. Smith, University of Edinburgh, King's Buildings, West Mains Road, Edinburgh EH9 3JQ. Tel: 0131-650 5890
OXFORD CENTRE FOR MOLECULAR SCIENCES
Director, Prof. J. E. Baldwin, FRS, New Chemistry Laboratory, University of Oxford, South Parks Road, Oxford OX1 3QT. Tel: 01865-275654
SUSSEX CENTRE FOR NEUROSCIENCE
Director, Prof. M. O'Shea, School of Biological Sciences, University of Sussex, Brighton BN1 9QG. Tel: 01273-678055

SCOTTISH AGRICULTURAL AND BIOLOGICAL RESEARCH INSTITUTES

HANNAH RESEARCH INSTITUTE, Ayr KA6 5HL. Tel: 01292-476013. *Director*, Prof. M. Peaker, FRS

MACAULAY LAND USE RESEARCH INSTITUTE,
Craigiebuckler, Aberdeen AB15 8QH. Tel: 01224-318611.
Director, Prof. T. J. Maxwell, FRSE
MOREDUN RESEARCH INSTITUTE, 408 Gilmerton Road,
Edinburgh EH17 7JH. Tel: 0131-664 3262. *Director*, Prof.
Q. A. McKellar
ROWETT RESEARCH INSTITUTE, Greenburn Road,
Bucksburn, Aberdeen AB21 9SB. Tel: 01224-712751.
Director, Prof. W. P. T. James, CBE, FRSE
SCOTTISH CROP RESEARCH INSTITUTE (SCRI),
Invergowrie, Dundee DD2 5DA. Tel: 01382-562731.
Director, Prof. J. Hillman, FRSE
BIOMATHEMATICS AND STATISTICS SCOTLAND
(BioSS) (Administered by SCRI), University of
Edinburgh, James Clerk Maxwell Building, The King's
Buildings, Mayfield Road, Edinburgh EH9 3JZ. Tel: 0131-
650 4900. *Director*, R. A. Kempton

COUNCIL FOR THE CENTRAL LABORATORY OF THE RESEARCH COUNCILS (CCLRC)
Chilton, Didcot, Oxon OX11 0QX
Tel 01235-821900

The CCLRC was set up in April 1995 and is responsible for
the Daresbury and Rutherford Appleton Laboratories,
which provide advanced facilities and specialist expertise
to support academic and industrial research in the physical
and life sciences.
Chairman and Chief Executive, Dr P. R. Williams, CBE

DARESBURY LABORATORY, Daresbury, Warrington,
Cheshire WA4 4AD. Tel: 01925-603000
RUTHERFORD APPLETON LABORATORY, Chilton, Didcot,
Oxon OX11 0QX. Tel: 01235-821900

ECONOMIC AND SOCIAL RESEARCH COUNCIL (ESRC)
Polaris House, North Star Avenue, Swindon SN2 1UJ
Tel 01793-413000

The purpose of the ESRC is to promote and support
research and postgraduate training in the social sciences; to
advance knowledge and provide trained social scientists; to
provide advice on, and disseminate knowledge and
promote public understanding of, the social sciences.
Chairman, Dr B. Smith, OBE
Chief Executive, Prof. R. Amann

RESEARCH CENTRES

CAMBRIDGE GROUP FOR THE HISTORY OF POPULATION
AND SOCIAL STRUCTURE, 27 Trumpington Street,
Cambridge CB2 1QA. Tel: 01223-333181. *Director*, Prof.
R. Smith
CENTRE FOR BUSINESS RESEARCH, Department of
Applied Economics, University of Cambridge,
Sidgwick Avenue, Cambridge CB3 9DE. Tel: 01223-
335248. *Director*, A. Hughes
CENTRE FOR ECONOMIC LEARNING AND SOCIAL
EVOLUTION, Department of Economics, University
College London, 8 Alfred Place, London WC1E 6BT. Tel:
0171-380 7027. *Research Director*, Prof. K. Binmore
CENTRE FOR ECONOMIC PERFORMANCE, London School
of Economics, Houghton Street, London WC2A 2AE. Tel:
0171-955 7284. *Director*, Prof. R. Layard

CENTRE FOR HOUSING RESEARCH AND URBAN STUDIES,
Department of Urban Studies, University of Glasgow,
25 Bute Gardens, Glasgow G12 8RS. Tel: 0141-330 4121.
Director, Prof. P. A. Kemp
CENTRE FOR FISCAL POLICY, Institute for Fiscal Studies,
7 Ridgmount Street, London WC1E 7AE. Tel: 0171-636
3784. *Director*, Prof. R. Blundell
CENTRE FOR INTERNATIONAL EMPLOYMENT RELATIONS
RESEARCH, School of Industrial and Business Studies,
University of Warwick, Coventry CV4 7AL. Tel: 01203-
524265. *Director*, Prof. K. Sisson
CENTRE FOR ORGANIZATION AND INNOVATION, Institute
of Work Psychology, University of Sheffield, Sheffield
S10 2TN. Tel: 0114-276 5656. *Director*, Prof. T. Wall
CENTRE FOR RESEARCH IN DEVELOPMENT,
INSTRUCTION AND TRAINING, Department of
Psychology, University of Nottingham, Nottingham
NG7 2RD. Tel: 0115-951 5311. *Director*, Prof. D. J. Wood
CENTRE FOR RESEARCH IN ETHNIC RELATIONS,
University of Warwick, Coventry CV4 7AL. Tel: 01203-
523523. *Director*, Prof. Z. Layton-Henry
CENTRE FOR RESEARCH INTO ELECTIONS AND SOCIAL
TRENDS, Social and Community Planning Research,
35 Northampton Square, London EC1V 0AX. Tel: 0171-
250 1866. *Director*, Prof. R. Jowell
CENTRE FOR RESEARCH INTO SOCIAL INTEGRATION AND
EXCLUSION, London School of Economics, Houghton
Street, London WC2A 2AE. Tel: 0171-405 7686. *Director*, J.
Hills
CENTRE FOR RESEARCH ON INNOVATION AND
COMPETITION, Faculty of Economic and Social
Studies, University of Manchester M13 9PL. Tel: 0161-
275 2000. *Director*, Prof. S. Metcalfe; Manchester School
of Management, UMIST, Manchester M60 1QD. Tel:
0161-236 3311. *Director*, Prof. R. Coombs
CENTRE FOR SOCIAL AND ECONOMIC RESEARCH ON THE
GLOBAL ENVIRONMENT, School of Environmental
Sciences, University of East Anglia, Norwich NR4 7TJ.
Tel: 01603-593176. *Director*, Prof. K. Turner
CENTRE FOR THE STUDY OF AFRICAN ECONOMIES,
Institute of Economics and Statistics, University of
Oxford, St Cross Building, Manor Road, Oxford OX1 3UL.
Tel: 01865-271084. *Director*, Prof. P. Collier
CENTRE FOR THE STUDY OF GLOBALIZATION AND
REGIONALIZATION, Department of Political Science,
University of Warwick, Coventry CV4 7AL. Tel: 01203-
523916. *Director*, Prof. R. Higgott
CENTRE ON SCIENCE, TECHNOLOGY, ENERGY AND
ENVIRONMENT POLICY, SPRU, Mantell Building,
Falmer, Brighton BN1 9RF. Tel: 01273-686758. *Director*,
Ms. M. Sharp
COMPLEX PRODUCT SYSTEM INNOVATION CENTRE,
SPRU, Mantell Building, University of Sussex, Brighton
BN1 9RF. Tel: 01273-686758. *Director*, Dr M. Hobday;
CENTRIM, University of Brighton, Brighton BN1 9PH.
Tel: 01273-642188. *Director*, H. Rush
FINANCIAL MARKETS CENTRE, London School of
Economics, Houghton Street, London WC2A 2AE. Tel:
0171-955 7275. *Director*, Prof. D. Webb
HUMAN COMMUNICATION RESEARCH CENTRE,
University of Edinburgh, 2 Buccleuch Place, Edinburgh
EH8 9LW. Tel: 0131-650 4444. *Director*, Prof. K. Stenning
RESEARCH CENTRE ON MICRO-SOCIAL CHANGE,
University of Essex, Wivenhoe Park, Colchester, Essex
CO4 3SQ. Tel: 01206-872957. *Director*, Prof. J. Gershuny
TRANSPORT STUDIES UNIT, Centre for Transport
Studies, University College London, Gower Street,
London WC1E 6BT. Tel: 0171-391 1580. *Director*, Dr
P. Goodwin

RESOURCE CENTRES

BUSINESS PROCESS RESOURCE CENTRE, Warwick Manufacturing Group, University of Warwick, Coventry cv4 7AL. Tel: 01203-524173. *Director,* Dr S. Manton

CENTRE FOR APPLIED SOCIAL SURVEYS, Social and Community Planning Research, 35 Northampton Square, London ECIV OAX. Tel: 0171-250 1866. *Director,* R. Thomas

CENTRE FOR ECONOMIC POLICY RESEARCH, 25–28 Old Burlington Street, London WIX ILB. Tel: 0171-734 9110. *Director,* Prof. R. Portes

ESRC DATA ARCHIVE, University of Essex, Wivenhoe Park, Colchester, Essex co4 3SQ. Tel: 01206-872006. *Director,* Prof. D. Lievesley

INTERNATIONAL BIBLIOGRAPHY OF THE SOCIAL SCIENCES, British Library of Political and Economic Science, London School of Economics, Houghton Street, London WC2A 2AE. Tel: 0171-955 7000. *Director,* Ms L. Brindley

QUALITATIVE DATA ARCHIVAL RESOURCE CENTRE, Department of Sociology, University of Essex, Wivenhoe Park, Colchester, Essex co4 3SQ. Tel: 01206-873333. *Director,* Prof. P. Thompson

RESOURCE CENTRE FOR ACCESS TO DATA IN EUROPE, Department of Geography, University of Durham, Durham DHI 3HP. Tel: 0191-374 7350. *Director,* Prof. R. Hudson

ENGINEERING AND PHYSICAL SCIENCES RESEARCH COUNCIL (EPSRC)
Polaris House, North Star Avenue, Swindon SN2 IET
Tel 01793-444000

The purpose of the EPSRC is to encourage and support all basic and strategic research and training in UK higher education institutions in the natural and physical sciences and engineering. It no longer has any research institutions. *Chairman,* Dr A. Rudge, OBE, FRS, F.Eng. *Chief Executive,* Prof. R. Brook, OBE

INTERDISCIPLINARY RESEARCH CENTRES

The EPSRC supports eight interdisciplinary research centres (IRCs) based at universities throughout the UK and specializing in strategic research areas. These were originally funded for a ten-year period (which expires in 1998 for the first IRC and 2000 for the last). It is envisaged that after the ten-year period the IRCs will seek funding from the EPSRC as well as obtaining money from other sources, e.g. industry, to make up their budgets.

CENTRE FOR PROCESS SYSTEMS ENGINEERING – University College and Imperial College, London

IRC FOR SEMICONDUCTOR MATERIALS – Imperial College London, Universities of Oxford and Sheffield, University College London

IRC IN BIOMEDICAL MATERIALS – Queen Mary and Westfield College, London Hospital Medical College, Royal Free Hospital School of Medicine, Royal National Orthopaedic Hospital

IRC IN MATERIALS FOR HIGH PERFORMANCE APPLICATIONS – Universities of Birmingham and Swansea

IRC IN SUPERCONDUCTIVITY – University of Cambridge

OPTOELECTRONICS RESEARCH CENTRE – University of Southampton

POLYMER SCIENCE AND TECHNOLOGY IRC – Universities of Bradford, Leeds and Durham

SURFACE SCIENCE IRC – Universities of Liverpool and Manchester

MEDICAL RESEARCH COUNCIL (MRC)
20 Park Crescent, London WIN 4AL
Tel 0171-636 5422

The purpose of the MRC is to promote medical and related biological research. The council employs its own research staff and funds research by other institutions and individuals, complementing the research resources of the universities and hospitals. *Chairman,* Sir David Plastow *Chief Executive,* Prof. G. K. Radda, CBE, D.phil., FRS *Chairman, Neurosciences and Mental Health Board,* Dr T. W. Robbins *Chairman, Molecular and Cellular Medicine Board,* Prof. L. K. Borysiewicz *Chairman, Physiological Medicine and Infections Board,* Prof. A. M. McGregor, MD, FRCP *Chairman, Health Services and Public Health Research Board,* Prof. A. Haines

NATIONAL INSTITUTE FOR MEDICAL RESEARCH, The Ridgeway, Mill Hill, London NW7 IAA. Tel: 0181-959 3666. *Director,* Sir John Skehel, PH.D., FRS

CLINICAL SCIENCES CENTRE, Royal Postgraduate Medical School, Du Cane Road, London W12 ONN. Tel: 0181-743 2030. *Assistant Director,* J. E. Cope, PH.D.

LABORATORY OF MOLECULAR BIOLOGY, Hills Road, Cambridge CB2 2QH. Tel: 01223-248011. *Director,* R. Henderson, PH.D., FRS

RESEARCH UNITS

ANATOMICAL NEUROPHARMACOLOGY UNIT, Mansfield Road, Oxford OXI 3TH. Tel: 01865-271865. *Hon. Director,* Prof. A. D. Smith, D.Phil.

APPLIED PSYCHOLOGY UNIT, 15 Chaucer Road, Cambridge CB2 2EF. Tel: 01223-355294. *Director (acting),* Sir Dai Rees, FRS

BBSRC/MRC NEUROPATHOGENESIS UNIT, Ogston Building, West Mains Road, Edinburgh EH9 3JF. Tel: 0131-667 5204. *Director,* J. Bourne

BIOCHEMICAL AND CLINICAL MAGNETIC RESONANCE UNIT, University Department of Biochemistry, South Parks Road, Oxford OXI 3QU. Tel: 01865-275274. *Hon. Director,* P. Styles, D.phil.

BIOSTATISTICS UNIT, Institute of Public Health, University Forvie Site, Robinson Way, Cambridge CB2 2SR. Tel: 01223-330366. *Hon. Director,* Prof. N. E. Day, PH.D.

BRAIN METABOLISM UNIT, University Department of Pharmacology, 1 George Square, Edinburgh EH8 9JZ. Tel: 0131-650 3543. *Director,* Prof. G. Fink, MD, D.phil., FRSE

CANCER TRIALS OFFICE, 5 Shaftesbury Road, Cambridge CB2 2BW. Tel: 01223-311110

CELL MUTATION UNIT, University of Sussex, Falmer, Brighton BNI 9RR. Tel: 01273-678123. *Director,* Prof. B. A. Bridges, PH.D., FIBIOL.

CELLULAR IMMUNOLOGY UNIT, Sir William Dunn School of Pathology, Oxford OXI 3RE. Tel: 01865-275594. *Director (acting),* D. W. Mason

CENTRE FOR BRAIN REPAIR, E. D. Adrian Building, University Forvie Site, Robinson Way, Cambridge CB2 2PY. Tel: 01223-331160. *Chairman,* Prof. D. A. S. Compston, MD, FRCP

CENTRE FOR MECHANISMS OF HUMAN TOXICITY, Hodgkin Building, University of Leicester, PO Box 138, Lancaster Road, Leicester LE1 9HN. Tel: 0116-252 5525. *Director*, Prof. G. C. K. Roberts, ph.d.
CENTRE FOR MOLECULAR SCIENCES, New Chemistry Laboratory, South Parks Road, Oxford OX1 3QT. Tel: 01865-275627. *Director*, Prof. J. E. Baldwin, FRS
CENTRE FOR PROTEIN ENGINEERING, MRC Centre, Hills Road, Cambridge CB2 2QH. Tel: 01223-248011. *Director*, Prof. A. Fersht, ph.d., FRS
CHILD PSYCHIATRY UNIT, Institute of Psychiatry, De Crespigny Park, Denmark Hill, London SE5 8AF. Tel: 0171-703 5411. *Hon. Director*, Prof. Sir Michael Rutter, CBE, FRS, MD, FRCP, FRCPsych.
COGNITIVE DEVELOPMENT UNIT, 4 Taviton Street, London WC1H 0BT. Tel: 0171-387 4692. *Director*, Prof. J. Morton, ph.d.
CYCLOTRON UNIT, MRC Clinical Sciences Centre, RPMS Hammersmith Hospital, Du Cane Road, London W12 0NN. Tel: 0181-740 3162. *Director*, T. Jones, D.SC., MD
DUNN NUTRITION UNIT, Downhams Lane, Milton Road, Cambridge CB4 1XJ. Tel: 01223-426356. *Director*, R. G. Whitehead, CBE, ph.d.
ENVIRONMENTAL EPIDEMIOLOGY UNIT, Southampton General Hospital, Southampton SO16 6YD. Tel: 01703-777624. *Director*, Prof. D. J. P. Barker, MD, ph.d., FRCP, FRCOG
EPIDEMIOLOGY AND MEDICAL CARE UNIT, Wolfson Institute of Preventive Medicine, St Bartholomew's and the Royal London Hospital School of Medicine and Dentistry, Charterhouse Square, London EC1M 6BQ. Tel: 0171-982 6000. *Director*, Prof. T. W. Meade, CBE, DM, FRCP
HUMAN BIOCHEMICAL GENETICS UNIT, The Galton Laboratory, University College London, Wolfson House, 4 Stephenson Way, London NW1 2HE. Tel: 0171-387 7050. *Director*, Prof. D. A. Hopkinson, MD
HUMAN GENETICS UNIT, Western General Hospital, Crewe Road, Edinburgh EH4 2XU. Tel: 0131-332 2471. *Director*, Prof. N. D. Hastie, ph.d., FRSE
HUMAN GENOME MAPPING PROJECT RESOURCE CENTRE, Hinxton Hall, Hinxton, Cambridge CB10 1RQ. Tel: 01223-494500. *Manager*, K. Gibson, ph.d.
HUMAN MOVEMENT AND BALANCE UNIT, Institute of Neurology, National Hospital for Neurology and Neuro-surgery, Queen Square, London WC1 3BG. Tel: 0171-837 3611. *Hon. Director*, Prof. C. D. Marsden, D.SC., FRCP, FRS
IMMUNOCHEMISTRY UNIT, University Department of Biochemistry, South Parks Road, Oxford OX1 3QU. Tel: 01865-275354. *Director*, Prof. K. B. M. Reid, ph.d.
INSTITUTE FOR ENVIRONMENT AND HEALTH, University of Leicester, PO Box 138, Lancaster Road, Leicester LE1 9HN. Tel: 0116-223 1600. *Director*, Prof. L. Smith, ph.d.
INSTITUTE OF HEARING RESEARCH, University of Nottingham, Nottingham NG7 2RD. Tel: 0115-922 3431. *Director*, Prof. M. P. Haggard, ph.d.
INSTITUTE OF MOLECULAR MEDICINE, John Radcliffe Hospital, Headington, Oxford OX3 9DU. Tel: 01865-222443. *Hon. Director*, Prof. Sir David Weatherall, MD, FRCP, FRCPath., FRS
INTERDISCIPLINARY RESEARCH CENTRE FOR COGNITIVE NEURO-SCIENCE, University Laboratory of Physiology, Parks Road, Oxford OX1 3PT. Tel: 01865-272470. *Director*, Prof. C. Blakemore, FRS
INTERDISCIPLINARY RESEARCH CENTRE IN CELL BIOLOGY, MRC Laboratory for Molecular Cell Biology, University College London, Gower Street, London WC1E 6BT. Tel: 0171-380 7806. *Director*, Prof. C. R. Hopkins, ph.d.

MAMMALIAN GENETICS UNIT, Harwell Site, Chilton, Didcot, Oxon OX11 0RD. Tel: 01235-834393. *Director*, B. Cattanach, D.SC., FRS
MEDICAL SOCIOLOGY UNIT, 6 Lilybank Gardens, Glasgow G12 8QQ. Tel: 0141-357 3949. *Director*, Prof. S. Macintyre, ph.d.
MOLECULAR HAEMATOLOGY UNIT, Institute of Molecular Medicine, John Radcliffe Hospital, Headington, Oxford OX3 9DU. Tel: 01865-222359. *Hon. Director*, Prof. Sir David Weatherall, MD, FRCP, FRCPath., FRS
MOLECULAR IMMUNOPATHOLOGY UNIT, MRC Centre, University Medical School, Hills Road, Cambridge CB2 2QH. Tel: 01223-245133. *Hon. Director*, Prof. P. J. Lachmann, ph.d., SC.D., FRCP, FRCPath., FRS
MOUSE GENOME CENTRE, Harwell Site, Chilton, Didcot, Oxon OX11 0RD. Tel: 01235-834393. *Director*, Prof. S. Brown, ph.d.
MRC CENTRE, CAMBRIDGE, Hills Road, Cambridge CB2 2QH. Tel: 01223-248011. *Head of Centre*, M. B. Davies, ph.d.
MRC CENTRE, OXFORD, Manor House, John Radcliffe Hospital, Headington, Oxford OX3 9DU. Tel: 01865-222124. *Head of Centre*, D. McLaren, ph.d.
MRC LABORATORIES, THE GAMBIA, PO Box 273, Banjul, The Gambia, W. Africa. *Director*, Prof. K. McAdam, FRCP
MRC LABORATORIES, JAMAICA, University of the West Indies, Mona, Kingston 7, Jamaica. *Director*, Prof. G. R. Serjeant, CMG, MD, FRCP
MUSCLE AND CELL MOTILITY UNIT, Division of Biomedical Sciences, King's College London, 26–29 Drury Lane, London WC2B 5RL. Tel: 0171-836 8851. *Hon. Director*, Prof. R. M. Simmons, ph.d.
NEUROCHEMICAL PATHOLOGY UNIT, Newcastle General Hospital, Westgate Road, Newcastle upon Tyne NE4 6BE. Tel: 0191-273 5251. *Director*, Prof. J. A. Edwardson, ph.d.
PROTEIN PHOSPHORYLATION UNIT, Department of Biochemistry, Medical Sciences Institute, University of Dundee, Dundee DD1 4HN. Tel: 01382-344241. *Hon. Director*, Prof. P. Cohen, ph.d., FRS, FRSE
RADIATION AND GENOME STABILITY UNIT, Harwell Site, Chilton, Didcot, Oxon OX11 0RD. Tel: 01235-834393. *Director*, D. Goodhead, D.phil.
REPRODUCTIVE BIOLOGY UNIT, Centre for Reproductive Biology, 37 Chalmers Street, Edinburgh EH3 9EW. Tel: 0131-229 2575. *Director*, Prof. A. S. McNeilly, ph.d., D.SC., FRSE
SOCIAL, GENETIC AND DEVELOPMENTAL PSYCHIATRY RESEARCH CENTRE, Institute of Psychiatry, De Crespigny Park, Denmark Hill, London SE5 8AF. Tel: 0171-740 5121. *Director*, Sir Michael Rutter, CBE, FRS, FRCP, FRCPsych.
TOXICOLOGY UNIT, Hodgkin Building, University of Leicester, PO Box 138, Lancaster Road, Leicester LE1 9HN. Tel: 0116-252 5600. *Director*, Prof. L. Smith, ph.d.
VIROLOGY UNIT, Institute of Virology, Church Street, Glasgow G11 5JR. Tel: 0141-330 4017. *Director*, Prof. D. J. McGeoch

NATURAL ENVIRONMENT RESEARCH COUNCIL (NERC)
Polaris House, North Star Avenue, Swindon SN2 1EU
Tel 01793-411500

The purpose of the NERC is to promote and support research, survey, long-term environmental monitoring and related postgraduate training in terrestrial, marine and freshwater biology, and Earth, atmospheric, hydrological, oceanographic and polar sciences and Earth observation; to advance knowledge and technology, and to provide services and trained scientists and engineers; to provide advice, disseminate knowledge and promote public understanding in these fields.
Chairman, J. C. Smith, F.Eng., FRSE
Chief Executive, Prof. J. R. Krebs, FRS

CENTRES/SURVEYS

BRITISH ANTARCTIC SURVEY, High Cross, Madingley Road, Cambridge CB3 0ET. Tel: 01223-251400. *Director*, Dr D. Drewry
BRITISH GEOLOGICAL SURVEY, Kingsley Dunham Centre, Nicker Hill, Keyworth, Nottingham NG12 5GG. Tel: 0115-936 3100. *Director*, Dr P. Cook, CBE
CENTRE FOR COASTAL AND MARINE SCIENCE
Director, Dr B. Bayne (based at Plymouth Marine Laboratory)
  PLYMOUTH MARINE LABORATORY, Prospect Place, West Hoe, Plymouth PL1 3DH. Tel: 01752-633100. *Director*, Prof. R. F. Mantoura
  PROUDMAN OCEANOGRAPHIC LABORATORY, Bidston Observatory, Birkenhead L43 7RA. Tel: 0151-653 8633. *Director*, Dr B. S. McCartney
  DUNSTAFFNAGE MARINE LABORATORY, PO Box 3, Oban, Argyll PA34 4AD. Tel: 01631-562244. *Director*, Dr G. B. Shimmield
CENTRE FOR ECOLOGY AND HYDROLOGY
Director, Prof. W. B. Wilkinson (based at Institute of Hydrology)
  INSTITUTE OF FRESHWATER ECOLOGY, The Ferry House, Far Sawrey, Ambleside, Cumbria LA22 0LP. Tel: 015394-42468. *Director*, Prof. A. D. Pickering
  INSTITUTE OF HYDROLOGY, Maclean Building, Crowmarsh Gifford, Wallingford, Oxon OX10 8BB. Tel: 01491-838800. *Director*, Dr J. Wallace
  INSTITUTE OF TERRESTRIAL ECOLOGY, Monks Wood, Abbots Ripton, Huntingdon PE17 2LS. Tel: 01487-773381. *Director*, Prof T. M. Roberts
  INSTITUTE OF VIROLOGY AND ENVIRONMENTAL MICROBIOLOGY, Mansfield Road, Oxford OX1 3SR. Tel: 01865-512361. *Director*, Dr P. Nuttall
SOUTHAMPTON OCEANOGRAPHY CENTRE, University of Southampton, Empress Dock, Southampton SO14 3ZH. Tel: 01703-596666. *Director*, Dr J. Shepherd

UNITS

SEA MAMMAL RESEARCH UNIT, Gatty Marine Laboratory, University of St Andrews, St Andrews, Fife KY16 8LB. Tel: 01334-463472. *Head*, Dr. P. Hammond
UNIT OF AQUATIC BIOCHEMISTRY, School of Natural Sciences, Stirling University, Stirling FK9 4LA. Tel: 01786-473171. *Director*, Prof. J. R. Sargent, FRSE
UNIT OF COMPARATIVE PLANT ECOLOGY, University of Sheffield, Sheffield S10 2TN. Tel: 0114-276 8555. *Director*, Prof. J. P. Grime

ENVIRONMENTAL SYSTEMS SCIENCE CENTRE, Department of Geography, Reading University, Whiteknights, Reading RG6 2AB. Tel: 01734-318741. *Director*, Prof. R. Gurney
CENTRE FOR POPULATION BIOLOGY, Imperial College, Silwood Park, Ascot, Berks SL5 7PY. Tel: 01344-294354. *Director*, Prof. J. Lawton, FRS
ATMOSPHERIC CHEMISTRY MODELLING SUPPORT UNIT, University Chemical Laboratory, University of Cambridge, Lensfield Road, Cambridge CB2 1EP. Tel: 01223-336473. *Director*, Dr J. A. Pyle
JOINT CENTRE FOR MESOSCALE METEOROLOGY, Department of Meteorology, University of Reading, 2 Earley Gate, Whiteknights, Reading RG6 2AU. Tel: 0118-931 8957. *Director*, Prof. A. J. Thorpe
CENTRE FOR GLOBAL ATMOSPHERIC MODELLING, Department of Meteorology, University of Reading, 2 Earley Gate, Whiteknights, Reading RG6 2AU. Tel: 0118-931 8315. *Director*, Prof. A. O'Neill

PARTICLE PHYSICS AND ASTRONOMY RESEARCH COUNCIL (PPARC)
Polaris House, North Star Avenue, Swindon SN2 1SZ
Tel 01793-442000

The purpose of the PPARC is to support research into elementary particles and the fundamental forces of nature, planetary and solar research, including space physics, and astronomy, astrophysics and cosmology. It funds research in the universities and is responsible for funding both national and international facilities, including the European Laboratory for Particle Physics (CERN) and the European Space Agency. In July 1997 the Government announced that the work of the two Royal Observatories was to be concentrated in a new UK Astronomy Technology Centre (UKATC) at Edinburgh.
Chairman, Dr P. Williams, CBE
Chief Executive, Prof. K. Pounds, CBE, FRS
ROYAL GREENWICH OBSERVATORY, Madingley Road, Cambridge CB3 0EZ. Tel: 01223-374000. *Director*, Dr J. V. Wall
ROYAL OBSERVATORY, EDINBURGH, Blackford Hill, Edinburgh EH9 3HJ. Tel: 0131-668 8100. *Director*, S. G. Pitt
ISAAC NEWTON GROUP OF TELESCOPES, Apartado de Coreos 321, Santa Cruz de la Palma, Tenerife 38780, Canary Islands. Tel: 00 3422-411048. *Head*, Dr S. Unger
JOINT ASTRONOMY CENTRE, 660 N A'ohoku Place, University Park, Hilo, Hawaii 96720. Tel: 00 808-961 3756. *Head*, Prof. I. Robson

Research and Technology Organizations

The following industrial and technological research bodies are members of the Association of Independent Research and Technology Organizations (AIRTO). Members' activities span a wide range of disciplines from life sciences to engineering. Their work includes basic research, development and design of innovative products or processes, instrumentation testing and certification, and technology and management consultancy. AIRTO publishes a directory to help clients identify the organizations which might be able to assist them.

AIRTO, PO Box 330, Cambridge CB5 8DU. Tel: 01223-167831. *Secretary-General*, J. Bennett

ADVANCED MANUFACTURING TECHNOLOGY RESEARCH INSTITUTE, Hulley Road, Macclesfield, Cheshire SK10 2NE. Tel: 01625-425421. *Managing Director*, D. Palethorpe

AIRCRAFT RESEARCH ASSOCIATION LTD, Manton Lane, Bedford MK41 7PF. Tel: 01234-350681. *Chief Executive*, B. Timmins

ASSOCIATION FOR INFORMATION MANAGEMENT (ASLIB), Information House, 20–24 Old Street, London ECIV 9AP. Tel: 0171-253 4488. *Chief Executive*, R. Bowes

BHR GROUP LTD (*Fluid mechanics and process technology*), Cranfield, Bedford MK43 0AJ Tel: 01234-750422. *Chief Executive*, I. Cooper

BIBRA INTERNATIONAL (*Assessment of toxicity of food and chemicals to humans*), Woodmansterne Road, Carshalton, Surrey SM5 4DS. Tel: 0181-652 1000. *Director*, Dr S. E. Jaggers

BLC (THE LEATHER TECHNOLOGY CENTRE), Leather Trade House, Kings Park Road, Moulton Park, Northants NN3 6JD. Tel: 01604-494131. *Chief Executive*, Dr K. Alexander

BRITISH GLASS, Northumberland Road, Sheffield S10 2UA. Tel: 0114-268 6201. *Director-General*, Dr W. Cook

BRITISH MARITIME TECHNOLOGY LTD, Orlando House, 1 Waldegrave Road, Teddington, Middx TW11 8LZ. Tel: 0181-943 5544. *Chief Executive*, D. Goodrich

BRF INTERNATIONAL (*Alcoholic beverages*), Lyttel Hall, Coopers Hill Road, Nutfield, Surrey RH1 4HY. Tel: 01737-822272. *Director-General*, Prof. R. Righelato

BRITISH TEXTILE TECHNOLOGY GROUP, Wira House, West Park Ring Road, Leeds LS16 6QL. Tel: 0113-259 1999, Shirley House, Didsbury, Manchester M20 8RB. Tel: 0161-445 8141. *Chief Executive*, A. King

BUILDING RESEARCH ESTABLISHMENT, Garston, Watford WD2 7JR. Tel: 01923-664206. *Managing Director*, Dr. M. Wyatt

BUILDING SERVICES RESEARCH AND INFORMATION ASSOCIATION, Old Bracknell Lane West, Bracknell, Berks RG12 7AH. Tel: 01344-426511. *Chief Executive*, G. J. Baker

CAMBRIDGE CONSULTANTS LTD (*Products, systems and manufacturing processes design and development*), Science Park, Milton Road, Cambridge CB4 4DW. Tel: 01223-420024. *Chief Executive*, Dr J. P. Auton

CAMBRIDGE REFRIGERATION TECHNOLOGY (CRT), 140 Newmarket Road, Cambridge CB5 8HE. Tel: 01223-365101. *Technical Director*, R. D. Heap

CAMPDEN AND CHORLEYWOOD FOOD RESEARCH ASSOCIATION, Chipping Campden, Glos GL55 6LD. Tel: 01386-842000. *Director-General*, Prof. C. Dennis

CERAM (BRITISH CERAMIC RESEARCH LTD), Queen's Road, Penkhull, Stoke-on-Trent ST4 7LQ. Tel: 01782-845431. *Chief Executive*, Dr N. E. Sanderson

CIRIA (CONSTRUCTION INDUSTRY RESEARCH AND INFORMATION ASSOCIATION), 6 Storey's Gate, London SWIP 3AU. Tel: 0171-222 8891. *Director-General*, Dr P. L. Bransby

CRL (*Specialist products, technology licences, intellectual property rights services, research and development*), Dawley Road, Hayes, Middx UB3 1HH. Tel: 0181-848 9779. *Managing Director*, Dr J. White

CUTLERY AND ALLIED TRADES RESEARCH ASSOCIATION, Henry Street, Sheffield S3 7EQ. Tel: 0114-276 9736. *Director of Research*, R. C. Hamby

EA TECHNOLOGY (*Use and distribution of electricity*), Capenhurst, Chester CH1 6ES. Tel: 0151-339 4181. *Chief Executive*, Dr S. F. Exell

ERA TECHNOLOGY LTD (*Electronic, electrical, materials and structural engineering*), Cleeve Road, Leatherhead, Surrey KT22 7SA. Tel: 01372-367000. *Chief Executive*, M. J. Withers

FABRIC CARE RESEARCH ASSOCIATION, Forest House Laboratories, Knaresborough Road, Harrogate, N. Yorks HG2 7LZ. Tel: 01423-885977. *Managing Director*, C. Tebbs

FURNITURE INDUSTRY RESEARCH ASSOCIATION, Maxwell Road, Stevenage, Herts SG1 2EW. Tel: 01438-313433. *Managing Director*, H. Davies

HR WALLINGFORD GROUP LTD (*Hydroinformatics and engineering*), Howbery Park, Wallingford, Oxon OX10 8BA. Tel: 01491-835381. *Chief Executive*, Dr J. Weare, OBE

INTERNATIONAL RESEARCH AND DEVELOPMENT LTD (*Materials, joining and electro-mechanical systems*), Shields Road, Newcastle upon Tyne NE6 2YD. Tel: 0191-275 2800. *General Manager*, R. Potts

LABORATORY OF THE GOVERNMENT CHEMIST, Queens Road, Teddington, Middx TW11 0LY. Tel: 0181-943 7300. *Chief Executive and Government Chemist*, Dr R. Worswick

LEATHERHEAD FOOD RESEARCH ASSOCIATION, Randalls Road, Leatherhead, Surrey KT22 7RY. Tel: 01372-376761. *Director*, Dr M. P. J. Kierstan

MATERIALS ENGINEERING RESEARCH LABORATORY LTD, Tamworth Road, Hertford SG13 7DG. Tel: 01992-500120. *Managing Director*, Dr A. Stevenson

MINERAL INDUSTRY RESEARCH ORGANIZATION, Expert House, Sandford Street, Lichfield, Staffs WS13 6QA. Tel: 01543-262957. *Director*, N. Roberts

MOTOR INDUSTRY RESEARCH ASSOCIATION, Watling Street, Nuneaton, Warks CV10 0TU. Tel: 01203-355000. *Managing Director*, J. R. Wood

MOTOR INSURANCE REPAIR RESEARCH CENTRE, Colthorp Lane, Thatcham, Berks RG19 4NP. Tel: 01635-868855. *Chief Executive*, M. Smith

THE NATIONAL COMPUTING CENTRE LTD, Oxford House, Oxford Road, Manchester M1 7ED. Tel: 0161-228 6333. *Managing Director*, C. Pearse

NATIONAL PHYSICAL LABORATORY, 1 Queens Road, Teddington, Middx TW11 0LW. Tel: 0181-977 3222. *Deputy Director*, Dr A. Wallard

PAINT RESEARCH ASSOCIATION, 8 Waldegrave Road, Teddington, Middx TW11 8LD. Tel: 0181-977 4427. *Managing Director*, J. A. Bernie

PERA GROUP (*Multi-disciplinary research, design, development and consultancy*), Middle Aston House, Middle Aston, Oxon OX6 3PT. Tel: 01869-347755. *Chief Executive*, R. A. Armstrong

PIRA INTERNATIONAL (*Paper and board, printing, publishing and packaging*), Randalls Road, Leatherhead, Surrey KT22 7RU. Tel: 01372-802000. *Managing Director*, B. W. Blunden, OBE

RAPRA TECHNOLOGY LTD (*Rubber and plastics*), Shawbury, Shrewsbury SY4 4NR. Tel: 01939-250383; North East Centre, 18 Belasis Court, Belasis Technology Park, Billingham TS23 4AZ. Tel: 01642-370406. *Chief Executive*, Dr P. Extance

SATRA FOOTWEAR TECHNOLOGY CENTRE, Satra House, Rockingham Road, Kettering, Northants NN16 9JH. Tel: 01536-410000. *Chief Executive*, Dr R. E. Whittaker

SIRA LTD (*Measurement, instrumentation, control and optical systems technology*), South Hill, Chislehurst, Kent BR7 5EH. Tel: 0181-467 2636. *Managing Director*, R. A. Brook

SMITH INSTITUTE (*Mathematics and computing*), PO Box 183, Guildford, Surrey GU2 5GG. Tel: 01483-579108. *Director*, Dr L. A. Warren

SMITH SYSTEM ENGINEERING LTD, Surrey Research Park, Guildford, Surrey GU2 5YP. Tel: 01483-442000. *Managing Director*, Dr T. Black

STEEL CONSTRUCTION INSTITUTE, Silwood Park, Ascot, Berks SL5 7QN. Tel: 01344-23345. *Director*, Dr G. Owens

TRADA TECHNOLOGY LTD (*Timber and wood-based products*), Stocking Lane, Hughenden Valley, High Wycombe, Bucks HP14 4NA. Tel: 01494-563091. *Managing Director*, A. Abbott

TRANSPORT RESEARCH LABORATORY, Old Wokingham Road, Crowthorne, Berks RG45 6AU. Tel: 01344-773131. *Chief Executive*, G. Clarke

TWI (*Welding*), Abington Hall, Abington, Cambridge CB1 6AL. Tel: 01223-891162. *Chief Executive*, A. B. M. Braithwaite, OBE

WRC PLC (*Water, waste water and environmental management*), PO Box 16, Marlow, Bucks SL7 2HD. Tel: 01491-571531. *Managing Director*, Dr J. Moss

Chemical Elements

Element	Symbol	Atomic Number	Element	Symbol	Atomic Number	Element	Symbol	Atomic Number
Actinium	Ac	89	Hafnium	Hf	72	Promethium	Pm	61
Aluminium	Al	13	Helium	He	2	Protactinium	Pa	91
Americium	Am	95	Holmium	Ho	67	Radium	Ra	88
Antimony	Sb	51	Hydrogen	H	1	Radon	Rn	86
Argon	Ar	18	Indium	In	49	Rhenium	Re	75
Arsenic	As	33	Iodine	I	53	Rhodium	Rh	45
Astatine	At	85	Iridium	Ir	77	Rubidium	Rb	37
Barium	Ba	56	Iron	Fe	26	Ruthenium	Ru	44
Berkelium	Bk	97	Krypton	Kr	36	Samarium	Sm	62
Beryllium	Be	4	Lanthanum	La	57	Scandium	Sc	21
Bismuth	Bi	83	Lawrencium	Lr	103	Selenium	Se	34
Boron	B	5	Lead	Pb	82	Silicon	Si	14
Bromine	Br	35	Lithium	Li	3	Silver	Ag	47
Cadmium	Cd	48	Lutetium	Lu	71	Sodium	Na	11
Caesium	Cs	55	Magnesium	Mg	12	Strontium	Sr	38
Calcium	Ca	20	Manganese	Mn	25	Sulphur	S	16
Californium	Cf	98	Mendelevium	Md	101	Tantalum	Ta	73
Carbon	C	6	Mercury	Hg	80	Technetium	Tc	43
Cerium	Ce	58	Molybdenum	Mo	42	Tellurium	Te	52
Chlorine	Cl	17	Neodymium	Nd	60	Terbium	Tb	65
Chromium	Cr	24	Neon	Ne	10	Thallium	Tl	81
Cobalt	Co	27	Neptunium	Np	93	Thorium	Th	90
Copper	Cu	29	Nickel	Ni	28	Thulium	Tm	69
Curium	Cm	96	Niobium	Nb	41	Tin	Sn	50
Dysprosium	Dy	66	Nitrogen	N	7	Titanium	Ti	22
Einsteinium	Es	99	Nobelium	No	102	Tungsten (Wolfram)	W	74
Erbium	Er	68	Osmium	Os	76	Uranium	U	92
Europium	Eu	63	Oxygen	O	8	Vanadium	V	23
Fermium	Fm	100	Palladium	Pd	46	Xenon	Xe	54
Fluorine	F	9	Phosphorus	P	15	Ytterbium	Yb	70
Francium	Fr	87	Platinum	Pt	78	Yttrium	Y	39
Gadolinium	Gd	64	Plutonium	Pu	94	Zinc	Zn	30
Gallium	Ga	31	Polonium	Po	84	Zirconium	Zr	40
Germanium	Ge	32	Potassium	K	19			
Gold	Au	79	Praseodymium	Pr	59			

Sports Bodies

* Governing body for the sport

Sports Councils

CENTRAL COUNCIL OF PHYSICAL RECREATION, Francis House, Francis Street, London SW1P 1DE. Tel: 0171-828 3163. *General Secretary*, M. Denton

THE ENGLISH SPORTS COUNCIL, 16 Upper Woburn Place, London WC1H 0QP. Tel: 0171-273 1500. *Chairman*, Sir Rodney Walker

SCOTTISH SPORTS COUNCIL, Caledonia House, South Gyle, Edinburgh EH12 9DQ. Tel: 0131-317 7200. *Chief Executive*, F. A. L. Alstead, CBE

SPORTS COUNCIL FOR NORTHERN IRELAND, House of Sport, Upper Malone Road, Belfast BT9 5LA. Tel: 01232-381222. *Chief Executive*, E. McCartan

SPORTS COUNCIL FOR WALES, Sophia Gardens, Cardiff CF1 9SW. Tel: 01222-300500. *Chief Executive*, L. Tatham

UK SPORTS COUNCIL, Walkden House, 3–10 Melton Street, London NW1 2EB. Tel: 0171-380 8000. *Chief Executive*, H. Wells

Alpine Skiing

*BRITISH SKI FEDERATION, 258 Main Street, East Calder, Livingston, W. Lothian EH53 0FF. Tel: 01506-884343. *Chief Executive*, M. Jardine

Angling

*NATIONAL FEDERATION OF ANGLERS, Halliday House, Egginton Junction, Derbys DE65 6GU. Tel: 01283-734735. *Chief Administration Officer*, W. Hall

Archery

*GRAND NATIONAL ARCHERY SOCIETY, National Agricultural Centre, 7th Street, Stoneleigh, Kenilworth, Warks CV8 2LG. Tel: 01203-696631. *Chief Executive*, J. S. Middleton

Association Football

*THE FOOTBALL ASSOCIATION, 16 Lancaster Gate, London W2 3LW. Tel: 0171-262 4542. *Chief Executive*, R. H. G. Kelly

*FOOTBALL ASSOCIATION OF WALES, Plymouth Chambers, 3 Westgate Street, Cardiff CF1 1DD. Tel: 01222-372325. *Secretary-General*, D. G. Collins

THE FOOTBALL LEAGUE LTD, 319 Clifton Drive South, Lytham St Annes, Lancs FY8 1JG. Tel: 01253-729421. *Secretary*, J. D. Dent

*IRISH FOOTBALL ASSOCIATION, 20 Windsor Avenue, Belfast BT9 6FF. Tel: 01232-669458. *General Secretary*, D. I. Bowen

IRISH FOOTBALL LEAGUE, 96 University Street, Belfast BT7 1HE. Tel: 01232-242888. *Secretary*, H. Wallace

*SCOTTISH FOOTBALL ASSOCIATION, 6 Park Gardens, Glasgow G3 7YF. Tel: 0141-332 6372. *Chief Executive*, J. Farry

SCOTTISH FOOTBALL LEAGUE, 188 West Regent Street, Glasgow G2 4RY. Tel: 0141-248 3844. *Secretary*, P. Donald

Athletics

AMATEUR ATHLETIC ASSOCIATION OF ENGLAND, 225A Bristol Road, Edgbaston, Birmingham B5 7UB. Tel: 0121-440 5000. *Chairman*, D. Cropper

ATHLETICS ASSOCIATION OF WALES, Morfa Athletics Stadium, Upper Bank, Landore, Swansea SA1 7DF. Tel: 01792-456237. *National Administrator*, Mrs B. Currie

*BRITISH ATHLETIC FEDERATION, 225A Bristol Road, Edgbaston, Birmingham B5 7UB. Tel: 0121-440 5000. *Chairman*, K. Rickhuss

NORTHERN IRELAND AMATEUR ATHLETIC FEDERATION, Athletics House, Old Coach Road, Belfast BT9 5PR. Tel: 01232-602707. *Secretary*, J. Allen

SCOTTISH ATHLETICS FEDERATION, Caledonia House, South Gyle, Edinburgh EH12 9DQ. Tel: 0131 317 7320. *Administrator*, N. F. Park

Badminton

*BADMINTON ASSOCIATION OF ENGLAND LTD, National Badminton Centre, Bradwell Road, Loughton Lodge, Milton Keynes MK8 9LA. Tel: 01908-568822. *Chief Executive*, S. Baddeley

*SCOTTISH BADMINTON UNION, Cockburn Centre, 40 Bogmoor Place, Glasgow G51 4TQ. Tel: 0141-445 1218. *Chief Executive*, Miss A. Smillie

*WELSH BADMINTON UNION, Fourth Floor, 3 Westgate Street, Cardiff CF1 1ND. Tel: 01222-222082. *Coaching Development Manager*, L. Williams

Baseball

*BRITISH BASEBALL FEDERATION, PO Box 45, Hessle, E. Yorks HU13 0YQ. Tel: 01482-643551. *Secretary*, Ms W. Macadam

Basketball

*BASKETBALL ASSOCIATION OF WALES, Connies House, Rhymney River Bridge Road, Cardiff CF3 7YZ. Tel: 01222-454395. *Administrator*, F. M. Daw

*ENGLISH BASKETBALL ASSOCIATION, 48 Bradford Road, Stanningley, Leeds LS28 6DF. Tel: 0113-236 1166. *Chief Executive*, S. Catton

*SCOTTISH BASKETBALL ASSOCIATION, Caledonia House, South Gyle, Edinburgh EH12 9DQ. Tel: 0131-317 7260. *Chairman*, W. D. McInnes

Billiards

*WORLD LADIES BILLIARDS AND SNOOKER ASSOCIATION, 26 Welbeck Road, Wisbech, Cambs PE13 2JY. Tel: 01945-589589. *Chairman*, Ms M. Fisher

*WORLD PROFESSIONAL BILLIARDS AND SNOOKER ASSOCIATION, 27 Oakfield Road, Clifton, Bristol BS28 2AT. Tel: 0117-974 4491. *Chief Executive*, J. McKenzie

Bobsleigh

*BRITISH BOBSLEIGH ASSOCIATION, The Chestnuts, 85 High Street, Codford, Warminster, Wilts BA12 0ND. Tel: 01985-850064. *General Secretary*, Ms H. Alderman

Bowls

*BRITISH ISLES BOWLING COUNCIL, 28 Woodford Park, Lurgan, Co. Armagh BT66 7HA. Tel: 01762-322036. *Hon. Secretary*, W. A. Gracey

*BRITISH ISLES INDOOR BOWLS COUNCIL, 9 Highlight Lane, Barry CF62 8AA. Tel: 01446-733978. *Hon. Secretary*, J. R. Thomas, MBE

*BRITISH ISLES WOMEN'S BOWLING COUNCIL, 2 Case Gardens, Seaton, Devon EX12 2AP. Tel: 01297-21317. *Hon. Secretary*, Mrs N. Colling, MBE

*BRITISH ISLES WOMEN'S INDOOR BOWLS COUNCIL, 3 Scirocco Close, Moulton Park, Northampton NN3 6AP. Tel: 01604-494163. *Hon. Secretary*, Mrs M. E. Ruff

*ENGLISH BOWLING ASSOCIATION, Lyndhurst Road, Worthing, W. Sussex BNII 2AZ. Tel: 01903-820222. *Secretary*, G. D. Shaw

*ENGLISH INDOOR BOWLING ASSOCIATION, David Cornwell House, Bowling Green, Leicester Road, Melton Mowbray, Leics LEI3 ODA. Tel: 01664-481900. *Secretary*, D. N. Brown

*ENGLISH WOMEN'S BOWLING ASSOCIATION, 2 Case Gardens, Seaton, Devon EXI2 2AP. Tel: 01297-21317. *Hon. Secretary*, Mrs N. Colling, MBE

*ENGLISH WOMEN'S INDOOR BOWLING ASSOCIATION, 3 Scirocco Close, Moulton Park, Northampton NN3 6AP. Tel: 01604-494163. *Secretary*, Mrs M. E. Ruff

Boxing
*AMATEUR BOXING ASSOCIATION OF ENGLAND LTD, Crystal Palace National Sports Centre, London SEI9 2BB. Tel: 0181-778 0251. *Secretary*, C. Brown

*BRITISH AMATEUR BOXING ASSOCIATION, 96 High Street, Lochee, Dundee DD2 3AY. Tel: 01382-611412. *Chief Executive*, F. Hendry

*BRITISH BOXING BOARD OF CONTROL LTD, Jack Petersen House, 52A Borough High Street, London SEI IXW. Tel: 0171-403 5879. *General Secretary*, J. Morris

Canoeing
*BRITISH CANOE UNION, Adbolton Lane, West Bridgford, Nottingham NG2 5AS. Tel: 0115-982 1100. *Chief Executive*, P. Owen

Chess
*BRITISH CHESS FEDERATION, 9A Grand Parade, St Leonard's-on-Sea, E. Sussex TN38 ODD. Tel: 01424-442500. *Manager*, Mrs G. White

Clay Pigeon Shooting
*CLAY PIGEON SHOOTING ASSOCIATION, Earlstrees Court, Earlstrees Road, Corby, Northants NNI7 4AX. Tel: 01536-443566. *Director*, E. G. Orduna

Cricket
*ENGLAND AND WALES CRICKET BOARD, Lord's, London NW8 8QZ. Tel: 0171-432 1200. *Chief Executive*, T. Lamb
MCC, Lord's, London NW8 8QN. Tel: 0171-289 1611. *Secretary*, R. Knight

Croquet
*CROQUET ASSOCIATION, c/o The Hurlingham Club, Ranelagh Gardens, London SW6 3PR. Tel: 0171-736 3148. *Secretary*, P. W. P. Campion

Cycling
*BRITISH CYCLING FEDERATION, National Cycling Centre, Stuart Street, Manchester MII 4DQ. Tel: 0161-230 2301. *Chief Executive*, J. Hendry

*ROAD TIME TRIALS COUNCIL, 77 Arlington Drive, Pennington, Leigh, Lancs WN7 3QP. Tel: 01942-603976. *National Secretary*, P. Heaton

Diving
*GREAT BRITAIN DIVING FEDERATION, PO Box 222, Batley, W. Yorks WFI7 8XD. Tel: 01924-422322. *Director of Administration*, J. Cryer

Equestrianism
*BRITISH EQUESTRIAN FEDERATION, British Equestrian Centre, Stoneleigh Park, Kenilworth, Warks CV8 2LR. Tel: 01203-696697. *Director-General*, Col. J. D. Smith-Bingham

*BRITISH HORSE TRIALS ASSOCIATION, British Equestrian Centre, Stoneleigh Park, Kenilworth, Warks CV8 2LR. Tel: 01203-696697. *Director*, Maj. T. Taylor

Eton Fives
*ETON FIVES ASSOCIATION, 74 Clarence Road, St Albans, Herts ALI 4NG. Tel: 01727-837099. *Secretary*, R. Beament

Fencing
*BRITISH FENCING ASSOCIATION, 1 Baron's Gate, 33–35 Rothschild Road, London W4 5HT. Tel: 0181-742 3032. *General Secretary*, Miss G. Kenneally

Gliding
*BRITISH GLIDING ASSOCIATION, Kimberley House, Vaughan Way, Leicester LEI 4SE. Tel: 0116-253 1051. *Secretary*, B. Rolfe

Golf
*LADIES' GOLF UNION, The Scores, St Andrews, Fife KYI6 9AT. Tel: 01334-475811. *Secretary*, Mrs J. Hall
*ROYAL AND ANCIENT GOLF CLUB OF ST ANDREWS, Golf Place, St Andrews, Fife KYI6 9JD. Tel: 01334-472112. *Secretary*, M. F. Bonallack, OBE

Greyhound Racing
*NATIONAL GREYHOUND RACING CLUB LTD, Twyman House, 16 Bonny Street, London NWI 9QD. Tel: 0171-267 9256. *Chief Executive*, F. Melville

Gymnastics
*BRITISH GYMNASTICS, Ford Hall, Lilleshall National Sports Centre, Newport, Shropshire TFI0 9NB. Tel: 01952-820330. *General Secretary*, D. Minnery

Hockey
*ENGLISH HOCKEY ASSOCIATION, The Stadium, Silbury Boulevard, Milton Keynes MK9 INR. Tel: 01908-689290. *Chief Executive*, S. P. Baines
*SCOTTISH HOCKEY UNION, 48 Pleasance, Edinburgh EH8 9TJ. Tel: 0131-650 8170. *Chairman*, P. Monaghan
*WELSH HOCKEY UNION, 80 Woodville Road, Cathays, Cardiff CF2 4ED. Tel: 01222-233257. *Executive Secretatry*, J. G. Williams

Horse-racing
*BRITISH HORSERACING BOARD, 42 Portman Square, London WIH OEN. Tel: 0171-396 0011. *Chief Executive*, R. T. Ricketts
THE JOCKEY CLUB, 42 Portman Square, London WIH OEN. Tel: 0171-486 4921. *Senior Steward*, Sir Thomas Pilkington, Bt.

Ice Hockey
*BRITISH ICE HOCKEY ASSOCIATION, 2nd Floor Suite, 517 Christchurch Road, Boscombe, Bournemouth BHI 4AG. Tel: 01202-303946. *General Secretary*, D. Pickles

Ice Skating
*NATIONAL ICE SKATING ASSOCIATION OF THE UK LTD, 15–27 Gee Street, London ECIV 3RE. Tel: 0171-253 3824. *Chief Executive*, Ms C. Godsall

Judo
*BRITISH JUDO ASSOCIATION, 7A Rutland Street, Leicester LEI IRB. Tel: 0116-255 9669. *Office Manager*, Mrs S. Startin

Lacrosse
*ENGLISH LACROSSE ASSOCIATION, 4 Western Court, Bromley Street, Digbeth, Birmingham B9 4AN. Tel: 0121-773 4422. *Chief Executive Officer*, D. Shuttleworth
*ENGLISH LACROSSE UNION, 70 High Road, Rayleigh, Essex SS6 7AD. Tel: 01268-770758. *Hon. Secretary*, R. Balls

Lawn Tennis
*LAWN TENNIS ASSOCIATION, The Queen's Club, London WI4 9EG. Tel: 0171-381 7000. *Secretary*, J. C. U. James

Lugeing
*GREAT BRITAIN LUGE ASSOCIATION, 1 Highfield House, Hampton Bishop, Hereford HR1 4JN. Tel: 01432-271982. *General Secretary,* J. G. Evans

Martial Arts
MARTIAL ARTS DEVELOPMENT COMMISSION, PO Box 381, Erith, Kent DA8 1TF. Tel: 01322-431440. *Office Administrator,* Mrs E. Jewell

Motor Sports
*AUTO-CYCLE UNION, ACU House, Wood Street, Rugby, Warks CV21 2YX. Tel: 01788-540519. *Chief Executive,* G. Wilson
MOTORCYCLE CIRCUIT RACING CONTROL BOARD (MCRCB), PO Box 72, Castle Donington, Derbys DE74 2ZO, Tel: 01332-853822. *Manager,* D. R. Barnfield
*RAC MOTOR SPORTS ASSOCIATION LTD, Motor Sports House, Riverside Park, Colnbrook, Slough SL3 0HG. Tel: 01753-681736. *Chief Executive,* J. R. Quenby
*SCOTTISH AUTO CYCLE UNION LTD, Block 2, Unit 6, Whiteside Industrial Estate, Bathgate, W. Lothian EH48 2RX. Tel: 01506-630262. *Secretary,* A. M. Brownlie

Mountaineering
*BRITISH MOUNTAINEERING COUNCIL, 177–179 Burton Road, West Didsbury, Manchester M20 2BB. Tel: 0161-445 4747. *General Secretary,* R. Payne

Multi-Sport Bodies
BRITISH OLYMPIC ASSOCIATION, 1 Wandsworth Plain, London SW18 1EH. Tel: 0181-871 2677. *General Secretary,* S. Clegg
BRITISH UNIVERSITIES SPORTS ASSOCIATION, 8 Union Street, London SE1 1SZ. Tel: 0171-357 8555. *Chief Executive,* G. Gregory-Jones
COMMONWEALTH GAMES COUNCIL FOR ENGLAND, Tavistock House South, Tavistock Square, London WC1H 9JZ. Tel: 0171-388 6643. *General Secretary,* Miss A. Hogbin
COMMONWEALTH GAMES FEDERATION, Walkden House, 3–10 Melton Street, London NW1 2EB. Tel: 0171-383 5596. *Hon. Secretary,* D. Dixon, CVO

Netball
*ALL ENGLAND NETBALL ASSOCIATION LTD, Netball House, 9 Paynes Park, Hitchin, Herts SG5 1EH. Tel: 01462-442344. *Chief Executive,* Mrs E. M. Nicholl
*NORTHERN IRELAND NETBALL ASSOCIATION, House of Sport, Upper Malone Road, Belfast BT9 5LA. Tel: 01232-381222. *Secretary,* Mrs R. McWhinney
*SCOTTISH NETBALL ASSOCIATION, 24 Ainslie Road, Hillington Business Park, Hillington, Glasgow G52 4RU. Tel: 0141-570 4016. *Administrator,* Ms M. Martin
*WELSH NETBALL ASSOCIATION, 50 Cathedral Road, Cardiff CF1 9LL. Tel: 01222-237048. *President,* Miss P. Nicholas

Orienteering
*BRITISH ORIENTEERING FEDERATION, Riversdale, Dale Road North, Darley Dale, Matlock, Derbys DE4 2HX. Tel: 01629-734042. *Secretary-General,* D. Locke

Polo
*THE HURLINGHAM POLO ASSOCIATION, Winterlake, Kirtlington, Kidlington, Oxon OX5 3HG. Tel: 01869-350044. *Secretary,* J. W. M. Crisp

Rackets and Real Tennis
*TENNIS AND RACKETS ASSOCIATION, c/o The Queen's Club, Palliser Road, London W14 9EQ. Tel: 0171-386 3447/8. *Chief Executive,* Brig. A. D. Myrtle, CB, CBE

Rifle Shooting
*NATIONAL RIFLE ASSOCIATION, Bisley Camp, Brookwood, Woking, Surrey GU24 0PB. Tel: 01483-797777. *Chief Executive,* Col. C. C. C. Cheshire, OBE
*NATIONAL SMALL-BORE RIFLE ASSOCIATION, Lord Roberts House, Bisley Camp, Brookwood, Woking, Surrey GU24 0NP. Tel: 01483-476969. *Secretary,* Lt.-Col. J. D. Hoare

Rowing
*AMATEUR ROWING ASSOCIATION LTD, The Priory, 6 Lower Mall, London W6 9DJ. Tel: 0181-748 3632. *National Manager,* Mrs R. Napp
HENLEY ROYAL REGATTA, Regatta Headquarters, Henley-on-Thames, Oxon RG9 2LY. Tel: 01491-572153. *Secretary,* R. S. Goddard
SCOTTISH AMATEUR ROWING ASSOCIATION, 18 Daniel McLauchlin Place, Kirkintilloch, Glasgow G66 2LH. Tel: 0141-775 0522. *Secretary,* Miss R. Clarke
*WELSH AMATEUR ROWING ASSOCIATION, c/o Monmouth School, Monmouth NP5 3XP. Tel: 01600-713143. *Secretary,* M. R. Christmas

Rugby Fives
*RUGBY FIVES ASSOCIATION, The Old Forge, Sutton Valence, Maidstone, Kent ME17 3AW. Tel: 01622-842278. *General Secretary,* M. F. Beaman

Rugby League
*BRITISH AMATEUR RUGBY LEAGUE ASSOCIATION, West Yorkshire House, 4 New North Parade, Huddersfield HD1 5JP. Tel: 01484-544131. *Chief Executive,* M. F. Oldroyd
*THE RUGBY FOOTBALL LEAGUE, Red Hall, Red Hall Lane, Leeds LS17 8NB. Tel: 0113-232 9111. *Chief Executive,* M. P. Lindsay

Rugby Union
*IRISH RUGBY FOOTBALL UNION, 62 Lansdowne Road, Ballsbridge, Dublin 4, Republic of Ireland. Tel: 00 353-1-668 4601. *Secretary,* P. R. Browne
IRISH WOMEN'S RUGBY UNION, 110 Georgian Village, Castleknock, Dublin 15, Republic of Ireland. Tel: 00 353-1-821 4237. *Secretary,* Ms R. Hanley
*RUGBY FOOTBALL UNION, Twickenham TW1 1DZ. Tel: 0181-892 8161. *Secretary,* vacant
RUGBY FOOTBALL UNION FOR WOMEN (ENGLAND), 33 Rice Mews, St Thomas, Exeter EX2 9AY. Tel: 01635-278177. *Secretary,* Ms. S. Eakers
*SCOTTISH RUGBY UNION, Murrayfield, Edinburgh EH12 5PJ. Tel: 0131-346 5000. *Chief Executive,* I. A. L. Hogg
SCOTTISH WOMEN'S RUGBY UNION, 11 Bavelaw Crescent, Penicuik, Midlothian EH26 9AX. Tel: 01968-673355. *Chairperson,* Ms M. Sharp
*WELSH RUGBY UNION, PO Box 22, Hodge House, St Mary Street, Cardiff CF1 1DY. Tel: 01222-390111. *Secretary,* R. Jasinski
WELSH WOMEN'S RUGBY UNION, 40 Wolseley Street, Pilwenlly, Newport NP9 2HP. Tel: 01633-220249. *Secretary,* Ms. F. Margerison

Snooker
*WORLD LADIES BILLIARDS AND SNOOKER ASSOCIATION, 26 Welbeck Road, Wisbech, Cambs PE13 2JY. Tel: 01945-589589. *Chairman,* Ms M. Fisher
*WORLD PROFESSIONAL BILLIARDS AND SNOOKER ASSOCIATION, 27 Oakfield Road, Clifton, Bristol BS28 2AT. Tel: 0117-974 4491. *Company Secretary,* M. Veal

Speedway
*SPEEDWAY CONTROL BOARD LTD, ACU Headquarters, Wood Street, Rugby, Warks cv21 2yx. Tel: 01788-540096. *Manager,* D. Hughes

Squash Rackets
*SCOTTISH SQUASH, Caledonia House, South Gyle, Edinburgh eh12 9dq. Tel: 0131-317 7343. *Secretary,* N. Brydon
*SQUASH RACKETS ASSOCIATION, PO Box 1106, London w3 0zd. Tel: 0181-746 1616. *Chief Executive,* M. Hammond
*WELSH SQUASH RACKETS FEDERATION, PO Box 56, Penarth cf64 1xp. Tel: 01222-704096. *Chairman,* S. Osborne

Sub-Aqua
*BRITISH SUB-AQUA CLUB, Telfords Quay, Ellesmere Port, Cheshire l65 4fy. Tel: 0151-350 6200. *Chairman,* C. Allen

Swimming
*AMATEUR SWIMMING ASSOCIATION, Harold Fern House, Derby Square, Loughborough, Leics le11 5al. Tel: 01509-618700. *Chief Executive,* D. Sparkes
*SCOTTISH AMATEUR SWIMMING ASSOCIATION, Holmhills Farm, Greenlees Road, Cambuslang, Glasgow g72 8dt. Tel: 0141-641 8818. *Administration Manager,* Mrs E. Mackenzie
*WELSH AMATEUR SWIMMING ASSOCIATION, Wales Empire Pool, Wood Street, Cardiff cf1 1pp. Tel: 01222-342201. *Hon. General Secretary,* G. Robins

Table Tennis
*ENGLISH TABLE TENNIS ASSOCIATION, Queensbury House, Havelock Road, Hastings, E. Sussex tn34 1hf. Tel: 01424-722525. *Chief Executive,* R. Yule

Volleyball
*ENGLISH VOLLEYBALL ASSOCIATION, 27 South Road, West Bridgford, Nottingham ng2 7ag. Tel: 0115-981 6324. *Chief Executive Officer,* Mrs G. Harrison
*SCOTTISH VOLLEYBALL ASSOCIATION, 48 Pleasance, Edinburgh eh8 9tj. Tel: 0131-556 4633. *Director,* N. S. Moody
*WELSH VOLLEYBALL ASSOCIATION, 9 St Dennis Road, Heath, Cardiff cf4 4na. Tel: 01222-758427. *Secretary,* Ms T. Shaw

Walking
*RACE WALKING ASSOCIATION, Hufflers, Heard's Lane, Shenfield, Brentwood, Essex cm15 0sf. Tel: 01277-220687. *Hon. Secretary,* P. J. Cassidy

Water Skiing
*BRITISH WATER SKI FEDERATION, 390 City Road, London ec1v 2qa. Tel: 0171-833 2855. *Executive Officer,* Ms G. Hill

Weightlifting
*BRITISH AMATEUR WEIGHTLIFTERS ASSOCIATION, 3 Iffley Turn, Oxford ox4 4du. Tel: 01865-200339. *Hon. Secretary,* W. Holland, obe

Wrestling
*BRITISH AMATEUR WRESTLING ASSOCIATION, 41 Great Clowes Street, Salford, Manchester m7 1rq. Tel: 0161-832 9209. *National Development Officer,* R. Tomlinson

Yachting
*ROYAL YACHTING ASSOCIATION, RYA House, Romsey Road, Eastleigh, Hants so50 9ya. Tel: 01703-627400. *Secretary-General,* R. Duchesne, obe

The Commonwealth Games

The Games were originally called the British Empire Games. From 1954 to 1966 the Games were known as the British Empire and Commonwealth Games, and from 1970 to 1974 as the British Commonwealth Games. Since 1978 the Games have been called the Commonwealth Games.

BRITISH EMPIRE GAMES

I	Hamilton, Canada	1930
II	London, England	1934
III	Sydney, Australia	1938
IV	Auckland, New Zealand	1950

BRITISH EMPIRE AND COMMONWEALTH GAMES

V	Vancouver, Canada	1954
VI	Cardiff, Wales	1958

VII	Perth, Australia	1962
VIII	Kingston, Jamaica	1966

BRITISH COMMONWEALTH GAMES

IX	Edinburgh, Scotland	1970
X	Christchurch, New Zealand	1974

COMMONWEALTH GAMES

XI	Edmonton, Canada	1978
XII	Brisbane, Australia	1982
XIII	Edinburgh, Scotland	1986
XIV	Auckland, New Zealand	1990
XV	Victoria, Canada	1994
XVI	Kuala Lumpur, Malaysia	1998
XVII	Manchester, England	2002

Clubs

LONDON CLUBS

ALPINE CLUB (1857), 55 Charlotte Road, London EC2A 3QT. Tel: 0171-613 0755. *Hon. Secretary*, G. D. Hughes

AMERICAN WOMEN'S CLUB (1899), 68 Old Brompton Road, London SW7 3LQ. Tel: 0171-589 8292. *Secretary*, Mrs S. Byrnes

ANGLO-BELGIAN CLUB (1955), 60 Knightsbridge, London SW1X 7LF. Tel: 0171-235 2121. *Secretary*, Baronne van Havre

ARMY AND NAVY CLUB (1837), 36 Pall Mall, London SW1Y 5JN. Tel: 0171-930 9721. *Secretary*, Maj. D. B. Taylor

ARTS CLUB (1863), 40 Dover Street, London W1X 3RB. Tel: 0171-499 8581. *Secretary*, Ms J. Downing

ARTS THEATRE CLUB (1927), 50 Frith Street, London W1V 5TE. Tel: 0171-287 9236. *Hon. Secretary*, S. Labisko

THE ATHENAEUM (1824), 107 Pall Mall, London SW1Y 5ER. Tel: 0171-930 4843. *Secretary*, R. T. Smith

AUTHORS' CLUB (1892), 40 Dover Street, London W1X 3RB. Tel: 0171-499 8581. *Secretary*, Mrs A. de la Grange

BEEFSTEAK CLUB (1876), 9 Irving Street, London WC2H 7AT. Tel: 0171-930 5722. *Secretary*, Sir John Lucas-Tooth, Bt.

BOODLE'S (1762), 28 St James's Street, London SW1A 1HJ. Tel: 0171-930 7166. *Secretary*, R. J. Edmonds

BROOKS'S (1764), St James's Street, London SW1A 1LN. Tel: 0171-493 4411. *Secretary*, G. Snell

BUCK'S CLUB (1919), 18 Clifford Street, London W1X 1RG. Tel: 0171-734 6896. *Secretary*, Capt. P. G. J. Murison, RN

CALEDONIAN CLUB (1891), 9 Halkin Street, London SW1X 7DR. Tel: 0171-235 5162. *Secretary*, P. J. Varncy

CANNING CLUB (1910), 94 Piccadilly, London W1V 0BP. Tel: 0171-499 5163. *Secretary*, T. M. Harrington

CARLTON CLUB (1832), 69 St James's Street, London SW1A 1PJ. Tel: 0171-493 1164. *Secretary*, R. N. Linsley

CAVALRY AND GUARDS CLUB (1893), 127 Piccadilly, London W1V 0PX. Tel: 0171-499 1261. *Secretary*, N. J. Walford

CHELSEA ARTS CLUB (1891), 143 Old Church Street, London SW3 6EB. Tel: 0171-376 3311. *Secretary*, D. Winterbottom

CITY LIVERY CLUB (1914), 20 Aldermanbury, London EC2V 7HP. Tel: 0171-814 0200. *Hon. Secretary*, J. C. F. B. Byllam-Barnes

CITY OF LONDON CLUB (1832), 19 Old Broad Street, London EC2N 1DS. Tel: 0171-588 7991. *Secretary*, G. S. Jones

CITY UNIVERSITY CLUB (1895), 50 Cornhill, London EC3V 3PD. Tel: 0171-626 8571. *Secretary*, Miss R. C. Graham

EAST INDIA CLUB (1849), 16 St James's Square, London SW1Y 4LH. Tel: 0171-930 1000. *Secretary*, J. G. F. Stoy

FARMERS CLUB (1842), 3 Whitehall Court, London SW1A 2EL. Tel: 0171-930 3751. *Secretary*, Gp Capt G. P. Carson

FLYFISHERS' CLUB (1884), 69 Brook Street, London W1Y 2ER. Tel: 0171-629 5958. *Secretary*, Cdr. T. Boycott, OBE, RN

GARRICK CLUB (1831), 15 Garrick Street, London WC2E 9AY. Tel: 0171-379 6478. *Secretary*, M. J. Harvey

GREEN ROOM CLUB (1877), 9 Adam Street, London WC2N 6AA. Tel: 0171-836 7453. *Secretary*, Ms J. Mander

GROUCHO CLUB (1985), 45 Dean Street, London W1V 5AP. Tel: 0171-439 4685. *Company Secretary*, Miss Z. Noordin

HURLINGHAM CLUB (1869), Ranelagh Gardens, London SW6 3PR. Tel: 0171-736 8411. *Secretary*, P. H. Covell

KENNEL CLUB (1873), 1–5 Clarges Street, London W1Y 8AB. Tel: 0171 493 6651. *Chief Executive*, R. French

LANSDOWNE CLUB (1934), 9 Fitzmaurice Place, London W1X 6JD. Tel: 0171-629 7200. *Secretary*, Lt.-Cdr. T. P. Havers

LONDON ROWING CLUB (1856), Embankment, Putney, London SW15 1LB. Tel: 0181-788 1400. *Hon. Secretary*, N. A. Smith

MCC (MARYLEBONE CRICKET CLUB) (1787), Lord's Cricket Ground, London NW8 8QN. Tel: 0171-289 1611. *Secretary*, R. D. V. Knight

NATIONAL CLUB (1845), c/o The Carlton Club, 69 St James's Street, London SW1A 1PJ. Tel: 0171-493 1164. *Hon. Secretary*, I. A. Sowton

NATIONAL LIBERAL CLUB (1882), Whitehall Place, London SW1A 2HE. Tel: 0171-930 9871. *Secretary*, S. J. Roberts

NAVAL AND MILITARY CLUB (1862), 94 Piccadilly, London W1V 0BP. Tel: 0171-499 5163. *Secretary*, Cdr. J. A. Holt, MBE, RN

NAVAL CLUB (1946), 38 Hill Street, London W1X 8DP. Tel: 0171-493 7672. *Chief Executive*, Capt. R. J. Husk, CBE, RN

NEW CAVENDISH CLUB (1984), 44 Great Cumberland Place, London W1H 8BS. Tel: 0171-723 0391. *Secretary*, J. Malone-Lee

DEN NORSKE KLUB (1924), Norway House, 21–24 Cockspur Street, London SW1Y 5BN. Tel: 0171-930 4084. *Secretary*, Ms J. P. Okkenhaug

ORIENTAL CLUB (1824), Stratford House, Stratford Place, London W1N 0ES. Tel: 0171-629 5126. *Secretary*, S. C. Doble

PORTLAND CLUB (1816), 42 Half Moon Street, London W1Y 7RD. Tel: 0171-499 1523. *Secretary*, J. Burns, CBE

PRATT'S CLUB (1841), 14 Park Place, London SW1A 1LP. Tel: 0171-493 0397. *Secretary*, G. Snell

QUEEN'S CLUB (1886), Palliser Road, London W14 9EQ. Tel: 0171-385 3421. *Secretary*, J. A. S. Edwardes

RAILWAY CLUB (1899), Room 208, 25 Marylebone Road, London NW1 5JS. Tel: 0173-781 2175. *Hon. Secretary*, A. G. Wells

REFORM CLUB (1836), 104–105 Pall Mall, London SW1Y 5EW. Tel: 0171-930 9374. *Secretary*, R. A. M. Forrest

ROEHAMPTON CLUB (1901), Roehampton Lane, London SW15 5LR. Tel: 0181-876 5505. *Chief Executive*, M. Yates

ROYAL AIR FORCE CLUB (1918), 128 Piccadilly, London W1V 0PY. Tel: 0171-499 3456. *Secretary*, P. N. Owen

ROYAL AUTOMOBILE CLUB (1897), 89–91 Pall Mall, London SW1Y 5HS. Tel: 0171-930 2345. *General Secretary*, Col. N. A. Johnson, OBE

ROYAL OCEAN RACING CLUB (1925), 20 St James's Place, London SW1A 1NN. Tel: 0171-493 2248. *General Manager*, D. J. Minords, OBE

ROYAL OVER-SEAS LEAGUE (1910), Over-Seas House, Park Place, St James's Street, London SW1A 1LR. Tel: 0171-408 0214. *Director-General*, R. F. Newell

ROYAL THAMES YACHT CLUB (1775), 60 Knightsbridge, London SW1X 7LF. Tel: 0171-235 2121. *Secretary*, Capt. D. Goldson, RN

St Stephen's Constitutional Club (1870), 34 Queen Anne's Gate, London swiH 9AB. Tel: 0171-222 1382. *Secretary*, L. D. Mawby

Savage Club (1857), 1 Whitehall Place, London SWIA 2HD. Tel: 0171-930 8118. *Hon. Secretary*, D. Stirling

Savile Club (1868), 69 Brook Street, London WIY 2ER. Tel: 0171-629 5462. *Secretary*, N. Storey

Ski Club of Great Britain (1903), The White House, 57–63 Church Road, Wimbledon SW19 5DQ. Tel: 0181-410 2000. *Managing Director*, Ms C. Stuart-Taylor

Thames Rowing Club (1860), Embankment, Putney, London SW15 ILB. Tel: 0181-788 0798. *Hon. Secretary*, J. McConnell

Travellers Club (1819), 106 Pall Mall, London SWIY 5EP. Tel: 0171-930 8688. *Secretary*, M. S. Allcock

Turf Club (1868), 5 Carlton House Terrace, London SWIY 5AQ. Tel: 0171-930 8555. *Secretary*, Col. J. G. B. Rigby, OBE

United Oxford and Cambridge University Club (1972), 71 Pall Mall, London SWIY 5HD. Tel: 0171-930 5151. *Secretary*, G. R. Buchanan

University Women's Club (1886), 2 Audley Square, South Audley Street, London WIY 6DB. Tel: 0171-499 2268. *Secretary*, J. Robson

Victoria Club (1863), 1 North Court, Great Peter Street, London SWIP 3LL. Tel: 0171-222 2357. *Secretary*, Ms S. David

Victory Services Club (1907), 63–79 Seymour Street, London W2 2HF. Tel: 0171-723 4474. *General Manager*, G. F. Taylor

White's (1693), 37–38 St James's Street, London SWIA IJG. Tel: 0171-493 6671. *Secretary*, D. C. Ward

Wig and Pen Club (1908), 229–230 Strand, London WC2R IBA. Tel: 0171-583 7255. *Chairman*, B. Coral

CLUBS OUTSIDE LONDON

Bath: Bath and County Club (1865), Queen's Parade, Bath BAI 2NJ. Tel: 01225-423732. *Secretary*, R. M. Lockert

Birmingham: The Birmingham Club (1872), Winston Churchill House, 8 Ethel Street, Birmingham B2 4BG. Tel: 0121-643 3357. *Hon. Secretary*, T. R. Pepper

St Paul's Club (1859), 34 St Paul's Square, Birmingham B3 1QZ. Tel: 0121-236 1950. *Hon. Secretary*, E. A. Fellowes

Bishop Auckland: The Club (1868), 1 Victoria Avenue, Bishop Auckland, Co. Durham DL14 7JH. Tel: 01388-603219. *Hon. Secretary*, R. Kellett

Blackburn: District and Union Club (1849), Northwood, 1 West Park Road, Blackburn BB2 6DE. Tel: 01254-51474. *Hon. Secretary*, B. Haydock

Bristol: Clifton Club (1882), 22 The Mall, Clifton, Bristol BS8 4DS. Tel: 0117-973 5527. *Secretary*, M. G. M. Henry

Cambridge: Cambridge University Amateur Dramatic Club (1855), ADC Theatre, Park Street, Cambridge CB5 8AS. Tel: 01223-359547. *Secretary*, Ms F. Beauman

The Union (1815), Bridge Street, Cambridge CB2 1UB. Tel: 01223-361521. *Chief Clerk*, Ms S. Finding

Canterbury: Kent and Canterbury Club (1868), The Elms, 17 Old Dover Road, Canterbury CT1 3JB. Tel: 01227-462181. *Secretary*, K. D. Bassey

Cheltenham: New Club (1874), 2 Montpellier Parade, Cheltenham GL50 1UD. Tel: 01242-523285. *Hon. Secretary*, N. S. Parrack

Chichester: Regnum Club (1862), 45A South Street, Chichester, W. Sussex PO19 IDS. Tel: 01243-780219. *Chairman*, M. Milburn

Durham: County Club (1890), 52 Old Elvet, Durham DHI 3HJ. Tel: 0191-384 8156. *Secretary*, Mrs C. Arnot

North Bailey Club (1842), 24 North Bailey, Durham DHI 3EW. Tel: 0191-384 3724. *Secretary*, Mrs E. M. Hardcastle

Guildford: The County Club, 158 High Street, Guildford GUI 3HJ. Tel: 01483-560677. *Hon. Secretary*, R. W. D. Hemingway

Henley-on-Thames: Leander Club (1818), Henley-on-Thames, Oxon RG9 2LP. Tel: 01491-575782. *Hon. Secretary*, J. Beveridge

Phyllis Court Club (1906), Marlow Road, Henley-on-Thames, Oxon RG9 2HT. Tel: 01491-570500. *Secretary*, R. Edwards

Hove: Hove Club (1882), 28 Fourth Avenue, Hove, E. Sussex BN3 2PJ. Tel: 01273-730872. *Secretary*, J. L. C. Young

Leamington Spa: Tennis Court Club (1846), 50 Bedford Street, Leamington Spa, Warks CV32 5DT. Tel: 01926-424977. *Hon. Secretary*, P. J. Lloyd

Leeds: The Leeds Club (1849), 3 Albion Place, Leeds LS1 6JL. Tel: 0113-242 1591. *Administrator*, Mrs I. Sigsworth

Leicester: Leicestershire Club (1873), 9 Welford Place, Leicester LEI 6ZH. Tel: 0116-254 0399. *Secretary*, T. M. Bedingfield

Liverpool: The Athenaeum (1797), Church Alley, Liverpool LI 3DD. Tel: 0151-709 7770. *Secretary*, N. Platt

Macclesfield: Old Boys' and Park Green Club, 7 Churchside, Macclesfield, Cheshire SK10 IHG. Tel: 01625-423292. *Hon. Secretary*, M. J. Garrity

Manchester: St James's Club, St James's House, Charlotte Street, Manchester MI 4DZ. Tel: 0161-236 2235. *Hon. Secretary*, B. A. Drewitt

Newcastle upon Tyne: Northern Constitutional Club (1882), 37 Pilgrim Street, Newcastle upon Tyne NEI 6QE. Tel: 0191-232 0884. *Hon. Secretary*, J. L. Browne

Northampton: Northampton and County Club (1873), George Row, Northampton NNI IDF. Tel: 01604-32962. *Secretary*, J. Green

Norwich: Norfolk Club (1770), 17 Upper King Street, Norwich NR3 IRB. Tel: 01603-610652. *Secretary*, G. G. Hardaker

Nottingham: Nottingham and Notts United Services Club (1920), Newdigate House, Castle Gate, Nottingham NGI 6AF. Tel: 0115-912 6220. *Secretary*, K. Goodman

Oxford: Frewen Club (1869), 98 St Aldate's, Oxford OXI IBT. Tel: 01865-243816. *Hon. Secretary*, B. R. Boyt

Vincent's Club (1863), 1A King Edward Street, Oxford OXI 4HS. Tel: 01865-722984. *Steward*, H. Dean

Paignton: Paignton Club (1882), The Esplanade, Paignton, Devon TQ4 6ED. Tel: 01803-559682. *Hon. Secretary*, P. Grafton

Shrewsbury: Salop Club (1974), The Old House, Dogpole, Shrewsbury SYI IEP. Tel: 01743-362182. *Secretary*, J. W. Rouse

Stourbridge: Stourbridge Old Edwardian Club (1898), Drury Lane, Stourbridge, West Midlands DY8 IBL. Tel: 01384-395635. *Hon. Secretary*, D. J. Lucas

Teddington: Royal Canoe Club (1866), Trowlock Island, Teddington, Middx TWII 9QZ. Tel: 0181-977 5269. *Hon. Secretary*, Mrs J. S. Evans

WALES

Cardiff: Cardiff and County Club (1866), Westgate Street, Cardiff CFI IDA. Tel: 01222-220846. *Hon. Secretary*, Cdr. J. E. Payn, RD

SCOTLAND

Aberdeen: ROYAL NORTHERN AND UNIVERSITY CLUB (1854/ 1889, amal. 1979), 9 Albyn Place, Aberdeen AB10 1YE. Tel: 01224-583292. *Secretary,* Miss R. A. Black

Ayr: AYR COUNTY CLUB (1872), Savoy Park Hotel, Racecourse Road, Ayr KA7 2UT. Tel: 01292-266112. *Hon. Secretary,* G. A. Hay

Edinburgh: CALEDONIAN CLUB, 32 Abercromby Place, Edinburgh EH3 6QE. Tel: 0131-557 2675. *Secretary,* P. Walker

NEW CLUB (1787), 86 Princes Street, Edinburgh EH2 2BB. Tel: 0131-226 4881. *Secretary,* A. D. Orr Ewing

Glasgow: GLASGOW ART CLUB (1867), 185 Bath Street, Glasgow G2 4HU. Tel: 0141-248 5210. *Secretary,* L. J. McIntyre

ROYAL SCOTTISH AUTOMOBILE CLUB (1899), 11 Blythswood Square, Glasgow G2 4AG. Tel: 0141-221 3850. *Secretary,* J. C. Lord

WESTERN CLUB (1825), 32 Royal Exchange Square, Glasgow G1 3AB. Tel: 0141-221 2016. *Secretary,* D. H. Gifford

NORTHERN IRELAND

Belfast: ULSTER REFORM CLUB (1885), 4 Royal Avenue, Belfast BT1 1DA. Tel: 01232-323411. *Secretary,* Miss M. P. Mackintosh

Londonderry: NORTHERN COUNTIES CLUB (1880), 24 Bishop Street, Londonderry BT48 6PP. Tel: 01504-262012. *Hon. Secretary,* N. Dykes

CHANNEL ISLANDS

Guernsey: UNITED CLUB (1870), Pier Steps, St Peter Port, Guernsey GY1 2LW. Tel: 01481-725722. *Hon. Secretary,* G. D. E. Chaloner

Jersey: VICTORIA CLUB (1853), Beresford Street, St Helier, Jersey JE2 4WN. Tel: 01534-23381. *Secretary,* W. A. F. Hurst

---

YACHT CLUBS

Bembridge: BEMBRIDGE SAILING CLUB (1886), Embankment Road, Bembridge, IOW PO35 5NR. Tel: 01983-872237. *Secretary,* Lt.-Col. M. J. Samuelson, RM

Birkenhead: ROYAL MERSEY YACHT CLUB (1844), Bedford Road East, Rock Ferry, Birkenhead, Merseyside L42 1LS. Tel: 0151-645 3204. *Hon. Secretary,* P. A. Bastow

Bridlington: ROYAL YORKSHIRE YACHT CLUB (1847), 1 Windsor Crescent, Bridlington, E. Yorks YO15 3HX. Tel: 01262-672041. *Secretary,* J. H. Evans

Burnham-on-Crouch: ROYAL CORINTHIAN YACHT CLUB (1872), The Quay, Burnham-on-Crouch, Essex CM0 8AX. Tel: 01621-782105. *Hon. Secretary,* B. Stanford

Chichester: CHICHESTER YACHT CLUB (1965), Chichester Yacht Basin, Birdham, Chichester, W. Sussex PO20 7EJ. Tel: 01243-512918. *Secretary,* Mrs V. A. Allan

Cowes: ROYAL YACHT SQUADRON (1815), The Castle, Cowes, IOW PO31 7QT. Tel: 01983-292191. *Secretary,* Maj. R. P. Rising, RM

Dover: ROYAL CINQUE PORTS YACHT CLUB (1872), 5 Waterloo Crescent, Dover, Kent CT16 1LA. Tel: 01304-206262. *Secretary,* Mrs C. A. Partridge

Fowey: ROYAL FOWEY YACHT CLUB (1881), Whitford Yard, Fowey, Cornwall PL23 1BH. Tel: 01726-833573. *Hon. Secretary,* M. E. J. Harrison

Ipswich: ROYAL HARWICH YACHT CLUB (1843), Woolverstone, Ipswich IP9 1AT. Tel: 01473-780319. *Secretary,* Cdr. J. A. Adams, RD

Dartmouth: ROYAL DART YACHT CLUB (1866), Priory Street, Kingswear, Dartmouth, Devon TQ6 0AB. Tel: 01803-752496. *Hon. Secretary,* R. Hine-Haycock

Leigh-on-Sea: ESSEX YACHT CLUB (1890), HQS Bembridge, Foreshore, Leigh-on-Sea, Essex SS9 1BD. Tel: 01702-78404. *Hon. Secretary,* Ms L. Kelly

London: THE CRUISING ASSOCIATION (1908), CA House, 1 Northey Street, Limehouse Basin, London E14 8BT. Tel: 0171-537 2828. *General Secretary,* Mrs. L. Hammett

ROYAL THAMES YACHT CLUB (1775), 60 Knightsbridge, London SW1X 7LF. Tel: 0171-235 2121. *Secretary,* Capt. D Goldson, RN

Lowestoft: ROYAL NORFOLK AND SUFFOLK YACHT CLUB (1859), Royal Plain, Lowestoft, Suffolk NR33 0AQ. Tel: 01502-566726. *General Manager,* A. Donovan

Lymington: ROYAL LYMINGTON YACHT CLUB (1922), Bath Road, Lymington, Hants SO41 3SE. Tel: 01590-672677. *Secretary,* Gp Capt. J. D. Hutchinson

Plymouth: ROYAL PLYMOUTH CORINTHIAN YACHT CLUB (1877), Madeira Road, Plymouth PL1 2NY. Tel: 01752-664327. *Hon. Secretary,* V. J. De Boo

ROYAL WESTERN YACHT CLUB OF ENGLAND (1827), Queen Anne's Battery, Plymouth PL4 0TW. Tel: 01752-660077. *Chief Executive,* J. Lewis

Poole: EAST DORSET SAILING CLUB (1875), 352 Sandbanks Road, Poole, Dorset BH14 8HY. Tel: 01202-706111. *Hon. Secretary,* Mrs T. Neely

PARKSTONE YACHT CLUB (1895), Pearce Avenue, Poole, Dorset BH14 8EH. Tel: 01202-743610. *Secretary,* D. E. Norman

POOLE HARBOUR YACHT CLUB (1949), 38 Salterns Way, Lilliput, Poole, Dorset BH14 8JR. Tel: 01202-707321. *Secretary,* J. N. J. Smith

POOLE YACHT CLUB (1865), New Harbour Road West, Hamworthy, Poole, Dorset BH15 4AQ. Tel: 01202-672687. *Secretary/Manager,* Miss L. Clark

Portsmouth: ROYAL NAVAL CLUB AND ROYAL ALBERT YACHT CLUB (1867), 17 Pembroke Road, Portsmouth PO1 2NT. Tel: 01705-824491. *Secretary,* J. Dalmeny

Ramsgate: ROYAL TEMPLE YACHT CLUB (1857), 6 Westcliff Mansions, Ramsgate, Kent CT11 9HY. Tel: 01843-591766. *Hon. Secretary,* M. Moore

Southampton: ROYAL AIR FORCE YACHT CLUB (1932), Riverside House, Rope Walk, Hamble, Southampton SO31 4HD. Tel: 01703-452208. *Secretary,* Mrs S. E. Fullwood

ROYAL SOUTHAMPTON YACHT CLUB, 1 Channel Way, Ocean Village, Southampton SO14 3QF. Tel: 01703-223352. *Secretary,* A. M. Paterson

ROYAL SOUTHERN YACHT CLUB (1837), Rope Walk, Hamble, Southampton SO31 4HB. Tel: 01703-453271. *Secretary,* Mrs. J. A. Atkins

Torquay: ROYAL TORBAY YACHT CLUB (1863), Beacon Hill, Torquay, Devon TQ1 2BQ. Tel: 01803-292006. *Club Administrator,* R. M. Porteous

Westcliff-on-Sea: THAMES ESTUARY YACHT CLUB (1895), 3 The Leas, Westcliff-on-Sea, Essex SS0 7ST. Tel: 01702-345967. *Hon. Secretary,* D. G. Brown

Weymouth: ROYAL DORSET YACHT CLUB (1875), 11 Custom House Quay, Weymouth, Dorset DT4 8BG. Tel: 01305-786258. *Secretary,* Mrs K. Mead

Windermere: ROYAL WINDERMERE YACHT CLUB (1860), Fallbarrow Road, Bowness-on-Windermere, Windermere, Cumbria LA23 3DJ. Tel: 015394-43106. *Hon. Secretary,* P. V. Barraclough

Yarmouth: ROYAL SOLENT YACHT CLUB (1878), Yarmouth, IOW PO41 0NS. Tel: 01983-760256. *Secretary*, Mrs S. Tribe

WALES

Beaumaris: ROYAL ANGLESEY YACHT CLUB (1802), 6–7 Green Edge, Beaumaris, Anglesey LL58 8BY. Tel: 01248-810295. *Hon. Secretary*, J. E. de Leyland-Berry
Caernarfon: ROYAL WELSH YACHT CLUB (1847), Porth-Yr-Aur, Caernarfon LL55 1SW. Tel: 01286-672599. *Hon. Secretary*, J. H. Long
Penarth: PENARTH YACHT CLUB (1880), The Esplanade, Penarth, Vale of Glamorgan CF64 3AU. Tel: 01222-708196. *Hon. Secretary*, R. S. McGregor
Swansea: BRISTOL CHANNEL YACHT CLUB (1875), 744 Mumbles Road, Mumbles, Swansea SA3 4EL. Tel: 01792-366000. *Hon. Secretary*, R. L. Morgan

SCOTLAND

Dundee: ROYAL TAY YACHT CLUB (1885), 34 Dundee Road, Broughty Ferry, Dundee DD5 1LX. Tel: 01382-477516. *Hon. Secretary*, S. Buchanan
Edinburgh: ROYAL FORTH YACHT CLUB (1868), Middle Pier, Granton Harbour, Edinburgh EH5 1HF. Tel: 0131-552 8560. *Hon. Secretary*, C. D. Hurn
Helensburgh: ROYAL WESTERN YACHT CLUB (1875), Edenbank, 66 Colquhoun Street, Helensburgh, Argyll and Bute G84 9JP. *Hon. Secretary*, D. W. Pritty
Oban: ROYAL HIGHLAND YACHT CLUB (1881), Raslie House, Slockavullin, Argyll PA31 8QG. Tel: 01546-510261. *Secretary*, Mrs A. Wood
Rhu: ROYAL NORTHERN AND CLYDE YACHT CLUB (1824, amal. 1978), Rhu, Helensburgh, Argyll and Bute G84 8NG. Tel: 01436-820322. *Hon. Secretary*, B. C. Staig

NORTHERN IRELAND

Bangor: ROYAL ULSTER YACHT CLUB (1866), 101 Clifton Road, Bangor, Co. Down BT20 5HY. Tel: 01247-270568. *Secretary*, Mrs V. F. M. Boyd

CHANNEL ISLANDS

Jersey: ROYAL CHANNEL ISLANDS YACHT CLUB (1862), Le Boulevard, Bulwarks, St Aubin, Jersey JE3 8GW. Tel: 01534-41023. *Hon. Secretary*, D. C. Dale

Societies and Institutions

Although this section is arranged in alphabetical order, organizations are usually listed by the keyword in their title. The date in parenthesis after the organization's title is the year of its foundation.

ABBEYFIELD SOCIETY (1956), Abbeyfield House, 53 Victoria Street, St Albans, Herts AL1 3UW. Tel: 01727-857536. Housing for elderly people. *Chief Executive*, F. Murphy

ACCOUNTANTS, ASSOCIATION OF CHARTERED CERTIFIED (1904), 29 Lincoln's Inn Fields, London WC2A 3EE. Tel: 0171-396 5751. *Chief Executive*, Mrs A. L. Rose

ACCOUNTANTS IN ENGLAND AND WALES, INSTITUTE OF CHARTERED (1880), Chartered Accountants' Hall, PO Box 433, Moorgate Place, London EC2P 2BJ. Tel: 0171-920 8100. *Secretary*, A. J. Colquhoun

ACCOUNTANTS, INSTITUTE OF COMPANY (1974), 40 Tyndalls Park Road, Bristol BS8 1PL. Tel: 0117-973 8261. Also 80 Portland Place, London W1N 4DP. *Director-General*, B. T. Banks

ACCOUNTANTS, INSTITUTE OF FINANCIAL (1916), Burford House, 44 London Road, Sevenoaks, Kent TN13 1AS. Tel: 01732-458080. *Chief Executive*, J. M. Dean

ACCOUNTANTS OF SCOTLAND, INSTITUTE OF CHARTERED (1854), 27 Queen Street, Edinburgh EH2 1LA. Tel: 0131-225 5673. *Chief Executive*, P. W. Johnston

ACCOUNTING TECHNICIANS, ASSOCIATION OF (1980), 154 Clerkenwell Road, London EC1R 5AD. Tel: 0171-837 8600. *Secretary*, Ms J. Scott Paul

ACE STUDY TOURS (formerly Association for Cultural Exchange), Babraham, Cambridge CB2 4AP. Tel: 01223-835055. *General Secretary*, P. B. Barnes

ACTION RESEARCH (1952), Vincent House, Horsham, W. Sussex RH12 2DP. Tel: 01403-210406. *Director-General*, Mrs A. Luther

ACTORS' BENEVOLENT FUND (1882), 6 Adam Street, London WC2N 6AA. Tel: 0171-836 6378. *General Secretary*, Mrs R. Stevens

ACTORS' CHARITABLE TRUST (1896), 255–256 Africa House, 64–78 Kingsway, London WC2B 6BD. Tel: 0171-242 0111. *General Secretary*, B. Batchelor

ACTORS' CHURCH UNION (1899), St Paul's Church, Bedford Street, London WC2E 9ED. Tel: 0171-836 5221. *Senior Chaplain*, Canon W. Hall

ACTUARIES IN SCOTLAND, FACULTY OF (1856), 17 Thistle Street, Edinburgh EH2 1DF. Tel: 0131-220 4555. *Secretary*, W. W. Mair

ACTUARIES, INSTITUTE OF (1848), Staple Inn Hall, High Holborn, London WC1V 7QJ. Tel: 0171-242 0106. *Secretary-General*, G. B. L. Campbell

ADMINISTRATIVE MANAGEMENT, INSTITUTE OF (1915), 40 Chatsworth Parade, Petts Wood, Orpington, Kent BR5 1RW. Tel: 01689-875555. *Chief Executive*, Prof. G. Robinson

ADULT SCHOOL ORGANIZATION, NATIONAL (1899), MASU Centre, Gaywood Croft, Cregoe Street, Birmingham B15 2ED. Tel: 0121-622 3400. *General Secretary*, Mrs P. C. Dean

ADVERTISING, INSTITUTE OF PRACTITIONERS IN (1927), 44 Belgrave Square, London SW1X 8QS. Tel: 0171-235 7020. *Director-General*, N. Phillips

ADVERTISING STANDARDS AUTHORITY (1962), 2 Torrington Place, London W1E 7HW. Tel: 0171-580 5555. *Director-General*, Mrs M. Alderson

AERONAUTICAL SOCIETY, ROYAL (1866), 4 Hamilton Place, London W1V 0BQ. Tel: 0171-499 3515. *Director*, R. J. Kennett

AFRICAN INSTITUTE, INTERNATIONAL (1926), SOAS, Thornhaugh Street, Russell Square, London WC1H 0XG. Tel: 0171-323 6035. *Hon. Director*, Prof. P. Spencer

AFRICAN MEDICAL AND RESEARCH FOUNDATION, 11 Old Queen Street, London SW1H 9JA. Tel: 0171-233 0066. *Executive Director*, A. Heroys

AGE CONCERN CYMRU, 4th Floor, 1 Cathedral Road, Cardiff CF1 9SD. Tel: 01222-371566. *Director*, R. W. Taylor

AGE CONCERN ENGLAND (1940), Astral House, 1268 London Road, London SW16 4ER. Tel: 0181-679 8000. *Director-General*, Ms S. Greengross, OBE

AGE CONCERN NORTHERN IRELAND (1976), 3 Lower Crescent, Belfast BT7 1NR. Tel: 01232-245729. *Director*, C. J. Common

AGE CONCERN SCOTLAND (1943), 113 Rose Street, Edinburgh EH2 3DT. Tel: 0131-220 3345. *Director*, Ms M. O'Neill

AGEING, CENTRE FOR POLICY ON (1947), 25–31 Ironmonger Row, London EC1V 3QP. Tel: 0171-253 1787. *Director*, Dr G. Dalley

AGEING, RESEARCH INTO (1978), Baird House, 15–17 St Cross Street, London EC1N 8UN. Tel: 0171-404 6878. *Director*, Mrs E. Mills

AGRICULTURAL BENEVOLENT INSTITUTION, ROYAL (1860), Shaw House, 27 West Way, Oxford OX2 0QH. Tel: 01865-724931. *Chief Executive*, Air Cdre R. B. Duckett, CVO, AFC

AGRICULTURAL BENEVOLENT INSTITUTION, ROYAL SCOTTISH (1897), Ingliston, Edinburgh EH28 8NB. Tel: 0131-333 1023. *Director*, I. C. Purves-Hume

AGRICULTURAL ENGINEERS ASSOCIATION (1875), Samuelson House, Paxton Road, Orton Centre, Peterborough PE2 5LT. Tel: 01733-371381. *Director-General*, J. Vowles

AGRICULTURAL SOCIETY, EAST OF ENGLAND, East of England Showground, Peterborough PE2 6XE. Tel: 01733-234451. *Chief Executive*, T. Gibson, OBE

AGRICULTURAL SOCIETY OF ENGLAND, ROYAL (1838), National Agricultural Centre, Stoneleigh Park, Kenilworth, Warks CV8 2LZ. Tel: 01203-696969. *Chief Executive*, C. Runge

AGRICULTURAL SOCIETY OF THE COMMONWEALTH, ROYAL (1957), 55 Sleaford Street, London SW8 5AB. Tel: 0171-978 1301. *Hon. Secretary*, F. R. Francis, CVO, MBE

AGRICULTURAL SOCIETY, ROYAL ULSTER (1826), The King's Hall, Balmoral, Belfast BT9 6GW. Tel: 01232-665225. *Chief Executive*, W. H. Yarr, OBE

AIR LEAGUE (1909), Broadway House, Tothill Street, London SW1H 9NS. Tel: 0171-222 8463. *Director*, Gp Capt. E. R. Cox

ALCOHOLICS ANONYMOUS (1947), PO Box 1, Stonebow House, Stonebow, York YO1 2NJ. Tel: 01904-644026. *General Secretary*, J. Keeney

ALEXANDRA ROSE DAY (1912), 2A Ferry Road, Barnes, London SW13 9RX. Tel: 0181-748 4824. *National Director*, Mrs G. Greenwood

ALLIANCE PARTY OF NORTHERN IRELAND (1970), 88 University Street, Belfast BT7 1HE. Tel: 01232-324274. *Party Leader*, Lord Alderdice

ALLOTMENT AND LEISURE GARDENERS, NATIONAL SOCIETY OF (1930), Hunters Road, Corby, Northants NN17 5JE. Tel: 01536-266576. *National Secretary*, G. W. Stokes

ALMSHOUSES, NATIONAL ASSOCIATION OF (1946), Billingbear Lodge, Carter's Hill, Wokingham, Berks RG40 5RU. Tel: 01344-52922. *Director*, Maj.-Gen. A. deC. L. Leask

ALZHEIMER'S DISEASE SOCIETY (1979), Gordon House, 10 Greencoat Place, London SW1P 1PH. Tel: 0171-306 0606. *Executive Director*, H. Cayton

AMNESTY INTERNATIONAL UNITED KINGDOM (1961), 99–119 Rosebery Avenue, London EC1R 4RE. Tel: 0171-814 6200. *Director*, D. Bull

ANAESTHETISTS OF GREAT BRITAIN AND IRELAND, ASSOCIATION OF (1932), 9 Bedford Square, London WC1B 3RA. Tel: 0171-631 1650. *Hon. Secretary*, Dr D. J. Wilkinson

ANCIENT BUILDINGS, SOCIETY FOR THE PROTECTION OF (1877), 37 Spital Square, London E1 6DY. Tel: 0171-377 1644. *Secretary*, P. Venning, FSA

ANCIENT MONUMENTS SOCIETY (1924), St Ann's Vestry Hall, 2 Church Entry, London EC4V 5HB. Tel: 0171-236 3934. *Secretary*, M. J. Saunders

ANGLO-ARAB ASSOCIATION (1961), The Arab British Centre, 21 Collingham Road, London SW5 0NU. Tel: 0171-373 8414. *Executive Director*, A. Lee

ANGLO-BELGIAN SOCIETY (1982), 5 Hartley Close, Bickley, Kent BR1 2TP. Tel: 0181-467 8442. *Hon. Secretary*, P. R. Bresnan

ANGLO-BRAZILIAN SOCIETY (1943), 32 Green Street, London W1Y 3FD. Tel: 0171-493 8493. *Secretary*, Mrs M. Lee

ANGLO-DANISH SOCIETY (1924), 25 New Street Square, London EC4A 3LN. Tel: 01753-884846. *Chairman*, H. Castenskiold, OBE

ANGLO-NORSE SOCIETY (1918), 25 Belgrave Square, London SW1X 8QD. Tel: 0171-591 5500. *Chairman*, Dame Gillian Brown, DCVO, CMG

ANIMAL CONCERN (1988), 62 Old Dumbarton Road, Glasgow G3 8RE. Tel: 0141-334 6014. *Organizing Secretary*, J. F. Robins

ANIMAL HEALTH TRUST (1942), PO Box 5, Newmarket, Suffolk CB8 7DW. Tel: 01638-661111. *Director*, A. J. Higgins, PH.D.

ANTHROPOLOGICAL INSTITUTE, ROYAL (1843), 50 Fitzroy Street, London W1P 5HS. Tel: 0171-387 0455. *Director*, J. C. M. Benthall

ANTHROPOSOPHICAL SOCIETY IN GREAT BRITAIN (1923), Rudolf Steiner House, 35 Park Road, London NW1 6XT. Tel: 0171-723 4400. *General Secretary*, N. C. Thomas

ANTIQUARIES OF LONDON, SOCIETY OF (1717), Burlington House, Piccadilly, London W1V 0HS. Tel: 0171-734 0193. *General Secretary*, D. Morgan Evans, FSA

ANTIQUARIES OF SCOTLAND, SOCIETY OF (1780), Royal Museum of Scotland, Chambers Street, Edinburgh EH1 1JF. Tel: 0131-225 7534. *Director*, Mrs F. Ashmore, FSA

ANTIQUE DEALERS' ASSOCIATION, BRITISH (1918), 20 Rutland Gate, London SW7 1BD. Tel: 0171-589 4128. *Secretary-General*, Mrs E. J. Dean

ANTI-SLAVERY INTERNATIONAL (1839), Unit 4, Stableyard, Broomgrove Road, London SW9 9TL. Tel: 0171-924 9555. *Director*, M. Dottridge

ANTI-VIVISECTION: BRITISH UNION FOR THE ABOLITION OF VIVISECTION (1898), 16A Crane Grove, London N7 8LB. Tel: 0171-700 4888. *Director*, M. Baker

ANTI-VIVISECTION SOCIETY, NATIONAL (1875), 261 Goldhawk Road, London W12 9PE. Tel: 0181-846 9777. *Director*, Ms J. Creamer

APOSTLESHIP OF THE SEA (1920), Stella Maris, 66 Dock Road, Tilbury, Essex RM18 7BX. Tel: 01375-850801. *National Director*, T. J. MacGuire

APOTHECARIES OF LONDON, SOCIETY OF (1617), 14 Black Friars Lane, London EC4V 6EJ. Tel: 0171-236 1189. *Clerk*, R. J. Stringer

ARBITRATORS, CHARTERED INSTITUTE OF (1915), 24 Angel Gate, City Road, London EC1V 2RS. Tel: 0171-837 4483. *Secretary-General*, K. Harding

ARCHAEOLOGICAL ASSOCIATION, CAMBRIAN (1846), The Laurels, Westfield Road, Newport, Gwent NP9 4ND. Tel: 01633-262449. *General Secretary*, Dr J. M. Hughes

ARCHAEOLOGICAL INSTITUTE, ROYAL (1843), c/o Society of Antiquaries of London, Burlington House, Piccadilly, London W1V 0HS. *Secretary*, J. G. Coad, FSA

ARCHAEOLOGY, COUNCIL FOR BRITISH (1944), Bowes Morrell House, 111 Walmgate, York YO1 2UA. Tel: 01904-671417. *Director*, R. K. Morris

ARCHITECTS AND SURVEYORS INSTITUTE (1926), St Mary House, 15 St Mary Street, Chippenham, Wilts SN15 3WD. Tel: 01249-444505. *Chief Executive*, C. G. A. Nash, OBE

ARCHITECTS BENEVOLENT SOCIETY (1850), 43 Portland Place, London W1N 3AG. Tel: 0171-580 2823. *Hon. Secretary*, R. Roth

ARCHITECTS IN SCOTLAND, ROYAL INCORPORATION OF (1922), 15 Rutland Square, Edinburgh EH1 2BE. Tel: 0131-229 7545. *Secretary*, S. Tombs

ARCHITECTS REGISTRATION BOARD (1931), 73 Hallam Street, London W1N 6EE. Tel: 0171-580 5861. *Registrar*, D. W. Smart

ARCHITECTS, ROYAL INSTITUTE OF BRITISH (1834), 66 Portland Place, London W1N 4AD. Tel: 0171-580 5533. *President*, Dr F. Duffy

ARCHITECTURAL ASSOCIATION INC. (1847), 34–36 Bedford Square, London WC1B 3ES. Tel: 0171-636 0974. *Secretary*, E. Le Maistre

ARCHITECTURAL HERITAGE FUND (1976), Clareville House, 26–27 Oxendon Street, London SW1Y 4EL. Tel: 0171-925 0199. *Secretary*, Lady Weir

ARCHIVISTS, SOCIETY OF (1947), Information House, 20–24 Old Street, London EC1V 9AP. Tel: 0171-253 5087. *Executive Secretary*, P. S. Cleary

ARK ENVIRONMENTAL FOUNDATION (1988), Suite 640–643, Linen Hall, 162–168 Regent Street, London W1R 5TB. Tel: 0171-439 4567. *Co-ordinator*, Ms N. Malone

ARLIS/UK AND IRELAND (THE ART LIBRARIES SOCIETY) (1969), 18 College Road, Bromsgrove, Worcs B60 2NE. Tel: 01527-579298. *Administrator*, Ms S. French

BIRMINGHAM AND MIDLAND INSTITUTE (1854) and PRIESTLEY LIBRARY (1779), Margaret Street, Birmingham B3 3BS. Tel: 0121-236 3591. *Administrator and General Secretary*, P. A. Fisher

BLIND, GUIDE DOGS FOR THE, *see* GUIDE DOGS FOR THE BLIND ASSOCIATION

BLIND, NATIONAL LIBRARY FOR THE (1882), Far Cromwell Road, Bredbury, Stockport, Cheshire SK6 2SG. Tel: 0161-494 0217. *Chief Executive*, Ms M. Bennett

BLIND PEOPLE, ACTION FOR (1857), 14—16 Verney Road, London SE16 3DZ. Tel: 0171-732 8771. *Chief Executive*, S. Remington

BLIND, ROYAL LONDON SOCIETY FOR THE (1838), Dorton House, Seal, Sevenoaks, Kent TN15 0ED. Tel: 01732-761477. *Chief Executive*, P. Talbot

BLIND, ROYAL NATIONAL COLLEGE FOR THE (1872), College Road, Hereford HR1 1EB. Tel: 01432-265725. *Principal*, C. Housby-Smith, PH.D.

BLIND, ROYAL NATIONAL INSTITUTE FOR THE, *see* ROYAL NATIONAL INSTITUTE FOR THE BLIND

BLIND, ROYAL SCHOOL FOR THE, *see* SEEABILITY

BLOOD SERVICE, NATIONAL (1948), Oak House, Reeds Crescent, Watford, Herts WD1 1QH. Tel: 01923-486800. *Chief Executive*, J. Adey

BLOOD TRANSFUSION ASSOCIATION, SCOTTISH NATIONAL (1940), c/o Scottish National Blood Transfusion Service, Ellen's Glen Road, Edinburgh EH17 7QT. Tel: 0131-664 2317. *Secretary*, W. Mack

BLUE CROSS (1897), Shilton Road, Burford, Oxon OX18 4PF. Tel: 01993-822651. *Secretary and Chief Executive*, A. Kennard, MBE

BODLEIAN, FRIENDS OF THE (1925), Bodleian Library, Oxford OX1 3BG. Tel: 01865-277022/277234. *Secretary*, G. Groom

BOOK AID INTERNATIONAL (1954), 39—41 Coldharbour Lane, London SE5 9NR. Tel: 0171-733 3577. *Director*, Mrs S. Harrity, MBE

BOOKSELLERS ASSOCIATION OF GREAT BRITAIN AND IRELAND (1895), Minster House, 272 Vauxhall Bridge Road, London SW1V 1BA. Tel: 0171-834 5477. *Chief Executive*, T. E. Godfray

BOOK TRADE BENEVOLENT SOCIETY (1967), Dillon Lodge, The Retreat, Kings Langley, Herts WD4 8LT. Tel: 01923-263128. *Chief Executive*, D. Hicks

BOOK TRUST (1986), Book House, 45 East Hill, London SW18 2QZ. Tel: 0181-870 9055. *Executive Director*, B. Perman

BORN FREE FOUNDATION (1984), Cherry Tree Cottage, Coldharbour, Dorking, Surrey RH5 6HA. Tel: 01306-712091. *Director*, W. Travers

BOTANICAL SOCIETY OF SCOTLAND, c/o Royal Botanic Garden, Inverleith Row, Edinburgh EH3 5LR. Tel: 0131-552 7171. *Hon. General Secretary*, R. Galt

BOTANICAL SOCIETY OF THE BRITISH ISLES (1836), c/o Department of Botany, The Natural History Museum, Cromwell Road, London SW7 5BD. Tel: 0171-938 8701. *Hon. General Secretary*, R. Gwynn Ellis

BOY SCOUTS ASSOCIATION, *see* SCOUT ASSOCIATION

BOYS' AND GIRLS' CLUBS OF NORTHERN IRELAND (1940), 2nd Floor, 38 Dublin Road, Belfast BT2 7HN. Tel: 01232-241924. *General Secretary*, K. Culbert

BOYS' BRIGADE (1883), Felden Lodge, Hemel Hempstead, Herts HP3 0BL. Tel: 01442-231681. *Brigade Secretary*, S. Jones, OBE

BREWING, INSTITUTE OF (1886), 33 Clarges Street, London W1Y 8EE. Tel: 0171-499 8144. *Chief Executive*, P. W. E. Istead

BRIDEWELL ROYAL HOSPITAL (1553), Witley, Godalming, Surrey GU8 5SG. Tel: 01428-682371. *Clerk*, G. Goddard

BRITAIN-NEPAL SOCIETY (1960), 3C Gunnersbury Avenue, London W5 3NH. Tel: 0181-992 0173. *Hon. Secretary*, Mrs P. Mellor

BRITAIN-RUSSIA CENTRE and BRITISH EAST WEST CENTRE (1959), 14 Grosvenor Place, London SW1X 7HW. Tel: 0171-235 2116. *Director*, Dr I. Elliot

BRITISH AND FOREIGN SCHOOL SOCIETY (1808), Richard Mayo Hall, Eden Street, Kingston upon Thames, Surrey KT1 1HZ. Tel: 0181-546 2379. *Secretary*, new appointment awaited

BRITISH EXECUTIVE SERVICE OVERSEAS (1976), 164 Vauxhall Bridge Road, London SW1V 4RB. Tel: 0171-630 0644. *Chief Executive*, G. Ramsey, CBE

BRITISH INSTITUTE IN EASTERN AFRICA (1959), 20—22 Queensberry Place, London SW7 2DZ. Tel: 0171-584 4653. *London Secretary*, Mrs J. Moyo

BRITISH INSTITUTE OF ARCHAEOLOGY AT ANKARA (1948), 31—34 Gordon Square, London WC1H 0PY. Tel: 0171-388 2361. *Director*, Dr R. J. Matthews

BRITISH INSTITUTE OF PERSIAN STUDIES (1961), c/o The British Academy, 20—21 Cornwall Terrace, London NW1 4QP. *Assistant Secretary*, Ms J. Dryden

BRITISH INTERPLANETARY SOCIETY (1933), 27—29 South Lambeth Road, London SW8 1SZ. Tel: 0171-735 3160. *Executive Secretary*, Ms S. A. Jones

BRITISH ISRAEL WORLD FEDERATION (1919), 8 Blades Court, Deodar Road, London SW15 2NU. Tel: 0181-877 9010. *Secretary*, A. E. Gibb

BRITISH LEGION, ROYAL (1921), 48 Pall Mall, London SW1Y 5JY. Tel: 0171-973 7200. *Secretary-General*, Brig. I. G. Townsend

BRITISH LEGION SCOTLAND, ROYAL (1921), New Haig House, Logie Green Road, Edinburgh EH7 4HR. Tel: 0131-557 2782. *General Secretary*, Maj.-Gen. J. D. MacDonald, CB, CBE

BRITISH MEDICAL ASSOCIATION (1832), BMA House, Tavistock Square, London WC1H 9JP. Tel: 0171-387 4499. *Chairman*, Dr A. W. Macara

BRITISH NATIONAL PARTY (1982), PO Box 117, Welling, Kent DA16 3DW. Tel: 0374-454893. *Chairman*, J. Tyndall

BRITISH RED CROSS (1870), 9 Grosvenor Crescent, London SW1X 7EJ. Tel: 0171-235 5454. *Director-General*, M. R. Whitlam

BRITISH SCHOOL OF ARCHAEOLOGY IN JERUSALEM (1919), 21 Buccleuch Place (Top Flat), The University of Edinburgh, Edinburgh EH8 9LN. Tel: 0131-650 3975. *President*, P. R. S. Moorey, PH.D., FBA

BUDDHIST SOCIETY (1924), 58 Eccleston Square, London SW1V 1PH. Tel: 0171-834 5858. *General Secretary*, R. C. Maddox

BUDGERIGAR SOCIETY (1925), 49—53 Hazelwood Road, Northampton NN1 1LG. Tel: 01604-24549. *General Secretary*, D. Whittaker

BUILDING, CHARTERED INSTITUTE OF (1834), Englemere, King's Ride, Ascot, Berks SL5 7TB. Tel: 01344-630700. *Chief Executive*, K. Banbury

BUILDING ENGINEERS, ASSOCIATION OF (1925), Jubilee House, Billing Brook Road, Weston Favell, Northampton NN3 8NW. Tel: 01604-404121. *Chief Executive,* D. Gibson

BUILDING SERVICES ENGINEERS, CHARTERED INSTITUTE OF (1897), 222 Balham High Road, London SW12 9BS. Tel: 0181-675 5211. *Secretary,* A. V. Ramsay

BUILDING SOCIETIES ASSOCIATION (1936), 3 Savile Row, London WIX IAF. Tel: 0171-437 0655. *Director-General,* A. Coles

BUSINESS AND PROFESSIONAL WOMEN UK LTD (1938), 23 Ansdell Street, London W8 5BN. Tel: 0171-938 1729. *General Secretary,* Mrs M. Owen

BUSINESS ARCHIVES COUNCIL (1934), The Clove Building, 4 Maguire Street, London SE1 2NQ. Tel: 0171-407 6110. *Secretary-General,* Ms W. S. Quinn

BUSINESS IN THE COMMUNITY (1982), 44 Baker Street, London W1M 1DH. Tel: 0171-224 1600. *Chief Executive,* Ms J. Cleverdon, CBE

BUSINESS SOFTWARE ALLIANCE (1989), 79 Knightsbridge, London SW1X 7RB. Tel: 0171-245 0304. *Managing Director,* Mrs E. Knight

CADET FORCE ASSOCIATION, COMBINED (1952), E Block, The Duke of York's HQ, London SW3 4RR. Tel: 0171-730 9733/4. *Secretary,* Brig. R. B. MacGregor-Oakford, CBE, MC

CAFOD (CATHOLIC FUND FOR OVERSEAS DEVELOPMENT) (1962), Romero Close, Stockwell Road, London SW9 9TY. Tel: 0171-733 7900. *Director,* J. Filochowski

CALOUSTE GULBENKIAN FOUNDATION (1956), 98 Portland Place, London W1N 4ET. Tel: 0171-636 5313. *Director,* B. Whitaker

CAMBRIDGE PRESERVATION SOCIETY (1929), Wandlebury Ring, Gog Magog Hills, Babraham, Cambridge CB2 4AE. Tel: 01223-243830. *Secretary,* D. J. Carrott

CAMERON FUND (1971), Tavistock House North, Tavistock Square, London WC1H 9HR. Tel: 0171-388 0796. *Secretary,* Mrs J. Martin

CAMPAIGN FOR NUCLEAR DISARMAMENT (CND) (1958), 162 Holloway Road, London N7 8DQ. Tel: 0171-700 2393. *Chair,* D. Knight

CANCER CARE, MARIE CURIE, *see* MARIE CURIE CANCER CARE

CANCER CARE FOR CHILDREN, SARGENT (1968), 14 Abingdon Road, London W8 6AF. Tel: 0171-565 5100. *Chief Executive,* Mrs D. Yeo

CANCER RELIEF, MACMILLAN (1911), Anchor House, 15–19 Britten Street, London SW3 3TZ. Tel: 0171-351 7811. *Chief Executive,* N. Young

CANCER RESEARCH CAMPAIGN, 10 Cambridge Terrace, London NW1 4JL. Tel: 0171-224 1333. *Director-General,* Prof. J. G. McVie

CANCER RESEARCH FUND, IMPERIAL (1902), PO Box 123, Lincoln's Inn Fields, London WC2A 3PX. Tel: 0171-242 0200. *Director-General,* Dr P. Nurse, FRS

CANCER RESEARCH: ROYAL CANCER HOSPITAL, INSTITUTE OF, 17A Onslow Gardens, London SW7 3AL. Tel: 0171-352 8133. *Chief Executive,* Prof. P. B. Garland

CANCER UNITED PATIENTS, BRITISH ASSOCIATION OF (BACUP) (1985), 3 Bath Place, Rivington Street, London EC2A 3JR. Tel: 0171-696 9003. Cancer Information Service: 0800-181199 or 0171-613 2121. *Chief Executive,* Mrs J. Mossman

CARERS NATIONAL ASSOCIATION (1988), Ruth Pitter House, 20–25 Glasshouse Yard, London EC1A 4JS. Tel: 0171-490 8818. *Chief Executive,* Ms J. Pitkeathley, OBE

CARNEGIE DUNFERMLINE TRUST (1903), Abbey Park House, Dunfermline, Fife KY12 7PB. Tel: 01383-723638. *Secretary,* W. C. Runciman

CARNEGIE HERO FUND TRUST (1908), Abbey Park House, Dunfermline, Fife KY12 7PB. Tel: 01383-723638. *Secretary,* W. C. Runciman

CARNEGIE UNITED KINGDOM TRUST (1913), Comely Park House, Dunfermline, Fife KY12 7EJ. Tel: 01383-721445. *Secretary,* C. J. Naylor, OBE

CATHEDRALS FABRIC COMMISSION FOR ENGLAND (1949), Fielden House, Little College Street, London SW1P 3SH. Tel: 0171-222 3793. *Secretary,* Dr R. Gem

CATHOLIC ENQUIRY OFFICE (1954), The Chase Centre, 114 West Heath Road, London NW3 7TX. Tel: 0181-458 3316. *Secretary,* Fr J. O'Toole

CATHOLIC RECORD SOCIETY (1904), c/o 12 Melbourne Place, Wolsingham, Co. Durham DL13 3EH. Tel: 01388-527747. *Hon. Secretary,* Dr L. Gooch

CATHOLIC TRUTH SOCIETY (1868), 192 Vauxhall Bridge Road, London SW1V 1PD. Tel: 0171-834 4392. *General Secretary,* F. Martin

CATHOLIC UNION OF GREAT BRITAIN (1872), St Maximilian Kolbe House, 63 Jeddo Road, London W12 9EE. Tel: 0181-749 1321. *Secretary,* P. H. Higgs

CATTLE ASSOCIATION, NATIONAL, 60 Kenilworth Road, Leamington Spa, Warks CV32 6JX. Tel: 01926-337378. *Secretary,* Miss K. S. Brake

CATTLE BREEDER'S CLUB LTD, BRITISH (1945), 16A Swan Street, Loughborough, Leics LE11 0BL. Tel: 01509-261810. *Secretary,* M. J. Peasnall

CENTRAL AND CECIL HOUSING TRUST (1926), 2 Priory Road, Kew, Richmond, Surrey TW9 3DG. Tel: 0181-940 9828/9. *Secretary,* G. Brighton

CENTRAL BUREAU FOR EDUCATIONAL VISITS AND EXCHANGES (1948), 10 Spring Gardens, London SW1A 2BN. Tel: 0171-389 4004. *Director,* A. H. Male

CENTREPOINT (1969), Bewlay House, 2 Swallow Place, London W1R 7AA. Tel: 0171-629 2229. *Chief Executive,* V. O. Adebowale

CHADWICK TRUST (1895), Department of Civil and Environmental Engineering, University College, Gower Street, London WC1E 6BT. Tel: 0171-380 7327/7766. For the promotion of health and prevention of disease. *Secretary to the Trustees,* I. K. Orchardson, PH.D.

CHANTREY BEQUEST (1875), Royal Academy of Arts, Burlington House, Piccadilly, London W1V 0DS. Tel: 0171-439 7438. *Secretary,* P. Rodgers

CHARITIES AID FOUNDATION (1974), Kings Hill, West Malling, Kent ME19 4TA. Tel: 01732-520000. *Chief Executive,* M. Brophy

CHEMICAL ENGINEERS, INSTITUTION OF (1922), Davis Building, 165–189 Railway Terrace, Rugby, Warks CV21 3HQ. Tel: 01788-578214. *Chief Executive,* Dr T. J. Evans

CHEMISTRY, ROYAL SOCIETY OF, Burlington House, Piccadilly, London W1V 0BN. Tel: 0171-437 8656. *Secretary-General,* Dr T. D. Inch

CHESHIRE (LEONARD) FOUNDATION, *see* LEONARD CHESHIRE FOUNDATION

CHESS FEDERATION, BRITISH (1904), 9A Grand Parade, St Leonards-on-Sea, E. Sussex TN38 0DD. Tel: 01424-442500. *Manager*, Mrs G. White

CHEST, HEART AND STROKE ASSOCIATION, *see* STROKE ASSOCIATION

CHILDBIRTH TRUST, NATIONAL (1956), Alexandra House, Oldham Terrace, London W3 6NH. Tel: 0181-992 8637. *Director*, Ms C. Swarbrick

CHILDREN 1ST (ROYAL SCOTTISH SOCIETY FOR PREVENTION OF CRUELTY TO CHILDREN) (1884), Melville House, 41 Polwarth Terrace, Edinburgh EH11 1NU. Tel: 0131-337 8539. *Chief Executive*, A. M. M. Wood, OBE

CHILDREN'S SOCIETY (1881), Edward Rudolf House, Margery Street, London WC1X 0JL. Tel: 0171-837 4299. *Chief Executive*, I. Sparks

CHINA ASSOCIATION (1889), Swire House, 59 Buckingham Gate, London SW1E 6AJ. Tel: 0171-821 3220. *Executive Director*, D. F. L. Turner

CHIROPODISTS AND PODIATRISTS, SOCIETY OF (1945), 53 Welbeck Street, London W1M 7HE. Tel: 0171-486 3381. *General Secretary*, J. G. C. Trouncer

CHIROPRACTIC ASSOCIATION, BRITISH (1925), 29 Whitley Street, Reading, Berks RG2 0EG. Tel: 01734-757557. *Executive Director*, Miss S. A. Wakefield

CHOIRS SCHOOLS ASSOCIATION (1921), The Minster School, Deangate, York YO1 2JA. Tel: 01904-624900. *Administrator*, Ms W. Jackson

CHRISTIAN AID (1945), PO Box 100, London SE1 7RT. Tel: 0171-620 4444. *Director*, Revd M. H. Taylor

CHRISTIAN EDUCATION COUNCIL, NATIONAL (1809), 1020 Bristol Road, Selly Oak, Birmingham B29 6LB. Tel: 0121-472 4242. *General Secretary*, vacant

CHRISTIAN EDUCATION MOVEMENT (1965), Royal Buildings, Victoria Street, Derby DE1 1GW. Tel: 01332-296655. *Director*, Revd Dr S. Orchard

CHRISTIAN EVIDENCE SOCIETY (1870), St Stephen's House, St Stephen's Crescent, Brentwood, Essex CM13 2AT. Tel: 01277-214623. *Administrator*, Mrs G. M. Ryeland

CHRISTIAN KNOWLEDGE, SOCIETY FOR PROMOTING (SPCK) (1698), Holy Trinity Church, Marylebone Road, London NW1 4DU. Tel: 0171-387 5282. *General Secretary*, P. Chandler

CHRISTIANS AND JEWS, COUNCIL OF (1942), Drayton House, 30 Gordon Street, London WC1H 0AN. Tel: 0171-388 3322. *Director*, P. Mendel

CHURCH ARMY (1882), Independents Road, London SE3 9LG. Tel: 0181-318 1226. *Chief Secretary*, Capt. P. Johanson

CHURCH BUILDING SOCIETY, INCORPORATED (1818), Fulham Palace, London SW6 6EA. Tel: 0171-736 3054. *Secretary*, M. W. Tippen

CHURCH EDUCATION CORPORATION, Bedgebury School, Goudhurst, Cranbrook, Kent TN17 2SH. Tel: 01580-211630. *Secretary*, Col. C. G. Champion

CHURCH HOUSE, THE CORPORATION OF (1888), Church House, Dean's Yard, London SW1P 3NZ. Tel: 0171-222 5261. *Secretary*, C. D. L. Menzies

CHURCH LADS' AND CHURCH GIRLS' BRIGADE (1891), 2 Barnsley Road, Wath upon Dearne, Rotherham, S. Yorks S63 6PY. Tel: 01709-876535. *General Secretary*, J. S. Cresswell

CHURCH MISSION SOCIETY (1799), Partnership House, 157 Waterloo Road, London SE1 8UU. Tel: 0171-928 8681. *General Secretary*, Ms D. K. Witts

CHURCH MONUMENTS SOCIETY (1979), The Royal Armouries, Tower of London, London EC3N 4AB. Tel: 0171-480 6358. *Hon. Secretary*, C. J. Easter

CHURCH MUSIC, ROYAL SCHOOL OF (1927), Cleveland Lodge, Westhumble, Dorking, Surrey RH5 6BW. Tel: 01306-877676. *Director*, H. Bramma

CHURCH OF ENGLAND PENSIONS BOARD (1926), 7 Little College Street, London SW1P 3SF. Tel: 0171-222 2091. *Secretary*, R. G. Radford

CHURCH SOCIETY, INTERCONTINENTAL (ICS) (1823), 175 Tower Bridge Road, London SE1 2AQ. Tel: 0171-407 4588. *International Director*, Revd Canon J. R. Moore

CHURCH UNION (1859), Faith House, 7 Tufton Street, London SW1P 3QN. Tel: 0171-222 6952. *House Manager*, Mrs J. Miller

CHURCHES, COUNCIL FOR THE CARE OF (1921), Fielden House, Little College Street, London SW1P 3SH. Tel: 0171-222 3793. *Secretary*, Dr T. Cocke

CHURCHES FOR BRITAIN AND IRELAND, COUNCIL OF (1942), Inter-Church House, 35–41 Lower Marsh, London SE1 7RL. Tel: 0171-620 4444. *General Secretary*, Revd J. P. Reardon

CHURCHES, FRIENDS OF FRIENDLESS (1957), St Ann's Vestry Hall, 2 Church Entry, London EC4V 5HB. Tel: 0171-236 3934. *Hon. Director*, M. Saunders

CHURCHES MAIN COMMITTEE (1941), Fielden House, Little College Street, London SW1P 3JZ. Tel: 0171-222 4984. *Secretary*, D. Taylor Thompson, CB

CHURCHES TOGETHER IN ENGLAND (1990), Inter-Church House, 35–41 Lower Marsh, London SE1 7RL. Tel: 0171-620 4444. *General Secretary*, Revd B. Snelson

CHURCHES TOGETHER IN SCOTLAND, ACTION OF (1990), Scottish Churches House, Kirk Street, Dunblane FK15 0AJ. Tel: 01786-823588. *General Secretary*, Revd M. Craig

CHURCHILL SOCIETY (1990), 18 Grove Lane, Ipswich IP4 1NR. Tel: 01473-221607.

CITIZEN'S ADVICE BUREAUX, NATIONAL ASSOCIATION OF (1931), Myddelton House, 115–123 Pentonville Road, London N1 9LZ. Tel: 0171-833 2181. *Chief Executive*, Ms A. Abraham

CITY BUSINESS LIBRARY, Brewers Hall Garden, London EC2V 5BX. Tel: 0171-638 8215

CITY PAROCHIAL FOUNDATION (1891), 6 Middle Street, London EC1A 7PH. Tel: 0171-606 6145. *Clerk*, T. Cook

CIVIC TRUST (1957), 17 Carlton House Terrace, London SW1Y 5AW. Tel: 0171-930 0914. *Director*, M. Gwilliam

CIVIL ENGINEERS, INSTITUTION OF (1818), 1 Great George Street, London SW1P 3AA. Tel: 0171-222 7722. *Director-General*, R. S. Dobson, OBE, FEng.

CIVIL LIBERTIES, NATIONAL COUNCIL FOR, *see* LIBERTY

CLASSICAL ASSOCIATION (1903), Department of Classics, University of Keele, Keele, Newcastle under Lyme, Staffs ST5 5BG. Tel: 01782-583048. *Hon. Treasurer*, R. Wallace

CLEAR AIR AND ENVIRONMENTAL PROTECTION, NATIONAL SOCIETY FOR (1899), 136 North Street, Brighton BN1 1RG. Tel: 01273-326313. *Secretary-General*, Dr T. Crossett

CLERGY ORPHAN CORPORATION (1749), 57B Tufton Street, London SW1P 3QL. Tel: 0171-222 1812. *Secretary*, Miss J. Buncher

CLERKS OF WORKS OF GREAT BRITAIN INC., INSTITUTE OF (1882), 41 The Mall, London W5 3TJ. Tel: 0181-579 2917/8. *Secretary*, A. P. Macnamara

COACHING CLUB (1871), West Compton House, West Compton, Shepton Mallet, Somerset BA4 4PD. Tel: 01749-890633. *Secretary*, D. H. Clarke

COLITIS AND CROHN'S DISEASE, NATIONAL ASSOCIATION FOR (1979), PO Box 205, St Albans, Herts AL1 1AB. Tel: 01727-844296. *Director*, R. Driscoll

COMMERCE, BRITISH CHAMBER OF (1860), Manning House, 22 Carlisle Place, London SW1P 1JA. Tel: 0171-565 2000. *Director-General*, R. G. Taylor, CBE

COMMERCE AND INDUSTRY, LONDON CHAMBER OF (1881), Swan House, 33 Queen Street, London EC4R 1AP. Tel: 0171-248 4444. *Chief Executive*, S. G. Sperryn

COMMERCE AND MANUFACTURES, EDINBURGH CHAMBER OF (1786), 3 Randolph Crescent, Edinburgh EH3 7UD. Tel: 0131-225 5851. *Chief Executive*, D. I. Brown

COMMERCE AND MANUFACTURES, GLASGOW CHAMBER OF (1783), 30 George Square, Glasgow G2 1EQ. Tel: 0141-204 2121. *Chief Executive*, G. Runcie

COMMERCE, ASSOCIATION OF SCOTTISH CHAMBERS OF, Conference House, The Exchange, 152 Morrison Street, Edinburgh EH3 8EB. Tel: 0131-477 8025. *Director*, L. Gold

COMMERCE, CANADA-UNITED KINGDOM CHAMBER OF (1921), 38 Grosvenor Street, London ODP. Tel: 0171-258 6572. *Executive Director*, M. Hall

COMMERCIAL TRAVELLERS' BENEVOLENT INSTITUTION (1849), Gable End, Mill Hill Road, Arnesby, Leicester LE8 5WG. Tel: 0116-247 8647. *Secretary*, M. N. Bown

COMMISSIONAIRES, THE CORPS OF (1859), Market House, 85 Cowcross Street, London EC1M 6BP. Tel: 0171-490 1125. *Managing Director*, C. J. Salt

COMMUNICATORS IN BUSINESS, BRITISH ASSOCIATION OF (1949), 3 Locks Yard, High Street, Sevenoaks, Kent TN13 1LT. Tel: 01732-459331. *Director*, A. F. Brobyn

COMPLEMENTARY AND ALTERNATIVE MEDICINE, COUNCIL FOR (1985), 179 Gloucester Place, London NW1 6DX. Tel: 0171-724 9103. *Secretary*, Ms C. Daglish

COMPLEMENTARY MEDICINE, INSTITUTE FOR (1856), PO Box 194, London SE16 1QZ. Tel: 0171-237 5165. *Director*, A. Baird

COMPOSERS' GUILD OF GREAT BRITAIN (1945), The Penthouse, 4 Brook Street, London W1Y 1AA. Tel: 0171-629 0886. *General Secretary*, Ms N. Moskovic

COMPUTER SOCIETY, BRITISH (1957), 1 Sanford Street, Swindon SN1 1HJ. Tel: 01793-417417. *Chief Executive*, G. Kirkpatrick

CONSERVATION OF HISTORIC AND ARTISTIC WORKS, INTERNATIONAL INSTITUTE FOR (1950), 6 Buckingham Street, London WC2N 6BA. Tel: 0171-839 5975. *Secretary-General*, D. Bomford

CONSERVATION VOLUNTEERS, BRITISH TRUST FOR (BTCV) (1970), 36 St Mary's Street, Wallingford, Oxon OX10 0EU. Tel: 01491-839766. *Chief Executive*, T. O. Flood

CONSULTANTS BUREAU, BRITISH (1965), 1 Westminster Palace Gardens, 1–7 Artillery Row, London SW1P 1RJ. Tel: 0171-222 3651. *Director*, C. Adams, CBE

CONSULTING ECONOMISTS' ASSOCIATION, INTERNATIONAL (1986), 3 St George's Court, Putney Bridge Road, London SW15 2PA. Tel: 0181-875 9960. *Chairman*, Dr N. Harris

CONSULTING ENGINEERS, ASSOCIATION OF (1913), Alliance House, 12 Caxton Street, London SW1H 0QL. Tel: 0171-222 6557. *Chief Executive*, H. C. Woodrow

CONSULTING SCIENTISTS, ASSOCIATION OF (1958), Gaw House, Alperton Lane, Wembley Middx HA0 1WU. Tel: 0181-991 4883. *Hon. Secretary*, A. Brewster

CONSUMERS' ASSOCIATION (1957), c/o The Association for Consumer Research, 2 Marylebone Road, London NW1 4DF. Tel: 0171-830 6000. *Director*, Ms S. McKechnie, OBE

CONTEMPORARY APPLIED ARTS (1948), 2 Percy Street, London W1P 9FA. Tel: 0171-436 2344. *Director*, Ms M. La Trobe-Bateman

CONVENIENCE STORES, ASSOCIATION OF (1890), Federation House, 17 Farnborough Street, Farnborough, Hants GU14 8AG. Tel: 01252-515001. *Chief Executive*, T. Dixon

CONVEYANCERS, COUNCIL FOR LICENSED (1986), 16 Glebe Road, Chelmsford, Essex CM1 1QG. Tel: 01245-349599. *Director*, Mrs V. Eden

CO-OPERATIVE PARTY, Victory House, 10–14 Leicester Square, London WC2H 7QH. Tel: 0171-439 0123. *Secretary*, P. Clarke

CO-OPERATIVE UNION LTD (1869), Holyoake House, Hanover Street, Manchester M60 0AS. Tel: 0161-832 4300. *Chief Executive*, D. L. Wilkinson

CO-OPERATIVE WHOLESALE SOCIETY (CWS) LTD (1863), PO Box 53, New Century House, Manchester M60 4ES. Tel: 0161-834 1212. *Chief Executive*, G. J. Melmoth

COPYRIGHT COUNCIL, BRITISH (1953), 29–33 Berners Street, London W1P 4AA. Tel: 0181-371 9993. *Secretary*, Mrs H. Rosenblatt

CORONERS' SOCIETY OF ENGLAND AND WALES (1846), 44 Ormond Avenue, Hampton, Middx TW12 2RX. Tel: 0181-979 6805. *Hon. Secretary*, M. J. G. Burgess

CORPORATE TREASURERS, ASSOCIATION OF (1979), Ocean House, 10–12 Little Trinity Lane, London EC4V 2AA. Tel: 0171-213 9728. *Director-General*, J. Wagener

CORPORATE TRUSTEES, ASSOCIATION OF (1974), The Glen House, 43 Surrey Road, Westbourne, Bournemouth, Dorset BH4 9HR. Tel: 01202-761112. *Secretary*, R. J. Payne

CORRESPONDENCE COLLEGES, ASSOCIATION OF BRITISH (1955), 6 Francis Grove, London SW19 4DT. Tel: 0181-544 9559. *Secretary*, Mrs H. Owen

CORRYMEELA COMMUNITY (1965), Corrymeela House, 8 Upper Crescent, Belfast BT7 1NT. Tel: 01232-325008. *Leader*, Revd T. Williams

COTTON GROWING ASSOCIATION, BRITISH (1904), Knowle Hill Park, Fairmile Lane, Cobham, Surrey KT11 2PD. Tel: 01932-861000. *Managing Director*, P. R. Walters

COUNCIL FOR THE PROTECTION OF RURAL ENGLAND, *see* CPRE

COUNCIL SECRETARIES AND SOLICITORS, ASSOCIATION OF (1974, merged 1996), 11 Rectory Road, Frampton Cotterell, Bristol BS17 2BN. Tel: 01454-775883. *Hon. Secretary*, R. King

COUNSEL AND CARE (1954), Twyman House, 16 Bonny Street, London NW1 9PG. Tel: 0171-485 1550. Advice Line: 0171-485 1566. *General Manager,* J. Smith

COUNTRY HOUSES ASSOCIATION (1955), Suite 10, Aynhoe Park, Aynho, Banbury, Oxon OX17 3BQ. Tel: 01869-812800. *Chief Executive,* A. R. A. Bennett

COUNTRY LANDOWNERS ASSOCIATION (1907), 16 Belgrave Square, London SW1X 8PQ. Tel: 0171-235 0511. *Director-General,* J. A. Anderson

COUNTRYSIDE ALLIANCE (1930), Old Town Hall, 367 Kennington Road, London SE11 4PT. Tel: 0171-582 5432. *Chief Executive,* R. Hanbury-Tenison, OBE

COUNTY CHIEF EXECUTIVES, ASSOCIATION OF (1974), PO Box 9, Shire Hall, Warwick CV34 4RR. Tel: 01926-412559. *Hon. Secretary,* I. G. Caulfield

COUNTY EMERGENCY PLANNING OFFICERS' SOCIETY, *see* EMERGENCY PLANNING

COUNTY SECRETARIES, SOCIETY OF, *see* COUNCIL SECRETARIES AND SOLICITORS, ASSOCIATION OF

COUNTY SURVEYORS' SOCIETY (1884), c/o Director of Environment, Gloucestershire County Council, Shire Hall, Bearland, Glos GL1 2TH. Tel: 01452 426191. *Hon. Secretary,* R. C. Wigginton

COUNTY TREASURERS, SOCIETY OF (1903), County Hall, West Bridgford, Nottingham NG2 7QP. Tel: 0115-977 4906. *Hon. Secretary,* R. Latham

CPRE (COUNCIL FOR THE PROTECTION OF RURAL ENGLAND) (1926), Warwick House, 25 Buckingham Palace Road, London SW1W 0PP. Tel: 0171-976 6433. *Director,* Ms F. Reynolds

CRAFTS COUNCIL (1971), 44A Pentonville House, London N1 9BY. Tel: 0171-278 7700. *Director,* T. Ford

CRISIS (1967), 1st Floor, Challenger House, 42 Adler Street, London E1 1EE. Tel: 0171-377 0489. *Director,* S. Ghosh

CROSSLINKS (1922), 251 Lewisham Way, London SE4 1XF. Tel: 0181-691 6111. *General Secretary,* Revd R. Bowen

CRUEL SPORTS, THE LEAGUE AGAINST (1924), 83–87 Union Street, London SE1 1SG. Tel: 0171-403 6155. *Joint Chief Officers,* G. Sirl; J. Bryant

CRUELTY TO ANIMALS, SOCIETY FOR THE PREVENTION OF, *see* ROYAL and SCOTTISH

CRUELTY TO CHILDREN, SOCIETY FOR THE PREVENTION OF, *see* CHILDREN 1ST and NATIONAL

CRUSE BEREAVEMENT CARE (1959), 126 Sheen Road, Richmond, Surrey TW9 1UR. Tel: 0181-940 4818. Bereavement Line: 0181-332 7227. *Director,* R. Pearce

CURWEN INSTITUTE (1875), 5 Bigbury Close, Styvechale, Coventry CV3 5AJ. Tel: 01203-413010. *Director,* J. Dowding

CWMNI URDD GOBAITH CYMRU (1922), Swyddfa'r Urdd, Aberystwyth, Dyfed SY23 1EN. Tel: 01970-623744. *Chief Executive,* J. O'Rourke

CYCLISTS' TOURING CLUB (1878), Cotterell House, 69 Meadrow, Godalming, Surrey GU7 3HS. Tel: 01483-417217. *Director,* A. Harlow

CYMMRODORION, THE HONOURABLE SOCIETY OF (1751), 30 Eastcastle Street, London W1N 7PD. Tel: 0171-631 0502. *Hon. Secretary,* J. Samuel

CYSTIC FIBROSIS TRUST (1964), Alexandra House, 5 Blyth Road, Bromley, Kent BR1 3RS. Tel: 0181-464 7211. *Chief Executive,* Ms R. Barnes

CYTUN (CHURCHES TOGETHER IN WALES) (1990), Tŷ John Penri, 11 St Helen's Road, Swansea SA1 4AL. Tel: 01792-460876. *General Secretary,* Revd N. A. Davies

DAIRY FARMERS, ROYAL ASSOCIATION OF BRITISH (1876), Dairy House, 60 Kenilworth Road, Leamington Spa, Warks CV32 6JX. Tel: 01926 887477. *Chief Executive,* P. M. Gilbert

DAIRY TECHNOLOGY, SOCIETY OF (1943), 72 Ermine Street, Huntingdon, Cambs PE18 6EZ. Tel: 01480-450741. *National Secretary,* Mrs R. Gale

DATA (DESIGN AND TECHNOLOGY ASSOCIATION), 16 Wellesbourne House, Walton Road, Wellesbourne, Warks CV35 9JB. Tel: 01789-470007. *Chairman,* Dr R. V. Peacock, OBE

D-DAY AND NORMANDY FELLOWSHIP (1968), 9 South Parade, Southsea, Hants PO5 2JB. Tel: 01705-812180. *Hon. Secretary,* Mrs L. R. Reed

DEAF, COMMONWEALTH SOCIETY FOR THE (SOUND SEEKERS) (1959), 134 Buckingham Palace Road, London SW1W 9SA. Tel: 0171-259 0200. *Chairman,* F. R. Rutter

DEAF ASSOCIATION, BRITISH (formerly British Deaf and Dumb Association) (1890), 1 Worship Street, London EC2A 2AB. Tel: 0171-588 3520. *Chief Executive,* J. McWhinney

DEAF CHILDREN, ROYAL SCHOOL FOR (1792), Victoria Road, Margate, Kent CT9 1NB. Tel: 01843-227561. *Secretary,* J. C. Gunnell, OBE

DEAF PEOPLE, FOLEY HOUSE RESIDENTIAL HOME FOR (1851), Foley House, 115 High Garrett, Braintree, Essex CM7 5NU. Tel: 01376-326652. *Director,* Mrs N. Hartard

DEAF PEOPLE, ROYAL ASSOCIATION IN AID OF (1841), 27 Old Oak Road, London W3 7HN. Tel: 0181-743 6187. *General Secretary,* B. Edmond

DEAF PEOPLE, ROYAL NATIONAL INSTITUTE FOR (1911), 19–23 Featherstone Street, London EC1Y 8SL. Tel: 0171-296 8000. *Chief Executive,* J. Strachan

DEFENCE STUDIES, ROYAL UNITED SERVICES INSTITUTE FOR (1831), Whitehall, London 2ET. Tel: 0171-930 5854. *Director,* Rear-Adm. R. Cobbold, CB

DEMOCRATIC LEFT (1991), 6 Cynthia Street, London N1 9JF. Tel: 0171-278 4443. *Secretary,* Ms N. Temple

DENTAL ASSOCIATION, BRITISH (1880), 64 Wimpole Street, London W1M 8AL. Tel: 0171-935 0875. *Chief Executive,* J. M. G. Hunt

DENTAL COUNCIL, GENERAL (1956), 37 Wimpole Street, London W1M 8DQ. Tel: 0171-486 2171. *Chief Executive and Registrar,* Mrs R. M. Hepplewhite

DENTAL HOSPITALS OF THE UNITED KINGDOM, ASSOCIATION OF (1942), Birmingham Dental Hospital, St Chad's Queensway, Birmingham B4 6NN. Tel: 0121-236 8611 ext.5732. *Hon. Secretary,* Mrs P. Harrington

DESIGN AND INDUSTRIES ASSOCIATION (1915), Business Design Centre, 52 Upper Street, London N1 0QH. Tel: 0171-288 6212. *Chairman,* G. Adams

DESIGNERS, CHARTERED SOCIETY OF (1930), 32–38 Saffron Hill, London EC1N 8FH. Tel: 0171-831 9777. *Director,* B. Lymbery

DESIGNERS FOR INDUSTRY, FACULTY OF ROYAL (1936), RSA, 8 John Adam Street, London WC2N 6EZ. Tel: 0171-930 5115. *Administrator,* Ms J. Thackray

DIABETIC ASSOCIATION, BRITISH (1934), 10 Queen Anne Street, London W1M 0BD. Tel: 0171-323 1531. *Director-General,* M. Cooper

DICKENS FELLOWSHIP (1902), Dickens House, 48 Doughty Street, London WC1N 2LF. Tel: 0171-405 2127. *Hon. General Secretary,* E. G. Preston

DIRECTORS, INSTITUTE OF (1903), 116 Pall Mall, London SWIY 5ED. Tel: 0171-839 1233. *Director-General,* T. Melville-Ross

DIRECTORS OF PUBLIC HEALTH, ASSOCIATION OF (1982), Walsall Health Authority, Lichfield House, 27–31 Lichfield Street, Walsall, West Midlands WSI ITE. Tel: 01922-720255. *Hon. Secretary,* Dr S. Ramaiah

DIRECTORY PUBLISHERS ASSOCIATION (1970), 93A Blenheim Crescent, London WII 2EQ. Tel: 0171-221 9089. *Secretary,* Ms R. Pettit

DISPENSING OPTICIANS, ASSOCIATION OF BRITISH (1925), 6 Hurlingham Business Park, Sulivan Road, London SW6 3DU. Tel: 0171-736 0088. *Registrar,* D. S. Baker

DISTRICT SECRETARIES, ASSOCIATION OF, *see* COUNCIL SECRETARIES AND SOLICITORS, ASSOCIATION OF

DITCHLEY FOUNDATION, Ditchley Park, Enstone, Chipping Norton, Oxon OX7 4ER. Tel: 01608-677346. *Director,* Sir Michael Quinlan, GCB

DOWNS SYNDROME ASSOCIATION (1970), 155 Mitcham Road, London SW17 9PG. Tel: 0181-682 4001

DOWSERS, BRITISH SOCIETY OF (1933), Sycamore Barn, Hastingleigh, Ashford, Kent TN25 5HW. Tel: 01233-750253. *Secretary,* M. D. Rust

DRAINAGE AUTHORITIES, ASSOCIATION OF (1937), The Mews, 3 Royal Oak Passage, High Street, Huntingdon, Cambs PE18 6EA. Tel: 01480-411123. *Secretary,* D. Noble

DRINKING FOUNTAIN AND CATTLE TROUGH ASSOCIATION, METROPOLITAN (1859), Oaklands, 5 Queensborough Gardens, Chislehurst, Kent BR7 6NP. Tel: 0181-467 1261. *Secretary,* R. P. Baber

DRIVING SOCIETY, BRITISH (1957), 27 Dugard Place, Barford, Warwick CV35 8DX. Tel: 01926-624420. *Secretary,* Mrs J. M. Dillon

DRUG DEPENDENCE, INSTITUTE FOR THE STUDY OF (ISDD) (1968), 32 Loman Street, London SEI OEE. Tel: 0171-920 1211. *Director,* Mr A. Bradley

DUKE OF EDINBURGH'S AWARD SCHEME (1956), Gulliver House, Madeira Walk, Windsor, Berks SL4 1EU. Tel: 01753-810753. *Director,* M. F. Hobbs, CBE

DYERS AND COLOURISTS, SOCIETY OF (1884), PO Box 244, Perkin House, 82 Grattan Road, Bradford BDI 2JB. Tel: 01274-725138. *General Secretary,* K. M. McGhee

DYSLEXIA INSTITUTE (1972), 133 Gresham Road, Staines, Middlesex TW18 2AJ. Tel: 01784-463851. *Executive Director,* Mrs E. J. Brooks

EARLY CHILDHOOD EDUCATION, BRITISH ASSOCIATION FOR (1923), 111 City View House, 463 Bethnal Green Road, London E2 9QY. Tel: 0171-739 7594. *Secretary,* Mrs B. Boon

EATING DISORDERS ASSOCIATION (1989), Sackville Place, 44 Magdalen Street, Norwich NR3 1JE. Tel: 01603-619090. Helpline: 01603-621414. *Director,* J. Vincent

ECCLESIASTICAL HISTORY SOCIETY (1961), Department of Medieval History, University of Glasgow, Glasgow G12 8QQ. Tel: 0141-330 4087. *Secretary,* M. J. Kennedy

ECCLESIOLOGICAL SOCIETY (1839), Underedge, Back Lane, Hathersage, Sheffield S30 1AR. Tel: 01433-650833. *Hon. Secretary,* Prof. K. H. Murta

EDITH CAVELL AND NATION'S FUND FOR NURSES (1917), Flints, Petersfield Road, Winchester, Hants SO23 0JD. Tel: 01962-860900. *Administrator,* Mrs A. Rich

EDITORS, GUILD OF (1946), Bloomsbury House, 74–77 Great Russell Street, London WCIB 3DA. Tel: 0171-636 7014. *Secretary,* Ms V. L. Hird

EDUCATION OFFICERS' SOCIETY, COUNTY (1889), Education Department, Northamptonshire County Council, PO Box 149, County Hall, Northampton NNI 1AU. Tel: 01604-236250. *Secretary,* J. R. Atkinson

EDUCATION OFFICERS, SOCIETY OF (1971), Boulton House, 17–21 Chorlton Street, Manchester MI 3HY. Tel: 0161-236 5766. *General Secretary,* A. Collier

EDUCATIONAL RESEARCH IN ENGLAND AND WALES, NATIONAL FOUNDATION FOR (1946), The Mere, Upton Park, Slough SLI 2DQ. Tel: 01753-574123. *Director,* Dr S. Hegarty

EGYPT EXPLORATION SOCIETY (1882), 3 Doughty Mews, London WCIN 2PG. Tel: 0171-242 1880. *Secretary,* Dr P. A. Spencer

ELECTORAL REFORM SOCIETY, 6 Chancel Street, London SEI OUU. Tel: 0171-928 1622. *President,* Baroness Seear

ELECTRICAL ENGINEERS, INSTITUTION OF (1871), Savoy Place, London WC2R OBL. Tel: 0171-240 1871. *Secretary,* J. C. Williams, PH.D., FENG.

ELGAR FOUNDATION (1973), 23 Meadow Hill Road, King's Norton, Birmingham B38 8DE. Tel: 0121-458 2747. *Secretary to the Trustees,* J. G. Hughes

ELGAR SOCIETY (1951), c/o 29 Van Diemens Close, Chinnor, Oxon OX9 4QE. Tel: 01844-354096. *Hon. Secretary,* Ms W. Hillary

EMERGENCY PLANNING SOCIETY (1966), Emergency Planning Officer, London Borough of Brent, Pyramid House, Forthway, Wembley, Middx HA9 OLJ. Tel: 0181-908 7035. *Hon. Secretary,* K. D. Gosling

ENABLE (SCOTTISH SOCIETY FOR THE MENTALLY HANDICAPPED) (1954), 7 Buchanan Street, Glasgow GI 3HL. Tel: 0141-226 4541. *Director,* N. Dunning

ENERGY ASSOCIATION, BRITISH (1924), 34 St James's Street, London SWIA 1HD. Tel: 0171-930 1211. *Director,* M. Jefferson

ENERGY, INSTITUTE OF (1927), 18 Devonshire Street, London WIN 2AU. Tel: 0171-580 7124. *Secretary,* J. E. H. Leach

ENERGY SAVING TRUST (1992), 11–12 Buckingham Gate, London SWIE 6LB. Tel: 0171-931 8401. *Chief Executive,* Dr E. Lees

ENGINEERING COUNCIL, THE (1981), 10 Maltravers Street, London WC2R 3ER. Tel: 0171-240 7891. *Director-General,* M. Heath

ENGINEERING DESIGNERS, INSTITUTION OF (1945), Courtleigh, Westbury Leigh, Westbury, Wilts BA13 3TA. Tel: 01373-822801. *Secretary,* M. J. Osborne

ENGINEERING INDUSTRIES ASSOCIATION (1941), Broadway House, Tothill Street, London SWIH 9NS. Tel: 0171-222 2367. *Chief Executive,* Ms J. Moore

ENGINEERS, INSTITUTION OF BRITISH (1928), Royal Liver Building, 6 Hampton Place, Brighton BNI 3DD. Tel: 01273-734274. *Secretary,* Ms J. Busby

ENGINEERS, SOCIETY OF (1854), Guinea Wiggs, Nayland, Colchester, Essex CO6 4NF. Tel: 01206-263332. *Secretary,* Mrs L. C. A. Wright

ENGLISH ASSOCIATION (1906), University of Leicester, University Road, Leicester LEI 7RH. Tel: 0116-252 3982. *Secretary,* Ms H. Lucas

ENGLISH FOLK DANCE AND SONG SOCIETY (1932), Cecil Sharp House, 2 Regent's Park Road, London NW1 7AY. Tel: 0171-485 2206. *Chief Executive*, N. Thompson

ENGLISH PLACE-NAME SURVEY (1923), Grey College, Durham DH1 3LG. Tel: 0191-374 2960. *Hon. Director*, V. E. Watts, FSA

ENGLISH-SPEAKING UNION OF THE COMMONWEALTH (1918), Dartmouth House, 37 Charles Street, London W1X 8AB. Tel: 0171-493 3328. *Director-General*, Mrs V. Mitchell

ENTOMOLOGICAL SOCIETY OF LONDON, ROYAL (1833), 41 Queen's Gate, London SW7 5HR. Tel: 0171-584 8361. *Registrar*, G. G. Bentley

ENVIRONMENTAL HEALTH, CHARTERED INSTITUTE OF (1883), Chadwick Court, 15 Hatfields, London SE1 8DJ. Tel: 0171-928 6006. *Chief Executive*, M. Cooke

ENVIRONMENT COUNCIL (1969), 21 Elizabeth Street, London SW1W 9RP. Tel: 0171-824 8411. *Chief Executive*, S. Robinson

EPILEPSY ASSOCIATION, BRITISH (1949), Anstey House, 40 Hanover Square, Leeds LS3 1BE. Tel: 0113-243 9393/ 0800-309030. *Chief Executive*, P. Lee

EPILEPSY, NATIONAL SOCIETY FOR (1892), Chalfont St Peter, Gerrards Cross, Bucks SL9 0RJ. Tel: 01494-601300. *Chief Executive*, D. Bennett

EQUESTRIAN FEDERATION, BRITISH (1972), British Equestrian Centre, Stoneleigh Park, Kenilworth, Warks CV8 2LR. Tel: 01203-696697. *Director-General*, Col. J. D. Smith-Bingham

ESPERANTO ASSOCIATION OF BRITAIN (1977), 140 Holland Park Avenue, London W11 4UF. Tel: 0171-727 7821. *Office Manager*, M. McClelland

ESTATE AGENTS, NATIONAL ASSOCIATION OF (1962), Arbon House, 21 Jury Street, Warwick CV34 4EH. Tel: 01926-496800. *Chief Executive*, H. Dunsmore-Hardy

ESTATE AGENTS, OMBUDSMAN FOR CORPORATE (1990), Beckett House, 4 Bridge Street, Salisbury, Wilts SP1 2LX. Tel: 01722-333306. *Ombudsman*, T. D. G. Quayle, CB

EUGENICS SOCIETY, *see* GALTON INSTITUTE

EVANGELICAL ALLIANCE (1846), Whitefield House, 186 Kennington Park Road, London SE11 4BT. Tel: 0171-582 0228. *General Director*, Revd J. Edwards

EVANGELICAL LIBRARY (1928), 78A Chiltern Street, London W1M 2HB. Tel: 0171-935 6997. *Librarian*, S. J. Taylor

EXPORT, INSTITUTE OF (1935), Export House, 64 Clifton Street, London EC2A 4HB. Tel: 0171-247 9812. *Director-General*, I. J. Campbell

EX-SERVICES LEAGUE, BRITISH COMMONWEALTH (1921), 48 Pall Mall, London SW1Y 5JG. Tel: 0171-973 7263. *Secretary-General*, Lt.-Col. S. Pope, OBE, RM

EX-SERVICES MENTAL WELFARE SOCIETY (1919), Broadway House, The Broadway, London SW19 1RL. Tel: 0181-543 6333. *Director*, Brig. A. K. Dixon

FABIAN SOCIETY (1884), 11 Dartmouth Street, London SW1H 9BN. Tel: 0171-222 8877. *General Secretary*, S. Twigg

FAIR ISLE BIRD OBSERVATORY TRUST (1948), Fair Isle Bird Observatory, Fair Isle, Shetland ZE2 9JU. Tel: 01595-760258. *Administrator*, M. Newell

FALSE MEMORY SOCIETY, BRITISH (1993), Bradford on Avon, Wilts BA15 1NF. Tel: 01225-868682. *Director*, R. Scotford

FAMILY HISTORY SOCIETIES, FEDERATION OF (1974), The Benson Room, Birmingham and Midland Institute, Margaret Street, Birmingham B3 3BS. *Administrator*, Mrs P. A. Saul

FAMILY MEDIATION, NATIONAL (THE NATIONAL ASSOCIATION OF FAMILY MEDIATION AND CONCILIATION SERVICES) (1982), 9 Tavistock Place, London WC1H 9SN. Tel: 0171-383 5993. *Director*, Ms T. Fisher

FAMILY PLANNING ASSOCIATION (1939), 2–12 Pentonville Road, London N1 9FP. Tel: 0171-837 5432. *Chief Executive*, Ms A. Weyman

FAMILY WELFARE ASSOCIATION (1869), 501–505 Kingsland Road, London E8 4AU. Tel: 0171-254 6251. *Chief Executive*, Ms H. Dent

FAUNA AND FLORA INTERNATIONAL (1903), Great Eastern House, Tenison Road, Cambridge CB1 2DT. Tel: 01223-461471. *Director*, M. Rose

FELLOWSHIP HOUSES TRUST (1937), Clock House, 192 High Road, Byfleet, Surrey KT14 7RN. Tel: 01932-343172. *Secretary*, Mrs A. J. Elliot

FIELD ARCHAEOLOGISTS, INSTITUTE OF (1982), University of Manchester, Oxford Road, Manchester M13 9PL. Tel: 0161-275 2304. *Director*, P. Hinton

FIELD STUDIES COUNCIL (1943), Preston Montford, Montford Bridge, Shrewsbury SY4 1HW. Tel: 01743-850674. *Director*, A. D. Thomas

FILM CLASSIFICATION, BRITISH BOARD OF (1912), 3 Soho Square, London W1V 6HD. Tel: 0171-439 7961. *Director*, vacant

FIRE ENGINEERS, INSTITUTION OF (1918), 148 New Walk, Leicester LE1 7QB. Tel: 0116-255 3654. *General Secretary*, D. W. Evans

FIRE PROTECTION ASSOCIATION (1946), Melrose Avenue, Borehamwood, Herts WD6 2BJ. Tel: 0181-207 2345. *Director*, S. Kidd

FIRE SERVICES NATIONAL BENEVOLENT FUND (1943), Marine Court, Fitzalan Road, Littlehampton, W. Sussex BN17 5NF. Tel: 01903-736063. *General Manager*, C. W. Pile

FLAG INSTITUTE (1971), 10 Vicarage Road, Chester CH2 3HZ. Tel: 01244-351335. *Director*, Dr W. G. Crampton

FLEET AIR ARM OFFICERS' ASSOCIATION (1957), 94 Piccadilly, London W1V 0BP. Tel: 0171-499 0360. *Chairman*, Capt. A. A. Hensher, MBE, RN

FOLKLORE SOCIETY, c/o University College, Gower Street, London WC1E 6BT. Tel: 0171-387 5894. *Hon. Secretary*, Dr J. Simpson

FOOD FROM BRITAIN (1983), 123 Buckingham Palace Road, London SW1W 9SA. Tel: 0171-233 5111. *Chairman*, G. John, CBE

FOOD SCIENCE AND TECHNOLOGY, INSTITUTE OF (1964), 5 Cambridge Court, 210 Shepherd's Bush Road, London W6 7NJ. Tel: 0171-603 6316. *Chief Executive*, Ms H. G. Wild

FORCES HELP SOCIETY AND LORD ROBERTS WORKSHOPS, *see* SSAFA FORCES HELP

FOREIGN PRESS ASSOCIATION IN LONDON (1888), 11 Carlton House Terrace, London SW1Y 5AJ. Tel: 0171-930 0445. *Secretary*, Ms D. Crole

FORENSIC SCIENCE SOCIETY (1959), Clarke House, 18A Mount Parade, Harrogate, N. Yorks HG1 1BX. Tel: 01423-506068. *Hon. Secretary*, Dr A. R. W. Forrest

FORENSIC SCIENCES, BRITISH ACADEMY OF (1959), Anaesthetic Unit, The Royal London Hospital, Whitechapel, London E1 1BB. Tel: 0171-377 9201. *Secretary-General*, Dr P. J. Flynn

FORESTERS, INSTITUTE OF CHARTERED (1982), 7A St Colme Street, Edinburgh EH3 6AA. Tel: 0131-225 2705. *Executive Director*, Mrs M. W. Dick

FORESTRY ASSOCIATION, COMMONWEALTH (1921), c/o Oxford Forestry Institute, South Parks Road, Oxford OX1 3RB. Tel: 01865-275072. *Chairman*, Dr J. S. Maini

FORESTRY SOCIETY OF ENGLAND, WALES AND NORTHERN IRELAND, ROYAL (1882), 102 High Street, Tring, Herts HP23 4AF. Tel: 01442-822028. *Director*, J. E. Jackson, PH.D.

FORESTRY SOCIETY, ROYAL SCOTTISH (1854), The Stables, Dalkeith Country Park, Dalkeith, Midlothian EH22 2NA. Tel: 0131-660 9480. *Director*, M. Osborne

FOUNDRYMEN, INSTITUTE OF BRITISH (1904), Bordesley Hall, The Holloway, Alvechurch, Birmingham B48 7QA. Tel: 01527-596100. *Secretary*, G. A. Schofield

FRANCO-BRITISH SOCIETY (1924), Room 623, Linen Hall, 162–168 Regent Street, London W1R 5TB. Tel: 0171-734 0815. *Executive Secretary*, Mrs M. Clarke

FREE CHURCH FEDERAL COUNCIL (1940), 27 Tavistock Square, London WC1H 9HH. Tel: 0171-387 8413. *General Secretary*, Revd G. H. Roper

FREEDOM ASSOCIATION (1975), 35 Westminster Bridge Road, London SE1 7JB. Tel: 0171-928 9925. *Office Manager*, Mrs P. North

FREEMASONS: GRAND LODGE OF ANTIENT FREE AND ACCEPTED MASONS OF SCOTLAND (1736), Freemasons' Hall, 96 George Street, Edinburgh EH2 3DH. Tel: 0131-225 5304. *Grand Master Mason of Scotland*, The Lord Burton

FREEMASONS: UNITED GRAND LODGE OF ENGLAND (1717), Freemasons' Hall, Great Queen Street, London WC2B 5AZ. Tel: 0171-831 9811. *Grand Master*, HRH The Duke of Kent, KG, GCMG, GCVO

FREEMEN OF ENGLAND AND WALES (1966), Glenrise, Churchfields, Stonesfield, Witney, Oxon OX8 8PP. Tel: 01993-891414. *President*, R. J. M. Bishop

FREEMEN OF THE CITY OF LONDON, GUILD OF (1908), PO Box 153, 40A Ludgate Hill, London EC4M 7DE. Tel: 0171-223 7638. *Clerk*, Col. D. Ivy

FREEMEN OF THE CITY OF YORK, GILD OF (1953), 29 Albermarle Road, York YO2 1EW. Tel: 01904-653698. *Hon. Clerk*, R. Lee

FREEMEN'S GUILD, CITY OF COVENTRY (1946), 47 Brownshill Green Road, Coventry CV6 2AP. Tel: 01203-333980. *Hon. Clerk*, K. Talbot

FRIENDLY SOCIETIES, ASSOCIATION OF (1887), Royex House, Aldermanbury Square, London EC2V 7HR. Tel: 0171-606 1881. *General Secretary*, Miss M. Poole

FRIENDS OF CATHEDRAL MUSIC (1956), 26 Dumbrells Court, North End, Ditchling, W. Sussex BN6 8TG. Tel: 01273-842903. *Secretary*, V. Waterhouse

FRIENDS OF THE EARTH (1971), 26–28 Underwood Street, London N1 7JQ. Tel: 0171-490 1555. *Director*, C. Secrett

FRIENDS OF THE ELDERLY (1905), 42 Ebury Street, London SW1W 0LZ. Tel: 0171-730 8263. *Chief Executive*, Mrs S. Levett

FRIENDS OF THE NATIONAL LIBRARIES (1931), c/o The British Library, London WC1B 3DG. Tel: 0171-412 7559. *Hon. Secretary*, M. Borrie, OBE, FSA

FURNITURE HISTORY SOCIETY (1964), 1 Mercedes Cottages, St John's Road, Haywards Heath, W. Sussex RH16 4EH. Tel: 01444-413845. *Membership Secretary*, Dr B. Austen

GALLIPOLI ASSOCIATION (1915), Earleydene Orchard, Earleydene, Ascot, Berks SL5 9JY. Tel: 01344-26523. *Hon. Secretary*, J. C. Watson Smith

GALTON INSTITUTE (1907), 19 Northfields Prospect, London SW18 1PE. Tel: 0181-874 7257. *General Secretary (acting)*, Mrs V. Barter

GAMBLERS ANONYMOUS (1954), PO Box 88, London SW10 0EU. Tel: 0171-384 3040

GAME CONSERVANCY TRUST (1969), Fordingbridge, Hants SP6 1EF. Tel: 01425-652381. *Director-General*, Dr G. R. Potts

GARDEN HISTORY SOCIETY (1965), 77 Cowcross Street, London EC1M 6BP. Tel: 0171-608 2409. *Director*, Ms L. Wigley

GARDENERS' ASSOCIATION, THE GOOD (1968), Pinetum, Churcham, Glos GL2 8AD. Tel: 01452-750402. *Hon. Director*, D. Wilkin

GARDENERS' ROYAL BENEVOLENT SOCIETY (1839), Bridge House, 139 Kingston Road, Leatherhead, Surrey KT22 7NT. Tel: 01372-373962. *Chief Executive*, K. Moller

GARDENS SCHEME CHARITABLE TRUST, NATIONAL (1927), Hatchlands Park, East Clandon, Guildford, Surrey GU4 7RT. Tel: 01483-211535. *Director*, Lt.-Col. T. A. Marsh

GAS CONSUMERS COUNCIL (1986), 6th Floor, Abford House, 15 Wilton Road, London SW1V 1LT. Tel: 0171-931 0977. *Director*, Ms S. Slipman, OBE

GAS ENGINEERS, INSTITUTION OF (1863), 21 Portland Place, London W1N 3AF. Tel: 0171-636 6603. *Chief Executive*, Mrs S. M. Razne

GEMMOLOGICAL ASSOCIATION AND GEM TESTING LABORATORY OF GREAT BRITAIN (1931), 27 Greville Street, (Saffron Hill entrance), London EC1N 8SU. Tel: 0171-404 3334. *Director*, Dr R. R. Harding

GENEALOGICAL RESEARCH SOCIETY, IRISH (1936), c/o The Irish Club, 82 Eaton Square, London SW1W 9AJ. Tel: 0171-235 4164. *Hon. Librarian*, J. G. Chartres

GENEALOGISTS AND RECORD AGENTS, ASSOCIATION OF (1968), 29 Badgers Close, Horsham, W. Sussex RH12 5RU.

GENEALOGISTS, SOCIETY OF (1911), 14 Charterhouse Buildings, Goswell Road, London EC1M 7BA. Tel: 0171-251 8799. *Director*, A. J. Camp

GENERAL PRACTITIONERS, ROYAL COLLEGE OF (1952), 14 Princes Gate, London SW7 1PU. Tel: 0171-581 3232. *Secretary*, Dr W. Reith

GENTLEPEOPLE, GUILD OF AID FOR (1904), 10 St Christopher's Place, London W1M 6HY. Tel: 0171-935 0641.

GEOGRAPHICAL ASSOCIATION, 343 Fulwood Road, Sheffield S10 3BP. Tel: 0114-267 0666. *Senior Administrator*, Miss F. M. Soar

GEOGRAPHICAL SOCIETY, ROYAL and THE INSTITUTE OF BRITISH GEOGRAPHERS (1830), 1 Kensington Gore, London SW7 2AR. Tel: 0171-591 3000. *President*, The Earl of Selborne, KBE, FRS

GEOGRAPHICAL SOCIETY, ROYAL SCOTTISH (1884), Graham Hills Building, 40 George Street, Glasgow G1 1QE. Tel: 0141-552 3330. *Director*, Dr D. M. Munro

GEOLOGICAL SOCIETY (1807), Burlington House, Piccadilly, London WIV OJU. Tel: 0171-434 9944. *Chief Executive Officer*, E. Nickless

GEOLOGISTS' ASSOCIATION (1858), Burlington House, Piccadilly, London WIV 9AG. Tel: 0171-434 9298. *Executive Secretary*, Mrs S. Stafford

GEORGIAN GROUP (1937), 6 Fitzroy Square, London WIP 6DX. Tel: 0171-387 1720. *Secretary*, N. Burton

GIFTED CHILDREN, NATIONAL ASSOCIATION FOR (1966), Elder House, Milton Keynes MK9 ILR. Tel: 01908-673677. *Executive Director*, P. Carey

GILBERT AND SULLIVAN SOCIETY (1924), 1 Nethercourt Avenue, Finchley, London N3 IPS. *Hon. Secretary*, Ms M. Bowden

GINGERBREAD (1970), 16–17 Clerkenwell Close, London ECIR OAA. Tel: 0171-336 8183. An association for one-parent families and their children. *Chief Executive*, Ms L. Sewell

GIRL GUIDES, *see* GUIDE ASSOCIATION

GIRLS' BRIGADE, Girls' Brigade House, 62 Foxhall Road, Didcot, Oxon OXII 7BQ. Tel: 01235-510425. *Brigade Secretary*, Mrs S. P. Bunting

GIRLS' FRIENDLY SOCIETY IN ENGLAND AND WALES (1875), 126 Queens Gate, London SW7 5LQ. Tel: 0171-589 9628. *General Secretary*, Mrs H. Crompton

GIRLS' VENTURE CORPS AIR CADETS (1964), Redhill Aerodrome, Kings Mill Lane, South Nutfield, Redhill RHI 5JY. Tel: 01737-823345. *Corps Director*, Mrs M. A. Rowland

GLASS ENGRAVERS, GUILD OF (1975), 19 Wildwood Road, London NWII 6UL. Tel: 0181-731 9352

GLASS TECHNOLOGY, SOCIETY OF (1916), Thornton, 20 Hallam Gate Road, Sheffield SIO 5BT. Tel: 0114-266 3168. *Administration Manager*, Ms J. Costello

GLIDING ASSOCIATION, BRITISH (1930), Kimberley House, Vaughan Way, Leicester LEI 4SE. Tel: 0116-253 1051. *Secretary*, B. Rolfe

GOAT SOCIETY, BRITISH (1879), 34–36 Fore Street, Bovey Tracey, Newton Abbot, Devon TQI3 9AD. Tel: 01626-833168. *Secretary*, Ms S. Knowles

GRAPHOLOGISTS, BRITISH INSTITUTE OF (1983), 24–26 High Street, Hampton Hill, Hampton, Middx TWI2 IPD. Tel: 01932-351429. *Chairman*, E. Rees

GREEK INSTITUTE (1969), 34 Bush Hill Road, London N2I 2DS. Tel: 0181-360 7968. *Director*, Dr K. Tofallis

GREEN PARTY (1973), 1A Waterlow Road, London NI9 5NJ. Tel: 0171-272 4474. *Executive Chair*, Ms J. Jones

GREENPEACE UK (1971), Canonbury Villas, London NI 2PN. Tel: 0171-865 8100. *Executive Director*, The Lord Melchett

GUIDE ASSOCIATION (1910), 17–19 Buckingham Palace Road, London SWIW OPT. Tel: 0171-834 6242. *Chief Guide*, Miss B. Towle

GUIDE DOGS FOR THE BLIND ASSOCIATION (1931), Hillfields, Burghfield Common, Reading, Berks RG7 3YG. Tel: 0118-983 5555. *Chief Executive*, Mrs G. Peacock

GULBENKIAN FOUNDATION, *see* CALOUSTE GULBENKIAN FOUNDATION

GURKHA WELFARE TRUST (1969), 3rd Floor, 88 Baker Street, London WIM 2AX. Tel: 0171-707 1925. *Director*, E. D. Powell-Jones

HAEMOPHILIA SOCIETY (1950), Chesterfield House, 385 Euston Road, London NWI 3AU. Tel: 0171-380 0600. *Director of Services and Development*, G. Barker

HAIG HOMES (1928), Alban Dobson House, Green Lane, Morden, Surrey SM4 5NS. Tel: 0181-648 0335. *General Secretary*, J. B. Holt

HAKLUYT SOCIETY (1846), c/o Map Library, The British Library, Great Russell Street, London WCIB 3DG. Tel: 01986-788359. *Hon. Secretary*, A. P. Payne

HANSARD SOCIETY FOR PARLIAMENTARY GOVERNMENT (1944), St Philips Building North, Sheffield Street, London WC2A 2EX. Tel: 0171-955 7478. *Director*, D. Harris

HARD OF HEARING, BRITISH ASSOCIATION OF THE, *see* HEARING CONCERN

HARVEIAN SOCIETY OF EDINBURGH (1782), Respiratory Medicine Unit, Department of Medicine, The Royal Infirmary, Edinburgh EH3 9YW. Tel: 0131-536 2351. *Joint Secretaries*, A. B. MacGregor; Prof. N. J. Douglas

HARVEIAN SOCIETY OF LONDON (1831), Lettson House, 11 Chandos Street, London WIM OEB. Tel: 0171-580 1043. *Executive Secretary*, M. C. Griffiths, TD

HEALTH AUTHORITIES AND TRUSTS, NATIONAL ASSOCIATION OF (1974), Birmingham Research Park, Vincent Drive, Birmingham BI5 2SQ. Tel: 0121-471 4444. *Director*, P. Hunt, OBE

HEALTH CARE ASSOCIATION, BRITISH (1931), 24A Main Street, Garforth, Leeds LS25 IAA. Tel: 0113-232 0903. *Chief Executive*, Mrs C. Bell

HEALTH EDUCATION, INSTITUTE OF (1962), Department of Oral Health and Development, University Dental Hospital, Higher Cambridge Street, Manchester MI5 6FH. Tel: 0161-275 6610. *Hon. Secretary*, Prof. A. S. Blinkhorn

HEALTH, GUILD OF (1904), Edward Wilson House, 26 Queen Anne Street, London WIM 9LB. Tel: 0171-580 2492. *General Secretary*, Revd A. Lynn

HEALTH SERVICES MANAGEMENT, INSTITUTE OF (1902), 39 Chalton Street, London NWI IJD. Tel: 0171-388 2626. *Director*, Ms K. Caines

HEARING CONCERN (BRITISH ASSOCIATION OF THE HARD OF HEARING) (1948), 7–11 Armstrong Road, London W3 7JL. Tel: 0181-743 1110. *Director*, C. J. Meyer, OBE

HEART FOUNDATION, BRITISH (1963), 14 Fitzhardinge Street, London WIH 4DH. Tel: 0171-935 0185. *Director-General*, Maj.-Gen. L. F. H. Busk, CB

HEDGEHOG PRESERVATION SOCIETY, BRITISH (1982), Knowbury House, Knowbury, Ludlow, Shropshire SY8 3LQ. Tel: 01584-890287. *Founder*, Maj. A. H. Coles, TD

HELLENIC STUDIES, SOCIETY FOR THE PROMOTION OF (1879), Senate House, Malet Street, London WCIE 7HU. Tel: 0171-323 9590. *Secretary*, Mrs F. J. Fisher-Hunt

HELP THE AGED (1960), St James's Walk, Clerkenwell Green, London ECIR OBE. Tel: 0171-253 0253. *Director-General*, C. M. Lake, CBE

HERALDIC AND GENEALOGICAL STUDIES, INSTITUTE OF (1961), 79–82 Northgate, Canterbury, Kent CTI IBA. Tel: 01227-768664. *Registrar*, J. Palmer

HERALDRY SOCIETY (1947), PO Box 32, Maidenhead, Berks SL6 3FD. Tel: 0118-932 0210. *Secretary*, Mrs M. Miles, MBE, RD

HERPETOLOGICAL SOCIETY, BRITISH (1947), c/o Zoological Society of London, Regent's Park, London NWI 4RY. Tel: 0181-452 9578. *Secretary*, Mrs M. Green

HISPANIC AND LUSO BRAZILIAN COUNCIL (1943), Canning House, 2 Belgrave Square, London SWIX 8PJ. Tel: 0171-235 2303. *Director-General*, J. Amey

HISTORICAL ASSOCIATION (1906), 59A Kennington Park Road, London SE11 4JH. Tel: 0171-735 3901. *Chief Executive*, Mrs M. Stiles

HISTORIC HOUSES ASSOCIATION (1973), 2 Chester Street, London SW1X 7BB. Tel: 0171-259 5688. *Director-General*, R. Wilkin

HISTORICAL SOCIETY, ROYAL (1868), University College London, Gower Street, London WC1E 6BT. Tel: 0171-387 7532. *Executive Secretary*, Mrs J. N. McCarthy

HOME FARM TRUST (1962), Merchants House, Wapping Road, Bristol BS1 4RW. Tel: 0117-927 3746. *Director-General*, C. Carey

HOMEOPATHIC ASSOCIATION, BRITISH (1902), 27A Devonshire Street, London W1N 1RJ. Tel: 0171-935 2163. *General Secretary*, Mrs E. Segall

HONG KONG ASSOCIATION (1961), Swire House, 59 Buckingham Gate, London SW1E 6AJ. Tel: 0171-821 3220. *Executive Director*, D. F. L. Turner

HOROLOGICAL INSTITUTE, BRITISH (1858), Upton Hall, Upton, Newark, Notts NG23 5TE. Tel: 01636-813795. *Secretary*, Ms H. Bartlett

HOROLOGICAL SOCIETY, ANTIQUARIAN (1953), New House, High Street, Ticehurst, Wadhurst, E. Sussex TN5 7AL. Tel: 01580-200155. *Secretary*, Mrs P. Hossbach

HORSE SOCIETY, BRITISH (1947), British Equestrian Centre, Stoneleigh Park, Kenilworth, Warks CV8 2LR. Tel: 01203-696697. *Chief Executive*, Col. T. Eastwood

HOSPITAL FEDERATION, INTERNATIONAL (1947), 4 Abbot's Place, London NW6 4NP. Tel: 0171-372 7181. *Director-General*, Dr E. N. Pickering

HOSPITALITY ASSOCIATION, BRITISH (1907), Queens House, 55–56 Lincoln's Inn Fields, London WC2A 3BH. Tel: 0171-404 7744. *Chief Executive*, J. Logie

HOSPITAL SATURDAY FUND (1873), 24 Upper Ground, London SE1 9PQ. Tel: 0171-928 6662. *Chief Executive*, K. R. Bradley

HOSPITAL SAVING ASSOCIATION, Hambledon House, Andover, Hants SP10 1LQ. Tel: 01264-353211. *Chief Executive*, J. A. Young

HOTEL AND CATERING INTERNATIONAL MANAGEMENT ASSOCIATION (1971), 191 Trinity Road, London SW17 7HN. Tel: 0181-672 4251. *Chief Executive*, D. Wood

HOUSING AID SOCIETY, CATHOLIC (1956), 209 Old Marylebone Road, London NW1 5QT. Tel: 0171-723 7273. *Director*, Ms R. Rafferty

HOUSING AND TOWN PLANNING COUNCIL, NATIONAL (1900), 14–18 Old Street, London EC1V 9AB. Tel: 0171-251 2363. *Director*, K. MacDonald

HOUSING, CHARTERED INSTITUTE OF, Octavia House, Westwood Business Park, Westwood Way, Coventry CV4 8JP. Tel: 01203-694966. *Chief Executive*, Ms C. Laird

HOUSE OF ST BARNABAS-IN-SOHO (1846), 1 Greek Street, London W1V 6NQ. Tel: 0171-437 1894. For homeless women in London. *Director*, Ms S. Dixon

HOVERCRAFT SOCIETY (1971), 24 Jellicoe Avenue, Alverstoke, Gosport, Hants PO12 2PE. Tel: 01705-584371. *Chairman*, J. Gifford

HOWARD LEAGUE FOR PENAL REFORM (1866), 708 Holloway Road, London N19 3NL. Tel: 0171-281 7722. *Director*, Ms F. Crook

HUGUENOT SOCIETY OF GREAT BRITAIN AND IRELAND (1885), The Huguenot Library, University College, Gower Street, London WC1E 6BT. Tel: 0171-380 7094. *Hon. Secretary*, Mrs M. Bayliss

HUMANE RESEARCH TRUST (1974), Brook House, 29 Bramhall Lane South, Bramhall, Stockport, Cheshire SK7 2DN. Tel: 0161-439 8041. *Chairman*, K. Cholerton

HUMANIST ASSOCIATION, BRITISH (1963), 47 Theobald's Road, London WC1X 8SP. Tel: 0171-430 0908. *Executive Director*, R. Ashby

HUMAN RIGHTS, BRITISH INSTITUTE OF (1970), King's College London, Strand, London WC2R 2LS. Tel: 0171-873 2352. *Director*, Dr J. J. Busuttil

HYDROGRAPHIC SOCIETY (1972), c/o University of East London, Longbridge Road, Dagenham, Essex RM8 2AS. Tel: 0181-597 1946. *Hon. Secretary*, R. Naylor

HYMN SOCIETY OF GREAT BRITAIN AND IRELAND (1936), St Nicholas Rectory, Glebe Fields, Curdworth, Sutton Coldfield, West Midlands B76 9ES. Tel: 01675-470384. *Secretary*, Revd M. Garland

ICAN (INVALID CHILDREN'S AID NATIONWIDE) (1888), Barbican Citygate, 1–3 Dufferin Street, London EC1Y 8NA. Tel: 0171-374 4422. *Director*, B. J. Jones

IMMIGRATION ADVISORY SERVICE (1970), County House, 190 Great Dover Street, London SE1 4YB. Tel: 0171-357 6917. 24-hour line: 0171-378 9191. *Chief Executive*, K. Best

INDEPENDENT BRITAIN, CAMPAIGN FOR AN (1976), 81 Ashmole Street, London SW8 1NF. Tel: 0181-340 0314. *Hon. Secretary*, Sir Robin Williams, Bt.

INDEPENDENT SCHOOL BURSARS' ASSOCIATION (1933), 5 Chapel Close, Old Basing, Basingstoke, Hants RG24 7BY. Tel: 01256-330369. *General Secretary*, M. J. Sant

INDEPENDENT SCHOOLS CAREERS ORGANIZATION (1942), 12A Princess Way, Camberley, Surrey GU15 3SP. Tel: 01276-21188. *National Director*, G. W. Searle

INDEPENDENT SCHOOLS INFORMATION SERVICE (1972), 56 Buckingham Gate, London SW1E 6AG. Tel: 0171-630 8793. *Director*, D. J. Woodhead

INDEPENDENT SCHOOLS JOINT COUNCIL (1974), Grosvenor Gardens House, 35–37 Grosvenor Gardens, London SW1W 0BS. Tel: 0171-630 0144. *General Secretary*, Dr A. B. Cooke, OBE

INDEXERS, SOCIETY OF (1957), 1 Mermaid House, Mermaid Court, London SE1 1HR. Tel: 0171-403 4947. *Secretary*, Mrs C. Shuttleworth

INDUSTRIAL SOCIETY (1918), Robert Hyde House, 48 Bryanston Square, London W1H 7LN. Tel: 0171-262 2401. *Chief Executive*, T. Morgan

INDUSTRY AND PARLIAMENT TRUST, 1 Buckingham Place, London SW1E 6HR. Tel: 0171-976 5311. *Director*, F. R. Hyde-Chambers

INDUSTRY CHURCHES FORUM (formerly Industrial Churches Fellowship) (1877), 86 Leadenhall Street, London EC3A 3DH. Tel: 0171-283 6120. *Chairman*, Revd Canon B. Brown

INDUSTRY TRAINING ORGANIZATIONS, NATIONAL COUNCIL OF (1988), 10 Meadowcourt, Amos Road, Sheffield S9 1BX. Tel: 0114-261 9926. *Administrator*, J. Maisari

INFANT DEATHS, FOUNDATION FOR THE STUDY OF (1971), 14 Halkin Street, London SW1X 7DB. Tel: 0171-235 0965. Cot death helpline: 0171-235 1721. *Secretary-General*, Mrs J. Epstein

INFORMATION SCIENTISTS, INSTITUTE OF (1958), 44–45 Museum Street, London WC1A 1LY. Tel: 0171-831 8003. *Director*, E. Hyams

INNER WHEEL CLUBS IN GREAT BRITAIN AND IRELAND, ASSOCIATION OF (1934), 51 Warwick Square, London SW1V 2AT. Tel: 0171-834 4600. *Secretary*, Miss J. Dobson

INSOLVENCY, SOCIETY OF PRACTITIONERS OF (1990), Halton House, 20–23 Holborn, London EC1N 2JE. Tel: 0171-831 6563. *General Secretary*, R. M. Stancombe

INSURANCE AND INVESTMENT BROKERS' ASSOCIATION, BRITISH, BIIBA House, 14 Bevis Marks, London EC3A 7NT. Tel: 0171-623 9043. *Chairman*, A. Gavaghan

INSURANCE BROKERS REGISTRATION COUNCIL, 63 St Mary Axe, London EC3A 8MB. Tel: 0171-621 1061. *Registrar*, Miss E. J. Rees

INSURANCE INSTITUTE, CHARTERED (1897), 20 Aldermanbury, London EC2V 7HY. Tel: 0181-989 8464. *Director-General*, D. E. Bland, PH.D.

INSURERS, ASSOCIATION OF BRITISH (1985), 51 Gresham Street, London EC2V 7HQ. Tel: 0171-600 3333. *Director-General*, M. Boléat

INTERNATIONAL AFFAIRS, ROYAL INSTITUTE OF (1920), Chatham House, 10 St James's Square, London SW1Y 4LE. Tel: 0171-957 5700. *Director*, Sir Timothy Garden, KCB

INTERNATIONAL FRIENDSHIP LEAGUE (1931), 3 Creswick Road, London W3 9HE. *Secretary*, Miss. J. Nelson

INTERNATIONAL POLICE ASSOCIATION (British Section) (1950), 1 Fox Road, West Bridgford, Nottingham NG2 6AJ. Tel: 0115-981 3638. *Chief Executive Officer*, A. F. Carter

INTERNATIONAL STUDENTS HOUSE (1962), 229 Great Portland Street, London W1N 5HD. Tel: 0171-631 8300. *Executive Director*, P. Anwyl

INTERSERVE (1852), 325 Kennington Road, London SE11 4QH. Tel: 0171-735 8227. *National Director*, R. Clark

INTER VARSITY CLUBS, ASSOCIATION OF (1946), 2nd Floor, Grosvenor House, 94–96 Grosvenor Square, Manchester M1 7HL. Tel: 0161-273 2316. *Secretary*, D. Bousfield

INVALIDS-AT-HOME (1966), 17 Lapstone Gardens, Kenton, Harrow, Middx HA3 0EB. Tel: 0181-907 1706. *Executive Officer*, Mrs S. Lomas

INVISIBLES, BRITISH (1983), 6th Floor, Windsor House, 39 King Street, London EC2V 8DQ. Tel: 0171-600 1198. *Director-General*, The Hon. Mrs A. Wright

INVOLVEMENT AND PARTICIPATION ASSOCIATION (1884), 42 Colebrooke Row, London N1 8AF. Tel: 0171-354 8040. *Director*, B. C. Stevens

IRAN SOCIETY (1936), 2 Belgrave Square, London SW1X 8PJ. Tel: 0171-235 5122. *Chairman*, M. Noël-Clarke

ITRI (formerly International Tin Research Institute) (1932), Kingston Lane, Uxbridge, Middx UB8 3PJ. Tel: 01895-272406. *Director*, R. Bedder

JACQUELINE DU PRÉ MUSIC BUILDING APPEAL (1988), St Hilda's College, Oxford OX4 1DY. Tel: 01865-276803. *Chairman*, Dr J. H. Mellanby

JAPAN ASSOCIATION (1950), Swire House, 59 Buckingham Gate, London SW1E 6AJ. Tel: 0171-821 3221. *Executive Director*, D. F. L. Turner

JERUSALEM AND THE MIDDLE EAST CHURCH ASSOCIATION (1887), 1 Hart House, The Hart, Farnham, Surrey GU9 7HA. Tel: 01252-726994. *Secretary*, Mrs V. Wells

JEWISH HISTORICAL SOCIETY OF ENGLAND (1893), 33 Seymour Place, London W1H 5AP. Tel: 0171-723 5852. *Hon. Secretary*, C. M. Drukker

JEWISH PEOPLE, CHURCH'S MINISTRY AMONG (1809), 30c Clarence Road, St Albans, Herts AL1 4JJ. Tel: 01727-833114. *General Director*, Revd Dr W. Riggans

JEWISH YOUTH, ASSOCIATION FOR (part of Norwood Ravenswood) (1899), Norwood House, Harmony Way, Victoria Road, London NW4 2BZ. Tel: 0181-203 3030. *Head*, E. Finestone

JOURNALISTS, CHARTERED INSTITUTE OF (1883), 2 Dock Offices, Surrey Quays Road, London SE16 2XU. Tel: 0171-252 1187. *General Secretary*, C. J. Underwood

JUSTICE (British Section of the International Commission of Jurists) (1957), 59 Carter Lane, London EC4V 5AQ. Tel: 0171-329 5100. *Director*, Ms A. Owers

JUSTICES' CLERKS' SOCIETY (1839), The Magistrates' Court, 107 Dale Street, Liverpool L2 2JQ. Tel: 0151-255 0790. *Hon. Secretary*, M. Marsh

KING EDWARD'S HOSPITAL FUND FOR LONDON (THE KING'S FUND) (1897), 11–13 Cavendish Square, London W1M 0AN. Tel: 0171-307 2400. *Chief Executive*, Dr R. J. Maxwell, CBE

KING GEORGE'S FUND FOR SAILORS (1917), 8 Hatherley Street, London SW1P 2YY. Tel: 0171-932 0000. *Director-General*, Capt. M. J. Appleton, RN

KIPLING SOCIETY (1927), Tree Cottage, 2 Brownleaf Road, Brighton, E. Sussex BN2 6LB. Tel: 01273-303719. *Hon. Secretary*, J. W. M. Smith

LADIES IN REDUCED CIRCUMSTANCES, SOCIETY FOR THE ASSISTANCE OF (1886), Lancaster House, 25 Hornyold Road, Malvern, Worcs WR14 1QQ. Tel: 01684-574645.

LANDSCAPE INSTITUTE (1929), 6–8 Barnard Mews, London SW11 1QU. Tel: 0171-738 9166. *Director-General*, S. Royston

LAND-VALUE TAXATION AND FREE TRADE, INTERNATIONAL UNION FOR, 177 Vauxhall Bridge Road, London SW1V 1EU. Tel: 0171-834 4266. *Hon. Secretary*, Mrs B. P. Sobrielo

LANGUAGE LEARNING, ASSOCIATION FOR (1990), 150 Railway Terrace, Rugby CV21 3HN. Tel: 01788-546443. *Secretary-General*, Mrs C. Wilding

LAW REPORTING FOR ENGLAND AND WALES, INCORPORATED COUNCIL OF (1865), 3 Stone Buildings, Lincoln's Inn, London WC2A 3XN. Tel: 0171-242 6471. *Secretary*, J. Cobbett

LEAGUE OF THE HELPING HAND (1908), Petersham Hollow, 226 Petersham Road, Petersham, Richmond, Surrey TW10 7AL. Tel: 0181-940 7303. *Secretary*, Mrs I. Goodlad

LEAGUE OF WELLDOERS (1893), 119–133 Limekiln Lane, Liverpool L5 8SN. Tel: 0151-207 1984. *Warden and Secretary*, Mrs C. Fell

LEATHER AND HIDE TRADES' BENEVOLENT INSTITUTION (1860), 60 Wickham Hill, Hurstpierpoint, Hassocks, W. Sussex BN6 9NP. Tel: 01273-843488. *Secretary*, Mrs G. M. Stapleton, MBE

LEGAL EXECUTIVES, INSTITUTE OF (1892), Kempston Manor, Kempston, Bedford MK42 7AB. Tel: 01234-841000. *Chief Executive*, R. Ball

LEONARD CHESHIRE FOUNDATION (1955), 26–29 Maunsel Street, London SW1P 2QN. Tel: 0171-828 1822. *Director-General*, J. Stanford

LEPROSY MISSION (ENGLAND AND WALES) (1874), Goldhay Way, Orton Goldhay, Peterborough PE2 5GZ. Tel: 01733-370505. *Executive Director*, Revd J. A. Lloyd, PH.D.

LEUKAEMIA RESEARCH FUND (1962), 43 Great Ormond Street, London WC1N 3JJ. Tel: 0171-405 0101. *Executive Director*, D. L. Osborne

LIBERAL PARTY (1877; relaunched 1989), Gayfere House, 22 Gayfere Street, London SW1 3HP. Tel: 0171-233 2124. *Directors*, M. Oborski; D. Green

LIBERTY (NATIONAL COUNCIL FOR CIVIL LIBERTIES) (1934), 21 Tabard Street, London SE1 4LA. Tel: 0171-403 3888. *Director*, J. Wadham

LIBRARY ASSOCIATION (1877), 7 Ridgmount Street, London WC1E 7AE. Tel: 0171-636 7543. *Chief Executive*, R. Shimmon

LIFEBOATS, *see* ROYAL NATIONAL LIFEBOAT INSTITUTION

LIGHT HORSE BREEDING SOCIETY, NATIONAL (1885), 96 High Street, Edenbridge, Kent TN8 5AR. Tel: 01732-866277. *General Secretary*, G. W. Evans

LINGUISTS, INSTITUTE OF (1910), Saxon House, 48 Southwark Street, London SE1 1UN. Tel: 0171-940 3100. *Director*, Ms E. H. F. Ostarhild

LINNEAN SOCIETY OF LONDON (1788), Burlington House, Piccadilly, London W1V 0LQ. Tel: 0171-434 4479. *President*, Prof. Sir Ghillean Prance, FRS

LIONS CLUBS INTERNATIONAL (BRITISH ISLES AND IRELAND) (1949), 257 Alcester Road South, Kings Heath, Birmingham B14 6BT. Tel: 0121-441 4544. *Office Manager*, Mrs J. Davis

LISTENING LIBRARY, 12 Lant Street, London SE1 1QH. Tel: 0171-407 9417. *Chief Executive*, T. Taylor

LLOYD'S OF LONDON, 1 Lime Street, London EC3M 7HA. Tel: 0171-327 1000. *Chief Executive*, R. Sandler

LLOYD'S PATRIOTIC FUND (1803), Lloyd's, Lime Street, London EC3M 7HA. Tel: 0171-327 5925. *Secretary*, Mrs L. Harper

LLOYD'S REGISTER OF SHIPPING, 71 Fenchurch Street, London EC3M 4BS . Tel: 0171-709 9166. *Chairman*, P. C. K. O'Ferrall, OBE

LOCAL AUTHORITY CHIEF EXECUTIVES, SOCIETY OF (1974), PO Box 21, Archway Road, Huyton, Knowsley, Merseyside L36 9YU. Tel: 0151-443 3931. *Executive Officer*, Ms S. Rheinlander

LOCAL COUNCILS, NATIONAL ASSOCIATION OF (1947), 109 Great Russell Street, London WC1B 3LD. Tel: 0171-637 1865. *Director*, P. Clayden, OBE

LOCAL GOVERNMENT ASSOCIATION (1974), 26 Chapter Street, London SW1P 4ND. Tel: 0171-834 2222. *Chief Executive*, B. Briscoe

LOCAL GOVERNMENT INTERNATIONAL BUREAU (1913), *also* Council of European Municipalities and Regions (British Section) and International Union of Local Authorities (British Section) (1951), 35 Great Smith Street, London SW1P 3BJ. Tel: 0171-222 1636. *Secretary-General*, J. Smith

LOCAL HISTORY, BRITISH ASSOCIATION FOR (1843), 24 Lower Street, Harnham, Salisbury, Wilts SP2 8EY. Tel: 01722-332158. *Secretary*, M. Cowan

LONDON APPRECIATION SOCIETY (1932), 14 Hill View, 2–4 Primrose Hill Road, London NW3 3AX. *Chairman*, Miss V. C. Colin-Russ

LONDON CITY MISSION (1835), 175 Tower Bridge Road, London SE1 2AH. Tel: 0171-407 7585. *General Secretary*, Revd J. McAllen

LONDON COURT OF INTERNATIONAL ARBITRATION (LCIA) (1892), Hulton House, 6th Floor, 161–166 Fleet Street, London EC4A 2DY. Tel: 0171-936 3530. *Executive Director*, Ms M. May, CBE

LONDON FLOTILLA (1937), 40 Endlesham Road, London SW12 8JL. Tel: 0181-673 1879. *Hon. Secretary*, Lt.-Cdr. H. C. R. Upton, RD

LONDON GOVERNMENT, ASSOCIATION OF (1964), 36 Old Queen Street, London SW1H 9JF. Tel: 0171-222 7799. *Chief Executive*, M. Pilgrim

LONDON LIBRARY, THE (1841), 14 St James's Square, London SW1Y 4LG. Tel: 0171-930 7705. *Librarian*, A. S. Bell

LONDON MAGISTRATES' CLERKS' ASSOCIATION (1889), c/o Thames Magistrates' Court, 58 Bow Road, London E3 4DJ. Tel: 0181-980 1000 ext. 3708. *Hon. Chairman*, J. Mulhern

LONDON PLAYING FIELDS SOCIETY (1890), Boston Manor Playing Field, Boston Gardens, Brentford, Middx TW8 9LR. Tel: 0181-560 3667. *Secretary*, D. Northwood

LONDON SOCIETY (1912), 4th Floor, Senate House, Malet Street, London WC1E 7HU. Tel: 0171-580 5537. *Hon. Secretary*, Mrs B. Jones

LORD'S DAY OBSERVANCE SOCIETY (1831), 6 Sherman Road, Bromley, Kent BR1 3JH. Tel: 0181-313 0456. *General Secretary*, J. G. Roberts

LOTTERIES COUNCIL (1979), Windermere House, Kendal Avenue, London W3 0XA. Tel: 0181-896 2333. *Hon. Secretary*, G. Wilson, CBE

LUNG FOUNDATION, BRITISH (1985), 78 Hatton Garden, London EC1N 8JR. Tel: 0171-831 5831. *Chief Executive*, B. Walden

MAGISTRATES' ASSOCIATION (1920), 28 Fitzroy Square, London W1P 6DD. Tel: 0171-387 2353. *Secretary*, Ms S. Dickinson

MAILING PREFERENCE SERVICE (1983), 5 Reef House, Plantation Wharf, London SW11 3UF. Tel: 0345-034599. To limit direct mail: Freepost 22, London W1E 7EZ. *Chief Executive*, Ms K. Beckett

MAIL USERS' ASSOCIATION (1976), 70 Main Road, Hermitage, Near Emsworth, W. Sussex PO10 8AX. Tel: 0976-710315. *Chairman*, D. Thomas

MANAGEMENT, INSTITUTE OF (1992), Management House, Cottingham Road, Corby, Northants NN17 1TT. Tel: 01536-204222. *Director-General*, R. Young

MANAGEMENT AND PROFESSIONAL STAFFS, ASSOCIATION OF (1972), Parkgates, Bury New Road, Prestwich, Manchester M25 0JW. Tel: 0161-773 8621. *Executive Secretary*, A. J. Casey

MANAGEMENT SERVICES, INSTITUTE OF, 1 Cecil Court, London Road, Enfield, Middx EN2 6DD. Tel: 0181-363 7452.

MANIC DEPRESSION FELLOWSHIP (1983), 8–10 High Street, Kingston upon Thames, Surrey KT1 1EY. Tel: 0181-974 6550. *Director*, Ms M. Fulford

MANORIAL SOCIETY OF GREAT BRITAIN (1906), 104 Kennington Road, London SE11 6RE. Tel: 0171-735 6633. *Hon. Chairman*, R. A. Smith

MANPOWER SOCIETY (1969), 39 Apple Tree Walk, Climping, Littlehampton, W. Sussex BN17 5QN. Tel: 01903-731728. *Administrator*, Mrs H. Gale

MARIE CURIE CANCER CARE (1948), 28 Belgrave Square, London SW1X 8QG. Tel: 0171-235 3325. Scottish Office: 21 Rutland Street, Edinburgh EH1 2AH. Tel: 0131-229 8332. *Chief Executive*, Sir Nicholas Fenn, GCMG

MARINE ARTISTS, ROYAL SOCIETY OF (1939), 17 Carlton House Terrace, London SW1Y 5BD. Tel: 0171-930 6844. *Secretary*, Ms S. Robinson

MARINE BIOLOGICAL ASSOCIATION OF THE UK (1884), Citadel Hill, Plymouth PL1 2PB. Tel: 01752-633331. *Secretary*, Prof. M. Whitfield

MARINE ENGINEERS, INSTITUTE OF (1889), The Memorial Building, 76 Mark Lane, London EC3R 7JN. Tel: 0171-481 8493. *Secretary*, J. E. Sloggett, OBE

MARINE SCIENCE, SCOTTISH ASSOCIATION FOR (1914), PO Box 3, Oban, Argyll PA34 4AD. Tel: 01631-562244. *Director*, Dr G. B. Shimmield

MARINE SOCIETY (1756), 202 Lambeth Road, London SE1 7JW. Tel: 0171-261 9535. *Director*, Capt. J. J. Howard

MARIO LANZA EDUCATIONAL FOUNDATION (1976), 1 Kenton Gardens, Minster, Ramsgate, Kent CT12 4EN. *Hon. Secretary*, Mrs W. Stilwell

MARKET AUTHORITIES, NATIONAL ASSOCIATION OF BRITISH (1948), NABMA House, 21 Tarnside Road, Orrell, Wigan, Lancs WN5 8RN. Tel: 01695-623860. *Secretary*, J. Edwards

MARKETING, CHARTERED INSTITUTE OF (1911), Moor Hall, Cookham, Maidenhead, Berks SL6 9QH. Tel: 01628-427500. *Director-General*, S. Cuthbert

MARK MASTER MASONS, GRAND LODGE OF (1856), Mark Masons' Hall, 86 St James's Street, London SW1A 1PL. Tel: 0171-839 5274. *Grand Master*, HRH Prince Michael of Kent, KCVO

MARRIAGE CARE (formerly the Catholic Marriage Advisory Council) (1946), Clitherow House, 1 Blythe Mews, Blythe Road, London W14 0NW. Tel: 0171-371 1341. *Chief Executive*, Mrs M. Corbett

MASONIC BENEVOLENT INSTITUTION, ROYAL (1842), 20 Great Queen Street, London WC2B 5BG. Tel: 0171-405 8341. *Chief Executive*, Miss J. Reynolds

MASONIC TRUST FOR GIRLS AND BOYS (1985), 31 Great Queen Street, London WC2B 5AG. Tel: 0171-405 2644. *Secretary*, Lt.-Col. J. C. Chambers

MASTERS OF WINE, INSTITUTE OF (1955), Five Kings House, 1 Queen Street Place, London EC4R 1QS. Tel: 0171-236 4427. *Executive Director*, J. F. Casson

MATERIALS, INSTITUTE OF (1985), 1 Carlton House Terrace, London SW1Y 5DB. Tel: 0171-839 4071. *Chief Executive*, Dr B. A. Rickinson

MATERNAL AND CHILD WELFARE LTD, NATIONAL ASSOCIATION FOR (1911), 1st Floor, 40–42 Osnaburgh Street, London NW4 3ND. Tel: 0171-383 4117. *Administrator*, Mrs V. A. Farebrother

MATERNITY ALLIANCE (1980), 45 Beech Street, London EC2P 2LX. Tel: 0171-588 8583. *Director*, Ms C. Gowridge

MATHEMATICAL ASSOCIATION (1871), 259 London Road, Leicester LE2 3BE. Tel: 0116-270 3877. *Executive Secretary*, Ms H. Whitby

MATHEMATICS AND ITS APPLICATIONS, INSTITUTE OF (1964), Catherine Richards House, 16 Nelson Street, Southend-on-Sea, Essex SS1 1EF. Tel: 01702-354020. *Executive Secretary*, Dr A. M. Lepper

ME ASSOCIATION (1976), 4 Corringham Road, Stanford-le-Hope Essex SS17 0AH. Tel: 01375-642466. *Administrator*, Ms M. Moore

MEASUREMENT AND CONTROL, INSTITUTE OF (1944), 87 Gower Street, London WC1E 6AA. Tel: 0171-387 4949. *Secretary*, M. J. Yates

MECHANICAL ENGINEERS, INSTITUTION OF (1847), 1 Birdcage Walk, London SW1H 9JJ. Tel: 0171-222 7899. *Director-General*, Dr R. Pike

MEDIC-ALERT FOUNDATION, 1 Bridge Wharf, 156 Caledonian Road, London N1 9UU. Tel: 0171-833 3034. *Chief Executive*, Miss J. Friend

MEDICAL COUNCIL, GENERAL (1858), 178 Great Portland Street, London W1N 6JE. Tel: 0171-580 7642. *Chief Executive and Registrar*, F. M. Scott, TD

MEDICAL FOUNDATION FOR THE CARE OF VICTIMS OF TORTURE (1986), 96–98 Grafton Road, London NW5 3EJ. Tel: 0171-813 7777. *Director*, Ms H. Bamber

MEDICAL SOCIETY OF LONDON (1773), Lettsom House, 11 Chandos Street, London W1M 0EB. Tel: 0171-580 1043. *Registrar*, M. C. Griffiths, TD

MEDICAL WOMEN'S FEDERATION (1917), Tavistock House North, Tavistock Square, London WC1H 9HX. Tel: 0171-387 7765. *Hon. Secretary*, Dr S. Glendinning

MEMORIAL FUND FOR DISASTER RELIEF, Europa House, 13–17 Ironmonger Row, London EC1V 3QN. Tel: 0171-250 1700. *Director*, D. Childs

MENCAP (THE ROYAL SOCIETY FOR MENTALLY HANDICAPPED CHILDREN AND ADULTS) (1946), 123 Golden Lane, London EC1Y 0RT. Tel: 0171-454 0454. *Chief Executive*, F. Heddell

MENSA LTD, BRITISH (1946), Mensa House, St Johns Square, Wolverhampton WV2 4AH. Tel: 01902-772771. *General Manager*, D. Chatten

MENTAL AFTER CARE ASSOCIATION (1879), 25 Bedford Square, London WC1B 3HW. Tel: 0171-436 6194. *Chief Executive*, G. Hitchon

MENTAL HEALTH FOUNDATION (1949), 37 Mortimer Street, London W1N 8JU. Tel: 0171-580 0145. *Director*, Ms J. McKerrow

MENTAL HEALTH, NATIONAL ASSOCIATION FOR, *see* MIND

MENTAL HEALTH, SCOTTISH ASSOCIATION FOR (1923), Cumbrae House, 15 Carlton Court, Glasgow G5 9JP. Tel: 0141-429 4800. *Chief Executive*, Ms S. M. Barcus

MENTALLY HANDICAPPED, SCOTTISH SOCIETY FOR THE, *see* ENABLE

MERCHANT NAVY WELFARE BOARD (1948), 19–21 Lancaster Gate, London W2 3LN. Tel: 0171-723 3642. *General Secretary*, Capt. D. A. Parsons

METAL TRADES BENEVOLENT SOCIETY, ROYAL (1843), Brooke House, 4 The Lakes, Bedford Road, Northampton NN4 7YD. Tel: 01604-22023. *General Secretary*, A. N. Nisbet

METEOROLOGICAL SOCIETY, ROYAL (1850), 104 Oxford Road, Reading, Berks RG1 7LJ. Tel: 01734-568500. *Executive Secretary*, R. P. C. Swash

METROPOLITAN HOSPITAL-SUNDAY FUND (1872), 45 Westminster Bridge Road, London SE1 7JB. Tel: 0171-922 0200. *Secretary*, H. F. Doe

MIDDLE EAST ASSOCIATION (1961), Bury House, 33 Bury Street, St James's, London SW1Y 6AX. Tel: 0171-839 2137. *Director-General*, B. P. Constant

MIDWIVES, ROYAL COLLEGE OF (1881), 15 Mansfield Street, London W1M 0BE. Tel: 0171-872 5100. *General Secretary*, Mrs K. Davis

MIGRAINE ASSOCIATION, BRITISH (1858), 178A High Road, Byfleet, West Byfleet, Surrey KT14 7ED. Tel: 01932-352468. *Director,* Mrs A. Turner

MIGRAINE TRUST (1965), 45 Great Ormond Street, London WC1N 3HZ. Tel: 0171-278 2676. *Director,* Ms A. Rush

MILITARY HISTORICAL SOCIETY, National Army Museum, Royal Hospital Road, London SW3 4HT. Tel: 01980-630613. *Chairman,* D. Wood

MIND (THE NATIONAL ASSOCIATION FOR MENTAL HEALTH), Granta House, 15–19 Broadway, London E15 4BQ. Tel: 0181-519 2122. *Chief Executive,* Ms J. Clements

MINERALOGICAL SOCIETY (1876), 41 Queen's Gate, London SW7 5HR. Tel: 0171-584 7516. *Hon. General Secretary,* Dr B. A. Cressey

MINES OF GREAT BRITAIN, FEDERATION OF SMALL, 29 King Street, Newcastle under Lyme, Staffs ST5 1ER. Tel: 01782-614618. *Secretary,* R. W. Bladen

MINIATURE PAINTERS, SCULPTORS AND GRAVERS, ROYAL SOCIETY OF (1895), 1 Knapp Cottages, Wyke, Gillingham, Dorset SP8 4NQ. Tel: 01747-825718. *Executive Secretary,* Mrs P. Henderson

MINING AND METALLURGY, THE INSTITUTION OF (1892), 44 Portland Place, London W1N 4BR. Tel: 0171-580 3802. *Secretary,* M. J. Jones

MINING ENGINEERS, INSTITUTION OF (1889), Danum House, 6A South Parade, Doncaster, S. Yorks DN1 2DY. Tel: 01302-320486. *Secretary,* Dr G. J. M. Woodrow

MISSING PERSONS HELPLINE, NATIONAL (1992), Roebuck House, 284–286 Upper Richmond Road West, London SW14 7JE. Tel: 0181-392 2000. Helpline: 0500-700700. *Co-Founders,* Ms M. Asprey; Ms J. Newman

MISSION TO DEEP SEA FISHERMEN, ROYAL NATIONAL (1881), 43 Nottingham Place, London W1M 4BX. Tel: 0171-487 5101. *Chief Executive,* A. D. Marsden

MISSIONS TO SEAMEN (1856), St Michael Paternoster Royal, College Hill, London EC4R 2RL. Tel: 0171-248 5202. *Secretary-General,* Revd Canon G. Jones

MODERN CHURCHPEOPLE's UNION (1898), MCU Office, 25 Birch Grove, London W3 9SP. Tel: 0181-992 2333. *General Secretary,* Revd N. P. Henderson

MONUMENTAL BRASS SOCIETY (1887), Lowe Hill House, Stratford St Mary, Colchester, Essex CO7 6JX. Tel: 01206-337239. *Hon. Secretary,* H. M. Stuchfield

MORAVIAN MISSIONS, LONDON ASSOCIATION IN AID OF (1817), Moravian Church House, 5–7 Muswell Hill, London N10 3TJ. Tel: 0181-883 3409. *Secretary,* Ms J. Morten

MOTHERS' UNION (1876), Mary Sumner House, 24 Tufton Street, London SW1P 3RB. Tel: 0171-222 5533. *Chief Executive,* Mrs A. Ridler

MOTOR INDUSTRY, INSTITUTE OF THE, Fanshaws, Brickendon, Hertford SG13 8PQ. Tel: 01992-511521. *Secretary,* F. W. Janes

MOUNTBATTEN MEMORIAL TRUST (1979), 1 Grosvenor Crescent, London SW1X 7EF. Tel: 0171-235 5231 ext 255. *Director,* J. Boyd-Brent

MOUNTBATTEN TRUST, THE EDWINA (1960), 1 Grosvenor Crescent, London SW1X 7EF. Tel: 0171-235 5231 ext 255. *Secretary,* J. Boyd-Brent

MULTIPLE SCLEROSIS SOCIETY (1953), 25 Effie Road, London SW6 1EE. Tel: 0171-610 7171. Helpline: 0171-371 8000. *Chief Executive,* P. Cardy

MUNICIPAL ENGINEERS, ASSOCIATION OF, Institution of Civil Engineers, Great George Street, London SW1P 3AA. Tel: 0171-222 7722. *Director,* A. Bhogal

MUSEUMS ASSOCIATION (1889), 42 Clerkenwell Close, London EC1R 0PA. Tel: 0171-608 2933. *Director,* M. Taylor

MUSIC HALL SOCIETY, BRITISH (1963), Brodie and Middleton Ltd, 68 Drury Lane, London WC2B 5SP. Tel: 0171-836 3289/0. *Hon. Secretary,* Mrs D. Masterton

MUSICIANS BENEVOLENT FUND (1921), 16 Ogle Street, London W1P 8JB. Tel: 0171-636 4481. *Secretary,* Ms H. Faulkner

MUSICIANS, INCORPORATED SOCIETY OF (1882), 10 Stratford Place, London W1N 9AE. Tel: 0171-629 4413. *Chief Executive,* N. Hoyle

MUSICIANS OF GREAT BRITAIN, ROYAL SOCIETY OF (1738), 10 Stratford Place, London W1N 9AE. Tel: 0171-629 6137. *Secretary,* Mrs M. Gibb

MUSIC INFORMATION CENTRE, BRITISH (1967), 10 Stratford Place, London W1N 9AE. Tel: 0171-499 8567. *Directors,* M. Greenall; T. Morgan

MUSIC SOCIETIES, NATIONAL FEDERATION OF (1935), Francis House, Francis Street, London SW1P 1DE. Tel: 0171-828 7320. *Chief Executive,* R. Jones

NABC - CLUBS FOR YOUNG PEOPLE (1925), 371 Kennington Lane, London SE11 5QY. Tel: 0171-793 0787. *National Director,* C. Groves

NABS (formerly National Advertising Benevolent Society) (1913), 199–205 Old Marylebone Road, London NW1 5QP. Tel: 0171-723 8028. *Director,* Ms H. Tridgell

NACRO (NATIONAL ASSOCIATION FOR THE CARE AND RESETTLEMENT OF OFFENDERS) (1966), 169 Clapham Road, London SW9 0PU. Tel: 0171-582 6500. *Chief Executive,* Ms H. Edwards

NATIONAL BENEVOLENT INSTITUTION (1812), 61 Bayswater Road, London W2 3PG. Tel: 0171-723 0021. *Secretary,* Gp Capt. D. St J. Homer, MVO

NATIONAL COUNCIL FOR VOLUNTARY ORGANIZATIONS, *see* VOLUNTARY ORGANIZATIONS, NATIONAL COUNCIL FOR

NATIONAL COUNCIL OF WOMEN OF GREAT BRITAIN (1895), 36 Danbury Street, London N1 8JU. Tel: 0171-354 2395. *President,* Mrs G. Wedekind

NATIONAL DEMOCRATS (formerly National Front) (1967), PO Box 2269, London E6 3RF. Tel: 0181-471 6872. *Chairman,* I. Anderson

NATIONAL EXTENSION COLLEGE (1963), 18 Brooklands Avenue, Cambridge CB2 2HN. Tel: 01223-316644. *Director,* Dr R. Morpeth

NATIONAL SOCIETY (1811), Church House, Great Smith Street, London SW1P 3NZ. Tel: 0171-222 1672. For promoting religious education. *General Secretary,* G. Duncan

NATIONAL SOCIETY FOR THE PREVENTION OF CRUELTY TO CHILDREN (NSPCC) (1884), 42 Curtain Road, London EC2A 3NH. Tel: 0171-825 2500. *Director,* J. Harding

NATIONAL TRUST, THE (1895), 36 Queen Anne's Gate, London SW1H 9AS. Tel: 0171-222 9251. *Chairman,* C. Nunneley

NATIONAL TRUST FOR SCOTLAND (1931), 5 Charlotte Square, Edinburgh EH2 4DU. Tel: 0131-226 5922. *Chairman,* H. L. Melville

NATIONAL UNION OF STUDENTS (1922), Nelson Mandela House, 461 Holloway Road, London N7 6LJ. Tel: 0171-272 8900. *National President*, D. Trainer

NATIONAL VIEWERS' AND LISTENERS' ASSOCIATION (1964), All Saints House, High Street, Colchester CO1 1UG. Tel: 01206-561155. *General Secretary*, J. C. Beyer

NATIONAL WOMEN'S REGISTER (1960), 3A Vulcan House, Vulcan Road North, Norwich NR6 6AQ. Tel: 01603-406767. *National Organizer*, Mrs M. Dodkins

NATURALISTS' ASSOCIATION, BRITISH (1905), 1 Bracken Mews, London E4 7UT. *Hon. Membership Secretary*, Mrs Y. H. Griffiths

NAUTICAL RESEARCH, SOCIETY FOR (1911), c/o National Maritime Museum, Greenwich, London SE10 9NF. *Hon. Secretary*, Lt.-Cdr. W. J. R. Gardner

NAVAL ARCHITECTS, ROYAL INSTITUTION OF (1860), 10 Upper Belgrave Street, London SW1X 8BQ. Tel: 0171-235 4622. *Secretary*, T. Blakeley

NAVAL, MILITARY AND AIR FORCE BIBLE SOCIETY (1780), Radstock House, 3 Eccleston Street, London SW1W 9LZ. Tel: 0171-730 2155. *General Secretary*, J. M. Hines

NAVIGATION, ROYAL INSTITUTE OF (1947), 1 Kensington Gore, London SW7 2AT. Tel: 0171-589 5021. *Director*, Gp Capt. D. W. Broughton, MBE

NAVY RECORDS SOCIETY (1893), c/o Dept. of War Studies, King's College, The Strand, London WC2R 2LS. *Hon. Secretary*, Dr A. D. Lambert

NCH ACTION FOR CHILDREN (1869), 85 Highbury Park, London N5 1UD. Tel: 0171-226 2033. *Chief Executive*, D. Mead

NEEDLEWORK, ROYAL SCHOOL OF (1872), Apartment 12A, Hampton Court Palace, East Molesey, Surrey KT8 9AU. Tel: 0181-943 1432. *Principal*, Mrs E. Elvin

NEWCOMEN SOCIETY (1920), The Science Museum, London SW7 2DD. Tel: 0171-589 1793. For the study of the history of engineering and technology. *Executive Secretary*, C. Ellam

NEWSPAPER PRESS FUND (1864), Dickens House, 35 Wathen Road, Dorking, Surrey RH4 1JY. Tel: 01306-887511. *Director*, P. W. Evans

NEWSTRAID BENEVOLENT SOCIETY (1839), PO Box 306, Dunmow, Essex CM6 1HY. Tel: 01371-874198. *President*, A. Cameron

NOISE ABATEMENT SOCIETY (1959), PO Box 518, Eynsford, Dartford, Kent DA4 0LL. Tel: 01322-862789. *Chairman*, J. Connell, OBE

NON-SMOKERS, NATIONAL SOCIETY OF, *see* QUIT

NORWOOD RAVENSWOOD (formerly Norwood Childcare) (1795), Broadway House, 80–82 The Broadway, Stanmore, Middx HA7 4HB. Tel: 0181-954 4555. *Executive Directors*, Ms N. Brier; S. Brier

NOTARIES' SOCIETY (1907), 7 Lower Brook Street, Ipswich IP4 1AF. Tel: 01473-214762. *Secretary*, A. G. Dunford

NUCLEAR ENERGY SOCIETY, BRITISH (1962), 1–7 Great George Street, London SW1P 3AA. Tel: 0171-222 7722. *Executive Officer*, A. Tillbrook

NUFFIELD FOUNDATION (1943), 28 Bedford Square, London WC1B 3EG. Tel: 0171-631 0566. *Director*, A. Tomei

NUFFIELD PROVINCIAL HOSPITALS TRUST (1939), 59 New Cavendish Street, London WIM 7RD. Tel: 0171-485 6632. *Secretary*, J. Wyn Owen, CB

NURSES' NATIONAL HOME, RETIRED (1934), Riverside Avenue, Bournemouth BH7 7EE. Tel: 01202-396418. *Chairman*, G. J. Rowlett

NURSES, ROYAL NATIONAL PENSION FUND FOR, Burdett House, 15 Buckingham Street, London WC2N 6ED. Tel: 0171-839 6785. *General Manager*, V. G. West

NURSING, MIDWIFERY AND HEALTH VISITING, ENGLISH NATIONAL BOARD FOR, Victory House, 170 Tottenham Court Road, London WIP 0HA. Tel: 0171-388 3131. *Chief Executive Officer*, A. P. Smith

NURSING, MIDWIFERY AND HEALTH VISITING, UK CENTRAL COUNCIL FOR, 23 Portland Place, London WIN 4JT. Tel: 0171-637 7181. *Registrar and Chief Executive*, Ms S. Norman

NURSING, MIDWIFERY AND HEALTH VISITING, WELSH NATIONAL BOARD FOR, 2nd Floor, Golate House, 101 St Mary Street, Cardiff CF1 1DX. Tel: 01222-261400. *Chief Executive*, D. A. Ravey

NURSING, MIDWIFERY AND HEALTH VISITING FOR NORTHERN IRELAND, NATIONAL BOARD FOR, Centre House, 79 Chichester Street, Belfast BT1 4JE. Tel: 01232-238152. *Chief Executive*, Prof. O. D'A. Slevin

NURSING, MIDWIFERY AND HEALTH VISITING FOR SCOTLAND, NATIONAL BOARD FOR, 22 Queen Street, Edinburgh EH2 1NT. Tel: 0131-226 7371. *Chief Executive*, Mrs L. Mitchell

NURSING, ROYAL COLLEGE OF (1916), 20 Cavendish Square, London WIM 0AB. Tel: 0171-409 3333. *General Secretary*, Miss C. Hancock

NUTRITION FOUNDATION, BRITISH (1967), High Holborn House, 52–54 High Holborn, London WC1V 6RQ. Tel: 0171-404 6504. *Director-General*, Dr B. A. Wharton

NUTRITION SOCIETY (1941), 10 Cambridge Court, 210 Shepherds Bush Road, London W6 7NJ. Tel: 0171-602 0228. *Hon. Secretary*, Dr J. D. Oldham

OBSTETRICIANS AND GYNAECOLOGISTS, ROYAL COLLEGE OF (1929), 27 Sussex Place, London NW1 4RG. Tel: 0171-262 5425. *President*, Dr N. Patel

OCCUPATIONAL HEALTH AND SAFETY AGENCY, *see* OHSA

OCCUPATIONAL SAFETY AND HEALTH, INSTITUTION OF (1946), The Grange, Highfield Drive, Wigston, Leics LE18 1NN. Tel: 0116-257 3100. *Chief Executive*, J. R. Barrell, OBE

OFFICERS' ASSOCIATION, THE (1920), 48 Pall Mall, London SW1Y 5JY. Tel: 0171-930 0125. *General Secretary*, Brig. P. D. Johnson

OFFICERS' PENSIONS SOCIETY (1946), 68 South Lambeth Road, London SW8 1RL. Tel: 0171-820 9988. *General Secretary*, Maj.-Gen. P. R. F. Bonnet, CB, MBE

OHSA (formerly Occupational Health and Safety Agency), Communications HQ, Dacre House, 17–19 Dacre Street, London SW1H 0DH. Tel: 0171-222 1202. *Managing Director*, Ms W. Gill

OIL PAINTERS, ROYAL INSTITUTE OF (1883), 17 Carlton House Terrace, London SW1Y 5BD. Tel: 0171-930 6844. *Secretary*, B. Bennett

ONE-PARENT FAMILIES, NATIONAL COUNCIL FOR, 255 Kentish Town Road, London NW5 2LX. Tel: 0171-267 1361. *Director*, Ms K. Pappenheim

OPAS (PENSIONS ADVISORY SERVICE) (1982), 11 Belgrave Road, London SW1V 1RB. Tel: 0171-233 8080. *Deputy Chief Executive*, Mrs P. A. Green

OPEN-AIR MISSION (1853), 19 John Street, London WC1N 2DL. Tel: 0171-405 6135. *Secretary*, A. J. Greenbank

OPEN SPACES SOCIETY (1865), 25A Bell Street, Henley-on-Thames, Oxon RG9 2BA. Tel: 01491-573535. *General Secretary*, Miss K. Ashbrook

OPERATIC AND DRAMATIC ASSOCIATION, NATIONAL (1899), NODA House, 1 Crestfield Street, London WC1H 8AU. Tel: 0171-837 5655. *Chief Executive,* M. Thorburn

OPSIS (NATIONAL ASSOCIATION FOR THE EDUCATION, TRAINING AND SUPPORT OF BLIND AND PARTIALLY SIGHTED PEOPLE) (1992), Gretton House, 43 Hatton Garden, London EC1N 8EE. Tel: 0171-405 6697. *Secretary-General,* C. Binks

OPTICAL COUNCIL, GENERAL (1958), 41 Harley Street, London W1N 2DJ. Tel: 0171-580 3898. *Registrar,* R. Wilshin

OPTOMETRISTS, COLLEGE OF, 10 Knaresborough Place, London SW5 0TG. Tel: 0171-373 7765. *Secretary,* P. D. Leigh

ORDERS AND MEDALS RESEARCH SOCIETY (1942), 123 Turnpike Link, Croydon CRO 5NU. Tel: 0181-680 2701. *General Secretary,* N. G. Gooding

ORIENTAL CERAMIC SOCIETY (1921), 30B Torrington Square, London WC1E 7LJ. Tel: 0171-636 7985. *Secretary,* Mrs J. Martin

ORNITHOLOGISTS' CLUB, SCOTTISH (1936), 21 Regent Terrace, Edinburgh EH7 5BT. Tel: 0131-556 6042. *Secretary,* Ms S. Laing

ORNITHOLOGISTS' UNION, BRITISH (1858), c/o The Natural History Museum, Akeman Street, Tring, Herts HP23 6AP. Tel: 01442-890080. *Administrative Secretary,* Mrs G. Bonham

ORNITHOLOGY, BRITISH TRUST FOR (1932), The National Centre for Ornithology, The Nunnery, Thetford, Norfolk IP24 2PU. Tel: 01842-750050. *Director,* Dr J. J. D. Greenwood

ORTHOPAEDIC ASSOCIATION, BRITISH (1918), c/o The Royal College of Surgeons, 35–43 Lincoln's Inn Fields, London WC2A 3PN. Tel: 0171-405 6507. *Chief Executive,* D. C. Adams

OSTEOPATHIC MEDICINE, LONDON COLLEGE OF, 8–10 Boston Place, London NW1 6QH. Tel: 0171-262 5250. *Clinic Manager,* Mrs A. Dalby

OSTEOPATHS, GENERAL COUNCIL AND REGISTER OF (1936), 56 London Street, Reading, Berks RG1 4SQ. Tel: 01734-576585. *Secretary,* Dr D. C. Weeks

OSTEOPOROSIS SOCIETY, NATIONAL (1986), PO Box 10, Radstock, Bath BA3 3YB. Tel: 01761-471771. *Office Manager,* Mrs H. Kingman

OUTWARD BOUND TRUST (1941), PO Box 1219, Windsor, Berks SL4 1XR. Tel: 01753-730060. *Director,* M. Hobbs, CBE

OVERSEAS DEVELOPMENT INSTITUTE (1960), Portland House, Stag Place, London SW1E 5DP. Tel. 0171-393 1600. *Director,* S. Maxwell

OVERSEAS SERVICE PENSIONERS' ASSOCIATION (1960), 138 High Street, Tonbridge, Kent TN9 1AX. Tel: 01732-363836. *Secretary,* D. F. B. Le Breton, CBE

OVERSEAS SETTLEMENT (1925), Church of England Board for Social Responsibility, Great Smith Street, London SW1P 3NZ. Tel: 0171-222 9011. *Administration Secretary,* Miss P. J. Hallett

OXFAM UK/IRELAND (1942), 274 Banbury Road, Oxford OX2 7DZ. Tel: 01865-311311. *Director,* D. Bryer, CMG

OXFORD PRESERVATION TRUST (1927), 10 Turn Again Lane, St Ebbes, Oxford OX1 1QL. Tel: 01865-242918. *Secretary,* Mrs M. Haynes

OXFORD SOCIETY (1932), 41 Wellington Square, Oxford OX1 2JF. Tel: 01865-270088. *Secretary (acting),* T. J. Lewis

PAEDIATRICS AND CHILD HEALTH, ROYAL COLLEGE OF (1928), 5 St Andrews Place, Regents Park, London NW1 4LB. Tel: 0171-486 6151. *Hon. Secretary,* Dr K. Dodd

PAINTER-PRINTMAKERS, ROYAL SOCIETY OF (1880), Bankside Gallery, 48 Hopton Street, London SE1 9JH. Tel: 0171-928 7521. *President,* Prof. D. Carpanini

PAINTERS IN WATER COLOURS, ROYAL INSTITUTE OF (1831), 17 Carlton House Terrace, London SW1Y 5BD. Tel: 0171-930 6844. *Secretary,* T. Hunt

PALAEONTOLOGICAL ASSOCIATION (1957), c/o Lapworth Museum, School of Earth Sciences, University of Birmingham, Birmingham B15 2TT. Tel: 0121-414 4173. *Secretary,* Dr P. Smith

PARENTS AT WORK (1985), 45 Beech Street, Barbican, London EC2Y 8AD. Tel: 0171-628 3578. *Joint Chief Executives,* Ms S. Jackson; Ms S. Monk

PARKINSON'S DISEASE SOCIETY OF THE UNITED KINGDOM (1969), 22 Upper Woburn Place, London WC1H 0RA. Tel: 0171-383 3513. *Chief Executive,* B. A. Brooking, MBE

PARLIAMENTARY AND SCIENTIFIC COMMITTEE (1939), 16 Great College Street, London SW1P 3RX. Tel: 0171-222 7085. *Administrative Secretary,* Dr A. Whitehouse

PASTORAL PSYCHOLOGY, GUILD OF (1936), PO Box 1107, London W3 6ZP. Tel: 0181-993 8366. *Administrator,* Mrs N. Stanley

PATENT AGENTS, CHARTERED INSTITUTE OF (1882), Staple Inn Buildings, High Holborn, London WC1V 7PZ. Tel: 0171-405 9450. *Secretary,* M. C. Ralph

PATENTEES AND INVENTORS, INSTITUTE OF (1919), Suite 505A Triumph House, 189 Regent Street, London W1R 7WF. Tel: 0171-434 1818. *Secretary,* R. Magnus

PATHOLOGISTS, ROYAL COLLEGE OF, 2 Carlton House Terrace, London SW1Y 5AF. Tel: 0171-930 5863. *President,* Prof R. N. M. MacSween

PATIENTS ASSOCIATION (1963), 8 Guilford Street, London WC1N 1DT. Tel: 0171-242 3460. *General Manager,* C. Gritzner

PDSA (PEOPLE'S DISPENSARY FOR SICK ANIMALS) (1917), Whitechapel Way, Priorslee, Telford, Shropshire TF2 9PQ. Tel: 01952-290999. *Director-General,* M. R. Curtis, MBE

PEACE COUNCIL, NATIONAL (1908), 88 Islington High Street, London N1 8EG. Tel: 0171-354 5200.

PEAK AND NORTHERN FOOTPATHS SOCIETY (1894), 15 Parkfield Drive, Tyldesley, Manchester M29 8NR. Tel: 0161-790 4383. *Hon. General Secretary,* D. Taylor

PEARSON'S HOLIDAY FUND, PO Box 123, Bishops Waltham, Southampton SO32 1ZE. Tel: 01489-893260. *General Secretary,* R. Heasman

PEDESTRIANS ASSOCIATION (1929), 126 Aldersgate Street, London EC1A 4JQ. Tel: 0171-490 0750. *Chairman,* Ms F. Lawson

PEN, INTERNATIONAL (1921), 9–10 Charterhouse Buildings, Goswell Road, London EC1M 7AT. Tel: 0171-253 4308. English Centre, 7 Dilke Street, London SW3 4JE. Tel: 0171-352 6303. World association of writers. *International Secretary,* A. Blokh

PENSION FUNDS LTD, NATIONAL ASSOCIATION OF (1923), 12–18 Grosvenor Gardens, London SW1W 0DH. Tel: 0171-730 0585. *Director-General,* Dr A. Robinson

PENSIONS ADVISORY SERVICE, *see* OPAS

PERFORMING RIGHT SOCIETY LTD (1914), 29–33 Berners Street, London W1P 4AA. Tel: 0171-580 5544. *Chief Executive*, J. Hutchinson

PERIODICAL PUBLISHERS ASSOCIATION LTD (1913), Queens House, 28 Kingsway, London WC2B 6JR. Tel: 0171-404 4166. *Chief Executive*, I. Locks

PESTALOZZI CHILDREN'S VILLAGE TRUST (1959), Sedlescombe, Battle, E. Sussex TN33 0RR. Tel: 01424-870444. *Director*, M. Phillips

PETROLEUM, INSTITUTE OF (1913), 61 New Cavendish Street, London W1M 8AR. Tel: 0171-467 7100. *Director-General*, I. Ward

PHARMACEUTICAL SOCIETY OF GREAT BRITAIN, ROYAL (1841), 1 Lambeth High Street, London SE1 7JN. Tel: 0171-735 9141. *Secretary and Registrar*, J. Ferguson, OBE

PHARMACOLOGICAL SOCIETY, BRITISH (1931), 16 Angel Gate, City Road, London EC1V 2PT. Tel: 0171-417 0113. *Hon. General Secretary*, Prof. N. G. Bowery

PHILOLOGICAL SOCIETY (1842), School of Oriental and African Studies, University of London, Thornhaugh Street, London WC1H 0XG. Tel: 0171-637 2388. *Hon. Secretary*, Prof. R. J. Hayward

PHILOSOPHY, ROYAL INSTITUTE OF (1925), 14 Gordon Square, London WC1H 0AG. Tel: 0171-387 4130. *Director*, Prof. A. O'Hear

PHOTOGRAPHY, BRITISH INSTITUTE OF PROFESSIONAL (1901), Fox Talbot House, Amwell End, Ware, Herts SG12 9HN. Tel: 01920-464011. *Chief Executive*, A. Mair

PHYSICAL RECREATION, CENTRAL COUNCIL OF (1935), Francis House, Francis Street, London SW1P 1DE. Tel: 0171-828 3163/4. *General Secretary*, M. Denton

PHYSICIANS, ROYAL COLLEGE OF (1518), 11 St Andrews Place, London NW1 4LE. Tel: 0171-935 1174. *President*, Prof. K. G. M. M. Alberti, FRCP

PHYSICIANS AND SURGEONS OF GLASGOW, ROYAL COLLEGE OF (1599), 232–242 St Vincent Street, Glasgow G2 5RJ. Tel: 0141-221 6072. *President*, Prof. N. Mackay

PHYSICIANS OF EDINBURGH, ROYAL COLLEGE OF (1681), 9 Queen Street, Edinburgh EH2 1JQ. Tel: 0131-225 7324. *President*, Prof. J. D. Cash

PHYSICS AND ENGINEERING IN MEDICINE, INSTITUTE OF, 4 Campleshon Road, York YO2 1PE. Tel: 01904 610821. *General Secretary*, R. W. Neilson

PHYSICS, INSTITUTE OF (1874), 76 Portland Place, London W1N 4AA. Tel: 0171-470 4800. *Chief Executive*, Dr A. D. W. Jones

PHYSIOLOGICAL SOCIETY (1876), PO Box 11319, London WC1E 7JF. Tel: 0171-631 1456. *Hon. Secretary*, Prof. P. Stanfield

PHYSIOTHERAPY, CHARTERED SOCIETY OF (1894), 14 Bedford Row, London WC1R 4ED. Tel: 0171-306 6666. *Secretary*, P. Lambden

PIG ASSOCIATION, BRITISH (1884), 7 Rickmansworth Road, Watford WD1 7HE. Tel: 01923-234377/230421. *Chief Executive*, G. E. Welsh

PILGRIM TRUST (1930), Fielden House, Little College Street, London SW1P 3SH. Tel: 0171-222 4723. *Director*, Miss G. Nayler

PILGRIMS OF GREAT BRITAIN (1902), c/o 32 Old Queen Street, London SW1H 9HP. Tel: 0171-222 0232. *Hon. Secretary*, M. P. S. Barton

PLAIN ENGLISH CAMPAIGN (1979), PO Box 3, New Mills, High Peak SK22 4QP. Tel: 01663-744409. *Director*, Ms C. Maher, OBE

PLANT ENGINEERS, INSTITUTION OF, 77 Great Peter Street, London SW1P 2EZ. Tel: 0171-233 2855. *Secretary*, P. F. Tye

PLAYING FIELDS ASSOCIATION, NATIONAL (1925), 25 Ovington Square, London SW3 1LQ. Tel: 0171-584 6445. *Director*, Ms E. Davies

PLUNKETT FOUNDATION (1919), 23 Hanborough Business Park, Long Hanborough, Oxford OX8 8LH. Tel: 01993-883636. *Director*, E. Parnell

POETRY SOCIETY (1909), 22 Betterton Street, London WC2H 9BU. Tel: 0171-240 4810. *Director*, C. Meade

POLICY STUDIES INSTITUTE (1978), 100 Park Village East, London NW1 3SR. Tel: 0171-468 0468. *Director*, Ms P. Meadows

POLIO FELLOWSHIP, BRITISH (1939), Ground Floor, Unit A, Eagle Office Centre, The Runway, South Ruislip, Middx HA4 6SE. Tel: 0181-842 1898. *General Secretary*, M. Drake

POLITE SOCIETY (1986), 6 Norman Avenue, Henley-on-Thames, Oxon RG9 1SG. Tel: 01491-572794. *Hon. Secretary*, Miss G. Mackenzie

PONY CLUB (1929), National Agricultural Centre, Stoneleigh Park, Kenilworth, Warks CV8 2LR. Tel: 01203-696697. *Chief Executive*, Lt. Col. T. W. Kopanski

PORTRAIT PAINTERS, ROYAL SOCIETY OF (1891), 17 Carlton House Terrace, London SW1Y 5BD. Tel: 0171-930 6844. *Secretary*, P. Brason

POST OFFICE USERS' NATIONAL COUNCIL (1970), 6 Hercules Road, London SE1 7DN. Tel: 0171-928 9458. *Secretary*, K. Hall

PRAYER BOOK SOCIETY (1975), St James Garlickhythe, Garlick Hill, London EC4V 2AL. Tel: 01923-824278. *Chairman*, C. A. A. Kilmister

PRECEPTORS, COLLEGE OF (1846), Coppice Row, Theydon Bois, Epping, Essex CM16 7DN. Tel: 01992-812727. *Chief Executive Officer*, T. Wheatley

PRE-SCHOOL LEARNING ALLIANCE, 69 Kings Cross Road, London WC1X 9LL. Tel: 0171-833 0991. *Chief Executive Officer*, Ms M. Lochrie

PRESS UNION, COMMONWEALTH (1909), 17 Fleet Street, London EC4Y 1AA. Tel: 0171-583 7733. *Director*, R. MacKichan

PREVENTION OF ACCIDENTS, ROYAL SOCIETY FOR THE (1916), Edgbaston Park, 353 Bristol Road, Birmingham B5 7ST. Tel: 0121-248 2000. *Chief Executive*, Dr J. Hooper

PRINCESS LOUISE SCOTTISH HOSPITAL (Erskine Hospital) (1916), Bishopton, Renfrewshire PA7 5PU. Tel: 0141-812 1100. For disabled ex-servicemen and women. *Chief Executive*, Col. M. F. Gibson, OBE

PRINCESS ROYAL TRUST FOR CARERS (1990), 16 Byward Street, London EC3R 5BA. Tel: 0171-480 7788. *Chief Executive*, D. Butler

PRINCE'S SCOTTISH YOUTH BUSINESS TRUST (1989), 6th Floor, Mercantile Chambers, 53 Bothwell Street, Glasgow G2 6TS. Tel: 0141-248 4999. *Director*, D. W. Cooper

PRINCE'S TRUST (1976) and ROYAL JUBILEE TRUSTS (1935, 1977), 18 Park Square East, London NW1 4LH. Tel: 0171-543 1234. *Director*, T. Shebbeare, CVO

PRINCE'S YOUTH BUSINESS TRUST, 18 Park Square East, London NW1 4LH. Tel: 0171-543 1234. *Chief Executive*, R. Street

PRINTERS' CHARITABLE CORPORATION (1827), 7 Cantelupe Mews, Cantelupe Road, East Grinstead, W. Sussex RH19 3BG. Tel: 01342-318882. *Director*, Ms T. Searle

PRINTING HISTORICAL SOCIETY (1964), St Bride Institute, Bride Lane, London EC4Y 8EE. *Hon. Secretary*, P. Wickens

PRINTING, INSTITUTE OF (1961), 8A Lonsdale Gardens, Tunbridge Wells, Kent TN1 1NU. Tel: 01892-538118. *Secretary-General*, D. Freeland

PRISONERS ABROAD (1978), 72–82 Rosebery Avenue, London EC1R 4RR. Tel: 0171-833 3467. *Director*, C. Laurenzi

PRISON VISITORS, NATIONAL ASOCIATION OF (1922), 29 Kimbolton Road, Bedford MK40 2PB. Tel: 01234-359763. *General Secretary*, Mrs A. G. McKenna

PRIVATE LIBRARIES ASSOCIATION (1957), Ravelston, South View Road, Pinner, Middx HA5 3YD. *Hon. Secretary*, F. Broomhead

PROCURATORS IN GLASGOW, ROYAL FACULTY OF (1600), 12 Nelson Mandela Place, Glasgow G2 1BT. Tel: 0141-552 3422. *Clerk*, A. J. Campbell

PROFESSIONAL CLASSES AID COUNCIL (1921), 10 St Christopher's Place, London W1M 6HY. Tel: 0171-935 0641.

PROFESSIONAL ENGINEERS, UK ASSOCIATION OF (1969), Hayes Court, West Common Road, Bromley BR2 7AU. Tel: 0181-462 7755. *National Secretary*, J. M. Dalgleish

PROFESSIONAL FOOTBALLERS' ASSOCIATION, 2 Oxford Court, Bishopsgate, Manchester M2 3WQ. Tel: 0161-236 0575. *Chief Executive*, G. Taylor

PROFESSIONS SUPPLEMENTARY TO MEDICINE, COUNCIL FOR, Park House, 184 Kennington Park Road, London SE11 4BU. Tel: 0171 582 0866. *Registrar (acting)*, Dr P. Burley

PROTECTION OF UNBORN CHILDREN, SOCIETY FOR THE (1967), Phyllis Bowman House, 5–6 St Matthew Street, London SW1P 2JT. Tel: 0171-222 5845. *National Director*, J. Smeaton

PROTESTANT ALLIANCE (1845), 77 Ampthill Road, Flitwick, Bedford MK45 1BD. Tel: 01525-712348. *General Secretary*, Dr S. J. Scott-Pearson

PSORIASIS ASSOCIATION (1968), 7 Milton Street, Northampton NN2 7JG. Tel: 01604-711129. *National Secretary*, Mrs L. Henley

PSYCHIATRISTS, ROYAL COLLEGE OF (1971), 17 Belgrave Square, London SW1X 8PG. Tel: 0171-235 2351. *President*, Dr R. Kendell

PSYCHICAL RESEARCH, SOCIETY FOR (1882), 49 Marloes Road, London W8 6LA. Tel: 0171-937 8984. *Secretary*, Ms E. J. O'Keeffe

PSYCHOLOGICAL SOCIETY, BRITISH (1901), St Andrews House, 48 Princess Road East, Leicester LE1 7DR. Tel: 0116-254 9568. *Executive Secretary*, C. V. Newman, PH.D.

PUBLIC FINANCE AND ACCOUNTANCY, CHARTERED INSTITUTE OF (1885), 3 Robert Street, London WC2N 6BH. Tel: 0171-543 5600. *Chief Executive*, D. Adams

PUBLIC HEALTH AND HYGIENE, ROYAL INSTITUTE OF (1937), 28 Portland Place, London W1N 4DE. Tel: 0171-580 2731. *Secretary*, Gp Capt. R. A. Smith

PUBLIC RELATIONS, INSTITUTE OF (1948), The Old Trading House, 15 Northburgh Street, London EC1V 0PR. Tel: 0171-253 5151. *Executive Director*, J. B. Lavelle

PUBLIC TEACHERS OF LAW, SOCIETY OF (1908), Faculty of Law, Kings College London, Strand, London WC2R 2LS. Tel: 0171-873 2452. *Hon. Secretary*, Prof. D. Hayton

PURCHASING AND SUPPLY, CHARTERED INSTITUTE OF (1967), Easton House, Easton on the Hill, Stamford, Lincs PE9 3NZ. Tel: 01780-756777. *Director-General*, P. Thomson

PURE WATER ASSOCIATION, NATIONAL (1960), Meridan, Cae Goody Lane, Ellesmere, Shropshire SY12 9DW. Tel: 01691-623015. *Secretary*, N. Brugge

QUAKER SOCIAL RESPONSIBILITY AND EDUCATION, Friends House, 173–177 Euston Road, London NW1 2BJ. Tel: 0171-663 1000. *General Secretary*, Ms B. Smith

QUALITY ASSURANCE, INSTITUTE OF, PO Box 712, 61 Southwark Street, London SE1 1SB. Tel: 0171-401 7227. *Secretary-General*, D. G. Campbell

QUARRIERS HOMES (1871), Bridge of Weir, Renfrewshire PA11 3SA. Tel: 01505-612224. *Director*, G. E. Lee

QUARRYING, INSTITUTE OF (1917), 7 Regent Street, Nottingham NG1 5BS. Tel: 0115-941 1315. *Secretary*, M. J. Arthur

QUEEN ELIZABETH'S FOUNDATION FOR DISABLED PEOPLE (1967), Leatherhead Court, Leatherhead, Surrey KT22 0BN. Tel: 01372-842204. *Director*, M. B. Clark, PH.D.

QUEEN'S ENGLISH SOCIETY (1972), 20 Jessica Road, London SW18 2QN. Tel: 0171-371 7530. *Hon. Secretary*, Miss P. Raper

QUEEN'S NURSING INSTITUTE (1887), 3 Albemarle Way, London EC1V 4JB. Tel: 0171-490 4227. *Director*, Mrs P. Bagnall

QUEEN VICTORIA CLERGY FUND (1897), Church House, Dean's Yard, London SW1P 3NZ. Tel: 0171-222 5261. *Secretary*, C. D. L. Menzies

QUEEN VICTORIA SCHOOL (1908), Dunblane, Perthshire FK15 0JY. Tel: 01786-822288. *Headmaster*, B. Raine

QUEKETT MICROSCOPICAL CLUB (1865), Flat 3, Romagna, 101 Truro Road, London N22 4DL. *Hon. Business Secretary*, Miss P. Hamer

QUIT (NATIONAL SOCIETY OF NON-SMOKERS) (1926), Victory House, 170 Tottenham Court Road, London W1P 0HA. Tel: 0171-388 5775. Freephone helpline: 0800-002200. *Chief Executive*, P. McCabe

RADAR (ROYAL ASSOCIATION FOR DISABILITY AND REHABILITATION) (1977), 12 City Forum, 250 City Road, London EC1V 8AF. Tel: 0171-250 3222. *Director*, B. Massie, OBE

RADIOLOGISTS, ROYAL COLLEGE OF (1934), 38 Portland Place, London W1N 4JQ. Tel: 0171-636 4432. *President*, Dr M. J. Brindle

RADIOLOGY, BRITISH INSTITUTE OF (1897), 36 Portland Place, London W1N 4AT. Tel: 0171-580 4317. *Chief Executive*, Ms M. A. Piggott

RAIL USERS' CONSULTATIVE COMMITTEE, CENTRAL (1948), Clements House, 14–18 Gresham Street, London EC2V 7NL. Tel: 0171-505 9090. *Secretary*, M. Patterson

RAILWAY AND CANAL HISTORICAL SOCIETY, 17 Clumber Crescent North, The Park, Nottingham NG7 1EY. Tel: 0115-941 4844. *Hon. Secretary*, G. H. R. Gwatkin

RAILWAY BENEVOLENT INSTITUTION (1858), Foundation House, 7–11 Macon Court, Herald Drive, Crewe, Cheshire CW1 6WA. Tel: 01270-251316. *Director*, B. R. Whitnall

RAINER FOUNDATION (1876), 89 Blackheath Hill, London
SE10 8TJ. Tel: 0181-694 9497. Provides community-
based services for young people who are homeless,
offending or in difficulty with their families. *Chief
Executive*, Ms N. Varma

RAMBLERS' ASSOCIATION (1935), 1–5 Wandsworth Road,
London SW8 2XX. Tel: 0171-339 8500. *Director*,
A. Mattingly

RARE BREEDS SURVIVAL TRUST (1973), National
Agricultural Centre, Stoneleigh Park,
Kenilworth, Warks CV8 2LG. Tel: 01203-696551.
Executive Director, G. L. H. Alderson

RATHBONE COMMUNITY INDUSTRY (1919), 1st Floor, The
Excalibur Building, 77 Whitworth Street, Manchester
M1 6EZ. Tel: 0161-236 5358. Learning Difficulties
Helpline: 0161-236 1877. Helps people with learning
difficulties. *Chief Executive*, Ms A. Weinstock, CBE

RECORD SOCIETY, SCOTTISH (1897), Department of
Scottish History, University of Glasgow, Glasgow
G12 8QH. Tel: 0141-339 8855 ext 5682. *Hon. Secretary*,
J. Kirk, PH.D.

RECORDS ASSOCIATION, BRITISH (1932), c/o London
Metropolitan Archives, 40 Northampton Road, London
EC1R 0HB. Tel: 0171-833 0428. *Hon. Secretary*, Mrs E.
Hughes

RED CROSS SOCIETY, BRITISH, *see* BRITISH RED CROSS

RED POLL CATTLE SOCIETY (1888), The Market Hill,
Woodbridge, Suffolk IP12 4LU. Tel: 01394-380643.
Secretary, P. Ryder-Davies

REFRIGERATION, INSTITUTE OF (1899), Kelvin House, 76
Mill Lane, Carshalton, Surrey SM5 2JR. Tel: 0181-
647 7033. *Secretary*, M. J. Horlick

REFUGEE COUNCIL, BRITISH (1981), Bondway House,
3–9 Bondway, London SW8 1SJ. Tel: 0171-820 3000. *Chief
Executive*, N. Hardwick

REGIONAL STUDIES ASSOCIATION (1965), Wharfdale
Projects, 15 Micawber Street, London N1 7TB. Tel: 0171-
490 1128. *Director*, Mrs S. Hardy

REGULAR FORCES EMPLOYMENT ASSOCIATION (1885), 49
Pall Mall, London SW1Y 5JG. Tel: 0171-321 2011. *Chief
Executive*, Maj.-Gen. M. F. L. Shellard, CBE

RELATE: NATIONAL MARRIAGE GUIDANCE (1938),
Herbert Gray College, Little Church Street, Rugby,
Warks CV21 3AP. Tel: 01788-573241. *Chief Executive*, Ms S.
Bowler

RENT OFFICERS AND RENTAL VALUES, INSTITUTE OF
(1966), Beaufort House, Hamble Lane, Bursledon,
Southampton SO31 8BR. Tel: 01703-403716. *General
Secretary*, A. E. Corcoran

RESEARCH DEFENCE SOCIETY (1908), 58 Great
Marlborough Street, London W1V 1DD. Tel: 0171-
287 2818. *Executive Director*, Dr M. Matfield

RETIREMENT PENSIONS ASSOCIATIONS, NATIONAL
FEDERATION OF (1938), Thwaites House, Railway
Road, Blackburn BB1 5AX. Tel: 01254-52606. *General
Secretary*, R. Stansfield

REVENUES, RATING AND VALUATION, INSTITUTE OF
(1882), 41 Doughty Street, London WC1N 2LF. Tel: 0171-
831 3505. *Director*, C. Farrington

RICHARD III SOCIETY (1924), 4 Oakley Street, London
SW3 5NN. Tel: 0171-351 3391. *Secretary*, Miss E. M. Nokes

ROAD SAFETY OFFICERS, INSTITUTE OF (1971), 31
Heather Grove, Hollingworth, Hyde, Cheshire SK14 8JL.
Tel: 0161-474 4876. *Secretary*, B. Wilkinson

ROAD TRANSPORT ENGINEERS, INSTITUTE OF (1945), 22
Greencoat Place, London SW1P 1PR. Tel: 0171-630 1111.
Chief Executive, A. F. Stroud

ROMAN STUDIES, SOCIETY FOR THE PROMOTION OF
(1910), Senate House, Malet Street, London WC1E 7HU.
Tel: 0171-323 9583. *Secretary*, Dr H. M. Cockle

ROTARY INTERNATIONAL IN GREAT BRITAIN AND
IRELAND (1914), Kinwarton Road, Alcester, Warks
B49 6BP. Tel: 01789-765411. *Secretary*, D. Morehen

ROUND TABLES OF GREAT BRITAIN AND IRELAND,
NATIONAL ASSOCIATION OF (1927), Marchesi House, 4
Embassy Drive, Edgbaston, Birmingham B15 1TP. Tel:
0121-456 4402. *General Secretary*, R. H. Renold

ROYAL AIR FORCE BENEVOLENT FUND (1919), 67
Portland Place, London W1N 4AR. Tel: 0171-580 8343.
Controller, Air Chief Marshal Sir Roger Palin, KCB, OBE

ROYAL AIR FORCES ASSOCIATION (1943), 43 Grove Park
Road, London W4 3RX. Tel: 0181-994 8504. *Secretary-
General*, J. G. Hargreaves, CBE

ROYAL ALEXANDRA AND ALBERT SCHOOL (1758), Gatton
Park, Reigate, Surrey RH2 0TW. Tel: 01737-642576.
Secretary, Wg Cdr. N. J. Wright

ROYAL ALFRED SEAFARERS' SOCIETY (1865), Weston
Acres, Woodmansterne Lane, Banstead, Surrey SM7 3HB.
Tel: 01737-352231. *General Secretary*, A. R. Quinton

ROYAL ARMOURED CORPS WAR MEMORIAL
BENEVOLENT FUND (1946), c/o RHQ RTR, Bovington
Camp, Wareham, Dorset BH20 6JA. Tel: 01929-403331.
Secretary, Maj. A. Henzie (retd), MBE

ROYAL ARTILLERY ASSOCIATION, Artillery House, Front
Parade, Royal Artillery Barracks, Woolwich, London
SE18 4BH. Tel: 0181-781 3005. *General Secretary*, Lt.-Col.
M. J. Darmody

ROYAL ASIATIC SOCIETY (1823), 60 Queen's Gardens,
London W2 3AF. Tel: 0171-724 4741/2. *Secretary*, T. N.
Guina

ROYAL BRITISH LEGION, *see* BRITISH LEGION, ROYAL

ROYAL CALEDONIAN SCHOOLS EDUCATIONAL TRUST
(1815), 80A High Street, Bushey, Watford, Herts
WD2 3DE. Tel: 0181-421 8845. *Chief Executive*, J. Horsfield

ROYAL CELTIC SOCIETY (1820), 23 Rutland Street,
Edinburgh EH1 2RN. Tel: 0131-228 6449. *Secretary*, J. G.
Cameron, WS

ROYAL CHORAL SOCIETY (1871), Unit 9, 92 Lots Road,
London SW10 0QD. Tel: 0171-376 3718. *Administrator*,
G. Tonge

ROYAL ENGINEERS ASSOCIATION, RHQ Royal Engineers,
Brompton Barracks, Chatham, Kent ME4 4UG. Tel:
01634-847005. *Controller*, Lt.-Col. J. W. Ray (retd)

ROYAL ENGINEERS, INSTITUTION OF (1875), Brompton
Barracks, Chatham, Kent ME4 4UG. Tel: 01634-842669.
Secretary, Col. M. R. Cooper

ROYAL HIGHLAND AND AGRICULTURAL SOCIETY OF
SCOTLAND (1784), Royal Highland Centre, Ingliston,
Edinburgh EH28 8NF. Tel: 0131-333 2444. *Chief Executive*,
H. W. Davies

ROYAL HORTICULTURAL SOCIETY (1804), PO Box 313, 80
Vincent Square, London SW1P 2PE. Tel: 0171-834 4333.
Secretary, D. P. Hearn

ROYAL HOSPITAL FOR NEURO-DISABILITY (1854), West
Hill, London SW15 3SW. Tel: 0181-780 4500. *Chief
Executive*, V. J. Beauchamp

ROYAL HUMANE SOCIETY (1774), Brettenham House, Lancaster Place, London WC2E 7EP. Tel: 0171-836 8155. *Secretary*, Maj.-Gen. C. Tyler, CB

ROYAL INSTITUTION (1799), 21 Albemarle Street, London W1X 4BS. Tel: 0171-409 2992. *Director*, Prof. P. Day, FRS

ROYAL LIFE SAVING SOCIETY UK (1891), Mountbatten House, Studley, Warks B80 7NN. Tel: 01527-853943. *Director-General*, S. Lear

ROYAL LITERARY FUND (1790), 144 Temple Chambers, Temple Avenue, London EC4Y 0DA. Tel: 0171-353 7150. *Secretary*, Mrs F. M. Clark

ROYAL MEDICAL BENEVOLENT FUND (1836), 24 King's Road, London SW19 8QN. Tel: 0181-540 9194. *Secretary*, Mrs G. A. R. Wells

ROYAL MEDICAL SOCIETY (1737), Students Centre, 5/5 Bristo Square, Edinburgh EH8 9AL. Tel: 0131-650 2672. *Senior President*, C. Parsons

ROYAL MICROSCOPICAL SOCIETY (1839), 37–38 St Clements, Oxford OX4 1AJ. Tel: 01865-248768. *Administrator*, P. B. Hirst

ROYAL MUSICAL ASSOCIATION (1874), Department of Music, The University of Leeds, Leeds LS2 9JT. *President*, J. Rushton

ROYAL NATIONAL INSTITUTE FOR THE BLIND (1868), 224 Great Portland Street, London W1N 6AA. Tel: 0171-388 1266. *Director-General*, I. Bruce

ROYAL NATIONAL LIFEBOAT INSTITUTION (1824), West Quay Road, Poole, Dorset BH15 1HZ. Tel: 01202-663000. *Director*, B. Miles, CBE, RD

ROYAL NAVAL AND ROYAL MARINES CHILDREN'S TRUST (1834), HMS Nelson, Portsmouth PO1 3HH. Tel: 01705-81/455. *Secretary*, Mrs M. Bateman

ROYAL NAVAL ASSOCIATION (1950), 82 Chelsea Manor Street, London SW3 5QJ. Tel: 0171-352 6764. *General Secretary*, Capt. R. McQueen

ROYAL NAVAL BENEVOLENT SOCIETY FOR OFFICERS (1739), 1 Fleet Street, London EC4Y 1PD. Tel: 0171 353 4080 ext 471. *Secretary*, Capt. I. B. Sutherland

ROYAL NAVAL BENEVOLENT TRUST (1922), Castaway House, 311 Twyford Avenue, Portsmouth PO2 8PE. Tel: 01705-690112. *Chief Executive*, Cdr. J. Owens

ROYAL NAVY OFFICERS, ASSOCIATION OF (1920), 70 Porchester Terrace, London W2 3TP. Tel: 0171-402 5231. *Secretary*, Lt.-Cdr. I. M. P. Coombes

ROYAL OVER-SEAS LEAGUE (1910), Over-Seas House, Park Place, St James's Street, London SW1A 1LR. Tel: 0171-408 0214. *Director-General*, R. F. Newell

ROYAL PATRIOTIC FUND CORPORATION (1854), 40 Queen Anne's Gate, London SW1H 9AP. Tel: 0171-233 1894. *Secretary*, Brig. T. G. Williams, CBE

ROYAL PHILATELIC SOCIETY LONDON (1869), 41 Devonshire Place, London W1N 1PE. Tel: 0171-486 1044. *Hon. Secretary*, Prof. B. S. Jay

ROYAL PHOTOGRAPHIC SOCIETY (1853), The Octagon, Milsom Street, Bath BA1 1DN. Tel: 01225-462841. *Secretary-General*, B. Lane

ROYAL PINNER SCHOOL FOUNDATION, 110 Old Brompton Road, London SW7 3RA. Tel: 0171-373 6168. *Secretary*, D. Crawford

ROYAL SAILORS' RESTS (1876), 5 St Georges Business Centre, St Georges Square, Portsmouth PO1 1EY. Tel: 01705-296096. *Executive Director*, Revd J. Martin

ROYAL SOCIETY FOR ASIAN AFFAIRS (1901), 2 Belgrave Square, London SW1X 8PJ. Tel: 0171-235 5122. *Secretary*, Mrs H. McKeag

ROYAL SOCIETY FOR THE ENCOURAGEMENT OF ARTS, MANUFACTURES AND COMMERCE (RSA) (1754), 8 John Adam Street, London WC2N 6EZ. Tel: 0171-930 5115. *Chairman*, R. Onians

ROYAL SOCIETY FOR THE PREVENTION OF CRUELTY TO ANIMALS (RSPCA) (1824), Causeway, Horsham, W. Sussex RH12 1HG. Tel: 01403-264181. *Director-General*, P. R. Davies, CB

ROYAL SOCIETY FOR THE PROTECTION OF BIRDS (RSPB) (1889), The Lodge, Sandy, Beds SG19 2DL. Tel: 01767-680551. *Chief Executive*, Miss B. S. Young

ROYAL SOCIETY OF HEALTH (1876), RSH House, 38 St George's Drive, London SW1V 4BH. Tel: 0171-630 0121.

ROYAL SOCIETY OF LITERATURE (1823), 1 Hyde Park Gardens, London W2 2LT. Tel: 0171-723 5104. *Secretary*, Mrs M. Fergusson

ROYAL SOCIETY OF MEDICINE (1805), 1 Wimpole Street, London W1M 8AE. Tel: 0171-290 2901. *Executive Director*, Dr A. Grocock

ROYAL SOCIETY OF ST GEORGE (1894), 127 Sandgate Road, Folkestone, Kent CT20 2BL. Tel: 01303-241795. *General Secretary*, Lt.-Cdr. D. Odell

ROYAL STAR AND GARTER HOME FOR DISABLED SAILORS, SOLDIERS AND AIRMEN (1916), Richmond upon Thames, Surrey TW10 6RR. Tel: 0181-940 3314. *Chief Executive*, I. Lashbrooke

ROYAL STATISTICAL SOCIETY (1834), 12 Errol Street, London EC1Y 8LX. Tel: 0171-638 8998. *Executive Secretary*, I. J. Goddard

ROYAL TANK REGIMENT BENEVOLENT FUND (1919), RHQ RTR, Bovington Camp, Wareham, Dorset BH20 6JA. Tel. 01929-403331. *Regimental Secretary*, Maj. A. Henzie, MBE

ROYAL TELEVISION SOCIETY (1927), Holborn Hall, 100 Gray's Inn Road, London WC1X 8AL. Tel: 0171-430 1000. *Executive Director*, M. Bunce

ROYAL UNITED KINGDOM BENEFICENT ASSOCIATION (1863), 6 Avonmore Road, London W14 8RL. Tel: 0171-602 6274. *Director*, W. Rathbone

RURAL ENGLAND, COUNCIL FOR THE PROTECTION OF, *see* CPRE

RURAL SCOTLAND, ASSOCIATION FOR THE PROTECTION OF (1926), 3rd Floor, Gladstone's Land, 483 Lawnmarket, Edinburgh EH1 2NT. Tel: 0131-225 7012/3. *Manager*, Mrs E. J. Garland

RURAL WALES, CAMPAIGN FOR THE PROTECTION OF (1928), Tŷ Gwyn, 31 High Street, Welshpool, Powys SY21 7YD. Tel: 01938-552525. *Director*, M. Williams

SAFETY COUNCIL, BRITISH (1957), National Safety Centre, 70 Chancellor's Road, London W6 9RS. Tel: 0181-741 1231. *Director-General*, Sir Neville Purvis, KCB

SAILORS' FAMILIES' SOCIETY (1821), Newland, Hull HU6 7RJ. Tel: 01482-342331. *Chief Executive*, G. J. Powell

SAILORS' SOCIETY, BRITISH AND INTERNATIONAL (1818), 3 Orchard Place, Southampton SO14 3AT. Tel: 01703-337333. *General Secretary*, G. Chambers

ST DEINIOL'S RESIDENTIAL LIBRARY (1902), Hawarden, Deeside, Flintshire CH5 3DF. Tel: 01244-532350. *Warden and Chief Librarian*, Revd P. B. Francis

St Dunstan's, PO Box 4XB, 12–14 Harcourt Street, London WIA 4XB. Tel: 0171-723 5021. For men and women blinded in the Services. *Chief Executive*, G. B. J. Frost

St John Ambulance (1887), 1 Grosvenor Crescent, London SWIX 7EF. Tel: 0171-235 5231. *Executive Director*, L. Martin

Sales and Marketing Management, Institute of (1966), NatWest House, 31 Upper George Street, Luton LUI 2RD. Tel: 01582-411130. *Chief Executive*, B. Edwards

Salmon and Trout Association (1903), Fishmongers' Hall, London Bridge, London EC4R 9EL. Tel: 0171-283 5838. *Director*, C. W. Poupard

Saltire Society (1936), 9 Fountain Close, 22 High Street, Edinburgh EHI ITF. Tel: 0131-556 1836. *Administrator*, Mrs K. Munro

Samaritans (1953), 10 The Grove, Slough SLI IQP. Tel: 01753-532713. Telephone numbers in local directories or ring 0345-909090. *Chief Executive*, S. Armson

SANE: The Mental Health Charity (1986), 199–205 Old Marylebone Road, London NWI 5QP. Tel: 0171-724 6520. Saneline: 0345-678000. *Chief Executive*, Ms M. Wallace, MBE

Save Britain's Heritage (1975), 68 Battersea High Street, London SWII 3HX. Tel: 0171-228 3336. *Secretary*, R. Pollard

Save the Children Fund (1919), 17 Grove Lane, London SE5 8RD. Tel: 0171-703 5400. *Director-General*, M. Aaronson

Schizophrenia Fellowship, National (NSF) (1970), 28 Castle Street, Kingston upon Thames, Surrey KTI ISS. Tel: 0181-547 3937. *Chief Executive*, B. Mehta

School Library Association (1937), Liden Library, Barrington Close, Liden, Swindon SN3 6HF. Tel: 01793-617838. *Executive Secretary*, Ms K. Lemaire

Schoolmasters, Society of (1798), Dolton's Farm, Woburn, Milton Keynes MKI7 9HX. Tel: 01525-290093. *Secretary*, Mrs B. A. Skipper

Schoolmistresses and Governesses Benevolent Institution (1843), Queen Mary House, Manor Park Road, Chislehurst, Kent BR7 5PY. Tel: 0181-468 7997. *Director*, L. I. Baggott

Science, British Association for the Advancement of (1831), 23 Savile Row, London WIX 2NB. Tel: 0171-973 3500. *Chief Executive*, Dr P. Briggs

Science Education, Association for (1963), College Lane, Hatfield, Herts ALIO 9AA. Tel: 01707-267411. *Chief Executive*, Dr D. S. Moore

SCOPE (formerly The Spastics Society) (1952), 12 Park Crescent, London WIN 4EQ. Tel: 0171-636 5020. *Chief Executive*, R. P. Brewster

Scotch Whisky Association (1919), 20 Atholl Crescent, Edinburgh EH3 8HF. Tel: 0131-222 9200. *Director-General*, H. Morison

Scottish Chiefs, Standing Council of (1952), Hope Chambers, 52 Leith Walk, Edinburgh EH6 5HW. Tel: 0131-554 6321. *General Secretary*, G. A. Way of Plean

Scottish Church History Society (1922), St Serf's Manse, 1 Denham Green Terrace, Edinburgh EH5 3PG. Tel: 0131-552 4059. *Hon. Secretary*, Revd Dr P. H. Donald

Scottish Corporation, Royal (1611), 37 King Street, London WC2E 8JS. Tel: 0171-240 3718. *Chief Executive*, Wg Cdr. A. Robertson

Scottish Country Dance Society, Royal (1923), 12 Coates Crescent, Edinburgh EH3 7AF. Tel: 0131-225 3854. *Secretary*, Miss G. S. Parker

Scottish Genealogy Society (1953), Library and Family History Centre, 15 Victoria Terrace, Edinburgh EHI 2JL. Tel: 0131-220 3677. *Hon. Secretary*, Miss J. P. S. Ferguson

Scottish History Society (1886), Department of Scottish History, 17 Buccleuch Place, University of Edinburgh, Edinburgh EH8 9LN. Tel: 0131-650 4030. *Hon. Secretary*, Dr S. Boardman

Scottish Landowners' Federation (1906), 25 Maritime Street, Edinburgh EH6 5PW. Tel: 0131-555 1031. *Director*, Dr M. S. Hankey

Scottish Law Agents Society, Ivy Cottage, Commonside, Hawick TD9 0LB. Tel: 01450-850360. *Secretary (acting)*, K. W. Cramond

Scottish National Institution for the War Blinded (1915), PO Box 500, Gillespie Crescent, Edinburgh EHIO 4HZ. Tel: 0131-229 1456. *Secretary*, J. B. M. Munro

Scottish National War Memorial (1927), The Castle, Edinburgh EHI 2YT. Tel: 0131-226 7393. *Secretary*, Lt.-Col. H. D. R. Mackay

Scottish Society for the Prevention of Cruelty to Animals (1839), Braehead Mains, 603 Queensferry Road, Edinburgh EH4 6EA. Tel: 0131-339 0222. *Chief Executive*, J. Morris, CBE

Scottish Society for the Protection of Wild Birds (1927), Foremount House, Kilbarchan, Renfrewshire PAIO 2EZ. Tel: 01505-702419. *Secretary*, Dr J. A. Gibson

Scottish Wildlife Trust (1964), Cramond House, Kirk Cramond, Cramond Glebe Road, Edinburgh EH4 6NS. Tel: 0131-312 7765. *Director*, D. J. Hughes-Hallett

Scout Association (1907), Baden-Powell House, Queen's Gate, London SW7 5JS. Tel: 0171-584 7030. *Chief Scout*, W. G. Purdy

Scribes and Illuminators, Society of (1921), 6 Queen Square, London WCIN 3AR. Tel: 01483-894155. *Hon. Secretary*, Ms C. Turvey

Scripture Gift Mission Incorporated (1888), Radstock House, 3 Eccleston Street, London SWIW 9LZ. Tel: 0171-730 2155. *International Director*, R. Kennedy

Scripture Union (1867), 207–209 Queensway, Bletchley, Milton Keynes MK2 2EB. Tel: 01908-856000. *Chief Executive*, P. Kimber

Sea Cadet Association (1895), 202 Lambeth Road, London SEI 7JF. Tel: 0171-928 8978. *General Secretary*, Capt. R. M. Parker, RN

Seamen's Boy's Home, British (1863), Outdoor Educational Activity Centre, Grenville House, Berry Head Road, Brixham, Devon TQ5 9AF. Tel: 01803-852797. *Secretary*, R. M. Williams

Seamen's Christian Friend Society (1846), 48 South Street, Alderley Edge, Cheshire SK9 7ES. Tel: 01625-590010. *Director*, M. J. Wilson

Seamen's Pension Fund, Royal (1919), 65 High Street, Ewell, Epsom, Surrey KTI7 IRX. Tel: 0181-393 5873. *Secretary*, D. Barker

Secretaries and Administrators, Institute of Chartered (1891), 16 Park Crescent, London WIN 4AH. Tel: 0171-580 4741. *Chief Executive*, M. J. Ainsworth

SECULAR SOCIETY LTD, NATIONAL (1866), Bradlaugh House, 47 Theobald's Road, London WC1X 8SP. Tel: 0171-404 3126. *General Secretary*, K. P. Wood

SEEABILITY (formerly Royal School for the Blind) (1799), 56–66 Highlands Road, Leatherhead, Surrey KT22 8NR. Tel: 01372-373086. *Chief Executive*, R. M. Perkins

SELDEN SOCIETY (1887), Faculty of Laws, Queen Mary College, Mile End Road, London E1 4NS. Tel: 0171-975 5136. To encourage the study and advance the knowledge of the history of English law. *Secretary*, V. Tunkel

SENSE (THE NATIONAL DEAFBLIND AND RUBELLA ASSOCIATION) (1955), 11–13 Clifton Terrace, London N4 3SR. Tel: 0171-272 7774. *Chief Executive*, R. Clark

SHAFTESBURY HOMES AND ARETHUSA (1843), 3 Rectory Grove, London SW4 0DX. Tel: 0171-720 8709. *Director*, Capt. N. C. Baird-Murray, CBE, RN

SHAFTESBURY SOCIETY (1844), 16 Kingston Road, London SW19 1JZ. Tel: 0181-239 5555. Provides care and education services to people with learning and/or physical disabilities, and support for poor or disadvantaged people. *Chief Executive*, Ms F. Beckett

SHELLFISH ASSOCIATION OF GREAT BRITAIN (1904), Fishmongers' Hall, London Bridge, London EC4R 9EL. Tel. 0171-283 8305. *Director*, E. Edwards, OBE, PH.D.

SHELTER (THE NATIONAL CAMPAIGN FOR HOMELESS PEOPLE) (1966), 88 Old Street, London EC1V 9HU. Tel: 0171-505 2000. *Director*, C. Holmes

SHERLOCK HOLMES SOCIETY OF LONDON (1951), 64 Graham Road, London SW19 3SS. Tel: 0181-540 7657. *General Secretary*, T. J. K. Owen

SHIPBROKERS, INSTITUTE OF CHARTERED (1911), 3 St Helen's Place, London EC3A 6EJ. Tel: 0171-628 5559. *Director*, Mrs B. Fletcher

SHIRE HORSE SOCIETY (1878), East of England Showground, Peterborough PE2 6XE. Tel: 01733-234451. *Secretary*, T. Gibson, OBE

SHRIEVALTY ASSOCIATION (1971), Office of the High Sheriffs, Duncombe Place, York YO1 2DY. Tel: 01904-634771. *Secretary*, J. H. N. Towers

SIGHT SAVERS INTERNATIONAL (ROYAL COMMONWEALTH SOCIETY FOR THE BLIND) (1950), Grosvenor Hall, Bolnore Road, Haywards Heath, W. Sussex RH16 4BX. Tel: 01444-412424. *Executive Director*, R. Porter

SIMPLIFIED SPELLING SOCIETY (1908), Tailours, High Road, Chigwell, Essex IG7 6DL. Tel: 0181-501 0405. *Chairman*, C. J. H. Jolly

SIR OSWALD STOLL FOUNDATION (1916), 446 Fulham Road, London SW6 1DT. Tel: 0171-385 2110. *Director*, R. C. Brunwin

SMALL BUSINESSES, FEDERATION OF (1974), 2 Catherine Place, London SW1E 6HF. Tel: 0171-233 7900. *Hon. National Chairman*, Mrs P. McAlester

SMALL FARMERS' ASSOCIATION (1979), PO Box 18, Woodbridge, Suffolk IP13 0QP. Tel: 0171-249 4790. *Chairman*, J. Morford

SOCIAL CONCERN, NATIONAL COUNCIL FOR, Montague Chambers, Montague Place, London SE1 9DA. Tel: 0171-403 0977. *Director*, P. Carlin

SOCIALIST PARTY OF GREAT BRITAIN (1904), 52 Clapham High Street, London SW4 7UN. Tel: 0171-622 3811. *General Secretary*, Ms J. Carter

SOCIAL WORKERS, BRITISH ASSOCIATION OF (1970), 16 Kent Street, Birmingham B5 6RD. Tel: 0121-622 3911. *Director*, C. C. Walsh

SOIL ASSOCIATION (1946), 86 Colston Street, Bristol BS1 5BB. Tel: 0117-929 0661. *Director*, P. Holden

SOLDIERS' AND AIRMEN'S SCRIPTURE READERS ASSOCIATION (1838), Havelock House, Barrack Road, Aldershot, Hants GU11 3NP. Tel: 01252-310033. *General Secretary*, Lt.-Col. M. Hitchcott

SOLDIERS' WIDOWS, ROYAL CAMBRIDGE HOME FOR (1851), 82–84 Hurst Road, East Molesey, Surrey KT8 9AH. Tel: 0181-979 3788. *Superintendent*, Mrs I. O. Yarnell

SOLICITORS IN THE SUPREME COURT OF SCOTLAND, SOCIETY OF (1784), SSC Library, Parliament House, 11 Parliament Square, Edinburgh EH1 1RF. Tel: 0131-225 6268. *Secretary*, I. L. S. Balfour

SOROPTIMIST INTERNATIONAL OF GREAT BRITAIN AND IRELAND (1923), 127 Wellington Road South, Stockport SK1 3TS. Tel: 0161-480 7686. *Executive Officer*, Ms K. Heward

SOS SOCIETY, *see* 2CARE

SOUTH AMERICAN MISSION SOCIETY (1844), Allen Gardiner House, Pembury Road, Tunbridge Wells, Kent TN2 3QU. Tel: 01892-538647. *General Secretary*, Rt. Revd D. R. J. Evans

SOUTH WALES INSTITUTE OF ENGINEERS (1857), Empire House, Mount Stuart Square, Cardiff CF1 6DN. Tel: 01222-481726. *Hon. Secretary*, R. E. Lindsay

SPEAKERS CLUBS, ASSOCIATION OF (1971), 28 High Street, Auchterarder, Perthshire PH3 1DF. Tel: 01764-662457. *National Secretary*, D. Williams

SPINA BIFIDA AND HYDROCEPHALUS, ASSOCIATION FOR (ASBAH), 42 Park Road, Peterborough PE1 2UQ. Tel: 01733-555988. *Executive Director*, A. Russell

SPORT AND THE ARTS, FOUNDATION FOR (1991), PO Box 20, Liverpool L13 1HB. Tel: 0151-259 5505. *Secretary to the Trustees*, G. Endicott

SPORTS MEDICINE, INSTITUTE OF (1963), Room 212, University College London Medical School, Charles Bell House, 67–73 Riding House Street, London W1P 7LD. Tel: 0171-813 2832. *Hon. Secretary*, Dr W. T. Orton

SPURGEON'S CHILD CARE (1867), 74 Wellingborough Road, Rushden, Northants NN10 9TY. Tel: 01933-412412. *Chief Executive*, D. C. Culwick

SSAFA FORCES HELP (1885, merged 1997), 19 Queen Elizabeth Street, London SE1 2LP. Tel: 0171-403 8783. *Controller*, Maj.-Gen. P. Sheppard, CB, CBE

STANDING CONFERENCE OF NATIONAL AND UNIVERSITY LIBRARIES (SCONUL) (1950), 102 Euston Street, London NW1 2HA. Tel: 0171-387 0317. *Secretary*, A. J. C. Bainton

STATISTICIANS, INSTITUTE OF, *see* ROYAL STATISTICAL SOCIETY

STEWART SOCIETY (1899), 17 Dublin Street, Edinburgh EH1 3PG. Tel: 0131-557 6824. *Hon. Secretary*, Mrs M. Walker

STRATEGIC PLANNING SOCIETY (1967), 17 Portland Place, London W1N 3AF. Tel: 0171-636 7737. *Office Manager*, J. Mainee

STRATEGIC STUDIES, INTERNATIONAL INSTITUTE FOR (1958), 23 Tavistock Street, London WC2E 7NQ. Tel: 0171-379 7676. *Director*, Dr J. Chipman

STROKE ASSOCIATION (1899), Stroke House, Whitecross Street, London EC1Y 8JJ. Tel: 0171-490 7999.

STRUCTURAL ENGINEERS, INSTITUTION OF (1908), 11 Upper Belgrave Street, London SW1X 8BH. Tel: 0171-235 4535. *Chief Executive*, Dr J. W. Dougill, FEng.

STUDENT CHRISTIAN MOVEMENT (1889), Westhill College, 14–16 Weoley Park Road, Selly Oak, Birmingham B29 6LL. Tel: 0121-471 2404. *Administrator*, Ms S. Cowley

SUFFOLK HORSE SOCIETY (1878), The Market Hill, Woodbridge, Suffolk IP12 4LU. Tel: 01394-380643. *Secretary*, P. Ryder-Davies

SURGEONS OF EDINBURGH, ROYAL COLLEGE OF (1505), Nicolson Street, Edinburgh EH8 9DW. Tel: 0131-527 1600. *Executive Secretary*, Miss A. Campbell, FRCSEd.

SURGEONS OF ENGLAND, ROYAL COLLEGE OF (1800), 35–43 Lincoln's Inn Fields, London WC2A 3PN. Tel: 0171-405 3474. *Secretary*, R. H. E. Duffett

SURVEYORS, ROYAL INSTITUTION OF CHARTERED (1868), 12 Great George Street, London SW1P 3AD. Tel: 0171-222 7000. *Chief Executive*, Ms C. Makin

SURVIVAL INTERNATIONAL (1969), 11–15 Emerald Street, London WC1N 3QT. Tel: 0171-242 1441. *Director*, S. Corry

SUZY LAMPLUGH TRUST (1986), 14 East Sheen Avenue, London SW14 8AS . Tel: 0181-392 1839. *Executive Secretary*, P. Lamplugh

SWEDENBORG SOCIETY (1810), 20–21 Bloomsbury Way, London WC1A 2TH. Tel: 0171-405 7986. *Secretary*, Miss M. G. Waters

TALKING BOOKS FOR THE HANDICAPPED AND HOSPITAL PATIENTS, *see* LISTENING LIBRARY

TAVISTOCK INSTITUTE, THE (1947), 30 Tabernacle Street, London EC2A 4DD. Tel: 0171-417 0407. *Institute Secretary*, J. Margarson

TAXATION, CHARTERED INSTITUTE OF (1930), 12 Upper Belgrave Street, London SW1X 8BB. Tel: 0171-235 9381. *Secretary-General*, R. A. Dommett

TEACHERS OF HOME ECONOMICS AND TECHNOLOGY, NATIONAL ASSOCIATION OF (1896), Hamilton House, Mabledon Place, London WC1H 9BJ. Tel: 0171-387 1441. *General Secretary*, G. Thompson

TEACHERS OF MATHEMATICS, ASSOCIATION OF (1952), 7 Shaftesbury Street, Derby DE23 8YB. Tel: 01332-346599. *Hon. Secretary*, Ms A. Gammon

TEACHERS OF THE DEAF, BRITISH ASSOCIATION OF (1977), 41 The Orchard, Leven, Beverley, E. Yorks HU17 5QA. Tel: 01865-792890. *Hon. Secretary*, P. A. Simpson

TEACHERS' UNION, ULSTER (1919), 94 Malone Road, Belfast BT9 5HP. Tel: 01232-662216. *General Secretary*, D. Allen

TELECOMMUNICATION USERS' ASSOCIATION (1965), Woodgate Studios, 2–8 Games Road, Cockfosters, Herts EN4 9HN. Tel: 0181-449 8844. *Executive Chairman*, W. E. Mieran

TEMPERANCE COUNCIL, NATIONAL UNITED (1880), Alliance House, 12 Caxton Street, London SW1H 0QS. Tel: 0181-444 5004. *General Secretary*, Mrs G. O. Stretton

TEMPERANCE FRIENDLY SOCIETY, ORDER OF THE SONS OF (1855), 176 Blackfriars Road, London SE1 8ET. Tel: 0171-928 7384. *Secretary*, Mrs M. C. Scroby

TEMPERANCE LEAGUE, BRITISH NATIONAL (1834), Westbrook Court, 2 Sharrow Vale Road, Sheffield S11 8YZ. Tel: 0114-267 9976. *Executive Director*, A. Willis

TEMPERANCE SOCIETY, ROYAL NAVAL (1876), 5 St George's Business Centre, St George's Square, Portsmouth PO1 3EY. Tel: 01705-296096. *General Secretary*, A. A. Lockwood, MBE

TEMPLETON FOUNDATION (1973), 18 Eastgate Gardens, Taunton, Somerset TA1 1RD. Tel: 01823-324522. *UK Representative*, Mrs N. Pearse

TERRENCE HIGGINS TRUST (1982), 52–54 Grays Inn Road, London WC1X 8JU. Tel: 0171-831 0330. Helpline: 0171-242 1010. *Chairman*, N. Partridge

TERRITORIAL, AUXILIARY AND VOLUNTEER RESERVE ASSOCIATIONS, COUNCIL OF (1908), Centre Block, Duke of York's HQ, London SW3 4SG. Tel: 0171-730 6122. *Secretary*, Maj.-Gen. W. A. Evans, CB

TEXTILE INSTITUTE, THE (1910), 10 Blackfriars Street, Manchester M3 5DR. Tel: 0161-834 8457. *Chief Executive*, R. G. Denyer

THEATRE RESEARCH, SOCIETY FOR (1948), c/o The Theatre Museum, 1E Tavistock Street, London WC2E 7PA. *Joint Hon. Secretaries*, Ms E. Cottis; Ms F. Dann

THEATRES TRUST (1976), 22 Charing Cross Road, London WC2H 0HR. Tel: 0171-836 8591. *Director*, P. Longman

THEATRICAL FUND, ROYAL (1839), 11 Garrick Street, London WC2E 9AR. Tel: 0171-836 3322. *Secretary*, Mrs R. M. Oliver

THEOSOPHICAL SOCIETY IN ENGLAND (1875), 50 Gloucester Place, London W1H 4EA. Tel: 0171-935 9261. *General Secretary*, Miss L. Storey

THISTLE FOUNDATION (1945), Niddrie Mains Road, Edinburgh EH16 4EA. Tel: 0131-661 3366. *Director*, Ms J. Fisher

THOMAS CORAM FOUNDATION FOR CHILDREN (formerly The Foundling Hospital) (1739), 40 Brunswick Square, London WC1N 1AZ. Tel: 0171-278 2424. *Director*, Dr G. Pugh

TIDY BRITAIN GROUP (1953), The Pier, Wigan WN3 4EX. Tel: 01942-824620. *Director-General*, Prof. G. Ashworth, CBE

TOC H (1915), 1 Forest Close, Wendover, Aylesbury Bucks HP22 6BT. Tel: 01296-623911. *Director*, M. Lyddiard

TOURIST BOARD, ENGLISH, Thames Tower, Black's Road, London W6 9EL. Tel: 0181-846 9000. *Chief Executive*, T. Bartlett

TOURIST BOARD, NORTHERN IRELAND, St Anne's Court, 59 North Street, Belfast BT1 1NB. Tel: 01232-231221. *Chief Executive*, I. G. Henderson

TOURIST BOARD, SCOTTISH (1969), 23 Ravelston Terrace, Edinburgh EH4 3EU. Tel: 0131-332 2433. *Chief Executive*, T. Buncle

TOURIST BOARD, WALES, Brunel House, 2 Fitzalan Road, Cardiff CF2 1UY. Tel: 01222-499909. *Chief Executive*, J. French

TOWN AND COUNTRY PLANNING ASSOCIATION (1899), 17 Carlton House Terrace, London SW1Y 5AS. Tel: 0171-930 8903/4/5. *Director*, vacant

TOWN PLANNING INSTITUTE, ROYAL (1914), 26 Portland Place, London W1N 4BE. Tel: 0171-636 9107. *Secretary-General*, R. Upton

TOWNSWOMEN'S GUILDS (1929), Chamber of Commerce House, 75 Harborne Road, Birmingham B15 3DA. Tel: 0121-456 3435. *National Secretary*, Mrs P. Wilkes

TOYNBEE HALL (1884), 28 Commercial Street, London E1 6LS. Tel: 0171-247 6943. *Chief Executive*, A. Prescott

TRADE MARK AGENTS, INSTITUTE OF (1934), Canterbury House, 2–6 Sydenham Road, Croydon CR0 9XE. Tel: 0181-686 2052. *Secretary*, Mrs M. J. Tyler

TRADING STANDARDS ADMINISTRATION, INSTITUTE OF (1881), 3–5 Hadleigh Business Centre, 351 London Road, Hadleigh, Essex SS7 2BT. Tel: 01702-559922. *Chief Executive*, A. J. Street

TRANSLATION AND INTERPRETING, INSTITUTE OF (1986), 377 City Road, London EC1V 1NA. Tel: 0171-713 7600. *President*, Sir Rowland Whitehead, Bt

TRANSPORT ADMINISTRATION, INSTITUTE OF (1944), 32 Palmerston Road, Southampton SO14 1LL. Tel: 01703-631380. *Director*, J. K. Millar

TRANSPORT, CHARTERED INSTITUTE OF (1919), 80 Portland Place, London W1N 4DP. Tel: 0171-636 9952. *Director*, Mrs S. Gross

TRAVEL AGENTS, ASSOCIATION OF BRITISH (ABTA) (1950), 55–57 Newman Street, London W1P 4AH. Tel: 0171-637 2444. *Chief Executive*, I. Reynolds

TREE COUNCIL (1974), 51 Catherine Place, London SW1E 6DY. Tel: 0171-828 9928. *Director*, R. Osborne

TREE FOUNDATION, INTERNATIONAL (formerly Men of the Trees) (1922), Sandy Lane, Crawley Down, W. Sussex RH10 4HS. Tel: 01342-712536. *Chairman*, S. G. Keys

TROPICAL MEDICINE AND HYGIENE, ROYAL SOCIETY OF (1907), Manson House, 26 Portland Place, London W1N 4EY. Tel: 0171-580 2127. *Hon. Secretaries*, Dr D. C. Barker; Dr W. R. C. Weir

TURNER SOCIETY (1975), BCM Box Turner, London WC1N 3XX. *Chairman*, E. Joll

2CARE (formerly The SOS Society) (1929), 11–13 Harwood Road, London SW6 4QP. Tel: 0171-371 0118. Residential and nursing homes for the elderly, and psychiatric rehabilitation centres. *Chief Executive*, Miss E. C. R. O'Sullivan

UFAW (UNIVERSITIES FEDERATION FOR ANIMAL WELFARE) (1926), 8 Hamilton Close, South Mimms, Potters Bar, Herts EN6 3QD. Tel: 01707-658202. *Director*, Dr J. K. Kirkwood

UK INDEPENDENCE PARTY, 80 Regent Street, London W1R 5PE. Tel: 0171-434 4559. *Secretary*, Ms B. Bullen

UNBORN CHILDREN, SOCIETY FOR THE PROTECTION OF, *see* PROTECTION OF UNBORN CHILDREN

UNITED KINGDOM ALLIANCE (1863), 176 Blackfriars Road, London SE1 8ET. Tel: 0171-928 1538. *General Secretary*, Revd B. Kinman

UNITED NATIONS ASSOCIATION OF GREAT BRITAIN AND NORTHERN IRELAND (1945), 3 Whitehall Court, London SW1A 2EL. Tel: 0171-930 2931. *Director*, M. C. Harper

UNITED REFORMED CHURCH HISTORY SOCIETY (1972), 86 Tavistock Place, London WC1H 9RT. Tel: 0171-916 2020. *Hon. Secretary*, Revd E. J. Brown

UNITED SOCIETY FOR CHRISTIAN LITERATURE (1799), Robertson House, Leas Road, Guildford, Surrey GU1 4QW. Tel: 01483-577877. *General Secretary*, Dr A. Marriage

UNITED SOCIETY FOR THE PROPAGATION OF THE GOSPEL (USPG) (1701), Partnership House, 157 Waterloo Road, London SE1 8XA. Tel: 0171-928 8681. *Secretary*, vacant

UNIVERSITIES OF THE UNITED KINGDOM, COMMITTEE OF VICE-CHANCELLORS AND PRINCIPALS OF THE (1918), Woburn House, 20 Tavistock Square, London WC1H 9HQ. Tel: 0171-419 4111. *Chief Executive*, Ms D. Warwick

UNIVERSITY AND COLLEGE LECTURERS, ASSOCIATION OF (1973), 104 Albert Road, Southsea, Hants PO5 2SN. Tel: 01705-818625. *Chief Executive*, Ms C. Cheesman

VALUERS AND AUCTIONEERS, INCORPORATED SOCIETY OF (1968), 3 Cadogan Gate, London SW1X 0AS. Tel: 0171-235 2282. *Chief Executive*, H. Whitty

VEGAN SOCIETY (1944), Donald Watson House, 7 Battle Road, St Leonards-on-Sea, E. Sussex TN37 7AA. Tel: 01424-427393. *Information Officer*, Ms A. Rofe

VEGETARIAN SOCIETY OF THE UNITED KINGDOM LTD, Parkdale, Dunham Road, Altrincham, Cheshire WA14 4QG. Tel: 0161-928 0793. *Chief Executive*, Ms T. Fox

VENEREAL DISEASES, MEDICAL SOCIETY FOR THE STUDY OF (1922), The Royal Society of Medicine, 1 Wimpole Street, London W1M 8AE. Tel: 0171-290 3904. *Hon. Secretary*, Dr A. J. Ro

VERNACULAR ARCHITECTURE GROUP (1953), 16 Falna Crescent, Coton Green, Tamworth, Staffs B79 8JS. Tel: 01827-69434. *Hon. Secretary*, R. A. Meeson

VETERINARY ASSOCIATION, BRITISH (1881), 7 Mansfield Street, London W1M 0AT. Tel: 0171-636 6541. *Chief Executive*, J. H. Baird

VETERINARY SURGEONS, ROYAL COLLEGE OF (1844), Belgravia House, 62–64 Horseferry Road, London SW1P 2AF. Tel: 0171-222-2001. *President*, N. T. Gorman

VICTIM SUPPORT (NATIONAL ASSOCIATION OF VICTIMS SUPPORT SCHEMES) (1979), National Office, Cranmer House, 39 Brixton Road, London SW9 6DZ. Tel: 0171-735 9166. *Director*, Ms H. Reeves, OBE

VICTORIA CROSS AND GEORGE CROSS ASSOCIATION, Room 028, The Old War Office, London SW1A 2EU. *Chairman*, Col. B. S. T. Archer, GC, OBE

VICTORIA INSTITUTE (PHILOSOPHICAL SOCIETY OF GREAT BRITAIN), 41 Marne Avenue, Welling, Kent DA16 2EY. Tel: 0181-303 0465. *Chairman of Council*, T. C. Mitchell

VICTORIAN SOCIETY (1958), 1 Priory Gardens, Bedford Park, London W4 1TT. Tel: 0181-994 1019. *Director*, Dr W. Filmer-Sankey

VICTORY (SERVICES) ASSOCIATION LTD AND CLUB (1907), 63–79 Seymour Street, London W2 2HF. Tel: 0171-723 4474. *General Manager*, G. F. Taylor

VIKING SOCIETY FOR NORTHERN RESEARCH (1892), Department of Scandinavian Studies, University College, Gower Street, London WC1E 6BT. Tel: 0171-380 7176. *Hon. Secretaries*, Prof. M. P. Barnes; Dr J. Jesh

VOLUNTARY ORGANIZATIONS, NATIONAL COUNCIL FOR (1919), Regents Wharf, 8 All Saints Street, London N1 9RL. Tel: 0171-713 6161. *Chief Executive*, S. Etherington

VOLUNTARY ORGANIZATIONS, SCOTTISH COUNCIL FOR (1943), 18–19 Claremont Crescent, Edinburgh EH7 4QD. Tel: 0131-556 3882. *Director*, M. Sime

VSO (VOLUNTARY SERVICE OVERSEAS) (1958), 317 Putney Bridge Road, London SW15 2PN. Tel: 0181-780 7500. *Director*, D. Green

WAR ON WANT (1952), Fenner Brockway House, 37–39 Great Guildford Street, London SE1 0ES. Tel: 0171-620 1111. *Director*, Ms M. Lynch

WASTE MANAGEMENT, INSTITUTE OF (1898), 9 Saxon Court, St Peter's Gardens, Northampton NN1 1SX. Tel: 01604-20426. *Chief Executive*, M. J. Philpott

WATER AND ENVIRONMENTAL MANAGEMENT, CHARTERED INSTITUTION OF (1987), 15 John Street, London WCIN 2EB. Tel: 0171-831 3110. *Executive Director*, R. A. Bispham

WATERCOLOUR SOCIETY, ROYAL (1804), Bankside Gallery, 48 Hopton Street, London SEI 9JH. Tel: 0171-928 7521. *Secretary*, Ms J. Dixey

WELLBEING (1964), 27 Sussex Place, London NWI 4SP. Tel: 0171-262 5337. Health research charity for women and babies. *Director*, Mrs C. Lebus

WELLCOME TRUST (1936), The Wellcome Building, 183 Euston Road, London NWI 2BE. Tel: 0171-611 8888. *Director*, Dame Bridget Ogilvie, DBE

WESLEY HISTORICAL SOCIETY (1893), 34 Spiceland Road, Northfield, Birmingham B31 INJ. Tel: 0121-475 4914. *General Secretary*, Dr E. D. Graham

WEST LONDON MISSION (1887), 19 Thayer Street, London WIM 5LJ. Tel: 0171-935 6179. *Superintendent*, Revd D. S. Cruise

WESTMINSTER FOUNDATION FOR DEMOCRACY (1992), Clutha House, 10 Storey's Gate, London SWIP 3AY. Tel: 0171-976 7565. *Chief Executive*, Ms A. Jones

WES (WORLD-WIDE EDUCATION SERVICE) (1888), Canada House, 272 Field End Road, Eastcote, Ruislip, Middx HA4 9NA. Tel: 0181-866 4400. *Head of Consultancy*, Mrs T. Mulder-Reynolds

WILDFOWL AND WETLANDS TRUST (1946), The New Grounds, Slimbridge, Glos GL2 7BT. Tel: 01453-890333. *Director-General*, Dr M. Owen

WILDLIFE TRUSTS (1912), Waterside South, Lincoln LN5 7JR. Tel: 01522-544400. *Director-General*, Dr S. Lyster

WILLIAM MORRIS SOCIETY AND KELMSCOTT FELLOWSHIP (1918), Kelmscott House, 26 Upper Mall, London W6 9TA. Tel: 0181-741 3735. *Hon. Secretary*, P. Faulkner

WINE AND SPIRIT ASSOCIATION OF GREAT BRITAIN AND NORTHERN IRELAND (*c.* 1825), Five Kings House, 1 Queen Street Place, London EC4R IXX. Tel: 0171-248 5377. *Director*, P. Lewis

WOMEN, SOCIETY FOR PROMOTING THE TRAINING OF (1859), The Rectory, Main Street, Great Casterton, Stamford, Lincs PE9 4AP. Tel: 01780-764036. *Hon. Secretary*, Revd B. Harris

WOMEN ARTISTS, SOCIETY OF (1855), Westminster Gallery, Westminster Central Hall, Storey's Gate, London SWIH 9NU. *President*, Prof. B. Tate

WOMEN GRADUATES, BRITISH FEDERATION OF (1907), 4 Mandeville Courtyard, 142 Battersea Park Road, London SWII 4NB. Tel: 0171-498 8037. *Secretary*, Mrs A. B. Stein

WOMEN'S ENGINEERING SOCIETY (1920), Imperial College of Science and Technology, Department of Civil Engineering, Imperial College Road, London SW7 2BU. Tel: 0171-594 6025. *Secretary*, Mrs C. MacGillivray

WOMEN'S INSTITUTES, NATIONAL FEDERATION OF (1915), 104 New Kings Road, London SW6 4LY. Tel: 0171-371 9300. *General Secretary*, Mrs J. Osborne

WOMEN'S INSTITUTES OF NORTHERN IRELAND, FEDERATION OF (1932), 209–211 Upper Lisburn Road, Belfast BTIO OLL. Tel: 01232-301506/601781. *General Secretary*, Mrs I. A. Sproule

WOMEN'S NATIONWIDE CANCER CONTROL CAMPAIGN (1964), Suna House, 128–130 Curtain Road, London EC2A 3AR. Tel: 0171-729 4688/1735. Helpline: 0171-729 2229. *Administrator*, Miss J. Harding

WOMEN'S ROYAL NAVAL SERVICE BENEVOLENT TRUST (1942), 311 Twyford Avenue, Portsmouth PO2 8PE. Tel: 01705-655301. *General Secretary*, Mrs S. Torabella

WOMEN'S ROYAL VOLUNTARY SERVICE (WRVS), Milton Hill House, Milton Hill, Abingdon, Oxfordshire OX13 6AF. Tel: 01235-442900. *National Chairman*, Lady Toulson

WOMEN'S RURAL INSTITUTES, SCOTTISH (1917), 42 Heriot Row, Edinburgh EH3 6ES. Tel: 0131-225 1724. *General Secretary*, Mrs A. Peacock

WOMEN'S TRANSPORT SERVICE (FANY) (1907), Mercury House, Duke of York's Headquarters, London SW3 4RX. Tel: 0171-730 2058. *Corps Commander*, Mrs A. Whitehead, OBE

WOODLAND TRUST (1972), Autumn Park, Dysart Road, Grantham, Lincs NG31 6LL. Tel: 01476-581111. *Chief Executive*, M. J. Townsend

WOOD PRESERVING AND DAMP-PROOFING ASSOCIATION, BRITISH (1930), 6 The Office Village, 4 Romford Road, London E15 4EA. Tel: 0181-519 2588. *Director*, Dr C. R. Coggins

WORKERS' EDUCATIONAL ASSOCIATION, Temple House, 17 Victoria Park Square, London E2 9PB. Tel: 0181-983 1515. *General Secretary*, R. Lochrie

WORLD EDUCATION FELLOWSHIP (1921), International Headquarters, 58 Dickens Rise, Chigwell, Essex IG7 6NY. Tel: 0181-281 7122. *General Secretary*, G. John

WORLD ENERGY COUNCIL (1924), 34 St James's Street, London SWIA IHD. Tel: 0171-930 3966. *Secretary-General*, I. D. Lindsay

WORLD MISSION, COUNCIL FOR (1977), 32–34 Great Peter Street, London SWIP 2DB. Tel: 0171-222 4214. *General Secretary*, D. P. Niles, PH.D.

WORLD SHIP SOCIETY (1946), 101 The Everglades, Hempstead, Gillingham, Kent ME7 3PZ. Tel: 01634-372015. *Secretary*, J. Poole

WORLD SOCIETY FOR THE PROTECTION OF ANIMALS (1981), 2 Langley Lane, London SW8 ITJ. Tel: 0171-793 0540. *Chief Executive*, A. Dickson

WRITERS TO HM SIGNET, SOCIETY OF (1532), Signet Library, Parliament Square, Edinburgh EHI IRF. Tel: 0131-225 4923. *Clerk*, A. M. Kerr

WWF-UK (WORLD WIDE FUND FOR NATURE) (1961), Panda House, Weyside Park, Godalming, Surrey GU7 IXR. Tel: 01483-426444. *Director*, Dr R. Pellew

YEOMANRY BENEVOLENT FUND (1902), 10 Stone Buildings, Lincoln's Inn, London WC2A 3TG. Tel: 0171-831 6727. *Secretary*, Mrs C. W. Chrystie

YORKSHIRE AGRICULTURAL SOCIETY (1837), Great Yorkshire Showground, Harrogate, N. Yorks HG2 8PW. Tel: 01423-541000. *Chief Executive*, R. T. Keigwin

YORKSHIRE SOCIETY (1812), 35 Waldorf Heights, Camberley, Surrey GU17 9JH. Tel: 01276-36342. Educational trust making grants to students of all ages. *Secretary*, G. G. Prince, TD

YOUNG FARMERS' CLUBS, NATIONAL FEDERATION OF, YFC Centre, National Agricultural Centre, Stoneleigh Park, Kenilworth, Warks CV8 2LG. Tel: 01203-696544. *Chief Executive*, B. Loughran

YOUNG MEN'S CHRISTIAN ASSOCIATION (YMCA) (1844), National Council of YMCAs, 640 Forest Road, London E17 3DZ. Tel: 0181-520 5599. *National Secretary*, N. Nightingale

YOUNG WOMEN'S CHRISTIAN ASSOCIATION OF GREAT BRITAIN (YWCA) (1855), Clarendon House, 52 Cornmarket Street, Oxford OXI 3EJ. Tel: 01865-726110. *Chief Executive*, Ms G. Tishler

YOUTH ACTION, NORTHERN IRELAND (1944), Hampton, Glenmachan Park, Belfast BT4 2PJ. Tel: 01232-760067. *Director*, P. Graham

YOUTH CLUBS UK (1911), Kirby House, 20–24 Kirby Street, London ECIN 8TS. Tel: 0171-242 4045. *Chief Executive*, J. Bateman

YOUTH HOSTELS ASSOCIATION (ENGLAND AND WALES) (1930), Trevelyan House, 8 St Stephen's Hill, St Albans, Herts ALI 2DY. Tel: 01727-855215. *Chief Executive*, C. Logan

YOUTH HOSTELS ASSOCIATION OF NORTHERN IRELAND (1931), 22 Donegall Road, Belfast BT12 5JN. Tel: 01232-324733. *Hon. Secretary*, N. O'Reilly

YOUTH HOSTELS ASSOCIATION, SCOTTISH (1931), 7 Glebe Crescent, Stirling FK8 2JA. Tel: 01786-891400. *General Secretary*, W. Forsyth

ZOOLOGICAL SOCIETY, NORTH OF ENGLAND (1934), Chester Zoo, Upton by Chester, Chester CH2 ILH. Tel: 01244-380280. *Director*, Dr G. McGregor Reid

ZOOLOGICAL SOCIETY OF LONDON (1826), Regent's Park, London NWI 4RY. Tel: 0171-722 3333. *Director-General*, R. D. A. Burge

ZOOLOGICAL SOCIETY OF SCOTLAND, ROYAL (1913), Scottish National Zoological Park, Edinburgh Zoo, 134 Corstorphine Road, Edinburgh EH12 6TS. Tel: 0131-334 9171. *Director*, Prof. R. J. Wheater, OBE, FRSE

LOCAL HISTORY AND ARCHAEOLOGICAL SOCIETIES

ENGLAND

Berkshire: BERKSHIRE ARCHAEOLOGICAL SOCIETY. *Hon. Secretary*, L. J. Over, 43 Laburnham Road, Maidenhead, Berks SL6 4DE. Tel: 01628-31225.

Buckinghamshire: BUCKINGHAMSHIRE ARCHAEOLOGICAL SOCIETY. *Hon. Secretary*, G. J. Aylett, County Museum, Church Street, Aylesbury, Bucks HP20 2QP. Tel: 01296-20984.

Cambridgeshire: CAMBRIDGE ANTIQUARIAN SOCIETY. *Hon. Secretary*, Mrs S. Oosthuizen, Board of Continuing Education, Madingley Hall, Madingley, Cambs CB3 8AQ.

Cheshire: CHESTER ARCHAEOLOGICAL SOCIETY. *Secretary*, Dr D. J. P. Mason, FSA, Ochr Cottage, Porch Lane, Hope Mountain, Caergwrle, Flintshire LL12 9LS. Tel: 01978-760834.

Cornwall: CORNWALL ARCHAEOLOGICAL SOCIETY. *Hon. Secretaries*, Mrs Hammond; B. Hammond, 7 Porthmeor Road, Holmbush, St Austell, Cornwall PL25 3LT. Tel: 01726-74763.

Cumberland and Westmorland: CUMBERLAND AND WESTMORLAND ANTIQUARIAN AND ARCHAEOLOGICAL SOCIETY. *Hon. Secretary*, R. Hall, 1 High Tenterfell, Kendal, Cumbria LA9 4PG. Tel: 01539-773540.

Derbyshire: DERBYSHIRE ARCHAEOLOGICAL SOCIETY. *Hon. Secretary*, I. Mitchell, 68 Myrtle Avenue, Long Eaton, Nottingham NG10 3LY. Tel: 0115-972 9029.

Devonshire: DEVON ARCHAEOLOGICAL SOCIETY. *Hon. Secretary*, H. Bishop, RAM Museum, Queen Street, Exeter, Devon EX4 3RX. Tel: 01392-265858.

Dorset: DORSET NATURAL HISTORY AND ARCHAEOLOGICAL SOCIETY. *Secretary*, R. M. de Peyer, Dorset County Museum, Dorchester, Dorset DTI IXA. Tel: 01305-262735.

Durham: DURHAM AND NORTHUMBERLAND ARCHITECTURAL AND ARCHAEOLOGICAL SOCIETY. *Hon. Secretary*, S. Cousins, 24 Toll House Road, Durham DHI 4HU. Tel: 0191-384 2724.

Essex: ESSEX SOCIETY FOR ARCHAEOLOGY AND HISTORY. *Secretary*, Dr C. Thornton, Hollytrees Museum, High Street, Colchester COI IUG. Tel: 01206-271458.

Gloucestershire: BRISTOL AND GLOUCESTERSHIRE ARCHAEOLOGICAL SOCIETY. *Hon. Secretary*, D. J. H. Smith, FSA, 22 Beaumont Road, Gloucester GL2 0EJ. Tel: 01452-302610.

Hampshire: HAMPSHIRE FIELD CLUB AND ARCHAEOLOGICAL SOCIETY. *Hon. Secretary*, D. Allen, c/o Andover Museum, 6 Church Close, Andover, Hants SPIO IDP. Tel: 01264-366283.

Herefordshire: WOOLHOPE NATURALISTS' FIELD CLUB. *Hon. Secretary*, J. W. Tonkin, FSA, Chy an Whyloryon, Wigmore, Leominster, Herefordshire HR6 9UD. Tel: 01568-770356.

Hertfordshire: EAST HERTFORDSHIRE ARCHAEOLOGICAL SOCIETY. *Hon. Secretary*, Mrs M. C. Readman, 1 Marsh Lane, Stanstead Abbots, Ware, Herts SG12 8HH. Tel: 01920-870664.

ST ALBANS AND HERTFORDSHIRE ARCHITECTURAL AND ARCHAEOLOGICAL SOCIETY. *Hon. Secretary*, B. E. Moody, 24 Rose Walk, St Albans, Herts AL4 9AF. Tel: 01727-853204

Isle of Wight: ISLE OF WIGHT NATURAL HISTORY AND ARCHAEOLOGICAL SOCIETY. *Hon. Secretary*, Mrs T. Goodley, Island Countryside Centre, Rylstone Gardens, Shanklin, Isle of Wight PO37 6RG. Tel: 01983-867016.

Kent: KENT ARCHAEOLOGICAL SOCIETY. *Hon. General Secretary*, A. I. Moffat, Three Elms, Woodlands Lane, Shorne, Gravesend, Kent DAI2 3HH.

Leicestershire: LEICESTERSHIRE ARCHAEOLOGICAL AND HISTORICAL SOCIETY. *Hon. Secretary*, Dr A. D. McWhirr, The Guildhall, Leicester LEI 5FQ. Tel: 0116-270 3031.

London and Middlesex: CITY OF LONDON ARCHAEOLOGICAL SOCIETY. *Hon. Secretary*, Ms M. Bowen, 34 College Cross, London NI IPR. Tel: 0171-609 2930.

LONDON AND MIDDLESEX ARCHAEOLOGICAL SOCIETY. *Hon. Secretary*, M. Curtis, 34 Alexandra Road, Wimbledon, London SW19 7JZ. Tel: 0181-879 7109.

Norfolk: NORFOLK AND NORWICH ARCHAEOLOGICAL SOCIETY. *Hon. General Secretary*, R. Bellinger, 30 Brettingham Avenue, Norwich NR4 6XG. Tel: 01603-455913.

Northumberland and Tyne and Wear: SOCIETY OF ANTIQUARIES OF NEWCASTLE UPON TYNE. *Secretary*, N. Hodgson, Black Gate, Castle Garth, Newcastle upon Tyne NEI IRQ. Tel: 0191-261 5390.

SUNDERLAND ANTIQUARIAN SOCIETY. *Hon. Secretary*, Mrs V. M. Stevens, 16 Grizedale Court, Seaburn Dene, Sunderland SR6 8JP. Tel: 0191-548 7541.

Oxfordshire: OXFORDSHIRE ARCHITECTURAL AND HISTORICAL SOCIETY. *Hon. Secretary*, Dr A. J. Dodd, 53 Radley Road, Abingdon, Oxon OX14 3PN. Tel: 01235-525960.

Shropshire: SHROPSHIRE ARCHAEOLOGICAL AND
HISTORICAL SOCIETY. *Chairman,* J. B. Lawson, Westcott
Farm, Pontesbury, Shrewsbury SY5 0SQ. Tel: 01743-
790531.
Somerset: SOMERSET ARCHAEOLOGICAL AND NATURAL
HISTORY SOCIETY. *Hon. Secretary,* Dr I. J. Sinclair,
Taunton Castle, Taunton, Somerset TA1 4AD. Tel:
01823-272429.
Staffordshire: CITY OF STOKE-ON-TRENT MUSEUM
ARCHAEOLOGICAL SOCIETY. *Chairman,* E. E. Royle, City
Museum and Art Gallery, Hanley, Stoke-on-Trent
ST1 3DW. Tel: 01782-202173.
Suffolk: SUFFOLK INSTITUTE OF ARCHAEOLOGY AND
HISTORY. *Hon. Secretary,* E. A. Martin, Oak Tree Farm,
Finborough Road, Hitcham, Ipswich IP7 7LS. Tel: 01449-
741266.
Surrey: SURREY ARCHAEOLOGICAL SOCIETY. *Hon.
Secretaries,* Mrs Graham; K. J. Graham, Castle Arch,
Guildford, Surrey GU1 3SX. Tel: 01483-32454.
Sussex: SUSSEX ARCHAEOLOGICAL SOCIETY. *Chief
Executive,* J. Manley, Bull House, 92 High Street,
Lewes, E. Sussex BN7 1XH. Tel: 01273-486260.
Warwickshire: BIRMINGHAM AND WARWICKSHIRE
ARCHAEOLOGICAL SOCIETY. *Hon. Secretary,* Miss S.
Middleton, c/o Birmingham and Midland Institute,
Margaret Street, Birmingham B3 3BS.
Wiltshire: WILTSHIRE ARCHAEOLOGICAL AND NATURAL
HISTORY SOCIETY. *Secretary,* Cdr P. M. M. Coston,
Devizes Museum, 41 Long Street, Devizes, Wilts
SN10 1NS. Tel: 01380-727369.
Worcestershire: WORCESTERSHIRE ARCHAEOLOGICAL
SOCIETY. *Hon. Secretary,* T. J. Bridges, Queen Elizabeth
House, Trinity Street, Worcester WR1 2PW. Tel: 01905-
722369.
Yorkshire: HALIFAX ANTIQUARIAN SOCIETY. *Hon. Secretary,*
Dr J. A. Hargreaves, 7 Hyde Park Gardens, Haugh Shaw
Road, Halifax, W. Yorks HX1 3AH. Tel: 01422-250780.
THORESBY SOCIETY. *Hon. Secretary,* B. Harrison,
Claremont, 23 Clarendon Road, Leeds LS2 9NZ.
YORKSHIRE ARCHAEOLOGICAL SOCIETY. *Hon. Secretary,*
Ms J. Heron, Claremont, 23 Clarendon Road, Leeds
LS2 9NZ. Tel: 0113-245 7910.

SCOTLAND

AYRSHIRE ARCHAEOLOGICAL AND NATURAL HISTORY
SOCIETY. *Hon. Secretary,* Dr T. Mathews, 10 Longlands
Park, Ayr KA7 4RJ. Tel: 01292-441915.
DUMFRIESSHIRE AND GALLOWAY NATURAL HISTORY
AND ANTIQUARIAN SOCIETY. *Hon. Secretary,* M. White,
Smithy Cottage, Crocketford Road, Milton, Dumfries
D92 8QT.
HAWICK ARCHAEOLOGICAL SOCIETY. *Hon. Secretary,* I. W.
Landles, Orrock House, Stirches Road, Hawick,
Roxburghshire TD9 7HF. Tel: 01450-375546.
INVERNESS FIELD CLUB. *Hon. Secretary,* Miss I. McLean, 6
Drumblair Crescent, Inverness IV2 4RG. Tel: 01463-
234702.

WALES

Dyfed: CEREDIGION ANTIQUARIAN SOCIETY. *Hon.
Secretary,* Mrs M. T. Burdett-Jones, Skomer, Llanbadarn
Road, Aberystwyth, Ceredigion SY23 3QW. Tel: 01970-
612342.
Powys: POWYSLAND CLUB. *Hon. Secretary,* Miss P. M.
Davies, Llygad y Dyffryn, Llanidloes, Powys SY18 6JD.
Tel: 01686-412277.

CHANNEL ISLANDS

SOCIÉTÉ JERSIAISE, ARCHAEOLOGICAL SECTION. *Hon.
Secretary,* Mrs D. Shute, La Hougue Bie Museum,
Grouville, Jersey. Tel: 01534-58314.

International Organizations

ASSOCIATION OF SOUTH EAST ASIAN NATIONS
70 A. Jl. Sisingamangaraja Kebayoran Baru, Jakarta Selatan, PO Box 2072, Jakarta, Indonesia

The Association of South East Asian Nations (ASEAN) was formed in 1967 with the aims of fostering economic growth, social progress and cultural development, and ensuring regional stability.

The heads of government meeting, which convenes every three years, is ASEAN's highest authority. Its main policy-making body is the annual meeting of foreign ministers of the member countries, which appoints the secretary-general. The founding members are Indonesia, Malaysia, the Philippines, Singapore and Thailand. Brunei and Vietnam joined in 1984 and 1995 respectively. ASEAN voted in May 1997 to admit Cambodia, Laos and Myanmar.

The heads of government summit in 1992 agreed to set up the ASEAN Free Trade Area (AFTA) in 2008, progress towards which began in 1993 with the introduction of a common preferential tariff. In 1994 it was decided to bring foward the date for AFTA implementation to 2003, with Vietnam likely to join by 2006.

At the 1995 annual summit, a South East Asia nuclear weapon-free zone was declared by ASEAN, Cambodia, Laos and Myanmar.
Secretary-General, Dato' Ajit Singh (Malaysia)

BANK FOR INTERNATIONAL SETTLEMENTS
Centralbahnplatz 2, 4002 Basle, Switzerland
Tel: Basle 280 8080; fax: Basle 280 9100

The objectives of the Bank for International Settlements (founded in 1930) are to promote co-operation between central banks; to provide facilities for international financial operations; and to act as trustee or agent in international financial settlements entrusted to it. There are 41 members. The London agent is the Bank of England, and the Governor of the Bank of England is a member of the Board of Directors, in which administrative control is vested.
Chairman of the Board of Directors and President of the Bank for International Settlements, Alfons Verplaetse (Belgium)

CAB INTERNATIONAL
Wallingford, Oxon OX10 8DE
Tel: 01491-832111; fax: 01491-833508

CAB International (formerly the Commonwealth Agricultural Bureaux) was founded in 1929. It generates, disseminates and applies scientific knowledge in support of sustainable development, with an emphasis on the needs of developing countries. The organization is owned and governed by its 40 member governments, each represented on an Executive Council. A Governing Board provides guidance to management on policy issues.

CABI has five institutes: mycology, entomology, parasitology, biological control and information science. These undertake taxonomic research, offer pest and disease diagnostic services, characterize biodiversity, develop sustainable crop protection practices, test new drugs against human diseases, and provide training and information services. The organization publishes books, journals and newsletters and produces bibliographic databases on agriculture, forestry, allied disciplines and aspects of human health. It also undertakes contracted scientific research and provides consultancy services and information support to developing countries.
Director-General, J. Gilmore

CARIBBEAN COMMUNITY AND COMMON MARKET
PO Box 10827, Georgetown, Guyana
Tel: Georgetown 69281; fax: Georgetown 67816

The Caribbean Community and Common Market (CARICOM) was established in 1973 with three objectives: economic co-operation through the Caribbean Common Market, the co-ordination of foreign policy among the member states, and the provision of common services and co-operation in matters such as health, education, culture, communications and industrial relations.

The supreme organ is the Conference of Heads of Government, which determines policy, takes strategic decisions and is responsible for resolving conflicts and all matters relating to the founding treaty. The Community Council of Ministers consists of ministers of government responsible for CARICOM affairs and any other ministers designated by member states and is responsible for strategic planning in the areas of economic integration, functional co-operation and external relations. The principal administrative arm is the Secretariat, based in Guyana. The Bureau of the Conference of Heads of Government is the executive body. It comprises the Chairman of the Conference, the outgoing Chairman and the Secretary-General, who are authorized to initiate proposals and to secure the implementation of CARICOM decisions.

The 14 member states are Antigua and Barbuda, The Bahamas (which is not a member of the Common Market), Barbados, Belize, Dominica, Grenada, Guyana, Jamaica, Montserrat, St Christopher and Nevis, St Lucia, St Vincent and the Grenadines, Suriname and Trinidad and Tobago. The British Virgin Islands and the Turks and Caicos Islands are associate members. The Dominican Republic, Haiti, Mexico, Puerto Rico and Venezuela have observer status.
Secretary-General, Edwin W. Carrington

THE COMMONWEALTH

The Commonwealth is a voluntary association of 53 sovereign independent states together with their associated states and dependencies. All of the states were formerly parts of the British Empire or League of Nations (later UN) mandated territories, except for Mozambique which was admitted as a unique case because it was surrounded by Commonwealth nations.

The status and relationship of member nations were first defined by the Inter-Imperial Relations Committee of the 1926 Imperial Conference, when the six existing dominions (Australia, Canada, the Irish Free State, Newfoundland, New Zealand and South Africa) were described as 'autonomous Communities within the British Empire, equal in status, in no way subordinate one to another in any aspect of their domestic or external affairs, though united by a common allegiance to the Crown and freely associated as Members of the British Commonwealth of Nations'. This formula was given legal substance by the Statute of Westminster 1931.

This concept of a group of countries owing allegiance to a single Crown changed in 1949 when India decided to become a republic. Her continued membership of the Commonwealth was agreed by the other members on the basis of her 'acceptance of The King as the symbol of the free association of its independent member nations and as such the head of the Commonwealth'. This paved the way for other republics to join the association in due course. Member nations agreed at the time of the accession of Queen Elizabeth II to recognize Her Majesty as the new Head of the Commonwealth. However, the position is not vested in the British Crown.

THE MODERN COMMONWEALTH

As the UK's former colonies joined, initially with India and Pakistan in 1947, the Commonwealth was transformed from a grouping of all-white dominions into a multi-racial association of equal, sovereign nations. It increasingly focused on promoting development and racial equality, most notably imposing sanctions against South Africa in the 1970s over its policy of apartheid.

The new goals of advocating democracy, the rule of law, good government, human rights and social justice were enshrined in the Harare Commonwealth Declaration (1991), which formed the basis of new membership guidelines agreed in Cyprus in 1993. The heads of government meeting in Auckland, New Zealand, in 1995 adopted the Millbrook Commonwealth Action Programme to implement the Harare principles and suspended Nigeria for its anti-democratic behaviour. South Africa attended its first summit, having been readmitted.

MEMBERSHIP

Membership of the Commonwealth involves acceptance of the association's basic principles and is subject to the approval of existing members. There are 53 members at present. (The date of joining the Commonwealth is shown in parenthesis.)

*Antigua and Barbuda (1981)	India (1947)
*Australia (1931)	*Jamaica (1962)
*The Bahamas (1973)	Kenya (1963)
Bangladesh (1972)	Kiribati (1979)
*Barbados (1966)	Lesotho (1966)
*Belize (1981)	Malawi (1964)
Botswana (1966)	Malaysia (1957)
Brunei (1984)	The Maldives (1982)
Cameroon (1995)	Malta (1964)
*Canada (1931)	Mauritius (1968)
Cyprus (1961)	Mozambique (1995)
Dominica (1978)	Namibia (1990)
The Gambia (1965)	Nauru (1968)
Ghana (1957)	*New Zealand (1931)
*Grenada (1974)	†Nigeria (1960)
Guyana (1966)	

Pakistan (1947)	Tanzania (1961)
*Papua New Guinea (1975)	Tonga (1970)
*St Christopher and Nevis (1983)	Trinidad and Tobago (1962)
*St Lucia (1979)	*Tuvalu (1978)
*St Vincent and the Grenadines (1979)	Uganda (1962)
	*United Kingdom
Seychelles (1976)	Vanuatu (1980)
Sierra Leone (1961)	Western Samoa (1970)
Singapore (1965)	Zambia (1964)
*Solomon Islands (1978)	Zimbabwe (1980)
South Africa (1931)	*Realms of Queen Elizabeth II
Sri Lanka (1948)	†Suspended in 1995
Swaziland (1968)	

Nauru and Tuvalu are special members, with the right to participate in all functional Commonwealth meetings and activities, but not to attend meetings of Commonwealth heads of government.

Countries which have left the Commonwealth
Fiji (1987)
Republic of Ireland (1949)
Pakistan (1972, rejoined 1989)
South Africa (1961, rejoined 1994)

Of the 53 member states, 16 have Queen Elizabeth II as head of state, 32 are republics, and five have national monarchies.

In each of the realms where Queen Elizabeth II is head of state (except for the UK), she is personally represented by a Governor-General, who holds in all essential respects the same position in relation to the administration of public affairs in the realm as is held by Her Majesty in Britain. The Governor-General is appointed by The Queen on the advice of the government of the state concerned.

INTERGOVERNMENTAL AND OTHER LINKS

The main forum for consultation is the Commonwealth heads of government meetings held biennially to discuss international developments and to consider co-operation among members. The UK was the venue of the October 1997 meeting. Decisions are reached by consensus, and the views of the meeting are set out in a communiqué. There are also annual meetings of finance ministers and frequent meetings of ministers and officials in other fields, such as education, health, labour, law, women's affairs, agriculture, youth and science. Intergovernmental links are complemented by the activities of some 300 Commonwealth non-governmental organizations linking professionals, sportsmen and sportswomen, and interest groups, forming a 'people's Commonwealth'. The Commonwealth Games take place every four years.

Assistance to other Commonwealth countries normally has priority in the bilateral aid programmes of the association's developed members (Australia, Britain, Canada and New Zealand), who direct about 30 per cent of their aid to other member countries. Developing Commonwealth nations also assist their poorer partners, and many Commonwealth voluntary organizations promote development.

COMMONWEALTH SECRETARIAT

The Commonwealth has a secretariat, established in 1965 in London, which is funded by all member governments. This is the main agency for multilateral communication between member governments on issues relating to the Commonwealth as a whole. It promotes consultation and co-operation, disseminates information on matters of common concern, organizes meetings including the biennial summits, co-ordinates Commonwealth activities, and provides technical assistance for economic and social development through the Commonwealth Fund for Technical Co-operation.

The Commonwealth Foundation was established by Commonwealth governments in 1966 as an autonomous body with a board of governors representing Commonwealth governments that fund the Foundation. It promotes and funds exchanges and other activities aimed at strengthening the skills and effectiveness of professionals and non-government organizations. It also promotes culture, rural development, social welfare and the role of women.

COMMONWEALTH SECRETARIAT, Marlborough House, Pall Mall, London SW1Y 5HX. Tel: 0171-839 3411.
   Secretary-General, Chief Emeka Anyaoku (Nigeria)
COMMONWEALTH FOUNDATION, Marlborough House, Pall Mall, London SW1Y 5HY. Tel: 0171-930 3783.
   Director, Dr Humayun Khan (Pakistan)
COMMONWEALTH INSTITUTE, Kensington High Street, London W8 6NQ. Tel: 0171-603 4535. *Director-General*, S. Cox

COMMONWEALTH OF INDEPENDENT STATES

The Commonwealth of Independent States (CIS) is a multilateral grouping of 12 sovereign states which were formerly constituent republics of the USSR. It was formed by Russia, Ukraine and Belorussia on 8 December 1991, the remaining republics, apart from the Baltic states and Georgia, joining on 21 December. Georgia joined in December 1993. Azerbaijani and Moldovan membership effectively lapsed, because of non-ratification, until September 1993 and April 1994 respectively. The CIS charter, signed in 1993, formally established the functions of the organization and the obligations of its member states.

The CIS acts as a co-ordinating mechanism for foreign, defence and economic policies, and is a forum for addressing those problems which have specifically arisen from the break-up of the USSR. These matters are addressed in more than 50 inter-state, intergovernmental co-ordinating and consultative statutory bodies.

STRUCTURE

The two supreme CIS bodies are the Council of Heads of State and the Council of Heads of Government. The Council of Heads of State is the highest organ of the CIS and meets not less than twice yearly. In theory it is chaired by the heads of state of the members in (Russian) alphabetical order, although in March 1997 President Yeltsin of Russia was given a second consecutive term. The Council of Heads of Government meets not less than once every three months to co-ordinate military and economic activity. Other important bodies are the Council of Heads of Collective Security (defence ministers), the Joint Staff for Co-ordinating Military Co-operation, the CIS Inter-Parliamentary Assembly, the Economic Arbitration Court and the Co-ordinating Consultative Committee. Administrative support is provided by the Executive Secretariat based in Minsk.

DEFENCE CO-OPERATION

On becoming member states of the CIS, the 11 original states agreed to recognize their existing borders, respect one another's territorial integrity and reject the use of military force or other forms of coercion to settle disputes between them. Agreement was also reached on fulfilling all the international treaty obligations of the former USSR,

and on a unified central control for nuclear weapons and other strategic forces, together with the establishment of CIS joint armed forces.

The members agreed on a central CIS command for all nuclear weapons, the control over which was passed to CIS commander-in-chief Marshal Shaposhnikov in December 1991. All tactical nuclear weapons had been transferred to Russia by May 1992. An agreement was reached with the USA in May 1992 by the four republics with strategic nuclear weapons (Russia, Ukraine, Belarus, Kazakhstan) on implementing the strategic arms reduction talks (START) treaty previously signed by the USA and USSR, and the START I treaty was ratified by the five parties between October 1992 and February 1994. Under this agreement Ukraine, Belarus and Kazakhstan agreed to eliminate all their strategic nuclear weapons over a seven-year period and Russia has agreed to reduce its strategic nuclear weapons.

A CIS high command and a joint conventional force were created in 1992 to operate in parallel with member states' own armed forces. In the same year, a Treaty on Collective Security was signed by six states and a joint peacemaking force, to intervene in CIS conflicts, was agreed upon by nine states. Deployment of these forces was made conditional on consensus in the Council of Heads of State. Fear of Russian domination by some states (Ukraine, Moldova, Turkmenistan) led to the downgrading of the high command into a Joint Staff for Co-ordinating Military Co-operation in 1993. Russia responded by concluding bilateral and multilateral agreements with other CIS states under the supervision of the Council of Heads of Collective Security (established 1993). These have been gradually upgraded into CIS agreements under the umbrella of the Treaty on Collective Security, enabling Russia to station troops in ten of the other 11 CIS states (not Ukraine), and giving Russian forces *de facto* control of virtually all of the former USSR's external borders. Only Ukraine and Moldova remain outside the defence co-operation framework and have not signed the Treaty on Collective Security. In November 1995, the ten agreed to recreate a joint air defence system.

ECONOMIC CO-OPERATION

In 1991 11 republics signed a treaty forming an economic community. The principles of the treaty were embodied within the CIS and formed the basis of its economic co-operation. Members agreed to refrain from economic actions that would damage each other and to co-ordinate economic and monetary policies. A Co-ordinating Consultative Committee, an economic arbitration court and an inter-state bank were established. A single monetary unit, the rouble, was originally agreed upon by all member states, and the members recognized that the basis of recovery for their economies was private ownership, free enterprise and competition.

Russia effectively forced the collapse of the rouble zone in July 1993 by withdrawing all pre-1993 roubles and forcing the remaining states using roubles to accept Russian monetary control or introduce their own currencies, which all did apart from Tajikistan. The resulting economic collapse of the non-Russian economies led to renewed interest in economic co-operation and the signing of a Treaty on Economic Union in September 1993. The 11 CIS members who have signed the Treaty (Ukraine is an associate member of the economic union) are committed to a common market without internal barriers to trade, common fiscal policies and an eventual currency union with currencies semi-fixed against the rouble. In order to facilitate faster economic integration 11 states (not Turkmenistan) agreed in October 1994 to establish an

Inter-state Economic Committee, and in May 1995 a monetary committee to facilitate payments in different currencies was agreed. Belarus has withdrawn its currency and rejoined Russia and Tajikistan in the rouble zone. A treaty creating a common market was signed by Kazakhstan, Kyrgyzstan, Russia and Belarus in March 1996, with other CIS states excluded from membership.

THE COUNCIL OF EUROPE
67075 Strasbourg, France
Tel: Strasbourg 8841 2000; fax: Strasbourg 8841 2780

The Council of Europe was founded in 1949. Its aim is to achieve greater unity between its members, to safeguard their European heritage and to facilitate their progress in economic, social, cultural, educational, scientific, legal and administrative matters, and in the furtherance of pluralist democracy, human rights and fundamental freedoms.

The 40 members are Albania, Andorra, Austria, Belgium, Bulgaria, Croatia, Cyprus, Czech Republic, Denmark, Estonia, Finland, France, Germany, Greece, Hungary, Iceland, the Republic of Ireland, Italy, Latvia, Liechtenstein, Lithuania, Luxembourg, Macedonia (Former Yugoslav Republic of), Malta, Moldova, the Netherlands, Norway, Poland, Portugal, Romania, Russia, San Marino, Slovakia, Slovenia, Spain, Sweden, Switzerland, Turkey, the UK and Ukraine. 'Special guest status' has been granted to Armenia, Azerbaijan, Belarus, Bosnia-Hercegovina and Georgia. Turkey's membership was suspended from April 1995 to September 1996 over its military offensive against Kurdish guerrillas in northern Iraq.

The organs are the Committee of Ministers, consisting of the foreign ministers of member countries, who meet twice yearly, and the Parliamentary Assembly of 286 members, elected or chosen by the national parliaments of member countries in proportion to the relative strength of political parties. There is also a Joint Committee of Ministers and Representatives of the Parliamentary Assembly.

The Committee of Ministers is the executive organ. The majority of its conclusions take the form of international agreements (known as European Conventions) or recommendations to governments. Decisions of the Ministers may also be embodied in partial agreements to which a limited number of member governments are party. Member governments accredit Permanent Representatives to the Council in Strasbourg, who are also the Ministers' Deputies. The Committee of Deputies meets every month to transact business and to take decisions on behalf of Ministers.

The Parliamentary Assembly holds three week-long sessions a year. Its 13 permanent committees meet once or twice between each public plenary session of the Assembly. The Congress of Local and Regional Authorities of Europe each year brings together mayors and municipal councillors in the same numbers as the members of the Parliamentary Assembly.

One of the principal achievements of the Council of Europe is the European Convention on Human Rights (1950) under which was established the European Commission and the European Court of Human Rights, which were merged in 1993. The reorganized European Court of Human Rights sits in chambers of seven judges or exceptionally as a grand chamber of 17 judges. Litigants must exhaust legal processes in their own country before bringing cases before the court.

Among other conventions and agreements are the European Social Charter, the European Cultural Convention, the European Code of Social Security, the European Convention on the Protection of National Minorities, and conventions on extradition, the legal status of migrant workers, torture prevention, conservation, and the transfer of sentenced prisoners. Most recently, the specialized bodies of the Venice Commission and Demosthenes have been set up to assist in developing legislative, administrative and constitutional reforms in central and eastern Europe.

Non-member states take part in certain Council of Europe activities on a regular or *ad hoc* basis; thus the Holy See participates in all the educational, cultural and sports activities. The European Youth Centre is an educational residential centre for young people. The European Youth Foundation provides youth organizations with funds for their international activities.

Secretary-General, Daniel Tarschys (Sweden)
Permanent UK Representative, HE Roger Beetham, CMG, LVO, *apptd* 1993

THE ECONOMIC COMMUNITY OF WEST AFRICAN STATES
Secretariat Building, Asokoro, Abuja, Nigeria
Tel: Abuja 523 1858

The Economic Community of West African States (ECOWAS) was founded in 1975 and came into operation in 1977. It aims to promote the cultural, economic and social development of West Africa through mutual co-operation. A revised ECOWAS Treaty was signed in 1993 and came into effect on 30 July 1995. It makes the prevention and control of regional conflicts an aim of ECOWAS and provides for the imposition of a community tax and for the establishment of a regional parliament, an economic and social council, and a court of justice.

Measures undertaken by ECOWAS include the gradual elimination of barriers to the movement of goods, people and services between member states and the improvement of regional telecommunications and transport.

The supreme authority of ECOWAS is vested in the annual summit of heads of government of all 16 member states. A Council of Ministers, two from each member state, meets biannually to monitor the organization and make recommendations to the summit. ECOWAS operates through a Secretariat, headed by the Executive Secretary. In addition there is a financial controller, an external auditor, the Disputes Tribunal and the Defence Council.

A Fund for Co-operation, Compensation and Development, situated at Lomé, Togo, finances development projects and provides compensation to member states who have suffered losses as a result of ECOWAS's policies, particularly trade liberalization.

An ECOWAS Monitoring Group (ECOMOG) peace-keeping force has been involved in attempts to restore peace in Liberia (1990–6) and Sierra Leone (1997).

Executive Secretary, Edouard Benjamin

THE EUROPEAN BANK FOR RECONSTRUCTION AND DEVELOPMENT
One Exchange Square, London EC2A 2EH
Tel: 0171-338 6000; fax: 0171-338 6100

The charter of the European Bank for Reconstruction and Development (EBRD) was signed by 40 countries, the

European Commission and the European Investment Bank in May 1990 and was inaugurated in April 1991.

The aim of the EBRD is to facilitate the transformation of the states of central and eastern Europe (Albania, Bulgaria, Czech Republic, Estonia, Hungary, Latvia, Lithuania, Poland, Romania, Slovakia, the republics of the former USSR and former Yugoslavia) from centrally-planned to free-market economies, and to promote multi-party democracy, entrepreneurial initiative, and respect for human rights and the environment.

The EBRD provides technical assistance, training and investment in the upgrading of infrastructure; privatization; the strengthening of legal systems; gaining foreign direct investment; the creation of modern financial systems; nuclear safety; tourism; the exploitation of natural resources; and the restructuring of state industries. The EBRD's assistance is weighted towards the private sector; no more than 40 per cent of its investment can be made in state-owned concerns. It works in co-operation with its members, private companies, and international organizations such as the OECD, the IMF, the World Bank and the UN specialized agencies.

The EBRD has an initial subscribed capital of 10 billion ECU, which the Board of Governors agreed to double in April 1996, of which 30 per cent is paid in. The EBRD is also able to borrow on world capital markets. Its major subscribers are the USA, 10 per cent; Britain, France, Germany, Italy and Japan, 8.5 per cent each; central and eastern European states, 11.9 per cent. The EBRD offers a range of financing instruments including loans, equity investments and guarantees. In 1995 the EBRD approved 134 projects, totalling ECU 2,855 million; the total number of projects approved since its establishment is 451, involving ECU 10,400 million of EBRD funds.

The EBRD has 60 members. The highest authority is the Board of Governors; each member appoints one Governor and one Alternate. The Governors delegate most powers to a 23-member Board of Directors; the Directors are responsible for the EBRD's operations and budget, and are elected by the Governors for three-year terms. The Governors also elect the President of the Board of Directors, who acts as the Bank's president, for a four-year term. A Secretary-General liaises between the Directors and EBRD staff.

President of the Board of Directors, Jacques de Larosière (France)
UK Executive Director, Robert Graham-Harrison
Secretary-General, Antonio Maria Costa (Italy)

EUROPEAN FREE TRADE ASSOCIATION
9–11 rue de Varembé, 1211 Geneva 20, Switzerland
Tel: Geneva 749 1111
74 rue de Trèves, 1040 Brussels, Belgium

The European Free Trade Association (EFTA) was established in 1960 by Austria, Denmark, Norway, Portugal, Sweden, Switzerland and the UK, and was subsequently joined by Finland, Iceland and Liechtenstein. Six members have left to join the European Union: Denmark and the UK (1972), Portugal (1985), Austria, Finland and Sweden (1994). The existing members are Iceland, Liechtenstein, Norway and Switzerland.

The first objective of EFTA was to establish free trade in industrial goods between members; this was achieved in 1966. Its second objective was the creation of a single market in western Europe and in 1972 EFTA signed free trade agreements with the EC covering trade in industrial

goods; the remaining tariffs on industrial products were abolished in 1984.

An agreement on the creation of the European Economic Area (EEA), an extension of the EC single market to the EFTA states, was signed in 1992 and entered into force on 1 January 1994. Switzerland rejected EEA membership in a referendum in 1992 and Liechtenstein joined on 1 May 1995 after adapting its customs union with Switzerland.

EFTA has expanded its relations with other non-EU states in recent years and free trade agreements have been signed with Turkey (1991), Israel, Poland and Romania (1992), Bulgaria, Hungary, the Czech Republic and Slovakia (1993), and Estonia, Latvia, Lithuania and Slovenia (1995). In addition, EFTA has signed declarations of economic co-operation with Albania (1992), Egypt, Morocco and Tunisia (1995), the Former Yugoslav Republic of Macedonia and the PLO (1996).

The EFTA Council is the principle organ of the Association. It generally meets twice a month at the level of heads of the permanent national delegations to the EFTA Secretariat in Geneva and twice a year at ministerial level.

Secretary-General, Kjartan Jóhannsson (Iceland)

EUROPEAN ORGANIZATION FOR NUCLEAR RESEARCH (CERN)
CH-1211 Geneva 23, Switzerland
Tel: Geneva 767 4101; fax: Geneva 785 0247

The Convention establishing the European Organization for Nuclear Research (CERN) came into force in 1954. CERN promotes European collaboration in high energy physics of a scientific, rather than a military nature.

The member countries are Austria, Belgium, the Czech Republic, Denmark, Finland, France, Germany, Greece, Hungary, Italy, the Netherlands, Norway, Poland, Portugal, Slovakia, Spain, Sweden, Switzerland and the UK. Israel, Russia, Turkey, the EU Commission and UNESCO have observer status.

The Council is the highest policy-making body and comprises two delegates from each member state. There is also a Committee of the Council comprising a single delegate from each member state (who is also a Council member) and the chairmen of the scientific policy and finance advisory committees. The Council is chaired by the President who is elected by the Council in Session. The Council also elects the Director-General, who is responsible for the internal organization of CERN. The Director-General heads a workforce of approximately 3,000, including physicists, craftsmen, technicians and administrative staff. At present over 6,500 physicists use CERN's facilities.

The member countries contribute to the budget in proportion to their net national revenue. The 1997 budget was SFr 873 million.

President of the Council, Prof. Luciano Maiani (Italy)
Director-General (1994–9), Prof. Christopher Llewellyn-Smith (UK)

EUROPEAN SPACE AGENCY
8–10 rue Mario Nikis, 75738 Paris, France
Tel: Paris 5369 7400; fax: Paris 5369 7424

The European Space Agency (ESA) was created in 1975 by the merger of the European Space Research Organization

(ESRO) and the European Launcher Development Organization (ELDO). Its aims include the advancement of space research and technology, the implementation of a long-term European space policy and the co-ordination of national space programmes.

The member countries are Austria, Belgium, Denmark, Finland, France, Germany, Republic of Ireland, Italy, Netherlands, Norway, Spain, Sweden, Switzerland and the UK. Canada is a co-operating state.

The agency is directed by a Council composed of the representatives of the member states; its chief officer is the Director-General.

Director-General, Antonio Rodotà, *apptd* 1997

FOOD AND AGRICULTURE ORGANIZATION
OF THE UNITED NATIONS
Viale delle Terme di Caracalla, 00100 Rome, Italy
Tel: Rome 52251; fax: Rome 5225 3152

The Food and Agriculture Organization (FAO) is a specialized UN agency, established in 1945. It assists rural populations by raising levels of nutrition and living standards, and by encouraging greater efficiency in food production and distribution. It collects, analyses and disseminates information on agriculture and natural resources. The FAO also advises governments on national agricultural policy and planning; its Investment Centre, together with the World Bank and other financial institutions, helps to prepare development projects. The FAO's field programme covers a range of activities, including strengthening crop production, rural and livestock development, and conservation.

The FAO's top priorities are sustainable agriculture, rural development and food security. The Organization attempts to ensure the availability of adequate food supplies, stability in the flow of supplies and the securing of access to food by the poor. The FAO monitors potential famine areas. The Office for Special Relief Operations channels emergency aid from governments and other agencies, and assists in rehabilitation. The Technical Co-operation Programme provides schemes for countries facing agricultural crises.

The FAO had 175 members (174 states and the EU) as at May 1997. It is governed by a biennial conference of its members which sets a programme and budget. The budget for 1996–7 is US$650 million, funded by member countries in proportion to their gross national products. The FAO is also funded by the UN Development Programme, donor governments and other institutions.

The Conference elects a Director-General and a 49-member Council which governs between conferences. The Regular and Field Programmes are administered by a Secretariat, headed by the Director-General. Five regional, five sub-regional and 80 national offices help administer the Field Programme.

Director-General, Jacques Diouf (Senegal)
UK Representative, D. Sands Smith, British Embassy, Rome

INMARSAT
99 City Road, London ECIY IAX
Tel: 0171-728 1773; fax: 0171-728 1779

Inmarsat (formerly the International Mobile Satellite Organization) was founded in 1979 as the International Maritime Satellite Organization and began operations in 1982. Inmarsat is an internationally-owned co-operative

which operates a system of satellites to provide global mobile communications. Inmarsat satellite terminals are used world-wide on ships, in aircraft and on land for telephone, facsimile, telex and e-mail data, as well as maritime safety, position reporting and distress communications.

Inmarsat comprises three bodies: the Assembly, the Council and the Directorate. The Assembly is composed of representatives of the 80 member countries, each having one vote. It meets every two years to review activities and objectives, and to make recommendations to the Council. The Council is the main decision-making body and consists of representatives of the 18 members with the largest investment shares, and four members representing the interests of developing countries who are elected to the Council on the basis of geographical representation. Members have voting powers equal to their investment shares. The Council meets at least three times a year and oversees the activities of the Directorate, the permanent staff of Inmarsat.

Director-General, Warren Grace (Australia)

INTERNATIONAL ATOMIC ENERGY
AGENCY
Vienna International Centre, Wagramerstrasse 5,
PO Box 100, 1400 Vienna, Austria
Tel: Vienna 2060; fax: Vienna 20607

The International Atomic Energy Agency (IAEA) was established in 1957. It is an intergovernmental organization which reports to, but is not a specialized agency of, the UN.

The IAEA aims to enhance the contribution of atomic energy to peace, health and prosperity, and to ensure that any assistance that it provides is not used for military purposes. It establishes atomic energy safety standards and offers services to its member states for the safe operation of their nuclear facilities and for radiation protection. It is the focal point for international conventions on the early notification of a nuclear accident, assistance in the case of a nuclear accident, civil liability for nuclear damage, physical protection of nuclear material, and nuclear safety. The IAEA also encourages research and training in nuclear power. It is additionally charged with drawing up safeguards and verifying their use in accordance with the Nuclear Non-Proliferation Treaty (NPT) 1968, the Treaty for the Prohibition of Nuclear Weapons in Latin America (Tlatelolco Treaty) 1968, the Treaty on a South Pacific Nuclear Free Zone (Rarotonga Treaty), and the African Nuclear Weapon-Free Zone Treaty (Pelindaba Treaty) 1996. Together with the Food and Agriculture Organization and the World Health Organization, the IAEA established an International Consultative Group on Food Irradiation in 1983.

The IAEA concluded a safeguards agreement with North Korea in April 1992 and began inspections to verify that its nuclear programme was for peaceful purposes only. In June 1994 the IAEA informed the UN Security Council that North Korea had violated its NPT obligations and all technical aid to North Korea was suspended. North Korea resigned from the IAEA in June 1994, but permitted IAEA inspections under the terms of an agreement with the USA which enabled the IAEA to resume safeguards inspections.

The IAEA had 124 members as at May 1997. A General Conference of all its members meets annually to decide policy, a programme and a budget (1997, US$222 million), as well as electing a Director-General and a 35-member Board of Governors. The Board meets four times a year to

formulate policy which is implemented by the Secretariat under a Director-General.
Director-General, Hans Blix (Sweden)
Permanent UK Representative, Dr John Freeman, Jaurèsgasse 12, 1030 Vienna, Austria

INTERNATIONAL CIVIL AVIATION ORGANIZATION
1000 Sherbrooke Street West, Montreal, Quebec, Canada H3A 2R2
Tel: Montreal 954 8221; fax: Montreal 954 6376

The International Civil Aviation Organization (ICAO) was founded with the signing of the Chicago Convention on International Civil Aviation in 1944, and became a specialized agency of the United Nations in 1947. It sets international technical standards and recommended practices for all areas of civil aviation, including airworthiness, air navigation, traffic control and pilot licensing. It encourages uniformity and simplicity in ground regulations and operations at international airports, including immigration and customs control. The ICAO also promotes regional air navigation, plans for ground facilities, and collects and distributes air transport statistics worldwide. It is dedicated to improving safety and to the orderly development of civil aviation throughout the world.

The ICAO had 185 members as at 21 December 1996. It is governed by an assembly of its members which meets at least once every three years. A Council of 33 members is elected, which represents leading air transport nations as well as less developed countries. The Council elects the President, appoints the Secretary-General and supervises the organization through subsidiary committees, serviced by a Secretariat.
President of the Council, Dr Assad Kotaite (Lebanon)
Secretary-General, Dr Philippe Rochat (Switzerland)
UK Representative, D. S. Evans, CMG, Suite 14.15, 999 University Street, Montreal, Quebec, Canada H3C 5J9

INTERNATIONAL CONFEDERATION OF FREE TRADE UNIONS
Boulevard Emile Jacqmain 155 B1, B-1210 Brussels, Belgium
Tel: Brussels 224 0211; fax: Brussels 203 0756

The International Confederation of Free Trade Unions (ICFTU) was created in 1949. It aims to establish, maintain and promote free trade unions, and to promote peace with economic security and social justice.

Affiliated to the ICFTU are 195 individual unions and representative bodies in 137 countries and territories. There were 124 million members on 29 November 1996.

The Congress, the supreme authority of the ICFTU, convenes at least every four years. It is composed of delegates from the affiliated trade union organizations. The Congress elects an Executive Board of 49 members which meets not less than once a year. The Board establishes the budget and receives suggestions and proposals from affiliates as well as acting on behalf of the Confederation. The Congress also elects the General Secretary.
General Secretary, Bill Jordan (UK)
UK Affiliate, TUC, Congress House, 23–28 Great Russell Street, London WC1B 3LS. Tel: 0171-636 4030

INTERNATIONAL CRIMINAL POLICE ORGANIZATION
200 Quai Charles de Gaulle, 69006 Lyon, France
Tel: Lyon 7244 7000

The International Criminal Police Commission (Interpol) was set up in 1923 to establish an international criminal records office and to harmonize extradition procedures. From 1 January 1998 the organization will comprise 177 member states.

Interpol's aims are to promote co-operation between criminal police authorities, and to support government agencies concerned with combating crime, whilst respecting national sovereignty. It is financed by annual contributions from the governments of member states.

Interpol's policy is decided by the General Assembly which meets annually; it is composed of delegates appointed by the member states. The 13-member Executive Committee is elected by the General Assembly from among the member states' delegates, and is chaired by the President, who has a four-year term of office. The permanent administrative organ is the General Secretariat, headed by the Secretary-General, who is appointed by the General Assembly.
Secretary General, Raymond Kendall, QPM (UK)
UK OFFICE, NCIS-Interpol, Spring Gardens, Tinworth Street, London SE11 5EH. Tel: 0171-238 8000. *UK Representative*, vacant

INTERNATIONAL ENERGY AGENCY
9 rue de la Fédération, 75739 Paris Cedex 15, France
Tel: Paris 4057 6554; fax: Paris 4057 6559

The International Energy Agency (IEA), founded in 1974, is an autonomous agency within the framework of the Organization for Economic Co-operation and Development (OECD). The IEA had 24 member countries at May 1997.

The IEA's objectives include improvement of energy co-operation world-wide, increased efficiency, development of alternative energy sources and the promotion of relations between oil producing and oil consuming countries. The IEA also maintains an emergency system to alleviate the effects of severe oil supply disruptions.

The main decision-making body is the Governing Board composed of senior energy officials from member countries. Various standing groups and special committees exist to facilitate the work of the Board. The IEA Secretariat, with a staff of energy experts, carries out the work of the Governing Board and its subordinate bodies. The Executive Director is appointed by the Board.
Executive Director, Robert Priddle (UK)

INTERNATIONAL FUND FOR AGRICULTURAL DEVELOPMENT
107 Via del Serafico, 00142 Rome, Italy
Tel: Rome 519 3328

The establishment of the International Fund for Agricultural Development (IFAD) was proposed by the 1974 World Food Conference and IFAD began operations as a UN specialized agency in 1977. Its purpose is to mobilize additional funds for agricultural and rural development projects in developing countries that benefit the poorest rural populations; provide employment and additional income for poor farmers; reduce malnutrition; and improve food distribution systems.

IFAD had 160 members as at February 1997. Membership is divided into three lists: List A (OECD countries), List B (OPEC countries), and List C (developing countries) which is subdivided into C1 (Africa), C2 (Africa, Asia and the Pacific) and C3 (Latin America and the Caribbean). All powers are vested in a Governing Council of all member countries. It elects an 18-member Executive Board (with 17 alternate members) responsible for IFAD's operations. The Council meets annually and elects a President who is also chairman of the Board. He is assisted by a Vice-President and three Assistant Presidents.

At the end of December 1996 IFAD's loan portfolio comprised commitments of US$4,956.2 million for 462 approved projects in 110 developing countries. In 1996 the Executive Board approved 33 projects, including loans worth US$435.7 million.

President, Fawzi H. Al-Sultan (Kuwait)

INTERNATIONAL LABOUR ORGANIZATION
4 route des Morillons, 1211 Geneva 22, Switzerland
Tel: 0171-828 6401; fax: 0171-233 5925

The International Labour Organization (ILO) was established in 1919 as an autonomous body of the League of Nations and became the UN's first specialized agency in 1946. The ILO aims to increase employment, improve working conditions, raise living standards and encourage democratic development. It sets minimum international labour standards through the drafting of international conventions. Member countries are obliged to submit these to their domestic authorities for ratification, and thus undertake to bring their domestic legislation in line with the conventions. Members must report to the ILO periodically on how these regulations are being implemented. The ILO plays a major role in helping developing countries achieve economic stability and job expansion through its wide-ranging programme of technical co-operation. The ILO is also the world's principal resource centre for information, analysis and guidance on labour and employment. The organization aims to improve working and living conditions throughout the world and to support the transition to democracy and market economics under way in many states.

The ILO had 174 members as at May 1997. It is composed of the International Labour Conference, the Governing Body and the International Labour Office. The Conference of members meets annually, and is attended by national delegations comprising two government delegates, one worker delegate and one employer delegate. It formulates international labour conventions and recommendations, provides a forum for discussion of world employment and social issues, and approves the ILO's programme and budget (1997–8, US$569.08 million).

The 56-member Governing Body, composed of 28 government, 14 worker and 14 employer members, acts as the ILO's executive council. Ten governments, including Britain, hold seats on the Governing Body because of their industrial importance. There are also various regional conferences and advisory committees. The International Labour Office acts as a secretariat and as a centre for operations, publishing and research.

Director-General, Michel Hansenne (Belgium)
UK OFFICE, Vincent House, Vincent Square, London
SW1P 2NB. Tel: 0171-828 6401

INTERNATIONAL MARITIME ORGANIZATION
4 Albert Embankment, London SE1 7SR
Tel: 0171-735 7611; fax: 0171-587 3210

The International Maritime Organization (IMO) was established as a UN specialized agency in 1948. Owing to delays in treaty ratification it did not commence operations until 1958. Originally it was called the Inter-Governmental Maritime Consultative Organization (IMCO) but changed its name in 1982.

The IMO fosters intergovernmental co-operation in technical matters relating to international shipping, especially with regard to safety at sea. It is also charged with preventing and controlling marine pollution caused by shipping and facilitating marine traffic. The IMO is responsible for convening maritime conferences and drafting marine conventions. It also provides technical aid to countries wishing to develop their activities at sea.

The IMO had 155 members as at May 1997. It is governed by an Assembly comprising delegates of all its members. It meets biennially to formulate policy, set a budget (1996–7, £36.6 million), vote on specific recommendations on pollution and maritime safety and elect the Council. The Council fulfils the functions of the Assembly between sessions and appoints the Secretary-General. It consists of 32 members: eight from the world's largest shipping nations, eight from the nations most dependent on seaborne trade, and 16 other members to ensure a fair geographical representation. The Maritime Safety Committee, through its sub-committees, makes reports and recommendations to the Council and the Assembly. There are a number of other specialist subsidiary committees, including one for marine environmental protection.

The IMO acts as the secretariat for the London Convention (1972) which regulates the disposal of land-generated waste at sea.

Secretary-General, William A. O'Neil (Canada)

INTERNATIONAL MONETARY FUND
700 19th Street NW, Washington DC 20431, USA

The International Monetary Fund (IMF) was established in 1944, at the UN Monetary and Financial Conference held at Bretton Woods, New Hampshire. Its Articles of Agreement entered into force in 1945 and it began operations in 1946.

The IMF exists to promote international monetary co-operation, the expansion of world trade, and exchange stability, and to eliminate foreign exchange restrictions. The IMF advises members on their economic and financial policies; promotes policy co-ordination among the major industrial countries; and gives technical assistance in central banking, balance of payments accounting, taxation, and other financial matters. The IMF serves as a forum for members to discuss important financial and monetary issues and seeks the balanced growth of international trade and, through this, high levels of employment, income and productive capacity. As at April 1997 the IMF had 181 members. Sudan's and the Democratic Republic of Congo's voting rights have been suspended.

Upon joining the IMF, a member is assigned a 'quota', based on the member's relative standing in the world economy and its balance of payments position, that determines its capital subscription to the Fund, its access to IMF resources, its voting power, and its share in the allocation of Special Drawing Rights (SDRs). Quotas are reviewed every five years and adjusted accordingly. Since the Ninth General Review of quotas in 1994, total Fund quotas stand at SDR 145.3 billion. The SDR, an international reserve asset issued by the IMF, is calculated daily on a basket of usable currencies and is the IMF's unit of account; on 30 April 1997, SDR 1 equalled US$1.36553. SDRs are allocated at intervals to supplement members' reserves and thereby improve international financial liquidity.

IMF financial resources derive primarily from members' capital subscriptions, which are equivalent to their quotas. In addition, the IMF is authorized to borrow from official lenders. It may also draw on a line of credit of SDR 18.5 billion from various countries under the so-called General Arrangements to Borrow (GAB). Periodic charges are also levied on financial assistance. At the end of April 1997, total outstanding IMF credits amounted to SDR 34.5 billion.

The IMF is not a bank and does not lend money; it provides temporary financial assistance by selling a member's SDRs or other members' currencies in exchange for the member's own currency. The member can then use the purchased currency to alleviate its balance of payments difficulties. The IMF's credit under its regular facilities is made available to members in tranches or segments of 25 per cent of quota. For first credit tranche purchases, members are required to demonstrate reasonable efforts to overcome their balance of payments difficulties. There are no performance criteria and the total amount is repaid in three and a quarter to five years. Upper credit tranche purchases are normally associated with stand-by arrangements. These typically cover periods of one to two years. They focus on macroeconomic policies aimed at overcoming balance of payment difficulties and are required to meet certain performance criteria. Repurchases are made in three and a quarter to five years.

The IMF supports long-term efforts at economic reform and transformation, such as the re-establishment of market economies in the countries of eastern Europe and the former Soviet Union. In addition, the IMF supports medium-term programmes under the extended Fund facility, which generally runs for three years (sometimes up to four years) and is aimed at overcoming balance of payments difficulties stemming from macroeconomic and structural problems. Members experiencing a temporary balance of payments shortfall have access to the compensatory and contingency financing facility. The IMF also offers credits to low-income countries engaged in economic reform through its structural adjustment facility (SAF) and enhanced structural adjustment facility (ESAF). As at 30 April 1997, SDR 5.8 billion in SAF and ESAF loans is outstanding.

The IMF is headed by a Board of Governors, comprising representatives of all members, which meets annually. The Governors delegate powers to 24 Executive Directors, who are appointed or elected by member countries. The Executive Directors operate the Fund on a daily basis under a Managing Director, whom they elect.

Managing Director, Michel Camdessus (France)

UK Executive Director, Gus O'Donnell, Room 11-120, IMF, 700 19th Street NW, Washington DC 20431

INTERNATIONAL RED CROSS AND RED CRESCENT MOVEMENT
17 avenue de la Paix, 1211 Geneva, Switzerland
Tel: 0171-201 5008; fax: 0171-235 5194

The International Red Cross and Red Crescent Movement is composed of three elements. The International Committee of the Red Cross (ICRC), the organization's founding body, was formed in 1863. It aims to negotiate between warring factions and to protect and assist victims of armed conflict. It also seeks to ensure the application of the Geneva Conventions with regard to prisoners of war and detainees.

The International Federation of Red Cross and Red Crescent Societies was founded in 1919 to contribute to the development of the humanitarian activities of national societies, to co-ordinate their relief operations for victims of natural disasters, and to care for refugees outside areas of conflict. There are Red Cross and Red Crescent Societies in 170 countries, with a total membership of 250 million.

The International Conference of the Red Cross and Red Crescent meets every four years, bringing together delegates of the ICRC, the International Federation and the national societies, as well as representatives of nations bound by the Geneva Conventions.

President of the ICRC, Cornelio Sommaruga

BRITISH RED CROSS, 9 Grosvenor Crescent, London SW1X 7EJ. Tel: 0171-201 5008. *Director-General*, Michael R. Whitlam.

INTERNATIONAL TELECOMMUNICATIONS SATELLITE ORGANIZATION
3400 International Drive NW, Washington DC 20008–3098, USA
Tel: Washington DC 944 7835; fax: Washington DC 944 7890

The International Telecommunications Satellite Organization (Intelsat) was formed in 1964. It owns and operates the world-wide commercial communications satellite system which is composed of over 20 satellites and more than 4,000 antennas which connect over 180 countries, territories and dependencies. Intelsat provides international and domestic voice/data and video services.

Each of the 140 member states contributes to the capital costs of the organization in proportion to its investment share, which is based on its relative usage of the system.

There is a four-tier hierarchy. The Assembly of Parties to the agreement meets every two years to consider long-term objectives and is composed of representatives of the member governments. The Meeting of Signatories annually considers the financial, technical and operational aspects of the system. The Board of Governors has 28 members; INTELSAT Management is the permanent staff of the organization and is headed by a Director-General who reports to the Board of Governors.

Director-General, Irving Goldstein (USA)

INTERNATIONAL TELECOMMUNICATION UNION
Place des Nations, 1211 Geneva 20, Switzerland

The International Telecommunication Union (ITU) was founded in Paris in 1865 as the International Telegraph

Union and became a UN specialized agency in 1947. It promotes international co-operation and sets standards and regulations for the interconnection of telecommunications systems of all kinds. It assists the development of telecommunications in developing countries by providing technical assistance, management, investment financing and network installation. The ITU adopts international regulations and treaties to allocate the radio frequency spectrum and registers radio frequency assignments in order to avoid harmful interference between radio stations of different countries. It also governs and allocates the use of the geostationary-satellite orbit and collects and disseminates telecommunications information.

The ITU had 187 member states and 433 members (scientific and industrial companies, broadcasters, public and private operators, and international organizations) as at June 1997. The supreme authority is the Plenipotentiary Conference, composed of representatives of all the members, which meets once every four years. It elects the Administrative Council of 46 members which meets annually to supervise the Union and set the budget (1996–7, SFr 295 million). The Conference also elects the Secretary-General, who heads the General Secretariat. The ITU is structured into three sectors: the radiocommunication sector, including world and regional radiocommunication conferences, radiocommunication assemblies and the Radio Regulations Board; the telecommunication standardization sector; and the telecommunication development sector.

Secretary-General, Dr P. Tarjanne (Finland)

LEAGUE OF ARAB STATES
Maidane Al-Tahrir, Cairo, Egypt
Tel: 0171-629 0044; fax: 0171-493 7943

The purpose of the League of Arab States, founded in 1945, is to ensure co-operation among member states and protect their independence and sovereignty, to supervise the affairs and interests of Arab countries, to control the execution of agreements concluded among the member states, and to promote the process of integration among them. The League considers itself a regional organization and has observer status at the United Nations.

Member states are Algeria, Bahrain, Comoros, Djibouti, Egypt, Iraq, Jordan, Kuwait, Lebanon, Libya, Mauritania, Morocco, Oman, Palestine, Qatar, Saudi Arabia, Somalia, Sudan, Syria, Tunisia, UAE and Yemen.

Member states participate in various specialized agencies of the League whose role is to develop specific areas of co-operation between Arab states. These include: the Arab Organization for Mineral Resources; the Arab Monetary Fund; the Arab Satellite Communications Organization; the Arab Academy of Maritime Transport; the Arab Bank for Economic Development in Africa; the Arab League Educational, Cultural and Scientific Organization, and the Council of Arab Economic Unity.

Secretary-General, Dr Ahmed Esmat Abdel-Meguid (Egypt)
UK OFFICE, 52 Green Street, London W1Y 3RH. Tel: 0171-629 0044

NORDIC COUNCIL
Tyrgatan 7, Box 19506, Stockholm 10432, Sweden

The Nordic Council was established in March 1952 as an advisory body on economic and social co-operation, comprising parliamentary delegates from Denmark, Ice-

land, Norway and Sweden. It was subsequently joined by Finland (1955), and representatives from the Faröes (1970), the Åland Islands (1970), and Greenland (1984).

Co-operation is regulated by the Treaty of Helsinki signed in 1962. This was amended in 1971 to create the Nordic Council of Ministers, which discusses all matters except defence and foreign affairs. Matters are given preparatory consideration by a Committee of Co-operation Ministers' Deputies and joint committees of officials. Decisions of the Council of Ministers, which are taken by consensus, are binding, although if ratification by member parliaments is required, decisions only become effective following parliamentary approval. The Council of Ministers is advised by the Nordic Council, to which it reports annually. There are Ministers for Nordic Co-operation in every member government.

The Nordic Council, comprising 87 voting delegates nominated from member parliaments and about 80 non-voting government representatives, meets twice a year in plenary sessions. The full Council chooses an 11-member Praesidium, comprising two delegates from each sovereign member and one party group-nominated delegate, which conducts business between sessions. A Secretariat, located in Stockholm and headed by a Secretary-General, liaises with the Council of Ministers and provides administrative support, as well as acting as a publishing house and information centre. The Council of Ministers has a separate Secretariat, based in Copenhagen.

SECRETARIAT TO THE NORDIC COUNCIL, Tyrgatan 7, S-10432 Stockholm, Sweden. *Secretary-General*, Anders Wenström (Sweden)

SECRETARIAT OF NORDIC COUNCIL OF MINISTERS, Store Strandgade 18, 1255 Copenhagen K, Denmark. *Secretary-General*, Per Stenback (Finland)

NORTH ATLANTIC TREATY ORGANIZATION
Brussels 1110, Belgium
Tel: Brussels 728 4111; fax: Brussels 728 4579

The North Atlantic Treaty (Treaty of Washington) was signed in 1949 by Belgium, Canada, Denmark, France, Iceland, Italy, Luxembourg, the Netherlands, Norway, Portugal, the UK and the USA. Greece and Turkey acceded to the Treaty in 1952, the Federal Republic of Germany in 1955 (the reunited Germany acceded in October 1990), and Spain in 1982.

The North Atlantic Treaty Organization (NATO) is the structural framework for a defensive political and military alliance designed to provide common security for its members through co-operation and consultation in political, military and economic as well as scientific and other non-military fields.

STRUCTURE

The North Atlantic Council (NAC), chaired by the Secretary-General, is the highest authority of the Alliance and is composed of permanent representatives of the 16 member countries. It meets at ministerial level (foreign ministers) at least twice a year. The permanent representatives (ambassadors) head national delegations of advisers and experts. Defence matters are dealt with by the Defence Planning Committee (DPC), composed of representatives of all member countries. The DPC also meets at ministerial level (defence ministers) at least twice a year. Nuclear matters are dealt with in the Nuclear Planning Group (NPG), composed of representatives of all countries except for France (Iceland being an observer). The

NPG meets regularly at Permanent Representatives level and twice a year at ministerial level (defence ministers). The NATO Secretary-General chairs the Council, the DPC and the NPG.

The Council and DPC are forums for constant inter-governmental consultation and are the main decision-making bodies within the Alliance. They are assisted by an International Staff, divided into five divisions: political affairs; defence planning and policy; defence support; infrastructure, logistics and civil emergency planning; scientific and environmental affairs.

The senior military authority in NATO, under the Council and DPC, is the Military Committee composed of the Chief of Defence Staffs of each member country except Iceland, which has no military and may be represented by a civilian. The Military Committee, which is assisted by an integrated international military staff, also meets in permanent session with permanent military representatives and is responsible for making recommendations to the Council and DPC on measures considered necessary for the common defence of the NATO area and for supplying guidance on military matters to the major NATO commanders. The Chairman of the Military Committee, elected for a period of two to three years, represents the committee on the Council.

The strategic area covered by the North Atlantic Treaty is divided between two major NATO commands (MNCs), European and Atlantic; and three major subordinate commands (MSCs) within Allied Command Europe, South, Central and North-West. There is also a Regional Planning Group (Canada and the United States).

The major NATO commanders are responsible for the development of defence plans for their respective areas, for the determination of force requirements and for the deployment and exercise of the forces under their command. The major NATO commanders report to the Military Committee. From 1995 the reorganized NATO force structure consists of three components: the Allied Rapid Reaction Corps of four divisions, with air and sea components (the majority of which are British forces); the main defence force of four corps (one Danish-German, one Dutch-German, two US-German); and the augment-ation forces of reserves and territorials.

Post-Cold War Developments

In response to the new security environment arising from the demise of the Warsaw Pact and the end of the Cold War in 1990, NATO issued a Declaration of Peace and Co-operation in 1991, and published a new strategic concept which introduced organizational changes and force reductions of around 30 per cent.

The North Atlantic Co-operation Council (NACC) was established in 1991 to form closer security links with eastern European and former Soviet states. Its role was to facilitate closer official and informal ties on security and related issues between its 38 member states (Finland has observer status). In May 1997 NATO members agreed to replace the NACC with the Euro-Atlantic Partnership Council (EAPC) which, like the NACC, will focus on defence planning, defence industry conversion, defence management and force structuring, and the democratic concepts of civilian-military relations. The EAPC will provide the framework for consultations and co-operation under the Partnership for Peace (PFP) programme, a form of associate membership launched in 1994. NATO will consult with any PFP partner which perceives a direct threat to its territorial integrity, political independence or security. Most of the 27 PFP partners send liaison officers to NATO headquarters in Brussels and to the Partnership Co-ordination Cell in Mons, Belgium, and participate in joint military exercises co-ordinated by NATO. EAPC membership will be open to all former NACC members and PFP participants. It will meet monthly at ambassadorial level in Brussels and twice a year at foreign minister and defence minister level.

In 1994, NATO announced that it would consider admitting new members, and a summit in July 1997 considered applications (see Events of the Year). The most likely new members are Poland, the Czech Republic and Hungary. Russian opposition to this proposed expansion was tempered by the signing of a Founding Act on Mutual Relations, Co-operation and Security on 27 May 1997 which provided for the creation of a Permanent Joint Council. Russia will have ambassadorial representation at NATO, attend NATO meetings and have equal status in preparing for peacekeeping operations. It will have no right to veto NATO actions.

In June 1996 the NAC proposed the creation of combined joint task forces which would provide European NATO members with a framework for operations without US involvement, under the auspices of the WEU. The strengthened role for Europeans was also credited with prompting France to announce that it would re-establish a permanent military mission to NATO, which had been closed in 1966. A French representative attended a meeting of NATO defence ministers in June 1996.

From 1992 until the end of 1995, NATO provided support for UN peacekeeping efforts in the former Yugo-slavia. With the signing of the Bosnian peace agreement in December 1995, a NATO-led multinational Implementa-tion Force (IFOR) embarked on Operation Joint Endeav-our to implement the peace accord. IFOR was replaced by the Sustaining Force (SFOR) in December 1996.

Secretary-General and Chairman of the North Atlantic Council, of the DPC and of the NPG, Javier Solana (Spain)
UK Permanent Representative on the North Atlantic Council, Sir John Goulden, KCMG
Chairman of the Military Committee, Gen. Klaus Naumann (Germany)
Supreme Allied Commander, Europe, Gen. Wesley Clark (USA)
Supreme Allied Commander, Atlantic, Gen. John Sheehan (USA)

ORGANIZATION FOR ECONOMIC CO-OPERATION AND DEVELOPMENT

2 rue André-Pascal, 75116 Paris
Tel: Paris 4524 9820; fax: Paris 4524 1795

The Organization for Economic Co-operation and Devel-opment (OECD) was formed in 1961 to replace the Organization for European Economic Co-operation. It is the instrument for international co-operation among industrialized member countries on economic and social policies. Its objectives are to assist its member govern-ments in the formulation and co-ordination of policies designed to achieve high, sustained economic growth while maintaining financial stability, to contribute to world trade on a multilateral basis and to stimulate members' aid to developing countries.

The members are Australia, Austria, Belgium, Canada, the Czech Republic, Denmark, Finland, France, Germany, Greece, Hungary, Iceland, Republic of Ireland, Italy, Japan, Republic of Korea, Luxembourg, Mexico, the Netherlands, New Zealand, Norway, Poland, Portugal, Spain, Sweden, Switzerland, Turkey, the UK and the USA.

The Council is the supreme body of the organization. It is composed of one representative for each member country and meets at permanent representative level under the chairmanship of the Secretary-General, or at ministerial level (usually once a year) under the chairmanship of a minister elected annually. Decisions and recommendations are adopted by the unanimous agreement of all members. An executive committee comprising 14 members of the Council is chosen annually, although most of the OECD's work is undertaken in over 200 specialized committees and working parties. Five autonomous or semi-autonomous bodies are associated in varying degrees to the Organization: the Nuclear Energy Agency, the International Energy Agency, the Development Centre, the Centre for Educational Research and Innovation, and the European Conference of Ministers of Transport. These bodies, the committees and the Council are serviced by an international Secretariat headed by the Secretary-General.

Secretary-General, Donald J. Johnston (Canada)
UK Permanent Representative, HE Peter Vereker, 19 rue de Franqueville, Paris 75116

ORGANIZATION FOR SECURITY AND CO-OPERATION IN EUROPE
Kärntner Ring 5–7, A-1010 Vienna, Austria
Tel: Vienna 5143 6190; fax: Vienna 514 3696

The Organization for Security and Co-operation in Europe (OSCE) was launched in 1975 (as the Conference on Security and Co-operation in Europe (CSCE)) under the Helsinki Final Act. This established agreements between NATO members, Warsaw Pact members, and neutral and non-aligned European countries covering security in Europe; economic, scientific, technological and environmental co-operation; and humanitarian principles. Further conferences were held at Belgrade (1977–8), Madrid (1980–3) and Vienna (1986–9).

With the end of the Cold War, it was decided that the CSCE should be institutionalized to provide a new security framework for Europe. The Charter of Paris for a New Europe, signed on 21 November 1990, committed members to support multi-party democracy, free-market economics, the rule of law, and human rights. The signatories also agreed to regular meetings of heads of government, ministers and officials. The first institutionalized heads of state and government summit was held in Helsinki in December 1992, at which the Helsinki Document was adopted. This declared the CSCE to be a regional organization and defined the structures of the organization. The summit also appointed a High Commissioner on National Minorities. At its December 1994 summit the CSCE was renamed the Organization for Security and Co-operation in Europe.

Three structures have been established: the Ministerial Council of foreign ministers, the central decision-making and governing body, which meets at least once a year; the Senior Council, which prepares work for the Ministerial Council, carries out its decisions and is responsible for the overview, management and co-ordination of OSCE activities and meets at least three times a year; and the Permanent Council, which is responsible for the day-to-day operational tasks of the OSCE and is the regular body for political consultation, meeting weekly. The chairmanship of the Ministerial Council, Senior Council and Permanent Council rotates among participating states with the Senior Council meeting in Prague and the Permanent Council in Vienna.

The OSCE is also underpinned by four permanent institutions: a Secretariat (Vienna); a Forum for Security Co-operation (Vienna), which meets weekly to discuss arms control, disarmament and security-building measures; an Office for Democratic Institutions and Human Rights (Warsaw), which is charged with furthering human rights, democracy and the rule of law; and an office of the High Commissioner on National Minorities (The Hague), which identifies ethnic tensions that might endanger peace and promotes their resolution. There is also a documentation and conference centre in Prague, an OSCE Parliamentary Assembly with a secretariat based in Copenhagen, and a Court of Conciliation and Arbitration in Geneva.

In June 1991 the CSCE agreed upon new crisis prevention mechanisms to prevent or manage violent conflict between and within member countries. In an attempt to put these mechanisms into place, the OSCE has established monitoring missions in ten OSCE countries, has sent an assistance group to Chechenia, co-ordinates the international presence in Albania and is organizing a peacekeeping force in Nagorno-Karabakh. The OSCE supervised the general election in Bosnia-Hercegovina in 1996 and the municipal elections in September 1997. A Joint Consultative Group of the OSCE promotes the objectives and implementation of the Conventional Armed Forces in Europe (CFE) Treaty (1990) which limits conventional ground and air forces.

The OSCE has 55 participating states: Albania, Andorra, Armenia, Austria, Azerbaijan, Belarus, Belgium, Bosnia-Hercegovina, Bulgaria, Canada, Croatia, Cyprus, Czech Republic, Denmark, Estonia, Finland, France, Georgia, Germany, Greece, Hungary, Iceland, Ireland, Italy, Kazakhstan, Kyrgyzstan, Latvia, Liechtenstein, Lithuania, Luxembourg, Macedonia (Former Yugoslav Republic of), Malta, Moldova, Monaco, the Netherlands, Norway, Poland, Portugal, Romania, Russia, San Marino, Slovakia, Slovenia, Spain, Sweden, Switzerland, Tajikistan, Turkey, Turkmenistan, UK, Ukraine, USA, Uzbekistan, the Vatican and Yugoslavia (suspended from activities July 1992).

Chair of the OSCE: Denmark (1997); Poland (1998)
Secretary-General of the OSCE, Giancarlo Aragona (Italy)
Director of the Office for Democratic Institutions and Human Rights, Gérard Stoudmann (Switzerland)
OSCE High Commissioner on National Minorities, Max van der Stoel (Netherlands)

ORGANIZATION OF AFRICAN UNITY
PO Box 3243, Addis Ababa, Ethiopia
Tel: Addis Ababa 517700; fax: Addis Ababa 511299

The Organization of African Unity (OAU) was established in 1963 and has 53 members; Morocco suspended its participation in 1985 in protest at the Polisario-proclaimed Saharan Arab Democratic Republic (SADR), representing Western Sahara, being admitted as a member. The OAU aims to further African unity and solidarity, to co-ordinate political, economic, social and defence policies, and to eliminate colonialism in Africa.

The chief organs are the Assembly of heads of state or government, which is the supreme organ of the OAU and meets once a year to consider matters of common African concern and to co-ordinate the Organization's policies; the Council of foreign ministers, which is the Organization's executive body responsible for the implementation of the Assembly's policies, and which meets twice a year; and the Commission of Mediation, Conciliation and Arbitration which promotes the peaceful settlement of disputes between member countries. The main administrative body is the General Secretariat, based in Addis Ababa, headed by a Secretary-General who is elected by the Assembly for a four-year term.

The Council set a biennial budget of US$61.45 million in 1996; US$30.6 million was allocated for 1996–7 and US$30.85 million for 1997–8. Substantial budgetary arrears due to delays in the payment of national contributions has meant that the OAU continually faces difficulties in furthering its aims. Most OAU programmes were suspended in November 1994 after unpaid contributions reached US$77 million although arrears had dropped to US$38.3 million by June 1995. In June 1991 the Assembly adopted an African Economic Community Treaty which envisages establishment of the Economic Community after ratification by two-thirds of the OAU's membership. In June 1993 a mechanism was created for conflict prevention, management and resolution, and a peace fund was established.

Secretary-General, Salim Ahmed Salim (Tanzania)

ORGANIZATION OF AMERICAN STATES
17th Street and Constitution Avenue NW, Washington DC 20006, USA
Tel: Washington DC 458 3000

Originally founded in 1890 for largely commercial purposes, the Organization of American States (OAS) adopted its present name and charter in 1948. The charter entered into force in 1951 and was amended in 1967, 1985 and 1996; the 1992 Protocol of Washington will enter into force upon ratification by two-thirds of member states.

The OAS aims to strengthen the peace and security of the continent; to promote and consolidate representative democracy with due respect for the principle of non-intervention; to prevent possible causes of difficulties and to ensure the peaceful resolution of disputes arising among its member states; to provide for common action on the part of those states in the event of aggression; to seek the resolution of political, judicial and economic problems that may arise among them; to promote, by co-operative action, their economic, social and cultural development; and to achieve an effective limitation of conventional weapons so that resources can be devoted to economic and social development.

Policy is determined by the annual General Assembly, which is the supreme authority and elects the Secretary-General for a five-year term. The Meeting of Consultation of ministers of foreign affairs considers urgent problems on an *ad hoc* basis. The Permanent Council, comprising one representative from each member state, promotes friendly inter-state relations, acts as an intermediary in case of disputes arising between states and oversees the General Secretariat, the main administrative body. The Inter-American Council for Integral Development was created in January 1996 by the ratification of the Protocol of Managua to promote sustainable development.

The 35 member states are Antigua and Barbuda, Argentina, Bahamas, Barbados, Belize, Bolivia, Brazil, Canada, Chile, Colombia, Costa Rica, Cuba, Dominica, Dominican Republic, Ecuador, Grenada, Guatemala, Guyana, Haiti, Honduras, Jamaica, Mexico, Nicaragua, Panama, Paraguay, Peru, St Christopher and Nevis, St Lucia, St Vincent and the Grenadines, El Salvador, Suriname, Trinidad and Tobago, Uruguay, USA and Venezuela. The European Union and 39 non-American states have permanent observer status.

Secretary-General, Dr César Gaviria Trujillo (Colombia)

ORGANIZATION OF ARAB PETROLEUM EXPORTING COUNTRIES
PO Box 20501, Safat 13066, Kuwait
Tel: Kuwait 484 4500; fax: Kuwait 481 5747

The Organization of Arab Petroleum and Exporting Countries (OAPEC) was founded in 1968. Its objectives are to promote co-operation in economic activities, to safeguard members' interests, to unite efforts to ensure the flow of oil to consumer markets, and to create a favourable climate for the investment of capital and expertise.

The Ministerial Council is composed of oil ministers from the member countries and meets twice a year to determine policy, to direct activities and to approve the budgets and accounts of the General Secretariat and the Judicial Tribunal. The Judicial Tribunal is composed of seven part-time judges who rule on disputes between member countries and disputes between countries and oil companies. The executive organ of OAPEC is the General Secretariat.

The members are Algeria, Bahrain, Egypt, Iraq, Kuwait, Libya, Qatar, Saudi Arabia, Syria and the United Arab Emirates. Tunisia's membership has been inactive since 1987.

Secretary-General, Abdel-Aziz A. Al-Turki

ORGANIZATION OF THE ISLAMIC CONFERENCE
PO Box 178, Jeddah 21411, Saudi Arabia

The Organization of the Islamic Conference (OIC) was established in 1971 with the purpose of generating solidarity and co-operation between Islamic countries. It also has the specific aims of co-ordinating efforts to safeguard the Muslim holy places, supporting the formation of a Palestinian state, assisting member states to maintain their independence, co-ordinating the views of member states in international forums such as the UN, and improving co-operation in the economic, cultural and scientific fields.

The OIC has three central organs, supreme among them the Conference of the Heads of State which meets once every three years to discuss issues of importance to Islamic states. The Conference of Foreign Ministers meets annually to prepare reports for the Conference of Heads of State. The General Secretariat carries out administrative tasks. It is headed by a Secretary-General who is elected by the Conference of Foreign Ministers for a non renewable four-year term.

In addition to this structure, the OIC has several subsidiary bodies and specialized bodies. These include the Islamic Solidarity Fund, to aid Islamic institutions in member countries, and the Islamic Development Bank, to finance development projects in poorer member states. An Islamic Court of Justice is planned. The OIC runs various offices to organize the economic boycott of Israel.

The achievement of the OIC's aims has often been prevented by political rivalry and conflicts between member states, such as the Iran-Iraq war and the Iraqi invasion of Kuwait. Egypt's membership was suspended from 1979 to 1984 because of its peace treaty with Israel. Saudi Arabia, the main source of funding, exercises great influence within the OIC. Since 1991 the OIC has become more united and has spoken out against violence against Muslims in India, the Occupied Territories and Bosnia-Hercegovina. From 1993 to 1995 the OIC co-ordinated the offering of troops to the UN by Muslim states to protect Muslim areas of Bosnia-Hercegovina.

The Organization has 54 members (53 sovereign Muslim states in Africa, the Middle East, central and south-east Asia and Europe, plus the Palestine Liberation Organization) and three observers, the Central African Republic, Togo and Turkish Northern Cyprus. It has an annual budget of £5 million.

Secretary-General, Azzedine Laraki (Morocco)

ORGANIZATION OF THE PETROLEUM EXPORTING COUNTRIES
Obere Donaustrasse 93, 1020 Vienna, Austria
Tel: Vienna 21112

The Organization of the Petroleum Exporting Countries (OPEC) was created in 1960 as a permanent intergovernmental organization with the principal aims of unifying and co-ordinating the petroleum policies of its members, determining ways of protecting their interests individually and collectively, and ensuring the stabilization of prices in international oil markets with a view to eliminating unnecessary fluctuations. Since 1982 OPEC has attempted (only partially successfully) to impose overall production limits and production quotas in an attempt to maintain stable oil prices. In the first quarter of 1996 the overall production quota was 24,520,000 barrels per day.

The supreme authority is the Conference of Ministers of oil, mines and energy of member countries, which meets at least twice a year to formulate policy. The Board of Governors, nominated by member countries, directs the management of OPEC and implements conference resolutions. The Secretariat carries out executive functions under the direction of the Board of Governors.

The member states are Algeria, Indonesia, Iran, Iraq, Kuwait, Libya, Nigeria, Qatar, Saudi Arabia, UAE and Venezuela. Ecuador withdrew in 1992 and Gabon in 1995.

Secretary-General, HE Dr Rilwanu Lukman (Nigeria)

SOUTH PACIFIC COMMISSION
BP D5, Nouméa Cedex, New Caledonia
Tel: Nouméa Cedex 262000; fax: Nouméa Cedex 263818

The South Pacific Commission is a technical assistance agency with programmes in agriculture and plant protection, fisheries and marine resources, community health, socio-economic and statistical services, and community education services.

The South Pacific Commission (SPC) was established in 1947 by Australia, France, the Netherlands, New Zealand, the UK and the USA with the aim of promoting the economic and social stability of the islands in the region. The SPC now numbers 26 member states and territories: the four remaining founder states (the Netherlands and the UK have withdrawn), in which no programmes are run, and the other 22 states and territories of Melanesia, Micronesia and Polynesia.

The governing body is the South Pacific Conference, which meets every two years. The Director-General is the chief executive.

Director-General, Bob Dun (Australia)
Deputy Directors-General, Jimmie Rodgers (Solomon Islands); Lourdes Pangelinan (Guam)

THE UNITED NATIONS
UN Plaza, New York, NY 10017, USA

The United Nations (UN) is an intergovernmental organization of member states, dedicated through signature of the UN Charter to the maintenance of international peace and security and the solution of economic, social and political problems through international co-operation.

The UN was founded as a successor to the League of Nations and inherited many of its procedures and institutions. The name 'United Nations' was first used in the Washington Declaration 1942 to describe the 26 states which had allied to fight the Axis powers. The UN Charter developed from discussions at the Moscow Conference of the foreign ministers of China, the UK, the USA and the Soviet Union in 1943. Further progress was made at Dumbarton Oaks, Washington, in 1944 during talks involving the same states. The role of the Security Council was formulated at the Yalta Conference in 1945. The Charter was formally drawn up by 50 allied nations at the San Francisco Conference between April and 26 June 1945, when it was signed. Following ratification the UN came into effect on 24 October 1945, which is celebrated annually as United Nations Day. The UN flag is light blue with the UN emblem centred in white.

The principal organs of the UN are the General Assembly, the Security Council, the Economic and Social Council, the Trusteeship Council, the Secretariat and the International Court of Justice. The Economic and Social Council and the Trusteeship Council are auxiliaries, charged with assisting and advising the General Assembly and Security Council. The official languages used are Arabic, Chinese, English, French, Russian and Spanish. Deliberations at the International Court of Justice are in English and French only.

MEMBERSHIP

Membership is open to all countries which accept the Charter and its principle of peaceful co-existence. New members are admitted by the General Assembly on the recommendation of the Security Council. The original membership of 51 states has grown to 185:

Afghanistan	Bulgaria
Albania	Burkina
Algeria	Burundi
Andorra	Cambodia
Angola	Cameroon
Antigua and Barbuda	*Canada
*Argentina	Cape Verde
Armenia	Central African Rep.
*Australia	Chad
Austria	*Chile
Azerbaijan	*China
The Bahamas	*Colombia
Bahrain	Comoros
Bangladesh	Congo, Democratic Rep.
Barbados	Congo, Rep. of
*Belarus	*Costa Rica
*Belgium	Côte d'Ivoire
Belize	Croatia
Benin	*Cuba
Bhutan	Cyprus
*Bolivia	*Czech Republic
Bosnia-Hercegovina	*Denmark
Botswana	Djibouti
*Brazil	Dominica
Brunei	*Dominican Republic

*Ecuador
*Egypt
Equatorial Guinea
Eritrea
Estonia
*Ethiopia
Federated States of
   Micronesia
Fiji
Finland
*France
Gabon
Gambia
Georgia
Germany
Ghana
*Greece
Grenada
*Guatemala
Guinea
Guinea-Bissau
Guyana
*Haiti
*Honduras
Hungary
Iceland
*India
Indonesia
*Iran
*Iraq
Ireland, Republic of
Israel
Italy
Jamaica
Japan
Jordan
Kazakhstan
Kenya
Korea, D. P. Rep. (North)
Korea, Rep. of (South)
Kuwait
Kyrgyzstan
Laos
Latvia
*Lebanon
Lesotho
*Liberia
Libya
Liechtenstein
Lithuania
*Luxembourg
Macedonia (The Former
   Yugoslav Republic of)
Madagascar
Malawi
Malaysia
Maldives
Mali
Malta
Marshall Islands
Mauritania
Mauritius
*Mexico
Moldova
Monaco
Mongolia
Morocco
Mozambique
Myanmar (Burma)
Namibia

Nepal
*Netherlands
*New Zealand
*Nicaragua
Niger
Nigeria
*Norway
Oman
Pakistan
Palau
*Panama
Papua New Guinea
*Paraguay
*Peru
*Philippines
*Poland
Portugal
Qatar
Romania
*Russian Federation
Rwanda
St Christopher and Nevis
St Lucia
St Vincent and the
   Grenadines
*El Salvador
Samoa
San Marino
São Tomé and Príncipe
*Saudi Arabia
Senegal
Seychelles
Sierra Leone
Singapore
*Slovakia
Slovenia
Solomon Islands
Somalia
*South Africa
Spain
Sri Lanka
Sudan
Suriname
Swaziland
Sweden
*Syria
Tajikistan
Tanzania
Thailand
Togo
Trinidad and Tobago
Tunisia
*Turkey
Turkmenistan
Uganda
*Ukraine
United Arab Emirates
*United Kingdom
*United States of America
*Uruguay
Uzbekistan
Vanuatu
*Venezuela
Vietnam
Yemen
*Yugoslavia (suspended)
Zambia
Zimbabwe

*Original member (i.e. from 1945). From 25 October 1971 'China' was taken to mean the People's Republic of China. Czechoslovakia was an original member in 1945 and a member until 31 December 1992; the successor states of the Czech Republic and Slovakia were admitted as members in January 1993.

The Russian Federation took over the membership of the Soviet Union in the Security Council and all other UN organs on 24 December 1991. Belarus (formerly Belorussia) and the Ukraine on becoming independent sovereign states continued their existing memberships of the UN, both having been granted separate UN membership in 1945 as a concession to the Soviet Union.

OBSERVERS

Permanent observer status is held by the Holy See and Switzerland. The Palestine Liberation Organization has special observer status.

NON-MEMBERS

A number of countries are not members, usually due to their small size and limited financial resources. Notable exceptions include Switzerland, which follows a policy of absolute neutrality, and Taiwan, which was replaced by the People's Republic of China in 1971. The others are Kiribati, Nauru, Tonga, Tuvalu and the Holy See.

THE GENERAL ASSEMBLY
UN Plaza, New York, NY 10017, USA

The General Assembly is the main deliberative organ of the UN. It consists of all members, each entitled to five representatives but having only one vote. The annual session begins on the third Tuesday of September, when the President is elected, and usually continues until mid-December. Special sessions are held on specific issues and emergency special sessions can be called within 24 hours.

The Assembly is empowered to discuss any matter within the scope of the Charter, except when it is under consideration by the Security Council, and to make recommendations. Under the 'uniting for peace' resolution, adopted in 1950, the Assembly may also take action to maintain international peace and security when the Security Council fails to do so because of a lack of unanimity of its permanent members. Important decisions, such as those on peace and security, the election of officers, the budget, etc., need a two-thirds majority. Others need a simple majority. The Assembly has effective power only over the internal operations of the UN itself; external recommendations are not legally binding.

The work of the General Assembly is divided among six main committees, on each of which every member has the right to be represented: disarmament and international security; economic and financial; social, humanitarian and cultural; special political issues and decolonization (including non-self governing territories); administrative and budgetary; and legal. In addition, the General Assembly appoints *ad hoc* committees to consider special issues, such as human rights, peacekeeping, disarmament and international law. All committees consider items referred to them by the Assembly and recommend draft resolutions to its plenary meeting.

The Assembly is assisted by a number of functional committees. The General Committee co-ordinates its proceedings and operations, while the Credentials Committee verifies the credentials of representatives. There are also two standing committees, the Advisory Committee on Administration and Budgetary Questions and the Committee on Contributions, which suggests the scale of members' payments to the UN.

President of the General Assembly (1996), Ismail Razali (Malaysia)

The Assembly has created a large number of specialized bodies over the years, which are supervised jointly with the Economic and Social Council. They are supported by UN and voluntary contributions from governments, non-governmental organizations and individuals. These organizations include:

THE CONFERENCE ON DISARMAMENT (CD)
Palais des Nations, 1211 Geneva 10, Switzerland
Established by the UN as the Committee on Disarmament in 1962, the CD is the single multilateral disarmament negotiating forum. The present title of the organization was adopted in 1984. There were 40 members as at June 1994.

A Chemical Weapons Convention was agreed in Paris in 1993 and came into force in April 1997 after being ratified by 87 countries. It bans the use, production, stockpiling and transfer of all chemical weapons. All US and Russian weapons must be destroyed within 15 years of the Convention entering into force and all other states' weapons must be destroyed within ten years.
Secretary-General, Vladimir Petrovsky (Russia)
UK Representative, I. Soutar, 37–39 rue de Vermont, 1211 Geneva 20, Switzerland

THE UNITED NATIONS CHILDREN'S FUND (UNICEF)
3 UN Plaza, New York, NY 10017, USA
Established in 1947 to assist children and mothers in the immediate post-war period, UNICEF now concentrates on developing countries. It provides primary health-care and health education. In particular, it conducts programmes in oral hydration, immunization against leading diseases, child growth monitoring, and the encouragement of breast-feeding. Its operations are often conducted in co-operation with the World Health Organization (WHO).
Executive Director, Carol Bellamy (USA)

THE UNITED NATIONS DEVELOPMENT PROGRAMME (UNDP)
1 UN Plaza, New York, NY 10017, USA
Established in 1966 from the merger of the UN Expanded Programme of Technical Assistance and the UN Special Fund, UNDP is the central funding agency for economic and social development projects around the world. Much of its annual expenditure is channelled through UN specialized agencies, governments and non-governmental organizations.
Administrator, James G. Speth (USA)

THE UNITED NATIONS HIGH COMMISSIONER FOR REFUGEES (UNHCR)
Centre William Rappard, 154 rue de Lausanne, PO Box 2500, 1211 Geneva 2, Switzerland
Established in 1951 to protect the rights and interests of refugees, it organizes emergency relief and longer-term solutions, such as voluntary repatriation, local integration or resettlement.
High Commissioner, Sadako Ogata (Japan)
UK OFFICE, 76 Westminster Palace Gardens, London
SWIP IRL. Tel: 0171-222 3065

THE UN RELIEF AND WORKS AGENCY FOR PALESTINE REFUGEES IN THE NEAR EAST (UNRWA)
Vienna International Centre, Wagramerstrasse 5, PO Box 100, 1400 Vienna, Austria
Established in 1949 to bring relief to the Palestinians displaced by the Arab-Israeli conflict.
Commissioner-General, Ilter Turkman (Turkey)

THE UNITED NATIONS HIGH COMMISSIONER FOR HUMAN RIGHTS
Established in 1993 to secure respect for, and prevent violations of human rights by engaging in dialogue with governments and international organizations. Responsible for the co-ordination of all UN human rights activities.
High Commissioner, Mary Robinson (Ireland)

Other bodies include:
THE UN CENTRE FOR HUMAN SETTLEMENTS (Habitat), PO Box 30030, Nairobi, Kenya
THE UN CONFERENCE ON TRADE AND DEVELOPMENT (UNCTAD), Palais des Nations, 1211 Geneva 10, Switzerland
THE DEPARTMENT OF HUMANITARIAN AFFAIRS (DHA), Palais des Nations, 1211 Geneva 10, Switzerland
THE INTERNATIONAL SEABED AUTHORITY, Kingston, Jamaica
THE UN ENVIRONMENT PROGRAMME (UNEP), PO Box 30552, Nairobi, Kenya
THE UN POPULATION FUND (UNFPA), 220 East 42nd Street, New York, NY 10017, USA
THE UN INSTITUTE FOR THE ADVANCEMENT OF WOMEN (INSTRAW), PO Box 21747, Santo Domingo, Dominican Republic
THE UN UNIVERSITY (UNU), Toho Seimei Building, 15–1, Shibuya, 2-Chome, Shibuya-ku, Tokyo 150, Japan
THE WORLD FOOD COUNCIL (WFC), Via delle Terme di Caracalla, 00100 Rome, Italy
THE WORLD FOOD PROGRAMME (WFP), Via delle Terme di Caracalla, 00100 Rome, Italy

BUDGET OF THE UNITED NATIONS
The budget adopted for the biennium 1996–7 was US$2,510 million. The scale of assessment contributions of 88 UN members is set at the minimum 0.01 per cent. The ten largest assessments are: USA, 25 per cent; Japan, 12.45; Germany, 8.93; Russia, 6.91; France, 6.00; UK, 5.02; Italy, 4.29; Canada, 3.11; Spain, 1.98; Australia, 1.51.

THE SECURITY COUNCIL
UN Plaza, New York, NY 10017, USA

The Security Council is the senior arm of the UN and has the primary responsibility for maintaining world peace and security. It consists of 15 members, each with one representative and one vote. There are five permanent members, China, France, Russia, the UK and the USA, and ten non-permanent members. Each of the non-permanent members is elected for a two-year term by a two-thirds majority of the General Assembly and is ineligible for immediate re-election. Five of the elective seats are allocated to Africa and Asia, one to eastern Europe, two to Latin America and two to western Europe and remaining countries. Procedural questions are determined by a simple majority vote. Other matters require a majority inclusive of the votes of the permanent members; they thus have a right of veto. The abstention of a permanent member does not constitute a veto. The presidency rotates each month by state in (English) alphabetical order. Parties to a dispute, other non-members and individuals can be invited to participate in Security Council debates but are not permitted to vote. In 1997 the ten non-permanent members were: Chile, Egypt, Guinea-Bissau, Poland, Republic of Korea (*term expires 31 December 1997*), Costa Rica, Japan, Kenya, Portugal, Sweden (*term expires 31 December 1998*).

The Security Council is empowered to settle or adjudicate in disputes or situations which threaten international peace and security. It can adopt political, economic and military measures to achieve this end. Any matter considered to be a threat to or breach of the peace or an act of aggression can be brought to the Security Council's attention by any member state or by the Secretary-General. The Charter envisaged members placing at the disposal of the Security Council armed forces and other facilities which would be co-ordinated by the Military Staff Committee, composed of military representatives of the five permanent members. The Security Council is also supported by a Committee of Experts, to advise on procedural and technical matters, and a Committee on Admission of New Members.

Owing to superpower disunity, the Security Council rarely played the decisive role set out in the Charter; the Military Staff Committee was effectively suspended from 1948 until 1990, when a meeting was convened during the Gulf Crisis on the formation and control of UN-supervised armed forces. However, at an extraordinary meeting of the Security Council in January 1992, heads of government laid plans to transform the UN in light of the changed post-Cold War world. The Secretary-General was asked to draw up a report on enhancing the UN's preventive diplomacy, peacemaking and peacekeeping ability. The report, *An Agenda for Peace*, was produced in June 1992 and centred on the establishment of a UN army composed of national contingents on permanent standby, as envisaged at the time of the UN's formation.

PEACEKEEPING FORCES

The Security Council has established a number of peace-keeping forces since its foundation, comprising contingents provided mainly by neutral and non-aligned UN members. Current forces include: the UN Truce Supervision Organization (UNTSO), Israel, 1948; the UN Military Observer Group in India and Pakistan (UNMO-GIP), 1949; the UN Peacekeeping Force in Cyprus (UNFICYP), 1964; the UN Disengagement Observer Force (UNDOF), Golan Heights, Syria, 1974; the UN Interim Force in Lebanon (UNIFIL), 1978; the UN Iraq-Kuwait Observation Mission (UNIKOM), 1991; the UN Mission for the Referendum in Western Sahara (MINUR-SO), 1991; the UN Observer Mission in Georgia (UN-OMIG), 1993; the UN Observer Mission in Liberia (UNOMIL), 1993; the UN Observer Mission in Guatemala (MINUGA), 1994; the UN Observer Mission in Tajikistan (UNMOT), 1994; the UN Preventive Deployment Force (UNPREDEP), Former Yugoslav Republic of Macedonia, 1995; the UN Angola Verification Mission III (UNAVEM III), 1995; the UN Mission in Bosnia-Hercegovina (UNMIBH), 1995; the UN Transitional Administration for Eastern Slavonia (UNTAES), 1996; the UN Mission of Observers in Prevlaka (UNMOP), 1996.

THE ECONOMIC AND SOCIAL COUNCIL
UN Plaza, New York, NY 10017, USA

The Economic and Social Council is responsible under the General Assembly for the economic and social work of the UN and for the co-ordination of the activities of the 15 specialized agencies and other UN bodies. It makes reports and recommendations on economic, social, cultural, educational, health and related matters, often in consultation with non-governmental organizations, passing the reports to the General Assembly and other UN bodies. It also drafts conventions for submission to the Assembly and calls conferences on matters within its remit.

The Council consists of 54 members, 18 of whom are elected annually by the General Assembly for a three-year term. Each has one vote and can be immediately re-elected on retirement. A President is elected annually and is also eligible for re-election. One substantive session is held annually and decisions are reached by simple majority vote of those present.

The Council has established a number of standing committees on particular issues and several commissions. Commissions include: Statistical, Human Rights, Social Development, Sustainable Development, Status of Women, Crime Prevention and Criminal Justice, Narcotic Drugs, Science and Technology for Development, and Population; and Regional Economic Commissions for Europe, Asia and the Pacific, Western Asia, Latin America and Africa.

THE TRUSTEESHIP COUNCIL
UN Plaza, New York, NY 10017, USA

The Trusteeship Council supervised the administration of territories within the UN Trusteeship system inherited from the League of Nations. It consists of the five permanent members of the Security Council. With the independence of the Republic of Palau in October 1994, all eleven trusteeships have now progressed to independence or merged with neighbouring states and the Trusteeship Council suspended its operations on 1 November 1994.

THE SECRETARIAT
UN Plaza, New York, NY 10017, USA

The Secretariat services the other UN organs and is headed by a Secretary-General elected by a majority vote of the General Assembly on the recommendation of the Security Council. He is assisted by an international staff, chosen to represent the international character of the organization. The Secretary-General is charged with bringing to the attention of the Security Council any matter which he considers poses a threat to international peace and security. He may also bring other matters to the attention of the General Assembly and other UN bodies and may be entrusted by them with additional duties. As chief administrator to the UN, the Secretary-General is present in person or via representatives at all meetings of the other five main organs of the UN. He may also act as an impartial mediator in disputes between member states.

The power and influence of the Secretary-General has been determined largely by the character of the office-holder and by the state of relations between the superpowers. The thaw in these relations since the mid-1980s has increased the effectiveness of the UN, particularly in its attempts to intervene in international disputes. It helped to end the Iran-Iraq war and sponsored peace in Central America. Following Iraq's invasion of Kuwait in 1990 the UN took its first collective security action since the Korean War. UN action to protect the Kurds in northern Iraq has widened its legal authority by breaching the prohibition on its intervention in the essentially domestic affairs of states. Currently the UN is involved in peacekeeping, aid distribution and negotiations in the former Yugoslavia; and is addressing the global problems of Aids and environmental destruction.

Secretary-General, Kofi Annan, apptd 1996 (Ghana)

UNDER-SECRETARIES-GENERAL

Administration and Management, Joseph Connor (USA)
Chef de Cabinet, Iqbqal Riza (Pakistan)
Development Support and Management Services, Jin Yongjian (China)
Humanitarian Affairs, Yasushi Akashi (Japan)
Legal Affairs and UN Legal Counsel, Hans Corell (Sweden)
Peacekeeping Operations, Bernard Miyet (France)

Policy Co-ordination and Sustainable Development, Nitin Desai (India)
Political Affairs, Sir Kieran Prendergast (UK)

FORMER SECRETARIES-GENERAL
1946–53	Trygve Lie (Norway)
1953–61	Dag Hammarskjöld (Sweden)
1961–71	U Thant (Burma)
1971–81	Kurt Waldheim (Austria)
1981–91	Javier Pérez de Cuéllar (Peru)
1991–6	Boutros Boutros-Ghali (Egypt)

INTERNATIONAL COURT OF JUSTICE
The Peace Palace, 2517 KJ The Hague, The Netherlands

The International Court of Justice is the principal judicial organ of the UN. The Statute of the Court is an integral part of the Charter and all members of the UN are *ipso facto* parties to it. The Court is composed of 15 judges, elected by both the General Assembly and the Security Council for nine-year terms which are renewable. Judges may deliberate over cases in which their country is involved. If no judge on the bench is from a country which is a party to a dispute under consideration, that party may designate a judge to participate *ad hoc* in that particular deliberation. If any party to a case fails to adhere to the judgment of the Court, the other party may have recourse to the Security Council.
President, Mohammed Bedjaoui (Algeria) (2006)
Vice-President, Stephen M. Schwebel (USA) (2006)
Judges, Carl-August Fleischhauer (Germany) (2003); Gilbert Guillaume (France) (2000); Geza Herczegh (Hungary) (2003); Rosalyn Higgins (UK) (2000); Shi Jiuyong (China) (2003); Pieter H. Kooijmans (Netherlands) (2006); Abdul G. Koroma (Sierra Leone) (2003); Shigeru Oda (Japan) (2003); Gonzalo Parra-Aranguren (Venezuela) (2000); Raymond Ranjeva (Madagascar) (2000); José Francisco Rezek (Brazil) (2006); Christopher G. Weeramantry (Sri Lanka) (2000); Vladlen S. Vereshchetin (Russia) (2006)

INTERNATIONAL WAR CRIMES TRIBUNAL FOR THE FORMER YUGOSLAVIA
Churchill Plein 1, PO Box 13888, 2501 EW The Hague, The Netherlands

In February 1993, the Security Council voted to establish a war crimes tribunal for the former Yugoslavia to hear cases covering grave breaches of the Geneva Conventions and crimes against humanity. The Court was inaugurated in November 1993 in The Hague with 11 judges elected by the UN General Assembly from 11 states, divided into two trial chambers of three judges each and an appeal chamber of five judges. The court is unable to force suspects to stand trial but is empowered to pass verdicts in the absence of suspects and can put suspects under an 'act of accusation' which prevents them from leaving their own country.
    In October 1995, the tribunal formally charged the Bosnian Serb leaders Radovan Karadzic and Gen. Ratko Mladic, and the Croatian Serb President Milan Martic and 21 others with genocide and crimes against humanity. As at January 1997 only one of the 75 suspected war criminals to be indicted has been imprisoned.
President, Antonio Cassese (Italy)
Chief Prosecutor, Louise Arbour (Canada)

INTERNATIONAL CRIMINAL TRIBUNAL FOR RWANDA
In November 1994, the UN Security Council voted to establish a tribunal to try those responsible for genocide and other violations of international humanitarian law in Rwanda between 1 January and 31 December 1994. The

tribunal, based in Arusha, Tanzania, is empowered to try the most senior people responsible for the massacre. It formally opened in November 1995 to consider 463 indictments.
Chief Prosecutor, Louise Arbour (Canada)

SPECIALIZED AGENCIES

Fifteen independent international organizations, each with its own membership, budget and headquarters, carry out their responsibilities in co-ordination with the UN under agreements made with the Economic and Social Council. An entry for each appears elsewhere in the International Organizations section. They are: the Food and Agriculture Organization of the UN; International Civil Aviation Organization; International Fund for Agricultural Development; International Labour Organization; International Maritime Organization; the International Monetary Fund; International Telecommunications Union; UN Educational, Scientific and Cultural Organization; UN Industrial Development Organization; Universal Postal Union; World Bank (International Bank for Reconstruction and Development, International Development Agency, International Finance Corporation); World Health Organization; World Intellectual Property Organization; and World Meteorological Organization. The International Atomic Energy Agency and the World Trade Organization are linked to the UN but are not specialized agencies.

UK MISSION TO THE UNITED NATIONS
One Dag Hammarskjöld Plaza, 885 Second Avenue, New York, NY 10017, USA
Permanent Representative to the United Nations and Representative on the Security Council, Sir John Weston, KCMG, *apptd* 1995
Deputy Permanent Representative, S. J. Gomersall, CMG

UK MISSION TO THE OFFICE OF THE UN AND OTHER INTERNATIONAL ORGANIZATIONS IN GENEVA
37–39 rue de Vermont, 1211 Geneva 20, Switzerland
Permanent UK Representative, R. M. J. Lyne, CMG, *apptd* 1997
Deputy Permanent Representatives, Sir John Ramsden, Bt. (*Head of Chancery*); P. R. Jenkins (*Economic Affairs*)

UK MISSION TO THE INTERNATIONAL ATOMIC ENERGY AGENCY, THE UN INDUSTRIAL DEVELOPMENT ORGANIZATION AND THE UN OFFICE AT VIENNA
Jaurèsgasse 12, 1030 Vienna, Austria
Permanent UK Representative, Dr J. Freeman, *apptd* 1997
Deputy Permanent Representative, G. D. Cole

UN OFFICE AND INFORMATION CENTRE
Millbank Tower, 21–24 Millbank, London, SW1P 4QH
Tel: 0171-630 1981

UNITED NATIONS EDUCATIONAL, SCIENTIFIC AND CULTURAL ORGANIZATION
7 place de Fontenoy, 75352 Paris 07SP, France

The United Nations Educational, Scientific and Cultural Organization (UNESCO) was established in 1946. It promotes collaboration among its member states in education, science, culture and communication. It aims to further a universal respect for human rights, justice and the rule of law, without distinction of race, sex, language or religion, in accordance with the UN Charter.
    UNESCO runs a number of programmes to improve education and extend access to it. It provides assistance to ensure the free flow of information and its wider and better

balanced dissemination without any obstacle to freedom of expression, and to maintain cultural heritage in the face of development. It fosters research and study in all areas of the social and environmental sciences.

UNESCO had 186 member states as at July 1997. There are three associate members. The General Conference, consisting of representatives of all the members, meets biennially to decide the programme and the budget (1994–5, US$455,490,000). It elects the 51-member Executive Board, which supervises operations, and appoints a Director-General who heads a Secretariat responsible for carrying out the organization's programmes. In most member states national commissions liaise with UNESCO to execute its programme.

The UK withdrew from UNESCO in 1985 and was granted observer status in 1986. It rejoined on 1 July 1997.
Director-General, Federico Mayor Zaragoza (Spain)

UNITED NATIONS INDUSTRIAL DEVELOPMENT ORGANIZATION
Vienna International Centre, Wagramerstrasse 5, PO Box 300, A-1400 Vienna, Austria
Tel: Vienna 211310; fax: Vienna 232156

The United Nations Industrial Development Organization (UNIDO) was established in 1966 by the UN General Assembly to act as the central co-ordinating body for industrial activities within the UN. It became a UN specialized agency in 1985 with the aim of promoting the industrialization of developing countries, with special emphasis upon the manufacturing sector. To this end it provides technical assistance and advice, provides investment promotion and helps with planning. UNIDO assists both public and private sectors and has made its services available to former centrally planned economies in transition to a market economy.

UNIDO had 168 members as at June 1997. It is funded by the UN, member states and non-governmental organizations. A General Conference of all the members meets biennially to discuss strategy and policy, approve the budget (1996–7, US$181 million) and elect the Director General. The Industrial Development Board is composed of members from 53 member states and reviews implementation of the regular work programme and the budget, which is prepared by the Programme and Budget Committee.
Director-General, Mauricio de Maria y Campos (Mexico)
Permanent UK Representative, Dr John Freeman, British Embassy, Vienna

UNIVERSAL POSTAL UNION
Weltpoststrasse 4, 3000 Berne 15, Switzerland
Tel: Berne 350 3111

The Universal Postal Union (UPU) was established by the Treaty of Berne 1874, taking effect from 1875, and became a UN specialized agency in 1948. The UPU is an intergovernmental organization which exists to form and regulate a single postal territory of all member countries for the reciprocal exchange of correspondence without discrimination. It also assists and advises on the improvement of postal services.

The UPU had 189 members as at May 1997. A Universal Postal Congress of all its members is the UPU's supreme authority and meets every five years to review the Treaty. A Council of Administration composed of 41 members was

established by the 1994 Congress. It meets annually to ensure continuity between congresses, study regulatory developments and broad policies, approve the budget and examine proposed Treaty changes. A Postal Operations Council also meets annually to deal with specific technical and operational issues. The three UPU bodies are served by the International Bureau, a secretariat headed by a Director-General.

Funding is provided by members according to a scale of contributions drawn up by the Congress. The Council sets the annual budget (1997, SFr35,747,000) within a five-year figure decided by the Congress.
Director-General, Thomas E. Leavey (USA)

WESTERN EUROPEAN UNION
4 rue de la Régence, 1000 Brussels, Belgium

The Western European Union (WEU) originated as the Brussels Treaty Organization (BTO) established under the Treaty of Brussels, signed in 1948 by Belgium, France, Luxembourg, the Netherlands and the UK, to provide collective self-defence and economic, cultural and social collaboration amongst its signatories. With the collapse of the European Defence Community and the decision of NATO to incorporate the Federal Republic of Germany into the Western security system, the BTO was modified to become the WEU in 1954 with the admission of West Germany and Italy. However, owing to the overlap with NATO and the Council of Europe, the Union became largely defunct.

From the late 1970s onwards efforts were made to add a security dimension to the EC's European Political Co-operation. Opposition to these efforts from Denmark, Greece and Ireland led the remaining EC countries, all WEU members, to decide to reactivate the Union in 1984. Members committed themselves to harmonizing their views on defence and security and developing a European security identity, while bearing in mind the importance of transatlantic relations. Portugal and Spain joined the WEU in 1988, and Greece became a full member in 1995.

After much debate about its future, the EU Maastricht Treaty designated the WEU as the future defence component of the European Union. WEU foreign ministers agreed in the Petersberg Declaration 1992 to assign forces to WEU command for 'peacemaking' operations in Europe. In November 1992 the WEU's role as the common security dimension of the EU was enhanced when WEU ministers signed a declaration with remaining European NATO members to give them various forms of WEU membership. Iceland, Norway and Turkey became associate members; Ireland, Denmark, Austria, Finland and Sweden became observer members. In 1994 the WEU reached agreements with nine eastern European states (Estonia, Latvia, Lithuania, Poland, Czech Republic, Slovak Republic, Hungary, Romania and Bulgaria) under which they all became associate partners.

The WEU acts in accordance with positions adopted within the Atlantic Alliance, and relations between the WEU and NATO are developing on the basis of transparency and complementarity. WEU foreign ministers stated in the Luxembourg Declaration 1993 that the WEU is ready to participate in the future work of the NATO Alliance as its European pillar, and to co-operate to prevent the duplication of WEU and NATO actions.

The formation of a 'Eurocorps' based on the Franco-German brigade as a force answerable to the WEU was announced in 1992. The 'Eurocorps' was inaugurated in 1993 and became fully operational in 1995 with 51,000 troops comprising French, German, Belgian, Luxembourg and Spanish forces.

A Council of Ministers (foreign and defence) meets biannually in the capital of the presiding country; the presidency rotates biannually. A Permanent Council of the member states' permanent representatives meets weekly in Brussels. Associate members have the right to attend Permanent Council meetings. The Permanent Council is chaired by the Secretary-General and serviced by the Secretariat. A planning cell has been established to draw up contingency plans in the areas of humanitarian relief, peacekeeping and crisis management. The Assembly of the WEU is composed of 115 parliamentarians of member states and meets twice annually in Paris to debate matters within the scope of the revised Brussels Treaty.

Presidency (1997), France, Germany; (1998), Greece, Italy
Secretary-General, José Cutileiro (Portugal)
UK Representative on the Permanent Council, Sir John Goulden, KCMG
ASSEMBLY, 43 avenue du Président Wilson, 75775 Paris Cedex 16, France

THE WORLD BANK
1818 H Street NW, Washington DC 20433, USA

The World Bank, more formally known as the International Bank for Reconstruction and Development (IBRD), is a specialized agency of the UN. It developed from the international monetary and financial conference held at Bretton Woods, New Hampshire, in 1944 and was established by 44 nations in 1945 to encourage economic growth in developing countries through the provision of loans and technical assistance to their respective governments. The IBRD now has 178 members.

The Bank is owned by the governments of member countries and its capital is subscribed by its members. It finances its lending primarily from borrowing in world capital markets, and derives a substantial contribution to its resources from its retained earnings and the repayment of loans. The interest rate on its loans is calculated in relation to its cost of borrowing. Loans generally have a grace period of five years and are repayable within 20 years. The loans made by the Bank since its inception to 30 June 1994 totalled US$333,806.8 million to 110 countries. Total capital is US$170,003 million.

Originally directed towards post-war reconstruction in Europe, the Bank has subsequently turned towards assisting less-developed countries with the establishment of two affiliates, the International Finance Corporation (IFC) in 1956 and the International Development Association (IDA) in 1960. The IFC aids developing member countries by promoting the growth of the private sector of their economies and by helping to mobilize domestic and foreign capital for this purpose. The IFC's subscribed share capital was US$2,251 million at 30 June 1994. It is also empowered to borrow up to two and a half times the amount of its unimpaired subscribed capital and accumulated earnings for use in its lending programme. At 30 June 1994, the IFC had committed financing totalling more than US$14,316,215 million in about 162 countries.

The IDA performs the same function as the World Bank but primarily to less developed countries and on terms that bear less heavily on their balance of payments than IBRD loans. Eligible countries typically have a per capita gross national product of less than US$835 (1994). Funds (called credits to distinguish them from IBRD loans) come mostly in the form of subscriptions and contributions from the IDA's richer members and transfers from the net income of the IBRD. The terms for IDA credits, which bear no interest and are made to governments only, are ten-year grace periods and 35- or 40-year maturities. By 30 June 1994, the IDA had extended development credits totalling US$87,880 million to 157 countries.

The IBRD and its affiliates are financially and legally distinct but share headquarters. The IBRD is headed by a Board of Governors, consisting of one Governor and one alternate Governor appointed by each member country. Twenty-four Executive Directors exercise all powers of the Bank except those reserved to the Board of Governors. The President, elected by the Executive Directors, conducts the business of the Bank, assisted by an international staff. Membership in both the IFC (162 members) and the IDA (157 members) is open to all IBRD countries. The IDA is administered by the same staff as the Bank; the IFC has its own personnel but draws on the IBRD for administrative and other support. All share the same President.

In 1988 a third affiliate, the Multilateral Investment Guarantee Agency (MIGA) was formed. MIGA encourages foreign investment in developing states by providing investment guarantees to potential investors and advisory services to developing member countries. At 30 December 1994 128 countries were members of MIGA.

President (IBRD, IFC, IDA, MIGA), James D. Wolfensohn (USA)
UK Executive Director, A. O'Donnell, Room 11-120, IMF, 700 19th Street NW, Washington DC 20431
EUROPEAN OFFICE, 66 avenue d'Iena, 75116 Paris, France
JAPAN OFFICE, Kokusai Building 916, 1-1 Marunouchi 3-Chomse, Chiyoda-ku, Tokyo 100, Japan
UK OFFICE, New Zealand House, Haymarket, London SW1Y 4TQ

THE WORLD COUNCIL OF CHURCHES
PO Box 2100, 1211 Geneva 2, Switzerland
Tel: Geneva 791 6152

The World Council of Churches (WCC) was constituted in 1948 to promote unity among Christian churches. The 332 member churches have adherents in more than 100 countries. With the exception of Roman Catholicism, virtually all Christian traditions are represented.

The policies of the Council are determined by delegates of the member churches meeting in Assembly, roughly every seven years; the seventh Assembly was held in Canberra, Australia, in February 1991 and the eighth Assembly is scheduled to be held in Harare, Zimbabwe, in September 1998. More detailed decisions are taken by a 156-member Central Committee which is elected by the Assembly and meets, with the eight WCC Presidents, annually. The Central Committee in turn appoints a smaller Executive Committee and also nominates commissions to guide the various programmes.

General Secretary, Dr Konrad Raiser (Germany)

WORLD HEALTH ORGANIZATION
20 avenue Appia, 1211 Geneva 27, Switzerland
Tel: Geneva 791 2888

The UN International Health Conference, held in 1946, established the World Health Organization (WHO) as a UN specialized agency, with effect from 1948. It is dedicated to attaining the highest possible level of health for all. It collaborates with member governments, UN agencies and other bodies to improve health standards, control communicable diseases and promote all aspects of family and environmental health. It seeks to raise the standards of health teaching and training, and promotes research through collaborating research centres worldwide. Its other services include the *International Pharmacopoeia*, epidemiological surveillance, and the collation and publication of statistics. WHO activities are orientated to achieving 'Health for All'.

WHO had 191 members as at June 1996. It is governed by the annual World Health Assembly of members which meets to set policy, approve the budget (1996–7, US$1,900 million), appoint a Director-General, and adopt health conventions and regulations. It also elects 32 members who designate one expert to serve on the Executive Board. The Board effects the programme, suggests initiatives and is empowered to deal with emergencies. A Secretariat, headed by the Director-General, supervises the activities of six regional offices.
Director-General, Dr H. Nakajima (Japan)

WORLD INTELLECTUAL PROPERTY ORGANIZATION
34 chemin des Colombettes, 1211 Geneva 20, Switzerland
Tel: Geneva 338 9111

The World Intellectual Property Organization (WIPO) was established in 1967 by the Stockholm Convention, which entered into force in 1970. In addition to that Convention, WIPO administers 22 treaties, the principal ones being the Paris Convention for the Protection of Industrial Property and the Berne Convention for the Protection of Literary and Artistic Works. WIPO became a UN specialized agency in 1974.

WIPO promotes the protection of intellectual property throughout the world through co-operation among states, and the administration of various 'Unions', each founded on a multilateral treaty and dealing with the legal and administrative aspects of intellectual property.

Intellectual property comprises two main branches: industrial property (inventions, trademarks, industrial designs and appellations of origin); and copyright (literary, musical, photographic, audiovisual and artistic works, etc.). WIPO also assists creative intellectual activity and facilitates technology transfer, particularly to developing countries.

WIPO had 164 members as at May 1997. The biennial session of all its governing bodies sets policy, a programme and a budget (1996–7, SFr300 million) WIPO has three governing bodies: the General Assembly, composed of WIPO members who are also members of the Paris or Berne conventions; the Conference, composed of all WIPO members; and the Co-ordination Committee, composed of member states elected by members of WIPO and the Paris and Berne conventions. The General Assembly elects a Director-General, who heads the International Bureau (secretariat).

A separate International Union for the Protection of New Varieties of Plants (UPOV), established by convention in 1961, is linked to WIPO. It has 32 members.
Director-General, Dr Arpad Bogsch (USA)

WORLD METEOROLOGICAL ORGANIZATION
41 avenue Giuseppe Motta, PO Box 2300, 1211 Geneva 20, Switzerland

The World Meteorological Organization (WMO) was established as a UN specialized agency in 1950, succeeding the International Meteorological Organization founded in 1873. It facilitates co-operation in the establishment of networks for making meteorological, climatological, hydrological and geophysical observations, as well as their exchange, processing and standardization, and assists technology transfer, training and research. It also fosters collaboration between meteorological and hydrological services, and furthers the application of meteorology to aviation, shipping, environment, water problems, agriculture, etc.

The WMO had 179 member states and six member territories as at 30 December 1996. The supreme authority is the World Meteorological Congress of member states and member territories, which meets every four years to determine general policy, make recommendations and set a budget (1996–9, SFr255 million). It also elects 26 members of the 36-member Executive Council, the other members being the President and three Vice-Presidents of the WMO, and the Presidents of the six regional associations, who are ex-officio members. The Council supervises the implementation of Congress decisions, initiates studies and makes recommendations on matters needing international action. The WMO functions through six regional associations and eight technical commissions. Each of the regional associations has responsibility for co-ordinating meteorological activities within its region. The technical commissions study meteorological and hydrological problems, lay down the necessary methodologies and procedures, and make recommendations to the Executive Council and Congress. The Secretariat is headed by a Secretary-General, appointed by the Congress.
Secretary-General, G. O. P. Obasi (Nigeria)

WORLD TRADE ORGANIZATION
Centre William Rappard, 154 rue de Lausanne, 1211 Geneva 21, Switzerland
Tel: Geneva 739 5286; fax: Geneva 739 5458

The World Trade Organization was established on 1 January 1995 as the successor to the General Agreement on Tariffs and Trade (GATT). GATT was established in 1948 as an interim agreement until the charter of a new international trade organization could be drafted by a committee of the UN Economic and Social Council and ratified by member states. The charter was never ratified and GATT became the only regime for the regulation of world trade, evolving its own rules and procedures.

GATT was dedicated to the expansion of non-discriminatory international trade and progressively extended free trade via 'rounds' of multilateral negotiations. Eight 'rounds' were concluded: Geneva (1947), Annecy (1948), Torquay (1950), Geneva (1956), Dillon (1960–1), Kennedy (1964–7), Tokyo (1973–9) and Uruguay (1986–94). By the time that the measures of the Uruguay Round are fully implemented in 2002 the average duties on manufactured goods will have been reduced from 40 per cent in the 1940s to 3 per cent. The Final Act of the Uruguay Round was signed by trade ministers from the 128 GATT negotiating states and the EU in Marrakesh, Morocco, on 15 April 1994. It established the World Trade Organization (WTO) to supersede GATT and implement the Uruguay Round agreements.

The WTO is the legal and institutional foundation of the multilateral trading system. It provides the contractual obligations determining how governments frame and implement trade policy and provides the forum for the debate, negotiation and adjudication of trade problems. The WTO's principal aims are to liberalize world trade and place it on a secure basis, and it seeks to achieve this partly by an agreed set of trade rules and market access agreements and partly through further trade liberalization negotiations. The WTO also administers and implements a further 29 multilateral agreements in fields such as agriculture, textiles and clothing, services, government procurement, rules of origin and intellectual property.

The highest authority of the WTO is the Ministerial Conference composed of all members which meets at least once every two years. The General Council meets as required and acts on behalf of the Ministerial Conference in regard to the regular working of the WTO. Composed of all members, the General Council also convenes in two particular forms: as the Dispute Settlement Body, dealing with disputes between members arising from the Uruguay Round Final Act; and as the Trade Policy Review Body, conducting regular reviews of the trade policies of members. A secretariat of 450 staff headed by a Director-General services WTO bodies and provides trade performance and trade policy analysis.

As at April 1997 there were 131 WTO members, and a further 28 governments had applied to join the WTO. The WTO budget for 1997 was SFr115 million, with members' contributions calculated on the basis of their share of the total trade conducted by WTO members. The official languages of the WTO are English, French and Spanish.

Director-General, Renato Ruggiero (Italy)
Permanent UK Representative, N. C. R. Williams, CMG, 37–39 rue de Vermont, 1211 Geneva 20

The European Union

MEMBERS

State	Accession Date	Population (million)	GNP (US$ million)	GDP per head‡	Council Votes	EP Seats
Austria	1 January 1995	8.03	216,547	108	4	21
Belgium	1 January 1958*	10.08	250,710	112	5	25
Denmark	1 January 1973	5.21	156,027	116	3	16
Finland	1 January 1995	5.10	105,174	96	3	16
France	1 January 1958*	57.75	1,451,051	108	10	87
Germany	1 January 1958*†	81.41	2,254,343	111	10	99
Greece	1 January 1981	10.43	85,885	66	5	25
Ireland	1 January 1973	3.57	52,765	93	3	15
Italy	1 January 1958*	57.19	1,088,085	103	10	87
Luxembourg	1 January 1958*	0.40	16,876	169	2	6
Netherlands	1 January 1958*	15.38	371,039	107	5	31
Portugal	1 January 1986	9.83	96,689	67	5	25
Spain	1 January 1986	39.14	532,347	77	8	64
Sweden	1 January 1995	8.78	209,720	101	4	22
UK	1 January 1973	58.09	1,094,734	96	10	87
TOTAL		370.39	7,981,992		87	626

* Acceded to the European Coal and Steel Community (ECSC) on its formation in 1952
† Federal Republic of Germany (West) 1952/1958; German Democratic Republic (East) acceded on German reunification (3 October 1990)
‡ Expressed as purchasing power parities: EU average = 100. Figures are for 1995. *Source*: Eurostat
EP European Parliament

DEVELOPMENT

1950 Robert Schuman (French foreign minister) proposes that France and West Germany pool their coal and steel industries under a supranational authority (Schuman Plan)
1951 Paris Treaty signed by France, West Germany, Belgium, Italy, Luxembourg and the Netherlands establishes the European Coal and Steel Community (ECSC)
1952 ECSC treaty enters into force
1957 25 March: Treaty of Rome signed by the six, establishes the European Economic Community (EEC) and the European Atomic Energy Authority (EURATOM). Treaty aims to create a customs union; remove obstacles to free movement of capital, goods, people and services; establish common external trade policy and common agricultural and fisheries policies; co-ordinate economic policies; harmonize social policies; promote co-operation in nuclear research
1958 1 January: EEC and EURATOM begin operation. Joint Parliament and Court of Justice established for all three communities, and the Commission, Council of Ministers, Economic and Social Committee and Investment Bank for the EEC
1962 Common Agricultural Policy (CAP) agreed (*see* page 771)
1967 EEC, ECSC and EURATOM merge to form the European Communities (EC), with a single Council of Ministers and Commission
1968 EEC customs union completed Implementation of CAP completed
1970 Foreign policy co-ordination begins
1971 The Common Fisheries Policy comes into operation
1972 European Social Fund established
1974 Regular heads of governments summits begin

1975 'Own resources' funding of EC budget introduced (*see* pages 770–1)
UK renegotiates its terms of accession
European Regional Development Fund created
1979 European Monetary System (EMS) comes into operation (*see* page 772)
First direct elections to European Parliament (June)
1984 Fontainebleau summit settles UK annual budget rebate and agrees first major CAP reform
European Parliament elections (June)
1986 Single European Act (SEA) signed (*see* page 771)
European Political Co-operation (EPC) established (*see* page 772)
1988 Second major CAP reform
1989 European Parliament elections (June)
1991 Maastricht Treaty agreed (*see* page 772)
1992 31 December: Single internal market programme completed
1993 September: the exchange rate mechanism (ERM) of the EMS effectively suspended
1 November: The Maastricht Treaty enters into force, establishing the European Union (EU)
1994 1 January: European Economic Area (EEA) agreement comes into operation (*see* pages 771–2)
Norway rejects EU membership in referendum
1997 Amsterdam Treaty agreed

ENLARGEMENT AND EXTERNAL RELATIONS

The procedure for accession to the EU is laid down in the Treaty of Rome; states must be stable European democracies governed by the rule of law with free market economics. A membership application is studied by the Commission, which produces an Opinion. If the Opinion is positive, negotiations may be opened leading to an Accession Treaty which must be approved by all member state governments and parliaments, the European Parliament, and the applicant state's government and parliament. *Applicants:* Morocco (applied 1987/rejected 1987), Turkey (applied 1987/negative Opinion 1989), Cyprus (applied 1990/rejected 1993), Malta (applied 1990/negative Opinion 1993), Switzerland (applied 1992/no Opinion yet), Hungary (applied 1994/no Opinion yet), Poland (applied 1994/no Opinion yet), Bulgaria (applied 1995/no Opinion yet), Estonia (applied 1995/no Opinion yet), Latvia (applied 1995/no Opinion yet), Lithuania (applied 1995/no Opinion yet), Romania (applied 1995/no Opinion yet), Slovakia (applied 1995/no Opinion yet), the Czech Republic (applied 1996/no Opinion yet).

Apart from the EEA Agreement (*see* page 771), the EU has three types of agreements with other European and CIS states. 'Europe' Agreements commit the EU and signatory states to long-term political and economic integration, a free trade zone (apart from agriculture and labour movement) and eventual EU membership. Government representatives from the signatory states are entitled to attend one summit and two finance and foreign council meetings a year. 'Europe' agreements have been signed with Poland, Hungary (1991), Romania, Bulgaria, Czech Republic, Slovak Republic (1993), Estonia, Latvia and Lithuania (1995). Association agreements include a commitment to EU financial aid and to eventual membership; agreements have been signed with Malta (1971), Cyprus (1972), Turkey (1974) and Slovenia (1996). Partnership and co-operation agreements are based on regulating and improving political and economic relations and mutual trade concessions but exclude any possibility of membership. Agreements have been signed with Ukraine, Russia, Moldova (1994), Kyrgyzstan and Belarus (1995).

THE COUNCIL OF THE EUROPEAN UNION
175 rue de la Loi, 1048 Brussels, Belgium

The Council of the European Union (Council of Ministers) consists of ministers from the government of each of the member states. It formally comprises the foreign ministers of the member states but in practice the minister depends on the subject under discussion, e.g. when EC environment matters are under discussion, the meeting is informally known as the Environment Council. Council decisions are taken by qualified majority vote (in which members' votes are weighted), by a simple majority, or by unanimity. Council meetings are prepared by the Committee of Permanent Representatives (COREPER) of the member states, which acts as the 'gatekeeper' between national governments and the supranational EC, often negotiating on proposals with the Commission during the legislative process.

Unanimity votes are taken on issues such as taxation, budgets, foreign policy, the accession of new members, European Parliament electoral law, rights of free movement and residence, and some environment and transport policies. Qualified majority votes are taken on Single Market laws and harmonization, environment policy, health and safety, transport policy, overseas aid, research and development, culture, consumer protection, education and training, the development of a single currency and social policy. Member states have weighted votes in the Council loosely proportional to their relative population sizes (*see* introductory table), with a total of 87 votes. For a proposal from the Commission to pass, it must receive 62 votes; 26 votes are necessary to block a proposal, and 23

votes constitute a temporary blocking minority. For other proposals to be passed they must receive 62 votes cast by at least ten member states.

The European Council, comprising the heads of government of the member states, meets twice a year to provide overall policy direction. The presidency of the EC is held in rotation for six-month periods, setting the agenda for and chairing all Council meetings. The presidency provides the incumbent nation with an opportunity to pursue its own policy priorities. The European Council holds a summit in the country holding the presidency at the end of its period in office. The holders of the presidency for the years 1997–9 are:

1997 Netherlands, Luxembourg
1998 UK, Austria
1999 Germany, Finland

OFFICE OF THE UNITED KINGDOM PERMANENT REPRESENTATIVE TO THE EUROPEAN COMMUNITIES
avenue d'Auderghem, 1040 Brussels, Belgium
Ambassador and UK Permanent Representative, HE Sir Stephen Wall, KCMG, LVO, *apptd* 1995
Minister and Deputy Permanent Representative, D. Bostock

THE EUROPEAN COMMISSION
200 rue de la Loi, 1049 Brussels, Belgium

The Commission consists of 20 Commissioners, two each from France, Germany, Italy, Spain and the UK, and one each from the remaining member states. The members of the Commission are appointed for five-year renewable terms by the agreement of the member states; the present Commission came into office on 23 January 1995 and in future the five-year term will run concurrently with the term of the European Parliament. The President and Vice-Presidents are elected by the Commissioners from among their number. The Commissioners pledge sole allegiance to the EC. The Commission initiates and implements EC legislation and is the guardian of the EC treaties. It is the exponent of Community-wide interests rather than the national preoccupations of the Council. Each Commissioner is supported by advisers and oversees whichever of the 24 departments, known as Directorates-General (DGs), is assigned to him. Each Directorate-General is headed by a Director-General. The Commission has a total staff of around 15,000 civil servants.

COMMISSIONERS *as at June 1997*

President

Secretariat-General; Forward Studies Unit; Inspectorate-General; Legal Services; Spokesman's Service; Joint Interpreting and Conference Service; Security Office; Overall responsibility for monetary matters, common foreign and security policy, institutional questions and intergovernmental conference, Jacques Santer (Luxembourg)

Vice-Presidents

External Relations with the Mediterranean, the Middle East, Latin America and parts of Asia, Manuel Marin (Spain)
External Relations with North America, Australia, Japan, New Zealand, China, South Korea, Taiwan, Hong Kong, Macao, Common Commercial Policy, Relations with the OECD and WTO, Sir Leon Brittan (UK)

Members

Industrial Affairs, Information Technology and Telecommunications, Martin Bangemann (Germany)

Immigration, Interior and Judicial Affairs, Financial Control, Anti-Fraud Measures, Relations with the Ombudsman, Anita Gradin (Sweden)

Agriculture and Rural Development, Franz Fischler (Austria)

Budget, Personnel and Administration, Translation, Erkki Liikanen (Finland)

Economic and Financial Affairs, Monetary matters, Credit and Investments, Statistical Office, Yves-Thibault de Silguy (France)

Energy and Euratom Supply Agency, Small and Medium Enterprises, Tourism, Christos Papoutis (Greece)

Institutional Questions, Intergovernmental Conference, Relations with the European Parliament, Culture and Audiovisual, Publications Office, Openness, Communications and Information, Marcelino Oreja (Spain)

Transport, Neil Kinnock (UK)

Regional Policy, Relations with the Committee of the Regions, Cohesion Fund, Monika Wulf-Mathies (Germany)

Science, Research and Development, Joint Research Centre, Human Resources, Education, Training and Youth, Edith Cresson (France)

Competition, Karel Van Miert (Belgium)

External Relations with Central and Eastern Europe, the former Soviet Union and other European states, Common Foreign and Security Policy, External Service, Hans van den Broek (Netherlands)

External Relations with African, Caribbean and Pacific states, Lomé Convention, João de Deus Pinheiro (Portugal)

Social Affairs and Employment, Relations with the Economic and Social Committee, , Padraig Flynn (Ireland)

Fisheries, Consumer Policy, EC Humanitarian Office, Emma Bonino (Italy)

Environment, Nuclear Safety, Ritt Bjerregaard (Denmark)

Internal Market, Financial Services, Customs, Taxation, Mario Monti (Italy)

Secretary-General, Carlo Trojan (Netherlands)

THE EUROPEAN PARLIAMENT

The European Parliament (EP) originated as the Common Assembly of the ECSC; it acquired its present name in 1962. Members (MEPs) were initially appointed from the membership of national parliaments; direct elections to the Parliament were first held in 1979. Elections to the Parliament are held on differing bases throughout the EC; British MEPs are elected on a first-past-the-post system, except in Northern Ireland which uses proportional representation. The latest elections were held in June 1994, when the Parliament expanded from 518 to 567 seats to include representatives from the former East Germany and concurrent increases in other member states' representatives. It expanded to 626 seats on 1 January 1995 with the accession of Austria, Finland and Sweden to the EU. For total number of seats per member and political groupings, see table below. MEPs serve on 20 committees, which scrutinize draft EC legislation and the activities of the Commission. A minimum of 12 plenary sessions a year are held in Strasbourg and Brussels, committees meet in Brussels, and the Secretariat's headquarters is in Luxembourg.

The EP has gradually expanded its influence within the EU through the Single European Act, which introduced the co-operation procedure, and the Maastricht Treaty, which extended the co-operation procedure and introduced the co-decision procedure (see Legislative Process).

EUROPEAN PARLIAMENT POLITICAL GROUPINGS

	PES	EPP	UFE	ELDR	EUL/NGL	Green	ERA	IEN	Ind.	Total
Austria	6	7	–	1	–	1	–	–	6	21
Belgium	6	7	–	6	–	2	1	–	3	25
Denmark	4	3	–	5	–	–	–	4	–	16
Finland	4	4	–	5	2	1	–	–	–	16
France	15	12	17	1	7	1	12	11	11	87
Germany	40	47	–	–	–	12	–	–	–	99
Greece	10	9	2	–	4	–	–	–	–	25
Ireland	1	4	7	1	–	2	–	–	–	15
Italy	18	15	24	4	5	4	2	–	15	87
Luxembourg	2	2	–	1	–	–	1	–	–	6
Netherlands	7	9	2	10	–	1	–	2	–	31
Portugal	10	9	3	–	3	–	–	–	–	25
Spain	21	30	–	2	9	–	2	–	–	64
Sweden	7	5	–	3	3	4	–	–	–	22
UK	63	18	–	2	–	–	2	1	1	87
TOTAL	214	181	55	41	33	28	20	18	36	626

PES Party of European Socialists (including British Labour Party, Northern Ireland Social Democratic and Labour Party, Italian Democratic Left Party) Socialist, Social Democratic and Labour parties

EPP European People's Party (including British Conservative Party, Northern Ireland Official Unionist Party, Spanish Popular Party, French UDF, Irish Fine Gael, Swedish Moderate Party) Christian Democrats and Conservatives

UFE Union for Europe (including Forza Italia Party, French Gaullists, Irish Fianna Fáil, Greek Political Spring Party, Portuguese Centre Party)

ELDR European Liberal Democratic and Reformist Group (including British Liberal Democratic Party, Portuguese Social Democrats) centre and liberal parties

EUL/ NGL Confederal Group of the European United Left/Nordic Green Left (French, Greek and Portuguese Communist Parties, Italian Refounded Communist Party, some Spanish regionalists, Danish, Swedish, Finnish, Greek, Italian and Spanish Green/Left parties)

Green Green and Ecologist parties

ERA European Radical Alliance (Scottish National Party, French Radicals of the Left, Italian Radical Party, Belgian Flemish and Spanish regionalists)

IEN Independent Europe of the Nations Group (French Other Europe Group, Dutch and Danish Euro-sceptics)

Ind Independents (Italian National Alliance, French National Front, Belgian Vlaams Blok, Northern Ireland Democratic Unionist Party)

It has general powers of supervision over the Commission, and consultation and co-decision with the Council; it votes to approve a newly appointed Commission and can dismiss it at any time by a two-thirds majority. Under the Maastricht Treaty it has the right to be consulted on the appointment of the new Commission and can veto its appointment. It can reject the EU budget as a whole, alter non-compulsory expenditure not specified in the EU primary legislation, and can question the Commission's management of the budget and call in the Court of Auditors. Although the EP cannot directly initiate legislation, its reports can spur the Commission into action. In accordance with the Maastricht Treaty the EP appointed an ombudsman in October 1995, to provide citizens with redress against maladministration by EU institutions.

The Parliament's organization is deliberately biased in favour of multi-national political groupings, recognition of a political grouping in the parliament entitling it to offices, funding, representation on committees and influence in debates and legislation. A political grouping with members from only one country needs a minimum of 29 members for recognition, whereas one with members from two countries needs 23 members, a grouping with members from three countries needs 18 members, and a grouping with members from four or more countries needs only 14 members.

PARLIAMENT , Palais de l'Europe, 67006 Strasbourg Cedex, France; 97–113 rue Belliard, 1047 Brussels, Belgium
SECRETARIAT , Centre Européen, Kirchberg, L-2929 Luxembourg
President, José Maria Gil-Robles Gil-Delgado (Spain)
Ombudsman, Jacob Söderman (Finland), 1 avenue du Président Robert Schuman, BP403, F-67001, Strasbourg, France
(For a full list of British MEPs, *see* pages 268–9)

THE LEGISLATIVE PROCESS

The core of the EU policymaking process is a dialogue between the Commission, which initiates and implements policy, and the Council of Ministers, which takes policy decisions. A degree of democratic control is exercised by the European Parliament.

The original legislative process is known as the consultative procedure. The Commission drafts a proposal which it submits to the Council and to the Parliament. The Council then consults the Economic and Social Committee (ESC), the Parliament and the Committee of the Regions; the Parliament may request that amendments are made. With or without these amendments, the proposal is then adopted by the Council and becomes law.

Under the Single European Act (SEA), changes were made to the legislative process, particularly in strengthening the role of the Parliament by the introduction of the co-operation procedure. The Parliament now has a second reading of proposals in some fields, and after the second reading its rejection of a proposal can only be overturned by a unanimous decision of the Council. The Maastricht Treaty extends the scope of the co-operation procedure, which now applies to Single Market laws and harmonization, trans-European networks, development policy, the social fund, and some aspects of transport, environment, research, social policy and competition policy.

The SEA introduced the assent procedure, whereby an absolute majority of the Parliament must vote to approve laws in certain fields before they are passed. Issues covered by the assent procedure include foreign treaties, accession treaties, international agreements with budgetary implications, citizenship, residence rights, the CAP, and regional and structural funds.

The Maastricht Treaty introduced the co-decision procedure; if, after the Parliament's second reading of a proposal, the Council and Parliament fail to agree, a conciliation committee of the two will reach a compromise. If a compromise is not reached, the Parliament can reject the legislation by the vote of an absolute majority of its members. The Amsterdam Treaty extended co-decision to all areas covered by qualified majority voting.

The Council issues the following legislation:
– Regulations, which are binding in their entirety and directly applicable to all member states; they do not need to be incorporated into national law to come into effect
– Directives, which are less specific, binding as to the result to be achieved but leaving the method of implementation open to member states; a directive thus has no force until it is incorporated into national law
– Decisions, which are also binding but are addressed solely to one or more member states or individuals in a member state
– Recommendations
– Opinions, which are merely persuasive

The Council also has certain budgetary powers, including the power to reject the budget as a whole and to increase expenditure or redistribute money within sectors.

THE COMMUNITY BUDGET

The principles of funding the European Community budget were established by the Treaty of Rome and remain with modifications to this day. There is a legally binding limit on the overall level of resources (known as 'own resources') that the Community can raise from its member states; this limit is defined as a percentage of gross national product (GNP). Budget revenue and expenditure must balance and there is therefore no deficit financing. The own resources decision, which came into effect in 1975, states that there are four sources of Community funding under which each member state makes contributions: levies charged on agricultural imports into the Community from non-member states; customs duties on imports from non-member states; contributions based on member states' shares of a notional Community harmonized VAT base; and contributions based on member states' shares of Community GNP. The latter is the budget-balancing item and covers the difference between total expenditure and the revenue from the other three sources. Since 1984 the UK has had an annual rebate equivalent to 66 per cent of the difference between what the UK contributes to the budget and what it receives. This was introduced to compensate the UK for disproportionate contributions caused by its high proportion of agricultural and non-agricultural imports from non-member states and its relatively small receipts from the Common Agricultural Policy, the most important portion of Community expenditure.

BUDGET 1997

	Billion ECU*	As % of total
Agriculture	41.3	50.9
Regional and Social	26.3	32.4
External Action	4.8	5.9
Administration	4.3	5.3
Research and Technology	3.2	3.9
Consumer Protection, Industry, Internal Market	0.7	0.9
Energy and Environment	0.2	0.2
Foreign and Security Policy	0.3	0.4
TOTAL	81.1	99.9

EC Budget by Member State 1995 (*billion ECU**)

	Contributions		Receipts	Net gain‡
Germany	20.83	(27.6%)	7.89	− 12.94
France	11.98	(15.9%)	10.15	− 1.83
UK	9.55	(12.7%)	4.53	− 5.02
Italy	7.05	(9.3%)	5.80	− 1.25
Netherlands	4.14	(5.5%)	2.34	− 1.80
Spain	3.42	(4.5%)	10.86	+ 7.44
Belgium	2.64	(3.5%)	2.37	− 0.27
Austria	1.87	(2.5%)	0.86	− 1.01
Sweden	1.70	(2.3%)	0.72	− 0.98
Denmark	1.25	(1.7%)	1.60	+ 0.35
Greece	1.04	(1.4%)	4.47	+ 3.43
Finland	0.94	(1.2%)	0.72	− 0.22
Portugal	0.92	(1.2%)	3.25	+ 2.33
Ireland	0.83	(1.1%)	2.55	+ 1.72
Luxembourg	0.16	(0.2%)	0.12	− 0.04
Total	68.32	(90.6%)	58.23	—

* 1 ECU = £0.68 as at 10 September 1997
‡ Net contributor (−)/net recipient (+)

Under the Edinburgh summit agreement (December 1992) the EC budget will rise in stages from 1.2 per cent of Community (Union) GNP in 1992 to 1.27 per cent in 1999.

THE COMMON AGRICULTURAL POLICY

The Common Agricultural Policy (CAP) was established to increase agricultural production, provide a fair standard of living for farmers and ensure the availability of food at reasonable prices. This aim is achieved by a number of mechanisms:
− import levies (the EC sets a target price for a particular product in the Community, the world price is monitored and if it falls below the guide price, an import levy can be imposed equivalent to the difference between the two)
− intervention purchase (if the price of a product falls below the level indicated by the Council, member states must purchase supplies of the product, provided that they are of suitable quality)
− export subsidies (the EC pays a food exporter a subsidy equivalent to the difference between the price at which the product is bought in the EC and the lower sale price on the world market)
  These measures stimulated production but also placed increasing demands on the EC budget which were exacerbated by the increase in EC members and yields enlarged by technological innovation; CAP now accounts for almost 50 per cent of EC expenditure. To surmount these problems reforms were agreed in 1984, 1988 and 1992.
  The 1984 reforms created the system of co-responsibility levies: farm payments to the EC by volume of product sold. This system was supplemented by national quotas for particular products, such as milk. The 1988 reforms emphasized 'set-aside', whereby farmers are given direct grants to take land out of production as a means of reducing surpluses. Originally aimed at cereal farmers, who were allowed to set aside between 15 per cent and 100 per cent of their land, the set aside reforms were extended in 1993 for another five years and to every farm in the EC, which must set aside at least 18 per cent of its land. The 1992 reforms are based on the reduction of target prices for cereals, beef and dairy produce. These are being reduced by 29 per cent, 15 per cent and 5 per cent respectively, and the amount of money spent by the EC on the three mechanisms will fall. By 1995 successive CAP reforms had virtually eliminated EU food mountains.
  Under the Uruguay round agreement of GATT concluded in 1993, the EU must, over a six-year period

from 1 January 1995, reduce its import levies by 36 per cent, reduce its domestic subsidies by 20 per cent, reduce its export subsidies by 36 per cent in value, and reduce its subsidized exports by 21 per cent in volume.

THE SINGLE MARKET

Throughout the 1970s and early 1980s, EC members became concerned at the slow growth of the European economy. Although tariffs and quotas had been removed between member states, the EC was still separated into a number of national markets by a series of non-tariff barriers. It was to overcome these internal barriers to trade that the concept of the Single Market was developed. The measures to be undertaken were outlined in the Cockfield report (1985) and codified in the Single European Act (SEA) 1986, which came into force in 1987 with a target date of 31 December 1992 for completion.
  The SEA includes articles removing obstacles that distort the internal market: the elimination of frontier controls; the mutual recognition of professional qualifications; the harmonization of product specifications, largely by the mutual recognition of national standards; open tendering for public procurement contracts; the free movement of capital; the harmonization of VAT and excise duties; and the reduction of state aid to particular industries. The SEA changed the legislative process within the EC, particularly with the introduction of qualified majority voting in the Council of Ministers for some policy areas, and the introduction of the assent procedure in the European Parliament. The SEA also extends EC competence into the fields of technology, the environment, regional policy, monetary policy and external policy. The Single Market came into effect on 1 January 1993 and is expected to result in at least a 5 per cent increase in the collective GNP of EC member states. The full implementation of the elimination of frontier controls and the harmonization of taxes have, however, been repeatedly delayed.

THE EUROPEAN ECONOMIC AREA (*see also* EFTA, page 749)

The EC Single Market programme spurred European non-member states to open negotiations with the EC on preferential access for their goods, services, labour and capital to the Single Market. Principal among these states were European Free Trade Association (EFTA) members who opened negotiations on extending the Single Market to EFTA by the formation of the European Economic Area (EEA) encompassing all 19 EC and EFTA states. Agreement was reached in May 1992 but the operation of the EEA was delayed by its rejection in a Swiss referendum, necessitating an additional protocol agreed by the remaining 18 states. The EEA came into effect on 1 January 1994 after ratification by 17 member states (Liechtenstein joined on 1 May 1995 after adapting its customs union with Switzerland).
  Austria, Finland and Sweden joined the EU itself on 1 January 1995, leaving only Norway, Iceland and Liechtenstein as the non-EU EEA members. Under the EEA agreement, the three states are to adopt the EU's *acquis communautaire*, apart from in the fields of agriculture, fisheries, and coal and steel.
  The EEA is controlled by regular ministerial meetings and by a joint EU-EFTA committee which extends relevant EU legislation to EEA states. Apart from single market measures, there is co-operation in education, research and development, consumer policy and tourism. An EFTA Court of Justice has been established in Luxembourg and an EFTA Surveillance Authority in

Brussels to supervise the implementation of the EEA Agreement.

THE EUROPEAN MONETARY SYSTEM

The European monetary system (EMS) began operation in March 1979 with three main purposes. The first was to establish monetary stability in Europe, initially in exchange rates between EC member state currencies, and in the longer term to be part of a wider stabilization process, overcoming inflation and budget and trade deficits. The second purpose was to overcome the constraints resulting from the interdependence of EC economies, and the third was to aid the long-term process of European monetary integration. All EC member state currencies are members of the EMS.

The EMS has three components: the ECU; the exchange rate mechanism (ERM); and the credit mechanisms. The ECU is a monetary unit, the value of which is calculated as a basket of set amounts of each member state currency. The relative weighting given to each currency in the ECU basket is proportional to the size of an EU member's economy and the state's share of EU trade. The German Deutsche Mark (DM) has the largest weighting of 32 per cent. The ECU is used for officially fixing the central rates in the ERM and as a means of settlement among central banks in the EMS.

The ERM is the central component of the EMS. Officially all member currencies of the ERM have a central rate against the ECU, the anchor of the mechanism. In practice, the Deutsche Mark has become the anchor currency, with all other currencies' central rates expressed against the DM. Central banks are obliged to maintain their currencies within set margins of their central rate (either 2.25 per cent or 6 per cent above or below) by intervening in the foreign currency markets. Currencies may be revalued or devalued by up to 10 per cent by agreement with all other ERM members. To do this, central banks co-ordinate their actions and can use the credit mechanisms to borrow money from each other and from the Central European Monetary Co-operation Fund where they each deposit 20 per cent of their reserves. Financial assistance is available to central banks over very short-term, short-term and medium-term periods.

Five currencies (Deutsche Mark, French franc, Belgian franc, Dutch guilder, Danish krone) joined the ERM with 2.25 per cent fluctuation margins, and two currencies (Irish punt and Italian lira) with 6 per cent margins in 1979. Subsequently the punt and lira reduced to 2.25 per cent margins. The Spanish peseta (1989), UK pound sterling (1990) and Portuguese escudo (1992) joined the ERM with 6 per cent margins. The pound and the lira were forced out of the mechanism by speculation in September 1992; the lira rejoined in November 1996. Speculation forced the widening of the fluctuation margins to 15 per cent from August 1993 for six of the remaining ERM member currencies (the Deutsche Mark and Dutch guilder remain within 2.25 per cent margins). By April 1994 the French franc, Belgian franc, Irish punt and Danish krone were informally operating within 2.25 per cent fluctuation margins again. The Austrian schilling joined the ERM in January 1995, operating within 15 per cent margins.

THE MAASTRICHT TREATY

The Treaty on European Union was agreed at a meeting of the European Council in Maastricht, the Netherlands, in December 1991. It came into effect in November 1993 following ratification by the member states.

Three 'pillars' formed the basis of the new treaty:
- the European Community with its established institutions and decision-making processes
- a Common Foreign and Security Policy (see below) with the Western European Union as the potential defence component of the EU
- co-operation in justice and home affairs, with the Council of Ministers to co-ordinate policies on asylum, immigration, conditions of entry, cross-border crime, drug trafficking and terrorism

The Treaty established a common European citizenship for nationals of all member states and introduced the principle of subsidiarity whereby decisions are taken at the most appropriate level: national, regional or local. It extended EC competency into the areas of environmental and industrial policies, consumer affairs, health, and education and training, and extended qualified majority voting in the Council of Ministers to cover areas which had previously required a unanimous vote. The powers of the European Parliament over the budget and over the Commission were also enhanced and a co-decision procedure enabled the Parliament to override decisions made by the Council of Ministers (see page 770). A separate protocol to the Maastricht Treaty on social policy was adopted by 11 states and incorporated into the Amsterdam Treaty in 1997 following adoption by the UK. The Amsterdam Treaty was the culmination of a 15-month intergovernmental conference to review the Maastricht Treaty. See Events of the Year.

COMMON FOREIGN AND SECURITY POLICY

The Common Foreign and Security Policy (CFSP) was created as a pillar of the EU by the Maastricht Treaty (see above). It adopted the machinery of the European Political Co-operation (EPC) framework which it replaced and was charged with providing a forum for member states and EU institutions to consult on foreign affairs.

The CFSP system is headed by the European Council, which provides general lines of policy. Specific policy decisions are taken by the Council of Foreign Ministers, which meets at least four times a year to determine areas for joint action. The foreign minister of the state holding the EU presidency initiates action, manages the CFSP and represents it abroad. He is supported by a secretariat based in Brussels and is advised by the past and future holders of the presidency, forming a so-called troika. The Council of Ministers is supported by the Political Committee which meets monthly, or within 48 hours if there is a crisis, to prepare for ministerial discussions. A group of correspondents, designated diplomats in each member's foreign ministry, provides day-to-day contact.

The Amsterdam Treaty introduced qualified majority voting for foreign affairs and created a high representative on CFSP to act as a spokesperson.

ECONOMIC AND MONETARY UNION

The Maastricht Treaty set in motion timetables for achieving economic and monetary union (EMU) and a single currency (the euro). EMU member states will be chosen in spring 1998 on the basis of their economic performance in 1997. On 1 January 1999 member states will fix their exchange rates against each other and against the euro, the European Central Bank will begin operating and the euro will replace the ecu. Euros will circulate alongside national currencies for six months from 1

January 2002, after which national currencies will be abolished.

Member states have to conform to, or be close to conforming to and moving towards, the following criteria:
- the budget deficit should be 3 per cent or less of gross domestic product (GDP)
- total national debt must not exceed 60 per cent of GDP
- inflation should be no more than 1.5 per cent above the average rate of the three best performing economies in the EU
- long-term interest rates should be no more than 2 per cent above the average of the three best performing economies in the EU in the previous 12 months
- applicants must have been a member of the ERM for two years without having realigned or devalued their currency

The table below indicates progress towards achieving the qualifying criteria for economic and monetary union. Budget deficit/surplus, national debt and interest rate figures are based on estimates for 1996.

A growth and stability pact was agreed in Dublin in December 1996 which establishes penalties to be imposed on EMU members with high budget deficits. Governments with deficits exceeding 3 per cent of GDP will receive a warning and will be obliged to pay up to 0.5 per cent of their GDP into a fund after ten months. This will become a fine if the budget deficit is not rectified within two years. A member state with negative growth will be allowed to apply for an exemption from the fine in 'exceptional circumstances', e.g. a recession whereby GDP had fallen by 0.75 per cent or more during one year.

A special protocol was agreed allowing the UK to 'opt out' of a single currency if it so wishes in January 1999. Denmark also secured an 'opt-out' from the single currency.

THE SCHENGEN AGREEMENT

The Schengen Agreement was signed by France, Germany, Belgium, Luxembourg and the Netherlands in 1990 to replace an accord on border controls agreed in Schengen, Luxembourg, in 1985. The Agreement committed the five states to abolishing internal border controls and erecting external frontiers against illegal immigrants, drug traffickers, terrorists and organized crime.

Subsequently signed by Spain and Portugal, the Agreement was ratified by the seven signatory states and entered into force in March 1995 with the removal of frontier,

passport, customs and immigration controls. Provisional agreement was reached in June 1995 between the signatory states and the Nordic Union on a merger of the two frontier-free zones, enabling Denmark, Finland and Sweden to become full members in December 1996. Italy became a member in June 1997; Austria and Greece have applied for membership.

The Schengen Agreement originated as an intergovernmental agreement but is to become part of the EU following the signing of the Amsterdam Treaty.

THE ECONOMIC AND SOCIAL COMMITTEE
2 rue Ravenstein, 1000 Brussels, Belgium

The Economic and Social Committee (ESC) is an advisory and consultative body. The ESC has 222 members, who are nominated by member states. It is divided into three groups: employers, workers, and other interest groups such as consumers, farmers and the self-employed. It issues opinions on draft EC legislation and can bring matters to the attention of the Commission, Council and Parliament; it has a key role in providing specialist and technical input.
President, Tom Jenkins (UK)

THE EUROPEAN COURT OF AUDITORS
12 rue A. De Gasperi, L-1615 Luxembourg

The European Court of Auditors, established in 1977, is responsible for the audit of the legality and regularity as well as of the sound financial management of the resources managed by the European Communities and Community bodies. The Court of Auditors may also submit observations on specific questions and deliver opinions. The Court of Auditors draws up an annual report and a statement of assurance on the accounts and underlying operations of the Communities. The Maastricht Treaty designated the Court of Auditors as a full institution of the European Union, enabling it to take other institutions to the Court of Justice. It has 15 members appointed for six-year terms by the Council of Ministers following consultation with the European Parliament.
President, Bernhard Friedmann (Germany)

PROGRESS TOWARDS MEETING EMU CRITERIA

State	Budget deficit*	National debt*	Inflation rate (%)	Interest rate (%)†	Year of joining ERM
Austria	−5.1	69.3	2.2	6.6	1995
Belgium	−3.4	132.7	2.0	6.8	1979
Denmark	−1.0	81.6	2.4	7.6	1979
Finland	−3.0	62.5	2.0	7.7	1996
France	−4.2	55.0	1.8	6.6	1979
Germany	−3.9	60.1	1.5	6.3	1979
Greece	−7.9	113.3	7.4	13.3	—
Ireland	−2.6	80.0	2.3	8.0	1979
Italy	−6.8	121.4	4.4	10.4	1979–92, 1996
Luxembourg	—	6.7	1.8	6.8	1979
Netherlands	−3.5	79.5	2.3	6.5	1979
Portugal	−4.5	72.6	3.5	9.1	1992
Spain	−4.7	65.5	3.6	9.9	1989
Sweden	−4.5	79.5	2.8	8.8	—
UK	−3.8	49.7	2.8	8.1	1990–2

* percentage of GDP
† as at March 1996
Source: IMF

COURT OF JUSTICE OF THE EUROPEAN COMMUNITIES
L–2925 Luxembourg

The European Court superseded the Court of Justice of the ECSC and is common to the three European Communities. It exists to safeguard the law in the interpretation and application of the Community treaties, to decide on the legality of decisions of the Council of Ministers or the Commission, and to determine infringements of the treaties. Cases may be brought to it by the member states, the Community institutions, firms or individuals. Its decisions are directly binding in the member countries, and the Maastricht Treaty enhanced the Court's powers by permitting it to impose fines on member states. The 15 judges and nine advocates-general of the Court are appointed for renewable six-year terms by the member governments in concert. During 1996, 423 new cases were lodged at the court, 280 cases were concluded and 193 judgments were delivered.

Composition of the Court, in order of precedence, with effect from 7 October 1996:

G. C. Rodríguez Iglesias (*President*); G. F. Mancini (*President of the 2nd and 6th Chambers*); J. C. Moitinho de Almeida (*President of the 3rd and 5th Chambers*); J. L. Murray (*President of the 4th Chamber*); A. M. La Pergola (*First Advocate-General*); L. Sevón (*Judge*); C. N. Kakouris (*Judge*); C. O. Lenz (*Advocate-General*); F. G. Jacobs (*Advocate-General*); G. Tesauro (*Advocate-General*); P. J. G. Kapteyn (*Judge*); C. Gulman (*Judge*); D. A. O. Edward (*Judge*); G. Cosmas (*Advocate-General*); J.-P. Puissochet (*Judge*); P. Léger (*Advocate-General*); G. Hirsch (*Judge*); M. B. Elmer (*Advocate-General*); P. Jann (*Judge*); H. Ragnemalm (*Judge*); N. Fennelly (*Advocate-General*); D. Ruiz-Jarabo Colomer (*Advocate-General*); M. Wathelet (*Judge*); R. Schintgen (*Judge*); R. Grass (*Registrar*)

COURT OF FIRST INSTANCE
L-2925 Luxembourg

Established under powers conferred by the Single European Act, the Court of First Instance started to exercise its functions at the end of October 1989. It had jurisdiction to hear and determine certain categories of cases brought by natural or legal persons, in particular cases brought by European Community officials, or cases on competition law. By a Council decision of 1993 the court had its jurisdiction enlarged to hear and determine all actions brought by natural or legal persons. During 1995, 253 new cases were lodged at the court, 198 cases were concluded and 98 judgments were delivered.

Composition of the Court, in order of precedence, for the judicial year 1996–7:

A. Saggio (*President of the Court and of the 1st Chamber*); B. Vesterdorf (*President of the 3rd Chamber*); R. García-Valdecasas y Fernández (*President of the 5th Chamber*); K. Lenaerts (*President of the 4th Chamber*); C. W. Bellamy (*President of the 2nd Chamber*); C. P. Briët (*Judge*); A. Kalogeropoulos (*Judge*); V. Tiili (*Judge*); P. Lindh (*Judge*); J. Azizi (*Judge*); A. Potocki (*Judge*); R. Moura-Ramos (*Judge*); J. D. Cooke (*Judge*); M. Jaeger (*Judge*); H. Jung (*Registrar*)

THE EUROPEAN INVESTMENT BANK
100 Boulevard Konrad Adenauer, L-2950 Luxembourg

The European Investment Bank (EIB) was set up in 1958 under the terms of the Treaty of Rome to finance capital investment projects promoting the balanced development of the European Community.

It grants long-term loans to private and public enterprises, public authorities and financial institutions, to finance projects which further the economic development of less advanced regions (Assisted Areas); improvement of European communications; environmental protection; attainment of the EU's energy policy objectives; modernization of enterprises, co-operation between undertakings in the different member states, and the activities of small and medium-sized enterprises.

EIB activities have also been extended outside member countries as part of the EU's development co-operation policy, under the terms of different association or co-operation agreements with 12 countries in the Mediterranean region, 11 in central and eastern Europe, 30 in Latin America and Asia, and, under the Lomé Conventions, 70 in Africa, the Caribbean and the Pacific.

The Bank's total financing operations in 1996 amounted to 23,200 million ECU, of which 20,900 million was for investment in the EU and 2,300 million for investment outside the EU. Between 1992 and 1996 the EIB made available a total of more than £9,000 million for investment in the UK.

The members of the EIB are the 15 member states of the EU, who have all subscribed to the Bank's capital of 62,013 million ECU. The bulk of the funds required by the Bank to carry out its tasks are borrowed on the capital markets of the EU and non-member countries, and on the international market.

As it operates on a non-profit-making basis, the interest rates charged by the EIB reflect the cost of the Bank's borrowings and closely follow conditions on world capital markets.

The Board of Governors of the EIB consists of one government minister nominated by each of the member countries, usually the finance minister, who lay down general directives on the policy of the Bank and appoint members to the Board of Directors (24 nominated by the member states, one by the European Commission), which takes decisions on the granting and raising of loans and the fixing of interest rates. A Management Committee, composed of the Bank's President and seven Vice-Presidents, also appointed by the Board of Governors, is responsible for the day-to-day operations of the Bank. The President and Vice-Presidents also preside as Chairman and Vice-Chairmen at meetings of the Board of Directors.

President, Sir Brian Unwin, KCB

Vice-Presidents, Wolfgang Roth; Panagiotis-Loukas Gennimatas; Massimo Ponzellini; Louis Martí; Ariane Obolensky; Rudolf de Korte; Claes de Neergaard

UK OFFICE: 68 Pall Mall, London SW1Y 5ES. Tel: 0171-343 1200

NEW INSTITUTIONS AND AGENCIES

The Maastricht Treaty, together with the 1993 Brussels Council summit, established a number of new institutions and agencies:

THE COMMITTEE OF THE REGIONS
79 rue Belliard, 1040 Brussels, Belgium

The Committee of the Regions (COR) is an advisory and consultative body established to redress the lack of a role for regional and local authorities in the EU democratic system. The COR is composed of 222 appointed and indirectly elected members, of whom half are from large regions and half are from small local authorities, who meet five times each year for two days. The COR delivers opinions on policies affecting regions, such as trans-border transport links, economic and social cohesion, education and training, social policy, culture and regional policy.
President, Maragrll Emerr (Spain)

THE EUROPEAN MONETARY INSTITUTE
29 Kaiserstrasse, 60311 Frankfurt-am-Main, Germany

The European Monetary Institute was established to co-ordinate member states' monetary policy during stage II of economic and monetary union (EMU), which began on 1 January 1994; to oversee preparation for a transfer to a single currency; and to create the right conditions for the third and final stage of EMU. The EMI consists of the governors of the central banks of the 15 EU member states, who form the EMI Council, and support staff. The council meets monthly to assess how well member governments are meeting the criteria laid down by the Maastricht Treaty for achieving economic convergence.
President, Baron Alexandre Lamfalussy (Belgium)

THE EUROPEAN DRUGS AGENCY
Raamweg 47, 2596HN The Hague, The Netherlands

The European Drugs Agency (EUROPOL) was estab-lished as an information clearing house engaged in surveillance of drug trafficking. It is staffed by 80 personnel seconded from member states' police, gendarmeries and customs forces, housed in 15 national liaison offices linked to their respective national police computers; the working language is English. Its remit has been expanded from co-ordinating cross-border drug-trafficking investigations to include combating illegal immigration rackets, trade in nuclear materials, cross-border car theft and any associated money laundering. EUROPOL has no legal powers of its own and can only operate through member states' police and customs forces. At present it operates on an *ad hoc* basis as its convention has yet to be agreed and ratified by the member states.
Co-ordinator, Juergen Storbeck (Germany)

Other bodies include:
THE EUROPEAN MEDICINE EVALUATION AGENCY, London
THE EUROPEAN TRADEMARK OFFICE, Alicante
THE EUROPEAN AGENCY FOR HEALTH AND SAFETY AT WORK, Bilbao
THE EUROPEAN OFFICE FOR VETERINARY AND PLANT HEALTH INSPECTION, Dublin
THE EUROPEAN DRUGS OBSERVATORY, Lisbon
THE EUROPEAN FOUNDATION FOR TRAINING, Turin
THE EUROPEAN CENTRE FOR THE DEVELOPMENT OF VOCATIONAL TRAINING, Salonika
THE EUROPEAN ENVIRONMENT AGENCY, Copenhagen
THE EUROPEAN TRANSLATION AGENCY, Luxembourg

EUROPEAN COMMUNITY INFORMATION

EUROPEAN COMMISSION REPRESENTATIVE OFFICES
ENGLAND, 8 Storey's Gate, London SW1P 3AT. Tel: 0171-973 1992

WALES, 4 Cathedral Road, Cardiff CF1 9SG. Tel: 01222-371631
SCOTLAND, 9 Alva Street, Edinburgh EH2 4HP. Tel: 0131-225 2058
NORTHERN IRELAND, Windsor House, 9–15 Bedford Street, Belfast BT2 7EG. Tel: 01232-240708
REPUBLIC OF IRELAND, 39 Molesworth Street, Dublin 2
USA, 2100 M Street NW (Suite 707), Washington DC 20037; 1 Dag Hammarskjöld Plaza, 254 East 47th Street, New York, NY 10017
CANADA, Inn of the Provinces, Office Tower (Suite 1110), 350 Sparks Street, Ottawa, Ontario, KIR 7SA
AUSTRALIA, 18 Alakana Street, Yarralumia, ACT 2600, and a number of other cities

UK EUROPEAN PARLIAMENT INFORMATION OFFICE
2 Queen Anne's Gate, London SW1H 9AA Tel: 0171-227 4300

There are European Information Centres, set up to give information and advice to small businesses, in 24 British towns and cities. A number of universities maintain European Documentation Centres.

Countries of the World

WORLD AREA AND POPULATION

The total population of the world in mid-1990 was estimated at 5,292 million, compared with 3,019 million in 1960 and 2,070 million in 1930.

Continent, etc.	Area sq. miles '000	sq. km '000	Estimated population mid-1990
Africa	11,704	30,313	642,000,000
North America[1]	8,311	21,525	276,000,000
Latin America[2]	7,933	20,547	448,000,000
Asia[3]	10,637	27,549	3,113,000,000
Europe[4]	1,915	4,961	498,000,000
Former USSR	8,649	22,402	289,000,000
Oceania[5]	3,286	8,510	26,500,000
TOTAL	52,435	135,807	5,292,000,000

[1] Includes Greenland and Hawaii
[2] Mexico and the remainder of the Americas south of the USA
[3] Includes European Turkey, excludes former USSR
[4] Excludes European Turkey and former USSR
[5] Includes Australia, New Zealand and the islands inhabited by Micronesian, Melanesian and Polynesian peoples
Source: UN Demographic Yearbook 1990 (pub. 1992)

A United Nations report *The Sex and Age Distribution of the World Populations* (revised 1994) puts the world's population in the late 20th and the 21st centuries at the following levels (medium variant data):

1995	5,716.4m	2030	8,670.6m
2000	6,158.0m	2040	9,318.2m
2010	7,032.3m	2050	9,833.2m
2020	7,887.8m		

The population forecast for the years 2000 and 2050 is:

Continent, etc.	Estimated population (million) 2000	2050
Africa	831.596	2,140.844
North America[1]	306.280	388.997
Latin America[2]	523.875	838.527
Asia	3,753.846	5,741.005
Europe	729.803	677.764
Oceania	30.651	46.070
TOTAL	6,158.051	9,833.207

[1] Includes Bermuda, Greenland, and St Pierre and Miquelon
[2] Mexico and the remainder of the Americas south of the USA

AREA AND POPULATION BY CONTINENT

No complete survey of many countries has yet been achieved and consequently accurate area figures are not always available. Similarly, many countries have not recently, or have never, taken a census. The areas of countries given below are derived from estimated figures published by the United Nations. The conversion factors used are:
(i) to convert square miles to square km, multiply by 2.589988
(ii) to convert square km to square miles, multiply by 0.3861022
Population figures for countries are derived from the most recent estimates available. Accurate and up-to-date data for the populations of capital cities are scarce, and definitions of cities' extent differ. The figures given below are the latest estimates available.

Ψ   seaport

AFRICA

COUNTRY/TERRITORY	AREA sq. miles	sq. km	POPULATION	CAPITAL	POPULATION OF CAPITAL
Algeria	919,595	2,381,741	27,325,000	Ψ Algiers	1,740,461
Angola	481,354	1,246,700	10,674,000	Ψ Luanda	475,328
Benin	43,484	112,622	5,387,000	Ψ Porto Novo	179,138
Botswana	224,607	581,730	1,443,000	Gaborone	133,468
Burkina Faso	105,792	274,000	9,889,000	Ouagadougou	634,479
Burundi	10,747	27,834	6,134,000	Bujumbura	235,440
Cameroon	183,569	475,442	12,871,000	Yaoundé	653,670
Cape Verde	1,557	4,033	417,000	Ψ Praia	80,000
Central African Republic	240,535	622,984	3,235,000	Bangui	473,817
Chad Republic	495,755	1,284,000	6,214,000	Ndjaména	179,000
The Comoros	863	2,235	630,000	Moroni	17,267
Congo, Dem. Rep.	905,567	2,345,409	42,552,000	Kinshasa	2,778,281
Congo, Rep. of	132,047	342,000	2,516,000	Brazzaville	596,200
Côte d'Ivoire	124,503	322,463	13,695,000	Yamoussoukro	126,191
Djibouti	8,958	23,200	566,000	Ψ Djibouti	340,700
Egypt	386,662	1,001,449	58,978,000	Cairo	13,000,000
Equatorial Guinea	10,830	28,051	389,000	Ψ Malabo	30,418
Eritrea	45,406	117,600	3,437,000	Asmara	358,100
Ethiopia	426,373	1,104,300	54,938,000	Addis Ababa	2,316,400

Country/Territory	Area sq. miles	sq. km	Population	Capital	Population of Capital
Gabon	103,347	267,667	1,283,000	Ψ Libreville	251,000
Gambia	4,361	11,295	1,081,000	Ψ Banjul	109,986
Ghana	92,098	238,533	17,434,227	Ψ Accra	738,498
Guinea	94,926	245,857	6,501,000	Ψ Conakry	763,000
Guinea-Bissau	13,948	36,125	1,050,000	Ψ Bissau	109,214
Kenya	224,081	580,367	29,292,000	Nairobi	1,400,000
Lesotho	11,720	30,355	1,996,000	Maseru	288,951
Liberia	43,000	111,369	2,700,000	Ψ Monrovia	421,053
Libya	679,362	1,759,540	4,899,000	Ψ Tripoli	1,000,000
Madagascar	226,669	587,041	14,303,000	Antananarivo	377,600
Malawi	45,747	118,484	9,461,000	Lilongwe	233,973
Mali	478,841	1,240,192	10,462,000	Bamako	658,275
Mauritania	395,956	1,025,520	2,211,000	Nouakchott	850,000
Mauritius	720	1,865	1,142,513	Ψ Port Louis	144,970
Mayotte (Fr.)	144	372	94,410	Mamoundzou	12,000
Morocco	172,414	446,550	26,590,000	Ψ Rabat	1,220,000
Western Sahara	102,703	266,000	272,000	Laayoune	96,784
Mozambique	309,495	801,590	16,500,000	Ψ Maputo	882,601
Namibia	318,261	824,292	1,500,000	Windhoek	125,000
Niger	489,191	1,267,000	8,846,000	Niamey	392,169
Nigeria	356,669	923,768	108,467,000	Abuja	378,671
Réunion (Fr.)	969	2,510	644,000	St Denis	121,999
Rwanda	10,169	26,338	7,750,000	Kigali	156,000
St Helena (UK)	47	122	5,644	Ψ Jamestown	1,332
Ascension Island	34	88	1,111	Ψ Georgetown	—
Tristan da Cunha	38	98	288	Ψ Edinburgh of the Seven Seas	—
São Tomé and Príncipe	372	964	125,000	Ψ São Tomé	43,420
Senegal	75,755	196,722	8,102,000	Ψ Dakar	1,641,358
Seychelles	176	455	74,000	Ψ Victoria	24,324
Sierra Leone	27,699	71,740	4,402,000	Ψ Freetown	469,776
Somalia	246,201	637,657	9,077,000	Ψ Mogadishu	1,000,000
South Africa	471,445	1,221,031	40,436,000	Pretoria / Ψ Cape Town	525,583 / 854,616
Sudan	967,500	2,505,813	28,947,000	Khartoum	924,505
Swaziland	6,704	17,363	832,000	Mbabane	38,290
Tanzania	364,900	945,087	28,846,000	Dodoma	88,474
Togo	21,925	56,785	3,928,000	Ψ Lomé	366,476
Tunisia	63,170	163,610	8,733,000	Ψ Tunis	1,394,749
Uganda	93,065	241,038	20,621,000	Kampala	750,000
Zambia	290,586	752,614	9,196,000	Lusaka	982,362
Zimbabwe	150,872	390,757	11,150,000	Harare	1,189,103

AMERICA

North America

Country/Territory	Area sq. miles	sq. km	Population	Capital	Population of Capital
Canada	3,849,670	9,970,599	29,248,000	Ottawa	974,077
Greenland (Den.)	840,004	2,175,600	55,700	Ψ Godthåb	12,483
Mexico	756,066	1,958,201	93,008,000	Mexico City	15,017,685
St Pierre and Miquelon (Fr.)	93	242	6,000	Ψ St Pierre	5,416
United States	3,540,321	9,169,389	265,284,000	Washington DC	6,919,572

Central America and the West Indies

Anguilla (UK)	35	91	8,960	The Valley	1,400
Antigua and Barbuda	171	442	65,000	Ψ St John's	22,342
Aruba (Neth.)	75	193	71,000	Ψ Oranjestad	25,000
Bahamas	5,358	13,878	284,000	Ψ Nassau	172,196
Barbados	166	430	261,000	Ψ Bridgetown	108,000
Belize	8,763	22,696	211,000	Belmopan	44,087
Bermuda (UK)	20.59	53	60,075	Ψ Hamilton	2,277
Cayman Islands (UK)	100	259	35,000	Ψ George Town	20,000
Costa Rica	19,730	51,100	3,071,000	San José	1,186,417
Cuba	42,804	110,861	10,960,000	Ψ Havana	2,160,368
Dominica	290	751	71,000	Ψ Roseau	16,243
Dominican Republic	18,816	48,734	7,760,000	Ψ Santo Domingo	1,540,786

Country/Territory	Area sq. miles	sq. km	Population	Capital	Population of Capital
Grenada	133	344	92,000	Ψ St George's	4,788
Guadeloupe (Fr.)	658	1,704	421,000	Ψ Basse Terre	29,522
Guatemala	42,042	108,889	10,322,000	Guatemala City	1,675,589
Haiti	10,714	27,750	7,041,000	Ψ Port-au-Prince	690,168
Honduras	43,277	112,088	5,770,000	Tegucigalpa	670,100
Jamaica	4,244	10,991	2,496,000	Ψ Kingston	103,962
Martinique (Fr.)	425	1,102	375,000	Ψ Fort de France	97,814
Montserrat (UK)	38	98	6,500	Ψ Plymouth	2,500
Netherlands Antilles (Neth.)	308	800	207,333	Ψ Willemstad	50,000
Nicaragua	50,193	130,000	4,401,000	Managua	608,020
Panama	29,157	75,517	2,631,013	Ψ Panama City	445,902
Puerto Rico (USA)	3,427	8,875	3,733,000	Ψ San Juan	437,745
St Christopher and Nevis	101	261	41,000	Ψ Basseterre	14,161
St Lucia	238	616	141,000	Ψ Castries	56,000
St Vincent and the Grenadines	150	388	111,000	Ψ Kingstown	33,694
El Salvador	8,124	21,041	5,641,000	San Salvador	422,570
Trinidad and Tobago	1,981	5,130	1,257,000	Ψ Port of Spain	50,878
Turks and Caicos Is. (UK)	166	430	19,000	Ψ Grand Turk	4,000
Virgin Islands:					
British (UK)	59	153	16,108	Ψ Road Town	3,983
US (USA)	134	347	101,809	Ψ Charlotte Amalie	11,756
South America					
Argentina	1,073,512	2,780,400	34,180,000	Ψ Buenos Aires	10,686,163
Bolivia	424,165	1,098,581	7,237,000	La Paz	784,976
Brazil	3,286,488	8,511,965	153,725,000	Brasilia	1,601,094
Chile	292,134	756,626	13,994,000	Santiago	5,257,937
Colombia	439,737	1,138,914	34,520,000	Bogotá	8,000,000
Ecuador	109,484	283,561	11,221,000	Quito	1,387,887
Falkland Islands (UK)	4,700	12,173	2,621	Ψ Stanley	1,636
French Guiana (Fr.)	34,749	90,000	141,000	Ψ Cayenne	41,164
Guyana	83,000	214,969	825,000	Ψ Georgetown	250,000
Paraguay	157,048	406,752	4,700,000	Asunción	502,000
Peru	496,225	1,285,216	23,088,000	Lima	6,483,901
South Georgia (UK)	1,580	4,092	—	—	—
Suriname	63,037	163,265	418,000	Ψ Paramaribo	200,970
Uruguay	68,500	177,414	3,167,000	Ψ Montevideo	1,383,660
Venezuela	352,145	912,050	21,177,000	Caracas	2,784,042

ASIA

Country/Territory	Area sq. miles	sq. km	Population	Capital	Population of Capital
Afghanistan	251,772	652,090	18,879,000	Kabul	1,424,400
Bahrain	268	694	549,000	Ψ Manama	136,999
Bangladesh	55,598	143,998	117,787,000	Dhaka	3,397,187
Bhutan	18,147	47,000	1,614,000	Thimphu	15,000
Brunei	2,226	5,765	305,100	Bandar Seri Begawan	49,902
Cambodia	69,898	181,035	10,600,000	Ψ Phnom Penh	832,000
China[1]	3,705,408	9,596,961	1,208,842,000	Beijing (Peking)	7,362,426
Hong Kong (China)	415	1,075	6,311,000	—	—
India	1,269,346	3,287,590	918,570,000	New Delhi	301,297
Indonesia	735,358	1,904,569	192,217,000	Ψ Jakarta	8,500,000
Iran	630,577	1,633,188	59,275,359	Tehran	6,750,043
Iraq	169,235	438,317	19,925,000	Baghdad	3,841,268
Israel[2]	8,130	21,056	5,383,000	Tel Aviv	1,812,100
West Bank and Gaza Strip	2,406	6,231	1,635,000	Gaza City	120,000
Japan	143,939	372,801	124,961,000	Tokyo	8,080,286
Jordan	37,738	97,740	5,198,000	Amman	1,270,000
Kazakhstan	1,049,156	2,717,300	17,027,000	Alma-Ata	1,198,000
Korea, D.P.R. (North)	46,540	120,538	23,483,000	Pyongyang	2,000,000
Korea, Rep. of (South)	38,330	99,274	44,606,000	Seoul	10,229,000
Kuwait	6,880	17,818	1,575,983	Ψ Kuwait City	400,000
Kyrgyzstan	76,642	198,501	4,596,000	Bishkek	627,800
Laos	91,429	236,800	4,605,300	Vientiane	132,253
Lebanon	4,015	10,400	2,915,000	Ψ Beirut	1,500,000
Macao (Port.)	6	15.5	395,000	Ψ Macao	—
Malaysia	127,320	329,758	20,103,000	Kuala Lumpur	1,145,075

Country/Territory	Area sq. miles	sq. km	Population	Capital	Population of Capital
Maldives	115	298	256,157	Ψ Malé	62,973
Mongolia	604,829	1,566,500	2,363,000	Ulan Bator	515,100
Myanmar (Burma)	261,218	676,552	45,555,000	Ψ Yangon (Rangoon)	2,513,023
Nepal	56,827	147,181	21,360,000	Kathmandu	419,073
Oman	82,030	212,457	2,077,000	Ψ Muscat	400,000
Pakistan	307,374	796,095	126,610,000	Islamabad	350,000
Philippines	115,831	300,000	67,038,000	Ψ Manila	8,594,150
Qatar	4,247	11,000	540,000	Ψ Doha	217,294
Saudi Arabia	830,000	2,149,640	17,451,000	Riyadh	1,800,000
Singapore	239	618	3,400,000	—	—
Sri Lanka	25,332	65,610	17,865,000	Sri Jayawardenapura	2,026,000
Syria	71,498	185,180	13,844,000	Damascus	1,549,000
Taiwan	13,800	35,742	21,450,183	Taipei	2,607,010
Tajikistan	55,251	143,100	5,513,400	Dushanbe	602,000
Thailand	198,115	513,115	60,700,000	Ψ Bangkok	5,876,000
Turkey[3]	299,158	774,815	61,183,000	Ankara	3,103,000
Turkmenistan	188,456	488,100	3,808,900	Ashkhabad	407,000
United Arab Emirates	32,278	83,600	2,377,453	Abu Dhabi	450,000
Uzbekistan	172,742	447,400	21,206,800	Tashkent	2,094,000
Vietnam	128,066	331,689	72,510,000	Hanoi	3,056,146
Yemen	203,850	527,968	15,800,000	Sana'a	972,000

[1] Including Tibet
[2] Including East Jerusalem, the Golan Heights and Israeli citizens on the West Bank
[3] Including Turkey in Europe

EUROPE

Country/Territory	Area sq. miles	sq. km	Population	Capital	Population of Capital
Albania	11,099	28,748	3,414,000	Tirana	244,153
Andorra	175	453	64,479	Andorra la Vella	16,151
Armenia	11,506	29,800	3,548,000	Yerevan	1,254,400
Austria	32,378	83,859	8,047,000	Vienna	1,593,000
Azerbaijan	33,436	86,600	7,553,000	Ψ Baku	1,149,000
Belarus	80,155	207,600	10,265,000	Minsk	1,681,000
Belgium	11,783	30,519	10,080,000	Brussels	960,324
Bosnia-Hercegovina	19,735	51,129	3,527,000	Sarajevo	115,631
Bulgaria	42,823	110,912	8,443,000	Sofia	1,189,641
Croatia	34,022	88,117	4,504,000	Zagreb	867,717
Cyprus	3,572	9,251	734,000	Nicosia	186,400
Czech Republic	30,450	78,864	10,333,000	Prague	1,216,513
Denmark	16,639	43,094	5,251,027	Ψ Copenhagen	1,752,078
Faroe Islands	540	1,399	43,700	Ψ Tórshavn	16,218
Estonia	17,413	45,100	1,464,100	Talinn	427,510
Finland	130,559	338,145	5,095,000	Ψ Helsinki	1,016,291
France	212,934	551,500	57,747,000	Paris	9,319,367
Georgia	26,911	69,700	5,401,000	Tbilisi	1,268,000
Germany	137,735	356,733	81,410,000	Berlin	3,472,009
Gibraltar (UK)	2.5	6.5	27,337	Ψ Gibraltar	—
Greece	50,961	131,990	10,426,000	Athens	3,027,331
Hungary	35,920	93,032	10,261,000	Budapest	2,002,121
Iceland	39,768	103,000	269,735	Ψ Reykjavik	104,258
Ireland, Republic of	27,136	70,283	3,626,087	Ψ Dublin	952,700
Italy	116,320	301,268	57,193,000	Rome	2,693,383
Latvia	24,942	64,600	2,529,600	Riga	840,000
Liechtenstein	62	160	31,000	Vaduz	5,072
Lithuania	25,174	65,200	3,707,200	Vilnius	580,000
Luxembourg	998	2,586	412,800	Luxembourg	75,800
Macedonia, Former Yugoslav Republic of	9,925	25,713	2,142,000	Skopje	448,229
Malta	122	316	376,335	Ψ Valletta	7,184
Moldova	13,912	36,018	4,335,000	Kishinev	667,100
Monaco	0.4	1	31,000	Monaco-Ville	27,063
Netherlands	15,770	40,844	15,500,000	Ψ Amsterdam	1,095,739
Norway[1]	125,050	323,877	4,369,957	Ψ Oslo	758,949
Poland	124,808	323,250	38,613,000	Warsaw	1,643,000
Portugal[2]	35,514	91,982	9,830,000	Ψ Lisbon	2,561,225

Country/Territory	Area sq. miles	sq. km	Population	Capital	Population of Capital
Romania	92,043	238,391	22,600,000	Bucharest	2,037,278
Russia[3]	6,592,850	17,075,400	147,976,400	Moscow	8,745,000
San Marino	23	61	25,515	San Marino	4,251
Slovakia	18,932	49,035	5,347,000	Bratislava	448,785
Slovenia	7,816	20,251	1,942,000	Ljubljana	330,000
Spain[4]	195,365	505,992	39,481,991	Madrid	3,084,673
Sweden	173,732	449,964	8,780,000	Ψ Stockholm	1,532,803
Switzerland	15,940	41,284	6,995,000	Berne	322,855
Ukraine	233,090	603,700	52,100,000	Kiev	2,642,700
United Kingdom[5]	94,248	244,101	58,606,000	Ψ London	6,904,600
England	50,351	130,410	48,903,000	—	—
Wales	8,015	20,758	2,917,000	Ψ Cardiff	303,000
Scotland	30,420	78,789	5,137,000	Ψ Edinburgh	448,000
Northern Ireland	5,461	14,144	1,649,000	Ψ Belfast	297,000
Vatican City State	0.2	0.44	1,000	Vatican City	766
Yugoslavia, Fed. Rep. of	39,506	102,350	10,515,000	Belgrade	1,136,786

[1] Excludes Svalbard and Jan Mayen Islands (approx. 24,101 sq. miles (62,422 sq. km) and 3,000 population)
[2] Includes Madeira (314 sq. miles) and the Azores (922 sq. miles)
[3] Includes Russia in Asia
[4] Includes Balearic Islands, Canary Islands, Ceuta and Melilla
[5] Excludes Isle of Man (221 sq. miles (572 sq. km), 69,788* population), and Channel Islands (75 sq. miles (194 sq. km), 142,949* population)

OCEANIA

Country/Territory	Area sq. miles	sq. km	Population	Capital	Population of Capital
American Samoa (USA)	77	199	46,773	Ψ Pago Pago	3,519
Australia	2,966,153	7,682,300	18,423,900	Canberra	307,100
Norfolk Island	14	36	1,772	Ψ Kingston	—
Fiji	7,055	18,274	784,000	Ψ Suva	141,273
French Polynesia (Fr.)	1,544	4,000	215,000	Ψ Papeete	36,784
Guam (USA)	210	544	133,152	Agaña	1,139
Kiribati	280	726	77,000	Tarawa	17,921
Marshall Islands	70	181	54,000	Dalap-Uliga-Darrit	20,000
Micronesia, Fed. States of	271	701	104,000	Palikir	—
Nauru	8	21	11,000	Ψ Nauru	—
New Caledonia (Fr.)	7,172	18,575	183,000	Ψ Noumea	97,581
New Zealand	103,736	268,675	3,642,500	Ψ Wellington	325,700
Cook Islands	93	241	18,904	Avarua	—
Niue	100	259	2,239	Alofi	—
Ross Dependency[1]	175,000	453,248	—	—	—
Tokelau	5	12	1,500	—	—
Northern Mariana Islands (USA)	179	464	58,846	Saipan	52,706
Palau (USA)	175	454	17,000	Koror	10,493
Papua New Guinea	178,704	462,840	3,997,000	Ψ Port Moresby	123,624
Pitcairn Islands (UK)	1.9	5	42	—	—
Samoa	1,097	2,842	164,000	Ψ Apia	36,000
Solomon Islands	11,157	28,896	366,000	Ψ Honiara	40,000
Tonga	288	747	98,000	Ψ Nuku'alofa	29,018
Tuvalu	10	25	9,000	Ψ Funafuti	2,856
Vanuatu	4,706	12,190	165,000	Ψ Port Vila	26,100
Wallis and Futuna Islands (Fr.)	77	199	14,000	Ψ Mata-Utu	—

[1] Includes permanent shelf ice

THE ANTARCTIC

The Antarctic is generally defined as the area lying within the Antarctic Convergence, the zone where cold northward-flowing Antarctic sea water sinks below warmer southward-flowing water. This zone is at about latitude 50° S. in the Atlantic Ocean and latitude 55°–62° S. in the Pacific Ocean. The continent itself lies almost entirely within the Antarctic Circle, an area of about 13.66 million sq. km (5.3 million sq. miles), 99.67 per cent of which is permanently ice-covered. The average thickness of the ice is 2,450 m (7,100 ft) but in places exceeds 4,500 m (14,500 ft). Some mountains protrude, the highest being Vinson Massif, 4,897 m (16,067 ft). The ice amounts to some 30 million cubic km (7.2 million cubic miles) and represents more than 90 per cent of the world's fresh water.

Along 43 per cent of the Antarctic coastline, land-ice flowing outwards forms extensive ice shelves, fragments of which break off to form tabular icebergs, leaving ice-cliffs up to 50 m (150 ft) high. Much of the sea freezes in winter, forming fast ice which breaks up in summer and drifts north as pack ice.

The most conspicuous physical features of the continent are its high inland plateau (much of it over 3,000 m (10,000 ft)), the Transantarctic Mountains (which together with the large embayments of the Weddell Sea and Ross Sea mark the approximate boundary between East and West Antarctica), and the mountainous Antarctic Peninsula and off-lying islands which extend northwards towards South America.

CLIMATE

On land, summer temperatures range from just above freezing around the coast to − 34° C (about − 30° F) on the plateau, and in winter from − 20° C (about − 4° F) on the coast to − 65° C (about − 85° F) inland. Over a large area the maxima do not exceed − 15° C (+5° F).

Precipitation is scant over the plateau but amounts to 25–76 cm (10–30 in) (water equivalent) along the coast and some scientific stations are permanently buried by snow. Some rain falls over the more northerly areas in summer. Gravity winds on the plateau slopes and cyclonic storms further north can both exceed 160 km/h (100 m.p.h.) and gusts have been known to reach 240 km/h (150 m.p.h.). Visibility can be reduced to zero in blizzards.

FLORA AND FAUNA

Although a small number of flowering plants, ferns and clubmosses occur on the sub-Antarctic islands, only two (a grass and a pearlwort) extend south of 60° S. Antarctic vegetation is dominated by lichens and mosses, with a few liverworts, algae and fungi. Most of these occur around the coast or on islands, but lichens and some mosses also occur inland.

The only land animals are tiny insects and mites with nematodes, rotifers, and tardigrades in the mosses, but large numbers of seals, penguins and other sea-birds go ashore to breed in the summer. The emperor penguin is the only species which breeds ashore throughout the winter. By contrast, the Antarctic seas abound with life, a wide variety of invertebrates (including krill) and fish providing food for the seals, penguins and other birds, and a residual population of whales.

In 1994 the International Whaling Commission agreed to establish a whale sanctuary around Antarctica in which commercial whaling will be banned for ten years. The sanctuary will cover all sea areas south of 60°S. latitude, apart from the south-west Atlantic and south-east Pacific where it will be south of 40°S. latitude.

POTENTIAL RESOURCES

In the 180 years from Captain James Cook's circumnavigation of the Antarctic in 1772–5 to the mid-1950s, expeditions to the Antarctic made major contributions to geographical and scientific knowledge of the area.

Increasing pressure on the world's food and mineral supplies has stimulated interest in the potential resources even in the extremely hostile polar environment. Minerals may be present in great variety but not in commercially exploitable concentrations in accessible localities. There are indications that off-shore hydrocarbons may be present but mostly below great depths of stormy, ice-infested seas.

Currently, the chief interest is in marine protein, including the shrimp-like krill already fished commercially by Japan and Poland. Research to ensure management of stocks of this organism is being continued by international groups, but it is estimated that they could sustain a yield equal to the present total annual world fish catch.

THE ANTARCTIC TREATY

The International Geophysical Year 1957–8 gave great impetus to Antarctic research, increasing the number of stations from 17 to 44 and the number of nations involved in research from four to 12 by 1957. The co-operative scientific effort proved so fruitful that the 12 nations involved (Argentina, Australia, Belgium, Chile, France, Japan, New Zealand, Norway, South Africa, the Soviet Union, the UK and the USA) pledged themselves to promote scientific and technical co-operation unhampered by politics, and the Antarctic Treaty was signed by the 12 states in 1959.

The 12 signatories to the treaty agreed to establish free use of the Antarctic continent for peaceful scientific purposes; to freeze all territorial claims and disputes in the Antarctic; to ban all military activities in the area; and to prohibit nuclear explosions and the disposal of radioactive waste. Since then additional agreements have been reached to promote conservation and regulate tourism, waste disposal and pollution.

The Antarctic Treaty was defined as covering areas south of latitude 60° S., excluding the high seas but including the ice shelves, and came into force in 1961. It has since been signed by a further 31 states, 14 of which are active in the Antarctic and have therefore been accorded consultative status, bringing the number of consultative parties to 26. In 1991 a protocol to the treaty was adopted by the signatory states which introduced a range of measures to protect Antarctica's environment and prohibit mineral exploitation and mining.

TERRITORIAL CLAIMS

Under the provisions of the Antarctic Treaty all territorial claims and disputes were frozen without the acceptance or denial of the claims of the various claimants. The US and Soviet governments also made it clear that although they had not made any specific territorial claims, they did not relinquish the right to make such claims.

Seven states have made claims in the Antarctic: Argentina claims the part of Antarctica between 74° W. and 25° W.; Chile that part between 90° W. and 53° W.; Britain claims the British Antarctic Territory, an area of 1,093,390 sq. km (422,158 sq. miles) between 20° and 80° W.

longitude; France claims Terre Adélie, 432,000 sq. km (166,800 sq. miles) between 136° and 142° E.; Australia claims the Australian Antarctic Territory, 6,120,000 sq. km (2,320,000 sq. miles) between 160° and 45° E. longitude excluding Terre Adélie; Norway claims Queen Maud Land between 20° W. and 45° E.; and New Zealand claims the Ross Dependency, 450,000 sq. km (175,000 sq. miles) between 160° E. and 150° W. longitude. The Argentinian, British and Chilean claims overlap while the part of the continent between 90° W. and 150° W. is unclaimed by any state.

SCIENTIFIC RESEARCH

There were 35 permanently occupied stations in 1995–6 operated by the following nations: Argentina (6), Australia (3), Brazil (1), Chile (3), China (2), France (1), Germany (1), India (1), Japan (2), New Zealand (1), Poland (1), Russia (4), South Africa (1), South Korea (1), UK (2), Ukraine (1), Uruguay (1), USA (3, including one at the South Pole).

The staff of these stations and summer field-workers are the only people present on the continent and off-lying islands. There are no indigenous inhabitants.

LARGEST CITIES OF THE WORLD

In most cases figures refer to urban agglomerations (Ψ seaport)

	Population			Population
Mexico City, Mexico	15,047,685		Manila, Philippines	8,594,150
Cairo, Egypt	13,000,000	Ψ	Jakarta, Indonesia	8,500,000
Ψ Bombay/Mumbai, India	12,571,720		Delhi, India	8,419,084
Ψ Calcutta, India	10,916,272		Tokyo, Japan	8,080,286
Ψ Buenos Aires	10,686,163		Bogotá, Colombia	8,000,000
Seoul, South Korea	10,229,000		Istanbul, Turkey	7,784,100
São Paulo, Brazil	9,646,187		Beijing, China	7,362,426
Paris, France	9,319,367	Ψ	New York, USA	7,333,253
Ψ Shanghai, China	8,760,000	Ψ	Karachi, Pakistan	7,183,000
Moscow, Russia	8,745,000			

Currencies of the World
AND EXCHANGE RATES AGAINST £ STERLING

Franc CFA = Franc de la Communauté financière africaine
Franc CFP = Franc des Comptoirs français du Pacifique
*Official exchange rate; all other rates are market rates

COUNTRY/TERRITORY	MONETARY UNIT	AVERAGE RATE TO £ 30 August 1996	AVERAGE RATE TO £ 5 September 1997
Afghanistan	Afghani (Af) of 100 puls	Af 7424.25	Af 7531.12
Albania	Lek (Lk) of 100 qindarka	Lk 170.523	Lk 242.978
Algeria	Algerian dinar (DA) of 100 centimes	DA 81.9872	DA 95.1300
American Samoa	Currency is that of the USA	US$ 1.5630	US$ 1.5855
Andorra	French and Spanish currencies in use	—	—
Angola	Readjusted kwanza (Kzrl) of 100 lwei	Kzrl 49678.4	Kzrl 407676.4
Anguilla	East Caribbean dollar (EC$) of 100 cents	EC$ 4.2201	EC$ 4.2809
Antigua and Barbuda	East Caribbean dollar (EC$) of 100 cents	EC$ 4.2201	EC$ 4.2809
Argentina	Peso of 10,000 australes	Pesos 1.5609	Pesos 1.5847
Armenia	Dram of 100 louma	Dram 654.585	Dram 794.494*
Aruba	Aruban florin	Florins 2.7978	Florins 2.8381
Ascension Island	Currency is that of St Helena	at parity with £ sterling	
Australia	Australian dollar ($A) of 100 cents	$A 1.9754	$A 2.1703
Norfolk Island	Currency is that of Australia	$A 1.9754	$A 2.1703
Austria	Schilling of 100 Groschen	Schilling 16.2535	Schilling 20.1585
Azerbaijan	Manat of 100 gopik	Manat 6727.15	Manat 6262.72*
The Bahamas	Bahamian dollar (B$) of 100 cents	B$ 1.5630	B$ 1.5855
Bahrain	Bahrain dinar (BD) of 1,000 fils	BD 0.5893	BD 0.5977
Bangladesh	Taka (Tk) of 100 poisha	Tk 65.4898	Tk 70.6341
Barbados	Barbados dollar (BD$) of 100 cents	BD$ 3.1437	BD$ 3.1889
Belarus	Rouble of 100 kopeks	Roubles 26852.4	Roubles 68710.7*
Belgium	Belgian franc (or frank) of 100 centimes (centiemen)	Francs 47.5621	Francs 59.1551
Belize	Belize dollar (BZ$) of 100 cents	BZ$ 3.1260	BZ$ 3.1710
Benin	Franc CFA	Francs 790.270	Francs 964.080
Bermuda	Bermuda dollar of 100 cents	$ 1.5630	$ 1.5855
Bhutan	Ngultrum of 100 chetrum (Indian currency is also legal tender)	Ngultrum 55.7523	Ngultrum 58.0294
Bolivia	Boliviano ($b) of 100 centavos	$b 8.0182	$b 8.3715
Bosnia-Hercegovina	Dinar of 100 paras	—	—
Botswana	Pula (P) of 100 thebe	P 5.4508	P 5.8511
Brazil	Real of 100 centavos	Real 1.5888	Real 1.7330
Brunei	Brunei dollar (B$) of 100 sen (fully interchangeable with Singapore currency)	$ 2.1995	$ 2.4021
Bulgaria	Lev of 100 stotinki	Leva 329.012	Leva 2857.07
Burkina Faso	Franc CFA	Francs 790.270	Francs 964.080
Burundi	Burundi franc of 100 centimes	Francs 338.437	Francs 562.187
Cambodia	Riel of 100 sen	Riel 3594.90	Riel 4785.04
Cameroon	Franc CFA	Francs 790.270	Francs 964.080
Canada	Canadian dollar (C$) of 100 cents	C$ 2.1386	C$ 2.1930
Cape Verde	Escudo Caboverdiano of 100 centavos	Esc 129.602	Esc 154.142
Cayman Islands	Cayman Islands dollar (CI$) of 100 cents	CI$ 1.3303	CI$ 1.3131
Central African Republic	Franc CFA	Francs 790.270	Francs 964.080
Chad	Franc CFA	Francs 790.270	Francs 964.080
Chile	Chilean peso of 100 centavos	Pesos 641.846	Pesos 657.824
China	Renminbi Yuan of 10 jiao or 100 fen	Yuan 12.9828	Yuan 13.1413
Hong Kong	Hong Kong dollar (HK$) of 100 cents	HK$ 12.0863	HK$ 12.2837
Colombia	Colombian peso of 100 centavos	Pesos 1628.65	Pesos 1880.09
Comoros	Comorian franc (KMF) of 100 centimes	Francs 593.921	Francs 726.996
Congo, Dem. Rep. of	New Zaïre of 100 makuta	Zaïre 77999.2	Zaïre 218006.2
Congo, Rep. of	Franc CFA	Francs 790.270	Francs 964.080
Costa Rica	Costa Rican colón (₡) of 100 céntimos	₡ 329.715	₡ 375.779
Côte d'Ivoire	Franc CFA	Francs 790.270	Francs 964.080
Croatia	Kuna of 100 lipas	Kuna 8.1782	Kuna 10.1121
Cuba	Cuban peso of 100 centavos	Pesos 1.5630	Pesos 33.2955
Cyprus	Cyprus pound (C£) of 100 cents	C£ 0.7164	C£ 0.8458
Czech Republic	Koruna (Kčs) of 100 haléřu	Kčs 40.5380	Kčs 54.3629

Country/Territory	Monetary Unit	Average Rate to £ 30 August 1996	Average Rate to £ 5 September 1997
Denmark	Danish krone of 100 øre	Kroner 8.9275	Kroner 10.9075
Faroe Islands	Currency is that of Denmark	Kroner 8.9275	Kroner 10.9075
Djibouti	Djibouti franc of 100 centimes	Francs 250.080	Francs 281.775
Dominica	East Caribbean dollar (EC$) of 100 cents	EC$ 4.2201	EC$ 4.2809
Dominican Republic	Dominican Republic peso (RD$) of 100 centavos	RD$ 21.7023	RD$ 22.3476
Ecuador	Sucre of 100 centavos	Sucres 5125.86	Sucres 6536.22*
Egypt	Egyptian pound (£E) of 100 piastres or 1,000 millièmes	£E 5.3123	£E 5.3879
Equatorial Guinea	Franc CFA	Francs 790.270	Francs 964.080
Eritrea	Ethiopian currency is in use	EB 9.0654	EB 10.6609
Estonia	Kroon of 100 sents	Kroons 18.5316	Kroons 22.9141
Ethiopia	Ethiopian birr (EB) of 100 cents	EB 9.0654	EB 10.6609
Falkland Islands	Falkland pound of 100 pence	*at parity with £ sterling*	
Fiji	Fiji dollar (F$) of 100 cents	F$ 2.1799	F$ 2.3163
Finland	Markka (Mk) of 100 penniä	Mk 6.9845	Mk 8.5887
France	Franc of 100 centimes	Francs 7.9027	Francs 9.6408
French Guiana	Currency is that of France	Francs 7.9027	Francs 9.6408
French Polynesia	Franc CFP	Francs 143.981	Francs 176.241
Gabon	Franc CFA	Francs 790.270	Francs 964.080
The Gambia	Dalasi (D) of 100 butut	D 15.3643	D 15.9057
Georgia	Lari of 100 tetri	—	—
Germany	Deutsche Mark (DM) of 100 Pfennig	DM 2.3098	DM 2.8647
Ghana	Cedi of 100 pesewas	Cedi 2633.66	Cedi 3472.25
Gibraltar	Gibraltar pound of 100 pence	*at parity with £ sterling*	
Greece	Drachma of 100 leptae	Drachmae 369.415	Drachmae 451.519
Greenland	Currency is that of Denmark	Kroner 8.9275	Kroner 10.9075
Grenada	East Caribbean dollar (EC$) of 100 cents	EC$ 4.2201	EC$ 4.2809
Guadeloupe	Currency is that of France	Francs 7.9027	Francs 9.6408
Guam	Currency is that of USA	US$ 1.5630	US$ 1.5855
Guatemala	Quetzal (Q) of 100 centavos	Q 9.5038	Q 9.6459
Guinea	Guinea franc of 100 centimes	Francs 1558.31	Francs 1759.90
Guinea-Bissau	Franc CFA	Pesos 28190.3	Francs 964.080
Guyana	Guyana dollar (G$) of 100 cents	G$ 217.101	G$ 225.934
Haiti	Gourde of 100 centimes	Gourdes 23.2178	Gourdes 26.1766
Honduras	Lempira of 100 centavos	Lempiras 18.8654	Lempiras 20.6115
Hungary	Forint of 100 fillér	Forints 235.958	Forints 311.939
Iceland	Icelandic króna (Kr) of 100 aurar	Kr 103.471	Kr 114.568
India	Indian rupee (Rs) of 100 paisa	Rs 55.7523	Rs 58.0294
Indonesia	Rupiah (Rp) of 100 sen	Rp 3660.55	Rp 4653.45
Iran	Rial	Rials 4689.00	Rials 4756.50
Iraq	Iraqi dinar (ID) of 1,000 fils	ID 0.4860	ID 0.4929*
Ireland, Rep. of	Punt (IR£) of 100 pence	IR£ 0.9630	IR£ 1.0672
Israel	Shekel of 100 agora	Shekels 4.9060	Shekels 5.5770
Italy	Lira of 100 centesimi	Lire 2358.53	Lire 2792.53
Jamaica	Jamaican dollar (J$) of 100 cents	J$ 53.5328	J$ 54.6205
Japan	Yen of 100 sen	Yen 169.742	Yen 192.171
Jordan	Jordanian dinar (JD) of 1,000 fils	JD 1.1094	JD 1.1249
Kazakhstan	Tenge	Tenge 106.597	Tenge 120.260
Kenya	Kenya shilling (Ksh) of 100 cents	Ksh 88.9348	Ksh 100.481
Kiribati	Australian dollar ($A) of 100 cents	$A 1.9754	$A 2.1703
Korea, North	Won of 100 chon	Won 3.3605	Won 3.4881
Korea, South	Won of 100 jeon	Won 1280.49	Won 1437.26
Kuwait	Kuwaiti dinar (KD) of 1,000 fils	KD 0.4678	KD 0.4838
Kyrgyzstan	Som	—	—
Laos	Kip (K) of 100 at	K 1437.96	K 1523.67
Latvia	Lats of 100 santimes	Lats 0.8502	Lats 0.9287
Lebanon	Lebanese pound (L£) of 100 piastres	L£ 2441.41	L£ 2439.29
Lesotho	Loti (M) of 100 lisente	M 7.0140	M 7.4384
Liberia	Liberian dollar (L$) of 100 cents	L$ 1.5630	L$ 1.5855
Libya	Libyan dinar (LD) of 1,000 dirhams	LD 0.5557	LD 0.6081
Liechtenstein	Swiss franc of 100 rappen (or centimes)	Francs 1.8718	Francs 2.3467
Lithuania	Litas	Litas 6.2520	Litas 6.3429
Luxembourg	Luxembourg franc (LF) of 100 centimes (Belgian currency is also legal tender)	LF 47.5621	LF 59.1551
Macao	Pataca of 100 avos	Pataca 12.4867	Pataca 12.6877

Country/Territory	Monetary Unit	Average Rate to £ 30 August 1996	Average Rate to £ 5 September 1997
Macedonia (Former Yugoslav Republic of)	Dinar of 100 paras	Dinars 63.2940	Dinars 89.2816
Madagascar	Franc malgache (FMG) of 100 centimes	FMG 6017.55	FMG 7848.22
Malawi	Kwacha (K) of 100 tambala	K 23.9139	K 27.3118
Malaysia	Malaysian dollar (ringgit) (M$) of 100 sen	M$ 3.8978	M$ 4.6713
Maldives	Rufiyaa of 100 laaris	Rufiyaa 18.3965	Rufiyaa 18.6613
Mali	Franc CFA	Francs 790.270	Francs 964.080
Malta	Maltese lira (LM) of 100 cents or 1,000 mils	LM 0.5594	LM 0.6337
Marshall Islands	Currency is that of USA	US$ 1.5630	US$ 1.5855
Martinique	Currency is that of France	Francs 7.9027	Francs 9.6408
Mauritania	Ouguiya (UM) of 5 khoums	UM 214.233	UM 246.142
Mauritius	Mauritius rupee of 100 cents	Rs 31.6430	Rs 34.6749
Mayotte	Currency is that of France	Francs 7.9027	Francs 9.6408
Mexico	Peso of 100 centavos	Pesos 11.8585	Pesos 12.3733
Federated States of Micronesia	Currency is that of USA	US$ 1.5630	US$ 1.5855
Moldova	Leu	Leu 7.2445	Leu 7.2457
Monaco	French franc of 100 centimes	Francs 7.9027	Francs 9.6408
Mongolia	Tugrik of 100 möngö	Tugriks 729.406	Tugriks 1244.24
Montserrat	East Caribbean dollar (EC$) of 100 cents	EC$ 4.2201	EC$ 4.2809
Morocco	Dirham (DH) of 100 centimes	DH 13.4903	DH 15.5997
Mozambique	Metical (MT) of 100 centavos	MT 17412.6	MT 18226.1
Myanmar	Kyat (K) of 100 pyas	K 9.1519	K 9.8541
Namibia	Namibian dollar of 100 cents	*at parity with SA Rand*	
Nauru	Australian dollar ($A) of 100 cents	$A 1.9754	$A 2.1703
Nepal	Nepalese rupee of 100 paisa	Rs 87.5671	Rs 90.2942
The Netherlands	Gulden (guilder) or florin of 100 cents	Guilders 2.5893	Guilders 3.2267
Netherlands Antilles	Netherlands Antilles guilder of 100 cents	Guilders 2.7978	Guilders 2.8381
New Caledonia	Franc CFP	Francs 143.981	Francs 176.241
New Zealand	New Zealand dollar (NZ$) of 100 cents	NZ$ 2.2644	NZ$ 2.4912
Cook Islands	Currency is that of New Zealand	NZ$ 2.2644	NZ$ 2.4912
Niue	Currency is that of New Zealand	NZ$ 2.2644	NZ$ 2.4912
Tokelau	Currency is that of New Zealand	NZ$ 2.2644	NZ$ 2.4912
Nicaragua	Córdoba (C$) of 100 centavos	C$ 13.3918	C$ 15.2761
Niger	Franc CFA	Francs 790.270	Francs 964.080
Nigeria	Naira (N) of 100 kobo	N 34.3860	N 34.7003*
Northern Mariana Islands	Currency is that of USA	US$ 1.5630	US $1.5855
Norway	Krone of 100 øre	Kroner 10.0138	Kroner 11.7812
Oman	Rial Omani (OR) of 1,000 baiza	OR 0.6019	OR 0.6105
Pakistan	Pakistan rupee of 100 paisa	Rs 55.6184	Rs 64.1803
Palau	Currency is that of the USA	US$ 1.5630	US$ 1.5855
Panama	Balboa of 100 centésimos (US notes are also in circulation)	Balboa 1.5630	Balboa 1.5855
Papua New Guinea	Kina (K) of 100 toea	K 2.0512	K 2.2554
Paraguay	Guaraní (Gs) of 100 céntimos	Gs 3243.23	Gs 3448.46
Peru	New Sol of 100 cénts	New Sol 3.8607	New Sol 4.1960
The Philippines	Philippine peso (P) of 100 centavos	P 40.9428	P 50.8946
Pitcairn Islands	Currency is that of New Zealand	NZ$ 2.2644	NZ$ 2.4912
Poland	Złoty of 100 groszy	Złotys 4.2803	Złotys 5.5532
Portugal	Escudo (Esc) of 100 centavos	Esc 236.873	Esc 290.543
Puerto Rico	Currency is that of USA	US$ 1.5630	US$ 1.5855
Qatar	Qatar riyal of 100 dirhams	Riyals 5.6909	Riyals 5.7723
Réunion	Currency is that of France	Francs 7.9027	Francs 9.6408
Romania	Leu (Lei) of 100 bani	Lei 4798.41	Lei 11851.6
Russia	Rouble of 100 kopeks	Roubles 8384.71	Roubles 9260.91
Rwanda	Rwanda franc of 100 centimes	Francs 507.037	Francs 478.907
St Christopher and Nevis	East Caribbean dollar (EC$) of 100 cents	EC$ 4.2201	EC$ 4.2809
St Helena	St Helena pound (£) of 100 pence	*at parity with £ sterling*	
St Lucia	East Caribbean dollar (EC$) of 100 cents	EC$ 4.2201	EC$ 4.2809
St Pierre and Miquelon	Currency is that of France	Francs 7.9027	Francs 9.6408
St Vincent and the Grenadines	East Caribbean dollar (EC$) of 100 cents	EC$ 4.2201	EC$ 4.2809
El Salvador	El Salvador colón (₡) of 100 centavos	₡ 13.6841	₡ 13.8811
Samoa	Tala (S$) of 100 sene	WS$ 3.8069	S$ 4.1515

COUNTRY/TERRITORY	MONETARY UNIT	AVERAGE RATE TO £ 30 August 1996	AVERAGE RATE TO £ 5 September 1997
San Marino	San Marino and Italian currencies are in circulation	Lire 2358.53	Lire 2792.53
São Tomé and Príncipe	Dobra of 100 centavos	Dobra 3727.96	Dobra 3781.62
Saudi Arabia	Saudi riyal (SR) of 20 qursh or 100 halala	SR 5.8621	SR 5.9465
Senegal	Franc CFA	Francs 790.270	Francs 964.080
Seychelles	Seychelles rupee of 100 cents	Rs 7.7916	Rs 8.0861
Sierra Leone	Leone (Le) of 100 cents	Le 1359.81	Le 1236.69
Singapore	Singapore dollar (S$) of 100 cents	S$ 2.1995	S$ 2.4021
Slovakia	Koruna (Kčs) of 100 haléru	Kčs 47.8356	Kčs 55.3197
Slovenia	Tolar (SIT) of 100 stotin	Tolars 205.460	Tolars 268.058
Solomon Islands	Solomon Islands dollar (SI$) of 100 cents	SI$ 5.5526	SI$ 5.8184
Somalia	Somali shilling of 100 cents	Shillings 4095.06	Shillings 4154.01
South Africa	Rand (R) of 100 cents	R 7.0140	R 7.4384
Spain	Peseta of 100 céntimos	Pesetas 195.445	Pesetas 241.694
Sri Lanka	Sri Lankan rupee of 100 cents	Rs 86.9029	Rs 94.3373
Sudan	Sudanese dinar (SD) of 10 pounds	SD 225.072	SD 244.167
Suriname	Suriname guilder of 100 cents	Guilders 640.830	Guilders 635.785
Swaziland	Lilangeni (E) of 100 cents (South African currency is also in circulation)	E 7.0140	E 7.4384
Sweden	Swedish krona of 100 öre	Kronor 10.3397	Kronor 12.3493
Switzerland	Swiss franc of 100 rappen (or centimes)	Francs 1.8718	Francs 2.3467
Syria	Syrian pound (S$) of 100 piastres	S£ 65.5679	S£ 63.4200
Taiwan	New Taiwan dollar (NT$) of 100 cents	NT$ 42.9317	NT$ 45.3730
Tajikistan	Tajik rouble (TJR) of 100 tanga	TJR 83.8471	—
Tanzania	Tanzanian shilling of 100 cents	Shillings 906.540	Shillings 976.589
Thailand	Baht of 100 satang	Baht 39.5518	Baht 58.7825
Togo	Franc CFA	Francs 790.270	Francs 964.080
Tonga	Pa'anga (T$) of 100 seniti	T$ 1.9754	T$ 2.1703
Trinidad and Tobago	Trinidad and Tobago dollar (TT$) of 100 cents	TT$ 9.2860	TT$ 9.6795
Tristan da Cunha	Currency is that of the UK	—	—
Tunisia	Tunisian dinar of 1,000 millimes	Dinars 1.4974	Dinars 1.8103
Turkey	Turkish lira (TL) of 100 kurus	TL 135613.7	TL 269281.4
Turkmenistan	Manat	—	—
Turks and Caicos Islands	US dollar (US$)	US$ 1.5630	US$ 1.5855
Tuvalu	Australian dollar ($A) of 100 cents	$A 1.9754	$A 2.1703
Uganda	Uganda shilling of 100 cents	Shillings 1667.72	Shillings 1744.05
Ukraine	Hryvna of 100 kopiykas	Ka 275869.6	Hryvnas 2.9494
United Arab Emirates	UAE dirham of 100 fils	Dirham 5.7407	Dirham 5.8234
United Kingdom	Pound sterling (£) of 100 pence	£ 1.00	£ 1.00
United States of America	US dollar (US$) of 100 cents	US$ 1.5630	US$ 1.5855
Uruguay	New Uruguayan peso of 100 centésimos	Pesos 12.9651	Pesos 15.4586
Uzbekistan	Sum	—	—
Vanuatu	Vatu of 100 centimes	Vatu 173.313	Vatu 186.479
Vatican City State	Italian currency is legal tender	Lire 2358.53	Lire 2792.53
Venezuela	Bolívar (Bs) of 100 céntimos	Bs 742.425	Bs 786.606
Vietnam	Dông of 10 hào or 100 xu	Dông 17223.5	Dông 18545.6
Virgin Islands, British	US dollar (US$) (£ sterling and EC$ also circulate)	US$ 1.5630	US$ 1.5855
Virgin Islands, US	Currency is that of the USA	US$ 1.5630	US$ 1.5855
Wallis and Futuna Islands	Franc CFP	Francs 143.981	Francs 176.241
Yemen	Riyal of 100 fils	Riyals 218.820	Riyals 206.115
Yugoslavia	New dinar of 100 paras	New Dinars 7.6879	New Dinars 9.0507
Zambia	Kwacha (K) of 100 ngwee	K 1985.01	K 2100.00
Zimbabwe	Zimbabwe dollar (Z$) of 100 cents	Z$ 16.1615	Z$ 18.9626

Time Zones

Standard time differences from the Greenwich meridian

+   hours ahead of GMT
−   hours behind GMT
*   may vary from standard time at some part of the year (Summer Time or Daylight Saving Time)
h   hours
m   minutes

	h	*m*
Afghanistan	+ 4	30
*Albania	+ 1	
Algeria	+ 1	
*Andorra	+ 1	
Angola	+ 1	
Anguilla	− 4	
Antigua and Barbuda	− 4	
Argentina	− 3	
Armenia	+ 4	
Aruba	− 4	
Ascension Island	0	
*Australia	+10	
Broken Hill area (NSW)	+ 9	30
Lord Howe Island	+10	30
Northern Territory	+ 9	30
*South Australia	+ 9	30
Western Australia	+ 8	
*Austria	+ 1	
*Azerbaijan	+ 4	
*Azores	− 1	
*Bahamas	− 5	
Bahrain	+ 3	
Bangladesh	+ 6	
Barbados	− 4	
*Belarus	+ 2	
*Belgium	+ 1	
Belize	− 6	
Benin	+ 1	
*Bermuda	− 4	
Bhutan	+ 6	
Bolivia	− 4	
*Bosnia-Hercegovina	+ 1	
Botswana	+ 2	
Brazil		
Acre	− 5	
*eastern, including all coast and Brasilia	− 3	
Fernando de Noronha Island	− 2	
*western	− 4	
British Antarctic Territory	− 3	
British Indian Ocean Territory	+ 5	
Diego Garcia	+ 6	
British Virgin Islands	− 4	
Brunei	+ 8	
*Bulgaria	+ 2	
Burkina Faso	0	
Burundi	+ 2	
Cambodia	+ 7	
Cameroon	+ 1	
Canada		
*Alberta	− 7	
*British Columbia	− 8	
*Labrador	− 4	
*Manitoba	− 6	

	h	*m*
*New Brunswick	− 4	
*Newfoundland	− 3	30
*Northwest Territories		
east of 85° W.	− 5	
85° W.–102° W.	− 6	
west of 102° W.	− 7	
*Nova Scotia	− 4	
*Ontario		
east of 90° W.	− 5	
west of 90° W.	− 6	
*Prince Edward Island	− 4	
*Quebec		
east of 63° W.	− 4	
west of 63° W.	− 5	
Saskatchewan	− 6	
*Yukon	− 8	
*Canary Islands	0	
Cape Verde	− 1	
Cayman Islands	− 5	
Central African Republic	+ 1	
Chad	+ 1	
*Chatham Island	+12	45
*Chile	− 4	
China	+ 8	
Christmas Island (Indian Ocean)	+ 7	
Cocos Keeling Islands	+ 6	30
Colombia	− 5	
Comoros	+ 3	
Congo (Dem. Rep.)		
east	+ 2	
west	+ 1	
Congo (Rep. of)	+ 1	
Cook Islands	− 10	
Costa Rica	− 6	
Côte d'Ivoire	0	
*Croatia	+ 1	
*Cuba	− 5	
*Cyprus	+ 2	
*Czech Republic	+ 1	
*Denmark	+ 1	
Djibouti	+ 3	
Dominica	− 4	
Dominican Republic	− 4	
Ecuador	− 5	
Galápagos Islands	− 6	
*Egypt	+ 2	
Equatorial Guinea	+ 1	
Eritrea	+ 3	
*Estonia	+ 2	
Ethiopia	+ 3	
*Falkland Islands	− 4	
*Faröe Islands	0	
Fiji	+12	
*Finland	+ 2	
*France	+ 1	
French Guiana	− 3	
French Polynesia	−10	
Marquesas Islands	− 9	30
Gabon	+ 1	
The Gambia	0	
*Georgia	+ 4	
*Germany	+ 1	
Ghana	0	
*Gibraltar	+ 1	
*Greece	+ 2	
*Greenland	− 3	

	h	*m*
Danmarkshavn	0	
Mesters Vig	0	
*Scoresby Sound	− 1	
*Thule area	− 4	
Grenada	− 4	
Guadeloupe	− 4	
Guam	+10	
Guatemala	− 6	
Guinea	0	
Guinea Bissau	0	
Guyana	− 4	
*Haiti	− 5	
Honduras	− 6	
*Hungary	+ 1	
Iceland	0	
India	+ 5	30
Indonesia		
Bali	+ 8	
Flores	+ 8	
Irian Jaya	+ 9	
Java	+ 7	
Kalimantan (south and east)	+ 8	
Kalimantan (west and central)	+ 7	
Molucca Islands	+ 9	
Sulawesi	+ 8	
Sumatra	+ 7	
Sumbawa	+ 8	
Tanimbar	+ 9	
Timor	+ 8	
*Iran	+ 3	30
*Iraq	+ 3	
*Ireland, Republic of	0	
*Israel	+ 2	
*Italy	+ 1	
Jamaica	− 5	
Japan	+ 9	
*Jordan	+ 2	
*Kazakhstan		
western (Aktau)	+ 4	
central (Atyrau)	+ 5	
eastern	+ 6	
Kenya	+ 3	
Kiribati	+12	
Kiritimati Island	−10	
Korea, North	+ 9	
Korea, South	+ 9	
Kuwait	+ 3	
*Kyrgyzstan	+ 5	
Laos	+ 7	
*Latvia	+ 2	
*Lebanon	+ 2	
Lesotho	+ 2	
Liberia	0	
*Libya	+ 1	
*Liechtenstein	+ 1	
*Lithuania	+ 2	
*Luxembourg	+ 1	
Macao	+ 8	
*Macedonia (Former Yug. Rep. of)	+ 1	
Madagascar	+ 3	
*Madeira	0	
Malawi	+ 2	
Malaysia	+ 8	
Maldives	+ 5	

	h	*m*		*h*	*m*
Mali	0		El Salvador	− 6	
*Malta	+ 1		Samoa	−11	
Marshall Islands	+12		Samoa, American	−11	
Ebon Atoll	−12		*San Marino	+ 1	
Martinique	− 4		São Tomé and Príncipe	0	
Mauritania	0		Saudi Arabia	+ 3	
Mauritius	+ 4		Senegal	0	
Mexico	− 6		Seychelles	+ 4	
central	− 7		Sierra Leone	0	
western	− 8		Singapore	+ 8	
Micronesia			*Slovakia	+ 1	
Caroline Islands	+10		*Slovenia	+ 1	
Kosrae	+11		Solomon Islands	+11	
Pingelap	+11		Somalia	+ 3	
Pohnpei	+11		South Africa	+ 2	
*Moldova	+ 2		South Georgia	− 2	
*Monaco	+ 1		*Spain	+ 1	
*Mongolia	+ 8		Sri Lanka	+ 6	30
Montserrat	− 4		Sudan	+ 2	
Morocco	0		Suriname	− 3	
Mozambique	+ 2		Swaziland	+ 2	
Myanmar	+ 6	30	*Sweden	+ 1	
*Namibia	+ 1		*Switzerland	+ 1	
Nauru	+12		*Syria	+ 2	
Nepal	+ 5	45	Taiwan	+ 8	
*Netherlands	+ 1		Tajikistan	+ 5	
Netherlands Antilles	− 4		Tanzania	+ 3	
New Caledonia	+11		Thailand	+ 7	
*New Zealand	+12		Togo	0	
Nicaragua	− 6		Tonga	+13	
Niger	+ 1		Trinidad and Tobago	− 4	
Nigeria	+ 1		Tristan da Cunha	0	
Niue	−11		Tunisia	+ 1	
Norfolk Island	+11	30	*Turkey	+ 2	
Northern Mariana Islands	+10		Turkmenistan	+ 5	
*Norway	+ 1		*Turks and Caicos Islands	− 5	
Oman	+ 4		Tuvalu	+12	
Pakistan	+ 5		Uganda	+ 3	
Palau	+ 9		*Ukraine	+ 2	
Panama	− 5		*Simferopol	+ 3	
Papua New Guinea	+10		United Arab Emirates	+ 4	
*Paraguay	− 4		United States		
Peru	− 5		*Alaska, east of		
Philippines	+ 8		169° 30′ W.	− 9	
*Poland	+ 1		*Aleutian Islands, west		
*Portugal	0		of 169° 30′ W.	−10	
Puerto Rico	− 4		eastern time	− 5	
Qatar	+ 3		*central time	− 6	
Réunion	+ 4		Hawaii	−10	
*Romania	+ 2		*mountain time	− 7	
*Russia			*Pacific time	− 8	
Zone 1	+ 2		Uruguay	− 3	
Zone 2	+ 3		Uzbekistan	+ 5	
Zone 3	+ 4		Vanuatu	+11	
Zone 4	+ 5		*Vatican City State	+ 1	
Zone 5	+ 6		Venezuela	− 4	
Zone 6	+ 7		Vietnam	+ 7	
Zone 7	+ 8		Virgin Islands (US)	− 4	
Zone 8	+ 9		Yemen	+ 3	
Zone 9	+10		*Yugoslavia (Fed. Rep. of)	+ 1	
Zone 10	+11		Zambia	+ 2	
Zone 11	+12		Zimbabwe	+ 2	
Rwanda	+ 2				
St Helena	0				
St Christopher and Nevis	− 4				
St Lucia	− 4				
*St Pierre and Miquelon	− 3				
St Vincent and the					
Grenadines	− 4				

Source: reproduced with permission from data produced by HM Nautical Almanac Office

Countries of the World: A–Z

AFGHANISTAN
Da Afghanistan Jamhuriat

AREA – 251,772 sq. miles (652,090 sq. km). Neighbours: Iran (west), Pakistan (south), Tajikistan, Uzbekistan and Turkmenistan (north), Pakistan and China (east)

POPULATION – 18,879,000 (1994 UN estimate): Pushtuns (38 per cent) predominate in the south and west; Tajiks (25 per cent); Hazaras (19 per cent) in the centre; Uzbeks (6 per cent) in the north; Aimaqs (4 per cent); Baluchis (0.5 per cent). The principal languages are Dari (a form of Persian) and Pushtu

CAPITAL – Kabul (population, 1,424,400, 1988)

MAJOR CITIES – Kandahar 225,500; Herat 177,300; Mazar-i-Sharif 130,600; Jalalabad 55,000 (1988 UN estimates)

CURRENCY – Afghani (Af) of 100 puls

NATIONAL ANTHEM – Soroud-e-Melli

NATIONAL DAY – 19 August

NATIONAL FLAG – Three horizontal stripes of green, white, black with the national arms in the centre in gold

LIFE EXPECTANCY (years) – male 43.00; female 44.00

POPULATION DENSITY – 29 per sq. km (1994)

Mountains, chief among which are the Hindu Kush, cover three-quarters of the country. There are three great river basins, the Oxus, Helmand, and Kabul. The climate is dry, with extreme temperatures.

HISTORY AND POLITICS

The constitutional monarchy, introduced by the 1964 constitution, was overthrown by a coup in 1973. The country was ruled by presidential decree until 1977 when Mohammad Daoud was elected president. He was overthrown in 1978 by the armed forces and power was handed to the People's Democratic Party of Afghanistan (PDPA). In December 1979 Soviet troops invaded Afghanistan and installed Babrak Karmal as head of state. Armed Islamic resistance groups, the mujahidin, fought against Soviet and Afghan forces until the withdrawal of Soviet troops in 1988. Mujahidin opposition to the Homeland Party (formerly PDPA) government continued until the government collapsed in April 1992. Mujahidin forces overran Kabul bringing an end to the war, and declared an Islamic state. The main factions of the mujahidin are:
– Jamiat-i-Islami, led by Burhanuddin Rabbani and Ahmad Shah Massoud; roughly 60,000 troops; ethnic Tajiks; possibly supported by Tajikistan, India and Iran
– Hezb-i-Islami, led by Gulbardin Hekmatyar; roughly 50,000 troops; ethnic Pushtuns
– National Islamic Movement, led by Gen. Rashid Dostum; 65,000 troops; ethnic Uzbeks; possibly supported by Russia and Iran
– Hezb-i-Wahdat, led by Abdul Karim Khalili; more than 100,000 troops; possibly supported by Iran.

The new government appointed Rabbani as interim president although the mujahidin coalition was divided over the election of a permanent president. Fighting resumed in December 1992 between Hezb-i-Islami, supported by the Hezb-i-Wahdat, and Jamiat-i-Islami. A cease-fire and power sharing agreement under which Rabbani remained president and Hekmatyar became head of a transitional government collapsed in October 1993. In the winter of 1994–5, Hezb-i-Islami and Hezb-i-Wahdat suffered heavy defeats at the hands of the Taliban (armed Islamic students), which extended its power across half of the country. In March 1996, Hekmatyar and Rabbani agreed to combine their forces against the Taliban but failed to prevent the Taliban from seizing Kabul in September 1996. The forces of the former government were forced northwards. A Supreme Council for the Defence of Afghanistan was formed by the four main mujahidin factions which together controlled one-third of Afghanistan. The Taliban, thought to be backed by Pakistan and Saudi Arabia, imposed strict Sharia law in Kabul; women, formerly 70 per cent of the workforce, were banned from working. In May 1997 the Taliban temporarily gained control of Mazar-i-Sharif after forming an alliance with Gen. Abdul Malik who had defected from the opposition. The alliance enabled the Taliban to oust Gen. Dostum from the north of the country leaving Jamiat-i-Islami as the only active opposition. *See also* Events of the Year.

POLITICAL SYSTEM

There are 32 provinces, 17 of which are under Taliban control and governed through an interim council (*shura*).

EMBASSY OF THE ISLAMIC STATE OF AFGHANISTAN
31 Prince's Gate, London SW7 1QQ
Tel 0171-589 8891
Ambassador Extraordinary and Plenipotentiary, new appointment awaited
Minister-Counsellor and Chargé d'Affaires, Ahmad Wali Masud

BRITISH EMBASSY
Karte Parwan, Kabul
Staff were withdrawn from post in February 1989.
Ambassador is now resident in Islamabad.

ECONOMY

The economy has been devastated by the political upheavals of the last 16 years. Agriculture and sheep raising are traditionally the principal industries. Silk, woollen and hair cloths and carpets are manufactured. Salt, silver, copper, coal, iron, lead, rubies, lapis lazuli, gold, chrome, barite, uranium, and talc are found.

There are thought to be considerable fuel reserves. US and Saudi Arabian companies have attempted to negotiate with the Taliban and mujahidin for permission to construct an oil pipeline from Pakistan to Turkmenistan crossing Afghanistan.

In 1995 heroin worth £50,000 million was produced. Afghanistan is also the world's second largest producer of opium; the Taliban impose a 10 per cent tax on opium sales.

GDP – US$17,953 million (1992); US$2,195 per capita (1992)

INFLATION RATE – estimated to be 400 per cent in 1996

TRADE

Trade is now largely limited to narcotics, but in the past exports have been Persian lambskins (Karakul), dried fruits, nuts, cotton, raw wool, carpets, spice and natural gas, while the imports are chiefly oil, cotton yarn and piece goods, tea, sugar, machinery and transport equipment.

In 1991 imports totalled US$616 million and exports US$188 million. There was a current account deficit of US$143 million in 1989.

Trade with UK	1995	1996
Imports from UK	£7,156,000	£7,581,000
Exports to UK	415,000	2,693,000

COMMUNICATIONS

Main roads run from Kabul to Kandahar, Herat, Maimana via Mazar-i-Sharif and Faizabad via Khanabad. Roads cross the border with Pakistan at Chaman and via the Khyber Pass, and there are roads from Herat to the borders of Central Asia and Iran.

In 1982 the Afghan and Uzbek shores of the River Oxus were linked by a road and rail bridge which joins the Afghan port of Hairatan and the Uzbek port of Termez.

EDUCATION

Education is free and nominally compulsory, elementary schools having been established in most centres; there are secondary schools in large urban areas and four universities, in Kabul (established 1932), Jalalabad (established 1962), Balkh and Herat (both established 1988). Kabul's 26 newspapers were closed by the Taliban and women were prohibited from teaching or studying at schools and universities.

ILLITERACY RATE – 68.5 per cent
ENROLMENT (percentage of age group) – primary 29 per cent (1993); tertiary 1.7 per cent (1990)

ALBANIA
Republika e Shqipërisë

AREA – 11,099 sq. miles (28,748 sq. km). Neighbours: Montenegro (north), Serbia and Macedonia (east), Greece (south)
POPULATION – 3,414,000 (1994 UN estimate). Muslim (70 per cent), Greek Orthodox (20 per cent), Roman Catholic (10 per cent)
CAPITAL – Tirana (population, 244,153, 1990)
CURRENCY – Lek (Lk) of 100 qindarka
NATIONAL DAY – 28 November
NATIONAL FLAG – Black two-headed eagle on a red field
LIFE EXPECTANCY (years) – male 69.60; female 75.50
POPULATION GROWTH RATE – 1.2 per cent (1994)
POPULATION DENSITY – 119 per sq. km (1994)
URBAN POPULATION – 36.7 per cent (1991)
ENROLMENT (percentage of age group) – tertiary 9.5 per cent (1993)

HISTORY AND POLITICS

Albania was under Turkish suzerainty from 1468 until 1912, when independence was declared. After a period of unrest, a republic was declared in 1925, and in 1928 a monarchy. The King went into exile in 1939 when the country was occupied by the Italians; Albania was liberated in November 1944. Elections in 1945 resulted in a Communist-controlled Assembly; the King was deposed in absentia and a republic declared in January 1946.

From 1946 to 1991 Albania was a one-party, Communist state. In March 1991 multiparty elections were won by the Socialist Party (the renamed Communist Party of Labour) and a coalition government was formed in June 1991. In December 1991 the Democratic Party withdrew from the government and won new elections which were held in March 1992. A coalition government was formed with the Social Democrat and Republican parties. In April 1992 the Democratic Party leader Dr Sali Berisha was elected by parliament as Albania's first non-Communist president.

The general election on 26 May 1996 was marred by allegations of ballot-rigging and voter intimidation. A re-run on 16 June was boycotted by opposition parties, enabling the Democratic Party to win 122 of the 140 seats in parliament. Legislative elections held in June 1997 were won by a Socialist-led coalition. President Berisha resigned following the announcement of the result.

INSURGENCY

Rioting broke out in January 1997 following the collapse of several pyramid investment schemes. Anti-government protests spread, taking the form of armed rebellion, particularly in the south. A state of emergency was declared on 2 March and an interim government held power until legislative elections could take place. A 6,000-strong multinational force arrived in April to oversee the distribution of aid.

HEAD OF STATE
President, Prof. Rexhep Medjani, *elected by parliament* 24 July 1997

COUNCIL OF MINISTERS *as at July 1997*
Prime Minister, Fatos Nanto (SP)
Deputy PM, Bashkim Fino (SP)
Agriculture and Food, Lufter Xhuveli (AP)
Culture, Youth and Sports, Arta Dade (SP)
Defence, Sabit Brokaj (SP)
Education and Science, Et'hem Ruka (SP)
Finance, Arben Malaj (SP)
Foreign Affairs, Paskal Milo (SDP)
Health and Environment, Leonard Solis (HRUP)
Interior, Neritan Ceka (DAP)
Justice, Thimio Kondi (Ind.)
Labour, Social Affairs and Women, Elmaz Sherifi (SP)
Ministers of State, Ermelinda Meksi (SP) (*Economic Cooperation and Development*); Arben Imami (DAP) (*Legislative Reform and Relations with People's Assembly*)
Public Economy and Privatization, Ylli Buffi (SP)
Public Works and Transport, Gaqo Apostoli (SDP)
Secretaries of State, Perikli Teta (DAP) (*Defence Policy*); Maqo Lakrori (SP) (*Euro-Atlantic Integration*); Ndre Legisi (SP) (*Interior*); Lush Përpali (SP) (*Local Government*)
Trade and Tourism, new appointment awaited

AP Agrarian Party; DAP Democratic Alliance Party; DP Democratic Party; HRUP Human Rights Union Party; SDP Social Democratic Party; SP Socialist Party.

EMBASSY OF THE REPUBLIC OF ALBANIA
4th Floor, 38 Grosvenor Gardens, London SWIW OEB
Tel 0171-730 5709
Ambassador Extraordinary and Plenipotentiary, new appointment awaited

BRITISH EMBASSY
Rruga Vaso Pasha, 7–1, Tirana
Tel: Tirana 34973/4/5
Ambassador Extraordinary and Plenipotentiary, HE Andrew Tesoriere, apptd 1996

DEFENCE

The Army has 859 main battle tanks, 103 armoured personnel carriers and 860 artillery pieces. The Navy has two submarines and 37 patrol and coastal combatant vessels at six bases. The Air Force has 98 combat aircraft.

MILITARY EXPENDITURE – 2.8 per cent of GDP (1995)
MILITARY PERSONNEL – 67,500: Army 45,000, Navy 2,500, Air Force 6,500, Paramilitaries 13,500
CONSCRIPTION DURATION – 12 months

ECONOMY

Much of the country is mountainous and nearly a half is covered by forest. The main crops are wheat, maize, sugar beet, potatoes and fruit. There are large chromium deposits. The principal industries are agricultural product processing, textiles, oil products and cement.

Since April 1992, the government has imposed austerity measures in an attempt to reduce the budget deficit and to cut inflation which stood at 23 per cent in 1994. The currency stabilized with strong growth in 1994 signalling a brief recovery from the economic collapse of 1988–92. The economy faltered again in 1996–7 with a rapid drop in retail sales and a decline in the value of the lek. Up to US$1,200 million worth of personal savings were lost in the collapse of several fraudulent pyramid savings schemes in January 1997.

Remittances from 500,000 overseas workers remain an important source of revenue. Albania has received $1 billion in aid from Western donors and was promised £2,800 million in food and medical aid by the EU in March 1997.

GNP – US$2,199 million (1995); US$670 per capita (1995)
GDP – US$1,417 million (1992); estimated to be US$2,300 million (1996); US$197 per capita (1992)
UNEMPLOYMENT – 9.1 per cent (1991)
TOTAL EXTERNAL DEBT – US$709 million (1995)

TRADE

Exports include crude oil, minerals (bitumen, chrome, nickel, copper), tobacco, fruit and vegetables. In 1994 Albania had a trade deficit of US$460 million and a current account deficit of US$157 million.

TRADE WITH UK	1995	1996
Imports from UK	£7,555,000	£14,664,000
Exports to UK	1,017,000	318,000

ALGERIA
Al-Jumhuriya al-Jazairiya ad-Dimuqratiya ash-Shabiya

AREA – 919,595 sq. miles (2,381,741 sq. km)
POPULATION – 27,325,000 (1994 UN estimate); 22,971,558 (1987 census)
CAPITAL – ΨAlgiers (population, 1,740,461, 1977; now roughly 3,250,000). It is one of the principal ports of the Mediterranean
MAJOR CITIES – ΨOran; Constantine; ΨAnnaba; Blida; Serif; Sidi-Bel-Abbès; Tlemcen; ΨMostaganem; ΨSkikda; ΨBejaia and Tizi Ouzou
CURRENCY – Algerian dinar (DA) of 100 centimes
NATIONAL ANTHEM – Qassaman
NATIONAL DAY – 1 November
NATIONAL FLAG – Divided vertically green and white with a red crescent and star over all in the centre
LIFE EXPECTANCY (years) – male 65.75; female 66.34
POPULATION GROWTH RATE – 2.2 per cent (1994)
POPULATION DENSITY – 11 per sq. km (1994)
ILLITERACY RATE – 38.4 per cent
ENROLMENT (percentage of age group) – primary 95 per cent (1994); secondary 55 per cent (1994); tertiary 11.4 per cent (1992)

HISTORY AND POLITICS

Algeria was annexed to France in 1842, with the departments of Algiers, Oran and Constantine forming an integral part of France. President de Gaulle declared Algeria independent in July 1962 following an eight-year armed rebellion by the (Arab) Front de Libération Nationale (FLN), whose leader, Ben Bella, was elected president in 1963. Ben Bella was deposed in 1965 by a military junta presided over by Col. Boumediène, who was formally elected president in 1976. Boumediène died in 1978 and was succeeded by Chadli Bendjedid.

A new constitution agreed by referendum in 1989 moved Algeria towards pluralism. However, the 1991 legislative elections were abandoned in anticipation of the success of the opposition Islamic Salvation Front (FIS), which had campaigned on a radical 'Islamist' platform. The Army forced President Bendjedid to resign and a military-backed Higher Committee of State (HCS), headed by former FLN veteran Mohammed Boudiaf, took power. The HCS declared a state of emergency in 1992 which was extended indefinitely in 1993. The FIS was banned in 1992 but continued to operate covertly and was suspected of assassinating Boudiaf in June 1992.

A national reconciliation conference in January 1994 was boycotted by the FIS but nevertheless it appointed Gen. Liamine Zeroual as president to replace the HCS, which disbanded itself. Zeroual was elected president for a five-year term in November 1995. Multiparty elections on 5 June 1997 were won by a newly-formed pro-Zeroual party, National Democratic Rally (RND), which captured 155 seats. Hamas (Movement for a Society of Peace) (MSP) won 69 seats; the FLN 64 seats; Annahda (Renaissance Movement) 34; Rally for Culture and Democracy 19; Socialist Forces Front 19.

INSURGENCY

Since the abortive elections in 1992, the FIS-backed Islamic Salvation Army (AIS) and the more extreme Armed Islamic Group (GIA) have waged an armed campaign against the military regime in favour of an Islamic state. The two groups have targeted the military and security forces, their secular supporters in the population, and foreign expatriates; the military has killed and detained thousands of Islamic militants and sentenced hundreds to death. More than 60,000 people have died in the fighting, including 300 people during Ramadan in 1997.

POLITICAL SYSTEM

A referendum on 28 November 1996 approved the creation of a new second chamber, the *Majlis el-Umma* (Council of the Nation). One-third of its members will be appointed by the president. The referendum also approved amendments to the constitution to ban political parties based on religion and to make Islam the state religion.

HEAD OF STATE

President, Gen. Liamine Zeroual, *elected* November 1995

GOVERNMENT as at June 1997

Prime Minister, Ahmed Ouyahia (RND)
Agriculture and Fisheries, Boulahaouadjeb Benalia (FLN)
Communications and Culture, Habib Chawki Hamraoui (RND)
Energy and Mines, Youcef Yousfi (RND)
Equipment, National and Regional Development, Abderrahmane Belayat (FLN)
Finance, Abdelkrim Harchaoui (RND)
Foreign Affairs, Ahmed Attaf (RND)
Health and Population, Yahia Guidoum (RND)
Higher Education and Scientific Research, Amar Tou (FLN)
Housing, Abdelkader Bounekraf (FLN)
Industry and Restructuring, Abdelmajid Menasra (MSP)
Interior, Local Communities, Environment, Mostefa Benmansour (RND)
Justice, Mohamed Adami (RND)

Labour, Social Services and Vocational Training, Hacene Laskri
  (RND)
National Education, Boubakeur Benbouzid (RND)
National Solidarity and Family Matters, Rabea Mercherchene
  (RND)
Posts and Telecommunications, Mohamed-Salah Youyou
  (RND)
Religious Affairs, Bouabdellah Ghlamallah (RND)
Small and Medium-Sized Enterprises, Bouguerra Soltani
  (MSP)
Tourism and Handicrafts, Abdelkader Bengrina (MSP)
Trade, Bakhti Belaib (RND)
Transport, Sid Ahmed Boulil (MSP)
War Veterans, Said Abadou (RND)
Youth and Sports, Mohammed Aziz Derouaz (RND)

ALGERIAN EMBASSY
54 Holland Park, London WII 3RS
Tel 0171-221 7800
Ambassador Extraordinary and Plenipotentiary, HE Ahmed
  Benyamina, apptd 1996

BRITISH EMBASSY
7 Chemin des Glycines,
BP08, Alger-Gare 16000, Algiers
Tel: Algiers 692411
Ambassador Extraordinary and Plenipotentiary, HE François
  Gordon, apptd 1996

DEFENCE

The Army has 960 main battle tanks, 680 armoured
personnel carriers and 416 artillery pieces. The Navy has
two submarines, three frigates and 24 patrol and coastal
vessels. The Air Force has 180 combat aircraft and 60
armed helicopters.
MILITARY EXPENDITURE – 2.5 per cent of GDP (1995)
MILITARY PERSONNEL – 164,900: Army 107,000, Navy
  6,700, Air Force 10,000, Paramilitaries 41,200
CONSCRIPTION DURATION – 18 months

ECONOMY

The main industry is the hydrocarbons industry. Oil and
natural gas are pumped from the Sahara to terminals on the
coast before being exported; the gas is first liquefied at
liquefaction plants at Skikda and Arzew, although pipelines serve Libya and Italy direct. In November 1996 a 750-
mile gas pipeline to Spain was opened which will enable
Algeria to double its gas exports to Morocco, Spain,
Germany and France. Its initial annual capacity of 8,000
million cubic metres is projected to rise to 20,000 million
cubic metres a year by 2000.
  Other major industries include a steel industry, motor
vehicles, building materials, paper making, chemical
products and metal manufactures. Most major industrial
enterprises are still under state control.
  From 1965 to 1989 the economy was centrally planned
and state-controlled in most sectors. Economic reform,
begun in 1987, was speeded up in 1988 and now includes
industrial and financial sectors. In April 1994 the government finally accepted full economic reform and liberalization under a reform programme agreed with the IMF.
The government has cut the budget deficit, devalued the
currency and freed price controls.
GNP – US$44,609 million (1995); US$1,600 per capita
  (1995)
GDP – US$56,150 million (1992); US$1,743 per capita
  (1992)
ANNUAL AVERAGE GROWTH OF GDP – –5.3 per cent
  (1982)
INFLATION RATE – 29.8 per cent (1995)
UNEMPLOYMENT – 23.8 per cent (1992)

TOTAL EXTERNAL DEBT – US$32,610 million (1995)

TRADE

Export earnings come mainly from crude oil and liquefied
natural gas sales.
  In 1991 Algeria had a trade surplus of US$5,468 million
and a current account surplus of US$2,367 million. In 1993
imports totalled US$7,770 million and exports US$10,230
million.

TRADE WITH UK	1995	1996
Imports from UK	£64,277, 000	£70,939,000
Exports to UK	244,279,000	202,428,000

ANDORRA
Principat d'Andorra

AREA – 175 sq. miles (453 sq. km). Neighbours: Spain and
  France
POPULATION – 64,479 (1996); less than one-quarter of the
  population are native Andorrans. The official language
  is Catalan, but French and Spanish (Castilian) are also
  spoken. The established religion is Roman Catholicism
CAPITAL – Andorra la Vella (population, 16,151, 1986)
CURRENCY – French and Spanish currencies in use
NATIONAL DAY – 8 September
NATIONAL FLAG – Three vertical bands, blue, yellow, red;
  Andorran coat of arms frequently imposed on central
  (yellow) band but not essential
POPULATION GROWTH RATE – 5.3 per cent (1994)
POPULATION DENSITY – 143 per sq. km (1994)
URBAN POPULATION – 95.6 per cent (1991)

HISTORY AND POLITICS

Andorra is a small, neutral principality formed by a treaty
in 1278. The first elections under the new constitution
were held in December 1993, and on 20 January 1994 the
first sovereign government of Andorra took office.

POLITICAL SYSTEM

Under a new constitution promulgated in May 1993,
Andorra became an independent, democratic parliamentary co-principality, with sovereignty vested in the people
rather than in the two co-princes, as was previously the
case. The constitution enables Andorra to establish an
independent judiciary and to carry out its own foreign
policy, whilst its people may now join trade unions and
political parties. The two co-princes, the president of the
French Republic and the Spanish Bishop of Urgel, remain
heads of state but now only have the power to veto treaties
with France and Spain which affect the state's borders and
security. The co-princes are represented by Permanent
Delegates of whom one is the French Prefect of the
Pyrénées Orientales Department at Perpignan and the
other is the Spanish Vicar-General of the Diocese of Urgel.
They are in turn represented in Andorra la Vella by two
resident Viguiers known as the Viguier Français and the
Viguier Episcopal.
  Andorra has a unicameral legislature of 28 members
known as the *Consell General de las Valls d'Andorra* (Valleys of
Andorra General Council). Fourteen members are elected
on a national list basis and 14 in seven dual-member
constituencies based on Andorra's seven parishes. The
Council appoints the head of the executive government,
who designates the members of his government.

Viguier Français, Jean Ive Caullet
Viguier Episcopal, Nemesi Marqués

EXECUTIVE GOVERNMENT *as at June 1997*
President, Marc Forné Molné
Culture, Pere Canturri Montanya
Economy, Enric Casadevall Medrano
Education, Youth and Sports, Carme Sala Sansa
Environment and Tourism, Enric Pujal Areny
Finance, Susagna Arasanz Serra
Foreign Affairs, Albert Pintat Santolària
Interior, Lluís Montanya Tarrés
Presidency, Estanislau Sangrà Cardona
Public Works, Josep Garrallà Rossell
Sanitation and Public Health, Josep Maria Goicoechea
  Utrillo

ANDORRAN DELEGATION, 63 Westover Road, London
  SW18 2RF. Tel: 0181-874 4806
BRITISH AMBASSADOR – HE David Brighty, CMG, CVO,
  resident at Madrid

ECONOMY

Potatoes are produced in the highlands and tobacco in the valleys. The economy is largely based on tourism, banking, commerce, tobacco, construction and forestry; a third of the country is classified as forest. Andorra has negotiated a customs union with the European Union which came into force in 1991. The economy is now diversifying rapidly into offshore financial services.

GDP – US$738 million (1992); US$17,781 per capita
(1992)

TRADE WITH UK	1995	1996
Imports from UK	£13,043,000	£19,096,000
Exports to UK	8,000	3,394,000

COMMUNICATIONS

A road into the valleys from Spain is open all year round, and that from France is closed only occasionally in winter. There are two radio stations in Andorra, one privately owned and Radio Andorra, operated by the government.

ANGOLA
República de Angola

AREA – 481,354 sq. miles (1,246,700 sq. km). Neighbours: Democratic Republic of Congo (north and east), Zambia (east) and Namibia (south). The enclave of Cabinda is separated from the rest of Angola by the Democratic Republic of Congo and also borders on the Republic of Congo
POPULATION – 10,674,000 (1994 UN estimate)
CAPITAL – ΨLuanda (population, 475,328, 1970)
CURRENCY – Kwanza (Kzrl) of 100 lwei
NATIONAL ANTHEM – Angola Avante
NATIONAL DAY – 11 November (Independence Day)
NATIONAL FLAG – Red and black with a yellow star, machete and cog-wheel
LIFE EXPECTANCY (years) – male 44.90; female 48.10
POPULATION GROWTH RATE – 1.6 per cent (1994)
POPULATION DENSITY – 9 per sq. km (1994)
ILLITERACY RATE – 59.0 per cent
ENROLMENT (percentage of age group) – tertiary 0.7 per cent (1991)

HISTORY AND POLITICS

After a Portuguese presence of five centuries, and an anti-colonial war since 1961, Angola became independent on 11

November 1975 in the midst of civil war. Soviet-Cuban military assistance to the Popular Movement for the Liberation of Angola (MPLA) enabled it to defeat its rivals early in 1976. The MPLA government remained under pressure from the National Union for the Total Independence of Angola (UNITA) guerrilla movement, led by Dr Jonas Savimbi. In 1988 a cease-fire between South African, Cuban and Angolan forces took place and an agreement providing for the withdrawal of South African and Cuban troops by July 1991 was signed. A peace agreement was signed between the government and UNITA in 1991, and multiparty legislative and presidential elections took place in 1992, with the MPLA and its leader, Dos Santos, winning UNITA refused to accept the results and the civil war resumed in 1993.

Fighting continued until UNITA and the MPLA government signed a peace agreement (the Lusaka Protocol) under UN mediation in November 1994. By September 1996 more than 70,000 UNITA troops had been confined by the UN peacekeeping force, UNAVEM III, although many subsequently fled. A government of nationl reconciliation was formed in April 1997 with 70 UNITA legislators due to take up their seats in parliament although Savimbi rejected an offer of the vice-presidency and refused to enter Luanda. Heavy fighting resumed in May 1997 following the fall from power of President Mobutu of Zaïre, one of Savimbi's key supporters. *See also* Events of the Year.

SECESSION
In the northern enclave of Cabinda, the Front for the Liberation of the Cabinda Enclave (FLEC) fought a 20-year war of independence until the signing of a cease-fire agreement with the government in September 1995, which was followed by the initialling of a peace agreement in April 1996.

POLITICAL SYSTEM
The MPLA, formerly a Marxist-Leninist party, was the sole legal party until early 1991 when a multiparty system was adopted. The constitution declares Angola to be a democratic state and provides for a president, who appoints a Council of Ministers to assist him, and a 220-member National Assembly. In November 1996 the National Assembly adopted a constitutional amendment extending its mandate for between two and four years.

HEAD OF STATE
President, José Eduardo Dos Santos, *re-elected* 30 September 1992

EMBASSY OF ANGOLA
98 Park Lane, London W1Y 3TA
Tel 0171-495 1752
Ambassador Extraordinary and Plenipotentiary, HE António
  Da Costa Fernandes, apptd 1993

BRITISH EMBASSY
Rua Diogo Cão 4 (Caixa Postal 1244), Luanda
Tel: Luanda 334582/3
Ambassador Extraordinary and Plenipotentiary, HE Roger
  Hart, apptd 1995

DEFENCE

The army has 400 main battle tanks, 100 armoured personnel carriers and 300 artillery pieces. The Navy has five patrol vessels at three bases. The Air Force has 36 combat aircraft and 26 armed helicopters.
MILITARY EXPENDITURE – 4.8 per cent of GDP (1995)
MILITARY PERSONNEL – 106,900: Army 90,000, Navy 2,000, Air Force 5,500, Paramilitaries 9,400

ECONOMY

Angola has valuable oil and diamond deposits and exports of these two commodities account for over 90 per cent of total exports. Principal agricultural crops are cassava, maize, bananas, coffee, palm oil and kernels, cotton and sisal. Coffee, sisal, maize and palm oil are exported; exports also include mahogany and other hardwoods from the tropical rain forests in the north of the country.

The government is attempting to reform the socialist economy by free market reforms but is making little progress, with high inflation and a collapsing economy, together with the loss of most diamond-producing areas to UNITA.

In 1993 Angola had a trade surplus of US$1,438 million and a current account deficit of US$669 million.

GNP – US$4,442 million (1995); US$410 per capita (1995)
GDP – US$11,182 million (1992); US$18 per capita (1992)
TOTAL EXTERNAL DEBT – US$11,482 million (1995)

TRADE WITH UK	1995	1996
Imports from UK	£29,387,000	£45,631,000
Exports to UK	22,408,000	8,852,000

ANTIGUA AND BARBUDA
State of Antigua and Barbuda

AREA – 171 sq. miles (442 sq. km); Antigua 108 sq. miles (279 sq. km); Barbuda 62 sq.miles (160 sq. km); Redonda ½sq. mile (1.2 sq. km)
POPULATION – 65,000 (1994 UN estimate); 65,962, Antigua 64,562, Barbuda 1,400 (official census 1991)
CAPITAL – ΨSt John's (population, 22,342, 1991)
MAJOR TOWNS – The town of Barbuda is Codrington
CURRENCY – East Caribbean dollar (EC$) of 100 cents
NATIONAL ANTHEM – Fair Antigua and Barbuda
NATIONAL DAY – 1 November (Independence Day)
NATIONAL FLAG – Red with an inverted triangle divided black over blue over white, with a rising gold sun on the white band
POPULATION GROWTH RATE – 0.4 per cent (1994)
POPULATION DENSITY – 147 per sq. km (1994)
MILITARY EXPENDITURE – 0.8 per cent of GDP (1995)

Antigua is part of the Leeward Islands in the eastern Caribbean It is distinguished from the rest of the Leeward group by its absence of high hills and forest, and a drier climate than most of the West Indies. Barbuda, formerly a possession of the Codrington family, is very flat, mainly scrub-covered, with a large lagoon.

HISTORY AND POLITICS

Antigua was first settled by the English in 1632, and was granted to Lord Willoughby by Charles II. It became internally self-governing in 1967 and fully independent on 1 November 1981.

The Antigua Labour party won the general election of March 1994 and a fifth successive term of office with 11 seats in the House of Representatives compared to five seats for the United Progressive Party.

POLITICAL SYSTEM

Antigua and Barbuda is a constitutional monarchy with Queen Elizabeth II as Head of State, represented by the Governor-General. There is a Senate of 17 appointed members and a House of Representatives of 17 members elected every five years. The Attorney-General may be appointed.

Governor-General, HE Sir James Carlisle, GCMG

CABINET *as at May 1997*
Prime Minister, Foreign Affairs, Social Affairs, Lester Bird
Agriculture, Lands, Fisheries, Planning and Co-operatives; Finance and Social Security, John St Luce
Education, Youth, Sports, Community Development, Bernard Percival
Health and Civil Service Affairs, Samuel Aymer
Justice, Legal Affairs and Attorney-General, Radford Hill
Labour and Home Affairs, Adolphus Freeland
Prime Minister's Office, Henderson Simon
Public Utilities, Public Works, Energy, Robin Yearwood
Tourism, Culture, Environment, Dr Rodney Williams
Trade, Industry, Commerce, Consumer Affairs, Hilroy Humphreys

HIGH COMMISSION FOR ANTIGUA AND BARBUDA
15 Thayer Street, London WIM 5LD
Tel 0171-486 7073/5
High Commissioner, HE Ronald Sanders, CMG, apptd 1995

BRITISH HIGH COMMISSION
11 Old Parham Road (PO 483), St John's
Tel: St John's 4620 008/9
High Commissioner, HE Richard Thomas, CMG, resident at Bridgetown, Barbados
Resident High Commissioner, M. Maxwell, MVO

ECONOMY

Tourism and related services account for 60 per cent of GDP and employ 40 per cent of the workforce. For many years sugar was the dominant crop but is no longer produced. Agricultural production includes livestock, sea island cotton, mixed market gardening and fishing. An offshore banking centre has been developed.

In 1993 Antigua and Barbuda had a current account deficit of US$19 million and a trade deficit of US$229 million.

GNP – US$453 million (1994); US$6,970 per capita (1994)
GDP – US$436 million (1992); US$6,646 per capita (1992)
ANNUAL AVERAGE GROWTH OF GDP – 3.4 per cent (1993)
INFLATION RATE – 1.0 per cent (1985)

TRADE WITH UK	1995	1996
Imports from UK	£23,272,000	£36,792,000
Exports to UK	1,517,000	3,207,000

ARGENTINA
República Argentina

AREA – 1,073,512 sq. miles (2,780,400 sq. km). Neighbours: Bolivia (north), Paraguay, Brazil and Uruguay (north-east), Chile (west) from which it is separated by the Cordillera de los Andes
POPULATION – 34,180,000 (1994 UN estimate); 32,370,298 (1991 census). The language is Spanish
CAPITAL – ΨBuenos Aires (population, 10,686,163, 1991); metropolitan area 2,960,976
MAJOR CITIES – ΨRosario (894,645); Córdoba (1,148,305); ΨLa Plata (640,344); ΨMar del Plata (519,707); San Miguel de Tucumán (622,348); Mendoza (773,559)
CURRENCY – Peso of 10,000 australes
NATIONAL ANTHEM – ¡Oid Mortales! (Hear, oh mortals!)
NATIONAL DAY – 25 May
NATIONAL FLAG – Horizontal bands of blue, white, blue; gold sun in centre of white band

LIFE EXPECTANCY (years) – male 68.17; female 73.09
POPULATION GROWTH RATE – 1.2 per cent (1994)
POPULATION DENSITY – 12 per sq. km (1994)

Argentina occupies the greater portion of the southern part of the South American continent, and extends from Bolivia to Cape Horn.

HISTORY AND POLITICS

The estuary of La Plata was discovered in 1515 by Juan Díaz de Solís and the region was subsequently colonized by the Spanish. Spain ruled the territory from the 16th century until 1810. In 1816, after a long campaign of liberation conducted by General José de San Martín, independence was declared by the Congress of Tucumán.

President Juan Domingo Perón was overthrown in 1955, and there followed 18 years of instability until 1973 when he was recalled from exile. Perón died within a year and was succeeded by his widow, Vice-President María Estela Martínez de Perón. A coup led to the establishment of a military junta in 1976. Following the Falkland Islands defeat in 1982 the President, Gen. Galtieri, resigned and the Army appointed Gen. Bignone. A civilian president was elected in 1983. Presidential elections in 1989 were won by the Justicialist Party (Perónist) candidate Carlos Menem. The Justicialist Party held 135 seats in the Chamber of Deputies following the legislative elections in May 1995.

POLITICAL SYSTEM

The 1853 constitution was amended in 1994. Power is vested in the president who appoints the Cabinet and is directly elected for a once-renewable four-year term. A presidential candidate must win at least 45 per cent of the vote, or 40 per cent with a 10 per cent lead over the nearest challenger, to gain victory. The legislature consists of a 72-member (three for each province) Senate and a 259-member Chamber of Deputies. A third of the Senate is elected every three years and half of the Chamber of Deputies is elected every two years. Senators serve for a nine-year term and Deputies for a four-year term.

The republic is divided into 23 provinces, each with an elected Governor and legislature, and one federal district (Buenos Aires), with an elected mayor and autonomous government.

HEAD OF STATE

President, Dr Carlos Saúl Menem, *elected* May 1989, *re-elected* 14 May 1995
Vice-President, Dr Carlos Federico Ruckauf

CABINET *as at April 1997*

Defence, Jorge Domínguez
Economy and Public Works, Roque Fernández
Education and Culture, Susana Decibe
Foreign Affairs, Guido Di Tella
Health and Social Welfare, Alberto José Mazza
Interior, Carlos Corach
Justice, Raúl Granillo Ocampo
Labour and Social Security, José Armando Caro-Figueroa

EMBASSY OF THE ARGENTINE REPUBLIC
65 Brook Street, London WIY IYE
Tel 0171-318 1300
Ambassador Extraordinary and Plenipotentiary, HE Rogelio Pfirter, apptd 1995
Defence Attaché, Col. Héctor José Gallardo
Counsellor (Economic and Commercial Affairs), Gustavo Martino

BRITISH EMBASSY
Dr Luis Agote 2412, 1425 Buenos Aires
Tel: Buenos Aires 8037 070/1
Ambassador Extraordinary and Plenipotentiary, HE William Marsden, CMG, apptd 1997
Deputy Head of Mission and Minister, Dominic Asquith
Defence and Air Attaché, Gp Capt. D. McDonnell, OBE
Naval and Military Attaché, Col. H. Massey
First Secretary (Commercial), H. Wiles
Cultural Attaché and British Council Representative, M. Potter, Marcelo T. de Alvear 590, 1058 Buenos Aires
BRITISH CHAMBER OF COMMERCE, Av. Corrientes 457, 10 piso, 1043 Buenos Aires

DEFENCE

The Army has 296 main battle tanks, 717 armoured infantry fighting vehicles and armoured personnel carriers, 41 helicopters and 231 artillery pieces. The Navy has three submarines, six destroyers, seven frigates, 14 patrol and coastal vessels, 31 combat aircraft and 15 armed helicopters. The Air Force has 202 combat aircraft, and 14 armed helicopters.
MILITARY EXPENDITURE – 1.7 per cent of GDP (1995)
MILITARY PERSONNEL – 103,740: Army 36,000, Navy 24,500, Air Force 12,000, Paramilitaries 31,240
CONSCRIPTION DURATION – Ended 1 April 1995

ECONOMY

A large proportion of the land is still held in large estates devoted to cattle raising but the number of small farms is increasing. The principal crops are wheat, maize, oats, barley, rye, linseed, sunflower seed, alfalfa, sugar, fruit and cotton. Argentina is pre-eminent in the production of beef, mutton and wool. Total oil production for 1995 was 38,152,906 tonnes. There is a refinery in San Lorenzo (Santa Fé province). Natural gas is also produced. Coal, lead, zinc, tungsten, iron ore, sulphur, mica and salt are the other chief minerals being exploited. There are small worked deposits of beryllium, manganese, bismuth, uranium, antimony, copper, kaolin, arsenate, gold, silver and tin. Coal is produced at the Rio Turbio mine in the province of Santa Cruz.

Meat-packing is one of the principal industries; flour-milling, sugar-refining, and the wine industry are also important. In recent years progress has been made by the textile, plastic and machine tool industries and engineering, especially in the production of motor vehicles and steel manufactures.

The Menem government introduced an economic reform programme in 1991 involving the privatization of most state-owned industries, widespread deregulation, exchange-rate stabilization and lower trade barriers. This led to economic growth, increased foreign investment and much lower inflation. Despite an austerity programme introduced in April 1995 in the wake of the Mexican economic crisis, the pace of growth slowed in 1995–6. The peso has been pegged to the US dollar since 1991.
GNP – US$278,431 million (1995); US$8,030 per capita (1995)
GDP – US$167,267 million (1992); US$6,912 per capita (1992)
ANNUAL AVERAGE GROWTH OF GDP – 7.4 per cent (1994)
INFLATION RATE – 3.4 per cent (1995)
UNEMPLOYMENT – 18.8 per cent (1995)
TOTAL EXTERNAL DEBT – US$89,747 million (1995)

TRADE

The chief imports are machinery, industrial and transport equipment, chemicals, metals and plastics. The chief exports are vegetable products, processed foods, minerals, live animals and oils. Argentina's main trading partners are Brazil and the USA.

In 1993 Argentina had a trade deficit of US$2,428 million and a current account deficit of US$7,452 million. In 1995 imports totalled US$20,123 million and exports US$20,967 million.

TRADE WITH UK	1995	1996
Imports from UK	£233,682,000	£331,631,000
Exports to UK	252,265,000	285,487,000

COMMUNICATIONS

The 25,386 miles of railway are state-owned. The combined national and provincial road network totals approximately 137,000 miles of which 23,180 miles are surfaced.

CULTURE AND EDUCATION

The literature of Spain is part of the culture. There is little indigenous literature before the break from Spain, but all branches have flourished since the latter half of the 19th century. About 450 daily newspapers are published in Argentina, including seven major ones in the city of Buenos Aires. The English language newspaper is the *Buenos Aires Herald* (daily).

Education is compulsory for the seven grades of primary school (six to 13). Secondary schools (14 to 17+) are available in and around Buenos Aires and in most of the important towns in the interior of the country. Most secondary schools are administered by the Central Ministry of Education in Buenos Aires, while primary schools are administered by the Central Ministry or by Provincial Ministries of Education. Private schools, of which there are many, are also loosely controlled by the Central Ministry. The total number of universities is over 50 with 24 national, 25 private and a small number of provincial universities.

ILLITERACY RATE – 3.8 per cent

ENROLMENT (percentage of age group) – primary 95 per cent (1991); secondary 59 per cent (1991); tertiary 35.8 per cent (1994)

ARMENIA
Hayastany Hanrapetoutioun

AREA – 11,506 sq. miles (29,800 sq. km). Neighbours: Azerbaijan (east and south-west), Georgia (north), Iran (south) and Turkey (west)

POPULATION – 3,548,000 (1994 UN estimate). Armenians 93.8 per cent, Kurds 1.7 per cent and Russians 1.6 per cent. Azerbaijanis formed 2.6 per cent of the population, but most fled or were expelled after the outbreak of war with Azerbaijan. There are also Ukrainians, Greeks and Assyrians. The Armenian diaspora numbers some 5,300,000. Armenian is the official language, though Russian is widely spoken and understood. The main religion is Armenian Orthodox Christian (Armenian Church centred in Etchmiadzin). Armenia adopted Christianity as its official religion in AD 301, the first state in the world to do so

CAPITAL – Yerevan (population, 1,254,400, 1990)

CURRENCY – Dram of 100 louma

NATIONAL DAY – 21 September (Independence Day)

NATIONAL FLAG – Three horizontal stripes of red, blue and orange

LIFE EXPECTANCY (years) – male 68.66; female 75.51

POPULATION GROWTH RATE – 0 per cent (1994)

POPULATION DENSITY – 119 per sq. km (1994)

URBAN POPULATION – 68.5 per cent (1992)

Armenia lies between the Black and Caspian Seas, occupying the south-western part of the Caucasus region of the former Soviet Union. It is very mountainous, consisting of several vast tablelands surrounded by ridges. The climate is continental, dry and cold, but the Ararat valley has a long, hot and dry summer.

HISTORY AND POLITICS

Armenia was first unified in 95 BC but was divided between the Persian and Byzantine Empires in AD 387 and then conquered in the 11th century by the Seljuk Turks and the Mongols. In the 16th century most of Armenia was incorporated into the Ottoman Empire. In 1639 the country was divided again, the easternmost portions, now the republic of Armenia, becoming part of the Persian Empire. In 1828 eastern Armenia became part of the Russian Empire while western Armenia remained under Ottoman rule. The Ottomans launched pogroms against the Armenians from 1894 onwards, and in 1915 to 1918 massacred 1,500,000 Armenians.

Armenia declared its independence on 28 May 1918, but was crushed and divided between Turkish and Soviet forces in 1920, with the area under Soviet control proclaimed a Soviet Socialist Republic on 29 November 1920. The Soviet government was overthrown by a nationalist revolt in 1921 but reinstated by the Red Army a few months later. In early 1922 Armenia acceded to the USSR.

An Armenian nationalist movement swept to power in national elections in mid-1990. In a referendum in 1991, 99 per cent of the electorate voted for independence, which was declared on 21 September 1991.

FOREIGN RELATIONS

The dispute between the (ethnic Armenian) Nagorno-Karabakh forces supported by Armenia and the Azeri government over Nagorno-Karabakh erupted into all-out war in May 1992, when Nagorno-Karabakh forces breached Azerbaijan's defences to form a land bridge to Armenia. By the end of summer 1992 all of Nagorny-Karabakh was under Armenian control. Continued victories over Azeri forces in 1992–3 brought all Azeri territory that separated Nagorny-Karabakh from Armenia and all mountainous Azeri territory around Nagorny-Karabakh, an estimated 10 per cent of Azeri territory, under the control of Nagorny-Karabakh Armenians. Armenia claims this territory as historically Armenian land arbitrarily given to Azerbaijan by Stalin in 1921–2. A cease-fire agreement between Armenia, Azerbaijan and Nagorny-Karabakh was reached in May 1994.

POLITICAL SYSTEM

In April 1995, a law was passed creating a 190-member National Assembly, to be elected every four years by a combined constituency and party-list system. In the first elections to the new body in July 1995, the ruling Republican coalition led by the Pan-Armenian National Movement won a majority of seats. A new constitution was approved by a referendum in July 1995.

Armenia is divided into 11 Administrative Regions.

HEAD OF STATE

President, Levon Ter-Petrosyan, *elected* 16 October 1991, *re-elected* 23 September 1996

CABINET *as at June 1997*

Prime Minister, Robert Kocharian

Communications, Grigor Pokhpatyan
Culture, Armen Smbatian
Defence, Vazgen Sargsyan
Director of State Taxation Agency, Pavel Safryan
Director of Statistics, State Register and Analysis Department,
   Eduard Agadzhanov
Economy, Vahram Avanesyan
Education and Science, Artashes Petrossian
Energy and Fuel, Gagik Martirossian
Environment, Souren Avetissian
Finance, Armen Darbinian
Foreign Affairs, Alexander Arzoumanian
Industry, Ashot Safarian
National Security, Serzh Sargsyan
Justice, Marat Alexanyan
Public Health, Ara Babloyan
Social Security, Employment and Refugees, Hranoush Hakobian
Trade Services and Tourism, Garnik Nanagulian
Transport, Henrikh Kochinyan
Urban Planning and Construction, Felix Pirumyan

Chairman of the National Assembly, Babken Ararktsyan

EMBASSY OF THE REPUBLIC OF ARMENIA
25A Cheniston Gardens, London W8 6TG
Tel 0171-938 5415
Ambassador Extraordinary and Plenipotentiary, new
   appointment awaited

BRITISH EMBASSY
28 Charents Street, Yerevan
Tel: Yerevan 151 841/2
Ambassador Extraordinary and Plenipotentiary, HE Dr John
   Mitchiner, apptd 1996

DEFENCE

The Army has 102 main battle tanks, 240 armoured
infantry fighting vehicles and armoured personnel carriers, 225 artillery pieces, six combat aircraft and seven
armed helicopters.

Russia maintains 4,300 army personnel in Armenia. An
agreement on military co-operation with Russia was
signed in May 1996 which paved the way for joint military
exercises. A protocol was also signed on the establishment
of coalition troops in Transcaucasia and the planned use of
Russian and Armenian armed forces as part of coalition
troops in cases of mutual interest.
MILITARY EXPENDITURE – 4.4 per cent of GDP (1995)
MILITARY PERSONNEL – 57,600: Army 56,600,
   Paramilitaries 1,000
CONSCRIPTION DURATION – 18 months

ECONOMY

The Armenian economy has been badly affected by the
1988 earthquake which devastated much of the country,
and by the Azeri and Turkish economic embargos which
have been in place since 1988. The main trade and
transportation routes now lie via Georgia and Iran.

Armenia has a strong agricultural sector in low-lying
areas, where industrial and fruit crops are grown. Grain is
grown in the hills and the country is also noted for its wine
and brandy. There are large copper ore and molybdenum
deposits and other minerals. The country also has developed chemicals, industrial vehicles and textiles
industries.

The government introduced a programme of economic
reforms in November 1994 with IMF support, including
the liberalization of prices, stabilization of the currency,
privatization, and reducing the budget deficit.

In 1994 Armenia had a trade deficit of US$181 million
and a current account deficit of US$106 million.
GNP – US$2,752 million (1995); US$730 per capita (1995)
GDP – US$6,391 million (1992); US$88 per capita (1992)
TOTAL EXTERNAL DEBT – US$374 million (1995)

	1995	1996
TRADE WITH UK		
Imports from UK	£918,000	£3,856,000
Exports to UK	173,000	283,000

CULTURE AND EDUCATION

The Armenian alphabet was established in AD 405. Major
writers include the poets Frick (13th century), Nahapet
Kuchak (16th century) and Sayat-Nova (18th century).
The composer Aram Khachaturian (1903–78) was
Armenian.
ILLITERACY RATE – 0.4 per cent
ENROLMENT (percentage of age group) – tertiary 48.9 per
   cent (1991)

AUSTRALIA
The Commonwealth of Australia

AREA AND POPULATION*

States and Territories	Area (sq. km)	Resident population 31 December 1996p
New South Wales (NSW)	801,600	6,240,900
Queensland (Qld)	1,727,200	3,374,300
South Australia (SA)	984,000	1,476,800
Tasmania (Tas.)	67,800	474,200
Victoria (Vic.)	227,600	4,581,600
Western Australia (WA)	2,525,500	1,782,700
Australian Capital Territory (ACT)	2,400	308,500
Northern Territory (NT)	1,346,200	184,900
Total	7,682,300	18,423,900

* estimated
p preliminary

POPULATION OF ABORIGINAL AND TORRES STRAIT
ISLANDER ORIGIN (*1991 census*)

	Number	% of state population
New South Wales	70,019	1.20
Queensland	70,124	2.40
South Australia	16,232	1.14
Tasmania	8,885	0.20
Victoria	16,735	0.40
Western Australia	41,779	2.54
Australian Capital Territory	1,775	0.63
Northern Territory	39,916	22.70
Total	265,459	1.60

	1995	1996
Permanent arrivals	96,970	92,500
Permanent departures	27,870	28,480

CAPITAL – Canberra, in the Australian Capital Territory.
   Estimated population at 30 June 1996 was 307,100. It has
   been the seat of government since 1927
CURRENCY – Australian dollar ($A) of 100 cents
NATIONAL ANTHEM – Advance Australia Fair
NATIONAL DAY – 26 January (Australia Day)
NATIONAL FLAG – The British Blue Ensign with five stars
   of the Southern Cross in the fly and the white
   Commonwealth Star of seven points beneath the Union
   Flag

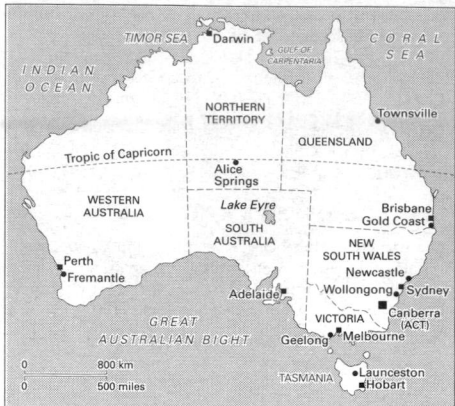

LIFE EXPECTANCY (years) – male 74.99; female 80.86
POPULATION GROWTH RATE – 1.1 per cent (1994)
POPULATION DENSITY – 2 per sq. km (1994)
URBAN POPULATION – 85.4 per cent (1986)

Australia is a continent in the southern hemisphere. The highest point is Mt. Kosciusko (2,228 m) and the lowest, Lake Eyre (−15 m). Climatic conditions range from the alpine to the tropical. Two-thirds of the continent is arid or semi-arid although good rainfalls (over 800 mm annually) occur in the northern monsoonal belt and along the eastern and southern highland regions.

HISTORY AND POLITICS

Australia was discovered in the 18th century and was colonized by the British, initially as a penal colony. The Commonwealth of Australia was inaugurated on 1 January 1901, at which time Australia gained dominion status within the British Empire. Australia became independent within the British Commonwealth by the 1931 Statute of Westminster.

POLITICAL SYSTEM

The government is that of a federal commonwealth within the Commonwealth, the executive power being vested in the Sovereign (through the Governor-General), assisted by a federal government. Under the constitution the federal government has acquired and may acquire certain defined powers as surrendered by the states, residuary legislative power remaining with the states. The right of a state to legislate on any matter is not abrogated except in connection with matters exclusively under federal control, but where a state law is inconsistent with a law of the Commonwealth the latter prevails to the extent of the inconsistency.

Parliament consists of Queen Elizabeth II, the Senate and the House of Representatives. The constitution provides that the number of members of the House of Representatives shall be, as nearly as practicable, twice the number of senators. Members of the Senate are elected for six years by universal suffrage, half the members retiring every third year. Each of the six states returns 12 senators, and the Australian Capital Territory and the Northern Territory two each. The House of Representatives, similarly elected for a maximum of three years, contains members proportionate to the population, with a minimum of five members for each state. There are now 148 members in the House of Representatives, including one

member for the Northern Territory and two for the Australian Capital Territory.

The High Court exercises jurisdiction over all matters arising under the constitution, all matters arising between the states and between residents of different states, matters to which the Commonwealth of Australia is a party, matters arising under any treaty, and matters affecting foreign representatives in Australia. The High Court also hears appeals from the Federal Court and from the Supreme Courts of states and territories.

The Federal Court of Australia has jurisdiction over important industrial, trade practices, intellectual property, administrative law, admiralty law and bankruptcy matters. It also acts as a court of appeal for decisions from the Australian Capital Territory Supreme Court and certain decisions of state Supreme Courts exercising federal jurisdiction. Each state has its own judicature of supreme, superior and minor courts for criminal and civil cases.

GOVERNOR-GENERAL

Governor-General, HE Sir William Deane, AC, KBE, *assumed office* 16 February 1996

CABINET *as at July 1997*

Prime Minister, John Howard
Deputy Prime Minister, Trade, Tim Fischer
Communications and the Arts, Sen. Richard Alston
Defence, Ian McLachlan
Employment, Education, Training and Youth Affairs, Sen. Amanda Vanstone
Finance, John Fahey
Foreign Affairs, Alexander Downer
Health and Family Services, Dr Michael Wooldridge
Industry, Science and Tourism, John Moore
Leader of the Government in the Senate, Environment, Sen. Robert Hill
Leader of the House, Industrial Relations, Peter Reith
Primary Industries and Energy, John Anderson
Social Security, Minister Assisting the Prime Minister for the Status of Women, Sen. Jocelyn Newman
Transport and Regional Development, John Sharp
Treasurer, Peter Costello

President of the Senate, Sen. Kerry Sibraa
Speaker, House of Representatives, Stephen Martin

AUSTRALIAN HIGH COMMISSION

Australia House, Strand, London WC2B 4LA
Tel 0171-379 4334
High Commissioner, HE Neal Blewett, apptd 1994
Deputy High Commissioner, R. McGovern
Minister-Counsellor, C. J. Walsh *(Industry, Science and Technology)*
Head of Defence Staff, Brig. P. L. McGuiness

BRITISH HIGH COMMISSION

Commonwealth Avenue, Yarralumla, Canberra, ACT 2600
Tel: Canberra 270 6666
High Commissioner, HE Sir Roger John Carrick, KCMG, LVO, apptd 1995
Deputy High Commissioner, A. J. Pocock
First Secretary, B. J. Davidson *(Economic and Agricultural)*
Defence and Naval Adviser and Head of British Defence Liaison Staff, Cdre P. C. Wykeham-Martin
Consuls-General, S. J. Hiscock *(Brisbane)*; G. Finlayson *(Melbourne)*; M. J. Horne *(Perth)*; P. Morrice *(Sydney)*
Cultural Adviser and British Council Representative, J. Potts, OBE, Edgecliff Centre, 401/203 New South Head Road (PO Box 88), Edgecliff, Sydney, NSW 2027

DEFENCE

The Army has 71 main battle tanks, 591 armoured personnel carriers and armoured infantry fighting vehicles, 385 artillery pieces, three aircraft and 25 armed helicopters. The Navy has four submarines, three destroyers, eight frigates, 15 patrol and coastal vessels and 23 armed helicopters. There are bases at Sydney, Cockburn Sound, Cairns and Darwin. The Air Force has 126 combat aircraft.

MILITARY EXPENDITURE – 2.5 per cent of GDP (1995)
MILITARY PERSONNEL – 57,800: Army 26,000, Navy 14,700, Air Force 17,100

ECONOMY

The wide range of climatic and soil conditions has resulted in a diversity of crops. Generally, cereal crops (excluding rice and sorghum) are widely grown, while other crops are confined to specific locations in a few states. However, scant or erratic rainfall, limited potential for irrigation and unsuitable soils or topography have restricted intensive agriculture.

Significant mineral resources include bauxite, coal, copper, crude petroleum, gems, gold, ilmenite, iron ore, lead, limestone, manganese, nickel, rutile, salt, silver, tin, tungsten, uranium, zinc and zircon. In 1995 241,834,000 tonnes of coal, 27,031,036 tonnes of crude oil, 29,761 cubic metres of natural gas, 142,936,000 tonnes of iron ore, 365,000 tonnes of copper, 455,000 tonnes of lead, 253,084 kilograms of gold were produced.

In 1994 the government had a budget deficit equivalent to 2.96 per cent of GDP.

GNP – US$337,909 million (1995); US$18,720 per capita (1995)
GDP – US$304,803 million (1992); US$16,715 per capita (1992)
ANNUAL AVERAGE GROWTH OF GDP – 3.1 per cent (1995)
INFLATION RATE – 4.6 per cent (1995)
UNEMPLOYMENT – 8.5 per cent (1995)

TRADE

In 1995-6 the main exports were coal and gas (12 per cent); gold (7 per cent); aluminium and aluminium oxide (7 per cent); iron, iron ore and steel (6 per cent); petroleum oils and products (4 per cent); wheat (4 per cent); wool (3 per cent). The major imports are motor vehicles and parts (9 per cent); (computer technology (5 per cent); petroleum oils (6 per cent); telecommunications equipment (3 per cent); aircraft and spacecraft (3 per cent).

Australia's main trading partners are the USA, Japan, New Zealand, the south-east Asian 'tiger' economies, Germany and the UK.

In 1994 Australia had a trade deficit of US$3,199 million and a current account deficit of US$15,224 million. In 1995 imports totalled US$61,286 million and exports US$53,074 million.

Trade with UK	1995	1996
Imports from UK	£2,121,352,000	£2,465,635,000
Exports to UK	1,110,448,000	1,296,021,000

COMMUNICATIONS

There are six government-owned railway systems, operated by the State Rail Authority of NSW, Victorian Railways, Queensland Government Railways, Western Australian Government Railways, the State Transport Authority of Southern Australia, and the Australian National Railways Commission (ANRC). The ANRC incorporates the former Commonwealth Railways system, and the Tasmanian and non-metropolitan South Australian railways (urban rail services in Southern Australia remain the responsibility of the State Transport Authority).

The Northern Territory has three main ports: Darwin, and the private mining ports of Gove and Groote Eylandt. Most freight in the Territory is moved by road trains. These are massive trucks hauling two or three trailers, having a net capacity of about 100 tonnes and measuring up to 45 metres in length.

EDUCATION

Education is administered by the state governments and is compulsory between the ages of five or six and 15 years. It is available at government schools controlled by the state education department and at private or independent schools, some of which are denominational. Tertiary education is available through universities, and technical and further education colleges. New South Wales has ten universities, South Australia three, the University of Tasmania in Tasmania, Victoria nine and Western Australia four.

ENROLMENT (percentage of age group) – primary 98 per cent (1993); secondary 81 per cent (1993); tertiary 40.9 per cent (1994)

THE NORTHERN TERRITORY

The Northern Territory has a total area of 519,770 sq. miles (1,346,200 sq. km),. The estimated population of the Northern Territory in December 1996 was 184,900.

GOVERNMENT

The administration was taken over by the Commonwealth on 1 January 1911 from the State of South Australia. The Northern Territory (Self-Government) Act 1978 established the Northern Territory as a body politic from 1 July 1978, with Ministers having control over and responsibility for Territory finances and the administration of the functions of government.

The Northern Territory elects one member to the federal House of Representatives and two members to the Senate.

SEAT OF ADMINISTRATION – Darwin
Administrator, Dr Neil R. Conn
Chief Minister, Shane L. Stone

ECONOMY

Northern Territory's economy is based on the exploitation of its natural resources of minerals, land and fisheries and on tourist attractions. The agricultural and horticultural industries are also beginning to contribute an increasing amount to Territory output. The beef cattle industry continues to be the major user of pastoral lands.

Mining and energy resource development has played a major part in the development of the Northern Territory and in 1993–4 the total value of production was $A1,028 million. The Territory is a leading uranium producer and contains 20 per cent of the developed world's low-cost uranium reserves. Large-scale production of zinc-lead concentrate commenced in 1994. The value of oil and gas production for 1993–4 was $A342 million.

Tourism is a major growth industry and generates over $A603 million annually.

EXTERNAL TERRITORIES

ASHMORE AND CARTIER ISLANDS

Ashmore Islands (known as Middle, East and West Islands) and Cartier Island are situated in the Indian Ocean 850 km and 790 km west of Darwin respectively. The islands are uninhabited.

Great Britain took formal possession of the Ashmores in 1878 and Cartier was annexed in 1909. In 1931 the islands were placed under the authority of the Commonwealth of Australia, and were accepted in 1933 under the name of the Territory of Ashmore and Cartier Islands. The territory is administered by the Commonwealth Government. In 1983 Ashmore Reef was declared a national nature reserve.

THE AUSTRALIAN ANTARCTIC TERRITORY

The Australian Antarctic Territory was established in 1933 by an Order in Council which placed under the government of the Commonwealth of Australia all the islands and territories, other than Adélie Land, which are situated south of the latitude 60° S. and lying between 160° E. longitude and 45° E. longitude. The Order came into force in 1936. The territory is administered by the Antarctic Division of the Department of the Environment, Sport and Territories, which, since 1948, has organized yearly expeditions to Antarctica, known as Australian National Antarctic Research Expeditions (ANARE). There are nine scientific research stations.

CHRISTMAS ISLAND

Christmas Island is situated in the Indian Ocean about 1,408 km NW of North West Cape in Western Australia, and has an area of 135 sq. km. Population (1991 census) is 1,275, largely consisting of mineworkers and government employees. There is no indigenous population. The island became an Australian territory in 1958, having previously been administered as part of the colony of Singapore.

The Administrator is responsible to the Australian Minister for Sport, Territories and Local Government in Canberra. The Shire of Christmas Island (SOCI) has nine elected members. SOCI is responsible for municipal functions and services on the island.

The island has extensive deposits of phosphates, the extraction of which has traditionally been the major economic activity. The deposits of low grade phosphate ore are now being extracted by a private mining company. The other major commercial activity is the operation of a casino and resort complex.

Administrator, Graham Nicholls (*acting*)

COCOS (KEELING) ISLANDS

The Cocos (Keeling) Islands are two separate atolls (North Keeling Island and, 24 km to the south, the main atoll) comprising some 27 small coral islands with a total area of about 14 sq. km, situated in the Indian Ocean. The main islands of the southern atoll are West Island (about 9 km in length); Home Island, where the Cocos Malay community lives; Direction Island, Horsburgh and South Island. The population as at 30 June 1991 was 647.

The islands were declared a British possession in 1857. All land in the islands was granted to George Clunies-Ross and his heirs by Queen Victoria in 1886. In 1955 the islands, which had been governed through the British colonies of Ceylon (from 1878), the Straits Settlements (1886) and Singapore (1903), were accepted as a Territory of Australia. In 1978 the Australian Government purchased all Clunies-Ross land and property interests except for the family home and grounds. Between 1979 and 1984 most of the land was transferred to the Cocos (Keeling) Islands Council, the local government body established in 1979 which was replaced by the Shire of the Cocos (Keeling) Islands in July 1992. In 1993 the federal government purchased the last of the remaining grounds.

The Cocos (Keeling) Islands Act 1955 provided the legal framework for the political and administrative arrangements in the territory. On 6 April 1984 the Cocos community, in a UN supervised Act of Self-Determination, chose to integrate with Australia. The islands are administered by the Australian Government through the Department of the Environment, Sport and Territories in Canberra.

The territory has a limited economic base. In 1986–7 the copra industry suffered severe losses and in 1987 ceased production. Tourism is being developed.

Administrator, Maureen Ellis (*acting*)

CORAL SEA ISLANDS TERRITORY

The Coral Sea Islands Territory lies east of Queensland between the Great Barrier Reef and longitude 156° 06′ E., and between latitudes 12° and 24° S. It comprises scattered islands, spread over a sea area of 780,000 sq. km. The islands are formed mainly of coral and sand, and most are extremely small, with no permanent fresh water. There is a manned meteorological station in the Willis Group but the remaining islands are uninhabited. Two national nature reserves were designated in the Territory in 1982.

The Australian Government bases its claim to the islands on numerous acts of sovereignty since early this century and enacted the Coral Sea Islands Act 1969 which declares the islands a territory of the Commonwealth of Australia. The Department of the Environment, Sport and Territories, Canberra, is responsible for the administration of the territory.

HEARD ISLAND AND McDONALD ISLANDS

The Heard and McDonald islands, about 4,100 km south-west of Fremantle, comprise all the islands and rocks lying between 52° 30′ and 53° 30′ S. latitude and 72° and 74° 30′ E. longitude. Sovereignty over the islands was transferred by the UK to the Commonwealth of Australia in 1947. The Heard Island and McDonald Islands Act 1953 provides for the government of the islands as one territory. The islands are administered by the Department of the Environment, Sport and Territories.

NORFOLK ISLAND

Norfolk Island is situated in the South Pacific Ocean. It is about 8 km long by 5 km wide, with an area of 3,455 hectares. The climate is mild and subtropical. Resident population at the 1996 census was 1,772.

The island, discovered by Captain Cook in 1774, served as a penal colony from 1788 to 1814 and 1825 to 1855. In 1856, 194 descendants of the *Bounty* mutineers accepted an invitation to leave Pitcairn and settle on Norfolk Island, which led to Norfolk Island becoming a separate settlement under the jurisdiction of the Governor of New South Wales. In 1897 Norfolk Island became a dependency of NSW and in 1914 a territory of Australia. From that date, Norfolk Island has been regarded as an integral part of Australia.

In 1979 Norfolk Island gained a substantial degree of self-government. Wide powers are exercised by a nine-member Legislative Assembly. The Act preserves the Commonwealth's responsibility for Norfolk Island as a territory under its authority, with the Minister for the Environment, Sport and Territories as the responsible Minister.

The island is a popular tourist resort, and a large proportion of the population depends on tourism and its ancillaries for employment.

The seat of government and administration offices are in Kingston.

Administrator, A. J. Messner

AUSTRALIAN STATES

NEW SOUTH WALES

New South Wales comprises an area of 309,433 sq. miles (801,427 sq. km) (exclusive of 939 sq. miles of Australian Capital Territory which lies within its borders). The preliminary estimated resident population at 31 December 1996 was 6,240,900.

STATE CAPITAL – ΨSydney, on the shores of Port Jackson. Sydney Harbour extends inland for 21 km; the total area of water is about 55 sq. km. The preliminary estimated resident population in 1996 of the Sydney statistical division was 3,821,400.

GOVERNMENT

New South Wales was first colonized as a British possession in 1788, and after progressive settlement a partly elective legislature was established in 1843. In 1855 responsible government was granted, the present constitution being founded on the Constitution Act of 1902. New South Wales federated with the other states of Australia in 1901.

The executive authority is vested in a Governor (appointed by the Crown), assisted by a Council of Ministers. The legislature consists of the Legislative Council of 42 members, elected by popular vote, and the Legislative Assembly of 99 members elected for a maximum period of four years.
Governor of New South Wales, HE Gordon Samuels, AC
Lt.-Governor and Chief Justice of NSW, A. M. Gleeson, AC
Premier, Bob Carr

NEW SOUTH WALES GOVERNMENT OFFICE IN LONDON, Australia House, Strand, London WC2B 4LA. Tel: 0171-887 5246

ECONOMY

A large area is suitable for sheep-raising, the principal breed of sheep being the merino, which was introduced in 1797. The principal minerals are coal, lead, zinc, gold, rutile, copper and zircon. The turnover in the mining industry in 1995–6 was $A4,987.3 million.

LORD HOWE ISLAND

Lord Howe Island, which is part of New South Wales, has an area of 6.37 sq. miles (16.5 sq. km) and a population of 340 in 1996. The island is of volcanic origin, Mount Gower reaching an altitude of 866 m. The affairs of the Island are administered by the Lord Howe Island Board

QUEENSLAND

Queensland comprises the whole north-eastern portion of the Australian continent and possesses an area (including offshore islands) of 668,997 sq. miles (1,732,700 sq. km). At 31 December 1996 the estimated resident population numbered 3,374,300.
STATE CAPITAL – ΨBrisbane is situated on the Brisbane River. The estimated resident population of the Brisbane statistical division at 30 June 1996 was 1,525,500.

GOVERNMENT

Queensland was constituted a separate colony with responsible government in 1859, having previously formed part of New South Wales. The executive authority is vested in a Governor (appointed by the Crown), aided by an Executive Council of 18 members. Parliament consists of a Legislative Assembly of 89 members.

Governor of Queensland, HE Mary Marguerite Leneen Forde, AC
Premier, R. E. Borbidge

AGENT-GENERAL'S OFFICE IN LONDON, 392 Strand, London WC2R 0LZ. Tel: 0171-836 1333. *Agent-General*, D. A. McManus

ECONOMY

Queensland is Australia's major beef-producing state. In March 1994, there were 9.7 million beef cattle in the state, which constituted 42 per cent of Australia's total meat cattle. In 1994–5, Queensland's coal, coke and briquette exports were valued at $A4,124.5 million. The major metallic minerals mined in 1994–5 were bauxite (9.3 million tonnes), copper concentrate (749,260 tonnes), gold bullion (41,770 kilograms) and lead concentrate (299,382 tonnes). The total value of all minerals produced in Queensland in 1994–5 was $A5,430.4 million.

SOUTH AUSTRALIA

South Australia has a total area of 380,070 sq. miles (984,376 sq. km). At 31 December 1996, the resident population was estimated to be 1,479,153.
STATE CAPITAL – ΨAdelaide, estimated resident population at 30 June 1996, 1,086,532.

GOVERNMENT

South Australia was proclaimed a British province in 1836, and in 1851 a partially elective legislature was established. The present constitution rests upon a law of 24 October 1856, the executive authority being vested in a Governor appointed by the Crown, aided by a Council of 13 Ministers.

Parliament consists of a Legislative Council of 22 members elected for eight years, one half retiring every four years; and a House of Assembly of 47 members, elected for a maximum duration of four years.
Governor of South Australia, HE Sir Eric Neal, AC, CVO, *assumed office* 1996
Lt.-Governor, Dr Basil Hetzel, AC, *assumed office* 1992
Premier, John Wayne Olsen

AGENT-GENERAL'S OFFICE IN LONDON, 115 Strand, London WC2R 0AJ. *Agent-General*, G. Walls

TASMANIA

Tasmania is an island state situated in the Southern Ocean off the south-eastern extremity of the mainland. It is separated from the mainland by Bass Strait and incorporates King Island and the Furneaux group of islands which are in the strait. It has an area of 26,383 sq. miles (68,331 sq km). Macquarie Island, situated at about 900 miles north of the Antarctic Continent, is a dependency of Tasmania. The estimated resident population at 31 December 1996 was 474,200.
STATE CAPITAL – ΨHobart, founded 1804. Population (30 June 1996) (metropolitan area), 195,000.

GOVERNMENT

The island was first settled by a British party from New South Wales in 1803, becoming a separate colony in 1825. In 1851 a partly elective legislature was inaugurated, and in 1856 responsible government was established. In 1901 Tasmania became a state of the Australian Commonwealth. Executive authority is vested in a Governor appointed by the Crown, but is exercised by Cabinet Ministers responsible to the legislature, of which they are members. Parliament consists of a Legislative Council of 19 members, elected for six years, and a House of Assembly of 35 members, elected by proportional representation for four years in five seven-member constituencies.

Governor of Tasmania, HE Sir Guy Montague Greene AC, KBE

Premier, Tony Rundle

ECONOMY

Tasmania produces the most electrical energy per head of population of the Australian states. Most of it is derived from water power, with a total installed generator capacity of over 2,500,000 kW. Due to its low-cost electricity, Tasmania has large plants producing ferro-manganese and newsprint.

The quantity of timber (excluding firewood) cut in 1995–6 was 4,470,900 cubic metres. The chief ores mined are those containing copper, tin, iron, silver, zinc and lead. The chief manufactures for export are refined metals, agricultural products, textiles, paper, confectionery, wood chips and sawn timber.

VICTORIA

Victoria comprises the south-east corner of Australia, at the part where its mainland territory projects furthest into the southern latitudes. Its area is 87,876 sq. miles (227,600 sq. km). The estimated resident population at 31 December 1996 was 4,581,600.

STATE CAPITAL – ΨMelbourne had a resident population at 30 June 1996 estimated at 3,248,800.

GOVERNMENT

Victoria was originally known as the Port Phillip District of New South Wales and was created a separate colony in 1851, with a partially elective legislature. In 1855 responsible government was conferred.

The executive authority is vested in a Governor, appointed by the Crown, aided by an Executive Council of Ministers. Parliament consists of a Legislative Council of 44 members, elected for the 22 provinces for two terms of the Legislative Assembly, one half retiring every four years at a general election; and a Legislative Assembly of 88 members, elected for a maximum duration of four years. Voting is compulsory.

Governor of Victoria, HE James A. Gobbo

Lt.-Governor, Adrienne E. Clarke

Premier, Jeff Kennett

AGENT-GENERAL'S OFFICE IN LONDON, Victoria House, Melbourne Place, Strand, London WC2B 4LG. *Agent-General,* Alan J. Brown

ECONOMY

Minerals raised include oil and natural gas, brown coal, limestone, clays and stone for construction material. Production of brown coal in 1993–4 was 48,214 million tonnes. Production from Victorian natural gas and crude oil fields in 1993–4 was 17,221 megalitres of crude oil and 4,999 gigalitres of natural gas.

WESTERN AUSTRALIA

Western Australia has an area of 975,920 sq. miles (2,527,621 sq. km). At 31 December 1996 the estimated resident population was 1,782,700.

STATE CAPITAL – ΨPerth, on the north bank of the Swan River estuary, 12 miles from Fremantle. Estimated resident population (30 June 1996) of Perth statistical division, including the port of ΨFremantle, 1,282,800.

GOVERNMENT

Western Australia was first settled in 1829, and in 1870 it was granted a partially elective legislature. In 1890 responsible government was granted.

The executive is vested in a Governor appointed by the Crown and aided by a Council of Ministers. Parliament consists of a Legislative Council and a Legislative Assembly, elected by adult suffrage subject to qualifications of residence and registration. There are 34 members in the Legislative Council elected for a period of four years. The Legislative Assembly has 57 members, who are elected for a term of four years.

Governor of Western Australia, Maj.-Gen. Philip M. Jeffery, AO, MC

Lt.-Governor, D. K. Malcolm, QC

Premier, Richard Court

EUROPEAN OFFICE, Western Australia House, 115 Strand, London WC2R 0AJ. *Agent-General,* C. E. Griffiths

ECONOMY

The forests contain some of the finest hardwoods in the world. In 1995 135,966,000 tonnes of iron, 12,512 megalitres of crude oil, 189,353 kilograms of gold, 5,827 gigalitres of natural gas and 23,452,000 carats of diamonds were produced. The ex-mine value of all minerals (excluding construction materials) produced in 1995 was $A14,582 million.

Source: for demographic, economic and education statistics, Australian Bureau of Statistics.

AUSTRIA
Republik Österreich

AREA – 32,378 sq. miles (83,859 sq. km). Neighbours: the Czech Republic and Slovakia (north), Italy and Slovenia (south) Hungary (east), Germany (north-west), Switzerland and Liechtenstein (west)

POPULATION – 8,047,000 (1995 estimate); 7,813,000 (1991 census). The language is German, but the rights of the Slovene- and Croat-speaking minorities in Carinthia, Styria and Burgenland are protected. The predominant religion is Roman Catholicism

CAPITAL – Vienna, on the Danube (population, 1,593,000, 1995 estimate)

MAJOR CITIES – Graz (237,810); Linz (203,044); Innsbruck (118,112); Salzburg (143,978); Klagenfurt (89,415), 1991

CURRENCY – Schilling of 100 Groschen

NATIONAL ANTHEM – Land der Berge, Land am Strome (Land of mountains, land on the river)

NATIONAL DAY – 26 October

NATIONAL FLAG – Three equal horizontal stripes of red, white, red

LIFE EXPECTANCY (years) – male 72.87; female 79.35

POPULATION GROWTH RATE – 1.0 per cent (1994)

POPULATION DENSITY – 96 per sq. km (1994)

URBAN POPULATION – 64.6 per cent (1991)

HISTORY AND POLITICS

The Republic of Austria was established in 1918 on the break-up of the Austro-Hungarian Empire. In March 1938 Austria was incorporated into Nazi Germany under the name *Ostmark.* After the liberation of Vienna in 1945, the Republic of Austria was reconstituted within the 1937 frontiers and a freely-elected government took office in December 1945. The country was divided into four zones occupied respectively by the UK, USA, USSR and France, while Vienna was jointly occupied by the four Powers. In 1955 the Austrian State Treaty was signed by the foreign ministers of the four Powers and of Austria. This treaty recognized the re-establishment of Austria as a sovereign, independent and democratic state, having the same frontiers as on 1 January 1938. Austria acceded to the European Union on 1 January 1995.

After the general election of 17 December 1995 the Social Democrats and the People's Party formed a coalition government.

POLITICAL SYSTEM

There is a bicameral national assembly; the lower house (*Nationalrat*) has 183 members and the upper house (*Bundesrat*) has 64 members. There is a 4 per cent qualification for parliamentary representation.

There are nine provinces: Burgenland, Carinthia, Lower Austria, Upper Austria, Salzburg, Styria, Tyrol, Vienna, and Vorarlberg.

HEAD OF STATE
President of the Republic of Austria, Dr Thomas Klestil, *took office* 8 July 1992

CABINET *as at June 1997*
Chancellor, Viktor Klima (SPÖ)
Vice Chancellor, Foreign Affairs, Wolfgang Schüssel (ÖVP)
Agriculture and Forestry, Wilhelm Molterer (ÖVP)
Defence, Werner Fasslabend (ÖVP)
Economic Affairs, Johann Farnleitner (ÖVP)
Education and Cultural Affairs, Elisabeth Gehrer (ÖVP)
Environment, Youth and Family, Martin Bartenstein (ÖVP)
Finance, Rudolf Edlinger (SPÖ)
Interior, Karl Schlögl (SPÖ)
Justice, Nikolaus Michalek (Ind.)
Labour, Health and Social Affairs, Eleonore Hostasch (SPÖ)
Science and Transport, Caspar Einem (SPÖ)
Women's Affairs and Consumer Protection, Barbara Prammer (SPÖ)
SPÖ Social Democratic Party; ÖVP People's Party; Ind. Independent

AUSTRIAN EMBASSY
18 Belgrave Mews West, London SW1X 8HU
Tel 0171–235 3731
Ambassador Extraordinary and Plenipotentiary, Eva Nowotny, apptd 1997
Minister, Dr Herbert Krauss
Defence Attaché, Brig. H. Rüdiger Sulzgruber
Consul-General, Hella Naumann
Commercial Counsellor and Trade Commissioner, Dr Rudolf Engel

BRITISH EMBASSY
Jaurèsgasse 12, 1030 Vienna
Tel: Vienna 716130
Ambassador Extraordinary and Plenipotentiary, HE Sir Anthony Figgis, KCVO, CMG, apptd 1996
Deputy Head of Mission, Counsellor and Consul-General, I. Cliffe, OBE
Defence Attaché, Lt.-Col. A. Manton
First Secretary (Economic), W. Brandon

BRITISH CONSULAR OFFICES – There is a consular office at Vienna, and Honorary Consulates at Bregenz, Graz, Innsbruck and Salzburg.

BRITISH COUNCIL REPRESENTATIVE, M. Evans, Schenkenstrasse 4, A–1010 Vienna

DEFENCE

The Army has 170 main battle tanks, 483 armoured personnel carriers and 295 artillery pieces. The Air Force has 53 combat aircraft.

MILITARY EXPENDITURE – 1.0 per cent of GDP (1995)
MILITARY PERSONNEL – 55,800: Army 51,500, Air Force 4,300
CONSCRIPTION DURATION – Seven to eight months plus refresher training

ECONOMY

Austria produces wheat, rye, barley, oats, maize, potatoes, sugar beet and turnips. Timber forms a valuable source of Austria's indigenous wealth, about 47 per cent of the total land area consisting of forest areas.

In 1995, 17,173,000 foreign tourists visited Austria. Foreign exchange receipts from tourism were a major contribution to the balance of payments.

In 1994 Austria had a current account deficit of US$2,452 million and a trade deficit of US$8,869 million.
GNP – US$216,547 million (1995); US$26,890 per capita (1995)
GDP – US$165,121 million (1992); US$23,725 per capita (1992)
ANNUAL AVERAGE GROWTH OF GDP – 1.8 per cent (1995)
INFLATION RATE – 2.3 per cent (1995)
UNEMPLOYMENT – 4.5 per cent (1995)

TRADE

Main exports are processed goods (iron and steel, other metal goods, textiles, paper and cardboard products), machinery and transport equipment, other finished goods (including clothing), raw materials, chemical products and foodstuffs. Main imports are machinery and transport equipment, processed goods, chemical products, foodstuffs, fuel and energy. Austria's main trading partners are Germany, Italy, France and Switzerland.

Trade with UK	1995	1996
Imports from UK	£1,068,300,000	£1,209,400,000
Exports to UK	883,900,000	1,082,100,000

COMMUNICATIONS

Internal communications are partly restricted because of the mountainous nature of the country, although there is now a network of 1,567 km of *Autobahn* between major cities which also links up with the German and Italian networks. The railways are state-owned and in 1993 had 5,605 km of track, 58.8 per cent of which is electrified. Of the 425 km of waterways, 350 km are navigable and there is considerable trade through the Danube ports by both local and foreign shipping. There are six commercial airports catering for 5,527,600 passengers in 1995.

There are four national radio and two national television channels, together with three national and twelve regional newspapers.

EDUCATION

Education is free and compulsory between the ages of six and 15 and there are good facilities for secondary, technical and professional education. There are 12 state-maintained universities and six colleges of art.

ENROLMENT (percentage of age group) – primary 100 per cent; secondary 91 per cent; tertiary 43.2 per cent (1993)

AZERBAIJAN
Azarbaijchan Respublikasy

AREA – 33,436 sq. miles (86,600 sq. km). Neighbours: Iran (south), Armenia (west) and Georgia and Russia (north)
POPULATION – 7,553,000 (1996 estimate): 83 per cent Azeri, 6 per cent Russian and 6 per cent Armenian. There are also Kurds, Jews, Georgians and Turks. There are more Azeris in Iran than in Azerbaijan. The population is predominantly Shia Muslim although it was heavily secularized during the Soviet era
CAPITAL – ΨBaku (population, 1,149,000, 1990)
CURRENCY – Manat of 100 gopik
NATIONAL DAY – 28 May (Independence Day)
NATIONAL FLAG – Three horizontal stripes of blue, red and green with a white crescent and eight-pointed star in the centre
LIFE EXPECTANCY (years) – male 66.60; female 74.20
POPULATION GROWTH RATE – 1.1 per cent (1994)
POPULATION DENSITY – 86 per sq. km (1994)
URBAN POPULATION – 54.2 per cent (1989)

Azerbaijan occupies the eastern part of the Caucasus region of the former Soviet Union, on the shore of the Caspian Sea. The north-eastern part of the republic is taken up by the south-eastern end of the main Caucasus ridge, its south-western part by the smaller Caucasus hills, and its south-eastern corner by the spurs of the Talysh Ridge. Its central part is a depression irrigated by the River Kura and the lower reaches of its tributary the Araks. Sheltered by the mountains from the humid west winds blowing from the Black Sea, Azerbaijan has a continental climate.

Azerbaijan has 64 administrative districts and also includes the Nakhichevan Autonomous Republic, which is geographically separated from the rest of Azerbaijan by Armenia and borders on Iran and Turkey, and the Nagorno-Karabakh Autonomous Province.

HISTORY AND POLITICS

The territory that is now Azerbaijan was successively part of the Assyrian, Persian, Median and Greek empires. With the influx of Huns and Khazars in the first century BC, the Turkic Azerbaijani people evolved and formed an independent state. This was invaded by the Arab Caliphates in the seventh century AD and under their 300-year rule Islam was introduced and became the dominant religion. In the 16th century Azerbaijan was again invaded by Persia and became a Persian province. The country was divided during the Russo-Persian wars of the early 19th century, the northern portion (the present-day Azerbaijan) becoming part of the Russian Empire and the southern portion remaining Persian and subsequently Iranian.

In 1918 the Azerbaijan Democratic Republic was established. It was overthrown by Communists in 1918 and Azerbaijan acceded to the USSR in 1922.

In January 1990, the Azerbaijani Popular Front took power from the local Communist Party and declared independence from the Soviet Union. Soviet troops overthrew the Popular Front and restored the Communist regime under President Ayaz Mutalibov. This government declared Azerbaijan's independence in August 1991. Mutalibov won the presidential election held in September 1991, but he was forced to resign by widespread civil unrest. At the presidential election in June 1992 the Popular Front leader Abulfaz Elchibey was elected.

Popular discontent at military defeats caused Elchibey to flee Baku in June 1993 and the former Azerbaijani

Communist Party First Secretary Heydar Aliyev took over the presidency. The new regime was confirmed in office in a referendum in August and Aliyev won the presidential election in October 1993.

In November 1995, elections were held to the *Milli Majlis* (parliament), which had been increased to 125 seats: 100 directly elected and 25 allocated by proportional representation. The New Azerbaijan party, founded by Aliyev, won 70 per cent of the vote and a majority of seats.

SECESSION

In 1988 fighting broke out in the predominantly Armenian-populated region of Nagorny-Karabakh between Soviet Azerbaijani forces and ethnic Armenians demanding unification with Armenia. In late 1993 Nagorno-Karabakh forces captured all of the region, together with all Azeri territory separating the region from Armenia (20 per cent of Azeri territory). Azeri forces pushed back the Nagorno-Karabakh forces in early 1994 before a cease-fire agreement was signed in May 1994. Peace talks have been held under the auspices of the OSCE. Twenty per cent of Azeri territory remains under the control of Nagorno-Karabakh forces. Between 500,000 and one million Azeris have been displaced by the fighting.

POLITICAL SYSTEM

A new constitution was approved by a referendum in November 1995, which created a presidential republic with executive power to be exercised by the president and with legislative power vested in the Milli Majlis.

HEAD OF STATE

President, Heydar Aliyev, *assumed office* 18 June 1993, *elected* 3 October 1993

GOVERNMENT *as at June 1997*

Prime Minister, Artur Rasizade
First Deputy Prime Minister, Abbas Abbasov
Deputy Prime Ministers, Tofig Azizov; Elchin Efendiyev; Izzet Rustamov; Abid Sharifov
Agriculture, Irshad Aliyev
Communications, Siruz Abbasbeyli
Culture, Polad Byulbyulogly
Defence, Lt.-Gen. Safar Abiyev
Economy, Namik Nasrullayev
Education, Lidiya Rasulova
Finance, Fikret Yusifov
Foreign Affairs, Hasan Hasanov
Foreign Economic Relations, Gudrat Guliyev
Health, Ali Insanov
Internal Affairs, Ramil Usubov
Justice (acting), Sudaba Hasanova
Labour and Social Protection of the Population, Ali Nagiyev
Media and Information, Siruz Tebrizli

National Security, Namig Abbasov
Trade, Miri Gambarov
Youth and Sports, Abulfaz Karayev

AZERBAIJANI EMBASSY
4 Kensington Court, London W8 5DL
Tel 0171-938 3412
Ambassador Extraordinary and Plenipotentiary, HE Mahmud
  Mamed-Kuliyev, apptd 1994

BRITISH EMBASSY
2 Izmir Street, Baku 370065
Tel: Baku 985558
Ambassador Extraordinary and Plenipotentiary, HE David R.
  Thomas, apptd 1997

DEFENCE

The Army has 300 main battle tanks, 431 armoured
infantry fighting vehicles, 149 armoured personnel carriers and 302 artillery pieces. The Navy is based at Baku,
with a share of the former Soviet Caspian Fleet Flotilla,
comprising two frigates and 15 patrol and coastal vessels.
The Air Force has 46 combat aircraft and 18 attack
helicopters.
MILITARY EXPENDITURE – 5.0 per cent of GDP (1995)
MILITARY PERSONNEL – 110,700: Army 57,300, Navy
  2,200, Air Force 11,200, Paramilitaries 40,000
CONSCRIPTION DURATION – 17 months

ECONOMY

Azerbaijan was heavily industrialized as part of the
Russian Empire. Industry is dominated by oil and natural
gas extraction and related industries centred on Baku and
Sumgait and the large oil deposits in the Caspian Sea,
estimated at more than 6,000 million barrels. Five contracts to explore and exploit oilfields in the Caspian Sea
have been signed since 1994.
   The republic is also rich in mineral resources, with iron,
copper, lead and salt, and is important as a cotton-growing
area and a silkworm-breeding area.
   The Azeri economy was devastated by the war although
it is now showing signs of reovery. Inflation is still over 10
per cent a year; growth is forecast to be over 5 per cent in
1997.
GNP – US$3,601 million (1995); US$480 per capita (1995)
GDP – US$12,422 million (1992); US$178 per capita
  (1992)
TOTAL EXTERNAL DEBT – US$321 million (1995)

TRADE WITH UK	1995	1996
Imports from UK	£13,906,000	£30,145,000
Exports to UK	6,080,000	2,238,000

CULTURE AND EDUCATION

Azerbaijan was the birthplace of the prophet Zoroaster,
who founded one of the first monotheistic religions in the
world. The country has witnessed a succession of three
religions: Zoroastrianism, Christianity and Islam.
   Azeri is one of the Turkic languages. Previously written
in the Russian script, Azeri in the Latin script was adopted
as the official language in December 1992. In the 18th and
19th centuries Azerbaijani literature produced the poets
and dramatists Vagif, Vazekhi, Zakir, Akhundov and
Vezirov.
ILLITERACY RATE – 0.4 per cent
ENROLMENT (percentage of age group) – tertiary 19.8 per
  cent (1993)

THE BAHAMAS
The Commonwealth of The Bahamas

AREA – 5,358 sq. miles (13,878 sq. km)
POPULATION – 284,000 (1996 estimate)
CAPITAL – ΨNassau (population, 172,196, 1996 estimate)
CURRENCY – Bahamian dollar (B$) of 100 cents
NATIONAL ANTHEM – March on, Bahamaland
NATIONAL DAY – 10 July (Independence Day)
NATIONAL FLAG – Horizontal stripes of aquamarine, gold
  and aquamarine, with a black equilateral triangle on the
  hoist
LIFE EXPECTANCY (years) – male 68.32; female 75.28
POPULATION GROWTH RATE – 1.6 per cent (1994)
POPULATION DENSITY – 20 per sq. km (1994)
URBAN POPULATION – 83.5 per cent (1990)
MILITARY EXPENDITURE – 0.6 per cent of GDP (1995)
MILITARY PERSONNEL – 860: Navy

The Bahamas extend from the coast of Florida on the
north-west almost to Haiti on the south-east. The group
consists of 700 islands, of which 30 are inhabited, and 2,400
cays. The principal islands include: Abaco, Acklins, Andros, Berry Islands, Bimini, Cat Island, Crooked Island,
Eleuthera, Exuma, Grand Bahama, Harbour Island, Inagua, Long Island, Mayaguana, New Providence (on which
is located the capital, Nassau), Ragged Island, Rum Cay,
San Salvador and Spanish Wells. San Salvador was the first
landfall in the New World of Christopher Columbus on 12
October 1492.

HISTORY AND POLITICS

The Bahamas were settled by the British and became a
Crown colony in 1717. Taken over in 1782 by the Spanish,
the Treaty of Versailles in 1783 restored them to the
British. The Bahamas gained independence on 10 July
1973.
   A general election held in March 1997 was won by the
Free National Movement which defeated the Progressive
Liberal Party. The Free National Movement won 34 seats
in the House of Assembly and the Progressive Liberal
Party six seats.

POLITICAL SYSTEM
The head of state is Queen Elizabeth II who is represented
in the islands by a Governor-General. There is an
appointed Senate of 16 members and an elected House of
Assembly of 40 members.

Governor-General, HE Sir Orville Turnquest, GCMG, QC,
  apptd 1994

CABINET *as at June 1997*

Prime Minister, Hubert A. Ingraham
Deputy Prime Minister, National Security, Frank H. Watson
Agriculture and Fisheries, Dr Earl Deveaux
Attorney-General, Justice, Tennyson R. G. Wells
Consumer Welfare and Aviation, Pierre V. Dupuch
Education, Sen. Dame Ivy L. Dumont, DCMG
Finance and Planning, William C. Allen
Foreign Affairs, Janet G. Bostwick
Health and Environment, Sen. Dr Ronald Knowles
Labour, Immigration and Training, Theresa Moxey-
  Ingraham
Public Works, Tommy Turnquest
Social Development and Housing, Algernon Allen
Tourism, Cornelius A. Smith
Transport, James F. Knowles

President of the Court of Appeal, Sir Joaquim Gonsalves-
  Sabola, KCMG
Chief Justice, Dame Joan Sawyer

BAHAMAS HIGH COMMISSION
Bahamas House, 10 Chesterfield Street, London W1X 8AH
Tel 0171-408 4488
High Commissioner, HE Arthur A. Foulkes, apptd 1992

BRITISH HIGH COMMISSION
PO Box N-7516, Nassau
Tel: Nassau 325 7471
High Commissioner, HE Peter Young, MBE, apptd 1996

ECONOMY

Tourism employs about half of the labour force and
provides about half of government revenue and about half
the country's foreign exchange earnings. International
banking and trust business is also important. The absence
of any direct taxation and internal stability have enabled
the country to become one of the world's leading offshore
financial centres.

   Agricultural production is mainly of fresh vegetables,
fruit, meat and eggs for the domestic market, and crawfish,
mostly for export. Reserves of aragonite, limestone and salt
are being commercially exploited. Freeport is the country's leading industrial centre, with a pharmaceutical and
chemicals plant, an oil trans-shipment and storage
terminal, and port and bunkering facilities. There are also
a brewery and a rum distillery on New Providence.
GNP – US$3,297 million (1995); US$11,940 per capita
  (1995)
GDP – US$3,064 million (1992); US$11,587 per capita
  (1992)
ANNUAL AVERAGE GROWTH OF GDP – 4.9 per cent (1987)
INFLATION RATE – 1.4 per cent (1994)
UNEMPLOYMENT – 13.3 per cent (1994)

TRADE

The imports are chiefly foodstuffs, manufactured articles,
building materials, vehicles and machinery, chemicals and
petroleum. The chief exports are rum, petroleum, hor-
mones, salt, crawfish and aragonite.
   In 1993 the Bahamas had a trade deficit of US$760
million and a current account deficit of US$68 million.

Trade with UK	1995	1996
Imports from UK	£30,912,000	£18,825,000
Exports to UK	33,029,000	62,769,000

COMMUNICATIONS

The main ports are Nassau (New Providence), Freeport
(Grand Bahama), Matthew Town (Inagua). International
air services are operated from Abaco, Bimini, Eleuthera,
Exuma, Grand Bahama and New Providence. About 50
smaller airports and landing strips facilitate services
between the islands, the services being mainly provided
by Bahamasair, the national carrier. There are roads on the
larger islands, and roads are under construction on the
smaller islands. There are no railways.

EDUCATION

Education is compulsory between the ages of five and 16.
More than 60,000 students are enrolled in Ministry of
Education and independent schools in New Providence
and the Family Islands.
ILLITERACY RATE – 1.8 per cent
ENROLMENT (percentage of age group) – primary 95 per
  cent (1993); secondary 87 per cent (1993); tertiary 17.5
  per cent (1985)

BAHRAIN
Dawlet al-Bahrein

AREA – 268 sq. miles (694 sq. km)
POPULATION – 549,000 (1994 UN estimate); about 70 per
  cent are Bahraini; about 40 per cent of the Bahrainis are
  Sunni Muslims, the remaining 60 per cent being Shias;
  the ruling family and many of the most prominent
  merchants are Sunnis
CAPITAL – ΨManama (population, 136,999, 1991 census)
CURRENCY – Bahrain dinar (BD) of 1,000 fils
NATIONAL DAY – 16 December
NATIONAL FLAG – Red, with vertical serrated white bar
  next to staff
LIFE EXPECTANCY (years) – male 66.83; female 69.43
POPULATION GROWTH RATE – 3.1 per cent (1994)
POPULATION DENSITY – 791 per sq. km (1994)
URBAN POPULATION – 88.4 per cent (1991)
ILLITERACY RATE – 14.8 per cent
ENROLMENT (percentage of age group) – primary 100 per
  cent (1994); secondary 85 per cent (1994); tertiary 20.2
  per cent (1993)

Bahrain consists of a group of low-lying islands situated
about half-way down the Gulf, some 20 miles off the east
coast of Saudi Arabia. The largest of these, Bahrain island,
is about 30 miles long and 10 miles wide at its broadest,
with the capital, Manama, situated on the north shore. The
second largest, Muharraq, with the town and Bahrain
International Airport, is connected to Manama by a
causeway 1½ miles long. Bahrain is connected by causeway
to Saudi Arabia.

INSURGENCIES

Since 1994 Shi'ite protestors demanding the re-establishment of the National Assembly have regularly clashed
with security forces and Shi'ite leaders have been detained.
Opponents of the government have engaged in a sustained
bombing campaign.

POLITICAL SYSTEM

Bahrain is a constitutional monarchy and has been fully
independent since 1971, when British protectorate status
was ended. The 1973 constitution provides for a National
Assembly but this was dissolved in 1975. A 30-member
Consultative Council was established in January 1993. A
new Council composed of 40 members was appointed in
September 1996.

HEAD OF STATE

HH The Amir of Bahrain, Shaikh Isa bin Sulman Al-Khalifa,
  GCMG, *born* 1932; *acceded* 16 December 1961
Crown Prince (and C.-in-C., Bahrain Defence Force), HE Shaikh
  Hamad bin Isa Al Khalifa, KCMG

CABINET *as at June 1997*

Prime Minister, HH Shaikh Khalifa bin Salman Al-Khalifa
Agriculture and Public Works, HE Majid Jawad Al-Jishi
Amiri Court Affairs, HH Shaikh Ali bin Isa Al-Khalifa
Cabinet Affairs and Information, HE Mohammed Ebrahim
  Al-Mutawa
Chairman of the Consultative Council, Ebrahim Mohammed
  Humaidan
Commerce, HE Ali Saleh Abdulla Al-Saleh
Defence, HE Maj.-Gen. Shaikh Khalifa bin Ahmed Al-
  Khalifa
Education, HE Abdul-Aziz bin Mohammed Al-Fadhil
Electricity and Water, HE Abdulla Mohammed Juma

Finance and National Economy, HE Ebrahim Abdul-Karim Mohammed
Foreign Affairs, HE Shaikh Mohammed bin Mubarak Al-Khalifa
Health, HE Dr Faisal Radhi Al Mousawi
Housing, Municipalities and Environment, Shaikh Khalid bin Abdulla Al-Khalifa
Interior, HE Shaikh Mohammed bin Khalifa Al-Khalifa
Justice and Islamic Affairs, HE Shaikh Abdulla bin Khaled Al-Khalifa
Labour and Social Affairs, HE Abdul-Nabi Al-Sho'ala
Minister of State, HE Jawad Salem Al-Orayed
Oil and Industry, HE Shaikh Isa bin Ali Al-Khalifa
Transport, HH Shaikh Ali bin Khalifa bin Sulman Al-Khalifa

EMBASSY OF THE STATE OF BAHRAIN
98 Gloucester Road, London SW7 4AU
Tel 0171–370 5132
Ambassador Extraordinary and Plenipotentiary, HE Shaikh Abdul-Aziz bin Mubarak Al-Khalifa, apptd 1996

BRITISH EMBASSY
21 Government Avenue, Manama 306, PO Box 114
Tel: Manama 534404
Ambassador Extraordinary and Plenipotentiary, HE Ian Lewty, apptd 1996

BRITISH COUNCIL REPRESENTATIVE, J. Shorter, AMA Centre, PO Box 452, Manama 356

DEFENCE

The Army has 106 main battle tanks, 240 armoured personnel carriers and 49 artillery pieces. The Navy, based at Mina Sulman, has ten patrol and coastal vessels. The Air Force has 24 combat aircraft and 24 armed helicopters.
MILITARY EXPENDITURE – 5.2 per cent of GDP (1995)
MILITARY PERSONNEL – 11,000: Army 8,500, Navy 1,000, Air Force 1,500

ECONOMY

The largest sources of revenue are oil production and refining. The Bahrain field, discovered in 1932, is wholly owned by the Bahrain National Oil Co. The Sitra refinery derives about 70 per cent of its crude oil by submarine pipeline from Saudi Arabia. Bahrain also has a half share with Saudi Arabia in the profits of the offshore Abu Sa'afa field. A reservoir of unassociated gas has recently been developed on Bahrain island.

Heavy industry is currently limited to the Aluminium Bahrain (ALBA) smelter, the Gulf Petrochemical Industries Co. (GPIC) producing ammonia and methanol, the Gulf Aluminium Rolling Mill (GARMCO), and the Arab Shipbuilding and Repair Yard (ASRY), operating dry dock facilities up to 500,000 tons. There are a number of small to medium-sized industrial units.

The state has developed as a financial centre. Apart from several commercial banks, many international banks have been licensed as offshore banking units; there are also money brokers and merchant banks.
GNP – US$4,525 million (1995); US$7,840 per capita (1995)
GDP – US$4,156 million (1992); US$8,188 per capita (1992)
ANNUAL AVERAGE GROWTH OF GDP – 2.3 per cent (1994)
INFLATION RATE – 0.8 per cent (1994)

TRADE WITH UK	1995	1996
Imports from UK	£150,757,000	£161,180,000
Exports to UK	26,379,000	20,677,000

COMMUNICATIONS

Bahrain International airport is one of the main air traffic centres of the Gulf; it is the headquarters of Gulf Air, and a stopping point on routes between Europe and Australia and the Far East for other airlines. A causeway links Bahrain to Saudi Arabia.

A world-wide telephone and telex service, by satellite and cable, is operated by Bahrain Telecommunications Company.

BANGLADESH
Ghana Praja Tantri Bangladesh

AREA – 55,598 sq. miles (143,998 sq. km)
POPULATION – 117,787,000 (1994 UN estimate); 108,000,000 (1991 census). The state language is Bengali. Use of Bengali is compulsory in all government departments. English is understood and is used widely as an unofficial second language. The faith of 88 per cent of the population is Islam and 10.5 per cent Hinduism. Islam has been declared the state religion
CAPITAL – Dhaka (population, 3,397,187, 1991 census)
CURRENCY – Taka (Tk) of 100 poisha
NATIONAL ANTHEM – Amar Sonar Bangla
NATIONAL DAY – 26 March (Independence Day)
NATIONAL FLAG – Red circle on a bottle-green ground
LIFE EXPECTANCY (years) – male 56.91; female 55.97
POPULATION GROWTH RATE – 2.1 per cent (1994)
POPULATION DENSITY – 818 per sq. km (1994)
URBAN POPULATION – 13.8 per cent (1986)
MILITARY EXPENDITURE – 1.8 per cent of GDP (1995)
MILITARY PERSONNEL – 167,000: Army 101,000, Navy 10,000, Air Force 6,500, Paramilitaries 49,500

The country is crossed by a network of rivers, including the eastern arms of the Ganges, the Jamuna (Brahmaputra) and the Meghna, flowing into the Bay of Bengal. The climate is tropical and monsoon; hot and extremely humid during the summer, and mild and dry during the short winter.

HISTORY AND POLITICS

Prior to becoming East Pakistan, Bangladesh had been the province of East Bengal and the Sylhet district of Assam of British India. The territory acceded to Pakistan in August 1947, which became a republic on 23 March 1956. Bangladesh achieved its independence from Pakistan on 16 December 1971, following the conclusion of the Indo-Pakistan war. Pakistan and Bangladesh accorded one another mutual recognition in 1974.

In 1975 a one-party presidential system was introduced, with Prime Minister Sheikh Mujibur Rahman assuming the presidency under martial law until he was assassinated in 1975. A presidential election in 1978 was won by Maj.-Gen. Zia Rahman, who lifted martial law and introduced a multiparty presidential system of government. Zia was assassinated in 1981. He was replaced by Justice Abdus Sattar, who was overthrown in 1982 in a coup led by the then Chief of Army Staff, Gen. Ershad. Following parliamentary elections in 1986, a civilian Cabinet was appointed and Gen. Ershad was elected president. Popular unrest forced Gen. Ershad's resignation in December 1990 and parliamentary elections were held in February 1991. The Bangladesh Nationalist Party (BNP) won the largest number of seats and the BNP leader, Begum Khaleda Zia, was sworn in as prime minister. In August 1991 Parliament approved a constitutional amendment returning Bangladesh to parliamentary rule.

In December 1994, the opposition parties resigned from parliament and organized a series of mass rallies and strikes in demand of an independent caretaker government to oversee fresh elections. Public disorder persisted despite a general election in February 1996 which was won by the BNP, although turnout was a mere 5 per cent. In March 1996, Prime Minister Zia agreed to new elections, to be supervised by an interim 11-member ruling council led by former Supreme Court Chief Justice Muhammad Habibur Rahman. The fresh elections in June 1996 produced a majority for the Awami League under Prime Minister Sheikh Hasina Wajed.

POLITICAL SYSTEM

There is a unicameral parliament (*Jatiya Sangshad*) of 330 members which can amend the constitution by a two-thirds majority. The country is divided into six administrative divisions, sub-divided into 64 districts.

HEAD OF STATE
President, Shahabuddin Ahmed, *sworn in* 9 October 1996

CABINET *as at May 1997*

Prime Minister, Armed Forces Division, Cabinet Division, Special
    Affairs, Defence, Establishment, Sheikh Hasina Wajed
Agriculture and Food, Matia Chowdhury
Commerce and Industry, Tofail Ahmed
Communications, Anwar Hossain Manju
Education, Science and Technology, A. S. H. K. Sadeque
Environment and Forests, Syeda Sajeda Chowdhury
Finance, S. A. M. S. Kibria
Foreign Affairs, Abdus Samad Azad
Health and Family Welfare, Salahuddin Yousuf
Home Affairs, Maj. (retd) Rafiqul Islam Bir Uttam
Law, Justice and Parliamentary Affairs, Abdul Matin Khasru
Local Government, Rural Development and Co-operatives,
    Mohammad Zillur Rahman
Post and Telecommunications, Housing and Public Works,
    Mohammad Nasim
Power, Energy and Mineral Resources, Lt.-Gen. (retd)
    Nooruddin Khan
Shipping, A. S. M. Abdur Rob
Water Resources, Abdur Razzak

BANGLADESH HIGH COMMISSION
28 Queen's Gate, London sw7 5JA
Tel 0171–584 0081
High Commissioner, HE Mahmood Ali, apptd 1997
Deputy High Commissioner, Munshi Faiz Ahmad
Defence Adviser, Brig. A. M. Mahmuduzzaman
Economics Minister, new appointment awaited

BRITISH HIGH COMMISSION
United Nations Road, Baridhara Dhaka
PO Box 6079, Dhaka-12
Tel: Dhaka 882705
High Commissioner, HE David Walker, CMG, CVO, apptd 1996
Deputy High Commissioner, M. McIntosh
Defence Adviser, Col. J. M. Philips

BRITISH COUNCIL REPRESENTATIVE, T. Cowin, 5 Fuller
Road (PO Box 161), Dhaka 1000

ECONOMY

Between 1991–5, the government implemented an IMF economic reform plan which delivered stable prices and inflation, and reduced the budget deficit from 8 per cent of GDP in 1989 to 5.3 per cent in 1993.

Bangladesh is self-sufficient in food production. Agricultural products include rice, wheat, tobacco, tea, oil seeds, pulses and sugar cane. The chief industries are jute, cotton, tea, leather, pharmaceuticals, fertilizer, sugar, prawn fishing, natural gas. Garment manufacturing is the main export, earning £1,400 million in 1994–5, 63 per cent of total foreign exchange earnings. Remittances sent home by Bangladeshis abroad are of considerable significance to the economy.

GNP – US$28,599 million (1995); US$240 per capita
    (1995)
GDP – US$26,280 million (1992); US$208 per capita
    (1992)
ANNUAL AVERAGE GROWTH OF GDP – 4.4 per cent (1995)
INFLATION RATE – 5.8 per cent (1995)
TOTAL EXTERNAL DEBT – US$16,370 million (1995)

TRADE

In 1993 Bangladesh had a current account surplus of US$197 million and a trade deficit of US$1,283 million. In 1995 imports totalled US$6,496 million and exports US$3,173 million.

TRADE WITH UK	1995	1996
Imports from UK	£89,145,000	£71,557,000
Exports to UK	231,644,000	279,573,000

COMMUNICATIONS

Principal seaports are Chittagong and Mongla. The Bangladesh Shipping Corporation has been set up by the Government to operate the Bangladesh merchant fleet. The principal airports are Dhaka (Zia International) and Chittagong. The international airline, Bangladesh Biman, serves Europe, the Middle East, South and South-East Asia, and an internal network.

There are about 6,880 miles of roads; 4,724 miles are metalled. There are 1,720 miles of railway track.

EDUCATION

Primary education is free and planned to be universal by 2000. There are 11 universities.
ILLITERACY RATE – 61.9 per cent
ENROLMENT (percentage of age group) – primary 70 per cent; secondary 18 per cent; tertiary 3.9 per cent (1990)

BARBADOS

AREA – 166 sq. miles (430 sq. km); nearly 21 miles long by
    14 miles broad
POPULATION – 261,000 (1994 UN estimate)
CAPITAL – ΨBridgetown in the parish of St Michael
    (population, 108,000, 1990)
MAJOR TOWNS – Oistins in Christ Church, Holetown in St
    James and Speightstown in St Peter
CURRENCY – Barbados dollar (BD$) of 100 cents
NATIONAL ANTHEM – In Plenty and in Time of Need
NATIONAL DAY – 30 November (Independence Day)
NATIONAL FLAG – Three vertical stripes, dark blue, gold
    and dark blue, with a trident head on gold stripe
LIFE EXPECTANCY (years) – male 67.15; female 72.46
POPULATION GROWTH RATE – 0.3 per cent (1994)
POPULATION DENSITY – 607 per sq. km (1994)
MILITARY EXPENDITURE – 0.7 per cent of GDP (1995)

Barbados is the most easterly of the Caribbean islands. The land rises in a series of terraced tablelands to the highest point, Mt Hillaby (1,116 ft). The annual average temperature is 26.6°C (79.8°F) with rainfall varying from a yearly average of 75 inches in the high central district to 50 inches in the low-lying coastal areas.

HISTORY AND POLITICS

The first inhabitants of Barbados were Arawak Indians but the island was uninhabited when first settled by the British in 1627. It was a Crown Colony from 1652 until it became an independent state within the Commonwealth on 30 November 1966.

The last general election took place on 6 September 1994 and seats in the House of Assembly were distributed as follows: Barbados Labour Party 19, Democratic Labour Party 8, National Democratic Party 1.

POLITICAL SYSTEM

The legislature consists of the Governor-General, a Senate and a House of Assembly. The Senate comprises 21 Senators appointed by the Governor-General, of whom 12 are appointed on the advice of the prime minister, two on the advice of the Leader of the Opposition and seven by the Governor-General at his/her discretion to represent religious, economic or social interests. The House of Assembly comprises 28 members elected every five years by adult suffrage.

There are 11 administrative areas (parishes): St Michael, Christ Church, St Andrew, St George, St James, St John, St Joseph, St Lucy, St Peter, St Philip and St Thomas.

Governor-General, HE Sir Clifford Husbands, GCMG, KA, apptd 1996

CABINET *as at July 1997*

Prime Minister, Finance and Economic Affairs, Civil Service, Owen Arthur
Deputy Prime Minister, Foreign Affairs, Tourism and International Transport, Billie Miller
Agriculture and Rural Development, Rawle Eastmond
Attorney-General and Home Affairs, David Simmons, QC
Education, Youth and Culture, Mia Mottley
Health and Environment, Elizabeth Thompson
Industry and Commerce, Sen. Reginald Farley
International Trade, Sen. Phillip Goddard
Labour, Community Development and Sport, Rudolph Greenidge
Minister of State, Foreign Affairs, International Transport and Tourism, Ronald Toppin
Minister of State, Prime Minister's Office, Sen. Glyne Murray
Public Works, Transport and Housing, George Payne

BARBADOS HIGH COMMISSION

1 Great Russell Street, London WC1B 3JY
Tel 0171–631 4975
High Commissioner, HE Peter Simmons, apptd 1995
Deputy High Commissioner, H. Yearwood
First Secretary (Commercial), K. Campbell

BRITISH HIGH COMMISSION

Lower Collymore Rock, PO Box 676, Bridgetown C
Tel: Bridgetown 436 6694
High Commissioner, HE Richard Thomas, CMG, apptd 1994
Deputy High Commissioner, P. J. Mathers, LVO
Defence Adviser, Capt. I. M. Hime
First Secretary, P. Curwen

JUDICATURE

There is a Supreme Court of Judicature consisting of a High Court and a Court of Appeal. In certain cases a further appeal lies to the Judicial Committee of the Privy Council. The Chief Justice and Puisne Judges are appointed by the Governor-General on the recommendation of the prime minister and after consultation with the Leader of the Opposition.

Chief Justice, Sir Denys Williams, KCMG

ECONOMY

The economy is based on tourism, sugar and light manufacturing. In 1995, 442,107 tourists visited Barbados and 484,670 cruise ship passengers. Chief exports are sugar and its by-products, chemicals, electronic components and clothing.

GNP – US$1,745 million (1995); US$6,560 per capita (1995)
GDP – US$1,596 million (1992); US$6,078 per capita (1992)
ANNUAL AVERAGE GROWTH OF GDP – –4.0 per cent (1991)
INFLATION RATE – 1.9 per cent (1995)
UNEMPLOYMENT – 19.7 per cent (1995)
TOTAL EXTERNAL DEBT – US$597 million (1995)

TRADE WITH UK	1995	1996
Imports from UK	£101,144,000	£35,538,000
Exports to UK	25,639,000	65,524,000

COMMUNICATIONS

Barbados has some 965 miles of roads, of which about 917 miles are asphalted. The Grantley Adams International airport is situated at Seawell, 12 miles from Bridgetown. Bridgetown, the only port of entry, has a deep-water harbour with berths for eight ships, but oil is pumped ashore at Spring Garden and at an Esso installation on the West Coast. Barbados has a colour television service, three radio broadcasting services, and a wired broadcasting service.

EDUCATION

Education is free in government schools. There are 105 primary schools, 22 government secondary schools and 15 approved government secondary schools.
ILLITERACY RATE – 2.6 per cent
ENROLMENT (percentage of age group) – primary 78 per cent (1991); secondary 75 per cent (1989); tertiary 28.1 per cent (1994)

BELARUS
Respublika Belarus

AREA – 80,155 sq. miles (207,600 sq. km). Neighbours: Latvia and Lithuania (north), Russia (east), Ukraine (south) and Poland (west)
POPULATION – 10,265,000 (1995 official estimate), 78 per cent Belarusian, 13 per cent Russian, 4 per cent Polish and 3 per cent Ukrainian, with smaller numbers of Jews and Lithuanians. Belarusian, a Slavonic language written in the Cyrillic script, and Russian have equal official language status. Most of the population are Belarusian Orthodox with a minority of Roman Catholics
CAPITAL – Minsk (population, 1,681,000, 1993 estimate); the administrative centre of the CIS
MAJOR CITIES – Gomel, Vitebsk, Brest, Grodno
CURRENCY – Rouble of 100 kopeks
NATIONAL ANTHEM – The former Soviet national anthem but with the words omitted
NATIONAL DAY – 3 July (Independence Day)
NATIONAL FLAG – Red with a green strip along the lower edge, and in the hoist a vertical red and white ornamental pattern
LIFE EXPECTANCY (years) – male 64.92; female 75.45
POPULATION GROWTH RATE – 0.2 per cent (1994)

POPULATION DENSITY – 50 per sq. km (1994)
URBAN POPULATION – 67.8 per cent (1992)

Belarus is situated in the western part of the European area of the former USSR. The main rivers are the upper reaches of the Dnieper, of the Niemen and of the Western Dvina. Much of the land is a plain, with many lakes, swamps and marshy areas. The climate is continental with mild, humid winters and relatively cool and rainy summers.

HISTORY AND POLITICS

In the ninth century AD the Kievan Rus state was a unified state encompassing all the Russian, Ukrainian and Belarusian populations. After being absorbed into Lithuania in the 13th and 14th centuries, the Belarusian nationality, language and culture flourished until it came under Polish rule in the mid-16th century. Two hundred years of Polish rule followed until Belarus was re-absorbed into the Russian Empire.

Much of Belarus was under German control at the time of the Russian revolution and it was not until German forces withdrew that a Byelorussian Soviet Socialist Republic was declared on 1 January 1919. Western Belarus was ceded to Poland after the Soviet defeat in the Polish-Soviet war of 1919–20, and was not recovered until Soviet forces occupied the area under the 1939 Nazi-Soviet Pact. Belarus was devastated by the German invasion in the Second World War; 25 per cent of the population was killed and thousands deported.

Belarus issued a Declaration of State Sovereignty on 27 July 1990 and declared its independence from the Soviet Union after the failed coup in Moscow in August 1991.

After the failed Moscow coup, Stanislav Shuskevich became Belarusian leader at the head of a coalition of Communists and democrats. Until 1994, however, parliament and the government remained under the control of former Communists, who thwarted all attempts at economic and political reform. Shuskevich was forced to resign in January 1994 and was replaced by Gen. Mecheslav Grib who pursued closer political, economic and trade relations with Russia. Alexander Lukashenko won a presidential election in July 1994 and appointed a reformist government.

FOREIGN RELATIONS

An agreement was signed with Russia in April 1996 to form a Commonwealth of Sovereign Republics. In April 1997 a treaty of union was signed with Russia. It provided for the creation of a supreme council, chaired by the state presidents on a two-year rotating basis, which will co-ordinate foreign affairs and economic and defence co-operation.

POLITICAL SYSTEM

A referendum held on 24 November 1996 extended the president's tenure to seven and a half years and gave him/her authority to appoint half the members of the constitutional court and the electoral commission. It approved the formation of a new bicameral national assembly, comprising a 110-member House of Representatives (lower chamber) and a 64-member Council of the Republic (upper chamber). Eight members of the upper chamber are appointed by the president, the rest are indirectly elected by members of the local soviets in each region.

The republic is divided into six regions (*oblasts*): Brest, Gomel, Grodno, Minsk, Mogilev and Vitebsk.

HEAD OF STATE

President, Alexander Lukashenko, *elected* 10 July 1994

COUNCIL OF MINISTERS *as at June 1997*

Prime Minister, Syargei Ling
First Deputy Prime Minister, Pyotr Prakapovich
Deputy Prime Ministers, Uladzimir Garkun; UladzimirKokaraw; Uladzimir Rusakevich; Vasil Dalgalyow; Genadz Navitsky
Agriculture and Food, Vasil Lyavonaw
Architecture and Construction, Viktar Vyatrow
CIS Affairs, Ivan Bambiza
Communications, Uladzimir Gancharenka
Culture, Alyaksandr Sasnowsky
Defence, Lt.-Gen. Alyaksandr Chumakow
Economy, Uladzimir Shymaw
Education, Vasil Strazhaw
Emergency Situations, Ivan Kenik
Enterprise and Investment, Alyaksandr Sazonaw
Foreign Affairs, Ivan Antanovich
Foreign Economic Relations, Mikhail Marynich
Forestry, Valyantsin Zoryn
Fuel and Energy, Valyantsin Gerasimaw
Health, Igar Zelyankevich
Housing and Municipal Services, Barys Batura
Industry, Anatol Kharlap
Internal Affairs, Maj.-Gen. Valyantsin Agalets
Justice, Genadz Varantsow
Labour, Ivan Lyakh
Natural Resources and Environmental Protection, Mikhail Rusy
Social Protection, Volga Dargel
Sport and Tourism, Uladzimir Makeychyk
State-owned Property and Privatization, Vasil Novak
Statistics and Analysis, Uladzimir Nichyparovich
Trade, Pyotar Kazlow

EMBASSY OF THE REPUBLIC OF BELARUS
6 Kensington Court, London W8 5DL
Tel 0171-937 3288
Ambassador Extraordinary and Plenipotentiary, HE Uladzimir Shchasny, apptd 1995

BRITISH EMBASSY
37 Karl Marx Street, Minsk 220030
Tel: Minsk 292303/4/5
Ambassador Extraordinary and Plenipotentiary, HE Jessica Pearce, apptd 1995

DEFENCE

Belarus has on its territory 18 SS-25 Intercontinental Ballistic Missiles which it was due to return to Russia by 1997 for destruction under the terms of the START 1 Treaty, which it ratified in 1993 along with the Nuclear Non-Proliferation Treaty.

MILITARY EXPENDITURE – 3.3 per cent of GDP (1995)
MILITARY PERSONNEL – 76,200: Army 50,500, Air Force 25,700
CONSCRIPTION DURATION – 18 months

ECONOMY

Agricultural productivity was severely affected by nuclear fallout from the Chernobyl disaster in 1986 although Belarus is now self-sufficient in the production of foodstuffs. The manufacturing sector also declined as a result of the collapse of the Soviet centrally planned economic system, which had been relied on for cheap supplies of energy and raw materials. Energy from Russia is still the largest import.

Economic reform and privatization have been introduced and in May 1995 a customs union agreement with Russia took effect. A treaty was signed with Kazakhstan,

Kyrgyzstan and Russia in March 1996 aimed at the establishment of a single customs territory.

In 1996 the government had a budget deficit equivalent to 1.9 per cent of GDP.

GNP – US$21,356 million (1995); US$2,070 per capita (1995)
GDP – US$55,431 million (1992); US$460 per capita (1992)
UNEMPLOYMENT – 2.7 per cent (1995)
TOTAL EXTERNAL DEBT – US$1,648 million (1995)

TRADE WITH UK	1995	1996
Imports from UK	£22,570,000	£27,661,000
Exports to UK	20,981,000	13,596.000

EDUCATION

The national system comprises pre-school, general secondary, out-of-school, vocational training and trade schools, secondary specialized and higher education. General secondary education begins at the age of six. There are also 22 private educational institutions.
ILLITERACY RATE – 0.5 per cent
ENROLMENT (percentage of age group) – primary 97 per cent (1994); tertiary 42.4 per cent (1993)

BELGIUM
Royaume de Belgique

AREA – 11,783 sq. miles (30,519 sq. km). Neighbours: the Netherlands (north), France (south), and Germany and Luxembourg (east)
POPULATION – 10,080,000 (1994 UN estimate). Greater Brussels 949,070; Flanders 5,847,022; Wallonia 3,304,539, of whom 68,741 are German-speaking
CAPITAL – Brussels (population, 960,324, 1991 estimate)
MAJOR CITIES – ΨAntwerp, the chief port (933,813); Liège (594,699); ΨGhent (490,285); Louvain (442,685); Charleroi (120,206); Namur (273,897); Mons (252,990); Bruges (267,172)
CURRENCY – Belgian franc (or frank) of 100 centimes (centiemen)
NATIONAL ANTHEM – La Brabançonne
NATIONAL DAY – 21 July (Accession of King Leopold I, 1831)
NATIONAL FLAG – Three vertical bands, black, yellow, red
LIFE EXPECTANCY (years) – male 72.43; female 79.13
POPULATION GROWTH RATE – 0.3 per cent (1994)
POPULATION DENSITY – 330 per sq. km (1994)

The Meuse and its tributary, the Sambre, divide Belgium into two distinct regions, that in the west being generally level and fertile, while the tableland of the Ardennes, in the east, has mostly poor soil. The polders near the coast, which are protected by dykes against floods, cover an area of 193 sq. miles. The principal rivers are the Scheldt and the Meuse.

Belgium is divided between those who speak Dutch (the Flemings) and those who speak French (the Walloons). Dutch is recognized as the official language in the northern areas and French in the southern (Walloon) area and there are guarantees for the respective linguistic minorities. Brussels is officially bilingual. There is a small German-speaking area (Eupen and Malmédy) along the German border, east of Liège.The majority of Belgians are Roman Catholic.

HISTORY AND POLITICS

The kingdom formed part of the Low Countries (Netherlands) from 1815 until 14 October 1830, when a National Congress proclaimed its independence. On 4 June 1831, Prince Leopold of Coburg was chosen as the hereditary king. The separation from the Netherlands and the neutrality and inviolability of Belgium were guaranteed by a Conference of the European powers, and by the Treaty of London 1839. On 4 August 1914 the Germans invaded Belgium, in violation of the terms of the treaty, and this led the Allies to declare war. Eupen and Malmédy were ceded by Germany under the Versailles Treaty 1919. The kingdom was again invaded by Germany in 1940 and was occupied by Nazi troops until liberated by the Allies in September 1944.

The last general election was held on 21 May 1995. The results were as follows (seats):

Chamber of Deputies: CVP 29; PS 21; VLD (Flemish Liberals and Democrats) 21; SP 20; PRL-FDF (Liberal Reform Party-Democratic Front (Francophone)) 18; PSC 12; Vlaams Blok (Flemish Nationalist Party) 11; Ecolo (Francophone Ecology Party) 6; Agalev (Flemish Environmental Party) 5; VU (Flemish People's Union) 5; Front National (FN) 2.

Senate: of the 40 seats directly elected, CVP 7; SP 6; VLD 6; PRL-FDF 5; PS 5; PSC 3; Vlaams Blok 3; VU 2; Ecolo 2; Agalev 1. A further 31 Senators are indirectly elected or co-opted (*see* below).

POLITICAL SYSTEM

Belgium is a constitutional representative and hereditary monarchy with a bicameral legislature, consisting of the King, the Senate and the Chamber of Deputies. The parliamentary term is four years. Amendments to the constitution enacted since 1968 have devolved power to the regions. The national government retains competence only in foreign and defence policies, the national budget and monetary policy, social security, and the judiciary, legal and penal systems. The Senate has 71 seats, of which 40 are directly elected, 21 indirectly elected and ten co-opted by the Flemish and Francophone Communities. The Chamber of Deputies has 150 seats. There are four levels of sub-national government: community, regional, provincial, and communal.

There are four communities: Flemish; Francophone; Brussels; Germanophone. Each community has its own assembly, which elects the community government. At this level, Flanders is covered by the Flemish Community Assembly; Brussels is covered by its Joint Community Commission as well as the Flemish and Francophone Community Assemblies; most of Wallonia is covered by the Francophone Community Assembly and the areas of Wallonia in the German-speaking communities of Eupen and Malmédy are covered by the Germanophone Community Assembly.

At regional level, Belgium is divided into the regions of Wallonia, Brussels and Flanders. Each region has its own assembly and government.

There are ten provinces; five French-speaking in Wallonia (Hainaut, Liège, Luxembourg, Namur and French Brabant); and five Dutch-speaking in Flanders (Antwerp, East Flanders, West Flanders, Limbourg and Flemish Brabant). In addition, Belgium has 589 communes as the lowest level of local government.

There has been an increase in power of the regional governments at the expense of both the community and national levels. The Francophone Community Assembly and government is gradually losing power to the Walloon and Brussels regional governments, whilst the Flemish have amalgamated their community and regional governments to form one increasingly powerful Flanders government.

Minister-President of the Flemish Government, Luc Van den Brande (CVP)
Minister-President of the Walloon Regional Government, Robert Collignon (PS)

HEAD OF STATE

HM The King of the Belgians, King Albert II, *born* 6 June 1934; *succeeded* 9 August 1993; *married* 2 July 1959, Donna Paola Ruffo di Calabria, and has *issue* Prince Philippe (*see* below); Princess Astrid, *b*. 5 June 1962; Prince Laurent, *b*. 20 October 1963
Heir, HRH Prince Philippe Léopold Louis Marie, *born* 15 April 1960

CABINET *as at June 1997*

Prime Minister, Jean-Luc Dehaene (CVP)
Deputy P.M, Economic Affairs, Elio Di Rupo (PS)
Deputy P.M, Finance, Philippe Maystadt (PSC)
Deputy P.M, Interior Affairs, Johan Vande Lanotte (SP)
Deputy P.M, Budget, Herman Van Rompuy (CVP)
Agriculture and Small and Medium-Sized Enterprises, Karel Pinxten (CVP)
Civil Service, André Flahaut (PS)
Defence, Jean-Pol Poncelet (PSC)
Employment, Equal Opportunities, Miet Smet (CVP)
Foreign Affairs, Eric Derycke (SP)
Justice, Stefaan De Clerck (CVP)
Pensions and Public Health, Marcel Colla (SP)
Scientific Policy, Yvan Ylieff (PS)
Social Affairs, Magda De Galan (PS)
Transport, Michel Daerden (PS)

CVP Christian Social Party (Flemish); PS Socialist Party (Francophone); SP Socialist Party (Flemish); PSC Christian Social Party (Francophone)

BELGIAN EMBASSY
103 Eaton Square, London SW1W 9AB
Tel 0171-470 3700
Ambassador Extraordinary and Plenipotentiary, HE Lode Willems, apptd 1997
Minister-Counsellors, M. Vanmerk (*Political*); F. De Sutter (*Economic*)
Military, Naval and Air Attaché, Col. J. Bouzette

BRITISH EMBASSY
rue d'Arlon 85, 1040 Brussels
Tel: Brussels 287 6211
Ambassador Extraordinary and Plenipotentiary, HE David Colvin, CMG, apptd 1993
Deputy Ambassador, Counsellor and Consul-General, E. C. Glover, MVO
Counsellors (Commercial), M. T. Jones; I. McRory
Defence and Military Attaché, Gp Capt. D. C. Hencken
There are British Consular Offices at Brussels, Antwerp and Liège.
BRITISH COUNCIL REPRESENTATIVE TO BELGIUM AND LUXEMBOURG – Dr Ken Churchill, OBE, rue de la Charité 15, Liefdadigheidstraat 15, 1210 Brussels.
BRITISH CHAMBER OF COMMERCE FOR BELGIUM AND LUXEMBOURG (INC.), rue Joseph II 30, 1040 Brussels

DEFENCE

The Army has 334 main battle tanks, 539 armoured personnel carriers, 214 armoured infantry fighting vehicles, 278 artillery pieces and 78 helicopters. The Navy is based at Ostend and Zeebrugge and has two frigates and three helicopters. The Air Force has 132 combat aircraft.

The headquarters of NATO, SHAPE and the Western European Union Military Planning Cell are in Belgium; 1,345 US personnel are stationed in the country.
MILITARY EXPENDITURE – 1.7 per cent of GDP (1995)
MILITARY PERSONNEL – 45,050: Army 30,100, Navy 2,650, Air Force 12,300

ECONOMY

With no natural resources except coal, production of which has now ceased, industry is based largely on the processing for re-export of imported raw materials. Principal industries are steel and metal products, chemicals and petrochemicals, textiles, glass, and foodstuffs.

In an attempt to meet the Maastricht Treaty criteria for economic and monetary union, the government introduced a series of austerity packages in 1993–6 to try to reduce Belgian public debt.

In 1996 there was a budget deficit of 3.3 per cent of GDP and public debt was 130.6 per cent of GDP.
GNP – US$250,710 million (1995); US$24,710 per capita (1995)
GDP – US$198,708 million (1992); US$21,935 per capita (1992)
ANNUAL AVERAGE GROWTH OF GDP – 1.9 per cent (1995)
INFLATION RATE – 1.5 per cent (1995)
UNEMPLOYMENT – 9.3 per cent (1995)

TRADE

External trade figures relate to Luxembourg as well as Belgium since the two countries formed an economic union in 1921. The main trading partners are Germany, France and the Netherlands.

In 1993 Belgium and Luxembourg had a trade surplus of US$6,126 million and a current account surplus of US$12,588 million. In 1994 exports totalled US$136,864 million and imports US$125,297 million.

Trade with UK (Belgium and Luxembourg)

	1995	1996
Imports from UK	£7,880,300,000	£8,114,000,000
Exports to UK	7,631,300,000	8,096,000,000

COMMUNICATIONS

The railways are operated by the Belgian National Railways. Ship canals include Ghent-Terneuzen (18 miles, half in the Netherlands) by which ships up to 60,000 tons reach Ghent; Willebroek Rupel-Brussels (20 miles, by which ships drawing 18 ft reach Brussels from the sea); Bruges (from Zeebrugge on the North Sea to Bruges, 6 miles); Albert (79 miles), Liège to Antwerp for barges up to 1,350 tons. The River Meuse from the Dutch to the French frontiers, the River Sambre between Namur and Monceau, the River Scheldt from Antwerp to Ghent and the Brussels-Charleroi Canal are being widened or deepened to take barges up to 1,350 tons. Most maritime trade is carried in foreign shipping.

In 1986 there were 14,260 km of trunk road, of which about 1,550 km were motorways. The Belgian national airline Sabena operates regular services between Brussels and European centres, as well as intercontinental services worldwide.

CULTURE AND EDUCATION

The literature of France and the Netherlands is supplemented by an indigenous Belgian literary activity in both French and Dutch. Maurice Maeterlinck (1862–1949) was awarded the Nobel Prize for Literature in 1911. Emile Verhaeren (1855–1916) was a poet of international standing. Of contemporary Belgian writers, the most celebrated was Georges Simenon (1903–89).

Nursery schools provide free education for children from two and a half to six years. There are over 4,000 primary schools (6 to 12 years), more than 1,000 secondary schools offering a general academic education slightly over half of which are free institutions (predominantly Roman Catholic but subsidized by the state) and the remainder official institutions. The official school-leaving age is 18.

ENROLMENT (percentage of age group) – primary 96 per cent (1991); secondary 88 per cent (1991); tertiary 40.2 per cent (1990)

BELIZE

AREA – 8,763 sq. miles (22,696 sq. km). Neighbours: Mexico (north and north-west) and Guatemala (west and south)
POPULATION – 211,000 (1994 UN estimate); 205,000 (1993 census): 44 per cent Mestizo (Maya-Spanish); 30 per cent Creole; 11 per cent Maya; plus a number of East Indian and Spanish descent. The races are now inter-mixed.The majority of the population is Christian, about 58 per cent Catholic and 34 per cent Protestant. The official language and language of instruction is English. Spanish is also widely spoken and English Creole is the vernacular. There are also Garifuna and Maya speakers
CAPITAL – Belmopan (population, 44,087, 1991)
MAJOR CITIES – ΨBelize City (1993 census 46,342), the former capital; Corozal (7,420), San Ignacio (9,417), Dangriga (6,761), Orange Walk (11,573)
CURRENCY – Belize dollar (BZ$) of 100 cents. The Belize dollar is tied to the US dollar, BZ$2 = US$1
NATIONAL ANTHEM – Land of the Free
NATIONAL DAY – 21 September (Independence Day)
NATIONAL FLAG – Blue ground with red band along top and bottom edges, and in centre a white disc containing the coat of arms surrounded by a green garland
LIFE EXPECTANCY (years) – male 69.95; female 74.07
POPULATION GROWTH RATE – 2.8 per cent (1994)
POPULATION DENSITY – 9 per sq. km (1994)
URBAN POPULATION – 47.5 per cent (1994)
MILITARY EXPENDITURE – 2.6 per cent of GDP (1995)

The coastal areas are mostly flat and swampy with many islets but the country rises gradually towards the interior, which is mainly forest. The northern and western districts are hilly, and in the south the Maya Mountains and the Cockscombs form the backbone of the country, reaching a height of 3,700 feet at Victoria Peak. The climate is sub-tropical.

HISTORY AND POLITICS

Numerous ruins in the area indicate that Belize was heavily populated by the Maya Indians. The first British settlement was established in 1638 but was subject to repeated attacks by the Spanish, who claimed sovereignty until defeated by the Royal Navy and settlers in 1798. In 1871 the area was recognized by Britain as a colony and called British Honduras. In 1973 the colony was renamed Belize, and was granted independence on 21 September 1981.

The National Assembly was dissolved in June 1993 and in the ensuing elections the People's United Party government was defeated by the United Democratic Party.

FOREIGN RELATIONS

A long-standing territorial dispute with Guatemala was provisionally resolved in 1992 when the Guatemalan Congress and Supreme Court voted to recognize Belize and establish diplomatic relations. Guatemala still retains its claim, subject to arbitration by the International Court of Justice.

POLITICAL SYSTEM

Queen Elizabeth II is head of state, represented in Belize by a Governor-General. There is a National Assembly, comprising a House of Representatives (29 members elected for five years) and a Senate (nine members appointed by the Governor-General). Executive power is vested in the Cabinet, which is responsible to the National Assembly.

Governor-General, HE Sir Colville Norbert Young, GCMG, apptd 17 November 1993

CABINET *as at June 1997*
Prime Minister, Finance and Economic Development, Manuel Esquivel
Deputy PM, National Security, Attorney-General, Foreign Affairs, Dean O. Barrow
Agriculture and Fisheries, Russell García
Education, Public Service, Elodio Aragón
Energy, Science, Technology and Transport, Joseph Cayetano
Health and Sports, Ruben Campos
Home Affairs and Labour, Elito Urbina sen.
Housing, Urban Development and Co-operatives, Hubert Elrington
Human Resources, Women's Affairs and Youth Development, Philip S. W. Goldson
Natural Resources, Eduardo Juan
Tourism and Environment, Henry Young
Trade and Industry, Salvador Fernández
Works, Melvin Hulse jun.

BELIZE HIGH COMMISSION
22 Harcourt House, 19 Cavendish Square, London WIM 9AD
Tel 0171-499 9728
High Commissioner, HE Dr Ursula Barrow, apptd 1993

BRITISH HIGH COMMISSION
PO Box 91, Belmopan
Tel: Belmopan 22146/7
High Commissioner, HE Gordon Baker, apptd 1995

ECONOMY

About 30 per cent of the population is engaged in agriculture. The country is more or less self-sufficient in fresh beef, pork and poultry, but processed meat and dairy products are imported. About 25 per cent of timber production (mostly mahogany) is exported, and there is a large US market for lobster, conch and scale fish. Tourism is also a valuable source of income.

In 1993 Belize had a trade deficit of US$119 million and a current account deficit of US$49 million. In 1995 imports totalled US$258 million and exports US$139 million. The government had a budget deficit equivalent to 8.79 per cent of GDP in 1993.

GNP – US$568 million (1995); US$2,630 per capita (1995)
GDP – US$443 million (1992); US$2,364 per capita (1992)
ANNUAL AVERAGE GROWTH OF GDP – 3.7 per cent (1995)
INFLATION RATE – 2.9 per cent (1995)
UNEMPLOYMENT – 11.1 per cent (1994)
TOTAL EXTERNAL DEBT – US$261 million (1995)

Trade with UK	1995	1996
Imports from UK	£14,261, 000	£10,192,000
Exports to UK	47,010,000	47,863,000

COMMUNICATIONS

There is a government-operated radio service and three privately-owned radio stations but no official television service in the country. An automatic telephone service operated by Belize Telecommunications Ltd covers the whole country.

The principal airport is at Belize City and various airlines operate international flights to the USA and other Central American states. The main port is also Belize City, which has deep water quays. Several inland waterways are also navigable. There are 1,865 miles of road, including four main highways, but there is no railway system.

EDUCATION

Education is compulsory from six to 14 years of age. In 1992 primary education was provided by 241 schools, most of which are government-aided. Secondary education is provided by 40 secondary and post-secondary institutions. A University College of Belize has been established. There is an extra-mural faculty of the University of the West Indies, with a resident tutor.
ILLITERACY RATE – 29.7 per cent
ENROLMENT (percentage of age group) – primary 97 per cent; secondary 36 per cent (1994)

BENIN
République du Benin

AREA – 43,484 sq. miles (112,622 sq. km). Neighbours: Togo (west), Burkina Faso and Niger (north), Nigeria (east)
POPULATION – 5,387,000 (1994 UN estimate). The official language is French
CAPITAL – ΨPorto Novo (population, 179,138, 1992)
MAJOR TOWNS – ΨCotonou (487,020, 1992) is the principal commercial town and port
CURRENCY – Franc CFA of 100 centimes
NATIONAL DAY – 30 November
NATIONAL FLAG – Two horizontal stripes of yellow over red with a vertical green band in the hoist
LIFE EXPECTANCY (years) – male 45.92; female 49.29
POPULATION GROWTH RATE – 3.2 per cent (1994)

POPULATION DENSITY – 48 per sq. km (1994)
URBAN POPULATION – 35.7 per cent (1992)
MILITARY EXPENDITURE – 1.3 per cent of GDP (1995)
MILITARY PERSONNEL – 7,300: Army 4,500, Navy 150, Air Force 150, Paramilitaries 2,500
CONSCRIPTION DURATION – 18 months
ILLITERACY RATE – 63.0 per cent
ENROLMENT (percentage of age group) – primary 53 per cent (1991); tertiary 2.4 per cent (1993)

Benin (formerly known as Dahomey) has a short coastline of 78 miles on the Gulf of Guinea but extends northwards inland for 437 miles. The four main regions, running horizontally, are a narrow sandy coastal strip, a succession of inter-communicating lagoons, a clay belt and a sandy plateau in the north.

HISTORY AND POLITICS

Benin was placed under French administration in 1892 and became an independent republic within the French Community in December 1958; full independence outside the Community was proclaimed on 1 August 1960. Between 1963 and 1972 successive governments were overthrown by the military until a coup d'état in 1972 brought to power a Marxist-Leninist military government headed by Lt.-Col. Kérékou.

The government dropped Marxism-Leninism as the official ideology in 1989, revoked the constitution in March 1990 and changed the country's official name from the People's Republic of Benin to the Republic of Benin. The Revolutionary National Assembly (legislature) was replaced by a High Council of the Republic (HCR).

A pluralistic constitution was adopted in December 1990 and legislative and presidential elections were held in 1991. Nicéphore Soglo was sworn in as president and appointed a Benin Resistance Party (PRB)-dominated provisional government. Legislative elections to the 83-seat National Assembly in March 1995 gave the PRB and allies 32 seats and opposition parties 49 seats. Soglo was defeated by former military ruler Gen. Kérékou in a presidential election in March 1996.

HEAD OF STATE
President and Head of the Armed Forces, HE Gen. Mathieu Kérékou, *sworn in* 4 April 1996

CABINET *as at July 1997*
Prime Minister, Adrien Houngbedji
Civil Service, Yacoubou Assouma
Commerce, Artisans and Tourism, Gatien Houngbedji
Culture and Communication, Timothée Zannou
Defence, Sévérin Adjovi
Environment and Housing, Sahidou Dango-Nadey
Finance, Moïse Mensah
Foreign Affairs and Co-operation, Pierre Osho
Health, Social Protection and Women's Affairs, Marina d'Almeida-Massougbodji
Industry, Small and Medium-Sized Enterprises, Félix Adimi
Interior, Security and Administration, Théophile N'da
Justice, Legislation and Human Rights, Ismaël Tidjani Serpos
Mines, Energy and Water Resources, Emmanuel Golou
National Education and Scientific Research, Djidjoho Léonard Padonou
Planning, Economic Reconstruction and Employment Promotion, Albert Tevoejre
Public Works and Transport, Kamarou Fassassi
Rural Development, Jérôme Sacca Kina
Youth, Sports and Leisure, Damien Alahassa

EMBASSY OF THE REPUBLIC OF BENIN
87 Avenue Victor Hugo, 75116 Paris, France
Tel: Paris 4500 9882
Ambassador Extraordinary and Plenipotentiary, HE André-
Guy Ologoudou
HONORARY CONSULATE, 16 The Broadway, Stanmore,
Middx HA7 4DW. Tel: 081–954 8800. *Honorary Consul*,
Lawrence Landau

BRITISH AMBASSADOR, HE John T. Masefield CMG,
resident at Lagos, Nigeria

ECONOMY

The principal exports are cotton, palm products, groundnuts, shea-nuts, and coffee. Small deposits of gold, iron and
chrome have been found. Oil production started in 1983;
124,000 tonnes were produced in 1995.

In 1993 Benin had a trade deficit of US$239 million and a
current account deficit of US$52 million. In 1994 imports
totalled US$493 million and exports US$163 million.
GNP – US$2,034 million (1995); US$370 per capita (1995)
GDP – US$1,962 million (1992); US$435 per capita (1992)
ANNUAL AVERAGE GROWTH OF GDP – 6.0 per cent (1995)
INFLATION RATE – 14.5 per cent (1995)
TOTAL EXTERNAL DEBT – US$1,646 million (1995)

TRADE WITH UK	1995	1996
Imports from UK	£43,115,000	£43,636,000
Exports to UK	1,012,000,	3,097,000

BHUTAN
Druk-yul

AREA – 18,147 sq. miles (47,000 sq. km). Neighbours: Tibet
(north), India (west, south and east)
POPULATION – 1,614,000 (1994 UN estimate); about 80
per cent are Buddhists, the remainder (mostly the
Nepali Bhutanese) are Hindu. The official language for
administrative and religious purposes, is Dzongkha, a
variant of Tibetan, which functions as a lingua franca
amongst a variety of languages and dialects. Nepali
remains a recognized language and English remains the
medium of instruction and the working language of the
administration
CAPITAL – Thimphu (population, 15,000, 1987 estimate)
CURRENCY – Ngultrum of 100 chetrum (Indian currency
is also legal tender)
NATIONAL DAY – 17 December
NATIONAL FLAG – Saffron yellow and orange-red divided
diagonally, with dragon device in centre
LIFE EXPECTANCY (years) – male 49.10; female 52.40
POPULATION GROWTH RATE – 1.1 per cent (1994)
POPULATION DENSITY – 34 per sq. km (1994)
ILLITERACY RATE – 57.8 per cent

There is a mountainous northern region which is infertile
and sparsely populated, a central zone of upland valleys
where most of the population and cultivated land is found,
and in the south the densely forested foothills of the
Himalayas, which are mainly inhabited by Nepalese
settlers and indigenous tribespeople.

INSURGENCIES

In January 1989 the King introduced a code of national
etiquette designed to protect the national culture and
language from Nepali encroachment. These measures,
together with the granting of citizenship only to Nepalis
settled in Bhutan before 1958, led to an exodus of ethnic

Nepalis to Nepal, where about 80,000 live in camps. A low-
level insurgency has been waged in the south of the
country against the King's policies by ethnic Nepalis since
1990. Talks between the Nepali and Bhutan governments
continue in an attempt to resolve the fate of the refugees.

FOREIGN RELATIONS

Under a 1949 treaty Bhutan is guided by the advice of India
in regard to its external relations. It retains its own
diplomatic representatives and is a member of the UN. It
also receives from India an annual payment of Rs500,000
as compensation for portions of its territory annexed by the
British Government in India in 1864.

POLITICAL SYSTEM

Bhutan has a 150-member National Assembly which
meets twice a year. The ten-member Royal Advisory
Council, nominated by the King and the National Assem-
bly, acts as a consultative body when the National
Assembly is not in session. The King is also assisted by the
Lhengyal Sgungtsog (Cabinet). There are no political parties.

HEAD OF STATE

HM *The King of Bhutan*, Jigme Singye Wangchuk, *born* 11
November 1955; *succeeded his father* July 1972; *crowned* 2
June 1974
Heir, Crown Prince Jigme Gesar Namgyal Wangchuk,
designated 31 October 1988

CABINET MINISTERS *as at July 1997*

Representative of the King in the Ministry of Agriculture, HRH
Ashi Sonam Chhoden Wangchuck
Representative of the King in the Ministry of Communications,
HRH Ashi Dechen Wangmo Wangchuck
*Representative of the King in the Ministry of Health and
Education*, HRH N. Wangchuck
Cabinet Secretary, Foreign Affairs, Dawa Tsering
Finance, Dorji Tshering
Home Affairs, Dago Tshering
Planning, Chenkyab Dorji
Trade and Industry, Om Pradhan

ECONOMY

The economy is based on agriculture and animal husbandry, which engage over 90 per cent of the workforce in what
is largely a self-sufficient rural society. The principal food
crops are rice, wheat, maize and barley. Vegetables and
fruit are also produced. Bhutan is the world's largest
producer of cardamom, which forms its principal export to
countries other than India. Agriculture is, however,
limited by the country's mountainous topography and 60
per cent forest cover.

The mountains contain rich deposits of limestone,
gypsum, dolomite and graphite and small amounts of coal,
which are exported to India. A modest industrial base is
being developed. A distillery and cement, chemicals and
food-processing plants are in production; a forestry
industries complex is being expanded. Tourism and
postage stamps are increasingly important sources of
foreign exchange.

The government budget deficit was equivalnt to 0.26
per cent of GDP in 1993. In 1991 imports totalled US$102
million and exports US$72 million.
GNP – US$295 million (1995); US$420 per capita (1995)
GDP – US$312 million (1992); US$152 per capita (1992)
ANNUAL AVERAGE GROWTH OF GDP – 4.6 per cent (1990)
INFLATION RATE – 7.0 per cent (1994)
TOTAL EXTERNAL DEBT – US$87 million (1995)

TRADE

Over 90 per cent of foreign trade is with India. Principal exports are agricultural products, timber, cement and coal; main imports are textiles, cereals and consumer goods. Bhutan's airline, Druk Air, flies between Paro, New Delhi and Calcutta.

Trade with UK	1995	1996
Imports from UK	£2,428,000	£1,313,000
Exports to UK	492,000	394,000

BOLIVIA
República de Bolivia

AREA – 424,165 sq. miles (1,098,581 sq. km)
POPULATION – 7,237,000 (1994 UN estimate); 6,440,000 (1992 census), 12 per cent is of white European descent, 30 per cent mestizo (mixed European-Indian), 25 per cent Quechua Indian and 17 per cent Aymará Indian. The official language is Spanish, which is spoken by around 60 per cent of the population, with Quechua spoken by 25 per cent and Aymará by 15 per cent. Roman Catholicism was the state religion until disestablishment in 1961
CAPITAL – La Paz (population, 784,976, 1993 estimate)
MAJOR CITIES – Cochabamba (512,000); Oruro (183,000); Santa Cruz (694,000); Potosí (112,000); Sucre, the legal capital and seat of the judiciary (131,000); Tarija (90,000)
CURRENCY – Boliviano ($b) of 100 centavos
NATIONAL ANTHEM – Bolivianos, El Hado Propicio (Oh Bolivia, our long-felt desires)
NATIONAL DAY – 6 August (Independence Day)
NATIONAL FLAG – Three horizontal bands; red, yellow, green
LIFE EXPECTANCY (years) – male 57.74; female 61.00
POPULATION GROWTH RATE – 2.4 per cent (1994)
POPULATION DENSITY – 7 per sq. km (1994)
URBAN POPULATION – 57.5 per cent (1992)
MILITARY EXPENDITURE – 2.6 per cent of GDP (1995)
MILITARY PERSONNEL – 33,500: Army 25,000, Navy 4,500, Air Force 4,000
CONSCRIPTION DURATION – 12 months

The chief topographical feature is the great central plateau over 500 miles in length, at an average altitude of 12,500 feet above sea level, between the two great chains of the Andes, which traverse the country from south to north. The total length of the navigable rivers is about 12,000 miles, the principal rivers being the Itenez, Beni, Mamore and Madre de Dios.

HISTORY AND POLITICS

Bolivia won its independence from Spain in 1825 after a war of liberation led by Simon Bolivar (1783–1830), from whom the country derives its name. From 1964 to 1982 Bolivia was ruled by military juntas until civilian rule was restored.

Congressional and presidential elections were held in June 1993 with Gonzalo Sánchez of the opposition National Revolutionary Movement (MNR) winning the largest share of the vote in the presidential election but as no candidate won more than 50 per cent, the new President was chosen by congressional vote in August, when Gonzalo Sánchez was elected. The MNR emerged as the largest party in Congress, winning 52 out of 130 seats, and formed a government in coalition with the Civic Solidarity Union (20 seats) and the Free Bolivia Movement (7 seats).

POLITICAL SYSTEM

The constitution provides for a directly elected executive president who appoints the Cabinet The legislature (Congress) consists of a 27-member Senate and a 130-member Chamber of Deputies. Both the president and Congress are elected for five-year terms.

HEAD OF STATE

President of the Republic, Gonzalo Sánchez de Lozada, *inaugurated* 5 August 1993
Vice President, Victor Hugo Cardenas

CABINET *as at June 1997*
Economic Development, Jaime Villalobos
Education and Culture, Carlos Pimentel
Finance, Fernando Caudia
Foreign Affairs and Worship, Antonío Araníbar Quiroga
Health, Oscar Sandoval Moron
Human Development, Freddy Teodovich
Information, Guillermo Richter
Interior, Carlos Sanchez Berzain
Justice, René Blattman
Labour, Reynaldo Peters
National Defence, Jorge Otasevic Toledo
Presidency, José Guillermo Justiniano
Privatization, Alfonso Revollo
Sustainable Development, Moises Jarmusz

BOLIVIAN EMBASSY
106 Eaton Square, London SW1W 9AD
Tel 0171-235 2257/4248
Ambassador Extraordinary and Plenipotentiary, new appointment awaited

BRITISH EMBASSY
Avenida Arce 2732, (Casilla 694) La Paz
Tel: La Paz 357424
Ambassador Extraordinary and Plenipotentiary, HE David Ridgway, OBE, apptd 1995
Deputy Head of Mission, J. Gardner

There is an Honorary Consulate at Santa Cruz.

ECONOMY

Mining, natural gas, petroleum and agriculture are the principal industries. The ancient silver mines of Potosí are now worked chiefly for tin, but gold is obtained on the Eastern Cordillera of the Andes. Tin output, together with other minerals (copper, tungsten, antimony, lead, zinc, asbestos, wolfram, bismuth salt and sulphur), provides over one-third of exports. Small quantities of oil are produced for internal consumption, and gas (currently providing about a quarter of export income) is piped to Argentina; there are plans to build a pipeline to São Paulo, Brazil.

The economy deteriorated badly in the late 1970s and early 1980s, with a large external debt, and the collapse of world tin prices. In the mid-1980s economic reforms were introduced with privatization of some state-owned firms and the encouragement of foreign investment. Tin prices began to increase in 1989, but the industry remains uneconomic. Many workers took to growing coca, which has now become a significant export.

The peso was replaced in 1987 with the Boliviano of 1,000,000 old pesos in a successful effort to stem hyper-inflation. The economy and currency have stabilized.

In October 1996 the government signed an agreement with the South American Common Market (Mercosur) in an attempt to create a free trade zone within 18 years.

GNP – US$5,905 million (1995); US$800 per capita (1995)
GDP – US$5,919 million (1992); US$839 per capita (1992)
ANNUAL AVERAGE GROWTH OF GDP – 3.7 per cent (1995)

INFLATION RATE – 10.2 per cent (1995)
UNEMPLOYMENT – 3.6 per cent (1995)
TOTAL EXTERNAL DEBT – US$5,266 million (1995)

TRADE

Mineral exports represent about 35 per cent of total trade. Bolivia has now developed its own smelters and is exporting metals. The chief imports are wheat and flour, iron and steel products, machinery, vehicles and textiles.

In 1992 Bolivia had a trade deficit of US$432 million and a current account deficit of US$534 million. There was a government budget deficit equivalent to 1.86 per cent of GDP in 1993. In 1995 imports totalled US$1,424 million and exports US$1,101 million.

Trade with UK	1995	1996
Imports from UK	£17,042,000	£11,270,000
Exports to UK	14,732,000	39,142,000

COMMUNICATIONS

There are 2,200 miles of railways in operation including the lines from Corumbá to Santa Cruz. There is direct railway communication to the sea at Antofagasta, Arica, and Mollendo, and also to Buenos Aires. Communication with Peru is by road from La Paz via Copacabana and thence to the railhead at Puno. In 1993 Bolivia and Peru signed an agreement granting Bolivia a concession of 162 hectares at the southern Peruvian port of Ilo for 98 years to construct a free trade zone.

Commercial aviation is conducted by the national airline, Lloyd Aereo Boliviano and Transporte Aereo Militar between the major towns, and Lloyd Aereo Boliviano and a number of foreign airlines provide international flights to the USA, South and Central America and Europe.

Most towns have radio, telephone or telegraph communication with the main cities. There are 16 principal daily newspapers.

EDUCATION

Elementary education is compulsory and free and there are secondary schools in urban centres. Provision is also made for higher education; in addition to St Francisco Xavier's University at Sucre, founded in 1624, there are seven other universities, the largest being the University of San Andrés at La Paz, and ten private universities.
ILLITERACY RATE – 16.9 per cent
ENROLMENT (percentage of age group) – primary 91 per cent; secondary 29 per cent; tertiary 22.2 per cent (1990)

BOSNIA-HERCEGOVINA

AREA – 19,735 sq. miles (51,129 sq. km). Neighbours: Serbia (east), Montenegro (south-east), Croatia (north and west)
POPULATION – 3,527,000 (1994 UN estimate); 4.4 million (1991 census); 2,900,000 (1995 estimate); 44 per cent Muslims, 31 per cent Serbs and 17 per cent Croats
CAPITAL – Sarajevo (population, 415,631)
MAJOR CITIES – Tuzla, Banja Luka, Zenica, Vitez and Mostar
CURRENCY – Dinar of 100 paras
NATIONAL DAY – 1 March (anniversary of 1992 declaration of independence)
NATIONAL FLAG – White flag bearing a blue shield with a white diagonal and six gold fleurs-de-lys
LIFE EXPECTANCY (years) – male 69.55; female 75.11

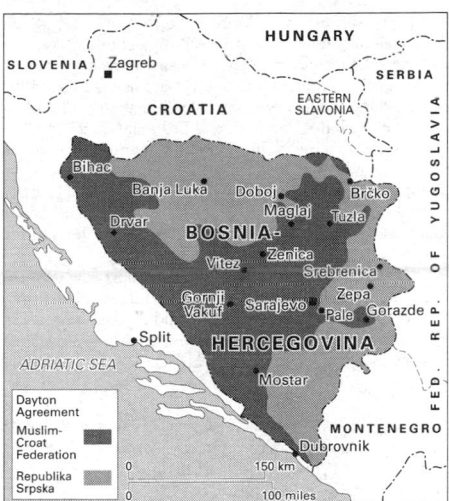

POPULATION GROWTH RATE – –5.0 per cent (1994)
POPULATION DENSITY – 69 per sq. km (1994)
MILITARY EXPENDITURE – 18.8 per cent of GDP (1995)
MILITARY PERSONNEL – Bosnian Muslim Army (BiH): 92,000; Croat Defence Council (HVO): 50,000; Bosnian Serb Army. 85,000
GDP – US$6,392 million (1992); US$3,639 per capita (1991)

HISTORY AND POLITICS

The country was settled by Slavs in the seventh century and conquered by the Ottoman Turks in 1463. Ruled by the Turks for over 400 years, the country came under Austro-Hungarian control in 1878. Austria-Hungary's annexation of Bosnia-Hercegovina in 1908 was never accepted by Serbia because of the large ethnic Serb population in the country, and the assassination of the heir to the Austro-Hungarian throne in Sarajevo by an ethnic Serb precipitated the First World War. Bosnia-Hercegovina became part of the 'Kingdom of Serbs, Croats and Slovenes' (renamed Yugoslavia in 1929) under the Versailles Treaty (1919). It was occupied by German and Axis forces between 1941 and 1945. At the end of the war Bosnia-Hercegovina came under Communist rule as part of the Socialist Federal Republic of Yugoslavia, which eventually collapsed with the secession of Slovenia and Croatia in 1991.

The Bosnia-Hercegovina government issued a declaration of sovereignty in October 1991 against the wishes of the ethnic Serb Democratic Party. Independence was declared on 1 March 1992 following a referendum which was boycotted by the Bosnian Serbs. Bosnia-Hercegovina was recognized as an independent state by the EC and USA in April 1992 and admitted to UN membership in May 1992.

THE WAR

Fighting broke out in March 1992 between the pro-independence Muslims and Bosnian Serbs who wanted to merge with the Serbian republic to form a Greater Serbia. The Bosnian Serbs, assisted by the Serb-dominated Federal Yugoslav Army (JNA) rapidly gained control of 70 per cent of Bosnia and in August 1992 declared their own 'Republika Srpska' with its capital at Pale. International pressure eventually forced the JNA to withdraw but it handed over its weapons to the Bosnian Serb forces.

The Bosnian government (Muslim) forces formed an alliance with Bosnian Croat and Croat forces in early 1992 which collapsed in 1993. The Muslims then came under fire from both Bosnian Serb and Bosnian Croat forces. In January 1993 the UN and EU attempted to negotiate an end to the war by proposing a peace plan at a conference in Geneva. The Vance-Owen plan was accepted by all parties including the Bosnian president Radovan Karadzic but was rejected by the Bosnian Serb parliament and the fighting continued.

The Bosnian Serbs began to shell Sarajevo and government-held enclaves following the collapse of a three-month détente between the Serbs and the Muslims which lasted until December 1993. The attack on the enclaves and the siege of Sarajevo prompted the UN to declare Srebrenica, Zepa, Gorazde, Sarajevo, Tuzla and Bihac 'safe areas'.

In August 1993 the Bosnian Croats declared a 'Republic of Herceg-Bosna', with its capital in Mostar, and following a cease-fire in February 1994 joined the government forces in a Muslim-Croat Federation.

A Bosnian Serb artillery attack on a Sarajevo market in February 1994 killed 68 people resulting in the imposition of a heavy weapons exclusion zone around the city by the UN and NATO. Bosnian Serb forces captured most of the enclave of Gorazde in April despite NATO air strikes. NATO widened its threat of air strikes to all UN 'safe areas' and galvanized the USA, Britain, France, Germany and Russia to form the Contact Group (CG) to co-ordinate peace efforts. The CG brought about a cease-fire in June 1994 and presented a peace plan, proposing a 51:49 division of territory between the Muslim-Croat Federation and the Bosnian Serbs. The Bosnian Serbs rejected the plan and the CG attempted to isolate them, with the support of Serbia, which had agreed to blockade Bosnian Serb forces in exchange for a relaxation of sanctions.

NATO air strikes against Bosnian Serbs in December 1994 resulted in the seizure of 350 UN peacekeepers, who were released as part of a cease-fire agreement in January. Bosnian Serbs retaliating against a Federation offensive in March resumed artillery attacks on Sarajevo, prompting a NATO bombing campaign and a second hostage crisis.

Fighting intensified in 1995, climaxing in a land-grab during the final months of the war. Bosnian Serb forces overran the UN safe areas of Zepa and Srebrenica in July, allegedly massacring thousands of fleeing Muslims, and then laid siege to the Bihac 'safe area' together with Croatian Serbs and rebel Muslims. Bosnian government and Croatian forces lifted the siege of Bihac in August, enabling a joint attack on Serb-held central Bosnia.

A Serb artillery attack on Sarajevo on 28 August which killed 37 people prompted NATO to bomb military and infrastructure targets and to issue an ultimatum to the Bosnian Serbs to remove their heavy weapons from around Sarajevo. The ultimatum was met by 20 September, following coercion from President Milosevic of Serbia.

The foreign ministers of Bosnia, Croatia and Serbia (rump Yugoslavia) met in Geneva in September 1995 and agreed to a US-sponsored peace accord. A cease-fire agreement was signed on 5 October and observed from 22 October, delayed by a Federation advance in the west and north-west, and Bosnian Serbs overrunning Tuzla.

THE PEACE AGREEMENT

The Presidents of Bosnia, Serbia and Croatia met in Dayton, Ohio, USA, for negotiations which culminated in an agreement on 21 November 1995. The Dayton Peace Treaty was signed in Paris on 14 December. It was agreed to preserve Bosnia as a single state with a 51:49 division of territory between the Bosnian and Croat Federation and the Republika Srpska (Bosnian Serbs). A Republican (national) government, presidency and democratically elected institutions, based in Federation-controlled Sarajevo, were provided for. The Bosnian Serbs agreed to return five Sarajevo suburbs to the Federation and were given access to the sea in a land-swap with Croatia. The Federation gained a land corridor between Sarajevo and Gorazde but was obliged to return Mrkonjic Grad to the Bosnian Serbs.

The Dayton agreement provided for the deployment of a 60,000-strong NATO-led Peace Implementation Force (IFOR) which took over from UNPROFOR on 20 December 1995 and was mandated until December 1996. IFOR was replaced by a 31,000-strong, NATO-led Stabilization Force (SFOR) which was mandated for 18 months.

Mostar, which had been divided during the war between the Muslims and Croats of the Federation and administered by the EU, held elections in June 1996. The EU withdrew in December 1996. Control of the northern town of Brcko is still contested but remains under Bosnian Serb control. The Bosnian Croat state of Hercog-Bosna ceased to exist on 17 December 1996. *See also* Events of the Year.

POLITICAL SYSTEM

Under the Dayton peace agreement, the Bosnian republican (national) government was made responsible for foreign affairs, currency, citizenship and immigration. Executive authority was vested in a democratically elected rotating presidential triumvirate comprising a representative from each community.

Legislative authority is vested in a bicameral parliament, the Assembly of Bosnia-Hercegovina, comprising a House of Peoples and a House of Representatives. The House of Peoples has 15 members, five from each community, who are selected by the House of Representatives. The House of Representatives has 42 members who were directly elected in September 1996. Two thirds of the members come from the Federation and one third from Republika Srpska. Within the Muslim-Croat Federation there is a 140-member House of Representatives and ten cantonal assemblies; in the Republika Srpska there is an 83-member People's Assembly.

HEADS OF STATE (FOR ALL BOSNIA)
Current President, Alija Izetbegovic (Muslim); *Presidency Members,* Momcilo Krajisnik (Serb); Kresimir Zubak (Croat), *elected* 14 September 1996

HEAD OF STATE OF THE FEDERATION
President, Vladimir Soljic (Croat), *elected by Federation House of Representatives* 18 March 1997
Vice-President, Ejup Ganic (Muslim)

HEAD OF STATE OF REPUBLIKA SRPSKA
President, Biljana Plavsic, *elected* 14 September 1996
Vice-President, Dragljub Mirjanic

COUNCIL OF MINISTERS (FOR ALL BOSNIA) *as at July 1997*
Co-Prime Ministers, Haris Silajdzic (Muslim); Boro Bosic (Serb)
Deputy Prime Minister, Neven Tomic (Croat)
Communications and Civilian Affairs, Spasoje Albijanic (Serb)
Foreign Affairs, Jadranko Prlic (Croat)
Foreign Trade and Economic Relations, Hasan Muratovic (Muslim)

FEDERATION CABINET *as at July 1997*
Prime Minister, Edhem Bicakcic (Muslim)
Deputy PM, Finance, Drago Bilandzija (Croat)
Agriculture, Water Management and Forestry, Ahmed Smajic
 (Muslim)
Defence, Ante Jelavic (Croat)
Education, Science, Culture and Sport, Fahrudin
 Rizvanbegovic (Muslim)
Energy, Mining and Industry, Izudin Kapetanovic (Muslim)
Environment, Ibrahim Morankic (Muslim)
Health, Bozo Ljubic (Croat)
Interior, Mehmed Zilic (Muslim)
Justice, Mate Tadic (Croat)
Social Welfare, Displaced Persons and Refugees, Rasim Kadic
 (Muslim)
Trade, Ile Krezo (Croat)
Transport and Communications, Rasim Gacanovic (Muslim)
Without Portfolio, Nikola Antunovic (Croat); Nedjeljko
 Despotevic (Serb)

REPUBLIKA SRPSKA GOVERNMENT *as at November 1996*
Prime Minister, Gojko Klickovic
Deputy PMs, Djuradj Banjac *(Economy and Finance);* Ostoja
 Kremenovic *(Internal Affairs);* Velibor Ostojic *(Social
 Affairs)*
Agriculture/Forestry and Water Management, Djojo Arsenovic
Construction, Urban Development and Utilities, Ratko
 Misanovic
Defence, Milan Ninkovic
Education/Science and Culture, Stevan Stevic
Finance, Ranko Travar
Foreign Affairs, Aleksa Buha
Foreign Economic Relations, Branko Stjepanovic
Health, Mirko Sosic
Industry and Energy, Milorad Skoko
Information, Svetlana Siljegovic
Internal Affairs, Dragan Kiljac
Justice, Branko Petric
Labour, Employment and Social Services, Vinko Kondic
Reconstruction and Development, Novak Kondic
Refugees and Displaced Persons, Ljubisa Vladusic
Religion, Dragan Davidovic
Sport, Rajko Popovic
Trade and Provisions, Mladen Cicovic
Transport and Communications, Nedeljko Laic
Veterans and Victims of War, Vojislav Gligic

EMBASSY OF THE REPUBLIC OF BOSNIA-HERCEGOVINA
4th Floor, Morley House, 314–22 Regent Street, London
WIR 5AB
Tel 0171-255 3758
Ambassador Extraordinary and Plenipotentiary, new
 appointment awaited

BRITISH EMBASSY
8 Tina Ujevica, Sarajevo
Tel: Sarajevo 663922
Ambassador Extraordinary and Plenipotentiary, HE Charles
 Crawford, apptd 1996

BRITISH COUNCIL REPRESENTATIVE, Sue Barnes

TRADE WITH UK	1995	1996
Imports from UK	£4,084,000	£16,644,000
Exports to UK	240,000	635,000

BOTSWANA
The Republic of Botswana

AREA – 224,607 sq. miles (581,730 sq. km). Neighbours:
 South Africa (south and east), Zimbabwe (north and
 north-east), Namibia (west)
POPULATION – 1,443,000 (1994 UN estimate). The
 national language is Setswana and the official language is
 English
CAPITAL – Gaborone (population, 133,468, 1991 census)
MAJOR CITIES – Francistown (55,244); Lobatse (26,052);
 Selebi-Phikwe (39,772)
CURRENCY – Pula (P) of 100 thebe
NATIONAL ANTHEM – Fatshe La Rona
NATIONAL DAY 30 September
NATIONAL FLAG – Light blue with a horizontal black
 stripe fimbriated in white across the centre
LIFE EXPECTANCY (years) – male 52.32; female 59.70
POPULATION GROWTH RATE – 2.6 per cent (1994)
POPULATION DENSITY – 2 per sq. km (1994)
URBAN POPULATION – 26.5 per cent (1993)
MILITARY EXPENDITURE – 7.1 per cent of GDP (1995)
MILITARY PERSONNEL – 7,500: Army 7,000, Air Wing 500

A plateau at a height of about 4,000 feet divides Botswana
into two main topographical regions. To the east of the
plateau streams flow into the Marico, Notwani and
Limpopo rivers; to the west lies a flat region comprising
the Kgalagadi Desert, the Okavango Swamps and the
Northern State Lands area. The climate is generally sub-
tropical.

HISTORY AND POLITICS

On 30 September 1966 the British Protectorate of Bechua-
naland became a republic within the Commonwealth
under the name Botswana.
 The last general election on 15 October 1994 was won
by the Botswana Democratic Party with 26 seats to the
Botswana National Front's 13 seats.

POLITICAL SYSTEM

The president is head of state and is elected by an absolute
majority in the National Assembly. He appoints as vice
president a member of the National Assembly who is
leader of government business in the National Assembly.
The Assembly consists of the president, 40 members
elected on a basis of universal adult suffrage, four specially
elected members, the Attorney-General (non-voting) and
the Speaker. Presidential and legislative elections are held
every five years. There is also a 15-member House of
Chiefs which considers legislation affecting the constitution and chieftaincy matters.

HEAD OF STATE
President, HE Sir Ketumile Masire, GCMG, *re-elected* 17
 October 1994 for a third five-year term

CABINET *as at July 1997*
The President
Agriculture, Roy Blackbeard
Assistant Ministers, R. Sebego *(Agriculture);* J. Mothibamela
 (Finance and Development Planning); M. N. Nasha, B.
 Mokgothu *(Local Government, Land and Housing)*
Commerce and Industry, George Kgoroba
Education, Dr Gaositwe Chiepe
Finance and Development Planning, Festus Mogae
Foreign Affairs, Lt.-Gen. Mompati Merafhe
Health, Chapson Butale

Labour and Home Affairs, Bahiti Temane
Local Government, Land and Housing, Patrick Balopi
Mineral Resources and Water Affairs, David Magang
Presidential Affairs, Ponatshengo Kedikilwe
Works, Transport and Communications, Daniel Kwelagobe

BOTSWANA HIGH COMMISSION
6 Stratford Place, London WIN 9AE
Tel 0171–499 0031
High Commissioner, HE Tuelonyana Ditlhabi-Oliphant,
apptd 1996

BRITISH HIGH COMMISSION
Private Bag 0023, Gaborone
Tel: Gaborone 352841 /2/3
High Commissioner, HE David Beaumont, apptd 1994

BRITISH COUNCIL REPRESENTATIVE, P. Mitchell British
High Commission Building, Queen's Road, The Mall,
PO Box 439, Gaborone

ECONOMY

Agriculture is predominantly pastoral. The national herd
is around 2.2 million cattle and one million sheep and goats.
Cattle rearing accounts for about 85 per cent of agricultural output and livestock products, particularly beef, are a
major source of foreign exchange earnings.

Mineral extraction and processing is now the major
source of income following the opening of large mines for
diamonds and copper-nickel. Botswana is one of the largest
producers of diamonds in the world, with diamonds
accounting for 80 per cent of export revenue. Large
deposits of coal have been discovered and are now being
mined. In 1995, Botswana produced 900,000 tonnes of coal,
21,029 tonnes of copper and 16,506,000 carats (15 per cent
of the world total) of diamonds. Manufacturing industry is
growing but it is still a small sector of the economy.
Tourism is the third largest industry with up to 400,000
visitors each year generating about 7 per cent of GDP.

In 1992 the government had a budget surplus equivalent
to 10.78 per cent of GDP. In 1994 imports totalled
US$1,638 million and exports US$1,845 million.
GNP – US$4,381 million (1995); US$3,020 per capita
(1995)
GDP – US$3,737 million (1992); US$3,003 per capita
(1992)
ANNUAL AVERAGE GROWTH OF GDP – 4.1 per cent (1994)
INFLATION RATE – 10.5 per cent (1995)
TOTAL EXTERNAL DEBT – US$699 million (1995)

Trade with UK	1995	1996
Imports from UK	£25,837,000	£23,444,000
Exports to UK	23,647,000	48,269,000

COMMUNICATIONS

The railway from Cape Town to Zimbabwe passes
through eastern Botswana. The main roads are the north-
south road, which closely follows the railway, and the road
running east–west that links Francistown and Maun. A
road from Nata to Kazungula provides a direct link to
Zambia from Botswana. Air services are provided on a
scheduled basis between the main towns.

EDUCATION

There are 657 primary schools, 163 community junior
secondary schools and 23 government and government-
aided senior secondary schools.Total enrolment in the
tertiary sector (teacher training establishments, colleges of
education and the University of Botswana) numbers 6,923.
ILLITERACY RATE – 30.2 per cent

ENROLMENT (percentage of age group) – primary 96 per
cent (1993); secondary 45 per cent (1993); tertiary 4.9 per
cent (1994)

BRAZIL
República Federativa do Brasil

AREA – 3,286,488 sq. miles (8,511,965 sq. km). Neighbours:
the Guianas, Colombia and Venezuela (north), Peru,
Bolivia, Paraguay, and Argentina (west), Uruguay
(south)
POPULATION – 153,725,000 (1994 UN estimate).
Portuguese is the national language but Italian, Spanish,
German, Japanese and Arabic are also spoken
CAPITAL – Brasilia (population, 1,601,094, 1994),
inaugurated 1960
MAJOR CITIES – São Paulo (9,646,187); ΨRio de Janeiro
(5,480,786), the former capital; Belo Horizonte
(2,029,160); ΨRecife (1,298,227); ΨSalvador
(2,075,275); ΨFortaleza (1,768,637), 1996 census
CURRENCY – Real of 100 centavos
NATIONAL ANTHEM – Ouviram do Ipirangas às Margens
Placidas (From peaceful Ypiranga's banks)
NATIONAL DAY – 7 September (Independence Day)
NATIONAL FLAG – Green with a yellow lozenge
containing a blue sphere studded with white stars, and
crossed by a white band with the motto *Ordem e Progresso*
LIFE EXPECTANCY (years) – male 64.04; female 68.68
POPULATION GROWTH RATE – 1.5 per cent (1994)
POPULATION DENSITY – 18 per sq. km (1994)

The north is mainly wide, low-lying, forest-clad plains.
The central areas are principally plateau land and the east
and south are traversed by successive mountain ranges
interspersed with fertile valleys. The principal ranges are
Serra do Mar, the Serra da Mantiqueira and the Serra do
Espinhaco along the east coast. The River Amazon flows
from the Peruvian Andes to the Atlantic.

HISTORY AND POLITICS

Brazil was discovered by the Portuguese navigator Pedro
Alvares Cabral in 1500 and colonized by Portugal in the
early 16th century. In 1822 it became independent under
Dom Pedro, son of King Joao VI of Portugal, who had been
forced to flee to Brazil during the Napoleonic Wars. In
1889, Dom Pedro II was dethroned and a republic was
proclaimed. In 1985 Brazil returned to democratic rule
after two decades of military government.

Fernando Cardoso of the Social Democratic Party, part
of the Liberal Front coalition, was elected outright in the
presidential election of October 1994. In the November
1994 legislative elections the Liberal Front won 33 Senate
seats, 175 seats in the Chamber of Deputies and nine state
governorships.

POLITICAL SYSTEM

The Federative Republic of Brazil is composed of the
federal district and 26 states. Under the 1988 constitution
the president, who heads the executive, is directly elected
for a single four-year term. The Congress consists of an 81-
member Senate (three senators per state elected for an
eight-year term) and a 517-member Chamber of Deputies
which is elected every four years; the number of deputies
per state depends upon the state's population. Each state
has a Governor, and a Legislative Assembly with a four-
year term.

HEAD OF STATE
President, Fernando Henrique Cardoso, *sworn in* 1 January 1995
Vice-President, Marco Antonio de Oliveira Maciel

CABINET *as at July 1997*
Administration, Luiz Carlos Bresser Pereira
Agriculture, Arlindo Porto
Air Force, Air Chief Marshal Brigadier Lélio Viana Lobo
Armed Forces, Gen. Benedito Onofre Bezerra Leonel
Army, Gen. Zenildo Gonzaga Zoroastro de Lucena
Communications, Sérgio Roberto Vieira da Motta
Culture, Francisco Correa Weffort
Education, Paulo Renato de Souza
Environment, Water Resources and Amazonia, Gustavo Krause Gonçalves Sobrinho
External Relations, Luiz Felipe Lampreia
Finance, Pedro Malan
Health, Carlos César Silva de Albuquerque
Industry, Trade and Tourism, Francisco Dornelles
Justice, Iris Resende
Labour, Paulo Paiva
Land Reform, Raul Jungmann
Mines and Energy, Raimundo Mendes de Brito
Minister Chief of Staff of the Presidency, Gen. Alberto Mendes Cardoso
Minister for the Civilian Cabinet, Clóvis de Barros Carvalho
Navy, Admiral Mauro Cesar Rodrigues Pereira
Planning and Budget, Antonio Kandir
Political Co-ordination, Luiz Carlos Santos
Social Security, Reinhold Stephanes
Sports, Edson Arantes do Nascimento (Pelé)
Transport, Alcides José Saldanha

BRAZILIAN EMBASSY
32 Green Street, London WIY 4AT
Tel 0171-499 0877
Ambassador Extraordinary and Plenipotentiary, HE Rubens Antonio Barbosa, LVO, apptd 1994
Military Attaché, Fernando Drubski de Campos
Counsellor (Financial and Economic Affairs), Bezerra Abbott Galvão

There is also a Brazilian Consulate-General in London and honorary consular offices at Cardiff and Glasgow.

BRITISH EMBASSY
Sector de Embaixadus Sul, Quadra 801, Conjunto K, CEP 70.408 Brasilia DF
Tel: Brasilia 225 2710
Ambassador Extraordinary and Plenipotentiary, HE Keith Haskell, CMG, CVO, apptd 1995
Deputy Head of Mission, Consul-General, J. A. Penney
Defence Attaché, Col. D. M. Black
First Secretary (Commercial), M. A. Patterson

There are British Consulates-General at Rio de Janeiro and São Paulo.

BRITISH COUNCIL REPRESENTATIVE, Howard Thompson, OBE, Edificio Morro Vermilho, Quadra 1. Bloco 21, SCS, 70399-900, Brasilia. Regional directors in Recife, Rio de Janeiro and São Paulo

BRITISH AND COMMONWEALTH CHAMBER OF COMMERCE IN SÃO PAULO, Rua Barão de Itapetininga 275, 7th Floor, 01042, São Paulo (*Postal Address*, PO Box 1621, 01000 São Paulo) and Rua Real Grandeza 99, 22281 Rio de Janeiro

DEFENCE

The Army has 61 main battle tanks, 823 armoured personnel carriers, 724 artillery pieces, three aircraft and 72 helicopters. The Navy has bases at Rio de Janeiro, Salvador, Natal, Belém, Rio Grande do Sul, Ladario and Manaus. It is equipped with five submarines, one aircraft carrier, three destroyers, 15 frigates, and 35 patrol and coastal vessels. Naval aviation has 38 armed helicopters, the Marines have six armoured personnel carriers and 31 artillery pieces. The Air Force has 280 combat aircraft and 29 armed helicopters.
MILITARY EXPENDITURE – 1.5 per cent of GDP (1995)
MILITARY PERSONNEL – 295,000: Army 195,000, Navy 50,000, Air Force 50,000
CONSCRIPTION DURATION – 12 months

ECONOMY

There are large mineral deposits including iron ore (hematite), manganese, bauxite, beryllium, chrome, nickel, tungsten, cassiterite, lead, gold, monazite (containing rare earths and thorium) and zirconium. Diamonds and precious and semi-precious stones are also found. The iron ore deposits of Minas Gerais are exceeded by those of the Amazon region, principally in the Carajás areas where deposits are estimated at 35,000 million tonnes.

Electric power production in 1994 was 52,000 m Kwh. In 1995, the total output of pig iron was 25,377,900 tonnes and production of crude petroleum was 35,965,658 tonnes. Brazil is the world's largest producer of coffee; the other main agriculture products are cassava, maize, soya, rice, wheat, black beans, potatoes, cotton, cocoa, tobacco and peanuts.

Since the return to civilian rule in 1985 successive governments have attempted to curb high inflation and large budget deficits. In February 1994 the government and Congress agreed the first balanced budget in 20 years and created a US$16 billion social emergency fund. An interim currency pegged to the US dollar, known as the Real Unit Value, was introduced in March 1994 and replaced by a new non-inflationary currency, the real, in July 1994.

By mid-1995 reduced inflation had brought economic stabilization and an increase in foreign exchange reserves to US$40,000 million. Privatization was reactivated and the oil industry, telecommunications, electricity supplies, gas distribution and coastal shipping have been opened to private investment. In 1994 Brazil signed an agreement to reschedule its US$52,000 million debt to 750 foreign commercial banks.
GNP – US$579,787 million (1995); US$3,640 per capita (1995)
GDP – US$473,846 million (1992); US$2,528 per capita (1992)
ANNUAL AVERAGE GROWTH OF GDP – 5.7 per cent (1994)
INFLATION RATE – 84.4 per cent (1995)
UNEMPLOYMENT – 6.2 per cent (1993)
TOTAL EXTERNAL DEBT – US$159,130 million (1995)

TRADE

Principal imports are fuel and lubricants, machinery, mineral products, chemicals, wheat, metals and metal manufactures. Principal exports are industrial goods, coffee, iron ore, soya, meat, steel and orange juice. In 1994 the Brazilian automobile industry produced 1,400,000 vehicles. Of these, 374,000 vehicles were exported. The main trading partners are the USA and the EU.

Trade with UK	1995	1996
Imports from UK	£674,502,000	£846,505,000
Exports to UK	986,520,000	983,041,000

COMMUNICATIONS

There are 1,670,148 km of highways and the route-length of railways is 30,129 km. There are ten international airports and internal air services are highly developed. There are 21,944 miles of navigable inland waterways. Rio de Janeiro and Santos are the two leading ports.

EDUCATION

The education system includes both public and private institutions. Public education is free at all levels.
ILLITERACY RATE – 16.7 per cent
ENROLMENT (percentage of age group) – primary 91 per cent; secondary 20 per cent; tertiary 11.4 per cent (1994)

BRUNEI
Negara Brunei Darussalam

AREA – 2,226 sq. miles (5,765 sq. km)
POPULATION – 305,100 (1996 official estimate): 66.9 per cent Malay, 15.2 per cent Chinese and 5.9 per cent indigenous races, 12 per cent European, Indian and other races. The majority are Sunni Muslims
CAPITAL – Bandar Seri Begawan (population, 49,902, 1994)
CURRENCY – Brunei dollar (B$) of 100 sen (fully interchangeable with Singapore currency)
NATIONAL ANTHEM – Allah Peliharakan Sultan (God Bless His Majesty)
NATIONAL DAY – 23 February
NATIONAL FLAG – Yellow with diagonal stripes of white over black and the arms in red all over the centre
LIFE EXPECTANCY (years) – male 70.13; female 72.69
POPULATION GROWTH RATE – 2.5 per cent (1994)
POPULATION DENSITY – 49 per sq. km (1994)
URBAN POPULATION – 66.6 per cent (1991)
MILITARY EXPENDITURE – 6.0 per cent of GDP (1995)
MILITARY PERSONNEL – 7,300: Army 3,900, Navy 700, Air Force 400, Paramilitaries 2,300
ILLITERACY RATE – 11.8 per cent
ENROLMENT (percentage of age group) – primary 90 per cent (1994); secondary 61 per cent (1994); tertiary 6.0 per cent (1992)

Brunei is situated on the north-west coast of the island of Borneo. It has a humid tropical climate.

HISTORY AND POLITICS

In 1959 the Sultan promulgated the first written constitution, which provides for a Privy Council, a Council of Ministers and a Legislative Council. On 1 January 1984 Brunei resumed full independence from Britain. A ministerial system of government was established with ministers being appointed by the Sultan and responsible to him. The Sultan presides over the Privy Council and the Council of Ministers. The Legislative Council was disbanded in 1984. The Sultan effectively rules by decree as a state of emergency has been in effect since a revolt in 1962.

HEAD OF STATE
HM The Sultan of Brunei, HM Sultan Haji Hassanal Bolkiah Mu'izzaddin Waddaullah, Sultan and Yang Di-Pertuan, GCB, *acceded* 1967, *crowned* 1 August 1968

COUNCIL OF MINISTERS *as at July 1997*
Prime Minister, Defence, Finance, HM The Sultan
Communications, Pehin Dato Haji Zakaria
Culture, Youth and Sports, Pehin Dato Haji Hussain
Development, Pengiran Dato Dr Ismail
Education, Pehin Dato Abdul Aziz
Foreign Affairs, HRH Prince Mohamed
Health, Dato Dr Johar
Industry and Primary Resources, Pehin Dato Abdul Rahman
Law, Pengiran Bahrin
Religious Affairs, Pehin Dato Mohammed Zain
Special Adviser to the Sultan, Home Affairs, Pehin Dato Haji Isa

BRUNEI DARUSSALAM HIGH COMMISSION
19–20 Belgrave Square, London SW1X 8PG
Tel 0171-581 0521
High Commissioner, HE Pehin Dato Jaya Abdul Latif, apptd 1997

BRITISH HIGH COMMISSION
Hong Kong and Shanghai Bank Building (3rd Floor), Jalan Pemancha, PO Box 2197 Bandar Seri Begawan
Tel: Bandar Seri Begawan 222231
High Commissioner, HE Ivan Callan, CMG, apptd 1994

BRITISH COUNCIL REPRESENTATIVE, T. Walsh, 45 Simpang 100, Jalan Tungku Link, Gadong 3192

ECONOMY

The economy is based on the production of oil and natural gas by Brunei Shell Petroleum. Royalties and taxes from these operations form the bulk of government revenue and have enabled the construction of free health, education and welfare services. The country has eight hospitals, 350 schools and one university. Brunei's main road connects the capital with Kuala Belait in the centre of the oil fields. Royal Brunei Airlines operates scheduled flights to the UK, Australia and throughout the Far East. Radio Television Brunei broadcasts one colour television and three radio channels from the capital.

In 1995 Brunei produced 7,738,000 tonnes of crude petroleum and 9,350 cubic metres of natural gas. In 1991 imports totalled US$1,111 million and exports US$2,480 million.
GNP – US$3,975 million (1994); US$14,240 per capita (1994)
GDP – US$3,683 million (1992); US$14,516 per capita (1992)

Trade with UK	1995	1996
Imports from UK	£254,282,000	£562,396,000
Exports to UK	125,918,000	291,711,000

BULGARIA
Republika Bulgaria

AREA – 42,823 sq. miles (110,912 sq. km). Neighbours: Romania (north), Serbia and the former Yugoslav Republic of Macedonia (west), Greece and Turkey (south)
POPULATION – 8,443,000 (1994 UN estimate). The language is Bulgarian, a Southern Slavonic tongue closely allied to Serbo-Croat and Russian with local admixtures of modern Greek, Albanian and Turkish words. The alphabet is Cyrillic. The predominant religion is the Bulgarian Orthodox Church
CAPITAL – Sofia (population, 1,189,641, 1992 estimate)

MAJOR CITIES – ΨVarna (314,357), on the Black Sea; ΨBourgas (210,788), on the Black Sea; Plovdiv (341,374); Roussé (186,869); Plévène (160,383); Stara Zagora (175,385); Slivène (144,045) and Dobritch (104,485); 1992 estimates
CURRENCY – Lev of 100 stotinki
NATIONAL DAY – 3 March
NATIONAL FLAG – Three horizontal bands, white, green, red
LIFE EXPECTANCY (years) – male 67.61; female 74.39
POPULATION GROWTH RATE – – 1.6 per cent (1994)
POPULATION DENSITY – 76 per sq. km (1994)
URBAN POPULATION – 67.2 per cent (1992)

HISTORY AND POLITICS

A principality of Bulgaria was created by the Treaty of Berlin 1878. In 1908 the country was declared an independent kingdom. In September 1944 a coup d'état gave power to the Fatherland Front, a coalition of Communists, Agrarians and Social Democrats. In August 1945, the main body of Agrarians and Social Democrats left the government. A referendum in September 1946 led to the abolition of the monarchy and the setting up of a republic.

The post-war period was dominated by the Communist Party (BCP), led by Todor Zhivkov. He was forced to resign in November 1989, and in January 1990 the National Assembly voted to abolish the BCP's constitutional guarantee of power. Multiparty elections to a Grand National Assembly (parliament) were held in June 1990 and won by the BCP, renamed the Bulgarian Socialist Party, which formed a government which lasted two months. A multiparty government was formed in December 1990 which began to implement a programme of economic and political reform.

A new constitution, enshrining democracy and the free market was adopted by the Grand National Assembly on 12 July 1991.

After legislative elections in October 1991 a coalition government of the Union of Democratic Forces (UDF) and the Turkish Movement for Rights and Freedom Party (MRF) was formed. The government was replaced in December 1992 by a weak government of non-party technocrats which also collapsed. The BSP won the ensuing general election in December 1994 and formed a government with the Agrarian National Union (ANU). In November 1996 the UDF candidate, Petar Stoyanov, became president. The following month the BSP Prime Minister Jan Videnov resigned following protests about falling standards of living. The UDF beat the BSP in the resulting elections in April 1997.

HEAD OF STATE
President, Petar Stoyanov, *elected* 3 November 1996

COUNCIL OF MINISTERS *as at July 1997*
Prime Minister, Ivan Kostov
Deputy PM, Industry, Aleksandur Bozhkov
Deputy PM, Regional and Urban Development, Evgeniy Bakhurdzhiev
Deputy PM, Education and Science, Veselin Metodiev
Agriculture, Forestry and Agrarian Reform, Ventsislav Vurbanov
Culture, Ema Moskova
Defence, Georgi Ananiev
Environment, Evdokiya Maneva
Finance, Muravey Radev
Foreign Affairs, Nadezhda Mikhaylova
Health, Petur Boyadzhiev
Interior, Bogomil Bonev
Justice and European Legal Integration, Vasil Gotsev

Labour and Social Policy, Ivan Neikov
State Administration, Mario Tagarinski
Trade and Tourism, Valentin Vasilev
Transport, Wilhelm Kraus

EMBASSY OF THE REPUBLIC OF BULGARIA
186–188 Queen's Gate, London SW7 5HL
Tel 0171–584 9400/9433
Ambassador Extraordinary and Plenipotentiary, HE Stefan Tafrov, apptd 1995
Counsellor (Commercial/Economic), D. Georgiev
Military, Air and Naval Attaché, Capt. Ivan Mladenov Yordanov

BRITISH EMBASSY
38 Boulevard Vassil Levski, Sofia
Tel: Sofia 492 3361/2
Ambassador Extraordinary and Plenipotentiary, HE Roger Short, MVO, apptd 1994
Deputy Head of Mission, Consul and First Secretary, J. F. Gunn
Defence Attaché, Col. M. I. V. Dore
First Secretary (Commercial), M. J. Carbine

BRITISH COUNCIL REPRESENTATIVE, K. Lewis, 7 Tulovo Street, 1504, Sofia

DEFENCE

The Army has 1,550 main battle tanks, 164 armoured infrantry fighting vehicles, 1,894 armoured personnel carriers and 2,052 artillery pieces. The Navy has two submarines, one frigate, 23 patrol and coastal vessels, and nine armed helicopters. The Air Force has 272 combat aircraft and 44 attack helicopters.
MILITARY EXPENDITURE – 3.3 per cent of GDP (1995)
MILITARY PERSONNEL – 81,800: Army 51,600, Navy 6,100, Air Force 20,100, Paramilitaries 4,000
CONSCRIPTION DURATION – 18 months

ECONOMY

The principal crops are wheat, maize, beet, tomatoes, tobacco, oleaginous seeds, fruit, vegetables and cotton. The livestock includes cattle, sheep, goats, pigs, horses, asses, mules and water buffaloes. Cadmium, coal, copper, pig iron, kaolin, lead, silver and zinc are produced.

Privatization has proceeded slowly, with only 30 to 40 large- and medium-sized enterprises being privatized by 1995. The lack of radical economic reform has hampered economic development; annual inflation in 1994–5 was 120 per cent and unemployment 20 per cent. In the first half of 1996, the lev lost 70 per cent of its value and food shortages were commonplace. The government responded by adopting a radical reform package including the closure of 70 state companies. The economy sunk further in the second half of 1996, with interest rates and inflation both reaching 300 per cent a year.
GNP – US$11,225 million (1995); US$1,330 per capita (1995)
GDP – US$17,712 million (1992); US$1,070 per capita (1992)
UNEMPLOYMENT – 11.1 per cent (1995)
TOTAL EXTERNAL DEBT – US$10,887 million (1995)

TRADE

The principal imports are fuels, minerals and metals, engineering goods and industrial equipment. The principal exports are agricultural produce, engineering goods and industrial equipment, industrial consumer goods, chemicals and fuels, minerals and metals.

The European Union and industralized nations are now Bulgaria's most important trade partners. In 1993 Bulgaria signed an Association Agreement with the EU, and EU duties on Bulgarian industrial goods were abolished by 1995 and levies on agricultural goods significantly lowered.

In 1994 Bulgaria had a trade surplus of US$152 million and a current account surplus of US$139 million. The principal trading partners are Russia and Germany.

Trade with UK	1995	1996
Imports from UK	£104,224,000	£87,260,000
Exports to UK	118,550,000	116,018,000

EDUCATION

Education is free and compulsory for children from seven to 15 years inclusive. There are three universities (at Sofia, Plovdiv and Veliko Turnovo), an American University and 21 higher educational establishments.

ILLITERACY RATE – 1.7 per cent

ENROLMENT (percentage of age group) – primary 83 per cent; secondary 58 per cent; tertiary 34.3 per cent (1994)

BURKINA FASO

AREA – 105,792 sq. miles (274,000 sq. km). Neighbours: Mali (west), Niger and Benin (east), Togo, Ghana and Côte d'Ivoire (south)

POPULATION – 9,889,000 (1994 UN estimate). The official language is French

CAPITAL – Ouagadougou (population, 634,479, 1991 estimate)

MAJOR CITIES – Bobo-Dioulasso (228,668); Koudougou (30,000)

CURRENCY – Franc CFA

NATIONAL DAY – 11 December

NATIONAL FLAG – Equal bands of red over green, with a yellow star in centre

LIFE EXPECTANCY (years) – male 45.84; female 49.01

POPULATION GROWTH RATE – 2.4 per cent (1994)

POPULATION DENSITY – 36 per sq. km (1994)

URBAN POPULATION – 14.9 per cent (1994)

MILITARY EXPENDITURE – 2.4 per cent of GDP (1995)

MILITARY PERSONNEL – 10,000: Army 5,600, Air Force 200, Paramilitaries 4,200

ILLITERACY RATE – 80.8 per cent

ENROLMENT (percentage of age group) – primary 32 per cent; secondary 7 per cent; tertiary 1.0 per cent (1993)

Burkina Faso (formerly Upper Volta) is an inland savannah state in West Africa. The largest tribe is the Mossi whose king, the Moro Naba, still wields a certain moral influence.

HISTORY AND POLITICS

Burkina Faso was annexed by France in 1896 and between 1932 and 1947 was administered as part of the Colony of the Ivory Coast. It decided on 11 December 1958 to remain an autonomous republic within the French Community; full independence outside the Community was proclaimed on 5 August 1960.

In 1966 the Army assumed power, a new constitution allowing for a partial return to civilian rule was adopted in 1970, but in 1974 this was suspended. Full legislative and presidential elections were held again in 1978.

Following a number of military coups, Capt. Blaise Compaoré seized power in 1987. A new constitution was adopted in 1991. Presidential elections were held in December 1991 and won by Capt. Compaoré in the face of a boycott by the main opposition parties, who were unhappy with the new constitution. Opposition parties also boycotted the legislative elections held in May 1992, which were won by Compaoré's Organization for Popular Democracy-Labour Movement (ODP-MT) party; it formed the government in coalition with several smaller parties.

HEAD OF STATE

President, Capt. Blaise Compaoré, assumed office October 1987, elected December 1991

COUNCIL OF MINISTERS as at July 1997

Prime Minister, Economy and Finance, Kadré Désiré Ouedraogo

Agriculture and Animal Resources, Michel Koutaba

Basic and Mass Education, Banworo Seydou Sanou

Civil Service and Administrative Organization, Juliette Bonkoungou

Communications and Culture, Mahamoudou Ouedraogo

Defence, Col. Badaye Fayama

Employment, Labour, Social Security, Elie Sare

Energy and Mines, Elie Ouedraogo

External Relations, Ablassé Ouedraogo

Health, Christophe Dabire

Integration and African Solidarity, Hermann Yameogo

Justice, Keeper of the Seals, Larba Yarga

Public Works, Housing, Town Planning, Joseph Kabore

Relations with Parliament, Thomas Sanou

Secondary and Higher Education, Scientific Research, Mélégué Maurice Traore

Social Affairs and Family, Bana Ouandaogo

Territorial Administration and Security, Yéro Boly

Trade, Industry and Cottage Industry, Talata Dominique Kafando

Transport and Tourism, Viviane Compaoré

Water and Environment, Salif Diallo

Youth and Sports, Joseph André Tiendrebeogo

EMBASSY OF BURKINA FASO

16 Place Guy d'Arezzo, 1060 Brussels, Belgium

Tel: Brussels 345 9912

Ambassador Extraordinary and Plenipotentiary, HE Youssouf Ouedraogo, apptd 1995, resident in Brussels

HONORARY CONSULATE, 5 Cinnamon Row, Plantation Wharf, London SW11 3TW. Tel: 0171-738 1800. Honorary Consul-General, S. G. Singer

BRITISH AMBASSADOR, HE Margaret Rothwell, CMG, resident at Abidjan, Côte d'Ivoire

ECONOMY

The principal industry is cattle and sheep rearing. Agriculture employs one fifth of the workforce and contributes 10 per cent of GDP. The chief exports are livestock, groundnuts, millet and sorghum. Small deposits of gold, manganese, copper, bauxite and graphite have been found.

In 1993 Burkina Faso had a trade deficit of US$367 million and a current account deficit of US$118 million.

GNP – US$2,417 million (1995); US$230 per capita (1995)

GDP – US$2,343 million (1992); US$258 per capita (1992)

ANNUAL AVERAGE GROWTH OF GDP – 13.1 per cent (1985)

INFLATION RATE – 7.4 per cent (1995)

TOTAL EXTERNAL DEBT – US$1,267 million (1995)

Trade with UK	1995	1996
Imports from UK	£8,881,000	£11,283,000
Exports to UK	398,000	1,015,000

BURUNDI
République de Burundi

AREA – 10,747 sq. miles (27,834 sq. km)
POPULATION – 6,134,000 (1994 UN estimate): 83 per cent Hutu, 15 per cent Tutsi. The official languages are Kirundi, a Bantu language, and French. Kiswahili is also used
CAPITAL – Bujumbura (formerly Usumbura) (population, 235,440, 1994)
MAJOR CITIES – Kitega (18,000)
CURRENCY – Burundi franc of 100 centimes
NATIONAL DAY – 1 July
NATIONAL FLAG – Divided diagonally by a white saltire into red and green triangles; on a white disc in the centre three red six-pointed stars edged in green
LIFE EXPECTANCY (years) – male 48.42; female 51.92
POPULATION GROWTH RATE – 2.9 per cent (1994)
POPULATION DENSITY – 220 per sq. km (1994)
URBAN POPULATION – 6.3 per cent (1990)
MILITARY EXPENDITURE – 5.3 per cent of GDP (1995)
MILITARY PERSONNEL – 22,000: Army 18,500, Paramilitaries 3,500
ILLITERACY RATE – 62.2 per cent
ENROLMENT (percentage of age group) – primary 51 per cent; secondary 5 per cent; tertiary 0.8 per cent (1992)

HISTORY AND POLITICS

Formerly a Belgian trusteeship under the United Nations, Burundi became independent as a constitutional monarchy on 1 July 1962. However, the monarchy was overthrown in 1966 and the country became a republic. In 1987 the government was overthrown by a Military Committee of National Redemption led by Maj. Pierre Buyoya.

Although most of the population is Hutu, political and military power has traditionally rested with the Tutsi minority. Hutu attempts to overthrow Tutsi rule have resulted in ethnic massacres since the 1960s. The National Unity and Progress Party (UPRONA) government attempted to introduce multiparty non-tribal politics in 1991–2. This was approved by national referendum in March 1992.

In June 1993 Melchior Ndadaye, a Hutu, was elected president and the opposition Front for Democracy in Burundi (FRODEBU) won the legislative elections. However, the identification of the FRODEBU government with Hutu interests led the Tutsi-dominated army to attempt a coup in October 1993 in which President Ndadaye was killed. The government regained control in December but two months of inter-racial fighting left 50,000–100,000 dead and 500,000, mainly Hutu, refugees in neighbouring states. Ndadye was succeeded by Cyprien Ntaryamira (Hutu), who was killed in April 1994.

FRODEBU and UPRONA agreed to form a coalition government in February 1994 with a Tutsi prime minister and Hutu president. The constitution was amended to specifiy that the 25-member Cabinet must include ten Tutsi, ten Hutu and five neutral ministers. However, the government was unable to halt attacks by the Tutsi-dominated army and Hutu militias on each other's communities. The fighting claimed 200,000 lives in 1993–5 and more than 100 lives a week in 1996.

In July 1996 the army again seized power and installed Maj. Pierre Buyoya (Tutsi) as president. Political parties were banned and the National Assembly was suspended until October 1996 when fewer than half its deputies attended. A multi-ethnic government of national unity was formed in August 1996. Clashes between the army and Hutu militias, and massacres of civilians have continued in 1997. Many Hutus remain in camps in Tanzania and the Democratic Republic of Congo. *See also* Events of the Year and Democratic Republic of Congo.

HEAD OF STATE
President, Maj. Pierre Buyoya, *appointed* 25 July 1996

COUNCIL OF MINISTERS *as at July 1997*
Prime Minister, Pascal Firmin Ndimira
Agriculture and Livestock, Damase Ntiranyibagira
Basic Education and Adult Literacy, Joseph Ndayisaba
Commerce, Industry and Tourism, Grégoire Banyiyezako
Communal Development, Pierre Bambasi
Communications, Pierre-Claver Ndayicariye
Defence, Lt.-Col. Firmin Sinzoyiheba
Development Planning and Reconstruction, Evariste Minani
Energy and Mines, Bernard Barandereka
Finance, Gérard Niyibigira
Foreign Affairs and Co-operation, Luc Rukingama
Health, Juma Kariburyo
Human Rights, Social Action and Women's Promotion, Christine Ruhaza
Institutional Reforms and Relations with the National Assembly, Eugène Nindorera
Interior and Public Security, Epitace Bayaganakandi
Justice, Térence Siniyunguruza
Public Service, Monique Ndakozé
Public Works and Equipment, Vital Nzobonimpa
Relocation and Resettlement of Displaced Persons and Refugees, Pascal Nkurunziza
Secondary Education, Higher Education and Scientific Research, Rogatien Ndoricimpa
Secretary of State with responsibility for Co-operation, Léonidas Havyarimana
Secretary of State with responsibility for Security, Prime Kaziguye
Territorial Management and Environment, Samuel Bigawa
Transport, Posts and Telecommunications, Vénérand Nzohabonayo
Work, Handicrafts and Professional Training, Barnabé Muteragiranwa
Youth, Sports and Culture, Bonaventure Gasutwa

EMBASSY OF THE REPUBLIC OF BURUNDI
Square Marie Louise 46, 1040 Brussels, Belgium
Tel: Brussels 2304535
Ambassador Extraordinary and Plenipotentiary, Ndoricampa Leonidas, resident in Brussels
BRITISH AMBASSADOR, HE Kaye Oliver, OBE, resident at Kigali, Rwanda

ECONOMY

The chief crop is coffee, representing about 80 per cent of export earnings. Cotton is the second most important crop. Mineral, tea, hide and skin exports are also important.

A total economic blockade was imposed by Cameroon, Ethiopia, Kenya, Rwanda, Tanzania, Uganda and Zaïre following the 1996 coup.
GNP – US$984 million (1995); US$160 per capita (1995)
GDP – US$1,228 million (1992); US$181 per capita (1992)
ANNUAL AVERAGE GROWTH OF GDP – 2.3 per cent (1992)
INFLATION RATE – 19.2 per cent (1995)
TOTAL EXTERNAL DEBT – US$1,157 million (1995)

TRADE WITH UK	1995	1996
Imports from UK	£3,339,000	£2,439,000
Exports to UK	3,670,000	2,712,000

CAMBODIA

AREA – 69,898 sq. miles (181,035 sq. km)
POPULATION – 10,600,000 (1997 estimate)
CAPITAL – ΨPhnom Penh (population, 832,000, 1997)
CURRENCY – Riel of 100 sen
NATIONAL ANTHEM – Nokoreach
NATIONAL DAY – 9 November (Independence Day)
NATIONAL FLAG – Three horizontal stripes of blue, red,
   blue, with the blue of double width and containing a
   representation of the temple of Angkor in white
LIFE EXPECTANCY (years) – male 50.10; female 52.90
POPULATION GROWTH RATE – 2.8 per cent (1994)
POPULATION DENSITY – 53 per sq. km (1994)
URBAN POPULATION – 12.6 per cent (1990)
MILITARY EXPENDITURE – 4.7 per cent of GDP (1995)
MILITARY PERSONNEL – 37,700: Army 36,000, Navy
   1,200, Air Force 500
CONSCRIPTION DURATION – Not implemented since
   1993
ILLITERACY RATE – 34.7 per cent
ENROLMENT (percentage of age group) – tertiary 1.4 per
   cent (1994)

HISTORY AND POLITICS

Cambodia became a French protectorate in 1863 and was
granted independence within the French Union as an
Associate State in 1949. Full independence was proclaimed
on 9 November 1953. From 1955 the political life of the
country was dominated by Prince Norodom Sihanouk,
first as king, then as head of government after he had
abdicated in favour of his father and finally (following his
father's death in 1960) as head of state. In March 1970
Prince Sihanouk was deposed and a Khmer Republic was
declared in October 1970.

In April 1975 Phnom Penh fell to the North Vietnamese-backed Khmer Rouge after a five-year civil war. A
new government led by Pol Pot, the leader of the Khmer
Rouge (Communist) party, was appointed and the state
was renamed Democratic Kampuchea. During Khmer
Rouge rule hundreds of thousands of Cambodians fled
into exile and an estimated two million were killed.

In December 1978 Vietnamese troops invaded Cambo-
dia, capturing Phnom Penh on 7 January 1979. The
following day the Cambodian National United Front for
National Salvation established a People's Revolutionary
Council. The state was renamed The People's Republic of
Kampuchea (PRK); in April 1989 it became the State of
Cambodia (SOC). With support from the Vietnamese
army, PRK forces won control of most of the country from
the forces of the Coalition Government of Democratic
Kampuchea (CGDK), formed in June 1982 by the Khmer
Rouge and two non-Communist groups. Following the
Vietnamese withdrawal in 1989, the resistance forces
regained ground.

In September 1990, the SOC and the CGDK established
a Supreme National Council. A permanent cease-fire
began on 23 June and peace agreements were signed on 23
October 1991. In March 1992 the United Nations Transitional Authority for Cambodia (UNTAC) assumed
authority from the SOC government in the run-up to the
May 1993 elections.

Multiparty elections were held in May 1993 for 120
National Assembly seats. Prince Sihanouk brokered a
coalition government agreement between FUNCINPEC
and the Cambodian People's Party (CPP) (the former SOC
party) under which he became head of state and FUN-

CINPEC and CPP leaders Prince Ranariddh and Hun Sen
became co-prime ministers. In September 1993 the National Assembly adopted a new constitution under which
Cambodia became a pluralist liberal democracy with a
constitutional monarchy. Prince Sihanouk was elected
king and he appointed a new government. Prince Ranariddh was ousted from power following a coup by soldiers
loyal to Hun Sen in July 1997. *See also* Events of the Year.

INSURGENCIES

In July 1994 the Royal Government outlawed the Khmer
Rouge, which responded by declaring a provisional
government. Large numbers of Khmer Rouge have
defected to the Royal Government including more than
2,500 Khmer Rouge members, led by Ieng Sary, who
formally joined the Royal Cambodian Armed Forces in
November 1996. Khmer Rouge leader Pol Pot was
captured by a group of defectors in June 1997.

About 3,000 Khmer Rouge members are still active in
northern Cambodia and control 5 per cent of the territory.
See also Events of the Year.

POLITICAL SYSTEM

Legislative power is vested in the National Assembly,
executive power in the Royal Government, with the King
having the power only to make appointments and declare a
state of emergency, in consultation with the government.

HEAD OF STATE

HM The King of Cambodia, Norodom Sihanouk, *elected by the
   Council of the Throne* 24 September 1993

BRITISH EMBASSY

29, Street 75, Phnom Penh
Tel: Phnom Penh 427124
Ambassador Extraordinary and Plenipotentiary, HE George
   Edgar, apptd 1997

ECONOMY

The economy is based on agriculture, fishing and forestry.
In addition to rice, which is the staple crop, the major

products are rubber, livestock, maize, timber, pepper, palm sugar, fresh and dried fish, kapok, beans, soya and tobacco. Rice and rubber used to be the main exports, though production was brought to a standstill by the hostilities.

Under the Khmer Rouge, the urban population was forced to work on the land, and re-establish plantations producing such crops as cotton, rubber and bananas. Following the Vietnamese invasion of 1978 the towns were repopulated and factories, in particular textile mills, iron smelting works and cement works, were put back in production.

A Cambodian Development Council was created in 1994 to encourage foreign investment although political instability has deterred investors.

GNP – US$2,718 million (1995); US$270 per capita (1995)
GDP – US$922 million (1992); US$105 per capita (1992)
TOTAL EXTERNAL DEBT – US$2,031 million (1995)

TRADE WITH UK	1995	1996
Imports from UK	£2,989,000	£3,343,000
Exports to UK	7,531,000	21,932,000

COMMUNICATIONS

The country had over 5,000 kilometres of roads, of which nearly half were hard-surfaced and passable in the rainy season, although now in a state of disrepair. There are two railways, one from Phnom Penh to the Thai border, the other from Phnom Penh to Kampot and Sihanoukville (Kompong Som), but operations and repairs are hindered by occasional Khmer Rouge attacks. Phnom Penh is on a river capable of receiving ships of up to 2,500 tons all the year round. The deep water port at Sihanoukville (Kompong Som) on the Gulf of Thailand can receive ships up to 10,000 tons. The port is linked to Phnom Penh by a modern highway.

CAMEROON
République du Cameroun

AREA – 183,569 sq. miles (475,442 sq. km). Neighbours: Nigeria (west), Chad and the Central African Republic (east), Republic of Congo, Gabon and Equatorial Guinea (south)
POPULATION – 12,871,000 (1994 UN estimate). French and English are both official languages and enjoy equal status
CAPITAL – Yaoundé (population, 653,670, 1986 estimate)
MAJOR CITIES – ΨDouala (1,029,736) is the commercial centre
CURRENCY – Franc CFA of 100 centimes
NATIONAL ANTHEM – O Cameroun, Berceau de Nos Ancêtres (O Cameroon, thou cradle of our forefathers)
NATIONAL DAY – 20 May
NATIONAL FLAG – Vertical stripes of green, red and yellow with single five-pointed yellow star in centre of red stripe
LIFE EXPECTANCY (years) – male 54.50; female 57.50
POPULATION GROWTH RATE – 2.8 per cent (1994)
POPULATION DENSITY – 27 per sq. km (1994)
MILITARY EXPENDITURE – 1.8 per cent of GDP (1995)
MILITARY PERSONNEL – 22,100: Army 11,500, Navy 1,300, Air Force 300, Paramilitaries 9,000
ILLITERACY RATE – 36.6 per cent
ENROLMENT (percentage of age group) – secondary 15 per cent (1980); tertiary 3.2 per cent (1990)

HISTORY AND POLITICS

The German colony of the Cameroons, established in 1884, was captured by British and French forces in 1916 and divided into the League of Nations-mandated territories (later UN trusteeships) of East (French) and West (British) Cameroon. On 1 January 1960 East Cameroon became independent as the Republic of Cameroon. This was joined on 1 October 1961 by the southern part of West Cameroon after a plebiscite held under United Nations auspices; the northern part joined Nigeria. Cameroon became a federal republic with separate East and West Cameroon state governments. After a plebiscite held in 1972, Cameroon became a unitary republic and a one-party state.

After extensive unrest, multiparty elections were held in March 1992, although they were boycotted by two of the main opposition parties. The ruling People's Democratic Movement emerged short of a parliamentary majority but formed a coalition government with a small opposition party, the Movement for the Defence of the Republic.

Presidential elections were held in October 1992 and won by the incumbent Paul Biya. The results were disputed by opponents and foreign observers, who accused the authorities of malpractice. In November a new coalition government was formed with the addition of the Union for Democracy and Progress and the Union of Peoples of Cameroon. Legislative and presidential elections were due to be held in 1997.

Cameroon joined the Commonwealth in November 1995.

POLITICAL SYSTEM

In May 1993 President Biya published a draft bill on constitutional reform providing for a Council of State, Senate and a Constitutional Court but rejecting a return to a federal state. In December 1995, a constitutional amendment was passed extending the president's term in office from five to seven years and authorizing a maximum of two terms. A Senate was also created.

HEAD OF STATE

President and Commander in Chief of the Armed Forces, Paul Biya, *acceded* 6 November 1982, *elected* 14 January 1984, *re-elected* 24 April 1988, 10 October 1992, *sworn in* 3 November 1992

CABINET *as at September 1996*

Prime Minister, Peter Mafany Musonge
Deputy PM, Territorial Administration, Gilbert Andze Tsoungui
Deputy PM, Housing and Town Planning, Hamadou Mustapha
Agriculture, Augustin Frederic Kodock
Civil Service and Administrative Reform, Sali Dairou
Communication, Augustin Kontchou Kouomegni
Culture, Isaie Charles Toko Mangan
Economy and Finance, Edouard Akame Mfoumouv
Environment and Forests, Joseph Mbede
External Relations, Ferdinand Leopold Oyone
Higher Education, Peter Agbor Tabi
Justice, Laurent Esso
Livestock, Fisheries and Animal Industries, Hamadjoda Adjoudji
Labour and Social Insurance, Simon Mbila
National Education, Robert Mbella Mbappe
Posts and Telecommunications, Dakolle Daissala
Public Health, Titus Edzoa
Public Works, Jean-Baptiste Bokam
Scientific and Technical Research, Bava Djingoer
Social and Women's Affairs, Yaou Aissatou

Superior State Control, Joseph Owona
Tourism, Pierre Souman
Trade and Industrial Development, Justin Ndioro
Transport, Joseph Tsanga Abanda
Water Resources and Energy, Andre Bello Mbele
Youth and Sports, Samuel Makon

EMBASSY OF THE REPUBLIC OF CAMEROON
84 Holland Park, London WII 3SB
Tel 0171–727 0771/3
Ambassador Extraordinary and Plenipotentiary, HE Samuel
   Libock Mbei, apptd 1995

BRITISH HIGH COMMISSION
Avenue Winston Churchill, BP 547 Yaoundé
Tel: Yaoundé 220545
High Commissioner, HE Nicholas McCarthy, MBE, apptd
   1996
There is also a British Consulate at Douala.
BRITISH COUNCIL DIRECTOR, Terence Humphreys,
   Avenue Charles de Gaulle (BP 818), Yaoundé

ECONOMY

Principal products are cocoa, coffee, bananas, cotton,
timber, groundnuts, aluminium, rubber and palm products.
Crude petroleum is also one of Cameroon's principal
products, although production dropped from 8.3 million
tonnes in 1990 to 5 million tonnes in 1995.

In 1993 most foreign donors suspended aid after an IMF
structural adjustment plan lapsed in 1992. The IMF agreed
to resume support of an improved economic reform
programme with the approval of standby credits totalling
US$214 million in 1994–5.

France, Spain and other European Union states are
Cameroon's main trading partners. In 1993 the govern-
ment had a budget deficit equivalent to 1.68 per cent of
GDP. There was a trade surplus of US$502 million and a
current account deficit of US$565 million. In 1994 exports
totalled US$1,360 million and imports US$728 million.
GNP – US$8,615 million (1995); US$650 per capita (1995)
GDP – US$13,373 million (1992); US$1,152 per capita
   (1992)
ANNUAL AVERAGE GROWTH OF GDP – 2.1 per cent (1990)
INFLATION RATE – 13.9 per cent (1995)
TOTAL EXTERNAL DEBT – US$9,350 million (1995)

TRADE WITH UK	1995	1996
Imports from UK	£25,234,000	£33,745,000
Exports to UK	31,328,000	42,682,000

CANADA

AREA AND POPULATION

Provinces or Territories (with official contractions)	Area (sq. miles)	Population, census 1996
Alberta (AB)	255,290	2,696,826
British Columbia (BC)	365,950	3,724,500
Manitoba (MB)	250,950	1,113,898
New Brunswick (NB)	28,360	738,133
Newfoundland and Labrador (NF)	156,650	551,792
Nova Scotia (NS)	21,420	909,282
Ontario (ON)	412,580	10,753,573
Prince Edward Island (PE)	2,180	134,557
Quebec (QC)	594,860	7,138,795
Saskatchewan (SK)	251,870	990,237
Yukon Territory (YT)	186,660	30,766
Northwest Territories (NT)	1,322,900	64,402
Total	3,849,670	28,846,761

Area figures include land and water area

CAPITAL – Ottawa (population, 974,077, 1992 estimate).
   The city population was 313,987 at the 1991 census and
   the population of the metropolitan area of Ottawa–Hull
   was estimated at 1,024,657 in 1995
CURRENCY – Canadian dollar (C$) of 100 cents
NATIONAL ANTHEM – O Canada
NATIONAL DAY – 1 July (Dominion Day)
NATIONAL FLAG – Red maple leaf with 11 points on white
   square, flanked by vertical red bars one-half the width of
   the square
LIFE EXPECTANCY (years) – male 73.02; female 79.79
POPULATION GROWTH RATE – 2.4 per cent (1994)
POPULATION DENSITY – 3 per sq. km (1994)
URBAN POPULATION – 76.6 per cent (1991)

Canada occupies the whole of the northern part of the
North American continent, with the exception of Alaska.
In eastern Canada, the southernmost point is Middle Island
in Lake Erie. Canada has six main physiographic divisions:
the Appalachian-Acadian region, the Canadian shield,
which comprises more than half the country, the St
Lawrence-Great Lakes lowland, the interior plains, the
Cordilleran region and the Arctic archipelago.

The climate of the eastern and central portions presents
greater extremes than in corresponding latitudes in
Europe, but in the south-western portion of the prairie
region and the southern portions of the Pacific slope the
climate is milder.

HISTORY AND POLITICS

Canada was originally discovered by Cabot in 1497 but its
history dates from 1534, when the French took possession
of the country. The first permanent settlement at Port
Royal (now Annapolis), Nova Scotia, was founded in 1605,
and Quebec was founded in 1608. In 1759 Quebec was
captured by British forces under General Wolfe and in
1763 the whole territory of Canada became a possession of
Great Britain by the Treaty of Paris 1763. Nova Scotia was
ceded in 1713 by the Treaty of Utrecht, the provinces of
New Brunswick and Prince Edward Island being subsequently formed out of it. British Columbia was formed
into a Crown colony in 1858, having previously been a part
of the Hudson Bay Territory, and was united to Vancouver
Island in 1866.

The constitution of Canada has its source in the British
North America Act of 1867 which formed a Dominion,
under the name of Canada, of the four provinces of
Ontario, Quebec, New Brunswick and Nova Scotia. To
this federation the other provinces have subsequently been
admitted: Manitoba (1870), British Columbia (1871),
Prince Edward Island (1873), Alberta and Saskatchewan
(1905) and Newfoundland (1949). In 1982, the constitution
was patriated (severed from the British parliament) with
the approval of all provinces except Quebec. In 1985, the
federal prime minister and the provincial premiers concluded the Meech Lake Accord which provided for
Quebec to be recognized as a distinct society within
Canada. However, two provincial legislatures withheld
approval and the accord did not come into force. In
Quebec, a referendum calling for sovereignty and a new
political and economic partnership was defeated in
October 1995.

In the federal election on 2 June 1997 the Liberal Party
was returned to power. The state of parties in the House of
Commons following the election was Liberals 155, Reform Party 60, Bloc Québécois 44, New Democrats 21,
Progressive Conservatives 20, Independent 1.

POLITICAL SYSTEM

Executive power is vested in a Governor-General appointed by the Sovereign on the advice of the Canadian government.

Parliament consists of a Senate and a House of Commons. The Senate consists of 104 members, nominated by the Governor-General, the seats being distributed between the various provinces.

The House of Commons has 301 members and is elected every five years at longest. Representation by provinces is at present: Newfoundland 7, Prince Edward Island 4, Nova Scotia 11, New Brunswick 10, Quebec 75, Ontario 103, Manitoba 14, Saskatchewan 14, Alberta 26, British Columbia 34, Northwest Territories 2, Yukon 1.

The judicature is administered by judges following the civil law in Quebec province and common law in other provinces. Each province has a Court of Appeal. All superior, county and district court judges are appointed by the Governor-General, the others by the Lieutenant-Governors of the provinces.

The highest federal court is the Supreme Court of Canada, which exercises general appellate jurisdiction throughout Canada in civil and criminal cases. There is one other federally constituted court, the Federal Court of Canada, which has jurisdiction on appeals from its trial division, from federal tribunals and reviews of decisions and references by federal boards and commissions.

GOVERNOR-GENERAL
Governor-General and Commander-in-Chief, HE Roméo Le Blanc, CC, CMM, CD

CABINET *as at July 1997*
Prime Minister, Jean Chrétien
Deputy Prime Minister, Herb Gray
Agriculture and Agri-Food, Lyle Vanclief
Canadian Heritage, Sheila Copps
Citizenship and Immigration, Lucienne Robillard
Environment, Christine Stewart
Federal Office of Regional Development-Quebec, Martin Cauchon
Finance, Paul Martin
Fisheries and Oceans, David Anderson
Foreign Affairs, Lloyd Axworthy
Health, Allan Rock
Human Resources Development, Pierre Pettigrew
Indian Affairs and Northern Development, Jane Stewart
Industry, John Manley
Infrastructure, Marcel Massé
Intergovernmental Affairs, Stéphane Dion
International Co-operation and the Francophonie, Diane Marleau
International Trade, Sergio Marchi
Justice and Attorney-General, Anne McLellan
Labour, Lawrence MacAulay
Leader of the Government in the House of Commons, Don Boudria
National Defence, Arthur Eggleton
National Revenue, Herb Dhaliwal
Natural Resources, Ralph Goodale
Public Works and Government Services, Alfonso Gagliano
Transport, David Collenette
Veterans Affairs, Fred Mifflin

CANADIAN HIGH COMMISSION
Macdonald House, 1 Grosvenor Square, London WIX OAB
Tel 0171-258 6600
High Commissioner, HE Roy MacLaren, apptd 1996
Deputy High Commissioner, Jacques Bilodeau
Minister, Tom MacDonald (*Commercial/Economic*)

Defence Adviser, Cdre D. Miller

BRITISH HIGH COMMISSION
80 Elgin Street, Ottawa KIP 5K7
Tel: Ottawa 237 1530
High Commissioner, HE Sir Anthony Goodenough, KCMG, apptd 1996
Deputy High Commissioner, L. J. Duffield
Counsellor, M. Uden (*Economic*)
Defence and Military Adviser, Brig. E. Springfield, CBE
CONSULATES-GENERAL – Montreal, Toronto, Vancouver
CONSULATES – Halifax, St John's, Winnipeg
BRITISH COUNCIL DIRECTOR, Dr S. Lewis (*Cultural Counsellor*)
BRITISH COUNCIL REPRESENTATIVE IN QUEBEC, S. Dawbarn, 1000 ouest rue de la Gauchetière, Montreal, Quebec H3B 4W5

DEFENCE

The Canadian armed forces are unified and organized into three functional commands: Land Force Command; Maritime Command; Air Command.

The Army (Land Forces) has 114 main battle tanks, 1,858 armoured personnel carriers and 269 artillery pieces. The Navy (Maritime Forces) has three submarines, four destroyers, 16 frigates and 14 patrol and coastal vessels. There are naval bases at Halifax and Esquimalt. The Air Force has 141 combat aircraft and 30 armed helicopters.

MILITARY EXPENDITURE – 1.6 per cent of GDP (1995)
MILITARY PERSONNEL – 70,500: Army 21,500, Navy 9,500, Air Force 16,400, Other 23,100

ECONOMY

About 7.3 per cent of the total land area is farmed. Over 60 per cent of this is under cultivation, the remainder being predominantly classified as unimproved pasture. More than 80 per cent of the cultivated land is in the prairie region of Western Canada.

Farm cash receipts from the sale of farm products in 1996 were C$28,379 million. Livestock and animal products contributed C$13,648 million; field crops C$13,846 million; grain and oilseed C$9,538 million.

Canada in 1995–6 produced pelts valued at C$83 million. Wildlife pelts made up 30.2 per cent of the total, with a value of C$25 million.

The marketed value of fish catches in 1994 was C$3,149 million (preliminary).

In 1991 about 42 per cent of the total land area was considered as inventoried forest area. The value of shipments and other revenue from forestry-related industries in 1994 was: logging $10,144.8 million; sawmill and planing mill products $15,075.9 million; shingle and shake $251.1 million, veneer and ply wood $1,402.9 million, and paper and allied products $25,647.8 million.

In 1995, Canada was the world's largest producer of zinc, potash and uranium, the second largest of nickel, asbestos, cadmium and elemental sulphur. The country is also rich in gold, copper, lead, molybdenum, platinum group metals, gypsum, cobalt, titanium concentrates, and aluminium. The total value of mineral production in 1996 was C$49,171.8 million.

Production of gold was 151,257 kg in 1995 and of silver 1,245,939 kg. Uranium production in 1995 was 10,518 tonnes.

GNP – US$573,695 million (1995); US$19,380 per capita (1995)
GDP – US$563,548 million (1992); US$20,600 per capita (1992)
ANNUAL AVERAGE GROWTH OF GDP – 2.3 per cent (1995)

INFLATION RATE – 2.2 per cent (1995)
UNEMPLOYMENT – 9.5 per cent (1995)

TRADE

The main exports in 1996 were passenger automobiles and chassis, motor vehicle parts except engines, lumber and softwood, crude petroleum, trucks, truck tractors and chassis, newsprint paper, other telecommunication and related equipment, wood pulp and similar pulp, natural gas, petroleum and coal products.. Trade with the USA accounts for about 79 per cent of total trade in merchandise.

In 1995 imports totalled US$168,426 million and exports US$192,197 million. In 1994 Canada had a trade surplus of US$12,202 million and a current account deficit of US$17,388 million.

Trade with UK	1995	1996
Imports from UK	£1,811,964,000	£1,974,524,000
Exports to UK	2,379,624,000	2,484,044,000

COMMUNICATIONS

In 1991 there were 290,194 km of federal and provincial territorial roads and highways and 85,563 km of railway track in operation.

The registered shipping on 1 January 1991 including inland vessels, was 43,787 vessels with gross tonnage 4,956,845. The bulk of canal shipping in Canada is handled through the two sections of the St Lawrence Seaway, which provide access to the Great Lakes for ocean-going ships.

EDUCATION

Education is under the control of the provincial governments, the cost of the publicly controlled schools being met by local taxation, aided by provincial grants. Education is compulsory between the ages of five or six and fifteen or sixteen.

In 1992–3 there were 16,063 elementary and secondary schools with 5,287,730 pupils. Of these, 1,515 were private schools, 383 federal schools and 19 special schools for the blind and deaf. In 1992–3 there were 69 degree-granting universities.

ILLITERACY RATE – 3.4 per cent
ENROLMENT (percentage of age group) – primary 97 per cent; secondary 91 per cent; tertiary 102.9 per cent (1993)

Source: for financial and economic statistics, Statistics Canada

YUKON TERRITORY

The area of the Territory is 186,660 sq. miles (483,447 sq. km), with a population of 30,766 (1996). Minerals, government and tourism are the chief industries, followed by transportation, communications and other utilities industries.

SEAT OF GOVERNMENT – Whitehorse, population (1991 census) 17,925

The Yukon Act 1970, as amended, provides for the administration of the Territory by a Commissioner acting under instructions given by the Governor-in-Council or the Minister of Indian Affairs and Northern Development. Legislative powers, analogous to those of a provincial government, are exercised by a Legislative Assembly of 17 members elected from electoral districts in the Territory. The Executive Council of the Assembly consists of the government leader as chairman and five elected members.

Commissioner, J. Gingell
Premier, John Ostashek

NORTHWEST TERRITORIES

The area of the Northwest Territories is 1,322,900 sq. miles (3,426,389 sq. km), with a population of 64,402 (1996). The Northwest Territories are subdivided into the regions of Baffin, Fort Smith, Inuvik, Keewatin, Kitikmeot. The chief industry is mining, particularly lead, zinc, gold, silver and oil exploration and natural gas.

SEAT OF GOVERNMENT – Yellowknife, population (1991 census) 15,179

There is a Legislative Assembly of 24 elected members, of which the Executive Council under the chairmanship of the government leader is the senior decision-making body of the government in the Territory.

In 1992 a referendum approved a plan to divide the Territories into two and to establish in one part a self-governing autonomous Inuit (Eskimo) populated territory known as Nunavat. Nunavat will comprise the present regions of Baffin, Keewatian and Kitikmeot and will be phased in over six years up to 1999. The territory will have its own government and legislature, though neither will have provincial status. It has a population of some 22,000, of which 80 per cent are Inuit, and covers some 850,000 sq. miles (2,201,500 sq. km).

Commissioner, D. Norris
Government Leader, N. Cournoyea

CANADIAN PROVINCES

ALBERTA

Alberta has an area of 255,290 sq. miles (661,198 sq. km), including about 6,485 sq. miles of water (16,796 sq. km), with a population of 2,696,826 (1996).

PROVINCIAL CAPITAL – Edmonton, city population 616,306, metropolitan area, 862,597. Other centres are Calgary (768,082), Lethbridge (63,053), Red Deer (60,075), Medicine Hat (46,783), St Albert (46,888), 1996.

GOVERNMENT

The Government is vested in a Lieutenant-Governor and Legislative Assembly composed of 83 members, elected for five years. The Progressive Conservative Party formed the last government.

Lt.-Governor, H. A. Olson
Premier, President of Executive Council, Ralph Klein

ECONOMY

The total GDP at factor cost in 1995 amounted to C$77,458 million. Preliminary estimates for mineral production in 1995 came to C$21,085 million. Of this total, crude oil and natural gas amounted to C$20,004 million.

The total value of manufacturing shipments (1995) was C$27,160 million. The leading industrial products are refined petroleum and coal products, meat and meat products, chemicals and chemical products, fabricated metal products, non-metallic mineral products and primary metals.

BRITISH COLUMBIA

British Columbia has an area of 365,950 sq. miles (947,806 sq. km), with a population of 3,724,500 (1996).

PROVINCIAL CAPITAL – ΨVictoria, metropolitan population 304,287. Other principal cities are ΨVancouver (metropolitan population 1,831,665), Prince George, Kamloops, Kelowna and Nanaimo.

GOVERNMENT

The government consists of a Lieutenant-Governor and an Executive Council together with a Legislative Assembly of 75 members. The New Democratic Party formed a government after a general election on 28 May 1996.
Lt.-Governor, Garde B. Gardom
Premier, Glen Clark

AGENT-GENERAL'S OFFICE IN LONDON, British Columbia House, 1 Regent Street, London SW1Y 4NS.
Agent-General, Paul King

ECONOMY

Service industries generate 72 per cent of provincial GDP and account for over 76 per cent of employment. Manufacturing activity is based largely on the processing of the output of the logging, mineral, fishing and agriculture industries.

British Columbia is the leading provincial producer of timber and sawmill products. Mining, the second most important non-service activity, is based on copper, zinc, lead, iron concentrates, molybdenum, coal, natural gas, crude petroleum, asbestos, gold and silver. Molybdenum production is approximately 96 per cent of the Canadian total.

The most important agricultural products are livestock, eggs and poultry, fruits and dairy products.

MANITOBA

Manitoba, originally the Red River settlement, is the central province of Canada. The province has a large area of prairie land but also has 401 miles (645 kilometres) of coastline on Hudson Bay, large lakes and rivers covering an area of 39,225 sq. miles (101,592 sq. km). The total area is 250,950 sq. miles (649,957 sq. km), with a population of 1,113,898 (1996).

PROVINCIAL CAPITAL   Winnipeg, population 652,355). Other cities are Brandon (38,567), Thompson (14,977), Portage la Prairie (13,186) and Flin Flon (7,119), 1991.

GOVERNMENT

The Lieutenant-Governor is The Queen's representative in Manitoba. There is a Legislative Assembly of 57 members, of which the Executive Council of Ministers are all members.

The Progressive Conservatives formed a majority government after a general election held on 25 April 1995.
Lt.-Governor, W. Yvon Dumont
Premier, Gary A. Filmon

ECONOMY

Of the total land area, 19,126,517 acres are in occupied farms. The estimated GDP value of agriculture in 1996 was C$5,971 million.

The chief manufacturing centres are Winnipeg, Brandon, Selkirk and Portage la Prairie. The largest manufacturing industry is the food and beverage industry, followed by transportation equipment and primary metal industries.

NEW BRUNSWICK

New Brunswick is one of the eastern maritime provinces. It has a total area of 28,360 sq. miles (73,452 sq. km), with a population of 762,602 (1997).

PROVINCIAL CAPITAL – Fredericton, population 78,950. Other cities are ΨSaint John (125,705); Moncton (113,491); Bathurst (25,415); Edmundston (22,624); Campbellton (16,867), 1996.

GOVERNMENT

Government is administered by a Lieutenant-Governor, an Executive Council, and an elected Legislative Assembly of 55 members. The Liberal Party formed a government following the last provincial election on 11 September 1995.
Lt-Governor, Marilyn Trenholm
Premier, Frank McKenna

ECONOMY

New Brunswick's largest manufacturing sectors are the paper and allied industries and the food and wood industries. Together these accounted in 1996 for 51.2 per cent of the total value of manufacturing shipments of C$7,849 million. Saint John has an ice-free port and is the principal manufacturing centre of the province.

Farmland amounted to 930,067 acres in 1996. Dairy products and potatoes are the leading agricultural products. Fishing is an important industry, employing 9,082 fishermen.

Zinc, lead, copper and coal deposits are mined in New Brunswick, which is the largest zinc producer in Canada. Antimony and potash are also produced. Total mineral production was valued at C$924,758,000 in 1996.

NEWFOUNDLAND AND LABRADOR

The island of Newfoundland is situated on the north-east side of the Gulf of St Lawrence, and is separated from the North American continent by the Straits of Belle Isle on the north-west and by Cabot Strait on the south-west. The island is about 510 km long and 508 km broad and is triangular in shape. It comprises an area of 43,008 sq. miles (111,390 sq. km). The population (inclusive of Labrador) is 551,792 (1996).

Labrador forms the most easterly part of the North American continent, and extends from Point St Charles, at the north east entrance to the Straits of Belle Isle on the south, to Cape Chidley, at the eastern entrance to Hudson's Straits on the north. It has an area of 113,641 sq. miles (294,328 sq. km), with a population of 29,190 (1996).

PROVINCIAL CAPITAL – ΨSt John's (Greater St John's population (1996) 174,051) is North America's oldest city. It is the principal port for the island of Newfoundland. Newfoundland's second city of Corner Brook (population (1996) 21,893) is situated on the west coast.

GOVERNMENT

The government is administered by a Lieutenant-Governor, aided by an Executive Council and a Legislative Assembly of 48 members elected for a term of five years. The Liberal Party formed a government following the last election on 22 February 1996.
Lt.-Governor, A. Maxwell House
Premier, Brian Tobin

ECONOMY

The main primary industries are fishing, forestry and mining. In 1996 shipments of fish products were valued at C$532 million; newsprint shipments at C$627 million; and mining (mainly iron ore) plus structural materials shipments at C$934 million. Total manufacturing shipments were valued at C$934 million. The hydroelectric plant on the Churchill river is the largest underground plant in the world, with a capacity of 5,225,000 kW.

Over 139 wells have been drilled off Newfoundland since 1965. Oil was discovered in 1979 on the Grand Banks. Oil production is expected to begin in the late 1990s, with a peak production of 125,000 barrels of oil a day.

NOVA SCOTIA

Nova Scotia is a peninsula which is connected to New Brunswick by a low isthmus about 28 km wide. It has an area of 21,420 sq. miles (55,477 sq. km), including 2,650 sq. km of lakes and rivers and 10,424 km of shoreline. No place is more than 56 km from the Atlantic Ocean. Population 909,282 (1996).

Cape Breton Island has been part of Nova Scotia since 1819. It is the centre of the steel manufacturing and coal mining industries.

PROVINCIAL CAPITAL – ΨHalifax, including the neighbouring city of Dartmouth, has a population of 184,484 (1996). The harbour, ice-free all year round, is the main Atlantic winter port of Canada. Other cities and towns include ΨSydney (25,860) and ΨGlace Bay (19,551).

GOVERNMENT

The government consists of a Lieutenant-Governor and a 52-member elected Legislative Assembly, from which the Executive Council is selected. The Lieutenant-Governor represents The Queen and is appointed by the Governor-in-Council. The Liberal Party formed the last government.
Lt.-Governor, J. James Kinley
Premier, John Savage

ECONOMY

Provincial GDP in 1996 was C$16,301 million, of which 12.1 per cent was produced by manufacturing.

The estimated value of commodity production in 1996 was: minerals C$597,472,000; fish and shellfish C$494,000,000; farm production C$355,069,000. The total value of manufacturing shipments was C$6,134 million.

Forest land covers 73 per cent of the land area and most is privately owned. Forest-based industries employed an average of 11,200 in 1996, and contributed C$975,400,000 to the Nova Scotia economy.

ONTARIO

Ontario has a total area of 412,580 sq. miles (1,068,577 sq. km), with a population of 10,753,573 (1996).

PROVINCIAL CAPITAL – ΨToronto (metropolitan, census 1991, 3,893,046). Other major urban areas are: Ottawa, the national capital (313,987); ΨHamilton (599,760); London (381,522); ΨWindsor (262,075); Kitchener (356,421) and Sudbury (157,613).

GOVERNMENT

The government is vested in a Lieutenant-Governor and a Legislative Assembly of 130 members elected for five years.

The last legislative election was held on 8 June 1995 and won by the Progressive Conservatives who formed a government.
Lt.-Governor, Henry N. R. Jackman
Premier, Michael Harris

ECONOMY

Ontario is the chief manufacturing province in Canada, producing 50 per cent of all manufactured goods. Major industries are iron and steel, metal fabrication, machinery, electricals and chemicals. Toronto is also a major centre of finance and service industry.

Agricultural production had a gross value of C$6,030 million and total net farm income was C$1,180 million. Productive forested lands cover 39.9 million hectares. Paper and allied industries are by far the most important sector of Ontario's forest industry.

Ontario's natural resources include basic minerals such as copper, iron ore, zinc, sulphur, gold, nickel and platinum. Total value of the mineral production in 1992 was estimated at C$4,800 million.

PRINCE EDWARD ISLAND

Prince Edward Island lies in the southern part of the Gulf of St Lawrence. It is about 225 km in length, and from 6 to 64 km in breadth; its area is 2,180 sq. miles (5,646 sq. km), and its population 134,557 (1996).

PROVINCIAL CAPITAL – ΨCharlottetown, population 32,531 (1996), on the shore of Hillsborough Bay, which forms a good harbour.

GOVERNMENT

The government is vested in a Lieutenant-Governor, an Executive Council, and Legislative Assembly of 27 members elected for a term of up to five years. After the election of 18 November 1996 the Progressive Conservatives formed a government.
Lt.-Governor, Gilbert R. Clements
Premier, Patrick G. Binns

ECONOMY

Approximately 46.8 per cent of the total area of the province is farmland. The value of farm cash receipts in 1996 was C$294,400,000, of which 46.9 per cent was from the sale of potatoes. Dairy, beef and hogs are also important agriculture products. Fish landings were valued at C$104,700,000 in 1996 of which 62.9 per cent was of lobster.

The total value of manufacturing shipments was C$687.5 million in 1995, of which 68.5 per cent was in the food products industry. A major summer economic activity is tourism. Non-resident tourists spent an estimated C$171 million in the province in 1996.

QUEBEC

Quebec has an estimated area of 594,860 sq. miles (1,540,680 sq. km) with a population (1996 census) of 7,138,795, of which about 80 per cent are French-speaking.

PROVINCIAL CAPITAL – ΨQuebec, population 167,264 (1996). Other important cities are ΨMontreal, the commercial centre, (1,016,376); Laval (330,393); Longueuil (127,977); Gatineau (100,702); Montreal-Nord (81,581); Sherbrooke (76,786); La Salle (72,079).

GOVERNMENT

The government of the province is vested in a Lieutenant-Governor, a Council of Ministers and a National Assembly of 125 members elected for five years. The last provincial election on 12 September 1994 was won by the Parti Québécois which formed a government.
Lt.-Governor, Lise Thibault
Prime Minister, Lucien Bouchard

AGENT-GENERAL'S OFFICE IN LONDON, 59 Pall Mall, London SW1Y 5JH. *Agent-General,* Richard Guay

ECONOMY

Total estimated value of shipments in the manufacturing industries in 1996 was C$105,374 million. Forests cover 757,900 sq. km, of which 527,698 sq. km are productive. In 1996 farm receipts totalled C$4,613,241,000. In 1995 47,787 tonnes of fish, to the value of C$177,165,000 were landed.

Minerals to the value of C$3,314,855,000 were mined in 1996. This included gold, copper and asbestos.

SASKATCHEWAN

Saskatchewan lies between Manitoba to the east and Alberta to the west and has an area of 251,870 sq. miles (652,340 sq. km). The population is 990,237 (1996). Saskatchewan extends along the Canada–USA boundary for 393 miles (632 km) and northwards for 761 miles (1,224 km). Its northern width is 276 miles (440 km).

PROVINCIAL CAPITAL – Regina. Population (estimated 1995), 178,726. Other cities are Saskatoon (189,745), Moose Jaw (33,803), Prince Albert (33,507) and Yorkton (15,574).

GOVERNMENT

The government is vested in the Lieutenant-Governor, with a Legislative Assembly of 58 members. The Legislative Assembly is elected for roughly five years. The New Democrats formed the current government.

Lt.-Governor, Jack Wiebe
Premier, Roy Romanow, QC

CAPE VERDE
República de Cabo Verde

AREA – 1,557 sq. miles (4,033 sq. km). Comprising the Windward Islands (Santo Antão, São Vicente, Santa Luzia, São Nicolau, Boa Vista and Sal) and Leeward Islands (Maio, São Tiago, Fogo and Brava)
POPULATION – 417,000, (1995 estimate), the majority of whom are Roman Catholic
CAPITAL – ΨPraia (population, 80,000, 1995 estimate)
CURRENCY – Escudo Caboverdiano of 100 centavos
NATIONAL DAY – 5 July (Independence Day)
NATIONAL FLAG – Blue with three horizontal stripes of white, red, white near the bottom; over all on these near the hoist a ring of ten yellow stars
LIFE EXPECTANCY (years) – male 63.53; female 71.33
POPULATION GROWTH RATE – 2.7 per cent (1994)
POPULATION DENSITY – 94 per sq. km (1994)
URBAN POPULATION – 44.1 per cent (1990)
MILITARY EXPENDITURE – 1.8 per cent of GDP (1995)
MILITARY PERSONNEL – 1,100: Army 1,000, Air Force 100
CONSCRIPTION DURATION – Selective
ILLITERACY RATE – 28.4 per cent
ENROLMENT (percentage of age group) – primary 100 per cent; secondary 22 per cent (1993)

HISTORY AND POLITICS

The islands, colonized *c.*1460, achieved independence from Portugal on 5 July 1975 under the nationalist party of Guinea Bissau and Cape Verde. A federation of the islands with Guinea Bissau was planned but this was dropped following the 1980 coup in Guinea Bissau.

The republic was a one-party state under the African Party for the Independence of Cape Verde (PAICV) until the constitution was amended in 1990. Multiparty elections, held in January 1991, were won by the opposition Movement for Democracy (MPD). The MPD government was re-elected in December 1995 with 50 of the 72 seats in the National Assembly. President António Mascarenhas Monteiro was re-elected unopposed in February 1996.

HEAD OF STATE
President, António Mascarenhas Gomes Monteiro, *assumed office* 22 March 1991, *re-elected* 18 February 1996

COUNCIL OF MINISTERS *as at July 1997*
Prime Minister, Carlos Wahnon de Carvalho Veiga
Adjoint-Minister of the Prime Minister, José António Mendes dos Reis
Agriculture, Food and Environment, José António Pinto Monteiro
Economic Co-ordination, António Gualberto do Rosario
Education, Science and Culture, José Livramento Monteiro Alves de Brito
Foreign Affairs, Amilcar Spencer Lopes
Health and Social Promotion, João Ferreira Medina
Infrastructure and Transport, Armindo Gregório Ferreira
Justice and Internal Administration, Simão Gomes Monteiro
National Defence, Minister of Presidence of the Ministers' Council, Úlpio Napoleão Fernandes
Sea, Maria Nobre Morais Querido Semedo
Secretary of State, Culture, António Jorge Delgado
Secretary of State, Decentralization, César de Barbosa e Almeida
Secretary of State, Fight Against Poverty, Manuela de Jesus Alves Silva Gomes
Secretary of State, Finance, José Ulisses Correia e Silva
Secretary of State, Foreign Affairs and Co-operation, José de Jesus
Secretary of State, Public Administration, Ana Pinto Almeida Fernandes
Secretary of State, Tourism, Industry and Trade, Alexandre Dias Monteiro
Secretary of State, Youth and Sports, Victor Ascencão de Pinto Osório

EMBASSY OF THE REPUBLIC OF CAPE VERDE
44 Koninginnegracht, 2514 AD, The Hague, The Netherlands
Tel: The Hague 3469623
Ambassador Extraordinary and Plenipotentiary, new appointment awaited

BRITISH AMBASSADOR, HE David Snoxell, resident at Dakar, Senegal
There is a British Consulate on São Vicente.

ECONOMY

The islands have little rain and agriculture is mostly confined to irrigated inland valleys. The chief products are bananas and coffee (for export), maize, sugarcane and nuts. Fish and shellfish are important exports. Salt is obtained on Sal, Boa Vista and Maio; volcanic rock is also mined for export.

In January 1993 the government announced a programme of reform to institute a change to a market economy and to privatize most industry within four years. In 1993 imports totalled US$154 million and exports US$4 million.

The main ports are Praia and Mindelo, and there is an international airport on Sal.

GNP – US$366 million (1995); US$960 per capita (1995)
GDP – US$363 million (1992); US$1,002 per capita (1992)
TOTAL EXTERNAL DEBT – US$216 million (1995)

TRADE WITH UK	1995	1996
Imports from UK	£4,465,000	£6,942,000
Exports to UK	584,000	803,000

CENTRAL AFRICAN REPUBLIC
République Centrafricaine

AREA – 240,535 sq. miles (622,984 sq. km). Neighbours: Cameroon, Chad, Sudan, Democratic Republic of Congo
POPULATION – 3,235,000 (1994 UN estimate)
CAPITAL – Bangui (population, 473,817, 1984 estimate)
CURRENCY – Franc CFA of 100 centimes
NATIONAL DAY – 1 December
NATIONAL FLAG – Four horizontal stripes, blue, white, green, yellow, crossed by central vertical red stripe with a yellow five-pointed star in top left-hand corner
LIFE EXPECTANCY (years) – male 46.87; female 51.88
POPULATION GROWTH RATE – 2.5 per cent (1994)
POPULATION DENSITY – 5 per sq. km (1994)
MILITARY EXPENDITURE – 1.8 per cent of GDP (1995)
MILITARY PERSONNEL – 4,950: Army 2,500, Air Force 150, Paramilitaries 2,300
CONSCRIPTION DURATION – Two years
ENROLMENT (percentage of age group) – primary 58 per cent (1989); tertiary 1.4 per cent (1989)

HISTORY AND POLITICS

In December 1958 the French colony of Ubanghi Shari elected to remain within the French Community and adopted the title of the Central African Republic. It became fully independent on 17 August 1960. The first President David Dacko was overthrown in 1966 by the then Col. Bokassa. In December 1976, President Bokassa proclaimed himself Emperor and renamed the country the Central African Empire. In 1979 Bokassa was deposed by Dacko in a bloodless coup and the country reverted to a republic. President Dacko surrendered power in 1981 to Gen. André Kolingba, who instituted military rule until 1985, when a civilian-dominated Cabinet was appointed. In November 1986 a referendum was held which approved a new constitution and the establishment of a one-party state.

Multiparty presidential and legislative elections were held in October 1992 but were annulled due to irregularities. President Kolingba formed a coalition government in December 1992 and another in February 1993. Presidential and legislative elections held in 1993 were won by Ange-Felix Patasse (MLPC), and the Central African People's Liberation Party (MLPC). The MLPC formed a coalition government in October 1993.

POLITICAL SYSTEM

Constitutional reforms were passed in a national referendum in December 1994 which created a constitutional court, introduced elected local assemblies, extended the presidential mandate to a maximum of two six-year terms and subordinated the government to the president.

INSURGENCY

The army is divided between southerners loyal to former President Gen. Kolingba and northerners loyal to President Patasse. The 1,500 French troops stationed near Bangui have been called upon to quell frequent mutinies by Gen. Kolingba's supporters.

HEAD OF STATE

President, Ange-Felix Patasse, *elected* 19 September 1993

COUNCIL OF MINISTERS *as at July 1997*

Prime Minister, Michel Gbezera-Bria (Ind.)
Agriculture and Livestock, Charles Massi (MLPC)
Civil Service, Labour and Training, Jean-Claude Ngouandja (FPP)
Communication, Thierry Inifolo-van del Boss (PLD)
Defence and Restructuring the Army, Pascal Kado (MLPC)
Economic Reform, Planning and International Co-operation, Christophe Mbremaidou (CN)
Environment Water, Forests, Hunting and Fishing, Joseph Nyomba (MDREC)
Finance and Budget, Anicet Georges Dologuele (MLPC)
Foreign Affairs, Jean Mette Yapende (MLPC)
Higher Education, Scientific and Technological Research, Theophile Touba (RDC)
Housing, Planning and Construction, Clement Belibanga (ADP)
Human Rights, Promotion of Democratic Culture and National Reconciliation, Laurent Gomina-Pampali (Ind.)
Industry and Trade, Simon Bongolape (MDD)
Justice, Marcel Metefara (MLPC)
Mines and Energy, Joseph Agbo (MLPC)
National Education, Albert Mberio (MLPC)
Post and Telecommunications, Michel Bindo (RDP)
Promotion of Family, Social Affairs, National Solidarity, Eliane Mokodopo (MESAN)
Public Health and Population, Dr Fernand Djengbot (RDC)
Public Works and Regional Development, Jacquescon Mazette (MLPC)
Relations with Parliament, Charles Armel Doubane (ADP)
Territorial Administration and Public Security, Gen. François Djader Bedaya (Ind.)
Tourism, Arts and Culture, Gaston Beina-Gbadi (PLD)
Transport and Civil Aviation, Andre Gombacko (FPP)
Youth and Sport, Bertin Bea (MDD)

MLPC Movement for the Liberation of the Central African People; PLD Liberal Democratic Party; MESAN Movement for the Social Evolution of Black Africa; CN National Convention; RDC Central African Democratic Rally; ADP Alliance for Democracy and Progress; FPP Patriotic Front for Progress; MDD Movement for Democracy and Development; MDREC Democratic Movement for the Renaissance and Evolution of the Central African Republic; Ind. Independent

EMBASSY OF THE CENTRAL AFRICAN REPUBLIC
30 rue des Perchamps, 75016, Paris
Tel: Paris 4224 4256
Ambassador Extraordinary and Plenipotentiary, new appointment awaited
BRITISH AMBASSADOR, HE Nicholas McCarthy, OBE, resident at Yaoundé, Cameroon
Honorary Consul, J. Y. Lauge, BP 977, Bangui

ECONOMY

In an effort to revive an ailing economy, the government began in 1986 to streamline the civil service, increase tax revenues, and reduce price controls. The IMF approved a US$23 million credit to support economic reform in 1994. Cotton, diamonds, coffee and timber are the major exports.

In 1992 there was a trade deficit of US$42 million and a current account deficit of US$57 million. In 1995 exports totalled US$187 million and imports US$189 million.
GNP – US$1,123 million (1995); US$340 per capita (1995)
GDP – US$1,507 million (1992); US$514 per capita (1992)
INFLATION RATE – 24.6 per cent (1994)
TOTAL EXTERNAL DEBT – US$944 million (1994)

TRADE WITH UK	1995	1996
Imports from UK	£638,000	£749,000
Exports to UK	192,000	87,000

CHAD
République du Tchad

AREA – 495,755 sq. miles (1,284,000 sq. km). Neighbours: Niger and Cameroon (west), Libya (north), Sudan (east), Central African Republic (south)
POPULATION – 6,214,000 (1994 UN estimate)
CAPITAL – Ndjaména (population, 179,000, 1972 estimate)
CURRENCY – Franc CFA of 100 centimes
NATIONAL DAY – 13 April
NATIONAL FLAG – Vertical stripes, blue, yellow and red
LIFE EXPECTANCY (years) – male 45.93; female 49.12
POPULATION GROWTH RATE – 2.2 per cent (1994)
POPULATION DENSITY – 5 per sq. km (1994)
URBAN POPULATION – 21.7 per cent (1993)
MILITARY EXPENDITURE – 2.6 per cent of GDP (1995)
MILITARY PERSONNEL – 34,850: Army 25,000, Air Force 350, Paramilitaries 9,500
ILLITERACY RATE – 51.9 per cent
ENROLMENT (percentage of age group) – tertiary 0.8 per cent (1993)

HISTORY AND POLITICS

Chad became a member state of the French Community in 1958, and was proclaimed fully independent on 11 August 1960. The constitution was suspended in 1975 when President Tombalbaye was killed in a coup by Gen. Felix Malloum, who was overthrown in 1979. A Transitional Government of National Unity was replaced in 1982 by the government of Hissène Habré, but this was overthrown in 1990 in a coup led by Idriss Déby. Déby announced the adoption of a multiparty system, allowing the legalization of political parties in 1991 and 1992. A sovereign national conference held in 1993 elected a Higher Transitional Council (CST) to serve as the transitional legislature and appointed a transitional government in conjunction with President Déby. The CST has twice extended the transitional period by one year to allow sufficient time to organize elections. In March 1996, the government concluded the Franceville agreement with opposition parties which provided for a national cease-fire and an independent commission to oversee the election. A new constitution, establishing a unified, democratic state, was confirmed by a referendum. Déby won the first multiparty presidential elections in June and July 1996. Elections to the 125-member National Assembly in January and February 1997 were won by the pro-Déby Patriotic Salvation Movement (MPS).

FOREIGN RELATIONS

The Aouzou strip was claimed by Libya, which occupied the area from 1973 to 1994. A war over the territory ended in 1987. In 1990 Chad and Libya presented their claims to the International Court of Justice, which in 1994 awarded jurisdiction over the whole of the strip to Chad.

HEAD OF STATE
President, Idriss Déby, *took power* December 1990, *elected* 3 July 1996

GOVERNMENT *as at May 1997*
Prime Minister, Nassour Ouaidou Guelendouksia
Agriculture, Ali Mahamat Zene Ali Fadel
Basic and Secondary Education and Literacy, Abdelrahim Breme Hamit
Communication, Government Spokesman, Salibou Garba
Environment and Water, Edgar Ngarbaroum

Finance, Economy, Planning and Territorial Development, Bichara Cherif Daoussa
Foreign Affairs and Co-operation, Mahamat-Saleh Annadif
Higher Education and Scientific Research, Adoum Goudja
Industrial, Commercial and Arts and Craft Development, Pahimi Padacke Albert
Interior, Security and Decentralization, Youssouf Togoimi
Justice, Nadjita Beassoumal
Livestock, Mahamat Nouri
Mines, Energy and Oil, Pascal Yoadimaji
Minister of State, Public Works, Transportation, Housing and Urban Development, Saleh Kebzabo
National Defence and Reinsertion, Mahamat Nimir Hamatta
Posts and Telecommunications, Mahamat Ahmat Karambal
Public Health Kedellah Younous Hamit
Public Service, Labour, Employment Promotion and Modernization, Ousman Djidda
Social Action and Family, Monique Ngaralbaye

EMBASSY OF THE REPUBLIC OF CHAD
Boulevard Lambermont 52, 1030 Brussels, Belgium
Tel: Brussels 215 1975
Ambassador Extraordinary and Plenipotentiary, HE Ramadane Barma, apptd 1994

BRITISH AMBASSADOR, HE Nicholas McCarthy, OBE, resident at Abuja, Nigeria
Honorary Consul, E. Abtour, BP877, Avenue Charles de Gaulle, Ndjaména

ECONOMY

About 90 per cent of the workforce is occupied in agriculture, fishing and forestry. There is an oilfield in Kanem and salt is mined around Lake Chad, but the most important activities are cotton growing (mostly in the south) and animal husbandry (in central areas). Raw cotton and meat are the main exports.

The IMF approved a loan of US$74 million in 1995. In 1993 Chad had a trade deficit of US$66 million and a current account deficit of US$84 million. In 1994 imports totalled US$185 million and exports US$156 million.
GNP – US$1,144 million (1995); US$180 per capita (1995)
GDP – US$1,212 million (1992); US$243 per capita (1992)
ANNUAL AVERAGE GROWTH OF GDP – –5.6 per cent (1987)
INFLATION RATE – 40.4 per cent (1994)
TOTAL EXTERNAL DEBT – US$908 million (1995)

TRADE WITH UK	1995	1996
Imports from UK	£1,939,000	£3,708,000
Exports to UK	3,173,000	1,180,000

CHILE
República de Chile

AREA – 292,134 sq. miles (756,626 sq. km)
POPULATION – 13,994,000 (1994 UN estimate). The main groups are: indigenous Araucanian Indians, Fuegians, Rapanui and Changos; Spanish settlers and their descendants; mixed Spanish Indians; and European immigrants. Because of extensive intermarriage only a few indigenous Indians are racially separate - the language is Spanish, with admixtures of local words of Indian origin. The main religion is Roman Catholicism
CAPITAL – Santiago (population, 5,257,937)
MAJOR CITIES – ΨValparaíso (282,040); Concepción (331,027); Temuco (243,561); ΨAntofagasta (110,000); ΨValdivia (122,168), ΨPunta Arenas (113,666), on the Straits of Magellan, is the southernmost city in the world

CURRENCY – Chilean peso of 100 centavos
NATIONAL ANTHEM – Canción Nacional de Chile
NATIONAL DAY – 18 September (National Anniversary)
NATIONAL FLAG – Two horizontal bands, white, red; in
    top sixth a white star on blue square, next staff
LIFE EXPECTANCY (years) – male 68.54; female 75.59
POPULATION GROWTH RATE – 1.5 per cent (1994)
POPULATION DENSITY – 18 per sq. km (1994)
URBAN POPULATION – 85.3 per cent (1993)

Chile lies between the Andes (5,000 to 15,000 feet above
sea level) and the shores of the South Pacific, extending
coastwise from the arid north around Arica to Cape Horn.
The extreme length of the country is about 2,800 miles,
with an average breadth, north of 41°, of 100 miles.
    Island possessions include the Juan Fernández group
(three islands) about 360 miles from Valparaíso; one of
these islands is the reputed scene of Alexander Selkirk's
(Robinson Crusoe) shipwreck. Easter Island, about 2,000
miles away in the South Pacific Ocean, contains stone
platforms and hundreds of stone figures.

HISTORY AND POLITICS

Chile was discovered by Spanish adventurers in the 16th
century and remained under Spanish rule until 1810, when
the first autonomous government was established. Full
independence was consolidated in 1818 after a revolutionary war.
    A Marxist, Salvador Allende, was elected president in
1970, but was overthrown in a military coup in 1973.
    In 1981, Gen. Pinochet was sworn in to serve as
president until 1989; a plebiscite to permit a second eight-
year term of office was rejected in 1988. Presidential and
congressional elections were held in 1989, beginning the
transition to full democracy. Gen. Pinochet remains
Commander-in-Chief of the Armed Forces until 1998.
    Presidential and legislative elections were held in 1993.
Eduardo Frei won the presidential election and his ruling
Coalition for Democracy (centre and centre-left parties)
won 70 Chamber of Deputies seats and 22 of the Senate
seats.

POLITICAL SYSTEM

Executive power is held by the president, legislative
power is exercised by a Congress which comprises a Senate
of 47 Senators (38 elected and nine appointed) and a
Chamber of Deputies of 120 elected members. A joint
session of Congress in 1994 reduced the presidential term
from eight to six years with no possibility of re-election.
    Chile is divided into 12 regions and the Metropolitan
Area.

HEAD OF STATE
President of the Republic, Eduardo Frei Ruiz-Tagle, *elected* 11
    December 1993, *sworn in* 11 March 1994

CABINET *as at July 1997*
Agriculture, Carlos Mladinic
Defence, Edmundo Pérez Yoma
Economy, Alvaro García
Education, José Pablo Arrellano
Energy, Alejandro Jadresic
Finance, Eduardo Aninat
Foreign Affairs, José Miguel Insulza
Housing, Edmundo Hermosilla
Interior, Carlos Figueroa
Justice, Soledad Alvear
Labour and Social Security, Jorge Arrate
Mining, Benjamín Teplisky
National Properties, Adriana del Piano

Planning and Development, Roberto Pizarro
Public Health, Alex Figueroa
Public Works, Ricardo Lagos
Secretary-General of the Government, José Joaquín Brunner
Secretary-General of the Presidency, Juan Villarzú
Transport, Claudio Hohmann
Women's Affairs, Josefina Bilbao

EMBASSY OF CHILE
12 Devonshire Street, London WIN 2DS
Tel 0171–580 6392
Ambassador Extraordinary and Plenipotentiary, HE Mario
    Artaza, apptd 1996

BRITISH EMBASSY
Avenida El Bosque Norte 0125
Casilla 72-D, Santiago 9
Tel: Santiago 231 3737
Ambassador Extraordinary and Plenipotentiary, HE Glynne
    Evans, CMG, apptd 1997
Deputy Head of Mission, Counsellor and Consul-General, D.
    Roberts
Defence Attaché, Capt. P. Ellis
First Secretary (Commercial), T. Torlot
CONSULAR OFFICES – Antofagasta, Arica, Concepción,
    Santiago, Punta Arenas, Valparaíso.

BRITISH COUNCIL DIRECTOR, D. Stokes (*Cultural Attaché*),
    Eliodoro Yañez 832, Casilla 115 Correa 55, Santiago
British-Chilean Chamber of Commerce, Av. Suecia
    155-C, Casilla 536, Santiago

DEFENCE

The Army has 119 main battle tanks, 20 armoured infantry
fighting vehicles, 310 armoured personnel carriers and 126
artillery pieces. The Navy has four submarines, five
destroyers, four frigates, 23 patrol and coastal vessels, 16
combat aircraft and ten armed helicopters. The Air Force
has 110 combat aircraft.
MILITARY EXPENDITURE – 3.8 per cent of GDP (1995)
MILITARY PERSONNEL – 120,900: Army 51,700, Navy
    24,000, Air Force 14,000, Paramilitaries 31,200
CONSCRIPTION DURATION – One to two years

ECONOMY

Economic reforms during the late 1970s and 1980s, with
large-scale privatization and deregulation, have made
Chile the most successful economy in Latin America. The
economy has grown by 50 per cent in ten years, with
economic growth averaging 7 per cent a year in 1987–94.
    Cereals, vegetables, fruit, tobacco, hemp and vines are
grown extensively and livestock accounts for nearly 40 per
cent of agricultural production. Sheep farming predominates in the extreme south. There are large timber tracts in
the central and southern zones which produce timber,
cellulose and wood for export. Industrial-scale fishing
makes Chile the fifth largest producer in terms of catch.
    Chile is rich in copper-ore, iron-ore and nitrates, and has
the only commercial production of nitrate of soda (Chile
saltpetre) from natural resources in the world. There are
large deposits of high grade sulphur. Oil and natural gas are
produced in the Magallanes area, but domestic production
is now declining. Production figures for 1995 were: coal
1,484,867 tonnes; copper 2,488,100 tonnes; crude petroleum 552,019 tonnes; natural gas 2,104,000 cu. metres.
    In 1994 the government had a budget surplus equivalent
to 1.63 per cent of GDP and a current account deficit of
US$757 million.
GNP – US$59,151 million (1995); US$4,160 per capita
    (1995)

GDP – US$35,285 million (1992); US$3,030 per capita (1992)
ANNUAL AVERAGE GROWTH OF GDP – 8.5 per cent (1995)
INFLATION RATE – 8.2 per cent (1995)
UNEMPLOYMENT – 4.7 per cent (1995)
TOTAL EXTERNAL DEBT – US$25,562 million (1995)

TRADE

The principal exports are minerals, timber and metal products, fish products, vegetables, fruit and wool. The principal imports are sugar and other food products, industrial raw materials, machinery, equipment and spares, oil fuels, lubricants and transportation equipment. In 1994 there was a trade surplus of US$659 million. In 1995 imports totalled US$15,914 million and exports US$16,039 million.

Trade with UK	1995	1996
Imports from UK	£170,949,000	£166,129,000
Exports to UK	299,959,000	377,549,000

COMMUNICATIONS

With the improvement of the roads an increasing share of internal transportation is moving by road and rail, although shipping is still important. The road system is about 65,000 km in length.

A railway line runs from Valparaíso through La Calera and Santiago to Puerto Montt. With the completion of a section of 435 miles from Corumba, Brazil, to Santa Cruz, Bolivia, the Trans-Continental Line will link the Chilean Pacific port of Arica with Rio de Janeiro on the Atlantic. A line runs from Antofagasta to Salta (Argentina).

Domestic air traffic is carried by Linea Aerea Nacional (LAN) and LADECO, which also operate internationally, and smaller regional carriers.

CULTURE AND EDUCATION

The Nobel Prize for Literature was awarded in 1945 to Gabriela Mistral, for Chilean verse and prose, and in 1971 to the poet Pablo Neruda.

Elementary education is free and compulsory. There are eight state universities (three in Santiago, two in Valparaíso, one each in Antofagasta, Concepción and Valdivia), and many private universities.
ILLITERACY RATE – 4.8 per cent
ENROLMENT (percentage of age group) – primary 86 per cent (1994); secondary 54 per cent (1994); tertiary 26.7 per cent (1993)

CHINA
Zhonghua Renmin Gongheguo   The People's Republic of China

AREA – 3,705,408 sq. miles (9,596,961 sq. km)
POPULATION – 1,208,842,000 (1994 UN estimate). A census (the fourth) was held in 1990 and recorded a total population of 1,130 million. About 6 per cent of the population belong to around 55 ethnic minorities. Among the largest are the Zhuang of Guangxi, the Uygurs of Xinjiang, the Tibetans and the Mongols. The indigenous religions are Confucianism, Taoism and Buddhism. There are also Muslims (officially estimated at about 12 million) and Christians (unofficially estimated at about 50 million)
CAPITAL – Beijing (Peking) (population, 7,362,426, 1990)
MAJOR CITIES – ΨShanghai 8,760,000; Harbin 3,100,000; Tianjin 4,970,000; Chengdu 2,670,000; Shenyang 3,860,000; Nanjing 2,430,000; Wuhan 3,860,000; Changchun 2,400,000; Chongqing 3,780,000; Xian 2,360,000; Guangzhou (Canton) 3,560,000; Dalian 2,330,000; Qingdao 2,240,000, 1993
CURRENCY – Renminbi Yuan of 10 jiao or 100 fen
NATIONAL ANTHEM – March of the Volunteers
NATIONAL DAY – 1 October (Founding of People's Republic)
NATIONAL FLAG – Red, with large gold five-point star and four small gold stars in crescent, all in upper quarter next staff
LIFE EXPECTANCY (years) – male 66.70; female 70.45
POPULATION GROWTH RATE – 1.1 per cent (1994)
POPULATION DENSITY – 126 per sq. km (1994)
URBAN POPULATION – 26.2 per cent (1990)

HISTORY AND POLITICS

China was ruled by imperial dynasties for over 20 centuries until revolutionaries led by Sun Yat-sen forced the Emperor to abdicate on 10 October 1911. Neither the new Nationalist Party (Kuomintang (KMT)) government nor the emergent Chinese Communist Party (CCP) were able to unify China, or to agree on the basis for further reform. Warlord infighting rendered China weak, enabling Japan to occupy Manchuria and all the important northern and coastal areas of China by 1939. Japan's occupation was ended by its defeat by the allies in 1945.

The Communists' initial five-year co-operation with the KMT ended in 1927, although the KMT was unable to suppress the CCP. The CCP had successfully politicized the rural population, setting up a 'Soviet Republic' in Jiangxi in the early 1930s, but were forced to flee by the KMT and began the 'Long March' to Shanxi in 1934. The Communists established control over large areas of China in the early 1940s, seizing the territory abandoned by Japan in 1945. Civil war lasted until 1949 when the CCP, led by Mao Zedong (Mao Tse-tung), inaugurated the People's Republic of China (PRC), and the KMT under Chiang K'ai-shek went into exile in Taiwan. The USA continued to recognize the Chiang Kai-shek regime as the rightful government of China until 1971, when the PRC took over China's membership of the United Nations from Taiwan.

Under Mao Zedong China was ruled on the basis of four 'cardinal principles': Marxist–Leninist–Maoist thought, the Socialist Road, the dictatorship of the proletariat, and the leadership of the CCP. Mao's 'Great Leap Forward' (1958–61) was an attempt to industrialize rural areas which resulted in a famine in which 30–40 million people died. The country was plunged into chaos during the Cultural Revolution (1966–70) when the Red Guards were used to rid the country of 'rightist elements'.

Following the death of Mao Zedong in 1976, the disgraced Deng Xiaoping was recalled. In 1977 he was elected Vice-Chairman of the CCP, becoming the dominant force within the party by eliminating leftist influence, rehabilitating fallen leaders and promoting an 'open door' policy of economic liberalization. The Congresses of 1982 and 1987 reaffirmed Deng's policies, and in 1987 most of the revolutionary generation were replaced in the top posts by younger, more liberal supporters of reform.

Student-led pro-democracy demonstrations in April and May 1989, centred on Tiananmen Square in Beijing, ended on 3–4 June when the army took control of Beijing, killing thousands of protesters. This strengthened the position of hardliners within the leadership, who re-adopted policies of centralization based on Marxist ideology. Deng retired from his last official post in November 1989 but retained effective control until late 1994.

At Deng's instigation during 1992 the emphasis switched back to economic reform and the power of the

```
0        800 km
0        500 miles
```

RUSSIA

Lake Baikal

KAZAKHSTAN

Lake Balkhash

Darkhan•
Erdenet•   Choibalsan
Ulan Bator•   Harbin•

MONGOLIA

Shenyang•

•Urumqi   N. KOREA

KYRGYZSTAN   Beijing   •Dalian
                          (Peking)■
                          Tianjin•   S. KOREA

                   Taiyuan•

                          Qingdao•   YELLOW
                                       SEA
         Lanzhou•

C H I N A   •Xian   Nanjing•
                                          •Shanghai

    TIBET   Chengdu•   EAST
                            •Wuhan   CHINA
     Lhasa•   •Chongqing   SEA

NEPAL   Taipei•
     (BHUTAN)

INDIA   TAIWAN
         BANGLA-   •Kunming   Guangzhou   Kaohsiung•
         DESH   (Canton)
                          MACAO   •Hong
                          (PORT.)   Kong
              MYANMAR   VIETNAM   SOUTH
              (BURMA)   CHINA
     Bay of   LAOS   SEA
     Bengal   HAINAN
                          (CHINA)

hardliners waned. The 14th Party Congress in 1992 endorsed Deng's calls for faster, bolder economic reforms and his 'socialist market economy'. However, austerity measures to combat inflation have seen official unemployment rise to around five million, with a further 50–100 million migrant labourers unemployed, causing peasant unrest. A degree of central control has been reasserted over the free-market coastal regions, especially their tax revenues, in an attempt to prevent a repetition of the political unrest of 1989.

Deng died on 19 February 1997 and his designated successor, Jiang Zemin, assumed the mantle of leader. Jiang's grip on power is tenuous however, and a rival may emerge at the 15th Party Congress in October 1997.

INSURGENCIES

Separatists from the Uygur Muslim minority group in Xinjiang Autonomous Region have demonstrated against Han rule. They have claimed responsibility for bomb attacks in the provincial capital, Urumqi, and in Beijing.

POLITICAL SYSTEM

Under the 1982 constitution, the National People's Congress is the highest organ of state power. It is elected for a term of five years and is supposed to hold one session a year. It is empowered to amend the constitution, make laws, select the president and vice-president and other leading officials of the state, approve the national economic plan, the state budget and the final state accounts, and to decide on questions of war and peace. The State Council is the highest organ of the state administration. It is composed of the Premier, the Vice-Premiers, the State Councillors, heads of Ministries and Commissions, the Auditor-General and the Secretary-General. Command over the armed forces is vested in the Central Military Commission.

Deputies to Congresses at the primary level are 'directly elected' by the voters 'through a secret ballot after democratic consultation'. This is now extended to county level. These Congresses elect the deputies to the Congress at the next higher level. Deputies to the National People's Congress are elected by the People's Congresses of the provinces, autonomous regions and municipalities directly under the central government, and by the armed forces.

Local government is conducted through People's Governments at provincial, municipal and county levels. Autonomous regions, prefectures and counties exist for national minorities and are described as self-governing.

HEAD OF STATE

President of the People's Republic of China, Jiang Zemin, *elected* April 1993

Vice President, Rong Yiren
Chairman of the Standing Committee of the Eighth National People's Congress, Qiao Shi
Chairman of the Central Military Commission, Jiang Zemin

STATE COUNCIL *as at July 1997*

Premier, Li Peng
Vice-Premiers, Qian Qichen; Li Lanqing; Zhu Rongji; Zou Jiahua; Wu Bangguo; Jiang Chunyun
State Councillors, Li Tieying; Chi Haotian; Song Jian; Li Guixian; Ismail Amat; Peng Peiyun; Luo Gan; Chen Junsheng

MINISTERS

Agriculture, Liu Jiang
Chemical Industry, Gu Xiulian
Civil Affairs, Doje Cering
Coal Industry, Wang Senhao
Communications, Huang Zhendong
Construction, Hou Jie
Culture, Liu Zhongde
Defence, Chi Haotian
Electronics Industry, Hu Qili
Finance, Liu Zhongli
Foreign Affairs, Qian Qichen
Foreign Trade and Economic Co-operation, Wu Yi
Forestry, Xu Youfang
Geology and Mineral Resources, Song Ruixiang
Internal Trade, Chen Bangzhu
Justice, Xiao Yang
Labour, Li Boyong
Machine Industry, He Guangyuan
Metallurgical Industry, Liu Qi
Personnel, Song Defu
Posts and Telecommunications, Wu Jichuan
Power Industry, Shi Dazhen
Public Health, Chen Minzhang
Public Security, Tao Siju
Radio, Film and Television, Sun Jiazheng
Railways, Han Zhubin
State Security, Jia Chunwang
Supervision, Cao Qingze
Water Resources, Niu Maosheng

MINISTERS IN CHARGE OF STATE COMMISSIONS

Economics and Trade, Wang Zhongyu
Education, Zhu Kaixuan
Family Planning, Peng Peiyun
Nationalities Affairs, Ismail Amat
Physical Culture and Sports, Wu Shaozu
Planning, Chen Jinhua
Restructuring Economy, Li Tieying
Science, Technology and Industry for National Defence, Ding
    Henggao
Science and Technology, Song Jian
Auditor-General, Guo Zhenqian
Secretary-General, Luo Gan

President of the People's Bank of China, Dai Xianglong

THE CHINESE COMMUNIST PARTY

General Secretary, Jiang Zemin
Politburo Standing Committee, Jiang Zemin; Li Peng; Li
    Ruihuan; Zhu Rongji; Liu Huaqing; Hu Jintao
Politburo of the Central Committee, Tian Jiyun; Jiang Zemin;
    Li Tieying; Li Ruihuan; Liu Huaqing; Zhu Rongji; Hu
    Jintao; Ding Guangen; Qian Qichen; Jiang Chunyun; Li
    Lanqing; Wei Jianxing; Wu Bangguo; Xie Fei; Yang
    Baibing; Zou Jiahua; Li Peng; Huang Ju *(full members)*;
    Wen Jiabao; Wang Hanbin *(alternate members)*
Secretariat of the Central Committee, Jiang Zemin; Ding
    Guangen; Hu Jintao; Wei Jianxing; Ren Jianxin; Wen
    Jiabao; Wu Bangguo; Jiang Chunyun *(full members)*
Membership, 52,000,000 (1993)

EMBASSY OF THE PEOPLE'S REPUBLIC OF CHINA

49–51 Portland Place, London WIN 4JL
Tel 0171–636 0288/5726
Ambassador Extraordinary and Plenipotentiary, HE Ma
    Zhengang, apptd 1997
Minister-Counsellor, Lu Kexing *(Commercial)*
Defence Attaché, Maj.-Gen. Yan Kunsheng

BRITISH EMBASSY

11 Guang Hua Lu, Jian Guo Men Wai, Beijing 100 600
Tel: Beijing 6532 1961/4
Ambassador, HE Anthony Galsworthy, CMG, apptd 1997
Minister, Consul-General and Deputy Head of Mission, A. D.
    Sprake
Counsellors, S. Featherstone (*Political and Economic*); C. Segar
    (*Commercial*); M. Davidson (*Cultural, and British Council
    Representative*)
Defence, Military and Air Attaché, Brig. K. O. Winfield
CONSULATE-GENERAL – Shanghai

DEFENCE

All three military arms are parts of the People's Liberation
Army (PLA). China has at least 17 intercontinental and 70
intermediate range land-based, and 12 submarine-laun-
ched nuclear ballistic missiles. The Army has up to 8,500
main battle tanks, 4,500 armoured personnel carriers and
armoured infantry fighting vehicles, and more than 14,500
artillery pieces.

The Navy has 63 submarines, 18 destroyers, 36 frigates,
830 patrol and coastal vessels, 605 combat aircraft and 20
armed helicopters. The Air Force has 4,970 combat aircraft.

MILITARY EXPENDITURE – 5.7 per cent of GDP (1995)
MILITARY PERSONNEL – 3,535,000: Army 2,200,000, Navy
    265,000, Air Force 470,000, Paramilitaries 600,000
CONSCRIPTION DURATION – Three to four years

ECONOMY

Economic liberalization in the early 1980s reduced central
planning and broadened the role of the market, which has
led to an explosion in manufacturing, concentrated in
China's coastal regions. Foreign direct investment, especially from Hong Kong and Taiwan, has mushroomed and
enabled the construction of a significant industrial base
and transport infrastructure. In the coastal regions the
economy has become a free market in all but name, with
several stock markets and Shanghai's emergence as a
financial centre. The economy is prone to bouts of 'over-
heating', fuelled by excessive investment in capital construction, which has required austerity measures in
1993–5 in an attempt to control inflation. By 1994, 50–60
per cent of industrial output was produced by private or
collective firms which employed a total of 120 million
people.

Agriculture remains of great importance, with 70 per
cent of the population still living in rural areas. Agricultural policies have devolved responsibility for agricultural
production to individual households.

Cereals, with peas and beans, are grown in the northern
provinces, and rice, tea and sugar in the south. Rice is the
staple food of the inhabitants. Cotton (mostly in valleys of
the Yangtze and Yellow Rivers), tea (in the west and south),
with hemp, jute and flax, are the most important crops.
Livestock is raised in large numbers. Sericulture is one of
the oldest industries. Cottons, woollens and silks are
manufactured in large quantities.

Coal, iron ore, tin, antimony, wolfram, bismuth and
molybdenum are abundant. Oil is produced in several
northern provinces, particularly in Heilongjiang and
Shandong, and off-shore deposits are being sought in co-
operation with western and Japanese companies.

In 1993 the government had a budget deficit equivalent
to 2.25 per cent of GDP and a current account deficit of
US$12,399 million.

GNP – US$744,890 million (1995); US$620 per capita
    (1995)

GDP – US$444,311million (1992); US$378 per capita (1992)
ANNUAL AVERAGE GROWTH OF GDP – 11.9 per cent (1994)
INFLATION RATE – 16.9 per cent (1995)
UNEMPLOYMENT – 2.8 per cent (1994)
TOTAL EXTERNAL DEBT – US$118,090 million (1995)

TRADE

Foreign trade and external economic relations have grown enormously since 1978. In 1995, import tariffs were cut to an average 23 per cent in line with China's attempts to join the World Trade Organization. The principal exports are animals and animal products, oil, textiles, ores, metals, tea, electronics and manufactured goods. The principal imports are motor vehicles, machinery, chemical fertilizer, plants, aircraft, books, paper and paper-making materials, chemicals, metals and ores, and dyes.
In 1993 China had a trade deficit of US$10,654 million. In 1995 imports totalled US$129,113 million and exports US$148,797 million.

Trade with UK	1995	1996
Imports from UK	£824,403,000	£738,514,000
Exports to UK	1,937,869,000	2,202,081,000

COMMUNICATIONS

There are more than 53,400 km of railway lines and 1,041,100 km of highway (1991). In addition, internal civil aviation has been developed, with routes totalling more than 471,900 km.
In the past the principal means of communication east to west was by the rivers, the most important of which are the Yangtze (Changjiang) (3,400 miles), the Yellow River (Huanghe) (2,600 miles) and the West River (Xihe) (1,650 miles). These, together with the network of canals connecting them, are still much used but their overall importance has declined. Coastal port facilities are being improved and the merchant fleet expanded.
Postal services and telecommunications have developed in recent years and it is claimed that 95 per cent of all rural townships are on the telephone and that postal routes reach practically every production brigade headquarters.

EDUCATION

Primary education lasts five years and secondary education lasts five years (three years in junior middle school and two years in senior middle school). There are over 1,000 universities, colleges and institutes.
ILLITERACY RATE – 18.5 per cent
ENROLMENT (percentage of age group) – primary 96 per cent (1993); tertiary 3.8 per cent (1993)

CULTURE

The Chinese language has many dialects, notably Cantonese, Hakka, Amoy, Foochow, Changsha, Nanchang, Wu (Shanghai) and the northern dialect. The Common Speech or *putonghua* (often referred to as Mandarin) is based on the northern dialect. The Communists have promoted it as the national language and it is taught throughout the country. As *putonghua* encourages the use of the spoken language in writing, the old literary style and ideographic form of writing has fallen into disuse. Since 1956 simplified characters have been introduced to make reading and writing easier. In 1958 the National People's Congress adopted a system of romanization known as pinyin.
Chinese literature is one of the richest in the world. Paper has been employed for writing and printing for nearly 2,000 years. The Confucian classics which formed the basis of traditional Chinese culture date from the Warring States period (fourth to third centuries BC), as do the earliest texts of Taoism. Histories, philosophical and scientific works, poetry, literary and art criticism, novels and romances survive from most periods.
The most important among the newspapers and magazines are the *People's Daily* and the twice-monthly *Qiushi*, which replaced *Red Flag* as the CCP's mouthpiece in 1989.

TIBET

Tibet is a plateau seldom lower than 10,000 feet, which forms the northern frontier of India (boundary imperfectly demarcated), from Kashmir to Burma, but is separated therefrom by the Himalayas. The area is estimated at 463,000 sq. miles with a population of 2,260,000 in 1993.
From 1911 to 1950, Tibet was virtually an independent country though its status was never officially so recognized. In 1950 Chinese Communist forces invaded eastern Tibet. In 1951 an agreement was reached whereby the Chinese army was allowed entry into Tibet, and a Communist military and administrative headquarters was set up. A series of revolts against Chinese rule culminated in 1959 in a rising in Lhasa, the capital. Fighting continued for several days before the rebellion was crushed and military rule was imposed. The Dalai Lama fled to India where he and his followers were granted political asylum and established a government in exile.
In 1964 the Dalai Lama was declared a traitor, and both he and the Panchen Lama were dismissed, marking the end of co-operation between the Chinese government and the traditional religious authorities. Tibet became an Autonomous Region of China in 1965. Martial law was declared in Tibet in 1989 after serious unrest, and sporadic outbursts of unrest continue.
The Panchen Lama died in 1989. China rejected the Dalai Lama's choice of successor, who is believed to have been executed, and enthroned its own candidate.

HONG KONG

AREA – 415 sq. miles (1,075 sq. km)
POPULATION – 6,311,000 (1996)
CURRENCY – Hong Kong dollar (HK$) of 100 cents
NATIONAL FLAG – Red, with a white bauhinia flower of five petals each containing a red star
LIFE EXPECTANCY (years) – male 75.21; female 80.74
POPULATION GROWTH RATE – 1.5 per cent (1994)
POPULATION DENSITY – 5,639 per sq. km (1994)
URBAN POPULATION – 93.1 per cent (1986)

Hong Kong, consisting of more than 230 islands and of a portion of the mainland (Kowloon and the New Territories) on the south-east coast of China, is situated at the eastern side of the mouth of the Pearl River. Hong Kong Island is about 11 miles (18 km) long and from two to five miles (three to eight km) broad. It is separated from the mainland by a narrow strait.
The climate is sub-tropical, tending towards the temperate for nearly half the year. The mean monthly temperature ranges from 16° C to 29° C. The average annual rainfall is 2,214 mm, of which nearly 80 per cent falls between May and September. Tropical cyclones occur between May and November, causing high winds and heavy rain.

HISTORY AND POLITICS

Hong Kong Island was first occupied by Great Britain in 1841 and formally ceded by the Treaty of Nanking in 1842. Kowloon was acquired by the Peking Convention of 1860 and the New Territories, consisting of a peninsula in the southern part of the Guangdong province together with adjacent islands, by a 99-year lease signed on 9 June 1898.

On 19 December 1984 the UK and China signed a Joint Declaration in which it was agreed that China would resume sovereignty over Hong Kong on 1 July 1997. In the run-up to the 1997 handover, the Chinese government's insistence on a greater say in the running of the colony and Governor Patten's plan for an extension of democracy prompted acrimonious disputes. The Chinese government refused to accept the reforms and replaced the Legislative Council with a Provisional Legislative Council (see below).

Hong Kong became, with effect from 1 July 1997, a Special Administrative Region (SAR) of the People's Republic of China.

The Joint Declaration which took effect in May 1985 guarantees: the free movement of goods and capital; the retention of Hong Kong's free port status, separate customs territory and freely convertible currency; the protection of property rights and foreign investment; the right of free movement to and from Hong Kong; Hong Kong's autonomy in the conduct of its external commercial relations and its own monetary and financial policies; and judicial independence. Hong Kong's constitution is the Basic Law which was passed by China's National People's Congress in 1990 and guarantees that the SAR's social and economic systems will remain unchanged for 50 years.

POLITICAL SYSTEM

Hong Kong is administered by the Hong Kong government, headed by the Chief Executive, who is aided by an Executive Council and a Provisional Legislative Council. The Executive Council consists of three ex-officio members (the Chief Secretary, the Financial Secretary and the Attorney-General) together with ten other members.

The Provisional Legislative Council consists of 60 members and replaced the Legislative Council (Legco). Both the Chief Executive and the Provisional Legislative Council were elected by a 400-strong committee which in turn was chosen by a 150-member Preparatory Committee, headed by the Chinese foreign minister, from a shortlist drawn up by China. The President of the Legislative Council is elected by the members. The next legislative elections are due to be held in May 1998 and will use a proportional representation system in five geographical constituencies, each with three to five seats. Thirty members will be elected in functional constituencies and ten more from a committee.

The Urban Council provides services relating to public health and sanitation, culture and recreation in the urban area. A Regional Council was set up in 1986 to provide similar services in the New Territories. There are also 18 district boards (nine in the urban areas and nine in the New Territories) which are statutory bodies that provide a forum for public consultation and participation in the administration of the districts.

Chief Executive, Tung Chee-hwa, *sworn in* 1 July 1997

EXECUTIVE COUNCIL *as at July 1997*

Non-official Members, Dr Chung Sze-yuen *(convenor)*; Dr Raymond Ch'ien; Chung Shui-ming; Nellie Fong; Charles Lee; Antony Leung; Leung Chun-ying; Tam Yiu-chung; Henry Tang; Rosanna Wong; Yang Ti-liang
Ex-officio Members, Anson Chan; Donald Tsang; Elsie Leung

GOVERNMENT SECRETARIAT *as at July 1997*

Administrative Secretary, Anson Chan
Financial Secretary, Donald Tsang
Justice, Elsie Leung

Broadcasting, Culture and Sport, Chau Tak-hay
Civil Service, Lam Woon-kwong
Commissioner Against Corruption, Lily Yam
Commissioner of Customs and Excise, Lawrence Li
Commissioner of Police, Eddie Hui
Constitutional Affairs, Michael Suen
Director of Audit, Dominic Chan
Director of Immigration, Regina Ip
Economic Services, Stephen Ip
Education and Manpower, Joseph Wong
Financial Services, Rafael Hui
Health and Welfare, Katherine Fok Lo, OBE
Home Affairs, Michael M. Y. Suen
Housing, Dominic Wong
Planning, Environment and Lands, Bowen Leung
Security, Peter Lai
Trade and Industry, Denise Yue
Transport, Nicholas Ng
Treasury, Kwong Ki-chi
Works, Benedict Kwong
Speaker of the Provisional Legislative Council, Rita Fan

BRITISH CONSUL-GENERAL, F. Cornish, LVO, CMG, 1 Supreme Court Road, Central, (PO Box 528), Hong Kong. Tel: Hong Kong 2901 3000

BRITISH COUNCIL REPRESENTATIVE, T. Buchanan, Easey Commercial Building, 225 Hennessy Road, Wanchai, Hong Kong

HONG KONG GOVERNMENT OFFICE, 6 Grafton Street, London WIX 3LB. Tel: 0171 499 9821. *Commissioner*, Sir David Ford, KBE, LVO, *apptd* 1993

ECONOMY

The main economic sector is the services industry, especially financial services. It employs roughly half the workforce and contributed 84 per cent to GDP in 1995. The manufacturing sector contributed 8.8 per cent to GDP and accounts for about 13 per cent of total employment. Up to 80 per cent of manufacturing output is eventually exported. Light consumer goods, such as electronics, plastics, electrical products, watches and clocks, accounted for 31 per cent of total domestic exports in 1995. Textiles and clothing, Hong Kong's traditional leading industries, accounted for 39 per cent of exports in 1996.

Diversification in terms of products and markets continues to be the main feature of recent industrial development, as are industrial partnerships with overseas companies. The economy is based on export rather than the domestic market.

Tourism is very important to the economy; over 12 million people visited Hong Kong in 1996.

GNP – US$142,332 million (1995); US$22,990 per capita (1995)

GDP – US$78,775 million (1992); US$16,567 per capita (1992)

INFLATION RATE – 9.2 per cent (1995)
UNEMPLOYMENT – 3.2 per cent (1995)

TRADE

In 1995 imports totalled US$192,774 million and exports US$173,754 million. Hong Kong's principal customers for its domestic products, in order of value of trade, were China, USA, Singapore, Germany and Japan. China was its principal supplier.

Trade with UK	1995	1996
Imports from UK	£2,656,583,000	£2,923,391,000
Exports to UK	3,538,821,000	4,072,935,000

COMMUNICATIONS

Hong Kong has one of the world's finest natural harbours, and it is the busiest container port in the world, with eight terminals, as well as large modern cargo and liner terminals. Dockyard facilities include eight floating drydocks, the largest being capable of docking vessels up to 150,000 tonnes deadweight. A new 17-berth container port will open in stages between 1997 and 2003.

Hong Kong International Airport, Kai Tak, situated to the east of the Kowloon peninsula, is regularly used by over 63 international airlines, providing nearly 3,000 scheduled passenger and cargo services each week. During 1995, over 21 million passengers and 1,458,000 tonnes of freight arrived and departed by air. A new international airport is being built on reclaimed land off Lantau Island at Chek Lap Kok and is planned to become operational by April 1998. It will be capable of handling 35 million passengers and 1.5 million tonnes of cargo annually.

EDUCATION

Free education for children up to the age of 15 is compulsory. Post-secondary education is provided by six universities and one college. The Open Learning Institute of Hong Kong provides university education. There are also seven technical institutes and the Hong Kong Institute of Education.

ILLITERACY RATE – 7.8 per cent

ENROLMENT (percentage of age group) – primary 95 per cent (1980); secondary 61 per cent (1980); tertiary 22.7 per cent (1993)

COLOMBIA
República de Colombia

AREA – 439,737 sq. miles (1,138,914 sq. km). Neighbours: Venezuela (north and east), Brazil (south-east), Peru (south), Ecuador (south-west), Panama (north-west)

POPULATION – 34,520,000 (1994 UN estimate). The language is Spanish. Roman Catholicism is the established religion

CAPITAL – Bogotá (population, 8,000,000, 1992)

MAJOR CITIES – Medellín (2,400,000); Cali (1,800,000); ΨBarranquilla (1,400,000), the major port on the Caribbean; ΨCartagena (700,000), Bucaramanga (350,000); ΨBuenaventura (130,000), the major port on the Pacific

CURRENCY – Colombian peso of 100 centavos

NATIONAL ANTHEM – Oh gloria inmarcesible

NATIONAL DAY – 20 July (National Independence Day)

NATIONAL FLAG – Broad yellow band in upper half, surmounting equal bands of blue and red

LIFE EXPECTANCY (years) – male 66.36; female 72.26

POPULATION GROWTH RATE – 1.7 per cent (1994)

POPULATION DENSITY – 30 per sq. km (1994)

URBAN POPULATION – 67.2 per cent (1985)

Colombia lies in the extreme north-west of South America, having a coastline on both the Caribbean Sea and Pacific Ocean.

The country is divided by the Cordillera de los Andes into a coastal region in the north and west and extensive plains in the east. The eastern range of the Colombian Andes is a series of vast tablelands. This temperate region is the most densely peopled portion of the country. The principal rivers are the Magdalena, Guaviare, Cauca, Atrato, Caquetá, Putumayo and Patia.

HISTORY AND POLITICS

The Colombian coast was visited in 1502 by Columbus, and in 1536 a Spanish expedition penetrated the interior and established a government. The country remained under Spanish rule until 1819 when Simón Bolivar established the Republic of Colombia, consisting of the territories now known as Colombia, Panama, Venezuela and Ecuador. In 1829–30 Venezuela and Ecuador withdrew, and in 1831 the remaining territories formed the Republic of New Granada. The name was changed to the Granadine Confederation in 1858, to the United States of Colombia in 1861 and to the Republic of Colombia in 1866. Panama seceded in 1903.

During the early 1950s Colombia suffered a period of virtual civil war between the supporters of the Conservative and the Liberal parties. From 1957 to 1974 the country was governed under the 'National Front' agreement with an alternating presidency and equal numbers of ministerial posts. The alternation of the presidency ended in 1974 and parity in appointments in 1978. Thereafter, the constitution lays down that government portfolios and administrative appointments shall be divided proportionally among the two major parties in Congress.

Elections to a constitutional convention were held in 1990, in which the former guerrilla movement M19 gained 30 per cent of the vote and a new constitution was promulgated in 1991. Congressional elections to the 102-seat Senate and 163-seat House of Representatives were last held in March 1994 and saw the re-emergence of the traditional parties. The Liberal Party won 89 seats, the Social Conservative Party (PSC) 56 seats and M19 two seats. In the Senate elections the Liberal Party won 52 seats, the PSC 21 seats and M19 one seat. In the 1994 presidential election the Liberal candidate Ernesto Samper narrowly defeated the PSC candidate. President Samper appointed a Liberal–PSC coalition government in August 1994.

INSURGENCIES

Colombia is dogged by insurgency from left-wing guerrillas and from the drugs cartels centred on Cali. In 1989–94 the government reached peace agreements with four left-wing guerrilla groups, including M19 and the Current of Socialist Revolution (CRS), although the Simón Bolivar National Guerrilla Co-ordinating Board remains active. The security threat from the Medellín drugs cartel effectively ended with the death of Pablo Escobar, the cartel leader, in December 1993. In 1995, the government came under suspicion of having links with the cartel and President Samper was accused of authorizing the use of cartel money to fund his 1994 election campaign.

HEAD OF STATE

President, Dr Ernesto Samper-Pizano, *elected* 19 June 1994, *sworn in* 7 August 1994

CABINET *as at July 1997*

Agriculture and Rural Development, Antonio Gómez Merlano
Communications, Saulo Arboleda
Economic Development, Orlando Cabrales Martínez
Environment, Eduardo Verano de la Rosa
Finance and Public Credit, José Antonio Ocampo Gaviria
Foreign Affairs, María Emma Mejía
Foreign Trade, Carlos Ronderos Torres
Health, María Teresa Forero de Saade
Interior, Carlos Holmes Trujillo
Justice and Law, Almabeatriz Renjifo
Labour and Social Security, Iván Moreno Rojas
Mines and Energy, Rodrigo Villamizar
National Defence, Gilberto Echeverry Mejía

National Education, Jaime Niño Diez
Transport, José Enrique Rizo Pombo

COLOMBIAN EMBASSY
Flat 3A, 3 Hans Crescent, London SWIX OLR
Tel 0171–589 9177/5037
Ambassador Extraordinary and Plenipotentiary, HE Dr Carlos
Lemos-Simmonds, apptd 1995

BRITISH EMBASSY
Torre Propaganda Sancho, Calle 98 No. 9–03 Piso 4,
Bogotá
Tel: Bogotá 218 5111
Ambassador Extraordinary and Plenipotentiary, HE Sir Arthur
L. Coltman, KBE, CMG, apptd 1994
BRITISH CONSULAR OFFICES – Barranquilla, Bogotá, Cali
and Medellín
BRITISH COUNCIL DIRECTOR, K. Board, Calle 87 No.
12–79, Bogotá DE
COLOMBO-BRITISH CHAMBER OF COMMERCE, Apartado
Aereo 054 728, Av. 39 No. 13–62, Bogotá DE

DEFENCE

The Army has 12 light tanks, 80 armoured personnel
carriers, and 130 artillery pieces. The Navy has two
submarines, four frigates, 37 patrol and coastal vessels, two
aircraft and two helicopters at eight bases. The Air Force
has 74 combat aircraft and 75 armed helicopters.
MILITARY EXPENDITURE – 2.0 per cent of GDP (1995)
MILITARY PERSONNEL – 146,300: Army 121,000, Navy
18,000, Air Force 7,300
CONSCRIPTION DURATION – 12–18 months

ECONOMY

Coal, natural gas and hydroelectricity resources are
largely unexploited, although development of coal is being
given priority. In 1995 26.1 million tonnes of coal and 30.1
million tonnes of crude petroleum were produced. Since
1993 oil reserves of 1,000 million barrels and large gas
reserves have been discovered.

The hydrocarbon sector accounts for over half of the
mining output, precious metals (gold, platinum and silver)
and iron ore accounting for the remainder. Other mineral
deposits include nickel, bauxite, copper, gypsum, limestone, phosphates, sulphur and uranium. Colombia is also
the world's largest producer of emeralds and has deposits of
other precious and semi-precious stones.

A wide variety of crops are grown, principally coffee.
Other major cash crops are sugar, bananas, cut flowers and
cotton. Cattle are raised in large numbers, and meat and
cured skins and hides are also exported.

The government has encouraged diversification to
reduce dependence on coffee as the major export and this
has led to the growth of new export-orientated industries,
particularly textiles, paper products and leather goods.
Stimulus to the economy has been provided by loans from
the World Bank and IADB for project development,
particularly in the power sector (in which hydroelectric
projects have predominated) and for telecommunications.

Since the late 1980s the government has introduced
trade liberalization and privatization measures which have
effectively freed foreign exchange transactions, increased
foreign competition, ended protectionism and reduced
inflation.

In 1993 the government had a budget deficit of 0.55 per
cent of GDP. There was a current account surplus of
US$912 million in 1992. In March 1997 Colombia was
blacklisted by the USA for failing to curb levels of drug
production sufficiently.

GNP – US$70,263 million (1995); US$1,910 per capita
(1995)
GDP – US$42,600 million (1992); US$1,300 per capita
(1992)
ANNUAL AVERAGE GROWTH OF GDP – 5.3 per cent (1995)
INFLATION RATE – 21.0 per cent (1995)
TOTAL EXTERNAL DEBT – US$20,760 million (1995)

TRADE

Principal exports are petroleum and derivatives, coffee,
bananas, cut flowers, clothing and textiles, ferro-nickel
and coal. Principal trading partners are USA, the EU and
Latin America.

In 1995 imports totalled US$13,853 million and exports
US$9,764 million.

Trade with UK	1995	1996
Imports from UK	£145,244,000	£177,767,000
Exports to UK	174,109,000	211,476,000

COMMUNICATIONS

The Andes make surface transport difficult so air transport
is used extensively. There are daily air services between
Bogotá and all the principal towns, as well as frequent
services to other countries. The 'Atlantic Railway' links the
departmental lines running down to the River Magdalena,
and completes the connection between Bogotá and Santa
Marta. Although the railways are in a poor state, there are
about 2,600 miles of rail in use at present. The road
network consists of 105,201 km of roads of all types, of
which 21,800 km are classified as main trunk and transver-
sal roads. A canal to link the Pacific Ocean and the
Caribbean Sea has been planned.

There are three national television channels.

CULTURE AND EDUCATION

There is a flourishing press in urban areas and a national
literature supplements the rich inheritance from the time
of Spanish colonial rule. State education is free. There are
27 universities.
ILLITERACY RATE – 8.7 per cent
ENROLMENT (percentage of age group) – primary 87 per
cent; secondary 46 per cent; tertiary 17.5 per cent (1994)

THE COMOROS
République Fédérale Islamique des Comores

AREA – 863 sq. miles (2,235 sq. km). The Comoro
archipelago includes the islands of Great Comoro,
Anjouan, Mayotte and Moheli and certain islets in the
Indian Ocean
POPULATION – 630,000 (1994 UN estimate), mostly
Muslim
CAPITAL – Moroni (population, 17,267, 1980), on Great
Comoro
CURRENCY – Comorian franc of 100 centimes. The Franc
CFA / Franc of 100 centimes is also used
NATIONAL DAY – 6 July (Independence Day)
NATIONAL FLAG – Green ground, with a white crescent
and four white stars, horns towards the fly. The name of
Allah, in Arabic script in the upper fly and the name of
Mohammed in the lower hoist
LIFE EXPECTANCY (years) – male 55.50; female 56.50
POPULATION GROWTH RATE – 3.7 per cent (1994)
POPULATION DENSITY – 282 per sq. km (1994)
URBAN POPULATION – 28.5 per cent (1991)
ILLITERACY RATE – 42.7 per cent

ENROLMENT (percentage of age group) – primary 51 per cent (1993); tertiary 0.5 per cent (1990)

HISTORY AND POLITICS

The islanders voted for independence from France in December 1974 and three islands became independent on 6 July 1975. The island of Mayotte opposed independence and has remained under French administration.

An election in 1993 brought President Djohar's PDR party to power. Djohar was temporarily ousted in a coup attempt by mercenaries led by former French colonel Bob Denard in September 1995 which was thwarted by French troops. While Djohar was abroad for medical attention, the Prime Minister of the newly installed unity government, Caabiel Yachroutou, declared himself interim president and refused to acknowledge Djohar's authority, resulting in the formation of a rival government. Djohar returned to the Comoros in January 1996 but was prohibited from contesting the March 1996 presidential election, which was won by Mohammad Taki Abdoulkarim of the National Union for Democracy in the Comoros. Taki dissolved the National Assembly and legislative elections were held in December 1996 although boycotted by the opposition FAR.

POLITICAL SYSTEM

In October 1996 a new constitution was approved by referendum. The president may be elected for an unlimited number of six-year terms and has the authority to appoint a prime minister and Governors, and reports to the Federal Assembly.

Each island is administered by a Governor, assisted by up to four Commissioners whom he appoints, and has an elected Legislative Council.

HEAD OF STATE

President, Mohammad Taki Abdoulkarim, *sworn in* 25 March 1996

GOVERNMENT *as at October 1996*

Prime Minister, Tajiddine Ben Said Massonde
Agricultural Production and the Environment, Said Ali Mohamed
Defence, Mouhdar Ahmed Charif
Education, Professional Training, Francophone Affairs, Culture, Youth, Sports and Scientific Research, Mouzaoir Abdallah
Finance, Economy, Budget and Internal Trade, Said Ali Kemal
Foreign Affairs, Co-operation and External Trade, Said Omar Said Ahmed
Industry, Works and Mining Research, Madi Ahmada
Interior and Information, Said Mohamed Said Hassan
Justice and Islamic Affairs, Mohamed Abdul Wahab
Territorial Development, Housing and Town Planning, Soidri Salim Madi
Public Health, Population and Social Affairs, Halidi Abderenane Ibrahim
Tourism, Transport, Posts and Telecommunications, Omar Tamou

BRITISH AMBASSADOR, HE Robert Dewar, resident at Antananarivo, Madagascar

ECONOMY

The most important products are vanilla, copra, cloves and essential oils, which are the principal exports; cacao, sisal and coffee are also cultivated. Great Comoro is well forested and produces some timber.
GNP – US$237 million (1995); US$470 per capita (1995)
GDP – US$252 million (1992); US$466 per capita (1992)
TOTAL EXTERNAL DEBT – US$203 million (1995)

TRADE WITH UK	1995	1996
Imports from UK	£2,021,000	£907,000
Exports to UK	13,000	68,000

REPUBLIC OF CONGO
République du Congo

AREA – 132,047 sq. miles (342,000 sq. km). Neighbours: Gabon (west) and the Democratic Republic of Congo (east)
POPULATION – 2,516,000 (1994 UN estimate)
CAPITAL – Brazzaville (population, 596,200, 1984)
MAJOR CITIES – ΨPointe Noire (350,000)
CURRENCY – Franc CFA of 100 centimes
NATIONAL DAY – 15 August
NATIONAL FLAG – Divided diagonally into green, yellow and red bands
LIFE EXPECTANCY (years) – male 48.91; female 53.77
POPULATION GROWTH RATE – 3.0 per cent (1994)
POPULATION DENSITY – 7 per sq. km (1994)
MILITARY EXPENDITURE – 1.7 per cent of GDP (1995)
MILITARY PERSONNEL – 15,000: Army 8,000, Navy 800, Air Force 1,200, Paramilitaries 5,000
ILLITERACY RATE – 25.1 per cent

HISTORY AND POLITICS

Formerly the French colony of Middle Congo, the Congo became a member state of the French Community on 28 November 1958 and fully independent on 17 August 1960.

In 1968, a National Council of army officers took power and created the Parti Congolais du Travail (PCT) and the People's Republic of the Congo the following year. After popular pressure, the PCT abandoned its monopoly of power and renounced Marxism in 1990. A transitional government was formed in January 1991 and a national conference suspended the constitution, stripped President Sassou-Nguesso of all powers and formed itself into the Higher Council of the Republic (CSR). In December 1991 the CSR adopted a new multiparty constitution with a directly-elected president and a bicameral parliament. The new constitution was approved by a referendum in March 1992 and in the ensuing presidential and legislative elections the Pan-African Union for Social Democracy (UPADS) emerged as the largest party in both the Senate and the National Assembly.

The lack of a parliamentary majority forced President Lissouba to call fresh elections in May and June 1993. These too were won by the UPADS but the results were disputed by opposition groups and violence broke out between the armed forces and armed supporters of the URD (Union for Democratic Renewal)-PCT opposition alliance. Fighting resumed until February 1994, when it was agreed to call in an international panel to examine the 1993 election results. The panel annulled the results in nine seats, for which by-elections were held in April 1995. A new UPADS-dominated government was appointed in January 1995 which included URD members who had left the opposition alliance. A multiparty Cabinet was appointed in September 1996. In June 1997 fighting broke out between forces of President Lissouba and former president Sassou-Nguesso. *See also* Events of the Year.

HEAD OF STATE

President, Pascal Lissouba, *elected* 16 August 1992

CABINET *as at July 1997*
Prime Minister, Charles David Ganao

Ministers of State, Martin Mberi *(Decentralization, Communication, Urban Development and Housing);* Col. Philippe Bikinkita *(Interior and Security);* Victor Tamba-Tamba *(Transport and Civil Aviation)*
Agriculture, Water and Forest Resources, Fisheries, Prosper Koyo
Civil Service and Territorial Administration, Marius Mouambenga
Commerce, Consumption and Small and Medium-sized Enterprises, Joseph Hondjuila Miokono
Economy, Planning and Finance, Nguila Moungounga-Nkombo
Energy, Jean Itadi
Equipment and Public Works, Lambert Galibali
Foreign Affairs and Co-operation, Francophonie, Destin-Arsène Tsaty-Boungou
Higher and Technical Education, Martial Vincent De Paul Ikounga
Hydrocarbons and Mines, Benoît Koukebene
Industrial Development, Raymond Vincent Ombaka Ekori
Justice, Joseph Ouabari
Labour and Vocational Training, Théophile Obenga
National Defence, Gen. François Ayayen
Posts and Telecommunications, Alphonse Nkoua
Primary and Secondary Education, Sylvain Mackosso-Macrosso
Public Health, Gaston Bikandou
Scientific Research, Anaclet Tsomambet
Tourism and Environment, Gabriel Matsiona
Women's Integration into Development, Marie Thérèse Avemeka
Youth, Sports and Civic Service, Henri Okemba

EMBASSY OF THE REPUBLIC OF CONGO
37 bis rue Paul Valéry, 75116 Paris, France
Tel: Paris 4500 6057
Ambassador Extraordinary and Plenipotentiary, HE Pierre-Michel Nguimbi, apptd 1996

HONORARY CONSULATE, Alliance House, 12 Caxton Street, London SW1H 0QS. Tel: 0171-222 7575. *Honorary Consul,* L. Muzzu

BRITISH AMBASSADOR, Marcus Hope, resident at Kinshasa, Democratic Republic of Congo
HONORARY CONSULATES – Brazzaville and Pointe Noire

ECONOMY

Congo has its own oil deposits, producing about 9 million tonnes annually. It also produces lead, zinc and gold. The principal agricultural products are timber, cassava, sugar cane and yams. Imports are mainly of machinery.
    In 1993 Congo had a trade surplus of US$617 million and a current account deficit of US$507 million. In 1996 the UN approved a three-year loan of US$100 million and the Paris Club cancelled 67 per cent of the debt owed to it by Congo.
GNP – US$1,784 million (1995); US$680 per capita (1995)
GDP – US$2,802 million (1992); US$1,428 per capita (1992)
ANNUAL AVERAGE GROWTH OF GDP – 1.8 per cent (1989)
INFLATION RATE – 2.0 per cent (1993)
TOTAL EXTERNAL DEBT – US$6,032 million (1995)

TRADE WITH UK	1995	1996
Imports from UK	£18,426,000	£29,000,000
Exports to UK	5,229,000	22,698,000

DEMOCRATIC REPUBLIC OF CONGO

AREA – 905,567 sq. miles (2,345,409 sq. km)
POPULATION – 42,552,000 (1994 UN estimate). The population was 34,671,607 at the 1985 census, composed almost entirely of Bantu groups, divided into roughly 300 semi-autonomous tribes. Minorities include Sudanese, Nilotes, Pygmies and Hamites, as well as refugees from Angola. Swahili, a Bantu dialect with an admixture of Arabic, is the nearest approach to a common language in the east and south, while Lingala is the language of a large area along the river and in the north, and Kikongo of the region between Kinshasa and the sea. French is the language of administration
CAPITAL – Kinshasa (population, 2,664,309, 1985)
MAJOR CITIES – Kananga (601,239); Kisangani (310,705); Likasi (146,394); Lubumbashi (403,623); ΨMatadi (143,598); Mbandaka (134,495)
CURRENCY – New zaïre of 100 makuta
NATIONAL DAY – 24 November
NATIONAL FLAG – Blue with a large yellow five-pointed star in the centre and five small yellow five-pointed stars in a vertical line down the hoist
LIFE EXPECTANCY (years) – male 50.40; female 53.66
POPULATION GROWTH RATE – 4.5 per cent (1994)
POPULATION DENSITY – 18 per sq. km (1994)
URBAN POPULATION – 39.5 per cent (1985)
MILITARY EXPENDITURE – 2.0 per cent of GDP (1995)
ILLITERACY RATE – 22.7 per cent
ENROLMENT (percentage of age group) – primary 54 per cent (1993); secondary 17 per cent (1993); tertiary 1.9 per cent (1990)

The Democratic Republic of Congo (formerly Zaïre) is Africa's second largest state. Apart from the coastal district in the west which is fairly dry, the rainfall averages between 60 and 80 inches. The average temperature is about 27°C, but in the south the winter temperature can fall nearly to freezing point. Extensive forest covers the central districts.

HISTORY AND POLITICS

The state of the Congo, founded in 1885, became a Belgian colony in 1908 and was administered by Belgium until independence in 1960. Mobutu Sésé Seko, formerly commander-in-chief of the Congolese National Army, came to power in a coup in 1965 and was elected president in 1970. Legislative power was vested in a unicameral National Legislative Council, elected for a five-year term by compulsory direct and universal suffrage with candidates proposed by the sole legal political party, Mouvement Populaire de la Révolution (MPR).
    Political reforms were announced in April 1990 and President Mobutu called a National Conference to draft a new constitution although the government refused to grant it sovereign status. Mobutu accepted an opposition-dominated government under Prime Minister Etienne Tshisekedi in October 1991. His attempts to replace this with MPR-dominated governments failed and the National Conference confirmed the Tshisekedi government as legitimate in August 1992.
    From 1992 to 1995 President Mobutu and the opposition were locked in a power struggle. In January 1994 President Mobutu dissolved the government and endorsed the formation of a High Council of the Republic–Parliament of Transition (HCR–PT) with a mandate of choosing a new prime minister. On 9 April 1994 President Mobutu promulgated a Transitional Constitutional Act which regulated a 15-month period of transition to democracy.

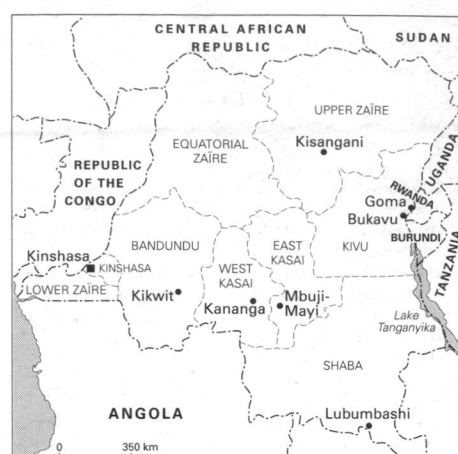

In July 1995 the HCR–PT voted to extend the transition period by a further two years.

In October 1996 fighting broke out between Zaïrean Tutsis (*Banyamulenge*) and the Zaïrean army in North and South Kivu provinces which had received an influx of Hutu refugees from Rwanda. The pro-Hutu army attempted to expel the Tutsis from the region but found themselves outgunned by the rebels, under the leadership of Laurent Kabila, who were backed by the Rwandan and Ugandan governments. Kabila's Alliance of Democratic Forces for the Liberation of Congo-Zaïre (AFDL) captured Kinshasa in May 1997 and President Mobutu fled. Zaïre was renamed the Democratic Republic of Congo. *See also* Events of the Year.

SECESSION

Since 1992 ethnic Katangans have been forcing ethnic Kasai mineworkers and their families out of the southern region of Shaba (Katanga) in a wave of ethnic violence which is a repeat of the Katanga secessionist war in 1960. In December 1993 the Governor of Shaba declared total autonomy and announced the reversion of the region's name to Katanga.

POLITICAL SYSTEM

President Kabila announced a two-year transitional period before elections in April 1999. A Constituent Council is to be set up to draft a new constitution that will be approved or rejected in a referendum in December 1998. Political parties have been banned.

There are 11 regions, each under a Governor and provincial administration: Bas-Zaïre (provincial capital, Matadi); Bandundu (Bandundu); Equateur (Mbandaka); Haut-Zaïre (Kisangani); Kinshasa (Kinshasa); Maniema (Kindu); North Kivu (Goma); South Kivu (Bukavu); Shaba (Katanga) (Lubumbashi); East Kasai (Mbuji-Mayi); West Kasai (Kananga).

HEAD OF STATE

President and Minister of Defence, Laurent Désiré Kabila, *sworn in* 29 May 1997

CABINET *as at July 1997*

Agriculture, Paul Bandoma
Civil Service, Justine Mpoyo Kasa-Vubu
Defence, The President
Economy, Industry and Commerce, Pierre Victoir Mpoyo
Energy, Pierre Lokombe Kitete
Environment and Tourism, Eddy Angulu
Finance, Mawapanga Mwana Nanga
Foreign Affairs, Bizima Karaha
Health, Dr Jean-Baptiste Sondji
Home Affairs, Kongolo Mwenze
Information and Cultural Affairs, Raphaël Ghenda
International Co-operation, Thomas Kanza
Justice, Célestin Luangi
Mines, Matukulo Kambale
National Education, Kamara Wa Kahikara
Planning and Development, Babi Mbaye
Post and Telecommunications, Kinkela Vinkasi
Public Works, Tshubaka Bisikuabo
Reconstruction, Etienne Richard Mbaya
Transport, Henri Mova Sakani
Youth and Sports, Tshibal Mutombo

EMBASSY OF THE DEMOCRATIC REPUBLIC OF CONGO
26 Chesham Place, London SW1X 8HH
Tel 0171-235 6137
Ambassador Extraordinary and Plenipotentiary, new appointment awaited

BRITISH EMBASSY
Avenue des Trois 'Z', Gombe, Kinshasa
Tel: Kinshasa 34775
Ambassador Extraordinary and Plenipotentiary, Marcus L. H. Hope, apptd 1996
CONSULATE – Kisangani

ECONOMY

The cultivation of oil palms is widespread, palm oil being the most important agricultural cash product though it is no longer exported. Coffee, rubber, cocoa and timber are the most important agricultural exports. The production of cotton, pyrethrum and copal is increasing. The country is rich in minerals, particularly Shaba (Katanga) province. Copper is widely exploited, and industrial diamonds and cobalt are also produced. Oil deposits are exploited off the Zaïre estuary and reef-gold is mined in the north-east of the country.

There is a wide variety of small secondary industries, the main products being foodstuffs, beverages, tobacco, textiles, leather, wood products, cement and building materials, metallurgy, small river craft and bicycles. There are reserves of hydroelectric power and the Inga dam on the river Zaïre supplies electricity to Matadi, Kinshasa and Shaba.

Rampant hyperinflation and corruption have left the economy and the state's finances in a parlous state. Multilateral and bilateral aid was greatly reduced because of President Mobutu's refusal to leave office.

In 1993 the government had a budget deficit equivalent to 13.72 per cent of GDP.
GNP – US$5,313 million (1995); US$120 per capita (1995)
GDP – US$3,617 million (1992); US$93 per capita (1992)
ANNUAL AVERAGE GROWTH OF GDP – – 10.5 per cent (1992)
INFLATION RATE – 541.9 per cent (1995)
TOTAL EXTERNAL DEBT – US$13,137 million (1995)

TRADE

The chief exports are copper, crude oil, coffee, diamonds, rubber, cobalt, gold, cassiterite, zinc and other metals.

In 1994 imports totalled US$382 million and exports US$419 million

Trade with UK	1995	1996
Imports from UK	£15,671,000	£17,090,000
Exports to UK	11,350,000	14,754,000

COMMUNICATIONS

There are approximately 20,500 km of roads (earth-surfaced) of national importance, and 6,000 km of railways. The country has four international and 40 principal airports.

COSTA RICA
República de Costa Rica

AREA – 19,730 sq. miles (51,100 sq. km). Neighbours: Nicaragua, Panama

POPULATION – 3,071,000 (1994 UN estimate); mainly of European origin. The language is Spanish

CAPITAL – San José (population, 1,186,417, 1994 estimate)

MAJOR CITIES – Alajuela (44,358); ΨPuntarenas (37,390); ΨLimón (67,784)

CURRENCY – Costa Rican colón (₡) of 100 céntimos

NATIONAL ANTHEM – Himno Nacional de Costa Rica

NATIONAL DAY – 15 September

NATIONAL FLAG – Five horizontal bands, blue, white, red, white, blue (the red band twice the width of the others with emblem near staff)

LIFE EXPECTANCY (years) – male 72.89; female 77.60

POPULATION GROWTH RATE – 2.3 per cent (1994)

POPULATION DENSITY – 60 per sq. km (1994)

URBAN POPULATION – 44.0 per cent (1994)

MILITARY EXPENDITURE – 0.3 per cent of GDP (1995)

ILLITERACY RATE – 5.2 per cent

ENROLMENT (percentage of age group) – primary 90 per cent (1994); secondary 43 per cent (1994); tertiary 30.3 per cent (1991)

The coastal lowlands have a tropical climate but the interior plateau, with a mean elevation of 4,000 feet, enjoys a temperate climate.

HISTORY AND POLITICS

For nearly three centuries (1530–1821) Costa Rica was under Spanish rule. In 1821 the country obtained its independence, although from 1824 to 1839 it was one of the United States of Central America.

In 1948 the Army was abolished, the President declaring it unnecessary. The main political parties are the Social Christian Unity Party (PUSC) and the National Liberation Party (PLN). The last presidential and legislative elections were held on 6 February 1994 when PLN candidate José Maria Figueres won the presidential election, and the PLN won 28 seats and the PUSC 25 seats in the Legislative Assembly.

POLITICAL SYSTEM

Executive power is vested in the president, who is head of state and government, with legislative power vested in the 57-member Legislative Assembly. Under the constitution both the President and the members of the Legislative Assembly are elected for a single four-year term and may not be re-elected.

HEAD OF STATE

President, José Maria Figueres Olsen, *took office* 8 May 1994

MINISTERS *as at July 1997*

Vice-President, Minister for the Presidency, Rodrigo Oreamuno

Agriculture and Livestock, Ricardo Garrón

Culture, Youth and Sports, Dr Arnoldo Mora

Finance, Francisco de Paula Gutierrez

Economy, José León Desanti

Education, Eduardo Doryam

Foreign Affairs, Dr Fernando Naranjo

Foreign Trade, José Rossi

Health, Dr Herman Weinstok

Housing, Rebecca Grynspan

Information, Alejandro Soto

Interior, Justice, Maureen Clark

Labour, Farid Ayales

Natural Resources, Energy and Mines, Rene Castro

Planning, Dr Leonardo Garnier

Public Works and Transport, Rodolfo Silva

Science and Technology, vacant

Security, Laura Chinchilla

Tourism, Carlos Roesch

COSTA RICAN EMBASSY

Flat 1, 14 Lancaster Gate, London W2 3LH

Tel 0171-706 8844

Ambassador Extraordinary and Plenipotentiary, HE Jorge Borbón, apptd 1994

BRITISH EMBASSY

Apartado 815, Edificio Centro Colón (11th Floor), San José 1007

Tel: San José 221 5566

Ambassador Extraordinary and Plenipotentiary and Consul-General, HE Richard Jackson, CVO, apptd 1995

ECONOMY

Agriculture is the chief industry and the principal products are coffee, bananas, sugar and cattle (for meat). Other crops are cocoa, rice, maize, potatoes, hemp, pineapple, casava, ginger, chaw chaw, melon and flowers. Industrial activity is principally in the manufacturing sector and manufactured goods include foodstuffs, textiles and clothing, plastic goods, pharmaceuticals, fertilizers and electrical equipment. Tourism became the main source of foreign exchange revenue in 1992.

In 1994 the government had a budget deficit equivalent to 5.71 per cent of GDP. There was a current account deficit of US$470 million in 1993.

GNP – US$8,884 million (1995); US$2,610 per capita (1995)

GDP – US$6,157 million (1992); US$1,977 per capita (1992)

ANNUAL AVERAGE GROWTH OF GDP – 2.5 per cent (1995)

INFLATION RATE – 23.2 per cent (1995)

UNEMPLOYMENT – 5.2 per cent (1995)

TOTAL EXTERNAL DEBT – US$3,800 million (1995)

TRADE

The chief exports are manufactured goods and other products, coffee, bananas, cocoa and sugar. The chief imports are machinery, including transport equipment, manufactures, chemicals, fuel and mineral oils and foodstuffs. In 1993 there was a trade deficit of US$666 million. In 1995 imports totalled US$3,274 million and exports US$2,611 million.

Trade with UK	1995	1996
Imports from UK	£23,271,000	£36,030,000
Exports to UK	78,515,000	93,051,000

COMMUNICATIONS

The chief ports are Limón on the Atlantic coast, through which passes most of the coffee exported, and Caldera on the Pacific coast. The railway system is 500 miles long and nationalized. LACSA is the national airline, operating flights throughout Central and South America, the Caribbean and USA, besides internal flights to local airports by SANSA.

CÔTE D'IVOIRE
République de Côte d'Ivoire

AREA – 124,503 sq. miles (322,463 sq. km). Neighbours: Guinea and Liberia (west), Mali and Burkina Faso (north), Ghana (east)
POPULATION – 13,695,000 (1994 UN estimate): 39 per cent Muslim, 28 per cent Christian (mainly Roman Catholic) and 17 per cent maintain traditional beliefs. The official language is French
CAPITAL – Yamoussoukro (population, 126,191, 1988), the political and administrative capital since 1983
MAJOR CITIES – ΨAbidjan (2,700,000), the economic and financial centre
CURRENCY – Franc CFA of 100 centimes
NATIONAL ANTHEM – L'Abidjanaise
NATIONAL DAY – 7 August
NATIONAL FLAG – Three vertical stripes, orange, white and green
LIFE EXPECTANCY (years) – male 49.69; female 52.38
POPULATION GROWTH RATE – 3.9 per cent (1994)
POPULATION DENSITY – 42 per sq. km (1994)
URBAN POPULATION – 45.6 per cent (1993)
MILITARY EXPENDITURE – 1.0 per cent of GDP (1995)
MILITARY PERSONNEL – 16,200: Army 6,800, Navy 900, Air Force 700, Paramilitaries 7,800
CONSCRIPTION DURATION – Six months
ILLITERACY RATE – 59.9 per cent
ENROLMENT (percentage of age group) – primary 52 per cent (1991); tertiary 3.1 per cent (1990)

The climate is equatorial in the south and west, which are mainly forested; tropical in the centre and east, which are savannah regions with trees; dry and tropical in the north, which is a grassy savannah region.

HISTORY AND POLITICS

Although French contact was made in the first half of the 19th century, Côte d'Ivoire became a colony only in 1893 and was finally pacified in 1912. It decided on 5 December 1958 to remain an autonomous republic within the French Community; full independence outside the Community was proclaimed on 7 August 1960.

The PDCI won multiparty elections held in November 1990 amid allegations of electoral fraud; opposition protests continue. After having been president since independence in 1960, President Houphouët-Boigny died in December 1993 and was replaced by the parliamentary speaker Henri Konan-Bédié. Konan-Bédié was elected by an overwhelming majority following an opposition party boycott in the October 1995 presidential election. The PDCI won 148 of the 175 seats in the November 1995 elections to the National Assembly.

POLITICAL SYSTEM

Côte d'Ivoire has a presidential system of government and a single-chamber National Assembly of 175 members. Although the constitution provides for a multiparty system, it was not until 1990 that any party other than the ruling PDCI party was authorized.

HEAD OF STATE
President, Henri Konan-Bédié, *took office* 7 December 1993, *elected* 22 October 1995

CABINET *as at July 1997*
Prime Minister, Planning and Industrial Development, Daniel Kablan Duncan
Agriculture and Animal Resources, Lambert Kouassi Konan
Commerce, Nicholas Kouassi Akon
Commodities, Guy-Alain Emmanuel Gauze
Communications, Government Spokesperson, Danielle Boni-Claverie
Culture, Bernard Zadi Zahourou
Defence, Bandama N'Gatta
Economic Infrastructure, Ezan Akele
Economy and Finance, Niamien N'Goran
Employment and Civil Service, Social Welfare, Atchi Atsin
Family and Women's Promotion, Albertine Gnanazan Epie
Foreign Affairs, Amara Essy
Handicrafts, Lacine Gon Coulibaly
High Commissioners, Tchere Seka *(Development in Mountainous Areas)*; Ahmadou Ahmed Timite *(Development of Central and Northern Areas)*; Eugene Kindo Bouadi *(Tourism)*; Toure Sekou *(Water)*
Higher Education, Scientific Research and Technological Innovation, Saliou Toure
Housing, Living Conditions and Environment, Albert Kacou Tiapani
Interior and National Integration, Emile Constant Bombet
Justice and Public Freedom, Kouakou Brou
Mines and Petroleum, Rear-Adm. Lamine Fadiga
Minister-Delegates, Safiatou Françoise Ba N'Da *(Energy and Transport)*; Ahoua N'Doli Theophile *(Planning and Industrial Development)*
National Education and Basic Training, Pierre Kipre
National Solidarity, Laurent Dona Fologo
Presidential Affairs, Faustin Kouame
Promotion of Young Farmers, Amadou Ouattara
Relations with Institutions, Ahoua N'Guetta Timothee
Secretary-General of the Government, Adolphe Kadjo Djidji
Security, Marcel Dibonan Koné
Sports, Siguide Soumahoro
Technical Education and Professional Training, Zakpa Komenan
Yamoussoukro, Jean Konan Banny
Youth Promotion and Civil Education, Vlami Bi Dou

EMBASSY OF THE REPUBLIC OF CÔTE D'IVOIRE
2 Upper Belgrave Street, London SW1X 8BJ
Tel 0171–235 6991
Ambassador Extraordinary and Plenipotentiary, HE Kouadio Adjoumani, apptd 1997

BRITISH EMBASSY
Immeuble Les Harmonies, 01 BP 2581, Abidjan 01
Tel: Abidjan 226850
Ambassador Extraordinary and Plenipotentiary, HE Margaret I. Rothwell, CMG, apptd 1990

ECONOMY

Côte d'Ivoire became wealthy in the 1970s because of the high prices of its two principal export earners, coffee and cocoa. In the late 1980s the economy contracted considerably as its exports deteriorated in competitiveness and its rivals devalued their currencies while the franc CFA remained pegged to the French franc. An economic reform and stabilization programme began in 1989 under IMF auspices which has brought down inflation, increased investment and led to GDP growth. The devaluation of the CFA franc in January 1994 has increased exports considerably and restored a trade surplus. For the 1994–6 period Côte d'Ivoire has received US$467 million in credit support from the IMF.

The principal exports are coffee, cocoa, timber, palm oil, sugar, rubber, pineapples, bananas, and cotton. There are a few deposits of diamonds and minerals including manganese and iron. Oil and gas deposits began to be exploited in 1995.

There was a trade surplus of US$1,072 million in 1993 and a current account deficit of US$1,229 million.

GNP – US$9,248 million (1995); US$660 per capita (1995)
GDP – US$12,418 million (1992); US$1,069 per capita (1992)
ANNUAL AVERAGE GROWTH OF GDP – 3.5 per cent (1981)
INFLATION RATE – 14.3 per cent (1995)
TOTAL EXTERNAL DEBT – US$18,952 million (1995)

TRADE WITH UK	1995	1996
Imports from UK	£49,428,000	£54,165,000
Exports to UK	101,737,000	91,470,000

CROATIA

AREA – 34,022 sq. miles (88,117 sq. km). Neighbours: Slovenia, Hungary, the rump Federal Yugoslav state, Bosnia-Hercegovina
POPULATION – 4,504,000 (1994 UN estimate); 4,784,265 (1991 census): 78 per cent Croat, 12 per cent Serb, 2 per cent Yugoslav. Also Hungarians, Italians, Albanians, Czechs, Ukrainians and Jews. Roman Catholic 76.5 per cent, Eastern Orthodox 11.1 per cent, Protestant 1.4 per cent, Muslim 1.2 per cent. The majority language is Croatian in the Latin script. Serbs use Serbian in the Cyrillic script
CAPITAL – Zagreb (population, 867,717, 1991)
MAJOR CITIES – Split (200,459) Rijeka (167,964) and Osijek (129,792), 1991
CURRENCY – Kuna of 100 lipas
NATIONAL ANTHEM – Lijepa naša domovina (Our Beautiful Homeland)
NATIONAL DAY – 30 May (Statehood Day)
NATIONAL FLAG – Three horizontal stripes of red, white, blue, with the national arms over all in the centre
LIFE EXPECTANCY (years) – male 68.29; female 75.63
POPULATION GROWTH RATE – –1.5 per cent (1994)
POPULATION DENSITY – 51 per sq. km (1994)
URBAN POPULATION – 54.3 per cent (1991)
ILLITERACY RATE – 2.4 per cent
ENROLMENT (percentage of age group) – primary 82 per cent; secondary 66 per cent; tertiary 27.1 per cent (1994)

Croatia is divided into three major geographic regions: the Pannonian region in the north, the central mountain belt, and the Adriatic coast region of Istria and Dalmatia which has 1,185 islands and islets and 1,104 miles (1,778 km) of coastline.

HISTORY AND POLITICS

Croatia was part of the Austro-Hungarian Empire from 1526 to 1918. On 29 October 1918 the Croatian parliament declared Croatia independent and soon after Croatia joined with Slovenia, Bosnia-Hercegovina, Serbia and Montenegro to form the 'Kingdom of Serbs, Croats and Slovenes' (renamed Yugoslavia in 1929). From 1941 to 1945 Yugoslavia was occupied by the Axis powers, with Italy and Hungary annexing parts of Croatia and a pro-

Nazi Croat puppet state being established in the remainder of Croatia and Bosnia-Hercegovina. The armed extremists of this state (Ustashe) engaged in fierce fighting with Serbian royalists, Communist partisans and pro-Allied Croat partisans.

At the end of the war Yugoslavia was re-established as a federal republic under Communist rule but gradually disintegrated following the death of the wartime partisan leader Josep Tito in 1980. When Croatia informed Belgrade of its independence in June 1991, the Federal Yugoslav Army (JNA) intervened against local defence forces to prevent the disintegration of the federation. Croatia's ethnic Serb minority, which rejected Croatia's independence, began fighting with the Croat defence forces. By September 1991 this had escalated into war between Croatia and Serbia, which had assumed control of the JNA.

The war in Croatia continued until January 1992 when a cease-fire was declared. The JNA and Serb forces had secured control of virtually all ethnic Serb areas in Croatia. Four UN protected areas, Northern and Southern Krajina and Eastern and Western Slavonia, were created from the Serb-controlled areas in Croatia and UN troops arrived to police the areas. The JNA withdrew from Croatia but the ethnic Serb forces refused to disarm.

In April and May 1990 Croatia's first free, democratic elections were won by the Croatian Democratic Union (HDZ) of Dr Franjo Tudjman. A new constitution was adopted by parliament in December 1990 and a referendum in May 1991 backed independence from Yugoslavia. Croatia declared its independence on 30 May 1991.

The HDZ won a majority of seats in the October 1995 elections to the Chamber of Deputies and in the April 1997 elections to the Chamber of Districts.

SECESSION

Croatia's ethnic Serbs voted to establish a Republic of Serbian Krajina (RSK) in 1993 and elected President Milan Martic in January 1994. Fighting between Croatian Serbs and government troops continued until a cease fire agreement was concluded in the UN-protected areas of Slavonia and Krajina in April 1994. A new mandate agreed for the UN Confidence Rebuilding Operation (UNCRO) was annulled in Western Slavonia following the capture of the area by Croatian forces in May 1995. The government seized the whole of Krajina in August 1995 prompting the withdrawal of 10,000 UNCRO peacekeepers and the flight of 150,000 Serbs. The last Croatian Serb-held area of Eastern Slavonia agreed in November 1995 to its eventual reintegration into Croatia in 1997–8. A 5,000-strong UN force was dispatched to the area in 1996 to oversee the formation of a two-year transitional government. In April 1996, the regional council of Eastern Slavonia, the sole remaining component of the RSK, appointed Goran Hadzic as president. The council was dissolved and replaced by a regional assembly based in Vukovar.

FOREIGN RELATIONS

An agreement to normalize relations with Yugoslavia was signed in August 1996. Croatia was sworn in as a member of the Council of Europe in November 1996.

POLITICAL SYSTEM

Executive power is vested in a president and government. The president is directly elected for five-year terms. Legislative power is vested in the bicameral parliament (Sabor), comprising the 68-member Chamber of Districts and the 127-member Chamber of Deputies.

Croatia is divided into 20 counties; each county elects three members to the Chamber of Districts. Counties are composed of groups of districts and function both as units of local government and as regional offices for the central administration. There are 102 districts.

HEAD OF STATE
President, Franjo Tudjman, *elected* May 1990, *re-elected* 2 August 1992, 15 June 1997

CABINET *as at July 1997*
Prime Minister, Zlatko Matesa
Deputy PMs, Borislav Skegro *(Economy and Finance)*; Dr Mate Granic *(Foreign Affairs)*; Dr Jure Radic *(Reconstruction and Development)*; Dr Ivica Kostovic *(Humanitarian Issues and Science)*; Ljerka Mintas-Hodak *(Domestic Policy and Public Services)*
Administration, Davorin Mlakar
Agriculture and Forestry, Zlatko Dominkovic
Co-ordination and Emigration, Marijan Petrovic
Culture, Bozo Biskupic
Defence, Gojko Susak
Economy, Nenad Porges
Education and Sport, Ljilja Vokic
Finance, Bozo Prka
Health, Dr Andrija Hebrang
Interior, Ivan Penic
Justice, Miroslav Separovic
Labour and Social Welfare, Joso Skara
Maritime Affairs, Transport and Communications, Zeljko Luzavec
Privatization and Property Management, Milan Kovac
Tourism, Nico Bulic
Urban Planning, Construction and Housing, Marko Sirac
Without Portfolio, Branko Mocibob

EMBASSY OF THE REPUBLIC OF CROATIA
21 Conway Street, London WIP 5HL
Tel 0171-387 2022
Ambassador Extraordinary and Plenipotentiary, HE Andrija Kojaković, apptd 1997

BRITISH EMBASSY
Vlaska 121/III Floor, PO Box 454, 4100 Zagreb
Tel: Zagreb 455 5310
Ambassador Extraordinary and Plenipotentiary, HE Colin Munro, apptd 1997
BRITISH CONSULATES – Split and Dubrovnik
BRITISH COUNCIL DIRECTOR, R. Evans, PO Box 55, 10001, Zagreb

DEFENCE

The Army has 250 main battle tanks, 150 armoured personnel carriers, 100 armoured infantry fighting vehicles and 2,500 artillery pieces. The Air Force has 25 combat aircraft and 15 armed helicopters. The Navy has two submarines and nine patrol and coastal combatants at five bases.
MILITARY EXPENDITURE – 12.6 per cent of GDP (1995)
MILITARY PERSONNEL – 64,700: Army 63,000, Navy 1,100, Air Force 600
CONSCRIPTION DURATION – Ten months

ECONOMY

Production was severely hampered during the conflict in 1991–5; the material damage was estimated by the government to be US$27 billion, with the loss of 13,583 lives. Large areas of farmland were destroyed and the tourist industry, which provided one third of total foreign exchange earnings in 1990, was decimated.
Shipbuilding and fishing are major industries on the Adriatic coast. Inland there is a light manufacturing sec-

tor, food-processing industries, bauxite deposits, thermal mineral springs, hydroelectric potential, and agriculture based on grain, horticulture, livestock and tobacco. Textiles is one of the most important industries employing more than 17 per cent of the population. In April 1996, Croatia agreed to pay 29.5 per cent of Yugoslavia's debt, totalling US$1.45 billion.
In 1995 Croatia had a trade deficit of US$969 million. There was a current account surplus of US$102 million in 1994. In 1995 imports totalled US$7,582 million and exports US$4,633 million.
GNP – US$15,508 million (1995); US$3,250 per capita (1995)
GDP – US$17,200 million (1995); US$5,319 per capita (1992)
INFLATION RATE – 4.1 per cent (1995)
UNEMPLOYMENT – 16.8 per cent (1993)
TOTAL EXTERNAL DEBT – US$3,662 million (1995)

TRADE

Trade with UK	1995	1996
Imports from UK	£231,512,000	£135,333,000
Exports to UK	36,725,000	37,066,000

CUBA
República de Cuba

AREA – 42,804 sq. miles (110,861 sq. km)
POPULATION – 10,960,000 (1994 UN estimate). The language is Spanish
CAPITAL – ΨHavana (population, 2,160,368, 1992 estimate)
MAJOR CITIES – ΨSantiago (425,787), Santa Clara (202,190), Camagüey (291,122), Holguín (241,100) and Guantánamo (204,836)
CURRENCY – Cuban peso of 100 centavos
NATIONAL ANTHEM – Al Combate, Corred Bayameses (To battle, men of Bayamo)
NATIONAL DAY – 1 January (Day of Liberation)
NATIONAL FLAG – Five horizontal bands, blue and white (blue at top and bottom) with red triangle, close to staff, charged with five-point star
LIFE EXPECTANCY (years) – male 72.89; female 76.80
POPULATION GROWTH RATE – 0.8 per cent (1994)
POPULATION DENSITY – 99 per sq. km (1994)
URBAN POPULATION – 74.3 per cent (1992)

HISTORY AND POLITICS

The island was visited by Columbus in 1492. Early in the 16th century the island was conquered by the Spanish, and for almost four centuries remained under Spanish rule. Separatist agitation culminated in the closing years of the 19th century in open warfare. In 1898 the USA intervened and demanded the evacuation of Cuba by Spanish forces. The Spanish–American war led to the abandonment of the island, which came under American military rule from 1899 until 1902, when an autonomous government was inaugurated with an elected president, and bicameral legislature.
A revolution led by Dr Fidel Castro overthrew the government of Gen. Batista in 1959. In 1965 the Communist Party of Cuba was formed to succeed the United Party of the Socialist Revolution; it is the only authorized political party. A new Socialist constitution came into force in 1976 and indirect elections to the National Assembly of People's Power were subsequently held. The

first direct elections to the 589-member National Assembly were held in February 1993; all candidates were officially approved by the Communist Party and ran for election unopposed. The 14 provincial assemblies were elected in the same manner. The fifth congress of the Cuban Communist Party was due to be held in October 1997.

HEAD OF STATE

President of Council of State, Dr Fidel Castro Ruz, *appointed* 2 November 1976, *re-elected* 15 March 1993 for a five-year term

COUNCIL OF STATE *as at July 1997*

President, Dr Fidel Castro Ruz
First Vice-President, Raúl Castro Ruz
Vice-Presidents, Carlos Lage Dávila, Juan Almeida Bosque; Abelardo Colomé Ibarra; Esteban Lazo Bernandez; Dr José Ramon Machado Ventura
Secretary, Dr José Miyai Barrucco

COUNCIL OF MINISTERS *as at July 1997*

President, Dr Fidel Castro Ruz
First Vice-President, Revolutionary Armed Forces, Raúl Castro Ruz
Vice-Presidents, Dr Carlos Rafael Rodríguez; Osmany Cienfuegos Gormarán; Pedro Miret Prieto; José Ramón Fernández Alvárez; José Luis Rodríguez García; Adolfo Diaz Suárez
Secretary, Carlos Lage Dávila
Ministers, Alfredo Jordán Morales (*Agriculture*); Marcos J. Portal León (*Base Industry*); Gen. Silvano Colás Sánchez (*Communications*); Juan M. Junco del Pino (*Construction*); José M. Cañete Alvárez (*Construction Materials Industry*); Abel Prieto Jiménez (*Culture*); Barbara Castillo Cuesta (*Domestic Trade*); José Luis Rodríguez García (*Economy*

and Planning); Luís Ignacio Gómez Gutiérrez (*Education*); Manuel Millares Rodríguez (*Finance and Prices*), Orlando Felipe Rodríguez Romay (*Fishing*); Alejandro Roca Iglesias (*Food Industry*); Ibrahim Ferradaz Garcia (*Foreign Investment and Economic Co-operation*); Roberto Robaina (*Foreign Relations*); Ricardo Cabrisas Ruíz (*Foreign Trade*); Wilfredo López Rodríguez (*Government*); Fernando Vecino Alegret (*Higher Education*); Gen. Abelardo Colomé Ibarra (*Interior*); Roberto Ignacio González Planas (*Iron and Steel, Machine and Electronics Industries*); Roberto Díaz Selelonge (*Justice*); Salvador Valdes Mesa (*Labour and Social Security*); Jesús Pérez Othon (*Light Industry*); Dr Carlos Dotres Martinez (*Public Health*); Rosa Elena Simeón Negrín (*Science, Technology and Environment*); Nelson Torres Pérez (*Sugar Industry*); Osmany Cienfuegos Gorriarán (*Tourism*); Alvaro Pérez Morales (*Transport*)

EMBASSY OF THE REPUBLIC OF CUBA
167 High Holborn, London WC1V 6PA
Tel 0171–240 2488
Ambassador Extraordinary and Plenipotentiary, Rodney Alejandro López Clemente, apptd 1995

BRITISH EMBASSY
e7 ma Y 17, Miramar, Havana.
Tel: Havana 331771
Ambassador Extraordinary and Plenipotentiary, HE Philip McLean, CMG, apptd 1994

DEFENCE

The Army has 1,500 main battle tanks, 400 armoured infantry fighting vehicles, 700 armoured personnel carriers and 740 artillery pieces. The Navy has two submarines, two frigates and 15 patrol and coastal bessels at six bases. The Air Force has 130 combat aircraft and 45 armed helicopters.

The last former Soviet combat personnel left Cuba in 1993, but 810 Russian military advisers remain to operate military intelligence facilities. The United States has 1,650 naval personnel at Guantánamo Bay Naval Base, which has been leased since before the 1959 revolution.

MILITARY EXPENDITURE – 2.8 per cent of GDP (1995)
MILITARY PERSONNEL – 115,000: Army 85,000, Navy 5,000, Air Force 10,000, Paramilitaries 15,000
CONSCRIPTION DURATION – Two years

ECONOMY

After the revolution virtually all land and industrial and commercial enterprises were nationalized. Following the curtailing of Cuba's privileged trading relationships with the Soviet bloc in 1989, the economy deteriorated sharply. GDP fell by 75 per cent between 1989 and 1994, and the government was forced to introduce reforms. Since 1993, the government has legalized the holding of US dollars by private individuals, permitted private enterprise, cut subsidies to loss-making state industries, allowed prices for some goods and services to rise, and introduced income tax. State farms have been transformed into co-operatives run by private individuals and permitted to sell 20 per cent of produce on the open market, but remain relatively unproductive. In 1995, foreign investors were permitted to buy property and own Cuban-based companies, with British and Canadian firms becoming involved in the oil and mining industries.

Austerity measures imposed in 1993 enabled the economy to grow by 0.7 per cent in 1994 and 2.5 per cent in 1995. Sugar is still the mainstay of the economy and the principal source of foreign exchange; production dropped from 8.04 million tons in 1989–90 to 4 million tons in 1993–4. Domestic oil production is rising and reached 1.285 million tonnes in 1995.

The tourism industry has expanded since 1986. In 1993 544,000 tourists visited Cuba, generating US$700 million in gross income.

GDP – US$13,464,million (1992); US$1,534 per capita (1992)

TRADE

Cuba's exports dropped from US$8.1 billion in 1989 to US$1.7 billion in 1993 while imports declined by 73 per cent. Trade between Cuba and the former socialist economies of Europe is now less than 10 per cent of pre-1989 levels. A trade deal was signed with Russia in 1995 providing for the exchange of sugar for oil. The US trade and economic embargo remains in force. Principal exports are sugar, nickel, seafood, citrus fruits, tobacco and rum.

Trade with UK	1995	1996
Imports from UK	£19,160,000	£24,504,000
Exports to UK	8,184,000	19,378,000

COMMUNICATIONS

There are 12,700 km of railway track, of which 5,000 km are in public service. In 1986 there were 13,247 km of road. At present scheduled international air services run to Central and South American countries and Europe.

CULTURE AND EDUCATION

The press and broadcasting are under the control of the government. Education is compulsory and free. In 1964 illiteracy was officially declared to be eliminated.

ILLITERACY RATE – 4.3 per cent
ENROLMENT (percentage of age group) – primary 100 per

cent (1994); secondary 58 per cent (1993); tertiary 13.9 per cent (1994)

CYPRUS
Kypriaki Dimokratia / Kibris Cumhuriyeti

AREA – 3,572 sq. miles (9,251 sq. km)
POPULATION – 734,000 (1994 UN estimate): 84.7 per cent Greek, 12.3 per cent Turkish. Greek and Turkish are official languages
CAPITAL – Nicosia (Lefkosia) (population in the government-controlled area, 186,400)
MAJOR CITIES – ΨLimassol; ΨFamagusta; ΨLarnaca; Paphos; Kyrenia
CURRENCY – Cyprus pound (C£) of 100 cents
NATIONAL ANTHEM – Ode to Freedom
NATIONAL DAY – 1 October (Independence Day)
NATIONAL FLAG – White with a gold map of Cyprus above a wreath of olive
LIFE EXPECTANCY (years) – male 74.64; female 79.05
POPULATION GROWTH RATE – 1.9 per cent (1994)
POPULATION DENSITY – 79 per sq. km (1994)
ILLITERACY RATE – 5.6 per cent
ENROLMENT (percentage of age group) – primary 96 per cent; secondary 92 per cent; tertiary 17.0 per cent (1994)

The climate is Mediterranean, with a hot dry summer and a variable warm winter.

HISTORY AND POLITICS

Cyprus came under British administration from 1878, and was formally annexed to Britain in 1914 on the outbreak of war with Turkey. From 1925 to 1960 it was a Crown Colony. Following the launching in 1955 of an armed campaign by EOKA in support of union with Greece, a state of emergency was declared which lasted for four years. An agreement was signed on 19 February 1959 between the United Kingdom, Greece, Turkey, and the Greek and Turkish Cypriots which provided that Cyprus would be an independent republic.

The island became independent on 16 August 1960. The constitution provided for a Greek Cypriot president and a Turkish Cypriot vice-president. The constitution proved unworkable and led to intercommunal trouble. The UN Peace-Keeping Force in Cyprus (UNFICYP) was set up in 1964.

A general election was held for the House of Representatives (Greek Cypriot and 24 vacant Turkish Cypriot seats) on 26 May 1996, resulting in the parties gaining the following seats: Democratic Rally-Liberal Party 20; AKEL (Communist) 19; Democratic Party (DIKO) 10; EDEK (Socialist) 5; Free Democrats 2. The last presidential election was held in 1993 and won by Glafcos Clerides of the Democratic Rally-Liberal Party.

DIVISION

In 1974, mainland Greek officers under instructions from the military junta in Athens launched a coup and installed a former EOKA member, Nikos Sampson, as president. Turkey invaded northern Cyprus and occupied over a third of the island. In 1975 a 'Turkish Federated State of Cyprus' under Rauf Denktash was declared in this area, its constitution being approved by referendum. In 1983 a 'Declaration of Statehood' was issued which purported to establish the 'Turkish Republic of Northern Cyprus'. The declaration was condemned by the UN Security Council and only Turkey has recognized the new 'state'. In 1985 a referendum in the north of Cyprus approved a constitution for the 'Turkish Republic of Northern Cyprus', Denktash was elected president and a general election was held. Denktash was re-elected in 1990 and April 1995, and general elections were held in 1990 and 1993.

HEAD OF STATE
President, Glafcos Clerides, *elected* 14 February 1993

COUNCIL OF MINISTERS *as at July 1997*

Agriculture, Environment and Natural Resources, Costas Petrides
Commerce, Industry and Tourism, Kyriacos Christophi
Communications and Works, Leontios Ierodiaconou
Defence, Costas Eliades
Education and Culture, Georghios Hadjinicolaou
Finance, Christodoulos Christodoulou
Foreign Affairs, Dr Yiannakis Cassoulides
Government Spokesman, Manolis Christofides
Health, Christos Solomis
Interior, Dinos Michaelides
Justice and Public Order, Nicos Koshis
Labour and Social Insurance, Andreas Moushouttas

CYPRUS HIGH COMMISSION
93 Park Street, London W1Y 4ET
Tel 0171-499 8272
High Commissioner, HE Vanias Markides, apptd 1995
Counsellors, G. Vyrides (*Consular Affairs*); K. Avgoustinos (*Cultural Affairs*); A. Georgiades (*Commerce*)

BRITISH HIGH COMMISSION
Alexander Pallis Street (PO Box 1978), Nicosia
Tel: Nicosia 2-473131
High Commissioner, HE David Madden, CMG, apptd 1994
Counsellor and Deputy High Commissioner, J. S. Buck
Defence Adviser, Col. A. C. Taylor
First Secretary (Commercial), W. Preston

BRITISH COUNCIL DIRECTOR, Robert Ness, PO Box 5654, 3 Museum Street, 1097 Nicosia

BRITISH SOVEREIGN AREAS
The UK retained full sovereignty and jurisdiction over two areas of 99 square miles in all: Akrotiri–Episkopi–Paramali and Dhekelia–Pergamos–Ayios Nicolaos–Xylophagou. The British Administrator of these areas is appointed by The Queen and is responsible to the Secretary of State for Defence. The combined total of army and RAF personnel stationed in the areas is 3,900.
Administrator of the British Sovereign Areas, Air Vice-Marshal P. Millar

DEFENCE
The National Guard has 52 main battle tanks, 27 armoured infantry fighting vehicles, 200 armoured personnel carriers and 86 artillery pieces. Turkey has 35,000 troops in northern Cyprus.
MILITARY EXPENDITURE – 4.5 per cent of GDP (1995)

ECONOMY
Agriculture employs 12 per cent of the workforce. Main products are citrus fruits, grapes and vine products, meat, milk, potatoes and other vegetables. Manufacturing, construction, distribution and other service industries are other major employers. Tourism is the main growth industry with over two million tourists producing C£1,200 million in foreign exchange earnings in 1995; it contributed 25 per cent of GDP and employed 25 per cent of the workforce. Over 5,000 foreign firms and individuals

have registered as offshore companies in Cyprus, and 20 per cent of the world's ships are Cypriot registered.
In 1993 the government had a budget deficit equivalent to 2.4 per cent of GDP.
GDP – US$6,042 million (1992); US$9,273 per capita (1992)
ANNUAL AVERAGE GROWTH OF GDP – 5.0 per cent (1995)
INFLATION RATE – 2.6 per cent (1995)
UNEMPLOYMENT – 2.6 per cent (1995)

TRADE
The UK is the main trading partner, taking 29 per cent of exports in 1994 and supplying 12 per cent of imports. In 1995 imports totalled US$3,694 million and exports US$1,229 million.

Trade with UK	1995	1996
Imports from UK	£307,438,000	£290,735,000
Exports to UK	156,451,000	158,728,000

CZECH REPUBLIC
Česká Republika

AREA – 30,450 sq. miles (78,864 sq. km). Neighbours: Poland (north-east), Germany (west and north-west), Austria (south), Slovakia (south-east)
POPULATION – 10,333,000 (1994 UN estimate), 10,302,000 (1991 census): 95 per cent Czech, 3 per cent Slovak. Czech is the official language. The majority of the population is Roman Catholic, with a small Protestant minority
CAPITAL – Prague (Praha) on the Vltava (Moldau) (population, 1,216,513, 1994 estimate)
MAJOR CITIES – Brno (Brün) (391,093); Ostrava (331,241); Plzeň (174,676)
CURRENCY – Koruna (Kčs) of 100 haléřu
NATIONAL ANTHEM – Kde Domov Můj (Where is my Motherland)
NATIONAL DAY – 28 October
NATIONAL FLAG – White over red horizontally with a blue triangle extending from the hoist to the centre of the flag
LIFE EXPECTANCY (years) – male 69.28; female 76.35
POPULATION GROWTH RATE – –0.1 per cent (1994)
POPULATION DENSITY – 131 per sq. km (1994)
URBAN POPULATION – 75.3 per cent (1991)

The Czech Republic is composed of Bohemia and Moravia. Bohemia is surrounded by mountain ranges while Moravian land stretches to the Danubian basin.

HISTORY AND POLITICS
The area which is now the Czech Republic came under the rule of the Habsburg dynasty in 1526 and remained part of the Austro-Hungarian Empire until 1918. Austrian attempts to Germanize the Czech lands in the 18th and 19th centuries led to the rise of Czech nationalism in the late 19th century. The independence of Czechoslovakia was proclaimed on 28 October 1918 following an amalgamation of Bohemia, Moravia, Slovakia and Ruthenia and was confirmed by the Versailles Peace Conference in 1919.
Czechoslovakia was forced to cede the ethnic German Sudetenland to Nazi Germany in 1938 after the Munich Agreement. German forces invaded the Czech Republic in March 1939 and incorporated it into Germany while Slovakia became a puppet state. The Czech Republic was liberated by Soviet and American forces in May 1945. The pre-war democratic Czechoslovak state was re-established

in 1945, having ceded Ruthenia to the Soviet Union. The Communists took power in a coup in 1948 and remained in power until 1989.

In 1968 the Communist Party under Alexander Dubček embarked on a political and economic reform programme (the Prague Spring). The reforms were suppressed following an invasion by Warsaw Pact troops on the night of 20 August 1968, and were abandoned when Gustáv Husák became leader of the Communist Party in 1969.

Mass protests in November 1989 led to the resignation of the Communist Party Central Committee. The Party was forced to concede its monopoly of power and on 10 December a new government was appointed in which only half the ministers were Communists. Husák resigned as president and was replaced by the dissident writer Václav Havel. Free elections were held in June 1990 in which the Communist Party was defeated.

In late 1992 the leaders of the Czech and Slovak republics agreed to dissolve the federation and form two sovereign states; this took effect on 1 January 1993.

The elections of June 1992 had returned the Civil Democratic Party (ODS) as the largest party in the Czech parliament, and it formed a coalition government with three other centre-right parties in July 1992 which was sworn in as the government of the Czech Republic on 1 January 1993. The former federal President Havel was elected president. Following the general election of 31 May 1996, the ODS and its coalition partners, two seats short of a majority, agreed to slow the rate of privatization in return for support from the opposition Social Democrats.

POLITICAL SYSTEM

The constitution vests legislative power in the bicameral parliament, comprising a 200-member Chamber of Deputies elected for a four-year term and an 81-member Senate elected for a six-year term, one-third being renewed every two years. The president is elected by parliament for a five-year term. Executive power is held by the prime minister and Council of Ministers. A two-thirds majority in parliament is necessary to amend the constitution, and federal laws remain in place unless superseded by Czech ones. A Constitutional Court has been established comprising 15 judges nominated by the president for ten-year terms with Senate approval.

HEAD OF STATE

President, Václav Havel, *elected* 26 January 1993, *sworn in* 2 February 1993

COUNCIL OF MINISTERS *as at July 1997*

Prime Minister, Václav Klaus (ODS)
Agriculture, Josef Lux (KDU-ČSL)
Culture, Jaromír Talíř (KDU-ČSL)
Defence, Miloslav Výborný (KDU-ČSL)
Development of Regions, Towns and Municipalities, Tomáš Kvapil (KDU-ČSL)
Education, Jiří Gruša (ODS)
Environment, Jiří Skalický (ODA)
Finance, Ivan Pilip (ODS)
Foreign Affairs, Josef Zieleniec (ODS)
Health, Jan Stráský (ODS)
Industry and Trade, Karel Kühnl (ODA)
Interior, Jan Ruml (ODS)
Justice, Vlasta Parkánová (ODA)
Labour and Social Affairs, Jindřich Vodička (ODS)
Transport, Martin Říman (ODS)
Without Portfolio, Pavel Bratinka (ODA)

ODS Civic Democratic Party; KDU-ČSL Christian Democratic Union-Czech People's Party; ODA Civic Democratic Alliance

EMBASSY OF THE CZECH REPUBLIC

26–30 Kensington Palace Gardens, London w8 4QY
Tel 0171–243 1115
Ambassador Extraordinary and Plenipotentiary, new appointment awaited
Minister-Counsellor, Milan Jakobec
Military Attaché, Col. Milan Skalický
Counsellor (Commercial), Karel Antropius

BRITISH EMBASSY

Thunovská 14, 11800 Prague 1
Tel: Prague 10439
Ambassador Extraordinary and Plenipotentiary, HE David Broucher, apptd 1997
Deputy Head of Mission, J. M. Cresswell
Defence Attaché, Col. W. E. Nowosielski-Slopowron
First Secretary (Commercial), M. L. Connor
Cultural Attaché, M. O'Neill (*British Council Director*)

DEFENCE

The army has 953 main battle tanks, 951 armoured infantry fighting vehicles, 412 armoured personnel carriers and 830 artillery pieces. The Air Force has 126 combat aircraft and 36 attack helicopters. The Czech Republic has been accepted for membership of Nato.

MILITARY EXPENDITURE – 2.8 per cent of GDP (1995)
MILITARY PERSONNEL – 45,600: Army 28,000, Air Force 16,000, Paramilitaries 1,600
CONSCRIPTION DURATION – 12 months

ECONOMY

Under Communist rule industry was state-owned and nearly all agricultural land was cultivated by state or co-operative farms. An economic reform programme began in 1990 to produce a free-market economy, and the government of the Czech Republic has continued to follow the policies of the former federal government. This has necessitated a restrictive monetary policy to stem inflation and a restructuring of industry to be competitive, and these were major reasons for the break with Slovakia. As a result, foreign investment (US$4,000 million in 1989–94) and private enterprises have grown and reliance on trade with the former Soviet bloc countries has ended. By late 1995 over 90 per cent of the economy had been privatized, with two-thirds of the population owning shares.

A trade-liberalizing association agreement with the EU is in operation. The Czech Republic applied for membership of the EU in January 1996.

A customs union between the Czech and Slovak Republics is in place but separate currencies were introduced in February 1993 following speculation. The Koruna was made fully convertible in October 1995.

Principal agricultural products are sugar beet, potatoes and cereal crops; the timber industry is also very important. Having been the major industrial area of the Austro-Hungarian Empire, the country has long been industrialized, and machinery, industrial consumer goods and raw materials are major exports.

In 1994 the government had a budget surplus equivalent to 0.88 per cent of GDP. In 1995 imports totalled US$26,444 million and exports US$21,647 million.

GNP – US$39,990 million (1995); US$3,870 per capita (1995)
GDP – US$25,193 million (1992); US$2,623 per capita (1992)
ANNUAL AVERAGE GROWTH OF GDP – 4.8 per cent (1995)

INFLATION RATE – 9.1 per cent (1995)
UNEMPLOYMENT – 3.4 per cent (1995)
TOTAL EXTERNAL DEBT – US$16,576 million (1995)

TRADE WITH UK	1995	1996
Imports from UK	£567,923,000	£714,613,000
Exports to UK	321,497,000	372,796,000

EDUCATION

Education is compulsory and free for all children from the ages of six to 16. There are seven universities of which the oldest and most famous is Charles University in Prague (founded 1348).
ENROLMENT (percentage of age group) – tertiary 19.2 per cent (1994)

CULTURE

The Reformation gave a widespread impetus to Czech literature, the writings of Jan Hus (martyred in 1415 as a religious and social reformer) familiarizing the people with Wyclif's teaching. This lasted until the close of the 17th century when Jan Amos Komensky or Comenius (1592–1670) was expelled from the country. Under Austrian rule and with the pursuit of Germanization, there was a period of stagnation until the national revival in the 19th century. Authors of international reputation include Jaroslav Hašek (1883–1923), Jaroslav Seifert (1901–86, Nobel Prize for Literature, 1985), Václav Havel (b. 1936) and Milan Kundera (b. 1929).

DENMARK
Kongeriget Danmark

AREA – 16,639 sq. miles (43,094 sq. km)
POPULATION – 5,251,027 (1996 estimate)
CAPITAL – ΨCopenhagen (population, 1,752,078, 1996 estimate)
MAJOR CITIES – ΨÅrhus 209,404; ΨOdense 143,029; ΨÅlborg 116,567; Esbjerg 73,149; Randers 55,515
CURRENCY – Danish krone of 100 øre
NATIONAL ANTHEMS – Kong Kristian; Det er et yndigt land
NATIONAL DAY – 5 June (Constitution Day)
NATIONAL FLAG – Red, with white cross
LIFE EXPECTANCY (years) – male 72.35; female 77.78
POPULATION GROWTH RATE – 0.3 per cent (1994)
POPULATION DENSITY – 121 per sq. km (1994)

Denmark is a kingdom, consisting of the islands of Zealand, Funen, Lolland, etc., the peninsula of Jutland, the outlying island of Bornholm in the Baltic, and the Faröes and Greenland.

HISTORY AND POLITICS

On 25 January 1993 a coalition government of the Social Democrat, Centre Democrat, Social Liberal and Christian People's Party was sworn in after the previous Conservative-Liberal coalition had resigned. After the last parliamentary election on 21 September 1994, a new coalition government of the Social Democrat, Social Liberal and Centre Democrat parties was formed.

POLITICAL SYSTEM

The legislature consists of one chamber, the *Folketing*, of not more than 179 members, including two for the Faröes and two for Greenland, which is elected for a four-year term. The voting age is 18 with voting based on a proportional representation system with a 2 per cent threshold for parliamentary representation.

HEAD OF STATE

HM The Queen of Denmark, Queen Margrethe II, KG, *born* 16 April 1940, *succeeded* 14 January 1972, *married* 10 June 1967, Count Henri de Monpezat (Prince Henrik of Denmark), and *has issue* Crown Prince Frederik (*see* below); Prince Joachim, *born* 7 June 1969; *married* 18 November 1995, Miss Alexandra Manley (Princess Alexandra of Denmark)
Heir, HRH Crown Prince Frederik, *born* 26 May 1968

CABINET *as at July 1997*

Prime Minister, Poul Nyrup Rasmussen (S)
Business and Industry, Jan Trøjborg (S)
Culture, Ebbe Lundgaard (RV)
Defence, Hans Haekkerup (S)
Development Co-operation, Poul Nielson (S)
Economic Affairs and Nordic Co-operation, Marianne Jelved (RV)
Education and Ecclesiastical Affairs, Ole Vig Jensen (RV)
Environment and Energy, Svend Auken (S)
Finance, Mogens Lykketoft (S)
Food, Agriculture and Fisheries, Henrik Dam Christensen (S)
Foreign Affairs, Niels Helveg Petersen (RV)
Housing and Building, Ole Løvig Simonsen (S)
Interior and Health, Birte Weiss (S)
Justice, Frank Jensen (S)
Labour, Jytte Andersen (S)
Research, Jytte Hilden (S)
Social Affairs, Karen Jespersen (S)
Taxation, Carsten Koch (S)
Transport, Bjørn Westh (S)

S Social Democrat Party; RV Social Liberal Party

ROYAL DANISH EMBASSY
55 Sloane Street, London SW1X 9SR
Tel 0171–333 0200
Ambassador Extraordinary and Plenipotentiary, HE Ole Lønsmann Poulsen, apptd 1996
Counsellor (Commercial), Gunner Tetler
Defence Attaché, Capt. P. Grooss

BRITISH EMBASSY
36–40 Kastelsvej, DK-2100 Copenhagen
Tel: Copenhagen 3526 4600
Ambassador Extraordinary and Plenipotentiary, HE Andrew
Bache, CMG, apptd 1996
Counsellor and Deputy Head of Mission, F. X. Gallagher, OBE
Defence Attaché, Cmdr. W. T. Wiseman, RN
First Secretary (Commercial), D. T. Cox

BRITISH CONSULATES – Åbenraa, Ålborg, Århus, Esbjerg,
Fredericia, Herning, Odense, Rønne (Bornholm);
Tórshavn (Faröe Islands); Godthåb (Nuuk) (Greenland)

BRITISH COUNCIL REPRESENTATIVE, Dr M. Sorensen-
Jones, Gammel Mont 123, 1117 Copenhagen K

DEFENCE

The Army has 353 main battle tanks, 50 armoured infantry
fighting vechicles, 568 armoured personnel carriers, 246
artillery pieces and 12 attack helicopters. The Navy has
five submarines, three frigates and 41 patrol and coastal
vessels at two bases. The Air Force has 66 combat aircraft.
MILITARY EXPENDITURE – 1.8 per cent of GDP (1995)
MILITARY PERSONNEL – 32,900: Army 19,000, Navy
6,000, Air Force 7,900
CONSCRIPTION DURATION – Four to 12 months

ECONOMY

Of the labour force, in 1995 37.7 per cent was employed in
the private retailing sector; 30.5 per cent in the public
sector; 21 per cent in manufacturing and building and 4.7
per cent in agriculture. The chief agricultural products are
pigs, cattle, dairy products, poultry and eggs, seeds, cereals
and sugar beet; manufactures are mostly based on imported raw materials but there are also considerable
imports of finished goods. Denmark is self-sufficient in oil
and natural gas.
GNP – US$156,027 million (1995); US$29,890 per capita
(1995)
GDP – US$132,974 million (1992); US$ 27,626 per capita
(1992)
ANNUAL AVERAGE GROWTH OF GDP – 2.6 per cent
(1995); forecast to be 2.9 per cent in 1997
INFLATION RATE – 2.1 per cent (1995); forecast to be 2.3
per cent in 1997
UNEMPLOYMENT – 7.0 per cent (1995); forecast to be 6.0
per cent in 1997

TRADE

The principal imports are industrial raw materials, consumer goods, construction inputs, machinery, raw materials, vehicles and textile products. The chief exports are
manufactured articles, agricultural and dairy products.
Germany and Sweden are Denmark's main trading partners.

Trade with UK	1995	1996
Imports from UK	£1,996,100,000	£2,111,700,000
Exports to UK	2,075,200,000	2,239,400,000

COMMUNICATIONS

In 1996, the Danish mercantile fleet numbered 584 ships of
more than 100 gross tonnage. There were 3,000 km of
railway, 85 per cent of which belonged to the state and 15
per cent to privately-owned companies. A rail tunnel and
bridge linking the islands of Zealand and Funen was
opened in June 1997.

CULTURE AND EDUCATION

The Danish language is akin to Swedish and Norwegian.
Danish literature, ancient and modern, embraces all forms
of expression, familiar names being Hans Christian Andersen (1805–75), Søren Kierkegaard (1813–55) and Karen
Blixen (1885–1962). Some 38 newspapers are published in
Denmark; eight daily papers are published in Copenhagen.
Education is free and compulsory. Special schools are
numerous, commercial, technical and agricultural pre-
dominating. There are universities at Copenhagen (founded in 1479), Århus (1928), Odense (1966), Roskilde (1972)
and Ålborg (1974).
ENROLMENT (percentage of age group) – primary 99 per
cent (1993); secondary 87 per cent (1992); tertiary 44.8
per cent (1993)

THE FARÖE ISLANDS

The Faröes, or Sheep Islands have an area of 540 sq. miles
(1,399 sq. km) and a population (1995) of 43,700. The
capital is Tórshavn.
Since 1948 the Faröes have had a degree of home rule.
The islands are governed by a *Løgting* of 32 members and a
Landsstyre of four members which deals with special Faröes
affairs, and send two representatives to the *Folketing* at
Copenhagen. The Faröes are not part of the EU.
The main industries are agriculture, fishing, fish- farm-
ing, whaling and the public sector; tourism is growing in
importance.
Prime Minister, Edmund Joensen

Trade with UK	1995	1996
Imports from UK	£8,334,000	£15,499,000
Exports to UK	79,435,000	116,630,000

GREENLAND

Greenland has a total area of 840,004 sq. miles
(2,175,600 sq. km), of which about 16 per cent is ice-free,
and a population (1995) of 55,700. It is divided into three
provinces: West, North and East. The capital is Godthåb
(Nuuk).
Greenland attained a status of internal autonomy in
May 1979 and a government (*Landsstyre*) was established. It
has a *Landsting* of 31 members and sends two representatives to the *Folketing* at Copenhagen. Greenland negotiated its withdrawal from the EU, without discontinuing
relations with Denmark, and left on 1 February 1985.
The traditional industries of fishing, sealing, whaling
and reindeer herding are the most important sectors of the
economy, together with public services and administration. Mineral and oil prospecting revealed deposits of lead,
zinc, iron ore, oil, gas and uranium. Commercial exploitation of these resources has begun. The trade of Greenland
is mainly under the management of the Grønlands Handel.
The USA has acquired certain rights to maintain air bases
in Greenland.
Premier, Lars Emil Johansen

Trade with UK	1995	1996
Imports from UK	£1,884,000	£2,772,000
Exports to UK	9,549,000	9,666,000

DJIBOUTI
Jumhouriyya Djibouti

AREA – 8,958 sq. miles (23,200 sq. km). Neighbours: Eritrea,
Ethiopia, Somalia

POPULATION – 566,000 (1994 UN estimate), 520,000 (1991 census), mostly Afar or Issas
CAPITAL – ΨDjibouti (population, 340,700, 1991)
CURRENCY – Djibouti franc of 100 centimes
NATIONAL DAY – 27 June (Independence Day)
NATIONAL FLAG – Blue over green with white triangle in the hoist containing a red star
LIFE EXPECTANCY (years) – male 46.72; female 50.00
POPULATION GROWTH RATE – 2.3 per cent (1994)
POPULATION DENSITY – 24 per sq. km (1994)
MILITARY EXPENDITURE – 5.3 per cent of GDP (1995)
MILITARY PERSONNEL – 12,600: Army 8,000, Navy 200, Air Force 200, Paramilitaries 4,200
GDP – US$563 million (1992); US$1,238 per capita (1992)
TOTAL EXTERNAL DEBT – US$260 million (1995)
ILLITERACY RATE – 53.8 per cent
ENROLMENT (percentage of age group) – primary 32 per cent (1994); secondary 11 per cent (1985); tertiary 0.1 per cent (1992)

The climate is harsh and much of the country is semi-arid desert.

HISTORY AND POLITICS

Formerly French Somaliland and then the French Territory of the Afars and the Issas, the Republic of Djibouti became independent on 27 June 1977. The sole legal party was formerly the *Rassemblement Populaire pour le Progrès* (RPP, the Popular Rally for Progress). A multiparty constitution was adopted by referendum in 1992 and subsequent multiparty elections held in December 1992 were won by the ruling RPP with 77 per cent of the vote and all 65 seats in the Chamber of Deputies. President Aptidon was re-elected for a fourth six-year term in 1993. However, less than half the electorate voted in either election and the Front for the Restoration of Unity and Democracy (FRUD) boycotted both.

INSURGENCY

Armed FRUD rebels, their support based among ethnic Afars, have been fighting the government since 1991 in protest at the concentration of political power in the hands of the Somali-speaking Issas. A formal peace agreement with the government was signed by the majority faction of FRUD in December 1994 and FRUD was recognized as a political party in March 1996. A minority faction has condemned the agreement and continues to fight.

HEAD OF STATE

President, Hassan Gouled Aptidon, *elected* 1977, *re-elected* 1981, 1987 and 9 May 1993

CABINET *as at July 1997*

Prime Minister, Planning and Land Development, Barkat Gourad Hamadou
Agriculture and Water Resources, Ougoureh Kifle Ahmed
Civil Service and Administrative Reform, Mohamed Dini Farah
Commerce and Tourism, Rifki Abdulkader
Finance and Economy, Mohamed Ali Mohamed
Foreign Affairs and Co-operation, Mohamed Moussa Chehem
Health and Social Affairs,Ali Mohamed Daoud
Industry, Energy and Mines, Ali Abdi Farah
Interior and Regional Administration, Idris Harbi Farah
Justice and Islamic Affairs, Hassan Farah Miguil
Labour and Training, Osman Robleh Daich
National Defence, Abdallah Chirwa Djibril
National Education, Ahmed Guire Waberi
Public Works, Construction and Housing, Atayeh Ismail Waiss

Transport, Communications, Port and Maritime Affairs, Salah Omar Hildid
Youth, Sports and Culture, Mohamed Balad Abdon

EMBASSY OF THE REPUBLIC OF DJIBOUTI
26 rue Emile Ménier, 75116 Paris, France
Tel: Paris 4727 4922
Ambassador Extraordinary and Plenipotentiary, HE Ahmed Omar Farah, apptd 1991

BRITISH AMBASSADOR, HE Gordon Wetherell, resides at Addis Ababa, Ethiopia

BRITISH CONSULATE
PO Box 81, 9–11 Rue de Geneve, Djibouti
Honorary Consul, P. Lambrecht

The French continue to maintain army, navy and air force bases in Djibouti, with a total strength of 3,400 personnel. Djibouti has an excellent port, an international airport, and a railway line runs to Addis Ababa.

TRADE WITH UK	1995	1996
Imports from UK	£13,699,000	£12,911,000
Exports to UK	62,000	74,000

DOMINICA
The Commonwealth of Dominica

AREA – 290 sq. miles (751 sq. km)
POPULATION – 71,000 (1994 UN estimate). English is the official language although Creole French is more commonly used
CAPITAL – ΨRoseau (population, 16,243, 1991)
MAJOR TOWNS – Portsmouth (3,620)
CURRENCY – East Caribbean dollar (EC$) of 100 cents
NATIONAL ANTHEM – Isle of Beauty
NATIONAL DAY – 3 November (Independence Day)
NATIONAL FLAG – Green ground with a cross overall of yellow, black and white stripes, and in the centre a red disc charged with a Sisserou parrot in natural colours within a ring of ten green stars
POPULATION GROWTH RATE – 0.0 per cent (1994)
POPULATION DENSITY – 95 per sq. km (1994)

Dominica, in the Lesser Antilles, lies in the Windward Islands group 95 miles south of Antigua. It is about 29 miles long and 16 miles wide. The island is of volcanic origin and very mountainous, and the soil is very fertile. The temperature varies, according to the altitude, from 13° to 29°C.

HISTORY AND POLITICS

The island was discovered by Columbus in 1493, when it was a stronghold of the Caribs, who remained virtually the sole inhabitants until the French established settlements in the 18th century. It was captured by the British in 1759 but passed back and forth between France and Britain until 1805, after which British possession was not challenged. From 1871 to 1939 Dominica was part of the Leeward Islands Colony, then from 1940 the island was a unit of the Windward Islands group. Internal self-government from 1967 was followed on 3 November 1978 by independence as a republic.

The last general election was held on 12 June 1995 and won by the Dominica United Workers' Party, which captured 11 seats, with five seats each going to the Dominica Freedom Party and the Dominica Labour Party.

POLITICAL SYSTEM

Executive authority is vested in the president, who is elected by the House of Assembly for not more than two terms of five years. Parliament consists of the president and the House of Assembly (21 representatives elected by universal adult suffrage for a five-year term) and nine senators, five of whom are appointed on the advice of the prime minister and the other four on the advice of the Leader of the Opposition.

HEAD OF STATE

President, HE Crispin Sorhaindo, OBE, *elected* 4 October 1993, *took office* 25 October 1993

CABINET *as at July 1997*

Prime Minister, External Affairs, Legal Affairs and Labour, Edison James
Agriculture and the Environment, Peter Carbon
Communications, Works and Housing, Earl Williams
Community Development and Women's Affairs, Gertrude Roberts
Education, Sports and Youth Affairs, Ronald Green
Finance, Industry and Planning, Julius Timothy
Health and Social Security, Doreen Paul
Tourism, Ports and Employment, Sen. Norris Prevost
Trade and Marketing, Norris Charles

HIGH COMMISSION FOR THE COMMONWEALTH OF DOMINICA

1 Collingham Gardens, London SW5 0HW
Tel 0171–370 5194/5
High Commissioner, HE George Williams, apptd 1996
BRITISH HIGH COMMISSIONER, HE Richard Thomas, CMG, resides at Bridgetown, Barbados

BRITISH CONSULATE
PO Box 6, Roseau
Honorary Consul, R. W. Duckworth

ECONOMY

Agriculture is the principal occupation, with tropical and citrus fruits the main crops. Products for export are bananas, lime juice, lime oil, bay oil, copra and rum. Forestry, fisheries and agro-processing are being encouraged. The only commercially exploitable mineral is pumice, used chiefly for building purposes. Manufacturing consists largely of the processing of agricultural products although there have been attempts to diversify into light industry.

GNP – US\$218 million (1995); US\$2,990 per capita (1995)
GDP – US\$175 million (1992); US\$2,594 per capita (1992)
ANNUAL AVERAGE GROWTH OF GDP – 1.8 per cent (1993)
INFLATION RATE – 1.6 per cent (1994)
TOTAL EXTERNAL DEBT – US\$93 million (1995)

TRADE WITH UK	1995	1996
Imports from UK	£9,038,000	£11,166,000
Exports to UK	15,324,000	19,110,000

DOMINICAN REPUBLIC
República Dominicana

AREA – 18,816 sq. miles (48,734 sq. km). Neighbours: Haiti and Cuba (west), Puerto Rico (east)
POPULATION – 7,760,000 (1994 UN estimate). The language is Spanish
CAPITAL – ΨSanto Domingo (population, 1,540,786, 1981)

MAJOR CITIES – Santiago de los Caballeros (550,372); La Vega (385,043); San Francisco De Macoris (235,544); San Juan (239,957); San Cristóbal (446,132), 1981 census
CURRENCY – Dominican Republic peso (RD\$) of 100 centavos
NATIONAL FLAG – Divided into blue and red quarters by a white cross
NATIONAL ANTHEM – Quisqueyanos Valientes, Alcemos (Brave men of Quisqueya, let's raise our song)
NATIONAL DAY – 27 February (Independence Day 1844)
LIFE EXPECTANCY (years) – male 67.63; female 71.69
POPULATION GROWTH RATE – 2.0 per cent (1994)
POPULATION DENSITY – 159 per sq. km (1994)
URBAN POPULATION – 61.2 per cent (1994)
MILITARY EXPENDITURE – 1.3 per cent of GDP (1995)
MILITARY PERSONNEL – 24,500: Army 15,000, Navy 4,000, Air Force 5,500
ILLITERACY RATE – 17.9 per cent
ENROLMENT (percentage of age group) – primary 81 per cent (1994); secondary 22 per cent (1994); tertiary 18.0 per cent (1985)

The Dominican Republic, the eastern part of the island of Hispaniola (Haiti is the western part), is the oldest European settlement in America. The climate is tropical in the lowlands and semi-tropical to temperate in the higher altitudes.

HISTORY AND POLITICS

Santo Domingo was discovered by Columbus in 1492, and was a Spanish colony until 1821. In 1822 it was subjugated by the neighbouring Haitians who remained in control until 1844, when the Dominican Republic was proclaimed. The country was occupied by American marines from 1916 until 1924. Gen. Rafael Trujillo ruled from 1930 until 1961.

President Juan Bosch held office from December 1962 to September 1963, when he was deposed by a military junta. A left-wing revolt in favour of ex-President Bosch in April 1965 developed into civil war lasting until September the same year when Bosch's supporters were defeated by the arrival of US troops and a provisional president was elected. A presidential election in May 1994 was won by the incumbent President Balaguer. Balaguer was replaced by opposition Dominican Liberation Party (PLD) candidate, Leonel Fernández, who defeated the ruling Christian Social Reform Party (PRSC) candidate, Jacinto Peynado, in a run-off election on 30 June 1996.

POLITICAL SYSTEM

Executive power is vested in the president, who is directly elected for four-year terms and appoints the Cabinet. Legislative power is exercised by the Congress, which has a term of four years concurrent with the presidency. The Congress comprises the Senate of 30 senators, one for each province and one for Santo Domingo, and the 120-member Chamber of Deputies.

HEAD OF STATE
President, Leonel Fernández, *elected* 30 June 1996
Vice-President, Dr Jaime David Fernández Mirabal

CABINET *as at July 1997*

Agriculture, Frank Rodríguez
Armed Forces, Gen. Paulino Luna
Attorney-General, Abel Rodríguez del Orbe
Education, Ligia Amada Melo de Cardona
Finance, Daniel Toribio
Foreign Affairs, Eduardo Latorre
Health, Alejandra Guzman

Industry and Commerce, Luis Manuel Bonetti
Information, Miguel Guerrero
Interior, Norge Botello
Labour, Rafael Albuquerque
Public Works and Communications, Jaime Durán
Sport, Juan Marichal
Tourism, Felucho Jiménez
Without Portfolio, Lidio Cadet; Ramón Ventura Carnejo

EMBASSY OF THE DOMINICAN REPUBLIC
15 Brechin Place, London, SW7 4QB
Ambassador Extraordinary and Plenipotentiary, HE Dr Pedro
   Padilla, apptd 1997

BRITISH EMBASSY
Edificio Corominas Pepin, Ave 27 de Fabrero No 233, Santo
Domingo
Tel: Santo Domingo 472 7671/7373
Ambassador Extraordinary and Plenipotentiary, HE Dick
   Thomson, apptd 1995
BRITISH CONSULAR OFFICES – Santo Domingo, Puerto
   Plata.

ECONOMY

Since 1990 the government has successfully reduced
inflation and increased output. Large amounts of foreign
debt have been paid off but unemployment remains high.
State subsidies were ended in 1995 in an attempt to reduce
the budget deficit.
   Sugar, coffee, cocoa, and tobacco are the most important
crops. Other products are peanuts, maize, rice, bananas,
molasses, salt, cement, ferro-nickel, gold, silver, cattle, sisal
products, honey and chocolate. Light industry produces
beer, tinned foodstuffs, glass products, textiles, soap,
cigarettes, construction materials, plastic articles, shoes,
papers, paint, rum, matches and peanut oil.
   In 1993 the government had a budget surplus equivalent
to 0.03 per cent of GDP.
GNP – US$11,390 million (1995); US$1,460 per capita
   (1995)
GDP – US$7,617 million (1992); US$1,092 per capita
   (1992)
ANNUAL AVERAGE GROWTH OF GDP – 4.7 per cent (1995)
INFLATION RATE – 12.5 per cent (1995)
TOTAL EXTERNAL DEBT – US$4,259 million (1995)

TRADE

The chief imports are machinery, foodstuffs, iron and steel,
cotton textiles and yarns, mineral oils (including petrol),
motor vehicles, chemical and pharmaceutical products,
electrical equipment and accessories, construction
material, paper and paper products, and rubber and rubber
products. The chief exports are sugar, coffee, cocoa,
tobacco, chocolate, molasses, bauxite, ferro-nickel and
gold.
   In 1993 there was a trade deficit of US$1,607 million and
a current account deficit of US$161 million. In 1995
imports totalled US$2,976 million and exports US$765
million.

Trade with UK	1995	1996
Imports from UK	£27,946,000	£27,322,000
Exports to UK	24,343,000	25,725,000

COMMUNICATIONS

There are over 4,000 miles of roads and a direct road from
Santo Domingo to Port-au-Prince, the capital of Haiti, but
that part of it in the border area has fallen into disuse. The
frontier has been closed since 1967, except for the section
crossed by the main road linking the two capitals. A

telephone system connects all the principal towns. There
are more than 90 commercial broadcasting stations and six
television stations.
   There are two national airlines with an international
airport 18 miles to the east of the capital and one near
Puerto Plata on the north coast.

ECUADOR
República del Ecuador

AREA – 109,484 sq. miles (283,561 sq. km)
POPULATION – 11,221,000 (1994 UN estimate),
   descendants of the Spanish, aboriginal Indians, and
   Mestizos. Spanish is the principal language but Quechua
   is also a recognized language and is spoken by most
   Indians
CAPITAL – Quito (population, 1,387,887, 1991 estimate)
MAJOR CITIES – ΨGuayaquil (1,531,229), the chief port;
   Cuenca (332,117)
CURRENCY – Sucre of 100 centavos
NATIONAL DAY – 10 August (Independence Day)
NATIONAL FLAG – Three horizontal bands, yellow, blue
   and red (the yellow band twice the width of the others);
   emblem in centre
LIFE EXPECTANCY (years) – male 67.32; female 72.49
POPULATION GROWTH RATE – 2.2 per cent (1994)
POPULATION DENSITY – 40 per sq. km (1994)
URBAN POPULATION – 58.5 per cent (1994)
MILITARY EXPENDITURE – 3.4 per cent of GDP (1995)
MILITARY PERSONNEL – 57,100: Army 50,000, Navy
   4,100, Air Force 3,000
CONSCRIPTION DURATION – 12 months

Ecuador is an equatorial state of South America. It extends
across the Western Andes, the highest peaks being Chim-
borazo (20,408 ft) and Ilinza (17,405 ft) in the Western
Cordillera; and Cotopaxi (19,612 ft) and Cayambe
(19,160 ft) in the Eastern Cordillera. Ecuador is watered
by the Upper Amazon, and by the rivers Guayas, Mira,
Santiago, Chone, and Esmeraldas on the Pacific coast.
There are extensive forests.

HISTORY AND POLITICS

The former kingdom of Quito was conquered by the Incas
of Peru in the 15th century. Early in the 16th century
Pizarro's conquests led to the inclusion of the present
territory of Ecuador in the Spanish Vice-royalty of Quito.
Independence was achieved in a revolutionary war which
culminated in the battle of Mount Pichincha (1822).
   After seven years of military rule, Ecuador returned to
democracy in 1979. In the 1992 legislative election a loose
coalition of parties enabled President Ballén to introduce a
programme of economic reform, financial liberalization
and privatization. This, together with reductions in state
spending, caused social unrest in 1992–4 and led to the
government's defeat in the May 1994 legislative elections.
In the July 1996 elections the ruling Social Christian Party
won a majority of seats. A populist, Abdala Bucaram, was
elected president in July 1996, and appointed a coalition
government. Bucaram was ousted by the legislature on the
grounds of insanity and replaced firstly by Vice-President
Arteaga and then by the Speaker of the National Congress
Fabián Alarcón. Presidential elections are due to be held in
August 1998.

FOREIGN RELATIONS

The border with Peru was demarcated by a 1942 treaty which was partly revoked by Ecuador in 1960 in relation to a disputed 50-mile stretch. An inconclusive four-week border war was fought with Peru in February 1995 until a cease-fire was signed on 1 March 1995. A 54-mile demilitarized zone was agreed in July 1995.

POLITICAL SYSTEM

The 1978 constitution provides for an elected president and vice-president who serve for a single four-year term. There is a unicameral National Congress which meets for two months a year and has 77 members, 12 of whom are elected on a national basis every four years and 65 on a provincial basis every two years. Voting is compulsory for all literate and voluntary for all illiterate citizens over the age of 18. The republic is divided into 21 provinces.

HEAD OF STATE

President (acting), Fabián Alarcón Rivera, *sworn in* 12 February 1997
Vice-President, Rosalia Arteaga

CABINET *as at July 1997*

Agriculture, Alfredo Saltos Guale
Defence, Gen. (retd) Ramiro Ricaurte
Education and Culture, Mario Jaramillo
Energy and Mines, Raul Baca Carbo
Finance, Carlos Davalos
Foreign Affairs, José Ayala Lasso
Government and Police Force, Cesar Verduga
Health, Guillermo Wagner
Industry, Commerce, Integration and Fishing, Benigno Sotomayor
Labour and Human Resouces, Edgar Rivadeneira
Public Works and Communications, Estuardo Hidalgo Bifarini
Social Welfare, Gustavo Baquero
Urbanization and Housing, Diego Ponce
Tourism, Juana Vallejo

EMBASSY OF ECUADOR

Flat 3B, 3 Hans Crescent, London SW1X 0LS
Tel 0171–584 1367
Ambassador Extraordinary and Plenipotentiary, HE Patricio Maldonado, apptd 1994

BRITISH EMBASSY

Av. González Suárez, 111 (Casilla 314), Quito
Tel: Quito 560670
Ambassador Extraordinary and Plenipotentiary, HE John Forbes-Meyler, apptd 1997
BRITISH CONSULAR OFFICES – Cuenca, Galápagos and Guayaquil

BRITISH COUNCIL REPRESENTATIVE, Anthony Deyes, Av. Amazonas 1646, Orellana (Casilla 17078829), Quito

ECONOMY

Agriculture is the most important sector of the economy, supporting nearly 50 per cent of the population and contributing 14.5 per cent of GDP and 19.5 per cent of exports. The main products for export are fish, bananas, which provide a third of agricultural exports, cocoa and coffee. Other important crops are sugar, corn, soya, rice, cotton, African palm, vegetables, fruit and timber. The main imports are manufactured goods and machinery.

The economy was transformed by the discovery in 1972 of major oil fields in the Oriente area which are evacuated by a trans-Andean pipeline to the port of Balao. Ecuador withdrew from OPEC in 1992 in order to raise its production to 19,303,000 tonnes in 1994.

GNP – US$15,997 million (1995); US$1,390 per capita (1995)
GDP – US$11,535 million (1992); US$1,142 per capita (1992)
ANNUAL AVERAGE GROWTH OF GDP – 2.3 per cent (1995)
INFLATION RATE – 22.9 per cent (1995)
UNEMPLOYMENT – 7.1 per cent (1994)
TOTAL EXTERNAL DEBT – US$13,957 million (1995)

TRADE WITH UK	1995	1996
Imports from UK	£52,825,000	£41,430,000
Exports to UK	20,390,000	29,150,000

COMMUNICATIONS

There are 23,256 km of permanent roads and 5,044 km of roads which are only open during the dry season. There are about 750 miles of railway. Ten commercial airlines operate international flights and there are internal services between all important towns. Two daily newspapers are published at Quito and four at Guayaquil.

EDUCATION

Elementary education is free and compulsory. There are ten universities (three at Quito, three at Guayaquil, and one each at Cuenca, Machala, Loja and Portoviejo), polytechnic schools at Quito and Guayaquil and eight technical colleges in other provincial capitals.
ILLITERACY RATE – 9.9 per cent
ENROLMENT (percentage of age group) – tertiary 20.0 per cent (1990)

GALÁPAGOS ISLANDS

The Galápagos (Giant Tortoise) Islands, forming the province of the Archipelago de Colón, were annexed by Ecuador in 1832. The archipelago lies in the Pacific, about 500 miles from the mainland. There are 12 large and several hundred smaller islands with a total area of about 3,000 sq. miles and an estimated population (1982) of 6,119. The capital is San Cristóbal, on Chatham Island. Although the archipelago lies on the equator, the temperature of the surrounding water is well below equatorial average owing to the Humboldt current. The province consists for the most part of National Park Territory, where unique marine birds, iguanas, and the giant tortoises are conserved. There is some local subsistence farming; the main industry, apart from tourism, is tuna and lobster fishing.

EGYPT
Al-Jumhuriyat Misr al-Arabiya

AREA – 386,662 sq. miles (1,001,449 sq. km). Neighbours: Sudan (south), Libya (west), Gaza Strip and Israel (east)
POPULATION – 58,978,000 (official estimate 1995). The largest, or 'Egyptian' element, is a Hamito-Semite race. A second element is the *Bedouin*, or nomadic Arabs of the Western and Arabian deserts, who are now mainly semi-sedentary tent-dwellers. The third element is the *Nubian* of the Nile Valley of mixed Arab and Negro blood. Over 90 per cent of the population are Muslims of the Sunni denomination, and most of the rest Coptic Christians. Arabic is the official language
CAPITAL – Cairo (population, 13,000,000, 1994 estimate), stands on the Nile about 14 miles from the head of the delta

MAJOR CITIES – ΨAlexandria (3,419,000, 1994 official estimate), founded 332 BC by Alexander the Great, was the capital for over 1,000 years; Ismailia (400,000); ΨPort Said (526,000); Asyût (300,000); Faiyûm (180,000); ΨSuez (458,000)

CURRENCY – Egyptian pound (£E) of 100 piastres or 1,000 millièmes

NATIONAL DAY – 23 July (Anniversary of Revolution in 1952)

NATIONAL FLAG – Horizontal bands of red, white and black, with an eagle in the centre of the white band

LIFE EXPECTANCY (years) – male 62.86; female 66.39

POPULATION GROWTH RATE – 2.3 per cent (1994)

POPULATION DENSITY – 58 per sq. km (1994)

URBAN POPULATION – 44.0 per cent (1994)

ILLITERACY RATE – 48.6 per cent

ENROLMENT (percentage of age group) – primary 89 per cent; secondary 65 per cent; tertiary 16.9 per cent (1993)

Egypt comprises Egypt proper, the peninsula of Sinai and a number of islands in the Gulf of Suez and Red Sea, of which the principal are Jubal, Shadwan, Gafatin and Zeberged (or St John's Island).

The country is mainly flat but there are mountainous areas in the south-west, along the Red Sea coast and in the south of the Sinai peninsula; the highest peak is Mt Catherina (8,668 ft). Most of the land is desert and the Nile valley and delta were the only fertile areas until the opening of the Aswan Dam allowed areas of desert to be reclaimed. West of the Nile Valley is the Western desert, containing some depressions whose springs irrigate oases. The Eastern Desert between the Nile and the mountains along the Red Sea coast is mostly plateaux dissected by wadis (dry water-courses).

HISTORY AND POLITICS

The unification of the kingdoms of Lower and Upper Egypt under the Pharaohs c.3100 BC marked the establishment of the Egyptian state, with Memphis as its capital. Egypt was ruled for nearly 2,800 years by a succession of 31 Pharaonic dynasties which built the pyramids at Gizeh. A period of Hellenic rule began in 332 BC, followed by a period of rule by Rome (30 BC to AD 324) and then by the Byzantine Empire. In AD 640 Egypt was subjugated by Arab Muslim invaders. In 1517 the country was incorporated in the Ottoman Empire, under which it remained until the early 19th century. A British Protectorate over Egypt lasted from 1914 to 1922, when Sultan Ahmed Fuad was proclaimed King of Egypt. In 1953 the monarchy was deposed and Egypt became a republic.

In 1956, as a result of Egypt's trade agreements with Communist countries, Britain and the USA withdrew offers of financial aid and in retaliation President Nasser seized the assets of the Suez Canal Company. Egyptian occupation of the Canal Zone while repulsing an Israeli attack was used as a pretext for military action by Britain and France in support of their Suez Canal Company interests. A cease-fire and Anglo-French withdrawal were negotiated by the UN.

The Israeli invasion of 1956 overran the Sinai peninsula but six months later Israel withdrew. However, mounting tension culminated in a second invasion of Sinai (the Six Day War in June 1967) and occupation of the peninsula by Israel. Egypt's attempt to recapture the territory (the Yom Kippur War in October 1973) was unsuccessful but Sinai was returned to Egypt in 1982 under the treaty of 1979 which resulted from the Camp David talks and formally terminated a 31-year-old state of war between the two countries.

The ruling National Democratic Party won the general election held in November and December 1995. President Mubarak was nominated by the legislature to run unopposed for a third six-year term in July 1993, and was elected in October.

INSURGENCY

Militant Muslim fundamentalists re-emerged in 1992, carrying out attacks on Coptic Christians, tourists, government ministers, civil servants and the security forces. Attacks continued in 1993–6 and are concentrated in Upper Egypt and the Cairo area. The government has reacted vigorously to the armed campaign with the arrest of 20,000 militants.

POLITICAL SYSTEM

The constitution of 1971 provides for an executive president who appoints the Council of Ministers and determines government policy. The president is elected by the legislature every six years. The legislature is the People's Assembly which has 454 members, 444 of whom are elected, the remaining ten nominated by the president. The Shura Council or Consultative Assembly (258 members) has an advisory role.

HEAD OF STATE

President, Muhammad Hosni Mubarak, *elected* 1981, *re-elected* 1987, 13 October 1993

COUNCIL OF MINISTERS *as at July 1997*

Prime Minister, Planning, International Co-operation, Dr Ahmed Kamal el-Ganzouri

Deputy PM, Agriculture and Land Reclamation, Yousef Amin Wali

Cabinet Affairs, Tala'at Sayyed Ahmad Hammad

Culture, Farouk Hosni Abdel Aziz

Defence and Military Production, Field Marshal Mohammad Hussein Tantawi Soliman

Economy, Yousef Boutros Ghali

Education, Hussein Kamel Bahauddin

Electricity and Energy, Mohammad Maher Othman Abaza

Environment, Nadia Riyad Makram Ebeid

Finance, Dr Mohieddin Abu Bakr Al Ghareeb

Foreign Affairs, Amr Mahmoud Moussa

Health, Dr Ismail Awadallah Sallam

Higher Education and Scientific Research, Mofeed Mahmoud Shehab

Housing and Public Utilities, Mohamed Ibrahim Soliman

Information, Mohammad Safwat el-Sharif

Insurance and Social Affairs, Mervat Mehana el-Telawi

Interior, Hassan Mohamed Al Alfi

Justice, Farouk Seif el-Nasr

Local Government, Dr Mahmoud el-Sherif Sayeed Ahmad

Manpower and Emigration, Ahmad Ahmad Al Amawy

Military Production, Dr Mohammad Al-Ghamrawi Daoud Hassan

Oil, Dr Hamdi Abdel Wahab Al Banbi

Planning, Dr Zafer Selim Al Beshri

Public Business Sector, Dr Atef Mohamed Ebeid

Public Works and Water Resources, Dr Mahmoud Abdel Halim Abu Zeid

Religious Affairs (Waqfs), Dr Mahmoud Hamdi

Rural Development, Dr Mahmoud Sherif

Supply and Trade, Dr Ahmed Ahmad Gowaili

Tourism, Dr Mamdouh Ahmad Al-Beltagui

Transport and Communications, Soliman Metwalli Soliman

EMBASSY OF THE ARAB REPUBLIC OF EGYPT
26 South Street, London WIY 6DD
Tel 0171-499 2401

Ambassador Extraordinary and Plenipotentiary, new
appointment awaited
Ministers Plenipotentiary, Aly-Galal Bassiouny (*Deputy Chief
of Mission*); Samiha Abou Steit (*Consul-General*); Ahmed
Nafeh (*Consular Affairs*); Ismail Roushdy (*Commercial*)
Defence Attaché, Brig. Ibrahim El Shayeb
Cultural Counsellor, Samir Youssef El-Sayad

BRITISH EMBASSY
Ahmed Ragheb Street, Garden City, Cairo
Tel: Cairo 354 0850
Ambassador Extraordinary and Plenipotentiary, HE David
Blatherwick, CMG, OBE, apptd 1995
Counsellor and Deputy Head of Mission, R. E. Makepeace
Defence and Military Attaché, Col. A. Snook, OBE
First Secretaries, P. Byrde (*Consul*); A. D. F. Henderson
(*Commercial*)
BRITISH CONSULAR OFFICES − Consulate-General,
Alexandria; *Consulates*, Luxor, Suez, Port Said
BRITISH COUNCIL DIRECTOR, D. Marler OBE (Cultural
First Secretary), 192 Sharia el Nil, Agouza, Cairo

DEFENCE

The Army has 4,690 main battle tanks, 1,549 armoured
infantry fighting vehicles, 3,748 armoured personnel
carriers and 1,247 artillery pieces. The Navy has one
destroyer, six frigates, 43 patrol and coastal vessels and 14
armed helicopters. The Air Force has 567 combat aircraft
and 103 armed helicopters.
MILITARY EXPENDITURE − 4.3 per cent of GDP (1995)
MILITARY PERSONNEL − 590,000: Army 310,000, Navy
20,000, Air Force 30,000, Air Defence Command
80,000, Paramilitaries 150,000
CONSCRIPTION DURATION − Three years

ECONOMY

Despite increasing industrialization, agriculture remains
the most important economic activity, employing over 45
per cent of the labour force and producing 17 per cent of
exports. Egypt is still a net importer of foodstuffs,
especially grain, and a food security programme has been
set up with the aim of achieving self-sufficiency. The main
cash crop is cotton, of which Egypt is one of the world's
main producers. Other important crops are maize, rice,
sugar cane, wheat, beans, citrus fruit and other fruits and
vegetables are also grown.

With its considerable reserves of petroleum and natural
gas, and the hydroelectric power produced by the Aswan
and High Dams, Egypt is self-sufficient in energy. The
production of petroleum provides 60−65 per cent of total
exports, and supports a refining industry. The major
manufacturing industries are food processing, motor cars,
electrical goods, steel, chemical products, yarns and
textiles. In 1996 more than two million tourists visited
Egypt.

In 1993 the government had a budget surplus equivalent
to 1.7 per cent of GDP and a current account surplus of
US$2,299 million.
GNP − US$45,507 million (1995); US$790 per capita
(1995)
GDP − US$45,012 million (1992); US$746 per capita
(1992)
ANNUAL AVERAGE GROWTH OF GDP − 4.6 per cent (1995)
INFLATION RATE − 8.3 per cent (1995)
UNEMPLOYMENT − 11.0 per cent (1994)
TOTAL EXTERNAL DEBT − US$34,116 million (1995)

TRADE

The main imports are wheat, flour, wood and trucks. The
main exports are crude petroleum, cotton, cotton yarn,
oranges, rice and cotton textiles.

In 1993 Egypt had a trade deficit of US$6,378 million.

Trade with UK	1995	1996
Imports from UK	£383,541,000	£431,424,000
Exports to UK	246,619,000	281,502,000

COMMUNICATIONS

The road and rail networks link the Nile valley and delta
with the main development areas east and west of the river.
The Suez Canal was reopened in 1975 and a two-stage
development project begun to widen and deepen the canal
to allow the passage of larger shipping and to permit two-
way traffic. Port Said and Suez have been reconstructed
and the port of Alexandria is being improved.

EQUATORIAL GUINEA
República de Guinea Ecuatorial

AREA − 10,830 sq. miles (28,051 sq. km)
POPULATION − 389,000 (1994 UN estimate)
CAPITAL − ΨMalabo on the island of Bioko (population,
30,418, 1983 estimate)
MAJOR TOWN − ΨBata is the principal town and port of
Rio Muni
CURRENCY − Franc CFA of 100 centimes
NATIONAL DAY − 12 October
NATIONAL FLAG − Three horizontal bands, green over
white over red; blue triangle next staff; coat of arms in
centre of white band
LIFE EXPECTANCY (years) − male 44.86; female 47.78
POPULATION GROWTH RATE − 2.8 per cent (1994)
POPULATION DENSITY − 14 per sq. km (1994)
URBAN POPULATION − 37.0 per cent (1991)
MILITARY EXPENDITURE − 1.3 per cent of GDP (1995)
MILITARY PERSONNEL − 1,320: Army 1,100, Navy 120, Air
Force 100
ILLITERACY RATE − 21.5 per cent

Equatorial Guinea consists of the island of Bioko, in the
Bight of Biafra about 20 miles from the west coast of Africa,
Annonbón Island in the Gulf of Guinea, the Corisco Islands
(Corisco, Elobey Grande and Elobey Chico), and Rio
Muni, a mainland area between Cameroon and Gabon.

HISTORY AND POLITICS

Formerly colonies of Spain, the territories now forming
Equatorial Guinea were constituted as two provinces of
Metropolitan Spain in 1959, became autonomous in 1963
and fully independent in 1968.

In 1979 President Macias was deposed by a revolutionary military council headed by Col. Obiang Nguema.
Constitutional amendments in 1982 provided for legislative elections, which were held in 1983 and 1988, but all
candidates were presidential nominees.

A multiparty political system under a new constitution
was approved by a referendum in 1991 and ten opposition
parties have been legalized, operating alongside the ruling
Equatorial Guinea Democratic Party (PDGE). A National
Pact was agreed and signed in March 1993 but when
legislative elections were held in November they were
boycotted by most of the electorate and opposition parties.
The PDGE won 68 out of 80 National Assembly seats and
formed a government. In the February 1996 election, the

President claimed to have won more than 99 per cent of the vote. Most opposition parties boycotted the ballot.

HEAD OF STATE
President of the Supreme Military Council and Minister of Defence, Brig.-Gen. Teodoro Obiang Nguema Mbasogo, *took office* August 1979, *re-elected* June 1989, February 1996

MINISTERS *as at July 1997*
Prime Minister, Angel Serafin Seriche Dougan
Deputy P.M, Civil Service and Administrative Reform, Francisco Javier Ngomo Mbengono
Minister of State, Employment and Social Security, Carmelo Modu Akuse Bindang
Minister of State, Foreign Affairs and Co-operation, Miguel Oyono Ndong Mifuma
Minister of State, Interior, Julio Ndong Ela Mangue
Minister of State, Missions at the Presidency, Alejandro Evuna Owono
Minister of State, Fishing and Forestry, Anatolio Ndong Mba
Minister of State, Youth and Sports, Francisco Pascual Eyegue Obama Asue
Minister of State, Planning and Economic Development, Government Spokesperson, Antonio Fernando Nve Ngu
Agriculture and Livestock, Vidal Choni Becoba
Culture, Tourism and Francophonie, Pedro Cristino Bufribfri
Education and Science, Richard Mangue Obama Nfube
Finance and Economy, Marcelino Oyono Ntutumu
Health and Environment, Dario Tadeo Ndong Olumo
Information, Santos Pascual Bikomo Nangwande
Industry, Small and Medium-sized Enterprises, Constantino Ekong Nsue
Justice and Religions, Ignacio Milam Tang
Mines and Energy, Juan Olo Mba Nseng
Public Works, Housing and Urban Development, Pedro Nsue Obama Angono
Relations with Parliament and Legislative Co-ordination, Antonio Pascual Oko Ebobo
Secretary-General of the Presidency, Salomon Nguema Owono
Transport and Communications, Elias Ovono Nguema
Women's Integration, Social Affairs, Margarita Alene Mba

EMBASSY OF THE REPUBLIC OF EQUATORIAL GUINEA
6 Rue Alfred de Vigny, 75008, Paris
Tel: Paris 4766 4433
Ambassador Extraordinary and Plenipotentiary, new appointment awaited

BRITISH AMBASSADOR, HE Nicholas McCarthy, OBE, resident at Yaoundé, Cameroon

ECONOMY

The chief products are cocoa, coffee and wood. Production has declined and except for cocoa there is little commercial agriculture. The economy is heavily dependent on outside aid, principally from Spain. Oil and gas deposits exist but remain largely unexploited. Equatorial Guinea entered the 'franc zone' in 1985.
GNP – US$152 million (1995); US$380 per capita (1995)
GDP – US$173 million (1992); US$502 per capita (1992)
INFLATION RATE – 4.0 per cent (1993)
TOTAL EXTERNAL DEBT – US$293 million (1995)

TRADE WITH UK	1995	1996
Imports from UK	£347,000	£1,504,000
Exports to UK	94,000	108,000

ERITREA

AREA – 45,406 sq. miles (117,600 sq. km). Neighbours: Sudan (north and north-west), Ethiopia (south and south-west), Djibouti (south-east)
POPULATION – 3,437,000 (1994 UN estimate), roughly half Coptic Christian (mainly highlanders) and half Muslim (mainly lowlanders). English and Arabic are the main languages. There are nine indigenous language groups: Afar; Bilen; Hadareb; Kunama; Nara; Rashida; Saho; Tigre; Tigrinya
CAPITAL – Asmara (population, 358,100, 1990 estimate)
MAJOR TOWNS – ΨMassawa; ΨAssab
CURRENCY – Ethiopian currency is in use
NATIONAL DAY – 24 May (Independence Day)
NATIONAL FLAG – Divided into three triangles; the one based on the hoist is red and bears a gold olive wreath; the upper triangle is green and the lower one light blue
LIFE EXPECTANCY (years) – male 48.85; female 52.06
POPULATION GROWTH RATE – 2.7 per cent (1994)
POPULATION DENSITY – 29 per sq. km (1994)
MILITARY EXPENDITURE – 5.7 per cent of GDP (1995)
ENROLMENT (percentage of age group) – primary 27 per cent; secondary 12 per cent; tertiary 1.0 per cent (1994)

HISTORY AND POLITICS

Eritrea was colonized by Italy in the late 19th century and was the base for the 1936 Italian invasion of Abyssinia (Ethiopia). After the Italian defeat in East Africa in 1941 by British and Commonwealth forces, Eritrea became a British protectorate. This lasted until 15 September 1952 when Eritrea was federated with Ethiopia. The Ethiopian Emperor Haile Selassie incorporated Eritrea as a province of Ethiopia in 1962. An armed campaign for independence began in the 1970s, first against Emperor Haile Selassie's forces and from 1974 against the Mengistu regime.

In 1991 the Mengistu government was overthrown by the Eritrean People's Liberation Front (EPLF) and the Ethiopian People's Revolutionary Democratic Front (EPRDF). The new EPRDF-led government in Ethiopia agreed to an Eritrean referendum on independence which was held in April 1993 and recorded a 99 per cent vote in favour. Independence was declared on 24 May 1993.

FOREIGN RELATIONS
Eritrea claims the three Hanish Islands in the Red Sea, the largest of which, Hanish al Kabir, was seized from Yemen in December 1995. The land border with Djibouti is also disputed. Eritrean troops briefly seized Lesser Hanish in August 1996 but withdrew within days.

POLITICAL SYSTEM
At independence the provisional government became the transitional government of Eritrea to govern for a maximum of four years while a new constitution is drafted. At the end of the transition period multiparty elections are to be held. During the transition period legislative power is vested in the National Assembly and executive power in the State Council appointed and chaired by the President. In 1994 the EPLF transformed itself into a political party, the People's Front for Democracy and Justice (PFDJ), and the National Assembly was changed for the remainder of the transition period to comprise 75 PFDJ central council members and 75 elected members.

HEAD OF STATE
President, Chairman of the National Assembly, Isaias Afwerki, *elected by National Assembly* 22 May 1993

STATE COUNCIL *as at July 1997*
Chairman, The President
Agriculture, Arefaine Berhe
Construction, Abraha Asfaha
Defence, Gen. Sebhat Ephrem
Education, Osman Saleh Mahmoud
Energy and Mining, Tesfay Gebraselassie
Finance, Gebreselassie Yosief
Foreign Affairs, Haile Weldetensae
Health, Dr Saleh Meki
Information, Beraki Gebreselassie
Justice, Fozia Hashim
Labour and Social Welfare, Ogbe Abraha
Land, Water Resources and Environment, Dr Tesfay
    Girmatsien
Local Government, Mahmoud Ahmed Sherifo
Marine Resources, Petros Solomon
Tourism, Ahmed Haji Ali
Trade and Industry, Ali Said Abdella
Transport and Communications, Saleh Idris Kekia

EMBASSY OF THE STATE OF ERITREA
15–17 avenue Wolvendael, 1180 Brussels, Belgium
Tel: Brussels 374 4434
Ambassador Extraordinary and Plenipotentiary, HE Andebrhan
    Weldegiorgis, apptd 1996
BRITISH AMBASSADOR, HE Gordon Wetherell, resides at
    Addis Ababa, Ethiopia

BRITISH CONSULATE
PO Box 997, Asmara
Tel: Asmara 411 4242
Honorary Consul, Dr R. B. Hicks
BRITISH COUNCIL DIRECTOR – Dr Negusse Araya, PO
    Box 997, Asmara

ECONOMY

Since 1991 the government has attempted to rebuild
industry, agriculture and infrastructure which were devastated by the war of independence. The rebuilding
programme has focused on the ports of Massawa and
Assab, the roads from the ports to Ethiopia, and the railway
from Massawa to Sudan via Asmara. Before 1962 Eritrea
was one of the most industrialized areas of Africa and some
industry remains, producing textiles and footwear. The
government hopes to base the rebuilding of the economy
on the return of well-educated exiles, international aid and
investment, the development of tourism along the coast,
and the diversification of the economy away from agriculture.
GDP – US$376 million (1992); US$53 per capita (1992)

TRADE WITH UK	1995	1996
Imports from UK	£768,000	£2,348,000
Exports to UK	41,000	39,000

ESTONIA
The Republic of Estonia

AREA – 17,413 sq. miles (45,100 sq. km). Neighbours:
    Russia (east), Latvia (south)
POPULATION – 1,464,100 (1997 UN estimate): 64.6 per
    cent Estonian, 28.5 per cent Russian, 2.6 per cent
    Ukrainian, 1.5 per cent Belarusian, 0.7 per cent Finnish,
    others 1.9 per cent. The majority religion is Lutheran,
    with Russian Orthodox and Baptist minorities. Estonian
    is the first language of 64.2 per cent and Russian of 28.7
    per cent

CAPITAL – Tallinn (population, 427,510, 1996 estimate)
MAJOR TOWNS AND CITIES – Tartu (103,424); Narva
    (76,354); Kohtla-Järve (69,919)
CURRENCY – Kroon of 100 sents
NATIONAL ANTHEM – Mu Isamaa, mu onn ja rõõm (My
    Native Land, My Joy, Delight)
NATIONAL DAY – 24 February (Independence Day)
NATIONAL FLAG – Three horizontal stripes of blue, black,
    white
LIFE EXPECTANCY (years) – male 64.05; female 75.03
POPULATION GROWTH RATE – – 1.2 per cent (1994)
POPULATION DENSITY – 33 per sq. km (1994)
URBAN POPULATION – 70.4 per cent (1993)
MILITARY EXPENDITURE – 5.3 per cent of GDP (1995)
MILITARY PERSONNEL – 3,450: Army 3,300, Navy 150
CONSCRIPTION DURATION – 12 months

Estonia includes 1,500 islands in the Baltic Sea and the
Gulf of Riga. Forests cover roughly 20 per cent of the
country, which also has many lakes. The climate is mild
and maritime.

HISTORY AND POLITICS

Estonia, a former province of the Russian Empire, declared
its independence on 24 February 1918. A war of independence was fought against the German army until November 1918, and then against Soviet forces until the peace
treaty of Tartu was signed in 1920. By this treaty the Soviet
Union recognized Estonia's independence.

The Soviet Union annexed Estonia in 1940 under the
terms of the Molotov-Ribbentrop pact with Germany.
Estonia was occupied when Germany invaded the Soviet
Union during the Second World War. In 1944 the Soviet
Union recaptured the country from Germany and con-
firmed its annexation.

The Estonian Supreme Soviet in November 1989
declared the republic to be sovereign and its 1940 annexation by the Soviet Union to be illegal. In February 1990 the
leading role of the Communist Party was abolished, and
following multiparty elections in March 1990 a period of
transition to independence was inaugurated. Independence was declared on 20 August 1991.

Presidential and legislative elections were held in
September 1992 on the basis of special provisions different
from the 1992 constitution. The president was directly
elected for a four-year term and the Riigikogu for a three-
year term. A radical right-wing coalition government was
elected which held power until September 1994. At the
legislative election of March 1995 a centre-left government of the Coalition Party and Rural People's Union
(KMÜ) and the Centre Party was formed; the government
collapsed in October 1995. A new coalition government
formed by the KMÜ and the Reform Party lasted until the
withdrawal of the Reform Party in November 1996, after
which the KMÜ formed a minority government.

POLITICAL SYSTEM

Legislative power is exercised by the unicameral *Riigikogu*
of 101 members elected by proportional representation
every four years. The president is elected for a five-year
term by the Riigikogu by a two-thirds majority or, if no
candidate receives this majority after three rounds of
voting, by an electoral body composed of Riigikogu
members and local government officials. Executive authority is vested in a prime minister who is nominated by
the president and who forms a government. Members of
the government need not be members of the Riigikogu.

Estonia is divided into 46 towns and 15 districts for local
administration purposes.

HEAD OF STATE
President, Lennart Meri, *elected* 5 October 1992, *re-elected* 20
   September 1996

GOVERNMENT *as at July 1997*
Prime Minister, Mart Siimann
Agriculture, Andres Varik
Culture, Jaak Allik
Defence, Andrus Öövel
Economic Affairs, Jaak Leiman
Education, Mait Klaassen
Environment, Villu Reiljan
Finance, Mart Opmann
Foreign Affairs, Toomas Hendrik Ilves
Interior, Robert Lepikson
Justice, Paul Varul
Social Affairs, Tiiu Aro
Transport and Communications, Raivo Vare
Without Portfolio, Peep Aru; Andra Veidemann *(European
   Affairs)*

EMBASSY OF THE REPUBLIC OF ESTONIA
16 Hyde Park Gate, London SW7 5DG
Tel 0171-589 3428
Ambassador Extraordinary and Plenipotentiary, HE Raul Mälk,
   apptd 1996

BRITISH EMBASSY
Kentmanni 20, Tallinn EE0100
Tel: Tallinn 631 3353
Ambassador Extraordinary and Plenipotentiary, HE Timothy
   Craddock, apptd 1997
BRITISH COUNCIL REPRESENTATIVE, C. Campbell, Vana
   Posti 7, Tallinn

ECONOMY

Since 1992 the government has introduced free-market
reforms, privatization and restructuring. Privatization has
gained momentum with foreign direct investment quad-
rupling in 1994. Estonia has no outstanding debt to Russia
but is still dependent on Russian natural gas supplies.

Agriculture and dairy-farming are a major sector of the
economy, the main products being rye, oats, barley, flax,
potatoes, meat, milk, butter and eggs.

Light industry is the other major sector, concentrating
on textiles, clothing and footwear, forestry, wood and
paper products, and food and fish processing. Some heavy
industry exists, mostly chemicals and the manufacture of
power equipment.

There was a budget deficit equivalent to 2.01 per cent of
GDP in 1993.
GNP – US$4,252 million (1995); US$2,860 per capita
   (1995)
GDP – US$7,036 million (1992); US$728 per capita (1992)
ANNUAL AVERAGE GROWTH OF GDP – – 7.8 per cent
   (1993)
INFLATION RATE – 28.9 per cent (1995)
UNEMPLOYMENT – 8.9 per cent (1994)
TOTAL EXTERNAL DEBT – US$309 million (1995). The
   IMF approved a standby credit of US$20 million in July
   1996.

TRADE

Although Estonia signed a free trade deal with Russia in
1992, it has greatly reduced its trade with the former Soviet
states. In 1994 over 70 per cent of trade was with EU and
EFTA states and Estonia's trade rose by 50 per cent. Free
trade and association agreeements with the EU came into
effect in 1995; Estonia has applied for membership of the
EU.

In 1994 there was a trade deficit of US$361 million and a
current account deficit of US$170 million.

Trade with UK	1995	1996
Imports from UK	£29,665,000	£55,421,000
Exports to UK	111,840,000	144,150,000

COMMUNICATIONS

Freedom of the press is guaranteed in the constitution, and
the state monopoly on television and radio ended soon
after independence. All newspapers have been privatized
and broadcasting channels are in the process of being
privatized. Russian-language news and programmes are
provided on Estonian Television. There are five Estonian
and three Russian-language daily newspapers.

EDUCATION

Estonia has a three-tier education system, consisting of
primary level (four years), secondary level (six years) and
university level (four to six years). Primary- and
secondary-level education is compulsory.
ILLITERACY RATE – 0.2 per cent
ENROLMENT (percentage of age group) – primary 90 per
   cent (1994); secondary 80 per cent (1993); tertiary 24.0
   per cent (1994)

ETHIOPIA
Federal Democratic Republic of Ethiopia

AREA – 426,373 sq. miles (1,104,300 sq. km). Neighbours:
   Sudan (north-west), Kenya (south), Djibouti and
   Somalia (east), Eritrea (north-east)
POPULATION – 54,938,000 (1994 UN estimate). About
   one-third are of Semitic origin (Amharas and Tigreans)
   and the remainder mainly Oromos (40 per cent), Somalis
   (6 per cent) and Afar (4 per cent). Amharas, Tigreans and
   many Oromos are Ethiopian Orthodox Christians. The
   Afar people in the north and the Somalis in the south-
   east, as well as some Oromos, are Muslim. Amharic is the
   most widely used of the 70 languages
CAPITAL – Addis Ababa (population, 2,316,400, 1994
   estimate)
MAJOR CITIES – Dire Dawa (population, 194,587, 1994
   estimate)
CURRENCY – Ethiopian birr (EB) of 100 cents
NATIONAL ANTHEM – Ityopya, Ityopya Kidemi
NATIONAL DAY – 28 May
NATIONAL FLAG – Three horizontal bands: green, yellow,
   red, in the centre a blue disc, containing a yellow
   pentagram
LIFE EXPECTANCY (years) – male 45.93; female 49.06
POPULATION GROWTH RATE – 3.2 per cent (1994)
POPULATION DENSITY – 50 per sq. km (1994)
URBAN POPULATION – 15.0 per cent (1994)
MILITARY EXPENDITURE – 2.1 per cent of GDP (1995)

HISTORY AND POLITICS

The Hamitic culture was heavily influenced by Semitic
immigration from Arabia at about the time of Christ.
Christianity was introduced in the fourth century. The
empire attained its zenith in the sixth century under the
Axum rulers but was checked by Islamic expansion from
the east. Modern Ethiopia dates from 1855 when Theodore
established supremacy over the various tribes. The last
emperor was Haile Selassie who reigned from 1930 until
1974, when he was deposed by the armed forces. After ten

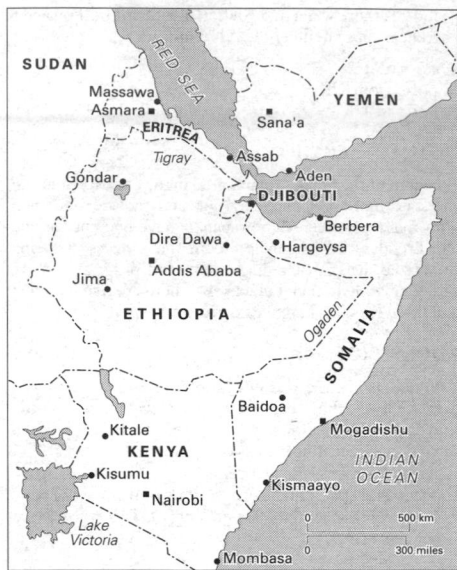

years of military rule, a Workers' Party on the Soviet model was formed with Lt.-Col. Mengistu Haile Mariam as General Secretary. The People's Democratic Republic of Ethiopia was established under a new constitution in 1987 with Lt.-Col. Mengistu as president. Armed insurgencies by the Eritrean People's Liberation Front (EPLF) and the Ethiopian People's Revolutionary Democratic Front (EPRDF), originating in Tigre, brought down Mengistu's government in May 1991.

A transitional administration comprising the EPRDF and other opposition groups formed a Council of Representatives which governed until 1995 under President Meles Zenawi. In 1994, the Council agreed on a draft federal constitution which was adopted by an elected Constituent Assembly on 8 December 1994. Multiparty elections in May and June 1995 were won by the EPRDF, which gained 80 per cent of the seats in the newly-created 526-seat Council of People's Representatives; a 117-member Federal Council to represent the 22 ethnic groups was also created. The Council of People's Representatives elected Dr Negasso Gidaola to the non-executive office of president and Meles Zenawi as prime minister. The Federal Democratic Republic of Ethiopia was proclaimed on 22 August 1995.

POLITICAL SYSTEM

The constitution provides for a federal government responsible for foreign affairs, defence and economic policy, and for nine regional administrations (Tigre, Afar, Amara, Oromia, Somai, Benshangui, Gambela, Harer and Southern), with a degree of autonomy and the right to secede.

HEAD OF STATE
President, Dr Negasso Gidada, *elected by the Council of People's Representatives* 22 August 1995

FEDERAL GOVERNMENT *as at July 1997*
Prime Minister, Meles Zenawi
Deputy PMs, Tamirat Layne *(Defence)*; Kassu Illala *(Economic Affairs)*
Agriculture, Seifu Ketema
Economic Development and Co-operation, Girma Birru

Education, Genet Zewdie
Finance, Sufiyan Ahmed
Foreign Affairs, Seyoum Mesfin
Health, Dr Adem Ibrahim
Information and Culture, Michael Chamo
Justice, Mahteme Solomon
Labour and Social Affairs, Hassan Abdela
Mines and Energy, Ezedin Ali
Trade and Industry, Kasahun Ayele
Transport and Communications, Abdulmejid Hussien
Water Resources, Shiferaw Jarso
Works and Urban Development, Haile Assegde

EMBASSY OF ETHIOPIA
17 Prince's Gate, London SW7 1PZ
Tel 0171-589 7212/3/4/5
Ambassador Extraordinary and Plenipotentiary, HE Dr Solomon Gidada, apptd 1992
Counsellor, Osman Beshir (*Commercial*)

BRITISH EMBASSY
Fikre Mariam Abatechan Street (PO Box 858), Addis Ababa
Tel: Addis Ababa 161 2354
Ambassador Extraordinary and Plenipotentiary, HE Gordon Wetherell, apptd 1997
Deputy Head of Mission and First Secretary, C. O. Pigott

BRITISH COUNCIL REPRESENTATIVE, M. Sargent, Artistic Building, Adwa Avenue (PO Box 1043), Addis Ababa

ECONOMY

The post-Mengistu government implemented a programme of free-market economic reform which reduced government spending and inflation. The currency was devalued, the civil service reduced and the army cut by two-thirds. Western states have responded with debt relief and loans. An agreement waiving customs levies was concluded with Eritrea in April 1995.

Agriculture accounts for approximately 40 per cent of GDP, 85 per cent of exports and 80 per cent of total employment. The major food crops are teff, maize, barley, sorghum, wheat, pulses and oil seeds. Famine conditions in 1984–5 recurred to a lesser extent in 1992. However, agricultural liberalization has led to dramatic progress in food production.

Manufacturing industry accounts for less than 9 per cent of GDP and is heavily dependent on agriculture. Ethiopia's known, but as yet largely unexploited, natural resources include gold, platinum, copper and potash. Traces of oil and natural gas have been found.

In 1994 the government had a budget deficit equivalent to 8.46 per cent of GDP. In 1993 there was a trade deficit of US$507 million and a current account deficit of US$54 million.
GNP – US$5,722 million (1995); US$100 per capita (1995)
GDP – US$5,774 million (1992); US$53 per capita (1992)
ANNUAL AVERAGE GROWTH OF GDP – –6.0 per cent (1991)
INFLATION RATE – 10.0 per cent (1995)
TOTAL EXTERNAL DEBT – US$5,221 million (1995)

TRADE

The chief imports by value are machinery and transport equipment, manufactured goods and chemicals; the principal exports by value are coffee, oil seeds, hides and skins, and pulses.

Trade with UK	1995	1996
Imports from UK	£53,337,000	£49,377,000
Exports to UK	15,928,000	26,260,000

COMMUNICATIONS

A network of roads in rural areas links the major cities with each other, with the Sudanese and Kenyan borders and through Eritrea to the Red Sea coast. The Ethiopian and Eritrean governments negotiated an agreement in 1992 which guarantees Ethiopia access to the Red Sea via the ports of Assab and Massawa.

There is a railway link from Addis Ababa to Djibouti. Ethiopian Airlines maintains regular services from Addis Ababa to many provincial towns, throughout Africa and to Europe.

EDUCATION

Elementary and secondary education are provided by government schools in the main centres of population; there are also mission schools. The National University (founded 1961) co-ordinates the institutions of higher education. There is a separate university at Alemaya (agricultural).

ILLITERACY RATE – 64.5 per cent
ENROLMENT (percentage of age group) – primary 21 per cent (1993); tertiary 0.7 per cent (1991)

FIJI
Matanitu Ko Viti – Republic of Fiji

AREA – 7,055 sq. miles (18,274 sq. km)
POPULATION – 784,000 (1994 UN estimate), 715,373 (1986 census): 48.6 per cent Indians, 46.2 per cent Fijians, and 5.2 per cent other races. Since the 1987 coup many ethnic Indians have left and by 1994 Melanesian Fijians formed the largest population group
CAPITAL – ΨSuva (population, 141,273, 1986), on the island of Viti Levu
CURRENCY – Fiji dollar (F$) of 100 cents
NATIONAL ANTHEM – God Bless Fiji
NATIONAL DAY – 10 October (Fiji Day)
NATIONAL FLAG – Light blue ground with Union flag in top left quarter and the shield of Fiji in the fly
LIFE EXPECTANCY (years) – male 60.72; female 63.87
POPULATION GROWTH RATE – 1.7 per cent (1994)
POPULATION DENSITY – 43 per sq. km (1994)
URBAN POPULATION – 38.7 per cent (1987)
MILITARY EXPENDITURE – 1.5 per cent of GDP (1995)
MILITARY PERSONNEL – 3,590: Army 3,300, Navy 290
ILLITERACY RATE – 8.4 per cent
ENROLMENT (percentage of age group) – primary 99 per cent (1992); tertiary 11.9 per cent (1991)

Fiji is composed of roughly 332 islands (about 100 permanently inhabited) and over 500 islets in the South Pacific, about 1,100 miles north of New Zealand. The group extends 300 miles from east to west and 300 miles north to south. The International Date Line has been diverted to the east of the island group. The largest islands are Viti Levu and Vanua Levu. The main groups of islands are Lomaiviti, Lau and Yasawas. The climate is tropical without extremes of heat.

HISTORY AND POLITICS

Fiji was a British colony from 1874 until 10 October 1970 when it became an independent state and a member of the Commonwealth.

A coalition under Dr Timoci Bavadra won a general election in April 1987, but was overthrown by the military on 14 May by Lt.-Col. Sitiveni Rabuka. An Advisory Council was set up as an interim government, but it too was overthrown on 25 September 1987. On 7 October Rabuka declared Fiji a republic; the Governor-General resigned on 15 October; Fiji's Commonwealth membership lapsed and another interim government was formed.

The Fijian Political Party led by Rabuka won the general elections in May 1992 and February 1994 and has formed a coalition government with the General Voters Party.

POLITICAL SYSTEM

The 1990 constitution established the political dominance of the Melanesian community within the judiciary and a bicameral parliament. The parliament consists of a Senate of 34 members appointed by the president, of which 24 seats are reserved for Melanesian Fijians, one for the Polynesian island of Rotuma and nine for other races. The House of Representatives has 70 seats; 37 reserved for Melanesians, 27 for Indians, one for Rotuma, and five for other races. The presidency and the premiership can only be held by Melanesians. The president is elected by the (Melanesian) Great Council of Chiefs.

HEAD OF STATE
President, Ratu Sir Kamisese Mara, GCMG, KBE, *inaugurated* 18 January 1994

CABINET *as at August 1997*
Prime Minister, Fijian Affairs, Multi-ethnic Affairs, Regional Development, Maj.-Gen. Sitiveni Rabuka, OBE
Agriculture, Fisheries and Forests, Militoni Leweniqila
Assistant Minister to the Prime Minister with Special Responsibilities in Fijian Affairs, Multi-ethnic Affairs and Regional Development, Lagisoa Delana
Attorney-General, Justice, Ratu Etuate Tavai
Commerce, Trade, Industry and Public Enterprises, Isimeli Bose
Education, Women and Culture, Taufa Vakatale
Finance and Economic Development, Berenado Vunibobo, CBE
Foreign Affairs, Sen. Filipe Bole, CBE
Health and Social Welfare, Leo Smith
Home Affairs and Immigration, Col. Paul Manueli, OBE
Labour and Industrial Relations, Vincent Lobendahn
Lands, Mining and Energy, Ratu Timoci Vesikula
Minister with Special Responsibilities in the Prime Minister's Office, Jonetani Kaukimoce
Public Works, Infrastructure, Transport, Information, Broadcasting, Television and Telecommunications, Ratu Inoke Kubuabola
Tourism and Civil Aviation, David Pickering, CBE
Urban Development, Housing and Environment, Vilisoni Cagimaivei
Youth, Employment Opportunities and Sports, Jim Ah Koy, OBE

EMBASSY OF THE REPUBLIC OF FIJI
34 Hyde Park Gate, London SW7 5DN
Tel 0171-584 3661
Ambassador Extraordinary and Plenipotentiary, HE Filimone Jitoko, apptd 1996

BRITISH EMBASSY
Victoria House, 47 Gladstone Road, PO Box 1355, Suva
Tel: Suva 311033
Ambassador Extraordinary and Plenipotentiary, HE Michael Peart, CMG, LVO, apptd 1995

ECONOMY

The economy is primarily agrarian. The principal cash crop is sugar cane, which is the main export, followed by coconuts, ginger and copra. A variety of other fruit, vegetables and root crops are also grown, and self-sufficiency in rice is a major aim. Forestry, fishing and beef production are being encouraged in order to diversify the economy. The processing of agricultural, marine and timber products are the main industries, along with gold mining and textiles. Tourism is second only to sugar as a money-earner.

In 1993 the government had a budget deficit equivalent to 4.87 per cent of GDP.

GNP – US$1,895 million (1995); US$2,440 per capita (1995)
GDP – US$1,280 million (1992); US$1,904 per capita (1992)
ANNUAL AVERAGE GROWTH OF GDP – 6.7 per cent (1990)
INFLATION RATE – 2.2 per cent (1995)
UNEMPLOYMENT – 5.4 per cent (1995)
TOTAL EXTERNAL DEBT – US$253 million (1995)

TRADE

The chief imports are foodstuffs, machinery, mineral fuels, chemicals, beverages, tobacco and manufactured articles. Chief exports are sugar, coconut oil, gold, lumber, garments, molasses, ginger and canned fish.

In 1993 there was a trade deficit of US$210 million and a current account surplus of US$13 million. In 1995 imports totalled US$864 million and exports US$607 million.

Trade with UK	1995	1996
Imports from UK	£6,770,000	£7,362,000
Exports to UK	82,020,000	89,508,000

COMMUNICATIONS

Fiji is one of the main aerial crossroads in the Pacific, providing services to New Zealand, Australia, Tonga, Western Samoa, Vanuatu, the Solomon Islands, Kiribati, Tuvalu, New Caledonia and American Samoa. Fiji has three ports of entry, at Suva, Lautoka and Levuka. There are 5,100 km of roads.

FINLAND
Suomen Tasavalta

AREA – 130,559 sq. miles (338,145 sq. km)
POPULATION – 5,095,000 (1994 UN estimate). Finnish and Swedish are both official languages, 93.6 per cent speaking Finnish as their first language and 6.2 per cent Swedish. Lapp is spoken by the 2,500 Lapps who live in the far north. The population is predominantly Lutheran
CAPITAL – ΨHelsinki (Helsingfors) (population, 1,016,291, 1993 estimate)
MAJOR CITIES – Tampere (Tammerfors) (242,785); ΨTurku (Åbo) (249,890); Espoo (Esbo) (180,851); Vantaa (Vanda) (160,158); Ψ Oulu (Oleåborg) (144,656), 1993 estimates
CURRENCY – Markka (Mk) of 100 penniä
NATIONAL DAY – 6 December (Independence Day)
NATIONAL FLAG – White with blue cross
LIFE EXPECTANCY (years) – male 70.93; female 78.87
POPULATION GROWTH RATE – 0.5 per cent (1994)
POPULATION DENSITY – 15 per sq. km (1994)
URBAN POPULATION – 64.0 per cent (1993)

The Åland archipelago (Ahvenanmaa), a group of small islands at the entrance to the Gulf of Bothnia, covers about 572 square miles, with a population (1994) of 25,158 (95.2 per cent Swedish-speaking). The islands have semi-autonomous status.

HISTORY AND POLITICS

Finland was part of the Swedish Empire from the Middle Ages until it was ceded to Russia in 1809 and became an autonomous grand duchy of the Russian Empire. Finland became independent after the Russian revolution of 1917, but was forced to cede around one-tenth of its land to the Soviet Union and to resettle 10 per cent of its population under the Treaty of Paris (1947). A Soviet-Finnish Co-operation Treaty forced Finland to demilitarize its Soviet border, to enter into a barter trade agreement and to adopt a stance of neutrality. These terms lasted until the demise of the Soviet Union in 1991.

The present government took office in April 1995. The five parties in the ruling coalition are the Social Democratic Party, the National Coalition Party (conservative), the Left-wing Alliance, the Swedish People's Party, and the Green League, with a total of 145 out of 200 seats.

Finland joined the European Union on 1 January 1995 following a referendum in October 1994 in which accession was approved by 57 per cent in Finland and by 74 per cent in a separate Åland Islands referendum.

POLITICAL SYSTEM

Under the constitution there is a unicameral legislature, the *Eduskunta*, composed of 200 members elected by universal suffrage. The highest executive power is held by the president who is directly elected for a period of six years. The first direct elections for the presidency were held in 1994, the president having previously been elected by an electoral college.

HEAD OF STATE
President, Martti Ahtisaari, *inaugurated* 1 March 1994

CABINET *as at July 1997*
Prime Minister, Paavo Lipponen (SDP)
Deputy PM, Finance, Sauli Niinistö (NCP)
Administration, Jouni Backman (SDP)

Agriculture and Forestry, Kalevi Hemilä (Ind.)
Culture, Youth, Universities, Science, Claes Andersson (LA)
Defence, Anneli Taina (NCP)
Education, Olli-Pekka Heinonen (NCP)
Environment, Development Co-operation, Pekka Haavisto
(Green)
Europe, Ole Norrback (SPP)
Finance, PM's Office, Arja Alho (SDP)
Foreign Affairs, Tarja Halonen (SDP)
Interior, Jan-Erik Enestam (SPP)
Justice, Kari Häkämies (NCP)
Labour, Liisa Jaakonsaari (SDP)
Labour Protection, Social and Health Services, Equality Affairs,
Terttu Huttu (LA)
Social Affairs and Health, Housing and Building, Sinikka
Mönkäre (SDP)
Trade and Industry, Antti Kalliomäki (SDP)
Transport, Tuula Linnainmaa (NCP)

SDP Social Democratic Party; NCP National Coalition
Party; LA Left-wing Alliance; SPP Swedish People's Party;
Green Green League

EMBASSY OF FINLAND
38 Chesham Place, London SW1X 8HW
Tel 0171-838 6200
Ambassador Extraordinary and Plenipotentiary, HE Pertti
Salolainen, apptd 1996
Minister, Kirsti Eskelinen
Counsellor (Commercial), Marcus Moberg
Defence Attaché, Col. H. Strang

BRITISH EMBASSY
Itäinen Puistotie 17, 00140 Helsinki
Tel: Helsinki 2286 5100
Ambassador Extraordinary and Plenipotentiary, HE Gavin
Hewitt, CMG, apptd 1997
Deputy Head of Mission and Counsellor, D. J. Gowan
First Secretary (Commercial), H. B. Formstone, OBE
Defence Attaché, Lt.-Col. S. W. L. Strickland

BRITISH CONSULAR OFFICES – Helsinki, Jyväskylä,
Kotka, Kuopio, Oulu, Pori, Tampere, Turku, Vaasa,
Mariehamn

BRITISH COUNCIL REPRESENTATIVE, Tuija Talvitie,
Hakaniemenkatu 2, 00530 Helsinki

DEFENCE

The Army has 232 main battle tanks, 1,098 armoured
infantry fighting vehicles and armoured personnel carriers, and 810 artillery pieces. The Navy has 14 patrol and
coastal vessels. The Air Force has 118 combat aircraft.
MILITARY EXPENDITURE – 2.0 per cent of GDP (1995)
MILITARY PERSONNEL – 32,500: Army 26,000, Navy
2,500, Air Force 4,000
CONSCRIPTION DURATION – Eight to 11 months

ECONOMY

Finland produces a wide range of capital and consumer
goods. Timber and timber-based products account for a
third of exports, but the importance of metal-working,
shipbuilding and engineering has grown. The textile
industry is well developed and the glass, ceramics and
furniture industries enjoy international reputations. Other
important industries are rubber, plastics, chemicals and
pharmaceuticals, footwear, foodstuffs and electronic
equipment.
The Finnish economy was adversely affected by declining trade with the former Soviet bloc, together with the
world-wide economic recession, causing GDP to fall by 15

per cent, and output by 13 per cent, in 1990–3 before
exports and the currency strengthened in 1994–5. The
markka joined the ERM in August 1996.
In 1996, the budget deficit was equivalent to 3.3 per cent
of GDP and public debt was 61.3 per cent of GDP.
GNP – US$105,174 million (1995); US$20,580 per capita
(1995)
GDP – US$123,005 million (1992); US$21,756 per capita
(1992)
ANNUAL AVERAGE GROWTH OF GDP – 4.2 per cent
(1995); estimated to be 4.1 per cent in 1997
INFLATION RATE – 1.0 per cent (1995); estimated to be 2.0
per cent in 1997
UNEMPLOYMENT – 17.4 per cent (1995); estimated to be
15.3 per cent in 1997

TRADE

The principal imports are raw materials, machinery and
manufactured goods. The special barter-trade relationship
with the former Soviet Union collapsed in 1991 and
exports to the countries of the former Soviet Union fell
from 20 per cent of the total in the early 1980s to 5 per cent
in 1994.
In 1994 there was a trade surplus of US$7,651 million
and a current account surplus of US$1,068 million. In 1995
imports totalled US$28,114 million and exports
US$39,573 million.

Trade with UK	1995	1996
Imports from UK	£1,630,900,000	£1,729,300,000
Exports to UK	2,345,200,000	2,467,600,000

COMMUNICATIONS

There are 9,000 km of railroad, railway connections with
Sweden and Russia, and passenger boat connections with
Sweden, Germany, Poland, Russia and the Baltic states.
There are also passenger/cargo services between Britain
and Helsinki, Kotka and other Finnish ports. External air
services are maintained by most European airlines.

CULTURE AND EDUCATION

Newspapers, books, plays and films appear in both Finnish
and Swedish. There is a vigorous modern literature. F. E.
Sillanpää, who died in 1964, was awarded the Nobel Prize
for Literature in 1939. In 1994 there were 60 daily
newspapers (12 Swedish).
Primary education (co-educational comprehensive
school) is free and compulsory for children from seven to
16 years.
ENROLMENT (percentage of age group) – secondary 93 per
cent (1990); tertiary 63.2 per cent (1993)

FRANCE
La République Française

AREA – 212,934 sq. miles (551,500 sq. km)
POPULATION – 57,747,000 (1994 UN estimate);
57,218,000 (Metropolitan France), and 58,745,000
including overseas departments (1992 official estimate)
CAPITAL – Paris (population, 9,319,367, 1990), on the
Seine
MAJOR CITIES – Lyon (1,262,000); ΨMarseille
(1,231,000); Lille (959,000); ΨBordeaux (696,000);
Toulouse (650,000); Nice (516,000); Nantes (496,000);
Toulon (437,000); Grenoble (404,000); Strasbourg
(388,000). The chief towns of Corsica are ΨAjaccio
(58,315) and ΨBastia (52,446)

CURRENCY – Franc of 100 centimes
NATIONAL ANTHEM – La Marseillaise
NATIONAL DAY – 14 July (Bastille Day 1789)
NATIONAL FLAG – The tricolour, three vertical bands, blue, white, red (blue next to flagstaff)
LIFE EXPECTANCY (years) – male 72.91; female 81.13
POPULATION GROWTH RATE – 0.4 per cent (1994)
POPULATION DENSITY – 105 per sq. km (1994)
URBAN POPULATION – 74.0 per cent (1990)

HISTORY AND POLITICS

There are dolmens and menhirs in Brittany, prehistoric remains and cave drawings in Dordogne and Ariège, and throughout France various megalithic monuments erected by primitive tribes, predecessors of Iberian invaders from Spain (now represented by the Basques), Ligurians from northern Italy and Celts or Gauls from the valley of the Danube. Julius Caesar found Gaul 'divided into three parts' and described three political groups: Aquitanians south of the Garonne, Celts between the Garonne and the Seine and Marne, and Belgae from the Seine to the Rhine. Roman remains are plentiful throughout France in the form of aqueducts, arenas, triumphal arches, etc. The celebrated Norman and Gothic cathedrals, including Notre Dame in Paris and those of Chartres, Reims, Amiens, Bourges, Beauvais, Rouen, etc., have survived invasions and bombardments with only partial damage, and many of the Renaissance and the 17th- and 18th-century chateaux survived the French Revolution.

The state of the parties in the Senate at August 1996 was: Rassemblement pour la République (RPR) 102; Socialists 78; Centrist Union (UDC) 64; Republican and Independent Union (RI) 47; Democratic and European Rally (RDE) 26; Communists 15; Independents 9.

In the last elections to the National Assembly in May and June 1997 the Socialist Party (PS) won 241 seats, the Gaullist Rassemblement pour la République (RPR) 134, Union pour la Démocratie Française (UDF) 108, Communists (PCF) 38, Independent Left 21, Independent Right 14, Radical Socialist Party 12, Green Party 7, National Front 1, Independent 1.

POLITICAL SYSTEM

The legislature consists of the National Assembly of 577 deputies (555 for Metropolitan France and 22 for the overseas departments and territories) and the Senate of 321 Senators (296 for Metropolitan France, 13 for the overseas departments and territories and 12 for French citizens

abroad). One-third of the Senate is indirectly elected every three years.

The prime minister is appointed by the president, as is the Council of Ministers on the prime minister's recommendation. They are responsible to the legislature, but as the executive is constitutionally separate from the legislature, ministers may not sit in the legislature and must hand over their seats to a substitute.

France is divided into 95 departments, including the island of Corsica, in the Mediterranean off the west coast of Italy.

HEAD OF STATE
President of the French Republic, Jacques Chirac, *elected* 7 May 1995, *took office* 17 May 1995

COUNCIL OF MINISTERS *as at June 1997*
Prime Minister, Lionel Jospin
Agriculture and Fisheries, Louis Le Pensec
Capital Works, Transport and Housing, Jean–Claude Gayssot
Civil Service, Administrative Reform and Decentralization, Emile Zuccarelli
Culture and Communication, Government Spokesperson, Catherine Trautmann
Defence, Alain Richard
Economy, Finance and Industry, Dominique Strauss-Kahn
Employment and Solidarity, Martine Aubry
Foreign Affairs, Hubert Vedrine
Interior, Jean-Pierre Chevenement
Justice, Elisabeth Guigou
National Education, Research and Technology, Claude Allegre
Relations with Parliament, Daniel Vaillant
Town and Country Planning and the Environment, Dominique Voynet
Youth and Sport, Marie-George Buffet

President of the Senate, René Monory
President of the National Assembly, Laurent Fabius

FRENCH EMBASSY
58 Knightsbridge, London SW1X 7JT
Tel 0171-201 1000
Ambassador Extraordinary and Plenipotentiary, HE Jean Gueguinou, apptd 1993
Minister-Counsellor, G. Keller
Defence Attaché, Contre-Amiral Y. de Kersauson
Cultural Counsellor, O. Poivre D'Arvor
Minister-Counsellor (Economic and Commercial Affairs), O. Louis

BRITISH EMBASSY
35 rue du Faubourg St Honoré, 75383 Paris Cedex 08
Tel: Paris 4451 3100
Ambassador Extraordinary and Plenipotentiary, HE Sir Michael Jay, KCMG, apptd 1996
Minister, Michael Pakenham, CMG
Defence and Air Attaché, Air Cdre P. H. Eustace
Counsellor, V. Caton (*Finance and Economic*)
First Secretary and Consul-General, K. C. Moss

BRITISH CONSULAR OFFICES – Bordeaux, Biarritz, Toulouse, Lille, Boulogne, Calais, Dunkirk, Lyon, Marseille, Nice, Paris, Cherbourg, Le Havre, Nantes, St Malo; overseas in Cayenne (French Guiana), Papeete (French Polynesia), Fort de France (Martinique), Pointe à Pitre (Guadeloupe) and St Denis (Réunion)

BRITISH COUNCIL DIRECTOR, C. Gamble, 9/11 rue de Constantine, 75007 Paris
FRANCO-BRITISH CHAMBER OF COMMERCE, 8 rue Cimarosa, 75116 Paris. *President,* R. Lyon. *Vice-President,* B. Cordery, OBE

DEFENCE

The Army has 880 main battle tanks, 4,553 armoured personnel carriers and armoured infantry fighting vehicles, 1,306 artillery pieces, two aircraft and 645 helicopters.

The Navy has 17 submarines (including five nuclear-powered ballistic missile submarines with a total of 80 ballistic missiles, and six nuclear-powered submarines), one aircraft carrier, one cruiser, four destroyers, 36 frigates and 36 patrol and coastal vessels, 69 combat aircraft (including 36 short- to medium-range nuclear attack aircraft) and 40 armed helicopters. The Navy has four domestic and five overseas bases.

The Air Force has 547 combat aircraft including 45 short-range nuclear attack aircraft and 15 strategic bombers, and 18 intermediate-range ballistic missiles.

France deploys 52,257 armed forces personnel abroad; 15,000 in Germany; 20,300 in French Overseas Departments and Territories; 8,800 in former French colonies in Africa; and 8,157 on UN and peacekeeping duties.

MILITARY EXPENDITURE – 3.1 per cent of GDP (1995)
MILITARY PERSONNEL – 388,500: Army 236,600, Navy 63,300, Air Force 88,600
CONSCRIPTION DURATION – Ten months. Conscription is to be phased out over six years, beginning in 1997

ECONOMY

Viniculture is extensive, regions famous for their wines including Bordeaux, Burgundy and Champagne. Production of wine in 1995 was 5,300,000 tonnes. Cognac, liqueurs and cider are also important products.

Oil is produced from fields in the Landes area, but France is a net importer of crude oil, for processing by its important oil-refining industry. Natural gas is produced in the foothills of the Pyrenees.

Heavy industries include oil-refining and the production of iron and steel, and aluminium. In 1995 production of pig iron was 13,154,000 tonnes and steel 18,104,000 tonnes. Other important industries produce chemicals, tyres, aluminium, textiles, paper products and processed food. Engineering products include motor vehicles, and television and radio sets.

In 1993 the conservative government announced the privatization of most public sector companies, which was expected to generate F300,000 million over five years.

The Banque de France was made independent in 1994 with the formation of a nine-member monetary policy council to define and implement monetary policy independent of the government.

In 1995–6, the government sought to introduce austerity measures to enable France to meet the Maastricht criteria for European monetary union. Cost cutting reforms targeted the welfare budget, provoking a series of strikes by public-sector workers and students in December 1995 and early 1996. Concessions to the unions, tax cuts, and a high level of public debt make it unlikely that France will reduce the budget deficit to the required 3 per cent in 1997.

In 1996 the government had a budget deficit equivalent to 4.2 per cent of GDP.

GNP – US$1,451,051 million (1995); US$24,990 per capita (1995)
GDP – US$1,215,251 million (1992); US$23,149 per capita (1992)
ANNUAL AVERAGE GROWTH OF GDP – 2.2 per cent (1995); forecast to be 2.4 per cent in 1997
INFLATION RATE – 1.8 per cent (1995); forecast to be 1.6 per cent in 1997
UNEMPLOYMENT – 11.6 per cent (1995); forecast to be 12.1 per cent in 1997

TRADE

The principal imports are raw materials for the heavy and manufacturing industries (e.g. oil, minerals, chemicals), machinery and precision instruments, agricultural products, chemicals and vehicles. Raw materials, semi-manufactured and manufactured goods, chemicals and vehicles are also the principal exports. Most of France's trade is done with other EU countries.

In 1994 there was a trade surplus of US$9,132 million and a current account surplus of US$8,832 million. In 1995, imports totalled US$274,972 million and exports US$286,694 million.

Trade with UK	1995	1996
Imports from UK	£14,442,200,000	£16,190,100,000
Exports to UK	15,498,400,000	16,624,500,000

COMMUNICATIONS

The length of roads in 1996 was 964,356 km, of which 7,396 km were motorways.

The railroad system is extensive. The length of lines open for traffic in 1996 was 31,940 km.

The French mercantile marine consisted in 1995 of 208 ships of a total of 4,300,000 tonnes which transported 91,500,000 tonnes of freight.

CULTURE AND EDUCATION

French is the official language. The work of the French Academy, founded in 1635, has established *le bon usage*, equivalent to 'The Queen's English' in Britain. French authors have been awarded the Nobel Prize for Literature on 12 occasions and include R. F. A. Sully-Prudhomme (1901), Anatole France (1921), André Gide (1947), François Mauriac (1952), Albert Camus (1957), Jean Paul Sartre (1964) and Claude Simon (1985).

Education is compulsory, free and secular from six to 16. Schools may be single sex or co-educational. Primary education is given in nursery schools, primary schools and *collèges d'enseignement général* (four-year secondary modern course); secondary education in *collèges d'enseignement technique, collèges d'enseignement secondaire* and *lycées* (seven-year course leading to one of the five *baccalauréats*). Special schools are numerous.

There are many *grandes écoles* in France which award diplomas in many subjects not taught at university, especially applied science and engineering. Most of these are state institutions but have a competitive system of entry, unlike universities. There are universities in 24 towns including 13 in Paris and the immediate area.

In 1993 the government gave German official parity with French in Alsace schools.

ENROLMENT (percentage of age group) – primary 99 per cent; secondary 90 per cent; tertiary 49.7 per cent (1993)

OVERSEAS DEPARTMENTS

Greater powers of self-government were granted to French Guiana, Guadeloupe, Martinique and Réunion in 1982. These former colonies had enjoyed departmental status since 1946 and the status of regions since 1974. Their directly-elected Assemblies operate in parallel with the existing, indirectly constituted Regional Councils. The French government is represented by a Prefect in each.

FRENCH GUIANA – Situated on the north-eastern coast of South America, French Guiana is flanked by Suriname on the west and by Brazil on the south and east. Area, 34,749 sq. miles (90,000 sq. km). Population (1994) 141,000. Capital, ΨCayenne (41,164). Under the administration of French

Guiana is a group of islands (St Joseph, Ile Royal and Ile du Diable), known as Iles du Salut.
Prefect, P. Dartout

Trade with UK	1995	1996
Imports from UK	£3,734,000	£11,713,000
Exports to UK	591,000	1,149,000

GUADELOUPE – A number of islands in the Leeward Islands group of the West Indies, consisting of the two main islands of Guadeloupe (or Basse-Terre) and Grande-Terre, with the adjacent islands of Marie-Galante, La Désirade and Îles des Saintes, and the islands of St Martin and St Barthélemy over 150 miles to the north-west. Area, 658 sq. miles (1,7049 sq. km). Population (1994) 421,000. Capital ΨBasse Terre (29,522) in Guadeloupe. Other towns are ΨPointe à Pitre (26,000) in Grande-Terre and ΨGrand Bourg (6,611) in Marie-Galante.
Prefect, M. Diefenbacher

Trade with UK	1995	1996
Imports from UK	£6,896,000	£10,029,000
Exports to UK	211,000	68,000

MARTINIQUE – An island situated in the Windward Islands group of the West Indies, between Dominica in the north and St Lucia in the south. Area, 425 sq. miles (1,102 sq. km). Population (1994) 375,000. Capital ΨFort de France (97,814). Other towns are ΨTrinité (11,214) and ΨMarin (6,104).
Prefect, J.-F. Cordet

Trade with UK	1995	1996
Imports from UK	£13,839,000	£16,422,000
Exports to UK	14,000	196,000

RÉUNION – Réunion, which became a French possession in 1638, lies in the Indian Ocean, about 569 miles east of Madagascar and 110 miles south-west of Mauritius. Area, 969 sq. miles (2,510 sq. km). Population (1994) 644,000. Capital, St Denis (121,999). Other towns are Saint-Paul (71,669) and Saint-Pierre (58,846). The smaller, uninhabited islands of Bassas da India, Europa, Îles Glorieuses, Juan de Nova and Tromelin are administered from Réunion.
Prefect, R. Pommies

Trade with UK	1995	1996
Imports from UK	£15,345,000	£15,374,000
Exports to UK	2,278,000	2,910,000

TERRITORIAL COLLECTIVITÉS

MAYOTTE – Area, 144 sq. miles (372 sq. km). Population (1991 census) is 94,410. Capital, Mamoundzou (12,000). Part of the Comoros Islands group, Mayotte remained a French dependency when the other three islands became independent as the Comoros Republic in 1975. Since 1976 the island has been a *collectivité territoriale*, an intermediate status between Overseas Department and Overseas Territory.
Prefect, P. Boisadam

Trade with UK	1995	1996
Imports from UK	£5,064,000	£5,823,000
Exports to UK	312,000	447,000

ST PIERRE AND MIQUELON – Area 93 sq. miles (242 sq. km). Population (1990) 6,000. Capital, ΨSt Pierre (5,416). Two small groups of islands off the coast of Newfoundland. Became a *collectivité territoriale* in 1985.
Prefect, J.-F. Carenco

Trade with UK	1995	1996
Imports from UK	£561,000	£1,542,000
Exports to UK	25,000	—

OVERSEAS TERRITORIES

FRENCH POLYNESIA – Five archipelagos in the south Pacific, comprising the Society Islands (Windward Islands group includes Tahiti, Moorea, Makatea, Mehetia, Tetiaroa, Tubuai Manu; Leeward Islands group includes Huahine, Raiatea, Tahaa, Bora-Bora, Maupiti), the Tuamotu Islands (Rangiroa, Hao, Turéia, etc.), the Gambier Islands (Mangareva, etc.), the Tubuai Islands (Rimatara, Rurutu, Tubuai, Raivavae, Rapa, etc.) and the Marquesas Islands (Nuku-Hiva, Hiva-Oa, Fatu-Hiva, Tahuata, Ua Huka, etc.). Area, 1,544 sq. miles (4,000 sq. km). Population (1994) 215,000. Capital, ΨPapeete (36,784) in Tahiti. Economy based on tourism and exports of copra, coffee, vanilla, citrus fruits and cultured pearls.
High Commissioner, P. Roncière

Trade with UK	1995	1996
Imports from UK	£6,078,000	£6,327,000
Exports to UK	235,000	207,000

NEW CALEDONIA – A large island in the western Pacific, 700 miles east of Queensland. Dependencies are the Isles of Pines, the Loyalty Islands (Mahé, Lifou, Urea, etc.), the Bélep Archipelago, the Chesterfield Islands, the Huon Islands and Walpole. New Caledonia was discovered in 1774 and annexed by France in 1854; from 1871 to 1896 it was a convict settlement. A referendum in 1987 on the question of independence was boycotted by the indigenous Kanaks, and New Caledonia therefore voted to remain French. However, a new independence referendum has been promised for 1998. In 1995, the territory was divided into three provinces, each with a provincial assembly which combined to form the Territorial Assembly. In elections in July 1995, Kanaks won majorities in North province and the Loyalty Islands, whereas pro-French settlers won a majority in the South province. Area, 7,172 sq. miles (18,575 sq. km). Population (1994) 183,000. Capital ΨNoumea (97,581). It is one of the world's largest producers of nickel.
High Commissioner, D. Bur

Trade with UK	1995	1996
Imports from UK	£9,006,000	£10,529,000
Exports to UK	9,534,000	10,891,000

SOUTHERN AND ANTARCTIC TERRITORIES – Created in 1955 from former Réunion dependencies, the territory comprises the islands of Amsterdam (25 sq. miles) and St Paul (2.7 sq. miles), the Kerguelen Islands (2,700 sq. miles) and Crozet Islands (116 sq. miles) archipelagos and Adélie Land (116,800 sq. miles) in the Antarctic continent. The only population are members of staff of the scientific stations.

WALLIS AND FUTUNA ISLANDS – Two groups of islands (the Wallis Archipelago and the Îles de Hoorn) in the central Pacific, north-east of Fiji. Area, 77 sq. miles (199 sq. km). Population (1990 census) 14,000. Capital, Mata-Utu on Uvea, the main island of the Wallis group.
Supreme Administrator, C. Pierret

Trade with UK	1995	1996
Imports from UK	£17,000	£20,000
Exports to UK	—	—

THE FRENCH COMMUNITY

The constitution of the Fifth French Republic, promulgated in 1958, envisaged the establishment of a French Community of States. A number of the former French states in Africa have seceded from the Community but for all practical purposes continue to enjoy the same close links with France as those that remain formally members. Most former French African colonies are closely linked to France by financial, technical and economic agreements.

GABON
République Gabonaise

AREA – 103,347 sq. miles (267,667 sq. km). Neighbours: Equatorial Guinea and Cameroon (north), Republic of Congo (east and south)
POPULATION – 1,283,000 (1994 UN estimate)
CAPITAL – ΨLibreville (population, 251,000)
CURRENCY – Franc CFA of 100 centimes
NATIONAL ANTHEM – La Concorde
NATIONAL DAY – 17 August
NATIONAL FLAG – Horizontal bands, green, yellow and blue
LIFE EXPECTANCY (years) – male 51.86; female 55.18
POPULATION GROWTH RATE – 2.8 per cent (1994)
POPULATION DENSITY – 5 per sq. km (1994)
URBAN POPULATION – 73.2 per cent (1993)
MILITARY EXPENDITURE – 1.7 per cent of GDP (1995)
MILITARY PERSONNEL – 4,700: Army 3,200, Navy 500, Air Force 1,000
ILLITERACY RATE – 36.8 per cent

HISTORY AND POLITICS

Gabon elected on 28 November 1958 to remain an autonomous republic within the French Community and gained full independence on 17 August 1960.

A national conference was held in March 1990 to demand the legalization of opposition parties. Multiparty elections held in autumn 1990 were won by the ruling Parti Démocratique Gabonais (PDG), amid allegations of fraud. The PDG formed a coalition government, although the other parties left the government in 1991 in protest at PDG domination. A presidential election in 1993 was won by the incumbent, President Bongo of the PDG, amid accusations of corruption, which led to riots in Libreville. In September 1994, the government and opposition parties signed the Paris Agreement, which provided for a new coalition government and parliamentary elections. The reforms were approved in a referendum on 23 July 1995. The elections, held in December 1996, returned the PDG to power.

POLITICAL SYSTEM

The constitution provides for an executive president directly elected for a seven-year term, who appoints the Council of Ministers. There is a 120-member National Assembly and a 91-member Senate.

HEAD OF STATE
President, El Hadj Omar Bongo, *assumed office* December 1967, *re-elected* 1973, 1979, 1986 and 5 December 1993

COUNCIL OF MINISTERS *as at July 1997*
Prime Minister, Dr Paulin Obame Nguema
Minister of State, Agriculture, Livestock and Rural Economy, Emmanuel Ondo Methogo
Minister of State, Education, Women, Paulette Missambo

Minister of State, Equipment and Construction, Zacharie Myboto
Minister of State, Foreign Affairs and Co-operation, Casimir Oyé Mba
Minister of State, Interior, Antoine Mboumbou Miyakou
Minister of State, Justice, Marcel Eloi Rahandi Chambrier
Minister of State, Labour, Human Resources and Training, Jean-Rémy Pendy-Bouyiki
Minister of State, Lands, Housing, Welfare, Jean-François Ntoutoume-Emane
Civil Service and Administrative Reform, Patrice Ziengui
Commerce and Industry, Martin Fidèle Magnaga
Finance and Economy, Marcel Doupamby Matoka
Higher Education and Scientific Research, Lazare Digombé
Merchant Marine and Fishing, Joachim Mahotes Magouindi
Mining, Energy and Oil, Paul Toungui
National Defence and Security, Gen. Idriss Ngari
National Education, Communication, Culture and Arts, Jacques Adiahénot
Planning, Environment and Tourism, Jean Ping
Public Health and Population, Faustin Boukoubi
Relations with Parliament, André Mba Obame
Social Affairs, National Solidarity and the Family, Pierre-Claver Zeng Ebome
Transport and Civil Aviation, Gen. Albert Ndjavé-Ndjoy
Water, Forests and Reafforestation, André Dieudonné Berre
Youth, Sports and Leisure, Alexandre Sambat

EMBASSY OF THE REPUBLIC OF GABON
27 Elvaston Place, London SW7 5NI
Tel 0171–823 9986
Ambassador Extraordinary and Plenipotentiary, HE Honorine Dossou-Naki, apptd 1996

BRITISH AMBASSADOR, HE N. M. McCarthy, OBE, resident in Yaoundé, Cameroon

ECONOMY

The economy is heavily dependent on oil and, to a much lesser extent, other mineral resources, including manganese and uranium. Gabon has considerable timber reserves (particularly Okoumé) with 80 per cent of the country still forested, although production has stagnated in recent years.

The economy experienced considerable growth from the mid-1970s onwards but after 1986 was adversely affected by the fall in oil prices. Revenue has increased in the 1990s following oil exploitation at Rabi-Kounga.

In 1993 there was a trade surplus of US$1,305 million and a current account deficit of US$269 million.
GNP – US$3,759 million (1995); US$3,490 per capita (1995)
GDP – US$4,607 million (1992); US$3,932 per capita (1992)
INFLATION RATE – 36.2 per cent (1994)
TOTAL EXTERNAL DEBT – US$4,492 million (1995)

TRADE WITH UK	1995	1996
Imports from UK	£25,358,000	£20,900,000
Exports to UK	5,948,000	8,433,000

THE GAMBIA
The Republic of the Gambia

AREA – 4,361 sq. miles (11,295 sq. km). Neighbour: Senegal, which surrounds the Gambia except at the coast
POPULATION – 1,081,000 (1994 UN estimate), mainly Wolof, Mandinka and Fula peoples who originally migrated from the north and east

CAPITAL – ΨBanjul (population, 109,986, 1980 estimate)
CURRENCY – Dalasi (D) of 100 butut
NATIONAL ANTHEM – For The Gambia, Our Homeland
NATIONAL DAY – 18 February (Independence Day)
NATIONAL FLAG – Horizontal stripes of red, blue and
    green, separated by narrow white stripes
LIFE EXPECTANCY (years) – male 43.41; female 46.63
POPULATION GROWTH RATE – 4.0 per cent (1994)
POPULATION DENSITY – 96 per sq. km (1994)
MILITARY EXPENDITURE – 3.8 per cent of GDP (1995)
MILITARY PERSONNEL – 800: Army 800

The Gambia is named after the Gambia River, which it
straddles for over 200 miles inland from the west coast of
Africa. The climate is Sahelian, with a dry season between
October and May and heavy rainfall in July and August.

HISTORY AND POLITICS

The Gambia River basin was part of the region dominated
in the tenth to 16th centuries by the Songhai and Mali
kingdoms centred on the upper Niger. The Portuguese
reached the Gambia River in 1447; English merchants
began to trade along the river from 1588. Merchants from
France, Courland (now Latvia) and the Netherlands also
established trading posts. In 1816 the British stationed a
garrison on an island at the river mouth which became the
capital of a small British-administered colony. In 1889
France agreed that the British rights along the upper river
should extend 10 km on either bank. British administration
was extended from the Colony to this Protectorate. The
Gambia became independent within the Commonwealth
on 18 February 1965, and a republic on 24 April 1970.

In July 1994 junior army officers launched a coup which
ousted the President and the government, and a military
council was formed. The coup leader, Lt. (later Capt.)
Jammeh, assumed the presidency, the constitution was
suspended and a civilian-military government was formed
to rule in conjunction with the Ruling Military Council. A
referendum approved a new constitution in August 1996,
Jammeh was elected president the following month and
the Ruling Military Council was dissolved. A pro-pre-
sidential party won 33 of the 49 seats in the new parliament
in a legislative election in January 1997.

FOREIGN RELATIONS

The relationship with Senegal remains an important factor
in political and economic policy. Moves towards a closer
association were accelerated after an abortive coup in 1981
was put down with the help of Senegalese troops. In 1982
the Senegambia Confederation was instituted but following disagreements it was dissolved in 1989. A treaty of
friendship and co-operation was signed with Senegal in
1991.

POLITICAL SYSTEM

The constitution gives enhanced powers to the president
who is elected for an indefinite term.

HEAD OF STATE

President, Defence, Capt. Yayah Jammeh, *took power* 23 July
1994, *elected* 26 September 1996
Vice-President, Health and Women's Affairs, Isatou Njie Saidy

CABINET *as at July 1997*

The President
The Vice-President
Agriculture and National Resources, Musa Mbenga
Attorney-General, Justice, Awa Sisay Sabally
Education, Satang Jow
Finance and Economic Affairs, Dominic Mendy

Foreign Affairs, Modou Njie
Interior, Momodou Bojang
Lands and Local Government, Yankuba Touray
Presidency, Edward Singhateh
Tourism and Culture, Susan Waffa-Ogoo
Trade, Industry and Employment, Famara Jatta
Works, Communication and Information, Ebrima Ceesay
Youth and Sports, Kaba Bojo

GAMBIA HIGH COMMISSION
57 Kensington Court, London w8 5DG
Tel 0171-937 6316
High Commissioner, HE John P. Bojang, apptd 1997

BRITISH HIGH COMMISSION
48 Atlantic Road, Fajara (PO Box 507), Banjul
Tel: Banjul 495133
High Commissioner, HE J. Wilde, apptd 1995

ECONOMY

Agriculture accounts for 75 per cent of employment and
contributes 40 per cent of GDP. The chief product,
groundnuts, is also the most important export item,
forming over 80 per cent of domestic exports. Other crops
are rice, millet, sorghum, maize and cotton. Fishing and
livestock industries are being developed. Thirty per cent of
the country's basic food requirements are imported.

Manufactures are limited to groundnut processing,
minor metal fabrications, paints, furniture, soap and
bottling. Tourism is developing quickly. Trade through
the Gambia, re-exporting imported goods to neighbouring
countries, is an important element in the economy.
GNP – US$354 million (1995); US$320 per capita (1995)
GDP – US$318 million (1992); US$374 per capita (1992)
ANNUAL AVERAGE GROWTH OF GDP – –4.1 per cent
    (1995)
INFLATION RATE – 7.0 per cent (1995)
TOTAL EXTERNAL DEBT – US$426 million (1995)

TRADE WITH UK	1995	1996
Imports from UK	£13,591,000	£16,443,000
Exports to UK	3,119,000	3,207,000

COMMUNICATIONS

There is an international airport at Yundum, 17 miles from
Banjul, with scheduled services flying to other West
African states and to the UK and Belgium. Banjul is the
main port. Internal communication is by road and river.
There are five broadcasting stations and a UHF telephone
service linking Banjul with the principal towns in the
provinces. There is one television station.

EDUCATION

There are 24 secondary schools (eight high and 16
technical). Two high schools provide A-level education.
Gambia College provides post-secondary courses in
education, agriculture, public health and nursing. There
are seven vocational training institutions. Higher education and advanced training courses are taken outside The
Gambia, currently by over 200 students.
ILLITERACY RATE – 61.4 per cent
ENROLMENT (percentage of age group) – primary 55 per
    cent; secondary 18 per cent; tertiary 1.6 per cent (1992)

GEORGIA
Sakartvelos Respublika

AREA – 26,911 sq. miles (69,700 sq. km). Neighbours:
Russia (north), Azerbaijan (south-east), Armenia
(south), Turkey (south-west)

POPULATION – 5,401,000 (1995 official estimate): 70 per
cent Georgian, 8 per cent Armenian, 6 per cent Russian,
6 per cent Azerbaijani and 3 per cent Ossetians, with
smaller groups of Abkhazians, Greeks, Ukrainians, Jews
and Kurds. The majority religion is the Georgian
Orthodox Church. There is also a small Muslim
minority. Georgian, Russian and Armenian are the most
commonly used languages. Georgian is one of the oldest
languages in the world to have been continually in use,
the alphabet having emerged in the third century BC

CAPITAL – Tbilisi (population, 1,268,000, 1990 estimate)

MAJOR CITIES – Batumi (150,000); Sukhumi (capital of
Abkhazia) (125,000)

CURRENCY – Lari of 100 tetri

NATIONAL DAY – 26 May (Independence Day)

NATIONAL FLAG – Cherry red with a canton in the upper
hoist divided black over white

LIFE EXPECTANCY (years) – male 68.10; female 75.70

POPULATION GROWTH RATE – –0.1 per cent (1994)

POPULATION DENSITY – 78 per sq. km (1994)

URBAN POPULATION – 55.4 per cent (1989)

MILITARY EXPENDITURE – 3.4 per cent of GDP (1995)

MILITARY PERSONNEL – 13,000: Army 10,000, Navy
2,000, Air Force 1,000

CONSCRIPTION DURATION – Two years

ILLITERACY RATE – 0.5 per cent

ENROLMENT (percentage of age group) – primary 82 per
cent (1994); tertiary 41.5 per cent (1994)

Georgia occupies the north-western part of the Caucasus
region of the former Soviet Union. It contains the two
autonomous republics of Abkhazia and Adjaria and the
disputed region of South Ossetia (Tskhinvali).

Georgia is mountainous, with the Greater Caucasus in
the north and the Lesser Caucasus in the south. Western
Georgia has a mild and damp climate, eastern Georgia is
more continental and dry. The Black Sea shore and the
Rioni lowland are subtropical.

HISTORY AND POLITICS

The Georgians formed two states, Colchis and Iberia, on
the edge of the Black Sea around 1000 BC. After centuries
of invasions by Arabs, Turks and Khazars, Georgia entered
its 'Golden Age' in the 12th century AD when trade,
irrigation and communications were developed. Invasions
by the Khazars and Mongols led to the division of Georgia
into several states. These struggled against the Turkish
and the Persian Empires from the 16th to the 18th
centuries, gradually turning to the Russian Empire for
protection and support. Eastern Georgia signed a treaty of
alliance with Russia which recognized Russian supremacy
in 1783 and joined the Russian Empire in 1801, followed
soon after by Western Georgia.

In the late 19th century nationalist and Marxist movements competed for limited political influence under
autocratic Russian rule. One of the most prominent
Marxist activists was Iosif Dzhugashvili (Josef Stalin).
After the Russian revolution of 1917, a nationalist government came to power in Georgia supported by allied
intervention forces. In 1921 Soviet forces occupied Tbilisi,
and in 1922 Georgia joined the Soviet Union as part of the
Transcaucasian Soviet Socialist Republic.

In March 1990 the Georgian Supreme Soviet declared
illegal the treaties of 1921–2 by which Georgia had joined
the Soviet Union. The Communist Party's monopoly on
power was abolished and in multiparty elections held in
October and November 1990 the nationalist leader Zviad
Gamsakhurdia was elected president. Georgia declared its
independence from the Soviet Union in May 1991 and was
admitted to UN membership on 31 July 1992.

Gamsakhurdia's government faced armed opposition
from 1991 onwards. Defeat in the ensuing civil war in
Tbilisi led to Gamsakhurdia's overthrow in January 1992,
with a military council taking power until March 1992,
when a state council was appointed with the former Soviet
foreign minister Eduard Shevardnadze as chairman. Fighting continued throughout 1992 and 1993. In October 1992
Shevardnadze was elected head of state and Chairman of
the Parliament, and a loose alliance of pro-Shevardnadze
parties formed a government.

Gamsakhurdia returned to western Georgia in September 1993, a month after economic chaos had forced the
government to resign. President Shevardnadze assumed
full executive powers at the head of an emergency council,
but failed to prevent the advance of Gamsakhurdia's rebels
because most government forces were engaged in Abkhazia. Shevardnadze was forced to accept Russian
armaments and troops to defeat the rebellion and in return
agreed to join the CIS. Presidential and legislative
elections, held on 5 November 1995, were won by
President Shevardnadze and his Citizens' Union of Georgia party.

SECESSION

In late 1990 the South Ossetians took up arms against
Georgian rule in an attempt to join North Ossetia, itself
part of Russia. The South Ossetian provincial parliament
voted in November 1992 to secede from Georgia and join
Russia. The province's status remains unresolved since
June 1992 when fighting stopped and a joint Russian-
Georgian-Ossetian peacekeeping force was dispatched.

Representatives of the South Ossetian and Georgian
governments met in April 1996 to agree security and
confidence-building measures. South Ossetia was renamed Tskhinvali under Georgia's 1995 constitution.
Presidential elections in South Ossetia were won by
Ludvig Chibirov, the chair of the Supreme Council, in
November 1996.

In July 1992 the Abkhazian republican parliament
declared Abkhazia independent. Fighting broke out between Georgian forces and Abkhazian separatists supported by Russian arms and irregulars; Georgian forces were
defeated and were forced to withdraw in September 1993.
Negotiations under Russian auspices led to an Abkhaz-
Georgian cease-fire and separation of forces agreement
being signed in May 1994 and the deployment of 2,500
Russian UN peacekeepers on the Abkhaz-Georgian border. In November 1994 the Abkhaz Supreme Soviet
declared Abkhazia's independence again and elected
Vladislav Ardzinba as president. Abkhazia was given
autonomous republic status under the 1995 constitution;
this was rejected by the republican parliament. Elections to
the self-declared Abkhaz People's Assembly were held in
November 1996.

FOREIGN RELATIONS

In 1994 Georgia signed a ten-year Treaty of Friendship
and Co-operation with Russia which gained a decisive say
in Georgian economic policy and maintains four major
military bases in the country. The Georgian parliament
ratified CIS membership on 1 March 1994.

POLITICAL SYSTEM

A new constitution was promulgated in 1995 which provided for a federal republic with a unicameral legislature; and a popularly elected president who serves a maximum of two five-year terms.

HEAD OF STATE

President, Eduard Shevardnadze, *elected* 11 October 1992, *re-elected* 5 November 1995

CABINET *as at May 1997*

Prime Minister, Zurab Zhvaniani
Agriculture, Bakur Gulua
Communications and Post, Fridon Injia
Culture, Valeri Asatiani
Defence, Vardiko Nadibaidze
Economy, Vladimer Papava
Education, Tamaz Kvachantiradze
Environment, Nino Chkobadze
Finance, Mikhail Chkuaseli
Foreign Affairs, Irakliu Menagarishvili
Health, Avtandil Jobenadze
Industry, Tamaz Agladze
Interior, Kakha Targamadze
Minister of State, Nicoloz Lekishvili
Refugees, Valeri Vashakidze
Social Security, Tnegiz Gazdeliani
State Property Management, Avtandil Silagadze
State Security, Shota Kviraia
Trade and Foreign Economic Relations, Konstantine Zaldastanishvili
Urbanization and Building, Merab Chkhenkeli

EMBASSY OF THE REPUBLIC OF GEORGIA
3 Hornton Place, London, w8 4lz
Tel 0171–937 8233
Ambassador Extraordinary and Plenipotentiary, HE Teimuraz Mamatsashvili, apptd 1995

BRITISH EMBASSY
Metechi Palace Hotel, 380003 Tbilisi
Tel: Tbilisi 955497
Ambassador Extraordinary and Plenipotentiary, HE Stephen Nash, apptd 1995

ECONOMY

The economy was brought to the brink of collapse by civil and secessionist wars and the ending of former Soviet trading relationships. Industrial production fell by 70 per cent between 1991 and 1995. Although Georgia has deposits of coal, they have not been exploited and it is desperately short of energy supplies. A large proportion of production is stolen by black marketeers, whilst the tourist industry on the Black Sea coast has been destroyed by the fighting. The only productive sector of the economy is agriculture, with a concentration on viniculture, tea and tobacco-growing and citrus fruits.

Economic performance improved in 1995 with inflation dropping from 7,500 per cent in 1994 to 2 per cent per month in 1995. Reforms included the introduction of a new currency in October 1995, and new legislation permitting the private ownership of arable land and stricter bank regulation. GDP has experienced negative growth since the late 1980s.

GNP – US$2,358 million (1995); US$440 per capita (1995)
GDP – US$13,465 million (1992); US$144 per capita (1992)

TOTAL EXTERNAL DEBT – US$1,189 million (1995)

TRADE WITH UK	1995	1996
Imports from UK	£2,842,000	£3,784,000
Exports to UK	1,185,000	579,000

GERMANY
Bundesrepublik Deutschland – Federal Republic of Germany

AREA – 137,735 sq. miles (356,733 sq. km)
POPULATION – 81,410,000 (1994 UN estimate). The estimated population (March 1993) is 81,075,000, of whom 65,400,000 live in the former West and 15,700,000 in the former East Germany. In 1994 there were 28,197,000 Protestants, 27,909,797 Roman Catholics, 2,700,000 Muslims and 53,797 Jews

Land	Population (1995)	Minister-President (July 1997)
Baden-Württemberg	10.3m	Erwin Teufel (CDU)
Bavaria	11.9m	Dr Edmund Stoiber (CSU)
Berlin	3.5m	Eberhard Diepgen (CDU)*
Brandenburg	2.5m	Dr Manfred Stolpe (SPD)
Bremen	0.7m	Dr Henning Scherf
Hamburg	1.7m	Dr Henning Voscherau (SPD)*
Hesse	6.0m	Hans Eichel (SPD)
Lower Saxony	7.7m	Gerhard Schröder (SPD)
Mecklenburg-Western Pomerania	1.8m	Dr Berndt Seite (CDU)
North Rhine-Westphalia	17.8m	Dr Johannes Rau (SPD)
Rhineland-Palatinate	4.0m	Kurt Beck (SPD)
Saarland	1.1m	Oskar Lafontaine (SPD)
Saxony	4.8m	Prof. Kurt Biedenkopf (CDU)
Saxony-Anhalt	2.8m	Dr Reinhard Höppner (SPD)
Schleswig-Holstein	2.7m	Heide Simonis (SPD)
Thuringia	2.5m	Dr Bernhard Vogel (CDU)

*Berlin, *Govening Mayor*; Bremen, *Mayor*; Hamburg, *First Mayor*.

CDU Christian Democratic Union; CSU Christian Social Union; SPD Social Democratic Party

CAPITAL – Berlin (population, 3,472,009, 1996). The seat of government and parliament is to be transferred from Bonn to Berlin by 2000
MAJOR CITIES – Hamburg (1,705,872); Munich (1,244,676); Cologne (963,817); Frankfurt am Main (652,412); Essen (617,955); Dortmund (600,918); Stuttgart (588,482); Düsseldorf (572,638); Bremen (549,182); Duisburg (536,106); Hannover (524,823); Leipzig (481,121); Nuremberg (495,845); Dresden (474,443), 1996
CURRENCY – Deutsche Mark (DM) of 100 Pfennig
NATIONAL ANTHEM – Einigkeit und Recht und Freiheit (Unity and right and freedom)
NATIONAL DAY – 3 October (Anniversary of 1990 Unification)
NATIONAL FLAG – Horizontal bars of black, red and gold
LIFE EXPECTANCY (years) – male 71.81; female 78.37 (West Germany, 1985–7)
POPULATION GROWTH RATE – 0.6 per cent (1994)
POPULATION DENSITY – 228 per sq. km (1994)
URBAN POPULATION – 76.3 per cent (1990)

HISTORY AND POLITICS

The term 'deutsch' (German) was probably first used in the eighth century and described the language spoken in the

The Federal Republic of Germany (FRG) was created out of the three western zones in 1949. A Communist government was established in the Soviet zone (henceforth the German Democratic Republic (GDR)). In 1961 the Soviet zone of Berlin was sealed off, and the Berlin Wall was built along the zonal boundary, partitioning the western sectors of the city from the eastern.

Soviet-initiated reform in eastern Europe during the late 1980s led to unrest in the GDR. The mass exodus of its citizens to the west via Hungary and Czechoslovakia culminated in the opening of the Berlin Wall in November 1989 and the collapse of Communist government. The 'Treaty on the Final Settlement with Respect to Germany', concluded between the FRG, GDR and the four former occupying powers in September 1990, unified Germany with effect from 3 October 1990 as a fully sovereign state. Economic and monetary union preceded formal union on 1 July 1990. Unification is constitutionally the accession of Berlin and the five reformed *Länder* of the GDR to the FRG, which remains in being. The first government of the new Germany took office in January 1991 following all-German elections on 2 December 1990.

The distribution of seats following the last election for the Bundestag on 16 October 1994 was: Christian Democratic Union, 244; Social Democrats, 252; Free Democrats, 47; Christian Social Union, 50; Democratic Socialists, 30; The Greens, 49.

POLITICAL SYSTEM

The Basic Law provides for a president, elected by a Federal Convention (electoral college) for a five-year term, a lower house (*Bundestag*) of 672 members elected by direct universal suffrage for a four-year term of office, and an upper house (*Bundesrat*) composed of 79 members appointed by the governments of the *Länder* in proportion to *Lander* populations, without a fixed term of office.

Germany is a federal republic composed of 16 states (*Länder*) (ten from the former West, five from the former East and Berlin). Each *Land* has its own directly elected legislature and government led by Minister Presidents (prime ministers) or equivalents. The 1949 Basic Law vests executive power in the *Länder* governments except in those areas reserved for the federal government.

Judicial authority is exercised by the Federal Constitutional Court, the federal courts provided for in the Basic Law and the courts of the Länder.

HEAD OF STATE

Federal President, Professor Roman Herzog, *born* 1934, *elected* 23 May 1994, *sworn in* 1 July 1994

CABINET *as at July 1997*

Federal Chancellor, Dr Helmut Kohl (CDU)
Deputy Chancellor, Foreign Affairs, Dr Klaus Kinkel (FDP)
Agriculture, Jochen Borchert (CDU)
Defence, Volker Rühe (CDU)
Economic Co-operation and Development, Carl-Dieter Spranger (CSU)
Economy, Dr Günter Rexrodt (FDP)
Education, Research and Technology, Dr Jürgen Rüttgers (CDU)
Environment, Dr Angela Merkel (CDU)
Family and Elderly, Women and Youth, Claudia Nolte (CDU)
Federal Chancellery, Friedrich Bohl (CDU)
Finance, Dr Theodor Waigel (CSU)
Health, Horst Seehofer (CSU)
Interior, Manfred Kanther (CDU)
Justice, Prof. Edzard Schmidt-Jortzig (FDP)
Labour and Social Affairs, Dr Norbert Blüm (CDU)
Posts and Telecommunications, Dr Wolfgang Bötsch (CSU)

eastern part of the Frankish realm. The first German realm was the Holy Roman Empire, established in AD 962 when Otto I of Saxony was crowned Emperor. The Empire endured until 1806, but the achievement of a national state was prevented by fragmentation into small principalities and dukedoms.

The Empire was replaced by a loose association of sovereign states known as the German Confederation, which was dissolved in 1866 and replaced by the Prussian-dominated North German Federation. Prussia had translated its earlier economic predominance into political hegemony by the annexation of the duchies of Schleswig and Holstein from Denmark in 1864 and a decisive defeat of Austria in 1866 (the Seven Weeks' War). After the Franco-Prussian War of 1870–1, which resulted in the defeat of France and the cession of Alsace and part of Lorraine, the south German principalities united with the northern federation to form a second German Empire, the King of Prussia being proclaimed Emperor in 1871.

Defeat in the First World War led to the abdication of the Emperor, and the country became a republic. The Treaty of Versailles (1919) returned Alsace-Lorraine to France, and large areas in the east were lost to Poland. The world economic crisis of 1929 contributed to the collapse of the Weimar Republic and the subsequent rise to power of the National Socialist movement of Adolf Hitler, who became Chancellor in 1933.

After concluding a Treaty of Non-Aggression with the Soviet Union in August 1939, Germany invaded Poland (1 September 1939), precipitating the Second World War, which lasted until 1945. Hitler committed suicide on 30 April 1945. On 8 May 1945, Germany unconditionally surrendered.

THE POST-WAR PERIOD

Germany was divided into American, French, British and Soviet zones of occupation. Supreme authority was exercised by the respective Commanders-in-Chief, and jointly through the Control Council of the four Commanders, with Berlin under joint administration. The USSR withdrew from the Control Council in 1948 and the rift divided Germany *de facto* into east and west.

Regional Planning, Housing and Urban Development, Prof.
Klaus Töpfer (CDU)
Transport, Matthias Wissmann (CDU)
CDU Christian Democratic Union; CSU Christian Social
Union; FDP Free Democratic Party.

EMBASSY OF THE FEDERAL REPUBLIC OF GERMANY
23 Belgrave Square, London SW1X 8PZ
Tel 0171-824 1300
Ambassador Extraordinary and Plenipotentiary, new
appointment awaited
Minister, Peter von Butler
Minister-Counsellor, Paul von Maltzahn
Counsellors, F. Burbach (*Cultural Affairs*); R. Lüdeking
(*Economic Affairs*)
Defence Attaché, Brig.-Gen. Eckart Fischer

BRITISH EMBASSY
Friedrich-Ebert-Allée 77, 53113 Bonn
Tel: Bonn 91670
Ambassador Extraordinary and Plenipotentiary, HE HE Paul
Lever, CMG, apptd 1997
Deputy Head of Mission, Minister, R. F. Cooper, MVO
Defence Attaché, Brig. B. R. Isbell, MBE
Counsellor (Economic), Dr P. Collecott
Counsellor (Management and Consular), S. C. Johns

BRITISH EMBASSY OFFICE, BERLIN
Unter den Linden 32/34, 0-10117 Berlin
Tel: Berlin 201 840
Counsellor, Deputy Head of Mission, D. L. Corner
Minister, A. Ford, CMG
First Secretary (Commercial), S. R. Dannreutyer

BRITISH CONSULATES-GENERAL – Düsseldorf, Frankfurt,
Hamburg, Munich, Stuttgart
BRITISH CONSULATES – Bremen, Hannover, Kiel and
Nuremberg

BRITISH COUNCIL REPRESENTATIVE, K. Dobson, OBE,
Hahnenstrasse 6, 50667 Köln. Offices at Berlin, Leipzig,
Hamburg and Munich

BRITISH CHAMBER OF COMMERCE, Neumarkt 14,
D-5000 Köln 1. *Director*, Herr Heumann

DEFENCE

The Army has 2,988 main battle tanks, 6,378 armoured
personnel carriers and armoured infantry fighting vehicles, 2,228 artillery pieces, and 205 attack helicopters.
The Navy has 17 submarines, three destroyers, 11
frigates, 36 patrol and coastal vessels, 54 combat aircraft
and 17 armed helicopters. The Air Force has 489 combat
aircraft.
There remain 123,550 NATO personnel in Germany
(USA 75,450; UK 28,100; Belgium 2,000; France 15,000;
Netherlands 3,000).
During 1993 both the Constitutional Court and the
Bundestag agreed that German armed forces may operate
outside Germany and the NATO area in UN and other
peacekeeping operations for the first time since 1945. In
1994 the Constitutional Court ruled that German forces
could serve in armed peacemaking missions.
MILITARY EXPENDITURE – 2.0 per cent of GDP (1995)
MILITARY PERSONNEL – 358,400: Army 252,800, Navy
28,500, Air Force 77,100. Under the terms of the Treaty
of Unification, the German armed forces have been
limited to 370,000 active personnel since the end of 1994
CONSCRIPTION DURATION – Ten months

ECONOMY

Germany has a predominantly industrial economy. Principal industries are coal mining, iron and steel production,
machine construction, the electrical industry, the manufacture of steel and metal products, chemicals, automobile
production, electronics, textiles, and the processing of
foodstuffs.
In 1995, Germany produced 246,400,000 tonnes of coal
and 2,882,000 tonnes of crude petroleum.
After a mini-boom generated by new East German
demand in 1990 and 1991, Germany entered its most
severe recession since the war induced by the costs of
reunification. In 1993 a 'Solidarity Pact' was agreed by
federal and länder governments, opposition parties, and
employers and trade unions, to take effect from 1995. The
pact lays down the basis of future funding transfers to the
East based on a 7.5 per cent rise in income taxes, wage
restraint in the West, more private investment in the East,
and the distribution of the funding burden between the
federal and länder governments. The pact was supplemented in August 1993 by reductions in Western social
security payments for the 1994–6 period, and by a petrol
tax levy. The economy returned to export-led growth in
1994 with a GDP growth rate of 2.8 per cent but re-entered
recession in May 1996 when unemployment also surpassed four million (10.8 per cent), having averaged 9.4 cent in
1995. The government, under pressure to meet the criteria
for European monetary union in 1999, announced proposed spending cuts of 2.5 per cent for 1996, which met
strong disapproval from the unions.
GNP – US$2,252,343 million (1995); US$27,510 per
capita (1995)
GDP – US$1,732,088 million (1992); US$24,157 per capita
(1992)
ANNUAL AVERAGE GROWTH OF GDP – 1.9 per cent
(1995); expected to be 2.4 per cent in 1997
INFLATION RATE – 1.8 per cent (1995)
UNEMPLOYMENT – 12.9 per cent (1995); expected to be 10
per cent in 1997

Trade with UK	1995	1996
Imports from UK	£19,224,100,000	£19,753,800,000
Exports to UK	24,889,600,000	25,560,400,000

COMMUNICATIONS

In 1995 the state-owned railways measured 40,209 km of
which 17,054 km were electrified, and the privately owned
railways totalled approximately 2,807 km. Classified roads
measured 228,604 km in 1995, of which motorways were
11,143 km. Merchant shipping under the German flag in
1994, amounted to 5,696,088 tonnes gross. Inland waterways are 6,929 km long.

EDUCATION

School attendance is compulsory between the ages of six
and 18 and comprises nine years full-time education at
primary and main schools and three years of vocational
education on a part-time basis. The secondary school
leaving examination (*Abitur*) entitles the holder to a place
of study at a university or another institution of higher
education.
Children below the age of 18 who are not attending a
general secondary or a full-time vocational school have
compulsory day-release at a vocational school.
The largest universities are in Munich, Berlin, Hamburg, Bonn, Frankfurt and Cologne.
ENROLMENT (percentage of age group) – primary 97 per
cent; secondary 86 per cent; tertiary 35.6 per cent (1993)

CULTURE

Modern (or New High) German has developed from the time of the Reformation to the present day, with differences of dialect in Austria, Alsace, Luxembourg, Liechtenstein and the German-speaking cantons of Switzerland.

The literary language is usually regarded as having become fixed by Luther and Zwingli at the Reformation, since which time many great names occur in all branches, notably philosophy, from Leibnitz (1646–1716) to Kant (1724–1804), Fichte (1762–1814), Schelling (1775–1854) and Hegel (1770–1831); drama, from Goethe (1749–1832) and Schiller (1759–1805) to Gerhart Hauptmann (1862–1946); and poetry, Heine (1797–1856). Seven German authors have received the Nobel Prize for Literature: Theodor Mommsen (1902), R. Eucken (1908), P. Heyse (1909), Gerhart Hauptmann (1912), Thomas Mann (1929), N. Sachs (1966) and Heinrich Böll (1972).

GHANA
The Republic of Ghana

AREA – 92,098 sq. miles (238,533 sq. km). Neighbours: Burkina Faso (north), Côte d'Ivoire (west), Togo (east)

POPULATION – 17,434,227 (1997 estimate); most are Sudanese Negroes, although Hamitic strains are common in the north. The official language is English. The principal indigenous language group is Akan, of which Twi and Fanti are the most commonly used. Ga, Ewe and languages of the Mole-Dagbani group are common in certain regions. Most Ghanaians are Christians, although there is a substantial Muslim minority in the north

CAPITAL – ΨAccra (population, 738,498, 1970), Greater Accra Region (including Tema) 1,781,100 (1990 estimate)

MAJOR CITIES – Kumasi; Tamale; ΨSekondi-Takoradi; ΨCape Coast; Sunyani; Ho; Koforidua; Wa; ΨWinneba

CURRENCY – Cedi of 100 pesewas

NATIONAL FLAG – Equal horizontal bands of red over gold over green; five-point black star on gold stripe

NATIONAL ANTHEM – God Bless our Homeland Ghana

NATIONAL DAY – 6 March (Independence Day)

LIFE EXPECTANCY (years) – male 54.22; female 57.84

POPULATION GROWTH RATE – 3.0 per cent (1994)

POPULATION DENSITY – 71 per sq. km (1994)

MILITARY EXPENDITURE – 1.2 per cent of GDP (1995)

MILITARY PERSONNEL – 7,500: Army 5,000, Navy 1,000, Air Force 1,000, Paramilitaries 500

ILLITERACY RATE – 35.5 per cent

ENROLMENT (percentage of age group) – tertiary 1.4 per cent (1990)

HISTORY AND POLITICS

First reached by Europeans in the 15th century, the constituent parts of Ghana came under British administration at various times, the original Gold Coast Colony being constituted in 1874; Ashanti in 1901; and the Northern Territories Protectorate in 1901. The territory of Trans-Volta-Togoland, part of the former German colony of Togo, was mandated to Britain by the League of Nations after the First World War, and remained under British administration as a United Nations Trusteeship after the Second World War. After a plebiscite in 1956, under UN auspices, the territory was integrated with the Gold Coast Colony. The former Gold Coast Colony and associated territories became the independent state of Ghana on 6 March 1957 and became a republic in 1960.

Since 1966 Ghana has experienced long periods of military rule (1966–9, 1972–9, 1982–92) interspersed with short-lived civilian governments. A coup in 1979 led to the formation of an Armed Forces Revolutionary Council chaired by Flt. Lt. Jerry Rawlings. Civilian rule was restored in 1979 but overthrown on 31 December 1981, when another coup brought Flt. Lt. Rawlings back to power.

A referendum in April 1992 approved a new multiparty constitution and the legalization of political parties. The National Democratic Congress (NDC) was established as a political party from the ruling Provisional National Defence Council. Flt. Lt. Rawlings won the presidential election in November 1992 and the NDC won parliamentary elections in December 1992, which were boycotted by most opposition parties and most of the electorate. The Fourth Republic was declared on 7 January 1993 and a new government nominated by the president and approved by parliament took office in March 1993. As executive president, Flt. Lt. (retd) Rawlings also chairs the Cabinet. The presidential term is four years, renewable only once. In the December 1996 legislative elections the NDC retained its absolute majority; President Rawlings was also re-elected.

For political and administrative purposes Ghana is divided into ten regions, each headed by a Regional Minister who is the representative of the central government.

HEAD OF STATE
President, Flt. Lt. (retd) Jerry John Rawlings, *took power* 31 December 1981, *elected* 3 November 1992, *re-elected* 7 December 1996
Vice-President, Prof. John Evans Atta Mills

CABINET as at July 1997
Communications, Ekow Spio-Garbrah
Defence, Alhaji Mahama Iddrisu
Education, Dr Christine Amoako-Nuamah
Employment and Social Welfare, Alhaji Mohammed Mumuni
Environment, Science and Technology, J. E. Afful
Finance, Kwame Peprah
Food and Agriculture, Dr Kwabena Adjei
Foreign Affairs (acting), Kwamena Ahwoi
Health, Dr Eunice Brookman-Amissah
Interior, Nii Okaidja Adamafio
Justice and Attorney-General, Dr Obed Asamoah
Lands and Forestry, Cletus Avoka
Local Government, Kwamena Ahwoi
Mines and Energy, Fred Ohene-Kena
Parliamentary Affairs, J. H. Owusu-Acheampong
Roads and Transport, Edward Salia
Tourism, Vida Yeboah
Trade and Industry, Dr John Abu
Minister of State, Kofi Totobi-Quakyi
Works and Housing, Isaac Adjei-Mensah
Youth and Sports, E. T. Mensah

GHANA HIGH COMMISSION
104 Highgate Hill, London N6 5HE
Tel 0181-342 8686
High Commissioner, new appointment awaited
Acting High Commissioner, Patrick Hayford
Defence Adviser, Capt. Nii Coleman
Counsellor, A. K. Budu-Amoako (*Trade*)

BRITISH HIGH COMMISSION
PO Box 296, Osu Link, Accra
Tel: Accra 221665
High Commissioner, HE Ian Mackley, CMG, apptd 1996
Deputy High Commissioner, I. C. Orr
Defence Adviser, Lt.-Col. A. R. Gale, MBE
First Secretary (Commercial), W. F. Somerset

BRITISH COUNCIL DIRECTOR, C. Stevenson, Liberia Road
(PO Box 771), Accra. There is also an office in Kumasi.

ECONOMY

Agriculture is the basis of the economy, employing 70 per
cent of the work-force. Crops include cocoa, the largest
single source of revenue, rice, cassava, avocado pears,
oranges and pineapples, groundnuts, corn, millet, oil
palms, yams, maize and vegetables. Livestock is raised in
uncultivated areas. Attempts are being made to diversify
agricultural production, with cash crops such as coffee and
tobacco being cultivated for export. Fishing is important in
coastal areas and in the Volta lake and river system.

Manganese production ranks among the world's largest,
with 186,902 tonnes of ore being produced in 1995;
diamonds and bauxite are also produced. The Ashanti
Goldfields Corporation is one of the world's largest
producers and was privatized in 1994 with estimated gold
reserves of 20.3 million ounces. Some 30,000 persons are
employed by the mining companies.

Small-scale traditional industries include tailoring,
goldsmithing and carpentry. Priority has been given in
recent years to establishing a number of manufacturing
industries and a modern industrial complex has developed
in the Accra-Tema area. Tourism is also important.

Since 1966 the Volta Dams at Akosombo and Kpong
have generated hydroelectric power for the processing of
bauxite and fed a power transmission network for most of
Ghana, Togo and Benin.

Under the Economic Recovery Programme (ERP) in
place since 1983, the economy has achieved a growth rate
of 6 per cent a year for the past decade and paid off a large
proportion of its foreign debt; debt servicing had fallen to
23 per cent of export earnings in 1993.

GNP – US$6,719 million (1995); US$390 per capita (1995)
GDP – US$6,792 million (1992); US$398 per capita (1992)
ANNUAL AVERAGE GROWTH OF GDP – 5.0 per cent (1993)
INFLATION RATE – 59.5 per cent (1995)
TOTAL EXTERNAL DEBT – US$5,874 million (1995)

TRADE

Principal exports are cocoa, timber, minerals and gold.
Principal imports are road vehicles, manufacturing equipment, petroleum and raw materials.

Trade with UK	1995	1996
Imports from UK	£240,081,000	£299,791,000
Exports to UK	163,812,000	190,386,000

COMMUNICATIONS

The Kotoka Airport at Accra is an international airport and
Ghana Airways is the national airline. There are also
internal airports at Takoradi, Kumasi, Sunyani, and
Tamale.

There are 20,000 miles of motorable roads, of which
2,335 miles are bitumenized. There are 600 miles of
railway, linking Accra and the principal ports of Takoradi
and Tema with their hinterlands, the mining centres and
with each other.

Takoradi Harbour consists of seven quay berths: one is
leased specially for manganese exports. Tema Harbour has
ten berths for larger ocean-going vessels and the largest dry

dock on the West African coast. An oil berth has also been
built to serve the refinery at Tema.

GREECE
Elliniki Dimokratia

AREA – 50,961 sq. miles (131,990 sq. km). Neighbours:
Albania, the Former Yugoslav Republic of Macedonia
and Bulgaria (north), Turkey (east)
POPULATION – 10,426,000 (1994 UN estimate), 10,256,464
(1991 census); over 97 per cent are adherents of the
Greek Orthodox Church, which is the state religion
CAPITAL – Athens (population 3,027,331, 1981); including
ΨPiraeus and suburbs, 3,096,775 (1991 census)
MAJOR CITIES – ΨThessaloniki (Salonika) (739,998);
ΨPatras (172,763); ΨHeraklion (Crete) (127,600);
ΨVolos (115,732); Larissa (113,426); ΨCanea (Crete)
(65,519); ΨKavalla (58,576); ΨRhodes (43,619)
CURRENCY – Drachma of 100 leptae
NATIONAL ANTHEM – Imnos Eis Tin Eleftherian (Hymn
to Freedom)
NATIONAL DAY – March 25 (Independence Day)
NATIONAL FLAG – Blue and white stripes with a white
cross on a blue field in the canton
LIFE EXPECTANCY (years) – male 74.61; female 79.96
POPULATION GROWTH RATE – 0.6 per cent (1994)
POPULATION DENSITY – 79 per sq. km (1994)
URBAN POPULATION – 58.9 per cent (1991)

The main areas are: Macedonia (which includes Mt Athos
and the island of Thasos), Thrace (including the island of
Samothrace), Epirus, Thessaly, Continental Greece
(which includes the island of Euboea and the Sporades),
Crete and the Peloponnese. The main island groups are the
Sporades (of which the largest is Skyros), the Dodecanese
or Southern Sporades (Rhodes, Astypalaia, Karpathos,
Kassos, Nisyros, Kalymnos, Leros, Patmos, Kos, Symi,
Khalki, Tilos), the Cyclades (about 200, including Syros,
Andros, Tinos, Mykonos, Naxos, Paros, Santorini, Milos
and Serifos), the Ionian Islands (Corfu, Paxos, Levkas,
Ithaca, Cephalonia, Zante and Cerigo), the Aegean Islands
(Chios, Lesbos, Limnos and Samos). In Crete from about
3000 to 1400 BC a civilization flourished which spread its
influence throughout the Aegean, and the ruins of the
palace of Minos at Knossos afford evidence of astonishing
comfort and luxury.

HISTORY AND POLITICS

Greece was under Turkish rule from the mid-15th century
until a war of independence (1821–7) led to the establishment of a Greek kingdom in the Peloponnese in 1829. The
remainder of Greece gradually became independent until
the Dodecanese were returned by Italy in 1947. After
heavy resistance to the Nazi German occupation of
1941–4, a civil war between monarchist and Communist
groups lasted from 1946 to 1949, and tension between
right-wing and radical groups continued after 1949. In
1967 right-wing elements in the army seized power and
established a military regime (the 'Greek Colonels'). The
King went into voluntary exile in 1967; in 1974 the
monarchy was abolished and a republic established.

Unrest in Athens in 1973–4 intensified after the
government was involved in the overthrow of President
Makarios of Cyprus in July 1974, and led the Colonels to
surrender power. Konstantinos Karamanlis (prime minister 1955–63) returned from exile to form a provisional
government, and the first elections for ten years were held

in 1974. The restoration of the monarchy was rejected by referendum on 8 December 1974 and Greece became a republic.

The most recent general election was held on 22 September 1996 with the Panhellenic Socialist Party (PASOK) winning 162 seats, the New Democracy Party (Christian Democrats) 108 seats, the Communist Party 11 seats, the Coalition of the Left and Progress ten seats, and the Democratic Social Movement nine seats.

POLITICAL SYSTEM

In 1986 most executive power was transferred from the president to the government and the president became a ceremonial figure. The unicameral 300-member Chamber of Deputies (*Vouli*) is elected for a four-year term by universal adult suffrage under a system of proportional representation, with a three per cent threshold for parliamentary representation.

HEAD OF STATE

President of the Hellenic Republic, Constantine
  Stephanopoulos, *elected by parliament* 8 March 1995

CABINET *as at July 1997*

Prime Minister, Costas Simitis
Aegean, Elisabeth Papazoi
Agriculture, Stephanos Tzoumakas
Culture, Evangelos Venizelos
Development, Vasso Papandreou
Education and Religious Affairs, Gerasimos Arsenis
Environment, Town Planning and Public Works, Costas
  Laliotis
Foreign Affairs, Theodoros Pangalos
Health and Welfare, Costas Geitonas
Interior, Public Administration and Decentralization, Alekos
  Papadopoulos
Justice, Evangelos Yiannopoulos
Labour and Social Security, Miltiades Papaioannou
Macedonia and Thrace, Phillipos Petsalnikos
Merchant Marine, Stavros Soumakis
National Defence, Akis Tsohatzopoulos
National Economy and Finance, Yiannos Papantoniou
Press and Media, Dimitris Reppas
Public Order, George Romeos
Transport and Communications, Haris Kastanidis

EMBASSY OF GREECE
1A Holland Park, London W11 3TP
Tel 0171-229 3850
Ambassador Extraordinary and Plenipotentiary, HE Vassilis
  Zafiropoulos, apptd 1996
Defence Attaché, Capt. N. Kostakis
Minister (Consular Affairs), G. Costoulas
Counsellor, A. Missa-Kerkentzes (*Economic Affairs*)

HONORARY CONSULATES – Belfast, Birmingham,
  Edinburgh, Falmouth, Glasgow, Leeds and
  Southampton

BRITISH EMBASSY
1 Ploutarchou Street, 10675 Athens
Tel: Athens 723 6211
Ambassador Extraordinary and Plenipotentiary, HE Sir
  Michael Llewellyn Smith, KCVO, CMG, apptd 1996
Deputy Head of Mission, Counsellor and Consul-General, P. J.
  Millet
Defence and Military Attaché, Brig. W. A. McMahon
First Secretary (Commercial), G. G. Thomas

BRITISH CONSULAR OFFICES – Athens, Corfu, Patras, Kos,
  Rhodes, Salonika, Heraklion (Crete) and Syros

BRITISH COUNCIL DIRECTOR, P. Chenery, 17 Plateia
  Philikis Etairias (PO Box 3488), Kolonaki Square,
  Athens 10210. There is also an office at Salonika.

BRITISH-HELLENIC CHAMBER OF COMMERCE, 25 Vas.
  Sofias Avenue, GR-106 74 Athens. Tel: 72 10 361

DEFENCE

The Army has 1,735 main battle tanks, 844 armoured personnel carriers and armoured infantry fighting vehicles, and 1,878 artillery pieces. The Navy has eight submarines, four destroyers, ten frigates, 42 patrol and coastal vessels and 15 armed helicopters. The Air Force has a total of 388 combat aircraft.

Greece maintains 2,250 army personnel in Cyprus. There are 437 US military personnel stationed in Greece.

MILITARY EXPENDITURE – 4.6 per cent of GDP (1995)
MILITARY PERSONNEL – 168,300: Army 122,000, Navy
  19,500, Air Force 26,800
CONSCRIPTION DURATION – Up to 21 months

ECONOMY

The principal minerals are nickel, bauxite, iron ore, iron pyrites, manganese magnesite, chrome, lead, zinc and emery, and prospecting for petroleum is being carried on. The chief industries are textiles (cotton, woollen and synthetics), chemicals, cement, glass, metallurgy, shipbuilding, domestic electrical equipment and footwear, the production of aluminium, nickel, iron and steel products, tyres, chemicals, fertilizers and sugar (from locally-grown beet). Food processing and ancillary industries are also growing.

The development of the country's electric power resources, irrigation and land reclamation schemes, and the exploitation of lignite resources for fuel and industrial purposes are also being carried out. Tourism has developed rapidly, with over 10 million visitors in 1994.

Though there has been a substantial measure of industrialization, agriculture still employs about a fifth of the working population and contributes 12 per cent of GDP. The most important agricultural products are tobacco, wheat, cotton, sugar, rice, fruit (olives, peaches, vines, oranges, lemons, figs, almonds and currant-vines). Exports of fresh fruit, currants and vegetables are an important contributor to the economy.

The 1989–93 New Democracy government followed an IMF austerity programme of privatization and reduction of the public sector. This has been partially reversed by the PASOK government, which has slowed privatization.

Further austerity measures imposed in an attempt to meet the EU's economic and monetary union criteria have prompted strikes.

GNP – US$85,885 million (1995); US$8,210 per capita (1995)
GDP – US$68,522 million (1992); US$7,686 per capita (1992)
ANNUAL AVERAGE GROWTH OF GDP – 2.0 per cent (1995)
INFLATION RATE – 9.3 per cent (1995)
UNEMPLOYMENT – 10.0 per cent (1995)

Trade with UK	1995	1996
Imports from UK	£990,200,000	£1,090,400,000
Exports to UK	403,900,000	368,800,000

COMMUNICATIONS

The 2,650 km of railways are state-owned, with the exception of the Athens–Piraeus Electric Railway. Roads total over 35,500 km, of which about 25 per cent are national highways and just under 30,000 km are provincial roads. The Greek mercantile fleet numbers 1,864 ships over 100 tons gross with a total tonnage of 53,778,128 tons gross. Athens has direct airline links with Australasia, North America, most countries in Europe, Africa and the Middle East.

EDUCATION

Education is free and compulsory from the age of six to 15 and is maintained by state grants. There are ten universities: Athens, Thessaloniki, Patras, Thrace, Ioannina, Piraeus, Aegean, Ionian, Thessaly and Crete. There are several other institutes of higher learning, mostly in Athens.
ILLITERACY RATE – 3.3 per cent
ENROLMENT (percentage of age group) – primary 91 per cent; secondary 86 cent; tertiary 42.5 per cent (1993)

CULTURE

Greek civilization emerged c.1300 BC and the poems of Homer, which were probably current c.800 BC, record the struggle between the Achaeans of Greece and the Phrygians of Troy (1194 to 1184 BC).

The spoken language of modern Greece is descended from the Common Greek of Alexander the Great's empire. *Katharevousa*, a conservative literary dialect evolved by Adamantios Corais (Diamant Coray) (1748–1833) and used for official and technical matters, has been phased out. Novels and poetry are mostly in *dimotiki*, a progressive literary dialect which owes much to John Psicharis (1854–1929). The poets Solomos, Palamas, Cavafy and Sikelianos have won a European reputation. George Seferis (1963) and Odysseus Elytis (1979) have won the Nobel Prize for Literature.

GRENADA
The State of Grenada

AREA – 133 sq. miles (344 sq. km)
POPULATION – 92,000 (1994 UN estimate), 95,000 (1992 census)
CAPITAL – ΨSt George's (population, 4,788, 1981)

CURRENCY – East Caribbean dollar (EC$) of 100 cents
NATIONAL DAY – 7 February (Independence Day)
NATIONAL FLAG – Divided diagonally into yellow and green triangles within a red border containing six yellow stars, a yellow star on a red disc in the centre and a nutmeg on the green triangle in the hoist
POPULATION GROWTH RATE – 0.3 per cent (1994)
POPULATION DENSITY – 267 per sq. km (1994)

The island is about 21 miles long and 12 miles wide. Also a part of Grenada are some of the Grenadines islets, the largest of which is Carriacou, 13 square miles in area.

HISTORY AND POLITICS

Discovered by Columbus in 1498, and named Conception, Grenada was originally colonized by France and was ceded to Great Britain by the Treaty of Versailles 1783. It became an Associated State in 1967 and an independent nation within the Commonwealth on 7 February 1974.

The government was overthrown in 1979 by the New Jewel Movement and a People's Revolutionary Government was set up. In October 1983 disagreements within the PRG led to the death of Prime Minister Maurice Bishop, whose government was replaced by a Revolutionary Military Council. These events prompted the intervention of Caribbean and US forces. The Governor-General installed an advisory council to act as an interim government until a general election was held in December 1984. A phased withdrawal of US forces was completed by June 1985.

The general election held on 20 June 1995 was won by the New National Party led by Dr Keith Mitchell, with eight seats in the House of Representatives to the National Democratic Congress's five seats.

POLITICAL SYSTEM

Queen Elizabeth II is head of state and is represented by a Governor-General. Legislative power is vested in a bicameral parliament consisting of an elected 15-member House of Representatives and a nine-member Senate appointed by the Governor-General.

Justice is administered by the Organization of Eastern Caribbean States (OECS) Supreme Court, which is composed of a High Court of Justice and a two-tier Court of Appeals, and by Magistrates' Courts. The final court of appeal remains the UK Privy Council.

Governor-General, HE Sir Daniel Williams, GCMG ,QC, apptd 1996

CABINET *as at July 1997*

Prime Minister, Finance, Trade and Industry, External Affairs, National Security, Information, National Mobilization, Carriacou and Petit Martinique Affairs, Dr Keith Mitchell
Minister of State, Agriculture, Forestry, Lands and Fisheries, Michael Baptiste
Minister of State, Carriacou and Petit Martinique Affairs, Sen. Elvin Nimrod
Minister of State, Communications, Works and Public Utilities, Oliver Archibald
Minister of State, Finance, Sen. Patrick Bubb
Minister of State, Health and Environment, Sen. Dr. Roger Radix
Minister of State, Youth, Sports, Culture and Community Development, Willan Dewsbury
Agiculture, Lands, Forestry and Fisheries, Mark Isaac
Communications, Works and Public Utilities, Sen. Gregory Bowen
Education and Labour, Sen. Lawrence Joseph
Health and Environment, Grace Duncan

Housing, Social Security, Women's Affairs, Laurina Waldron
Legal Affairs, Local Government, Foreign Affairs, Dr Raphael
Fletcher
Tourism, Civil Aviation and Co-operatives, Sen. Joslyn
Whiteman
Youth, Sports, Culture and Community Development, Adrian
Mitchell

GRENADA HIGH COMMISSION
1 Collingham Gardens, London SW5 0HW
Tel 0171-373 7809
High Commissioner, HE Marcelle Gairy, apptd 1997

BRITISH HIGH COMMISSIONER, HE Richard Thomas,
CMG, resides at Bridgetown, Barbados

ECONOMY

The economy is principally agrarian, with cocoa, nutmegs
and bananas the major crops. Fruit and vegetables are
grown and a little livestock raised for domestic consumption. The fishing industry is being developed. Manufacturing consists of processing agricultural products and the
production of textiles, concrete, aluminium and handicrafts.

Tourism is the main foreign exchange earner. A hotel
expansion programme is taking place. The number of
cruise ship calls to Grenada in 1995 was 438, bringing
249,879 out of a total of 357,836 tourists.
GNP – US$271 million (1995); US$2,980 per capita (1995)
GDP – US$208 million (1992); US$2,380 per capita (1992)
ANNUAL AVERAGE GROWTH OF GDP – 0.6 per cent (1992)
INFLATION RATE – 3.0 per cent (1995)
TOTAL EXTERNAL DEBT – US$113 million (1995)

TRADE

In 1993 Grenada had a trade deficit of US$91 million and a
current account deficit of US$28 million.

Trade with UK	1995	1996
Imports from UK	£7,582,000	£7,503,000
Exports to UK	3,311,000	1,767,000

GUATEMALA
República de Guatemala

AREA – 42,042 sq. miles (108,889 sq. km)
POPULATION – 10,322,000 (1994 UN estimate). The
language is Spanish, but 40 per cent of the population
speak an Indian language
CAPITAL – Guatemala City (population, 1,675,589, 1990
estimate)
MAJOR CITIES – Quezaltenango (100,000); ΨPuerto
Barrios (23,000); Mazatenango (21,000); Antigua
(30,000)
CURRENCY – Quetzal (Q) of 100 centavos
NATIONAL ANTHEM – Guatemala Feliz (Guatemala be
praised)
NATIONAL DAY – 15 September
NATIONAL FLAG – Three vertical bands, blue, white, blue;
coat of arms on white stripe
LIFE EXPECTANCY (years) – male 55.11; female 59.43
POPULATION GROWTH RATE – 2.9 per cent (1994)
POPULATION DENSITY – 95 per sq. km (1994)
URBAN POPULATION – 38.5 per cent (1994)
MILITARY EXPENDITURE – 1.4 per cent of GDP (1995)
MILITARY PERSONNEL – 44,200: Army 42,000, Navy
1,500, Air Force 700
CONSCRIPTION DURATION – 30 months

ILLITERACY RATE – 44.4 per cent
ENROLMENT (percentage of age group) – primary 58 per
cent (1980); secondary 13 per cent (1980); tertiary 8.1 per
cent (1985)

Guatemala is traversed from west to east by mountains
containing volcanic summits rising to 13,000 feet above sea
level; earthquakes are frequent. There are numerous
rivers. The climate is hot and malarial near the coast,
temperate in the higher regions.

HISTORY AND POLITICS

Guatemala was under Spanish rule from 1524 until 1821
when it became independent. It formed part of the
Confederation of Central America from 1823 to 1839.

After military coups in 1963, 1982 and 1983, civilian rule
was restored with the election of a Constituent Assembly
in 1984 and the promulgation of a new constitution in 1985.

In May 1993 President Serrano partially suspended the
constitution and attempted to rule by decree but was
effectively ousted by the army on 1 June. Ramiro de León
Carpio was elected president by Congress to serve out
Serrano's term to January 1996.

President de León continued the attempt to curb
political corruption and in November 1993 forced Congress and the Supreme Court to dissolve themselves and to
agree to constitutional changes, including reducing the
presidential term to four years, which were ratified by a
referendum in January 1994. Legislative elections to a
smaller 80-seat National Congress were held in August
1994 and the new Congress elected 13 new Supreme Court
judges in October 1994. Elections to the National Congress on 12 November 1995 were won by the National
Advancement Party (PAN) which won 43 seats to the
Guatemalan Republican Front's 21. The presidential
election in January 1996 was won by Alvaro Arzú of the
PAN.

Executive power is vested in the directly elected
president, who appoints the Cabinet and is assisted by the
vice-president. Legislative authority is vested in the
National Congress.

The republic is divided into 22 departments.

INSURGENCY

Since 1960 the armed forces have been fighting insurgency
by the left-wing, mainly Mayan Indian, guerrillas of the
Guatemalan Revolutionary National Unity Movement
(URNG). Some 150,000 have been killed in the fighting.
Government-URNG negotiations began in 1991 and have
continued since, leading to a reduction in fighting and
agreements in 1993. In March 1994 a human rights accord
was reached under which a 300-strong UN Observer
Mission (MINUGUA) was established in November 1994
to supervise the implementation of government-URNG
accords. An accord recognizing the rights of the indigenous
population was signed in March 1995. Representatives of
the four rebel groups comprising the URNG signed a
peace treaty with the government in December 1996
under which they are to become a political party.

HEAD OF STATE
President, Alvaro Arzú Irigoyen, *sworn in* 14 January 1996
Vice-President, Luis Flores Asturias

GOVERNMENT *as at July 1997*
The President
The Vice-President
Agriculture, Mariano Ventura
Communications, Fritz García Gallont
Defence, Gen. Julio Balconi

Economy, Juan Mauricio Wurmser
Education, Roberto Moreno Godoy
Energy, Leonel López Rodas
Finance, José Alejandro Arevalo
Foreign Affairs, Eduardo Stein
Interior, Rodolfo Mendoza
Labour, Héctor Cifuentes Mendoza
Public Health and Social Security, Marco Tulio Sosa
Secretary-General of the Presidency, Carlos García

EMBASSY OF GUATEMALA
13 Fawcett Street, London SW10 9HN
Tel 0171-351 3042
Ambassador Extraordinary and Plenipotentiary, HE Fernando
    Andrade Díaz-Duran, apptd 1996

BRITISH EMBASSY
Edificio Centro Financiero (7th Floor), Seventh Avenue
5–10, Zone 4, Guatemala City
Tel: Guatemala City 3321601
Ambassador Extraordinary and Plenipotentiary, HE Peter
    Newton, apptd 1995
BRITISH CONSULATE – Puerto Barrios

ECONOMY

Agriculture provides 25 per cent of GDP. Roughly 95 per
cent of the rural population is landless and 2 per cent of the
population owns 65 per cent of the land. The principal
export is coffee, other articles being manufactured goods,
sugar, bananas, cotton, beef and essential oils. The chief
imports are petroleum, vehicles, machinery and foodstuffs.
    The chief seaports are San José de Guatemala and
Champerico on the Pacific and Santo Tomás de Castilla
and Puerto Barrios on the Atlantic side.
    In 1994 the government had a budget deficit equivalent
to 1.18 per cent of GDP. In 1993 there was a trade deficit of
US$1,021 million and a current account deficit of US$702
million. In 1994 imports totalled US$2,604 million and
exports US$1,522 million.
GNP – US$14,255 million; US$1,340 per capita (1995)
GDP – US$8,309 million (1992); US$1,071 per capita
    (1992)
ANNUAL AVERAGE GROWTH OF GDP – 4.0 per cent (1994)
INFLATION RATE – 10.9 per cent (1994)
TOTAL EXTERNAL DEBT – US$3,275 million (1995)

TRADE WITH UK	1995	1996
Imports from UK	£31,103,000	£27,878,000
Exports to UK	14,898,000	19,635,000

GUINEA
République de Guinée

AREA – 94,926 sq. miles (245,857 sq. km) Neighbours:
    Guinea-Bissau, Sierra Leone, Senegal, Mali, Côte
    d'Ivoire, Liberia
POPULATION – 6,501,000 (1994 UN estimate), mostly of
    the Fullah, Malinké and Soussou tribes
CAPITAL – ΨConakry (population, 763,000)
MAJOR CITIES – Kankan; Kindia; N'Zérékoré; Mamou;
    Siguiri; Labé
CURRENCY – Guinea franc of 100 centimes
NATIONAL DAY – 2 October (Anniversary of
    Proclamation of Independence)
NATIONAL FLAG – Three vertical stripes of red, yellow
    and green
LIFE EXPECTANCY (years) – male 44.00; female 45.00
POPULATION GROWTH RATE – 3.0 per cent (1994)

POPULATION DENSITY – 26 per sq. km (1994)
MILITARY EXPENDITURE – 1.4 per cent of GDP (1995)
MILITARY PERSONNEL – 19,300: Army 8,500, Navy 400,
    Air Force 800, Paramilitaries 9,600
CONSCRIPTION DURATION – Two years
ILLITERACY RATE – 64.1 per cent
ENROLMENT (percentage of age group) – primary 40 per
    cent (1993); secondary 9 per cent (1985); tertiary 1.1 per
    cent (1990)

HISTORY AND POLITICS

Guinea was separated from Senegal in 1891 and administered by France as a separate colony until 1958. On 2
October 1958 Guinea became an independent republic.
    M. Sékou Touré assumed office as head of the new
government, and was elected president in 1961. The death
of President Sékou Touré in 1984 was followed by a
military coup. Guinea was ruled by a military government
directed by a Military Committee for National Recovery
(CMRN). A new constitution, providing for the end of
military rule, was approved by referendum in 1990.
    In January 1991 the CMRN was dissolved and a mixed
civilian-military Transitional Committee for National
Recovery (CTRN) was established which appointed a
new government. Disturbances throughout 1991 led by
trade unions and opposition parties caused the government to introduce a full multiparty system in April 1992,
since when 40 opposition parties have been legalized. A
presidential election held in 1993 was won by the incumbent President Conté with 51 per cent of the vote amid
opposition claims of electoral fraud. Legislative elections
in June 1995 were won by President Conté's Party of Unity
and Progress (PUP), which gained 71 of the 114 National
Assembly seats.

HEAD OF STATE
President, Maj.-Gen. Lansana Conté, *took power* 3 April 1984,
    elected 19 December 1993

COUNCIL OF MINISTERS *as at May 1997*
Prime Minister, Economy, Finance and Planning, Sidya Touré
Agriculture, Water and Forests, Jean-Paul Sarr
Communications and Culture, Alpha Diallo
Economy and Finance, Ibrahima Kassory Fofana
Employment and Civil Service, Germain Doualamou
Fishing and Animal Husbandry, Boubacar Barry
Foreign Affairs, Lamine Kamara
Justice, Maurice Zogbélémou Togba
National Education and Scientific Research, Kozo Zoumanigui
Natural Resources and Energy, Facinet Fofana
Planning and Co-operation, Ousmane Kaba
Private Sector, Industry and Commerce, Madi Kaba Camara
Public Health, Kandjoura Drame
Public Works and Environment, Cellou Diallo
Secretary-General to the President, Almamy Fodé Sylla
Security, Moussa Sampil
Social Affairs, Promotion of Women and Children, Saran Daraba
Technical Education and Vocational Training, Almamy Diaby
Territorial Administration and Decentralization, Assifat
    Dorank Diasseny
Transport, Tourism and Hotels, Cellou Dalen Diallo
Urbanization and Housing, Alpha Ousmane Diallo
Youth, Sport and Civil Education, Koumba Diakite

EMBASSY OF THE REPUBLIC OF GUINEA
51 rue de la Faisanderie, 75061 Paris, France
Tel: Paris 4704 8148/4553 8545
Ambassador Extraordinary and Plenipotentiary, HE Ibrahima
    Sylla, apptd 1997

BRITISH CONSULATE
BP 834 Conakry, Guinea
British Ambassador, HE David Snoxell, resident at Dakar, Senegal

ECONOMY

The principal products are bauxite, alumina, iron ore, palm kernels, millet, rice, coffee, bananas, pineapples and rubber. Deposits of iron ore, gold, diamonds and uranium have been discovered. Principal imports are cotton goods, manufactured goods, tobacco, petroleum products, sugar, rice, flour and salt; exports, bauxite, alumina, iron ore, diamonds, coffee, hides, bananas, palm kernels and pineapples.

In 1993 Guinea had a trade deficit of US$22 million and a current account surplus of US$65 million.

GNP – US$3,593 million (1995); US$550 per capita (1995)
GDP – US$3,041 million (1992); US$490 per capita (1992)
TOTAL EXTERNAL DEBT – US$3,242 million (1995)

TRADE WITH UK	1995	1996
Imports from UK	£16,643,000	£19,911,000
Exports to UK	2,983,000	1,064,000

GUINEA-BISSAU
República da Guiné-Bissau

AREA – 13,948 sq. miles (36,125 sq. km). Neighbours: Senegal, Guinea
POPULATION – 1,050,000 (1994 UN estimate). The main ethnic groups are the Balante, Malinké, Fulani, Mandjako and Pepel
CAPITAL ΨBissau (population, 109,214, 1979)
CURRENCY – Franc CFA
NATIONAL DAY – 24 September (Independence Day)
NATIONAL FLAG – Horizontal bands of yellow over green with vertical red band in the hoist charged with a black star
LIFE EXPECTANCY (years) – male 41.92; female 45.12
POPULATION GROWTH RATE – 2.1 per cent (1994)
POPULATION DENSITY – 29 per sq. km (1994)
MILITARY EXPENDITURE – 3.0 per cent of GDP (1995)
MILITARY PERSONNEL – 9,250: Army 6,800, Navy 350, Air Force 100, Paramilitaries 2,000
CONSCRIPTION DURATION – Selective
ILLITERACY RATE – 45.1 per cent
ENROLMENT (percentage of age group) – primary 45 per cent (1987); secondary 3 per cent (1980); tertiary 0.5 per cent (1988)

HISTORY AND POLITICS

Guinea-Bissau, formerly Portuguese Guinea, achieved independence on 24 September 1974. Following a coup led by Maj. (now Brig.-Gen.) Vieira in 1980, the Assembly was suspended and a Revolutionary Council was established. Under a new constitution adopted in 1984, the Revolutionary Council became a 15-member Council of State and an Assembly of 150 members was set up. The ruling African Party for the Independence of Guinea and Cape Verde (PAIGC) voted to introduce a multiparty system in January 1991. Ten opposition parties have been legalized since November 1991. Legislative elections to a new 100-seat legislature were held on 3 July 1994 and won by the PAIGC, which took 64 seats. Brig.-Gen. Vieira won the second round of the presidential election on 7 August 1994 with 52 per cent of the votes

HEAD OF STATE
Chairman of the Republic, C.-in-C. of the Armed Forces, Brig.-Gen. João Bernardo Vieira, *took power* November 1980, *elected* June 1989, *re-elected for a five-year term* 7 August 1994

COUNCIL OF MINISTERS *as at June 1997*
Prime Minister, Carlos Correia
Culture, Youth and Sports, Ibrahima Sow
Defence, Samba Lamine Mane
Economy and Finance, Issuf Sanha
Energy, Carlos Pinho Brandao
Equipment, João Gomes Cardoso
Foreign Affairs and Co-operation, Fernando Delfim da Silva
Interior, Francisca Pereira
Justice and Labour, Daniel Ferreira
National Education, Odette Semedo
Presidency, Malal Sane
Public Health, Brandao Gomes Co
Public Works, Armando Antonio Napoko
Rural Development, Natural Resources and Environment, Avito José da Silva
Social Affairs and Women's Promotion, Nharebat Ninçaia N'Tchasso
Territorial Administration, Nicandro Pereira Barreto
Veterans' Affairs, Arafan Mane

EMBASSY OF THE REPUBLIC OF GUINEA-BISSAU
94 Rue St Lazare, Paris 9, France
Tel: Paris 4526 1851
Ambassador Extraordinary and Plenipotentiary, new appointment awaited

BRITISH CONSULATE
Mavegro Int., CP100, Bissau
British Ambassador, HE David Snoxell, resident at Dakar, Senegal

ECONOMY

Guinea-Bissau produces rice, coconuts, groundnuts and palm oil products. Cattle are raised, and there are bauxite deposits in the south. The government has started to introduce free market reforms.

In 1993 the trade deficit was US$38 million and the current account deficit was US$65 million. In 1995 imports totalled US$70 million and exports US$23 million.

GNP – US$265 million (1995); US$250 per capita (1995)
GDP – US$249 million (1992); US$133 per capita (1992)
ANNUAL AVERAGE GROWTH OF GDP – 3.0 per cent (1993)
INFLATION RATE – 45.4 per cent (1995)
TOTAL EXTERNAL DEBT – US$894 million (1995)

TRADE WITH UK	1995	1996
Imports from UK	£1,889,000	£1,695,000
Exports to UK	60,000	94,000

GUYANA
The Co-operative Republic of Guyana

AREA – 83,000 sq. miles (214,969 sq. km). Neighbours: Venezuela, Brazil and Suriname
POPULATION – 825,000 (1994 UN estimate): 51 per cent East Indian (mainly rural), 30 per cent African (mainly urban), Amerindians, Europeans, Chinese and people of mixed descent; 50 per cent Christian, 35 per cent Hindu; less than 10 per cent Muslim. Guyana is the only English-speaking country in South America
CAPITAL – ΨGeorgetown (population, 250,000)

MAJOR TOWNS – Linden (35,000); ΨNew Amsterdam (25,000); Corriverton (24,000)
CURRENCY – Guyana dollar (G$) of 100 cents
NATIONAL ANTHEM – Dear Land of Guyana
NATIONAL DAYS – 26 May (Independence Day); 23 February (Republic Day)
NATIONAL FLAG – Green with a yellow, white-bordered triangle based on the hoist and surmounted by a red, black-bordered triangle
LIFE EXPECTANCY (years) – male 62.44; female 68.02
POPULATION GROWTH RATE – 0.9 per cent (1994)
POPULATION DENSITY – 4 per sq. km (1994)
MILITARY EXPENDITURE – 1.1 per cent of GDP (1995)

HISTORY AND POLITICS

Guyana (formerly British Guiana) became independent on 26 May 1966, with a Governor-General appointed by Queen Elizabeth II. It became a republic on 23 February 1970.

Presidential and general elections were held on 5 October 1992 after proper voter registration lists and electoral machinery had finally been established after many years. In the presidential election Dr Cheddi Jagan defeated the incumbent Desmond Hoyte and in the legislative election Jagan's People's Progressive Party (PPP) defeated the People's National Congress (PNC) which had governed since independence. Jagan died in March 1997 and was replaced by former Prime Minister Samuel Hinds.

POLITICAL SYSTEM

The 1980 constitution provides for an executive president who serves a five-year term, a first vice-president and prime minister, and a National Assembly of 65 members, of which 53 are elected nationally by proportional representation and 12 are regional representatives.

The Supreme Court of Judicature consists of a Court of Appeal and a High Court. There are also Courts of Summary Jurisdiction. The Court of Appeal consists of the Chancellor as President, the Chief Justice and Justices of Appeal. The High Court consists of the Chief Justice, as President, and nine Puisne Judges. It is a court with unlimited jurisdiction in civil matters.

HEAD OF STATE
Executive President, Samuel Hinds, *sworn in* 6 March 1997

CABINET *as at July 1997*
The Executive President
First Vice-President, Prime Minister, Janet Jagan
Second Vice-President, Agriculture, Reepu Daman Persaud
Amerindian Affairs, Vilbert de Souza
Attorney-General, Legal Affairs, Bernard de Santos
Education and Cultural Development, Dale Bisnauth
Finance, Bharrat Jagdeo
Foreign Affairs, Clement Rohee
Health, Gail Teixeira
Home Affairs, Feroze Mohamed
Information, Moses Nagamootoo
Labour, Human Services and Social Security, Dr Henry Jeffrey
Office of the President, George Fung-on
Public Works, Communications and Regional Development, Anthony Xavier
Regional and Local Government, Clinton Collymore; Harripersaud Nokta
Trade, Tourism and Industry, Michael Shree Chan

GUYANA HIGH COMMISSION
3 Palace Court, Bayswater Road, London W2 4LP
Tel 0171-229 7684
High Commissioner, HE Laleshwar Singh, apptd 1993

BRITISH HIGH COMMISSION
44 Main Street (PO Box 10849), Georgetown
Tel: Georgetown 65881/4
High Commissioner, HE David J. Johnson, CMG, CVO, apptd 1993

ECONOMY

Agriculture is the prinicpal economic activity. The economy is based almost entirely on the main export items of Demerara sugar, rice, shrimps, gold, bauxite and alumina. Diamonds are also mined, timber and rum are produced. There is some cattle ranching in the savanna country, and oil deposits have been found there. The fishing industry is being expanded. Industry is fairly small-scale. Much emphasis is now being placed on eco-tourism. Foreign aid covers much of the government deficit.

The USA, Canada, the UK, Trinidad and Tobago, and Netherlands Antilles are Guyana's main trading partners.
GNP – US$493 million (1995); US$590 per capita (1995)
GDP – US$293 million (1992); US$296 per capita (1992)
ANNUAL AVERAGE GROWTH OF GDP – 8.2 per cent (1993)
INFLATION RATE – 2.6 per cent (1992)
TOTAL EXTERNAL DEBT – US$2,105 million (1995)

TRADE WITH UK	1995	1996
Imports from UK	£33,946,000	£33,984,000
Exports to UK	72,821,000	91,558,000

COMMUNICATIONS

Georgetown and New Amsterdam are the principal ports, though bauxite ships also sail to Linden, on the Demerara, and Everton, on the Berbice. There are no public railways and the few roads are confined mainly to the coastal areas. Paved roads total about 430 miles out of a total network of 1,459 miles. Air transport is the easiest form of communication between the coast and the interior. The state-owned national airline is called Guyana Airways.

There is a state-owned radio broadcasting station which operates two channels and a fledgling television service.

EDUCATION

Education is compulsory between the ages of five and 14; nursery, primary and secondary schooling are free. The government assumed total control of the education system in 1976 and made education free. The government instituted fees for study at the University of Guyana in 1994.

There are several technical and vocational institutions, as well as some 30 adult education schools. There are also a number of technical and vocational institutions not under the aegis of the Ministry of Education.
ILLITERACY RATE – 1.9 per cent
ENROLMENT (percentage of age group) – tertiary 9.3 per cent (1992)

HAITI
République d'Haïti

AREA – 10,714 sq. miles (27,750 sq. km)
POPULATION – 7,041,000 (1994 UN estimate) of which 90 per cent are black and 10 per cent mulatto (mixed race). Both French and Creole are regarded as official languages. French is the language of government and the press but it is only spoken by the educated mulatto minority. The usual language is Creole
CAPITAL – ΨPort-au-Prince (population, 690,168, 1990 estimate)
MAJOR CITIES – ΨCap Haitien (54,691); Gonaives (36,736); Les Cayes (27,222); Jérémie (25,117)
CURRENCY – Gourde of 100 centimes
NATIONAL ANTHEM – La Dessalinienne
NATIONAL DAY – 1 January
NATIONAL FLAG – Horizontally blue over red
LIFE EXPECTANCY (years) – male 54.95; female 58.34
POPULATION GROWTH RATE – 2.1 per cent (1994)
POPULATION DENSITY – 254 per sq. km (1994)
URBAN POPULATION – 32.0 per cent (1994)
MILITARY EXPENDITURE – 2.1 per cent of GDP (1995)
ILLITERACY RATE – 55.0 per cent
ENROLMENT (percentage of age group) – primary 26 per cent (1990); tertiary 1.1 per cent (1985)

The Republic of Haiti occupies the western third of the Caribbean island of Hispaniola. The climate is tropical with high humidity and an almost constant temperature.

HISTORY AND POLITICS

Haiti was a French slave colony under the name of Saint-Domingue from 1697 until 1791, when French rule was overthrown in a revolt led by Toussaint L'Ouverture, who made himself Governor-General. French rule was restored by Napoleon in 1802 but in 1803 French forces surrendered to a British naval blockade and on 1 January 1804 the colony was declared independent as Haiti by Jean Jacques Dessalines. Dessalines became Emperor of Haiti but was assassinated in 1806.

Haiti was under US military occupation from 1915 to 1934. Dr François 'Papa Doc' Duvalier was elected in 1957 and became life president in 1964. He was succeeded in 1971 by his son Jean-Claude 'Baby Doc' Duvalier who fled to France in 1986 in the face of sustained popular unrest. Five years of military government followed until Father Jean-Bertrand Aristide, leader of the National Front for Change and Democracy, won a free presidential election in 1990.

Aristide fled to the USA following a military coup in September 1991. The UN and OAS imposed an oil and arms embargo and froze the military élite's foreign assets, which forced the regime to negotiate the Governor's Island Agreement in July 1993. The Agreement provided for Aristide's return and led to the lifting of UN sanctions, but in September 1993 the military reneged on the agreement and the UN reimposed sanctions, and imposed a naval blockade and a total economic, trade and travel ban. In September 1994 a UN negotiating team reached an agreement with the regime on President Aristide's return and the flight of the military junta members abroad. The UN sanctions were lifted and Aristide returned on 15 October and appointed a new government. UN forces of the UNMIH (UN Mission in Haiti) took over responsibility for internal security and retraining Army personnel on 31 March 1995. The last US soldiers left in April 1996. Elections to the 27-member Senate and 83-member Chamber of Deputies in June to August 1995 were won by the pro-Aristide Lavalas party. The presidential election on 17 December 1995 was won by the Lavalas candidate René Préval.

HEAD OF STATE
President, René Préval, *sworn in* 7 February 1996

CABINET *as at July 1997*
Prime Minister, Rony Smarth
Agriculture, Gérald Mathurin
Commerce, Fresel Germain
Culture, Raoul Peck
Economy and Finance, Fred Joseph
Education, Jacques Edouard Alexis
Environment, Yves Andre Wainright
Foreign Affairs, Fritz Longchamp
Haitians Abroad, Paul Dejean
Interior, Jean-Joseph Moliere
Justice, Pierre Max Antoine
Planning, Jean-Erick Dérice
Public Health and Population, Rudolphe Malebranche
Secretaries of State, Astride Foucher Gardere (*Judicial Reform*); Adeline Chancy (*Literacy*); Robert Manuel (*Public Security*); Maryse Penette (*Tourism*); Evans Lescouflair (*Youth and Sport*)
Social Affairs, Pierre-Denis Amédée
Women's Affairs, Ginette Cherubin

BRITISH AMBASSADOR, HE A. R. Thomas, CMG, resident at Kingston, Jamaica

ECONOMY

Coffee accounts for about 32 per cent of total exports. Cocoa is the second largest export earner. Corn, sorghum and rice are also grown. Increased production of tropical fruits and vegetables is being encouraged.

Items such as leather goods, textiles, electronic components and sports equipment are manufactured, using imported raw materials, for re-export. Principal imports are raw materials for the export assembly sector, foodstuffs, machinery, vehicles, mineral oils and textiles.

Privatization of several large state enterprises and a programme of land redistribution have begun.

In 1993 Haiti had a trade deficit of US$185 million and a current account deficit of US$78 million. In 1995 imports totalled US$652 million and exports US$105 million.
GNP – US$1,777 million (1995); US$250 per capita (1995)
GDP – US$2,233 million (1992); US$235 per capita (1992)
ANNUAL AVERAGE GROWTH OF GDP – 3.8 per cent (1995)
INFLATION RATE – 25.5 per cent (1995)
TOTAL EXTERNAL DEBT – US$807 million (1995)

TRADE WITH UK	1995	1996
Imports from UK	£13,466,000	£9,732,000
Exports to UK	1,254,000	1,789,000

COMMUNICATIONS

The main roads are asphalted and secondary roads are fair. Air services are maintained between the capital and the principal provincial towns and to the USA and Caribbean and South American countries. The principal towns and villages are connected by telephone and/or telegraph. There are several commercial radio stations and two television stations at Port-au-Prince.

HOLY SEE, *see* VATICAN CITY STATE

HONDURAS
República de Honduras

AREA – 43,277 sq. miles (112,088 sq. km). Neighbours: Guatemala, Nicaragua, El Salvador
POPULATION – 5,770,000 (1994 UN estimate) of mixed Spanish and Indian blood. The Garifunas in the north are of West Indian origin. The language is Spanish, although English is the first language of many in the islands and on the north coast
CAPITAL – Tegucigalpa (population, 670,100, 1991 estimate)
MAJOR CITIES – San Pedro Sula (325,900); ΨLa Ceiba (77,100); ΨPuerto Cortes (32,500); Choluteca (63,200); ΨTela (24,000)
CURRENCY – Lempira of 100 centavos
NATIONAL ANTHEM – Tu Bandera Es Un Lampo De Cielo (Your flag is a heavenly light)
NATIONAL DAY – 15 September
NATIONAL FLAG – Three horizontal bands, blue, white, blue (with five blue stars on white band)
LIFE EXPECTANCY (years) – male 65.43; female 70.06
POPULATION GROWTH RATE – 3.1 per cent (1994)
POPULATION DENSITY – 51 per sq. km (1994)
URBAN POPULATION – 46.7 per cent (1994)
MILITARY EXPENDITURE – 1.3 per cent of GDP (1995)
MILITARY PERSONNEL – 24,300: Army 16,000, Navy 1,000, Air Force 1,800, Paramilitaries 5,500
CONSCRIPTION DURATION – Ended 1995

The country is mountainous, being traversed by the Cordilleras, with peaks rising to 1,500 and 2,400 metres above sea level. Rainfall is seasonal, May to October being wet and November to April dry.

HISTORY AND POLITICS

Discovered and settled by the Spanish in the 16th century, Honduras formed part of the Spanish American dominions until 1821 when independence was proclaimed. Under military government from 1972, Honduras returned to civilian rule in 1981 with an executive presidency, a 128-seat unicameral Congress, and a multiparty system based on the Liberal Party and the National Party. The last presidential and legislative elections were held on 28 November 1993 and won by the Liberal Party, which formed a new government in January 1994.

The country is divided into 18 departments.

HEAD OF STATE
President of the Republic, Carlos Roberto Reina, *elected* 28 November 1993, *sworn in* 27 January 1994
Vice-Presidents, Walter López Reyes; Juan de la Cruz Avelar; Guadalupe Jerezano

CABINET *as at January 1997*

Agriculture and Livestock, Ricardo Arias
Communications and Public Works, Luis Carlos Zelaya
Culture, Rodolfo Pastor Fasquelle
Defence, Col. José Luis Núñez Beneth
Economic Planning, Guillermo Molina Chocano
Economy, Fernando García
Education, Zenobia Rodas de León Gómez
Environment, Carlos Medina
Finance, Juan Ferrera
Foreign Affairs, Delmer Urbizo Panting
Health, Dr Enrique Samayoa
Interior and Justice, Efraín Moncada Silva
Labour and Social Security, Cecilio Zavala Méndez

Natural Resources, Jerónimo Sandoval
President of the Central Bank, Dr Hugo Noé Pino

EMBASSY OF HONDURAS
115 Gloucester Place, London WIH 3PJ
Tel 0171-486 4880
Ambassador Extraordinary and Plenipotentiary, new appointment awaited

BRITISH EMBASSY
Apartado Postal 290, Tegucigalpa
Tel: Honduras 320612/18
Ambassador Extraordinary and Plenipotentiary, HE P. R. Holmes, apptd 1995
BRITISH CONSULATE – San Pedro Sula

ECONOMY

Three-quarters of the country is covered by pine forests. Agriculture and cattle raising is mainly confined to the fertile coastal plain on the Caribbean and the extensive valleys in the Comayagua and Olancho regions of the interior. The Mosquitia tropical forest covers the area from the coast to the border with Nicaragua and provides valuable reserves of timber. Lead, zinc and silver are mined on a small scale.

The chief exports are coffee, bananas, frozen meat and timber, the most important woods being pine, mahogany and cedar. Other products are tobacco, beans, maize, rice, cotton, palm oil, sugar cane, cement, shrimps, lobsters and tropical fruits.

In 1993 Honduras had a trade deficit of US$91 million and a current account deficit of US$309 million. In 1995 imports totalled US$1,219 million and exports US$1,061 million.
GNP – US$3,566 million (1995); US$600 per capita (1995)
GDP – US$6,422 million (1992); US$536 per capita (1992)
ANNUAL AVERAGE GROWTH OF GDP – 3.6 per cent (1995)
INFLATION RATE – 29.5 per cent (1995)
UNEMPLOYMENT – 3.2 per cent (1995)
TOTAL EXTERNAL DEBT – US$4,567 million (1995)

TRADE WITH UK	1995	1996
Imports from UK	£15,537,000	£12,203,000
Exports to UK	18,130,000	13,772,000

COMMUNICATIONS

There are about 1,004 km of railway in operation, chiefly to serve the banana plantations and the Caribbean ports. There are 17,947 km of roads, of which 2,613 km are paved. There are 33 smaller airstrips and four international airports, Tegucigalpa, San Pedro Sula, La Ceiba and Roatan (Bay Island).

The chief ports are Puerto Cortes, Tela and La Ceiba on the north coast, through which passes the bulk of the trade with the USA and Europe. Puerto Castilla is being developed as a deep-water container port, and San Lorenzo is also experiencing rapid growth.

EDUCATION

Primary and secondary education is free, primary education being compulsory, and the government has launched a campaign to eradicate illiteracy.
ILLITERACY RATE – 27.3 per cent
ENROLMENT (percentage of age group) – primary 90 per cent (1993); secondary 21 per cent (1991); tertiary 9.3 per cent (1994)

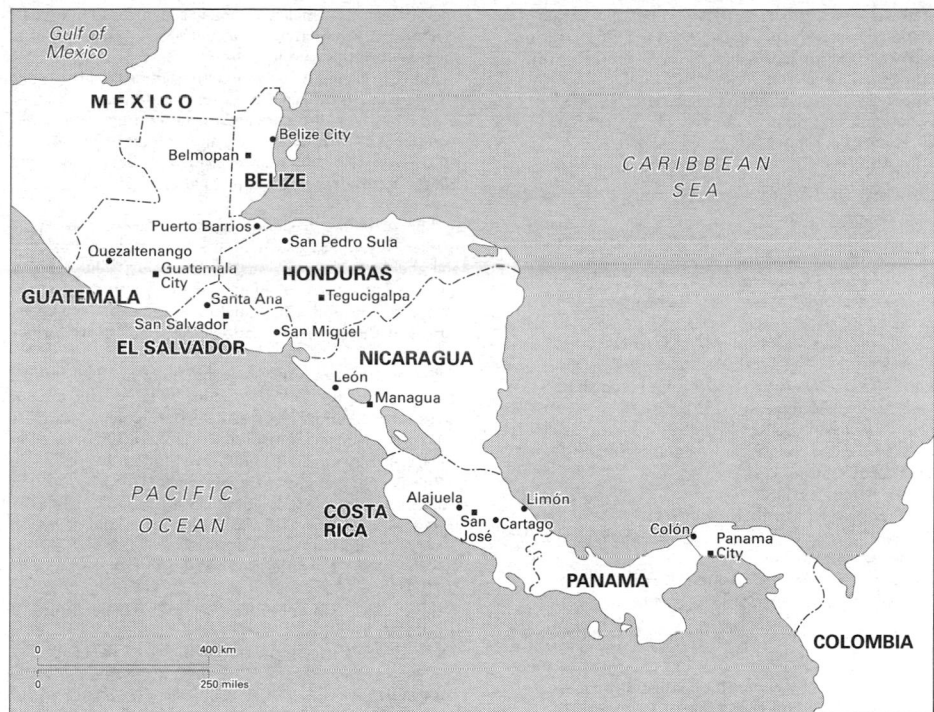

HUNGARY
Magyar Köztársaság

AREA – 35,920 sq miles (93,032 sq km) Neighbours:
Slovakia (north), Ukraine and Romania (east), the rump
Yugoslav Federal state and Croatia (south), and Slovenia
and Austria (west)

POPULATION – 10,261,000 (1994 UN estimate). There are
minorities of gypsies (4.8 per cent), ethnic Germans (1.9
per cent) and Slovaks (0.9 per cent). About two-thirds of
the population are Roman Catholic and the remainder
mostly Calvinist

CAPITAL – Budapest, on the Danube, (population,
2,002,121, 1993 estimate)

MAJOR CITIES – Miskolc (192,000), Debrecen (215,000);
Szeged (177,000) and Pécs (169,000)

CURRENCY – Forint of 100 fillér

NATIONAL ANTHEM – Isten Áldd Meg A Magyart (God
Bless the Hungarians)

NATIONAL DAYS – 15 March, 20 August, 23 October

NATIONAL FLAG – Red, white, green (horizontally)

LIFE EXPECTANCY (years) – male 64.53; female 73.81

POPULATION GROWTH RATE – –0.3 per cent (1994)

POPULATION DENSITY – 110 per sq. km (1994)

URBAN POPULATION – 63.8 per cent (1993)

HISTORY AND POLITICS

Hungary, reconstituted as a kingdom in 1920 after having
been declared a republic on 17 November 1918, joined the
Anti-Comintern Pact in February 1939 and entered the
Second World War on the side of Germany in 1941. On 20
January 1945 a Hungarian provisional government of
liberation signed an armistice under the terms of which the
frontiers of Hungary were withdrawn to the 1937 limits.

After the liberation, a coalition of parties carried out
land reform and nationalization. By 1949 the Communists
had succeeded in gaining a monopoly of power and by 1952
practically the entire economy had been 'socialized'.

Divisions within the Communist Party and popular
demand for free elections and Soviet troop withdrawals
grew from July 1956 onwards. An uprising on 23 October
involving fighting between demonstrators and factory
workers, and the State Security Police was quelled by
Soviet forces the following morning. By 30 October the
Soviets had withdrawn from Budapest and on 3 November
an all-party coalition government under Imre Nagy was
formed. This government was overthrown and the
attempted revolution suppressed by a renewed attack by
Soviet forces on Budapest on 4 November. The formation
of a new Hungarian Revolutionary Worker Peasant
(Communist) government under János Kádár was announced the same day.

From 1968 the government gradually introduced economic reforms and some political liberalization. Kádár was
forced to resign in May 1989. In October 1989 the National
Assembly (*Országgyülés*) approved an amended constitution which described Hungary as an independent, democratic state. The 386-seat National Assembly is elected on
a mixed first past the post and proportional representation
basis with a five per cent threshold for representation. The
first free multiparty elections took place in March and
April 1990 and were won by the (conservative) Hungarian
Democratic Forum.

The last general election in May 1994 was won by the
former ruling Communist Party, reconstituted as the
Hungarian Socialist Party. A coalition government of the
Hungarian Socialist Party and the Alliance of Free Demo-

crats was sworn in on 15 July 1994. The composition of the National Assembly in August 1995 was: Hungarian Socialist Party (HSP) 209, Alliance of Free Democrats (AFD) 70, Hungarian Democratic Forum 21, Independent Smallholders Party 26, Christian Democratic People's Party 22, Federation of Young Democrats-Hungarian Civic Party 20, Hungarian Democratic People's Party 15.

HEAD OF STATE
President, Árpád Göncz, *sworn in* 3 August 1990, *re-elected by parliament* 19 June 1995

CABINET *as at July 1997*
Prime Minister, Gyula Horn (HSP)
Deputy Prime Minister, Interior, Gábor Kuncze (AFD)
Agriculture, Frigyes Nagy (HSP)
Culture and Education, Bálint Magyar (AFD)
Defence, György Keleti (HSP)
Environment and Regional Protection, Dr Ferenc Baja (HSP)
Finance, Péter Medgyessy (HSP)
Foreign Affairs, László Kovács (HSP)
Industry and Commerce, Szabolcs Fazakas (Ind.)
Justice, Pál Vastagh (HSP)
Labour, Péter Kiss (HSP)
Public Welfare, Dr Mihály Kökény (HSP)
Transport, Telecommunications and Water Management, Dr Károly Lotz (AFD)
Without Portfolio, István Nikolits (HSP) (*Civil Secret Services*); Judit Csiha (HSP) (*Privatization*)

HSP Hungarian Socialist Party; AFD Alliance of Free Democrats; Ind. Independent

EMBASSY OF THE REPUBLIC OF HUNGARY
35 Eaton Place, London SWIX 8BY
Tel 0171–235 4048/7191
Ambassador Extraordinary and Plenipotentiary, HE Tádé Alföldy, apptd 1995
Minister Plenipotentiary, Sándor Juhász.
Counsellor and Consul-General, Dr Péter Kallós
Commercial Counsellor, Dr Jenő Hámori
Defence and Military Attaché, Col. László Hajdú

BRITISH EMBASSY
Harmincad Utca 6, Budapest V
Tel: Budapest 266–2888
Ambassador Extraordinary and Plenipotentiary, HE Christopher Long, CMG, apptd 1995
Counsellor and Deputy Head of Mission, C. Prentice, CVO
Defence Attaché, Col. H. Stephens
First Secretary (Commercial), S. C. Martin
First Secretary (Management) and Consul, I. H. Davies

BRITISH COUNCIL DIRECTOR, P. Dick, OBE, Benczur Utca 26, H–1068 Budapest VI

DEFENCE

The Army has 835 main battle tanks, 1,540 armoured infantry fighting vehicles and armoured personnel carriers and 840 pieces of artillery. The Air Force has 127 combat aircraft and 59 attack helicopters. Hungary will join Nato by April 1999.
MILITARY EXPENDITURE – 1.4 per cent of GDP (1995)
MILITARY PERSONNEL – 64,300: Army 48,000, Air Force 16,300
CONSCRIPTION DURATION – 12 months

ECONOMY

Agriculture accounts for 14 per cent of GDP and 23 per cent of exports. In 1993, 6 per cent of the land area was owned by state farms and 47 per cent was within co-operative farms, which will remain a feature of Hungarian agriculture. Production is concentrated on maize, wheat, sugar beet, barley, rye and oats.

Industry is mainly based on imported raw materials but Hungary has its own coal, bauxite, considerable deposits of natural gas, some iron ore and oil. Output figures in 1995 were: coal 14,461,000 tonnes; aluminium 34,900 tonnes; rolled steel 1,865,000 tonnes; crude petroleum 1,669,000 tonnes. Natural gas production totalled 5,365 million cubic metres.

The economy has suffered from the loss of export markets in the Soviet Union and the former Yugoslavia, and the transition to a market economy. The 1990–4 government embarked upon the privatization of state-owned concerns, the deregulation of the command economy and the return of nationalized land to its former owners.

Privatization and the establishment of small businesses proved successful in 1990–4, aided by large-scale foreign investment. Some 40 per cent of state enterprises have been privatized and they produced 55 per cent of GDP in 1994. Hungary joined the OECD in March 1996.

In 1994 Hungary had a trade deficit of US$3,716 million and a current account deficit of US$4,054 million. In 1995 imports totalled US$15,073 million and exports US$12,540 million.
GNP – US$41,129 million (1995); US$4,120 per capita (1995)
GDP – US$27,775 million (1992); US$3,378 per capita (1992)
ANNUAL AVERAGE GROWTH OF GDP – 1.5 per cent (1995); estimated to be 3.2 per cent in 1997
INFLATION RATE – 28.3 per cent (1995); estimated to be 17.6 per cent in 1997
UNEMPLOYMENT – 10.3 per cent (1995)
TOTAL EXTERNAL DEBT – US$31,248 million (1995)

Trade with UK	1995	1996
Imports from UK	£295,859,000	£347,111,000
Exports to UK	371,571,000	423,294,000

EDUCATION

There are five types of schools under the Ministry of Education: kindergartens for age three to six, general schools for age six to 14 (compulsory), vocational schools (15–18), secondary schools (15–18), universities and adult training schools (over 18).
ILLITERACY RATE – 0.8 per cent
ENROLMENT (percentage of age group) – primary 93 per cent (1994); secondary 73 per cent (1994); tertiary 16.9 per cent (1993)

CULTURE

Magyar, or Hungarian, is one of the Finno-Ugrian languages. Hungarian literature began to flourish in the second half of the 16th century. Among the greatest writers of the 19th and 20th centuries are Mihály Vörösmarty (1800–55), Sándor Petőfi (1823–49), János Arany (1817–82), Imre Madách (1823–64), Kálmán Mikszáth (1847–1910), Endre Ady (1877–1918), Attila József (1905–37), Mihály Babits (1883–1941), Dezső Kosztolányi (1885–1936), Gyula Illyes (1902–83), János Pilinszky (1921–81) and Sándor Weöres (1913–89).

ICELAND
Island

AREA – 39,768 sq. miles (103,000 sq. km)
POPULATION – 269,735 (1996). Some 92.2 per cent of the population are members of the (Lutheran) Church of Iceland
CAPITAL – ΨReykjavik (population, 104,258, 1995)
MAJOR CITIES – ΨAkureyri; Kópavogur; ΨHafnarfjördur; Keflavík; Westmann Islands; Akranes; Isafjördur; ΨSiglufjördur
CURRENCY – Icelandic króna (Kr) of 100 aurar
NATIONAL ANTHEM – O Gud Vors Lands (Our Country's God)
NATIONAL DAY – 17 June
NATIONAL FLAG – Blue, with white-bordered red cross
LIFE EXPECTANCY (years) – male 76.85; female 80.75
POPULATION GROWTH RATE – 1.1 per cent (1994)
POPULATION DENSITY – 3 per sq. km (1994)
URBAN POPULATION – 91.3 per cent (1993)

HISTORY AND POLITICS

Iceland was uninhabited before the ninth century, when settlers came from Norway. For several centuries a form of republican government prevailed, with an annual assembly of leading men called the *Althing*, but in 1262 Iceland became subject to Norway, and later to Denmark. During the colonial period, Iceland maintained its cultural integrity but a deterioration in the climate, together with frequent volcanic eruptions and outbreaks of disease, led to a serious drop in living standards and to a decline in the population to little more than 40,000. In the 19th century a struggle for independence led to home rule in 1918 and to independence as a republic in 1944.

The parliamentary (*Althing*) elections on 8 April 1995 gave the Independence Party 25 seats, Progressives 15, Social Democratic Party 7, People's Alliance 9, Awakening of the Nation 4, and Women's Alliance 3. A coalition government of the Independence Party and the Progressive Party was formed after the election.

HEAD OF STATE
President, Olafur Ragnar Grimsson, *elected* 29 June 1996

CABINET *as at July 1997*

Prime Minister, Statistical Bureau of Iceland, David Oddsson (IP)
Agriculture and Environment, Gudmundur Bjarnason (PP)
Communications, Halldór Blöndal (IP)
Education and Culture, Björn Bjarnason (IP)
Finance, Fridrik Sophusson (IP)
Fisheries, Justice and Ecclesiastical Affairs, Thorsteinn Pálsson (IP)
Foreign Affairs and External Trade, Halldór Ásgrímsson (PP)
Health and Social Security, Ingibjörg Pálmadóttir (PP)
Social Affairs, Páll Pétursson (PP)
Trade and Industry, Finnur Ingólfsson (PP)
(PP)

IP Independence Party; PP Progressive Party

EMBASSY OF ICELAND
1 Eaton Terrace, London SW1W 8EY
Tel 0171–730 5131
Ambassador Extraordinary and Plenipotentiary, HE Benedikt Ásgeirsson, apptd 1995

BRITISH EMBASSY
Laufásvegur 49, 101 Reykjavík
Tel: Reykjavík 551 15883/4
Ambassador Extraordinary and Plenipotentiary and Consul-General, HE James McCulloch, apptd 1996
CONSULATE – Akureyri

ECONOMY

Iceland has considerable resources of hydroelectric and geothermal energy. It is estimated that exploitation of these two resources represents only about 11 per cent of that economically exploitable. Heavy industry includes an aluminium smelter, a nitrogen fertilizer factory, a cement factory, a diatomite plant and a ferro-silicon plant.

The major sectors of the economy are fishing and fish processing, manufacturing, agriculture, energy production, government and the public sector, and tourism, which is of growing importance with 200,835 visitors in 1996.

As a member of the European Free Trade Association (EFTA), Iceland has become a member of the European Economic Area (EEA) which extends most of the provisions of the EU's single market to EFTA states.

In 1993 Iceland had a trade surplus of US$181 million and a current account deficit of US$6 million. In 1995 imports totalled US$1,756 million and exports US$1,804 million

GNP – US$6,686 million (1995); US$24,950 per capita (1995)
GDP – US$5,854 million (1992); US$25,436 per capita (1992)
ANNUAL AVERAGE GROWTH OF GDP – 2.2 per cent (1995)
INFLATION RATE – 1.7 per cent (1995)
UNEMPLOYMENT – 4.9 per cent (1995)

TRADE

The principal exports are fish and fish products, ferro-silicon and aluminium; the chief imports are consumer durables, capital goods, petroleum products, transport equipment, textiles, foodstuffs, animal feeds, timber, and alumina.

Trade with UK	1995	1996
Imports from UK	£138,103,000	£153,975,000
Exports to UK	251,887,000	267,876,000

COMMUNICATIONS

At 1 January 1996, the mercantile marine consisted of 1,021 registered vessels (160,371 gross tons). There are regular shipping services between Reykjavík and Felixstowe, Humber ports, Europe and the USA.

A regular air service is maintained by Icelandair between Glasgow and London and Reykjavík. There are also air services to Scandinavia, USA, Germany, France and Luxembourg.

Road communications are adequate in summer but greatly restricted by snow in winter. Only roads in town centres and key highways are metalled, the rest being of gravel, sand and lava dust. The climate and terrain make first-class surfaces for highways out of the question. There are no railways.

There are three television channels (one public, two private) and several private and public radio stations.

CULTURE

The ancient Norraena (or Northern tongue) has close affinities to Anglo-Saxon and as spoken and written in Iceland today differs little from that introduced into the island in the ninth century. There is a rich literature with two distinct periods of development, from the mid-11th to the late 13th century and from the early 19th century to the present.

Enrolment (percentage of age group) – tertiary 28.8 per cent (1993)

INDIA
The Republic of India

Area – 1,269,346 sq. miles (3,287,590 sq. km)

Population – 918,570,000 (1994 UN estimate), 846,302,688 (1991 census): Hindu (82.6 per cent), the rest being Muslim (11.4 per cent), Christian (2.4 per cent), Sikh (2.0 per cent), Buddhist (0.7 per cent) and Jain (0.5 per cent). The official languages are Hindi in the Devanagari script and English, though 17 regional languages also are recognized for adoption as official state languages

Capital – New Delhi (population, 301,297; 8,419,084 including Delhi/Dilli), 1991)

Major Cities – Ahmadabad (3,297,655); Bangalore (4,086,548); ΨBombay/Mumbai (12,571,720); ΨCalcutta (10,916,272); Hyderabad (4,280,261); Kanpur (2,111,284); Lucknow (1,642,134); ΨMadras/Chinnai (5,361,468); Pune (2,485,014), 1991

Currency – Indian rupee (Rs) of 100 paisa

National Anthem – Jana-gana-mana

National Day – 26 January (Republic Day)

National Flag – A horizontal tricolour with bands of deep saffron, white and dark green in equal proportions. In the centre of the white band appears an Asoka wheel in navy blue

Life Expectancy (years) – male 57.70; female 58.10

Population Growth Rate – 2.4 per cent (1994)

Population Density – 279 per sq. km (1994)

Urban Population – 26.3 per cent (1993)

Illiteracy Rate – 48.0 per cent

Enrolment (percentage of age group) – tertiary 6.0 per cent (1990)

India has three well-defined regions: the mountain range of the Himalayas, the Indo–Gangetic plain, and the southern peninsula. The main mountain ranges are the Himalayas (over 29,000 feet) and the Western and Eastern Ghats (over 8,000 feet). Major rivers include the Ganges, Indus, Krishna, Godavari and Mahanadi.

Temperatures vary over the country between averages of about 10°C and 33°C, reaching over 38°C in some parts during the hot season. There are similar variations in rainfall, from only a few inches a year falling in the western Thar Desert to over 400 inches in Meghalaya.

HISTORY AND POLITICS

The Indus civilization was fully developed by *c.*2500 BC but collapsed *c.*1750 BC, and was replaced by an Aryan civilization from the west. Arab invasions of the north-west began in the seventh century and Muslim, Hindu and Buddhist states developed until the establishment of the Mogul dynasty in 1526. The British East India Company established settlements throughout the 17th century; clashes with the French and native princes led to the British government taking control of the company in 1784 and gradually extending sovereignty over the whole sub-continent. The separate dominions of India and Pakistan became independent within the Commonwealth on 15 August 1947 and India became a republic in 1950.

Between 1947 and 1996, India was ruled by the Congress (I) Party for all but four years (March 1977–January 1980,

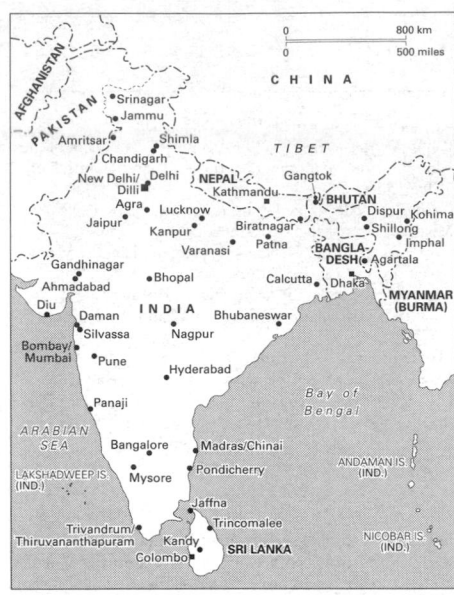

November 1989–June 1991). Congress (I) has been led by members of the Nehru-Gandhi dynasty for most of the post-independence period: Prime Ministers Jawaharlal Nehru (1947–64), Indira Gandhi (1966–1977, 1980–84) and Rajiv Gandhi (1984–89). Indira Gandhi was assassinated by Sikh extremists seeking an independent Sikh state in Punjab; her son Rajiv was assassinated by Sri Lankan Tamils.

The last parliamentary elections to the Lok Sabha in April and May 1996, were won by the Hindu nationalist Bharatiya Janata Party (BJP) which formed a government which lasted only 13 days before resigning on 28 May in the face of an imminent vote of no confidence. A United Front coalition of Communist and low-caste parties led by H. D. Deve Gowda assumed office on 1 June 1996. Deve Gowda was replaced as prime minister by Inder Kumar Gujral following a Congress (I) threat to withdraw its support.

Secession

The Hindu Maharaja of Kashmir signed his state's instrument of accession to India in October 1947, two months after India and Pakistan became independent. This was disputed by Pakistan, on the basis that the majority of the state's population was Muslim. After three Indian-Pakistani wars, a line of control was agreed under the 1972 Simla agreement (China has also occupied some of Kashmir since the 1962 Sino-Indian war). The line was rejected by armed groups which have waged a campaign of violence against the Hindu population and against Indian security forces. Kashmir was placed under direct rule in 1990 but state assembly elections, held in September 1996, were won by Jammu and Kashmir National Conference.

Insurgencies

Groups of Bodo separatists in Assam have been fighting for a separate Bodoland since the 1980s.

Foreign Relations

India and Pakistan have fought three major wars since independence, in 1947–8, 1965 and 1971. Since 1985 they have continued a low-level war at altitude for control of the Siachen glacier in Kashmir.

POLITICAL SYSTEM

Executive power is vested in the president, elected for a five-year term by an electoral college consisting of the elected members of the Union and State legislatures. The president appoints the prime minister and, on the latter's advice, the ministers, and can dismiss them. The Council of Ministers is collectively responsible to the Lok Sabha (lower house). The vice-president is ex-officio chairman of the Rajya Sabha (upper house).

Legislative power rests with the president, the Rajya Sabha (245 members serving six-year terms) and the Lok Sabha (545 members). Twelve members of the Rajya Sabha are presidential nominees, the rest are indirectly elected representatives of the State and Union Territories. The 530 members of the Lok Sabha representing the States are directly elected by universal adult franchise, and 15 representatives of the Union Territories are chosen, for a maximum term of five years.

The Supreme Court consists of the Chief Justice and not more than 25 other judges, appointed by the President. It is the highest court in respect of all constitutional matters and the final Court of Appeal and is situated in New Delhi. Each state or group of states also has a High Court with a hierarchy of subordinate courts. The judges of the High Court of a state are appointed by the president.

HEAD OF STATE

President of the Republic of India, Kocheril Raman Narayanan, elected 17 July 1997
Vice-President, Krishan Khant

COUNCIL OF MINISTERS *as at July 1997*

Prime Minister, Atomic Energy, Personnel, Public Grievances and Pensions, Health and Family Welfare, Planning and Programme Implementation, Inder Kumar Gujral
Agriculture, Chaturanan Mishra
Chemicals and Fertilizers, M. Arunachalam
Civil Aviation, C. M. Ibrahim
Communications, Beni Prasad Verma
Defence, Mulayam Singh Yadav
Environment and Forests, Prof. Saifuddin Soz
Finance, P. Chidambaran
Home Affairs, Indrajit Gupta
Human Resource Development, S. R. Bommai
Industry, Murasoli Maran
Information and Broadcasting, S. Jaipal Reddy
Parliamentary Affairs and Tourism, Srikanta Kumar Jena
Petroleum and Natural Gas, Janeshwar Mishra
Railways, Ram Vilas Paswan
Rural Areas and Employment, Yerran Naidu
Steel and Mines, Birendra Prasad Baishya
Surface Transport, T. G. Venkatraman
Textiles, R. L. Jalappa
Welfare, Balwant Singh Ramoowalia

INDIAN HIGH COMMISSION

India House, Aldwych, London WC2B 4NA
Tel 0171–836 8484
High Commissioner, HE Dr L. M. Singhvi, apptd 1991
Deputy High Commissioner, P. K. Singh
First Secretaries, Devi Charan Bansal (*Commerce*); Rajiv Kumar (*Consular*); Anup Ranjan Basu (*Culture*)
Military Adviser, Brig. R. Dhir
CONSULATES-GENERAL – Birmingham; Glasgow

BRITISH HIGH COMMISSION

Chanakyapuri, New Delhi 110021
Tel: New Delhi 687 2161
High Commissioner, HE Sir David Gore-Booth, KCMG, apptd 1996
Deputy High Commissioner and Minister, Dr D. Carter

Deputy High Commissioners, M. C. Bates (*Bombay*); S. M. Scaddan (*Calcutta*); S. H. Palmer (*Madras*)
Defence and Military Adviser, Brig. R. A. Draper, OBE
Counsellor (Economic and Commercial), W. Morris
Minister for Cultural Affairs and British Council Representative, C.W. Perchard, OBE

BRITISH COUNCIL – offices at New Delhi, Bombay, Calcutta and Madras. British Council libraries at these four centres and British libraries at Ahmadabad, Bangalore, Bhopal, Hyderabad, Lucknow, Patna, Pune and Trivandrum

STATES AND TERRITORIES OF THE UNION

There are 25 States and seven Union Territories. Each state is headed by a Governor, who is appointed by the President and holds office for five years, and by a Council of Ministers. All states have a Legislative Assembly, and some have also a Legislative Council, elected directly by adult suffrage for a maximum period of five years.

The Union Territories are administered, except where otherwise provided by Parliament, by the president acting through an Administrator or Lieutenant-Governor, or other authority appointed by him.

(Capital in parenthesis)	Area (sq. km)	Population (1991 census)
STATES		
Andhra Pradesh (Hyderabad)	275,100	66,304,854
Arunachal Pradesh (Itanagar)	83,700	858,392
Assam (Dispur)	78,400	22,414,322
Bihar (Patna)	173,900	86,374,465
Goa (Panaji)	3,700	1,168,622
Gujarat (Gandhinagar)	196,000	41,309,582
Haryana (Chandigarh)	44,200	16,463,648
Himachal Pradesh (Shimla)	55,700	5,170,877
Jammu and Kashmir* (Srinagar/Jammu)	222,200	5,987,389
Karnataka (Bangalore)	191,800	44,977,201
Kerala (Trivandrum)	38,900	29,011,237
Madhya Pradesh (Bhopal)	443,500	66,135,862
Maharashtra (Bombay/Mumbai)	307,700	78,937,187
Manipur (Imphal)	22,300	1,826,714
Meghalaya (Shillong)	22,400	1,774,778
Mizoram (Aizawl)	21,100	686,217
Nagaland (Kohima)	16,600	1,209,549
Orissa (Bhubaneswar)	155,700	31,659,736
Punjab (Chandigarh)	50,400	20,190,795
Rajasthan (Jaipur)	342,700	44,005,990
Sikkim (Gangtok)	7,100	405,550
Tamil Nadu (Madras/Chinnai)	130,100	55,638,318
Tripura (Agartala)	10,500	2,744,827
Uttar Pradesh (Lucknow)	294,400	139,112,287
West Bengal (Calcutta)	88,800	67,982,732
UNION TERRITORIES		
Andaman and Nicobar Is. (Port Blair)	8,200	280,661
Chandigarh	114	642,015
Dadra and Nagar Haveli (Silvassa)	500	138,477
Daman and Diu	112	101,586
Delhi	1,500	9,420,644
Lakshadweep (Kavaratti)	30	51,681
Pondicherry	500	807,785

* The area figure includes those parts occupied by Pakistan and China, which are claimed by India, but the population figure excludes the population of these areas, where the census was not taken. The state's capital is at Srinagar in summer and Jammu in winter.

DEFENCE

The Army has 3,500 main battle tanks, 507 armoured infantry fighting vehicles and armoured personnel carriers and 4,175 artillery pieces. The Navy has 19 submarines, 2 aircraft carriers, five destroyers, 19 frigates, 44 patrol and coastal vessels, 68 combat aircraft and 75 armed helicopters. It has nine bases including one under construction. The Air Force has 778 combat aircraft and 34 armed helicopters.

India exploded its first nuclear weapon in 1974 and is since believed to have acquired a stockpile of nuclear arms. In 1993–4 India successfully test-fired its intermediate-range 'Agni' and 'Prithvi' ballistic missiles.

MILITARY EXPENDITURE – 2.5 per cent of GDP (1995)
MILITARY PERSONNEL – 1,152,500: Army 980,000, Navy 55,000, Air Force 110,000, Paramilitaries 7,500

ECONOMY

Agriculture supports about 65 per cent of the population, and contributes nearly 29 per cent of GDP. Production has grown by 2.6 per cent each year since 1951, remaining slightly ahead of the 2 per cent increase necessary to keep pace with the rising population. Food crops occupy three-quarters of the total cultivated area. The main food crops are rice, cereals (principally wheat) and pulses. The major cash crops include sugar cane, jute, cotton and tea. Other products include oil seeds, spices, groundnuts, soya bean, tobacco, rubber and coffee. Livestock is raised, principally for dairy purposes or for the hides.

Industry is based on the exploitation and processing of mineral resources, principally coal, oil and iron, and on the production of textiles. The coal industry reached an output in 1995 of 285,500,000 tonnes; production of crude petroleum was 34,456,000 tonnes. Steel production is mainly in the hands of the public sector, with five public and one private sector integrated steel plants producing 20,291,000 tonnes of ingot steel in 1995. The engineering industry, heavy and light, is increasingly being privatized.

The manufacture of paper, cement, pharmaceuticals, chemicals, fertilizers, petrochemicals, motor vehicles and commercial vehicles has been expanded. Other principal manufactures are those derived from agricultural products, textiles, jute goods, sugar, leather, which along with tea, tobacco, rubber, fish, and iron ore and concentrates are major exports.

India abandoned 40 years of centralized planning in 1991 and introduced free market reforms. Subsidies were cut, state corporations privatized and the economy opened up to foreign competition and investment. To integrate India into the international trading system proper, the 1993–5 budgets floated the rupee, cut interest rates and duties on imports, reduced subsidies to farmers, restructured the taxation system, removed industrial controls and dismantled protectionist structures.

The reforms have been successful, encouraging high levels of foreign investment, a fall in inflation, a 24 per cent increase in exports, a rise in foreign currency reserves from US$1,000 million to US$16,000 million in 1996, improved agricultural efficiency and an increase in the average annual industrial growth rate from 1 per cent to 12 per cent.

In 1995 imports totalled US$34,522 million and exports US$30,484 million.

GNP – US$319,660 million (1995); US$340 per capita (1995)
GDP – US$319,542 million (1992); US$306 per capita (1992)
ANNUAL AVERAGE GROWTH OF GDP – 6.3 per cent (1994)
INFLATION RATE – 10.2 per cent (1995)
TOTAL EXTERNAL DEBT – US$93,766 million (1995)

TRADE WITH UK	1995	1996
Imports from UK	£1,682,709,000	£1,706,606,000
Exports to UK	1,435,481,000	1,610,996,000

COMMUNICATIONS

The International Airports Authority manages five international airports: Palam (Delhi), Sahar (Bombay), Dum Dum (Calcutta), Meenambakkam (Madras) and Trivandrum. The other 88 aerodromes are controlled and operated by the Civil Aviation Department of the government. The national airlines are Indian Airlines (internal) and Air India (international).

The railways are grouped into nine administrative zones, Southern, Central, Western, Northern, North-Eastern, North-East Frontier, Eastern, South-Eastern and South-Central with a total track length of 62,660 km, about 19 per cent of which is electrified. The total length of the road network is 2,065,209 km of which 964,072 km is surfaced.

The chief seaports are Bombay/Mumbai, Calcutta, Haldia, Madras/Chinnai, Mormugao, Cochin, Visakhapatnam, Kandla, Paradip, Mangalore and Tuticorin; these handled a cargo of 179.3 million tonnes in 1993–4. There are 139 minor working ports with varying capacity.

INDONESIA
Republik Indonesia

AREA – 735,358 sq. miles (1,904,569 sq. km)
POPULATION – 192,217,000 (1994 UN estimate)
CAPITAL – ΨJakarta (population, 8,500,000)
MAJOR CITIES – (Java) ΨSurabaya (2,027,913), ΨSemarang (1,026,671), Bandung (1,462,637); (Sumatra) Palembang (787,187), Medan (1,378,955); (Sulawesi) ΨUjung Pandang (709,038); (Kalimantan) Banjarmasin (381,286), ΨPontianak (304,778), (Moluccas) Ambon (208,898); (Nusa Tenggara) Kupang (329,371); (Irian Jaya) Jayapura (107,164)
CURRENCY – Rupiah (Rp) of 100 sen
NATIONAL ANTHEM – Indonesia Raya (Great Indonesia)
NATIONAL DAY – 17 August (Anniversary of Proclamation of Independence)
NATIONAL FLAG – Equal bands of red over white
LIFE EXPECTANCY (years) – male 61.00; female 64.50
POPULATION GROWTH RATE – 1.7 per cent (1994)
POPULATION DENSITY – 101 per sq. km (1994)
URBAN POPULATION – 30.9 per cent (1990)
ILLITERACY RATE – 16.2 per cent
ENROLMENT (percentage of age group) – primary 97 per cent (1993); secondary 37 per cent (1992); tertiary 9.3 per cent (1992)

Indonesia comprises the islands of Java, Madura, Sumatra, the Riouw-Lingga archipelago, Bangka and Billiton, part of the island of Borneo (Kalimantan), Sulawesi (formerly Celebes), the Molucca Islands, the islands of Bali, Lombok, Sumbawa, Sumba, Flores, Timor and others comprising the provinces of East and West Nusa Tenggara and the western half of the island of New Guinea (Irian Jaya).

HISTORY AND POLITICS

From the early part of the 17th century much of the Indonesian archipelago was under Dutch rule. Following the Second World War, during which the archipelago was occupied by the Japanese, a strong nationalistic movement formed and after sporadic fighting all the former Dutch

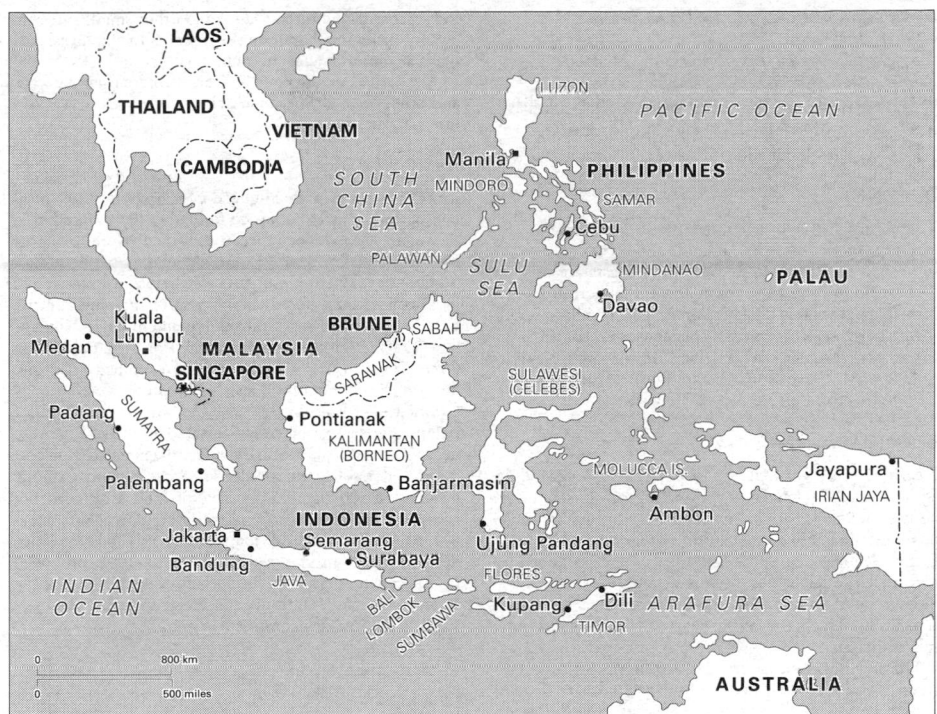

East Indies except western New Guinea became independent as Indonesia on 27 December 1949. Western New Guinea became part of Indonesia in 1963 under the name West Irian (now Irian Jaya), this interpretation being confirmed in an 'Act of Free Choice' in July 1969.

The Army Minister Gen. Suharto assumed effective political power in March 1966. Gen. Suharto was appointed president in 1968 and has been reappointed by the People's Consultative Assembly (composed of the House of People's Representatives (*Dewan Perwakilan Rakyat*) together with 500 government, regional and party appointees) at each presidential election since. The House of People's Representatives is composed of 425 elected members and 75 military appointees. The military has effectively ruled since 1966 through its political organization Golkar.

Only three parties may legally contest elections. Golkar won 74 per cent of the votes cast in the general election on 29 May 1997. The next presidential election is scheduled to be held in 1998.

INSURGENCIES

Besides East Timor (*see* page 896), there are two armed secessionist movements based on ethnic and nationalist groups, which are fighting perceived Javanese domination. In Irian Jaya government forces are fighting the Papua Independent Organization (OPM) guerrillas who claim the 1969 referendum was rigged and oppose Indonesian settlement. In northern Sumatra the Free Aceh Movement is active.

HEAD OF STATE

President, Gen. Suharto, *appointed acting president* March 1967; *confirmed as president* 28 March 1968, *re-elected* 1973, 1978, 1983, 1988 and March 1993
Vice-President, Try Sutrisno, *elected* March 1993

CABINET *as at July 1997*

Co-ordinating Ministers, Gen. (retd) Soesilo Soedarman (*Political and Security Affairs*); Saleh Afiff (*Economy*); Maj.-Gen. Azwar Anas (*Public Welfare*); Ir Hartarto (*Production and Distribution*)
Ministers, Lt.-Gen. (retd) Yogi Memet (*Internal Affairs*); Ali Alatas (*Foreign Affairs*); Gen. Edi Sudrajat (*Defence and Security*); Oesman Oetojo (*Justice*); Mr Hartono (*Information*); Mar'ie Muhammad (*Finance*); Tungki Ariwibowo (*Trade and Industry*); Sjarifuddin Baharsyah (*Agriculture*); Lt.-Gen. Ida Bagus Sujana (*Mines and Energy*); Radinal Mochtar (*Public Works*); Haryanto Dhanutirto (*Communications*); Abdul Latief (*Manpower*); Siswono Yudohusodo (*Transmigration*); Joop Ave (*Tourism, Posts and Telecommunications*); Wardiman Joyonegoro (*Education and Culture*); Dr Suyudi (*Health*); Tarmizi Taher (*Religious Affairs*); Prof. Endang Suweno (*Social Affairs*); Jamaludin Suryohadikasumo (*Forestry*); Subiakto Cakrawerdaya (*Co-operatives and Small Businesses*); Dr Murdiono (*Minister and State Secretary*)
In addition there are 14 ministers of state.

INDONESIAN EMBASSY

38 Grosvenor Square, London WIX 9AD
Tel 0171–499 7661
Ambassador Extraordinary and Plenipotentiary, new appointment awaited
Minister, H. Sudirman (*Deputy Chief of Mission*)
Commercial Attaché, Andreas Anugerah

BRITISH EMBASSY

Jalan M. H. Thamrin 75, Jakarta 10310
Tel: Jakarta 330904
Ambassador Extraordinary and Plenipotentiary, HE Robin Christopher, CMG, apptd 1997

Deputy Ambassador, Counsellor and Consul-General,
  Q. M. Quayle
Counsellor (Commercial/Development), P. J. Johnstone
Defence Attaché, Col. D. S. Mac Farlane
BRITISH CONSULAR OFFICES – Jakarta, Medan, Surabaya
BRITISH COUNCIL DIRECTOR, Dr N. Kemp, S Widjojo
  Centre, Jalan Jenderal Sudirman 71, Jakarta 12190

DEFENCE

The Army has 200 armoured personnel carriers, 181 artillery pieces, and 11 aircraft. The Navy has two submarines, 17 frigates, 57 patrol and coastal vessels, 24 combat aircraft and 14 armed helicopters. There are seven principal naval bases. The Air Force has 77 combat aircraft.
MILITARY EXPENDITURE – 1.6 per cent of GDP (1995)
MILITARY PERSONNEL – 311,200: Army 235,200, Navy 43,000, Air Force 21,000, Paramilitaries 12,000
CONSCRIPTION DURATION – Two years

ECONOMY

Nearly 70 per cent of the population is engaged in agriculture and related production. Copra, kapok, nutmeg, pepper and cloves are produced, mainly by smallholders; palm oil, sugar, fibres and cinchona are produced by large estates. Rubber, tea, coffee and tobacco are produced by both in large quantities. Rice is a staple food and Java, Sulawesi and Sumatra are important producers. Production has risen rapidly in recent years and the country is now self-sufficient.

Oil and liquefied natural gas are the most important assets, the export of which constitutes around 80 per cent of export earnings. Timber is the second largest foreign exchange earner after oil.

Indonesia is rich in minerals, particularly tin, of which the country is the world's third biggest producer; coal, nickel and bauxite are the other principal mineral products. There are also considerable deposits of gold, silver, manganese phosphates and sulphur.

Indonesia is aiming to diversify its economy to reduce its dependence on oil and gas exports, with particular emphasis on agriculture, heavy engineering (shipbuilding) and high technology (aerospace).

Principal exports are petroleum, textiles and clothing, timber, natural gas and rubber. Principal imports are machinery and transport equipment, electrical equipment and chemicals.

In 1993 the government had a budget surplus equivalent to 0.59 per cent of GDP. There was a trade surplus of US$8,231 milllion and a current account deficit of US$2,016 million. In 1995 imports totalled US$40,918 million and exports US$45,417 million.
GNP – US$190,105 million (1995); US$980 per capita (1995)
GDP – US$121,085 million (1992); US$671 per capita (1992)
ANNUAL AVERAGE GROWTH OF GDP – 7.5 per cent (1994)
INFLATION RATE – 9.4 per cent (1995)
TOTAL EXTERNAL DEBT – US$107,831 million (1995)

TRADE WITH UK	1995	1996
Imports from UK	£525,499,000	£828,268,000
Exports to UK	903,867,000	980,680,000

COMMUNICATIONS

There are railway systems in Java and Sumatra linking the main towns. There are about 50,000 miles of roads.

Sea communications are maintained by the state-run shipping companies Djakarta-Lloyd (ocean-going) and Pelni (coastal and inter-island) and other small concerns. Transport by small craft on the rivers of the larger islands plays an important part in trade.

Air services are operated by Garuda Indonesian Airways and other local airlines, and Jakarta is served by various international services.

EAST TIMOR

East Timor was a Portuguese colony from 1702 until Portuguese control collapsed following the 1974 coup in Portugal. An independence war waged by the Marxist Fretilin (Revolutionary Front for an Independent East Timor) developed into a civil war between Fretilin and local conservative forces in 1975. After gaining control, Fretilin declared East Timor independent on 27 November 1975 and this was recognized by Portugal. Indonesian forces invaded East Timor on 7 December 1975 and declared East Timor Indonesia's 27th province.

Since 1975 Fretilin has waged an armed campaign for independence; resistance has left 200,000 East Timorese dead. About 150,000 Muslims have been settled in East Timor alongside the predominantly Roman Catholic population (80 per cent in 1975). The UN does not recognize the annexation and considers Portugal to exercise sovereignty still. A massacre of pro-independence demonstrators in the capital, Dili, in 1991 provoked international outrage. Fighting between Fretilin and the Indonesian army continues despite the imprisonment of Fretilin's leader, Xanana Gusmao in 1993.

IRAN
Jomhuri-e-Islami-e-Iran

AREA – 630,577 sq. miles (1,633,188 sq. km). Neighbours: Armenia, Azerbaijan, Turkmenistan (north), Afghanistan (north-east), Pakistan (south-east), Iraq (south-west), Turkey (north-west)
POPULATION – 59,275,359 (1996 census): 99 per cent Muslims (Shia 91 per cent and Sunni 8 per cent) with small minorities of Zoroastrians, Bahais, Jews, and Armenian and Assyrian Christians. The official language is Persian. Turkish, Kurdish, Arabic, Lori, Guilani, Mazandarani and Baluchi are also spoken
CAPITAL – Tehran, (population 6,750,043, 1994 estimate)
MAJOR CITIES – Mashhad (1,964,489); Esfahan (1,220,595); Tabriz (1,166,203); Shiraz, (1,042,801); Ahwaz (828,380); Qom (780,453), 1994
CURRENCY – Rial
NATIONAL ANTHEM – Sorood-e Jomhoori-e Eslami
NATIONAL DAY – 11 February
NATIONAL FLAG – Three horizontal stripes of green, white, red, with the slogan *Allahu Akbar* repeated 22 times along the edges of the green and red stripes, and the national emblem in the centre
LIFE EXPECTANCY (years) – male 58.38; female 59.70
POPULATION GROWTH RATE – 2.3 per cent (1994)
POPULATION DENSITY – 37 per sq. km (1994)
URBAN POPULATION – 57.5 per cent (1993)

Iran is mostly an arid tableland, encircled, except in the east, by mountains, the highest in the north rising to 18,934 ft. The central and eastern portion is a vast salt desert.

HISTORY AND POLITICS

Iran was ruled from the end of the 18th century by Shahs of the Qajar dynasty. In 1925 the last of the dynasty, Sultan

Ahmed Shah, was deposed in his absence by the National Assembly, which handed executive power to Prime Minister Reza Khan. Reza Khan was elected Shah as Reza Shah Pahlavi by the Constituent Assembly in December 1925. In 1941 Reza Shah abdicated in favour of the Crown Prince, who ascended the throne as Mohammed Reza Shah Pahlavi.

In January 1979, the Shah left Iran, handing over power to the Prime Minister, who was ousted by Ayatollah Khomeini, the spiritual leader of the Shia Muslims, on his return from exile. Following a national referendum, an Islamic Republic was declared on 1 April 1979. A new constitution, providing for a president, prime minister, Consultative Assembly, and leadership by Ayatollah Khomeini, was approved by referendum in December 1979. In June 1989 Khomeini died and President Khamenei was appointed Leader of the Islamic Republic. Rafsanjani was elected president in July 1989, and the post of prime minister was abolished. In the 1992 elections to the *Majlis* (consultative assembly), candidates supporting President Rafsanjani won over 200 of the 270 seats. However, in the 1993 presidential election, President Rafsanjani received only 63 per cent of the vote (compared with 94 per cent in 1989) and only 56 per cent of the electorate voted. The elections in March and April 1996 saw the conservative Society of Combatant Clergy lose overall control of the Majlis due to gains by the Servants of Iran's Construction.

FOREIGN RELATIONS

Iran was at war with Iraq following the Iraqi invasion of Iran in September 1980. International efforts to end the fighting resulted in a cease-fire in August 1988. In August 1990 Iraq accepted Iran's conditions for settling the conflict, including a return to the 1975 border, but a formal peace treaty has not been signed.

POLITICAL SYSTEM

The leader of the republic is elected by the Council of Experts whose 83 members are popularly elected every eight years. The president, who is the chief executive, is directly elected for a four-year term and may only be re-elected once. Ministers are nominated by the president and must obtain a vote of confidence in the Majlis. The Majlis comprises 270 representatives who are directly elected for a four-year term. Laws passed by the Majlis must be approved by the 12-member Guardian Council.

Leader of the Islamic Republic, Ayatollah Seyed Ali Khamenei, *appointed* June 1989
President, Seyed Mohammad Khatami, *elected* 23 May 1997
First Vice-President, Masumeh Ebtekar

COUNCIL OF MINISTERS *as at July 1997*

Vice-Presidents, Seyed Ataollah Mohajerani (*Legal and Parliamentary Affairs*); Reza Amrollahi (*Atomic Energy*); Massoud Razavi (*State Employment and Administrative Affairs*); Mohammad Hashemi (*Executive Affairs*); Mehdi Manafi (*Environmental Protection*); Seyyed Mostafa Hashemi-Taba (*Physical Education*)
Agriculture, Issa Kalantari
Commerce, Yahya Al-Eshaq
Construction Crusade, Gholam Reza Forouzesh
Co-operatives, Gholem Reza Shafei
Culture and Higher Education, Dr Hashemi Golpeygani
Defence, Mohammed Forouzandeh
Economy and Finance, Morteza Mohammed Khan
Education, Mohammad Ali Najafi
Energy, Bizhan Namdar Zanganeh
Foreign Affairs, Ali Akbar Velayati

Health, Ali Reza Marandi
Housing and Urban Development, Abbas Ahmad Akhundi
Industries, Mohammad Reza Nematzadeh
Intelligence, Ali Fallahian
Interior, Ali Mohammad Besharati
Islamic Culture and Guidance, Mostafa Mir-Salim
Justice, Mohammad Esmail Shoushtari
Labour and Social Affairs, Hossein Kamali
Mines and Metals, Mohammad Hossein Mahloujchi
Oil, Gholamreza Aghazadeh
Posts, Telephones and Telegraphs, Mohammad Gharrazi
Roads and Transport, Ali Akbar Torkan

EMBASSY OF THE ISLAMIC REPUBLIC OF IRAN
16 Prince's Gate, London SW7 1PT
Tel 0171-225 3000
Chargé d'Affaires, G. Ansari

BRITISH EMBASSY
143 Ferdowsi Avenue, PO Box 11365–4474, Tehran 11344
Tel: Tehran 675011
Counsellor and Chargé d'Affaires, Jeffrey R. James, CMG, apptd 1993
First Secretary (Commercial), A. F. Bedford

DEFENCE

The Army has 1,440 main battle tanks, 950 armoured personnel carriers and armoured infantry fighting vehicles, more than 2,000 artillery pieces, 50 aircraft and 100 attack helicopters. The Navy has two submarines, two destroyers, three frigates, 48 patrol and coastal vessels and nine armed helicopters. There are six naval bases. The Air Force has some 295 combat aircraft, of which only about 50 per cent are serviceable due to the US armaments embargo, in operation since 1979.
MILITARY EXPENDITURE – 3.9 per cent of GDP (1995)
MILITARY PERSONNEL – 513,000: Army 345,000, Revolutionary Guard Corps 120,000, Navy 18,000, Air Force 30,000
CONSCRIPTION DURATION – 24 months

ECONOMY

Privatization began in 1991 but since 1993 its pace has been reduced by the government due to rising unemployment. Iran's support for international terrorism and its alleged nuclear weapons programme prompted the USA to impose a full trade and investment embargo in June 1995, and to impose sanctions on foreign companies investing more than £26 million a year in Iran's energy sector, in July 1996. However, in August 1996, Turkey signed a £13 billion deal to buy Iranian gas and for the construction of a gas pipeline.

Agricultural output rose following the end of the Iran–Iraq war and an attempt is being made to reduce dependence on food imports. Wheat is the principal crop; other important crops are barley, rice, cotton, sugar beet, fruit, nuts and vegetables. Wool is also a major product.

The oilfields, which lie in south-western Iran, were nationalized in 1951. From 1957 until the 1979 revolution a consortium of eight foreign oil companies was responsible for the production, refining and sale of oil but in July 1979 the National Iranian Oil Company assumed full control. Oil production was 180,911,000 tonnes in 1995.

Apart from oil, the principal industrial products are carpets, textiles, sugar, cement and other construction materials, ginned cotton, vegetable oil and other food products, leather and shoes, metal manufactures, pharmaceuticals, motor vehicles, fertilizers and plastics.

In 1994 the government had a budget deficit equivalent to 0.13 per cent of GDP.

GDP – US$600,007 million (1992); US$13,561 per capita (1992)
ANNUAL AVERAGE GROWTH OF GDP – 1.9 per cent (1994)
INFLATION RATE – 49.6 per cent (1995)
TOTAL EXTERNAL DEBT – US$21,935 million (1995)

TRADE

Imports are mainly industrial and agricultural machinery, motor vehicles and motor vehicle components for assembly, iron and steel (including manufactures), electrical machinery and goods, foodstuffs and certain textile fabrics and yarns. The principal exports, apart from oil and gas, are carpets and fruit. Japan, Germany, France and Italy are Iran's main trading partners.

Trade with UK	1995	1996
Imports from UK	£332,614,000	£396,561,000
Exports to UK	125,834,000	118,771,000

COMMUNICATIONS

Tehran is the centre of a network of highways linking the major towns, ports, the Caspian Sea and the national frontiers.

The Trans-Iranian Railway runs from Bandar Turcoman, on the Caspian Sea, via Tehran to Bandar Khomeini, on the Persian Gulf. Other lines link Tehran with Tabriz and Mashhad; Tabriz to Julfa; Zahedan to Quetta; Ahvaz to Khorramshahr; Qom to Kerman; and Bandar Turcoman to Gorgan. The rail system is linked to the Turkish system via Van. A track between Mashhad and Tedzhen in Turkmenistan, opened in May 1996, has re-established the ancient Silk Road between China and the Mediterranean.

There is an international airport at Tehran (Mehrabad), and airports at all the major provincial centres. The national airline, Iranair, is government-owned and operates international and domestic routes.

EDUCATION AND CULTURE

Since 1943 primary education has been compulsory and free. There are 57 universities in Iran. The educational system has been reformed following the revolution.

Persian or Farsi is an Indo-European language with many Arabic elements added; the alphabet is mainly Arabic, with writing from right to left. Among the great names in Persian literature are those of Abu'l Kásim Mansúr, or Firdausi (AD 939–1020), Omar Khayyám, the astronomer-poet (died AD 1122), Muslihu'd-Din, known as Sa'di (born AD 1184), and Shems-ed-Din Muhammad, or Hafiz (died AD 1389).

ILLITERACY RATE – 27.7 per cent
ENROLMENT (percentage of age group) – primary 79 per cent (1985); tertiary 12.7 per cent (1994)

IRAQ
Al-Jumhouriya al-'Iraqia

AREA – 169,235 sq. miles (438,317 sq. km). Neighbours: Turkey (north and north-east), Syria (east)
POPULATION – 19,925,000 (1994 UN estimate), 16,278,316 (1987 census). The official language is Arabic. Minority languages include Kurdish (about 15 per cent), Turkic and Aramaic
CAPITAL – Baghdad (population, 3,841,268, 1987)
MAJOR CITIES – ΨBasra; Mosul; Kirkuk
CURRENCY – Iraqi dinar (ID) of 1,000 fils
NATIONAL DAY – 17 July (Revolution Day)

NATIONAL FLAG – Three horizontal stripes of red, white, black; on the white stripe three stars and the slogan *Allahu Akbar* all in green
LIFE EXPECTANCY (years) – male 77.43; female 78.22
POPULATION GROWTH RATE – 3.4 per cent (1994)
POPULATION DENSITY – 45 per sq. km (1994)
URBAN POPULATION – 69.9 per cent (1990)
ILLITERACY RATE – 29.2 per cent
ENROLMENT (percentage of age group) – primary 79 per cent (1992); secondary 37 per cent (1992); tertiary 12.6 per cent (1990)

In 1993 the border between Iraq and Kuwait was formally demarcated, moving a few hundred metres northwards and giving part of the port of Umm Qasr to Kuwait. The rivers Euphrates (1,700 miles) and Tigris (1,150 miles) rise in Turkey and traverse Iraq to their junction at Qurna, from where the Euphrates flows the 70 miles to the Gulf.

HISTORY AND POLITICS

Iraq is the site of the remains of several ancient civilizations: one site at Tel Hassuna, near Shura, dates back to 5000 BC; Tel Abu Shahrain near 'Ur of the Chaldees' is the site of the Sumerian city of Eridu; the ancient city of Hillah, 70 miles south of Baghdad, is near the site of Babylon and the Tower of Babel. Mosul governorate covers a great part of the ancient kingdom of Assyria, the ruins of Ninevah, the Assyrian capital, being visible on the banks of the Tigris, opposite Mosul. Qurna, at the junction of the Tigris and Euphrates, is traditionally supposed to be the site of the Garden of Eden.

Under the Treaty of Lausanne (1923), Turkey renounced sovereignty over Mesopotamia. A provisional government was set up in 1920, and in 1921 the Emir Faisal was elected King of Iraq. The country was a monarchy until July 1958, when King Faisal II was assassinated. From 1958 Iraq has been under the rule of the Ba'ath Party.

The Arab Ba'ath Socialist Party held a majority of Assembly seats following the 1989 elections; no party affiliations were ascribed in the results of the most recent election, held on 24 March 1996.

FOREIGN RELATIONS

Iraq invaded Iran in September 1980 and was at war until the August 1988 cease-fire. In 1990 Iraq accepted Iran's conditions for peace, including a return to the 1975 border, but a formal peace treaty has not been signed.

Iraq invaded Kuwait on 2 August 1990 and declared Kuwait a province of Iraq. The UN Security Council declared the annexation void. After months of diplomatic attempts to secure an Iraqi withdrawal from Kuwait, an alliance of NATO and Middle East countries launched an offensive in January 1991 and liberated Kuwait in February 1991.

INSURGENCIES

Following the allied victory in Kuwait in February 1991, rebellion broke out in the Kurdish north and the Shi'ite south. Although the revolt was quickly suppressed, Iraqi attacks on Kurdish civilians led Western governments to set up a security zone and a UN safe haven in northern Iraq to protect them. An air exclusion zone north of the 36th parallel was also established. Saddam Hussein withdrew his administration from Kurdish northern Iraq in October 1991, enabling the Kurds to establish a de facto administration with its capital at Arbil. In 1992 the Kurds voted for a 100-seat parliament and a 'political leader'. The Kurdish Democratic Party (KDP) and the Patriotic Union of Kurdistan (PUK) both gained 50 seats and a coalition government was formed. Trading difficulties, fuel and food shortages, and land disputes led to fighting between the two parties. A cease-fire lasted from September 1995 to August 1996 when the KDP invited Iraqi troops to invade the safe haven. Another cease-fire was signed in October 1996. There are 25,000 KDP members and 12,000 PUK members. *See also* Events of the Year.

Although the Shi'ite revolt in southern Iraq was defeated in April 1991, a low-level insurgency continued in the southern marshlands. Continued Iraqi bombing of Shi'ite refugees in these areas led to an air exclusion zone being established south of the 32nd parallel in August 1992, patrolled by US, British and French aircraft. Since then the Iraqi regime has systematically drained the southern marshes by canal construction and river diversion; with continued ground offensives, this had effectively ended the Shi'ite rebellion by late 1994.

POLITICAL SYSTEM

According to the provisional constitution, the highest state authority is the Revolutionary Command Council (RCC), which elects the president from among its members. A constitutional amendment approved in September 1995 provided for the confirmation of the RCC's choice of president by the National Assembly and by a popular referendum. The president appoints the Council of Ministers. Legislative authority is shared by the RCC and the 250-member National Assembly, which is elected every four years by universal adult suffrage. Following the amendment to the constitution, a referendum on a further seven-year term for President Saddam was approved by a claimed 99.96 per cent of voters on 15 October 1995.

HEAD OF STATE

President, Saddam Hussein, *assumed office* 16 July 1979, *reappointed* 17 October 1995
Vice Presidents, Taha Yassin Ramadhan; Taha Mohieddin Maaruf

REVOLUTIONARY COMMAND COUNCIL

Chairman, The President
Vice-Chairman, Izzat Ibrahim
Head of the Presidential Office, Ahmed Hussein Khudayyir
Members, Taha Yassin Ramadhan; Tariq Aziz; Mohammed Hamza al-Zubeidi; Gen. Ali Hassan al-Majeed; Mizban Khider Hadi; Taha Mohieddin Maaruf

CABINET *as at June 1997*

The President
Deputy Prime Ministers, Tariq Aziz; Taha Yassin Ramadhan; Mohammed Hamza al-Zubeidi
Agriculture and Irrigation, Abdulillah Hameed Mahmoud Saleh
Culture and Information, Abd-al-Ghani Abd-al-Ghafur
Defence, Lt-Gen. Sultan Hashim Ahmed
Education, Abduljabbar Tawfig Mohammed
Finance, Hikmat Mezban Ibrahim
Foreign Affairs, Mohammed Saaed al-Sahhaf
Health, Umeed Madhat Mubarak
Higher Education and Scientific Research, Humam Abdel-Khaliq Ghafuras
Housing and Construction, Maan Abdullah Sarsam
Industry and Minerals, Adnan Abdul-Majeed Jassim
Interior, Muhammad Zimam Abdul-Razzaq
Irrigation, Mohamoud Diyab al-Ahmad
Justice, Shabib al-Maliki
Labour and Social Affairs, Latif Nassif Jassem
Oil, Lt.-Gen. Amir Muhammad Rashid
Religious Endowments and Religious Affairs, Abdul-Muneim Ahmed Saleh
Trade, Muhammed Mahdi Salih

Transport and Communications, Ahmed Murtada Ahmed Khalil

IRAQI DIPLOMATIC MISSION IN LONDON

Since Iraq's breach of diplomatic relations with Britain in February 1991, the Jordanian Embassy has handled Iraqi interests in the UK.

BRITISH DIPLOMATIC REPRESENTATION

The British Embassy was closed in January 1991. The Russian Embassy has since handled British interests in Iraq.

DEFENCE

The Army has roughly 2,700 main battle tanks, 2,900 armoured personnel carriers and armoured infantry fighting vehicles, 1,950 artillery pieces and 120 armed helicopters. The Navy has one frigate and seven patrol and coastal vessels at two bases.

In 1991, the UN demanded the destruction of all weapons of mass destruction and their means of production as a prerequisite for the lifting of sanctions. By mid-1995 it was believed that nearly all these weapons had been destroyed and a long-term monitoring operation was under way to ensure production did not restart. In late 1995, evidence of a ballistic missile programme and large biological weapons stockpiles was discovered.
MILITARY EXPENDITURE – 14.8 per cent of GDP (1995)
MILITARY PERSONNEL – 417,500: Army 350,000, Navy 2,500, Air Force 30,000, Paramilitaries 35,000
CONSCRIPTION DURATION – 18 – 24 months

ECONOMY

Increasing industrialization is taking place but production has been hampered by war damage and sanctions. Iraq's major industry is oil production which was nationalized in 1972 and usually accounts for approximately 98 per cent of the total government revenue and 45 per cent of GNP. Production was 3.5 million barrels per day in 1979 but has been reduced by war damage from the Iran–Iraq and Gulf wars, the closure of Syrian, Turkish and Saudi pipelines and UN economic sanctions. A £2.2 million deal with Russia was signed in March 1997 to develop the Qurnah oilfield in southern Iraq.

Agricultural production is important, with two harvests usually gathered in a year, depending on rainfall. Salinity and soil erosion limit productivity.

The UN imposed economic sanctions and a world-wide ban on Iraqi oil exports in August 1990. In May 1996, Iraq agreed to a UN-proposed 'oil-for-food' deal, permitting the sale of £2.6 billion of oil a year to buy food and medicine. Limited oil exports resumed in December 1996. Thirty per cent of the revenue will pay for reparations to Gulf War victims, up to 15 per cent will provide aid to Iraqi Kurds.
GDP – US$26,141 million (1992); US$3,556 per capita (1992)
ANNUAL AVERAGE GROWTH OF GDP – –7.2 per cent (1989)

TRADE

The principal imports are normally iron and steel, military equipment, building materials, mechanical and electrical machinery, motor vehicles, textiles and clothing, essential foodstuffs and raw industrial materials. The chief exports are normally crude petroleum, dates, raw wool, raw hides and skins and raw cotton.

Trade with UK	1995	1996
Imports from UK	£5,044,000	£10,927,000
Exports to UK	164,000	105,000

COMMUNICATIONS

The port of Basra has not been used since the outbreak of hostilities with Iran in 1980. Continuous dredging of the Shatt-al-Arab has also been suspended by hostilities and the channel has seriously silted. The port of Umm Qasr on the Kuwaiti border, which was developed for freight and sulphur handling and includes a container terminal, was opened in late 1993. All external borders, except that of Jordan, are closed to Iraqi traffic.

There is an international airport at Baghdad. Iraqi Airways provided flights between Baghdad and London, and other international airlines operated to Europe. Iraqi Republican Railways provided regular passenger and goods services between Basra, Baghdad and Mosul. There is also a metre gauge rail line connecting Baghdad with Khanaqin, Kirkuk and Arbil.

Iraqi communications were greatly affected by the Gulf War; large numbers of bridges were destroyed and the railway system extensively disrupted.

REPUBLIC OF IRELAND
Poblacht Na hEireann

AREA – 27,136 sq. miles (70,283 sq. km)

POPULATION – 3,626,087 (1996 census). At the 1991 census religious adherence was: Roman Catholic, 3,228,327; Church of Ireland, 89,187; Presbyterians, 13,199; Methodists, 5,037; others, 189,969. Irish is the first official language and English is recognized as a second official language, but is more commonly used

CAPITAL – ΨDublin (*Baile Atha Cliath*), (population, 952,700, 1996 census)

MAJOR CITIES – ΨCork (180,000); ΨLimerick (79,100); ΨGalway (57,400); Waterford (44,200), 1996 census

CURRENCY – Punt (IR£) of 100 pence

NATIONAL ANTHEM – Amhrán na BhFiann (The Soldier's Song)

NATIONAL DAY – 17 March (St Patrick's Day)

NATIONAL FLAG – Equal vertical stripes of green, white and orange

LIFE EXPECTANCY (years) – male 72.30; female 77.87

POPULATION GROWTH RATE – 0.5 per cent (1994)

POPULATION DENSITY – 51 per sq. km (1994)

URBAN POPULATION – 57.0 per cent (1991)

MILITARY EXPENDITURE – 1.2 per cent of GDP (1995)

MILITARY PERSONNEL – 12,700: Army 10,500, Navy 1,100, Air Force 1,100

CONSCRIPTION DURATION – Voluntary, three-year terms

Ireland is separated from Scotland by the North Channel and from England and Wales by the Irish Sea and St George's Channel. The greatest length of the island, from north-east to south-west (Torr Head to Mizen Head), is 302 miles, and the greatest breadth, from east to west (Dundrum Bay to Annagh Head), is 174 miles. On the north coast of Achill Island (Co. Mayo) are the highest cliffs in the British Isles, 2,000 feet sheer above the sea.

The highest point is Carrantuohill (3,414 ft). The principal river is the Shannon (240 miles), which drains the central plain. The Slaney flows into Wexford Harbour, the Liffey to Dublin Bay, the Boyne to Drogheda, the Lee to Cork Harbour, the Blackwater to Youghal Harbour, and the Suir, Barrow and Nore to Waterford Harbour.

The principal hydrographic feature is the loughs; the Shannon chain of Allen, Boderg, Forbes, Ree and Derg, and the Erne chain of Gowna, Oughter, Lower Erne, and Erne; Melvin, Gill, Gara and Conn in the north-west; and Corrib and Mask (joined by a hidden channel) in the west.

The Republic of Ireland is divided into four provinces of 26 counties: Leinster (Carlow, Dublin, Kildare, Kilkenny, Laoighis, Longford, Louth, Meath, Offaly, Westmeath, Wexford and Wicklow); Munster (Clare, Cork, Kerry, Limerick, Tipperary and Waterford); Connacht (Galway, Leitrim, Mayo, Roscommon and Sligo); and part of Ulster (Cavan, Donegal and Monaghan).

HISTORY AND POLITICS

The first inhabitants of Ireland, hunters from mainland Britain, arrived in 7,000 BC, and were joined by Celts from central Europe from the sixth century BC until about the time of Christ. The introduction of Christianity in the fifth century is traditionally associated with St Patrick and inspired 300 years of rich cultural achievements. The Vikings, who established most of the major towns, including Dublin and Cork, invaded around AD 800 and controlled Ireland until their defeat at the Battle of Clontarf (1014) by Brian Boru, who had become king of all Ireland in 1002.

In the 12th century the Norman English invaded at the invitation of Dermod MacMurrough, the deposed king of Leinster, and established feudal control over most of the island; this lasted for 300 years. King Henry VIII of England reconquered Ireland and in 1541 declared himself king of Ireland, the first English monarch to do so. Protestantism was introduced but failed to take root, except in Ulster where English and Scottish Presbyterians settled during the reign of James I (1603–25). A rebellion initiated by Ulster Catholics in 1641 was ruthlessly crushed by Oliver Cromwell's army. Catholicism was repressed and further Protestant colonization encouraged. Following the abdication of the Catholic King James II in 1688, Irish Protestants supported William of Orange's accession to the throne. James II was defeated in Ireland, most famously at the Battle of the Boyne (1690), and Protestant ascendancy was restored, enduring throughout the 18th century.

The Irish parliament was granted independence in 1782, although the Dublin administration was still appointed by the king. The parliament was abolished by the Act of Union in 1801 following a rebellion by the Society of the United Irishmen in 1798, and subsequently Irish MPs sat at Westminster. Demands for the restoration of the Irish parliament and home rule for Ireland were successful in 1914, but were delayed when World War I broke out. A rebellion, the Easter Rising of 1916, was suppressed by the British, fuelling support for the *Sinn Féin* party, which won the 1918 election in Ireland and withdrew from the British parliament to form a legislature in Dublin under the leadership of Éamon de Valera. The resulting two-year war of independence between the Irish Republican Army and British forces ended in a truce, followed by negotiations leading to the signing of the Anglo-Irish Treaty in December 1921. The island was partitioned, the 26 counties of the Irish Free State accepting dominion status within the British Empire, while six of the nine counties of Ulster, where the majority Protestant population opposed home rule, remained part of the United Kingdom, governed by a Northern Ireland parliament.

Civil war broke out between the new Irish government and opponents of the treaty until a truce was reached in May 1923. Constitutional links between the Irish Free State and the UK were gradually removed by the Irish parliament and a new constitution enacted in 1937 declared the Irish Free State a sovereign, independent state with a republican government. However, it continued in association with the states of the British Commonwealth until 1949, when the last constitutional links with Britain were severed and the state was renamed the Republic of Ireland.

The composition of the Dáil Eireann following the last general election on 6 June 1997 was: Fianna Fáil 77, Fine Gael 54; Labour 17; Democratic Left 4; Progressive Democrats 4; Green Party 2; Sinn Fein 1; others 7. Fianna Fail and the Progressive Democrats formed a coalition government.

POLITICAL SYSTEM

The 1937 constitution declares the national territory to be the whole island of Ireland, but that pending the reintegration of the national territory, laws enacted by Parliament will apply in the area which constituted the Irish Free State, i.e. not in the six counties of Northern Ireland.

The president (*Uachtarán na hÉireann*) is directly elected for a term of seven years, and is eligible for a second term. The president is aided and advised by a Council of State.

The National Parliament (*Oireachtas*) consists of the president, House of Representatives (*Dáil Éireann*) and Senate (*Seanad Éireann*). Dáil Éireann is composed of 166 members elected for a five-year term on a basis of proportional representation by means of the single transferable vote. Seanad Éireann is composed of 60 members, of whom 11 are nominated by the taoiseach and 49 are elected, six by institutions of higher education and 43 from panels of candidates established on a vocational basis.

Executive power is vested in the government subject to the constitution. The government is responsible to the Dáil. The taoiseach is appointed by the president on the nomination of the Dáil. The other members of the government are appointed by the president on the nomination of the taoiseach with the previous approval of

the Dáil. The taoiseach appoints a member of the government to be his deputy (the *tánaiste*).

The judicial system comprises courts of first instance and a court of final appeal called the Supreme Court (*Cúirt Uachtarach*). The courts of first instance include a High Court (*Ard-Chúirt*) and courts of local and limited jurisdiction, with a right of appeal as determined by law. The High Court alone has original jurisdiction to consider the question of the validity of any law having regard to the provisions of the constitution. The Supreme Court has appellate jurisdiction from decisions of the High Court.

HEAD OF STATE
President, Mary Robinson, *assumed office* 3 December 1990

CABINET *as at July 1997*
Taoiseach (PM), Bertie Ahern
Tánaiste (Deputy PM), *Enterprise and Employment*, Mary Harney
Agriculture, Food and Forestry, Joe Walsh
Arts, Culture and the Gaeltacht, Síle de Valera
Attorney-General, David Byrne
Defence, David Andrews
Education, Michael Martin
Environment, Noel Dempsey
Finance, Charlie McCreevy
Foreign Affairs, Ray Burke
Health, Brian Cowen
Justice and Equality, Law Reform, John O'Donoghue
Marine, Michael Woods
Minister of State, Government Chief Whip, Séamus Brennan
Minister of State to the Government, Robert Molloy
Social Welfare, Dermot Ahern
Tourism and Trade, Jim McDaid
Transport, Energy and Communications, Mary O'Rourke

IRISH EMBASSY
17 Grosvenor Place, London SW1X 7HR
Tel 0171-235 2171
Ambassador Extraordinary and Plenipotentiary, HE Edward Barrington, apptd 1995
Counsellor, E. Carcy (*Economic and Commercial*)

BRITISH EMBASSY
31 Merrion Road, Dublin 4
Tel: Dublin 205 3700
Ambassador Extraordinary and Plenipotentiary, HE Veronica Sutherland, CMG, apptd 1995
Counsellor and Deputy Head of Mission, R. I. Clarke
Defence Attaché, Col. S. D. Lambe, CBE
First Secretary (Commercial), R. N. J. Baker

BRITISH COUNCIL REPRESENTATIVE, Harold Fish, OBE, Newmount House, 22/24 Lower Mount Street, Dublin 2

ECONOMY

Although industry has expanded greatly since Ireland's entry into the European Community in 1973, agriculture remains important; in 1996, 10 per cent of the workforce was employed in agriculture. The main crops are wheat, barley, potatoes and sugar beet. Agriculture has benefited considerably from the EU Common Agricultural Policy and support funds but has suffered from the drift of the rural population to urban areas and abroad.

Industry accounted for about 38 per cent of GNP and about 27 per cent of employment in 1996. The traditional brewing, spirits and food-processing sectors have expanded and have been joined by the manufacture of textiles, chemicals, pharmaceuticals, electronics, office machinery and transportation equipment. The services sector is currently the fastest-growing sector of the economy and accounted for 58 per cent of GNP and 62 per cent of employment in 1996. Tourism is the most important part of the service sector and in recent years has provided substantial revenue, with over four million visitors in 1995.

The lack of energy resources has been minimised over the past 15 years by the discovery of two natural gas fields off the south coast, which now supply all the country's natural gas needs but are expected to be depleted by around 2000, and by the opening of seven government-funded milled peat power-generating stations. Hydro-electric power from the Shannon barrage and other schemes is also important but Ireland still imports 54 per cent of oil and coal for power generation.

Metal content of ores raised (1996) was lead, 45,300 tonnes; zinc, 164,200 tonnes; silver 14,700,000 grammes. An estimated 15,500 persons were employed in the fisheries in 1996.

Animal products, dairy products and livestock, especially cattle, are the main exports. The UK, USA, Germany, France and Japan are Ireland's main trading partners.

In 1993 Ireland had a trade surplus of US$8,172 million and a current account surplus of US$3,735 million. In 1995 imports totalled US$32,300 million and exports US$43,681 million.

GNP – US$52,765 million (1995); US$14,710 per capita (1995)
GDP – US$48,161 million (1992); US$14,484 per capita (1992)
ANNUAL AVERAGE GROWTH OF GDP – 10.3 per cent (1995)
INFLATION RATE – 2.5 per cent (1995)
UNEMPLOYMENT – 12.15 per cent (1995)

Trade with UK	1995	1996
Imports from UK	£7,331,300,000	£8,272,700,000
Exports to UK	6,651,500,000	6,825,000,000

COMMUNICATIONS

In 1996 there were 1,945 km of railway operated by *Iarnród*. In 1995 the number of ships with cargo which arrived at Irish ports was 15,890 (45,968,000 net registered tons); of these 2,438 (7,962,000 net registered tons) were of Irish nationality.

Shannon Airport, Co. Limerick, is on the main trans-atlantic air route. In 1995 the airport handled 1,571,385 passengers. Dublin Airport serves the cross-channel and European services operated by the Irish national airline Aer Lingus and other airlines. In 1995 the airport handled 8,024,894 passengers. In 1995 Cork Airport handled 971,319 passengers.

EDUCATION

Primary education is directed by the state, with the exception of 64 private primary schools. There were 3,317 state-aided primary schools in 1995–6.

In 1995–6 there were 445 recognized secondary schools under private management (mainly religious orders), and 246 vocational schools. There were 16 state comprehensive schools and 61 community schools.

Third-level education is catered for by seven university colleges, and also by third-level courses offered by the technical colleges and regional technical colleges and other third-level institutions.

ENROLMENT (percentage of age group) – primary 100 per cent; secondary 84 per cent; tertiary 36.4 per cent (1993)

ISRAEL
Medinat Israel

AREA – 8,130 sq. miles (21,056 sq. km). Neighbours: Lebanon (north), Syria (north-east), Jordan and the West Bank (east), the Gaza Strip and the Egyptian province of Sinai (south-west)
POPULATION – 5,383,000 (1994 UN estimate): roughly 82 per cent Jewish, 14 per cent Arab Muslims, 2.5 per cent Christians of which 90 per cent are Arab, and 2 per cent Druze. Since independence Israel has had a policy of granting an immigration visa to every Jew who expresses a desire to settle in Israel. Between 1948 and 1992, 2.3 million immigrants had entered Israel from over 100 different countries. Hebrew and Arabic are the official languages. Arabs are entitled to transact all official business with government departments in Arabic
CAPITAL – Most of the government departments are in Jerusalem, population 662,700 (1995 estimate). A resolution proclaiming Jerusalem as the capital of Israel was adopted by the *Knesset* in 1950. It is not, however, recognized as the capital by the UN because East Jerusalem is part of the Occupied Territories captured in 1967. The UN and international law continues to reject the Israeli annexation of East Jerusalem and considers the pre-1950 capital Tel Aviv (population, 1,812,100) to be the capital
MAJOR CITIES – ΨHaifa (and district 491,000) and Beersheba (and district 122,000)
CURRENCY – Shekel of 100 agora
NATIONAL ANTHEM – Hatikvah (The Hope)
NATIONAL FLAG – White, with two horizontal blue stripes, the Shield of David in the centre
LIFE EXPECTANCY (years) – male 74.75; female 78.40
POPULATION GROWTH RATE – 3.6 per cent (1994)
POPULATION DENSITY – 256 per sq. km (1994)
URBAN POPULATION – 89.8 per cent (1993)

Israel comprises the hill country of Galilee and parts of Judea and Samaria, rising to heights of nearly 4,000 ft; the coastal plain from the Gaza strip to north of Acre, including the plain of Esdraelon running from Haifa Bay to the south-east which divides the hill region; the Negev, a semi-desert triangular-shaped region, extending from a base south of Beersheba, to an apex at the head of the Gulf of Aqaba; and parts of the Jordan valley, including the Hula region, Tiberias and the south-western extremity of the Dead Sea.

The principal river is the Jordan, which rises from three main sources in Israel, the Lebanon and Syria, and flows through the Hula valley, Lake Tiberias/Kinneret (Sea of Galilee) and the Jordan Valley into the Dead Sea, falling 1,517 ft from Hulata to the Dead Sea. The other principal rivers are the Yarkon and Kishon. The Dead Sea is a lake (shared between Israel, the West Bank and Jordan), 1,286 ft below sea-level; it has no outlet, the surplus being carried off by evaporation.

The climate is variable, modified by altitude and distance from the sea, with hot summers and rainy winters.

HISTORY AND POLITICS

The Ottoman Empire province of Palestine was captured by British forces in 1917, the same year that the British Government issued the Balfour Declaration which 'viewed with favour the establishment of a national home for the Jewish people in Palestine'. The Balfour Declaration's terms were enshrined in Britain's League of Nations mandate over Palestine, leading to steady Jewish

immigration in the inter-war years and a post-1945 flood by Nazi concentration camp survivors. The Arab Palestinian population revolted against Jewish immigration from 1936 onwards, while Jewish groups conducted a terrorist campaign against the British administration from 1945 onwards.

In 1947 Britain announced its withdrawal from Palestine with effect from May 1948, handing over to the UN responsibility for resolving the conflict between Arabs and Jews. Both sides ignored the UN partition plan; on the withdrawal of British forces on 14 May 1948 the State of Israel was proclaimed and the first Arab-Israeli war began. By the time of the January 1949 cease-fire Israeli forces controlled all of the former mandate territory apart from the West Bank (and East Jerusalem) and the Gaza Strip, which had come under Jordanian and Egyptian control respectively.

During the 1967 Six-Day War Israel captured the West Bank and the Gaza Strip, together with Sinai from Egypt and the Golan Heights from Syria, and annexed East Jerusalem. Israel held on to its gains in the 1973 Yom Kippur War. The Golan Heights were annexed in 1981; Sinai was returned to Egypt in 1982 in accordance with the 1979 Israeli–Egyptian peace treaty, and the South Lebanon Security Zone was established after the 1982–5 invasion of Lebanon. The annexations of East Jerusalem and the Golan Heights remain unrecognized internationally.

The Labour leader of the coalition government formed after the 1992 general election, Yitzhak Rabin, was assassinated by a Jewish extremist on 4 November 1995, and was replaced by Foreign Minister Shimon Peres. A general election on 29 May 1996, the first to have separate ballots for the prime minister and legislature, was won by Likud leader Benjamin Netanyahu, although no party

gained outright control of the Knesset. Netanyahu formed an eight-party coalition government which commanded 66 seats in the Knesset.

FOREIGN RELATIONS

A peace process started in October 1991 in Madrid led to agreements with the Palestine Liberation Organization (*see* page 905), and with Jordan on 14 September 1993. A full peace agreement with Jordan was signed on 26 October 1994 and provides for the return to Jordan of land occupied by Israel since 1967 in the southern Araba valley (completed 9 February 1995).

Intermittent peace talks with Syria have stumbled over control of the Golan Heights and Israel's role in southern Lebanon.

POLITICAL SYSTEM

Israel is a sovereign democratic republic with executive power vested in a prime minister and Cabinet, and legislative power in a unicameral legislature (*Knesset*) of 120 members elected by proportional representation for a maximum term of four years. The prime minister is elected separately from the legislature. The president is head of state and is elected by the Knesset for a maximum of two five-year terms.

HEAD OF STATE

President of Israel, Ezer Weizmann, *elected* 24 March 1993, *inaugurated* 13 May 1993

CABINET *as at July 1997*

Prime Minister, Construction and Housing, Benjamin Netanyahu (L)
Deputy PM, Agriculture and Rural Development, Environment, Rafael Eitan (L)
Deputy PM, Foreign Affairs, David Levy (L)
Deputy PM, Education, Culture and Sport, Zevulun Hammer (NRP)
Deputy PM, Tourism, Moshe Katsav (L)
Communications, Limor Livnat (L)
Defence, Yitzhak Mordechai (L)
Finance, Prof. Yaacov Ne'eman (Ind.)
Health, Yehoshua Matza (L)
Immigrant Absorption, Yuli Edelstein (YB)
Industry and Trade, Natan Sharansky (YB)
Interior and Religious Affairs, Eli Suissa (S)
Justice, Tzachi Hanegbi (L)
Labour and Social Affairs, Eliyahu Yishai (S)
National Infrastructure, Ariel Sharon (L)
Public Security, Avigdor Kahalani (TW)
Science, Michael Eitan (L)
Transportation, Yitzhak Levy (NRP)

L Likud; NRP National Religious Party; S Shas; TW Third Way; YB Yisrael Ba'aliya; Ind. Independent

EMBASSY OF ISRAEL
2 Palace Green, Kensington, London w8 4QB
Tel 0171–957 9500
Ambassador Extraordinary and Plenipotentiary, HE Moshe Raviv, apptd 1993
Minister Plenipotentiary, A. Magid
Defence Attaché, Brig.-Gen. I. Chen
Minister, M. Bar-On (*Consular*)
Counsellor, A. Wohl (*Commercial*)

BRITISH EMBASSY
192 Hayarkon Street, Tel Aviv 63405
Tel: Tel Aviv 5249171
Ambassador Extraordinary and Plenipotentiary,
HE David G. Manning, CMG, apptd 1995

Counsellor, Consul-General and Deputy Head of Mission, S.
Pease
Defence and Military Attaché, Col. E. Houstoun, OBE
First Secretary (Commercial), W. W. Magor
CONSULATE-GENERAL – East Jerusalem (Occupied
Territories); Consular Offices – Tel Aviv, Eilat

BRITISH COUNCIL DIRECTOR, H. Brookes, 140 Hayarkon
Street, PO Box 3302, Tel Aviv 61032
ISRAEL -BRITISH CHAMBER OF COMMERCE, 76 IBN Guirol
Street, Tel Aviv 64162

DEFENCE

Israel is believed to have a nuclear capacity of around 100
warheads which could be delivered by aircraft and Jericho
I and II missiles.

The Army has 4,300 main battle tanks, more than 9,000
armoured personnel carriers and 1,550 artillery pieces.
The Navy has two submarines and 55 patrol and coastal
vessels at three bases. The Air Force has 449 combat
aircraft and 116 armed helicopters.
MILITARY EXPENDITURE – 9.2 per cent of GDP (1995)
MILITARY PERSONNEL – 175,000: Army 134,000, Navy
9,000, Air Force 32,000
CONSCRIPTION DURATION – 21–48 months (Jews and
Druze only)

ECONOMY

The country is generally fertile although water supply for
irrigation restricts production. Agriculture accounts for 5
per cent of GNP and 4 per cent of exports.

The 'Jaffa' orange is produced in large quantities for
export, along with other summer fruits, seasonal vegetables and glasshouse crops. Olives are cultivated, mainly for
the production of oil. The main winter crops are wheat,
barley and various kinds of pulses, while in summer
sorghum, millet, maize, sesame and summer pulses are
grown. Beef, cattle and poultry farming have been developed. Tobacco and medium staple cotton are now grown.

In value polished diamonds account for about 23 per
cent of total exports. Amongst the most important industries are textiles, foodstuffs and chemicals (mainly fertilizers and pharmaceuticals). Metal-working and science-
based industries are sophisticated and technologically
advanced and include the aircraft and military industries.
Other important manufacturing industries include plastics, rubber, cement, glass, paper and oil refining. Industry
accounts for 30 per cent of GNP and 60 per cent of exports.

In 1994 the government had a budget deficit equivalent
to 3.11 per cent of GDP.
GNP – US$87,875 million (1995); US$15,920 per capita
(1995)
GDP – US$63,154 million (1992); US$13,522 per capita
(1992)
ANNUAL AVERAGE GROWTH OF GDP – 6.5 per cent (1994)
INFLATION RATE – 10.0 per cent (1995)
UNEMPLOYMENT – 6.9 per cent (1995)

TRADE

The principal imports are foodstuffs, crude oil, machinery
and vehicles, iron, steel and manufactures thereof, and
chemicals. The principal exports are metal machinery,
electronic goods, chemicals, rubber, plastics, textiles, food
and beverages, minerals, citrus produce and polished
diamonds.

In 1994 Israel had a trade deficit of US$6,141 million and
a current account deficit of US$4,008 million. In 1995
imports totalled US$29,632 million and exports
US$19,028 million.

Trade with UK	1995	1996
Imports from UK	£1,108,455,000	£1,265,773,000
Exports to UK	692,156,000	831,845,000

COMMUNICATIONS

Israel State Railways serves Haifa, Tel Aviv, Jerusalem,
Lod, Nahariya, Beersheba, Dimona, Ashdod and intermediate stations with a network of 528 km. There were
12,823 km of paved road in 1986. A major road building
programme has been underway in the West Bank since
1992.

The chief ports are Haifa and Ashdod on the Mediterranean, and Eilat on the Red Sea; Acre has an anchorage for
small vessels. The chief international airport is Ben
Gurion between Tel Aviv and Jerusalem.

EDUCATION

Education from six to 16 years is free and compulsory. The
law also provides for working youth age 16–18, who for
some reason have not completed their education, to be
exempted from work in order to do so. There are seven
universities including two engineering and technological
institutes.
ILLITERACY RATE – 4.4 per cent
ENROLMENT (percentage of age group) – tertiary 34.2 per
cent (1993)

CULTURE

Important historic sites in Israel include: Jerusalem – the
Church of the Holy Sepulchre, the Al Aqsa Mosque and
Dome of the Rock standing on the remains of the Temple
Mount of Herod the Great of which the Western (wailing)
Wall is a fragment, the Church of the Dormition and the
Coenaculum on Mount Zion, Ein Karem, Church of the
Visitation, Church of St John the Baptist; Galilee – the Sea,
Church and Mount of the Beatitudes, ruins of Capernaum
and other sites connected with the life of Christ; Mount
Tabor – Church of the Transfiguration; Nazareth – Church
of the Annunciation, and other Christian shrines associ-
ated with the childhood of Christ; there are also numerous
sites dating from biblical and medieval days, such as
Ascalon, Caesarea, Atlit, Massada, Megiddo and Hazor.

PALESTINIAN AUTONOMOUS AREAS

AREA – The total area is 2,406 sq. miles (6,231 sq. km). The
area which is fully autonomous is 159 sq. miles (412 sq.
km), of which the Gaza Strip is 136 sq. miles (352 sq. km)
and the Jericho enclave 23 sq. miles (60 sq. km). The
partially autonomous area is the remainder of the West
Bank, some 2,247 sq. miles (5,819 sq. km). The UN and
the international community also recognize East
Jerusalem as part of the Occupied Territories
POPULATION – 1,635,000 (1992 estimate), of whom
660,000 live in the Gaza Strip, 40,000 in Jericho, and
935,000 in the remainder of the West Bank. In addition
there are 141,000 Jewish settlers in the West Bank and
4,000 in the Gaza Strip who remain under Israeli
administration and jurisdiction. Some 90 per cent of
Palestinians are Muslim (the vast majority Sunni) and 10
per cent are Christians
CAPITAL – Although Palestinians claim East Jerusalem as
their capital, the administrative capital has been
established in Gaza City (120,000)
MAJOR TOWNS – Khan Yunis and Rafah in the Gaza Strip;
Nablus, Hebron, Jericho, Ramallah and Bethlehem on
the West Bank

FLAG – Three horizontal stripes of black, white, green with a red triangle based on the hoist (the PLO flag)
NATIONAL ANTHEM – Biladi, Biladi (My Country, My Country)

HISTORY AND POLITICS

Israel captured the Gaza Strip, East Jerusalem and the West Bank during the 1967 Six-Day War and annexed East Jerusalem. After the war the Israeli government began to establish settlements in the Occupied Territories. Palestinian resistance to Israeli rule was led by the Palestine Liberation Organization (PLO) which was established in 1964. Frustration at continued Israeli occupation led to the start of the *intifada*, a campaign of sustained unrest, in 1987. When the 1991 Madrid peace process stalled, Israeli and PLO officials engaged in secret negotiations in Norway which led to the signing of the 'Declaration of Principles on Interim Self-Government Arrangements' on 13 September 1993. Under this agreement the PLO renounced terrorism and recognized Israel's right to exist in secure borders, while Israel recognized the PLO as the legitimate representative of the Palestinian people.

The Declaration of Principles established a timetable for progress towards a final settlement: negotiations leading to an Israeli military withdrawal from the Gaza Strip and Jericho by 13 April 1994, when power was to be transferred to a nominated Palestinian National Authority (PNA); elections to a new Palestinian Council, which would also exercise control over six policy areas in the rest of the West Bank (culture, tourism, health, education, social welfare, direct taxation), and the Israeli military administration dissolved by 13 July 1994; negotiations on a permanent settlement, including Jewish settlers and East Jerusalem, to begin by 13 April 1996; and a permanent settlement to be in place by 13 April 1999.

The timetable has slipped, with the Israeli military not finally redeploying in the Gaza Strip and withdrawing from Jericho until 18 May 1994, when the five-year period of interim self-government under the PNA began.

Israel and the Palestinians struggled to reach agreement on the extension of self-rule until 28 September 1995, when the 'Oslo B' or Taba Accord was signed which provided for Israeli withdrawal from six towns and 85 per cent of Hebron; the extension of self-rule to most of the West Bank by 1998; the release of 5,300 Palestinian prisoners; and the striking out of the demand for Israel's destruction from the PLO's charter. On 29 December 1995 an agreement was reached on the transfer of 17 areas of civilian power to the PNA in Hebron.

Implementation of the agreement began with the release of 1,100 Palestinian prisoners in October 1995; Israeli troops left Ramallah, the last of the six West Bank towns, on 27 December 1995 and the inaugural Palestinian National Council meeting on 23 April 1996 voted to amend the PLO charter. The final element of the Declaration of Principles, the 'final status talks' opened in Taba, Egypt, on 5 May 1996 to decide the final status of the West Bank, Gaza and Jerusalem. The election of a Likud-led government opposed to the establishment of a Palestinian state resulted in a deadlock in negotiations in 1997 and delays in the withdrawal of Israeli troops from Hebron.

Legislative elections on 20 January 1996 were won by the mainstream al-Fatah faction of the PLO, with its leader Yasser Arafat winning 88.1 per cent of the vote to become the leader. *See also* Events of the Year.

POLITICAL SYSTEM

The Oslo B accord laid down the political structure of the nascent Palestinian state. Executive authority is vested in the Palestinian National Authority which is headed by a popularly elected leader (*rais*). Legislative authority is vested in the 88-member Palestinian Council which is directly elected by means of a first-past-the-post system, and itself elects the four-fifths of the PNA not appointed by the leader.

PALESTINIAN NATIONAL AUTHORITY *as at July 1997*
Leader, Yasser Arafat
Agriculture, Abdul Jawad Saleh
Civil Affairs, Jamil Tarifi
Culture and Arts, Yasser Abed Rabbo
Economy and Trade, Maher al-Masri
Education, Yaser Amro
Finance, Muhamad Zuhdi Nashashibi
Health, Dr Riyad Za'noun
Higher Education, Dr Hanan Ashrawi
Housing, Abdul Rahman Hamad
Industry, Bashir Barghouthi
Information, Yasser Abed Rabbo
Interior, vacant
Justice, Freih Abu Meddien
Labour, Dr Samir Ghosheh
Local Government, Sa'eb Erekat
Planning and International Co-operation, Nabil Sha'ath
Post and Telecommunication, Imad Falouji
Public Works, Azzam al-Ahmad
Social Affairs, Intisar al-Wazir
Supplies, Abdul Aziz Shaheen
Transport, Ali Qawasmi
Tourism and Archaeology, Elias Freij
Waqf and Religious Affairs, Hassan Tahboob
Youth and Sports, vacant

BRITISH CONSULATE-GENERAL
19 Nashashibi Street, PO Box 19690, East Jerusalem 97200
Consul-General, R. J. Dalton

BRITISH COUNCIL DIRECTOR, P. Skelton, OBE (*Cultural Attaché*), Al-Nuzha Building, 2 Abu Obeida Street, PO Box 19136, Jerusalem

ITALY
Repubblica Italiana

AREA – 116,320 sq. miles (301,268 sq. km). Neighbours: Switzerland and Austria (north), Slovenia (east), France (west)

POPULATION – 57,193,000 (1994 UN estimate). The language is Italian, a Romance language derived from Latin. It is spoken in its purest form in Tuscany, but there are numerous dialects, showing variously French, German, Spanish and Arabic influences. Sard, the dialect of Sardinia, is accorded by some authorities the status of a distinct Romance language

CAPITAL – Rome (population, 2,693,383, 1991). The Eternal City was founded, according to legend, by Romulus in 753 BC. It was the centre of Latin civilization and capital of the Roman Republic and Roman Empire

MAJOR CITIES – Milan (1,371,008); ΨNaples (1,054,601); Turin (961,916); ΨGenoa (675,639); Bologna (404,322); Florence (402,316); *Sicily,* ΨPalermo (697,162); *Sardinia,* ΨCagliari (203,254), 1991 census

CURRENCY – Lira of 100 centesimi
NATIONAL ANTHEM – Inno di Mameli
NATIONAL DAY – 2 June
NATIONAL FLAG – Vertical stripes of green, white and red
LIFE EXPECTANCY (years) – male 73.50; female 80.03

POPULATION GROWTH RATE – –0.2 per cent (1994)
POPULATION DENSITY – 190 per sq. km (1994)
URBAN POPULATION – 96.6 per cent (1991)

Italy consists of a peninsula, the islands of Sicily, Sardinia, Elba and about 70 other small islands. The peninsula is for the most part mountainous, but between the Apennines, which form its spine, and the east coastline are two large fertile plains: Emilia/Romagna in the north and Apulia in the south. The Alps divide Italy from France, Switzerland, Austria and Slovenia. Partly within the Italian borders are Monte Rosa (15,217 ft), the Matterhorn (14,780 ft) and several peaks from 12,000 to 14,000 ft. The chief rivers are the Po (405 miles), flowing through Piedmont, Lombardy and the Veneto; the Adige (Trentino and Veneto); the Arno (Florentine plain); the Tiber (flowing through Rome to Ostia).

HISTORY AND POLITICS

Italian unity was accomplished under the House of Savoy after a struggle from 1848 to 1870 in which Mazzini (1805–72), Garibaldi (1807–82) and Cavour (1810–61) were the principal figures. It was completed when Lombardy was ceded by Austria in 1859 and Venice in 1866, and through the evacuation of Rome by the French in 1870. In 1871 the King of Italy entered Rome, and that city was declared to be the capital.

A fascist regime came to power in 1922 under Benito Mussolini, known as Il Duce (The Leader), who was prime minister from 1922 until 25 July 1943, when the regime was abolished. Mussolini was captured by Italian partisans while attempting to escape across the Swiss frontier and killed on 28 April 1945.

In fulfilment of a promise given in April 1944 that he would retire when the Allies entered Rome, a decree was signed in June 1944 by King Victor Emmanuel III under which Prince Umberto, his son, became Lieutenant-General of the Realm. The King remained head of the House of Savoy and retained the title King of Italy until his abdication in May 1946, when he was succeeded by the Crown Prince. A general election was held in June 1946, together with a referendum on the future of the monarchy, in which a majority favoured a republic and the royal family left the country.

Political instability and widespread corruption, often with Mafia links, led to public disenchantment with the major political parties. Their support collapsed in the April 1992 general election, which produced an increase in support for Northern League and anti-Mafia parties. The so-called 'clean hands' investigation into corruption and Mafia links that began in Milan in February 1992 has led to the arrest by magistrates of thousands of politicians and businessmen.

The first general election under the new electoral system, on 27–28 March 1994, resulted in victory for the right-wing Freedom Alliance composed of the new Forza Italia party, the Northern League and the National Alliance. The Forza Italia leader and millionaire businessman Silvio Berlusconi formed a government in May 1994. The coalition government collapsed on 21 December 1994 following Berlusconi's indictment on charges of bribery and corruption. The independent Treasury minister Lamberto Dini formed a government of technocrats in January 1995. Dini resigned on 11 January 1996 and a general election on 21 April 1996 was won by the left-wing Olive Tree alliance led by the Democratic Party of the Left, whose leader, Romano Prodi, became prime minister. The government won 157 seats in the Senate and 284 seats in the Chamber of Deputies where it required the support of the Communist Refoundation to win a vote of confidence.

POLITICAL SYSTEM

The constitution provides for the election of the president for a seven-year term by an electoral college which consists of the two houses of the parliament (the Chamber of Deputies and the Senate) sitting in joint session, together with three delegates from each region (one in the case of the Valle d'Aosta). The president, who must be over 50 years of age, has the right to dissolve one or both houses after consultation with the Speakers. Members of both houses were elected wholly by proportional representation until 1993. Now 75 per cent (232) of the 315 elected seats in the Senate are elected on a first-past-the-post basis and the remaining elected seats are filled by proportional representation. There are 11 life senators, who are past presidents and prime ministers. In the Chamber of Deputies 75 per cent (472) of seats are elected on a first-past-the-post basis, and 25 per cent (158) by proportional representation, with a 4 per cent threshold for parliamentary representation.

HEAD OF STATE

President, Oscar Luigi Scalfaro, elected by electoral college 25 May 1992

COUNCIL OF MINISTERS as at July 1997

Prime Minister, Romano Prodi (IPP)
Deputy P.M., Culture, Walter Veltroni (DPL)
Agriculture, Michele Pinto (IPP)
Defence, Beniamino Andreatta (IPP)
Education, Luigi Berlinguer (DPL)
Environment, Edo Ronchi (Green)
Equal Opportunities, Anna Finocchiaro (DPL)
Family and Social Affairs, Livia Turco (DPL)
Finance, Vincenzo Visco (DPL)
Foreign Affairs, Lamberto Dini (IR)
Foreign Trade, Augusto Fantozzi (IR)
Health, Rosaria Bindi (DPL)
Industry, Pierluigi Bersani (DPL)
Interior, Giorgio Napolitano (DPL)
Justice, Giovanni Maria Flick (Ind.)
Labour, Tiziano Treu (IR)
Post and Telecommunications, Antonio Maccanico

Public Works, Paolo Costa (Ind.)
Regional Affairs, Franco Bassanini (DPL)
Transport, Claudio Burlando (DPL)
Treasury, Budget, Carlo Azeglio Ciampi (Ind.)

DPL Democratic Party of the Left; IPP Italian Popular Party; IR Italian Renewal; Ind. Independent

ITALIAN EMBASSY
14 Three Kings Yard, Davies Street, London WIY 2EH
Tel 0171-312 2200
Ambassador Extraordinary and Plenipotentiary,
HE Dr Paolo Galli, apptd 1995
Minister-Counsellor, A. Armellini
Defence Attaché, P. Rizzo
Cultural Attaché, Prof. B. Bini
Consul-General, L. Savoia
First Counsellor, A. Cevese (*Commercial*)
CONSULAR OFFICES – Bedford, Edinburgh, Manchester

BRITISH EMBASSY
Via XX Settembre 80A, 00187 Rome
Tel: Rome 482-5441
Ambassador Extraordinary and Plenipotentiary,
HE Thomas L. Richardson, CMG, apptd 1996
Deputy Head of Mission, K. G. Bloomfield
Defence and Military Attaché, Brig. J. A. Anderson
*Director-General for British Trade Development in Italy and
Consul-General,* C. De Chassiron (*Milan*)
Counsellor (Economic and Commercial), T. G. Paxman

CONSULATES-GENERAL – Milan, Naples
CONSULATES – Rome, Bari, Florence, Genoa, Trieste,
Turin, Venice, Messina, Brindisi, Palermo, Cagliari

BRITISH COUNCIL REPRESENTATIVE, R. Alford, OBE,
Palazzo del Drago, Via Quattro Fontane 20,
00184 Rome. There are British Council Offices at
Milan, Bologna and Naples

BRITISH CHAMBER OF COMMERCE, Via San Paolo 7,
20121 Milan

DEFENCE

The Army has 1,164 main battle tanks, 2,954 armoured personnel carriers and 1,939 artillery pieces. The Navy has eight submarines, one aircraft carrier, one cruiser, four destroyers, 26 frigates, 16 patrol and coastal vessels, five combat aircraft and 74 armed helicopters. There are ten naval bases. The Air Force has 314 combat aircraft.
MILITARY EXPENDITURE – 1.8 per cent of GDP (1995)
MILITARY PERSONNEL – 471,450: Army 167,250, Navy
44,000, Air Force 68,000, Paramilitaries 192,200
CONSCRIPTION DURATION – 12 months

ECONOMY

Italy is generally poor in mineral resources but deposits of natural methane gas and oil have been discovered, mainly south of Sicily, and rapidly exploited. Production of lignite has also increased. Other minerals include iron ores and pyrites, mercury (over one-quarter of the world production), lead, zinc and aluminium. Rich gold veins were discovered in Sardinia in May 1996. Marble is a traditional product of the Massa Carrara district.

Agricultural production is concentrated in Tuscany, Emilia-Romagna, Sicily and the whole of the southern third of the country. The principal products are wine, tobacco, citrus fruits, tomatoes, almonds, sugar beet, wheat and maize.

Tourism is centred on Rome, Florence, Venice, the Alps, Sicily, the Adriatic coast and the Bay of Naples. The commercial and banking services are concentrated in Rome and in Milan, where the stock market is located.

The state-owned sector of Italian industry is still important, dominated by the holding companies IRI (mechanical, steel, airlines), ENI (petrochemicals), and ENEL (electricity). Industry is centred around Milan (steel, machine tools, motor cars), Turin (motor cars, steel, roller bearings, textiles), Rome (light industries), Venice (shipbuilding, paper, mechanical equipment, electrical goods, woollens), Bologna/Florence (food industry, footwear and textiles, reproduction furniture, glassware, pottery, ceramics), Naples, Bari (valves, vehicle bodies, tyres), Taranto (steel, oil refining), Trieste (shipbuilding) and Cagliari (aluminium production, petrochemicals).

Government economic policy has in recent years focused on introducing austerity measures to enable Italy to join the first wave of countries joining the EU's economic and monetary union.

In 1994 the government had a budget deficit equivalent to 10.51 per cent of GDP, there was a trade surplus of US$35,497 million and a current account surplus of US$14,301 million. In 1995 imports totalled US$204,062 million and exports US$231,336 million.

Italy's chief exports are industrial and agricultural machinery, textiles and clothing, transport and electrical equipment and chemicals. Chief imports are chemicals, transport and electrical equipment, metals and energy. Italy's main trading partners are Germany, France, the UK, the USA and Switzerland.
GNP – US$1,088,085 million (1995); US$19,020 per capita (1995)
GDP – US$1,120,826 million (1992); US$21,177 per capita (1992)
ANNUAL AVERAGE GROWTH OF GDP – 3.0 per cent (1995); forecast to be 2.2 per cent in 1997
INFLATION RATE – 5.2 per cent (1995); forecast to be 3.0 per cent in 1997
UNEMPLOYMENT – 12 per cent (1995); forecast to be 11.5 per cent in 1997

TRADE WITH UK	1995	1996
Imports from UK	£7,436,500,000	£7,659,900,000
Exports to UK	7,834,300,000	8,949,200,000

COMMUNICATIONS

The main railway system is state-run by the *Ferrovia dello Stato*. A network of motorways (*autostrade*) covers the country, built and operated mainly by the IRI state holding company and ANAS, the state highway authority. Alitalia, the principal international and domestic airline, is also state-controlled by the IRI group. Other smaller companies, including ATI (an Alitalia subsidiary) and Air Mediterranea, operate on domestic routes. Genoa is the major port, handling about one-third of Italy's foreign trade.

EDUCATION

Education is free and compulsory between the ages of six and 14; this comprises five years at primary school and three in the 'middle school', of which there are about 8,000. Pupils who obtain the middle school certificate may seek admission to any 'senior secondary school', which may be a lyceum with a classical or scientific or artistic bias, or an institute directed at technology (of which there are eight different types), trade or industry (including vocational schools), or teacher-training. Courses at the lyceums and technical institutes usually last for five years and success in the final examination qualifies for admission to university.

There are 35 state and 14 private universities, some of ancient foundation; those at Bologna, Modena, Parma and Padua were started in the 12th century. University education is not free, but entrants with higher qualifications are charged reduced fees according to a sliding scale.

In general, schools, lyceums and universities are financed by local taxation and central government grants.

ILLITERACY RATE – 1.9 per cent
ENROLMENT (percentage of age group) – tertiary 37.3 per cent (1993)

CULTURE

Florence, the capital of Tuscany, was one of the greatest cities in Europe from the 11th to the 16th centuries, and the cradle of the Renaissance. Under the Medici family in the 15th century flourished many of the greatest names in Italian art, including Filippo Lippi, Botticelli, Donatello and Brunelleschi, and in the 16th century Michelangelo and Leonardo da Vinci.

Italian literature (in addition to Latin literature, which is the common inheritance of western Europe) is one of the richest in Europe, particularly in its golden age (Dante, 1265–1321; Petrarch, 1304–74; Boccaccio, 1313–75) and in the Renaissance (Ariosto, 1474–1533; Machiavelli, 1469–1527; Tasso, 1544–95). Notable in modern Italian literature are Manzoni (1785–1873), Carducci (1835–1907) and Gabriele d'Annunzio (1864–1938). The Nobel Prize for Literature has been awarded to Italian authors on five occasions: G. Cariducci (1906), Signora G. Deledda (1926), Luigi Pirandello (1934), Salvatore Quasimodo (1959) and Eugenio Montale (1975).

ISLANDS

CAPRI.
EOLIAN ISLANDS, including Lipari; area 116 sq. km; population 18,636.
FLEGREAN ISLANDS, including Ischia; area 60 sq. km; population 51,883.
PANTELLERIA ISLAND (part of Trapani Province) in the Sicilian Narrows; area 31 sq. miles; population 9,601.
THE PELAGIAN ISLANDS (Lampedusa, Linosa and Lampione) are part of the province of Agrigento; area 8 sq. miles; population 4,811.
PONTINE ARCHIPELAGO, including Ponza; area 10 sq. km; population 2,515.
TREMITI ISLANDS; area 3 sq. km; population 426.
THE TUSCAN ARCHIPELAGO (including Elba); area 293 sq. km; population 31,861.

JAMAICA

AREA – 4,244 sq. miles (10,991 sq. km)
POPULATION – 2,496,000 (1994 UN estimate)
CAPITAL – ΨKingston (population, 103,962, 1991)
MAJOR CITIES – ΨMontego Bay; Ocho Rios; Spanish Town; Mandeville; May Pen
CURRENCY – Jamaican dollar (J$) of 100 cents
NATIONAL ANTHEM – Jamaica, Land We Love
NATIONAL DAY – First Monday in August (Independence Day)
NATIONAL FLAG – Gold diagonal cross forming triangles of green at top and bottom, triangles of black at hoist and in fly
LIFE EXPECTANCY (years) – male 71.41; female 75.82
POPULATION GROWTH RATE – 0.8 per cent (1994)
POPULATION DENSITY – 227 per sq. km (1994)

MILITARY EXPENDITURE – 0.6 per cent of GDP (1995)
MILITARY PERSONNEL – 3,170: Army 3,000, Air Wing 170
ILLITERACY RATE – 15.0 per cent
ENROLMENT (percentage of age group) – primary 100 per cent; secondary 64 per cent; tertiary 5.9 per cent (1992)

Jamaica is divided into three counties (Surrey, Middlesex and Cornwall) and 14 parishes. The island consists mainly of coastal plains, divided by the Blue Mountain range in the east and the hills and limestone plateaux in the central and western areas of the interior. The central chain of the Blue Mountains is over 6,000 feet above sea level, and the Blue Mountain Peak is 7,402 feet.

HISTORY AND POLITICS

The island was discovered by Columbus in 1494, and occupied by Spain from 1509 until 1655 when an English expedition under Admiral Penn and General Venables captured the island. In 1670 it was formally ceded to England by the Treaty of Madrid. Jamaica became an independent state within the Commonwealth on 6 August 1962.

At the general election of 30 March 1993, the People's National Party won 52 seats and the Jamaica Labour Party won 8.

POLITICAL SYSTEM

Queen Elizabeth II is the head of state, represented by the Governor-General. The legislature consists of a Senate of 21 nominated members and a House of Representatives consisting of 60 members elected by universal adult suffrage.

Governor-General, HE Sir Howard Felix Hanlon Cooke, GCMG, GCVO, apptd 1991

CABINET *as at July 1997*

Prime Minister, Percival J. Patterson, QC
Deputy PM, Foreign Affairs and Foreign Trade, Seymour Mullings
Agriculture and Mining, Horace Clarke
Education, Youth and Culture, Burchell Whiteman
Environment and Housing, Easton Douglas
Finance and Planning, Dr Omar Davies
Health, Dr Peter Phillips
Industry, Investments and Commerce, Dr Paul Robertson
Labour, Social Security and Sports, Portia Simpson
Legal Affairs, Attorney-General, Arnold Nicholson
Local Government and Works, Roger Clarke
National Security and Justice, K. D. Knight
Public Utilities, Transport and Energy, Robert Pickersgill
Tourism, Francis Tulloch

JAMAICAN HIGH COMMISSION
1–2 Prince Consort Road, London SW7 2BZ
Tel 0171-823 9911
High Commissioner, HE Derick Heaven, apptd 1994
Deputy High Commissioners, O. Singh; J. K. Pringle, CBE (*Trade*)
Minister-Counsellor, L. Wilks (*Consular Affairs*)
Defence Adviser, B. Blake

BRITISH HIGH COMMISSION
PO Box 575, Trafalgar Road, Kingston 10
Tel: Kingston 926 9050
High Commissioner, HE Richard Thomas, CMG, apptd 1995
Deputy High Commissioner, J. Malcolm
Defence Adviser, Col. A. Moorby
First Secretary (Management/Consular), P. Duffy

BRITISH COUNCIL REPRESENTATIVE IN THE CARIBBEAN, D. Tarr, 4th Floor, PCMB Building, 64 Knutsford Boulevard, PO Box 575, Kingston 5

ECONOMY

Alumina, bananas, bauxite and sugar are the main exports. Earnings from sugar in 1992 amounted to US$82.5 million, bauxite and alumina US$560 million and bananas US$39.6 million. Other exports include garments, processed food products, limestone and ornamental horticultural products.

Since 1989 the PNP government has introduced economic reforms including the abolition of price subsidies, the removal of foreign exchange controls and the introduction of a 10 per cent consumption tax. Jamaica is a popular tourist resort, attracting 1,563,097 visitors during 1992. Actual foreign exchange receipts from tourism amounted to US$850 million in 1992.

In 1993 Jamaica had a trade deficit of US$822 million and a current account deficit of US$214 million. In 1995 imports totalled US$2,757 million and exports US$1,414 million.

GNP – US$3,803 million (1995); US$1,510 per capita (1995)
GDP – US$4,223 million (1992); US$1,236 per capita (1992)
ANNUAL AVERAGE GROWTH OF GDP – 0.7 per cent (1993)
INFLATION RATE – 19.9 per cent (1995)
UNEMPLOYMENT – 15.9 per cent (1992)
TOTAL EXTERNAL DEBT – US$4,270 million (1995)

Trade with UK	1995	1996
Imports from UK	£69,771,000	£67,749,000
Exports to UK	149,076,000	151,410,000

COMMUNICATIONS

There are several excellent harbours, Kingston being the principal port. The island has 2,944 miles of main roads and 7,264 miles of subsidiary roads.

There are two international airports, the Norman Manley International Airport on the south coast serving Kingston, and Sangster Airport on the north coast serving the major tourist areas. In addition there are licensed aerodromes at Port Antonio, Ocho Rios, Mandeville and Negril. There are 16 privately owned, seven public and two military airstrips. Air Jamaica, the national airline, operates international services; Air Jamaica Express and Tropical Airways operate scheduled internal and regional services.

JAPAN
Nihon Koku – Land of the Rising Sun

AREA – 143,939 sq. miles (372,801 sq. km)
POPULATION – 124,961,000 (1994 UN estimate). The principal religions are Mahayana Buddhism and Shinto. About 1 per cent of Japanese are Christians
CAPITAL – Tokyo (population, 8,080,286, 1993 estimate)
MAJOR CITIES – ΨYokohama (3,265,000); ΨOsaka (2,481,000); ΨNagoya (2,091,000); Sapporo (1,719,000); ΨKobé (1,479,000); Kyoto, the ancient capital (1,391,000); ΨFukuoka (1,221,000), 1994
CURRENCY – Yen of 100 sen
NATIONAL ANTHEM – Kimigayo
NATIONAL DAY – 23 December (the Emperor's Birthday)
NATIONAL FLAG – White, charged with sun (red)
LIFE EXPECTANCY (years) – male 76.25; female 82.51
POPULATION GROWTH RATE – 0.3 per cent (1994)
POPULATION DENSITY – 331 per sq. km (1994)
URBAN POPULATION – 77.4 per cent (1990)

Japan consists of four large islands: *Honshu* (or Mainland) 88,839 sq. miles (230,448 sq. km), *Shikoku*, 7,231 sq. miles (18,757 sq. km), *Kyushu*, 16,170 sq. miles (42,079 sq. km), *Hokkaido*, 30,265 sq. miles (78,508 sq. km), and many small islands (including Okinawa).

The interior is very mountainous, and crossing the mainland from the Sea of Japan to the Pacific is a group of volcanoes, mainly extinct or dormant. Mount Fuji, the most sacred mountain of Japan, is 12,370 ft high and has been dormant since 1707, but volcanoes which are active include Mount Aso in Kyushu. There are frequent earthquakes, mainly along the Pacific coast near the Bay of Tokyo. The climate varies from sub-tropical in the south to cool temperate in the north.

HISTORY AND POLITICS

According to tradition, Jimmu, the first Emperor of Japan, ascended the throne on 11 February 660 BC. Under the *Meiji* constitution (1889), the monarchy is hereditary in the male heirs of the Imperial house.

After the unconditional surrender to the allied nations (14 August 1945), Japan was occupied by Allied forces under General MacArthur. A Japanese peace treaty became effective on 28 April 1952. Japan then resumed her status as an independent power.

The (conservative) Liberal Democratic Party (LDP) governed Japan almost without interruption from the Second World War until 1993. During the 1990s public disenchantment at political corruption led to a loss of support for the LDP and the formation of several splinter parties. Support for the new parties caused the LDP to lose its majority at the 1993 election, following which a seven-party coalition formed a government.

The government led by Morihiro Hosokawa (JNP) reached a compromise with the LDP-controlled House of Councillors to phase out corporate donations to individual MPs by 2000. State funding for political parties was introduced and the electoral system altered. The LDP returned to power in June 1994 in coalition with the SDPJ and Sakigake parties, with SDPJ leader Tomiichi Murayama becoming Japan's first socialist prime minister. The five reformist opposition parties (JNP, JRP, Komeito, DSP, USDP) merged in November 1994 to form the New Frontier Party (NFP) (Shinshinto) as a rival centre-right conservative party to the LDP. Murayama resigned in January 1996 and was replaced by LDP leader Ryutaro Hashimoto.

The LDP won 239 seats in the House of Representatives in the election of October 1996, the first to be contested under the new electoral system. A minority LDP government was formed with SDP and Sakigake parliamentary support. Prime Minister Hashimoto was elected to a second term. The standing of the other parties was: NFP 156; Democratic Party 52; Japan Communist Party 26; SDP 15; Sakigake 2; Democratic Reform Party 1; Independent 9.

POLITICAL SYSTEM

Legislative authority rests with the bicameral *Diet*, which comprises a 500-member House of Representatives, and a 252-member House of Councillors. The House of Representatives chooses the prime minister from among its ranks, ratifies treaties and passes budget bills. Since 1996, 200 of its members are elected by proportional representation in 11 regional blocks and 300 in single-member, first-past-the-post constituencies. All members serve four-year terms. The House of Councillors elects half its members every three years for six-year terms. Unlike the lower House it cannot be dissolved by the prime minister.

Executive authority is vested in the Cabinet which is responsible to the legislature.

HEAD OF STATE

His Imperial Majesty The Emperor of Japan, Emperor Akihito, *born* 23 December 1933; *succeeded* 8 January 1989; *enthroned* 12 November 1990; *married* 10 April 1959, Miss Michiko Shoda, and has *issue:* the Crown Prince; Prince Fumihito, *born* 30 November 1965; and Princess Sayako, *born* 18 April 1969

Heir, HRH Crown Prince Naruhito Hironomiya, *born* 23 February 1960, *married* 9 June 1993 Miss Masako Owada

CABINET *as at July 1997*

Prime Minister, Ryutaro Hashimoto
Agriculture, Forestry and Fisheries, Takao Fujimoto
Chief Cabinet Secretary, Seiroku Kajiyama
Construction, Shizuka Kamei
Director-General, Defence Agency, Fumio Kyuma
Director-General, Economic Planning Agency, Taro Aso
Director-General, Environment Agency, Michiko Ishii
Director-General, Hokkaido and Okinawa Development Agencies, Jitsuo Inagaki
Director-General, Management and Co-ordination Agency, Kabun Muto
Director-General, National Land Agency, Kosuke Ito
Director-General, Science and Technology Agency, Riichiro Chikaoka
Education, Takashi Kosugi
Finance, Hiroshi Mitsuzuka
Foreign Affairs, Yukihiko Ikeda
Health and Welfare, Jun'ichiro Koizumi
Home Affairs, Katsuhiko Shirakawa
International Trade and Industry, Shinji Sato
Justice, Isao Matsuura
Labour, Yutaka Okano
Posts and Telecommunications, Hisao Horinouchi
Transport, Makoto Koga

EMBASSY OF JAPAN
101–104 Piccadilly, London WIV 9FN
Tel 0171-465 6500
Ambassador Extraordinary and Plenipotentiary, HE Hiroaki Fujii, apptd 1994
Ministers, S. Numata; M. Amano (*Commercial*); Y. Matsuo (*Financial*); M. Kohno (*Consul-General*); M. Muto (*Cultural*)
Defence Attaché, Capt. M. Shimada

BRITISH EMBASSY
No. 1 Ichiban-cho, Chiyoda-ku, Tokyo 102
Tel: Tokyo 5211-1100
Ambassador Extraordinary and Plenipotentiary, HE David J. Wright, KCMG, LVO, apptd 1996
Ministers, C. T. W. Humfrey; J. E. W. Kirby (*Financial*)
Counsellors, D. A. Warren (*Commercial*); P. V. Rollitt (*Management and Consul-General*)
Defence and Naval Attaché, Capt. N. D. V. Robertson
CONSULATES GENERAL – Tokyo, Osaka
HONORARY CONSULATES – Fukuoka, Hiroshima, Nagoya

BRITISH COUNCIL REPRESENTATIVE, M. Barrett, OBE (*Cultural Attaché*), 2 Kagurazaka 1-Chome, Shinjuku-ku, Tokyo 162

BRITISH CHAMBER OF COMMERCE, No. 16 Kowa Building, 1–9–20 Akasaka, Minato-ku, Tokyo 107

DEFENCE

The constitution prohibits the maintenance of armed forces, although internal security forces were created in the 1950s and their mission was extended in 1954 to include the defence of Japan against aggression. In the 1990s legislation was passed permitting the armed forces limited participation in UN peacekeeping missions and allowing them to enter foreign conflicts in order to rescue Japanese nationals.

The Ground Self-Defence Force (GSDF) has 1,130 main battle tanks, 940 armoured personnel carriers and infantry fighting vehicles, 780 artillery pieces, 20 aircraft and 80 attack helicopters. The Maritime Self-Defence Force (MSDF) has 17 submarines, nine destroyers, 50 frigates, 110 combat aircraft and 99 armed helicopters at five bases. The Air Self-Defence Force (ASDF) has 379 combat aircraft.

The USA has 44,660 personnel stationed in Japan. Following an agreement in December 1996 the USA is due to vacate 21 per cent of the land it occupies in Japan and close part or all of 11 military facilities.
MILITARY EXPENDITURE – 1.1 per cent of GDP (1995)
MILITARY PERSONNEL – 235,500: Army 148,000, Navy 43,000, Air Force 44,500

ECONOMY

Owing to the mountainous nature of the country less than 20 per cent of its area can be cultivated and only 14 per cent is used for agriculture; 67 per cent is wooded. The soil is only moderately fertile but intensive cultivation secures good crops. Tobacco, tea, potatoes, rice, maize, wheat and other cereals are all cultivated. Rice is the staple food of the people. Fruit is abundant and pigs and chickens are widely reared.

Mineral resources include gold, silver, copper, lead, zinc, iron chromite, white arsenic, coal, sulphur, petroleum, salt and uranium. However, iron ore, coal and crude oil are among the principal imports.

Japan is one of the most highly industrialized nations in the world, with the whole range of modern light and heavy industries, including steel, aerospace, computers, office machinery, motor vehicles, electronics, metals, machinery, chemicals, textiles (cotton, silk, wool and synthetics), cement, pottery, glass, rubber, lumber, paper, oil refining and shipbuilding.
GNP – US$4,963,587 million (1995); US$39,640 per capita (1995)
GDP – US$3,092,219 million (1992); US$29,387 per capita (1992)
ANNUAL AVERAGE GROWTH OF GDP – 0.1 per cent (1993)
INFLATION RATE – –0.1 per cent (1995)
UNEMPLOYMENT – 3.2 per cent (1995)

TRADE

Being deficient in natural resources, Japan has had to develop a complex foreign trade. Principal imports in 1993 consisted of machinery and equipment (19.4 per cent), foodstuffs (16.4 per cent), petroleum (11.6 per cent), chemicals (7.5 per cent), metal ores and scrap (2.9 per cent). Principal exports consist of machinery and equipment (76 per cent, of which motor vehicles comprise 16.1 per cent), iron and steel (4.0 per cent), chemicals (5.6 per cent), textile goods (2.3 per cent) and ships (1.4 per cent).

In 1994 Japan had a trade surplus of US$145,930 million and a current account surplus of US$129,240 million. In 1995 imports totalled US$335,882 million and exports US$443,116 million. The USA, China, Australia, Hong Kong, South Korea, Taiwan and Singapore are Japan's main trading partners.

Trade with UK	1995	1996
Imports from UK	£3,782,955,000	£4,263,666,000
Exports to UK	9,613,810,000	8,994,299,000

COMMUNICATIONS

Japan National Railways was privatized in 1987 and is known as Japan Railways (JR). There are six regional companies and one goods company. Shinkansen (bullet train) tracks are currently being expanded. The opening in 1988 of the Seikan rail tunnel and the Seto Ohashi rail bridge means that the four major islands are now linked for the first time.

The merchant fleet had a shipping capacity of 25.4 million gross tons and 10,091 vessels in 1992, making it the largest in the world in terms of number of vessels and third in terms of tonnage.

EDUCATION

Education at elementary (six-year course) and lower secondary (three-year course) schools is free, compulsory and co-educational. The (three-year) upper secondary schools are attended by 96.7 per cent of the age group.

There are two- or three-year junior colleges and four-year universities. Some of the universities have graduate schools. In 1993 there were 1,129 universities and junior colleges, most of which are privately maintained. The most prominent universities are the seven state universities of Tokyo, Kyoto, Tohoku (Sendai), Hokkaido (Sapporo), Kyushu (Fukuoka), Osaka and Nagoya, and the two private universities of Keio and Waseda.

ENROLMENT (percentage of age group) – primary 100 per cent (1994); secondary 97 per cent (1990); tertiary 29.1 per cent (1990)

CULTURE

Japanese is said to be one of the Uro-Altaic group of languages and remained a spoken tongue until the fifth or seventh centuries AD, when Chinese characters came into use. Japanese who have received school education can read and write the Chinese characters in current use (about 1,800) and also the syllabary characters called Kana.

JORDAN
Al-Mamlaka al Urduniya al-Hashemiyah

AREA – 37,738 sq. miles (97,740 sq. km). Neighbours: Syria (north), Israel (west), Saudi Arabia (south), Iraq (east)

POPULATION – 5,198,000 (1994 UN estimate); 4,095,579 (1994 census). The majority are Sunni Muslims and Islam is the religion of the state; however, freedom of belief is guaranteed by the constitution

CAPITAL – Amman (population, 1,270,000, 1994)

CURRENCY – Jordanian dinar (JD) of 1,000 fils

NATIONAL ANTHEM – Long Live the King

NATIONAL DAY – 25 May (Independence Day)

NATIONAL FLAG – Three horizontal stripes of black, white, green and a red triangle based on the hoist, containing a seven-pointed white star

LIFE EXPECTANCY (years) – male 66.16; female 69.84

POPULATION GROWTH RATE – 5.0 per cent (1994)

POPULATION DENSITY – 53 per sq. km (1994)

ILLITERACY RATE – 13.4 per cent

ENROLMENT (percentage of age group) – primary 89 per cent (1992); secondary 42 per cent (1989); tertiary 24.5 per cent (1989)

HISTORY AND POLITICS

After the defeat of Turkey in the First World War, the Amirate of Transjordan was established in the area east of the River Jordan as a state under British mandate. The mandate was terminated after the Second World War and the Amirate, still ruled by its founder the Amir Abdullah, became the Hashemite Kingdom of Jordan. Following the 1948–9 war between Israel and the Arab states, that part of Palestine remaining in Arab hands (the West Bank and East Jerusalem, but excluding Gaza) was, with Palestinian agreement, incorporated into the Hashemite Kingdom. King Abdullah was assassinated in 1951; his son Talal ruled briefly but abdicated in favour of King Hussein in 1952.

The West Bank has been under Israeli occupation since its capture from Jordan in the 1967 war, and East Jerusalem was annexed by Israel in 1967. In 1988 Jordan severed its legal and administrative ties with the occupied West Bank, but did not formally renounce sovereignty over the area. As a result of the wars of 1948–9 and 1967 there are about one million Palestinian refugees and displaced persons living in East Jordan, about 200,000 of whom live in refugee and displaced persons camps established by the UN Relief and Works Agency (UNRWA). In addition there are 300,000 self-supporting Palestinians in East Jordan.

The first multiparty parliamentary elections since 1956 were held in 1993, traditionalists and centrists winning 59 seats and the Islamic Action Front 16 seats. The next elections are due to be held in November 1997.

FOREIGN RELATIONS

The Middle East peace process begun in 1991 led to Jordan signing an agreement on a 'common agenda' for peace with Israel in 1993. Intensive bilateral negotiations continued throughout 1993–4 with Israel agreeing to return two narrow strips of territory in the Arava desert seized in 1967. On 25 July 1994 King Hussein and the Israeli Prime Minister signed a framework agreement for peace which ended the state of war existing since 1948. The first Israeli–Jordanian border crossing was opened between

Eilat and Aqaba in August 1994. A full peace treaty was signed on 26 October 1994 which established full diplomatic and economic relations between the two states. It included agreements on sharing water from the Jordan and Yarmouk rivers; co-operating in the fields of commerce, transport, tourism, communications, energy and agriculture; and granted King Hussein custodianship of Islamic holy sites in Jerusalem. Israeli forces completed their withdrawal from Jordanian land in the Arava valley on 9 February 1995.

POLITICAL SYSTEM

The constitution provides for a senate of 40 members (all appointed by the King) and an elected House of Representatives which until 1988 had 60 members representing both the East and West Banks. Legislation passed in 1989 stipulated that in future elections seats would be contested on the East Bank only. The first parliamentary elections since 1967 took place in 1989 to a new 80-member House of Representatives.

The King appoints the members of the Council of Ministers. Crown Prince Hassan normally acts as regent when King Hussein is abroad. In 1991 a new national charter was formulated which lifted the ban on political parties, imposed in 1957.

HEAD OF STATE

His Majesty The King of the Jordan, King Hussein, GCVO, born 14 November 1935, *succeeded* on the abdication of his father, King Talal, 11 August 1952, *assumed constitutional powers* 2 May 1953, on coming of age
Crown Prince, Prince Hassan, third son of King Talal of Jordan, *born* 1947, *appointed Crown Prince* 1 April 1965

COUNCIL OF MINISTERS *as at August 1997*

Prime Minister, Defence, Foreign Affairs, Dr Abdel Salam Majali
Agriculture, Mijhem Khreishah
Awqaf and Islamic Affairs, Dr Abdul Salam Al Abbadi
Culture and Youth, Dr Qassem Abu Ein
Education, Dr Munther Al Masri
Energy and Mineral Resources, Muhammad Saleh Hourani
Finance, Suleiman Hafez
Foreign Affairs, Dr Fayez Tarawneh
Health, Dr Ashraf Kurdi
Higher Education, Dr Munthir Masri
Industry, Trade and Supply, Dr Hani Mulqi
Information, Dr Samir Mutawe
Interior, Nathir Rashid
Justice, Riyad Shak'a
Labour, Dr Saleh Khasawneh
Minister of State for Prime Ministry Affairs, Sa'ed Eddin Jum'a
Municipal, Rural and Environmental Affairs, Dr Tawfiq Kreishan
Planning, Dr Rima Khalaf-Hneidi
Public Works and Housing, Nasser Lawzi
Services and Administrative Development, Dr Abdullah Ensour
Social Development, Dr Mohammed Khair Mamser
Tourism and Antiquities, Aqel Beltaji
Transport and Telecommunication, Dr Bassam Saket
Water and Irrigation, Munther Haddadin

EMBASSY OF THE HASHEMITE KINGDOM OF JORDAN
6 Upper Phillimore Gardens, London W8 7HB
Tel 0171-937 3685
Ambassador Extraordinary and Plenipotentiary, HE Fouad Ayoub, apptd 1991
Defence Attaché, Brig. Ahmad Batayneh

BRITISH EMBASSY
Abdoun (PO Box 87), Amman
Tel: Amman 823100
Ambassador Extraordinary and Plenipotentiary, HE Christopher Battiscombe, CMG, apptd 1997
Counsellor, S. P. Collis *(Deputy Head of Mission and Consul-General)*
Defence Attaché, Col. T. R. Dumas, OBE
First Secretary, D. G. Tunstall, MBE *(Management)*
BRITISH COUNCIL DIRECTOR, Dr D. Burton, Rainbow Street (PO Box 634), Amman 11118

DEFENCE

The Army has 1,051 main battle tanks, 1,135 armoured personnel carriers and armoured infantry fighting vehicles, and 485 artillery pieces. The Navy has five patrol and coastal vessels at its base at Aqaba. The Air Force has 97 combat aircraft and 24 armed helicopters
MILITARY EXPENDITURE – 6.7 per cent of GDP (1995)
MILITARY PERSONNEL – 128,650: Army 90,000, Navy 650, Air Force 8,000, Paramilitaries 30,000

ECONOMY

The main agricultural areas are the Jordan Valley, the hills overlooking the valley, and the flatter country to the south of Amman and around Madaba and Irbid. However, several large farms, which depend for irrigation on water pumped from deep aquifers, have been established in the southern desert area. The rest of the country is desert and semi-desert. The principal crops are wheat, barley, vegetables, olives and fruit (mainly grapes and citrus fruits). Agricultural production has increased considerably in recent years due to improvements in production and irrigation techniques.

Important industrial products are raw phosphates (1995, 4.9 million tonnes) and potash (1995, 1.06 million tonnes), most of which is exported, together with fertilizers and pharmaceuticals. The Trans-Arabian oil pipeline (Tapline) runs through north Jordan from Saudi Arabia to the Lebanese port of Sidon. A branch pipeline, together with oil trucked by road from Iraq, feeds a refinery at Zerqa (production 1994, 2.9 million tons) which meets most of Jordan's requirements for refined petroleum products. Sufficient reserves of natural gas have been discovered in the north-east to produce electricity for the national grid since 1989. No significant reserves of oil have been found.

Tourism has developed, principally in Amman, Aqaba, Zerka Ma'in and on the shores of the Dead Sea.

The peace with Israel, including a preferential trade agreement signed in October 1995, has created a mini-boom, with a 40 per cent rise in tourism and 25 per cent rise in exports.

In 1993 the government had a budget surplus equivalent to 1.83 per cent of GDP, there was a trade deficit of US$1,899 million and a current account deficit of US$629 million. In 1995 imports totalled US$3,698 million and exports US$1,769 million.
GNP – US$6,354 million (1995); US$1,510 per capita (1995)
GDP – US$4,383 million (1992); US$1,106 per capita (1992)
ANNUAL AVERAGE GROWTH OF GDP – 6.4 per cent (1995)
INFLATION RATE – 2.4 per cent (1995)
TOTAL EXTERNAL DEBT – US$7,944 million (1995)

TRADE WITH UK	1995	1996
Imports from UK	£119,597,000	£140,044,000
Exports to UK	24,894,000	25,081,000

COMMUNICATIONS

Amman is linked to Aqaba, Damascus, Baghdad and Jeddah by roads which are of considerable importance in the overland trade of the Middle East.

The former Hejaz Railway runs from Syria through Jordan, and is used mainly for freight between Amman and Damascus. The Aqaba railway carries phosphate rock from the mines of al Hasa and al Abiad to Aqaba. A total of 2,485 vessels called at Aqaba in 1994, and 10,572,300 tons of cargo were handled.

The Royal Jordanian Airline operates from Amman to Aqaba and has an extensive network of routes to the Middle East, Europe, North America and the Far East.

KAZAKHSTAN
Kazak Respublikasy

AREA – 1,049,156 sq. miles (2,717,300 sq. km). Neighbours: Russia (north and west), Turkmenistan, Uzbekistan and Kyrgyzstan (south), China (east)

POPULATION – 17,027,000 (1994 UN estimate): Kazakhs (43 per cent), Russians (36 per cent), Ukrainians (5 per cent) and ethnic Germans (4 per cent), with smaller numbers of Tatars, Uzbeks, Koreans and Belarusians. The Russian population is concentrated in the north of the country, where it forms a significant majority, and in Alma Ata. The majority of ethnic Kazakhs are Sunni Muslims, and this is the main religion of the republic. Kazakh (one of the Turkic languages) became the official language in 1993 and Russian was given a special status as the 'social language between peoples'. Otherwise each ethnic group uses its own language

CAPITAL – Alma-Ata (Almaty), (population, 1,198,000, 1993 estimate).The Kazakh parliament voted in 1994 to move the capital to the central town of Akmola by 2000

MAJOR CITIES – Karaganda (596,000); Chimkent (447,000), 1993 estimates

CURRENCY – Tenge

NATIONAL DAY – 25 October (Republic Day)

NATIONAL FLAG – Dark blue with a sun and a soaring eagle in the centre all in gold, and a red vertical ornamentation stripe near the hoist

LIFE EXPECTANCY (years) – male 63.83; female 73.06

POPULATION GROWTH RATE – 0.5 per cent (1994)

POPULATION DENSITY – 6 per sq. km (1994)

URBAN POPULATION – 56.9 per cent (1993)

ILLITERACY RATE – 0.4 per cent

ENROLMENT (percentage of age group) – tertiary 33.6 per cent (1994)

Kazakhstan occupies the northern part of what was Soviet Central Asia. It stretches from the Volga and the Caspian Sea in the west to the Altai and Tienshan mountains in the east. The country consists of arid steppes and semi-deserts, flat in the west, hilly in the east and mountainous in the south-east (Southern Altai and Tienshan mountains). The main rivers are the Irtysh, the Ural, the Syr-Darya and the Ili. The climate is continental and very dry.

HISTORY AND POLITICS

Kazakhstan was inhabited by nomadic tribes before being invaded by Ghenghiz Khan and incorporated into his empire in 1218. After his empire disintegrated, feudal towns emerged based on large oases. These towns affiliated and established a Kazakh state in the late 15th century which engaged in almost continuous warfare with the marauding Khanates on its southern border. After appeal-ing to Russia for aid and protection, in 1731 Kazakhstan acceded to the Russian Empire under a voluntary act of accession.

The First World War brought privation to Kazakhstan, leading to an uprising in 1916 against the conscription of male Kazakhs. After the 1917 Russian revolution, Kazakhstan came under the control of White Russian forces until 1919. On 26 August 1920 a constitution was signed under which Kazakhstan became a Soviet Socialist Republic. Under Soviet rule in the 1920s and 1930s there was rapid industrial development and the traditional nomadic way of life disappeared. The Kazakhs suffered greatly in the Stalinist purges, the merchant and religious classes being murdered and thousands dying in the desert on collective farms. Other nationalities, such as Tatars and Germans, were forcibly transported to Kazakhstan by Stalin. Kazakhstan was the last of the former USSR republics to declare its independence (16 December 1991).

The Communist-derived Congress of People's Unity of Kazakhstan (SNEK) won the March 1994 legislative elections which were ruled invalid by the Constitutional Court. The President responded by dissolving the Supreme Kenges in March 1995. Elections to the new legislature were held in December 1995; the requirement for candidates to achieve an absolute majority made run-offs necessary. A referendum on 29 April 1995 extended President Nazarbayev's term until 2000.

POLITICAL SYSTEM

Under the constitution adopted on 28 January 1993, executive power is vested in the president and government. The president must be a Kazakh speaker and has the power to appoint the prime minister, other senior ministers and all ambassadors. The parliament does not have the power to impeach the president but the president can dissolve parliament.

A new constitution approved by referendum on 30 August 1995 granted the president the power to dissolve the legislature and to rule by decree. It also nominated Kazakh as the sole official language; prohibited dual citizenship; and created a new bicameral legislature composed of a 40-member Senate and a 67-member Majlis. The Constitutional Court, which opposed the new constitution, was replaced by a Constitutional Council which was made subject to presidential veto.

HEAD OF STATE

President, Nursultan Nazarbayev, *elected* 1 December 1991, *confirmed in office until 2000 by referendum* 29 April 1995

GOVERNMENT *as at August 1997*

Prime Minister, Akezhan Kazhegeldin

First Vice-Premier, Akhmetzhan Yesimov

Vice-Premiers, Dyusembai Duisenov; Zhanybek Karibzhanov; Alexander Pavlov; Imangali Tasmagambetov

Agriculture, Amangeldy Akhymbekov

Construction and Housing, Askar Kulibayev

Culture and Education, Imangali Tasmagambekov

Defence, Mukhtar Altynbaev

Ecology and Biological Resources, Nikolai Bayev

Economics, Umirzak Shukeyev

Finance, Alexander Pavlov

Foreign Affairs, Kasymzhomart Tokayev

Geology and Mineral Resources, Serikbek Daukeyev

Health, Vassily Devyatko

Industry and Trade, Khairulla Ospanov

Internal Affairs, Kairbek Suleimenov

Justice, Konstantin Kolpakov

Labour and Social Protection, Natalia Korzhova

Oil and Gas, Nurlan Balgimbayev
Power Engineering and Natural Resources, Viktor Khrapunov
Science, Vladimir Shkolnik
Transport and Communications, Yury Lavrinenko
Youth Affairs, Tourism, Physical Culture and Sport, Temerkan Dosmukhambetov

EMBASSY OF THE REPUBLIC OF KAZAKHSTAN
33 Thurloe Square, London SW7 2SD
Tel 0171-581 4646
Ambassador Extraordinary and Plenipotentiary,
HE Kanat Saudabaev, apptd 1997

BRITISH EMBASSY
U1 Furmanova 173, Alma-Ata
Tel: Alma-Ata 506191
Ambassador Extraordinary and Plenipotentiary,
HE Douglas B. McAdam, apptd 1996

BRITISH COUNCIL DIRECTOR, E. White, Panfilov 158, 480046

DEFENCE

In 1993–4 Kazakhstan established its own armed forces from forces that were formerly under joint CIS control with Russia. An agreement signed with Russia in January 1995 provides for eventual reunification of the two states' armed forces. The CIS mutual defence treaty of 1993, to which Kazakhstan is a signatory, retains a common air defence force, while Kazakh forces also take part in the CIS peacekeeping force along the Tajikistan–Afghanistan border. A military union with a joint staff is being formed in co-operation with Kyrgyzstan and Uzbekistan. Kazakhstan ratified the Start 1 Treaty in 1992 and signed the Nuclear Non-Proliferation Treaty in December 1994. By 1996, all nuclear warheads had been returned to Russia although Kazakhstan retained 48 SS-18 intercontinental ballistic missiles.

The Army has 630 main battle tanks and 1,000 artillery pieces. The Caspian Sea Flotilla, which Kazakhstan shares with Russia and Turkmenistan, operates under Russian command. The Air Force has 141 combat aircraft.
MILITARY EXPENDITURE – 3.0 per cent of GDP (1995)
MILITARY PERSONNEL – 62,500: Army 25,000, Air Force 15,000, Paramilitaries 22,500

ECONOMY

Kazakhstan is rich in minerals, with copper, lead, gold, uranium, chromium, silver, zinc, iron ore, coal, oil and natural gas. In 1995 production of coal was 82.2 million tonnes and iron ore was 2.3 million tonnes. The oil and gas industry, concentrated in the west of the country, is being expanded by foreign investment, which is also being used to explore two large fields in the Caspian Sea: Karachaganak (gas), with reserves of 16,000 million cubic feet; and Tengiz (oil), with reserves of 6,000–9,000 million barrels.

An agreement was signed with Russia, Oman and eight oil companies in April 1996 to begin the construction of a pipeline between Russia and Kazakhstan. Oil production in 1995 was 20 million tonnes. Industry is dominated by food processing and mining and metals production; textiles, steel and tractors are also produced. The main centres of the metal industry are in the Altai mountains, in Chimkent, north of Lake Balkhash and in central Kazakhstan.

Agriculture, including stock-raising, is highly developed, particularly in the central and south-west of the republic. Grain is grown in the north and north-east, and cotton and wool produced in the south and south-east. A record grain crop was grown in 1992 and 1.5 million tonnes of meat produced in 1993.

In March 1993 the government announced a three-year privatization programme under which most state-owned enterprises were to be sold by means of a voucher system. Small businesses and retail outlets have been sold at auction since 1992. The economy was weakened by the ending of preferential trading links to other CIS states at the break-up of the Soviet Union although a single market was formed with Kyrgyzstan and Uzbekistan in 1994. A treaty on further economic and humanitarian co-operation, as well as a customs union, was signed with Belarus, Kyrgyzstan and Russia in March 1996.

GNP – US$22,143 million (1995); US$1,330 per capita (1995)
GDP – US$62,797 million (1992); US$607 per capita (1992)
UNEMPLOYMENT – 1.0 per cent (1993)
TOTAL EXTERNAL DEBT – US$3,712 million (1995)

TRADE WITH UK	1995	1996
Imports from UK	£26,561,000	£33,653,000
Exports to UK	48,902,000	47,375,000

KENYA
Jamhuri ya Kenya

AREA – 224,081 sq. miles (580,367 sq. km). Neighbours: Somalia (east), Ethiopia (north), Sudan (north-west), Uganda (west), Tanzania (south)
POPULATION – 29,292,000 (1994 UN estimate). The main tribal groups are the Kikuyu, Luhya, Luo, Kalenjin, Kamba and Masai. The official languages are Swahili, which is generally understood throughout Kenya, and English; numerous indigenous languages are also spoken
CAPITAL – Nairobi (population, 1,400,000, 1989 estimate)
CURRENCY – Kenya shilling (Ksh) of 100 cents
NATIONAL DAY – 12 December (Independence Day)
NATIONAL FLAG – Horizontally black, red and green with the red fimbriated in white, and with a shield and crossed spears all over in the centre
LIFE EXPECTANCY (years) – male 54.18; female 57.29
POPULATION DENSITY – 50 per sq. km (1994)
MILITARY EXPENDITURE – 2.3 per cent of GDP (1995)
MILITARY PERSONNEL – 24,200: Army 20,500, Navy 1,200, Air Force 2,500
ILLITERACY RATE – 21.9 per cent
ENROLMENT (percentage of age group) – primary 91 per cent (1980); tertiary 1.6 per cent (1990)

HISTORY AND POLITICS

Kenya became an independent state and a member of the British Commonwealth on 12 December 1963 and a republic in 1964. In 1982 the government introduced amendments to the constitution making the country a one-party state, with Kenya African National Union (KANU) as the ruling party. In December 1991 the government yielded to internal and international pressure and introduced a multiparty democracy.

Multiparty presidential and legislative elections were held in December 1992 which were won by President Moi and KANU respectively, amid opposition claims that the elections were not free and fair which were supported by the Commonwealth observers. In the unicameral National Assembly of 200 seats, KANU has 107 seats (95 elected and 12 nominated by the President) and the three major opposition parties have 85 seats between them. KANU formed a new government on 13 January 1993 and parliament reopened on 22 March 1993 but was boycotted by two of the main opposition parties for three months. Elections are due to be held in 1997.

The country is divided into eight provinces (Central, Coast, Eastern, Nairobi, Nyanza, North Eastern, Rift Valley, Western).

HEAD OF STATE
President and C.-in-C. Armed Forces, Daniel T. arap Moi, *took office* 14 October 1978, *re-elected* 1979, 1983, 1988 and 29 December 1992

CABINET *as at June 1997*
The President
Vice-President, Planning and National Development, Prof. George Saitoti
Agriculture, Livestock and Marketing, Darius Mbela
Attorney-General, Amos Wako
Commerce and Industry, Joshua Angatia
Co-operative Development, Kamwithi Munyi
Cultural and Social Services, Nyiva Mwenda
Education, Joseph Kamotho
Energy, Kirugi M'Mukindia
Environment and Natural Resources, Henry Kosgei
Finance, W. Musalia Mudavadi
Foreign Affairs and International Co-operation, Stephen Kalonzo Musyoka
Health, Gen. Jackson Mulinge
Home Affairs and National Heritage, William Ole Ntimana
Information and Broadcasting, Johnstone Makau
Labour and Manpower Development, Philip Masinde
Land Reclamation, Regional and Water Development, S. Nyachae
Lands and Settlement, Noah Katana Ngala
Local Government, Francis Lotodo
Ministers of State in the President's Office, Nicholas K. Biwott; J.K. Koech
Public Works and Housing, Jonathan Ngeno
Research, Technical Training and Technology, Hussein Maalima Mohamed
Tourism and Wildlife, Dr P. K. Momanyi
Transport and Communication, Wilson Ndolo Ayah

KENYA HIGH COMMISSION
45 Portland Place, London WIN 4AS
Tel 0171-636 2371
High Commissioner, HE Mwanyengela Ngali, apptd 1996
Defence Attaché, Col. E. Sifuma
Commercial Attaché, D. Mbogua

BRITISH HIGH COMMISSION
Bruce House, Standard Street, PO Box 30465 Nairobi
Tel: Nairobi 335944
High Commissioner, HE Jeffrey James, CMG apptd 1997
Deputy High Commissioner, A. Tucker
Defence Adviser, Col. T. Merritt, OBE
First Secretary (Commercial), S. Martin
First Secretary (Consular), J. Dunlop
CONSULAR OFFICES – Nairobi, Mombasa, Malindi
BRITISH COUNCIL REPRESENTATIVE, B. Harvey, (PO Box 40751) ICEA Building, Kenyatta Avenue, Nairobi. There are offices at Kisumu and Mombasa

ECONOMY

Agriculture provides about 52 per cent of total export earnings (excluding processed oil products). The great variation in altitude and ecology provides conditions under which a wide range of crops can be grown. These include wheat, barley, pyrethrum, coffee, tea, sisal, coco-nuts, cashew nuts, cotton, maize and a wide variety of tropical and temperate fruits and vegetables. The total area of well-farmed land on which concentrated mixed farming can be practised is small and the remainder is arid or semi-arid country but population pressure and the need to increase agricultural production for export has led to attempts to develop such areas.

Mineral production consists of soda ash, salt and lime-stone. Hydroelectric power has been developed, particularly on the Upper Tana River. Kenya is now almost self-sufficient in electric power generation but the connection with Owen Falls in Uganda is still in being.

There has been considerable industrial development over the last 15 years and Kenya has a variety of industries processing agricultural produce and manufacturing products from local and imported raw materials. New industries are steel, textile mills, dehydrated vegetable processing and motor tyre manufacture. Smaller schemes have added to the country's consumer goods manufacturing base. There is an oil refinery in Mombasa supplying both Kenya and Uganda, and a fuel pipeline now connects Mombasa and Nairobi.

In 1994 the government had a budget deficit equivalent to 3.69 per cent of GDP.

GNP – US$7,583 million (1995); US$280 per capita (1995)
GDP – US$8,837 million (1992); US$332 per capita (1992)
ANNUAL AVERAGE GROWTH OF GDP – 3.9 per cent (1994)
INFLATION RATE – 0.8 per cent (1995)
TOTAL EXTERNAL DEBT – US$7,381 million (1995)

TRADE

Principal exports are coffee and tea, which account for 33 per cent of total export earnings. Also exported are fruit, vegetables, and crude animal and vegetable material. Petroleum products account for about 37 per cent of imports; other imports are manufactured goods, particularly machinery, transport equipment, metals, pharmaceuticals and chemicals.

In 1993 Kenya had a trade deficit of US$239 million and a current account surplus of US$124 million. In 1995 imports totalled US$2,948 million and exports US$1,856 million.

Trade with UK	1995	1996
Imports from UK	£244,347,000	£241,132,000
Exports to UK	162,198,000	191,262,000

COMMUNICATIONS

The Kenya Railways Corporation has 1,700 miles of railway open to traffic. There are also 39,000 miles of road, of which 5,000 are bitumen surfaced. Trans-border links with Tanzania were reopened in 1985 with rail services for freight and steamer services for passengers and freight. The principal port is Mombasa, operated by the Kenya Ports Authority. International air services operate from airports at Nairobi and Mombasa.

KIRIBATI
Ribaberikin Kiribati

AREA – 280 sq. miles (726 sq. km)
POPULATION – 77,000 (1994 UN estimate); predominantly Christian
CAPITAL – Tarawa (population, 17,921, 1978)
CURRENCY – Australian dollar ($A) of 100 cents
NATIONAL ANTHEM – Teirake Kain Kiribati (Stand Kiribati)

NATIONAL DAY – 12 July (Independence Day)
NATIONAL FLAG – Red, with blue and white wavy lines in base, and in the centre a gold rising sun and a flying frigate bird
POPULATION GROWTH RATE – 1.7 per cent (1994)
POPULATION DENSITY – 106 per sq. km (1994)

Kiribati, the former Gilbert Islands, became an independent republic in 1979. Kiribati comprises 36 islands: the Gilberts Group (17) including Banaba (formerly Ocean Island), the Phoenix Islands (8), and the Line Islands (11), which are situated in the south-west central Pacific around the point at which the International Date Line cuts the Equator. The total land area is spread over some 2 million square miles of ocean. Few of the atolls are more than half a mile in width or more than 12 feet high. The vegetation consists mainly of coconut palms, breadfruit trees and pandanus.

HISTORY AND POLITICS

The president is head of state as well as head of government and is elected nationally. There is a House of Assembly of 41 members (39 elected and two appointed: the Attorney-General and a representative of Banaba Island). Executive authority is vested in the Cabinet. The last legislative election was held in July 1994, and the last presidential election, on 30 September 1994, was won by Teburoro Tito.

HEAD OF STATE
President, Foreign Affairs, Teburoro Tito, *sworn in* 1 October 1994
Vice-President, Home Affairs, Rural Development, Tewareka Tentoa

CABINET *as at August 1997*
The President
The Vice-President
Commerce, Industry and Tourism, Tim Taekiti
Education, Training and Technology, Teiraoi Tetabea
Environment and Social Development, Tewarekoa Bodrau
Finance and Economic Planning, Beniamina Tiinga
Health and Family Planning, Kataotika Tekee
Information, Communications and Transport, Manraoi Kaiea
Labour, Employment and Co-operatives, Tanieru Awerika
Line and Phoenix Islands, Timbo Kariki
Natural Resources Development, Willie Tokataake
Works and Energy, Emile Schutz

HONORARY CONSULATE
The Great House, Llanddewi Rhydderch,
Monmouthshire, NP7 9UY
Tel 0171-222 6952
Honorary Consul, M. Walsh

BRITISH HIGH COMMISSIONER, HE Michael Peart, CMG, LVO, apptd 1995, resident at Suva, Fiji

ECONOMY

Many people still practise a semi-subsistence economy, the main staples of their diet being coconuts and fish.

The principal imports are foodstuffs, consumer goods, machinery and transport equipment. The principal exports are copra and fish.
GNP – US$73 million (1995); US$920 per capita (1995)
GDP – US$38 million (1992); US$528 per capita (1992)

TRADE WITH UK	1995	1996
Imports from UK	£431,000	£231,000
Exports to UK	3,000	10,000

COMMUNICATIONS

Air communication exists between most of the islands and is operated by Air Tungaru, a statutory corporation. Air Marshall Islands operates a weekly service between Majuro, Tarawa, Funafuti and Nadi, and Air Nauru between Tarawa, Nauru and Nadi. Inter-island shipping is operated by a statutory corporation, the Shipping Corporation of Kiribati.

EDUCATION AND SOCIAL WELFARE

The government maintains a teacher training college and a secondary school. Five junior secondary schools are maintained by missions. Throughout the republic there are about a hundred primary schools. The total enrolment of children of school age is about 16,000. The Marine Training School at Tarawa trains seamen for service with overseas shipping lines.

There is a general hospital at Tarawa. The other inhabited islands have dispensaries.

KOREA

Korea's southern and western coasts are fringed with innumerable islands, of which the largest, forming a province of its own, is Cheju. The Korean language is of the Ural-Altaic Group. Its script, Hangul, was invented in the 15th century; prior to this Chinese characters alone were used. Despite the great cultural influence of the Chinese, Koreans have developed and preserved their own cultural heritage.

HISTORY

The Korean peninsula was first unified in AD 676 when Silla, having emerged as the dominant tribal state, drove out the Chinese. The Kim dynasty was succeeded by the Wang dynasty in 918. The last native dynasty (Yi) ruled from 1392 until 1910 when Japan formally annexed Korea. The country remained part of the Japanese Empire until the defeat of Japan in 1945, when it was occupied by troops of the USA and the USSR, the 38th parallel being fixed as the boundary between the two zones of occupation.

Attempts to reunite Korea failed and the issue was referred to the UN General Assembly. The UN in November 1947 resolved that elections should be held for a National Assembly which, when elected, should set up a government. The Soviet government refused to comply and a UN commission was only allowed to operate south of the 38th parallel.

A general election was held on 10 May 1948, and the first National Assembly met in Seoul on 31 May. The Assembly passed a constitution on 12 July and on 15 August 1948 the republic was formally inaugurated and American military government came to an end. Meanwhile, in the Soviet-occupied zone north of the 38th parallel the Democratic People's Republic had been established with its capital at Pyongyang. A Supreme People's Soviet was elected in September 1948, and a Soviet-style constitution adopted.

THE KOREAN WAR
Korea remained divided along the 38th parallel until June 1950, when North Korean forces invaded South Korea. In response to Security Council recommendations, 16 nations, including the USA and the UK, came to the aid of the Republic of Korea. China entered the war on the side of North Korea in November 1950. The fighting was ended

by an armistice agreement signed on 27 July 1953. By this agreement (which was not signed by the Republic of Korea), the line of division between North and South Korea remained close to the 38th parallel, and a Military Armistice Commission (MAC) was established to monitor the cease-fire. North Korea and China withdrew from the MAC in 1994.

Talks between North and South Korea on the reunification of the country have taken place intermittently. A non-aggression accord was signed between the North and South in 1991 and an agreement on the denuclearization of the Korean peninsula was reached in 1992. A summit of North and South Korean Presidents was scheduled for July 1994 but Kim Il-sung died before it could take place.

DEMOCRATIC PEOPLE'S REPUBLIC OF KOREA
Chosun Minchu-chui Inmin Kongwa-guk

AREA – 46,540 sq. miles (120,538 sq. km)
POPULATION – 23,483,000 (1994 UN estimate)
CAPITAL – Pyongyang (approximate population, 2,000,000)
CURRENCY – Won of 100 chon
NATIONAL ANTHEM – A Chi Mun Bin No Ra I Gang San (Shine bright, oh dawn, on this land so fair)
NATIONAL DAY – 16 February (Kim Jong-il's birthday)
NATIONAL FLAG – Red with white fimbriations and blue borders at top and bottom; a large red star on a white disc near the hoist
LIFE EXPECTANCY (years) – male 67.70; female 73.95
POPULATION GROWTH RATE – 1.9 per cent (1994)
POPULATION DENSITY – 195 per sq. km (1994)

POLITICAL SYSTEM

The constitution of the Democratic People's Republic of Korea provides for a Supreme People's Assembly, presently consisting of 687 deputies, which is elected every five years by universal suffrage. The Assembly elects a president for a five-year term, and the Central People's Committee. In turn, the Central People's Committee directs the Administrative Council which implements the policy formulated by the Committee. The Administrative Council (51 members), the government of North Korea, includes the prime minister and various ministers. In practice, however, the country is ruled by the Korean Workers' Party which elects a Central Committee; this in

turn appoints a Politburo. The senior ministers of the Administrative Council are all members of the Communist Party Central Committee and the majority are also members of the Politburo. Kim Il-sung, who had been head of the state, party and military since the country's inception in 1948, died on 8 July 1994. His son Kim Jong-il has not yet assumed his father's positions.

HEAD OF STATE
President, vacant
Vice-Presidents, Kim Yong-ju; Kim Pyong-sik; Pak Song-ch'ol; Yi Chong-ok

Politburo of the Central Committee, Kim Jong-il (*full member and member of the presidium*); Kim Yong-ju; Yi Chong-ok; Pak Song-chol; Kim Yong-nam; Kye Ung-tae; So Yun-sok; Chon Pyong-ho; Han Song-yong (*full members*); Li Son-sil; Hong Song-nam; Choe Tae Pok; Kim Chol-man; Choe Yong-nim; Ying Hyong-sop; Yon Hyong-muk; Hong Sok-hyong (*alternate members*)

ADMINISTRATION COUNCIL *as at August 1997*
Prime Minister, Kang Song-san
Deputy Prime Ministers, Hong Song-nam; Kim Yun-hyok; Kim Chang-ju; Kong Jin-tae (*Chairman, Public Welfare Commission*); Chang Chol (*Culture and Art*); Kim Yong-nam (*Foreign Affairs*); Kim Bok-sin (*Chairman, Light Industry Commission*); Kim Hwan (*Chemical Industry*); Choe Yong-rim (*Metals Industry*)

MINISTERS
Atomic Energy Industry, Pak Yong-nam
Building Materials Industry, Li Buek-ha
City Management, Li Chol-bong
Coal Industry, Kim Ri-ryong
Construction, Cho Yun-hui
Defence, vacant
External Economic Affairs, Li Seong-dae
Finance, Yun Gi-jong
Forestry, Kim Jae-yul
Labour Administration, Li Jae-yun
Local Industry, Kim Song-gu
Machine Building Industry, Kwak Pom-gi
Marine, O Song-ryol
Mining Industry, Kim Phyong-gil

DEFENCE

The Army has 3,400 main battle tanks, 2,200 armoured personnel carriers and 10,200 artillery pieces. The Navy has 25 submarines, three frigates and about 417 patrol and coastal vessels at 16 bases. The Air Force has 611 combat aircraft.

Between 1992 and 1994 North Korea embarked on a clandestine nuclear weapons programme despite being a signatory of the Nuclear Non-Proliferation Treaty (NPT). The NPT's enforcing arm, the International Atomic Energy Authority (IAEA), was repeatedly refused access to inspect military installations. North Korea threatened to withdraw from the NPT, carrying out its threat in June 1994 following an IAEA report that North Korea was attempting to reprocess plutonium for use in nuclear weapons. An agreement was signed with the USA on 21 October 1994 under which North Korea vowed to remain a party to the NPT; to permit IAEA inspections; and to switch to light-water reactors unsuitable for plutonium production. In return the USA agreed to establish diplomatic and economic relations and to pay for interim energy requirements. The IAEA verified the halting of North Korea's nuclear programme in November

1994 although a final settlement was only achieved in June 1995.

MILITARY EXPENDITURE – 25.2 per cent of GDP (1995)

MILITARY PERSONNEL – 1,169,000: Army 923,000, Navy 46,000, Air Force 85,000, Paramilitaries 115,000

CONSCRIPTION DURATION – Three to ten years

ECONOMY

North Korea is rich in minerals and industry was developed, but the economy has stagnated owing to poor planning and a shortage of foreign exchange. The current economic crisis was precipitated by the curtailment of barter trade with the Soviet Union after 1991, and the end of subsidized oil and grain from China. Industrial output has collapsed, with industry operating at one-third of capacity. The economy has been sustained by foreign exchange sent by ethnic Koreans in Japan.

In 1995–7, a slump in agricultural production was exacerbated by widespread flooding which devastated the rice harvest and threatened potential famine.

Under the nuclear agreement, North Korea is to receive 500,000 tons of oil a year and is hoping to export manganese to the USA; it has lifted the embargo on the import of US commodities.

GDP – US$19,554 million (1992)

TRADE WITH UK	1995	1996
Imports from UK	£22,266,000	£23,625,000
Exports to UK	173,000	231,000

REPUBLIC OF KOREA
Daehanminkuk

AREA – 38,330 sq. miles (99,274 sq. km)

POPULATION – 44,606,000 (1996). There is freedom of religion; the largest religion is Buddhism (13 million), with large minorities of Christians (8 million Protestants, 2.2 million Roman Catholics) and Confucianists (4.7 million)

CAPITAL – Seoul (population, 10,229,000, 1995)

MAJOR CITIES – ΨPusan (3,814,000), Taegu (2,449,000); ΨInchon (2,308,000)

CURRENCY – Won of 100 jeon

NATIONAL ANTHEM – Aegukka

NATIONAL DAY – 15 August (Independence Day)

NATIONAL FLAG – White with a red and blue yin-yang in the centre, surrounded by four black trigrams

LIFE EXPECTANCY (years) – male 67.66; female 75.67

POPULATION GROWTH RATE – 0.9 per cent (1994)

POPULATION DENSITY – 448 per sq. km (1994)

URBAN POPULATION – 74.4 per cent (1990)

HISTORY AND POLITICS

The Republic of Korea was not officially recognized by any former Communist bloc country until 1989, and not by the People's Republic of China until 1992.

The most recent elections to the National Assembly in April 1996 produced no outright majority although the ruling New Korea Party (formerly Democratic Liberal Party) was able to form a government following defections from opposition parties. In the most recent presidential election of December 1992, long-time opposition leader Kim Young-sam was victorious. In February 1993 he named the first wholly civilian government in 32 years.

POLITICAL SYSTEM

A new constitution was adopted in 1988 following a year of political unrest. The president, who is head of state, chief of the executive and commander-in-chief of the armed forces, is directly elected for a single term of five years. He appoints the prime minister with the consent of the National Assembly, and members of the State Council (Cabinet) on the recommendation of the prime minister. The president is also empowered to take wide-ranging measures in an emergency, including the declaration of martial law, but must obtain the agreement of the National Assembly. The National Assembly of 299 members is directly elected for a four-year term.

HEAD OF STATE

President, Kim Young-sam, *elected* 18 December 1992, *took office* 25 February 1993

CABINET *as at August 1997*

Prime Minister, Koh Kun

Deputy PM, Finance, Economy, Kang Kyong-shik

Deputy PM, National Unification, Kwon O-kie

Agriculture and Forestry, Jeong Shi-chae

Construction and Transportation, Lee Hwan-kyun

Culture and Sports, Song Tae-ho

Defence, Kim Dong-jin

Director, National Security Planning Agency, Kwon Young-hae

Education, Ahn Byung-young

Environment, Kang Hyon-wook

First Minister of State for Political Affairs, Shin Kyung-shik

Foreign Affairs, Yoo Chong-ha

Government Administration, Kim Han-kyu

Health and Welfare, Sohn Hak-kyu

Home Affairs, Kang Won-tae

Information, Oh In-whan

Information and Communication, Kang Bong-kyun

Justice, Choi Sang-yup

Labour Affairs, Jin Nyum

Legislation, Song Jong-eui

Maritime Affairs and Fisheries, Shin Sang-woo

Patriots' and Veterans' Affairs, Park Sang-bum

Science and Technology, Kwon Sook Il

Second Minister of State for Political Affairs, Kim Yun-duk

Trade, Industry and Energy, Lim Chang-yuel

EMBASSY OF THE REPUBLIC OF KOREA

60 Buckingham Gate, London SW1E 6AJ

Ambassador Extraordinary and Plenipotentiary, HE Choi Dong-jin, apptd 1996

Defence Attaché, Capt. Jang Kil Joo

Consul, Jong Kug Lee

Counsellor, Chil Doo Kim *(Commercial Affairs)*

BRITISH EMBASSY

No. 4, Chung-Dong, Chung-Ku, Seoul 100

Tel: Seoul 735–7341/3

Ambassador Extraordinary and Plenipotentiary, HE Stephen Brown, apptd 1997

Counsellor (Economic) and Deputy Head of Mission, D. R. Marsh

Defence and Military Attaché, Brig. C. D. Parr, OBE

First Secretary (Commercial), D. F. Graham

There is a Trade Office and an Honorary British Consul at Pusan.

BRITISH COUNCIL REPRESENTATIVE, T. Toney, 1st Floor, Anglican Church Building, 3–7 Chung Dong, Choong-ku, Seoul 100–120. There is also an office at Pusan

BRITISH CHAMBER OF COMMERCE, c/o Chartered Bank, 1st and 2nd Floors, Samsung Building, 50, 1-Ka Ulchi Ro, Chung-Ku, Seoul

DEFENCE

The Army has 2,050 main battle tanks, 2,460 armoured personnel carriers, 4,500 artillery pieces and 143 armed helicopters.

The Navy has four submarines, seven destroyers, 33 frigates, 122 patrol and coastal vessels, 23 combat aircraft, 47 armed helicopters, 60 main battle tanks and 60 armoured personnel carriers. There are eight naval bases. The Air Force has 461 combat aircraft.

The USA maintains 35,910 personnel in the country.
MILITARY EXPENDITURE – 3.4 per cent of GDP (1995)
MILITARY PERSONNEL – 660,000: Army 548,000, Navy 60,000, Air Force 52,000
CONSCRIPTION DURATION – 26–30 months

ECONOMY

The soil is fertile but arable land is limited by the mountainous nature of the country. Staple agricultural products are rice, barley and other cereals, beans, tobacco and hemp. Fruit-growing, sericulture and the growing of the medicinal root ginseng are also practised. The fishing industry is a major contributor to both food supply and exports.

Korea is deficient in mineral resources, except for deposits of coal on the east coast and tungsten. There are some prospects of discovering oil in the sea between Korea and Japan.

Land redistribution and US aid (US$6,000 million from 1945 to 1978) enabled the rapid industrialization of South Korea in the 1950s and 1960s. Former land owners formed *chaebols* (industrial conglomerates) which benefited from a highly-educated workforce and import substitution policies. From 1961 to 1979 exports increased by an average of 10 per cent a year. Despite a decline in aid and a brief slowdown in the early 1980s and early 1990s, growth has been maintained, averaging 7.8 per cent in 1985 to 1994. Major industries now include shipbuilding, construction, iron and steel, textiles, electrical and electronic goods, footwear, passenger vehicles and railway rolling stock. The 1994–8 five-year economic plan includes the liberalization of foreign exchange rates and capital markets, the deregulation of interest rates and the easing of regulations on foreign exchange holdings by companies.

In 1994 the government had a budget surplus equivalent to 0.32 per cent of GDP; there was a trade deficit of US$3,146 million and a current account deficit of US$4,095 million. In 1995 imports totalled US$135,119 million and exports US$125,058 million.
GNP – US$435,137 million (1995); US$9,700 per capita (1995)
GDP – US$277,373 million (1992); US$6,721 per capita (1992)
UNEMPLOYMENT – 2.0 per cent (1995)
TOTAL EXTERNAL DEBT – US$54,542 million

TRADE WITH UK	1995	1996
Imports from UK	£1,153,116,000	£1,303,560,000
Exports to UK	1,561,775,000	2,038,376,000

COMMUNICATIONS

In 1995 there were 37,493 km of paved road. Seoul and Pusan have subway systems and there are 6,558 km of railway lines. Korean Air and Asiana operate regular flights to Europe, the USA, the Middle East and south-east Asia. Pusan and Inchon are the major ports with Pusan serving the industrial areas of the south-east. Inchon, 28 miles from Seoul, serves the capital, but development and operation at Inchon are hampered by a tidal variation of 9–10 metres.

EDUCATION

Primary education is compulsory for six years from the age of six. Secondary and higher education is extensive with the option of middle school to age 15 and high school to age 18.
ILLITERACY RATE – 2.0 per cent
ENROLMENT (percentage of age group) – primary 93 per cent; secondary 95 per cent; tertiary 54.8 per cent (1995)

KUWAIT
Dowlat al-Kuwait

AREA – 6,880 sq. miles (17,818 sq. km)
POPULATION – 1,575,983 (1995 census): 41.6 per cent were Kuwaiti citizens, the remainder being other Arabs, Iranians, Indians and Pakistanis. The total Western population was 14,240. Islam is the official religion, though religious freedom is constitutionally guaranteed. The official language is Arabic, and English is widely spoken as a second language
CAPITAL – ΨKuwait City (population, 400,000, 1975) population (excluding suburbs) 400,000
CURRENCY – Kuwaiti dinar (KD) of 1,000 fils
NATIONAL DAY – 25 February
NATIONAL FLAG – Three horizontal stripes of green, white and red, with black trapezoid next to staff
LIFE EXPECTANCY (years) – male 71.77; female 73.32
POPULATION GROWTH RATE – –6.8 per cent (1994)
POPULATION DENSITY – 91 per sq. km (1994)
MILITARY EXPENDITURE – 11.8 per cent of GDP (1995)
MILITARY PERSONNEL – 20,300: Army 11,000, Navy 1,800, Air Force 2,500, Paramilitaries 5,000
CONSCRIPTION DURATION – Voluntary, conscripts two years

In 1993 the UN settled the dispute between Kuwait and Iraq, moving the border some few hundred metres northwards. Kuwait has since completed a 130 mile ditch, sand wall and barbed wire system along its border.

Kuwait has a dry, desert climate with summer extending from April to September. The mean temperature varies between 29–45°C in summer, and 8–18°C in winter. Humidity rarely exceeds 60 per cent except in July and August.

HISTORY AND POLITICS

Although Kuwait had been independent for some years, the 'exclusive agreement' of 1899 between the Sheikh of Kuwait and the British government was formally abrogated by an exchange of letters dated 19 June 1961. Iraq invaded Kuwait on 2 August 1990 and it was liberated on 26 February 1991 by an alliance of Western and Arab forces. Iraq built up its armed forces on Kuwait's border in October 1994, until it was deterred by the arrival of US and British forces. Iraq formally recognized the sovereignty and territorial integrity of Kuwait as well as the UN-demarcated border in November 1994. Roughly 600 Kuwaitis are still held in Iraq.

Voting took place for a new National Assembly in October 1996. Pro-government candidates won 19 of the 25 seats, although all were independent.

POLITICAL SYSTEM

Under the constitution legislative power is vested in the Amir and the 50-member National Assembly, and executive power in the Amir and the Cabinet. The sixth National Assembly was dissolved in July 1986. Following popular pressure after the liberation, elections for the National Assembly were held in October 1992. The electorate consists of all Kuwaiti male nationals over 21 whose families have lived in the Emirate since before 1921.

There are five governorates: Capital, Hawally, Ahmadi, Jara and Al Farwaniya.

HEAD OF STATE

HH The Amir of Kuwait, Sheikh Jaber al-Ahmad al Jaber Al-Sabah, *born* 1928, acceded 31 December 1977
Crown Prince, HH Sheikh Saad al-Abdullah al-Salem al-Sabah

CABINET *as at August 1997*

Prime Minister, HH The Crown Prince
First Deputy PM, Foreign Affairs, Sheikh Sabah al-Ahmad al-Jaber
Second Deputy PM, Finance, Nasser Abdulla Al-Rodhan
Deputy PM, Defence, Sheikh Salem Sabah Al-Salem Al-Sabah
Commerce and Industry, Jassem Abdullah Al-Mudhaf
Communications, Electricity and Water, Jassem Mohamad Al-Aoun
Education and Higher Education, Abdullah Yousef Al-Ghunaim
Information, Health (acting), Saud Nasser Al-Sabah
Interior, Sheikh Mohammad Khaled Al-Hamad Al-Sabah
Justice, Awqaf and Islamic Affairs, Mohammad Dhaifallah Sharar
Labour and Social Affairs, Ahmad Khalid al-Kolaib
Minister of State for Cabinet Affairs, Abdul-Aziz Dakhil Al-Dakhil
Oil, Issa Mohammad Al-Mazidi
Planning and Administrative Development Affairs, Ali Fahd Al-Zumei
Public Works, Housing Affairs, Abdullah Rashed Al-Hajri

EMBASSY OF THE STATE OF KUWAIT
45–46 Queen's Gate, London SW7 5JN
Tel 0171-589 4533
Ambassador Extraordinary and Plenipotentiary, HE Khaled al-Duwaisan, GCVO, apptd 1993
Cultural Attaché, Prof. Ibraheem Al-Refaie

BRITISH EMBASSY
PO Box 2 Safat, 13001 Safat, Kuwait
Tel: Kuwait 2403334/6
Ambassador Extraordinary and Plenipotentiary, HE Graham H. Boyce, CMG, apptd 1996
Counsellor and Deputy Head of Mission, J. Jenkins, LVO
First Secretaries, L. Hartley (*Management and Consul*); M. Hurley (*Commercial*)
Defence Attaché, Col. G. Sayle, OBE
BRITISH COUNCIL REPRESENTATIVE, C. Reuter, 2 al Arabi Street (PO Box 345), 13004 Safat, Mansouriyah

ECONOMY

Despite the desert terrain, 8.4 per cent of land is under cultivation, fruit and vegetables being the main crops. Shrimp fishing is becoming important.

The oil industry was brought into government ownership in 1975. Since reorganization in 1980, the national industry has been run by the Kuwait Petroleum Corporation.

Oil installations were extensively damaged when Iraqi forces set light to oil wells prior to their retreat. Oil exports were resumed in July 1991 and production (including output from the neutral zone) reached 2,000,000 barrels per day in 1993, in line with the quota allocated by OPEC (compared to a production capacity of 2,200,000 barrels

per day before the Iraqi invasion). Capacity is 2,500,000 barrels per day.

Before the Iraqi invasion Kuwait had six power stations capable of generating 7,200 MW of electricity. Associated desalination capacity, on which the country largely depends for water, was 118 million gallons a day; reserves stored up to 2,000 million barrels. All six power stations were damaged during the Iraqi occupation. Essential services were restored after liberation and after substantial investment electricity and water distillation capacity was restored to pre-invasion levels in 1995.

GNP – US$28,941 million (1995); US$17,390 per capita (1995)
GDP – US$20,300 million (1992); US$11,017 per capita (1992)
ANNUAL AVERAGE GROWTH OF GDP – –9.6 per cent (1992)
INFLATION RATE – 0.4 per cent (1993)

TRADE

Oil is the major export. Non-oil exports, mainly to Asian countries and the Indian sub-continent, have included chemical fertilizers, ammonia and other chemicals, metal pipes, shrimps and building materials. Re-exports to neighbouring states traditionally accounted for a major proportion of non-oil exports but were brought to a halt by the Iraqi invasion. Major trading partners are Japan, the USA and Western Europe.

In 1994 Kuwait had a trade surplus of US$5,221 million and a current account surplus of US$3,763 million. In 1995 imports totalled US$7,139 million and exports US$13,036 million.

Trade with UK	1995	1996
Imports from UK	£550,870,000	£579,097,000
Exports to UK	151,377,000	179,865,000

COMMUNICATIONS

Ports and airport were damaged during the Iraqi occupation, but have reopened since liberation. There is a network of dual-carriageway roads and more are under construction. Telecommunications and postal services are conducted by the government. Its earth satellite station and telecommunications network were severely damaged during the Iraqi occupation but domestic and international telephone services have been fully restored.

SOCIAL WELFARE

The government invested its considerable oil revenues in comprehensive social services. Education and medical treatment are free. Kuwait University opened in 1966, and in 1987–8 had 15,602 students. In 1987–8 there were over 489,000 pupils at government and private schools. These numbers have declined along with the total population since the Iraqi invasion and a number of schools did not reopen after Kuwait's liberation.

ILLITERACY RATE – 21.4 per cent
ENROLMENT (percentage of age group) – primary 64 per cent (1994); secondary 56 per cent (1993); tertiary 24.2 per cent (1994)

KYRGYZSTAN
Kyrgyz Respublikasy

AREA – 76,642 sq. miles (198,501 sq. km). Neighbours: Kazakhstan (north), China (east), Tajikistan (south and south-west), Uzbekistan (west)

POPULATION – 4,596,000 (1994 UN estimate): 52.4 per cent Kirghiz (Turkic origin), 21.5 per cent Russian and 12.9 per cent Uzbek, with smaller numbers of Ukrainians, Germans, Tatars and Kazakhs. Islam is the main religion. Kirghiz is a Turkic language which was given an alphabet in the 1930s and became the official language after independence. Russian is an equal official language in the fields of science, industry and the health service, and in all regions where there is a large Russian population. Otherwise the ethnic groups use their own languages

CAPITAL – Bishkek (population, 627,800, 1991 estimate; 616,000, 1989 census)

CURRENCY – Som (introduced on 10 May 1993 at rate of 1:200 against the Rouble)

NATIONAL DAY – 31 August (Independence Day)

NATIONAL FLAG – Red with a rayed sun containing a representation of a yurt, all in gold

LIFE EXPECTANCY (years) – male 64.60; female 72.74

POPULATION GROWTH RATE – 1.1 per cent (1994)

POPULATION DENSITY – 23 per sq. km (1994)

URBAN POPULATION – 39.0 per cent (1994)

MILITARY EXPENDITURE – 3.5 per cent of GDP (1995)

MILITARY PERSONNEL – Army 7,000

CONSCRIPTION DURATION – 12–18 months

Kyrgyzstan (formerly Kirghizia) is mountainous, the major part being covered by the ridge of the Central Tienshan, while the Pamir-Altai system occupies its southern part. There are a number of spacious mountain valleys, the Alai, Susamyr and others. Kyrgyzstan is divided into six administrative regions.

HISTORY AND POLITICS

The Kirghiz people were first mentioned in Chinese chronicles in the second millennium BC. They are a merger of two ethnic groups, a Turkic-speaking people driven into the area by the Mongols from the River Yenisei area of Central Asia, and indigenous peoples who spoke a similar language. After a long period under Mongol, Chinese and Persian rule, the Kirghiz became part of the Russian Empire in the 1860s and 1870s. Kyrgyzstan became part of the Soviet Union in 1920 and underwent some industrialization.

Kyrgyzstan declared independence just after the failed Moscow coup on 31 August 1991.

Ethnic tensions between the rural nomadic Kirghiz, the urban Russians and the wealthy Uzbeks who own many businesses and form the majority in the second largest town of Osh, are never far from the surface. By presidential decree the sphere of official usage of the Russian language has been expanded to encourage Russians to remain, and a treaty on dual citizenship has been signed with Russia. The government is also committed to the fair representation of ethnic Russians in the civil service.

President Akaev had difficulty in introducing economic reforms because of obstruction by the bureaucracy and the *Uluk Kenesh* (parliament) over the reforms enshrined in the constitution. The President won a referendum on his plans for greater economic reform in January 1994. Elections to the new parliament, the *Zhogorku Kenesh*, were held in February 1995. A new government was appointed by the President in February 1996 in the wake of the referendum increasing his powers.

POLITICAL SYSTEM

A new constitution was adopted on 5 May 1993 by the Uluk Kenesh which requires the country's adherence to moral and international principles of law and human rights and to the values of Islam. President Akaev transferred the role of head of government from himself to the prime minister although a referendum in February 1996 gave the president the power to appoint all senior officials except the prime minister, whose appointment requires legislative approval. A referendum in October 1994 overwhelmingly supported the abolition of the Uluk Kenesh and its replacement by a smaller bicameral parliament composed of a 35-member Legislative Assembly and a 70-member People's Assembly.

HEAD OF STATE

President, Askar Akaev, *elected* 12 October 1991, *re-elected* 24 December 1995

GOVERNMENT *as at August 1997*

Prime Minister, Apas Jumagulov

First Deputy PM, Kemelbek Nanaev

Deputy PMs, Bekbolot Talgarbekov (*Agrarian Policy*); Mira Jangarachova (*Sociocultural Policy*)

Agriculture and Water Conservancy, Karimshar Abdimomunov

Architecture and Construction, Alexander Moiseyev

Communications, Abdyzhapar Tagayev

Co-operation with CIS States, Yan Fisher

Defence, Murzakan Subanov

Education, Sciences and Culture, Askar Kakeyev

Emergency Situations and Civil Defence, Mambetzhunus Abylov

Environmental Protection, Kulubek Bokonbayev

Finance, Talaibek Koichumanov

Foreign Affairs, Roza Otunbayeva

Health, Naken Kasiyev

Industry and Foreign Trade, Andrei Iordan

Interior, Omurbek Kutuyev

Justice, Larisa Gutnichenko

Labour and Social Security, Asylgul Abdurekhmenova

National Security, Valery Verchagin (*acting*)

Transport and Communications, Zhantoro Satybaldiev

BRITISH AMBASSADOR, HE Douglas B. McAdam, resident at Alma Ata, Kazakhstan

ECONOMY

Agriculture is the main sector of the economy, with sugar beet, cotton and sheep the main products. Private ownership of land was legalized in 1997. Industry is concentrated in the food-processing, textiles, timber and mining fields. Hydroelectric power is abundant and Kyrgyzstan has reserves of gold, coal, mercury and uranium, although only gold has so far been exploited and is the country's largest export.

The government introduced the som in May 1993 to break the link with the depreciating rouble, the cause of high inflation in 1992 and early 1993. The President and government have also made the Central Bank independent of government and parliamentary control. However, the country needs direct foreign investment desperately and has had most of its trading links with other Central Asian republics reduced because of their refusal to accept payments in soms, although this has been ameliorated by the signing of an economic union agreement with Kazakhstan and Uzbekistan in February 1994. Subsidized goods supplies from Russia have also been reduced. In March 1996, a treaty was signed with Belarus, Kazakhstan and Russia enhancing economic co-operation and working towards a single customs territory.

GNP – US$3,158 million (1995); US$700 per capita (1995)

GDP – US$9,865 million (1992); US$177 per capita (1992)

TOTAL EXTERNAL DEBT – US$610 million (1995)

TRADE WITH UK	1995	1996
Imports from UK	£4,086,000	£5,565,000
Exports to UK	846,000	344,000

CULTURE AND EDUCATION

Until the 1930s the Kirghiz language had an oral tradition of literature which included the epic poem *Manas*, which tells the history of the Kirghiz people. Internationally, one of the best-known writers of the former Soviet Union is the Kirghiz writer Chingiz Aitmatov (1928–).
ILLITERACY RATE – 0.4 per cent
ENROLMENT (percentage of age group) – tertiary 20.1 per cent (1993)

LAOS
Satharanarath Pasathipatai Pasason Lao

AREA – 91,429 sq. miles (236,800 sq. km). Neighbours: China (north), Vietnam (north-east and east), Cambodia (south), Thailand (west), Myanmar (north-west)
POPULATION – 4,605,300 (1995 census)
CAPITAL – Vientiane (population, 132,253, 1966; 120,000, 1984 estimate)
CURRENCY – Kip (K) of 100 at
NATIONAL DAY – 2 December
NATIONAL FLAG – Blue background with a central white circle, framed by two horizontal red stripes
LIFE EXPECTANCY (years) – male 49.50; female 52.50
POPULATION GROWTH RATE – 3.0 per cent (1994)
POPULATION DENSITY – 20 per sq. km (1994)
MILITARY EXPENDITURE – 4.2 per cent of GDP (1995)
MILITARY PERSONNEL – 37,000: Army 33,000, Navy 500, Air Force 3,500
CONSCRIPTION DURATION – 18 months minimum
ILLITERACY RATE – 43.4 per cent
ENROLMENT (percentage of age group) – primary 68 per cent; secondary 18 per cent; tertiary 1.5 per cent (1993)

HISTORY AND POLITICS

The kingdom of Lane Xang, the Land of a Million Elephants, was founded in the 14th century but broke up at the beginning of the 16th century into the separate kingdoms of Luang Prabang and Vientiane and the principality of Champassac, which together came under French protection in 1893. In 1945 the Japanese staged a coup and suppressed the French administration. In 1947 Laos became a constitutional monarchy under King Sisvang Vong, and an independent sovereign state in 1953. The next 22 years in Laos were marked by power struggles and civil war, eventually won by the North Vietnamese-backed Pathet Lao, a Communist-dominated organization.

The Lao People's Democratic Republic was proclaimed in December 1975 following victory by the Pathet Lao and the abdication of the King. A president and Council of Ministers were installed, and a 45-member Supreme People's Council was appointed to draft a constitution, which was approved in 1991. The Lao People's Revolutionary Party (LPRP) is the sole legal political organization. A general election to the 85-member National Assembly established by the 1991 constitution was held on 20 December 1992; all the candidates were approved by the LPRP. The President, Prime Minister and Council of Ministers were confirmed in their posts by the National Assembly on 22 February 1993.

HEAD OF STATE
President, Nouhak Phonmsavan, *elected by Supreme People's Assembly* 25 November 1992

COUNCIL OF MINISTERS *as at May 1997*
Prime Minister, Gen. Khamtai Siphandone
Deputy PMs, Khamphoui Keoboualapha; Bounnhang Vorachit
Agriculture and Forestry, Dr Siene Saphangthong
Commerce, Sompadith Volasane
Communications, Transport, Posts and Construction, Phao Bounnaphol
Education, Phimmasone Leuangkhamma
Finance, Saysomphone Phonvihane
Foreign Affairs, Somsavat Lengsavat
Governor of the National Bank, Pany Yathotou
Head of the President's Office, Thongdam Chanthapon
Health, Dr Pommeck Daraloy
Industry, Soulivong Dalavong
Information and Culture, Osakan Thammatheva
Interior, Lt.-Gen. Asang Laoli
Justice, Khamouane Boupha
Labour and Social Welfare, Thongloun Sisoulith
Minister, and Head of the Office of the Council of Ministers, Cheuang Sombounkhanh
National Defence and Supreme Commander of the Lao People's Army, Lt.-Gen. Choummali Saygnasone
President of the Supreme People's Assembly, Samane Vignaket

EMBASSY OF THE LAO PEOPLE'S DEMOCRATIC REPUBLIC
74 Avenue Raymond-Poincaré 75116 Paris
Tel: Paris 4553 0298
Ambassador Extraordinary and Plenipotentiary, HE Kamphan Simmalavong, apptd 1995

BRITISH AMBASSADOR, HE Sir James Hodge, KCVO, CMG, resident at Bangkok, Thailand

ECONOMY

A 'new economic mechanism' programme was introduced in 1986 which began the liberalization of the economy, with greater autonomy for state enterprises, the relaxation of price controls and the encouragement of private business and investors. These reforms have produced a market-orientated economic system which has increased growth and reduced inflation. The economy is dominated by the agricultural sector, which contributed 60 per cent of real GDP in 1994, when 1.5 million tons of paddy rice was produced. Laos is also the world's third largest producer of opium.

Although Laos is one of the poorest states in the world, there is potential for increased hydroelectric power exports to Thailand and there are unexploited deposits of iron ore, gold, bauxite and lignite. Foreign capital investment in infrastructure began with the 1994 opening of the Friendship Bridge over the Mekong river border with Thailand which links road routes from Singapore to China. Hydroelectric power is the main export, followed by wood.

In 1993 Laos had a trade deficit of US$148 million and a current account deficit of US$53 million. In 1995 imports totalled US$587 million and exports US$348 million.
GNP – US$1,694 million (1995); US$350 per capita (1995)
GDP – US$962 million (1992); US$269 per capita (1992)
TOTAL EXTERNAL DEBT – US$2,165 million (1995)

TRADE WITH UK	1995	1996
Imports from UK	£3,472,000	£5,264,000
Exports to UK	13,993,000	6,988,000

LATVIA
The Republic of Latvia

AREA – 24,942 sq. miles (64,600 sq. km). Neighbours: Estonia (north), Lithuania and Belarus (south), the Russian Federation (east)

POPULATION – 2,529,600 (1995): 54.8 per cent Latvian, 32.8 per cent Russian, 4.0 per cent Belarusian, with small Ukrainian and Polish minorities. The main religions are Lutheran, Roman Catholic and Russian Orthodox. The majority (54.8 per cent) have Latvian as their first language and 32.8 per cent Russian. Education is in Latvian and Russian. Public sector employees must pass language tests in Latvian to a level commensurate with the nature of their employment. The right of minorities to use their mother tongue has been acknowledged

CAPITAL – Riga (population, 840,000, 1995)

MAJOR CITIES – Daugavpils (120,200); Liepaja (100,200); Jelgava (71,100); Jurmala (59,300); and Ventspils (47,000)

CURRENCY – Lats of 100 santimes

NATIONAL ANTHEM – Dievs, svētī Latviju (God bless Latvia)

NATIONAL DAY – 18 November (Independence Day 1918)

NATIONAL FLAG – Crimson, with a white horizontal stripe across the centre

LIFE EXPECTANCY (years) – male 61.61; female 73.84

POPULATION GROWTH RATE – –1.2 per cent (1994)

POPULATION DENSITY – 39 per sq. km (1994)

URBAN POPULATION – 69.0 per cent (1993)

HISTORY AND POLITICS

Latvia came under the control of the German Teutonic Knights at the end of the 13th century. During the next few centuries the country endured sporadic invasions by the Swedes, Poles and Russians. By 1795 Latvia was entirely under Russian control. On 18 November 1918 Latvia declared its independence and this was confirmed by the Versailles Treaty in 1919. Several years of fighting with the new Soviet Russia ensued until a peace treaty was signed under which Soviet Russia renounced all claims to Latvian territory.

The Soviet Union annexed Latvia in 1940 under the terms of the Molotov-Ribbentrop pact with Germany. Latvia was invaded and occupied when Germany invaded the Soviet Union during the Second World War. In 1944 the Soviet Union recaptured Latvia from Germany and confirmed its annexation, though this was never accepted as legal by most states.

In 1988 the Popular Front of Latvia was formed to campaign for greater sovereignty and democracy for Latvia. It won the elections to the Supreme Council in 1989, and on 4 May 1990 the Supreme Council declared the independent republic of Latvia to be, *de jure*, still in existence. Agitation in Latvia against Soviet rule led in 1990 and early 1991 to clashes between independence supporters and Latvian Communists and the Soviet military. Violence reached a peak in January 1991 with deaths caused by Soviet Interior Ministry troops and attacks on Baltic border posts. A national referendum was held in March 1991 in which 73 per cent voted in favour of independence, and this was declared on 21 August 1991. The State Council of the Soviet Union recognized the independence of Latvia on 10 September 1991.

After the 31 September–1 October 1995 general election nine political parties were represented in the *Saéima*.

No party had a clear majority, but a coalition of Saimnieks, Latvia's Way and six other parties formed a government.

POLITICAL SYSTEM

Executive authority is vested in a prime minister and Cabinet of Ministers. Legislative power is exercised by the unicameral parliament (Saéima), which comprises 100 deputies elected for three-year terms by proportional representation with a 4 per cent threshold for parliamentary representation. The deputies elect a president of state, who in turn appoints the prime minister. The prime minister appoints, and the Saéima approves, the Cabinet of Ministers.

The electorate and citizenship had been restricted to descendants of Latvian citizens before the 1940 Soviet occupation and to those who can pass the required Latvian language tests, until 1994 when a law was passed enabling naturalization of long-term residents.

HEAD OF STATE
President, Guntis Ulmanis, *elected* 7 July 1993, *re-elected* 18 June 1996

COUNCIL OF MINISTERS *as at May 1997*
Prime Minister, Andris Šķēle (Ind.)
Deputy PMs, Juris Kaksītis (DPS); Anatolijs Gorbunovs *(Environmental Protection and Regional Development)* (LC)
Agriculture, Roberts Dilba (LZS)
Culture, Rihards Piks (LZS)
Defence, Talavs Jundzis
Economy, Guntars Krasts (TB)
Education and Science, Juris Celmiņš (DPS)
EU Affairs, Aleksandrs Kiršteins (LNNK)
Finance, Roberts Zīle (TB)
Foreign Affairs, Valdis Birkavs (LC)
Interior, Dainis Turlais (DPS)
Justice, Defence (acting), Dzintars Rasnacs (TB)
Transport, Vilis Krištopāns (LC)
Welfare, Vladimirs Makārovs (TB)

DPS Democratic Party Saimnieks; LC Latvia's Way; LNNK Latvia's National Conservative Party; LZS Latvia's Farmers' Union; TB For Father and Freedom; Ind. Independent

EMBASSY OF THE REPUBLIC OF LATVIA
45 Nottingham Place, London WIM 3FE
Tel 0171-312 0040
Ambassador Extraordinary and Plenipotentiary, HE Normans Penke, apptd 1997

BRITISH EMBASSY
5, Alunana Iela Street, Riga LV1010
Tel: Riga 733 8126
Ambassador Extraordinary and Plenipotentiary, HE Nicholas R. Jarrold, apptd 1996

BRITISH COUNCIL DIRECTOR, I. Stewart, Lazaretes iela 3, Riga LV-1010

DEFENCE

The Army has 13 armoured personnel carriers and 26 artillery pieces, the Navy has 18 patrol craft at two bases and the Air Force has two aircraft and five helicopters.

All remaining Russian forces withdrew from Latvia on 31 August 1994 except for those stationed at the anti-ballistic missile early-warning radar at Skrunda, which will continue to operate until 1999.

MILITARY EXPENDITURE – 3.2 per cent of GDP (1995)
MILITARY PERSONNEL – 3,000: Army 1,750, Navy 1,000, Air Force 250
CONSCRIPTION DURATION 18 months

ECONOMY

Attempts to move from a command economy to a market economy resulted in low growth and high unemployment in the early 1990s. Economic independence from the CIS was largely achieved, however. The government has initiated a privatization process which has made many industrial facilities available for purchase both by Latvian and foreign private investors. By the end of 1993, 20 per cent of economic production and 40 per cent of agricultural production had been privatized.

Latvia is an agricultural exporter, specializing in cattle and pig breeding, dairy farming and crops, including sugar beet, flax, cereals and potatoes. Natural resources include limestone, gypsum, peat and timber.

Industry was organized to contribute to the centralized Soviet economy and is specialized in certain areas. These include the production of electric and diesel trains, telephones, telephone exchange equipment, food processing, agricultural machinery, and timber and paper products.

Tourism is being developed, capitalizing on its beach resorts, nature reserves and parks. Latvia is also geographically well-placed for the development of transport services.

GNP – US$5,708 million (1995); US$2,270 per capita (1995)
GDP – US$11,392 million (1992); US$460 per capita (1992)
ANNUAL AVERAGE GROWTH OF GDP – –1.6 per cent (1995)
INFLATION RATE – 25.0 per cent (1995)
UNEMPLOYMENT – 6.6 per cent (1995)
TOTAL EXTERNAL DEBT – US$462 million (1995)

TRADE

Russia remains one of the most important trading partners for Latvia. In 1994, 41 per cent of exports went to the CIS, 40 per cent to the EU and EFTA states, and 6 per cent to Lithuania and Estonia. Of total imports, 38 per cent came from the CIS, 17 per cent from the EU, 13 per cent from Lithuania and Estonia, 11 per cent from EFTA states. The main imports are oil and energy, and the main exports are wood and wood products, artificial fibres, meat, dairy products and rolled ferrous metals.

In 1995 imports totalled US$1,810 million and exports US$1,283 million.

Trade with UK	1995	1996
Imports from UK	£40,058,000	£78,986,000
Exports to UK	170,411,000	307,121,000

COMMUNICATIONS

Latvia has a reasonably well-developed railway (2,397 km) and road (18,834 km) system, along which a significant proportion of exports from CIS republics are transported to western Europe. Latvia is also being developed as a transportation route from Scandinavia to central and southern Europe. Several warm-water ports exist, of which two, Riga and Ventspils, are developed for commercial transport. The national airline, Latvijas Aviolinijas, operates regular flights to Russia, Scandinavia and Europe.

CULTURE AND EDUCATION

The Latvian language belongs to the Baltic branch of the Indo-European languages, and as such is distinct from Russian. The Latin alphabet is used. Independent Latvian literature appeared in the late 18th and early 19th centuries and played a role in the fight for independence in 1918.

There are 15 higher education institutions, of which four are universities.
ILLITERACY RATE – 0.3 per cent
ENROLMENT (percentage of age group) – primary 81 per cent; secondary 78 per cent; tertiary 21.8 per cent (1994)

LEBANON
Al-Jumhouriya al-Lubnaniya

AREA – 4,015 sq. miles (10,400 sq. km)
POPULATION – 2,915,000 (1994 UN estimate): 30 per cent Christian, 6 per cent Druze, 4 per cent Armenian. Arabic is the official language, and French and English are also widely used
CAPITAL – ΨBeirut (population, 1,500,000, 1991)
MAJOR CITIES – Ψ Tripoli (200,000); ΨSidon (100,000); ΨTyre (70,000); Zahlé (30,000)
CURRENCY – Lebanese pound (L£) of 100 piastres
NATIONAL ANTHEM – Kulluna Lil Watan Lil'ula Lil'alam (We all belong to the homeland)
NATIONAL DAY – 22 November
NATIONAL FLAG – Horizontal bands of red, white and red with a green cedar of Lebanon in the centre of the white band
LIFE EXPECTANCY (years) – male 66.60; female 70.50
POPULATION GROWTH RATE – 3.3 per cent (1994)
POPULATION DENSITY – 280 per sq. km (1994)

HISTORY AND POLITICS

Lebanon became an independent state in 1920, administered under French mandate until 22 November 1943. Powers were transferred to the Lebanese government from January 1944 and French troops were withdrawn in 1946.

In 1975, fighting broke out in Beirut between Maronite, Sunni and Shia factions, the latter supported by Palestinian guerrillas based in Lebanon. In 1976 the Arab Deterrent Forces, composed mainly of Syrian troops, imposed a cease-fire but fighting resumed and continued until the end of the civil war in 1990. In 1978 Israeli forces invaded but withdrew some months later, handing over their positions, except for a belt in the south, to the UN Interim Force in Lebanon (UNIFIL). In 1982 Israeli forces again invaded, penetrating as far as Beirut. Although the bulk of Israeli troops withdrew from southern Lebanon in 1985, a buffer zone controlled by the Israeli-backed South Lebanon Army (SLA), a Christian militia, was established along the Israeli–Lebanon border. Syrian forces are deployed in west Beirut and in the north and the east of the country.

The Taif Accord 'for national conciliation', drawn up by an Arab League-appointed committee, gained the approval of most Lebanese MPs in 1989, but was resisted by Gen. Aoun, who insisted on an immediate withdrawal of the 35,000 Syrian troops in Lebanon. The Lebanese government with the backing of Syrian troops ousted Gen. Aoun in October 1990 and a new government incorporating the main militia leaders was formed in December 1990. Since then the government has attempted to clear the militias from the Greater Beirut area and restore its authority throughout most of the country. The Beqa'a valley remains under Syrian control and the South Lebanon Security Zone under Israeli control. All militias have been disarmed apart from Hezbollah and the SLA. Since 1993 the Lebanese Army has deployed in southern villages alongside UNIFIL forces but has not disarmed Hezbollah forces, who are financed, armed and trained by

Syria and Iran to continue fighting against Israel and the SLA.

Low-level fighting continued throughout 1993–7. In April 1996, Israel began a two-week missile bombardment of Hezbollah targets in Beirut and southern Lebanon. The mission, code-named 'Grapes of Wrath', was in retaliation for suicide attacks and Hezbollah strikes against Israel's northern cities. An agreement was reached on 15 April to confine hostilities to southern Lebanon.

The first parliamentary elections since 1972 were held between August and October 1992. The 128-seat National Assembly was directly elected by universal suffrage and divided equally between Christians and Muslims. The polls were widely boycotted in Christian areas because of the continuing presence of Syrian troops, in breach of the Taif Accord. A government was formed under Prime Minister Rafic Al-Hariri in October 1992 which has focused on the economy and reconstruction. National Assembly elections were held in August and September 1996.

HEAD OF STATE

President of the Republic of Lebanon, Elias Hrawi, *took office* 25 November 1989 (term extended by three years by National Assembly on 19 October 1995)

CABINET *as at August 1997*

Prime Minister, Post and Telecommunications, Finance, Rafic Al-Hariri
Deputy PM, Interior, Michel El-Murr
Administrative Reform, Boharah Merhej
Agriculture, Chawki Fakhouri
Culture and Higher Education, Fawzi Hobeish
Displaced People, Walid Joumblatt
Economy and Trade, Yassine Jaber
Emigrants, Talal Arslan
Environment, Akram Chhayeb
Foreign Affairs, Fares Boueiz
Health, Sleiman Franjieh
Housing and Co-operatives, Mahmoud Abou Hamdan
Industrial Affairs, Nadim Salem
Industry and Petroleum, Shahi Barsoumian
Information, Basem Al-Sabaa
Justice, Bahij Tabbarah
Labour, Asaad Hardan
Ministers of State, Fouad Siniora *(Finance)*; Elias Hanna; Ghazi Seifeddine
Municipalities and Rural Affairs, Hagop Damarjian
National Defence, Mohsen Dalloul
National Education, Jean Obeid
Public Works, Ali Harajli
Social Affairs, Ayoub Hmayed
Tourism, Nicholas Fattouch
Transport, Omar Meskaoui
Vocational and Technical Education, Farouk Al-Barbir
Water and Electricity Resources, Elias Hobeika

LEBANESE EMBASSY

21 Kensington Palace Gardens, London W8 4QM
Tel 0171–229 7265/6
Ambassador Extraordinary and Plenipotentiary, HE Mahmoud Hammoud, apptd 1990

BRITISH EMBASSY

Autostrade Jal El Dib, Coolrite Building (PO Box 60180), Beirut
Tel: Beirut 406330
Ambassador Extraordinary and Plenipotentiary, HE David MacLennan, apptd 1996

BRITISH COUNCIL DIRECTOR, A. Malamah-Thomas, MBE, Sidani Street, Azar Building, Beirut

DEFENCE

The Army has 300 main battle tanks, 1,057 armoured personnel carriers and 150 artillery pieces. The Navy has 14 patrol and coastal vessels at three bases. The Air Force has three combat aircraft and four armed helicopters.

There are a 4,491-strong UN peacekeeping force, 35,000 Syrian troops and 150 Iranian Revolutionary Guards operating in Lebanon.

MILITARY EXPENDITURE – 5.3 per cent of GDP (1995)
MILITARY PERSONNEL – 61,900: Army 47,500, Navy 600, Air Force 800, Paramilitaries 13,000
CONSCRIPTION DURATION – 12 months

ECONOMY

Fruits are the most important products and include citrus fruit, apples, grapes, bananas and olives. There is some light industry, mostly for the production of consumer goods, but most factories are still in need of reconstruction because of the civil war.

A ten-year plan has been initiated to repair war damage and to restore Lebanon's position as a regional financial services and light industrial centre. The 1993–2002 reconstruction plan is estimated to cost US$12,900 million in total, of which US$7,600 million is to come from foreign loans and grants and US$5,300 million from budget surpluses. It is to concentrate on rebuilding housing, transport, utilities, services, education and health services, and aiding industry and agriculture.

A plan to reconstruct the commercial centre of Beirut has been started, with the issue in January 1994 of US$650 million of shares in the US$1,800 million Solidère company which will reconstruct the 400-acre site. The government has also obtained US$1,600 million in loans and grants for its national reconstruction programme, mainly from Arab states and international agencies.

Operation 'Grapes of Wrath' halted the resurgence of business confidence in Beirut and set back the redevelopment of the infrastructure. The World Bank provided US$50 million to compensate for the damage caused by the operation. More than US$300 million of aid was pledged at a reconstruction conference in December 1996.

GNP – US$10,673 million (1995); US$2,660 per capita (1995)
GDP – US$4,287 million (1992); US$1,496 per capita (1992)
INFLATION RATE – 6.8 per cent (1994)
TOTAL EXTERNAL DEBT – US$2,966 million (1995)

TRADE

Principal imports are gold and precious metals, machinery and electrical equipment, textiles and yarns, vegetable products, iron and steel goods, and motor vehicles. There had been a gradual decline in the overall amount of imports as a result of continued instability.

Principal exports include gold and precious metals, fruits and vegetables, textiles, building materials, furniture, plastic goods, foodstuffs, tobacco and wine.

At one time there was a considerable transit trade through Beirut into the Arab hinterland. Lebanon is the terminal for two oil pipelines, one formerly belonging to the Iraq Petroleum Company, debouching at Tripoli, the other belonging to the Trans Arabian Pipeline Company, at Sidon. These lines have not functioned for some years.

Trade with UK	1995	1996
Imports from UK	£175,616,000	£173,766,000
Exports to UK	14,198,000	12,200,000

COMMUNICATIONS

The railways are not functioning as a result of the civil war. There is an international airport at Beirut, served by the national carrier MEA and other airlines. An internal service operates from Beirut to Tripoli.

ARCHAEOLOGY

Lebanon has some important historical remains, notably Baalbek (Heliopolis) which contains the ruins of first- to third-century Roman temples and Jbeil (Byblos), one of the oldest continuously inhabited towns in the world, and ancient Tyre.

EDUCATION

There are six universities in Beirut, the American and the French universities, and the Lebanese National University, the Beirut University College, the Kaslik Saint Esprit University and the Arab University, with the University of Balamand situated near Tripoli. There are several institutions for vocational training, and there is a good provision throughout the country of primary and secondary schools, among which are a great number of private schools.
ILLITERACY RATE – 7.6 per cent
ENROLMENT (percentage of age group) – tertiary 28.9 per cent (1991)

LESOTHO
'Muso oa Lesotho

AREA – 11,720 sq. miles (30,355 sq. km). Neighbour: South Africa which completely surrounds Lesotho
POPULATION – 1,996,000 (1994 UN estimate)
CAPITAL – Maseru (population, 288,951, 1986)
CURRENCY – Loti (M) of 100 lisente
NATIONAL ANTHEM – Pina ea Sechaba
NATIONAL DAY – 4 October (Independence Day)
NATIONAL FLAG – Diagonally white over blue over green with the white of double width, and an assegai and knobkerrie on a Basotho shield in brown in the upper hoist
LIFE EXPECTANCY (years) – male 58.00; female 63.00
POPULATION GROWTH RATE – 2.7 per cent (1994)
POPULATION DENSITY – 66 per sq. km (1994)
MILITARY EXPENDITURE – 5.5 per cent of GDP (1995)
MILITARY PERSONNEL – Army 2,000

HISTORY AND POLITICS

Lesotho (formerly Basutoland) became a constitutional monarchy within the Commonwealth on 4 October 1966. The independence constitution was suspended in 1970 and the country was governed by a Council of Ministers headed by Leabua Jonathan until the establishment of a nominated National Assembly in 1974.

Jonathan's government was overthrown in 1986, and executive and legislative powers were conferred on the King, to be advised by the Military Council and Council of Ministers led by Maj.-Gen. Justin Lekhanya. In March 1990 King Moshoeshoe II's powers were formally revoked and in November the King was deposed and replaced by his son, who assumed the title of Letsie III. Maj.-Gen. Lekhanya was overthrown in 1991 in a coup led by Col. Elias Ramaema. Elections were held in March 1993 and the Basotho Congress Party (BCP) won all 65 seats in the new National Assembly. A BCP government led by Ntsu Mokhele was formed, King Letsie III swore allegiance to a new multiparty democratic constitution and the Military Council was dissolved.

On 17 August 1994 King Letsie III and sections of the military mounted a coup attempt and announced the dismissal of the government and the dissolution of parliament. After mediation, the government, which had refused to leave office, was restored by the King. King Letsie also announced his intention to abdicate in favour of his father, Moshoeshoe II, who was restored on 25 January 1995. When King Moshoeshoe II died in a car crash on 15 January 1996 King Letsie III again ascended to the throne.

The country is divided into ten administrative districts. In each district there is a district secretary who co-ordinates all government activity in the area, working in co-operation with hereditary chiefs.

HEAD OF STATE
HM The King of Lesotho, King Letsie III, *acceded* February 1996

COUNCIL OF MINISTERS *as at August 1997*
Prime Minister, Defence, Public Service, Dr Ntsu Mokhehle
Deputy PM, Home Affairs, Local Government, Rural and Urban Development, Pakalitha Mosisili
Agriculture, Co-operatives and Youth Affairs, Mopshatla Mabitle
Education, Lesao Lehohla
Finance and Development Planning, Victor Ketso
Foreign Affairs, Kelebone Maope
Health and Social Welfare, Tefo Mabote
Information and Broadcasting, Monyane Moleleki
Justice, Human Rights, Law and Constitutional Affairs, Sephiri Motanyane
Labour and Employment, Not'si Molopo
Natural Resources, Shakhane Robong Mokhehle
Tourism, Sport and Culture, Pasho Mochesane
Trade and Industry, Lira Motete
Transport and Communications, Mamoshebi Kabi
Works, Mohaila Mohale

HIGH COMMISSION FOR THE KINGDOM OF LESOTHO
7 Chesham Place, London SW1X 8HN
Tel 0171-235 5686
High Commissioner, HE Benjamin Masilo, apptd 1996

BRITISH HIGH COMMISSION
PO Box 521, Maseru 100
Tel: Maseru 313961
High Commissioner, HE Peter J. Smith, OBE, apptd 1996

BRITISH COUNCIL REPRESENTATIVE, S. Cwepe, Hobson's Square, PO Box 429, Maseru 100

ECONOMY

The economy is based on agriculture and animal husbandry, and the adverse balance of trade (mainly consumer and capital goods) is offset by the earnings of the large numbers of the population who work in South Africa. Apart from some diamonds, Lesotho has few natural resources and only small-scale industrial development. The Lesotho National Development Corporation was set up to promote the development of industry, mining, trade and tourism. Work has commenced on the Highlands Water Scheme designed to provide water for the Vaal industrial zone in South Africa and hydroelectricity for Lesotho. Drilling is being carried out for oil. A National Park has been established at Sehlabathebe in the Maluti mountains. A number of light manufacturing and processing industries have recently been established.

The main sources of revenue are customs and excise duty.

In 1993 Lesotho had a trade deficit of US$778 million and a current account surplus of US$22 million.
GNP – US$1,519 million (1995); US$770 per capita (1995)
GDP – US$598 million (1992); US$387 per capita (1992)
TOTAL EXTERNAL DEBT – US$659 million (1995)

TRADE WITH UK	1995	1996
Imports from UK	£1,324,000	£1,864,000
Exports to UK	399,000	60,000

COMMUNICATIONS

A tarred road links Maseru to several of the main lowland towns, and this is being extended in the south of the country. The mountainous areas are linked by tarred, gravelled and earth roads and tracks. Roads link border towns in South Africa with the main towns in Lesotho. Maseru is also connected by rail with the main Bloemfontein–Natal line of the South African Railways. Scheduled international air services are operated daily between Maseru and Johannesburg and other scheduled international flights are to Gabarone, Harare, Manzini and Maputo. There are around 30 airstrips. Internal scheduled services are operated by the Lesotho Airways Corporation. The telephone network is fully automated in all urban centres. Radio telephone communication is used extensively in the remote rural areas.

EDUCATION

Most schools are mission-controlled, the government providing grants for salaries and buildings. There are over 1,000 primary and over 100 secondary schools; few areas lack a school and there is a literacy rate of about 70 per cent. Increasing emphasis is being laid on agricultural and vocational education. The National University of Lesotho at Roma was established as a university in 1975.
ILLITERACY RATE – 28.7 per cent
ENROLMENT (percentage of age group) – primary 65 per cent (1994); secondary 17 per cent (1993); tertiary 2.3 per cent (1993)

LIBERIA
Republic of Liberia

AREA – 43,000 sq. miles (111,369 sq. km). Neighbours: Guinea (north), Côte d'Ivoire (east), Sierra Leone (north-west)
POPULATION – 2,700,000 (1994 UN estimate). The official language is English. Over 16 ethnic languages are spoken
CAPITAL – ΨMonrovia (population, 421,053, 1984)
MAJOR CITIES – ΨBuchanan (Grand Bassa); ΨGreenville (Sinoe); ΨHarper (Cape Palmas)
CURRENCY – Liberian dollar (L$) of 100 cents
NATIONAL ANTHEM – All Hail, Liberia, Hail
NATIONAL DAY – 26 July
NATIONAL FLAG – Alternate horizontal stripes (five white, six red), with five-pointed white star on blue field in upper corner next to flagstaff
LIFE EXPECTANCY (years) – male 45.80; female 44.00
POPULATION GROWTH RATE – 2.9 per cent (1994)
POPULATION DENSITY – 24 per sq. km (1994)
URBAN POPULATION – 44.2 per cent (1994)
MILITARY EXPENDITURE – 3.2 per cent of GDP (1995)
ILLITERACY RATE – 61.7 per cent

HISTORY AND POLITICS

Liberia was founded by the American Colonization Society in 1822 as a colony for freed American slaves, and has been recognized since 1847 as an independent state.

William V. S. Tubman, President since 1944, died in 1971 and was succeeded by Dr Tolbert. The constitution was suspended following a military coup in 1980 during which Tolbert was killed. M/Sgt. Samuel Doe assumed power as chairman of a military council. A new constitution was endorsed by a referendum in 1984. Doe and his party, the National Democratic Party of Liberia (NDPL) won the elections held in 1985, amid allegations of electoral fraud, and a civilian government was formally installed in 1986.

CIVIL WAR

A rebel incursion in 1989 by the National Patriotic Front of Liberia (NPFL) led by Charles Taylor developed into a full-scale civil war in 1990. A five-nation ECOWAS peacekeeping force (known as ECOMOG) landed in Monrovia in an effort to end the conflict but in September 1990 President Doe was killed, having refused to step down.

The Interim Government of National Unity (IGNU) was formed in August 1990 in The Gambia and arrived in Monrovia in November. An agreement to establish a cease-fire and confine troops to barracks under ECOMOG supervision broke down in October 1992 when the NPFL attempted to seize Monrovia. In response ECOMOG assumed a more offensive role, driving NPFL forces out of Monrovia's suburbs. By March 1993 the NPFL had been driven into eastern parts of Liberia and peace negotiations between the warring factions had begun. Under UN-sponsored negotiations a peace agreement was signed by the IGNU, NPFL and another rebel group, ULIMO, on 25 July 1993 which brought about a cease-fire on 1 August. Interim President Amos Sawyer was due to be replaced within one month by a five-member Council of State to govern the country during a transitional period, together with a 35-member transitional legislature including members from all three factions. The Council of State and legislature did not take power until March 1994 and the transitional government of IGNU, NPFL and ULIMO members not until May 1994.

Continued fighting and the fracturing of the three factions led to further negotiations and an agreement in December 1994 on a new Council of State. A Council of State comprising the faction leaders was inaugurated on 1 September 1995 and a transitional government formed. Fighting resumed briefly in April 1996, although a cease-fire in July 1996 enabled legislative elections to be held in July 1997 which were won by the NPFL.

HEAD OF STATE
President, Charles Taylor, *elected* 19 July 1997

EMBASSY OF THE REPUBLIC OF LIBERIA
2 Pembridge Place, London W2 4XB
Tel 0171-221 1036
Minister-Counsellor, Chargé d'Affaires, Ishmael Grant

BRITISH EMBASSY
The British Embassy in Monrovia was closed in March 1991.

ECONOMY

Before the civil war began principal exports were iron ore, crude rubber, timber, uncut diamonds, palm kernels, cocoa and coffee, but the civil war has resulted in the suspension of most economic activity.

GDP – US$854 million (1992); US$354 per capita (1992)
ANNUAL AVERAGE GROWTH OF GDP – 2.7 per cent (1987)
INFLATION RATE – 9.1 per cent (1989)
TOTAL EXTERNAL DEBT – US$2,127 million (1995)

TRADE WITH UK	1995	1996
Imports from UK	£8,456,000	£6,095,000
Exports to UK	544,000	11,707,000

COMMUNICATIONS

The artificial harbour and free port of Monrovia was
opened in 1948. There are nine ports of entry, including
three river ports. Robertsfield International Airport is
under NPFL control and not yet in use. Spriggs Payne
airfield, on the outskirts of Monrovia, normally used for
internal flights, is currently being used for flights to other
West African countries.

LIBYA
Al-Jamahiriya Al-Arabiya
Al-Libiya Al-Shabiya Al-Ishtirakiya Al-Uthma

AREA – 679,362 sq. miles (1,759,540 sq. km). Neighbours:
Egypt and Sudan (east), Chad and Niger (south), Algeria
and Tunisia (west)
POPULATION – 4,899,000 (1994 UN estimate). The people
of Libya are principally Arab with some Berbers in the
west and some Tuareg tribesmen in the Fezzan. Islam is
the official religion but other religions are tolerated. The
official language is Arabic
CAPITAL – ΨTripoli (population, 1,000,000, 1991
estimate)
MAJOR CITIES – ΨBenghazi (500,000); ΨMisurata
(200,000); Sirte (100,000)
CURRENCY – Libyan dinar (LD) of 1,000 dirhams
NATIONAL DAY – 1 September
NATIONAL FLAG – Libya uses a plain emerald green flag
LIFE EXPECTANCY (years) – male 61.58; female 65.00
POPULATION DENSITY – 3 per sq. km
ILLITERACY RATE – 23.8 per cent
ENROLMENT (percentage of age group) – primary 97 per
cent (1992); secondary 62 per cent (1980); tertiary 16.4
per cent (1991)

Vast sand and rock deserts, almost completely barren,
occupy the greater part of Libya. The southern part of the
country lies within the Sahara Desert. There are few rivers
and as rainfall is irregular outside parts of Cyrenaica and
Tripolitania, good harvests are rare.
The ancient ruins in Cyrenaica, at Cyrene, Ptolemais
(Tolmeta) and Apollonia, are outstanding, as are those at
Leptis Magna, 70 miles east, and at Sabratha, 40 miles west
of Tripoli. An Italian expedition found in the south-west of
the Fezzan a series of rock-paintings more than 5,000 years
old.

HISTORY AND POLITICS

Libya was occupied by Italy in 1911–12 in the course of the
Italo-Turkish War, and under the Treaty of Ouchy 1912
sovereignty over the province was transferred by Turkey
to Italy. In 1939 the four provinces of Libya (Tripoli,
Misurata, Benghazi and Derna) were incorporated in the
national territory of Italy as *Libia Italiana*. After the Second
World War Tripolitania and Cyrenaica were placed
provisionally under British and the Fezzan under French
administration, and in conformity with a resolution of the
UN General Assembly in 1949, Libya became on 24

December 1951 the first independent state to be created by
the UN. The monarchy was overthrown by a revolution in
1969 and the country was declared a republic. It was ruled
by the Revolutionary Command Council (RCC) under
the leadership of Colonel Muammar Gadhafi.
In 1977 a new form of direct democracy, the 'Jamahiriya'
(state of the masses) was promulgated and the official name
of the country was changed to Socialist People's Libyan
Arab Jamahiriya. Since a reorganization in 1979 neither
Col. Gadhafi nor his former RCC colleagues have held
formal posts in the administration. Gadhafi continues to
hold the ceremonial title 'Leader of the Revolution'.

POLITICAL SYSTEM

At local level authority is vested in about 1,500 Basic and 14
Municipal People's Congresses which appoint Popular
Committees to execute policy. Officials of these congresses and committees, together with representatives from
unions and other organizations, form the General People's
Congress, which normally meets for about a week each
year. In addition, a number of extraordinary sessions are
held throughout the year. This is the highest policy-
making body in the country.
The General People's Congress appoints its own General Secretariat and the General People's Committee,
whose members head the government departments which
execute policy at national level. The Secretary of the
General People's Committee has functions similar to those
of a prime minister.

*Leader of the Revolution and Supreme Commander of the Armed
Forces,* Col. Muammar al-Gadhafi

SECRETARIAT OF THE GENERAL PEOPLE'S CONGRESS *as at
August 1997*

Secretary, Zanati Muhammad al-Zentani
Assistant Secretary, Abdulhamid Seid al-Zanati; Noura
Ramadane Busfreta *(Women's Affairs)*
Secretary, Affairs of People's Congresses,
Ahmed Mohamed Ibrahim
Secretary, Affairs of People's Committees, Dr Albagdadi Ali
Mahmoudi
Secretary, Trade Unions, Abdallah Idriss Ibrahim
Secretary, Foreign Affairs, Saad Mujber

GENERAL PEOPLE'S COMMITTEE (CABINET)

Secretary-General (Premier), Abdulmagid Gaoud
Agriculture, Ali Ben Ramdan
Animal Resources, Massoud Said Abousawa
Communication and Transport, Azzeddine Henshiri
Economy, Planning and Trade, Dr Abdulhafid Zletni
Education and Scientific Research, Dr Mehdi Moftah
Emberish
Energy, Abdalla Salem Albadri
Finance, Dr Mohammed Beit Elmal
Foreign Liaison, Omar al-Muntasser
Health and Social Security, Sleiman Alghamari
Housing and Services, Moubarak Abdallah Shamekh
Industry and Mining, Moftah Azouz
Information, Culture and Mobilization of the Masses, Faouzia
Shallabi
Justice, Mohamed Belqassem Zouei
Marine Resources, Béchir Ramadan Abougenah
Professional Development and Labour, Maatouk Mohamed
Maatouk
Public Security, Mohamed Mahmoud Hejazi
Tourism, Elboukhari Salem Hoda
Unity, Jamma Mahdi Alfazzani
Youth and Sport, Ali Moussa Shairi

LIBYAN DIPLOMATIC MISSION IN LONDON

Since the break of diplomatic relations with Libya in April 1984, the Royal Embassy of Saudi Arabia has handled Libyan interests in Britain.

BRITISH EMBASSY

British interests are currently handled by the British Interests Section of the Italian Embassy, Sharia Uahran 1 (PO Box 4206), Tripoli.

DEFENCE

The Army has 2,210 main battle tanks, 1,990 armoured infantry fighting vehicles and armoured personnel carriers, and 1,170 artillery pieces. The Navy has four submarines, two frigates, 36 patrol and coastal vessels, and 30 armed helicopters at six bases. The Air Force has 420 combat aircraft and 52 armed helicopters.

Libya is alleged to have built at least one chemical weapons plant. The USA claims that a plant at Rabta, closed in 1990, was reopened in 1995, and that a plant has been constructed near Tahunah, south of Tripoli.

As part of the UN economic sanctions imposed in April 1992 there is a total embargo on arms sales to Libya.
MILITARY EXPENDITURE – 5.5 per cent of GDP (1995)
MILITARY PERSONNEL – 65,000: Army 35,000, Navy 8,000, Air Force 22,000
CONSCRIPTION DURATION – Selective conscription, one to two years

ECONOMY

Economic sanctions were imposed on Libya in April 1992 by the UN Security Council following Libya's failure to hand over two suspects in the bombing of Pan-Am flight 103 over Lockerbie, Scotland, in 1988. The UN imposed additional sanctions in December 1993, including freezing assets abroad and restricting imports of spare parts and equipment for the oil and aviation sectors. All the sanctions remain in place and are renewed every 120 days. The USA also enacted legislation in July 1996 penalizing foreign companies that invest more than £26 million a year in Libya's energy sector.

Agriculture is confined mainly to the coastal areas of Tripolitania and Cyrenaica, where barley, wheat, olives, almonds, citrus fruits and dates are produced, and to the areas of the oases, many of which are well supplied with springs supporting small fertile areas. Among the important oases are Jaghbub, Ghadames, Jofra, Sebha, Murzuq, Brak, Ghat, Jalo and the Kufra group in the south-east.

The main industry is oil and gas production. There are pipelines from Zelten to the terminal at Mersa Brega, from Dahra to Ras-es-Sider, from Amal to Ras Lanuf, and from the Intisar field to Zueitina. In 1995, 66.6 million tonnes of crude oil was produced. A major petrochemical complex has been built at Ras Lanuf where a refinery and ethylene plant began operations in 1985. The construction of an iron and steel plant at Misurata has been completed. Economic constraints have delayed some projects, particularly since Libya decided in 1983 to go ahead with a major irrigation scheme, the 'Great Man-Made River'.

Libya has technical assistance agreements with a number of countries, and also employs large numbers of foreign labourers and experts.
GDP – US$32,876 million (1992); US$6,121 per capita (1992)

TRADE

Exports are dominated by crude oil, but some wool, cattle, sheep and horses, olive oil, and hides and skins are also exported. Principal imports are foodstuffs, including sugar, tea and coffee, and most construction materials and consumer goods. After the revolution the private sector was virtually eliminated and Libya became a state trading country with imports controlled by state monopolies. In 1988, however, reforms were implemented which have allowed a small private sector to be re-established.

Trade with UK	1995	1996
Imports from UK	£227,369,000	£248,818,000
Exports to UK	131,787,000	150,380,000

COMMUNICATIONS

The coastal road running from the Tunisian frontier through Tripoli to Benghazi, Tobruk and the Egyptian border serves the main population centres. Main roads also link the provincial centres, and the oil-producing areas of the south with the coastal towns.

There are airports at Tripoli and Benghazi (Benina), Tobruk, Mersa Brega, Sebha, Ghadames and Kufra regularly used by commercial airlines. Since April 1992 a UN embargo on air links with Libya has been in force.

LIECHTENSTEIN
Fürstentum Liechtenstein

AREA – 62 sq. miles (160 sq. km). Neighbours: Austria, Switzerland
POPULATION – 31,000 (1994 UN estimate). The language of the principality is German
CAPITAL – Vaduz (population, 5,072, 1993)
CURRENCY – Swiss franc of 100 rappen (or centimes)
NATIONAL ANTHEM – Oben am Jungen Rhein (High on the Rhine)
NATIONAL DAY – 15 August
NATIONAL FLAG – Equal horizontal bands of blue over red; gold crown on blue band near staff
LIFE EXPECTANCY (years) – male 66.07; female 72.94
POPULATION GROWTH RATE – 1.4 per cent (1994)
POPULATION DENSITY – 192 per sq. km (1994)
ILLITERACY RATE – 0.3 per cent

HISTORY AND POLITICS

The Patriotic Union and Progressive Citizens' parties have governed the country in coalition since 1938. There is a threshold of 8 per cent for parties to gain representation in the Landtag. At the general election on 31 January and 2 February 1997 the Patriotic Union won 13 seats, Progressive Citizens' Party 11, and Free List 2. The Patriotic Union is the the first government to face an opposition since 1938.

HEAD OF STATE

HSH The Prince of Liechtenstein, Hans Adam II, *born* 14 February 1945; *succeeded* 13 November 1989; *married* 30 July 1967, Countess Marie Kinsky; and has *issue*: Prince Alois (*see* below); Prince Maximilian, *b.* 16 May 1969; Prince Constantin, *b.* 15 March 1972; Princess Tatjana, *b.* 10 April 1973
Heir, HSH Prince Alois, *b.* 11 June 1968, *married* 1993 Duchess Sophie of Bavaria; and has *issue*: Prince Wenzel, *b.* 24 May 1995

MINISTRY *as at June 1997*

Prime Minister, Finance, Construction, Dr Mario Frick
Education, Environment, Transportation, Norbert Marxer

Foreign Affairs, Family and Equal Opportunities, Culture and Sport, Andrea Willi
Internal Affairs, Economy, Health and Welfare, Michael Ritter
Justice, Heinz Frommelt

DIPLOMATIC REPRESENTATION

Liechtenstein is represented in diplomatic and consular matters in the United Kingdom by the Swiss Embassy.

BRITISH AMBASSADOR, Christopher Hulse, CMG, resident at Berne, Switzerland

ECONOMY

The main industries are high and ultra-high vacuum engineering, the semi-conductor industry, roller bearings, fastenings and securing systems, artificial teeth, heating and hot water equipment, synthetic fibres, woollen and homespun fabrics.

In 1991 Liechtenstein became a member of the European Free Trade Association, and as such is a party to the European Economic Area (EEA) Agreement with the EU which came into force on 1 January 1994. In December 1992 in separate referenda, Switzerland voted against EEA membership while Liechtenstein voted in favour. After adapting its customs union with Switzerland, and again voting in favour of joining the EEA in a referendum on 9 April 1995, Liechtenstein joined the EEA on 1 May 1995.
GDP – US$1,430 million (1992); US$54,607 per capita (1992)

LITHUANIA
Lietuva

AREA – 25,174 sq. miles (65,200 sq. km). Neighbours: Latvia (north), Belarus (east and south), Poland and the Kaliningrad region of the Russian Federation (south-west)
POPULATION – 3,707,200 (1997): 81.6 per cent Lithuanian, 8.2 per cent Russian, 6.9 per cent Polish, 1.5 per cent Belarusian, 1 per cent Ukrainian. The majority are Roman Catholic, with Russian Orthodox and Lutheran minorities. Lithuanian is the state language, spoken by 80 per cent, with Russian, Polish and Belarusian minorities
CAPITAL – Vilnius (population, 580,000, 1997)
MAJOR CITIES – Kaunas (421,600); Klaipéda (204,300), 1993 estimates
CURRENCY – Litas, pegged to the dollar, US$1= 4 litas
NATIONAL ANTHEM – Tautiška Giesmé (The National Song)
NATIONAL DAY – 16 February (Independence Day)
NATIONAL FLAG – Three horizontal stripes of yellow, green, red
LIFE EXPECTANCY (years) – male 63.27; female 75.04
POPULATION GROWTH RATE – 0.0 per cent (1994)
POPULATION DENSITY – 57 per sq. km (1994)
URBAN POPULATION – 68.0 per cent (1994)

Lithuania lies in the middle and lower basin of the river Nemunas. Along the coast is a lowland plain which rises inland to form uplands in east and central Lithuania. These uplands, the Middle Lowlands, give way to the Baltic Highlands in east and south-east Lithuania; the highest point is 294 m (965 ft). There is a network of rivers and over 2,800 lakes, which mainly lie in the east of the country. The climate varies between maritime and continental.

HISTORY AND POLITICS

The first independent Lithuanian state emerged as the Kingdom of Lithuania in 1251, and over the next few centuries acted as a buffer state between Germans to the west and Mongols and Tartars to the east. After forming a joint Commonwealth and Kingdom with Poland in 1561, Lithuania was taken over by the Russian Empire in the partitions of Poland that occurred in 1772, 1792 and 1795.

Lithuania declared its independence from the Russian Empire on 16 February 1918 and then fought against German and Soviet forces until its independence was recognized by the Versailles Treaty (1919) and the peace treaty signed with the Soviet Union on 12 July 1920. The Soviet Union annexed Lithuania in 1940 under the terms of the Molotov–Ribbentrop pact with Germany. Lithuania was invaded and occupied when Germany invaded the Soviet Union during the Second World War. In 1944 the Soviet Union recaptured the country and confirmed its annexation, though this was never accepted as legal by most states.

In December 1989 public pressure forced the Lithuanian Communist Party to agree to multiparty elections, which were held in February 1990. These were won by the nationalist Sajudis movement, and the Supreme Council (parliament) declared the restoration of independence on 11 March 1990. Clashes occurred throughout 1990 between Lithuanians and Soviet military forces. Over 90 per cent of the population voted for independence in a referendum in February 1991. The Soviet Union recognized the independence of Lithuania on 10 September 1991.

The ruling Lithuanian Democratic Labour Party (former Communist Party) was defeated in a legislative election in October 1996. The Homeland Union (Conservative Party) and the Christian Democratic Party formed a coalition government.

FOREIGN RELATIONS

Lithuania applied for membership of the EU in December 1995; a treaty of association with the EU was ratified by parliament on 20 June 1996.

POLITICAL SYSTEM

Under the 1992 constitution, executive authority is vested in the government, consisting of the prime minister, who is appointed by the president with the approval of the *Seimas*, and ministers appointed upon the recommendation of the prime minister. The government is accountable to the Seimas, and presidential powers are under strict parliamentary control.

Legislative power is exercised by the Seimas, which is a unicameral parliament of 141 members elected for four-year terms. Seventy-one members are elected in first-past-the-post constituencies and 70 by proportional representation, with a 5 per cent threshold for representation. The constitution bans an alignment of Lithuania with any post-Soviet eastern alliance.

Lithuania is divided into 11 cities and 44 rural districts. Each has a municipal council elected by the local population for a period of three years.

The judicial system comprises the Constitutional Court (consisting of nine judges appointed for terms of nine years), the Supreme Court, Court of Appeal, district and local courts. For the investigation of administrative, labour, family and other litigations, specialized courts may be established pursuant to law. Supreme legal supervision is exercised by the Prosecutor-General and by local prosecutors under his supervision.

HEAD OF STATE

President, Algirdas Brazauskas, *elected* 14 February 1993 for a five-year term

GOVERNMENT *as at July 1997*

Prime Minister, Gediminas Vagnorius
Agriculture, Vytautas Petras Knašys
Communications and Information, Rimantas Pleikys
Construction and Urban Planning, Algis Čaplikas
Economics, Vincas Kęstutis Babilius
Environmental Protection, Imantas Lazdinis
European Affairs, Laima Liucija Andrikiene
Finance, Algirdas Šemeta
Foreign Affairs, Algirdas Saudargas
Health, Juozas Galdikas
Internal Affairs, Vidmantas Žiemelis
Justice, Vytautas Pakalniškis
National Defence, Česlovas Vytautas Stankevičius
Public Administration Reform and Local Government Affairs, Kęstutis Skrebys
Social Security and Labour, Irena Degutiene
Transport, Algis Žvaliauskas

EMBASSY OF LITHUANIA
84 Gloucester Place, London WIH 3HN
Tel 0171-486 6401
Ambassador Extraordinary and Plenipotentiary, HE Justas Paleckis, apptd 1996

BRITISH EMBASSY
2 Antakalnio, 2055 Vilnius
Tel: Vilnius 222 2070
Ambassador Extraordinary and Plenipotentiary, HE Thomas Macan, apptd 1994

BRITISH COUNCIL REPRESENTATIVE, V. Ziukiene, Vilniaus 39/6,2600 Vilnius

DEFENCE

The Army has 10 armoured personnel carriers; the Navy has two frigates and five patrol and coastal vessels based at Klaipeda; the Air Force has three helicopters but no combat aircraft. The last Russian troops withdrew in 1993.
MILITARY EXPENDITURE – 2.4 per cent of GDP (1995)
MILITARY PERSONNEL – 5,100: Army 4,200, Navy 350, Air Force 550
CONSCRIPTION DURATION – 12 months

ECONOMY

The economy was largely agricultural prior to rapid industrialization during the Soviet era. The transition from a centralized to a free-market economy has taken place against the background of a decline in GDP in 1992 of 35 per cent. GDP began to grow again in 1994. A privatization programme begun in 1991 ran into difficulties over the restitution of agricultural land and the modernization of state-owned industries, but progress in the sale of small enterprises has been quick and successful. In 1997 the privatization of communication, energy and transport companies was begun.

In 1996 agriculture and forestry accounted for 13 per cent of GDP, the chief products being beef, pork, rye, oats, wheat, flax, barley, sugar beet and potatoes. The main industries are chemicals and petrochemicals, food processing, wood products, building materials, textiles, leather goods, machinery, machine tools and household appliances.
GNP – US$7,070 million (1995); US$1,900 per capita (1995)
GDP – US$12,943 million (1992); US$686 per capita (1992)
ANNUAL AVERAGE GROWTH OF GDP – 2.6 per cent (1995)
INFLATION RATE – 39.7 per cent (1995)
UNEMPLOYMENT – 7.3 per cent (1995)
TOTAL EXTERNAL DEBT – US$802 million (1995)

TRADE

Trade with the West is gradually increasing at the expense of trade with the former Soviet Union. In 1996 45 per cent of Lithuania's trade was with CIS states, 33.4 per cent with the EU and 1.6 per cent with EFTA. The Lithuanian economy is still heavily dependent on Russian supplies of oil, gas and metals.

In 1995 imports totalled US$3,083 million and exports US$2,707 million.

Trade with UK	1995	1996
Imports from UK	£49,435,000	£83,539,000
Exports to UK	173,387,000	184,542,000

COMMUNICATIONS

Lithuania has 1,483 miles (2,393 km) of state roads. There is a relatively well-developed railway system of 1,240 miles (2,000 km) running east-west and north-south and linking the major towns with Vilnius and Klaipéda, the main international port. Vilnius has an international airport and there are smaller ones at Kaunas, Palanga and Siauliai.

CULTURE AND EDUCATION

Lithuanian culture and literature are closely linked to the national liberation movements of the 19th and early 20th centuries, and the literature of Lithuanians who went into exile during the Soviet era.

Lithuania re-established a national education system in 1990. Education begins at age 6–7 years, with the system comprising elementary schools (four years), nine-year schools (five years), and secondary schools (three years). The language of instruction is predominantly Lithuanian, but there are also Russian and Polish schools. There are 105 vocational schools and 65 colleges. Lithuania has six universities and eight other institutes of higher education. Vilnius University, founded in 1579, is one of the oldest universities in eastern Europe.

ILLITERACY RATE – 0.5 per cent
ENROLMENT (percentage of age group) – secondary 81 per cent; tertiary 26.7 per cent (1994)

LUXEMBOURG
Grand-Duché de Luxembourg

AREA – 998 sq. miles (2,586 sq. km). Neighbours: Germany, Belgium and France
POPULATION – 412,800 (1996), nearly all Roman Catholic. The officially designated 'national language' is Letzebuergesch (Luxembourgish), a mainly spoken language. French and German are the official languages for written purposes, and French is the language of administration
CAPITAL – Luxembourg (population, 75,800, 1996), a dismantled fortress
CURRENCY – Luxembourg franc (LF) of 100 centimes (Belgian currency is also legal tender). The Luxembourg franc is linked in a currency union with the Belgian franc
NATIONAL ANTHEM – Ons Hémécht (Our homeland)
NATIONAL DAY – 23 June
NATIONAL FLAG – Three horizontal bands, red, white and blue
LIFE EXPECTANCY (years) – male 70.61; female 77.87
POPULATION GROWTH RATE – 1.2 per cent (1994)
POPULATION DENSITY – 155 per sq. km (1994)
ENROLMENT (percentage of age group) – primary 81 per cent; secondary 66 per cent; tertiary 2.6 per cent (1985)

HISTORY AND POLITICS

Established as an independent state under the sovereignty of the King of the Netherlands as Grand Duke by the Congress of Vienna in 1815, Luxembourg formed part of the Germanic Confederation from 1815 to 1866, and was included in the German 'Zollverein'. In 1867 the Treaty of London declared it a neutral territory. On the death of the King of the Netherlands in 1890 it passed to the Duke of Nassau.

The territory was invaded and overrun by the Germans at the beginning of the war in 1914 but was liberated in 1918. By the Treaty of Versailles (1919), Germany renounced its former agreements with Luxembourg and in 1921 an economic union was formed with Belgium. The Grand Duchy was again invaded and occupied by Germany in 1940, and liberated in 1944.

FOREIGN RELATIONS

The constitution was modified in 1948 and the stipulation of permanent neutrality was abandoned. Luxembourg is now a signatory of the Brussels and North Atlantic Treaties, and also a member of the EU. Luxembourg is a member of the Belgium-Netherlands-Luxembourg Customs Union (Benelux 1960).

POLITICAL SYSTEM

There is a Chamber of 60 deputies, elected by universal suffrage for five years. Legislation is submitted to the Council of State. The last general election was held on 12 June 1994 and a coalition government was installed.

HEAD OF STATE

HRH The Grand Duke of Luxembourg, Grand Duke Jean, KG, *born* 5 January 1921; *succeeded* (on the abdication of his mother) 12 November 1964; *married* 9 April 1953 Princess Joséphine-Charlotte of Belgium, and has *issue*, three sons and two daughters
Heir, HRH Prince Henri, *born* 16 April 1955, *married* 14 February 1981, Maria Teresa Mestre, and has *issue*, Prince Guillaume, *b.* 11 November 1981; Prince Felix, *b.* 3 June 1984; Prince Louis, *b.* 3 August 1986; Princess Alexandra, *b.* 2 February 1991; Prince Sébastien, *b.* 16 April 1992, Princess Gabriella, *b.* 26 March 1994

CABINET *as at August 1997*

Prime Minister, Minister of State, Employment, Finance and Treasury, Jean-Claude Juncker (CD)
Deputy PM, Foreign Affairs, Trade, Overseas Aid and Development, Jacques Poos (SOC)
Agriculture, Rural Development, Small Businesses, Housing and Tourism, Fernand Boden (CD)
Economy, Public Works, Energy, Robert Goebbels (SOC)
Education, Cultural and Religious Affairs, Erna Hennicot-Schoepges (CD)
Environment, Health, Johny Lahure (SOC)
Family, Women and the Disabled, Marie-Josée Jacobs (CD)
Home Affairs, Civil Service and Administrative Reforms, Michel Wolter (CD)
Justice, Budget, Relations with Parliament, Marc Fischbach (CD)
Land Planning, Defence, Youth and Sports, Alex Bodry (SOC)
Social Security, Transport, Post and Communication, Mady Delvaux-Stehres (SOC)
CD Christian Social People's Party; SOC Luxembourg Socialist Workers' Party

EMBASSY OF LUXEMBOURG
27 Wilton Crescent, London SW1X 8SD
Tel 0171-235 6961
Ambassador Extraordinary and Plenipotentiary, HE Joseph Weyland, apptd 1993

BRITISH EMBASSY
14 Boulevard F. D. Roosevelt, L-2450 Luxembourg Ville
Tel: Luxembourg 229864
Ambassador Extraordinary and Plenipotentiary, HE John N. Elam, CMG, apptd 1994

DEFENCE

For legal reasons, NATO's squadron of 18 E-3A Sentry airborne early warning aircraft is registered in Luxembourg.
MILITARY EXPENDITURE – 0.9 per cent of GDP (1995)
MILITARY PERSONNEL – Army 800

ECONOMY

The country has an important iron and steel industry and is an important financial centre.
GNP – US$16,876 million (1995); US$41,210 per capita (1995)
GDP – US$9,438 million (1992); US$31,343 per capita (1992)
ANNUAL AVERAGE GROWTH OF GDP – 3.7 per cent (1995)
INFLATION RATE – 1.9 per cent (1995)
UNEMPLOYMENT – 2.8 per cent (1995)

TRADE WITH UK
(Belgium and Luxembourg)

	1995	1996
Imports from UK	£7,880,300,000	£8,114,000,000
Exports to UK	7,631,300,000	8,096,000,000

MACEDONIA (FORMER YUGOSLAV REPUBLIC OF)

AREA – 9,925 sq. miles (25,713 sq. km). Neighbours: Federal Republic of Yugoslavia (north), Bulgaria (east), Greece (south), Albania (west)

POPULATION – 2,142,000 (1994 UN estimate); 1,936,877 (1994 census): 66.5 per cent Macedonian, 22.9 per cent Albanian, 4.0 per cent ethnic Turks, 2.3 per cent gypsies, 2.3 per cent Serbs and 0.4 per cent Vlachs. The census results are disputed by the ethnic Albanians and Serbs. Macedonian Orthodox Christianity is the majority religion, with a Muslim minority. The main language is Macedonian (a south Slavic language), which is written in the Cyrillic script

CAPITAL – Skopje (population, 448,229, 1991)

MAJOR CITIES – Bitola (84,002); Prilep (70,152); Kumanov (69,231)

CURRENCY – Dinar of 100 paras

NATIONAL ANTHEM – Today over Macedonia

NATIONAL FLAG – Red with an eight-rayed sun displayed over the whole field

LIFE EXPECTANCY (years) – male 68.80; female 74.95

POPULATION GROWTH RATE – 1.4 per cent (1994)

POPULATION DENSITY – 83 per sq. km (1994)

URBAN POPULATION – 58.1 per cent (1991)

MILITARY EXPENDITURE – 7.8 per cent of GDP (1995)

MILITARY PERSONNEL – Army 10,400

CONSCRIPTION DURATION – Nine months

ENROLMENT (percentage of age group) – primary 87 per cent; secondary 49 per cent; tertiary 17.1 per cent (1994)

HISTORY AND POLITICS

From the ninth to the 14th centuries AD Macedonia was ruled alternately by the Bulgars and the Byzantine Empire. In the middle of the 14th century the area was conquered by the Turks and remained under the Ottoman Empire for over 500 years. After the defeat of Turkey in the two Balkan wars of 1912–13 the geographical area of Macedonia was divided, the major part becoming Serbian (the areas of the present-day Macedonia) and the remainder given to Greece and Bulgaria. In 1918 on the formation of the Kingdom of the Serbs, Croats and Slovenes (later Yugoslavia), Serbian Macedonia was incorporated into Serbia as South Serbia. When Yugoslavia was reconstituted in 1944 as a Communist federal republic under President Tito, Macedonia became a constituent republic.

Multiparty elections for the 120-seat assembly held in November and December 1990 produced the first non-Communist government since the Second World War. The electorate overwhelmingly approved Macedonian sovereignty and independence in a referendum and independence was declared on 18 September 1991.

Presidential and legislative elections were held in October 1994, and the presidential election was won by the incumbent, Kiro Gligorov. The parliamentary elections to the 120-seat Sobranie (National Assembly) were marred by allegations of ballot-rigging and partially boycotted by the Democratic Party and the nationalist UMRO party. The elections were won by the ruling Alliance for Macedonia (a coalition of the Social Democrat, Liberal and

Socialist parties) with 95 seats; the ethnic Albanian parties won 19 seats, and independents six. A coalition government was formed in December 1994 by the Social Democratic Alliance of Macedonia, the Party of Democratic Prosperity (an ethnic Albanian party) and the Socialist Party of Macedonia.

FOREIGN RELATIONS

A new constitution was adopted in November 1991 and then amended at the EC's request to make it clear that Macedonia had no territorial claim on its neighbours. Macedonia applied for EC recognition in December 1991 but was refused because of Greece's objections to the state's name, flag and currency which, according to the Greek government, amounted to a territorial claim on the Greek province of Macedonia. The peaceful withdrawal of the Yugoslav Army (JNA) from Macedonia was completed in April 1992.

Tensions between Macedonia and its neighbours grew in late 1992, with Greece imposing a virtual economic blockade and Albania alleging discrimination against ethnic Albanians. Fearing conflict, the UN sent 1,000 peacekeepers in 1992–3 to man border posts with Serbia and Albania. A full UN peacekeeping force, the UN Preventive Deployment Force (UNPREDEP) was established in March 1995.

Macedonia gained UN membership on 8 April 1993 following a compromise with Greece by which it is temporarily known as the 'Former Yugoslav Republic of Macedonia' (FYROM). Greece subsequently reopened its border to Macedonian trade in September 1993, but reimposed its economic blockade in February 1994 after the majority of EU states established diplomatic relations with Macedonia. An agreement was signed in September 1995 under which Greece agreed to lift the embargo on 15 October 1995 in exchange for Macedonia removing the contentious Star of Vergina from its flag.

HEAD OF STATE

President, Kiro Gligorov, elected 27 January 1991, re-elected 16 October 1994

GOVERNMENT as at June 1997

Prime Minister, Branko Crvenovski (SDSM)

Agriculture, Forestry and Water Management, Kiro Dokuzovski (SDSM)

Culture, Slobodan Unkovski (SDSM)

Defence, Blagoja Handziski

Development, Menef Neziri (PDP)

Economy, Boris Rikalovski (SDSM)

Education and Physical Culture, Sofija Todorova (SDSM)

Finance, Taki Fiti (SDSM)

Foreign Affairs, Blagoj Handziski (SDSM)

Health, Petar Ilijevski (SPM)

Interior, Tomislav Cokrevski (SDSM)

Justice, Gjorgji Spasov (SDSM)

Labour and Social Policy, Naser Ziberi (PDP)

Science, Aslan Selmani (PDP)

Transport and Communications, Abdelmenaf Bedzeti (PDP)

Urbanism, Civil Engineering and Environment, Trome Trombev (SDSM)

Without Portfolio, Dimitar Buzlevski (SDSM), Dzemail Hajdari (PDP), Vlado Naumovski (SPM), Zlatka Popovska (SPM)

SDSM Social Democratic Alliance of Macedonia; PDP Party of Democratic Prosperity; SPM Socialist Party of Macedonia

EMBASSY OF THE FORMER YUGOSLAV REPUBLIC OF
MACEDONIA
10 Harcourt House, 19A Cavendish Square, London
WIM 9AD
Tel 0171-499 5152
Ambassador Extraordinary and Plenipotentiary, HE Stevo
  Crevenovski, apptd 1997

BRITISH EMBASSY
Veljko Vlahovíc 26, 9100 Skopje
Tel: Skopje 116772
Ambassador Extraordinary and Plenipotentiary, HE Mark
  Dickinson, apptd 1997

ECONOMY

The economy was decimated by the UN trade sanctions
against the rump Yugoslavia (from May 1992 until
November 1995), with which Macedonia had conducted
60 per cent of its trade. The Greek economic blockade
(from February 1994 until October 1995) deprived Macedonia of most of its oil supplies and industry survived on
imports from Turkey and Bulgaria. Macedonia is attempting to transform its economy to a market-orientated one
and to introduce privatization. Output and GDP have
fallen significantly since 1990. Foreign investment has
been minimal because of the lack of international recognition.
  In 1991 41.2 per cent of GDP was produced by industry
and mining and 14 per cent by agriculture. Mineral
resources include nickel, lead, zinc, manganese and iron
ore. The main industrial sectors are basic metal industries,
chemicals, textiles and food processing. Important agricultural crops are wheat, tobacco, rice, wine, lamb, cotton and
sugar beet.
GNP – US$1,813 million (1995); US$860 per capita (1995)
GDP – US$4,495 million (1992); US$3,285 per capita
  (1992)
UNEMPLOYMENT – 35.6 per cent (1995)
TOTAL EXTERNAL DEBT – US$1,213 million (1995)

TRADE WITH UK	1995	1996
Imports from UK	£18,079,000	£17,955,000
Exports to UK	5,323,000	9,282,000

MADAGASCAR
Repoblika n'i Madagaskar

AREA – 226,669 sq. miles (587,041 sq. km)
POPULATION – 14,303,000 (1994 UN estimate). The
  people are of mixed Malayo-Polynesian, Arab and
  African origin. There are sizeable French, Chinese and
  Indian communities. The official languages are
  Malagasy and French
CAPITAL – Antananarivo (population, 377,600, 1971
  estimate)
MAJOR CITIES – ΨToamasina (230,000), the chief port;
  ΨMahajanga (200,000); Fianarantsoa (300,000);
  ΨAntsiranana (220,000)
CURRENCY – Franc malgache (FMG) of 100 centimes
NATIONAL DAY – 26 June (Independence Day)
NATIONAL FLAG – Equal horizontal bands of red (above)
  and green, with vertical white band by staff
LIFE EXPECTANCY (years) – male 55.00; female 58.00
POPULATION DENSITY – 24 per sq. km (1994)
MILITARY EXPENDITURE – 1.1 per cent of GDP (1995)
MILITARY PERSONNEL – 21,000: Army 20,000, Navy 500,
  Air Force 500
CONSCRIPTION DURATION – 18 months

ILLITERACY RATE – 54.3 per cent
ENROLMENT (percentage of age group) – tertiary 3.5 per
  cent (1992)

Madagascar lies 240 miles off the east coast of Africa and is
the fourth largest island in the world.

HISTORY AND POLITICS

Madagascar (known from 1958 to 1975 as the Malagasy
Republic) became a French protectorate in 1895, and a
French colony in 1896 when the former queen was exiled.
Republican status was adopted on 14 October 1958, and
independence was proclaimed on 26 June 1960.
  The post-independence civilian government was re-
placed by a military government in 1975 and the following
month martial law was declared. A Supreme Council of the
Revolution under Capitaine de Frégate (subsequently
Admiral) Didier Ratsiraka was established.
  In November 1991, after six months of agitation against
his one-party socialist rule, President Ratsiraka relinquished executive power to a new prime minister, Guy
Razanamasy. However, the President retained his official
position and the main opposition grouping, the *Forces Vives*,
established a rival government led by Albert Zafy. In
December 1991 a transitional government including
Forces Vives and Razanamasy supporters was formed to
draft a new constitution, which was approved by referendum in August 1992. Presidential elections were held in
two rounds in November 1992 and February 1993, Albert
Zafy emerging victorious with 67 per cent of the vote. He
became the first president of the Third Republic, which
also came into being at the same time.
  A legislative election held in June 1993 was won by
Forces Vives and allied parties, with Forces Vives member
Francisque Ravony being elected prime minister by
parliament in August 1993. The new constitution declares
Madagascar to be a unitary state and reduces the executive
powers of the president, although the president acquired
the power to appoint the prime minister following a
referendum in September 1995. President Zafy was
impeached in September 1996 and defeated in a presidential election in November and December 1996 by former
president Ratsiraka.

HEAD OF STATE
President, Adm. Didier Ratsiraka, *elected* 29 December 1996

COUNCIL OF MINISTERS *as at August* 1997

Prime Minister, Pascal Rakotomavo
Deputy PMs, Pierrot Rajaonarivelo *(Decentralization and the*
  Budget); Tantely Andrianarivo *(Finance and the Economy)*;
  Herizo Razafimahaleo *(Foreign Affairs)*
Agriculture, Ranjakason
Armed Forces, Gen. Marcel Ranjeva
Basic and Secondary Education, Jacquit Simon
Civil Service, Work and Social Legislation, Abel Jean Désiré
  Ratovonelinjafy
Commerce and Consumption, Auguste Paraina
Energy and Mines, Charles Rasoza
Environment, Colette Vaohita
Fishing, Abdallah Houssen
Health, Henriette Rahantalalao
Higher Education, Prof. Ange Andrianarisoa
Industrialization and Craftsmanship, Manassé
  Esoavelomandroso
Information, Culture and Communication, Fredo Betsimifira
Interior, Col. Jean Jacques Rasolondraibe
Justice, Anaclet Imbiki
Livestock, Capt. Ndrianasolo
Population and Solidarity, Ernest Njara

Post and Telecommunications, Ny Hasina Andriamanjato
Private Sector and Privatization, Constant Horace
Public Works, Col. Emile Tsaranazy
Rural Development and Towns, Herivelona Ramanantsoa
Scientific Research, Lila Ratsifandriamanana
Secretaries of State, Ben Marouf Azaly *(Public Security);* Gen.
    Jean Paul Bory *(Police)*
Technical Education and Professional Development, Boniface
    Levelo
Tourism, Juliette Raharisoa
Transport and Meteorology, Naivo Ramamonjisoa
Water and Forests, Rija Rajohnson
Youth and Sport, Lina Andriamifidimanana

EMBASSY OF THE REPUBLIC OF MADAGASCAR
4 avenue Raphael, 75016 Paris, France
Tel: Paris 4504 6211
Ambassador Plenipotentiary and Extraordinary, new
    appointment awaited

HONORARY CONSULATE OF THE REPUBLIC OF
MADAGASCAR
16 Lanark Mansions, Pennard Road, London W12 8DT
Tel 0181-746 0133
Honorary Consul, Stephen Hobbs

BRITISH EMBASSY
1st Floor, Immeuble 'Ny Havana', Cite de 67 Ha,
BP 167, Antananarivo
Tel: Antananarivo 27749
Ambassador Extraordinary and Plenipotentiary, HE Robert S.
    Dewar, apptd 1996

ECONOMY

The economy is still largely based on agriculture, which
accounts for three-quarters of its exports. Development
plans have placed emphasis on increasing agricultural and
livestock production, the improvement of communications, the exploitation of mineral deposits and the creation
of small industries.

In 1993 the government had a budget deficit equivalent
to 4.77 per cent of GDP. In 1995 imports totalled US$532
million and exports US$364 million.

GNP – US$3,178 million (1995); US$230 per capita (1995)
GDP – US$2,924 million (1992); US$243 per capita (1992)
ANNUAL AVERAGE GROWTH OF GDP – 2.1 per cent (1993)
INFLATION RATE – 49.1 per cent (1995)
TOTAL EXTERNAL DEBT – US$4,302 million (1995)

TRADE WITH UK	1995	1996
Imports from UK	£7,203,000	£6,430,000
Exports to UK	15,236,000	22,372,000

MALAWI
Dziko La Malawi

AREA – 45,747 sq. miles (118,484 sq. km). Neighbours:
    Tanzania (north-east), Zambia (west), Mozambique
    (south)
POPULATION – 9,461,000 (1994 UN estimate). The official
    languages are Chichewa and English
CAPITAL – Lilongwe (population, 233,973, 1987)
MAJOR CITIES – Blantyre, incorporating Blantyre and
    Limbe, (331,588 1987), the major commercial and
    industrial centre; Mzuzu; Thyolo; Mulanje; Mangochi;
    Salima; Dedza; Zomba, the former capital
CURRENCY – Kwacha (K) of 100 tambala
NATIONAL ANTHEM   O God Bless Our Land of Malawi
NATIONAL DAY – 6 July (Independence Day)

NATIONAL FLAG – Horizontal stripes of black, red and
    green, with rising sun in the centre of the black stripe
LIFE EXPECTANCY (years) – male 43.51; female 46.75
POPULATION GROWTH RATE – 3.3 per cent (1994)
POPULATION DENSITY – 80 per sq. km (1994)
URBAN POPULATION – 18.1 per cent (1994)
MILITARY EXPENDITURE – 1.2 per cent of GDP (1995)
MILITARY PERSONNEL – 10,800: Army 9,800,
    Paramilitaries 1,000

Malawi lies in south-eastern Africa. Much of the eastern
border of Malawi is formed by Lake Malawi (formerly
Lake Nyasa), which covers nearly half of the north of the
country. The valley of the River Shire runs south from the
lake, its watershed with the Zambezi lying on the western
border with Mozambique and its tributary, the Ruo, with
lakes Chinta and Chirwa, lying on the eastern border with
Mozambique. The north and centre are plateaux, and the
south highlands.

HISTORY AND POLITICS

Malawi (formerly Nyasaland) assumed internal self-government on 1 February 1963, and became independent on
6 July 1964. It became a republic on 6 July 1966.

In 1991–2 Life President Hastings Banda, who had
ruled since independence, came under increasing pressure
to introduce a multiparty democratic system of government. In May 1992 aid donors tied new loans to improvements in the human rights record and moves to multiparty
democracy. A referendum was held on the adoption of a
multiparty democracy in June 1993 and approved by 63
per cent of voters. President Banda and the Malawi
Congress Party refused to resign but parliament passed a
law to amend the constitution to allow multiparty politics
and Banda announced a political amnesty to allow exiles to
return. Multiparty presidential and legislative elections
held in May 1994 were won by Bakili Muluzi and the
United Democratic Front (UDF) respectively. Foreign
and multilateral aid has since been restored. A coalition
UDF-Alliance for Democracy (AFORD) government was
formed although AFORD withdrew from the coalition in
June 1996.

POLITICAL SYSTEM

There is a Cabinet consisting of the president and
ministers. The National Assembly consists of 177 members, each elected by universal suffrage, and usually meets
three times a year. A new multiparty constitution took
effect on 17 May 1994. It ends the idea of the life
presidency, reduces presidential powers, establishes the
posts of first and second vice-president and provides for a
Senate, to come into being by May 1999.

HEAD OF STATE
President, Bakili Muluzi, *elected* 17 May 1994, *sworn in* 21
    May 1994
Vice-President, Defence, Justin Malewezi

CABINET *as at July 1997*
The President
The Vice-President
Agriculture and Irrigation, Aleke Banda
Attorney-General, Justice, Cassim Chilumpha
Commerce and Industry, Matembo Nzunda
Defence, Joseph Kubwalo
Education, Brown Mpinganjira
Energy and Mining, Revd Dumbo Lemani
Foreign Affairs, Dr Mapopa Chipeta
Forestry, Fisheries and Environmental Affairs, Mayinga
    Mkandawire

Health and Population, Harry Thomson
Home Affairs, Melvin Moyo
Information, Sam Mpasu
Labour and Vocational Training, Kaliyoma Phumisa
Lands, Housing, Physical Planning and Surveys, Peter Fatchi
Local Government and Sports, Chakakala Chaziya
Minister of State, Edda Chitalo
Ministers of State, Preisdents Office, Robson Makuwira,
   Bundaunda Phiri
National Heritage, Richard Sembereka
Tourism, Parks and Wildlife, Patrick Mbewe
Transport, Kamangadazi Chambao
Water Development, Edward Bwanali
Women, Youth and Community Services, Lilian Patel
Works and Supplies, Abdul Pilani

MALAWI HIGH COMMISSION
33 Grosvenor Street, London WIX ODE
Tel 0171-491 4172/7
High Commissioner, HE Jake Muwamba, apptd 1995

BRITISH HIGH COMMISSION
PO Box 30042, Lilongwe 3
Tel: Lilongwe 782400
High Commissioner, HE John F. Martin, CMG, apptd 1993

BRITISH COUNCIL REPRESENTATIVE, J. Kennedy, Plot
   No. 13/20, City Centre, PO Box 30222, Lilongwe 3

ECONOMY

The economy is largely agricultural, with maize the main
subsistence crop. Tobacco, sugar, tea, groundnuts and
cotton are the main cash crops and principal exports. There
are two sugar mills. A number of light manufacturing
industries have been established, mainly in agricultural
processing, clothing/textiles and building materials.

In 1993 Malawi had a current account deficit of US$96
million. In 1994 imports totalled US$491 million and
exports US$325 million.

GNP – US$1,623 million (1995); US$170 per capita (1995)
GDP – US$2,099 million (1992); US$184 per capita (1992)
ANNUAL AVERAGE GROWTH OF GDP – –9.3 per cent
   (1994)
INFLATION RATE – 34.7 per cent (1994)
TOTAL EXTERNAL DEBT – US$2,140 million (1995)

TRADE WITH UK	1995	1996
Imports from UK	£13,449,000	£20,558,000
Exports to UK	16,188,000	16,062,000

COMMUNICATIONS

A single-track railway runs from Mchinji on the Zambian
border, through Lilongwe and Salima on Lake Malawi
(itself served by two passenger and a number of cargo
boats) through to Blantyre. The route south to the
Mozambique port of Beira was severed by the Mozambican civil war, but the route to Nacala in Mozambique is
open again. There are 12,215 km of roads in Malawi of
which about 21.8 per cent are bituminized. There is an
international airport 26 km from Lilongwe, which handles
regional and intercontinental flights.

EDUCATION

Primary education is the responsibility of local authorities
in both urban and rural areas, although policy, curricula
and inspection are the responsibility of the Ministry of
Education and Culture. The Ministry is also responsible
for secondary schools, technical education and primary
teacher training. Religious bodies, with government assistance, still play an important part in these fields. The

University of Malawi was opened in 1965 and has five
constituent colleges.
ILLITERACY RATE – 43.6 per cent
ENROLMENT (percentage of age group) – primary 92 per
   cent (1994); secondary 2 per cent (1994); tertiary 0.8 per
   cent (1993)

MALAYSIA
Persekutuan Tanah Malaysia

AREA – 127,320 sq. miles (329,758 sq. km)
POPULATION – 20,103,000 (1995); 16,921,300 (1988
   census): Malays (53 per cent), Chinese (35 per cent), and
   those of Indian and Sri Lankan origin, as well as the
   indigenous races of Sarawak and Sabah. Bahasa Malaysia
   (Malay) is the sole official language, but English, various
   dialects of Chinese, and Tamil are also widely spoken.
   There are a few indigenous languages widely spoken in
   Sabah and Sarawak. Islam is the official religion of
   Malaysia, each ruler being the head of religion in his
   state (except in Sabah and Sarawak). The Yang di-
   Pertuan Agung is the head of religion in Melaka and
   Penang. The constitution guarantees religious freedom
CAPITAL – Kuala Lumpur (population, 1,145,075, 1991)
CURRENCY – Malaysian dollar (ringgit) (M$) of 100 sen
NATIONAL ANTHEM – Negara-Ku
NATIONAL DAY – 31 August (*Hari Kebangsaan*)
NATIONAL FLAG – Equal horizontal stripes of red (seven)
   and white (seven); 14-point yellow star and crescent in
   blue canton
LIFE EXPECTANCY (years) – male 68.68; female 73.04
POPULATION GROWTH RATE – 2.3 per cent (1994)
POPULATION DENSITY – 59 per sq. km (1994)
URBAN POPULATION – 50.6 per cent (1991)
ILLITERACY RATE – 16.5 per cent
ENROLMENT (percentage of age group) – tertiary 9.6 per
   cent (1993)

Malaysia comprises the 11 states of peninsular Malaya plus
Sabah and Sarawak. It occupies two distinct regions, the
Malay peninsula which extends from the isthmus of Kra to
the Singapore Strait, and the north-west coastal area of the
island of Borneo. Each is separated from the other by the
South China Sea.

The year is commonly divided into the south-west and
north-west monsoon seasons. Rainfall averages about 100
inches throughout the year. The average daily temperature varies from 21° C to 32° C, though in higher areas
temperatures are lower and vary widely.

HISTORY AND POLITICS

The Federation of Malaya became an independent coun-
try within the Commonwealth on 31 August 1957. On 16
September 1963 the federation was enlarged by the
accession of the states of Singapore, Sabah (formerly
British North Borneo) and Sarawak, and the name of
Malaysia was adopted from that date. On 9 August 1965
Singapore seceded from the federation.

The National Front (Barisan Nasional) Coalition led by
Dr Mahathir Muhammad won a fourth term in office in a
general election held on 25 April 1995, winning 162 of the
192 seats.

POLITICAL SYSTEM

The constitution provides for a strong federal government
and a degree of autonomy for the state governments. It

created a constitutional Supreme Head of the Federation (HM the *Yang di-Pertuan Agung*) and a Deputy Supreme Head (HRH *Timbalan Yang di-Pertuan Agung*) to be elected for a term of five years by the rulers from among their number. The Malay rulers are either chosen or succeed to their position in accordance with the custom of the particular state. In other states of Malaysia, choice of the head of state is at the discretion of the Yang di-Pertuan Agung after consultation with the Chief Minister of the state.

The Federal Parliament consists of two houses, the Senate and the House of Representatives. The Senate (*Dewan Negara*) consists of 68 members, 26 elected by the Legislative Assemblies of the States (two from each) and 42 appointed by the Yang di-Pertuan Agung. The House of Representatives (*Dewan Rakyat*) consists of 192 members elected by universal adult suffrage with a common electoral roll.

According to the constitution, each state shall have its own constitution not inconsistent with the federal constitution, with the ruler or governor acting on the advice of an Executive Council appointed on the advice of the Chief Minister and a single-chamber Legislative Assembly. The Legislative Assemblies are fully elected on the same basis as the Federal Parliament.

The judicial system consists of a Federal Court and two High Courts, one in peninsular Malaysia and one for Sabah and Sarawak. The Federal Court comprises a president, the two Chief Justices of the High Courts and other judges. It possesses appellate, original and advisory jurisdiction.

Each of the High Courts consists of a Chief Justice and not less than four other judges. In peninsular Malaysia the subordinate courts consist of the sessions courts and the magistrates' courts. In Sabah/Sarawak the magistrates' courts constitute the subordinate courts.

HEAD OF STATE

Supreme Head of State, HM Tuanku Jaafar Ibni Al-Marhum Tuanku Abdul Rahman (Yang Dipertuan Besar of Negeri Sembilan), *sworn in* 26 April 1994, *crowned* 22 September 1994

Deputy Supreme Head of State, HRH Sultan Salahuddin Abdul Aziz Shah Al-Haj ibni Almarhum Sultan Hishamuddin Alam Shah Al-Haj (Sultan of Selangor)

CABINET *as at June 1997*

Prime Minister, Home Affairs, Datuk Seri Dr Mahathir Muhammad
Deputy PM, Finance, Datuk Seri Anwar Ibrahim
Agriculture, Datuk Dr Sulaiman Haji Daud
Culture, Arts and Tourism, Datuk Sabbaruddin Chik
Defence, Datuk Syed Hamid Syed Jaafar Albar
Domestic Trade and Consumer Affairs, Dato Megat Junid Megat Ayob
Education, Datuk Seri Mohamad Najib Tun Abdul Razak
Energy, Telecommunications and Post, Datuk Leo Moggie Anak Irok
Entrepreneur Development, Datuk Mustapa Mohamed
Foreign Affairs, Dato Abdullah Haji Ahmad Badawi
Health, Chua Jui Meng
Housing and Local Government, Datuk Ting Chew Peh
Human Resources, Datuk Lim Ah Lek
Information, Dato Mohamed Rahmat
International Trade and Industry, Datuk Seri Rafidah Aziz
Land and Co-operative Development, Dato Osu Haji Sukam
National Unity and Social Development, Datin Paduka Zaleha Ismail
Primary Industries, Datuk Seri Dr Lim Kheng Yaik

Prime Minister's Department, Datuk Abang Abu Bakar Abang Haji Mustapha; Dato Dr Haji Abdul Hamid Haji Othman; Sen. Datuk Chong Kah Kiat
Rural Development, Dato Haji Annuar Haji Musa
Science, Technology and Environment, Datuk Law Hieng Ding
Transport, Datuk Seri Dr Ling Liong Sik
Works, Datuk Seri S. Samy Vellu
Youth and Sports, Tan Sri Dato Haji Muhyiddin Yasin

NOTE: Tunku/Tengku, Tun, Tan Sri, and Datuk/Dato are titles. Tunku/Tengku is equivalent to Prince. Tun denotes membership of the highest order of Malaysian chivalry. Tan Sri and Datuk/Dato (Datuk Seri in Perak and Datu in Sabah) are the equivalent of a knighthood. The wife of a Tun is styled Toh Puan, that of a Tan Sri is styled Puan Sri and of a Datuk, Datin. Tuan or Encik is equivalent to Mr and Puan is equivalent to Mrs.

MALAYSIAN HIGH COMMISSION
45 Belgrave Square, London SW1X 8QT
Tel 0171-235 8033
High Commissioner, HE Dato Kamarudin Abu, apptd 1992
Deputy High Commissioner, Jasmi Muhammad Yusoff
Defence Adviser, Col. Kamaruddin Mattan
Trade Commissioner (Commercial), Z. M. Perai

BRITISH HIGH COMMISSION
185 Jalan Ampang (PO Box 11030), 50450 Kuala Lumpur
Tel: Kuala Lumpur 248 2122
High Commissioner, HE David Moss, CMG, apptd 1994
Deputy High Commissioner, T. N. Byrne
Counsellor (Commercial/Economic), H. Parkinson
Defence Adviser, Col. M. B. Cooper

BRITISH COUNCIL DIRECTOR, T. Edmundson, PO Box 10539, Jalan Bukit Aman, Kuala Lumpur 50916. There are also offices at Johore Bahru, Kota Kinabalu (Sabah) and Kuching (Sarawak).

STATES

The 13 states of the Federation of Malaysia are:

State	Capital	Population (1988 census)
ΨJohore	Johore Bahru	2,007,300
Kedah	Alor Setar	1,353,500
Kelantan	Kota Bahru	1,150,400
ΨMelaka	Melaka	560,700
Negri Sembilan	Seremban	694,100
ΨPahang	Kuantan	1,001,200
ΨPenang	Georgetown	1,103,200
Perak	Ipoh	2,143,200
Perlis	Kangar	179,700
ΨSabah	Kota Kinabalu	1,371,000
ΨSarawak	Kuching	1,501,000
ΨSelangor	Shah Alam	1,878,300
ΨTerengganu	Kuala Terengganu	705,200

Federal Territories	
Kuala Lumpur	} 1,182,700
Labuan	

DEFENCE

The Army has 816 armoured infantry fighting vehicles and armoured personnel carriers and 127 artillery pieces. The Royal Malaysian Navy has six frigates, 37 patrol and coastal vessels and 12 armed helicopters at five bases. The Royal Malaysian Air Force has 79 combat aircraft and 12,500 personnel.

Australia maintains an infantry company and an air force detachment in Malaysia.

MILITARY EXPENDITURE – 4.5 per cent of GDP (1995)
MILITARY PERSONNEL – 132,500: Army 90,000, Navy
12,000, Air Force 12,500, Paramilitaries 18,000

ECONOMY

From being an agriculturally-based economy reliant on
raw materials exports at independence, Malaysia has
undergone an industrialization programme and now
produces clothing, textiles, rubber goods, electronics,
office equipment, cars, household appliances, semi- conductors, food processing and chemicals. Under the New
Economic Policy of 1970–90, the economy grew at an
average rate of 6.7 per cent a year. The National Development Policy 1990–2000 is seen as the second stage in
making Malaysia a fully-developed industrial state by
2020. Economic growth in 1990–5 has averaged 8.0 per
cent a year. The 1996–2000 five-year plan aims to achieve
8 per cent GDP growth and to keep unemployment at no
more than 2.8 per cent. In 1995 44 per cent of GDP was
produced by services, 35 per cent by manufacturing and 13
per cent by agriculture.

In 1994 the government had a budget surplus equivalent
to 3.91 per cent of GDP.

GNP – US$78,321 million (1995); US$3,890 per capita
(1995)
GDP – US$50,160 million (1992); US$3,087 per capita
(1992)
ANNUAL AVERAGE GROWTH OF GDP – 8.7 per cent (1994)
INFLATION RATE – 5.3 per cent (1995)
UNEMPLOYMENT – 2.8 per cent (1995)
TOTAL EXTERNAL DEBT – US$34,352 million (1995)

TRADE

Malaysia is the largest exporter of natural rubber, tin, palm
oil and tropical hardwoods. Other major export commodities are manufactured and processed products, petroleum,
oil, and other minerals, palm kernel oil, tea and pepper.
Exports of major commodities were (1995): manufactured
goods 78 per cent, agricultural products 12 per cent,
minerals, oil and gas 6 per cent. Imports consist mainly of
machinery and transport equipment, manufactured goods,
foods, mineral fuels, chemicals and inedible crude materials.

In 1993 Malaysia had a trade surplus of US$3,011
million and a current account deficit of US$2,411 million.
In 1995 imports totalled US$77,751 million and exports
US$74,045 million.

Trade with UK	1995	1996
Imports from UK	£1,189,582,000	£1,160,025,000
Exports to UK	1,487,884,000	2,380,115,000

MALDIVES
Dhivehi Jumhooriyya

AREA – 115 sq. miles (298 sq. km)
POPULATION – 256,157 (1996). The people are Sunni
Muslims and the Maldivian (Dhivehi) language is akin
to Elu or old Sinhalese
CAPITAL – ΨMalé (population, 62,973, 1995)
CURRENCY – Rufiyaa of 100 laaris
NATIONAL ANTHEM – Qaumee Salaam
NATIONAL DAY – 26 July
NATIONAL FLAG – Green field bearing a white crescent,
with wide red border
LIFE EXPECTANCY (years) – male 67.15; female 66.60
POPULATION GROWTH RATE – 3.2 per cent (1994)

POPULATION DENSITY – 825 per sq. km (1994)
URBAN POPULATION – 25.9 per cent (1990)
ILLITERACY RATE – 6.8 per cent

The Maldives are a chain of coral atolls 400 miles to the
south-west of Sri Lanka, stretching north for about 600
miles from just south of the Equator. There are about 19
coral atolls comprising over 1,200 islands, 198 of which are
inhabited. No point in the entire chain of islands is more
than eight feet above sea-level.

HISTORY AND POLITICS

Until 1952 the islands were a sultanate under the protection of the British Crown. Internal self-government was
achieved in 1948 and full independence in 1965. The
Maldives became a special member of the Commonwealth
in 1982 and a full member in 1985.

The Maldives form a republic which is elective. There is
a legislature, the *Citizens' Majlis*, with representatives
elected from all the atolls. The life of the Majlis is five
years. The government consists of a Cabinet, which is
responsible to the Majlis.

HEAD OF STATE
President, HE Maumoon Abdul Gayoom, *elected* 1978, *re-
elected* 1983, 1989, 1 October 1993

CABINET *as at August 1997*

Atolls Administration, Majlis Speaker, Abdulla Hameed
Attorney-General, Dr Mohamed Munawwar
Construction and Public Works, Umar Zahir
Defence and National Security, Finance and Treasury, The
President
Education, Dr Mohamed Latheef
Fisheries and Agriculture, Hassan Sabir
Foreign Affairs, Fathuhulla Jameel
Health, Ahmed Abdulla
Home Affairs and Housing, Abdulla Jameel
Information, Arts and Culture, Ibrahim Manik
Justice, Ahmed Zahir
Ministers of State, Anbaree Abdul Sattar *(Defence and National
Security)*; Arif Hilmy *(Finance and Treasury)*; Mohamed
Hussain
Planning, Human Resources and Environment, Abdul Rasheed
Hussain *(Presidential Affairs)*
Tourism, Ibrahim Hussain Zaki
Trade, Industries and Labour, Abdulla Yameen
Transport and Communications, Ismail Shafeeu
Women's Affairs and Social Welfare, Rashida Yoosuf
Youth and Sports, Mohamed Zahir Hussain

HIGH COMMISSION OF THE REPUBLIC OF MALDIVES
22 Nottingham Place, London WIM 3FB
High Commissioner, new appointment awaited

BRITISH HIGH COMMISSIONER, HE David E.Tatham,
CMG, resident at Colombo, Sri Lanka

ECONOMY

The vegetation of the islands is coconut palms with some
scrub. Hardly any cultivation of crops is possible and
nearly all food to supplement the basic fish diet has to be
imported. The principal industry is fishing and considerable quantities of fish and dried fish are exported to Japan
and Sri Lanka. The tourist industry is expanding rapidly
(338,733 visitors in 1996). Fishing and tourism together
account for about 30 per cent of GDP. The Maldives
National Ship Management Ltd (MNSML) has a fleet of
nine merchant ships. There is an international airport at
Malé.

In 1993 the Maldives had a trade deficit of US$139 million and a current account deficit of US$48 million. In 1995 imports totalled US$268 million and exports US$50 million.

GNP – US$251 million (1995); US$990 per capita (1995)
GDP – US$164 million (1992); US$782 per capita (1992)
ANNUAL AVERAGE GROWTH OF GDP – 7.2 per cent (1995)
INFLATION RATE – 20.2 per cent (1993)
TOTAL EXTERNAL DEBT – US$155 million (1995)

Trade with UK	1995	1996
Imports from UK	£3,850,000	£5,895,000
Exports to UK	8,879,000	7,549,000

MALI
République du Mali

AREA – 478,841 sq. miles (1,240,192 sq. km)
POPULATION – 10,462,000 (1994 UN estimate)
CAPITAL – Bamako (population, 658,275, 1987)
MAJOR CITIES – Gao; Kayes; Mopti; Sikasso; Segou; Timbuktu (all regional capitals)
CURRENCY – Franc CFA of 100 centimes
NATIONAL DAY – 22 September
NATIONAL FLAG – Vertical stripes of green (by staff), yellow and red
LIFE EXPECTANCY (years) – male 55.24; female 58.66
POPULATION DENSITY – 8 per sq. km (1994)
URBAN POPULATION – 22.0 per cent (1987)
MILITARY EXPENDITURE – 2.4 per cent of GDP (1995)
MILITARY PERSONNEL – 12,350: Army 7,350, Paramilitaries 5,000
CONSCRIPTION DURATION – Two years
ILLITERACY RATE – 69.0 per cent
ENROLMENT (percentage of age group) – primary 23 per cent (1993); secondary 5 per cent (1990); tertiary 0.8 per cent (1990)

HISTORY AND POLITICS

Formerly the French colony of Soudan, the territory elected on 24 November 1958 to remain an autonomous republic within the French Community. It associated with Senegal in the Federation of Mali, which was granted full independence on 20 June 1960. The Federation was effectively dissolved in August 1960 by the secession of Senegal. The title of the Republic of Mali was adopted in September 1960.

The regime of Modibo Keita was overthrown in 1968 by a group of army officers who formed a National Liberation Committee and appointed a prime minister. Moussa Traoré assumed the functions of head of state. A new civil constitution came into being in 1979.

President Traoré was overthrown in March 1991 by troops led by Lt.-Col. Toure. A military National Reconciliation Committee joined with democratic parties to form a Transitional Committee for the Salvation of the People which suspended the constitution and dissolved the Mali People's Democratic Union (UPDM), formerly the sole party. A transitional government was formed in April 1991. A new constitution was approved by a national referendum in January 1992. The new constitution provided for a multiparty political system, and legislative elections were held in February and March 1992 with the Alliance for Democracy in Mali (ADEMA) emerging victorious. Alpha Konaré, the ADEMA leader, won the presidential elections in April 1992 and appointed a government dominated by ADEMA members. ADEMA won legislative elections in July 1997.

HEAD OF STATE
President, Alpha Oumar Konaré, *elected* 1992, *re-elected* 11 May 1997

CABINET *as at May 1997*
Prime Minister, Ibrahim Boubacar Keita
Armed Forces and Veterans, Mamadou Ba
Civil Service, Labour and Employment, Boubacar Diarra
Culture and Communications and Government Spokesman, Bakary Koniba Traore
Finance and Commerce, Souleymane Cisse
Health, Solidarity and Pensioners, Modibo Sidibe
Justice, Cheikna Kamissoko
Mines, Energy and Water Resources, Cheickna Seydou Diawara
Minister of State, Foreign Affairs, Malians Abroad and African Integration, Dioncounda Traore
Primary Education, Adama Sammassekou
Public Works and Transport, Mohamed Ag Erlaf
Rural Development and Environment, Modibo Traore
Secondary and Higher Education and Scientific Research, Moustapha Dicko
Territorial Administration and Security, Lt.-Col. Sada Samake
Tourism and Crafts, Fatou Haidara
Urbanization and Housing, Sy Kadiatou Sow
Youth and Sports, Boubacar Coulibaly

EMBASSY OF THE REPUBLIC OF MALI
Avenue Molière 487, 1060 Brussels, Belgium
Tel: Brussels 3457432
Ambassador Extraordinary and Plenipotentiary, HE N'Tji Traoré, apptd 1993; resident at Brussels

BRITISH AMBASSADOR, HE David Snoxell, resident at Dakar, Senegal
BRITISH CONSULATE – Bamako

ECONOMY

Mali's principal exports are gold, groundnuts, cotton fibres, meat and dried fish. Mali rejoined the CFA Franc Zone in 1984.

In 1993 Mali had a trade deficit of US$120 million and a current account deficit of US$244 million.

GNP – US$2,410 million (1995); US$250 per capita (1995)
GDP – US$2,747 million (1992); US$284 per capita (1992)
ANNUAL AVERAGE GROWTH OF GDP – –0.2 per cent (1991)
INFLATION RATE – 12.4 per cent (1995)
TOTAL EXTERNAL DEBT – US$3,066 million (1995)

Trade with UK	1995	1996
Imports from UK	£24,074,000	£24,335,000
Exports to UK	225,000	681,000

MALTA
Repubblika ta' Malta

AREA – 122 sq. miles (316 sq. km)
POPULATION – 376,335 (1995). The Maltese are mainly
   Roman Catholic. The Maltese language is of Semitic
   origin and held by some to be derived from the
   Carthaginian and Phoenician tongues. Maltese and
   English are the official languages of administration.
   Maltese is the official language in all the courts of law
   and the language of general use in the islands
CAPITAL – ΨValletta (population, 7,184, 1995 census)
CURRENCY – Maltese lira (LM) of 100 cents or 1,000 mils
NATIONAL ANTHEM – L-Innu Malti
NATIONAL DAYS – 31 March (Freedom Day); 8
   September (Lady of Victories); 7 June; 21 September
   (Independence Day); 13 December (Republic Day)
NATIONAL FLAG – Two equal vertical stripes, white at the
   hoist and red at the fly. A representation of the George
   Cross is carried edged with red in the canton of the white
   stripe
LIFE EXPECTANCY (years) – male 72.99; female 77.81
POPULATION GROWTH RATE – 0.7 per cent (1994)
POPULATION DENSITY – 1,152 per sq. km (1994)
MILITARY EXPENDITURE – 1.1 per cent of GDP (1995)
MILITARY PERSONNEL – 1,950

Malta lies in the Mediterranean Sea, 58 miles (93 km) from
Sicily and about 180 miles (288 km) from the African coast.
It is about 17 miles (27 km) in length and 9 miles (14.5 km)
in breadth. Malta also includes the islands of Gozo (area
25.9 sq. miles (67 sq. km)), Comino and minor islets.

HISTORY AND POLITICS

Malta was in turn held by the Phoenicians, Carthaginians,
Romans and Arabs. In 1090 it was conquered by Count
Roger of Normandy and in 1530 handed over to the
Knights of St John. In 1565 it sustained the famous siege,
when the Turks were successfully withstood by Grand-
master La Valette. The Knights fortified the islands and
built Valletta before being expelled by Napoleon in 1798.
The Maltese rose against the French garrison soon afterwards and the island was subsequently blockaded by the
British fleet. The Maltese people requested the protection
of the British Crown in 1802 on condition that their rights
would be respected. The islands were finally annexed to
the British Crown by the Treaty of Paris in 1814.
    Malta was again besieged during the Second World War.
From June 1940 to the end of the war, 432 members of the
garrison and 1,540 civilians were killed by enemy aircraft.
The island was awarded the George Cross for gallantry on
15 April 1942.
    On 21 September 1964 Malta became an independent
state within the Commonwealth, and on 13 December
1974 a republic within the Commonwealth.
    Elections to the unicameral parliament of 65 members
are held every five years by a system of proportional
representation.
    The Malta Labour Party was elected in the general
election in October 1996, winning 35 seats to the Nationalist Party's 34.

FOREIGN RELATIONS

Malta applied for EC membership in 1990 and in June 1993
the Commission issued its Opinion that Malta should be
accepted as a member subsequent to the implementation of
a series of economic reforms. In October 1996 the Labour
government announced its intention to withdraw Malta's

EU application and its participation in NATO's partnership for peace programme.

HEAD OF STATE
President, Dr Ugo Mifsud Bonnici, *took office* 4 April 1994

CABINET *as at August 1997*
Prime Minister, Dr Alfred Sant
Deputy PM, Foreign Affairs, Environment, Dr George Vella
Agriculture and Fisheries, Noel Farrugia
Economic Affairs and Industry, Dr John Attard Montalto
Education and National Culture, Evarist Bartolo
Finance and Commerce, Leo Brincat
Health, Care of the Elderly and Family Affairs, Dr Michael
   Farrugia
Housing, Freddie Portelli
Justice and Local Councils, Dr Charles Mangion
Office of the Prime Minister, Joseph Mizzi
Public Works and Construction, Charles Buhagiar
Social Welfare, Prof. Edwin Grech
Tourism, Karmenu Vella
Transport and Ports, Joseph Debono Grech

MALTA HIGH COMMISSION
Malta House, 36–38 Piccadilly, London WIV OPQ
Tel 0171-292 4800
High Commissioner, HE Richard Matrenza, apptd 1997

BRITISH HIGH COMMISSION
7 St Anne Street, Floriana (PO Box 506), Malta
Tel: Floriana 233134/8
High Commissioner, HE Graham R. Archer, CMG, apptd 1995

BRITISH COUNCIL REPRESENTATIVE, A. Bradley, c/o
   British High Commission

ECONOMY

Agriculture and fisheries contributed 2.8 per cent of GDP
in 1996. Principal products are animal products, vegetables, fruit (especially grapes), flowers and cuttings.
    The island's leading industry is the state-owned Malta
Drydocks, employing about 3,350 people. The main port
of Grand Harbour handled traffic of 1.15 million tonnes
between October 1996 and May 1997. Malta Freeport was
opened in 1990 in the southern port of Marsaxlokk and
comprises a container distribution centre, an oil products
terminal and warehouse facilities. A second container
terminal is being built.
    In 1994 manufacturing employed 22.1 per cent of the
workforce and accounted for 24 per cent of GDP.
Industries include food processing, textiles, footwear and
clothing, plastics and chemical products, electronic equipment, machinery and components.
    Tourism has assumed primary importance, with
1,053,788 tourists visiting the island in 1996. In 1996
2,443,502 passengers passed through Malta airport.
    In 1995 imports totalled US$2,977 million and exports
US$1,887 million.
GDP – US$2,553 million (1992); US$7,536 per capita
   (1992)
ANNUAL AVERAGE GROWTH OF GDP – 4.3 per cent (1992)
INFLATION RATE – 4.0 per cent (1995)
UNEMPLOYMENT – 4.5 per cent (1993)
TOTAL EXTERNAL DEBT – US$955 million (1995)

TRADE

The principal imports are foodstuffs (mainly wheat, meat
and bullocks, milk and fruit), fodder, beverages and
tobacco, fuels, chemicals, textiles and machinery (industrial, agricultural and transport). The chief exports are

processed food, electronics, textiles, and other manufactures.

Trade with UK	1995	1996
Imports from UK	£284,346,000	£242,572,000
Exports to UK	79,790,000	94,910,000

EDUCATION

Education is compulsory between the ages of five and 16 and is free at all levels. Secondary education in state schools is provided in secondary schools, junior lyceums and trade schools. There are ten junior lyceums, 18 secondary schools and five centres catering for low achievers.

A Junior College, administered by the University of Malta, prepares students specifically for a university course. Tertiary education is available at the University of Malta. There are also schools administered by the Catholic Church and other private schools.

ILLITERACY RATE – 8.7 per cent

ENROLMENT (percentage of age group) – primary 99 per cent; secondary 83 per cent; tertiary 20.0 per cent (1993)

MARSHALL ISLANDS
Republic of the Marshall Islands

AREA – 70 sq. miles (181 sq. km)

POPULATION – 54,000 (1994 UN estimate): 99 per cent are Micronesian. Over half the population is under 15. About 60 per cent of the population is concentrated on the two atolls of Majuro and Kwajalein. The population is Christian, primarily Protestant but with a substantial Catholic minority. The principal Protestant denomination is the United Church of Christ. Marshallese and English are the official languages

CAPITAL – Dalap-Uliga-Darrit, on Majuro Atoll (population, 20,000)

MAJOR TOWNS – Ebeye (9,200)

CURRENCY – Currency is that of USA

NATIONAL DAY – 21 October (Compact Day)

NATIONAL FLAG – Blue with a diagonal ray divided white over orange running from the lower hoist to the upper fly; in the canton a white sun

LIFE EXPECTANCY (years) – male 59.06; female 62.96

POPULATION GROWTH RATE – 3.9 per cent (1994)

POPULATION DENSITY – 299 per sq. km (1994)

The Republic of the Marshall Islands consists of 29 atolls and five islands in the central Pacific. The islands and atolls form two parallel chains running north-west to south-east: the Ratak (Sunrise) chain and the Ralik (Sunset) chain. The largest atoll is Kwajalein in the Ralik chain. The atolls are coral and the islands are volcanic. None of the islands rises more than a few metres above sea level. The climate is hot and humid with little seasonal variation in temperature.

HISTORY AND POLITICS

The Marshall Islands were claimed by Spain in 1592 but were left undisturbed by the Spanish Empire for 300 years. In 1886 the Marshall Islands formally became a German protectorate. On the outbreak of the First World War in 1914, Japan took control of the islands on behalf of the Allied powers, and after the war administered the territory as a League of Nations mandate. During the Second World War US armed forces seized the islands from the Japanese after intense fighting. In 1947 the USA entered into agreement with the UN Security Council to administer

the Micronesia area, of which the Marshall Islands are a part, as the UN Trust Territory of the Pacific Islands.

The islands became internally self-governing in 1979, and the US Trusteeship administration came to an end on 21 October 1986, when a Compact of Free Association between the USA and the Republic of the Marshall Islands came into effect. By this agreement the USA recognized the Republic of the Marshall Islands as a fully sovereign and independent state. The UN Security Council terminated the UN Trust Territory of the Pacific in relation to the Marshall Islands and recognized its independence in December 1990.

FOREIGN RELATIONS

The Republic of the Marshall Islands has no defence forces. The Compact of Free Association places full responsibility for defence of the Marshall Islands on the USA. The US Department of Defence retains control of islands within Kwajalein Atoll where it has a missile test range.

POLITICAL SYSTEM

The republic is a democracy based on a parliamentary system of government. The executive is headed by the president, who is elected by the *Nitijela* from among its members. The president serves for a four-year term. The legislature has two chambers, the Council of Iroij of 12 members and the Nitijela of 33 members. The Nitijela is the law-making chamber, to which the president and government are accountable. The Council of Iroij has an advisory role.

There are 24 local government districts, each of which usually consists of an elected council, a mayor and appointed local officials.

HEAD OF STATE
President, Imata Kabua, *elected* 14 January 1997

GOVERNMENT *as at June 1997*
The President
Education, Philip Muller
Finance, Ruben Zackras
Foreign Affairs, Thomas Kijner
Health and Environment, Henchi Balos
Internal Affairs, Brenson Wase
Justice, Luckner Abner
Public Works, Antonio Eliu
Resources and Development, Amsa Jonathan
Social Services, Christopher Locak
Transport and Communications, Kunio Lemari

BRITISH AMBASSADOR, HE Vernon Scarborough, resident at Suva, Fiji

ECONOMY

The economy is a mixture of subsistence and a service-based sector. About half the working population is engaged in agriculture and fishing, with coconut oil and copra production comprising 90 per cent of total exports. The service sector is based in Majuro and Ebeye and concentrated in banking and insurance, construction, transportation and tourism. Direct US aid under the Compact accounts for two-thirds of the islands' budget. The islands charge large foreign (mainly Japanese) fishing fleets licences for fishing tuna in the waters around the islands. Japanese fleets pay some US$3 million a year. The USA and Japan are the major trading partners.

GNP – US$88 million (1994)

GDP – US$69 million (1992); US$1,618 per capita (1992)

Trade with UK	1995	1996
Imports from UK	£3,271,000	£2,562,000
Exports to UK	364,000	383,000

COMMUNICATIONS

Air Marshall Islands provides air services within the islands and to Hawaii. Continental Air Micronesia serves Majuro and Kwajalein with flights to Hawaii and Guam. Majuro also has shipping links to Hawaii, Australia, Japan and throughout the Pacific.

SOCIAL WELFARE

Majuro and Ebeye have hospitals run by the government with aid from the US Public Health Service. Each outer island community has a health assistant.

The state school system provides education up to age 18, but only 25 per cent of students proceed beyond elementary level because of inadequate resources.

MAURITANIA
République Islamique de Mauritanie

Area – 395,956 sq. miles (1,025,520 sq. km). Neighbours: Senegal (south), Mali (east), Algeria and the Western Sahara (north)
Population – 2,211,000 (1994 UN estimate). The official languages are French and Arabic
Capital – Nouakchott (population, 850,000)
Currency – Ouguiya (UM) of 5 khoums
National Day – 28 November
National Flag – Yellow star and crescent on green ground
Life Expectancy (years) – male 49.90; female 53.10
Population Growth Rate – 2.5 per cent (1994)
Population Density – 2 per sq. km (1994)
Military Expenditure – 1.9 per cent of GDP (1995)
Military Personnel – 17,650: Army 15,000, Navy 500, Air Force 150, Paramilitaries 2,000
Conscription Duration – Two years
Illiteracy Rate – 62.3 per cent
Enrolment (percentage of age group) – tertiary 4.1 per cent (1993)

HISTORY AND POLITICS

Mauritania elected on 28 November 1958 to remain within the French Community as an autonomous republic. It became fully independent on 28 November 1960. In 1972 Mauritania left the Franc Zone.

Mauritania and Morocco occupied the Western Sahara territory in February 1976 when Spain formally relinquished it and in April 1976 agreed on a new frontier dividing the territory between them. In August 1979, Mauritania relinquished all claim to the southern sector of the Western Sahara after a three-year war against Polisario Front guerrillas.

After a military coup in 1978, Mauritania was ruled by a Military Committee for National Salvation (CMSN). In April 1991 President Ould Taya announced a political amnesty and a referendum on the constitution, followed by multiparty elections for a reconvened Senate and National Assembly. The constitution was approved in July 1991. Multiparty elections to the Senate and National Assembly were held in March 1992 and won by the Republican Democratic and Social Party (PRDS) led by President Ould Taya. The President appointed a Cabinet of PRDS

members in April 1992 but the legitimacy of the new government was undermined by the boycott of the elections by the main opposition grouping, the Union of Democratic Forces (UDF).

Legislative elections in October 1996 were won by the PRDS after the UDF pulled out after the first round accusing the government of fraud.

Head of State
President, Col. Maaouya Ould Sidi Ahmed Taya, *took power* 12 December 1984, *elected* 17 January 1992

Cabinet *as at June 1997*
Prime Minister, Cheihk el Avia Ould Mohamed Khouna
Civil Service, Labour, Youth and Sports, Baba Ould Sidi
Commerce, Handicrafts and Tourism, Abour Demba Sow
Communications and Relations with Parliament, Rachid Ould Saleh
Culture, Islamic Affairs, Khattry Ould Jiddou
Defence, Yeslem Ould Vil
Education, Sgheyer Ould M'Bare
Equipment and Transport, Mohamed Deina Sow
Finance, Camara Ali Gueladio
Fisheries and Maritime Economy, Beijel Ould Houmeid
Foreign Affairs and Co-operation, Sow Abou Demba
Health and Social Affairs, Mohamed Mahmoud Ould Dahmane
Interior, Posts and Telecommunications, Baba Ould Alewa
Justice, Mohamed Lemine Salem Ould Dah
Mines and Industry, N'gaide Lemine Kayou
Planning, Mohamed Ould Amar
Rural Development and the Environment, Ahmed Salem Ould Salek
Trade, Handicrafts and Tourism, Abdallahi Ould Neme
Water and Energy, Mohamed Ahmed Kelly Ould Cheikh Sidya

Embassy of the Islamic Republic of Mauritania
5 rue de Montevideo, Paris XVIe, France
Tel: Paris 45048854
Ambassador Extraordinary and Plenipotentiary, Dah Ould Abdi, apptd 1996

British Ambassador, HE William H. Fullerton, cmg, resident at Rabat, Morocco

ECONOMY

The main source of potential wealth lies in rich deposits of iron ore around Zouérate, in the north of the country, and rich fishing grounds off the coast.

In 1993 Mauritania had a trade surplus of US$3 million and a current account deficit of US$139 million.
GNP – US$1,049 million (1995); US$460 per capita (1995)
GDP – US$1,235 million (1992); US$571 per capita (1992)
Inflation Rate – 9.3 per cent (1993)
Total External Debt – US$2,467 million (1995)

Trade with UK	1995	1996
Imports from UK	£6,026,000	£14,150,000
Exports to UK	14,579,000	13,982,000

MAURITIUS

Area – 720 sq. miles (1,865 sq. km)
Population – 1,142,513 (1996 estimate): Asiatic races (Hindus 51.8 per cent, Muslims 16.5 per cent, Chinese 2.8 per cent), and persons of European (mainly French) extraction, mixed and African descent (28.6 per cent). English is the official language but French may be used

in the National Assembly and lower law courts. Creole is the most commonly used language and several Indian languages are also used

CAPITAL – ΨPort Louis (population, 144,970, 1994 estimate)

MAJOR TOWNS – Beau Bassin-Rose Hill (97,050); Curepipe (76,971); Vacoas-Phoenix (94,558) and Quatre Bornes (73,870), 1994 estimates

CURRENCY – Mauritius rupee of 100 cents

NATIONAL ANTHEM – Glory to thee, Motherland

NATIONAL DAY – 12 March

NATIONAL FLAG – Red, blue, yellow and green horizontal stripes

LIFE EXPECTANCY (years) – male 66.39; female 73.86

POPULATION GROWTH RATE – 1.0 per cent (1994)

POPULATION DENSITY – 541 per sq. km (1994)

URBAN POPULATION – 43.7 per cent (1993)

MILITARY EXPENDITURE – 0.5 per cent of GDP (1995)

MILITARY PERSONNEL – Paramilitaries 1,300

Mauritius is an island group lying in the Indian Ocean, 550 miles east of Madagascar. The climate is sub-tropical and maritime, with a wide range of rainfall and temperature resulting from the mountainous nature of the island. Humidity is high throughout the year.

HISTORY AND POLITICS

Mauritius was discovered in 1511 by the Portuguese; the Dutch visited it in 1598 and named it Mauritius after Prince Maurice of Nassau. From 1638 to 1710 it was held as a Dutch colony and in 1715 the French took possession but did not settle it until 1721. Mauritius was taken by a British force in 1810 and became a Crown Colony. It became an independent state within the Commonwealth on 12 March 1968 and a republic on 12 March 1992.

The last general election was held on 20 December 1995. The present government is a coalition of the Partides Travailleurs Mauricien (PTM) and the Militant Mauritian Movement (MMM) which holds 60 seats.

POLITICAL SYSTEM

The president is head of state and is elected by the members of the National Assembly. The prime minister, appointed by the president, is the member of the National Assembly who appears to the president best able to command the support of the majority of members of the Assembly. Other ministers are appointed by the president acting in accordance with the advice of the prime minister.

The National Assembly has a normal term of five years and consists of 62 elected members (the island of Mauritius is divided into 20 three-member constituencies and Rodrigues returns two members), and eight specially-elected members. Of the latter, four seats go to the 'best loser' of whichever communities in the island are under-represented in the Assembly after the general election and the four remaining seats are allocated on the basis of both party and community.

HEAD OF STATE

President, Cassam Uteem, *elected* June 1992

COUNCIL OF MINISTERS *as at June 1997*

Prime Minister, Defence and Home Affairs, External Communications and Information Technology, Rodrigues and Outer Islands, Dr Navinchandra Ramgoolam

Deputy PM, Foreign Affairs, International and Regional Co-operation, Paul Raymond Berenger

Agriculture and Natural Resources, Dr Arvin Boolell

Arts, Culture and Leisure, Dhurma Gian Nath

Attorney-General, Justice, Human Rights and Corporate Affairs, Abdool Razack Mahomed Ameen Peeroo

Civil Service Affairs, Tsang Fan Hin Tsang Mang Kin

Economic Planning, International Trade and Telecommunications, Rajkeswur Purryag

Education, Science and Technology, James Burty David

Environment and Quality of Life, Rajesh Anand Bhagwan

Finance, Dr Vasant Kumar Bunwaree

Fisheries, Co-operatives and Marine Resources Development, Motee Ramdass

Health, Ramsamy Chedumbarum Kadress Pillay

Housing and Land Development, Alan Ganoo

Human Resource Development and Institutional Reform, Samioullah Lauthan

Industry and Commerce, Jayakrishna Cuttaree

Labour and Industrial Relations, Louis Steven Obeegadoo

Land Transport, Shipping and Public Safety, Dr Ahmed Rashid Beebeejaun

Local Government and Public Utilities, Devanand Virahsawmy

Public Infrastructure, Dr Siddick Mohummud Chady

Social Security and National Solidarity, Marie-Thérèse Joceline Minerve

Tourism, José Arunasalon

Women, Family Welfare and Child Development, Indira Savitree Thacoor-Sidaya

Youth and Sport, Sachindev Mahess Kumar Soonarane

MAURITIUS HIGH COMMISSION
32–33 Elvaston Place, London SW7 5NW
Tel 0171-581 0294/5
High Commissioner, HE Sir Satcam Boolell, QC, apptd 1996

BRITISH HIGH COMMISSION
Les Cascades Building, Edith Cavell Street, Port Louis (PO Box 1063)
Tel: Port Louis 211 1361
High Commissioner, HE James Daly apptd 1997

BRITISH COUNCIL DIRECTOR, S. Ponnappa, PO Box 111, Rose Hill

ECONOMY

About 55 per cent of the total sugar crop is produced on plantations, while smaller owners cultivate about 24 per cent of the land under cane. Tea and tobacco are also grown commercially but on a smaller scale than sugar. Production in 1996 was: sugar, 560,138 tonnes; tea (manufactured), 2,497 tonnes; tobacco (leaves), 878 tonnes. In 1994 production of molasses, mainly for export, was 138,421 tonnes. Other products include alcohol, rum, denatured spirits, perfumed spirits and vinegar.

The bulk of the island's requirements in manufactured products still has to be imported. However, the Mauritius Export Processing Zone (MEPZ) scheme, introduced in 1971, has attracted investment from overseas and the number of export-orientated enterprises had risen from ten in 1971 to 481 in 1996. The biggest firms are in clothing manufacture, particularly woollen knitwear, but the range of goods produced includes toys, plastic products, leather goods, diamond cutting and polishing, watches, television sets and telephones.

Tourism is a major source of income, with an estimated 486,867 tourists in 1996. France is the most important source of tourists, followed closely by the neighbouring French island of Réunion.

In 1994 the government had a budget deficit equivalent to 0.29 per cent of GDP.

GNP – US$3,815 million (1995); US$3,380 per capita (1995)

GDP – US$2,825 million (1992); US$2,765 per capita (1992)

ANNUAL AVERAGE GROWTH OF GDP – 5.4 per cent (1993)
INFLATION RATE – 6.0 per cent (1995)
TOTAL EXTERNAL DEBT – US$1,801 million (1995)

TRADE

Most foodstuffs and raw materials have to be imported from abroad. Apart from local consumption (about 36,500 tonnes a year), the sugar produced is exported, mainly to Britain.

In 1993 Mauritius had a trade deficit of US$254 million and a current account deficit of US$92 million. In 1995 imports totalled US$1,959 million and exports US$1,537 million.

Trade with UK	1995	1996
Imports from UK	£71,018,000	£73,417,000
Exports to UK	345,149,000	344,161,000

COMMUNICATIONS

Port Louis, on the north-west coast, handles the bulk of the island's external trade. A bulk sugar terminal capable of handling the total crop began operating in 1980. The international airport is located at Plaisance about five miles from Mahébourg. There are seven daily newspapers and 15 weeklies, mostly in French. The Mauritius Broadcasting Corporation operates television and radio broadcasting in the country. There is a satellite communications ground station near Port Louis.

EDUCATION

Primary and secondary education are free and primary education is compulsory. There are a number of training facilities offering vocational training. The Institute of Education is responsible for training primary and secondary school teachers and for curriculum development. The University of Mauritius had 2,496 students in 1996–7.
ILLITERACY RATE – 17.1 per cent
ENROLMENT (percentage of age group) – primary 94 per cent; tertiary 4.8 per cent (1993)

RODRIGUES AND DEPENDENCIES

Rodrigues, formerly a dependency but now part of Mauritius, is about 350 miles east of Mauritius, with an area of 40 square miles. Population (1996) 35,019. Cattle, salt fish, sheep, goats, pigs, maize and onions are the principal exports. The island is administered by an Island Secretary.
Island Secretary, B. Juggoo

The islands of Agalega and St Brandon are dependencies of Mauritius. Total population (1996) 170.

MEXICO
Estados Unidos Mexicanos

AREA – 756,066 sq. miles (1,958,201 sq. km)
POPULATION – 93,008,000 (1994 UN estimate). Spanish is the official language and is spoken by about 95 per cent of the population. There are five main groups of Indian languages (Náhuatl, Maya, Zapotec, Otomí, Mixtec) and 59 dialects derived from them
CAPITAL – Mexico City (population, 15,047,685, 1990)
MAJOR CITIES – Guadalajara (2,846,000); Monterrey (2,521,697); Puebla (1,454,526); León (956,070); Torreón (876,4560); Toluca (827,339); Ciudad Juarez (797,679); Tijuana (742,686); Tijuana (742,686), 1990 census

CURRENCY – Peso of 100 centavos
NATIONAL ANTHEM – Mexicanos, Al Grito De Guerra (Mexicans, to the war cry)
NATIONAL DAY – 16 September (Proclamation of Independence)
NATIONAL FLAG – Three vertical bands in green, white, red, with the Mexican emblem (an eagle on a cactus devouring a snake) in the centre
LIFE EXPECTANCY (years) – male 62.10; female 66.00
POPULATION GROWTH RATE – 1.9 per cent (1994)
POPULATION DENSITY – 47 per sq. km (1994)

The Sierra Nevada, known in Mexico as the Sierra Madre, and Rocky Mountains continue south from the northern border with the USA, running parallel to the west and east coasts. The interior consists of an elevated plateau between the two ranges. In the west is the peninsula of Lower California, separated from the mainland by the Gulf of California. The main rivers are the Rio Grande (Rio Bravo) del Norte, which forms part of the northern boundary and is navigable for about 70 miles from its mouth in the Gulf of Mexico, and the Rio Grande de Santiago, the Rio Balsas and Rio Papaloapan.

HISTORY AND POLITICS

Present-day Mexico and Guatemala were once the centre of a civilization which flowered in the periods from AD 500 to 1100 and 1300 to 1500 and collapsed before the army of Spanish adventurers under Hernán Cortés in the years following 1519. Pre-Columbian Mexico was divided between different Indian cultures, each of which has left distinctive archaeological remains. The best-known of these are Chichén Itzá, Uxmal, Bonampak and Palenque, in Yucatán and Chiapas (Maya); Teotihuacán, renowned for the Pyramid of the Sun in the Valley of Mexico (Teotihuacáno); Monte Albán and Mitla, near Oaxaca (Zapotec); El Tajín in the state of Veracruz (Totonac); and Tula in the state of Hidalgo (Toltec). The last and most famous Indian culture, the Aztec, based on Tenochtitlán, suffered more than the others at the hands of the Spanish and very few Aztec monuments remain.

After the conquest, the Spanish appointed a Viceroy to rule their new dominions, which they called New Spain. The country was largely converted to Christianity and a distinctive colonial civilization, representing a marriage of Indian and Spanish traditions, developed. In 1810 a revolt began against Spanish rule. This was finally successful in 1821, when a precarious independence was proclaimed.

Friction with the USA led to the war of 1845–8, at the end of which Mexico was forced to cede the northern provinces of Texas, California and New Mexico. In 1862 Mexican insolvency led to invasion by French forces which installed Archduke Maximilian of Austria as Emperor. The empire collapsed with the execution of the Emperor in 1867 and the austere reformer Juárez restored the republic. Juárez's death was followed by the dictatorship of Porfirio Díaz, which saw an enormous increase in foreign, particularly British and American, investment in the country. In 1910 began the Mexican Revolution which reformed the social structure and the land system, curbed the power of foreign companies and ushered in the independent industrial Mexico of today.

There are nine registered political parties, of which the largest is the Partido Revolucionario Institucional (PRI) which has constituted the governing party for more than 60 years. The main opposition parties are Partido de Acción Nacional (PAN) and Partido de la Revolución Democrática (PRD). On 6 July 1997 voting took place in the first fully democratic elections for the Chamber of Deputies, a quarter of the Senate, six state governorships and the

Mayor of Mexico. The PRI lost control of the Chamber of Deputies.

INSURGENCIES

An armed revolt of Zapatista peasant Indians in the southern state of Chiapas in January 1994 highlighted continuing charges against the PRI of corruption and fraud, and these continued up to the August 1994 elections.

A further armed revolt by the Zapatista National Liberation Army (ZNLA) in Chiapas from December 1994 to February 1995 caused a political and economic crisis. President Zedillo introduced political reforms agreed with the PAN and PRD, making the electoral commission fully independent and providing for the re-examination of contentious elections by impartial observers. Negotiations with the Zapatistas produced a preliminary agreement on indigenous rights in February 1996 and are still ongoing.

New guerrilla groups, the People's Revolutionary Army (EPR) and the Popular Insurgency Revolutionary Army (ERIP) emerged in 1996.

POLITICAL SYSTEM

Congress consists of a Senate of 128 members, elected for six years, and of a Chamber of Deputies, at present numbering 500, elected for three years. The chief executive of the government is the president, who is elected for a six-year term and may not be re-elected.

The country is divided into 31 states and the federal district of Mexico City.

HEAD OF STATE

President, Dr Ernesto Zedillo Ponce de León, *elected* 4 June 1994, *took office* 1 December 1994

CABINET *as at July 1997*

Agrarian Reform, Arturo Warman Gryj
Agriculture, Rural Development and Livestock, Francisco Labastida Ochoa
Attorney-General, Jorge Madrazo Cuéllar
Attorney of Justice for Mexico City, Lorenzo Thomas Torres
Communication and Transport, Carlos Ruiz Sacristan
Comptroller-General, Arsenio Farell
Defence, Gen. Enrique Cervantes Aguirre
Education, Miguel Limon Rojas
Energy, Jesús Reyes Heroles
Finance and Public Credit, Guillermo Ortiz Martínez
Fishing, Environment and Natural Resources, Julia Carabias Lillo
Foreign Affairs, José Angel Gurría Treviño
Health, Juan Ramón de la Fuente Ramírez
Interior, Emilio Chuayffet
Labour and Social Welfare, Javier Bonilla
Mayor of Mexico City, Cuauhtémoc Cárdenas
Naval Affairs, Adm. José Ramón Lorenzo Franco
Social Development, Carlos Rojas Gutiérrez
Tourism, Silvia Hernández Enríquez
Trade and Industry, Herminio Blanco

MEXICAN EMBASSY

42 Hertford Street, London WIY 7TF
Tel 0171-499 8586
Ambassador Extraordinary and Plenipotentiary, HE Santiago Oñate, apptd 1997
Minister, Deputy Ambassador, J. Brito-Moncada
Military Attaché, Gen. F. A. Meza-Castro
Minister, Consul-General, J. Ibarra
Counsellor, F. Estandía-González (*Commercial*)

BRITISH EMBASSY

Calle Río Lerma 71, Colonia Cuauhtémoc,
06500 Mexico City
Tel: Mexico City 207 2089
Ambassador Extraordinary and Plenipotentiary, HE Adrian J. Beamish, CMG, apptd 1994
Deputy Head of Mission, Minister-Counsellor and Consul-General, Dr P. Tibber
Defence Attaché, Col. J. Watson
First Secretary (*Commercial*), A. Stephens

CONSULAR OFFICES – Mexico City, Acapulco, Cancun, Ciudad Juárez, Guadalajara, Mérida, Monterrey, Oaxaca, Tampico, Tijuana, Veracruz

BRITISH COUNCIL DIRECTOR, A. Curry, Maestro Antonio Caso 127, Col. San Rafael, Delegación Cuauhtemoc, (PO Box 30-588), Mexico 06470 DF

BRITISH CHAMBER OF COMMERCE, British Trade Centre, Rio de la Plata 30, Col. Cuauhtemoc, CP 06500, Mexico City DF, *Manager,* Stephen Grant

DEFENCE

The Army has with 274 armoured personnel carriers and 123 artillery pieces. The Navy has three destroyers, two frigates, 103 patrol and coastal vessels, and nine combat aircraft. There are 21 naval bases. The Air Force has 97 combat aircraft and 25 armed helicopters.

MILITARY EXPENDITURE – 0.9 per cent of GDP (1995)
MILITARY PERSONNEL – 175,000: Army 130,000, Navy 37,000, Air Force 8,000
CONSCRIPTION DURATION – 12 months (four hours per week) by lottery

ECONOMY

The principal crops are maize, beans, rice, wheat, sugar cane, coffee, cotton, tomatoes, chillies, tobacco, chick-peas, groundnuts, sesame, alfalfa, vanilla, cocoa and many kinds of fruit. The maguey, or Mexican cactus, yields several fermented drinks, mezcal and tequila (distilled) and pulque (undistilled). Another species of the plant supplies sisal-hemp (henequen). The forests contain mahogany, rosewood, ebony and chicle trees. Agriculture employs an estimated 20 per cent of the working population.

The principal industries are mining and petroleum, although there has been considerable expansion of both light and heavy industries; exports of manufactured goods now average about 56 per cent of total exports. The steel industry expanded steadily until recently and current production is around 7.9 million tons. In 1995, 931,000 motor vehicles were produced, of which 779,000 were for export.

The mineral wealth is great, and principal minerals are gold, silver, copper, lead, zinc, quicksilver, iron and sulphur. Substantial reserves of uranium have been found. Mexico produces 25 per cent of the world's supply of fluorspar.

Oil exports were 1.5 million barrels per day in 1996. Daily production of natural gas is approximately 3 billion cubic feet. Oil reserves have increased substantially due to discoveries in the Gulf of Campeche. A refinery at Tula is the nation's largest; and new refineries in Monterrey, State of Nuevo León, and Salina Cruz, State of Oaxaca, are under construction.

Political and economic uncertainty in late 1994 caused a crisis of confidence in the economy by foreign investors and a run on the peso. Insolvency and defaulting on the foreign debt was only averted by a US$50,000 million loan package from the USA and international institutions. Since January 1995 the government has introduced austerity measures, increasing interest rates and petrol taxes, curbing pay levels and reducing public expenditure in an attempt to keep inflation and debt levels under control and to rein back a runaway trade deficit. In June 1997 the government announced a three-year National Programme for the Financing of Development intended to stimulate the economy. Mexico repaid the last of its debt to the USA in 1997.

Mexico joined GATT in 1986 and the OECD in 1994.

GNP – US$304,596 million (1995); US$3,320 per capita (1995)

GDP – US$259,971 million (1992); US$3,736 per capita (1992)

ANNUAL AVERAGE GROWTH OF GDP – –6.9 per cent (1995)

INFLATION RATE – 35.0 per cent (1995)

UNEMPLOYMENT – 4.7 per cent (1995)

TOTAL EXTERNAL DEBT – US$165,743 million (1995)

TRADE

Major imports include computers, auto assembly material, electrical parts, auto and truck parts, powdered milk, corn and sorghum, transport, sound-recording and power-generating equipment, chemicals, industrial machinery, pharmaceuticals and specialized appliances. Principal exports include oil, automobiles, auto engines, fruits and vegetables, shrimps, coffee, computers, cattle, glass, iron and steel pipes, and copper. The main trading partners are the USA (65.6 per cent), EU (15 per cent), Latin America (5.2 per cent) and Japan (5 per cent). The North American Free Trade Agreement, to which Mexico is a signatory, came into effect on 1 January 1994, significantly increasing Mexico's trade.

In 1994 Mexico had a trade deficit of US$18,465 million and a current account deficit of US$28,784 million. In 1995 imports totalled US$46,887 million and exports US$48,430 million.

Trade with UK	1995	1996
Imports from UK	£276,753,000	£317,428,000
Exports to UK	298,124,000	334,765,000

COMMUNICATIONS

Veracruz, Tampico and Coatzacoalcos are the chief ports on the Atlantic, and Guaymas, Mazatlán, Puerto Lázaro Cárdenas, Acapulco, Salina Cruz and Puerto Madero on the Pacific. Work is proceeding on the reorganization and re-equipment of the whole rail system. Total track length of the railways was 240,186 km in 1990. Mexico City may be reached by at least three highways from the USA, and from the south from Yucatán as well as on two principal highways from the Guatemalan border.

There are 1,113 airports and landing fields in Mexico, of which 18 are equipped to handle long-distance flights. There are 166 airline companies, including two of the major, now private, national airlines, Mexicana de Aviación and Aeroméxico.

Teléfonos de México, now privatized, controls about 98 per cent of all telephone services.

EDUCATION

Education is divided into primary, secondary and superior levels.

ILLITERACY RATE – 10.4 per cent

ENROLMENT (percentage of age group) – primary 99 per cent (1993); secondary 46 per cent (1990); tertiary 13.8 per cent (1993)

FEDERATED STATES OF MICRONESIA

AREA – 271 sq. miles (701 sq. km)

POPULATION – 104,000 (1994 UN estimate). Pohnpei: population, 31,000; capital, Kolonia; Chuuk (Truk): population, 52,000; capital, Moen; Yap: population, 12,000; capital, Colonia; Kosrae: population, 6,500; capital, Lelu. The population is Micronesian and predominantly Christian. English (official) and eight other languages are used in different parts of the Federated States: Yapese, Ulithian, Woleaian, Ponapean, Nukuoran, Kapingamarangi, Trukese and Kosraen

FEDERAL CAPITAL – Palikir, on Pohnpei

CURRENCY – Currency is that of USA

NATIONAL FLAG – United Nations blue with four white stars in the centre

POPULATION GROWTH RATE – 1.0 per cent (1994)

POPULATION DENSITY – 149 per sq. km (1994)

The Federated States of Micronesia comprise more than 600 islands extending 2,900 km (1,800 miles) across the archipelago of the Caroline Islands in the western Pacific Ocean. The islands vary geologically from mountainous islands to low coral atolls. The climate is tropical. Storms are common between August and December, and typhoons between July and November.

HISTORY AND POLITICS

The Spanish Empire claimed sovereignty over the Caroline Islands until 1899, when Spain withdrew from her Pacific territories and sold her possessions in the Caroline Islands to Germany. The Caroline Islands became a German protectorate until the outbreak of the First World War in 1914, when Japan took control of the islands on behalf of the Allied powers. After the war Japan continued to administer the territory under a League of Nations mandate. During the Second World War, US armed forces took control of the islands from the Japanese. In 1947 the USA entered into agreement with the UN Security Council to administer the Micronesia area, of which the Federated States of Micronesia were a part, as the UN Trust Territory of the Pacific Islands.

The US Trusteeship administration came to an end on 3 November 1986, when a Compact of Free Association between the USA and the Federated States of Micronesia came into effect. By this agreement the USA recognized the Federated States of Micronesia as a fully sovereign and independent state. The independence of the Federated States of Micronesia was recognized by the UN in December 1990.

POLITICAL SYSTEM

The Federated States of Micronesia is a federal republic of four constituent states: Chuuk, Kosrae, Pohnpei and Yap. The constitution separates the executive, legislative and judicial branches. There is a bill of rights and provision for traditional rights.

The executive comprises a federal president and vice-president, both of whom must be chosen from amongst the four nationally-elected senators. There is a single- chamber Congress of 14 members, four members elected on a nation-wide basis and ten members elected from congressional districts apportioned by population.

Each of the constituent states has its own government and legislative system.

The Compact of Free Association places full responsibility for the defence of the Federated States of Micronesia on the USA.

The judiciary is headed by the Supreme Court, which is divided into trial and appellate divisions. Below this, each state has its own judicial system.

HEAD OF STATE
President, Jacob Nena (Kosrae)
Vice-President, Leo Falcalm (Pohnpei)

CABINET *as at June 1997*

Administrative Services, Kapily Capelle
Attorney-General, Camillo Noket
Budget, Patrick McGanzie
Education, Catalino Cantero
External Affairs, Asterio Takesy
Finance, John Ehsa
Human Resources, Eliuel Pretrick
Planning and Statistics, Bermin Weilbacher
Resources and Development, Sabastian Anefal
Transport and Communications, Robert Weilbacher

BRITISH AMBASSADOR, HE V. M. Scarborough, resident at Suva, Fiji

ECONOMY

The economy is dependent mainly on subsistence agriculture and government spending. Copra and fish are the two main exports. The majority of the working population is engaged in government administration, subsistence farming, fishing, copra production and the growing tourist industry.
GNP – US$215 million (1995)
GDP – US$254 million (1992); US$2,484 per capita (1992)

TRADE WITH UK	1995	1996
Imports from UK	£105,000	£19,000
Exports to UK	30,000	—

MOLDOVA
Republica Moldovenească

AREA – 13,912 sq. miles (36,018 sq. km). Neighbours: Ukraine (north, east and south-east), Romania (west)
POPULATION – 4,335,000 (1996 official estimate): 65 per cent are Moldovan, 14.2 per cent Ukrainian and 13 per cent Russian, together with smaller numbers of Gagauz (ethnic Turks), Jews and Bulgarians. Most of the population are adherents of the Romanian Orthodox Church. Moldovan was made the official language (written in the Latin script) in 1989 but the use of Russian and Ukrainian in official business is permitted
CAPITAL Kishinev (population, 667,100)
CURRENCY – Leu (plural lei)
NATIONAL DAY – 27 August (Independence Day)
NATIONAL FLAG – Vertical stripes of blue, yellow, red, with the national arms in the centre
LIFE EXPECTANCY (years) – male 64.28; female 70.99
POPULATION GROWTH RATE – -0.1 per cent (1994)
POPULATION DENSITY – 129 per sq. km (1994)
URBAN POPULATION – 46.9 per cent (1992)
MILITARY EXPENDITURE – 3.7 per cent of GDP (1995)
MILITARY PERSONNEL – 15,300: Army 10,600, Air Force 1,300, Paramilitaries 3,400
CONSCRIPTION DURATION – Up to 18 months
ILLITERACY RATE – 1.1 per cent
ENROLMENT (percentage of age group) – tertiary 30.4 per cent (1994)

HISTORY AND POLITICS

A Moldovan feudal state was established in the 14th century when Slavic tribes who had previously lived under Roman and Byzantine rule integrated with Slavic tribes from further east. In the 15th century a Moldovan principality was formed which entered into military and political alliances with Muscovy before being absorbed into the Turkish Empire in the 16th century. Moldova became the site of many Russo-Turkish battles and skirmishes in the 18th century before the area between the Dniester and Prut rivers (later known as Bessarabia) was annexed to the Russian Empire by the Bucharest Peace Treaty of 1812.

After the Russian Revolution in 1917, Bessarabia came under the control of White Russian forces and was annexed to Romania under the Versailles Peace Treaty (1919). In 1924 the Moldavian Autonomous Soviet Socialist Republic (ASSR) was established on the east bank of the Dniester river as part of Soviet Ukraine. In August 1940 the Soviet Union forced Romania to cede Bessarabia and the Moldavian Soviet Socialist Republic was formed from the fusion of the majority of Bessarabia (the southernmost parts were incorporated into the Ukraine) with the Moldavian ASSR.

Moldova (formerly Moldavia) declared its independence from the USSR in August 1991. Reunification with Romania was defeated in a referendum on 6 March 1994, following which the Moldovan parliament voted to join the CIS. In July 1994 the Moldovan parliament adopted a new constitution which defines Moldova as a 'presidential parliamentary republic' based on political pluralism. It also provides for autonomous status for the Gagauz and Transdniester regions, with the Gagauz region having its own elected National Assembly.

The Moldovan Popular Front government, which came to power in the 1990 legislative elections to the 380-seat Supreme Soviet, was replaced in July 1992 by a government of national accord led by the Peasant Democratic Party. The former Communists of the Agrarian Democratic Party were returned to power in the legislative election of February 1994 and formed a coalition government with the Socialist Party. Parliament now has 104 seats and is elected by proportional representation. President Petru Lucinschi replaced former Communist president Mircea Snegur in presidential elections in November–December 1996.

INSURGENCIES

After independence was declared, the majority ethnic Romanian (Moldovan) population expressed a wish to rejoin Romania. This alienated the ethnic Ukrainian and Russian populations, who formed a majority east of the Dniester, and they declared their independence from Moldova as the Transdniester republic in December 1991. The Moldovan government refused to recognise this and in 1992 a war was waged between government forces and Transdniester forces, who were supported by the former Soviet 14th Army stationed in Transdniester and by Cossack volunteers from Russia.

A mainly Russian CIS peacekeeping force (later changed to a joint Russian-Moldovan-Transdniester force) was deployed in July 1992 and a cease-fire has held since August 1992. Although no political solution has been finalized and a state of armed truce remains, the Moldovan government in February 1994 agreed to a CSCE plan for the Transdniester area to have a high degree of autonomy within Moldova but no independent or federal status. In October 1994 the Russian and Moldovan presidents signed an agreement on the withdrawal of the 14th Army over a three-year period, the first troops leaving in February 1996.

A referendum in Transdniester on 24 December 1995 approved independence. President Igor Smirnov was re-elected in presidential elections in Transdniester in December 1996.

HEAD OF STATE
President, Petru Lucinschi, *elected* 1 December 1996

GOVERNMENT *as at August 1997*
Prime Minister, Ion Chubuk
Deputy PMs, Ion Gutzu *(Economics and Reform)*; Valeriu Bulgar
Agriculture and Foodstuffs, George Lungu
Culture, Gennadie Chobanu
Defence, Valery Pasat
Economics and Reform, Ion Gutsu
Education, Youth and Sport, Yakob Popovich
Finance, Valeriu Chitan
Foreign Affairs, Mihai Popov
Industry and Trade, Grigore Triboi
Information, Science and Communications, Ion Cassian
Internal Affairs, Mikhai Plemedyale
Justice, Vasile Sturza
Minister of State, Nikolae Chernomaz
National Security, Tudor Botnaru
Privatization, Iurie Badir
Public Health, Mikhail Magdei
Social Protection, Dumitru Nidelcu
Territorial Development, Communal Economy and Construction, Mikhail Severovan
Transport and Roads, Vasile Iouv

MOLDOVAN AMBASSADOR, HE Tudor Botnaru, resident at Brussels
BRITISH AMBASSADOR, HE Sir Andrew Wood, KCMG, resident at Moscow

ECONOMY

The main sector is agriculture, especially viniculture, fruit-growing and market gardening. Industry is small and concentrated east of the Dniester. Severe drought in 1992, the severance of most trading ties with former Soviet republics, war damage and reductions in Russian fuel deliveries paralysed the economy from 1992 to 1994. An economic reform programme began in summer 1993; a privatization programme, completed in November 1995, sold off 1,132 large enterprises and 613 shops by means of voucher auctions. Moldova is dependent on Russia for energy supplies.
GNP – US$3,996 million (1995); US$920 per capita (1995)
GDP – US$11,856 million (1992); US$257 per capita (1992)
UNEMPLOYMENT – 1.0 per cent (1995)
TOTAL EXTERNAL DEBT – US$691 million (1995)

TRADE WITH UK	1995	1996
Imports from UK	£2,248,000	£3,181,000
Exports to UK	301,000	866,000

MONACO
Principauté de Monaco

AREA – 0.4 sq. miles (1 sq. km)
POPULATION – 31,000 (1994 UN estimate). Only 5,000 residents have full Monégasque citizenship and thus the right to vote
CAPITAL – Monaco-Ville (population, 27,063, 1982)

CURRENCY – French franc of 100 centimes
NATIONAL ANTHEM – Hymne Monégasque
NATIONAL DAY – 19 November
NATIONAL FLAG – Two equal horizontal stripes, red over white
POPULATION GROWTH RATE – 0.8 per cent (1994)
POPULATION DENSITY – 20,805 per sq. km (1994)

A small principality on the Mediterranean, with land frontiers joining France at every point, Monaco is divided into the districts of Monaco-Ville, La Condamine, Font-vielle and Monte Carlo.

HISTORY AND POLITICS

The principality, ruled by the Grimaldi family since 1297, was abolished during the French Revolution and re-established in 1815 under the protection of the kingdom of Sardinia. In 1861 Monaco came under French protection.
The 1962 constitution, which can be modified only with the approval of the National Council, maintains the traditional hereditary monarchy and guarantees freedom of association, trade union freedom and the right to strike. Legislative power is held jointly by the Prince and a unicameral, 18-member National Council elected by universal suffrage. Executive power is exercised by the Prince and a four-member Council of Government, headed by a Minister of State. The judicial code is based on that of France.

HEAD OF STATE
HSH The Prince of Monaco, Prince Rainier III Louis-Henri-Maxence Bertrand, *born* 31 May 1923, *succeeded* 9 May 1949; *married* 19 April 1956, Miss Grace Patricia Kelly (died 14 September 1982) and *has issue* Prince Albert (*see* below); Princess Caroline Louise Marguerite, *born* 23 January 1957; and Princess Stephanie Marie Elisabeth, *born* 1 February 1965
Heir, HRH Prince Albert Alexandre Louis Pierre, *born* 14 March 1958

President of the Crown Council, Charles Ballerio
President of the National Council, Dr Jean-Louis Campora
Minister of State, Michel Lévêque, *appointed* 1997

CONSULATE-GENERAL OF MONACO
4 Cromwell Place, London SW7 2JE
Tel 0171-225 2679
Consul-General, I. B. Ivanovic

BRITISH CONSUL -GENERAL, I. Davies, apptd 1997, resident at Marseilles, France

ECONOMY

The whole available ground is built over so that there is no cultivation, though there are some notable public and private gardens. The economy is based on real estate revenues, the financial sector and tourism (over 250,000 visitors a year). Monaco has a small harbour (30 ft alongside quay) and the import duties are the same as in France.
GDP – US$596 million (1992); US$23,082 per capita (1992)

MONGOLIA
State of Mongolia

AREA – 604,829 sq. miles (1,566,500 sq. km). Neighbours: Russia (north), China (south)
POPULATION – 2,363,000 (1994 UN estimate). Mongolians also live in China and in the neighbouring regions of

Russia, especially the Mongolian Buryat Autonomous Region

CAPITAL – Ulan Bator (population, 515,100, 1987 estimate)

CURRENCY – Tugrik of 100 möngö

NATIONAL DAY – 11 July.

NATIONAL FLAG – Vertical tri-colour red, blue, red and in the hoist the traditional Soyombo symbol in gold

LIFE EXPECTANCY (years) – male 62.32; female 65.00

POPULATION GROWTH RATE – 2.0 per cent (1994)

POPULATION DENSITY – 2 per sq. km (1994)

URBAN POPULATION – 57.1 per cent (1989)

MILITARY EXPENDITURE – 2.4 per cent of GDP (1995)

MILITARY PERSONNEL – 17,300: Army 15,500, Paramilitaries 1,800

CONSCRIPTION DURATION – 12 months

ILLITERACY RATE – 1.3 per cent

ENROLMENT (percentage of age group) – primary 78 per cent; secondary 56 per cent; tertiary 13.6 per cent (1994)

Mongolia, which is almost entirely at least 1,000 metres above sea level, forms part of the central Asiatic plateau and rises towards the west in the mountains of the Mongolian Altai and Hangai ranges. The Hentai range, situated to the north-east of the capital Ulan Bator, is lower. The Gobi region covers much of the southern half of the country and contains sand deserts interspersed with semi-desert. There are several long rivers and many lakes but good water is scarce as much of the lake water is salty. The climate is harsh, with a short mild summer giving way to a long winter when temperatures can drop as low as −50°C.

HISTORY AND POLITICS

Mongolia, under Genghis Khan the conqueror of China and much of Asia, was for many years a buffer state between Tsarist Russia and China, although it was under general Chinese suzerainty. The Chinese Revolution in 1911 led to a declaration of autonomy under Chinese suzerainty which was confirmed by the Sino-Russian Treaty of Kiakhta (1915) but cancelled by a unilateral Chinese declaration in 1919. Later the country became a battle-ground of the Russian civil war, and Soviet and Mongolian troops occupied Ulan Bator in 1921; this was followed by another declaration of independence. In 1924 the Soviet Union in a treaty with China again recognized the latter's sovereignty over Mongolia, but this was never properly exercised because of China's preoccupation with internal affairs and later by the war with Japan. The Mongolian People's Republic was formally established in 1924. Under the Yalta Agreement, President Chiang Kai-shek of China agreed to a plebiscite, held in 1945, in which the Mongolians declared their desire for independence and this was formally recognized by China.

The Mongolian People's Revolutionary Party (MPRP) was the sole political party from 1924 to 1990. Demonstrations in favour of political and economic reform began in December 1989 and led to changes in the MPRP leadership in March 1990. The MPRP's constitutionally guaranteed monopoly of power was subsequently relinquished, and the introduction of a multiparty system was approved by the Great People's Hural (parliament). The MPRP won the first multiparty elections, held in July 1990. Since then, and following Moscow's lead, Mongolia has embarked on a programme of political and economic reforms.

The most recent legislative election, held on 30 June 1996, was won by the Democratic Union Coalition (Mongolian National Democratic Party and Mongolian Social Democratic Party) which won 50 seats. The country's first direct presidential election was held in 1993 and won by the incumbent Punsalmaagiyn Ochirbat, who stood as an opposition candidate after the MPRP refused to endorse him as its candidate. Ochirbat was ousted in May 1997 by the leader of the MPRP, Natsagiin Bagabandi.

The country and three city districts (Ulan Bator, Darkhan and Erdenet) are divided into 21 *aimaks* (provinces) and beneath these into 258 *somons* (districts), and these form the basis of the state organization of the country. The last remaining former Soviet armed forces personnel were withdrawn in late 1992.

POLITICAL SYSTEM

A new constitution was approved in January 1992 which enshrines the concepts of democracy, a mixed economy, free speech and neutrality in foreign affairs. The Great and Little Hurals were abolished, and a new unicameral Great Hural became the legislative body of the country. Members of the Great Hural are elected for four-year terms by a simple majority amounting to at least 25 per cent of the votes cast.

HEAD OF STATE

President, Natsagiin Bagabandi, *elected* 18 May 1997

CABINET *as at July 1997*

Prime Minister, Mendsaihany Enkhsahan

Agriculture and Industry, L. Nyamsambuu

Defence, D. Dorligjav

Education, C. Lhagvajav

External Relations, S. H. Altangezel

Environment, T. Adiyasuren

Finance, P. Tsagaan

Health and Social Security, L. Zorig

Infrastructure Development, G. Nyamdavaa

Justice, J. Amarsanaa

Chairman of the Great Hural, Radnaasumbereliin Gonchigdorj

EMBASSY OF MONGOLIA

7 Kensington Court, London W8 5DL

Tel 0171-937 0150

Ambassador Extraordinary and Plenipotentiary, HE Tsedenjavyn Suhbaatar, apptd 1997

BRITISH EMBASSY

30 Enkh Taivny Gudamzh (PO Box 703), Ulan Bator 13

Tel: Ulan Bator 358133

Ambassador Extraordinary and Plenipotentiary, HE John Durham, apptd 1997

ECONOMY

Traditionally the Mongolians led a nomadic life tending flocks of sheep, goats, horses, cows and camels. With the coming of the Communist regime, and especially after 1952, great efforts were made to settle the population but a proportion still live nomadically or semi-nomadically in the traditional *ger* (circular tent). Collectivization at the end of the 1950s into huge *negdels* (co-operatives) and state farms hastened the process of settlement, but within these the herdsmen and their families still move with their *gers* from pasture to pasture as the seasons change. Total livestock was 25 million in 1993.

The semi-desert areas of the Gobi region provide pasture for sheep, goats, camels, horses and some cattle. In the steppe areas to the north of the Gobi pasturage is better and livestock more abundant. Even further north, in the better-watered provinces, grain, fodder and vegetable crops are grown.

Although the economy remains predominantly pastoral, factories have started up, coal, copper and molybdenum are mined and the electricity industry has been developed.

Ulan Bator and Darkhan are the main seats of industry, which includes lime, cement and building materials, a flour mill and a power station. Choibalsan is also being developed industrially.

Mongolia's economic difficulties stem from its small labour force, and its undeveloped infrastructure. Communication is still difficult as there are very few tarmac roads and horses are still the characteristic means of transport for the rural population. The trans-Mongolian railway links Mongolia with both China and Russia. All trade barriers were abolished in May 1997.

GNP – US$767 million (1995); US$310 per capita (1995)
GDP – US$1,935 million (1992); US$479 per capita (1992)
ANNUAL AVERAGE GROWTH OF GDP – – 11.6 per cent (1992)
INFLATION RATE – 87.6 per cent (1994)
TOTAL EXTERNAL DEBT – US$512 million (1995)

TRADE

Foreign trade was formerly dominated by the Soviet Union and other eastern bloc countries. Following the collapse of the COMECON trading system, trade with Western countries, Japan and South Korea is increasing. Since January 1991, trade has been in hard currency, causing particular strain. The principal exports are animal by-products (especially wool, hides and furs) and cattle.

In 1994 imports totalled US$223 million and exports US$324 million.

Trade with UK	1995	1996
Imports from UK	£3,023,000	£2,518,000
Exports to UK	1,960,000	11,696,000

MOROCCO
Al-Mamlaka Al-Maghrebia

AREA – 172,414 sq. miles (446,550 sq. km)
POPULATION – 26,590,000 (1994 UN estimate). Arabic is the official language. Berber is the vernacular, mainly in the mountain regions. French and Spanish are also spoken, mainly in the towns. Islam is the state religion
CAPITAL – ΨRabat (population, 1,220,000, 1993 estimate)
MAJOR CITIES – ΨCasablanca (2,943,000); Marrakesh (602,000); Fez (564,000); Oujda (331,000); Meknes (401,000); ΨAgadir (137,000), 1993 estimates
CURRENCY – Dirham (DH) of 100 centimes
NATIONAL DAY – 3 March (Anniversary of the Throne)
NATIONAL FLAG – Red, with green pentagram (the Seal of Solomon)
LIFE EXPECTANCY (years) – male 61.58; female 65.00
POPULATION GROWTH RATE – 2.1 per cent (1994)
POPULATION DENSITY – 60 per sq. km (1994)
URBAN POPULATION – 51.1 per cent (1994)

Morocco is traversed in the north by the Rif mountains and, in a south-west to north-east direction, by the Middle Atlas, the High Atlas, the Anti-Atlas and the Sarrho ranges. Much of the country is desert. The north-westerly point of Morocco is the peninsula of Tangier dominated by the Jebel Mousa which, with the rocky eminence of Gibraltar, was known to the ancients as the Pillars of Hercules, the western gateway of the Mediterranean.

HISTORY AND POLITICS

Morocco became an independent sovereign state in 1956, following joint declarations made with France on 2 March 1956 and with Spain on 7 April 1956. The Sultan of

Morocco, Sidi Mohammad ben Youssef, adopted the title of King Mohammad V.

Legislative elections were held in June–September 1993, with the centre-right four-party Entente National coalition winning 154 seats and the leftist six-party Bloc Démocratique winning 120 seats. After both coalitions had been unable to form a government, King Hassan appointed a government of technocrats and independents in November 1993. In February 1995 the King replaced this with a government of the Entente National and technocrats. Diplomatic relations with Israel were opened in September 1994.

POLITICAL SYSTEM

The 1992 constitution states that Morocco is a democratic constitutional monarchy. The King nominates the prime minister and, on the latter's recommendation, appoints the members of the Council of Ministers. The government is responsible both to parliament and to the King. The unicameral legislature (Chamber of Representatives) has 333 members, 222 elected by direct universal suffrage (including five representing overseas workers) and 111 members elected by electoral colleges representing local government, industry, agriculture, professional and trade union groups. The replacement of the Chamber of Representatives with a directly-elected bicameral legislature has been proposed by the King and was approved by referendum on 13 September 1996.

Effective political power remains with the King despite the constitutional changes of October 1992 enhancing the prime minister's and legislature's powers.

HEAD OF STATE
HM The King of Morocco, King Hassan II (Moulay Hassan Ben Mohammed), born 9 July 1929; acceded 3 March 1961
Heir, HRH Crown Prince Sidi Mohamed, born 21 August 1963

COUNCIL OF MINISTERS as at July 1997
Prime Minister, Foreign Affairs and Co-operation, Abdellatif Filali
Agriculture and Agricultural Investment, Hassan Abouyoub
Communications, Alaoui Mdaghri
Culture, Abdellah Azmani
Employment and Social Affairs, Aminie Demnati
Energy and Mines, Abdeliatif Guerraoui
Environment, Dr Noureddine Benomar Alami
Finance and Foreign Investment, Mohamed Kabbaj
Foreign Trade, Mohamed Alami
Higher Education and Scientific Research, Driss Khalil
Housing, Said Fassi
Interior, Driss Basri
Justice, Abderrahmane Amalou
Minister of State, Ahmed Alaoui
National Education, Rachid Ben Mokhtar
Post and Telecommunications, Hamza Kettani
Privatization, Abderrahmane Saaidi
Professional Development, Adessalam Beroual
Public Health, Dr Ahmed Alami
Public Works, Abdelaziz Meziane Belfkih
Relations With Parliament, Abdessalam Baraka
Religious Endowments and Islamic Affairs, Abdelkebir M'Daghri Alaoui
Sea Fisheries and the Merchant Marine, Mostafa Sahel
Secretary-General of the Government, Abdessadek Rabiah
Tourism, Mohamed Alaoui M'Hamdi
Trade, Industry and Handicrafts, Driss Jettou
Transport, Said Ameskane
Youth and Sport, Ahmed Meziane

EMBASSY OF THE KINGDOM OF MOROCCO
49 Queen's Gate Gardens, London SW7 5NE
Tel 0171–581 5001/4
Ambassador Extraordinary and Plenipotentiary, HE Khalil
Haddaoui, apptd 1991

BRITISH EMBASSY
17 Boulevard de la Tour Hassan (BP 45), Rabat
Tel: Rabat 7209 05/6
Ambassador Extraordinary and Plenipotentiary, HE William H.
Fullerton, CMG, apptd 1996
CONSULATE-GENERAL/COMMERCIAL OFFICE –
Casablanca
CONSULATES - Agadir, Marrakesh, Tangier

BRITISH COUNCIL DIRECTOR, Dr M. Phillips, BP 427, 36
rue Tanger, Rabat
BRITISH CHAMBER OF COMMERCE, 1st Floor, 185
Boulevard Zerktouni, Casablanca. Tel: 256920

DEFENCE

The Army has 524 main battle tanks, 100 light tanks, 900
armoured infantry fighting vehicles and armoured personnel carriers, and 331 artillery pieces.

The Navy has one frigate and 2 patrol and coastal
combatant vessels at five bases. The Air Force has 112
combat aircraft and 24 armed helicopters.

Morocco deploys 2,000 troops in the United Arab
Emirates. The UN has some 398 personnel in Western
Sahara pending the referendum. Polisario deploys
3,000–6,000 troops in Western Sahara with Algerian-
supplied and captured Moroccan tanks, armoured person-
nel carriers, anti-tank and anti-aircraft weapons.
MILITARY EXPENDITURE – 4.3 per cent of GDP (1995)
MILITARY PERSONNEL – 224,000: Army 175,000, Navy
6,000, Air Force 13,000, Paramilitaries 30,000
CONSCRIPTION DURATION – 18 months

ECONOMY

Morocco's main sources of wealth are agricultural and
mineral. The latest development plan (1987 onwards)
emphasizes social improvement, industrial development,
agriculture, fisheries and tourism. Economic reform has
also been implemented to reduce debt and inflation. A
large-scale privatization programme has attracted substantial foreign investment.

Agriculture employs more than 40 per cent of the
working population. The main agricultural exports are
fruit and vegetables, with cereals and sugar beet produced
and sheep reared for domestic consumption. Cork and
wood-pulp are the most important commercial forest
products. Esparto grass is also produced. There is a fishing
industry and substantial quantities of canned fish, mainly
sardines and fishmeal, are exported.

For a developing country Morocco has a large industrial
sector. The main sectors are chemicals, textiles and leather
goods, food processing and cement production. Manufacturing industries are centred in Casablanca, Fez, Tangier
and Safi.

Morocco's mineral exports are phosphates, fluorite,
barite, manganese, iron ore, lead, zinc, cobalt, copper and
antimony. Morocco possesses nearly three-quarters of the
world's estimated reserves of phosphates. There are oil
refineries at Mohammedia and Sidi Kacem handling about
four million tonnes of crude oil a year.

Tourism is of increasing importance to the economy,
with development concentrated in Agadir and Marrakesh.
In 1993, 2,945,700 foreign tourists visited Morocco. Workers' remittances, US$1,959 million in 1993, are also
important to the economy.

GNP – US$29,545 million (1995); US$1,110 per capita
(1995)
GDP – US$26,425 million (1992); US$1,079 per capita
(1992)
ANNUAL AVERAGE GROWTH OF GDP – 11.5 per cent
(1994)
INFLATION RATE – 6.1 per cent (1995)
UNEMPLOYMENT – 16.0 per cent (1992)
TOTAL EXTERNAL DEBT – US$22,147 million (1995)

TRADE

The main imports are petroleum products, motor vehicles,
building materials, agricultural and other machinery,
chemical products, sugar, green tea and other foodstuffs.
The EU, with which an association agreement was signed
in November 1995, is Morocco's largest trading partner.
The main exports are textiles, phosphates and phosphoric
acid, fertilizers, citrus fruits, and fish and seafoods.

In 1993 Morocco had a trade deficit of US$1,466 million
and a current account surplus of US$36 million. In 1995
imports totalled US$8,563 million and exports US$4,824
million.

Trade with UK	1995	1996
Imports from UK	£271,114,000	£281,575,000
Exports to UK	253,752,000	303,998,000

COMMUNICATIONS

Railroads cover 1,175 miles (1,893 km), linking the major
towns. An extensive network of 9,880 miles (15,900 km) of
well-surfaced roads covers all the main towns. There are
air services between Casablanca, Tangier, Agadir (seasonal), Marrakesh and London, and also between Tangier and
Gibraltar connecting with London. Royal-Air-Maroc
operates internal services and services to 36 states in
Europe, Africa and Asia.

EDUCATION

There are government primary, secondary and technical
schools. In 1991 there were 4,890 government schools. At
Fez there is a theological university of great repute in the
Muslim world. There is a secular university at Rabat.
Schools for special denominations, Jewish and Catholic,
are permitted and may receive government grants. Amer-
ican schools operate in Rabat and Casablanca.
ILLITERACY RATE – 56.3 per cent
ENROLMENT (percentage of age group) – primary 69 per
cent; secondary 30 per cent; tertiary 10.0 per cent (1994)

WESTERN SAHARA

Formerly the Spanish Sahara, the territory was split
between Morocco and Mauritania in 1976 after Spain
withdrew in December 1975. In 1976 the Polisario Front
(Frente Popular para la Liberación de Saguia y Río de Oro)
declared Western Sahara to be an independent state, the
Saharan Arab Democratic Republic, and formed a government led by Bouchraya Bayoune which remains in exile.
The Polisario Front has been recognized as the legitimate
government of Western Sahara by over 70 states and the
Organization of African Unity. In 1979 Mauritania renounced its claim to its share of the territory, which was
added by Morocco to its area.

In 1988, Morocco and the Polisario Front accepted a UN
peace plan under which a cease-fire came into effect in
September 1991. A referendum to determine the future of
the area was to have been held in January 1992 but has not
yet taken place because the Moroccan government and
Polisario have not agreed on the referendum terms or voter
eligibility. The UN Security Council intervened to break

the impasse, passing a resolution which stipulates that the referendum should be a straight choice between independence or integration with Morocco. A further resolution provided for the drawing up of a new voter registration list. Voter identification began in August 1994 but the failure to agree on eligibility prompted the UN to threaten the suspension of the UN Mission for the Referendum in Western Sahara (MINURSO), which had been deployed since 1991.

MOZAMBIQUE
República de Moçambique

AREA – 309,495 sq. miles (801,590 sq. km). Neighbours: Swaziland (south), South Africa (south and west), Zimbabwe (west), Zambia and Malawi (north-west), Tanzania (north)
POPULATION – 16,500,000 (1995 official estimate). The official language is Portuguese
CAPITAL – ΨMaputo (population, 882,601, 1986 estimate)
MAJOR CITIES – ΨBeira (264,202); ΨNacala (182,505), 1986 estimates
CURRENCY – Metical (MT) of 100 centavos
NATIONAL DAY – 25 June (Independence Day)
NATIONAL FLAG – Horizontally green, black, yellow with white fimbriations; a red triangle based on the hoist containing the national emblem
LIFE EXPECTANCY (years) – male 44.88; female 48.01
POPULATION GROWTH RATE – 4.0 per cent (1994)
POPULATION DENSITY – 21 per sq. km (1994)
MILITARY EXPENDITURE – 3.7 per cent of GDP (1995)
MILITARY PERSONNEL – 15,750: Army 11,000, Navy 750, Air Force 4,000
ILLITERACY RATE – 59.9 per cent
ENROLMENT (percentage of age group) – primary 41 per cent; secondary 7 per cent; tertiary 0.4 per cent (1993)

HISTORY AND POLITICS

Mozambique, discovered by Vasco da Gama in 1498 and colonized by Portugal, achieved independence on 25 June 1975. It was a Marxist one-party (Frelimo) state until a multiparty system was adopted in 1990. The legislative assembly has 250 members.

Following two years of negotiations, the Frelimo government and rebel Mozambican National Resistance (Renamo) signed a peace agreement in October 1992 which ended 16 years of civil war. Under the peace agreement, demobilization of government and Renamo troops was due to begin within one month of parliamentary ratification of the peace accord (which occurred on 9 October 1992) although the belated arrival of the UN Operation for Mozambique (ONUMOZ) delayed demobilization until 1994.

Presidential and legislative elections were held on 27–29 October 1994. The incumbent, Joaquim Chissano of Frelimo, won the presidential election in the first round with 53 per cent of the vote. Frelimo also won the legislative election, gaining 129 seats to Renamo's 112 seats and the Democratic Union's 9 seats. The last ONUMOZ troops left in January 1995.

Mozambique was admitted to the Commonwealth on 13 November 1995 as a special case, because of its close links with Commonwealth countries.

HEAD OF STATE
President, Joaquim Alberto Chissano, *sworn in* November 1986, *elected* 29 October 1994

COUNCIL OF MINISTERS *as at July 1997*
Prime Minister, Pascoal Mocumbi
Agriculture and Fisheries, Carlos Rosario
Culture, Youth and Sports, José Mateus Katupha
Education, Arnaldo Nhavoto
Environment, Bernardo Ferraz
Finance, Tomas Salomao
Foreign Affairs and Co-operation, Leonardo Simão
Health, Aurelio Zihao
Industry, Trade and Tourism, Oldemiro Baloi
Justice, José Abudo
Labour, Guilherme Mavila
Mineral Resources and Energy, John Kachamila
Ministers in the President's Office, Eneias Comiche (*Economic and Social Affairs*); Francisco Madeira (*Parliamentary Affairs*); Almerindo Manhenje (*Defence, Security Affairs and Interior*)
National Defence, Aguiar Real Mazula
Public Works and Housing, Roberto White
Social Affairs, Filipe Manjate *(acting)*
State Administration, Alfredo Gamito
Transport and Communications, Paulo Muxanga

HIGH COMMISSION FOR THE REPUBLIC OF MOZAMBIQUE
21 Fitzroy Square, London WIP 5HJ
Tel 0171–383 3800
High Commissioner, HE Dr Eduardo José Baciao Koloma, apptd 1996

BRITISH HIGH COMMISSION
Av. Vladimir I Lenine 310, CP 55, Maputo
Tel: Maputo 420111/2/5/6/7
High Commissioner, HE Bernard J. Everett, apptd 1996

BRITISH COUNCIL DIRECTOR, P. Woods, PO Box 4178, Maputo

ECONOMY

The basis of the economy is subsistence agriculture, but there is an industrial sector based mainly in Beira and Maputo. There are substantial coal deposits in Tete province and an offshore gas field at Pande. The government launched an economic rehabilitation programme in 1987 to attract foreign investment and boost production. Economic subsidies have been removed and an IMF reform programme is being implemented. The economy is still heavily dependent on aid. A five-year plan has been launched with the priorities of rural development, education, health and land reform.
GNP – US$1,353 million (1995); US$80 per capita (1995)
GDP – US$1,340 million (1992); US$65 per capita (1992)
ANNUAL AVERAGE GROWTH OF GDP – 5.7 per cent (1994)
INFLATION RATE – 54.4 per cent (1995)
TOTAL EXTERNAL DEBT – US$5,781 million (1995)

TRADE

The main exports are shellfish, cotton, sugar, cashew nuts, copra, tea and sisal. In 1995 exports totalled US$169 million and imports US$784 million. Mozambique's main trading partners are Portugal, Spain and France.

Trade with UK	1995	1996
Imports from UK	£13,274,000	£14,421,000
Exports to UK	1,922,000	2,195,000

MYANMAR
Pyidaungsu Myanma Naingngandaw – Union of Myanmar

AREA – 261,218 sq. miles (676,552 sq. km). Neighbours:
Bangladesh, India (west), China, Laos and Thailand
(east)

POPULATION – 45,555,000 (1994 UN estimate).The
indigenous inhabitants are of similar racial types and
speak languages of the Tibeto-Burman, Mon-Khmer
and Thai groups. The three significant non-indigenous
elements are Indians, Chinese and those from
Bangladesh. Burmese is the official language, but
minority languages include Shan, Karen, Chin, Kayah
and the various Kachin dialects. English is spoken in
educated circles. Buddhism is the religion of 85 per cent
of the people, with 5 per cent Animists, 4 per cent
Muslims, 4 per cent Hindus and less than 3 per cent
Christians

CAPITAL – ΨYangon (Rangoon) (population, 2,513,023,
1983)

MAJOR CITIES – Mandalay (532,949); Mawlamyine/
Moulmein (219,961); Pathein/Bassein (144,096)

CURRENCY – Kyat (K) of 100 pyas

NATIONAL DAY – 4 January

NATIONAL FLAG – Red, with a canton of dark blue, inside
which are a cogwheel and two rice ears surrounded by 14
white stars

LIFE EXPECTANCY (years) – male 57.89; female 63.14

POPULATION GROWTH RATE – 2.1 per cent (1994)

POPULATION DENSITY – 67 per sq. km (1994)

HISTORY AND POLITICS

The Union of Burma (the name was officially changed to
the Union of Myanmar in 1989) became an independent
republic outside the British Commonwealth on 4 January
1948 and remained a parliamentary democracy for 14
years. In 1962 the army took power and suspended the
parliamentary constitution. A Revolutionary Council of
senior officers under Gen. Ne Win instituted a socialist
state.

After months of popular demonstrations and a series of
presidents during 1988, Gen. Saw Maung, leader of the
armed forces, assumed power in September 1988. The
People's Assembly, the Council of State and the Council of
Ministers were abolished and replaced by the State Law
and Order Restoration Council (SLORC). The constitution was effectively abrogated.

A People's Assembly Election Law was published in
1989 committing the SLORC to hold multiparty elections.
These were held on 27 May 1990, resulting in a majority
for the National League for Democracy (NLD) even
though its leader Aung San Suu Kyi had been under house
arrest since July 1989. The SLORC refused to transfer
power to a civilian government and large numbers of NLD
MPs and supporters were detained. Others fled to the
border areas with Thailand where an exile government led
by Sein Win, the National Coalition Government of the
Union of Burma (NCGUB), was set up. However, following the replacement of Saw Maung by Than Shwe as
SLORC chairman and prime minister in April 1992, the
government began a dialogue with some elements of the
opposition. A Constitutional Convention of delegates
appointed by the SLORC to discuss a future constitution
convened in January 1993 and has continued fitfully since,
but with minimal progress. The SLORC released Aung
San Suu Kyi (who won the Nobel Peace Prize in 1991) on

10 July 1995 but many others remain in detention or under
house arrest.

Myanmar is comprised of seven states (Chin, Kachin,
Kayin (Karen), Kayah, Mon, Rakhine, Shan) and seven
divisions (Irrawaddy, Magwe, Mandalay, Pegu, Yangon
(Rangoon), Sagaing, Tenasserim).

INSURGENCIES

Since independence in 1948 the government has fought
various armed insurgent groups, the largest of which were
derived from the Kachin, Karen, Karenni, and Wa ethnic
groups but the Shan, Mon, Arakan and Chin ethnic
minorities have also formed armed groups.

Since 1992, as a result of government offensives, 15
ethnic groups have signed cease fire agreements with the
government, including the Kachin Independence Army,
the Karenni National People's Liberation Front and the
Shan State Liberation Organization in 1994, and Mon
rebels in July 1995. In 1995–6, government forces launched successful offensives against the Karen National
Union, the Karenni National Progressive Party and the
Mong Tai army, whose leader, the drugs warlord Khun Sa,
surrendered in January 1996.

STATE LAW AND ORDER RESTORATION COUNCIL

Chairman, Gen. Than Shwe
Vice-Chairman, Gen. Maung Aye

Members, Vice-Adm. Maung Maung Khin; Lt.-Gen. Tin
Tun; Lt.-Gen. Aung Ye Kyaw; Lt.-Gen. Phone Myint;
Lt.-Gen. Sein Aung; Lt.-Gen. Chit Swe; Lt.-Gen. Kyaw
Ba; Lt.-Gen. Maung Thint; Lt.-Gen. Myint Aung; Lt.-
Gen. Mya Thinn; Lt.-Gen. Tun Kyi; Lt.-Gen. Aye
Thaung; Lt.-Gen. Myo Nyunt; Lt.-Gen. Maung Hla;
Lt.-Gen. Kyaw Min; Maj.-Gen. Soe Myint
Secretaries, Lt.-Gen. Khin Nyunt; Lt.-Gen. Tin Oo

CABINET *as at August 1997*
Prime Minister, Defence, Gen. Than Shwe
Deputy PMs, Vice-Adm. Maung Maung Khin; Lt.-Gen. Tin
Tun
Agriculture an Irrigation, Lt.-Gen. Myint Aung
Borders and Ethnic Groups, Lt.-Gen. Maung Thint
Communication, Post and Telecommunications, U Soe Tha
Construction, Maj.-Gen. Saw Tun
Co-operatives, U Than Aung
Culture, U Aung San
Education, U Pan Aung
Energy, U Khin Maung Thein
Finance and Revenue, Brig.-Gen. Win Tin
Foreign Affairs, U Ohn Gyaw
Forestry, Lt.-Gen. Chit Swe
Health, U Saw Tun
Home Affairs, Lt.-Gen. Mya Thinn
Hotels and Tourism, Lt.-Gen. Kyaw Ba
Immigration and Population, Lt.-Gen. Maung Hla
Industry, Lt.-Gen. Sein Aung, Maj.-Gen. Kyaw Than
Information, Maj.-Gen. Aye Kyaw
Labour, Maj.-Gen. Saw Lwin
Livestock, Breeding and Fisheries, U Aung Thaung
Mines, Lt.-Gen. Kyaw Min
National Planning and Economic Development, Brig.-Gen.
David Abel
Prime Minister's Office, Brig.-Gen. Lun Maung, Col. Pe
Thein, U Than Shwe
Railways, U Win Sein
Religious Affairs, Lt.-Gen. Myo Nyunt
Science and Technology, U Thaung
Social Welfare, Relief and Resettlement, Maj.-Gen. Soe Myint
Sport, Col. Sein Win
Trade, Lt.-Gen. Tun Kyi
Transport, Lt.-Gen. Thein Win

EMBASSY OF THE UNION OF MYANMAR
19A Charles Street, Berkeley Square, London WIX 8ER
Tel 0171-499 8841
Ambassador Extraordinary and Plenipotentiary, HE U Win
Aung, apptd 1996

BRITISH EMBASSY
80 Strand Road (Box No. 638), Yangon
Tel: Yangon 95300
Ambassador Extraordinary and Plenipotentiary, HE Robert A.
E. Gordon, OBE, apptd 1995
Cultural Attaché and British Council Director, C. Harrison

DEFENCE

The Army has 26 main battle tanks, 270 armoured
personnel carriers and 246 artillery pieces. The Navy has
58 patrol and coastal vessels at six bases.
MILITARY EXPENDITURE – 6.2 per cent of GDP (1995)
MILITARY PERSONNEL – 321,000: Army 300,000, Navy
12,000, Air Force 9,000

ECONOMY

The chief sources of revenue are profits on state trading,
taxes and duties; the chief heads of expenditure are
defence, education and police.

Three-quarters of the population depend on agriculture; the chief products are rice, oilseeds (sesamum and
groundnut), maize, millet, cotton, beans, wheat, grain, tea,
sugar-cane, tobacco, jute and rubber.

Myanmar is rich in minerals, including petroleum, lead,
silver, tungsten, zinc, tin, wolfram and gemstones. Production of crude petroleum in 1995 totalled 823,000 tonnes.
There are refineries at Chauk, the main oilfield, Syriam
and Mann. Major reserves of natural gas have been
discovered in the Martaban Gulf, production of which
totalled 1,290 million cubic metres in 1994–5. Timber
production is also an important industry and timber is a
major export.

A new ministry was established in 1992 with the task of
attracting 500,000 tourists; less than 10,000 visited in 1991
but visitors and revenues are increasing. Visit Yangon Year
was launched in November 1996. Foreign hotels have
opened in Yangon and Mandalay.

In 1993 the government began to open the economy to
foreign investment, signing 50 joint ventures in the fields of
oil and gas exploration, hotel construction and forestry.

Myanmar is thought to be the world's leading producer
of opium with an estimated annual output of 2,600 tons.

In July 1997, Myanmar became a member of ASEAN. In
1997 the EU stripped Myanmar of trading privileges and
the USA imposed economic sanctions.

In 1993 the government had a budget deficit equivalent
to 2.21 per cent of GDP. In 1995 imports totalled US$1,335
million and exports US$846 million.

GDP – US$26,313 million (1992); US$866 per capita
(1992)
ANNUAL AVERAGE GROWTH OF GDP – 9.8 per cent (1995)
INFLATION RATE – 25.2 per cent (1995)
TOTAL EXTERNAL DEBT – US$5,771 million (1995)

TRADE WITH UK	1995	1996
Imports from UK	£15,244,000	£21,421,000
Exports to UK	9,283,000	13,732,000

COMMUNICATIONS

The Irrawaddy and its chief tributary, the Chindwin, are
important waterways, the main stream being navigable 900
miles from its mouth and carrying much traffic. The chief
seaports are Yangon (Rangoon), Mawlamyine (Moulmein), Akyab (Sittwe) and Pathein (Bassein).

The railway network covers 2,764 route miles, extending to Myitkyina on the Upper Irrawaddy. There are 2,452
miles of highways and 11,767 miles of other main roads.
The airport at Mingaladon, about 13 miles north of Yangon
(Rangoon), only handles limited international air traffic.

EDUCATION

Most children attend primary school, and about six million
are currently enrolled; in middle and high schools, enrolment is about two million. There are five universities, at
Yangon (Rangoon), Mandalay, Taunggyi, Sagaing and
Mawlamyine (Moulmein). Under the universities are
three affiliated degree colleges and the Workers' College,
Yangon. There are also 14 two-year colleges affiliated to
the universities, spread throughout the country.

Vocational training is provided at 16 teachers' training
institutes, seven government technical institutes, 14 technical high schools, 15 agricultural institutes and schools,
and 34 vocational schools for handicrafts, etc.
ILLITERACY RATE – 16.9 per cent
ENROLMENT (percentage of age group) – tertiary 5.1 per
cent (1993)

NAMIBIA
The Republic of Namibia

AREA – 318,261 sq. miles (824,292 sq. km). Neighbours: Angola (north), South Africa (south), Botswana (east), Zambia and Zimbabwe (north-east)

POPULATION – 1,500,000 (1994 UN estimate). The main population groups are: Ovambo (587,000), Kavango (110,000), Damara (89,000), Herero (89,000), whites (78,000), Nama (57,000), coloured (48,000), Caprivians (44,000), Bushmen (34,000), Rehoboth Baster (29,000), Tswana (7,000). English is the official language, with Afrikaans, German and local languages also in use

CAPITAL – Windhoek (population 125,000, 1990)

MAJOR TOWNS – Swakopmund (15,500); Rehoboth (15,000); Rundu (15,000); Keetmanshoop (14,000), 1990

CURRENCY – Namibian dollar of 100 cents at parity to South African rand

NATIONAL DAY – 21 March (Independence Day)

NATIONAL FLAG – Divided diagonally blue, red and green with the red fimbriated in white; a gold twelve-rayed sun in the upper hoist

LIFE EXPECTANCY (years) – male 57.50; female 60.00

POPULATION GROWTH RATE – 2.7 per cent (1994)

POPULATION DENSITY – 2 per sq. km (1994)

URBAN POPULATION – 32.3 per cent (1991)

MILITARY EXPENDITURE – 2.7 per cent of GDP (1995)

MILITARY PERSONNEL – 8,000: Army 8,000

ILLITERACY RATE – 24.2 per cent

ENROLMENT (percentage of age group) – primary 91 per cent; secondary 35 per cent; tertiary 8.2 per cent (1994)

HISTORY AND POLITICS

The German protectorate of South West Africa from 1880 to 1915, Namibia was administered until the end of 1920 by the Union of South Africa. Under the terms of the Treaty of Versailles, the territory was entrusted to South Africa with full powers of administration and legislation over the territory. After the dissolution of the League of Nations and in the absence of a trusteeship agreement, South Africa informed the UN that it would continue to administer South West Africa.

In 1971 the International Court of Justice at The Hague delivered a majority opinion that the continued presence of South Africa was illegal. The South African government rejected this opinion, but accepted the principle that the territory should attain independence. Elections for 72 seats in Namibia's first nationally elected body took place under UN supervision on 7–11 November 1989. The South West Africa People's Organization (SWAPO) won 41 seats, the Democratic Turnhalle Alliance 21 seats, other parties ten seats. Independence was declared on 21 March 1990. Namibia joined the Commonwealth on independence.

Previously a British and South African colony separate from German South West Africa/Namibia, Walvis Bay was governed from August 1992 by the joint South African-Namibian Walvis Bay Administrative Body until 28 February 1994, when South Africa renounced its claim to sovereignty over the enclave and it became part of Namibia.

Presidential and legislative elections were held on 7–8 December 1994 and won by the incumbent, Sam Nujoma, and by SWAPO respectively. In the 72-seat National Assembly SWAPO has 53 seats, the Democratic Turnhalle Alliance 15 seats, and other parties four seats.

POLITICAL SYSTEM

Constitutionally defined as a multiparty, secular, democratic republic, Namibia has an executive president as head of state who exercises the functions of government with the assistance of a Cabinet headed by a prime minister. The president is directly elected for a maximum of two five-year terms. Legislative authority lies with the National Assembly, which is the lower house of a bicameral parliament; an upper house (National Council) representing regional councils was elected in November 1992 and inaugurated in January 1993. Each of the 13 regional councils appoints two representatives to the National Council. The main function of the National Council is to review and consider legislation from the National Assembly. Under a system of proportional representation, elections to the National Assembly are to take place every five years, or earlier if decided by the president. Members of the National Council hold their seats for six years. The constitution can only be changed by a two-thirds majority in the National Assembly.

HEAD OF STATE

President, Dr Sam Nujoma, *elected* 16 February 1990, *re-elected* 8 December 1994

CABINET *as at June 1997*

Prime Minister, Hage Geingob

Deputy PM, Revd Hendrik Witbooi

Agriculture, Water and Rural Development, Helmut Angula

Basic Education and Culture, John Mutorwa

Defence, Philemon Mwalima

Environment and Tourism, Gert Hanekom

Finance, Nangolo Mbumba

Fisheries and Marine Resources, Hifikepunye Pohamba

Foreign Affairs, Theo-Ben Gurirab

Health and Social Services, Dr Libertine Amathila

Higher Education, Vocational Training, Science and Technology, Nahas Angula

Home Affairs, Jerry Ekandjo

Information and Broadcasting, Ben Amadhila

Justice, Ngarikutuke Tjiriange

Labour and Manpower Development, Moses Garoeb

Lands, Resettlement and Rehabilitation, Richard Kapelwa-Kabajani

Mines and Energy, Andimba Toivo ya Toivo

Prisons and Correctional Services, Marco Hausiku

Regional and Local Government and Housing, Libertine Amadhila

Trade and Industry, Hidipo Hamutenya

Works, Transport and Communication, Hampie Plichta

Youth and Sport, Pendukeni Ithana

HIGH COMMISSION OF THE REPUBLIC OF NAMIBIA
6 Chandos Street, London WIM 0LQ.
Tel 0171-636 6244
High Commissioner, HE Benjamin Ulenga, apptd 1996

BRITISH HIGH COMMISSION
116 Robert Mugabe Avenue, Windhoek 9000
Tel: Windhoek 223022
High Commissioner, HE Robert H. G. Davies, apptd 1996

BRITISH COUNCIL REPRESENTATIVE, D. Crowe, PO Box 24224, 74 Bülowstrasse, Windhoek 9000

ECONOMY

Mining (mainly diamonds and uranium), agriculture and fisheries account for over 40 per cent of GDP. Most of the labour force is employed in the agricultural sector. Large deposits of diamonds along the coast and offshore along the sea bed are estimated at between 1,500 and 3,000 million carats. Walvis Bay and Lüderitz are the main ports.

The government's 'First National Development Plan' envisages growth of 5 per cent a year from 1995 to 2000. In 1994 there was a trade surplus of US$118 million and a current account surplus of US$150 million. In 1994 imports totalled US$1,196 million and exports US$1,321 million.

GNP – US$3,098 million (1995); US$2,000 per capita (1995)
GDP – US$2,374 million (1992); US$1,601 per capita (1992)
ANNUAL AVERAGE GROWTH OF GDP – 5.4 per cent (1994)
INFLATION RATE – 10.8 per cent (1994)

TRADE WITH UK	1995	1996
Imports from UK	£5,983,000	£6,892,000
Exports to UK	26,635,000	25,280,000

NAURU
The Republic of Nauru

AREA – 8 sq. miles (21 sq. km)
POPULATION – 11,000 (1994 UN estimate); 8,042 (1983 census): Nauruans 4,964; other Pacific Islanders 2,134; Asians 682; Caucasians 262. About 43 per cent of Nauruans are adherents of the Nauruan Protestant Church and there is a Roman Catholic mission on the island. The main languages are English and Nauruan
CAPITAL – ΨNauru
CURRENCY – Australian dollar ($A) of 100 cents
NATIONAL DAY – 31 January (Independence Day)
NATIONAL FLAG – Twelve-point star (representing the 12 original Nauruan tribes) below a gold bar (representing the Equator), all on a blue ground
POPULATION GROWTH RATE – 2.4 per cent (1994)
POPULATION DENSITY – 524 per sq. km (1994)

HISTORY AND POLITICS

From 1888 until the First World War Nauru was administered by Germany. In 1920 it became a British Empire-mandated territory under the League of Nations, administered by Australia. A trusteeship superseding the mandate was approved in 1947 by the UN and Nauru continued to be administered by Australia until it became independent on 31 January 1968. It was announced in November 1968 that a special form of membership of the Commonwealth had been devised for Nauru at the request of its government.

POLITICAL SYSTEM

Parliament has 18 members including the Cabinet and Speaker. Voting is compulsory for all Nauruans over 20 years of age, except in certain specified instances. Elections are held every three years. The Cabinet is chosen by the president, who is elected by the parliament from amongst its members, and comprises not fewer than five nor more than six members including the president.

A Supreme Court of Nauru is presided over by the Chief Justice. The District Court, which is subordinate to the Supreme Court, is presided over by a Resident Magistrate. Both the Supreme Court and the District Court are courts of record. The Supreme Court exercises both original and appellate jurisdiction.

HEAD OF STATE

President, External Affairs, Finance and the Public Sector, Kinza Clodumar, *elected by parliament* 13 February 1997

CABINET *as at August 1997*
Health and Youth Affairs, Ludwig Scotty
Internal Affairs, Sports, Assistance to the President, Vinson Detenamo
Island Development, Industry, Civil Aviation, Education, Bernard Dowiyogo
Justice, Vassal Gadoengin
Works and Community Services, Derog Gioura

BRITISH HIGH COMMISSIONER, HE Michael Peart, CMG, LVO, resident at Suva, Fiji

ECONOMY

The only fertile areas are in the narrow coastal belt and local requirements of fruit and vegetables are mostly met by imports. The economy is heavily dependent on the extraction of phosphate, of which the island has one of the world's richest deposits. In 1995 178,415 tonnes of phosphate rock was exported. The industry has been run since 1970 by the Nauru Phosphate Corporation. Considerable investments have been made abroad with the royalties on phosphate exports to provide for a time when production declines. In 1993 an agreement was signed with Australia for compensation to cover damage caused by phosphate mining during the Australian mandate and trusteeship periods. The compensation package is worth some £50 million (a portion of which will be paid by the UK and New Zealand governments), composed of a £33 million payment and a 20-year package of health and education programmes.

Air Nauru operates air services throughout the Pacific region and to Australia, New Zealand, Japan, Singapore and the Philippines.

TRADE WITH UK	1995	1996
Imports from UK	£1,195,000	£912,000
Exports to UK	134,000	116,000

SOCIAL WELFARE

Nauru has a hospital service and other medical and dental services. There is also a maternity and child welfare service.

Education is available in nine primary and two secondary schools on the island with a total enrolment of about 1,600 pupils receiving primary education and 500 secondary education.

NEPAL

AREA – 56,827 sq. miles (147,181 sq. km). Neighbours: China (north), India (south, west and east)
POPULATION – 21,360,000 (1994 UN estimate). The inhabitants are of mixed stock, with Mongolian characteristics prevailing in the north and Indian in the south. The official religion is Hinduism; 87 per cent of the population are Hindus, 8 per cent Buddhist and 3 per cent Muslim. Gautama Buddha was born in Nepal
CAPITAL – Kathmandu (population, 419,073, 1991)
MAJOR CITIES – Biratnagar (130,129); Patan (117,023); Bhadgaon (61,122), 1991
CURRENCY – Nepalese rupee of 100 paisa
NATIONAL ANTHEM – May Glory Crown Our Illustrious Sovereign
NATIONAL DAYS – 18 February (National Democracy Day); 28 December (The King's Birthday)

NATIONAL FLAG – Double pennant of crimson with blue border on peaks; white moon with rays in centre of top peak; white quarter sun, recumbent in centre of bottom peak
LIFE EXPECTANCY (years) – male 50.88; female 48.10
POPULATION GROWTH RATE – 4.1 per cent (1994)
POPULATION DENSITY – 145 per sq. km (1994)
MILITARY EXPENDITURE – 1.0 per cent of GDP (1995)
MILITARY PERSONNEL – 43,000: Army 42,800, Air Force 200
ILLITERACY RATE – 72.5 per cent
ENROLMENT (percentage of age group) – tertiary 4.8 per cent (1993)

Nepal lies between India and the Tibet Autonomous Region of China on the slopes of the Himalayas, and includes Mount Everest (29,028 ft).

The southern region, the Terai, was covered with jungle but has been more widely cultivated recently. It forms about 23 per cent of the total land area and nearly 44 per cent of the population live there. The central belt is hilly, but with many fertile valleys, leading up to the snowline at about 16,000 feet. The hills account for 42 per cent of the area and about 48 per cent of the population. The remainder of the country, the Himalayan region, consists of high mountains which are sparsely inhabited. The country is drained by three great river systems rising within and beyond the Himalayan mountain ranges and eventually flowing into the Ganges in India.

HISTORY AND POLITICS

Nepal was originally divided into numerous hill clans and petty principalities but emerged as a nation in the middle of the 18th century when it was unified by the warrior Raja of Gorkha, Prithvi Narayan Shah, who founded the present Nepalese dynasty. In 1846 power was seized by Jung Bahadur Rana after a massacre of nobles, and he was the first of a line of hereditary Rana prime ministers who ruled Nepal for 104 years. During this time the role of the monarchs was mainly ceremonial.

In 1950–1 a revolutionary movement broke the hereditary power of the Ranas and restored the monarchy to its former position. After ten years, during which various parties and individuals tried their hand at government, King Mahendra proscribed all political parties and assumed direct powers in 1960, with the object of leading a united country to democracy. In 1962 he introduced a new constitution embodying a tiered, partyless system of panchyat (council) democracy.

Mass agitation for political reform led in April 1990 to the lifting of the ban on political parties and the abolition of the panchyat system. A new constitution was promulgated in November 1990 establishing a multiparty, parliamentary system of government and a constitutional monarchy.

Elections in May 1991 were won by the Nepali Congress Party, which formed a government. This was brought down by a no-confidence vote in July 1994. Elections in November 1994 produced no overall control for any party and the United Marxist Leninist Party formed a minority government as the largest party. This government was brought down by a no-confidence vote in June 1995 and was replaced by a coalition government of the Congress Party, right-wing Rashtriya Prajatrantra and royalist Sandbhavana Parishad parties.

POLITICAL SYSTEM

The King retains joint executive power with the Council of Ministers. The bicameral legislature consists of a 205-member House of Representatives and a 60-member National Council, including ten royal nominees.

HEAD OF STATE

HM The King of Nepal, King Birendra Bir Bikram Shah Dev, *born* 28 December 1945; *succeeded* 31 January 1972; *crowned* 24 February 1975; *married* February 1970, HM Queen Aishwatya Rajya Laxmi Devi Shah
Heir, HRH Crown Prince Dipendra Bir Bikram Shah Dev, *born* 27 June 1971

CABINET *as at July 1997*

Prime Minister, Royal Palace Affairs, Defence, Water Resources, Land Reform and Management, Science and Technology, Lokendra Bahadur Chand
Deputy PM, Home Affairs, Bamdev Gautam
Agriculture, Ramkrishna Acharya
Commerce, Buddhiman Tamang
Education, Devi Prasad Ojha
Finance, Rabindra Nath Sharma
Foreign Affairs, Dr Prakash Chandra Lohani
Forestry and Soil Conservation, Rameshwor Raya Yadav
General Administration, Siddhi Lal Singh
Health, Radhakrishna Mainali
Housing and Planning, Kamal Thapa
Industry, Keshav Prasad Badal
Information and Communications, Jhalanath Khanal
Labour, Mukunda Neupane
Law and Justice, Prem Bahadur Singh
Local Development, Amrit Kumar Bohara
Parliamentary Affairs, Ashok Kumar Rai
Population and Environment, Vidya Devi Bhandari
Supplies, Gajendra Narayan Singh
Tourism and Civil Aviation, Salim Mian Ansari
Women and Social Welfare, Sahana Pradhan
Works and Transport, Bharatmohan Adhikari
Youth, Sports and Culture, Bishnu Prasad Poudyal
Without Portfolio, Sarbendra Nath Shukla, Bhim Bahadur Kadayat
Ministers of State, Rakam Chemjong *(Information and Communications);* Dr Bharat Kumar Pradhan *(Health);* Prem Bahadur Bhandari *(Agriculture);* Rajiv Parajuli *(Water Resources),* Mahesh Chaudhari *(Local Development),* Mahendra Raya Yadav *(Works and Transport);* Tul Bahadur Gurung *(Industry);* Bhojraj Joshi *(Education);* Khobhari Raya Yadav *(Housing and Physical Planning)*

ROYAL NEPALESE EMBASSY

12A Kensington Palace Gardens, London W8 4QU
Tel 0171–229 1594/6231
Ambassador Extraordinary and Plenipotentiary, HE Dr Singha B. Basnyat, apptd 1997

BRITISH EMBASSY

Lainchaur Kathmandu, PO Box 106
Tel: Kathmandu 410583
Ambassador Extraordinary and Plenipotentiary, HE Lloyd B. Smith, CMG, apptd 1995

BRITISH COUNCIL REPRESENTATIVE, S. Evans, (PO Box 640), Kantipath, Kathmandu

ECONOMY

Nepal exports carpets, jute, handicrafts, garments, hides and skins, medicinal herbs, cardamom, pulses, tea, etc., and imports textiles, machinery and parts, transport equipment, medicine, construction materials etc. Tourism is the single largest commercial earner of foreign exchange. Nepal's main trading partners are India, Germany, USA and China (Hong Kong).

In 1993 Nepal had a trade deficit of US$462 million and a current account deficit of US$223 million. In 1995 imports totalled US$1,374 million and exports US$348 million.

GNP – US$4,391 million (1995); US$200 per capita (1995)
GDP – US$3,307 million (1992); US$144 per capita (1992)
ANNUAL AVERAGE GROWTH OF GDP – 7.3 per cent (1994)
INFLATION RATE – 7.6 per cent (1995)
TOTAL EXTERNAL DEBT – US$2,398 million (1995)

Trade with UK	1995	1996
Imports from UK	£7,618,000	£10,438,000
Exports to UK	4,562,000	8,123,000

COMMUNICATIONS

The total length of roads is 9,534 km. Most of the major roads have been built since the 1960s, often with aid from India and China. Kathmandu is connected by road with India and Tibet. Internally, the road network links Kathmandu to Kodari and Pokhara, and Pokhara to Sunauli. A road between Mugling and Naryanghat has further improved communications between Kathmandu and the Terai. The East–West Highway (Mahendra Raj Marg) running along the entire length of the country is complete except for the Banbasa-Mahakali section.

Royal Nepal Airlines operates an extensive network of domestic flights, and there are international flights to Europe, the Middle East and throughout Asia.

Telecommunication services, both domestic and international, are available. Television was introduced in 1984.

THE NETHERLANDS
Koninkrijk der Nederlanden

AREA – 15,770 sq. miles (40,844 sq. km)
POPULATION – 15,500,000 (1996). The language is Dutch, a West Germanic language of Saxon origin closely akin to Old English and Low German. It is spoken in the Netherlands and the northern part of Belgium (Flanders). It is also used in the Netherlands Antilles
CAPITAL – ΨAmsterdam (population, 1,095,739, 1993 estimate)
SEAT OF GOVERNMENT – The Hague (Den Haag or, in full, 's-Gravenhage), population 694,190, 1993 estimates
MAJOR CITIES – ΨRotterdam (1,071,872); Utrecht (544,582); Eindhoven (392,070); Tilburg (236,259); Haarlem (213,919); Groningen (209,822), 1993 estimates
CURRENCY – Gulden (guilder) or florin of 100 cents
NATIONAL ANTHEM – Wilhelmus
NATIONAL FLAG – Three horizontal bands of red, white and blue
LIFE EXPECTANCY (years) – male 74.21; female 80.20
POPULATION GROWTH RATE – 0.7 per cent (1994)
POPULATION DENSITY – 377 per sq. km (1994)
URBAN POPULATION – 60.5 per cent (1993)

The Kingdom of the Netherlands is a maritime country of western Europe, situated on the North Sea, consisting of 12 provinces (Eastern and Southern Flevoland being amalgamated to form the twelfth province). The land is generally flat and low, intersected by numerous canals and connecting rivers. The principal rivers are the Rhine, Maas, Yssel and Scheldt.

HISTORY AND POLITICS

In 1815 the Netherlands became a constitutional kingdom under King William I, a descendant of the house of Orange-Nassau.

The most recent election to the Second Chamber was held on 3 May 1994 and resulted in a three-party centre-left coalition of the Labour Party, People's Party and Democrats 66. The state of the parties as at August 1996 was: Labour Party (PvdA) 37; Christian Democratic Appeal (CDA) 34; People's Party for Freedom and Democracy (VVD) 31; Democrats 66 (D66) 24; Green Left 5; others 19. A legislative election is due to be held in 1998.

POLITICAL SYSTEM

The States-General consists of the *Eerste Kamer* (First Chamber) of 75 members, elected for four years by the Provincial Council; and the *Tweede Kamer* (Second Chamber) of 150 members, elected for four years by voters of 18 years and upwards. Members of the *Tweede Kamer* are paid.

HEAD OF STATE

HM The Queen of the Netherlands, Queen Beatrix Wilhelmina Armgard, KG, GCVO, *born* 31 January 1938; *succeeded* 30 April 1980, upon the abdication of her mother Queen Juliana; *married* 10 March 1966, HRH Prince Claus George Willem Otto Frederik Geert of the Netherlands, Jonkheer van Amsberg; and has *issue*, Prince Willem (*see* below); Prince Johan Friso, *b.* 25 September 1968; Prince Constantijn Christof, *b.* 11 October 1969
Heir, HRH Prince Willem Alexander, *b.* 27 April 1967

CABINET *as at August 1997*

Prime Minister, Minister of General Affairs, Wim Kok (PvdA)
Deputy PM, Home Affairs, Hans Dijkstal (VVD)
Deputy PM, Foreign Affairs, Hans van Mierlo (D66)
Agriculture, Nature Management and Fisheries, J. van Aartsen (VVD)
Defence, Netherlands Antilles and Aruba Affairs, Joris Voorhoeve (VVD)
Development Co-operation, Jan Pronk (PvdA)
Economic Affairs, G. J. Wijers (D66)
Education, Culture and Science, Dr Jo Ritzen (PvdA)
Finance, Gerrit Zalm (VVD)
Housing, Physical Planning and Environment, M. De Boer (PvdA)
Justice, Winnie Sorgdrager (D66)
Social Affairs and Employment, Ad Melkert (PvdA)

Transport and Public Works, Annemarie Jorritsma-Lebbink (VVD)
Welfare, Health and Sport, Dr E. Borst-Eilers (D66)

VVD People's Party for Freedom and Democracy; D66 Democrats 66; PvdA Labour Party

ROYAL NETHERLANDS EMBASSY
38 Hyde Park Gate, London SW7 5DP
Tel 0171–584 5040
Ambassador Extraordinary and Plenipotentiary, HE Jan Herman van Roijen, apptd 1995
Ministers Plenipotentiary, G. C. M. van Pallandt; R. Brouwer (*Economic*)
Consul-General, H. Nijenhuis
Defence, Naval and Air Attaché, Capt. J. J. Blok

BRITISH EMBASSY
Lange Voorhout 10, The Hague, 2514 ED
Tel: The Hague 427 0427
Ambassador Extraordinary and Plenipotentiary, HE Rosemary Spencer, CMG, apptd 1996
Counsellors, P. S. Dimond (*Deputy Head of Mission*); C. W. Robins (*Commercial and Consul-General*)
Defence and Naval Attaché, Capt. P. J. Organ, RN
CONSULATE-GENERAL – Amsterdam
CONSULATE – Willemstad (Curaçao); Vice-Consulate – Philipsburg (St Maarten) (both Netherlands Antilles)

BRITISH COUNCIL DIRECTOR, T. Butchard, Keizersgracht 269, 1016 ED Amsterdam

NETHERLANDS-BRITISH CHAMBER OF COMMERCE, The Dutch House, 307–308 High Holborn, London WC1V 7LS

UK OFFICE IN THE HAGUE, Holland Trade House, Bezuidenhoutseweg 181, 2594 AH The Hague

DEFENCE

The Army has 734 main battle tanks, 1,353 armoured infantry fighting vehicles and armoured personnel carriers, and 722 artillery pieces. The Navy has four submarines, four destroyers, 12 frigates, 13 combat aircraft and 22 armed helicopters. The Air Force has 108 combat aircraft and 12 armed helicopters.

The armed forces are almost entirely committed to NATO.

MILITARY EXPENDITURE – 2.2 per cent of GDP (1995)
MILITARY PERSONNEL – 58,700: Army 32,350, Navy 14,000, Air Force 12,350
CONSCRIPTION DURATION – abolished in August 1996

ECONOMY

The chief agricultural products are potatoes, wheat, rye, barley, sugar beet, cattle, pigs, milk and milk products, cheese, butter, poultry, eggs, beans, peas, vegetables, fruit, flower bulbs, plants and cut flowers and there is an important fishing industry.

Among the principal industries are engineering, electronics, nuclear energy, petrochemicals and plastics, road vehicles, aircraft and defence equipment, shipbuilding repair, steel, textiles of all types, electrical appliances, metal ware, furniture, paper, cigars, sugar, liqueurs, beer, clothing etc.

In 1994 the government had a budget deficit equivalent to 0.5 per cent of GDP.

GNP – US$371,039 million (1995); US$24,000 per capita (1995)
GDP – US$293,542 million (1992); US$21,130 per capita (1992)
ANNUAL AVERAGE GROWTH OF GDP – 2.3 per cent (1995)

INFLATION RATE – 1.9 per cent (1995)
UNEMPLOYMENT – 7.1 per cent (1995)

TRADE

The Dutch are traditionally a trading nation. Trade, banking and shipping are of particular importance to the economy. The geographical position of the Netherlands, at the mouths of the Rhine, Meuse and Scheldt, brings a large volume of transit trade to and from the interior of Europe to Dutch ports. Principal trading partners are Germany, Belgium/Luxembourg and France.

In 1994 the Netherlands had a trade surplus of US$14,416 million and a current account surplus of US$11,249 million. In 1995 imports totalled US$176,123 million and exports US$195,516 million.

Trade with UK	1995	1996
Imports from UK	£11,639,300,000	£12,709,300,000
Exports to UK	10,854,300,000	11,680,900,000

COMMUNICATIONS

The total extent of navigable rivers including canals is 5,052 km. The total length of the railway system is 2,757 km, of which 1,991 km are electrified. The mercantile marine in 1995 consisted of 385 ships of total 2,903,000 gross registered tons. The total of kilometres flown by KLM (Royal Dutch Airlines) in 1991–2 was 188 million km.

There are six national papers, four of which are morning papers, and there are many regional daily papers.

EDUCATION

Primary and secondary education is given in both denominational and state schools and is compulsory.

The principal universities are at Leiden, Utrecht, Groningen, Amsterdam (two), Nijmegen, Maastricht and Rotterdam, and there are technical universities at Delft, Eindhoven, Enschede and Wageningen (agriculture).

ENROLMENT (percentage of age group) – primary 93 per cent (1993); secondary 86 per cent (1992); tertiary 47.1 per cent (1993)

OVERSEAS TERRITORIES

ARUBA

Aruba covers an area of 75 sq. miles (193 sq. km) and has a population (1994) of 71,000. The island was from 1828 part of the Dutch West Indies and from 1845 part of the Netherlands Antilles. On 1 January 1986 it became a separate territory within the Kingdom of the Netherlands. The 1983 Constitutional Conference agreed that Aruba's separate status would last for ten years from 1986, after which the island would become fully independent. In 1994 this decision was changed and it was decided that Aruba will retain its separate status within the Kingdom of the Netherlands.

Governor, O. L. Koolman
Prime Minister, J. H. A. Eman

CAPITAL – ΨOranjestad (population 25,000); and Sint Nicolaas (17,000)
CURRENCY – Aruban florin

ECONOMY – The economy of Aruba is based largely on tourism. In 1995 there were 612,916 tourists

TRADE WITH UK	1995	1996
Imports from UK	£58,816,000	£50,684,000
Exports to UK	3,605,000	3,675,000

NETHERLANDS ANTILLES

The Netherlands Antilles comprise the islands of Curaçao, Bonaire, part of St Martin, St Eustatius, and Saba in the West Indies. The islands cover an area of 308 sq. miles (800 sq. km) with a population (1995) of 207,333 (Curaçao 151,448, Bonaire 14,218, St Martin 38,567, St Eustatius 1,900, Saba 1,200). The Netherlands Antilles, which have a 22-member federal parliament, are largely self-governing under the terms of the Realm Statute which took effect in 1954.

Governor, Dr Jaime Saleh
Prime Minister, Miguel Pourier

CAPITAL – ΨWillemstad (on Curaçao) (pop. 50,000)
CURRENCY – Netherlands Antilles guilder of 100 cents

ECONOMY – The economy of the Netherlands Antilles is based on small manufacturing industries. The soil is too poor to permit large-scale agriculture and most products for consumption and industrial raw materials must be imported. Tourism is also important, with 752,000 tourists and 757,000 cruise-ship day trippers in 1995

TRADE WITH UK	1995*	1996*
Imports from UK	£18,615,000	£33,513,000
Exports to UK	14,378,000	6,535,000

*Curaçao

NEW ZEALAND

AREA – 103,736 sq. miles (268,675 sq. km)
POPULATION – 3,642,500 (1995): 79 per cent European stock, 13 per cent Maori, 5 per cent other Pacific Islanders. The main religion is Christianity. In 1991 the principal denominations were Anglican 22.1 per cent, Presbyterian 16.3 per cent, Roman Catholic 15 per cent, Methodist 4.2 per cent, Baptist 2.1 per cent

Islands	Area (sq. miles)	Population at 31 March 1993
North Island	44,281	2,604,200
South Island	58,093	890,100
Other islands	1,362	
Total	103,736	3,494,300
Territories		
Tokelau	5	1,700 (a)
Niue	100	2,239
Cook Islands	93	18,300 (b)
Ross Dependency	175,000	

(a) 1994
(b) 1991

CAPITAL – ΨWellington (population, 325,700, 1992 estimate)
MAJOR CITIES – ΨAuckland (929,300); ΨChristchurch (318,100); ΨDunedin (112,400); Hamilton (153,800); Ψ Napier-Hastings (110,200)
CURRENCY – New Zealand dollar (NZ$) of 100 cents
NATIONAL ANTHEM – God Save The Queen/God Defend New Zealand
NATIONAL DAY – 6 February (Waitangi Day)
NATIONAL FLAG – Blue ground, with Union Flag in top left quarter, four five-pointed red stars with white borders on the fly
LIFE EXPECTANCY (years) – male 72.86; female 78.74
POPULATION GROWTH RATE – 1.0 per cent (1994)
POPULATION DENSITY – 13 per sq. km (1994)
URBAN POPULATION – 84.9 per cent (1991)

New Zealand consists of a number of islands in the South Pacific Ocean, and also has administrative responsibility for the Ross Dependency in Antarctica. The two larger islands, North Island and South Island, are separated by a relatively narrow strait. The remaining islands are much smaller and widely dispersed.

Much of the North and South Islands is mountainous. The principal range is the Southern Alps, extending the entire length of the South Island and having its culminating point in Mount Cook/Mount Aoraki (12,349 ft). The North Island mountains include several volcanoes, two of which are active. Of the numerous glaciers in the South Island, the Tasman (18 miles long by 1 wide), the Franz Josef and the Fox are the best known. The more important rivers include the Waikato (270 miles in length), Wanganui (180), and Clutha (210) and lakes include Taupo, 234 sq. miles in area; Wakatipu, 113; and Te Anau, 133.

New Zealand includes, in addition to North and South Islands: Chatham Islands (Chatham, Pitt, South East Islands and some rocky islets, combined area, 965 sq. km (373 sq. miles), largely uninhabited); Stewart Island (area 1,746 sq. km (674 sq. miles), largely uninhabited); the Kermadec Group (Raoul or Sunday, Macaulay, Curtis Islands, L'Esperance, and some islets; population 9–10, all government employees at a meteorological station); Campbell Island, used as a weather station; the Three Kings (discovered by Tasman on the Feast of the Epiphany); Auckland Islands; Antipodes Group; Bounty Islands; Snares Islands and Solander.

New Zealand has a temperate marine climate, but with abundant sunshine. The mean temperature ranges from 15°C in the north to about 9°C in the south. Rainfall in the North Island ranges from 35 to 70 inches and in the South Island from 25 to 45 inches.

HISTORY AND POLITICS

The discoverers and first colonists of New Zealand were Polynesian people, ancestors of the modern-day Maori. The ninth century is generally considered to be the date of the first settlement; by the 13th or 14th century there were well-established settlements. The first European to discover New Zealand was a Dutch navigator, Abel Tasman, who sighted the coast in 1642 but did not land. It was the British explorer James Cook who circumnavigated New Zealand and landed in 1769. Largely as a result of increased British emigration, the country was annexed by the British government in 1840. The British Lieutenant-Governor, William Hobson, proclaimed sovereignty over the North Island by virtue of the Treaty of Waitangi, signed by him and many Maori chiefs, and over the South Island and Stewart Island by right of discovery.

In 1841 New Zealand was created a separate colony distinct from New South Wales. In 1907 the designation was changed to 'The Dominion of New Zealand'. The constitution rests upon the Constitution Act 1852 and other imperial statutes. A 1986 Constitution Act brought a number of statutory constitutional provisions. The Statute of Westminster was formally adopted by New Zealand in 1947.

Following the general election of 12 October 1996, the state of the parties in the House of Representatives was: National Party (NP) 44 seats, Labour 37, New Zealand First (NZF) 17, The Alliance 13, Association of Consumers and Tax Payers (ACT) 8, United Party 1. The National Party and New Zealand First formed a coalition government.

POLITICAL SYSTEM

The executive authority is entrusted to a Governor-General appointed by the Crown and aided by an Executive Council, within a unicameral legislature, the House of Representatives. The House of Representatives consists of 99 members elected for three years. There are four Maori electorates. In a referendum in 1992 the electorate voted in favour of the introduction of a mixed-member proportional representation system to replace the first-past-the-post system. From the October 1996 election onwards there will be 120 House of Representatives seats, of which 60 will be elected by the first-past-the-post system and 55 by proportional representation on a party list basis. The number of Maori electorates will be increased to five.

The judicial system comprises a High Court, a Court of Appeal and district courts having both civil and criminal jurisdiction.

GOVERNOR-GENERAL

Governor-General and Commander-in-Chief, HE Sir Michael Hardie Boys, KCMG, *sworn in* March 1996

THE EXECUTIVE COUNCIL *as at June 1997*

The Governor-General
Prime Minister, Jim Bolger (NP)
Deputy P.M, Treasurer, Winston Peters (NZF)
Agriculture, Forestry, International Trade, Lockwood Smith (NP)
Attorney-General, Defence, War Pensions, Audit Department, Paul East (NP)
Commerce, Fisheries, Lands, Industry, John Luxton (NP)
Education, Leader of the House, Wyatt Creech (NP)
Employment, Peter McCardle (NP)
Environment, Simon Upton (NP)
Finance, Revenue, Bill Birch (NP)
Foreign Affairs, Trade, Pacific Island Affairs, Disarmament and Arms Control, Don McKinnon (NP)
Health, Bill English (NP)
Housing, Tourism, Sport, Fitness and Leisure, Murray McCully (NP)
Justice, Courts, Waitangi Negotiations, Doug Graham (NP)
Labour, Immigration, Energy, Business Development, Max Bradford (NP)
Maori Affairs, Racing, Tau Henare (NZF)
Police, Internal Affairs, Civilian Defence, Jack Elder (NZF)
Research, Science and Technology, Communications, Information Technology and Statistics, Maurice Williamson (NP)
Social Welfare, Roger Sowry (NP)
State Services, State-Owned Enterprises, Transport, Accident Rehabilitation and Compensation Insurance, Jenny Shipley (NP)
Valuation Department, Public Trust Office, John Delamere (NZF)

NEW ZEALAND HIGH COMMISSION

New Zealand House, Haymarket, London SW1Y 4TQ
Tel 0171-930 8422
High Commissioner, HE Dr Richard Grant, apptd 1997
Deputy High Commissioner, M. Chilton
Minister, J. Waugh (*Commercial*)
Head, Defence Staff, Brig. I. Duthie
First Secretary, G. Rush (*Cultural Affairs*)

BRITISH HIGH COMMISSION

44 Hill Street (PO Box 1812), Wellington 1
Tel: Wellington 4726-049
High Commissioner, HE Robert J. Alston, CMG, apptd 1994
Deputy High Commissioner, C. H. Salvesen
Counsellor, A. W. Turquet
Defence Adviser, Col. P. R. Barry, CBE
First Secretary, M. A. Capes (*Commercial*)

Consul-General and Director of Trade Promotion, J. Smith-Laittan (*resides at Auckland*)
CONSULATE-GENERAL – Auckland
CONSULATE – Christchurch

BRITISH COUNCIL DIRECTOR, P. Smith

BRITISH CHAMBER OF COMMERCE FOR AUSTRALIA AND NEW ZEALAND, PO Box 141, Manuka, ACT 2603, Australia; UK OFFICE, Suite 615, 6th Floor, The Linen Hall, 162–168 Regent Street, London W1R 5TB

DEFENCE

The Army has 78 armoured personnel carriers and 34 artillery pieces. The Navy has three frigates, four patrol and coastal vessels and five armed helicopters. The Air Force has 42 combat aircraft.
MILITARY EXPENDITURE – 1.7 per cent of GDP (1995)
MILITARY PERSONNEL – 9,870: Army 4,500, Navy 2,150, Air Force 3,220

ECONOMY

Since 1984 economic reforms have changed the economy from a highly regulated, nationalized and protected economy with a large welfare state to an economy at the forefront of market economics. Finance market and labour market deregulation, privatization, VAT reform, the introduction of private sector principles in the civil service, health service and education, the ending of agricultural subsidies and the near elimination of import tariffs have all occurred. The Reserve Bank has been made independent, with a contract to keep inflation below 2 per cent. Centralized wage-bargaining has ended and widespread means-testing has been introduced throughout the welfare state, so that only the very poor receive free or subsidized healthcare and other benefits.

Agricultural production is dominated by cattle- and sheep-rearing, for meat, wool, dairy products and other by-products, such as skins, leather, etc.

Non-metallic minerals such as coal, clay, limestone and dolomite are more important than metallic ones. Coal output in 1995 was 3,300,000 tonnes. Of the metals, the most important are gold and ironsand. Natural gas deposits in the offshore Taranaki Maui field and onshore fields are increasingly being exploited and used for electricity generation and as a premium fuel. Hydroelectric power is used to generate 96 per cent of the country's electricity.

Manufacturing has become increasingly important to the economy over the past decade and is based on food processing, machinery production, motor vehicle assembly, chemicals, electrical and electronic goods, and paper and printing. Tourism is the fastest growing sector of the economy, with 1,385,907 visitors in 1994–5.

In 1994 the government had a budget deficit equivalent to 0.84 per cent of GDP. In 1993 New Zealand had a trade surplus of US$1,714 million and a current account deficit of US$1,251 million. In 1995 imports totalled US$13,958 million and exports US$13,736 million.
GNP – US$51,655 million (1995); US$14,340 per capita (1995)
GDP – US$43,928 million (1992); US$12,003 per capita (1992)
ANNUAL AVERAGE GROWTH OF GDP – 1.9 per cent (1995)
INFLATION RATE – 3.8 per cent (1995)
UNEMPLOYMENT – 6.3 per cent (1995)

TRADE

New Zealand's largest trading partners are Australia, Japan, USA and the UK. New Zealand exports to the UK include butter and cheese, wool, lamb, hides, skins and leather.

Trade with UK	1995*	1996*
Imports from UK	£437,451,000	£471,820,000
Exports to UK	576,587,000	631,973,000

*Includes Niue, Tokelau and Cook Islands

COMMUNICATIONS

The national railway system is owned and operated by the privately-owned Tranz Rail Ltd. In June 1995, there were 4,439 route km of railway in operation.

During 1991–2 the vessels entered from overseas ports numbered 3,282 (gross tonnage 27,983,000) and those cleared for overseas 3,298 (gross tonnage 27,508,000). In December 1995 there were 2,977 ships registered in New Zealand (gross tonnage 482,180).

Domestic flights in 1990 carried 4,502,000 passengers and 47,700 tonnes of freight. International flights carried 3,129,000 passengers, 134,074 tonnes of freight and 5,082 tonnes of mail.

In June 1995 there were 91,875 km of maintained roads.

EDUCATION

Schools are free and attendance is compulsory between the ages of six and 15. There are 2,246 state and 66 private primary schools and 320 state secondary schools. There are seven universities and 25 polytechnics.

ENROLMENT (percentage of age group) – primary 99 per cent; secondary 95 per cent; tertiary 59.8 per cent (1994)

TERRITORIES

TOKELAU (OR UNION ISLANDS)

Tokelau is a group of atolls, Fakaofo, Nukunonu and Atafu, with a total land area of 5 sq. miles and a population of 1,500 (1996). It was proclaimed part of New Zealand as from 1 January 1949. A Council of Faipule, composed of one elected representative from each atoll, was established in August 1992 to govern Tokelau when the council of elders (General Fono) was not in session. The position of *Ulu-o-Tokelau* (leader) was also established in 1992 and is rotated among the three Faipale members annually. Administrative responsibility for Tokelau lies with the Administrator but in January 1994 his powers were delegated to the General Fono and Council of Faipale. The Tokelau Amendment Act, passed by the New Zealand Parliament in 1996, conferred legislative power on the General Fono. New Zealand provides substantial aid (NZ$5.0 million in year ended 30 June 1994), to meet administrative, social, economic and development requirements. Tokelau receives revenue from the granting of fishing rights in its economic zone.

Administrator, Lindsay Watt
Ulu-o-Tokelau (1998), Kuresa Nasau

THE ROSS DEPENDENCY

The Ross Dependency, placed under the jurisdiction of New Zealand in 1923, is defined as all the Antarctic islands and territories between 160° E. and 150° W. longitude which are situated south of the 60° S. parallel, including Edward VII Land and portions of Victoria Land. Since 1957 a number of research stations have been established in the Dependency.

ASSOCIATED STATES

COOK ISLANDS

Included in the realm of New Zealand since June 1901, the Cook Islands group consists of the islands of Rarotonga,

Aitutaki, Mangaia, Atiu, Mauke, Mitiaro, Manuae, Takutea, Palmerston, Penrhyn or Tongareva, Manihiki, Rakahanga, Suwarrow, Pukapuka or Danger, and Nassau. The total population of the group was 18,904 in 1996.

The Queen has a representative on the islands, as does the New Zealand government. Since 1965 the islands have been in free association with New Zealand and enjoyed complete internal self-government, executive power being in the hands of a Cabinet consisting of the Prime Minister and eight other ministers. There is a 25-member Legislative Assembly. New Zealand has an obligation to assist with foreign affairs and defence if requested. The New Zealand citizenship of the Cook Islanders is embodied in the constitution.

The chief industries are tourism, financial services, clothing, agriculture, and black pearls. The New Zealand Government continues to give development aid to the Cook Islands.

HM Representative, Apenera Short, OBE
Prime Minister, Sir Geoffrey Henry, KBE
New Zealand High Commissioner, James Kember

NIUE

The population of Niue was 2,239 at the November 1991 census. A New Zealand High Commissioner is stationed at Niue, which since 1974 has been self-governing in free association with New Zealand. New Zealand is responsible for external affairs and defence, and continues to give financial aid. Executive power is in the hands of a Premier and a Cabinet of three drawn from the Assembly of 20 members. The Assembly is the supreme legislative body.

New Zealand High Commissioner, W. Searell

NICARAGUA
República de Nicaragua

AREA – 50,193 sq. miles (130,000 sq. km)
POPULATION – 4,401,000 (1994 UN estimate); three-quarters are of mixed blood, another 15 per cent are white, mostly of pure Spanish descent, and the remaining 10 per cent are West Indians or Indians. The latter group includes the Misquitos, who live on the Atlantic coast. The official language is Spanish and the majority are Roman Catholic, although the English language and the Moravian Church are widespread on the Atlantic coast
CAPITAL – Managua (population, 608,020, 1979 estimate)
MAJOR CITIES – Chinandega (144,291); Granada (72,640); León (158,577); Masaya (78,308)
CURRENCY – Córdoba (C$) of 100 centavos
NATIONAL ANTHEM – Salve A Tí Nicaragua (Hail, Nicaragua)
NATIONAL DAY – 15 September
NATIONAL FLAG – Horizontal stripes of blue, white and blue, with the Nicaraguan coat of arms in the centre of the white stripe
LIFE EXPECTANCY (years) – male 64.80; female 67.71
POPULATION GROWTH RATE – 3.2 per cent (1994)
POPULATION DENSITY – 34 per sq. km (1994)
URBAN POPULATION – 62.8 per cent (1994)
ILLITERACY RATE – 34.3 per cent
ENROLMENT (percentage of age group) – primary 79 per cent (1994); secondary 26 per cent (1993); tertiary 9.7 per cent (1992)

HISTORY AND POLITICS

The eastern coast of Nicaragua was touched by Columbus in 1502, and was overrun by Spanish forces in 1518. It formed part of the Spanish Captaincy-General of Guate mala until 1821, when its independence was secured. In 1927 Augusto Cesar Sandino began a guerrilla war against the occupation of Nicaragua by US Marines, which continued until they were expelled in 1933. Sandino was assassinated by Anastasio Somoza, director of the National Guard, and in 1936 Somoza assumed the presidency. He was succeeded by his sons Luis and Anastasio Somoza, until 1979 when the family and the National Guard were overthrown by guerrillas of the Sandinista National Liberation Front (FSLN).

After ten years in power and a ten-year civil war against US-backed Contra guerrillas, the Sandinistas lost their parliamentary majority in elections held in February 1990. A coalition of former opposition parties, Unión Nacional de Opositora (UNO), gained 51 seats to the Sandinistas' 39 seats in the 92-seat National Assembly and formed a government, with UNO leader Violeta Chamorro as President. With the defeat of the Sandinistas, the civil war came to an end.

President Chamorro and the UNO were forced to compromise with the Sandinistas, who controlled the trade unions, and to leave the armed forces and police under Sandinista control. Resentment among the UNO coalition members came to a head in December 1992 when UNO deputies tried to oust Chamorro from power. Chamorro ordered the police to seize the National Assembly and negotiated a new governing majority in the National Assembly of 39 Sandinistas and nine loyal UNO deputies, forcing the remaining 42 UNO deputies and Vice-President Godoy into opposition. A further 19 UNO deputies formed the Democratic Christian Union (UDC) in January 1994, which joined the governing coalition. A deadlock over constitutional reforms was broken in July 1995 when President Chamorro conceded the curbing of presidential powers. The president's term of office was reduced from six to five years with a maximum of two terms. Power over taxation and international treaties has been transferred to the National Assembly.

The Liberal Alliance won the legislative election in October 1996 although the Nationalist Liberal Party left the Alliance in May 1997.

HEAD OF STATE
President, Arnoldo Alemán Lacayo *sworn in* 10 January 1997
Vice-President, Enrique Bolanos

COUNCIL OF MINISTERS *as at June 1997*
Agriculture, Cario de Franco
Attorney-General, Julio Centeno
Construction and Transport, Edgard Quintana
Defence, Jaime Cuadra
Economy and Development, Martin Aguado
Education, Humberto Belli Pereira
Environment and Natural Resources, Roberto Stadhagen
Health, Lombardo Martínez Cabezas
Interior, José Antonio Alvarado
Finance, Estebán Duque-Estrada
Foreign Co-operation, David Robleto
Foreign Affairs, Emilio Alvárez-Montalvan
Labour, Wilfredo Navarro
Presidency, Lorenzo Guerrero
President of the Central Bank, Noel Ramírez
Social Action, Jamilet Bonilla
Tourism, Pedro Joaquín Chamorro

NICARAGUAN DIPLOMATIC REPRESENTATION
The Embassy of Nicaragua closed in May 1997 although a consulate-general is due to open.

BRITISH EMBASSY
PO Box A-169, Plaza Churchill, Reparto 'Los Robles', Managua
Tel: Managua 780014
Ambassador and Consul-General, HE Roy Osbourne, apptd 1997

DEFENCE

The Army has 130 main battle tanks, 102 armoured personnel carriers and 142 artillery pieces. The Navy has 15 patrol and coastal vessels at four bases. The Air Force has 15 armed helicopters. Under the Sandinista government, Nicaragua maintained armed forces of over 120,000 personnel. Since 1990, active armed forces personnel has fallen to 12,000 and service is now voluntary. The Army has 10,000 personnel. The Navy has a strength of 800, with 12 patrol and coastal vessels. The Air Force has 1,200 personnel and 15 armed helicopters.
MILITARY EXPENDITURE – 1.8 per cent of GDP (1995)
MILITARY PERSONNEL – 17,000: Army 15,000, Navy 800, Air Force 1,200

ECONOMY

After the civil war the UNO government began to transform the Sandinistas' socialist economy into a free-market one. An agreement was reached with the IMF in April 1994 which provided US$662 million in credits; the Paris club pledged US$1.5 billion in June 1995.

The country is mainly agricultural. The major crops are peanuts, cotton, coffee, sugarcane, tobacco, sesame and bananas. Beans, rice, maize and ipecacuanha, livestock and timber production are also important. However, fishing, forestry, grain and cattle production are still recovering from the civil war in the main growing areas. Nicaragua possesses deposits of gold and silver.

In 1994 the government had a budget deficit equivalent to 4.5 per cent of GDP. In 1994 Nicaragua had a trade deficit of US$434 million and a current account deficit of US$729 million. In 1995 imports totalled US$949 million and exports US$525 million.
GNP – US$1,659 million (1995); US$380 per capita (1995)
GDP – US$1,471 million (1992); US$371 per capita (1992)
ANNUAL AVERAGE GROWTH OF GDP – 4.2 per cent (1995)
INFLATION RATE – 10.9 per cent (1995)
UNEMPLOYMENT – 14.0 per cent (1991)
TOTAL EXTERNAL DEBT – US$9,287 million (1995)

TRADE
Considerable quantities of foodstuffs are imported as well as cotton goods, jute, iron and steel, machinery and petroleum products. The chief exports are peanuts, sesame seed, cotton, coffee (30 per cent of total export earnings), beef, gold, sugar, cottonseed and bananas.

Trade with UK	1995	1996
Imports from UK	£7,334,000	£5,924,000
Exports to UK	8,265,000	3,433,000

COMMUNICATIONS

Transport, except on the Pacific slope, is still difficult but many new roads have been opened. The Inter-American Highway runs between the Honduras and the Costa Rican borders; the inter-oceanic highway runs from the Corinto on the Pacific coast via Managua to Rama, where there is a natural waterway to Bluefields on the Atlantic. The main airport is at Managua. The chief port is Corinto on the Pacific. There are 252 miles of railway, all on the Pacific side of the country. There are 51 radio stations and five television stations in Managua. An automatic telephone system has been installed in major cities.

There are four daily newspapers published at Managua, apart from the official Gazette (*La Gaceta*). There are universities at León and Managua.

NIGER
République du Niger

AREA – 489,191 sq. miles (1,267,000 sq. km). Neighbours: Algeria and Libya (north), Chad (east), Nigeria and Benin (south), Mali and Burkina (west). Apart from a small region along the Niger Valley in the south-west near the capital, the country is entirely savannah or desert

POPULATION – 8,846,000 (1994 UN estimate): Hausa (54 per cent) in the south, Songhai and Djerma in the south-west, Fulani, Beriberi–Manga, and nomadic Tuareg in the north. The official language is French

CAPITAL – Niamey (population, 392,169, 1988 census)

CURRENCY – Franc CFA of 100 centimes

NATIONAL DAY – 18 December

NATIONAL FLAG – Three horizontal stripes, orange, white and green with an orange disc in the middle of the white stripe

LIFE EXPECTANCY (years) – male 44.90; female 48.14

POPULATION GROWTH RATE – 3.4 per cent (1994)

POPULATION DENSITY – 7 per sq. km (1994)

URBAN POPULATION – 15.3 per cent (1988)

MILITARY EXPENDITURE – 0.9 per cent of GDP (1995)

MILITARY PERSONNEL – 7,800: Army 5,200, Air Force 100, Paramilitaries 2,500

CONSCRIPTION DURATION – Two years

ILLITERACY RATE – 86.4 per cent

ENROLMENT (percentage of age group) – primary 25 per cent (1990); secondary 6 per cent (1990); tertiary 0.3 per cent (1980)

HISTORY AND POLITICS

The first French expedition arrived in 1891 and the country was fully occupied by 1914. It decided on 18 December 1958 to remain an autonomous republic within the French Community; full independence outside the Community was proclaimed on 3 August 1960.

The 1960 constitution provided for a presidential system of government and a single-chamber National Assembly. In 1974 Lt.-Col. Seyni Kountché seized power, suspended the constitution, dissolved the National Assembly and suppressed all political organizations. He set up a Supreme Military Council with himself as president. President Kountché died in 1987 and was succeeded by his cousin, Col. Ali Saibou.

In August 1991, a national conference of all groups voted to suspend the constitution and stripped President Saibou of all powers. A transitional government held office until a legislative election was held in February 1993. The former ruling party, the National Movement for a Development Society (MNSD), emerged as the largest party, although the Alliance of Forces for Change (AFC) formed the government. Mahamane Ousmane of the AFC won the presidential election in March.

The defection of one of the main AFC parties from the government in late 1994 led to a parliamentary election in January 1995 which was won by the MNSD and allied parties. The President and government were overthrown in a military coup led by Col. Ibrahim Barre Mainassara on 27 January 1996. Power was assumed by a National Salvation Council, which suspended the constitution, appointed a civilian Cabinet and created a transitional legislature until presidential and parliamentary elections could be held. A new constitution was promulgated on 12 May 1996 and the ban on political parties was lifted. Brig.-Gen. Mainassara was elected president on 8 July 1996. The pro-Mainassara National Union of Independents for Democratic Renewal won the largest number of seats in legislative elections in November 1996.

INSURGENCY

An ethnic Tuareg-based insurgency began in the north of Niger in November 1991, leading the government to impose a state of emergency in April 1992. The insurgency by the Front for the Liberation of Aïr and Azawad (FLAA) aimed to gain greater local autonomy for the Tuaregs, a change to regional boundaries, the demilitarization of the north and the teaching of the Tuareg language, Tamashek. In 1993 two groups, the Front for the Liberation of Tamoust (FLT) and the Revolutionary Army of Northern Niger (RANN) split from the FLAA in protest at its entry into negotiations with the government. An interim peace agreement was signed between the government and all Tuareg groups in Ouagadougou in October 1994, and a peace accord ending the conflict and providing for a peace process was signed on 24 April 1995.

HEAD OF STATE
President, Brig.-Gen. Ibrahim Barre Mainassara, *sworn in* 7 August 1996

CABINET *as at June 1997*
Prime Minister, Amadou Boubacar Cisse
Ministers of State, Sanoussi Tambari Jackou *(African Integration and Citizens Overseas)*; Aissata Moumouni *(National Education)*; Andre Salifou *(Relations with Parliament)*
Agriculture, Akoli Daouel
Civil Service, Labour and Employment, Seyni Ali Gado
Commerce, Ibrahim Koussou
Communications, Culture, Government Spokesman, Inoussa Ousseini
Director of the Cabinet, Mahamane Sani Bako
Equipment and Infrastructure, Chako Cherif
External Relations, Ibrahim Assane Mayaki
Health, Sambo Abdoulaye Mariama
Higher Education and Research and Technology, Prof. Hamidou Arouna Sidikou
Industrial Development and Energy, Kada Labo Aboubacar
Interior and Territorial Development, Omar Idi Ango
Justice and Human Rights, Boubey Oumarou
Mines, Mai Manga Boukar
National Defence, Ousmane Issoufou Oubandawaki
Social Development, Population, Promotion of Women and Protection of Children, Rabi Daddy Gaoh
Tourism and Artisans, Diallo Aissa Abdoulaye
Transport, Souley Abdoulaye
Water and Environment, Brah Mamane
Youth, Sport and National Solidarity, Abdoul Ramane Seydou

EMBASSY OF THE REPUBLIC OF NIGER
154 rue de Longchamp, 75116, Paris
Tel: Paris 4504 8060
Ambassador Extraordinary and Plenipotentiary, HE Mariama Hima, apptd 1997

BRITISH AMBASSADOR, HE Margaret I. Rothwell, CMG, resident at Abidjan, Côte d'Ivoire

ECONOMY

The cultivation of groundnuts and the production of livestock are the main industries and provide two of the main exports. A company formed by the government, the French Atomic Energy Authority and private interests is exploiting uranium deposits at Arlit, and this is the main export. There is also some oil exploration which has found signs of oil in the eastern desert. Gold deposits exist north-west of Niamey.

In 1993 Niger had a trade deficit of US$6 million and a current account deficit of US$29 million.

GNP – US$1,961 million (1995); US$220 per capita (1995)
GDP – US$2,605 million (1992); US$329 per capita (1992)
ANNUAL AVERAGE GROWTH OF GDP – –6.3 per cent (1981)
INFLATION RATE – 10.6 per cent (1995)
TOTAL EXTERNAL DEBT – US$1,633 million (1995)

Trade with UK	1995	1996
Imports from UK	£3,809,000	£3,785,000
Exports to UK	14,000	113,000

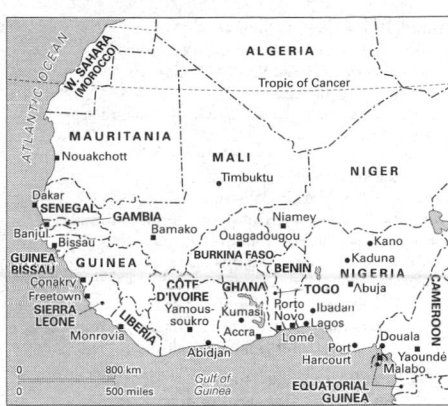

NIGERIA
Federal Republic of Nigeria

AREA – 356,669 sq. miles (923,768 sq. km). Neighbours: Benin (west), Niger (north), Cameroon (east)
POPULATION – 108,467,000 (1994 UN estimate); 88,514,501 (1991 census). The main ethnic groups are Hausa/Fulani, Yoruba and Ibo, and the principal languages are English, Hausa, Yoruba and Ibo. Over half the population are Muslim, these being concentrated in the north and west. In the southern areas in particular there are many Christians
CAPITAL – Abuja, (population, 378,671), declared the federal capital in 1991
MAJOR CITIES – Lagos, the former capital; Benin City; Enugu; Ibadan; Kaduna; Kano; Port Harcourt
CURRENCY – Naira (N) of 100 kobo
NATIONAL ANTHEM – Arise, O Compatriots
NATIONAL DAY – 1 October (Independence Day)
NATIONAL FLAG – Three equal vertical bands, green, white and green
LIFE EXPECTANCY (years) – male 48.81; female 52.01
POPULATION GROWTH RATE – 3.0 per cent (1994)
POPULATION DENSITY – 117 per sq. km (1994)
URBAN POPULATION – 16.1 per cent (1988)

A belt of mangrove swamp forest lies along the entire coastline. North of this there is a zone of tropical rain forest and oil-palms. North of the rain forest, the country rises and the vegetation changes to open woodland and savannah. In the extreme north the country is semi-desert. The Niger, Benue, and Cross are the main rivers. The climate is tropical. The rainy season is from about April to October. During the dry season the cool *harmattan* wind blows from the desert.

HISTORY AND POLITICS

The Federation of Nigeria attained independence as a member of the Commonwealth on 1 October 1960 and became a republic in 1963. Originally regional in structure, the Federation is now divided into 36 states and the Federal Capital Territory.

In 1966 the military took power; in 1979 civil rule was restored after elections at national and state level. After similar elections in 1983 the new administration was overthrown by the military on 31 December, this regime itself being overthrown in August 1985. A 28-member Armed Forces Ruling Council (AFRC) was sworn in and governed in conjunction with a Council of Ministers until January 1993, when they were replaced by a National Defence and Security Council (NDSC) and a civilian Transitional Council respectively to govern the country until a handover to civilian government. A presidential election on 11 June is generally believed to have been won by Chief Moshood Abiola of the Social Democratic Party but the military government declared the election invalid. The military government resigned on 26 August, handing power to the Transitional Council.

Continued instability led Defence Minister Gen. Sanni Abacha to launch a military coup on 17 November 1993 and install himself as head of state. A (military) Provisional Ruling Council and (civilian) Federal Executive Council were established to govern the country until a new constitution is passed. Strikes and pro-democracy demonstrations continued in support of Chief Moshood Abiola, who returned from exile in June 1994 to establish a rival government, for which he has been imprisoned.

The National Constitutional Conference (NCC) convened by Gen. Abacha in June 1994 announced in January 1995 that Gen. Abacha should have an open-ended term of office. An attempted coup was defeated in March 1995 and political activity was restored in June, when the NCC presented the draft of a new constitution to Gen. Abacha. The military regime vowed to hand over power to an elected government in October 1998.

FOREIGN RELATIONS

Nigeria was suspended from the Commonwealth on 11 November 1995, following the execution of nine human rights activists.

HEAD OF STATE
Chairman of the Provisional Ruling Council and Federal Executive Council, Commander-in-Chief of the Armed Forces, Gen. Sanni Abacha, *took power* 17 November 1993

FEDERAL EXECUTIVE COUNCIL *as at August 1997*
Chairman, Minister of Defence, Gen. Sanni Abacha
Vice-Chairman, Chief of General Staff, Lt.-Gen. D. O. Diya
Agriculture, Gambo Jimata
Aviation, Air Cdre. Ita Udoh-Ime
Commerce and Tourism, Rear Adm. J. O. Ayinla
Communications, Maj.-Gen. Tajudeen Olarenwaju
Education, Mohammad Liman
Federal Capital Territory, Lt.-Gen. J. Useni
Finance, Chief Anthony Ani
Foreign Affairs, Chief Tom Ikimi

Health, Ikechukwa Madubuike
Industries, Lt.-Gen. Muhammadu Haladu
Information and Culture, Walter Ofonagoro
Interior, Babagana Kingibe
Justice and Attorney-General, Michael Agbamuche
Labour, Uba Ahmed
National Planning, Ayo Ogunlade
Petroleum Resources, Chief Dan Etete
Power and Steel, Bashir Dalhatu
Science and Technology, Brig.-Gen. Samuel Momah
Solid Mineral Resources, Kaloma Ali
Transport, Maj.-Gen. Ibrahim Gumel
Water Resources, Aliyu Yelwa
Women's and Social Affairs, Judith Attah
Works and Housing, Maj.-Gen. Abdulkarim Adisa
Youth and Sports, Chief Jim Nwobodo

NIGERIA HIGH COMMISSION
9 Northumberland Avenue, London WC2N 5BX
Tel 0171-839 1244
Acting High Commissioner, U. O. Okeke
Minister, A. A. Ella

BRITISH HIGH COMMISSION
Shehu Shangari Way (North), Maitama, Abuja
Tel: Abuja 5232011
11 Eleke Crescent, Victoria Island, Lagos
Tel: Lagos 2619531
High Commissioner, HE Graham Burton, CMG, apptd 1997
Deputy High Commissioner and Counsellor (Political), R. A.
  Pullen
Counsellor (Economic and Commercial), D. D. Pearey
LIAISON OFFICES – Kaduna, Kano, Port Harcourt, Ibadan

BRITISH COUNCIL DIRECTOR, Dr J. Hawkins, 11
  Kingsway Road, Ikoyi (PO Box 3702), Lagos. Branch
  offices at Enugu, Ibadan, Kaduna and Kano City

DEFENCE

The Army has 200 main battle tanks, 380 armoured
personnel carriers, and 458 artillery pieces. The Navy has
one frigate, 51 patrol and coastal vessels and two helicopters at six bases. The Air Force has 92 combat aircraft and
15 armed helicopters.
MILITARY EXPENDITURE – 2.9 per cent of GDP (1995)
MILITARY PERSONNEL – 77,100: Army 62,000, Navy
  5,600, Air Force 9,500

ECONOMY

Nigeria was a predominantly agricultural country until
the early 1970s when oil became the principal source of
export revenue (over 90 per cent). Since 1981 oil revenues
have fallen to half their peak level and austerity measures
were introduced in 1982. Recent governments have
attempted to stimulate greater self-reliance by encouraging non-oil exports and the use of local rather than
imported raw materials.

The government introduced economic reforms in
January 1995, including lifting exchange controls and
ending foreign investment controls in Nigerian or jointly-
owned firms. Economic recovery has been hampered by
the suspension of aid and development programmes
following the execution of nine human rights activists in
November 1995.

Three oil refineries are in operation at Port Harcourt,
Warri and Kaduna, and steel plants at Warri and Ajaokuta.
Other projects include natural gas liquefaction, petrochemicals, fertilizers, power stations and irrigation
schemes. Tin and calumbite mining on the Jos plateau,
textiles and coal mining are also important.

GNP – US$28,411 million (1995); US$260 per capita
  (1995)
GDP – US$35,852 million (1992); US$256 per capita
  (1992)
ANNUAL AVERAGE GROWTH OF GDP – 1.3 per cent (1994)
INFLATION RATE – 72.8 per cent (1995)
TOTAL EXTERNAL DEBT – US$35,055 million (1995)

TRADE

The principal exports are oil, groundnuts, palm products,
tin, cocoa, rubber and timber. In 1995 imports totalled
US$29,987,000 million and exports US$34,179,000 million.

Trade with UK	1995	1996
Imports from UK	£431,502,000	£432,972,000
Exports to UK	181,038,000	293,749,000

COMMUNICATIONS

The Nigerian railway system, which is controlled by the
Nigerian Railway Corporation, has 2,178 route miles of
lines. The principal international airlines operate from
Lagos, Kano and Port Harcourt. A network of internal air
services connects the main centres. The principal seaports
are served by a number of shipping lines, including the
Nigerian National Line. A nationwide television and radio
network is being developed, with each state eventually
having its own television and radio station.

EDUCATION

A programme was introduced in 1976 intended to achieve
universal primary education. There are 37 universities (24
federal, 12 state and one military).
ILLITERACY RATE – 42.9 per cent
ENROLMENT (percentage of age group) – tertiary 3.3 per
  cent (1985)

NORWAY
Kongeriket Norge

AREA – 125,050 sq. miles (323,877 sq. km) of which
  Svalbard and Jan Mayen have a combined area of 24,355
  sq. miles (63,080 sq. km). Neighbours: Sweden, Finland,
  Russia
POPULATION – 4,369,957 (1996)
CAPITAL – ΨOslo (population, 758,949, 1993 estimate)
MAJOR CITIES – ΨTrondheim (142,927); ΨBergen
  (221,717); ΨKristiansand (68,609); ΨStavanger
  (103,590)
CURRENCY – Krone of 100 øre
NATIONAL ANTHEM – Ja, vi elsker dette landet (Yes, we
  love this country)
NATIONAL DAY – 17 May (Constitution Day)
NATIONAL FLAG – Red, with white-bordered blue cross
LIFE EXPECTANCY (years) – male 74.24; female 80.25
POPULATION GROWTH RATE – 0.5 per cent (1994)
POPULATION DENSITY – 13 per sq. km (1994)
URBAN POPULATION – 72.0 per cent (1990)

The coastline is deeply indented with numerous fjords and
fringed with rocky islands. The surface is mountainous,
consisting of elevated and barren tablelands separated by
deep and narrow valleys. At the North Cape the sun does
not appear to set from the second week in May to the last
week in July, causing the phenomenon known as the
Midnight Sun; conversely, there is no apparent sunrise
from about 18 November to 23 January. During the long

winter nights are seen the Northern Lights or Aurora Borealis.

HISTORY AND POLITICS

The kingdom of Norway was founded in AD 872. From 1397 to 1814 Norway was united with Denmark and from 1814 with Sweden. The union with Sweden was dissolved on 7 June 1905 when Norway regained complete independence.

The centre-right coalition government collapsed in October 1990 because of a dispute over whether to apply for membership of the European Community and was replaced by a minority Labour government. This was returned to power in the general election held on 13 September 1993 (*see* Stop-press).

FOREIGN RELATIONS

The Storting voted in November 1992 to apply to join the European Community. Negotiations with the EU concluded on 1 March 1994 with a proposed accession date of 1 January 1995, subject to parliamentary and national referendum ratifications. However, in a national referendum on 28 November 1994 the electorate voted against joining the EU by 52.4 per cent to 47.6 per cent.

POLITICAL SYSTEM

Under the 1814 constitution, the 165-member *Storting* elects one-quarter of its members to constitute the *Lagting* (Upper Chamber), the other three-quarters forming the *Odelsting* (Lower Chamber).

HEAD OF STATE

HM The King of Norway, King Harald V, GCVO, born 21 February 1937; *succeeded* 17 January 1991, on the death of his father King Olav V; *married* 29 August 1968, Sonja Haraldsen, and has *issue*, Prince Haakon Magnus (*see* below), and Princess Martha Louise, *born* 22 September 1971

Heir, HRH Crown Prince Haakon Magnus, *born* 20 July 1973

CABINET *as at June 1997*

Prime Minister, Thorbjørn Jagland
Agriculture, Dag Terje Andersen
Church, Education and Research, Reidar Sandal
Cultural Affairs, Turid Birkeland
Defence, Jørgen Kosmo
Development Co-operation, Kari Nordheim-Larsen
Environment, Thorbjørn Berntsen
Family and Children's Affairs, Sylvia Brustad
Finance, Jens Stoltenberg
Fisheries, Karl Schjøtt-Pedersen
Foreign Affairs, Bjørn Tore Godal
Health, Gudmund Hernes
Justice and Police, Liv-Gerd Valla
Local Government and Labour, Kjell Opseth
Oil and Energy, Ranveig Frøiland
Social Affairs, Hill-Marta Solberg
Trade and Industry, Grete Knudsen
Transport and Communications, Sissel Rønbeck
Without Portfolio, Bendik Rugaas

ROYAL NORWEGIAN EMBASSY

25 Belgrave Square, London SW1X 8QD
Tel 0171-591 5500
Ambassador Extraordinary and Plenipotentiary, HE Kjell Colding, CMG, apptd 1996
Defence Attaché, Capt. T. Seim
First Secretary, I. Brusell (*Consular*)
Counsellor, S. Lindtvedt (*Commercial*)

BRITISH EMBASSY

Thomas Heftyesgate 8, 0244 Oslo
Tel: Oslo 552400
Ambassador Extraordinary and Plenipotentiary, HE Mark Elliott, CMG, apptd 1994
Counsellor, D. G. Blunt (*Deputy Head of Mission and Consul-General*)
First Secretary, C. M. Sweney (*Economic and Commercial*)
Defence and Naval Attaché, Lt.-Col. P. D. T. Irvine, OBE

BRITISH CONSULAR OFFICES – Oslo; Honorary Consulates at Alesund, Bergen, Harstad, Haugesund, Kristiansand (South), Kristiansund (North), Stavanger, Tromsø, Trondheim

BRITISH COUNCIL REPRESENTATIVE, R. Olsen, Fridtjof Nansens Plass 5, 0160, Oslo 1

DEFENCE

Norway is a member of NATO and the headquarters of Allied Forces Northern Europe is situated near Oslo. The Army has 170 main battle tanks, 223 armoured infantry fighting vehicles and armoured personnel carriers and 346 artillery pieces. The Navy has 12 submarines, four frigates and 28 patrol and coastal vessels at four bases. The Air Force has 80 combat aircraft.

MILITARY EXPENDITURE – 2.6 per cent of GDP (1995)
MILITARY PERSONNEL – 29,000: Army 14,700, Navy 6,400, Air Force 7,900
CONSCRIPTION DURATION – 12 months

ECONOMY

The cultivated area is about 10,826 sq. km, 3.5 per cent of the total surface area. Forests cover nearly 23 per cent; the rest consists of highland pastures or uninhabitable mountains. The chief agricultural products are grain, potatoes, root vegetables, milk, furs and timber.

The Gulf Stream causes the sea temperature to be higher than the average for the latitude, which brings shoals of herring and cod into the fishing grounds. The quantity of fish caught by Norwegian fishing vessels is greater than that of any other European country except Russia.

The chief industries are oil production and transport, construction, electricity supply, manufactures, agriculture and forestry, fisheries, mining, production of metals and ferro-alloys, and shipping. Industries providing both manufactured products and services for the development of North Sea oil and gas resources have become increasingly important. In 1995 139,228,000 tonnes of crude oil were produced, of which 121,680,000 tonnes were exported. Manufactures are aided by great resources of hydroelectric power. Actual production in 1995 amounted to 112,348 GWh.

GNP – US$136,077 million (1995); US$31,250 per capita (1995)
GDP – US$110,726 million (1992); US$26,331 per capita (1992)
ANNUAL AVERAGE GROWTH OF GDP – 3.3 per cent (1995)
INFLATION RATE – 2.5 per cent (1995)
UNEMPLOYMENT – 4.9 per cent (1995)

TRADE

The chief imports are raw materials, motor vehicles, chemicals, ships and machinery, foods and textiles. Exports consist chiefly of crude oil and gas, manufactured goods, fish and fish products (as canned fish, whale oils), pulp, paper, iron ore and pyrites, nitrate of lime, stone, calcium carbide, aluminium, ferro-alloys, zinc, nickel, cyanamides, etc.

Trade with UK	1995	1996
Imports from UK	£1,998,499,000	£2,066,273,000
Exports to UK	4,325,432,000	4,984,405,000

COMMUNICATIONS

The total length of railways open at the end of 1995 was 4,023 km, excluding private lines. There are 90,262 km of public roads in Norway (including urban streets). Scheduled internal air services are operated by Scandinavian Airlines System (SAS) on behalf of Det Norske Luftfartselskap (DNL), by Braathens South American and Far East Airtransport (SAFE), and by Widerøes Flyveselskap AS. The mercantile marine in 1994 consisted of 1,642 vessels of 21,745,000 gross tons (vessels above 100 gross tons, excluding fishing boats, floating whaling factories, tugs, salvage vessels, icebreakers and similar types of vessel). In 1993 there were 149 daily newspapers.

CULTURE AND EDUCATION

The Norwegian language in both its present forms is closely related to other Scandinavian languages. Independence from Denmark (1814) and resurgent nationalism led to the development of 'new Norwegian' based on dialects, which now has equal official standing with 'bokmål', in which Danish influence is more obvious. Ludvig Holberg (1684–1754) is regarded as the father of Norwegian literature, though the modern period begins with the writings of Henrik Wergeland (1808–45). Some of the famous names are Henrik Ibsen (1828–1906), Bjørnstjerne Bjørnson (1832–1910), Nobel Prizewinner in 1903, and the novelists Jonas Lie (1833–1908), Alexander Kielland (1849–1906), Knut Hamsun (1859–1952) and Sigrid Undset (1882–1949), the latter two also Nobel Prizewinners. Old Norse literature is among the most ancient and richest in Europe.

Education from six to 16 is free and compulsory in the 'basic schools', and free from 16 to 19 years. The majority of the pupils receive post-compulsory schooling at 'upper secondary' schools, regional colleges akin to polytechnics (98), universities (five) and seven other university-level specialist colleges.

ENROLMENT (percentage of age group) – primary 99 per cent; secondary 92 per cent; tertiary 54.4 per cent (1993)

TERRITORIES

SVALBARD

The Svalbard archipelago lies between 74° and 81° N. and between 10° and 35° E., with an estimated area of 24,295 sq. miles. The archipelago consists of the main island, Spitsbergen (15,200 sq. miles), North East Land, the Wiche Islands, Barents and Edge Islands, Prince Charles Foreland, Hope Island, Bear Island and many islands in the neighbourhood of the main group. Glaciers cover 60 per cent of the land area. South Cape is 355 miles from the Norwegian coast. Transit from Tromsø to Green Harbour takes two to three days.

The sovereignty of Norway over the archipelago was recognized by other nations in 1920 and in 1925 Norway assumed sovereignty. The 3,700 inhabitants are mainly engaged in coal-mining, but the islands are also visited by hunters for seals, foxes and polar bears.

JAN MAYEN ISLAND

Jan Mayen, an island in the Arctic Ocean (70° 49' to 71° 9' N. and 7° 53' to 9° 5' W.) was joined to Norway by law in 1930.

NORWEGIAN ANTARCTIC TERRITORIES

BOUVET ISLAND (54° 26' S. and 3° 24' E.) was declared a dependency of Norway in 1930

PETER THE FIRST ISLAND (68° 48' S. and 90° 35' W.), was declared a dependency of Norway in 1931

PRINCESS RAGNHILD LAND (from 70° 30' to 68° 40' S. and 24° 15' to 33° 30' E.) has been claimed as Norwegian since 1931

QUEEN MAUD LAND – In 1939 the Norwegian Government declared the area between 20° W. and 45° E., adjacent to Australian Antarctica, to be Norwegian territory

---

OMAN
The Sultanate of Oman

AREA – 82,030 sq. miles (212,457 sq. km). Neighbours: Yemen, Saudi Arabia and the UAE (west)

POPULATION – 2,077,000 (1994 UN estimate). The inhabitants of the north are mostly Arab, though there are large communities of Hindus, Khojas and Baluch, in addition to Omanis of Zanzibari origin, especially around Salalah. However, in the mountains the inhabitants are either of pure Arab descent or belong to tribes of pre-Arab origin, the Qarra and Mahra, who speak their own dialects of Semitic origin

CAPITAL – ΨMuscat (population, 400,000)

MAJOR CITIES – ΨMutrah and Ruwi, the commercial centres; ΨSur; ΨBarka, ΨSohar, on the northern coast; Salalah, the main town of Dhofar

CURRENCY – Rial Omani (OR) of 1,000 baiza

NATIONAL DAY – 18 November

NATIONAL FLAG – Red with a white panel in the upper fly and a green one in the lower fly; in the canton the national emblem in white

LIFE EXPECTANCY (years) – male 67.70; female 71.80

POPULATION GROWTH RATE – 0.9 per cent (1994)

POPULATION DENSITY – 10 per sq. km (1994)

Oman lies at the eastern corner of the Arabian peninsula. Sharjah and Fujairah (UAE) separate the main part of Oman from the northernmost part of the state, a peninsula extending into the Strait of Hormuz.

The north and the south of Oman are divided by nearly 400 miles of desert. The Batinah, the coastal plain, is fertile. The Hajjar is a mountain spine running from north-west to south-east and for the most part barren, but valleys penetrate the central massif which are irrigated by wells or a system of underground canals called *falajs* which tap the water table. The two plateaus leading from the western slopes of the mountains descend to the Empty Quarter of the Arabian Desert. Dhofar, the southern province, is the only part of the Arabian peninsula to be touched by the south-west monsoon. Temperatures are more moderate than in the north.

HISTORY AND POLITICS

A State Consultative Council established in 1981 was replaced by Sultanic decree in 1991 by a *Majlis A'shura*, or State Advisory Council. This body, meeting twice a year, consists of a representative from each of the 59 wilayats, or governorates, of the Sultanate. The Council has the right to review legislation, question ministers and make policy proposals. Effective political power remains with the Sultan, who rules by decree and is advised by the Cabinet, which he appoints.

In November 1996 the Sultan decreed Oman to be a hereditary absolute monarchy and announced that a Council of State would be established.

HEAD OF STATE

HM The Sultan of Oman, Sultan HM Qaboos Bin-Said, *succeeded* on deposition of Sultan Said bin Taimur, 23 July 1970

COUNCIL OF MINISTERS *as at June 1997*

Prime Minister, Foreign Affairs, Defence and Finance, The Sultan

Personal Representative of HM The Sultan, HH Sayyid Thuwainy bin Shihab Al Said

Deputy P.M, HH Sayyid Fahad bin Mahmood al Said

Minister of State and Governor of Dhofar, HE Sayyid Mussellam bin Ali Al Busaidi

Minister of State and Governor of Muscat, HE Sayyid Al Mutassim bin Hamoud Al Busaidi

Minister of State for Development Affairs, HE Mohammed bin Moosa al Yousef

Minister of State for Foreign Affairs, HE Yousuf bin Alawi bin Abdullah

Minister of State for Legal Affairs, HE Mohammed bin Ali al Alawi

Civil Service, HE Shaikh Abdullaziz bin Matar al-Azizi

Commerce and Industry, HE Maqbool bin Ali bin Sultan

Communications, HE Salim bin Abdullah Al Ghazali

Defence, HE Sayyid Badr bin Sa'oud bin Hareb al Busaidi

Divan of Royal Court, HE Sayyid Saif bin Hamed bin Sa'oud

Economy, Agriculture and Fisheries, HE Mohammed bin Abdallah bin Zaher al Hinai

Education, Youth, HE Saud bin Ibrahim bin Saud al-Busa'di

Electricity and Water, HE Shaikh Mohammed bin Ali Al Qatabi

Health, HE Dr Ali bin Mohammed bin Moosa

Higher Education, HE Yahya bin Mahfoodh al Manthri

Housing, HE Malik bin Suleiman al Ma'amari

Information, HE Abdul Aziz bin Mohammed al Rowas

Interior, HE Alib bin Hamud bin Ali al-Busaidi

Justice, Awqaf and Islamic Affairs, HE Hamoud bin Abdullah Al Harthi

National Heritage and Culture, HH Sayyid Faisal bin Ali al Said

Palace Office Affairs, HE Gen. Ali bin Majid Al Ma'amari

Petroleum and Minerals, HE Said bin Ahmed bin Said al Shanfari

Post, Telegraphs and Telephones, HE Ahmed bin Sweidan al Baluchi

Regional Municipalities and Environment, HE Shaikh Amer bin Shuwain al Hosni

Social Affairs and Labour, HE Ahmed bin Mohammed bin Salim Al Isa'ee

Water Resources, HE Hamed bin Said Al Aufi

EMBASSY OF THE SULTANATE OF OMAN
167 Queen's Gate, London SW7 5HE
Tel 0171-225 0001
Ambassador Extraordinary and Plenipotentiary, HE Hussain Ali Abdullatif, apptd 1995
Minister Plenipotentiary, Ghassan Ibrahim Shaker
Military Attaché, Gp Capt Said Hassan Al-Shedad

BRITISH EMBASSY
PO Box 300, Muscat
Tel: Muscat 693-77
Ambassador Extraordinary and Plenipotentiary, HE Richard John Muir, CMG, apptd 1994
Counsellor, N. J. Guckian (*Deputy Head of Mission*)
Defence and Military Attaché, Brig. M. I. Keun

First Secretary (Commercial), P. Williams
Consul, G. Brown

BRITISH COUNCIL DIRECTOR, C. Bruton, PO Box 73, Muscat. There are also offices at Salalah and Sohar

DEFENCE

The Army has 91 main battle tanks, 63 armoured personnel carriers and 97 artillery pieces. The Navy has one corvette and 12 patrol and coastal vessels at five bases. The Air Force has 46 combat aircraft.
MILITARY EXPENDITURE – 15.1 per cent of GDP (1995)
MILITARY PERSONNEL – 39,800: Army 25,000, Navy 4,200, Air Force 4,100, Royal Household 6,500

ECONOMY

Although there is considerable cultivation in the fertile areas and cattle are raised on the mountains, the backbone of the economy is the oil industry. Petroleum Development (Oman) Ltd (owned 60 per cent by Oman Government and 34 per cent by Shell) began exporting oil in 1967. Concessions (off and on shore) are held by several major international companies. The current level of oil production is about 650,000 barrels per day, planned to increase to 700,000.

A gas turbine power station operates at Rusail, where there is also a 200-plot industrial estate. There is a power station and a desalination plant near Muscat and flour, animal feed, cement and copper production facilities.

In 1994 the government had a budget deficit equivalent to 11.17 per cent of GDP. In 1993 there was a current account deficit of US$1,069 million.
GNP – US$10,578 million (1995); US$4,820 per capita (1995)
GDP – US$12,284 million (1992); US$7,051 per capita (1992)
ANNUAL AVERAGE GROWTH OF GDP – 3.5 per cent (1994)
TOTAL EXTERNAL DEBT – US$3,107 million (1995)

TRADE

Trade is mainly with the UAE, UK, Japan, the Netherlands, USA, Germany, France and India. Chief imports are machinery, cars, building materials, food and telecommunications equipment.

In 1995 imports totalled US$4,248 million. In 1993 Oman had a trade surplus of US$1,336 million.

Trade with UK	1995	1996
Imports from UK	£447,922,000	£415,750,000
Exports to UK	74,232,000	86,993,000

COMMUNICATIONS

Port Qaboos at Matrah has eight deep-water berths which have been constructed as part of the harbour facilities. A modern telecommunications service to the main population centres and an international service are operated by the General Telecommunications Organization. There are good tarmac roads linking most main population centres of the country with the coast and with the towns of the UAE, though only a trunk road links the north and south of Oman.

SOCIAL WELFARE AND EDUCATION

For many years the Sultanate was a poor country but the advent of oil revenues and the change of regime in 1970 led to the initiation of a wide-ranging development programme, especially concerned with health, education and communications. There are now nearly 50 hospitals with

around 3,400 beds; 823 schools, with 387,000 pupils, were in operation in 1992.
ENROLMENT (percentage of age group) – primary 72 per cent (1994); secondary 52 per cent (1993); tertiary 4.9 per cent (1992)

PAKISTAN
Islami Jamhuriya-e-Pakistan

AREA – 307,374 sq. miles (796,095 sq. km). Neighbours: Iran, Afghanistan, China, the disputed territory of Kashmir, India
POPULATION – 126,610,000 (1994 UN estimate); 83,780,000 (1981 census): 95 per cent Muslim, 3.5 per cent Christian, about 1 per cent Hindu, and 0.5 per cent Buddhist. Urdu is the national language, but is only spoken by a small minority of the population. The most widely used language is Punjabi, followed by Sindi and Pushto. English is used in business, government and higher education
CAPITAL – Islamabad (population, 350,000)
MAJOR CITIES – ΨKarachi (7,183,000); Lahore (4,072,000)
CURRENCY – Pakistan rupee of 100 paisa
NATIONAL ANTHEM – Quami Tarana
NATIONAL DAYS – 23 March (Pakistan Day), 14 August (Independence Day)
NATIONAL FLAG – Green with a white crescent and star, and a white vertical strip in the hoist
LIFE EXPECTANCY (years) – male 59.04; female 59.20
POPULATION GROWTH RATE – 3.1 per cent (1994)
POPULATION DENSITY – 159 per sq. km (1994)
URBAN POPULATION – 28.2 per cent (1991)

Running through Pakistan are five great rivers, the Indus, Jhelum, Chenab, Ravi and Sutlej. The upper reaches of these rivers are in Kashmir, and their sources in the Himalayas.

HISTORY AND POLITICS

Pakistan was constituted as a Dominion under the Indian Independence Act 1947, becoming a republic on 23 March 1956. Until 1972 Pakistan consisted of two geographical units, West and East Pakistan, separated by about 1,100 miles of Indian territory. East Pakistan's insistence on complete autonomy led to civil war, which broke out on 25 March 1971 and continued until December 1971 when a cease-fire was arranged. The independence of East Pakistan as Bangladesh was proclaimed in April 1972. Under the 1972 Simla Agreement with India, a line of control was established in Kashmir; Pakistan controls an area of 33,653 sq. miles (87,159 sq. km) to the north and west of the line.
The armed forces under Gen. Zia-ul-Haq assumed power in 1977 and martial law was in force from July 1977 to March 1985. Gen. Zia declared himself President in September 1978, but was killed in a plane crash in August 1988. The Pakistan People's Party (PPP) won the election to the National Assembly and Benazir Bhutto became Prime Minister. In August 1990 the President dissolved the National Assembly and dismissed the Bhutto Cabinet. Elections were held in October 1990 and won by the Islamic Democratic Alliance, led by Mian Muhammad Nawaz Sharif.
In July 1993, the Army intervened to end a power struggle between President Ishaq Khan and Prime Minister Sharif by replacing them with a caretaker administration until new elections were held in October. These were won by the PPP and Benazir Bhutto resumed the premiership. The PPP candidate Farooq Leghari was elected president by an electoral college of the National and provincial assemblies.
The Bhutto government was dismissed by the President in November 1996 for alleged corruption and economic mismanagement. Elections held in February 1997 were won by the Pakistan Muslim League with 134 seats; the PPP won only 18 seats.

INSURGENCY
Since early 1994 there has been civil disorder in Sind province, especially in Karachi, in two conflicts: armed militants of the Mohajir Qaumi Movement (MQM) Party, which represents Urdu-speaking Indian Muslims who fled from India at partition and their descendants, are fighting for an autonomous Karachi province; and there is an armed conflict between Shia and Sunni fundamentalists.

POLITICAL SYSTEM
In January 1997 the interim government set up a Council for Defence and National Security including members of the Cabinet and armed forces to advise on foreign, defence and economic policies.
The National Assembly amended the constitution in April 1997 to remove from the president the power to dismiss the government and dissolve parliament.

HEAD OF STATE
President, Farooq Ahmad Khan Leghari, *elected* 13 November 1993

FEDERAL CABINET *as at August 1997*
Prime Minister, Mian Muhammad Nawaz Sharif
Commerce, Muhammad Ishaq Dar
Communications, Muhammad Azam Khan Hoti
Culture, Sports, Tourism, Youth Affairs, Labour, Manpower and Overseas Pakistanis, Sheikh Rashid Ahmed
Education, Syed Ghaus Ali Shah
Finance, Economic Affairs, Statistics, Planning and Development, Sartaj Aziz
Food, Agriculture and Livestock, Mian Abdul Sattar Laleka
Foreign Affairs, Gohar Ayub Khan
Health, Makhdoom Muhammad Javed Hashmi
Industries and Production, Dr Khalid Maqbool Siddiqui
Information and Media Development, Mushahid Hussain Syed
Interior, Shujaat Hussain
Kashmir Affairs and Northern Areas and States, and Frontier Regions, Lt.-Gen. (retd) Malik Abdul Majeed
Law, Justice, Human Rights and Parliamentary Affairs, Khalid Anwar
Parliamentary Affairs, Mian Muhammad Yaseen Khan Wattoo
Petroleum and Natural Resources, Inter-Provincial Co-ordination, Nisar Ali Khan
Population Welfare, Syeda Abida Hussain
Railways, Sardar Muhammad Yaqub Khan Nasar
Religious Affairs, Zakat and Ushar and Minorities Affairs, Raja Muhammad Zafar-ul-Haq
Water and Power, Raja Nadir Pervaiz Khan
Ministers of State, Syed Ahmed Mehmud *(Environment, Local Government and Rural Development)*; Muhammad Siddique Khan Kanju *(Foreign Affairs)*; Asghar Ali Shah *(Housing and Works)*; Capt. Haleem Ahmed Siddiqui *(Water and Power)*; Tahmina Daultana *(Women's Development, Social Welfare and Special Education)*

HIGH COMMISSION FOR PAKISTAN
35–36 Lowndes Square, London SWIX 9JN
Tel 0171-235 2044

High Commissioner, HE Mian Riaz Samee, apptd 1997
Deputy High Commissioner, Javed Iqbal
Consul-General, M. Nisar
Defence and Naval Attaché, Cdre A. U. Khan
Counsellor, A. Azeem (*Commercial*)

BRITISH HIGH COMMISSION
Diplomatic Enclave, Ramna 5, PO Box 1122, Islamabad
Tel: Islamabad 822131/5
High Commissioner, HE D. Dain, CMG, apptd 1994
Deputy High Commissioners, J. W. Watt (*Islamabad*);
E. W. Callway (*Karachi*)
Counsellor (Economic and Commercial), S. N. Evans, OBE
Counsellor, A. J. C. Boyd
Defence and Military Adviser, Brig. R. D. O'Lone
DEPUTY HIGH COMMISSION – Karachi
CONSULATE – Lahore

BRITISH COUNCIL REPRESENTATIVE, P. Elborn, OBE, PO
Box 1135, Islamabad. There are offices at Karachi,
Lahore and Peshawar

DEFENCE

In August 1994 former Prime Minister Nawaz Sharif stated
that Pakistan had constructed a nuclear weapon, although
the government denies US allegations that China is
assisting in the manufacture of a medium-range missile
system.

The Army has 2,050 main battle tanks, 850 armoured
personnel carriers, 1,820 artillery pieces and 20 attack
helicopters. The Navy has nine submarines, three destroyers, eight frigates, 13 patrol and coastal vessels, four combat
aircraft and 12 armed helicopters based at Karachi. The Air
Force has 430 combat aircraft.
MILITARY EXPENDITURE – 6.5 per cent of GDP (1995)
MILITARY PERSONNEL – 834,000: Army 520,000, Navy
22,000, Air Force 45,000, Paramilitaries 247,000

ECONOMY

The economy is based on agriculture. The principal crops
are cotton, rice, wheat and sugar cane. Pakistan has one of
the longest irrigation systems in the world. The total area
irrigated is 42.5 million acres. There are large deposits of
rock salt.

Pakistan also produces hides and skins, leather, wool,
fertilizers, paints and varnishes, soda ash, paper, cement,
fish, carpets, sports goods, surgical appliances and engineering goods, including switchgear, transformers, cables
and wires.

An agreement was reached in 1993 with the IMF for a
three-year loan of US$1,320 million on implementation of
an austerity and structural adjustment programme. This
has led to the lowering of the foreign debt, inflation and the
budget deficit (5.5 per cent of GDP in 1994–5). The IMF
suspended the agreement in February 1995 after the
government announced its proposed budget, although a
US$596 million standby credit was negotiated in Decem-
ber 1995, before austerity measures were reintroduced.

In 1996 foreign exchange reserves fell below the
US$1,000 million floor decreed by the IMF and the
economy went into a severe recession. Attempts to impose
taxes resulted in industrial action and capital flight. The
Sharif government announced an economic revival programme in March 1997 including tax and tariff reductions.

In 1994 the government had a budget deficit equivalent
to 6.94 per cent of GDP. In 1993 there was a current
account deficit of US$2,935 million.
GNP – US$59,991 million (1995); US$460 per capita
(1995)

GDP – US$54,673 million (1992); US$452 per capita
(1992)
ANNUAL AVERAGE GROWTH OF GDP – 4.0 per cent (1994)
INFLATION RATE – 12.3 per cent (1995)
UNEMPLOYMENT – 4.8 per cent (1994)
TOTAL EXTERNAL DEBT – US$30,152 million (1995)

TRADE

Principal imports are petroleum products, machinery,
fertilizers, transport equipment, edible oils, chemicals and
ferrous metals. Principal exports are raw cotton, cotton
yarn and cloth, carpets, rice, petroleum products, synthetic
textiles, leather, and fish.

In 1995 imports totalled US$11,461 million and exports
US$7,992 million.

Trade with UK	1995	1996
Imports from UK	£340,382,000	£344,507,000
Exports to UK	363,068,000	390,923,000

COMMUNICATIONS

The main seaport is Karachi. The main airports are at
Karachi, Islamabad, Lahore, Peshawar and Quetta. Pakistan International Airlines operates air services between
the principal cities as well as abroad. There are 179,752 km
of roads and 8,163 km of rail track.

EDUCATION

Education consists of five years of primary education (five
to nine years), three years of middle or lower secondary
(general or vocational), two years of upper secondary, two
years of higher secondary (intermediate) and two to five
years of higher education in colleges and universities.
Education is free to upper secondary level.
ILLITERACY RATE – 62.2 per cent
ENROLMENT (percentage of age group) – tertiary 2.9 per
cent (1990)

PALAU
Republic of Palau

AREA – 175 sq. miles (454 sq. km)
POPULATION – 17,000 (1994 UN estimate); 15,122
(1990 census); 13,900 live on Koror and Babelthaup. The
population is Micronesian, and predominantly Roman
Catholic with a Protestant minority. Both Palauan and
English are official languages
CAPITAL Koror (population, 10,493, 1994)
CURRENCY – Currency is that of the USA
NATIONAL FLAG – Light blue with a yellow disc set near
the hoist
POPULATION GROWTH RATE – 3.1 per cent (1994)
POPULATION DENSITY – 37 per sq. km (1994)

The Republic of Palau consists of 340 islands and islets in
the western Pacific Ocean, of which eight are inhabited.
Part of the Caroline Islands group, the Palau archipelago
stretches over 400 miles (644 km) between 2° and 8°N., and
131° and 138°E. Koror island is about 810 miles (1,300 km)
south-west of Guam and about 530 miles (852 km) south-
east of Manila.

The islands vary in terrain from the highly mountainous
to low coral atolls. The climate is tropical with a rainy
season lasting from June to October; the average temperature is 27°C (80°F).

HISTORY AND POLITICS

Spain acquired sovereignty over the Caroline Islands, of which the Palau archipelago is part, in 1886. After defeat in the Spanish-American war of 1898, Spain sold its remaining Pacific possessions, including Palau, to Germany in 1899. On the outbreak of the First World War in 1914 Japan took control of Palau on behalf of the Allied powers, and Japanese administration was confirmed in a League of Nations mandate in 1921. During the Second World War Allied forces gained control of the archipelago after intense fighting. In 1947 the USA entered into agreement with the UN Security Council to administer the Micronesia area, including Palau, as the UN Trust Territory of the Pacific Islands.

In July 1978 the Palau electorate voted in a referendum not to join the new Federated States of Micronesia and instead became a separate part of the UN Trust Territory. A Compact of Free Association was signed with the USA in 1982, which allowed the entry of US nuclear waste and weapons into Palau in contravention of the 1979 constitution. A referendum in November 1993 amended the constitution to enable the implementation of the Compact on 1 October 1994. Under this agreement the USA recognized the Republic of Palau as a fully sovereign and independent state and the UN Trust Territory of the Pacific Islands was terminated. Palau was admitted to UN membership in December 1994.

The last presidential and legislative elections were held in November 1992.

POLITICAL SYSTEM

Under the 1981 constitution, Palau is a democracy with separate executive, legislative and judicial branches of government. Executive power is vested in the president and vice-president, who are elected for four-year terms; the president appoints the Cabinet. There is a bicameral legislature (*Olbiil Era Kekulau*) composed of the 16-member House of Delegates (one member elected from each of the 16 constituent states) and the 14-member Senate. There is also a Council of Chiefs to advise the President on matters concerning traditional law and customs. The judiciary consists of a Supreme Court, a National Court and lesser courts. Each of the 16 component states have their own elected governors and legislatures.

The Compact of Free Association places responsibility for the defence of Palau on the USA for 50 years.

HEAD OF STATE

President, Kuniwo Nakamura, *elected* 4 November 1992
Vice-President, Tommy Remengesau

ECONOMY

The economy remains heavily dependent on US financial support, which the USA is committed to giving under the Compact. Fisheries, tourism, subsistence agriculture and government service are the main areas of employment. Agricultural products include coconuts and copra, and Palau earns significant revenue from the sale of fishing licences to foreign fleets fishing for tuna. Tourism is being developed; there were 26,000 visitors in 1989.

The USA carried out an infrastructure improvement programme in the 1970s and 1980s. There are now three airports on Koror, Peleliu and Angaur which have daily flights from Guam operated by Continental Air Micronesia. Ocean freight services to Palau are provided by two shipping lines to the port at Koror. A communications centre on Arakabesang Island handles international telephone, telex, cable and facsimile communications. There is a privately owned television station and a government-operated radio station.

EDUCATION AND SOCIAL WELFARE

There is a free public school system which, together with independent missionary schools, provides primary and secondary education. A tertiary technical school has been established on Koror since 1969. General medical and dental care is provided by a public hospital and a medical clinic.

PANAMA
República de Panama

AREA – 29,157 sq. miles (75,517 sq. km)
POPULATION – 2,631,013 (1995 estimate). Spanish is the official language
CAPITAL – ΨPanama City (population, 445,902, 1994)
CURRENCY – Balboa of 100 centésimos (US notes are also in circulation)
NATIONAL ANTHEM – Alcanzamos Por Fin La Victoria (Victory is ours at last)
NATIONAL DAY – 3 November
NATIONAL FLAG – Four quarters; white with blue star (top, next staff), red (in fly), blue (below, next staff) and white with red star
LIFE EXPECTANCY (years) – male 70.85; female 75.00
POPULATION GROWTH RATE – 1.9 per cent (1994)
POPULATION DENSITY – 34 per sq. km (1994)
URBAN POPULATION – 55.1 per cent (1994)
MILITARY EXPENDITURE – 1.3 per cent of GDP (1995)
ILLITERACY RATE – 9.2 per cent
ENROLMENT (percentage of age group) – primary 91 per cent (1990); secondary 51 per cent (1990); tertiary 27.5 per cent (1994)

HISTORY AND POLITICS

After a revolt in 1903, Panama declared its independence from Colombia and established a separate government. After 1968, control of Panama was increasingly taken over by Gen. Omar Torrijos, commander of the National Guard, following a military coup. In 1978 Gen. Torrijos withdrew from the government, and Dr Aristides Royo was elected President by the Assembly of Representatives.

An attempt in February 1988 by President Delvalle to remove Gen. Noriega as Commander of the Defence Forces failed. Noriega ousted Delvalle and replaced him with Manuel Solis Palma. Presidential elections were held in May 1989 but Noriega annulled the results and on 15 December he assumed power formally as head of state. On 20 December US troops invaded Panama to oust Noriega. Guillermo Endara, believed to have won the May elections, was installed as president. In December 1991 the Legislative Assembly approved a change to the constitution which abolished the armed forces.

The most recent presidential election, on 8 May 1994, was won by Ernesto Pérez Balladares of the Democratic Revolutionary Party (PRD) who appointed the government.

POLITICAL SYSTEM

Legislative power is vested in a unicameral Legislative Assembly of 72 members; executive power is held by the president, assisted by two elected vice-presidents and an appointed Cabinet. Elections are held every five years under a system of universal and compulsory adult suffrage.

HEAD OF STATE

President, Ernesto Pérez Balladares, *elected* 8 May 1994,
sworn in 1 September 1994
First Vice-President, Tomas Gabriel Altamirano Duque
Second Vice-President, Felipe Alejandro Virzi

CABINET *as at June 1997*

Agricultural Development, Carlos Sousa-Lennox
Commerce and Industry, Raul Arango
Economy and Planning, Dr Guillermo Chapman
Education, Dr Pablo Thalassinos
Finance and Treasury, Miguel Heras Castro
Foreign Affairs, Ricardo A. Arias
Health, Aida de Rivera
Housing, Dr Francisco Sánchez Cárdenas
Interior and Justice, Raúl Montenegro
Labour and Social Welfare, Mitchell Doens
Presidency, Olmedo Miranda
Public Works, Luis Blanco

EMBASSY OF THE REPUBLIC OF PANAMA

48 Park Street, London WIY 3PD
Tel 0171-493 4646
Ambassador Extraordinary and Plenipotentiary, new
appointment awaited

BRITISH EMBASSY

Torre Swiss Bank, Calle 53 (Apartado 889) Zona 1, Panama
City, Panama 1
Tel: Panama City 269 0866
Ambassador Extraordinary and Plenipotentiary, HE William B.
Sinton, apptd 1996

ECONOMY

The soil is moderately fertile, but nearly one-half of the
land is uncultivated. The chief crops are bananas, sugar,
coconuts, cacao, coffee and cereals. The shrimping industry plays an important role in the economy. In 1992
tourism became the principal foreign currency earner,
ahead of bananas. A railway joins the Atlantic and Pacific
oceans.

In 1993 the government had a budget surplus equivalent
to 4.34 per cent of GDP.
GNP – US$7,235 million (1995); US$2,750 per capita
(1995)
GDP – US$5,958 million (1992); US$2,386 per capita
(1992)
ANNUAL AVERAGE GROWTH OF GDP – 3.7 per cent (1994)
INFLATION RATE – 1.0 per cent (1995)
UNEMPLOYMENT – 13.7 per cent (1995)
TOTAL EXTERNAL DEBT – US$7,180 million (1995)

TRADE

Imports are mostly manufactured goods, machinery,
lubricants, chemicals and foodstuffs. Exports are bananas,
petroleum products, shrimps, sugar, meat and fishmeal.

In 1994 Panama had a trade deficit of US$902 million
and a current account deficit of US$331 million.

Trade with UK †	1995	1996
Imports from UK	£67,975,000	£66,942,000
Exports to UK	2,553,000	11,186,000

†Including Colon Free Zone

THE PANAMA CANAL ZONE

With effect from 1 October 1979 the Canal Zone (647 sq.
miles) was disestablished, with all areas of land and water
within the Zone reverting to Panama. By the 1977 treaty
with the USA, the USA is allowed the use of operating
bases for the Panama Canal, together with several military
bases, but the Republic of Panama is sovereign in all such
areas. Control of the Canal will revert to Panama at noon
on 31 December 1999.

DEPENDENCIES

Taboga Island (area 4 sq. miles) is a popular tourist resort
some 12 miles from the Pacific entrance to the Panama
Canal.

Tourist facilities have also been developed in the Las
Perlas Archipelago in the Gulf of Panama, particularly on
the island of Contadora.

There is a penal settlement at Guardia on the island of
Coiba (area 19 sq. miles) in the Gulf of Chiriqui.

PAPUA NEW GUINEA

AREA – 178,704 sq. miles (462,840 sq. km)
POPULATION – 3,997,000 (1994 UN estimate)
CAPITAL – ΨPort Moresby (population, 123,624, 1980)
MAJOR CITIES – Goroka; Lae; Madang; Mount Hagen;
Rabaul; Wewak
CURRENCY – Kina (K) of 100 toea
NATIONAL ANTHEM – Arise All You Sons
NATIONAL DAY – 16 September (Independence Day)
NATIONAL FLAG – Divided diagonally red (fly) and black
(hoist); on the red a soaring Bird of Paradise in yellow
and on the black five white stars of the Southern Cross
LIFE EXPECTANCY (years) – male 55.16; female 56.68
POPULATION GROWTH RATE – 1.9 per cent (1994)
POPULATION DENSITY – 9 per sq. km (1994)
MILITARY EXPENDITURE – 1.3 per cent of GDP (1995)
MILITARY PERSONNEL – 3,700: Army 3,200, Navy 400, Air
Force 100
ILLITERACY RATE – 27.8 per cent
ENROLMENT (percentage of age group) – tertiary 3.2 per
cent (1995)

The country has many island groups, principally the
Bismarck Archipelago, a portion of the Solomon Islands,
the Trobriands, the D'Entrecasteaux Islands and the
Louisade Archipelago. The main islands of the Bismarck
Archipelago are New Britain, New Ireland and Manus.
Bougainville is the largest of the Solomon Islands within
Papua New Guinea.

Papua New Guinea lies within the tropics and has a
typically monsoonal climate. Temperature and humidity
are uniformly high throughout the year.

HISTORY AND POLITICS

New Guinea was sighted by Portuguese and Spanish
navigators in the early 16th century, but remained largely
isolated from the rest of the world. In 1884 a British
Protectorate, British New Guinea, was proclaimed over
the southern coast of New Guinea (Papua) and the adjacent
islands, which were annexed outright in 1888. In 1906 the
Territory of British New Guinea was placed under the
authority of Australia.

In 1884 Germany had formally taken possession of
certain northern areas, later known as the Trust Territory
of New Guinea. In 1914 the German areas were occupied
by Australian troops and remained under military administration until 1921, when they became a League of
Nations mandate administered by Australia. New Guinea
was administered under the mandate and Papua under the
Papua Act until the invasion by the Japanese in 1942 when
the civil administration was suspended until the Japanese
surrendered in 1945.

From 1970 there was a gradual assumption of powers by the Papua New Guinea government, culminating in formal self-government in December 1973. Papua New Guinea achieved full independence within the Commonwealth on 16 September 1975.

Prime Minister Chan resigned in March 1997 following a dispute with the army over the use of mercenaries to attack rebels on Bougainville. A coalition government was formed by Pangu, the People's Progress Party and the People's National Congress following elections in June 1997.

INSURGENCIES

Separatist aspirations, dormant since independence, re-emerged in 1989 when the Bougainville Revolutionary Army (BRA) mounted a successful insurrection. Government security forces withdrew from the island, enabling the BRA to declare an independent republic in May 1990. A peace accord was signed in January 1991, although the question of Bougainville's status was left unresolved. Fighting resumed and government forces returned to the island in October 1992, subsequently capturing 90 per cent of rebel-held territory. The government launched a new offensive in June 1996 after peace talks failed to produce a breakthrough. At least 7,000 people, mostly civilians, have died as a result of the insurrection.

POLITICAL SYSTEM

Elections are held every five years. The Parliament comprises 109 elected members, 20 from regional electorates, the remainder from open electorates. The Governor-General is appointed by Parliament for a six-year term. Provincial governments were abolished in August 1995, and replaced with councils combining local and national politicians and headed by an appointed governor.

Governor-General, HE Sir Wiwa Korowi, GCMG, *appointed* 18 November 1991

NATIONAL EXECUTIVE COUNCIL *as at August 1997*

Prime Minister, Bill Skate
Deputy PM, Planning and Implementation, Chris Haiveta
Agriculture and Livestock, Andrew Baing
Bougainville Affairs, Sam Akoital
Commerce and Industry, Nakikus Konga
Communications, Simeon Wai
Defence, Mao Zemming
Education, Culture and Science, Gabriel Dusava
Environment and Conservation, Robert Sakias
Finance, Roy Yaki
Fisheries, Kala Swokin

Foreign Affairs, Kilroy Genia
Forests, Dokta Fabian Pok
Health, Ludger Mondo
Home Affairs, Youth and Women, Muki Taranupi
Housing, Robert Nagle
Industrial Relations, Samson Napo
Internal Affairs, Thomas Palika
Justice, Jacob Wama
Lands, Viviso Seravo
Mining, Ian Ling Stuckey
Minister of State, Sir Pita Lus
Petroleum and Energy, Castan Maibawa
Provincial and Local Government, Simon Kaumi
Public Service, Iaro Lasaro
Trade and Tourism, Michael Nali
Transport and Civil Aviation, Philemon Embel
Works, Dibara Yagabo

PAPUA NEW GUINEA HIGH COMMISSION
3rd Floor, 14 Waterloo Place, London SW1R 4AR
Tel 0171-930 0922/7
High Commissioner, HE Sir Kina Bona, KBE, apptd 1995

BRITISH HIGH COMMISSION
PO Box 212, Waigani NCD 131, Port Moresby
Tel: Port Moresby 325 1677
High Commissioner, HE Robert Low, CBE, apptd 1994

ECONOMY

Until the 1970s the economy was based almost entirely on agriculture, principally copra, cocoa, tea, coffee, palm oil, rubber, groundnuts, spices and timber. A variety of commercial agricultural developments co-exist with the traditional rural economy. In 1995, the government initiated an austerity programme intended to reduce the budget deficit, privatize state assets and eliminate trade tariffs.

There are extensive mineral deposits throughout Papua New Guinea, including copper, gold, silver, nickel, chromite, bauxite and possibly commercial deposits of oil and gas. In 1972, Bougainville Copper Pty Ltd (BCL) began mining in the North Solomons province, producing copper, silver and gold. The Bougainville copper mine closed indefinitely in 1989 because of the unrest on the island. It had provided more than 15 per cent of the country's annual revenue and accounted for 40 per cent of export earnings.

Industry includes processing of primary products, and brewing, bottling and packaging, paint, plywood, and metal manufacturing and the construction industries.

In 1993 the government had a budget deficit equivalent to 5.7 per cent of GDP, there was a current account surplus of US$554 million and a trade surplus of US$1,370 million. In 1995 imports totalled US$1,451 million and exports US2,654 million.

GNP – US$4,976 million (1995); US$1,160 per capita (1995)

GDP – US$3,830 million (1992); US$1,058 per capita (1992)

ANNUAL AVERAGE GROWTH OF GDP – 14.4 per cent (1993)

INFLATION RATE – 2.9 per cent (1994)

TOTAL EXTERNAL DEBT – US$2,431 million (1995)

TRADE WITH UK	1995	1996
Imports from UK	£10,849,000	£7,976,000
Exports to UK	97,391,000	107,149,000

COMMUNICATIONS

Air Niugini operates regular air services to other countries in the region. Internal air services are also operated by Air Niugini. Several shipping companies operate cargo services to Australia, Europe, the Far East and USA. There are very limited cargo and passenger services between Papua New Guinea main ports, outports, plantations and missions. Road communications are very limited, the most important road being that linking Lae with the populous highlands. Papua New Guinea is linked by international cable to Australia, Guam, Hong Kong, Kota Kinabalu, the Far East and USA. Telecommunications are widely available.

PARAGUAY
República del Paraguay

AREA – 157,048 sq. miles (406,752 sq. km)

POPULATION – 4,700,000 (1994 UN estimate). Spanish is the official language of the country but outside the larger towns Guaraní, the language of the largest single group of original Indian inhabitants, is widely spoken, and is also an official language

CAPITAL – Asunción (population, 502,000)

MAJOR CITIES – Ciudad del Este (98,491); Concepción (25,607); Encarnación (31,445); P. Juan Caballero (41,475)

CURRENCY – Guaraní (Gs) of 100 céntimos

NATIONAL ANTHEM – Paraguayos, República O Muerte (Paraguayans, republic or death)

NATIONAL DAY – 15 May

NATIONAL FLAG – Three horizontal bands, red, white, blue with the National seal on the obverse white band and the Treasury seal on the reverse white band

LIFE EXPECTANCY (years) – male 66.30; female 70.83

POPULATION GROWTH RATE – 2.7 per cent (1994)

POPULATION DENSITY – 12 per sq. km (1994)

URBAN POPULATION – 50.3 per cent (1992)

MILITARY EXPENDITURE – 1.4 per cent of GDP (1995)

MILITARY PERSONNEL – 20,200: Army 14,900, Navy 3,600, Air Force 1,700

CONSCRIPTION DURATION – One to two years

Paraguay is an inland subtropical state of South America, situated between Argentina, Bolivia and Brazil. It is a country of grassy plains and forested hills. In the angle formed by the Paraná-Paraguay confluence are extensive marshes, one of which, known as Neembucú (or endless) is drained by Lake Ypoa, a large lagoon south-east of the capital. The Chaco, lying between the rivers Paraguay and Pilcomayo and bounded on the north by Bolivia, is a flat plain, rising uniformly towards its western boundary to a height of 1,140 feet; it suffers much from floods and still more from drought, but the building of dams and reservoirs has converted part of it into good pasture for cattle.

HISTORY AND POLITICS

In 1535 Paraguay was settled as a Spanish possession. In 1811 it declared its independence from Spain.

Gen. Alfredo Stroessner, dictator from 1954, was overthrown in February 1989 by Gen. Andrés Rodríguez, who was elected President in May 1989. In May 1991, the first free municipal elections were held, and elections to the parliament were held in December 1991. Amendments to the constitution came into effect in June 1992. The last presidential and legislative elections were held on 9 May 1993. The presidential election was won by Juan Carlos Wasmosy (Colorado Party). In the legislative election, the distribution of seats in the senate was: the ruling Colorado Party (ANR-PC) 20; Authentic Radical Liberal Party (PLRA) 17; National Encounter (EN) eight. In the Chamber of Deputies, the distribution of seats was: ANR-PC 40, PLRA 32, EN eight. An attempt by Gen. Lino Oviedo to oust the President was thwarted in April 1996.

POLITICAL SYSTEM

The constitution provides for a two-chamber legislature consisting of a 45-member Senate and an 80-member Chamber of Deputies. Deputies are elected on a regional basis, the number of seats allocated to each regional department being directly proportional to the department's population. Voting is compulsory for all citizens over 18. The president is elected for a five-year term and may not be re-elected. The vice-president may only contest the presidency if he resigns his post six months before the election. The president appoints the Cabinet, which exercises all the functions of government.

HEAD OF STATE

President, Juan Carlos Wasmosy, elected 9 May 1993, sworn in 15 August 1993

CABINET *as at June 1997*

Agriculture and Livestock, Juan Borgognon
Education, Vicente Sarubbi
Finance, Miguel Maidana
Foreign Affairs, Ruben Melgarejo Lan Zoni
Industry and Commerce, Ubaldo Scavone
Interior, Atilio Fernandez
Justice and Labour, Sebastian Gonzalez
National Defence, Hugo Estigarribia Elizeche
Public Health and Social Welfare, Andrés Vidovich
Public Works and Communications, Gustavo Pedrozo

EMBASSY OF PARAGUAY
Braemar Lodge, Cornwall Gardens, London sw7 4aq
Tel 0171-937 1253
Ambassador Extraordinary and Plenipotentiary, new appointment awaited

BRITISH EMBASSY
Calle Presidente Franco 706 (PO Box 404), Asunción
Tel: Asunción 444472
Ambassador Extraordinary and Plenipotentiary and Consul-General, HE Graham Pirnie, apptd 1995

ECONOMY

President Rodríguez introduced an economic liberalization programme which has been continued by the Wasmosy government. This has reduced foreign debt and attracted foreign investment. About three-quarters of the population are engaged in agriculture and cattle raising. Cassava, sugar cane, soya, corn, cotton and wheat are the main agricultural products. The forests contain many varieties of timber which find a good market abroad.

Paraguay's rivers give it considerable hydroelectric capacity. There is a hydroelectric power station at Acaray which exports surplus power to Argentina and Brazil. Joint projects have been undertaken with Brazil, on a hydro-electric dam at Itaipú (the largest in the world), and with Argentina, at Yacyretá.

In 1993 the government had a budget surplus equivalent to 1.16 per cent of GDP.

GNP – US$8,158 million (1995); US$1,690 per capita (1995)
GDP – US$5,486 million (1992); US$1,300 per capita (1992)
ANNUAL AVERAGE GROWTH OF GDP – 4.2 per cent (1995)
INFLATION RATE – 13.4 per cent (1995)
UNEMPLOYMENT – 4.4 per cent (1994)
TOTAL EXTERNAL DEBT – US$2,288 million (1995)

TRADE

The chief imports are machinery; fuels and lubricants; transport and accessories; and drinks and tobacco. The chief exports are soya beans, cotton fibres, meat and coffee.

In 1993 Paraguay had a trade deficit of US$1,019 million and a current account deficit of US$603 million. In 1994 imports totalled US$2,370 million and exports US$817 million.

Trade with UK	1995	1996
Imports from UK	£66,430,000	£55,019,000
Exports to UK	3,468,000	15,802,000

COMMUNICATIONS

There are direct shipping services from Asunción to Europe and the USA, and river steamer services for internal transport and to Argentina. Eight airlines operate services from Asunción. There are 27,741 km (1990) of asphalted roads in Paraguay, connecting Asunción with São Paulo (26 hours) via the Bridge of Friendship and Foz de Yguazú, and with Buenos Aires (24 hours) via Puerto Pilcomayo, and about 4,050 miles of earth roads liable to be closed or to become impassable in wet weather. A 1,000 km road links Asunción with the Bolivian border. Rail services, with train ferries, provide internal and international links. Four daily and five weekly newspapers are published in Asunción.

EDUCATION

Education is free and compulsory. There is a National University in Asunción and a Catholic University.
ILLITERACY RATE – 7.9 per cent
ENROLMENT (percentage of age group) – primary 90 per cent (1994); secondary 34 per cent (1994); tertiary 9.9 per cent (1993)

PERU
República del Peru

AREA – 496,225 sq. miles (1,285,216 sq. km)
POPULATION – 23,088,000 (1994 UN estimate). Spanish, the language of the original Spanish stock from which the governing and professional classes are mainly recruited is an official language, together with Quechua and Aymará. Quechua and Aymará are spoken by more than half the population

CAPITAL – Lima (including ΨCallao, population, 6,483,901, 1993 census)
MAJOR CITIES – Arequipa (820,471); Trujillo (508,715)
CURRENCY – New Sol of 100 cénts
NATIONAL ANTHEM – Somos Libres, Seámoslo Siempre (We are free, let us remain so forever)
NATIONAL DAY – 28 July (Anniversary of Independence)
NATIONAL FLAG – Three vertical stripes of red, white, red
LIFE EXPECTANCY (years) – male 62.77; female 66.56
POPULATION GROWTH RATE – 1.7 per cent (1994)
POPULATION DENSITY – 18 per sq. km (1994)
URBAN POPULATION – 70.1 per cent (1993)

The country is traversed throughout its length by the Andes, running parallel to the Pacific coast. There are three main regions, the Costa, west of the Andes, the Sierra or mountain ranges of the Andes, which include the Punas or mountainous wastes below the region of perpetual snow, and the Montaña or Selva, which is the vast area of jungle stretching from the eastern foothills of the Andes to the eastern frontiers of Peru. The coastal area, lying upon and near the Pacific, is not tropical though close to the Equator, being cooled by the Humboldt Current.

HISTORY AND POLITICS

Peru was conquered in the early 16th century by Francisco Pizarro (1478–1541). He subjugated the Incas (the ruling caste of the Quechua Indians), who had started their rise to power some 500 years earlier, and for nearly three centuries Peru remained under Spanish rule. A revolutionary war of 1821–4 established its independence, declared on 28 July 1821. A military junta ruled Peru from 1968 until 1980 when civilian government was restored.

In April 1992 President Fujimori, faced with increasing terrorist violence, suspended the constitution, dissolved Congress and began to govern by decree. A programme of market-orientated economic reform, new anti-terrorist measures, and a streamlining of the executive, legislative and judicial institutions was undertaken. In November 1992 a legislative election was held to an 80-seat Democratic Constituent Congress (CCD) which was installed as an interim legislature and constituent assembly to write a new constitution. Parties supporting Fujimori's suspension of the constitution gained a majority in the CCD. In January 1993 the 1979 constitution was re-established and the CCD declared Fujimori constitutional head of state. The CCD produced a new constitution which was endorsed in a national referendum in October 1993.

Parliamentary and presidential elections were held on 9 April 1995, with President Fujimori winning the first round of the presidential election outright and his Cambio 90-Nueva Mayoría Party winning 67 out of 120 seats in the new Congress.

INSURGENCIES

Since the late 1970s the government has faced violence from drug organizations and insurgencies from two leftist guerrilla movements, the Maoist Sendero Luminoso (Shining Path) and the Movimiento Revolucionario Tupac Amaru (MRTA). Some areas of the country remain under states of emergency, but the capture of the leaders of both groups in 1992 and the anti-terrorist clampdown from 1992 to 1994 has reduced violence considerably. The Shining Path continues to launch attacks on security forces and infrastructure and has engaged in mass intimidation and execution campaigns in rural areas, with fighting having left 30,000 dead.

In 1996–7 the MRTA re-emerged, overrunning the residence of the Japanese ambassador and seizing hostages. *See also* Events of the Year.

POLITICAL SYSTEM

The constitution, promulgated in December 1993, provides for the president to be able to serve two terms rather than one, as previously; the introduction of the death penalty for terrorists; and the formation of a new 120-member unicameral Congress. A constitutional panel approved a Bill in August 1996, allowing President Fujimori to stand for a third term in office.

HEAD OF STATE

President of the Republic, Alberto Fujimori, *assumed office* 28 July 1990, *re-elected* 9 April 1995, *sworn in* 28 July 1995

CABINET *as at July 1997*

Advancement of Women and Human Development, Dr Miriam Schenone Ordinola
Agriculture, Rodolfo Muñante Sanguinetti
Defence, Gen. Cesar Saucedo Sanchez
Economy and Finance, Jorge Camet Dickman
Education, Domingo Palermo Cabrejos
Energy and Mines, Alberto Pandolfi Arbulu
Fisheries, Ludvick Mayer Cornejo
Foreign Affairs, Eduardo Ferrero Costa
Health, Marino Costa Bauer
Industry, Tourism, Integration and International Trade, Gustavo Caillaux
Interior, Gen. José Villanueva Ruesta
Justice, Alfredo Quispe Correa
Labour and Social Promotion, Jorge González Izquierdo
Presidency, Daniel Hokama Tokashiki
Transport, Communications, Housing and Construction, Elsa Carrera de Escalante

EMBASSY OF PERU
52 Sloane Street, London SWIX 9SP
Tel 0171-235 1917/2545/3802
Ambassador Extraordinary and Plenipotentiary, HE Eduardo Ponce-Vivanco, apptd 1995

BRITISH EMBASSY
Edificio El Pacifico Washington, Piso 12, Plaza Washington (PO Box 854), Lima 100
Tel: Lima 334738
Ambassador Extraordinary and Plenipotentiary, HE John Illman, apptd 1995
CONSULAR OFFICE – Lima
HONORARY CONSULATES – Arequipa, Cusco, Iquitos, Piura, Trujillo

BRITISH COUNCIL DIRECTOR, C. Brown, PO Box No. 14-0114, Calle Alberto Lynch 110, San Isidro, Lima 27

DEFENCE

The Army has 300 main battle tanks, 272 armoured personnel carriers, 276 artillery pieces, 13 aircraft and 59 helicopters. The Navy has eight submarines, two cruisers, one destroyer, four frigates, seven patrol and coastal vessels, seven combat aircraft and 14 armed helicopters at eight bases. The Air Force has 89 combat aircraft and 23 armed helicopters.
MILITARY EXPENDITURE – 1.6 per cent of GDP (1995)
MILITARY PERSONNEL – 125,000: Army 85,000, Navy 25,000, Air Force 15,000
CONSCRIPTION DURATION – Two years

ECONOMY

The chief products of the coastal belt are cotton, sugar and petroleum. There are large tracts of land suitable for cultivation and stock-raising (cattle, sheep, llamas, alpacas and vicuñas) on the eastern slopes of the Andes, and in the mountain valleys maize, potatoes and wheat are grown. The jungle area is a source of timber and petroleum. Other major crops are fruit, vegetables, rice, barley, grapes and coffee. The mountains contain rich mineral deposits and mineral exports include lead, zinc, copper, iron ore and silver. Peru is normally the world's largest exporter of fishmeal.

Since 1990 the government has launched a radical free-market restructuring programme which has rebuilt the foreign exchange reserves from virtually zero, reduced inflation from 7,600 per cent a year in 1990 to 11.1 per cent in 1995, cut subsidies and import tariffs, freed interest rates and privatized most state firms. Foreign investment has been encouraged and has grown dramatically. The economic recovery has increased the gap between rich and poor.

In 1994 the government had a budget surplus equivalent to 3.04 per cent of GDP.
GNP – US$55,019 million (1995); US$2,310 per capita (1995)
GDP – US$37,312 million (1992); US$1,991 per capita (1992)
ANNUAL AVERAGE GROWTH OF GDP – 7.0 per cent (1995)
INFLATION RATE – 11.1 per cent (1995)
UNEMPLOYMENT – 7.1 per cent (1995)
TOTAL EXTERNAL DEBT – US$30,831 million (1995)

TRADE

The principal imports are machinery and chemicals and pharmaceutical products. The chief exports are minerals and metals, fishmeal, sugar, cotton and coffee.
In 1993 Peru had a trade deficit of US$580 million and a current account deficit of US$1,800 million. In 1995 imports totalled US$9,224 million and exports US$5,575 million.

Trade with UK	1995	1996
Imports from UK	£57,500,000	£62,876,000
Exports to UK	122,645,000	130,434,000

COMMUNICATIONS

In recent years the coastal and sierra zones have been opened up by means of roads and air routes. There is air communication, as well as communication by protracted land routes, with the tropical and eastern zones which lie east of the Andes towards the borders of Brazil. The Andean Highway forms a link between the Pacific, the Amazon and the Atlantic. The Pan-American Highway runs along the Peruvian coast connecting it with Ecuador and Chile. The Inter-Ocean Corridor linking the port of Matarani and Buenos Aires will be opened soon.

The railway is administered by the government. There is also steam navigation on the Ucayali and Huallaga, and in the south on Lake Titicaca. Air services are maintained throughout Peru, and many international services call at Lima.

EDUCATION

Education is compulsory and free between five and 16.
ILLITERACY RATE – 11.3 per cent
ENROLMENT (percentage of age group) – primary 88 per cent (1993); secondary 46 per cent (1993); tertiary 30.9 per cent (1994)

THE PHILIPPINES
Repúblika ng Pilipinas

AREA – 115,831 sq. miles (300,000 sq. km)
POPULATION – 67,038,000 (1994 UN estimate). The
inhabitants are basically of Malay stock, with a
considerable admixture of Spanish and Chinese blood in
many localities. The Chinese minority is estimated at
500,000, with smaller numbers of Spanish, American
and Indian. About 90 per cent are Christian,
predominantly Roman Catholics. Most of the remainder
are Muslims, in the south, and indigenous animists,
mainly in Luzon and parts of Mindanao. The official
languages are Filipino and English. Filipino is based on
Tagalog, one of the Malay–Polynesian languages.
English, which is the language of government and of
instruction in secondary and university education, is
spoken by at least 44 per cent of the population. Spanish
is now spoken by a very small minority
CAPITAL – ΨManila (population, 8,594,150, 1994)
MAJOR CITIES – Bacolod (328,648); ΨCebu (613,184);
ΨDavao (819,525); ΨIloilo (287,711); ΨZamboanga
(433,328), 1989 estimates
CURRENCY – Philippine peso (P) of 100 centavos
NATIONAL ANTHEM – Bayang Magiliw
NATIONAL DAY – 12 June (Independence Day 1898)
NATIONAL FLAG – Equal horizontal bands of blue (above)
and red; gold sun with three stars on a white triangle next
staff
LIFE EXPECTANCY (years) – male 63.10; female 66.70
POPULATION GROWTH RATE – 2.2 per cent (1994)
POPULATION DENSITY – 223 per sq. km (1994)
URBAN POPULATION – 44.9 per cent (1994)

There are eleven larger islands and 7,079 other islands.
The principal islands (area in sq. miles) are: Luzon (40,422);
Mindoro (3,759); Mindanao (36,538); Leyte (2,786); Samar
(5,050); Cebu (1,703); Negros (4,906); Bohol (1,492);
Palawan (4,550); Masbate (1,262); Panay (4,446). Other
groups are the Sulu islands (capital, Jolo), Babuyanes and
Batanes; the Calamian islands; and Kalayaan Islands.

HISTORY AND POLITICS

The Portuguese navigator Magellan came to the Philippines in 1521 and was killed by the natives of Mactan, a
small island near Cebu. In 1565 Spain undertook the
conquest of the country, which was named Filipinas after
Philip II of Spain. In 1896 the Filipinos revolted against
Spanish rule and declared their independence on 12 June
1898. In the Spanish–American War of 1898, Manila was
captured by American troops with the help of Filipinos and
the islands were ceded to the USA by the Treaty of Paris in
1898. Despite a rebellion against US rule between 1899 and
1902, the Americans remained in control of the country
until 1946. The Republic of the Philippines came into
existence on 4 July 1946.

Ferdinand Marcos was president from 1965 to 1986.
Although he gained a majority of votes in the official count
of a presidential election in February 1986, the election
was marred by widespread electoral abuse and his rival,
Mrs Corazón Aquino, launched a campaign of non-violent
civil disturbance which gained wide support. On 25 February Marcos fled to Hawaii. Mrs Aquino took over as
president and survived seven coup attempts.

Fidel Ramos was elected president on 11 May 1992 and
has overcome the problems that plagued President Aquino,
namely military coup attempts and legislative obstruc-
tiveness. A presidential election is due to be held in 1998;

the Supreme Court has ruled out the possibility of
President Ramos standing for a second six-year term.

Legislative elections to both houses of Congress were
held on 8 May 1995 when the coalition of the Lakas ng
Edsa, National Union of Christian Democrats and Laban
ng Demokratikong Pilipino won majorities in both houses.
Leban ng Demokratikong Pilipino subsequently withdrew
from the ruling coalition.

INSURGENCIES

On 2 September 1996, the government signed an agreement with the Moro National Liberation Front (MNLF)
on the creation of an autonomous Muslim region in
Mindanao, Palawan, Sulu and Basilan, ending a 24-year
rebellion which had left more than 120,000 people dead.
The Moro Islamic Liberation Front (MILF), a radical
breakaway group, threatened an upsurge in violence to
disrupt the agreement. The Communist New People's
Army (NPA) maintains a presence in eastern Mindanao,
Negros, Samar, Bicol, the mountains of northern Luzon
and Bataan. The NPA signed a cease-fire agreement with
the government in December 1993; peace talks are
continuing.

The 900-strong Islamic fundamentalist Abu Sayyaf
group killed over 100 people in an attack on Ipil in April
1995.

POLITICAL SYSTEM

A new constitution was approved by referendum in 1987
and came into force that July. Legislative authority is
vested in a bicameral elected Congress comprising a
House of Representatives of 250 members and a 24-
member Senate.

The Autonomous Region of Mindanao consists of four
provinces: Sulu, Tawitawi, Lanao del Sur and Maguinada-
nao. There is a 24-member regional assembly and a
Governor.

HEAD OF STATE
President, Fidel V. Ramos, *assumed office* 30 June 1992
Vice-President, Joseph Estrada

CABINET *as at August 1997*
Agriculture, Salvador Escudero
*Director-General of the National Economic Development Agency,
    Socio-Economic Planning*, Cielito Habito
Education, Culture and Sport, Ricardo Gloria
Energy, Francisco Viray
Environment and Natural Resources, Victor Ramos
Finance, Roberto de Ocampo
Foreign Affairs, Domingo Siazon
Health, Dr Carmencita Reodica
Interior and Local Government, Robert Barbers
Justice, Teofisto Guingona
Labour and Employment, Leonardo Quisumbing
National Defence, Gen. Renato de Villa
Press and Presidential Spokesman, Hector Villanueva
Public Works and Highways, Gregorio Vigilar
Science and Technology, William Padolina
Social Welfare and Development, Lina Laigo
Tourism, Mina Gabor
Trade and Industry, Cesar Bautista
Transport and Communications, Arturo Enrile

EMBASSY OF THE PHILIPPINES
9A Palace Green, London w8 4QE
Tel 0171-937 1600
Ambassador Extraordinary and Plenipotentiary, HE Jesus P.
    Tambunting, apptd 1993
Defence Attaché, Col. E. Abu
Counsellor and Consul-General, E. Castro
Commercial Counsellor, P. Sales

BRITISH EMBASSY

Locsin Building, 6752 Ayala Avenue, Corner Makati Avenue, 1226 Makati, Metro Manila (PO Box 2927 MCPO)
Tel: Manila 816 7116
Ambassador Extraordinary and Plenipotentiary, HE Adrian Thorpe, CMG, apptd 1995
Deputy Head of Mission, M. Reilly
Defence Attaché, Gp Capt. P. G. Wildman
First Secretary, E. McEvoy *(Commercial)*

BRITISH COUNCIL DIRECTOR, Dr K. Bailey, 10F Taipan Place, Emerald Avenue, Ortigas Complex, Pasig City, Manila

DEFENCE

The Army has 464 armoured infantry fighting vehicles and armoured personnel carriers, and 242 artillery pieces. The Navy has one frigate, 54 patrol and coastal vessels and eight combat aircraft at three bases. The Air Force has 43 combat aircraft and 104 armed helicopters.
MILITARY EXPENDITURE – 1.6 per cent of GDP (1995)
MILITARY PERSONNEL – 107,500: Army 68,000, Navy 23,000, Air Force 16,500

ECONOMY

The Philippines is predominantly agricultural, the chief products being rice, coconuts, maize, coffee, sugar cane, abaca (manila hemp), fruits, tobacco and lumber. There is, however, an increasing number of manufacturing industries and it is the policy of the government to diversify its economy. There are also deposits of nickel, iron, copper, gold and silver.

The Philippines has been bypassed by the economic growth of most of the rest of south-east Asia since the 1960s, mainly because of the incompetence and corruption of the Marcos regime. President Ramos has, however, restored economic growth and increased electricity generation to resolve the energy crisis. An economic reform programme of liberalization, privatization and deregulation has also been put in place and has led to increased exports, increased foreign investment, and a reduction in inflation.

In 1993 the government had a budget deficit equivalent to 1.48 per cent of GDP.
GNP – US$71,865 million (1995); US$1,050 per capita (1995)
GDP – US$43,748 million (1992); US$807 per capita (1992)
ANNUAL AVERAGE GROWTH OF GDP – 4.8 per cent (1995)
INFLATION RATE – 8.1 per cent (1995)
UNEMPLOYMENT – 8.4 per cent (1995)
TOTAL EXTERNAL DEBT   US$39,445 million (1995)

TRADE

Principal exports are sugar, coconut oil, copper concentrate, lumber and copra, together with increasingly important manufactured exports such as electronics products and clothing. The major trading partners are the USA, Japan, Taiwan and Hong Kong.

In 1993 the Philippines had a trade deficit of US$6,222 million and a current account deficit of US$3,289 million. In 1995 imports totalled US$28,337 million and exports US$17,502 million.

Trade with UK	1995	1996
Imports from UK	£432,397,000	£395,311,000
Exports to UK	352,425,000	895,486,000

COMMUNICATIONS

The highway system covers about 161,709 kilometres. The Philippine National Railway used to operate 1,282 km of track, but a greater part of this is being rebuilt. There are 94 ports of entry and 164,404 vessels of various types totalling 50,467,000 tons are engaged in inter-island traffic. There are 82 national airports and 137 privately operated airports. Philippine Air Lines has regular flights throughout the Far East, to the USA and Europe, in addition to inter-island services.

EDUCATION

Secondary and higher education is extensive and there are 37 private universities recognized by the government, including the Dominican University of Santo Tomas (founded in 1611). There are also 296 state-supported colleges and universities, including the University of the Philippines, founded 1908.
ILLITERACY RATE – 5.4 per cent
ENROLMENT (percentage of age group) – primary 97 per cent; secondary 60 per cent; tertiary 26.8 per cent (1993)

POLAND
Rzeczpospolita Polska

AREA – 124,808 sq. miles (323,250 sq. km). Neighbours: Russia (north), Germany (west), the Czech Republic and Slovakia (south), Belarus, Ukraine and Lithuania (east)
POPULATION – 38,643,000 (1995). Roman Catholicism is the religion of 95 per cent of the inhabitants
CAPITAL – Warsaw (population, 1,643,000), on the Vistula
MAJOR CITIES – Bydgoszcz (385,400); Gdansk (757,300); Katowice (359,000); Kraków (744,200); Łódź (835,800); Poznan (582,800); Szczecin (418,300); Wroclaw (641,400)
CURRENCY – Zloty of 100 groszy
NATIONAL ANTHEM – Jeszcze Polska Nie Zginela (Poland has not yet been destroyed)
NATIONAL DAY – 3 May
NATIONAL FLAG – Equal horizontal stripes of white (above) and red
LIFE EXPECTANCY (years) – male 66.11; female 75.27
POPULATION GROWTH RATE – 0.3 per cent (1994)
POPULATION DENSITY – 119 per sq. km (1994)
URBAN POPULATION – 62.1 per cent (1992)

HISTORY AND POLITICS

The Polish Commonwealth ceased to exist in 1795 after three successive partitions in 1772, 1793 and 1795 in which Prussia, Russia and Austria shared. The Republic of Poland, reconstituted within the limits of the old Polish Commonwealth, was proclaimed at Warsaw in November 1918, and its independence guaranteed by the signatories of the Treaty of Versailles.

German forces invaded Poland on 1 September 1939; on 17 September, Russian forces invaded eastern Poland, and on 21 September 1939 Poland was declared by Germany and Russia to have ceased to exist. At the end of the war a coalition government was formed in which the Polish Workers' Party played a large part. In December 1948, the Polish Workers' Party and the Polish Socialist Party merged to form the Polish United Workers' Party (PUWP). A new constitution modelled on the Soviet constitution was adopted in 1952, and was modified in 1976.

Steep price rises in 1980 prompted strikes which forced the government to allow independent trade unions, including 'Solidarity' led by Lech Walesa. The unions agitated for further reforms although their activities were suspended when martial law was in force from December 1981 until July 1983.

A wave of strikes resulted in talks between Walesa and the PUWP early in 1989. Multiparty parliamentary elections were held in the summer of 1989, following which the PUWP ceased to be the ruling party. The post-Communist governments have introduced a market economy but economic difficulties and a fragmented Parliament have led to a succession of short-lived governments.

Elections held on 19 September 1993 resulted in six parties gaining representation in the 460-seat *Sejm*: Democratic Left Alliance (SLD) 171 seats; Polish Peasant Party (PSL) 132 seats; Freedom Union (UW) 74 seats; Labour Union (UP) 41 seats; Confederation for an Independent Poland (KPN) 22 seats; Reform Bloc 16 seats; German minority parties 4 seats. In the 100-member Senate the results were: SLD 37; PSL 36; Solidarity 10; UW 4; others 13. The SLD (dominated by reformist Communists) returned to power after four years by forming a coalition government with the PSL and UP parties.

Legislative elections are due to be held in September 1997 (*see* Stop-press).

Foreign Relations

Poland was invited to join NATO in July 1997. It has also been approved by the European Commission for membership of the EU.

Political System

On 25 May 1997 a new constitution was approved by a referendum to replace the 'small constitution' which was in force from 1992–95. The president appoints the prime minister and has the right to be consulted over the appointment of the foreign, defence and interior ministers. There is a 5 per cent threshold for representation for parties in the Sejm and 8 per cent for alliances (except for minority groups). The Senate is elected on a provincial basis.

Head of State

President, Aleksander Kwaśniewski, *elected* 19 November 1995, *sworn in* 23 December 1995

Council of Ministers *as at June 1997*

Prime Minister, Wlodzimierz Cimoszewicz (SLD)
Deputy PM, Agriculture, Jaroslaw Kalinowski (PSL)
Deputy PM, Finance, Marek Belka (Ind.)
Deputy PM, Treasury, Miroslaw Pietrewicz (PSL)
Communications, Andrzej Zieliński (Ind.)
Culture and Arts, Zdzislaw Podkański (PSL)
Defence, Stanislaw Dobrzański (PSL)
Economy, Wieslaw Kaczmarek (SLD)
Education, Jerzy Wiatr (SLD)
Environmental Protection, Natural Resources and Forestry, Stanislaw Zelichowski (PSL)
Foreign Affairs, Dariusz Rosati (Ind.)
Health and Social Welfare, Jacek Zochowski (Ind.)
Internal Affairs and Administration, Leszek Miller (SLD)
Justice, Lech Kubicki (Ind.)
Labour and Social Policy, Tadeusz Zieliński (Ind.)
Transport and Maritime Economy, Boguslaw Liberadzki (Ind.)

PSL Polish Peasant Party; SLD Democratic Left Alliance; Ind. Independent

EMBASSY OF THE REPUBLIC OF POLAND
47 Portland Place, London WIN 4JH
Tel 0171-580 4324/9
Ambassador Extraordinary and Plenipotentiary, HE Ryszard Stemplowski, apptd 1994
Defence Attaché, Cdr. I. Goreczny
Consul-General, J. Starosciak
Minister, P. Kozerski *(Commercial)*

BRITISH EMBASSY
No. 1 Aleja Róz, 00-556 Warsaw
Tel: Warsaw 628 1001/5
Ambassador Extraordinary and Plenipotentiary, HE Christopher O. Hum, CMG, apptd 1996
Counsellor, W. A. Harrison (*Deputy Head of Mission*)
Defence and Air Attaché, Gp Capt M. Mitchell
Counsellor (Commercial and Consul-General), S. D. Pattison
HONORARY CONSULATES – Gdansk, Katowice, Poznan, Szczecin, Wroclaw

BRITISH COUNCIL DIRECTOR, E. Pugh, Al. Jerozolimskie 59, 00–697 Warsaw

DEFENCE

The Army has 1,721 main battle tanks, 1,455 armoured infantry fighting vehicles and armoured personnel carriers and 1,581 artillery pieces. The Navy has three submarines, one destroyer, one frigate, 33 patrol and coastal vessels, 30 combat aircraft and ten helicopters at five bases. The Air Force has 437 combat aircraft and 22 attack helicopters.
MILITARY EXPENDITURE – 2.5 per cent of GDP (1995)
MILITARY PERSONNEL – 248,500: Army 178,700, Navy 17,800, Air Force 52,000
CONSCRIPTION DURATION – 18 months

ECONOMY

Poland is well endowed with mineral resources; there are large reserves of brown coal (14,100 million tons) in central and south-western Poland and hard coal (65 million tons) in Upper Silesia and the Walbrzych and Lublin regions; sulphur, copper, zinc, lead, natural gas and salt are also produced. In 1994, there were 18.6 million hectares of arable land, 73 per cent of which was privately owned.

In 1990, the government embarked upon a series of measures designed to introduce a free-market economy. However, growth did not resume until 1992 and the public backlash against rising food prices and unemployment prompted the government to overstep the budgetary limits agreed with international creditors. The IMF prescribed a 'shock therapy' of allowing bankruptcy and ending of state subsidies to reduce the deficit. Further IMF credits followed the passing of an austerity budget and the introduction of a mass privatization bill for 600 state-owned firms in 1993.

The transition to a market economy has been painful, with unemployment rising from 6.3 per cent in 1990 to 13.1 per cent in 1995. Industrial output has improved and the rate of growth of GDP has increased although inflation remains high.

Poland's major imports are petroleum, textiles, and industrial and electrical equipment. Its major exports are fruits and vegetables, clothing, coal, non-ferrous metals, iron and steel, furniture and transport equipment. Germany is Poland's main trading partner.

In 1993 there was a trade deficit of US$3,505 million and a current account deficit of US$5,788 million. In 1995 imports totalled US$29,050 million and exports US$22,892 million.
GNP – US$107,829 million (1995); US$2,790 per capita (1995)

GDP – US$58,408 million (1992); US$2,356 per capita (1992)
ANNUAL AVERAGE GROWTH OF GDP – 7.0 per cent (1995); estimated to be 5.7 per cent in 1996
INFLATION RATE – 26.8 per cent (1995), estimated to be 19.9 per cent in 1996
UNEMPLOYMENT – 13.1 per cent (1995)
TOTAL EXTERNAL DEBT – US$42,291 million (1995)

TRADE WITH UK	1995	1996
Imports from UK	£944,672,000	£1,350,985,000
Exports to UK	638,077,000	599,862,000

EDUCATION

Elementary education (ages seven to 15) is compulsory and free. Secondary education is optional and free. There are universities at Kraków, Warsaw, Poznan, Lódź, Wroclaw, Lublin and Toruń and a number of other towns.
ENROLMENT (percentage of age group) – primary 97 per cent (1994); secondary 83 per cent (1994); tertiary 27.5 per cent (1993)

CULTURE

Polish is a western Slavonic tongue, the Latin alphabet being used. Major writers include Henryk Sienkiewicz (1846–1916), Nobel Prizewinner for Literature in 1905; Boleslaw Prus (1847–1912); Stanislaw Reymont (1868–1925), Nobel Prizewinner in 1924; Czeslaw Milosz, Nobel Prizewinner in 1980; and Wislawa Szymborske, Nobel Prizewinner in 1996.

PORTUGAL
República Portuguesa

AREA – 35,514 sq. miles (91,982 sq. km)
POPULATION – 9,830,000 (1994 UN estimate); 9,862,700 (including the Azores and Madeira) (1991 census). The language is Portuguese, a Romance language with admixtures of Arabic and other idioms
CAPITAL – ΨLisbon (population, 2,561,225, 1991)
MAJOR CITIES – ΨOporto (1,683,000)
CURRENCY – Escudo (Esc) of 100 centavos
NATIONAL ANTHEM – A Portuguesa
NATIONAL DAY – 10 June
NATIONAL FLAG – Divided vertically into unequal parts of green and red with the national emblem over all on the line of division
LIFE EXPECTANCY (years) – male 70.77; female 78.01
POPULATION GROWTH RATE – –0.2 per cent (1994)
POPULATION DENSITY – 107 per sq. km (1994)
URBAN POPULATION – 48.2 per cent (1991)

HISTORY AND POLITICS

Portugal was a monarchy from the 12th century until 1910, when an armed rising in Lisbon drove King Manuel II into exile and a republic was set up. A period of political instability ensued until the military stepped in and abolished political parties in 1926. The constitution of 1933 gave formal expression to the corporative 'Estado Novo' (New State) which was personified by Dr Salazar, Prime Minister 1932–68. Dr Caetano succeeded Salazar as prime minister in 1968 but his failure to liberalize the regime or to conclude the wars in the African colonies resulted in his government's overthrow by a military coup on 25 April 1974. There was great political turmoil between April 1974 and July 1976 but with the failure of

an attempted coup by the extreme left in November 1975 the situation stabilized.

In the general election held on 1 October 1995, the Socialist Party (PS) won 112 seats, the Social Democrats (PSD) 88 seats, the Christian Democrats (CDS/PP) 15 seats, and the Communist Coalition (CDU) 15 seats. The Socialist candidate, Jorge Sampaio, won the January 1996 presidential election.

POLITICAL SYSTEM

Under the 1976 constitution, amended in 1982 and 1989, the president, elected for a five-year term by universal adult suffrage, appoints the prime minister and, on the latter's recommendation, the members of the Council of Ministers. Legislative authority is vested in the 230-member Assembly of the Republic, elected by a system of proportional representation every four years. The president retains certain limited powers to dismiss the government, dissolve the Assembly or veto laws.

HEAD OF STATE

President of the Republic, Jorge Sampaio, *elected* 1996, *inaugurated* 9 March 1996

COUNCIL OF MINISTERS *as at July 1997*

Prime Minister, António Guterres
Agriculture, Food and Fisheries, Fernando Gomes da Silva
Assistant to the PM, Jorge Almeida Coelho
Culture, Manuel Maria Carrilho
Defence, António Vitorino
Economy, Daniel Bessa
Education, Marçal Grilo
Employment, Maria João Rodrigues
Environment, Maria Elisa Ferreira
Finance, António Sousa Franco
Foreign Affairs, Jaime Gama
Health, Maria de Belém Henriques de Pina
Home Affairs, Alberto Costa
Justice, José Vera Jardim
Planning and Territorial Administration, João Cravinho
Public Works, António Borrani Teixeira
Science and Technology, José Rebelo Cago
Social Security, Eduardo Ferro Rodrigues

PORTUGUESE EMBASSY

11 Belgrave Square, London SWIX 8PP
Tel 0171-235 5331
Ambassador Extraordinary and Plenipotentiary, new appointment awaited
Minister-Counsellor and Consul-General, A. de Almeida Ribeiro
Minister-Counsellor, J Ramos-Pinto
Defence Attaché, Rear-Adm. A. Bettencourt

BRITISH EMBASSY

Rua de S. Bernardo 33, 1200 Lisbon
Tel: Lisbon 3924000
Ambassador Extraordinary and Plenipotentiary, HE Roger Westbrook, CMG, LVO, apptd 1995
Counsellor, A. F. Smith *(Deputy Head of Mission)*
Defence Attaché, Cdr. R. Goddard
First Secretaries, P. Sinkinson *(Commercial);* C. Gibson, MVO, *(Consul)*
CONSULATES – Oporto, Portimão, Funchal (Madeira), Ribeira Grande (Azores), Macao
BRITISH COUNCIL DIRECTOR, B. Jefferson, OBE, Rua de Sao Marçal 174, 1294 Lisbon. There are also offices at Cascais, Coimbra and Oporto
BRITISH PORTUGUESE CHAMBER OF COMMERCE, Rua da Estrela 8, 1200 Lisbon and Rua Sa de Bandeira 784–20E, Frente, 4000 Oporto

DEFENCE

The Army has 186 main battle tanks, 350 armoured personnel carriers and 318 artillery pieces. The Navy has three submarines, 11 frigates and 29 patrol and coastal vessels at four bases. The Air Force has 90 combat aircraft.

Lisbon is the base of the NATO Iberian Atlantic Command and the USA maintains 1,155 personnel in mainland Portugal and on the Azores.

MILITARY EXPENDITURE – 2.9 per cent of GDP (1995)
MILITARY PERSONNEL – 90,400: Army 29,700, Navy 12,500, Air Force 7,300, Paramilitaries 40,900
CONSCRIPTION DURATION – Four to 18 months

ECONOMY

The chief agricultural products are cork, potatoes, maize, wheat, rice, vegetables, olives, olive oil, figs, citrus fruits, almonds, timber, port wine and table wines. There are extensive forests of pine, cork, eucalyptus and chestnut covering about 20 per cent of the total area of the country. The principal mineral products are pyrites, wolfram, uranium, iron ores, copper and sodium and calcium minerals.

The country is moderately industrialized. The principal manufactures are textiles, clothing and footwear, machinery (including electrical machinery and transport equipment), pulp and paper, pharmaceuticals, foodstuffs, chemicals, fertilizers, wood, cork, furniture, cement, glassware and pottery. There are a modern steelworks and two large shipbuilding and repair yards at Lisbon and Setúbal, working mainly for foreign shipowners. There are several hydroelectric power stations and a new thermal power station.

Since joining the EC (EU) in 1986 Portugal has been adjusting its economy to the European single market, and to the economic and monetary union criteria laid down in the Maastricht Treaty. The escudo joined the ERM in April 1992.

GNP – US$96,689 million (1995); US$9,740 per capita (1995)
GDP – US$61,628 million (1992); US$8,534 per capita (1992)
ANNUAL AVERAGE GROWTH OF GDP – 2.4 per cent (1995)
INFLATION RATE – 4.1 per cent (1995)
UNEMPLOYMENT – 5.5 per cent (1993)

TRADE

The principal imports are cereals, meat, raw and semi-manufactured iron and steel, industrial machinery, chemicals, crude oil, motor vehicles and raw materials for textiles. The principal exports are textiles, footwear, timber, pulp, automotive parts, cork, electrical and other machinery, and chemicals.

In 1993 Portugal had a trade deficit of US$6,636 million and a current account surplus of US$947 million. In 1995 imports totalled US$32,322 million and exports US$22,584 million.

Trade with UK	1995	1996
Imports from UK	£1,391,300,000	£1,598,900,000
Exports to UK	1,397,200,000	1,564,800,000

COMMUNICATIONS

There are international airports at Lisbon and Oporto, and at Faro in the Algarve. Four morning and one evening daily newspapers are published in Lisbon and four morning newspapers in Oporto. There are six main weekly newspapers.

EDUCATION

Education is free and compulsory for nine years from the age of six. Secondary education is mainly conducted in state lyceums, commercial and industrial schools, but there are also private schools. There are also military, naval, technical, polytechnic and other special schools. There are universities at Coimbra (founded in 1290), Oporto, Lisbon, Braga, Aveiro, Vila Real, Faro, Evora and in the Azores.

ILLITERACY RATE – 10.4 per cent
ENROLMENT (percentage of age group) – primary 100 per cent (1991); tertiary 34.5 per cent (1993)

AUTONOMOUS REGIONS

Madeira and The Azores are two administratively autonomous regions of Portugal, having locally elected assemblies and governments.

MADEIRA

Madeira is a group of islands in the Atlantic Ocean about 520 miles south-west of Lisbon, and consists of Madeira, Porto, Santo and three uninhabited islands (Desertas). The total area is 314 sq. miles (813 sq. km), with a population of 271,400 (1989). ΨFunchal in Madeira, the largest island (270 sq. miles), is the capital (population 44,111); Machico (10,905).

THE AZORES

The Azores are a group of nine islands (Flores, Corvo, Terceira, São Jorge, Pico, Faial, Graciosa, São Miguel and Santa Maria) in the Atlantic Ocean, with a total area of 922 sq. miles (2,387 sq. km), and a population of 255,100 (1989). ΨPonta Delgada, on São Miguel, is the capital of the group (population 137,700). Other ports are ΨAngra, in Terceira (55,900) and ΨHorta (16,300).

OVERSEAS TERRITORY

MACAO

Macao, situated at the mouth of the Pearl River, comprises a peninsula and the islands of Coloane and Taipa, having an area of six sq. miles (15.5 sq. km), with a population (UN estimate 1994) of 395,000. Macao became a Portuguese colony in 1557; in a Sino-Portuguese treaty of 1887 China recognized Portugal's sovereignty over Macao. An agreement to transfer the administration of Macao to the Chinese authorities was signed on 13 April 1987. Macao will become a 'special administrative region' (SAR) of China when transferred on 20 December 1999. The final session of the Macao SAR Basic Law Drafting Committee was held in Beijing in January 1993 and approved the Basic Law which will serve as Macao's constitution after 1999.

Macao is subject to Portuguese constitutional law but otherwise enjoys autonomy. The Governor is appointed by the Portuguese president and there is a 23-member legislative assembly, which has a three-year term. The assembly comprises seven members appointed by the Governor; eight directly elected, and eight indirectly elected by business associations.

Macao's major industry is textile manufacturing, which accounts for 62 per cent of all exports. Most government revenue, however, comes from gambling. Port Macao is served by British, Portuguese and Dutch shipping lines and has regular services to Hong Kong, some 35 miles away.

Governor, Gen. Vasco Rocha Vieira

TRADE WITH UK	1995	1996
Imports from UK	£15,963,000	£14,097,000
Exports to UK	55,079,000	54,656,000

QATAR
Dawlat Qatar

AREA – 4,247 sq. miles (11,000 sq. km)
POPULATION – 540,000 (1994 UN estimate). Most of the population is concentrated in the urban district of Doha. Only a small minority still pursue the traditional life of the semi-nomadic tribesmen and fisherfolk
CAPITAL – ΨDoha (population, 217,294, 1986)
MAJOR CITIES – Dukhan; Khor; ΨUmm Said; Wakra
CURRENCY – Qatar riyal of 100 dirhams
NATIONAL DAY – 3 September
NATIONAL FLAG – White and maroon, white portion nearer the mast; vertical indented line comprising 17 angles divides the colours
LIFE EXPECTANCY (years) – male 68.75; female 74.20
POPULATION GROWTH RATE – 2.6 per cent (1994)
POPULATION DENSITY – 49 per sq. km (1994)
MILITARY EXPENDITURE – 4.4 per cent of GDP (1995)
MILITARY PERSONNEL – 11,800: Army 8,500, Navy 1,800, Air Force 1,500
ILLITERACY RATE – 20.6 per cent
ENROLMENT (percentage of age group) – primary 81 per cent (1993); secondary 69 per cent (1993); tertiary 27.5 per cent (1994)

The state of Qatar covers the peninsula of Qatar in the Gulf from approximately the northern shore of Khor al Odaid to the eastern shore of Khor al Salwa.

HISTORY AND POLITICS

Qatar was one of nine independent emirates in the Gulf in special treaty relations with the UK until 1971. On 2 April 1970 a provisional constitution for Qatar was proclaimed, providing for the establishment of a Council of Ministers and for the formation of a Consultative Council to assist the Council of Ministers in running the affairs of the state. There are no political parties or legislature. The Amir, who had ruled since 22 February 1972, was overthrown on 27 June 1995 by his son and heir, who assumed power as Amir the same day. A coup attempt was thwarted in February 1996.

HEAD OF STATE
HH Amir of Qatar, Minister of Defence and Commander-in-Chief of Armed Forces, Sheikh Hamad bin Khalifa Al-Thani, KCMG, *assumed power* 27 June 1995

COUNCIL OF MINISTERS *as at August 1997*
Prime Minister, Interior, HH Sheikh Abdulla bin Khalifa Al-Thani
Civil Service Affairs and Housing, HE Sheikh Falah bin Jassim Al-Thani
Communications and Transport, HE Sheikh Ahmed bin Nasser Al-Thani
Education and Culture, HE Dr Mohamed Abdulrahim Kafoud
Electricity and Water, Justice (acting), HE Ahmed Mohamed Ali Al-Subaie
Endowments and Islamic Affairs, HE Ahmed Abdulla Al-Merri
Energy and Industry, HE Abdulla bin Hamad Al-Attiyah
Finance, Economy and Trade, HE Sheikh Mohamed bin Khalifa Al-Thani
Foreign Affairs, HE Sheikh Hamad bin Jassem bin Jabr Al-Thani
Minister of State, Cabinet Affairs, HE Sheikh Mohamed bin Khalid Al-Thani
Minister of State, Foreign Affairs, HE Ahmed Abdulla Al-Mahmoud
Minister of State, Interior Affairs, Sheikh Abdullah bin Khalid Al-Thani
Ministers of State, HE Sheikh Hamad bin Suhaim Al-Thani; HE Sheikh Ahmed bin Saif Al-Thani; HE Sheikh Hamad bin Abdulla Al-Thani; HE Sheikh Hassan bin Abdullah Al-Thani
Municipal Affairs and Agriculture, HE Ali bin Saeed Al-Khayarin
Public Health, HE Dr Abdulrahman Salem Al-Kawari

EMBASSY OF THE STATE OF QATAR
1 South Audley Street, London W1Y 5DQ
Tel 0171-493 2200
Ambassador Extraordinary and Plenipotentiary, HE Ali M. Jaidah, apptd 1993

BRITISH EMBASSY
PO Box 3, Doha
Tel: Doha 421991
Ambassador Extraordinary and Plenipotentiary, HE D. Wright, OBE, apptd 1997

BRITISH COUNCIL DIRECTOR, J. Gildea, 93 Al Sadd Street, (PO Box 2992), Doha

ECONOMY

Although Qatar is a desert country, there are gardens and smallholdings near Doha and to the north, and encouragement is being given to the development of agriculture.

The Qatar General Petroleum Corporation is the state-owned company controlling Qatar's interests in oil, gas and petrochemicals. The corporation is responsible for Qatar's oil production onshore and offshore. The production level for Qatar agreed in OPEC is currently 364,000 b.p.d. The large reserves of natural gas in the North Field came into production in September 1991. A 50,000 b.p.d. oil refinery was commissioned in 1984 to increase domestic refinery capacity.

Current industries include a steel mill, a fertilizer plant, a cement factory, a petrochemical complex and two natural gas liquids plants. With the exception of the cement works at Umm Bab, all these industries are at Umm Said, about 30 miles south of Doha. Qatar is also expanding its infrastructure, including electrical generation and water distillation, roads, houses, and government buildings, although reduced demand for crude oil in international markets has led to a downturn in the economy and a slower rate of development than hitherto.

In 1994 imports totalled US$1,927 million.
GNP – US$7,448 million (1995); US$11,600 per capita (1995)
GDP – US$7,594 million (1992); US$16,497 per capita (1992)
INFLATION RATE – 4.4 per cent (1991)

TRADE WITH UK	1995	1996
Imports from UK	£146,289,000	£191,848,000
Exports to UK	14,950,000	10,502,000

COMMUNICATIONS

Regular air services provided by Gulf Air and Qatar Airways connect Qatar with the other Gulf states, the Middle East, the Indian sub-continent, Africa and Europe. The Qatar Broadcasting Service transmits on medium, shortwave, and VHF.

ROMANIA
România

AREA – 92,043 sq. miles (238,391 sq. km)
POPULATION – 22,600,000 (1997 estimate); 22,810,035 (1992 census): 89.4 per cent Romanian, 7.1 per cent Hungarian, 1.7 per cent gypsy, 0.3 per cent German, 0.3 per cent Ukrainian, 0.04 per cent Jews and others. Religious affiliation: Orthodox 86.8 per cent, Roman Catholic 5 per cent, Reformed 3.5 per cent, Greek Catholic 1 per cent. Romanian is a Romance language with many archaic forms and with admixtures of Slavonic, Turkish, Magyar and French words
CAPITAL – Bucharest (population, 2,037,278, 1996), on the Dimbovita
MAJOR CITIES – ΨBrăila (235,243); Braşov (319,908); Constanţa (346,830); Craiova (310,838); Cluj-Napoca (332,297); Iasi (346,613); Ploiesti (253,623); Timisoara (332,277)
CURRENCY – Leu (Lei) of 100 bani
NATIONAL ANTHEM – Desteapta-te, romane (Awake ye, Romanian)
NATIONAL DAY – 1 December
NATIONAL FLAG – Three vertical bands, blue, yellow, red
LIFE EXPECTANCY (years) – male 66.56; female 73.17
POPULATION GROWTH RATE – –0.5 per cent (1994)
POPULATION DENSITY – 95 per sq. km (1994)
URBAN POPULATION – 54.5 per cent (1993)

HISTORY AND POLITICS

Romania has its origin in the union of the Danubian principalities of Wallachia and Moldavia in 1859. Although under nominal Turkish suzerainty, Alexandru Ioan Cuza was elected ruler of both territories effectively unifying them. The name Romania was adopted in 1862. Full independence was proclaimed on 9 May 1877 and was formally recognized under the Treaty of Berlin (1878) which awarded part of the territory of Dobrogea to Romania and allowed the Russians to reannex Southern Bessarabia. In 1881 Romania was recognized as a kingdom.

In 1918 the populations of Bessarabia, Bukovina, Transylvania and Banat voted in favour of union with Romania, these additions being confirmed by the Versailles Treaty (1919). In 1940 the Soviet government compelled Romania to cede Bessarabia and Northern Bukovina and the Herta Land. In the same year north-western Transylvania was ceded to Hungary and southern Dobrogea to Bulgaria.

In 1947 King Michael was forced to abdicate and Romania became 'The Romanian People's Republic'. The leading political force from the Second World War until 1989 was the Romanian Communist Party. A revolution in December 1989 led to the overthrow of Nicolae Ceauşescu, president since 1965. A provisional government abolished the leading role of the Communist Party and held free elections in May 1990.

In the elections held in November 1996 the Romanian Democratic Convention (CDR) candidate, Prof. Emil Constantinescu, was elected president and three coalitions (the CDR, the Social Democratic Union (USD), and the Democratic Union of the Romanian Magyars (UDMR)) combined to form a government.

POLITICAL SYSTEM

A new constitution adopted in 1991 formally makes Romania a multiparty democracy and endorses human rights and a market economy. The parliament comprises the Chamber of Deputies with 343 seats, of which 15 are reserved for ethnic minorities other than Hungarians, and the Senate with 143 seats.

HEAD OF STATE
President of the Republic, Prof. Emil Constantinescu, *elected* 17 November 1996

GOVERNMENT *as at June 1997*
Prime Minister, Victor Ciorbea (CDR)
Minister of State, Finance, Mircea Ciumara (CDR)
Minister of State, Foreign Affairs, Adrian Severin (USD)
Minister of State, Industry and Trade, Călin Popescu-Tăriceanu (CDR)
Minister of State, Reform and Privatization, Ulm Spineanu (CDR)
Agriculture, Dinu Gavrilescu (CDR)
Communications, Sorin Pantiş (CDR)
Culture, Ion Caramitru (CDR)
Defence, Victor Babiuc (USD)
Education, Virgil Petrescu (CDR)
Health, Stefan Iosif Drăgulescu (CDR)
Interior, Gavril Dejeu (CDR)
Justice, Valeriu Stoica (CDR)
Labour and Social Protection, Alexandru Athanasiu (USD)
Public Works and Physical Planning, Nicolae Noica (CDR)
Relations with Parliament, Bogdan Niculescu Duvăz (USD)
Research and Technology, Bogdan Bujor Teodoriu (USD)
Tourism, Birtalan Akos (UDMR)
Transport, Traian Băsescu (USD)
Water, Forestry and Environmental Protection, Ioan Oltean (USD)
Youth and Sport, Marin Sorin Stănescu (CDR)

EMBASSY OF ROMANIA
Arundel House, 4 Palace Green, London W8 4QD
Tel 0171-937 9666
Ambassador Extraordinary and Plenipotentiary, HE Radu Onofrei, apptd 1997
Defence Attaché, Col. Vasile Huică
Counsellor, C. Soare (*Economic*)
Second Secretary, A. Gheorge (*Consular*)

BRITISH EMBASSY
24 Strada Jules Michelet, 70154 Bucharest
Tel: Bucharest 312 0303
Ambassador Extraordinary and Plenipotentiary, HE Christopher Crabbie, CMG, apptd 1996
Counsellor, Deputy Head of Mission, R. Publicover
Defence Attaché, Lt.-Col. R. Owen, OBE
First Secretary (Commercial), N. Sheppard

BRITISH COUNCIL DIRECTOR, H. Meixner, Calea Dorobantilor 14, Bucharest

DEFENCE

The Army has 1,255 main battle tanks, 1,882 armoured personnel carriers and armoured infantry fighting vehicles and 1,359 artillery pieces. The Navy has one submarine, one destroyer, five frigates, 77 patrol and coastal vessels, seven helicopters, 120 main battle tanks and 120 artillery pieces at six bases. The Air Force has 368 combat aircraft and 16 attack helicopters.
MILITARY EXPENDITURE – 3.1 per cent of GDP (1995)
MILITARY PERSONNEL – 195,900: Army 129,800, Navy 18,500, Air Force 47,600
CONSCRIPTION DURATION – 12–18 months

ECONOMY

Romania is among the most fertile areas in Europe. Agriculture employs 35 per cent of the workforce and contributes 20 per cent of GDP. The principal crops are cereals, vegetables, flax and hemp. Vines and fruits are also grown. The forests of the mountainous regions are extensive, and the timber industry is important.

There are plentiful supplies of natural gas, together with various mineral deposits including coal, iron ore, bauxite, lead, zinc, copper and uranium in quantities which allow a substantial part of the requirements of industry to be met from local resources. Production of crude oil was 6,712,000 tonnes in 1995.

The economy inherited from the totalitarian regime was characterized in 1990 by state-owned and co-operative ownership, excessive centralization, rigid planning and low efficiency. After the revolution the government opted for a slow pace of reform with subsidized production resulting in budget and trade deficits, high inflation and currency depreciation. In 1994, after inflation had surpassed 300 per cent annually and unemployment 10 per cent, Romania agreed to implement an IMF austerity package to gain access to loans of US$700 million.

The government elected in 1996 vowed to institute a programme of reform including the acceleration of restructuring and privatization of state-owned companies, reduction of subsidies, full liberalization of prices and monetary stability.

In 1993 the government had a budget deficit equivalent to 0.5 per cent of GDP.

GNP – US$33,488 million (1995); US$1,480 per capita (1995)

GDP – US$28,785 million (1992); US$833 per capita (1992)

ANNUAL AVERAGE GROWTH OF GDP – 4.0 per cent (1994)
INFLATION RATE – 32.2 per cent (1995)
UNEMPLOYMENT – 8.0 per cent (1995)
TOTAL EXTERNAL DEBT – US$6,653 million (1995)

TRADE

The main imports are machines and equipment, mineral fuels, textiles, clothing and leather goods, and chemicals and plastics. The main exports are textiles, clothing and leather goods, metallurgical products, equipment, minerals, agricultural and food products. Germany, Italy, Russia, France and South Korea are Romania's most important trading partners.

In 1994 Romania had a trade deficit of US$330 million and a current account deficit of US$259 million. In 1995 imports totalled US$9,424 million and exports US$7,548 million.

Trade with UK	1995	1996
Imports from UK	£176,770,000	£210,284,000
Exports to UK	173,844,000	182,024,000

COMMUNICATIONS

In 1995 there were 11,376 km of railway track, 34 per cent of which was electrified, and 72,859 km of public roads. The main national roads largely follow the railway lines and almost all lead to the capital. The principal ports are Constanta (on the Black Sea), Sulina (on the Danube Estuary), Galati, Braila, Giurgiu and Turnu Severin. The Danube and the Black Sea are linked by a canal completed in 1984.

EDUCATION

Education is free and primary and secondary education are compulsory. There are state universities in seven cities, 66 private universities, six polytechnics, two commercial academies, and five agricultural colleges.

ILLITERACY RATE – 2.1 per cent
ENROLMENT (percentage of age group) primary 94 per
cent (1994); secondary 72 per cent (1994); tertiary 12.9 per cent (1993)

RUSSIA
Rossiiskaya Federatsiya – Russian Federation

AREA – 6,592,850 sq. miles (17,075,400 sq. km). Neighbours: Norway, Finland, Estonia, Latvia, Belarus and Ukraine (west),Georgia, Azerbaijan, Kazakhstan, China, Mongolia and North Korea (south). The Kaliningrad enclave borders Lithuania and Poland

POPULATION – 147,976,400 (1997 estimate): 87.5 per cent Russian, 3.5 per cent Tatar, 2.7 per cent Ukrainian, 1.3 per cent ethnic German, 1.1 per cent Chavash, 0.9 per cent Bashkir, 0.7 per cent Belarusian and 0.7 per cent Mordovian. There are another six minorities with populations of over half a million and more than 130 nationalities in total. The Russian Orthodox Church is the predominant religion, though the Tatars are Muslims and there are Jewish communities in Moscow and St Petersburg

CAPITAL – Moscow (population, 8,745,000, 1993 estimate), founded about 1147, became the centre of the rising Moscow principality and in the 15th century the capital of the whole of Russia (Muscovy). In 1325 it became the seat of the Metropolitan of Russia. In 1703 Peter the Great transferred the capital to St Petersburg, but on 14 March 1918 Moscow was again designated as the capital

MAJOR CITIES – ΨSt Petersburg (4,799,000, 1997), from 1914 to 1924 Petrograd and from 1924 to 1991 Leningrad). Other cities: Nizhny-Novgorod/Gorky (1,438,000); Novosibirsk/Novonikolayevsk (1,436,000); Yekaterinburg/Sverdlovsk (1,367,000); Samara/Kuibyshev (1,257,000); Omsk (1,148,000); Chelyabinsk (1,143,000); Ufa (1,083,000); Perm/Molotov (1,091,000); Kazan (1,094,000); Rostov-on-Don (1,020,000), 1990

CURRENCY – Rouble of 100 kopeks
NATIONAL ANTHEM – The Patriotic Song
NATIONAL DAY – 12 June (Independence Day)
NATIONAL FLAG – Three horizontal stripes of white, blue, red
LIFE EXPECTANCY (years) – male 58.91; female 71.88
POPULATION GROWTH RATE – 0.0 per cent (1994)
POPULATION DENSITY – 9 per sq. km (1994)
URBAN POPULATION – 73.2 per cent (1993)
ILLITERACY RATE – 0.5 per cent
ENROLMENT (percentage of age group) – primary 94 per cent; tertiary 43.3 per cent (1994)

Russia occupies three-quarters of the land area of the former Soviet Union.

The Russian Federation comprises 89 members: 49 regions (*oblast*) – Amur, Archangel, Astrakhan, Belgorod, Bryansk, Chelyabinsk, Chita, Irkutsk, Ivanovo, Kaliningrad, Kaluga, Kamchatka, Kemerovo, Kirov, Kostroma, Kurgan, Kursk, Leningrad, Lipetsk, Magadan, Moscow, Murmansk, Nizhny-Novgorod, Novgorod, Novosibirsk, Omsk, Orel, Orenburg, Penza, Perm, Pskov, Rostov, Ryazan, Sakhalin, Samara, Saratov, Smolensk, Sverdlovsk, Tambov, Tomsk, Tula, Tver, Tyumen, Ulyanovsk, Vladimir, Volgograd, Vologda, Voronezh, Yaroslavl; six autonomous territories (*krai*) – Altai, Khabarovsk, Krasnodar, Krasnoyarsk, Primorye, Stavropol; 21 republics – Adygeia, Altai, Bashkortostan, Buryatia, Chechen, Chuvash, Daghestan, Ingush, Kabardino-Balkar, Kalmykia, Karachaevo-Cherkess, Karelia, Khakassia, Komi, Mari-El, Mordovia,

North Ossetia (Alania), Sakha, Tatarstan, Tyva, Udmurt; ten autonomous areas – Agin-Buryat, Chukot, Evenki, Khanty-Mansi, Komi-Permyak, Koryak, Nenets, Taimyr, Ust-Orda-Buryat, Yamal-Nenets; two cities of federal status – Moscow, St Petersburg; and one autonomous Jewish region, Birobijan.

There are three principal geographic areas: a low-lying flat western area stretching eastwards up to the Yenisei and divided in two by the Ural ridge; the eastern area between the Yenisei and the Pacific, consisting of a number of tablelands and ridges; and a southern mountainous area. Russia has a very long coastline, including the longest Arctic coastline in the world (about 17,000 miles).

The most important rivers are the Volga, the Northern Dvina and the Pechora, the Neva, the Don and the Kuban in the European part, and in the Asiatic part, the Ob, the Irtysh, the Yenisei, the Lena and the Amur, and, further north, Khatanga, Olenek, Yana, Indigirka, Kolyma and Anadyr. Lake Baikal in eastern Siberia is the deepest lake in the world.

HISTORY AND POLITICS

The Gregorian calendar was not introduced until 14 February 1918. For the events surrounding the 1917 revolutions the dates given here are the Gregorian calendar dates in use in the rest of the world at the time, with the dates in the Julian calendar (os) in parenthesis.

Russia was formally created from the principality of Muscovy and its territories by Tsar Peter I (The Great) (1682–1725), who initiated its territorial expansion, introduced western ideas of government and founded St Petersburg. By the end of Peter the Great's reign, the Baltic territories (modern-day Estonia and Latvia) had been annexed from Sweden and Russia had become the dominant military power of north-eastern Europe. In the 18th century the partitions of Poland and wars with Turkey brought the territories of modern-day Lithuania, Belarus, Ukraine and the Crimea under Russian control, and the colonization of Siberia east of the Urals began in earnest. Russia overran the Caucasus region (modern-day Armenia, Azerbaijan and Georgia) in the early 19th century, seized Finland from Sweden in 1809 and Bessarabia from Turkey in 1812. Throughout the remainder of the 19th century Russia subdued and annexed the inde-

pendent Muslim states which later formed the five Central Asian republics.

Discontent caused by autocratic rule, the poor conduct of the military in the First World War and wartime privation led to a revolution which broke out on 12 March (27 February os) 1917. Tsar Nicholas II abdicated three days later and a provisional government was formed; a republic was proclaimed on 14 September (1 September os) 1917. A power struggle ensued between the provisional government and the Bolshevik Party which controlled the Soviets (councils) set up by workers, soldiers and peasants. This led to a second revolution on 7 November (25 October os) 1917 in which the Bolsheviks, led by Lenin, seized power.

The Bolshevik (Communist) Party withdrew from the First World War under the Treaty of Brest-Litovsk (March 1918), surrendering large areas of territory. Armed resistance to Communist rule developed into an all-out civil war between 'red' Bolshevik forces and 'white' monarchist and anti-Communist forces which lasted until the end of 1922. During the civil war, Russia had been declared a Soviet Republic and other Soviet republics had been formed in Ukraine, Byelorussia and Transcaucasia. These four republics merged to form the Union of Soviet Socialist Republics (USSR) on 30 December 1922.

The Nazi-Soviet pact of August 1939 and the Second World War resulted in further territorial expansion, regaining much of the territory lost in or after 1918, as well as extending Soviet influence to the countries of eastern Europe liberated by Soviet troops. The USSR lost 26 million combatants and civilians in the war.

Joseph Stalin emerged as the undisputed party leader in 1928. He introduced a policy of rapid industrialization under a series of five-year plans, brought all sectors of industry under government control, abolished private ownership and enforced the collectivization of agriculture. He eliminated potential political opponents through purges and show trials, and total political repression lasted until his death in 1953.

Repression lessened under Khrushchev and Brezhnev, but the Communist Party remained dominant in all walks of life. This was the state of affairs when Mikhail Gorbachev became Soviet leader in March 1985. Gorbachev introduced the policies of *perestroika* (complete restructuring) and *glasnost* (openness) in order to revamp the economy, which had stagnated since the 1970s, to root out corruption and inefficiency, and to end the Cold War and its attendant arms race. The retreat from total control by the Communist Party unleashed ethnic and nationalist tensions.

On 19 August 1991 a coup was attempted by hardline elements of the Communist Party, the armed forces and the state security service (KGB) in an attempt to reimpose Communist control on the USSR. The coup was defeated by reformist and democratic political groups under the leadership of Russian President Yeltsin. Mikhail Gorbachev returned to Moscow although it became clear that effective political power was in the hands of the republican leaders, especially Russian President Yeltsin, and the Soviet Union began to break up as the constituent republics declared their independence. Gorbachev resigned as Soviet President on 25 December 1991 and on 26 December 1991 the USSR formally ceased to exist.

Russia was recognized as an independent state by the EC and USA in January 1992; it took over the Soviet Union's seat at the UN in December 1991.

A new Russian Federal Treaty was signed on 13 March 1992 between the central government and the autonomous republics. Tatarstan refused to sign the Treaty and in April 1992 declared its 'independence'. In February 1994 Tatarstan signed its own agreement with the federal government on the basis of being a 'state united with Russia'. Similarly, after declaring its 'independence' in March 1992, Bashkortostan signed a treaty with the Federation in August 1994 giving it considerable legislative and economic autonomy.

Elections to the Federal Assembly were held on 12 December 1993 and resulted in the pro-reform Russia's Democractic Choice bloc emerging as the largest party in the State Duma. The state of the parties in the State Duma following the December 1995 election was: Communist Party 157 seats; Our Home is Russia 55; Liberal Democratic Party 51; Yabloko 45; Agrarian Party 20; Russia's Democratic Choice 9; Power to the People 9; Congress of Russian Communities 5; Independents 77; others 22. The first round of voting in the presidential election on 16 June 1996 gave President Yeltsin a marginal lead over Communist Party candidate Gennadi Zyuganov. President Yeltsin offered the third-placed candidate, Gen. Aleksandr Lebed, the position of National Security Adviser and secretary of the presidential Security Council. Gen. Lebed accepted and stepped down from the presidential race, enabling President Yeltsin to win the second ballot on 3 July 1996. Lebed was dismissed in October 1996.

POLITICAL SYSTEM

The present constitution came into force on 22 December 1993. It enshrines the right to private ownership and the freedoms of press, speech, association, worship and travel, and states that Russia is a multiparty democracy. The president is head of state and of government, head of the Security Council and commander-in-chief of the armed forces and may declare war or declare a state of emergency or martial law (subject to confirmation by the Federation Council). He may chair Cabinet meetings, determine basic government policy, veto legislation, issue decrees and directives, call referendums, dismiss the government, and nominate senior judges, the prosecutor-general and the Central Bank Governor. The president nominates the prime minister and deputy prime ministers, who must be approved by the State Duma.

The president is directly elected for a maximum of two four-year terms, and may only be impeached on the grounds of treason or serious crime after rulings in both the Supreme and Constitutional Courts and two-thirds majorities in both houses of parliament. The prime minister takes over from the president in the event that he is unable to fulfil his duties.

Legislative power is vested in the Federal Assembly, comprising the Federation Council (upper house) of 178 members, two elected by each of the 89 members of the Russian Federation; the State Duma (lower house) of 450 members, of which 225 are elected by constituencies on a first-past-the-post basis and 225 by proportional representation, with a 5 per cent threshold for representation. State Duma deputies may not serve as ministers. The Council is composed of two representatives from each constituent territory of the Federation: the head of the legislative and the head of the executive body.

The State Duma, elected for four-year terms, oversees government appointments, has the power to reject the government's fiscal and monetary policies, may pass votes of no confidence in the government (which the president may ignore on the first vote), and cannot be dissolved less than one year after its election.

The judicial system consists of a Constitutional Court of 19 members appointed for a 12-year term which protects and interprets the constitution and decides if laws are compatible with it. The Supreme Court adjudicates in criminal and civil laws cases. The Arbitration Court deals with commercial disputes between companies. The new code of civil law came into force in January 1995.

INSURGENCIES

The Chechen republic declared its 'independence' in November 1991 after a nationalist coup in the republic which brought former Soviet Air Force General Dudayev to power as republican president. Chechenia refused to sign the Russian Federal Treaty in March 1992 and a constitutional stalemate ensued. Civil war began in early 1994 between Gen. Dudayev's forces and armed opposition forces of the 'Provisional Chechen Council', tacitly supported by the Russian government. On 9 December 1994 President Yeltsin ordered the Russian military to retake the republic. Chechen forces were finally forced out of Grozny in early February.

A peace accord was signed on 30 July 1995 which provided for the disarming of rebels and the withdrawal of Russian troops. The agreement collapsed in October 1995, however, and a state of emergency was declared by the Russian government. The Russian-approved candidate was elected head of state of Chechenia on 17 December 1995 and concluded an autonomy accord with Russia giving the region autonomous status within the Federation. The rebels rejected the accord and intensified their insurrection, attacking Grozny in March 1996. President Yeltsin's new National Security Adviser, Gen. Aleksandr Lebed, resumed negotiations with the rebels in August 1996, reaching an agreement to cease hostilities and to delay a decision on Chechenia's final status until 2001. The last Russian troops were withdrawn in January 1997 when presidential and legislative elections were also held in Chechenia. A treaty renouncing the use of force to resolve Chechenia's status was signed between President Maskhadov and President Yeltsin in May 1997. (*See also* Events of the Year).

In November 1992 President Yeltsin imposed direct rule in the autonomous republics of Ingush and North Ossetia after Ingush forces attacked North Ossetia; a state of emergency was declared in the two autonomous republics in March 1993; it remains in place.

FOREIGN RELATIONS

A union treaty was signed by the presidents of Russia and Belarus in April 1997. Both countries will retain sovereignty and territorial integrity although citizens of the two countries will also be citizens of the Union.

A Founding Act was signed by Russia and NATO in May 1997 which lays down the principles of post-Cold War co-operation. A joint permanent council is to be set up.

HEAD OF STATE

President, Boris Yeltsin, *elected* 12 June 1991, *re-elected* 3 July 1996, *inaugurated* 9 August 1996

GOVERNMENT *as at July 1997*

Prime Minister, Viktor Chernomyrdin

First Deputy PMs, Anatoly Chubais *(Finance)*; Boris Nemtsov *(Fuel and Power)*

Deputy PMs, Viktor Khlystun *(Agriculture and Foodstuffs)*; Alfred Kokh *(Chairman of the State Property Committee)*; Yakov Urinson *(Economics)*; Anatoly Kulikov *(Interior)*; Oleg Sysuyev *(Labour and Social Development)*; Vladimir Bulgak; Valery Serov

Atomic Energy, Viktor Mikhailov

CIS Affairs, vacant

Civil Defence, Disaster Relief, Sergei Shoigu

Culture, Yevgeny Sidorov

Defence, Igor Sergeyev

Foreign Affairs, Yevgeni Primakov

Foreign Economic Relations and Trade, Mikhail Fradkov

General and Vocational Education, Vladimir Kinelev

Justice, Sergei Stepashin

Nationalities and Federal Affairs, Vyacheslav Mikhailov

Natural Resources, Viktor Orlov

Railways, Nikolai Aksenko

Russian Federation, Head of Government Staff, Vladimir Babichev

Science and Technology, Vladimir Fortov

Transport, Nikolai Tsakh

Without Portfolio, Yevgeni Yasin

EMBASSY OF THE RUSSIAN FEDERATION

13 Kensington Palace Gardens, London w8 4QX

Tel 0171-229 3628

Ambassador Extraordinary and Plenipotentiary, HE Yuri Fokine, apptd 1997

Minister-Counsellor, G. Gventsadze

Defence Attaché, Lt.-Gen. V. N. Pronin

Trade Representative, N. B. Teliatnikov

BRITISH EMBASSY

Sofiiskaya Naberezhnaya 14, Moscow 109072

Tel: Moscow 956 7200

Ambassador Extraordinary and Plenipotentiary, HE Sir Andrew Wood, KCMG, apptd 1995

Minister and Deputy Head of Mission, A. Longrigg, CMG

Defence and Air Attaché, Air Cdre M. L. Freenan, CBE

Counsellor (Commercial), A. R. Brenton

Consuls-General: I. Kydd (Moscow); J. W. Guy, OBE (St Petersburg)

CONSULATE-GENERAL – St Petersburg

BRITISH COUNCIL DIRECTOR, T. Andrews, Biblioteka Inostrannoi Literaturi, Ulitsa Nikolo-Yamskaya 1, Moscow 109189. There are also offices at St Petersburg and Ekaterinburg

DEFENCE *(see also* CIS entry, pages 747–8)

Since the demise of the Soviet Union the Russian armed forces have been considerably reduced but remain among the most powerful in the world.

The Strategic Nuclear Forces have 34 nuclear-powered ballistic missile submarines with 540 missiles, 800 intercontinental ballistic missiles, 1,820 armoured personnel carriers, 750 helicopters, 66 long-range bomber aircraft and 100 anti-ballistic missiles.

The Army has 16,800 main battle tanks, 25,700 armoured personnel carriers and armoured infantry fighting vehicles, 18,400 artillery pieces and 2,450 helicopters. The Navy has 99 submarines, one aircraft carrier, 24 cruisers, 21 destroyers, two anti-submarine vessels, 120 frigates, 134 patrol and coastal vessels, 396 combat aircraft and 250 armed helicopters. The Air Force has 1,775 combat aircraft.

Russia maintains a joint air defence force with the five Central Asian republics, maintains joint armed forces of 11,000 personnel with Turkmenistan, and was due to establish a joint armed forces with Kazakhstan by the end of 1995. It also deploys forces in Armenia (4,300), Georgia (8,500), Moldova (6,400) and Tajikistan (12,000). Russia is the world's third largest contributor to peacekeeping operations. An agreement with Ukraine on the division on the Black Sea Fleet was signed in May 1997.

MILITARY EXPENDITURE – 3.82 per cent of GDP (1997)

MILITARY PERSONNEL – 1,444,000: Missile Forces 122,000, Army 460,000, Navy 190,000, Air Force 320,000, Paramilitaries 352,000

CONSCRIPTION DURATION – 18–24 months. Due to be ended by 2000

ECONOMY

Under the Soviet regime, an essentially agrarian economy in 1917 was transformed by the early 1960s into the second strongest industrial power in the world. However, by the early 1970s the concentration of resources on the military-industrial complex was causing the civilian economy to stagnate. This was exacerbated by the bureaucratic inefficiency of the centrally planned economic system and the poor distribution system. It was in an attempt to solve these problems that Gorbachev introduced economic restructuring (*perestroika*). Free market reforms were introduced, including the legalization of small private businesses, the reduction of state control over the economy, and denationalization and privatization. In May 1992 most state subsidies were abolished and price liberalization was introduced. The first stage of mass privatization of state industries began in October 1992 and the central distribution system was abolished with effect from 1 January 1993.

However, the abolition of central planning before a fully free market system was in place resulted in economic confusion. By the end of the first stage of mass privatization in June 1994 an estimated 35–40 per cent of enterprises had been privatized. On 27 October 1993 President Yeltsin issued a decree allowing the unrestricted buying and selling of land for the first time since 1917. The second stage of mass privatization was launched on 1 July 1994 and consists of the sale of residual government shares in most companies. By February 1996, 80 per cent of the economy had been privatized.

The restructuring of state enterprises has not been successful. In January 1992 economic 'shock therapy' was introduced to end hyperinflation and restore government reserves by liberalizing prices and restructuring firms to end their reliance on state subsidies. The policy was only partially implemented in 1992–4 due to parliamentary resistance. As a result industrial production declined (15.5 per cent in 1993), hyperinflation continued (900 per cent in 1993) and the rouble tumbled.

From 1994 to 1996, the economy began to stabilize with economic reforms judged to have become irreversible. Industrial output and GDP fell by 3 per cent and 4 per cent respectively in 1995, compared with 21 per cent and 18.6 per cent in 1994, a result of the government having finally gained control of the money supply. Agricultural production declined by more than 10 per cent in 1995, whereas arms sales grew by 62 per cent, rising to US$6,000 million from US$3,700 million in 1994.

Russia has received considerable international aid since 1993. In April 1993 a rescheduling of Russia's US$80 billion foreign debt was announced, which saved US$15 billion in repayments. A further US$39.5 billion was rescheduled in 1994–5. The G7 summit in Tokyo in April 1994 pledged aid of US$43 billion for structural reform and rouble stabilization, conditional on political and economic reforms. In 1995 the IMF provided US$6,800 million in standby credit to cover part of the budget deficit. A further three-year credit of US$10,087 million, granted in February 1996, was made conditional on the government maintaining spending limits.

Russia has some of the richest mineral deposits in the world. Coal is mined in the Kuznetsk area, in the Urals, south of Moscow, in the Donets basin and in the Pechora area in the north. Oil is produced in the northern Caucasus, between the Volga and the Urals, and in western Siberia, which also has large deposits of natural gas. Coal and gas deposits in Siberia and the far east (especially Yakutia) are currently being developed. The Ural mountains contain high-quality iron ore, manganese, copper, aluminium, gold, platinum, precious stones, salt, asbestos, pyrites, coal, oil, etc. Iron ore is also mined near Kursk, Tula, Lipetsk, in several areas in Siberia and in the Kola Peninsula. Nonferrous metals are found in the Altai, in eastern Siberia, in the northern Caucasus, in the Kuznetsk basin, in the far east and in the far north.

The vast area and the great variety in climatic conditions is reflected in the structure of agriculture. In the far north reindeer breeding, hunting and fishing are predominant. Further south, timber industry is combined with grain growing. In the southern half of the forest zone and in the adjacent forest-steppe zone, the acreage under grain crops is larger and the structure of agriculture more complex. Between the Volga and the Urals cericulture is predominant (particularly summer wheat), followed by cattle breeding. Beyond the Urals is another important grain-growing and stock-breeding area in the southern part of the western Siberian plain. The southern steppe zone is the main wheat granary of Russia, containing also large acreages under barley, maize and sunflowers. In the extreme south cotton is cultivated. Vine, tobacco and other southern crops are grown on the Black Sea shore of the Caucasus.

Moscow and St Petersburg are still the two largest industrial centres in the country, but new industrial areas have been developed in the Urals, the Kuznetsk basin, in Siberia and the far east. Most of the oil produced in the former USSR came from Russia; half the annual output comes from Tyumen Oblast in western Siberia. All industries are represented in Russia, including iron and steel and engineering.

GNP – US$331,948 million (1995); US$2,240 per capita (1995)

GDP – US$890,980 million (1992); US$827 per capita (1992)

INFLATION RATE – 197.4 per cent (1995)

UNEMPLOYMENT – 8.3 per cent (1995)

TOTAL EXTERNAL DEBT – US$120,461 million (1995)

TRADE

Russia's main trading partners are Ukraine, Germany and the USA. Trade in 1996 was worth more than US$133,000 million, 5.2 per cent more than in 1995. In 1995 imports totalled US$57,965 million and exports US$79,045 million.

Trade with UK	1995	1996
Imports from UK	£870,387,000	£1,009,250,000
Exports to UK	965,870,000	1,274,785,000

COMMUNICATIONS

The European area of Russia is well served by railways, St Petersburg and Moscow being the two main focal points of rail routes. The centre and south have a good system of north-south and east-west lines, but the eastern part (the Volga lands), traversed by trunk lines between Europe and Asia, lacks north-south routes. In Asia, there are still large areas, notably in the far north and Siberia, with few or no railways. In the northern part of European Russia, the North Pechora Railway has been completed, while in the far east a second Trans-Siberian line (the Baikal-Amur Railway) is partially in use; it follows a more northerly alignment than the earlier Trans-Siberian and terminates in the Pacific port of Sovetskaya Gavan.

The most important ports (Taganrog, Rostov and Novorossiisk) lie around the Black Sea and the Sea of Azov. The northern ports (St Petersburg, Murmansk and Archangel) are, with the exception of Murmansk, icebound during winter. Several ports have been built along the Arctic Sea route between Murmansk and Vladivostok and are in regular use every summer. The far eastern port of Vladivostok, the Pacific naval base of Russia, is kept open by icebreakers all the year round.

Inland waterways, both natural and artificial, are of great importance in the country, although some of them are icebound in winter (from two and a half months in the south to six months in the north). The great rivers of European Russia flow outwards from the centre, linking all parts of the plain with the chief ports, an immense system of navigable waterways which carried about 690 million tons of freight in 1988. They are supplemented by a system of canals which provide a through traffic between the White, Baltic, Black and Caspian Seas. The most notable are the White Sea-Baltic Canal, the Moscow-Volga Canal and the Volga-Don Canal linking the Baltic and the White Seas in the north to the Caspian Sea, the Black Sea and the Sea of Azov in the south.

CULTURE

Russian is a branch of the Slavonic family of languages and is written in the Cyrillic script.

Before the westernization of Russia under Peter the Great (1682–1725), Russian literature consisted mainly of folk ballads (*byliny*), epic songs, chronicles and works of moral theology. The 18th and 19th centuries saw the development of poetry and fiction. Poetry reached its zenith with Alexander Pushkin (1799–1837), Mikhail Lermontov (1814–41), Alexander Blok (1880–1921), the 1958 Nobel Prize laureate Boris Pasternak (1890–1960), Vladimir Mayakovsky (1893–1930) and Anna Akhmatova (1888–1966). Fiction is associated with the names of Nikolai Gogol (1809–52), Ivan Turgenev (1818–83), Fyodor Dostoevsky (1821–81), Leo Tolstoy (1828–1910), Anton Chekhov (1860–1904), Maxim Gorky (1868–1936), Ivan Bunin (1870–1953), Mikhail Bulgakov (1891–1940), Mikhail Sholokhov (1905–84) and Alexander Solzhenitsyn (b.1918).

Great names in music include Glinka (1804–57), Borodin (1833–87), Mussorgsky (1839–81), Rimsky-Korsakov (1844–1908), Rubinstein (1829–94), Tchaikovsky (1840–93), Rachmaninov (1873–1943), Skriabin (1872–1915), Prokofiev (1891–1953), Stravinsky (1882–1971), Shostakovich (1906–75) and Alfred Schnittke (b.1934).

RWANDA
Republika y'u Rwanda

AREA – 10,169 sq. miles (26,338 sq. km). Neighbours: Burundi (south), Democratic Republic of Congo (west), Uganda (north), Tanzania (east)

POPULATION – 7,750,000 (1994 UN estimate): Hutus 90 per cent, Tutsis 9 per cent, Twa (pygmy) 1 per cent. Kinyarwanda, French and English are the official languages

CAPITAL – Kigali (population, 156,000)

CURRENCY – Rwanda franc of 100 centimes

NATIONAL DAY – 1 July

NATIONAL FLAG – Three vertical bands, red, yellow and green with letter R on yellow band

LIFE EXPECTANCY (years) – male 45.10; female 47.70

POPULATION GROWTH RATE – 1.9 per cent (1994)

POPULATION DENSITY – 294 per sq. km (1994)

URBAN POPULATION – 5.4 per cent (1991)

MILITARY EXPENDITURE – 4.4 per cent of GDP (1995)

MILITARY PERSONNEL – Army 33,000

ILLITERACY RATE – 39.5 per cent

ENROLMENT (percentage of age group) – primary 71 per cent (1991); secondary 8 per cent (1991); tertiary 0.4 per cent (1985)

HISTORY AND POLITICS

The majority Hutu population rebelled against Tutsi feudal rule (under the Belgian colonial authority) in 1959–61, leading to the massacre of thousands of Tutsis. Large numbers fled into exile in Uganda. A referendum held in September 1961 showed the majority of the population were opposed to the retention of the monarchy, which was abolished in October 1961. Rwanda became an independent republic on 1 July 1962, with Gregoire Kayibanda as head of state. He was deposed in 1973 and replaced by a military government under Maj.-Gen. Juvénal Habyarimana, who established a one-party state.

Armed Tutsi exiles repeatedly attempted to invade Rwanda in the 1960s and 1970s but were defeated by the predominantly Hutu army. Continued Hutu-Tutsi conflict left thousands dead over a period of 30 years. In October 1990 Rwanda was invaded by the Rwandan Patriotic Front (RPF) of exiled Tutsis and moderate Hutus, who forced the one-party MRND (National Revolutionary Movement for Development) government to end its monopoly of power and introduce a multiparty constitution in 1991. After the government reneged on a 1992 peace agreement, the RPF advanced on Kigali and forced the government to restart negotiations, which led to the August 1993 Arusha peace accord. The accord provided for a transitional period under a broad-based government including the RPF until the 1995 elections, with UN forces in the country throughout the period.

During the transitional period, President Habyarimana, who had retained the interim presidency, died on 6 April 1994 in a plane crash widely believed to have been caused by a rocket attack by extremist sections of the Hutu army. The Hutu army and armed militia, the *interahamwe*, then carried out a preplanned act of genocide against the Tutsi minority and moderate Hutus; 500,000 people were massacred in three months. The civil war restarted and the RPF gradually re-established its control over the country, forcing the defeated government forces and two million Hutu refugees into exile, while another 1.2 million Hutus fled to the French 'safe zone' in the south-west. On 18 July 1994 the RPF declared victory and established a broad-based government of national unity in which moderate Hutus were given the presidency and premiership and the RPF took eight of the 22 seats.

Some 50,000–60,000 Hutu refugees died of disease in refugee camps in eastern Zaïre in August–September 1994. The remainder have since been prevented from returning to Rwanda by the Hutu army and militia forces. French troops withdrew from their 'safe zone' in the south-west of Rwanda in September 1994 and were replaced by RPF forces who gradually returned most refugees in the zone to their homes. UN forces (UNAMIR II) were deployed to deter revenge attacks by Tutsis on Hutus, although their mandate expired in March 1996.

In April 1995, 200,000 Hutu refugees remained in camps in the south-west controlled by armed Hutu militia members. RPF forces attacked the camps and broke the militia control in fighting which killed hundreds of people before the return of refugees was completed. In August the Zaïrean government began the forcible repatriation of some of the over one million Hutu refugees who, it felt, were destabilizing eastern Zaïre. However, after thousands had fled to the countryside rather than return to Rwanda, international pressure forced the Zaïrean government to agree to a voluntary repatriation programme organized by the UN High Commissioner for Refugees (UNHCR). In November 1994 the UN Security Council established the International Criminal Tribunal for Rwanda to prosecute those responsible for genocide and other international humanitarian law violations between 1 January and 31 December 1994. An estimated 200,000 Tutsi refugees who fled to Uganda in the 1960s and 1970s have returned to Rwanda. By December 1995, 500,000 refugees remained in Tanzania, and one million in Zaïre.

The 70-member Transitional National Assembly provided for by the Arusha agreement began operation on 12 December 1994 with the extremist Hutu MRND excluded. However, tensions between Tutsis and moderate Hutus in the government remain, with Prime Minister Twagiramungu and four other ministers being dismissed in August 1995 after criticizing the lack of power-sharing by the RPF and the security situation in the country. *See also* Democratic Republic of Congo.

HEAD OF STATE
President, Pasteur Bizimungu, *sworn in* 19 July 1994
Vice-President, Defence, Maj.-Gen. Paul Kagame

GOVERNMENT *as at August 1997*

The President
The Vice-President
Prime Minister, Pierre Celestin Rwigyema
Agriculture, Livestock, Environment and Rural Development, Dr Augustin Iyamuremye
Commerce, Industry and Co-operatives, Bonaventure Niyibizi
Communications, Charles Ntakirutinka
Cottage Industries, Mining and Tourism, Marc Rugenera
Education, Dr Joseph Karemera
Finance and Economic Planning, Jean Berchmas Birara
Foreign Affairs and International Co-operation, Dr Anastase Gasana
Gender, Family and Social Affairs, Aloysia Inyumba
Health, Dr Vincent Biruta
Information, Jean Nepomuscene Nayinzira
Interior, Communal Development and Resettlement, Shakh Abdulkarim Harelimana
Justice, Faustin Nteziryayo
Ministers of State, Jean Pierre Bizimana *(Education);* Dr Donat Kaberuka *(Finance and Economic Planning);* Beatrie Sebatware Panda *(Internal, Communal Development and Resettlement);* Gerald Zirimwabagabo *(Agriculture, Livestock, Environment and Rural Development)*
President's Office, Patrick Mazimhaka

Public Service and Labour, Joseph Nsengimana
Youth, Sports and Vocational Training, Dr Jacques Bihozagara

EMBASSY OF THE REPUBLIC OF RWANDA
Uganda House, 58-59 Trafalgar Square, London WC2N 5DX
Tel: 0171-930 2570
Ambassador Extraordinary and Plenipotentiary, Dr Zac
   Nsenga, apptd 1996

BRITISH EMBASSY
Parcelle No. 1071, Kimihurura, Kigali
Tel: Kigali 84098
Ambassador Extraordinary and Plenipotentiary, HE Kaye W.
   Oliver, OBE, apptd 1996

ECONOMY

Coffee, tea and sugar are grown. Tin, hides, bark of quinine
and extract of pyrethrum flowers are also exported.
   In 1993 imports totalled US$285 million and exports
US$56 million.
GNP – US$1,128 million (1995); US$180 per capita (1995)
GDP – US$2,394 million (1992); US$216 per capita (1992)
ANNUAL AVERAGE GROWTH OF GDP – 0.5 per cent (1992)
INFLATION RATE – 12.4 per cent (1993)
TOTAL EXTERNAL DEBT – US$1,008 million (1995)

Trade with UK	1995	1996
Imports from UK	£4,825,000	£4,170,000
Exports to UK	1,841,000	2,478,000

ST CHRISTOPHER AND NEVIS
The Federation of St Christopher and Nevis

AREA – 101 sq. miles (261 sq. km)
POPULATION – 41,000 (1994 UN estimate)
CAPITAL – ΨBasseterre (population, 14,161, 1980)
MAJOR TOWNS – ΨCharlestown (1,200), the chief town of
   Nevis
CURRENCY = East Caribbean dollar (EC$) of 100 cents
NATIONAL ANTHEM – Oh Land of Beauty
NATIONAL DAY – 19 September (Independence Day)
NATIONAL FLAG – Three diagonal bands, green, black and
   red; each colour separated by a stripe of yellow. Two
   white stars on the black band
LIFE EXPECTANCY (years) – male 65.10; female 70.08
POPULATION GROWTH RATE – –0.6 per cent (1994)
POPULATION DENSITY – 157 per sq. km (1994)
ILLITERACY RATE – 2.7 per cent

The state of St Christopher and Nevis is located at the
northern end of the eastern Caribbean. It comprises the
islands of St Christopher (St Kitts) (68 sq. miles) and Nevis
(36 sq. miles). The central area of St Christopher is forest-
clad and mountainous, rising to the 3,792 ft. Mount
Liamuiga. Nevis is separated from the southern tip of St
Christopher by a strait two miles wide and is dominated by
Nevis Peak, 3,232 ft.

HISTORY AND POLITICS

St Christopher was the first island in the British West
Indies to be colonized (1623). The Territory of St
Christopher and Nevis became a State in Association with
Britain in 1967. The State of St Christopher and Nevis
became an independent nation on 19 September 1983.
   In the July 1995 election to the National Assembly, the
Labour Party won seven seats, and the People's Action
Movement won one seat. Of the three seats reserved for
Nevis, the Concerned Citizens Movement won two seats
and the Nevis Reformation Party won one seat.

POLITICAL SYSTEM
Under the constitution, Queen Elizabeth II is head of state,
represented in the islands by the Governor-General.
There is a central government with a ministerial system,
the head of which is the prime minister of St Christopher
and Nevis, and a National Assembly located on St
Christopher. The National Assembly is composed of the
Speaker, three senators (nominated by the prime minister
and the Leader of the Opposition) and 11 elected repres-
entatives. On Nevis there is a Nevis Island Administration,
the head being styled Premier of Nevis, and a Nevis Island
Assembly of five elected and three nominated members.
Governor-General, HE Sir Cuthbert Montraville Sebastian,
   GCMG, OBE, apptd 1996

CABINET *as at August 1997*
*Prime Minister, Finance, National Security, Planning,
   Information, Foreign Affairs,* Dr Denzil Douglas
*Deputy PM, Trade and Industry, Caricom Affairs, Youth, Sports
   and Community Affairs,* Sam Condor
Agriculture, Lands and Housing, Timothy Harris
Attorney-General, Delano Bart
Communications, Works, Public Utilities and Posts, Cedric
   Liburd
Culture, Environment and Tourism, G. A. Dwyer Astaphan
Education, Labour and Social Security, Rupert Herbert
Health and Women's Affairs, Dr Earl Asim Martin

HIGH COMMISSION FOR ST CHRISTOPHER AND NEVIS
10 Kensington Court, London W8 5DL
Tel 0171-937 9522
High Commissioner for the Eastern Caribbean States, HE Aubrey
   Hart, apptd 1994

BRITISH HIGH COMMISSIONER, HE R. Thomas, CMG,
   resident at Bridgetown, Barbados

ECONOMY
The economy of the islands has been based on sugar for
over three centuries. Tourism (210,000 visitors in 1994)
and light industry, concentrating on brewing, food processing, clothing and electronics, are now being developed.
The economy of Nevis centres on small peasant farmers,
but a sea-island cotton industry is being developed for
export.
   The main exports are sugar, lobsters and electrical
equipment. Foodstuffs, energy, machinery and transport
equipment are the main imports.
   In 1993 St Christopher and Nevis had a trade deficit of
US$57 million and a current account deficit of US$21
million.
GNP – US$212 million (1995); US$5,170 per capita (1995)
GDP – US$135 million (1992); US$3,114 per capita (1992)
ANNUAL AVERAGE GROWTH OF GDP – 4.0 per cent (1993)
INFLATION RATE – 2.6 per cent (1994)
TOTAL EXTERNAL DEBT – US$56 million (1995)

Trade with UK	1995	1996
Imports from UK	£9,104,000	£9,387,000
Exports to UK	8,671,000	2,929,000

COMMUNICATIONS

Basseterre is a port of registry and has deep water harbour
facilities. Golden Rock airport, on St Kitts, can take most
large jet aircraft; Newcastle airstrip on Nevis can take
small aircraft and has night landing facilities. The sea ferry
route from Basseterre to Charlestown is 11 miles

ST LUCIA

AREA – 238 sq. miles (616 sq. km)
POPULATION – 141,000 (1994 UN estimate)
CAPITAL – ΨCastries (population, 56,000, 1989)
CURRENCY – East Caribbean dollar (EC$) of 100 cents
NATIONAL ANTHEM – Sons and Daughters of Saint Lucia
NATIONAL DAY – 22 February (Independence Day)
NATIONAL FLAG – Blue, bearing in centre a device of
   yellow over black over white triangles having a common
   base
LIFE EXPECTANCY (years) – male 68.00; female 74.80
POPULATION GROWTH RATE – 1.5 per cent (1994)
POPULATION DENSITY – 227 per sq. km (1994)

St Lucia, the second largest of the Windward group is 27
miles in length, with an extreme breadth of 14 miles. It is
mountainous, its highest point being Mt Gimie (3,145 ft)
and for the most part it is covered with forest and tropical
vegetation.

HISTORY AND POLITICS

Possession of St Lucia was fiercely disputed and it
constantly changed hands between the British and the
French. It became independent within the Commonwealth
on 22 February 1979.
   The St Lucia Labour Party defeated the ruling United
Workers' Party in a general election on 23 May 1997,
winning all but one of the seats in the House of Assembly.

POLITICAL SYSTEM

The head of state is Queen Elizabeth II, represented in the
island by a St Lucian Governor-General, and there is a
bicameral legislature. The Senate has 11 members, six
appointed by the ruling party, three by the Opposition and
two by the Governor-General. The House of Assembly,
which has a life of five years, has 17 elected members and a
Speaker, who may be elected from outside the House.

Governor-General, HE Sir George Mallet, GCMG,CBE, apptd
   1996

CABINET *as at June 1997*

Prime Minister, Finance, Planning, Development, Home Affairs,
   Kenny Anthony
*Deputy PM and Minister for Education, Human Resource
   Development, Youth and Sports,* Mario Michel
Agriculture and Fisheries, Environment, Cassius Elias
Commerce and Industry, Consumer Affairs, Walter François
Communications, Works, Transport and Public Utilities, Calixte
   George
*Community Development,Culture, Local Government and Co-
   operatives,* Damian Greaves
Foreign Affairs, International Trade, George Odlum
Health, Human Services, Family Affairs, Women, Sarah Flood
Legal Affairs, Labour, Home Affairs, Velon John
*Parliamentary Secretary in the Ministry of Aviation and
   Financial Services,* Menissa Rambally
*Parliamentary Secretary in the Ministry of Communications,
   Works, Transport and Public Utilities,* Cyprian Lansiquot
Tourism, Civil Aviation, Philip Pierre

HIGH COMMISSION FOR ST LUCIA
10 Kensington Court, London W8 5DL
Tel 0171-937 9522
High Commissioner for the Eastern Caribbean States, HE Aubrey
   Hart, apptd 1994

OFFICE OF THE BRITISH HIGH COMMISSION
Derek Walcott Square, PO Box 227, Castries
Tel: Castries 4522484
High Commissioner, HE R.Thomas, CMG, resident at
   Bridgetown, Barbados
Acting High Commissioner, M. Growcott

ECONOMY

The economy is mainly agrarian, with manufacturing
based on the processing of agricultural products. Principal
crops are bananas, coconuts, cocoa, mangoes, avocado
pears, breadfruit, spices, root crops such as cassava and
yams, and citrus fruit. Attempts are being made to diversify
the economy, in particular through greater industrialization. Tourism is also of increasing importance, with
204,000 visitors to the island in 1989.
GNP – US$532 million (1995); US$3,370 per capita (1995)
GDP – US$278 million (1992); US$2,206 per capita (1992)
ANNUAL AVERAGE GROWTH OF GDP – 6.6 per cent (1992)
INFLATION RATE – 2.7 per cent (1995)
TOTAL EXTERNAL DEBT – US$128 million (1995)

TRADE

The principal exports are bananas, coconut products
(copra, edible oils, soap), cardboard boxes, beer, and textile
manufactures. The chief imports are flour, meat, machinery, building materials, motor vehicles, cotton piece goods,
petroleum and fertilizers.
   In 1993 St Lucia had a trade deficit of US$144 million
and a current account deficit of US$42 million.

Trade with UK	1995	1996
Imports from UK	£70,076,000	£18,156,000
Exports to UK	45,993,000	52,186,000

ST VINCENT AND THE GRENADINES

AREA – 150 sq. miles (388 sq. km)
POPULATION – 111,000 (1994 UN estimate)
CAPITAL – ΨKingstown (population, 33,694)
CURRENCY – East Caribbean dollar (EC$) of 100 cents
NATIONAL ANTHEM – St Vincent, Land So Beautiful
NATIONAL DAY – 27 October (Independence Day)
NATIONAL FLAG – Three vertical bands, of blue, yellow
   and green, with three green diamonds in the shape of a
   'V' mounted on the yellow band
POPULATION GROWTH RATE – 0.9 per cent (1994)
POPULATION DENSITY – 286 per sq. km (1994)

The territory of St Vincent includes certain of the
Grenadines, a chain of small islands stretching 40 miles
across the Caribbean Sea between Grenada and St Vincent,
some of the larger of which are Bequia, Canouan, Mayreau,
Mustique, Union Island, Petit St Vincent and Prune Island.

HISTORY AND POLITICS

St Vincent was discovered by Christopher Columbus in
1498. It was granted by Charles I to the Earl of Carlisle in
1627 and after subsequent grants and a series of occupations alternately by the French and English, it was finally
restored to Britain in 1783. St Vincent achieved full
independence within the Commonwealth as St Vincent
and the Grenadines on 27 October 1979.
   The governing New Democratic Party won 12 seats and
the United Labour Party three seats at the election held in
February 1994.

POLITICAL SYSTEM

Queen Elizabeth II is head of state, represented by a Governor-General. The House of Assembly consists of 15 elected members and four Senators appointed by the government and two by the Opposition. It is presided over by a Speaker elected by the House from within or without it.

Governor-General, HE Sir David Jack, GCMG, MBE, *sworn in* 20 September 1989

CABINET *as at August 1997*

Prime Minister, Finance and Planning, Sir James Mitchell, KCMG

Deputy PM, Attorney-General, Justice, Ecclesiastical Affairs and Information, Carl Joseph

Agriculture and Labour, Allan Cruickshank

Communications and Works, Monty Roberts

Culture, Education and Women's Affairs, John Horne

Foreign Affairs and Tourism, Alpian Allen

Health and the Environment, Yvonne Francis-Gibson

Housing, Local Government, Community Development, Youth and Sports, Louis Jones

Minister of State in the PM's Office, Stephanie Browne

Parliamentary Secretaries, Stuart Nanton (*Foreign Affairs and Tourism*), Alfred Bynoe (*Housing, Local Government, Community Development, Youth and Sports*)

Trade, Industry and Consumer Affairs, Bernard Wyllie

HIGH COMMISSION FOR ST VINCENT AND THE GRENADINES
10 Kensington Court, London w8 5DL
Tel 0171-937 9522
High Commissioner for the Eastern Caribbean States, HE Aubrey Hart, apptd 1994

BRITISH HIGH COMMISSION
Granby Street (PO Box 132), Kingstown
Tel: St Vincent 457 1701/2
High Commissioner, HE Richard Thomas, CMG, resident at Bridgetown, Barbados
Acting High Commissioner, B. Robertson

ECONOMY

This is based mainly on agriculture but tourism (155,068 visitors in 1992) and manufacturing industries have been expanding. The main products are bananas, arrowroot, coconuts, cocoa, spices and various kinds of food crops. The main imports are foodstuffs (meat, rice, beverages), textiles, lumber, cement and other building materials, fertilizers, motor vehicles and fuel.

In 1993 St Vincent and the Grenadines had a trade deficit of US$60 million and a current account deficit of US$42 million. In 1994 imports totalled US$135 million and exports US$43 million.

GNP – US$253 million (1995); US$2,280 per capita (1995)
GDP – US$213 million (1992); US$1,771 per capita (1992)
ANNUAL AVERAGE GROWTH OF GDP – 1.4 per cent (1993)
INFLATION RATE – 1.9 per cent (1995)
TOTAL EXTERNAL DEBT – US$206 million (1995)

TRADE WITH UK	1995	1996
Imports from UK	£7,215,000	£7,719,000
Exports to UK	22,242,000	21,091,000

EL SALVADOR
República de El Salvador

AREA – 8,124 sq. miles (21,041 sq. km)
POPULATION – 5,641,000 (1994 UN estimate). The language is Spanish
CAPITAL – San Salvador (population, 422,570, 1992)
MAJOR CITIES – Santa Ana (417,000); San Miguel (157,838); Ψ Acajutia; Ψ La Libertad; Ψ La Unión (Cutuco)
CURRENCY – El Salvador colón (₡) of 100 centavos
NATIONAL ANTHEM – Saludemos La Patria Orgullosos (Let us proudly hail the Fatherland)
NATIONAL DAY – 15 September
NATIONAL FLAG – Three horizontal bands, sky blue, white, sky blue; coat of arms on white band
LIFE EXPECTANCY (years) – male 50.74; female 63.89
POPULATION GROWTH RATE – 2.2 per cent (1994)
POPULATION DENSITY – 268 per sq. km (1994)
URBAN POPULATION – 44.8 per cent (1989)
MILITARY EXPENDITURE – 1.8 per cent of GDP (1995)
MILITARY PERSONNEL – 28,400: Army 25,700, Navy 1,100, Air Force 1,600
CONSCRIPTION DURATION – 12 months

El Salvador extends along the Pacific coast of Central America for 160 miles. The surface of the country is very mountainous, many of the peaks being extinct volcanoes. Much of the interior has an average altitude of 2,000 feet. The climate varies from tropical to temperate. There is a wet season from May to October, and a dry season from November to April. Earthquakes are frequent, the most recent being in October 1986.

HISTORY AND POLITICS

El Salvador was conquered in 1526 by Pedro de Alvarado, and formed part of the Spanish viceroyalty of Guatemala until 1821. It is divided into 14 Departments.

Decades of military rule ended in March 1982 when a Constituent Assembly was elected. Subsequent presidential and parliamentary elections were boycotted by the FMLN (Farabundo Martí National Liberation Front) guerrilla movement. Conflict between the guerrillas and the government continued throughout the 1980s until negotiations culminated in a peace plan signed in January 1992. A cease-fire took effect on 1 February and began a nine-month transition period which ended in December 1992 when the FMLN finished its disarmament and became a political party. A 'Truth Commission', established under UN auspices to investigate human rights abuses in the 1980–91 period, reported in March 1993. The report caused a political crisis when it declared that 15 senior army commanders should be removed. The government was reluctant to do so but came under economic pressure from the USA, which withheld aid for reconstruction until the officers were dismissed on 1 July 1993.

The UN Observer Mission in El Salvador (ONUSAL) monitored the 1992–4 transition process, overseeing the final destruction of FMLN arms in August 1993 and the presidential, parliamentary and local elections held in March and April 1994. Armando Calderón Sol of the ruling right-wing ARENA party won the presidential election. ARENA won 39 of the Legislative Assembly's 84 seats and formed a government with other right-wing parties; the FMLN won 21 seats.

ARENA won marginally more seats than the FMLN in legislative elections in March 1997. A presidential election is due to be held in 1999.

HEAD OF STATE
President, Armando Calderón Sol, *assumed office* 1 June 1994
Vice-President, Minister of the Presidency, Enrique Borgo
  Bustamante

CABINET *as at August 1997*
The Vice President
Agriculture, Ricardo Quiñonez
Defence and Public Security, Gen. Jaime Guzmán Morales
Economy, Eduardo Zablah Touche
Education, Cecilia Gallardo de Cano
Finance, Manuel Hinds
Foreign Affairs, Ramón González
Interior, Mario Acosta Oertell
Justice, Dr Rubén Antonio Mejía Peña
Labour and Social Security, Eduardo Tomasino
Public Health, Dr Eduardo Interiano
Public Works, Roberto Bara

EMBASSY OF EL SALVADOR
Tennyson House, 159 Great Portland Street, London WIN
  5FD
Tel 0171-436 8282
Ambassador Extraordinary and Plenipotentiary, HE Manuel
  Gutiérrez Ruiz, apptd 1996

BRITISH EMBASSY
PO Box 1591, San Salvador
Tel: San Salvador 263 6527
Ambassador Extraordinary and Plenipotentiary, HE Ian
  Gerken, LVO, apptd 1995

ECONOMY

The principal cash crops are coffee, cotton, chemical
products, sugarcane and shrimps. However, cotton and
sugar production have decreased as a result of the civil war.
Also cultivated are maize, sesame, indigo, rice, balsam, etc.
In the lower altitudes towards the east, sisal is produced
and used in the manufacture of coffee and cereal bags. The
Salvadorean Coffee Company, sugar exports and the
banking system are being privatized.
  Existing factories make textiles, clothing, construc-
tional steel, furniture, cement and household items.
  In 1994 the government had a budget deficit equivalent
to 0.79 per cent of GDP.
GNP – US$9,057 million (1995); US$1,610 per capita
  (1995)
GDP – US$5,566 million (1992); US$1,109 per capita
  (1992)
ANNUAL AVERAGE GROWTH OF GDP – 6.1 per cent (1995)
INFLATION RATE – 10.0 per cent (1995)
UNEMPLOYMENT – 7.7 per cent (1995)
TOTAL EXTERNAL DEBT – US$2,583 million (1995)

TRADE

Chief exports are coffee, cotton, sugar, shrimps, sisal,
alsam, meat, towels, hides and skins. The chief imports are
chemicals, fertilizers, pharmaceutical goods, petroleum,
manufactured goods, industrial and electronic machinery
and equipment, vehicles and consumer goods.
  In 1995 imports totalled US$2,853 million and exports
US$998 million. In 1993 there was a trade deficit of
US$1,035 million and a current account deficit of US$118
million.

Trade with UK	1995	1996
Imports from UK	£22,737,000	£18,900,000
Exports to UK	3,419,000	5,724,000

COMMUNICATIONS

The Executive Autonomous Port Commission (CEPA)
administers the ports of Cutuco, La Unión, Acajutla, and
the railways through FENADESAL. There are 6,089 miles
(9,800 km) of paved roads. There are good roads between
Acajutla and the capital (60 miles), and between the capital
and Guatemala City. The Pan-American Highway from
the Guatemalan frontier follows this route and continues
to the Honduran frontier. The El Salvador international
airport can receive jet aircraft with daily flights to other
Central American capitals, Mexico, and five US cities.
There are 100 broadcasting stations and six television
stations. Five daily newspapers are published in San
Salvador and four in the provinces.

EDUCATION

Primary education is nominally compulsory, but the
number of schools and teachers available is too small to
enable education to be given to all children of school age.
ILLITERACY RATE – 28.5 per cent
ENROLMENT (percentage of age group) – primary 70 per
  cent (1992); secondary 15 per cent (1989); tertiary 15.4
  per cent (1993)

SAMOA
Ole Malo Tutoatasi o Samoa – Independent State of Samoa

AREA – 1,097 sq. miles (2,842 sq. km)
POPULATION – 164,000 (1994 UN estimate); 162,000
  (1989 census), the largest numbers being on Upolu
  (114,980) and Savai'i (43,150). The Samoans are a
  Polynesian people, though the population also includes
  other Pacific Islanders, Euronesians, Chinese and
  Europeans. The main languages are Samoan and
  English. The islanders are Christians of different
  denominations
CAPITAL – ΨApia (population, 36,000, 1989), on Upolu.
  Robert Louis Stevenson died and was buried at Apia in
  1894
CURRENCY – Tala (S$) of 100 sene
NATIONAL ANTHEM – The Banner of Freedom
NATIONAL DAY – 1 June (Independence Day)
NATIONAL FLAG – Red with a blue canton bearing five
  white stars of the Southern Cross
LIFE EXPECTANCY (years) – male 61.00; female 64.30
POPULATION GROWTH RATE – 0.0 per cent (1994)
POPULATION DENSITY – 58 per sq. km (1994)

Samoa consists of the islands of Savai'i, Upolu, Apolima,
Manono, Fanuatapu, Namua, Nuutele, Nuulua and Nuu-
safee. All the islands are mountainous. Upolu, the most
fertile, contains the harbours of Apia and Mulifanua, and
Savai'i the harbour of Salelologa.

HISTORY AND POLITICS

Formerly administered by New Zealand (latterly with
internal self-government), Western Samoa became fully
independent on 1 January 1962. The state was treated as a
member country of the Commonwealth until its formal
admission on 28 August 1970. A constitutional amendment came into effect on 4 July 1997 changing the state's
name to the Independent State of Samoa.
  Suffrage was made universal following a referendum
held in 1990. After elections held on 26 April 1996, the seats
in the *Fono* were: Human Rights Protection Party 26;

Samoan National Development Party 13; Independents 10.

POLITICAL SYSTEM

The 1962 constitution provides for a head of state to be elected by the 49-member legislative assembly, the *Fono*, for a five-year term. Initially two of the four Paramount chiefs jointly held the office of head of state for life. When one of the chiefs died in April 1963, Malietoa Tanumafili II became head of state for life. The head of state's functions are analogous to those of a constitutional monarch. Executive government is carried out by a Cabinet of Ministers.

HEAD OF STATE

Head of State for Life, HH Malietoa Tanumafili II, GCMG, CBE, *since* 15 April 1963
Deputy Head of State, Hon. Mataafa Faasuamaleaui Puela

CABINET *as at June 1997*

Prime Minister, Foreign Affairs, Tofilau Eti Alesana
Deputy PM, Finance, Tuilaepa Malielegaoi
Agriculture, Forestry, Fisheries and Meteorological Services, Molioo Teofilo
Education, Fiame Naomi Mataafa
Health, Misa Telefoni
Justice, Solia Papu Vaai
Labour, Polataivao Fosi
Lands, Survey and Environment, Tuala Tagaloa
Post and Telecommunications, Leafa Vitale
Public Works, Luagalau Kamu
Transport, Hans Joachim Keil
Women's Affairs, Leniu Avamagalo
Youth, Sports and Culture, Leota Lu II

SAMOA HIGH COMMISSION
Avenue Franklin D. Roosevelt 123, 1050 Brussels
Tel: Brussels 660 8454
High Commissioner, HE Tauiliili Uili Meredith, apptd 1997

BRITISH HIGH COMMISSIONER, HE Robert Alston, CMG, resident at Wellington, New Zealand
HONORARY CONSULATE   PO Box 2029, Apia

ECONOMY

Agriculture is the basis of the economy, the principal cash crops (and exports) being coconuts (copra), cocoa and bananas. Other agricultural exports include coffee, timber, tropical fruits and seeds. Efforts are being made to develop fishing on a commercial scale. Manufacturing is very small in scope and concerned largely with processing agricultural products, but is being encouraged by the government. Tourism is increasing rapidly.

In 1993 Samoa had a trade deficit of US$81 million and a current account deficit of US$39 million. In 1995 imports totalled US$95 million and exports US$9 million.
GNP – US$184 million (1995); US$1,120 per capita (1995)
ANNUAL AVERAGE GROWTH OF GDP – 0.5 per cent (1983)
INFLATION RATE – 1.0 per cent (1995)
TOTAL EXTERNAL DEBT – US$162 million (1995)

	1995	1996
TRADE WITH UK		
Imports from UK	£567,000	£1,264,000
Exports to UK	16,000	12,000

SAN MARINO
Repubblica di San Marino

AREA – 23 sq. miles (61 sq. km). Neighbour: Italy
POPULATION – 25,515 (1996). The official language is Italian and the religion is Roman Catholic
CITY – San Marino (population, 4,251, 1994), on the slope of Monte Titano
CURRENCY – San Marino and Italian currencies are in circulation
NATIONAL DAY – 3 September
NATIONAL FLAG – Two horizontal bands, white, blue (with coat of arms of the republic in centre)
LIFE EXPECTANCY (years) – male 73.16; female 79.12
POPULATION GROWTH RATE – 1.5 per cent (1994)
POPULATION DENSITY – 402 per sq. km (1994)
URBAN POPULATION – 91.4 per cent (1993)
GDP – US$476 million (1992); US$21,099 per capita (1992)
UNEMPLOYMENT – 3.9 per cent (1995)

HISTORY AND POLITICS

San Marino is a small republic in the hills near Rimini, on the Adriatic, founded, it is said, by a pious stonecutter of Dalmatia in the fourth century. The republic resisted Papal claims and those of neighbouring dukedoms during the 15th to 18th centuries, and its integrity and sovereignty is recognized and respected by Italy.

A coalition government of the Christian Democratic Party and the Socialist Party took office in March 1992, and was returned in the general election of 31 May 1993.

The principal products are wine, cereals, and fruits, and the main industries are tourism, metals, machinery, textiles and food.

POLITICAL SYSTEM

Executive power is vested in the Congress of State composed of ten ministries under the presidency of the two heads of state, who are elected at six-monthly intervals (every April and October). Legislative power is exercised by the 60-member Great and General Council which is elected for a term of five years. A Council of Twelve forms in certain cases a Supreme Court of Justice.

HEADS OF STATE
Regents, Two 'Capitani Reggenti'

CONGRESS OF STATE *as at July 1997*

Commerce and Relations with Local Councils, Ottaviano Rossi
Communications, Transport, Tourism and Sport, Augusto Casali
Education, Justice and Culture, Pier Marino Menicucci
Finance and Budget, Planning and Information, Clelio Galassi
Foreign and Political Affairs, Gabriele Gatti
Health and Social Security, Sante Canducci
Industry, Handicrafts and Economic Co-operation, Fiorenzo Stolfi
Internal Affairs, Antonio Lazzaro Volpinari
Labour and Co-operation, Claudio Podeschi
Territory, Environment and Agriculture, Luciano Ciavatta

CONSULATE-GENERAL IN LONDON
166 High Holborn, London WC1V 6TT
Tel 0171-836 7744
Consul-General, vacant

BRITISH CONSUL-GENERAL, R. J. Griffiths, OBE, resident at Florence, Italy

TRADE

Trade with UK	1995	1996
Imports from UK	£5,091,000	£8,557,000
Exports to UK	2,285,000	4,140,000

SÃO TOMÉ AND PRÍNCIPE
República Democrática de São Tomé e Príncipe

AREA – 372 sq. miles (964 sq. km)
POPULATION – 125,000 (1994 UN estimate)
CAPITAL – ΨSão Tomé (population, 43,420, 1991)
CURRENCY – Dobra of 100 centavos
NATIONAL DAY – 12 July (Independence Day)
NATIONAL FLAG – Horizontal stripes of green, yellow, green, the yellow of double width and bearing two black stars; and a red triangle in the hoist
POPULATION GROWTH RATE – 2.0 per cent (1994)
POPULATION DENSITY – 129 per sq. km (1994)
ILLITERACY RATE – 42.6 per cent

The islands of São Tomé and Príncipe are situated in the Gulf of Guinea, off the west coast of Africa.

HISTORY AND POLITICS

The islands became independent on 12 July 1975. A multi-party constitution was approved by referendum in August 1990. The Movement for the Liberation of São Tomé and Príncipe-Social Democratic Party (MLSTP-PSD), which had been the sole legal party since independence, was defeated by the opposition Democratic Convergence Party (PCD) in legislative elections held on 20 January 1991. Miguel Trovoada, an independent, was elected president on 3 March 1991. The President dismissed governments in 1992 and 1994 because of mounting criticism of economic reforms. A legislative election on 2 October 1994 was won by the MLSTP-PSD with 27 seats in the 55-seat National Assembly to the PCD's 14 seats. The MLSTP-PSD formed a government but this was dismissed on 15 August 1995 after five junior army officers launched a bloodless military coup, arrested the President and suspended parliament and the constitution. The EU threatened to suspend all aid and the officers relinquished power on 21 August after Angolan mediation. The President, government, parliament and constitution were restored and the officers were granted an amnesty.

A government of national unity incorporating opposition party members, was appointed on 5 January 1996. Prime Minister Almeida tendered his resignation on 29 March 1996, but agreed to continue until a presidential election could be held. President Trovoada was re-elected in June 1996. In September 1996 the government lost a vote of confidence in the National Assembly and a coalition government was installed.

HEAD OF STATE
President and Commander-in-Chief of the Armed Forces, Miguel Trovoada, *elected* 3 March 1991, *re-elected* July 1996, *inaugurated* 3 September 1996

COUNCIL OF MINISTERS *as at July 1997*
Prime Minister, Raul Braganca Neto
Agriculture and Fishing, Hermenegildo de Assuncao Sousa e Santos
Commerce, Cosme Afonso Rita
Defence, Joao Bexiga
Education, Albertino Sequeira Braganca
Foreign Affairs, Homero Jeronimo Salvaterra

Health, Eduardo Neto Matos
Justice, Amaro de Couto
Planning, Finance, Acacio Elba Bonfim
Social Affairs, Arlindo Afonso de Carvalho

EMBASSY OF THE DEMOCRATIC REPUBLIC OF SÃO TOMÉ AND PRÍNCIPE
Square Montgomery, 174 avenue de Tervuren, 1150 Brussels
Tel: Brussels 734 8966
Ambassador Extraordinary and Plenipotentiary, new appointment awaited

HONORARY CONSULATE
42 North Audley Street, London W1A 4PY
Tel 0171-499 1995
Honorary Consul, vacant

BRITISH CONSULATE
Residencial Avenida, Av. Da Independencia CP 257
British Ambassador, HE Roger D. Hart, resident at Luanda, Angola
Honorary Consul, J. Gomes

ECONOMY

The economy is heavily dependent on tourism and agriculture, with cacao being the main product.

In 1993 imports totalled US$22 million and exports US$5 million.
GNP – US$45 million (1995); US$350 per capita (1995)
GDP – US$57 million (1992); US$218 per capita (1992)
TOTAL EXTERNAL DEBT – US$277 million (1995)

TRADE WITH UK	1995	1996
Imports from UK	£2,297,000	£2,185,000
Exports to UK	85,000	260,000

SAUDI ARABIA
Al Mamlaka al Arabiya as-Sa'udiyya

AREA – 830,000 sq. miles (2,149,640 sq. km). Neighbours: UAE (east), Jordan, Iraq and Kuwait (north), Yemen and Oman (south)
POPULATION – 17,451,000 (1994 UN estimate); 16,929,294 (1992 census). Islam is the only permitted religion
CAPITAL – Riyadh (population, 1,800,000, 1991)
MAJOR CITIES – Jeddah (1.5 million); Buraydah; Dammam; Hofuf; Mecca; Medina; Tabuk
CURRENCY – Saudi riyal (SR) of 20 qursh or 100 halala
NATIONAL ANTHEM – Long live our beloved King
NATIONAL DAY – 23 September (proclamation and unification of the Kingdom, 1932)
NATIONAL FLAG – Green oblong, white Arabic device in centre: 'There is no God but God and Muhammad is the Prophet of God', and a white scimitar beneath the lettering
LIFE EXPECTANCY (years) – male 68.39; female 71.41
POPULATION GROWTH RATE – 4.0 per cent (1994)
POPULATION DENSITY – 8 per sq. km (1994)

Saudi Arabia comprises almost the whole of the Arabian peninsula, with the exception of Yemen, Oman, the UAE and Qatar. The Nejd ('plateau') extends over the centre of the peninsula, including the Nafud and Dahna deserts. The Hejaz ('the boundary') extends along the Red Sea coast to Asir and contains the holy towns of Mecca (Makkah) and Medina (Madinah). Asir ('inaccessible') is so named for its mountainous terrain, and, with the coastal plain of the Tihama, lies along the southern Red Sea coast from the

Hejaz to the border with Yemen. It is the only region to enjoy substantial rainfall. The east and south-east of the country are lower-lying and largely desert.

Mecca (Al-Makkah), about 60 km east of Jeddah, is the birthplace of the Prophet Muhammad, and contains the Great Mosque, within which is the Kaaba (*Ka'abah*) or sacred shrine of the Muslim religion. This is the focus of the annual Hajj ('pilgrimage'). Medina (Al-Madinah) Al Munawwarah ('The City of Light'), some 300 km north of Mecca, is celebrated as the first city to embrace Islam and as the Prophet Muhammad's burial place.

HISTORY AND POLITICS

In the 18th century Nejd was an independent state governed from Diriya, and the stronghold of the Wahhabis, a puritanical Islamic sect. It subsequently fell under Turkish rule; in 1913 Abdul Aziz Ibn Saud threw off Turkish rule and captured the Turkish province of Al Hasa. In 1920 he captured the Asir and in 1921 the Jebel Shammar territory of the Rashid family. In 1925 he completed the conquest of the Hejaz. Great Britain recognized Abdul Aziz Ibn Saud as the independent ruler, King of the Hejaz and of Nejd and its Dependencies, in 1927. The name was changed to the Kingdom of Saudi Arabia in September 1932.

INSURGENCIES

Opposition to the Al-Saud regime has been growing, fuelled by the economic downturn. Attacks on government and US military targets, including a bomb which killed 19 people at a US Air Force base in June 1996, have been blamed on Islamic militants.

POLITICAL SYSTEM

Saudi Arabia is a hereditary monarchy, ruled by the sons and grandsons of Abdul Aziz Ibn Saud, in accordance with the Sharia law of Wahhabi Islam. The line of succession passes from brother to brother according to age, although several sons of Ibn Saud renounced their right to the throne. All sons and grandsons of Ibn Saud must be consulted before a new king accedes the throne.

In 1992 King Fahd announced a new Basic Law for the system of government based on Sharia law and including rules to protect personal freedoms. The constitution is defined as the Holy Koran (*Qur'an*) and the *Sunnah* (the teachings and sayings of the Prophet Muhammad). The

King and the Council of Ministers (established in 1953) retain executive power. A consultative council (*Majlis-al-Shura*) of a chairman and 60 members appointed by the King was set up to share power with, and question, the government and to make recommendations to the King. The Majlis-al-Shura began meeting in December 1993 and debates government policy in the areas of the budget, defence, foreign and social affairs. Members of the ruling Al-Saud family are excluded from membership of the Council, which has a four-year term and takes decisions by majority vote. Cabinet ministers have terms of four years, with the possibility of a two-year extension.

In 1993 the country was reorganized into 13 provinces: Riyadh; Mecca (Makkah); Medina (Madinah); Al Qasim; Eastern; Asir; Tabuk; Hail; Northern Border; Jizan; Najran; Baha; Jouf. Each province has a governor appointed by the King and a council of prominent local citizens to advise the governor on local government, budgetary and planning issues.

The judicial system is based on Sharia law, administered by the Justice Ministry through the Sharia courts: general courts, courts of first instance, the High Sharia Court and the Appeals Court. The highest court of appeal is the Council of Ministers whose decision, signed by the King, is final and absolute.

HEAD OF STATE

Custodian of the Two Holy Mosques and HM The King of Saudi Arabia, King Fahd bin Abdul Aziz Al Saud, *born* 1921, *ascended the throne* 1 June 1982
HRH Crown Prince, Prince Abdullah bin Abdul Aziz Al Saud

COUNCIL OF MINISTERS *as at June 1997*

Prime Minister, HM The King
First Deputy Prime Minister and Commander of the National Guard, HRH The Crown Prince
Second Deputy Prime Minister, Defence and Aviation, HRH Prince Sultan bin Abdul Aziz Al Saud
Agriculture and Water, Dr Abdullah bin Abdul Aziz bin Muammar
Commerce, Osama bin Jaafar al Faqih
Communications, Dr Nasser bin Mohammed Al Salloum
Education, Mohammed bin Ahmad al-Rashid
Finance and National Economy, Dr Ibrahim bin Abdul Aziz Al Assaf
Foreign Affairs, HRH Prince Saud al-Faisal bin Abdul Aziz
Health, Osama bin Abdul-Majid Aziz Shobokshi
Higher Education, Dr Khalid al-Angari
Industry and Electricity, Dr Hashem bin Abdullah Yamani
Information, Dr Fouad bin Abdul-Salam Farisi
Interior, HRH Prince Naif bin Abdul Aziz Al Saud
Islamic Affairs, Awqafs and Guidance, Dr Abdul Mohsen Al-Turki
Justice, Dr Abdallah bin Ibrahim Al Shaikh
Labour and Social Affairs, Mousaed bin Mohammed al-Sunani
Municipal and Rural Affairs, Mohammed bin Ibrahim al-Jarallah
Petroleum and Mineral Resources, Ali bin Ibrahim al-Nouaimi
Planning, Dr Abdul Wahab al-Attar
Pilgrimage, Dr Mahmoud Safr
Post, Telegraphs and Telecommunications, Ali bin Talal al-Jehani
Public Works and Housing, HRH Prince Mit'ab bin Abdul Aziz Al Saud

ROYAL EMBASSY OF SAUDI ARABIA
30 Charles Street, London W1X 7PM
Tel 0171-917 3000
Ambassador Extraordinary and Plenipotentiary, HE Dr Ghazi Algosaibi, apptd 1992

Minister Plenipotentiary, Dr Mohammed Rajah Al-Hussainy
Defence Attaché, Brig. A. H. Al-Bassam
Cultural Attaché, A. M. Al-Nasser
Commercial Attaché, M. A. Al-Sheddi

BRITISH EMBASSY
PO Box 94351, Riyadh 11693
Tel: Riyadh 488 0077
Ambassador Extraordinary and Plenipotentiary, HE Andrew F.
   Green, CMG, apptd 1996
Counsellors, W. C. Patey *(Deputy Head of Mission and Consul-
   General)*; R. Northern, MBE *(Commercial)*
Defence and Military Attaché, Brig. W. E. Strong
First Secretary and Consul, S. Lovett
CONSULATE-GENERAL – PO Box 393, Jeddah 21411.
   Consul-General, L. E. Walker, OBE, LVO
TRADE OFFICE – Dhahran/Al Khobar, PO Box 88,
   Dhahran Airport 31932

BRITISH COUNCIL DIRECTOR, A. Lewis, Olaya Main
   Road, Al Mousa Centre, Tower B (PO Box 58012),
   Riyadh 11594. There are also offices in Jeddah,
   Dammam and Jubail

DEFENCE

The Army has 765 main battle tanks, 2,820 armoured
personnel carriers and armoured infantry fighting vehicles, 448 artillery pieces and 43 helicopters. The Navy has
eight frigates, 29 patrol and coastal vessels and 23 armed
helicopters at eight bases. The Air Force has 301 combat
aircraft and 12 armed helicopters.

Saudi Arabia is base to the Gulf Co-operational Council
Peninsula Shield Force of 7,000 troops. The USA, UK and
France station aircraft and support units in the country to
patrol the air exclusion zone in southern Iraq.
MILITARY EXPENDITURE – 10.6 per cent of GDP (1995)
MILITARY PERSONNEL – 189,500: Army 70,000, Navy
   13,500, Air Force 18,000, National Guard 77,000,
   Paramilitaries 11,000

ECONOMY

Saudi Arabia's revenue has been lower since the drop in
world oil prices from the mid-1980s onwards, and in the
1990s financial reserves have been used up to meet budget
deficits. In addition the country has had the cost of the
1990–1 Gulf War, estimated at US$60,000 million. The
1995 budget was in deficit by SR15,000 million, or 4.0 per
cent of GDP, following spending cuts of 20 per cent in 1994
and increases in local petrol and utilities prices in an
attempt to achieve a balanced budget.

Outside the manufacturing centres which have grown
up around many towns, most of the population are engaged
in agriculture. The productivity of traditional dryland
farming is supplemented by extensive irrigation, desalination and use of aquifers, so that agricultural production has
increased greatly over the past 20 years.

The principal industry is oil extraction and processing,
which produced 33 per cent of GDP in 1992. Oil was first
found in commercial quantities in 1938. About 97 per cent
of the total is extracted by Saudi Aramco, formerly the
Arabian–American Oil Company. Aramco's 66-year lease
will terminate in 1999 but the company was effectively
nationalized in 1980. Proven oil reserves of 260,110 million
barrels account for about one-quarter of the world's proven
reserves. The country is the world's largest oil exporter and
supplied 12 per cent of world demand in 1993. Recoverable
gas reserves of 181.65 trillion cubic feet, in fields associated
with crude oil and those separate from it, are beginning to
be exploited. Mineral exploitation of gold, silver, copper

and other minerals is also beginning, with gold production
of 5.1 tonnes in 1995.

The government, in a series of five-year development
plans since 1970, has actively encouraged the establishment of manufacturing industries in the country. Industries have developed in the fields of construction materials,
metal fabrication, simple machinery and electrical equipment, food and beverages, textiles, chemicals and plastics.
Investment in industrial gases, intermediate petrochemicals, light engineering and machinery is encouraged.

Eight industrial centres have been established, the
principal ones at Jubail and Yanbu, financed by the state
agency Saudi Arabian Basic Industries Corporation.
Linked by gas and oil pipelines, both have petrochemical
complexes producing ethylene and methanol; six of the
seven plants on-stream are joint ventures with American
and Japanese companies.

The state agency Petromin operates nine refineries with
a capacity of 1,800,000 b.p.d., producing petrol, fuel and
diesel oil, liquefied petroleum gas, jet fuel, kerosene and
asphalt.
GNP – US$133,540 million (1995); US$7,040 per capita
   (1995)
GDP – US$91,499 million (1992); US$5,927 per capita
   (1992)
ANNUAL AVERAGE GROWTH OF GDP – 0.5 per cent (1994)
INFLATION RATE – 4.9 per cent (1995)

TRADE

Oil remains the main source of receipts in the balance of
payments. The leading suppliers of imports are USA,
Japan, Germany, the UK, Italy and France and the chief
customers for exports are Japan, France, USA and Singapore. There is a total ban on the importation of alcohol,
pork products, firearms, and items regarded as non-Islamic
or pornographic.

In 1993 there was a trade surplus of US$19,150 million
and a current account deficit of US$14,218 million. In 1994
imports totalled US$23,338 million. Exports totalled
US$42,395 in 1993.

Trade with UK	1995	1996
Imports from UK	£1,644,356,000	£2,482,981,000
Exports to UK	£720,783,000	£752,605,000

COMMUNICATIONS

There is one railway line from Dammam on the Gulf of
Riyadh which was opened in 1951 and is operated by the
Saudi Government Railway Organization, carrying
around 400,000 passengers and 1.8 million tons of goods
per year. The line is being extended to the port of Jubail on
the Gulf. A network of 80,000 miles of roads, including an
expressway system, connects all the cities and main towns.
There are 21 ports, of which the five major ones are
Dammam and Jubail (Gulf) and Jeddah, Yanbu and Jizan
(Red Sea). The 15.5 mile-long King Fahd Causeway
completed in 1986 connects the Eastern Province to the
state of Bahrain and is the world's second longest causeway.

The government-owned Saudi Arabian Airlines (Saudia)
operate scheduled services to 22 domestic airports. There
are international airports at Dhahran (King Fahd), Jeddah
(King Abdul Aziz), and Riyadh (King Khalid). Saudia have
an extensive overseas operation, and a large number of
international airlines operate into the country.

Telecommunications are being rapidly expanded with
1.78 million telephone lines in 1995 and seven earth
stations linked to the Intelsat system, allowing direct
dialling to 185 countries.

EDUCATION

With the exception of a few schools for expatriate children, all schools are government-supervised and are segregated for boys and girls. There are universities in Jeddah, Mecca, Riyadh (branches in Abha and Qassim), Dammam (branch at Hofuf) and Dhahran, and there are Islamic universities in Medina and Riyadh together with 83 tertiary colleges. There is great emphasis on vocational training, provided at literacy and artisan skill training centres and more advanced industrial, commercial and agricultural education institutes. Education from kindergarten to university is free, with more than 22,000 schools in 1996.
ILLITERACY RATE – 37.2 per cent
ENROLMENT (percentage of age group) – primary 63 per cent; secondary 37 per cent; tertiary 13.9 per cent (1993)

SENEGAL
République du Sénégal

AREA – 75,755 sq. miles (196,722 sq. km). Neighbours: Mauritania (north), Mali (east), Guinea-Bissau and Guinea (south), the Gambia
POPULATION – 8,102,000 (1994 UN estimate)
CAPITAL – ΨDakar (population, 1,641,358, 1994)
CURRENCY – Franc CFA of 100 centimes
NATIONAL DAY – 4 April
NATIONAL FLAG – Three vertical bands, green, yellow and red; a green star on the yellow band
LIFE EXPECTANCY (years) – male 48.30; female 50.30
POPULATION GROWTH RATE – 1.9 per cent (1994)
POPULATION DENSITY – 41 per sq. km (1994)
URBAN POPULATION – 42.9 per cent (1993)
MILITARY EXPENDITURE – 1.9 per cent of GDP (1995)
MILITARY PERSONNEL – 13,350: Army 12,000, Navy 700, Air Force 650
CONSCRIPTION DURATION – Two years
ILLITERACY RATE – 66.9 per cent
ENROLMENT (percentage of age group) – primary 50 per cent (1993); tertiary 3.4 per cent (1992)

HISTORY AND POLITICS

Formerly a French colony, Senegal elected in 1958 to remain within the French Community as an autonomous republic. It became independent as part of the Federation of Mali in June 1960 and seceded to form the Republic of Senegal in September 1960. President Diouf was re-elected in the first round of presidential elections in February 1993 with 58.4 per cent of the vote. The legislative election in May 1993 was won by the ruling Parti Socialiste (PS), which secured 84 seats, with the Parti Démocratique Sénégalais (PDS) winning 27 seats, and other parties nine seats. A coalition PS-PDS government was formed in March 1995 to settle political instability.

INSURGENCIES

There is an insurgent separatist movement (Movement of Democratic Forces of Casamance (MFDC)) in the southern Casamance region. A cease-fire between the government and MFDC was signed in July 1993 but a political agreement has still to be reached and clashes continue.

FOREIGN RELATIONS

A border dispute with Mauritania was defused in early 1992 when the border was reopened and diplomatic relations restored.

POLITICAL SYSTEM

In 1963 a new constitution was approved giving executive powers to the president. There are 16 officially recognized political parties. A general election for the National Assembly of 120 seats (70 elected by proportional representation and 50 on a majority basis) is held every five years. The president announced on 31 December 1995 that a Senate would be created to serve as an upper house.

HEAD OF STATE
President, Abdou Diouf, *installed* 1981, *re-elected* 1988, 21 February 1993

GOVERNMENT *as at June 1997*
Prime Minister, Habib Thiam
Ministers of State, Moustapha Niasse (*Foreign Affairs and Expatriates*); Robert Sagna (*Agriculture*); Ousmane Dieng (*Presidential Services*); Abdoulaye Wade (*Presidency*)
Armed Forces, Cheikh Hamidou Kane
Commerce and Handicrafts, Idrissa Seck
Communications, Serigne Diop
Culture, Abdoulaye Kane
Economy, Finance and Planning, Papa Ousmane Sakho
Employment, Labour and Professional Training, Assane Diop
Energy, Mines and Industry, Magued Diouf
Environment and Conservation of Nature, Abdoulaye Bathily
Equipment and Land Transport, Landing Sané
Fisheries and Sea Transport, Alassane Dialy N'diaye
Interior, Abdourahmane Sow
Justice, Jacques Baudin
Modernization, Babacar Néné Mbaye
National Education, André Sonko
Public Health and Social Action, Ousmane Ngom
Scientific Research and Technology, Marie-Louise Corea
Tourism and Air Transport, Tidiane Sylla
Towns, Daour Cisse
Water Resources, Mamadou Faye
Women, Children and Family Welfare, Aminata Mbengue Ndiaye
Youth and Sports, Ousmane Paye

EMBASSY OF THE REPUBLIC OF SENEGAL
2nd Floor, Norway House, 21–24 Cockspur Street, London SW1Y 5BN
Tel 0171-930 7606
Ambassador Extraordinary and Plenipotentiary, HE Gabriel Alexandre Sar, apptd 1993

BRITISH EMBASSY
BP 6025, Dakar
Tel: Dakar 237392
Ambassador Extraordinary and Plenipotentiary, HE David Snoxell, apptd 1997

BRITISH COUNCIL REPRESENTATIVE, R. Budd, 34–36 Blvd. de la République, Immeuble Sonatel, BP 6232, Dakar

ECONOMY

Senegal's principal exports are groundnuts (raw and processed) and phosphates. Tourism is also of growing importance as a revenue earner.

In 1993 there was a trade deficit of US$383 million and a current account deficit of US$305 million. In 1994 imports totalled US$704 million and exports US$340 million.
GNP – US$5,070 million (1995); US$600 per capita (1995)
GDP – US$5,820 million (1992); US$812 per capita (1992)
ANNUAL AVERAGE GROWTH OF GDP – –1.5 per cent (1989)
INFLATION RATE – 7.9 per cent (1995)
TOTAL EXTERNAL DEBT – US$3,845 million (1995)

Trade with UK	1995	1996
Imports from UK	£32,217,000	£34,882,000
Exports to UK	8,485,000	13,350,000

SEYCHELLES
The Republic of Seychelles

AREA – 176 sq. miles (455 sq. km)
POPULATION – 74,000 (1994 UN estimate)
CAPITAL – ΨVictoria (population, 24,324, 1987), on Mahé
CURRENCY – Seychelles rupee of 100 cents
NATIONAL ANTHEM – Koste Seselwa (Seychellois Unite)
NATIONAL DAY – 18 June
NATIONAL FLAG – Five rays extending from the lower hoist over the whole field, coloured blue, yellow, green, white and red
LIFE EXPECTANCY (years) – male 65.26; female 74.05
POPULATION GROWTH RATE – 1.5 per cent (1994)
POPULATION DENSITY – 162 per sq. km (1994)
MILITARY EXPENDITURE – 3.9 per cent of GDP (1995)
MILITARY PERSONNEL – 1,300: Army 300, Paramilitaries 1,000
ILLITERACY RATE – 15.6 per cent

Seychelles, in the Indian Ocean, consists of 115 islands spread over 400,000 sq. miles of ocean. There is a relatively compact granitic group, 32 islands in all, with high hills and mountains (highest point about 2,972 ft), of which Mahé is the largest and most populated (90 per cent of the population live on Mahé); and the outlying coralline group, for the most part only a little above sea-level. Although only 4° S. of the Equator, the climate is pleasant though tropical.

HISTORY AND POLITICS

Proclaimed French territory in 1756, the Mahé group was settled as a dependency of Mauritius from 1770, was captured by a British ship in 1794, and changed hands several times between 1803 and 1814, when it was finally assigned to Great Britain. In 1903 these islands, together with the coralline group, were formed into a separate colony. On 29 June 1976, the islands became an independent republic within the Commonwealth. A coup d'état took place in 1977. Seychelles was a one-party state from 1979 until 1991, when a multiparty democratic system was proposed by the President.

In presidential and legislative elections held in July 1993, President René was re-elected and the Seychelles People's Progressive Front formed a government after winning 27 of the National Assembly seats, to the Democratic Party's five.

POLITICAL SYSTEM

A new constitution was adopted in a referendum in June 1993. Under the new constitution multiparty politics was institutionalized, a National Assembly of 33 members (22 elected by constituencies, 11 by proportional representation) was established and the presidential mandate was set at five years, renewable three times.

HEAD OF STATE

President, France Albert René, *assumed office* 5 June 1977; *elected* 1979; *re-elected* 1984, 1989, 27 July 1993
Vice-President, Finance, Communication and Defence, James Michel

COUNCIL OF MINISTERS *as at July 1997*

The Vice-President
Administration and Manpower, Joseph Belmont
Agriculture and Fisheries, Esmé Juneau
Community Development, Dolor Ernesta
Education and Culture, Patrick Pillay
Employment and Social Affairs, William Herminie
Environment, Planning and Foreign Affairs, vacant
Health, Jacquelin Dugasse
Industry, Ralph Adam
Local Government, Youth and Sports, Sylvette Pool
Tourism and Transport, Simone de Comarmond

SEYCHELLES HIGH COMMISSION
Box No. 4PE, 2nd Floor, Eros House, 111 Baker Street, London WIM IFE
Tel 0171-224 1660
High Commissioner, new appointment awaited

BRITISH HIGH COMMISSION
Victoria House, PO Box 161 Victoria, Mahé
Tel: Victoria 225225
High Commissioner, HE Peter Thomson, CVO, apptd 1994

ECONOMY

The economy is based on tourism, fishing, small-scale agriculture and manufacturing, and the re-export of fuel for aircraft and ships. Deep sea tuna fishing by foreign fleets under licence, improved trans-shipment and other port facilities at Victoria, exports from a tuna canning factory and the export of fresh and frozen fish, attract growing revenues. The government is attempting to reduce the reliance on tourism, which generates 70 per cent of foreign exchange earnings, by promoting the country as an offshore haven for financial services.
GNP – US$487 million (1995); US$6,620 per capita (1995)
GDP – US$395 million (1992); US$5,684 per capita (1992)
ANNUAL AVERAGE GROWTH OF GDP – 2.2 per cent (1991)
INFLATION RATE – – 0.3 per cent (1995)
TOTAL EXTERNAL DEBT – US$164 million (1995)

TRADE

The principal imports are foodstuffs, beverages, tobacco, mineral fuels, manufactured items, building materials, machinery and transport equipment.

In 1994 imports totalled US$206 million and exports US$52 million.

Trade with UK	1995	1996
Imports from UK	£19,217,000	£16,975,000
Exports to UK	9,827,000	9,249,000

SIERRA LEONE
The Republic of Sierra Leone

AREA – 27,699 sq. miles (71,740 sq. km). Neighbours: Guinea (north-west, north, north-east), Liberia (south-east)
POPULATION – 4,402,000 (1994 UN estimate). The south is inhabited by peoples whose languages fall into the Mende group; the north by the Temne and smaller groups such as the Limba, Loko, Koranko and Susu
CAPITAL – ΨFreetown (population, 469,776, 1985)
CURRENCY – Leone (Le) of 100 cents
NATIONAL ANTHEM – High We Exalt Thee, Realm of the Free
NATIONAL DAY – 27 April (Independence Day)

NATIONAL FLAG – Three horizontal stripes of leaf green, white and cobalt blue
LIFE EXPECTANCY (years) – male 37.47; female 40.58
POPULATION GROWTH RATE – 2.4 per cent (1994)
POPULATION DENSITY – 61 per sq. km (1994)
MILITARY EXPENDITURE – 5.7 per cent of GDP (1995)
MILITARY PERSONNEL – 15,000: Army 14,000, Navy 200, Paramilitaries 800

HISTORY AND POLITICS

In the late 18th century a project was begun to settle destitute Africans from England on Freetown peninsula. In 1808 the settlement was declared a Crown colony and became the main base in West Africa for enforcing the 1807 Act outlawing the slave trade. The colony was also used as a settlement for Africans from North America and the West Indies, and Africans rescued from slave ships also settled there. In 1896 a Protectorate was declared over the hinterland.

In 1951 a new constitution was set up that united the colony of Freetown and the Protectorate and on 27 April 1961 Sierra Leone became a fully independent state within the Commonwealth. In 1971 a republican constitution was adopted and Dr Siaka Stevens became the first executive president. In 1978 Sierra Leone became a one-party state, following approval by Parliament and a referendum.

In September 1991 a new multiparty constitution was adopted and an interim government formed until a general election could be held. This government was overthrown by a coup on 29 April 1992. Captain Valentine Strasser became head of state, the House of Representatives was dissolved and all political activity was suspended. A Cabinet was appointed to govern the country until promised multiparty elections. In July 1992 Strasser abolished the Cabinet and appointed a Council of State Secretaries to co-ordinate the day-to-day running of government. Capt. Strasser was ousted in a bloodless coup on 16 January 1996 by his deputy, Brig.-Gen. Julius Maada Bio. The military government finally surrendered power to a civilian government on 29 March 1996, following legislative elections on 26 – 27 February and a run-off election for the presidency on 15 March.

The Sierra Leone People's Party (SLPP) won 27 seats to the 68-member National Assembly and formed a government with the support of the People's Democratic Party and the Democratic Centre Party. The SLPP's candidate, Ahmad Tejan Kabbah, won the presidential contest, attracting 59.4 per cent of the vote.

In May 1997 army officers led by Major Johnny Koromah seized power. President Kabbah fled and a 20-member Armed Forces Revolutionary Council was set up with Koromah as chairman and Revolutionary United Front (RUF) leader Foday Sankoh as vice-chairman.

INSURGENCY

Since May 1991 government forces have been fighting the RUF whose aim is to force all foreigners out of the country and to nationalize the mining sector. Talks between the RUF and the civilian government produced an interim cease-fire on 23 April 1996, and a 'final cease-fire' in May. The civil war has claimed more than 10,000 lives and displaced more than half the population.

HEAD OF STATE

President, Johnny Paul Koromah, *seized power* 25 May 1997

SIERRA LEONE HIGH COMMISSION
33 Portland Place, London WIN 3AG
Tel 0171-636 6483/4/5/6
High Commissioner, HE Prof Cyril Foray, apptd 1996

BRITISH HIGH COMMISSION
Spur Road, Freetown
Tel: Freetown 223961
High Commissioner, HE Alan Hunt, CMG, apptd 1997

BRITISH COUNCIL DIRECTOR, P. Hilken, OBE, PO Box 124, Tower Hill, Freetown

ECONOMY

The 1996 military government cracked down on corruption, liberalized the foreign exchange system and reduced inflation from 120 per cent to 25 per cent. The government's economic and financial reform programme for 1994 – 6 has been approved by the IMF, which has provided a credit of US$163 million to support it.

On the Freetown peninsula, farming is largely confined to the production of cassava and crops such as maize and vegetables for local consumption. In the hinterland the principal agricultural product is rice, which is the staple food of the country, and cash crops such as cocoa, coffee, palm kernels and ginger.

The economy depends largely on mineral exports, mainly diamonds, gold, bauxite and rutile, the production of which has been disrupted by the insurgency. Diamond exports provided Le 1,254.5 million in 1989.

In 1994 the government had a budget deficit equivalent to 5.5 per cent of GDP. In 1995 imports totalled US$135 million and in 1994 exports US$115 million.
GNP – US$762 million (1995); US$180 per capita (1995)
GDP – US$501 million (1992); US$169 per capita (1992)
ANNUAL AVERAGE GROWTH OF GDP – –2.8 per cent (1995)
INFLATION RATE – 26.0 per cent (1995)
TOTAL EXTERNAL DEBT – US$1,226 million (1995)

TRADE WITH UK	1995	1996
Imports from UK	£26,319,000	£32,624,000
Exports to UK	4,774,000	5,709,000

COMMUNICATIONS

Since the phasing out of the railway system in 1974 the road network has been developed considerably and there are now 5,000 miles of roads in the country, over 2,000 miles being surfaced. A bridge has been constructed over the Mano River linking Sierra Leone and Liberia.

The Freetown international airport is situated at Lungi. The main port is Freetown, which has one of the largest natural harbours in the world, and where there is a deep water quay. There are smaller ports at Pepel, Bonthe and Niti.

Radio is operated by the government. Broadcasts are made in several of the indigenous languages, in addition to English and French.

EDUCATION

Technical education is provided in the two government technical institutes, situated in Freetown and Kenema, in two trade centres and in the technical training establishments of the mining companies. Teacher training is carried out at the University of Sierra Leone, six colleges in the provinces and in the Milton Margai Training College near Freetown.
ILLITERACY RATE – 68.6 per cent
ENROLMENT (percentage of age group) – tertiary 1.3 per cent (1990)

SINGAPORE

AREA – 239 sq. miles (618 sq. km)
POPULATION – 3,400,000 (1996): Chinese 77.3 per cent, Malays 14.1 per cent, Indians (including those of Pakistani, Bangladeshi and Sri Lankan origin) 7.3 per cent and 1.3 per cent from other ethnic groups. Malay, Mandarin, Tamil and English are the official languages. At least eight Chinese dialects are used. Malay is the national language and English is the language of administration. The religions are Buddhism 31.9 per cent, Taosim 21.9 per cent, Islam 14.9 per cent, Hinduism 3.3 per cent
CURRENCY – Singapore dollar (S$) of 100 cents
NATIONAL ANTHEM – Majulah Singapura
NATIONAL DAY – 9 August
NATIONAL FLAG – Horizontal bands of red over white; crescent with five five-point stars on red band near staff
LIFE EXPECTANCY (years) – male 74.02; female 78.33
POPULATION GROWTH RATE – 2.0 per cent (1994)
POPULATION DENSITY – 4,741 per sq. km (1994)
MILITARY EXPENDITURE – 5.9 per cent of GDP (1995)
MILITARY PERSONNEL – 53,900: Army 45,000, Navy 2,900, Air Force 6,000
CONSCRIPTION DURATION – 24–30 months
ILLITERACY RATE – 8.9 per cent
ENROLMENT (percentage of age group) – primary 99 per cent (1980); tertiary 35.2 per cent (1994)

Singapore consists of the island of Singapore and 59 islets. Singapore island is 26 miles long and 14 miles in breadth and is situated just north of the Equator off the southern extremity of the Malay peninsula, from which it is separated by the Straits of Johore. A causeway crosses the three-quarters of a mile to the mainland. The climate is hot and humid. Rainfall averages 240 cm a year and temperature ranges from 24° to 32° C (76°–89° F).

HISTORY AND POLITICS

Singapore, where Sir Stamford Raffles first established a trading post under the East India Company in 1819, was incorporated with Penang and Malacca to form the Straits Settlements in 1826. The Straits Settlements became a Crown colony in 1867. Singapore fell into Japanese hands in 1942 and civil government was not restored until 1946, when it became a separate colony. Internal self-government was introduced in 1959. Singapore became a state of Malaysia in September 1963, but left Malaysia and became an independent sovereign state within the Commonwealth on 9 August 1965. Singapore adopted a republican constitution from that date.

After the general election of 2 January 1997 the People's Action Party (PAP) had 81 seats in Parliament.

POLITICAL SYSTEM

There is a Cabinet collectively responsible to an 87-member (81 elected and six nominated by the president) Parliament. In November 1991 the constitution was amended to provide for a directly-elected president, elected for a six-year term, with enlarged powers and the ability to veto government decisions relating to internal security, the budget, financial reserves and the appointment of senior civil servants. The president appoints the prime minister and, on his advice, the members of the Cabinet.

HEAD OF STATE
President, Ong Teng Cheong, elected 28 August 1993, took office 2 September 1993

CABINET as at June 1997
Prime Minister, Goh Chok Tong
Senior Minister, PM's Office, Lee Kuan Yew, GCMG, CH
Deputy PM, Defence, Dr Tony Tan Keng Yam
Deputy PM, PM's Office, Brig.-Gen. Lee Hsien Loong
Communications, Mah Bow Tan
Community Development, Abdullah Tarmugi
Education, Rear-Adm. Teo Chee Hean
Finance, Dr Richard Hu Tsu Tau
Health and Environment, Yeo Cheow Tong
Home Affairs, Wong Kan Seng
Information and the Arts, Brig.-Gen. George Yong-Boon Yeo
Labour, Dr Lee Boon Yang
Law and Foreign Affairs, Prof. S. Jayakumar
National Development, Lim Hng Kiang
Trade and Industry, Lee Yock Suan
Without Portfolio, Lim Boon Heng

HIGH COMMISSION FOR THE REPUBLIC OF SINGAPORE
9 Wilton Crescent, London SW1X 8RW
Tel 0171-235 8315
High Commissioner, HE J. Y. Pillay, apptd 1996
Counsellor, Jimmy Tin Chew Chua
First Secretary, Kheng Hian Philip Ho (Commercial)

BRITISH HIGH COMMISSION
Tanglin Road, Singapore 247919
Tel: Singapore 4739333
High Commissioner, HE Alan Hunt, CMG, apptd 1997
Deputy High Commissioner and Counsellor (Economic/ Commercial), A. Gooch
Defence Adviser, Gp Capt J. M. Collier

BRITISH COUNCIL DIRECTOR, Dr J. Grote, OBE, 30 Napier Road, Singapore 1025

ECONOMY

Historically Singapore's economy was based on the sale and distribution of raw materials from surrounding countries and on entrepot trade in finished products. An industrialization programme was launched in 1968 and manufacturing industries have been established, including shipbuilding and repairing, iron and steel, transport equipment, textiles, footwear, wood products, microelectronics, televisions, computers, telecommunications equipment, office machinery, audio equipment, scientific instruments, detergents, confectionery, pharmaceuticals, petroleum products, etc. Singapore has also become an important financial services centre with significant insurance and foreign exchange markets, a stock exchange, 132 commercial banks and 75 merchant banks and an oil-refining centre. Singapore's major trading partners are the USA, Malaysia, the EU, Hong Kong and Japan.

In 1993 Singapore had a trade deficit of US$6,417 million and a current account surplus of US$2,039 million. In 1995 imports totalled US$124,507 million and exports US$118,268 million.
GNP – US$79,831 million (1995); US$26,730 per capita (1995)
GDP – US$39,520 million (1992); US$16,621 per capita (1992)
ANNUAL AVERAGE GROWTH OF GDP – 10.1 per cent (1994)
INFLATION RATE – 1.7 per cent (1995)
UNEMPLOYMENT – 2.7 per cent (1995)

Trade with UK	1995	1996
Imports from UK	£2,068,581,000	£2,144,680,000
Exports to UK	2,205,799,000	2,572,600,000

COMMUNICATIONS

Singapore is one of the largest and busiest seaports in the world, with six terminals, deep water wharves and ship repairing facilities. Ships also anchor in the roads, unloading into lighters. In 1994, the total volume of cargo handled was 290,100,000 tonnes. More than 500 shipping lines use the port, with 104,014 ship arrivals in 1995.

The international airport is at Changi, in the east of the island, with Singapore Airlines operating flights to 40 countries and 23,200,000 passengers using the airport in 1995. There are 67 km of metre gauge railway connected to the Malaysian rail system by the causeway across the Straits of Johore, and 3,027 km of roads.

There are 19 radio and four television channels operated by the Singapore Broadcasting Corporation in the four official languages, and three private broadcasting stations.

SLOVAKIA
Slovenská Republika – The Republic of Slovakia

AREA – 18,932 sq. miles (49,035 sq. km). Neighbours: Poland (north), Ukraine (east), Hungary (south), Austria (south-west), the Czech Republic (west)

POPULATION – 5,347,000 (1994 UN estimate): 85.7 per cent are ethnic Slovaks, 10.8 per cent ethnic Hungarians, 1.4 per cent gypsy, 1.1 per cent Czech, with smaller numbers of Ruthenians, Ukrainians and Germans. The population is mainly Christian, some 60 per cent Roman Catholic and 6 per cent Protestant. The main languages are Slovak, Hungarian and Czech

CAPITAL – Bratislava (population, 448,785, 1993), on the Danube

MAJOR CITIES – Košice (238,454); Žilina (86,373); Prešov (92,013); Banská Bystríca (78,321)

CURRENCY – Koruna (Kčs) of 100 haléru

NATIONAL ANTHEM – Nad Tatrou sa blýska (Storm over the Tatras)

NATIONAL DAYS – 1 January (Establishment of Slovak Republic); 5 July (Day of the Slav Missionaries); 29 August (Slovak National Uprising); 1 September (Constitution Day)

NATIONAL FLAG – Three horizontal stripes of white, blue, red with the arms all over near the hoist

LIFE EXPECTANCY (years) – male 66.64; female 75.44

POPULATION GROWTH RATE – 0.2 per cent (1994)

POPULATION DENSITY – 109 per sq. km (1994)

URBAN POPULATION – 57.1 per cent (1992)

ENROLMENT (percentage of age group) – tertiary 18.7 per cent (1994)

The Tatry (Tatras) mountains in the centre and north of Slovakia reach heights of 2,600 m (8,530 ft). The major river is the Váh which flows from the Tatry mountains to join the Danube at the Hungarian border. The climate is continental.

HISTORY AND POLITICS (*see also* Czech Republic)

At the end of the 11th century Slovakia became part of the Hungarian state when the Magyars gained control of the area. After the Hungarians were defeated at the battle of Moháč in 1526, most of Hungary (including part of Slovakia) was occupied by the Turks, with the remainder of Hungary and Slovakia being incorporated into the Austrian Empire. With the establishment of the Austro-Hungarian monarchy in 1867, Slovakia again came under Hungarian control. The attempted Magyarization of Slovakia gave impetus to the national revival which had begun in 1848–9, and when the First World War came many Slovaks fought with the allies. Amalgamated into the republic of Czechoslovakia on 28 October 1918, Slovakia became independent in March 1939 as a Nazi puppet state when Germany invaded the Czech lands. Slovakia was liberated by Soviet forces in 1945 and returned to Czechoslovakia. The formation of a federal republic between the Czech lands and Slovakia was the only Prague Spring reform to survive the Soviet invasion of 1968. Following the collapse of Communist rule at federal and republic level in 1989, nationalist feeling grew even stronger and the Czech and Slovak republics began to negotiate the dissolution of the federation into two sovereign states in 1992. Dissolution took effect on 1 January 1993.

A coalition government of the Movement for a Democratic Slovakia (HZDS) and Slovak National Party (SNS) was sworn in on 12 January 1993 but lost its majority in the National Council when the SNS left the government. Increasing criticism of the economic policy and authoritarian style of the HZDS government led ten HZDS members to form a new party which, in alliance with three other parties, brought down the government by a no-confidence vote in March 1994. The four-party coalition then formed a government which was approved by President Kováč on 16 March 1994.

Legislative elections on 30 September and 1 October 1994, however, returned the HZDS to power at the head of a three-party coalition with the Association of Slovak Workers (ZRS) and the Slovak National Party (SNS) which took office on 13 December 1994. Antagonism between President Kováč and Prime Minister Mečiar resulted in transferral of the role of Commander-in-Chief of the Armed Forces from the president to the government in June 1995.

The state of the parties in the National Council following the 1994 election was: HZDS 61; Democratic Left Party (SDL) 18; Christian Democratic Movement (KDH) 17; Hungarian Coalition 17; Democratic Union (DU) 15; ZRS 13; SNS 9.

POLITICAL SYSTEM

The constitution vests legislative power in the National Council of 150 members elected for a four-year term by proportional representation with a five per cent threshold for parliamentary representation. The president is elected for a five-year term by the National Council; executive power is held by the prime minister and Cabinet. Minority rights are enshrined in the constitution but discrimination is claimed by the ethnic Hungarian population.

Referenda on NATO membership and a directly-elected presidency were held in May 1997 but were ruled invalid due to low turnout.

HEAD OF STATE
President, Michal Kováč, *elected* 15 February 1993

GOVERNMENT *as at July 1997*

Prime Minister, Vladimír Mečiar (HZDS)
Deputy PMs, Sergej Kozlík (HZDS) *(Economy and Finance)*; Katarína Tóthová (HZDS) *(Legislature and Media)*; Jozef Kalman (ZRS) *(Social, Industrial and Trade Union Relations)*

Agriculture, Peter Baco (HZDS)
Construction and Public Works, Ján Mráz (ZRS)
Culture, Ivan Hudec (HZDS)
Defence, Ján Sitek (SNS)
Economy, Karol Česnek (Ind.)
Education and Science, Eva Slavkovská (SNS)
Environment, Jozef Zlocha (ZRS)
Foreign Affairs, Zdenka Kramplová (Ind.)
Health, Ľubomír Javorský (HZDS)
Interior, Gustáv Krajči (HZDS)
Justice, Jozef Liščák (ZRS)
Labour, Social Affairs and Family, Oľga Keltošová (HZDS)
Privatization, Peter Bisák (ZRS)
Transport, Post and Telecommunications, J. Jasovský

HZDS Movement for a Democratic Slovakia; ZRS Association of Slovak Workers; SNS Slovak National Party; Ind. Independent

EMBASSY OF THE SLOVAK REPUBLIC
25 Kensington Palace Gardens, London W8 4QY
Tel 0171-243 0803
Ambassador Extraordinary and Plenipotentiary, Igor Slobodnik, apptd 1997

BRITISH EMBASSY
Panska 16, 81101 Bratislava
Tel: Bratislava 531 9632
Ambassador Extraordinary and Plenipotentiary, HE Peter Harborne, apptd 1995

BRITISH COUNCIL DIRECTOR, S. Wallace-Shaddad, PO Box 68, Panská 17, 81499 Bratislava

DEFENCE

The Army has 478 main battle tanks, 749 armoured personnel carriers and armoured infantry fighting vehicles and 383 artillery pieces. The Air Force has 125 combat aircraft and 19 attack helicopters.
MILITARY EXPENDITURE – 2.8 per cent of GDP (1995)
MILITARY PERSONNEL – 40,570: Army 25,000, Air Force 12,220, Paramilitaries 3,350
CONSCRIPTION DURATION – 12 months

ECONOMY

From independence until mid-1994 Slovakia faced economic difficulties because of the structure of its centrally-planned and inefficiently managed economy, reliant on state-subsidized heavy industries with low productivity, and because of the ambivalent attitude to reform of the HZDS government. The HZDS faced increasing problems in 1993 as output, exports and foreign currency reserves fell and unemployment and inflation increased. In July 1993 the Slovak Crown was devalued by 10 per cent in return for an IMF loan of US$89 million. Economic reform policies, including macro-economic stabilization, price liberalization, currency convertibility and extensive privatization were continued, though at a slower rate than in the Czech Republic. Firms have been privatized by a voucher system, transfer, public auction, restoration to former owners, or transformation into joint-stock companies.

In mid-1994, however, the economic situation stabilized as the Moravčik government implemented a second round of privatization. The election of a HZDS-led government in October 1994 slowed the pace of reform. Natural resources include brown coal, natural gas, iron ore, antimony, lead, zinc and magnesite.

In 1993 Slovakia had a trade deficit of US$912 million and a current account deficit of US$580 million. In 1994

imports totalled US$6,823 million; exports totalled US$8,552 in 1995.
GNP – US$15,848 million (1995); US$2,950 per capita (1995)
GDP – US$11,315 million (1992); US$2,085 per capita (1992)
ANNUAL AVERAGE GROWTH OF GDP – 7.4 per cent (1995)
INFLATION RATE – 9.9 per cent (1995)
UNEMPLOYMENT – 13.1 per cent (1995)
TOTAL EXTERNAL DEBT – US$5,827 million (1995)

TRADE WITH UK	1995	1996
Imports from UK	£76,764,000	£103,549,000
Exports to UK	67,509,000	65,491,000

SLOVENIA
Republika Slovenija

AREA – 7,816 sq. miles (20,251 sq. km). Neighbours: Austria (north), Hungary (north-east), Croatia (east and south), Italy (west)
POPULATION – 1,942,000 (1994 UN estimate). The population is mostly Slovenian. There are small Hungarian (0.5 per cent) and Italian (0.1 per cent) minorities, together with a Romany population. About 1,075 refugees from the former Yugoslavia remain in Slovenia. The main religion is Roman Catholicism. Slovene is the official language, together with Hungarian and Italian in ethnically mixed regions
CAPITAL – Ljubljana (population, 330,000)
MAJOR CITIES – Maribor (103,113); Celje (39,782); Kranj (36,770); ΨKoper (24,495), the only port, 1994
CURRENCY – Tolar (SIT) of 100 stotin
NATIONAL ANTHEM – Zdravljica (A Toast)
NATIONAL DAY – 25 June (Statehood Day)
NATIONAL FLAG – Three horizontal stripes of white, blue, red, with the arms in the upper hoist
LIFE EXPECTANCY (years) – male 69.54; female 77.38
POPULATION GROWTH RATE – –0.7 per cent (1994)
POPULATION DENSITY – 96 per sq. km (1994)
URBAN POPULATION – 50.4 per cent (1993)
MILITARY EXPENDITURE – 1.5 per cent of GDP (1995)
MILITARY PERSONNEL – Army 9,550

Slovenia is a small mountainous state which is the most northerly of the former Yugoslav republics. The two major rivers are the Sava and the Drava. There is a short coastline in the south-west 29 miles (46 km) in length on the Adriatic. The climate is a mixture of Mediterranean, continental and alpine.

HISTORY AND POLITICS

The area that is now Slovenia came under the control of the Habsburg Empire in the 15th century and remained so until the defeat of the Austro-Hungarian Empire in 1918. On 27 October 1918 Slovenia became part of the state of Slovenes, Croats and Serbs (later Yugoslavia) and this was confirmed by the Versailles Treaty (1919). Slovenia was reduced in size, however, by the Italian annexation of the western third of the country and the Austrian annexation of parts of the north. In 1941 Yugoslavia was invaded by German forces and Slovenia was divided between Germany, Italy and Hungary. Slovenia was reformed as a constituent republic of the federal Yugoslav state in May 1945. After a dispute with Italy and nine years of international administration, the Adriatic coast and hinterland were returned to Slovenia in 1954 and Italy retained Trieste.

Slovenian fears of Serbian dominance led the Slovene Assembly in 1989 to amend the republican constitution to lay the basis of a sovereign state. The first democratic elections, held in April 1990, were won by the pro-independence 'Demos' coalition. In a referendum in December 1990, 88 per cent of the electorate voted for independence, which was declared on 25 June 1991. A ten-day war with the Yugoslav National Army followed before the Army called off hostilities and withdrew.

Legislative elections were held on 10 November 1996. Liberal Democracy of Slovenia won the most seats and formed a coalition government.

FOREIGN RELATIONS

Slovenia signed an association agreement and applied for membership of the EU in June 1996.

POLITICAL SYSTEM

Executive power is vested in the prime minister and Cabinet of Ministers. Legislative authority is held by a bicameral parliament, composed of the 90-member National Assembly (lower house) and 40-member National Council (upper house). The National Assembly is elected on a proportional representation basis, with one seat each reserved for the Italian and Hungarian minorities. The National Council has 22 elected and 18 appointed members (six by non-profit making organizations, four by employers, four by employees and four by farmers, small businessmen and independent professionals).

HEAD OF STATE

President, Milan Kučan, *elected* April 1990, *re-elected for a five-year term* 6 December 1992

CABINET *as at August 1997*

Prime Minister, Janez Drnovšek (LDS)
Deputy PM, Marjan Podobnik (SLS)
Agriculture, Food and Forestry, Ciril Smrkolj (SLS)
Co-ordination of Social Activities Bodies, Janko Kušar (DeSUS)
Culture, Jožef Školč (LDS)
Defence, Tit Turnšek (LDS)
Economic Affairs, Metad Dragonja (LDS)
Economic Relations and Development, Marjan Senjur (SLS)
Education and Sports, Slavko Gaber (LDS)
Environment, Dr Pavle Gantar (LDS)
European Affairs, Igor Bavcar (LDS)
Finance, Mitja Gaspari (LDS)
Foreign Affairs, Zoran Thaler (LDS)
Health, Marjan Jereb (SLS)
Interior, Mirko Bandelj (LDS)
Justice, Tomaž Marušič (SLS)
Labour, Family and Social Affairs, Anton Rop (LDS)
Local Government, Božo Grafenauer (SLS)
Science and Technology, Lojze Marinček (SLS)
Transport and Communications, Anton Bergauer (SLS)

LDS Liberal Democracy of Slovenia; SLS Slovene People's Party; DeSUS Democratic Party of Pensioners of Slovenia

EMBASSY OF SLOVENIA

11–15 Wigmore Street, London WIH 9LA
Tel 0171-495 7775
Ambassador Extraordinary and Plenipotentiary, new appointment awaited

BRITISH EMBASSY

4th Floor, Trg Republike 3, 61-000 Ljubljana
Tel: Ljubljana 1257191
Ambassador Extraordinary and Plenipotentiary, HE David Lloyd, OBE, apptd 1997

BRITISH COUNCIL DIRECTOR, F. King, Štefanova 1/III, 61000 Ljubljana

ECONOMY

Slovenia's economy has emerged as the most stable of the former Yugoslav economies and the least affected by the end of central planning. Although it has lost its captive export market and cheap supplies of raw materials from Serbia, Slovenia is one of the richest former Communist countries. It has successfully re-orientated its exports towards Western markets, with 65 per cent of exports going to EU states in 1996. By mid-1996, 91 per cent of companies were in the private sector.

In 1995 agriculture contributed 5 per cent to the total value of GDP, industry 34 per cent and services 61 per cent. The main agricultural products are potatoes, wheat, corn, apples, wine, meat and milk. The major manufacturing sectors are metal-working, electronics, textiles, automotive parts, chemicals, glass products and food-processing. Tourism (worth roughly US$1,000 million in 1996) and transport are major export earners, with 1,400,000 tourists visiting in 1991.

In 1994 Slovenia had a trade deficit of US$146 million and a current account surplus of US$492 million. In 1995 imports totalled US$9,452 and exports US$8,286 million.

GNP – US$16,328 million (1995); US$8,200 per capita (1995)
GDP – US$14,672 million (1992); US$8,298 per capita (1992); estimated to be US$18,580 and US$9,348 per capita in 1995
ANNUAL AVERAGE GROWTH OF GDP – 4.9 per cent (1995); forecast to be 4 per cent in 1997
INFLATION RATE – 12.6 per cent (1995)
UNEMPLOYMENT – 7.4 per cent (1995)
TOTAL EXTERNAL DEBT – US$3,489 million (1995)

TRADE WITH UK	1995	1996
Imports from UK	£122,397,000	£131,714,000
Exports to UK	113,956,000	109,111,000

COMMUNICATIONS

Important road and rail communications cross the country from west to east (Milan–Ljubljana–Budapest), and north to south (Munich–Ljubljana–Zagreb–Belgrade–Athens). There are international airports at Ljubljana, Maribor and Portoroz (Adriatic Coast). Koper is an important shipment point for goods from Austria, Hungary, the Czech Republic and Slovakia.

EDUCATION

Education is compulsory and free between the ages of seven and 14. There are 821 primary schools (age seven–14), 152 secondary or middle schools (age 14–19), 30 colleges and two universities (Ljubljana and Maribor).
ILLITERACY RATE – 0.5 per cent
ENROLMENT (percentage of age group) – primary 96 per cent; tertiary 30.1 per cent (1994)

SOLOMON ISLANDS

AREA – 11,157 sq. miles (28,896 sq. km)
POPULATION – 366,000 (1994 UN estimate); 328,723 (1991 census). English is the official language; there are over 80 local languages
CAPITAL – ΨHoniara (population, 40,000, 1991)
CURRENCY – Solomon Islands dollar (SI$) of 100 cents

NATIONAL ANTHEM – God Bless our Solomon Islands
NATIONAL DAY – 7 July (Independence Day)
NATIONAL FLAG – Blue over green divided by a diagonal
yellow band, with five white stars in the top left quarter
LIFE EXPECTANCY (years) – male 59.90; female 61.40
POPULATION GROWTH RATE – 3.4 per cent (1994)
POPULATION DENSITY – 13 per sq. km (1994)

Forming a scattered archipelago of mountainous islands
and low-lying coral atolls, the Solomon Islands stretches
about 900 miles in a south-easterly direction from the
Shortland Islands to the Santa Cruz islands. The six biggest
islands are Choiseul, New Georgia, Santa Isabel, Guadal-
canal, Malaita and Makira. They are characterized by
thickly-forested mountain ranges intersected by deep,
narrow valleys.

HISTORY AND POLITICS

The origin of the present Melanesian inhabitants is
uncertain. European interest in the islands began in the
mid-16th century and continued intermittently for about
300 years, when the inauguration of sugar plantations in
Queensland and Fiji (which created a need for labour) and
the arrival of missionaries and traders led to increased
European interest in the region. Great Britain declared a
Protectorate in 1893 over the Southern Solomons, adding
the Santa Cruz group in 1898 and 1899. The islands of the
Shortland groups were transferred from Germany to Great
Britain by treaty in 1900. The Solomon Islands achieved
internal self- government in 1976, and became indepen-
dent in July 1978.

A four-party National Coalition government led by
Francis Billy Hilly took power after winning 24 of the 47
seats in the legislative election of 26 May 1993. Hilly was,
however, forced to resign as prime minister in October
1994 after his coalition lost its parliamentary majority. On
7 November the National Parliament elected Solomon
Mamaloni as prime minister and he formed a new
government. Parliament was dissolved in June 1997 and a
caretaker government headed by Prime Minister Mamaloni was put in place until elections could be held.

POLITICAL SYSTEM

The Solomon Islands is a constitutional monarchy. Queen
Elizabeth II is represented locally by the Governor-
General. Executive authority is exercised by the Cabinet.
Legislative power is vested in a unicameral National
Parliament of 47 members, elected for a four-year term.

Governor-General, HE Sir Moses Pitakaka, GCMG, apptd
1994

CABINET *as at September 1997*

Prime Minister, Bartholomew Ulufa'alu
Deputy PM, Transport, Works and Utilities/Communications,
Sir Baddeley Devesi, GCMG, GCVO
Agriculture and Fisheries, Dr Steven Aumanu
Commerce and Tourism, Enele Kwainairara
Development Planning, Fred Fono
Education and Training, Ronnie Mannie
Finance, Mannassah Sogavare
Foreign Affairs and Trade, Patteson Oti
Forests, Environment and Conservation, Hilda Kari
Health and Medical Services, Dick Warakohia
Home Affairs, Revd Leslie Boseto
Lands and Housing, Jackson Piasi
Mines and Energy, Walton Naeson
Police and National Security, Lester Saomasi
Provincial Government, Japhet Waipora
Women, Youth and Sports, Roben Mesepitu

HIGH COMMISSION OF THE SOLOMON ISLANDS
Boulevard Saint Michel 28, Box 23, 1040 Brussels
Tel: Brussels 2732 7085
High Commissioner, HE Robert Sisilo, apptd 1996

HONORARY CONSULATE
19 Springfield Road, London SW19 7AL
Tel 0181-296 0232
Honorary Consul, Edward Nielsen, OBE

BRITISH HIGH COMMISSION
Telekon House, Mendana Avenue (PO Box 676), Honiara
Tel: Honiara 21705/6
High Commissioner, HE Brian N. Connelly, apptd 1996

ECONOMY

The main imports are foodstuffs, consumer goods, machinery and transport materials. Principal exports are
timber, fish, copra, and palm oil. Fisheries exports for 1992
totalled SI$88.1m, timber SI$110.4m and copra SI$22.7m.
Other exports include cocoa and marine shells. In 1993
imports totalled US$101 million and exports US$94
million. In 1994 exports totalled US$142 million.
GNP – US$341 million (1995); US$910 per capita (1995)
GDP – US$200 million (1992); US$606 per capita (1992)
ANNUAL AVERAGE GROWTH OF GDP – –5.1 per cent
(1987)
INFLATION RATE – 9.6 per cent (1995)
TOTAL EXTERNAL DEBT – US$158 million (1995)

Trade with UK	1995	1996
Imports from UK	£1,014,000	£2,111,000
Exports to UK	8,602,000	6,573,000

COMMUNICATIONS

Solomon Airlines operates international services to other
Pacific states and Australia. Air Niugini flies from Port
Moresby to Honiara. There are about 52 miles of secondary and minor roads in the urban areas of Honiara, Auki and
Gizo. In the rural areas there are some 800 miles of road,
including those in private plantations, forestry areas and
roads built and maintained by councils. Telekom, a
company jointly owned by Cable and Wireless and the
Solomon Islands government, operates the international
and domestic telephone circuits from a ground station in
Honiara via the Intelsat Pacific Ocean communication
satellite.

SOMALIA
Jamhuuriyadda Diimoqraadiga ee Soomaaliya

AREA – 246,201 sq. miles (637,657 sq. km). Neighbours:
Djibouti, Ethiopia and Kenya (west)
POPULATION – 9,077,000 (1994 UN estimate)
CAPITAL – ΨMogadishu (population, 1,000,000, 1987
estimate)
MAJOR CITIES – ΨBerbera (15,000); Boroma (65,000);
Burao (15,000); Hargeisa (20,000); ΨKisimayu (60,000)
CURRENCY – Somali shilling of 100 cents
NATIONAL DAY – under review
NATIONAL FLAG – Five-pointed white star on blue ground
LIFE EXPECTANCY (years) – male 45.41; female 48.60
POPULATION GROWTH RATE – 1.1 per cent (1994)
POPULATION DENSITY – 14 per sq. km (1994)
URBAN POPULATION – 23.5 per cent (1987)
ENROLMENT (percentage of age group) – primary 8 per
cent; secondary 3 per cent; tertiary 2.1 per cent (1985)

HISTORY AND POLITICS

British rule in Somaliland lasted from 1887 until 1960, except for a short period in 1940–1 when the Protectorate was occupied by Italian forces. Somalia, formerly an Italian colony, was occupied by British forces in 1941. In 1950 it was placed under Italian administration by a resolution of the UN; this trusteeship lasted until the British protectorate and the trust territory became independent as the Somali Democratic Republic on 1 July 1960. In 1969, the armed forces seized power and established a ruling Revolutionary Council under Siad Barre's leadership.

Siad Barre was overthrown by rebels in January 1991, sparking civil war between rival clan-based movements. The United Somali Congress (USC) seized control in Mogadishu and formed an interim administration under Ali Mahdi Mohammed, which was contested by the Somali Salvation Democratic Front (SSDF), the Somali Patriotic Movement (SPM) and the Somali Democratic Movement (SDM). In the north, the Somali National Movement formed a rival administration under its leader, Abourahman Ahmed Ali. Fighting between the USC and supporters of the Somali National Alliance (SNA) of Gen. Mohammed Aideed devastated Mogadishu and large parts of the south, exacerbating famine conditions. The UN Operation in Somalia (UNOSOM) proved ineffective in securing aid distribution routes and was replaced on 9 December 1992 by a UN-approved, US-led, United Task Force (UNITAF) which, having secured distribution routes, attempted to confiscate weapons, provoking retaliatory attacks from the factions.

On 4 May 1993, UNITAF handed over to a 28,000-strong UN force (UNOSOM). Clashes between the UN force, attempting to broker a settlement, and the SNA left 90 UN troops and 2,000 Somalis dead between June and November 1993. Western troops withdrew from the UN operation in March 1994, leaving UN troops from India, Pakistan and Egypt, which were easily overrun by the Somali factions.

The UN Security Council voted to withdraw its troops in March 1995, enabling Gen. Aideed's militia to take control of the city's port and airport. On 12 June 1995, Gen. Aideed was ousted as SNA leader by a joint USC-SNA congress which nominated Osman Ali Ato as its leader. Gen. Aideed responded by declaring himself president on 15 June 1995. Gen. Aideed died of gunshot wounds in July 1996 and was replaced by his son, Hussein Aideed. Fighting between the factions continued in 1996–7 despite a brief cease-fire in October 1996. Aideed and Ato met for peace negotiations in May 1997.

INSURGENCIES

Civil war broke out in May 1988 between the government and the opposition Somali National Movement (SNM) in the north of the country. With the downfall of Siad Barre, the SNM took control of the north-west (the former British Somaliland Protectorate) and in May 1991 declared unilateral independence as the 'Somaliland Republic'. A government and legislature was formed which elected Mohamed Ibrahim Egal as president in May 1993.

SOMALI DIPLOMATIC REPRESENTATION
The Embassy closed in January 1992.

BRITISH DIPLOMATIC REPRESENTATION
The British Embassy in Mogadishu closed in January 1991.

ECONOMY

Livestock raising is the main occupation and there is a modest export trade in livestock, skins and hides. Italy, the Gulf States and Saudi Arabia import the bulk of the banana crop, the second biggest export. Due to UN aid and pacification of the countryside, the harvest improved from 10 per cent of normal in 1992 to 50 per cent in 1993.

GDP – US$546 million (1992); US$36 per capita (1992)
ANNUAL AVERAGE GROWTH OF GDP – 10.1 per cent (1987)
INFLATION RATE – 81.9 per cent (1988)
TOTAL EXTERNAL DEBT – US$2,678 million (1995)

TRADE WITH UK	1995	1996
Imports from UK	£3,714,000	£4,614,000
Exports to UK	23,000	10,000

SOUTH AFRICA
Republiek van Suid-Afrika – Republic of South Africa

AREA – 471,445 sq. miles (1,221,031 sq. km). Neighbours: Namibia (north-west), Botswana and Zimbabwe (north), Mozambique and Swaziland (north-east), Lesotho, which is completely surrounded by South Africa
POPULATION – 40,436,000 (1994 UN estimate); 43,800,000 (1995 estimate): 78.9 per cent African, 11 per cent White, 7.9 per cent Coloured, 2.2 per cent Asian. The interim constitution designates 11 official languages: Afrikaans; English; Ndebele; Sesotho sa Leboa; Sesotho; Si Swati (Swazi); Tsonga; Tswana; Venda; Xhosa; Zulu. Afrikaans and English are to remain the languages of record although any citizen may correspond official business in his own language. Afrikaans is descended from old Dutch and is the language of the Afrikaner and Coloured populations
CAPITAL – The seat of the government is Pretoria (population, 525,583, 1991); the seat of the legislature is ѰCape Town (population, 854,616, 1991)
MAJOR CITIES – Johannesburg (1,609,408); ѰDurban, the largest seaport (982,075); ѰPort Elizabeth (651,993); ѰEast London (167,002); Pietermaritzburg (192,417), 1985
CURRENCY – Rand (R) of 100 cents
NATIONAL ANTHEMS – Die Stem Van Suid-Afrika (The Call of South Africa); Nkosi Sikele'i Afrika (God Bless Africa)
NATIONAL DAY – 27 April (Freedom Day)
NATIONAL FLAG – Divided red over blue by a horizontal white-fimbriated green Y; in the hoist a black triangle fimbriated in yellow
LIFE EXPECTANCY (years) – male 60.01; female 66.00
POPULATION GROWTH RATE – 2.2 per cent (1994)
POPULATION DENSITY – 33 per sq. km (1994)
URBAN POPULATION – 56.6 per cent (1991)
ILLITERACY RATE – 18.2 per cent
ENROLMENT (percentage of age group) – primary 96 per cent; secondary 52 per cent; tertiary 15.9 per cent (1994)

South Africa occupies the southernmost part of the African continent from the courses of the Limpopo, Marico, Molopo, Nosop and Orange Rivers to the Cape of Good Hope, with the exception of Lesotho, Swaziland and the extreme south of Mozambique. To the west, east and south lie the south Atlantic and southern Indian Oceans. Some 1,192 miles (1,920 km) to the south-east of Capetown lie Prince Edward and Marion Islands, part of South Africa since 1947.

The Orange, with its tributary the Vaal, is the principal river, rising in the Drakensberg and flowing into the Atlantic near the border with Namibia. The Limpopo, or

Crocodile River, in the north, rises in the Transvaal and flows into the Indian Ocean through Mozambique.

The climate is subtropical, dry and sunny moderated by the warm temperate winds from the Atlantic and Indian Oceans. Moist hot air masses from the Indian Ocean are the chief source of rainfall for most of the country.

HISTORY AND POLITICS

Hunter-gatherers, the San (Bushmen) and Khoikhoi (Hottentots) inhabited southern Africa from c.8,000 BC. Their descendants, and those of Bantu-speaking peoples who had migrated south, occupied the area when the Portuguese navigator Bartolomeu Dias charted the coast in 1488.

The colony of the Cape of Good Hope was founded by the Dutch at Cape Town in 1652 and remained a Dutch colony until Britain took possession of it in 1795. Restored to Dutch rule in 1803, it was again taken by Britain in 1806 and this was confirmed by the London Convention of 1814. A rejection of British liberalism and the desire to keep slaves led to the movement of large numbers of Boers (the descendants of Dutch settlers) north-eastwards in the years following 1834. This 'Great Trek' led to the foundation of the Orange Free State and Transvaal republics by the Boers, which were recognized by Britain in 1853–4. Natal was annexed to Cape Colony by the British in 1844 and then formed as a separate colony in 1856, to which Zululand was added in 1897 after the British victory in the Zulu wars. Transvaal and the Orange Free State (renamed the Orange River Colony) became British colonies after the Boer defeat in the Second Boer War 1899–1902. The self-governing colonies of the Cape of Good Hope, Natal, the Transvaal and the Orange River Colony became united in 1910 under the name of the Union of South Africa. Independence within the Commonwealth was gained in 1931 under the Statute of Westminster. South Africa left the Commonwealth and became a republic on 31 May 1961, largely as a result of international condemnation of apartheid and of the Sharpeville massacre.

From 1948, when the Afrikaner National Party came to power, South Africa's social and political structure was based on apartheid, a policy of racial segregation. Opposition protests culminated in the Sharpeville massacre in 1960; the African National Congress (ANC) and other opposition groups were subsequently banned. A new wave of opposition climaxed in 1976 with uprisings in Soweto, in which hundreds were shot dead. In 1984 renewed rioting in the black townships and continuing unrest led to the declaration of a state of emergency in July 1985 in 36

districts, and nationwide from 12 June 1986; it was renewed annually until 1990.

As part of its policy of apartheid, the government established a number of black 'homelands'. Six areas (Gazankulu, Lebowa, KwaNdbele, KaNgwane, Qwaqwa and KwaZulu) were designated as self-governing states. A further four (Bophuthatswana, Ciskei, Transkei and Venda) were regarded as independent republics by the South African government but never recognized as such by the UN.

MOVES TO DEMOCRACY

The first moves to reform apartheid came into effect in 1984, when a new constitution extended the franchise to the Coloured and Indian populations. Coloureds and Indians elected members to a three-house parliament, Coloured and Indian houses being added to the existing white chamber. However, whites retained effective political power and blacks remained excluded.

In 1989, F. W. de Klerk became president of South Africa and accelerated the process of reform. In 1990, the ban on the ANC and restrictions on other anti-apartheid groups were lifted; Nelson Mandela, the main ANC political detainee, was released. In 1991 the laws implementing apartheid were effectively abolished. In 1992 a referendum amongst the white electorate on continued political reform and a new constitution reached by negotiation was approved by 69 per cent to 31 per cent.

On 20 December 1991, the Convention on a Democratic South Africa (CODESA) talks between the government, ANC, Inkatha Freedom Party and other political, business and church groups, opened. CODESA reached agreement on the establishment of an inter-racial administration and the formation of a five-year coalition government following a multiracial election. On 7 September 1993, the delegates agreed to form a multiparty Transitional Executive Council (TEC), which became effective in December 1993. An interim constitution was agreed on 17 November and adopted by parliament on 22 December.

In the country's first multiracial general election held on 26–29 April 1994 the results in the National Assembly were (seats): African National Congress (ANC) 62.7 per cent (252), National Party (NP) 20.4 per cent (82), Inkatha Freedom Party (IFP) 10.5 per cent (43), Freedom Front (FF) 2.2 per cent (nine), Democratic Party (DP) 1.7 per cent (seven), Pan Africanist Congress (PAC) 1.3 per cent (five), African Christian Democratic Party 0.4 per cent (two). In the Senate the ANC gained 60 seats, the NP 17, IFP five, FF five, DP three.

The new parliament has passed two significant pieces of legislation to settle the legacy of the apartheid era. In November 1994 the Restitution of Land Rights Act was passed which established a Land Claims Commission and a Land Claims Court to restore the rights of those dispossessed of their land since the 1913 Land Act. In June 1995 the Promotion of National Unity and Reconciliation Act was passed which established a Truth Commission covering the apartheid era, with a remit to assess confessions, grant amnesties for political crimes and set compensation for victims. The first hearing opened on 15 April 1996.

POLITICAL SYSTEM

The interim constitution establishes a democratic, multiparty state, and will remain in force until 1999, when the final constitution will take effect. The final constitution, agreed by the Constituent Assembly (composed of the National Assembly and Senate) on 8 May 1996, retains the existing political structure but replaces the Senate with a National Council of Provinces, rejects the representation of minority parties in the Cabinet and incorporates a Bill of Rights.

Under the interim constitution the ten homelands have been reincorporated in South Africa. Executive power is vested in a president and Cabinet, with the president elected by parliament; two deputy presidents appointed by parties with over 20 per cent of the vote; and a Cabinet and government of national unity to last five years composed of all parties gaining over 5 per cent of the vote. Legislative power is vested in a bicameral parliament, a directly elected 400-member National Assembly elected by proportional representation, and an indirectly elected 90-member Senate composed of ten members elected by each of the nine regional legislatures.

The interim constitution also established, in February 1995, a constitutional court of 11 members to adjudicate in disputes between the three tiers of government, to interpret and certify amendments to the constitution, to ensure that all executive, legislative and judicial actions conform to the new Bill of Rights, to decide on the validity of the final constitution, and to protect all rights and freedoms.

The four former provinces (Cape Province, Natal, Orange Free State, Transvaal) have been replaced by nine new regions (Western Cape, Northern Cape, Eastern Cape, Free State, North-West, KwaZulu/Natal, Gauteng, Northern Province, Eastern Transvaal). Each region has its own Prime Minister, a legislature of between 30 and 100 seats elected by proportional representation, and its own constitution. At local government level, new multiracial municipal councils have their seats allocated on a 30 per cent white, 30 per cent non-white and 40 per cent non-racial basis.

HEAD OF STATE
President, Nelson Rolihlahla Mandela, OM, *elected by parliament* 9 May 1994, *sworn in* 10 May 1994
Executive Deputy President, Thabo Mbeki (ANC)

CABINET *as at June 1997*
Agriculture and Land Affairs, Derek Hanekom (ANC)
Arts, Culture, Science and Technology, Lionel Mtshali (IFP)
Correctional Services, Dr Sipo Mzimela (IFP)
Defence, Joe Modise (ANC)
Education, Dr Sibusiso Bengu (ANC)
Environmental Affairs and Tourism, Dr Pallo Jordan (ANC)
Finance, Trevor Manuel (ANC)
Foreign Affairs, Alfred Nzo (ANC)
Health, Dr Nkosazana Dlamini-Zuma (ANC)
Home Affairs, Dr Mangosuthu Buthelezi (IFP)
Housing, Sankie Mthembi-Mahanyele (ANC)
Justice and Intelligence Services, Dullah Omar (ANC)
Labour, Tito Mboweni (ANC)
Mineral and Energy Affairs, Penuell Maduna (ANC)
Post, Telecommunications and Broadcasting, Jay Naidoo (ANC)
Provincial Affairs and Constitutional Development, Valli Moosa (ANC)
Public Enterprises, Stella Sigcau (ANC)
Public Services and Administration, Dr Zola Skweyiya (ANC)
Public Works, Jeff Radebe (ANC)
Safety and Security, Sidney Mufamadi (ANC)
Sport and Recreation, Steve Tshwete (ANC)
Trade and Industry, Alec Erwin (ANC)
Transport, Mac Maharaj (ANC)
Water and Forestry, Prof. Kader Asmal (ANC)
Welfare and Population Development, Geraldine Fraser-Moleketi (ANC)

HIGH COMMISSION FOR THE REPUBLIC OF SOUTH AFRICA
South Africa House, Trafalgar Square, London WC2N 5DP
Tel 0171-451 7299
High Commissioner, HE Mendi Msimang, apptd 1995
Deputy High Commissioner, H. Mahlangu
Minister (Economic), S. Pretorius
Counsellors, B. C. Bam; D. Seals; S. van Heerden; L. Hanekom (*Consul-General*)
Defence and Naval Adviser, Cdre J. Vorster

BRITISH HIGH COMMISSION
255 Hill Street, Pretoria 0002
Tel: Pretoria 433121
91 Parliament Street, Cape Town 8001
Tel: Cape Town 4617220
High Commissioner, HE Maeve Fort, CMG, apptd 1996
Counsellor, Deputy High Commissioner, M. J. Lyall-Grant
Counsellor (Political), D. Woods
Defence and Military Adviser, Brig. M. Wildman
Consul-General and Director of Trade Promotion (Johannesburg), P. Longworth
CONSULATE-GENERAL – Johannesburg
CONSULATES – Cape Town and Durban
HONORARY CONSULS – Port Elizabeth, East London

Cultural Attaché and British Council Representative, L. Phillips, OBE, 76 Juta Street, (PO Box 30637), Braamfontein 2017, Johannesburg. There is also an office in Cape Town.

DEFENCE

The armed forces are engaged in the formation of a new South African National Defence Force (SANDF) from the merger of the South African Defence Forces (SADF), the Umkhonto we Sizwe (MK) armed wing of the ANC, the Azanian People's Liberation Army (APLA) of the PAC, and the defence forces of the four former independent homelands. White conscription is being phased out and the SANDF will be a fully professional force.

The Army has 50 main battle tanks, 3,160 armoured personnel carriers and armoured infantry fighting vehicles and 370 artillery pieces. The Navy has three submarines and 12 patrol and coastal vessels at two bases. The Air Force has 234 combat aircraft and 14 armed helicopters.
MILITARY EXPENDITURE – 2.9 per cent of GDP (1995)
MILITARY PERSONNEL – 131,900: Army 118,000, Navy 5,500, Air Force 8,400
CONSCRIPTION DURATION – Voluntary service of two to six years followed by service in the Part-Time Force (PTF)

ECONOMY

Mining is of great importance, producing 9 per cent of GDP in 1995. It is the largest source of foreign exchange. The principal minerals produced are gold, coal, diamonds, copper, iron ore, manganese, lime and limestone, uranium, platinum, fluorspar, andalusite, zinc, zirconium, vanadium, titanium, nickel, lead and chrome ore. South Africa is the world's largest producer of gold, platinum, diamonds, chrome ore, manganese and vanadium, and has the world's largest reserves of chrome ore, manganese, vanadium and andalusite.

Agriculture, forestry and fishing accounted for 4.5 per cent of GDP in 1995. Over 50 per cent of land is pasture so livestock farming is widespread and meat and wool important products. Principal crops are maize, sugarcane, fruits and vegetables, wheat, sorghum, sunflower seeds and groundnuts. Cotton is widely grown because of its suitability to the climate, and viticulture is also widespread.

Industries, concentrated most heavily around Johannesburg, Pretoria and the major ports, process foodstuffs, metals and non-metallic mineral products, produce oil from coal, and also produce beverages and tobacco, motor vehicles, chemicals and chemical products, machinery, textiles and clothing, and paper and paper products. Manufacturing industry contributed 25 per cent of GDP in 1995.

Energy production is based upon coal and natural gas and the production of synthetic liquid fuel from coal. One nuclear power station is in operation and others are planned. South Africa exports electricity through its electric grid connections to all states in southern Africa. The economy has suffered from recession, industrial unrest, drought, the fall in the world gold price and foreign disinvestment. An austerity programme launched in 1985 reduced the national debt to 70 per cent of GDP and enabled the government in September 1993 to announce the repayment of the US$5,000 million foreign debt over an eight-year period.

The first budget of the new government in June 1994 included a one-off 5 per cent levy on corporations and wealthy individuals. Argument over the cost of the ANC's reconstruction and development programme (RDP), including increased spending on education, health care, new homes and electrification, led to a run on the rand and a crisis in foreign exchange and gold reserves, necessitating a scaling-down of expenditure.

In 1994 the government had a budget deficit equivalent to 8.67 per cent of GDP. In 1993 South Africa had a trade surplus of US$5,781 million and a current account surplus of US$1,804 million. In 1995 imports totalled US$30,555 million and exports US$27,860 million.

GNP – US$130,918 million (1995); US$3,160 per capita (1995)

GDP – US$99,620 million (1992); US$2,882 per capita (1992)

ANNUAL AVERAGE GROWTH OF GDP – 3.3 per cent (1995)

INFLATION RATE – 8.7 per cent (1995)

UNEMPLOYMENT – 4.5 per cent (1995)

TRADE

Principal exports are gold, base metals and metal products, coal, diamonds, food (especially fruit), chemicals, machinery and transport equipment, and wool. Principal imports are machinery, chemicals, motor vehicles, metals and metal products, food, inedible raw materials and textiles.

American and EU sanctions, in place since 1986, were lifted in July 1991 and January 1992 respectively. The longer-standing UN finance, oil and arms embargoes were lifted in October 1993, December 1993 and April 1994 respectively.

South Africa's main trading partners are Germany, the USA, the UK and Japan.

Trade with UK	1995	1996
Imports from UK	£1,830,397,000	£1,880,800,000
Exports to UK	1,113,064,000	1,220,706,000

COMMUNICATIONS

There are international airports at Johannesburg, Durban and Cape Town. South African Airways operates international services to Europe, South America, the Far East, Africa, Australia and the USA, and it is the principal operator of domestic flights. The largest seaport is Durban, Natal. Other major ports are Cape Town, Port Elizabeth, East London, Saldanha Bay and Mossel Bay in Cape Province and Richards Bay, Natal. The national railway system, and most long-distance passenger and freight road transport are run by independent companies. The six landlocked states of Botswana, Lesotho, Swaziland, Zimbabwe, Zambia and Malawi make extensive use of South African Railways for foreign trade.

SPAIN
España

AREA – 195,365 sq. miles (505,992 sq. km). Neighbours: Portugal (west), France (north)

POPULATION – 39,481,991 (1996 census)

CAPITAL – Madrid (population, 3,084,673, 1996)

MAJOR CITIES – ΨBarcelona (1,624,000); Valencia (753,000); Seville (659,000); Zarogoza (586,000); ΨMálaga (512,000), 1991

CURRENCY – Peseta of 100 céntimos

NATIONAL ANTHEM – Marcha Real Española

NATIONAL DAY – 12 October

NATIONAL FLAG – Three horizontal stripes of red, yellow, red, with the yellow of double width

LIFE EXPECTANCY (years) – male 73.40; female 80.49

POPULATION GROWTH RATE – 0.1 per cent (1994)

POPULATION DENSITY – 77 per sq. km (1994)

URBAN POPULATION – 64.1 per cent (1991)

The interior of the Iberian peninsula consists of an elevated tableland surrounded and traversed by mountain ranges: the Pyrenees, the Cantabrian Mountains, the Sierra de Guadarrama, Sierra Morena, Sierra Nevada, Montes de Toledo, etc. The principal rivers are the Duero, the Tajo, the Guadiana, the Guadalquivir, the Ebro and the Miño.

HISTORY AND POLITICS

Spain was a monarchy until 1931, when King Alfonso XIII left the country and a republic was proclaimed. A provisional government, drawn from the various republican and socialist parties, was formed. In July 1936 a counter-revolution broke out in military garrisons in Spanish Morocco and spread throughout Spain. The principal leader was Gen. Franco, leader of the Military-Fascist fusion, or *Falange*. Civil war ensued until March 1939, when the Popular Front governments in Madrid and Barcelona surrendered to the Nationalists (as Gen. Franco's followers were then named). Gen. Franco became president and ruled the country until his death in 1975, when, according to his wishes, he was succeeded as head of state by Prince Juan Carlos of Bourbon (grandson of Alfonso XIII) and Spain again became a monarchy. The first free election was held on 15 June 1977.

The general election of June 1993 was won by the PSOE (Spanish Socialist Workers' Party), which formed a minority government with the support of the Catalan and Basque nationalists. The withdrawal of nationalist support following the government's embroilment in the anti-terrorist GAL scandal forced Prime Minister González to call an early general election, on 3 March 1996. The Popular Party (PP) won 156 seats in the Congress of Deputies, defeating the PSOE which won 141 seats. The PP formed a minority government with the support of the Catalan nationalists.

INSURGENCIES

The Basque separatist terrorist organization ETA (*Euzkadi ta Azkatasuna* – Basque Nation and Liberty) has since its formation in 1959 carried out a terrorist campaign of bombings, shootings and kidnappings against the Spanish state and its security forces in an attempt to gain independence for the Basque country. ETA rejected regional

autonomy for the Basque country in 1979 as insufficient and continued its campaign, but increased co-operation between French and Spanish security forces and an alleged illegal anti-terrorist campaign organized by the Spanish state under the acronym GAL (*Grupos Antiterroristas de Liberación*) had greatly weakened ETA by the early 1990s. Most of its leaders were caught and jailed in 1992; the conflict has left 700–800 dead and 600 ETA members in jail.

POLITICAL SYSTEM

Under the 1978 constitution there is a bicameral *Cortes Generales* comprising a 350-member Congress of Deputies elected for a maximum term of four years, which elects the prime minister; and a Senate consisting of 208 directly elected representatives of the provinces, islands, and Ceuta and Melilla, and 44 representatives appointed by the assemblies of the autonomous regions.

Since the promulgation of the 1978 constitution, 19 autonomous regions have been established, with their own parliaments and governments. These are Andalucia, Aragon, Asturias, Balearics, the Basque country, Canaries, Castilla-La Mancha, Castilla-Leon, Cantabria, Cataluña, Ceuta, Extremadura, Galicia, Madrid, Melilla, Murcia, Navarre, La Rioja and Valencia. The Basque country, incorporating the three provinces of Álava, Guipúzcoa and Vizcaya, has the authority to raise taxes and is responsible for social services, culture and the Basque language within the region. In addition Madrid and Barcelona have special autonomous status, but not the same degree of autonomy as the autonomous regions.

HEAD OF STATE

HM The King of Spain, King Juan Carlos I de Borbón y Borbón, KG, GCVO, *born* 5 January 1938, *acceded to the throne* 22 November 1975, *married* 14 May 1962, Princess Sophie of Greece *and has issue* Infante Felipe (*see* below); Infanta Elena Maria Isabel Dominga, *born* 20 December 1963; and Infanta Cristina Federica Victoria Antonia, *born* 13 June 1965

Heir, HRH The Prince of the Asturias (Infante Felipe Juan Pablo Alfonso y Todos los Santos), *born* 30 January 1968

CABINET *as at August 1997*

Prime Minister, José María Aznar López

Deputy PMs, Francisco Alvárez-Cascos Fernández (*Presidency*); Rodrigo de Rato y Figaredo (*Economy and Finance*)

Agriculture, Food and Fisheries, Loyola de Palacio del Valle-Lersundi

Defence, Eduardo Serra Rexach

Development, Rafael Arias-Salgado y Montalvo

Education and Culture, Esperanza Aguirre y Gil de Biedma

Environment, Isabel Tocino Biscarolasaga

Foreign Affairs, Abel Matutes Juan

Health and Consumer Affairs, José Manuel Romay Beccaría

Industry and Energy, Josep Piqué i Camps

Interior, Jaime Mayor Oreja

Justice, Margarita Mariscal de Gante

Labour and Social Affairs, Javier Arenas Bocanegra

Public Administration, Mariano Rajoy Brey

SPANISH EMBASSY

39 Chesham Place, London SW1X 8SB

Tel 0171-235 5555

Ambassador Extraordinary and Plenipotentiary, HE Don Alberto Aza Arias, apptd 1993

Minister Counsellor, Don Pablo Barrios Almanzor

Defence Attaché, Lt.-Col. D. L. Diaz-Ripoll

Ministers, Don L. E. Valera (*Consul*); Dr D. de Lario (*Cultural*)

Counsellor, Don J. García-Valverde (*Commercial*)

BRITISH EMBASSY

Calle de Fernando el Santo 16, 28010 Madrid

Tel: Madrid 319 0200

Ambassador Extraordinary and Plenipotentiary, HE Anthony Brighty, CMG, CVO, apptd 1994

Minister, Deputy Head of Mission, J. A. Dew

Counsellors, M. H. Conner (*Commercial*); C. J. Ingham (*Economic and Community Affairs*); M. Ramscar

Defence and Naval Attaché, Capt. P. Pacey

Consuls-General, D. G. Alexander, MBE (*Madrid*); J. R. Cowling (*Barcelona*); M. McLoughlin (*Bilbao*)

CONSULATES-GENERAL – Madrid, Barcelona, Bilbao

CONSULATES – Alicante, Málaga, Palma de Mallorca, Las Palmas, Seville, Tenerife

VICE-CONSULATES – Ibiza, Menorca

HONORARY CONSULATES – Santander, Tarragona, Vigo

BRITISH COUNCIL DIRECTOR, P. Taylor, OBE, Paseo del General Martinez, Campos 31, 28100 Madrid. There are offices in Barcelona, Bilbao, Las Palmas, Palma, Segovia, Seville and Valencia

BRITISH CHAMBER OF COMMERCE, Plaza de Santa Barbara 10, 1st Floor, 28004 Madrid; Paseo de Gracia 11, Barcelona 7; Alameda de Mazarredo 5, Bilbao 1

DEFENCE

The Army has 682 main battle tanks, 1,995 armoured personnel carriers, 1,304 artillery pieces and 28 attack helicopters. The Navy has eight submarines, one aircraft carrier, 17 frigates, 31 patrol and coastal vessels, 20 combat aircraft and 25 armed helicopters at seven bases. The Air Force has 187 combat aircraft.

The USA maintains 3,000 naval and 220 air force personnel in Spain.

MILITARY EXPENDITURE – 1.5 per cent of GDP (1995)

MILITARY PERSONNEL – 281,800: Army 142,200, Navy 36,100, Air Force 28,500, Paramilitaries 75,000

CONSCRIPTION DURATION – Nine months

ECONOMY

The expansion of the economy and accession to the EU have led to changes in Spanish agriculture. It accounted for 3.5 per cent of GDP in 1993 and employs over 10 per cent of the working population. The country is generally fertile, and olives, oranges, lemons, almonds, pomegranates, bananas, apricots, tomatoes, peppers, cucumbers and grapes are cultivated. Other agricultural products include wheat, barley, oats, rice, hemp and flax. The vine is cultivated widely; in the south-west, around Jerez, sherry and tent wines are produced. The fishing industry is important.

Spain's mineral resources of coal, iron, wolfram, copper, zinc, lead and iron ores are exploited. Output of coal in 1994 was 29.5 million tonnes; output of steel (1988) 11.9 million tonnes.

The principal industrial goods are cars, steel, ships, manufactured goods, textiles, chemical products, footwear and other leather goods. Tourism is a major industry; in 1993 an estimated 57,259,000 tourists visited Spain.

The government is attempting to reform the economy so that it will meet the convergence criteria laid down for entry into a future EU economic and monetary union. The budget deficit was reduced from 6.7 per cent of GDP in 1994 to 5.8 per cent in 1995. The weak peseta had to be devalued by 7 per cent in the exchange rate mechanism in March 1995. The government announced spending cuts of £1,000 million and froze public sector workers' wages in an attempt to reduce spending to 3 per cent of GDP by 1997. A privatization programme was begun in 1996 which will be completed by 2000.

In 1994 Spain had a trade deficit of US$14,581 million and a current account deficit of US$6,832 million. In 1995 imports totalled US$115,019 million and exports US$91,716 million.

GNP – US$532,347 million (1995); US$13,580 per capita (1995)

GDP – US$506,702 million (1992); US$14,697 per capita (1992)

ANNUAL AVERAGE GROWTH OF GDP – 3.0 per cent (1995)
INFLATION RATE – 4.7 per cent (1995)
UNEMPLOYMENT – 22.9 per cent (1995)

TRADE

The principal imports are cotton, tobacco, cellulose, timber, coffee and cocoa, food products, fertilizers, dyes, machinery, motor vehicles and agricultural tractors, wool and petroleum products. The principal exports include cars, petroleum products, iron ore, cork, salt, vegetables, fruits, wines, olive oil, potash, mercury, pyrites, tinned fruit and fish, tomatoes and footwear.

Trade with UK	1995	1996
Imports from UK	£4,123,900,000	£6,371,600,000
Exports to UK	5,800,100,000	4,730,700,000

EDUCATION

Education is free for those aged six to 18, and compulsory up to the age of 14. Private schools (30 per cent of primary and 60 per cent of secondary schools) have to fulfil certain criteria to receive government maintenance grants. There are 33 public sector universities, the oldest of which, Salamanca, was founded in 1218. Other ancient foundations are Valladolid (1346), Barcelona (1430), Zaragoza (1474), Santiago (1495), Valencia (1500), Seville (1505), Madrid (1508), Granada (1531), Oviedo (1604). Private universities are Deusto in Bilbao, Navarra in Pamplona, one in Madrid and one in Salamanca.
ILLITERACY RATE – 2.9 per cent
ENROLMENT (percentage of age group) – primary 100 per cent (1992); secondary 90 per cent (1992); tertiary 44.1 per cent (1993)

CULTURE

Castilian is the language of more than three-quarters of the population of Spain. Basque, said to have been the original language of Iberia, is spoken in Vizcaya, Guipúzcoa and Álava. Catalan is spoken in Provençal Spain, and Galician, spoken in the north-western provinces, is akin to Portuguese. The governments of these regions actively encourage use of their local languages.

The literature of Spain is one of the oldest and richest in the world, the *Poem of the Cid*, the earliest of the heroic songs of Spain, having been written about 1140. The outstanding writings of its golden age are those of Miguel de Cervantes Saavedra (1547–1616), Lope Felix de Vega Carpio (1562–1635) and Pedro Calderón de la Barca (1600–81). The Nobel Prize for Literature has five times been awarded to Spanish authors: J. Echegaray (1904), J. Benavente (1922), Juan Ramón Jiménez (1956), Vicente Aleixandre (1977) and Camilo José Cela (1989).

ISLANDS AND ENCLAVES

The Balearic Isles form an archipelago off the east coast of Spain. There are four large islands (Majorca, Minorca, Ibiza and Formentera), and seven smaller (Aire, Aucanada, Botafoch, Cabrera, Dragonera, Pinto and El Rey). The total area is 1,935 sq. miles (5,011 sq. km), with a population of 685,088. The archipelago forms a province of Spain, the capital being ΨPalma in Majorca, pop. 304,422.

The Canary Islands are an archipelago in the Atlantic, off the African coast, consisting of seven islands and six mostly uninhabited islets. The total area is 2,807 sq. miles (7,270 sq. km), with a population of 1,444,626. The Canary Islands form two provinces of Spain: Las Palmas, comprising Gran Canaria, Lanzarote (38,500), Fuerteventura (19,500) and the islets of Alegranza, Roque del Este, Roque del Oeste, Graciosa, Montaña Clara and Lobos, with seat of administration at ΨLas Palmas (366,454) in Gran Canaria; and Santa Cruz de Tenerife, comprising Tenerife, La Palma (76,000), Gomera (31,829), and Hierro (10,000), with seat of administration at ΨSanta Cruz in Tenerife, population estimate 190,784.

Isla de Faisanes is an uninhabited Franco-Spanish condominium, at the mouth of the Bidassoa in La Higuera bay.

ΨCeuta is a fortified post on the Moroccan coast, opposite Gibraltar. The total area is 5 sq. miles (13 sq. km), with a population of 70,864.

ΨMelilla is a town on a rocky promontory of the Rif coast, connected with the mainland by a narrow isthmus. Population 58,449. Ceuta and Melilla are autonomous regions of Spain.

OVERSEAS TERRITORIES

Spanish settlements on the Moroccan seaboard are:
Peñón de Alhucemas, a bay including six islands, population 366
Peñón de la Gomera (or Peñón de Velez), a fortified rocky islet, population 450
The Chaffarinas (or *Zaffarines*), a group of three islands near the Algerian frontier, population 610

SRI LANKA
Sri Lanka Prajatantrika Samajawadi Janarajaya

AREA – 25,332 sq. miles (65,610 sq. km)
POPULATION – 17,865,000 (1994 UN estimate): 74 per cent Sinhalese, 12.6 per cent Sri Lankan Tamils, 5.6 per cent

Indian Tamils, 7.1 per cent Sri Lankan Moors, 0.7 per cent Burghers, Malays and others. The religion of the majority is Buddhism (69.3 per cent), then Hinduism (15.5 per cent), Islam (7.6 per cent), and Christianity (7.5 per cent). The national languages are Sinhala and Tamil

CAPITAL – Sri Jayawardenapura (population, 2,026,000, 1993); ΨColumbo (population, 615,000, 1993) is the commercial capital

MAJOR CITIES – Kandy (1,269,000); ΨJaffna (879,000); ΨGalle (971,000); ΨTrincomalee (323,000)

CURRENCY – Sri Lankan rupee of 100 cents

NATIONAL ANTHEM – Namo Namo Matha (We all stand together)

NATIONAL DAY – 4 February (Independence Day)

NATIONAL FLAG – On a dark red field, within a golden border, a golden lion passant holding a sword in its right paw, and a representation of a *bo*-leaf, issuing from each corner; and to its right, two vertical stripes of saffron and green also placed within a golden border, to represent the minorities of the country

LIFE EXPECTANCY (years) – male 67.78; female 71.66

POPULATION GROWTH RATE – 1.3 per cent (1994)

POPULATION DENSITY – 272 per sq. km (1994)

ILLITERACY RATE – 9.8 per cent

ENROLMENT (percentage of age group) – tertiary 6.1 per cent (1994)

Sri Lanka (formerly Ceylon) is an island in the Indian Ocean, off the southern tip of India and separated from it by the narrow Palk Strait. Forests, jungle and scrub cover the greater part of the island. In areas over 2,000 ft above sea level grasslands (*patanas* or *talawas*) are found. One of the highest peaks in the central massif is Adam's Peak (7,360 ft), a place of pilgrimage for Buddhists, Hindus and Muslims.

The climate is warm throughout the year, with a high relative humidity. The two main monsoon seasons are mid-May to September (south-west) and November to March (north-east).

HISTORY AND POLITICS

The Portuguese landed in Ceylon in the early 16th century and founded settlements, eventually conquering much of the country. Portuguese rule lasted 150 years; in 1658 it gave way to that of the Dutch East India Company until 1796. The maritime provinces of Ceylon were ceded by the Dutch to the British in 1798, becoming a British Crown Colony in 1802. With the annexation of the Kingdom of Kandy in 1815, all Ceylon came under British rule.

Ceylon became a self-governing state and a member of the British Commonwealth on 4 February 1948. A republican constitution was adopted in 1972 and the country was renamed Sri Lanka (meaning 'Resplendent Island').

Eight provincial councils were set up in 1988 under the Indo-Sri Lankan peace accord in an attempt to diffuse ethnic tension. Since then, except for the temporarily merged North-East province, all provinces have had elected provincial councils.

In the general election of 16 August 1994 the ruling United National Party (UNP) was defeated by the People's Alliance led by Chandrika Bandaranaike Kumaratunga. The People's Alliance, a coalition of seven parties, won 105 seats; the UNP 94 seats; and other parties, mainly Muslim and moderate Tamils, 26 seats. The People's Alliance formed a government with the support of the Sri Lankan Muslim Congress and moderate Tamil parties. Prime Minister Kumaratunga won the presidential election on 9 November 1994 with 62 per cent of the vote after the UNP candidate Gamini Dissanayake was assassinated by Tamil

Tiger terrorists. President Kumaratunga handed over the premiership to her mother, the former Prime Minister Sirimavo Bandaranaike.

In August 1995 the government proposed constitutional changes intended to form a federal state with eight autonomous regions (one covering the Tamil north-east). Each region would have its own elected legislature, executive and judicial branch of government, a police force, and powers devolved from the central government. The package must be passed by a two-thirds parliamentary majority and a national referendum.

INSURGENCIES

The Liberation Tigers of Tamil Eelam (LTTE) guerrilla group has been fighting Sri Lankan forces for control of the Tamil majority areas in the north and east of the country since 1983.

The People's Alliance government came to power on a platform of negotiating a peaceful settlement, to include full autonomy for the Tamil-majority areas. Peace negotiations opened in September 1994, leading to a formal cease-fire with the LTTE which began on 8 January 1995. Fighting resumed in April 1995 after the LTTE had unilaterally broken the cease-fire and negotiations had broken down. A government offensive, launched in October 1995, forced the LTTE to retreat, enabling the government to regain control of Jaffna town in December. The rebels rejected the offer of an amnesty and devolution, and heavy fighting and bomb attacks continued. A second government offensive in April 1996 gained control over almost the entire northern Jaffna peninsula, although the rebels counter-attacked, briefly seizing a government military base in July 1996. The LTTE has up to 10,000 personnel.

POLITICAL SYSTEM

In 1978 a new constitution introduced a system of proportional representation. Legislative power is exercised by the parliament, executive power being exercised by the president and Cabinet.

HEAD OF STATE

President, Buddha Sasana, Defence, Finance, Planning, Ethnic Affairs and National Integration, Chandrika Bandaranaike Kumaratunga, *elected* 9 November 1994, *sworn in* 12 November 1994

CABINET *as at June 1997*

The President

Prime Minister, Sirimavo Bandaranaike

Agriculture and Land, D. M. Jayaratne

Co-operation Development, D. Wickremasinghe

Forestry and Environment, Nandimitra Ekanayake

Health and Indigenous Medicine, Nimal Siripala De Silva

Housing and Urban Development, Indika Gunawardena

Justice and Constitutional Affairs, Ethnic and National Integration, G. L. Peiris

Labour, John Seneviratne *(acting)*

Livestock Development and Estates Infrastructure, S. Thondaman

Mahaweli Development, Maithripala Srisena

Media, Post and Telecommunications, Mangala Samaraweera

Planning, Implementation and Parliamentary Affairs, Jeyaraj Fernandopulle

Power and Irrigation, Col. Anuruddha Ratwatte

Provincial Councils and Local Government, Alavi Maulana

Public Administration, Home Affairs, Plantation Industries, Ratnasiri Wickremanayake

Shipping, Energy, M. H. M. Ashroff

Social Services, Berty Premanand Dissanayake

Tourism and Aviation, Dharmasiri Senanayake
Transport and Highways, A. Fowzie
Vocational Training and Rural Industries, Amarasiri
Dodangoda
Welfare, D. Dissanayaka
Women's Affairs, Hema Ratnayake

HIGH COMMISSION FOR THE DEMOCRATIC SOCIALIST
REPUBLIC OF SRI LANKA
13 Hyde Park Gardens, London W2 2LU
Tel 0171-262 1841
High Commissioner, HE Sarath Wickremesinghe, apptd 1995
Deputy High Commissioner, C. Wagiswara
Ministers, A. Karunaratne *(Consular);* T. Ariyaratne
(Commercial)
First Secretary, C. Obeyesekera *(Defence)*

BRITISH HIGH COMMISSION
Galle Road 190, Kollupitiya (PO Box 1433), Colombo 3
Tel: Colombo 437336
High Commissioner, HE David Tatham, CMG, apptd 1996
Deputy High Commissioner, P. C. Gregory-Hood
Defence Adviser, Lt.-Col. T. J. O'Donnell, MBE
First Secretary (Commercial and Economic), C. Haslam

BRITISH COUNCIL DIRECTOR, P. Ellwood, 49 Alfred
House Gardens, PO Box 753, Colombo 3

DEFENCE

The Army has 25 main battle tanks, 51 armoured personnel
carriers and armoured infantry fighting vehicles and 50
artillery pieces. The Navy has 40 patrol and coastal vessels
at seven bases. The Air Force has 24 combat aircraft and 15
armed helicopters.
MILITARY EXPENDITURE – 4.9 per cent of GDP (1995)
MILITARY PERSONNEL – 130,300: Army 95,000, Navy
10,300, Air Force 10,000, Paramilitaries 15,000

ECONOMY

The staple products are tea, rubber, copra, spices and gems.
There is increasing emphasis on local production of food,
especially rice, and plans for the large-scale production of
sugarcane, cotton and citrus fruits.
The manufacturing sector has grown considerably over
the past few years and produces ceramic ware, vegetable
oils and by-products, paper, tobacco, tanning and leather
goods, plywood, cement, chemicals, beverages, sugar,
flour, salt, textiles and garments, ilmenite, tiles, tyres,
fertilizers, clothing, jewellery and hardware and there is a
petroleum refinery. By the end of 1996 1,953 foreign
investment projects had been approved. Tourism attracts
roughly 400,000 visitors annually.
Since regaining control of Jaffna, the government has
requested £178 million in foreign aid to fund a three-year
programme of reconstruction.
In 1994 the government had a budget deficit equivalent
to 8.55 per cent of GDP. In 1994 Sri Lanka had a trade
deficit of US$871 million and a current account deficit of
US$547 million. In 1995 imports totalled US$5,185 million
and exports US$3,798 million.
GNP – US$12,616 million (1995); US$700 per capita
(1995)
GDP – US$8,674 million (1992); US$542 per capita (1992)
ANNUAL AVERAGE GROWTH OF GDP – 4.8 per cent (1991)
INFLATION RATE – 7.7 per cent (1995)
UNEMPLOYMENT – 12.5 per cent (1995)
TOTAL EXTERNAL DEBT – US$8,230 million (1995)

TRADE WITH UK	1995	1996
Imports from UK	£156,409,000	£148,339,000
Exports to UK	205,652,000	232,088,000

COMMUNICATIONS

There are over 61,200 miles of roads in Sri Lanka and a
government-run railway system with 1,230 miles of lines.
A satellite earth station at Padukka provides telecommunication links world-wide. The principal airport is at
Katunayake, 19 miles north of Colombo. Air Lanka
operates 69 flights weekly to the Gulf States, the Maldives,
western Europe and throughout the Far East.

SUDAN
Al-Jamhuryat es-Sudan Al-Democratia

AREA – 967,500 sq. miles (2,505,813 sq. km). Neighbours:
Egypt (north), Eritrea and Ethiopia (east), Kenya,
Uganda and the Democratic Republic of Congo (south),
Central African Republic, Chad, and Libya (west)
POPULATION – 28,947,000 (1994 UN estimate). Arab and
Nubian peoples populate the north and centre, Nilotic
and Negro peoples the south. Arabic is the official
language and Islam the state religion, although the
Nilotics of the Bahr el Ghazal and Upper Nile valleys
are generally Animists or Christians
CAPITAL – Khartoum (population, 924,505, 1994). The
combined population of Khartoum, Khartoum North
and Omdurman (excluding refugees and displaced
people) is estimated at 3,000,000
CURRENCY – Sudanese dinar (SD) of 10 pounds
NATIONAL ANTHEM – Nahnu Djundullah (We are the
army of God)
NATIONAL DAY – 1 January (Independence Day)
NATIONAL FLAG – Three horizontal stripes of red, white
and black with a green triangle next to the hoist
LIFE EXPECTANCY (years) – male 51.58; female 54.37
POPULATION GROWTH RATE – 2.9 per cent (1994)
POPULATION DENSITY – 12 per sq. km (1994)
URBAN POPULATION – 27.1 per cent (1994)
MILITARY EXPENDITURE – 4.3 per cent of GDP (1995)
MILITARY PERSONNEL – 104,000: Army 85,000, Navy
1,000, Air Force 3,000, Paramilitaries 15,000
CONSCRIPTION DURATION – Three years

The White Nile, as the Bahr el Jebel, flows through Sudan
from Nimule to Wadi Halfa. The Blue Nile flows from
Lake Tana on the Ethiopian plateau through Sudan to join
the White Nile at Khartoum. The next confluence of
importance is at Atbara where the main Nile is joined by
the River Atbara. Between Khartoum and Wadi Halfa lie
five of the six cataracts.

HISTORY AND POLITICS

The Anglo-Egyptian Condominium over Sudan was
established in 1899 and ended when the Sudan House of
Representatives, on 19 December 1955, declared Sudan a
fully independent sovereign state. A republic was proclaimed on 1 January 1956, and was recognized by Great
Britain and Egypt. Sudan was under military rule from
1958 to 1964; under the rule of a revolutionary council
headed by Col. Gaafar Mohamed El Nimeri from 1969
until April 1985 when the army command deposed
Nimeri; and experienced a third military coup in June
1989 when the civilian government, in power since 1986,
was overthrown by Brig.-Gen. Omar Hassan Ahmad al-

Bashir. The constitution was suspended and parliament was replaced by a 15-member ruling junta (Revolutionary Command Council) who exercised control over a Cabinet. The ruling junta appointed Gen. al-Bashir as head of state on 16 October 1993 and then dissolved itself. Presidential and legislative elections were held in March 1996. President al-Bashir was elected with 75.7 per cent of the vote having faced no serious contender. Hassan al-Tourabi of the fundamentalist National Islamic Front (NIF) was elected president of the 269-member National Assembly, although political parties had officially been banned from contesting the elections.

INSURGENCIES

Nearly 17 years of insurrection in the southern provinces ended in 1972 with the signing of an agreement recognizing southern regional autonomy within the Sudanese state. However, insurrection resumed in 1983 and since then there has been civil war in the regions of Eastern and Western Equatoria in the south of the country between government forces and the Christian and Animist majority in the area, organized into the Sudan People's Liberation Army (SPLA). Although the Islamic government has officially stated that it is not attempting to introduce Sharia law in the south, the Sharia affects the two million Christians in northern areas.

Between 1991 and 1994 the SPLA was split into four factions based on tribal groups. The two principal factions were SPLA-Torit led by the original SPLA leader John Garang, and SPLA-United led by Rick Machar. By early 1994 government forces controlled most of the towns and roads in the region and launched the largest offensive since 1983, forcing the SPLA factions to resort to guerrilla tactics. Garang's SPLA-Torit faction made considerable advances against government forces in late 1995 and early 1996. In April 1996, the government signed a peace treaty with the South Sudan Independence Movement and SPLA-United who agreed to relinquish any hope of independence. SPLA-Torit rejected the agreement. In 1997 five rebel factions signed peace deals with the government; SPLA-Torit made advances in the south having been strengthened by its alliance with the National Democratic Alliance.

The warfare has left an estimated 1.4 million dead, including 300,000 who died in the war-induced famine in 1988 and thousands in a similar situation in 1994. Some three million refugees have fled the fighting, either to the north, to neighbouring states or to the far south near the Ugandan border. The fighting has left large areas of the south desolate and uninhabitable.

FOREIGN RELATIONS

The government has developed close relations with Iran and is believed by western states to support international terrorism and have Iranian Revolutionary Guards' bases on its territory. Supported and dominated by the NIF, the government has since 1989 turned Sudan into an Islamic state. In August 1993 the USA placed Sudan on a list of countries sponsoring terrorism and suspended all trade apart from humanitarian goods. In 1995 Sudan's relations with its neighbours, notably Egypt, Eritrea and Uganda, deteriorated as they consider that Sudan is arming Islamic and insurgent groups in their states. In April 1996 the UN imposed sanctions on Sudan for failing to extradite three people suspected of attempting to assassinate President Mubarak of Egypt in Ethiopia in June 1996.

HEAD OF STATE

President, Prime Minister, Lt.-Gen. Omar Hassan Ahmad al-Bashir, *appointed* 16 October 1993, *elected* 17 March 1996

First Vice-President, Deputy Prime Minister, Maj.-Gen. Zubeir Mohammed Saleh
Vice-President, Maj.-Gen. George Kongor

CABINET *as at September 1997*

Agriculture and Forests, Dr Nafie Ali Nafie
Animal Resources, Musa Al-Muk Kur
Aviation, Maj.-Gen. (retd) AlTigani Adam Tahir
Cabinet Affairs, Brig. (retd) Salah-Eddin Karar
Culture and Information, Brig. Al-Tayeb Ibrahim Mohamed Kheir
Defence, Lt.-Gen. Hassan Abdul-Rahman
Education, Dr Kabashor Koko
Energy and Mining, Dr Awad Ahmed Al Jaz
Environment and Tourism, Mohamed Tahir Eila
Federal Relations, Dr Ali El Haj
Finance and National Economy, Abdul Wahab Osman
Foreign Affairs, Ali Osman Mohamed Taha
Health, Ihsan Al Ghabshawi
Higher Education and Scientific Research, Dr Abdul-Wahab Abdul Rahim Bob
Industry, Badr-Eldin Suleiman
Interior and Adviser on Security Affairs, Brig. Bakri Hassan Salih
Irrigation, Dr Yacoub Musa Abu Shora
Justice, Abdul Basit Sabdarat
Presidency, Brig. Abdul-Rahim Mohamed Hussein
Public Service, Angelo Beda
Roads and Communications, Maj.-Gen. (retd) Al-Hadi Bushra
Social Planning, Mohamed Osman Khalifa
Trade, Osman El Hadi Ibrahim
Transport, Maj.-Gen. (retd) Al-Bino Akol Akol

EMBASSY OF THE REPUBLIC OF THE SUDAN
3 Cleveland Row, London SW1A 1DD
Tel 0171-839 8080
Ambassador Extraordinary and Plenipotentiary, HE Sayed Omer Yousif Bireedo, apptd 1995

BRITISH EMBASSY
PO Box 801, Khartoum
Tel: Khartoum 777105
Ambassador Extraordinary and Plenipotentiary, HE Alan Goulty, apptd 1995

BRITISH COUNCIL DIRECTOR, D. Sloan, 14 Abu Sin Street (PO Box 1253), Khartoum.

ECONOMY

Agriculture provides employment for over half the labour force and contributes over one-third of GDP. It is based on large and medium-sized public sector irrigation projects with small-scale private irrigation schemes providing mostly fruit and vegetables. Mechanized and traditional agriculture is practised in areas of sufficient rainfall. The principal grain crops are *dura* (great millet) and wheat, the staple food of the population. Sesame and groundnuts are other important food crops, which also yield an exportable surplus, and a promising start has been made with castor seed. The principal export crop is cotton, both long-staple cotton and short and medium-staple cotton. Sudan also produces the bulk of the world's supply of gum arabic. Sugar is an increasingly important crop, although Sudan still has to achieve self sufficiency in its production.

Livestock is the mainstay of the nomadic Arab tribes of the desert and the Negro tribes of the swamp and wooded grassland country in the south. Production has been affected by drought, famine and civil war.

The manufacturing sector contributes less than 8 per cent to GDP and provides employment for 4 per cent of the work-force. The main manufacturing enterprises are food processing, textiles, shoes, cigarettes and batteries.

In 1992 Sudan had a trade deficit of US$597 million and a current account deficit of US$506 million.

GDP – US$29,594 million (1992); US$186 per capita (1992)

INFLATION RATE – 101.4 per cent (1993)

TOTAL EXTERNAL DEBT – US$17,623 million (1995)

TRADE

The principal exports are cotton, livestock, gum arabic and other agricultural produce. The chief imports are petroleum goods and other raw materials, machinery and equipment, transport and equipment, medicines and chemicals.

Trade with UK	1995	1996
Imports from UK	£44,222,000	£57,818,000
Exports to UK	10,183,000	8,814,000

COMMUNICATIONS

The railway system, adversely affected by the civil war, has a route length of about 3,200 miles. Nile river services between Khartoum and Juba have been interrupted by the southern insurrection. Port Sudan is the country's main seaport. Sudan Airways flies services from Khartoum to other parts of the Sudan and to other African states, Europe and the Middle East.

EDUCATION

School education is free for most children but not compulsory, beginning with six years of primary education, followed by three years of secondary education at general secondary schools, the more academic higher secondary schools or vocational schools. The medium of instruction is Arabic. English is no longer taught in schools since new Arabization legislation came into effect in 1991.

Khartoum University has ten faculties. There is a branch of Cairo University in Khartoum, an Islamic University at Omdurman and universities at Wad Medani and Juba. In addition to the universities there are various technical post-secondary institutes as well as professional and vocational training establishments.

ILLITERACY RATE – 49.4 per cent

ENROLMENT (percentage of age group) – tertiary 3.0 per cent (1990)

SURINAME
Republiek Suriname

AREA – 63,037 sq. miles (163,265 sq. km). Neighbours: French Guiana (east), Brazil (south), Guyana (west)

POPULATION – 418,000 (1994 UN estimate). The official language is Dutch, the native language Sranang Tongo, and other widely-used languages are Hindustani and Javanese

CAPITAL – ΨParamaribo (population, 200,970, 1993)

CURRENCY – Suriname guilder of 100 cents

NATIONAL DAY – 25 November

NATIONAL FLAG – Horizontal stripes of green, white, red, white, green, with a five-pointed yellow star in the centre

LIFE EXPECTANCY (years) – male 67.80; female 72.78

POPULATION GROWTH RATE – 0.9 per cent (1994)

POPULATION DENSITY – 3 per sq. km (1994)

MILITARY EXPENDITURE – 3.9 per cent of GDP (1995)

MILITARY PERSONNEL – 1,800: Army 1,400, Navy 240, Air Force 160

ILLITERACY RATE – 7.0 per cent

HISTORY AND POLITICS

Formerly known as Dutch Guiana, Suriname remained part of the Netherlands West Indies until 25 November 1975, when it achieved complete independence. The civilian government was ousted in 1980 by the military who appointed a predominantly civilian government in 1982. According to the 1987 constitution, a National Assembly of 51 members elects the president.

President Shankar was overthrown in a military coup, instigated by Lt.-Col. Desi Bouterse, in December 1990; Johan Kraag, a supporter of Bouterse, was installed as president. Elections to the National Assembly were held in May 1991. The New Front for Democracy and Development, a coalition comprising opposition groups, won 30 of the 51 seats, but failed to gain the necessary two-thirds majority to appoint the president. In September 1991 a special sitting of a United People's Assembly elected New Front leader Ronald Venetiaan as president and he formed a government which amended the constitution to limit the power of the military.

The New Front won the most seats in the elections to the National Assembly on 23 May 1996 but failed to win a majority sufficient to appoint the president, and a coalition government headed by the National Democratic Party was formed.

HEAD OF STATE

President, Jules Wijdenbosch, *inaugurated* 14 September 1996

Vice-President, Pretaapnarain Radhakishun

CABINET *as at August 1997*

Agriculture, Animal Husbandry and Fisheries, Saimin Redjosentono (KTPI)

Defence, Ramon Dwarka-Panday (KTPI)

Education, Tjan Gobardhan (BVD)

Foreign Affairs, Faried Pierkhan (BVD)

Finance, Motilal Mungra (BVD)

Internal Affairs, Sonny Kertowidjojo (KTPI)

Justice and Police, Paul Sjak Sie (NDP)

Labour, Errol Snijders (NDP)

Planning and International Co-operation, Ernie Brunings (HPP)

Public Health, Elias Khodabaks (HPP)

Public Works, Rudolf Mangal (HPP)

Regional Development, Yvonne Raveles-Resida (NDP)

Social Affairs and Housing, Soewarto Moestadja (KTPI)

Trade and Industry, Robby Dragman (KTPI)

Transportation, Communication and Tourism, Dick De Bie (NDP)

BVD Movement for Renewal and Change; HPP Renewed Progressive Party; KTPI Party for Union and Harmony; NDP National Democratic Party

EMBASSY OF THE REPUBLIC OF SURINAME

2 Alexander Gogelweg, The Hague, The Netherlands

Tel: The Hague 365 0844

Ambassador Extraordinary and Plenipotentiary, HE Evert Guillaume Azimullah, apptd 1994

BRITISH AMBASSADOR, HE David Johnson, CVO, resident at Georgetown, Guyana

BRITISH CONSULATE, c/o VSH United Buildings, Van't Hogerhuystraat, PO Box 1300, Paramaribo. *Honorary Consul*, J. J. Healy, MBE

ECONOMY

Suriname has large timber resources. Rice and sugarcane are the main crops. Bauxite is mined, and is the principal export. Principal trading partners are the Netherlands, USA and Norway.

In 1994 Suriname had a trade surplus of US$99 million and a current account surplus of US$59 million.

GNP – US$360 million (1995); US$880 per capita (1995)
GDP – US$1,863 million (1992); US$6,408 per capita (1992)
ANNUAL AVERAGE GROWTH OF GDP – –4.5 per cent (1993)
INFLATION RATE – 235.6 per cent (1995)
UNEMPLOYMENT – 12.7 per cent (1994)

Trade with UK	1995	1996
Imports from UK	£7,536,000	£12,168,000
Exports to UK	22,992,000	14,764,000

SWAZILAND
Umbuso we Swatini

AREA – 6,704 sq. miles (17,363 sq. km). Neighbours: South Africa (north, west and south), Mozambique (east)
POPULATION – 832,000 (1994 UN estimate)
CAPITAL – Mbabane (population, 38,290, 1986)
MAJOR TOWNS – Manzini (30,000); Big Bend; Mhlambanyati; Mhlume; Nhlangano; Pigg's Peak; Simunye
CURRENCY – Lilangeni (E) of 100 cents (South African currency is also in circulation). Swaziland is a member of the Common Monetary Area and its unit of currency *Emalangeni* (singular *Lilangeni*) has a par value with the South African rand
NATIONAL ANTHEM – Ingoma Yesive
NATIONAL DAY – 6 September (Independence Day)
NATIONAL FLAG – Blue with a wide crimson horizontal band bordered in yellow across the centre, bearing a shield and two spears horizontally
LIFE EXPECTANCY (years) – male 42.90; female 49.50
POPULATION GROWTH RATE – 2.0 per cent (1994)
POPULATION DENSITY – 48 per sq. km (1994)
URBAN POPULATION – 22.8 per cent (1986)
ILLITERACY RATE – 23.3 per cent
ENROLMENT (percentage of age group) – primary 95 per cent (1994); secondary 37 per cent (1994); tertiary 5.1 per cent (1993)

The broken mountainous Highveld along the western border, with an average altitude of 4,000 ft, is densely forested, mainly with conifers and eucalyptus; the Middleveld, averaging about 2,000 ft, is a mixed farming area including cotton and pineapples; and the Lowveld in the east was mainly scrubland until the introduction of large sugar-cane plantations. Four rivers, the Komati, Usutu, Mbuluzi and Ngwavuma, flow from west to east.

HISTORY AND POLITICS

The Kingdom of Swaziland came into being on 25 April 1967 under a self-government constitution and became an independent kingdom, headed by HM Sobhuza II, in membership of the Commonwealth on 6 September 1968.

POLITICAL SYSTEM

A new government system was introduced in 1978 and amended in 1992–3 under which the King, assisted by his appointed Cabinet, holds considerable executive, legisla-tive and judicial authority. In addition, there is a bicameral legislative body comprising a Senate and a House of Assembly. Each of the 55 traditional *Tinkhundla* (chieftaincies) are directly elected and become members of the House of Assembly. The King appoints ten members to the House of Assembly, making 65 in all, who then elect ten members of their own number to the Senate. To these are added 20 senators appointed by the King, bringing the full membership of the Senate to 30. All political parties are banned.

Pro-democracy protests in 1996 drew concessions from King Mswati III, who promised to review the ban on political parties and to establish a People's Parliament and a National Council, although their functions were not defined.

HEAD OF STATE

King of Swaziland, HM King Mswati III, *inaugurated* 25 April 1986

CABINET *as at July 1997*

Prime Minister, Dr Barnabas Dlamini
Deputy Prime Minister, Dr Sishayi Nxumalo
Agriculture and Co-operatives, Sen. Chief Dambuza Lukhele
Economic Planning and Development, Albert Shabangu
Education, Solomon Dlamini
Enterprise and Employment, Revd Absalom Dlamini
Finance, Themba Masuku
Foreign Affairs and Trade, Sen. A. Khoza
Health and Social Welfare, Sen. Dr Phetsile Dlamini
Home Affairs, Sen. Prince Guduza
Housing and Urban Development, John Carmichael
Justice and Constitutional Development, Chief Maweni Simelane
Natural Resources and Energy, Majahenkhaba Dlamini
Public Service and Information, Muntu Mswane
Public Works and Transport, Dumsane Masango
Tourism and Communications, Musa Nkambule

KINGDOM OF SWAZILAND HIGH COMMISSION
20 Buckingham Gate, London SW1E 6LB
Tel 0171-630 6611
High Commissioner, HE Revd Percy Mngomezulu, apptd 1994

BRITISH HIGH COMMISSION
Allister Miller Street, Mbabane
Tel: Mbabane 42581/4
High Commissioner, HE John F. Doble, OBE, apptd 1996

BRITISH COUNCIL DIRECTOR, F. Mahundla

ECONOMY

Manufacturing was announced to have replaced agriculture as the dominant sector in 1988.

In 1993 Swaziland had a trade deficit of US$125 million and a current account deficit of US$37 million. In 1995 imports totalled US$1,060 million and exports US$833 million.

GNP – US$1,051 million (1995); US$1,170 per capita (1995)
GDP – US$792 million (1992); US$1,205 per capita (1992)
ANNUAL AVERAGE GROWTH OF GDP – 5.1 per cent (1994)
INFLATION RATE – 14.7 per cent (1995)
TOTAL EXTERNAL DEBT – US$251 million (1995)

Trade with UK	1995	1996
Imports from UK	£3,033,000	£2,104,000
Exports to UK	39,714,000	40,322,000

COMMUNICATIONS

Swaziland's railway is about 150 miles long and connects with the Mozambique port of Maputo and the South African railway network to Richards Bay. A rail line to the north-west border provides a link to Komatipoort. Most passenger and goods traffic is carried by privately-owned motor transport services. There are scheduled air services by Royal Swazi National Airways to southern and eastern Africa. International telecommunications and television services are provided through a satellite earth station, and there is also a national telephone network.

SWEDEN
Konungariket Sverige

Area – 173,732 sq. miles (449,964 sq. km). Neighbours: Norway (west and north-west), Finland (east)
Population – 8,780,000 (1994 UN estimate); 8,745,109 (1993 census). The state religion is Lutheran Protestant, to which over 95 per cent officially adhere
Capital – ΨStockholm (population, 1,532,803, 1993)
Major Cities – ΨGothenburg (Göteborg) (437,313); ΨMalmö (237,438); Uppsala (178,011)
Currency – Swedish krona of 100 öre
National Anthem – Du Gamla, Du Fria (Thou ancient, thou freeborn)
National Day – 6 June (Day of the Swedish Flag)
National Flag – Yellow cross on a blue ground
Life Expectancy (years) – male 75.49; female 80.79
Population Growth Rate – 0.6 per cent (1994)
Population Density – 20 per sq. km (1994)
Urban Population – 83.4 per cent (1990)

HISTORY AND POLITICS

In the general election held on 18 September 1994 the four-party centre-right coalition of the Moderate, Liberal, Centre and Christian Democratic Parties was defeated by the Social Democrats, who formed a minority government. (The Social Democratic Party has been in government, either alone or in coalition, continuously since 1932, apart from 1936, 1976–82 and 1991–4.) Prime Minister Ingvar Carlsson retired in March 1996, and was replaced by Göran Persson.

Foreign Relations

Sweden applied for EU membership in July 1991 and negotiations on entry were successfully concluded on 1 March 1994. The Accession Treaty was ratified in a national referendum on 13 November 1994 by 52.3 per cent to 46.8 per cent and by a parliamentary vote on 15 December, enabling Sweden to accede to the EU on 1 January 1995.

Political System

Sweden is a constitutional monarchy, with the monarch retaining purely ceremonial functions as head of state. Under the Act of Succession 1810 (with amendments) the throne is hereditary in the House of Bernadotte. The constitution is based upon the Instrument of Government 1974, which amended the 1810 Act and removed from the monarch the roles of appointing the prime minister and signing parliamentary bills into law. A 1979 amendment vested the succession in the monarch's eldest child irrespective of sex.

Executive power is vested in the prime minister and Council of Ministers. There is a unicameral legislature

(*Riksdag*) of 349 members elected by universal suffrage on a proportional representation basis (with a 4 per cent threshold for representation) for four years. The Council of Ministers (*Statsråd*) is responsible to the *Riksdag*.

Sweden is divided into 24 counties (*län*) and 288 municipalities (*kommun*).

Head of State

HM The King of Sweden, Carl XVI Gustaf, kg, *born* 30 April 1946, *succeeded* 15 September 1973, *married* 19 June 1976 Fräulein Silvia Renate Sommerlath and has *issue*, Crown Princess Victoria (*see* below); Prince Carl Philip Edmund Bertil, Duke of Värmland, *born* 13 May 1979; Princess Madeleine Thérèse Amelie Josephine, Duchess of Hälsingland and Gästrikland, *born* 10 June 1982

Heir, HRH Crown Princess Victoria Ingrid Alice Désirée, Duchess of Västergötland, *born* 14 July 1977

Council of Ministers *as at June 1997*

Prime Minister, Göran Persson
PM's Office, Thage Peterson
Agriculture, Food and Fisheries, Annika Ahnberg
Culture, Marita Ulvskog
Defence, Bjorn von Sydow
Education and Science, Carl Tham
Environment, Anna Lindh
Finance, Erik Åsbrink
Foreign Affairs, Lena Hjelm-Wallén
Health and Social Affairs, Maj-Inger Klingvall
Home Affairs, Jörgen Andersson
Industry and Commerce, Leif Pagrotsky
Justice, Laila Freivalds
Labour, Margareta Winberg
Transport and Communications, Ines Uusmann

SWEDISH EMBASSY
11 Montagu Place, London WIH 2AL
Tel 0171-917 6400
Ambassador Extraordinary and Plenipotentiary, HE Mats
Bergquist, apptd 1997
Minister (Economic), Mårten Grunditz
Military Attaché, Col. G. Diurlin
Consul-General, G. Dannerljung

BRITISH EMBASSY
Skarpögatan 6–8, S115 93 Stockholm
Tel: Stockholm 671 9000
Ambassador Extraordinary and Plenipotentiary, HE Robert
Bone, CMG, apptd 1995
Counsellor, Consul-General and Deputy Head of Mission, E. C.
Robson
Counsellor (Economic and Commercial), A. R. Murray
Defence and Air Attaché, Wg Cdr. P. McCullum
CONSULAR OFFICES – Stockholm, Gothenburg
HONORARY CONSULATES – Gothenburg, Malmö,
Sundsvall

BRITISH COUNCIL REPRESENTATIVE , Dr P. Spaven,
Strandagen 57A, S-115 23 Stockholm
BRITISH-SWEDISH CHAMBER OF COMMERCE,
Grevgatan 34, 11453 Stockholm

DEFENCE

The Army has 244 main battle tanks, 978 armoured
personnel carriers and armoured infantry fighting vehi
cles, 956 artillery pieces and 109 helicopters. The Navy has
14 submarines, 22 patrol and coastal vessels, one combat
aircraft and 14 armed helicopters at four bases. The Air
Force has 412 combat aircraft.

Sweden has a policy of non-alignment in peace and
neutrality in war, and it maintains a 'total defence' which
includes peacetime organizations for civil, economic and
psychological defence.
MILITARY EXPENDITURE – 2.9 per cent of GDP (1995)
MILITARY PERSONNEL – 62,600: Army 43,100, Navy
10,000, Air Force 9,500
CONSCRIPTION DURATION – Seven to 12 months

ECONOMY

Less than 10 per cent of the land area is farmland and less
than 3 per cent of the labour force is employed in farming
although Sweden is more than 80 per cent self-sufficient in
food.

Industrial prosperity is based on natural resources:
forests, mineral deposits and water power. The forests
cover about half the total land surface and sustain timber,
finished wood products, pulp and paper milling industries.
The mineral resources include iron ore, lead, zinc, sulphur,
granite, marble, precious and heavy metals (the latter not
exploited) and extensive deposits of low grade uranium
ore. Industries based on mining are important but it is the
general engineering industry that provides the basis of
Sweden's exports, especially specialized machinery and
systems, motor vehicles, aircraft, electrical and electronic
equipment, pharmaceuticals, plastics and chemical industries.

Apart from water power (hydroelectricity supplies 15
per cent of energy needs) Sweden has no significant
indigenous resources of conventional hydrocarbon fuels
and relies for 50 per cent of its energy needs upon imported
oil and coal. Around half of Sweden's electricity is
generated by nuclear power but as a result of a referendum
in 1980 the nuclear programme is to be discontinued in the
future. Small supplies of natural gas are imported from

Denmark into southern Sweden, with the pipeline being
extended to Gothenburg.

Sweden experienced a deep recession between 1990 and
1993 during which time GDP declined by 5 per cent and
employment by 10 per cent. The centre-right government, elected in 1991, introduced austerity measures and
free market economic policies of privatization, deregulation, the ending of state subsidies, trade union legislation, a
floating exchange rate, central bank independence and tax
reform. Further budget cuts and reductions in the public
sector, local government, and the welfare state, together
with tax increases, have been implemented by the Social
Democratic government. The aim is to reduce the
unsustainable levels of public spending and reduce the
budget deficit to 5 per cent of GDP by 1998.

In 1994 the government had a budget deficit equivalent
to 13.17 per cent of GDP. In 1994 Sweden had a trade
surplus of US$9,583 million and a current account surplus
of US$826 million. In 1995 imports totalled US$64,438
million and exports US$79,908 million.
GNP – US$209,720 million (1995); US$23,750 per capita
(1995)
GDP – US$219,975 million (1992); US$28,291 per capita
(1992)
ANNUAL AVERAGE GROWTH OF GDP – 3.0 per cent
(1995); expected to be 2 per cent in 1997
INFLATION RATE – 2.5 per cent (1995)
UNEMPLOYMENT – 7.7 per cent (1995)

TRADE

About 45 per cent of industrial output is exported, mainly
in the form of cars, trucks, machinery, electrical and
communications equipment. Sweden conducts 70 per cent
of its trade with EFTA and the rest of the EU.

Trade with UK	1995	1996
Imports from UK	£4,286,400,000	£4,212,100,000
Exports to UK	3,894,800,000	4,509,200,000

COMMUNICATIONS

The total length of railroads is 11,745 km. The road
network is over 400,000 km in length. The mercantile
marine amounted in 1992 to 3,037,000 gross tonnage.
Regular domestic air traffic is maintained by the Scandinavian Airlines System and by Linjeflyg. Regular European and intercontinental air traffic is maintained by the
Scandinavian Airlines System.

EDUCATION

The state system provides nine years' free and compulsory
schooling from the age of seven to 16 in the comprehensive
elementary schools. Over 90 per cent continue into further
education of two to four years' duration in the upper
secondary schools and a unified higher education system
administered in six regional areas containing one of the
universities: Uppsala (founded 1477); Lund (1668); Stockholm (1878); Gothenburg (1887); Umeå (1963) and Lin-
köping (1967). At present there are 33 institutions of
higher education including three technical universities in
Stockholm, Gothenburg and Luleå, and the Karolinska
Institute in Stockholm, which specializes in medicine and
dentistry.
ENROLMENT (percentage of age group) – primary 99 per
cent; secondary 93 per cent; tertiary 40.1 per cent (1993)

CULTURE

Swedish belongs, with Danish and Norwegian, to the
North Germanic language group. Swedish literature dates
back to King Magnus Eriksson, who codified the old

Swedish provincial laws in 1350. With his translation of the Bible, Olaus Petri (1493–1552) formed the basis for the modern Swedish language. Literature flourished during the reign of Gustavus III, who founded the Swedish Academy in 1786. Notable Swedish writers include Almquist (1795–1866), Strindberg (1849–1912) and Lagerlöf (1858–1940), Nobel Prizewinner in 1909. Contemporary authors include Lagerquist (1891–1974), Nobel Laureate in 1951, Martinson (1904–78) and Johnson (1900–76), Nobel Laureates jointly in 1974. The Swedish scientist Alfred Nobel (1833–96) founded the Nobel Prizes for literature, science and peace.

SWITZERLAND
Schweizerische Eidgenossenschaft – Confédération Suisse – Confederazione Svizzera

AREA – 15,940 sq. miles (41,284 sq. km). Neighbours: France (west and north-west), Germany (north), Austria (east), Italy (south)

POPULATION – 6,995,000 (1994 UN estimate): 46.1 per cent Roman Catholic, 40 per cent Protestant, 5 per cent other religions and 8.9 per cent without religion. The official languages are German (the first language of 63.7 per cent), French (19.2 per cent), Italian (7.6 per cent) and Romansch (0.6 per cent). German is the dominant language in 19 of the 26 cantons; French in Fribourg, Jura, Geneva, Neuchâtel, Valais and Vaud; Italian in Ticino; and Romansch in parts of the Grisons

CAPITAL – Berne (population, 322,855, 1993)

MAJOR CITIES – Geneva (433,692); Lausanne (282,652); Lucerne (178,851) Winterthur (115,076); Zürich (918,328), 1993

CURRENCY – Swiss franc of 100 rappen (or centimes)

NATIONAL ANTHEM – Trittst im Morgenrot Daher (Radiant in the morning sky)

NATIONAL DAY – 1 August

NATIONAL FLAG – Square and red, bearing a couped white cross

LIFE EXPECTANCY (years) – male 74.70; female 81.40

POPULATION GROWTH RATE – 1.0 per cent (1994)

POPULATION DENSITY – 169 per sq. km (1994)

URBAN POPULATION – 68.0 per cent (1993)

Switzerland, the Helvetia of the Romans, is the most mountainous country in Europe. The Alps, from 5,000 to 15,217 ft in height, occupy its southern and eastern frontiers and the chief part of its interior; the Jura mountains rise in the north-west. The Alps occupy 61 per cent, and the Jura mountains 12 per cent of the country. The highest peak, Mont Blanc, Pennine Alps (15,782 ft) is partly in France and partly in Italy; Monte Rosa (15,217 ft) and Matterhorn (14,780 ft) are partly in Switzerland and partly in Italy. The highest wholly Swiss peaks are Dufourspitze (15,203 ft), Finsteraarhorn (14,026), Aletschhorn (13,711), Jungfrau (13,671), Mönch (13,456), Eiger (13,040), Schreckhorn (13,385), and Wetterhorn (12,150) in the Bernese Alps, and Dom (14,918), Weisshorn (14,803) and Breithorn (13,685). The Swiss lakes include Lakes Maggiore, Zürich, Lucerne, Neuchâtel, Geneva, Constance, Thun, Zug, Lugano, Brienz and the Walensee.

HISTORY AND POLITICS

On 22 October 1995, the ruling coalition, comprising the Social Democrats, the Swiss People's Party, the Radical Democratic Party and the Christian Democrats, in power

since 1959, was re-elected with 162 of the 200 seats in the National Council.

FOREIGN RELATIONS

The Federal Council voted in 1992 to apply for European Community membership. The European Economic Area (EEA) Treaty between the EC and EFTA, which extends the provisions of the EC single internal market to EFTA states, was defeated in a national referendum on 6 December 1992. Switzerland is consequently the only EFTA state outside the EEA.

POLITICAL SYSTEM

The federal government consists of the Federal Assembly of two chambers, a National Council (*Nationalrat*) of 200 members, and a States Council (*Ständerat*) of 46 members (two from each canton and one from each demi-canton). Members of the National Council are elected for four years, elections taking place in October. The executive power is in the hands of a Federal Council (*Bundesrat*) of seven members, elected for four years by the Federal Assembly and presided over by the president of the Confederation. Each year the Federal Assembly elects from the Federal Council the president and the vice-president. Not more than one of the same canton may be elected a member of the Federal Council; however, there is a tradition that Italian- and French-speaking areas should between them be represented on the Federal Council by at least two members.

Switzerland is a federal republic. There are 23 cantons, three of which are subdivided, making 26 in all. Each canton has its own government.

FEDERAL COUNCIL

President of the Swiss Confederation (1997) *and Head of Justice and Police*, Arnold Koller

Vice-President (1997) *and Foreign Affairs*, Flavio Cotti

Economic Affairs, Jean-Pascal Delamuraz

Finance, Kaspar Villiger

Home Affairs, Ruth Dreifuss

Military, Adolf Ogi

Transport, Communications and Energy, Moritz Leuenberger

EMBASSY OF SWITZERLAND

16–18 Montagu Place, London WIH 2BQ

Tel 0171-616 6000

Ambassador Extraordinary and Plenipotentiary, HE François Nordmann, apptd 1994

Minister, R. Reich

Defence Attaché, Col. W. Knüsli

Consul-General, R. Müller

Counsellor, D. Furgler (*Economic and Financial*)

CONSULATE-GENERAL – Manchester

BRITISH EMBASSY
Thunstrasse 50, 3005 Berne
Tel: Berne 3525021/6
Ambassador Extraordinary and Plenipotentiary, HE
Christopher Hulse, CMG, OBE, apptd 1997
Counsellor and Deputy Head of Mission, J. Nichols
Commercial Attaché, B. Haessig
Defence Attaché, Lt.-Col. The Lord Crofton
CONSULATES-GENERAL – Geneva, Zürich
CONSULAR OFFICES – Berne (at Embassy), Lugano,
Montreux,Valais
DIRECTORATE OF BRITISH EXPORT PROMOTION –
Consulate-General Office, Dufourstrasse 56, 8008
Zürich

BRITISH COUNCIL DIRECTOR , C. Morrissey, Sennweg 2,
PO Box 532, 3000, Berne 15

BRITISH-SWISS CHAMBER OF COMMERCE, Freiestrasse
155, 8032 Zürich
SWISS-BRITISH SOCIETIES: Berne, *President,* Dr
H. Beriger; Zürich, *President,* J.-P. Müller; Basle,
President, Dr C. Grey

DEFENCE

The Army has 742 main battle tanks, 1,343 armoured
personnel carriers and armoured infantry fighting vehicles, 796 artillery pieces and 60 helicopters. The Air Corps,
which is part of the Army, has 153 combat aircraft.
MILITARY EXPENDITURE – 1.9 per cent of GDP (1995)

ECONOMY

Agriculture is followed chiefly in the valleys and the
central plateau, where cereals, flax, hemp, and tobacco are
produced, and fruits and vegetables as well as grapes are
grown. Dairying and stock-raising are the principal industries, about 3,000,000 acres being under grass for hay and
2,000,000 acres pasturage. The forests cover about 28 per
cent of the whole surface.

The chief manufacturing industries comprise engineering and electrical engineering, metal-working, chemicals
and pharmaceuticals, textiles, watchmaking, woodwork-
ing, foodstuffs, printing and publishing, and footwear.
Banking, insurance and tourism are major industries.

Some 5.9 per cent of the work-force is employed in
agriculture, 34.7 per cent in industry and 59.4 per cent in
services.
GNP – US$286,014 million (1995); US$40,630 per capita
(1995)
GDP – US$225,822 million (1992); US$35,606 per capita
(1992)
ANNUAL AVERAGE GROWTH OF GDP 0.7 per cent (1995)
INFLATION RATE – 1.8 per cent (1995)
UNEMPLOYMENT – 3.3 per cent (1995)

TRADE

The principal imports are machinery, electrical and electronic equipment, textiles, motor vehicles, non-ferrous
metals, chemical elements, clothing, food, medicinal and
pharmaceutical products. The principal exports are machinery, chemical elements, non-ferrous metals, watches,
electrical and electronic equipment, textiles, dyeing, tanning and colouring equipment.

In 1993 Switzerland had a trade surplus of US$2,237
million and a current account surplus of US$16,696
million. In 1995 imports totalled US$76,985 million and
exports US$77,649 million.

Trade with UK	1995	1996
Imports from UK	£2,759,325,000	£3,205,206,000
Exports to UK	5,157,507,000	5,417,807,000

COMMUNICATIONS

There were in 1993, 5,029 km of railway tracks (Swiss
Federal Railways, 2,990 km; privately owned railways
2,039 km). At the end of 1993 the total length of motorways
was 1,530 km. The merchant marine consisted at June
1990 of 20 vessels with a total gross tonnage of 287,487
tonnes. In 1989, goods handled at Basle Rhine ports
amounted to 8,845,162 tonnes. In 1990, 163 lake and river
vessels (excluding the Rhine) transported 12 million
passengers and 500 tonnes of freight. Swiss airlines have a
network covering 348,762 km (1990) and in 1990 carried
17,100,000 passengers. Swissair, the national airline, flies
to and from the airports at Zürich, Geneva and Basle.

The Swiss electorate voted in a February 1994 referendum for a ban on foreign lorries using alpine roads,
which will be phased in over ten years. From 2005 onwards
foreign lorries will have to use two new north-south road-
rail tunnels.

EDUCATION

Education is controlled by cantonal and communal
authorities. Primary education is free and compulsory.
School age varies, generally seven to 14, with secondary
education from age 12 to 15. Special schools make a feature
of commercial and technical instruction. Universities are
Basle (founded 1460), Berne (1834), Fribourg (1889),
Geneva (1873), Lausanne (1890), Zürich (1832), and
Neuchâtel (1909), the technical universities of Lausanne
and Zürich and the economics university of St Gall.
ENROLMENT (percentage of age group) – primary 100 per
cent (1992); secondary 79 per cent (1992); tertiary 30.6
per cent (1993)

CULTURE

Modern authors who have achieved international fame
include Karl Spitteler (1845–1924) and Hermann Hesse
(1877–1962), awarded the Nobel Prize for Literature in
1919 and 1946 respectively.

In 1993 there were 96 daily newspapers published (78
German, 17 French, four Italian).

SYRIA
Al-Jamhouriya Al-Arabia as-Souriya

AREA – 71,498 sq. miles (185,180 sq. km). Neighbours:
Lebanon (west), Israel and Jordan (south-west), Iraq
(east), Turkey (north)
POPULATION – 13,844,000 (1994 UN estimate); mostly
Muslim. Arabic is the principal language, but Kurdish,
Turkish and Armenian are spoken among significant
minorities and a few villages still speak Aramaic, the
language spoken by Christ and the Apostles. English has
taken over from French as the main foreign language
CAPITAL – Damascus (population, 1,549,000, 1994)
MAJOR CITIES – Aleppo (1,542,000); Hama (273,000);
Homs (558,000); ΨLatakia, the principal port (303,000),
1994 estimates
CURRENCY – Syrian pound (S$) of 100 piastres
NATIONAL DAY – 17 April
NATIONAL FLAG – Red over white over black horizontal
bands, with two green stars on central white band
LIFE EXPECTANCY (years) – male 64.42; female 68.05
POPULATION GROWTH RATE – 3.3 per cent (1994)

POPULATION DENSITY – 75 per sq. km (1994)
URBAN POPULATION – 51.4 per cent (1994)

The Orontes flows northwards from the Lebanon range across the northern boundary to Antakya (Antioch, Turkey). The Euphrates crosses the northern boundary near Jerablus and flows through north-eastern Syria to the boundary of Iraq.

The region is rich in historical remains. Damascus (Dimishq ash-Sham) is said to be the oldest continuously inhabited city in the world (although Aleppo disputes this claim), having existed as a city for over 4,000 years. The city contains the Omayed Mosque, the Tomb of Saladin, and the 'street which is called Straight' (Acts 9:11), while to the north-east is the Roman outpost of Dmeir and further east is Palmyra. On the Mediterranean coast at Amrit are ruins of the Phoenician town of Marath, and also ruins of Crusaders' fortresses at Markab, Sahyoun, and Krak des Chevaliers. At Tartous the cathedral of Our Lady of Syria, built by the Knights Templars in the 12th and 13th centuries, has been restored as a museum. One of the oldest alphabets in the world has been discovered at Ugarit (Ras Shamra), a Phoenician village near the port of Latakia. Hittite cities dating from 2000 to 1500 BC, have been explored on the west bank of the Euphrates at Jerablus and Kadesh.

HISTORY AND POLITICS

Once part of the Ottoman Empire, Syria came under French mandate after the First World War. Syria became an independent republic during the Second World War; the first independently elected parliament met in August 1943, but foreign troops were in occupation until April 1946. Syria remained an independent republic until 1958, when it became part, with Egypt, of the United Arab Republic. It seceded from the United Arab Republic in September 1961.

Elections to the 250-seat People's Council in August 1994 resulted in a large majority for the National Progressive Front which won 167 seats and is dominated by the Ba'ath Party, its allies being the Arab Socialist Union, Socialist Unionist Movement, Arab Socialist Party and Syrian Communist Party. Independents won 83 seats.

POLITICAL SYSTEM

A new constitution was promulgated in 1973. This declared that Syria is a democratic, popular socialist state, and that the Arab Socialist Renaissance (Ba'ath) Party, which has been the ruling party since 1963, is the leading party in the state and society.

HEAD OF STATE

President, Lt.-Gen. Hafez Al-Assad, *assumed office* 14 March 1971, *re-elected* 1978, 1985, 3 December 1991
Vice-Presidents, Abdel Halim Khaddam, Rifaat Al-Assad, Zuhair Masharqa

MINISTERS *as at September 1997*

Prime Minister, Mahmoud Al-Zubi
Deputy PM, Defence, Maj.-Gen. Mustafa Tlass
Deputy PM, Economic Affairs, Salim Yassin
Deputy PM, Social Services, Rashid Akhtarini
Agriculture and Agrarian Reform, Asaad Mustafa
Awqaf (Religious Endowments), Muhammad Ziadei
Communications, Radwan Martini
Construction, Majid Ezzou Ruhaibani
Culture, Najah Al-Attar
Economy and Foreign Trade, Muhammad Al-Imady
Education, Ghassan Halabi
Electricity, Mounib Saaem Al-daher

Environment, Abdel-Hamid Al-Munajjid
Finance, Khaled Mahayni
Foreign Affairs, Farouk Al-Shara
Health, Iyad Al-shatti
Higher Education, Salha Sunkar
Housing and Utilities, Hussam Al-safadi
Industry, Ahmed Nezam Al-ddin
Information, Muhammad Salman
Interior, Muhammad Harba
Irrigation, Abdel-Rahman Al-madani
Justice, Hussein Hassoun
Local Administration, Yahya Abu Asali
Oil and Mineral Resources, Muhammad Maher Jamal
Planning, Abdel-Rahim Al-Sebai
Presidential Affairs, Wahib Al-Fadel
Social Affairs and Labour, Ali Khalil
Supply and Internal Trade, Nadim Akkash
Tourism, Danho Daoud
Transport, Mufid Abdel-Karim

EMBASSY OF THE SYRIAN ARAB REPUBLIC
8 Belgrave Square, London SW1X 8PH
Tel 0171-245 9012
Ambassador Extraordinary and Plenipotentiary, new appointment awaited

BRITISH EMBASSY
Kotob Building, 11 rue Mohammad Kurd Ali, Malki, Damascus (PO Box 37)
Tel: Damascus 3712561
Ambassador Extraordinary and Plenipotentiary, HE Basil Eastwood, CMG, apptd 1996
CONSULATE – Aleppo

BRITISH COUNCIL DIRECTOR, Dr P. Clark, OBE, Ground Floor, Tasheen Tabaa' Building, Abd Almalek Bin Marwan Street, Malki, PO Box 33105, Damascus

DEFENCE

The Army has 4,600 main battle tanks, 3,810 armoured personnel carriers and armoured infantry fighting vehicles and 2,080 artillery pieces. The Navy has three submarines, two frigates, 27 patrol and coastal vessels and 29 armed helicopters at three bases. The Air Force has 579 combat aircraft and 100 armed helicopters.

Syria maintains a force of some 35,000 men in Lebanon; 1,061 UN troops are deployed on the Golan Heights.
MILITARY EXPENDITURE – 6.8 per cent of GDP (1995)
MILITARY PERSONNEL – 421,000: Army 315,000, Navy 6,000, Air Force 40,000, Air Defence Command 60,000
CONSCRIPTION DURATION – 30 months

ECONOMY

Agriculture is the principal source of production; wheat and barley are the main cereal crops, but the cotton crop is the highest in value. Tobacco is grown in the maritime plain in Sahel, the Sahyoun and the Djebleh district of Latakia. Large areas are coming under cultivation in the north-east of the country as a result of irrigation from the Thawra dam. There are an increasing number of light assembly plants as Syria's industrialization programme develops. Skins and hides, leather goods, wool and silk, textiles, cement, vegetable oil, glass, soap, sugar, plastics and copper and brass utensils are produced. Oil has been found at Karachuk and other parts in the north-eastern corner of the country and production of high quality reserves is proceeding in the region of Deir ez Zor. Syria produces nearly 400,000 barrels per day at present. A pipeline has been built to the Mediterranean port of Banias, via Homs. Two oil refineries are in production at Homs

and Banias. Syria also has gas reserves, deposits of phosphate and rock salt, and produces asphalt.
GNP – US$15,780 million (1995); US$1,120 per capita (1995)
GDP – US$29,254 million (1992); US$2,489 per capita (1992)
ANNUAL AVERAGE GROWTH OF GDP – 6.2 per cent (1994)
INFLATION RATE – 9.2 per cent (1994)
UNEMPLOYMENT – 6.8 per cent (1991)
TOTAL EXTERNAL DEBT – US$21,138 million (1995)

TRADE

The principal imports are foodstuffs (fruit, vegetables, cereals, meat and dairy products, tea, coffee and sugar), mineral and petroleum products, yarn and textiles, iron and steel manufactures, machinery, chemicals, pharmaceuticals, fertilizers and timber. Exports include raw cotton, oil, cereals, fruit, phosphates, cement, livestock and dairy products, other foodstuffs, textiles and raw wool.
In 1993 Syria had a trade deficit of US$322 million and a current account deficit of US$607 million. In 1995 imports totalled US$4,616 million and exports US$3,970 million.

Trade with UK	1995	1996
Imports from UK	£84,593,000	£100,085,000
Exports to UK	89,768,000	88,924,000

COMMUNICATIONS

Although railway lines run from Damascus to both Beirut and Amman, train services go only to Amman as much of the Lebanese line has been dismantled. A track has been opened connecting Homs with Damascus. A track links Homs, Hamah, Aleppo, Deir ez Zor and Qamishliye to the Iraq frontier. Branch lines connect the ports of Tartous and Latakia to the system and another line runs from Aleppo down the Euphrates valley to Deir ez Zor and thence north to Qamishliye, with a branch going to the Euphrates dam. All the principal towns in the country are connected by roads which vary from modern dual carriageways to narrow country lanes. An internal air service operates between all major towns. The main international airport is at Damascus and there are also flights from Aleppo.
There are three daily newspapers and several periodicals in Arabic published in Damascus, and also a daily newspaper in English.

EDUCATION

Education is under state control and although a few of the schools are privately owned, they all follow a common syllabus. Elementary education is free at state schools and is compulsory from the age of seven. Secondary education is not compulsory and is free only at the state schools. There are universities at Damascus, Aleppo, Tishrin, Latakia and the Ba'ath University, Homs.
ILLITERACY RATE – 29.2 per cent
ENROLMENT (percentage of age group) – primary 93 per cent (1994); secondary 40 per cent (1994); tertiary 17.6 per cent (1992)

TAIWAN
Chung-hua Min-kuo

AREA – 13,800 sq. miles (35,742 sq. km)
POPULATION – 21,450,183 (1996). Mandarin Chinese has been the official language since 1949. Now Taiwanese, spoken by 85 per cent of the population, is growing in importance

CAPITAL – Taipei (population, 2,607,010, 1996)
MAJOR CITIES – ΨKaohsiung (1,432,289); ΨKeelung (373,863), Taichung (873,514);Tainan (710,658), 1996
CURRENCY – New Taiwan dollar (NT$) of 100 cents
NATIONAL DAY – 10 October
NATIONAL FLAG – Red, with blue quarter at top next staff, bearing a 12-point white sun

An island in the China Sea, Taiwan, formerly Formosa, lies 90 miles east of the Chinese mainland. The eastern part of the main island is mountainous and forested. Mt Morrison (Yu Shan) (13,035 ft) and Mt Sylvia (Tz'ukaoshan) (12,972 ft) are the highest peaks. The western plains are watered by many rivers.
Territories include the Pescadores Islands (50 sq. miles), some 35 miles west of Taiwan, as well as Quemoy (68 sq. miles) and Matsu (11 sq. miles) which are only a few miles from mainland China.

HISTORY AND POLITICS

Settled for centuries by the Chinese, the island was ceded by China to Japan in 1895 and remained part of the Japanese empire until Japan's defeat in 1945. Nationalist Kuomintang (KMT) leader Gen. Chiang Kai-shek withdrew to Taiwan in 1949, towards the end of the war against the Communist regime in mainland China, after which the territory continued under his presidency until his death in 1975. He was succeeded as president by his son Gen. Chiang Ching-kuo who ruled until his death in 1988, when Vice-President Lee Teng-hui was appointed president. Martial law was lifted in 1987 after 38 years.
In 1991, President Lee announced that the 'period of Communist rebellion' on the Chinese mainland was over, recognizing *de facto* the People's Republic of China. The announcement also ended emergency measures which had frozen political life on Taiwan since 1949. In 1991–2 power shifted away from mainlanders to native Taiwanese with the forcible retirement of the 'Senior Parliamentarians' who had retained their seats since being elected on the mainland in 1948. The new parliament, the Legislative Yuan, gained control of the budget, of law-making and of the appointment of the prime minister. A general election to the Legislative Yuan in December 1995 was won by the KMT with 85 of the 164 seats; the pro-independence Democratic Progressive Party won 54 seats, the pro-reunification New Party won 21 seats; and independents and minor parties the remaining four seats.
The incumbent, President Lee, won the first democratic presidential election on 23 March 1996, with 54 per cent of the vote. His running-mate, former Prime Minister Lien Chan, was reappointed and holds the posts of vice-president and prime minister concurrently.

FOREIGN RELATIONS

Taiwan (Nationalist China) held China's seat on the UN Security Council until 25 October 1971 when it was replaced by the People's Republic of China.

POLITICAL SYSTEM

Constitutional reforms passed by the Legislative Yuan in July 1994 provide for the president and vice-president to be directly elected for four-year terms (previously the president was elected by parliament).

HEAD OF STATE

President, Lee Teng-hui, *appointed* 13 January 1988, *elected by parliament* 21 March 1990, *elected* 23 March 1996
Vice-President, Lien Chan

EXECUTIVE YUAN *as at July 1997*
Prime Minister, Lien Chan
Deputy PM, Hsu Li-teh
Ministers of State, Shirley Guo, Lin Chen-kuo, Su Chi, Chao Shou-po, Lin Feng-cheng, Yang Shih-chien, Tu Teh-chi, Tsai Cheng-wen
Minister of State, Economic Affairs, Wang Chih-kang
Minister of State, Education, Wu Jin
Minister of State, Finance, Paul Chiu
Minister of State, Foreign Affairs, Chang Hsiao-yen
Minister of State, Justice, Liao Cheng-hao
Minister of State, Mongolian and Tibetan Affairs, Lee Hou-kao
Minister of State, National Defence, Chiang Chung-ling
Minister of State, Overseas Chinese Affairs, Chu Chi-ying
Minister of State, Transport and Communications, Tsay Jaw-yang
Central Personnel Administration, Cheng Kang-chin
Directorate-General of Budget, Accounting and Statistics, Wei Duan
Government Information Office, Lee Ta-wei
Health, Chang Po-ya
Interior, Yeh Chin-fong

Chairs of Councils:
Agriculture, Peng Tso-kuei
Atomic Energy, Hu Ching-piao
Construction and Planning Administration, Huang Nan-yuan
Cultural Affairs, Lin Cheng-chih
Economic Planning and Development, Chiang Pin-kung
Environmental Protection Administration, Tsai Hsung-hsiung
Labour Affairs, Hsu chieh-kwei
Mainland Affairs, Chang King-yuh
Research, Huang Ta-chou
Science, Liu Chao-shiuan
Youth, Wu Wan-lan

TAIPEI REPRESENTATIVE OFFICE , 50 Grosvenor Gardens, London, SWIW OEB

BRITISH COUNCIL REPRESENTATIVE, Tom Buchanan, 7th Floor, Fu Key Building, 99 Jen Ai Road, Section 2, Taipei 10625

DEFENCE

The Army has 630 main battle tanks, 1,175 armoured personnel carriers and armoured infantry fighting vehicles, 1,375 artillery pieces, 20 aircraft and 200 helicopters. The Navy has four submarines, 18 destroyers, 18 frigates, 98 patrol and coastal vessels, 31 combat aircraft and 21 armed helicopters at three bases. The Air Force has 392 combat aircraft.
MILITARY EXPENDITURE – 5.0 per cent of GDP (1995)
MILITARY PERSONNEL – 376,000: Army 240,000, Navy 68,000, Air Force 68,000
CONSCRIPTION DURATION – Two years

ECONOMY

The soil is very fertile, producing sugar, rice, sweet potatoes, tea, bananas, pineapples and tobacco. Mineral resources are meagre. Taiwan produces one-tenth of its coal needs and some natural gas. There are important fisheries. The principal seaports are ΨKeelung and ΨKaohsiung situated in the north and south of the island.
Over the past 30 years Taiwan has transformed itself from a mainly agricultural country to one of the fastest growing industrial economies in Asia. A series of six-year plans has expanded the industrial base; important sectors are steel, shipbuilding, chemicals, cement, machinery, plastic and rubber goods, electrical equipment and textiles. In 1996 agriculture contributed 3.3 per cent of GDP,

manufacturing 35.7 per cent and services 61.1 per cent. Continued trade surpluses have led to one of the largest foreign exchange reserves of any country in the world. Direct shipping between Taiwan and China, which had been suspended in 1949, resumed in April 1997.
In 1996 imports totalled US$102,400 million and exports US$115,900 million.

TRADE
The principal exports are electronic goods, machinery, metal goods, textiles, plastic products and toys and games. The main imports are oil, chemicals, machinery and natural resources. The main trading partners are the USA, Japan, Hong Kong, Germany, the UK and Canada.

Trade with UK	1995	1996
Imports from UK	£961,933,000	£941,241,000
Exports to UK	1,726,761,000	2,088,483,000

TAJIKISTAN
Respublika i Tojikiston

AREA – 55,251 sq. miles (143,100 sq. km). Neighbours: Uzbekistan (west and north-west), Kyrgyzstan (north-east), China (east), Afghanistan (south)
POPULATION – 5,513,400 (1997); 5,093,000 (1989 census): 62 per cent Tajik, 23 per cent Uzbek and 8 per cent Russian, with smaller numbers of Tatars, Kirghiz, Germans and Ukrainians. The people are predominantly Sunni Muslim. The main languages are Tajik (62 per cent), Uzbek (23 per cent), Russian (8 per cent). Tajik is close to the Farsi spoken in Iran
CAPITAL – Dushanbe (population, 602,000, 1990)
CURRENCY – Tajik rouble (TJR) of 100 tanga
NATIONAL DAY – 9 September (Independence Day)
NATIONAL FLAG – Three horizontal stripes of red, white and green with the white of double width and charged with a crown and seven stars, all in gold
LIFE EXPECTANCY (years) – male 66.80; female 71.70
POPULATION GROWTH RATE – 2.8 per cent (1994)
POPULATION DENSITY – 41 per sq. km (1994)
URBAN POPULATION – 28.5 per cent (1993)
MILITARY EXPENDITURE – 6.9 per cent of GDP (1995)
MILITARY PERSONNEL – Army 5,200
ILLITERACY RATE – 0.3 per cent
ENROLMENT (percentage of age group) – tertiary 24.8 per cent (1992)

The republic includes the Gorno-Badakhstan Autonomous Province and the Kulyab, Kurgan-Tyubinsk and Khodzhent Provinces. The country is mountainous with the Pamir highlands in the east and the high ridges of the Pamir-Altai system in the centre. Plains are formed by wide stretches of the Syr-Darya valley in the north and of the Amu-Darya in the south. The country has areas prone to earthquakes, and a continental climate.

HISTORY AND POLITICS

The area that is now Tajikistan was invaded and conquered by Alexander the Great in the fourth century BC. The area remained under Greek and Greco-Persian rule for 200 years until the Kingdom of Kusha was established, based on Bacharia (Bukhara). Tajikistan was invaded by the Arabs in the seventh century AD and by the Samanid Persians in the ninth century AD. The Tajik cities of Bukhara and Samarkand became two of the most important cultural and educational centres in the Islamic world.

The Tajiks lived under the control of various feudal emirates until the area was subsumed within the Russian Empire in 1868. At the time of the Russian revolution in 1917 the central Asian emirates attempted to re-establish their independence. Soviet power was re-established in northern Tajikistan by 1 April 1918, when the Turkestan Soviet Socialist Republic was formed, and the Bukhara emirate was overthrown by Soviet forces in 1920. In 1924 the Tajikistan Autonomous Soviet Socialist Republic was formed as part of the Uzbek Republic before Tajikistan was given full republican status within the Soviet Union in 1929. Stalin deprived the Tajiks of Bukhara and Samarkand, which remained in Uzbekistan, and during Soviet rule 1,000,000 Uzbeks and 800,000 Russians were settled in Tajikistan.

Tajikistan declared independence from the Soviet Union on 9 September 1991 and became a UN member on 2 March 1992. Tension between President Nabiev's supporters and the opposition Islamic and democratic groups led to armed clashes in 1992 and Nabiev was forced to resign on 7 September 1992. The Islamic-Democratic alliance formed a government in September but civil war broke out as forces loyal to the former Communist regime rebelled against the new government. By early November pro-Communist forces controlled virtually all the country and the Supreme Soviet installed Imamali Rakhmonov as its Speaker and head of state. Fighting continued but by March 1993 the Islamic-Democratic forces had been defeated by government and Russian Army units and driven across the border into Afghanistan.

Fighting resumed in July between Russian and Tajik government forces and the Afghan-based rebels, leading to the establishment of a CIS peacekeeping force on the Tajik-Afghan border to contain continuing rebel attacks. Negotiations between the government and opposition began in April 1994 in Moscow, bringing about a cease-fire in October 1994 to allow for presidential and parliamentary elections. The elections were boycotted by most opposition groups and fighting restarted along the Afghan border in early 1995. A peace agreement was signed in December 1996 which provided for the formation of a national reconciliation commission, a general amnesty and an exchange of prisoners.

A new democratic constitution which re-established the presidency was approved by parliament in July 1994 and by the electorate in a national referendum on 6 November 1994. On the same day the presidential election was won by acting head of state Imamali Rakhmonov amid a boycott by most opposition parties. Legislative elections to the new 181-seat Supreme Assembly (*Madjlisi Oli*) were held on 26 February 1995 and won by the ruling (former Communist) People's Party of Tajikistan amid another opposition boycott. The election was condemned as undemocratic by the OSCE monitoring team. Administratively Tajikistan is divided into two regions and one autonomous region.

HEAD OF STATE

President, Imamali Rakhmonov, *elected by Supreme Soviet* 19 November 1992, *elected* 6 November 1994

GOVERNMENT *as at August 1997*

Prime Minister, Yakhia Azimov
First Deputy PM, Yuri Posonov
Deputy PMs, Okil Okilov; Kholisjon Temurjanov; Jamoliddin Mansurov; Kadriddin Giasov
Agriculture, Kurbon Turaiev
Ambassador to Russia, Ramazan Mirzoyev
Bakery, Bekmurod Urakov
Chair of State Property Committee, Davlatov Matlubkhon

Communications, Ibrahim Usmanov
Culture and Information, Bobkhon Makhmadov
Defence, Sherali Khairullayev
Economy and Foreign Economic Relations, Rustam Mirzoiev
Education, Munira Inoyatova
Environmental Protection, Ismail Davlatov
Finance, Anvarzho Muzaffarov
Foreign Affairs, Talbak Nazarov
Health, Alamkhon Ahmedov
Industry, Shavkat Umarov
Interior, Khomidin Sharipov
Justice, Shavkat Ismailov
Labour, Shukurgan Zukhurov
Land Improvement and Water Conservancy, Ismat Eshmirzoev
Social Security, Abdusator Jabarov
Trade and Material Resources, Khakim Saliyev
Transport, Fariddun Muhiddinov

BRITISH AMBASSADOR, HE Alexander Bergne, OBE, apptd 1997, resident in Tashkent, Uzbekistan

ECONOMY

In January 1994 Tajikistan entered into a monetary union with Russia and exchanged its old roubles for post-1993 new Russian roubles. Effectively monetary control was handed over to the Russian central bank and a large amount of economic sovereignty to the Russian government in exchange for a US$100 million loan from Russia. This was needed to prevent an economic collapse caused by 40 per cent of the budget being spent on the civil war. The Tajik rouble was introduced to replace the Russian rouble in May 1995. The economy is being reformed and privatization undertaken in order to attract foreign investment.

Agriculture is the major sector of the economy, concentrating on cotton-growing and cattle-breeding. Tajikistan also has rich mineral deposits of mercury, lead, zinc and oil, is a source of uranium, and has estimated gold reserves of 16 million ounces. Industry specializes in the production of clothing and textiles.

GNP – US$1,976 million (1995); US$340 per capita (1995)
GDP – US$7,935 million (1992); US$103 per capita (1992)
TOTAL EXTERNAL DEBT – US$665 million (1995)

TRADE WITH UK	1995	1996
Imports from UK	£4,754,000	£1,598,000
Exports to UK	138,000	64,000

TANZANIA

Jamhuri ya Muungano wa Tanzania – United Republic of Tanzania

AREA – 364,900 sq. miles (945,087 sq. km). Neighbours: Kenya and Uganda (north), Mozambique (south), Malawi and Zambia (south-west), Rwanda, Burundi and the Democratic Republic of Congo (west)
POPULATION – 28,846,000 (1994 UN estimate). Africans form a large majority, with European, Asian, and other non-African minorities. The African population consists mostly of tribes of mixed Bantu race. Swahili is the national and official language. The use of English is widespread both for educational and government purposes
CAPITAL – Dodoma (population, 88,474, 1988)
MAJOR CITIES – ΨDar es Salaam (1,096,000), the economic and administrative centre; Mbeya (194,000); Mwanza (252,000); ΨTanga (172,000), 1985 estimates
CURRENCY – Tanzanian shilling of 100 cents

NATIONAL ANTHEM – Mungu Ibariki Afrika (God Bless Africa)
NATIONAL DAY – 26 April (Union Day)
NATIONAL FLAG – Green (above) and blue; divided by diagonal black stripe bordered by gold, running from bottom (next staff) to top (in fly)
LIFE EXPECTANCY (years) – male 47.00; female 50.00
POPULATION GROWTH RATE – 3.0 per cent (1994)
POPULATION DENSITY – 33 per sq. km (1994)
URBAN POPULATION – 20.8 per cent (1990)
MILITARY EXPENDITURE – 2.7 per cent of GDP (1995)
MILITARY PERSONNEL – 34,600: Army 30,000, Navy 1,000, Air Force 3,600
CONSCRIPTION DURATION – Two years

Tanzania comprises Tanganyika, on the mainland of east Africa and the island of Zanzibar. The greater part of the country is occupied by the central African plateau from which rise, among others, Mt Kilimanjaro (19,340 ft), the highest point on the continent of Africa, and Mt Meru (14,974 ft). The Serengeti National Park covers an area of 6,000 sq. miles in the Arusha, Mwanza and Mara Regions.

HISTORY AND POLITICS

Tanganyika became an independent state and a member of the British Commonwealth on 9 December 1961, and a republic within the Commonwealth on 9 December 1962. Zanzibar, comprising the islands of Zanzibar, Pemba and Mafia, was formerly ruled by the Sultan of Zanzibar and was a British Protectorate until 10 December 1963 when it became an independent state within the Commonwealth. On 26 April 1964 Tanganyika united with Zanzibar to form the United Republic of Tanzania.

The sole legal political party from 1977 to 1992 was the Chama Cha Mapinduzi (CCM). In 1992 President Mwinyi and the CCM leadership agreed to amend the constitution to allow multiparty politics. In June 1992 President Mwinyi endorsed a bill legalizing multiparty politics, with the stipulation that all parties must be active in both the mainland and in Zanzibar and that parties must not be formed on regional, religious, tribal or racial grounds.

The first multiparty presidential and parliamentary elections were held in October and November 1995. The CCM's candidate, Salmin Amour, was elected president of Zanzibar and his party won 26 seats in the Zanzibar House of Representatives. The Civic United Front gained 24 seats. Benjamin Mkapa of the CCM was elected Union president. The CCM won 186 of the 232 elected seats in the National Assembly.

POLITICAL SYSTEM

The president and vice-president are directly elected and may only serve two terms. The National Assembly contains 275 members, of whom 182 are elected from mainland constituencies and 50 from Zanzibar, 37 seats are reserved for women and are distributed to parties in ratio to their share of seats, five are nominated by the Zanzibar government and one is reserved for the Attorney-General. The Speaker may either be elected from among the members or be an additional member. Constituency members are elected by popular vote at a general election held at a maximum of five-yearly intervals.

Although Zanzibar has its own president, government and 50-member House of Representatives, Tanganyika is governed by the government of the Union. The president of Zanzibar is also a member of the Union Cabinet.

HEAD OF STATE

President of the United Republic, Benjamin Mkapa, *elected* 23 November 1995

Vice-President, Dr Omar Ali Juma

CABINET *as at July 1997*
The President
The Vice-President
Prime Minister, Frederick Sumaye
Agriculture and Co-operatives, Paul Kimiti
Communication and Transport, William Kusila
Community Development, Women's Affairs and Children, Mary Michael Nagu
Defence and National Service, Edgar Maokola Majogo
Education and Culture, Prof. Juma Athuman Kapuya
Energy and Minerals, Dr Abdallah Omar Kigoda
Finance, Daniel Yona
Foreign Affairs and International Co-operation, Jakaya Mrisho Kikwete
Health, Dr Aaron Chiduo
Home Affairs, Ali Ameir Muhammed
Industries and Trade, Dr William Shija
Justice and Constitutional Affairs, Harith Bakari Mwapachu
Labour and Youth Development, Sebastian Rukiza Kinyondo
Land, Housing and Urban Development, Gideon Cheyo
Natural Resources and Tourism, Zakia Meghji
Science, Technology and Higher Education, Jackson Makweta
Water, Pius Yasebasi Ng'wadu
Works, Anna Abdallah

HIGH COMMISSION FOR THE UNITED REPUBLIC OF TANZANIA
43 Hertford Street, London W1Y 8DB
Tel 0171-499 8951/4
High Commissioner, HE Dr Abdulkader A. Shareef, apptd 1995

BRITISH HIGH COMMISSION
Hifadhi House, Samora Avenue (PO Box 9200), Dar es Salaam
Tel: Dar es Salaam 117659/64
High Commissioner, HE Alan Montgomery, CMG, apptd 1995

BRITISH COUNCIL DIRECTOR, Robert Sykes, Ohio Samora Avenue (PO Box 9100), Dar es Salaam

ECONOMY

The economy is based mainly on the production and export of primary produce and the growing of foodstuffs for local consumption. The islands of Zanzibar and Pemba produce a large part of the world's supply of cloves and clove oil; and coconuts, coconut oil and copra are also produced. The mainland's chief export crops are coffee, cotton, sisal, tea, tobacco, cashew nuts and diamonds. The most important minerals are diamonds. Hides and skins are another valuable export. Industry is largely concerned with the processing of raw material for either export or local consumption. There are also secondary manufacturing industries, including factories for the manufacture of leather and rubber footwear, knitwear, razor blades, cigarettes and textiles, and a wheat flour mill.

In 1993 Tanzania had trade deficit of US$838 million and a current account deficit of US$408 million. In 1995 imports totalled US$1,619 million and exports US$639 million.

GNP – US$3,703 million (1995); US$120 per capita (1995)
GDP – US$2,745 million (1992); US$98 per capita (1992)
ANNUAL AVERAGE GROWTH OF GDP – 3.0 per cent (1994)
INFLATION RATE – 27.4 per cent (1995)
TOTAL EXTERNAL DEBT – US$7,333 million (1995)

TRADE WITH UK	1995	1996
Imports from UK	£87,412,000	£81,851,000
Exports to UK	27,480,000	28,983,000

COMMUNICATIONS

The main ports are Dar es Salaam, Tanga, Mtwara, Zanzibar, Mkoani and Wete, in addition to Mwanza, Musoma and Bukoba on Lake Victoria and Kigoma on Lake Tanganyika. Coastal shipping services connect the mainland to Zanzibar, and lake services are operated on Lake Tanganyika and Lake Malawi with neighbouring countries. The principal international airports are Dar es Salaam and Kilimanjaro. Other airports include Zanzibar, Arusha, Mwanza and Tanga. There are two railway systems; one connecting Dar es Salaam to Zambia, and the second having two main lines running from Dar es Salaam, one to northern Tanzania and Kenya and the other to Lakes Tanganyika and Victoria.

EDUCATION

The school system is administered in Swahili but the government is making efforts to improve English standards for the purposes of secondary and higher education. All Tanzanian secondary schools are expected to include practical subjects in the basic course. For higher education Tanzanian students go to the University of Dar es Salaam, Sokoine University of Agriculture in Morogoro, other African universities, or to universities and colleges outside Africa.

ILLITERACY RATE – 32.2 per cent
ENROLMENT (percentage of age group) – primary 50 per cent (1993); tertiary 0.3 per cent (1985)

THAILAND
Prathes Thai– Kingdom of Thailand

AREA – 198,115 sq. miles (513,115 sq. km). Neighbours: Malaysia (south), Myanmar (west), Laos and Cambodia (north-east)

POPULATION – 60,700,000 (1997 census). The principal language is Thai, a monosyllabic, tonal language of the Indo-Chinese linguistic family, with a vocabulary strongly influenced by Sanskrit and Pali. It is written in an alphabetic script derived from ancient Indian scripts. Significant minorities speak Chinese (in urban areas), Lao (in the north-east), Khmer (in the east) and Malay (in the far south). The principal religion is Buddhism (94.37 per cent), with 3.95 per cent Muslims, 0.53 per cent Christians and 1.15 per cent other religions

CAPITAL – ΨBangkok (population, 5,876,000, 1993)
MAJOR CITIES – Chiang Mai (167,000); Thon Buri (187,000); Muang Khon Kaen (206,000); Nakhon Ratchasima (278,000); Songkhla (243,000)
CURRENCY – Baht of 100 satang
NATIONAL ANTHEM – Pleng Chart
NATIONAL DAY – 5 December (The King's Birthday)
NATIONAL FLAG – Five horizontal bands, red, white, dark blue, white, red (the blue band twice the width of the others)
LIFE EXPECTANCY (years) – male 63.82; female 68.85
POPULATION GROWTH RATE – 1.4 per cent (1994)
POPULATION DENSITY – 116 per sq. km (1994)
URBAN POPULATION – 18.7 per cent (1990)

Thailand, formerly known as Siam, is divided geographically into four: the centre is a plain; to the north-east there is a plateau area and to the north-west mountains. The south of Thailand consists of a narrow mountainous peninsula. The principal rivers are the Chao Phraya in the central plains, and the Mekong on the northern and north-eastern borders.

HISTORY AND POLITICS

Thailand became a constitutional monarchy in 1932. Following a military coup in February 1991, a new constitution was approved under which the military would appoint the members of the Senate and so enshrine its place in Thai politics. Parties aligned with the military won the general election in March 1992, but opposition to the government grew and mass demonstrations held in Bangkok, with the help of the King, forced the government from power. Military power was curbed, the 1978 constitution was restored and the interim government sacked military chiefs.

Parliamentary elections in September 1992 resulted in a majority for 'democratic parties', i.e. those not allied with the military. Chuan Leekpai became prime minister at the head of a coalition which implemented a series of reforms in education, land tenure and the constitution. Some 600,000 families were granted land title rights, the voting age was reduced to 18, the appointed Senate was reduced to a maximum of two-thirds of the number of House of Representatives' seats and anti-corruption laws were introduced. In a general election on 17 November 1996 New Aspiration became the largest party in the House of Representatives and formed a six-party coalition government.

POLITICAL SYSTEM

The 1978 constitution (as amended) provides for a National Assembly consisting of a 260-member Senate appointed by the prime minister and a 391-member House of Representatives elected by universal adult suffrage for a term of four years.

HEAD OF STATE

HM The King of Thailand, King Bhumibol Adulyadej, *born* 1927; *succeeded his brother* 9 June 1946; *married* 28 April 1950 Princess Sirikit Kitiyakara; *crowned* 5 May 1950; and has *issue*, Princess Ubolratana, *born* 6 April 1951; Crown Prince Vajiralongkorn (*see* below); Princess Maha Chaki Sirindhorn, *born* 2 April 1955; Princess Chulabhorn, *born* 4 July 1957

Heir, HRH Crown Prince Vajiralongkorn, *born* 28 July 1952; *married* 3 January 1977 Soamsawali Kitiyakra

CABINET *as at July 1997*

Prime Minister, Defence, Gen. Chavalit Yongchaiyudh (NA)
Deputy PM, Samak Sundaravej (PT)
Deputy PM, Education, Sukavich Rangsitpol (NA)
Deputy PM, Industry, Korn Dabbaransi (CP)
Deputy PM, Public Health, Montree Pongpanit (SA)
Ministers to the Prime Minister's Office, Chingchai Mongcolram (NA); Piyanat Watcharaporn (NA); Werakorn Khumprakob (NA); Rakkiat Sukthana (SA); Sompong Amornvivat (CP); Bhokin Balakula (NA)
Agriculture and Co-operatives, Shucheep Hansaward (NA)
Commerce, Narongchai Akrasaranee (NA)
Finance, Thanong Bidaya (Ind.)
Foreign Affairs, Prachuab Chayasarn (CP)
Interior, Sanoh Thienthong (NA)
Justice, Suwit Khunkitti (SA)
Labour and Social Welfare, Chatchai Earsakul (NA)
Science, Technology and Environment, Yingpan Manasikarn (PT)
Transport and Communications, Suwat Liptapanlop (CP)
University Affairs, Montree Danphaiboon (NA)

CP Chart Pattana; NA New Aspiration; SA Social Action; PT Prachakorn Thai; Ind. Independent

ROYAL THAI EMBASSY
29–30 Queen's Gate, London SW7 5JB
Tel 0171-589 0173
Ambassador Extraordinary and Plenipotentiary, HE Sir Vidhya
    Rayananonda, KCVO, apptd 1994
Minister and Deputy Head of Mission, A. Chabchitrchaidol
Defence Attaché, Gp Capt. A. Ganchanahirun
Minister Counsellor, S. Jaovisidha (*Commercial*)

BRITISH EMBASSY
Thanon Witthayu, Bangkok 10330
Tel: Bangkok 2530 1919
Ambassador Extraordinary and Plenipotentiary, HE Sir James
    Hodge, KCVO, CMG, apptd 1996
Deputy Ambassador and Counsellor, P. Sizeland
Defence Attaché, Col. J. D. Fielden, LVO, MBE
Counsellor (Commercial), M. J. Greenstreet
Consul, P. Whiten

CONSULATE – Chang Mai

BRITISH COUNCIL DIRECTOR, Dr J. Richards, OBE, 254
    Chula Long Lorn Soi 64,, Siam Square, Phayathai Road,
    Pathumwan, Bangkok 10330. There is also an office in
    Chiang Mai

BRITISH CHAMBER OF COMMERCE, BP Building 18th
    Floor, Unit 1810, 54 Asoke Road (Sukhumvit 21),
    Bangkok 10110

DEFENCE

The Army has 253 main battle tanks, 940 amoured
personnel carriers, 409 artillery pieces and four attack
helicopters. The Navy has 12 frigates, 60 patrol and coastal
vessels, 61 combat aircraft and seven armed helicopters at
five bases. The Air Force has 212 combat aircraft.
MILITARY EXPENDITURE – 2.5 per cent of GDP (1995)
MILITARY PERSONNEL – 254,000: Army 150,000, Navy
    64,000, Air Force 40,000
CONSCRIPTION DURATION – Two years

ECONOMY

The agricultural sector employs more than half of the
labour force. In 1995 it contributed 11 per cent of GDP.
Rice remains the most important crop, accounting for 60
per cent of the area planted. The other main crops are
sugar, maize, sorghum, cassava, rubber, tobacco, kenaf and
jute. In recent years the production of livestock and
poultry, especially pigs and chickens for export, has gained
importance. There is a large fishing industry with more
than 20,000 vessels registered. Fish and prawn farming is
popular in many inland areas. A ban on hardwood export
has resulted in the decline of the forestry industry.
    Onshore oil and offshore gas were discovered in the late
1970s; crude oil production began in 1983. The predicted
surplus of natural gas has led the government to designate
an area on the east coast as the future centre of the
petrochemical industry. Another energy resource is lignite, which is found mainly in the north and is being used
increasingly for electricity production. Mineral resources
are mainly tin, tungsten, lead, antimony and iron. Among
these tin is the most important. In 1995 mining contributed
1.3 per cent of GDP.
    Since 1960 the government has actively promoted
industrial investment by means of tax relief and other
incentives to local and foreign investors. Initially industries established under this scheme were import-substitut-
ing but the emphasis has shifted now to export-oriented
industries. Important sectors are textiles, transportation
vehicles and equipment, construction materials, brewing,
petroleum refining, electrical appliances, plastics, compu-

ters and parts, and integrated circuits. In 1995 manufacturing contributed 29.1 per cent of GDP. The service sector is
large, the banking system contributing greatly to the
economy, and since 1982 tourism has been the main
foreign exchange earner. In 1995 there were 6,951,600
foreign visitors.
    In 1994 the government had a budget surplus equivalent
to 1.88 per cent of GDP.
GNP – US$159,630 million (1995); US$2,740 per capita
    (1995)
GDP – US$98,819 million (1992); US$1,967 per capita
    (1992)
ANNUAL AVERAGE GROWTH OF GDP – 8.5 per cent (1994)
INFLATION RATE – 5.1 per cent (1994)
UNEMPLOYMENT – 1.5 per cent (1993)
TOTAL EXTERNAL DEBT – US$56,789 million (1995)

TRADE

Thailand's main exports are rice, tapioca and tapioca
products, garments, rubber, computers and parts, cars,
integrated circuit boards, precious stones, pearls and other
ornaments, maize, canned sea food, fabrics, sugar and tin.
Main imports are crude oil, chemicals and pharmaceuticals, electrical and non-electrical machinery and spare
parts, industrial machinery, iron and steel, diesel oil and
other fuel oil, vehicle and transport equipment.
    In 1993 Thailand had a trade deficit of US$4,146 million
and a current account deficit of US$6,928 million. In 1995
imports totalled US$73,654 million and exports
US$56,440 million.

Trade with UK	1995	1996
Imports from UK	£836,622,000	£974,064,000
Exports to UK	1,039,849,000	1,187,872,000

COMMUNICATIONS

The road network, totalling 56,903 km in 1993, reaches all
parts of the country. Most of the smaller towns and bigger
villages are now served by paved roads. Navigable waterways have a length of about 1,100 km in the dry season and
1,600 km in the wet season. About 4,450 km of state-owned
railways were open to traffic in 1989. Main lines run from
Bangkok to the Cambodian border, the ferry terminal on
the River Mekong opposite Vientiane, Chiang Mai and to
Hat Yai, whence lines run down both sides of the Malay
peninsula to Singapore. A new line to Sattahip on the east
coast is being constructed. Bangkok is the international
airport, though airports at Chiang Mai, Phuket and Hat Yai
also receive international flights. Most major provincial
towns have airports. A mass transit system has been
planned for Bangkok.
    There are two important ports in the country. Bangkok,
which is a river port, can serve vessels up to 27 ft draught.
The deep-sea port at Sattahip caters for larger vessels.
Phuket and Songkhla deep-water ports have already been
completed and are the first to be managed privately under a
ten-year concession.

EDUCATION

Primary education is compulsory and free, and secondary
education in government schools is free. Private universities and colleges are playing an increasing role in higher
education. Out of 43 universities and other similar higher
institutes of learning, 21 are private.
ILLITERACY RATE – 6.2 per cent
ENROLMENT (percentage of age group) – tertiary 20.6 per
    cent (1994)

TOGO
République Togolaise

AREA – 21,925 sq. miles (56,785 sq. km). Neighbours: Ghana (west), Burkina Faso (north) Benin (east)
POPULATION – 3,928,000 (1994 UN estimate). The official language is French; Ewe is spoken by about 47 per cent
CAPITAL – ΨLomé (population, 366,476, 1983)
CURRENCY – Franc CFA of 100 centimes
NATIONAL DAY – 13 January (National Liberation Day)
NATIONAL FLAG – Five alternating green and yellow horizontal stripes; a quarter in red at top next staff bearing a white star
LIFE EXPECTANCY (years) – male 53.23; female 56.82
POPULATION GROWTH RATE – 2.7 per cent (1994)
POPULATION DENSITY – 69 per sq. km (1994)
MILITARY EXPENDITURE – 2.5 per cent of GDP (1995)
MILITARY PERSONNEL – 6,950: Army 6,500, Navy 200, Air Force 250
CONSCRIPTION DURATION – Two years
ILLITERACY RATE – 48.3 per cent
ENROLMENT (percentage of age group) – primary 69 per cent (1993); secondary 18 per cent (1990); tertiary 3.1 per cent (1994)

HISTORY AND POLITICS

The first president of Togo, Sylvanus Olympio, was assassinated in 1963. His successor was overthrown by an army coup d'état in 1967 and the army commander Lt.-Col. (later Gen.) Eyadéma named himself president. President Eyadéma came under increasing popular pressure to introduce reforms in 1990 and in October the *Rassemblement du peuple togolais* (RPT), the sole legal party, approved plans for a new constitutional conference after pro-democracy riots. Riots broke out again in March 1991 in protest at the slow pace of reform, and in April the government was forced to concede a political amnesty, the introduction of a multiparty constitution and a national conference. In August 1991 the national conference stripped President Eyadéma of all powers, banned the RPT and elected Kokou Koffigoh as prime minister of an interim government. The national conference set a date of 9 February 1992 for a referendum on a new constitution.

From the second half of 1991 onwards the political situation became progressively more unstable. Troops loyal to President Eyadéma three times attempted to overthrow the Koffigoh government (October, November and December 1991) but were frustrated by pro-democracy supporters. Continued political violence in 1992 between the army and pro-democracy groups and among rival opposition parties forced the postponement of the referendum until September 1992, when a new multiparty constitution was agreed. In November Eyadéma, who had regained the position of head of state in August 1992, ordered the Army to crush civil unrest and a general strike against his rule. In February 1993, as political violence continued, Koffigoh and Eyadéma agreed on the formation of a crisis government, which the national conference and the Collective Democratic Opposition-2 (COD-2) declared illegal.

President Eyadéma won a presidential election in August 1993 that was boycotted by opposition parties and declared rigged by international monitors. Legislative elections to the 81-seat National Assembly were held in February 1994 and won by the opposition alliance of the Action Committee for Renewal (CAR) (36 seats) and the Togolese Union for Democracy (UTD) (7 seats), while the

RPT and allied parties won 38 seats. However, Eyadéma persuaded UTD leader Edem Kodjo to form a coalition UTD-RPT government in April 1994, the RPT retaining a majority of Cabinet seats. The CAR returned to the National Assembly in August 1995, following a nine-month boycott prompted by a Supreme Court decision invalidating the election of some CAR candidates.

HEAD OF STATE
President, Gen. Gnassingbé Eyadéma, *assumed office* 14 April 1967; *re-elected* 1986, August 1993

CABINET *as at June 1997*
Prime Minister, Kwasi Klutse
Agriculture, Livestock and Fisheries, Kokou Dake Dogbe
Communications and Civic Education, Solitoki Esso
Decentralization, Urban Development and Housing, Koffiui Victor Ayassou
Economy and Finance, Barry Moussa Barque
Education and Scientific Research, Kodjo Edo Maurille Agbobli
Environment and Forest Resources, Yao Komlavi
Foreign Affairs and Co-operation, Koffi Panou
Industry and Commerce, Elome Kwami Dadzie
Industry and State Enterprises, Payadowa Boukpessi
Interior and Security, Col. Seyi Memene
Justice, Ephrem Dorkenoo
Mines, Supply, Transport, Posts and Telecommunications, Tchamdja Andjo
National Defence, Yaginim Birokotipou
Planning and Regional Development, Tcha Gouni Ati-Atcha
Promotion of Labour and Civil Service, Sambiani Liwab
Public Health, Koffi Sama
Relations with the National Assembly, Komi Dotse Amoudokpo
Social Welfare and Women's Affairs, Kissem Tchangai-Walla
Technical Education, Bamouni Somolou Stanislas Temele
Tourism and Leisure, Daro Elia
Youth, Culture and Sports, Kouami Agbogboli Ihoul

EMBASSY OF TOGO
The Embassy of Togo closed in September 1991

BRITISH AMBASSADOR, HE Ian Mackley, CMG, resident in Accra, Ghana
There is a Consulate (BP 20050) and a Commercial Office (BP 60958 BE) in Lomé.

ECONOMY

Although the economy remains largely agricultural, exports of phosphates have superseded agricultural products as the main source of export earnings. Other exports include palm kernels, copra and manioc. The production of phosphates entirely for export was taken over completely by the government in 1974. The IMF approved a loan of US$95 million in September 1994 to support the 1994–7 economic reform programme. In May 1995, France cancelled US$33.68 million of Togo's debt and rescheduled a further US$37.64 million.

In 1993 Togo had a trade deficit of US$34 million and a current account deficit of US$98 million. In 1995 imports totalled US$384 million and exports US$209 million.
GNP – US$1,266 million (1995); US$310 per capita (1995)
GDP – US$1,792 million (1992); US$559 per capita (1992)
ANNUAL AVERAGE GROWTH OF GDP – 0.1 per cent (1990)
INFLATION RATE – – 1.0 per cent (1993)
TOTAL EXTERNAL DEBT – US$1,486 million (1995)

TRADE WITH UK	1995	1996
Imports from UK	£11,781,000	£20,039,000
Exports to UK	2,671,000	4,459,000

TONGA
Kingdom of Tonga

AREA – 288 sq. miles (747 sq. km)
POPULATION – 98,000 (1994 UN estimate)
CAPITAL – ΨNuku'alofa (population, 29,018, 1986), on
   Tongatapu
CURRENCY – Pa'anga (T$) of 100 seniti
NATIONAL ANTHEM – E, 'Otua Mafimafi (Oh, Almighty
   God Above)
NATIONAL DAY – 4 June (Emancipation Day)
NATIONAL FLAG – Red with a white canton containing a
   couped red cross
POPULATION GROWTH RATE – 0.4 per cent (1994)
POPULATION DENSITY – 131 per sq. km (1994)
URBAN POPULATION – 30.7 per cent (1986)

Tonga, or the Friendly Islands, comprises a group of
islands situated in the southern Pacific some 450 miles
east-south-east of Fiji. The largest island, Tongatapu, was
discovered by Tasman in 1643. Most of the islands are of
coral formation, but some are volcanic (Tofua, Kao and
Niuafoou or 'Tin Can' Island).

HISTORY AND POLITICS

The Kingdom of Tonga is an independent constitutional
monarchy within the Commonwealth. Prior to 4 June 1970
it had been a British-protected state for 70 years. The
constitution provides for a government consisting of the
Sovereign, an appointed privy council which functions as a
Cabinet, a legislative assembly and a judiciary. The 30-
member legislative assembly comprises the 11-member
privy council, nine hereditary nobles elected by their
peers, and nine popularly elected representatives who hold
office for three years. The most recent election took place
in January 1996.

HEAD OF STATE
King of Tonga, HM King Taufa'ahau Tupou IV, GCMG,
   GCVO, KBE, *born* 4 July 1918, *acceded* 16 December 1965
Heir, HRH Crown Prince Tupouto'a

CABINET *as at June 1997*

Prime Minister, Agriculture, Fisheries, Forest and Marine, Baron
   Vaea of Houma
Deputy PM, Education and Civil Aviation, Dr S. Langi
   Kavaliku
Attorney-General, Justice, Tevita P. Tupou
Finance, Tutoatasi Fakafanua
Foreign Affairs and Defence, HRH Crown Prince Tupouto'a
Governor of Vava'u, Tu'i'afitu
Health, Dr S. Tapa
Labour, Commerce and Industries, Dr Giulio Masaso Paunga
Lands, Survey, and Natural Resources, Governor of Ha'apai,
   Fakafanua
Police, Prisons and Fire Services, Clive Edwards
Works and Disaster Relief, J. C. Cocker

TONGA HIGH COMMISSION
36 Molyneux Street, London W1H 6AB
Tel 0171-724 5828
High Commissioner, HE 'Akosita Fineanganofo, apptd 1996

BRITISH HIGH COMMISSION
PO Box 56, Nuku'alofa
Tel: Nuku'alofa 21020
High Commissioner, HE Andrew Morris, apptd 1994

ECONOMY

The economy is primarily agricultural; the main crops are
coconuts, bananas, vanilla, yams, taro, cassava, groundnuts,
squash pumpkins and other fruits. Fish is an important
staple food, though recent shortfalls have led to canned fish
being imported. Industry is based on the processing of
agricultural produce, and the manufacture of foodstuffs,
clothing and sports equipment.
GNP – US$170 million (1995); US$1,630 per capita (1995)
GDP – US$108 million (1992); US$1,280 per capita (1992)
ANNUAL AVERAGE GROWTH OF GDP – 4.8 per cent (1994)
INFLATION RATE – 1.4 per cent (1995)
TOTAL EXTERNAL DEBT – US$70 million (1995)

TRADE
The principal exports are copra, squash, other coconut
products, tropical root crops, bananas, knitwear, leather
goods and fibreglass boats.

Trade with UK	1995	1996
Imports from UK	£3,010,000	£3,727,000
Exports to UK	113,000	30,000

TRINIDAD AND TOBAGO
The Republic of Trinidad and Tobago

AREA – 1,981 sq. miles (5,130 sq. km)
POPULATION – 1,257,000 (1994 UN estimate). The
   language is English. Roman Catholicism, Protestantism,
   Hinduism and Islam are all practised
CAPITAL – ΨPort of Spain (population, 50,878, 1990)
MAJOR CITIES – San Fernando (34,300), the emerging
   industrial centre of Trinidad; Symbol1;Scarborough,
   the main town of Tobago
CURRENCY – Trinidad and Tobago dollar (TT$) of 100
   cents
NATIONAL DAYS – 31 August (Independence Day)
NATIONAL FLAG – Black diagonal stripe bordered with
   white stripes, running from top by staff, all on a red field
LIFE EXPECTANCY (years) – male 66.88; female 71.62
POPULATION GROWTH RATE – 0.6 per cent (1994)
POPULATION DENSITY – 245 per sq. km (1994)
MILITARY EXPENDITURE – 1.3 per cent of GDP (1995)
MILITARY PERSONNEL – Army 1,400

Trinidad, the most southerly of the West Indian islands,
lies seven miles off the north coast of Venezuela. The
island is about 50 miles in length by 37 miles in width. Two
mountain systems, the Northern and Southern Ranges,
stretch across almost its entire width and a third, the
Central Range, lies diagonally across its middle portion;
otherwise the island is mostly flat.
   Tobago lies 19 miles north-east of Trinidad. The island
is 32 miles long at its widest point, and 11 miles wide.
   Corozal Point and Icacos Point, the north-west and
south-west extremities of Trinidad, enclose the Gulf of
Paria. West of Corozal Point lie several islands, of which
Chacachacare, Huevos, Monos and Gaspar Grande are the
most important.
   The climate is tropical. There is a dry season from
December to May, and a wet season from June to
November broken by a short dry season (the *Petite Careme*)
in September and October.

HISTORY AND POLITICS

Trinidad was discovered by Columbus in 1498, was
colonized in 1532 by the Spaniards, capitulated to the

British in 1797, and was ceded to Britain under the Treaty of Amiens 1802. Tobago was discovered by Columbus in 1498. Dutch colonists arrived in 1632; Tobago subsequently changed hands numerous times until it was ceded to Britain by France in 1814 and amalgamated with Trinidad in 1888.

The Territory of Trinidad and Tobago became an independent state and a member of the British Commonwealth on 31 August 1962, and a republic in 1976.

The most recent general election on 6 November 1995 produced 17 seats each for the ruling People's National Movement (PNM) and the United National Congress (UNC). The UNC formed a coalition government with the National Alliance for Reconstruction (NAR) which held the remaining two seats.

POLITICAL SYSTEM

The president is elected for five years by all members of the Senate and the House of Representatives. The House of Representatives has 36 members, elected by universal adult suffrage, and the Senate has 31, of whom 16 are appointed on the advice of the prime minister, six on the advice of the Leader of the Opposition and nine at the discretion of the president. Legislation was passed in September 1980 which afforded Tobago a degree of self-administration through the 15-member Tobago House of Assembly.

HEAD OF STATE
President, HE Arthur N. R. Robinson, *elected* February 1997

CABINET *as at July 1997*
Prime Minister, Basdeo Panday
Agriculture, Lands and Marine Resources, Dr Reeza Mohammed
Attorney-General, Ramesh Maharaj
Culture and Women's Affairs, Daphne Phillips
Education, Dr Adesh Nanan
Energy, Finbar Ganga
Finance, Brian Kuei Tung
Foreign Affairs, Ralph Maraj
Health, Dr Hamza Rafeeq
Housing, John Humphrey
Labour and Co-operatives, Harry Partap
Legal Affairs, Kamla Persad-Bissessar
Local Government, Dhanraj Singh
National Security, Joseph Theodore
Planning and Development, Trevor Sudama
Public Administration and Information, Wade Mark
Public Utilities, Ganga Singh
Social Development, Manohar Ramsaran
Sport and Youth Affairs, Pamela Nicholson
Trade, Industry and Consumer Affairs, Mervyn Assam
Works and Transport, Sadeeq Baksh

HIGH COMMISSION OF THE REPUBLIC OF TRINIDAD AND TOBAGO
42 Belgrave Square, London SWIX 8NT
Tel 0171-245 9351
High Commissioner, HE Sheelagh de Osuna, apptd 1996

BRITISH HIGH COMMISSION
19 St Clair Ave, St Clair, Port of Spain
Tel: Port of Spain 622 2748
High Commissioner, HE Leo G. Faulkner, apptd 1996

ECONOMY

Trinidad and Tobago's main source of revenue is from oil. Production of domestic crude was 47 million barrels in 1996. Trinidad has large reserves of natural gas, and reserves are estimated to be in the region of 45 years at the

current rates of production. An integrated steel plant, two anhydrous ammonia plants, four methanol plants, one urea plant and one iron carbide plant have been constructed at Point Lisas. An industrial complex, including an iron and steel production plant, is developing around San Fernando.

Fertilizers, tyres, clothing, soap, furniture and foodstuffs are manufactured locally while motor vehicles, radios, TV sets, and electro-domestic equipment are assembled from parts, mainly from Japan. The main agricultural products are sugar, cocoa, coffee, horticultural products, and teak.

In 1993 Trinidad and Tobago had a trade surplus of US$547 million and a current account surplus of US$113 million. In 1995 imports totalled US$1,713 million and exports US$2,456 million.

GNP – US$4,851 million (1995); US$3,770 per capita (1995)
GDP – US$5,158 million (1992); US$4,302 per capita (1992)
ANNUAL AVERAGE GROWTH OF GDP – –1.7 per cent (1993)
INFLATION RATE – 8.8 per cent (1994)
UNEMPLOYMENT – 17.2 per cent (1995)
TOTAL EXTERNAL DEBT – US$2,556 million (1995)

Trade with UK	1995	1996
Imports from UK	£103,434,000	£83,792,000
Exports to UK	43,600,000	53,139,000

COMMUNICATIONS

There are some 6,436 km of all-weather roads in Trinidad and Tobago. The only general cargo port is Port of Spain but there are specialized port facilities elsewhere for crude oil, refinery products, sugar, bauxite and cement. Regular shipping services call and many inter-island craft use the port. Another rapidly growing port is at Port Point Lisas where new industries powered by local natural gas are located. International scheduled airlines, including the national airline, Trinidad and Tobago Airways (BWIA) Corporation, use Piarco International Airport. Caribbean Airways flies between Trinidad and Tobago.

EDUCATION

Education is free at all state-owned and government-assisted denominational schools and certain faculties at the University of the West Indies. In addition there are various private teaching establishments. Attendance is compulsory for children aged six to 12 years, after which attendance at free secondary schools is determined by success in the common entrance examination at 11 years. There are three technical institutes, two teachers' training colleges, and one of the three branches of the University of the West Indies is located in Trinidad. A medical teaching complex at Mt Hope operates in collaboration with the University of the West Indies.
ILLITERACY RATE – 2.1 per cent
ENROLMENT (percentage of age group) – primary 88 per cent (1992); secondary 65 per cent (1992); tertiary 7.6 per cent (1993)

TUNISIA
Al-Djoumhouria Attunusia

AREA – 63,170 sq. miles (163,610 sq. km). Neighbours: Algeria (west), Libya (south)
POPULATION – 8,733,000 (1994 UN estimate)
CAPITAL – ΨTunis (population, 1,394,749, 1984)

MAJOR CITIES – ΨBizerta (394,670); ΨSfax (577,992); ΨSousse (322,491); Gabes; Kairouan; Menzel Bourguiba
CURRENCY – Tunisian dinar of 1,000 millimes
NATIONAL ANTHEM – Himat Al Hima
NATIONAL DAY – 20 March
NATIONAL FLAG – Red with a white disc containing a red crescent and star
LIFE EXPECTANCY (years) – male 66.85; female 68.68
POPULATION GROWTH RATE – 2.0 per cent (1994)
POPULATION DENSITY – 53 per sq. km (1994)
URBAN POPULATION – 58.0 per cent (1990)
MILITARY EXPENDITURE – 2.0 per cent of GDP (1995)
MILITARY PERSONNEL – 45,000: Army 27,000, Navy 4,500, Air Force 3,500, Paramilitaries 10,000
CONSCRIPTION DURATION – 12 months
ILLITERACY RATE – 33.3 per cent
ENROLMENT (percentage of age group) – primary 99 per cent (1994); secondary 23 per cent (1980); tertiary 12.0 per cent (1994)

HISTORY AND POLITICS

A French Protectorate from 1881 to 1956, Tunisia became an independent sovereign state on 20 March 1956. In 1957 the Constituent Assembly abolished the monarchy and elected M. Bourguiba president of the Republic. In March 1975 the National Assembly proclaimed M. Bourguiba as president for life. He was deposed on 7 November 1987 and succeeded by President Zine el-Abidine Ben Ali. Presidential and legislative elections were held in April 1989. The Rassemblement Constitutionnel Démocratique (RCD) won all 141 seats in the National Assembly, which were contested by seven parties; President Ben Ali was elected with 99 per cent of the vote. Electoral changes enacted in September 1993 provide for opposition parties to be represented in the National Assembly; the Assembly has been expanded to 163 seats, 19 of which are reserved, on a proportional basis, for those parties not winning any of the 144 first-past-the-post seats. Presidential and legislative elections held in March 1994 were won by President Ben Ali, the only candidate, and the RCD, which won all 144 constituency seats. Diplomatic relations were opened with Israel in October 1994.

The country is divided into 23 regions (*gouvernorats*) each administered by a governor.

HEAD OF STATE
President, Zine el-Abidine Ben Ali, *took office* 7 November 1987, *elected* 2 April 1989, *re-elected* 21 March 1994

CABINET *as at June 1997*
Prime Minister, Hamed Karoui
Agriculture, Mabtouk Bahri
Communications, Ahmed Fria
Culture, Abdelbaki Hermassi
Defence, Habib ben Yahia
Director of Presidential Office, Mohammed Jegham
Economic Development, Taoufik Baccar
Education, Hatem Ben Othman
Environment and Land Development, Mohamed Mehdi Melika
Equipment and Housing, Ali Chaouch
Family and Women's Affairs, Neziha Zarrouk
Finance, Mohamed el Jeri
Foreign Affairs, Abderrahim Zouari
Health, Hedi Mhenni
Higher Education, Dali Jazi
Industry, Slaheddine Bouguerra
Interior, Mohammed Ben Rajab

International Co-operation and Foreign Investment, Mohammed Ghannouchi
Justice, Abdallah Kallel Sadok Chaabane
Religious Affairs, Ali Chebbi
Secretary-General of the Government, Ridha Grira
Social Affairs, Chedli Neffati
State Property, Mustapha Bouaziz
Tourism and Handicrafts, Slaheddine Maaoui
Trade, Mondher Zenaidi
Transport, Sadok Rabeh
Vocational Training and Employment, Moncer Rouissi
Youth and Childhood Welfare, Raouf Najja

TUNISIAN EMBASSY
29 Prince's Gate, London SW7 1QG
Tel 0171-584 8117
Ambassador Extraordinary and Plenipotentiary, HE Saida Chtioui, apptd 1996

BRITISH EMBASSY
5 Place de la Victoire, Tunis 1015 RP
Tel: Tunis 134 1444
Ambassador Extraordinary and Plenipotentiary and Consul-General, HE Richard Edis, CMG, apptd 1995
First Secretary, B. Bennett (*Deputy Head of Mission*)
HONORARY CONSULATE – Sfax

BRITISH COUNCIL DIRECTOR, J. McKenzie (*Cultural Attaché*)

ECONOMY

The valleys of the northern region support large flocks and herds and contain rich agricultural areas in which wheat, barley, and oats are grown. Vines and olives are extensively cultivated. Some oil has been discovered and crude oil production in 1994 was 4.5 million tons. Gas has also been discovered off the east coast but is only exploited in small quantities. Tourism is the main foreign exchange earner.

In 1993 Tunisia had a trade deficit of US$2,073 million and a current account deficit of US$905 million. In 1995 imports totalled US$7,903 million and exports US$5,475 million.
GNP – US$16,369 million (1995); US$1,820 per capita (1995)
GDP – US$13,829 million (1992); US$1,851 per capita (1992)
ANNUAL AVERAGE GROWTH OF GDP – 3.5 per cent (1995)
INFLATION RATE – 6.2 per cent (1995)
TOTAL EXTERNAL DEBT – US$9,938 million (1995)

TRADE

The chief exports are crude oil, phosphates, olive oil, finished textiles, and fruit. The chief imports are machinery and equipment, foodstuffs, petroleum products, and textiles. France remains the main trading partner.

Tunisia became an associate of the EC in 1969 and signed a new agreement with the EC in 1976. In May 1995 a new EU-Tunisian partnership agreement was signed which aims to modernize Tunisia's economy and improve its competitiveness with a view to creating a future free trade zone with the EU.

Trade with UK	1995	1996
Imports from UK	£83,667,000	£83,257,000
Exports to UK	55,690,000	65,829,000

TURKEY
Türkiye Cumhuriyeti

AREA – 299,158 sq. miles (774,815 sq. km). Neighbours: Greece (west), Bulgaria (north), Georgia, Armenia and Iran (east), Syria and Iraq (south)
POPULATION – 61,183,000 (1994 UN estimate); 56,473,035 (1990 census). Islam ceased to be the state religion in 1928 but 98.99 per cent of the population are Muslim. The main religious minorities, which are concentrated in Istanbul and on the Syrian frontier, are Greek Orthodox, Armenian, Syrian Christian, and Jewish
CAPITAL – Ankara (Angora), in Asia (population, 3,103,000, 1994). Ankara (or Ancyra) was the capital of the Roman Province of *Galatia Prima*, and a marble temple (now in ruins), dedicated to Augustus, contains the *Monumentum (Marmor) Ancyranum*, inscribed with a record of the reign of Augustus Caesar
MAJOR CITIES – ΨIstanbul (7,784,100); ΨIzmir (2,411,500); Adana (1,519,800); Bursa (1,381,300); Gaziantep (973,800); Konya (1,069,400), 1994 estimates. Istanbul, in Europe, is the former capital. The Roman city of Byzantium, it was selected by Constantine the Great as the capital of the Roman Empire about AD 328 and renamed Constantinople. Istanbul contains the celebrated church of St Sophia, which, after becoming a mosque, was made a museum in 1934. It also contains Topkapi, former palace of the Ottoman Sultans, which is also a museum
CURRENCY – Turkish lira (TL) of 100 kurus
NATIONAL ANTHEM – Istiklal Marşi (The Independence March)
NATIONAL DAY – 29 October (Republic Day)
NATIONAL FLAG – Red, with white crescent and star
LIFE EXPECTANCY (years) – male 63.26; female 66.01
POPULATION GROWTH RATE – 2.2 per cent (1994)
POPULATION DENSITY – 79 per sq. km (1994)
URBAN POPULATION – 63.5 per cent (1994)

Turkey lies partly in Europe and partly in Asia. Turkey in Europe consists of Eastern Thrace, including the cities of Istanbul and Edirne, and is separated from Asia by the Bosporus at Istanbul and by the Dardanelles (about 40 miles in length with a width varying from one to four miles), Turkey in Asia comprises the whole of Asia Minor or Anatolia.

HISTORY AND POLITICS

On 29 October 1923 the National Assembly declared Turkey a republic and elected Gazi Mustafa Kemal (later known as Kemal Ataturk) president. In 1945 a multiparty system was introduced but in 1960 the government was overthrown by the armed forces. A new constitution was adopted in 1961 and a civilian government took office. Civilian governments remained in power until September 1980 when mounting problems with the economy and terrorism led to a military takeover.

Following the general election in November 1983 the military leadership handed over power to a civilian government. President Özal died on 17 April 1993 leading to the election by parliament of Süleyman Demirel as president. Tansu Çiller formed a government which was sworn in on 25 June when Çiller became the first woman Turkish prime minister. The CHP withdrew from the government, forcing Çiller to resign on 20 September 1995. Following elections on 24 December 1995, the Islamist Welfare Party (Refah Parisi (RP)) won the most seats but was unable to form a government, enabling the True Path Party and the Motherland Party to form a coalition. The administration lasted until 24 May 1996 when True Path withdrew following corruption allegations against its leader, Tansu Çiller. The RP and True Path Party formed a coalition government on 28 June 1996. The government resigned under pressure from the military and was replaced in June 1997 by a new coalition led by Mesut Yilmaz, leader of the Motherland Party.

The RP has 158 seats in the Grand National Assembly, the True Path Party 135, the Motherland Party 132, the Democratic Left Party 76, and the National Action Party 49.

INSURGENCIES

Since 1984 Turkey has been fighting armed guerrillas of the Marxist Kurdish Workers Party (PKK) in the southeast of the country where Kurds are the majority population. The PKK has an estimated strength of 10,000 operating from bases in Lebanon, northern Iraq and Syria, with the latter giving tacit support and finance. The southeast remains under martial law. Since May 1993 the Turkish army has attempted to destroy the PKK by launching land and air raids against PKK bases in Syria and northern Iraq.

POLITICAL SYSTEM

A new constitution, extending the powers of the president, was approved in 1982. It provided for the separation of powers between the legislature, executive and judiciary, and the holding of free elections to the unicameral Grand National Assembly, which now has 550 members elected every five years.

Turkey is divided for administrative purposes into 76 *il* with subdivisions into *ilçe* and *nahiye*. Each *il* has a governor (*vali*) and elective council.

HEAD OF STATE

President, Süleyman Demirel, *elected by parliament for a seven-year term* 16 May 1993

GOVERNMENT *as at July 1997*

Prime Minister, Mesut Yılmaz (ANAP)
Deputy PM, Minister of State, Bülent Ecevit (DSP)
Deputy PM, National Defence, Ismet Sezgin
Ministers of State, Güneş Taner (ANAP); Hüsamettin Özkan (DSP); Yücel Seçkiner (ANAP); Işilay Saygin (ANAP); Hikmet Sami Türk (DSP); Mehmet Salih Yildirim (ANAP); Rifat Serdaroğlu (DTP); Metin Gürdere (ANAP); Şükrü Sina Gürel (DSP); Ahat Andican (ANAP); Işin Çelebi (ANAP); Mustafa Yilmaz (DSP); Refaiddin Şahin (DTP); Burhan Kara (ANAP); Cavit Kavak (ANAP); Eyüp Aşik (ANAP); Rustu Kazim Yucelen (ANAP); Hasan Gemici (DSP); Mehmet Batalli (DTP)
Agriculture and Rural Affairs, Mustafa Taşar (ANAP)
Culture, Istemihan Talay (DSP)
Education, Hikmet Uluğbay (DSP)
Energy and Natural Resources, Cumhur Ersümer (ANAP)
Environment, Imren Aykut (ANAP)
Finance and Customs, Zekeriya Temizel (DSP)
Foreign Affairs, Ismail Cem (DSP)
Forestry, Ersin Taranoğlu (ANAP)
Health, Halil Ibrahim Özsoy (ANAP)
Interior, Murat Başeşgioglu (ANAP)
Justice, Oltan Sungurlu (ANAP)
Labour and Social Security, Nami Çağan (DSP)
Public Works and Housing, Yaşar Topçu (ANAP)
Tourism, Ibrahim Gürdal (ANAP)
Trade and Industry, Yalim Erez (Ind.)
Transport, Necdet Menzir (DTP)

ANAP Motherland Party; DSP Democratic Left Party; DTP Democratic Turkey Party; Ind. Independent

TURKISH EMBASSY
43 Belgrave Square, London SW1X 8PA
Tel 0171-393 0202
Ambassador Extraordinary and Plenipotentiary, HE Özdem Sanberk, apptd 1995
Minister Counsellor, Mehmet Akat

BRITISH EMBASSY
Sehit Ersan Caddesi 46/A, Cankaya, Ankara
Tel: Ankara 468 6230/42
Ambassador Extraordinary and Plenipotentiary, HE David Logan, CMG, apptd 1997
Counsellor, Deputy Head of Mission, H. Mortimer
First Secretary, A. T. MacDermott *(Commercial)*
Defence and Military Attaché, Brig. A. V. Twiss
Consul-General (Istanbul), P. Hunt

CONSULATE-GENERAL – Istanbul
VICE-CONSULATE – Izmir
HONORARY CONSULATES – Antalya, Bodrum, Iskenderun, Marmaris, Mersin

BRITISH COUNCIL DIRECTOR, C. Gobby, Kirklangic Sokak 9, Gazi Osman Pasa, Ankara 06700

BRITISH CHAMBER OF COMMERCE OF TURKEY INC., Mesrutiyet Caddessi No. 34, Tepebasi Beyoğlu, Istanbul (*postal address*, PO Box 190 Karaköy, Istanbul)

DEFENCE

The Army has 4,280 main battle tanks, 4,116 armoured personnel carriers and armoured infantry fighting vehicles, 4,341 artillery pieces and 43 attack helicopters. The Navy has 15 submarines, five destroyers, 16 frigates, 50 patrol and coastal vessels and 14 armed helicopters at eight bases. The Air Force has 434 combat aircraft.

Between 150,000 and 200,000 troops are stationed in the south-east of the country fighting Kurdish guerrillas.

Since its invasion of Cyprus in 1974, Turkey has maintained forces in the north of the island and at present has 30,000 men stationed there.

As a member of NATO, Turkey is host to the Head-quarters Allied Land Forces South-Eastern Europe and the Sixth Allied Tactical Air Force Headquarters. US (2,950 personnel), UK (230 personnel) and French (150 personnel) air force detachments are based at Incirlik air base in southern Turkey to patrol the air exclusion zone over northern Iraq.
MILITARY EXPENDITURE – 3.6 per cent of GDP (1995)
MILITARY PERSONNEL – 819,000: Army 525,000, Navy 51,000, Air Force 63,000, Paramilitaries 180,000
CONSCRIPTION DURATION – 18 months

ECONOMY

Agricultural production accounts for some 16 per cent of GDP. About 50 per cent of the working population are in the rural sector. The principal crops are wheat, barley, rice, tobacco, sugar beet, tea, olives, grapes, figs and hazelnuts. With the exception of wheat, which is mostly grown on the arid central Anatolian plateau, most of the crops are grown on the fertile littoral. Tobacco, sultana and fig cultivation is centred around Izmir, where substantial quantities of cotton are also grown. The main cotton area is in the Cukurova plain around Adana. The forests which lie between the littoral plain and the Anatolian plateau contain beech, pine, oak, elm, chestnut, lime, plane, alder, box, poplar and maple.

After agriculture, Turkey's most important industry is based on the considerable mineral wealth which is, however, comparatively unexploited. The main export minerals are chromite and boron.

The bulk of the country's requirements in sugar, cotton, woollen and silk textiles, and cement, is produced locally. Other industries include vehicle assembly, paper, glass and glassware, iron and steel, leather and leather goods, sulphur refining, canning and rubber goods, soaps and cosmetics, pharmaceutical products, and prepared foodstuffs.

A customs union with the EU came into force on 1 January 1996 which was expected to boost the economy, although Greece succeeded in suspending an EU aid package of US$480 million in February 1996. A gas deal worth £14,800 million was signed with Iran in August 1996 which provided for a 20-year supply of Iranian gas.

In 1993 the government had a budget deficit equivalent to 6.87 per cent of GDP.
GNP – US$169,452 million (1995); US$2,780 per capita (1995)
GDP – US$159,815 million (1992); US$2,647 per capita (1992)
ANNUAL AVERAGE GROWTH OF GDP – 7.3 per cent (1995)
INFLATION RATE – 93.6 per cent (1995)
UNEMPLOYMENT – 6.6 per cent (1995)
TOTAL EXTERNAL DEBT – US$73,592 million (1995)

TRADE

The main imports are machinery, crude oil and petroleum products, iron and steel, vehicles, medicines and dyes, chemicals, fertilizers and electrical appliances. Agricultural commodities (cotton, tobacco, fruits, nuts, livestock) represent 47 per cent of total exports. Other exports are minerals, textiles, glass and cement.

In 1993 Turkey had a trade deficit of US$14,162 million and a current account deficit of US$6,380 million. In 1995 imports totalled US$35,710 million and exports US$21,600 million.

Trade with UK	1995	1996
Imports from UK	£1,157,777,000	£1,565,938,000
Exports to UK	794,890,000	932,876,000

COMMUNICATIONS

The rail network is run by the State Railways Administration. The total length of lines in operation (1993) is 10,386 km. In 1993, there were 59,770 km of roads. The Bosporus is spanned by two bridges; plans are being drawn up for a third fixed link between the two continents. By the end of 1988 the number of ships over 18 gross tons was 3,805. The state airline (THY) operates all internal services and has services to Europe, the Far East, Africa, North America and the Middle East. Most of the leading European airlines operate services to Istanbul and some also to Ankara.

EDUCATION

Education is free, secular and compulsory at primary level. There are elementary, secondary and vocational schools. There are 27 universities in Turkey, including six in Istanbul, five in Ankara, two in Izmir, and one each in Erzurum and Trabzon.
ILLITERACY RATE – 17.7 per cent
ENROLMENT (percentage of age group) – primary 90 per cent; secondary 56 per cent; tertiary 19.6 per cent (1993)

CULTURE

Turkish was written in Arabic script until 1926 when a version of the Roman alphabet reflecting Turkish phonetics was substituted for use in official correspondence and in 1928 for universal use, with Arabic numerals as used throughout Europe. The revolution of 1908 led to the introduction of native literature free from foreign influences and adapted to the understanding of the people.

TURKMENISTAN
Turkmenostan Respublikasy

AREA – 188,456 sq. miles (488,100 sq. km). Neighbours: Iran (south), Afghanistan (south-east), Uzbekistan (east and north), Kazakhstan (north-west)

POPULATION – 3,808,900 (1997 estimate); 4,483,000 (1996 census): 77 per cent Turkoman, 6.7 per cent Russian, 9.2 per cent Uzbek, together with smaller numbers of Kazakhs, Tatars, Ukrainians and Armenians. Most of the population are Sunni Muslims. The main languages are Turkmenian (72 per cent), Russian (9 per cent), Uzbek (9 per cent). Turkmenian is one of the Turkic languages

CAPITAL – Ashkhabad (population, 407,000, 1990)

CURRENCY – Manat

NATIONAL DAY – 28 October (Independence Day)

NATIONAL FLAG – Green with a vertical carpet pattern near the hoist in black, white and wine-red; and in the lower part of the carpet design two laurel branches; in the upper hoist a crescent and five stars, all in white

LIFE EXPECTANCY (years) – male 61.80; female 68.40

POPULATION GROWTH RATE – 2.2 per cent (1994)

POPULATION DENSITY – 8 per sq. km (1994)

URBAN POPULATION – 45.2 per cent (1989)

MILITARY EXPENDITURE – 1.9 per cent of GDP (1995)

MILITARY PERSONNEL – Army 18,000

ILLITERACY RATE – 0.3 per cent

ENROLMENT (percentage of age group) tertiary 21.8 per cent (1990)

The republic comprises five regions: Ashkhabad; Chardjou; Krasnovodsk; Mary; and Tashauz. The country is a low-lying plain fringed by hills in the south. Ninety per cent of the plain is taken up by the Obe Kara-Kum (Black Sands) desert. The climate is hot and dry.

HISTORY AND POLITICS

Situated at the crossroads of Central Asia, the area that is now Turkmenistan has been invaded and occupied by many empires: Persian; Greek under Alexander the Great; Parthian; Mongol. A Turkmenian nation was established in the 15th century but remained riven with dissent and divided between warring emirates. From the early 19th century until 1886 Turkmenistan was gradually incorporated into the Russian Empire. Soviet control over Turkmenistan was established on 30 April 1918 when it became an Autonomous Soviet Socialist Republic. The banks, cotton refineries and oil and gas fields were nationalized before a civil war broke out in July 1918, sparked by the intervention of British troops from Iran and India. The war ended in 1920 with the withdrawal of the interventionist forces; Turkmenistan became a full republic of the Soviet Union in February 1925.

Turkmenistan declared its independence from the Soviet Union on 27 October 1991 and gained UN membership on 2 March 1992.

The autocratic government of President Niyazov has prevented any effective political opposition or free press through harassment and the continuation of authoritarianism. The political leadership has rejected political plural-

ism and instead a cult of personality has developed around President Niyazov. The Supreme Soviet voted on 30 December 1993 to extend the term of President Niyazov to 2002 and this was confirmed by a 99.99 per cent vote in a referendum on 15 January 1994. The Communist Party, renamed the Democratic Party, remains in power. Legislative elections to the *Khalk Maslakhaty* were won by the Democratic Party.

FOREIGN RELATIONS

In 1992 joint Turkmen–Russian armed forces of 34,000 army and air force personnel were established and remain in operation. In late 1993 Turkmen–Russian agreements were signed allowing Russian troops to protect the borders with Iran and Afghanistan; Russian citizens to undergo military training in Turkmenistan; Turkmen officers to train in Russia; and Turkmenistan to bear the cost of Russian forces in the country. Agreement on dual citizenship for ethnic Russians in Turkmenistan was also reached. In December 1993 Turkmenistan signed the CIS charter to become a full CIS member and in January 1994 became a member of the CIS economic union.

POLITICAL SYSTEM

The constitution passed on 18 May 1992 declares the president head of state and government and provides for a bicameral legislature of the existing Supreme Soviet (renamed the *Majlis*) and a 60-member (50 directly elected and ten appointed) supervisory upper house, the *Khalk Maslakhaty* (People's Council).

HEAD OF STATE

President, Saparmurad Niyazov, *elected* 27 October 1990, *re-elected* 21 June 1992, *appointed head of government* 18 May 1992, *elected by referendum for an eight-year term* 15 January 1994

COUNCIL OF MINISTERS *as at April 1997*

Prime Minister, The President
Deputy PM, Agriculture, Pirkuli Odeyev
Deputy PM, Culture, Orazgeldy Aidogdyiev
Deputy PM, Education, Mukhamed Abalakov
Deputy PM, Foreign Affairs, Boris Shikmuradov
Deputy PMs, Reedjep Saparov; Ilaman Shykhyiev
Automobile Transport and Roads Maintenance, Senkuly Rakhmanov
Chairman of the Majlis, Sakhat Muradov
Communications, Ashirberdy Cherkezov
Construction and Architecture, Allaberdy Tekaiev
Defence, Dangatar Kopekov
Foreign Economic Relations, Mired Orazov
Health, Chary Kuliev
Industry and Building Materials, Kakadzhan Tashliyev
Interior, Kurbanmukhamed Kasymov
Justice, Tagandurdy Khallyev
Land Improvement and Water Conservancy, Alexander Dodonov
Nature Management and Environmental Protection, Pirdzham Gurbanov
Oil, Gas and Mineral Resources, Gochmurad Nadzhanov
Power Engineering and Industry, Saparmurad Nuryev
Social Affairs, vacant
Textile Industry, Begench Nepesov
Trade, Halnazar Agakhanov

EMBASSY OF TURKMENISTAN

2nd Floor South, St George's House, 14/17 Wells Street, London WIP 3FP
Tel 0171-255 1071
Ambassador Extraordinary and Plenipotentiary, HE Murad Chariev, apptd 1997

BRITISH EMBASSY
3rd Floor, Office Building, Ak Altin Plaza Hotel, Ashkhabad
Ambassador Extraordinary and Plenipotentiary, HE Neil Hook,
MVO, apptd 1995

ECONOMY

The large reserves of natural gas and the foreign revenue
that they earn make the country economically viable and
have enabled the government to maintain low stable prices
for all basic commodities and utilities.

Cotton cultivation, stock-raising and mineral extraction are the principal industries, together with natural gas
production and the long-established silk industry. Some
fisheries exist along the Caspian sea coast. Arable land is
irrigated by the Niyazov canal, which cuts through the
Kara Kum desert. There are estimated reserves of some
700 million tonnes of oil and 8,000,000 million cubic
metres of natural gas. Natural gas is exported by pipeline to
Ukraine and western Europe and another pipeline is being
built through Iran and Turkey to Europe. Turkmenistan is
to export 5,000 million cubic metres of gas to Russia in
1997.

A new railroad links Turkmenistan with Iran.
GNP – US$4,125 million (1995); US$920 per capita (1995)
GDP – US$10,268 million (1992); US$381 per capita
    (1992)
TOTAL EXTERNAL DEBT – US$393 million (1995)

TRADE WITH UK	1995	1996
Imports from UK	£3,902,000	£6,265,000
Exports to UK	738,000	619,000

TUVALU

AREA – 10 sq. miles (25 sq. km)
POPULATION – 9,000 (1994 UN estimate). About 1,500
    Tuvaluans work overseas, mostly in Nauru, or as
    seamen. The people are almost entirely Polynesian. The
    principal languages are Tuvaluan and English. The
    entire population is Christian, predominantly
    Protestant
CAPITAL – ΨFunafuti (population, 2,856)
CURRENCY – The Australian dollar ($A) of 100 cents is
    legal tender. In addition there are Tuvalu dollar and cent
    coins in circulation
NATIONAL ANTHEM – Tuvalu Mo Te Atua (Tuvalu for
    the Almighty)
NATIONAL DAY – 1 October (Independence Day)
NATIONAL FLAG – Light blue ground with Union flag in
    top left quarter and nine five-pointed gold stars in the fly
POPULATION GROWTH RATE – 0.0 per cent (1994)
POPULATION DENSITY – 346 per sq. km (1994)

Tuvalu comprises nine coral atolls situated in the south-
west Pacific around the point at which the International
Date Line cuts the Equator. Few of the atolls are more than
12 ft above sea level or more than half a mile in width. The
vegetation consists mainly of coconut palms.

HISTORY AND POLITICS

Tuvalu, formerly the Ellice Islands, formed part of the
Gilbert and Ellice Islands Colony until 1 October 1975,
when separate constitutions came into force. Separation
from the Gilbert Islands was implemented on 1 January
1976. On 1 October 1978 Tuvalu became a fully independent state within the Commonwealth.

In December 1996 the government of Kamuta Lataasi
lost a confidence vote in parliament.

POLITICAL SYSTEM

The constitution provides for a prime minister and four
other ministers, who must be members of the 12-member
elected parliament. The prime minister presides at meetings of the Cabinet, which consists of the five Ministers and
is attended by the Attorney-General. Local government
services are provided by elected Island Councils.

Governor-General, HE Toomu Sione
Prime Minister, Bikenibeu Paeniu
BRITISH HIGH COMMISSIONER, HE Michael Peart, CMG,
    LVO, resides at Suva, Fiji

ECONOMY

Most people still practise a subsistence economy, the main
staples of the diet being coconuts and fish. The main
imports are foodstuffs, consumer goods and building
materials. The only export is copra, though philatelic sales
provide a major source of revenue and handicraft sales are
increasing. However, Tuvalu is almost entirely dependent
on foreign aid.

Funafuti has a grass strip airfield from which a service
operates regularly to Fiji and Kiribati, and is also the only
port.
GDP – US$9 million (1992); US$713 per capita (1992)

TRADE WITH UK	1995	1996
Imports from UK	£268,000	£306,000
Exports to UK	—	584,000

SOCIAL WELFARE

All islands are served by a dispensary and a primary school.
A maritime training school caters for 60 boys a year. There
is a 30-bed hospital at Funafuti.

UGANDA
Republic of Uganda

AREA – 93,065 sq. miles (241,038 sq. km). Neighbours:
    Democratic Republic of Congo (west), Sudan (north),
    Kenya (east), Tanzania and Rwanda (south)
POPULATION – 20,621,000 (1994 UN estimate). The
    official language is English. The main local vernaculars
    are of Bantu, Nilotic and Hamitic origins. Ki-Swahili is
    generally understood
CAPITAL – Kampala (population, 750,000, 1990)
MAJOR CITIES – Jinja (45,000); Mbale (28,000); Masaka
    (29,000)
CURRENCY – Uganda shilling of 100 cents
NATIONAL ANTHEM – Oh Uganda
NATIONAL DAY – 9 October (Independence Day)
NATIONAL FLAG – Six horizontal stripes of black, yellow,
    red, with a white disc in the centre containing the badge
    of a crested crane
LIFE EXPECTANCY (years) – male 43.57; female 46.19
POPULATION GROWTH RATE – 3.5 per cent (1994)
POPULATION DENSITY – 86 per sq. km (1994)
URBAN POPULATION – 1.3 per cent (1991)
MILITARY EXPENDITURE – 2.6 per cent of GDP (1995)
MILITARY PERSONNEL – 50,000: National Resistance
    Army 50,000

Large parts of Lakes Victoria, Edward and Albert (Mobu-
to) are within Uganda's boundaries, as are Lakes Kyoga,
Kwania, George and Bisina (formerly Salisbury) and the
course of the River Nile from its outlet from Lake Victoria
to the Sudan border at Nimule.

Despite its tropical location, the climate is tempered by its situation some 3,000 ft above sea level, and well over that altitude in the highlands of the Western and Eastern Regions. Uganda has three National Parks and a fourth (Lake Mburo) has been designated.

HISTORY AND POLITICS

Uganda became an independent state within the Commonwealth on 9 October 1962, after some 70 years of British rule. A republic was instituted in 1967, under an executive president assisted by a Cabinet of Ministers.

Early in 1971 an army coup took place and Maj.-Gen. Idi Amin, the army commander, proclaimed himself head of state. In 1979, following uprisings and military intervention by Tanzania, President Amin was overthrown. Dr Milton Obote became president in 1980 but was ousted by a military coup in 1985. A military council was installed but the National Resistance Movement led by Yoweri Museveni captured Kampala in January 1986, securing control of the rest of the country in the following few months. Yoweri Museveni was sworn in as president in January 1986.

President Museveni won the first direct presidential election on 9 May 1996. Supporters of the President won a majority of seats in legislative elections on 27 June. The ban on political party activity will continue until 2000.

POLITICAL SYSTEM

A Constituent Assembly was elected in March 1994 to draft a new constitution. The constitution, promulgated on 8 October 1995, endorsed the existing non-party political system. The National Resistance Council, the legislature, was replaced by a new 276-seat National Assembly.

HEAD OF STATE

President, Yoweri Museveni, *sworn in* 29 January 1986, *elected* 9 May 1996
Vice-President Agriculture, Animal Industry and Fisheries, Speciosa Wandira Kazibwe

CABINET *as at July 1997*

The Vice-President
Prime Minister, Kintu Musoke
First Deputy PM, Foreign Affairs, Eriya Kategaya
Second Deputy PM, Tourism, Wildlife and Antiquities, Brig. Moses Ali
Third Deputy PM, Labour and Social Services, Paul Orono Etiang
Attorney-General, Justice, Bart Katureebe
Education and Sports, Amanya Mushega
Finance, Joash Mayanja-Nkangi
Gender and Community Development, Hajati Janoti B. Mukwaya
Health, Dr Crispus W. C. B. Kiyonga
Information, Dr Ruhakana-Rugunda
Internal Affairs, Maj. Tom Butime
Lands, Housing and Urban Development, Francis Ayume
Local Government, Bidandi-Ssali
Natural Resources, Gerald Ssendaula
Planning and Economic Development, Richard Kaijuka
Public Services, Prof. A. Nsibambi
Trade and Industry, Henry Muganwa Kajura
Works, Transport and Communications, John Nasasira

UGANDA HIGH COMMISSION

Uganda House, 58–59 Trafalgar Square, London WC2N 5DX
Tel 0171–839 5783
High Commissioner, HE Prof. George Kirya, apptd 1990
Deputy High Commissioner, D. Ssozi

Minister Counsellor, E. Byaruhanga
Financial Attaché, A. Bamweyana

BRITISH HIGH COMMISSION

10–12 Parliament Avenue, PO Box 7070, Kampala
Tel: Kampala 257054/9
High Commissioner, HE Michael Cook, apptd 1997
Deputy High Commissioner, P. Rouse, MBE
Defence Adviser, Lt.-Col. N. Lewis, MBE

BRITISH COUNCIL DIRECTOR, R. Wilkins (*Cultural Attaché*)

ECONOMY

Since 1988 the government has been successful in implementing an IMF recovery programme. The civil service and army have been reduced in size, foreign investment encouraged, and property returned to Asians expelled by Idi Amin. In October 1994 the IMF approved a US$175 million loan to support the government's economic reform programme over the next three years. In February 1995 the Paris Club of bilateral official aid donors agreed to write off two-thirds of Uganda's debt to them. A World Bank sponsored debt relief programme is due to be implemented in April 1998 which will reduce Uganda's foreign debt by US$388 million.

The principal export earner is coffee, over 90 per cent of all exports. Attempts are being made to increase production of tobacco, cocoa, cotton and tea for export. Hydroelectricity is produced from the Owen Falls power station, some of which is exported to Kenya. The principal food crops are plantains, bananas, cassava, sweet potatoes, potatoes, maize and sorghum; livestock raising and inshore fishing are also important.

In 1993 Uganda had a trade deficit of US$278 million and a current account deficit of US$107 million. In 1995 imports totalled US$1,051 million and exports US$461 million.

GNP – US$4,668 million (1995); US$240 per capita (1995)
GDP – US$3,376 million (1992); US$153 per capita (1992)
ANNUAL AVERAGE GROWTH OF GDP – 9.4 per cent (1994)
TOTAL EXTERNAL DEBT – US$3,564 million (1995)

TRADE WITH UK	1995	1996
Imports from UK	£49,105,000	£50,751,000
Exports to UK	11,136,000	14,867,000

COMMUNICATIONS

There is an international airport at Entebbe, and eight other airfields around the country. Having no sea coast, Uganda is dependent upon rail and road links to Mombasa and Dar es Salaam for its trade. Over 5,000 km of the country's roads are currently being rehabilitated. A railway network joins the capital to the western, eastern and northern centres.

EDUCATION

Education is a joint undertaking by the government, local authorities and voluntary agencies. In 1988 Uganda had an estimated 7,905 primary schools, 774 secondary schools and various technical training institutions. There are four universities, Makerere University in Kampala, the Uganda Martyrs University, and at Mbale and Mbarara.
ILLITERACY RATE – 38.2 per cent
ENROLMENT (percentage of age group) – tertiary 1.3 per cent (1993)

UKRAINE
Ukraina

AREA – 233,090 sq. miles (603,700 sq. km). Neighbours: Belarus (north), Russia (north and east), Romania and Moldova (south-west), Hungary, Slovakia and Poland (west)

POPULATION – 52,100,000 (1996 estimate); 51,471,000 (1989 census): 73 per cent Ukrainian, 22 per cent Russian, with smaller numbers of Jews, Belarusians, Moldovans, Tatars, Poles, Hungarians and Greeks. The two main religions are Roman Catholicism and Orthodox. The Orthodox rite is divided between the Russian Orthodox Church with its Patriarch in Moscow and the Autocephalous Orthodox Church of the Ukraine with its own Patriarch in Kiev. There are also large numbers of Reformed Protestants in the Transcarpathian region and a sizeable Jewish community in Kiev. The main languages are Ukrainian (73 per cent) and Russian (22 per cent). Ukrainian is an Eastern Slavonic language related to Russian and Belarusian

CAPITAL – Kiev (population, 2,642,700, 1992)

MAJOR CITIES – Dnepropetrovsk (1,189,900); Donetsk (1,121,400); Kharkov (1,621,600); ΨOdessa (1,095,000), 1992 estimates

CURRENCY – Hryvna of 100 kopiykas

NATIONAL DAY – 24 August (Independence Day)

NATIONAL FLAG – Two horizontal stripes of blue over yellow

LIFE EXPECTANCY (years) – male 66.14; female 75.17

POPULATION GROWTH RATE – 0.0 per cent (1994)

POPULATION DENSITY – 86 per sq. km (1994)

URBAN POPULATION – 68.0 per cent (1993)

ILLITERACY RATE – 1.2 per cent

ENROLMENT (percentage of age group) – tertiary 45.9 per cent (1991)

The area of the present Ukraine is larger than that of the Ukrainian Soviet Republic formed in 1917–19 because of the westward territorial expansion of the former Soviet Union in the 1939–45 period and the addition of the Crimea from Russia in 1954. Ukraine now consists of 25 regions: Cherkassy, Chernigov, Chernovtsy, Crimea, Dnepropetrovsk, Donetsk, Ivano-Frankovsk, Kharkov, Kherson, Khmelnitsky, Kiev, Kirovograd, Lugansk, Lvov, Nikolayev, Odessa, Poltava, Rovno, Sumy, Ternopol, Transcarpathia, Vinnitsa, Volhynia, Zaporozhye and Zhitomir.

Most of Ukraine forms a plain with small elevations. The Carpathian mountains lie in the south-western part of the republic. The main rivers are the Dnieper with its tributaries, the Southern Bug and the Northern Donets (a tributary of the Don). The climate is moderate with relatively mild winters (particularly in the south-west) and hot summers.

HISTORY AND POLITICS

The earliest Russian state was formed in the middle reaches of the Dnieper River with its capital at Kiev in the ninth century AD. The state united the two large Slav states of Kiev and Novgorod and established the first common Russian language and nationality. The state lasted until Kiev fell to the Mongols in 1240. For the next four centuries Ukraine was invaded and ruled by Tatars, Turks, Poles, Hungarians and Lithuanians. In 1648 the Ukrainians threw off Polish rule to become independent and increasingly allied with Russia (formerly Muscovy). During the

reign of Catherine the Great of Russia (1763–96) Ukraine and the Crimea came under Russian control.

By the time of the Treaty of Brest-Litovsk in March 1918, most of Ukraine had been occupied by German and Austrian forces. The Treaty forced the Soviet government in Moscow to cede parts of western Ukraine to Germany and Austria-Hungary and accept the independence of the remainder. After the defeat of Germany in 1918, Ukraine became a battleground in the Russian civil war before the imposition of Soviet rule in 1922. Ukraine became a constituent republic of the USSR on 30 December 1922.

Ukraine declared itself independent of the Soviet Union, subject to a referendum, after the failed Moscow coup in August 1991. The referendum was held on 1 December 1991 and 90 per cent of the electorate voted for independence.

Political power in Ukraine in 1991–4 rested with the former Communists, led by President Leonid Kravchuk, in loose alliance with the Rukh nationalist party. This has limited political and economic change, although Leonid Kuchma, prime minister 1992–3, began to introduce economic reforms. Kuchma resigned in September 1993 after the Supreme Council obstructed his reform programme and President Kravchuk effectively took over the government.

In the legislative elections to the 450-seat Supreme Council in March to November 1994, the western regions of Ukraine voted for nationalist and reformist candidates while the eastern regions voted for Communist and allied ones; the result was a majority of Communist and allied candidates, plus 'independents' who were mainly agricultural and industrial managers tied to the status quo. In the June 1994 presidential election Kuchma defeated President Kravchuk.

A power struggle soon developed between President Kuchma and the Supreme Council. Kuchma's reformist government lost a no confidence vote in the Supreme Council but the President refused to dismiss it, and in June 1995 secured the passing of a 'constitutional treaty' by the Supreme Council. This gives the president the power to appoint the government without reference to the Supreme Council and allows greater presidential power to rule by decree. These changes were incorporated into a new constitution adopted by the Supreme Council on 28 June 1996. The constitution also provides for the Supreme Council to be renamed the People's Council (*Narodna Rada*) and for the creation of a Constitutional Court. Legislative elections are due to be held in March 1998 and a presidential election in October 1999.

INSURGENCIES

The Crimean parliament voted to make Crimea an autonomous republic in September 1991, which was accepted by Kiev, but then voted for independence in May 1992, which was not accepted and was suspended. A Russian nationalist, Yuri Meshkov, was elected President of Crimea in January 1994 and the Crimean parliament in May 1994 restored the suspended 1992 constitution declaring sovereignty. A constitutional and political crisis in Crimea caused by a power struggle between President Meshkov and the Crimean parliament from September 1994 onwards was resolved by Ukrainian intervention in March 1995. Direct presidential rule over Crimea was imposed in April 1995, to be lifted in August following elections to the Crimean parliament which saw a dramatic drop in support for pro-Russian parties. Arkady Demydenko was appointed Prime Minister of Crimea on 26 February 1996.

A referendum in June 1994 in the Donbass region of eastern Ukraine in favour of closer economic ties with

Russia and making Russian an official language was overwhelmingly passed, as was one in the Crimea in favour of dual Russian–Ukrainian citizenship.

FOREIGN RELATIONS

Since the demise of the Soviet Union, Russia and Ukraine have clashed over defence issues. All strategic nuclear weapons were placed under a central CIS command in December 1991, but on the abolition of the central command in July 1993 the government claimed possession of all nuclear weapons on its territory. Despite international pressure, the Supreme Council only ratified the START I Treaty in February 1994 and the Nuclear Non-Proliferation Treaty in November 1994.

Under a January 1994 USA–Russia–Ukraine Treaty, Ukraine agreed to transfer its nuclear arsenal to Russia for dismantling over a seven-year period. This was completed in May 1996. In return Ukraine has received a territorial guarantee from Russia, a cancellation of a large part of its debt to Russia, and nuclear security guarantees from Russia and the USA. Ukraine will also receive low-grade uranium from Russia for use in its power stations; and economic and technical aid from the USA.

In May 1997 a treaty of friendship and co-operation was signed with Russia. Agreement was also reached over the division of the former Soviet Black Sea Fleet. Russia is to gain four-fifths of the fleet and will rent most of the port of Sevastopol. The rent will be used to pay off part of Ukraine's debt to Russia.

HEAD OF STATE

President, Leonid Kuchma, *elected* 10 July 1994, *sworn in* 19 July 1994

CABINET *as at June 1997*

Prime Minister, Vasyl Durdynets
Deputy PMs, Mikhail Zubets *(Agro-Industrial Complex);* Sergei Tigipko *(Economic Reform Issues);* Ivan Kuras *(Humanitarian Issues)*
Coal Industry, Yuriy Rusantsov
Culture, Dmytro Ostapenko
Defence, Alexander Kuzmuk
Economy, Yury Yekhanurov
Education, Mykhailo Zgurovsky
Emergency Situations and Protection of the Population Against the Consequences of the Chernobyl Accident, Valery Kalchenko
Energy, Yuri Bochkaryov
Environmental Protection and Nuclear Safety, Yuriy Kostenko
Family and Youth, Syuzanna Stanik
Finance, Igor Mityukov
Fisheries, Mykola Shvedenko
Foreign Affairs, Gennadi Udovenko
Foreign Economic Relations and Trade, Serhiy Osyka
Forestry, Valeriy Samoplavsky
Health, Andrei Serdyuk
Industry, Valeriy Mazur
Information, Zinovy Kulik
Interior, Yuriy Kravchenko
Justice, Serhiy Holovaty
Labour, Nikolai Beloblotsky
Machine Building, Military Industrial Complex and Conversion, Vasyl Gureyev
Minister of State, Anatoly Minchenko
Science and Technologies, Vladimir Seminozhenko
Social Protection of the Population, Pyotr Ovcharenko
Statistics, vacant
Transport, Mykola Kruhlov

Chairman of the Supreme Council, Alexander Moroz

UKRAINIAN EMBASSY
78 Kensington Park Road, London W11 2PL
Tel 0171-727 6312
Ambassador Extraordinary and Plenipotentiary, HE Prof. Sergui Komissarenko, apptd 1992
Minister Plenipotentiary, Dr Y. Sergeyev
Counsellor (Economic and Commercial), Dr B. Savchuk

BRITISH EMBASSY
252025 Kiev Desyatinna 9
Tel: Kiev 462 0011
Ambassador Extraordinary and Plenipotentiary, HE Roy Reeve, apptd 1995
Consul-General and Deputy Head of Mission, S. Butt
Defence Attaché, Capt. L. Merrick
First Secretary (Commercial), T. Abbott-Watt

BRITISH COUNCIL DIRECTOR – T. Sholtz *(acting)*, 9/1 Bessarabska Ploshcha, Flat 9, Kiev 252004

DEFENCE

The Army has 4,026 main battle tanks, 6,919 armoured personnel carriers and armoured infantry fighting vehicles, 3,727 artillery pieces and 270 attack helicopters. The Navy has three submarines, four principal surface combat vessels and five patrol and coastal vessels at four bases. The Air Force has 789 combat aircraft and 24 attack helicopters.
MILITARY EXPENDITURE – 3.0 per cent of GDP (1995)
MILITARY PERSONNEL – 363,800: Army 187,800, Navy 16,000, Air Force 124,000, Paramilitaries 36,000
CONSCRIPTION DURATION – 18 months to two years

ECONOMY

Throughout 1991–4 the Communist-led government and legislature obstructed economic reform and economic mismanagement resulted. The economy came close to collapse because of hyperinflation caused by the printing of money to support uneconomic enterprises and to pay strikers' wage demands. Industrial output and GDP fell dramatically, while Russia threatened to cut all oil and gas supplies as Ukraine could not pay in hard currency. Ukraine has joined the CIS economic union as an associate member and is likely to seek full membership for access to better trading relations with Russia.

President Kuchma has, since September 1994, introduced a wide-ranging economic reform programme. Ukraine has received large amounts of foreign aid in support of its economic reform programme and for the closure of the Chernobyl nuclear plant which suffered a partial melt-down in 1986. In May 1995 the IMF approved a standby loan of US$867 million; in December 1995 the G7 countries and the IAEA agreed to grant Ukraine US$500 million in exchange for the closure of Chernobyl by 2000; and the USA granted US$1,200 million in February 1996. An aid package worth US$3,000 million was approved by international donors in October 1996.

Ukraine is still in disagreement with Russia over the division of assets and debts of the former Soviet Union. A large proportion of Ukraine's debt to Russia has been paid by granting Russian enterprises shares in Ukrainian firms which are to be privatized; the remainder of the debt has been rescheduled. Russia accounts for 40 per cent of Ukraine's trade turnover and supplies all its oil needs and more than half of its industrial raw materials and components. Agreement was reached with Turkey in June 1997 to build an oil pipeline which will reduce Ukraine's dependence on Russia.

The southern part of the country contains a coal-mining and iron and steel industrial area which was the largest in the former Soviet Union. Ukraine also contains engineering and chemical industries and ship-building yards on the Black Sea coast. Ukrainian agricultural production is good with large areas under cultivation with wheat, cotton, flax and sugar beet; stock-raising is very important. There are large deposits of coal and salt in the Donets Basin, of iron ore in Krivoy Rog and near Kerch in the Crimea, of manganese in Nikopol, and of quicksilver in Nikitovka.

The major ports are Odessa, Nikolayev, Kerch and Sevastopol.

In 1995 imports totalled US$11,379 million and exports US$11,567 million.

GNP – US$84,084 million (1995); US$1,630 per capita (1995)
GDP – US$219,738 million (1992); US$358 per capita (1992)
INFLATION RATE – 376.7 per cent (1995)
TOTAL EXTERNAL DEBT – US$8,434 million (1995)

TRADE WITH UK	1995	1996
Imports from UK	£111,106,000	£141,896,000
Exports to UK	22,941,000	23,875,000

UNITED ARAB EMIRATES
Al-Imarat Al-Arabiya Al-Muttahida

AREA – 32,278 sq. miles (83,600 sq. km) approximately
POPULATION – 2,377,453 (1995), of which 75 per cent are expatriates. The official language is Arabic, and English is widely spoken. The established religion is Islam
CAPITAL – Abu Dhabi (population, 450,000)
CURRENCY – UAE dirham of 100 fils (Dh)
NATIONAL DAY – 2 December
NATIONAL FLAG – Horizontal stripes of green over white over black with vertical red stripe in the hoist
LIFE EXPECTANCY (years) – male 72.95; female 75.27
POPULATION GROWTH RATE – 2.7 per cent (1994)
POPULATION DENSITY – 22 per sq. km (1994)

The United Arab Emirates is situated in the south-east of the Arabian peninsula. Six of the emirates lie on the shore of the Gulf between the Musandam peninsula in the east and the Qatar peninsula in the west while the seventh, Fujairah, lies on the Gulf of Oman. The climate varies between hot and humid in May to September and mild with erratic rainfall in October to April.

HISTORY AND POLITICS

The United Arab Emirates (formerly the Trucial States) is composed of seven emirates (Abu Dhabi, Ajman, Dubai, Fujairah, Ras al-Khaimah, Sharjah and Umm al-Qaiwain) which came together as an independent state on 2 December 1971 when they ended their individual special treaty relationships with the British government (Ras al-Khaimah joined the other six on 10 February 1972). On independence the Union Government assumed full responsibility for all internal and external affairs apart from some internal matters that remained the prerogative of the individual emirates.

FOREIGN RELATIONS

Relations with Iran remain strained over Iran's illegal occupation of three UAE islands in the Gulf (Abu Musa and the Two Tunbs).

POLITICAL SYSTEM

Overall authority lies with the Supreme Council of the seven emirate rulers, each of whom also governs in his own territory. The president and vice-president are elected every five years by the Supreme Council from among its members. The Supreme Council appoints the Council of Ministers. A 40-member Federal National Council, drawn proportionately from each emirate and composed of appointees of the rulers, studies draft laws referred to it by the Council of Ministers. Each emirate also has its separate government, with Abu Dhabi having an executive council chaired by the Crown Prince.

The legal system consists of both secular and religious courts guided by the Islamic philosophy of justice. Individual emirates retain their own penal codes and courts alongside a federal court system and penal code.

HEAD OF STATE
President, HH Sheikh Zayed bin Sultan al-Nahyan (*Abu Dhabi*), *elected* 1971, *re-elected* 1976, 1981, 1986, 1991, October 1996
Vice-President, Prime Minister, HH Sheikh Maktoun bin Rashid al-Maktoum (*Dubai*)

SUPREME COUNCIL
The President
The Vice-President
HH Sheikh Sultan bin Mohammed al-Qassimi (*Sharjah*)
HH Sheikh Saqr bin Mohammed al-Qassimi (*Ras Al-Khaimah*)
HH Sheikh Hamid bin Mohammed al-Sharqi (*Fujairah*)
HH Sheikh Humaid bin Rashid al-Nuaimi (*Ajman*)
HH Sheikh Rashid bin Ahmed al-Mualla (*Umm al-Qaiwain*)

COUNCIL OF MINISTERS *as at July 1997*
The Vice-President
Deputy PM, Sheikh Sultan bin Zayed al-Nahyan
Agriculture, Saeed Mohammed Al-Ragabani
Communications, Ahmed Humaid Al-Tayer
Defence, HH Gen. Sheikh Mohammed bin Rashid Al-Maktoum
Economy and Commerce, HH Sheikh Fahim bin Sultan Al Qassimi
Education and Youth, Dr Abdul Aziz Al-Sharhan
Electricity and Water, Humaid bin Nasser al-Owais
Financial and Industrial Affairs, Dr Mohammed Khalfan bin Kharbash
Foreign Affairs, Rashid Abdullah Al-Nuaimi
Health, Hamad Abdul Rahman Al-Madfa
Higher Education and Scientific Research, HH Sheikh Nahyan bin Mubarak Al-Nahyan
Information and Culture, HH Sheikh Abdullah bin Zayed Al-Nayhan
Interior, Lt.-Gen. Dr Mohammed Saeed Al-Badi
Justice, Islamic Affairs and Endowments, Mohammed Nakhira Al-Dhaheri
Labour and Social Affairs, Humaid Al-Tayer
Minister of State for Cabinet Affairs, Saeed Khalfan Al-Gaith
Minister of State for Finance and Industry, Dr Mohammed Khalfan bin Kharbash
Minister of State for Foreign Affairs, Sheikh Hamdan bin Zayed Al Nahyan
Minister of State for Supreme Council Affairs, Sheikh Majed bin Saeed Al-Nuaimi
Petroleum and Mineral Resources, Obeid bin Saif Al Nasiri
Planning, Sheikh Humaid bin Ahmed Al-Mualla
Public Works and Housing, Rakkad bin Salem Al Rakkad

EMBASSY OF THE UNITED ARAB EMIRATES
30 Princes Gate, London SW7 1PT
Tel 0171–5811281
Ambassador Extraordinary and Plenipotentiary, HE Easa Saleh Al-Gurg, CBE, apptd 1991
Military Attaché, Col. B. S. B. Al-Noaimi
Cultural Attaché, A. Al-Marri

BRITISH EMBASSIES
PO Box 248, Abu Dhabi
Tel: Abu Dhabi 326600
Ambassador Extraordinary and Plenipotentiary, HE Anthony
Harris, CMG, LVO, apptd 1994
Counsellor and Deputy Head of Mission, P. Morgan
Defence and Military Attaché, Col. C. J. Copeland

PO Box 65, Dubai
Tel: Dubai 521070
Counsellor and Consul-General, C. Wilton
Deputy Head of Post, Consul and First Secretary (Commercial), H.
Dunnachie, MBE

BRITISH COUNCIL REPRESENTATIVES
Abu Dhabi – R. Sykes, PO Box 46523, Abu Dhabi
Dubai – G. McCulloch (*Cultural Attaché*)

DEFENCE

The Army has 201 main battle tanks, 918 armoured
personnel carriers and armoured infantry fighting vehicles, and 257 artillery pieces. The Navy has one frigate and
19 patrol and coastal vessels. The Air Force has 99 combat
aircraft and 42 armed helicopters.
MILITARY EXPENDITURE – 4.8 per cent of GDP (1995)
MILITARY PERSONNEL – 64,500: Army 59,000, Navy
1,500, Air Force 4,000

ECONOMY

The UAE is the Gulf's third largest oil producer after Saudi
Arabia and Iran. It has an OPEC quota of 2,161,000 barrels
per day (bpd), and has oil reserves of 200,000 million
barrels and gas reserves of 200,000,000 million cubic feet.
Oil production in 1994 accounted for 33 per cent of GDP.
Other important sectors of the economy are government,
re-exporting, construction, manufacturing (aluminium,
cement, chemicals, fertilizers, ship repair), finance and
insurance services, and transport and communications.
Tourism is growing in importance. Agricultural production (vegetables, dates, fruit, milk, eggs, poultry,
flowers, olives, animal husbandry) has increased significantly due to large-scale water desalination and irrigation
projects, with 250,000 hectares of agricultural land in 1996.
There is no personal or corporate taxation apart from on
oil companies and foreign banks.
Fourteen major ports, of which nine are modern
container terminals, handled 35 million tonnes of cargo in
1993. Six international airports (Dubai, Abu Dhabi,
Sharjah, Ras al-Khaimah, Fujairah, Al Ain) are in operation.
Oil revenues over the past 30 years have enabled the
government to invest heavily in education, health and
social services, housing, transport and communications
infrastructure, and agriculture, and enabled the UAE's
citizens to have one of the highest GDPs per capita in the
world.
In 1993 imports totalled US$19,520 million.
GNP – US$42,806 million (1995); US$17,400 per capita
(1995)
GDP – US$33,344 million (1992); US$20,758 per capita
(1992)
ANNUAL AVERAGE GROWTH OF GDP – 2.7 per cent (1992)

Trade with UK	1995	1996
Imports from UK	£1,184,136,000	£1,394,106,000
Exports to UK	281,041,000	380,903,000

EDUCATION AND SOCIAL WELFARE

In 1995–6 there were 615 government schools, where
education is free; and 390 private schools. The Emirates
University is based at Al Ain (Abu Dhabi); there are also
three Colleges of Technology (Abu Dhabi, Dubai, Al Ain).
There were 33 government and 14 private hospitals in
1994.
ILLITERACY RATE – 20.8 per cent
ENROLMENT (percentage of age group) – primary 100 per
cent (1994); secondary 83 per cent (1994); tertiary 10.5
per cent (1992)

THE EMIRATES

ABU DHABI

Abu Dhabi is by far the largest emirate, with an area of
30,888 sq. miles (80,000 sq. km) stretching from Khor al-
Odaid in the west to the borders with Dubai in the Jebel Ali
area. It includes six villages in the Buraimi oasis, the other
three being part of the Sultanate of Oman, and a number of
settlements in the Liwa oasis system. The population of the
Emirate (1995) is 928,360.

AJMAN AND UMM AL-QAIWAIN

Ajman (100 sq. miles, 259 sq. km) and Umm al-Qaiwain
(300 sq. miles, 777 sq. km) are the smallest emirates in area;
they have populations (1995) of 118,812 and 35,157
respectively. Both lie on the Gulf coast although Ajman
has two inland enclaves at Manama and Masfut.

DUBAI

Dubai is the second largest emirate both in size (1,506 sq.
miles, 3,900 sq. km) and in population, which is (1995)
674,101. The town of Dubai is the main port for the UAE.
Dubai's prosperity was established by this trade long
before the discovery of oil in 1966.

FUJAIRAH

Fujairah, with an area of 502 sq. miles (1,300 sq. km) and a
population (1995) of 76,254, is the most remote of the seven
emirates, lying on the Gulf of Oman coast and only
connected by a metal road to the rest of the country.
Largely agricultural, its population is spread between the
slopes of the inland Hajar mountain range and the town of
Fujairah itself, together with a number of smaller settlements on the comparatively fertile plain on the coast.

RAS AL-KHAIMAH

Ras al-Khaimah has an area of 656 sq. miles (1,700 sq. km)
and a population (1995) of 144,430, of whom more than half
live in the town. An ancient sea-port, near to which
archaeological remains have been found, Ras al-Khaimah
is the most agricultural of the emirates, producing
vegetables, dates, fruit and tobacco.

SHARJAH

Sharjah, with an area of 1,004 sq. miles (2,600 sq. km) and a
population (1995) of 400,339, has declined from its former
position as principal town in the area. Sharjah is connected
by metalled roads to all the other northern emirates.

UNITED STATES OF AMERICA

AREA – 3,540,321 sq. miles (9,169,389 sq. km). Neighbours:
Canada (north), Mexico (south)
POPULATION – 265,284,000 (1996 estimate)
CAPITAL – Washington DC (population, 6,919,572, 1992).
The area of the District of Columbia (with which the
City of Washington is considered co-extensive) is 61 sq.
miles, with a resident population (1992 estimate) of
585,221. The District of Columbia is governed by an
elected mayor and City Council

MAJOR CITIES –ΨNew York (7,333,253); ΨLos Angeles (3,448,613); ΨChicago (2,731,743); ΨHouston (1,702,086); ΨPhiladelphia (1,524,249); ΨSan Diego (1,151,977); Phoenix (1,048,949); Dallas (1,022,830); San Antonio (998,905); ΨDetroit (992,038), 1994 estimates

CURRENCY – US dollar (US$) of 100 cents

NATIONAL ANTHEM – The Star-Spangled Banner

NATIONAL DAY – 4 July (Independence Day)

NATIONAL FLAG – Thirteen horizontal stripes, alternately red and white, with blue canton in the fly showing 50 white stars in nine horizontal rows of six and five alternately (known as the Star-Spangled Banner)

LIFE EXPECTANCY (years) – male 72.00; female 78.90

POPULATION GROWTH RATE – 1.1 per cent (1994)

POPULATION DENSITY – 28 per sq. km (1994)

URBAN POPULATION – 75.2 per cent (1990)

The coastline has a length of about 2,069 miles on the Atlantic, 7,623 miles on the Pacific, 1,060 miles on the Arctic, and 1,631 miles on the Gulf of Mexico.

The principal river is the Mississippi-Missouri-Red (3,710 miles long), traversing the whole country to its mouth in the Gulf of Mexico; its main affluents are the Yellowstone, Platte, Arkansas, and Ohio rivers. The chain of the Rocky Mountains separates the western portion of the country from the remainder. West of these, bordering the Pacific coast, the Cascade Mountains and Sierra Nevada form the outer edge of a high tableland, consisting in part of stony and sandy desert and partly of grazing land and forested mountains, and including the Great Salt Lake, which extends to the Rocky Mountains. In the eastern states large forests still exist, the remnants of the forests which formerly extended over all the Atlantic slope. The highest point is Mount McKinley (20,320 ft) in Alaska, and the lowest point of dry land is in Death Valley (Inyo, California), 282 ft below sea-level.

AREA AND POPULATION

	Total land area 1990 (sq. miles)	Population census 1990
The United States (a)	3,536,278	248,709,873
Outlying areas under US jurisdiction	4,043	3,847,309
Territories	4,027	3,847,116
Puerto Rico	3,427	3,522,037
Guam	210	133,152
US Virgin Islands	134	101,809
American Samoa	77	46,773
Northern Mariana Is.	179	43,345
Other possessions	16	193
Population abroad (b)	–	925,845
TOTAL	3,540,321	253,483,027

(a) the 50 states and the Federal District of Columbia
(b) excludes US citizens temporarily abroad on business

RESIDENT POPULATION BY RACE 1990 (Thousands)

White	199,686.1
Black	29,986.1
*American Indian	1,959.2
Chinese	1,645.5
Filipino	1,406.8
Japanese	847.6
Asian Indian	815.4
Korean	798.8
Vietnamese	614.5
Other Asian	780.0
Pacific Islander	365.0
All other races	9,804.8
†Hispanic origin	22,354.1
Cuban	1,043.9
Mexican	13,495.9
Puerto Rican	2,727.8
Other Hispanic	5,086.4
TOTAL	248,709.9

*Includes Eskimo and Aleut
†Persons of Hispanic origin may be of any race

IMMIGRATION

From 1820 to 1996, 63,140,227 immigrants were admitted to the United States. Total number of immigrants in 1996 was 915,900, of which 402,309 came from North and South America (163,572 from Mexico), 307,807 from Asia and 141,581 from Europe.

HISTORY AND POLITICS

The area which is now the USA was first inhabited by nomadic hunters who probably arrived from Asia c.30,000 BC. The first (failed) European colony was founded by Sir Walter Raleigh in 1585. By 1733 there were 13 British colonies, composed largely of religious non-conformists who had left Britain to escape persecution; the French and Spanish had also founded colonies. Relations between the colonies reflected tensions and conflicts between the European powers in the 17th and 18th centuries; from 1689 to 1763 the French, with native Indians, frequently attacked British settlements. In accordance with the Peace of Paris (1763) Britain returned Cuba and the Philippines to Spain and received Florida in return and France ceded New Orleans and (until 1800) Louisiana to Spain.

The War of Independence broke out in 1775 largely because of the colonists' objection to being taxed by, but having no representation in, the British Parliament. The forces of the British government were defeated with French, Spanish and Dutch assistance. The Declaration of Independence which inaugurated the United States of America was signed on 4 July 1776; Britain recognized American sovereignty in 1783. The first federal constitution was drawn up in 1787; ten amendments, termed the Bill of Rights, were added in 1791. The 13 original states of the Union ratified the constitution between 1787 and 1790. Vermont, Kentucky and Tennessee were admitted in the 1790s but most of the states acceded in the 19th century as the opening up of the centre and west led to the creation of new states and European or neighbouring countries ceded or sold their territories to the USA.

The Civil War (1861-5) was fought over the issue of slavery, which was integral to the economy of the southern states but was opposed by the northern states. The northern states defeated the Confederacy of southern states (South Carolina, Georgia, Alabama, Florida, Mississippi, Louisiana), all of which had seceded from the Union between 1860 and 1861; they all re-entered the Union by 1870. From 1866 Negroes were given full rights as citizens.

The USA emerged as a world economic and military superpower in the 20th century and played a decisive role in the two world wars, in which it was engaged between 1917 and 1918, and between 1941 and 1945. Its economic and military (including nuclear) supremacy gave the USA a key role in shaping the post-war world. The USA facilitated the rebuilding of Europe through the Marshall Plan, oversaw the creation of the United Nations, International Monetary Fund and International Bank for Reconstruction and Development, and underpinned the new liberal world economy. The USA contended for global supremacy with the USSR and the two superpowers engaged in a costly arms race and 'cold war' fought by proxy in the Third World. The USA's opposition to communism led it into wars in Korea (1950-3) and Vietnam (1964-73). President Richard Nixon initiated détente with Russia and China in the early 1970s but was forced to resign in 1974 over corruption allegations (Watergate).

POLITICAL SYSTEM

By the constitution of 17 September 1787 (to which amendments were added in 1791, 1798, 1804, 1865, 1868, 1870, 1913, 1920, 1933, 1951, 1961, 1964, 1967, 1971 and 1992), the government of the United States is entrusted to three separate authorities: the executive (the president and Cabinet), the legislature (Congress) and the judicature.

The president is indirectly elected by an electoral college every four years. There is also a vice-president, who, should the president die, becomes president for the remainder of the term. The tenure of the presidency is limited to two terms.

The president, with the consent of the Senate, appoints the Cabinet officers and all the chief officials. He makes recommendation of a general nature to Congress, and when laws are passed by Congress he may return them to Congress with a veto. But if a measure so vetoed is again passed by both Houses of Congress by two-thirds majority in each House, it becomes law, notwithstanding the objection of the president. The president must be at least 35 years of age and a native citizen of the United States.

Presidential elections

Each state elects (on the first Tuesday after the first Monday in November of the year preceding the year in which the presidential term expires) a number of electors (members of the electoral college), equal to the whole number of Senators and Representatives to which the state may be entitled in the Congress. The electors for each state meet in their respective states on the first Monday after the second Wednesday in December following, and vote for a president by ballot. The ballots are then sent to Washington, and opened on 6 January by the President of the Senate in the presence of Congress. The candidate who has received a majority of the whole number of electoral votes cast is declared president for the ensuing term. If no one has a majority, then from the highest on the list (not exceeding three) the House of Representatives elects a president, the votes being taken by states, the representation from each state having one vote. A presidential term begins at noon on 20 January.

HEAD OF STATE

President of the United States, William Jefferson Blythe IV Clinton, *born* 19 August 1946, *elected* 1994, *re-elected* 1996. Democrat

Vice-President, Albert Gore, jun., *born* 31 March 1948

THE CABINET *as at August 1997*

Administrator, Environmental Protection Agency, Carol Browner
Agriculture, Daniel Glickman
Ambassador to the UN, Bill Richardson
Attorney-General, Janet Reno
Commerce, William Daley
Defence, William Cohen
Director, Office of Management and Budget, Franklin Raines
Education, Richard Riley
Energy, Federico Pena
Health and Human Services, Donna Shalala
Housing and Urban Development, Andrew Cuomo
Interior, Bruce Babbitt
Labour, Alexis Herman
National Security Adviser, Samuel Berger
Secretary of State, Madeleine Albright
Trade Representative, Charlene Barshefsky
Transportation, Rodney Slater
Treasury, Robert Rubin
Veterans' Affairs, Jesse Brown
White House Chief of Staff, Erskine Bowles

Other senior positions:
Director of CIA, George Tenet
Director, Office of National Drug Control Policy, Gen. Barry McCaffrey
Director of FBI, Louis Freeh
Chairman, Federal Reserve Board of Governors, Alan Greenspan

THE STATES OF THE UNION

The United States of America is a federal republic consisting of 50 states and the federal District of Columbia and of organized territories. Of the present 50 states, 13 are original states, seven were admitted without previous organization as territories, and 30 were admitted after such organization.

STATE (with date and *order* of admission)	LAND AREA sq. m.	POPULATION (1990 census)	CAPITAL	GOVERNOR (end of term in office)	
Alabama (Ala.) (1819) *(22)*	50,750	4,040,587	Montgomery	Fob James *(R)*	(1998)
Alaska (1959) *(49)*	570,374	550,043	Juneau	Tony Knowles *(D)*	(1998)
Arizona (Ariz.) (1912) *(48)*	113,642	3,665,228	Phoenix	J. Fife Symington *(R)*	(1998)
Arkansas (Ark.) (1836) *(25)*	52,075	2,350,725	Little Rock	Mike Huckabee *(R)*	(1998)
California (Calif.) (1850) *(31)*	155,973	29,760,021	Sacramento	Pete Wilson *(R)*	(1998)
Colorado (Colo.) (1876) *(38)*	103,729	3,294,394	Denver	Roy Romer *(D)*	(1998)
Connecticut (Conn.) § (1788) *(5)*	4,845	3,287,116	Hartford	John Rowland *(R)*	(1998)
Delaware (Del.) § (1787) *(1)*	1,955	666,168	Dover	Tom Carper *(D)*	(2000)
Florida (Fla.) (1845) *(27)*	53,997	12,937,926	Tallahassee	Lawton Chiles *(D)*	(1998)
Georgia (Ga.) § (1788) *(4)*	57,919	6,478,216	Atlanta	Zell Miller *(D)*	(1998)
Hawaii (1959) *(50)*	6,423	1,108,229	Honolulu	Ben Cayetano *(D)*	(1998)
Idaho (1890) *(43)*	82,751	1,006,749	Boise	Phil Batt*(R)*	(1998)
Illinois (Ill.) (1818) *(21)*	55,593	11,430,602	Springfield	Jim Edgar *(R)*	(1998)
Indiana (Ind.) (1816) *(19)*	35,870	5,544,159	Indianapolis	Frank O'Bannon *(D)*	(2000)
Iowa (1846) *(29)*	55,875	2,776,755	Des Moines	Terry Branstad *(R)*	(1998)
Kansas (Kan.) (1861) *(34)*	81,823	2,477,574	Topeka	Bill Graves *(R)*	(1998)
Kentucky (Ky.) (1792) *(15)*	39,732	3,685,296	Frankfort	Paul Patton *(D)*	(1999)
Louisiana (La.) (1812) *(18)*	43,566	4,219,973	Baton Rouge	Murphy Foster *(R)*	(1999)
Maine (Me.) (1820) *(23)*	30,865	1,227,928	Augusta	Angus King *(I)*	(1998)
Maryland (Md.) § (1788) *(7)*	9,775	4,781,468	Annapolis	Parris Glendening *(D)*	(1998)
Massachusetts (Mass.) § (1788) *(6)*	7,838	6,016,425	Boston	William Weld *(R)*	(1998)
Michigan (Mich.) (1837) *(26)*	56,809	9,295,297	Lansing	John Engler *(R)*	(1998)
Minnesota (Minn.) (1858) *(32)*	79,617	4,375,099	St Paul	Arne Carlson *(R)*	(1998)
Mississippi (Miss.) (1817) *(20)*	46,914	2,573,216	Jackson	Kirk Fordice *(R)*	(1999)
Missouri (Mo.) (1821) *(24)*	68,898	5,117,073	Jefferson City	Mel Carnahan *(D)*	(2000)
Montana (Mont.) (1889) *(41)*	145,556	799,065	Helena	Marc Racicot *(R)*	(2000)
Nebraska (Neb.) (1867) *(37)*	76,878	1,578,385	Lincoln	Ben Nelson *(D)*	(1998)
Nevada (Nev.) (1864) *(36)*	109,806	1,201,833	Carson City	Robert J. Miller *(D)*	(1998)
New Hampshire (NH) § (1788) *(9)*	8,969	1,109,252	Concord	Jeanne Shaheen *(D)*	(1998)
New Jersey (NJ) § (1787) *(3)*	7,419	7,730,188	Trenton	Christine Whitman *(R)*	(1997)
New Mexico (NM) (1912) *(47)*	121,365	1,515,069	Santa Fé	Gary Johnson *(R)*	(1998)
New York (NY) § (1788) *(11)*	47,224	17,990,455	Albany	George Pataki *(R)*	(1998)
North Carolina (NC) § (1789) *(12)*	48,718	6,628,637	Raleigh	James B. Hunt, jun. *(D)*	(2000)
North Dakota (ND) (1889) *(39)*	68,994	638,800	Bismarck	Edward Schafer *(R)*	(2000)
Ohio (1803) *(17)*	40,953	10,847,115	Columbus	George Voinovich *(R)*	(1998)
Oklahoma (Okla.) (1907) *(46)*	68,679	3,145,585	Oklahoma City	Frank Keating *(R)*	(1998)
Oregon (Ore.) (1859) *(33)*	96,003	2,842,321	Salem	John Kitzhaber *(D)*	(1998)
Pennsylvania (Pa.) § (1787) *(2)*	44,820	11,881,643	Harrisburg	Tom Ridge *(R)*	(1998)
Rhode Island (RI) § (1790) *(13)*	1,045	1,003,464	Providence	Lincoln Almond *(R)*	(1998)
South Carolina (SC) § (1788) *(8)*	30,111	3,486,703	Columbia	David Beasley *(R)*	(1998)
South Dakota (SD) (1889) *(40)*	75,896	696,004	Pierre	William Janklow *(R)*	(1998)
Tennessee (Tenn.) (1796) *(16)*	41,220	4,877,185	Nashville	Don Sundquist *(R)*	(1998)
Texas (1845) *(28)*	261,914	16,986,510	Austin	George W. Bush *(R)*	(1998)
Utah (1896) *(45)*	82,168	1,722,850	Salt Lake City	Mike Leavitt *(R)*	(2000)
Vermont (Vt.) (1791) *(14)*	9,249	562,758	Montpelier	Howard Dean *(D)*	(1998)
Virginia (Va.) § (1788) *(10)*	39,598	6,187,358	Richmond	George Allen *(R)*	(1997)
Washington (Wash.) (1889) *(42)*	66,581	4,866,692	Olympia	Gary Locke *(D)*	(2000)
West Virginia (W. Va.) (1863) *(35)*	24,087	1,793,477	Charleston	Cecil Underwood *(D)*	(2000)
Wisconsin (Wis.) (1848) *(30)*	54,314	4,891,769	Madison	Tommy Thompson *(R)*	(1998)
Wyoming (Wyo.) (1890) *(44)*	97,105	453,588	Cheyenne	Jim Geringer *(R)*	(1998)
Dist. of Columbia (DC) (1791)	61	606,900	—	Marion Barry *(D)* *(Mayor)*	

OUTLYING TERRITORIES AND POSSESSIONS

American Samoa	77	46,773	Pago Pago	Tauese Sunia *(D)*	(2000)
Guam	210	133,152	Agaña	Carl Gutierrez *(D)*	(1998)
Northern Mariana Islands	179	43,345	Saipan	Froilan C. Tenorio *(D)*	(1998)
Puerto Rico	3,427	3,522,037	San Juan	Dr Pedro J. Rossello *(D)*	(2000)
US Virgin Islands	134	101,809	Charlotte Amalie	Roy Schneider *(I)*	(1998)

§The 13 original states
D Democratic Party; *I* Independent; *R* Republican Party

UNITED STATES EMBASSY
24 Grosvenor Square, London WIA IAE
Tel 0171-499 9000
Ambassador Extraordinary and Plenipotentiary, HE Philip
  Lader, apptd 1997
Deputy Chief of Mission, R. Bradtke
Defence and Naval Attaché, Capt. J. Mader
Minister-Counsellors, L. M. Dent, jun. (*Administrative*);
  C. A. Ford (*Commercial*); M. N. Robinson (*Consular*)

BRITISH EMBASSY
3100 Massachusetts Avenue NW, Washington DC 20008
Tel: Washington DC 462 1340
Ambassador Extraordinary and Plenipotentiary, HE
  Christopher Meyer, CMG, apptd 1997
Ministers, S. Wright; H. P. Evans (*Economic*); J. Taylor
  (*Defence Material*); K. Pang, C. Jackson (Hong Kong
  Economic and Trade Affairs)
Head of British Defence Staff and Defence Attaché, Maj.-Gen. C.
  Vyvyan, CBE
Counsellor, R. French (*Management and Consul-General*)
Consul-General (*New York*) *and Director-General of Trade and
  Investment*, J. Ling, CMG
Cultural Attaché and British Council Director, D. Evans

BRITISH CONSULATES-GENERAL – Atlanta, Boston,
  Chicago, Houston, Los Angeles, New York and San
  Francisco
BRITISH CONSULATES – Anchorage, Charlotte,
  Cleveland, Dallas,Denver, Kansas City, Miami,
  Minneapolis, Nashville, New Orleans, Philadelphia,
  Portland, St Louis, Salt Lake City, Seattle and Puerto
  Rico
BRITISH-AMERICAN CHAMBER OF COMMERCE, 275
  Madison Avenue, New York 10016; UK OFFICE, Suite
  201, High Holborn, London WCIV 6RR

THE CONGRESS

Legislative power is vested in two houses, the Senate and
the House of Representatives. The Senate has 100
members, two Senators from each state, elected for the
term of six years, and each Senator has one vote.
Representatives are chosen in each state, by popular vote,
for two years.

The House of Representatives consists of 435 Representatives, a resident commissioner from Puerto Rico and
a delegate each from American Samoa, the District of
Columbia, Guam and the Virgin Islands.

Members of the 10th Congress were elected on 5
November 1996. The 105th Congress is constituted as
follows:

Senate – Republicans 55; Democrats 45; total 100
House of Representatives Republicans 227; Democrats 207;
  Independent 1; total 435

President of the Senate, The Vice-President
Senate Majority Leader, Trent Lott (*R*), *Mississippi*
Speaker of the House of Representatives, Newton Gingrich (*R*),
  Georgia
Secretary of the Senate, Gary Sisco
Clerk of the House of Representatives, Robin H. Carle

THE JUDICATURE

The federal judiciary consists of three sets of federal courts:
the Supreme Court at Washington DC, consisting of a
Chief Justice and eight Associate Justices, with original
jurisdiction in cases where a state is a party to the suit, and
with appellate jurisdiction from inferior federal courts and
from the judgments of the highest courts of the states; the

United States Courts of Appeals, dealing with appeals from
district courts and from certain federal administrative
agencies, and consisting of 168 circuit judges within 13
circuits; the 94 United States district courts served by 575
district court judges.

THE SUPREME COURT
US Supreme Court Building, Washington DC 20543

Chief Justice, William H. Rehnquist, *Arizona*, apptd 1986

Associate Justices
John Paul Stevens, *Illinois*, apptd 1975
Sandra Day O'Connor, *Arizona*, apptd 1981
Antonin Scalia, *Virginia*, apptd 1986
Anthony M. Kennedy, *California*, apptd 1988
David H. Souter, *New Hampshire*, apptd 1990
Clarence Thomas, *Georgia*, apptd 1991
Ruth Bader Ginsburg, *New York*, apptd 1993
Stephen Breyer, *Massachusetts*, apptd 1994

Clerk of the Supreme Court, William K. Suter

In 1995 there were 13,862,700 recorded offences: murder
and non-negligent manslaughter 21,610; forcible rape
97,470; robbery 580,510; aggravated assault 1,099,210;
burglary 2,593,800; larceny-theft 7,997,700; motor vehicle
theft 1,472,400.

DEFENCE

Each military department is separately organized and
functions under the direction, authority and control of the
Secretary of Defence. The Air Force has primary responsibility for the Department of Defence space development
programmes and projects.

Under strategic command the USA has 432 submarine-
launched ballistic missiles, 550 inter-continental ballistic
missiles, 128 heavy nuclear-capable bombers and 90
strategic defence interceptor aircraft together with multiple intelligence satellites, radars and early warning systems
throughout the world.

The Army has 10,497 main battle tanks, 30,583 armoured infantry fighting vehicles and armoured personnel
carriers, 8,160 artillery pieces, 300 aircraft and 1,476 armed
helicopters.

The Navy has 17 strategic submarines, 78 tactical
submarines, 12 aircraft carriers, 31 cruisers, 52 destroyers,
49 frigates, 25 patrol and coastal vessels, 347 amphibious
and support ships, 1,728 combat aircraft and 487 armed
helicopters.

The Marine Corps has 403 main battle tanks, 1,322
amphibious armoured vehicles and 789 artillery pieces.
The Air Force has 178 long-range strike aircraft, 2,626
tactical combat aircraft and 218 helicopters.

The major deployments of US personnel overseas are:
Germany (63,377); South Korea (37,213); Japan (37,137);
Italy (12,192); UK (11,562); Panama (6,101); Turkey
(3,056); Saudi Arabia (2,541).
MILITARY EXPENDITURE – 3.8 per cent of GDP (1995)
MILITARY PERSONNEL – 1,483,800: Army 495,000, Navy
  426,700, Marine Corps 173,900, Air Force 388,200

Secretary of Defence (*in the Cabinet*), William Cohen
Chairman, Joint Chiefs of Staff, Gen. Henry Shelton

ECONOMY AND FINANCE

In 1995 central government budget receipts totalled
US$1,351.5 billion and outlays US$1,515.4 billion. The
largest items of expenditure were: defence US$271.9
billion; social security US$335.8 billion, income security
US$220.1 billion, debt interest US$232.2 billion. Social
welfare expenditure was US$1,363,884 million in 1993

including US$657,328 million (US$2,515 per capita) spent on social insurance, US$331,910 million (US$1,274 per capita) spent on education and US$74,503 million (US$286 per capita) spent on health.

At the end of September 1992 the total gross federal debt stood at US$4,002,062 million.

GNP – US$7,100,007 million (1995); US$26,980 per capita (1995)

GDP – US$5,575,429 million (1992); US$23,332 per capita (1992)

ANNUAL AVERAGE GROWTH OF GDP – 2.0 per cent (1995)

INFLATION RATE – 2.8 per cent (1995)

UNEMPLOYMENT – 5.6 per cent (1995)

GROSS DOMESTIC PRODUCT BY INDUSTRY 1994

	US$ millions
Private industries	6,000,021
Agriculture, forestry, fisheries	117,848
Mining	90,058
Construction	269,232
Manufacturing	1,197,098
Transportation and public utilities	606,354
Wholesale trade	461,863
Retail trade	609,908
Finance, insurance, and real estate	1,273,678
Services	1,342,720
Government and government enterprises	931,336
Statistical discrepancy	31,262
TOTAL	12,931,378

AGRICULTURE

The total number of farms in 1997 was 2,058,910, with a total area of land in farms of 968,338,000 acres, and an average acreage per farm of 470 acres. Principal crops are corn for grain, soybeans, wheat, hay, cotton, tobacco, grain sorghums, potatoes, oranges and barley. Gross income from farming in 1996 was US$233 billion. Cash income from all crops in 1996 was US$109 billion and from livestock and livestock products US$92.9 billion.

MINERALS

The value of non-fuel raw mineral production in 1996 totalled an estimated US$38 billion. Mineral exports in 1996 were valued at US$33 billion, and imports at US$49 billion. In 1996 the following quantities of minerals were produced: iron ore 62,132,000 tons; marketable phosphate rock 45,400,000 tons; copper 1,910,000 tons; zinc 575,000 tons; lead 418,000 tons.

ENERGY

Production in 1995 was 71.12 quadrillion BTU, principally coal, natural gas and crude oil. Coal accounted for almost half of energy exports of 4.58 quadrillion BTU. Imports were 22.48 quadrillion BTU, of which crude oil was 15.63 quadrillion BTU, to meet consumption of 90.94 quadrillion BTU (quadrillion=10^{15}).

TRADE

In 1994 the USA had a trade deficit of US$166,360 million and a current account deficit of US$156,157 million. In 1995 imports totalled US$770,958 million and exports US$584,743 million.

Trade with UK	1995	1996
Imports from UK	£17,949,473,000	£19,833,631,000
Exports to UK	20,268,863,000	23,011,494,000

COMMUNICATIONS

In 1994 there were 3.9 million miles of public roads and streets, of which 3.09 million miles were in rural areas and 813,591 miles were in urban areas. Surfaced roads and streets account for 59.8 per cent of the total. An estimated total of US$90,074 million was spent in 1994 on roads and streets in the United States.

The ocean-going merchant marine on 1 April 1997 consisted of 490 vessels of 1,000 gross tons and over, of which 296 were privately-owned and 194 were government-owned ships. There were 140 ships in the National Defence Reserve Fleet of inactive government-owned vessels.

According to preliminary figures, US domestic and international scheduled airlines in 1996 carried 581,18,585 passengers over 578,611,749 revenue passenger miles. Operating revenues of all US scheduled airlines were US$101,598,692,005 in 1996. Total operating expenses rose to US$95,387,159,915 in 1996. Scheduled operations showed a net operating profit of US$6,211,532,090 in 1996.

EDUCATION

All the states and the District of Columbia have compulsory school attendance laws. In general, children are obliged to attend school from seven to 16 years of age.

Most of the revenue for public elementary and secondary school purposes comes from federal, state, and local governments. Less than three per cent comes from gifts and from tuition and transportation fees.

Among the better-known universities are: Harvard, founded at Cambridge, Mass. in 1636, and named after John Harvard of Emmanuel College, Cambridge, England, who bequeathed to it his library and a sum of money in 1638; Yale, founded at New Haven, Connecticut, in 1701; Princeton, NJ, founded 1746.

ILLITERACY RATE – 0.5 per cent

ENROLMENT (percentage of age group) – primary 100 per cent; secondary 90 per cent; tertiary 79.7 per cent (1993)

US TERRITORIES, ETC

Responsibility for territorial affairs generally is centred in the Office of the Assistant Secretary, Territorial and International Affairs, Department of the Interior, Washington DC.

As well as the territories mentioned below, the USA also exercises sovereignty over the following:

JOHNSTON ATOLL – two small islands, less than 1 sq. mile in area, to the south-west of Hawaii; administered by the US Air Force

MIDWAY ISLANDS – two islands (area, 3 sq. miles), at the western end of the Hawaiian chain; administered by the US Navy

WAKE ISLANDS – area about 3 sq. miles and average elevation of less than 3 metres, lying about 2,300 miles west of Hawaii; administered by the US Air Force

Certain small guano islands, rocks or keys, considered as appertaining to the USA

THE COMMONWEALTH OF PUERTO RICO

AREA – 3,427 sq. miles (8,875 sq. km)

POPULATION – 3,733,000 (1996 estimate); 3,522,037 (1990 census). The majority of the inhabitants are of Spanish descent, and Spanish and English are the official languages

CAPITAL – ΨSan Juan, population of the municipality (1990), 437,745. Other major towns are: Bayamón (220,262); ΨPonce (187,749); Carolina (177,806)

Puerto Rico (Rich Port) is an island of the Greater Antilles group in the West Indies.

Puerto Rico was discovered in 1493 by Columbus and explored by Ponce de León in 1508. It was a Spanish possession until 1898, when the USA took formal possession as a result of the Spanish-American War.

The 1952 constitution establishes the Commonwealth of Puerto Rico with full powers of local government. The Legislative Assembly consists of two elected houses; the Senate of 27 members and the House of Representatives of 51 members. The term of the Legislative Assembly is four years. The Governor is popularly elected for a term of four years. Residents of Puerto Rico are US citizens. Puerto Rico is represented in Congress by a Resident Commissioner, elected for a term of four years, who has a seat in the House of Representatives but not a vote, although he has a right to vote on those committees of which he is a member. A plebiscite on the future constitutional status of Puerto Rico was held on 14 November 1993 in which 48 per cent voted to maintain the existing Commonwealth status, 46 per cent voted for full US statehood and 4 per cent for independence.

Principal crops are sugar cane, coffee, vegetables, fruits and tobacco. Most valuable areas of manufacturing are chemicals and allied products, metal products and machinery, and food processing.

Governor, Dr Pedro J. Rossello

Trade with UK	1995	1996
Imports from UK	£466,196,000	£307,035,000
Exports to UK	81,961,000	104,799,000

GUAM

AREA – 210 sq. miles (544 sq. km)
POPULATION – 133,152 (1990 estimate); mostly of Chamorro stock mingled with Filipino and Spanish blood. The Chamorro language belongs to the Malayo-Polynesian family, but with considerable admixture of Spanish. Chamorro and English are the official languages and most residents are bilingual
CAPITAL – Agaña. Port of entry, ΨApra

Guam is the largest of the Mariana Islands, in the north Pacific Ocean.

Guam was occupied by the Japanese in December 1941 but was recaptured by US forces in 1944. Under the Organic Act of Guam 1950, Guam has statutory powers of self-government, and Guamanians are US citizens. A 21-member unicameral legislature is elected biennially. The Governor and Lieutenant Governor are popularly elected. A non-voting Delegate is elected to serve in the US House of Representatives. There is also a District Court of Guam, with original jurisdiction in cases under federal law.

Guam's two main sources of revenue are tourism and US military spending.

Governor, Carl Gutierrez
Lt.-Governor, Frank Blas

AMERICAN SAMOA

AREA – 77 sq. miles (199 sq. km)
POPULATION – 46,773 (1990 estimate)
CAPITAL – ΨPago Pago (population, 3,519)

American Samoa consists of the islands of Tutuila, Anu'u, Ofu, Olesega, Ta'u, Rose and Swains Islands. Tutuila, the largest of the group, has an area of 52 sq. miles and a magnificent harbour at Pago Pago. The remaining islands have an area of about 24 sq. miles. Tuna and copra are the chief exports.

American Samoans are US nationals, but some have acquired citizenship through service in the United States armed forces or other naturalization procedure. The 1960 constitution grants American Samoa a measure of self-government, with certain powers reserved to the US Secretary of the Interior. There is a bicameral legislature with popularly elected Representatives and Governors and a popularly elected Governor. A non-voting Delegate is elected to serve in the US House of Representatives.

Governor, Tauese Sunia

THE VIRGIN ISLANDS

AREA – 134 sq. miles (347 sq. km)
POPULATION – 101,809 (1990)
CAPITAL – ΨCharlotte Amalie (population, 11,756,1980), on St Thomas

The US Virgin Islands were purchased from Denmark and proclaimed US territory in 1917. There are three main islands, St Thomas (28 sq. miles), St Croix (84 sq. miles), St John (20 sq. miles) and about 50 small islets or cays, mostly uninhabited.

Under the provisions of the Revised Organic Act of the Virgin Islands 1954, legislative power is vested in the Legislature, a unicameral body composed of 15 senators popularly elected for two-year terms. The Governor is popularly elected. Virgin Islanders are US citizens. A non-voting Delegate is elected to serve in the US House of Representatives. A referendum is to take place at a future date to determine the future political status of the islands.

Governor, Roy Schneider
Lt.-Governor, Derek M. Hodge

Trade with UK	1995	1996
Imports from UK	£4,018,000	£4,739,000
Exports to UK	95,000	164,000

NORTHERN MARIANA ISLANDS

AREA – 179 sq. miles (464 sq. km)
POPULATION – 58,846 (1995 census)
SEAT OF GOVERNMENT – Saipan (population, 52,706, 1995 census)
The USA administered the Northern Mariana Islands as part of a UN Trusteeship until the trusteeship agreement was terminated in 1986, bringing fully into effect a 1976 congressional law establishing a commonwealth of the Northern Mariana Islands. Most of the residents became US citizens. There is a popularly elected bicameral legislature and a popularly elected Governor.

Governor, Froilan C. Tenorio
Lt.-Governor, Jesus Borja

THE PANAMA CANAL

As a result of the Panama Canal Treaty 1977, the Canal Zone was disestablished, with all jurisdiction over the former Canal Zone reverting to Panama with effect from 1 October 1979. Under the treaty, the United States is allowed the use of operating areas for the Panama Canal, together with several military bases, although the Republic of Panama is sovereign in all such areas. The Panama Canal Commission, an arm of the US Government, will continue to operate the canal until noon on 31 December 1999.

In the fiscal year 1996, the total number of transits by ocean-going commercial traffic was 13,536; canal net tons totalled 226,884,859; cargo tons totalled 198,067,990.

URUGUAY
República Oriental del Uruguay

AREA – 68,500 sq. miles (177,414 sq. km)
POPULATION – 3,167,000 (1994 UN estimate);
predominantly of Spanish and Italian descent. Spanish is
the official language. Many Uruguayans are Roman
Catholics. There is no established church
CAPITAL – ΨMontevideo (population, 1,383,660, 1992)
MAJOR CITIES – Melo; Mercedes; Minas; ΨPaysandú;
Punta del Este; Rivera; Salto
CURRENCY – New Uruguayan peso of 100 centésimos
NATIONAL ANTHEM – Orientales, La Patria O La Tumba
(Uruguayans, the fatherland or death)
NATIONAL DAY – 25 August (Declaration of
Independence, 1825)
NATIONAL FLAG – Four blue and five white horizontal
stripes surcharged with sun on a white ground in the top
corner, next flagstaff
LIFE EXPECTANCY (years) – male 68.43; female 74.88
POPULATION GROWTH RATE – 0.6 per cent (1994)
POPULATION DENSITY – 18 per sq. km (1994)
URBAN POPULATION – 89.9 per cent (1994)
MILITARY EXPENDITURE – 2.6 per cent of GDP (1995)
MILITARY PERSONNEL – 26,520: Army 17,600, Navy
5,000, Air Force 3,000, Paramilitaries 920

The country consists mainly of undulating grassy plains.
The principal river is the Rio Negro (with its tributary the
Yi), flowing from north-east to south-west into the Rio
Uruguay. The climate is temperate.

HISTORY AND POLITICS

Uruguay (or the *Banda Oriental*, as the territory lying on the
eastern bank of the Uruguay River was then called) resisted
all attempted invasions of the Portuguese and Spanish
until the early 17th century; 100 years later the Portuguese
settlements were captured by the Spanish. From 1726 to
1814 the country formed part of Spanish South America. In
1814 the armies of the Argentine Confederation captured
the capital and annexed the province; afterwards it was
annexed by Portugal and became a province of Brazil. In
1825, the country threw off Brazilian rule. This action led
to war between Argentina and Brazil which was settled by
the mediation of the UK, Uruguay being declared an
independent state in 1828. In 1830 a republic was inaugurated.
    General elections held in 1984 marked the return to
civilian rule after 11 years of presidential rule with military
support. The first fully free presidential and legislative
elections since 1971 were held in 1989, and were won by
the *Partido Nacional Blanco*. After the 1994 elections a
coalition government of the Colorado Party and the
Partido Nacional Blanco was appointed by President
Sanguinetti (Colorado Party).

POLITICAL SYSTEM

Under the constitution the president (who may serve only
a single term) appoints a council of 11 ministers and a
Secretary (Planning and Budget Office), and the vice-
president presides over Congress. The Congress consists
of a Chamber of 99 deputies and a Senate of 30 members
(plus the vice-president), elected for five years by proportional representation.
    The republic is divided into 19 Departments, each with
an elected governor and legislature.

HEAD OF STATE
President, Dr Julio Maria Sanguinetti, *elected* 27 November
    1994, *took office* 1 March 1995
Vice-President, Dr Hugo Batalla

CABINET *as at August 1997*
Economy and Finance, Luis Mosca
Education and Culture, Samuel Lichtensztejn
Foreign Affairs, Alvaro Ramos
Housing, Territorial Regulation and Environment, Juan
    Chiruchi
Industry, Energy and Mines, Dr Julio Herrera
Interior, Dr Didier Operti
Labour and Social Security, Ana Lía Piñeyrua
Livestock, Agriculture and Fisheries, Carlos Gasparri
National Defence, Dr Raúl Iturria
Public Health, Dr Raúl Bustos
Secretary, Planning and Budget Office, Ariel Davrieux
Tourism, Benito Stern
Transport and Public Works, Lucio Caceres

EMBASSY OF THE ORIENTAL REPUBLIC OF URUGUAY
2nd Floor, 140 Brompton Road, London SW3 1HY
Tel 0171-584 8192
Ambassador Extraordinary and Plenipotentiary, HE Juan
    Enrique Fischer, apptd 1993

BRITISH EMBASSY
Calle Marco Bruto 1073, Montevideo 11300 (PO Box
16024)
Tel: Montevideo 623650
Ambassador Extraordinary and Plenipotentiary, HE Robert
    Hendrie, apptd 1994

BRITISH-URUGUAYAN CHAMBER OF COMMERCE,
    Avenida Labertador Brig. Gen., Lavalleja 1641, P2-OF
    201, Montevideo

ECONOMY

The economy is based on agriculture, primarily livestock.
There are just over 9 million cattle and just under 24
million sheep. Wheat, barley, maize, linseed, sunflower
seed and rice are cultivated. In addition to wool, meat
packing, other foodstuffs (citrus, wine, beer), fishing and
textile industries are of importance.
    Industrial development continues and, in addition to the
greatly augmented textile industry, includes tyres, sheet-
glass, three-ply wood, cement, leather-curing, beet-sugar,
plastics, household consumer goods, edible oils and the
refining of petroleum and petroleum products. There are
some ferrous minerals, not extracted at present. Non-
ferrous exploited minerals include clinker, dolomite,
marble and granite.
    In 1994 the government had a budget deficit equivalent
to 2.94 per cent of GDP.
GNP – US$16,458 million (1995); US$5,170 per capita
    (1995)
GDP – US$9,060 million (1992); US$3,523 per capita
    (1992)
ANNUAL AVERAGE GROWTH OF GDP – –2.4 per cent
    (1995)
INFLATION RATE – 42.2 per cent (1995)
UNEMPLOYMENT – 10.2 per cent (1995)
TOTAL EXTERNAL DEBT – US$5,307 million (1995)

TRADE

The major exports are meat and by-products, wool and by-
products, hides and bristle and agricultural products. The
principal imports are raw materials, construction materials, oils and lubricants, automotive vehicles, kits and

machinery. Principal trading partners are Brazil, USA and Argentina.

In 1993 Uruguay had a trade deficit of US$387 million and a current account deficit of US$227 million. In 1995 imports totalled US$2,867 million and exports US$2,117 million.

Trade with UK	1995	1996
Imports from UK	£56,833,000	£66,251,000
Exports to UK	62,379,000	78,357,000

COMMUNICATIONS

There are about 11,300 km of national highways, and 2,993 km of standard gauge railway in use. Passenger rail services were cancelled in 1988 and services are now limited to cargo transport; services are state-run. A state-owned airline, PLUNA, provides international services, and internal passenger and limited freight services are provided by TAMU, another state-owned airline, using principally military aircraft and personnel. The international airport of Carrasco lies 12 miles outside Montevideo. The River Uruguay is navigable from its estuary to Salto, 200 miles north, and the Negro is also navigable for a considerable distance.

EDUCATION

Primary and secondary education is compulsory and free, and technical and trade schools and evening courses for adult education are state controlled. The university at Montevideo (founded in 1849) has ten faculties and a new university has been built at Salto.

ILLITERACY RATE – 2.7 per cent
ENROLMENT (percentage of age group) – primary 94 per cent (1994); tertiary 27.3 per cent (1992)

UZBEKISTAN
Ozbekiston Respublikasy

AREA – 172,742 sq. miles (447,400 sq. km). Neighbours: Kazakhstan (north), Kyrgyzstan and Tajikistan (east), Afghanistan and Turkmenistan (south), Kazakhstan (west)
POPULATION – 21,206,800 (1995 estimate): 71 per cent Uzbek, 8 per cent Russian, 5 per cent Tajik and 4 per cent Kazakh, with smaller numbers of Tatars, Kara-Kalpaks, Koreans, Ukrainians and Kirghiz. The predominant religion is Sunni Muslim. Islam is tolerated within strict bounds; it is allowed to play no part in politics. The principal language is Uzbek (71 per cent) with Russian (8 per cent), Tajik (5 per cent) and Kazakh (4 per cent). Uzbek is one of the Turkic group of languages. In June 1994 the government approved a six-year programme for the transfer of the Uzbek language to a Latin script
CAPITAL – Tashkent (population, 2,094,000, 1990)
MAJOR CITY – Samarkand (388,000), which contains the Gur-Emir (Tamerlane's Mausoleum), completed in 1400 by Ulugbek, Tamerlane's astronomer grandson
CURRENCY – Sum (Som) of 100 tiyin
NATIONAL DAY – 1 September (Independence Day)
NATIONAL FLAG – Three horizontal stripes of blue, white, green, with the white fimbriated in red; on the blue near the hoist a crescent and twelve stars, all in white
LIFE EXPECTANCY (years) – male 66.00; female 72.10
POPULATION GROWTH RATE – 2.1 per cent (1994)
POPULATION DENSITY – 50 per sq. km (1994)
URBAN POPULATION – 40.6 per cent (1989)

MILITARY EXPENDITURE – 3.6 per cent of GDP (1995)
MILITARY PERSONNEL – 45,000: Army 25,000, Air Force 4,000, Paramilitaries 16,000
CONSCRIPTION DURATION – 18 months
ILLITERACY RATE – 0.3 per cent
ENROLMENT (percentage of age group) – tertiary 31.8 per cent (1992)

Uzbekistan occupies the south-central part of former Soviet Central Asia, lying between the high Tienshan Mountains and the Pamir highlands in the east and south-east and sandy lowlands in the west and north-west. Uzbekistan consists of the Kara-Kalpak Autonomous Republic and 12 regions: Andizhan, Bokhara, Dzhizak, Ferghana, Kashkadar, Khorezm, Namangan, Navoi, Samarkand, Surkhan-Darya, Syr-Darya and Tashkent. Most of the country is a plain with huge waterless deserts, and several large oases which form the main centres of population and economic life. The climate is continental and dry.

HISTORY AND POLITICS

Between the sixth and fourth centuries BC the area that is now Uzbekistan was under the control of the Persians and then Alexander the Great. In the 14th century the area became the centre of a great Muslim empire under Tamerlane and then his grandson Ulugbek, following whose murder the state disintegrated. By the beginning of the 19th century three independent Khanates, Khiva, Kokand and Bukhara, existed in what is now Uzbekistan. These were gradually annexed to the Russian Empire by the middle of the 19th century. In November 1917 a Communist revolution broke out in Tashkent and parts of Uzbekistan were included in the Turkestan Soviet Republic at its formation in 1918. The remainder of Uzbekistan was under the rule of the independent states of Khiva and Bukhara, which had re-emerged in 1918, until they were defeated by the Red Army and Soviet rule was established throughout the area in 1921. Under Soviet rule a massive land irrigation programme was implemented to allow the cultivation of cotton.

Uzbekistan declared its independence from the Soviet Union on 1 September 1991. Its independence was confirmed in a referendum on 29 December and recognized internationally. Elections to the new *Oliy Majilis* were held on 25 December 1994 and won by the ruling People's Democratic Party and its allies with a total of 205 seats.

The government of President Karimov is formed by the former Communist Party, which has renamed itself the People's Democratic Party. Despite the constitutionally guaranteed freedom of religion and thought, and respect for human rights and multiparty democracy, censorship is still widely used and little political opposition is tolerated. The main opposition parties, Erk (Freedom) and Birlik (Unity) nationalist party, have been continually banned since the introduction of the multiparty constitution in December 1992. In March 1995 President Karimov's hold on power was confirmed when his term of office was extended to 2000 by a national referendum.

INSURGENCIES

Uzbek nationalism has caused violent clashes with Tajiks in the Ferghana valley in recent years. The ability to speak Uzbek is now a condition of appointment to government posts. This has severely disrupted the civil service and public sector, mostly staffed by ethnic Russians.

FOREIGN RELATIONS

President Karimov is attempting to form close ties with Turkey in the cultural and business spheres, and in 1994 began to strengthen economic ties with Russia again. Uzbek forces have been deployed in Tajikistan since late 1992 to help maintain the government and defeat the Islamic forces.

POLITICAL SYSTEM

A new constitution was adopted by the Supreme Soviet in December 1992 under which the president and government hold executive power. The president may serve a maximum of two five-year terms and has the power to dissolve the 250-member Supreme Assembly (*Oliy Majilis*), which may not remove or impeach the president.

HEAD OF STATE

President, Islam Karimov, *elected* 29 December 1991, *elected by referendum for a five-year term* 26 March 1995

CABINET *as at August 1997*

Chairman of the Cabinet, The President
Prime Minister, Utkur Sultanov
First Deputy Prime Minister, Ismoil Jurabekov
Deputy PMs, Bakhtier Khamidov *(Macroeconomics);* Alisher Azizkhojaev; Victor Chjen; Dilbar Ghulamova; Rustam Junusov; Kayim Khakkulov; Kamiljan Rakhimov; Mirabror Usmanov
Communal Services, Victor Mikhailov
Communications, Abuwahid Jurabaev
Cultural Affairs, Khairulla Juraev
Defence, Maj.-Gen. Rustam Ahmedov
Education, Jura Yuldashev
Foreign Affairs, Abdulaziz Kamilov
Foreign Economic Relations, Elyor Ghaniev
Health, Shavkat Karimov
Higher and Secondary Specialized Education, Akil Salimov
Interior, Zakir Almatov
Justice, Sirojiddin Mirsafaev
Labour, Akiljon Abidov
Power and Electrification, Valeriy Ataev
Social Security, Bakhodir Umursakov
Water Resources and Land Improvement, Marks Jumaniazov

EMBASSY OF THE REPUBLIC OF UZBEKISTAN
41 Holland Park, London WII 2RP
Tel: 0171-229 7679
Ambassador Extraordinary and Plenipotentiary, HE Fatih Teshbaev, apptd 1997

BRITISH EMBASSY
Ul. Gogolya 67, Tashkent 700000
Tel: Tashkent 406288
Ambassador Extraordinary and Plenipotentiary, HE Barbara Hay, MBE, apptd 1995

ECONOMY

Uzbekistan is attempting to integrate its economy with that of Kazakhstan, with which it signed an economic agreement in January 1994 to allow the free circulation of goods, services and capital and the co-ordination of credit and finance policies, budgets, taxation and customs duties. Uzbekistan is also a member of the CIS economic union and in March 1994 signed an economic treaty with Russia to provide for mutually convertible currencies and to enhance private business links. In 1994–5 the government embarked on an economic reform programme under which subsidies on foodstuffs and transport were abolished and those on public utilities reduced. Peasant farmers have been granted private plots of land and inflation has been reduced.

Uzbekistan's economy is based on intensive agricultural production, and especially cotton production, made possible by extensive irrigation schemes. In addition there are some agricultural and textile machinery plants and several chemical combines. Large and previously underdeveloped mineral resources have begun to be exploited; these include gold, natural gas, oil, copper, lead, zinc and coal. A sizeable oilfield was discovered in the Ferghana Valley in 1992. The Muruntao mine is the largest open-cast gold mine in the world, producing 75 million tonnes per year.
GNP – US$21,979 million (1995); US$970 per capita (1995)
UNEMPLOYMENT – 0.4 per cent (1995)
TOTAL EXTERNAL DEBT – US$1,630 million (1995)

TRADE WITH UK	1995	1996
Imports from UK	£15,073,000	£38,188,000
Exports to UK	1,611,000	2,587,000

VANUATU
Ripablik Blong Vanuatu

AREA – 4,706 sq. miles (12,190 sq. km)
POPULATION – 165,000 (1994 UN estimate). About 95 per cent are Melanesian, the rest being mostly Micronesian, Polynesian and European. The national language is Bislama, but English and French are also official languages
CAPITAL – ΨPort Vila (population, 26,100, 1993), on Efate
MAJOR TOWNS – Luganville (8,800, 1993), on Espiritu Santo
CURRENCY – Vatu of 100 centimes
NATIONAL ANTHEM – Nasonal sing sing blong Vanuatu
NATIONAL DAY – 30 July (Independence Day)
NATIONAL FLAG – Red over green with a black triangle in the hoist, the three parts being divided by fimbriations of black and yellow, and in the centre of the black triangle a boar's tusk overlaid by two crossed fern leaves
LIFE EXPECTANCY (years) – male 63.48; female 67.34
POPULATION GROWTH RATE – 2.9 per cent (1994)
POPULATION DENSITY – 14 per sq. km (1994)
URBAN POPULATION – 18.2 per cent (1989)
ILLITERACY RATE – 47.1 per cent
ENROLMENT (percentage of age group) – primary 74 per cent (1989); secondary 17 per cent (1991)

Vanuatu is situated in the South Pacific Ocean. It includes 13 large and some 70 small islands, of coral and volcanic origin, including the Banks and Torres Islands in the north. The principal islands are Vanua Lava, Espiritu Santo, Maewo, Pentecost, Ambae, Malekula, Ambrym, Epi, Efate, Erromango, Tanna and Aneityum. Most islands are mountainous and there are active volcanoes on several. The climate is oceanic tropical, moderated by the south-east trade winds which blow between May and October. At other times winds are variable and cyclones may occur.

HISTORY AND POLITICS

Vanuatu, the former Anglo-French Condominium of the New Hebrides, became an independent republic within the Commonwealth on 30 July 1980. Parliament consists of 46 members elected for a term of four years. A Council of Chiefs advises on matters of custom. Executive power is held by the prime minister (elected from and by parliament) and a Council of Ministers who are responsible to parliament. The president is elected for a five-year term by the presidents of the six provincial governments and the members of parliament.

HEAD OF STATE
President, HE Jean-Marie Leye, *elected* 2 March 1994

COUNCIL OF MINISTERS *as at June 1997*
Prime Minister, Serge Vohor (UMP)
Deputy PM, Trade and Commerce, Barak Sope (MPP)
Agriculture, Amos Adeng (UMP)
Education, Louis Carlot (UMP)
Finance, Willie Jimmy (UMP)
Foreign Affairs, Vital Soksok (UMP)
Health, Charley Nako (UMP)
Home Affairs, Robert Karie (NUP)
Justice, Culture and Women's Affairs, Fr Walter Lini (NUP)
Lands and Natural Resources, Sato Kilman (MPP)
Transport and Public Works, Samson Bue (UMP)

MPP Melanesian Progressive Party; NUP National United Party; UMP Union of Moderate Parties

HIGH COMMISSIONER TO GREAT BRITAIN, vacant, resident at Port Vila, Vanuatu

BRITISH HIGH COMMISSION
PO Box 567, Port Vila
Tel: Vila 23100
High Commissioner, HE Malcolm Hilson, apptd 1997

ECONOMY

Most of the population is employed on plantations or in subsistence agriculture. Subsistence crops include yams, taro, manioc, sweet potato and breadfruit; principal cash crops are copra, cocoa and coffee. Large numbers of cattle are kept on the plantations and beef is the second largest export. Principal exports are copra, meat (frozen, tinned and chilled), timber and cocoa.

Tourism is an important revenue earner, and the absence of direct taxation has led to growth in the finance and associated industries.

In 1993 Vanuatu had a trade deficit of US$47 million and a current account deficit of US$21 million. In 1994 imports totalled US$89 million and in 1995 exports totalled US$28 million.
GNP – US$202 million (1995); US$1,200 per capita (1995)
GDP – US$160 million (1992); US$1,149 per capita (1992)
ANNUAL AVERAGE GROWTH OF GDP – 3.8 per cent (1993)
INFLATION RATE – 2.2 per cent (1995)
TOTAL EXTERNAL DEBT – US$48 million (1995)

TRADE WITH UK	1995	1996
Imports from UK	£277,000	£271,000
Exports to UK	1,162,000	1,176,000

VATICAN CITY STATE
Stato della Città del Vaticano

AREA – 0.2 sq. miles (0.44 sq. km)
POPULATION – 1,000 (1994 UN estimate)
CAPITAL – Vatican City (population, 766, 1988)
CURRENCY – Italian currency is legal tender
NATIONAL DAY – 22 October (Inauguration of present Pontiff)
NATIONAL FLAG – Square flag; equal vertical bands of yellow (next staff), and white; crossed keys and triple crown device on white band
POPULATION GROWTH RATE – 0.0 per cent (1994)
POPULATION DENSITY – 2,273 per sq. km (1994)

The office of the ecclesiastical head of the Roman Catholic Church (Holy See) is vested in the Pope, the Sovereign Pontiff. For many centuries the Sovereign Pontiff exercised temporal power but by 1870 the Papal States had become part of unified Italy. The temporal power of the Pope was in suspense until the treaty of 1929 which recognized the full and independent sovereignty of the Holy See in the City of the Vatican.

Sovereign Pontiff, His Holiness Pope John Paul II (Karol Wojtyla), *born* at Wadowice (Krakow, Poland), 18 May 1920, *elected* Pope in succession to Pope John Paul I, 16 October 1978
Secretary of State, Cardinal Angelo Sodano, *appointed* December 1990

APOSTOLIC NUNCIATURE
54 Parkside, London SW19 5NE
Tel 0181-946 1410
Apostolic Nuncio, HE Archbishop Pablo Puente, apptd 1997

BRITISH EMBASSY TO THE HOLY SEE
91 Via Condotti, I–00187 Rome
Tel: Rome 6992 3561
Ambassador Extraordinary and Plenipotentiary, HE Mark Pellen, apptd 1997

TRADE WITH UK	1995	1996
Imports from UK	£1,528,000	£2,160,000
Exports to UK	—	8,000

VENEZUELA
República de Venezuela

AREA – 352,145 sq. miles (912,050 sq. km). Neighbours: Colombia (west), Guyana (east), Brazil (south)
POPULATION – 21,177,000 (1994 UN estimate): 67 per cent Mestizo, 21 per cent white, 10 per cent black and 2 per cent Indian. Spanish is the language of the country. About 96 per cent of the population is Roman Catholic
CAPITAL – Caracas (population, 2,784,042, 1990)
MAJOR CITIES – ΨMaracaibo (1,660,233); Valencia (1,225,342); Barquisimeto (793,565); Maracay (449,180), 1997 estimates
CURRENCY – Bolívar (Bs) of 100 céntimos
NATIONAL ANTHEM – Gloria Al Bravo Pueblo (Glory to the brave people)
NATIONAL DAY – 5 July
NATIONAL FLAG – Three horizontal stripes of yellow, blue, red with an arc of seven white stars on the blue stripe
LIFE EXPECTANCY (years) – male 66.68; female 72.80
POPULATION GROWTH RATE – 2.3 per cent (1994)
POPULATION DENSITY – 23 per sq. km (1994)
URBAN POPULATION – 84.1 per cent (1990)

Included in the area of the South American republic of Venezuela are 72 islands off the coast, with a total area of about 14,650 sq. miles, the largest being Margarita (area, about 400 sq. miles), which is politically associated with Tortuga, Cubagua and Coche to form the state of Nueva Esparta.

The mountains are the Eastern Andes and Maritime Andes, running south-west to north-east. The main range is known as the Sierra Nevada de Mérida, and contains Pico Bolívar (16,411 ft) and Picacho de la Sierra (15,420 ft). The principal river is the Orinoco, with innumerable affluents, the main river exceeding 1,600 miles in length. The upper waters of the Orinoco are united with those of the Rio Negro (a Brazilian tributary of the Amazon) by a natural river or canal, known as the Casiquiare. The coastal regions contain many lagoons and lakes, of which Maracaibo (area 8,296 sq. miles) is the largest lake in South America.

The climate is tropical, except where modified by altitude or tempered by sea breezes.

HISTORY AND POLITICS

Venezuela gained independence from Spain in 1830.

Carlos Andrés Pérez of the (Social Democratic) Democratic Action (AD) party won the December 1988 presidential election and the AD emerged as the largest party in both houses in the Congressional elections. President Pérez's government successfully introduced a series of free market economic reforms which led to impressive economic growth but increasing social problems. Two military coup attempts in 1992 were defeated but President Pérez resigned in May 1993 after the Supreme Court indicted him on corruption charges. Former President Rafael Caldera won the ensuing presidential election in December 1993 but his National Convergence coalition of 17 parties failed to gain majorities in either house of Congress, where the traditional AD and COPEI (Social Christian) parties remained strong. President Caldera took office in February 1994.

POLITICAL SYSTEM

Under the 1961 constitution, executive power is held by the president, who also appoints the Council of Ministers. Legislative power is exercised by a bicameral National Congress, comprising a 204-member Chamber of Deputies and a Senate of 49 elected members plus the former presidents of constitutional governments as life members. The president and National Congress are directly elected for concurrent five-year terms.

Venezuela is divided into 22 states, one federal territory and a federal district.

HEAD OF STATE

President, Rafael Caldera Rodríguez, *elected* 5 December 1993, *sworn in* 2 February 1994

COUNCIL OF MINISTERS *as at July 1997*

Agriculture, Raul Alegrett
Defence, Vice-Adm. Tito Rincón Bravo
Education, Antonio Luis Cardenas
Energy, Erwin José Arrieta
Environment, Rafael Martínez Monro
Family Affairs, Carlos Altimari
Federal District Governor, Abdón Vivas Terán
Finance, Luis Raul Matos
Foreign Affairs, Miguel Angel Burelli
Health and Social Security, Pedro Rincón Gutiérrez
Home Affairs, José Guillermo Andueza
Justice, Hilarión Cardozo
Labour, María Bernardoni De Govea
Ministers of State, Fernando Egaña *(Central Information Office);* Guido Arnal *(Science and Technology)*
Presidents, Ricardo Combellas *(Commission for the Reform of the State);* Oscar Sambrano *(National Council for Culture);* Teodoro Petkoff *(Planning);* Alberto Poletto *(Venezuelan Investment Fund);* Hermman Soriano *(Venezuelan Tourist Corporation)*
Secretary of the Presidency, Asdrúbal Aguiar
Trade and Industry, Freddy Rojas Parra
Transport and Communications, Moises Orozco Graterol
Urban Development, Francisco Gonzalez

VENEZUELAN EMBASSY
1 Cromwell Road, London SW7 2HW
Tel 0171-584 4206/7

Ambassador Extraordinary and Plenipotentiary, HE Roy Chaderton-Matos, apptd 1996
Defence Attaché, Capt. A. Sánchez-Vegas-Pérez

BRITISH EMBASSY
Apartado 1246, Caracas 1010–A
Tel: Caracas 993 4111
Ambassador Extraordinary and Plenipotentiary, HE Richard Wilkinson, CVO, apptd 1997
Deputy Head of Mission, Donald Maclaren of Maclaren
Defence Attaché, Capt. K. Ridland
First Secretary (Commercial), A. Goodworth

CONSULAR OFFICES – Caracas, Maracaibo, Margarita, Mérida

BRITISH COUNCIL DIRECTOR, P. de Quincey, Apartado 65131, Caracas 1065

BRITISH-VENEZUELAN CHAMBER OF COMMERCE, Apartado 5713, Caracas 1010. Torre Británica, Piso 10, Letra E, Av. José Félix Sosa, Altamira Sur, Caracas 1060

DEFENCE

The Army has 70 main battle tanks, 290 armoured personnel carriers, 107 artillery pieces and five attack helicopters. The Navy has two submarines, six frigates, six patrol and coastal vessels, four combat aircraft and eight armed helicopters at La Guaira. The Air Force has 104 combat aircraft and 27 armed helicopters.

MILITARY EXPENDITURE – 1.1 per cent of GDP (1995)
MILITARY PERSONNEL – 79,000: Army 34,000, Navy 15,000, Air Force 7,000, National Guard 23,000
CONSCRIPTION DURATION – 30 months

ECONOMY

The government of President Caldera has promised to moderate the free market reforms which provided impressive GDP growth in 1990–2 but saw recession in 1993–4. The oil industry accounted for 21.3 per cent of GNP in 1992, manufacturing 16.8 per cent, commerce 11.7 per cent, government 8.7 per cent and construction 7.4 per cent. A banking crisis in 1994 which necessitated a government rescue of private banks caused the budget deficit to increase drastically, inflation to soar and the currency to collapse. The government announced a two-year economic stabilization programme in September 1994, reintroducing exchange and currency controls, raising taxes and domestic petrol prices, attracting foreign investment, reactivating the privatization programme and reducing government spending. The programme failed to rejuvenate the economy, compelling President Caldera to launch a second stabilization plan in April 1996 as a means of securing an IMF standby credit of US$1,000 million. The programme introduced large increases in petrol prices and the total dismantling of foreign exchange controls.

Products of the tropical forest region include orchids, wild rubber, timber, mangrove bark, balata gum and tonka beans. Agricultural products include corn, bananas, cocoa beans, coffee, cotton, rice, maize, sugar, sesame, groundnuts, potatoes, tomatoes, other vegetables, sisal and tobacco. There is an extensive beef and dairy farming industry. Despite substantial improvements in agriculture, Venezuela is heavily reliant upon food imports, which constitute about 60 per cent of total consumption.

The principal industry is that of petroleum, although daily production in the oilfields (nationalized 1976) has steadily declined since 1973 in line with Venezuela's conservation policies. There are eight refineries. The Orinoco heavy oil belt is being developed; estimates put

recoverable resources at 70,000 million barrels in the
Orinoco region.

Aluminium is the second highest source of foreign
exchange after petroleum. The Venezuelan state holds the
majority stake in both the principal producing companies,
Venalum and Alcasa, and is moving towards a consolidation of the industry. Rich iron ore deposits in eastern
Venezuela have been developed. The government-owned
steel mill at Matanzas uses local iron ore and obtains its
electric power from hydroelectric installations on the
Caroni River. A mill at Ciudad Guayana produces
centrifugally-cast iron pipe. Other industry includes a
wide variety of manufacturing and component assembly,
principally petrochemicals, gold, diamonds, clothing and
foodstuffs.

In 1994 the government had a budget deficit equivalent
to 4.31 per cent of GDP.

GNP – US$65,382 million; US$3,020 per capita (1995)
GDP – US$56,961 million (1992); US$2,994 per capita
(1992)
Annual Average Growth of GDP – 2.2 per cent (1995)
Inflation Rate – 59.9 per cent (1995)
Unemployment – 10.3 per cent (1995)
Total External Debt – US$35,842 million (1995)

Trade

Apart from oil the main exports are bauxite, iron ore,
agricultural products and basic manufactures. The main
imports are machinery and transport equipment, chemicals and foodstuffs. Some 50 per cent of trade is conducted
with the USA.

In 1993 Venezuela had a trade surplus of US$2,958
million and a current account deficit of US$2,223 million.
In 1995 imports totalled US$11,978 million and exports
US$18,324 million.

Trade with UK	1995	1996
Imports from UK	£178,784,000	£180,255,000
Exports to UK	204,167,000	189,104,000

COMMUNICATIONS

There are about 93,471 km of roads, 29,954 km of them
paved. The state has now acquired all but a very few of the
railway lines, whose total length is only some 363 km. Road
and river communications have made railways of negligible importance in Venezuela except for carrying iron ore
in the south-east, though the government is expanding the
network.

The Orinoco is navigable for ocean-going ships (up to
40 ft draught) for 150 miles upstream, by large steamers for
700 miles, and by smaller vessels some 900 miles upstream.
There are seven Venezuelan airlines which between them
have a comprehensive network of internal and international flights.

EDUCATION

Education is free and compulsory between the ages of five
and 14. There are more than ten universities in Venezuela,
five in Caracas and the others in Maracaibo, Mérida,
Valencia, Cumaná and Barquisimeto.
Illiteracy Rate – 8.9 per cent
Enrolment (percentage of age group) – primary 88 per
cent (1992); secondary 20 per cent (1992); tertiary 28.5
per cent (1991)

VIETNAM
Công Hòa Xã Hôi Chu Nghĩa Viêt Nam

Area – 128,066 sq. miles (331,689 sq. km). Neighbours:
China (north), Laos and Cambodia (west)
Population – 72,510,000 (1994 UN estimate)
Capital – Hanoi (population, 3,056,146, 1989)
Major Cities – Hai Phong (456,000); Ho Chi Minh City
(3,169,000)
Currency – Dông of 10 hào or 100 xu
National Anthem – Tien Quan Ca (The troops are
advancing)
National Day – 2 September
National Flag – Red, with yellow five-point star in
centre
Life Expectancy (years) – male 63.66; female 67.89
Population Growth Rate – 2.3 per cent (1994)
Population Density – 219 per sq. km (1994)
Urban Population – 19.5 per cent (1994)
Illiteracy Rate – 6.3 per cent
Enrolment (percentage of age group) – primary 95 per
cent (1980); tertiary 3.2 per cent (1993)

HISTORY AND POLITICS

Following the end of the war in Vietnam in 1975, North
and South Vietnam were reunified in 1976 under the name
of the Socialist Republic of Vietnam. The national flag,
anthem and capital of North Vietnam were adopted, and
Saigon was renamed Ho Chi Minh City.

A new National Assembly of 365 members was elected
in August 1992 and convened in September when it elected
Le Duc Anh as president and, in October, approved the
composition of the new government headed by Vo Van
Kiet.

Political System

Effective power lies with the Vietnamese Communist
Party (VCP), its highest executive body being the Central
Committee, elected by a Party Congress on a national
basis. The Politburo and the Secretariat of the Central
Committee exercise the real power.

A new constitution was adopted in June 1992 which
reaffirmed Communist Party rule but also formalized free
market economic reforms. The constitution increased the
powers of the president and replaced the Council of
Ministers by a prime minister and Cabinet.

Head of State
President, Le Duc Anh, elected by National Assembly 23
September 1992
Vice President, Nguyen Thi Binh

Cabinet as at June 1997
Prime Minister, Vo Van Kiet
Deputy PMs, Phan Van Khai; Nguyen Khanh; Tran Duc
Luong
Agriculture and Rural Development, Nguyen Cong Tan
Child Protection, Tran Thi Thanh Thanh
Construction, Ngo Xuan Loc
Culture and Information, Nguyen Khoa Diem
Education and Training, Prof. Tran Hong Quan
Ethnic Minorities and Mountain Regions, Hoang Duc Nghi
Finance, Nguyen Sinh Hung
Foreign Affairs, Nguyen Manh Cam
General Inspector of the State Inspectorate, Ta Huu Thanh
Government Personnel and Organization, Do Quang Trung
Government Secretariat, Lai Van Cu
Governor of the State Bank, Cao Sy Kiem

Industry, Dang Vu Chu
Interior, Le Minh Huong
Justice, Nguyen Dinh Loc
Labour, War Invalids and Social Affairs, Tran Dinh Hoan
National Defence, Gen. Doan Khue
Planning and Investment, Tran Xuan Gia
Population and Family Planning, Mai Ky
Public Health, Dr Do Nguyen Phuong
Science, Technology and Environment, Pham Gia Khiem
Trade, Le Van Triet
Water Resources, Ta Quang Ngoc
Youth Affairs, Ha Quang Du

EMBASSY OF THE SOCIALIST REPUBLIC OF VIETNAM
12–14 Victoria Road, London w8 5RD
Tel 0171-937 1912/8564
Ambassador Extraordinary and Plenipotentiary, HE Huynh
   Ngoc An, apptd 1994

BRITISH EMBASSY
Central Building, 31 Hai Ba Trung, Hanoi
Tel: Hanoi 825 2510
Ambassador Extraordinary and Plenipotentiary, HE David Fall,
   apptd 1997

CONSULATE-GENERAL – Ho Chi Minh City

BRITISH COUNCIL DIRECTOR, I. Simm (*Cultural Attaché*)

DEFENCE

The Army has 1,300 main battle tanks, 1,400 armoured
personnel carriers and armoured infantry fighting vehicles, and 2,330 artillery pieces. The Navy has eight frigates
and 52 patrol and coastal vessels at seven principal bases.
The Air Force has 196 combat aircraft and 33 armed
helicopters.
MILITARY EXPENDITURE – 4.3 per cent of GDP (1995)
MILITARY PERSONNEL – 557,000: Army 500,000, Navy
   42,000, Air Force 15,000
CONSCRIPTION DURATION – Two to three years

ECONOMY

Vietnam experienced economic difficulties following the
imposition of socialist reforms in the south after 1975.
However, economic reforms, known as 'Doi Moi' liberalization, were instituted after the Sixth Party Congress
(1986) and have had significant success. The state's share of
control has fallen to 60 per cent of industry, 40 per cent of
services and 2 per cent of agriculture, which is now mainly
run by family farms. This has led to a significant improvement in agricultural production, with Vietnam becoming a
major rice exporter.
   Foreign investment has been actively encouraged and
has expanded greatly since the USA dropped its opposition
to IMF and World Bank loans and aid to Vietnam in 1993
and ended its trade embargo in 1994. Investment was
further boosted by the US decision in July 1995 to establish
full diplomatic and economic relations and by Vietnam's
accession to ASEAN in August 1995. Oil production
(mainly offshore) has increased to 110,000 barrels per day
and large natural gas reserves have been found offshore,
though these are also claimed by China.
   In 1994 imports totalled US$5,000 million and exports
US$3,600 million.
GNP – US$17,634 million (1995); US$240 per capita
   (1995)
GDP – US$7,451 million (1992); US$131 per capita (1992)
TOTAL EXTERNAL DEBT – US$26,495 million (1995)

TRADE WITH UK	1995	1996
Imports from UK	£60,442,000	£49,557,000
Exports to UK	106,943,000	160,008,000

YEMEN
Al-Jamhuriya Al-Yamaniya

AREA – 203,850 sq. miles (527,968 sq. km). Neighbours:
   Saudi Arabia (north), Oman (east)
POPULATION – 15,800,000 (1995 census)
CAPITAL – Sana'a (population, 972,000, 1995)
MAJOR CITY – Ψ Aden (562,000), the former capital of
   South Yemen
CURRENCY – Riyal of 100 fils
NATIONAL DAY – 22 May
NATIONAL FLAG – Horizontal bands of red, white and
   black
LIFE EXPECTANCY (years) – male 49.90; female 50.40
POPULATION GROWTH RATE – 2.9 per cent (1994)
POPULATION DENSITY – 24 per sq. km (1994)
URBAN POPULATION – 26.4 per cent (1994)
ENROLMENT (percentage of age group) – tertiary 4.4 per
   cent (1991)

Included in the state of Yemen are the offshore islands of
Perim and Kamaran in the Red Sea, and Socotra in the Gulf
of Aden. The border with Saudi Arabia is unclear and
remains in dispute; only the north-west corner of it is
delineated, by the 1934 Taif Accord. The highlands and
central plateau, and the highest portions of the maritime
range in the south, form the most fertile part of Arabia, with
abundant but irregular rainfall. The north is largely
composed of mountains and desert, and rainfall is generally
scarce.

HISTORY AND POLITICS

Turkish occupation of North Yemen (1872–1918) was
followed by the rule of the Hamid al-Din dynasty until a
revolution in 1962 overthrew the monarchy and the
Yemen Arab Republic was declared. The People's Republic of South Yemen was set up in 1967 when the British
government ceded power to the National Liberation
Front, bringing to an end 129 years of British rule in Aden
and some years of protectorate status in the hinterland.
Negotiations towards merging the two states began in 1979
and unification was proclaimed on 22 May 1990. The
constitution was approved by referendum in May 1991. A
five-member Presidential Council comprising former
senior government figures of the separate states was
formed for the period of transition.
   A general election for the House of Representatives
took place on 27 April 1993. Of the total of 301 seats, 122
were won by the General People's Congress (GPC, former
ruling party in the North), 62 by the Islamic Islah (Alliance
for reform) party and 56 by the Yemeni Socialist Party
(YSP, former ruling party in the South). The three parties
formed a coalition government and the House of Representatives asked the Presidential Council to remain in
office.
   Continued political tensions and a power struggle
between the former Northern and Southern Yemen elites
in mid-1993, coupled with arguments over the distribution
of oil revenues and the alleged assassination of Southern
ministers led YSP leaders to withdraw to Aden in August
1993. A reconciliation pact signed in February 1994 by
President Saleh and Vice-President al-Beedh was never
implemented and, after sporadic clashes, a civil war broke

out on 5 May 1994 between the unmerged Northern and Southern forces. The Southern leadership declared secession on 20 May but fled when Aden was captured by victorious Northern forces on 7 July, bringing the civil war to an end.

After the civil war a coalition government of the General People's Congress and the Islamic Islah was formed, an amnesty for the secessionists declared (with the exception of key YSP leaders) and the constitution amended. The Presidential Council was abolished and will be replaced from 1999 with a directly elected president. Gen. Saleh was elected president by the House of Representatives for a five-year term. Multiparty democracy, a free market economy and Sharia law are enshrined in the constitution.

A general election held on 27 April 1997 was won by the ruling General People's Congress.

HEAD OF STATE
President, Gen. Ali Abdullah Saleh, *took office* 22 May 1990, *elected* 1 October 1994
Vice-President, Maj. Gen. Abd Rabbah Mansour Hadi

COUNCIL OF MINISTERS *as at July 1997*
Chairman, Dr Faraj Saeed Bin Ghanem
Deputy PM, Foreign Affairs, Dr Abdulkarim Al-Eryani
Agriculture and Water Resources, Ahmed Salem Al Gabali
Civil Service and Administrative Reform, Mohamed Ahmed Al-Gonaid
Construction, Housing and Urban Planning, Abdullah Hussein Al-Dafee
Culture and Tourism, Abdulmalek Mansour
Defence, Col. Mohamed Dhaifallah Mohamed
Education, Dr Yahya Mohamed Abdullah Al-Shuaibi
Endowments and Guidance, Ahmed Mohamed Al-Shami
Expatriates Abroad, Abdullah Saleh Saba'a
Finance, Alawi Salih Assalami
Fisheries, Ahmed Musaed Hussein
Industry, Ahmed Mohamed Sofan
Information, Abdulrahman Al-Akawa'a
Interior, Col. Hussein Mohamed Arab
Justice, Isamael Ahmed Al-Wazir
Labour and Vocational Training, Mohamed Mohamed Attayeb
Legal and Council of Ministers' Affairs, Abdullah Ahmed Ghanem
Local Administration, Sadeq Amin Aburas
Minister of State for the Affairs of the Council of Ministers, Dr Ahmed Ali Al-Bushari
Oil and Mineral Resources, Mohamed Al-Khadem Al-Wajeeh
Planning and Development, Abdulkader Bajammal
Power and Water, Ali Hamid Sharaf
Public Health, Dr Abdullah Abdulwali Nasher
Social Security and Social Affairs, Mohamed Abdullah Al-Bitani
Telecommunications, Ahmed Mohamed Al-Anisi
Trade and Provisions, Abdulrahman Mohamed Ali Othman
Transport, Brig. Abdulmalik Assyani
Youth and Sports, Abdulwahab Raweh

EMBASSY OF THE REPUBLIC OF YEMEN
57 Cromwell Road, London SW7 2ED
Tel 0171-584 6607
Ambassador Extraordinary and Plenipotentiary, HE Dr Hussein Abdullah Al-Amri, apptd 1995

BRITISH EMBASSY
PO Box 1287, Sana'a
Tel: Sana'a 264 081
Ambassador Extraordinary and Plenipotentiary, HE Victor Henderson, apptd 1997

BRITISH COUNCIL DIRECTOR, B. McSharry, MBE, As-Sabain Street No. 7 (PO Box 2157), Sana'a

DEFENCE
The Army has 1,125 main battle tanks, 830 armoured personnel carriers and armoured infantry fighting vehicles and 512 artillery pieces. The Navy has 15 patrol and coastal vessels at two bases. The Air Force has 65 combat aircraft and six attack helicopters.
MILITARY EXPENDITURE – 3.9 per cent of GDP (1995)

ECONOMY
The civil war has seriously damaged the country's economy, already weakened since 1991 by the loss of US$2,000 million in annual remittances from 800,000 Yemeni workers in Saudi Arabia, who were sent home because of Yemen's perceived support for Iraq in the Gulf War. However, the war had little effect on oil production, which averages roughly 400,000 barrels per day (bpd). The refinery at Aden was damaged in the civil war and is working at reduced capacity. An agreement was signed with the French oil company Total in September 1995 for the exploitation of liquefied natural gas over a 25-year period and the construction of a gas liquefication plant by 2000. Despite the production of oil Yemen remains one of the poorest states in the world. The critical economic situation obliged the government in 1995 to begin implementing a series of IMF and World Bank-prescribed reforms. The IMF approved a 15-month standby credit of US$184 million in March 1996. In June 1997 international donors pledged US$1,800 million to assist the government's economic reform programme.

Agriculture is the main occupation of the inhabitants. This is largely of a subsistence nature, sorghum, sesame and millet being the chief crops, with wheat and barley widely grown at the higher elevations. Exports include cotton, coffee, fruit and vegetables, hides and skins.

In 1994 Yemen had a trade deficit of US$52 million and current account deficit of US$74 million.
GNP – US$4,044 million (1995); US$260 per capita (1995)
GDP – US$8,449 million (1992); US$715 per capita (1992)
INFLATION RATE – 12.8 per cent (1984)
TOTAL EXTERNAL DEBT – US$6,212 million (1995)

TRADE WITH UK	1995	1996
Imports from UK	£66,825,000	£74,152,000
Exports to UK	4,113,000	8,418,000

YUGOSLAVIA
Federativna Republika Jugoslavije – Federal Republic of Yugoslavia

AREA – 39,506 sq. miles (102,350 sq. km). Neighbours: Hungary (north), Romania and Bulgaria (east), the Former Yugoslav Republic of Macedonia (south), Albania (south-west), Bosnia-Hercegovina and Croatia (west)
POPULATION – 10,515,000 (1994 UN estimate): 66 per cent are Serb and Montenegrin, 18 per cent Albanian, 8 per cent Muslim, 4 per cent Hungarian, with smaller numbers of Yugoslavs (no ethnic group), Croats and Bulgarians. The majority religion is Serbian Orthodox, with significant Muslim and small Roman Catholic minorities. The main language is Serbian (Serbo-Croat) (74 per cent), with Albanian and Hungarian minorities. Serbo-Croat is a South Slav language written in the Cyrillic script

CAPITAL – Belgrade (population, 1,136,786, 1991)
MAJOR CITIES – Kragujevac (164,823); Niš (230,711);
    Novi Sad (257,685); Podgorica (132,290), the capital of
    Montenegro; Priština (210,040); Subotica (154,611),
    1981
CURRENCY – New dinar of 100 paras
NATIONAL ANTHEM – Hej, Slaveni, Jošte Živi Reǒ Naših
    Dedova (Oh! Slavs, our ancestors' words still live)
NATIONAL DAY – 27 April
NATIONAL FLAG – Three horizontal stripes of blue,
    white, red
LIFE EXPECTANCY (years) – male 69.50; female 74.49
POPULATION GROWTH RATE – 0.0 per cent (1994)
POPULATION DENSITY – 103 per sq. km (1994)
ILLITERACY RATE – 2.1 per cent
ENROLMENT (percentage of age group) – primary 69 per
    cent (1990); secondary 62 per cent (1990); tertiary 18.3
    per cent (1993)

The climate is continental. Montenegro and southern
Serbia are extremely mountainous, while the north is
dominated by the low-lying plains of the Danube. The
major rivers are: the Danube, which flows through the
north of Serbia to Romania and Bulgaria; the Sava, which
flows eastwards from Bosnia to join the Danube at
Belgrade; the Drina, which flows along most of the
Serbian–Bosnian border to join the Sava; and the Morava,
which flows from the extreme south to join the Danube in
the north.

HISTORY AND POLITICS

Serbia emerged from the rule of the Byzantine Empire in
the 13th century to form a large and prosperous state in the
Balkans. Defeat by the Turks in 1389 led to almost 500
years of Turkish rule. After gaining autonomy within the
Ottoman Empire in 1815, Serbia became fully independent in 1878 and a kingdom in 1881. Montenegro was part
of the Serbian state before it was conquered by the Turks in
1355; it became independent in 1851. At the end of the First
World War Serbia and Montenegro joined with the former
Austro-Hungarian provinces of Slovenia, Croatia and
Bosnia-Hercegovina to form the 'Kingdom of Serbs,
Croats and Slovenes' which was proclaimed on 1 December 1918 under the rule of the Serbian royal house. The
state was renamed Yugoslavia in 1929. In 1941–5 Yugoslavia was occupied by Axis forces which were fought by
Communist and royalist Chetnik partisans supplied by
Allied forces. In 1945 with the defeat of Nazi Germany,
Yugoslavia was reformed as a Communist federal republic
under the presidency of partisan leader Josip Tito.

Tito died in 1980 and the delicate political balance of a
rotating federal presidency was unable to contain the
growing nationalist movements after his death. Efforts by
the six republican presidents to negotiate a new federal or
confederal structure for the country failed in 1991. On 25
June 1991 Slovenia and Croatia declared their independence from Yugoslavia. Intervention by the Federal
Yugoslav Army (JNA) against local defence forces to
prevent the disintegration of the federation failed and
within two months the ethnically homogeneous Slovenia
had negotiated its independence.

In Croatia the ethnic Serb minority refused to accept
Croatia's independence and fighting began in July 1991
between Croat Defence Forces and Serbian guerrillas
backed by the JNA. By September 1991 this had escalated
into war between Croatia and Serbia. The war in Croatia
continued until January 1992 when the EU and the UN
were able to bring about a cease-fire (see Croatia).

Bosnia-Hercegovina adopted a memorandum on state
sovereignty on 15 October 1991 and independence was
affirmed in a referendum on 1 March 1992. Independence
was supported by the ethnic Muslims and Croats but
rejected by the ethnic Serbs and fighting between Muslims
and Serbs broke out in March 1992. The JNA intervened
against the Muslims but in May 1992 withdrew to Serbia
and Montenegro.

On 27 April 1992 the two remaining republics of the
former Socialist Federal Republic of Yugoslavia, Serbia
and Montenegro, announced the formation of a new
Yugoslav federation, which they invited Serbs in Croatia
and Bosnia-Hercegovina to join. The new federation
remains unrecognized internationally.

The last federal legislative elections were held in
November 1996. The Serbian Socialist Party emerged as
the largest party in the federal legislature and formed a
coalition government with Yugoslav United Left and New
Democracy.

POLITICAL SYSTEM

The Federal Republic has a bicameral parliament with a
138-seat (108 Serbian, 30 Montenegrin) lower house, the
Chamber of Citizens, and a 40-seat (20 Serbian, 20
Montenegrin) upper house, the Chamber of Republics.
Executive power is vested in a federal president and
government.

HEAD OF STATE

Federal President, Slobodan Milosevic, *elected by parliament*
    15 July 1997

FEDERAL GOVERNMENT *as at June 1997*

Prime Minister, Dr Radoje Kontic
Deputy PMs, Nikola Sainovic; Vojin Djukanovic; Danko
    Djunic; Dr Vladan Kutlesic
Agriculture, Nedeljko Sipovac
Co-operation with International Financial Organizations, Dr
    Nebojsa Maljkovic
Defence, Pavle Bulatovic
Development, Science and the Environment, Dr Jagos Zelenovic
Domestic Trade, Milorad Miskovic
Economy, Dr Rade Filipovic
Finance, Bozidar Gazivoda
Foreign Affairs, Milan Milutinovic
Foreign Trade, Borislav Vukovic
Interior, Zoran Sokolovic
Justice, Zoran Knezevic
Labour, Health and Welfare, Miroslav Ivanisevic
Sport, Zoran Bingulac
Telecommunications, Dojcilo Radojevic

Transport, Dejan Drobnjakovic
Without Portfolio, Jugoslav Kostic

EMBASSY OF YUGOSLAVIA
5 Lexham Gardens, London w8 5JJ
Tel 0171-370 6105
Ambassador Extraordinary and Plenipotentiary, HE Dr Milos
    Radulovic, apptd 1996
Minister-Counsellor, R. Bogojevic
Defence Attaché, Capt. M. Ladicorbic

BRITISH EMBASSY
Generala Ždanova 46, 11000 Belgrade
Tel: Belgrade 645055
Ambassador Extraordinary and Plenipotentiary, HE Ivor
    Roberts, CMG
Deputy Head of Mission and First Secretary (Political), Dr D.
    Landsman
Defence Attaché, Col. J. H. Crosland
First Secretary (Commercial), D. A. Slinn

BRITISH COUNCIL REPRESENTATIVE, J. McGrath,
    Generala Ždanova 34-Mazanin (Post Fah 248), 11001
    Belgrade

MONTENEGRO
AREA – 5,331 sq. miles (13,812 sq. km)
POPULATION – 615,000: 62 per cent Montenegrin, 14.5 per
    cent Muslim, 6.5 per cent Albanian and 3 per cent Serb
CAPITAL – Podgorica (population, 117,875, 1991)

The Montenegrin Social Democrat Party (former Communists) won multiparty elections in November 1996 for
the 85-seat republican assembly and formed a government.
A presidential election is due to be held on 5 October 1997.

President, Momir Bulatovic, *elected* 11 January 1993
Prime Minister, vacant

SERBIA
AREA – 34,175 sq. miles (88,538 sq. km)
POPULATION – 9,300,000, of whom 66 per cent are Serbs
CAPITAL – Belgrade (population, 1,136,786, 1991)

Serbia includes the provinces of Kosovo (population 1.6
million), of great historic importance to Serbs, and
Vojvodina (population 2 million); the autonomy of both
was ended in September 1990. Kosovo, with its capital at
Priština, is predominantly Albanian (90 per cent). In
defiance of the Serbian authorities, ethnic Albanians held
parliamentary and presidential elections in May 1992,
which were won respectively by the Democratic League of
Kosovo and its leader Ibrahim Rugova. Tension between
Albanians and Serbs remains very high. Vojvodina, with its
capital at Novi Sad, has a large Hungarian minority (21 per
cent).
    The Socialist Party of Serbia (SPS) (formerly the
Communists) emerged as the largest party in multiparty
elections for the 250-seat National Assembly, held in
December 1992 and formed a coalition government with
the Serbian Radical Party (SRS). The coalition broke
down in September 1993. In the ensuing parliamentary
election on 19 December 1993 the SPS gained 123 seats,
three seats short of a majority, and formed a minority
government. Presidential and legislative elections are due
to be held in September 1997.

President, vacant
Prime Minister, Mirko Marjanovic

DEFENCE

The Army has 1,360 main battle tanks, 629 armoured
personnel carriers and armoured infantry fighting vehicles
and 720 artillery pieces. The Navy has four submarines,
four frigates and 34 patrol and coastal vessels at four bases.
The Air Force has 204 combat aircraft and 71 armed
helicopters.
MILITARY EXPENDITURE – 22.1 per cent of GDP (1995)
MILITARY PERSONNEL   113,900: Army 90,000, Navy
    7,200, Air Force 16,700
CONSCRIPTION DURATION – 12–15 months

ECONOMY

Since 1991 the economy has been devastated by the wars in
Croatia and Bosnia-Hercegovina, by the UN economic
sanctions and trade embargo, and because of the lack of
free-market reforms. Most factories have closed. Only the
evasion of UN sanctions and the country's agricultural
self-sufficiency have kept it afloat. In 1993 hyperinflation
became rampant because the government continued to
print money to finance the wars and subsidize industries.
By December 1993 inflation had reached 21,000 per cent a
month, the tax system had collapsed, output was one-third
of pre-war levels, industry was working at one-quarter of
capacity and the dinar had been devalued ten times. In
January 1994 a successful economic stabilization package
was introduced with a new superdinar pegged at one-to-
one parity with the Deutsche Mark. The UN voted to lift
economic sanctions on 22 November 1995 following the
conclusion of the Dayton Peace Accord on Bosnia.
Industrial production remains extremely low.
GDP – US$27,684 million (1992); US$3,840 per capita
    (1992)
ANNUAL AVERAGE GROWTH OF GDP – –2.0 per cent
    (1988)
INFLATION RATE – 117.4 per cent (1991)
TOTAL EXTERNAL DEBT – US$13,839 million (1995)

TRADE WITH UK	1995	1996
Imports from UK	£9,970,000	£32,518,000
Exports to UK	560,000	13,855,000

ZAMBIA
Republic of Zambia

AREA – 290,586 sq. miles (752,614 sq. km)
POPULATION – 9,196,000 (1994 UN estimate)
CAPITAL – Lusaka (population, 982,362, 1990)
MAJOR CITIES – Chipata; Kabwe; Kasama; Livingstone;
    Mansa; Mazabuka; Mbala; Mongu; Ndola; Solwezi;
    Chililabombwe; Chingola; Kalulushi; Kitwe; Luanshya;
    Mufulira, the last six towns being the main centres in the
    copper belt
CURRENCY – Kwacha (K) of 100 ngwee
NATIONAL ANTHEM – Stand and Sing of Zambia, Proud
    and Free
NATIONAL DAY – 24 October (Independence Day)
NATIONAL FLAG – Green with three small vertical stripes,
    red, black and orange (next fly); eagle device on green
    above stripes
LIFE EXPECTANCY (years) – male 50.70; female 53.00
POPULATION GROWTH RATE – 3.3 per cent (1994)
POPULATION DENSITY – 12 per sq. km (1994)
URBAN POPULATION – 42.0 per cent (1990)
MILITARY EXPENDITURE – 1.9 per cent of GDP (1995)
MILITARY PERSONNEL – 21,600: Army 20,000, Air Force
    1,600
ILLITERACY RATE – 21.8 per cent
ENROLMENT (percentage of age group) – primary 69 per
    cent (1994); tertiary 2.0 per cent (1990)

Zambia lies on the plateau of Central Africa. With the
exception of the valleys of the Zambezi, the Luapula, the

Kafue and the Luangwa rivers, and the Luano valley, elevations vary from 3,000 to 5,000 feet above sea level, but in the north-east the plateau rises to occasional altitudes of over 6,000 feet. Although Zambia lies within the tropics, and fairly centrally in the African land mass, its elevation relieves it from extremely high temperatures and humidity.

HISTORY AND POLITICS

Northern Rhodesia came under British rule in 1889. It achieved internal self-government when the Federation of Rhodesia and Nyasaland was dissolved in 1963 and became an independent republic within the Commonwealth on 24 October 1964 under the name of Zambia.

Zambia was a one-party state (the United National Independence Party) from 1973 until 1990, when pressure from opposition groups led to a new constitution (August 1991) and multiparty legislative and presidential elections in October 1991. The Movement for Multiparty Democracy (MMD) won 125 of the 150 seats in parliament, and the MMD candidate Frederick Chiluba defeated Kenneth Kaunda, who had ruled since independence, in the presidential election. A constitutional amendment was approved by the president in May 1996 requiring presidential candidates to be third-generation Zambians, thereby excluding former President Kaunda who had returned to politics in June 1995.

HEAD OF STATE
President, Frederick J. Chiluba, *elected* October 1991, *re-elected* 18 November 1996
Vice-President, Brig.-Gen. Godfrey Miyanda

CABINET *as at June 1997*
Agriculture, Food and Fisheries, Edith Nawakwi
Commerce, Trade and Industry, Alfeyo Hambayi
Community Development and Social Services, Newstead Zimba
Defence, Benjamin Mwila
Education, Dr Syamukayumbu Syamujaya
Energy and Water Development, Suresh Desai
Environment and Natural Resources, William Harrington
Finance and Economic Development, Ronald Penza
Foreign Affairs, Prof. Lawrence Shimba
Health, Dr Katele Kalumba
Home Affairs, Chitalu Sampa
Information and Broadcasting Services, David Mpamba
Labour and Social Security, Dr Peter Machungwa
Land, Dawson Lupunga
Legal Affairs, Vincent Malambo
Local Government and Housing, Bennie Mwiinga
Mines and Mineral Development, Gen. Christon Tembo
Science, Technology and Vocational Training, Enock Kavindele
Sport, Youth and Child Development, Samuel Miyanda
State House, Eric Silwamba
Tourism, Amusa Mwanamwabwa
Without Portfolio, Michael Sata
Works and Supply, Keli Walubita

HIGH COMMISSION FOR THE REPUBLIC OF ZAMBIA
2 Palace Gate, London w8 5NG
Tel 0171-589 6655
High Commissioner, new appointment awaited
Defence Adviser, Brig.-Gen. M. G. Lisita

BRITISH HIGH COMMISSION
Independence Avenue (PO Box 50050), 15 101 Ridgeway, Lusaka
Tel: Lusaka 251133
High Commissioner, HE Patrick Nixon, CMG, OBE, apptd 1993
Deputy High Commissioner, B. S. Jones, LVO
First Secretary (Commercial/Consular), R. Clark

BRITISH COUNCIL DIRECTOR, M. Fryars, Heroes Place, Cairo Road (PO Box 34571), Lusaka

ECONOMY

The MMD government has begun the transformation of the state-controlled economy into a free market system with the sale and privatization of large sectors of the economy. Aid and investment have poured into the country, foreign exchange controls have been removed, the Kwacha floated and prices freed. The free market economic reforms introduced since 1991 by the MMD government have revolutionized the economy, which had been highly regulated and protected from competition. Price subsidies and tariffs have been lowered or abolished and public sector wages frozen but inflation and interest rates have increased, causing hardships. Increased imports have affected manufacturing and agricultural production.

Principal products are maize, sugar, groundnuts, cotton, livestock, vegetables and tobacco.

Following the reforms initiated by the government, the US government wrote off K59,000 million of debt in 1993. The IMF lifted its suspension of Zambia, in place since September 1987; loans worth US$1,300 million were subsequently approved.

In 1994 exports totalled US$758 million.
GNP – US$3,605 million (1995); US$400 per capita (1995)
GDP – US$3,989 million (1992); US$258 per capita (1992)
ANNUAL AVERAGE GROWTH OF GDP – –1.8 per cent (1991)
INFLATION RATE – 53.7 per cent (1994)
TOTAL EXTERNAL DEBT – US$6,853 million (1995)

TRADE WITH UK	1995	1996
Imports from UK	£49,819,000	£51,544,000
Exports to UK	19,460,000	17,726,000

ZIMBABWE
Republic of Zimbabwe

AREA – 150,872 sq. miles (390,757 sq. km). Neighbours: Zambia (north), Mozambique (east), South Africa (south), Botswana and Namibia (west)
POPULATION – 11,150,000 (1994 UN estimate); 10,400,000 (1992 census)
CAPITAL – Harare (population, 1,189,103, 1992)
MAJOR CITIES – Bulawayo (population, 621,742), the largest town in Matabeleland; Chitungwiza; Gweru; Hwange; Kadoma; Kwe Kwe; Masvingo; Mutare
CURRENCY – Zimbabwe dollar (Z$) of 100 cents
NATIONAL ANTHEM – Ngaikomberarwe Nyika Ye Zimbabwe (Blessed be the country of Zimbabwe)
NATIONAL DAY – 18 April (Independence Day)
NATIONAL FLAG – Seven horizontal stripes of green, yellow, red, black, red, yellow, green; a white, black-bordered, triangle based on the hoist containing the national emblem
LIFE EXPECTANCY (years) – male 58.00; female 62.00
POPULATION GROWTH RATE – 4.4 per cent (1994)
POPULATION DENSITY – 29 per sq. km (1994)
MILITARY EXPENDITURE – 4.2 per cent of GDP (1995)
MILITARY PERSONNEL – 43,000: Army 39,000, Air Force 4,000

HISTORY AND POLITICS

Southern Rhodesia was granted responsible government in 1923. An illegal declaration of independence on 11 November 1965 was finally terminated on 12 December 1979. Following elections in February 1980 the country became independent on 18 April 1980 as the Republic of Zimbabwe, a member of the British Commonwealth.

The independence constitution was amended in 1987, making the presidency an executive post. The president is popularly elected for a six-year term, appoints the Cabinet and can veto parliamentary bills. The legislature became unicameral in 1990 and the House of Assembly has 150 members: 120 elected, eight provincial governors, ten traditional chiefs and 12 others appointed by the president. A merger agreement between the ZANU (PF) and ZAPU parties was signed in 1987 with a view to the eventual creation of a one-party state. The new party is known as ZANU-PF. The latest general election was held in April 1995 and ZANU-PF won 118 of the 120 elective seats, although it lost a by-election in November 1995. President Mugabe was re-elected for a six-year term in March 1996, following the withdrawal of the other two contenders.

The country is divided into eight provinces: Manicaland, Masvingo, Matabeleland North, Matabeleland South, Midlands, Mashonaland West, Central and East.

HEAD OF STATE

Executive President, Robert Gabriel Mugabe, *elected* 30 December 1987, *re-elected* March 1990, March 1996

CABINET *as at June 1997*

The President
Vice-Presidents, Simon Muzenda; Dr Joshua Nkomo
Agriculture, vacant
Defence, Moven Mahachi
Education, Gabriel Machinga
Environment and Tourism, Chenhamo Chimutingwende
Finance, Dr Herbert M. Murerwa
Foreign Affairs, Dr Stanislaus Mudenge
Health and Child Welfare, Dr Timothy Stamps
Higher Education, Ignatius Chombo
Home Affairs, Dumiso Dabengwa
Industry and Commerce, Dr Nathan M. Shamuyarira
Information, Posts and Telecommunications, Joyce Mujuru
Justice, Legal and Parliamentary Affairs, Emmerson Mnangagwa
Labour, Public Service and Social Welfare, Florence L. Chitauro
Lands and Water Resources, Kumbirai Kangai
Local Government, Rural and Urban Development, John Nkomo
Mines, Dr Swithun T. Mombeshora
National Affairs, Employment Creation and Co-operatives, Tenjiwe Lesabe
National Security, Dr Sidney Sekeramayi
Planning, Richard Hove
President's Office, Cephas Msipa
Public Construction and National Housing, Enos Chikowore
Sports, Recreation and Culture, Dr Witness Mangwende
Transport and Energy, Simon Moyo
Without Portfolio, Dr Eddison J. M. Zvobgo; Joseph Msika

HIGH COMMISSION OF THE REPUBLIC OF ZIMBABWE
Zimbabwe House, 429 Strand, London WC2R 0SA
Tel 0171-836 7755
High Commissioner, HE Dr Ngoni Togarepi Chideya, apptd 1993
Minister-Counsellors, A. Nyazika; J. Mupamhanga
Defence Adviser, Lt.-Col. E. Zabanyana
First Secretary, B. Mutoti (*Commercial*)

BRITISH HIGH COMMISSION
Corner House, Samora Machel Avenue (PO Box 4490), Harare
Tel: Harare 772990
High Commissioner, HE Martin J. Williams, CVO, OBE, apptd 1995
Deputy High Commissioner, I. Hay-Campbell
Defence Adviser, Col. A. Reed Screen, OBE

First Secretaries, A. R. Ashcroft (*Commercial*); G. M. Johnson (*Consular*)

BRITISH COUNCIL DIRECTOR, Dr J. Eyres, OBE, 23 Jason Moyo Avenue (PO Box 664), Harare

ECONOMY

Ten years of socialism and central planning in 1980–90, coupled with a period of drought, brought the economy to crisis point before free market economic reforms were introduced in 1990 under the auspices of a World Bank-enhanced structural adjustment programme. This has involved the removal of food subsidies, the floating of the currency, opening the market to imports, and reducing subsidies. The programme has been partly implemented but the economy remains highly regulated and the civil service and armed forces have not been reduced sufficiently. The Supreme Court approved government plans to seize 12 million acres of white-owned farmland in June 1996.

The country is endowed with minerals, water, forests, wildlife and other resources. The agricultural sector is well-developed, accounts for 68 per cent of GDP and employs 70 per cent of the workforce. Tobacco remains the most important crop in terms of export (Zimbabwe is the largest exporter in the world), and maize the most important for domestic consumption. Agriculture has diversified in recent years with horticultural products (especially roses and tulips), fruit and vegetables becoming important export earners. Other crops include wheat, cotton, and sugar. Beef is exported to the EU.

The manufacturing sector is very dependent on the agricultural sector for raw materials. Industry is also dependent on imports e.g. fuel oil, steel products and chemicals, as well as heavy machinery and items of transport. The mining sector, although contributing a relatively small portion to GDP, is important to the economy as a foreign exchange earner. Almost all mineral production is exported. Gold is the most important mineral, others are asbestos, diamonds, silver, nickel, copper, chrome ore, tin, iron ore and cobalt. There is a successful ferro-chrome industry and a substantial steel works which has been heavily subsidized by government. Platinum mining is about to begin following a £160 million investment by an Australian firm.

Tourism is of growing importance, with more than 1,000,000 visitors in 1995.

In 1993 Zimbabwe had a trade surplus of US$122 million and a current account deficit of US$116 million. In 1994 imports totalled US$2,241 million and exports US$1,885 million.

GNP – US$5,933 million (1995); US$540 per capita (1995)
GDP – US$6,019 million (1992); US$473 per capita (1992)
ANNUAL AVERAGE GROWTH OF GDP – −2.8 per cent (1991)
INFLATION RATE – 22.6 per cent (1995)
TOTAL EXTERNAL DEBT – US$4,885 million (1995)

TRADE WITH UK	1995	1996
Imports from UK	£87,696,000	£103,819,000
Exports to UK	149,344,000	136,516,000

EDUCATION

Since independence, a policy of free primary education and accelerated expansion at secondary level has resulted in rapidly expanding enrolment. Over 80 per cent of schools are government-aided schools. The University of Zimbabwe was founded in 1955.

ILLITERACY RATE – 14.9 per cent
ENROLMENT (percentage of age group) – tertiary 6.1 per cent (1992)

British Dependent Territories

ANGUILLA

Anguilla is a flat coralline island in the Caribbean, about 16 miles in length, three and a half miles in breadth at its widest point and its area is about 35 sq. miles (91 sq. km). The island is covered with low scrub and fringed with white coral-sand beaches. The climate is pleasant, with temperatures in the range of 24–30° C throughout the year.

POPULATION – The population (1992 census) is 8,960.

CAPITAL – The Valley (population 1,400).

CURRENCY – East Caribbean dollar (EC$) of 100 cents.

FLAG – British Blue Ensign with the coat of arms and three dolphins in the fly.

GOVERNMENT

Anguilla has been a British colony since 1650. For much of its history it was linked administratively with St Christopher, but three months after the Associated State of Saint Christopher (St Kitts)-Nevis-Anguilla came into being in 1967, the Anguillans repudiated government from St Kitts. A Commissioner was installed in 1969 and in 1976 Anguilla was given a new status and separate constitution. Final separation from St Kitts and Nevis was effected on 19 December 1980 and Anguilla reverted to a British dependency. A new constitution was introduced in 1982, providing for a Governor, an Executive Council comprising four elected Ministers and two ex-officio members (the Attorney-General and Permanent Secretary, Finance), and an 11-member legislative House of Assembly presided over by a Speaker.

The 1982 Constitution (Amendment) Order 1990 came into operation on 30 May 1990. Among the new constitutional provisions are a Deputy Governor (who replaces the Permanent Secretary (Finance) in the Executive Council and the Legislature), a Parliamentary Secretary, Leader of Opposition and Deputy Speaker.

Governor, HE Robert Harris, *apptd* 1997
Deputy Governor, vacant

EXECUTIVE COUNCIL *as at June 1997*

Chairman, The Governor
Chief Minister and Minister of Tourism, Lands, Agriculture and Fisheries, Hubert Hughes
Attorney-General, Kurt De Freitas
Communications, Public Utilities and Works, Albert Hughes
Finance and Economic Development, Victor Banks
Social Services, Edison Baird
Member, The Deputy Governor

ECONOMY

Low rainfall limits agricultural output and export earnings are mainly from sales of fish and lobsters. Tourism has developed rapidly in recent years and accounts for most of the island's economic activity. In 1996 there were 37,498 tourists and a further 48,741 day visitors.

TRADE WITH UK	1995	1996
Imports from UK	£2,059,000	£2,688,000
Exports to UK	14,000	46,000

ASCENSION
— *see* St Helena

BERMUDA

The Bermudas, or Somers Islands, are a cluster of about 100 small islands (about 20 of which are inhabited) situated in the west of the Atlantic Ocean, the nearest point of the mainland being Cape Hatteras in North Carolina, about 570 miles distant. The total area is approximately 20.59 sq. miles (53 sq. km).

POPULATION – The population (1994) is 60,075.

CAPITAL – ΨHamilton (population 1993, 2,277).

CURRENCY – Bermuda dollar of 100 cents.

FLAG – British Red Ensign with the shield of arms in the fly.

GOVERNMENT

The colony derives its name from Juan Bermudez, a Spaniard, who sighted it before 1515. No settlement was made until 1609 when Sir George Somers, who was shipwrecked there on his way to Virginia, colonized the islands.

Internal self-government was introduced in 1968. There is a Senate of 11 members and an elected House of Assembly of 40 members. The Governor retains responsibility for external affairs, defence, internal security and the police, although administrative matters for the police service have been delegated to the Minister of Labour, Home Affairs and Public Safety. Independence from the UK was rejected in a referendum in August 1995.

The last general election was held on 5 October 1993. The United Bermuda Party holds 22 seats, and the Progressive Labour Party 18 seats.

Governor and Commander-in-Chief, HE John T. Masefield, *apptd* 1997
Deputy Governor, Peter Willis

CABINET *as at May 1997*

Premier, Pamela F. Gordon
Deputy Premier, Education and Human Affairs, C. Jerome Dill
Community and Cultural Affairs, Sen. Yvette V. A. Swan
Environment, Planning and Natural Resources, J. Irving Pearman
Finance, E. G. Grant Gibbons
Health and Social Services, Clarence R. Terceira
Labour, Home Affairs and Public Safety, Quinton L. Edness
Legislative Affairs and Women's Issues, Sen. Lynda Milligan-Whyte
Technology and Information, John Barritt
Tourism and Marine Services, A. David Dodwell
Transport and Aviation Services, Wayne L. Furbert
Works and Engineering, Parks and Housing, C. V. Jim Woolridge
Youth Development, Sports and Recreation, David Dyer

President of the Senate, A. S. Jackson, CBE
Speaker of the House of Assembly, Ernest DeCouto
Chief Justice, Austin Ward, QC

ECONOMY

The islands' economic structure is based on tourism, the major industry, and international company business, attracted by the low level of taxation and sophisticated telecommunications system. In 1996 a total of 576,628 visitors arrived by air and cruise ship.

Locally manufactured concentrates, perfumes, cut flowers and pharmaceuticals are the islands' leading exports. Little food is produced except vegetables and fish, other foodstuffs being imported.

In November 1995, the US, UK and Canadian governments handed over 1,500 acres of land (roughly 10 per cent of the colony), to the government. The land, which had been used for military bases, included an airport on St David's Island.

TRADE WITH UK	1995	1996
Imports from UK	£17,316,000	£19,032,000
Exports to UK	3,085,000	7,150,000

COMMUNICATIONS

One daily and two weekly newspapers are published in Bermuda. Three commercial companies operate radio and television services, including a cable-television system. The Bermuda Telephone Company and Cable and Wireless provide telecommunications links to more than 140 countries.

EDUCATION

Free elementary education was introduced in 1949. Free secondary education was introduced in 1965 for those children in the aided and maintained schools who were below the upper limit of the statutory school age of 18 (from 1969 onwards).

THE BRITISH ANTARCTIC TERRITORY

The British Antarctic Territory was designated in 1962 and consists of the areas south of 60°S. latitude which were previously included in the Falkland Islands Dependencies. The territory includes the South Orkney Islands, the South Shetland Islands, the mountainous Antarctic Peninsula (highest point Mount Jackson, 13,620 ft, in Palmer Land) and all adjacent islands, and the land mass extending to the South Pole. The territory has no indigenous inhabitants and the British population consists of the scientists and technicians who man the British Antarctic Survey stations. The number averages about 60 to 70 in winter, but increases considerably in the southern hemisphere's summer months with the arrival of field scientists. Argentina, Brazil, Chile, China, Korea (South), Poland, USA, Russia, Spain, Ukraine and Uruguay also have scientific stations in the territory.

The first two British Antarctic Survey stations were established in the South Shetland Islands in 1944, and by 1956 the number of stations had risen to 12. Due to the completion of field work in some areas and increased mobility, this number has now been reduced to four. These are Rothera (Adelaide Island), Halley (Caird Coast) and, in summer only, Fossil Bluff (George VI Sound) and Signy Island (South Orkney Islands). Fifteen other stations have been established but are at present unoccupied.

The territory is administered by a Commissioner, resident in London.

Commissioner (non-resident), Anthony J. Longrigg, CMG, *apptd* 1995

THE BRITISH INDIAN OCEAN TERRITORY

The British Indian Ocean Territory was established by an Order in Council in 1965 and included islands formerly administered from Mauritius and the Seychelles. The islands of Farquhar, Desroches and Aldabra became part of the Seychelles when it became independent in 1976; since then the Territory has consisted of the islands of the Chagos Archipelago only.

The Chagos Archipelago consists of six main groups of islands situated on the Great Chagos Bank and covering some 21,000 sq. miles (54,389 sq. km). The largest and most southerly of the Chagos Islands is Diego Garcia, a sand cay with a land area of about 17 sq. miles approximately 1,100 miles east of Mahé, used as a joint naval support facility by Britain and the USA.

The other main island groups of the archipelago, Peros Banhos (29 islands with a total land area of 4 sq. miles) and Salomon (11 islands with a total land area of 2 sq. miles) are uninhabited. The islands have a tropical maritime climate, with average temperatures between 25° C and 29° C in Diego Garcia, and rainfall in the whole archipelago of 90–100 inches a year.

FLAG – Divided horizontally into blue and white wavy stripes, with the Union Flag in the canton and a crowned palm-tree over all in the fly.

Commissioner, Bruce Dinwiddy, *apptd* 1996
Administrator, Louise Savill, *apptd* 1996

TRADE WITH UK	1995	1996
Imports from UK	£1,924,000	£1,869,000
Exports to UK	—	30,000

THE BRITISH VIRGIN ISLANDS

The Virgin Islands are situated at the eastern extremity of the Greater Antilles, divided between the UK and the USA. Those of the group which are British number 46, of which 11 are inhabited, and have a total area of about 59 sq. miles (153 sq. km). The principal islands are Tortola, the largest (area, 21 sq. miles), Virgin Gorda (8¼ sq. miles), Anegada (15 sq. miles) and Jost Van Dyke (3½ sq. miles).

Apart from Anegada, which is a flat coral island, the British Virgin Islands are hilly, being an extension of the Puerto Rico and the US Virgin Islands archipelago. The highest point is Sage Mountain on Tortola which rises to a height of 1,780 feet.

The islands lie within the trade winds belt and possess a sub-tropical climate. The average temperature varies from 22°–28° C in winter to 26°–31° C in summer. Average annual rainfall is 53 inches.

POPULATION – The 1991 census showed a total population of 16,108: Tortola (13,225); Virgin Gorda (2,431); Anegada (162); Jost Van Dyke (140); and other islands (144).

CAPITAL – ΨRoad Town, on the south-east of Tortola. Population 3,983.

CURRENCY – The US dollar (US$) of 100 cents is legal tender.

FLAG – British Blue Ensign with the shield of arms in the fly.

GOVERNMENT

Under the 1977 constitution the Governor, appointed by the Crown, remains responsible for defence and internal security, external affairs and the civil service but in other matters acts in accordance with the advice of the Executive Council. The Executive Council consists of the Governor as Chairman, one ex-officio member (the Attorney-General), the Chief Minister and three other ministers. The Legislative Council consists of a Speaker chosen from outside the Council, one ex-officio member (the Attorney-General), and 13 elected members returned from ten electoral districts.

Governor, HE David P. Mackilligin, CMG, *apptd* 1995
Deputy Governor, M. Elton Georges, OBE

EXECUTIVE COUNCIL *as at June 1997*

Chairman, The Governor
Chief Minister and Minister of Finance, Ralph O'Neal, OBE
Attorney-General, Dancia Penn
Communications and Works, Alvin Christopher
Health, Education and Welfare, Eileene L. Parsons
Natural Resources and Labour, Oliver Cills

Puisne Judge (resident), Justice Stanley Moore

ECONOMY

Tourism is the main industry but the financial centre is growing steadily in importance. Other industries include a rum distillery, three stone-crushing plants and factories manufacturing concrete blocks and paint. The major export items are fresh fish, gravel, sand, fruit and vegetables; exports are largely confined to the US Virgin Islands. Chief imports are building materials, machinery, cars and beverages.

TRADE WITH UK	1995	1996
Imports from UK	£5,399,000	£5,048,000
Exports to UK	994,000	12,935,000

COMMUNICATIONS

The principal airport is on Beef Island, linked by bridge to Tortola, and an extended runway of 3,600 ft enables larger aircraft to call. There is a second airfield on Virgin Gorda and a third on Anegada. There are direct shipping services to the UK and the USA and fast passenger services connect the main islands by ferry.

THE CAYMAN ISLANDS

The Cayman Islands consist of three islands, Grand Cayman, Cayman Brac, and Little Cayman, with a total area of 100 sq. miles (259 sq. km). About 150 miles south of Cuba, the islands are divided from Jamaica, 180 miles to the south-east, by the Cayman Trench, the deepest part of the Caribbean. The nearest point on the US mainland is Miami in Florida, 450 miles to the north. Cooled by trade winds, the annual average temperature and rainfall are 27.2° C and 50.7 inches respectively.

POPULATION – Population (estimate 1996) 35,000, of which most live on Grand Cayman.

CAPITAL – ΨGeorge Town, in Grand Cayman, population (estimate 1996) 20,000.

CURRENCY – Cayman Islands dollar (CI$) of 100 cents, which is fixed at CI$ = US$1.20.

FLAG – British Blue Ensign with the arms on a white disc in the fly.

GOVERNMENT

The colony derives its name from the Carib word for the crocodile, 'caymanas', which appeared in the log of the first English visitor to the islands, Sir Francis Drake. Although tradition has it that the first settlers arrived in 1658, the first recorded settlers arrived in 1666–71. The first recorded permanent settlers followed the first land grant by Britain in 1734. The islands were placed under direct control of Jamaica in 1863. When Jamaica became independent in 1962, the islands opted to remain under the British Crown.

The constitution provides for a Governor, a Legislative Assembly and an Executive Council, and effectively allows a large measure of self-government. Unless there are exceptional reasons, the Governor accepts the advice of the Executive Council, which comprises three official members and five ministers elected from the 15 elected members of the Assembly. The official members also sit in the Assembly. The Governor has responsibility for the police, civil service, defence and external affairs. The Governor handed over the presidency of the Legislative Assembly to the Speaker in 1991. The normal life of the Assembly is four years, with a general election next due in November 2000.

Governor, HE John W. Owen, MBE, *apptd* 1995

EXECUTIVE COUNCIL *as at June 1997*

President, The Governor
Chief Secretary, J. Ryan, MBE
Agriculture, Environment, Communications and Works, J. McLean, OBE
Attorney-General, R. H. Coles
Community Development, Sports, Women's Affairs, Youth and Culture, W. M. Bush
Education, Aviation and Planning, T. M. Bodden, OBE
Financial Secretary, G. A. McCarthy, OBE
Health, Drug Abuse Prevention and Rehabilitation, A. S. Eden
Tourism, Commerce and Transport, T. C. Jefferson, OBE

Speaker of Legislative Assembly, Capt. M. Kirkconnell, MBE

CAYMAN ISLANDS GOVERNMENT OFFICE, 6 Arlington Street, London SW1A 1RE. Tel: 0171-491 7772.
Government Representative, T. Russell, CMG, CBE

ECONOMY

With a complete absence of direct taxation, the Cayman Islands has become successful over the past 25 years as an offshore financial centre. With representation from 62 countries, there were, at the end of 1996, 648 banks and trust companies, of which local offices were maintained by 107. In addition, there were 498 licensed insurance companies and 34,000 registered companies. The Cayman Islands stock exchange opened in January 1997. Tourism, with an emphasis on scuba diving, has also been developed successfully. There were 373,200 visitors by air and 771,068 cruise ship callers in 1996.

The two industries support a heavy imbalance in trade resulting from the need to import most of what is consumed and used on the islands, and have created a thriving local economy in which the GDP reached an estimated US$1,023.8 million (US$29,251 per capita) in 1996. Import duty and fees from financial centre operations have provided revenue enabling the government to undertake heavy investment in education (which is provided free to all four- to 16-year olds), health and other social programmes.

TRADE WITH UK	1995	1996
Imports from UK	£10,621,000	£17,284,000
Exports to UK	1,330,000	1,372,000

FALKLAND ISLANDS

The Falkland Islands, the only considerable group in the South Atlantic, lie about 300 miles east of the Straits of Magellan. They consist of East Falkland (area 2,610 sq. miles; 6,759 sq. km), West Falkland (2,090 sq. miles; 5,413 sq. km) and over 100 small islands. Mount Usborne (E. Falkland), the loftiest peak, rises 2,312 feet above sea level. The islands are chiefly moorland.

The climate is cool. At Stanley the mean monthly temperature varies between 19° C in January and 2° C in July.

POPULATION – The population, excluding the British garrison, was 2,221 at April 1996.

CHIEF TOWN – ΨStanley, population (1996) 1,636. Stanley is about 8,103 miles from Britain.

CURRENCY – Falkland pound of 100 pence.

FLAG – British Blue Ensign with the arms on a white disc in the fly.

GOVERNMENT

The Falklands were sighted first by Davis in 1592, and then by Hawkins in 1594; the first known landing was by Strong in 1690. A settlement was made by France in 1764; this was subsequently sold to Spain, but the latter country recognized Great Britain's title to a part at least of the group in 1771. The first British settlement was established in 1766. After Argentina declared independence from Spain, the Argentine government in 1820 proclaimed its sovereignty over the Falklands and a settlement was founded in 1826. The settlement was destroyed by the Americans in 1831. In 1833 occupation was resumed by the British for the protection of the seal-fisheries, and the islands were permanently colonized. Argentina continued to claim sovereignty over the islands (known to them as las Islas Malvinas), and in pursuance of this claim invaded the islands on 2 April 1982 and also occupied South Georgia. A naval and military force dispatched from Great Britain recaptured South Georgia on 25 April and after landing at San Carlos Bay on 21 May, recaptured the islands from the Argentines, who surrendered on 14 June 1982. A British naval and military garrison of 1,700 personnel remains in the area. A military zone of 55 miles (previously 80) remains around the islands within which Argentinian naval and air forces may not intrude.

Under the 1985 constitution, the Governor is advised by an Executive Council consisting of three elected members of the Legislative Council and two ex-officio members, the Chief Executive and the Financial Secretary. The Legislative Council consists of eight elected members and the same two ex-officio members.

Governor and Chairman of the Executive Council, HE Richard Peter Ralph, CMG, CVO, apptd 1996
Chief Executive, A. M. Gurr
Attorney General, D. G. Lang, QC

Commander, British Forces, Falkland Islands, Brig. I. D. S. Campbell
Financial Secretary, D. F. Howatt
FALKLAND ISLANDS GOVERNMENT OFFICE, Falkland House, 14 Broadway, London SW1H 0BH. Tel: 0171-222 2542. *Government Representative*, Miss S. Cameron

ECONOMY

The economy was formerly based solely on agriculture, principally sheep farming with a little dairy farming for domestic requirements and crops for winter fodder. Since the establishment of an interim conservation and management fishing zone around the islands in 1987 and the consequent introduction of a licensing regime for vessels fishing within the 200-mile zone, the economy has diversified. Income from the associated fishing activities, mainly for illex squid, is now the largest source of revenue. The increase in government revenue from fishing licences has led to the establishment of a substantial health, education and welfare system with a well-equipped hospital in Stanley, free education until the age of 16 and further education in the UK paid for by the Falklands government. The islands are now self-financing except for defence. Chief imports are provisions, alcoholic beverages, timber, clothing and hardware. Tourism is a small but expanding industry.

In 1993 the Falkland Islands government announced a 200-mile oil exploration zone around the islands. In September 1995 the UK and Argentina signed an agreement which provided for a joint commission to co-ordinate exploration of the oil field. Exploration licences were issued in October 1996 with exploration drilling expected to begin in 1998. In 1995–6 the government had a budget deficit of £5 million.

TRADE WITH UK	1995	1996
Imports from UK	£15,665,000	£19,932,000
Exports to UK	4,721,000	5,568,000

GIBRALTAR

Gibraltar is a rocky promontory with a total area of 2½ sq. miles (6.5 sq km) and a height of 1,396 ft at its greatest elevation. It juts southwards from the south-east coast of Spain, with which it is connected by a low isthmus. It is about 20 miles (32 km) from the opposite coast of Africa. The town stands at the foot of the promontory on the west side.

POPULATION – The population at the end of 1996 was 27,337.

CURRENCY – Gibraltar pound of 100 pence.

FLAG – White with a red stripe along the lower edge; over all a red castle with a key hanging from its gateway.

GOVERNMENT

Gibraltar was captured in 1704, during the war of the Spanish Succession, by a combined Dutch and English force, and was ceded to Great Britain by the Treaty of Utrecht (1713). Several attempts have been made to retake it, the most celebrated being the great siege of 1779 to 1783, when General Eliott held it for three years and seven months against a combined French and Spanish force. The Treaty of Utrecht stipulates that if Britain ever relinquishes its colonial rights over Gibraltar the colony would return to Spain. In a 1967 referendum on the colony's status, 12,000 people voted to remain a British Dependent Territory and 44 voted to join Spain. Spain closed the border with Gibraltar from 1969 to 1985 and refused to engage in any trade.

The 1969 constitution makes provision for certain domestic matters to devolve on a local government of ministers appointed from among elected members of the House of Assembly. The House of Assembly consists of an independent Speaker, 15 elected members, the Attorney-General and the Financial and Development Secretary.

The Governor retains responsibility for external affairs, defence, internal security and financial security, while the local government is responsible for other domestic matters. The Gibraltar government has recently been pressing for more local autonomy especially in its relations with the EU, and this has led to tension with the UK and Spanish governments. Gibraltar is part of the EU (with the UK government responsible for enforcing EU directives affecting Gibraltar) but is not a fully-fledged member. The Gibraltar Social Democrats won the last election in May 1996.

Governor and Commander-in-Chief, HE the Rt. Hon. Sir Richard Luce
Commander British Forces, HM Naval Base, Gibraltar, Cdre A. J. S. Taylor
Deputy Governor, M. Robinson, CMG
Attorney-General, R. Rhoda
Chief Justice, D. Schoffield
Chief Minister, Peter Caruana
Speaker, J. Alcantara

ECONOMY

Gibraltar has an extensive shipping trade and is a popular shopping centre and tourist resort. The chief sources of revenue are the port dues, the rent of the Crown estate in the town, and duties on consumer items. The free port tradition of Gibraltar is still reflected in the low rates of import duty. A financial services industry is expanding, based on Gibraltar's status as an offshore financial centre. However, many jobs have been lost as a result of reductions in the British naval and military presence.

A total of 4,222 merchant ships (79.2 million gross registered tons aggregate) entered the port during 1996. There are 49.9 km of roads.

TRADE WITH UK	1995	1996
Imports from UK	£79,579,000	£87,110,000
Exports to UK	10,598,000	4,225,000

EDUCATION

Education is compulsory and free for children between the ages of four and 15 whose parents are ordinarily resident in Gibraltar. Scholarships are available for higher education in Britain. The total enrolment in government schools was 4,638 in December 1996.

MONTSERRAT

Montserrat is about 11 miles long and seven miles wide, with an area of 38 sq. miles (98 sq. km). Fertile and green, it is volcanic with several hot springs. About two-thirds of the island is mountainous, the rest capable of cultivation.
POPULATION – Population (estimate 1997) is 6,500.
CHIEF TOWN – ΨPlymouth, population 2,500.
CURRENCY – East Caribbean dollar (EC$) of 100 cents.

FLAG – British Blue Ensign with the shield of arms in the fly.

GOVERNMENT

Discovered by Columbus in 1493, Montserrat became a British colony in 1632. The first settlers were predominantly Irish indentured servants from St Kitts. Montserrat was captured by the French in 1664, 1667 and 1782 but the island reverted to Britain within a few years on each occasion and was finally assigned to Great Britain in 1783.

A ministerial system was introduced in Montserrat in 1960. The Executive Council is presided over by the Governor and is composed of four elected members (the Chief and three other Ministers) and two ex-officio members (the Attorney-General and the Financial Secretary). The four Ministers are appointed from the members of the political party or coalition holding the majority in the Legislative Council. The Legislative Council consists of the Speaker, two ex-officio members (the Attorney-General and the Financial Secretary), two nominated members and seven elected members. Following elections in November 1996 the elected element of the legislature comprised the following parties: Movement for National Reconstruction (MNR) 2; People's Progressive Alliance (PPA) 2; National Progressive Party 1; Independents 2.

Governor, HE Anthony Abbott, MBE, *apptd* 1997

EXECUTIVE COUNCIL *as at June 1997*
President, The Governor
Chief Minister and Minister of Finance and Economic Development, David Brandt
Agriculture, Trade and the Environment, P. Austin Bramble
Attorney-General, Gerrel Thom
Communications and Works, Rupert Weckes
Education, Health, Community Services and Labour, Adelina Tuitt
Financial Secretary, C. T. John, OBE

Speaker of the Legislative Council, Dr H. A. Fergus, CBE

ECONOMY

The economy, which consists of tourism, related construction activities, offshore business services and agriculture, has been seriously affected by relocation to the north of the island due to volcanic activity.

TRADE WITH UK	1995	1996
Imports from UK	£2,554,000	£3,106,000
Exports to UK	4,720,000	7,944,000

PITCAIRN ISLANDS

Pitcairn, a small volcanic island 1.9 sq. miles (5 sq. km) in area, is the chief of a group of islands situated about midway between New Zealand and Panama in the South Pacific Ocean. The island rises in cliffs to a height of 1,100 feet and access from the sea is possible only at Bounty Bay, a small rocky cove, and then only by surf boats. The other three islands of the group (Henderson lying 105 miles east-north-east of Pitcairn, Oeno lying 75 miles north-west and Ducie lying 293 miles east) are all uninhabited.

Mean monthly temperatures vary between 66° F (19° C) in August and 75° F (24° C) in February and the average annual rainfall is 80 inches. With an equable climate, the island is very fertile and produces both tropical and sub-tropical trees and crops.

POPULATION – At 31 December 1996 the population was 42. Since 1887 the islanders have all been adherents of the Seventh-day Adventist Church.

FLAG – British Blue Ensign with the arms in the fly.

GOVERNMENT

First settled in 1790 by the Bounty mutineers and their Tahitian companions, Pitcairn was left uninhabited in 1856 when the entire population was resettled on Norfolk Island. The present community are descendants of two parties who, not wishing to remain on Norfolk, returned to Pitcairn in 1859 and 1864 respectively.

Pitcairn became a British settlement under the British Settlement Act 1887, and was administered by the Governor of Fiji from 1952 until 1970, when the administration was transferred to the British High Commission in New Zealand and the British High Commissioner was appointed Governor. The local Government Ordinance of 1964 provides for a Council of ten members of whom six are elected.

Governor of Pitcairn, Henderson, Ducie and Oeno Islands, HE Robert J. Alston, CMG (*British High Commissioner to New Zealand*)
Island Magistrate and Chairman of Island Council, J. Warren

ECONOMY

The islanders live by subsistence gardening and fishing. Wood carvings and other handicrafts are sold to passing ships and to a few overseas customers. Other than small fees charged for gun and driving licences there are no taxes and government revenue is derived almost solely from the sale of postage stamps and income from investments. Communication with the outside world is maintained by cargo vessels travelling between New Zealand and Panama which call at irregular intervals, and by means of a satellite service providing telephone, telex and fax facilities.

SOCIAL WELFARE

Education is compulsory between the ages of five and 15. Secondary education in New Zealand is encouraged by the administration, which provides scholarships and bursaries. Medical care is provided by a registered nurse when a doctor is not present.

ST HELENA AND DEPENDENCIES

ST HELENA

St Helena is situated in the South Atlantic Ocean, 955 miles south of the Equator, 702 miles south-east of Ascension, 1,140 miles from the nearest point of the African continent, 1,800 miles from the coast of South America, 1,694 miles from Cape Town. It is $10\frac{1}{2}$ miles long, $6\frac{1}{2}$ broad, and encloses an area of 47 sq. miles (122 sq. km).

St Helena is of volcanic origin, and consists of numerous rugged mountains, the highest rising to 2,700 feet (820 m), interspersed with picturesque ravines. Although within the tropics, the south-east trade winds keep the temperature mild and equable.

POPULATION – The population (1987) is 5,644.
CAPITAL– ΨJamestown. Population (1987) 1,332.
CURRENCY – St Helena pound (£) of 100 pence.
FLAG – British Blue Ensign with the shield of arms in the fly.

GOVERNMENT

St Helena was discovered by the Portuguese navigator, Joao da Nova Castella, in 1502 (probably on St Helena's Day) and remained unknown to other European nations until 1588. It was used as a port of call for vessels of all nations trading to the East until it was annexed by the Dutch in 1633. It was never occupied by them, however, and the English East India Company seized it in 1659. From 1815 to 1821 the island was lent to the British government as a place of exile for the Emperor Napoleon Bonaparte who died in St Helena on 5 May 1821, and in 1834 it was annexed to the British Crown.

The government of St Helena is administered by a Governor, with the aid of a Legislative Council, consisting of a Speaker, three ex-officio members (Chief Secretary, Financial Secretary and Attorney-General) and 12 elected members. Five committees of the Legislative Council are reponsible for general oversight of the activities of government departments and have in addition a wide range of statutory and administrative functions. The Governor is also assisted by an Executive Council of the three ex-officio members and the chairmen of the Council committees.

Governor, HE David L. Smallman, LVO, *apptd* 1995
Attorney-General, vacant
Chief Administrative Health Officer, R. Essex
Chief Agriculture and Forestry Officer, C. J. Lomas
Chief Auditor, vacant
Chief Development Officer, K. M. Thomas
Chief Education Officer, J. Price
Chief Employment and Social Services Officer, vacant
Chief Engineer, J. Jacobson
Chief Finance Officer, D. H. Wade
Chief Justice, G. W. Martin, OBE
Chief Personnel Officer, S. I. Ellick
Chief Secretary, J. G. Perrott
Deputy Secretary, E. C. Yon
Financial Secretary, M. J. Young
Postmistress, Ms I. Henry

ECONOMY

St. Helena receives an annual grant from the UK which amounted to £3.2 million in 1997. The only significant export is canned and frozen fish. The other exports are a small amount of high quality coffee and cottage industry products (including lace, decorative woodwork and beadwork). James's Bay, on the north-west of the island, possesses a good anchorage. There is as yet no airport or airstrip.

TRADE WITH UK	1995	1996
Imports from UK	£9,144,000	£7,698,000
Exports to UK	446,000	386,000

ASCENSION

The small island of Ascension lies in the South Atlantic some 750 miles north-west of the island of St Helena. It is a rocky peak of purely volcanic origin. The highest point (Green Mountain), some 2,817 ft, is covered with lush vegetation and has a farm of some ten acres, producing vegetables and livestock. The island is a breeding area for green turtles and for the sooty tern, or wideawake. Other wildlife includes feral donkeys and cats, and francolin partridge.

POPULATION – The resident population in March 1997 totalled 1,111, of whom 771 were from St Helena, 110 from the UK and 230 from the USA. The residents consist of the employees and families of the British organizations, of the contractors of the US Air Force and RAF and of the St Helena government.

British forces returned to the island in April 1982 in support of operations in the Falkland Islands. At present there are about 25 RAF personnel on the island supporting the air link to the Falklands.

CAPITAL – Georgetown.

GOVERNMENT

Ascension was discovered by Joao da Nova Castella in 1501 and two years later was visited on Ascension Day by Alphonse d'Albuquerque, who gave the island its present name. It was uninhabited until the arrival of Napoleon in St Helena in 1815 when a small British naval garrison was stationed on the island. As HMS *Ascension* it remained under the supervision of the Board of Admiralty until 1922, when it was made a dependency of St Helena.

The British Foreign Secretary appoints the Administrator who is responsible to the Governor resident in St Helena. There is a small police force, bank and post office. The British organizations through Ascension Island Services (AIS) provide and operate various common services for the island (school, hospital, public works etc).

Administrator, Roger Huxley, *apptd* 1995

COMMUNICATIONS

Cable and Wireless PLC operates the international telephone and cable services and maintains an internal telephone service. The BBC opened its Atlantic relay station broadcasting to Africa and South America in 1967. There is a monthly shipping service and two flights a week by RAF Tristars which transit Ascension en route to the Falkland Islands.

TRISTAN DA CUNHA

Tristan da Cunha is the chief island of a group of islands in the South Atlantic which lies some 1,260 nautical miles (2,333 km) south-south-west of St Helena. It has an area of 38 sq. miles (98 sq. km). Inaccessible Island lies 20 nautical miles south-west and has an area of 4 sq. miles (10 sq. km), and the three Nightingale Islands lie 20 nautical miles south of Tristan da Cunha and have an area of three-quarters of a sq. mile (2 sq. km). Gough Island lies some 230 nautical miles south-south-east of Tristan da Cunha and has an area of 35 sq. miles (91 sq. km).

All the islands are volcanic and steep-sided with cliffs or narrow beaches. Tristan itself has a single volcanic cone rising to 6,760 feet (2,060 m) and a narrow north-western coastal plain on which the settlement of Edinburgh is situated.

Inaccessible Island is a lofty mass of rock with sides two miles in length; the island is the resort of penguins and sea-birds. Cultivation was started in 1937 but has been abandoned.

The Nightingale Islands are three in number, of which the largest is one mile long and three-quarters of a mile wide, and rises in two peaks, 960 and 1,105 feet above sea level respectively. The smaller islands, Stoltenhoff and Middle Isle, are little more than huge rocks. Seals, penguins, and sea-birds visit these islands.

Gough Island is about eight miles long and four miles broad. It is the resort of penguins, sea-elephants, fur seals and sea-birds and has valuable guano deposits.

Gough and Inaccessible islands are nature reserves and access is strictly limited.

The islands have a warm-temperate oceanic climate which is damp and windy. Rainfall averages 66 inches a year on the coast of Tristan da Cunha.

POPULATION – Population in 1997 was 288, in the settlement of Edinburgh on Tristan da Cunha. In addition, there is a meteorological station maintained on Gough Island by the South African government. Inaccessible Island and the Nightingale Islands are uninhabited.

CAPITAL – Edinburgh of the Seven Seas.

CURRENCY – Pound sterling.

HISTORY

Tristan da Cunha was discovered in 1506 by a Portuguese admiral (Tristão da Cunha) after whom it was named. In 1760 a British naval officer visited the islands and gave his name to Nightingale Island. In 1816 the group was annexed to the British Crown and a garrison was placed on Tristan da Cunha, but this force was withdrawn in 1817. Corporal William Glass remained at his own request with his wife and two children. This party, with two others, formed a settlement. In 1827 five women from St Helena, and afterwards others from Cape Colony, joined the party.

Due to its position on a main sailing route the colony thrived, with an economy based on trading with whalers, sealers and other passing ships. However, the replacement of sail by steam and the opening of the Suez Canal in the late 19th century led to decline.

In October 1961 a volcano, believed to have been extinct for thousands of years, erupted and the danger of further volcanic activity led to the evacuation of inhabitants to the UK. An advance party returned to Tristan da Cunha in 1963 and subsequently the main body of the islanders returned to the island.

GOVERNMENT

In 1938 Tristan da Cunha and the neighbouring islands of Inaccessible, Nightingale and Gough were made dependencies of St Helena. They are administered by the Governor of St Helena through a resident Administrator, with headquarters at Edinburgh. Under a constitution introduced in 1985, the Administrator is advised by an Island Council of eight elected members, of whom one must be a woman, and three appointed members. There is universal suffrage at 18. Elections are held every three years.

Administrator, Brendan Dalley, *apptd* 1994

ECONOMY

The island is financially self-sufficient. The main industries are crayfish fishing, fish-processing and agriculture, with the shore-based fishing industry having been developed with the construction of the boat harbour in 1967 and the re-establishment of the lobster factory in 1966. There are no taxes, income being derived from the royalties from the rock lobster fishery around the islands, interest from the reserve fund, and the sales of stamps and handicrafts. Apart from the fishing industry, the other main employer is the administration itself. There is one hospital with a resident medical officer, and a school catering for children up to age 15. Healthcare and education are free for the islanders.

COMMUNICATIONS

Scheduled visits to the island are restricted to about six calls a year by fishing vessels from Cape Town and annual calls of the RMS *St Helena* and the *SA Agulhas*, also from Cape Town. A wireless station on the island is in daily contact with Cape Town and a radio-telephone service was established in 1969, the same year that electricity was introduced to all the islanders' homes. A marine satellite system providing direct dialling telephone, telex and fax facilities was installed in 1992.

SOUTH GEORGIA AND THE SOUTH SANDWICH ISLANDS

South Georgia is an island 800 miles east-south-east of the Falkland group, with an area of 1,580 sq. miles. The population comprises a small military garrison and a civilian harbour master at King Edward Point, and staff of the British Antarctic Survey at Bird Island, to the north-west of South Georgia.

The South Sandwich Islands lie some 470 miles south-east of South Georgia. The group is a chain of uninhabited, actively volcanic islands about 150 miles long, with a wholly Antarctic climate.

The present constitution came into effect in 1985. It provides for a Commissioner who, for the time being, is the officer administering the government of the Falkland Islands.

In 1993 the UK government decreed an extension of Crown sovereignty and jurisdiction from 12 miles around South Georgia and the South Sandwich Islands to 200 miles around each in order to preserve marine stocks.

Commissioner for South Georgia and the South Sandwich Islands, Richard Ralph, cvo, *apptd* 1996

TURKS AND CAICOS ISLANDS

The Turks and Caicos Islands are about 50 miles south-east of the Bahamas of which they are geographically an extension. There are over 30 islands, of which eight are inhabited, covering an estimated area of 166 sq. miles (430 sq. km). The principal island and seat of government is Grand Turk.

The islands lie in the trade wind belt. The average temperature varies from 24°–27° C in the winter to 29°–32° C in the summer and humidity is generally low. Average rainfall is 21 inches a year.

POPULATION – The population in 1995 was estimated to be 19,000 (Grand Turk 4,000).

FLAG – British Blue Ensign with the shield of arms in the fly.

GOVERNMENT

A constitution was introduced in 1988, and amended in 1993, which provides for an Executive Council and a Legislative Council. The Executive Council is presided over by the Governor and comprises the Chief Minister and five elected Ministers, together with the ex-officio Chief Secretary and Attorney-General.

At the general election of 31 January 1995, the People's Democratic Movement won eight seats and the Progressive National Party five seats in the Legislative Council.

Governor, HE John P. Kelly, lvo, mbe, *apptd* 1996

EXECUTIVE COUNCIL *as at May 1997*

President, The Governor
Attorney-General, D. F. Ballantyne
Chief Minister, D. H. Taylor
Chief Secretary, Ms C. Astwood, mbe
Ministers, S. Harvey; O. Skippings; H. Ewing; C. Selver; S. Rigby

ECONOMY

The most important industries are fishing, tourism and offshore finance. The islands were visited by 79,000 tourists in 1995.

TRADE WITH UK	1995	1996
Imports from UK	£1,437,000	£924,000
Exports to UK	58,000	660,000

COMMUNICATIONS

The principal airports are on the islands of Grand Turk, Providenciales and South Caicos. Air services link Providenciales and Grand Turk with Miami, the Bahamas, Haiti and the Dominican Republic. An internal air service provides a regular service between the principal islands. There are direct shipping services to the USA (Miami). A comprehensive telephone and telex service is provided by Cable and Wireless (WI) Ltd.

Events of the Year

1 September 1996 to 31 August 1997

BRITISH AFFAIRS

SEPTEMBER 1996

15. A British engineer who had been kidnapped by guerrillas in Colombia in February 1996 was released. **16.** Roderick Wright resigned as the Roman Catholic Bishop of Argyll and the Isles after going into hiding with a woman from his diocese; he was later revealed to be the father of a 15-year-old son by another woman. **19.** The Government abandoned plans to slaughter 147,000 cattle after the European Commission agreed to examine new scientific evidence that BSE would die out naturally by 2001. **23.** The Liberal Democrat conference opened in Brighton. **30.** The Labour Party conference opened in Blackpool. Mandy Allwood, who had been expecting octuplets, miscarried three of the babies; on 2 October she lost the remaining five babies.

OCTOBER 1996

3. Baroness Turner of Camden was sacked as Labour's front bench spokesman in the House of Lords after she defended her role as a director of a lobbying firm, Ian Greer Associates, which had been accused of making inappropriate payments to MPs. **8.** The Conservative Party conference opened in Bournemouth. **12.** The Conservative MP Peter Thurnham, who had resigned the party whip in February 1996, said that he was joining the Liberal Democrats. **16.** The Cullen report on the murders in Dunblane in March 1996 was published; its recommendations included a ban on some handguns, improved security in schools and tighter control of adults working in youth clubs. The Government published a White Paper in response to the report (*see* page 1165). On 18 November a House of Commons motion to impose a total ban on handguns was defeated by 25 votes. **17.** The Rt. Revd Derek Rawcliffe was sacked as an assistant bishop in the diocese of Ripon because he had performed 'marriage' ceremonies for homosexual couples. **23.** The state opening of Parliament took place. New scientific evidence was published which showed an increased likelihood that a new strain of CJD was caused by eating beef from cattle infected with BSE. **27–29.** Six people died as gales and heavy rain hit many parts of Britain. **28.** The Queen and the Duke of Edinburgh arrived in Thailand for a five-day state visit. **29.** Manton Junior School in Worksop, Notts, closed because of strike action by teachers who refused to teach a ten-year-old boy they judged

to be out of control; the school reopened on 11 November. School inspectors began an emergency inspection of The Ridings School in Halifax, W. Yorks, where teachers had threatened to strike unless 60 'unteachable' pupils were excluded; on 31 October the school was closed down. It reopened on 6 November with a new head teacher, who excluded 12 pupils and suspended 23 others. The Education Secretary (Gillian Shephard) said that corporal punishment was a useful deterrent; the Prime Minister (John Major) said that it would not be brought back in state schools.

NOVEMBER 1996

4. The Prince of Wales arrived in Kiev for a nine-day official visit to the Ukraine and Central Asia. **11.** Millions of people observed a two-minute silence at 11 a.m. to mark Armistice Day. **12.** The European Court of Justice ruled that Britain was obliged to adopt a directive imposing a maximum 48-hour working week. **14.** The Government said that 2,000 troops would be sent to eastern Zaïre to help avert the impending humanitarian disaster (*see* below); the mission was put on hold on 19 November after the refugees had returned to Rwanda. **15.** The Stone of Scone, which had been part of the coronation seat in Westminster Abbey since the 14th century, was returned to Scotland; a ceremony was held at Edinburgh Castle on 30 November to mark its return. **16.** A controversial service to mark the 20th anniversary of the Lesbian and Gay Christian Movement was held at Southwark Cathedral, London. **19.** Staff in universities and higher education institutions staged a one-day strike over pay. **20.** The Audit Commission published a report, *Misspent Youth,* which said that the criminal justice system for young offenders was inefficient, slow and unnecessarily expensive. A report commissioned by local organizations on the Bradford riots in June 1995 found that a violent minority was directly to blame for the riots but that a minor incident had spiralled out of control because of arrogance and ignorance on the part of the police. **25.** Many of the details of the forthcoming Budget statement were leaked to the *Daily Mirror;* they were returned to the Government without being published. **26.** The Chancellor of the Exchequer (Kenneth Clarke) presented his Budget statement to the House of Commons (*see* page 1153). **26–28.** Police prevented lorries from entering Dover and Ramsgate because of long delays in ferry crossings caused by a blockade of the French Channel ports by striking French lorry drivers. The blockade in Calais was temporarily lifted on 28 November to enable 200 lorries to return to Britain and the dispute was settled on 29 November. **26 November–19 December.** Fifteen people died and about 50 were hospitalized in a food poisoning epidemic caused by E-coli 0157 which affected about 400 people in central Scotland; five more people had died by June 1997.

DECEMBER 1996

3. The Archbishop of Canterbury (George Carey) arrived in Rome for his first official visit to the Vatican. **5.** The Chancellor of the Exchequer denied that he had threatened to resign if the Prime Minister changed the Government's 'wait and see' approach to the establishment of a single European currency. **9.** A bill proposing that women should have equal rights to succeed to the throne was introduced into the House of Lords; in an unprecedented move caused by expressions of opposition from peers, it was allowed to proceed only after a vote. **10.** The Armed Forces Minister (Nicholas Soames) said that MPs had been misinformed by the Ministry of Defence over the extent to which troops had been exposed to organophosphate pesticides during the Gulf War. **11.** David Willetts resigned as Paymaster-General after the publication of a report by the House of Commons committee on standards and privileges which said that he had 'dissembled' when giving evidence on the 'cash for questions' controversy; the committee said that in future evidence from MPs would be taken on oath. **12.** The Government lost its majority when Labour won the Barnsley East by-election (*see* page 268). **13.** Labour won the Merseyside West by-election for the European Parliament; the turnout of 11.4 per cent was the lowest for a parliamentary election since the Second World War. **16.** The Government reinstated plans for a selective slaughter of about 100,000 cattle which could have been exposed to BSE. **17.** Labour and the Liberal Democrats accused the Government of cheating by 'double pairing' three absent MPs in a vote in the House of Commons on 16 December; they suspended the 'pairing' system indefinitely. **18.** The Duke of Edinburgh said in a radio interview that the Firearms Bill going through the House of Lords was unreasonable and drew an analogy between guns and a cricket bat as offensive weapons; he later apologised for any offence caused by his remarks.

JANUARY 1997

5. The Conservative MP Jerry Hayes denied newspaper allegations that he had had a homosexual relationship with an 18-year-old boy in 1991. **9.** The Prime Minister led a trade delegation to Calcutta at the beginning of a six-day tour of south Asia which included celebrations to mark the 50th anniversary of Indian independence. **11.** Nine women were ordained as the first women priests in the Anglican Church in Wales at a service in Bangor Cathedral. **13.** Two security guards were injured when a letter bomb exploded at the London headquarters of *al-Hayat*, an Arab newspaper. Diana, Princess of Wales

arrived in Angola for a four-day visit on behalf of the Red Cross during which she called for a world-wide ban on anti-personnel land-mines. **15.** The Government gave approval for a second runway at Manchester Airport. **16.** The Government became a minority administration after the death of the Conservative MP Iain Mills. It ceased to be in a minority when the Labour MP Martin Redmond died on 20 January. **20.** The Royal Yacht *Britannia* sailed from Portsmouth on its last official voyage. On 22 January the Defence Secretary (Michael Portillo) said that a new royal yacht would be built at a cost of £60 million. On 25 January the Shadow Chancellor (Gordon Brown) said that if the Labour Party were elected to government it would look at alternative ways of funding the new yacht. **30.** The Government announced the establishment of an independent Food Safety Council.

FEBRUARY 1997

4. A British human rights monitor working for the UN was shot dead in Rwanda. **5.** A midweek National Lottery draw was introduced. **7.** The chief executive of Ashworth high security hospital was suspended after allegations of paedophile activity and misuse of drugs and alcohol at the hospital. **17.** In the House of Commons an Opposition motion of censure on the Agriculture Minister (Douglas Hogg) over his handling of the BSE crisis was defeated by 320 votes to 307. **25.** President Weizman of Israel arrived in Britain for a three-day state visit, the first by an Israeli head of state. **27.** Labour won the Wirral South by-election (*see* page 268).

MARCH 1997

6. The Government denied that it had sought to suppress a highly critical draft report on hygiene standards at abattoirs in the UK which had been drawn up by the Meat Hygiene Service in early 1996. **8.** The Conservative MP Sir George Gardiner, who had been deselected by his constituency party in February 1997, announced that he had resigned the Conservative whip and joined the Referendum Party. **17.** The Prime Minister announced that the general election would be held on 1 May 1997. **18.** Britain signed an agreement with Russia in Moscow under which the countries agreed to co-operate on military training and exchange information on new weapons. **24.** The former Scottish Office minister Allan Stewart stood down as a candidate in the general election after newspaper allegations of an extra-marital relationship. **26.** The former Northern Ireland minister Tim Smith resigned as a candidate in the General Election; he had previously admitted receiving payments from the businessman Mohamed Al Fayed and failing to declare them. Neil Hamilton, one of the other MPs allegedly involved in the 'cash for questions' controversy, resisted Opposition pressure to stand down. **29.** The chairman of the Scottish Conservative Party, Sir Michael Hirst, resigned; on 30 March a newspaper published

allegations that he had had an extra-marital homosexual relationship.

APRIL 1997

4. The Hebridean island Eigg was bought by its 64
inhabitants for £1.5 million. 6. The BBC correspondent Martin Bell said that he would stand in Tatton,
Cheshire, against Neil Hamilton (*see* above) as an
'anti-sleaze' candidate if Mr Hamilton did not stand
down; the Labour and the Liberal Democrat candidates had agreed to withdraw in Mr Bell's favour. On
7 April Mr Hamilton was confirmed as the Conservative candidate in the election. 8. A report by
Prof. Hugh Pennington into the E-Coli outbreak in
Scotland was published; the Government accepted
its 32 recommendations for improving meat hygiene in shops, abatoirs and farms. A report, *Unemployment and the Future of Work*, by a working party
representing 11 Christian denominations was published; it said that work was central to the Christian
understanding of the human condition and should
not be regarded by political parties as an optional
extra. 12. Rioting broke out in Trafalgar Square,
London, after demonstrators tried to break through
a security cordon at Downing Street. 16. The Prime
Minister made a television broadcast in which he
appealed for support for his 'wait and see' policy on a
single European currency. On 17 April he said that
Conservative back-benchers would be given a free
vote if the Cabinet were to recommend that Britain
join a single currency. 19. Firefighters in Essex held
the first of several 24-hour strikes over spending
cuts. 21. The President of the European Commission, Jacques Santer, was accused of intervening in
the UK election campaign after saying that European integration would continue and that Euro-
sceptics were 'doom merchants'. 23. Up to 1,000
lorries were forced to queue on the M20 in Kent
because they could not enter Dover owing to a
blockade of three French Channel ferry ports by
fishermen protesting at an EU ruling on fishing-net
mesh sizes.

MAY 1997

1. The Labour Party gained 44.4 per cent of the vote
in the general election and won 418 seats, a majority
of 179 in the House of Commons; it is the largest
majority ever held by Labour and the largest
majority for a single party since 1924. The Conservatives gained 31.4 per cent of the vote and won
165 seats; it was their lowest share of the vote since
1832 and they won no seats in Scotland or Wales.
The Liberal Democrats gained 17.2 per cent of the
vote and won 46 seats, their highest number since
1929. The turnout was 71 per cent, the lowest since
1935. The number of women elected more than
doubled to 120. (For the full results of the general
election, *see* pages 236–68.) Local elections were
also held to county councils and some unitary
authorities in England. 2. John Major resigned as
leader of the Conservative Party. The Labour
leader Tony Blair was invited by The Queen to

form a government and became the youngest
British prime minister since 1812; he was officially
sworn in as prime minister the following day. 3. The
former Deputy Prime Minister Michael Heseltine
was admitted to hospital with chest pains and said
that he would not be a candidate in the contest for
the leadership of the Conservative Party. 12. A
British woman who had entered into a surrogate
pregnancy for a Dutch couple said that she had had
an abortion because she felt that they showed a lack
of commitment; on 14 May she said that she was still
pregnant but would keep the baby herself. 13. The
official report of the inquiry into the fire in the
Channel Tunnel in November 1996 was published;
it said that Eurotunnel had failed to act on warnings
of fundamental weaknesses in its safety systems.
The Foreign Secretary (Robin Cook) said that
Britain would rejoin Unesco. 14. The state opening
of Parliament took place. The Speaker (Betty
Boothroyd) said that MPs who did not swear the
oath of allegiance to The Queen (i.e. Sinn Fein MPs)
would not be allowed to use facilities in the House
of Commons. 15. The ban on trade union membership at GCHQ imposed in 1984, was lifted. 18. A
police investigation was launched after allegations
in the *News of the World* that a new Labour MP,
Mohammed Sarwar, had bribed an opponent during
the general election campaign; on 19 May Mr
Sarwar issued a libel writ against the newspaper. 19.
In the House of Commons Ann Widdecombe, the
former prisons minister, criticized the former
Home Secretary and Conservative Party leadership
candidate, Michael Howard, over the sacking of the
director-general of the Prison Service, Derek
Lewis, in October 1995; she also said that Mr
Howard had misled Parliament about the earlier
decision to remove the governor of Parkhurst
prison, John Marriott, from his post. 21. The
Foreign Secretary said that Britain would destroy
its stock of anti-personnel land-mines by 2005. Sir
Archibald Hamilton was elected chairman of the
Conservative MPs' 1922 Committee. 22. The
Education and Employment Secretary (David
Blunkett) said that nursery school vouchers would
be abolished from September 1997 and that free
nursery places would be available for every four-
year-old from September 1998. 28. The Defence
Secretary (George Robertson) announced a review
of Britain's defence needs and the role of the armed
forces. 29. The Prime Minister held talks with
President Clinton at Downing Street.

JUNE 1997

2. In a speech the Prime Minster outlined plans to
help unemployed people find work, and said that
people who declined offers of help could lose up to
40 per cent of their benefits. The National Heritage
Secretary (Chris Smith) ordered the directors of
Camelot, the National Lottery operator, to forgo
their large pay rises and bonuses; on 6 June the
directors said that they would donate some of the
money to charity. 3. A 54-year-old woman gave

birth to twins in London after becoming pregnant by *in vitro* fertilization. **10.** In the first round of the election for the leadership of the Conservative Party, Kenneth Clarke gained 49 votes, William Hague 41, John Redwood 27, Peter Lilley 24 and Michael Howard 23; Mr Lilley and Mr Howard withdrew from the contest. **11.** MPs voted to ban .22 pistols, making the ownership of all handguns illegal from the autumn of 1997. **16.** At the European summit in Amsterdam, Britain negotiated the right to retain control over its own visa, asylum and immigration policies. **17.** In the second round of the Conservative leadership election, Kenneth Clarke gained 64 votes, William Hague 62 and John Redwood 38; Mr Redwood was therefore eliminated. **18.** The Labour MP Bob Wareing was suspended by the Parliamentary Labour Party for allegedly failing to declare a financial interest in the House of Commons register. **19.** In the final round of the Conservative leadership election, William Hague gained 92 votes and Kenneth Clarke 70; 36-year-old Mr Hague therefore became the youngest leader of the Conservative Party since 1783. **23.** The Queen and the Duke of Edinburgh arrived in Canada at the start of a 12-day visit. **30.** The Prince of Wales, the Prime Minister and the Foreign Secretary attended ceremonies in Hong Kong to mark the return of the colony to China.

July 1997

2. Gordon Brown presented his first Budget statement to the House of Commons (*see* page 1159). **3.** The Parliamentary Commissioner for Standards (Sir Gordon Downey) published his report on allegations that MPs had accepted cash from the businessman Mohamed Al Fayed in return for furthering his interests through their House of Commons activities; the report found that five former Conservative MPs (Neil Hamilton, Tim Smith, Sir Andrew Bowden, Sir Michael Grylls and Michael Brown) had accepted money from Mr Al Fayed and failed to declare their interests. **7.** President Mandela of South Africa arrived in Britain for a four-day state visit. **9–11.** British Airways cabin crew held a strike over a pay restructuring deal imposed in May 1997. **12.** Diana, Princess of Wales began a controversial holiday with Princes William and Harry on board a yacht belonging to Mohamed Al Fayed. At the end of July she went on a private cruise with Mr Al Fayed's son Dodi, leading to rumours of a romance between the couple. **15.** The Queen and the Duke of Edinburgh held a garden party at Buckingham Palace to mark their 50th wedding anniversary; it was attended by 4,000 other couples who married in 1947. **22.** The Government published a White Paper setting out its proposals for an elected Welsh assembly (*see* page 1167). The Prime Minister announced that the leader of the Liberal Democrats (Paddy Ashdown) and four other Liberal Democrats would be invited to serve on a new Cabinet committee to discuss the constitution and other areas of mutual concern. **23.**

The report of an enquiry into higher education headed by Sir Ron Dearing was published; it said that there should be a higher level of investment, that the limits on numbers entering higher education should be abolished, that teaching standards should be improved and nationally-agreed qualifications standards should be introduced, and that students and graduates should make a greater contribution towards the costs of higher education. The Education and Employment Secretary (David Blunkett) said that grants towards students' maintenance costs would be replaced by an increased student loan and that there would be a means-tested parental contribution of £1,000 a year towards tuition fees from October 1998. **24.** The Government published a White Paper setting out its proposals for a Scottish parliament (*see* page 1167). **28.** The Labour MP for Paisley South, Gordon McMaster, was found dead; he left a suicide note blaming several colleagues for spreading false rumours about his health and sexuality. **29.** The Government published proposals for a Greater London Authority with an elected mayor. **31.** The Conservatives won the Uxbridge by-election (*see* page 268).

August 1997

3. The Government said that it favoured a £50 million refit for the royal yacht *Britannia*, to be financed by the private sector. **5.** After allegations of a conflict of interest, the Minister for Trade and Competitiveness in Europe (Lord Simon of Highbury) said that he would sell his £2 million portfolio of BP shares. **5–6.** Torrential rain caused flooding in south-west England and Wales. **8.** Diana, Princess of Wales arrived in Bosnia on a visit to highlight the campaign for a world-wide ban on anti-personnel land-mines. **7.** The owners of the last working tin mine in Cornwall, South Crofty, said that it would close by the end of 1997. **19.** After an enquiry by the chief whip, the Labour MP for West Renfrewshire, Tommy Graham, was suspended from the parliamentary party for alleged 'verbal attacks' on colleagues and for bringing the party into disrepute. **23.** The Secretary of State for International Development (Clare Short) criticized the government of Montserrat for raising unrealistic expectations of the financial help available from Britain for evacuation from the island because of the eruption of the Soufrière Hills volcano. On 27 August evacuation plans were scaled down because fewer people than expected wished to leave the island. **31.** Diana, Princess of Wales died in the early hours of the morning from injuries sustained in a car crash in Paris; Dodi Fayed, with whom she had dined at the Ritz hotel, and the chauffeur were also killed and a bodyguard was seriously injured. The driver of the car, which was being chased by *paparazzi* and was travelling at great speed, was reported to have had more than three times the legal alcohol limit in his blood. The Prince of Wales flew to Paris with the Princess's sisters and accompanied her body back to

RAF Northolt. Thousands of flowers were laid by mourners at the royal palaces and books of condolence were opened. The Princess's body lay privately in the Chapel Royal at St James's Palace until the day before the funeral. Campaigning in the Scottish and Welsh referendums was suspended. On 2 September seven of the *paparazzi* were charged with involuntary manslaughter and failing to assist at the scene of an accident. An official memorial fund was set up for donations to the Princess's favourite charities. On 4 September the royal family returned from Balmoral and The Queen broadcast to the nation from Buckingham Palace. On 5 September the Princess's coffin was taken to Kensington Palace. On 6 September it was borne on a gun carriage to Westminster Abbey, where the funeral was held at 11 a.m. During the service the Princess's brother, Earl Spencer, delivered a tribute to his sister in which he attacked the press for hounding her and said that her blood family would ensure that her sons were raised as she would have wanted. After the funeral a minute's silence was observed throughout the UK. The Princess was buried in a private ceremony on an island in a lake in the grounds of the Spencer family estate at Althorp, Northants.

NORTHERN IRELAND AFFAIRS

September 1996

3. A senior member of the INLA was shot dead. **23.** Ten tons of explosives were found by police in a storage unit in Hornsey, north London. An IRA terrorist suspect was shot dead by police in a raid on a guesthouse in west London, and five more suspects were detained in other raids in London. **30.** UDA prisoners withdrew their support for the loyalist cease-fire.

October 1996

7. Thirty-four people were injured when two IRA car bombs exploded inside Thiepval barracks, the Army's Northern Ireland headquarters, at Lisburn; one soldier later died. **15.** The opening agenda for all-party talks was agreed after the UUP and the SDLP devised a formula by which the decommissioning of weapons would be discussed alongside the main negotiations. **29.** A leading member of the UVF who had been suspended from the organization was shot dead in Belfast.

November 1996

7. Peter McMullen was sentenced in York to 14 years' imprisonment for his part in the bombing of an army base at Ripon, N. Yorks, in 1974; he was released because he had spent more than nine years in custody in the USA fighting extradition. **21.** A 600 lb car bomb planted by the Continuity Council of the IRA, a splinter group, was defused outside the RUC headquarters in Londonderry. **26.** The Prime Minister was reported to have rejected proposals for securing an IRA cease-fire put forward in early

October by the leader of the SDLP (John Hume) and the president of Sinn Fein (Gerry Adams). On 28 November Mr Major published a statement which said that Sinn Fein would be admitted to all-party talks if the IRA restored its cease-fire and ceased all paramilitary activities; the issue of weapons decommissioning would be handled during the talks. **29.** A 1,000 lb IRA bomb was found near the Drumadd army base, Co. Armagh, and was defused.

December 1996

8. Sean O'Callaghan, a former IRA leader who turned informer, was granted an early release from prison after serving eight years for committing two murders. **20.** A policeman was shot and wounded by the IRA while acting as a bodyguard to a Unionist politician visiting his son in a children's hospital in Belfast. **22.** An IRA member was injured when a bomb believed to have been planted by the UDA exploded in his car in Belfast. **28.** A bomb attached to the car of a leading member of Sinn Fein was defused in Londonderry.

January 1997

1. A 1,000 lb IRA bomb was found in the grounds of Belfast Castle. **6.** A police officer was injured when an IRA rocket was fired at a security post outside the Royal Courts of Justice, Belfast. **12.** Two unexploded IRA mortar bombs fired at a security base in Co. Fermanagh were defused. **18.** Two IRA mortar bombs were fired at an RUC patrol in Co. Down. **20.** A bomb planted by loyalist paramilitaries exploded under a van in Co. Antrim. **26.** Three off-duty soldiers escaped injury when an IRA bomb destroyed their car in Co. Down. **27.** The Government said that the Ulster Democratic Party and the Progressive Unionist Party would not be ejected from the all-party talks because although the loyalist cease-fire was under strain the parties had not breached the Mitchell principles of non-violence. **28.** Two IRA mortar devices were fired at a patrol in west Belfast. **30.** The North report into ways of preventing sectarian violence at marches was published; its recommendations included the establishment of an independent Parades Commission with the power to decide whether or not a march should take place.

February 1997

12. A soldier was shot dead by the IRA in Bessbrook, Co. Armagh.

March 1997

3. A bomb was found outside Sinn Fein offices in Co. Monaghan. **5.** The all-party talks were suspended until after the general election. **10.** The Northern Ireland Forum for Political Dialogue was suspended until after the general election. **14.** A Roman Catholic man was shot dead at his home in west Belfast. **24.** A 40-foot-long tunnel dug by IRA prisoners was discovered at the Maze prison, Co.

Antrim. **26.** A terrorist suspect was shot by police after a small bomb exploded outside a police station in Co. Tyrone. Two IRA bombs exploded near the railway station in Wilmslow, Cheshire; there were no casualties. **29.** A 1,000 lb bomb was found and defused near an army base in Co. Down. **30.** The Shadow Northern Ireland Secretary (Mo Mowlam) said that Sinn Fein could be invited to join all-party talks from June 1997 if the IRA were to call a cease-fire and an end to 'punishment beatings' with immediate effect. An IRA training camp was discovered near the border in Co. Monaghan. A policeman was shot and wounded by the IRA in Co. Armagh.

APRIL 1997

3. IRA bombs were found beneath two junctions of the M6 north of Birmingham. **5.** The Grand National was postponed after coded IRA bomb threats were received in Liverpool (*see also* Sport below). **6.** A Roman Catholic church in Co. Antrim was burnt down by loyalists. **7.** A Roman Catholic church in Co. Armagh was burnt down by loyalists. **9.** A Roman Catholic man was wounded by a suspected loyalist gunman in north Belfast. **10.** A policewoman was wounded by an IRA gunman in Londonderry. **13.** Eight Roman Catholic families were forced to flee their homes in north Belfast when they were attacked by loyalists. **18.** A small IRA bomb exploded near Leeds station; there were no casualties. Crewe, Stoke-on-Trent and Doncaster stations were also closed after IRA bomb threats were received. **21.** Four railway stations in central London, and Gatwick, Luton and Stansted airports were closed after IRA bomb threats were received. **25.** A small IRA bomb exploded near the M6 north of Birmingham. **28.** A Roman Catholic man was severely beaten by loyalists in Co. Armagh; he died on 8 May. **29.** Loyalist prisoners rioted at the Maze prison. Parts of the M1, the M3, the M25, the M26 and the M27 were closed after bomb threats were received; a section of the M25 was kept open in spite of a coded warning having been received.

MAY 1997

1. Sinn Fein won two seats in the general election: West Belfast and Mid-Ulster. **2.** Mo Mowlam was appointed Secretary of State for Northern Ireland and visited Belfast. **9.** An off-duty police officer was shot dead in a Belfast bar. **12.** A Roman Catholic man was shot dead in Co. Londonderry. **16.** The Prime Minister (Tony Blair) made his first visit to Northern Ireland and said that government officials were prepared to hold talks with Sinn Fein representatives. **18.** Violence broke out when an Apprentice Boys' march was prevented by the RUC from marching through the mainly nationalist village of Dunloy, Co. Antrim. **21.** Talks between government officials and Sinn Fein representatives took place in Belfast. **22.** In the local elections Sinn Fein became the joint largest party on Belfast City Council with the Ulster Unionists, who lost control

of the council for the first time; on 2 June Alban Maginness (SDLP) became the first nationalist Lord Mayor.

JUNE 1997

1. An off-duty policeman was kicked to death by loyalists outside a public house in Co. Antrim. A controlled explosion was carried out on a 1,000 lb bomb abandoned by the IRA in west Belfast. **3.** The multi-party talks at Stormont resumed. The Loyalist Volunteer Force and the republican Continuity Army Council were proscribed. **11.** Bobby Bates, a former member of the UVF and the 'Shankill Butchers' gang, was shot dead by the UDA in Belfast. The Queen visited Northern Ireland. **16.** Two policemen were shot dead by the IRA in Co. Armagh; talks between government officials and Sinn Fein representatives were called off. **21.** Three people were injured when a car bomb believed to have been planted by loyalists exploded in Belfast. **25.** The Prime Minister said that detailed talks on the future of Northern Ireland would begin in September 1997 and conclude in May 1998, with any agreement to be put to the people of Northern Ireland in a referendum. He also said that an independent commission would be set up to make proposals for decommissioning weapons during the negotiations, and that Sinn Fein had been told that it would be invited to take part in the talks six weeks after an unequivocal IRA cease-fire had been declared. **26.** A grenade was thrown at an RUC patrol in north Belfast.

JULY 1997

6. An Orange Order parade was allowed to march down the mainly nationalist Garvaghy Road near Drumcree, Co. Antrim; there was rioting overnight in many parts of Northern Ireland. **7.** A member of the UDA was killed when a bomb he was defusing blew up in south Belfast. Rioting continued overnight in Belfast and elsewhere. **9.** An extra infantry battalion was sent to Northern Ireland. **11.** The Orange Order said that four marches planned for 12 July would be rerouted or cancelled. Four members of a police and army patrol were shot and injured by the IRA in north Belfast. **15.** An 18-year-old Roman Catholic woman was shot dead as she slept at the home of her Protestant boyfriend in Co. Antrim. **18.** Gerry Adams said that he had called on the IRA to restore its cease-fire. **19.** The IRA announced an unequivocal restoration of its 1994 cease-fire from 12 noon on 20 July. **22.** The leader of the Democratic Unionist Party (Dr Ian Paisley) left the multi-party talks in protest at the Government's proposals for arms decommissioning; the leader of the UK Unionist Party (Robert McCartney) also subsequently left the talks. **31.** A 1,000 lb bomb believed to have been abandoned by a republican splinter group was defused by the Army in Co. Fermanagh.

AUGUST 1997

6. Mo Mowlam met a Sinn Fein delegation including Gerry Adams and Martin McGuinness at Stormont. **9.** Violence broke out in Londonderry during an Apprentice Boys' parade. **26.** The British and Irish governments said that an international disarmament commission would be set up in time for the scheduled opening of detailed talks on 15 September. **28.** Security sources said that an IRA bomb factory had been found near Crosskeys, Co. Cavan, in mid-August, but that it had not been used since the cease-fire declaration. **29.** Mo Mowlam announced that she had decided to invite Sinn Fein to enter the talks process.

ACCIDENTS AND DISASTERS

SEPTEMBER 1996

6. Hurricane Fran hit North and South Carolina, USA; about 22 people were killed. **10.** Typhoon Sally hit the coast of southern China; more than 110 people were killed. **11.** Hurricane Hortense hit Puerto Rico; at least ten people were killed. **25.** All 32 people on board a Dutch aeroplane were killed when it crashed off the coast of Holland.

OCTOBER 1996

2. All 70 people on board a Peruvian airliner were feared dead after it crashed off the coast near Lima. **8.** Four people were killed when a Russian cargo plane crashed outside Turin airport, Italy. **17.** At least 83 football fans were killed and 180 injured in a stampede at a world cup match in Guatemala City. **22.** Five people, including the vice-chairman of Chelsea FC, Matthew Harding, were killed in a helicopter crash in Cheshire. Thirty people were killed when a cargo plane crashed in Ecuador. **27.** At least 70 people were killed when a block of flats collapsed in Cairo. **31.** All 96 people on board a Brazilian airliner were killed when it crashed in São Paulo.

NOVEMBER 1996

6. At least 700 people were killed when a cyclone hit southern India. **10.** An earthquake registering 3.8 on the Richter scale hit western Cornwall. **12.** All 351 people on board were killed when two aircraft crashed in mid-air west of New Delhi, India. An earthquake registering 6.4 on the Richter scale hit southern Peru; at least 15 people were killed and 700 injured. **18.** Fire broke out on a freight train in the Channel Tunnel; passenger services restarted on 4 December after new safety arrangements had been agreed between Eurotunnel and the Channel Tunnel Safety Authority; a limited car shuttle service restarted on 10 December and freight services resumed on 15 June 1997. **20.** All 290 people on board a boat which set off from Haiti for the USA on 3 November were reported to have

drowned. **21.** Forty-five people were killed and at least 80 injured when fire broke out in an office block in Hong Kong. **23.** A hijacked Ethiopian plane crashed into the Indian Ocean off the Comoros Islands; 125 people were killed and 50 people survived.

DECEMBER 1996

8. A KLM plane crash-landed off the runway at Heathrow airport; there were no serious injuries. **15.** About 65 people were injured when a 68,000-ton freighter crashed into a riverside complex in New Orleans, USA. **29.** Two people died when they fell through the ice on a frozen lake at Aveley, Essex.

JANUARY 1997

9. At least 20 people died and hundreds were hospitalized when poisonous gas leaked from a lorry in Lahore, Pakistan. **12.** Two young brothers were drowned after their boat capsized in the Bristol Channel. **14.** A bus crash in Cairo killed at least 39 people.

FEBRUARY 1997

4. Two military helicopters crashed into each other in northern Israel, killing 73 soldiers. Four people were injured when a goods train was derailed near Bexley station, Kent. **19.** Three people died when their yacht capsized in stormy seas off the Isle of Wight. **23.** About 165 people were killed in a fire at a religious conference at Baripada, India. **28.** Earthquakes measuring 6.6 on the Richter scale hit southwestern Pakistan and north-western Iran; at least 165 people were killed.

MARCH 1997

10. Three people were killed and 62 injured in two pile-ups in fog on the M42 near Alvechurch, Hereford and Worcester. Four fishermen were drowned when their boat capsized 100 miles off the Scottish coast. Three fishermen drowned when their boat capsized off the Cornish coast. **28.** At least 20 people were feared drowned when a boat carrying Albanian refugees collided with an Italian warship in the Adriatic. **31.** At least 18 people were killed and 87 injured when a train was derailed in Navarre, Spain. In Shropshire two scout leaders were killed when a rocky overhang collapsed as they sat round a camp fire.

APRIL 1997

11. Turin Cathedral, Italy, was badly damaged by fire; the shroud of Turin was undamaged. **15.** At least 200 Muslim pilgrims were killed and 1,000 injured when fire broke out in an encampment near Mecca, Saudi Arabia. **20.** Five young men were killed when the stolen car they were in crashed in Salford while being chased by a police van.

MAY 1997

5. An 11-year-old boy was drowned and two others were missing presumed dead after being cut off by tides on marshland near Cleethorpes, Lincs. **10.** At least 1,560 people were killed and 200 villages were destroyed when an earthquake registering 7.1 on the Richter scale hit north-eastern Iran. **28.** At least 29 people were killed when tornadoes hit Texas, USA.

JUNE 1997

9. At least 150 people were killed in a landslide in the Yangshanzhou region of south-west China. **13.** Fifty-eight people died in a fire at a cinema in Delhi, India. **26.** Up to 23 people were killed when the Chances Peak volcano in the Soufrière Hills in Montserrat erupted.

JULY 1997

2. Serious flooding hit parts of northern Scotland after 3 inches of rain fell in 36 hours. **7.** Three British teenagers were killed and 24 other passengers were injured when a school coach crashed into a ravine in the French Alps. **6–28.** At least 100 people died in flooding caused by heavy rain in Poland, Germany and the Czech Republic; the River Oder burst through dykes on 17 July and flooded villages around Frankfurt an der Oder, eastern Germany. **9.** At least 67 people were killed when an earthquake registering 6.9 on the Richter scale hit central and eastern Venezuela. **11.** At least 78 people died in a fire that destroyed a hotel in Pattaya, Thailand. **26.** Nine people were killed and at least 55 injured when a light aircraft crashed at an air show in Ostend, Belgium. **30.** Twenty people were killed in a landslide at the Thredbo mountain resort in the Kosciusko National Park, Australia; a man who had been trapped in a small cavity was rescued on 2 August.

AUGUST 1997

5. Two hundred and twenty-two people were killed when a Korean Air jumbo jet crashed on the island of Guam in the north Pacific. **18–21.** At least 140 people were killed when Typhoon Winnie hit eastern China.

ARTS, SCIENCE AND MEDIA

SEPTEMBER 1996

3. Express Newspapers merged the editorial operation of the *Daily Express* and the *Sunday Express;* Sue Douglas resigned as editor of the *Sunday Express.* **9.** The Jerwood prize for painting was awarded to John Hubbard. **11.** The Bridgewater Hall, the new home of the Hallé Orchestra, opened in Manchester.

OCTOBER 1996

23. Bally Sagoo's single *Dil Cheez* became the first Asian-language record to enter the Top 40 pop charts. **29.** Graham Swift won the Booker Prize for his novel *Last Orders.* Works of art stolen from Jews by the Nazis in pre-war Austria went on auction in Vienna.

NOVEMBER 1996

16. The Russian space probe Mars 96 failed two hours after it was launched from Kazakhstan; it crashed into the Pacific Ocean on 18 November. **20.** *Crash,* a film featuring characters who derive sexual pleasure from car crashes, was banned from West End cinemas. **21.** Stephen Hodder won the RIBA Building of the Year award for his centenary building at Salford University. **25.** The European Court of Human Rights upheld the decision of British censors to ban the video film *Visions of Ecstasy,* based on the life of St Teresa of Avila, on the grounds that it could be blasphemous. **28.** The Turner Prize for modern art was awarded to the video artist Douglas Gordon.

DECEMBER 1996

5. A 52-year-old woman gave birth to her daughter's baby in Darlington, Co. Durham, after being artificially inseminated. **10.** After a meeting with the Heritage Secretary (Virginia Bottomley) the BBC, the Independent Television Commission (ITC) and the Broadcasting Standards Council (BSC) agreed to tighten their codes on screen violence.

JANUARY 1997

6. The first Top 50 chart of easy listening and compilation 'crossover' albums was published. **7.** A programme in which the future of the monarchy was debated in front of thousands of people at the National Exhibition Centre, Birmingham, was broadcast on ITV; it was widely criticized for being rowdy and trivializing the issue. **16.** A government report was published which said that xenotransplantation (the transplant of animal tissue into humans) was acceptable in principle but that further research was required to ensure that there was no risk of animal diseases being transmitted in the process. The DJ Chris Evans resigned from the Radio 1 *Breakfast Show.* Fourteen radio and television stations banned records by the pop group East 17 after its lead singer, Brian Harvey, said that Ecstasy was a safe drug which made users feel good; the following day he was sacked by his fellow band members. **17.** A new concert hall, the Waterfront Hall, opened in Belfast. **21.** Seamus Heaney won the Whitbread Book of the Year award for his volume of poetry *The Spirit Level.* **23.** The Arts Council of England announced a 'stabilization programme' of one-off grants to 15 arts organizations in financial difficulties.

FEBRUARY 1997

6. The auction house Sotheby's said that it had suspended two employees after allegations that a vendor in Italy had been encouraged to smuggle a painting to London; the Department of Trade and Industry launched an inquiry into the implications of the allegations for the London art market. **20.** The National Heritage Memorial Fund announced grants totalling £137 million for national and local museums and galleries from the Lottery Heritage Fund. **23.** Scientists in Scotland announced that they had produced a sheep which was the world's first clone of an adult animal.

MARCH 1997

13. The Restrictive Practices Court ruled that the Net Book Agreement, which bound bookshops to sell books at prices set by publishers and which collapsed in October 1995, was anti-competitive and should be abolished. **18.** The controversial film *Crash* was cleared for general release by the British Board of Film Classification. **19.** The designer Tadao Ando was awarded the RIBA Royal Gold Medal for architecture. **22.** The comet Hale-Bopp reached its closest point to the Earth. **25.** The British film *The English Patient* won nine awards at the Oscars ceremony in Hollywood. GEC-Marconi said that the Marconi Collection of historic items relating to the early days of radio broadcasting would be given to the Science Museum. **30.** The fifth and final terrestrial television channel in Britain, Channel 5, went on the air.

APRIL 1997

16. The writer Will Self was sacked by the *Observer* after allegations that he had taken drugs on board a plane carrying the Prime Minister to a campaign engagement; he was recruited by the *Independent on Sunday*. **17.** The trustees of Sudeley Castle, Glos, sold Poussin's *Temps Calme* to the Getty Museum in California for £15 million. **22.** The ITC reprimanded ITV for swamping its output with soap operas and dramas at the expense of documentaries and arts programmes. **24.** It was reported that a 63-year-old woman who had lied to doctors about her age had become the world's oldest-ever mother when she gave birth in California in November 1996 after *in vitro* fertilization.

MAY 1997

3. Fire broke out at the Royal Academy, London; no paintings were damaged. The UK won the Eurovision Song Contest in Dublin with *Love Shine a Light* by Katrina and the Waves. **4.** The National Heritage Secretary (Chris Smith) said that the Elgin Marbles were an integral part of the British Museum's collections and would not be returned to Greece. **6.** Pandurang Shastri Athavale was awarded the Templeton Prize for Progress in Religion. **7.** BSkyB, BT, Midland Bank and Matsushita Electric launched British Interactive Broadcasting, a service which will provide 200 digital channels for satellite viewers from April 1998 and digital interactive services from autumn 1998. **13.** Genista McIntosh resigned as chief executive of the Royal Opera House because of a stress-related illness; she was replaced by the Secretary-General of the Arts Council, Mary Allen. **15.** The Arts Council awarded a total of £92.25 million of lottery funding to three consortia to set up film studios and make 90 British films; a fourth franchise was not awarded.

JUNE 1997

4. The Canadian writer Anne Michaels was awarded the Orange prize for her first novel, *Fugitive Pieces*. **5.** The Globe Theatre in London, a replica of the theatre of Shakespeare's time, opened for its first full season. **9.** The new Hereford Cathedral library was named Building of the Year by the Royal Fine Art Commission and British Sky Broadcasting. **10.** The Hatton Gallery in Newcastle upon Tyne was saved from closure by a donation of £250,000 from the novelist Catherine Cookson. **11.** The journal Nature published scientific research which showed a genetic basis for differences in the social behaviour of men and women. The artist Rachel Whiteread refused an invitation to join the Royal Academy. **20.** BSkyB agreed to sell its 33 per cent stake in British Digital Broadcasting (BDB) after reportedly being told by the ITC that it would not grant a digital terrestrial licence to BDB as long as BSkyB was an equity partner in the venture. On 24 June BDB was awarded three digital television licences. **22.** The Chinese mezzo-soprano Guang Yang won the Cardiff Singer of the World competition. **24.** Twenty-six museums and galleries in Britain were designated by the National Heritage Secretary (Chris Smith) as being pre-eminent because of the richness and variety of their collections. **25.** The ITV company Yorkshire-Tyne Tees agreed to a take-over by Granada. The space station Mir was damaged when it collided with a supply ship while practising a docking manoeuvre. In New York, a charity auction of evening dresses belonging to Diana, Princess of Wales raised about £2 million.

JULY 1997

4. A robot explorer from the Pathfinder mission landed on Mars and sent back pictures of the planet's surface. The Science Minister (John Battle) said that the Royal Greenwich Observatory in Cambridge would close. **28.** The Secretary of State for Culture, Media and Sport (Chris Smith) said that the levy paid by Channel 4 to ITV would be phased out.

AUGUST 1997

5. A Soyuz rocket was launched from Kazakhstan to carry out repair work on the space station Mir. On 18 August a computer failure caused Mir to lose its orientation; on 22 August two cosmonauts succeeded in repairing the power system. **16.** The Old Vic theatre, London, was put up for sale. **23.** The new Oasis album *Be Here Now* became the fastest-selling record in British music history after selling 696,000 copies in two days. **25.** The space station Mir temporarily lost the use of its oxygen generators.

BUSINESS AND ECONOMIC AFFAIRS

SEPTEMBER 1996

2. Morgan Grenfell Asset Management suspended three European investment funds and a senior unit trust manager, Peter Young, because of suspected financial irregularities; another manager was suspended on 5 September. On 18 September Mr Young was sacked for gross misconduct. **10**. RJB Mining announced plans for the first new pit in Britain since privatization with the creation of about 500 jobs. **13**. The FT-SE 100 index reached a record high of 3,967.9. **23**. Lloyds TSB announced plans to take over Lloyds Abbey Life. **30**. HMSO was sold to National Publishing for £54 million.

OCTOBER 1996

2. The FT-SE 100 index closed at a record high of 4,015.1, the first time equities had traded above 4,000. **3**. P&O European Ferries and Stena Line announced a £400 million joint venture. British Gas rejected a package of new price controls proposed by the gas industry regulator covering its Transco subsidiary; it called for a Monopolies and Mergers Commission inquiry. **7**. Eurotunnel announced restructuring proposals agreed with its bankers in order to reduce its £8.7 billion debt; on 14 October it said that its Le Shuttle operation would be split off from Railway Services. On 22 October it announced 657 job losses. **8**. The Scottish Secretary (Michael Forsyth) announced that the South Korean conglomerate Hyundai would create a £2.4 billion microchip complex in Scotland. **15**. Sterling reached its highest level against the Deutschmark for 22 months when it rose to DM 2.4375. **17**. Marjorie Scardino was appointed head of the media group Pearson. **22**. Cable and Wireless announced plans to restructure the cable television industry. **25**. Sainsbury, the supermarket group, announced plans to launch its own bank. **30**. Bank base rates were raised to 6 per cent.

NOVEMBER 1996

3. British Telecom announced a £13 billion merger with the American telecommunications group MCI. **4**. The fund management company Invesco announced a £1 billion merger with the American company Aim Management Group. **19**. Sterling rose to DM 2.5176. **24**. Carlton Communications bought Westcountry Television for £85 million. **26**. Pearson bought the American publisher Putnam Berkley for $336 million.

DECEMBER 1996

3. The Government sold most of its remaining shares in utility companies. **6**. The FT-SE 100 index fell 88.2 points to 3,963.0, its worst fall in a single day for four years. **9**. The proposed take-over by Bass of Carlsberg-Tetley was referred to the Monopolies and Mergers Commission. **17**. The Treasury select committee of the House of Commons published a report highly critical of the role of the Bank of England in the collapse of Barings Bank in February 1995. **18**. The American company Entergy launched a £1.27 billion agreed offer for London Electricity. **24**. Northern Electric was taken over by the American company CE Electric. **31**. The FT-SE 100 index closed at a record high of 4,118.5.

JANUARY 1997

15. Ford announced that production of the Escort at its plant at Halewood, Merseyside would be phased out, resulting in at least 1,300 job losses; after threats of industrial action the company said on 7 February that production at the factory would continue and that job losses would be reduced to 980. The Rail Regulator (John Swift) said that Railtrack's level of investment in the railway network was 'wholly unacceptable'. **27**. The department stores group House of Fraser announced the closure of three stores and the loss of 1,000 jobs. **28**. The Ministry of Defence said that its £400 million food supply contract had been awarded to Booker Foodservice Group, with the resulting loss of 2,000 jobs at the former supplier, Naafi.

FEBRUARY 1997

7. Virgin Railways was selected as preferred bidder for the West Coast main line rail franchise. **13**. The FT-SE 100 index closed at a record high of 4,327.1. **16**. A pact allowing open competition in world telecommunications was signed by 68 countries in Switzerland. **17**. British Gas was split into two companies: BG, which runs the pipeline business and oil and gas exploration and production; and Centrica, which runs the trading and service operation. **17**. National Express was awarded the franchise for Central Trains. **18**. Granada sold the Welcome Break motorway service chain to Investcorp for £476 million. **20**. Railtrack published plans for a ten-year network management system and pledged £16 billion of investment for the period. **24**. Yorkshire Electricity accepted a £1.5 billion take-over bid from an American energy group, Yorkshire Holdings. **25**. National Express was awarded the franchise for ScotRail. **28**. NatWest Markets suspended its global head of options; on 13 March it suspended four other senior employees and said that a £90 million 'black hole' had been discovered in its derivatives operations.

MARCH 1997

4. Littlewoods put its 135 high street stores up for sale and said that it intended to concentrate on the home shopping market. **11**. Ian Hopkins, the former head of group treasury and risk at Barings Bank, was declared by the Securities and Futures Authority to be unfit to be a director because of his role in the bank's collapse in February 1995. **17**. The FT-SE 100 index closed 51 points down at 4,373.3 after the announcement of the date of the general election. **19**. British Steel announced plans to cut 10,000 jobs over the next five years.

APRIL 1997

1. The FT-SE 100 index closed 64.8 points down at 4,248.1 following big losses on Wall Street over Easter. **8**. Tesco announced pre-tax profits of £750 million. **15**. Sterling's average international value, measured by the trade-weighted index, rose to 100.1. **16**. Morgan Grenfell was fined a record £2 million by IMRO and ordered to pay £1 million costs for breaching unit trust rules. **17.** The Co-operative Wholesale Society (CWS) suspended two senior executives over a suspected serious breach of trust. On 18 April the CWS was granted a High Court injunction preventing Andrew Regan, a financier who had been stalking the CWS, from using confidential CWS information. On 24 April Mr Regan's take-over bid collapsed and the CWS launched a private criminal prosecution against him.

May 1997

6. Bank base rates were raised to 6.25 per cent; the Chancellor of the Exchequer (Gordon Brown) said that in future the Bank of England would have operational responsibility for setting interest rates to achieve inflation targets set by the Government and in support of the Government's economic policy. Richard Branson sold the Virgin Radio group to Capital Radio for £65 million. **7.** ICI said that it was to buy Unilever's speciality chemicals division for £5 billion and sell £3 billion of its existing businesses. **8.** Sterling fell to DM 2.7673 after rumours that the Government had plans to re-enter the ERM at at rate of DM 2.50. On 12 May the Chancellor of the Exchequer denied that there were any such plans. **12.** Grand Metropolitan and Guinness announced a £24 billion merger plan. **13.** The FT-SE 100 index closed at a record high of 4,691.0. **20.** The Chancellor of the Exchequer said that an enhanced Securities and Investments Board would replace the existing regulatory framework for banking, insurance and pensions.

June 1997

5. Railtrack announced pre-tax profits of £346 million. **6.** The Bank of England raised bank base rates to 6.5 per cent. **10.** Scottish Media and Grampian Television announced a merger. **12.** The Chancellor of the Exchequer set a target inflation rate of 2.5 per cent and said that the Bank of England would be responsible for achieving it and would have to report publicly on any fluctuation greater than 1 per cent from the target. **13.** PacifiCorp tabled a $5 billion bid for The Energy Group; on 1 August the Trade and Industry Secretary (Margaret Beckett) referred the bid to the Monopolies and Mergers Commission. **18.** The Monopolies and Mergers Commission supported new price controls on BG's Transco pipeline business which had been proposed by Ofgas in 1996. **20.** In the USA, leading tobacco companies reached a settlement of most of the outstanding legal claims against them in return for payments totalling $368 billion over 25 years. **27.** Margaret Beckett ruled that Bass's planned take-over of Carlsberg-Tetley would be anti-competitive and against the public interest. **30.** Margaret Beckett launched a wide-ranging review of utility regulation. Sterling reached DM 2.9070, its highest level since 1992.

July 1997

1. The FT-SE 100 index closed up 123.7 points at 4,728.3, the biggest one-day gain since 1992. **2.** The Chancellor of the Exchequer made his Budget statement in the House of Commons (*see* page 1159). **3.** The FT-SE 100 index closed at a record high of 4,831.7. Lockheed Martin, the world's biggest defence group, announced a $11.6 billion merger with Northrop Grumman, one of its leading competitors. **10.** The Bank of England raised bank base rates to 6.75 per cent. The head of corporate finance and two directors at Hambros merchant bank left their jobs after it was found that Hambros had used confidential CWS documents while working on the aborted bid by Andrew Regan (*see* above). **16.** The FT-SE 100 index closed at a record high of 4,964.2. **17.** Littlewoods said that 19 of its larger shops would be sold to Marks and Spencer for £192.5 million. **21.** Brian Staples was ousted as chief executive of United Utilities. **22.** The supermarket chain Sainsbury's launched a mortgage with the mutual insurance company Standard Life. The rail and bus operator Stagecoach announced a 176 per cent increase in pre-tax profits to £120 million. Sterling reached DM 3.0393, its highest level since 1989. **23.** Members of the Nationwide Building Society voted by a large majority in support of directors who were opposed to proposals to convert the Society to a bank.

August 1997

6. The FT-SE 100 index closed at 5,026.2, the first time the index had gone above 5,000. Apple said that it had sold $150 million of non-voting shares to Microsoft. **7.** The Bank of England raised bank base rates to 7 per cent. Margaret Beckett announced plans to replace the Monopolies and Mergers Commission with a Competition Commission with more extensive powers. **18.** RJB Mining closed Asfordby A mine in Leicestershire on the grounds that it was unsafe and uneconomic. **28–29.** The stock markets in the Philippines, Bangkok, Kuala Lumpur and Singapore fell sharply.

CRIMES AND LEGAL AFFAIRS

September 1996

12. Peter Martin, the owner of a model agency, was sentenced in Manchester to 20 years' imprisonment for raping six girls and indecently assaulting five others between 1981 and 1994. **19.** The High Court ruled that no further charges would be brought against Kevin Maxwell over the collapse of the Maxwell publishing empire in 1991. **30.** On the day before the trial was due to open, Neil Hamilton, the former corporate affairs minister, dropped his libel action against the *Guardian* over its allegations that he had accepted money to ask questions in the House of Commons.

OCTOBER 1996

9. The conviction of Colin Wallace, who served ten years in prison in 1981–91 for the manslaughter of Jonathan Lewis, an antiques dealer, was quashed by the Court of Appeal. **11.** Michael Clarke, a British travel agent, was sentenced in the Philippines to 16 years' imprisonment for promoting child sex tourism. **16.** Stuart Morgan was sentenced in Worcester to life imprisonment for the murder of Celine Figard, a French student, in December 1995. **17.** Sixteen-year-old Learco Chindamo was ordered at the Central Criminal Court to be detained indefinitely for the murder of Philip Lawrence, the headmaster of St George's School, Maida Vale, London, in December 1995. Philip Lawrence's widow Frances subsequently called for a national movement to tackle violence and encourage civic values. The High Court ruled that Diane Blood, whose husband died of meningitis in March 1995, could not have his baby by artificial insemination because his written consent had not been obtained; on 6 February 1997 the Court of Appeal ruled that Mrs Blood could take the sperm out of the country to undergo artificial insemination and on 27 February the Human Fertilization and Embryology Authority withdrew its opposition. **30.** Ruth Neave was acquitted in Northampton of the murder of her six-year-old son Rikki in November 1994; she was sentenced to seven years' imprisonment for cruelty towards him and two of her other children.

NOVEMBER 1996

10. At least 13 people were killed and 26 injured when a bomb believed to have been planted by an organized crime group exploded in a cemetery in Moscow. **12.** Fr Adrian McLeish, a Roman Catholic priest, was sentenced in Newcastle to six years' imprisonment for sexually abusing four boys and sending and receiving pornographic material via the Internet. **14.** Two 13-year-old girls pleaded guilty in Newcastle to the manslaughter of 13-year-old Louise Allen at a funfair in Corby in April 1996; they were sentenced to two years in a secure unit for young offenders. **15.** The High Court ruled that the prison service had been incorrectly calculating the length of time prisoners given concurrent sentences should stay in prison. A Sikh independence campaigner who had been in Bedford prison since 1990 fighting deportation to India won his case at the European Court of Human Rights and was released from prison. **18.** Stephen Webber was sentenced in Exeter to life imprisonment for the murder of a stable-girl in Devon in October 1995. **20.** A man was shot dead by police after handcuffing himself to a supermarket manager and threatening him with a knife in Birmingham. **21.** Martin Bryant was sentenced in Tasmania to 35 terms of life imprisonment for murdering 35 people at Port Arthur, Tasmania, in April 1996. **22.** An 84-year-old man was found murdered at his home in Ramsgate; 12 handguns had been stolen from the house. **24.** A 17-year-old girl was found murdered in Monmouth.

28. John West, the brother of the mass murderer Frederick West, committed suicide during his trial on charges of raping his niece and other girls at 25 Cromwell Street in the late 1970s and early 1980s. Maria Hnatiuk was sentenced in Norwich to life imprisonment for the murder of Rachael Lean in September 1995. **29.** Peter Moore was sentenced in Mold to four terms of life imprisonment for murdering four men in North Wales between September and December 1995.

DECEMBER 1996

2. A car driver was stabbed to death in what was claimed to be a 'road rage' attack; his fiancée was later charged with the murder. **3.** Mark Weston was cleared in Oxford of the murder of Vikki Thompson in August 1995. **9.** Horrett Campbell was convicted in Stafford of the attempted murder of three children and four women whom he attacked with a machete in a school playground in Wolverhampton in July 1996; on 7 February he was ordered to be detained indefinitely in a secure mental hospital. **10.** A 74-year-old widow was stabbed to death at her home in Merseyside. **11.** In the High Court John McCarthy was awarded £200,000 damages for post-traumatic stress disorder resulting from seeing fans including his half-brother crushed to death at the Hillsborough disaster in 1989. **13.** In the High Court the longest-ever libel trial in Britain, in which the fast food chain McDonalds sued two environmentalists, ended after two and a half years. **16.** Samar Alami and Jawad Botmeh were sentenced at the Central Criminal Court to 20 years' imprisonment each for conspiring to cause explosions at the Israeli embassy and a Jewish organization in London in July 1994. **17.** The European Court of Human Rights ruled that the rights of Ernest Saunders, the former chairman of Guinness, had been violated by the prosecution's use at his fraud trial in 1990 of transcripts of interviews conducted by DTI inspectors under their powers of compulsion. Neil Owen was sentenced in Cardiff to life imprisonment for the rape and murder of 15-year-old Claire Hood in January 1995. Seventeen-year-old Darren Lawrence was ordered in Truro to be detained at Her Majesty's pleasure for the murder of a 72-year-old man in Cornwall in January 1996. **18.** Russell Causley was sentenced in Winchester to life imprisonment for the murder in 1985 of his wife, whose body was never found. **19.** In the High Court Brian McCord, a former Stockport County footballer, was awarded immediate interim damages of £50,000 against Swansea City FC and its captain, John Cornforth, in a negligence claim over an injury McCord sustained in a match in 1993 that ended his career.

JANUARY 1997

1. Seventeen-year-old Nicola Dixon was found beaten to death in Sutton Coldfield. **10.** Nine-year-old Zoe Evans went missing from her home in Warminster; on 3 February her stepfather was charged with her murder and on 26 February her body was found. **17.** The first trial of an alleged Nazi war criminal to be held in Britain collapsed at the Central Criminal Court because the defendant, Szymon Serafinowicz, was found to be unfit to stand trial as he was suffering from Alzheimer's disease. **23.** The trial in London of five IRA prisoners and an armed robber on charges of breaking out of Whitemoor prison in 1994 was halted because of publicity in the London *Evening Standard* which was deemed to be prejudicial. **25.** An art teacher was found murdered on a farm in north Devon; a British man suspected of the murder drowned himself in Western Australia on 28 January. **29.** At the Central Criminal Court Arthur Jackson admitted the manslaughter of Anthony Fletcher, whom he shot dead after raiding a bank in London in 1962. **30.** Edwin Hopkins was sentenced in Birmingham to life imprisonment for the murder of 15-year-old Naomi Smith in Nuneaton in September 1995.

FEBRUARY 1997

4. An intruder was stabbed to death with his own knife by a woman whom he had attacked in her home near Folkestone. **5.** The former American football star O. J. Simpson, who had been acquitted of murdering his ex-wife and her friend in 1994, was ordered to pay nearly £5.5 million in compensation after a jury at a civil trial in Santa Monica found that he was responsible for their deaths. He was later ordered to pay £15.2 million in punitive damages to the victims' relatives. **6.** Andrew Pountley was sentenced in Manchester to two terms of life imprisonment for the rape and murder of five-year-old Rosie McCann in Oldham in January 1996. **7.** Six people were killed by a gunman at a ski resort in Raurimu, New Zealand. Fourteen-year-old Brian Smith was ordered in Liverpool to be detained at Her Majesty's pleasure for the murder of nine-year-old Jade Matthews in Bootle in July 1996. **11.** A Roman Catholic priest was stabbed in the back by a man at his church in north London. **12.** David Howells was sentenced to life imprisonment for the murder of his wife in Huddersfield in August 1995; his teenage sons Glenn and John were also convicted of the murder and were ordered to be detained at Her Majesty's pleasure. **13.** At the inquest on the death of a black youth, Stephen Lawrence, in south London in 1993, the jury found that he had been killed by five white youths in an unprovoked racist attack; on 14 February the *Daily Mail* controversially published photographs of the youths under the headline 'Murderers'. A British au pair, Louise Woodward, was charged in Boston, USA, with the murder of a baby in her care. Dr Salim Najada was sentenced in Birmingham to 12 months' imprisonment for the manslaughter of a diabetic patient whose condition he had failed to diagnose and for perverting the course of justice by falsifying the patient's medical notes. **15.** Thirteen-year-old Billie-Jo Jenkins was found beaten to death at her home in Hastings; her foster father was subsequent-

ly charged with the murder. **17.** At the Central Criminal Court, Port Ramsgate Ltd was convicted of failing to ensure the safety of passengers over the collapse in September 1994 of a ferry walkway which killed six people. **19.** In a landmark judgment in the Court of Appeal, the Master of the Rolls (Lord Woolf) ruled that exemplary damages to victims of unlawful arrest and police assault should be limited to £50,000. **20.** The trial of Frank Williams, the head of the Williams Formula 1 motor racing team, and two of his colleagues on charges of manslaughter over the death of the Brazilian driver Ayrton Senna in the San Marino grand prix in May 1994 opened in Imola. **21.** James Robinson, Vincent Hickey and Michael Hickey, who were imprisoned in 1979 for the murder of 13-year-old Carl Bridgewater, were released on bail pending a full appeal after the Appeal Court heard that two policemen had allegedly fabricated a confession; a fourth man convicted of the murder, Patrick Molloy, had died in prison in 1981. On 30 July the convictions of the four were quashed. **23.** One man was shot dead and seven people were wounded when a man opened fire on the observation deck of the Empire State Building, New York; the gunman then shot himself. **25.** The body of nine-year-old Kayleigh Ward, who went missing from her home in Chester on 19 December 1996, was found on the bank of the River Dee in north Wales; on 26 February a man was charged with her murder. The European Court of Human Rights ruled that the human rights of a Falklands veteran, who was imprisoned for two years in 1991 after being court martialled, had been breached by the unfair nature of the court martial system. **27.** The Home Secretary (Michael Howard) published proposals for reforming the criminal justice system, including the removal of the automatic right to a jury trial for many suspects.

MARCH 1997

7. Keith Laverack, a senior social services manager, was sentenced in Chester to 18 years' imprisonment for the sexual abuse of children in his care over a period of 30 years. The High Court ruled that the Lord Chancellor (Lord Mackay of Clashfern) had acted unlawfully in setting a new court fee system in January 1997 that made no provision for waiving charges in cases of financial hardship. **10.** Trevor Clark, the former bursar of the Royal Academy, was sentenced in London to five years' imprisonment for the theft of nearly £400,000 from the Academy since 1987. **17.** Diego Cogolato was sentenced at the Central Criminal Court to six years' imprisonment for the murder of the fashion designer Ossie Clark, his former lover, in August 1996. The Court of Appeal quashed the conviction of Elizabeth Forsyth, a former aide to Asil Nadir, who served ten months in prison in 1996–7 for handling allegedly stolen money in 1989 before the collapse of Nadir's Polly Peck business empire. **18.** A British surgeon was shot dead by police in the Congo. **24.** Seventeen-year-old Sharon Carr was sentenced in

Winchester to life imprisonment for the murder of 18-year-old Katie Rackliff in June 1992. **26.** In a landmark judgment the Court of Appeal ruled that where women are capable of a decision they have the right to refuse medical intervention during labour even if the refusal could lead to the death of their baby. The first practising solicitors were appointed Queen's Counsel.

April 1997

3. Abbas Gokal, a former shipping magnate, was convicted at the Central Criminal Court on fraud charges relating to a £750 million debt to the Bank of Credit and Commerce International, which collapsed in 1991. He was later sentenced to 14 years' imprisonment. **11.** Eight teenagers were convicted at the Central Criminal Court of raping an Austrian tourist in London in September 1996; on 7 May the 14-year-old ringleader was ordered to be detained for 12 years. **22.** The European Court of Human Rights ruled that the human rights of a British transsexual, Stephen Whittle, had not been violated by the refusal to allow him to be named as the father of his girlfriend's child conceived by artificial insemination.

May 1997

13. The decapitated body of 14-year-old Kirsty Tidman, who had gone missing on 4 May, was found in the River Thames at Wapping; her cousin, Paul Pearson, had committed suicide after being questioned in connection with her disappearance and was believed to have committed the murder. **16.** Fred Hayworth was sentenced in Winchester to four terms of life imprisonment for murdering four of his nieces and nephews by setting fire to their home in Southampton, where his estranged wife had taken refuge, in May 1996. **20.** A jeweller was stabbed to death while attempting to stop a robbery at his shop in Cowbridge, Vale of Glamorgan. The High Court ruled that an 11-year-old girl could be adopted by a woman living in a lesbian relationship in spite of objections from the child's natural mother. **21.** The Home Secretary (Jack Straw) said that a chief crown prosecutor would be appointed for each police force area. In a landmark judgment the House of Lords ruled that a deaf woman was entitled to a disability living allowance towards the extra costs of employing an interpreter to enable her to lead as normal a social life as possible. **22.** Twelve-year-old Katerina Konev was found strangled at her home in west London after her father had chased away an intruder. **23.** Roger Saint, an approved foster carer who had been convicted of a paedophile offence in 1972, was sentenced in Chester to six and a half years' imprisonment for the sexual abuse of children in his care. **24.** In a case brought by a man whose estranged wife had decided to have an abortion, the Court of Appeal in Edinburgh ruled that an unborn baby has no right to life if the mother has chosen to have an abortion; the man was given leave to appeal to the House of

Lords but on 27 May he said he would not do so. On 29 May the baby was aborted. **30.** Two teenagers, Noel Sayles and Jason Honeyghon, were ordered at the Central Criminal Court to be detained at Her Majesty's pleasure for the murder of 16-year-old Danny Westmacott in 1996; the judge strongly criticized the many witnesses who had refused to give evidence.

June 1997

2. Timothy McVeigh was convicted in Denver, USA, of planting the bomb which killed 168 people at the federal building in Oklahoma City in April 1995. On 13 June the jury sentenced him to death. **12.** Five law lords upheld rulings by lower courts against the former Home Secretary (Michael Howard), who had set a 15-year minimum term of detention for the two boys who murdered James Bulger in February 1993. **13.** Martin Cody, a security guard, was convicted in Exeter of the manslaughter of Fleur Lombard, a firefighter, who died in a blaze started by Cody in a supermarket in Bristol in February 1996. **18.** Jonathan Tokeley-Parry was sentenced in London to six years' imprisonment for smuggling Egyptian artefacts into Britain disguised as tourist souvenirs. **19.** The fast food chain McDonald's was awarded £60,000 libel damages in the High Court against two campaigners who had claimed that the company caused starvation in the Third World and destroyed rain forests and who had defended themselves in the trial, which lasted 313 days, the longest trial in English legal history. **20.** In the High Court the former Conservative Cabinet minister Jonathan Aitken dropped his libel action against the *Guardian* newspaper and Granada Television over allegations relating to his Middle Eastern connections after the defence produced new evidence to support its case. On 26 June Mr Aitken resigned as a privy counsellor. Charlie Kray was convicted in London of supplying cocaine as part of a £39 million operation; he was sentenced to 12 years' imprisonment. **21.** A 22-year-old student was found strangled in a park in Northampton. **24.** Clive Jones was sentenced in Leeds to life imprisonment for the murder of Stevan Popovic in April 1996. **25.** The European Court of Human Rights upheld a complaint by the former assistant chief constable of Merseyside, Alison Halford, that her privacy had been breached by her employers when they bugged her telephone after she had launched a sex discrimination action against them in 1990; she was awarded £10,000 compensation. **30.** A series of interlinked drugs trials arising out of an 18-month investigation by customs officers codenamed Operation Stealer ended with the conviction of 13 people for smuggling cocaine and cannabis worth £65 million. On 14 July the defendants received prison sentences ranging up to 25 years.

2. Six IRA members were each sentenced at the Central Criminal Court to 35 years' imprisonment for plotting to bomb electricity supply stations in south-east England in 1996. 4. Paul Esslemont, who was sentenced in 1993 to eight years' detention for the manslaughter of Carl Kennedy, was released after the Court of Appeal quashed his conviction. 15. The fashion designer Gianni Versace was shot dead outside his mansion in Miami, Florida; on 24 July Andrew Cunanan, the man suspected of murdering Versace and four other men, was found shot dead on a house-boat at Miami Beach, having apparently committed suicide. 21. A nine-year-old boy was found murdered in Aberdeen. 22. Eighty-three-year-old Erich Priebke, who was arrested in Argentina in 1993, was sentenced by a military court in Rome to 15 years' imprisonment, with ten years' remission because of his age, for taking part in the massacre of 335 civilians in the Ardeatine Caves in southern Rome in March 1944; Karl Hass was given a ten-year sentence, with ten years' remission, for his part in the massacre. 23. Angela Lee, a registered child-minder, was sentenced in Leeds to five years' imprisonment for the manslaughter of a four-month-old baby who had been left in her care in February 1996. The Court of Appeal ruled that homosexuals should have the same tenancy succession rights as heterosexuals. 24. Sheila Bowler, who was convicted in 1993 of murdering her aunt by pushing her into a river near Rye, was released from prison pending a retrial when the Court of Appeal quashed the conviction. 25. The Roman Catholic diocese of Dallas, USA, was ordered to pay damages of £72 million to former altar boys who had been sexually abused by a priest; the diocese had been accused of ignoring indications of abuse and subsequently conspiring to cover up the scandal. 28. The Government announced an inquiry into the workings of the Crown Prosecution Service after criticism over its conduct of two cases involving deaths in police or prison custody. 29. Tracie Andrews was sentenced at Birmingham Crown Court to life imprisonment for the murder of her boyfriend Lee Harvey, who she said had been killed in a 'road rage' attack in December 1996. Pavlos Georgiou was convicted by a court in Cyprus of knowingly infecting his former lover Janette Pink with the Aids virus; he was sentenced to 15 months' imprisonment. 31. The Home Secretary (Jack Straw) announced an inquiry into the murder of the black teenager Stephen Lawrence in south London in 1993. Paul Cowdrey, an estate agent, was sentenced at Winchester Crown Court to life imprisonment for the murder of his wife in November 1996.

AUGUST 1997

6. A five-year-old boy was shot dead and his stepfather was seriously injured in Bolton in an attack apparently related to drug-dealing. A British church minister was beaten to death and his wife was badly injured by robbers in Hungary. 7. After a second trial, the footballers Bruce Grobbelaar, John Fashanu and Hans Segers were cleared at Winchester Crown Court of conspiring to throw football matches for cash; on 8 August Grobbelaar was cleared of a charge of accepting £2,000 to fix matches. Mark Litchfield, the captain of the sailing ship *Maria Asumpta*, was sentenced at Exeter Crown Court to 18 months' imprisonment for the manslaughter of three crew members who drowned when the ship sank off the coast of Cornwall in May 1995. 11. The Government published new guidelines on the naming of convicted paedophiles. 13. A British student was shot dead while hitch-hiking in Israel. A body was found in Coniston Water, Cumbria; it was later identified as Carol Park, who went missing in 1976; on 25 August her former husband was charged with her murder. 22. The body of 12-year-old Thomas Marshall, who had gone missing on 21 August, was found near Thetford, Norfolk. 27. A British teacher, Carole Leach, was found beaten to death at her home on the island of Eleuthera in the Bahamas.

ENVIRONMENT

OCTOBER 1996

2. The Transport Secretary (Sir George Young) confirmed that a Salisbury bypass would be built, but said that a tunnel to bypass Stonehenge was too expensive. 23. The largest wind farm in Europe opened at Carno, Powys.

NOVEMBER 1996

17. A study carried out for British Gas Properties found that there was enough derelict land in towns and cities to accommodate all the new homes needed in the next 20 years. 25. The Government published a Green Paper proposing to build 60 per cent of the 4.4 million new homes needed in the next 20 years on previously-developed land and 40 per cent on greenfield sites. A conference calling for action to reduce light pollution over Britain was held in London.

DECEMBER 1996

9. Leading environmental groups published a report, *High and Dry*, which said that 300 wildlife sites were under threat from policies pursued by water companies, industry and agriculture.

JANUARY 1997

2. In a landmark ruling, Hull County Court declared that a roadside hawthorn hedge was protected under a 1765 Enclosure Act. 15. A leaked memo written by a director of the nuclear waste disposal company Nirex cast doubt on the safety of the company's plans to bury nuclear waste 2,400 feet underground at Sellafield, Cumbria; on 17 March the Environment Secretary (John Gummer) refused the com-

pany planning permission. **18.** At least 1,500 tons of petrol were spilt in the English Channel when two tankers collided 40 miles off the Kent coast. **24.** The Road Traffic Reduction Bill, which would require local councils to take measures to reduce local traffic congestion, received an unopposed second reading in the House of Commons. **30.** A week-long underground protest against the A30 improvement scheme near Honiton, Devon, ended when the last activist, known as 'Swampy', was brought to the surface.

February 1997

9. Scores of oil-covered birds were rescued along the south coast of England.

March 1997

12. The Government published the final version of a National Air Quality Strategy including commitments to major reductions in the principal air pollutants by 2005.

April 1997

7. About 350 acres of Dartmoor national park were destroyed by fire. **9.** A report commissioned by the National Trust produced strong scientific evidence that deer suffer high levels of stress when hunted; the Trust banned deer-hunting on its land. **22.** A public inquiry into plans by the Army to expand its training area in the Northumberland National Park opened in Newcastle upon Tyne. **23.** More than 1,000 acres of heathland near St Ives, Cornwall, were destroyed by fire.

May 1997

1. The Institute of Hydrology said that rainfall in April had been 42 per cent of the long-term average and that Britain had experienced its longest period of low rainfall since records began in 1767. **4.** Pollution from an unknown source killed all aquatic life in a five-mile stretch of the River Medway in Kent. **6.** A report commissioned by the Department of the Environment showed a sharp decline in at least 12 varieties of farmland birds in the last 25 years; the report called for reduced use of chemicals and other changes in agricultural practice. **8.** A report in *New Scientist* said that a plume of radioactive water from the nuclear reprocessing plant at Sellafield had reached the Arctic. **15.** The National Heritage Memorial Fund awarded £57 million of Lottery money for the restoration of 48 urban parks. **19.** The Deputy Prime Minister (John Prescott) met representatives of the water industry and its regulators and announced mandatory targets for the repair of leaking pipes and a review of licences for abstractions causing significant environmental damage. **20.** Security men began to evict environmental protesters in trees and tunnels from the site of the planned second runway at Manchester airport.

June 1997

11. Greenpeace activists occupied Rockall, an uninhabited rock in the Atlantic Ocean, in protest at oil exploration in the region. **19.** The Convention on International Trade in Endangered Species voted in Harare, Zimbabwe, to permit a limited resumption of the ivory trade. **23-28.** A special session of the UN was held in New York to discuss progress towards meeting global environmental targets set at the 1992 Rio summit. **30.** The Government admitted that radioactive waste had been dumped in Beaufort's Dyke off the coast of Scotland in the 1950s and 1960s.

July 1997

10. Tens of thousands of people held a 'countryside rally' in Hyde Park, London, to protest against proposed legislation to ban fox-hunting. **16.** The Marine Accident Investigation Branch published a report highly critical of the handling of the *Sea Empress* disaster at Milford Haven in February 1996; the Environment Agency said that the port authority and the harbourmaster would be prosecuted. **28.** The Government cancelled two major road schemes, the Salisbury bypass and the A40 West London approach; five other schemes were approved and five were set aside for further consideration.

August 1997

19. BP launched a legal action for damages against Greenpeace over its disruption of BP's oil activities in the Atlantic; on 21 August the action was suspended after Greenpeace said that it would no longer interfere with oil production. **21.** The High Court advised the National Trust to reconsider its ban on deer-hunting on its land and granted West Country deer-hunts leave to seek a further hearing to challenge the ban's legality. The Secretary of State for the Environment, Transport and the Regions (John Prescott) published a consultation document outlining options to achieve an integrated transport policy that would reduce the use of private cars.

SPORT

September 1996

1. Damon Hill was dropped by the Williams motor racing team for the 1996–7 season. **3.** The England rugby union squad boycotted a training session organized by the RFU in order to attend a meeting of the English Professional Rugby Union Clubs (EPRUC), which had announced its intention of breaking away from the RFU. **5.** The RFU reached an agreement with the other home rugby unions which saved the Five Nations Championship. **13.** Members of the England rugby union squad gave their support to EPRUC and said that they were not available for selection for the national team run by the RFU. **21.** Leicestershire won the cricket county championship for the first time in 21 years. **28.** At Ascot, Frankie Dettori became the first jockey to win all seven races at a meeting.

October 1996

4. The Pakistan batsman Shahid Afridi scored 100 runs from 37 balls, the fastest-ever century in international one-day cricket, in a match against Kenya in Nairobi. **7.** Yorkshire County Cricket Club said that it would leave its Leeds ground, Headingley, and move to a new cricket complex near Wakefield by 2000. Steve Coppell was appointed manager of Manchester City FC; he resigned on 8 November because of stress. **9.** The Estonia football team failed to turn up for its world cup qualifying match against Scotland in Tallinn after the kick-off time was brought forward because of inadequate floodlights at the ground; FIFA later ruled that the match should be replayed. **13.** Damon Hill won the Japanese Grand Prix in Suzuka, becoming the Formula One world motor racing champion. **14.** Mark Tout, Britain's Olympic bobsleigh driver, was banned for life after testing positive for anabolic steroids. **20.** Wasim Akram hit 12 sixes in his innings of 257 not out for Pakistan against Zimbabwe in Sheikupura, the highest number of sixes ever scored in an individual Test innings; it was also the highest-ever score by a number eight batsman in a Test. **24.** Fourteen-year-old Hassan Raza was reported to have became the youngest-ever Test cricketer when he played for Pakistan against Zimbabwe in Faisalabad; doubts were later expressed about his alleged age.

November 1996

1. Paul Gascoigne's selection for the England football squad attracted controversy because of allegations that he had beaten his wife. **5.** Phil de Glanville was named England rugby union captain. **10.** Evander Holyfield became the first man since Muhammad Ali to be world boxing champion three times when he unexpectedly beat Mike Tyson in Las Vegas to win the WBA championship. **13.** The National Heritage Secretary (Virginia Bottomley) said that £50 million of lottery funding would be made available to support talented sportspeople, develop coaching and fund one-off major sporting events. **14.** Ian Botham was appointed technical adviser to the England cricket team on its overseas winter tour. **15.** The Aston Villa goalkeeper Mark Bosnich was fined £1,000 by the FA for making a Nazi salute to Tottenham fans as a joke during a game on 12 October. **19.** The former England football coach Terry Venables was appointed Australia's head coach from January 1997. **27.** The RFU and EPRUC reached agreement about the future competitive and financial structures of first-class rugby union.

December 1996

5. The England cricket team was beaten by the mainly amateur players of Mashonaland at the beginning of a tour of Zimbabwe. **12.** The Test and County Cricket Board was wound up; on 1 January 1997 it was replaced by the England and Wales Cricket Board. **15.** Damon Hill was named BBC Sports Personality of the Year. **17.** The Sports Council announced that a new national stadium would be built in Wembley, north London, and a new stadium and swimming complex would be built in Manchester in preparation for the 2002 Commonwealth Games. **22.** Peter Shilton became the first footballer to play in 1,000 League matches when he kept goal for Leyton Orient against Brighton. The first match of the cricket Test series between Zimbabwe and England in Bulawayo became the first Test ever to end in a draw with the scores level.

January 1997

2. The champion cyclist Miguel Induráin announced his retirement from competitive racing. **7.** Richard Branson took off from Marrakesh, Morocco, in an attempt to become the first person to fly non-stop around the world in a balloon; the balloon was brought down on 8 January in north-west Algeria after developing technical problems. Murray Kidd resigned as coach of the Ireland rugby union team; he was replaced by Brian Ashton. **8.** Kevin Keegan resigned as manager of Newcastle Utd FC; he was replaced by Kenny Dalglish. **9.** Tony Bullimore, a British competitor in the Vendée Globe round-the-world yacht race who had capsized in the Southern Pacific Ocean, was rescued by the Australian Navy after spending nearly five days sheltering in an air pocket in the upturned hull of his yacht. **18.** The Norwegian explorer Boerge Ousland completed the first solo unsupported crossing of Antarctica. **20.** An American balloonist, Steve Fossett, landed in India six days into an attempt to fly around the world. **24.** Peter Graf, the father of the tennis champion Steffi Graf, was sentenced in Germany to three years and nine months' imprisonment for evasion of more than £5 million of tax on his daughter's earnings. **25.** Martina Hingis became the youngest tennis player to win a singles Grand Slam title this century when she won the Australian Open. **28.** A cricket Test match between England and New Zealand in Auckland ended in a draw after a last-wicket stand of 106 by New Zealand.

February 1997

1. England made their highest-ever score in a rugby union home international match when they beat Scotland 41–13 at Twickenham; on 15 February they beat Ireland 46–6 in Dublin. The RFU and EPRUC signed a deal under which a new company (Newco) was set up to administer and market the top club competitions. **3.** A row broke out when UEFA said that it had given its backing in 1993 to

Germany's bid to stage the 2006 World Cup; the FA, which had launched a campaign to stage the tournament in England, said that it had been unaware of the decision. On 7 February UEFA said that it would consider England's bid. **8.** Lennox Lewis won the WBC heavyweight title in Las Vegas when his opponent, Oliver McCall, broke down in tears in the ring. **9.** England won their first overseas cricket Test match for two years when they beat New Zealand by an innings and 68 runs in Wellington. On 18 February they won their first overseas Test series for five years when they won the third Test in Christchurch. **19.** The Arsenal footballer Ian Wright clashed with the Manchester Utd goalkeeper Peter Schmeichel during and after a match at Highbury; it was later alleged that Schmeichel had made racist remarks to Wright and the incident was referred to the FA. Newcastle rugby union club bought Va'aiga Tuigamala from Wigan rugby league club for a record fee of £500,000. **20.** After a two-day inquiry the Jockey Club ruled that stewards at Haydock Park had not followed written procedures when the day's racing was cancelled on 16 October 1996 after protests from all the participating jockeys over the condition of the course. **27.** In a landmark ruling, the High Court granted the rugby union player Mark Jones an injunction allowing him to continue playing pending an appeal against his four-week suspension for fighting during a game.

MARCH 1997

1. The former champion jockey Willie Carson announced his retirement from racing. **4.** The jury failed to reach a verdict at the trial in Winchester of the footballers Bruce Grobbelaar, Hans Segers and John Fashanu on charges of match-fixing. **19.** At least six Manchester Utd football supporters were injured when police fired rubber bullets and tear gas before a match against Porto in Portugal. **22.** Fourteen-year-old Tara Lipinski became the youngest-ever world figure-skating champion when she won the title in Lausanne. **23.** The British yachtsman Pete Goss, who had made a 120-mile detour in order to save the life of a fellow competitor, finished the Vendée Globe round-the-world race. **26.** The England and Wales Cricket Board announced a sponsorship deal with Vodafone worth £13 million over four years. **27.** The Liverpool footballer Robbie Fowler was fined £900 by UEFA for wearing a T-shirt expressing support for striking dockers in a European Cup-Winners' Cup tie. **30.** Thirteen-year-old Luke McShane became the youngest-ever British International Chess Master. **31.** Martina Hingis became the youngest-ever world no. 1 tennis player at the age of 16 years and six months.

APRIL 1997

5. The Grand National was postponed after coded IRA bomb threats were received in Liverpool; Aintree was evacuated and thousands of racegoers spent the night in emergency accommodation while security checks were completed. The race was held on 7 April. **9.** The Newcastle rugby union player Nick Popplewell was fined £1,000 by his club for punching a Bedford player in a match on 5 April. **13.** Twenty-one-year-old Tiger Woods became the first black golfer to win the US Masters and its youngest-ever winner; he also scored the lowest-ever total (270) and won by the biggest-ever margin (12 strokes). **21.** Ronnie O'Sullivan scored the fastest-ever maximum break of 147 at the world snooker championships in Sheffield when he cleared the table in 5 minutes 20 seconds. **27.** The last rugby union match was played at Cardiff Arms Park before its redevelopment.

MAY 1997

2. Gianfranco Zola was named Footballer of the Year. **5.** Stephen Hendry, world snooker champion since 1992, was beaten in the final of the 1997 championships by Ken Doherty. **6.** Manchester Utd won the football Premiership for the fourth time in five years. The consultants Deloitte Touche put forward proposals for expanding the Football League to include the Vauxhall Conference clubs, with the third division enlarged and regionalized; the clubs rejected the proposals as unworkable. **7.** Rangers won the Scottish Premier League championship for the ninth successive year. Disaffected members of the RFU formed an RFU Reform Group headed by Fran Cotton, the Lions manager. **11.** The IBM computer Deep Blue beat the world chess champion Garry Kasparov $3\frac{1}{2}-2\frac{1}{2}$ in a match in New York. **12.** Susie Maroney became the first person officially to swim unassisted from Cuba to Florida. **13.** The Liverpool striker Stan Collymore was bought by Aston Villa for £7 million. Dick Best was sacked as Harlequins' director of rugby. **17.** Roberto di Matteo scored in 42 seconds in the match against Middlesbrough at Wembley, the quickest-ever goal in FA Cup final history. **18.** The Manchester Utd forward Eric Cantona announced his retirement from professional football. **19.** The Health Secretary (Frank Dobson) announced a ban on the sponsorship of sports events by tobacco companies. The FA's technical director (Howard Wilkinson) put forward proposals aimed at developing young footballing talent and ensuring the success of British international football. **27.** Four British women completed the last relay stage of the first all-female expedition to the North Pole.

JUNE 1997

2. Stephen Martin and David Mitchell became the first Britons to walk unaided to the North Pole. **5.** Australia slumped to 54−8 in the first Test against England at Edgbaston before being all out for 118. **8.** Gustavo Kuerten of Brazil, ranked 66 in the world, won the French Open tennis championships. **10.** The England football team won the Tournoi de France. **15.** The Canadian Formula 1 Grand Prix in Montreal was halted on the 50th lap after a crash in which the French driver Olivier Panis broke both his legs. 21. In the second Test against Australia, England were all out for 77 runs, their lowest total at Lord's since 1888; the Australian fast bowler Glenn McGrath took eight wickets for 38 runs. At the European Cup in Munich Linford Christie won the 100 metres in his last appearance for Great Britain; it was his eighth consecutive European Cup 100 metres victory and helped Great Britain's men's team to win the Cup for the first time since 1989. The British Lions won a Test series in South Africa for the first time since 1974 when they beat the Springboks 18–15 in Durban. 29. The former world heavyweight boxing champion Mike Tyson was disqualified in a title fight against Evander Holyfield in Las Vegas after biting off part of his opponent's ear; on 9 July he was banned from boxing, with permission to reapply for a licence after one year, and fined $3 million. Matches were played on the middle Sunday at Wimbledon for only the second time in the tournament's history after heavy rain earlier in the week.

JULY 1997

2. Two British men, Tim Henman and Greg Rusedski, reached the quarter-finals of Wimbledon for the first time since 1961. 3. The former Wimbledon champion Boris Becker played his last match at the championships, and lost to Pete Sampras on Centre Court. 5. Sixteen-year-old Martina Hingis became the youngest women's singles champion at Wimbledon since Lottie Dodd in 1887 when she beat Jana Novotna in the final. 11. Cliff Brittle was elected chairman of the RFU's management board. 13. Henry Akinwande was disqualified in a WBC heavyweight title fight against Lennox Lewis in Lake Tahoe after holding his opponent and refusing to fight. 20. Alistair Brown scored a record total of 203 in a Sunday league match for Hampshire against Surrey at Guildford. 30. The journalist and former Cabinet minister David Mellor was appointed head of a task force to investigate the problems facing football and to ensure that fans were treated fairly.

AUGUST 1997

5. The chairman of the England and Wales Cricket Board, Lord MacLaurin, proposed radical changes to the structure of professional cricket, including a three-group county championship and a 25-match national one-day league. At the world athletics championships in Athens, Michael Johnson won his third consecutive 400 metres title. 6. Sri Lanka set the highest total ever in a single innings in Test cricket when they scored 952 for six wickets against India in Colombo; Sanath Jayasuriya and Roshan Mahanama set a record Test partnership of 576, with Jayasuriya scoring 340 runs and Mahanama 225. 7. The former world and Olympic 400 metres hurdles champion Sally Gunnell and the former Olympic javelin champion Tessa Sanderson both announced their retirement from athletics. 9. The

former world and Olympic 100 metres champion Linford Christie announced his retirement from athletics. 10. Australia retained the Ashes after winning the fifth Test at Trent Bridge. 12. Robert Croft and Mark Ilott clashed as a NatWest Trophy semi-final match between Essex and Glamorgan at Chelmsford was cut short because of bad light; they were fined £1,000 each by their counties. 15. Jennifer Murray became the first woman to circumnavigate the globe in a helicopter. 17. The Secretary of State for Culture, Media and Sport (Chris Smith) said that football, rugby and cricket would be excluded from the planned British Academy of Sport because they could afford to fend for themselves. Ajay Jadeja and Mohammad Azharuddin set a record stand for one-day cricket of 223 runs for India in a match against Sri Lanka in Colombo.

APPOINTMENTS AND RESIGNATIONS

In addition to those mentioned above, the following appointments and resignations were announced:

1996

6 September: Adam Mills was appointed chief executive of London and Continental Railways

1997

6 January: Howard Wilkinson was appointed the first technical director of the Football Association

17 January: Graham Wallace was appointed chief executive of Cable and Wireless Communications

18 January: Peter Radford resigned as executive chairman of the British Athletic Federation

27 January: Michael Grade resigned as chief executive of Channel 4

27 February: Peter Leaver, QC, was appointed chief executive of the FA Premier League

10 March: Rosalind Wright was appointed director of the Serious Fraud Office

11 March: Faith Boardman was appointed chief executive of the Child Support Agency

13 March: David Graveney was appointed chairman of the England cricket selectors

27 March: Sir David English was appointed chairman of ITN

12 April: Peter Bamford resigned as managing director of W. H. Smith Retail; he was replaced by Beverley Hodson

2 May: The BBC's director of television and controller of BBC1, Michael Jackson, was appointed chief executive of Channel 4 in place of Michael Grade

13 May: Genista McIntosh resigned as chief executive of the Royal Opera House; she was replaced by Mary Allen

23 May: Alan Yentob was appointed director of television at the BBC
23 June: Bill Cockburn, the chief executive of W. H. Smith, was appointed group managing director of BT
2 July: Max Taylor was nominated as chairman of Lloyd's of London
1 August: Sir Richard Wilson was appointed Cabinet Secretary and head of the Home Civil Service from January 1998
5 August: Tony Hallett resigned as secretary of the Rugby Football Union
7 August: Sir Graeme Odgers resigned as chairman of the Monopolies and Mergers Commission
13 August: Ian Rickson was appointed artistic director of the Royal Court Theatre
20 August: Jack Rowell resigned as coach to the England rugby union team

---

AFRICA

SEPTEMBER 1996

5. President Zafy of Madagascar resigned after the High Constitutional Court confirmed his impeachment. **6.** South Africa's constitutional court rejected parts of the post-apartheid constitution. **24.** The armies of Rwanda and Zaïre exchanged fire across their mutual border. **26.** The military leader of the Gambia, Col. Yayah Jammeh, won the first presidential election under the new civilian constitution; the ruling military council was disbanded on 28 September.

OCTOBER 1996

10. A new constitution was approved by referendum in the Comoros. **11.** Gen. Magnus Malan, South Africa's former defence minister, was acquitted of murders alleged to have been committed in the apartheid era. **15.** The warring factions in Somalia declared a cease-fire with immediate effect. **21.** Fighting broke out between the Zaïrean army and Zaïrean Tutsis, causing more than 200,000 Rwandan Hutu refugees to flee from camps in eastern Zaïre. The mayor of Algiers was shot dead. **30.** Rwandan troops crossed into eastern Zaïre following the shelling of a Rwandan border town by Zaïrean soldiers. **31.** Zaïrean Tutsis and Rwandan troops captured Bukavu, the capital of Zaïre's South Kivu province.

NOVEMBER 1996

2. Zaïrean Tutsis and Rwandan troops captured Goma, the capital of Zaïre's North Kivu province. **15.** More than 500,000 Rwandan Hutu refugees in eastern Zaïre began to return to Rwanda after Hutu *Interahamwe* militia fled from the refugee camps. **18.** Frederick Chiluba was re-elected president of Zambia. **28.** Algerians voted in a referendum to approve a new constitution which bans religious parties, increases the powers of the presidency and creates a bicameral legislature.

DECEMBER 1996

5–11. Sixty people were killed by Islamic fundamentalists in Algeria. **8.** Rebel soldiers in the Central African Republic agreed to a cease-fire with government forces following a mutiny which began on 15 November. **15.** Thousands of Hutu refugees were forcibly repatriated to Rwanda from refugee camps in Tanzania.

JANUARY 1997

3. Two Hutus convicted of genocide were sentenced to death in Rwanda. **16.** A bomb exploded in Boufarik, Algeria, killing at least 14 people. **19.** A car bomb exploded in Algiers, killing at least 21 people; south-west of Algiers, 36 people were killed by Islamic fundamentalists. Hutu militia shot dead three Spanish aid workers in Rwanda. **20–21.** Islamic fundamentalists killed at least 98 people in Algeria. **31.** Thirty-one people were decapitated in Medea, Algeria, by men believed to be Islamic fundamentalists.

FEBRUARY 1997

6. Four people died in clashes between rioters and police in Johannesburg, South Africa. **18.** Armed men killed 33 people in a village south of Algiers. **24–25.** Islamic fundamentalists in Algeria killed 29 people.

MARCH 1997

2. Zaïrean rebels captured the town of Lubutu and the Tingi Tingi refugee camp, causing 160,000 refugees to flee. **12.** At least six people died during a demonstration by Zulus in Johannesburg to commemorate the deaths of eight Inkatha supporters in Johannesburg in 1994. The Nigerian government charged Nobel prize-winner Wole Soyinka and 14 other opponents of the regime with treason. **13.** Six people were arrested following an attempt to assassinate President Buyoya of Burundi. **15.** Zaïrean rebels captured the city of Kisangani. **18.** The parliament of Zaïre passed a motion of no confidence in Prime Minister Kengo wa Dondo; he was ousted by the military on 19 March. **19.** Islamic fundamentalists killed 32 people in Algeria.

APRIL 1997

2. Etienne Tshisekedi was appointed prime minister of Zaïre. **3–4.** More than 80 people were killed by Islamic fundamentalists in Algeria. **5.** Zaïrean rebels captured Mbuji-Mayi, the capital of Eastern Kasai region. **9.** Prime Minister Tshisekedi of Zaïre was arrested and Likulia Balongo was appointed as his successor; rebels captured Lubumbashi. **11.** The MPLA and UNITA formed a power-sharing government in Angola. **22.** Islamic fundamentalists murdered 93 people in Algeria; a further 42 were killed on 24 April. **25.** At least 21 people died when a bomb exploded beneath a passenger train near Algiers. **30.** The UN began an airlift of Rwandan Hutu refugees from Zaïre to Rwanda.

MAY 1997

4. President Mobutu of Zaïre and the rebel leader Laurent Kabila met unsuccessfully for peace talks on a South African ship at Pointe Noire in the Republic of Congo. Ninety-one Rwandan Hutu refugees died while being transported out of Zaïre by train. **7.** President Mobutu left Zaïre for a meeting of regional leaders in Gabon. **17.** Laurent Kabila declared himself head of state of the Democratic Republic of Congo, formerly Zaïre, and his troops took over the capital, Kinshasa. Former President Mobutu left the country. **23.** President Kabila announced a transitional government. **25.** President Kabbah of Sierra Leone was ousted in a coup led by army officers. **26.** President Kabila banned political parties from the new Democratic Republic of Congo.

JUNE 1997

5. The pro-government National Democratic Rally (RND) won 155 of the 380 seats in legislative elections in Algeria. **8.** A militia group attempted to seize Brazzaville and oust the government in the Republic of Congo. **11.** President Lissouba and the head of the militia, Gen. Sassou-Nguesso, called for a cease-fire in Brazzaville but fighting resumed on 15 June. **16.** An aid official claimed forces loyal to President Kabila had killed 250,000 refugees in the Democratic Republic of Congo. **18.** Fighting broke out in Uganda between government forces and rebels believed to be supported by former Zaïrean soldiers and Rwandan Hutus. **19.** Fifty-two people were killed in fighting in Sierra Leone.

JULY 1997

20. Charles Taylor won the presidential election in Liberia. **27.** Alliance for Democracy, the ruling party in Mali, won the legislative elections, which were boycotted by most opposition parties.

AUGUST 1997

7. Sudan government forces killed 400 members of the Sudan People's Liberation Army. **28.** The UN Security Council voted to impose sanctions on UNITA unless it complied with a UN-brokered peace accord. **28.** Islamic militants were blamed for the deaths of 98 civilians in Algeria.

THE AMERICAS

SEPTEMBER 1996

10. Susan McDougal, a former business partner of President Clinton, was imprisoned for contempt of court after refusing to testify about the President's alleged procurement of an illegal loan.

OCTOBER 1996

16. President Clinton and the Republican presidential nominee Robert Dole took part in the second of

two television debates. **20.** Arnoldo Alemán Lacayo won the presidential election in Nicaragua.

NOVEMBER 1996

5. Bill Clinton was re-elected president of the USA; the Republican Party retained control of the House of Representatives and the Senate.

DECEMBER 1996

17. President Bucaram of Ecuador survived an assassination attempt. MRTA guerrillas seized 460 hostages at the Japanese ambassador's residence in Lima, Peru, and demanded the release of their imprisoned leader; 38 hostages were released on 20 December and a further 225 hostages on the 23rd. **29.** Left-wing guerrillas in Guatemala signed a peace agreement with the government, ending 36 years of civil war.

JANUARY 1997

7. Newt Gingrich was re-elected Speaker of the US House of Representatives despite an investigation by the House ethics committee into alleged misuse of charitable donations. **20.** President Clinton was sworn in for a second term as president of the USA. **21.** Newt Gingrich was reprimanded by the House of Representatives and fined £180,000 for ethics violations involving the use of charitable donations for political purposes.

FEBRUARY 1997

6. The Ecuadorean legislature dismissed President Bucaram on the ground of mental incapacity and swore in Fabián Alarcón as acting president. **9.** The Ecuadorean legislature named vice-president Rosalia Arteaga as president; she resigned two days later and was replaced by Fabián Alarcón on 12 February.

MARCH 1997

4. MRTA guerrillas holding hostages at the Japanese embassy in Lima rejected an offer of asylum in Cuba. **6.** President Jagan of Guyana died; Samuel Hinds, the prime minister, was sworn in as his successor. **18.** President Clinton's nominee as director of the CIA, Anthony Lake, withdrew his nomination. **20.** David Saul, the prime minister of Bermuda, resigned. **25.** Pamela Gordon was elected prime minister of Bermuda. **27.** The bodies of 39 members of the Heaven's Gate sect were discovered in a house in California, USA, following a mass suicide.

APRIL 1997

14. James McDougal, a former business partner of President Clinton, was sentenced to three years' imprisonment for fraud. **22.** Peruvian armed forces stormed the Japanese ambassador's residence in Lima, releasing hostages held by MRTA guerrillas since 17 December and shooting dead all 14 rebels. **25.** The US Senate voted to ratify the Chemical Weapons Convention.

DIANA, PRINCESS OF WALES
1961–1997

MOTHER TERESA
1910–1997

Lady Diana Spencer and the Prince of Wales married in July 1981 (*Rex Features*)

The Princess was a tireless worker for charity; her last overseas engagement was a visit to victims of land-mines (*Rex Features*)

The Princess's companion in the final weeks of her life was Dodi Fayed, also a victim of the car crash which killed her (*Rex Features*)

The Princess's sons, Princes William and Harry, her brother Earl Spencer, the Prince of Wales and Prince Philip followed the Princess's coffin to Westminster Abbey, where her funeral was held on 6 September 1997 (*Rex Features*)

THE GENERAL ELECTION
The Labour Party won a landslide victory in May 1997 and formed the first Labour government for 18 years under Tony Blair (*Rex Features*)

CONSERVATIVE PARTY LEADERSHIP
John Major stepped down as leader of the Conservative Party after losing the general election in May 1997 (*top, Popperfoto*). The Conservative leader elected by MPs in June is William Hague (*below, Rex Features*)

NORTHERN IRELAND
There was rioting throughout Northern Ireland in July 1997 after an Orange Order march was allowed to pass through a nationalist area; the Orange Order rerouted or cancelled four subsequent marches.
In July the IRA announced a restoration of its 1994 cease-fire, in time for Sinn Fein to be invited to attend peace talks beginning in September (*PA News*)

HONG KONG
A British colony for 99 years, Hong Kong returned to Chinese sovereignty on 1 July 1997 (*Rex Features*)

ALBANIA
The collapse of pyramid investment schemes and consequent loss of people's savings provoked rioting and near civil war in Albania in spring 1997 (*Rex Features*)

THE MIDDLE EAST
Tension over the lack of progress in the peace settlement provoked a Palestinian bombing in Jerusalem in July 1997 that killed at least 13 people (*Popperfoto*)

CENTRAL AFRICA
Fighting between Zaïrean Tutsis and the Zaïrean army in eastern Zaïre in late 1996 caused Rwandan refugees in the area to flee; there were reports of mass killings (*AFP*)

COUP IN ZAÏRE
The ethnic fighting in eastern Zaïre developed into an uprising led by opponents of President Mobutu's rule. The rebels captured the capital in May 1997, ousting Mobutu and forming a new government (*Rex Features*)

FLOODING
Torrential rainfall in Europe in July 1997 caused widespread flooding in Poland, Germany and the Czech Republic; at least 100 people died (*Popperfoto*)

In Britain, there was also flooding and events such as the Glastonbury Festival and Wimbledon were affected (*Rex Features*)

MONTSERRAT ERUPTIONS
Volcanic activity on the Caribbean island of Montserrat increased in severity from spring 1997 and two-thirds of the island is now uninhabitable (*Associated Press*)

EXPEDITION TO MARS
A robot explorer from the Pathfinder mission to Mars landed on the planet's surface in July 1997 and started to send back pictures and other data (*Rex Features*)

COMET HALE-BOPP
the early part of 1997 the comet Hale-Bopp was visible in the night sky as it reached its closest point to
e Earth (*Rex Features*)

OBITUARIES
Deaths included (left to right): (*top*) Laurie Lee, Deng Xiaoping, Sir Laurens van der Post, Sir James Goldsmith (*Rex Features*); (*bottom*) Denis Compton (*Allsport*); Dorothy Lamour; James Stewart; Robert Mitchum (*Rex Features*)

Tommy Lawton (*centre*), England centre-forward, died in November 1996 (*Associated Press*)

WORLD HEAVYWEIGHT TITLE FIGHT
The fight between Mike Tyson and Evander Holyfield in June 1997 was stopped after Tyson bit off part of Holyfield's ear; Tyson was fined and banned from boxing for a year (*Allsport*)

YOUNG CHAMPIONS
Tiger Woods (*left*) became the first black golfer to win the US Masters and its youngest-ever winner in April 1997; in July Martina Hingis became the youngest women's singles champion at Wimbledon since 1887 (*Allsport*)

LIONS TRIUMPH IN SOUTH AFRICA
The British Lions won the rugby union test match series against South Africa in summer 1997 (*Allsport*)

THE ASHES
Although England made a good showing in the test matches, the Australians retained the Ashes
(*Hugh Routledge, Times Newspapers Ltd*)

MAY 1997

2. President Clinton and Republican leaders in Congress agreed to balance the federal budget by 2002. 27. The Supreme Court of the USA ruled that President Clinton could not claim constitutional immunity to avoid a sexual harassment lawsuit. 29. Three Supreme Court judges in Peru were dismissed after opposing a constitutional amendment which would allow President Fujimori to run for a third term in 2000.

JUNE 1997

2 The Liberal Party was returned to power in Canada, winning 155 of the 301 seats.

JULY 1997

6. The ruling Institutional Revolutionary Party lost control of the lower house of Congress in legislative elections in Mexico.

AUGUST 1997

18. President Clinton announced that the USA would support an international ban on land-mines. 23. The voluntary evacuation began of the island of Montserrat, two-thirds of which is now uninhabitable because of volcanic eruptions and which is threatened with further severe volcanic activity.

ASIA

SEPTEMBER 1996

2. The government of the Philippines signed a peace agreement with the Moro National Liberation Front, ending a 24-year rebellion. 8. A referendum in Okinawa, Japan, overwhelmingly approved a reduction in the US military presence on the island. 18. Eleven North Koreans were found dead and one was captured in South Korea following a failed attempt to infiltrate South Korea during which their submarine ran aground; a further seven were shot the following day and four bodies were discovered on 20 September. 21. Prime Minister Banharn Silpa-archa of Thailand announced his intention to resign. 22. Pro-China candidates won seven of the eight directly-elected seats in Macao's legislature. 23. Four gunmen murdered 21 people in a mosque in Multan, Pakistan, in a wave of violence which followed the killing of Prime Minister Bhutto's estranged brother. 26–27. Taliban forces in Afghanistan seized Kabul, driving government forces northwards; former President Najibullah was executed and a six-man interim ruling council set up. 29. Sri Lankan government troops seized the Tamil Tiger stronghold of Kilinochchi.

OCTOBER 1996

5. Taliban forces attacked the forces of the ousted Afghan government, led by Gen. Ahamd Shah Massoud, which had fled to the Panjshir Valley,

north of Kabul. 7. Protesters marched through Lahore to demand the resignation of Pakistan's Prime Minister Benazir Bhutto. 8. The forces of Gen. Rashid Dostum attacked Taliban troops near the Salang Pass, in north Afghanistan. Five divisions of the Khmer Rouge in Cambodia defected to the government. 10. Supporters of Gen. Massoud, Gen. Dostum and Abdul Karim Khalili formed a Supreme Defence Council for the Defence of Afghanistan to combine their forces against the Taliban. 12. The forces of Gen. Massoud gained control of the towns of Charikar and Jabal os-Siraj from the Taliban, which was forced to retreat. 16. The Taliban held peace talks with Gen. Dostum and Abdul Karim Khalili after Gen. Massoud warned the Taliban to leave Kabul. 20. The Liberal Democratic Party won the largest share of the votes in a general election in Japan. 30. Pro-democracy activist Wang Dan was sentenced to 11 years' imprisonment for conspiring to subvert the Chinese government.

NOVEMBER 1996

5. The President of Pakistan dismissed the government of Prime Minister Benazir Bhutto, dissolved the National Assembly and the state and provincial assemblies, and ordered the arrest of the interior minister Asif Ali Zardari, Benazir Bhutto's husband. 7. The Japanese *Diet* re-elected Prime Minister Ryutaro Hashimoto to head a minority Liberal Democratic government. 17. The New Aspiration Party won the largest number of seats in Thailand's general election. 25. Gen. Chavlit Yongchaiyudh was sworn in as prime minister of Thailand. 29. China and India signed a series of treaties designed to reduce tensions over their disputed comon border.

DECEMBER 1996

11. Tung Chee-Hwa was appointed Hong Kong's chief executive-designate, to take office in July 1997. 21. A 60-member provisional legislature for Hong Kong was selected in China. 25. A bomb exploded in Lhasa, Tibet. 26. The South Korean government pushed through controversial labour legislation, prompting widespread strikes. 30. Thirty-three people died when a bomb, thought to have been planted by Bodo separatists, exploded on a train in Assam, India.

JANUARY 1997

2. The ruling People's Action Party won 81 of the 83 seats in Singapore's general election. 3. The interim government in Pakistan established a Council for Defence and National Security, comprising the president and military leaders, to formulate foreign, defence and economic policy. 29. Fighting broke out between Dayaks and Madurese migrants in the Indonesian province of Kalimantan on Borneo; more than 300 people died.

FEBRUARY 1997

3. Nawaz Sharif was elected prime minister of Pakistan and his party, the Pakistan Muslim League, won a majority of seats in the National Assembly. 5–6. Nine people died in anti-Han Chinese riots in Yining, China. 12. Government troops in Myanmar launched an offensive against Karen National Union guerrillas; about 20,000 refugees fled to Thailand. 19. China's elder statesman Deng Xiaoping died. 21. The prime minister of North Korea, Kang Song San, was dismissed. 25. At least seven people were killed in three bomb explosions in Urumqi, China.

MARCH 1997

5. North and South Korea held their first talks for 25 years. 6. Fighting between government forces and Tamil Tiger rebels left 213 people dead in eastern Sri Lanka. Sher Bahadur Deuba resigned as prime minister of Nepal after his coalition government lost a vote of confidence in the legislature. 24. The Sri Lankan navy sank ten Tamil Tiger gunboats. 28. India and Pakistan began talks over Kashmir. 30. The Congress (I) Party withdrew its parliamentary support for the coalition government in India.

APRIL 1997

1. The National Assembly in Pakistan amended the constitution to remove the president's power to dismiss an elected government and to dissolve the National Assembly. 11. The Indian government lost a vote of confidence; H. D. Deve Gowda stayed on as caretaker prime minister. 20. Inder Kumar Gujral became prime minister of India after being elected leader of the ruling United Front coalition. 21. China imprisoned the abbot of the Tashilumpo, one of Tibet's senior religious leaders, for subversive activities. 22. The USA imposed economic sanctions at Myanmar in protest at alleged human rights violations. 27. Tamil Tiger rebels in Sri Lanka killed 22 soldiers and six policemen in two ambushes.

MAY 1997

18. Natsagiin Bagabandi, the leader of the former Communist Party, won the Mongolian presidential election. 24. The Taliban captured the northern town of Mazar-i-Sharif in Afghanistan, stronghold of the opposition alliance led by Gen. Dostum, who went into exile in Turkey. 25. A shopping mall was set alight during a riot in Banjarmasin, Indonesia, between supporters of rival political parties; 130 people were killed. 27. Hezb-i-Wahdat and forces loyal to Gen. Malik ousted the Taliban from Mazar-i-Sharif despite having earlier collaborated with the Taliban. 28–29. Fourteen people died in attacks by anti-government rebels in East Timor, Indonesia. 30. The forces of Gen. Massoud claimed to have recaptured much of northern Afghanistan from the Taliban.

JUNE 1997

18. The Khmer Rouge leader Pot Pot was reported to have surrendered to Khmer Rouge troops aligned with the Cambodian government. 23. India and Pakistan agreed to set up eight working parties to discuss outstanding disputes, including Kashmir.

JULY 1997

1. China assumed sovereignty of Hong Kong, hitherto a British colony. 6. Prince Ranariddh was ousted in Cambodia in a coup by troops loyal to co-Prime Minister Hun Sen. 16. North and South Korean troops exchanged fire across their mutual border.

AUGUST 1997

14. South Korea began shipping food to famine-stricken North Korea. 15. India celebrated 50 years of independence. 27. North Korea pulled out of talks with the USA on nuclear proliferation after demands for the repatriation of two defectors were rejected.

AUSTRALASIA AND THE PACIFIC

SEPTEMBER 1996

22. A cancer sufferer in Darwin, Australia, became the first person to die under the Northern Territory's voluntary euthanasia legislation.

OCTOBER 1996

4. The New Zealand government announced a £77.4 million deal with the Ngai Tahu tribe to settle a land claim. 12. The general election in New Zealand, the first to use a proportional representation system, produced no outright winner. 13. The head of the transitional government in the Papua New Guinea province of Bougainville, Theodore Miriung, was assassinated.

DECEMBER 1996

10. The National Party in New Zealand formed a coalition government with the New Zealand First party.

MARCH 1997

20. Rioting broke out in Port Moresby, Papua New Guinea; the Prime Minister, Sir Julius Chan, suspended a contract hiring British mercenaries to put down the nine-year rebellion on Bougainville. 24. The Australian government overturned the law permitting euthanasia in the Northern Territory. 26. Sir Julius Chan resigned as prime minister of Papua New Guinea; John Giheno was appointed caretaker prime minister the following day.

AUGUST 1997

28. The Australian parliament approved the holding of a national summit in 1998 or 1999 to decide on whether to become a republic.

EUROPE

SEPTEMBER 1996

5. The French government announced a programme of tax cuts intended to revive the economy. 15. The separatist leader Umberto Bossi declared the independence of the state of 'Padania' in northern Italy. 16. The Prime Ministers of Hungary and Romania signed a treaty in which they agreed to respect each other's borders and the rights of the Hungarian minority in Transylvania, Romania. France deactivated its land-based nuclear missiles. 22. A general election in Greece was won by the ruling socialist Pasok party whose leader, Costas Simitis, was reappointed prime minister.

OCTOBER 1996

8. The Pope underwent an operation to remove his appendix; it was announced that he is suffering from Parkinson's disease. A Turkish fighter jet crashed into the Aegean Sea after being attacked by Greek aircraft. 13. A Greek Cypriot was shot dead by Turkish soldiers in the buffer zone separating the Greek and Turkish communities in Cyprus. 17. French public sector workers staged a one-day strike in protest at government austerity measures. 23. The prime minister of Norway, Gro Harlem Brundtland, resigned. 27. Petar Stoyanov, the leader of the opposition Union of Democratic Forces, won the first round of Bulgaria's presidential election. The Labour Party won the general election in Malta.

NOVEMBER 1996

3. Petar Stoyanov was elected president of Bulgaria. The coalition led by the Serbian President Slobodan Milosevic won a majority of seats in elections to the lower chamber of the Federal Yugoslav parliament. 17. Emil Constantinescu was elected president of Romania.

DECEMBER 1996

3. A bomb exploded in a Paris train, killing four people. 21. Zhan Videnov resigned as prime minister of Bulgaria. 22. Greek farmers lifted a 25-day blockade of roads and ended a strike over pay.

JANUARY 1997

10. President Zhelev of Bulgaria announced that the former Communist Party would not be invited to form a new government after protesters attacked parliament. 15. Bulgaria's ruling Socialist Party agreed to hold elections by the end of the year but opposition demonstrations continued. 18. The

Austrian Chancellor, Franz Vranitzky, resigned. 20. Prime Minister Andris Šķēle of Latvia resigned. 21. Germany and the Czech Republic signed an accord apologizing to each other for their actions during and just after the Nazi era. 22. The Reform Party withdrew from the ruling coalition, prompting the collapse of the Estonian government. 26. Victims of failed pyramid investment schemes in Albania clashed with riot police in Tirana.

FEBRUARY 1997

3. Mario Frick was re-elected prime minister of Liechtenstein. 19. Spanish lorry drivers ended a 13-day strike over diesel prices and the retirement age. 28. King Michael of Romania returned to the country for his first official visit after 50 years in exile.

MARCH 1997

1. Prime Minister Aleksander Meksi of Albania resigned. 2. A state of emergency was declared in Albania; up to 12 people died in clashes with riot police. 3. President Berisha was re-elected by parliament despite unrest in Albania. 5. Prime Minister Necmettin Erbakan of Turkey signed a plan formulated by the military to limit Islamic radicalism. At least 15,000 demonstrators clashed with police in an attempt to prevent a convoy of radioactive waste from reaching a storage site in Gorleben, Germany. 9. President Berisha of Albania conceded opposition demands for a government of national unity and elections within two months. 10. Rebels in southern Albania rejected President Berisha's concessions and called for his resignation. German miners protested in Bonn against a government plan to close ten pits and cut jobs in the industry. 13. The German government reached an agreement with miners to provide an additional £110 million subsidy before 2000. 19. The Italian government declared a state of emergency following the arrival of more than 10,000 refugees from Albania. 28. The UN Security Council approved the formation of a multinational intervention force for Albania.

APRIL 1997

11. The first members of a 6,000-strong multinational intervention force arrived in Albania. 20. The Union of Democratic Forces defeated the ruling Socialist Party in a general election in Bulgaria.

MAY 1997

5–6. Ninety-three rebel Kurds and 12 Turkish government soldiers died in clashes in south-east Turkey. 9. Venetian separatists briefly occupied the campanile (bell-tower) in St Mark's Square before being arrested. 20. Greek Cypriots rioted in Nicosia following a UN-sponsored pop concert in the buffer zone separating the Greek and Turkish parts of the island. 25. Polish voters approved a new constitution in a referendum. 26. Prime Minister Alain

Juppé announced his resignation following a poor performance by the centre-right coalition government in the first round of France's legislative elections on 24 May.

JUNE 1997

1. The Socialist Party and its allies won an overall majority in France's legislative election, ousting the centre-right government. 6. Fianna Fail won the most seats in Ireland's general election and formed a coalition government with the Progressive Democrats. 15. Franjo Tudjman was elected president of Croatia for the third time. 20. President Demirel invited Mesut Yilmaz, leader of the Motherland Party, to form a new Turkish government. 27. A Socialist-led coalition won the first round of voting in a general election in Albania.

JULY 1997

9. Greece and Turkey announced a six-point peace agreement. 9–13. The leaders of Cyprus's Greek and Turkish communities met in New York State, USA, for talks on reuniting the island under a federal structure. 24. Rexhep Medjani was elected president of Albania by the legislature.

AUGUST 1997

25. Egon Krenz, the former Communist leader, was sentenced to six and a half years' imprisonment for his part in the killing of three people who were shot trying to escape East Germany.

COMMONWEALTH OF INDEPENDENT STATES

SEPTEMBER 1996

22. President Ter-Petrosyan of Armenia was elected for a second five-year term; the election was followed by accusations of corruption and by demonstrations.

OCTOBER 1996

17. President Yeltsin of Russia dismissed Gen. Lebed, National Security Adviser and secretary of the presidential Security Council, who was accused of planning a coup.

NOVEMBER 1996

5. President Yeltsin of Russia underwent a successful multiple heart bypass operation. 14. President Lukashenko of Belarus dismissed the chairman of the electoral commission who had criticized a referendum on the proposed constitution to be held later in the month. 18. Mikhail Chigir, the prime minister of Belarus, resigned because of his opposition to the referendum. 24. The referendum in Belarus endorsed a new constitution which increased the President's powers. 26. The supporters of President Lukashenko of Belarus set up a breakaway parliament.

DECEMBER 1996

14. A renegade Chechen guerrilla leader seized 22 Russian soldiers in Dagestan in an attempt to scupper the Chechen-Russian peace agreement. 16–17. Six Red Cross workers were shot dead in Chechenia, prompting the suspension of all Red Cross relief efforts. 23. President Yeltsin of Russia returned to work after an absence of nearly five months due to illness. 29. Russia withdrew its last troops from Chechenia.

JANUARY 1997

8. President Yeltsin of Russia was admitted to hospital suffering from pneumonia; he was discharged 13 days later. 27. Aslan Maskhadov was elected president of Chechenia.

MARCH 1997

11. President Yeltsin dismissed all but two members of the Russian government. 28. Leaders of the members of the Commonwealth of Independent States (CIS) met in Moscow.

APRIL 1997

2. Russia and Belarus signed a treaty of union providing for closer economic, political and military ties. 20. Fighting broke out between Armenian and Azerbaijani troops in the enclave of Nagorno-Karabakh.

MAY 1997

12. Russia and Chechenia signed a peace agreement formally ending the Chechen separatist war. 31. Russia and Ukraine signed a treaty agreeing to divide the Black Sea fleet and the port of Sebastapol.

AUGUST 1997

9. Fighting broke out between the forces of Col. Makhmud Khudoberdiyev and troops loyal to the Tajikistan government.

THE FORMER YUGOSLAVIA

SEPTEMBER 1996

14. Bosnians voted in a general election for a three-member presidency, a national House of Representatives, and assemblies for both the Srpska Republika and the Muslim-Croat Federation. The Muslim Party of Democratic Rights (SDA) rejected in advance the results from the Serb areas, which they claimed were invalid due to irregularities. 18. Bosnian President Alija Izetbegovic was declared to have won the most votes in the Bosnian presidential election, followed by Mladen Ivanic, a Serb, and Kresimir Zubak, a Croat.

OCTOBER 1996

1. The UN formally lifted sanctions against the Federal Republic of Yugoslavia.

NOVEMBER 1996

8. Gen. Ratko Mladic was dismissed as head of the Bosnian Serb armed forces by President Biljana Plavsic but only formally stepped down on 28 November. **12.** Serb police attacked Muslim civilians attempting to return to a village in a Bosnian Serb-occupied area of northern Bosnia. **29.** Drazen Erdemovic, a Bosnian Croat, was sentenced to ten years' imprisonment by the International War Crimes Tribunal for the Former Yugoslavia for participating in a massacre of Muslim civilians in July 1995.

DECEMBER 1996

4–5. A peace implementation conference on Bosnia-Hercegovina opened in London. **20.** The NATO-led Stabilization Force (SFOR) replaced IFOR as the international peacekeeping force in Bosnia-Hercegovina. **24–26.** Riot police clashed with protesters in Belgrade, Yugoslavia, following five weeks of protests against President Milosevic of Serbia.

JANUARY 1997

14. The electoral commission in Yugoslavia conceded that the opposition *Zajedno* coalition had won control of the city assemblies in Belgrade and Nis. **27.** The Yugoslav state municipal court upheld an earlier decision rejecting Zajedno's claim to have won control of Belgrade's city council; Zajedno took over control of the city council in Nis.

FEBRUARY 1997

4 President Milosevic of Serbia agreed to recognize the electoral victory of Zajedno in Belgrade following two days of violence. **11.** The Serbian parliament passed an emergency law recognizing opposition victories in municipal elections in November; opposition demonstrations continued. **14.** International arbitrators decided to retain international supervision of the disputed town of Brcko, Bosnia. **21.** Zoran Djindjic, the first non-socialist mayor of Belgrade, was sworn in.

MAY 1997

7. The International War Crimes Tribunal for the Former Yugoslavia found Dusan Tadic, a Bosnian Serb, guilty of crimes against humanity on 11 counts relating to the abuse of Muslims in detention camps in Bosnia in 1992.

JULY 1997

3. President Plavsic of the Republika Srpska dissolved the legislature and ordered new elections. **10.** British SFOR soldiers arrested one Bosnian Serb indicted on war crimes charges and shot dead another. **14.** Dusan Tadic, a Bosnian Serb war criminal, was sentenced to 20 years' imprisonment. **15.** Slobodan Milosevic was elected President of Yugoslavia.

AUGUST 1997

20. SFOR troops seized control of police stations in Banja Luka in an attempt to forestall a possible coup

against President Plavsic. **26.** The Republika Srpska parliament voted to remove the president's exclusive power over the army. **29.** A bomb exploded in a railway station in Banja Luka, killing one person.

EUROPEAN UNION

OCTOBER 1996

5. EU heads of government met in Dublin to review the Intergovernmental Conference. **13.** The People's Party gained the most votes in Austria's first direct election to the European Parliament, although the right-wing anti-Maastricht Freedom Party made dramatic gains. **14.** Finland joined the European monetary system. **16.** The European Commission approved a plan designed to penalize members of the future economic and monetary union (EMU) who run high budget deficits. **20.** The Centre Party, Social Democratic Party and National Coalition Party each won four seats in the Finnish elections to the European Parliament. **31.** The European Commission assented to a one-off payment by France Telecom to the French government as a means of reducing the country's budget deficit to comply with the criteria for membership of the EMU.

NOVEMBER 1996

7. The Europe of the Nations Group within the European Parliament was dissolved due to lack of members. **25.** Italy rejoined the European exchange rate mechanism (ERM).

DECEMBER 1996

12. The European Parliament approved a balanced budget of ECU 89 billion for 1997. **13–14.** EU heads of state agreed at a meeting in Dublin a 'stability pact', proposals to penalize members of the future EMU who exceed budget deficit targets. Ireland presented a draft revision of the Maastricht Treaty. **19.** Denmark, Finland and Sweden became full members of the Schengen group.

JANUARY 1997

14. José María Gil-Robles Gil-Delgado was elected president of the European Parliament.

FEBRUARY 1997

19. The European Parliament condemned the European Commission and the British government over their handling of the BSE crisis. **21.** The European Commission agreed to allow Italy to impose a one-off tax in order to reduce its budget deficit in preparation for EMU.

APRIL 1997

10. The EU severed diplomatic links with Iran following the conviction in Germany of four Iranians for the murder in 1992 of Iranian Kurdish leaders, which was thought to have been sanctioned by the Iranian government.

JUNE 1997

16–18. The European Council met in Amsterdam to review the Maastricht Treaty. In the Treaty of Amsterdam the members agreed:
– to transfer asylum and immigration policies from the justice and home affairs pillar to the community pillar of the EU
– to incorporate the Schengen Agreement gradually into the EU; the UK and Ireland will have an opt-out
– to include a chapter on employment in the treaty and to insert the Maastricht Treaty's social chapter fully into the treaty
– to extend majority voting to research, customs co-operation and fraud
– to increase the use of qualified majority voting in foreign policy and to appoint a high representative to act as a spokesperson on foreign affairs
– to give the European Parliament new powers of co-decision, to apply to all areas covered by qualified majority voting
25. The executive committee of the Schengen Agreement agreed to admit Italy.

JULY 1997

1. Luxembourg assumed the presidency of the EU. 16. The European Commission announced proposals to admit six new members and to reform the Common Agricultural Policy.

THE MIDDLE EAST

SEPTEMBER 1996

1. The UN postponed the implementation of the agreement allowing Iraq to sell oil and use the revenue to purchase food and humanitarian aid following Iraq's seizure of a Kurdish city in northern Iraq on 30 August. 3. Two US bombers launched cruise missiles at Iraqi targets in southern Iraq; the air exclusion zone in southern Iraq was extended from the 32nd to the 33rd parallel. 4. The new Israeli Prime Minister Benyamin Netanyahu held his first meeting with the Palestinian leader Yasser Arafat. American warships and jets fired cruise missiles at targets in southern Iraq. 5. Iraqi troops began to withdraw from the Kurdish safe haven in northern Iraq. Turkish aircraft attacked suspected Turkish Kurd bases inside the safe haven in northern Iraq; Turkey announced it would create a buffer zone on its border with Iraq to hinder attacks by Kurdish rebels. 8. Kurdish refugees fled to Iran following the capture of the towns of Degala and Koi Sanjak by the Iraqi-government backed Kurdistan Democratic Party (KDP). 9. The KDP captured the city of Sulaimaniya, the stronghold of the Patriotic Union of Kurdistan (PUK). 11–12. Iraqi troops fired on American aircraft patrolling the air exclusion zone in northern Iraq. 18. KDP forces in Iraq shelled a Kurdish refugee camp in Iran, killing four people.

25–27. Sixty-seven people died in clashes between Israeli security forces and Palestinians protesting against the reopening of a tunnel near the Al Aqsa mosque in east Jerusalem.

OCTOBER 1996

1–2. Prime Minister Netanyahu and Yasser Arafat met for an emergency summit in Washington, USA. 6. Peace talks between Israel and the Palestinians opened in Erez. 13. The PUK recaptured Sulaimaniya in northern Iraq from the KDP.

NOVEMBER 1996

26. The Iraqi government agreed to the terms of a UN deal to sell a limited amount of oil to buy food and humanitarian supplies; oil sales resumed 10 December.

DECEMBER 1996

11. Two Jewish settlers were killed by the Popular Front for the Liberation of Palestine near Ramallah on the West Bank. 12. An attempt was made to assassinate Uday Hussein, the son of President Saddam Hussein of Iraq; over 500 people were subsequently detained. 24. Two Israeli soldiers were killed by Hezbollah in southern Lebanon; a soldier had also been killed on 7 December. 31. A bomb exploded in Damascus, Syria, killing at least 15 people.

JANUARY 1997

1. An Israeli soldier opened fire in an Arab market in Hebron, injuring seven Palestinians. 6. Israeli and Palestinian officials agreed to the enlargement of an international observer force in Hebron. 15. Israel agreed to withdraw from 80 per cent of Hebron within ten days. 30. Three Israeli soldiers were killed by a bomb explosion in southern Lebanon.

FEBRUARY 1997

11. Israel began releasing 31 Palestinian women prisoners. 26. The Israeli government approved plans to build 2,500 new houses for Jews at Har Homa in east Jerusalem.

MARCH 1997

3. The UN Security Council decided to maintain sanctions against Iraq. The Israeli government approved plans to build more Jewish homes north of Jerusalem on land captured from Jordan in 1967. 7. The Israeli government agreed to withdraw its troops from nearly 10 per cent of the West Bank. 10. The chief Palestinian negotiator, Mahmoud Abbas, resigned in protest at the alleged inflexibility of the Israeli government. 13. A Jordanian soldier shot dead seven Israeli schoolgirls at Naharayim in the Jordan valley. 15. The Palestinian leader, Yasser Arafat, held a conference for international supporters of opposition to the building of new Israeli homes in east Jerusalem. 19. King Hussein of Jordan dismissed Prime Minister Abdel Karim Kabariti and appointed Abdel Salam Majali to the post. 20.

Palestinians in Bethlehem staged a protest against the construction of a settlement for Jews at Har Homa. **21.** A suicide bomber killed four people in Tel Aviv, Israel.

APRIL 1997

8. Three Palestinians died during clashes with Israeli settlers and police in Hebron. **15.** A fire broke out in a camp for pilgrims near Mecca, Saudi Arabia, killing 343 people.

MAY 1997

14. Turkish troops and members of the KDP began an offensive against the PKK in northern Iraq. **23.** Mohammed Khatami, a reformer, was elected president of Iran. **27.** President Mubarak of Egypt and Prime Minister Netanyahu of Israel met in an attempt to restart the Middle East peace process.

JULY 1997

30. Two Palestinian suicide bombers killed at least 13 people in a market in Jerusalem.

AUGUST 1997

18. Six people died when the Lebanese port of Sidon was shelled by the South Lebanon Army, a pro-Israeli militia force. **19.** Hezbollah guerrillas, based in southern Lebanon, launched rocket attacks on the Israeli town of Kiryat Shemona.

INTERNATIONAL RELATIONS

SEPTEMBER 1996

10. The United Nations (UN) general assembly approved the Comprehensive Test Ban Treaty despite opposition from India. **24.** China, France, Russia, the UK and the USA signed the Comprehensive Test Ban Treaty, although the treaty does not have legal status because of India's refusal to sign.

OCTOBER 1996

15. The Council of Europe agreed to admit Croatia as a member.

NOVEMBER 1996

19. The USA vetoed the reappointment of Boutros Boutros Ghali as Secretary-General of the United Nations. **24–25.** The Asia Pacific Economic Co-operation Forum convened in Manila, the Philippines.

DECEMBER 1996

10–11. NATO foreign ministers reaffirmed their commitment to expanding the organization at a meeting in Brussels. **17.** Kofi Annan was sworn in as UN Secretary-General.

FEBRUARY 1997

3. NATO offered Ukraine a charter agreement involving military co-operation and limited decision-making involvement.

MARCH 1997

13. The UN Secretary-General, Kofi Annan, announced that £76.8 million would be cut from the organization's £625 million budget for 1998–9. **20–21.** President Yeltsin of Russia and President Clinton of the USA met for talks in Helsinki, Finland, which focused on the proposed expansion of NATO. **24.** The EU agreed to strip Myanmar of its trading privileges because of its alleged use of forced labour and human rights abuses. Russia signed a £2.2 billion oil deal with Iraq despite a UN trade and investment embargo.

APRIL 1997

24. China, Russia, Kazakhstan, Kyrgzstan and Tajikistan signed an agreement to limit military activities along their borders.

MAY 1997

14. NATO reached agreement with Russia on the incorporation of the former Soviet states in eastern Europe into the NATO framework. **19.** The USA announced that China's most favoured nation trading status would be renewed. **21.** The UN adopted the Convention on the Law of the Non-Navigational Uses of International Watercourses, a treaty regulating the building of dams and the management of rivers that flow across borders. **27.** Russia signed a security agreement with the 16 NATO members at a meeting in Paris. Russia signed an agreement with the OECD intended to help Russia create a market economy and democratic institutions.

JUNE 1997

15. The heads of government of Bangladesh, Egypt, Indonesia, Iran, Malaysia, Nigeria, Pakistan and Turkey attended the inaugural ceremony of the Developing Eight group of nations in Istanbul, Turkey. **20–22.** The summit of the Eight (the G7 countries and Russia) convened in Denver, USA.

JULY 1997

1. The UK rejoined UNESCO. **8.** NATO agreed to admit the Czech Republic, Hungary and Poland by April 1999. **9.** NATO signed a security pact with Ukraine and inaugurated a Euro-Atlantic Partnership Council. **11.** Sierra Leone was suspended from attending Commonwealth meetings after questions were raised about the military government's respect for democracy. **23.** Laos and Myanmar were admitted as members of ASEAN; consideration of Cambodia's application for membership was suspended.

AUGUST 1997

21. Israel was invited to join the Commonwealth.

Obituaries

DIANA, PRINCESS OF WALES

Diana, Princess of Wales, the third and youngest daughter of Viscount Althorp (later the 8th Earl Spencer) and his first wife (later Mrs Frances Shand Kydd), was born on 1 July 1961 into a family with a long association with royalty; her father was a royal equerry, both of her grandmothers were friends of the Queen Mother, and one of her sisters married The Queen's private secretary.

Lady Diana Spencer first attracted media attention as a possible royal bride in the summer of 1980. Her engagement to the Prince of Wales was announced in February 1981 and the couple were married at St Paul's Cathedral, London, on 29 July 1981. Their first child, Prince William, was born in June 1982 and their second, Prince Harry, in September 1984. However, after some years of increasingly obvious marital strain and unhappiness, particularly on the Princess's part, the Prince and Princess formally separated in December 1992, divorcing in August 1996.

The Princess worked tirelessly for charity, particularly for children, the sick and the poor; her meetings and physical contact with AIDS and leprosy sufferers did much to dispel prejudice about both conditions. In the last year of her life the Princess backed the international campaign for a ban on anti-personnel land-mines and her support brought the issue to world attention; one of her last public engagements was a visit to land-mine victims in Bosnia.

From her engagement onwards, the Princess captured popular imagination, her spontaneity, compassion and rapport with ordinary people breaking through the traditional formality of royal engagements. These qualities, combined with glamour and charisma, attracted a world-wide adulation that fed upon and was fed by relentless media scrutiny of the Princess's life and relationships; this became increasingly intolerable to the Princess after her separation from the Prince of Wales. Media attention intensified in July 1997 when, following a holiday with her sons as guests of Mohamed Al Fayed, the Princess took further trips abroad with his son Dodi. It was during a high-speed drive through Paris pursued by *paparazzi* that their car crashed, killing Dodi Fayed and the chauffeur and leaving the Princess so severely injured that, despite a two-hour fight to resuscitate her, she died in the early hours of 31 August 1997, at the age of 36.

MOTHER TERESA

Mother Teresa was born Agnes Gonxha Bojaxhiu in Skopje (then in Albania) on 27 August 1910. She felt called to join a religious order and entered the Congregation of Loreto nuns, making her first vows in 1931, when she took the name Teresa, and her final vows in 1937. Sister Teresa taught for 17 years in Bengal, then, after receiving in 1946 a 'call' to work with the poorest of the poor, she left her congregation in 1948, undertook some months of medical training and moved to Calcutta, where she started a pavement school for *bustee* children. Former pupils of this school became the first postulants of her community, the Missionaries of Charity, which in 1952 opened its first home for dying destitutes; later, children's homes were also set up.

Although a woman of great humility, Mother Teresa had a formidable strength of purpose and refused to let officialdom or prejudice hinder her efforts to relieve the suffering of the destitute. She also understood the value of publicity in raising funds for the community's work. The growth in donations and in the size of her community as her fame spread enabled the Missionaries of Charity to undertake a wider range of activities, distributing free meals to the poor, starting medical clinics which provided free medicines, mobile clinics for leprosy and tubercular patients, night shelters, etc. Today the community has more than 3,000 novices and professed nuns supported by nearly 40,000 lay co-workers operating over 400 homes in nine countries. The first novitiate outside India was established in Southall, London, in 1971.

Mother Teresa was a tireless worker, even in later years. Despite poor health since 1989, when she began to suffer from heart trouble, she worked in the Calcutta home at the same tasks and keeping the same hours as the rest of the community until her health became too poor. She resigned from running the Missionaries of Charity in March 1997 because of her increasing frailty and died of heart failure in Calcutta on 5 September 1997, at the age of 87.

Agnew, Spiro, vice-president of the USA 1969-73, aged 77 – 17 September 1996

Aldaniti, racehorse and Grand National winner in 1981, aged 27 – March 1997

Allford, David, CBE, architect, aged 70 – 10 August 1997

Amery of Lustleigh, Lord (Julian), PC, Conservative MP for Preston North 1950-66 and Brighton Pavilion 1969-92, junior minister and Minister of State 1957-64, 1970-4, aged 77 – 3 September 1996

Amin, Mohamed, MBE, television cameraman, aged 53 – in a plane crash in the Comoros, 23 November 1996

Atkinson, Thomas, GC, aged 81 – 26 March 1997

Auckland, 9th Baron, aged 71 – 28 July 1997

Audley, 25th Lord, aged 83 – July 1997

Awdry, Revd Wilbert, OBE, clergyman and children's author who created Thomas the Tank Engine, aged 85 – 21 March 1997

Ayres, Lew, American actor, aged 88 – 30 December 1996

Baker, Sir Nicholas, Conservative MP for Dorset North 1979-97 and junior minister 1990-5, aged 58 – 25 April 1997

Bancroft, Lord, GCB, head of the Home Civil Service and Permanent Secretary to the Civil Service Department 1978-81, aged 73 – 19 November 1996

Banks, Lord, CBE, president of the Liberal Party 1968-9, deputy chief whip in the House of Lords 1977-83, aged 78 – 15 June 1997

Baseley, Godfrey, BBC producer who devised *The Archers* radio serial, aged 92 – 2 February 1997

Baxter, Jane, film and stage actress, aged 87 – 13 September 1996

Bell, Quentin, artist and author, aged 86 – 16 December 1996

Beloff, Nora, author and journalist, aged 78 – 12 February 1997

Bentine, Michael, CBE, comedian, member of *The Goon Show*, aged 74 – 26 November 1996

Bevan, David Gilroy, Conservative MP for Birmingham Yardley 1979-92, aged 68 – 12 October 1996

Bevins, Reginald, PC, Conservative MP for Liverpool Toxteth 1950-64, Postmaster-General 1959-64, aged 88 – 16 November 1996

Bidwell, Sydney, Labour MP for Ealing Southall 1966-92, aged 80 – 25 May 1997

Birk, Baroness (Alma), politician and journalist, aged 79 – 29 December 1996

Blishen, Edward, author and broadcaster, aged 76 – 13 December 1996

Bokassa, Jean-Bédel, ruler and self-styled emperor of the Central African Republic 1966-79, aged 75 – 3 November 1996

Borthwick, 23rd Lord, TD, farmer, aged 91 – 30 December 1996

Brown, Robert (Bob), Labour MP for Newcastle West 1966-83 and Newcastle North 1983-7, junior minister 1968-70, 1974-9, aged 75 – 3 September 1996

Brown, Sir William, CBE, managing director of Scottish Television 1966-90 and chairman of the Scottish Arts Council 1992-6, aged 67 – 29 December 1996

Burroughs, William S., American author, aged 83 – 2 August 1997

Cadogan, 7th Earl, MC, landowner and Jockey Club steward, aged 83 – 4 July 1997

Caesar, Irving, American lyricist, aged 101 – 17 December 1996

Calment, Jeanne, the world's oldest person, aged 122 – 4 August 1997

Calthorpe, 10th Baron, airline owner, novelist (as Peter Somerset) and theatrical backer, aged 69 – 23 May 1997

Calvin, Prof. Melvin, American chemist and Nobel laureate 1961, aged 85 – 8 January 1997

Carné, Marcel, French film director, aged 90 – 31 October 1996

Cassels, Field Marshal Sir James, GCB, KBE, DSO, Chief of the General Staff 1965-8, aged 89 – 13 December 1996

Chelmer, Lord, MC, TD, chairman of the Conservative Party executive committee 1957-65, joint treasurer 1965-77, aged 82 – 3 March 1997

Chester, Charlie, MBE, entertainer and radio broadcaster, aged 83 – 26 June 1997

Clydesmuir, 2nd Baron, KT, CB, MBE, TD, former governor of the Bank of Scotland and Lord Lieutenant of Lanarkshire 1963-92, aged 79 – 2 October 1996

Colnbrook, Lord (Humphrey Atkins), KCMG, PC, Conservative MP for Merton and Morden 1955-70, Spelthorne 1970-87, Secretary of State for Northern Ireland 1979-81, aged 74 – 4 October 1996

Compton, Denis, CBE, cricketer, aged 78 – 23 April 1997

Coral, Joe, bookmaker and former head of the Coral Leisure Group, aged 92 – 16 December 1996

Cordell, Alexander, novelist, aged 82 – found dead 9 July 1997

Cousteau, Jacques-Yves, French underwater explorer and film-maker, aged 87 – 25 June 1997

Craig, Charles, opera singer, aged 77 – 23 January 1997

Croft, 2nd Baron, art collector, aged 80 – 11 January 1997

Crowe, Dame Sylvia, DBE, landscape architect, aged 95 – 30 June 1997

Crowther, Leslie, CBE, actor and comedian, aged 63 – 28 September 1996

Cutler, Sir Horace, OBE, leader of the Greater London Council 1977-81, aged 84 – 2 March 1997

Danilova, Alexandra, Russian-born ballet dancer, aged 93 – 13 July 1997

Daresbury, 3rd Baron, chairman of Greenall Whitley 1969-71, aged 67 – 9 September 1996

de Kooning, Willem, Dutch-born artist, aged 92 – 19 March 1997

Deng Xiaoping, paramount leader of China since 1978 and economic modernizer, aged 92 – 19 February 1997

Doig, Peter, Labour MP for Dundee West 1963-79, aged 85 – 31 October 1996

Dolmetsch, Carl, CBE, musician, aged 85 – 11 July 1997

Donovan, Terence, photographer, aged 60 – 22 November 1996

Eccles, Sir John, FRS, Australian physiologist and Nobel laureate 1963, aged 94 – May 1997

Eckersley, Tom, RDI, graphic designer, aged 82 – 1 August 1997

Erdös, Paul, Hungarian-born mathematician, aged 83 – 20 September 1996

Fayed, Dodi, film producer and director of Harrods, aged 42 – 31 August 1997

Fenby, Eric, OBE, musician, amanuensis to Delius, aged 90 – 18 February 1997

Finsberg, Lord (Geoffrey), MBE, Conservative MP for Hampstead 1970-83, Hampstead and Highgate 1983-92, and junior minister, aged 70 – 8 October 1996

Fisher, Sir Nigel, MC, Conservative MP for Hitchin 1950-5, Surbiton 1955-74, Kingston-upon-Thames, Surbiton 1974-83, and junior minister 1962-4, aged 83 – 9 October 1996

Fraser, Ronald, actor, aged 66 – 13 March 1997

Furnival Jones, Sir Martin, CBE, director-general of MI5 1965-72, aged 84 – 1 March 1997

Garnett, John, CBE, director of the Industrial Society 1962-86, aged 76 – 14 August 1997

Gian Singh, VC, aged 76 – 6 October 1996

Gibbon, Gen. Sir John, GCB, OBE, aged 79 – 7 May 1997

Ginsberg, Allen, American poet, aged 70 – 5 April 1997

Gladwyn, 1st Baron (Gladwyn Jebb), GCMG, GCVO, CB, diplomat, an architect of the peacekeeping institutions of the post-war world, acting secretary-general of the UN 1946, Permanent British Representative at the UN 1950-4, Ambassador to France 1954-60, aged 96 – 24 October 1996

Glanusk, 4th Baron, aged 80 – 28 June 1997

Glover, Brian, actor, aged 63 – 24 July 1997

Goldsmith, Sir James, business tycoon and founder of the Referendum Party, aged 64 – 19 July 1997

Goold, Lord, chairman of the Scottish Conservative Party 1983-90, aged 63 – 27 July 1997

Granville, 5th Earl, MC, Lord Lieutenant of the Western Isles 1983-93, aged 77 – 31 October 1996

Green, Hughie, television presenter and entertainer, aged 77 – 3 May 1997

Grey of Codnor, 5th Baron, CBE, AE, aged 93 – 23 December 1996

Griffin, Admiral Sir Anthony, GCB, chairman of British Shipbuilders 1977-80, aged 75 – 16 October 1996

Hackforth, Norman, broadcaster, aged 87 – 14 December 1996

Hammond, Dame Joan, DBE, New Zealand-born opera singer, aged 86 – 26 November 1996

Hanff, Helene, American writer, aged 80 – 9 April 1997

Hankey, 2nd Baron, KCMG, KCVO, diplomat, aged 91 – 28 October 1996

Hanna, Vincent, broadcaster, aged 57 – 22 July 1997

Hanworth, 2nd Viscount, aged 80 – September 1996

Harding, Matthew, businessman, vice-chairman of Chelsea Football Club, aged 42, in a helicopter crash – 22 October 1996

Hardinge of Penshurst, 3rd Baron (George Hardinge), publisher, aged 75 – 14 July 1997

Harriman, Pamela, US Ambassador to France since 1993, aged 76 – 5 February 1997

Harvington, Lord, AE, PC, Conservative MP for St Pancras North 1937-45 and for Nantwich 1955-74, Deputy Speaker of the House of Commons 1970-4, aged 89 – 1 January 1997

Hassan, Sir Joshua, GBE, KCMG, LVO, QC, chief minister of Gibraltar 1964-9 and 1972-87, aged 81 – 1 July 1997

Herbison, Margaret (Peggy), Labour MP for North Lanark 1945-70, Minister of Pensions and National Insurance 1964-6 and Minister of Social Security 1966-7, the first woman to serve as Lord High Commissioner to the General Assembly of the Church of Scotland 1970-1, aged 89 – 29 December 1996

Herzog, Chaim, president of Israel 1983-93, aged 78 – 17 April 1997

Hill, Prof. Dame Elizabeth, DBE, first professor of Slavonic Studies at Cambridge University 1948-68, aged 96 – 17 December 1996

Hillaby, John, writer, naturalist and traveller, aged 79 – 19 October 1996

Hinton, Jack, VC, aged 87 – 28 June 1997

Hiss, Alger, American diplomat accused in 1950 of spying for the USSR in the 1930s, aged 92 – 15 November 1996

Hodge, Capt. Alexander (Sandy), GC, VRD, aged 80 – 4 January 1997

Hogan, Ben, American golfer, four times winner of the US Open Championship, aged 84 – 25 July 1997

Horder, 2nd Baron, publisher, aged 86 – 30 June 1997

Horner, John, general secretary of the Fire Brigades Union 1939-64, Labour MP for Oldbury and Halesowen 1964-70, aged 85 – 11 February 1997

Hughes, Pat, tennis player, aged 94 – 8 May 1997

Huxley, Elspeth, CBE, writer, aged 89 – 10 January 1997

Jagan, Cheddi, president of Guyana since 1992, aged 78 – 6 March 1997

Jak (Raymond Jackson), cartoonist, aged 70 – 27 July 1997

Jayewardene, Junius, executive president of Sri Lanka 1978-89, aged 90 – 1 November 1996

Jepson, Arthur, cricketer, footballer and umpire, aged 82 – 17 July 1997

John, Otto, German secret agent, aged 88 – 26 March 1997

Junor, John, editor of the *Sunday Express* 1954-86 and newspaper columnist, aged 78 – 3 May 1997

Kendrew, Sir John, CBE, FRS, biochemist and joint winner of the Nobel prize for chemistry 1962, aged 80 – 23 August 1997

Kinnaird, 13th Baron, aged 84 – 27 February 1997

Kitson, Alex, deputy general secretary of the Transport and General Workers' Union 1981-6, member of the Labour Party's National Executive Committee 1968-86, aged 75 – 2 August 1997

Lacoste, René, French tennis player, aged 92 – 12 October 1996

Lamour, Dorothy, American film actress, aged 81 – 23 September 1996

Launder, Frank, screenwriter and film director, aged 89 – 23 February 1997

Lawton, Tommy, former England and Everton footballer, aged 77 – 6 November 1996

Leadbitter, Edward (Ted), Labour MP for Hartlepool 1964-92, aged 77 – 24 December 1996

Leakey, Mary, archaeologist and anthropologist, aged 83 – 9 December 1996

Lee, Laurie, MBE, poet and author, aged 82 – 13 May 1997

Lewis, Sir Kenneth, Conservative MP for Rutland and Stamford 1959-83, Stamford and Spalding 1983-7, aged 81 – 2 July 1997

Listowel, 5th Earl, GCMG, PC, Labour politician and junior minister 1944-50, Governor-General of Ghana 1957-60, aged 90 – 12 March 1997

Manley, Michael, PC, prime minister of Jamaica 1972-80 and 1989-92, aged 72 – 7 March 1997

Mastroianni, Marcello, Italian film actor, aged 72 – 19 December 1996

May, Rt. Hon. Sir John, former Lord Justice of Appeal 1982-9, headed the inquiries into the cases of the Guildford Four and the Maguire Seven, aged 76 – 15 January 1997

Mayhew, Lord (Christopher), Labour MP for South Norfolk 1945-50 and for Woolwich East (later Greenwich, Woolwich East) 1951-74, junior minister 1946-50, Navy Minister 1964-6, journalist and broadcaster, aged 81 – 7 January 1997

McLaughlin, Patricia, CBE, Ulster Unionist MP for West Belfast 1955-64, aged 80 – 7 January 1997

McMaster, Gordon, MP, Labour and Co-operative MP for Paisley South since 1990, aged 37 – found dead 28 July 1997

Mills, Iain, MP, Conservative MP for Meriden since 1979, aged 56 – found dead 16 January 1997

Mitchum, Robert, American film actor, aged 79 – 1 July 1997

Murray, Ruby, Irish singer, aged 61 – 17 December 1996

Najibullah, Muhammad, president of Afghanistan 1986-92, aged 49 – executed 27 September 1996

Nancarrow, Conlan, American composer, aged 84 – 10 August 1997

Nation, Terry, television scriptwriter who invented the Daleks, aged 66 – 9 March 1997

Neckar, François, couturier, aged 92 – 6 December 1996

Nicholas, Sir Harry, OBE, general secretary of the Labour Party 1968-72, aged 92 – 15 April 1997

Normanton, Sir Tom, TD, Conservative MP for Cheadle 1970-87 and MEP 1973-89, aged 80 – 6 August 1997

Ogden, Eric, MP for Liverpool, West Derby 1964-83 (Labour 1964-81 and SDP 1981-3), aged 73 – 5 May 1997

Patchett, Terry, MP, Labour MP for Barnsley East since 1983, aged 56 – 11 October 1996

Pope, Dudley, naval historian and novelist, aged 71 – 25 April 1997

Porter, Barry, MP, Conservative MP for Bebington and Ellesmere Port 1979-83 and Wirral South since 1983, aged 57 – 3 November 1996

Portland, 11th Earl of, BBC producer, advertising producer and slogan-writer, aged 77 – 30 January 1997

Pritchett, Sir Victor, CH, CBE, short story writer, novelist and critic, aged 96 – 20 March 1997

Proops, Marjorie, OBE, journalist and agony aunt, aged about 85 – 10 November 1996

Prowse, Juliet, actress and dancer, aged 59 – 14 September 1996

Purcell, Edward, American astronomer and physicist, Nobel laureate in 1952, aged 84 – 7 March 1997

Redmond, Martin, MP, Labour MP for Don Valley since 1983, aged 59 – 20 January 1997

Reid, Beryl, OBE, actress, aged 76 – 13 October 1996

Riches, Gen. Sir Ian, KCB, DSO, Commandant-General of the Royal Marines 1959-62, aged 88 – 23 December 1996

Richter, Svyatoslav, Ukrainian classical pianist, aged 82 – 1 August 1997

Rippon of Hexham, Lord (Geoffrey), PC, QC, Conservative MP for Norwich South 1955-64, Hexham 1966-87, Chancellor of the Duchy of Lancaster 1970-4 and negotiator of the UK's entry into the Common Market, aged 72 – 28 January 1997

Roberts-Jones, Ivor, CBE, RA, sculptor, aged 83 – 9 December 1996

Roskill, Lord, PC, Lord of Appeal in Ordinary 1980-6, aged 85 – 4 October 1996

Rushton, Willie, comedian, satirist and cartoonist, aged 59 – 11 December 1996

Sagan, Carl, American astronomer and author, aged 62 – 20 December 1996

Salkind, Alexander, independent film producer, aged 75 – 8 March 1997

Saunders, Michael, CB, QC, Treasury Solicitor and head of the government legal service since 1995, aged 52 – 17 December 1996

Scott, Ronnie, jazz musician and nightclub owner, aged 69 – 23 December 1996

Seear, Baroness, PC, leader of the Liberal peers 1984-8, deputy leader of the Liberal Democrats in the House of Lords since 1988, aged 83 – 23 April 1997

Selby, 4th Viscount, aged 54 – 10 January 1997

Sherfield, 1st Baron (Sir Roger Makins), GCB, GCMG, FRS, Ambassador to the USA 1953-6, permanent secretary to the Treasury 1956-9, chairman of the Atomic Energy Authority 1960-4, chancellor of Reading University 1970-92, aged 92 – 9 November 1996

Shersby, Sir Michael, MP, Conservative MP for Uxbridge since 1972, aged 64 – 8 May 1997

Silverman, Julius, Labour MP for Birmingham Erdington, later Birmingham Aston, from 1945-83, aged 90 – 21 September 1996

Smallwood, Air Chief Marshal Sir Denis, GBE, KCB, DSO, DFC, aged 78 – 26 July 1997

Solti, Sir Georg, KBE, conductor, aged 84 – 5 September 1997

Somerset Fry, Plantagenet, writer, aged 65 – 10 September 1996

Sondes, 5th Earl, aged 56 – 2 December 1996

Stewart, James, American film actor, aged 89 – 2 July 1997

Stewart, Kenneth, Labour MEP for Merseyside since 1984, aged 71 – 3 September 1996

Sugden, Maj.-Gen. Francis, CB, CBE, Chief of Staff, British Army of the Rhine 1989-91 and Lieutenant-Governor of the Royal Hospital, Chelsea, since 1992, aged 59 – 6 August 1997

Tangye, Derek, author, aged 84 – 26 October 1996

Taylor of Gosforth, Lord (Peter), PC, Lord Chief Justice 1992-6, author of the report into the Hillsborough football disaster, aged 66 – 28 April 1997

Thomas, Clem, rugby player and journalist, aged 67 – 5 September 1996

Tikhonov, Nikolai, prime minister of the USSR 1980-5, aged 92 – 1 June 1997

Tinker, Jack, theatre critic of the *Daily Mail*, aged 58 – 28 October 1996

Tiny Tim, American popular singer, aged 74 – 30 November 1996

Todd, Lord, OM, D.SC., D.phil., FRS, organic chemist, Nobel laureate 1957 and president of the Royal Society 1975-80, aged 89 – 10 January 1997

Trevor, 4th Baron, aged 68 – January 1997

Trimlestown, 20th Baron, aged 69 – 19 August 1997

Tyrwhitt, Brig. Dame Mary, DBE, TD, founder-director of the Women's Royal Army Corps 1949-50, aged 93 – 13 February 1997

van der Post, Sir Laurens, CBE, writer and explorer, aged 90 – 16 December 1996

Vassall, John, Soviet spy, aged 76 – November 1996

Végh, Sándor, HON. CBE, Hungarian-born violinist, aged 91 – 8 January 1997

Versace, Gianni, Italian fashion designer, aged 50 – murdered 15 July 1997

Vickrey, William, American economist and Nobel laureate 1996, aged 82 – 11 October 1996

Wald, George, American biologist and winner of the Nobel Prize for medicine in 1967, aged 90 – April 1997

Wedgwood, Dame Veronica (C. V. Wedgwood), OM, DBE, FBA, historian, aged 86 – 9 March 1997

Weight, Carel, CH, CBE, RA, painter, aged 88 – 13 August 1997

Wilkinson, Prof. Sir Geoffrey, FRS, chemist and Nobel laureate 1973, aged 75 – 26 September 1996

Wilson, Jack, Olympic oarsman 1948, aged 82 – 16 February 1997

Wooller, Wilfred, Welsh rugby player and cricketer, aged 84 – 10 March 1997

Younger of Leckie, 3rd Viscount, OBE, TD, aged 90 – 25 June 1997

Zinnemann, Fred, Austrian-born film director, aged 89 – 14 March 1997

Archaeology

Stonehenge, a World Heritage Site and one of the best-known ancient monuments in the UK, has for many years posed intractable problems to those concerned with its conservation and ambience. These difficulties relate not least to the pressure of visitors and the proximity of modern roads making it impossible to demonstrate successfully the site's prehistoric setting. Any solution would be very expensive. To tackle the problems English Heritage developed a proposal for a £44 million park and visitor centre to re-establish a more appropriate setting for the monument. A bid for £22 million was submitted to the Millennium Commission. There was some surprise and more dismay when it was reported in June 1997 that this approach had failed. The English Heritage bid had the support of the National Trust, a major land-holder in the area, and the Tussauds Group which planned, so it was reported, a £10 million investment in an interpretation centre. Given the change in government, it was not clear whether the inclusion of a private sector partner had helped or hindered the application. Whatever the reasons for the rejection, the consequence is that the setting of Stonehenge, appreciated in the 18th century, investigated and partially protected in the 19th, studied but allowed to deteriorate in the 20th, will continue to present a challenge into the 21st century.

Ancient Thames

The construction of a rowing lake for Eton College at Dorney, Bucks, allowed archaeologists to investigate the valley floor of the Thames near Windsor Castle. As David Miles writes in *Minerva* (March/April 1997): 'The most important discovery is an ancient channel of the Thames, through which the river flowed in post-glacial times, from about 8000 BC until the Roman period when it became silted up and blocked. Unlike the modern Thames this arm has avoided the attentions of the dredgers. It is literally a waterlogged time-capsule.' During their investigations of the banks of the ancient channel archaeologists recovered evidence of Mesolithic sites of about 8000 BC and 6500 BC, which 'may be base camps or seasonal occupation sites used by mobile groups of hunter-gatherers who explored the forests of oak, elder, hazel and lime which then covered the landscape'. Evidence of early farmers was recovered dating from about 4000 BC with the remains of pits from which trees had been dug out. 'One mass of timberwork has proved to be a beaver dam of about 2000 BC.'

David Miles continues, 'The overbank alluviation has also protected rare evidence of the first farmers. Some of their activities were small-scale – flint knapping sites where one or two people crouched to make arrowheads, possibly for shooting wildfowl. Other deposits are massive, the silted hollows of earlier river channels were used as rubbish dumps or middens about 100 metres long. So far some 12,000 artefacts have been recovered but over ten times as many remain to be excavated before the construction of the lake begins in the spring of 1997. From about 4000 to 3000 BC there are complete smashed pottery vessels, notably carinated bowls, and polished stone axes, some perhaps ritually broken. Of particular importance is the mass of animal bone, evidence on an unusually large scale for the earliest domesticates in Britain. A mare and foal dating to the middle Bronze Age, about 1500 BC, are among the earliest horses to be found in these islands.' In addition to evidence of the earliest bridges across the Thames with radio-carbon dates to the later Bronze Age and the early Iron Age, that is, about 1300–600 BC, David Miles notes the 'carefully placed deposits in the edge of the river – pots and animal bones, and human remains in the channel. It is known that in the late Bronze Age, as the tradition of barrow burial declined, human bodies were placed in the river. Could these timber bridges have acted as mortuary platforms, like the ghats of the Ganges?'

Wood in Brochs

As the editor of *Current Archaeology* (no. 152, April 1997) remarks: 'Brochs are perhaps the most exotic and mysterious features of British archaeology, tall towers dating from the Iron Age and existing only in the north and west of Scotland.' In this review of recent work on brochs, attention is drawn to a specific problem; a number of small wooden tools and fragments were recovered from waterlogged lairs, yet the Western Isles are treeless. Analysed by Maisie Taylor, it was found that the wood used was North American tamarack larch which had been infested by the teredo mollusc, a warm-water creature. 'Thus a complicated story can be envisaged. The wood grew in around Newfoundland, where it fell into the sea. It was then carried down the coast of America to the Caribbean, where it went round and round the Sargasso Sea for a number of years, becoming thoroughly infested by the teredo. It was then caught up by the Gulf Stream, where it was carried across the Atlantic, up to the Western Isles, where it was eagerly seized upon by the inhabitants for their broch.' Some other woods were recovered, including willow, hazel, ash and pine but of particular interest was 'a piece of purging buckthorn. This is a tree that grows only in southern and eastern England and has long been valued for its magical and medicinal properties. What was it doing up in the Hebrides? Does this provide evidence for trade or at least some sort of contact between the Hebrides and southern England – was southern England exporting its magical drugs to the Western Isles?'

ROMAN SILVER DISH

A triangular, badly damaged fragment of a Roman silver dish was found near Ratley in south Warwickshire in September 1994, adjudged not to be treasure trove at an inquest held in June 1996 and subsequently donated to the Warwickshire Museum. Philip Wise of Warwickshire Museum reported on the piece in *Minerva* (September/October 1996), noting that despite its fragmentary state the dish 'has recently been confirmed as being of considerable importance for the study of Roman silverware in Britain'. Analysis by the British Museum shows that the silver is 96 per cent pure with small amounts of copper, gold and lead. It is estimated that the dish's original diameter was about 15 inches. 'The rim decoration is inspired by the cult of Bacchus, the Roman god of wine and poetry. The surviving motifs are a crossed carrying stick and throwing stick, a female mask, two pine trees, a griffin running to the right, and a tree. It is likely that these motifs form part of a frieze rather than a more formal hunting scene.'

The best parallels for the Ratley dish are from hoards buried in France during the third century, around AD 270–275, with the possibility that this dish was itself made in France. The Ratley silver dish was examined by Catherine Johns of the British Museum who is reported to consider the importance of the dish to lie 'in the fact that it was manufactured during the late second or third centuries. This makes it an unusual find from Roman Britain, where most of the hoards and single finds of Roman silver plate are of fourth-century date. Indeed, at present the Ratley dish is without parallel elsewhere in Britain.'

ROMAN WINE PRODUCTION

Excavations at Wollaston near Wellingborough have revealed Iron Age and Roman farms in the vicinity of the Roman town of Irchester, some two miles away. One of the farms posed a particular problem, as described by Ian Meadows in *Current Archaeology* (no. 150, November 1996), in the form of a series of broad and shallow parallel ditches, with flat bottoms and sharp vertical sides. Careful excavation 'revealed slight traces of what were probably the rootballs of plants'. Ian Meadows continues, 'It looked therefore as if the trenches had been used for the cultivation of plants in the centre requiring support from the posts along the outside.' As similar trench systems are known from the old wine-producing regions of Italy and, indeed, are described by Columella writing on agriculture in the first century AD, samples from the trench were checked for the necessary evidence. Although no plant remains were found grape-vine pollen was recovered by Dr Tony Brown of the Department of Geography at Exeter University. Ian Meadows concludes that 'The vineyard represents a major

capital investment by the original owner(s). Over six kilometres (four miles) of trench were dug and, on the basis of plant spacing at every 1.5 metres, there were at least 4,000 separate lines. This would allow for the production of about 15,000 bottles of white wine each year (nearly 2,300 gallons)... it looks as if we have the first conclusive evidence for viticulture in Roman Britain.'

STONE LIONESS

In January 1997 a team of professional archaeologists recovered a stone sculpture, the head of which had been spotted sticking out of the mud just before Christmas 1996 by the ferryman on the River Almond at Cramond, near Edinburgh, on the Firth of Forth. The object is described by Robert Lloyd Parry in *Minerva* (March/April 1997) as 'an early third-century AD Romano-British sandstone sculpture of a large feline, almost certainly a lioness, apparently devouring a human being'. It had been broken from its base, which was found nearby, and it was noted that 'The style is provincial rather than Classical, and the details of the face have Celtic elements.'

Although nothing exactly similar has been found in the British Isles before, the motif is known from elsewhere in the Roman world, especially from frontier locations. 'The Cramond sculpture is thought almost certainly to have come from a mausoleum, and, judging from its size, that of a person of some importance.' From the first construction of a Roman fort in about AD 142 until the Roman army retreated around AD 215, Cramond is known to have Roman associations and 'The latest find suggests that Cramond may have been more important than previously thought.'

THE DOCTOR'S GRAVE

In *Current Archaeology* (no. 153, July 1997) Philip Crummy reports that, 'The discovery in 1996 of an ancient board game with the pieces in play stirred up a great deal of interest. The game, dated to about AD 50, was in a grave in a quarry site at Stanway near Colchester. Nothing like this has been found before and the find caught the public imagination. However, lying on top of the board was something which in some ways is more remarkable. It is the first example of a medical kit from Britain (at least from a modern excavation), and it shows that the dead person had been a doctor.'

Having described the location and circumstances of the Stanway site, Philip Crummy continues, 'It was possible to work out how the burial had been made. A square pit was dug for the grave, the bottom being ledged so that one end was slightly deeper than the rest. A long wooden box was then placed in the deepest part of the grave so that it fitted tightly across one end. The gaming board was placed open and slightly askew inside the box. The pieces were set out in their starting positions, and a few pieces were moved as if a game had started. The cremated remains of the dead person were put on top of the board in a heap or in a bag. Then, either directly on the board or higher up on a shelf in the box were some medical instruments and a collection of metal rods. Two brooches, a bead, and some textiles (presumably as clothing or maybe blankets) were also put into the box. At the other end of the pit was a dinner service. Eleven pottery dishes and cups were carefully laid out to cover about a quarter of the floor of the pit. Food was presumably placed in and around the service. A Spanish amphora was set upright in a corner of the pit; one might expect an amphora in a grave to contain wine, but this is a type of amphora that normally contained salted fish or fish sauce. A flagon was put in the grave and then it was overlaid with something like a shelf, a tray or a low table. On top of this were placed a decorated samian bowl, a large copper-alloy handled pan, and a copper-alloy strainer bowl. The last object looked like a sort of teapot and was used in much the same way.'

Philip Crummy suggests 'that the site was more than simply a burial place but that it was more likely to have been primarily a special sacred area which included burials. As far as the Britons were concerned, physicians and Druids had much in common, at least in pre-Roman days. The Stanway enclosures were still in use in AD 60–61, at the time of the Boudican revolt, and the Druids were still a major influential force in the country at this time ... the presence of a doctor might allow some kind of Druidic connection, assuming of course (as the evidence does suggest) that he was a Briton rather than a Roman or a Greek.'

ROMAN GOLD COINS

An inquest decided in July 1997 that a hoard of late Roman gold coins found with a metal detector on farmland in West Sussex were treasure trove; in all the hoard consisted of 22 gold coins, 27 silver coins, two gold rings and 50 pieces of silver bullion. All the coins had been minted abroad with the earliest dating to AD 340 and the latest to AD 461; therefore the hoard must have been buried after the date of the latest coin minted. The date range spans the period during which the Romans withdrew from Britain in around AD 410. As reported in the media, the find is regarded as of particular significance because there is no evidence of coins being used in fifth-century Britain.

BOAR CREST HELMET

Although the existence of an Anglo-Saxon helmet with a model boar on its crest is attested in the Old English epic poem *Beowulf*, it is extremely rare in the archaeological record. Indeed, only one example had been found and that was discovered in 1861 in a burial at Benty Grange, Derbys. Great excitement, therefore, was occasioned by the discovery of a second example at Easter 1997 during an archaeological excavation in the Nene Valley near Wollaston, Northants. Not only are helmets with the boar crest rare, but so are the plainer metal

variety, with only two having been found, one at Sutton Hoo in Suffolk in 1939 and the other in Coppergate, York, in 1989.

An initial account of the Wollaston discovery is given by Leslie Webster and Ian Meadows in *Minerva* (July/August 1997). They report that the new helmet find comes from a rich male burial dating to the later seventh century. Although the grave has suffered some damage, sufficient remains to indicate a person buried there of high status, including a small bronze hanging bowl and a finely made sword. 'Alongside the left hip lay the most spectacular of the grave goods – an iron helmet surmounted by the three-dimensional figure of a boar. The helmet is of the same general type as the Sutton Hoo and York helmets, deriving ultimately from late Roman military parade helmets. Its iron cap is braced by two opposed iron crests, on the crossing of which the boar stands defiantly, a powerful symbol of strength and pugnacity. The longitudinal crest descends into the nasal guard, which, like the rest of the helmet, bears no additional decoration, in contrast to the more elaborate examples from Sutton Hoo and York. Cheek-pieces, complete with attachments for leather straps to tie beneath the chin, protected the face, and there seems to have been some kind of rod mail neck-guard.'

While much analysis and conservation needs to be carried out, the authors suggest something of the new discovery's significance: 'the apparent isolation of the burial, its setting under a mound, and its exploitation of a prominent topographical feature – a Roman road – for its location, is characteristic of a number of seventh-century Anglo-Saxon high-status warrior burials. This was a period of accelerated change in England – religious, political, social, and economic – and we may see in demonstrative burials such as this reflections of the aspirations and concerns of the local ruling class as they competed for territory and access to resources.'

WORCESTER CATHEDRAL

Press reports in July 1997 referred to the discovery of what archaeologists believe to have been the remains of the largest Anglo-Saxon cathedral in Britain, being demonstrated by the buried walls of a circular building some 80 feet in diameter in the grounds of the Norman cathedral at Worcester. After workmen digging a trench for a gas pipe came across the walls, archaeological investigations were put in hand by Christopher Guy, the cathedral archaeologist. The Anglo-Saxon cathedral had been built in AD 961 by Bishop St Oswald but his work was demolished in the 11th century on the orders of William the Conqueror. Because of the action of the Normans in superimposing their own constructions on Saxon sites, archaeology is crucially important in elucidating what remains are left. The remains suggest that the Anglo-Saxon cathedral at Worcester could have been larger even than those at Canterbury and Wells.

Norfolk Wall Paintings

What is hailed as 'the most important discovery of Romanesque wall painting in England for 20 years' is described by David Park and Stephen Heywood in *Minerva* (March/April 1997). Revealed in part in 1996 and now being researched and conserved, the wall-paintings are in the isolated parish church of Houghton-on-the-Hill, Norfolk, one of about 100 ruined churches in the county. Notwithstanding its designation as a ruin and its condition, the church is not redundant; it is part of a Norfolk County Council and English Heritage five-year scheme to repair some 20 of the most important of these churches. The authors report on the work to date at Houghton-on-the-Hill as follows: 'Most of the surviving painting is concentrated on the east wall of the nave, above and around the chancel arch. To the west of the arch is the Resurrection of the Dead, with an angel blowing the Last Trumpet, and tiny naked figures clambering out of their tombs. The narrow border above contains saints in roundels, each holding a scroll, while above is the most exciting survival of all: a monumental representation of the Trinity. Although much damaged, God can be seen enthroned in a triple mandorla, with Christ on the cross before him, and the dove of the Holy Spirit rising above Christ's outstretched arm. More uncovering remains to be carried out elsewhere in the nave, but a scene of Christ and another figure is visible on the north side, while intriguing remains on the west wall include the head of an evil figure represented in profile. Much of the significance of these paintings derives from their very early date.' As the style of the Houghton paintings is close to that of the 'Lewes Group' paintings at Hardham, Clayton, and elsewhere in Sussex, which were apparently executed by the same travelling workshop and date from *c.*1100, 'a dating of *c.*1090 seems most plausible for the Norfolk paintings'.

Plas Mawr

There was much media interest in May 1997 in the reopening of what has been described as Britain's finest surviving Elizabethan townhouse, Plas Mawr, Conwy, upon which Cadw has spent some £3 million for restoration purposes. The aim has been to return the building to the way it could have looked when it was finished in 1580 by Robert Wynn, trader, soldier and courtier. It is probable that Robert Wynn intended his home to reflect his wealth and status, but over the following 200 years the building declined, being divided into tenements. Acquired by the Cambrian Society in 1886 as its headquarters, it was put into the care of Cadw by the freeholder, Lord Mostyn, in 1993. It was reported in the press that the interior of the house had consumed hundreds of mature oak trees with the most serious damage being caused subsequently by deathwatch beetles. In addition to the fundamental structural restoration, the heraldic symbols of the Wynns and the house's ornate plasterwork were conserved.

Dudley Castle Condoms

One of the more unusual reports to appear in 1997 was in *Post-Medieval Archaeology* (vol. 30, 1996) entitled 'The archaeology of private life: the Dudley Castle condoms'. The paper is concerned with the analysis of the contents of a latrine excavated in the mid-1980s at Dudley Castle in the West Midlands. Its significance is that it was sealed during the demolition of the castle's defence in 1647, 'the intact deposit containing both the domestic and organic remains of the occupying royalist force which defended the castle under siege conditions between 1642 and 1646'. Analysis showed that there were 'fragments of ten individual animal-membrane condoms' representing 'the earliest definitive physical evidence for the use of animal-membrane condoms in post-medieval Europe, although at this early date it is impossible to know for sure whether they were designed as prophylactics for protection against venereal disease or as contraceptive devices'.

Scientific examination suggests that the condoms of the post-medieval period were probably made from animal intestine, with that of sheep or pig being the most likely. In an interesting discussion the authors remark that 'It was not until 1843, with the discovery of vulcanization (treating rubber with sulphur and heat to make it more durable), that technological advances made it possible to mass-produce reliable and cheap condoms. In the 1930s liquid latex replaced crepe rubber and production was intensified. Ironically it is only recently that modern condoms have approached the same "gossamer" quality of the animal-membrane sheaths of the 17th to 19th centuries.'

Wren's Fleet Bridge

Dr Simon Thurley, curator of the Historic Royal Palaces and the new director of the Museum of London from 1 September 1997, occasioned media interest in July 1997 when he brought to public attention the fact that what is left of the bridge designed by Sir Christopher Wren to go over the River Fleet remains in a sewer in central London. These relics are buried beneath Ludgate Circus in Holborn and are all that remain of Sir Christopher Wren's vision of turning London into a city with the canals and fine buildings more usually associated with Venice. The work of Dr Thurley together with specialists from the Museum of London and the Thames Water Authority again indicates how much remains in major cities still to be discovered, or if not discovered then reinterpreted.

Sir Christopher Wren canalized the River Fleet in 1677 after the Great Fire of London had destroyed most of the buildings in the city. The River Fleet had its source on Hampstead Heath, then flowed down through Farringdon into the Thames; it was the last stretch between Holborn and Blackfriars that Wren converted to a canal. However, his scheme to provide London with an equivalent of the Grand Canal failed, and in 1733, ten years after his death, it was bricked over. In all there were four bridges that once straddled the canal, the others, situated at Bridewell, Fleet Lane and Holborn, being flanked with warehouses, wharves and other buildings. Dr Thurley's work in rediscovering this bridge emphasizes how the city's rivers determined the layout of London, which is very far from the flat spread that it appears on the maps. Today the contours tend to be ignored and the Fleet valley is a good example of this in that it is sufficiently deep to be used by the Metropolitan Line underground trains between Kings Cross and Farringdon.

Treasure Trove

The annual report of the Treasure Trove Reviewing Committee for 1995–6 disclosed that during the year some 29 finds were brought to the attention of the committee, 26 of them being discovered by the use of metal detectors. Apart from coins, there were two items both dating from the late Bronze Age, i.e. about 1000–600 BC; they were a gold band from Cricklade and a gold 'dress fastener' from Cave Hill, Belfast. The latter case was significant as this was the first time the reviewing committee had considered a case from Northern Ireland, to which its remit has been extended. There were seven hoards containing ancient British coins, including some supplementary to other reported discoveries. There were also seven hoards of Roman coins, including 126 gold aurei from Didcot, Oxon, with coins dating from Nero to Antoninus Pius, the hoard being put into the ground in about AD 159. A hoard of Roman jewellery and coins was recovered at Bishop Cannings, Wilts, and this included a gold solidus of Gratian (AD 367–383), 1,569 silver siliquae and 5,837 bronze coins from Constantius II (AD 337–361) to Honorius (AD 393–423).

Two other hoards were composed of Anglo-Saxon coins and they were found in Bedale, N. Yorks, and Duddington, Northants. From the medieval period some nine silver pennies of Henry I were found in Toddington, Beds, and a group of 32 Short Cross, 11 Long Cross and four Scottish pennies were reportedly discovered in 'mid Norfolk'. The location of the find is not being made more specific to protect the site from damage.

Roman Names of English Towns and Cities

Bath	*Aquae Sulis*	Leicester	*Ratae Corieltauvorum*
Canterbury	*Durovernum Cantiacorum*	Lincoln	*Lindum*
Carlisle	*Luguvalium*	London	*Londinium*
Chelmsford	*Caesaromagus*	Manchester	*Mamucium*
Chester	*Deva*	Newcastle upon Tyne	*Pons Aelius*
Chichester	*Noviomagus Regnensium*	Pevensey	*Anderetium*
Cirencester	*Corinium Dobunnorum*	Rochester	*Durobrivae*
Colchester	*Camulodunum*	St Albans	*Verulamium*
Doncaster	*Danum*	Salisbury (Old Sarum)	*Sorviodunum*
Dorchester	*Durnovaria*	Silchester	*Calleva Atrebatum*
Dover	*Dubris*	Winchester	*Venta Belgarum*
Exeter	*Isca Dumnoniorum*	Wroxeter	*Viroconium Cornoviorum*
Gloucester	*Glevum*	York	*Eburacum*

Architecture

RIVER AND ROWING MUSEUM
Henley, Oxon
Architect: David Chipperfield Architects

This deceptively simple and serene building, completed and opened in 1997, provides an environment redolent with boat building and rowing references, for which sport Henley has long been regarded as a 'mecca', with its annual regatta a popular and traditional event of the summer season. Sited on the edge of Mill Meadow, among the water meadows along the southern bank of the River Thames and just upstream from the town centre of Henley, the museum offers a number of gallery spaces designed to house a collection of rowing hulls and an extensive range of exhibits illustrating the history of the sport of rowing and of the river itself. The building form takes its cue from the main exhibits: a long linear assembly of traditional pitched roof forms raised on pilotis above a raised timber deck, floating above the natural ground levels. The architect has placed the building tight up against a line of poplar trees that mark the course of a small stream crossing the meadows diagonally. The main vehicular approach follows the line of trees, crossing the stream and passing beneath a first-floor linking bridge to give access to the rear car park, from which pedestrian access is also gained.

The architectural design is based on a few simple but distinctive ideas: the raising of the long boat hall galleries to first-floor level and the predominantly solid introspective treatment of their enclosures; a contrasting transparent glazed ground storey, raised over a suspended timber deck; the use of traditional gabled pitched roof forms, allied to minimalist detailing and the finest quality materials to offer a modern reinterpretation of these traditional forms. Construction has been in two phases, the first being the larger and featuring two main gallery spaces at first-floor level, each of a different length, separated by a linear spine containing vertical circulation and smaller picture galleries. At ground-floor level the spine contains plant and public lavatories in addition to the lift, stairs and reception area. Each of the gallery spaces has a pitched roof clad in terned stainless steel sheet, incorporating a continuous glazed roof light over the whole length that allows natural light onto the sloping internal faces. A curved metal grille suspended below the ridge line internally reduces glare from the strip of glazing, and reflects light onto the plain white inner surfaces. The boat halls are for the most part windowless, the walls clad externally in horizontal oak boarding. The oak cladding, supplied to precise quality and moisture content standards, has a fine sawn face and

a machined bevel on each edge, but no further treatment has been necessary.

The oak cladding acts as a rain screen, with the boards open-jointed to allow for air movement and avoid the capillary attraction of water through closed joints. Each board, 160 × 20 mm in section, is fixed with pairs of stainless steel screws and slotted washers, each set into a circular sinking in the wood. The washers are set with slots aligned vertically to allow for natural shrinkage across the section of the oak boards. The underlying structural grid of latticed steel portal frames at 3.9 metre centres shows as a series of panels in the external cladding, with two panels per structural bay defined by a simple shadow gap line between the ends of adjacent boards. The paired fixings for each of the boards are located at close centres onto a subframe of Colombian pine, and the arrangement of the close boarded panels with their vertical rows of fixings, generates a subtle but sturdy surface, whose golden-brown colour will weather naturally to a silver-grey. At the eastern end of the longer northern boat hall the solid walls are sliced apart by a series of horizontal windows providing superb views of surrounding trees and out over the water meadows to the River Thames.

The lower storey is, in contrast, almost totally transparent, with floor to ceiling glass panels held in metal frames and shielded on the southern elevation by retractable sun blinds. At the heart of the plan at this level are the reception desk and foyer space. These are approached from both sides, from the south by an open, wide range of steps and from the north by a narrow pedestrian bridge crossing the stream under overhanging trees. This area provides a focal point for the meeting room, cafeteria, shop and library spaces, as well as a further gallery space. All have a view of the surroundings, and the adjoining external areas of raised oak decking, set flush with the main floor level to extend the floor plane out into the landscape.

The smaller, second phase building grows out of an extension of the central spine which forms a linking passage at first floor level to additional gallery and storage areas. At ground level there are further plant and storage areas and a caretaker's flat. The architecture of the exterior reflects that of phase one, but without the distinctive, steeply pitched gabled roof forms.

Throughout, the range of materials has been kept within very tight limits, and this has helped to create a sense of clarity, control and stillness. Great attention has been paid to simple and unadorned methods of detailing the junctions between materials. Yet there are also clear references to the craft traditions of boat building and yards, most obviously in the extended timber deck around the ground floor, with its glazed stainless steel framed railing, the use of oak boarding for the upper elevations, and the contrasting, vertically boarded access doors in the end of each boat hall which enable the long, beautifully crafted hulls of the exhibits to be brought into the galleries. This new museum is an important addition to the line of modern movement buildings that combines the technologies of the present with an understanding of the relevance of vernacular forms and traditional materials, and provides Henley with a superbly crafted and approachable environment in which to display the glories of its river-based heritage.

THE BRIDGEWATER HALL
Manchester
Architect: RHWL Partnership

Manchester's new international concert hall, the Bridgewater Hall, opened in September 1996 to critical acclaim. Designed specifically for the performance of symphonic and choral music, but adaptable to a range of other events, the concert hall provides a permanent home for the Hallé Orchestra, and a recording and performance base for other local orchestras and music groups. In recent years several new concert halls have been built in the UK as part of larger cultural and entertainment developments, such as at Birmingham's Centenary Square, but Bridgewater Hall is the first free-standing auditorium structure since the Royal Festival Hall of 1951. The hall is located on a site close to the city centre, between Lower Mosley Street and Great Bridgewater Street, with the G-Mex Exhibition Centre to the west. A new canal basin, fed by the Rochdale Canal, has been created on the east side to offer a peaceful waterside frontage as a contrast to the bustle of the city on the adjoining streets.

The form of the building is directly influenced by the auditorium volume, though the projecting angular forms clustered around it create a sense of dynamism and break down the overall scale so that the new building sits comfortably within its immediate urban context. The concert hall is sited on a north-south axis directed towards the spire of Manchester's Town Hall. This axis has influenced the planning of the ancillary spaces and circulation routes into separate and distinct zones. The vehicle arrival and set-down points, artists' entrance, loading dock and box-office facilities together with the main staircase and lifts are on the west side, facing onto Lower Mosley Street. The main public entrance is on the centre-line axis approached from the north under a dramatic glazed prow suspended from the auditorium roof. To the east, facing the quiet frontage of the canal basin, are the foyers and bars, function rooms and artists' dressing rooms; the public areas appear as a series of tall pointed radiating projections, fully glazed for maximum visibility both inwards and outwards.

The projecting forms of the superstructure enclose the limestone-clad walls of the auditorium,

and are themselves placed above a red sandstone plinth. Large areas of clear glazing to the foyers contrast with solid areas of silver-coated aluminium cladding panels to offices and ancillary accommodation. The auditorium walls project above these forms and support a curved pitched roof of stainless steel panels with a substantial overhang all round, rising to a soaring, pointed prow directly over the main entrance. The auditorium seats 2,400 people. It has been designed to achieve a balance between visual and acoustic criteria, to try and avoid the pitfalls of auditoria designed for aural perfection, and to provide the audience with a close relationship with the performers.

The adopted form, developed in conjunction with the acoustic design consultants Arup Acoustics, is a combination of aspects of the traditional 'shoe box' hall, such as the Vienna Musikverein and Amsterdam Concertgebouw halls, and the 'vineyard' form of separated tiers as exemplified by the Berlin Philharmonie. A feeling of intimacy and involvement has been achieved by dividing the audience into relatively small sections, each in its own space and with good sightlines onto the stage area. Rising spectacularly on the rear wall behind the stage is the great organ, with some 5,000 pipes, varying in length from about 32 feet to just two inches, designed in conjunction with the British organist Thomas Trotter and made in Denmark. It provides dramatic visual relief and interest in what is otherwise a generally sober decor. The finishes, including cherry veneered acoustic screens, red oak flooring and plain painted plaster, are restrained but of high quality. The auditorium roof is supported on free-standing circular columns at either side, and comprises two separate skins to minimize external noise penetration. The outer skin is clad with the stainless steel panels visible externally. The inner roof, the auditorium ceiling, is formed from two-way spanning steel roof trusses, the upper part of which are massive steel beams clad in concrete that support a series of stepped precast concrete infill ceiling panels. The lower tensile members of the truss are left exposed within the space like an inverted suspension bridge, a web of tension rods, struts and cast steel nodes carrying clusters of low voltage lights that mimic a starry night sky. Acoustic isolation of the structure at foundation level was important because of traffic vibration in the adjacent streets and in particular the tram route in Lower Mosley Street. The bases of the circular structural columns rest on giant isolation springs, visible in the services undercroft beneath the auditorium floor. This is the first time the technique has been used for a concert hall in this country.

Such a prestigious venue would not be complete without specially commissioned art work. The steeply inclined soffit of the rear of the auditorium, as it rises through the foyer levels wrapped around it, has been used as a backdrop for rippling coloured metal strips by the artist Deryck Healey. These are painted on the reverse in red, blue and yellow, the colours reflecting off the plain white plaster surface and varying according to the ambient lighting conditions throughout the day and night. Perhaps the most unexpected feature of the building is the separate, partially cylindrical glass-clad services tower at the junction of the two streets. This is set forward from the main building volume and attached by a giant metal-clad 'umbilical cord' to the upper level of the auditorium side wall. The outer curved wall of the five-storey structure is clad in vertical bands of U-shaped glass planks placed back to back to form a double-glazed, translucent blue skin that reveals the heating plant when the tower is illuminated at night. All major plant items, including the auditorium air-handling units, pumps, boilers, chillers and controls are housed here, with ductwork connections at high and low level. Treated air is circulated through plenums in each seating tier and thence to each seat through a floor grille, before being extracted through grilles at the top of the auditorium and returned to the tower via the high-level 'flying' connecting duct. The tower adds a distinctly industrial flavour to an unmistakeably civic building, and might be seen as a passing reference to the sturdy Victorian warehouse architecture to be found near the canal to the south.

At a total cost of £42 million, which includes the organ, services and supplies, Manchester has acquired a stunning concert facility of international rank, a long overdue successor to the outdated Free Trade Hall. The building will help to revitalize a substantial part of the city centre, and makes a dramatic focal point while fitting well into the robust urban context. The designers are to be congratulated on their response to stringent technological demands, one that should enable Manchester to realize its ambition of possessing a world-class concert hall and a worthy home for the Hallé Orchestra.

EXPERIMENTAL OFFICE BUILDING FOR BUILDING RESEARCH ESTABLISHMENT
Garston, Herts
Architect: Fielden Clegg Architects

This latest addition to the Building Research Establishment (BRE) site at Garston, near Watford, is a working experiment. It is part of BRE's long-standing commitment to foster designs and techniques for standard office buildings that will substantially reduce energy demands both in the construction and maintenance aspects of total 'energy costing'. This commitment has focused on a joint project between the BRE conservation support unit and a range of other companies (manufacturers, designers, public utilities and others), known as the 'energy-efficient office of the future' (EOF) project. Now redefined as 'environmental office of the future', the scheme's aim is to formulate good practice by investigating low-energy, comfortable and healthy workplaces for the 21st century and achieving appropriate energy

and environmental criteria for the year 2000 and beyond.

The opportunity to develop an EOF building arose with the relocation to Garston of the Fire Research Station, which needed new flexible office accommodation of some 1,300 square metres. BRE itself added a seminar block of 800 square metres containing a seminar room for 100 people, two smaller ones, a reception foyer and exhibition display space. The office accommodation is in a three-storey block forming one leg of the L-shaped building, linked to the three-storey seminar block by a full-height glazed lobby.

Among the main aims of the EOF project are the development of methods to exploit natural light and ventilation in buildings which otherwise would rely on air-conditioning, and to reduce energy demands, particularly electricity for lighting, air movement and cooling. Accordingly, the new office building is designed to make use of natural cross-ventilation from the prevailing south-westerly wind via openable windows on both sides of the building. The accommodation comprises open-plan office areas on the south side and cellular offices on the north side; a north-south orientation offers a helpful strategy for dealing with a number of environmental issues. North-facing offices can take advantage of north light and do not require solar control measures. East- and west-facing elevations are largely blank (here housing the two main staircases) and so eliminate glare and solar heat gain problems from low sun angles early and late in the day. Most of the environmental control devices are developed in the south-facing facade. Here, higher sun angles require horizontal louvres, blinds, projections and overhangs to cut off unwanted direct sunlight.

On days when air movement is slight, the natural ventilation is boosted by five external projecting ventilation towers, whose stack effect draws stale air out of the ground and first-floor offices to which they are connected. This creates a syphon, which draws in fresh air through the windows in the north facade. The second-floor space is separately vented by a series of north-facing clerestory windows set along the centre line of the building where the southern half of the roof is angled upwards. These windows allow daylight to penetrate the office floor, giving superior daylight levels to the lower floors. If the passive effect of the ventilation towers proves insufficient, fans set into the top of the stacks come into operation to increase exhaust rates. Between the ventilation towers, which also act as vertical sun-shielding fins, are suspended banks of translucent glass louvres. These are motorized and programmed to change their angle and intercept the sun's rays when they penetrate the office space. On dull days they are set at a horizontal angle to reflect light back onto the ceiling plane. The louvres are of toughened glass with a ceramic fritted underside to reduce glare and reflect light.

The most striking internal feature is the exposed concrete floor. This consists of a series of sinusoidal curved slabs supported on precast concrete beams. There are cast-in holes above and below the wave form slab to provide clear ventilation paths through the composite floor structure. The thermal mass of the floor slab is used for cooling purposes; cool night-time air is passed over it to pre-cool the structure for the following day. An innovative artificial lighting system has been installed using suspended fittings, each of which can be controlled from the central system as well as adjusted by each occupant, thus providing a high degree of flexibility. There is innovation too in the use of photovoltaic cells, which form an integral part of the south elevation on the blank walls to the small seminar rooms. These will generate power for the building, offsetting some of the normal power demand.

The principles of sustainable development have informed the design of many of the other elements of the building. Recycled materials have been used in the structure: reclaimed yellow London stock bricks for external cladding; wood block flooring salvaged from London's County Hall for the seminar block; and ready-mixed concrete for foundations, floor slabs and columns, using recycled crushed concrete aggregates, are examples. The pitched roof has thick timber decking, with high levels of insulation, to give a structure of high thermal mass with materials from a renewable resource. What is most striking about the building is the way in which all the major environmental issues, and the 'kit of parts' associated with them, have been incorporated in the final design. This is most obvious in the distinctive and highly engineered south elevation, dominated by the five glass block-faced ventilation towers. Each tower is surmounted by a tall stainless steel vent and rain hood three metres high, framing the gridded banks of glass louvres and window walls, and set off against the solid brick mass of the seminar block with its huge dark gridded solar panel filling the upper two storeys.

This display of functionalism organized with a feeling for balance and proportion lends further weight to an emerging architectural language of energy-efficient 'green' buildings. An initial assessment of the building's environmental contribution and performance, carried out under the criteria of the BRE's established Environmental Assessment Method (BREEAM), resulted in the award of the highest rating. BREEAM is a point-scoring system in which individual features contribute, depending on their energy significance, to an overall total which is then rated in a category. BRE staff have started to monitor the building's performance in use. The results will be disseminated for the benefit of the construction industry.

ST BARNABUS CHURCH
Dulwich, London
Architect: Hellmuth Obata and Kassabaum Inc

With traditional forms of church-going in decline and the range of alternative quests for spiritual enlightenment expanding, a commission for a new church has been something of a rarity in recent years. An opportunity arose in the parish of St Barnabus in December 1992, when the 100-year-old Victorian church, an imposing red-brick structure, was destroyed by fire. The new church is the result of a competition launched in January 1993 by the vicar and the parochial church council of the parish. The brief, developed by the parish, requested 'a new home for worship, prayer, learning, celebration, recreation and service to the community'. At the same time it called for a flexible, welcoming and comfortable environment for its users and a building that combined a respect for, and memory of, the past using contemporary materials and technology as an act of faith and hope for the future. The form of the realized building is relatively traditional in massing and layout, and reverts to the age-old tradition of orientation to the four cardinal points. The new church is sited further away from the road than the previous building and uses some of the walling from the old church to link past and present. Entrance to the new church is from a forecourt framed by the walls of the Barnabus Centre, a single-storey annexe of meeting rooms which survived the fire, and the new west end of church. The two are linked by a curving canopy and glazed screen leading to the narthex or gathering space beyond. From here doors open into the central nave and south aisle of the church, and give access to the other back-up areas and meeting rooms as well as an open south-facing courtyard area.

The layout of the church had to accommodate a number of different seating arrangements, for worship and other events. While the structure keeps a strong east-west axis, implying a 'nave' and side 'aisles', it is nevertheless primarily arranged for worship 'in the round'; the main altar is positioned centrally on the main axial crossing, beneath an innovative glass spire that allows light through the dominating barrel-vaulted shape of the main roof. The nave and aisle spaces are enclosed by eight brick piers, each one of a modified H-shape on plan, with one or more legs extended to create a longer wall plane on the east-west axis. The colour of the Baggeridge brick autumn russet stocks recalls the red bricks of the church's Victorian predecessor. The extended wall planes of the four central piers support deep paired beams, one pair each side of the nave. The spaces between are divided by cross panels that act as a huge louvre for the strip of clear glazed roof lights that runs along each side of the main roof, providing a source of indirect daylight into the body of the church. Further paired beams, of smaller dimensions, are set along the north and south walls, providing more indirect lighting at the perimeter.

The two inner pairs of beams and rooflights are linked by a barrel-vaulted ceiling set below the simple pitched roof and lined with slatted beech panels, whose warm tones harmonize well with the red brickwork. From the base of each outer beam a further half-barrel vault in the same finish curves down to the lower level of the perimeter walls. The building up of the volumes towards the central space, combined with the setting in and out of the massive wall planes around the crossing axis, emphasize the central focal point of the altar on its raised dais, and find their logical expression in the shaft of light and release of tension provided by the central glass spire.

The spire is a delicate planar glass structure, octagonal on plan and supported by a fine lattice framework of stainless steel; it rises from an octagonal solid base, clad in natural slate, to form a traditional landmark in the local setting. Internal fittings include an octagonal altar table in oak supported on eight massive oak legs with stainless steel junction elements, and purpose-made stacking benches. Designed to provide 400 seat spaces, the benches are flexible enough to accommodate half as many again at popular festivals and can be quickly cleared when required. A free-standing brick wall set between the piers at the east end supports the new organ with its case, and is framed and topped with specially commissioned stained-glass panels to a colourful abstract design by the artist Caroline Swash. At the opposite, west end of the main space, there is the baptismal font, salvaged from the wreckage of the old church. Beyond this a small chapel for daily prayer is sited on the central axis under its own roof at a lower level, but still with a timber-lined, barrel-vault interior. Glazed screens can be opened up to join this to the main space, and similarly to the four interconnecting meeting rooms on the north-south axis. These can also be opened up to provide a seating capacity of 650 for services at Easter and Christmas.

The architecture offers a contrast between mass and lightness and a modern interpretation of the traditional forms of ecclesiastical buildings. The pitched roof forms and the build-up of major and minor volumes provide a welcoming and recognizable image, especially when the internal vaults are lit up at night, with the glass spire assuming an incandescent quality, shining forth to the surrounding community. The architects have responded with dedication to the challenge of providing an appropriate centre of worship and community activity for a congregation aware of the past yet firmly focused on the spiritual needs of future generations.

WATERFRONT HALL
Lanyon Place, Laganside, Belfast
Architect: Robinson and McIlwaine

Lying to the east of City Hall on a previously derelict site on the banks of the River Lagan, Waterfront Hall is an important new civic building. It represents the main cultural element in a programme of urban renewal intended to reclaim the riverside and to forge stronger links between the river and the city centre. It also confirms a general mood of optimism about the city's future in the light of continuing political uncertainty. The site chosen for the new concert hall has been named Lanyon Place, in memory of the respected Belfast architect Charles Lanyon (1813-89), thus demonstrating an increasing awareness of the quality and value of the city's architectural heritage. Although designed primarily as an international standard concert hall for symphonic music, to be economically viable the hall has to cater for a wide variety of functions, not necessarily of a musical nature. To do this the 2,250-seat auditorium has an area of removable seating that can provide a clear 30 × 20 metre arena floor, while retaining the tiered gallery seating at upper levels. The auditorium can also provide full conference facilities, a stage-theatre grid with scenery-hoisting equipment and provisions for a proscenium arch, a cinema projection capability and even space for a 72-stop organ. The floors of the arena and concert platform area can also be raised and lowered if need be for musical or sporting events.

The range of possible uses has inevitably presented the architect and the acoustic consultant with the challenge of providing a high degree of acoustic quality for each of the different activities. The layout of the auditorium seating follows the 'vineyard terracing' principle established at Berlin's Philharmonie, in which the audience is separated into smaller interlocking terraced blocks, here arranged symmetrically around the central axis, to give a greater feeling of intimacy and rapport between audience and performers. The relative informality of the terraced approach to the auditorium seating is, however, in complete contrast to the external form of the building. Unlike the geometric projections of Manchester's Bridgewater Hall, the foyer and front-of-house facilities of Waterfront Hall are wrapped around the bulk of the auditorium and enclosed within a classical drum with a massive outward-leaning entablature, surmounted by a copper-clad shallow domed roof.

The architectural treatment of the walls of the drum takes several forms. At the main entrance, a cantilevered porte-cochère canopy of polished metal ribs canted upwards like wings, a simple trabeated arrangement of stone-clad columns and curved beams frames large areas of glazing, lighting the foyer areas behind. Where the back-of-house offices, servicing and performers' rooms are located, overlooking the riverside, the elevation reverts to a solid brick face punctuated by a grid of square window openings. Between the two, restaurant and bar areas erupt from the face of the drum in a three-storey projection pushing forwards towards the waterside. The curved outer face, describing a larger radius taken from the drum's centrepoint, is clad entirely in clear planar glazing, with a slight forward lean, and is secured by stainless steel patch fixings and angled metal brackets to the floor slabs. This transparency also extends to a glazed roof, and provides stunning views of the city, the river, and the surrounding countryside. Conversely any activity in the centre can be seen from surrounding areas, particularly at night. Partially floodlit at night, and with the projecting public spaces brightly lit, the building presents an imposing sight reflected in the waters of the Lagan river. The shallow flattened dome is visible from moderate distances. It is emphasized by a horizontally projecting stainless steel 'coronet' extending two metres beyond the vertical edge of the dome. The dome is illuminated around its circumference at night and forms a very satisfactory finishing touch to the bold but simple form of the building.

The foyer spaces derive considerable spatial complexity from the residual forms of the auditorium's terraced seating blocks, with their cantilevered soffits. The sense of drama is heightened by the cutting back of the upper-level foyer floors, which thus engage with the perimeter of the external drum rather than the bulk of the auditorium, to create a three-storey-high void that gives exciting vistas from floor to floor. At ground-floor level a marble staircase sweeps up to a half landing and thence by opposing symmetrical flights to the carpeted foyers above. Each foyer level offers a large interval bar area in the glazed extension overlooking the river. Great variety and interest is generated by the interplay of planes and voids in the front-of-house spaces, a preparation for the contrasting qualities of the auditorium. Glass bridges connect the galleries to the auditorium entry points and accentuate the variety of experience offered.

The acoustic qualities of the auditorium have been praised by performers. The 'vineyard' seating format creates its own vocabulary of acoustic devices, which include the perimeter walls to each of the terrace blocks. Carefully profiled and angled, they act as sound reflectors and provide an even distribution of short-delay reflected sound to the listeners. The auditorium as a whole is enclosed by vertical faceted walls which are spanned by a flat concrete soffit set sufficiently high to generate the right acoustic volume for the hall. Concentric rings of diffusing panels and acoustic reflectors are suspended from this soffit, with additional circular reflectors placed directly above the orchestra.

As the hall is on the flight path to Belfast City Airport, measures were needed to eliminate noise, and this has been done by using a double-skin concrete roof; the upper skin supports the flattened dome, the inner skin forms the auditorium ceiling. The weight of this roof, together with the lighting and theatrical paraphernalia housed at high level and in the roof space, is carried on four concrete columns; the large spans are resolved by means of a cruciform primary truss structure of two bowstring-shaped steel lattice girders of 56 metre span. The auditorium walls are also double-skinned, in high-density blockwork, to eliminate external noise. Early reactions have been that the acoustic performance of both envelope and auditorium is of top quality.

This new conference and concert centre, completed in December 1996 and opened on 17 January 1997, cost £32 million. Belfast City Council, as client, should feel richly rewarded for its investment, with a building of civic grandeur and national cultural significance that will contribute to the revival of the city's fortunes and attract to the province many of the world's leading orchestras.

The Seven Wonders of the World

I THE PYRAMIDS OF EGYPT

The pyramids are found from Gizeh, near Cairo, to a southern limit 60 miles (96 km) distant. The oldest is that of Zoser, at Saqqara, built c.2650 BC. The Great Pyramid of Cheops (built c.2580 BC) covers 13.12 acres (756 × 756 ft (230.4 × 230.4 m) at the base) and was originally 481 ft (146.6 m) in height

II THE HANGING GARDENS OF BABYLON

These adjoined Nebuchadnezzar's palace, 60 miles (96 km) south of Baghdad. The terraced gardens, ranging from 75 ft to 300 ft (25–90 m) above ground level, were watered from storage tanks on the highest terrace

III THE TOMB OF MAUSOLUS

Built at Halicarnassus, in Asia Minor, by the widowed Queen Artemisia about 350 BC. The memorial originated the term mausoleum

IV THE TEMPLE OF ARTEMIS AT EPHESUS

Ionic temple erected about 350 BC in honour of the goddess and burned by the Goths in AD 262

V THE COLOSSUS OF RHODES

A bronze statue of Apollo, set up about 280 BC. According to legend it stood at the harbour entrance of the seaport of Rhodes

VI THE STATUE OF ZEUS

Located at Olympia in the plain of Elis, and constructed of marble inlaid with ivory and gold by the sculptor Phidias, about 430 BC

VII THE PHAROS OF ALEXANDRIA

A marble watch tower and lighthouse on the island of Pharos in the harbour of Alexandria, built c.270 BC

Bequests to Charity

The list below represents some of the principal charitable bequests from wills published since the last edition. The exact values of residues of estates cannot be calculated accurately, since prior bequests, expenses and inheritance tax have to be deducted from the net figures given below.

The largest charitable bequest of the year was that of Humphrey Taylor, who left the residue of his estate for such charitable purposes as his trustees selected; his estate totalled over £9 million. Sarah Coleman and Revd Charles Borelli also left the residue of their estates similarly, in Revd Borelli's case, as the Roman Catholic Bishop of Arundel and Brighton decides. Harry Taylforth also left the residue of his £819,296 estate for charitable organizations selected by his trustees, to include those for the benefit of his local community in North Yorkshire. Other bequests benefiting local communities include those of Margaret Staffurth, Nancy Henagulph, Rose Hoenigsberg, and North Yorkshire builder Ronald Windle, whose bequests included a field and other property in Gargrave to be developed as low-cost housing for local inhabitants, specifying that the buildings should be predominantly of second-hand York stone.

The National Trust features prominently in the list, headed by the residue of the estate of Lord Airedale, while Mildred Cordeaux left the residue of her estate for the upkeep of Sheringham Hall in Norfolk. The Trust also received the residue of Marjorie Richmond's estate and half the estate of Michael Dransfield. Jean Fawcitt opened her will with the words 'I have revered my total inheritance since it was entrusted to my care by my parents Norman and Ethel Fawcitt and I now hope that their names will be perpetuated and grace an area of great natural beauty in accordance with the provisions of my will' and she left the residue of her estate to the National Trust for Scotland for the provision and preservation of such an area. She also left the Burn estate and adjoining woodland to the Royal Agricultural Society, directing that there should be no shooting or hunting over this land, that the badger sett be preserved, the woodland be kept in its natural state for wild birds and the estate maintained for the preservation of rare breeds of sheep.

In similar vein, Alan Wyndham Green left the residue of his estate to the Godinton Charitable Trust; he devoted his life to the conservation of his Jacobean home, Godinton Park, which had been bequeathed to him by his grandmother in 1953. Oxford colleges feature in several wills: Hildegarde Reynolds left all her estate to New College, Richard Saxby left a third of the residue of his estate to St Catherine's College, and Rosalind Hill left the residue of her estate to St Hilda's College. Arnold School in Blackpool shared the residue of the estate of William Procter with the Methodist Homes for the Aged and the National Trust, Reuben Hunt left a sixth of the residue of his estate to the Friends of Felsted School, and St Paul's School in London shared the estate of Lady Helmore with the Oxford Preservation Trust and Oxford Society. Helen Dykes left half the residue of her estate to Edinburgh University, for scholarships in homeopathic medicine, and she also left a quarter of the residue to the RNLI, for a lifeboat in Devon to be called *Alec and Christina Dykes*. Mary Lidbury also left the RNLI the residue of her estate for the provision of four lifeboats, two larger ones to be named *Charles Lidbury* and *Austin Lidbury* after her father and uncle, and two smaller ones to be named *Polly Lidbury* and *Bessie Lidbury* after her mother and aunt.

Manchester's Christie Hospital received the residue of the estate of Lady Margaret Holt, who left nearly £8 million. Edith Bloor also left the hospital a seventh of the residue of her estate, as well as bequests to departments in Victoria Hospital, Blackpool, and other local charities. Amnesty International features twice in the list, receiving half the residue of the estates of Norman Levitt and of Nina Nash. Cyril Oliver left the residue of his estate to the Save the Children Fund, stipulating that it should be invested in a wide spread of equities and unit trusts managed equally by Allied Dunbar and another 'notable investment manager', preferably Hambros Bank.

Margaret Dickinson, in addition to her estate, left the Lordship of the manor of Bisham and the right of presentation of All Saints Church, Bisham, to The Queen or, if not accepted, to the Council for the Preservation of Rural England and the Diocese of Oxford respectively. Jacquetta Hawkes, widow of the author J. B. Priestley, left £100,000 to the Royal Literary Fund, to be known as the J. B. Priestley Fund, and an oil painting of her husband by Michael Noakes to the National Portrait Gallery. Other estates not listed below include those of Beryl Reid, the actress and comedienne, who left an eighth of the residue of her £416,035 estate to the RSPCA for its Windsor and Staines branch, and Joyce Sharland, of Paignton, Devon, who left the residue of her estate (under £10,000) between the RSPCA in Torquay, the Save the Children Fund, two personal legatees and 'Bobby my bird'. Finally, Kenneth Jones, a London travel agent, left a number of charitable bequests and the residue of his estate between the Imperial Cancer Research Fund, RNLI and Seafarers Education Service. His will, made in 1989, is worthy of mention for a bequest of £35,000 to the British Railways Board for Special Projects, and his wish that 'my body to be cremated and the ashes to be consumed in the fires of a steam locomotive, preferably one operated by British

Rail Special Projects on a Sunday journey from Marylebone Station, and I wish a coach and refreshments to be provided for guests'.

Rt. Hon. Oliver James Vandeleur, Baron Airedale, of Ufford, Peterborough, £5,392,678 (the residue to the National Trust)

Leslie George Beaver, of Hove, E. Sussex, £1,738,055 (one fifth of the residue each to the Salvation Army and RNIB, three 25ths of the residue each to the National Trust, Imperial Cancer Research Fund and Spastics Society, and one 25th of the residue each to Barnardo's and the Children's Society)

Edith Bloor, of Thornton Cleveleys, Lancs, £2,119,974 (£100,000 to the endowment fund of the Haematology Unit and £75,000 each to the endowment funds of the Cardiac Surgery Unit and Cardiology Unit at Victoria Hospital, Blackpool, £30,000 to the Guide Dogs for the Blind Association, and the residue equally between Blackpool and Fylde Society for the Blind, Trinity Hospice, Blackpool, Salvation Army, Barnardo's, British Heart Foundation, Cancer Research Campaign, and the Christie Hospital, Manchester, for cancer research)

Revd Charles Vincent Borelli, of Farnham, Surrey, £1,566,118 (£200,000 to Holy Cross Hospital, Haslemere, £25,000 to the Southwark Brethren Charity, £10,000 to the Sisters of Providence, London NW3, and the residue to the Roman Catholic Bishop of Arundel and Brighton for such charitable purposes as he thinks fit)

Clara Broadbent, of Stalybridge, Cheshire, £1,142,514 (the residue equally between the Imperial Cancer Research Fund, Arthritis and Rheumatism Council, and St Matthew's Church, Stalybridge, for the upkeep of the fabric)

Herbert Clifford Brough, of Colwyn Bay, Clwyd, £2,616,686 (half his estate to Barnardo's, desiring it be used in the Liverpool area, three eighths of his estate to the Royal Liverpool Children's NHS Trust, and one eighth of his estate to the Royal Liverpool Philharmonic Society)

Daphne Austin Hanbury-Brown, of Eastergate, Chichester, £661,307 (the residue equally between the Humane Slaughter Association, Universities Federation for Animal Welfare, RSPCA, Compassion in World Farming and the Anglo-Italian Society for the Protection of Animals)

Eileen Mary Burton, of Bridge End, Warwick, £3,475,459 (the residue equally between the Imperial Cancer Research Fund, Leukaemia Research Fund, Cancer Relief Macmillan Fund and Arthritis and Rheumatism Council)

George William Chambers, of Sedbury, Chepstow, Monmouthshire, £2,166,736 (£10,000 to the National Trust, and the residue equally between the PDSA, RSPCA, National Society for Cancer Relief, RNLI, Imperial Cancer Research Fund, RNIB, BLESMA, RAF Benevolent Fund and the Army Benevolent Fund)

Betty Clowes, of Roland Gardens, London SW7, £265,558 (all her estate to the British Diabetic Association)

Mrs Peggy Christine Cole, of Sutton Coldfield, £2,089,994 (£100,000 to the Cole Charitable Trust and £50,000 to Christian Aid)

Sarah Ann Deary Coleman, of Newcastle upon Tyne, £2,325,422 (£50,000 to Newcastle University, for an engineering scholarship, and the residue for such charitable objects or purposes as her trustees select)

Mildred Jessie Cordeaux, of Hyde Park Gardens, London W2, £1,483,402 (£50,000 and the sale proceeds of her platinum wedding ring to the Imperial Cancer Research

Fund, £50,000 each to the Friends of the Elderly and Gentlefolk's Help, and the RNLI, for the upkeep of the Sheringham Lifeboat, Norfolk, and £150,000 and the residue of her estate to the National Trust, for the endowment and upkeep of Sheringham Hall)

Margaret Evelyn Dickinson, of Bisham Village, Marlow, Bucks, £2,610,610 (the residue equally between the Church of England Pensions Board, the Sue Ryder Home, Nettlebed, and the Thames Valley Hospice, Stoke Poges)

Michael Dransfield, of Sowerby, Thirsk, N. Yorks, £420,400 (half his estate to the National Trust)

Helen Christina Dykes, of Torquay, £3,236,699 (half the residue to Edinburgh University, for scholarships in homeopathic medicine, to be known as the Alexander Dykes Memorial Fund, one quarter of the residue to the RNLI, for a lifeboat in Devon to be called *Alec and Christina Dykes*, and one eighth of the residue each to Alzheimer's Disease Society and the Hahnemann Society, London, both for research projects bearing the name of Alexander and Christina Dykes)

Jean Margaret Fawcitt, of Harrogate, N. Yorks, £1,715,929 (the residue to the National Trust for Scotland, for the provision of an area or estate of great natural beauty in Scotland to be preserved for the nation in memory of her parents Norman and Ethel Fawcitt)

Arthur Geoffrey Langford Gerard, of Colwyn Bay, Clwyd, £1,396,137 (the residue equally between the Society for the Promotion of Christian Knowledge and the Church Missionary Society)

Alan Wyndham Green, of Godinton Park, Ashford, Kent, £5,238,637 (his effects not otherwise bequeathed to the Godinton House Preservation Trust, and the residue to the Godinton Charitable Trust)

Diana Winifred Green, of Macclesfield, Cheshire, £1,750,027 (the residue equally between the Police Benevolent Fund, Blue Cross, PDSA, Animal Health Trust, RSPB, Royal Veterinary College Animal Care Trust, Guide Dogs for the Blind Association, the Agricultural Benevolent Society and the National Trust)

Leslie Green, of Ferndale Road, London SW9, £542,080 (the residue to the Salvation Army)

Norah Patricia Margaret Hare, of Battle, E. Sussex, £589,818 (the residue equally between the Church of Our Lady and St Michael, Battle, the Association for the Propagation of the Faith, CAFOD, and All Saints Franciscan Friary, Urmston, Manchester)

Eva Elizabeth Healey, of Shepley, Huddersfield, W. Yorks, £496,213 (the residue to the Salvation Army, desiring her home be used as a convalescent or holiday home for retired or active Salvation Army officers, and the balance for its upkeep)

Margaret Eleanor, Lady Helmore, of Penn, Bucks, £1,349,390 (the residue equally between Oxford Preservation Trust, the Oxford Society, and St Paul's School, London)

Nancy Helen Henagulph, of Wokingham, Berks, £1,189,715 (certain land next to her house to Wokingham District Council to be used as a public park or recreational area, including the exercising of dogs, provided the young oaks and other trees there be preserved, and the residue equally between the Guide Dogs for the Blind Association, Blue Cross, Spastics Society, Barnardo's, RNLI, Marie Curie Memorial Foundation, National Deaf Children's Society, Woodland Trust, RSPB and World Wildlife Fund)

Lilian Grace Henson, of Gerrards Cross, Bucks, £1,383,761 (£50,000 to the Leprosy Mission, and the residue equally between the Scripture Gift Mission and the Austrian Bible Mission)

Rosalind Mary Theodosia Hill, of Radlett, Herts, £1,468,347 (the residue to St Hilda's College, Oxford)

Rose Hoenigsberg, of West Drayton, Middx, £603,902 (the residue to the London Borough of Hillingdon, for charitable purposes connected with the care of the elderly)

Lady Margaret Holt, of Sutton Scotney, Winchester, £7,965,686 (£20,000 to St Ann's Hospice, Heald Green, Cheshire, £10,000 each to Barnardo's and RUKBA, and the residue to Christie Hospital, Manchester, for cancer research)

Ethel Annie Hornell, of Hythe, Kent, £392,240 (all her estate to the RNLI)

Reuben Basil Hunt, of Earls Colne, Colchester, £2,760,273 (the residue equally between the Sue Ryder Foundation, Guide Dogs for the Blind Association, Hearing Dogs for the Deaf, British Wireless for the Blind Fund, Fight for Sight and the Friends of Felsted School)

Maj. John George Potter-Kirby, of Shipton by Beningborough, York, £3,113,643 (£10,000 each to 19 charities, and £10,000 and one sixth of the residue each to York Civic Trust, the Animal Health Trust, Army Benevolent Fund, Guide Dogs for the Blind Association, National Canine Defence League and the Gurkha Welfare Trust)

Agnes Mary Christabel Latham, of Pickering, N. Yorks, £741,841 (the residue equally between the RSPCA, RSPB, Imperial Cancer Research Fund, Royal National Mission to Deep Sea Fishermen, National Trust, National Library for the Blind, Scope, British Leprosy Relief Association, and the Fauna and Flora Preservation Society)

Emil Lechner, of Park Avenue, London NW10, £549,414 (the residue equally between Norwood Childcare, Jewish Care and the Imperial Cancer Research Fund)

Norman Levitt, of Hereford Road, London W2, £1,423,066 (the residue equally between Nightingale House Home for Aged Jews, London, and Amnesty International)

John Upton Lewin, of Brentford, Middx, £1,727,459 (the residue equally between the Imperial Cancer Research Fund and Cancer Research Campaign)

Mary Lidbury, of Brushford, Dulverton, Somerset, £2,506,035 (the residue to the RNLI, desiring it be used for two of its larger lifeboats, to be named *Charles Lidbury* and *Austin Lidbury*, and two smaller lifeboats to be named *Polly Lidbury* and *Bessie Lidbury*)

Arthur Francis Patrick McCullagh, of Wool, Wareham, Dorset, £1,295,399 (the residue equally between the Marie Curie Memorial Foundation, British Heart Foundation, Help the Aged, and the Brook Hospital for Animals, London)

Ethel Marks, of Brompton Road, London SW3, £2,104,953 (the residue to the Maurice Marks Charitable Trust)

Nina Adele Nash, of Hatfield, Herts, £1,355,603 (half the residue to Amnesty International, and half for such charities already indicated by her to her trustees, otherwise as they choose)

Lisbeth Margaret Nott, of Eastbourne, E. Sussex, £753,779 (the residue equally between the Cancer Relief Macmillan Fund and the National Asthma Campaign)

Cyril Frederick Oliver, of Coventry, £1,904,404 (the residue to the Save the Children Fund, the income to be used for the relief of distress of children in Third World countries)

Barbara Aileen Page, of Surbiton, Surrey, £1,068,468 (three quarters of the residue to Battersea Dogs Home and one quarter of the residue to the RNLI)

Jessie Jacquetta Priestley, of Leysbourne, Chipping Campden, Glos, £1,304,983 (£100,000 to the Royal Literary Fund, to be applied in accordance with her written wishes and to be known as the J. B. Priestley Fund)

William Procter, of Blackpool, £2,766,204 (the residue equally between the Methodist Homes for the Aged, for a home in Blackpool, the National Trust, and the Arnold School Development Fund, Blackpool)

Stanley Randall, of Bournemouth, Dorset, £1,017,041 (one sixth of the residue each to the RNLI, Guide Dogs for the Blind Association and RNIB)

Gwynneth Mary Rees, of Sketty, Swansea, £1,861,792 (three 26ths of the residue each to the Guide Dogs for the Blind Association and the PDSA, one 13th of the residue each to SPANA, RSPCA, NSPCC, Scope, St Dunstan's, and the Ty Olwen Continuing Care Unit at Morriston Hospital, Swansea, and one 26th of the residue each to Sight Savers International, Barnardo's, Ex-Services Mental Welfare Society, Imperial Cancer Research Fund, Parkinson's Disease Society, Swansea Mission to Seamen, Swansea District Society for Mentally Handicapped Children, and Swansea and District Friends of the Blind)

Hildegarde Johanna Reynolds, of West Byfleet, Surrey, £354,903 (all her estate to New College, Oxford, for scholarships in the name of her son Richard Douglas Reynolds)

Marjorie Cecil Richmond, of Timperley, Altrincham, Cheshire, £500,850 (the residue to the National Trust)

Carol Sims-Roberts, of Buxton, Berks, £1,182,737 (the residue to the RSPCA)

Malcolm Robinson, of Ashington, Northumberland, £467,169 (the residue equally between the North of England Cancer Research Campaign, Muscular Dystrophy Group and British Heart Foundation)

Richard Crabb Saxby, of Warwick Road, London W5, £546,808 (the residue equally between the Imperial Cancer Research Fund, the London Symphony Orchestra Sickness and Benevolent Association, and St Catherine's College, Oxford)

Laurance Leslie-Smith, of Ennismore Gardens, London SW7, £3,171,998 (£500,000 to the Weitzman Institute Foundation, London, £50,000 to British ORT, and the residue to the Jewish Philanthropic Association for Israel and the Middle East)

Marigold Geraldine Smith, of Allensmore, Hereford, £2,341,055 (the residue equally between the British Diabetic Association, and the PDSA, for its work in Wales and the Border counties)

Margaret Marion Ransford Staffurth, of Harrogate, N. Yorks, £2,611,358 (the residue equally between Harrogate Neighbours Housing Association, National Children's Homes, Papworth Village Settlement, Andover, the Bow Mission, London, Musicians Benevolent Fund, Royal Star and Garter Home, Richmond, Salvation Army, Great Ormond Street Hospital for Sick Children, London, and the Yorkshire Arthritis Research Trust)

Alice Standring, of Wilmslow, Cheshire, £1,433,028 (the residue equally between Alzheimer's Disease Society, St Ann's Hospice, Heald Green, and East Cheshire Hospice, Macclesfield)

Harold Jacob Stern, of Queensway, London W2, £1,204,770 (his properties 2 and 4 Pembridge Gardens, London W2, with all fixtures, fittings and furniture, to the Federation of Jewish Relief Organizations, and the residue equally between King David Foundation, Liverpool, Maghull Homes, Liverpool, Merseyside Jewish Welfare Council, Liverpool and District Home for Aged Jews, Liverpool Old Hebrew Congregation, Friends of the University of Liverpool, Liverpool Personal Service Society, Royal Liverpool Philharmonic Society, Central British Fund for World Jewish Relief, Artists General Benevolent Institution, Jews Temporary Shelter, London, Jewish Historical Society of England, Jewish Museum, London, Royal Society of Chemistry Benevolent Fund, the Oil and Colour Chemists Association, and Magdalen College Development Trust, Oxford)

Leonard Richard Stevens, of Effingham, Surrey, £1,696,129 (the residue equally between St Joseph's Hospice, London, Providence Row Night Refuge and Home, London, CAFOD, Catholic Truth Society, and 'the Catholic Children's Society Arundel and Brighton, Portsmouth and Southwark')

Noel Dudley Tayler Sutton, of Bournemouth, Dorset, £1,717,148 (£200,000 to the RNLI)

Edith Tagg, of Hyde, Cheshire, £359,313 (the residue equally between the RNIB, and the Christie Hospital, Manchester, to establish the Edith and Hiram Tagg and Samuel Fidler Gregson Memorial Fund, to benefit children and the elderly)

Jean Story Tatham, of Kirklinton, Carlisle, £1,068,865 (the residue equally between the Cumbrian committee of the Cancer Research Campaign, Multiple Sclerosis Society, Royal Masonic Hospital, National Equine Defence League, RNLI, RAF Benevolent Fund, Royal Naval Benevolent Trust, Arthritis and Rheumatism Council, Donkey Sanctuary, Sidmouth, British Heart Foundation, Newcastle upon Tyne, Penrith and District Royal British Legion, and Guide Dogs for the Blind Association, Carlisle branch)

Harry Taylforth, of Gargrave, Skipton, N. Yorks, £819,296 (the residue for such charitable institutions or organizations, including non-profit organizations operating for the benefit of the local community within the Craven District Council area, as his trustees select)

Humphrey Richardson Taylor, of Cheam, Surrey, £9,321,349 (the residue for such charitable objects or purposes as his trustees select)

Cdr Henry George Tidy, OBE, of Beaconsfield, Bucks, £1,089,692 (two 13ths of the residue to King George's Fund for Sailors, and one 13th of the residue each to the RNLI, Oxfam, National Trust, Imperial Cancer Research Fund, Children's Society, Help the Aged, British Red Cross, Barnardo's, RSPCA, NSPCC and RSPB)

Doris Lilian Warwick, of Richmond, Surrey, £1,312,551 (the residue equally between the Cancer Relief Macmillan Fund, International League for the Protection of Horses, RSPCA, and the British Red Cross, for famine and disaster relief)

Ronald Jackson Windle, of Gargrave, Skipton, N. Yorks, £1,507,536 (a five-acre field and other property in Gargrave for the building of low-cost housing for local inhabitants, to be built predominantly in second-hand York stone)

Doris Wood, of West Clandon, Surrey, £1,604,971 (£20,000 and one third of the residue each to the Cancer Research Campaign, the Stock Exchange Benevolent Fund and the Royal Masonic Benevolent Institution)

Peter Anthony Woodward, of Burnaby Crescent, London W4, £641,878 (the residue to the RNLI)

The National Debt

Net central government borrowing each year represents an addition to the National Debt. At the end of March 1996 the National Debt amounted to some £390,700 million of which about £18,325 million was in currencies other than sterling. Of the £372,350 million sterling debt, £267,000 million consisted of gilt-edged stock; of this, 31 per cent had a maturity of up to five years, 42 per cent a maturity of over five years and up to 15 years, and 27 per cent a maturity of over 15 years or undated. The remaining sterling debt was made up mainly of national savings (£53,800 million), certificates of tax deposits, Treasury bills, and Ways and Means advances (very short-term internal government borrowing).

Sizeable trust funds have been established over the past 50 years for the purpose of reducing the National Debt. The National Fund was established in 1927 with an original gift of £499,878. At 31 March 1997 was valued at £137,805,861; it is administered by Baring Trust Co. Ltd. The Elsie Mackay Fund was established in 1929 with an original gift of £527,809 to run for 45–50 years. It was wound up in 1979, when it was valued at £4,902,864. The John Buchanan Fund was established in 1932 with gifts totalling £36,702 to run for 50 years. It was wound up in 1982, when it was valued at £204,138.

Broadcasting

TELEVISION

A year of high-profile flops, accusations of 'dumbing down', creative conservatism and a widespread absence of strong new shows in many categories, 1996–7 saw British television relying heavily on proven winners. Demand for high audiences jeopardized quality as the main channels attempted to rise to the challenge of cable and satellite, and to a new, free-to-air terrestrial station, Channel 5, which finally arrived after several false starts. Broadcasters' minds were also preoccupied by the prospect of a new generation of digital channels.

Significantly, two of the year's outright successes were old favourites: *EastEnders*, which in April became the first soap ever to win the BAFTA award for best drama series, and a triple Christmas helping of the comedy drama *Only Fools and Horses*, starring David Jason as the wily wide-boy Del Boy. A record 24.3 million people watched the final episode of the *Only Fools and Horses* Yuletide trilogy, but that did not alter the fact that Del Boy and company, and the residents of Albert Square, were television stalwarts, crowd pleasers guaranteed to improve ratings when competition hots up. The safety-first mood prevalent in British television that saw the revival of such old chestnuts as *Poldark*, *The Liver Birds* and a repeat of *Till Death Us Do Part* during 1996–7 was due partly to the perceived threat of Channel 5, originally planned to start in January 1997 but delayed until Easter owing to transmission difficulties, a problem that continues to dog the new service. The arrival of the UK's first new terrestrial station for more than a decade failed to spur the established stations into a frenzy of original thinking. Instead, BBC1 and especially ITV reacted defensively to the newcomer.

In November ITV launched what it hoped would be a pre-emptive strike against Channel 5 with a fourth, Sunday evening, episode of *Coronation Street*, still the network's most popular show. But ratings for the extra programme fell short of those achieved during the week. The Street's makers, Granada Television, drafted in a new producer, Brian Park, who in the early months of 1997 attempted, with limited success, to reinvigorate the soap. Several of the serial's older characters, including Derek Wilson and Don Brennan, were written out. Storylines were beefed up. The aim was to broaden the Street's appeal to attract new, younger viewers. But perhaps, as some critics suggested, *Coronation Street* was losing touch with contemporary Britain and its preoccupations. By contrast, *EastEnders*, with its tougher, more inventive storylines and a line-up of characters battling with late 20th-century life-style issues, was, reviewers agreed, the soap to watch. Around 22 million viewers tuned in to witness Cindy Beale flee Albert Square following her adulterous affair with David Wicks, and large sections of the nation were desperate to discover who had sired Tiffany's baby. ITV, however, did have one surprise asset for soap fans. For years Yorkshire Television's rural saga *Emmerdale* had struggled to gain credibility with critics and sceptical audiences. While *Coronation Street* fought to maintain high standards, *Emmerdale*, adding a third weekly episode in January 1997, went from strength to strength, even attracting a significant following among younger audiences. This extra commitment to soap did not impress the regulator, the Independent Television Commission, which in its annual performance reviews, published in April, suggested that ITV needed to add more diversity to its peak-time schedules.

CHANNEL 5 GOES ON AIR

ITV's investment in soap opera was not justified by Channel 5's initial offerings. The Spice Girls, supposedly the epitome of modern womanhood, serenaded the newcomer onto the airwaves on Easter Sunday, but 'girl power' could not save the network from a critical drubbing. The consensus was that the established services had little to fear from their new rival, hamstrung by low programme budgets and a schedule laden with American imports. Writing in the *Independent*, Jasper Rees summed up the feelings of many when he said, 'By a random stroke of good luck half the nation has been deprived of adequate reception of Channel 5's float-past of derivative junk … There is more padding on this station than in all the cells in Broadmoor.'

Predictably, Channel 5 built its early evening schedule around a soap opera, *Family Affairs*. The show at least had the benefit of being produced in Britain, albeit by Grundy, the people responsible for *Neighbours*, yet, despite its concentration on sex, reviewers could find little of merit in the serial. More unusual was the new service's approach to news; its main evening bulletin was shown at 8.30 p.m., earlier than ITV's or BBC1's nightly résumés. Dispensing with television news's traditional presentation style, Channel 5's news was read by the former BBC presenter Kirsty Young, who, in another break with convention, wandered around the studio. The idea was to make the news accessible to the under-25s, in keeping with the network's 'modern mainstream' approach. In practice, Channel 5's news was fairly traditional in terms of the stories it covered.

Together with other aspects of the new arrival's programming, notably the game shows and celebrity gossip, this approach led to accusations of yet another example of 'dumbing down'. Throughout 1996—7 there was evidence of a new brashness in British television; Carlton's live debate on the monarchy, *Monarchy: The Nation Decides*, shown in January, divided opinion although many critics were convinced that it was not so much a debate on a matter of national importance as a 'slanging match' designed to arouse controversy and generate high ratings.

It is still early days for Channel 5 but after six months on air a relaunch seems almost inevitable. There is no doubt that it is a different kind of terrestrial service, having more in common with Sky Television than Britain's traditional networks.

RHODES FAILS TO CONQUER

Commentators detected a growing tendency for British television to underperform on many fronts during 1996—7, particularly in drama. *EastEnders* aside, the BBC suffered a succession of embarrassing failures. The most conspicuous was BBC1's *Rhodes*, a £10 million serialization of the life of the British imperialist Cecil Rhodes, with Martin Shaw as the eponymous empire builder. His performance was not as bad as the ratings suggested – a meagre four million. But reviewers agreed that the serial lacked coherence. Possibly even more disappointing was the long-awaited serialization of Joseph Conrad's novel, *Nostromo*, screened on BBC2 in the winter with an international cast including the Italian actor Claudio Amendola. Claudia Cardinale, Albert Finney and Colin Firth also starred. It looked ravishing but the narrative was too ponderous for even the most patient. Another BBC serialization of a classic novel, Sir Walter Scott's *Ivanhoe*, was greeted with dismay and ridicule by reviewers. While these ambitious dramatizations brought little credit to the BBC, whose drama department was in disarray following a leadership crisis, some of the corporation's more modest ventures in small-screen fiction were of high quality. Adaptations of George Eliot's *The Mill on the Floss* and Anne Brontë's *The Tenant of Wildfell Hall*, respectively in one and three parts, were widely regarded as sensitive treatments, well cast and convincingly told.

Responding to the BBC's earlier success with *Pride and Prejudice*, ITV, in autumn 1996, demonstrated that it too could translate Jane Austen to the small screen with flair. *Emma*, starring Kate Beckinsale, was generally welcomed. However, it lacked the impact of Granada's reworking of Daniel Defoe's *Moll Flanders*. As ever, Andrew Davies's script took several liberties with the text, adding a lesbian twist to what was already a raunchy tale. ITV's adaptation, featuring a full-bodied performance from Alex Kingston as Moll, left little to the imagination as one bedroom scene followed another. Undoubtedly, the programme was made with a view to overseas sales but several critics praised this less than reverential treatment of a literary classic. A triumph of a different kind for ITV was Jimmy McGovern's *Hillsborough*, a passionate account of the football stadium tragedy. Some reviewers objected to McGovern's meshing of fact and fiction, but the film sat comfortably within the impressive tradition of Granada drama-documentaries. Significantly, *Hillsborough* helped reopen an inquiry into police conduct during the incident. Nevertheless, there remained a feeling that ITV was still failing to take enough risks in drama and was relying too much on well-worn, long-running series such as *Heartbeat*, *London's Burning* and *Soldier Soldier*.

More worrying was British television's failure throughout 1996—7 to screen a wholly satisfactory, high-profile serial. The BBC's decision to repeat *Our Friends in the North* and *Pride and Prejudice* during summer 1997 only emphasized what was absent from the schedules. Similarly, Channel 4's repeat of *The Jewel in the Crown*, timed to coincide with the 50th anniversary of the end of the British Raj, was a reminder of how commercial pressures have scaled down ITV's ambitions in drama; *The Jewel in the Crown* was originally shown on ITV. It is impossible to imagine the network undertaking anything of this scale or subtlety in the late 1990s.

Another disappointment was, critics agreed, Chris Carter's eagerly awaited new series *Millennium*, his first since *The X Files*. ITV featured the programme in its summer schedule, but many commentators wondered what such a dark, nihilistic show, based on an investigator who reads the minds of criminals, was doing on a mainstream network. It would be wrong to dismiss all ITV drama as mere ratings fodder, recounting the activities of policemen and medical practitioners. *Reckless*, a bittersweet romance, was one of the year's most refreshing shows. But the tendency for ITV and the BBC to rely increasingly on star-driven vehicles was apparent throughout 1996—7. *Reckless* was no exception; its star was the ubiquitous Robson Green. This obsession, though, is hardly surprising. David Jason's popularity was highlighted again in February when *A Touch of Frost* drew more than 18 million viewers, a huge audience by any standards.

But perhaps one reason why BBC2's *This Life*, returning for an extended and possibly final run in 1997, became the cult drama of the year was because it started out with a cast of young unknown actors. For all its exaggerated hedonism and overdrawn view of the legal profession, *This Life* seemed to catch the mood of the times. Channel 4's outstanding drama of the year, Paula Milne's *The Fragile Heart* starring Nigel Hawthorne as a heart surgeon forced to face some uncomfortable truths, also proved that British television drama still has the courage to engage with ideas and kick against stereotypes.

SITCOM FALTERS

If the year threw up more than a few disappointments in drama, most commentators were equally despairing of the overall standards in comedy and entertainment. In fact, in its annual performance reviews the ITC rebuked ITV for allowing drama to dominate the schedules, effectively squeezing out situation comedy. Sitcom is possibly the most difficult of all television genres. It can also be expensive if star names are involved, with little prospect of lucrative sales abroad. This is presumably why Channel 5 has decided to ignore sitcom altogether. Nowadays ITV prefers to experiment with the less risky comedy drama hybrid. As with mainstream drama, a star name is usually involved, hence Yorkshire Television's promising new comedy drama *See You Friday*, starring Neil Pearson. The new LWT sitcom, *Holding the Baby*, featuring Nick Hancock as a single parent and shown in autumn 1996, gave ITV its biggest sitcom success for several years, but with ratings of only eight million and a mixed critical response, it was hardly a hit. More successful was *Cold Feet*, a stylish romantic comedy drama, winner of the Golden Rose of Montreux, television's top entertainment prize.

From autumn 1997 ITV is coming under new management with the departure of network director Marcus Plantin. A top priority for Mr Plantin's successor will be to secure a hit sitcom capable of taking on some of the BBC's ageing warhorses. But at least the corporation is still investing in new sitcoms, even if the results are erratic. *Chalk*, a new BBC1 series that attempted to do for the classroom what *Fawlty Towers* did for the hotel trade, received poor reviews but may eventually develop into something genuinely funny. Possibly the most successful of the BBC's new comedies was Jim Broadbent's portrayal of an incompetent bank manager in *The Peter Principle*. Compared with the slickness of America's *Friends* or *Frasier*, most reviewers agreed that the majority of British comedy failed to deliver enough laughs. Channel 4 was responsible for one of the year's funniest programmes, *Never Mind the Horrocks*, a sketch show featuring Jane Horrocks in a variety of roles. Other comedy highlights included BBC2's *The Fast Show*, BBC1's *Harry Enfield and Chums* and ITV's *An Evening with Lily Savage*.

DOCUMENTARIES MARGINALIZED

The BBC and Channel 4 made much of the running in factual programming. The ITC criticized ITV for its low provision of documentary and arts shows. More alarming still was the reduction in off-peak network documentaries and the narrowing of the range of subjects. Royalty and show business were favourite themes. *Hollywood Lovers*, following on from *Hollywood Women* and *Hollywood Pets*, provoked controversy when Yorkshire-Tyne Tees refused to screen the series because the company's managing director, Bruce Gyngell, considered it indecent. A more entertaining and perceptive view of celebrity was provided by *Elton John: Tantrums and Tiaras*, an unusually revealing film. Another enlightening look at the rich and famous was provided by BBC1

in *Ruby Wax Meets* … Ms Wax's encounter with the Duchess of York was compulsive viewing. Non-entertainment shows were also in retreat on BBC1. Most tellingly, *Panorama*, the BBC's flagship current affairs series, was shunted out of its traditional 9.30 p.m. slot to make way for *Birds of a Feather*; *Panorama* is now screened at 10 p.m. The channel's veteran arts programme *Omnibus* was also moved closer to the margins of the evening's viewing.

If these were other symptoms of 'dumbing down', what were audiences to make of the new mid-week lottery show, universally derided by critics, or the corporation's inept celebration of the 60th anniversary of BBC Television in *Auntie's All-Time Greats*, shown in autumn 1996? The world of broadcasting has changed beyond recognition since the television service was launched in 1936, but what would Lord Reith have made of an event that honoured Desmond Lynam in preference to Sir David Attenborough?

As ever, it was BBC2 which proved that the public service ethos still counted for something. The channel's flagship autumn documentary series, *The System*, provided audiences with a bleak insight into the twilight world of social security viewed from both sides of the desk. *American Vision*, a history of American art deftly presented by Robert Hughes, was another feather in BBC2's cap. However, a much publicized series on Britain's ruling classes, *The Aristocracy*, failed to live up to its hype. The documentary series *Modern Times* continued in impressive form, turning its attention to such topics as a Jewish marriage, Hong Kong and black America. Also notable was *Soho Stories*, a late-night glimpse of one of London's most exotic and eclectic neighbourhoods, using state-of-the-art cameras to capture intimate footage.

The Dimbleby brothers, David and Jonathan, acquitted themselves well, providing documentaries on India and Hong Kong respectively. The two broadcasters were also much in evidence during television's general election coverage. The 1997 election was relatively quiet from the broadcasters' perspective; their only mistake, perhaps, was to devote so much airtime to the hustings. *The Nine O'Clock News* extended its bulletins by 15 minutes during the campaign, which resulted in the defection of around a million viewers. Research conducted by the ITC suggested that viewers, especially women and first-time voters, felt that television had spent too many hours reporting and analysing the political battle.

DIGITAL DREAMS

Behind the cameras 1996–7 was a year of important changes as the three main independent television combines, Granada, Carlton and United, tightened their grip on the network via a succession of mergers and take-overs. Carlton and Granada abandoned their traditional rivalry to join forces in British Digital Broadcasting. The consortium beat competition from rival Digital Television Network to broadcast 15 commercial digital terrestrial channels planned to start in late 1998. The move was hailed as the biggest development in broadcasting since the introduction of colour television 30 years ago.

Possibly more significant in the short term was a series of changes in key jobs. In addition to Mr Plantin's resignation from ITV, Michael Grade, Channel 4's controversial chief executive, announced earlier in 1997 that he was leaving the industry. His place was taken by Michael Jackson, formerly director of television at the BBC where he also ran BBC1. There was widespread agreement that Mr Grade had allowed Channel 4 to lose its creative edge. BSkyB also suffered a crisis of confidence in the summer when its management team of Sam Chisholm and David Chance announced they were leaving. Their decision precipitated a rapid fall in the company's share price. Many commentators now believe that BSkyB's future lies in the hands of Rupert Murdoch's daughter Elisabeth, who joined the company in autumn 1996. Around 25 per cent of British homes are now able to receive the service, so BSkyB is well established. But with digital television imminent and the BBC about to enter the pay-TV market offering a series of specialist services, plus a 24-hour news operation to rival Sky's, the prospects for future growth look uncertain. Multi-channel television is now a force to be reckoned with in the UK, but there are signs that the appetite for niche services is limited. Granada's entry into the pay-TV market in the autumn was not a conspicuous success; one of Granada Sky Broadcasting's channels, Talk TV, announced this summer it would cease broadcasting.

RADIO

Most commentators agreed that 1996–7 was something of a new era for BBC Radio, which many believed would lose out to television in director-general John Birt's reorganization of the corporation announced in June 1996. These sweeping changes began to take effect in autumn 1996. New genre-based commissioning departments were set up, covering such key areas as music, in the newly formed BBC Broadcast division, now responsible for commissioning all radio and television programmes. As far as most listeners were concerned the effects of these changes were minimal. They did mean, however, that in the case of a major event, such as the 1997 Glastonbury music festival, Radio 1 and BBC2 could work in tandem rather than as rivals.

Of more concern to many people was how the new Radio 4 controller, James Boyle, would change Britain's best-loved broadcast network. Despite endless press speculation that Radio 4 would move down-market, the changes, finally announced in August 1997, were not as radical as many had feared.

Mr Boyle was convinced that there were still more people, perhaps as many as a million, who could be persuaded to become Radio 4 devotees. Of particular interest were the under-35s, as the proportion of older listeners tuning in had gradually increased during the past four years. The new strategy involved giving more prominence to flagship shows; from April 1998 *Today* will start 30 minutes earlier each day at 6 a.m. and *The Archers* will be extended by an extra episode on Sundays at 7 p.m. *Kaleidoscope, Breakaway, Afternoon Shift, Weekending* and *Mediumwave* were among the casualties. There was much debate over the fate of *Yesterday in Parliament*, but its future will not be decided until a review of all BBC news is completed later in the year. Meanwhile the full force of the controller's plans will not be known until the end of 1998.

Mr Boyle's decision to revive *Round Britain Quiz*, first broadcast in 1947, was welcomed by most critics. The new format, launched in August, was presented by Nick Clarke. Predictably there were accusations that the questions featured on the new *Round Britain Quiz* were not as demanding as they once were. Overall 1996–7 was a year of solid achievement at Radio 4, with audiences holding steady. One of the year's highlights was the drama, *Spoonface Steinberg*, a moving monologue from a young girl dying of cancer. The play drew a huge response from listeners. The Sony Best Drama Award, however, went to another Radio 4 programme, *Five Kinds of Silence*, about two sisters who killed their abusive father.

OUTRAGE IN AMBRIDGE

Storylines in *The Archers* sparked controversy. One of the radio soap's ex-producers, William Smethurst, dismissed the serial as 'a ferment of greed, sexual passion and family discord, racial hatred and rampant, radical feminism'. In October there were claims that Tony Parkin, the agricultural story editor, had resigned because he was unhappy with the way the soap was changing. The antics of some of its characters, such as Kate Aldridge smoking dope and taking Ecstasy, could have come straight from *Brookside*, although their treatment was a good deal more considered. But the storyline that really caught the listeners' imagination was more traditional. It concerned Eddie Grundy's battle and eventual triumph over his odious landlord Simon Pemberton. Passions were so aroused by this fictional showdown that in a *Today* discussion on the subject presenter Anna Ford used a four-letter word to describe the loathsome Pemberton. *Today* also aroused controversy in December 1996 when the programme's Personality of the Year contest was discredited after evidence of vote-rigging when 4,000 votes for John Major were disqualified. The year saw the departure of Nick Ross from the chair of *Call Nick Ross* after ten years. His successor was Edward Stourton. Cliff Morgan, the veteran presenter of *Sport on 4*, was another familiar voice who announced that he was leaving the station.

Anxieties over changes in the operations of the World Service continued to be expressed. Despite the Foreign Office agreeing to £5 million extra funding and the provision of additional safeguards to protect the service following the merger of its news-gathering activities with the corporation's domestic news directorate, critics still felt the character of the World Service was being destroyed from within.

RADIO 2 TRIUMPHS

The success story of BBC Radio was Radio 2. New developments included a Saturday comedy hour featuring Jasper Carrot and Griff Rhys Jones. Also joining the new look Radio 2 were Hugh Scully and Pam Ayers. Cynics suggested that the signing of such DJs as Bob Harris and Alan Freeman made the station resemble Radio 1 in exile. But controller Jim Moir's policy of wooing the over-40s with mellow rock, plus a bigger showcase for soul, was beginning to pay off. Evidence emerged that the decline in ratings may have been halted. In August 1997, Radio 2 recorded its highest share of the radio audience for two years, 13.2 per cent compared with Radio 1's 9.7 million.

The decline at Radio 1, below 10 per cent for the first time ever, was hardly surprising following the sacking of Chris Evans, its breakfast presenter, in January 1997. Evans's irreverent style had slowed the decline in Radio 1's ratings, but his turbulent reign finally came to an end after Matthew Bannister, the Radio 1 controller, refused to allow him extra time off to pursue his television career. Few doubted Evans's brilliance as an original voice but even his fans were becoming dismayed at what they regarded as his arrogance and lack of professionalism. Simon Mayo stepped in to fill the breakfast slot for a short time, but Mr Bannister decided to break with tradition and allow the show to come from Manchester, instead of London, where it was hosted by full-time replacements Mark Radcliffe and Marc 'Lard' Riley. As Radio 1 prepared for its 30th birthday celebrations in September 1997 there was speculation that its audience size could dip further still; a new London station, XFM, hopes to poach listeners from the network.

Radio 3 had a relatively quiet 12 months. However, certain critics continued to accuse the network of 'dumbing down', referring to the possibility that Radio 3 might emulate more popular stations and introduce a playlist. But there was praise for a number of new programmes, including *Private Passions*, winner of the Broadcasting Press Guild's radio prize. Writing in the *Sunday Times*, radio critic Paul Donovan said the series, a more erudite version of *Desert Island Discs*, proved it was possible to talk about music while avoiding jargon and cliché. For those who insisted that Radio 3 was too preoccupied with attempting to reduce Classic FM's audiences, controller Nicholas Kenyon had an answer. Launching in December what he described as Radio 3's 'most ambitious project to date',

Sounding the Century, Kenyon said: 'It's about time we stopped thinking of modern music as a problem and realized that our century has produced some of the most thrilling and moving music.' This celebration of 20th-century composers, kicking off in February 1997 with an acclaimed Stravinsky concert by Pierre Boulez, will run until the millennium. A more populist innovation was the BBC Proms in the Park in 1996, in which more than 25,000 people gathered in Hyde Park to enjoy a relay of the Last Night of the Proms beamed onto giant video screens.

INDEPENDENTS

At Classic FM the mood was less jubilant. The station underwent its biggest relaunch since going on air in September 1992. The service's credibility had begun to take a knock; its approach to serious music was seen, in some quarters, as part of the culture of sound-bites, cynically targeted at what Alan Bennett derided as 'Saga louts', a reference to the advertisements aimed at the over-50s who make up much of the audience. The station was under new management, having been taken over by Swindon-based commercial radio giant GWR in autumn 1995. Classic's new chief executive, Ralph Bernard, was determined to put the station back on a sound financial footing, increase station awareness and add one million new listeners. His first raft of changes included axing Paul Callan's *Celebrity Choice*, removing Andre Leon and Jane Markham as regular presenters and scaling down Susannah Simon's contribution. In such a competitive climate, with more than 200 UK stations now competing for audiences and still more planned for the future, Mr Bernard's task will not be easy; in fact Classic's audience share showed a slight increase, according to the latest industry figures, published in August, up from 3.1 to 3.3 million.

After the upheavals of the past, Talk Radio had a better year in 1996–7. Its audience figures, although still small, were at least static, no mean achievement in such a tough market. But perhaps more significant was research showing that its listeners – 2.2 million a week – stay tuned longer than those of the other commercial national networks. When Mr Boyle's reforms start to work their way through he will look with keen interest at what impact they are having on Talk's performance.

Conservation and Heritage

THE NATURAL ENVIRONMENT

Lewes Downs Incident

In April 1997 part of the chalk downs at Offham, near Lewes, E. Sussex, was ploughed by a farmer in order to attract the EC subsidy for growing flax. At £591 per hectare, this subsidy is more than the conservation agencies can pay in compensation, and, apparently because of a bureaucratic slip, it is available for any land suitable for growing flax, including Sites of Special Scientific Interest (SSSIs). English Nature, which is responsible for SSSIs, did not refer the case to the Secretary of State for the Environment since it considered that this particular SSSI was not important enough. However, the Environment Secretary, John Gummer, decided to intervene on his own initiative, perhaps conscious of unfavourable publicity attracted by this case during the general election campaign. A blocking order suspending further ploughing was served, and up to 200 volunteers, mostly local people, set about restoring the turf, inventing a new word, 'unploughing', in the process.

The Offham incident emphasizes the inadequacy of the 1981 Wildlife and Countryside Act which relies on the voluntary principle; essentially this means that SSSI owners can do as they like provided they tell English Nature first. English Nature can, in theory, purchase land, compulsorily if necessary, but in practice never does so for fear of upsetting the landowning community. The new Environment minister, Michael Meacher, has promised to review the legislation. The Government is also said to be taking another look at incentives for managing SSSIs to the 'favourable conservation status' standards specified in EC law, and also at using land owned by the Forestry Commission and Ministry of Defence in ways more sympathetic to nature conservation.

Habitats Directive

Wildlife Link, the environmental forum and watchdog body, criticized the Government for its slowness in implementing the 1992 EC Habitats Directive, which aims to establish a Europe-wide network of protected sites (Special Areas of Conservation or SACs) by the year 2000. Although the directive became law in the UK in June 1994 and a list of candidate sites was published in March 1995, their proposed boundaries are still confidential and details of how they were selected have still not been released. Several sites which seem to qualify under EC criteria were omitted, apparently because of existing permissions for development. These in-clude Cardiff Bay, where a barrage scheme will soon displace mudflats of value for wildlife, and Thorne Moors, which is being stripped of its peat by the fertilizer industry. In a test case brought by the RSPB over Lappell Bank in Kent, the European Court decided that it was unlawful for the Government to exclude a site on the grounds of proposed development. Notifying such sites would, however, involve the Government in paying out millions of pounds in compensation, and may be the main reason for its lack of haste.

Translocation

One means much favoured in recent years of apparently reconciling development and wildlife is to move the wildlife out of harm's way. Occasionally wild animals are rounded up and moved, as in a recent case involving badgers in Yeovil, but more often the habitat is dug up, turf by turf, and re-laid. This has come to be known as 'translocation'. Translocation enables developers to claim they have benefited the local environment. The evidence suggests, however, that most translocations are unsuccessful. Few of the cases examined by the Worldwide Fund for Nature in 1996 were found to have had clear objectives, and even fewer were monitored after removal. For example, an orchid-rich meadow at Solihull, moved to make way for a Tesco superstore, was promoted at the time as a great success, but in reality the receptor site has proved too wet and is now an unprepossessing field of sedges and rushes.

A still unpublished review of translocations by Dr James Bullock of the Institute of Terrestrial Ecology found a more successful example at Twyford Down, near Winchester. Here, chalk grassland turf removed from the path of the bypass has been transplanted onto the site of the former city ring road. Bullock attributed the success of the scheme to the dryness and shallowness of the soil, and hence the ease in which the turves could be lifted. By contrast, turves from the wet flood-meadow below the down lost some of their original interest when removed to the transplant site, probably because the degree of wetness has changed. Bullock concluded that translocation does not usually retain all the original features of the habitat, but that it is better than nothing if there is no other way of saving a habitat.

Birds

Seabirds suffered from the unrelenting rain at the height of their breeding season in June 1997, as well as from local shortages of sand-eels. At the RSPB's Bempton Cliff reserve in Yorkshire, thousands of kittiwake and guillemot chicks were swept from their ledges during unseasonable storms, while many puffin chicks drowned in their burrows on the Farne Isles. It was a better year for the ruddy duck, an attractive American stiff-tailed duck which has become well-established on English lakes and waterways since its escape from Slimbridge wildfowl centre 40 years ago. In the early 1990s, European bird groups including the RSPB had called for the ducks to be shot *en masse* to prevent them from mating with the closely related but much rarer white-headed duck of Spain and Turkey. A trial cull got underway, but some conservationists questioned the decision on scientific, economic and practical grounds. By 1997, the UK government agreed to call it off. As a compromise the ruddy duck will be listed as a quarry species, allowing sportsmen to shoot it.

DROUGHT AND ABSTRACTION

Drought rivalled road-building as the most contentious environmental issue of 1997. The demand for water has almost doubled over the past five years, while the inadequacies of Britain's water infrastructure are well-known. Increased water abstraction threatens the natural environment by reducing river flows and drying out ponds, marshes and fens, which can quickly turn into thickets of scrub, losing most of their wetland wildlife in the process. In 1996, English Nature published a report showing that of 166 wetland SSSIs investigated, 89 were 'at risk' from abstraction.

Many environmental organizations put forward possible solutions to the problem. The Biodiversity Challenge Group, a consortium of charities and government advisers, called for increased powers for the Environment Agency 'to implement a sustainable water resource strategy', including a review of abstraction licences. It also wants the regulatory body, Ofwat, to set environmental standards for the water companies. The Council for the Protection of Rural England weighed in with its views on the role of land-use planning for managing water resources more efficiently. English Nature recommended more phosphate-stripping plants to reduce the main source of pollution from sewage and agro-chemicals, and suggested that pumping in summer from rivers and aquifers be made 'prohibitively expensive'.

The Commons environment committee held an enquiry which rejected new reservoirs as a solution, and argued instead for reducing leakages and more efficient management of resources by the water companies. The new Labour Government proposes to hold a 'water summit' and says that it intends to place a legal duty on water companies to conserve water.

PROTECTED SPECIES

Every five years the list of legally protected wild animals and plants is revised and the latest review was under way at the time of going to press. To qualify for protection, a species must be considered to be threatened with extinction unless action is taken to save it. If it recovers well enough to be out of danger, or if it dies out altogether, it is taken off the list. The current review is considering 33 species for addition to the list, and one, the viper's bugloss moth, for removal on the grounds of its apparent extinction. Most of the proposed additions are of obscure mosses, lichens and invertebrates known only to specialists. A more substantial proposed addition is the basking shark, one of the world's largest fishes, of which there have been fewer sightings recently and which may be in danger from over-fishing. Protection for the water vole may be extended to its riverbank home. This once well-known rodent has declined seriously, probably from a combination of river engineering, water pollution and increased predation from mink. Protection from commercial collection may be extended to the still common bluebell on the grounds that some woods have been stripped of their native bluebells by bulb traders. Butterfly collectors may in future be denied the colourful marsh fritillary. Four rare toadstools (Royal Bolete, Sandy Stilt Puffball, Oak Polypore and Hedgehog Fungus) may become the first fungi other than lichens to be protected in the UK.

The legal protection provided under the 1981 legislation is generally of indirect benefit, since most of the species are not threatened by collecting or hunting. Listing helps to attract funding for research and habitat management, and also strengthens the conservation case at planning inquiries. However, legal listing is a time-consuming and relatively expensive exercise, and few prosecutions have resulted except in the case of bats and protected birds. The UK's Biodiversity Action Plan (BAP), which was approved by the Government in May 1996, is proving a more effective form of species protection, since it is geared towards specific targets and the improvement of the habitats of rare animals and plants, providing funds for the necessary action to reverse damaging declines. It is likely that in future the protected list will take second place to the BAP as a legal back-up in the rare cases of direct prosecution.

HEDGES

From June 1997, planning permission has been needed to remove hedges of particular wildlife or historic importance. To qualify for listing, a hedge must either mark a historical boundary, for example a parish; stand on an archaeological feature such as an ancient bank; contain five or more shrubs within a short section (as the oldest hedges usually do); or be home to a rare species. Local authorities can now not only refuse to allow a landowner to pull up the hedge but also oblige him to replace it if he does so. Unfortunately, many hedges were pulled up in anticipation of the law, and effective protection is also undermined by the requirement for local authorities to 'take into account the circumstances' of farmers or developers and by the fact that many authorities lack the knowledge to identify and preserve interesting hedges.

Meanwhile, an amateur lawyer, Colin Seymour, backed by Yorkshire Wildlife Trust, crowned a long series of successful legal challenges by saving a hedge near Scarborough. He was able to produce in evidence a 230-year-old Inclosure Act which required the owner to 'make and forever maintain' the hedge. The case has implications for hedgerow protection everywhere since many Inclosure Acts contain similar clauses.

BYPASSES

The Newbury bypass was under construction in 1997, and the campaigners moved elsewhere, for example to the A30 Fairmile bypass in Devon and to the extension to Manchester airport. In March 1997, the former Transport minister, Stephen Norris, admitted on a *Panorama* programme that the Newbury bypass might have been a mistake; it might have been better, he said, to opt for an improved route through the town. Signs of a fundamental change in roads policy came in July 1997, when the Salisbury bypass was cancelled by the new Government. The decision followed public concern about a road which would damage wildlife sites, including West Harnham Meadows, a proposed SAC, as well as attractive scenery, including Constable's famous view of Salisbury Cathedral. A scheme to widen parts of the M25 was also cancelled. Meanwhile the National Trust secured the cancellation of a proposed bypass which would have cut across its Golden Cap estate in Dorset. Plainly public opinion is now an important factor in deciding whether or not a road should be built, which did not used to be the case.

DEVELOPMENT

The Gwent Levels, a landscape of coastal marshes and grassland intersected with ditches or rhynes, is threatened by roadworks and industrial development. In what is described as 'the largest inward investment in Europe', the Korea-based Lucky Goldstar Group decided to build a £1.7 billion electronics factory at Newport, south Wales, bringing an expected 6,100 new jobs to the area and transforming the local economy. The development passed through the planning process with unprecedented speed. The 145-hectare factory complex is expected to obliterate some 22 hectares of the St Brides SSSI, one of the richest parts of the Gwent Levels, and a further 70 hectares of SSSI have been allocated for what the local council calls 'other proposed development'. Furthermore, permission has been given for the first section of a dual carriageway which, local conservationists believe, will inevitably drag further roadworks and housing developments into this sensitive area.

The implications for wildlife and countryside of the projected 4.4 million new homes to be built in Britain by the year 2016 have not fully sunk in. The housing schemes will cover an expected 170,000 hectares, an area roughly the size of Greater London, mainly in 'green-field' sites; they could be one of the greatest threats to Britain's wildlife during the next 20 years.

NATURE RESERVES

Several important sites were secured as nature reserves during 1997. The Wiltshire Wildlife Trust purchased, with the help of the Heritage Lottery Fund, the 62-hectare Clattinger Farm, one of the finest remaining areas of flower-rich natural meadowland. In Gloucestershire one of England's best-preserved ancient woods, the 300-hectare Lower Woods at Wickwar, also became a nature reserve.

In April 1997, the Scottish Wildlife Trust and the Highland Council joined with resident islanders to purchase the Hebridean island of Eigg for £1.5 million from its previous owner, a Hong Kong-based businessman; most of the funding came from an anonymous group of sympathizers. The new owners hope to combine economic development with nature conservation.

Less happy is the state of the National Nature Reserves (NNRs), which are run by Britain's three wildlife agencies (English Nature, Scottish Natural Heritage and the Countryside Council for Wales). The agencies are exploring ways of reducing expenditure on nature reserves, either by contracting out estate work or by persuading wildlife charities and others to take over their management. However, the charities are themselves pressed for resources, and are understandably reluctant to do the agencies' work for them. One famous NNR, Braunton Burrows in north Devon, was struck off the list after negotiations between English Nature and the owners broke down. English Nature had been refused permission to introduce grazing livestock, which it considered necessary to control scrub invasion. Another NNR, the Wyre Forest in Worcestershire, is to be handed back to the Forestry Commission as part of a cost-saving package, and English Nature is said to be seeking 'partners' for another 27 NNRs.

INTRODUCTIONS

A new informal body, 'Flora locale', has promised to keep an eye on so-called 'wildflower' seed mixes and to promote the sale of home-grown seed. Though commonly used in wildlife restoration schemes, the great majority of 'wildflower' seeds are in fact of foreign origin, partly because of cheaper labour costs in eastern Europe but also because Britain has no requirement to use material of local origin. Flora locale is convinced that responsible conservationists and restorers would prefer to use local material, even if they had to pay a little more for it. The body is therefore pressing for a certification scheme to display the exact source of seeds and plants.

Apart from the fraudulent aspects of foreign stock masquerading as native species, imported stock is a potential danger to native plants. There is the risk of hybridization, as with the native and introduced Spanish bluebells, and the danger that fast-growing, mass-produced crop varieties could outcompete native vegetation. The Ministry of Agriculture says it is now reviewing its policies on imported 'wild' plants.

THE BUILT ENVIRONMENT

The National Lottery continued to dominate conservation in 1996–7; the projected income for the Heritage Lottery Fund in 1997 was £260–280 million. With such a budget at its disposal, the Fund could afford to be generous.

The single largest grant, £25.136 million, went to the Kennet and Avon Canal, constructed between 1723 and 1810. The first grants under the Urban Parks Programme, designed to redress neglect of the great 19th-century municipal parks, allocated £9.1 million to 32 parks throughout the United Kingdom. Its grants in spring 1997 to museums and galleries included the following beneficiaries: the National Portrait Gallery (£11.9 million), the Wallace Collection (£7.243 million), the Courtauld Institute (£1.884 million), the Tate Gallery (£18.750 million for a Gallery of British Art at Millbank by 2001); the Manchester City Art Gallery (£15 million), the Manchester Museum (£12 million), the Museum of Science and Industry, also in Manchester (£8.8 million); the Museum of the History of Science, in Oxford (£1.195 million); and the National Waterways Museum in Gloucester (£1.140 million).

The Museum of Domestic Architecture and Design at Cats Hill, Herts, centred on the Silver Studio which between 1880 and the 1960s was one of the country's leading sources of decorative design, received £1.644 million. Sunderland Museum and Art Gallery, founded in 1846, was offered £3.750 million. For Reading Town Hall and Museum, based in one of Alfred Waterhouse's masterpieces, the grant was £3.854 million. The Russell Cotes Art Gallery in Bournemouth received £1.956 million, the Railway Heritage Centre at Swindon £7.960 million, the Museum of Hatting at Stockport £1.328 million, and the Welsh Slate Museum £1.610 million.

In a previous round of awards, the Down House Museum in Kent, the home of Charles Darwin from 1842 to 1882, had received £1.783 million and the Museum of Worcester Porcelain £1.770 million. In the summer of 1997 a grant of £18.250 million was offered towards the £96 million project to convert the south block of Somerset House in central London to display the Gilbert collection of silver and gold.

Smaller allocations included the Old Malt Cross Music Hall in Nottingham (£520,000); St Magnus the Martyr Church in the City of London for the conservation of its magnificent organ of 1712

(£112,000); St Patrick's Church, Castlederg, Co. Tyrone, (£500,000); the Holy Name of Jesus Church in Manchester (£437,800); the Crownhill Fort, Plymouth (£228,000); Dixon's Chimney in Carlisle, one of the tallest mill chimneys in the country (£191,300); the Waltham Abbey Royal Gunpowder Mills in Essex, in continuous use for the manufacture of gunpowder from 1665 to 1991 (£6.5 million), the West London Synagogue (£151,600); the Kent Tithe Map Project, to conserve and microfiche the county's collection of 615 tithe maps (£310,900); the Town Mill, Lyme Regis, Dorset (£221,500); St Giles's Church, Wrexham (£70,200); and Neville Street and Saddler Street, Durham, for the recobbling of the streets and the repair of buildings (£292,900). The New Steine in Brighton received £212,000 to reinstate the railings of this seafront square, first laid out in 1790. Pontefract market place, W. Yorks, was allocated £2.795 million, and Newhailes House, Musselburgh, built in 1696 by the architect James Smith, was allocated £8 million so that it could be taken into the care of the National Trust for Scotland. Churches saved from demolition included St Luke's, Newham, east London (£763,900); St Peter's, Wallsend, Tyne and Wear (£476,800); St James, Barrow-in-Furness, Cumbria (£439,000); and St Matthew's, Naburn, York (£165,000). Number 36 Craven Street, near Charing Cross station in central London, was the home between 1757 and 1775 of Benjamin Franklin, then Chief Agent for the American Colonies; it was allocated £528,750. Burslem Old Town Hall, Stoke-on-Trent, was offered a grant to allow it to be adapted to a museum of the history and future of ceramics.

NEW POWERS

Legislation which came into force in autumn 1997 greatly extended the potential for generosity on the part of the Heritage Lottery Fund. Hitherto, only local authorities and registered charities had been eligible to apply for grants. Thereafter virtually anyone could apply, whether private individual or commercial company. The Fund was also empowered to widen the range of projects it could subsidize to include pure research and the sponsorship of training. Grants in related areas included £250,000 to the Council of British Archaeology and the Imperial War Museum, among others, to record all defensive sites and structures erected in the UK in the 20th century, and £470,000 to the Public and Monuments Sculpture Association to record all examples of British public art and outdoor commemorative monuments built since the 17th century.

Although it had its budget slashed from £8 million to £5 million, the National Heritage Memorial Fund was still able to assist a variety of projects in the year under review. These included the purchase of the Lennox Boyd collection of 19th-century architectural prints, drawings and photographs for the British Architectural Library

(£55,000); the acquisition by the British Museum of two oak panels from King Henry III's painted chamber at the Palace of Westminster of 1263 (£375,000); £1 million towards the endowment of the Dulwich Picture Gallery; the purchase by the Victoria and Albert Museum of two drawings by Sir John Vanbrugh of the dome of Castle Howard (£11,467); the relocation to the National Museum of Wales of Robert Adam's late 18th-century organ case built for Wynnstay House (£121,000); and the restoration of six small windows containing 14th-century and 17th-century glass in St Mary's Church, Wimbledon.

The Arts Council has on occasion also been able to grant aid to historic buildings, albeit indirectly. In spring 1997 it offered a grant towards the conversion of the Grade I listed medieval church of St Margaret's, Walmgate, in York, to establish an international centre for the study of early music.

Projects rejected by the distributing bodies included the application to relocate the British Architectural Library to the Round House in Camden Town, London; the £20 million project for the re-creation of the 18th-century Pleasure Gardens at Vauxhall, south London; and the £10 million project to re-erect the Euston Arch.

STATE-FUNDED ORGANIZATIONS

Compared to the Heritage Lottery Fund, English Heritage, Historic Scotland, Cadw and the Department of the Environment for Northern Ireland, are small players in the field of grants. Unlike the Heritage Lottery Fund, however, they play a vital role in the identification and statutory protection of listed buildings and ancient monuments and as owners of buildings.

English Heritage has been faced with the prospect of a £40 million cut in its budget over a four-year period. About £1.8 million was restored to the body after Sir Jocelyn Stevens, its chairman, threatened to resign; in addition, English Heritage's role as adviser to the Heritage Lottery Fund brought in sufficient income to employ ten extra architects in 1997. There were, however, inevitable signs of retreat, both in overall grant levels and in the closure of English Heritage's building conservation training centre, opened in 1993, at Fort Brockhurst in Hampshire. Grants made during the year included £431,000 to the Assembly Rooms, Buxton, and £400,000 to Stanmer House, Brighton. English Heritage is also undertaking the purchase and repair of the long-derelict Grade I Danson Park at Bexley, Kent, designed by Sir Robert Taylor between 1763 and 1767 and purchased by Bexley Council in 1923 to serve as a museum, but abandoned to dereliction in the early 1940s.

In October 1996 English Heritage launched a joint grant scheme for churches and places of worship with the Heritage Lottery Fund, with each body contributing £10 million in the first year. In November 1996 it took over the conservation unit of the Department of National Heritage (now the Department of Culture, Media and Sport). The same month saw the launch of a travelling exhibition and catalogue, *Raising the Roofs of England,* intended to protect the surviving legacy of natural stone slates. English Heritage also decided to serve an urgent works notice on the owner of the Grade II* former Exe Vale Hospital at Exminster in Devon, built between 1842 and 1845, which has been in serious decay since 1989.

LISTING

English Heritage's broadest influence is not in terms of those historic buildings it owns or to which it offers grants, but those it advises the Secretary of State to list. In 1996, 1,807 historic buildings were added to the statutory lists, bringing the total to 450,351. In the year to March 1997 consent was given for the demolition of 61 listed buildings, compared with 51 in 1995; 291 buildings were 'delisted' in the same period. By December 1996 there were 8,592 conservation areas, of which 157 were designated in 1996, and 16,757 scheduled ancient monuments. At June 1997, 1,280 sites had been included in the register of historic parks and gardens, some 10 per cent of them listed as Grade I.

The most select list of all is the World Heritage List, administered by UNESCO. At present there are only 12 world heritage sites in the UK, although the Government has decided to apply for the same status in respect of Maritime Greenwich, in time for the planned millennium celebrations in the area.

A wide range of structures was given listed building protection in the course of 1996–7. These included a former firing-range at Belper, Derbys; the Kent home of Aymer Vallance, the architectural historian and friend of William Morris; a stone coffin rest at Baschurch, Shropshire; the late 19th-century school in London where, amid great controversy, the capital's first woodwork classes were held in 1885; the iron bridge at Culford School, Suffolk, designed in 1803 by Samuel Wyatt; the 1901 bridge at Highcliffe, Dorset, the first to be built in Britain in reinforced concrete; the first purpose-built museum of archaeology, at Driffield, E. Yorks; Alexandra Palace, north London, built in 1873–5 and previously rejected many times as a candidate for listing; several hundred buildings in Hampstead Garden Suburb; and the Ancient House in the High Street, West Malling, Kent, which has been upgraded from Grade II* to Grade I following confirmation of its 12th-century origins.

THREATS

Listing creates a presumption against demolition but does not rule it out altogether. In 1996 the number of listed buildings in England and Wales subject to an application to demolish was 260, compared with 246 in 1995 (and 693 in 1977). The principal threats in 1996 and 1997 were to a run of listed buildings near the cathedral at Blackburn, Lancs (application withdrawn); the remains of the former Assembly Rooms at Beverley, E. Yorks, latterly a cinema; Lawton Hall at Church Lawton, Cheshire, where a fire-gutted 18th-century mansion was threatened not by demolition but by a scheme to develop the grounds with new housing; a tithe barn at Crowle, Worcs; the Grand Theatre at Doncaster; the substantial Victorian wings of Barrington Park at Great Barrington, Glos (application refused); the former station at Oxford, an important early example of prefabrication; Sandown Hall at Wavertree, Liverpool (application refused); and a 1912 Edwardian Baroque cinema at Swansea (where the façade is to remain).

Churches threatened with demolition included St Mary's, Halifax (application refused); the residual tower and steeple of St James's, Burnley, of 1869; the 1878 former Roman Catholic church of St Joseph's in Caroline Street, Wigan, Lancs; and St Alban's Church, Cheetham, Manchester, which appears to have been saved after publicity brought forward a new user. Christchurch, Waterloo, in Merseyside, a masterpiece of 1869 by Paley and Austin, was saved by substantial grant offers from English Heritage and the Heritage Lottery Fund and the decision of the Church Commissioners to vest the building for preservation in perpetuity with the Churches Conservation Trust.

Public attention focused on St Ethelburga's, Bishopsgate, which was devastated by the IRA bomb in the City of London in 1993. Following the rejection by the City Corporation planning committee of radical proposals for 'rebuilding' the church with a wholly modern glazed façade, the new Bishop of London decided not to pursue that option but to reconstruct the church instead as a centre for reconciliation and peace. It was promised that the reconstruction would incorporate 'a traditional façade'.

The Conservative Government issued a consultation paper, *Protecting Our Heritage,* in 1996. This proposed, *inter alia,* that public consultation prior to the listing of buildings should be conducted but limited to post-war structures and those identified under the thematic building type surveys; that consideration should be given to a new form of listing for modern structures which would require a review every ten years; that the Scheduled Monument Consent regime should be handed over from the Secretary of State to local authorities; and that English Heritage's formal title, the Historic Buildings and Monuments Commission for England, should be abolished. The then National Heritage Secretary, Virginia Bottomley, also initiated a review of ecclesiastical exemption, to re-examine the freedom from listed building consent and conservation area consent controls enjoyed by the Church of England, the Church in Wales, the Baptist Church, the Methodist Church, the Roman Catholic Church and the United Reformed Church. The report was submitted to the new Government in September 1997.

WALES

In Wales, the Welsh Office published a new and extensively revised body of planning advice (Welsh Office circular 61/96), and the Welsh Affairs select committee of the House of Commons turned its attention to conservation in Wales. In its follow-up report to its first, influential, pronouncement in 1993, the committee welcomed the speeding-up of the resurveying of listed buildings, even if it still regretted the time-scale of ten years rather than the originally planned three years. It also welcomed the establishment of a regime of protection for redundant Anglican churches in Wales through the Friends of Friendless Churches, and urged the establishment of at least one building preservation trust together with the employment of suitably trained conservation staff within each local authority. It came to the view that Cadw, the Government's historic buildings agency in Wales, was understaffed.

SCOTLAND

Scotland's historic buildings do benefit from UK-wide organizations like the Heritage Lottery Fund, but the principal source of grant money and expertise is Historic Scotland. Its annual report for 1996–7, published in July 1997, summarizes some £12.4 million of grants to listed buildings, comprising some 145 projects, and £24,000 of grants to scheduled ancient monuments. Grant-aid has proved critical in facilitating major campaigns in the year which have resulted in the creation of a Motor Heritage Museum within the Grade A-listed Argyll Motor Works, Alexandria, and a National Piping Centre in the former Cowcaddens church and manse in Glasgow.

Historic Scotland is the principal adviser to the Secretary of State for Scotland on the identification of buildings to be protected through both the scheduling and listed buildings regimes. By 31 March 1997 the total of scheduled sites stood at 6,542 and the number of listed buildings at over 42,000.

Historic Scotland is also responsible for historic buildings in the direct care of the Government. The Bridge of Oich near Fort Augustus was a new vesting, in June 1996. There are also plans to spend a further £8 million on repairs to Stirling Castle by 2000. The report shows a dramatic increase in the number of visitors to Historic Scotland properties in the year, from 2.5 million to 2.9 million. Membership of the Friends of Historic Scotland stood at almost 40,000 at the end of the review period.

Dance

After many years of planning, fund-raising and controversy, the Royal Opera House finally closed on 14 July 1997 for a major refurbishment; it is due to reopen in autumn 1999. The closure marked the end of a year of turbulence unprecedented even for the Royal Opera House. When plans to build a temporary theatre on the south bank of the River Thames fell through, the only available last-minute option was to find a series of temporary venues in London for both the Royal Ballet and the Royal Opera, and to implement a programme of increased overseas touring.

The Royal Ballet, not for the first time but now with an almost startling clarity, has been treated as the second-class citizen within the state that constitutes the Royal Opera House. During the first part of the closure period, the Royal Opera will perform at five prestigious London venues and mount six new full-scale productions. The Royal Ballet will perform at the Labatt's Apollo in Hammersmith, west London – an unsuitable venue with no proper orchestra pit – and at the Royal Festival Hall – a venue recently abandoned by English National Ballet with a sigh of relief – and mount no new productions at all. If the hope was to attract new audiences to the Royal Ballet, this was undermined when ticket prices at the new venues were found to be in many cases higher than those at the Royal Opera House.

This treatment of the country's leading ballet company provoked angry protests. The Royal Opera House responded by promising new one-act works by the company later in 1998, though rumours abounded that there had been plans to disband the company altogether during the closure period. It also revealed a lack of understanding of the nature of a ballet company, and of how different the Royal Ballet is from the Royal Opera Company. Whereas the Royal Opera relies on starry guests to front its productions, the Royal Ballet is a complete entity with standards and traditions which have been built up over many years but which need to be constantly maintained if they are to be preserved. The whole episode has brought into the open what many in the ballet world have been saying privately for years – that the Royal Ballet should be an independent organization with its own theatre and a management that understands and supports the art of ballet. However, the sums of money that have been invested in the refurbishment of the Royal Opera House ensure that this will remain a pipe-dream for some years to come. The new theatre will at least provide better rehearsal facilities for the Royal Ballet and a studio theatre which should allow more new work to be performed. Lower ticket prices are also promised, but it remains to be seen how this can be achieved without higher government subsidy, which, the new Labour government has made clear, is unlikely to be forthcoming.

LOTTERY MANAGEMENT

In May 1997, before the row about the closure plans had died down, the new chief executive of the Royal Opera House, Genista McIntosh, resigned. The official reason given was a 'stress-related illness'; it quickly became apparent that Ms McIntosh, who had come to the Opera House from the National Theatre and whose appointment had been very well-received, had been unable to resolve the conflicting demands of the job. A respected and capable administrator was reduced to such a state after only months in the job. The Opera House swiftly decided that it wanted to appoint Mary Allen, the secretary-general of the Arts Council of England, as her successor, and that any delay in the appointment would result in a loss of confidence in the house. It therefore persuaded the Secretary of State for Culture, Media and Sport (Chris Smith) to allow the appointment to go ahead with no selection procedure. This means that the former chairman of the Arts Council's Lottery Fund (Lord Chadlington), who approved much of the £78.5 million award of lottery money to the Opera House for the refurbishment, is now chairman of the Opera House board, and the former secretary-general of the Arts Council, which has responsibility for funding the Opera House, is its chief executive. The leading players in this tragi-comedy were summoned to be questioned by a House of Commons select committee, and in June 1997 the Arts Council announced an inquiry into the relationship between the Council and the Opera House.

The Royal Opera House also came under fire for making 320 of its 820 staff redundant because of the closure. It was criticized too for using lottery funds towards the redundancy payments, although this had been explicitly allowed under the terms of the grant. In June 1997 it cancelled a new production of Verdi's *Macbeth* because it had allowed insufficient time for technical rehearsals (and because its technical staff by then were severely depleted). The season ended with promises of a bright new future in the refurbished house. The old house was beautifully 'put to sleep' by Darcey Bussell as the Lilac Fairy at the closure gala. It will take more than a kiss to reawaken it to its full glory.

INDEPENDENCE FOR BRB

Birmingham Royal Ballet, in what seemed a very auspicious move, became a fully independent organization in April 1997. The Arts Council of England had recommended in 1993 that the company should consider disaggregating itself from the Royal Opera House, and plans were set in motion.

The assets and operations of Birmingham Royal Ballet were transferred to a new incorporated company on 1 April 1997; the BRB Trust had been set up in 1996 to co-ordinate fund-raising activities. The company will however continue to maintain strong links with the Royal Opera House, and, more importantly, with the Royal Ballet School.

Scottish Ballet, mindful of these developments south of the border, was facing a fight for its survival at time of going to press. The Scottish Arts Council has been conducting negotiations about the future of the four national companies - the ballet, the opera, the national orchestra and the chamber orchestra - and favours the merger of the orchestras of the opera and ballet companies. Scottish Ballet withdrew from these negotiations in June 1997, arguing that to merge the orchestras would greatly increase its costs. Both Scottish Ballet and Scottish Opera tour extensively every year and a merged orchestra would make this both complicated and expensive. The Government has offered extra funding to the national companies, dependent on the merger, but the example of the shared orchestra at the Royal Opera House and the status of the Royal Ballet at Covent Garden would also seem to support Scottish Ballet's position. Scottish Ballet is therefore fighting to maintain its status as the independent national ballet company of Scotland; at a time when a separate Scottish Parliament seems likely to be established, this seems a fairly modest demand.

London City Ballet, which closed down in June 1996, rose phoenix-like from the ashes in August 1996 under the name City Ballet of London. Its indefatigable director, Harold King, secured sufficient sponsorship to set up a company comprising a core of 22 dancers which will be supplemented from time to time. The company has a new chairman and a new board of directors, and will perform classical and neo-classical works as well as commissioning as much as possible from new choreographers. It will adapt its repertoire to suit its new size and the venues in which it will perform, and it will not perform cut-down versions of the classics. It has already toured overseas, and brought Matthew Hart's production of *Cinderella* to London for a successful Christmas season.

PERFORMANCES

The actual performance of dance in the year under review sometimes seemed to be overshadowed by the various crises besetting the infrastructure of some of the leading dance companies. This was especially true in the case of the Royal Ballet. The company had a troubled year, with a largely unadventurous repertoire. It lost one of its leading male stars, Adam Cooper, who had scored such a success in the role of the swan in the Adventures in Motion Pictures' *Swan Lake* that he left the Royal Ballet to take the production to the USA and back into the West End of London. Two other leading dancers, Errol Pickford and his wife Benazir Hus-

sein, left to dance in Australia, and Cooper's girlfriend and one of the most exciting soloists in the company, Sarah Wildor, has taken leave of absence to dance with Cooper in the production of *Cinderella* to be staged by Adventures in Motion Pictures in autumn 1997. The two new one-act works presented by the company, *Two-Part Invention* by Ashley Page and *Amores* by Glen Tetley, both received a luke-warm response from the critics. Twyla Tharp's *Push Comes to Shove* was brought into the repertoire by Anthony Dowell, and served mainly to show the limitations of both the choreography and the leading dancer, Tetsuya Kumakawa. A planned production of Balanchine's *Apollo* was cancelled at short notice after a row over casting with the Balanchine Trust.

There were plenty of good performances in the classics, and welcome revivals of MacMillan's *The Prince of the Pagodas* and Bintley's *Consort Lessons*, but there was a poignant air to the gala held on 1 July to mark the 50th anniversary of the Royal Ballet School and the centenary year of the founder of the company and the school, Dame Ninette de Valois, who achieved such greatness with such limited resources. The Royal Ballet School itself was subsequently criticized for using outdated and inappropriate training methods, particularly at its junior school, White Lodge.

Birmingham Royal Ballet, under David Bintley's direction, is currently a greater credit to its founder. It mounted four new one-act works, including the popular and entertaining *Nutcracker Sweeties* by Bintley himself, and brought three important works into its repertoire: Ashton's *Les Patineurs*, MacMillan's *Song of the Earth* and Bintley's *Tombeaux*. Standards of dancing remained high, and Bintley has shown his determination to maintain a repertoire that is popular and creative while also incorporating great works from the past.

IN THE ROUND

Derek Deane at English National Ballet mounted one of the more controversial productions of the year when he created a *Swan Lake* which was danced in the round at the Royal Albert Hall, London, in summer 1997. This blockbuster provoked critical reaction ranging from great admiration to apoplectic fury; the reality probably deserved something between the two. It was an interesting and worthwhile experiment, and a surprisingly serious production in the circumstances. It served mainly to show why the traditional proscenium arch theatre is generally the best setting for ballet: productions are designed to be seen from the front, and the arch is an important device in creating a dramatic focus and ensuring that the audience becomes an entity in itself and provides the concentrated response necessary for an effective live performance. Deane's production was designed to be seen in the round, but could not overcome the obvious problems created by the setting. Moreover, presumably because of the difficulty of showing a double suicide leap in the middle of an arena with no wings, the production substituted a Soviet-style happy ending for the more usual and more powerful Western climax of redemption through sacrifice. This did not, however, seem to upset audiences unduly.

English National Ballet's season was also notable for the first performances by an English company of Balanchine's *Who Cares?*, and for the last performances by the company at the Royal Festival Hall, where it had mounted *The Nutcracker* every Christmas since 1952. Michael Corder's production of *Cinderella* deservedly won the Laurence Olivier award for the best new dance production of 1996.

Northern Ballet Theatre and Scottish Ballet joined the Royal Ballet in making *Romeo and Juliet* a mainstay of their repertoires for the season. Northern Ballet Theatre's production was mounted in 1991 by the young Italian choreographer Massimo Moricone and has proved a critical and popular success. The company's new work this year, *Dracula*, was praised for its designs by Lez Brotherston but otherwise panned. Scottish Ballet's *Romeo and Juliet* was John Cranko's version of 1962, which has long been regarded as one of the most important works by this now somewhat neglected British choreographer. The company also mounted two worthwhile new works, *The Four Seasons* and *Tam O'Shanter*.

Rambert Dance Company, whose dancers won the 1996 Laurence Olivier award for outstanding achievement in dance for the summer season at the London Coliseum, continued to attract praise for its attractive and accessible repertoire and outstanding dancing. It mounted well-received new works by Kim Brandstrup, Per Jonsson and Rambert's director, Christopher Bruce. Bruce has said, however, that he does not intend to stay with the company for more than a few years, because although the Arts Council grant has been increased there is simply not enough money for him to do the job properly and he has been forced to make artistic compromises. The former Royal Ballet dancer and choreographer Matthew Hart was a welcome recruit to the company and Paul Hoskins was appointed music director.

Dance Umbrella 1996 was launched with an extraordinary work by the American choreographer Stephan Koplowitz at the Natural History Museum, London. Entitled *Genesis Canyon*, the work is inspired by the design and purpose of the building and used dozens of dancers and several vocalists to spectacular effect. The festival also offered the world première of Richard Alston's *Okho* to Iannis Xenakis' score for djembes (large African drums), and the first performances of Siobhan Davies's *Affections*, set to six Handel arias. Davies, who is now celebrating 25 years as a choreographer, won a 1996 Prudential award for the arts, worth £50,000. In spite of the widespread critical acclaim for her work, Davies is unable to sustain a company on a full-time basis and can only assemble dancers for periods of a few months at a time to rehearse in

rented studios. This is in spite of a relaxation of the rules relating to lottery funding to help selected companies achieve greater financial stability, to support work by and for young people, to increase access to the arts and to invest in new work. Other notable works in the contemporary dance field during the year included Nigel Charnock's *The Message*, Shobana Jeyasingh's *Palimpsest*, Jonathan Burrows's *Quintet* and DV8's *Bound to Please*.

VISITORS

Major visiting companies in the year included Lindsay Kemp, with his new work *Variété* presented at the Hackney Empire, Antonio Gades with his production of *Carmen*, the young dancers of Nederlands Dans Theater 2, and the Kirov, which presented a highly successful season at the London Coliseum in summer 1997. Mark Morris finally brought his company to London, and the performances of his superb *L'Allegro, il Penseroso ed il Moderato*, in collaboration with English National Opera, at the London Coliseum in June 1997 were the highlight of the dance year in the capital.

One of the greatest ballerinas of the century, Alexandra Danilova, died on 13 July 1997 at the age of 93. She graduated from the Imperial Ballet School in St Petersburg (then Petrograd) into the Maryinsky company in 1920, and subsequently danced for Diaghilev's Ballets Russes. She also taught for many years at the School of American Ballet in New York at the invitation of George Balanchine. Anne Hewer, the former chairman of Scottish Ballet, died in July 1997. She was originally chairman of Western Theatre Ballet, which was founded in Bristol in 1957, and when a funding crisis threatened the company's future she was instrumental in transforming it into Scotland's national company and ensuring that it operated from a stable base north of the border.

In October 1996 the Arts Council announced a £25 million interim scheme to help subsidize dance and drama students who have been awarded discretionary grants by their local authorities to study at accredited training schools. This does not solve the problem of the many local authorities who do not award even discretionary grants, but it is a welcome recognition of the principle that talent, rather than parental means, will produce the great dancers of the future.

PRODUCTIONS

ROYAL BALLET
Founded 1931 as the Vic-Wells Ballet
Royal Opera House, Covent Garden, London WC2E 9DD
World premières:
Pavane pour une infante défunte (Christopher Wheeldon), 18 October 1996. A *pas de deux*. Music, Ravel; design, Bob Crowley. Dancers, Darcey Bussell and Jonathan Cope
    Two-Part Invention (Ashley Page), 26 November 1996. A one-act ballet. Music, Robert Moran and Prokofiev;

costume designs, Jon Morrell; set designs, Peter Mumford.
Cast led by Christina McDermott, Zenaida Yanowsky,
Leanne Benjamin, William Trevitt, Stuart Cassidy and
Adam Cooper
    Amores (Glen Tetley), 30 April 1997. A one-act ballet.
Music, Michael Torke; design, Nadine Baylis. Dancers,
Darcey Bussell, Deborah Bull, Leanne Benjamin, Stuart
Cassidy, Michael Nunn, William Trevitt
Company premières:
Push Comes to Shove (Twyla Tharp), 13 February 1997.
Music, Haydn and Joseph Lamb; design, Santo Loquasto.
Cast led by Tetsuya Kumakawa, Darcey Bussell and Sarah
Wildor
    Talisman pas de deux (Pyotr Gusev after Petipa), 5 July
1997. Music, Drigo. Dancers, Miyako Yoshida and Irek
Mukhamedov

Full length ballets from the repertoire: *Romeo and Juliet*
(MacMillan, 1965), *The Prince of the Pagodas* (MacMillan,
1989), *Cinderella* (Ashton, 1948), *Swan Lake* (Petipa/Ivanov,
prod. Dowell 1987), *The Sleeping Beauty* (Petipa, prod.
Dowell 1994), *La Bayadère* (Makarova after Petipa, 1980),
Anastasia (MacMillan, 1971).
    One-act ballets from the repertoire: *La Valse* (Ashton,
1958), *La Fin du jour* (MacMillan, 1979), *Daphnis and Chloë*
(Ashton, 1951), *Steptext* (Forsythe, 1985), *Winter Dreams*
(MacMillan, 1991), *Consort Lessons* (Bintley, 1983), *The
Judas Tree* (MacMillan, 1992), *Symphony in C* (Balanchine,
1947).
    A group of Royal Ballet dancers performed in Sheffield,
High Wycombe and Bath in March 1997 (the 'Dance Bites'
tour), performing *Pavane pour une infante défunte*, *Ebony
Concerto* (Page, 1995), and new works by Matthew Hart (*Cry
Baby Kreisler*), Ashley Page (*Room of Cooks*), Danny Sapsford
(*All Nighter*), William Tuckett (*The Magpie's Tower*) and
Cathy Marston (*Figure in Progress*).
    Dancers from the Royal Ballet took part in the Royal
Ballet School performance on 1 July 1997, which marked
the 50th anniversary of the school and the centenary year of
Dame Ninette de Valois. On 14 July 1997 company
members took part in a gala at the Royal Opera House to
mark the closure of the house for refurbishment.
    In addition to performances at the Royal Opera House,
the company toured to the USA (Orange County) and
Japan in May–June 1997. The repertoire on the tour was
*The Sleeping Beauty, La Valse, Pavane pour une infante défunte,
La Fin du jour, Daphnis and Chloë, Don Quixote* (Petipa, prod.
Baryshnikov 1978) and *Romeo and Juliet*. The company took
part in the Lincoln Center Festival in New York in July
1997, performing *The Prince of the Pagodas, Cinderella, La
Valse, Pavane pour une infante défunte, La Fin du jour* and
Daphnis and Chloe.

BIRMINGHAM ROYAL BALLET
Founded 1946 as the Sadler's Wells Opera Ballet
Birmingham Hippodrome, Thorp Street, Birmingham B5
4AU

World premières:
Le Baiser de la fée (James Kudelka), 26 September 1996.
Music, Stravinsky; design, Nadine Baylis. Cast led by
Sabrina Lenzi, Leticia Müller, Monica Zamora and
Michael O'Hare
    The Nutcracker Sweeties (David Bintley), 26 September
1996. Music, Tchaikovsky, arranged by Duke Ellington;
design, Jasper Conran. Cast led by Monica Zamora, Agnes
Oaks, Robert Parker, Chenca Williams, Joseph Cipolla
and Leticia Müller
    Sanctum (Lila York), 16 May 1997. Music, Ravel and
Christopher Rouse; design, Theoni V. Aldredge. Cast led
by Dorcas Walters and David Justin

Bright Young Things (Oliver Hindle), 29 May 1997.
Music, Gershwin; design, David Blight. Cast led by Leticia
Müller, Monica Zamora, Sergiu Pobereznic, Joseph
Cipolla and Chi Cao
Company premières:
Les Patineurs (Ashton), 26 September 1996. Music,
Meyerbeer; design, William Chappell. Given as part of
Birmingham's 'Towards the Millennium' festival, a
celebration of the 1960s. Cast led by Chi Cao, Sandra
Madgwick, Dorcas Walters, Catherine Batcheller, Yuri
Zhukov, Jessica Clarke and Anne Marie Little
    Song of the Earth (MacMillan, 1965), 25 February 1997.
Music, Mahler; design, Nicholas Georgiadis. Given as part
of Birmingham's 'Towards the Millennium' festival, a
celebration of the 1960s. Cast led by Joseph Cipolla,
Robert Parker and Leticia Müller
    Tombeaux (David Bintley), 15 May 1997. Music, Walton;
design, Jasper Conran. Cast led by Leticia Müller and
Andrew Murphy

Full length ballets from the repertoire: *Swan Lake* (Petipa/
Ivanov, prod. Wright and Samsova 1981), *The Nutcracker*
(Ivanov, prod. Wright, additional choreography by
Vincent Redmon, 1990), *The Sleeping Beauty* (Petipa, prod.
Wright 1984).
    One-act ballets from the repertoire: *Agon* (Balanchine,
1957), *Carmina Burana* (Bintley, 1995), *The Dream* (Ashton,
1964).
    On 29-31 May 1997 a choreographic project was
presented at the Birmingham Hippodrome on a bill with
Bright Young Things. It involved a collaboration between
choreographers from within the company, who staged
Mussorgsky's *Pictures at an Exhibition*. Students from the
theatre design course at the University of Central England
provided sets and costumes.
    In addition to four seasons at the Birmingham
Hippodrome, the company toured to Sunderland (two
seasons), Bradford, Bristol, Plymouth (three seasons),
Liverpool (two seasons), Southampton, Manchester and
London (the Royal Opera House).

ENGLISH NATIONAL BALLET
Founded 1950 as London Festival Ballet
Markova House, 39 Jay Mews, London SW7 2ES

World premières:
Swan Lake (Petipa/Ivanov, prod. Deane), 29 May 1997. A
production staged in the round at the Royal Albert Hall,
London. Music, Tchaikovsky; costumes, Peter Farmer.
Cast led by Altynai Assylmuratova and Roberto Bolle
    Cut to the Chase (Patrick Lewis), 24 June 1997. A one-act
work. Music, Steve Reich and John Adams; design, Peter
Mackintosh. Cast led by Monica Perego and Dmitri
Gruzdyev
    Perpetuum Mobile (Christopher Hampson), 24 June 1997.
A one-act work. Music, Bach; design, 'Fido'. Cast led by
Monica Perego, Dmitri Gruzdyev, Tamara Rojo and
Nathan Coppen
Company première:
Who Cares? (Balanchine), 17 February 1997. Music,
Gershwin; design, Ben Benson. Cast led by Giuseppe
Picone, Lisa Pavane and Monica Perego

Full-length ballets from the repertoire: *Coppélia* (Petipa and
Cecchetti, prod. Hynd 1985), *Alice in Wonderland* (Deane,
1995), *The Nutcracker* (Ivanov, prod. Stevenson 1972),
Giselle (Coralli/Perrot, prod. Deane 1994).
    One-act ballets and *pas de deux* from the repertoire:
Etudes (Lander, 1948), *My Brother, My Sisters* (MacMillan,
1978), *Grand Pas* from *Paquita* (Petipa/Deane), *Les Sylphides*
(Fokine, 1909), *Encounters* (Dean, 1996), *Three Preludes*
(Stevenson, 1969), *Impromptu* (Deane, 1982), and *pas de deux*

from *Swan Lake* (after Petipa), *The Sleeping Beauty* (Hynd), *Le Corsaire* (Petipa) and *Don Quixote* (after Petipa).

The full company toured to Liverpool, Southampton (three seasons), Manchester (three seasons), Leeds, Nottingham, London (Royal Festival Hall and Royal Albert Hall), Bristol and Birmingham.

In June–July 1997 the company split into two groups and went on two small-scale tours. One group toured *Encounters*, a selection of *pas de deux* (*Don Quixote*, *Alice in Wonderland* and *Swan Lake*) and *Who Cares?* to Swindon, Darlington, Dartford, Reading and Crawley. The other group toured a selection of *pas de deux* (*Don Quixote*, *The Sleeping Beauty*, *Le Corsaire*, *Impromptu* and *Swan Lake*), *Cut to the Chase*, *Perpetuum Mobile* and *Three Preludes* to Barnstaple, Bexhill-on-Sea, Scunthorpe, Barrow-in-Furness and Cambridge.

RAMBERT DANCE COMPANY
Founded 1926 as the Marie Rambert Dancers
94 Chiswick High Road, London W4 1SH

World premières:
Eidolon (Kim Brandstrup), 10 October 1996. Music, Kim Helweg; set design, Kim Brandstrup and Liz Reed; costumes, Sasha Keir
  Stream (Christopher Bruce), 6 December 1996. Music, Philip Chambon; design, Marian Bruce
  Port for Angels (Per Jonsson), 7 May 1997. Score, Lars Akerlund; design, Per Jonsson and Maria Heimer

Works from the repertoire: *Dark Elegies* (Tudor, 1937), *Quicksilver* (Bruce, 1996), *Kol Simcha* (Veldman, 1995), *Stabat Mater* (Cohan, 1975), *Swansong* (Bruce, 1987), *Rooster* (Bruce, 1991), *Moonshine* (Bruce, 1993), *Petite Mort* (Kylian, 1991), *Airs* (Taylor, 1978).

The company performed in High Wycombe, Sheffield, Carlisle, Aberdeen, Cardiff, Plymouth, Bristol, Blackpool, Oxford, Bournemouth, Cambridge, Canterbury, Norwich, Dartford, London (Peacock Theatre and a workshop at Riverside Studios), Brighton, Birmingham, Northampton and Edinburgh. It also performed in the USA and Canada in September 1996, with a repertoire of *Moonshine*, *Swansong*, *Rooster*, *Meeting Point* (Bruce, 1996), *Petite Mort*, *Axioma 7* (Naharin, 1991), *Kol Simcha* and *Stabat Mater*, and in Russia (including the first performances by a contemporary dance company at the Maryinsky Theatre, St Petersburg) in January 1997, with a repertoire of *Stream*, *Petite Mort* and *Rooster*.

RICHARD ALSTON DANCE COMPANY
Founded 1994
The Place, 17 Duke's Road, London WC1H 9AB

All works danced by the company are choreographed by Richard Alston unless otherwise stated.

World première:
Okho, 3 October 1996. Music, Iannis Xenakis; costumes, Elizabeth Baker. Cast led by Henri Oguike

Company premières:
Rumours, Visions (1994), 6 November 1996. Music, Benjamin Britten; costumes, Elizabeth Baker
  Amongst Shadows (Henri Oguike), 25 February 1997. Music, Dario Marinelli

Works from the repertoire: *Orpheus Singing and Dreaming* (1996), *Beyond Measure* (a reworking of *Bach Measures*, 1996), *Stardust* (premièred as *Sometimes I Wonder*, 1995), *Lachrymae* (1994).

The company performed in London (Royal Festival Hall), Epsom, Canterbury, Warwick, Swindon, Malvern, Manchester, Horsham, Nottingham, Newcastle upon Tyne, Oxford, Blackpool and Richmond (Surrey). It also toured to Cyprus in November 1996, with a repertoire of

Okho, *Stardust* and *Beyond Measure*; to China (Beijing and Guangzhou) in March 1997, with a repertoire of *Beyond Measure*, *Lachrymae* and *Okho*; and to Holland in June 1997 to perform *Okho* at the Xenakis Festival in Middelberg.

SCOTTISH BALLET
Founded 1956 as the Western Theatre Ballet
261 West Princes Street, Glasgow G4 9EE

World premières:
The Four Seasons (Robert Cohan), 27 August 1996. Music, Vivaldi; design, Norberto Chiesa. Cast led by Vladislav Bubnov, Nicci Theis, Campbell McKenzie, Anne Christie, Linda Packer, Robert Hampton, Rupert Jowett and Lorna Scott
  Tam O'Shanter (Lorna Scott), 27 June 1997. Music, Malcolm Arnold. Cast led by Robin Bernadet, Oliver Rydout, Anne Christie and Claire Robertson

Full-length ballets from the repertoire: *The Nutcracker* (Darrell after Ivanov, 1973), *Romeo and Juliet* (Cranko, 1962), *La Sylphide* (Bournonville, prod. Hans Brenaa 1973).
  One-act ballets from the repertoire: *Troy Game* (North, 1974), *Haydn Pieces* (Baldwin, 1995), *Shoals of Herring* (Maldoom, 1983), *Les Sylphides* (Fokine, 1909), *Vespri* (Prokovsky, 1973).

The full company performed in Glasgow (three seasons), Edinburgh (three seasons), Norwich, Stirling, Aberdeen (three seasons), Hull (two seasons), Blackpool, Woking, High Wycombe, Newcastle upon Tyne and Sheffield. In June–July 1997 it split into two groups and staged small-scale tours with a repertoire of *Les Sylphides*, *Shoals of Herring*, *Tam O'Shanter* and *Vespri*. The tours visited many small venues in Northern Ireland and Scotland.

Film

There were many films to savour in 1996–7 but it is unlikely to be remembered as a vintage year. Cinema-going as a leisure activity continued to grow at an impressive rate, helped by the new generation of multiplex cinemas. Yet as audiences expand, tastes appear to contract; few non-English language films made a significant impact either critically or commercially, while many of the new films from the revitalized UK film industry failed to reach the screen. American productions again dominated proceedings, and not just at the box-office; the American independent sector provided several of the year's most interesting and critically acclaimed films.

There was, however, a distinctly British flavour to the 1996 Academy Awards presented in March 1997, calling to mind Colin Welland's battle-cry 'The British are coming' in 1981, the year *Chariots of Fire* triumphed. Leading the charge was *The English Patient*, with an astonishing 12 nominations, nine of which were translated into actual awards. In that its writer/director and two of its main stars were from Britain, the film could technically be described as British. The fact that it was funded entirely by American money, however, while Mike Leigh's *Secrets and Lies*, the night's other big British film, was funded mainly with French money, are a telling comment on the continuing reluctance of British financiers to back feature films.

British talent, at least as far as the Oscars are concerned, is clearly recognized and valued. Of the five titles nominated for best film at the Oscars, two (*The English Patient* and *Secrets and Lies*) came from Britain, and *Fargo* was an American film made by the British production company Working Title. The Australian drama *Shine* was also nominated for this Oscar, leaving only one genuine Hollywood movie in the running, the comedy drama *Jerry Maguire*. Three Britons, none of them particularly well-known even at home, were among the five nominees for best actress: Brenda Blethyn for her affecting depiction of a downtrodden mother in *Secrets and Lies*, Kristin Scott Thomas for her sensuous performance in *The English Patient*; and Emily Watson for her astonishing performance in Lars von Trier's *Breaking the Waves*. Blethyn's co-star Marianne Jean-Baptiste was nominated for best supporting actress, confirming the depth of talent among British actors.

In critical terms there were some fine films to celebrate, not least the documentary of the year, *When We Were Kings*, the story of the near-legendary boxing encounter between Muhammad Ali and the then champion, George Foreman, in Zaïre in 1974. About an event which was much more than just a sporting encounter, this was the latest in a line of distinguished American documentaries willing to take on big subjects. After the Academy's snub of the magnificent *Hoop Dreams* in 1994, the award for *When We Were Kings* was especially welcome. Another memorable film was *Kolya*, the winner of the best foreign language film award. An affecting and deceptively simple tale of a lonely Czech cellist who befriends a small boy, set against the backdrop of Czechoslovakia's 'velvet revolution', the film heralded, in Jan Sverak, the finest new film-making talent to emerge from the former Communist bloc. The film certainly struck a chord in the director's native Czech Republic where it broke all box office records.

Geoffrey Rush's Oscar for best actor in *Shine* recognized one of year's finest films, a moving portrayal of a gifted pianist plagued by mental illness, based on the life of David Helfgott. Australia in recent years has produced a number of quirky and distinctive films, such as *Strictly Ballroom* and *Muriel's Wedding*. Though more serious in tone, *Shine* proved just as memorable, thanks to fine acting not just from the previously unknown Rush, but from a splendid cast, including Armin Mueller-Stahl as Helfgott's driven father. Director Scott Hicks showed the world a rare talent with this, his feature debut, and has now been signed up by Hollywood. Frances McDormand's best actress Oscar for her performance as a pregnant Swedish-American police chief in *Fargo* ensured that the film's makers, the Coen brothers, finally achieved Oscar recognition to match the critical acclaim for their work over the past decade.

The biggest surprise at the Oscars was the decision to award Juliette Binoche the Oscar for best supporting actress for her performance in *The English Patient*. Surprising not because Binoche did not deserve it, but because the favourite had been the veteran Lauren Bacall, whose appearance was the best thing about *The Mirror Has Two Faces*. One of the surprises among the nominations was *Sling Blade*, which was written by, directed by and starred the little-known Billy Bob Thornton. His memorable portrayal of a mentally challenged murderer looks set to establish him as a significant talent.

After the controversy at the 1995 awards when Revd Jesse Jackson led a protest at the lack of black nominees, it was fitting that Cuba Gooding, jun. should pick up the best supporting actor award for his role as a hot-headed American football player in Cameron Crowe's rousingly entertaining *Jerry Maguire*. Although this was a studio picture starring Tom Cruise, the world's top box office star, the film had some of the quirkiness and charm characteristic of the independent sector in which writer/director Crowe first made his name. It also showed that Cruise is a more accomplished and risk-taking actor than he has previously been given credit for, as his appearance in Stanley Kubrick's forthcoming *Eyes Wide Shut* looks set to confirm.

Another Oscar nominee of unusual versatility is Woody Harrelson who, since his days as the dim bartender in television's *Cheers*, has established himself in Hollywood as an actor capable of encompassing roles as diverse as the ten-pin bowler in the cheerily juvenile *Kingpin* and the controversial porn baron of the more serious *The People vs. Larry Flynt*. His co-star in that film, the singer Courtney Love in her first major film role, was a real find.

THE BRITISH ARE COMING

The film which dominated the Oscars, *The English Patient*, was an adaptation of the novel by Michael Ondaatje which was made only through the determination of its writer and director Anthony Minghella. Support from Miramax, the American independent production company, ensured that the project stayed alive when the original backers, one of Hollywood's big studios, pulled out after Minghella refused to cast a big-name star rather than the relatively unknown Kristin Scott Thomas in one of the lead roles. Minghella's decision was justified, though, when the film's three main stars received Oscar nominations.

The success of *The English Patient* coincided with a boom in British film production spurred by the injection of funding from the National Lottery. Over 120 feature films were made in 1996, compared with fewer than 80 the year before, and a new aura of optimism surrounded British film-making. However, few British films in late 1996 and early 1997 made much of an impact at the box-office, even if a few won critical acclaim. Certainly, nothing matched the success of *Trainspotting*, which took nearly £50 million at box-offices around the world, until summer 1997, when the unlikely saviour of a poor British cinema year turned out to be Mr Bean.

There were not many bright spots in between these two films but one exception was *Brassed Off*, which managed to be both a warm-hearted Ealing-type comedy about a northern brass band under threat and a harder-edged portrayal, Ken Loach-style, of a mining community devastated by pit closures. With attractive young British stars Ewan McGregor and Tara Fitzgerald in the lead and a terrific performance from Pete Postlethwaite, this was a film to savour.

Elsewhere there were a number of films which disappointed for one reason or another, *Fever Pitch*, *Twin Town* and *Fierce Creatures* for example, and it was only with the August 1997 release of *Bean*, subtitled *The Ultimate Disaster Movie*, that the optimistic mood among British film-makers looked like being justified at the box-office.

Based on the Mr Bean character developed with great success on television, the film took the bumbling naïf on a nightmare trip to the USA. The more upmarket critics found little to praise in a film predicated largely on slapstick, but audiences were quicker to respond to scenes in which the main character exploded a full sick bag on fellow aeroplane passengers and simulated intercourse (unwittingly) with a hot-air hand dryer, before destroying one of the world's greatest paintings with an ill-timed sneeze. *Bean*, whatever its merits as a work of art, was one of the funniest films of the year.

NEW TALENT

Bean was followed by another hit comedy, *The Full Monty*, which followed the attempts of six former steel workers from Sheffield to set themselves up as male strippers. Like *Brassed Off*, *The Full Monty* provided charming contemporary comedy within the context of a decayed industrial landscape. The result is a hilarious, occasionally moving and ultimately uplifting film which hit a nerve with audiences at home and abroad. Despite its studied unsentimentality, *The Full Monty*, like *Bean*, provided audiences with the feel-good factor which is usually the preserve of Hollywood.

Made by first-time director Peter Cattaneo and with no major stars (although Robert Carlyle as the lead character is well on the way to becoming one) *The Full Monty* had a chequered career, having been rejected by various British backers before Fox Searchlight, a division of the Hollywood studio, stepped in. Significantly, this meant that Fox's marketing muscle lay behind the release of the film. The real problem for British films lies not so much in the difficulty of finding financial backing as in the fact that distributors seem unwilling to give British films the chance to compete at the box-office. The success of *The Full Monty*, after the sort of marketing campaign and wide release usually afforded only to Hollywood films, supports claims that other British films could be as successful if only they were distributed and shown as widely as American films.

There is certainly no shortage of talented young British film-makers. Shane Meadows made his striking feature début, *Small Time*, for just under £50,000. It has echoes of Mike Leigh and Ken Loach in its funny, gritty, semi-improvised depiction of a gang of petty criminals in Nottingham. His talent was confirmed by his follow-up, *24/7*, made with a significantly bigger budget and with Bob Hoskins in the lead role. Unveiled in the newly instigated British Renaissance section of the Venice Film Festival in September 1997, this tale of a boxing coach trying to help the youths in his club was an immediate hit.

Michael Winterbottom's *Jude*, meanwhile, was a striking and hard-hitting version of Thomas Hardy's *Jude the Obscure* somewhat different from the usual run of period literary adaptations. The director's follow-up, *Welcome to Sarajevo*, was a world away in its subject matter, based on the journalist Michael Nicholson's experiences in the former Yugoslavia. But both films won critical acclaim for the director's uncompromising story-telling ability.

Literary adaptation of a more traditional variety, a mainstay of British cinema, could also be found, notably in Kenneth Branagh's star-studded *Hamlet* – all four hours of it. Purists will have been delighted, even if he did set the film in the 19th century. Shakespeare was given a wildly different treatment elsewhere in Australian director Baz Luhrman's remarkable version of *Romeo and Juliet*, a highly stylized and stylish resetting of the film in modern-day America, which nevertheless retained the bard's words. Leonardo DiCaprio, a striking Romeo, confirmed himself as one of Hollywood's brightest young talents.

HOLLYWOOD BLOCKBUSTERS

For all the positive noises being made by the British, Hollywood still dominates the box-office; American films account for over 80 per cent of the UK box-office. That is not necessarily a bad thing since Hollywood still produces the best popular cinema in the world, though the Hollywood studios appear to have lost their nerve a little, with a number of remakes and sequels among the intended blockbusters of the year. *Speed 2*, *Batman and Robin* and *The Saint*, with Val Kilmer ludicrously reprising Leslie Charteris's hero, were all turkeys. *The Lost World*, the sequel to *Jurassic Park*, the most successful film of all time, was one of the most commercially successful films of the year, but it never matched the impact of the first film.

The most successful film of the year at the box office was also one of the most enjoyable: *Men in Black*, based on a little-known comic book depicting the work of a group of undercover agents who monitor the aliens who live among us. Director Barry Sonnenfeld brought to the proceedings the mordant wit and snappy pace he first showed in *The Addams Family*, while the film's pairing of hard-nosed Tommy Lee Jones and brash young Will Smith worked a treat. Jones played beautifully on his irascible image, while Smith confirmed that he is the brightest young star in Hollywood. Audiences certainly seem to like him, since he has now starred in the biggest films of 1996 *(Independence Day)* and 1997.

Perhaps the most impressive feature of *Men in Black* was the film's use of special effects, in particular the creation of an array of splendid aliens by Rick Baker, master of the genre. With the notable exception of the cockroach-like baddy, its aliens were on the whole benign beings, if a little grumpy. The aliens of Tim Burton's *Mars Attacks!*, however, were irredeemably bad. Based on a series of bubblegum cards, *Mars Attacks!* featured little green men whose heads were encased in a glass dome. Their arrival on earth led to the systematic and gleeful destruction of some of the biggest names in Hollywood. Stars in Hollywood films are not supposed to die, but no-one told these aliens as the likes of Jack Nicholson, Danny DeVito, Pierce Brosnan, Michael J. Fox and Glenn Close met their ends in a variety of spectacular ways. America is

saved when it transpires that listening to Slim Whitman's version of 'When I'm Calling You' causes the aliens' brains to explode. The sheer silliness of such a premise is only part of the reason *Mars Attacks!* was such a treat. Director Tim Burton brought his usual off-the-wall style to the proceedings, and the gusto of the stellar cast is evident, in a satire more subtle and rich than it first seems.

Science fiction of the more epic variety was also on offer this year, notably in Luc Besson's *Fifth Element*, starring Bruce Willis, which appeared to combine the French director's undoubted visual flair with Hollywood's big-budget firepower. The result was certainly impressive to look at but, according to some, combined the worst of both worlds: the pretentiousness of French cinema and the vapidity of Hollywood. The effects were allegedly the most expensive ever, but it could not compete with the 20-year-old *Star Wars*. Re-released in a new edition, George Lucas's science fiction classic showed that it had stood the test of time, becoming one of the hits of the year and finding audiences not born when it was first released. Its sequel, *The Empire Strikes Back*, also did well, and ensured an audience for the series of prequels which Lucas is currently making in Britain, with Ewan McGregor as the young Obi-Wan Kenobi.

Action films remained popular, the pick of them being *Con Air*, about a group of dangerous prisoners who take a plane hostage before Nicolas Cage, a surprisingly convincing action hero, saves the day. Wolfgang Petersen's *Air Force One*, with Harrison Ford as an American president threatened by the Russians, incorporated notable effects but had a curiously Cold War feel to it. Elsewhere, with Russians and even South Africans now out of favour, the baddies were invariably British.

ANIMATION APPEAL

Films which appeal to family audiences are always in demand, and Disney's live-action remake of *101 Dalmatians* was better than most, with Glenn Close creating a memorable Cruella De Vil. *Matilda*, directed by and co-starring Danny DeVito, was a fine version of Roald Dahl's ever-popular book, while *Hercules*, the autumn 1997 release from Disney, was technically impressive but a little too eager to stress the contemporary relevance of its Greek hero. The depiction in the film of a themed shop stuffed with Hercules merchandise was a nice in-joke from a studio that tends to see its films as 90-minute advertisements for its tie-in products. But the animation, with significant input from the British cartoonist Gerald Scarfe, was impressive, even if it still lacks the quality of the hand-drawn classics of the 1940s and 1950s, as the re-released *The Lady and the Tramp* (made in 1955) demonstrated.

Hand-drawn but with no pretensions to artistic greatness, *Beavis and Butt-head Do America* was a hilarious feature-length adventure with the snickering adolescents better known from their MTV series. The boys' obsession with television (the film's narrative kicks off when their set is stolen), sex and matters lavatorial struck a chord with many who probably should know better. On that level, and as a satire of middle-American values, it provided one of the unexpected treats of the year.

Among other notable American films were two directed by British directors: *Evita* (directed by Alan Parker) was a visually stunning version of the Rice/ Lloyd Webber musical; while *Donnie Brasco* (directed by Mike Newell) was the year's best gangster movie with another matchless performance from Al Pacino. There were fine directorial debuts from three actors: Stanley Tucci's *Big Night* was the delightful tale of two brothers preparing for said evening at their Italian-American restaurant; Steve Buscemi's *Trees Lounge*, about a small-town loser trying to pull his life together, owed much to the godfather of American independent film-making, John Cassavetes; while John Cusack's *Grosse Pointe Blank*, was a rarity, a feel-good comedy about a contract killer.

Three of cinema's maverick talents, the Americans David Lynch and Abel Ferrara, and Canadian David Cronenberg, contributed some of the year's most distinctive films. Lynch's *Lost Highway* was a dark, nightmarish and often incomprehensible film, which made compelling viewing. Ferrara's double-bill of *The Funeral*, about a feuding mob family, and *The Addiction*, a modern-day vampire drama, were notable additions to this director's unique *oeuvre*, both featuring typically mesmeric performances by Christopher Walken.

Cronenberg's *Crash*, based on J. G. Ballard's 1973 novel whose characters are sexually aroused by car crashes, became a *cause célèbre* after its screening at the London Film Festival in November 1996. Invoking an arcane piece of legislation (based originally on the risk to the public of inflammable nitrate film) several local councils chose to ban *Crash*, including Westminster council, home to the West End's cinemas. It was eventually released in the spring and, once the controversy had died down, was considered an ambitious and occasionally disturbing film.

FESTIVALS

As films from the US independent sector, from Canada, Australia, Ireland and Britain make their mark, there seems to be little demand for foreign-language productions. This is reflected at the international film festivals where the great *auteurs* of world cinema have traditionally been showcased. These days, the Cannes, Venice and Berlin festivals are under intense pressure to show the latest mainstream Hollywood films. Distribution of foreign-language films is also affected by this trend. Neither of the two films which shared the Palme d'Or at the 1997 Cannes Festival – Japanese veteran Shohei Imamura's *The Eel*, about a man's relationship with an eel, and Iranian director Abbas Kiarostami's *The*

Taste of Cherries, about a man seeking help in order to commit suicide – is likely to receive a cinema release in the UK.

There were some notable films among those competing for the Palme d'Or, although yet again these were primarily North American in origin. The Canadian Atom Egoyan's *The Sweet Hereafter*, adapted from a Russell Banks novel about a community facing up to devastating coach crash, was a powerful piece of film-making, while the Taiwanese Ang Lee's *The Ice Storm*, starring Kevin Kline and Sigourney Weaver, and *LA Confidential*, an extremely stylish adaptation of the James Ellroy novel, both lingered in the mind. The most disturbing film was from Austria, Michael Haneke's *Funny Games*, in which a middle-class family holiday turns into a violent nightmare.

The Venice Festival in 1996, the last to be run by Gillo Pontecorvo, saw Neil Jordan's *Michael Collins* walk off with the Golden Lion award. A brilliant biography of the Irish hero, played by Liam Neeson, it provoked an outraged response from some commentators in the UK and broke all box office records in Ireland. Other films well-received at Venice included Jane Campion's *Portrait of a Lady* (although audiences elsewhere found this adaptation of Henry James's novel too slow), Barry Levinson's *Sleepers*, starring Robert De Niro, Dustin Hoffman and Brad Pitt, Georgian director Otar Ioseliani's *Brigands*, and, from Mexico, Arturo Ripstein's *Profundo carmesi* (*Deep Crimson*), a remake of the 1960s cult classic *The Honeymoon Killers*.

At the Berlin Festival in February 1997 it was once again an English-language film, Milos Forman's *The People vs. Larry Flynt*, which took the Golden Bear. *Mars Attacks!*, *The English Patient*, and *Romeo and Juliet* also attracted most of the interest, although Tsai Ming-Liang's *The River* won a Special Jury Prize, and the best director award went to Eric Heumann, the Frenchman better known as as a producer, for *Port Djema*, his film about a doctor in the Third World.

FILM AWARD WINNERS

ACADEMY AWARDS 1996

Best picture – *The English Patient*
Best director – Anthony Minghella, *The English Patient*
Best actor – Geoffrey Rush, *Shine*
Best actress – Frances McDormand, *Fargo*
Best supporting actor – Cuba Gooding jun., *Jerry Maguire*
Best supporting actress – Juliette Binoche, *The English Patient*
Best original screenplay – Ethan Coen, Joel Coen, *Fargo*
Best adapted screenplay – Billy Bob Thornton, *Sling Blade*
Best foreign language film – *Kolya,* Czech Republic
Best original musical or comedy score – Rachel Portman, *Emma*
Best original dramatic score – Gabriel Yared, *The English Patient*
Best original song – Sir Andrew Lloyd Webber, Sir Tim Rice, 'You Must Love Me', *Evita*
Best cinematography – *The English Patient*
Best art direction – *The English Patient*
Best costume design – *The English Patient*
Best film editing – *The English Patient*
Best sound – *The English Patient*
Best sound effects editing – *The Ghost and the Darkness*
Best visual effects – *Independence Day*
Best make-up – *The Nutty Professor*
Best animated short – *Quest*
Best documentary feature – *When We Were Kings*
Best short documentary – *Breathing Lessons: The Life and Work of Mark O'Brien*
Best live action short – *Dear Diary*
Honorary awards – Michael Kidd

BAFTA AWARDS 1996

Best film – *The English Patient*

Best actor – Geoffrey Rush, *Shine*
Best actress – Brenda Blethyn, *Secrets and Lies*
Best supporting actor – Paul Scofield, *The Crucible*
Best supporting actress – Juliette Binoche, *The English Patient*
Alex Korda award (British film of the year) – *Secrets and Lies*
The David Lean award (best achievement in direction) – Joel Coen, *Fargo*
Best film not in English – *Ridicule*
Best original screenplay – Mike Leigh, *Secret and Lies*
Best adapted screenplay – Anthony Minghella, *The English Patient*

CANNES FESTIVAL 1997

Palme d'Or – *The Eel; The Taste of Cherries*
Best director – Wong Kar-Wei, *Happy Together*
Best actor – Sean Penn, *She's So Lovely*
Best actress – Kathy Burke, *Nil by Mouth*
Grand Jury prize – *The Sweet Hereafter*

BERLIN FESTIVAL 1997

Best film (Golden Bear) – *The People vs. Larry Flynt*
Special Jury prize – *The River*
Best director – Raoul Ruiz, *Genealogies of a Crime;* Eric Heumann, *Port Djema*
Best actor – Leonardo DiCaprio, *William Shakespeare's Romeo and Juliet*
Best actress – Juliette Binoche, *The English Patient*

VENICE FESTIVAL 1997

Golden Lion – *Hana-Bi*
Special Gold Prize – *Ovosodo*
Best actor – Wesley Snipes, *One Night Stand*
Best actress – Robin Tunney, *Niagara, Niagara*

TELEVISION AWARD WINNERS

BAFTA AWARDS 1996

Best single drama – *Hillsborough*
Best drama series – *EastEnders*
Best drama serial – *Our Friends in the North*
Best light entertainment – *Shooting Stars*
Best comedy – *Only Fools and Horses*
Best actor – Nigel Hawthorne, *The Fragile Heart*
Best actress – Gina McKee, *Our Friends in the North*
Best comedy performance – David Jason, *Only Fools and Horses-Christmas Special*
Best light entertainment performance – John Bird, John Fortune, *Rory Bremner, Who Else?/ The Long Johns*
Best factual series – *The House*
Best arts programme (Huw Wheldon award) – *Leaving Home*
Best children's programme – *Shakespeare Shorts: Romeo and Juliet*
Flaherty documentary award – *Horizon: Fermat's Last Theorem*
Best news coverage – BBC *Newsnight* coverage of BSE
Best sports/events coverage – BBC1, *European Football Championships*
Best talk show – *Mrs Merton Christmas Show*
BAFTA Fellowship – Julie Christie, Woody Allen
The Richard Dimbleby award (for most important personal contribution on screen in factual television) – Robert Hughes

The Dennis Potter award – Peter Flannery
The Lew Grade award (for a significant and popular programme) – *Coronation Street*

ROYAL TELEVISION SOCIETY AWARDS 1996

Entertainment – *The Fast Show*
Situation comedy – *Only Fools and Horses*
Single documentary – *True Stories: Crime of the Wolf*
Documentary series – *The System*
Presenter – Cilla Black
Male actor – David Jason, *Only Fools and Horses*
Female actor – Stella Gonet, *Trip Trap*
Single drama – *Hillsborough*
Drama serial – *Our Friends in the North*
Drama series – *Ballykissangel*
TV performance – Paul Whitehouse, *The Fast Show*
Live sports coverage – BBC, *European Football Championships*
Sports news – ITN, *Channel Four News: Olympic Money*
Sports documentary – BBC, *Dickie Bird: A Rare Species*
Sports presenter – Andy Gray (Sky Sport)
Television journalist of the year – Colin Baker (ITN)
The Gold Medal – Michael Grade

Literature

In January 1997 the bookshop chain Waterstone's instituted a poll to find the 100 books of the 20th century that Britons regard most highly. Twenty-five thousand people responded by listing their top five. J. R. R. Tolkien's epic of elfland *The Lord of the Rings* controversially came out with the highest number of votes as the book of the century, and there were some unexpected inclusions. The best-selling cookery writer Delia Smith appeared at no. 83, beating such distinguished literary works as D. H. Lawrence's *The Rainbow*, George Orwell's *Down and Out in Paris and London*, Gunther Grass's *The Tin Drum*, Alexander Solzhenitsyn's *One Day in the Life of Ivan Denisovitch*, and Nelson Mandela's inspirational autobiography *Long Walk to Freedom*. Children's books were prominent; the list included four Roald Dahl books, Kenneth Grahame's *The Wind in the Willows*, A. A. Milne's *Winnie the Pooh*, and C. S. Lewis's *The Lion, The Witch and the Wardrobe*. Richard Adams's *Watership Down* and Tolkien's *The Hobbit* (both perceived as crossing over into adult literature) also appeared. There were nevertheless some highbrow choices on the list. James Joyce's *Ulysses* was at no. four and Gabriel García Márquez's *One Hundred Years of Solitude* came in eighth out of the 100. But among the 20th-century authors who went unmentioned were T. S. Eliot, Ernest Hemingway, Thomas Mann, Samuel Beckett, Jean-Paul Sartre, Martin Amis and Julian Barnes; also excluded were such admired texts as Doris Lessing's *The Golden Notebook* and Norman Mailer's *The Naked and the Dead*. It was later pointed out that the list closely corresponded to the Public Lending Right's list of the most borrowed library books of 1994 (which *The Lord of the Rings* also topped). The Top 100 received widespread media coverage and was the basis of promotions in many bookshops apart from the Waterstone's chain. It also brought some of the titles back onto the bestseller lists. This did not pacify the poll's detractors, among them Germaine Greer, who attacked the public's choice in *W*, Waterstone's own magazine.

Meanwhile there was dispute over great book no. four. In June 1997, Picador published a new edition of *Ulysses* edited by Danis Rose. Rose claimed that, as it had never been possible to publish the book without errors (every attempt at correction since 1922 added more, and with a book so dense with wordplay it was always hard to tell if an obscurity was intended or erroneous), he was introducing a new element: common sense. He argued that Joyce always strove to be both clear and accurate, and that errors that delighted academics with their opportunities for chasing reverberations were sometimes not only unintended but also against the spirit of the book. 'Joyce was the most careful of all authors. He went to infinite pains to clarify, to make things accurate and transparent. He didn't want fuzziness or imprecision in his own use of language.' Rose therefore made some 8–10,000 corrections (out of a total of 250,000 words), many of them 'rationalizing' punctuation, in 'an attempt to make *Ulysses* make sense from start to finish'. He corrected flaws, he said, that 'would impede readers, and make them search for subtleties that weren't intended'. It was supposed to 'free [readers] to search for the subtleties that did exist'. His edition was published with the subtitle 'A Reader's Edition' to emphasize his search for simplicity over scholarly obfuscation. *Ulysses*, he argued, had become too much the preserve of academics and he wanted it to find a large readership again, and to be recognized as fun rather than difficult.

Unfortunately, not everyone lauded these aims or approved of the means by which Rose sought to achieve them. The Joyce estate, in the person of Joyce's grandson Stephen Joyce, was not happy. Letters were sent by lawyers expressing concern about Rose's alterations, especially in the light of Picador's advertising, which described the edition as 'bold, brilliant, controversial'. The estate did not want the text tampered with unduly. However, copyright law meant that the Joyce estate's concerns could be ignored. On 1 January 1992, 50 years after his death, Joyce's works came out of copyright, allowing anyone to publish his work without the approval of the estate and without paying it any royalties. When in 1993, British law came into line with European law and extended copyright to 70 years after an author's death, Joyce's work went back into copyright and is owned by his estate again. However, the legislation extending copyright specified that any work that was on its way to publication between the expiry of the 50-year term of copyright and the introduction of the 70-year term could go ahead. Rose's work was contracted and largely carried out during this time so the estate had no power to stop him.

Rose expressed the view that his circumstances set an important precedent, since there could be objecting descendants in any academic sphere, with powers of censorship. He thought the estate was 'trying to stop the legitimate publication of a book', and did not think 'estates should have the right to prevent genuine scholarship – even to withhold documents ... Scholarship is openness.' If the Joyce estate had won, it would, claimed Rose, have 'put an end to research across the board'. The estate's opinion may have been ignored but that of the rest of the Joyce community could not be, and Rose had by no means an unqualified reception. One response in the *London Review of Books* concluded a scathing review with the assertion: '[Rose's] edition, if it can be called that, is a chastening example of how an excess of piety can turn into self-aggrandizing fantasy'. As ever, James Joyce's works arouse passionate argument, and Rose's Bloom may suffer withering blasts for some time to come.

ROYALTY

A casual observer might have assumed by late 1996 that there was no mileage left in books exposing the foibles and amorous adventures of the royal family. But Autumn 1996 brought not only the autobiography of Sarah, Duchess of York, *My Story*, but also two unofficial accounts of her life, Allan Starkie's *Fergie: Her Secret Life*, whose publication the Duchess tried to prevent with an injunction, and psychic Madame Vasso's *The Duchess of York: Uncensored*, which described tearful confidences. In February 1997 Michael O'Mara, publisher of Andrew Morton's books about Princess Diana, brought out *Princess Margaret* by Theo Aronson, billed as a 'revealing' biography of the first 'royal rebel'. April brought *Sophie's Kiss: The True Love Story of Prince Edward and Sophie Rhys-Jones* by Garth Gibbs and Sean Smith, who claimed to have 'the co-operation of friends of the couple'. In July, Brian Hoey's *Anne: Private Princess Revealed* promised 'a new insight into the private life' of the Princess Royal, including an account of the 'traumatic break-up' of her marriage to Mark Phillips. Despite their claims, none of these caused much commotion.

Among the most entertaining biographies of the year was Jeremy Lewis's 'authorized' life of Cyril Connolly (May), which was universally well received, and in which the subject's love of good literature and good gossip were matched by the biographer's own; Connolly's womanizing, though, was in a league of its own. The book which won the biography category of the 1996 Whitbread prizes was Diarmaid MacCulloch's life of Thomas Cranmer. At the time of publication it was less noticed by literary editors than were Hermione Lee's *Virginia Woolf* and Ray Monk's *Bertrand Russell: the Spirit*. It was, however, eventually beaten to the overall Whitbread prize by Seamus Heaney's latest collection of poetry, *The Spirit Level*, although Beryl Bainbridge's novel *Every Man for Himself* had been the bookies' favourite. ('For the first time I was disappointed' declared Bainbridge, after making several appearances on the shortlists for the major prizes.) Other noteworthy biographies included the investigative journalist Michael Crick's efficient and intelligent account of Michael Heseltine, published in February 1997. It was appreciated by reviewers, but contained no sensational revelations. Frances Spalding's life of Duncan Grant offered one more glimpse of Bloomsbury from the group's last surviving reliable witness following the death of Quentin Bell in December 1996. Bell's likeable last book, a collection of portraits of friends, *Elders and Betters*, was published posthumously in June 1997. In March Jacqueline du Pré's brother and sister, Hilary and Piers, told their version of her life, *A Genius in the Family*.

Perhaps the most remarkable books of the year were memoirs, of which none was more astonishing than *The Diving-bell and the Butterfly* by Jean-Dominique Bauby. A victim of locked in syndrome which paralysed all but his eyelids, Bauby dictated his book to Claude Mendibil, his editor at the Parisian publishing house Robert Laffont, by a system of blinks. The book climbed the bestseller lists after publication in Britain and was very enthusiastically reviewed. Critics felt that it was not merely a breathtaking achievement that the book was written at all, but that it was a work of exceptional literary quality in any circumstances. Bauby died just a few days after the book had come out in the UK. Other extraordinary memoirs included *The Kiss*, novelist Kathryn Harrison's true account of her four-year affair with her father. The book provoked some outraged reaction and debate about whether or not Harrison should have made the affair public knowledge, though the book was generally praised for its lack of sensationalism. And Gillian Slovo met a spy who was implicated in the murder of her mother, the South African political activist Ruth First, and wrote about the meeting and her relationship with her parents in her memoir *Every Secret Thing*.

AMERICAN LITERATURE

There was a new Saul Bellow, *The Actual*, a short novel about a high-school love that lasts a lifetime; the enamoured courts his first love again in old age. Reviewers admired its pared-down luminosity, and valued it as, if not among his best work, at least very good minor Bellow. The new Philip Roth, *American Pastoral*, is the first part of a trilogy devoted to three decades of American life. This volume covers the Sixties, and tells the story of a college athlete who marries a beauty queen in 1949 and lives a calm and conventional life until the days of Vietnam, when his wife becomes an urban terrorist. It was also well reviewed. There was a new work too from the third of America's pre-eminent triumvirate: a collection of short stories and articles from John Updike, *Golf Dreams*, which was a strong seller in hardback, while his last novel *In the Beauty of the Lilies* appeared on the paperback bestseller lists.

In the spring an epic-length novel came out from the reclusive Thomas Pynchon. Described by the author as 'an anti-historical counter-epic', *Mason and Dixon* reimagined the lives of the 18th-century British surveyors who divided Maryland from Pennsylvania with the line that a century later became the frontier of the Civil War. The book had mixed reviews; some found it hard-going, especially in its use of pastiche.

New works from British authors included Anita Brookner's *Visitors*, about the insensitivity of the young to the old and the married to the single. Reviewers cannot fault her on these themes, though there are those who do not care for them. Helen Dunmore, the winner of last year's Orange Prize, published a collection of short stories, tales of 'sex, estrangement and loss' entitled *Love of Fat Men*. Kate Atkinson, whose funny-sad northern family history *Behind the Scenes at the Museum* was the very readable Whitbread Book of the Year in 1995, was put to the daunting test of a second novel. *Human Croquet* was another tragi-comic saga of a mad family, more ambitious than her first, with Shakespearean echoes; some reviewers felt it was not entirely successful. Rachel Cusk, whose first novel *Saving Agnes* won the Whitbread first novel prize, entered Joanna Trollope territory with her third, *The Country Life*, a romantic comedy about a 29-year-old who kicks over the traces of her city existence and takes refuge in cold rustic comfort. Jonathan Coe garnered praise for *The House of Sleep*, set in a clinic for sufferers from sleeping disorders.

Among the frontrunners for the literary prizes in 1997 are John Banville's much admired novel *The Untouchable*, about an art historian who is also a spy, a protagonist inspired by Anthony Blunt but not meant to be him. Certainly a contender for the 1997 Booker prize, it earned excellent reviews. Other books tipped for the Booker were Jim Crace's *Quarantine* and Peter Carey's *Jack Maggs*.

Journalists often succumb to the temptation to make things up for a change. They used to write romances (Barbara Taylor Bradford, Sally Beauman, Penny Vincenzi) but death was this year's favourite subject. The media novel of the year was by Nicholas Coleridge, managing director of the magazine publisher Condé Nast, who penned a whodunnit *With Friends Like These* which, thanks to his connections, was widely reviewed, and which apparently contained disguised portraits of people in the magazine world. Jane Thynne, former media correspondent of the *Telegraph*, set out to supplement the fortune of her bestselling husband Philip Kerr with *Patrimony*, a romance and puzzle about the past of a poet; and television presenter Sarah Kennedy made her fiction début with a psychological thriller, *Charlotte's Friends*. Spouses Nicci Gerrard and Sean French pretended to be one person, Nicci French, for their co-authored murder mystery *The Memory Game*, which was praised for its atmosphere and the seamlessness of the joint literary effort.

It was a significant year for Indian writing. *The God of Small Things*, a first novel by a young woman, Arundhati Roy, attracted a huge amount of critical attention, and was launched with a big promotional campaign, although the theme of her book was anti-materialist and anti-ambitious. This novel was also considered a contender for the 1997 Booker prize. An extract from it appeared in a widely reviewed issue of Granta devoted to Indian fiction. Also, Vikram Chandra published a collection of short stories this year that attracted favourable reviews, and novelist Gita Mehta brought out a collection of non-fiction pieces about modern India. These factors combined to further the notion that some of the most interesting literature written in English today comes out of the sub-continent.

WORD OF MOUTH

One phenomenon of 1997 was the power of word-of-mouth to sell books. An outstanding example of this was Louis de Bernière's *Captain Corelli's Mandolin*; the author is quite publicity shy, but the word-of-mouth success of his book attracted media coverage which gave its sales a further boost. Another bestseller which, although substantially promoted, reached number one in the bestseller lists because everyone recommended it to their friends was Helen Fielding's hilarious and well-observed account of the life of a single thirtysomething woman, *Bridget Jones's Diary*.

Other notable bestsellers included Bill Bryson's vastly entertaining travel book about Britain, *Notes from A Small Island*, which, although published in paperback in August 1996, was still high in the bestseller lists a year later. Maeve Binchy's *The Glass Lake*, John Grisham's *The Runaway Jury* and Nicholas Evans' *The Horse Whisperer* all achieved paperback sales of one million copies, the last within nine months of publication (a feat last achieved by Sue Townsend's *The Secret Diary of Adrian Mole*). Dava Sobel's *Longitude* sustained its place in the lists, and was voted Book of the Year at the 1996 British Book Awards. Sobel's publisher Fourth Estate followed her success with two comparable non-fiction titles, Simon Singh's *Fermat's Last Theorem*, a study of the intractable mathematical problem and the science book of the year, backed up by a television documentary; and *The Perfect Storm* by Sebastian Junger, an account of a freak disaster off the coast of Massachusetts, a hellish event far stranger than fiction.

Several début novels were promoted hard this year to justify the sums the publishers paid for them: ex-McVities' executive Michael Cordy's scientific thriller *The Miracle Strain*, which made £2m internationally, financier John McLaren's bank heist thriller *Press Send*, and Lee Child's thriller *Killing Floor*, which earned a £150,000 advance and read like Kafka with violence.

The humour book of the past year was *Shooting Stars* by television comedians Vic Reeves and Bob Mortimer, which would have been the bestselling book of Christmas 1996 if sales had not been lost waiting for a reprint. The bestselling sports book was racing driver Damon Hill's *My Championship Year*, published to coincide with Hill's winning of the Formula One Drivers' World Championship in 1996. The year's most exceptional garden book, accompanying a Channel 4 documentary series, was *The Lost Gardens of Heligan*, Tim Smit's account of a wonder of Victorian horticulture and engineering rediscovered and restored to splendour after 70 years of neglect.

The 50th anniversary of the publication of *The Diary of Anne Frank* saw its republication in an unabridged edition, including material Anne's father excluded from the 1947 edition because it reflected badly on her relationship with her mother.

The book reached the top of the children's bestseller lists and climbed high on the general lists.

A pre-millennial spate of quasi-scholarly books claiming to discover miraculous truths began in 1982 with *The Holy Blood and the Holy Grail*, which asserted that Jesus's descendants were alive and living in France. More recent examples are *The Tomb of God*, *The Hiram Key* and *Keeper of Genesis*. The bestseller in the genre in 1997 was Michael Drosnin's *The Bible Code*, written by an American journalist and purportedly based on the work of an Israeli scholar. Its discovery was a code that could be applied to the Hebrew texts of the Bible and that revealed predictions of the future, among them the assassination of Yitzhak Rabin and the end of the world, now deferred. The book had a sustained appearance at the top of the bestseller list despite scholarly criticism. In September 1997 *The Truth Behind the Bible Code* by Dr Jeffrey Satinover countered Drosnin's claims.

CONTROVERSY

In January 1997, with the general election in the offing, Fourth Estate rushed out *Sleaze*, an investigation by *Guardian* journalists Ed Vulliamy and David Leigh into the affairs of Neil Hamilton, MP, and lobbyist Ian Greer; it followed Hamilton's withdrawal of his libel action against the *Guardian* over the paper's allegations that he had accepted cash for asking questions in Parliament. *Sleaze* was hyped as 'the book that will bring down the Government'. While a committee of enquiry was investigating the affair, Hamilton's solicitor sent letters to bookshop chains and several independents. The letter said that after the outcome of the enquiry was made public, Hamilton would 'review the remedies available to him against all those who have repeated or caused to be repeated the allegations'. The solicitor justified the threats implied by the letter thus: 'those who distribute defamatory material are at risk of being in the frame if action is taken later. We thought that, as a courtesy, it would be a good idea to draw that to people's attention'. Fourth Estate acted to indemnify booksellers against legal action – the *Guardian*, the owners of a 50 per cent share of Fourth Estate, agreed to foot the bill if legal action were taken against booksellers – and retaliated with a solicitor's letter to Mr Hamilton's solicitors saying: 'We give you notice that should our clients suffer any loss of sales of the book as a result of booksellers acting upon your letters and withdrawing the book from sale, our clients will seek to recover such loss against Mr Hamilton.' It is rare for individuals to threaten bookshops thus; among those few who have done so are David Irving, Robert Maxwell and the opponents of an anti-fascist magazine called *Searchlight*. The book, which was extracted in the *Guardian* and was the basis of a Channel 4 documentary, might indeed have helped to bring down the Government. It certainly did not help Mr Hamilton, who was defeated in the election by the independent candidate and former television journalist Martin Bell.

Another author caught up in political controversy was Will Self, who, while covering John Major's election campaign, was discovered to have taken heroin in the lavatories of the then prime minister's private plane. An undignified to and fro of denial and confession ended with his losing his newspaper job, but the controversy raised his profile when it came to promoting his new novel *Great Apes*.

The media kicked up a rumpus when one of the judges of the NCR award for non-fiction revealed that the judges did not necessarily read every word of all the submissions, or indeed any of every submission; other selectors whittled the list down for them. The mud seemed to fly in the direction of all the literary prizes; there was insistence from all sides that the job is generally properly done.

The announcement of the shortlist for the Library Association's Carnegie prize for children's literature caused a flurry of newspaper consternation over the darkness of the subjects. Among the selected books were Anne Fine's *The Tulip Touch*, Elizabeth Laird's *Secret Friends*, Michael Coleman's *Weirdo's War*, Jacqueline Wilson's *Bad Girls*, and Melvin Burgess's *Junk*, which between them involved bullying, arson, the death of a child on an operating table, and heroin addiction. Burgess's *Junk* was the overall winner, a book that chronicled the seduction and destruction of teenagers by heroin. The newspapers raised an eyebrow again, but no one in the know offered anything but enthusiasm for the choice.

The new edition of the Lonely Planet *Guide to Britain* caused consternation and generated a huge amount of publicity because the authors were less than impressed by their subject. About Coventry they were particularly damning, so what indignation there was came mostly from the Midlands, but the publishers insisted that this edition, unlike the first, two and a half years ago, reflected the new (post-election) optimism about Britain.

Several writers had their lifetime's achievement acknowledged in 1997. The honours list in June 1997 awarded an OBE to Michael Bond, the creator of Paddington Bear, for services to children's literature, and a CBE to playwright Tom Stoppard. In August 1997 the crime novelist Ruth Rendell was made a baroness, and she joins the House of Lords on the Labour benches.

The year saw the inauguration of World Book Day on 23 April 1997, organized at short notice and manifested largely as special promotions in bookshops. Plans for 1998 are already under way, and promise to have more impact. The organizers hope to build an annual event that makes a significant contribution to the encouragement of reading.

One significant contributor to the encouragement of reading by children, though much disapproved of in recent years, was Enid Blyton. The centenary of her birth in 1997 was celebrated with a debate at the Oxford Union (with tellers dressed as

Noddy and Big Ears), an academic conference at the Roehampton Institute, special exhibitions, new publishers' editions of the books, television programmes, commemorative stamps and a blue plaque. Enid Blyton's books may not be considered politically correct but they prove the enduring attraction of gripping story-telling.

LITERARY PRIZEWINNERS

Nobel Prize 1996 – Wislawa Szymborska

Commonwealth Writers Prize 1996 – Rohinton Mistry, *A Fine Balance*
First work – Vikram Chandra, *Red Earth and Pouring Rain*

Prix Goncourt 1996 – Pascale Roze, *Le Chasseur Zéro*

Booker Prize 1996 – Graham Swift, *Last Orders*

Whitbread Prize 1996: overall winner – Seamus Heaney, *The Spirit Level*
Novel – Beryl Bainbridge, *Every Man For Himself*
First novel – John Lanchester, *The Debt To Pleasure*
Biography – Diarmaid MacCulloch, *Thomas Cranmer: A Life*
Poetry – Seamus Heaney, *The Spirit Level*
Children's novel – Anne Fine, *The Tulip Touch*

David Higham Prize 1996 – Linda Grant, *The Cast Iron Shore*

Forward Prize 1996 (poetry) – John Fuller, *Stones and Fires*
First collection – Kate Clanchy, *Slattern*

William Hill Sports Book of the Year 1996 – Donald McRae, *Dark Trade: Lost in Boxing*

Smarties Prize 1996 (children's books):
Age 0–5 – Colin McNaughton, *Oops!*
Age 6–8 – Michael Morpurgo, *The Butterfly Lion*
Age 9–11 – Philip Pullman, *The Firework Maker's Daughter*

Crime Writers Association 1996:
Gold Dagger (fiction) – Ben Elton, *Popcorn*
Silver Dagger (fiction) – Peter Lovesey, *Bloodhounds*

British Book Awards 1996 – Dava Sobel, *Longitude*

Encore Prize 1996 (second novel) – David Flusfeder, *Like Plastic*

Orange Award 1997 (women writers) – Anne Michaels, *Fugitive Pieces*

NCR Award 1997 (non-fiction) – Orlando Figes, *A People's Tragedy: The Russian Revolution*

Somerset Maugham Prize 1997 – Rhidian Brook, *The Testimony of Taliesin*; Kate Clanchy, *Slattern*; Philip Hensher, *Kitchen Venom*; Francis Spufford, *I May Be Some Time*

Betty Trask Prize 1997 – Alex Garland, *The Beach*

McKitterick Prize 1997 (first novel by a writer over 40) – Patricia Duncker, *Hallucinating Foucault*

W. H. Smith Prize 1997 – Orlando Figes, *A People's Tragedy: The Russian Revolution*

Mail on Sunday/John Llewellyn Rhys Prize 1997 – Nicola Barker, *Heading Inland*

Cholmondeley Award 1997 (poetry) – Alison Brackenbury, Gillian Clarke, Tony Curtis, Anne Stevenson

Romantic Novel of the Year 1997 – Sue Gee, *The Hours of Night*

Carnegie Prize 1997 (children's) – Melvin Burgess, *Junk*

Kate Greenaway 1997 (children's illustrated) – Helen Cooper, *The Baby Who Wouldn't Go to Bed*

Nobel Prizes

For prize winners for the years 1901–93, *see* earlier editions of *Whitaker's Almanack*.

The Nobel Prizes are awarded each year from the income of a trust fund established by the Swedish scientist Alfred Nobel, the inventor of dynamite, who died on 10 December 1896 leaving a fortune of £1,750,000. The prizes are awarded to those who have contributed most to the common good in the domain of:

Physics – awarded by the Royal Swedish Academy of Sciences
Chemistry – awarded by the Royal Swedish Academy of Sciences
Physiology or Medicine – awarded by the Karolinska Institute
Literature – awarded by the Swedish Academy of Arts
Peace – awarded by a five-person committee elected by the Norwegian Storting
Economic Sciences (instituted 1969) – awarded by the Royal Swedish Academy of Sciences

The first awards were made in 1901 on the fifth anniversary of Nobel's death. The prizes are awarded every year on 10 December, the anniversary of Nobel's death.

The Trust is administered by the board of directors of the Nobel Foundation, Stockholm, consisting of five members and three deputy members. The Swedish Government appoints a chairman and a deputy chairman, the remaining members being appointed by the awarding authorities.

The awards have been distributed as follows:

PHYSICS
American 63, British 20, German 19 (1948–90, West German 8), French 11, Soviet 7, Dutch 6, Swedish 4, Austrian 3, Danish 3, Italian 3, Japanese 3, Canadian 2, Chinese 2, Swiss 2, Indian 1, Irish 1, Pakistani 1

CHEMISTRY
American 42, German 27 (1948–90, West German 10), British 24, French 7, Swiss 5, Swedish 4, Canadian 3, Dutch 3, Argentinian 1, Austrian 1, Belgian 1, Czech 1, Finnish 1, Hungarian 1, Italian 1, Japanese 1, Mexican 1, Norwegian 1, Soviet 1

PHYSIOLOGY OR MEDICINE
American 74, British 23, German 15 (1948–90, West German 4), French 7, Swedish 7, Swiss 6, Danish 5, Austrian 4, Belgian 4, Australian 3, Italian 3, Canadian 2, Dutch 2, Hungarian 2, Russian 2, Argentinian 1, Japanese 1, Portuguese 1, South African 1, Spanish 1

LITERATURE
French 12, American 10, British 8, Swedish 7, German 6 (1948–90, West German 1), Italian 5, Spanish 5, Danish 3, Irish 3, Norwegian 3, Polish 3, Soviet 3, Chilean 2, Greek 2, Japanese 2, Swiss 2, Australian 1, Belgian 1, Colombian 1, Czech 1, Egyptian 1, Finnish 1, Guatemalan 1, Icelandic 1, Indian 1, Israeli 1, Mexican 1, Nigerian 1, South African 1, Trinidadian 1, Yugoslav 1, Stateless 1

PEACE
American 17, Institutions 17, British 10, French 9, Swedish 5, German 4 (1948–90, West German 1), South African 4, Belgian 3, Israeli 3, Swiss 3, Argentinian 2, Austrian 2, East Timorese 2, Norwegian 2, Soviet 2, Burmese 1, Canadian 1, Costa Rican 1, Danish 1, Egyptian 1, Guatemalan 1, Irish 1, Italian 1, Japanese 1, Mexican 1, Palestinian 1, Polish 1, Tibetan 1, Vietnamese 1, Yugoslav 1

ECONOMICS
American 24, British 7, Norwegian 2, Swedish 2, Canadian 1, Dutch 1, French 1, German 1, Soviet 1

The Swedish Embassy (*see* page 1019) can provide a full list of winners.

Prize	1994	1995	1996
Physics	Prof. B. Brockhouse (Canadian) Prof. C. Shull (American)	Dr M. Perl (American) Dr F. Reines (American)	Prof. D. Lee (American) Prof. D. Osheroff (American) Prof. R. Richardson (American)
Chemistry	Prof. G. Olah (American)	P. Crutzen (Dutch) Dr M. Molina (Mexican) Dr S. Rowland (American)	Prof. R. Curl (American) Sir Harold Kroto, Kt., FRS (British) Prof. R. Smalley (American)
Physiology or Medicine	Dr A. Gilman (American) Dr M. Rodbell (American)	Dr E. Lewis (American) Dr C. Nuesslein-Volhard (German) Dr E. Wieschaus (American)	Prof. P. Doherty (Australian) Prof. R. Zinkernagel (Swiss)
Literature	K. Oe (Japanese)	S. Heaney (Irish)	W. Szymborska (Polish)
Peace	Y. Rabin (Israeli) Y. Arafat (Palestinian) S. Peres (Israeli)	Prof. J. Rotblat (British) The Pugwash Conference on Science and World Affairs	Bishop Carlos Belo (East Timorese) J. Ramos-Horta (East Timorese)
Economics	J. Harsanyi (American) J. Nash (American) R. Selten (German)	R. Lucas (American)	Prof. J. Mirrlees (British) Prof. W. Vickrey (Canadian)*

*Died on 11 October 1996

Opera

This was the golden jubilee season of the Royal Opera, which had opened, as the Covent Garden Opera Company, in January 1947 with a performance of *Carmen*. It was also the last season before the closure of the theatre for redevelopment, and was marked by a series of internal management crises. When it was announced that Sir Jeremy Isaacs, whose contract as general director of the Royal Opera House expired in September 1997, would leave at the end of 1996, Genista McIntosh, former executive director of the Royal National Theatre, was appointed chief executive of the Royal Opera House, taking up her post in January 1997. Four months later, Ms McIntosh resigned on the grounds of ill-health, and was replaced, without the usual recruitment procedure, by Mary Allen, former secretary-general of the Arts Council.

Lord Chadlington, a former member of the Arts Council, who became chairman of the board of directors in August 1996 in succession to Sir Angus Stirling, explained that this over-hasty appointment – as some critics considered it – was necessary, owing to the problems caused by the imminent closure of the House. Ms Allen took up her post in September 1997. Meanwhile, Chris Smith, Secretary of State for Culture, Media and Sport, ordered a select committee of MPs to look into the affairs of the Royal Opera House. Sitting at the end of July, the committee was told by Ms McIntosh that she had left, not because of ill-health, but because of the unhappiness and stress caused by 'managerial confusion' at the Opera House.

ARTISTIC SUCCESSES

In artistic terms, the jubilee season was a great success. Two well-loved singers celebrated the 25th anniversary of their first appearances with the company: Thomas Allen and Placido Domingo. During the season Allen, who had made his début in December 1971 as Donald in *Billy Budd*, sang four roles, Don Giovanni, the Baron in *Chérubin*, Cardinal Morone in *Palestrina* and Beckmesser in *Die Meistersinger*; Domingo, who also made his Covent Garden début in December 1971, as Cavaradossi, sang Siegmund in one performance of *Die Walküre* (his first Wagner role in London), conducted a performance of *Tosca*, and took the role of Gabriele Adorno in Verdi's original, 1857, version of *Simon Boccanegra*.

Although there were only two new productions, of Pfitzner's *Palestrina* and the 1857 *Simon Boccanegra*, both were highly praised by the critics and popular with the public. *Palestrina*, receiving its first fully professional stage performance in London, benefited from a superb cast, led by the American tenor Thomas Moser (making his Royal Opera début) in the title role. After the season ended on 14 July

1997, the company took the production of *Palestrina* to New York, where it was given its American stage première at the Metropolitan Opera on 21 July, during the Lincoln Center Festival. It was the Royal Opera's first visit to New York.

The original version of *Simon Boccanegra*, also receiving its London stage première during the Covent Garden Verdi Festival (May to July 1997), was equally well cast, with the Russian baritone Sergei Leiferkus in the title role and Domingo as Adorno, and even more successful. Another new production, of the original, 1847, version of *Macbeth*, had to be postponed because of 'diminution of resources and of space and time' for rehearsal, caused by the redevelopment, and was replaced by concert performances. The production will now be staged during the 2000 Verdi Festival, after the Royal Opera's return to Covent Garden's new, modernized stage and refurbished auditorium.

The 1996–7 season started with the first complete cycles of Richard Jones's production of *Der Ring des Nibelungen*, built up over the previous two seasons. The staging, substantially altered, was still found controversial by some, though Jones and his designer, Nigel Lowery, were awarded the *Evening Standard* award for artistic achievement in opera. There was no criticism of the musical performance, majestically conducted by musical director Bernard Haitink, who also conducted highly praised revivals of *Die Meistersinger von Nurnberg* and Janáček's *Kát'a Kabanová*; Haitink, who has renewed his contract with the Royal Opera, will lead the company back to Covent Garden in December 1999 with a new production of Verdi's *Falstaff*. Valery Gergiev, music director of the Kirov Opera in St Petersburg, conducted an exceptionally fine revival of *Lohengrin*.

The theatre closed on 14 July 1997, after a farewell gala, patronized by the Prince of Wales and Princess Margaret, and given by both the Royal Opera and the Royal Ballet. Relayed live on the Big Screen in the Covent Garden Piazza, and also televised on BBC2, this event was seen and heard – free of charge – by a very large audience. In August the company paid its first visit since 1961 to the Edinburgh International Festival (also celebrating its 50th anniversary) with a new production of Rameau's *Platée*, directed by the choreographer Mark Morris and conducted by Nicholas McGeegan, which will be seen in London at the Barbican Theatre in September 1997.

The Edinburgh programme also included a number of works given in the early years of the Festival. Verdi's *Macbeth* was the first opera performed in 1947, in a staging by Glyndebourne of the later, 1861 version; in 1997 the Royal Opera gave concert performances of the 1847 version, conducted by Sir Edward Downes. In 1950, Richard Strauss's *Ariadne auf Naxos* in the original 1912 version, with the opera preceded, not by the usual Prologue, but by Molière's *Le bourgeois gentilhomme* (substantially abridged), received its British première at Edinburgh, conducted by Sir Thomas Beecham; in 1997 Scottish Opera staged a new production of this version, directed by Martin Duncan and conducted by Richard Armstrong, which enters the repertoire in the 1997–8 season. Richard Jarman gave up his post as general director of Scottish Opera in 1997 and was succeeded by Ruth Mackenzie, the former executive director of the Nottingham Playhouse.

COLISEUM REPORT

English National Opera also experienced various crises during the 1996–7 season, mainly concerning the future of the company's home, the London Coliseum. The report on the feasibility study commissioned in the autumn of 1995 was published at the beginning of the 1996–7 season. Certain essential work at the Coliseum must be done in the near future in order to maintain its operating licence and fire certificate; the report then offered the options of minor refurbishment immediately, followed by major refurbishment in five years' time; or the building of a new theatre specifically intended for opera. The management appeared to be in favour of the second option, but the audience, including the critics, preferred the former. None of the sites proposed by the report was in the West End, while the Coliseum, despite its many inconveniences both in front of and behind the curtain, is greatly loved by many opera-goers.

ENO was without a music director during the whole season, as Paul Daniel, currently music director of Opera North, did not take up his appointment until August 1997. However, the standard of performance was kept reasonably high. The most notable new production was David Freeman's staging, the first by a British company, of Bernd-Alois Zimmermann's *Die Soldaten*, which requires huge musical and dramatic forces. Elgar Howarth conducted. Other new productions included popular versions of *La traviata*, directed by Jonathan Miller, and *The Italian Girl in Algiers*, staged by Howard Davies. Berlioz's *The Damnation of Faust*, directed by David Alden, was given a critical pasting for its production, although Mark Elder's musical direction was much praised.

The world première of Gavin Bryars' new opera, *Doctor Ox's Experiment*, based on a story by Jules Verne and due for performance in June 1997, had to be postponed for at least a year because of lack of funds. However, ENO's Contemporary Opera Studio, dedicated to the development and performance of new music theatre, had a full season working on, among other projects, *The Silver Tassie*, a new opera by Mark-Anthony Turnage, artistic consultant to the Studio and composer-in-association, due for performance in 1998, and a one-act chamber opera by Turnage, *The Country of the Blind*, based on a story by H. G. Wells. This was successfully premièred at the Aldeburgh Festival on 13 June 1997, and given its London première on 3 July at the Queen Elizabeth Hall, staged by Emma Jenkins, conducted by Nicholas Kok, with a virtuoso performance by the tenor Thomas Randle as Nunez, the mountain guide who stumbles on a lost community of blind people in the Andes.

LOTTERY CLIENTS

National Lottery rules were altered to allow a number of those organizations most deeply in debt to benefit from a so-called 'stabilization programme'. Companies already in receipt of lottery money for capital projects, like the Royal Opera, are not eligible, but ENO is to receive sufficient funds to 'close its current operating deficit', while Welsh National Opera gets £400,000 above its normal Arts Council grant to ensure that its English touring is not reduced. Despite financial difficulties, WNO presented an excellent season, with fine new productions of *Don Giovanni*, *Carmen* and *Simon Boccanegra* (the 1881 version), that all combined musical and dramatic interest.

Opera North, which gets £200,000 extra from the lottery, also in support of the company's touring programme, continued to maintain its high standards of performance. Gluck's *Iphigenia in Aulis* made a rare but enjoyable appearance, with Lynne Dawson in the title role; Annabel Arden's production of Monteverdi's *The Return of Ulysses*, in a performing edition by Paul Daniel much admired at the 1996 Buxton Festival, entered the Opera North repertoire, where it received similar critical appreciation; *Tannhäuser*, newly directed by David Fielding, was conducted by Paul Daniel and provided the climax to his highly successful tenure as music director of Opera North.

Daniel also conducted some performances of the revival of Britten's *Gloriana* (the others were conducted by James Holmes, Daniel's successor), with Dame Josephine Barstow in the title role; *Wozzeck* with Barstow as Marie; and a semi-staged concert version of Erich Wolfgang Korngold's one-act opera, *Violanta*, in commemoration of the composer's centenary; this was repeated at a promenade concert at the Royal Albert Hall in July 1997.

Another opera given at the Proms was Rossini's *Le Comte Ory*, one of two new productions at the 1997 Glyndebourne Festival; the other was Puccini's *Manon Lescaut*. Both these productions unfortunately lost their respective original protagonists not long before their respective first nights; though *Manon Lescaut* did not fully recover, *Le Comte Ory*, riotously staged by Jérôme Savary and enthusiastically conducted by Andrew Davis, was a huge success. Revivals of *The Makropoulos Case*, with Anya Silja again in the title role, and Handel's *Theodora*, which won the 1996 Royal Philharmonic Society Award for Opera, and an *Evening Standard* award for its director, Peter Sellars, were warmly praised by critics and public alike, while Britten's *Owen Wingrave*, first staged by the touring company, was successfully transferred to the main Festival.

There were no new productions by Glyndebourne Touring Opera in 1997, but earlier in the year, Glyndebourne Education mounted *Misper*, a new opera for and about young people, with music by John Lunn and libretto by Stephen Plaice. *Misper* had a cast of four adult professionals and 60 young people between the ages of ten and 16 from seven local East Sussex schools, who had all helped in the development of the story-line during various workshops; it was directed by Stephen Langridge and conducted by Andrea Quinn. Four performances, much enjoyed by performers and spectators, were given.

NOISE PROTEST

Now in its ninth year, Garsington Opera, playing in the garden of a Jacobean manor house, continued to explore the Haydn and later Richard Strauss operas that have characterized earlier seasons. However, the overture to the opening performance of *Le pescatrici* was accompanied by several instruments unknown to Haydn: a motor mower, hedge trimmers, car alarms and a light aeroplane. These were 'played' by residents of the nearby village in protest against what they considered excessive noise, although Leonard Ingrams, owner of the manor and director of the Opera, had obtained a performing licence from South Oxfordshire District Council and permission to continue for the next seven years.

Later performances of *Le pescatrici* and a revival of Mozart's *Così fan tutte* took place without incident, but the British stage première of Strauss's *Die Aegyptische Helena*, much more heavily scored, was judged to exceed the permitted noise level, and consequently Garsington Opera faced prosecution by the council for noise pollution. The six sold-out performances of *Die Aegyptische Helena*, directed and designed by David Fielding and conducted by Elgar Howarth, were much appreciated by audiences, and it would be a great pity if a solution to the problem were not found.

Sylvia Fisher, the Australian soprano who sang at Covent Garden from 1949 to 1973, died on 25 August 1996, aged 86. Her roles included Leonore in *Fidelio*, the Countess in *Le nozze di Figaro*, Senta in *Der fliegende Holländer*, Elsa in *Lohengrin*, Elisabeth in *Tannhäuser*, Isolde, Agathe in *Der Freischütz* and the Kostelnička in *Jenůfa*, but her finest interpretations were the Marschallin in *Der Rosenkavalier*, Sieglinde in *Die Walküre* and Mère Marie, which she sang in the British première of Poulenc's *Dialogues des Carmélits*. She also sang several roles in operas by Britten, Ellen Orford in *Peter Grimes*, Mrs Grose in *The Turn of the Screw*, the Female Chorus in *The Rape of Lucretia*, Queen Elizabeth in *Gloriana*, and Miss Wingrave, which she created in the TV production of *Owen Wingrave*. Myfanwy Piper, who provided Britten with texts for *The Turn of the Screw*, *Owen*

Wingrave and *Death in Venice*, died on 18 January 1997, aged 85.

Another soprano associated with Covent Garden, New Zealand-born Dame Joan Hammond, died on 26 November 1996 aged 86. She sang with the Carl Rosa Opera Company (1942–5) and at Covent Garden (1948–51). Her repertoire, mainly Italian, included Aida, Tosca, Mimi in *La bohème*, the title role of *Madama Butterfly* and Leonora in *Il trovatore*. She sang the title role of *Rusalka* in the professional British stage première of Dvořák's opera at Sadler's Wells in 1959. Dame Joan was awarded a golden disc in 1969 for her recording of 'O mio babbino caro' from *Gianni Schicchi*, which sold over a million copies.

Anna Pollak, the English mezzo-soprano who died on 28 November 1996 aged 84, spent the greater part of her career, from 1945 to 1962, at Sadler's Wells. Particularly convincing in trouser roles such as Cherubino, Hansel, Siebel in *Faust* and Prince Orlofsky in *Die Fledermaus*, she also sang Dorabella in *Così fan tutte*, Carmen, and the Secretary in Menotti's *The Consul*. She created Lady Nelson in Lennox Berkeley's *Nelson* and Mrs Strickland in John Gardner's *The Moon and Sixpence*. With the English Opera Group she created Bianca in *The Rape of Lucretia*, the title role of Berkeley's *Ruth* and various parts in Malcolm Williamson's *English Eccentrics*.

The New Zealand-born baritone Denis Dowling, who died on 23 September 1996, also spent his career mainly at Sadler's Wells (later ENO). He made his début with the company in 1939 as Herr Faninal in *Der Rosenkavalier*, and took his farewell in 1984 as Prince Nikolai Bolkonsky in Prokofiev's *War and Peace*. His wide repertoire, of more than 100 roles, included both Rossini's and Mozart's Figaro, Marcello in *La bohème*, Sharpless in *Madama Butterfly*, Doctor Malatesta in *Don Pasquale*, Guglielmo and Don Alfonso in *Così fan tutte*, Papageno in *The Magic Flute*, Gianni Schicchi, Dandini in *La Cenerentola*, Raimbaud in *The Count Ory* and many others. Though mainly a comic singer, he made a sinister Commandant in Janáček's *From the House of the Dead*.

Charles Craig, the London-born tenor who died on 23 January 1997, spent five years in the Covent Garden chorus before Sir Thomas Beecham sponsored his professional training. He sang with the Carl Rosa Opera Company (1953–7) in a variety of roles that included Gounod's Faust, Don Ottavio in *Don Giovanni*, the Duke in *Rigoletto*, the title role of Berlioz's *Benvenuto Cellini* and Des Grieux in Puccini's *Manon Lescaut*. Joining Sadler's Wells he added Manrico in *Il trovatore*, Samson in *Samson and Delilah*, the Prince in Dvořák's *Rusalka*, Andrea Chénier, Luigi in *Il tabarro*, Nadir in *The Pearl Fishers* and Bacchus in *Ariadne auf Naxos* to his repertoire. For Scottish Opera he sang Florestan in *Fidelio*, Siegmund in *Die Walküre* and Siegfried in *Götterdämmerung*.

Craig made his Covent Garden début in 1959 as Pinkerton in *Madama Butterfly*, followed by

Cavaradossi in *Tosca*, Turiddu in *Cavalleria rustica-na*, Radames in *Aida*, Arturo in *I puritani*, Calaf in *Turandot*, Canio in *Pagliacci* and Sergei in the British première of Shostakovich's *Lady Macbeth of the Mtsensk District* (1963). His finest role was the protagonist of Verdi's *Otello*, which he first sang in 1963 with Scottish Opera, then repeated throughout Europe and North America – but not in London until 1981, when he sang Otello with ENO, and also substituted for an indisposed tenor with the Royal Opera in Manchester. Finally, in 1983, he sang Otello at Covent Garden, this time standing in for Placido Domingo. He retired in 1985.

PRODUCTIONS

In the summaries of company activities shown below, the dates in brackets indicate the year that the current production entered the company's repertoire.

ROYAL OPERA
Founded 1946
Royal Opera House, Covent Garden, London WC2E 9DD
Productions from the repertoire: *Der Ring des Nibelungen* (1994–5), *La bohème* (1974), *Don Giovanni* (1992), *Tosca* (1964), *Turandot* (1984), *Chérubin* (1994), *Lohengrin* (1977), *Così fan tutte* (1995), *Die Meistersinger von Nürnberg* (1993), *Salome* (1995), *Otello* (1987), *L'elisir d'amore* (1975), *Elektra* (1990), *Kát'a Kabanová* (1994), *Simon Boccanegra* (1881 version) (1991), *Rigoletto* (1988)

New productions:
Palestrina (Pfitzner), 28 January 1997 (British professional stage première). Conductor, Christian Thielemann; director, Nikolaus Lehnhoff; designers, Tobias Hoheisel (set), Bettina Walter (costumes). Thomas Moser (Palestrina), Ruth Ziesak (Ighino), Randi Stene (Silla), René Pape (Pius IV), Thomas Allen (Morone), Kim Begley (Novagerio), Kurt Rydl (Madruschi), Alan Held (Borromeo), Nicolai Gedda (Abdisu), Sergei Leiferkus (Luna)
Simon Boccanegra (1857 version) (Verdi), 28 June 1997 (British stage première). Conductor, Mark Elder; director, Ian Judge; designers, John Gunter (set), Deirdre Clancy (costumes). Kallen Esperian (Amelia), Placido Domingo (Adorno), Sergei Leiferkus (Boccanegra), Jaako Ryhanen (Fiesco), Peter Sidhom (Paolo)

ENGLISH NATIONAL OPERA
Founded 1931
London Coliseum, St Martin's Lane, London WC2N 4BS
Productions from the repertoire: *A Midsummer Night's Dream* (1995), *Don Quixote* (1994), *The Cunning Little Vixen* (1988), *Rigoletto* (1982), *The Pearl Fishers* (1987), *The Mikado* (1986), *Der Rosenkavalier* (1994), *Figaro's Wedding* (1991), *Madam Butterfly* (1984), *Ariadne on Naxos* (1983), *Carmen* (1996), *Don Pasquale* (1995)

New productions:
La traviata (Verdi), 12 September 1996. Conductor, Steven Mercurio; director, Jonathan Miller; designers, Bernard Culshaw (set), Clare Mitchell (costumes). Rosa Mannion (Violetta), Nerys James (Flora), John Hudson (Alfredo), Christopher Robertson (Giorgio Germont), Andrew Greenan (Doctor Grenvil)
Die Soldaten (Bernd Alois Zimmermann), 19 November 1996 (British opera company première). Conductor, Elgar Howarth; director, David Freeman; designer, Sally Jacobs.

Lisa Saffer (Marie), Jon Garrison (Desportes), Roberto Salvatori (Stolzius), Jan Opalach (Wesener), Marie Angel (Countess of Roche), David Barrell (Major Haudy), Nicholas Folwell (Major Mary)
The Italian Girl in Algiers (Rossini), 18 January 1997. Conductor, Valentin Reymond; director, Howard Davies; designer, Tim Hatley. Della Jones (Isabella), Mary Hegarty (Elvira), Charles Workman (Lindoro), Alan Opie (Taddeo), Henry Runey (Mustafa)
Orpheus and Eurydice (Gluck), 3 March 1997. Conductor, Jane Glover; director, Martha Clarke; designers, John Conklin (set), Jane Greenwood (costumes). Michael Chance (Orpheus), Lesley Garrett (Eurydice), Helen Williams (Amor)
The Damnation of Faust (Berlioz), 7 April 1997. Conductor, Mark Elder; director, David Alden; designers, Roni Toren (set), Brigitte Gobbel (costumes). Bonaventura Bottone (Faust), Louise Winter (Marguerite), Willard White (Mephistopheles)
The Country of the Blind (Mark-Anthony Turnage), 13 June 1997 (world première by ENO Contemporary Opera Studio at the Aldeburgh Festival). Conductor, Nicholas Kok; director, Emma Jenkins; designer, Conor Murphy. Thomas Randle (Nunez), Regina Nathan (Medina), Keel Watson (The Elder)

OPERA NORTH
Founded 1978
Grand Theatre, 40 New Briggate, Leeds LS1 6NU
Productions from the repertoire: *Wozzeck* (1993), *The Marriage of Figaro* (1996), *Gloriana* (1994)

New productions:
Madama Butterfly (Puccini), 19 September 1996. Conductor, Marco Zambelli; director, Dalia Ibelhauptaite; designer, Oleg Cheintsis. Chen Sue (Butterfly), Liane Keegan (Suzuki), Mark Nicolson (Pinkerton), Peter Savidge (Sharpless), Mark Curtis (Goro)
Iphigenia in Aulis (Gluck), 30 September 1996. Conductor, Valentin Reymond; director, Tim Hopkins; designer, Nigel Lowery. Lynne Dawson (Iphigenia), Della Jones (Clytemnestra), Neill Archer (Achilles), Christopher Purves (Agamemnon)
Falstaff (Verdi), 16 January 1997. Conductor, Paul Daniel; director, Matthew Warchus; designer, Laura Hopkins. Andrew Shore (Falstaff), Rita Cullis (Alice Ford), Margaret Richardson (Nannetta), Yvonne Howard (Meg Page), Frances McCafferty (Mistress Quickly), Paul Nilon (Fenton), Robert Hayward (Ford)
The Return of Ulysses (Monteverdi), 15 April 1997. Conductor, Harry Bicket; director, Annabel Arden; designer, Tim Hatley. Alice Coote (Penelope), Nigel Robson (Ulysses), Therese Feighan (Minerva/Fortune), Frances McCafferty (Ericlea), Nicholas Sears (Telemachus), Jamie McDougall (Jove/Pisander), Mark Curtis (Eumaeus), Valentin Jar (Iro), Clive Bayley (Antinuous)
Tannhäuser (Wagner), 3 May 1997. Conductor, Paul Daniel; director/designer, David Fielding. Jeffrey Lawton (Tannhäuser), Rita Cullis (Elisabeth), Anne-Marie Owens (Venus), Keith Latham (Wolfram), Norman Bailey (Landgrave)
Così fan tutte (Mozart), 21 May 1997. Conductor, Claire Gibault; director, Tim Albery; designers, Matthew Howland, Robin Rawstorne (set), Tania Spooner (costumes). Susannah Glanville (Fiordiligi), Emma Selway (Dorabella), Linda Kitchen (Despina), Paul Nilon (Ferrando), William Dazeley (Guglielmo), Jonathan Best (Don Alfonso)
Performances were given at the Grand Theatre, Leeds,

and on tour at York, Manchester, Nottingham, Sheffield, Hull, Norwich, Sunderland, Blackpool and London (Royal Festival Hall).

SCOTTISH OPERA
Founded 1962
39 Elmbank Crescent, Glasgow G2 4PT

Productions from the repertoire: *Il trovatore* (1992), *La bohème* (1988), *The Cunning Little Vixen* (1980)

New productions:
Inés de Castro (James MacMillan), 23 August 1996 (world première). Conductor, Richard Armstrong; director, Jonathan Moore; designer, Chris Dyer. Helen Field (Inés de Castro), Elizabeth Byrne (Bianca), Anne Collins (Nurse/Old Woman), Jeffrey Lawton (Pedro), Jacek Strauch (Pacheco), Stafford Dean (The King)
    Idomeneo (Mozart), 3 October 1996. Conductor, Antoni Ros Marbá; director/designer, David McVicar. Lisa Milne (Ilia), Claire Rutter (Electra), Thomas Randle (Idomeneo), Toby Spence (Idamante), Peter Hoare (Arbace), Ian Storey (High Priest)
    Die Fledermaus (Johann Strauss), 12 February 1997. Conductor, Nicholas Braithwaite; director, Giles Havergal; designer, Kenny Miller. Janis Kelly (Rosalinda), Lisa Milne (Adele), Anne Howells (Orlofsky), Peter Evans (Eisenstein), Richard Coxon (Alfred), Andrew Hammond (Dr Falke), Andrew Slater (Colonel Frank)
    Samson et Dalila (Saint-Saëns), 23 April 1997. Conductor, Frédéric Chaslin; director/designer, Antony McDonald. Carolyn Sebron (Dalila), Mark Lundberg (Samson), Robert Hayward (High Priest), Christopher Purves (Abimelech)
    Performances were given in the Theatre Royal, Glasgow, and on tour at Edinburgh, Newcastle upon Tyne, Aberdeen and Inverness.

WELSH NATIONAL OPERA
Founded 1946
John Street, Cardiff CF1 4SP

Productions from the repertoire: *La bohème* (1984), *The Doctor of Myddfai* (1996), *Rigoletto* (1990), *Iphigénie en Tauride* (1992), *The Barber of Seville* (1986), *From the House of the Dead* (1982)

New productions:
Don Giovanni (Mozart), 14 September 1996. Conductor, Carlo Rizzi; director, Katie Mitchell; designer, Rae Smith. Davide Damiani (Don Giovanni), Arwel Huw Morgan (Leporello), Cara O'Sullivan (Donna Anna), Alwyn Mellor (Donna Elvira), Catrin Wyn Davies (Zerlina), Gwyn Hughes Jones (Don Ottavio), Davide Baronchelli (Masetto), Anthony Stuart Lloyd (Commendatore)
    Carmen (Bizet), 15 February 1997. Conductor, Robert Spano; directors, Patrice Caurier, Moshe Leiser; designers, Christian Fenouillat (set), Agostino Cavalca (costumes). Sara Fulgoni (Carmen), John Daszak (Don José), Alwyn Mellor (Micaela), Bruno Caproni (Escamillo)
    Simon Boccanegra (Verdi), 19 May 1997. Conductor, Carlo Rizzi; director, David Pountney; designers, Ralph Koltai (set), Sue Wilmington (costumes)
    Performances were given in the New Theatre, Cardiff, and on tour at Oxford, Birmingham, Plymouth, Southampton, Bristol, Liverpool, Swansea and Llandudno.

GLYNDEBOURNE FESTIVAL OPERA
Founded 1934
Glyndebourne, Lewes, East Sussex BN8 5UU

The Festival ran from 18 May to 24 August 1997. *Owen*

Wingrave (1995, touring company), *Le nozze di Figaro* (1994), *The Makropulos Case* (1995) and *Theodora* (1996) were revived.

New productions:
Manon Lescaut (Puccini), 18 May 1997. Conductor, John Eliot Gardiner; director, Graham Vick; designer, Richard Hudson. Adina Nitescu (Manon Lescaut), Patrick Denniston (Des Grieux), Roberto de Candia (Lescaut), Paolo Montarsolo (Géronte)
    Le Comte Ory (Rossini), 20 July 1997. Conductor, Andrew Davis; director, Jérôme Savary; designer, Ezio Toffolutti. Annick Massis (Comtesse Adèle), Diana Montague (Isolier), Marc Laho (Comte Ory), Ludovic Tézier (Raimbaud), Julien Robbins (Le Gouverneur)
GLYNDEBOURNE TOURING OPERA performed *Le Comte Ory* (1997), *Die Entführung aus dem Serail* (1980) and *The Makropulos Case* (1995) at Glyndebourne, Woking, Norwich, Oxford, Manchester, Plymouth, Southampton and Northampton, between 6 October and 11 December 1997.

GARSINGTON OPERA
Founded 1989
Garsington Manor, Garsington, Oxford OX44 9DH

The season ran from 9 June to 6 July 1997. *Così fan tutti* (1990) was revived.

New productions:
Le pescatrici (Haydn), 9 June 1997. Conductor, Wasfi Kani; director, Robert David MacDonald; designer, Tim Goodchild. Lynne Davies (Lesbina), Nicole Tibbels (Nerina), Patricia Bardon (Eurilda), Jeffrey Lloyd-Roberts (Burlotto), Aled Hall (Frisellino), Jozik Koc (Lindoro), Francesco Facini (Mastricco)
    Die Aegyptische Helena (Richard Strauss), 22 June 1997 (British stage première). Conductor, Elgar Howarth; director/ designer, David Fielding. Susan Bullock (Helena), Helen Field (Aithra), Rebecca de Pont Davies (Mussel), John Horton Murray (Menelaus), Roderick Earle (Altair), Nicholas Sears (Da-ud)

ENGLISH TOURING OPERA
Founded 1980 as OPERA 80

The Pearl Fishers and *Rigoletto* were toured to Richmond, Bath, Canterbury, Buxton, Basingstoke, Southsea, Crewe and High Wycombe between 16 October and 12 December 1996.
    The Marriage of Figaro and *The Pearl Fishers* were toured to Cambridge, Poole, Brighton, Lowestoft, Reading, Exeter, Yeovil, Ipswich, Crawley, Coventry, Lincoln, Darlington, Carlisle, Preston, Ulverston and Cheltenham between 18 February and 30 May 1997.

OPERA FACTORY
Founded 1982
South Bank Centre, London SE1

The Magic Flute was performed at the Queen Elizabeth Hall, London and toured to Birmingham, Reading, Barnstaple, Oxford, Malvern and Blackpool, between 4 September and 25 November 1996.

OPERA NORTHERN IRELAND
Founded 1982
35 Talbot Street, Belfast BT1 2LD

Autumn season 1996 at the Grand Opera House, Belfast: *Fidelio* (Beethoven), 14 September 1996. Conductor, Stephen Barlow; director, Matthew Francis; designer, Isabella Bywater. Suzanne Murphy (Leonore), Kate Ladner (Marzelline), John Horton Murray (Florestan), Keith Latham (Don Pizarro), Norman Bailey (Rocco), Philip Sheffield (Jaquino)

La traviata (Verdi), 15 September 1996. Conductor, Martin André; director, Stephen Medcalf; designer, Isabella Bywater. Rebecca Caine (Violetta), Richard Coxon (Alfredo), David Barrell (Germont)

Spring season 1997 at the Grand Opera House, Belfast:

Madama Butterfly (Puccini), 8 March 1997. Conductor, Stephen Barlow; director, Bliss Herbert; designer, Allen Charles Klein. Nancy Yuen (Butterfly), Kate McCarney (Suzuki), Mark Beudert (Pinkerton), Jonathan Veira (Sharpless), Christopher Gillett (Goro)

Masters of the Queen's (King's) Music

'Master of the King's Music' was the title given to the official who presided over the court band during the reign of Charles I. The first Master was appointed in 1626. Today the Master is expected to organize the music for state occasions and to write new music for them, although there are no fixed duties. The post is held for life and the Master receives an annual honorarium of £100.

Nicholas Lanier (1588–1666), appointed 1626
Louis Grabu (?–1674), appointed 1666
Nicholas Staggins (1650–1700), appointed 1674
John Eccles (1668–1735), appointed 1700
Maurice Greene (1695–1755), appointed 1735
William Boyce (1710–79), appointed 1755

John Stanley (1713–86), appointed 1779
Sir William Parsons (1746–1817), appointed 1786
William Shield (1748–1829), appointed 1817
Christian Kramer (?–1834), appointed 1829
François (Franz) Cramer (1772–1848), appointed 1834
George Anderson (?–1870), appointed 1848
Sir William Cusins (1833–93), appointed 1870
Sir Walter Parratt (1841–1924), appointed 1893
Sir Edward Elgar (1857–1934), appointed 1924
Sir Henry Walford Davies (1869–1941), appointed 1934
Sir Arnold Bax (1883–1953), appointed 1941
Sir Arthur Bliss (1891–1975), appointed 1953
Malcolm Williamson (1931–), appointed 1975

Parliament

Both Houses of Parliament returned from the summer recess on 14 October, when the Speaker of the House of Commons (Betty Boothroyd) made a statement on the 'very serious allegations widely made about the conduct of a number of MPs' during the recess, stressing that both the Committee on Standards and Privileges and the Parliamentary Commissioner for Standards (Sir Gordon Downey) would be given all the resources necessary to enable them to undertake fully and swiftly any investigation into the allegations. The Minister for Agriculture, Fisheries and Food (Douglas Hogg) responded to a private notice question from Labour's agriculture spokesman (Gavin Strang) on the future of the selective cattle slaughter programme that had been agreed at the European Council in Florence. He said that owing to further scientific findings during the summer, the Government was not proceeding with a selective cull for the time being. Further consultations would be carried out with the European Commission on the relaxing of export restrictions. Gavin Strang said that the decision to suspend the programme 'is adding to the uncertainty in the industry' and that the Minister 'had lost touch with the industry and was unable effectively to represent their interests in the European Union'. On 15 October the Speaker unusually approved a request for an emergency debate to be held the next day on allegations that improper pressure had been

brought to bear on members of the select committee on members' interests in 1994 by a government whip, David Willetts. On 16 October the Secretary of State for Scotland (Michael Forsyth) announced the publication of the report by Lord Cullen into the shootings at Dunblane primary school in March 1996 and the Government's response; in particular the Government would be introducing legislation covering the vetting and supervision of adults working with children. The Home Secretary (Michael Howard) made a further statement on the gun controls proposed in the report (*see* page 1165). The Opposition welcomed the ban on handguns and pledged its support but registered concern over the proposals to allow some handguns to remain in private ownership, albeit kept in licensed gun clubs. A motion introduced by Andrew Miller (Lab.) to refer the matter of the allegations of improper pressure being brought to bear on members of the select committee on members' interests by a government whip to the select committee on standards and privileges was approved without division.

NEW SESSION

On 17 October the 1995–6 session of Parliament ended. The 1996–7 session, the final one before the general election, was opened by The Queen on 23 October (for Queen's Speech, *see* below). During his

---

THE QUEEN'S SPEECH 1996

Legislation proposed in the Queen's Speech included measures:
– to improve discipline, raise standards, improve choice and diversity, give grant-maintained schools more power and extend the assisted places scheme (Education Bill)
– to implement the sentencing proposals from the April 1996 White Paper *Protecting the Public* (Crime (Sentences) Bill)
– to outlaw private ownership of handguns other than .22 pistols (Firearms (Amendment) Bill)
– to establish a National Crime Squad and a Criminal Records Agency for England and Wales (Police Bill)
– to abolish early release from prison, impose life sentences for second offences of serious violent or sexual assault and seven-year minimum sentences for third offence drug traffickers (Crime and Punishment (Scotland) Bill)
– to strengthen efforts to prevent, deter and detect benefit fraudsters by enabling comparison of databases and information sharing between different government agencies (Social Security Administration (Fraud) Bill)
– to implement the proposals in the October 1996 White Paper *Choice and Opportunity* (National Health Service (Primary Care) Bill)
– to create the rule-making powers necessary for the implementation of the Woolf report on access to justice (Civil Procedure Bill)
– to allow local authorities to reduce business rates on rural shops, to encourage community transport and crime

prevention measures in villages (Local Government and Rating Bill)
– to give greater protection to the coastal environment, implementing the measures identified after the *Braer* oil tanker incident in 1993 (Merchant Shipping and Maritime Security Bill)
– to reintroduce the Channel Tunnel Rail Link Bill for its final stages
– to allow the transfer of publicly owned crofting estates to crofting trusts (Transfer of Crofting Estates (Scotland) Bill)
– to put into effect in Northern Ireland the guidelines on decommissioning arrangements set out in the report from the International Body on Decommissioning in January 1996 (Northern Ireland Arms Decommissioning Bill)
– to relax the statutory constraints and allow lottery funding to be made available for a significantly wider range of heritage projects (National Heritage Bill)
For the first time the speech described bills which would be published in draft for consultation:
– a draft bill to help people meet their long-term care needs in old age
– a draft bill on the introduction of voluntary identity cards
Other bills promised 'if time allows' included:
– a Compensation Recovery Bill to include the ring-fencing of awards made for pain and suffering
– a Commonhold Bill to create a new form of property ownership for owners of flats

speech opening the debate on the Queen's Speech, the Prime Minister (John Major), responding to an offer from the Leader of the Opposition (Tony Blair), announced that two further bills would be brought forward by the Government covering the establishment of a register of paedophiles and measures to deal with harassment and stalking; it had been expected that these would be introduced as Private Members' Bills. Mr Major also said, 'Our legislative programme is a clear and practical set of measures to promote our aim of wider opportunity for all. We believe in choice, in personal responsibility and in opportunity. That thread has run through the past 17 years of Conservative Government. It runs through the current legislative programme in front of us and it will run through our plans and our programmes for the next Parliament also.' Tony Blair, although continuing to offer cross-party support for the efforts to work for a comprehensive and balanced peace in Northern Ireland, felt that 'we should not be debating a loyal address today; we should be having a general election…It is as if the Conservatives had just landed from Mars or as if they had been in exile for 17 years and had returned and discovered how shocking things really were … The Queen's Speech reflects a Government who see existing as all they have left to do … There is no leadership and no direction … This Queen's Speech shows that the Conservative Party has no vision for this country's future.' The Liberal Democrat leader (Paddy Ashdown) said, 'We see a programme for the next year that reveals a Government in their tormented and twilight days. It is a ragbag of irrelevant measures … driven more by what will wrong-foot the Opposition parties than by what is right for the country.' There followed the usual six days of debate. In the home affairs debate on 28 October the Home Secretary (Michael Howard) offered to consult all parties on the banning of specific categories of knives. A Labour amendment criticizing the education aspects of the speech was defeated by 297 votes to 283; during this day of debate the Secretary of State for Education and Employment (Gillian Shephard) confirmed her personal support for some forms of corporal punishment. A further Labour amendment noting the Government's broken promises on tax was defeated by 305 votes to 283. During this day of debate the Shadow Chancellor (Gordon Brown) committed a Labour Government to reducing VAT on fuel to 5 per cent in its first budget. A Liberal Democrat amendment regretting the shortcomings of the speech in respect of education, the National Health Service and crime prevention was defeated by 300 votes to 38. The speech itself was approved without division on 30 October. In the House of Lords a Labour amendment to the speech regretting the failure of the Government to manage the nation's affairs in a manner that preserves social cohesion and integrity was defeated on the same day by 158 votes to 103.

The hybrid Channel Tunnel Rail Link Bill to allow for the construction of the link, which had been carried over from the previous session of Parliament, completed its committee stage in the Lords on 31 October, when various government amendments were approved. Further government amendments were passed at report stage in the Lords on 21 November and the Commons approved the Lords amendments on 10 December. The Bill received royal assent on 18 December.

The Crime (Sentences) Bill to introduce mandatory and minimum custodial sentences was given a second reading in the Commons on 4 November. A Liberal Democrat amendment declining a second reading as the bill failed to protect the public adequately and would lead to the building of 12 new prisons was defeated by 165 votes to 25. The second reading itself was passed by 149 votes to 23. Remaining stages in the Commons were taken on 13 and 15 January. The debate on 13 January was adjourned by the government whips at 10 p.m. after discussion on new clause 6, when they accused the Opposition of filibustering. In the resumed debate, the third reading was passed by 229 votes to 21. During the bill's second reading in the Lords on 27 January several law lords spoke against the measure but it was passed without division. In committee on 13 February the Government was defeated when a new clause moved by Lord McIntosh of Haringey (Lab.) on conditions relating to mandatory and minimum custodial sentences (allowing judges to ignore the proposed mandatory sentence if they felt it would be unjust) was passed by 180 votes to 172. When the bill returned to the Commons for consideration of the Lords' amendments on 19 March, the Government did not seek to overturn its defeat and the bill received royal assent on 21 March.

The Crime and Punishment (Scotland) Bill, implementing similar proposals in Scotland to those proposed for England and Wales in the Crime (Sentences) Bill, was given a second reading in the Commons on 5 November, when an amendment from Labour was defeated by 288 votes to 267. The second reading itself was passed by 285 votes to 22. Having been taken in committee by a Scottish standing committee, the bill returned for remaining stages in the Commons on 20 and 29 January. On 20 January a new clause moved by Labour on women offenders was defeated by 292 votes to 291; the government whips adjourned further consideration at 10 p.m. In the resumed debate, the third reading was passed by 287 votes to 20. The second reading in the Lords was on 11 February. The Government was defeated in the third day of committee (10 March) when a new clause on community sentencing moved by Lord McCluskey (cross-bencher) was passed by 109 votes to 67. When the bill returned to the Commons for consideration of Lords amendments on 20 March, the Government did not seek to overturn its defeat and the bill received royal assent on 21 March.

A bill to establish a unified and simple set of civil proceedings as recommended in the Woolf report, the Civil Procedure Bill, had its second reading in the Lords on 5 November. The committee stage was taken on 20 November and completed in one day. On report on 9 December the Lord Chancellor (Lord Mackay of Clashfern) conceded many points to critics of the bill. The bill had an unopposed second reading in the Commons on 30 January and after one day in committee, had an unopposed third reading on 25 February, receiving royal assent on 27 February.

The Local Government and Rating Bill to provide rate relief for certain village shops and post offices, to encourage community transport schemes and to make grants to police authorities, had an unopposed second reading in the Commons on 6 November and completed an unopposed passage through the Commons on 23 January. The second reading in the Lords on 6 February was followed by the committee stage taken on 4 March and completed in one day. Unamended in the Lords, the bill received royal assent on 19 March.

The bill to improve waste management at ports, to authorize temporary exclusion zones at sea, to provide powers to charge ship owners for port state control inspections, for emergency response measures and for standard setting activity, to improve compensation payments for victims of marine pollution and to ensure that ships in UK waters were insured for third-party liabilities, the Merchant Shipping and Maritime Safety Bill, was given a second reading in the Lords on 7 November. The committee stage was taken on 25 and 26 November. The second reading in the Commons on 10 February was unopposed and only minor technical amendments were passed during the Commons stages. The bill received royal assent on 19 March.

On 12 November the President of the Board of Trade (Ian Lang) made a statement in the Commons on the judgement by the European Court of Justice, rejecting the British Government's case that the EC Working Time Directive (limiting the working week to 48 hours) should be annulled as it cut across the UK's right to opt out of the social chapter. He said that the Government would do everything it could to close the loophole in procedures that had allowed the directive through and would work to minimize the effect on businesses and jobs. The Prime Minister had indicated that he would insist that the Inter-Governmental Conference (IGC) tackled this question before all others or he would block any other progress. Labour's trade and industry spokeswoman (Margaret Beckett) accused the Government of wasting tax-payers' money to fight a court case it was always likely to lose, especially as the Government's own negotiator had failed to vote against the measure and had called the directive toothless. On 13 November the Government defeated an Opposition motion on its handling of the bovine spongiform encephalopathy

(BSE) crisis which had 'failed to protect the interests of UK consumers and producers' by 303 votes to 302. Labour's foreign affairs spokesman (Robin Cook) said, 'The crisis in our beef industry was made in Britain. The genius of the Government is that instead of solving the first crisis, they have paralleled it with a second crisis, our relations with Europe.' On 14 November the Secretary of State for Defence (Michael Portillo) made a statement on the decision in principle to send British troops to support the multinational UN force to protect humanitarian relief and promote refugee repatriation in Zaïre.

THE EDUCATION BILL

The Education Bill to give schools greater freedom to introduce or extend selection and specialization had its second reading in the Commons on 11 November, when an amendment from Labour refusing a second reading on the grounds that the bill was unacceptable and ineffective was defeated by 285 votes to 257. A motion to commit the bill to a special standing committee was defeated by 284 votes to 257. The Government was defeated in committee when an amendment covering grant-maintained schools' ability to enlarge their premises was passed. In attempting to overturn that defeat in the remaining stages debate on 27 January by introducing a new clause 3, relaxation of controls on enlargement of premises, the Government was caught in an ambush when the Opposition moved the vote on the new clause after only three minutes' debate and defeated it by 273 votes to 272. (It transpired next day that the vote had actually been tied at 272 votes each, in which case the Speaker would have been obliged to cast her vote with the Government, reversing the defeat of the new clause). The third reading was passed without division on 28 January. The second reading in the Lords was on 10 February. The Government was defeated in committee in the Lords on 24 February when a new clause on objections to notification of proposals which do not need to be published moved by Labour (which would seriously hamper the right of grant-maintained schools to increase the number of pupils they selected by ability) was passed by 111 votes to 94. The bill finished in committee in the Lords on 3 March but only after the Lords had sat until 3.05 a.m. On the second day of report stage on 19 March, the Government dropped the clauses relating to increasing the numbers of grant-maintained schools. When the bill returned to the Commons for consideration of Lords' amendments on 19 March, the Government did not seek to overturn its defeat and the bill received royal assent on 21 March.

The Police Bill, whose provisions included giving employers better access to the criminal records of those wishing to work with children or seeking other positions of trust, had its second reading in the Lords on 11 November. The Government was defeated on the second day in committee in the Lords on 2 December when an amendment to clause 100 moved by Lord Weatherill (cross-bencher) to exempt certain volunteers from the cost of meeting the conditions of obtaining criminal conviction certificates was passed by 137 votes to 135. On the first day of the report stage on 20 January the Government suffered two more defeats; first when a new clause moved by Lord McIntosh of Haringey to force chief constables to obtain permission from a special commissioner before carrying out electronic surveillance in people's homes was passed by 209 votes to 145, and then on a similarly intentioned but contradictory amendment to clause 91 moved by Lord Rodgers of Quarry Bank (LD) to insert the words 'circuit judge' was passed by 158 votes to 137. Business was adjourned when Lord McIntosh forced a division on an amendment to clause 106 and only 14 peers voted. The report stage was completed on 21 January. The Government narrowly avoided defeat on the third reading, when the vote on an amendment to clause 92 (authorizations to interfere with property, etc.) was tied at 161 votes each. The Lord Chancellor cast his vote for the Government in accordance with standing order no. 54. By the time of the second reading in the Commons on 12 February, an agreement had been reached with the Opposition over the defeats in the Lords on Part III of the bill (electronic surveillance) but the Home Secretary announced that the Government would be seeking to overturn the defeats on Part V (criminal conviction certificates). An amendment from the Liberal Democrats declining a second reading because the measure was unacceptable and ineffective was defeated by 264 votes to 41. In committee the Government came to an agreement over the 'bugging' clauses and overturned the defeat in the Lords over charging for certificates for volunteers. The third reading was passed without division on 19 March. The Commons accepted the Lords amendments on 20 March and the bill received royal assent on 21 March.

HANDGUN BAN

The Firearms (Amendment) Bill to ban the holding of certain handguns following the recommendations of the Cullen report into the Dunblane shootings had its second reading in the Commons on 12 November. Although the Shadow Home Secretary (Jack Straw) supported the bill as far as it went, an amendment moved by Sir Jerry Wiggin (C.) declining a second reading as the bill went beyond the recommendations of the Cullen report was defeated by 384 votes to 35. There was a government three-line whip but 31 Conservative MPs voted against. The committee on clauses 1 to 5 was taken on the floor of the House on 18 and 19 November, after the approval of a guillotine motion. On the first day the Home Secretary announced that more money would be available for compensation. Amendments moved by Sir Jerry Wiggin to water down the proposals were rejected. An amendment moved by Robert Hughes (C.) for a

complete ban on all handguns, supported by the Opposition front bench, was defeated by 306 votes to 281. On a three-line whip, four Conservative MPs voted against the Government (Terry Dicks, David Mellor, Hugh Dykes and Robert Hughes) and on a free vote 22 Labour MPs did not vote. Tony Blair announced that an incoming Labour Government would legislate for a total ban, on a free vote. The bill had two days in standing committee and at report stage on 4 December Sir Jerry Wiggin moved an amendment to widen the compensation package on offer to those affected by a ban but this was defeated by 299 votes to 113; 63 Conservative MPs defied the whip to vote against, with support from 22 Labour MPs, 24 Liberal Democrats and six MPs from other parties. The third reading was passed without division. At the second reading in the Lords on 16 December, a motion opposing the second reading moved by the Earl of Strafford (cross-bencher) was withdrawn. In committee in the Lords on 16 January a motion for instruction to withdraw clause 6 for further consideration moved by Lord Swansea (C.) was also withdrawn. Also in committee, on 21 January the Government was defeated when an amendment moved by the Earl of Shrewsbury (C.) to insert a new clause on compensation for gun clubs was passed by 158 votes to 135. At report stage on 4 February the Government suffered three defeats. The first was on clause 8 when an amendment moved by Lord Pearson of Rannoch (C.) to allow guns to be held in private homes if they were disassembled and the relevant parts stored in secure gun clubs was passed by 153 votes to 139; then a new clause to recompense owners of gun shops for business lost by the ban, moved by Lord Lester of Herne Hill (LD), was passed by 121 votes to 110; and finally a new clause to set up a centralized police register of licensed firearms holders moved by Lord Marlesford (C.) was passed by 57 votes to 53. In the Commons on 18 February the Government successfully overturned all the defeats it had suffered in the Lords but some 93 Conservative back-bench MPs (including five former Cabinet Ministers) voted in favour of retaining the Lords' amendment to increase compensation for gun clubs forced out of business (defeated by 319 votes to 140); some 81 voted for the amendment to allow compensation for dealers as well (defeated by 305 votes to 145); and some 92 voted for the amendment for concessions to allow small-calibre weapons to be kept at home (defeated by 394 votes to 115). The Lords accepted the Commons reasons for rejecting its amendments on 20 February, although attempts were made to change first the clause relating to guns being kept at home (moved by Lord Stoddart of Swindon (Lab.), and defeated by 197 votes to 24) and then the compensation arrangements for gun dealers (moved by Lord Lester (LD) and defeated by 160 votes to 24). The bill received royal assent on 27 February.

On 19 November the Secretary of State for Transport (Sir George Young) responded to a private notice question from Gwyneth Dunwoody (Lab.) on the fire aboard a Eurotunnel freight shuttle train the previous evening. He announced that the French authorities had begun a formal inquiry since the incident had occurred in the French part of the tunnel, that Eurotunnel's own investigation was under way and that the Channel Tunnel Safety Authority would be holding its own inquiry. On 20 November the Minister of State for the Armed Forces (Nicholas Soames), responding to a private notice question from one of Labour's defence team (John Reid) on the plans for the deployment of British troops to Zaïre, said that as the situation appeared to have eased substantially, the Government was consulting with partners before making any final decision on whether to commit troops to the area. In the meantime an extra £10 million had been provided by the Government to help meet the needs of the Great Lakes area.

The Social Security (Recovery of Benefits) Bill, to reform the compensation recovery scheme to allow victims of accident, injury or disease to retain their compensation for pain and suffering whilst ensuring that public funds did not subsidize the negligence of others, had its second reading in the Lords on 19 November. The measure was welcomed by all parties, completed all its stages in the Lords and moved to the Commons on 25 February, receiving royal assent on 19 March.

On 25 November the Chancellor of the Exchequer (Kenneth Clarke) made a statement on the regulations covering economic and monetary union (EMU) and clarifying the requirement for a full debate in the Commons. He promised this would take place before the EU summit in Dublin, when the issue would be on the agenda, and that he would enter a parliamentary scrutiny reserve on any discussion in EC Council of Finance Ministers, which would meet before any debate could be held. The Shadow Chancellor (Gordon Brown) accused him of saying one thing in Brussels but another back in Britain.

The bill to establish a fraud inspectorate, to empower local authorities to exchange information with each other and the DSS, and to give new powers to suspend benefit payments and to recover overpayments to landlords, the Social Security Administration (Fraud) Bill, received an unopposed second reading in the Commons on 25 November. Having completed its Commons stages, the bill had its second reading in the Lords on 17 February, where it was not amended and it received royal assent on 21 March.

THE BUDGET 1996

Kenneth Clarke presented his fourth Budget on 26 November (see page 1153). He said that the Budget was designed to provide 'high quality public services while securing the tax base and taking a further step towards the goal of a 20 pence basic rate of income tax' and to ensure that 'borrowing remains firmly on a downward path'. He continued, 'This Budget reduces public spending plans further, while providing more money for priority services. It makes responsible progress on our tax-cutting agenda, while getting borrowing down faster. This is not a reckless Budget on either tax or spending. In the run-up to Christmas I am not going to play Santa Claus but this year I am not going to play Scrooge either. I have one overriding aim, which is the lasting health of the economy ... to set this country on course to be the strongest industrial economy in Western Europe in years to come.' Opening the debate on the Budget, the Leader of the Opposition (Tony Blair) felt he had heard 'The last-gasp Budget of a Government whose time is up, who cannot be trusted with the future and who cannot make amends for the past. We have heard all their promises before ... There is nothing left for them to do, except go – and the sooner the better.' Paddy Ashdown thought it was 'The smoke and mirrors Budget, pretending to do what it does not ... Though the measures in the Budget may be small, the damage that it will do will be big ... Instead of consolidating the recovery that we have bought at such a high price, the Budget will place it at risk.' On the fifth day of the Budget debate the deputy leader of the Labour Party (John Prescott) introduced an amendment to reduce to 5 per cent the rate of VAT chargeable on domestic fuel. This was defeated by 317 votes to 312. An Opposition amendment rejecting the Budget as incompetent and mismanaged was defeated by 316 votes to 280, and the Budget itself was approved by 312 votes to 306. Specific votes were taken on hydrocarbon oils (passed by 316 votes to 43); air passenger duty (passed by 317 votes to 43); and income tax (passed by 316 votes to 35).

On 28 November the Scottish Secretary (Michael Forsyth) made a statement about the outbreak of E coli 0157 food poisoning in Lanarkshire the previous week which had affected over 130 elderly people, of whom five had died. He announced the setting-up of an expert group to investigate the circumstances of the outbreak. The Shadow Scottish Secretary (George Robertson) criticized the Government for the slow response in providing information to the public and called for the setting-up of a food services agency.

On 2 December the Welsh Secretary (William Hague) responded to a private notice question from Jon Owen Jones (Lab.) on the outbreak of meningitis at the University of Wales, Cardiff, which started in October, with a total of six cases, including two deaths. He would await the report of the local health authority before deciding whether to order any further inquiry. On 3 December the Chancellor reported to the Commons on the outcome of the EU Council of Finance Ministers that he had just attended, where political preparations had continued for the discussion of the EMU at the Dublin summit. No final conclusions had been reached due to decisions yet to be made on the operation of the proposed stability pact and the definition of an exceptional and temporary deficit for the purpose of Article 104(c). Whilst making a constructive contribution to the debate, he had, as promised,

THE BUDGET 1996

FISCAL OUTLOOK

Government spending plans for 1997–8 to be reduced by £1,900 million

Public sector investment cut by £700 million in 1996–7 and £1,700 million in 1997–8

Contingency reserve cut by £2,500 million in 1997–8

Public spending control total raised to £260,600 million in 1996–7 (a £500 million increase) and forecast to rise to £266,500 million in 1997–8

Public spending as a percentage of GDP estimated at 41 per cent in 1996–7 and 40 per cent in 1997–8

UK expected to meet the Maastricht criteria for European Monetary Union entry

Budget cuts taxes overall by £735 million in 1997–8, mostly in direct taxes. New measures to counter VAT fraud

Taxes and social security revenues projected to yield £265,600 million in 1996–7 and £282,100 million in 1997–8. General government receipts to rise from £280,900 million in 1996–7 to £299,400 million in 1997–8

PSBR to fall from £26,500 million in 1996–7 to £19,000 million in 1997–8

PSBR as a proportion of GDP would be 3.5 per cent in 1996–7 and 2.5 per cent in 1997–8

SPENDING

Public sector pay: pay agreements to be set on a basis of 2 per cent a year from 1997–8

Central government running costs raised by £230 million in 1997–8 and a further £356 million in 1998–9, then reduced in cash terms in each of the next two years

Benefit fraud: new programmes to tackle social security fraud and tax evasion to cost £800 million over next three years but to yield savings of £6,700 million

Social security: lone parent premium on income-related benefits and one-parent benefit no longer available to new claimants from April 1998. New restrictions on eligibility for housing and council tax benefit

Education and employment: spending on education in England to rise by £875 million in 1997–8, with £830 million going to schools (to include £50 million extra on school buildings). £100 million for projects to get long-term unemployed back to work

Transport: spending plans of £3,500 million over next three years. Increased role for private sector investment

Health: spending on patient services in NHS to rise by £1,600 million. Spending total for 1997–8 increased by £1,250 million on forecast. Private Finance Initiative to contribute £900 million over next three years

Home Office: increased spending on police in England and Wales of £220 million to allow for recruitment of

5,000 extra officers. Increased spending on prisons of £230 million

Private Finance Initiative: capital investment from PFI contracts expected to increase by £4,000 million a year by the end of the century

TAXATION

Corporation tax: main rate unchanged; small companies' rate cut to 23 per cent from April 1997

Business rates unchanged or reduced for small businesses

Employers' National Insurance contributions: lower earnings limit increased to £62 per week, upper earnings limit increased to £465 per week

Income tax: basic rate cut to 23 per cent and 20 per cent lower rate limit increased by £200. Personal allowances raised by £280; married couples' allowance raised by £40; blind person's allowance raised to £1,280

Inheritance tax: threshold raised to £215,000

Capital gains tax: annual exempt amount raised to £6,500 for individuals and to £3,250 for trusts

Insurance premium tax raised to 4 per cent

Profit-related pay schemes to be phased out from 1998 and withdrawn by 2000

Capital allowances on plant and machinery with an expected working life of 25 years or more reduced to 6 per cent

Petrol and diesel up by 3 pence a litre. Duty on environment-friendly sulphur-based fuels cut. Duty on road fuel gases to fall by 25 per cent. Vehicle Excise Duty cut by £500 for lorries meeting new low-emission standards but otherwise remains unchanged for lorries and is increased by £5 for cars

Airport tax doubled from November 1997 (£10 for European destinations, £20 elsewhere)

Tobacco duties increased: packet of 20 cigarettes up 15 pence, packet of cigars up 7 pence, hand rolling tobacco up in line with inflation

Duty on beer and wine unchanged. Duty on spirits cut by 4 per cent a bottle. Duty on alcopops raised by 8 pence a bottle

Customs and Excise powers to assess underpayments of VAT to be cut from six years' arrears to three

FORECAST

Rate of inflation expected to be 3 per cent by end of 1996 and on course to meet target rate of 2.5 per cent by end of 1997. Economy expected to grow more strongly. Exports forecast to grow rapidly

GDP forecast to rise by 2.5 per cent in 1996 and by 3.5 per cent in 1997. Consumer spending projected to rise by 3 per cent in 1996 and by 4.5 per cent in 1997. Current account expected to remain 'broadly in balance'

---

entered a parliamentary reserve on behalf of the UK and had not committed the Government to any agreements. During Prime Minister's Questions, immediately preceding the statement, John Major had pledged that he would fight the general election on the basis of 'wait and see' on the issue of Britain joining the single currency. Gordon Brown summed up the position as 'struggle as the Chancellor does to reconcile his party's interests with the British national interest, it is time for us to insist that the national interest comes first'. After a

sparsely attended adjournment debate on 6 December when Sir John Gorst (C.) raised the issue of emergency medical arrangements in Edgware, Sir John held a press conference to say that owing to the unsatisfactory nature of the replies he had received, the Government could no longer rely automatically upon his support. This technically put the Government in a minority of one.

The National Health Service (Primary Care) Bill to allow greater flexibility in medical and dental services for the provision of primary health care, whilst safeguarding the interests of patients and providing stability, was given a second reading in the Lords on 3 December, when it was given a qualified welcome by the Opposition. The second reading in the Commons was on 11 February when a Labour amendment declining a second reading because of the lack of consultation requirements in the measures proposed was defeated by 314 votes to 253. A motion to commit the bill to a special standing committee was defeated by 312 votes to 271. The third reading was passed without division and the bill received royal assent on 21 March.

The Northern Ireland Arms Decommissioning Bill giving effect to the six principles of arms decommissioning outlined in the Mitchell report, received an unopposed second reading in the Commons on 9 December. Labour stressed that they would facilitate the bill's speedy progress. It completed its Commons stages unamended on 16 January and had its second reading in the Lords on 30 January. It was not amended in the Lords and the bill received royal assent on 27 February.

On 9 December in the Lords, Lord Archer of Weston-super-Mare (C.) was given leave to present an humble address to The Queen to allow him to present a Private Member's Bill allowing automatic female succession to the throne by birth order, rather than only after male heirs. Normally passed 'on the nod', this procedural motion was put to the vote for the first time in 600 years and approved by 74 votes to 53. Lord Archer eventually presented his Succession to the Crown Bill on 18 February but it made no further progress. On 10 December the Armed Forces minister announced the provision of a further £1.3 million for research into Gulf War syndrome, involving some 18,000 British military personnel. He also apologized to the Commons for giving misinformation repeatedly over the extent to which British troops had been exposed to organophosphate pesticides; an internal Ministry of Defence enquiry had been launched to establish how such misinformation had been given repeatedly. The Paymaster-General (David Willetts) resigned his post after a report from the select committee on standards and privileges had called his integrity into question, following its enquiry into allegations that he had brought improper pressure to bear on members of the select committee on members' interests in 1994. On 11 and 12 December the Commons held the promised two-day debate on the European Union, covering economic and monetary union and the Inter-Governmental Conference, prior to the Dublin summit, but as the motion was on the adjournment of the House, there was no vote. On 13 December the Knives Bill, a Private Member's Bill to restrict the marketing of combat knives presented by Jimmy Wray (Lab.), had an unopposed second reading in the Commons. Supported by the Government, it received royal assent on 19 March. On 16 December the Prime Minister reported on the outcome of the Dublin summit, which had covered both EMU and the IGC. The conclusions of the summit on the stability pact, the legal status of the euro and the new voluntary ERM remained subject to a British parliamentary reserve. Tony Blair criticized the Prime Minister for failing to pull off a deal to lift the beef ban as he had promised and suggested that 'the whole affair has been handled with serial incompetence'. The Agriculture Minister (Douglas Hogg) then made a statement on the follow-up to the Florence agreement on BSE and the additional steps he proposed to take towards the eventual lifting of the ban on exports of beef from the UK. He announced an extension of the selective cull, to be completed within six months, and the certified herd scheme. The Labour agriculture spokesman, Gavin Strang, said 'He has completely failed to justify why the Government have taken six months to reach this point'. This was followed by the annual debate on the EU common fisheries policy (CFP). A Labour amendment to the motion calling the CFP a threat to the future of fishing was defeated by 316 votes to 305. The take note motion itself was passed by 316 votes to 304. After the vote there was a row when it emerged that government whips had offered three of the same pairs to both main Opposition parties (thus theoretically increasing their majority by three), and the Labour Party withdrew co-operation with the 'usual channels' for handling parliamentary business. On 17 December the President of the Board of Trade (Ian Lang) made a statement on the outcome of the first ministerial conference of the World Trade Organization, at which progress had been made on the three main British objectives: trade liberalization, IT tariffs and liberalizing basic telecommunications. The Home Secretary then made a statement on the outcome of the investigation into the centrifuge contamination at the Forensic Explosives Laboratory; this had concluded that no cases needed to be reopened as a result of the contamination. Jack Straw called for an oversight body or inspectorate to restore public confidence in the forensic science community.

The Protection from Harassment Bill to protect victims of stalking and harassment had an unopposed second reading in the Commons on 17 December. Jack Straw welcomed the measure and promised co-operation on its swift progress. The bill immediately went into committee of the whole House and the Government suffered a surprise defeat when an Opposition amendment to allow civil courts to impose a course of counselling on guilty parties was passed by 179 votes to 172. The Government later claimed that 14 Labour MPs had reneged on their pairing arrangements. The bill completed all its Commons stages on 18 December. The second reading in the Lords was on 24 January and the bill received royal assent on 21 March.

On 18 December the Attorney-General (Sir Nicholas Lyell) announced a new approach to public interest immunity in the light of the recommendations of the Scott report, with a change of practice in accordance with the view of the Lord

Chief Justice that it should only be claimed for the bare minimum of documents for which the claim of serious harm could be seen to be clearly justified. The Government remained committed to the principle that there should be maximum disclosure consistent with protecting essential public interests.

The Finance Bill implementing the proposals in the Budget had its second reading in the Commons on 14 January. An amendment declining a second reading as the bill failed to address the needs of the country, moved by the Shadow Chief Secretary to the Treasury (Alistair Darling), was defeated by 322 votes to 287. The second reading itself was passed by 314 votes to 30. The committee of the whole House on 22 and 23 January dealt with various clauses; during the remaining stages debate on 11 March the Government added new clauses on annuity business of insurance companies, consortium claims for group relief and futures and options: transactions with guaranteed returns. The third reading was passed by 202 votes to 21. The Lords considered the bill on 19 March and the bill received royal assent the same day.

On 15 January the Scottish Secretary made a statement on the publication of the interim report on the E coli outbreak in Scotland in November 1996. He had recommended further research but, on enforcement, had recommended urgent action to ensure that equivalent standards of hygiene applied to premises principally selling to the final customer as applied to premises subject to the Meat Products (Hygiene) Regulations and to ensure the physical separation of raw and cooked meats. George Robertson again called for the establishment of a food standards agency to ensure that food safety had the priority that the public expected. On 17 January the Public Entertainments Licences (Drug Misuse) Bill, a Private Member's Bill to give local authorities the power to close down clubs where there was a serious drugs problem presented by Barry Legg (C.), was given an unopposed second reading in the Commons. Supported by the Government, it received royal assent on 21 March.

On 21 January Teresa Gorman (C.) introduced a Private Member's Bill calling for a referendum on UK membership of the EU, but it stood no chance of making further progress. An Opposition motion expressing grave concern at the state of the NHS introduced by the Labour health spokesman (Chris Smith) was defeated by 319 votes to 312. An Opposition motion to annul the selective cull regulations, moved by Gavin Strang, was negatived. On 22 January the Defence Secretary announced plans for a publicly funded (£60 million) replacement for the royal yacht *Britannia*, to enter service in 2002. David Clark expressed some surprise at this unexpected announcement, made without any consultation. Back-bench MP Martin Redmond (Lab.) died on 20 January, leaving the Government and Opposition parties with an equal number of seats. On 24 January the Confiscation of Alcohol (Young Persons) Bill, a Private Member's Bill to restrict drinking by children in public places presented by Robert Spring (C.), had an unopposed second reading in the Commons. Supported by the Government, it received royal assent on 21 March.

On 28 January the Speaker made a statement on media coverage of members of the House and the review being carried out by the Parliamentary Commissioner for Standards and the select committee on standards and privileges. On 29 January the Minister of State at the Home Office (Ann Widdecombe) responded to a private notice question from Jeremy Corbyn (Lab.) on the 17 immigration detainees held at Rochester prison who were refusing food, with six of them refusing fluids as well. On 30 January the Northern Ireland Secretary (Sir Patrick Mayhew) announced the publication of the North report into parades and marches in Northern Ireland. The Government had accepted the seven fundamental principles of the report but would be consulting interested groups on the specific recommendations. Labour's Northern Ireland spokeswoman (Mo Mowlam) offered the Government the Opposition's full support and urged Sir Patrick to introduce legislation based on the report's recommendations. The leader of the Ulster Unionists (David Trimble) expressed concern that the report had failed to consider the underlying problem and that this to some extent undermined the whole approach. The Agriculture Minister made a statement on the appointment of an independent food safety council with membership drawn from a wide range of fields with an interest in the safety of food supply and whose chairman would be the Government's main advisor on food safety. Gavin Strang called the proposals belated and inadequate and 'no real substitute for an open and independent food standards agency with real authority'. On 31 January the Jurisdiction (Conspiracy and Incitement) Bill, a Private Member's Bill to give UK courts jurisdiction over acts of conspiracy and incitement in the UK but relating to acts intended to take place abroad presented by Nigel Waterson (C.) had an unopposed second reading in the Commons. Although supported by the Government, the bill was blocked on report by George Galloway (Lab.) on 14 February, when he forced a division on the third reading and only 26 MPs voted, and again on 28 February when only 20 MPs voted, and so the bill was lost. In the Lords on 31 January Lord Pearson of Rannoch (C.) successfully gained a second reading for his Private Member's Bill to remove the mechanism by which EC decisions were incorporated into UK law. The Government, as usual on back-bench bills, did not vote. The measure stood no chance of making any progress.

On 10 February the Health Secretary (Stephen Dorrell) announced the setting-up of a statutory inquiry into clinical policies and management at Ashworth Hospital following accusations of irregularities and possible paedophile activity in the hospital's personality disorder unit.

On 17 February, an Opposition motion censuring the Agriculture Minister for his and the Government's handling of the BSE crisis and calling for his salary to be reduced was moved by Gavin Strang but defeated by 320 votes to 307. In a debate on the constitution introduced by the Prime Minister on 20 February, Tony Blair suggested that any constitutional changes introduced by an incoming Labour administration would not be taken in committee on the floor of the House, as is the normal practice.

On 24 February an Opposition motion moved by the Labour health spokesman (Chris Smith) expressing deep concern at the continuing deterioration of the NHS was defeated by 311 votes to 281. On 25 February Sir George Young made a statement on proposals to privatize London Underground; no firm decisions had been made on the method but the Government was committed to ten principles as regards privatization, with safety as the top priority. The Labour transport spokesperson (Andrew Smith) called the statement 'the ultimate Tory abdication of responsibility for transport in London, neither equipping London for the future nor making good the mistakes of the past'. On 27 February the Home Secretary made a statement on improving the speed of justice in England and Wales and published the report from the review team set up the previous autumn, for consultation. They had made some 33 recommendations in five key areas, including bringing alleged offenders to court swiftly, youth courts and the right to trial by jury in all cases. Jack Straw welcomed many of the recommendations but felt that overall the real significance of the review was that it 'amounts to a catalogue of neglect and complacency on behalf of the Government in their running of the criminal justice system'.

On 5 March the Scottish Secretary responded to a private notice question from his Shadow, George Robertson, about possible nuclear contamination of carbon dioxide in fizzy drinks made in Ayrshire following the potential contamination of a tanker picking up the gas from Hunterston Nuclear Power Station; there appeared to be no risk to public health from this incident but he had asked the Scottish Environment Protection Agency and the Nuclear Installations Inspectorate for a full report. Mr Robertson urged the need for a full and open inquiry. The annual motion to approve the Prevention of Terrorism (Temporary Provisions) Act 1989 (Continuance) Order 1997 was passed by 304 votes to 13. The Labour Party line had been to abstain but 13 of its back-bench MPs voted against. On 6 March Douglas Hogg made a statement on the report by the Meat Hygiene Service on the state of hygiene in slaughterhouses, following comment in the press. He confirmed that there had been such a report but that it had not been published although the recommendations had been acted upon. Gavin Strang felt that the Government had to be open on food safety matters but that 'yet again, another

episode is leading the public to lose even more confidence in the Government on the subject of the safety of our food'. Douglas Hogg made a further statement about the standards of hygiene in British abattoirs on 12 March, following the leak of documents that seemed to suggest a crisis in the Meat Hygiene Service. He maintained that standards were improving. Gavin Strang said 'there is no confidence in him or in his Government as far as food safety issues are concerned'.

On 18 March the Prime Minister announced that Parliament would meet for prorogation on 21 March, prior to dissolution on 8 April, and called a general election for 1 May. The next two days of parliamentary business were dominated by trying to agree which parts of the Government's legislation could be passed and a row over the fact that the full report of the Parliamentary Commissioner for Standards into the allegations of misconduct made by the *Guardian* newspaper and Mr Al Fayed against a number of MPs (notably former Conservative minister Neil Hamilton), would not be ready for publication before the House rose. On 19 March the Commons approved without division a motion to set up a Northern Ireland Grand Committee. Some 16 bills received royal assent, including the Finance Bill. The Commons met for prorogation on 21 March and a further 25 bills received royal assent. Parliament was dissolved on 8 April.

THE NEW PARLIAMENT

Following its landslide victory on 1 May, the first Labour Government for 18 years took office with a parliamentary majority of 179. The State Opening of Parliament by The Queen took place on 14 May (for the Queen's Speech, *see* page 1157). In the debate on the Queen's Speech the Prime Minister (Tony Blair) said, 'Our mandate is clear – to modernize what is outdated, to make fair what is unjust, and to do both by the best means available irrespective of dogma or doctrine, without fear or favour. There is much to do.' He reaffirmed that 'Education should be our number one priority and it is.' He summed up the Queen's Speech as 'one of which my Government can be proud. It builds on the hope and optimism that the general election set coursing through the veins of our nation. It shows that change can come … It reflects the people's priorities. It shows the people's Government rebuilding trust between government and the governed.' The Leader of the Opposition (John Major) felt that 'the Government have a comprehensive mandate to introduce their programme, but I hope that they will be careful about how they use their substantial majority in the House … When the Government act sensibly, they will deserve cross-party support and I hope that they can expect such support when it is in the national interest; but when it is not, they can expect, and will certainly be given, vigorous opposition.' He also expressed disquiet about how Parliament was being bypassed, with arbitrary changes to Prime Minister's Question

THE QUEEN'S SPEECH 1997

The speech outlined 21 major bills and four White Papers for the session, which will last until October 1998. Education was to be 'the first priority' of the new Government and the central economic objectives would be 'high and stable levels of economic growth and employment to be achieved by ensuring opportunity for all'. Welfare-to-work would be the other central plank of the first session.

Early bills would include measures:
- to abolish the assisted places scheme and use the savings to reduce class sizes in primary schools (Education (Schools) Bill)
- to prohibit the possession of all small-calibre handguns (Firearms (Amendment) Bill)
- to allow the issue of appropriate credit approvals to local councils to take account of capital receipts set aside for debt repayment (Local Government Finance (Supplementary Credit Approvals) Bill)
- to clarify the powers of NHS trusts to enter into Private Finance Initiative contracts (National Health Service (Private Finance) Bill)
- to authorize the holding of referenda on devolution in Scotland and Wales and to stipulate the questions to be voted on (Referendums (Scotland and Wales) Bill)
- to allow the Bank to set short-term interest rates (Bank of England Bill)
- to introduce a prohibition approach to competition law similar to that contained in Articles 58/86 of the EC Treaty (Competition Bill)
- to introduce fast-track punishment for persistent young offenders, set up a National Youth Justice Board and local Youth Offender teams, and to introduce new court orders covering community safety, child protection, racial harassment and drink-related crime (Crime and Disorder Bill)
- to give effect to the EC data protection directive (Data Protection Bill)
- to raise standards in schools by developing early years provision, giving a new role for local education authorities, ending the grant-maintained programme and introducing foundation, community and aided schools, and establishing a General Teaching Council and mandatory qualifications for new teachers (Education Bill)

- to enable the UK to ratify any EC treaty amendments resulting from the Inter-Governmental Conference (European Communities (Amendment) Bill)
- to incorporate the European Convention on Human Rights into UK law
- to allow for a referendum on a new strategic authority for London (Greater London Authority (Referendum) Bill)
- to allow lottery funds to be used to promote education, health and other initiatives and set up a National Endowment for Science and Arts (National Lottery (Amendment) Bill)
- to provide for a statutory national minimum wage (dependent on the advice of the Low Pay Commission) (National Minimum Wage Bill)
- to introduce the Northern Ireland (Emergency Provisions) Act when current legislation expires in August 1998
- to implement the recommendations of the North report on parades and marches in Northern Ireland (Northern Ireland (Parades and Marches) Bill)
- to provide for the establishment of a Scottish Parliament (subject to outcome of the referendum)
- to provide for the establishment of a Welsh Assembly (subject to outcome of the referendum)
- to establish regional development agencies
- to introduce a new legal right to claim interest on late payment (Statutory Right to Interest on Debt Bill)
- to enable the UK to ratify the Comprehensive Test Ban Treaty Bill
- to remedy deficiencies in the existing immigration appeals procedures
- to simplify the decision-making process and to improve compliance and collection of National Insurance
- to introduce new economic tools for the management of the radio spectrum (Wireless Telegraphy (Radio Spectrum) Bill)

The White Papers will cover freedom of information, international development, the abolition of the internal market in the National Health Service, and tobacco advertising. These are in addition to the White Papers preceding the Education Bill (*Excellence in Schools, see* pages 1166–7) and the National Lottery (*The People's Lottery, see* page 1167).

Time being introduced without consultation and with changes to the role of the Bank of England over interest rates being announced before Parliament had even had a chance to consider the issue. The Liberal Democrat leader, Paddy Ashdown, said, 'I hope the Queen's Speech will mark the start not just of another Government, but of a decade that will bring the change, reform and modernization that our country needs so badly and for which it has waited for so long ... The Government's programme begins to address some of [the key challenges facing Britain] and for that reason we give it now a broad, if cautious, welcome.' During the five days of debate a Conservative amendment regretting the lack of a firm commitment to implement some of the criminal justice measures left over from the previous session was defeated by 422 votes to 151, and a further Conservative amendment regret-

ting the lack of any mention of the healthy economic climate that the Government had inherited was defeated by 446 votes to 156. A Liberal Democrat amendment regretting the absence of reference to such issues as greater environmental protection was defeated by 380 votes to 54. During the debate on the home affairs aspect of the speech (19 May) the former Home Office Minister Ann Widdecombe launched a stinging attack on her former boss Michael Howard for, amongst other things, misleading the House over the sacking of the director-general of the Prison Service. This was seen as an attempt to harm Howard's chances in the Conservative leadership election. The speech itself was approved by 421 votes to 151.

On 20 May the Chancellor of the Exchequer (Gordon Brown) made a statement on plans to set up an independent monetary policy committee within the Bank of England to decide on interest rates, to remove responsibility for banking supervision from the Bank of England and to reform the financial regulatory system around a restructured Security and Investments Board. The Shadow Chancellor (Kenneth Clarke) wondered why the announcement about the Bank of England committee had actually been made two weeks earlier, before the House had a chance to hear the statement, and whether the new Government 'were becoming contemptuous of Parliament and its procedures?' He also wondered why the decision had been taken so quickly, before the Bank had 'established a good track record of success in such matters' as had been promised by the Chancellor when in Opposition. On 21 May the first of the new, once-a-week, half-hour-long Prime Minister's Questions was held and many of the exchanges were about the way in which this change had been introduced without consultation.

The Referendums (Scotland and Wales) Bill to enable the holding of referenda on the setting-up of a Scottish Parliament and a Welsh Assembly had its second reading in the Commons on 22 and 23 May. An amendment moved by the Conservatives declining a second reading as the bill asked voters to give a blanket approval to proposals in advance of legislation was defeated by 406 votes to 155. The bill was committed to a committee of the whole House, which was taken on 3 and 4 June, along with all remaining stages. A guillotine motion limiting the committee debate to the two days was passed by 420 votes to 154, causing a row with the Opposition, which accused the Government of curtailing parliamentary scrutiny of the bill. The third reading was passed by 339 votes to 154. The second reading in the Lords was held on 17 June. The Government was defeated on the second day of committee on 3 July when an amendment to clause 2 moved by Lord Mackay of Ardbrecknish (C.), to ensure that the Scottish and Welsh referenda were held on the same day, was passed by 101 votes to 94. The Government was again defeated on the first day of the report stage on 21 July when an amendment to clause 1 also moved by Lord Mackay of Ardbrecknish, to limit the revenue-varying powers of the proposed Scottish Parliament to income tax, was passed by 149 votes to 132. After the third reading in the Lords on 29 July, the Government overturned those defeats in the Commons on 30 July, in another guillotined debate. The splitting of the dates for the referenda was overturned by 349 votes to 134, and the limiting of tax-varying powers by 330 votes to 131. Technical government amendments were also agreed at this stage. The Lords accepted the Commons reasons on 31 July and the bill received royal assent later the same day.

The Education (Schools) Bill abolishing the assisted places scheme had its second reading on 2 June, by 413 votes to 153. The bill was committed to a committee of the whole House, which was due to be completed on 5 June but the government whip

adjourned the debate at 1.15 a.m., accusing the Conservatives of filibustering. In the resumed debate on 10 June, the third reading was approved by 399 votes to 147. The second reading in the Lords was on 24 June. The Government was defeated on report on 17 July when an amendment to clause 2 moved by Baroness Byford (C.) to guarantee assisted places already given at preparatory schools up to the age of 13 rather than 11 (which the Conservatives claimed the Labour Party had promised in Opposition) was passed by 127 votes to 90. After the third reading in the Lords on 23 July the Government overturned this defeat in the Commons on 24 July by 286 votes to 120. It promised to use its discretion in honouring existing places. The bill received royal assent on 31 July.

The National Health Service (Private Finance) Bill to clarify the position of NHS trusts when it comes to signing Private Finance Initiative contracts had its second reading in the Lords on 3 June. It completed its passage through the Lords unamended and had an unopposed second reading in the Commons on 14 July. All other Commons stages were taken immediately and no amendments were made. The bill received royal assent on 15 July.

On 4 June Sir Peter Emery (C.), the former chairman of the Commons procedure select committee, had an adjournment debate to express concern at the way that the changes to Prime Minister's Question Time had been handled without consultation. The Commons agreed to set up a select committee to look at modernization of the House, to report to the House before the summer adjournment with its initial conclusions on ways in which the procedure for examining legislative proposals could be improved.

On 9 June the Secretary of State for Health (Frank Dobson) replied to a private notice question from Sir Peter Emery on the errors in the results of breast-screening scans carried out in Exeter and east Devon. An independent inquiry would be carried out and the Chief Medical Officer would review the breast-screening programme nationwide. In a Commons debate on the European Union on documents relating to the forthcoming Inter-Governmental Conference in Amsterdam, a Conservative amendment warning against fudging the criteria for EMU was defeated by 404 votes to 151. On 11 June the Chief Secretary to the Treasury (Alistair Darling) announced a comprehensive review of public spending beyond the next two years, in order to ensure clearly focused public spending. The review would take 12 months to complete and its conclusions would inform a new set of public spending plans for the rest of this Parliament. Terms of reference for each departmental review would be published in due course.

A bill to extend the handgun ban to all .22 pistols and revolvers, the Firearms (Amendment) Bill, had its second reading in the Commons on 11 June. An amendment from the Conservatives declining a

THE BUDGET 1997

FISCAL OUTLOOK

Government expenditure at £315,000 million for 1997–8.

Labour plan to keep within spending totals announced by the Conservatives in the November 1996 Budget (see page 1153) for first two years in government, but for 1998–9 part of the existing reserve (£2,200 million) within the control total will be allocated to health and education

No public expenditure survey in 1997: comprehensive spending review already announced

Ratio of government expenditure to GDP to be 39.5 per cent, 1.5 per cent lower than 1996–7

Total yield from tax changes to be £6,000 million in 1997–8 and £6,700 million in 1998–9, with the windfall tax on privatized utilities expected to raise £2,000 million in both years

Tax burden forecast to increase by 1 per cent in 1997–8, with government receipts expected to grow by 7.75 per cent in 1997–8, from 38.1 per cent of GDP to 38.7 per cent

PSBR forecast to be £10,900 million, £8,000 million lower than previously expected. Forecast to be £4,000 million in 1998–9

SPENDING

Welfare to work: £3,900 million to help provide work for the long-term unemployed and lone parents in particular. Total cost of £5,200 million up to 2002 to be financed by windfall tax. Programme to include: help for the long-term unemployed to find work, choosing from full-time education or training, a job in the voluntary sector, a job in the environmental task-force, or a job with an employer. There would be subsidies to employers to hire such people, £750 per person to finance training towards qualifications, and benefits reductions for people refusing any of the options. Lone parents whose youngest child was in the second term of full-time schooling would be offered help with job searches, training and, if necessary, with child-care. Scheme to be extended later to help the disabled and those on incapacity benefit. Creation of University for Industry for lifelong learning

Education: schools to receive £1,000 million from the contingency reserve for 1998–9 and £1,300 from the windfall tax over five years for infrastructure and IT equipment

Health: NHS to receive £1,200 million from the contingency reserve for 1998–9

Housing: local authorities to be allowed to reinvest £900 million of capital receipts from sale of council houses

TAXATION

Business taxation: main rate of corporation tax reduced to 31 per cent in April 1997 and to 21 per cent for small companies. Capital allowances for SMEs doubled for one year

Tax credits: payment of tax credits on dividends to pension schemes and UK companies to be abolished

Windfall tax: one-off tax to be applied to the profits of companies privatized by flotation and regulated by statute, to be levied on the difference between a company's privatization sale price and its imputed values over the subsequent four years

VAT on domestic fuel to be reduced from 8 per cent to 5 per cent from September 1997

North Sea gas levy to be abolished

Housing: MIRAS restricted to 10 per cent from April 1998. Stamp duty on the transfers of properties excluding shares increased 1.5 per cent on properties over £250,000 and to 2 per cent on properties over £500,000

Tax relief on private medical insurance for the over-60s abolished

Film producers will be able to write off 100 per cent of production or acquisition costs of pictures with budgets less than £15 million

Income tax: no change

Excise duties: tobacco duty up 19 pence on a packet of 20 cigarettes and 8 pence on a pack of small cigars from December 1997. In future average increase will be at least 5 per cent

Petrol and diesel increased by 4 pence a litre immediately

Alcohol and VED up in line with inflation (3 per cent) from January 1998

FORECAST

GDP forecast to grow by 3.25 per cent in 1997, falling back to 2.5 per cent in 1998. Consumer spending likely to remain buoyant

Underlying rate of inflation forecast at 2.5 per cent by end of 1997 and to go up to 2.75 per cent in 1998

Next Budget not to be until spring 1998

---

second reading because there was no justification for extending the ban was defeated by 384 votes to 173. The second reading itself was passed by 384 votes to 181, on a free vote. The bill was committed to a committee of the whole House, which was taken on 16 and 18 June. Discussion on 16 June was halted after clause 1, although the debate had been expected to resume after private business had been completed. All remaining stages were taken on 18 June and the third reading was approved by 350 votes to 164. The second reading in the Lords was on 30 June and it completed its Lords committee on 15 July.

On 12 June the Minister for Agriculture, Fisheries and Food (Dr Jack Cunningham) responded to a private notice question from Sir Teddy Taylor (C.) on the implications of the decision of the EU Veterinary Committee to reject proposals designed to relax the ban on UK beef exports. The Government was disappointed that the committee had asked for further clarification but was considering the points made and would give a detailed, technical response soon.

The Law Officers Bill, to allow business from the Attorney-General to be delegated to the Solicitor-General more easily, had its second reading in the Lords on 16 June. Unamended in the Lords, the bill was taken in one day in the Commons on 24 July and received royal assent on 31 July.

MAJOR BOWS OUT

Prime Minister's Question Time on 18 June saw the last appearance of John Major at the dispatch box as Leader of the Opposition. The Prime Minister reported on the outcome of the EC meeting in Amsterdam at which he had secured agreement to legal security to frontier controls, to preserving NATO and not the EU as the cornerstone of the defence of Europe, to a new deal for fishermen and to putting jobs at the top of the agenda for Europe. He concluded, 'We made Britain's voice heard at Amsterdam, because, for the first time for many years, Britain spoke as a united Government with a clear direction for Europe. We have proved to the people of Britain that we can get a better deal by being constructive and we have proved to Europe that Britain can be a leading player, setting a new agenda that faces the real challenges of a new century.' Mr Major accused the Prime Minister of making 'a series of concessions to the European Union. He has gained nothing that was not readily available and he has done nothing whatsoever to widen the Community and much to ensure that it is deepened. He has missed the opportunities of the summit.' The Agriculture Minister (Dr Jack Cunningham) made a statement about the agreement on the common fisheries policy concluded at the summit, with new British licences requiring at least 50 per cent of catches to be unloaded at British ports. From the Conservative front bench, Tony Baldry accused the Government of 'a complete sell-out of the UK fishing industry. The current proposals would not get rid of a single existing quota hopper.' On 20 June the Health Secretary (Frank Dobson) announced the setting-up of a comprehensive review of health-care in London, to report by the end of October 1997.

On 24 June the Prime Minister reported on the outcome of the G8 summit held in Denver, where there had been agreement on the need for structural reform in all the economies. As host of the next G8 summit in Birmingham, he had made it clear he wanted to concentrate on jobs and employability and the challenge of organized crime. In his first appearance at the dispatch box as the Leader of the Opposition, William Hague welcomed many aspects of the summit, particularly the participation by Russia and the conclusions on Hong Kong. On 25 June the Prime Minister made a statement on the Government's continuing search for peace and a political settlement in Northern Ireland, pledging that a settlement would be determined by the middle of 1998 even if Sinn Fein remained outside the substantive negotiations scheduled to begin in October.

On 30 June the junior minister for International Development (George Foulkes) responded to a private notice question from Diane Abbott (Lab.) on the Government's response to the devastating volcanic eruption on the Caribbean dependency of Montserrat. The Government had pledged a further £6.8 million of aid and had dispatched HMS *Liverpool* to the area. The Home Secretary (Jack Straw) made a statement about his decision to order an inquiry into new evidence on the Hillsborough disaster of April 1989 that may not have been available to the original inquiry.

LABOUR'S FIRST BUDGET

The new Chancellor of the Exchequer (Gordon Brown) presented his first Budget on 2 July (*see* page 1159). This was the first Budget in many years not to be presented on a Tuesday but the Prime Minister and other politicians had been attending the hand-over ceremony in Hong Kong earlier in the week.

The Chancellor said that the objective of the first Labour budget for 18 years was 'to achieve high and stable levels of growth and employment' and to reduce the deficit over five years, whilst remaining committed to the 'golden rule' – borrowing only to finance public investment and not to fund current expenditure. He went on, 'We are honouring our pledges to the British people. The measures I have announced today for stability, for investment, for employment opportunity for all and for education will make Britain better equipped to face the future with confidence … It is a Budget that equips Britain for the future – meeting the people's priorities. It is a people's Budget for Britain's future.' The Leader of the Opposition accused the Chancellor of producing a 'tax-raising Budget which breaks the central promises on which the Labour Party fought the last election. It flies in the face of the Prime Minister's assertion that no tax increases would be needed.' He criticized the windfall tax for hitting the ordinary man and woman in the street through the utility shares held by pension funds and insurance policies. He called the changes to advanced corporation tax 'another hammer blow against pensions and savings' and the scrapping of tax relief on private health insurance for the over-60s 'an utterly vindictive way in which to raise extra money for the Treasury'. Paddy Ashdown felt that 'in some ways the Budget can be applauded, but in the way that it fails our children's education and health service on which our families rely, it does not meet the immediate and urgent needs of our country'. He feared the windfall tax would hit ordinary people with pensions and savings. There was a dispute when the Government offered fewer days than usual for debate on the Budget and the non-sitting Friday (4 July) was reinstated to ensure that four days at least were available. On the second day of the debate the Secretary of State for Education and Employment (David Blunkett) outlined the details of the welfare-to-work schemes. At the end of the four days votes were taken on the windfall tax (approved by 342 to 196), hydrocarbon oil duties (335 to 137), vehicle excise duty (332 to 192), medical insurance premiums (377 to 113), pension fund tax credits (332 to 199) and stamp duty (367 to 147).

On 8 July the select committee on standards and privilege published the Downey report into allegations of misconduct by various former MPs, which found that several, including Neil Hamilton, had a case to answer. On 9 July the Prime Minister reported on the outcome of the NATO summit in Madrid during which it had been agreed to admit three new members, Poland, the Czech Republic and Hungary. On 10 July the Secretary of State for Defence (George Robertson) made a statement on the role played by British troops under NATO command in Bosnia in detaining two indicted war criminals, Simo Drlajaca and Milan Kovacevic. One British soldier had been wounded and Drlajaca had been shot dead in the exchanges. The Conservative defence spokesman (Sir George Young) offered the Government strong support for the action taken.

The Finance Bill implementing the proposals in the Budget was given a second reading in the Commons on 10 July by 314 votes to 179. The Shadow Chief Secretary (David Heathcoat-Amory) complained about the truncated timetable allowed for discussion and approval of the bill, which saw a guillotine motion approved by 342 votes to 175 for the committee of the whole House. The committee stage took place on 15 and 16 July and dealt with clauses relating to windfall tax, MIRAS, medical insurance premiums and pension fund tax credits, all of which were approved by large government majorities. Discussion in standing committee was also guillotined, as was consideration of remaining stages on 28 and 29 July, when the third reading was passed by 336 votes to 168. The Lords considered the bill on 31 July and it received royal assent later that day. In the Lords on 14 July the Lord Chancellor (Lord Irvine of Lairg), responding to a question about court fees, criticized 'fat cat' barristers who earned in excess of £1 million a year.

On 22 July the Welsh Secretary (Ron Davies) announced the publication of a White Paper *A Voice for Wales* outlining the Government's proposals for a democratically elected assembly in Wales in preparation for the referendum on 18 September. The Conservative constitutional spokesman (Michael Ancram) described the proposals as 'a mess'. The plans were discussed in a full day's debate on 25 July. During Prime Minister's Question Time on 23 July Paddy Ashdown was criticized for agreeing to join a Cabinet committee with four other members of his party to discuss 'policy issues of mutual interest'. The Prime Minister was also criticized from the Labour benches for the way in which he had set up the committee without consulting Parliament. On 23 July the Education and Employment Secretary (David Blunkett) announced the publication of the report of the National Committee of Inquiry into Higher Education. He said that the new deal it proposed addressed the funding problems of universities, protected free higher education for the less well-off,

ensured that no parent had to pay higher contributions and offered a fair deal for students and graduates. There was criticism of the decision to charge students up to £1,000 for their tuition. The Conservative education and employment spokesman (Stephen Dorrell) thought the statement would be 'met with widespread disappointment ... throughout the higher education world'. On 24 July the Scottish Secretary (Donald Dewar) announced the publication of a White Paper *Scotland's Parliament* outlining the Government's proposals for a Scottish Parliament in preparation for the referendum on 11 September. Michael Ancram called it 'a dangerous, damaging and dishonest document'. The plans were discussed in a full day's debate on 31 July; the Lords discussed both this and the Welsh proposals on 30 July. Later on 24 July the Opposition forced a vote on the European Community 1998 preliminary draft budget proposals, which would normally have been nodded through following consideration by the European standing committee; it was approved by 319 votes to 111. In the Lords on 25 July the Employment Rights (Dispute Resolution) Bill, a Private Member's Bill to amend the law relating to industrial tribunals and to rename them, introduced by Lord Archer of Sandwell (Lab.) had its second reading. The government chief whip (Lord Haskel) and the Opposition whip (Lord Burnham) indicated that they gave their full support to the measure, although several law lords expressed their concerns.

Prime Minister's Question Time on 30 July was dominated by Conservative attacks on the Minister for Trade and Competitiveness in Europe (Lord Simon of Highbury), the former chairman of BP who had taken a post in the Government, and how he had handled his large shareholdings in BP and other companies. The Home Secretary made a statement on plans for improving the criminal justice system in response to the Narey report; proposals included plans for tougher bail conditions, ending delays in cases coming to trial, a three-year minimum sentence for third-time domestic burglars, secure training orders for juvenile offenders, greater powers for probation supervision (including confiscation of passports), community safety orders and more help for the victims of crime. The Conservative home affairs spokesman (Dr Brian Mawhinney) welcomed the statement as 'acceptance of large parts of Conservative Government policy'.

Both the Commons and the Lords rose for the summer recess on 31 July. On the same day five bills, including the Finance Bill, received royal assent.

PUBLIC ACTS OF PARLIAMENT

This list commences with one Public Act which received the royal assent before September 1996. Those Public Acts which follow received the royal

assent after August 1996. The date stated after each Act is the date on which it came into operation; c. indicates the chapter number of each Act

Housing Act 1996, c.52, various dates, some to be appointed
Makes provision in connection with housing, including the rented sector, houses in multiple occupation, landlord and tenant matters, allocation of housing accommodation by local housing authorities; and for connected purposes

Public Order (Amendment) Act 1996, c.59, 17 October 1996
Amends the 1986 Act with regard to powers of arrest

Consolidated Fund (No. 2) Act 1996, c.60, 18 December 1996
Applies certain sums out of the Consolidated Fund to the service of the years ending on 31 March 1997 and 1998

Channel Tunnel Rail Link Act 1996, c.61, 18 December 1996
Provides for the construction, maintenance and operation of a railway between St Pancras in London and the Channel Tunnel portal at Folkestone; for the improvement of parts of the A2 and M2; and for compensation for blighted land

Theft (Amendment) Act 1996, c.62, 18 December 1996
Amends the 1968 Act following recommendations of the Law Commission by creating two new offences of dishonestly obtaining a money transfer by deception (this applies both to cheque and electronic transfers) and retaining credits from dishonest sources

Hong Kong Economic and Trade Office Act 1996, c.63, 18 December 1996
Provides for an Economic and Trade Office to be established in the UK from 1 July 1997 by the government of the Hong Kong Special Administrative Region; and confers certain privileges and immunities on this office

Horserace Totalisator Board Act 1997, c.1, 27 February 1997
Amends the Horserace Totalisator and Betting Levy Boards Act 1972 by conferring on the Horserace Totalisator Board the power to receive or negotiate bets made otherwise than by way of pool betting

Land Registration Act 1997, c.2, most provisions 27 April 1997, remaining provisions, days to be appointed
Amends the 1925 Act in order to strengthen the security provided by registration of title and to speed up the registration of land with unregistered title

Sea Fisheries (Shellfish) (Amendment) Act 1997, c.3, 27 February 1997
Amends the 1967 Act to make provision for fisheries of lobsters and other crustaceans

Telecommunications (Fraud) Act 1997, c.4, 27 April 1997
Amends the Telecommunications Act 1984 by making it illegal to possess or supply anything for fraudulent purposes in connection with the use of the telecommunications system

Firearms (Amendment) Act 1997, c.5, various dates, some to be appointed
Amends the Acts of 1968 to 1992 by prohibiting all handguns over .22 calibre and requiring that handguns of a lesser calibre be kept at registered gun clubs; and providing for connected purposes. (This in response to the Dunblane tragedy)

Local Government (Gaelic Names) (Scotland) Act 1997, c.6, 27 April 1997
Enables local authorities in Scotland to take a Gaelic name and vice versa

Northern Ireland Arms Decommissioning Act 1997, c.7, 27 February 1997
Makes provision in connection with Northern Ireland about the decommissioning of firearms ammunition and explosives

Town and Country Planning (Scotland) Act 1997, c.8, 27 May 1997
Consolidates with amendments, to give effect to recommendations of the Scottish Law Commission, enactments relating to town and country planning in Scotland

Planning (Listed Buildings and Conservation Areas) (Scotland) Act 1997, c.9, 27 May 1997
Consolidates with amendments to give effect to recommendations of the Scottish Law Commission enactments relating to buildings and areas of special architectural or historic interest

Planning (Hazardous Substances) (Scotland) Act 1997, c.10, 27 May 1997
Consolidates with amendments to give effect to recommendations of the Scottish Law Commission certain enactments relating to special controls in respect of hazardous substances

Planning (Consequential Provisions) (Scotland) Act 1997, c.11, 27 May 1997
Makes provision for repeals, consequential amendments, transitional measures and savings resulting from the consolidation of enactments in the Town and Country Planning (Scotland) Act 1997, the Planning (Listed Buildings and Conservation Areas) (Scotland) Act 1997, and the Planning (Hazardous Substances) (Scotland) Act 1997

Civil Procedure Act 1997, c.12, various dates
Amends the law about civil procedure in England and Wales by making provision for the establishment of a unified rule committee to consider the introduction of a single set of procedures for all civil litigation both in the High Court and in the county court; and for connected purposes

United Nations Personnel Act 1997, c.13, 27 April 1997
Gives effect to certain provisions of the Convention on the Safety of UN and Associated Personnel adopted by the UN in 1994. This has the effect of ensuring that even though an attack on such personnel were to take place outside the UK, the

perpetrator would be guilty of the same offence as if it had taken place in the UK

National Heritage Act 1997, c.14, day or days to be appointed
Amends the 1980 Act by extending the powers of the trustees of the National Heritage Memorial Fund to enable them to provide financial assistance for any project which appears to them to be of public benefit

Consolidated Fund Act 1997, c.15, 19 March 1997
Applies certain sums out of the Consolidated Fund to the service of the years ending on 31 March 1996 and 1997

Finance Act 1997, c.16, various dates
Amends certain duties, alters others and amends the law relating to the National Debt and the public revenue. For example, it amends the rules relating to the taxable element of a finance lease, restricts writing down allowances for long-life (over 25 years) assets, alters the anti-avoidance measures relating to transfer of assets abroad, increases the level before which a person has to register for VAT and the nil rate band for inheritance tax

Criminal Evidence (Amendment) Act 1997, c.17, 19 March 1997
Amends the Police and Criminal Evidence Act 1984 by extending the categories of persons from whom non-intimate body samples may be taken without consent to persons imprisoned or detained by virtue of pre-existing conviction for sexual offence and persons detained following acquittal on grounds of insanity or finding of unfitness to plead

Policyholders Protection Act 1997, c.18, various dates, some to be appointed
Amends the 1975 Act in relation to the insurance companies to which the Act applies, the eligibility of policyholders for protection, the protection of policyholders of companies in financial difficulties; and for purposes connected therewith

Pharmacists (Fitness to Practise) Act 1997, c.19, various dates, some to be appointed
Makes provision about finding registered pharmaceutical chemists unfit to practise due to ill health

British Nationality (Hong Kong) Act 1997, c.20, 19 March 1997
Allows British nationals in Hong Kong to acquire British citizenship provided that they qualify under one of several conditions, e.g. they were resident in Hong Kong immediately before 4 February 1997 and would otherwise have been stateless

Knives Act 1997, c.21, various dates, some to be appointed
Creates new offences in relation to the possession or marketing of knives or publications relating to knives; and for connected purposes

Architects Act 1997, c.22, day to be appointed
Consolidates enactments relating to architects in respect of the Architects Registration Board, professional standards and disciplinary procedures, and persons entitled to use the title architect

Lieutenancies Act 1997, c.23, 1 July 1997
Consolidates enactments relating to the lieutenancies in Great Britain and makes provision for deputy lieutenants and vice lord-lieutenants

Nurses, Midwives and Health Visitors Act 1997, c.24, 19 June 1997
Consolidates the 1979 Act and amending enactments

Justices of the Peace Act 1997, c.25, various dates
Consolidates the 1979 Act and related enactments in relation to, *inter alia*, commissions of the peace and petty session areas, magistrates' courts committees, and the appointment, removal and conditions of employment of JPs and justices' clerks

Transfer of Crofting Estates (Scotland) Act 1997, c.26, day to be appointed
Enables the Secretary of State to dispose of his crofting estates and certain other property to approved crofting bodies

Social Security (Recovery of Benefits) Act 1997, c.27, various dates, some to be appointed
Revokes and replaces the Social Security Administration Act 1992 Part IV by, *inter alia*, making compensators liable for all relevant social security benefits paid to victims of accident, injury or disease pending settlement; and for connected purposes

Merchant Shipping and Maritime Security Act 1997, c.28, various dates, some to be appointed
Amends the Merchant Shipping Act 1995; extends the powers of fire authorities to use fire brigades at sea; makes provision about piracy, and for various matters connected with shipping and maritime security

Local Government and Rating Act 1997, c.29, various dates, some to be appointed
Makes further provision about, *inter alia*, non-domestic rating; parishes and parish councils; and for connected purposes

Police (Property) Act 1997, c.30, 19 May 1997
Makes further provision as to the power of the police to retain unclaimed property and to dispose of property used, or intended for use, for criminal purposes

Appropriation Act 1997, c.31, 21 March 1997
Applies a sum out of the Consolidated Fund to the year ending 31 March 1998 and appropriates the supplies granted in this parliamentary session

Building Societies Act 1997, c.32, various dates, some to be appointed
Makes provision for amalgamating the Building Societies Investor Protection Board and the Deposit Protection Board into a single board, and the Building Societies Investor Protection Fund and the Deposit Protection Fund into a single fund; and for connected purposes

Confiscation of Alcohol (Young Persons) Act 1997, c.33, day to be appointed

Allows a constable to confiscate intoxicating liquor held by, or for use by, a young person in a public place or a place to which such young person has gained unlawful access

Contract (Scotland) Act 1997, c.34, 21 June 1997

Reforms the law of Scotland on the admissibility of extrinsic evidence to prove an additional express term or unilateral voluntary obligation of a contract; and for other purposes connected with contract law

Scottish Legal Services Ombudsman and Commissioner for Local Administration in Scotland Act 1997, c.35, various dates, some to be appointed

Makes further provision about the Scottish Legal Services Ombudsman and extends the jurisdiction of the Commissioner for Local Administration in Scotland

Flood Prevention and Land Drainage (Scotland) Act 1997, c.36, various dates, some to be appointed

Amends the Flood Prevention (Scotland) Act 1961 in relation to the flood prevention measures to be taken by local authorities; and for connected purposes

Welsh Development Agency Act 1997, c.37, 21 May 1997

Increases the financial limits of the Welsh Development Agency

Prisons (Alcohol Testing) Act 1997, c.38, 21 May 1997

Amends the Prison Act 1952 to enable prison officers to test prisoners for alcohol

Sexual Offences (Protected Material) Act 1997, c.39, day to be appointed

Regulates access by defendants and other persons to certain material in relation to proceedings for sexual offences, including victims' statements, photographs of victims and medical reports relating to victims

Protection from Harassment Act 1997, c.40, various dates, some to be appointed

Makes provision to protect persons from harassment and similar conduct

Building Societies (Distributions) Act 1997, c.41, 21 March 1997

Amends the law in respect of the distribution of assets on the takeover or conversion of a building society to protect the interest of beneficiaries in the case of trustee account holders

Police (Health and Safety) Act 1997, c.42, various dates, some to be appointed

Makes provision about the health and safety at work of members of the police forces, special constables, police cadets and other persons having the powers and privileges of a constable

Crime (Sentences) Act 1997, c.43, various dates, some to be appointed

Makes provision for mandatory sentences except in exceptional circumstances; and for other matters connected with sentencing and sentences

Education Act 1997, c.44, various dates, some to be appointed

Amends the 1996 Act in relation to school discipline and the supervision of external academic and vocational qualifications; and for connected purposes

Police (Insurance of Voluntary Assistants) Act 1997, c.45, 21 March 1997

Empowers the police authorities and Receiver for the Metropolitan Police District to insure people acting as voluntary assistants for police purposes

National Health Service (Primary Care) Act 1997, c.46, various dates, some to be appointed

Provides new arrangements in relation to the provision within the NHS of medical, dental or pharmaceutical and other services; and for connected purposes

Social Security Administration (Fraud) Act 1997, c.47, various dates, some to be appointed

Amends the Social Security Administration Act 1992 and the Social Security Administration (Northern Ireland) Act 1992 to allow the tax authorities to supply information for social security fraud prevention and verification; and for connected purposes

Crime and Punishment (Scotland) Act 1997, c.48, various dates, some to be appointed

Makes provision in Scotland, in relation to sentencing, criminal appeals, criminal procedure, evidence in criminal proceedings, early release of prisoners and criminal legal assistance; and for the remittance of offenders to courts in Scotland from England and Wales and Northern Ireland

Public Entertainments Licences (Drug Misuse) Act 1997, c.49, various dates, some to be appointed

Amends the Local Government (Miscellaneous Provisions) Act 1982 and the Local Government Act 1963 to permit local authorities to refuse applications for the renewal or transfer of entertainments licences or revocation of such licences relating to places at or near which controlled drugs are supplied or used

Police Act 1997, c.50, various dates, some to be appointed

Provides for the establishment and function of the National Criminal Intelligence Service and the National Crime Squad and makes provision about authorization of entry on and interference with property and with wireless telegraphy in the course of crime prevention or detection; and for other purposes connected with the police

Sex Offenders Act 1997, c.51, day or days to be appointed

Requires sex offenders to notify the police of any change of name or address and provides that a

British citizen or UK resident who commits a sexual offence in another jurisdiction shall have committed an offence under UK law

Police and Firemen's Pension Act 1997, c.52, various dates
Amends the Police Pensions Act 1976 and the Fire Services Act 1947 to make provision in respect of transfer values and other lump payments and to permit police authorities and fire authorities to provide information in respect of such schemes

Dangerous Dogs (Amendment) Act 1997, c.53, 8 June 1997
Amends the 1991 Act to give the court discretion not to order the destruction of a dog in certain circumstances

Road Traffic Reduction Act 1997, c.54, day to be appointed

Makes provision to require local authorities to make reports to the Secretary of State on the levels of local road traffic in their area and to forecast growth in those levels

Birds (Registration Charges) Act 1997, c.55, 21 March 1997
Provides for charges to be imposed for registration of sellers of dead wild birds and of certain captive wild birds

National Health Service (Private Finance) Act 1997, c.56, 15 July 1997
Makes provisions about the powers of NHS trusts to enter into agreements

Appropriation Act 1997, c. 57
Finance (No. 2) Act 1997, c. 58
Education (Schools) Act 1997, c. 59
Law Officers Act 1997, c. 60
Referendums (Scotland and Wales) Act 1997, c. 61

WHITE PAPERS, REPORTS, ETC.

Choice and Opportunity – Primary Care: The Future was presented to Parliament on 15 October 1996 by the Secretary of State for Health (Stephen Dorrell). It proposed measures to deregulate the provision of health-care services. The main proposals were:
– different types of GP contract to be piloted
– health authorities to be given greater flexibility when purchasing community pharmacy and optometry services
– local flexibility in primary care dentistry to be piloted

The Government's response to the Cullen report on the shootings in Dunblane in March 1996 was presented to Parliament on 16 October 1996 by the Home Secretary (Michael Howard). It accepted all the report's recommendations and made the following main proposals:
– all handguns over .22 calibre to be banned in England, Wales and Scotland
– all .22 pistols to be banned unless kept at licensed gun clubs; a police permit to be required for their removal
– all gun clubs to be required to be licensed
– all users of handguns to be required to have a firearms certificate
– guns purchased by mail order to be delivered to a gun dealer and given to the certificate-holder in person only
– the police to keep and exchange information on certificate-holders and those who have been refused a certificate, and to have the power to suspend any certificate without appeal

A White Paper in response to the House of Lords select committee's report on local government, *Building Trust*, was presented to Parliament by the Environment Secretary (John Gummer) on 4 November 1996. The main proposals were:

– to agree with the Local Government Association and the Welsh Local Government Association a statement of the role and status of local government in England and Wales and to develop further the guidelines for central government–local government relations
– to review the scope for local authorities to fulfil their community leadership role and to assess whether they should have a more general power of local competence
– to allow local authorities to experiment with their internal management structure
– to undertake research on public participation in local government
– to review arrangements for handling cross-departmental business affecting local government

Free Trade and Foreign Policy – A Global Vision was presented to Parliament by the Foreign Secretary (Malcolm Rifkind) and the Secretary of State for Trade and Industry (Ian Lang) on 11 November 1996. It said that Britain must continue to improve its competitiveness and seize the opportunities presented by world changes. It stated that the Government's objective was global free trade by 2020 and it set out a programme for achieving this, including the following:
– to press for further liberalization measures at the first World Trade Organization ministerial conference in December 1996
– to call for a new round of comprehensive multilateral negotiations
– to work in the OECD, the IMF and elsewhere for free flows of investment and capital

The National Health Service: a Service with Ambitions was presented to Parliament on 13 November 1996 by the Health Secretary (Stephen Dorrell). It promised that the NHS would remain a free service

funded from taxation. It sought improvements in the areas of information technology, professional development and quality management, and set out the following key objectives for the service:
– a well-informed public
– a seamless service
– decision-making based on the latest clinical evidence
– a highly trained and skilled workforce
– responsiveness to patients' needs

Learning to Compete: Education and Training for 14–19-Year-Olds was presented to Parliament by the Education and Employment Secretary (Gillian Shephard) on 9 December 1996. The main proposals were:
– an entitlement to learning credits for state-funded programmes to be introduced in September 1997 for all 14–21-year-olds
– Youth Training to be replaced by National Traineeships
– key skills to be promoted in education and training in order to improve the employability of young people
– a 'Relaunch' scheme to be introduced, focusing on local partnerships to provide more effective help for young people who are not learning or who are in danger of dropping out

The Governance of Public Bodies: a Progress Report was presented to Parliament by the Public Service Minister (Roger Freeman) on 12 February 1997. The main proposals were:
– all executive non-departmental public bodies (NDPBs) to be reviewed with a view to extending the Ombudsman's jurisdiction in this sector as widely as possible
– consideration to be given to bringing advisory bodies into the Ombudsman's jurisdiction for the first time
– a model code of practice to be drawn up for staff of NDPBs
– fuller and clearer guidance on codes of practice for board members of public bodies to be drawn up, covering in particular rules on conflicts of interest
– greater use to be made of consultative arrangements bringing together local public bodies and local authorities
– a National Consultative Forum to be set up to bring together key interests in public sector audit; the forum to be led by the National Audit Office, the Audit Commission and the Accounts Commission for Scotland

Pension Rights on Divorce was presented to Parliament by the Social Security Secretary (Peter Lilley) on 26 February 1997. The main proposals were:
– private pension rights and state earnings-related pension rights built up during a marriage to be included in assets to be considered when couples divorce, from April 2000
– divorcing couples to be given access to the information necessary for them to make an informed decision about whether or not to split pension rights
– any private pension rights transferred to be used to set up a separate pension
– any SERPS element transferred to be paid at retirement age
– the costs of transferring pension rights to be met by the divorcing couple
– if couples are unable to agree, the courts to have the right to impose a settlement

Social Services: Achievement and Challenge was presented to Parliament by the Health Secretary (Stephen Dorrell) on 12 March 1997. Its main proposals were:
– local authority social services departments no longer to run residential homes for the elderly and disabled or to provide services to them in their own homes, unless they can show that the private or voluntary sector cannot meet local need
– the role of local authorities usually to be restricted to assessing local residents' care requirements and purchasing care from the private or voluntary sector
– an independent inspectorate to be established to take over from local authorities the responsibility for regulating and monitoring care in private and voluntary homes
– elderly people to be offered vouchers to pay for some or all of the costs of private residential care, according to their assets
– greater stress to be laid on the responsibility of adults when making care decisions about children

Excellence in Schools was presented to Parliament by the Education and Employment Secretary (David Blunkett) on 7 July 1997. Its main targets and proposals, some requiring legislation and some issued as guidelines, were:
– an Early Years Forum to be established in each area to draw up plans for providing pre-school places for all four-year-olds
– class sizes to be kept to 30 or below for all children aged five, six and seven by 2002
– all five-year-olds to be assessed on entering school so that progress can be monitored
– literacy and numeracy to be given priority in primary schools, which would be expected to devote an hour every day to literacy (using the phonics teaching method) from September 1998 and to numeracy from September 1999
– 80 per cent of 11-year-olds to reach the standards expected for their age in English, and 75 per cent in mathematics, by 2002
– schools to be recategorized as community, foundation or aided
– 25 Education Action Zones to be set up in disadvantaged areas
– plans to allow some selection of pupils by general academic ability to be scrapped
– setting by ability to be the norm in secondary schools
– each local authority to have a development plan and to set approved performance targets every

three years for each age-group after local consultation; targets to be reviewed annually
- schools to be inspected at least once every six years, with a greater emphasis on classroom practice, but to be given less notice of inspection
- appraisal of teachers to be reviewed and streamlined procedures to be introduced for dismissing under-performing teachers
- each school's rate of improvement to be included in annual league tables
- failing schools which do not improve to be closed or given a 'fresh start'
- a new qualification to be introduced for aspiring head teachers, an induction year to be reintroduced for new teachers, and a new senior grade of Advanced Skills Teacher to be introduced
- home-school contracts to be introduced, covering discipline, homework and attendance; homework guidelines to be issued
- the Government to consult on new guidance on expelling pupils
- pupils turning 16 in the summer term to be compelled to finish the term

The People's Lottery was presented to Parliament by the Secretary of State for Culture, Media and Sport (Chris Smith) on 21 July 1997. It outlined plans to change the running of the National Lottery, and its main proposals were:
- a sixth 'good cause' to be created, called the New Opportunities Fund, to fund health, education and environmental initiatives
- a National Endowment for Science, Technology and the Arts (NESTA) to be created, which would be an independent body with a particular focus on multi media work
- £1 billion of lottery funds to be available to the New Opportunities Fund and NESTA by 2001
- distribution of lottery funds to be improved and made more efficient, with a more strategic approach based on assessment of need, decisions taken closer to the grass roots, and more priority given to health, education and the environment
- a new system for operating the lottery to be introduced, with unnecessary profit margins removed

A Voice for Wales was presented to Parliament by the Secretary of State for Wales (Ron Davies) on 22 July 1997. It outlined plans for setting up an elected Welsh assembly if devolution were supported in the referendum held on 18 September 1997. Its main proposals were:
- a 60-member assembly to be elected in May 1999, with 40 members each representing a constituency to be elected by majority vote and the remaining 20 members to be elected by proportional representation on the basis of party political lists; elections to be held every four years
- the assembly to have no tax-raising powers but to have powers to pass secondary legislation
- a leader to be elected from the majority party to chair an executive committee of ten

- The Queen to open the assembly
- the cost of establishing the assembly to be about £12–£15 million, and the annual running costs to be about £20 million
- the assembly to take over the Welsh Office's £7 billion budget; the Welsh Office civil servants to service the assembly
- the Government to abolish nine quangos after the passage of substantive legislation, and the assembly to review those remaining

Scotland's Parliament was presented to Parliament by the Secretary of State for Scotland (Donald Dewar) on 24 July 1997. It outlined plans for setting up a Scottish parliament if devolution were supported in the referendum held on 11 September 1997. Its main proposals were:
- a 129-member parliament to be elected in 1999, with 73 members each representing a constituency to be elected by majority vote and the remaining 56 members to be elected by proportional representation on the basis of party political lists; elections to be held every four years
- the parliament to have powers to raise or reduce the basic rate of income tax by up to three pence, if supported in the referendum; savings and dividend income to be exempted from the tax variation power
- Westminster to retain powers over such areas as foreign, economic, defence and security policy and the constitution; the Scottish parliament to have legislative powers in all other areas, including education, health, law, environment, economic development and local government
- a First Minister to be appointed by The Queen to head a Scottish Executive comprising ministers and law officers
- the cost of establishing the parliament to be about £10–£40 million, and the annual running costs to be about £20–£30 million
- the number of Scottish MPs at Westminster to be cut by about 12 by 2007
- the Secretary of State for Scotland to remain a Cabinet member and to be responsible for promoting communication between the Scottish and Westminster parliaments and for representing Scotland's interests in policy areas not devolved to the Scottish parliament
- the judicial committee of the Privy Council to be the arbiter in the event of a dispute between the two parliaments

The Queen's Awards

The Queen's Award for Export Achievement and The Queen's Award for Technological Achievement were instituted by royal warrant in 1976. The two separate awards took the place of The Queen's Award to Industry, which had been instituted in 1965. In 1992 the scheme was extended with the launch of a third award, The Queen's Award for Environmental Achievement.

The export and technological awards are designed to recognize and encourage outstanding achievements in exporting goods or services from the United Kingdom and in advancing process or product technology. The purpose of the environmental award is to recognize and encourage product and process development which has major benefits for the environment and which is commercially successful.

The awards differ from a personal royal honour in that they are given to a unit as a whole, management and employees working as a team. They may be applied for by any organization within the United Kingdom, the Channel Islands or the Isle of Man producing goods or services which meet the criteria for the awards. Eligibility is not influenced in any way by the particular activities, location or size of the unit applying. Units or agencies of central and local government with industrial functions, as well as research associations, educational institutions and bodies of a similar character, are also eligible provided that they can show they have contributed to industrial efficiency.

Each award is formally conferred by a grant of appointment and is symbolized by a representation of its emblem cast in stainless steel and encapsulated in a transparent acrylic block.

Awards are held for five years and holders are entitled to fly the appropriate award flag and to display the emblem on the packaging of goods produced in this country, on the goods themselves, on the unit's stationery, in advertising and on certain articles used by employees. Units may also display the emblem of any previous current awards during the five years.

Awards are announced on 21 April (the birthday of The Queen) and published formally in a special supplement to the London Gazette.

AWARDS OFFICE

All enquiries about the scheme and requests for application forms (completed forms must be returned by 31 October) should be made to: The Secretary, The Queen's Awards Office, 151 Buckingham Palace Road, London SW1W 9SS. Tel: 0171-222 2277.

EXPORT ACHIEVEMENT

The criterion upon which recommendations for an award for export achievement are based is a substantial and sustained increase in export earnings to a level which is outstanding for the products or services concerned and for the size of the applicant unit's operations. Account will be taken of any special market factors described in the application. Applicants for the award will be expected to explain the basis of the achievement (e.g. improved marketing organization or new initiative to cater for export markets) and this will be taken into consideration. Export earnings considered will include receipts by the applicant unit in this country from the export of goods produced in this country, and the provision of services to non-residents. Account will be taken of the overseas expenses incurred other than marketing expenses. Income from profits (after overseas tax) remitted to this country from the applicant unit's direct investments in its overseas branches, subsidiaries or associates in the same general line of business will be taken into account, but not receipts from profits on other overseas investments or by interest on overseas loans or credits.

In 1997, The Queen's Award for Export Achievement was conferred on the following concerns:

AGCO Ltd, Coventry
AgriSense BCS Ltd, Pontypridd
Agrisystems (Overseas) Ltd, Aylesbury, Bucks
Airwair Ltd, Rushden, Northants
Alwayse Engineering Ltd, Birmingham
Aquion Ltd, Rotherham
Astracast PLC, Birstall, W. Yorks
Avro International Aerospace (a division of British Aerospace Regional Aircraft Ltd), Stockport
Lawrence M. Barry and Co., London E16
Bartle Bogle Hegarty Ltd, London W1
Bass Beers Worldwide Ltd, Birmingham
Bionet Research Ltd, Camelford, Cornwall
Bisley Office Equipment Ltd, Woking, Surrey
Blease Medical Equipment Ltd, Chesham, Bucks
Borden Decorative Products Ltd, Wallcoverings Division, Darwen, Lancs
Bridgeport Machines Ltd, Leicester
British Steel PLC, London SE1
Business Monitor International Ltd, London EC4
Camborne Holdings Ltd, Mirfield, W. Yorks
The Chambers Candy Co. Ltd, Halesowen, W. Midlands
Computational Dynamics Ltd, London W10
Concept Systems Ltd, Edinburgh
Conren Ltd, Wrexham
Contract Chemicals Ltd, Prescot, Merseyside
Crestworth Trading Ltd, trading as 'Mathmos', London WC2
Davis and Dann Ltd, South Ruislip, Middx
James Dewhurst Ltd, Manufacturing Divisions, Accrington, Lancs
Electra Polymers and Chemicals Ltd, Tonbridge, Kent
Electrox (a division of 600 UK Ltd), Letchworth, Herts

Ellison Holdings PLC, Keighley, W. Yorks
ENTACO Ltd (English Needle and Fishing Tackle Co. Ltd), Studley, Warwicks
Eurocast Bar Ltd, Loughborough, Leics
European Gas Turbines Ltd, Industrial Gas Turbine Group, Lincoln
Exley Publications Ltd, Watford, Herts
Exsa (UK) Ltd, Texturizing Division, Garforth, Leeds
The Fin Machine Co. Ltd, Stockton-on-Tees
Financial Engineering Ltd, London W1
Fletcher Smith Ltd, Friar Gate, Derby
Fresh Catch Ltd, Peterhead, Aberdeenshire
GPT Public Networks Group, Coventry
Griffin-Woodhouse Ltd, Cradley Heath, W. Midlands
Harcros Chemicals UK Ltd, Durham Chemicals Division, Chester-le-Street, Co. Durham
Henrob Ltd, Flint
John Hogg Technical Solutions Ltd, Trafford Park, Manchester
IBM United Kingdom Ltd, Greenock site, Greenock
Iggesund Paperboard (Workington) Ltd, Workington, Cumbria
Innovative Technology Ltd, Royton, Oldham
International Gases and Chemicals Ltd, Newcastle-under-Lyme, Staffs
International KD Logistics and Technology Support Operations, Dagenham, Essex
International Systems and Communications Ltd, London SW1
Interpack Worldwide PLC, London NW10
Inveresk PLC, Dunfermline, Fife
J. C. Bamford Excavators Ltd, Backhoe Loader Division, Rocester, Staffs
JCB Earthmovers Ltd, Wheeled Loader Division, Rocester, Staffs
W. Jordan (Cereals) Ltd, Biggleswade, Beds
Keith Ceramic Materials Ltd, Belvedere, Kent
Kingston-SCL Ltd, Edinburgh
Lansing Linde Ltd, Basingstoke, Hants
Marks and Spencer PLC, London W1
Martin-Baker Aircraft Co. Ltd, Uxbridge, Middx
Matsushita Communication Industrial UK Ltd, Thatcham, Berks
Matsushita Electric (UK) Ltd, Pentwyn, Cardiff
Militair Aviation Ltd, Ringwood, Hants
Mivan Ltd, Antrim
Molins Tobacco Machinery Ltd, a division of Molins PLC, High Wycombe, Bucks
Morgan-Europe Ltd, Sheffield
Morrison Bowmore Distillers Ltd, Glasgow
NEC Semiconductors (UK) Ltd, Livingston, W. Lothian
Newbridge Networks Ltd, Newport
Nimbus Technology and Engineering, a division of Nimbus Communications International Ltd, Monmouth
Nortel Optoelectronics, a division of Nortel (Northern Telecom), Paignton, Devon
Novartis Grimsby, Grimsby, Lincs
Novocastra Laboratories Ltd, Newcastle upon Tyne
Oasis Art and Craft Products Ltd, Kidderminster
The Open University Business School, Milton Keynes, Bucks
Orkot Ltd, Rotherham
Orvec International Ltd, Kingston upon Hull
PFE International Ltd, Loughton, Essex
Pall Europe Ltd, Portsmouth, Hants
Panaz Ltd, Fence, Burnley, Lancs
Paralloy Ltd, Billingham, Co. Durham
Percell Group Ltd, Newport
Perfecseal Ltd, Londonderry

B. A. Peters PLC, Chichester, W. Sussex
Pfizer Ltd, Sandwich, Kent
Phoenix Engineering Co. Ltd, Chard, Somerset
Pipeline Integrity International, Cramlington, Northumberland
Pixel Power Ltd, Cambridge
Planit International Ltd, Ashford, Kent
Plessey Semiconductors Ltd, trading as GEC Plessey Semiconductors, Swindon, Wilts
Proton Textiles Ltd, London N22
RTA Wine Rack Company Ltd, Fakenham, Norfolk
Randox Laboratories Ltd, Crumlin, Co. Antrim
River Don Castings Ltd, Sheffield
Schwitzer (Europe) Ltd, Bradford
Shield Diagnostics Ltd, Dundee
Soil Machine Dynamics Ltd, Newcastle upon Tyne
Speedo International Ltd, Nottingham
Structural Polymer Systems Ltd, Cowes, Isle of Wight
Surface Technology Systems Ltd, Abercarn, Newport
Tensator Ltd, Milton Keynes, Bucks
Toyota Motor Manufacturing (UK) Ltd, Burnaston, Derbys
Turbosound, Partridge Green, W. Sussex
Urbanhurst Ltd, Sawbridgeworth, Herts
Victrex PLC, Thornton-Cleveleys, Lancs
Vitacalender, Salford
Wafer Technology Ltd, Milton Keynes, Bucks
Charles Wells Ltd, Bedford
Wolstenholme International Ltd, Blackburn, Lancs
Woodland Potteries Ltd, Stoke-on-Trent

TECHNOLOGICAL ACHIEVEMENT

The criterion upon which recommendations for an award for technological achievement are based is a significant advance, leading to increased efficiency, in the application of technology to a production or development process in British industry or the production for sale of goods which incorporate new and advanced technological qualities. An award is only granted for production or development processes which have achieved commercial success.

In 1997 The Queen's Award for Technological Achievement was conferred on the following concerns:

Amchem Company Ltd, Birmingham – *system for improving performance of microhole EDM machines*
Amersham Life Science (Amersham International PLC), Little Chalfont, Bucks – *solid phase scintillation assay technology*
Aspect Vision Care Ltd (Manufacturing Division), Southampton – *synchronized moulding of contact lenses*
Electrocraft Laboratories Ltd, Liss, Hants – *television test pattern generators (jointly with Snell and Wilcox Ltd)*
GPT Public Networks Group, Coventry – *SMA synchronous multiplexers*
ICG Ltd, Cheltenham, Glos – *ICG 350i series vertical drum scanners*
ICI Explosives Europe, Wigan, Lancs – *'Handibulk' system for mobile manufacture of bulk emulsion explosives*
Integrated Display Systems Ltd, Wallsend, Tyne and Wear – *belt tension measurement equipment*
Percell Group Ltd, Newport – *Tellermate electronic money counter*

Racal Avionics Ltd, London sw20 – *aeronautical satellite communications (SATCOM)*

Scapa Group, Advanced Products Division, Blackburn – *porous composite membrane constituent of paper machine press clothing*

Snell and Wilcox Ltd, Petersfield, Hants – *large screen display optimizer*

Snell and Wilcox Ltd, Petersfield, Hants – *television test pattern generators (jointly with Electrocraft Laboratories Ltd)*

VLSI Vision Ltd, Edinburgh – *miniature Complementary Metal Oxide Semiconductor (CMOS) cameras*

Whipp and Bourne, Rochdale, Lancs – *pole-mounted auto-recloser*

Zeneca LifeScience Molecules, Manchester – *technological innovation in the creation, development and commercialization of a biotransformation process for the production of the chiral chemical S-2-chloropropanoic acid (SCPA)*

ENVIRONMENTAL ACHIEVEMENT

The criterion upon which recommendations for an award for environmental achievement are based is a significant advance in the application by British industry of the development of products, technology or processes which offer major benefits in environmental terms compared to existing products, technology or processes. An award is only granted for products, technology or processes which have achieved commercial success.

In 1997 The Queen's Award for Environmental Achievement was conferred on the following concerns:

Autoflame Engineering Ltd, London se6 – *microprocessor-based fuel/air ratio control, incorporating exhaust gas analysis 3 parameter trim for industrial and commercial burners*

Cleveland Cascades, Middlesbrough – *loading chute that eliminates dust emissions and minimizes degradation and segregation of bulk materials*

European Gas Turbines Ltd, Industrial Gas Turbine Group, Lincoln – *dry low emissions combustor for EGT industrial gas turbines*

H. and R. Johnson Tiles Ltd, Stoke-on-Trent – *recycling of ceramic industry waste*

Laporte plc, Absorbents (Europe) Division, Widnes, Cheshire – *ferral, a new water purification coagulant minimizing waste*

Rolls-Royce Industrial and Marine Gas Turbines Ltd, Coventry – *dry low emissions combustion system for industrial aeroderivative gas turbines*

Sony Manufacturing Company UK, Pencoed, Mid Glamorgan – *development of an environmentally friendly machine soldering process*

Varn Products Company Ltd, Manchester – *removal of VOCs from the printing process*

Science and Discovery

Mars Landing

Towards the end of 1996 NASA launched two probes to explore the planet Mars. The first, *Mars Global Surveyor*, is designed to map the surface of the planet in greater detail than earlier probes and arrived in the vicinity of the planet on 11 September 1997. Although launched a month later, *Mars Pathfinder* arrived at the planet on 4 July and entered the thin atmosphere directly. It was gradually slowed down by atmospheric drag, parachutes and retro-rockets, and having lost most of its speed it fell to the surface, the capsule cushioned by huge airbags. After bouncing several times it came to rest in the region called Ares Vallis, the mouth of an ancient river channel. The probe automatically righted itself and then released the airbags. All except one of the bags fell clear of the probe but with a little manoeuvring the final one was jettisoned. The probe then deployed a six-wheeled vehicle weighing 11.5 kg onto the surface. The vehicle, named *Sojourner*, examined in detail some of the boulders and carried out experiments on the fine soil lying between the rocks. *Sojourner* carried a stereo camera and an X-ray spectrometer to determine the composition of the rocks and soil. *Sojourner*'s examinations are limited to a distance of 10 metres from the touchdown point at present, but longer excursions may be made later in the mission.

Early data shows that the geology of the planet is similar to that of the Earth. Chemical analysis of a rock labelled 'Barnacle Bill' has shown it to be richer in silicon than any meteorite believed to originate on Mars but it has a similar composition to terrestrial andesite. Photographs taken on the third day showed boulders stacked by currents and ripples in the soil. The evidence suggests that between 1 and 3 billion years ago the Ares Vallis was hundreds of feet under water, the site of a flood big enough to fill the Mediterranean basin on Earth. Now the area is completely dry. *Sojourner* recorded a maximum temperature of $-12°C$ and a minimum of $-76°C$. By mid July hundreds of photographs had been transmitted back to Earth and are currently being analysed.

Life on Mars?

The announcement in 1996 that evidence of life on Mars had been found in meteorite ALH 84001, discovered in the Allan Hills region in Antarctica, is being questioned. The strength of the claim lay in the carbonate globules found in the meteorite. Within the globules were tiny tubular structures that looked like fossil bacteria. The globules also contained the minerals magnetite and iron sulphide which are produced by some terrestrial bacteria and also polycyclic aromatic hydrocarbons (PAHs)

frequently formed during the decomposition of living organisms. This apparent evidence of the past existence of living organisms in a meteorite which was believed to have originated on Mars was taken as proof that there had been primitive life on the planet at some time in the past.

Doubt was cast on these conclusions at the time and subsequent work has shown that this had substance. Several scientists have examined a very thin section from one of the globules using an electron microscope. The internal structure of the magnetite was found to be rare in terrestrial magnetites and totally unknown in those produced by living organisms. The only source for such structures is thought to be fumaroles, volcanic vents that release hot gases, although more work is being carried out. Analysis was also carried out on the PAHs using a mass spectrometer and the results compared with similar analysis of the other meteorites found in the Antarctic ice. All the PAHs found in the original were also found in the ice samples and in other meteorites from the Antarctic region, including some that definitely did not come from Mars.

It is thought that the contamination of the meteorite occurred during the 12,000-year period that the meteorite lay on the Earth's surface. Data from the recently landed Mars probe *Pathfinder* should also help clarify matters.

Comet Hale Bopp

The brilliant display of Comet Hyakutake in 1996 followed by the appearance of a second and even brighter comet within a year excited an unusual degree of popular interest in astronomical matters. Comet Hale-Bopp has been exceptional right from the time it was discovered on 22 July 1995 by two amateurs, Alan Hale and Thomas Bopp. At that time the comet was still 7.15 astronomical units from the Sun. It passed through solar conjunction at the end of 1996 and emerged in the predawn sky in January 1997, brightening and rising higher day-by-day to produce a spectacular object during March and April, with a brilliant tail pointing virtually upwards. By late March and April is was also visible in the evening sky. Its rise to maximum brightness was not regular. During the first half of 1996 it increased in brightness as expected but for about four months from July it hardly brightened at all. After a brief spell of brightening it went quiet again during the latter half of December. Its nearest approach to the Earth took place on 22 March 1997 at a distance of 1.315 astronomical units.

As comets go, Hale-Bopp had a very large nucleus; estimates ranged from 10 km to 40 km. The dust tail remained dominant throughout the whole of spring 1997, a length of just over 40° being visible in very dark skies. Another prominent feature was the very straight, blue-coloured ion tail, with a length of about 16°. Astronomers stationed at La Palma, Canary Islands, recorded the existence of a third tail close to the ion tail. It was straight, about 6° long, and consisted of sodium ions. No satisfactory explanation has been put forward for this. As with Comet Hyakutake, X-ray emission was detected from the coma. The mechanism for this emission of X-rays is unclear at present, but it could be due to the scattering of solar X-rays in the coma or the product of X-ray emitting plasma from collisions between cometary and interplanetary dust. Spectra of the comet's dust envelope have revealed the presence of forsterite, a magnesium-rich silicate.

COMET CRASH ON JUPITER

The crash of Comet Shoemaker-Levy 9 on Jupiter in 1994 gave astronomers observational data about such events; until then data about cosmic impacts was mostly theoretical. At the time estimates of the frequency of cometary impacts on Jupiter ranged from 25 to 1,000 years, the former suggested by Brian Marsden of the Harvard-Smithsonian Center for Astrophysics and the higher value by Gene Shoemaker of the Geological Survey, Arizona.

Historical records of earlier impacts on Jupiter were searched and Isshi Tabe, a Japanese amateur astronomer, found in the Paris Observatory archives drawings and descriptions of an event in 1690 which seems similar to the 1994 impact. There have been instances in the past of the sudden appearances of spots, suggesting an impact, but the markings were too short-lived for comparison with the 1994 event. However, the 1690 observations are far more detailed and lend themselves to comparison.

The observer who described the 1690 event and made the drawings was Giovanni Cassini, the astronomer to Louis XIV of France and the leading astronomer of his time. Cassini recorded the sudden appearance of a round dark spot on 5 December 1690 and the slow changes in the spot over the next 18 days. The spot lengthened, spreading out along a parallel of latitude in exactly the same way as the 1994 event. Tabe analysed the drawings with a fellow amateur, Michiwo Jimbo, and Junichi Watanabe of the National Astronomical Observatory in Japan. All are convinced that Jupiter suffered an impact in 1690. Not all astronomers are convinced, but as Marsden commented, the similarity of Cassini's observations to those of 1994 seems almost too good to be true.

JUPITER'S MOONS

During the last year the *Galileo* spacecraft has made close fly-bys of Jupiter and its main satellites producing some fine photographs as well as information on the structure of the satellites.

On 6 September 1996 *Galileo* passed over Ganymede at a height of 262 km. It mapped Ganymede's north polar region and sent back details of its gravitational field and the newly discovered magnetosphere. Gannymede's surface is criss-crossed with ridges and grooves and the probe identified a relatively new crater. After taking long-distance photographs of Io, Amalthea, Europa and Callisto, *Galileo* made its third close approach to Jupiter and on 4 November it made a 1,200 km pass over Callisto. This and another pass in June 1997 provided much data about the satellite's surface which it is hoped will explain why Callisto's terrain is so heavily cratered, in contrast to that of the other satellites. Some data was transmitted back immediately but most was stored on tape for transmission at a later date. The limited data available so far suggests that Callisto has not suffered any internal melting. This means that there is no central core and that the satellite has a fairly undifferentiated structure.

Two low-level passes over Europa have shown it has a magnetic field, but one only about a quarter of the strength of that of Gannymede. A careful study of Europa's path taken as the satellite flew by has revealed that Europa has an outer shell of ice and water about 100 km thick but below this is a dense interior, thought to consist of a mixture of rock and metal or possibly a metal core surrounded by rock. Later information suggests that the ice layer is not as thick as first thought. Difficulties have prevented *Galileo* from taking photographs of the fourth of the major satellites, Io, to date but this is planned for late 1997.

VENUS'S TAIL

Planets which have strong magnetic fields, like the Earth and Jupiter, are protected to some extent from the solar wind, the streams of plasma pouring out of the Sun. However, Venus, lacking a magnetic field to deflect these ions, bears the full force of this radiation, resulting in the plasma bombarding the ions in the planet's upper atmosphere. This produces an ion-packed tail which extends outwards, away from the Sun. The existence of such a tail was first identified by NASA's *Pioneer Venus Orbiter* in the 1970s, when the spacecraft detected bursts of energetic particles at a distance of about 70,000 km from the planet. However, the extent of the tail is a surprise. Recent observations from the Solar and Heliospheric Observatory (SOHO) show that the tail stretches out at least 45 million km from Venus.

The spacecraft operates at the L1 libration point, some 1.5 million km from the Earth and during July 1996 it passed through the tail when it was roughly in line with the planet and the Sun. During a period of about five hours the satellite detected three bursts of oxygen and carbon ions, each lasting less than 45 seconds. Marcia Neugebauer, one of the research team, suggests that the spacecraft may have passed through three separate streams within the tail, or that it may have been a single filament flapping in the solar wind. There is a possibility that the tail is a bundle of narrow streams like those possessed by some comets. If this is so, it poses the problem of how such narrow plasma streams, which are unstable and dissipate quickly, can survive over such large distances.

KUIPER BELT FINDS

The Kuiper belt, the region of the solar system beyond the orbit of Neptune, contains thousands of small objects, most no more than a few hundred kilometres in diameter. Because they are so small and at such a great distance from the Sun, the objects appear to observers on Earth as exceedingly faint objects. The belt is thought to be the source of short period comets and so, from an astronomical point of view, these objects are of great importance. Researchers at the University of Arizona in Tucson, taking long exposures with the 100-metre Keck telescope in Hawaii, have analysed the spectrum of one of these objects. The object, known as 1993SC, appears to reflect long infra-red waves more strongly than short ones, a property which suggests the presence of long-chain hydrocarbons, tarry compounds sometimes found in meteorites.

The researchers also found that 1993SC absorbs light in the same infra-red bands as those recorded in the spectra of Pluto and Triton, the large satellite of Neptune. This is believed to be caused by methane ice. If this is the case, it implies that both Pluto and Triton were once members of the Kuiper belt and have changed very little since the solar system was formed.

The idea that some members of the Kuiper belt are covered with organic materials is strengthened by research on members of the 'Centaur' asteroids, a group of objects which lie beyond the orbit of Jupiter. A team at Vanderbilt University in Nashville, Tennessee, found that two of the Centaurs, 5145 Pholus and 1995 GO, were redder than any other asteroid in the solar system, a colour caused by organic compounds and pristine minerals. This suggests that they were until recently members of the Kuiper belt and so not subjected to the heating and collisions with other asteroids that can modify these surfaces. The exact nature of this red material is not known.

ASTEROID OR COMET?

It used to be thought that most asteroids (minor planets) orbited in a 'belt' between the orbits of Mars and Jupiter whilst comets were products of the Oort cloud on the outer edges of the solar system, travelling into the inner solar system when knocked out of the cloud by some disturbing influence. However, it is now accepted that many objects identified as asteroids are actually extinct comets. The case for this has been strengthened by analysis of an unusual object designated 1996PW, a small body some 8–15 km in diameter. It was discovered in August 1996 by the Near Earth Asteroid Tracking Team at the Jet Propulsion Laboratory. The general appearance of the object is asteroidal, with no coma or tail. Analysis of its orbit, however, revealed that it

has an eccentricity of 0.992 and a period of about 5,800 years. The aphelion distance (the point in its orbit when it is farthest away from the Sun) is approximately 645 astronomical units, a distance of about 100,000 million km. Such an aphelion distance is normally connected with the Oort cloud and its comets and this is the first instance in which an object in such an orbit has not been an active comet.

The possibility that asteroidal objects might be present in the Oort cloud was first suggested in 1979. Now Paul Weissman of the Jet Propulsion Laboratory and Harold Levison of Southwest Research Institute calculate that billions of asteroids from the normal asteroid belt have been flung out to the edges of the solar system after gravitational encounters with the main planets, in particular Jupiter. It is thought that these may constitute at least 1 per cent of the objects in the Oort cloud. Calculations show that it is feasible for asteroids to take up an orbit such as that of 1996PW roughly once every five years. Weissman believes that the 1996PW is a genuine asteroid and not a worn-out comet because although a comet from the Oort cloud could end up in such an orbit after about 100 visits to the Sun, during that period it would not have had time to expel all the gasses in its coma.

AGE OF THE UNIVERSE

Recent work to determine the age of the Universe has run up against the problem that the Universe seems to be younger than its oldest stars. Work in the field of cosmology depends on estimates of the distances of stars from the Earth. The apparent brightness of most stars cannot be used because of their great variation in size and absolute brightness. However, a certain class of stars known as Cepheid variables can be used because their absolute brightnesses are intimately connected to the periodicity of brightness changes which take place in the star. Therefore, if the distance of one of the Cepheids can be determined by an independent method, it becomes possible to measure the distance of any galaxy which contains such variables.

The distances of the nearest Cepheids can be calculated using the principle of parallax, by using the diameter of the Earth's orbit round the Sun as a base-line. Researchers at the University of Cape Town have used observations from the Hubble Space Telescope to calculate the distances of 200 Cepheids from the Earth. These stars are further away than previously thought. Clusters of very old stars often contain identifiable Cepheids and the new calculations indicate that these clusters are farther away and that the stars themselves must be more luminous. According to current evolution theories, the stars must be much younger than was thought, and their ages have consequently been reduced from 15 to 11 billion years. At the same time the revised calculations of distances raise the apparent age of the Universe to between 11 and 12 billion years. Although these values may not be absolutely correct, they go some way towards reconciling the apparent discrepancy between the age of the Universe and its oldest stars.

NEW LOCAL GALAXY

The Local Group of galaxies is dominated by the two massive spiral galaxies, our own Milky Way and the Andromeda galaxy. From the Earth the Andromeda galaxy is the brightest object outside the Milky Way and is visible to the naked eye in a dark sky. Other fainter, smaller galaxies in the Local Group, the so-called dwarf galaxies, are satellites to the dominant spiral structures and the number of dwarf galaxies that have been identified has increased so that there are now over 30 known members.

The Local Group provides an opportunity to explore the evolution of galaxies in greater detail than is possible for the more distant objects. The small galaxies, though difficult to locate owing to their extreme faintness, hold the key to questions about galaxy formation and the discovery of a new galaxy is of great interest.

Astronomers from the Royal Greenwich Observatory at Cambridge recently discovered a dwarf galaxy located in the southern constellation of the Antlia galaxy. The galaxy appears to be smooth and devoid of any obvious concentration of stars or clusters. It contains about a million stars in a volume about 5,000 light years across. It is about 3.3 million light years away, located in a region of space previously thought to be devoid of nearby galaxies. This relative isolation is important because it means the galaxy has not been disturbed or distorted by the gravitational pull of the dominant members of the Local Group. Astronomers hope the new discovery will provide them with data about the nature of undisturbed galaxies and the evolution of the Local Group as a whole.

MILKY WAY ANTIMATTER

Data from the Compton Gamma Ray Observatory (GRO) suggests that there is a giant, diffuse cloud of antimatter, measuring about 3,000 light years across, in the Milky Way at a distance of about 25,000 light years from the Earth. A team at Northwestern University used the GRO to scan several parts of the Milky Way in order to measure the energy spectrum of gamma rays. They found that gamma rays with energies of 511,000 electron volts were coming from a plume several degrees west of the centre of the galaxy, in the constellation of Sagittarius. Gamma rays with this energy are produced when an electron and a positron (a particle similar to an electron but having a positive instead of a negative charge, i.e. the electron's antimatter counterpart) collide and annihilate each other. This plume is separate from the large cloud of antimatter near to the centre of the galaxy and in the plane of the galaxy.

Positron-electron annihilation has been recorded in the past from the central region of the galaxy and the presence of positrons has been suspected in the jets of other active galaxies. It is thought that the Milky Way positrons may have emerged from a jet from the core of the galaxy, though if this explanation is correct, a second jet would be expected. Alternatively, the positrons may have been produced by radio-active elements formed from supernovae; this would explain the absence of a second jet on the other side of the galaxy. Whereas gamma rays have been observed for some time emerging from the core of the galaxy, the presence of such a large cloud clear of the galactic plane is a surprise. Another possible explanation is that this hot antimatter jet could be related to massive star formation taking place near the large black hole at the centre of the galaxy.

GROWTH OF SUPERGIANT

In February 1996 a Japanese amateur astronomer observed a rapidly brightening object in Sagittarius and over the following six months a team led by Bengt Gustafason used a telescope at the McDonald Observatory in Texas to log its behaviour. Now known as Sakurai's object, in honour of its discoverer, the star has grown from an object about the size of the Earth when first observed to one with a diameter some 80 times larger that that of the Sun. Initially a hot dwarf with a surface temperature of about 50,000°C, the object has evolved into a yellow supergiant with a surface temperature of a mere 6,000°C. The brightening has occurred because the increase in surface area more than compensates for the drop in temperature.

According to Martin Aslund of Uppsala Observatory in Sweden, this appears to be the fastest case of stellar evolution ever seen. He thinks that the star was once a red giant that started to shrink after running out of fuel. As it approached the white dwarf stage, in which a star is incapable of generating its own heat by nuclear reactions, it will have shrunk under its own gravitational force. The inner core, containing helium, carbon and oxygen, shrinks and generates sufficient heat to start helium burning. This generates more heat and the resulting convection currents move hot material to the surface and hydrogen into the core, where it is consumed. These processes are confirmed by the fivefold decrease in the amount of hydrogen and the fourfold increase in elements such as zinc, strontium and yttrium that have been recorded during the period in which the star has been under observation. In the star's core, the temperature reaches 100 million degrees, hot enough to free neutrons from their nuclei, a process known as the s-process. The onset of these nuclear reactions is responsible for the inflation of the star.

Aslund says that there are about six known born-again giants and claims that about 10 per cent of all stars like the Sun will go through a similar phase towards the end of their lives.

GAMMA RAY BURST PROGRESS

Gamma Ray Bursts (GRBs) were first discovered in the 1960s by the US *Vela* spy satellites designed to register gamma rays from nuclear explosions. GRBs consist of a sudden shower of penetrating photons lasting from a fraction of a second to a little over a minute. Located randomly over the sky, the source has been thought to be outside the Milky Way but it is difficult to record bursts on Earth because at such distances the bursts must emit more energy than a supernova. Pinpointing the location(s) of the source(s) of bursts has also been a problem as satellites could only specify the position of a burst to an accuracy of several degrees.

However, on 28 February 1997 a newly launched satellite, *BeppoSAX*, an Italian-Dutch satellite capable of a hundredfold improvement in positional accuracy, registered a burst from a source in the constellation of Orion. One of the two wide-field cameras saw an X-ray flash simultaneously with the gamma-ray monitor. Eight hours later other instruments on the satellite pinpointed a fading X-ray glow in the same part of the sky. This enabled the location of the source to be pinpointed to within 1 arcminute. Independently, astronomers from the University of Amsterdam announced that a very faint light source within the pinpointed area had faded from view between 28 February and 8 March. If the two events are connected, this will be the first transient optical signal associated with a GRB. Within hours of the 28 February outburst, John Telting used the William Herschel telescope on the Canary Islands to obtain a photograph of the region. Another photograph taken eight days later showed that an object recorded on the first photograph was no longer visible. In addition to the optical observations, the transient event was detected in the infrared but not at radio wavelengths. Two days later strong radio signals were recorded, but at shorter wavelengths emission was not received until 8 May. To gain more data about such events, a system of alerts between observatories has been set up.

Spin Rates in Black Holes

Scientists at the NASA Marshall Space Flight Center in Huntsville, Alabama, researching material lying close to black holes have put forward an explanation for the appearance of high-speed jets from the centres of many galaxies. When a massive star explodes, the material remaining collapses to form a black hole, where the gravitational force is so strong that any material within a certain distance (the event horizon) can never escape. The event horizon is typically only a few tens of kilometres in diameter. If the black hole is spinning, it drags space around with it but it is impossible to measure the spin directly. There is, however, a minimum distance at which matter can orbit a black hole without being drawn into the hole. This distance is closely related to the spin rate; the faster the black hole spins, the smaller is this distance.

Research centred on five objects in our galaxy thought to harbour black holes. Each of these objects has a companion star, the material from

which is being ripped away into the black hole through an accretion disc. This is so hot that it emits X-rays and the matter at the inner edge of the disc must be in the last stable orbit. The research team set up a computer model to study the emission of the X-ray spectrum in relation to the size of the accretion disc. With three of the objects, the inner edge of the accretion disc was well away from the event horizon and it was concluded that the black holes were spinning very slowly. In the other two cases, the inner edge of the disc almost grazes the event horizon and it is suggested that the black holes are spinning at close to the maximum rate permitted by the laws of physics. Studies of the objects have revealed the presence of jets of energetic particles shooting out from the poles. This supports the theory that jets associated with some quasars are in some way energized by the dynamo of a fast-spinning black hole at their centre.

Hydrogen Dims Hot Stars

Scientists at IBM claim to have solved a problem that has puzzled astronomers for over 75 years. In 1920 it was noticed that light from very hot stars dimmed at certain wavelengths. The cause was put down to unknown interstellar material absorbing the light but, despite improvements in equipment and increased knowledge, no link between the recorded dimming and any known interstellar molecules has since been found.

The missing wavelengths are known as the diffuse interstellar bands (DIBs) and over a spectrum ranging from 420 to 1300 nanometres more than 230 of these bands have been identified. James Glownia and Peter Sorokin of IBM tried to match the bands with such molecules as chlorophyll, fullerenes and freeze-dried bacteria, but none matched the DIB pattern in more than a few places. The possibility that molecular hydrogen, the commonest compound in space, might be the substance responsible for the dimming had been dismissed because hydrogen is not known to absorb light at any of the DIB wavelengths. However, research has shown that in unusual conditions a DIB photon can be absorbed as one of a pair of photons; if two photons hit the hydrogen molecule at the same time, their combined energy is exactly that needed to put one of its electrons into an excited state.

Glownia and Sorokin have calculated that it is theoretically possible to create a similar supply of trapped photons inside a cloud of molecular hydrogen if the cloud is between three and 30 light years from a hot young star. Most of the star's photons would pass straight through the cloud but some ultraviolet photons with wavelengths close to one of the DIBs would be scattered and virtually trapped within the cloud. This would produce the conditions enabling the hydrogen molecule to be excited.

SNOWBALLS FROM SPACE

In the late 1980s Louis Frank of the University of Iowa suggested that the Earth was continually being pelted by a 'gentle cosmic rain' containing simple organic compounds which were responsible for the development of life on our planet. This controversial theory was rejected at the time but new evidence suggests that Frank was right and that there is a continual stream of objects entering the Earth's upper atmosphere.

Satellite data released by NASA reveals that the Earth is bombarded by five and 30 icy objects every minute. One such object passed over Britain in September 1996. It was the size of a house and broke up more than 8,000 km above the Earth's surface. Generally these objects are melted by atmospheric friction and disintegrate at heights between 1,000 and 20,000 km, presenting no threat to astronauts or people on the Earth.

The source of the objects is a mystery. Cameras on board NASA's *Polar* spacecraft show that the objects are not condensing within our atmosphere and are possibly from the outer regions of the solar system. What is surprising is the size and frequency of the objects.

THE SUDBURY FEATURE

The extraordinary deposits of nickel ore at Sudbury, Ontario, had no satisfactory explanation until it was recognized that the feature was the remnants of an impact crater caused when an asteroid hit the area some 1.8 billion years ago, producing a crater about 140 km in diameter. However, this still left some of the geological features in the region unexplained. Recently John Spray of the University of New Brunswick examined the rocks beneath the crater in places where these rocks were exposed. He recognized a vein of distinctive glassy rock called pseudotachylyte, a type familiar from work on earthquakes.

With large earthquakes where there is slip along a fault up to a few metres, the heat generated by friction is sufficient to melt the adjacent rock to a depth of a few centimetres, forming pseudotachylyte. The extent of the pseudotachylyte in these cases is limited by the fact that the sliding rocks are pinned at both ends. At Sudbury, this glassy rock was found to be a kilometre thick and 45 kilometres wide, indicating that it was formed under drastically different conditions. Spray calculated that if large rocks slipped by hundreds of metres along an unpinned 'superfault', the friction was capable of melting a layer of rock about a kilometre thick in just a minute or two.

Spray believes that a superfault formed a few moments after the impact of the asteroid. The impact itself would have produced a massive steep-walled bowl-shaped crater with superfaults in the unstable walls. The crater would have been gravitationally unstable because of its size and the sides of the wall would have collapsed. Huge blocks of rock would have moved suddenly by hundreds of metres, heating the rock drastically enough to produce such a thick layer of pseudotachylyte.

MASS EXTINCTION THEORIES

The theory that the mass extinction of species, possibly including the dinosaurs, at the end of the Cretaceous period, 65 million years ago, was caused by a huge asteroid hitting the Earth in the Yucatán peninsula in Mexico is familiar to most people. Less well-known is that a more devastating extinction took place at the end of the Permian period, about 250 million years ago, which wiped out over 90 per cent of hard-shelled marine animals.

A number of theories have been advanced to explain the Permian extinction, such as massive volcanic eruptions or the depletion of oxygen in the oceans, but recent discoveries of shocked quartz, significant evidence of an asteroid impact at the end of the Cretaceous period, suggest that a similar impact occurred at the end of the Permian period.

Gregory Retallack of the University of Oregon in Eugene and colleagues have identified fractures in tiny quartz crystals found in rocks which existed at the end of the Permian period. They claim that this fracturing could only have been caused by an impact of a comet or asteroid. One of the team, David Krinsley, noticed that there was a sharp change in carbon isotope levels in rocks formed at the time of the Permian extinction, suggesting a marked drop in biodiversity lasting thousands of years. The shocked quartz that contained Krinsley's unusual abnormality came from mountains near Sydney. The shocked quartz was also found in rocks from the Transantarctic Mountains in Victoria Land, Antarctica. The researchers think that the shocked quartz is the result of an impact in an area covering south-east Australia and Antarctica, which at that time were joined. The impact might have triggered antipodal eruptions, i.e. eruptions at points diametrically on the opposite side of the Earth, as eruptions in Siberia are thought to have contributed to the Permian extinction. Certainly the massive volcanism which occurred in India at the end of the Cretaceous period was diametrically opposite the Yucatán impact. This theory about the cause of the Permian extinction is not widely accepted as yet but it has stimulated further research.

It is now generally accepted that the Cretaceous period ended at the time of the Yucatán impact some 65 million years ago, but it would appear that the Cretaceous may have started with a similar event. Christian Koeberl of the University of Vienna has studied rocks and formations around a huge crater discovered three years ago near the border between Botswana and South Africa. The feature, known as the Morokweng crater, is about 145 million years old, a date corresponding to the end of the Jurassic period and the start of the Cretaceous. The area contains a circular patch of dense rock and samples show an impact melt layer with a diameter of at least 75 km. About 3 per cent of the material in this layer has a meteoritic origin. Within the layer are crystals of zirconium silicate, which must have formed at the time of the impact. These have trapped the decay products of radioactive lead and plutonium, studies of which suggest an age for the rock of 144.7 to 147.7 million years.

The fossil record and other evidence indicate that about 20 per cent of all species were wiped out 145 million years ago. The impact may have caused this extinction through its dramatic effect on the climate, ejecting debris into the atmosphere and blocking out the Sun's light.

SPONGES AND EVOLUTION

Sponges have the simplest body stucture of all multicelled animals and therefore it has been assumed that they would have appeared very early in the history of evolution. However, the earliest undisputed sponge fossils have been dated to the time of the Cambrian explosion, which occurred after the era of the first animals that lived, the fragile, soft-bodied Ediacaran fauna, some 560 to 543 million years ago. Now a new discovery of sponge fossils in Mongolia has shown that sponges were in fact the earliest animals.

Martin Brasier and colleagues of Oxford University have discovered evidence of the existence of fossils in south-western Mongolia in rocks estimated to be at least 544 million years old. Measurements of carbon and strontium isotopes show that the rocks date back to the late Ediacaran time. Brasier found many spicules in chert, a rock rich in quartz which is capable of preserving very fine structures. The spicules are microscopic, spiked structures made of silica which stiffened the sponges. Brasier found a variety of spicules with shapes similar to modern sponges, showing conclusively that sponges existed early in the evolutionary timescale. He thinks that, because of the variety, sponges must have an even earlier record but no evidence of this has been preserved.

These fossil discoveries have thrown new light on evolution during the Ediacaran and Cambrian times. Brasier thinks that the Cambrian explosion took place over a longer period than previously thought and that there is a merging of the two periods. Although these newly identified fossils date to the Ediacaran time, the spicules come from water that was about 50–100 metres deep and rich in nutrients, whereas the Ediacaran fossils may have come from nutrient-poor, shallow water which may not have preserved spicules or the hard shells that mark the start of the Cambrian explosion. He also suggests that the fossils exist in Mongolia because continental drift made the region sink before rising waters covered the other regions.

EARLY BIRDS

How birds began to fly has puzzled scientists for over a century. Until recently the only evidence was the fossils of *Archaeopteryx*. *Archaeopteryx* lived about 150 million years ago and, apart from having

feathers, strongly resembled a type of dinosaur called theropods. It had long front limbs and because of the asymmetric shape of its feathers it is thought that it flew, although not in the manner of modern birds.

Chinese palaeontologists claim to have discovered a close relative of the *Archaeopteryx*. Named *Proarchaeopteryx robusta* by Ji Qiang, curator of the Geological Museum of China in Beijing, the turkey-sized fossil was found in lake-bed deposits in Liaoning province, a region which has provided many fossils of early birds. The fossil has feathered imprints on its tail. The feathers are symmetrical, making them more primitive than those of *Archaeopteryx*. It has much stronger legs and lighter arms although the general morphology of its hands and arms are very similar to those of *Archaeopteryx*. It is doubtful, however, that it could have flown. It was originally thought that feathers ran down its back but these are now thought to have been bristle-like filaments.

One theory of bird evolution is that birds evolved from small, fast-running theropods; another theory is that they developed from another type of dinosaur which lived in trees and then started to glide. This new find seems to strengthen the case for the former theory, except that there is some doubt about whether the tail feathers actually belonged to the bird. They are in the right position but not in the right direction to be attached to the tail. They could have been displaced after death but there is the possibility that they belonged to another animal. Also, there is some evidence that the rocks containing the fossil are younger than those that yielded *Archaeopteryx*. This aspect is currently being investigated.

THE FIRST SONGBIRDS

Studies of the fossils in the Tingamurra sediments some 160 km north-east of Brisbane, Australia, indicate that songbirds evolved in Australia more than 50 million years ago, about 2.5 million years before the oldest previously known songbird fossils, found in France and dating from the early Miocene period.

Walter Boles of the Australian Museum in Sydney, writing in a recent issue of *Emu*, the journal of the Royal Australasian Ornithologists Union, claims that the fossils include two ankle bones from a bird the size of a finch and part of the wing bone from a bird roughly the size of a thrush. Each fossil fragment has the characteristic knobs and bumps expected from a songbird of that kind but there is insufficient evidence to say what the bird looked like. However, it is thought that the bird was well advanced down the songbird line.

Potassium-argon dating indicates that the fossils are 54.6 million years old. This suggests that, far from having a derivative bird fauna, Australia was the country where songbirds first evolved. Boles thinks that just after the dinosaurs became extinct, birds such as pigeons, parrots and geese evolved in the southern hemisphere, rather than in the northern hemisphere. Fossils of these species have not been found with ages comparable to those of these songbirds.

The Tingamurra sediments are unique in Australia and cover a small area. In addition to the songbird fossils, they have yielded Australia's oldest frog, bat, marsupial and salamander, animals not previously thought to exist in the country. The local farmer allows access for digging only once a year so more surprises could emerge from the deposits. It is thought that the farm was once a billabong in which the fossils were preserved by highly alkaline water.

Storrs Olson of the Smithsonian Institution in Washington DC says that the discovery shows that all the bird groups existing today have evolved rapidly during the past 50 million years and that the appearance of birds in the northern hemisphere is a relatively recent event.

Dinosaur Museum

The discovery of dinosaur eggs would create little interest of itself but the discovery of thousands of eggs in one small location has produced a stir in palaeontological circles. An amateur palaeontologist, Alain Cabot, has discovered thousands of dinosaur eggs at a site near the town of Mèze in southern France. He found the first eggs towards the end of 1995 and since then he and a team of palaeontologists from the Institute of Evolutionary Science in nearby Montpellier have located thousands of nests, each nest containing between five and 15 eggs. Their ages lie between 71 and 65 million years, at which time the region was a tropical plain crossed by rivers. At the moment it is not clear which species of dinosaurs laid the eggs, but so far six different types of egg have been identified and it is hoped that the remains of unhatched foetuses will be found to enable researchers to identify the species of dinosaurs which lived in the area.

Research continues at the site, which is to become an open-air museum, as this is thought to be the only way to preserve and protect the nests. It will be the only museum of its kind in Europe.

Human Evolution

Fossils recently discovered at Atapuerca in northern Spain are challenging theories about the evolution of modern man from the early hominids. The current theory is that two early species of hominid, *H. habilis* and *H. rudolfensis* evolved into *H. erectus* and *H. ergaster*, and that during the period when *H. erectus* slipped into evolutionary obscurity in Asia, *H. ergaster* evolved into *H. heidelbergensis*, the hominid found at various locations in Africa and Europe and believed to be the common ancestor of the Neanderthals and of modern humans. However, the team led by José Bermúdez de Castro of the Museum of Natural Sciences in Madrid claims that a new species of human, *H. antecessor*, gave rise to *H. heidelbergensis*, and is therefore the last common ancestor of Neanderthals and of modern humans.

The new theory is based on studies of an incomplete set of facial bones of an 11-year-old child, the centre of whose face, it is claimed, is completely modern, being relatively flat compared to more primitive species. The lower and upper parts of the face, however, look primitive, and objections have also been raised that comparing adults with children is potentially misleading because the child's appearance might be just a passing phase in its development. Consequently, further evidence will be needed before the theory is fully accepted by anthropologists.

Early Toolmakers

Until recently the oldest records of the use of tools by early man were at sites in the Olduvai Gorge in Tanzania and Koobi Fora, Kenya. At these sites fossilized bones of the genus *Homo* were found with tools, estimated to be about 1.8 million years old. Now a jawbone and 20 stone tools have been found at a site in Ethiopia with an estimated age of 2.3 million years. William Kimbal, a palaeoanthropologist from the Institute of Human Origins in Berkeley, California, claims that the jawbone came from a member of the genus *Homo* and said that most of the tools were fist-sized river cobbles that had been chipped to a sharp edge, presumably to be used for chopping. Stone flakes were also present. Kimbel is unsure whether the tools were used by the owner of the jawbone but he has identified two stone tools which fitted exactly together, showing that they were made at the site rather than being deposited there by flowing water.

Kimbel and colleagues started exploring the Hadar region of Ethiopia in 1994 in the hope of throwing light on the gap in the fossil record of human evolution between two and three million years ago. On the first day two pieces of jawbone were found and Kimbel said that when they were put together it was immediately apparent that they were not from a primitive *Australopithecus* but something more closely related to modern man. As yet they have not been able to specify whether it belongs to *Homo habilis* or *H. rudolfensis*. Fortunately the find was located about 80 cm beneath a layer of volcanic ash, laser analysis of which has shown a date of 2.33 million years. The initial excavation covered only about 2 square metres but the scientists are expanding the excavation in the hope that they can find cut marks on bone, which would show that the tools were used at the site.

Man in South America

It used to be thought that man arrived in South America about 11,500 years ago but recent work by anthropologists shows that this date may be as much as 1,000 years too late. The revised date affects current ideas of how man spread over the American continent in general. Data from remains collected 20 years ago at a site in Chile known as Monte Verde indicated that wooden tools, bone and charcoal had a radio-carbon date of about 12,500 years, but the discoverer of the remains, Tom Dillehay, has only recently convinced colleagues that the dating is correct.

Migration into the American continent started during the last Ice Age when man crossed what is now the Bering Strait and then was a dry tundra known as Beringia. The route south would have been blocked by glaciers but eventually routes near the coast and possibly through the interior would have been found. However, it is not certain when this took place. Until recently the oldest accepted date for sites in Alaska was 12,000 years ago but between this date and 11,200 years ago nothing is known. After this time the Clovis people had colonized much of North America. If, as most anthropologists have assumed, the Clovis people were the first to colonize the Americas, no settlements should have been found in South America until much later. It was assumed that it would take about 1,000 years for migrants to cover the distance from Alaska to Chile. If sites in Chile have approximately the same age as those in Alaska, the accepted theory must be incorrect. Research is hampered by the fact that since the Ice Age the sea-level has risen nearly 100 metres so it is possible that evidence of settlements which would clarify understanding is covered by the sea.

ELVES AND SPRITES

Flashes in the upper atmosphere above thunder-storms were studied by NASA aircraft a few years ago and given the name 'sprites'. Californian scientists have since identified a second type of light flash occurring even higher in the strato-sphere. These flashes, called 'elves', appear at altitudes of about 90 km and are rings of light that move outwards, like ripples on a pond. The first images of this phenomenon were recorded a year ago, but as they last less than a thousandth of a second, it was difficult to obtain a detailed study.

In 1996 teams at Stanford University in Cali-fornia and Lockheed-Martin Research Laboratory in Palo Alto developed a detector consisting of ten sensitive photomultipliers, each pointing at a different part of the sky. Each detector was capable of recording flashes of light as short as 30 millionths of a second. The instrument was located at Yucca Ridge in Colorado, where the teams were able to track thunderstorms more than 600 km away. It was found that an elf formed about 150 microseconds after a lightning flash and that after a short delay another flash would appear, this second flash being fainter but longer lived. The instrument recorded that the elf expanded rapidly for about 220 micro-seconds, producing a ring of light more than 230 km in diameter.

The researchers believe that an elf is formed by a burst of radio-waves generated by the lightning flash. The intense electric field produced by the radio pulse as it passes through the ionosphere accelerates electrons which then collide with nitrogen molecules, producing a red light. This explanation is not accepted by Robert Roussel-

Dupre of the Los Alamos National Laboratory in New Mexico. He believes that the radio pulse is the real power source. Research continues.

BIRD MIGRATION

Birds migrate using the same routes each year, and differing routes are often taken by different types of birds. Birds have two navigation systems, one relying on the positions of the stars and the other on the Earth's magnetic field. It was thought that just one of these systems was enough for a systematic migration but recent work has shown that, at least in the case of garden warblers, both systems are required.

Wolfgang Wiltschko, a zoologist at Goethe University in Frankfurt, has shown that celestial rotation provides only a north-south axis but any deviation from that axis is coded with respect to the Earth's magnetic field. As autumn approaches, garden warblers from central Europe fly in a south-west direction to the Iberian peninsula; from there they fly south to Sierra Leone and then south-east towards South Africa. It is thought that although the birds are born with this instinct, it is necessary for them to relate it to an external reference system. To investigate this, two groups of chicks were exposed to an artificial sky with 16 fake stars rotating daily to imitate the real motion. One group was allowed to experience the Earth's magnetic field but the other was kept free of the field by neutralizing it with magnetic coils. When the birds were ready for migration in mid-August, the birds exposed to the stars and the Earth's magnetic field flew off in the expected south-west direction, but the other group oriented themselves virtually due south, which would have taken them over the Alps and the Central Sahara, a far more difficult journey. From this, it would appear that the birds need both the night sky and the magnetic field for a successful migration.

EARTHWORMS UNDER THREAT

During the last few decades native British earth-worms have been under attack from worms im-ported from overseas. The flatworm from New Zealand, *Artioposthia trianulata*, has spread through-out southern Scotland; the Australian flatworm, *Caenoplana alba*, seems to be more prevalent in southern England. The favourite food of these flatworms is the local earthworm. They can devour an earthworm in half an hour by secreting enzymes onto the worm and then sucking up the resulting soup. The decline in the earthworm population creates problems in fertilizing and aerating the soil, which flatworms do not do. It may also have an effect on the population of other wildlife, such as blackbirds and hedgehogs which rely heavily on earthworms for their food.

Now a third species of flatworm has been found, in Edinburgh; it is a completely new species. Hugh Jones of the University of Manchester thinks that it could have come from New Zealand because of its similarities with other known species. His studies reveal that this new species is just as voracious for earthworms as the other species and that it will pose an additional threat to earthworms should it become more widespread; at the moment only two specimens have been found and these are being kept in controlled conditions.

The two specimens were discovered in a garden west of Edinburgh in the summer of 1996 by Brian Gerard, a recently retired expert on worms at the Scottish Agricultural College in Edinburgh. He fed them on earthworms in a bed of moss. Taxonomists from Australia and New Zealand were unable to recognize the species. When one of the specimens died, Gerard killed the other and sent it to Jones for further study. Gerard still has an egg pouch, which he hopes may hatch and provide more information. He is also surveying the area where the new flatworms were originally found to see if further specimens can be located. Gerard thinks that this third species must be eradicated as quickly as possible. He commented that it is important to avoid making the same mistake as with New Zealand flatworms, when neither the Government nor anyone else did anything to control the spread of them until it was too late.

Mongooses Beat Snake Venom

It has always been thought that mongooses kill snakes solely by their ability to move quickly and avoid the lethal bite of the snake but studies show that mongooses are also immune to snake venom.

Sara Fuchs of the Immunology Department at the Weizmann Institute in Israel specializes in the physiology of the junctions between nerves and muscles. In a normal snake venom, the active compound, alpha-neurotoxin, operates by attaching itself to acetylcholine receptor molecules on the surface of muscle cells. The purpose of these receptors is to receive messages from nerves instructing them to relax or contract. The alpha-neurotoxin blocks the messages, thereby paralysing and then killing the victim. The shape of the receptor molecules in the mongoose makes it impossible for snake venom to attach itself to them. Consequently, the receptors can still transfer messages from the nerves to the muscles and are therefore immune to the venom. A similar process in snakes prevents them being poisoned by their own venom.

Fuchs is investigating other snake toxins to see if mongooses and snakes are protected from the effects by similar mechanisms. The ultimate aim of the study is to produce new anti-venom drugs which are more efficient and safer to use than the current drugs.

Synthetic Sea Shells

The swirls and spirals on sea shells are regarded as things of beauty but until recently have defied explanation. Creatures extract the calcium carbonate dissolved in sea water and then cement the mineral together with organic polymers such as proteins, polysaccharides on the membranes of their cells. Although the polymers act as templates, this does not explain how the resulting shells develop with logarithmic and Archimedean spirals.

A team from the University of Toronto, led by Geoffrey Ozin, working with colleagues from Imagetek Analytical Imaging, have recently created a random collection of tiny shells on a synthetic beach. They used tetraethyl silicate in place of calcium carbonate and a soap-like surfactant called cetyltrimethylammonium chloride in place of the organic polymers. These were mixed in water and a little hydrochloric acid to catalyse the reaction. After a week, shell-like structures were identified. Ozin thinks that each shell starts life as a hexagonalcylindrical liquid crystal which then evolves into a spiral or gyroid form as the silicate-based molecules are cemented together with varying degrees of curvature. Scanning electron micrographs of the shells were taken as they formed. The results showed many spirals and structures where two spirals are joined base to base. The images also showed corrugated ridges, channels and protuberances which are common features of natural shells. The work is of importance because it opens up the possibility of creating chemicals with specific rather than random shapes, with applications in fields such as catalysis, the separation of bacterial cells for analysis, and increasing the compatibility of surgical implants.

New 'Diamond'

The element carbon exists in graphite and diamond forms. Graphite is soft and its molecules consist of flat planes of carbon atoms, making it ideal for applications such as lubrication. Diamond, however, has a three-dimensional structure and is one of the hardest minerals known. Recently Benjamin Dorfman, a materials chemist at the Atomic Scale Design in New York, produced a new carbon-based compound with a structure that is a cross between that of graphite and diamond. It has properties which could make it one of the materials of the future.

Called Quasam, this new material has a molecular structure in which flat planes of carbon, as in graphite, are joined together in a three-dimensional lattice similar to that of diamond but consisting of silicon and oxygen atoms. It has a specific gravity of between 1.35 and 1.65, less than half that of diamond, but its hardness is about the bottom of the range for diamond. The planes of carbon are very small and are held rigidly in place by the network of silicon and oxygen atoms; this prevents sliding of the carbon planes. Pure quasam is an electrical insulator but because its overall structure can incorporate within its lattice up to 40 per cent by volume of metals such as iron and nickel, it should also be a good conductor. Quasam is highly resistant to chemical attack. It has virtually unchanging mechanical properties and a constant coefficient of thermal expansion up to 400°C.

Dorfman claims the new material to be the lightest hard substance known. It has potential uses in protective coatings, microscopic devices and small medical implants, as well as the more obvious applications in the aero and space industries.

Periods of Gestation or Incubation

The table shows approximate periods of gestation or incubation for some common animals and birds. In some cases the periods may vary and where doubt arises professional advice should be sought.

Species	Shortest period (days)	Usual period (days)	Longest period (days)
Human	240	273	313
Horse	305	336	340
Cow	273	280	294
Goat	147	151	155
Sheep	140	147–50	160
Pig	109	112	125
Dog	55	63	70
Cat	53	56	63
Rabbit	30	32	35
Goose	28	30	32
Turkey	25	28	28
Duck	28	28	32
Chicken	20	21	22
Pigeon	17	18	19
Canary	12	14	14
Guinea Pig	63	–	70
Rat	21	–	24
Mouse	18	–	19
Elephant		21–22 months	
Zebra		56 weeks	
Camel		45 weeks	

Theatre

In 1997 it looked as though British dominance of the musical was coming to an end. Neither Cameron Mackintosh nor Andrew Lloyd-Webber produced a major new work in London. Lloyd-Webber's *Whistle Down The Wind* made a swift, unsatisfactory appearance in Washington only, and later he announced that the Really Useful Company had made a £10 million loss this year. *Sunset Boulevard*, expected to be as successful as Lloyd-Webber's previous musicals, never appealed in the same way and was dogged by wrangles with its leading ladies. His musings that the high-tech blockbuster might have reached the end of its lifespan were stoutly contradicted by Mackintosh, who believes the crisis to be within the Lloyd-Webber organization and not general. In autumn 1996 Mackintosh reopened a reworked version of Boublil and Schönberg's *Martin Guerre* and although it is clearly not the huge hit of its predecessors *Les Misérables* and *Miss Saigon*, Mackintosh insists that five future productions world-wide are planned.

Signs that Broadway might be seizing the initiative back from London included the success of *Rent* in New York, a rock tragedy based on Puccini's *La bohème* which will open in London in 1998. *Beauty and the Beast*, a stage version of the Disney film and at £10 million London's most expensive musical ever, opened at the Dominion. The musical's lavish technical demands required the back wall of the theatre to be moved to house the necessary stage machinery, which needed a crew of 69 to operate it. The Disney organization plans further theatre versions of their films. Even the revivals were a success story for the Americans, especially *Damn Yankees*, the 1955 baseball musical which came into London in an American production recreating Bob Fosse's original choreography, with Jerry Lewis wearing the horns as the devil. *Smokey Joe's Café* was a more routine but popular trot through a non-stop medley of 1950s Americana.

Mackintosh was responsible for one small-scale new musical at the Donmar Warehouse. Called *The Fix*, it rummaged in the nauseous underbelly of American politics but was neither sharp enough to be satirical nor substantial enough to be taken seriously. More admired was the slick, powerful production by the Donmar's artistic director Sam Mendes. Mackintosh also provided some of the funds for the National Theatre's revival of *Lady in the Dark*, an obscure Hart/Ira Gershwin/Weill musical set in the 1940s with the unusual subject matter of therapy, Freud and the unconscious. It offered Maria Friedman the opportunity to shine in the leading role of a woman editor who cannot decide who she should marry. Elsewhere there were disasters; above all *Always*, a horribly gooey musical based on the love story of Edward VIII and Wallis Simpson which was popularly known as 'Wallis and Vomit'. *The Goodbye Girl*, based on the Neil Simon play of the same name and starring Gary Wilmot, waved farewell sooner than it would have liked.

The most enjoyable musical of the year, however, was a revival of a revival. Richard Eyre, who famously saved the National Theatre's financial bacon with his production of *Guys and Dolls* in the early 1980s, returned to Runyon/Loesser/Swerling/Burrows' great musical for his final year as artistic director. If it was a treat for him, it was also a treat for audiences, who were just as ecstatic about the cast of Imelda Staunton, Joanna Riding, Henry Goodman and Clarke Peters as they had been about the original cast. Led by Clive Rowe, 'Sit Down You're Rockin' the Boat' achieved the same number of rousing encores, and demand was so great for tickets that after a short run over Christmas 1996, the production returned later in the new year.

Lottery Effect

The National Lottery continued to have an effect, extending its remit to include the development of new audiences, participation in the arts, new work, work for young people, and training or professional development. Sadlers Wells Theatre was demolished and is to be redeveloped, mainly with lottery money. The National was wrapped in scaffolding as it went ahead with its plans to create a more impressive entrance and to make more of its riverside site. Essential money was found for the Royal Exchange company in Manchester, whose theatre was severely damaged by the bomb in June 1996. The Royal Court Theatre was closed for a £21 million overhaul, including the building of a restaurant stretching under Sloane Square. During the closure the company has occupied two West End theatres: the Duke of York's and the Ambassadors. The Duke of York's was thoroughly brutalized, the chandeliers and carpets removed in keeping with the plays produced within. The Ambassadors was converted into two spaces, one on stage and the other in the circle, although because of noise problems it was impossible for both theatres to be used simultaneously. Beneath the circle, the old stalls was converted into a bar with lopsided sofas and armchairs to cope with the sloping floor. Few productions at either theatre were conventionally staged. In summer 1997, the company's artistic director Stephen Daldry announced that he would be leaving in autumn 1998, after he had seen the company back into its old home, for a career as a producer and director of films. His successor will be Ian Rickson, an inhouse appointment, whose production of *The Weir* was one of the highlights of the year.

Much heralded was the opening of the Peter Hall Company at the Old Vic, a theatre which has struggled to find a role for itself since the departure of the National Theatre in the 1970s. Sir Peter was the founder of the Royal Shakespeare Company and the second artistic director of the National Theatre. Since leaving the National, he has worked on an *ad hoc* basis in the West End, with productions like *School for Wives* with Eric Sykes and Peter Bowles, and *A Streetcar named Desire* with Jessica Lange. David Mirvish, co-owner with his father of the Old Vic, offered Hall the opportunity to set up his own company again, without any of the bureaucracy of the National or the RSC. The company was given £700,000 by Mirvish, plus a rent-free theatre and staff. Unusually for these days, Hall set up a resident company of actors, including Felicity Kendal, Alan Howard, Michael Pennington and Denis Quilley and newcomers Victoria Hamilton and Dominic West, who signed up for a year. All productions took place within the same blue box set designed by John Gunter. It was hoped that audiences would be intrigued enough to come back and see the same names in different roles, as in the old days of repertory. Classics were performed from Tuesday to Saturday and new plays, with freshly recruited casts, on Sundays and Mondays, under the auspices of Dominic Dromgoole who made his name at the Bush.

To begin with, the repertoire was left sufficiently flexible for unsuccessful productions to be dropped and popular ones to be extended or for new plays to be transferred from their Sunday, Monday slot. However, the need for audiences to plan ahead meant that this flexibility had to be abandoned. The season opened with *Waste*, Harley Granville-Barker's neglected play about political ambition, with Michael Pennington as the politician whose career is ruined by an affair. The season was hailed by critics, who were delighted with Hall's courage in setting up such a company in the West End and with an ambitious repertoire that included *Waiting for Godot* (Hall returning to the play with which he made his name, creating a *cause célèbre* with the English première at the Arts Theatre in 1956), *The Provok'd Wife*, *The Seagull*, Caryl Churchill's *Cloud Nine*, David Rabe's *Hurlyburly*, and new plays by Sebastian Barry and Samuel Adamson. The perils of trying to run such a company without Arts Council subsidy became obvious, however, when David Mirvish revealed in June 1997, four months after the venture began, that he was already £1 million out of pocket. In August he announced that not only would the company have to move out in December 1997, but that he and his father intended to sell the Old Vic and retrench in Toronto. This development also threatens the National Theatre Studio where many young writers have emerged over the years. This is housed in a building next door to the Old Vic and also owned by the Mirvishes, who have allowed the Studio to stay there rent-free.

New Plays

This was a year of extraordinary vitality in new writing. Such energy has not been seen since the 1950s, although whether the plays have the same durability remains to be seen. David Hare celebrated his 50th birthday with a new play called *Amy's View* at the National Theatre and with a national tour and revival in the West End of his previous play *Skylight*, now starring Bill Nighy and Stella Gonet. *Amy's View* is a striking defence of theatre, borrowing its Home Counties, drawing-room setting from West End plays of the 1950s. In Richard Eyre's scrupulous production, Judi Dench played Esme, a larger-than-life, sometimes monstrous, actress of the old school, who comes into conflict with her son-in-law Dominic, a cultural pundit who cannot see the point of theatre in an age of film. Torn between the two is Amy, played by Samantha Bond (who looks remarkably like a young Dench) whose 'view' is her faith in love and understanding. It is only with her death that Esme and Dominic begin to understand each other. The play stretches over 15 years and Dench fascinatingly changes, relishing all facets of the character as her comfortable existence is blown apart. There are times when Hare appears to have written a piece of media punditry himself, but there is no doubt that the National's production will long be remembered for Dench's magnificent performance.

Another major opening was that of *Ashes to Ashes* by Harold Pinter in a Royal Court production at the Ambassadors directed by Pinter himself. The cast included Stephen Rea and Lindsay Duncan, an actress whose cool, tense beauty is ideally suited to Pinter and who went on to appear as Ruth in a revival of *The Homecoming* at the National. In an overwhelmingly beige room Rea's Devlin questions Duncan's Rebecca about her relationship with her previous lover with whom she used to engage in sado-masochistic rituals. Exploring links between sexuality and politics, the play also contains echoes of the Holocaust as Rebecca describes visits to a strange factory where the workers were so badly treated they were deprived even of toilets, and a dream she had of babies being torn away from their mothers and of crowds of people being shepherded into the sea in Dorset. Once again Pinter is trying to shake English complacency that such things could not happen here. He provoked, as usual, a mixed reaction; some were quick to claim the play as a masterpiece, while others felt that even an hour was too long for Pinter's heavily weighted, trance-like dialogue.

There was no doubt about the comedy of the year, although the playwright claimed that she thought she had written a tragedy when she collected her Evening Standard award. In autumn 1996, *Art* opened at Wyndhams Theatre, with Tom Courtenay, Albert Finney and Ken Stott in the cast and its producer, Sean Connery, in the audience. The play had already been performed all over Europe and its French author, Yasmina Reza, had already won a Molière, the French equivalent of an Olivier. The play concerns the deceptions of friendship, particularly male friendship, as revealed by the purchase of an almost completely white painting for a large sum of money by a would-be aesthete. His action is condemned by the more conservative of a trio of friends, who finds it hard to stay friends with anybody capable of such folly. The much put-upon third member of the group attempts to hold the trio together. The London production of *Art* provoked controversy, as supporters of modern art felt that the play was trying to strike a blow for philistinism in its ridicule of the white painting. The argument raged in the newspapers, most people feeling that the play was about friendship rather than a condemnation of art and that it was the English audiences who were to blame in their enthusiastic desire to seize every opportunity to laugh at the absurdity of a pure white painting.

Another crowd-puller in the West End, transferred from Nottingham Playhouse, was Ben Elton's *Popcorn*, his dramatization of his novel in which he takes issue with the multi-murder blockbusters that pour out of Hollywood in which the violence is supposed to be sexy and the sex inevitably gets violent. In *Popcorn* the Oscar-winning evening of a Hollywood director is turned into a nightmare when the two Mall murderers, who claim they have been inspired by his work, break into his luxurious home. Elton's attempt to create an old-fashioned farce with the moral message that we are all responsible for the entertainment that reaches our screens was popular with a young audience.

An unexpected hit came from the Royal Shakespeare Company. Peter Whelan's *The Herbal Bed* was based on the very little that is known about Shakespeare's daughter Susannah. She was married to the highly respected physician John Hall and was accused of committing adultery with a local haberdasher by her husband's former apprentice John Lane, who she sued for slander. Their house, Hall's Croft, where Whelan got the inspiration for his play, can be visited in Stratford today. Whelan creates a gripping love story which explodes into a nail-biting courtroom drama as Susannah's moral equivocation comes face-to-face with the Vicar-General's moral absolutism. The play first appeared in the Swan in Stratford, transferred to the Pit in November 1996 and then to the West End, where it settled in at the Duchess Theatre for a long run and won the lucrative Lloyds Private Banking award for 1996. There were other plays in the West End based on the lives of real people: Stephen Churchett's *Tom and Clem* about Tom Driberg and Clem Attlee at Potsdam 1945; Pam Gems' play about Marlene Dietrich, *Marlene*, with Sian Phillips as the diva; and the short-lived *Master Class*, by Terrence McNally, about Maria Callas.

At the National, Stephen Poliakoff followed up the success of *Sweet Panic* with *Blinded by the Sun*, in which he pursued his fascination with science and examined the world of pure research in 1990s Britain having to confront a world of press conferences, soundbites and dedication to market values. In the Cottesloe Frances de la Tour played the scientist, a creative genius who refuses to explain what she is investigating; Douglas Hodge, the nerd-like head of department who makes a living out of writing sceptical books about science; and Duncan Bell the scientist who succumbs disastrously to the pressure to produce results.

CLOSER

The main excitement of the year, however, was the number of young, mainly male, playwrights. For many the best new play of the year was *Closer*, written and directed by Patrick Marber at the Cottesloe with an outstanding cast of Ciaran Hinds, Clive Owen, Sally Dexter and Liza Walker. Marber pulled off the feat of writing a second play that was more interesting and more accomplished than his first, *Dealer's Choice. Closer*, including a scene in which one man picks up another on the Internet under the illusion that he is communicating with a woman, is about obsessional love, the conflict between honesty and kindness, and the gulf between men and women. More bad plays have probably been written on these subjects than any others, yet Marber's is astonishingly accomplished structurally and absolutely gripping from start to finish, even if the men are more complex, interesting characters than the women.

With a title like *Shopping and F***ing*, Mark Ravenhill's play inevitably caused controversy when it first appeared at the Royal Court at the Ambassadors in a production by Out of Joint. The title may have irritated some people but at least on a tour round the country audiences knew what to expect; gut-wrenching scenes of sado-masochistic sex were not to be taken lightly. Ravenhill's concern is for a society of low-lifers consumed by cheap culture, pot noodles, easy drugs and sexual transactions rather than relationships. The characters are vaguely aware that these things do not make for a satisfactory life without knowing how to escape. Unexpectedly, after a season at the Royal Court and a national and international tour, the play went into the Gielgud Theatre where it was a runaway success.

The Irish continued to have a powerful influence on British theatre, especially at the Royal Court which, with the help of associate director Garry Hynes, was quick to tap into the creative energy across the water. Martin McDonagh, who made such an impressive début the year before, returned with the Leenane Trilogy: *The Beauty Queen of Leenane*, *A Skull in Connemara* and *The Lonesome West*. The plays share not so much characters as a portrait of a rural part of Ireland as imagined by McDonagh, where grudges can be held for years and where most amusement is derived from others' misfortunes. Although born in Camberwell, McDonagh's parents were Irish and all but one of his plays have been co-produced by Druid, the touring company based in

Galway, and the Royal Court. Equally interesting is Conor McPherson, whose play *The Weir* was lovingly directed by Ian Rickson at the Royal Court. McPherson creates a detailed portrait (very different from McDonagh's) of life in a rural Irish community as gleaned from the conversation in a remote Irish bar. Three lonely men try to impress a young woman escaping from Dublin, by telling her ghost stories, only she turns out to have experienced the most haunting story of all. The performances, particularly Jim Norton's as an old codger, could hardly be faulted.

Ayub Khan-Din's *East is East* was another hit for the Royal Court, an autobiographical portrait of life in a mixed marriage in Salford with a father disturbed by news of war on the Indo-Pakistan border, and a mother trying to keep the peace between her husband and those children who are not impressed by the Muslim way of life. The comedy of this squabbling family was distinctly raucous. Other new plays that deserved attention were Joe Penhall's *Love and Understanding*, Samuel Adamson's *Grace Note* and Sebastian Barry's *Prayers from Sherkin*. From an older generation Simon Gray's *Life Support*, with Alan Bates as a raddled, fraudulent writer trying to yank his wife out of her vegetative state, was undramatic.

GLOBE OPENS

With the RSC no longer playing at the Barbican in the summer, Shakespearean revivals in London were unusually thin on the ground. Nevertheless, after the try-out season last summer, 1997 saw the official opening of Shakespeare's Globe, the post-humous realization of Sam Wanamaker's dream, with a celebratory opening night in front of The Queen. The visit of Cherie Blair and Hillary Clinton during the Clintons' visit to London also attracted media attention. Since 1996 the stage has been permanently fixed with its thatched roof, which is gaudily painted underneath and supported by marble-painted pillars. Behind is the balcony where musicians, actors and members of the audience mingle, as it is believed they did in the original Globe. Given the amount of rain, this was not the easiest of summers to open, although, unlike the Open Air Theatre, the actors and those members of the audience who choose to sit are always covered. It is only the groundlings standing in the centre for just £5 who feel the full force of the weather, as they certainly did on the opening night of *Henry V* when thunder and lightning added to the drama of the battle scenes. For all the fascination of the experiment, concentration is difficult for those who have come to see the plays rather than to experience an event; members of the audience are always on the move, the hawkers sell food, drink and plastic raincoats even during the performance, and the stewards noisily make sure that no one is blocking the fire exits. The irony is just how much attention increases as night falls and the anachronistic lighting takes over.

This is a space, however, that celebrates the art of the actor. David Freeman's production of *The Winter's Tale* suffered greatly from actors who did not have the vocal skills to command attention in a production that tended to work against the building. Far better was Richard Olivier's all-male production of *Henry V* with Mark Rylance as the king. The Chorus's opening lines requesting the audience to let its 'imaginary forces work' created a genuine frisson from the beginning. Rylance's sober, guilt-ridden Henry introduced some subtlety to counter-act the crowd-pleasing jingoism as the French paraded in their shining armour and splendid robes only to be roundly booed.

Back inside, it was a year for *King Lear*. Most unusually, Kathryn Hunter took on the part of the old king at the Leicester Haymarket and the Young Vic in Helena Kaut-Howson's production, which included an additional prologue set in an old people's home. Alan Howard played the part for the first time in Peter Hall's production at the Old Vic. But the major production of the year was Richard Eyre's at the Cottesloe, played in the traverse with Ian Holm as a diminutive king. Holm, who, until *Moonlight*, kept away from the stage for 16 years because of an attack of stagefright, was one of the great Lears of our time. Surrounded by similarly grizzled old men – Michael Bryant's Fool, David Burke's Kent and Timothy West's Gloucester – Holm was a hunched figure, drumming his fingers and cracking his whip in a impressive display of bullish authority. In a sudden gesture of common humanity, he impulsively removed all his clothes to hug Paul Rhys' similarly naked Edgar. The combination of this production and *Closer* in the Cottesloe meant that for much of the year the theatre was booked solid.

For the RSC in Stratford Alex Jennings played the Prince in a production of *Hamlet* by Matthew Warchus (hot from *Art*) that got rid of Fortinbras and Norway and began not on the ramparts but with a film of the young Hamlet playing with his father in the snow. The play was drastically cut to just three hours. The production had its supporters despite all the liberties with the text, most of all because of Jennings' performance as Hamlet, a young man stretched to breaking point. Adrian Noble's production of *Cymbeline* gave the play a rare exposure on the main stage, with Joanne Pearce as Imogen, Shakespeare's indefatigable heroine. Oddly for a play set in ancient Britain, the cast were all dressed in kimonos and flowing hair extensions and Anthony Ward's design included a Japanese catwalk that jutted out into the audience. The stage itself was dominated by a white billowing sail cloth in front of a rich blue background. It was a brave effort to see whether audiences can be persuaded to fill the main house for Shakespeare plays other than the eight that so regularly appear in the repertoire.

QUALITY REVIVALS

It is a tribute to the quality of London theatre that in a year notable for the number of new plays, there was no shortage of quality revivals, dominated by Anthony Page's production of *A Doll's House* at the Playhouse and Jonathan Kent's of *Ivanov* at the Almeida. In Page's production, produced by Thelma Holt, Nora was played by Janet McTeer, unusual casting in that she is 6 feet tall and not known for playing roles in which her character is patronized and patted on the head by her husband. But as Nora, McTeer was almost unbearable to watch as she twisted her hair round her fingers and played the little squirrel for her wilful, near-violent husband Torvald, played by Owen Teale. Frank McGuinness's translation came into its own in the final scene as Nora in vain sought from Torvald some understanding of her predicament, and then, in contrast with all the fussiness and simpering that had gone before, sat down and movingly explained as one adult to another why she had to leave. Because of Torvald's barely repressed violence the scene was even more electric than usual. The production, after a wrangle with Equity, went on to play on Broadway where it was a huge hit and both Page and McTeer won Tony awards.

For the revival of Chekhov's *Ivanov*, queues formed from as early as 3 a.m. in the morning outside the Almeida Theatre, the reason being that the titular role was played by Ralph Fiennes. Fine as Fiennes was in the role that is sometimes known as the Hamlet of the Steppes, there were many other reasons why this was a special evening. Far from making a grand entrance, the Oscar-winning star was sitting on the stage as the audience entered the auditorium for this early play, written when Chekhov was 27, which was so scorned by the playwright himself. It contains elements of the then fashionable farces, of Gogol's *The Government Inspector*, as well as looking forward to Chekhov's later, admittedly greater works. But as ever, Chekhov unpeels people's motives with an unflinching honesty and to exhilarating effect. The broad brushstrokes of Jonathan Kent's production and David Hare's energetic translation relished the meanness and stupidities of petit bourgeois provincial life and the cruel gusto of Count Shabyelski's cynicism (Oliver Ford Davies in his element). Ivanov is sunk in depression, unable to give his dying wife the love she needs, challenged by Lvov's superficial, priggish honesty, and surrounded by his grasping neighbours. The production successfully drew attention to a Chekhov play which has largely been ignored in favour of the much-performed later works.

The National's Olivier theatre was temporarily converted into a theatre in the round for Brecht's *Caucasian Chalk Circle*, creating an intimacy that had always been missing previously. Simon McBurney's production with Juliet Stevenson as Grusha, the peasant girl who travels through treacherous territories and risks her life in order to protect the Governor's child, was a great joy and a welcome return to the theatre for Stevenson after a long break. She brought her classical skills to an international cast, mostly members of Théâtre de Complicité who are used to working in a more physical fashion. Typically the company found unusual ways of depicting the frail rope bridges, the battles and the peasant wedding that Grusha encounters on her travels. Each actor played several parts and many of them several musical instruments, even Stevenson turning up as a fugitive member of the aristocracy; and McBurney, as well as directing, played Azdak, the filthy, drunken, foul-talking judge elected during the revolution who favours the poor and is not averse to the odd back-hander. The production may not have been quite ready at the beginning of its run, but by the end audiences were enthralled and giving the actors a standing ovation.

At Chichester, producer Duncan Weldon persuaded Kathleen Turner to cross the Atlantic to play Tallulah Bankhead in *Tallulah*. She was one of a number of American stars who appeared in England, including Lynne Redgrave in her one-woman show about her father Michael Redgrave, *Shakespeare for My Father*, Gene Wilder in *Laughter on the 23rd Floor*, Patti Lupone in *Master Class*, Jessica Lange in *A Streetcar Named Desire*, Jerry Lewis in *Damn Yankees* and Charlton Heston in *Love Letters*. They were usually quoted as saying that, despite the poor money, they felt the need to test themselves on the British stage. Some of them must have been glad to go home.

In Scarborough, the Stephen Joseph Theatre was under threat only three months after it had moved into a new complex with two theatres, a cinema, an education centre and bars and restaurants. There was the embarrassing possibility that this lottery-funded building would have to close after the local council threatened to cut the theatre's grant in order to have enough money to keep the town's public lavatories open. The heated debate in the town was reported in the media as a battle of luvvies versus lavvies. Fortunately some money was found in the town's tourism budget and the theatre was awarded an additional grant of £50,000 for five years; the lavatories too remained open.

Every two years the London International Festival of Theatre, organized by Rose Fenton and Lucy Neal, invites companies to the city from all over the world whose idea of theatre is very different from the standard West End production. The highlight of this year's festival was *Perioda Villa Villa* staged in a warehouse in Three Mills Island by De La Guarda from Buenos Aires. The company created an electrifying party atmosphere, a mixture of a rave, with all the appropriate lights and music, and a circus, with their acrobatic skills. The performers dived through a ceiling of paper, swung over the heads of the standing audience, and zig-zagged their way up a vertical wall. Once again LIFT proved that theatre can come in numerous guises.

PRODUCTIONS
September 1996 to August 1997

LONDON PRODUCTIONS

ADELPHI, WC2. *Sunset Boulevard*, since July 1993. (4 June) *Damn Yankees* (Richard Adler, Jerry Ross) with Jerry Lewis; director, Jack O'Brien

ALBERY, WC2 (17 September 1996) *Uncle Vanya*, transferred from Chichester. (25 November) *The Cherry Orchard*, RSC production transferred from Stratford. (17 April 1997) *The Goodbye Girl* (Neil Simon, adapt. Marvin Hamlisch, David Zippel) with Gary Wilmot, Ann Crumb; director, Rob Bettinson. (28 July) *Pygmalion* (Shaw) with Roy Marsden, Michael Elphick, Carli Norris; director, Ray Cooney

ALDWYCH, WC2 (6 November 1996) *Who's Afraid of Virginia Woolf?*, transferred from the Almeida. (14 April 1997) *Tom and Clem* (Stephen Churchett) with Michael Gambon, Alec McCowen, Sarah Woodward; director, Richard Wilson. (5 August) *Life Support* (Simon Gray) with Alan Bates, Georgina Hales; director, Harold Pinter

ALMEIDA, N1 (25 September 1996) *Who's Afraid of Virginia Woolf?* (Albee) with Diana Rigg, David Suchet, Clare Holman, Lloyd Owen; director, Howard Davies. (30 October) *Happy Days* (Beckett) with Rosaleen Linehan, Barry McGovern; director, Karel Reisz. (13 November) *Cyrano de Bergerac* (Rostand, trans. Edwin Morgan) with Tom Mannion; director, Gerry Mulgrew. (11 December) *A Midsummer Night's Dream* (Shakespeare) with Norman Rodway, Angela Thorne, Jason Watkins, Peter Bayliss; director, Jonathan Miller. (19 February 1997) *Ivanov* (Chekhov, adapt. David Hare) with Ralph Fiennes, Harriet Walter, Bill Paterson, Oliver Ford Davies; director, Jonathan Kent. (29 April) *Doña Rosita, The Spinster* (Lorca, trans. Peter Oswald) with Phoebe Nicholls, Clive Swift, Eleanor Bron, Celia Imrie; director, Phyllida Lloyd. (14 August) *Heartbreak House* (Shaw) with Emma Fielding, Patricia Hodge, Penelope Wilton, Richard Griffiths; director, David Hare

AMBASSADORS, WC2 (19 September 1996) *Ashes to Ashes* (Pinter) with Lindsay Duncan, Stephen Rea; director, Harold Pinter. (1 October) *Shopping and F***ing* (Mark Ravenhill), an Out of Joint production. (21 November) *East Is East* (Ayub Khan Din) with Nadim Sawalha, Linda Bassett, Zita Sattar, Paul Bazely, Jimi Mistry, Imran Ali; director, Kristine Landon-Smith. (5 December) *I Licked a Slag's Deodorant* (Jim Cartwright) with Polly Hemingway, Tim Potter; director, Jim Cartwright. (10 February 1997) *Backpay* (Tamantha Hammerschlag) with Dona Croll, Valerie Hunkins, Diane O'Kelly; director, Mary Peate (February) *Cockroach Who?* (Jess Walters) with Tameka Empson, Alicya Eyo, Nicola Stapleton; director, Caroline Hall. (12 March) *Attempts On Her Life* (Martin Crimp) with Ashley Jensen, David Fielder; director, Tim Albery. (23 April) *Bailegangaire* (Tom Murphy) with Rosaleen Linehan, Brid Breenan, Ruth McCabe; director, James Macdonald. (12 June) *Things Fall Apart*, transferred from Leeds. (June) *Ramzy Abul Majd* with Ahmad Abu Sal'oum, Hussam Abu Eshee. (4 July) *The Weir* (Conor McPherson) with Kieran Ahern, Brendan Coyle, Julia Ford, Jim Norton; director, Ian Rickson

APOLLO, W1 (11 December 1996) *The Official Tribute to the Blues Brothers*, revival of 1994 production. (20 March 1997) *Popcorn* (Ben Elton) with Patrick O'Kane, Dena Davis; director, Laurence Boswell

APOLLO VICTORIA, SW1. *Starlight Express*, since 1984

ARTS, WC2 (17 October 1996) *Never the Sinner* (John

Logan) with pupils and staff of King's College School, Wimbledon; director, Philip Swan. (11 November) *Darktales* (Tim Arthur) with Andrew Hall, Jamie Hinde; director, Karen Louise Hebden. (January 1997) *Showstopper* (Dan Rebellato) with Jackie Clune; director, Sarah Frankcom. (March) *Exposition* (Tom Minter) with Trevor Sellers, Niall Ashdown, Robert Miles; director, Areta Breeze. (20 June) *Twilight of the Golds* (Jonathan Tolins) with Jason Gould, Mark Hadfield; director, Polly James. (7 August) *Carnaby Street* (James Hall); director, Terry John Bates

BARBICAN, EC2 (12 September 1996) *A Midsummer Night's Dream*, revival of 1994 production. (23 October) *As You Like It*, transferred from Stratford. (6 November) *Macbeth*, transferred from Stratford. (4 December) *Troilus and Cressida*, transferred from Stratford. Closed for refurbishment from March to October 1997

THE PIT (13 September 1996) *Faust*, transferred from Stratford. (22 October) *In the Company of Men* (Edward Bond) with Karl Johnson, John Light; director, Edward Bond. (5 November) *The Herbal Bed*, transferred from Stratford. (3 December) *The Learned Ladies*, transferred from Stratford. (December) *The White Devil*, transferred from Stratford. (28 January 1997) *Three Hours After Marriage*, transferred from Stratford. (26 February) *The General From America*, transferred from Stratford. Closed for refurbishment from March to October 1997

BUSH, W12, closed for refurbishment 1996; performances at the Lyric Studio, Hammersmith. (January 1997) *All Of You Mine* (Richard Cameron) with Marion Bailey, Anne Carroll, David Hounslow, Andrew Dunn; director, Simon Usher. (21 February) *St Nicholas* (Conor McPherson) with Brian Cox; director, Conor McPherson. (4 April) *Language Roulette* (Daragh Carville), a Tinderbox Theatre production; director, Tim Loane. (May) *Love and Understanding* (Joe Penhall) with Paul Bettany, Nicholas Tennant, Celia Robertson; director, Mike Bradwell. (11 June) *Wishbones* (Lucinda Coxon) with Gawn Grainger, Amelda Brown, Madeline Newton, Jane Hazlegrove, Kevin McMonagle; director, Simon Usher. (25 July) *Goliath* (Bryony Lavery) with Nichola McAuliffe; director, Annie Castledine

CAMBRIDGE, WC2 (24 October 1996) *Grease*, transferred from the Dominion

COMEDY, WC2 (22 October 1996) *Talking Heads*, transferred from Chichester. (26 February 1997) *Birdy* (William Wharton, adapt. Naomi Wallace) with Rob Morrow, Matthew Wait; director, Kevin Knight. (May) *The School For Wives*, transferred from the Piccadilly. (August) *The Mysterious Mr Love* (Karoline Leach) with Susan Penhaligon, Paul Nicholas; director, Bob Tomson

CRITERION, W1. *The Complete Works of William Shakespeare (Abridged)* and *The Complete History of America (Abridged)*, since March 1996

DOMINION, WC1 (12 November 1996) *Scrooge: the Musical* (Leslie Bricusse, Anthony Newley) with Anthony Newley; director, Bob Tomson. (13 May 1997) *Beauty and the Beast* (Howard Ashman, Tim Rice, Alan Menken) with Julie-Alanah Brighten, Derek Griffiths, Barry Kames; director, Robert Jess Roth with Alasdair Harvey

DONMAR WAREHOUSE, WC2 (5 September 1996) *Pentecost* (Stewart Parker), a Rough Magic production. (10 October) *Fool for Love* (Shepard) with Barry Lynch, Lorraine Ashbourne; director, Ian Brown. (12 December) *Nine* (Fellini, adapt. Maury Yeston, Arthur Kopit) with Larry Lamb; director, David Leveaux. (11 March 1997) *Badfinger* (Simon Harris), a Thin Language Theatre Company production. (25 March) *Summer Begins* (David Eldridge) with Beatie Edney, Elizabeth Chadwick,

Heather Tobias, Gary Webster; director, Jonathan Lloyd. (9 April) *Halloween Night* (Declan Hughes) a Rough Magic Theatre Company production. (25 April) *The Fix* (John Dempsey, Dana P. Rowe) with John Barrowman, Kathryn Evans, Kristen Cummings; director, Sam Mendes. (25 June) *The Maids* (Genet) with Niamh Cusack, Kerry Fox; director, John Crowley. (14 August) *The Seagull* (Chekhov) with Cheryl Campbell, Denys Hawthorn, Mark Bazeley; director, Stephen Unwin

DRURY LANE THEATRE ROYAL, WC2. *Miss Saigon*, since 1989

DUCHESS, WC2 (16 April 1997) *The Herbal Bed*, RSC production transferred from The Pit

DUKE OF YORK'S, WC2 (16 October 1996) *Mojo*, revival of 1995 Royal Court Theatre production. (2 December) *The Beauty Queen of Leenane*, revival of March 1996 Royal Court Theatre Upstairs production. (13 February 1997) *The Shallow End* (Doug Lucie) with Julia Ford, Tony Doyle, Jane Asher, Nigel Terry; director, Robin Lefevre. (26 March) *East is East*, transferred from Theatre Royal, Stratford. (5 June) *The Censor* (Anthony Neilson) with Alastair Galbraith, Raquel Cassidy, Alison Newman; director, Anthony Neilson. (June) *This is a Chair* (Caryl Churchill) with Linus Roache, Amanda da Plummer, Desmond Barrit, Timothy Spall; director, Stephen Daldry. (26 July) *The Leenane Trilogy: The Beauty Queen of Leenane, A Skull in Connemara, The Lonesome West* (Martin McDonagh), a Royal Court and Druid Theatre co-production; director, Garry Hynes

FORTUNE, WC2. *The Woman in Black*, since 1989. (Sunday matinees) *Marie*, since 1995

GARRICK, WC2. *An Inspector Calls*, the 1992 National Theatre production, since 1995

GATE, W11 (20 September 1996) *Bug* (Tracy Letts) with Shannon Cochran, Michael Shannon, Marc Nelson. (29 October) *The Weavers* (Gerhart Hauptmann); director, Dominic Cooke. (29 November) *Swanwhite* (Strindberg) with Jules Melvin, Jason Morrell, Richenda Carey; director, Timothy Walker. (January 1997) *Strindberg's Chamber Plays: Storm* with John Grillo; director, Wils Wilson; *After the Fire* with Dudley Sutton; director, Loveday Ingram; *The Ghost Sonata* with Alan MacNaughtan; director, Georgina van Welie. (10 February) *Shakuntala* (Kalidasa, adapt. Peter Oswald) with Silas Carson, Will Keen, Lesley McGuire; director, Indhu Rubasingham. (18 April) *The Ubu Plays* (Alfred Jarry, trans. Kenneth McLeish) with Stephen Finegold, Joanna Holden; director, John Wright. (30 May) *The Birds* (Aristophanes, trans. Stephen Greenhorn); director, Gaynor MacFarlane. (2 July) *Candide* (Voltaire, trans. Murray Gold) with Justin Salinger; director, David Farr. (August) *Eve of Retirement* (Thomas Bernhard); director, David Fielding

GIELGUD, W1 (13 November 1996) *Old Wicked Songs*, transferred from Bristol. (27 February 1997) *Romance, Romance* (Keith Herman) with Caroline O'Connor, Mark Adam, Lindsay Hateley; director, Stephen Dexter. (26 June) *Shopping and F***ing*, transferred from the Ambassadors after tour. (13 August) *The Bible: the Complete Word of God (Abridged)*, a Reduced Shakespeare Company production

GLOBE, SE1 (14 June 1997) *Henry V* (Shakespeare) with Mark Rylance; director, Richard Olivier. (5 June) *The Winter's Tale* (Shakespeare) with Nicholas Le Provost; director, David Freeman. (August) *Umabatha* (Shakespeare's *Macbeth*, adapt. Welcome Msomi), a Johannesburg Civic Theatre production. (August) *A*

Chaste Maid in Cheapside (Thomas Middleton); director, Malcolm McKay. (August) *The Maid's Tragedy* (Beaumont, Fletcher); director, Lucy Bailey

GREENWICH, SE10 (23 October 1996) *Hamlet* (Shakespeare) with Michael Maloney; director, Philip Franks. (10 December) *The Adventures of Huckleberry Finn* (Twain, adapt. Matthew Francis) with Daniel Newman, Clive Llewellyn; director, Matthew Francis. (March 1997) *The Comic Mysteries* (Dario Fo), an Oxford Stage Company and Greenwich Theatre co-production; director, John Retallack. (29 April) *Absent Friends* (Ayckbourn); director, Michael Simkins. (11 June) *After October*, transferred from Chichester. (28 July) *Side by Side by Sondheim* with Dawn French, Kathryn Evans, Liza Sadovy, David Melak; director, Matthew Francis

HAMPSTEAD, NW3 (10 September 1996) *The Flight Into Egypt* (James Garner) with Paloma Baeza, Con O'Neill, Paul Jesson; director, John Dove. (29 October) *The Entertainer* (Osborne) with Michael Pennington; director, Stephen Rayne. (4 December) *The Eleventh Commandment* (David Schneider) with David Schneider, Sheila Steafel, Tracey Lynch, Jeffrey Segal; director, Matthew Lloyd. (27 January 1997) *Paper Husband* (Hannan Al-Shaykh) with Veronica Clifford, David Fielder; director, Gemma Bodinetz. (March) *The Positive Hour* (April de Angelis) with Margot Leicester, Robin Soans, Julia Lane, Kate Ashfield; director, Max Stafford-Clark. (15 April) *Cracked* (Daniel Hill) with David Horovitch, Mark Hadfield, Nigel Terry; director, Terry Johnson. (3 June) *All Things Considered* (Ben Brown) with Christopher Godwin, Susie Blake, Timothy Knightley, Jane Slavin; director, Alan Strachan. (July) *Chimps* (Simon Block) with Nicholas Woodeson, Fraser James, Darren Tighe, Ashley Jensen; director, Gemma Bodinetz

HAYMARKET THEATRE ROYAL, SW1 (11 October 1996) *Night Must Fall* (Emlyn Williams) with Jason Donovan, Rosemary Leach; director, John Tydeman. (7 November) *Shakespeare For My Father* (Lynn Redgrave) with Lynn Redgrave; director, John Clark. (30 December) *A Streetcar Named Desire* (Tennessee Williams) with Jessica Lange, Toby Stephens, Imogen Stubbs; director, Peter Hall. (1 April 1997) *Lady Windermere's Fan*, transferred from Manchester. (6 August) *An Ideal Husband*, revival of January 1996 production

HER MAJESTY'S, SW1. *The Phantom of the Opera*, since 1986

LONDON PALLADIUM, WC1. *Oliver!*, since 1994

LYCEUM, WC2 (19 November 1996) *Jesus Christ Superstar* (Rice, Lloyd Webber) with Steve Balsamo, Zubin Varla, Joanna Ampil; director, Gale Edwards

LYRIC, W1 (3 October 1996) *By Jeeves*, transferred from the Duke of York's Theatre. (8 April) *Marlene* (Pam Gems) with Sian Phillips, Lou Gish, Billy Mathias; director, Sean Mathias

LYRIC, W6 (18 September 1996) *Sarrasine* (Balzac, adapt. Neil Bartlett) with Bette Bourne, Beverley Klein, François Testory, Sara Kestelman; director, Neil Bartlett. (21 October) *Mrs Warren's Profession* (Shaw) with Maggie Stead, Catherine Cusack; director, Neil Bartlett. (18 December) *A Christmas Carol* (Dickens, adapt. Neil Bartlett) with Richard Briers; director, Neil Bartlett. (January 1997) *A Midsummer Night's Dream* (Shakespeare), a Tara Arts production; director, Jatinder Verma. (4 March) *The Message* with Paul Davies, Jan Knightly, Fern Smith; director, Nigel Charnock. (17 March) *The Fall of the House of Usherettes*, a Forkbeard Fantasy production; director, John Tellett. (23 April) *Out Cry* (Tennessee Williams), a Cheek by Jowl production; director, Timothy Walker. (May) *Titus Andronicus*, a Silviu Purcarete and Romanian National Theatre of Craiova production. (12 June) *The Winter's Tale* (Shakespeare), a Method and Madness production. (12 June) *Ghosts* (Ibsen), a Method and Madness Production

LYRIC STUDIO (3 October 1996) *Hector* (Corneille) with Jake Nightingale, Alex McSweeney, Esther Hall; director, Sydnee Blake. (25 October) *Buried Treasure* (David Ashton) with Alexander Morton, Jimmy Yuill; director, Robin Lefèvre. (20 November) *The Belle Vue* (von Horvath), an Actors Touring Company production. (5 December) *Dylan Thomas: Return Journey* with Bob Kingdom; *The Truman Capote Show* with Bob Kingdom. (February 1997) *Faust* (Goethe, adapt. Mark Ravenhill) with Alain Pelletier, Pete Bailie; director, Nick Philippou. (14 April) *70 Hill Lane* (Phelim McDermott) with Lee Simpson, Julian Crouch, Guy Dartnell; director, Phelim McDermott. (May) *The Duel* (Chekhov, adapt. Roger Ringrose, Tim Marchant) with Roger Ringrose, Jean-Benoit Blanc, Laura Jones, Victoria Plum. (18 July) *Her Sister's Tongue* (Janet Goddard), a Plain Clothes production; director, Jacquetta May. (August) *My Native Land* (Rodney Clark), a Scooting Owl Stage Company production; director, Ezra Hjalmarsson

MERMAID, EC4 (September 1996) *A Midsummer Night's Dream* (Shakespeare), a Yukio Ninagawa production. (28 November) *Le Cercle Invisible* with Jean Baptiste Thierrée, Victoria Chaplin

NEW LONDON, WC2. *Cats*, since 1981

OLD VIC, SE1. (28 January 1997) *Henry IV* (Shakespeare) with Timothy West, Samuel West, Gary Waldhorn; director, Stephen Unwin. (14 March) *Waste* (Granville Barker) with Michael Pennington, Felicity Kendal; director, Peter Hall. (21 March) *Cloud Nine* (Caryl Churchill) with Janine Duvitski, Tim McInnerny, Dominic West; director, Tom Cairns. (23 March) *Hurlyburly* (David Rabe) with Rupert Graves, Andy Serkis, Susannah Doyle; director, Wilson Milam. (9 May) *The Seagull* (Chekhov, trans. Tom Stoppard) with Victoria Hamilton, Felicity Kendal, Michael Pennington, Dominic West; director, Peter Hall (19 May) *Prayers of Sherkin* (Sebastian Barry) with Catherine Cusack, Patrick Kirwin, Julian Glover; director, John Dove. (23 June) *The Provok'd Wife* (Vanburgh) with Michael Pennington, Victoria Hamilton, Alison Steadman; director, Lindsey Posner. (27 June) *Waiting for Godot* (Beckett) with Ben Kingsley, Alan Howard, Greg Hicks; director, Peter Hall. (7 July) *Grace Note* (Samuel Adamson) with Geraldine McEwan; director, Dominic Dromgoole. (26 August) *King Lear* (Shakespeare) with Alan Howard, Victoria Hamilton, Greg Hicks; director, Peter Hall

OPEN AIR, Regent's Park, NW1 (27 May 1997) *A Midsummer Night's Dream* (Shakespeare) with Issy van Randwyck, Chook Sibtain, Michael Higgs, Ian Talbot; director, Rachel Kavanaugh. (June) *All's Well That Ends Well* (Shakespeare) with Frances Cuka, Nigel Planer; director, Helena Kaut-Howson. (25 July) *Kiss Me Kate* (Bella and Samuel Spewack, Cole Porter) a New Shakespeare Company production; director, Ian Talbot. (5 August) *Watership Down* (Richard Adams, adapt. Jacob Murray, Caroline Smith), a New Shakespeare Company production

PALACE, WC2. *Les Misérables*, since 1985

PHOENIX, WC1. *Blood Brothers*, since 1991

PICCADILLY, W1 (11 February) *The School For Wives* (Molière) with Peter Bowles, Carmen Silvera, Eric Sykes, Henry McGee; director, Peter Hall. (May) *Steaming* (Nell Dunn) with Jenny Eclair, Julie T. Wallace, Sheila Reid; director, Ian Brown. (19 June) *Elvis: the Musical* (Jack Good, Ray Cooney) with Michael Dimitri; director, Keith Strachan

PLAYHOUSE, WC2 (24 October 1996) *A Doll's House* (Ibsen) with Janet McTeer, Owen Teale; director, Anthony Page. (18 June 1997) *The Wood Demon* (Chekhov, adapt. Frank Dwyer, Nicholas Saunders) with Amanda Ryan, Philip Voss, Brian Protheroe, John Turner; director, Anthony Clark

PRINCE EDWARD, W1. *Martin Guerre*, since July 1996

PRINCE OF WALES, W1 (23 October 1996) *Smoky Joe's Café* (Leiber, Stoller) with Delee Lively, Stephanie Pope, Victor Trent Cook, B. J. Crosby; director, Jerry Zachs

QUEENS, W1 (3 October 1996) *Laughter on the 23rd Floor* (Neil Simon) with Gene Wilder; director, Roger Haines. (6 May 1997) *Master Class* (Terrence McNally) with Patti LuPone, David Maxwell Anderson; director, Leonard Foglia. (August) *Hurlyburly*, transferred from the Old Vic

ROYAL COURT and THEATRE UPSTAIRS, SW1. Closed for refurbishment 1996–7; performances at the Ambassadors and Duke of York theatres

ROYAL NATIONAL THEATRE, SE1, COTTESLOE (3 September 1996) *Blinded by the Sun* (Poliakoff) with Douglas Hodge, Frances de la Tour, Duncan Bell; director, Ron Daniels. (2 October) *Violin Time*, return of January 1996 production. (20 November) *Fair Ladies at a Game of Poem Cards* (Chikamatsu Monzaemon, adapt. Peter Oswald) with David Haig, Olwen Fouéré; director, John Crowley. (11 January 1997) *Light Shining in Buckinghamshire* (Caryl Churchill) with Patrick Brennan, Amelda Brown, Tim Crouch, Tina Gambe, Fergus Webster, Tim Welton; director, Mark Wing-Davey. (12 February) *Cardiff East* (Peter Gill) with Kenneth Cranham, Susan Brown, Matthew Rhys; director, Peter Gill. (27 March) *King Lear* (Shakespeare) with Ian Holm, Michael Bryant, Anne-Marie Duff, Barbara Flynn; director, Richard Eyre. (29 May) *Closer* (Patrick Marber) with Sally Dexter, Ciaran Hinds, Clive Owen, Liza Walker; director, Patrick Marber. (7 August) *Othello* (Shakespeare) with David Harewood, Simon Russell Beale, Clare Skinner; director, Sam Mendes

LYTTELTON (21 September 1996) *The Seven Streams of the River Ota* (Robert Lepage), an Ex Machina production; director, Robert Lepage. (31 October) *Death of a Salesman* (Miller) with Alun Armstrong, Colin Stinton, Mark Strong, Marjorie Yates; director, David Thacker. (7 January 1997) *The Cripple of Inishmaan* (Martin McDonagh) with Ruaidhri Conroy, Aisling O'Sullivan, Ray McBride; director, Nicholas Hytner. (23 January) *The Homecoming* (Pinter) with Keith Allen, Lindsay Duncan, Sam Kelly, Eddie Marsan; director, Roger Michell. (March) *Lady in the Dark* (Moss Hart, Ira Gershwin) with Maria Friedman, Adrian Dunbar, Paul Shelley, Steven Edward Moore; director, Francesca Zambello. (21 June) *Amy's View* (David Hare) with Judi Dench, Samantha Bond, Ronald Pickup, Eoin McCarthy; director, Richard Eyre

OLIVIER (17 September 1996) *The Oedipus Plays: Oedipus the King* and *Oedipus at Colonus* (Sophocles, trans. Ranjit Bolt) with Alan Howard, Suzanne Bertish, Pip Donaghy, Greg Hicks; director, Peter Hall. (9 October) *The Alchemist*, co-production transferred from Birmingham. (17 December) *Guys and Dolls* (Loesser) with Joanna Riding, Henry Goodman, Clarke Peters, Imelda Staunton; director, Richard Eyre. (21 April 1997) *The Caucasian Chalk Circle* (Brecht, adapt. Frank McGuinness) with Juliet Stevenson, Kulvinder Ghir, Simon McBurney, Tim McMullan, Bruce Myers, Hélène Patarot; director, Simon McBurney. (15 May) *Marat/Sade* (Peter Weiss, adapt. Geoffrey Skelton, Adrian Mitchell) with Corin Redgrave, David Calder, Anastasia Hille; director, Jeremy Sams

St Martins, wc2. *The Mousetrap*, since 1974

Savoy, wc2 (2 October 1996) *When We Are Married* (Priestley), transferred from Chichester. (2 December) *Plunder* (Ben Travers) with Griff Rhys Jones, Kevin McNally, Sara Crowe; director, Peter James. (18 March 1997) *The Importance of Being Oscar* (Michael MacLiammoir) with Simon Callow; director, Patrick Garland

Strand, wc2. *Buddy*, transferred from the Victoria Palace, since 1995

Theatre Royal, e15 (8 October 1996) *The Lodger* (Patrick Prior) with Murray Melvin, Lynn Farleigh; director, Philip Hedley. (February 1997) *East Is East*, transferred from the Ambassadors Theatre. (18 March) *Tickets and Ties: The African Tale* (Sesan Ogunledun) with Goda John, Usifu Jalloh, Tunde Euba; director, Femi Elufowoju. (June) *Throwaway* (Danny Miller) with Ian Dunn, Brian Stephen, Terence Beesley; director, Kate Williams

Tricycle, nw6 (10 October 1996) *Nuremberg*, revival of 1996 production. (11 October) *Srebrenica* (Nicolas Kent) with Jay Simpson; director, Nicolas Kent. (28 October) *The Gay Detective* (Gerard Stembridge) with Peter Hanly, Eddy Tighe. (December) *Sympathy for the Devil* (Roy Winston) with Ray Harrison Graham, Deborah A. Williams, Maria Oshodi, Jonathan Keeble; director, Ray Harrison Graham. (2 January 1997) *Beef, No Chicken* (Derek Walcott) a Talawa Theatre Company production; director, Yvonne Brewster. (3 February) *Kitchensink* (Paul Mercier) with Deirdre Molloy, Cathy Belton, Liam Carney, David Gorry; director, Paul Mercier. (3 April) *Kings* (Homer, trans. Christopher Logue) with Alan Howard. (28 April) *The Mai* (Marina Carr) with Judith Scott, Robert Gwilym, Lizzy McInerny, Julia Dearden; director, Nicolas Kent

Vaudeville, wc2 (13 September 1996) *Kindertransport* (Diane Samuels) with Diana Quick, Jean Boht, Sian Thomas; director, Abigail Morris. (9 December) *The Witches* (Roald Dahl, adapt. David Wood) with Katerina Jugati; director, David Wood. (30 June) *Skylight* (David Hare) with Stella Gonet, Bill Nighy; director, Richard Eyre

Victoria Palace, sw1 (June 1997) *Always* (William May, Jason Sprague) with Clive Carter, Jan Hartley; directors, Frank Hauser, Thommie Walsh

Whitehall (24 September 1996) *Cash on Delivery* (Michael Cooney) with Bradley Walsh, Nick Wilton, Frank Thornton, Brian Murphy, Jean Fergusson; director, Ray Cooney

Wyndham's, wc2 (15 October 1996) *Art* (Yasmina Reza, trans. Christopher Hampton) with Tom Courtenay, Albert Finney, Ken Stott; director, Matthew Warchus

Young Vic, se1 (27 September 1996) *Blood Wedding* (Lorca, trans. Ted Hughes) with Alexandra Gilbreath, Jasper Britton; director, Tim Supple. (4 December) *Beauty and the Beast*, with Liz May Brice, Simon Gregor; director, Laurence Boswell. (18 February 1997) *American Buffalo* (David Mamet) with Douglas Henshall, Neil Stuke, Nicholas Woodeson; director, Lindsay Posner. (April) *Animal Farm* (Orwell, adapt. Ian Woolridge) with David Whitaker, Jane Arnfield; director, Alan Lyddiard. (8 May) *My Mother Said I Never Should* (Charlotte Keatley), an Oxford Stage Company production; director, Dominic Cooke. (2 July) *King Lear*, transferred from Leicester

OUTSIDE LONDON

Birmingham: Repertory (16 September 1996) *The Alchemist* (Jonson) with Simon Callow, Josie Lawrence,

Tim Pigott-Smith, Geoffrey Freshwater; director, Bill Alexander. (29 November) *Pinocchio* (Carlo Collodi, adapt. Anthony Clark) with Neil Warhurst, Nigel Betts, Lorna Laidlaw, Simeon Truby; director Anthony Clark. (10 December) *Season's Greetings* (Ayckbourn) with Samantha Beckinsale; director, Gwenda Hughes. (11 February 1997) *The Merchant of Venice* (Shakespeare) with Cathy Tyson, David Schofield, Don Warrington; director, Bill Alexander. (May) *The Cherry Orchard* (Chekhov) with Estelle Kohler, Jack Klass, Burt Caesar, Joseph Jones; director, Janet Suzman. (20 June) *The Importance of Being Earnest* (Wilde) with Diane Fletcher, Candida Gubbins, Philip Bretherton; director, Terry Hands

Bristol: Old Vic (17 October 1996) *Old Wicked Songs* (Jon Marans) with Bob Hoskins, James Callis; director, Elijah Moshinsky. (November) *Marat/Sade* (Peter Weiss) with Terry Taplin; director, Andrew Hay. (April 1997) *The Amen Corner* (James Baldwin) with Cecilia Noble, Steve Toussaint; director, Paulette Randall

Chichester: Festival (September 1996) *Fortune's Fool* (Turgenev, adapt. Mike Poulton) with Alan Bates, Rachel Pickup, Benedick Bates, Desmond Barrit; director, Gale Edwards. (October) *Lock Up Your Daughters* (Lionel Bart) with George Cole, Sheila Hancock; director, Stephen Rayne. (18 April 1997) *The Admirable Crichton* (J. M. Barrie) with Michael Denison, Victoria Scarborough, Ian McShane; director, Michael Rudman. (2 May) *Lady Windermere's Fan* (Wilde) with Stephanie Beecham, Siri O'Neill, Tim Wallers, David Rintoul; director, Richard Cotterell. (13 June) *Blithe Spirit* (Coward) with Twiggy Lawson, Belinda Lang, Dora Bryan; director, Tim Luscombe. (10 July) *Divorce Me, Darling* (Sandy Wilson) with Ruthie Henshall, Marti Webb, Liliane Montevecchi; director, Paul Kerryson. (12 August) *Our Betters* (Somerset Maugham) with Rula Lenska, Nigel Davenport, Kathleen Turner; director, Michael Rudman

Minerva (September 1996) *The Handyman* (Ronald Harwood) with Frank Finlay, Francesca Hunt, Hugh Bonneville, Kate Lynn-Evans; director, Christopher Morahan. (15 May) *After October* (Rodney Ackland) with Nick Waring, Dorothy Tutin, Anna Quayle, Murray Melvin; director, Keith Baxter. (6 June) *Nocturne for Lovers* (Bruno Villien, adapt. Gavin Lambert) with Leslie Caron, David Abramovitz; director, Kado Kostzer. (27 June) *Tullulah!* (Sandra Ryan Heyward) with Kathleen Turner; director, Michael Rudman. (22 July) *Suzanna Andler* (Marguerite Duras, trans. Barbara Bray) with Julie Christie, Aden Gillett, Robert Hickson; director, Lindy Davies. (19 August) *Misalliance* (Shaw) with Sheila Reid, Joss Ackland, Tony Britton, Natalia Makarova; director, Frank Hauser

Edinburgh: Royal Lyceum (8 November 1996) *The Merchant of Venice* (Shakespeare) with Tom McGovern, Emily Mortimer; director, Kenny Ireland. (January 1997) *Dr Jekyll and Mr Hyde* (R. L. Stevenson, adapt. David Edgar) with Laurie Ventry; director, Kenny Ireland. (7 February) *Rebecca* (Du Maurier); director, Philip Franks

Glasgow: Citizens (October 1996) *Hamlet* (Shakespeare) with Cal MacAninch; director, Philip Prowse. (1 October) *Dracula* (Bram Stoker, adapt. Jon Pope) with Stuart Bowman; director, Jon Pope. (30 October) *Seascape* (Albee). (3 December) *The Wizard of Oz*, with Rachel Pittman; director, Giles Havergal. (January 1997) *The Country Wife* (Wycherley) with Henry Ian Cusick, Siobhan Stanley; director Anthony McDonald. (14 March) *Cat on a Hot Tin Roof* (Tennessee Williams) with Julie Saunders, Robert David Macdonald, Mark Bazeley; director, Philip Prowse

LEEDS: WEST YORKSHIRE PLAYHOUSE (11 September 1996) *The Crucible* (Miller); director, David Doiashvili. (15 October) *Popcorn*, transferred from Nottingham. (2 November) *A Perfect Ganesh* (Terrence McNally) with Prunella Scales, Eleanor Bron; director, Jude Kelly. (2 December) *Peter Pan*, revival of 1995 production. (30 January 1997) *Hamlet* (Shakespeare) with Michael Maloney, Zoe Waites. (March) *Landslide* (Andy de la Tour) with Jenna Russell, Christopher Ravenscroft, Deborah Norton, Raymond Coulthard; director, Gwenda Hughes. (13 March) *Hobson's Choice* (Harold Brighouse) with Jack Smethurst; director, Stuart Burge. (24 April) *The Wasp Factory* (Iain Banks, adapt. Malcolm Sutherland) with Tom Smith, Lucy Morgan, Martin Freeman; director, Malcolm Sutherland. (23 May) *Things Fall Apart* (Chinua Achebe, adapt. Biyi Bandele) with Yomi A. Michaels; director, Chuck Mike. (19 June) *Don Juan* (Molière, adapt. Edward Kemp) with Martin Marquez, Patrick Brennan; director, Toby Jones

COURTYARD (24 September 1996) *Office Suite: Green Forms* and *A Visit From Miss Prothero* (Alan Bennett) with Susan Wooldridge, Paola Dionisotti, Timothy Bateson; director, Jennie Darnell. (11 July) *Vanity Fair* (Thackeray, adapt. David Noble), a Community Company production; director, Michael Birch

LEICESTER: HAYMARKET (24 September 1996) *Marabou Stork Nightmares* (Irvine Walsh) with Jim Cunningham; director, Harry Gibson. (12 November) *Sweeney Todd* (Sondheim) with Dave Willetts, Jeanette Ranger; director, Paul Kerryson. (February 1997) *King Lear* (Shakespeare) with Kathryn Hunter, Marcello Magni, Hayley Carmichael; director, Helena Kaut-Howson. (1 May) *A Woman of No Importance* (Wilde) with Shirley Stelfox, Edmund Moriarty; director, Paul Kerryson. (22 August) *Heavenly Bodies* with David Dale, Guy Oliver Watts, Hazel Fernandes; director, Paul Kerryson

LIVERPOOL: PLAYHOUSE (November 1996) *Billy Liar* (Waterhouse, Willis) with Paul Basson; director, Richard Williams. (30 June 1997) *The Seagull* (Chekhov) with Cheryl Campbell, Denys Hawthorn, Mark Bazeley; director, Stephen Unwin. (1 August) *I'm Marrying Robbie Fowler* (John Chambers, Dave Simpson); director, Richard Williams

MANCHESTER: ROYAL EXCHANGE (September 1996) *All's Well That Ends Well* (Shakespeare). (November) *I Have Been Here Before* (Priestley) with David Horovitch; director, Marianne Elliott. (10 December) *Lady Windermere's Fan* (Wilde) with Rebecca Johnson, Gabrielle Drake, James Saxon, Simon Robson; director, Braham Murray. (6 March 1997) *The Road to Mecca* (Athol Fugard) with Ann Mitchell, Helen Schlesinger, William Russell; director, Gregory Hersov. (April) *The Candidate* (Paul Godfrey) with James Saxon, James Clyde, director, Braham Murray. (13 May) *Poor Super Man* (Brad Fraser); director, Marianne Elliott. (12 June) *The Illusion* (Corneille, adapt. Tony Kushner) with Julia Sawalha, Peter de Jersey, Trevor Baxter; director, Matthew Lloyd

MOLD: THEATR CLWYD (17 September 1996) *Silas Marner* (Eliot, adapt. Greg Cullen) with Johnson Willis, Nicola Reynolds; director, Tim Baker. (4 December) *The Snow Queen* (Andersen, adapt. Stuart Paterson); director, Lawrence Till. (April 1997) *The Servant of Two Masters* (Goldoni) with Billie-Claire Wright, Bob Goody, Melee Hutton, David Leonard; directors, Martin Duncan, Ultz. (7 June) *The Importance of Being Earnest* (Wilde)

NOTTINGHAM: PLAYHOUSE (3 September 1996) *Time and the Room* (Botho Strauss), a co-production with Edinburgh International Festival. (14 September 1996) *Popcorn* (Ben

Elton) with Vincenzo Nicoli, Patrick O'Kane, Dena Davis; director, Laurence Boswell. (20 November) *Elsinore* (Robert Lepage) with Robert Lepage. (7 February 1997) *As You Like It* (Shakespeare) with Stephen Mangan, Cate Hamer, Trilby James; director, David Pountney. (May) *The Servant of Two Masters*, transferred from Theatr Clwyd, Mold

PLYMOUTH: THEATRE ROYAL (5 September 1996) *Blue Murder* (Peter Nichols) with Anton Rodgers, Nichola McAuliffe, Barry Foster. (24 February) *A Chorus Line* (Hamlisch, Kleban) with Adam Faith. (August) *West Side Story*; director, Alan Johnson

SCARBOROUGH: STEPHEN JOSEPH (4 September 1996) *Dealing with Clair* (Martin Crimp); director, Connal Orton. (24 September) *Love Me Slender* (Vanessa Brooks); director, Auriol Smith. (4 December) *The Champion of Paribanou* (Ayckbourn) with Jonathan McGuinness, Pauline Turner; director, Alan Ayckbourn. (May 1997) *Things We Do for Love* (Ayckbourn) with Joanna Van Gyseghem, Sally Giles, Cameron Stewart, Barry McCarthy; director, Alan Ayckbourn. (21 May) *They're Playing Our Song* (Simon, Hamlisch, Sager); director, Alan Ayckbourn. (12 June) *The Farmer's Bride* (Ged McKenna); director, Alan Ayckbourn. (16 July) *Lucky Sods* (John Godber); director, Connal Orton. (26 August) *Fool to Yourself* (Robert Shearman); director, Alan Ayckbourn

SHEFFIELD: CRUCIBLE (4 October 1996) *Hay Fever* (Coward) with Jane How, Maria Charles, Peter McEnery; director, Deborah Paige. (November) *The Merchant of Venice* (Shakespeare) with David de Keyser, Niamh Linehan; director, Deborah Paige

SOUTHAMPTON: NUFFIELD (31 October 1996) *Three In A Bed: Bedtime Story* (O'Casey); *Waking Up* (Dario Fo); *Guiser Martin* (Robert Forrest). (7 February 1997) *The Comedy of Errors* (Shakespeare) with Anthony Pedley, Roy Boutcher, David Annen, Clive Flint; director, Patrick Sandford. (18 March) *The Caretaker* (Pinter) with Moray Treadwell, David Annen, Roger Lloyd Pack; director, Daniel Buckroyd. (11 April) *The Surprise Party* (Ivan Menchell) with Peter Duncan, Jessica Martin, Matthew Kelly; director, Patrick Sandford

STRATFORD: ROYAL SHAKESPEARE THEATRE (27 November 1996) *Much Ado About Nothing* (Shakespeare) with Siobhan Redmond, Alex Jennings; director, Michael Boyd. (19 December) *The Merry Wives of Windsor* (Shakespeare) with Leslie Phillips, Susannah York, Joanna McCallum, Cherry Morris; director, Ian Judge. (22 February 1997) *Cymbeline* (Shakespeare) with Joanne Pearce, Paul Freeman, Guy Henry; director, Adrian Noble. (8 May) *Hamlet* (Shakespeare) with Alex Jennings, Paul Freeman, Derbhle Crotty; director, Matthew Warchus

SWAN (26 November 1996) *Henry VIII* (Shakespeare) with Paul Jesson, Jane Lapotaire, Ian Hogg; director, Gregory Doran. (18 December) *Little Eyolf* (Ibsen) with Joanne Pearce, Robert Glenister; director, Adrian Noble. (22 February 1997) *Camino Real* (Tennessee Williams) with Peter Egan, Leslie Phillips, Susannah York; director, Steven Pimlott. (7 May) *The Spanish Tragedy* (Thomas Kyd) with Siobhan Redmond, Peter Wight, Robert Glenister, Patrice Naiambana; director, Michael Boyd

THE OTHER PLACE (14 November 1996) *Everyman* (anonymous, c.1500) with Joseph Mydell; directors, Kathryn Hunter, Marcello Magni. (March 1997) *The Mysteries: The Creation* and *The Passion* with David Ryall, Paul Hilton, Josette Bushell-Mingo; director, Katie Mitchell

Weather

JULY 1996

Rainfall totals were below normal generally for the third successive month. The 1st brought thunderstorms across southern England and on the 2nd heavy rain fell in the far west late in the day, with 44.0 mm (1.7 in) falling at Nantmor (Gwynedd). The 4th brought rain over northern Scotland. Showers continued generally on the 5th with thunder in parts of the Midlands and south-east England. Thunderstorms continued over southeast England on the 6th. The 7th brought thunder to the south coast but only scattered light showers. Rain fell over Northern Ireland and Scotland on the 8th. The 9th was generally dry but rain fell in Scotland on the 10th and in mainly western and northern areas of England and in Wales and Northern Ireland on the 11th. The 12th and 13th brought rain to the north of Scotland. A gust of 72 kt (83 mph) was recorded at Aonach Mor (Highland) on the 13th. The 14th to 20th were dry and fine everywhere while the 21st brought some fog to western areas. Heavy rain fell in Northern Ireland and Scotland on the 22nd when 36.2 mm (1.4 in) fell at Orsay (Strathclyde). The 24th brought thunderstorms to many areas of England and Wales and heavy rain fell over Scotland. In Cambridgeshire 57.3 mm (2.3 in) fell at Mepal and 55 mm (2.2 in) at Chatteris. More rain fell over England and Wales and Northern Ireland on the 28th when 37 mm (1.5 in) fell at Knockareven (Co. Fermanagh). Thunderstorms were widespread over the Midlands and southern England on the 29th.

Monthly mean temperatures were above normal over England and Wales. The highest temperature was 33.0°C (91.4°F) at St Helier (Jersey) on the 22nd and the lowest was 1.3°C (34.3°F) at Glenlivet (Moray) on the 16th.

Sunshine totals were above average over England and Wales. The highest daily total was 16.1 hours at Ringway (Gtr Manchester) on the 17th.

AUGUST 1996

Rainfall totals were slightly above normal over England and Wales. The 1st brought light showers to many areas, and to Scotland on the 2nd. The 3rd and 4th were fine and dry but on the 5th heavy rain fell in Northern Ireland and western Scotland when 72.3 mm (2.8 in) fell at Carmony (Co. Londonderry). The 6th brought heavy rain and thunderstorms to many areas; 64.5 mm (2.6 in) of rain fell at Pennerley (Shropshire) and a gust of 76 kt (87.5 mph) was recorded at The Needles (Isle of Wight). The 7th was mostly dry but rain fell mainly in the west on the 8th. Rain or drizzle fell widely on the 9th and 10th. Thunder occurred over southern England on the 11th when 84.7 mm (3.4 in) of rain fell at Stanton

(Suffolk). The 12th was mainly dry but a thunderstorm at Folkestone (Kent) produced 98.4 mm (3.9 in) of rain. The 13th and 14th were mostly dry. Fog was dense in places in southern England on the 16th. Rain fell in the Western Isles on the 17th and 18th. Rain fell mainly in western areas on the 19th and was widespread on the 20th when 51.0 mm (2.0 in) fell at Portrush (Co. Antrim). The 21st brought rain mainly over Scotland and heavy rain was widespread on the 22nd when 55.6 mm (2.2 in) fell at Poverty Bottom (E. Sussex) and 52.3 mm (2.1 in) fell at St Helier (Jersey). Thunder was widespread over England and Wales on the 23rd when 51.8 mm (2.0 in) of rain fell at Blagdon Hall (Avon). On the 26th, 67.9 mm (2.7 in) of rain fell at Bodfari (Clwyd) and 63.1 mm (2.5 in) at Graincliffe Reservoir (W. Yorks). Thunderstorms were widespread over England and Wales on the 27th and 28th when 51.4 mm (2.0 in) of rain fell at Coltishall (Norfolk). Heavy rain fell in south-east England on the 29th when 69.7 mm (2.7 in) fell at Hevingham (Norfolk). A heavy shower gave 76.4 mm (3.0 in) of rain at Feniton Court (Devon) on the 31st.

Monthly mean temperatures were above normal over England and Wales. The highest temperature was 31.8°C (89.2°F) at Nottingham on the 19th and the lowest was 2.1°C (35.8°F) at Tulloch Bridge (Highland).

Sunshine totals were above average over England and Wales. The highest daily sunshine was 14.5 hours at Poole (Dorset) on the 4th.

SEPTEMBER 1996

Rainfall totals were well below normal and it was the driest September since 1986. The 1st brought heavy rain to Scotland and northern England. The 3rd and 4th were mainly dry and the 5th to 7th were fine and dry while the 8th to 9th brought scattered showers or drizzle. On the 10th, 83.1 mm (3.3 in) of rain fell at Edern (Gwynedd). Rain was widespread on the 11th and 12th and fell over Scotland on the 14th but the 15th to 17th were fine and dry everywhere. Rain was widespread over southern England on the 19th and fell in coastal areas on the 20th. The 22nd was mainly dry but rain was widespread on the 24th to 26th. The 27th brought showers mainly over Scotland. The 28th was a wet day generally and 118.3 mm (4.7 in) of rain fell at Grasmere (Cumbria), 105.8 mm (4.2 in) at Bampton (Cumbria) and 91.0 mm (3.6 in) at Nantmor (Gwynedd). The 29th was another wet day generally and the 30th brought heavy rain to southern England when 94.7 mm (3.7 in) fell at Cray Reservoir (Oxon). Gusts of 75 kt (86 mph) were recorded at the Needles (Isle of Wight) on the 29th.

Monthly mean temperatures were above normal over England and Wales. The highest temperature was 25.7°C (78.3°F) at Leuchars (Fife) on the 2nd and the lowest was −2.0°C (28.4°F) at Aviemore (Highland) on the 19th.

Sunshine totals were above normal over England and Wales. The highest daily total was 12.6 hours at Cape Wrath (Highland) on the 5th.

OCTOBER 1996

Rainfall totals were generally around normal over England and Wales. Heavy rain fell in the northern half of the UK on the 2nd when 44.0 mm (1.7 in) fell at Kilmory (Highland). The 3rd was a wet day generally. Rain fell in northern areas on the 5th and more generally on the 6th when 32.5 mm (1.3 in) fell at Kilmory. The 7th brought rain or drizzle to Scotland while the 8th brought rain to southern England and the Midlands. The 10th was a mainly dry day. Heavy rain fell over Northern Ireland and Scotland on the 11th when 64.9 mm (2.6 in) fell at Eskdalemuir (Dumfries and Galloway). Further heavy rain fell over Scotland on the 12th. The 13th was mainly fine and dry but the 14th brought heavy rain to mainly western areas, when 30.0 mm (1.2 in) fell at Dumfries. On the 15th heavy rain fell over northern Scotland. The 17th was mainly dry but the 18th brought rain, heavy at times, to many areas. The 20th was a wet day generally and 36.7 mm (1.45 in) of rain fell at Nantmor (Gwynedd). The 21st and 23rd were mainly dry but the 24th brought heavy rain to many areas; 35.7 mm (1.4 in) fell at Orsay (Islay). The 26th brought rain to western areas and the 27th and 28th were wet generally, with 110.2 mm (4.3 in) of rain falling at Cray Reservoir (Oxon). Gusts of 76 kt (87 mph) were recorded in the Solent and at Portland Bill (Dorset) on the 28th. Rain fell in southern England on the 29th and in western areas on the 30th. The 31st was wet generally and 39.3 mm (1.55 in) of rain fell at Nantmor (Gwynedd).

Monthly mean temperatures were 1.1°C (1.92°F) above normal over England and Wales. The highest temperature recorded was 21.7°C (71.1°F) at Prestatyn (Clwyd) on the 24th and the lowest was −1.7°C (28.9°F) at Eskdalemuir (Dumfries and Galloway) on the 8th.

Sunshine totals were slightly higher than normal over England and Wales and the highest daily total was 10.7 hours at Swanage (Dorset) on the 2nd.

NOVEMBER 1996

Rainfall totals were generally well above normal. Rain or drizzle fell mainly in western areas on the 1st and 2nd, with 33.3 mm (1.3 in) falling at Greenock (Strathclyde) on the 2nd. Heavy rain fell over southern England on the 3rd when 37.2 mm (1.5 in) fell at Davidstow Moor (Cornwall). The 4th was a wet day generally and 42.6 mm (1.8 in) of rain fell at Fair Isle (Shetland). The 5th was also a generally wet day and 41.5 mm (1.6 in) fell at Knockareven (Co. Fermanagh). Gales were widespread on the 6th when gusts of 93 kt (107 mph) at Glen Ogle and Aonach Mor (Highland), 86 kt (99 mph) at the Needles (Isle of Wight) and 78 kt (90 mph) at

Greenock (Strathclyde), Great Dun Fell (Cumbria) and Capel Curig (Gwynedd) were recorded. Rain fell over northern Scotland on the 8th and heavy rain fell over southern counties on the 9th when 36.2 mm (1.4 in) fell at Eastbourne (E. Sussex). Persistent fog formed in the Vale of York and north-east England on the 10th and rain fell in many areas on the 11th. Rain fell mainly over Scotland on the 13th and drizzle was widely scattered on the 14th to 16th. Rain fell over England and Wales on the 17th. The 18th was mainly dry except for Cornwall but the 19th was wet in most areas with snow as far south as the Home Counties; 67 mm (2.6 in) of rain fell at Yorkshire Bridge (S. Yorks). The 21st was mainly dry while the 22nd produced rain or showers mainly in the south. The 23rd brought snow to northern England and Scotland and the 24th was wet everywhere with heavy snow over northern England and Scotland; 57.8 mm (2.3 in) of rain fell at Pembury (Kent) and 39 mm (1.5 in) fell at Weston-super-Mare (Somerset). The 26th was mainly dry but rain fell in western areas on the 27th and the 28th was wet everywhere in the evening when 35.9 mm (1.4 in) of rain fell at Bastreet (Cornwall).

Monthly mean temperatures were below normal over England and Wales. The highest temperature recorded was 18.1°C (64.6°F) at Heathrow (Gtr London) on the 2nd and the lowest was −11.7°C (10.9°F) at Altnaharra (Highland) on the 19th.

Sunshine totals were above normal over England and Wales. The highest daily total was 8.9 hours at Margate (Kent) on the 8th.

DECEMBER 1996

Rainfall totals were below normal over England and Wales. Heavy rain fell in south-western areas on the 2nd when 31.9 mm (1.3 in) of rain fell at Nantmor (Gwynedd), and the 3rd was a wet day generally with 44.6 mm (1.8 in) of rain falling at Eskdalemuir (Dumfries and Galloway). The 4th was wet in Scotland while the 5th and 6th were foggy over England and Wales. The 7th was a wet day over Northern Ireland and Scotland and 31.2 mm (1.2 in) of rain fell at Waterstein (Skye). On the 8th and 9th there was fog over England and Wales and rain over Scotland. Drizzle spread to most areas on the 12th. The 13th produced rain over southern England and northern Scotland and rain fell over southern parts on the 16th. The 17th brought dense fog to mainly central areas. Heavy rain fell over all areas on the 18th when 33.2 mm (1.3 in) fell at Fylingdales (N. Yorks) and on the 19th when 59.0 mm (2.3 in) fell at Yorkshire Bridge and 48.7 mm (1.9 in) at Donington-on-Bain (Lincs). Rain fell over much of England on the 20th. The 21st to 25th were generally fine and dry but the 26th brought rain or snow to northern areas. On the 27th snow fell as far south as the Channel coast east of the Isle of Wight. Snow showers were widespread over England and Wales on the 30th and in all areas on the 31st.

Monthly mean temperatures were 1.7°C (3.1°F) below normal over England and Wales. The highest temperature recorded was 13.8°C (56.8°F) at Guernsey on the 17th and the lowest was −12.8°C (9.0°F) at Altnaharra (Highland) on the 25th.

Sunshine totals were above average over England and Wales. The highest daily amount was 7.9 hours at Plymouth on the 25th and at St Helier (Jersey) on the 26th.

THE YEAR 1996

Rainfall totals were below normal and 1996 was the driest year since 1973. It was also a cool year with mean temperatures the lowest since 1987. Sunshine totals were near or slightly above normal over England and Wales. January was wet in the West Country and Northern Ireland, with flooding around Dawlish (Devon) on the 8th. On the 25th roads were blocked by snow in the West Country and Minehead was flooded. On the 26th, 15.2 cm (6 in) of snow fell in Sussex and Essex and the M4 was closed for a time. February was a wet month with heavy snowfall. On the 5th drifts were 3 m (10 ft) deep in the Channel Islands and on the 6th roads were blocked from Dorset to Strathclyde. On the 9th, 160 mm (6.3 in) of rain fell at Dumfries. Gales caused havoc on the 19th when Norfolk sea defences were breached. Rainfall in March was generally below normal. The 12th brought heavy snow and strong winds and there was flooding in Cumbria. It was the dullest March on record over Northern Ireland, the Orkney Islands and the Isle of Man. April was generally wet and at Prestwick (Strathclyde) it was the wettest since 1942. On the 4th the humidity fell to 16 per cent in London, the second lowest humidity ever recorded. Rain and thunderstorms were widespread during the month. Inverness (Highland) had its warmest April since 1914 and Eskdalemuir (Dumfries and Galloway) had its dullest since 1911. Rainfall in May was generally below normal but on the 19th rain and strong winds were widespread. On the 31st a gust of 103 kt (118.6 mph) was recorded on Cairngorm (Highland). Rainfall totals in June were generally below normal but on the 5th widespread flooding was caused by thunderstorms across southern England. In July rainfall was generally below normal and it was the third successive month drier than normal. Thunderstorms were a feature of the month. Rainfall totals were slightly above normal for August but the summer months (June, July and August) as a whole were drier than average. Thunderstorms were again a feature of the month and 98.4 mm (3.9 in) of rain fell at Folkestone (Kent) on the 12th. Temperature and sunshine levels were both above normal. September was a dry month and it was the driest September since 1986. The 28th was a very wet day and 118.3 mm (4.7 in) of rain fell at Grasmere and 105.8 mm (4.2 in) fell at Bampton (Cumbria). Temperature and sunshine levels were generally above normal. Rainfall totals for October were generally around normal but heavy rain fell at times and on the 28th, 110.2 mm (4.3 in) fell at Cray Reservoir (Oxon). Temperature and sunshine le-

vels were above normal and it was the fifth successive month with higher than normal temperatures. In November rainfall totals were well above normal. Gales were widespread on the 6th and heavy snow fell on the 24th. Temperatures were below normal but sunshine totals were above normal, making it the sunniest November since 1989. Rainfall was below normal in December but there were some heavy bursts of rain. Snow was widespread on the 30th and 31st. Temperatures were below normal but sunshine totals were above normal, making it the sunniest December since 1976.

JANUARY 1997

Rainfall totals were well below normal, particularly in western areas. Over England and Wales it was the driest January since 1779. On the 1st snow fell over many areas of England and Wales while the 2nd brought rain, sleet or snow to northern areas. The 3rd was very cold with some freezing fog in the Midlands. The 4th was mainly dry and cold but snow fell over south-east England. The 5th and 6th had wintry showers over mainly eastern areas. The 7th and 8th were cold and the 9th brought snow to southern counties when 6–10 cm (2–4 in) accumulated over Essex and Kent. Rain fell generally on the 11th when 30.2 mm (1.2 in) fell at Cape Wrath (Highland). Rain fell in many areas on the 12th but mainly over Scotland on the 13th and 14th, which were both windy days. Gusts of 110 kt (126.7 mph) at Cairngorm (Highland) on the 13th and 100 kt (115.2 mph) at Amersham (Bucks) on the 14th were recorded. The 15th and 16th brought fog to most parts of Wales and England. Rain fell in most places on the 17th and over Northern Ireland, Scotland and southern England on the 18th. Rain fell mainly over southern England and Wales on the 19th. The 21st brought rain to southern England and on the 22nd there was snow over northern England. The 23rd was mainly dry with patches of fog over England. The 24th brought rain to Scotland and western areas of Wales and northern England. The 26th brought rain to the far north and east of Scotland but was otherwise mostly dry. The 28th to 31st were mainly dry, although drizzle fell in southern areas on the 29th.

Monthly mean temperatures were generally below normal. The highest temperature recorded was 14.6°C (58.3°F) at Dyce (Grampian) on the 13th and the lowest was −15.2°C (4.6°F) at Shepshed (Leics) on the 3rd.

Sunshine totals were generally above normal and the highest daily total was 8.1 hours at St Helier (Jersey) on the 13th, at Wittering (Cambs) on the 28th, at Folkestone (Kent) on the 24th and at Margate (Kent) on the 25th.

FEBRUARY 1997

Rainfall totals were generally above normal over England and Wales. Rain fell mainly in the west on the 1st but the 2nd was fine and dry. On the 3rd heavy rain fell from mid-Wales northwards and 88.6 mm (3.5 in) fell at Mungrisdale (Cumbria), 87.3 mm (3.4 in) at Machynlleth (Powys) and 82.4 mm (3.2 in) at Langdon Brook (Cumbria). The 4th was generally wet but the 5th was dry and fine. Rain fell in Scotland on the 8th and in many areas on the 9th when 33.5 mm (1.3 in) fell at Nantmor (Gwynedd). There were gales in northern Scotland. The 10th brought gales to most of the country, with rain or snow in northern areas. The 11th was generally wet and 41 mm (1.6 in) of rain fell at Bastreet (Cornwall). On the 12th, 34.3 mm (1.35 in) of rain fell at Lybster (Highland). A gust of 80 kt (92 mph) was recorded at Portland Bill (Dorset) on the 13th. Rain was confined to southern England on the 14th. The 15th was generally fine but rain fell in most places on the 16th. Heavy rain fell almost everywhere on the 17th when 116.1 mm (4.6 in) fell at Burn Banks (Cumbria), 95.4 mm (3.8 in) at Nant-y-Ysfa (Gwent) and 94.4 mm (3.7 in) at Coniston (Cumbria). It was a very windy day with severe gales over the Scottish islands. A gust of 79 kt (91 mph) was recorded at Butt of Lewis (Hebrides). On the 19th gusts over 70 kt (81 mph) were recorded in many places; 94 kt (108 mph) was recorded at the Needles (Isle of Wight), 81 kt (93 mph) at Great Dun Fell (Cumbria) and 80 kt (92 mph) at Capel Curig (Gwynedd). Heavy rain fell almost everywhere, with 37.0 mm (1.5 in) falling at Eskdalemuir (Dumfries and Galloway). There were gales in the north and west on the 20th, with heavy rain in some places; 41.9 mm (1.7 in) fell at Eskdalemuir. The 21st was another windy day, with gales in the north and west. The 22nd was also windy and 35.2 mm (1.4 in) of rain fell at Waterstein (Skye) with gusts of 133 kt (153.2 mph) recorded at Cairngorm (Highland) and 113 kt (130.2 mph) at Cairnwell. The 23rd was windy with rain in many areas. Severe gales affected Scotland, Wales and southern England on the 24th and rain or showers fell everywhere. A gust of 94 kt (108 mph) was recorded at the Needles (Isle of Wight). Gales continued on the 25th. The 27th brought rain to northern England and Scotland and a gust of 85 kt (98 mph) was recorded at Ringway (Gtr Manchester). The 28th was mainly fine but thunder and hail were reported in the northern isles and the Hebrides.

Monthly mean temperatures were 2.9°C (5.2°F) above normal over England and Wales, making it the mildest February since 1990. The highest temperature was 15.2°C (59.4°F) at Guernsey on the 28th and the lowest was −7.0°C (19.4°F) at Benson (Oxon) and at Farnborough (Hants) on the 3rd.

Sunshine totals were around normal over England and Wales and the highest daily total was 9.4 hours at Bognor Regis (W. Sussex) on the 15th.

MARCH 1997

Rainfall totals were well below normal and it was the seventh driest March this century. The 1st was wet over Scotland and 40.4 mm (1.6 in) of rain fell at

Cape Wrath (Highland). The 2nd brought snow showers to Scotland. Both the 1st and 2nd were windy days, especially over Scotland. Gusts of 108 kt (124 mph) at Aonach Mor (Highland) and 84 kt (97 mph) at Great Dun Fell (Cumbria) on the 1st and 102 kt (117 mph) at Cairnwell (Highland) on the 2nd were recorded. Heavy rain fell over southern England on the 3rd when 46.6 mm (1.8 in) fell at Salcombe (Devon). The 6th was mainly dry with high winds in the north while the 7th brought rain to Northern Ireland and Scotland. A gust of 135 kt (155 mph) was recorded on Cairngorm (Highland) on the 6th. The 9th was foggy in many places but a temperature of 16.0°C (61°F) was recorded at Gatwick (Surrey). Fog was dense and persistent in some areas on the 10th and 11th. On the 12th, 85.5 mm (4.5 in) of rain at Larkhill (Wilts) and rain fell over western areas on the 13th. Heavy rain fell over Scotland on the 15th, with 37.2 mm (1.5 in) falling at Rackwick (Orkney). Scotland had rain on the 16th and rain or showers fell generally on the 18th, becoming widely scattered on the 19th and 20th. Rain fell over northern Scotland on the 21st and over northern England and Northern Ireland on the 22nd. Rain fell almost everywhere on the 24th and over mainly western areas on the 25th and 26th. A gust of 85 kt (98 mph) was recorded at Aberporth (Dyfed) on the 26th. The 27th brought gales to the far north where a gust of 66 kt (76 mph) was recorded at Lerwick (Shetland) and rain fell over Scotland and western areas. The 29th to 31st were mainly dry.

Monthly mean temperatures were 2.5°C (4.5°F) above normal over England and Wales. The highest temperature was 20.8°C (69.4°F) at Nantmor (Gwynedd) on the 11th and the lowest was -5.3°C (22.5°F) at Leeming (N. Yorks) on the 4th.

Sunshine totals were above normal over England and Wales. The highest daily total was 12.5 hours at Bastreet (Cornwall) on the 30th.

APRIL 1997

Rainfall totals were generally well below normal and East Anglia received only 14 per cent of its normal amount. Wales, however, received one-third of the normal total for the month on the 25th. There were gales in the north on the 2nd when a gust of 97 kt (112 mph) was recorded at Cairngorm (Highland). The 3rd brought snow to Scotland and rain and snow became heavier over Scotland on the 4th when 38 mm (1.5 in) fell at Lochranza (Arran). A gust of 72 kt (83 mph) was recorded at Great Dun Fell (Cumbria). Rain fell everywhere except southern England on the 5th but mainly over Scotland on the 6th. A gust of 76 kt (87 mph) was recorded at High Bradfield (S. Yorks) on the 5th. The 7th to 10th were mainly dry but light showers or drizzle fell over many areas on the 11th to 14th. The 15th and 16th were fine but drizzle fell in England and Wales on the 17th to 19th. Rain fell over Scotland on the 20th and over northern England on the 21st. Heavy rain fell over northern areas on the 23rd, when 34.5

mm (1.4 in) fell at Lochranza (Arran). Rain fell over Northern Ireland, Wales and northern England on the 24th and heavy rain fell over England and Wales on the 25th. Rain or drizzle fell nearly everywhere on the 26th and 27th. The 28th was a generally wet day but by the 30th the weather was generally fine and dry.

Monthly mean temperatures were above normal over England and Wales. The highest temperature was 21.7°C (71.1°F) at Bristol on the 9th and at Gatwick (Surrey) on the 10th. The lowest temperature was −6.8°C (19.8°F) at Glenlivet (Moray) on the 20th.

Sunshine totals were above normal over England and Wales. The highest daily total was 14.5 hours at Hayling Island (Hants) on the 30th.

MAY 1997

Rainfall totals were near or slightly above normal over England and Wales. The 1st and 2nd were mainly dry. The 4th was a wet day in many areas and 40.0 mm (1.6 in) of rain fell at Invergordon (Highland). The 5th was wet generally and 35.7 mm (1.4 in) of rain fell at Prestatyn (Clwyd). The 6th was showery with snow in the north and rain in the south; 15 cm (5.9 in) of snow lay around Halkyn (Clwyd). Rain or showers fell over most areas on the 7th to 9th with thunder in places. Thunderstorms and showers were again widespread on the 10th to 12th. A tornado and hail the size of golfballs were reported in Hampshire on the 12th. A gust of 93 kt (107 mph) was recorded at Gravesend (Kent) on the 14th. Heavy rain fell over East Anglia on the 15th and there were thunderstorms over southern areas on the 16th. A gust of 92 kt (106 mph) was recorded at Milford Haven (Dyfed) on the 16th. Heavy rain fell over Scotland on the 17th and thunder was widespread; 86.4 mm (3.4 in) of rain fell at Woburn Sands (Beds) and violent hail was reported at Aylesbury (Bucks). The 18th brought further heavy rain to Scotland when 40.4 mm (1.6 in) fell at Invergordon (Highland). Heavy rain fell over southern England and Wales on the 19th, with thunderstorms on the 20th when 33.0 mm (1.3 in) of rain fell at Shawbury (Shropshire). The 23rd and 24th were mainly dry but the 25th brought rain to Scotland. The 27th to 31st were mainly dry but isolated thunderstorms occurred on the 31st when 166.0 mm (6.5 in) of rain fell at Avon (Hants), 121.6 mm (4.8 in) at Belstone (Devon) and 103.4 mm (4.1 in) at Parracombe (Devon). Gusts of 102 kt (117 mph) at Rhyl (Clwyd) on the 29th and 100 kt (115 mph) at Walney Island (Cumbria) were recorded.

Monthly mean temperatures were generally above normal. The highest temperature recorded was 28.0°C (82.4°F) at Knockarevan (Co. Fermanagh) on the 31st. The lowest temperature was −5.2°C (22.6°F) at Loch Glascarnoch (Highland) on the 6th.

Sunshine totals were well above normal and the highest daily total was 16.0 hours at Morecambe (Lancs) on the 29th.

JUNE 1997

Rainfall totals were well above normal nearly everywhere and it was the wettest June over England and Wales since 1860. The month started mainly dry. The 5th brought heavy rain or showers to England and Wales and Northern Ireland, with scattered thunderstorms; 47.2 mm (1.9 in) of rain fell at Camborne (Cornwall). The 6th was wet everywhere with thunderstorms in eastern areas. Thunderstorms and showers were widespread on the 7th and 8th and a gust of 97 kt (112 mph) was recorded at Cairngorm (Highland) on the 7th. Rain fell in the west and south-west on the 10th but heavy rain was widespread on the 11th with thunderstorms over southern England, East Anglia and the Midlands. The 12th to 15th were mainly wet days. There were thunderstorms over south-east England on the 16th and over south-east and northern England on the 17th. The 18th brought rain to western areas and thunderstorms in East Anglia. The 19th and 20th were wet everywhere. The 21st was again wet, with hail and thunder over East Anglia and 46.8 mm (1.8 in) of rain at Hastings (E. Sussex). The 22nd and 23rd brought thunderstorms across southern England and a gust of 79 kt (90 mph) was recorded at Aonach Mor (Highland) on the 23rd. Heavy rain fell in western areas on the 24th, spreading to all areas on the 25th when 45.6 mm (1.8 in) fell at Fylingdales (N. Yorks). The 26th was another wet day and 73.2 mm (2.9 in) of rain fell at Liscombe (Somerset) and 58.7 mm (2.3 in) fell at Bognor Regis (W. Sussex). A gust of 82 kt (94 mph) was recorded at Wilsden (W. Yorks). The 27th was wet in the south. Rain fell over southern England on the 29th and the 30th was wet in northern areas; 59.0 mm (2.3 in) of rain fell at Bridlington (E. Yorks).

Monthly mean temperatures were mostly around normal over England and Wales. The highest temperature recorded was 27.2°C (81.0°F) at Gravesend (Kent) on the 6th and the lowest was −1.8°C (28.8°F) at Altnaharra (Highland) on the 16th.

Sunshine totals were below normal over England and Wales. The highest daily total was 16.0 hours at Cardiff (S. Glamorgan) on the 1st and at Lerwick (Shetland) and Cape Wrath (Highland) on the 4th.

AVERAGE AND GENERAL VALUES 1995-7 (JUNE)

	Rainfall (mm)				Temperature (°C)				Bright Sunshine (hrs per day)			
	Average 1961–90	1995	1996	1997	Average 1961–90	1995	1996	1997	Average 1961–90	1995	1996	1997
ENGLAND AND WALES												
January	77	161	63	14*	3.8	4.8	4.4	2.4*	1.6	1.6	0.8	1.7*
February	55	115	83	120*	3.8	6.5	2.7	6.5*	2.3	2.7	3.1	2.5*
March	63	67	43	31*	5.6	5.5	4.4	8.3*	3.5	5.2	2.1	4.3*
April	53	27	51	24*	7.7	8.9	8.3	8.8*	4.9	5.9	4.6	5.6*
May	56	49	57	72*	10.9	11.6	9.1	11.5*	6.2	6.8	6.0	7.8*
June	58	23	30	†	13.9	14.0	14.1	†	6.4	6.8	8.1	†
July	56	40	41	–	15.7	18.3	16.2	–	6.0	7.4	7.2	–
August	68	10	80	–	15.6	18.9	16.4	–	5.7	9.3	6.7	–
September	70	113	34	–	13.6	13.7	13.6	–	4.5	4.6	4.8	–
October	77	58	91	–	10.7	13.1	11.7	–	3.2	4.0	3.6	–
November	81	83	128*	–	6.6	7.8	6.0*	–	2.2	2.3	2.8*	–
December	82	84	54*	–	4.7	2.6	3.1*	–	1.5	1.4	1.7*	–
YEAR	796	828	755*	–	9.4	10.5	9.2*	–	4.0	4.0	4.3*	–
SCOTLAND												
January	117	227	89	56*	3.1	2.9	4.7	3.1*	1.3	1.3	0.9	1.3*
February	78	205	141	269*	3.1	3.9	2.5	4.8*	2.3	2.4	2.7	2.3*
March	94	143	60	136*	4.6	3.6	3.9	6.8*	3.2	3.3	2.2	3.3*
April	60	67	108	72*	6.5	7.0	7.4	7.8*	4.8	4.4	3.5	3.7*
May	67	84	78	112*	9.3	9.4	7.7	9.3*	5.6	5.8	6.1	5.8*
June	67	43	65	†	12.1	12.4	12.3	†	5.6	7.4	6.3	†
July	74	86	78	–	13.6	15.1	13.6	–	4.9	6.2	5.0	–
August	92	34	68	–	13.5	16.1	14.7	–	4.6	7.8	4.6	–
September	111	198	64	–	11.5	11.9	12.5	–	3.5	3.5	5.1	–
October	120	228	227	–	9.1	11.0	10.1	–	2.6	2.8	2.4	–
November	118	126	193*	–	5.3	6.9	4.1*	–	1.7	1.7	2.3*	–
December	116	56	98*	–	3.9	1.5	2.8*	–	1.0	1.6	1.3*	–
YEAR	1114	1497	1269*	–	7.9	8.5	8.0*	–	3.4	4.0	3.5*	–

* Provisional figures, subject to alteration by the Met Office
† Data not available from the Met Office at the time of going to press
Source: data provided by the Met Office

WEATHER RECORDS

WORLD RECORDS

Maximum air temperature	57.8°C/136°F
San Louis, Mexico, 11 August 1933	
Minimum air temperature	−89.2°C/−128.56°F
Vostok, Antarctica, 21 July 1983	
Greatest rainfall in one day	1870 mm/73.62 in
Cilaos, Isle de Réunion, 16 March 1952	
Greatest rainfall in one calendar month	9300 mm/366.14 in
Cherrapunji, Assam, July 1861	
Greatest annual rainfall total	22,990 mm/905.12 in
Cherrapunji, Assam, 1861	
Fastest gust of wind	201 knots/231 mph
Mt Washington Observatory, USA, 12 April 1934	

UNITED KINGDOM RECORDS

Maximum air temperature	37.1°C/98.8°F
Cheltenham, Glos, 3 August 1990	
Minimum air temperature	−27.2°C/−17°F
Braemar, Grampian, 11 February 1895 and 10 January 1982	
Greatest rainfall in one day	280 mm/11 in
Martinstown, Dorset, 18 July 1955	
Greatest annual rainfall total	6528 mm/257 in
Sprinkling Tarn, Cumbria, 1954	
Fastest gust of wind	150 knots/173 mph
Cairngorm, Highland, 20 March 1986	
Fastest low-level gust*	123 knots/141.7 mph
Fraserburgh, Grampian, 13 February 1989	
Highest mean hourly speed	92 knots/106 mph
Great Dun Fell, Cumbria, December 1974	
Highest low-level mean hourly speed*	72 knots/83 mph
Shoreham-by-Sea, Sussex, 16 October 1987	

* below 200 m/656 ft

WIND FORCE MEASURES

The *Beaufort Scale* of wind force has been accepted internationally and is used in communicating weather conditions. Devised originally by Admiral Sir Francis Beaufort in 1805, it now consists of the numbers 0–17, each representing a certain strength or velocity of wind at 10 m (33 ft) above ground in the open.

Scale no.	Wind Force	mph	knots
0	Calm	1	1
1	Light air	1–3	1–3
2	Slight breeze	4–7	4–6
3	Gentle breeze	8–12	7–10
4	Moderate breeze	13–18	11–16
5	Fresh breeze	19–24	17–21
6	Strong breeze	25–31	22–27
7	High wind	32–38	28–33
8	Gale	39–46	34–40
9	Strong gale	47–54	41–47
10	Whole gale	55–63	48–55
11	Storm	64–72	56–63
12	Hurricane	73–82	64–71
13	–	83–92	72–80
14	–	93–103	81–89
15	–	104–114	90–99
16	–	115–125	100–108
17	–	126–136	109–118

TEMPERATURE, RAINFALL AND SUNSHINE
At selected climatological reporting stations, July 1996–June 1997 and calendar year 1996

Ht   height (in metres) of station above mean sea level
°C   mean air temperature
Rain   total monthly rainfall
Sun   mean daily bright sunshine (hours)
Source: data provided by the Met Office

		July 1996			August 1996			September 1996			October 1996		
	Ht m	°C	Rain mm	Sun hrs	°C	Rain mm	Sun hrs	°C	Rain mm	Sun hrs	°C	Rain mm	Sun hrs
Lerwick	82	11.1	85.2	3.0	12.9	58.7	2.4	11.0	49.1	4.2	9.0	142.9	1.9
Stornoway	15	12.5	80.1	3.5	13.6	70.6	3.0	12.7	74.4	5.0	9.7	211.6	2.4
Dyce	65	14.3	70.6	5.7	14.9	46.6	5.2	12.6	30.1	4.3	10.2	100.9	3.1
Eskdalemuir	242	13.2	85.1	5.6	14.2	50.1	5.0	11.4	78.5	4.7	8.9	326.0	2.2
Aldergrove	68	15.0	59.0	5.2	14.7	70.4	3.6	13.4	27.4	5.5	10.8	121.1	2.1
Leeds	64	16.9	25.0	7.8	17.3	66.6	6.0	13.7	26.6	3.5	11.8	47.9	3.7
Valley	10	15.1	35.8	6.6	15.9	73.8	6.3	14.4	27.6	6.6	12.6	94.6	3.2
Elmdon	98	16.8	25.6	7.9	16.6	54.5	6.1	13.6	10.6	4.6	11.2	53.8	3.7
Skegness	6	16.6	28.3	9.2	16.8	72.3	6.5	14.1	11.4	4.4	11.7	65.7	4.3
Bristol	42	18.0	53.5	8.1	17.9	97.0	7.5	15.1	44.4	5.5	12.9	104.1	3.2
St Mawgan	103	15.8	41.2	7.5	15.8	79.4	8.0	14.1	53.4	6.6	12.6	117.2	3.2
Hastings	45	16.4	29.7	8.3	17.0	98.7	7.8	14.3	25.5	5.8	12.5	55.7	4.5

	November 1996			December 1996			The Year 1996			January 1997			February 1997		
	°C	Rain mm	Sun hrs	°C	Rain mm	Sun hrs	°C	Rain mm	Sun hrs	°C	Rain mm	Sun hrs	°C	Rain mm	Sun hrs
Lerwick	3.4	170.5	1.9	3.2	107.5	1.3	7.0	992.9	2.7	4.6	67.2	1.3	4.1	186.3	1.8
Stornoway	4.7	201.1	1.9	4.1	60.7	1.4	8.2	1098.5	3.0	5.0	56.8	1.6	4.9	277.4	2.4
Dyce	4.2	87.7	3.2	2.8	68.9	1.1	8.0	839.9	3.8	3.3	24.5	2.2	5.1	48.5	3.9
Eskdalemuir	2.7	190.9	2.3	1.0	130.0	1.2	7.0	1515.6	3.3	1.2	38.4	0.8	3.9	401.6	1.7
Aldergrove	5.4	91.2	2.7	3.8	61.0	1.5	8.9	888.1	3.7	4.3	22.0	1.0	5.6	85.0	2.6
Leeds	6.0	97.3	3.1	3.4	83.1	1.2	9.5	609.5	3.9	3.4	4.7	1.6	7.1	65.6	3.1
Valley	7.7	122.9	2.3	4.4	29.4	2.9	9.7	687.2	4.7	3.8	7.1	2.9	7.0	73.8	2.8
Elmdon	5.5	67.7	2.8	2.2	51.8	1.7	8.9	491.0	4.2	1.6	13.3	1.1	6.6	56.5	2.6
Skegness	6.1	87.3	3.6	3.8	52.7	2.1	9.2	464.1	4.7	2.7	10.7	1.5	6.4	46.6	2.8
Bristol	7.6	124.9	2.9	4.1	35.5	1.9	10.7	779.4	4.6	3.7	6.4	1.9	7.7	141.2	2.4
St Mawgan	8.1	200.1	2.5	4.7	39.4	2.5	10.2	1080.7	5.1	4.0	16.6	2.2	7.9	97.3	2.4
Hastings	7.3	117.3	3.6	4.1	38.9	1.5	9.8	593.8	5.2	2.1	18.4	2.0	6.2	67.4	2.1

	March 1997			April 1997			May 1997			June 1997		
	°C	Rain mm	Sun hrs	°C	Rain mm	Sun hrs	°C	Rain mm	Sun hrs	°C	Rain mm	Sun hrs
Lerwick	4.9	151.9	2.3	5.2	110.3	3.1	7.3	49.6	4.1	9.9	41.0	4.2
Stornoway	7.0	124.4	2.7	7.6	72.8	3.5	9.0	93.4	6.3	11.1	66.5	5.6
Dyce	7.4	41.3	4.7	8.0	29.7	3.4	9.0	136.2	5.2	11.6	140.3	5.1
Eskdalemuir	5.7	138.7	2.8	6.8	60.4	3.1	8.7	132.3	2.5	11.3	139.7	3.9
Aldergrove	7.4	37.0	2.8	8.8	31.6	2.6	11.0	99.0	7.5	12.8	64.0	5.7
Leeds	8.8	16.7	4.3	9.5	19.1	4.5	11.8	59.7	7.4	14.4	134.7	4.5
Valley	8.3	18.0	3.9	9.7	32.5	4.7	12.0	64.2	8.1	13.7	70.5	5.3
Elmdon	8.3	14.9	4.6	8.9	26.2	5.2	11.2	66.0	8.5	13.9	111.9	4.8
Skegness	8.1	16.6	4.3	8.4	18.7	4.5	11.0	36.2	8.1	14.0	122.1	5.4
Bristol	9.6	32.5	4.4	10.6	24.8	6.8	13.1	90.9	7.6	15.4	82.2	4.2
St Mawgan	8.8	30.4	4.3	9.8	19.2	9.3	12.4	66.4	9.3	13.7	119.8	4.4
Hastings	8.4	11.0	4.9	9.1	11.5	7.9	12.2	39.6	8.9	14.9	164.1	6.5

METEOROLOGICAL OBSERVATIONS London (Heathrow)

Temperature maxima and minima cover the 24-hour period 9–9 h; mean wind speed is 10 m above the ground; rainfall is for the 24 hours starting at 9 h on the day of entry; sunshine is for the 24 hours 0–24 h; averages are for the period 1961–90. *Source:* data provided by the Met Office

JULY 1996

	Temperature Max. °C	Min. °C	Wind knots	Rain mm	Sun hrs
Day 1	16.8	12.1	9.6	0.6	5.2
2	20.9	9.9	7.7	0.2	4.0
3	19.0	11.8	10.9	0.8	1.3
4	20.4	11.2	11.9	0.3	7.4
5	20.8	10.3	4.9	17.0	2.5
6	18.8	11.0	5.4	2.5	5.4
7	20.3	10.7	4.7	0.0	7.8
8	19.9	10.1	6.3	0.0	7.7
9	20.8	11.8	6.7	0.2	0.8
10	26.6	12.7	6.5	0.0	10.5
11	25.2	14.7	5.7	0.0	4.9
12	24.1	14.8	6.3	Trace	2.3
13	25.6	15.3	8.5	0.0	10.7
14	25.2	16.6	4.2	Trace	2.2
15	25.4	12.5	7.7	0.0	13.1
16	22.6	10.8	10.0	0.0	12.7
17	24.8	9.8	7.9	0.0	13.9
18	27.4	10.4	4.7	0.0	15.1
19	26.5	12.7	6.5	0.0	12.1
20	28.6	12.7	5.0	0.0	13.8
21	30.7	14.7	4.7	0.0	14.5
22	31.6	16.0	7.5	1.8	14.4
23	28.0	17.7	5.2	Trace	5.5
24	21.7	15.6	8.0	0.3	4.2
25	25.4	11.7	3.7	0.0	14.4
26	28.9	14.4	4.7	1.1	8.2
27	23.7	15.0	5.0	Trace	2.4
28	23.7	15.7	6.5	1.1	0.6
29	25.3	16.4	6.1	Trace	7.2
30	24.6	15.5	5.7	2.9	0.7
31	25.8	15.2	8.4	Trace	8.2
Total	–	–	–	28.8	233.7
Mean	24.2	13.3	6.7	1.0	7.6
Temp °F	75.6	55.9	–	–	–
Average	22.5	13.1	7.4	46.0	194.5

AUGUST 1996

	Temperature Max. °C	Min. °C	Wind knots	Rain mm	Sun hrs
Day 1	23.5	12.2	7.5	Trace	4.9
2	20.8	10.6	3.5	0.0	2.4
3	24.0	12.5	4.3	0.0	12.8
4	25.5	12.6	8.3	0.0	13.6
5	27.6	14.2	8.7	Trace	12.7
6	22.3	17.4	10.3	1.0	5.9
7	22.7	13.7	8.0	0.0	4.0
8	23.5	12.0	7.4	0.5	7.8
9	21.7	14.7	7.9	4.8	0.6
10	23.1	15.7	10.8	4.9	8.7
11	22.6	14.1	6.0	7.8	5.8
12	20.7	13.6	4.5	8.0	1.9
13	23.4	14.0	8.0	0.0	9.0
14	21.6	16.0	5.7	0.0	0.8
15	21.1	15.0	3.4	0.0	5.0
16	26.6	14.8	4.6	0.0	11.0
17	28.0	13.8	4.3	0.0	10.1
18	30.6	15.4	6.8	0.0	13.0
19	31.4	16.5	6.2	0.0	12.2
20	24.8	17.0	4.7	0.1	2.4
21	25.0	13.0	7.0	0.0	12.9
22	23.0	12.0	7.7	10.6	11.4
23	22.0	14.4	10.5	1.4	6.2
24	21.4	13.9	9.3	5.2	5.1
25	20.9	13.6	9.0	0.4	6.8
26	21.1	11.0	5.7	0.5	8.1
27	21.1	10.0	3.4	0.0	9.1
28	21.2	10.4	4.9	0.6	5.6
29	17.9	12.9	11.1	0.0	0.0
30	18.0	11.3	7.5	0.0	3.5
31	19.1	8.3	4.2	0.0	4.3
Total	–	–	–	45.8	217.6
Mean	23.2	13.5	6.9	1.5	7.1
Temp °F	73.7	56.3	–	–	–
Average	22.1	12.8	7.2	51.0	186.7

SEPTEMBER 1996

	Temperature Max. °C	Min. °C	Wind knots	Rain mm	Sun hrs
Day 1	21.5	9.5	3.3	0.0	10.4
2	22.6	14.6	2.8	5.2	0.9
3	21.6	15.0	6.3	Trace	4.2
4	19.2	14.5	8.1	0.0	2.1
5	23.4	13.8	8.8	Trace	9.3
6	21.9	10.2	5.1	0.0	11.5
7	20.7	11.4	4.9	0.0	3.7
8	20.6	13.0	6.8	0.3	2.7
9	19.5	12.2	8.1	Trace	4.1
10	17.6	11.7	5.5	Trace	0.3
11	20.0	8.9	4.2	Trace	3.0
12	18.1	12.2	8.0	0.0	6.1
13	18.6	7.8	6.2	0.0	10.0
14	19.6	6.1	2.4	0.0	10.7
15	23.0	6.9	2.7	0.0	11.3
16	22.6	9.5	6.8	0.0	11.0
17	19.7	10.6	10.0	Trace	10.6
18	16.6	9.5	10.4	4.1	1.5
19	14.3	9.5	9.5	1.5	0.4
20	15.0	9.2	8.3	Trace	0.0
21	17.1	12.0	8.0	0.0	4.4
22	16.0	9.8	5.3	0.0	0.0
23	15.5	10.1	3.7	Trace	0.4
24	18.9	4.7	4.1	Trace	6.7
25	19.6	9.0	3.3	Trace	3.3
26	17.9	10.0	8.7	Trace	2.0
27	21.2	12.2	7.7	0.3	5.6
28	20.5	10.4	9.5	0.5	5.7
29	18.9	13.6	14.2	3.1	0.0
30	15.6	12.8	4.5	7.0	0.1
31					
Total	–	–	–	22.0	142.0
Mean	19.3	10.7	6.6	0.8	4.8
Temp °F	66.7	51.3	–	–	–
Average	19.3	10.8	7.1	51.0	144.7

OCTOBER 1996

	Temperature Max. °C	Min. °C	Wind knots	Rain mm	Sun hrs
Day 1	17.1	7.8	4.0	Trace	8.2
2	18.4	5.4	2.5	0.0	9.7
3	16.5	9.8	8.9	1.1	0.1
4	16.2	8.0	7.5	2.6	8.1
5	14.9	6.6	5.5	0.5	8.3
6	13.4	5.8	3.3	0.4	0.0
7	16.5	9.4	2.2	0.0	0.2
8	18.0	12.3	1.7	8.8	0.4
9	16.1	9.5	4.4	0.0	4.7
10	15.4	9.8	2.7	0.0	8.9
11	16.2	5.4	4.1	0.0	2.8
12	17.5	9.2	6.3	0.0	4.7
13	19.6	11.6	9.7	0.0	8.5
14	20.4	11.0	7.5	1.2	3.6
15	16.0	10.6	6.9	0.1	8.2
16	15.4	7.7	6.7	0.1	7.3
17	15.1	6.0	2.3	3.6	9.1
18	16.6	5.8	8.3	1.6	2.0
19	16.7	7.4	7.3	0.1	5.9
20	17.0	11.3	8.2	2.7	0.0
21	16.4	11.9	4.0	Trace	6.0
22	18.0	10.0	4.5	0.0	3.1
23	20.5	8.6	7.0	0.0	8.8
24	19.4	9.0	5.5	Trace	2.9
25	17.9	12.6	7.7	2.8	4.1
26	15.9	8.4	6.9	4.4	5.3
27	17.0	10.7	13.4	2.2	0.0
28	17.0	12.5	18.1	0.9	4.5
29	12.2	10.1	9.3	0.0	6.9
30	11.8	2.9	5.6	2.0	0.0
31	15.5	7.5	10.0	0.3	0.0
Total	–	–	–	35.4	142.3
Mean	16.6	8.9	6.6	1.2	4.6
Temp °F	61.9	48.0	–	–	–
Average	15.4	8.0	7.2	58.0	107.2

NOVEMBER 1996

Day	Temperature Max. °C	Min. °C	Wind knots	Rain mm	Sun hrs
1	17.0	7.4	8.0	0.0	5.3
2	18.1	10.5	12.7	3.1	0.2
3	17.6	14.3	11.7	19.1	0.7
4	16.0	12.0	12.0	Trace	2.9
5	15.3	9.1	13.1	0.6	7.1
6	14.7	9.4	16.3	0.5	6.6
7	12.1	8.3	8.0	0.1	5.3
8	11.4	1.2	4.1	Trace	6.1
9	12.1	3.7	5.0	15.6	4.5
10	6.9	3.7	4.2	0.2	0.0
11	8.3	-1.5	2.4	Trace	2.2
12	9.3	0.5	10.0	0.5	0.0
13	8.8	2.6	4.1	0.0	7.1
14	9.2	-1.5	0.8	0.0	5.8
15	10.1	0.5	2.0	0.0	7.8
16	8.4	-1.7	2.3	2.5	3.4
17	9.4	1.1	4.8	6.3	0.0
18	6.7	2.5	4.9	9.4	6.9
19	7.2	-3.0	10.7	10.4	0.1
20	6.7	0.0	9.3	0.9	1.5
21	6.9	-0.7	3.6	0.0	8.0
22	7.6	-3.1	3.8	0.1	0.1
23	6.5	0.6	4.7	0.0	7.8
24	10.5	-0.8	6.7	13.6	0.0
25	9.7	0.7	7.4	0.1	3.2
26	7.6	3.7	5.5	0.0	4.9
27	6.3	0.8	3.3	0.0	1.3
28	11.2	-2.1	3.6	6.3	5.6
29	11.3	-0.4	9.1	1.5	0.1
30	11.0	4.3	7.5	0.2	3.0
Total	–	–	–	91.0	107.5
Mean	10.5	2.8	6.8	3.1	3.6
Temp °F	50.9	37.0	–	–	–
Average	10.4	4.1	8.0	55.0	68.1

DECEMBER 1996

Day	Temperature Max. °C	Min. °C	Wind knots	Rain mm	Sun hrs
1	12.2	2.9	7.1	0.1	0.0
2	10.6	4.7	8.6	6.0	4.3
3	13.2	3.9	12.6	0.3	0.0
4	10.0	2.6	7.5	0.0	7.0
5	8.7	-0.6	0.5	0.0	3.9
6	4.1	1.0	2.5	Trace	0.3
7	6.7	1.4	1.7	Trace	0.0
8	5.1	3.7	1.2	Trace	0.0
9	5.1	3.1	2.0	Trace	0.0
10	4.7	2.8	5.7	Trace	0.0
11	5.2	2.9	4.9	Trace	0.0
12	4.8	2.3	3.4	Trace	0.0
13	5.3	1.3	5.7	0.4	0.0
14	7.1	-3.3	3.4	Trace	2.8
15	8.6	-2.4	3.7	Trace	0.0
16	7.4	6.0	2.6	0.3	0.0
17	9.0	4.4	6.3	0.9	0.0
18	10.9	5.6	4.0	2.9	0.0
19	8.6	7.9	3.2	0.6	0.0
20	8.6	6.0	7.6	0.2	0.0
21	3.9	2.3	12.4	Trace	0.0
22	6.1	2.3	11.1	0.0	3.5
23	4.6	1.4	11.8	0.0	7.1
24	2.9	-0.9	12.0	0.1	6.0
25	5.0	-0.8	4.7	0.0	1.6
26	2.0	-3.0	4.7	0.2	6.0
27	4.1	-3.1	4.2	0.5	0.5
28	1.8	-1.4	6.4	0.0	6.9
29	4.2	-3.4	4.3	0.4	0.0
30	3.1	-2.0	7.7	0.1	2.0
31	-0.6	-3.4	12.2	Trace	5.7
Total	–	–	–	13.0	57.6
Mean	6.3	1.5	6.0	0.5	1.9
Temp °F	43.3	34.7	–	–	–
Average	8.0	2.3	8.1	57.0	46.2

JANUARY 1997

Day	Temperature Max. °C	Min. °C	Wind knots	Rain mm	Sun hrs
1	-1.7	-4.0	10.8	Trace	0.1
2	0.5	-5.5	4.0	0.0	6.9
3	0.1	-5.0	8.8	Trace	0.0
4	1.5	-2.9	11.3	Trace	0.0
5	2.5	-0.8	10.2	0.0	0.2
6	3.1	0.2	6.5	Trace	0.0
7	-0.2	-1.3	8.8	Trace	0.0
8	0.0	-3.4	8.3	Trace	0.0
9	1.4	-2.2	7.7	1.3	0.0
10	1.5	-0.6	5.3	Trace	0.0
11	7.1	-0.9	5.7	0.4	0.0
12	8.7	0.9	5.2	0.1	0.0
13	11.0	3.9	3.9	0.0	4.8
14	7.6	-0.6	1.9	0.0	7.1
15	2.4	-3.2	1.9	0.2	0.0
16	9.0	-2.8	5.0	Trace	7.5
17	8.1	1.4	5.7	1.5	0.0
18	8.8	5.2	5.7	2.1	0.1
19	5.9	3.7	4.9	0.1	0.0
20	7.5	3.0	5.1	Trace	1.4
21	6.2	1.7	8.0	3.4	5.4
22	8.6	2.0	5.0	1.1	0.0
23	8.7	3.9	3.3	0.1	0.9
24	11.1	1.8	2.0	0.0	5.6
25	11.2	0.5	3.8	0.0	7.8
26	8.6	1.0	3.0	0.0	7.2
27	7.6	0.4	3.0	Trace	0.0
28	8.4	0.4	3.3	Trace	4.3
29	5.9	2.6	5.9	Trace	0.0
30	5.2	3.4	9.3	0.0	0.0
31	5.5	3.2	9.3	0.0	0.0
Total	–	–	–	10.3	59.3
Mean	5.6	0.2	5.9	0.4	2.0
Temp °F	42.1	32.4	–	–	–
Average	7.1	1.4	8.5	52.0	51.7

FEBRUARY 1997

Day	Temperature Max. °C	Min. °C	Wind knots	Rain mm	Sun hrs
1	6.9	3.6	9.4	Trace	0.0
2	8.2	3.2	4.3	Trace	0.3
3	9.1	-3.0	5.9	Trace	6.5
4	9.6	-1.4	10.6	5.5	0.0
5	10.3	3.0	4.0	Trace	6.3
6	10.8	3.7	8.6	0.1	0.0
7	11.0	8.1	5.7	1.0	0.0
8	9.7	-2.4	2.2	Trace	4.3
9	11.9	-0.1	8.8	0.3	0.3
10	11.1	8.4	13.7	3.8	0.8
11	12.0	3.8	10.2	2.9	0.0
12	12.1	6.7	12.2	4.0	0.0
13	9.1	3.9	13.0	0.1	4.5
14	7.3	0.5	1.5	Trace	0.0
15	10.1	0.7	3.3	0.0	8.8
16	9.0	2.8	9.4	2.8	0.0
17	10.9	4.5	11.5	9.0	0.0
18	9.6	6.2	12.6	0.9	4.8
19	10.4	2.4	14.2	8.6	0.0
20	12.6	5.4	12.2	0.7	3.8
21	13.8	7.9	10.7	3.1	3.2
22	11.7	7.9	8.0	Trace	0.0
23	14.0	8.2	15.1	4.8	2.5
24	11.5	5.0	15.9	5.4	0.7
25	14.4	7.3	14.1	2.0	5.1
26	12.1	5.8	13.5	0.1	5.0
27	10.7	2.2	7.7	0.0	0.3
28	13.2	6.5	8.1	Trace	0.9
29					
30					
31					
Total	–	–	–	55.1	58.1
Mean	10.9	4.0	9.6	2.0	2.1
Temp °F	51.6	39.2	–	–	–
Average	7.5	1.5	8.8	35.0	67.3

MARCH 1997*

Day	Temperature Max. °C	Min. °C	Wind knots	Rain mm	Sun hrs
1	12.1	4.4	–	Trace	2.0
2	13.6	7.8	–	Trace	4.2
3	10.2	3.2	–	6.6	0.0
4	10.9	4.9	–	2.1	0.0
5	12.2	7.0	–	0.6	1.9
6	12.1	4.2	–	0.0	9.7
7	12.0	5.9	–	0.0	0.0
8	12.2	8.2	–	0.9	0.0
9	13.1	7.6	–	0.0	5.5
10	15.4	4.7	–	0.0	5.5
11	17.6	3.3	–	0.0	9.3
12	15.5	4.0	–	0.0	5.9
13	13.2	5.6	–	Trace	4.2
14	14.4	8.7	–	0.0	1.2
15	17.1	8.0	–	0.0	2.6
16	16.6	8.7	–	0.0	2.8
17	17.4	5.3	–	Trace	7.8
18	14.0	8.0	–	0.3	3.2
19	12.9	7.8	–	Trace	5.8
20	14.5	1.6	–	0.1	9.2
21	12.4	4.7	–	0.0	9.7
22	12.9	3.7	–	0.6	9.3
23	12.6	6.0	–	Trace	1.4
24	10.7	4.0	–	0.2	0.0
25	13.9	3.3	–	Trace	1.0
26	13.8	8.2	–	Trace	0.0
27	17.7	4.3	–	Trace	8.0
28	12.6	5.0	–	0.0	11.3
29	13.3	1.5	–	0.0	7.3
30	14.8	2.4	–	0.0	10.7
31	16.5	2.9	–	0.0	11.5
Total	–	–	–	11.4	151.0
Mean	13.9	5.4	8.0	0.4	4.9
Temp °F	57.0	41.7	–	–	–
Average	10.3	2.7	8.9	47.0	110.1

APRIL 1997*

Day	Temperature Max. °C	Min. °C	Wind knots	Rain mm	Sun hrs
1	17.2	3.2	–	0.0	11.5
2	17.7	4.5	–	0.0	7.5
3	14.9	6.7	–	0.0	5.0
4	13.8	3.4	–	Trace	9.1
5	17.7	7.0	–	Trace	4.8
6	14.5	8.1	–	0.0	7.0
7	15.0	2.5	–	0.0	11.6
8	17.3	2.9	–	0.0	9.8
9	20.5	4.2	–	0.0	10.0
10	21.3	4.7	–	0.0	11.4
11	16.0	6.5	–	0.0	4.6
12	13.7	1.2	–	0.0	11.7
13	17.3	6.2	–	0.0	8.5
14	15.5	6.4	–	0.0	0.8
15	13.4	6.7	–	0.0	12.3
16	15.1	2.4	–	0.0	11.4
17	14.7	7.6	–	Trace	6.7
18	11.9	2.4	–	0.1	3.2
19	9.9	5.6	–	Trace	2.1
20	10.4	1.0	–	0.0	9.5
21	13.9	–1.0	–	Trace	11.4
22	12.2	5.0	–	Trace	8.5
23	15.8	5.5	–	Trace	4.0
24	16.8	5.9	–	Trace	4.4
25	11.7	7.0	–	8.4	0.0
26	13.0	8.1	–	1.3	0.0
27	18.9	9.6	–	Trace	4.3
28	18.8	11.1	–	Trace	5.4
29	17.6	11.2	–	0.0	8.8
30	20.3	6.9	–	0.0	13.2
31					
Total	–	–	–	9.8	218.5
Mean	15.6	5.5	6.2	0.4	7.2
Temp °F	60.1	41.9	–	–	–
Average	13.1	4.7	8.5	45.0	146.9

MAY 1997*

Day	Temperature Max. °C	Min. °C	Wind knots	Rain mm	Sun hrs
1	22.7	8.0	–	0.0	13.7
2	25.8	9.4	–	0.0	13.8
3	23.7	10.3	–	0.0	7.3
4	20.1	12.7	–	0.2	3.9
5	18.5	11.6	–	6.8	4.1
6	9.1	4.2	–	Trace	9.3
7	12.9	–0.5	–	1.8	10.9
8	12.5	5.5	–	1.4	2.7
9	14.0	6.0	–	4.4	7.8
10	15.2	7.9	–	0.2	6.4
11	16.2	7.7	–	0.4	10.0
12	15.0	8.1	–	3.0	9.0
13	17.8	7.0	–	0.2	10.0
14	19.6	6.1	–	0.0	13.6
15	19.2	8.3	–	Trace	3.4
16	23.0	10.6	–	2.2	1.0
17	26.6	12.6	–	Trace	6.4
18	20.7	14.9	–	0.0	4.6
19	18.8	11.2	–	1.0	2.9
20	15.5	8.9	–	5.4	1.2
21	13.9	11.0	–	Trace	0.0
22	14.8	8.4	–	0.6	1.2
23	15.5	8.2	–	0.0	5.1
24	16.5	5.5	–	0.0	14.8
25	19.1	5.3	–	0.0	14.0
26	23.2	6.8	–	0.0	14.0
27	20.0	11.0	–	0.0	12.0
28	17.9	7.4	–	0.0	11.0
29	23.2	7.8	–	0.0	14.9
30	24.3	10.1	–	0.0	15.2
31	23.2	10.2	–	0.0	15.0
Total	–	–	–	28.2	259.2
Mean	18.8	8.5	–	1.0	8.4
Temp °F	65.8	47.3	–	–	–
Average	17.0	8.0	8.1	51.0	193.7

JUNE 1997*

Day	Temperature Max. °C	Min. °C	Wind knots	Rain mm	Sun hrs
1	19.7	11.2	–	Trace	15.2
2	22.1	12.6	–	0.0	9.5
3	22.8	10.1	–	0.0	8.3
4	22.8	9.7	–	0.0	10.7
5	26.7	12.6	–	0.4	4.5
6	25.9	14.4	–	11.8	3.6
7	24.0	15.9	–	0.0	7.0
8	22.2	14.0	–	2.4	11.7
9	22.8	10.2	–	0.0	7.6
10	26.3	14.4	–	2.8	4.7
11	24.5	16.6	–	4.6	2.0
12	19.6	15.3	–	0.0	3.3
13	22.6	14.5	–	Trace	7.1
14	18.0	13.0	–	Trace	1.2
15	19.0	10.7	–	0.2	6.0
16	20.3	11.1	–	Trace	5.0
17	20.4	11.8	–	1.8	5.1
18	21.4	11.7	–	3.4	7.3
19	16.8	12.2	–	1.6	0.7
20	16.0	7.5	–	3.8	3.2
21	18.9	11.9	–	7.4	9.5
22	18.1	11.5	–	4.6	3.9
23	19.9	12.2	–	0.4	7.1
24	19.0	10.2	–	3.0	6.3
25	16.0	11.9	–	4.8	0.0
26	16.1	13.0	–	21.0	0.1
27	13.5	11.9	–	4.6	0.0
28	16.2	11.0	–	Trace	0.1
29	18.2	11.2	–	Trace	0.2
30	16.6	11.6	–	Trace	0.5
31					
Total	–	–	–	78.6	151.6
Mean	20.3	12.2	–	2.7	5.1
Temp °F	68.5	54.0	–	–	–
Average	20.4	11.0	7.6	50.0	198.5

*Wind values for March to June were not available at the time of going to press

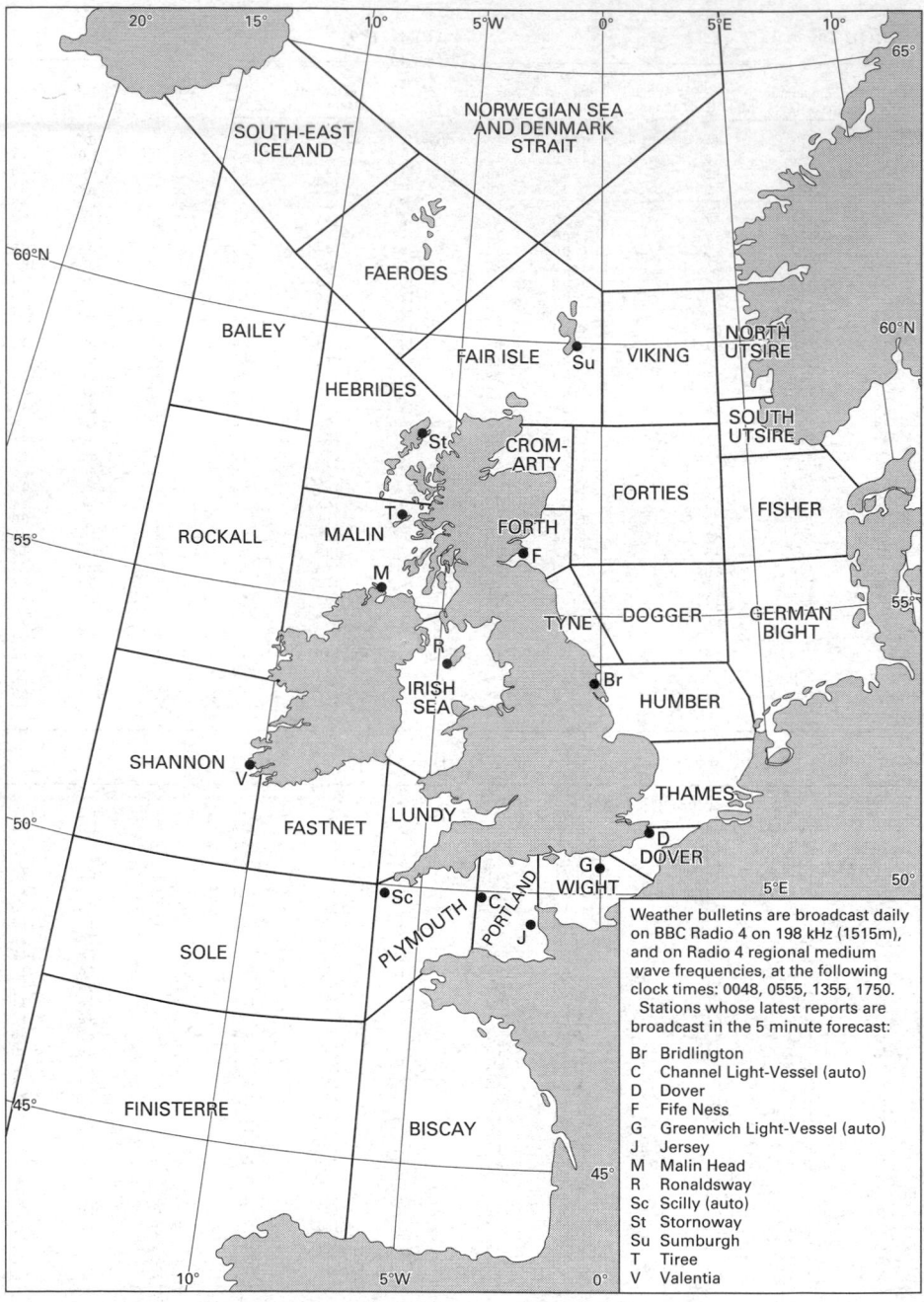

Weather bulletins are broadcast daily on BBC Radio 4 on 198 kHz (1515m), and on Radio 4 regional medium wave frequencies, at the following clock times: 0048, 0555, 1355, 1750.

Stations whose latest reports are broadcast in the 5 minute forecast:

Br Bridlington
C   Channel Light-Vessel (auto)
D   Dover
F   Fife Ness
G   Greenwich Light-Vessel (auto)
J   Jersey
M   Malin Head
R   Ronaldsway
Sc Scilly (auto)
St Stornoway
Su Sumburgh
T   Tiree
V   Valentia

Sports Results

For 1998 sports fixtures, *see* pages 12–13
For 1996–7 sporting events, *see* pages 1083–6

ALPINE SKIING

WORLD CUP 1996–7

MEN

Downhill: Luc Alphand (France), 779 points
Slalom: Thomas Sykora (Austria), 695 points
Giant Slalom: Michael Von Grünigen (Switzerland), 660 points
Super Giant Slalom: Luc Alphand (France), 351 points
Overall: Luc Alphand (France), 1,130 points

WOMEN

Downhill: Renate Götschl (Austria), 483 points
Slalom: Pernilla Wiberg (Sweden), 770 points
Giant Slalom: Deborah Compagnoni (Italy), 560 points
Super Giant Slalom: Hilde Gerg (Germany), 490 points
Overall: Pernilla Wiberg (Sweden), 1,960 points

Nations Cup: Austria, 11,959 points

WORLD CHAMPIONSHIPS 1997
Sestriere, Italy, February

MEN

Downhill: Bruno Kernen (Switzerland)
Slalom: Tom Stiansen (Norway)
Giant Slalom: Michael von Grünigen (Switzerland)
Super Giant Slalom: Atle Skaardal (Norway)
Combined Event: Kjetil-André Aamodt (Norway)

WOMEN

Downhill: Hilary Lindh (USA)
Slalom: Deborah Compagnoni (Italy)
Giant Slalom: Deborah Compagnoni (Italy)
Super Giant Slalom: Isolde Kostner (Italy)
Combined Event: Renate Götschl (Austria)

AMERICAN FOOTBALL

XXXI American Superbowl 1997 (New Orleans, 27 January): Green Bay Packers beat New England Patriots 35–21
World Bowl 1997 (Barcelona): Barcelona Dragons beat Rhein Fire 38–24
British Amateur final 1997: London O's beat Milton Keynes Pioneers 26–20 in overtime

---

ANGLING

NATIONAL COARSE CHAMPIONSHIPS 1996
Division: 1
Venue: River Witham; *no. of teams:* 84
Individual winner: R. Mitchell (Cambs and Isle of Ely), 23.850 kg
Team winners: Scunthorpe and District, 783 points

Division: 2
Venue: River Welland; *no. of teams:* 77
Individual winner: C. Willows (Cleethorpes AC), 19.970 kg
Team winners: Brighouse, 717 points

Division: 3
Venue: Tidal Trent; *no. of teams:* 71
Individual winner: C. Rhodes (Christchurch AC), 12.400 kg
Team winners: Rochdale AC, 634 points

Division: 4
Venue: Grand Union Canal; *no. of teams:* 75
Individual winner: D. Jarvis (Wymondham and District), 12.990 kg
Team winners: Team Shimano, 741 points

Division: 5
Venue: River Nene; *no. of teams:* 85
Individual winner: T. Tribe (JVAC Match Group), 8.520 kg
Team winners: Anchor Match Group, 803 points

Ladies' Championship
Venue: Middle Trent; *no. of competitors:* 128
Winner: R. Balcomb, 4.050 kg

WORLD CHAMPIONSHIPS 1997
Vallence, Hungary

Individual winner: A. Scotthorne (England), 19.711 kg
Team winners: Italy, 56½ points

ASSOCIATION FOOTBALL

LEAGUE COMPETITIONS 1996–7

ENGLAND AND WALES

Premiership
1. Manchester United, 75 points
2. Newcastle United, 68 points
Relegated: Sunderland, 40 points; Middlesbrough, 39 points*; Nottingham Forest, 34 points
* Three points deducted for failing to play a scheduled match against Blackburn Rovers

Division 1
1. Bolton Wanderers, 98 points
2. Barnsley, 80 points
Third promotion place: Crystal Palace
Relegated: Grimsby Town, 46 points; Oldham Athletic, 43 points; Southend United, 39 points

Division 2
1. Bury, 84 points
2. Stockport County, 82 points
Third promotion place: Crewe Alexandra
Relegated: Peterborough United, 47 points; Shrewsbury Town, 46 points; Rotherham United, 35 points; Notts County, 35 points

Division 3
1. Wigan Athletic, 87 points
2. Fulham, 87 points
3. Carlisle United, 84 points
Fourth promotion place: Northampton Town
Relegated: Hereford United, 47 points

GM Vauxhall Conference
Champions: Macclesfield Town, 90 points
Relegated: Bath City, 47 points; Bromsgrove Rovers, 41
    points; Altrincham, 39 points
League of Wales: Barry Town, 105 points
Women's Premier League: Arsenal

SCOTLAND
Premier Division
1. Rangers, 80 points
2. Celtic, 75 points
Relegated: Raith Rovers, 25 points

Division 1
1. St Johnstone, 80 points
2. Airdrieonians, 60 points (not promoted because lost a
    play-off against Hibernian)
Relegated: Clydebank, 28 points; East Fife, 14 points

Division 2
1. Ayr United, 77 points
2. Hamilton Academicals, 74 points
Relegated: Dumbarton, 35 points; Berwick Rangers, 23
    points

Division 3
1. Inverness Caledonian Thistle, 76 points
2. Forfar Athletic, 67 points
Bottom: Arbroath, 31 points

NORTHERN IRELAND
Irish League Championship: Crusaders, 46 points

CUP COMPETITIONS
ENGLAND
FA Cup final 1997 (Wembley, 17 May): Chelsea beat
    Middlesbrough 2–0
Coca Cola (League) Cup final 1997: Leicester City 1,
    Middlesbrough 1 a.e.t. *Replay:* Leicester City won 1–0
    a.e.t.
Auto Windscreens Shield final 1997: Carlisle United 0,
    Colchester United 0 a.e.t. Carlisle United won 4–3 on
    penalties
FA Vase final 1997: Whitby Town beat North Ferriby
    United 3–0
FA Trophy final 1997: Woking beat Dagenham and
    Redbridge 1–0 a.e.t.
Arthur Dunn Cup final 1997: Foresters beat Salopians 3–1
Charity Shield 1997: Manchester United 1, Chelsea 1 a.e.t.
    Manchester United won 4–2 on penalties
Women's FA Cup final 1997: Millwall Lionesses beat
    Wembley 1–0
Women's League Cup final 1997: Millwall Lionesses beat
    Everton 2–1

WALES
Welsh Cup final 1997: Barry Town beat Cwmbran Town
    2–1
League of Wales Cup final 1997: Bangor City 2, Barry Town
    2 a.e.t. Barry Town won 4–2 on penalties

SCOTLAND
Scottish Cup final 1997 (Ibrox, 24 May): Kilmarnock beat
    Falkirk 1–0
Coca Cola (League) Cup final 1996 (Celtic Park, 24
    November): Rangers beat Heart of Midlothian 4–3
League Challenge Cup final 1996: Stranraer beat St Johnstone
    1–0

NORTHERN IRELAND
Irish Cup final 1997: Glenavon beat Cliftonville 1–0

EUROPE
European Champions' Cup final 1997 (Munich): Borussia
    Dortmund beat Juventus 3–1
European Cup-Winners' Cup final 1997 (Rotterdam):
    Barcelona beat Paris St Germain 1–0
UEFA Cup final 1997: Schalke 1, Inter Milan 1 on agg.
    Schalke won 4–1 on penalties

INTERNATIONALS
WORLD CUP QUALIFYING MATCHES
1996
5 Oct	Riga	Latvia 0, Scotland 2
	Cardiff	Wales 1, Holland 3
	Belfast	N. Ireland 1, Armenia 1
9 Oct	Wembley	England 2, Poland 1
	Tallinn	Estonia failed to turn up for match against Scotland
9 Nov	Tbilisi	Georgia 0, England 2
	Eindhoven	Holland 7, Wales 1
	Nüremberg	Germany 1, N. Ireland 1
10 Nov	Ibrox Park	Scotland 1, Sweden 0
14 Dec	Cardiff	Wales 0, Turkey 0
	Belfast	N. Ireland 2, Albania 0

1997
11 Feb	Monte Carlo	Estonia 0, Scotland 0
12 Feb	Wembley	England 0, Italy 1
29 Mar	Kilmarnock	Scotland 2, Estonia 0
	Cardiff	Wales 1, Belgium 2
	Belfast	N. Ireland 0, Portugal 0
2 April	Celtic Park	Scotland 2, Austria 0
	Kiev	Ukraine 2, N. Ireland 1
30 April	Wembley	England 2, Georgia 0
	Gothenburg	Sweden 2, Scotland 1
	Yerevan	Armenia 0, N. Ireland 0
31 May	Katowice	Poland 0, England 2
8 June	Minsk	Belarus 0, Scotland 1
20 Aug	Belfast	N. Ireland 1, Germany 3
	Istanbul	Turkey 6, Wales 4
7 Sept	Aberdeen	Scotland 4, Belarus 1
10 Sept	Wembley	England 4, Moldova 0
	Zurich	Albania 1, N. Ireland 0

FRIENDLIES
1997
22 Jan	Palermo	Italy 2, N. Ireland 0
11 Feb	Belfast	N. Ireland 3, Belgium 0
	Cardiff	Wales 0, Rep. of Ireland 0
29 Mar	Wembley	England 2, Mexico 0
21 May	Bangkok	Thailand 0, N. Ireland 0
24 May	Old Trafford	England 2, S. Africa 1
27 May	Kilmarnock	Scotland 0, Wales 1
1 June	Valetta	Malta 2, Scotland 3
4 June	Nantes	England 2, Italy 0
7 June	Montpellier	France 0, England 1
10 June	Paris	Brazil 1, England 0

ATHLETICS

EUROPEAN CROSS-COUNTRY CHAMPIONSHIPS
Charleroi, Belgium, 15 December 1996

MEN
Individual: Jonathan Brown (GB), 32 min. 37 sec.

Team result: Portugal, 27 points

WOMEN
Individual: *Sara Wedlund (Sweden), 17 min. 04 sec.
Team result: France, 27 points
* Yulia Negura (Romania) finished first but was subsequently disqualified for failing a drugs test

AAA INDOOR CHAMPIONSHIPS
Birmingham, 25–26 January 1997

MEN

	min.	sec.
60 *metres:* Jason Livingston (Shaftesbury-Barnet)		6.58
200 *metres:* Jamie Baulch (Cardiff)		20.84
400 *metres:* Mark Hylton (Windsor, Slough and Eton)		46.24
800 *metres:* James Nolan (Ireland)	1	49.42
1,500 *metres:* Niall Bruton (Ireland)	3	49.23
3,000 *metres:* Darrius Burrows (Birchfield)	8	04.71
60 *metres hurdles:* Colin Jackson (Brecon)		7.54
3,000 *metres walk:* Andrew Penn (Coventry)	12	14.42

	metres
High jump: Mark Mandy (Ireland)	2.22
Pole vault: Kevin Hughes (Haringey)	5.20
Long jump: Steven Phillips (Rugby)	7.54
Triple jump: Oluwafemi Akinsanya (Peterborough)	16.37
Shot: Lee Newman (Belgrave)	18.10
Heptathlon: Brett Heath (Havering)	4,989 points

WOMEN

	min.	sec.
60 *metres:* Endurance Ojokolo (Essex Ladies)		7.27
200 *metres:* Katharine Merry (Birchfield)		23.50
400 *metres:* Phylis Smith (Sale)		52.85
800 *metres:* Hayley Parry (Swansea)	2	04.14
1,500 *metres:* Ann Griffiths (Sale)	4	18.86
3,000 *metres:* Angela Davies (Basingstoke)	9	26.04
60 *metres hurdles:* Denise Lewis (Birchfield)		8.41
3,000 *metres walk:* Sheila Black (Birchfield)	14	09.58

	metres
High jump: Debbi Marti (Bromley)	1.91
Pole vault: Janine Whitlock (Trafford)	3.70
Long jump: Jo Wise (Coventry)	6.41
Triple jump: Michelle Griffith (Windsor, Slough and Eton)	13.20
Shot: Judy Oakes (Croydon)	17.71
Pentathlon: Pauline Richards (Birchfield)	3,988 points

WORLD INDOOR CHAMPIONSHIPS
Paris, 7–9 March 1997

MEN

	min.	sec.
60 *metres:* Charalambos Papadias (Greece)		6.50
200 *metres:* Kevin Little (USA)		20.40
400 *metres:* Sunday Bada (Nigeria)		45.51
800 *metres:* Wilson Kipketer (Kenya)	1	42.67
1,500 *metres:* Hicham El Guerrouj (Morocco)	3	35.31
3,000 *metres:* Haile Gebrsilassie (Ethiopia)	7	34.71
60 *metres hurdles:* Anier Garcia (Cuba)		7.48
4 × 400 *metres relay:* USA	3	04.93

	metres
High jump: Charles Austin (USA)	2.35
Pole vault: Igor Potapovich (Kazakhstan)	5.40
Long jump: Ivan Pedroso (Cuba)	8.51
Triple jump: Yoel Garcia (Cuba)	17.30
Shot: Yuri Belonog (Ukraine)	21.02
Heptathlon: Robert Zmelik (Czech Republic)	6,228 points

WOMEN

	min.	sec.
60 *metres:* Gail Devers (USA)		7.06
200 *metres:* Ekaterini Koffa (Greece)		22.76
400 *metres:* Jearl Miles-Clark (USA)		50.96
800 *metres:* Maria Mutola (Mozambique)	1	58.96
1,500 *metres:* Yekaterina Podkopayeva (Russia)	4	05.19
3,000 *metres:* Gabriela Szabo (Romania)	8	45.75
60 *metres hurdles:* Michelle Freeman (Jamaica)		7.82
4 × 400 *metres relay:* Russia	3	26.84

	metres
High jump: Stefka Kostadinova (Bulgaria)	2.02
Pole vault: Stacy Dragila (USA)	4.40
Long jump: Fiona May (Italy)	6.86
Triple jump: Inna Lusovskaya (Russia)	15.01
Shot: Vita Pavlysh (Ukraine)	20.00
Pentathlon: Sabine Braun (Germany)	4,780 points

NATIONAL CROSS-COUNTRY CHAMPIONSHIPS
Havant, 8 March 1997

MEN (16 km)
Individual: Steffan White (Coventry Godiva), 45 min. 53 sec.
Team: Tipton Harriers, 162 points

WOMEN (6 km)
Individual: Andrea Whitcombe (Parkside Harrow), 21 min. 07 sec.
Team: Leeds City, 83 points

INTERNATIONAL CROSS-COUNTRY CHAMPIONSHIPS
Turin, 23 March 1997

MEN (12.33 km)
Individual: Paul Tergat (Kenya), 35 min. 11 sec.
Team: Kenya, 51 points

WOMEN (6.60 km)
Individual: Derartu Tulu (Ethiopia), 20 min. 53 sec.
Team: Ethiopia, 24 points

LONDON MARATHON
13 April 1997
Men: Antonio Pinto (Portugal), 2 hr. 07 min. 55 sec.
Women: Joyce Chepchumba (Kenya), 2 hr. 26 min. 51 sec.

EUROPEAN CUP
Munich, 21–22 June 1997

MEN

	min.	sec.
100 *metres:* Linford Christie (GB)		10.04
200 *metres:* Linford Christie (GB) and Georgios Panayiotopoulos (Greece), dead heat		20.56
400 *metres:* Roger Black (GB)		45.63
800 *metres:* Vebjörn Rodal (Norway)	1	47.54
1,500 *metres:* Fermin Cacho (Spain)	3	37.79
3,000 *metres:* Dieter Baumann (Germany)	7	41.08
5,000 *metres:* Gennaro Di Napoli (Italy)	13	38.33
3,000 *metres steeplechase:* Robert Hough (GB)	8	35.03
110 *metres hurdles:* Florian Schwarthoff (Germany)		13.20
400 *metres hurdles:* Fabrizio Mori (Italy)		48.93
4 × 100 *metres relay:* Italy		38.80
4 × 400 *metres relay:* Great Britain	2	59.46

	metres
High jump: Arturo Ortiz (Spain)	2.30
*Pole vault: Maksim Tarasov (Russia)	5.95
Long jump: Kiril Sosunov (Russia)	8.00
Triple jump: Jonathan Edwards (GB)	17.74
Shot: Oliver-Sven Buder (Germany)	20.41
Discus: Lars Riedel (Germany)	63.36
Hammer: Heinz Weis (Germany)	81.42
Javelin: Steve Backley (GB)	86.86

Team points: Great Britain 118, Germany 105, Russia 104, Italy 96, Spain 78, France 75, Norway 72½, Greece 71½
* Competition held indoors

WOMEN

	min.	sec.
100 *metres:* Natalya Voronova (Russia)		11.18
200 *metres:* Christine Arron (France)		22.89
400 *metres:* Grit Breuer (Germany)		50.38
800 *metres:* Yelena Afanasyeva (Russia)	1	59.93
1,500 *metres:* Kelly Holmes (GB)	4	04.79
3,000 *metres:* Roberta Brunet (Italy)	8	51.66
5,000 *metres:* Gabriela Szabo (Romania)	15	02.68
100 *metres hurdles:* Svetlana Laukhova (Russia)		12.94
400 *metres hurdles:* Sally Gunnell (GB)		54.57
4 × 100 *metres relay:* Russia		43.05
4 × 400 *metres relay:* Russia	3	24.10

	metres
High jump: Heike Balck (Germany)	1.94
Pole vault: Anzhela Balakhonova (Ukraine)	4.25
Long jump: Fiona May (Italy)	6.61
Triple jump: Inna Lasovskaya (Russia)	14.91
Shot: Astrid Kumbernuss (Germany)	20.64
Discus: Natalya Sadova (Russia)	67.72
Hammer: Olga Kuzenkova (Russia)	73.10
Javelin: Oksana Ovchinnikova (Russia)	67.16

Team points: Russia 127, Germany 112, Great Britain 86, Ukraine 80, France 77, Italy 77, Romania 71, Belarus 54

EUROPEAN CUP COMBINED EVENTS

MEN
Tallinn, 28–29 June 1997
Individual: Roman Sebrle (Czech Republic), 8,322 points
Team: Czech Republic, 24,416 points

WOMEN
Oulu, 28–29 June 1997
Individual: Irina Vostrikova (Russia), 6,298 points
Team: Russia, 18,651 points

BRITISH CHAMPIONSHIPS
Birmingham, 11–13 July 1997

MEN

	min.	sec.
100 *metres:* Ian Mackie (Pitreavie)		10.28
200 *metres:* Doug Walker (Newham)		20.63
400 *metres:* Iwan Thomas (Newham)		44.36
800 *metres:* Andy Hart (Coventry)	1	46.36
1,500 *metres:* John Mayock (Cannock)	3	39.69
5,000 *metres:* Adrian Passey (Bromsgrove)	13	38.21
3,000 *metres steeplechase:* Rob Hough (Sheffield)	8	41.44
110 *metres hurdles:* Tony Jarrett (Haringey)		13.33
400 *metres hurdles:* Chris Rawlinson (Belgrave)		49.69
10,000 *metres walk:* Andrew Penn (Coventry)	42	21.89

	metres
High jump: Brendan Reilly (Belgrave)	2.28
Pole vault: Paul Williamson (TVH)	5.40
Long jump: Steve Phillips (Birchfield)	7.58
Triple jump: Francis Agyepong (Shaftesbury)	16.48
Shot: Shaun Pickering (Haringey)	19.25
Discus: Bob Weir (Birchfield)	63.74
Hammer: Paul Head (Newham)	71.58
Javelin: Steve Backley (Cambridge)	86.20

WOMEN

	min.	sec.
100 *metres:* Simmone Jacobs (Shaftesbury)		11.50
200 *metres:* Katharine Merry (Birchfield)		23.19
400 *metres:* Donna Fraser (Croydon)		51.82
800 *metres:* Kelly Holmes (Army)	1	58.69
1,500 *metres:* Jo Pavey (Bristol)	4	18.57
5,000 *metres:* Paula Radcliffe (Bedford)	15	30.36
100 *metres hurdles:* Angela Thorp (Wigan)		13.34
400 *metres hurdles:* Sally Gunnell (Essex Ladies)		55.33
5,000 *metres walk:* Sylvia Black (Birchfield)	23	56.72

	metres
High jump: Debbie Marti (Bromley)	1.91
Pole vault: Janine Whitlock (Trafford)	4.00
Long jump: Jo Wise (Coventry)	6.47
Triple jump: Ashia Hansen (Shaftesbury)	14.10
Shot: Judy Oakes (Croydon)	18.42
Discus: Shelley Drew (Sutton)	58.16
Hammer: Sarah Moore (Bristol)	56.60
Javelin: Tessa Sanderson (Birchfield)	58.30

WORLD CHAMPIONSHIPS
Athens, 1–10 August 1997

MEN

	hr.	min.	sec.
100 *metres:* Maurice Green (USA)			9.86
200 *metres:* Ato Boldon (Trinidad and Tobago)			20.04
400 *metres:* Michael Johnson (USA)			44.12
800 *metres:* Wilson Kipketer (Denmark)		1	43.38
1,500 *metres:* Hicham El Guerrouj (Morocco)		3	35.83
5,000 *metres:* Daniel Komen (Kenya)		13	07.38
10,000 *metres:* Haile Gebrselassie (Ethiopia)		27	24.58
Marathon: Abel Anton (Spain)	2	13	16
3,000 *metres steeplechase:* Wilson Boit Kipketer (Kenya)		8	05.84
110 *metres hurdles:* Allen Johnson (USA)			12.93
400 *metres hurdles:* Stephane Diagana (France)			47.70
4 × 100 *metres relay:* Canada			37.86
4 × 400 *metres relay:* USA		2	56.47
20,000 *metres walk:* Daniel Garcia (Mexico)	1	21	43
50,000 *metres walk:* Robert Korzeniowski (Poland)	3	44	46

	metres
High jump: Javier Sotomayor (Cuba)	2.37
Pole vault: Sergei Bubka (Ukraine)	6.01
Long jump: Ivan Pedroso (Cuba)	8.42
Triple jump: Yoelvis Quesada (Cuba)	17.85
Shot: John Godina (USA)	21.44
Discus: Lars Riedel (Germany)	68.54
Hammer: Heinz Weis (Germany)	81.78
Javelin: Marius Corbett (S. Africa)	88.40
Decathlon: Tomas Dvorak (Czech Republic)	8,837 points

WOMEN

	hr.	min.	sec.
100 *metres:* Marion Jones (USA)			10.83
200 *metres:* Zhanna Pintusevich (Ukraine)			22.32
400 *metres:* Cathy Freeman (Australia)			49.77
800 *metres:* Ana Quirot (Cuba)		1	57.14
1,500 *metres:* Carla Sacramento			
(Portugal)		4	04.24
5,000 *metres:* Gabriela Szabo (Romania)		14	57.68
10,000 *metres:* Sally Barsosio (Kenya)		31	32.92
Marathon: Hiromi Suzuki (Japan)	2	29	48
100 *metres hurdles:* Ludmila Engquist			
(Sweden)			12.50
400 *metres hurdles:* Nezha Bidouane			
(Morocco)			52.97
4 × 100 *metres relay:* USA			41.47
4 × 400 *metres relay:* Germany		3	20.92
10,000 *metres walk* (*track*): Annarita Sidoti			
(Italy)		42	55.49

	metres
High jump: Hanne Haugland (Norway)	1.99
Long jump: Ludmila Galkina (Russia)	7.05
Triple jump: Sarka Kasparkova (Czech	
Republic)	15.20
Shot: Astrid Kumbernuss (Germany)	20.71
Discus: Beatrice Faumuina (New Zealand)	66.82
Javelin: Trine Hattestad (Norway)	68.78
Heptathlon: Sabine Braun (Germany)	6,739 points

AAA CHAMPIONSHIPS
Birmingham, 24–25 August 1997

MEN

	min.	sec.
100 *metres:* Jason Gardener (Wessex Bath)		10.31
200 *metres:* Marlon Devonish (Coventry)		20.65
400 *metres:* Kent Ulyatt (Norwich)		46.86
800 *metres:* James Nolan (Ireland)	1	51.47
1,500 *metres:* Richard Ashe (Hillingdon)	3	54.37
3,000 *metres:* Cormac Finnerty (Ireland)	8	08.83
5,000 *metres:* Kris Bowditch (Stoke)	13	53.12
3,000 *metres steeplechase:* Spencer Duval		
(Cannock)	8	45.91
110 *metres hurdles:* Damien Greaves		
(Newham)		14.02
400 *metres hurdles:* Charles Robertson-Adams		
(Telford)		51.01
10,000 *metres walk:* Philip King (Coventry)	42	32.32

	metres
High jump: Mark Mandy (Ireland)	2.20
Pole vault: Tim Thomas (Swansea)	5.30
Long jump: Steve Phillips (Rugby)	7.57
Triple jump: Francis Agyepong (Shaftesbury)	16.71
Shot: Stephan Hayward (Sale)	17.26
Discus: Bob Weir (Birchfield)	61.60
Hammer: Paul Head (Newham)	70.66
Javelin: Mark Robertson (Newham)	77.22

WOMEN

	min.	sec.
100 *metres:* Evadnie McKenzie (Ealing)		11.63
200 *metres:* Sharon Tunaley (Nottingham)		23.91
400 *metres:* Lorraine Hanson (Birchfield)		53.45
800 *metres:* Amanda Crowe (Lisburn)	2	04.66
1,500 *metres:* Diane Henaghan (Morpeth)	4	16.19
5,000 *metres:* Andrea Whitcombe (Parkside)	16	07.26
100 *metres hurdles:* Angela Thorp (Wigan)		13.56
400 *metres hurdles:* Keri Maddox (Sale)		57.69
5,000 *metres walk:* Olive Loughnane (Ireland)	24	09.18

	metres
High jump: Debbie Marti (Bromley)	1.90
Pole vault: Janine Whitlock (Trafford)	3.80
Long jump: Andrea Coore (Essex Ladies)	6.22
Triple jump: Katie Evans (Birchfield)	12.58
Shot: Judy Oakes (Croydon)	17.89
Discus: Jackie McKernan (Lisburn)	56.00
Hammer: Lyn Sprules (Hounslow)	61.18
Javelin: Karen Martin (RAF)	50.38

GRAND PRIX 1997 FINAL RESULTS

MEN

200 metres: Frankie Fredericks (Namibia)
800 metres: Wilson Kipketer (Denmark)
1 mile: Robert Andersen (Denmark)
5,000 metres: Khalid Boulami (Morocco)
3,000 metres steeplechase: Joseph Keter (Kenya)
110 metres hurdles: Mark Crear (USA)
Pole vault: Sergei Bubka (Ukraine)
Long jump: Ivan Pedroso (Cuba)
Discus: Lars Riedel (Germany)
Javelin: Jan Zelezny (Czech Republic)
Overall winner: Wilson Kipketer (Denmark)

WOMEN

200 metres: Marion Jones (USA)
800 metres: Ana Quirot (Cuba)
1 mile: Carla Sacramento (Portugal)
5,000 metres: Sally Barsosio (Kenya)
400 metres hurdles: Kim Batten (USA)
High jump: Inga Babakova (Ukraine)
Triple jump: Ashia Hansen (GB)
Shot: Astrid Kumbernuss (Germany)
Overall winner: Astrid Kumbernuss (Germany)

BADMINTON

WORLD CHAMPIONSHIPS 1997
Glasgow, May–June

Men's Singles: Peter Rasmussen (Denmark) beat Sun Jun
(China) 16–17, 18–13, 15–10
Women's Singles: Ye Zhaoying (China) beat Gong Zhichao
(China) 12–11, 11–8
Men's Doubles: Budiato Sigit and Chandra Wijaya
(Indonesia) beat Yap Kim Hock and Cheah Soon Kit
(Malaysia) 8–15, 18–17, 15–7
Women's Doubles: Gu Jun and Ge Fei (China) beat Tang
Yonghu and Qin Yiyuan (China) 15–1, 15–8
Mixed Doubles: Ge Fei and Liu Yong (China) beat Marlene
Thomsen and Jens Eriksen (Denmark) 15–5, 16–17,
15–4
Sudirman Cup final (team event): China beat S. Korea 5–0

ENGLISH NATIONAL CHAMPIONSHIPS 1997
Norwich, January–February

Men's Singles: Peter Knowles beat Steffan Pandya 15–1,
15–1
Women's Singles: Julia Mann beat Jo Muggeridge 12–11,
11–4
Men's Doubles: Simon Archer and Chris Hunt beat Nick
Ponting and John Quinn 15–6, 15–4
Women's Doubles: Nicky Beck and Jo Davies beat Julie
Bradbury and Jo Muggeridge 15–9, 15–4
Mixed Doubles: Joanne Goode and Simon Archer beat
Donna Kellogg and Chris Hunt 15–5, 15–2

SCOTTISH NATIONAL CHAMPIONSHIPS 1997
Edinburgh, February

Men's Singles: Jim Mailer beat Bruce Flockhart 10–15, 15–4, 15–11

Women's Singles: Anne Gibson beat Gillian Martin 11–4, 11–4

Men's Doubles: Russell Hogg and Kenny Middlemiss beat David Gilmour and Gordon Haldane 15–4, 9–15, 15–9

Women's Doubles: Elinor Middlemiss and Aileen Travers beat Alexis Blanchflower and Anne Gibson 15–3, 15–4

Mixed Doubles: Elinor Middlemiss and David Gilmour beat Alexis Blanchflower and Russell Hogg 15–6, 18–14

WELSH NATIONAL CHAMPIONSHIPS 1997
Tylorstown, February

Men's Singles: Richard Vaughan beat Geraint Lewis 15–5, 15–13

Women's Singles: Kelly Morgan beat Gail Davies 11–1, 11–0

Men's Doubles: Andrew Groves-Burke and Geraint Lewis beat Dayle Blencowe and Chris Davies 10–15, 15–8, 15–8

Women's Doubles: Kelly Morgan and Rachel Phipps beat Sarah Williams and Natasha Groves-Burke 15–2, 8–15, 15–4

Mixed Doubles: Kelly Morgan and Richard Vaughan beat Sarah Williams and Andrew Groves-Burke 15–7, 15–8

ALL-ENGLAND CHAMPIONSHIPS 1997
Birmingham, March

Men's Singles: Dong Jiong (China) beat Sun Jun (China) 15–9, 15–5

Women's Singles: Ye Zhaoying (China) beat Gong Zhichao (China) 11–1, 11–3

Men's Doubles: Ha Tae-Kwon and Kang Kyung-Jin (S. Korea) beat Jon Holst-Christensen and Michael Sogaard (Denmark) 15–11, 17–16

Women's Doubles: Ge Fei and Gu Jun (China) beat Eliza Zelin and Resiana Zelin (Indonesia) 15–6, 15–9

Mixed Doubles: Ge Fei and Liu Yong (China) beat Minarti Timur and Trikus Heryanto (Indonesia) 15–10, 15–2

BASKETBALL

MEN

Championship play-off final 1997: London Towers beat Leopards 89–88

League Trophy final 1997: London Towers beat Chester Jets 67–59

National Cup final 1997: Leopards beat Sheffield Sharks 87–79

National League Championship 1997: Leopards

WOMEN

Championship play-off final 1997: Sheffield Hatters beat Thames Valley 72–50

National Cup final 1997: Sheffield Hatters beat Rhondda Rebels 80–52

National League Championship 1997: Sheffield Hatters

BILLIARDS

World Matchplay Championship 1997: Robbie Foldvari (Australia) beat Geet Sethi (India) 4–2

UK Professional Championship 1997: Mike Russell (England) beat Sonic Multani (India) 2,476–580

BOWLS – INDOOR

MEN

WORLD CHAMPIONSHIPS 1997
Preston, January–February

Singles: Hugh Duff (Scotland) beat Andy Thomson (England) 7–4, 7–3, 7–4

Pairs: Mervyn King and Tony Allcock (England) beat Duncan Robinson and Brett Morley (England) 7–0, 5–7, 7–6, 7–4

NATIONAL CHAMPIONSHIPS 1997
Melton Mowbray, April

Singles: Robert Newman (Whiteknights) beat David Holt (Blackpool Borough) 21–20

Pairs: Handy Cross beat Watford 20–6

Triples: Bentham beat Kingsthorpe 19–16

Fours: Stanley beat Cyphers 20–11

BRITISH ISLES CHAMPIONSHIPS 1997
Balleymoney, March

Singles: Robert Marshall (Scotland) beat Neil Booth (Ireland) 21–18

Pairs: Wales beat Ireland 18–10

Triples: England beat Scotland 20–12

Fours: Scotland beat Ireland 25–13

Hilton Trophy (Home International Championship) 1997: England

Liberty Trophy (Inter-County Championship) final 1997: Nottinghamshire beat Cumbria 123–111

WOMEN

WORLD CHAMPIONSHIPS 1997
Llanelli, April

Singles: Norma Shaw (England) beat Caroline McAllister (Scotland) 3–2

NATIONAL CHAMPIONSHIPS 1997
York, February–March

Singles: Norma Shaw (Thornaby) beat Jayne Roylance (North Walsham) 21–9

Pairs: Nottingham beat Folkestone 19–15

Triples (two wood): Concordia beat Preston, Brighton 23–10

Triples (four wood): Cambridge Chesterton beat Egham 20–17

Fours: King George Field beat Richardson 22–13

BRITISH ISLES CHAMPIONSHIPS 1997
Perth, March

Singles: Sandy Hazell (England) beat Caroline McAllister (Scotland) 21–15

Pairs: England beat Wales 29–10

Triples: Wales beat Ireland 18–17

Fours: Wales beat Scotland 18–17

Home International Championship 1997: England

Atherly Trophy (Inter-County Championship) final 1997: Northamptonshire beat Middlesex 130–94

BOWLS – OUTDOOR

MEN

NATIONAL CHAMPIONSHIPS 1997
Worthing, August

Singles: Richard Brittan (Erdington Court, Warks) beat
  Martin Coles (Garston, Herts) 21–17
Pairs: Dorchester, Dorset beat Gosforth, Northumberland
  19–14
Triples: Wigton, Cumbria beat St Giles, Lincoln 15–13
Fours: Swindon Westlecot, Wilts beat Bridgwater BCL,
  Somerset 19–14

BRITISH ISLES CHAMPIONSHIPS 1997
Worthing, July

Singles: Jeremy Henry (Ireland) beat David Wilkins
  (Wales) 21–6
Pairs: Scotland beat England 28–11
Triples: Ireland beat Wales 17–16
Fours: Wales beat Ireland 20–13

Home International Championship 1997: Scotland
Middleton Cup (Inter-County Championship) final 1997:
  Norfolk beat Lancashire 113–109

WOMEN

NATIONAL CHAMPIONSHIPS 1997
Royal Leamington Spa, August

Singles (four woods): Margaret Price (Burnham, Bucks) beat
  Jean Baker (Blackwell, Derbys) 21–10
Singles (two woods): Katherine Hawes (Oxford City and
  County) beat Ann Parker (Carlton Conway, Notts)
  16–9
Pairs: Braintree, Essex beat Raynes Park, London 16–14
Triples: Skegness Vine beat Oxford City and County 29–3
Fours: Blackwell, Derbys beat Field Place, Worthing
  17–15

BRITISH ISLES CHAMPIONSHIPS 1997
Ayr, June

Singles: Margaret Johnston (Ireland) beat Ann Dainton
  (Wales) 25–11
Pairs: Scotland beat Wales 18–17
Triples: Ireland beat Scotland 23–11
Fours: England beat Ireland 27–18

Home International Championship 1997: Wales
Johns Trophy (Inter-County Championship) final 1997:
  Yorkshire beat Somerset 122–107

BOXING

PROFESSIONAL BOXING
as at 1 September 1997

WORLD BOXING COUNCIL (WBC) CHAMPIONS

Heavy: Lennox Lewis (GB)
Cruiser: Marcello Dominguez (Argentina)
Light-heavy: Roy Jones jun. (USA)
Super-middle: Robin Reid (GB)
Middle: Keith Holmes (USA)
Super-welter: Terry Norris (USA)
Welter: Oscar De La Hoya (USA)
Super-light: vacant
Light: Steve Johnston (USA)
Super-feather: Genaro Hernandez (Mexico)

Feather: Luisito Espinosa (Philippines)
Super-bantam: Daniel Zaragoza (Mexico)
Bantam: Sirimongkol Singmanssuk ('Thailand)
Super-fly: Gerry Penalosa (Philippines)
Fly: Chatchai Sasakul (Thailand)
Light-fly: Saman Sorjaturong (Thailand)
Straw: Ricardo Lopez (Mexico)

WORLD BOXING ASSOCIATION (WBA) CHAMPIONS

Heavy: Evander Holyfield (USA)
Cruiser: Nate Miller (USA)
Light-heavy: vacant
Super-middle: Frank Liles (USA)
Middle: Julio Cesar Green (USA)
Junior-middle: Laurent Bouduani (France)
Welter: Ike Quartey (Ghana)
Junior-welter: Khalid Rahilou (France)
Light: Olzubek Nazarov (Kyrgyzstan)
Junior-light: Yongsoo Choi (S. Korea)
Feather: Wilfredo Vasquez (Puerto Rico)
Junior-feather: Antonio Ceremeno (Venezuela)
Bantam: Nana Konadu (Ghana)
Junior-bantam: Yokthai Sith Oar (Thailand)
Fly: Jose Bonilla (Venezuela)
Light-fly: Pitchinoi Siriwat (Thailand)
Straw: Rosendo Alvarez (Nicaragua)

INTERNATIONAL BOXING FEDERATION (IBF)
CHAMPIONS

Heavy: Michael Moorer (USA)
Cruiser: Uriah Grant (USA)
Light-heavy: William Guthrie (USA)
Super-middle: Charles Brewer (USA)
Middle: Bernard Hopkins (USA)
Junior-middle: Raul Marquez (Mexico)
Welter: Felix Trinidad (Puerto Rico)
Junior-welter: Vince Phillips (USA)
Light: Shane Mosley (USA)
Junior-light: Arturo Gatti (USA)
Feather: Naseem Hamed (GB)
Junior-feather: Vuyani Bungu (S. Africa)
Bantam: Tim Austin (USA)
Junior-bantam: Johnny Tapia (USA)
Fly: Marc Johnson (USA)
Junior-fly: vacant
Mini-fly: Ratanapol Vorapin (Thailand)

BRITISH CHAMPIONS

Heavy: vacant
Cruiser: Johnny Nelson
Light-heavy: Crawford Ashley
Super-middle: Dean Francis
Middle: David Starie
Light-middle: Ryan Rhodes
Welter: Geoff McCreesh
Light-welter: vacant
Light: vacant
Super-feather: vacant
Feather: Paul Ingle
Super-bantam: Michael Brodie
Bantam: Drew Docherty
Fly: Adi Lewis

EUROPEAN CHAMPIONS

Heavy: Zeljko Mavrovic (Croatia)
Cruiser: Johnny Nelson (GB)
Light-heavy: Crawford Ashley (GB)
Super-middle: Andrey Shkalikov (Russia)
Middle: Hassine Cherifi (France)
Light-middle: Davide Ciarlante (Italy)

Welter: Andrei Pestriaev (Russia)
Light-welter: Soren Sondergaard (Denmark)
Light: Oscar Garcia Cano (Spain)
Super-feather: Djamel Lifa (France)
Feather: Billy Hardy (GB)
Super-bantam: Spencer Oliver (GB)
Bantam: Johnny Bredahl (Denmark)
Fly: David Guerault (France)

COMMONWEALTH CHAMPIONS

Heavy: Julius Francis (GB)
Cruiser: Darren Corbett (GB)
Light-heavy: Nicky Piper (GB)
Super-middle: Robert McCracken (GB)
Middle: Robert McCracken (GB)
Light-middle: Kevin Kelly (Australia)
Welter: vacant
Light-welter: Paul Burke (GB)
Light: David Odoi Tetteh (Ghana)
Super-feather: Justin Juuko (Uganda)
Feather: Jonjo Irwin (GB)
Super-bantam: vacant
Bantam: Paul Lloyd (GB)
Fly: Peter Culshaw (GB)

AMATEUR BOXING

AMATEUR BOXING ASSOCIATION (ABA)
CHAMPIONSHIP WINNERS 1997

Super-heavy (91+ kg): Audley Harrison
Heavy (91 kg): Blue Stevens
Light-heavy (81 kg): Paul Rogers
Middle (75 kg): Ian Cooper
Light-middle (71 kg): Chris Bessey
Welter (67 kg): Francis Barrett
Light-welter (63.5 kg): Richard Hatton
Light (60 kg): Mark Hawthorne
Feather (57 kg): Stephen Bell
Bantam (54 kg): Stephen Oates
Fly (51 kg): Michael Hunter
Light-fly (48 kg): Ian Napa

CHESS

PCA World Championship 1995: Garry Kasparov (Russia)
    beat Vishy Anand (India) 10.5–7.5
FIDE World Championship 1996: Anatoly Karpov (Russia)
    beat Gata Kamsky (USA) 10.5–7.5
Women's World Champion 1997: Harriet Hunt (GB)
British Champions 1997: Matthew Sadler and Michael
    Adams (joint champions)
British Women's Champion 1997: Harriet Hunt

CRICKET

TEST SERIES

ZIMBABWE V. ENGLAND

First Test (Bulawayo, 18–22 December 1996): Match
    drawn. Zimbabwe 376 and 234; England 406 and 204–6
Second Test (Harare, 26–30 December 1996): Match
    drawn. England 156 and 195–3; Zimbabwe 215

NEW ZEALAND V. ENGLAND

First Test (Auckland, 24–28 January 1997): Match drawn.
    New Zealand 390 and 248–9 dec.; England 521

Second Test (Wellington, 5–10 February 1997): England
    won by an innings and 68 runs. New Zealand 124 and
    191; England 383
Third Test (Christchurch, 14–18 February 1997): England
    won by 4 wickets. New Zealand 346 and 186; England
    228 and 307–6

ENGLAND V. AUSTRALIA

First Test (Edgbaston, 5–8 June 1997): England won by 9
    wickets. Australia 118 and 477; England 478–9 dec. and
    119–1
Second Test (Lord's, 19–23 June 1997): Match drawn.
    England 77 and 266–4 dec.; Australia 213–7 dec.
Third Test (Old Trafford, 3–7 July 1997): Australia won
    by 268 runs. Australia 235 and 395–8 dec.; England 162
    and 200
Fourth Test (Headingley, 24–28 July 1997): Australia won
    by an innings and 61 runs. England 172 and 268;
    Australia 501–9 dec.
Fifth Test (Trent Bridge, 7–10 August 1997): Australia
    won by 264 runs. Australia 427 and 336; England 313
    and 186
Sixth Test (The Oval, 21–23 August 1997): England won
    by 19 runs. England 180 and 163; Australia 220 and 104

OTHER TEST SERIES

India v. Australia (October 1996): India won 1–0
Pakistan v. Zimbabwe (October 1996): Pakistan won 1–0;
    one match drawn
India v. South Africa (November–December 1996): India
    won 2–1
Pakistan v. New Zealand (November–December 1996):
    New Zealand 1, Pakistan 1
Australia v. West Indies (November 1996–February 1997):
    Australia won 3–2
South Africa v. India (December 1996–January 1997):
    South Africa won 2–0; one match drawn
South Africa v. Australia (February–March 1997): Australia
    won 2-1
West Indies v. India (March–April 1997): West Indies won
    1–0; four matches drawn
New Zealand v. Sri Lanka (March 1997): New Zealand won
    2–0
Sri Lanka v. Pakistan (April 1997): Two matches, both
    drawn
West Indies v. Sri Lanka (June 1997): West Indies won 1–0;
    one match drawn
Sri Lanka v. India (August 1997): Two matches, both
    drawn
Zimbabwe v. New Zealand (September 1997): Two matches,
    both drawn

ONE-DAY INTERNATIONALS

ZIMBABWE V. ENGLAND

Bulawayo (15 December 1996): Zimbabwe won by 2
    wickets. England 152; Zimbabwe 153–8
Harare (1 January 1997): Zimbabwe won on scoring rate.
    Zimbabwe 200; England 179–7
Harare (3 January 1997): Zimbabwe won by 131 runs.
    Zimbabwe 249–7; England 118

NEW ZEALAND V. ENGLAND

Christchurch (20 February 1997): England won by 4
    wickets. New Zealand 222–6; England 226–6
Auckland (23 February 1997): England won on scoring rate.
    New Zealand 253–8; England 134–4
Napier (26 February 1997): Match tied. New Zealand 237;
    England 237–8
Auckland (2 March 1997): New Zealand won by 9 runs.
    New Zealand 153; England 144

Wellington (4 March 1997): New Zealand won by 28 runs. New Zealand 228–8; England 200

ENGLAND v. AUSTRALIA

Headingley (22 May 1997): England won by 6 wickets. Australia 170–8; England 175–4

The Oval (24 May 1997): England won by 6 wickets. Australia 249–6; England 253–4

Lord's (25 May 1997): England won by 6 wickets. Australia 269; England 270–4

INTERNATIONAL CUPS

World Series Cup final 1997: Pakistan beat West Indies 2–0

Sharjah Cup final 1997: Sri Lanka beat Pakistan by 4 wickets. Pakistan 214; Sri Lanka 215–6

ICC Trophy final 1997: Bangladesh beat Kenya by 2 wickets. Kenya 241–7; Bangladesh 166–8 (revised target set because of rain)

ZIMBABWE v. ENGLAND 1996 (Test Averages)

ZIMBABWE BATTING

	I	NO	R	HS	Av.
P. A. Strang	3	1	104	47*	52.00
A. D. R. Campbell	3	0	135	84	45.00
A. Flower	3	0	132	112	44.00
G. W. Flower	3	0	116	73	38.66
D. L. Houghton	3	0	100	37	33.33
A. C. Waller	3	0	69	50	23.00
G. J. Whittall	3	0	64	56	21.33
H. H. Streak	3	1	34	19	17.00
H. K. Olonga	3	0	0	0	0.00

Played in one match: E. A. Brandes, 9; B. C. Strang, 4*,3; M. H. Dekker, 2; S. V. Carlisle, 4,0
*Not out

ZIMBABWE BOWLING

	O	M	R	W	Av.
G. J. Whittall	42	13	69	5	13.80
P. A. Strang	116.4	27	259	10	25.90
H. H. Streak	89.1	20	240	8	30.00
H. K. Olonga	41	3	160	5	32.00

Also bowled: B. C. Strang, 17–5–54–0; G. W. Flower, 22–5–65–0; E. A. Brandes, 37–12–80–0

ENGLAND BATTING

	I	NO	R	HS	Av.
J. P. Crawley	3	1	166	112	83.00
A. J. Stewart	4	1	241	101*	80.33
N. V. Knight	4	0	197	96	49.25
N. Hussain	4	0	130	113	32.50
G. P. Thorpe	4	1	70	50*	23.33
P. C. R. Tufnell	2	1	11	9	11.00
R. D. B. Croft	2	0	21	14	10.50
M. A. Atherton	4	0	34	16	8.50
D. Gough	3	1	7	3*	3.50
A. D. Mullally	2	0	4	4	2.00

Played in one match: C. White, 9; C. E. W. Silverwood, 0
*Not out

ENGLAND BOWLING

	O	M	R	W	Av.
C. E. W. Silverwood	25	8	71	4	17.75
R. D. B. Croft	92	26	178	8	22.25
D. Gough	64	16	171	7	24.42
P. C. R. Tufnell	82.5	19	192	7	27.42
C. White	16	4	41	1	41.00
A. D. Mullally	64	16	150	3	50.00

NEW ZEALAND v. ENGLAND 1997 (Test Averages)

NEW ZEALAND BATTING

	I	NO	R	HS	Av.
D. L. Vettori	4	3	59	29*	59.00
S. P. Fleming	6	0	212	129	35.33
C. L. Cairns	6	0	208	67	34.66
N. J. Astle	6	1	172	102*	34.40
B. A. Pocock	6	0	182	70	30.33
B. A. Young	6	0	171	56	28.50
A. C. Parore	6	0	125	59	20.83
L. K. Germon	4	0	48	14	12.00
D. N. Patel	4	0	45	45	11.25
S. B. Doull	6	0	37	26	6.16
H. T. Davis	2	0	9	8	4.50
G. I. Allott	4	1	12	8*	4.00

Played in one match: M. J. Horne, 42,13; J. T. C. Vaughan, 3,2; D. K. Morrison, 6,14*
* Not out

NEW ZEALAND BOWLING

	O	M	R	W	Av.
D. L. Vettori	103.3	32	208	7	29.71
S. B. Doull	105.4	31	299	9	33.22
N. J. Astle	67	20	134	4	33.50
D. K. Morrison	24.4	4	104	3	34.66
G. I. Allott	61.4	11	197	5	39.40
D. N. Patel	68	16	151	3	50.33
J. T. C Vaughan	36	10	57	1	57.00
C. L. Cairns	52	11	146	2	73.00
H. T. Davis	36	8	93	1	93.00

Also bowled: B. A. Pocock, 2–0–10–0

ENGLAND BATTING

	I	NO	R	HS	Av.
M. A. Atherton	4	1	325	118	108.33
A. J. Stewart	4	0	257	173	64.25
G. P. Thorpe	4	0	247	119	61.75
D. G. Cork	4	1	121	59	40.33
P. C. R. Tufnell	3	2	38	19*	38.00
J. P Crawley	4	1	111	56	37.00
N. Hussain	4	0	117	64	29.25
R. D. B. Croft	2	0	31	31	15.50
N. V. Knight	4	0	56	29	14.00
A. R. Caddick	3	0	39	20	13.00
D. Gough	3	0	20	18	6.66

Played in one match: A. D. Mullally, 21; C. White, 0
* Not out

ENGLAND BOWLING

	O	M	R	W	Av.
R. D. B. Croft	90.1	27	162	10	16.20
D. Gough	127.3	31	361	19	19.00
A. R. Caddick	87.5	25	174	8	21.75
A. D. Mullally	53	22	102	3	34.00
P. C. R. Tufnell	132	47	242	7	34.57
C. White	25	5	77	2	38.50
D. G. Cork	98.5	21	300	7	42.85

Also bowled: G. P. Thorpe, 1–1–0–0

ENGLAND v AUSTRALIA 1997 (Test Averages)

ENGLAND BATTING

	I	NO	R	HS	Av.
G. P. Thorpe	11	2	453	138	50.33
N. Hussain	11	0	431	207	39.18
M. A. Ealham	6	3	105	53*	35.00
J. P. Crawley	9	1	243	83	30.37
M. A. Butcher	10	0	254	87	25.40
A. J. Stewart	12	1	268	87	24.36
M. A. Atherton	12	1	257	77	23.36
A. J. Hollioake	4	0	51	45	12.75
A. R. Caddick	8	2	59	26*	9.83
D. W. Headley	6	2	39	22	9.75
R. D. B. Croft	8	0	75	24	9.37
D. E. Malcolm	5	1	12	12	3.00
D. Gough	6	0	17	10	2.83

Played in one match: M. R. Ramprakash, 48,4; B. C. Hollioake, 28,2; P. J. Martin, 20,3; A. M. Smith, 4*,0; P. C. R. Tufnell, 1,0
* Not out

ENGLAND BOWLING

	O	M	R	W	Av.
P. C. R. Tufnell	47.4	22	93	11	8.45
M. A. Ealham	58.4	11	191	8	23.87
A. R. Caddick	179.5	27	634	24	26.41
A. J. Hollioake	19	2	55	2	27.50
D. W. Headley	131.2	20	444	16	27.75
D. Gough	142	27	511	16	31.93
B. C. Hollioake	15	2	83	2	41.50
D. E. Malcolm	93	19	307	6	51.16
R. D. B. Croft	161.5	41	439	8	54.87

Also bowled: M. A. Butcher, 2–0–14–0; P. J. Martin, 19–5–51–0; A. M. Smith, 23–2–89–0

AUSTRALIA BATTING

	I	NO	R	HS	Av.
P. R. Reiffel	6	3	179	54*	59.66
M. T. G. Elliott	10	0	556	199	55.60
R. T. Ponting	5	0	241	127	48.20
S. R. Waugh	10	0	390	116	39.00
G. S. Blewett	10	0	381	125	38.10
M. A. Taylor	10	0	317	129	31.70
I. A. Healy	10	1	225	63	25.00
M. E. Waugh	10	0	209	68	20.90
S. K. Warne	10	0	188	53	18.80
G. D. McGrath	8	6	25	20*	12.50
J. N. Gillespie	7	2	57	28*	11.40
M. G. Bevan	5	0	43	24	8.60
M. S. Kasprowicz	4	0	21	17	5.25

Played in one match: S. Young, 4*,0
* Not out

AUSTRALIA BOWLING

	O	M	R	W	Av.
M. E. Waugh	7	3	16	1	16.00
G. D. McGrath	249.5	67	701	36	19.47
J. N. Gillespie	91.4	20	332	16	20.75
M. S. Kasprowicz	93.3	19	310	14	22.14
S. K. Warne	237.1	69	577	24	24.04
P. R. Reiffel	112.1	28	293	11	26.63
M. G. Bevan	34.4	6	121	2	60.50

Also bowled: S. Young, 8–3–13–0; G. S. Blewett, 3–0–17–0; S. R. Waugh, 20–3–76–0

COUNTY CHAMPIONSHIP TABLE 1997

Order for 1996 in brackets	P	W	L	D	Bt	Bl	Pts
Glamorgan (10)	17	8	2	7	50	57	256
*Kent (4)	17	8	4	5	44	60	252
*Worcestershire (7)	17	6	3	8	49	54	228
Middlesex (9)	17	7	4	6	33	56	219
Warwickshire (8)	17	7	2	8	32	51	219
Yorkshire (6)	17	6	3	8	41	54	215
Gloucestershire (13)	17	6	6	5	35	60	206
Surrey (3)	17	5	5	7	39	52	192
Essex (5)	17	5	6	6	39	55	192
Leicestershire (1)	17	4	1	12	37	54	191
Lancashire (15)	17	5	6	6	34	54	186
Somerset (11)	17	3	3	11	38	64	183
Nottinghamshire (17)	17	4	3	10	26	55	175
Hampshire (14)	17	3	5	9	42	41	158
Northamptonshire (16)	17	3	5	9	33	48	156
Derbyshire (2)	17	2	9	6	32	59	141
Durham (18)	17	2	8	7	22	56	131
Sussex (12)	17	1	10	6	24	57	115

* Includes 8 points for batting last in a tied match

FIRST CLASS BATTING AVERAGES 1997
Qualifying requirement: 6 completed innings

	I	NO	R	HS	Av.
G. A. Hick	28	6	1,524	303*	69.27
S. P. James	30	4	1,775	162	68.26
M. P. Maynard	25	7	1,170	161*	65.00
R. T. Ponting	12	3	571	127	63.44
D. S. Lehmann	27	2	1,575	182	63.00
N. C. Johnson	18	5	819	150	63.00
G. P. Thorpe	23	4	1,160	222	61.05
M. T. G. Elliott	19	0	1,091	199	57.42
S. G. Law	28	2	1,482	175	57.00
M. R. Ramprakash	30	4	1,453	190	55.88
D. C. Nash	8	2	332	100	55.33
S. R. Waugh	17	0	924	154	54.35
T. A. Tweats	13	2	590	189	53.63
M. L. Hayden	30	3	1,446	235*	53.55
M. A. Ealham	30	10	1,055	139	52.75
H. Morris	28	4	1,262	233*	52.58
D. A. Leatherdale	25	8	886	129	52.11
R. J. Turner	28	7	1,069	144	50.90
K. J. Barnett	24	3	1,055	210*	50.23
G. D. Rose	26	9	852	191	50.11

*Not out

FIRST CLASS BOWLING AVERAGES 1997
Qualifying requirement: 20 wickets taken

	O	M	R	W	Av.
A. A. Donald	387.5	123	938	60	15.63
A. M. Smith	512.2	125	1,464	83	17.63
P. R. Reiffel	188.4	49	520	28	18.57
K. D. James	161.1	37	504	27	18.66
D. R. Brown	521.3	135	1,560	81	19.25
Saqlain Mushtaq	254.5	75	617	32	19.28
B. J. Phillips	282.1	73	877	44	19.93
P. M. Hutchison	233.1	56	741	37	20.02
S. K. Warne	433.4	112	1,154	57	20.24
J. H. Kallis	234.3	61	655	32	20.46
G. D. McGrath	363.4	104	1,012	49	20.65

	O	M	R	W	Av.
Azhar Mahmood	290.5	66	829	40	20.72
P. C. R. Tufnell	560.5	174	1,205	55	21.90
M. C. Ilott	332	91	946	43	22.00
M. M. Betts	329	77	1,085	49	22.14
Waqar Younis	441.4	83	1,551	68	22.80
S. L. Watkin	508.2	143	1,393	61	22.83
P. J. Hartley	170	39	532	23	23.13
P. J. Martin	474.2	136	1,342	58	23.13
J. P. Hewitt	439	97	1,393	60	23.21

Source for averages and county championship table: ECB/PA Cricket Record

OTHER RESULTS 1997

Benson and Hedges Cup final: Surrey beat Kent by 8 wickets. Kent 212–9; Surrey 215–2

NatWest Trophy final: Essex beat Warwickshire by 9 wickets. Warwickshire 170–8; Essex 171–1

Sunday League Champions: Warwickshire

MCC Trophy (Minor Counties knockout final): Norfolk beat Shropshire by 52 runs. Norfolk 279–4; Shropshire 227

Minor Counties Championship final: Devon beat Bedfordshire on run rate. Devon 216–5 and 180–8 dec.; Bedfordshire 119–9 and 251–6

National Club Championship final: Eastbourne beat Harrogate by 9 wickets. Harrogate 158; Eastbourne 159–1

National Village Championship final: Caldy beat Shipton-under-Wychwood by 56 runs. Caldy 166–9; Shipton-under-Wychwood 110

Varsity Match (one-day): Cambridge beat Oxford by 73 runs. Cambridge 297–6; Oxford 224

Varsity Match (three-day): Match drawn. Cambridge 358–8 dec. and 239–4 dec.; Oxford 272 and 249–8

CYCLING

World Cup series overall winner 1996: Johan Museeuw (Belgium), 162 points

Tour of Italy 1997: Ivan Gotti (Italy)

Tour de France 1997: Jan Ullrich (Germany)

Tour of Spain 1997: Alex Zülle (Switzerland)

World Open Road Race Championship 1996: Johan Museeuw (Belgium)

World Open Cyclo-Cross Championship 1997: Daniele Pontoni (Italy)

World Cyclo-Cross Cup series overall winner 1997: Adri Van Der Poel (Netherlands), 96 points

British Open Road Race Championship 1997: Jeremy Hunt (Banesto)

British Open Cyclo-Cross Championship 1997: Barrie Clarke (Team Raleigh)

Women's World Road Race Championship 1996: Barbara Heeb (Switzerland)

Women's National Road Race Championship 1997: Maria Lawrence (Team Ambrosia)

Women's British Open Cyclo-Cross Championship 1997: Caroline Alexander (Team Ritchey)

EQUESTRIANISM

SHOW JUMPING
World Cup final 1997: Hugo Simon on ET (Austria)

European Championships 1997:
   Individual: Ludger Beerbaum on Sprehe Ratina (Germany)
   Team: Germany

British Jumping Derby 1997 (Hickstead): John Popley on Sight and Sound Bluebird (GB)

THREE-DAY EVENTING
European Championships 1997 (Burghley):
   Individual: Bettina Overesch-Boker on Watermill Stream (Germany)
   Team: Great Britain

Badminton Horse Trials 1997: David O'Connor on Custom Made (USA)

British Open Horse Trials 1997 (Gatcombe Park): Andrew Hoy on Darien Powers (Australia)

ETON FIVES

County Championship final 1997: Middlesex beat Warwickshire 3–0

Amateur Championship (Kinnaird Cup) 1997: Edward Wass and James Halstead beat Robin Mason and Jonathan Mole 3–1

Holmwoods Schools' Championship 1997: St Olave's I

Barber Cup final 1997: Old Cholmeleians beat Old Salopians 2–1

League Championship (Douglas Keeble Cup) 1997: Old Salopians I

FENCING

MEN

WORLD CHAMPIONSHIPS 1997
Cape Town, July
Foil: Sergei Golubitsky (Ukraine)
Epée: Eric Srecki (France)
Sabre: Stanislaw Pozdniakov (Russia)
Team Foil: France
Team Epée: Cuba
Team Sabre: France

BRITISH CHAMPIONS 1997
Foil: Paul Walsh (Sussex House)
Epée: Quentin Berriman (Haverstock)
Sabre: Nick Fletcher (Salle Frohlich)
Team Foil: Sussex House 'A'
Team Epée: Haverstock

International Epée World Cup Series 1997: Michael Flegler (Germany)

Corble Cup 1997 (international sabre tournament): Philippe Daurelle (France)

WOMEN

WORLD CHAMPIONSHIPS 1997
Cape Town, July
Foil: Giovanna Trillini (Italy)
Epée: Miraide Garcia-Soto (Cuba)
Team Foil: Italy
Team Epée: Hungary

BRITISH CHAMPIONS 1997
Foil: Linda Strachan (Salle Paul)

Epée: Georgina Usher (Haverstock)
Sabre: Louise Bond-Williams (Stratford Swords)
Ipswich Cup 1997 (international epée world cup series):
Hajnalka Kiralay (Hungary)

GOLF (MEN)

THE MAJOR CHAMPIONSHIPS 1997

US Masters (Augusta, Georgia, 10–13 April): Tiger Woods
(USA), 270
US Open (Bethesda, Maryland, 12–15 June): Ernie Els (S.
Africa), 276
The Open (Royal Troon, 17–20 July): Justin Leonard
(USA), 272
US PGA Championship (Winged Foot, New York, 14–17
August): Davis Love III (USA), 269

PGA EUROPEAN TOUR 1996

German Masters (Motzener See): Darren Clarke (GB), 264
World Matchplay Championship (Wentworth): Ernie Els (S.
Africa) beat Vijay Singh (Fiji) 3 and 2
Volvo Masters (Valderrama): Mark McNulty (Zimbabwe),
276
European Tour Order of Merit 1996: 1. Colin Montgomerie
(GB); 2. Ian Woosnam (GB); 3. Robert Allenby
(Australia)

World Cup 1996 (Somerset West, S. Africa): Ernie Els (S.
Africa), 272
World Open Championship 1996 (Braselton, Georgia): Frank
Nobilo (New Zealand), 272
World Championship of Golf 1997 (Scottsdale, Arizona): Greg
Norman (Australia)

PGA EUROPEAN TOUR 1997

Johnnie Walker Classic (Hope Island, Australia): Ernie Els
(S. Africa), 278
Heineken Classic (Perth, Australia): Miguel Martin (Spain),
273
South African Open (Johannesburg): Vijay Singh (Fiji), 270
Dimension Data Pro-Am (Sun City, S. Africa): Nick Price
(Zimbabwe), 268
South African PGA (Johannesburg): Nick Price
(Zimbabwe), 269*
Dubai Desert Classic: Richard Green (Australia), 272*
Moroccan Open (Agadir): Clinton Whitelaw (S. Africa), 277
Portuguese Open (Aroeira): Michael Jonzon (Sweden), 269
Turespana Masters (Gran Canaria): José-Maria Olazabal
(Spain), 272
Madeira Island Open (Santo de Serra): Peter Mitchell (GB),
204
Cannes Open: Stuart Cage (GB), 270
Spanish Open (Madrid): Mark James (GB), 277*
Italian Open (Brescia): Bernhard Langer (Germany), 273
International Open (The Oxfordshire): Bernhard Langer
(Germany), 276
English Open (Hanbury Manor, Herts): Per-Ulrik
Johansson (Sweden), 269
PGA Championship (Wentworth): Ian Woosnam (GB), 275
Tournament Players' Open Championship of Europe
(Hamburg): Ross McFarlane (GB), 282
European Grand Prix (Slaley Hall): Colin Montgomerie
(GB), 270
German Open (Stuttgart): Ignacio Garrido (Spain), 271
French Open (Paris): Retief Goosen (S. Africa), 271
Irish Open (Druid's Glen): Colin Montgomerie (GB), 269
Loch Lomond World Invitational: Tom Lehman (USA), 265
Dutch Open (Hilversum): Sven Struver (Germany), 266

Scandinavian Masters (Barseback): Joakim Haeggman
(Sweden), 270
Czech Open (Karlstein): Bernhard Langer (Germany), 264
European Open (K Club, Co. Kildare): Per-Ulrik Johansson
(Sweden), 267
International Open (Munich): Robert Karlsson (Sweden),
264
European Masters (Crans-sur-Sierre): Costantino Rocca
(Italy), 266
Lancôme Trophy (Paris): Mark O'Meara (USA), 271
British Masters (Forest of Arden): Greg Turner (New
Zealand), 275

MAJOR TEAM EVENTS

Alfred Dunhill Cup final 1996 (St Andrews, 10–13 October):
USA beat New Zealand 2–1
World Cup 1996 (Somerset West, S. Africa): S. Africa, 547
Ryder Cup 1997 (Valderrama): Europe beat USA 14½–13½
Walker Cup 1997 (amateur) (Quaker Ridge, New York):
USA beat Great Britain and Ireland 18–6

AMATEUR CHAMPIONSHIPS

British Amateur Championship 1997 (Royal St George's):
Craig Watson (East Renfrewshire)
English Amateur Championship 1997 (Royal Liverpool):
Aaron Wainwright (Garforth)
Welsh Amateur Championship 1997 (Pyle and Kenfig): Jamie
Donaldson (Macclesfield)
Scottish Amateur Championship 1997 (Carnoustie): Craig
Hislop (Powfoot)
Brabazon Trophy (English Open Strokeplay) 1997 (Saunton):
David Park (Burghill Valley), 271
Welsh Open Strokeplay 1997 (Conwy): Gary Wolstenholme
(Kilworth Springs), 286
Scottish Open Strokeplay 1997 (Monifieth): D. B. Howard
(Cochrane Castle), 271
Lytham Trophy 1997 (Royal Lytham and St Anne's):
Graham Rankin (Palacerigg), 279
Berkshire Trophy 1997 (The Berkshire): Gary
Wolstenholme (Kilworth Springs), 275
International Match 1997 (La Manga): England beat Spain
16½–7½
Home International Championship 1997 (Burnham and
Berrow): England
Eisenhower Trophy (world amateur team championship) 1996
(Carmona, Philippines): Australia, 838
European Amateur Championship 1997 (Geneva): Didier De
Voogt (Belgium), 278
European Amateur Team Championship 1997 (Portmarnock):
Spain
President's Putter 1997 (Rye): Charlie Rotheroe (Oxford)
beat Simon Ellis (Cambridge) 3 and 2
Halford Hewitt Trophy 1997 (for public schools' old boys)
(Deal): Oundle beat Harrow 3–2
Varsity Match 1997 (Royal St George's): Oxford beat
Cambridge 11–4

* After a play-off

GOLF (WOMEN)

US Women's Open 1997 (Cornelius, Oregon): Alison
Nicholas (GB), 274
Women's World Championship 1996 (Seoul): Annika
Sorenstam (Sweden), 274

WPG EUROPEAN TOUR 1996

French Open (Arras): Trish Johnson (GB), 200
Italian Open (Il Picciola, Sicily): Laura Davies (GB), 282
Spanish Open (La Manga): Caryn Louw (S. Africa), 206
European Tour Order of Merit 1996: 1. Laura Davies (GB); 2. Helen Alfredsson (Sweden); 3. Trish Johnson (GB)

WPG EUROPEAN TOUR 1997

Estoril Open: Mandy Sutton (GB), 202
Tour Players' Classic (Tytherington): Karen Lunn (Australia), 283
Danish Open (Vejle): Laura Davies (GB), 207
Swiss Open (Lausanne): Marie-Laure de Lorenzi (France), 280*
Evian Masters: Hiromi Kobayashi (Japan), 274*
Irish Open (Luttrellstown): Patricia Meunier Lebouc (France), 284
German Open (Treudelberg): Joanne Mills (Australia), 283*
Championship of Europe (Gleneagles): Helen Alfredsson (Sweden), 276
British Open (Sunningdale): Karrie Webb (Australia), 269
Compaq Open (Osterakers, Stockholm): Annika Sorenstam (Sweden), 277
French Open (Paris): Karen Lunn (Australia), 281
Hennessy Cup (Cologne): Laura Davies (GB), 288

AMATEUR CHAMPIONSHIPS

British Open Championship 1997 (Cruden Bay): Alison Rose (GB)
English Amateur Championship 1997 (Saunton): Kim Rostron (Clitheroe)
Welsh Amateur Championship 1997 (Northop): Eleanor Pilgrim (Celtic Manor)
Scottish Amateur Championship 1997 (West Kilbride): Alison Rose (Stirling)
British Strokeplay 1997 (Silloth): Karen-Margrethe Juul (Denmark), 293
English Strokeplay 1997 (Hankley Common): Lynn Tupholme (Northcliff), 293
Welsh Strokeplay 1997 (Whitchurch, Cardiff). Kelly Edwards (Stafford Castle), 216
Scottish Strokeplay 1997 (Portland and Royal Troon): Kim Rostron (Clitheroe), 219*
Home International Championship 1997 (Lahinch): England
Espirito Santo Trophy (world amateur team championship) 1996 (Santa Elena, Philippines): S. Korea, 438
European Amateur Championship 1997 (Formby): Sylvia Cavalleri (Italy), 297
European Amateur Team Championship 1997 (Nordcenter, Finland): Sweden

* After a play-off

GREYHOUND RACING

Cesarewitch 1996 (Catford): Elbony Rose
St Leger 1996 (Wembley): Spring Rose
Oaks 1996 (Wimbledon): Annie's Bullet
Grand Prix 1996 (Walthamstow): Spring Rose
Gold Collar 1996 (Catford): Homeside Knight
Television Trophy 1997 (Hall Green): Thornfield Pride
Grand National 1997 (Hall Green): Tarn Bay Flash
Derby 1997 (Wimbledon): Some Picture
Scurry Gold Cup 1997 (Catford): Shoreham Beach
The Masters 1997 (Reading): Night Trooper
The Regency 1997 (Brighton): Million Percent

GYMNASTICS

WORLD CHAMPIONSHIPS 1997
Lausanne, September

MEN

World Champion: Ivan Ivankov (Belarus)
Individual Apparatus Champions:
Floor: Alexei Nemov (Russia)
Pommel Horse: Valeri Belenki (Germany)
Rings: Yuri Chechi (Italy)
Vault: Sergei Fedorchenko (Kazakhstan)
Parallel Bars: Zhang Jinjing (China)
High Bar: Jani Tanskanen (Finland)
World Team Champions 1997: China

WOMEN

World Champion: Svetlana Khorkina (Russia)
Individual Apparatus Champions:
Floor: Gina Gogean (Romania)
Beam: Gina Gogean (Romania)
Vault: Simona Amanar (Romania)
Assymetric Bars: Svetlana Khorkina (Russia)
World Team Champions 1997: Romania

BRITISH MEN'S CHAMPIONSHIPS 1996
Nottingham, November

British Champion: Lee McDermott (Woking)
Individual Apparatus Champions:
Floor: Dominic Brindle (City of Leeds)
Pommel Horse: Dominic Brindle (City of Leeds)
Rings: Dominic Brindle (City of Leeds)
Vault: Dominic Brindle (City of Leeds)
Parallel Bars: Dominic Brindle (City of Leeds)
High Bar: Lee McDermott (Woking)
British Men's Team Champions 1997 (Adam Shield): Woking

BRITISH WOMEN'S CHAMPIONSHIPS 1996
Guildford, October

British Champion: Lisa Mason (Huntingdon)
Individual Apparatus Champions:
Floor: Lisa Mason (Huntingdon)
Beam: Sharna Murray (Alderwood)
Vault: Gemma Cuff (Heathrow)
Assymetric Bars: Gabby Fuchs (Harrow)

BRITISH WOMEN'S CHAMPIONSHIPS 1997
Guildford, May

British Champion: Lisa Mason (Huntingdon)
Individual Apparatus Champions:
Floor: Annika Reeder (Basildon)
Beam: Gabby Fuchs (Harrow)
Vault: Gemma Cuff (Heathrow)
Assymetric Bars: Jennie Cox (Heathrow)
British Women's Team Champions 1997: Heathrow
British Rhythmics Champion 1997: Sarah McCann (Otley)

HOCKEY

MEN

National League 1997: Reading
Hockey Association Cup final 1997: Teddington beat Reading 2–1
National Indoor League 1997: Old Loughtonians

National Indoor Club Championship final 1997: St Albans beat East Grinstead 6–4
County Championship final 1997: Cheshire beat Sussex 5–1
Champions Trophy final 1996: Holland beat Pakistan 3–2
European Nations Indoor Cup final 1997: Germany beat Czech Republic 10–5
European Club Championship final 1997: HGC (Holland) beat Harvestehuder Hamburg (Germany) 4–3
European Indoor Club Championship final 1997: Harvestehuder Hamburg (Germany) beat Rot-Weiss Cologne (Germany) 6–5
European Cup Winners' Cup final 1997: Gladbacher (Germany) beat Reading (England) 7–2
Varsity Match 1997: Cambridge beat Oxford 2–0

WOMEN

National League 1997: Slough
AEWHA Cup final 1997: Hightown 2, Clifton 2. Hightown won 3–2 on penalties
National Indoor League 1997: Slough
County Championship final 1997: Gloucestershire beat Dorset 4–0
Champions Trophy final 1997: Australia beat Germany 2–1 a.e.t.
European Club Championship final 1997: Berliner (Germany) beat HGC (Netherlands) 2–1
European Indoor Club Championship final 1997: Russelsheim (Germany) beat Berlin (Germany) 7–6
European Cup Winners' Cup final 1997: SV Kampong (Netherlands) beat Ipswich (England) 4–1

HORSE-RACING

STATISTICS

WINNING FLAT OWNERS 1996

Godolphin	£1,852,814
Sheikh Mohammed	1,402,475
Hamdan Al-Maktoum	1,169,562
Khalid Abdulla	1,085,946
Maktoum Al-Maktoum	796,484
Wafic Said	785,570
Mollers Racing	606,405
Khalifa Dasmal	575,420
Cheveley Park Stud	458,260
Fahd Salman	366,541

WINNING FLAT TRAINERS 1996

Saeed bin Suroor	£1,962,598
Henry Cecil	1,935,053
John Gosden	1,099,450
Michael Stoute	1,097,248
Mark Johnston	1,091,020
Richard Hannon	986,135
John Dunlop	978,469
Paul Cole	894,126
Geoff Wragg	874,549
William Haggas	852,869

LEADING FLAT BREEDERS 1996

	Value
Sheikh Mohammed	£1,486,406
Juddmonte Farms	1,197,365
Gainsborough Stud Management Ltd	616,227
Cheveley Park Stud Ltd	609,925
Shadwell Estate Co Ltd	598,640
Khalifa Abdulla Dasmal	575,200
Darley Stud Management Inc	553,303
Gerald W. Leigh	385,679
Cyril Humphries	377,582
Lord Halifax	367,624

WINNING FLAT SIRES 1996

	Horses won	Races	Total value
Sadler's Wells (1981) by Northern Dancer	33	45	£1,015,174
Mtoto (1983) by Busted	19	27	832,743
Salse (1985) by Topsider	23	36	706,105
Diesis (1980) by Sharpen Up	20	28	698,993
Caerleon (1980) by Nijinsky	22	38	698,601
Cadeaux Genereux (1985) by Young Generation	26	42	620,967
Warning (1985) by Known Fact	28	35	613,397
Darshaan (1981) by Shirley Heights	12	17	562,651
Green Desert (1983) by Danzig	33	47	555,983
Woodman (1983) by Mr Prospector	13	18	513,882

WINNING FLAT JOCKEYS 1996

	1st	2nd	3rd	Unpl.	Total mts
Pat Eddery	186	137	96	463	882
Richard Quinn	149	117	124	492	882
Kieren Fallon	136	140	137	494	907
Jason Weaver	129	122	96	482	829
Frankie Dettori	123	75	61	311	570
Kevin Darley	113	120	104	530	867
John Reid	113	102	101	496	812
Seb Sanders	97	91	87	666	941
Ray Cochrane	86	83	71	387	627
Jimmy Fortune	83	78	113	513	787

WINNING NATIONAL HUNT JOCKEYS 1996–7

	1st	2nd	3rd	Unpl.	Total mts
Tony McCoy	190	150	78	267	665
Jamie Osborne	131	82	63	254	530
Richard Dunwoody	111	101	70	276	558
Richard Johnson	102	78	91	293	564
Norman Williamson	85	71	66	308	530
Peter Niven	84	57	50	188	379
Mick Fitzgerald	82	61	53	249	445
Adrian Maguire	81	72	61	184	398
Tony Dobbin	73	52	46	222	393
David Bridgwater	69	47	49	224	389

The above statistics are the copyright of *The Sporting Life*

...KES

...ket, 1 mile, 2 f

...(4y), (9st), W. Swinburn
...r Empereur (4y), (9st 4lb), S. Guillot
...rum (3y), (8st 10lb), J. Reid
...Sham (3y), (8st 8lb), P. Eddery

...CH

...wmarket, 2 miles and about 2 f

...ahsaylad (7y), (8st 12lb), J. Williams
...aptain's Guest (4y), (9st 9lb), A. Clark
...Old Red (5y), (7st 11lb), L. Charnock
...nchcailloch (7y), (7st 10lb), R. Ffrench

...SSY GOLD CUP

...Newbury, 3 miles and about 2½ f

99 Cogent (9y), (10st 8lb), D. Fortt
99 One Man (6y), (10st), A. Dobbin
199. Couldn't Be Better (8y), (10st 8lb), D. Gallagher
1996 Coome Hill (7y), (10st), J. Osborne

*KING GEORGE VI CHASE
(1937) Kempton, about 3 miles

1993 Barton Bank (7y), (11st 10lb), A. Maguire
1994 Algan (6y), (11st 10lb), P. Chevalier
†1995 One Man (8y), (11st 10lb), R. Dunwoody
1996 One Man (8y), (11st 10lb), R. Dunwoody

*CHAMPION HURDLE
(1927) Cheltenham, 2 miles and about ½ f

1994 Flakey Dove (8y), (11st 9lb), M. Dwyer
1995 Alderbrook (6y), (12st), N. Williamson
1996 Collier Bay (6y), (12st), G. Bradley
1997 Make A Stand (6y), (12st), A. McCoy

*QUEEN MOTHER CHAMPION CHASE
(1959) Cheltenham, about 2 miles

1994 Viking Flagship (7y), (12st), A. Maguire
1995 Viking Flagship (8y), (12st), C. Swan
1996 Klairon Davis (7y), (12st), F. Woods
1997 Martha's Son (10y), (12st), R. Farrant

*CHELTENHAM GOLD CUP
(1924) 3 miles and about 2½ f

1994 The Fellow (9y), (12st), A. Kondrat
1995 Master Oats (9y), (12st), N. Williamson
1996 Imperial Call (7y), (12st), C. O'Dwyer
1997 Mr Mulligan (9y), (12st), A. McCoy

LINCOLN HANDICAP
(1965) Doncaster, 1 mile

1994 Our Rita (5y), (8st 5lb), D. Holland
199. Roving Minstrel (4y), (8st 3lb), K. Darley
199. Stone Ridge (4y), (8st 12lb), D. O'Neill
199. Kuala Lipis (4y), (8st 6lb), T. Quinn

...ND NATIONAL
...) Liverpool, 4 miles and about 4 f

...Miinnehoma (11y), (10st 8lb), R. Dunwoody
...Royal Athlete (9y), (11st 10lb), J. Titley
...Rough Quest (10y), (10st 7lb), M. Fitzgerald
...Lord Gyllene (9y), (10st), A. Dobbin

...mes: 8 minutes 47.8 seconds by Mr Frisk in 1990;
...1.9 seconds by Red Rum in 1973

...D GOLD CUP
...own, 3 miles and about 5 f

...rs Island (8y), (10st), C. Swan
...Fleur (9y), (9st 10lb), R. Dunwoody
...A Lord (10y), (11st 10lb), C. Swan
...Lad (8y), (10st), Mr R. Nuttall

JOCKEY CLUB STAKES
(1894) Newmarket, 1½ miles

1994 Silver Wisp (5y), (8st 9lb), M. Hills
1995 Only Royale (6y), (8st 11lb), F. Dettori
1996 Riyadian (4y), (8st 9lb), T. Quinn
1997 Time Allowed (4y), (8st 6lb), J. Reid

KENTUCKY DERBY
(1875) Louisville, Kentucky, 1¼ miles

1994 Go for Gin, C. McCarron
1995 Thunder Gulch, G. Stevens
1996 Grindstone, J. Bailey
1997 Silver Charm, G. Stevens

PRIX DU JOCKEY CLUB
(1836) Chantilly, 1½ miles

1994 Celtic Arms (9st 2lb), G. Mossé
1995 Celtic Swing (9st 2lb), K. Darley
1996 Ragmar (9st 2lb), G. Mossé
1997 Peintre Célèbre (9st 2lb), O. Peslier

ASCOT GOLD CUP
(1807) Ascot, 2 miles and about 4 f

1994 Arcadian Heights (6y), (9st 2lb), M. Hills
1995 Double Trigger (4y), (9st), J. Weaver
1996 Classic Cliché (4y), (9st), M. Kinane
1997 Celeric (5y), (9st 2lb), P. Eddery

IRISH SWEEPS DERBY
(1866) Curragh, 1½ miles, for three year olds

1994 Balanchine (8st 11lb), F. Dettori
1995 Winged Love (9st), O. Peslier
1996 Zagreb (9st), P. Shanahan
1997 Desert King (9st), C. Roche

ECLIPSE STAKES
(1886) Sandown, 1 mile and about 2 f

1994 Ezzoud (5y), (9st 7lb), W. Swinburn
1995 Halling (4y), (9st 7lb), W. Swinburn
1996 Halling (5y), (9st 7lb), J. Reid
1997 Pilsudski (5y), (9st 7lb), M. Kinane

KING GEORGE VI AND QUEEN ELIZABETH DIAMOND STAKES
(1952) Ascot, 1 mile and about 4 f

1994 King's Theatre (3y), (8st 9lb), M. Kinane
1995 Lammtarra (3y), (8st 9lb), F. Dettori
1996 Pentire (4y), (9st 7lb), M. Hills
1997 Swain (5y), (9st 7lb), J. Reid

GOODWOOD CUP
(1812) Goodwood, about 2 miles

1994 Tioman Island (4y), (9st 5lb), T. Quinn
1995 Double Trigger (4y), (9st 5lb), J. Weaver
1996 Grey Shot (4y), (9st), P. Eddery
1997 Double Trigger (6y), (9st), M. Roberts

CAMBRIDGESHIRE HANDICAP
(1839) Newmarket, 1 mile

1994 Halling (3y), (8st 8lb), F. Dettori
1995 Cap Juluca (3y), (9st 10lb), R. Hughes
1996 Clifton Fox (4y), (8st 2lb), N. Day

PRIX DE L'ARC DE TRIOMPHE
(1920) Longchamp, 1½ miles

1994 Carnegie (3y), (8st 11lb), T. Jarnet
1995 Lammtarra (3y), (8st 11lb), F. Dettori
1996 Helissio (3y), (8st 11lb), O. Peslier

*National Hunt
†Run on 6 January 1996 because of bad weather

THE CLASSICS

ONE THOUSAND GUINEAS
(1814) Rowley Mile, Newmarket, for three-year-old fillies

Year	Winner	Betting	Owner	Jockey
1994	Las Meninas	12–1	R. Sangster	J. Reid
1995	Harayir	5–1	H. Al-Maktoum	R. Hills
1996	Bosra Sham	10–11	Wafic Said	P. Eddery
1997	Sleepytime	5–1	C. Wacker III	K. Fallon

Record time: 1 minute 36.71 seconds by Las Meninas in 1994

TWO THOUSAND GUINEAS
(1809) Rowley Mile, Newmarket, for three-year-olds

Year	Winner	Betting	Owner	Jockey	Trainer	
1994	Mister Baileys	16–1	P. Venner	J. Weaver	M. Johnston	2
1995	Pennekamp	9–2	Sheikh Mohammed	T. Jarnet	A. Fabre	11
1996	Mark of Esteem	8–1	Godolphin	F. Dettori	Saeed bin Suroor	13
1997	Entrepreneur	11–2	M. Tabor	M. Kinane	M. Stoute	16

Record time: 1 minute 35.08 seconds by Mister Baileys in 1994

THE DERBY
(1780) Epsom, 1 mile and about 4 f, for three-year-olds

The first winner was Sir Charles Bunbury's Diomed in 1780. The owners with the record number of winners are Lord Egremont, who won in 1782, 1804, 1805, 1807, 1826 (also won five Oaks); and the late Aga Khan, who won in 1930, 1935, 1936, 1948, 1952. Other winning owners are: Duke of Grafton (1802, 1809, 1810, 1815); Mr J. Bowes (1835, 1843, 1852, 1853); Sir J. Hawley (1851, 1858, 1859, 1868); the 1st Duke of Westminster (1880, 1882, 1886, 1899); and Sir Victor Sassoon (1953, 1957, 1958, 1960).

Record times are: 2 min. 32.31 sec. by Lammtarra in 1995; 2 min. 33.80 sec. by Mahmoud in 1936; 2 min. 33.84 sec. by Kahyasi in 1988; 2 min. 33.9 sec. by Reference Point in 1987.

The Derby was run at Newmarket in 1915–18 and 1940–5.

Year	Winner	Betting	Owner	Jockey	Trainer	No. of Runners
1994	Erhaab	7–2	H. Al-Maktoum	W. Carson	J. Dunlop	25
1995	Lammtarra	14–1	S. M. Al-Maktoum	W. Swinburn	Saeed bin Suroor	15
1996	Shaamit	12–1	Khalifa Dasmal	M. Hills	W. Haggas	20
1997	Benny The Dip	11–1	L. Knight	W. Ryan	J. Gosden	13

THE OAKS
(1779) Epsom, 1 mile and about 4 f, for three-year-old fillies

Year	Winner	Betting	Owner	Jockey	Trainer	No. of Runners
1994	Balanchine	6–1	M. Al-Maktoum	F. Dettori	H. Ibrahim	10
1995	Moonshell	3–1	M. Al-Maktoum/ Godolphin	F. Dettori	Saeed bin Suroor	10
1996	Lady Carla	100–30	Wafic Said	P. Eddery	H. Cecil	11
1997	Reams of Verse	5–6	Prince K. Abdulla	K. Fallon	H. Cecil	12

ST LEGER
(1776) Doncaster, 1 mile and about 6 f, for three-year-olds

Year	Winner	Betting	Owner	Jockey	Trainer
1994	Moonax	40–1	Sheikh Mohammed	P. Eddery	B. Hills
1995	Classic Cliché	100–30	Godolphin	F. Dettori	Saeed
1996	Shantou	8–1	Sheikh Mohammed	F. Dettori	J. Go
1997	Silver Patriarch	5–4	P. Winfield	P. Eddery	J. D

Record time: 3 minutes 1.60 seconds by Coronach in 1926 and Windsor Lad in 1934

1218 The Y

RESULTS

CHAMPION STA
(1877) Newma
1993 Derm
1994 Hatoo
1995 Spec
1996 Bos

CESAREW
(1839) Ne
1993 A
1994 C
199
199

"H
(

14
15
196
1997
Record
9 minut
*WHITBRI
(1957) SAR
1994 Sar
1995 Ush
1996 Cach
1997 Life c
Harwe

ICE HOCKEY

World Championship final 1997: Canada beat Sweden 2–1
Super League Championship play-off final 1997: Nottingham
  Panthers beat Sheffield Steelers 3–1
Super League Championship 1997: Cardiff Devils
Benson and Hedges Cup final 1996: Nottingham Panthers
  beat Ayr Scottish Eagles 5–3
Stanley Cup final 1997: Detroit beat Philadelphia 4–0

ICE SKATING

BRITISH CHAMPIONSHIPS 1995
Pairs: Lesley Rogers and Michael Aldred
Ice Dance: Marika Humphries and Philip Askew

BRITISH CHAMPIONSHIPS 1996
Guildford, November

Men: Neil Wilson
Women: Jenna Arrowsmith
Pairs: Lesley Rogers and Michael Aldred
Ice Dance: Marika Humphries and Philip Askew

EUROPEAN CHAMPIONSHIPS 1997
Paris, January

Men: Alexei Urmanov (Russia)
Women: Irina Slutskaya (Russia)
Pairs: Marina Eltsova and Andrei Bushkov (Russia)
Ice Dance: Oksana Gritschuk and Evgeny Platov (Russia)

WORLD CHAMPIONSHIPS 1997
Lausanne, March

Men: Elvis Stojko (Canada)
Women: Tara Lipinski (USA)
Pairs: Mandy Wötzel and Ingo Steuer (Germany)
Ice Dance: Oksana Gritschuk and Evgeny Platov (Russia)

JUDO

BRITISH NATIONAL CHAMPIONSHIPS 1996
Bath, December

MEN

Heavyweight (over 95 kg): Richard Blanes
Light-heavyweight (95 kg): Keith Davis
Middleweight (86 kg): Winston Gordon
Light-middleweight (78 kg): Neil Edwards
Lightweight (71 kg): Lee Burbridge
Featherweight (65 kg): Simon Moss
Bantamweight (60 kg): Sam Dunkley

WOMEN

Heavyweight (over 72 kg): Simone Callender
Light-heavyweight (72 kg): Joanne Melen
Middleweight (66 kg): Karen Powell
Light-middleweight (61 kg): Ruth Eddy
Lightweight (56 kg): Natalie Barry
Featherweight (52 kg): Elise Summers
Bantamweight (48 kg): Joyce Heron

LAWN TENNIS

MAJOR CHAMPIONSHIPS 1997
AUSTRALIAN OPEN CHAMPIONSHIPS
Melbourne, 13–26 January
Men's Singles: Pete Sampras (USA) beat Carlos Moya
  (Spain) 6–2, 6–3, 6–3
Women's Singles: Martina Hingis (Switzerland) beat Mary
  Pierce (France) 6–2, 6–2
Men's Doubles: Mark Woodforde (Australia) and Todd
  Woodbridge (Australia) beat Sebastien Lareau
  (Canada) and Alex O'Brien (USA) 4–6, 7–5, 7–5, 6–3
Women's Doubles: Martina Hingis (Switzerland) and
  Natasha Zvereva (Belarus) beat Lindsay Davenport
  (USA) and Lisa Raymond (USA) 6–2, 6–2
Mixed Doubles: Manon Bollegraf (Holland) and Rick
  Leach (USA) beat Larissa Neiland (Latvia) and John-
  Laffnie de Jager (S. Africa) 6–3, 6–7, 7–5

FRENCH OPEN CHAMPIONSHIPS
Paris, 26 May–8 June
Men's Singles: Gustavo Kuerten (Brazil) beat Sergei
  Bruguera (Spain) 6–3, 6–4, 6–2
Women's Singles: Iva Majoli (Croatia) beat Martina Hingis
  (Switzerland) 6–4, 6–2
Men's Doubles: Yevgeny Kafelnikov (Russia) and Daniel
  Vacek (Czech Republic) beat Mark Woodforde
  (Australia) and Todd Woodbridge (Australia) 7–6,
  4–6, 6–3
Women's Doubles: Gigi Fernandez (USA) and Natasha
  Zvereva (Belarus) beat Mary Joe Fernandez (USA) and
  Lisa Raymond (USA) 6–2, 6–3
Mixed Doubles: Rika Hiraki (Japan) and Mahesh Bhupathi
  (India) beat Lisa Raymond (USA) and Patrick
  Galbraith (USA) 6–4, 6–1

ALL-ENGLAND CHAMPIONSHIPS
Wimbledon, 23 June–6 July
Men's Singles: Pete Sampras (USA) beat Cedric Pioline
  (France) 6–4, 6–2, 6–4
Women's Singles: Martina Hingis (Switzerland) beat Jana
  Novotna (Czech Republic) 2–6, 6–3, 6–3
Men's Doubles: Todd Woodbridge and Mark Woodforde
  (Australia) beat Jacco Eltingh (Holland) and Paul
  Haarhuis (Holland) 7–6, 7–6, 5–7, 6–3
Women's Doubles: Gigi Fernandez (USA) and Natasha
  Zvereva (Belarus) beat Nicole Arendt (USA) and
  Manon Bollegraf (Holland) 7–6, 6–4
Mixed Doubles: Helena Sukova (Czech Republic) and Cyril
  Suk (Czech Republic) beat Larissa Neiland (Latvia)
  and Andrei Olkhovskiy (Russia) 4–6, 6–3, 6–4

US OPEN CHAMPIONSHIPS
New York, 25 August–7 September
Men's Singles: Patrick Rafter (Australia) beat Greg
  Rusedski (GB) 6–3, 6–2, 4–6, 7–5
Women's Singles: Martina Hingis (Switzerland) beat Venus
  Williams (USA) 6–0, 6–4
Men's Doubles: Yevgeny Kafelnikov (Russia) and Daniel
  Vacek (Czech Republic) beat Jonas Bjorkman (Sweden)
  and Nicklas Kulti (Sweden) 7–6, 6–3
Women's Doubles: Lindsay Davenport (USA) and Jana
  Novotna (Czech Republic) beat Gigi Fernandez (USA)
  and Natasha Zvereva (Belarus) 6–3, 6–4
Mixed Doubles: Manon Bollegraf (Netherlands) and Rick
  Leach (USA) beat Mercedes Paz (Argentina) and Pablo
  Albano (Argentina) 3–6, 7–5, 7–6

Grand Slam Cup 1996: Boris Becker (Germany) beat Goran Ivanisevic (Croatia) 6–3, 6–4, 6–4

Grand Slam Cup 1997: Pete Sampras (USA) beat Patrick Rafter (Australia) 6–2, 6–4, 7–5

TEAM CHAMPIONSHIPS

Davis Cup final 1996: France beat Sweden 3–2

LTA County Cup 1997:

Men: Hampshire and Isle of Wight

Women: Warwickshire

NATIONAL CHAMPIONSHIPS 1996

Telford, November

Men's Singles: Tim Henman (Oxon) beat Greg Rusedski (unattached) 6–7, 7–6, 6–4

Women's Singles: Julie Pullin (Sussex) beat Claire Taylor (Oxon) 6–3, 6–0

Men's Doubles: Andrew Richardson (Lincs) and Miles Maclagan (W. of Scotland) beat Danny Sapsford (Surrey) and Andrew Foster (Staffs) 7–6, 6–7, 11–9

Women's Doubles: Lorna Woodroffe (Surrey) and Julie Pullin (Sussex) beat Shirli-Ann Siddall (Dorset) and Mandy Wainwright (Essex) 7–6, 6–4

MOTOR CYCLING

---

500 CC GRAND PRIX 1996

Brazilian (Rio de Janeiro): Michael Doohan (Australia), Honda

Australian (Sydney): Loris Capirossi (Italy), Yamaha

Riders' Championship 1996: 1. Michael Doohan (Australia), Honda, 309 points; 2. Alex Criville (Spain), Honda, 245 points; 3. Luca Cadalora (Italy), Honda, 168 points

500 CC GRAND PRIX 1997

Malaysian (Kuala Lumpur): Michael Doohan (Australia), Honda

Japanese (Suzuka): Michael Doohan (Australia), Honda

Spanish (Jerez): Alex Criville (Spain), Honda

Italian (Mugello): Michael Doohan (Australia), Honda

Austrian (Zeltweg): Michael Doohan (Australia), Honda

French (Le Castellet): Michael Doohan (Australia), Honda

Dutch (Assen): Michael Doohan (Australia), Honda

San Marino (Imola): Michael Doohan (Australia), Honda

German (Nurburgring): Michael Doohan (Australia), Honda

Brazilian (Rio de Janeiro): Michael Doohan (Australia), Honda

British (Donington Park): Michael Doohan (Australia), Honda

Czech (Brno): Michael Doohan (Australia), Honda

Catalonian: Michael Doohan (Australia), Honda

Indonesian (Jakarta): Tadayuki Okada (Japan), Honda

Senior Manx Grand Prix 1997: Gary Carswell (Kawasaki)

Senior TT 1997, Isle of Man: Phillip McCallen (Honda)

Junior TT 1997, Isle of Man: Ian Simpson (Honda)

MOTOR RACING

FORMULA ONE GRAND PRIX 1996

Japanese (Suzuka): Damon Hill (GB), Williams-Renault

Drivers' World Championship 1996: 1. Damon Hill (GB), Williams-Renault, 97 points; 2. Jacques Villeneuve (Canada), Williams-Renault, 78 points; 3. Michael Schumacher (Germany), Ferrari, 59 points

Constructors' World Championship 1996: 1. Williams-Renault, 175 points; 2. Ferrari, 70 points; 3. Benetton-Renault, 68 points

FORMULA ONE GRAND PRIX 1997

Australian (Melbourne): David Coulthard (GB), McLaren-Mercedes

Brazilian (São Paulo): Jacques Villeneuve (Canada), Williams-Renault

Argentine (Buenos Aires): Jacques Villeneuve (Canada), Williams-Renault

San Marino (Imola): Heinz-Harald Frentzen (Germany), Williams-Renault

Monaco (Monte Carlo): Michael Schumacher (Germany), Ferrari

Spanish (Barcelona): Jacques Villeneuve (Canada), Williams-Renault

Canadian (Montreal): Michael Schumacher (Germany), Ferrari

French (Magny-Cours): Michael Schumacher (Germany), Ferrari

British (Silverstone): Jacques Villeneuve (Canada), Williams-Renault

German (Hockenheim): Gerhard Berger (Austria), Benetton Renault

Hungarian (Budapest): Jacques Villeneuve (Canada), Williams-Renault

Belgian (Spa-Francorchamps): Michael Schumacher (Germany), Ferrari

Italian (Monza): David Coulthard (GB), McLaren-Mercedes

Austrian (Zeltweg): Jacques Villeneuve (Canada), Williams-Renault

Luxembourg (Nurburgring): Jacques Villeneuve (Canada), Williams-Renault

Indianapolis 500 1997: Arie Luyendyk (Holland), G-Force-Aurora

Le Mans 24-hour Race 1997: Michele Alboreto (Italy), Stefan Johansson (Sweden) and T. Kristensen (Denmark), TWR Porsche

---

MOTOR RALLYING

1996

San Remo Rally: Colin McRae (GB), Subaru Impreza

Catalonia Rally: Colin McRae (GB), Subaru Impreza

Drivers' World Championship 1996: Tommi Makinen (Finland), Mitsubishi Lancer, 123 points

Manufacturers' World Championship 1996: Subaru, 401 points

National Champion 1996: Chris Mellors (GB), Ford Escort Cosworth

Hong Kong–Beijing Rally 1996: Ari Vatanen (Finland), Mitsubishi

RAC Rally 1996: Armin Schwarz (Germany), Toyota

1997

Dakar Rally: Kenjiro Shinozuka (Japan), Mitsubishi

Swedish Rally: Kenneth Eriksson (Sweden), Subaru Impreza

Safari Rally: Colin McRae (GB), Subaru Impreza

Rally of Portugal: Tommi Makinen (Finland), Mitsubishi Lancer

Catalunya Rally: Tommi Makinen (Finland), Mitsubishi
Lancer
Corsican Rally: Colin McRae (GB), Subaru Impreza
Argentine Rally: Tommi Makinen (Finland), Mitsubishi
Lancer
Acropolis Rally: Carlos Sainz (Spain), Ford Escort
New Zealand Rally: Kenneth Eriksson (Sweden), Subaru
Impreza
1,000 Lakes Rally (Jyvaskyla, Finland): Tommi Makinen
(Finland), Mitsubishi Lancer
Rally of Indonesia: Carlos Sainz (Spain), Ford Escort

National Champion 1997: Mark Higgins, Nissan Sunny
Monte Carlo Rally 1997: Piero Liatti (Italy), Subaru Impreza
China Rally 1997: Colin McRae (GB), Subaru Impreza
Rally of Thailand 1997: Colin McRae (GB), Subaru
Impreza

NETBALL

TESTS
1996
2 Nov	Birmingham	England 37, Jamaica 48
6 Nov	Manchester	England 37, Jamaica 50
9 Nov	Wembley Arena	England 43, Jamaica 46
11 Nov	Cardiff	Wales 48, Jamaica 75
13 Nov	Londonderry	N. Ireland 45, Jamaica 61

INTERNATIONALS
1997
25 Jan	Cardiff	Wales 29, England 87
26 Jan	Dublin	Rep. of Ireland 18, N. Ireland 74
8 Feb	Harlow	England 69, Rep. of Ireland 12
22 Feb	Belfast	N. Ireland 49, Wales 54
8 Mar	Cardiff	Wales 89, Rep. of Ireland 16
22 Mar	Belfast	N. Ireland 40, England 71
3 May	Bury	Scotland 61, Wales 28
16 July	Bloemfontein	S. Africa 40, England 38
21 July	Port Elizabeth	S. Africa 54, England 52
24 July	Cape Town	S. Africa 53, England 48
29 July	Windhoek	Namibia 29, England 67

Inter-County Championship final 1997: Essex Metropolitan
beat Bedfordshire 9–5
National Clubs Championship final 1997: Ipswich Ladies beat
Adelphi 72–58
English Counties League Championship 1997: Bedfordshire
National Clubs League Championship 1997: Wyvern

POLO

Prince of Wales's Trophy final 1997: Geebung beat Buffalos
10–9
Queen's Cup final 1997: Isla Carroll beat Black Bears 13–10
Warwickshire Cup final 1997: Black Bears beat Lovelocks
10–7
Gold Cup (British Open) final 1997: Labegorce beat Isla
Carroll 10–8
Westchester Cup 1997: Great Britain beat USA 12–9
Prince Philip Trophy 1997: Labegorce beat Black Bears
12–11
Arena Gold Cup 1997: Chopendoz beat Metropolitan 18–15
Arena European Nations 1997: England beat Holland 25–14
Varsity Match 1997: Cambridge beat Oxford 7–6

RACKETS

World Singles Champion: James Male (GB)
World Doubles Champions: Neil Smith and Shannon Hazell
(GB)
Professional Singles Championship final 1997: Peter Brake
(Queen's) beat David Makey (Marlborough) 3–0
British Open Singles Championship final 1997: Willie Boone
(GB) beat Matthew Windows (GB) 4–1
British Open Doubles Championship final 1997: Willie Boone
and Peter Brake (GB) beat Tim Cockroft and Rupert
Owen Browne (GB) 4–1
Amateur Singles Championship final 1996: James Male beat
Willie Boone 3–1
Amateur Doubles Championship final 1997: Tim Cockroft and
Rupert Owen-Browne beat Willie Boone and Matthew
Windows 4–1
National League 1997: Old Wellingtonians
Noel Bruce Cup final 1996 (public schools' old boys' doubles
championship): Eton (Willie Boone and Mark Hue
Williams) beat Wellington (Tim Cockroft and Toby
Sawrey-Cookson) 4–1
Public Schools' Singles Championship final 1996: Alexander
Titchener-Barrett (Harrow) beat Guy Smith-Bingham
(Eton) 3–1
Public Schools' Doubles Championship final 1997: Eton (Guy
Smith-Bingham and Hugo Loudon) beat Harrow
(Alexander Titchener-Barrett and Christopher
Wilson) 4–1
Varsity Match 1997: Oxford beat Cambridge 3–0

REAL TENNIS

World Singles Champion: Robert Fahey (Australia)
Professional Singles Championship final 1997: Lachie Deuchar
(Australia) beat Mike Gooding (GB) 3–0
Professional Doubles Championship final 1997: Lachie
Deuchar (Australia) and Mike Gooding (GB) beat Nick
Wood (GB) and Adam Phillips (GB) 3–1
British Open Singles Championship final 1996: Mike Gooding
(GB) beat Lachie Deuchar (Australia) 3–1
British Open Doubles Championship final 1996: Chris Bray
(GB) and Mike Happell (GB) beat Lachie Deuchar
(Australia) and Mike Gooding (GB) 3–2
Amateur Singles Championship final 1997: Julian Snow (GB)
beat Nigel Pendrigh (GB) 3–0
Amateur Doubles Championship final 1997: Julian Snow (GB)
and James Acheson-Gray (GB) beat Nigel Pendrigh
(GB) and Tim Goodale (USA) 3–1
Henry Leaf Cup final 1997 (public schools' old boys' doubles
championship): Charterhouse I (Nigel Pendrigh and
James Acheson-Gray) beat Haileybury I (William
Hollington and Ruaraidh Gunn) 2–1
Varsity Match 1997: Oxford beat Cambridge 5–1
Women's World Singles Championship final 1997: Penny
Lumley (GB) beat Sue Haswell (GB) 2–0
Women's World Doubles Championship final 1997: Penny
Lumley (GB) and Sue Haswell (GB) beat Kate
Leeming (Australia) and Fiona Deuchar (Australia)
2–0
Women's British Open Singles Championship final 1997: Penny
Lumley (GB) beat Sue Haswell (GB) 2–0
Women's British Open Doubles Championship final 1996: Penny
Lumley (GB) and Sue Haswell (GB) beat Sally Jones
(GB) and Alex Garside (GB) 2–0

Women's British Open Doubles Championship final 1997: Penny
Lumley (GB) and Sue Haswell (GB) beat Sally Jones
(GB) and Alex Garside (GB) 2–0

ROAD WALKING

BAF MEN's 20 KM WALK
Stoneleigh, 15 March 1997
Individual: Andy Penn (Coventry), 1 hr. 28 min. 41 sec.
Team: Road Hoggs, 34 points

BAF WOMEN's 10 KM WALK
Stoneleigh, 15 March 1997
Individual: Sylvia Black (Birchfield), 49 min. 39 sec.
Team: Sheffield, 17 points

WORLD RACE WALKING CUP
Prague, 19–20 April 1997
Men's 20 km (individual): Jefferson Perez (Ecuador), 1 hr.
18 min. 24 sec.
Men's 20 km (team): Russia, 431 points
Men's 50 km (individual): Jesus Garcia (Spain), 3 hr. 39 min.
54 sec.
Men's 50 km (team): Russia, 434 points
Women's 10 km (individual): Irina Stankina (Russia), 41 min.
52 sec.
Women's 10 km (team): Russia, 440 points

MEN's NATIONAL 10 MILES WALK
Victoria Park, London, 17 May 1997
Individual: Steve Partington (Manx), 1 hr. 15 min. 34 sec.
Team: Road Hoggs, 28 points

WOMEN's NATIONAL 10 MILES WALK
Victoria Park, London, 17 May 1997
Individual: Vicky Lupton (Sheffield), 1 hr. 25 min. 11 sec.
Team: Sheffield, 7 points

MEN's NATIONAL 20 MILES WALK
Leicester, 7 June 1997
Individual: Chris Cheeseman (Surrey), 2 hr. 34 min. 04 sec.
Team: Steyning, 15 points

MEN's NATIONAL 50 KM WALK
Stockport, 30 August 1997
Individual: Mark Easton (Surrey), 4 hr. 07 min. 45 sec.
Team: York, 21 points

WOMEN's NATIONAL 20 KM WALK
Stockport, 30 August 1997
Individual: Sylvia Black (Birchfield), 1 hr. 45 min. 48 sec.
Team: Steyning, 21 points

ROWING

WORLD CHAMPIONSHIPS 1997
Aiguebelette, France, September

MEN

Coxed pairs: USA
Coxless pairs: France
Coxed fours: France
Coxless fours: Great Britain
Single sculls: Jamie Koven (USA)
Double sculls: Germany
Quad sculls: Italy
Eights: USA

WOMEN

Coxless pairs: Canada
Coxless fours: Great Britain
Single sculls: Katya Khodotovitch (Belarus)
Double sculls: Germany
Quad sculls: Germany
Eights: Romania

NATIONAL CHAMPIONSHIPS 1997
Holme Pierrepont, July

MEN

Coxed pairs: Molesey
Coxless pairs: Queen's Tower
Coxed fours: NCRA/Newcastle University
Coxless fours: Cambridge University
Single sculls: Greg Searle (Molesey)
Double sculls: Tideway Scullers School
Quad sculls: NCRA/OUBC/Poplar/Queen's Tower
Eights: Nottingham

WOMEN

Coxless pairs: Edinburgh University/University of London
Coxed fours: Tideway Scullers School
Coxless fours: IC/Molesey/Queen's Tower/OUBC
Single sculls: Alison Sanders (City of Sheffield)
Double sculls: Hereford
Quad sculls: Thames
Eights: IC/Queen's Tower

THE 143rd UNIVERSITY BOAT RACE
Putney–Mortlake, 4 miles 1 f, 180 yd, 29 March 1997

Cambridge beat Oxford by 2 lengths; 17 min. 38 sec.
Cambridge have won 74 times, Oxford 68 and there has
been one dead heat. The record time is 16 min. 45 sec.,
rowed by Oxford in 1984

Women's Boat Race 1997 (Henley): Cambridge beat
Oxford by 1¼ lengths; 6 min. 30.5 sec.

HENLEY ROYAL REGATTA 1997

Grand Challenge Cup: Australian Institute of Sport and
NSW Institute of Sport (Australia) beat Berlin and
Tegel (Germany) by 3 lengths
Ladies' Challenge Plate: Nottinghamshire County and
Oxford Brookes University beat University of
Washington (USA) by 1 foot
Thames Challenge Cup: Nottingham A beat Neptune
(Ireland) by 2 feet
Temple Challenge Cup: Goldie beat Imperial College and
King's College by ¾ length
Princess Elizabeth Challenge Cup: St Paul's School beat
Canford School by 2½ lengths
Stewards' Challenge Cup: Leander Club and Oxford
University beat Nottinghamshire County by 2½ lengths
Prince Philip Challenge Cup: Eton Vikings and Leander Club
beat Nottinghamshire County and Newcastle
University by 1¼ lengths
Queen Mother Challenge Cup: Augusta (USA) beat Queen's
Tower and Poplar, Blackwall and District easily
Visitors' Challenge Cup: Oxford Brookes University beat
Imperial College and Charing Cross and Westminster
Medical School by 3¼ lengths
Wyfold Challenge Cup: Molesey A beat London Rowing
Club by 2¾ lengths
Britannia Challenge Cup: University of London beat Hansa
Hamburg (Germany) by 1½ lengths

Fawley Challenge Cup: Windsor Boys' School and Claire's Court School beat Mortlake Anglian and Alpha and Queen Elizabeth High School by ½ length

Silver Goblets and Nickalls' Challenge Cup: Rob Thatcher and Ben Hunt-Davis (GB) beat C. Fischer and S. Franke (Germany) easily

Double Sculls Challenge Cup: M. Free and D. Free (Australia) beat B. Klein and R. Weaver (USA) easily

Diamond Challenge Sculls: Greg Searle (Molesey) beat Peter Haining (Auriol Kensington) easily

Princess Royal Challenge Cup: Maria Brandin (Sweden) beat Guin Batten (GB), not rowed out

OTHER ROWING EVENTS

Cambridge Lents 1997: Men, Downing; *Women,* Emmanuel
Oxford Torpids 1997: Men, Oriel; *Women,* Osler-Green
Oxford Summer Eights 1997: Men, Oriel; *Women,* Osler-Green
Cambridge Mays 1997: Men, Downing; *Women,* Pembroke
Head of the River 1997: Men, Leander I; *Women,* Thames A
Doggett's Coat and Badge 1997: Michael Russell (Gravesend)
Wingfield Sculls 1997: Martin Kettle (Queen's Tower)
London Cup 1997: Greg Searle (Molesey)
Thames World Sculling Challenge 1996: Men, Merlin Vervoorn (Holland); *Women,* Guin Batten (GB)

RUGBY FIVES

National Singles Championship final 1996: Neil Roberts beat Wayne Enstone 15–6, 11–15, 15–6

National Doubles Championship final 1997: Wayne Enstone and Neil Roberts beat David Hebden and Ian Fuller 15–10, 15–4

National Club Championship 1997: Manchester YMCA

National Schools' Singles Championship final 1997: Chris Saltmarsh (Radley) beat Ben Lovett (Christ's Hospital) 9–11, 11–0, 11–4

National Schools' Doubles Championship final 1997: Radley (Chris Saltmarsh and Tom Maconie) beat Merchiston Castle (Adam Strang and Richard Swan) 11–8, 3–11, 11–2

Varsity Match 1997: Oxford beat Cambridge 281–157

RUGBY LEAGUE

TESTS

1996

5 Oct	Nadi	Fiji 4, Great Britain 72
18 Oct	Auckland	New Zealand 17, Great Britain 12
25 Oct	Palmerston North	New Zealand 18, Great Britain 15
1 Nov	Christchurch	New Zealand 32, Great Britain 12

OTHER COMPETITIONS

Challenge Cup final 1997 (Wembley, 3 May): St Helens beat Bradford Bulls 32–22

Premiership Trophy final 1997 (Old Trafford, 28 September): Wigan beat St Helens 33–20

Divisional Premiership final 1997: Huddersfield beat Hull Sharks 18–0

Stones Super League 1997: Bradford Bulls, 40 points

League Division 1 Championship 1997: Hull Sharks, 37 points

League Division 2 Championship 1997: Hunslet Hawks, 30 points

Varsity Match 1997: Cambridge beat Oxford 26–22

AMATEUR RUGBY LEAGUE 1996–7

County Championship: Ellenborough
National Inter-League Open Age Shield Competition: Humberside
National Cup Open Age Competition: Ellenborough
National League Premier Division Champions: West Hull

RUGBY UNION

FIVE NATIONS' CHAMPIONSHIP 1997

18 Jan	Murrayfield	Scotland 19, Wales 34
	Dublin	Ireland 15, France 32
1 Feb	Twickenham	England 41, Scotland 13
	Cardiff	Wales 25, Ireland 26
15 Feb	Dublin	Ireland 6, England 46
	Paris	France 27, Wales 22
1 Mar	Twickenham	England 20, France 23
	Murrayfield	Scotland 38, Ireland 10
15 Mar	Cardiff	Wales 13, England 34
	Paris	France 47, Scotland 20

	P	W	D	L	Points F	A	Total
France	4	4	0	0	129	77	8
England	4	3	0	1	141	55	6
Wales	4	1	0	3	94	106	2
Scotland	4	1	0	3	90	132	2
Ireland	4	1	0	3	57	141	2

OTHER INTERNATIONALS

1996

5 Oct	Rome	Italy 22, Wales 31
9 Nov	Murrayfield	Scotland 19, Australia 29
12 Nov	Dublin	Ireland 25, W. Samoa 40
23 Nov	Twickenham	England 54, Italy 21
	Dublin	Ireland 12, Australia 22
1 Dec	Cardiff	Wales 19, Australia 28
14 Dec	Twickenham	England 20, Argentina 18
	Murrayfield	Scotland 29, Italy 22
15 Dec	Cardiff	Wales 20, S. Africa 37

1997

4 Jan	Dublin	Ireland 29, Italy 37
11 Jan	Cardiff	Wales 34, USA 14
31 May	Buenos Aires	Argentina 20, England 46
7 June	Buenos Aires	Argentina 33, England 13
17 June	Harare	Zimbabwe 10, Scotland 55
6 July	Wilmington	USA 20, Wales 30
13 July	San Francisco	USA 23, Wales 28
19 July	Toronto	Canada 25, Wales 28
30 August	Wrexham	Wales 70, Romania 21

TESTS

1997

21 June	Cape Town	S. Africa 16, British Isles 25
28 June	Durban	S. Africa 15, British Isles 18
5 July	Johannesburg	S. Africa 35, British Isles 16
12 July	Sydney	Australia 25, England 6

European Club Cup final 1997 (Cardiff, 25 January): Brive beat Leicester 28–9

DOMESTIC COMPETITIONS

English League: Division 1, Wasps, 37 points; *Division 2,* Richmond, 40 points; *Division 3,* Exeter, 50 points; *Division 4 (north),* Worcester, 49 points; *Division 4 (south),* Newbury, 52 points

County Championship final 1997: Cumbria beat Somerset 21–13

Pilkington Cup final 1997: Leicester beat Sale 9–3

Scottish League: Division 1, Melrose, 28 points; *Division 2,*
    Edinburgh Academicals, 20 points; *Division 3,*
    Kirkcaldy, 24 points; *Division 4,* Gordonians, 24 points
Scottish Cup final 1997: Melrose beat Boroughmuir 31–23
Welsh League: Division 1, Pontypridd, 62 points; *Division 2,*
    Aberavon, 53 points; *Division 3,* Rumney, 52 points;
    Division 4, St Peter's, 47 points; *Division 5,* Ystrad
    Rhondda, 52 points
Welsh Challenge (Swalec) Cup final 1997: Cardiff beat
    Swansea 33–26
Irish League: Division 1, Shannon, 24 points; *Division 2,*
    Clontarf, 22 points; *Division 3,* Buccaneers, 19 points;
    Division 4, Suttonians, 18 points
Ulster Cup final 1997: Ballymena beat Malone 20–13
Services Championship 1997: Army beat Royal Navy 18–16;
    Army 35, Royal Air Force 35; Royal Air Force 24,
    Royal Navy 24
Varsity Match 1996: Cambridge beat Oxford 23–7
Middlesex Sevens final 1997: Barbarians beat Saracens 57-5

SHOOTING

128TH NATIONAL RIFLE ASSOCIATION IMPERIAL
MEETING
Bisley, July 1997

Queen's Prize: Anthony Ringer, 299.44 v-bulls
Grand Aggregate: Andrew Luckman, 597.88 v-bulls
Prince of Wales Prize: Richard Chase, 75.15 v-bulls
St George's Vase: D. Dodds, 149.22 v-bulls
Allcomers Aggregate: Jon Underwood, 323.54 v-bulls
National Trophy: England, 2,060.279 v-bulls
Kolapore Cup: Great Britain, 1,175.176 v-bulls
Chancellor's Trophy: Cambridge University, 1,155.147
    v-bulls
Musketeers Cup: Bath University, 581.62 v-bulls
Vizianagram Trophy: House of Commons, 491.28 v-bulls
County Long-Range Championship: Norfolk, 583.72 v-bulls
Mackinnon Challenge Cup: England, 1,162.152 v-bulls
The Ashburton: Sedbergh School, 480 points
The Elcho: Scotland, 1,723.176 v-bulls
The Albert: Alexander Henderson, 213.29 v-bulls
Hopton Challenge Cup: Stuart Collings, 959.105 v-bulls

CLAY PIGEON SHOOTING

World Sporting Championship 1997: Stuart Clarke (England)
International Cup (Down-the-Line) 1997: England, 5,910/
    6,000
British Open Down-the-Line Championship 1997: Derek
    Burnett (Ireland), 100/300
Mackintosh Trophy 1997: England
British Open Skeet Championship 1997: Alan Vesty, 100*
British Open Sporting Championship 1997: John Bidwell
Coronation Cup 1997: John Timmins, 376

* After a shoot-off

SNOOKER

1996
Benson and Hedges Championship: Brian Morgan (England)
    beat Drew Henry (Scotland) 9–8
Grand Prix: Mark Williams (Wales) beat Euan Henderson
    (Scotland) 9–5
Rothmans Grand Prix: Nigel Bond (England) beat Tony
    Drago (Malta) 7–3
World Cup: Scotland beat Republic of Ireland 10–7

UK Professional Championship: Stephen Hendry (Scotland)
    beat John Higgins (Scotland) 10–9
German Open: Ronnie O'Sullivan (England) beat Alain
    Robidoux (Canada) 9–7

1997
Welsh Open: Stephen Hendry (Scotland) beat Mark King
    (England) 9–2
Benson and Hedges Masters: Steve Davis (England) beat
    Ronnie O'Sullivan (England) 10–8
International Open: Stephen Hendry (Scotland) beat Tony
    Drago (Malta) 9–1
European Open: John Higgins (Scotland) beat John Parrott
    (England) 9–5
Thailand Open: Peter Ebdon (England) beat Nigel Bond
    (England) 9–7
Irish Masters: Stephen Hendry (Scotland) beat Darren
    Morgan (Wales) 9–8
British Open: Mark Williams (Wales) beat Stephen Hendry
    (Scotland) 9–2
World Championship: Ken Doherty (Ireland) beat Stephen
    Hendry (Scotland) 18–12
European League: Ronnie O'Sullivan (England) beat
    Stephen Hendry (Scotland) 10–8

Women's Welsh Regal Masters 1996: Kelly Fisher (England)
    beat Ann-Marie Farren (England) 4–1
Women's National Championship 1997: Karen Corr (England)
    beat Kelly Fisher (England) 3–2
Women's UK Championship 1997: Karen Corr (England) beat
    Kelly Fisher (England) 4–0
Women's Scottish Regal Masters 1997: Karen Corr (England)
    beat Kelly Fisher (England) 4–2

SPEEDWAY

World Champion 1996: Billy Hamill (USA)
Premier League Riders' Championship 1996: Sam Ermolenko
    (USA)

GRAND PRIX 1997

Czech (Prague): Greg Hancock (USA)
Swedish (Linkoping): Tomasz Gollob (Poland)
German (Landshut): Hans Nielsen (Denmark)
British (Bradford): Brian Andersen (Denmark)
Polish (Wroclaw): Greg Hancock (USA)
Danish (Vojens): Mark Loram (England)

World Champion 1997: Greg Hancock (USA)
World Team Cup final 1997: Denmark (Hans Nielsen and
    Tommy Knudsen), 24 points
World Championship, Overseas final 1997: Kelvin Tatum
    (England)
World Championship, British final 1997: Mark Loram
    (Bradford)
Elite League Knock-Out Cup final 1997: Eastbourne beat
    Poole 116–66

SQUASH RACKETS

MEN

World Open Championship final 1996: Jansher Khan
    (Pakistan) beat Rodney Eyles (Australia) 3–1
European Team Championship final 1997: England beat Wales
    4–0

British Open Championship final 1997: Jansher Khan
(Pakistan) beat Peter Nicol (Scotland) 3–2
National Championship final 1997: Mark Cairns (England)
beat Alex Gough (Wales) 3–0

WOMEN

World Open Championship final 1996: Sarah FitzGerald
(Australia) beat Cassie Jackman (GB) 3–0
World Team Championship final 1996: Australia beat England
2–1
European Team Championship final 1997: England beat
Germany 3–0
British Open Championship final 1997: Michelle Martin
(Australia) beat Sarah FitzGerald (Australia) 3–1
National Championship final 1997: Sue Wright (England)
beat Cassie Jackman (England) 3–1

SWIMMING

EUROPEAN CHAMPIONSHIPS 1997
Seville, August

MEN

50 metres freestyle: Alexander Popov (Russia)
100 metres freestyle: Alexander Popov (Russia)
200 metres freestyle: Paul Palmer (GB)
400 metres freestyle: Emiliano Brembilla (Italy)
1,500 metres freestyle: Emiliano Brembilla (Italy)
100 metres backstroke: Martin Lopez Zubero (Spain)
200 metres backstroke: Vladimir Selkov (Russia)
100 metres breaststroke: Alexander Goukov (Belarus)
200 metres breaststroke: Alexander Goukov (Belarus)
100 metres butterfly: Lars Frolander (Sweden)
200 metres butterfly: Franck Esposito (France)
200 metres medley: Marcel Wouda (Holland)
400 metres medley: Marcel Wouda (Holland)
4 × 100 metres freestyle relay: Russia
4 × 200 metres freestyle relay: Great Britain
4 × 100 metres medley relay: Russia

WOMEN

50 metres freestyle: Natalie Mescheriakova (Russia)
100 metres freestyle: Sandra Voelker (Germany)
200 metres freestyle: Michelle de Bruin (Ireland)
400 metres freestyle: Dagmar Hase (Germany)
800 metres freestyle: Kerstin Kielgass (Germany)
100 metres backstroke: Antje Buschschulte (Germany)
200 metres backstroke: Cathleen Rund (Germany)
100 metres breaststroke: Agnes Kovacs (Hungary)
200 metres breaststroke: Agnes Kovacs (Hungary)
100 metres butterfly: Mette Jacobsen (Denmark)
200 metres butterfly: Maria Pelaez (Spain)
200 metres medley: Oksana Verevka (Russia)
400 metres medley: Michelle de Bruin (Ireland)
4 × 100 metres freestyle relay: Germany
4 × 200 metres freestyle relay: Germany
4 × 100 metres medley relay: Germany

NATIONAL CHAMPIONSHIPS 1997
Crystal Palace, July

MEN

50 metres freestyle: Mark Foster (Bath University)
100 metres freestyle: Gavin Meadows (City of Leeds)
200 metres freestyle: James Salter (City of Edinburgh)
400 metres freestyle: Graeme Smith (Stockport Metro)
1,500 metres freestyle: Graeme Smith (Stockport Metro)

50 metres backstroke: Neil Willey (Barnet Copthall)
100 metres backstroke: Neil Willey (Barnet Copthall)
200 metres backstroke: Adam Ruckwood (City of
Birmingham)
50 metres breaststroke: Richard Maden (Rochdale
Aquabears)
100 metres breaststroke: Richard Maden (Rochdale
Aquabears)
200 metres breaststroke: Richard Maden (Rochdale
Aquabears)
50 metres butterfly: David Jones (Ealing)
100 metres butterfly: Stephen Parry (City of Liverpool)
200 metres butterfly: Stephen Parry (City of Liverpool)
200 metres medley: Tatsuya Kinugasa (City of Leeds)
400 metres medley: Tatsuya Kinugasa (City of Leeds)
4 × 100 metres freestyle relay: Portsmouth Northsea
4 × 200 metres freestyle relay: City of Leeds
4 × 100 metres medley relay: Loughborough Students

WOMEN

50 metres freestyle: Sue Rolph (City of Newcastle)
100 metres freestyle: Karen Pickering (Ipswich)
200 metres freestyle: Karen Pickering (Ipswich)
400 metres freestyle: Vicki Horner (Stockport Metro)
800 metres freestyle: Helen Billington (St Helens)
50 metres backstroke: Kathy Osher (Ealing)
100 metres backstroke: Sarah Price (Barnet Copthall)
200 metres backstroke: Helen Don-Duncan (Ashton Central)
50 metres breaststroke: Zoe Baker (City of Sheffield)
100 metres breaststroke: Linda Hindmarsh (City of Leeds)
200 metres breaststroke: Linda Hindmarsh (City of Leeds)
50 metres butterfly: Caroline Foot (York City Baths)
100 metres butterfly: Caroline Foot (York City Baths)
200 metres butterfly: Margaretha Pedder (Portsmouth
Northsea)
200 metres medley: Sue Rolph (City of Newcastle)
400 metres medley: Samantha Nesbit (Portsmouth
Northsea)
4 × 100 metres freestyle relay: City of Leeds
4 × 200 metres freestyle relay: City of Leeds
4 × 100 metres medley relay: Portsmouth Northsea

TABLE TENNIS

WORLD CHAMPIONSHIPS 1997
Manchester, April–May

Men's Singles: Jan-Ove Waldner (Sweden) beat Vladimir
Samsonov (Bulgaria) 3–0
Women's Singles: Deng Yaping (China) beat Wang Nan
(China) 3–1
Men's Doubles: Kong Linghui and Liu Guoliang (China)
beat Jan-Ove Waldner and Jorgen Persson (Sweden)
3–2
Women's Doubles: Deng Yaping and Yang Ying (China) beat
Li Ju and Wang Nan (China) 3–2
Mixed Doubles: Wu Na and Liu Guoliang (China) beat
Deng Yaping and Kong Linghui (China) 3–1
Men's Team Event: China beat France 3–1
Women's Team Event: China beat N. Korea 3–0

Men's World Cup final 1996: Liu Guo-liang (China) beat
Jan-Ove Waldner (Sweden) 3–1

ENGLISH NATIONAL CHAMPIONSHIPS 1997
Brighton, March

Men's Singles: Matthew Syed (Surrey) beat Alan Cooke
(Derbys) 3–0

Women's Singles: Nicola Deaton (Derbys) beat Helen
  Lower (Staffs) 3–0
Men's Doubles: Alan Cooke (Derbys) and Desmond
  Douglas (Warks) beat Chris Oldfield (Yorks) and Alex
  Perry (Devon) 2–0
Women's Doubles: Andrea Holt (Lancs) and Kubrat Owolabi
  (Middx) beat Helen Lower (Staffs) and Linda Radford
  (Essex) 2–1
Mixed Doubles: Andrea Holt (Lancs) and Alex Perry
  (Devon) beat Gemma Schwartz (Berks) and Terry
  Young (Berks) 2–0

VOLLEYBALL

MEN

World League final 1997: Italy beat Cuba 3–0
National League Championship 1997: Mizuno Malory
  Lewisham
National Cup final 1997: Tooting Aquila beat City of Stoke
  3–1

WOMEN

World Grand Prix 1997: Russia
National League Championship 1997: Britannia Music City
National Cup final 1997: London Malory beat Manchester
  United Salford 3–2

YACHTING

BT Global Challenge Round-the-World Race (set off from
  Southampton, 29 September 1996): Group 4 (Mike
  Golding) in 161 days, 5 hours and 25 minutes
Clipper Round-the-World Race (set off from Plymouth, 12
  October 1996): Ras Turner (GB) in Ariel, 31 points;
  arrived Plymouth 14 September 1997
Vendée Globe Single-Handed Non-Stop Round-the-World Race
  (set off from Les Sable d'Olonne, France, 3 November
  1996): Christophe Auguin (France) in Geodis, 105 days,
  20 hours, 31 minutes and 15 seconds
World Championships 1997 (Punta Ala, Italy): Gavin Brady
  (New Zealand) and Dee Smith (USA) in Thomas-I-
  Punkt
Admiral's Cup 1997: USA, 146.50 points
Fastnet Race 1997:
  Big boat class: Noon Madina (Italy)
  ILC 40 class: Pinta (Germany)
  Mumm 36 class: Bradamante (GB)

The Olympic Games

Venues of the modern Olympic Games

I	Athens, Greece	1896
II	Paris, France	1900
III	St Louis, USA	1904
*	Athens	1906
IV	London, Britain	1908
V	Stockholm, Sweden	1912
†VI	Berlin, Germany	1916
VII	Antwerp, Belgium	1920
VIII	Paris, France	1924
IX	Amsterdam, Netherlands	1928
X	Los Angeles, USA	1932
XI	Berlin, Germany	1936
†XII	Tokyo, Japan, then Helsinki, Finland	1940
†XIII	London, Britain	1944
XIV	London, Britain	1948
XV	Helsinki, Finland	1952
§XVI	Melbourne, Australia	1956
XVII	Rome, Italy	1960
XVIII	Tokyo, Japan	1964
XIX	Mexico City, Mexico	1968
XX	Munich, West Germany	1972
XXI	Montreal, Canada	1976
XXII	Moscow, USSR	1980
XXIII	Los Angeles, USA	1984
XXIV	Seoul, South Korea	1988
XXV	Barcelona, Spain	1992
XXVI	Atlanta, USA	1996
XXVII	Sydney, Australia	2000

WINTER OLYMPIC GAMES

I	Chamonix, France	1924
II	St Moritz, Switzerland	1928
III	Lake Placid, USA	1932
IV	Garmisch-Partenkirchen, Germany	1936
V	St Moritz, Switzerland	1948
VI	Oslo, Norway	1952
VII	Cortina d'Ampezzo, Italy	1956
VIII	Squaw Valley, USA	1960
IX	Innsbruck, Austria	1964
X	Grenoble, France	1968
XI	Sapporo, Japan	1972
XII	Innsbruck, Austria	1976
XIII	Lake Placid, USA	1980
XIV	Sarajevo, Yugoslavia	1984
XV	Calgary, Canada	1988
XVI	Albertville, France	1992
XVII	Lillehammer, Norway	1994
XVIII	Nagano, Japan	1998
XIX	Salt Lake City, USA	2002

* The 'Intercalated' Games
† These Games were scheduled but did not take place owing to
World Wars
§ Equestrian events were held in Stockholm, Sweden

Sports Records

All the world records given below have been accepted by the International Amateur Athletic Federation except those marked with an asterisk* which are awaiting homologation. Fully automatic timing to 1/100th second is mandatory up to and including 400 metres. For distances up to and including 10,000 metres, records will be accepted to 1/100th second if timed automatically, and to 1/10th if hand timing is used.

MEN'S EVENTS

TRACK EVENTS	hr.	min.	sec.
100 metres			9.84
Donovan Bailey, Canada, 1996			
200 metres			19.32
Michael Johnson, USA, 1996			
400 metres			43.29
Butch Reynolds, USA, 1988			
800 metres		1	41.11*
Wilson Kipketer, Denmark, 1997			
1,000 metres		2	12.18
Sebastian Coe, GB, 1981			
1,500 metres		3	27.37
Noureddine Morceli, Algeria, 1995			
1 mile		3	44.39
Noureddine Morceli, Algeria, 1993			
2,000 metres		4	47.88
Noureddine Morceli, Algeria, 1995			
3,000 metres		7	20.67
Daniel Komen, Kenya, 1996			
5,000 metres		12	39.74*
Daniel Komen, Kenya, 1997			
10,000 metres		26	27.85*
Paul Tergat, Kenya, 1997			
20,000 metres		56	55.6
Arturo Barrios, Mexico, 1991			
21,101 metres (13 miles 196 yards 1 foot)	1	00	00.0
Arturo Barrios, Mexico, 1991			
25,000 metres	1	13	55.8
Toshihiko Seko, Japan, 1981			
30,000 metres	1	29	18.8
Toshihiko Seko, Japan, 1981			
110 metres hurdles (3 ft 6 in)			12.91
Colin Jackson, GB, 1993			
400 metres hurdles (3 ft 0 in)			46.78
Kevin Young, USA, 1992			
3,000 metres steeplechase		7	55.72*
Bernard Barmasai, Kenya, 1997			

RELAYS	min.	sec.
4×100 metres		37.40
USA, 1992, 1993		
4×200 metres	1	19.11
Santa Monica TC, 1992		
4×400 metres	2	54.29
USA, 1993		
4×800 metres	7	03.89
GB, 1982		
4×1,500 metres	14	38.8
Federal Republic of Germany, 1977		

FIELD EVENTS	metres	ft	in
High jump	2.45	8	0½
Javier Sotomayor, Cuba, 1993			
Pole vault	6.14	20	1¾
Sergei Bubka, Ukraine, 1994			
Long jump	8.95	29	4½
Mike Powell, USA, 1991			
Triple jump	18.29	60	0¼
Jonathan Edwards, GB, 1995			
Shot	23.12	75	10¼
Randy Barnes, USA, 1990			
Discus	74.08	243	0
Jürgen Schult, GDR, 1986			
Hammer	86.74	284	7
Yuriy Sedykh, USSR, 1986			
Javelin	98.48	323	1
Jan Zelezny, Czech Rep., 1996			
Decathlon†	8,891 points		
Dan O'Brien, USA, 1992			

† Ten events comprising 100 m, long jump, shot, high jump, 400 m, 110 m hurdles, discus, pole vault, javelin, 1500 m

WALKING (TRACK)	hr.	min.	sec.
20,000 metres	1	17	25.6
Bernard Segura, Mexico, 1994			
29,572 metres (18 miles 660 yards)	2	00	00.0
Maurizio Damilano, Italy, 1992			
30,000 metres	2	01	44.1
Maurizio Damilano, Italy, 1992			
50,000 metres	3	40	57.9
Thierry Toutain, France, 1996			

WOMEN'S EVENTS

TRACK EVENTS	min.	sec.
100 metres		10.49
Florence Griffith-Joyner, USA, 1988		
200 metres		21.34
Florence Griffith-Joyner, USA, 1988		
400 metres		47.60
Marita Koch, GDR, 1985		
800 metres	1	53.28
Jarmila Kratochvilova, Czechoslovakia, 1983		
1,500 metres	3	50.46
Qu Yunxia, China, 1993		
1 mile	4	12.56
Svetlana Masterkova, Russia, 1996		
3,000 metres	8	06.11
Wang Junxia, China, 1993		
5,000 metres	14	36.45
Fernanda Ribeiro, Portugal, 1995		
10,000 metres	29	31.78
Wang Junxia, China, 1993		
100 metres hurdles (2 ft 9 in)		12.21
Yordanka Donkova, Bulgaria, 1988		
400 metres hurdles (2 ft 6 in)		52.61
Kim Batten, USA, 1995		

RELAYS	min.	sec.
4×100 metres		41.37
GDR, 1985		
4×200 metres	1	28.15
GDR, 1980		
4×400 metres	3	15.17
USSR, 1988		
4×800 metres	7	50.17
USSR, 1984		

FIELD EVENTS	metres	ft	in
High jump	2.09	6	10¼
Stefka Kostadinova, Bulgaria, 1987			
Pole vault	4.55	14	11
Emma George, Australia, 1997			
Long jump	7.52	24	8¼
Galina Chistiakova, USSR, 1988			
Triple jump	15.50	50	10¼
Inessa Kravets, Ukraine, 1995			
Shot	22.63	74	3
Natalya Lisovskaya, USSR, 1987			
Discus	76.80	252	0
Gabriele Reinsch, GDR, 1988			
Hammer	73.10	239	10
Olga Kuzenkova, Russia, 1997			
Javelin	80.00	262	5
Petra Felke, GDR, 1988			
Heptathlon†		7,291 points	
Jackie Joyner-Kersee, USA, 1988			

†Seven events comprising 100 m hurdles, shot, high jump, 200 m, long jump, javelin, 800 m

---

ATHLETICS NATIONAL (UK) RECORDS
AS AT 28 SEPTEMBER 1997

Records set anywhere by athletes eligible to represent Great Britain and Northern Ireland

MEN

TRACK EVENTS	hr.	min.	sec.
100 metres			9.87
Linford Christie, 1993			
200 metres			19.87
John Regis, 1994			
400 metres			44.36
Iwan Thomas, 1997			
800 metres		1	41.73
Sebastian Coe, 1981			
1,000 metres		2	12.18
Sebastian Coe, 1981			
1,500 metres		3	29.67
Sebastian Coe, 1985			
1 mile		3	46.32
Steve Cram, 1985			
2,000 metres		4	51.39
Steve Cram, 1985			
3,000 metres		7	32.79
David Moorcroft, 1982			
5,000 metres		13	00.41
David Moorcroft, 1982			
10,000 metres		27	23.06
Eamonn Martin, 1988			
20,000 metres		57	28.7
Carl Thackery, 1990			
20,855 metres	1	00	00.0
Carl Thackery, 1990			
25,000 metres	1	15	22.6
Ron Hill, 1965			
30,000 metres	1	31	30.4
Jim Alder, 1970			
3,000 metres steeplechase		8	07.96
Mark Rowland, 1988			
110 metres hurdles			12.91
Colin Jackson, 1993			
400 metres hurdles			47.82
Kriss Akabusi, 1992			

RELAYS	min.	sec.
4×100 metres		37.77
GB team, 1993		
4×200 metres	1	21.29
GB team, 1989		
4×400 metres	2	56.60
GB team, 1996		
4×800 metres	7	03.89
GB team, 1982		

FIELD EVENTS	metres	ft	in
High jump	2.37	7	9¼
Steve Smith, 1992, 1993			
Pole vault	5.75*	18	10¼
Nick Buckfield, 1997			
Long jump	8.23	27	0
Lynn Davies, 1968			
Triple jump	18.29	60	0¼
Jonathan Edwards, 1995			
Shot	21.68	71	1½
Geoff Capes, 1980			
Discus	65.22*	214	0
Perris Wilkins, 1997			
Hammer	77.54	254	5
Martin Girvan, 1984			
Javelin	91.46	300	1
Steve Backley, 1992			
Decathlon		8,847 points	
Daley Thompson, 1984			

WALKING (TRACK)	hr.	min.	sec.
20,000 metres	1	23	26.5
Ian McCombie, 1990			
30,000 metres	2	19	18
Christopher Maddocks, 1984			
50,000 metres	4	05	44.6
Paul Blagg, 1990			
26,037 metres (16 miles 315 yards)	2	00	00.0
Ron Wallwork, 1971			

WOMEN

TRACK EVENTS	min.	sec.
100 metres		11.10
Kathy Cook, 1981		
200 metres		22.10
Kathy Cook, 1984		
400 metres		49.43
Kathy Cook, 1984		
800 metres	1	56.21
Kelly Holmes, 1995		
1,500 metres	3	58.07
Kelly Holmes, 1997		
1 mile	4	17.57
Zola Budd, 1985		
3,000 metres	8	28.83
Zola Budd, 1985		
5,000 metres	14	45.51*
Paula Radcliffe, 1997		

		min.	sec.
10,000 metres		30	57.07
Liz McColgan, 1991			
100 metres hurdles			12.80
Angela Thorp, 1996			
400 metres hurdles			52.74
Sally Gunnell, 1993			

RELAYS	min.	sec.
4×100 metres		42.43
GB team, 1980		
4×200 metres	1	31.57
GB team, 1977		
4×400 metres	3	22.01
GB team, 1991		
4×800 metres	8	23.8
GB team, 1971		

FIELD EVENTS	metres	ft	in
High jump	1.95	6	4¾
Diana Elliott, 1982			
Pole vault	4.23	13	10½
Janine Whitlock, 1997			
Long jump	6.90	22	7¾
Beverley Kinch, 1983			
Triple jump	15.15*	49	8½
Ashia Hansen, 1997			
Shot	19.36	63	6¼
Judy Oakes, 1988			
Discus	67.48	221	5
Margaret Ritchie, 1981			
Hammer	64.90	212	11
Lorraine Shaw, 1995			
Javelin	77.44	254	1
Fatima Whitbread, 1986			
Heptathlon	6,736 points		
Denise Lewis, 1997			

*Awaiting ratification

SWIMMING WORLD RECORDS
AS AT 9 SEPTEMBER 1997

MEN	min.	sec.
50 metres freestyle		21.81
Tom Jager, USA		
100 metres freestyle		48.21
Alexander Popov, Russia		
200 metres freestyle	1	46.69
Giorgio Lamberti, Italy		
400 metres freestyle	3	43.80
Kieren Perkins, Australia		
800 metres freestyle	7	46.00
Kieren Perkins, Australia		
1,500 metres freestyle	14	41.66
Kieren Perkins, Australia		
100 metres breaststroke	1	00.60
Fred Deburghgraeve, Belgium		
200 metres breaststroke	2	10.16
Mike Barrowman, USA		
100 metres butterfly		52.27
Denis Pankratov, Russia		
200 metres butterfly	1	55.22
Denis Pankratov, Russia		
100 metres backstroke		53.86
Jeff Rouse, USA		
200 metres backstroke	1	56.57
Martin Lopez-Zubero, Spain		
200 metres medley	1	58.16
Jani Sievinen, Finland		

	min.	sec.
400 metres medley	4	12.30
Tom Dolan, USA		
4×100 metres freestyle relay	3	15.11
USA		
4×200 metres freestyle relay	7	11.95
CIS		
4×100 metres medley relay	3	34.84
USA		

WOMEN	min.	sec.
50 metres freestyle		24.51
Jingyi Le, China		
100 metres freestyle		54.01
Jingyi Le, China		
200 metres freestyle	1	56.78
Franziska van Almsick, Germany		
400 metres freestyle	4	03.85
Janet Evans, USA		
800 metres freestyle	8	16.22
Janet Evans, USA		
1,500 metres freestyle	15	52.10
Janet Evans, USA		
100 metres breaststroke	1	07.02
Penny Heyns, South Africa		
200 metres breaststroke	2	24.76
Rebecca Brown, Australia		
100 metres butterfly		57.93
Mary Meagher, USA		
200 metres butterfly	2	05.96
Mary Meagher, USA		
100 metres backstroke	1	00.16
Cihong He, China		
200 metres backstroke	2	06.62
Krisztina Egerszegi, Hungary		
200 metres medley	2	11.65
Lin Li, China		
400 metres medley	4	36.10
Petra Schneider, GDR		
4×100 metres freestyle relay	3	37.91
USA		
4×200 metres freestyle relay	7	55.47
GDR		
4×100 metres medley relay	4	01.67
China		

Travel Overseas

PASSPORT REGULATIONS

Applications for United Kingdom passports must be made on the forms obtainable from regional passport offices (addresses given below), main post offices, members of ARTAC WorldChoice Travel Agents and Lloyds Bank.

LONDON – Passport Office, Clive House, 70–78 Petty France, London SW1H 9HD

LIVERPOOL – Passport Office, 5th Floor, India Buildings, Water Street, Liverpool L2 0QZ

NEWPORT – Passport Office, Olympia House, Upper Dock Street, Newport, Gwent NP9 1XA

PETERBOROUGH – Passport Office, Aragon Court, Northminster Road, Peterborough PE1 1QG

GLASGOW – Passport Office, 3 Northgate, 96 Milton Street, Cowcaddens, Glasgow G4 0BT

BELFAST – Passport Office, Hampton House, 47–53 High Street, Belfast BT1 2QS

The above offices all use a single telephone number (0990-210410) to handle incoming calls, which are normally routed automatically to the nearest office unless all lines are busy, when the call will be rerouted to other offices. Recorded messages to deal with routine enquiries operate 24 hours a day.

The passport offices are open Monday–Friday 9 a.m. to 4.30 p.m. (8.15 a.m. to 4 p.m. in London). The Passport Office in London is also open for cases of emergency (e.g. death or serious illness) arising outside normal office hours between 4 p.m. and 6 p.m. Monday to Friday, between 10 a.m. and 7 p.m. on Saturdays, and between 9.30 a.m. and 2.30 p.m. on Sundays and Bank Holidays.

Straightforward, properly completed applications are processed within 15 working days from April to August, the busiest period, and within ten working days for the rest of the year. Applying in person does not guarantee that an application will be given priority.

Completed application forms should be posted, with the appropriate documents and fee, to the regional passport office indicated on the addressed envelope which is provided with each application form (an exception to this is the London office which is a calling-in office only). Accompanying cheques and postal orders should be crossed and made payable to 'The Passport Office'.

A passport cannot be issued or extended on behalf of a person already abroad; such persons should apply to the nearest British High Commission or Consulate.

UK passports are granted to:
(i)   British Citizens
(ii)   British Dependent Territories Citizens
(iii) British Nationals (Overseas)
(iv)   British Overseas Citizens
(v)   British subjects
(vi)   British Protected Persons

A passport granted to a child under 16 will normally be valid for an initial period of five years, after which it may be extended for a further five years with no extra charge. Children who have reached the age of 16 require a separate passport.

A passport granted to a person over 16 will normally be valid for ten years and will not be renewable. Thereafter, or if at any time the passport contains no further space for visas, a new passport must be obtained.

Completed application forms A and B should be countersigned by a Member of Parliament, justice of the peace, minister of religion, a professionally qualified person (e.g. doctor, engineer, lawyer, teacher), bank officer, established Civil Servant, police officer or a person of similar standing who has known the applicant for at least two years, and who is either a British Citizen, a British Dependent Territories Citizen, a British subject or a citizen of a Commonwealth country. A relative must not countersign the application. The applicant's birth certificate or previous British passport, and other documents in support of the statements made in the application must be produced at the time of applying.

If the applicant for a passport is a British national by naturalization or registration, the certificate proving this must be produced with the application, unless the applicant holds a previous UK passport issued after registration or naturalization.

The issue of passports including details of the holder's spouse has been discontinued, but existing family passports may be used until expiry. A spouse who is included in a family passport cannot travel on the passport without the holder.

In the case of children under the age of 16 requiring a separate passport, an application should be made by one of the parents on form B.

UK passports are generally available for travel to all countries. The possession of a passport does not, however, exempt the holder from compliance with any immigration regulations in force in British or foreign countries, or from the necessity of obtaining a visa where required.

WORKING ABROAD

A passport issued after 31 December 1982 showing the holder's national status as British Citizen will secure for the holder the right to take employment or to establish himself/herself in business or other self-employed activity in another member state of the European Union. A passport bearing the endorsement 'holder has the right of abode in the United Kingdom' where the holder so qualifies will also secure the same right. Employment permits are required in most other countries, even for casual labour. The nearest representative of the country concerned should be consulted. Local employment offices have a booklet entitled *Working Abroad*.

PHOTOGRAPHS

Duplicate unmounted photographs of the applicant must be sent. These photographs should be printed on normal thin photographic paper. They should measure 45 mm × 35 mm (1.77 in × 1.38 in) and should be taken full face without a hat. One photograph should be certified as a true likeness of the applicant by the person who countersigns the application form.

EXTENSION OF PASSPORTS

Applications for the extension of UK passports which have been valid for less than ten years must be made on form D.

AMENDMENTS AND ADDITIONS

Applications to make changes or add children to a UK passport must be made using form C.

48-PAGE PASSPORTS

The 48-page passport is intended to meet the needs of frequent travellers who fill standard passports well before the validity has expired. It is valid for ten years and costs £27.00.

VISAS

British nationals planning to travel overseas should enquire about visa requirements at the High Commission or consulate of their country of destination. (The address and telephone number of diplomatic representatives in the UK are given in the Countries of the World section of Whitaker.) Visa requirements may vary depending on the purpose or the length of the visit, and regulations are also liable to change, sometimes at short notice.

Overseas nationals who wish to enter the UK must satisfy the immigration officer at the port of arrival that they meet the requirements of the UK immigration rules. Separate rules apply to nationals of a member state of the European Economic Area (member states of the European Union and Iceland, Liechtenstein and Norway). Details are available from the nearest British mission (*see* the Countries of the World section of Whitaker).

Nationals from the following countries must have a valid visa issued prior to travel to the UK (before arrival), unless they are settled in the UK or are in the UK for some long-term purpose (more than six months) and returning within the period of a permission to stay granted previously:

Afghanistan; Albania; Algeria; Angola; Armenia; Azerbaijan; Bahrain; Bangladesh; Belarus; Benin; Bhutan; Bosnia-Hercegovina; Bulgaria; Burkina; Burundi; Cambodia; Cameroon; Cape Verde; Central African Republic; Chad; China; Colombia; Comoros; Democratic Republic of Congo; Republic of Congo; Côte d'Ivoire; Cuba; Djibouti; Dominican Republic; Ecuador; Egypt; Equatorial Guinea; Eritrea; Ethiopia; Fiji; Gabon; Gambia; Georgia; Ghana; Guinea; Guinea-Bissau; Guyana; Haiti; India; Indonesia; Iran; Iraq; Jordan; Kazakhstan; Kenya; Korea (North); Kuwait; Kyrgyzstan; Laos; Lebanon; Liberia; Libya; Macedonia (Former Yugoslav Republic of); Madagascar; Maldives; Mali; Mauritania; Mauritius; Moldova; Mongolia; Morocco; Mozambique; Myanmar (Burma); Nepal; Niger; Nigeria; Oman; Pakistan; Papua New Guinea; Peru; Philippines; Qatar; Romania; Russia; Rwanda; São Tomé and Príncipe; Saudi Arabia; Senegal; Sierra Leone; Somalia; Sri Lanka; Sudan; Suriname; Syria; Taiwan; Tajikistan; Tanzania; Thailand; Togo; Tunisia; Turkey; Turkmenistan; Uganda; Ukraine; United Arab Emirates; Uzbekistan; Vietnam; Yemen; Yugoslavia (Federal Republic of); Zambia.

A valid entry clearance is also required by people who are stateless or who hold a non-national travel document or passport issued by an authority not recognized by the UK.

Nationals of any country not listed above do not need an entry clearance to visit or study in the UK but must obtain entry clearance to settle, work or set up business. Entry clearances take the form of an entry certificate for non-visa Commonwealth nationals and non-visa foreign nationals.

UK entry clearances can be obtained from British Embassies, Consulates and High Commissions overseas. (The address and telephone number of British missions overseas are given in the Countries of the World section of Whitaker.)

IMMUNIZATION

In very general terms immunization against typhoid and polio, and protection against hepatitis A by immunoglobulin or vaccine should be considered for all countries where standards of hygiene and sanitation may be less than ideal. Protection against malaria, in the form of tablets, as well as measures to avoid mosquito bites, is advised for visits to malarious areas.

Immunization against yellow fever is compulsory for entry into some countries, either for all travellers or for those arriving from a yellow fever infected area, and is recommended for all travellers to infected areas.

Fuller details are set out in Department of Health leaflet *Health Advice for Travellers* (T5). Health care professionals can obtain up-to-date information about immunization recommendations from the Department of Health publication *Health Information for Overseas Travel* or from:

ENGLAND – Communicable Disease Surveillance Centre, 61 Colindale Avenue, London NW9 5EQ. Tel: 0181-200 6868

WALES – Welsh Office, Cathays Park, Cardiff CF1 3NQ. Tel: 01222-825111

SCOTLAND – Scottish Office Department of Health, St Andrew's House, Edinburgh EH1 3DG. Tel: 0131-556 8400; or The Communicable Diseases (Scotland) Unit, Ruchill Hospital, Bilsland Drive, Glasgow G20 9NB. Tel: 0141-946 7120

NORTHERN IRELAND – DHSS, Dundonald House, Upper Newtownards Road, Belfast BT4 3SF. Tel: 01232-520000

A doctor should be consulted at least eight weeks before departure, and will advise travellers and arrange vaccinations. If children will be travelling outside Europe, North America, Australia and New Zealand, the doctor should be informed, especially if they have not completed their full course of childhood immunization.

Details of free or reduced cost emergency medical treatment when visiting European countries, and countries with which the UK has reciprocal health arrangements, are set out in leaflet T5, available from some travel agents, local post offices or the Department of Health, PO Box 410, Wetherby, W. Yorks LS23 7LN. Tel: 0800-555777 (single copy orders).

Weights and Measures

SI UNITS

The Système International d'Unités (SI) is an international and coherent system of units devised to meet all known needs for measurement in science and technology. The system was adopted by the eleventh Conférence Générale des Poids et Mesures (CGPM) in 1960. A comprehensive description of the system is given in *SI The International System of Units*, HMSO. The British Standards describing the essential features of the International System of Units are *Specifications for SI units and recommendations for the use of their multiples and certain other units* (BS 5555:1993) and *Conversion Factors and Tables* (BS 350, Part 1:1974).

The system consists of seven base units and the derived units formed as products or quotients of various powers of the base units. Together the base units and the derived units make up the coherent system of units. In the UK the SI base units, and almost all important derived units, are realized at the National Physical Laboratory and disseminated through the National Measurement System.

BASE UNITS

metre (m) = unit of length
kilogram (kg) = unit of mass
second (s) = unit of time
ampere (A) = unit of electric current
kelvin (K) = unit of thermodynamic temperature
mole (mol) = unit of amount of substance
candela (cd) = unit of luminous intensity

DERIVED UNITS

For some of the derived SI units, special names and symbols exist; those approved by the CGPM are as follows:

hertz (Hz) = unit of frequency
newton (N) = unit of force
pascal (Pa) = unit of pressure, stress
joule (J) = unit of energy, work, quantity of heat
watt (W) = unit of power, radiant flux
coulomb (C) = unit of electric charge, quantity of electricity
volt (V) = unit of electric potential, potential difference, electromotive force
farad (F) = unit of electric capacitance
ohm (Ω) = unit of electric resistance
siemens (S) = unit of electric conductance
weber (Wb) = unit of magnetic flux
tesla (T) = unit of magnetic flux density
henry (H) = unit of inductance
degree Celsius (°C) = unit of Celsius temperature
lumen (lm) = unit of luminous flux
lux (lx) = unit of illuminance
becquerel (Bq) = unit of activity (of a radionuclide)
gray (Gy) = unit of absorbed dose, specific energy imparted, kerma, absorbed dose index
sievert (Sv) = unit of dose equivalent, dose equivalent index

The derived units include, as a special case (CIPM 1995), the supplementary units which may be treated as dimensionless within the SI.

radian (rad) = unit of plane angle
steradian (sr) = unit of solid angle

Other derived units are expressed in terms of base units and/or supplementary units. Some of the more commonly-used derived units are the following:

Unit of area = square metre (m^2)
Unit of volume = cubic metre (m^3)
Unit of velocity = metre per second ($m\,s^{-1}$)
Unit of acceleration = metre per second squared ($m\,s^{-2}$)
Unit of density = kilogram per cubic metre ($kg\,m^{-3}$)
Unit of momentum = kilogram metre per second ($kg\,m\,s^{-1}$)
Unit of magnetic field strength = ampere per metre ($A\,m^{-1}$)
Unit of surface tension = newton per metre ($N\,m^{-1}$)
Unit of dynamic viscosity = pascal second (Pa s)
Unit of heat capacity = joule per kelvin ($J\,K^{-1}$)
Unit of specific heat capacity = joule per kilogram kelvin ($J\,kg^{-1}\,K^{-1}$)
Unit of heat flux density, irradiance = watt per square metre ($W\,m^{-2}$)
Unit of thermal conductivity = watt per metre kelvin ($W\,m^{-1}\,K^{-1}$)
Unit of electric field strength = volt per metre ($V\,m^{-1}$)
Unit of luminance = candela per square metre ($cd\,m^{-2}$)

SI PREFIXES

Decimal multiples and submultiples of the SI units are indicated by SI prefixes. These are as follows:

multiples	*submultiples*
yotta (Y) $\times 10^{24}$	deci (d) $\times 10^{-1}$
zetta (Z) $\times 10^{21}$	centi (c) $\times 10^{-2}$
exa (E) $\times 10^{18}$	milli (m) $\times 10^{-3}$
peta (P) $\times 10^{15}$	micro (μ) $\times 10^{-6}$
tera (T) $\times 10^{12}$	nano (n) $\times 10^{-9}$
giga (G) $\times 10^{9}$	pico (p) $\times 10^{-12}$
mega (M) $\times 10^{6}$	femto (f) $\times 10^{-15}$
kilo (k) $\times 10^{3}$	atto (a) $\times 10^{-18}$
hecto (h) $\times 10^{2}$	zepto (z) $\times 10^{-21}$
deca (da) $\times 10$	yocto (y) $\times 10^{-24}$

METRIC UNITS

The metric primary standards are the metre as the unit of measurement of length, and the kilogram as the unit of measurement of mass. Other units of measurement are defined by reference to the primary standards.

MEASUREMENT OF LENGTH

Kilometre (km) = 1000 metres
Metre (m) is the length of the path travelled by light in vacuum during a time interval of 1/299 792 458 of a second
Decimetre (dm) = 1/10 metre
Centimetre (cm) = 1/100 metre
Millimetre (mm) = 1/1000 metre

MEASUREMENT OF AREA

Hectare (ha) = 100 ares
Decare = 10 ares

Are (a) = 100 square metres
Square metre = a superficial area equal to that of a square
  each side of which measures one metre
Square decimetre = 1/100 square metre
Square centimetre = 1/100 square decimetre
Square millimetre = 1/100 square centimetre

MEASUREMENT OF VOLUME

Cubic metre (m^3) = a volume equal to that of a cube each
  edge of which measures one metre
Cubic decimetre = 1/1000 cubic metre
Cubic centimetre (cc) = 1/1000 cubic decimetre
Hectolitre = 100 litres
Litre = a cubic decimetre
Decilitre = 1/10 litre
Centilitre = 1/100 litre
Millilitre = 1/1000 litre

MEASUREMENT OF CAPACITY

Hectolitre (hl) = 100 litres
Litre (l or L) = a cubic decimetre
Decilitre (dl) = 1/10 litre
Centilitre (cl) = 1/100 litre
Millilitre (ml) = 1/1000 litre

MEASUREMENT OF MASS OR WEIGHT

Tonne (t) = 1000 kilograms
Kilogram (kg) is equal to the mass of the international
  prototype of the kilogram
Hectogram (hg) = 1/10 kilogram
Gram (g) = 1/1000 kilogram
*Carat (metric) = 1/5 gram
Milligram (mg) = 1/1000 gram

*Used only for transactions in precious stones or pearls

METRICATION IN THE UK

The European Council Directive 80/181/EEC, as
amended by Council Directive 89/617/EEC, relates to
the use of units of measurement for economic, public
health, public safety or administrative purposes in the
member states of the European Union. The provisions of
the directives were incorporated into British law by the
Weights and Measures Act 1985 (Metrication) (Amendment) Order 1994 and the Units of Measurement Regulations 1994; these instruments amended the Weights and
Measures Act 1985. Parallel statutory rules amending
Northern Ireland weights and measures legislation were
made in May 1995.

The general effect of the 1994 and 1995 legislation is to
end the use of imperial units of measurement for trade,
replacing them with metric units – see below for timetable
for UK metrication. Imperial units can, however, be used in
addition to metric units, as supplementary indications.

IMPERIAL UNITS

The imperial primary standards are the yard as the unit of
measurement of length and the pound as the unit of
measurement of mass. Other units of measurement are
defined by reference to the primary standards. Most of
these units are no longer authorized for use in trade in the
UK – see below.

MEASUREMENT OF LENGTH

Mile = 1760 yards
Furlong = 220 yards
Chain = 22 yards

Yard (yd) = 0.9144 metre
Foot (ft) = 1/3 yard
Inch (in) = 1/36 yard

MEASUREMENT OF AREA

Square mile = 640 acres
Acre = 4840 square yards
Rood = 1210 square yards
Square yard (sq. yd) = a superficial area equal to that of a
  square each side of which measures one yard
Square foot (sq. ft) = 1/9 square yard
Square inch (sq. in) = 1/144 square foot

MEASUREMENT OF VOLUME

Cubic yard = a volume equal to that of a cube each edge of
  which measures one yard
Cubic foot = 1/27 cubic yard
Cubic inch = 1/1728 cubic foot

MEASUREMENT OF CAPACITY

Bushel = 8 gallons
Peck = 2 gallons
Gallon (gal) = 4.546 09 cubic decimetres
Quart (qt) = 1/4 gallon
*Pint (pt) = 1/2 quart
Gill = 1/4 pint
*Fluid ounce (fl oz) = 1/20 pint
Fluid drachm = 1/8 fluid ounce
Minim (min) = 1/60 fluid drachm

MEASUREMENT OF MASS OR WEIGHT

Ton = 2240 pounds
Hundredweight (cwt) = 112 pounds
Cental = 100 pounds
Quarter = 28 pounds
Stone = 14 pounds
*Pound (lb) = 0.453 592 37 kilogram
*Ounce (oz) = 1/16 pound
*†Ounce troy (oz tr) = 12/175 pound
Dram (dr) = 1/16 ounce
Grain (gr) = 1/7000 pound
Pennyweight (dwt) = 24 grains
Ounce apothecaries = 480 grains
Drachm (ʒ) = 1/8 ounce apothecaries
Scruple (℈) = 1/3 drachm

*Units of measurement still authorized for use for trade in the UK
†Used only for transactions in gold, silver or other precious metals, and
articles made therefrom

PHASING-OUT OF IMPERIAL UNITS IN THE UK

The Weights and Measures Act 1985 enacted the legal
units for the United Kingdom. It was amended to
implement the provisions of European Council Directive
80/181/EEC, as amended by Directive 89/617/EEC, by
the Weights and Measures Act 1985 (Metrication)
(Amendment) Order 1994 and the Units of Measurement
Regulations 1994, and by parallel statutory rules in
Northern Ireland in May 1995.

The effect of the amended legislation is to phase out the
use of imperial units for trade, replacing them with metric
units. With effect from 30 September 1995 imperial units
ceased to be authorized for use in the UK for economic,
public health, public safety and administrative purposes,
with the following exceptions:

Units of measurement authorized for use in specialized fields between 1 October 1995 and 31 December 1999

Unit	Field of application
fathom	Marine navigation
fluid ounce ⎫ pint ⎭	Beer, cider, water, lemonade, fruit juice in returnable containers
ounce ⎫ pound ⎭	Goods for sale loose from bulk
therm	Gas supply

Units of measurement authorized for use in specialized fields from 1 October 1995, without time limit

Unit	Field of application
inch ⎫ foot ⎪ yard ⎬ mile ⎭	Road traffic signs, distance and speed measurement
pint ⎰ ⎱	Dispense of draught beer or cider Milk in returnable containers
acre	Land registration
troy ounce	Transactions in precious metals

MEASUREMENT OF ELECTRICITY

Units of measurement of electricity are defined by the Weights and Measures Act 1985 as follows:

ampere (A) = that constant current which, if maintained in two straight parallel conductors of infinite length, of negligible circular cross-section and placed 1 metre apart in vacuum, would produce between these conductors a force equal to 2×10^{-7} newton per metre of length

ohm (Ω) = the electric resistance between two points of a conductor when a constant potential difference of 1 volt, applied between the two points, produces in the conductor a current of 1 ampere, the conductor not being the seat of any electromotive force

volt (V) = the difference of electric potential between two points of a conducting wire carrying a constant current of 1 ampere when the power dissipated between these points is equal to 1 watt

watt (W) = the power which in one second gives rise to energy of 1 joule

kilowatt (kW) = 1000 watts

megawatt (MW) = one million watts

WATER AND LIQUOR MEASURES

1 cubic foot = 62.32 lb
1 gallon = 10 lb
1 cubic cm = 1 gram
1000 cubic cm = 1 litre; 1 kilogram
1 cubic metre = 1000 litres; 1000 kg; 1 tonne
An inch of rain on the surface of an acre (43560 sq. ft) = 3630 cubic ft = 100.992 tons
Cisterns: A cistern $4 \times 2\frac{1}{2}$ feet and 3 feet deep will hold brimful 186.963 gallons, weighing 1869.63 lb in addition to its own weight

WATER FOR SHIPS
Kilderkin = 18 gallons
Barrel = 36 gallons
Puncheon = 72 gallons
Butt = 110 gallons
Tun = 210 gallons

BOTTLES OF WINE
Traditional equivalents in standard champagne bottles:
Magnum = 2 bottles
Jeroboam = 4 bottles
Rehoboam = 6 bottles
Methuselah = 8 bottles
Salmanazar = 12 bottles
Balthazar = 16 bottles
Nebuchadnezzar = 20 bottles

A quarter of a bottle is known as a *nip*
An eighth of a bottle is known as a *baby*

ANGULAR AND CIRCULAR MEASURES

60 seconds (″) = 1 minute (′)
60 minutes = 1 degree (°)
90 degrees = 1 right angle or quadrant
Diameter of circle × 3.141 6 = circumference
Diameter squared × 0.7854 = area of circle
Diameter squared × 3.141 6 = surface of sphere
Diameter cubed × 0.523 = solidity of sphere
One degree of circumference × 57.3 = radius*
Diameter of cylinder × 3.141 6; product by length or height, gives the surface
Diameter squared × 0.7854; product by length or height, gives solid content

*Or, one radian (the angle subtended at the centre of a circle by an arc of the circumference equal in length to the radius) = 57.3 degrees

MILLION, BILLION, ETC.

Value in the UK
Million	thousand × thousand	10^6
*Billion	million × million	10^{12}
Trillion	million × billion	10^{18}
Quadrillion	million × trillion	10^{24}

Value in USA
Million	thousand × thousand	10^6
*Billion	thousand × million	10^9
Trillion	million × million	10^{12}
Quadrillion	million × billion US	10^{15}

*The American usage of billion (i.e. 10^9) is increasingly common, and is now universally used by statisticians

NAUTICAL MEASURES

DISTANCE

Distance at sea is measured in nautical miles. The British standard nautical mile was 6080 feet but this measure has been obsolete since 1970 when the international nautical mile of 1852 metres was adopted by the Hydrographic Department of the Ministry of Defence. The cable (600 feet or 100 fathoms) was a measure approximately one-tenth of a nautical mile. Such distances are now expressed in decimal parts of a sea mile or in metres.

Soundings at sea were recorded in fathoms (6 feet). Depths are now expressed in metres on Admiralty charts.

SPEED

Speed is measured in nautical miles per hour, called knots. A ship moving at the rate of 30 nautical miles per hour is said to be doing 30 knots.

knots	m.p.h.	knots	m.p.h.
1	1.1515	9	10.3636
2	2.3030	10	11.5151
3	3.4545	15	17.2727
4	4.6060	20	23.0303
5	5.7575	25	28.7878
6	6.9090	30	34.5454
7	8.0606	35	40.3030
8	9.2121	40	46.0606

TONNAGE

Under the Merchant Shipping Act 1854, the tonnage of UK-registered vessels was measured in tons of 100 cubic feet. The need for a universal method of measurement led to the adoption of the International Convention on Tonnage Measurements of Ships 1969, which measures, in cubic metres, all the internal spaces of a vessel for the gross tonnage and those of the cargo compartments for the net tonnage. The convention has applied since July 1982 to new ships, ships which needed to be remeasured because of substantial alterations, and ships whose owners requested remeasurement. On 18 July 1994 the convention became mandatory and all vessels should have been remeasured by that date; however, there is a backlog and some vessels have not yet been remeasured.

DISTANCE OF THE HORIZON

The limit of distance to which one can see varies with the height of the spectator. The greatest distance at which an object on the surface of the sea, or of a level plain, can be seen by a person whose eyes are at a height of five feet from the same level is nearly three miles. At a height of 20 feet the range is increased to nearly six miles, and an approximate rule for finding the range of vision for small heights is to increase the square root of the number of feet that the eye is above the level surface by a third of itself. The result is the distance of the horizon in miles, but is slightly in excess of that in the table below, which is computed by a more precise formula. The table may be used conversely to show the distance of an object of given height that is just visible from a point on the surface of the earth or sea. Refraction is taken into account both in the approximate rule and in the table.

Height in feet	range in miles
5	2.9
20	5.9
50	9.3
100	13.2
500	29.5
1,000	41.6
2,000	58.9
3,000	72.1
4,000	83.3
5,000	93.1
20,000	186.2

TEMPERATURE SCALES

The SI (International System) unit of temperature is the kelvin, which is defined as the fraction $1/273.16$ of the temperature of the triple point of water (i.e. where ice, water and water vapour are in equilibrium). The zero of the Kelvin scale is the absolute zero of temperature. The freezing point of water is 273.15 K and the boiling point (as adopted in the International Temperature Scale of 1990) is 373.124 K.

The Celsius scale (formerly centigrade) is defined by subtracting 273.15 from the Kelvin temperature. The Fahrenheit scale is related to the Celsius scale by the relationships:

temperature $°F = (\text{temperature } °C \times 1.8) + 32$
temperature $°C = (\text{temperature } °F - 32) \div 1.8$

It follows from these definitions that the freezing point of water is 0°C and 32°F. The boiling point is 99.974°C and 211.953°F.

The temperature of the human body varies from person to person and in the same person can be affected by a variety of factors. In most people body temperature varies between 36.5°C and 37.2°C (97.7−98.9°F).

Conversion between scales

°C	°F	°C	°F	°C	°F
100	212	60	140	20	68
99	210.2	59	138.2	19	66.2
98	208.4	58	136.4	18	64.4
97	206.6	57	134.6	17	62.6
96	204.8	56	132.8	16	60.8
95	203	55	131	15	59
94	201.2	54	129.2	14	57.2
93	199.4	53	127.4	13	55.4
92	197.6	52	125.6	12	53.6
91	195.8	51	123.8	11	51.8
90	194	50	122	10	50
89	192.2	49	120.2	9	48.2
88	190.4	48	118.4	8	46.4
87	188.6	47	116.6	7	44.6
86	186.8	46	114.8	6	42.8
85	185	45	113	5	41
84	183.2	44	111.2	4	39.2
83	181.4	43	109.4	3	37.4
82	179.6	42	107.6	2	35.6
81	177.8	41	105.8	1	33.8
80	176	40	104	zero	32
79	174.2	39	102.2	− 1	30.2
78	172.4	38	100.4	− 2	28.4
77	170.6	37	98.6	− 3	26.6
76	168.8	36	96.8	− 4	24.8
75	167	35	95	− 5	23
74	165.2	34	93.2	− 6	21.2
73	163.4	33	91.4	− 7	19.4
72	161.6	32	89.6	− 8	17.6
71	159.8	31	87.8	− 9	15.8
70	158	30	86	−10	14
69	156.2	29	84.2	−11	12.2
68	154.4	28	82.4	−12	10.4
67	152.6	27	80.6	−13	8.6
66	150.8	26	78.8	−14	6.8
65	149	25	77	−15	5
64	147.2	24	75.2	−16	3.2
63	145.4	23	73.4	−17	1.4
62	143.6	22	71.6	−18	0.4
61	141.8	21	69.8	−19	− 2.2

PAPER MEASURES

Printing Paper	*Writing Paper*
516 sheets = 1 ream	480 sheets = 1 ream
2 reams = 1 bundle	20 quires = 1 ream
5 bundles = 1 bale	24 sheets = 1 quire

Brown Papers

	inches		*inches*
Casing	46 × 36	Imperial Cap	29 × 22
Double Imperial	45 × 29	Haven Cap	26 × 21
Elephant	34 × 24	Bag Cap	24 × 19½
Double Four Pound	31 × 21	Kent Cap	21 × 18

Printing Papers

	inches		*inches*
Foolscap	17 × 13½	Double Large Post	33 × 21
Double Foolscap	27 × 17	Demy	22½ × 17½
Quad Foolscap	34 × 27	Double Demy	35 × 22½
Crown	20 × 15	Quad Demy	45 × 35
Double Crown	30 × 20	Music Demy	20 × 15½
Quad Crown	40 × 30	Medium	23 × 18
Double Quad Crown	60 × 40	Royal	25 × 20
Post	19¼ × 15½	Super Royal	27½ × 20½
Double Post	31½ × 19½	Elephant	28 × 23
		Imperial	30 × 22

Writing and Drawing Papers

	inches		*inches*
Emperor	72 × 48	Copy or Draft	20 × 16
Antiquarian	53 × 31	Demy	20 × 15½
Double Elephant	40 × 27	Post	19 × 15¼
Grand Eagle	42 × 28¾	Pinched Post	18½ × 14¾
Atlas	34 × 26	Foolscap	17 × 13½
Colombier	34½ × 23½	Double Foolscap	26½ × 16½
Imperial	30 × 22	Double Post	30½ × 19
Elephant	28 × 23	Double Large Post	33 × 21
Cartridge	26 × 21	Double Demy	31 × 20
Super Royal	27 × 19	Brief	16½ × 13¼
Royal	24 × 19	Pott	15 × 12½
Medium	22 × 17½		
Large Post	21 × 16½		

INTERNATIONAL PAPER SIZES

The basis of the international series of paper sizes is a rectangle having an area of one square metre, the sides of which are in the proportion of $1:\sqrt{2}$. The proportions $1:\sqrt{2}$ have a geometrical relationship, the side and diagonal of any square being in this proportion. The effect of this arrangement is that if the area of the sheet of paper is doubled or halved, the shorter side and the longer side of the new sheet are still in the same proportion $1:\sqrt{2}$. This feature is useful where photographic enlargement or reduction is used, as the proportions remain the same.

Description of the A series is by capital A followed by a figure. The basic size has the description A0 and the higher the figure following the letter, the greater is the number of sub-divisions and therefore the smaller the sheet. Half A0 is A1 and half A1 is A2. Where larger dimensions are required the A is preceded by a figure. Thus 2A means twice the size A0; 4A is four times the size of A0.

Subsidiary Series

B sizes are sizes intermediate between any two adjacent sizes of the A series. There is a series of C sizes which is used much less. A is for magazines and books, B for posters, wall charts and other large items, C for envelopes particularly where it is necessary for an envelope (in C series) to fit into another envelope. The size recommended for business correspondence is A4.

Long sizes (DL) are obtainable by dividing any appropriate sizes from the two series above into three, four or eight equal parts parallel with the shorter side in such a manner that the proportion of $1:\sqrt{2}$ is not maintained, the ratio between the longer and the shorter sides being greater than $\sqrt{2}:1$. In practice long sizes should be produced from the A series only.

It is an essential feature of these series that the dimensions are of the trimmed or finished size.

A Series

	mm		*mm*
A0	841 × 1189	A6	105 × 148
A1	594 × 841	A7	74 × 105
A2	420 × 594	A8	52 × 74
A3	297 × 420	A9	37 × 52
A4	210 × 297	A10	26 × 37
A5	148 × 210		

B Series

	mm		*mm*
B0	1000 × 1414	B6	125 × 176
B1	707 × 1000	B7	88 × 125
B2	500 × 707	B8	62 × 88
B3	353 × 500	B9	44 × 62
B4	250 × 353	B10	31 × 44
B5	176 × 250		

C Series		DL	
	mm		*mm*
C4	324 × 229	DL	110 × 220
C5	229 × 162		
C6	114 × 162		

BOUND BOOKS

The book sizes most commonly used are listed below. Approximate centimetre equivalents are also shown. International sizes are converted to their nearest imperial size, e.g. A4 = D4; A5 = D8.

		inches	*cm*
Crown 32mo	C32	2½ × 3¾	6 × 9
Crown 16mo	C16	3¾ × 5	9 × 13
Foolscap 8vo	F8	4¼ × 6¾	11 × 17
Demy 16mo	D16	4⅜ × 5⅝	11 × 14
Crown 8vo	C8	5 × 7½	13 × 19
Demy 8vo	D8	5⅝ × 8¾	14 × 22
Medium 8vo	M8	5¾ × 9	15 × 23
Royal 8vo	R8	6¼ × 10	16 × 25
Super Royal 8vo	suR8	6¾ × 10	17 × 25
Foolscap 4to	F4	6¾ × 8½	17 × 22
Crown 4to	C4	7½ × 10	19 × 25
Imperial 8vo	Imp8	7½ × 11	19 × 28
Demy 4to	D4	8¾ × 11¼	22 × 29
Royal 4to	R4	10 × 12½	25 × 31
Super Royal 4to	suR4	10 × 13½	25 × 34
Crown Folio	Cfol	10 × 15	25 × 38
Imperial Folio	Impfol	11 × 15	28 × 38

Folio = a sheet folded in half
Quarto (4to) = a sheet folded into four
Octavo (8vo) = a sheet folded into eight
Books are usually bound up in sheets of 16, 32 or 64 pages. Octavo books are generally printed 64 pages at a time, 32 pages on each side of a sheet of quad.

CONVERSION TABLES FOR WEIGHTS AND MEASURES

Bold figures equal units of either of the columns beside them; thus: 1 cm = 0.394 inches and 1 inch = 2.540 cm

LENGTH			AREA			VOLUME			WEIGHT (MASS)		
Centimetres		Inches	Square cm		Square in	Cubic cm		Cubic in	Kilograms		Pounds
2.540	1	0.394	6.452	1	0.155	16.387	1	0.061	0.454	1	2.205
5.080	2	0.787	12.903	2	0.310	32.774	2	0.122	0.907	2	4.409
7.620	3	1.181	19.355	3	0.465	49.161	3	0.183	1.361	3	6.614
10.160	4	1.575	25.806	4	0.620	65.548	4	0.244	1.814	4	8.819
12.700	5	1.969	32.258	5	0.775	81.936	5	0.305	2.268	5	11.023
15.240	6	2.362	38.710	6	0.930	98.323	6	0.366	2.722	6	13.228
17.780	7	2.756	45.161	7	1.085	114.710	7	0.427	3.175	7	15.432
20.320	8	3.150	51.613	8	1.240	131.097	8	0.488	3.629	8	17.637
22.860	9	3.543	58.064	9	1.395	147.484	9	0.549	4.082	9	19.842
25.400	10	3.937	64.516	10	1.550	163.871	10	0.610	4.536	10	22.046
50.800	20	7.874	129.032	20	3.100	327.742	20	1.220	9.072	20	44.092
76.200	30	11.811	193.548	30	4.650	491.613	30	1.831	13.608	30	66.139
101.600	40	15.748	258.064	40	6.200	655.484	40	2.441	18.144	40	88.185
127.000	50	19.685	322.580	50	7.750	819.355	50	3.051	22.680	50	110.231
152.400	60	23.622	387.096	60	9.300	983.226	60	3.661	27.216	60	132.277
177.800	70	27.559	451.612	70	10.850	1147.097	70	4.272	31.752	70	154.324
203.200	80	31.496	516.128	80	12.400	1310.968	80	4.882	36.287	80	176.370
228.600	90	35.433	580.644	90	13.950	1474.839	90	5.492	40.823	90	198.416
254.000	100	39.370	645.160	100	15.500	1638.710	100	6.102	45.359	100	220.464

Metres		Yards	Square m		Square yd	Cubic m		Cubic yd	Metric tonnes		Tons (UK)
0.914	1	1.094	0.836	1	1.196	0.765	1	1.308	1.016	1	0.984
1.829	2	2.187	1.672	2	2.392	1.529	2	2.616	2.032	2	1.968
2.743	3	3.281	2.508	3	3.588	2.294	3	3.924	3.048	3	2.953
3.658	4	4.374	3.345	4	4.784	3.058	4	5.232	4.064	4	3.937
4.572	5	5.468	4.181	5	5.980	3.823	5	6.540	5.080	5	4.921
5.486	6	6.562	5.017	6	7.176	4.587	6	7.848	6.096	6	5.905
6.401	7	7.655	5.853	7	8.372	5.352	7	9.156	7.112	7	6.889
7.315	8	8.749	6.689	8	9.568	6.116	8	10.464	8.128	8	7.874
8.230	9	9.843	7.525	9	10.764	6.881	9	11.772	9.144	9	8.858
9.144	10	10.936	8.361	10	11.960	7.646	10	13.080	10.161	10	9.842
18.288	20	21.872	16.723	20	23.920	15.291	20	26.159	20.321	20	19.684
27.432	30	32.808	25.084	30	35.880	22.937	30	39.239	30.481	30	29.526
36.576	40	43.745	33.445	40	47.840	30.582	40	52.318	40.642	40	39.368
45.720	50	54.681	41.806	50	59.799	38.228	50	65.398	50.802	50	49.210
54.864	60	65.617	50.168	60	71.759	45.873	60	78.477	60.963	60	59.052
64.008	70	76.553	58.529	70	83.719	53.519	70	91.557	71.123	70	68.894
73.152	80	87.489	66.890	80	95.679	61.164	80	104.636	81.284	80	78.737
82.296	90	98.425	75.251	90	107.639	68.810	90	117.716	91.444	90	88.579
91.440	100	109.361	83.613	100	119.599	76.455	100	130.795	101.605	100	98.421

Kilometres		Miles	Hectares		Acres	Litres		Gallons	Metric tonnes		Tons (US)
1.609	1	0.621	0.405	1	2.471	4.546	1	0.220	0.907	1	1.102
3.219	2	1.243	0.809	2	4.942	9.092	2	0.440	1.814	2	2.205
4.828	3	1.864	1.214	3	7.413	13.638	3	0.660	2.722	3	3.305
6.437	4	2.485	1.619	4	9.844	18.184	4	0.880	3.629	4	4.409
8.047	5	3.107	2.023	5	12.355	22.730	5	1.100	4.536	5	5.521
9.656	6	3.728	2.428	6	14.826	27.276	6	1.320	5.443	6	6.614
11.265	7	4.350	2.833	7	17.297	31.822	7	1.540	6.350	7	7.716
12.875	8	4.971	3.327	8	19.769	36.368	8	1.760	7.257	8	8.818
14.484	9	5.592	3.642	9	22.240	40.914	9	1.980	8.165	9	9.921
16.093	10	6.214	4.047	10	24.711	45.460	10	2.200	9.072	10	11.023
32.187	20	12.427	8.094	20	49.421	90.919	20	4.400	18.144	20	22.046
48.280	30	18.641	12.140	30	74.132	136.379	30	6.599	27.216	30	33.069
64.374	40	24.855	16.187	40	98.842	181.839	40	8.799	36.287	40	44.092
80.467	50	31.069	20.234	50	123.555	227.298	50	10.999	45.359	50	55.116
96.561	60	37.282	24.281	60	148.263	272.758	60	13.199	54.431	60	66.139
112.654	70	43.496	28.328	70	172.974	318.217	70	15.398	63.503	70	77.162
128.748	80	49.710	32.375	80	197.684	363.677	80	17.598	72.575	80	88.185
144.841	90	55.923	36.422	90	222.395	409.137	90	19.798	81.647	90	99.208
160.934	100	62.137	40.469	100	247.105	454.596	100	21.998	90.719	100	110.231

Abbreviations

A Associate of
AA Alcoholics Anonymous / Automobile Association
AAA Amateur Athletic Association
AB Able-bodied seaman
ABA Amateur Boxing Association
abbr(ev) abbreviation
ABM Anti-ballistic missile
abr abridged
ac alternating current
a/c account
AC Aircraftman / (*Ante Christum*) Before Christ / Companion, Order of Australia
ACAS Advisory, Conciliation and Arbitration Service
ACT Australian Capital Territory
AD (*Anno Domini*) In the year of our Lord
ADC Aide-de-Camp
ADC (P) Personal ADC to The Queen
adj adjective
Adj Adjutant
ad lib (*ad libitum*) at pleasure
Adm Admiral / Admission
adv adverb
AE Air Efficiency Award
AEEU Amalgamated Engineering and Electrical Union
AEM Air Efficiency Medal
AFC Air Force Cross
AFM Air Force Medal
AG Adjutant-General / Attorney-General
AGM air-to-ground missile / annual general meeting
AH (*Anno Hegirae*) In the year of the Hegira
AI Artificial intelligence
AIDS Acquired immune deficiency syndrome
AIM Alternative Investment Market
alt altitude
am (*ante meridiem*) before noon
AM (*Anno mundi*) In the year of the world / amplitude modulation
amp ampere / amplifier
ANC African National Congress
anon anonymous
ANZAC Australian and New Zealand Army Corps
AO Air Officer / Officer, Order of Australia
AOC Air Officer Commanding
AONB Area of Outstanding Natural Beauty
AS Anglo-Saxon
ASA Advertising Standards Authority / Amateur Swimming Association
asap as soon as possible
ASB Alternative Service Book
ASEAN Association of South East Asian Nations
ASH Action on Smoking and Health
ASLEF Associated Society of Locomotive Engineers and Firemen
ASLIB Association for Information Management

ATC Air Training Corps
AUC (*ab urbe condita*) In the year from the foundation of Rome / (*anno urbis conditae*) In the year of the founding of the city
AUT Association of University Teachers
AV Audio-visual / Authorized Version (*of Bible*)
AVR Army Volunteer Reserve
AWOL Absent without leave
b born / bowled
BA Bachelor of Arts
BAA British Airports Authority / British Astronomical Association
BAF British Athletics Federation
BAFTA British Academy of Film and Television Arts
Bart Baronet
BAS Bachelor in Agricultural Science / British Antarctic Survey
BBC British Broadcasting Corporation
BBSRC Biotechnology and Biological Sciences Research Council
BC Before Christ / British Columbia
BCCI Bank of Credit and Commerce International
B Ch (D) Bachelor of (Dental) Surgery
BCL Bachelor of Civil Law
B Com Bachelor of Commerce
BD Bachelor of Divinity
BDA British Dental Association
BDS Bachelor of Dental Surgery
B Ed Bachelor of Education
BEM British Empire Medal
B Eng Bachelor of Engineering
BFI British Film Institute
BFPO British Forces Post Office
BL British Library
B Litt Bachelor of Letters *or* of Literature
BM Bachelor of Medicine / British Museum
BMA British Medical Association
B Mus Bachelor of Music
BOTB British Overseas Trade Board
Bp Bishop
B Pharm Bachelor of Pharmacy
B Phil Bachelor of Philosophy
Br(it) Britain / British
BR British Rail
Brig Brigadier
BSc Bachelor of Science
BSE Bovine spongiform encephalopathy
BSI British Standards Institution
BST British Summer Time
Bt Baronet
BTEC Business and Technology Education Council
B Th Bachelor of Theology
Btu British thermal unit
BVM (*Beata Virgo Maria*) Blessed Virgin Mary
BVMS Bachelor of Veterinary Medicine and Surgery

c (*circa*) about
C Celsius / Centigrade / Conservative
CA Chartered Accountant (*Scotland*)
CAA Civil Aviation Authority
CAB Citizens' Advice Bureau
Cantab (of) Cambridge
Cantuar. of Canterbury (*Archbishop*)
CAP Common Agricultural Policy
Capt Captain
Caricom Caribbean Community and Common Market
Carliol: of Carlisle (*Bishop*)
CB Companion, Order of the Bath
CBE Commander, Order of the British Empire
CBI Confederation of British Industry
CC Chamber of Commerce / Companion, Order of Canada / City Council / County Council / County Court
CCC County Cricket Club
CCF Combined Cadet Force
C Chem Chartered Chemist
CD Civil Defence / compact disc / Corps Diplomatique
Cdr Commander
Cdre Commodore
CDS Chief of the Defence Staff
CE Christian Era / Civil Engineer
C Eng Chartered Engineer
Cestr. of Chester (*Bishop*)
CET Central European Time / Common External Tariff
cf (*confer*) compare
CF Chaplain to the Forces
CFC Chlorofluorocarbon
CFS Chronic Fatigue Syndrome
CGC Conspicuous Gallantry Cross
CGM Conspicuous Gallantry Medal
CGS Centimetre-gramme-second (*system*) / Chief of General Staff
CH Companion of Honour
ChB/M Bachelor/Master of Surgery
CI Channel Islands / The Imperial Order of the Crown of India
CIA Central Intelligence Agency
Cicestr. of Chichester (*Bishop*)
CID Criminal Investigation Department
CIE Companion, Order of the Indian Empire
cif cost, insurance and freight
C-in-C Commander-in-Chief
CIPFA Chartered Institute of Public Finance and Accountancy
CIS Commonwealth of Independent States
CJD Creutzfeld-Jakob disease
C Lit Companion of Literature
CLJ Commander, Order of St Lazarus of Jerusalem
CM (*Chirurgiae Magister*) Master of Surgery
CMG Companion, Order of St Michael and St George

CND	Campaign for Nuclear Disarmament
c/o	care of
CO	Commanding Officer conscientious objector
COD	Cash on delivery
C of E	Church of England
COI	Central Office of Information
Col	Colonel
Con	Conservative
cons	consecrated
Cpl	Corporal
CPM	Colonial Police Medal
CPRE	Council for the Protection of Rural England
CPS	Crown Prosecution Service
CPVE	Certificate of Pre-Vocational Education
CRE	Commission for Racial Equality
CSA	Child Support Agency
CSE	Certificate of Secondary Education
CSI	Companion, Order of the Star of India
CVO	Commander, Royal Victorian Order
d	(*denarius*) penny
DBE	Dame Commander, Order of the British Empire
dc	direct current
DC	District Council District of Columbia
DCB	Dame Commander, Order of the Bath
D Ch	(*Doctor Chirurgiae*) Doctor of Surgery
DCL	Doctor of Civil Law
DCM	Distinguished Conduct Medal
DCMG	Dame Commander, Order of St Michael and St George
DCVO	Dame Commander, Royal Victorian Order
DD	Doctor of Divinity
DDS	Doctor of Dental Surgery
DDT	dichlorodiphenyl-trichloroethane
del	(*delineavit*) he/she drew it
DFC	Distinguished Flying Cross
DFEE	Department for Education and Employment
DFM	Distinguished Flying Medal
DG	(*Dei gratia*) By the grace of God Director-General
DH	Department of Health
DHA	District Health Authority
Dip Ed	Diploma in Education
Dip H E	Diploma in Higher Education
Dip Tech	Diploma in Technology
DJ	Disc jockey
DL	Deputy Lieutenant
D Litt	Doctor of Letters *or* of Literature
D Mus	Doctor of Music
DNA	deoxyribonucleic acid
DNB	*Dictionary of National Biography*
DNH	Department of National Heritage
do	(*ditto*) the same
DoE	Department of the Environment
DOS	Disk operating system (*computer*)
DP	Data processing
D Ph *or* D Phil	Doctor of Philosophy
DPP	Director of Public Prosecutions

Dr	Doctor
D Sc	Doctor of Science
DSC	Distinguished Service Cross
DSM	Distinguished Service Medal
DSO	Companion, Distinguished Service Order
DSS	Department of Social Security
DTI	Department of Trade and Industry
DTP	Desk-top publishing
Dunelm:	of Durham (*Bishop*)
DV	(*Deo volente*) God willing
E	East
Ebor:	of York (*Archbishop*)
EBRD	European Bank for Reconstruction and Development
EC	European Community
ECG	Electrocardiogram
ECGD	Export Credits Guarantee Department
ECSC	European Coal and Steel Community
ECU	European Currency Unit
ED	Efficiency Decoration
EEC	European Economic Community
EEG	Electroencephalogram
EFA	European Fighter Aircraft
EFTA	European Free Trade Association
eg	(*exempli gratia*) for the sake of example
EIB	European Investment Bank
EMS	European Monetary System
EMU	European Monetary Union
EOC	Equal Opportunities Commission
EPSRC	Engineering and Physical Sciences Research Council
ER	(*Elizabetha Regina*) Queen Elizabeth
ERD	Emergency Reserve Decoration
ERM	Exchange Rate Mechanism
ERNIE	Electronic random number indicator equipment
ESA	European Space Agency
ESP	Extra-sensory perception
ESRC	Economic and Social Research Council
ETA	*Euzkadi ta Askatasuna* (Basque separatist organization)
et al	(*et alibi*) and elsewhere (*et alii*) and others
etc	(*et cetera*) and the other things/ and so forth
et seq	(*et sequentia*) and the following
EU	European Union
Euratom	European Atomic Energy Commission
Exon:	of Exeter (*Bishop*)
f	(*forte*) loud
F	Fahrenheit Fellow of
FA	Football Association
FANY	First Aid Nursing Yeomanry
FAO	Food and Agriculture Organization (*UN*)
FBA	Fellow, British Academy
FBAA	Fellow, British Association of Accountants and Auditors
FBI	Federal Bureau of Investigation
FBIM	Fellow, British Institute of Management

FBS	Fellow, Botanical Society
FC	Football Club
FCA	Fellow, Institute of Chartered Accountants in England and Wales
FCCA	Fellow, Chartered Association of Certified Accountants
FCGI	Fellow, City and Guilds of London Institute
FCIA	Fellow, Corporation of Insurance Agents
FCIArb	Fellow, Chartered Institute of Arbitrators
FCIB	Fellow, Chartered Institute of Bankers Fellow, Corporation of Insurance Brokers
FCIBSE	Fellow, Chartered Institution of Building Services Engineers
FCII	Fellow, Chartered Insurance Institute
FCIPS	Fellow, Chartered Institute of Purchasing and Supply
FCIS	Fellow, Institute of Chartered Secretaries and Administrators
FCIT	Fellow, Chartered Institute of Transport
FCMA	Fellow, Chartered Institute of Management Accountants
FCO	Foreign and Commonwealth Office
FCP	Fellow, College of Preceptors
FD	(*Fidei Defensor*) Defender of the Faith
FE	Further Education
fec	(*fecit*) made this
FEng	Fellow, Royal Academy of Engineering
ff	(*fecerunt*) made this (*pl*)
ff	(*fortissimo*) very loud
FFA	Fellow, Faculty of Actuaries (*Scotland*) Fellow, Institute of Financial Accountants
FFAS	Fellow, Faculty of Architects and Surveyors
FFCM	Fellow, Faculty of Community Medicine
FFPHM	Fellow, Faculty of Public Health Medicine
FGS	Fellow, Geological Society
FHS	Fellow, Heraldry Society
FHSM	Fellow, Institute of Health Service Management
FIA	Fellow, Institute of Actuaries
FIBiol	Fellow, Institute of Biology
FICE	Fellow, Institution of Civil Engineers
FICS	Fellow, Institution of Chartered Shipbrokers
FIEE	Fellow, Institution of Electrical Engineers
FIERE	Fellow, Institution of Electronic and Radio Engineers
FIFA	International Association Football Federation
FIM	Fellow, Institute of Metals
FIMM	Fellow, Institution of Mining and Metallurgy
FInstF	Fellow, Institute of Fuel
FInstP	Fellow, Institute of Physics
FIQS	Fellow, Institute of Quantity Surveyors
FIS	Fellow, Institute of Statisticians
FJI	Fellow, Institute of Journalists
fl	(*floruit*) flourished
FLA	Fellow, Library Association
FLS	Fellow, Linnaean Society

FM — Field Marshal
frequency modulation
fo — folio
FO — Flying Officer
fob — free on board
FPhS — Fellow, Philosophical Society
FRAD — Fellow, Royal Academy of Dancing
FRAeS — Fellow, Royal Aeronautical Society
FRAI — Fellow, Royal Anthropological Institute
FRAM — Fellow, Royal Academy of Music
FRAS — Fellow, Royal Asiatic Society
Fellow, Royal Astronomical Society
FRBS — Fellow, Royal Botanic Society
Fellow, Royal Society of British Sculptors
FRCA — Fellow, Royal College of Anaesthetists
FRCGP — Fellow, Royal College of General Practitioners
FRCM — Fellow, Royal College of Music
FRCO — Fellow, Royal College of Organists
FRCOG — Fellow, Royal College of Obstetricians and Gynaecologists
FRCP — Fellow, Royal College of Physicians, London
FRCPath — Fellow, Royal College of Pathologists
FRCPE or
FRCPEd — Fellow, Royal College of Physicians, Edinburgh
FRCPI — Fellow, Royal College of Physicians, Ireland
FRCPsych — Fellow, Royal College of Psychiatrists
FRCR — Fellow, Royal College of Radiologists
FRCS — Fellow, Royal College of Surgeons of England
FRCSE or
FRCSEd — Fellow, Royal College of Surgeons of Edinburgh
FRCSGlas — Fellow, Royal College of Physicians and Surgeons of Glasgow
FRCSI — Fellow, Royal College of Surgeons in Ireland
FRCVS — Fellow, Royal College of Veterinary Surgeons
FREconS — Fellow, Royal Economic Society
FRGS — Fellow, Royal Geographical Society
FRHistS — Fellow, Royal Historical Society
FRHS — Fellow, Royal Horticultural Society
FRIBA — Fellow, Royal Institute of British Architects
FRICS — Fellow, Royal Institution of Chartered Surveyors
FRMetS — Fellow, Royal Meteorological Society
FRMS — Fellow, Royal Microscopical Society
FRNS — Fellow, Royal Numismatic Society
FRPharmS — Fellow, Royal Pharmaceutical Society
FRPS — Fellow, Royal Photographic Society
FRS — Fellow, Royal Society
FRSA — Fellow, Royal Society of Arts
FRSC — Fellow, Royal Society of Chemistry

FRSE — Fellow, Royal Society of Edinburgh
FRSH — Fellow, Royal Society of Health
FRSL — Fellow, Royal Society of Literature
FRTPI — Fellow, Royal Town Planning Institute
FSA — Fellow, Society of Antiquaries
FSS — Fellow, Royal Statistical Society
FSVA — Fellow, Incorporated Society of Valuers and Auctioneers
FT — *Financial Times*
FTI — Fellow, Textile Institute
FTII — Fellow, Chartered Institute of Taxation
FZS — Fellow, Zoological Society
GATT — General Agreement on Tariffs and Trade
GBE — Dame/Knight Grand Cross, Order of the British Empire
GC — George Cross
GCB — Dame/Knight Grand Cross, Order of the Bath
GCE — General Certificate of Education
GCHQ — Government Communications Headquarters
GCIE — Knight Grand Commander, Order of the Indian Empire
GCLJ — Knight Grand Cross, Order of St Lazarus of Jerusalem
GCMG — Dame/Knight Grand Cross, Order of St Michael and St George
GCSE — General Certificate of Secondary Education
GCSI — Knight Grand Commander, Order of the Star of India
GCVO — Dame/Knight Grand Cross, Royal Victorian Order
GDP — Gross domestic product
Gen — General
GHQ — General Headquarters
GM — George Medal
GMB — General, Municipal, Boilermakers and Allied Trades Union
GMT — Greenwich Mean Time
GNP — Gross national product
GNVQ — General National Vocational Qualification
GOC — General Officer Commanding
GP — General Practitioner
Gp Capt — Group Captain
GSA — Girls' Schools Association
GSO — General Staff Officer
HAC — Honourable Artillery Company
HB — His Beatitude
HBM — Her/His Britannic Majesty('s)
HCF — Highest common factor
Honorary Chaplain to the Forces
HE — Her/His Excellency
Higher Education
His Eminence
HGV — Heavy Goods Vehicle
HH — Her/His Highness
Her/His Honour
His Holiness
HIM — Her/His Imperial Majesty
HIV — Human immunodeficiency virus
HJS — (*hic jacet sepultus*) here lies buried
HM — Her/His Majesty('s)

HMAS — Her/His Majesty's Australian Ship
HMC — Headmasters' Conference
HMI — Her/His Majesty's Inspector
HML — Her/His Majesty's Lieutenant
HMS — Her/His Majesty's Ship
HMSO — Her/His Majesty's Stationery Office
HNC — Higher National Certificate
HND — Higher National Diploma
HOLMES — Home Office Large Major Enquiry System
Hon — Honorary
Honourable
hp — horse power
HP — Hire purchase
HQ — Headquarters
HRH — Her/His Royal Highness
HSE — Health and Safety Executive
(*hic sepultus est*) here lies buried
HSH — Her/His Serene Highness
HTR — High temperature reactor
HWM — High water mark
I — Island
IAAS — Incorporated Association of Architects and Surveyors
IAEA — International Atomic Energy Agency
IATA — International Air Transport Association
ibid — (*ibidem*) in the same place
IBRD — International Bank for Reconstruction and Development
ICAO — International Civil Aviation Organization
ICBM — Inter-continental ballistic missile
ICFTU — International Confederation of Free Trade Unions
ICJ — International Court of Justice
ICRC — International Committee of the Red Cross
id — (*idem*) the same
IDA — International Development Association
IDD — International direct dialling
ie — (*id est*) that is
IEA — International Energy Agency
IFAD — International Fund for Agricultural Development
IFC — International Finance Corporation
IHS — (*Iesus Hominum Salvator*) Jesus the Saviour of Mankind
ILO — International Labour Office/Organization
ILR — Independent local radio
IMF — International Monetary Fund
IMO — International Maritime Organization
Inc — Incorporated
incog — (*incognito*) unknown, unrecognized
INLA — Irish National Liberation Army
in loc — (*in loco*) in its place
Inmarsat — International Maritime Satellite Organization
INRI — (*Iesus Nazarenus Rex Iudaeorum*) Jesus of Nazareth, King of the Jews
inst — (*instant*) current month
Intelsat — International Telecommunications Satellite Organization
Interpol — International Criminal Police Commission
IOC — International Olympic Committee
IOM — Isle of Man

IOU	I owe you	LMSSA	Licentiate in Medicine and	MSc	Master of Science	
IOW	Isle of Wight		Surgery, Society of	MSF	Manufacturing, Science and	
IQ	Intelligence quotient		Apothecaries		Finance Union	
IRA	Irish Republican Army	loc cit	(*loco citato*) in the place cited	MTh	Master of Theology	
IRC	International Red Cross	log	logarithm	Mus B/D	Bachelor/Doctor of Music	
Is	Islands	Londin:	of London (*Bishop*)	MV	Merchant Vessel	
ISBN	International Standard Book	Long	Longitude		Motor Vessel	
	Number	LS	(*loco sigilli*) place of the seal	MVO	Member, Royal Victorian	
ISO	Imperial Service Order	LSA	Licentiate of Society of		Order	
ISSN	International Standard Serial		Apothecaries	MW	medium wave	
	Number	Lsd	(*Librae, solidi, denarii*) £,			
ITC	Independent Television		shillings and pence			
	Commission	LSE	London School of Economics	N	North	
ITN	Independent Television News		and Political Science	n/a	not applicable	
ITU	International	Lt	Lieutenant		not available	
	Telecommunication Union	LTA	Lawn Tennis Association	NAAFI	Navy, Army and Air Force	
ITV	Independent Television	Ltd	Limited (liability)		Institutes	
		LTh *or*		NASA	National Aeronautics and	
		L Theol	Licentiate in Theology		Space Administration	
JP	Justice of the Peace	LVO	Lieutenant, Royal Victorian	NAS/UWT	National Association of	
			Order		Schoolmasters/Union of	
		LW	long wave		Women Teachers	
K	Köchel numeration (*of Mozart's	LWM	Low water mark	NATO	North Atlantic Treaty	
	works*)				Organization	
KBE	Knight Commander, Order of			NB	New Brunswick	
	the British Empire	M	Member of		(*nota bene*) note well	
KCB	Knight Commander, Order of		Monsieur	NCIS	National Criminal Intelligence	
	the Bath	MA	Master of Arts		Service	
KCIE	Knight Commander, Order of	MAFF	Ministry of Agriculture,	NCO	Non-commissioned officer	
	the Indian Empire		Fisheries and Food	NEB	New English Bible	
KCLJ	Knight Commander, Order of	Maj	Major	nem con	(*nemine contradicente*) no one	
	St Lazarus of Jerusalem	max	maximum		contradicting	
KCMG	Knight Commander, Order of	MB	Bachelor of Medicine	NERC	Natural Environment	
	St Michael and St George	MBA	Master of Business		Research Council	
KCSI	Knight Commander, Order of		Administration	nes	not elsewhere specified	
	the Star of India	MBE	Member, Order of the British	NFT	National Film Theatre	
KCVO	Knight Commander, Royal		Empire	NFU	National Farmers' Union	
	Victorian Order	MC	Master of Ceremonies	NHS	National Health Service	
KG	Knight of the Garter		Military Cross	NI	National Insurance	
KGB	(*Komitet Gosudarstvennoi	MCC	Marylebone Cricket Club		Northern Ireland	
	Besopasnosti*) Committee of	MCh(D)	Master of (Dental) Surgery	NIV	New International Version (*of	
	State Security (USSR)	MD	Managing Director		Bible*)	
KKK	Ku Klux Klan		Doctor of Medicine	No	(*numero*) number	
KLJ	Knight, Order of St Lazarus of	MDS	Master of Dental Surgery	non seq	(*non sequitur*) it does not follow	
	Jerusalem	ME	Middle English	Norvic:	of Norwich (*Bishop*)	
ko	knock out (*boxing*)		Myalgic Encephalomyelitis	NP	Notary Public	
KP	Knight, Order of St Patrick	MEC	Member of Executive Council	NRA	National Rifle Association	
KStJ	Knight, Order of St John of	MEd	Master of Education	NS	New Style (*calendar*)	
	Jerusalem	mega	one million times		Nova Scotia	
Kt	Knight	MEP	Member of the European	NSPCC	National Society for the	
KT	Knight of the Thistle		Parliament		Prevention of Cruelty to	
kV	Kilovolt	MFH	Master of Foxhounds		Children	
kW	Kilowatt	Mgr	Monsignor	NSW	New South Wales	
kWh	Kilowatt hour	MI	Military Intelligence	NT	National Theatre	
		micro	one-millionth part		National Trust	
		milli	one-thousandth part		New Testament	
L	Liberal	min	minimum	NUJ	National Union of Journalists	
Lab	Labour	MIRAS	Mortgage Interest Relief at	NUM	National Union of	
Lat	Latitude		Source		Mineworkers	
lbw	leg before wicket	MLA	Member of Legislative	NUS	National Union of Students	
lc	lower case (*printing*)		Assembly	NUT	National Union of Teachers	
LCJ	Lord Chief Justice	MLC	Member of Legislative	NVQ	National Vocational	
LCM	Least/lowest common		Council		Qualification	
	multiple	MLitt	Master of Letters	NWT	Northwest Territory	
LD	Liberal Democrat	Mlle	Mademoiselle	NY	New York	
LDS	Licentiate in Dental Surgery	MLR	Minimum lending rate	NZ	New Zealand	
LEA	Local Education Authority	MM	Military Medal			
LHD	(*Literarum Humaniorum Doctor*)	Mme	Madame			
	Doctor of Humane Letters/	MN	Merchant Navy	OAPEC	Organization of Arab	
	Literature	MO	Medical Officer/Orderly		Petroleum Exporting	
Lib	Liberal	MoD	Ministry of Defence		Countries	
Lic	(*Licenciado*) lawyer (*Spanish*)	MoT	Ministry of Transport	OAS	Organization of American	
Lic Med	Licentiate in Medicine	MP	Member of Parliament		States	
Lit	Literary		Military Police	OAU	Organization of African Unity	
Lit Hum	(*Literae Humaniores*) Faculty of	mph	miles per hour	Ob *or* obit	died	
	classics and philosophy, Oxford	M Phil	Master of Philosophy	OBE	Officer, Order of the British	
Litt D	Doctor of Letters	MR	Master of the Rolls		Empire	
LJ	Lord Justice	MRC	Medical Research Council	OC	Officer Commanding	
LLB	Bachelor of Laws	MS	Master of Surgery	ODA	Overseas Development	
LLD	Doctor of Laws		Manuscript (*pl* MSS)		Administration	
LLM	Master of Laws		Multiple Sclerosis	OE	Old English	
LM	Licentiate in Midwifery				omissions excepted	

OECD   Organization for Economic Co-operation and Development

OED   *Oxford English Dictionary*

Offer   Office of Electricity Regulation

Ofgas   Office of Gas Supply

OFM   Order of Friars Minor (*Franciscans*)

Ofsted   Office for Standards in Education

OFT   Office of Fair Trading

Oftel   Office of Telecommunications

Ofwat   Office of Water Services

OHMS   On Her/His Majesty's Service

OM   Order of Merit

OND   Ordinary National Diploma

ONO   or near offer

ONS   Office for National Statistics

op   (*opus*) work

OP   Opposite prompt side (*of theatre*)

    Order of Preachers (*Dominicans*)

    out of print (*books*)

op cit   (*opere citato*) in the work cited

OPCS   Office of Population Censuses and Surveys

OPEC   Organization of Petroleum Exporting Countries

OPRAF   Office of Passenger Rail Franchising

OPS   Office of Public Service

ORR   Office of the Rail Regulator

OS   Old Style (*calendar*)

    Ordnance Survey

OSA   Order of St Augustine

OSB   Order of St Benedict

OSCE   Organization for Security and Co-operation in Europe

O StJ   Officer, Order of St John of Jerusalem

OT   Old Testament

OTC   Officers' Training Corps

Oxon   (of) Oxford

    Oxfordshire

p   page

p   (*piano*) softly

PA   Personal Assistant

    Press Association

PAYE   Pay as You Earn

pc   (*per centum*) in the hundred

PC   personal computer

    Police Constable

    politically correct

    Privy Counsellor

PCC   Press Complaints Commission

PDSA   People's Dispensary for Sick Animals

PE   Physical Education

Petriburg: of Peterborough (*Bishop*)

PFI   Private Finance Initiative

PGA   Professional Golfers Association

PGCE   Postgraduate Certificate of Education

PhD   Doctor of Philosophy

pinx(it)   he/she painted it

pl   plural

PLA   Port of London Authority

PLC   Public Limited Company

PLO   Palestine Liberation Organization

pm   (*post meridiem*) after noon

PM   Prime Minister

PMRAFNS   Princess Mary's Royal Air Force Nursing Service

PO   Petty Officer

    Pilot Officer

    Post Office

    postal order

POW   Prisoner of War

pp   pages

    (*per procurationem*) by proxy

PPARC   Particle Physics and Astronomy Research Council

PPS   Parliamentary Private Secretary

PR   Proportional representation

    Public relations

PRA   President of the Royal Academy

Pro tem   (*pro tempore*) for the time being

Prox   (*proximo*) next month

PRS   President of the Royal Society

PRSE   President of the Royal Society of Edinburgh

Ps   Psalm

PS   (*postscriptum*) postscript

PSBR   Public sector borrowing requirement

psc   passed Staff College

PSV   Public Service Vehicle

PTA   Parent-Teacher Association

Pte   Private

PTO   Please turn over

PVC   Polyvinyl chloride

QARANC   Queen Alexandra's Royal Army Nursing Corps

QARNNS   Queen Alexandra's Royal Naval Nursing Service

QB(D)   Queen's Bench (Division)

QC   Queen's Counsel

QED   (*quod erat demonstrandum*) which was to be proved

QGM   Queen's Gallantry Medal

QHC   Queen's Honorary Chaplain

QHDS   Queen's Honorary Dental Surgeon

QHNS   Queen's Honorary Nursing Sister

QHP   Queen's Honorary Physician

QHS   Queen's Honorary Surgeon

QMG   Quartermaster General

QPM   Queen's Police Medal

QS   Quarter Sessions

QSO   Quasi-stellar object (quasar)

    Queen's Service Order

quango   quasi-autonomous non-governmental organization

qv   (*quod vide*) which see

R   (*Regina*) Queen

    (*Rex*) King

RA   Royal Academy/Academician

    Royal Artillery

RAC   Royal Armoured Corps

    Royal Automobile Club

RADA   Royal Academy of Dramatic Art

RADC   Royal Army Dental Corps

RAE   Royal Aerospace Establishment

RAEC   Royal Army Educational Corps

RAeS   Royal Aeronautical Society

RAF   Royal Air Force

RAM   Random-access memory (*computer*)

    Royal Academy of Music

RAMC   Royal Army Medical Corps

RAN   Royal Australian Navy

RAOC   Royal Army Ordnance Corps

RAPC   Royal Army Pay Corps

RAVC   Royal Army Veterinary Corps

RBG   Royal Botanic Garden

RBS   Royal Society of British Sculptors

RC   Red Cross

    Roman Catholic

RCM   Royal College of Music

RCN   Royal Canadian Navy

RCT   Royal Corps of Transport

RD   Refer to drawer (*banking*)

    Royal Naval and Royal Marine Forces Reserve Decoration

    Rural Dean

RDI   Royal Designer for Industry

RE   Religious Education

    Royal Engineers

REME   Royal Electrical and Mechanical Engineers

Rep   Representative

    Republican

Rev(d)   Reverend

RFU   Rugby Football Union

RGN   Registered General Nurse

RGS   Royal Geographical Society

RHA   Regional Health Authority

RHS   Royal Horticultural Society

    Royal Humane Society

RI   Rhode Island

    Royal Institute of Painters in Watercolours

    Royal Institution

RIBA   Royal Institute of British Architects

RIP   (*Requiescat in pace*) May he/she rest in peace

RIR   Royal Irish Regiment

RL   Rugby League

RM   Registered Midwife

    Royal Marines

RMA   Royal Military Academy

RMN   Registered Mental Nurse

RMT   National Union of Rail, Maritime and Transport Workers

RN   Royal Navy

RNIB   Royal National Institute for the Blind

RNID   Royal National Institute for the Deaf

RNLI   Royal National Lifeboat Institution

RNMH   Registered Nurse for the Mentally Handicapped

RNR   Royal Naval Reserve

RNVR   Royal Naval Volunteer Reserve

RNXS   Royal Naval Auxiliary Service

RNZN   Royal New Zealand Navy

Ro   (*Recto*) on the right-hand page

ROC   Royal Observer Corps

Roffen: of Rochester (*Bishop*)

ROI   Royal Institute of Oil Painters

ROM   Read-only memory (*computer*)

RoSPA   Royal Society for the Prevention of Accidents

RP   Royal Society of Portrait Painters

rpm   revolutions per minute

RRC   Lady of Royal Red Cross

RSA   Republic of South Africa

    Royal Scottish Academician

    Royal Society of Arts

RSC   Royal Shakespeare Company

RSCN   Registered Sick Children's Nurse

RSE   Royal Society of Edinburgh

RSM   Regimental Sergeant Major

RSPB	Royal Society for the Protection of Birds
RSPCA	Royal Society for the Prevention of Cruelty to Animals
RSV	Revised Standard Version (*of Bible*)
RSVP	(*Répondez, s'il vous plaît*) Please reply
RSW	Royal Scottish Society of Painters in Watercolours
RTPI	Royal Town Planning Institute
RU	Rugby Union
RUC	Royal Ulster Constabulary
RV	Revised Version (*of Bible*)
RVM	Royal Victorian Medal
RWS	Royal Water Colour Society
RYS	Royal Yacht Squadron
s	second
	(*solidus*) shilling
S	South
SA	Salvation Army
	South Africa
	South America
	South Australia
SAE	stamped addressed envelope
Salop	Shropshire
Sarum:	of Salisbury (*Bishop*)
SAS	Special Air Service Regiment
SBS	Special Boat Squadron
SBN	Standard Book Number
ScD	Doctor of Science
SCM	State Certified Midwife
SDLP	Social Democratic and Labour Party
SEAQ	Stock Exchange Automated Quotations system
SEN	State Enrolled Nurse
SERPS	State Earnings Related Pension Scheme
SFO	Serious Fraud Office
SHMIS	Society of Headmasters and Headmistresses of Independent Schools
SI	(*Système International d'Unités*) International System of Units
	Statutory Instrument
sic	So written
Sig	Signature
	Signor
SJ	Society of Jesus (*Jesuits*)
SLD	Social and Liberal Democrats
SMP	Statutory Maternity Pay
SNP	Scottish National Party
SOE	Special Operations Executive
SOS	Save Our Souls (*distress signal*)
sp	(*sine prole*) without issue
spgr	specific gravity
SPQR	(*Senatus Populusque Romanus*) The Senate and People of Rome
SRN	State Registered Nurse
SRO	Self Regulating Organizations
SS	Saints
	Schutzstaffel (Nazi paramilitary organization)
	Steamship
SSC	Solicitor before Supreme Court (*Scotland*)
SSF	Society of St Francis
SSN	Standard Serial Number
SSP	Statutory Sick Pay
SSSI	Site of special scientific interest
STD	(*Sacrae Theologiae Doctor*) Doctor of Sacred Theology
	Subscriber trunk dialling
stet	let it stand (*printing*)

stp	Standard temperature and pressure
STP	(*Sacrae Theologiae Professor*) Professor of Sacred Theology
Sub Lt	Sub-Lieutenant
SVQ	Scottish Vocational Qualification
TA	Territorial Army
TB	Tuberculosis
TCCB	Test and County Cricket Board
TD	Territorial Efficiency Decoration
TEC	Training and Enterprise Council
TEFL	Teaching English as a foreign language
temp	temperature
	temporary employee
TES	*Times Educational Supplement*
TGWU	Transport and General Workers' Union
THES	*Times Higher Education Supplement*
TLS	*Times Literary Supplement*
TNT	trinitrotoluene (*explosive*)
trans	translated
trs	transpose (*printing*)
TRH	Their Royal Highnesses
TT	Teetotal
	Tourist Trophy (*motorcycle races*)
TUC	Trades Union Congress
TVEI	Technical and Vocational Education Initiative
U	Unionist
UAE	United Arab Emirates
uc	upper case (*printing*)
UCAS	Universities and Colleges Admissions Service
UCATT	Union of Construction, Allied Trades and Technicians
UDA	Ulster Defence Association
UDI	Unilateral Declaration of Independence
UDM	Union of Democratic Mineworkers
UDR	Ulster Defence Regiment
UEFA	Union of European Football Associations
UFF	Ulster Freedom Fighters
UFO	Unidentified flying object
UHF	ultra-high frequency
UK	United Kingdom
UKAEA	UK Atomic Energy Authority
UN	United Nations
UNESCO	United Nations Educational, Scientific and Cultural Organization
UNHCR	United Nations High Commissioner for Refugees
UNICEF	United Nations Children's Fund
UNIDO	United Nations Industrial Development Organization
Unita	National Union for the Total Independence of Angola
UPU	Universal Postal Union
URC	United Reformed Church
US(A)	United States (of America)
USDAW	Union of Shop, Distributive and Allied Workers
USM	Unlisted Securities Market

USSR	Union of Soviet Socialist Republics
UTC	Co-ordinated Universal Time system
UVF	Ulster Volunteer Force
v	(*versus*) against
VA	Vicar Apostolic
	Victoria and Albert Order
VAD	Voluntary Aid Detachment
VAT	Value added tax
VC	Victoria Cross
VCR	video cassette recorder
VD	Venereal disease
	Volunteer Officers' Decoration
VDU	Visual display unit
Ven	Venerable
VHF	very high frequency
VIP	Very important person
Vo	(*Verso*) on the left-hand page
VRD	Royal Naval Volunteer Reserve Officers' Decoration
VSO	Voluntary Service Overseas
VTOL	Vertical take-off and landing (*aircraft*)
W	West
WCC	World Council of Churches
WEA	Workers' Educational Association
WEU	Western European Union
WFTU	World Federation of Trade Unions
WHO	World Health Organization
WI	West Indies
	Women's Institute
Winton:	of Winchester (*Bishop*)
WIPO	World Intellectual Property Organization
WMO	World Meteorological Organization
WO	Warrant Officer
WRAC	Women's Royal Army Corps
WRAF	Women's Royal Air Force
WRNS	Women's Royal Naval Service
WRVS	Women's Royal Voluntary Service
WS	Writer to the Signet
YMCA	Young Men's Christian Association
YWCA	Young Women's Christian Association
Ψ	= seaport

Index

Stop-press

CHANGES SINCE PAGES WENT TO PRESS

ROYAL HOUSEHOLDS

Aide de Camp General – Gen. Sir Michael Walker replaces Gen. Sir Michael Rose

Gentleman Usher of the Sword of State – Adm. Sir Michael Layard appointed

Chaplains to The Queen – Ven. I. Russell appointed

PEERAGE

Viscount Samuel married

Viscount Tonypandy died (viscountcy extinct)

13th Lord Rollo died

Ms Valerie Amos gazetted Baroness Amos

Dame Jill Knight gazetted Baroness Knight of Collingtree

Norman Hogg gazetted Baron Hogg of Cumbernauld

Michael Levy gazetted Baron Levy

Richard Newby gazetted Baron Newby

Jeffrey Randall gazetted Baron Randall of St Budeaux

BARONETAGE AND KNIGHTAGE

Died: Sir Rudolf Bing, KBE; Sir Henry Boyne, CBE; Sir Henry Calley, DSO, DFC; Adm. Sir Derek Empson, GBE, KCB; Sir Edmond Falkiner, Bt.; Gen. Sir John Hackett, GCB, CBE, DSO, MC; Sir Guy Holland, Bt.; Sir Nigel Reed, CBE; Sir Charles Russell, Bt.; Sir Georg Solti, KBE

PRIVY COUNCIL

Viscount Tonypandy died

GOVERNMENT DEPARTMENTS AND PUBLIC OFFICES

British Film Commission – Steve Norris appointed commissioner and chief executive

Home Office – Colin Pickthall, MP, appointed parliamentary private secretary to Alun Michael; Brian Jenkins, MP, appointed parliamentary private secretary to Joyce Quin

Scottish Legal Aid Board – Ms M. Scanlan replaces Mrs P. Bowman

Parole Board – Ms Usha Prashar appointed chairman

Department of Social Security – Kate Hoey, MP, appointed parliamentary private secretary to Frank Field

The Treasury – Steve Robson appointed second permanent secretary; Adrian Montague appointed chief executive of Private Finance Task Force

LAW COURTS AND OFFICES

Lord Justice of Appeal – Mr Justice (Richard) Buxton replaces Sir Anthony McCowan (retired)

High Court appointments – Anthony Hughes (Family Division); Jeremy Sullivan (Queen's Bench Division)

Circuit judges – C. Bloom (Northern) appointed; Judge Davidson; Judge Potter (Midland and Oxford) retired

THE POLICE SERVICE

Sir John Wheeler appointed chairman of the Service Authorities for the National Crime Squad and the National Criminal Intelligence Service, which will come into operation in April 1998

National Criminal Intelligence Service – J. Abbott appointed director-general

North Yorkshire Police – chief constable D. Burke to retire

THE PRISON SERVICES

Prisons now designated also as Young Offender Institutions: Askham Grange; Cardiff; Chelmsford; Doncaster; Dorchester; Exeter; Gloucester; Hindley; Hull; Lewes; Low Newton; Northallerton; Norwich; Reading; Rochester; Swansea; Woodhill

DEFENCE

Army – Gen. Sir Michael Walker replaces Gen. Sir Michael Rose as Aide de Camp General

RAF – P. W. Henderson promoted air vice-marshal, to be Director-General, Support Management, HQ Logistics Command

CHURCH OF ENGLAND

Coventry – Rt. Revd Colin Bennetts (Area Bishop of Buckingham) to be Bishop of Coventry

Ely – Revd Canon John Beer to be Archdeacon of Huntingdon

Lincoln – Revd Canon Alastair Redfern to be Suffragan Bishop of Grantham

Southwark – Peter Price to be Area Bishop of Kingston upon Thames

Newcastle – Rt. Revd Martin Wharton (Area Bishop of Kingston upon Thames) to be Bishop of Newcastle

Ripon – Ven. Frank Weston (Archdeacon of Oxford) to be Suffragan Bishop of Knaresborough

Sheffield – Rt. Revd John Nicholls (Suffragan Bishop of Lancaster) to be Bishop of Sheffield

OTHER FAITHS

Judaism – Rabbi Dr C. H. Middleburgh to be executive director of the Union of Liberal and Progressive Synagogues

UNIVERSITIES

Sunderland - Sir David Puttnam to be chancellor

TRANSPORT

Railtrack – Gerald Corbett to be chief executive

TELECOMMUNICATIONS

BT – some charges increased from 18 September 1997

LOCAL GOVERNMENT

Lord Mayor of London 1997–8 – Alderman Richard Nichols, elected 29 September

TRADE UNIONS

President of the TUC 1997–8 – John Edmonds (GMB)

SPORTS BODIES

British Athletics Federation – D. Moorcroft to be chief executive

INTERNATIONAL ORGANIZATIONS

ASEAN – Laos and Myanmar became members 23 July 1997; Cambodia's application suspended

Countries of the World

Australia – Transport Minister John Sharp and Administrative Services Minister David Jull resigned 24 September

China – new Politburo standing committee of the Chinese Communist Party selected 19 September

Norway – general election held 15 September; incumbent coalition wins smaller share of vote and resigns, but remains as caretaker government until 13 October

Poland – Solidarity party wins majority of seats in election to legislature on 21 September and expected to form government

Yugoslavia – presidential and legislative elections in Serbia on 19 September

Sport

Olympic Games 2004 to be held in Athens

EVENTS – SEPTEMBER 1997

4. Three suicide bombs exploded in Jerusalem, killing seven people. **8.** More than 500 people were reported to have drowned when a ferry sank off the coast of Haiti. **9.** Sinn Fein leaders agreed at Stormont to abide by the Mitchell principles of democracy and non-violence. **11.** A referendum was held in Scotland; the turnout was about 62 per cent, of whom 74.3 per cent voted in favour of a Scottish parliament and 63.5 per cent in favour of the parliament having tax-raising powers. The IRA said that it would have problems with sections of the Mitchell principles; it ruled out any disarmament during the talks and rejected the principle of consent. **15.** Substantive talks opened at Stormont. None of the Unionist or loyalist parties attended; the UUP said that it required assurances that the IRA would hand over weapons during the talks. The first-class cricket counties voted 19–12 not to divide the county championship into two divisions. **16.** A 400 lb bomb believed to have been planted by a republican splinter group exploded in Co. Armagh; the UUP called for Sinn Fein's expulsion from the talks. The BBC announced plans to merge its television and radio news operations; after protests the plans were postponed. **17.** A referendum was held in Wales; the turnout was 50 per cent, of whom 50.3 per cent voted in favour of a Welsh assembly. The UUP, the Progressive Unionist Party and the Ulster Democratic Party re-entered negotiations at Stormont. Clive Woodward was appointed England rugby union coach. **18.** Ten people were killed in a gun and bomb attack on a bus in Cairo, Egypt. At the Royal Academy a controversial portrait of the child murderer Myra Hindley was damaged when protesters threw paint and eggs at it. **19.** Six people were killed and more than 160 injured when a passenger train crashed into a freight train in Southall, west London; a seventh person later died. Dennis Marks resigned as general director of English National Opera. **22–29.** Fires started by landowners attempting to clear forests in Indonesia caused heavy smog across the region. **23.** Unionist, loyalist, nationalist and republican leaders met face-to-face across the negotiating table at Stormont; the Unionists argued unsuccessfully that Sinn Fein should be expelled from the talks. A British nurse, Lucille McLauchlan, was sentenced in Saudi Arabia to 500 lashes and eight years' imprisonment for being an accessory to the murder of a colleague in December 1996. There were unconfirmed reports that a second British nurse, Deborah Parry, had been convicted of the murder and sentenced to death. The Foreign Secretary (Robin

Cook) made diplomatic representations aimed at preventing the sentences from being carried out. **24.** It was agreed at Stormont that the issue of decommissioning terrorist weapons would be dealt with by a new independent commission and that the substantive talks would concentrate on constitutional issues. **25.** A British team led by Andy Green set a new world land speed record of 714.144 m.p.h. The chairman of the Press Complaints Commission (Lord Wakeham) put forward proposals for a revised code of practice for newspapers to protect privacy and prevent intrusive photography. **26.** All 234 people on board were killed when an Indonesian airliner crashed near Medan, Sumatra. At least ten people were killed and the basilica of St Francis was badly damaged when an earthquake registering 5.5 on the Richter scale hit Assisi, Italy. The FT-SE 100 index closed at a record high of 5,226.3 and sterling fell to DM 2.8324 after rumours that the Government was adopting a more positive approach to EMU.

Obituaries

September

4 Jeffrey Bernard, journalist, aged 65
  Prof. Hans Eysenck, psychologist, aged 81
7 Mobutu Sese Seko, former president of Zaïre, aged 66
9 Gen. Sir John Hackett, aged 86
  Burgess Meredith, actor, aged 89
20 Adm. Sir Derek Empson, aged 78
22 Viscount Tonypandy (George Thomas), former Speaker of the House of Commons, aged 88